GW00703378

# Oxfor

## ENGLISH-ENGLISH-HINDI Dictionary

## अंग्रेज़ी-अंग्रेज़ी-हिंदी शब्दकोश

# Oxford

# ENGLISH-ENGLISH-HINDI Dictionary

## अंग्रेज़ी–अंग्रेज़ी–हिंदी शब्दकोश

***Editors***

**Dr Suresh Kumar**
**Dr Ramanath Sahai**

**OXFORD**
**UNIVERSITY PRESS**

**OXFORD**
UNIVERSITY PRESS
YMCA Library Building, Jai Singh Road, New Delhi 110001

Oxford University Press is a department of the University of Oxford.
It furthers the University's objective of excellence in research, scholarship,
and education by publishing worldwide in

Oxford New York
Auckland Cape Town Dar es Salaam Hong Kong Karachi
Kuala Lumpur Madrid Melbourne Mexico City Nairobi
New Delhi Shanghai Taipei Toronto

With offices in
Argentina Austria Brazil Chile Czech Republic France Greece
Guatemala Hungary Italy Japan Poland Portugal Singapore
South Korea Switzerland Thailand Turkey Ukraine Vietnam

Oxford is a registered trademark of Oxford University Press
in the UK and in certain other countries.

Published in India
by Oxford University Press

© Oxford University Press 2008
English base adapted from the *Oxford Student's Dictionary*,
© 2001, originally published
by Oxford University Press, Great Clarendon Street, Oxford

The moral rights of the author/s have been asserted.

Database right Oxford University Press (maker)

First published 2008
Eighteenth impression March 2011
This edition is published by arrangement with
Oxford University Press, Oxford
for sale throughout the world

All rights reserved. No part of this publication may be reproduced,
stored in a retrieval system, or transmitted, in any form or by any means,
without the prior permission in writing of Oxford University Press,
or as expressly permitted by law, or under terms agreed with the appropriate
reprographics rights organization. Enquiries concerning reproduction
outside the scope of the above should be sent to the Rights Department,
Oxford University Press, at the address above.

You must not circulate this book in any other binding or cover
and you must impose this same condition on any acquirer.

ISBN-13: 978-0-19-568962-4
ISBN-10: 0-19-568962-3

Illustrations by Agantuk

Typeset by Innovative Processors, New Delhi 110002
Printed in India by Manipal Press, Manipal
and published by Oxford University Press
YMCA Library Building, Jai Singh Road, New Delhi 110001

# विषय सूची

# भूमिका

अंग्रेज़ी-हिंदी शब्दकोशों की परंपरा में यह एक उच्चतर और विशिष्ट शब्दकोश है। शब्दार्थविज्ञान (सिमैंटिक्स) तथा शब्दकोशनिर्माण (लेक्सिकोग्राफ़ी) के अधुनातन सिद्धांतों और तकनीकों पर आधारित इस कोश में कोशीय सामग्री अंग्रेज़ी और हिंदी दोनों में समान रूप से दी गई है जिसके फलस्वरूप यह एक बृहत् **अंग्रेज़ी-अंग्रेज़ी-हिंदी शब्दकोश** बन गया है। अपने वर्तमान रूप में यह कोश अंग्रेज़ी के हिंदी भाषी छात्रों, अंग्रेज़ी-शिक्षकों और अनुवादकों के अतिरिक्त सामान्य पाठकों के लिए भी उपयोगी है।

शब्दकोश में संकलित शब्दसंग्रह का आकार बड़ा है। शीर्षशब्द, उपशीर्षशब्द, संबंधित शब्दावली (पर्याय, विलोम, व्युत्पन्न शब्द, मुहावरे, क्रियाओं के पदबंधीय रूप आदि), कुल मिलाकर 50 हज़ार प्रविष्टियाँ हैं। ये शब्द विभिन्न स्रोतों से लिए गए हैं। अंग्रेज़ी के अपने सामान्य और प्रचलित शब्दों के अतिरिक्त भारतीय भाषाओं से आगत सामान्य और विशिष्ट शब्द विभिन्न ज्ञानक्षेत्रों (जैसे कंप्यूटर विज्ञान, प्रबंधन शास्त्र, वाणिज्य, भूगोल, गणित शास्त्र, भौतिक व जैव विज्ञान एवं प्रौद्योगिकी, विधि, राजनीति शास्त्र आदि) के शब्द संकलित हैं। अन्य महत्त्वपूर्ण विशेषता है अर्थ का विशद स्पष्टीकरण। प्रविष्टि के अर्थ की व्याख्या करते हुए प्रायः एकाधिक उदाहरण-वाक्यों से उसे समझाया गया है। प्रविष्टि की आवश्यकता के अनुसार अर्थ की सुबोधता बढ़ाने के लिए आरेख और रेखांकन दिए गए हैं। संबंधित पर्याय और विलोम देते हुए उनके अर्थ-साम्य/भेद को समझाया गया है। उच्चारण-संकेत के साथ व्याकरण और प्रयोग संबंधी आवश्यक टिप्पणियाँ दी गई हैं। यथावश्यक रूप से प्रविष्टियों को ब्रिटिश/अमेरिकी अंग्रेज़ी, औपचारिक/अनौपचारिक, अपभाषा, प्राचीन प्रयोग आदि तथा संबंधित ज्ञानक्षेत्रों के लेबल दिए गए हैं।

शब्दकोश के हिंदी खंड में इस बात पर बल रहा है कि हिंदी भाषा की सहजता, स्वाभाविकता, उपयुक्तता, सम्प्रेषकता आदि के साथ उसकी 'आधुनिकता' का संरक्षण हो, और भाषासौष्ठव को सुरक्षित रखते हुए उसमें पारंपरिकता और खुलेपन का संतुलन बना रहे।

आशा है, अधुनातन युक्तियों से संपादित यह शब्दकोश प्रयोक्ताओं को अंग्रेज़ी भाषा की शब्दवली के संवर्धन, बोधन के परिमार्जन, और अभिव्यक्ति के संपोषण में सहायक होगा। कोश को अधिक उपयोगी बनाने के सुझावों का सदैव स्वागत है।

**सुरेश कुमार**

**रमानाथ सहाय**

# प्रयोग विधि

शीर्षशब्द अंग्रेज़ी में स्थूल अक्षरों में दिए गए हैं।

जहाँ **अमेरिकन वर्तनी** में भिन्नता मिलती है वहाँ कोष्ठक में *AmE* संकेत के बाद अमेरिकन वर्तनी दी गई है।

**paediatrics** (*AmE* **pediatrics**) /ˌpiːdiˈætrɪks ˌपीडिˈऐट्रिक्स् / *noun* [U] the area of medicine connected with the diseases of children चिकित्सा-शास्त्र का वह क्षेत्र जिसका संबंध बाल-रोगों से है ▶ **paediatric** (*AmE* **pediatric**) *adj.* बाल-चिकित्सा संबंधी

**शीर्षशब्द** सामान्यतया छोटे अक्षर से शुरू होते हैं किंतु व्यक्तिवाचक संज्ञा के रूप में आए शीर्षशब्द बड़े अक्षर से शुरू होते हैं।

**Parkinson's disease** /ˈpɑːkɪnsnz dɪziːz पाकिन्सन्ज़् डिज़ीज़् / *noun* [U] a disease that gets worse over a period of time and causes the muscles to become weak and the arms and legs to shake मांसपेशियों के दुर्बल हो जाने के कारण अंगों के काँपने का रोग; काँपा, कँपनी, झूलन रोग, पार्किसन्स डिज़ीज़

कहीं-कहीं **शीर्षशब्द** के ठीक ऊपर **1, 2** आदि लगे हुए मिलेंगे। इसका तात्पर्य यह है कि लिपि के अनुसार ये शब्द एक-से दिखाई पड़ते हैं किंतु उच्चारण या/और अर्थ की दृष्टि से वे भिन्न हैं।

कुछ शीर्षशब्द एक से ज़्यादा **शब्दभेदों** के रूप में प्रयुक्त होते हैं। यदि इनका विस्तृत विवरण देने से प्रविष्टि का आकार बहुत बड़ा हो जाता है तो इन शब्दभेदों को अलग-अलग प्रविष्टियाँ बना दी गई हैं और इन्हें संख्यांकित किया गया है।

**page**[1] /peɪdʒ पेज् / *noun* [C] **1** (*abbr.* **p**) one or both sides of a piece of paper in a book, magazine, etc. किसी पुस्तक, पत्रिका आदि का पन्ना; पृष्ठ *The letter was three pages long.* ○ ***the front page*** *of a newspaper* **2** (*computing*) a section of data or information that can be shown on a computer screen at any one time डाटा या सूचना का एक खंड जो किसी एक समय में कंप्यूटर के परदे पर प्रदर्शित किया जा सकता है ➪ **home page** देखिए।

**page**[2] /peɪdʒ पेज् / *verb* [T] to call sb by sending a message to a small machine (**a pager**) that sb carries, or by calling sb's name publicly through a device fixed to the wall (**a loudspeaker**) एक छोटी मशीन (पेजर) के माध्यम से किसी व्यक्ति को संदेश भेजकर बुलाना या उसके नाम से दीवार पर लगे लाउडस्पीकर द्वारा पुकारना

कुछ अंग्रेज़ी शब्दों के एक से ज़्यादा **रूप** या **वर्तनी** हो सकते हैं। सामान्य तौर पर प्रयुक्त होने वाला रूप/वर्तनी शीर्षशब्द बनाया गया है। अतिरिक्त रूप/वर्तनी कोष्ठक में दिए गए हैं।

**postbox** /ˈpəʊstbɒks पोस्ट्बॉक्स् / (*also* **letter box**, *AmE* **mailbox**) *noun* [C] a box in a public place where you put letters, etc. that you want to send पत्र पेटी (जिसमें भेजने-योग्य पत्र आदि डाले जाते हैं); लेटर बॉक्स ➪ **pillar box** देखिए।

**शीर्षशब्द** के ठीक बाद दो तिर्यक रेखाओं के बीच **उच्चारण** अंग्रेज़ी एवं देवनागरी लिपियों में दिया गया है।

**उच्चारण** की भिन्नताओं को कोष्ठक में दिया गया है। उच्चारण शैली में प्रयुक्त चिह्नों की पूर्ण सूची पृष्ठ xiii पर दी गई है।

**postman** /ˈpəʊstmən ˈपोस्ट्मन् / (*AmE* **mail man**) *noun* [C] (*pl.* **-men** /-mən -मन् /) a person whose job is to collect letters, packages, etc. and take them to people's houses डाकिया, चिट्ठीरसाँ, पत्रवाहक

उच्चारण के तुरंत बाद शब्द की व्याकरणिक कोटि (*noun, adj. prep.* आदि) का उल्लेख अंग्रेज़ी में तिर्यक अक्षरों में दिया गया है।

संज्ञा के गणनीय या अगणनीय रूप कोष्ठक में [C], [U] दिए गए हैं।

**patriarchy** /ˈpeɪtriɑːki ˈपेट्रिआकि / *noun* [C, U] (*pl.* **patriarchies**) a social system that gives power and control to men rather than women पितृतंत्र; पुरुष-प्रधान सामाजिक व्यवस्था ➪ **matriarchy** देखिए।

रूप-रचना में संज्ञा के अनियमित रूप कोष्ठक में दिए गए हैं।

**fiancé** (*feminine* **fiancée**) /fiˈɒnseɪ फ़िˈऑनसे / *noun* [C] a person who has promised to marry sb मँगेर या मँगेतर, वाग्दत्त या वाग्दत्ता *This is my fiancé Prem. We got engaged a few weeks ago.*

कुछ संज्ञाओं के स्त्रीलिंग/पुलिंग कोष्ठक में दिए गए हैं।

कहीं-कहीं संज्ञा के बाद [*sing.*] या [*pl.*] दिया गया है; इसका अर्थ यह है कि यह शब्द केवल एकवचन या बहुवचन में प्रयोग योग्य है।

**the Roman alphabet** *noun* [*sing.*] the letters A to Z, used especially in Western European languages, A से B तक रोमन वर्णमाला (विशेषतः पश्चिमी यूरोप की भाषाओं में प्रयुक्त)

क्रिया की वर्तनी में जहाँ अंतिम व्यंजन का द्वित्व होता है वहाँ कोष्ठक में संकेत दिया गया है।

क्रिया के सकर्मक या अकर्मक रूप कोष्ठक में [T], [I] दिए गए हैं।

**run**[1] /rʌn रन् / *verb* [I, T] (*pres. part.* **running**; *pt* **ran** /ræn रैन् /; *pp* **run**) **1** [I, T] to move using your legs, going faster than a walk दौड़ना (टाँगों के सहारे, चलने से अधिक तेज़, गति करना) *I had to run to catch the bus.* ○ *I often* ***go running*** *in the evenings* (= as a hobby). ○ *I ran nearly ten kilometres this morning.*

क्रिया के विभिन्न कालों के द्योतक शब्दों को अंग्रेज़ी एवं हिंदी उच्चारण समेत, कोष्ठक में *pres. part., pt, pp* आदि संकेतों के बाद दिया गया है।

कुछ शब्दभेदों का **संक्षिप्त रूप** दिया गया है। संक्षिप्त रूपों का पूर्ण रूप संक्षिप्ति सूची में पृष्ठ xvii पर दिया गया है।

**rosy** /ˈrəʊzi ˈरोज़ि / *adj.* (**rosier; rosiest**) **1** pink and pleasant in appearance गुलाबी और देखने में सुंदर *rosy cheeks* **2** full of good possibilities अनुकूल संभावनाओं से परिपूर्ण; उज्जवल *The future was looking rosy.*

विशेषण के तुलनात्मक और उत्तमावस्था रूप कोष्ठक में दिए गए हैं।

**व्याकरण से संबंधित** अन्य जानकारी व्याकरणिक कोटि के बाद तिर्यक अक्षरों में कोष्ठक में दिए गए हैं।

**rogue** /rəʊg रोग् / *adj.* (*only before a noun*) behaving differently from other similar people or things, often causing damage अपने सदृश व्यक्तियों या वस्तुओं से भिन्न आचरण करने वाला और प्रायः नुक़सानदेह *a rogue gene/program*

**विषय-लेबल** शब्द के विशिष्ट अर्थ के प्रयोग या व्यवहार क्षेत्र को दर्शाते हैं। ये लेबल शब्द के अर्थ से पहले संक्षिप्त या पूर्ण रूप में तिर्यक अक्षरों में, कोष्ठक में दिए गए हैं। पूर्ण लेबल सूची के लिए पृष्ठ xv देखिए।

**modular** /ˈmɒdjələ(r) ˈमॉड्यल(र्) / *adj.* (*technical*) (used about machines, buildings, etc.) consisting of separate parts or units that can be joined together (यंत्र, भवन आदि) जिसमें अनेक स्वतंत्र भाग या इकाइयाँ हों जिन्हें आवश्यकतानुसार जोड़ा जा सके

अर्थ को अंग्रेज़ी एवं हिंदी में अनेक शब्दों या वाक्यों से समझाया गया है।

**rosary** /ˈrəʊzəri ˈरोज़रि / *noun* [C] (*pl.* **rosaries**) a string of small round pieces of wood, etc. used by some Roman Catholics for counting prayers सुमिरनी, जयमाला (लकड़ी आदि के दानों की माला जिससे भक्त लोग प्रार्थनाओं की गिनती करते हैं)

प्रायः अर्थ को अधिक स्पष्ट करने के लिए कोष्ठक में अतिरिक्त जानकारी दी गई है।

एक शब्द में अर्थ तभी व्यक्त किया गया है जब उसकी अर्थछाया बिलकुल अंग्रेज़ी शब्द की अर्थछाया से मिलती हो।

**mixture** /ˈmɪkstʃə(r) ˈमिक्स्च(र्) / *noun* **1** [*sing.*] a combination of different things विभिन्न वस्तुओं का मिश्रण *Monkeys eat a mixture of leaves and fruit.* **2** [C, U] a substance that is made by mixing other substances together अनेक वस्तुओं को परस्पर मिलाकर बनाई गई एक वस्तु; मिश्रण *cake mixture ○ a mixture of eggs, flour and milk*

एक ही शब्द के एक से अधिक अर्थ हो सकते हैं। ऐसी स्थिति में अर्थों को 1, 2, 3 आदि संख्याएँ लगाकर पृथक किया गया है।

अर्थों को अधिकतर समुपयुक्त अंग्रेज़ी **उदाहरणों** से स्पष्ट किया गया है। उदाहरणों का मुद्रण तिर्यक अक्षरों में किया गया है। दो या ज़्यादा उदाहरणों को ○ चिह्न द्वारा अलग किया गया है।

**root²** /ruːt रूट् / *verb*

**PHR V** **root about/around (for sth)** to search for sth by moving things सामान इधर-उधर फैलाते हुए कुछ ढूँढ़ना *What are you rooting around in my desk for?*

**parenthesis** /pəˈrenθəsɪs पˈरेन्थसिस् / *noun*

**IDM** **in parenthesis** as an extra comment or piece of information अतिरिक्त टिप्पणी या सूचना के रूप में अंकित

शीर्षशब्द से संबंधित **उपवाक्यों**, **पदबंद क्रियाओं**, **मुहावरों** आदि को **PHR V**, **IDM** आदि संकेतों के बाद स्थूल वर्णरूप में दिया गया है।

**rot** /rɒt रॉट् / *verb* [I, T] (**ro*tt*ing; ro*tt*ed**) to go bad or make sth go bad as part of a natural process (किस चीज़) का सड़ना या ख़राब होना या को सड़ाना या ख़राब करना (प्राकृतिक प्रक्रिया के अंतर्गत) *Too many sweets will rot your teeth!* ✪ पर्याय **decay** ▶ **rot** *noun* [U] सड़न, विगलन

शीर्षशब्द से **संबंधित विलोम तथा पर्यायवाची** शब्दों को ✪ चिह्न के बाद स्थूल अक्षरों में दिया गया है।

शीर्षशब्द से व्युत्पन्न (प्रत्ययजनित) अथवा समासजनित शब्द, **उपशीर्ष शब्द** के रूप में ▶ चिह्न के बाद स्थूल अक्षरों में दिए गए हैं।

**patriot** /ˈpeɪtriət ˈपेट्रिअट् / *noun* [C] a person who loves his/her country and is ready to defend it against an enemy देशभक्त, राष्ट्रप्रेमी ▶ **patriotism** /ˈpeɪtriətɪzəm; ˈpæt- ˈपेट्रिअटिज़म्; ˈपैट्- / *noun* [U] देशभक्ति, राष्ट्रप्रेम

आवश्यकता पड़ने पर **उपशीर्षशब्द** के उच्चारण, उच्चारणभेद, वर्तनीभेद, व्याकरण, प्रयोग क्षेत्र आदि की सूचना शीर्षशब्द के समान दी गई है।

**patriotic** /ˌpeɪtriˈɒtɪk; ˌpæt-ˌपेट्रिˈऑटिक्; ˈपैट्- / *adj.* having or showing great love for your country देशभक्तिपूर्ण; राष्ट्रप्रेम से युक्त ▶ **patriotically** /-kli -कलि / *adv.* देशभक्ति के भाव से

**patio** /ˈpætiəʊ ˈपैटिओ / *noun* [C] (*pl.* **patios** /-əʊz -ओज़् /) a flat, hard area, usually behind a house, where people can sit, eat, etc. outside मकान के पीछे बना पक्का स्थान (जहाँ लोग खुले में उठ-बैठ, खा-पी सकते हैं) ➪ **balcony, verandah** और **terrace** देखिए।

शीर्षशब्द से संबंधित **अन्योन्य संदर्भ शब्दों** को ➪ चिह्न के बाद स्थूल अक्षरों में दिए गए हैं।

**pain**[1] /peɪn पेन् / *noun* **1** [C, U] the unpleasant feeling that you have when a part of your body has been hurt or when you are ill शरीर के किसी अंग पर चोट या किसी रोग से पीड़ित होने के कारण उत्पन्न दर्द; पीड़ा, वेदना *to* ***be in pain*** ○ *He screamed with pain.*

इन टिप्पणियों में शीर्षशब्द से संबंधित शब्दों के विभिन्न एवं सही प्रयोग को दर्शाया गया है।

शीर्षशब्द से संबंधित विभिन्न शब्दों पर **टिप्पणियाँ** NOTE संकेत के बाद स्क्रीन कोष्ठ में दी गई हैं।

NOTE एक दीर्घकालिक निरंतर दर्द के लिए शब्द **ache** का तथा अचानक हुए लघुकालिक तीव्र दर्दों के लिए शब्द **pain** का प्रयोग करते हैं। इसलिए हम सामान्यतया कहते हैं—*I've got earache/backache/toothache/a headache* किंतु—*He was admitted to hospital with pains in his chest.*

**possess** /pəˈzes पˈज़ेस् / *verb* [T] (*not used in the continuous tenses*) **1** (*formal*) to have or own sth किसी वस्तु को अधिकार में रखना या उस पर स्वामित्व होना *They lost everything they possessed in the fire.* ○ *Parul possesses a natural ability to make people laugh.* **2** to influence sb or to make sb do sth किसी के मन-मस्तिष्क को प्रभावित कर लेना या उसे कुछ करने के लिए मजबूर करना *What possessed you to say a thing like that!*

**व्याकरणिक टिप्पणियों** में उदाहरणों के द्वारा शब्दों के सही प्रयोगों को तिर्यक अक्षरों में दिखाया गया है।

**व्याकरण से संबंधित जानकारी** भी विस्तृत रूप से इन टिप्पणियों में दी गई हैं।

NOTE यद्यपि यह क्रिया सातत्यबोधक कालों (continuous tenses) में प्रयुक्त नहीं होती तथापि इसका (-ing युक्त) वर्तमान कृदंत (present participle) रूप काफ़ी प्रचलित है—*Any student possessing the necessary qualifications will be considered for the course.*

इस शब्दकोश में 200 से अधिक नामांकित चित्र दिए गए हैं।

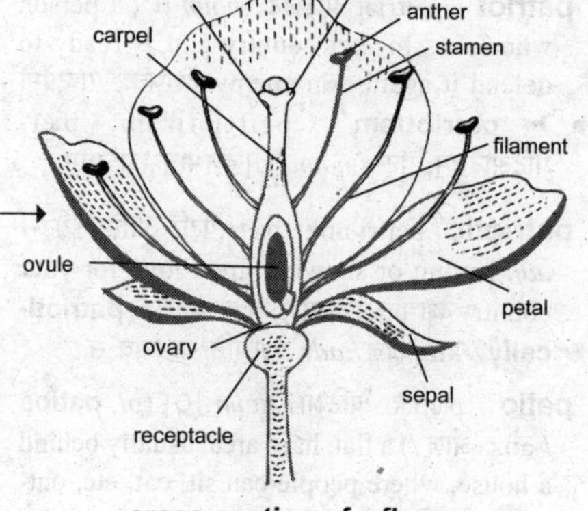


**cross-section of a flower**

नामांकित चित्रों द्वारा शब्दों के अर्थ को भली प्रकार चित्रित किया गया है, जिससे अर्थ स्पष्ट होता है।

# उच्चारण शैली

इस शब्दकोश में दी गई उच्चारण शैली International Phonetic Alphabet (IPA) शैली पर आधारित है। इस शैली में प्रत्येक ध्वनि के लिए एक विशेष चिह्न का प्रयोग किया जाता है। इन चिह्नों को देवनागरी लिपि में यथासंभव समान शैली में दिया गया है और इनकी विस्तृत सूची निम्नलिखित है–

**Consonants**

| IPA* symbol | Usage | Hindi symbol | Usage |
|---|---|---|---|
| p | cap /kæp/ | प् | / कैप् / |
| b | rub /rʌb/ | ब् | / रब् / |
| t | fit /fɪt/ | ट् | / फ़िट् / |
| d | red /red/ | ड् | / रेड् / |
| k | break /breɪk/ | क् | / ब्रेक् / |
| g | flag /flæg/ | ग् | / फ़्लैग् / |
| tʃ | rich /rɪtʃ/ | च् | / रिच् / |
| dʒ | badge /bædʒ/ | ज् | / बैज् / |
| f | life /laɪf/ | फ़् | / लाइफ़् / |
| v | wave /weɪv/ | व् | / वेव् / |
| θ | myth /mɪθ/ | थ़् | / मिथ़् / |
| δ | bathe /beɪδ/ | द़् | / बेद़् / |
| s | fuss /fʌs/ | स् | / फ़स् / |
| z | railings /ˈraɪlɪŋz/ | ज़् | / ˈरेलिङ्ज़् / |
| ʃ | fish /fɪʃ/ | श् | / फ़िश् / |
| ʒ | vision /ˈvɪʒn/ | श़् | / ˈविश़न् / |
| h | hat /hæt/ | ह | / हैट् / |
| m | fame /feɪm/ | म् | / फ़ेम् / |
| n | fin /fɪn/ | न् | / फ़िन् / |
| ŋ | ring /rɪŋ/ | ङ् | / रिङ् / |
| l | file /faɪl/ | ल् | / फ़ाइल् / |
| r | run /rʌn/ | र | / रन् / |
| (r) | for /fɔ:(r)/ | ऱ् | / फ़ॉ(ऱ्) / |
| j | granular /ˈgrænjələ(r)/ | य | / ˈग्रैन्यल(ऱ्) / |
| w | won /wʌn/ | व | / वन् / |

**Vowels and dipthongs**

| | | | |
|---|---|---|---|
| i | happy /hæpi/ | इ / ि | / हैपि / |
| ɪ | fig /fɪg/ | इ / ि | / फ़िग् / |
| i: | see /si:/ | ई / ी | / सी / |
| e | ten /ten/ | ए / े | / टेन् / |
| æ | cat /kæt/ | ऐ / ै | / कैट् / |
| ɑ: | far /fɑ:(r)/ | आ / ा | / फ़ार् / |
| ɒ | lot /lɒt/ | ऑ / ॉ | / लॉट् / |

| | | | |
|---|---|---|---|
| ɒ̃ | croissant /ˈkrwæsɒ̃/ | आ / ँ | /ˈक्रवैसाँ / |
| ɔ: | saw /sɔ:/ | ऑ / ॉ | / सॉ / |
| ʊ | put /pʊt/ | उ / ु | / पुट् / |
| u | actual /ˈæktʃuəl/ | उ / ु | /ˈऐक्चुअल् / |
| u: | too /tu:/ | ऊ / ू | / टू / |
| ʌ | cut /kʌt/ | अ | / कट् / |
| ɜ: | bird /bɜ:d/ | अ | / बड् / |
| ə | about; paper /ə'baʊt; 'peɪpə(r)/ | अ | / अ'बाउट्; 'पेप(र्) / |
| eɪ | fade /feɪd/ | ए / े | / फ़ेड् / |
| əʊ | go /gəʊ/ | ओ / ो | / गो / |
| aɪ | five /faɪv/ | आ + इ / ा + इ | / फ़ाइव् / |
| ɔɪ | boy /bɔɪ/ | ऑ + इ / ॉ + इ | / बॉइ / |
| aʊ | now /naʊ/ | आ + उ / ा + उ | / नाउ / |
| ɪə | near /nɪə(r)/ | इ + अ / ि + अ | / निअ(र्) / |
| eə | chair /tʃeə(r)/ | ए + अ / े + अ | / चेअ(र्) / |
| ʊə | pure /pjʊə(r) / | उ + अ / ु + अ | / प्युअ(र्) / |

**स्वराघात**

|ˈ| इस चिह्न के बाद आने वाले अक्षर-समूह (syllable) पर अधिक स्वराघात डाला जाता है। उदाहरण के लिए, शब्द **repeat** /rɪˈpi:t रिˈपीट् / में दूसरे अक्षर-समूह /ˈpi:t ˈपीट् / पर स्वाराघात आता है जबकि **rigid** /ˈrɪdʒɪd ˈरिजिड् / में पहले अक्षर-समूह (ˈrɪ ˈरि) पर स्वराघात आता है।

|ˌ| इस चिह्न के बाद बोले जाने वाले अक्षर-समूह पर अन्य अक्षर-समूहों से अधिक स्वाराघात डाला जाता है, परंतु उतना नहीं जितना |ˈ| के बाद बोले जाने वाले अक्षर-समूह पर डाला जाता है। उदाहरण के लिए, शब्द **residential** /ˌrezɪˈdenʃl ˌरेज़िˈडेन्शल् / में प्राथमिक स्वराघात दूसरे अक्षर-समूह (ˈden ˈडेन्) और गौण स्वराघात पहले अक्षर-समूह (ˌre ˌरे) पर डाला जाता है।

# लेबल सूची

| | |
|---|---|
| *also* | भी |
| *abbr.* | संक्षिप्त रूप |
| *chemistry* | रसायन शास्त्र |
| *compounds* | यौगिक शब्द |
| *computing* | कंप्यूटर विज्ञान |
| *exclamation* | विस्मयादिबोधक शब्द |
| *feminine* | स्त्रीलिंग |
| *figurative* | अलंकारिक |
| *formal* | औपचारिक |
| *geography* | भूगोल |
| *geology* | भूविज्ञान |
| *geometry* | रेखा गणित |
| *grammar* | व्याकरण |
| *humorous* | हास्यकर |
| *informal* | अनौपचारिक |
| *law* | क़ानूनी प्रयोग |
| *literary* | साहित्यिक |
| *mathematics* | गणित |
| *medical* | चिकित्सा |
| *music* | संगीत |
| *official* | आधिकारिक |
| *philosophy* | दर्शन शास्त्र |
| *slang* | अपभाषा |
| *spoken* | मौखिक |
| *symbol* | प्रतीक |
| *technical* | तकनीकी |
| *written* | लिखित |
| IDM (idiom) | मुहावरा |
| NOTE | टिप्पणी |
| PHR V (phrasal verb) | पदबंधीय क्रिया |

# व्याकरणिक कोटि

| | |
|---|---|
| active | कर्तृवाच्य |
| adjective | विशेषण |
| adverb | क्रियाविशेषण |
| auxiliary verb | सहायक क्रिया |
| comparative | तुलनापरक |
| conjunction | समुच्चयबोधक शब्द |
| continuous tense | सातत्यबोधक काल |
| countable noun | गणनीय संज्ञा |
| definite article | निश्चायक आर्टिकल (उपपद) |
| determiner | निर्धारक |
| direct object | प्रत्यक्ष कर्म |
| indefinite article | अनिश्चायक आर्टिकल |
| indirect object | अप्रत्यक्ष कर्म |
| infinitive | क्रियार्थक/संज्ञार्थक |
| intransitive verb | अकर्मक क्रिया |
| linking verb | संयोजक क्रिया |
| modal verb | वृत्तिवाचक क्रिया |
| negative | निषेधात्मक/निषेधवाचक |
| noun | संज्ञा |
| passive | कर्मवाच्य |
| past participle | भूत कृदंत |
| perfect tense | पूर्णताबोधक काल |
| past tense | भूतकाल |
| plural | बहुवचन |
| preposition | पूर्वसर्ग |
| present participle | वर्तमान कृदंत |
| positive | सकारात्मक |
| question | प्रश्न |
| short form | संक्षिप्त रूप |
| singular | एकवचन |
| strong form | प्रबल रूप |
| superlative | उत्तमावस्था |
| third person singular | अन्य पुरुष (एकवचन) |
| uncountable noun | अगणनीय संज्ञा |
| verb | क्रिया |

# संक्षिप्तियाँ

| | | |
|---|---|---|
| *abbr.* | abbreviation | संक्षिप्ति |
| *adj.* | adjective | विशेषण |
| *adv.* | adverb | क्रियाविशेषण |
| *AmE* | American English | अमेरिकी अंग्रेज़ी |
| *BrE* | British English | ब्रिटिश अंग्रेज़ी |
| [C] | countable noun | गणनीय संज्ञा |
| *conj.* | conjunction | समुच्चयबोधक शब्द |
| *det.* | determiner | निर्धारक |
| [I] | intransitive verb | अकर्मक क्रिया |
| *IndE* | Indian English | भारतीय अंग्रेज़ी |
| *pl.* | plural | बहुवचन |
| *pp* | past participle | भूत कृदंत |
| *pres. part.* | present participle | वर्तमान कृदंत |
| *pt* | past tense | भूतकाल |
| *prep.* | preposition | पूर्वसर्ग |
| sb | somebody | कोई (व्यक्ति) |
| sth | something | कुछ (वस्तु) |
| *3rd person sing.* | third person singular | अन्य पुरुष (एकवचन) |
| *sing.* | singular | एकवचनांत संज्ञा |
| [T] | transitive verb | सकर्मक क्रिया |
| TM | trade mark | ट्रेडमार्क |
| [U] | uncountable noun | अगणनीय संज्ञा |

# A a

**A, a**[1] /eɪ ए/ *noun* [C, U] (*pl.* **A's; a's** /eɪz एज़्/) **1** the first letter of the English alphabet अंग्रेज़ी वर्णमाला का पहला अक्षर, *'Anjali' begins with an 'A'.* **2** the highest mark given for an exam or piece of work किसी परीक्षा या कार्य के लिए दी जाने वाली उच्चतम श्रेणी *I got an 'A' for my essay.*

IDM **from A to B** from one place to another एक स्थान से दूसरे स्थान तक *All I need is a car that gets me from A to B.*

**a**[2] /ə; *strong form* eɪ अ; प्रबल रूप ए/ (*also* **an** /ən; *strong form* æn अन्; प्रबल रूप ऐन् /) *indefinite article*

NOTE **An** का प्रयोग स्वर ध्वनि के पूर्व किया जाता है।

**1** one एक *A cup of coffee, please.* ○ *We've got an apple, a banana and two oranges.* **2** used when you talk about one example of sth for the first time पहली बार किसी वस्तु या प्राणी के उल्लेख में प्रयुक्त *I saw a dog chasing a cat this morning.* ○ *Have you got a dictionary* (= any dictionary)? **3** used for saying what kind of person or thing sb/sth is किसी व्यक्ति या वस्तु के वर्ग की सदस्यता दर्शाने के लिए प्रयुक्त *He's a doctor.* ○ *'Is that an eagle?' 'No, it's a falcon.'* **4** (used with prices, rates, measurements) each (क़ीमतें, दरें और माप तोल बताने वाले प्रत्येक शब्द के साथ प्रयुक्त) प्रत्येक *I usually drink two litres of water a day.* ○ *twice a week* ○ *80 kilometres an hour.* **5** used with some expressions of quantity मात्रा या संख्या बताने वाले कुछ शब्दों के साथ प्रयुक्त *a lot of money* ○ *a few cars* **6** used when you are talking about a typical example of sth किसी वस्तु के प्रतिनिधि उदाहरण के उल्लेख के लिए प्रयुक्त *An elephant can live for up to eighty years.*

NOTE इस अर्थ के लिए बहुवचन रूप भी प्रयुक्त किया जा सकता है—*Elephants can live for up to eighty years.*

> NOTE Indefinite article के विषय में अधिक जानकारी के लिए इस शब्दकोश के अंत में **Quick Grammar Reference** देखिए।

**a-** /eɪ ए/ *prefix* (*in nouns, adjectives and adverbs*) not; without नहीं; के बिना *atheist* ○ *amoral*

**aback** /əˈbæk अˈबैक्/ *adv.*

PHR V **take sb aback** ➪ **take** देखिए।

**abacus** /ˈæbəkəs ˈऐबकस्/ *noun* [C] (*pl.* **abacuses**) a frame containing wires with small balls that move along them. It is used for counting एक ऐसा चौखटा जिसमें तार लगे होते हैं और उन तारों पर गोलियाँ घूमती हैं। यह चौखटा गिनने के काम में आता है; गिनतारा

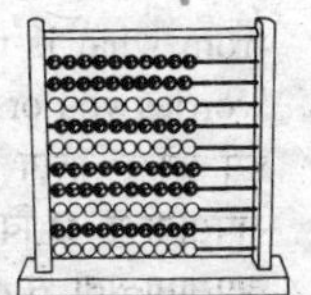

**abandon** /əˈbændən अˈबैन्डन् / *verb* [T] **1** to leave sb/sth that you are responsible for, usually permanently किसी प्राणी या वस्तु को, जिस का उत्तरदायित्व आप पर है, प्रायः सदा के लिए छोड़ देना *The bank robbers abandoned the car just outside the city.* **2** to stop doing sth without finishing it or without achieving what you wanted to do किसी काम को अधूरा या उद्देश्य प्राप्त किए बिना बीच में ही रोक देना *The search for the missing sailors was abandoned after two days.* ▶ **abandonment** *noun* [U] परित्याग

**abandoned** /əˈbændəned अˈबैन्डन्ड् / *adj.* left completely and no longer used or wanted अनचाही वस्तु को पूर्ण रूप से त्यागा या छोड़ा हुआ; परित्यक्त *an abandoned ship*

**abashed** /əˈbæʃt अˈबैश्ट् / *adj.* feeling guilty and embarrassed because of sth that you have done किए पर लज्जित व शर्मिंदा *'I'm sorry,' said Ali, looking abashed.*

**abate** /əˈbeɪt अˈबेट् / *verb* [I, T] to become less strong; to make sth less strong प्रकोप या प्रभाव का कम हो जाना या कम करना

**abattoir** /ˈæbətwɑː(r) ˈऐबट्वा(र्) / (*BrE*) = **slaughterhouse**

**abbess** /ˈæbes ˈऐबेस् / *noun* [C] a woman who is the head of a religious community for **nuns** ईसाई या धार्मिक साध्वी-समाज की प्रमुख (महिला)

**abbey** /ˈæbi ˈऐबि / *noun* [C] a large church together with a group of buildings where religious communities of **monks** or **nuns** live or used to live अनेक भवनों वाला बड़ा गिरजाघर जहाँ साधु-समाज और साध्वी समाज के सदस्य रहते हैं या कभी रहते थे

**abbot** /ˈæbət ˈऐबट् / *noun* [C] a man who is the head of a religious community for **monks** विशेषतः ईसाई धार्मिक साधु-समाज का प्रमुख (पुरुष)

**abbr.** (*also* **abbrev.**) *abbr.* = **abbreviation**

**abbreviate** /əˈbriːvieɪt अˈब्रीविएट् / *verb* [T] to make sth shorter, especially a word or phrase किसी शब्द या पदबंध को संक्षिप्त करना *'Kilometre' is usually abbreviated to 'km'.* ➪ **abridge** देखिए।

**abbreviation** /əˌbriːviˈeɪʃn अˌब्रीविˈएशन् / *noun* [C] a short form of a word or phrase किसी शब्द या पदबंध का संक्षिप्त रूप *In this dictionary 'sth' is the abbreviation for 'something'.*

**ABC** /ˌeɪ biː ˈsiː ˌए बी ˈसी / *noun* [*sing.*] **1** the alphabet; the letters of English from A to Z वर्णमाला; अंग्रेज़ी भाषा के A से Z तक वर्ण या अक्षर **2** the simple facts about sth किसी विषय के बारे में साधारण जानकारी या तथ्य *an ABC of Gardening*

**abdicate** /ˈæbdɪkeɪt ˈऐब्डिकेट् / *verb* **1** [I] to give up being King or Queen सम्राट या साम्राज्ञी के पद का त्याग करना *The Queen abdicated in favour of her son* (= her son became king). **2** [T] to give sth up, especially power or a position त्याग करना, विशेषतः अधिकार या पद का *to **abdicate responsibility*** (= to refuse to be responsible for sth) ▶ **abdication** /ˌæbdɪˈkeɪʃn ˌऐब्डिˈकेशन् / *noun* [C, U] पद या सत्ता का त्याग

**abdomen** /ˈæbdəmən ˈऐब्डमन् / *noun* [C] **1** a part of your body below the chest that contains the stomach, **bowels**, etc. छाती से नीचे का वह भाग जिसमें आमाशय (पेट) और आँतें होती हैं; उदर **2** the end part of an insect's body कीट के शरीर का पिछला भाग ➪ **thorax** देखिए। ▶ **abdominal** /æbˈdɒmɪnl ऐब्ˈडॉमिनल् / *adj.* उदरीय

**abduct** /æbˈdʌkt ऐब् ˈडक्ट् / *verb* [T] to take hold of sb and take him/her away illegally किसी को पकड़कर ग़ैर-क़ानूनी रूप से ले जाना; अपहरण करना ▶ **abduction** *noun* [C, U] अपहरण

**aberration** /ˌæbəˈreɪʃn ˌऐबˈरेशन् / *noun* [C, U] (*formal*) a fact, an action or a way of behaving that is not typical, and that may be unacceptable कोई तथ्य, कार्य या व्यवहार जो सामान्य से हटकर हो और जो अस्वीकार्य हो सकता हो

**abet** /əˈbet अˈबेट् / *verb* [T] (**abetting; abetted**) IDM **aid and abet** ➪ **aid**[2] देखिए।

**abhinaya** *noun* [U] (in Indian classical dance) the presentation of dramatic action silently through gestures and expressions (भारतीय शास्त्रीय नृत्य में) मूक हावभावों की नाटकीय प्रस्तुति *Even after so many years of performance his abhinaya lacks maturity.*

**abhor** /əbˈhɔː(r) अब्ˈहॉ(र्)/ *verb* [T] (**abhorring; abhorred**) to hate sth very much अत्यधिक घृणा करना

**abhorrence** /əbˈhɒrəns अब्ˈहॉरन्स् / *noun* [U] a strong feeling of hate; disgust घृणा की प्रबल भावना, जुगुप्सा

**abhorrent** /əbˈhɒrənt अब्ˈहॉरन्ट् / *adj.* that makes you feel hate or disgust घृणा या जुगुप्सा को उत्पन्न करने वाला *The idea of slavery is **abhorrent to** us nowadays.*

**abide** /əˈbaɪd अˈबाइड् / *verb*

IDM **can't/couldn't abide sb/sth/doing sth** to hate sb/sth; to not like sb/sth at all किसी व्यक्ति या वस्तु से घृणा करना; बिल्कुल ही पसंद न करना

PHR V **abide by sth** to obey a law, etc.; to do what sb has decided क़ानून आदि का पालन करना; निर्णय के अनुसार कार्य करते रहना

**ability** /əˈbɪləti अˈबिलटि/ *noun* [C, U] (*pl.* **abilities**) **(an) ability to do sth** the mental or physical power or skill that makes it possible to do sth किसी कार्य को पूरा करने की मानसिक या शारीरिक शक्ति; योग्यता, क्षमता *an ability to make decisions*

**abject** /ˈæbdʒekt ˈऐब्जेक्ट् / *adj.* **1** terrible and without hope अत्यधिक दयनीय और निराशाजनक *abject poverty/misery/failure* **2** without any pride or respect for yourself स्वाभिमान रहित *an abject apology*

**ablation** /əˈbleɪʃn अˈब्लेशन् / *noun* [U] (*technical*) the loss of material from a large mass of ice, snow or rock as a result of the action of the sun, wind or rain सूर्य, वायु या वर्षा के कारण बर्फ़ या चट्टान के बड़े खंड को पहुँची क्षति; अपक्षरण

**ablaze** /əˈbleɪz अˈब्लेज़् / *adj.* (*not before a noun*) burning strongly; completely on fire तेज़ी से जलता हुआ, पूरी तरह आग की लपेट में *Soldiers used petrol to **set** the building **ablaze**.*

**able** /ˈeɪbl ˈएबल् / *adj.* **1 able to do sth** (*used as a modal verb*) to have the ability, power, opportunity, time, etc. to do sth कुछ करने की योग्यता, शक्ति, अवसर, समय आदि होना *Will you be able to come to a meeting next week?* ○ *I was able to solve the problem quickly.*

> NOTE कर्मवाच्य (passive) में **can/could** का प्रयोग किया जाता है, न कि **able** का—*The arrangement can't be changed.* वृत्तिवाचक क्रियाओं (modal verbs) के विषय में अधिक जानकारी के लिए इस कोश में दिए **Quick Grammar Reference** देखें।

**2** (**abler** /ˈeɪblə(r) ˈएबल(र्) /; **ablest** /ˈeɪblɪst ˈएब्लिस्ट् /) clever; doing your job well चतुर; काम को अच्छे ढंग से करने योग्य *one of the ablest students in the class.* ○ *an able politician* ▶ **ably** /ˈeɪbli ˈएब्लि / *adv.* योग्यता से

**able-bodied** *adj.* physically healthy and strong; having full use of your body शारीरिक रूप से स्वस्थ एवं बलवान; अपने शरीर के पूरे प्रयोग में समर्थ

**abnormal** /æbˈnɔːml ऐब्ˈनॉमल् / *adj.* different from what is normal or usual, in a way that worries you or that is unpleasant सामान्य से कुछ इस प्रकार अलग कि अप्रिय लगे या परेशानी पैदा करे; अपसामान्य ✪ विलोम **normal** ▶ **abnormally** *adv.* अपसामान्यता से *abnormally high temperatures*

**abnormality** /ˌæbnɔːˈmæləti ˌऐब्नॉ ˈमैलटि / *noun* [C, U] (*pl.* **abnormalities**) something that is not normal, especially in a person's body सामान्य से भिन्न वस्तु, अवस्था आदि, विशेषतः शरीर का कोई अंग; असामान्यता *He was born with an abnormality of the heart.*

**aboard** /əˈbɔːd अˈबॉड् / *adv., prep.* on or onto a train, ship, aircraft or bus रेलगाड़ी, जहाज़, विमान या बस पर सवार *We climbed aboard the train and found a seat.* ○ *Welcome aboard this flight to Bangalore.*

**abode** /əˈbəʊd अˈबोड् / *noun* [*sing.*] (*written*) the place where you live घर; आवास; निवास स्थान
IDM **(of) no fixed abode/address** ➪ **fixed** देखिए।

**abolish** /əˈbɒlɪʃ अˈबॉलिश् / *verb* [T] to end a law or system officially किसी क़ानून या प्रथा को आधिकारिक रूप से समाप्त करना *When was capital punishment abolished here?*

**abolition** /ˌæbəˈlɪʃn ˌऐबˈलिश्न् / *noun* [U] the act of ending a law or system officially किसी क़ानून या प्रथा को आधिकारिक रूप से समाप्त करने का कार्य; से उन्मूलन *the abolition of slavery*

**abominable** /əˈbɒmɪnəbl अˈबॉमिनबल् / *adj.* very bad; shocking बहुत बुरा; घिनौना ▶ **abominably** /-əbli -अब्लि / *adv.* घिनौने रूप से

**Aborigine** /ˌæbəˈrɪdʒəni ˌऐबˈरिजनि / *noun* [C] **1** (*usually pl.*) a member of the race of people who were the original inhabitants of a country or region किसी देश या प्रदेश के मूल आदिवासी प्रजाति का सदस्य **2** a member of the race of people who were the original inhabitants of Australia ऑस्ट्रेलिया की मूल आदिवासी प्रजाति का सदस्य; ऑस्ट्रेलिया का मूल निवासी ▶ **aboriginal** *adj.* इन प्रजातियों से संबंधित *aboriginal traditions*

**abort** /əˈbɔːt अˈबॉट् / *verb* [T] **1** to end sth before it is complete किसी कार्य को पूरा होने के पूर्व समाप्त कर देना *The company aborted the project suddenly.* **2** end a pregnancy early in order to prevent a baby from developing and being born alive गर्भपात करवाना; भ्रूणहत्या करना

**abortion** /əˈbɔːʃn अˈबॉश्न् / *noun* [C, U] a medical operation that ends a pregnancy at an early stage गर्भपात कराने के लिए शल्य क्रिया *to have an abortion* ➪ **miscarriage** देखिए।

**abortionist** /əˈbɔːʃənɪst अˈबॉशनिस्ट् / *noun* a person who performs a medical operation, especially illegally, that causes a pregnancy to end earlier सामान्यतया अवैध गर्भपात में लिप्त शल्य चिकित्सक

**abortive** /əˈbɔːtɪv अˈबॉटिव् / *adj.* not completed successfully; failed निष्फल *He made two abortive attempts to escape from prison.*

**abound** /əˈbaʊnd अˈबाउन्ड् / *verb* [I] **1** to exist in large numbers बड़ी संख्या में विद्यमान होना *Animals abound in the forest.* **2 abound with sth** to contain large numbers of sth बड़ी मात्रा में समाए होना *The lake abounds with fish.*

**about**[1] /əˈbaʊt अˈबाउट् / *adv.* **1** (*AmE* **around**) a little more or less than; approximately लगभग *It's about three kilometres from here to the city.* ○ *I got home at about half past seven.* **2** (*informal*) almost; nearly क़रीब-क़रीब, लगभग *Dinner's just about ready.* **3** (*also* **around**) in many directions or places चारों ओर; इधर-उधर *I could hear people moving about upstairs.* ○ *Don't leave your clothes lying about all over the floor.* **4** (*also* **around**) (*used after certain verbs*) without doing anything in particular यों ही, कुछ विशेष न करते हुए *The kids spend most evenings **sitting about** bored.* **5** (*also* **around**) present in a place; existing (किसी स्थान में) उपस्थित; विद्यमान *It was very late and there were few people about.* ○ *There isn't much good music about these days.*
IDM **be about to do sth** to be going to do sth very soon (किसी क्रिया को) आरंभ करने को तैयार *The film's about to start.* ○ *I was just about to explain when she interrupted me.*

**about**[2] /əˈbaʊt अˈबाउट् / *prep.* **1** on the subject of के विषय में, के बारे में, के संबंध में *Let's talk about something else.* ○ *He told me **all about** his family.* **2** (*also* **around**) in many directions or places; in different parts of sth विभिन्न दिशाओं और स्थानों पर; इधर-उधर; यहाँ-वहाँ; किसी वस्तु के विभिन्न भागों में *We wandered about the town for an hour or two.* ○ *Lots of old newspapers were scattered about the room.* **3** in the character of sb/sth किसी व्यक्ति या वस्तु के स्वभाव में *There's something about him that I don't quite trust.*
IDM **how/what about...?** **1** (used when asking for information about sb/sth or for sb's opinion or wish) किसी की राय या इच्छा जानने या किसी से जानकारी माँगने के लिए प्रयुक्त *How about Rani? Have you heard from her lately?* ○ *I'm going to have chicken. What about you?* **2** (used when making a suggestion) (सुझाव देते समय प्रयुक्त) *What about going to a film tonight?*

**about-turn** (*AmE* **about-face**) *noun* [C] a complete change of opinion, plan or behaviour किसी विचार, योजना या व्यवहार में पूर्ण परिवर्तन *The government did an about-turn over tax.* ➪ **U-turn** देखिए।

**above** /ə'bʌv अ'बव़् / *prep., adj., adv.* **1** in a higher place उच्चतर स्थान में; ऊपर *The people in the flat above make a lot of noise.* ○ *The coffee is in the cupboard above the sink.* **2** in an earlier part (of sth written) (लिखित कथन के प्रसंग में) उपर्युक्त, पूर्वोक्त *Contact me at the above address* (= the address above). ✪ विलोम **below** NOTE ध्यान दें कि **below** का प्रयोग noun के पूर्व नहीं किया जाता है— *Contact me at the address below.* **3** more than a number, amount, price, etc किसी संख्या, राशि, क़ीमत आदि से अधिक *children aged 11 and above* ○ *You must get above 50 per cent to pass the exam.* ○ *above-average temperatures* ✪ विलोम **below** ➪ **over** देखिए। **4** with a higher position in an organization, etc. किसी संगठन आदि के उच्चतर पद पर *The person above me is the department manager.* ✪ विलोम **below** **5** too proud to do sth अभिमानवश किसी कार्य को तुच्छ समझना *He seems to think he's above helping with the cleaning.*

IDM **above all** (used to emphasize the main point) most importantly (मुख्य बिंदु पर बल देते समय प्रयुक्त) सर्वाधिक महत्त्वपूर्ण *Above all, stay calm!*

(**be**) **above board** (used especially about a business deal, etc.) honest and open (व्यावसायिक समझौते आदि के संदर्भ में प्रयुक्त) ईमानदार और निष्कपट

**above-mentioned** *adj.* (*only before a noun*) mentioned or named earlier in the same letter, book, etc. पत्र या पुस्तक में पूर्व निर्दिष्ट

**abrasion** /ə'breɪʒn अ'ब्रेश़न् / *noun* (*technical*) **1** [C] a damaged area of the skin where it has been rubbed against sth hard and rough त्वचा का वह भाग जो किसी कड़ी और खुरदरी वस्तु से रगड़ खाकर क्षतिग्रस्त हो गया हो **2** [U] damage to a surface caused by rubbing sth very hard against it किसी कठोर वस्तु से रगड़ खाने पर किसी सतह को पहुँची क्षति; अपघर्षण

**abrasive** /ə'breɪsɪv अ'ब्रेसिव़् / *adj.* **1** rough and likely to scratch खुरदरा और खरोंचदार *Do not use abrasive cleaners on the basin.* **2** (used about a person) rude and rather aggressive (किसी व्यक्ति के लिए प्रयुक्त) रूखा, अशिष्ट और लड़ाका

**abreast** /ə'brest अ'ब्रेस्ट् / *adv.* **abreast (of sb/sth)** next to or level with sb/sth and going in the same direction एक ही दिशा में जाने वाले लोगों या वस्तुओं के अग़ल-बग़ल या ठीक आगे-पीछे *The soldiers marched two abreast.*

IDM **be/keep abreast of sth** to have all the most recent information about sth किसी विषय पर नवीनतम जानकारी रखना

**abridge** /ə'brɪdʒ अ'ब्रिज़् / *verb* [T] to make sth (usually a book) shorter by removing parts of it किसी कथन (प्रायः पुस्तक) को, उसके कुछ अंश हटाकर, छोटा या संक्षिप्त करना ➪ **abbreviate** देखिए।

**abroad** /ə'brɔːd अ'ब्रॉड् / *adv.* in or to another country or countries विदेश में; विदेश को *They found it difficult to get used to living abroad.* ○ *She often **goes abroad** on business.*

**abrupt** /ə'brʌpt अ'ब्रप्ट् / *adj.* **1** sudden and unexpected आकस्मिक और अप्रत्याशित *an abrupt change of plan* **2** seeming rude and unfriendly (व्यवहार) रूखा और अमैत्रीपूर्ण ▶ **abruptly** *adv.* अप्रत्याशित ढंग से; रूखेपन से ▶ **abruptness** *noun* [U] आकस्मिकता

**abscess** /'æbses 'ऐब्सेस् / *noun* [C] a swelling on or in the body, containing a thick yellow liquid (**pus**) व्रण; शरीर के किसी भाग में मवाद भरा फोड़ा

**abscond** /əb'skɒnd अब्'स्कॉन्ड् / *verb* [I] (*formal*) **abscond (from sth) (with sth)** to run away from a place where you should stay, sometimes with sth that you should not take किसी स्थान से फ़रार होना; प्रपलायन करना *to abscond from prison* ○ *She absconded with all the company's money.*

**abseil** /'æbseɪl 'ऐब्सेल् / (*AmE* **rappel**) *verb* [I] to go down a steep cliff or rock while you are fastened to a rope, pushing against the rock with your feet रस्सी से बांधकर और पैरों को चट्टान पर टिकाते हुए सीधी खड़ी चट्टान से नीचे उतरना

**absence** /'æbsəns 'ऐब्सन्स् / *noun* **1** [C, U] a time when sb is away from somewhere; the fact of being away from somewhere किसी स्थान पर अनुपस्थित रहने का समय; किसी स्थान से दूर रहने की बात *Frequent absences due to illness meant he was behind with his work.* ○ *I have to make all the decisions in my boss's absence.* **2** [U] the fact of sth/sb not being there; lack किसी वस्तु या व्यक्ति के किसी स्थान पर न होने का तथ्य; अनुपस्थिति, अभाव, कमी ***In the absence of** a doctor, try to help the injured person yourself.* ✪ विलोम **presence**

**absent** /'æbsənt 'ऐब्सन्ट् / *adj.* **1 absent (from sth)** not present somewhere किसी स्थान पर अनुपस्थित *He was absent from work because of illness.* ✪ विलोम **present** **2** showing that you are not really looking at or thinking about what is happening around you ध्यान में कहीं और होना, अतएव वर्तमान से अनुपस्थित *an absent expression/stare* ▶ **absently** *adv.* बेमन से

**absentee** /ˌæbsən'tiː ˌऐब्सन्'टी / *noun* [C] a person who is not in the place where he/she should be अनुपस्थित या ग़ैर-हाज़िर व्यक्ति

**absenteeism** /ˌæbsən'tiːɪzəm ˌऐब्सन् 'टीइज़म् / *noun* [U] the problem of workers or students often not going to work or school कार्य स्थल या विद्यालय से आदतन अनुपस्थिति

**absent-minded** *adj.* often forgetting or not noticing things, because you are thinking about sth else भुलक्कड़, खोया-खोया; अन्यमनस्क ▸ **absent-mindedly** *adv.* अनमनेपन से

**absolute** /ˈæbsəluːt ˈऐब्सलूट्/ *adj.* **1** complete; total पूरा, समूचा, संपूर्ण *The trip was an absolute disaster.* **2** not measured in comparison with sth else बिना किसी से तुलना किए, स्वतंत्र रूप से; निरपेक्ष *Spending on health services has increased **in absolute terms**.*

**absolutely** *adv.* **1** /ˈæbsəluːtli ˈऐब्सलूट्लि/ completely; totally पूरी तरह से; सर्वथा *It's absolutely freezing outside!* ○ *He made absolutely no effort to help me.* **2** /ˌæbsəˈluːtli ˌऐब्सˈलूट्लि/ (used when you are agreeing with sb) yes; certainly (सहमति दर्शाने के लिए प्रयुक्त) हाँ; निश्चय ही, वाक़ई *'It is a good idea, isn't it?' 'Oh, absolutely!'*

**absolute majority** *noun* [C] (in an election) more than half of the total number of votes or winners (चुनाव में) पूर्ण बहुमत *A total of 280 seats are needed for an absolute majority in the National Assembly.*

**absolute zero** *noun* [U] the lowest temperature that is thought to be possible न्यूनतम संभव तापमान; निरपेक्ष शून्य तापमान; परम शून्य

**absolution** /ˌæbsəˈluːʃn ˌऐब्सˈलूश्न्/ *noun* [U] (especially in the Christian Church) a formal statement that a person is forgiven for what he or she has done wrong (विशेषतः ईसाई समुदाय में) अपराध या पाप करने वाले को क्षमादान की घोषणा

**absolve** /əbˈzɒlv अब्ˈज़ॉल्व्/ *verb* [T] **absolve sb (from/of sth)** to say formally that sb does not have to take responsibility for sth अपराध, पाप, उत्तरदायित्व आदि से मुक्त करना *The driver was absolved of any blame for the train crash.*

**absorb** /əbˈzɔːb; əbˈsɔːb अब्ˈज़ॉब्; अब्ˈसॉब्/ *verb* [T] **1 absorb sth (into sth)** to take in and hold sth (a liquid, heat, etc.) (द्रव पदार्थ, ताप आदि को) अपने में सोख लेना; अवशोषित करना *a drug that is quickly absorbed into the bloodstream* **2** to take sth into the mind and understand it किसी बात को मन में ले लेना और समझना; आत्मसात करना *I found it impossible to absorb so much information so quickly.* **3 absorb sth (into sth)** to take sth into sth larger, so that it becomes part of it अपने में समा लेना; अंतलीन करना *Over the years many villages have been absorbed into the city.* **4** to hold sb's attention completely or interest sb very much किसी के ध्यान या रुचि को आकृष्ट करना; तल्लीन या तन्मय करना *History is a subject that absorbs her.* **5** to reduce the effect of a sudden violent knock, hit, etc. अचानक पहुँचे तीव्र आघात के प्रभाव को कम करना *The front of the car is designed to absorb most of the impact of a crash.*

**absorbed** /əbˈzɔːbd; əbˈsɔːbd अब्ˈज़ॉब्ड्; अब्ˈसॉब्ड्/ *adj.* **absorbed (in sth)** giving all your attention to sth किसी विषय, काम आदि में अपना सारा ध्यान लगाना; तल्लीन हो जाना *He was absorbed in his work and didn't hear me come in.*

**absorbent** /əbˈzɔːbənt; əbˈsɔːbənt अब्ˈज़ॉबन्ट्; अब्ˈसॉबन्ट्/ *adj.* able to take in and hold liquid द्रव को सोख लेने की क्षमता रखते हुए *an absorbent cloth*

**absorbing** /əbˈzɔːbɪŋ; əbˈsɔːbɪŋ अब्ˈज़ॉबिङ्; अब्ˈसाबिङ्/ *adj.* holding all your interest and attention किसी की संपूर्ण रुचि या ध्यान को बनाऐ हुए *an absorbing book*

**absorption** /əbˈsɔːpʃn; -zɔːpʃn अब्ˈसॉप्श्न्; -ज़ॉप्श्न्/ *noun* [U] **1** the process of a liquid, gas or other substance being taken in द्रव, गैस या अन्य पदार्थ के अवशोषित होने की प्रक्रिया *Vitamin D is necessary to aid the absorption of calcium from food.* **2** the process of a smaller group, country, etc., becoming part of a larger group or country किसी छोटे दल, देश आदि का बड़े दल, देश आदि का भाग बनने की प्रक्रिया; अंतर्लयन *the absorption of immigrants into the host country* **3 absorption (in sth)** the fact of sb being very interested in sth so that it takes all his/her attention पूर्णतया तल्लीनता; तन्मयता *His work suffered because of his total absorption in sport.*

**abstain** /əbˈsteɪn अब्ˈस्टेन्/ *verb* [I] **1** *(formal)* **abstain (from sth/doing sth)** to stop yourself from doing sth that you enjoy अपने को संयम में रखना; परहेज़ करना *The doctor said I should abstain from smoking.* ▸ **abstinence** *noun* **2** (in a vote) to say that you are not voting either for or against sth (मतदान में) भाग न लेना; तटस्थ रहना *Two people voted in favour, two voted against and one abstained.* ▸ **abstention** *noun* तटस्थता

**abstainer** /əbˈsteɪnə(r) अब्ˈस्टेन(र्)/ *noun* [C] **1** a person who chooses not to vote either in favour of or against sth (मतदान में) मत न देने वाला व्यक्ति **2** a person who never drinks alcohol मदिरा से परहेज़ करने वाला व्यक्ति; मद्य का कभी न सेवन करने वाला व्यक्ति

**abstention** /əbˈstenʃn अब्ˈस्टेन्श्न्/ *noun* [C, U] an act of choosing not to vote either for or against sth मतदान में तटस्थ रहने की क्रिया

**abstinence** /ˈæbstɪnəns ˈऐब्स्टिनन्स् / *noun* [U] (*formal*) stopping yourself from having or doing sth that you enjoy भोग, विलास आदि से दूर रहने का आचरण *The doctor advised total abstinence from alcohol.* ▸ **abstain** *verb* संयम रखना

**abstract**[1] /ˈæbstrækt ˈऐब्स्ट्रैक्ट् / *adj.* existing only as an idea, not as a physical thing विचार या कल्पना मात्र में न कि कोई भौतिक वस्तु; अमूर्त *It is hard to imagine an abstract idea like 'eternity'.* ✪ विलोम **concrete**

**abstract**[2] /ˈæbstrækt ˈऐब्स्ट्रैक्ट् / *noun* [C] **1** an example of abstract art अमूर्त कला का उदाहरण **2** a short piece of writing that tells you the main contents of a book, speech, etc. किसी दस्तावेज़ का लिखित सारांश

**IDM** **in the abstract** only as an idea, not in real life केवल विचार रूप में न कि यथार्थ में

**abstract art** *noun* [U] art that does not show people or things as they really look, but which shows the artist's feelings about them ऐसी कला जो वस्तुओं को वैसा न दिखाए जैसी वे दिखाई पड़ती हैं बल्कि ऐसा कि जैसा कलाकार उसके बारे में सोचता है

**abstraction** /æbˈstrækʃn ऐब्ˈस्ट्रैक्श्न् / *noun* **1** [C, U] (*formal*) a general idea not based on any particular real person, thing or situation कोई सामान्य धारणा जिसका आधार कोई वास्तविक व्यक्ति, वस्तु या स्थिति न हो **2** [U] (*formal*) the state of thinking deeply about sth and not paying attention to what is around you विचारों में इस तरह मग्न रहने की अवस्था कि आसपास की गतिविधियों की तरफ़ ध्यान न जाए; तल्लीनता **3** [U, C] (*technical*) the act of removing sth from sth else किसी वस्तु को किसी अन्य वस्तु से अलग करना; पृथक्करण; सारग्रहण *water abstraction from rivers*

**abstract noun** *noun* [C] (*grammar*) a noun, for example 'goodness' or 'freedom', that refers to an idea or a general quality, not to a physical object भाववाचक संज्ञा

**absurd** /əbˈsɜːd अब्ˈसड् / *adj.* not at all logical or sensible; ridiculous जो बिल्कुल भी तर्कसंगत न हो; हास्यास्पद, बेतुका *It would be absurd to spend all your money on one book.* ▸ **absurdity** *noun* [C, U] (*pl.* **absurdities**) बेतुकापन, असंगति, बेतुकी या असंगत बात ▸ **absurdly** *adv.* असंगत रीति से

**abundance** /əˈbʌndəns अˈबन्डन्स् / *noun* [U, C, *sing.*] a very large quantity of sth किसी वस्तु की बहुत बड़ी मात्रा; बहुलता, प्रचुरता *These flowers grow here **in abundance**.* ○ *There is an abundance of wildlife in the forest.*

**abundant** /əˈbʌndənt अˈबन्डन्ट् / *adj.* existing in very large quantities; more than enough बहुत बड़ी मात्रा में विद्यमान, यथेष्ट से अधिक; भरपूर ▸ **abundantly** *adv.* पर्याप्त से अधिक मात्रा में

**abuse**[1] /əˈbjuːz अˈब्यूज़् / *verb* [T] **1** to use sth in a bad or dishonest way किसी वस्तु को बुरे या ग़लत ढंग से प्रयुक्त करना *The politician was accused of abusing his position in order to enrich himself.* **2** to say rude things to sb किसी को अपशब्द कहना; गाली देना **3** to treat sb badly, often violently किसी के प्रति बुरा बर्ताव करना; उग्रता से पेश आना *The girl had been physically abused.*

**abuse**[2] /əˈbjuːs अˈब्यूस् / *noun* **1** [C, U] using sth in a bad or dishonest way किसी वस्तु का बुरी तरह या ग़लत तरीक़े से प्रयोग *an abuse of power* ○ *the dangers of drug abuse* **2** [U] rude words, used to insult another person किसी अन्य व्यक्ति को अपमानित करने के लिए कहे गए अशिष्ट शब्द *The other driver leaned out of the car and **hurled abuse** at me.* ○ *racial abuse* **3** [U] bad, usually violent treatment of sb किसी अन्य व्यक्ति के साथ सामान्यतया उद्दंड एवं अशोभनीय व्यवहार *He subjected his children to verbal and physical abuse.* ○ *a victim of sexual abuse*

**abusive** /əˈbjuːsɪv अˈब्यूसिव् / *adj.* using rude language to insult sb किसी अन्य व्यक्ति को अपमानित करने के लिए अभद्र भाषा का प्रयोग *an abusive remark*

**abysmal** /əˈbɪzməl अˈबिज़्मल् / *adj.* very bad; of very poor quality बहुत बुरा; बहुत घटिया प्रकार का ▸ **abysmally** *adv.* बहुत बुरी तरह से

**abyss** /əˈbɪs अˈबिस् / *noun* [C] a very deep hole that seems to have no bottom बहुत गहरा गड्ढा जिसका अधस्तल मालूम न पड़े

**abyssal** /əˈbɪsəl अˈबिसल् / *adj.* (in geography) connected with the deepest parts of the ocean or the ocean floor (भूगोल में) महासागर के सबसे गहरे हिस्सों से संबंधित; रसातलीय

**AC** /ˌeɪˈsiː ˌएˈसी / *abbr.* **1** = **air conditioning** **2** = **alternating current**

**a/c** *abbr.* **1** = **account** **2** = **air conditioning**

**acacia** /əˈkeɪʃə अˈकेशा / (*also* **acacia tree**) *noun* [C] a tree with yellow or white flowers. There are several types of acacia trees, some of which produce a sticky liquid बबूल, कीकर जिसके पीले या सफ़ेद फूल होते हैं। इस पेड़ के अनेक प्रकार होते हैं; कुछ में से चिपचिपा द्रव निकलता है

**academic**[1] /ˌækəˈdemɪk ˌऐकˈडेमिक् / *adj.* **1** connected with education, especially in schools and universities शिक्षा से संबंधित, विशेषतया स्कूलों और विश्वविद्यालयों की शिक्षा से; शैक्षिक *The academic year begins in April.* **2** connected with subjects of interest to the mind rather than technical or practical subjects चिंतनप्रधान विषयों से संबंधित, न कि तकनीकी या व्यावहारिक विषयों से; वैदुषिक *academic subjects such as History* ✪ विलोम **non-academic** **3** not connected with reality; not affecting the facts of a situation अव्यावहारिक; वास्तविकता से असंबंधित; परिस्थिति को प्रभावित न करते हुए *academic* ▸ **academically** /ˌækəˈdemɪkli ˌऐकˈडेमिक्लि/ *adv.* शैक्षिक

**academic²** /ˌækəˈdemɪk ˌऐकˈडेमिक्/ *noun* [C] a person who teaches and/or does research at a university or college विश्वविद्यालय या महाविद्यालय में शिक्षक अथवा/और शोधक

**academician** /əˈkædmɪʃn अˌकैड्ˈमिश्न्/ *noun* [C] a member of an official group of people who are important in art, science or literature कला, विज्ञान या साहित्य के क्षेत्र में सुप्रतिष्ठित व्यक्तियों के मान्यता प्राप्त समुदाय का सदस्य

**academy** /əˈkædəmi अˈकैडमि/ *noun* [C] (*pl.* **academies**) **1** a school for special training विशेष प्रशिक्षण देने वाली संस्था *a military academy* **2** (*also* **Academy**) an official group of people who are important in art, science or literature कला, विज्ञान या साहित्य के क्षेत्र में सुप्रतिष्ठित व्यक्तियों का मान्यता प्राप्त अधिकारी वर्ग *the Indian Academy of Sciences*

**accede** /əkˈsiːd अक्ˈसीड्/ *verb* [I] **1 accede (to sth)** (*formal*) to agree to a request, demand, etc. किसी अनुरोध, माँग आदि को मान लेना *He acceded to demands for his resignation.* **2** to achieve a high position, especially to become king or queen उच्चतर पद प्राप्त करना, विशेषकर राजा या रानी का पद ▸ **accession** *noun* राज्यारोहण, पदग्रहण

**accelerate** /əkˈseləreɪt अक्ˈसेलरेट्/ *verb* [I, T] to go faster; to make sth go faster or happen more quickly गति का बढ़ना, किसी वस्तु, घटना आदि की गति को बढ़ाना *The driver slowed down for the bend then accelerated away.* ○ *to accelerate the pace of reform* ▸ **acceleration** /əkˌseləˈreɪʃn अक्ˌसेलˈरेश्न्/ *noun* [U] त्वरण, गतिवर्धन

**accelerator** /əkˈseləreɪtə(r) अक्ˈसेलरेट(र्)/ *noun* [C] the control in a vehicle that you press with your foot in order to make it go faster वाहन का वह नियंत्रक यंत्र जिसे वेग बढ़ाने के लिए पैर से दबाते हैं; एक्सेलरेटर

**accent** /ˈæksənt; -sent ˈऐक्सन्ट्; -सेन्ट्/ *noun* **1** [C, U] a particular way of pronouncing words that is connected with the country, area or social class that you come from शब्दों के उच्चारण का लहजा विशेष जो बोलने वाले के देश, निवासक्षेत्र या सामाजिक स्तर के दर्शाता है; स्वराघात *He speaks with a strong Bengali accent.* **2** [C] the greater force that you give to a particular word or part of a word when you speak बोलते समय शब्द विशेष या उस के किसी अंश पर दिया गया कुछ अधिक बल; ध्वनिबल *In the word 'because' the accent is on the second syllable.* **3** [C] (in writing) a mark, usually above a letter, that shows that it has to be pronounced in a certain way (लिखने में) किसी वर्ण पर लगा चिह्न जो यह संकेत करे कि इस वर्ण का विशेष ढंग से उच्चारण किया जाना है **4** [C] the particular importance that is given to sth किसी बात को दिया गया विशेष महत्त्व *In all our products the accent is on quality.*

**accentuate** /əkˈsentʃueɪt अक्ˈसेन्चुएट्/ *verb* [T] to emphasize sth or make sth easier to notice महत्त्व डालना या सुस्पष्ट बनाना *She uses make-up to accentuate her beautiful eyes.*

**accept** /əkˈsept अक्ˈसेप्ट्/ *verb* **1** [I, T] to agree to take sth that sb offers you (दी गई वस्तु को) स्वीकार या ग्रहण करना *Please accept this small gift.* ○ *Why won't you accept my advice?* **2** [I, T] to say yes to sth or to agree to sth सहमत होना, 'हाँ' करना; स्वीकार करना *Thank you for your invitation. I am happy to accept.* ○ *She has accepted the job.* **3** [I, T] to admit or recognize that sth unpleasant is true यह स्वीकार करना कोई बात अप्रिय होते हुए भी सत्य है *They refused to accept responsibility for the accident.* **4** [T] to allow sb to join a group, etc. किसी को दल आदि में शामिल होने देना *The university has accepted me on the course.*

**acceptable** /əkˈseptəbl अक्ˈसेप्टबल्/ *adj.* **1** that can be allowed जिसे माना जा सके; स्वीकार्य *One or two mistakes are acceptable but no more than that.* **2** good enough; satisfactory पर्याप्त, अच्छा; संतोषप्रद *We hope that you will consider our offer acceptable.* ✪ विलोम **unacceptable** ▸ **acceptability** /əkˌseptəˈbɪləti अक्ˌसेप्टˈबिलटि/ *noun* [U] स्वीकार्यता ▸ **acceptably** /-bli बलि/ *adv.* स्वीकार्य रूप से

**acceptance** /əkˈseptəns अक्ˈसेप्टन्स्/ *noun* [U, C] the act of accepting or being accepted स्वीकार करने या स्वीकार्य होने की क्रिया *His ready acceptance of the offer surprised me.* ○ *to **gain acceptance** in the group*

**access¹** /ˈækses ˈऐक्सेस्/ *noun* [U] **1 access (to sth)** a way of entering or reaching a place किसी स्थान में प्रवेश करने या वहाँ पहुँचने का रास्ता; प्रवेशमार्ग *Access to the garden is through the* *kitchen.* **2 access (to sth)** the chance or right to use or have sth किसी वस्तु को प्रयोग में लाने या प्राप्त करने का अवसर या अधिकार *Do you have access to a computer?* **3 access (to sb)** permission, especially legal or official, to see sb किसी से मिलने की अनुमति, जो प्रायः क़ानूनी या पूर्व स्वीकृत होती है *They are divorced, but he has regular access to the children.*

**access²** /ˈækses ˈऐक्सेस्/ *verb* [T] to find information on a computer कंप्यूटर में विशिष्ट जानकारी तक पहुँचना *Click on the icon to access a file.*

**accessible** /əkˈsesəbl अक्ˈसेसबल्/ *adj.* **1** possible to be reached or entered जहाँ पहुँचना या प्रवेश करना संभव हो; सुगम *The island is only accessible by boat.* **2** easy to get, use or understand सहजबोध्य या सहजगम्य *This television programme aims to make history more accessible to children.* ✪ विलोम **inaccessible** ► **accessibility** /əkˌsesəˈbɪləti अक्ˌसेसˈबिलटि/ *noun* [U] सुगमता *Computers have given people greater accessibility to information.*

**accession** /ækˈseʃn; ऐक्ˈसेशन्/ *noun* [U] the act of taking a very high position, especially as ruler of a country or head of sth किसी उच्च पद पर पहुँचने की क्रिया, विशेषतः किसी देश का राजा या संस्था का प्रमुख बनने की; पदारोहण, राज्यारोहण *the accession of Queen Elizabeth to the throne in 1952* ► **accede** *verb* कार्यभार या पद संभालना

**accessory** /əkˈsesəri अक्ˈसेसरि/ *noun* [C] (*pl.* **accessories**) **1** an extra item that is added to sth and is useful or attractive but not of great importance अतिरिक्त रूप से जुड़ने या लगने वाली वस्तु जो उपयोगी या सुंदर है परंतु अनिवार्य नहीं; साथ का पुरज़ा *The car has accessories such as an electronic alarm.* **2** [*usually pl.*] a thing that you wear or carry that matches your clothes, for example a piece of jewellery, a bag, etc. पहने हुए कपड़ों के साथ मेल खाने वाली वस्तु, जैसे कोई गहना, बैग आदि **3 an accessory (to sth)** (in law) a person who helps sb to do sth illegal (क़ानून में) ग़ैर-क़ानूनी काम में सहायक व्यक्ति *He was charged with being an accessory to murder.*

**accident** /ˈæksɪdənt ˈऐक्सिडन्ट्/ *noun* [C] an unpleasant event that happens unexpectedly and causes damage, injury or death दुर्घटना *I hope they haven't* ***had an accident****.* ○ *a fatal accident* (= when sb is killed)

IDM **by accident** by chance; without intending to संयोग से, अकस्मात; बिना किसी इरादे के *I knocked the vase over by accident as I was cleaning.*

**accidental** /ˌæksɪˈdentl ˌऐक्सिˈडेन्ट्ल्/ *adj.* happening by chance; not planned आकस्मिक; जिसकी कोई तैयारी न हो *Police do not know if the explosion was accidental or caused by a bomb.* ► **accidentally** /ˌæksɪˈdentəli ˌऐक्सिˈडेन्टलि/ *adv.* संयोगवश, जान-बूझकर नहीं *She accidentally took the wrong coat.*

**accident-prone** *adj.* often having accidents जहाँ प्रायः दुर्घटनाएँ घटें; दुर्घटना-आशंकित

**acclaim** /əˈkleɪm अˈक्लेम्/ *verb* [T] to express a very high opinion of sth/sb किसी (व्यक्ति या वस्तु) के प्रति आदर या प्रशंसा प्रकट करना; अभिनंदन करना a ***highly acclaimed*** *new film* ○ *The novel has been* ***acclaimed as*** *a modern classic.* ► **acclaim** *noun* [U] प्रशंसा, जय-जयकार

**acclamation** /ˌækləˈmeɪʃn ˌऐक्लˈमेशन्/ *noun* [U] (*formal*) loud and enthusiastic approval or welcome ज़ोरदार स्वागत या अभिनंदन

**acclimatize** (*also* **-ise**) /əˈklaɪmətaɪz अˈक्लाइमटाइज़्/ *verb* [I, T] **acclimatize (yourself/sb/sth) (to sth)** to get used to a new climate, a new situation, etc. so that it is not a problem anymore नए वातावरण, जलवायु का अभ्यस्त बनना या बनाना, नई परिस्थितियों के अनुकूल ढलना या ढालना; पर्यनुकूलन करना ► **acclimatization** (*also* **-isation**) əˌklaɪmətaɪˈzeɪʃn अˌक्लाइमटाइˈज़ेशन्/ *noun* [U] परिस्थिति-अनुकूलन ► **acclimatized** (*also* **-ised**) *adj.* परिस्थिति या वातावरण का अभ्यस्त

**accolade** /ˈækəleɪd ˈऐकलेड्/ *noun* [C] a comment, prize, etc. that you receive that shows people's high opinion of sth that you have done उपलब्धि पर समाज से मिलने वाली प्रशंसा, पुरस्कार आदि

**accommodate** /əˈkɒmədeɪt अˈकॉमडेट्/ *verb* [T] **1** to have enough space for sb/sth, especially for a certain number of people एक विशेष संख्या में लोगों के कहीं बैठने या ठहरने की पर्याप्त सुविधा होना *Each apartment can accommodate up to six people.* **2** to provide sb with a place to stay, live or work किसी व्यक्ति को कहीं रहने या काम करने के लिए स्थान देना *During the conference, you will be accommodated in a nearby hotel.* **3** (*formal*) to do or provide what sb wants or needs किसी की इच्छा या ज़रूरत को पूरा करना

**accommodating** /əˈkɒmədeɪtɪŋ अˈकॉमडेटिङ्/ *adj.* (used about a person) agreeing to do or provide what sb wants (व्यक्ति) किसी की इच्छा पूरी करने को तैयार

**accommodation** /əˌkɒməˈdeɪʃn अˌकॉमˈडेशन्/ *noun* **1** [U] a place for sb to live or stay रहने या

ठहरने का स्थान; आवास *We lived in rented accommodation before buying this house.* ○ *The price of the holiday includes flights and accommodation.*

NOTE ब्रिटिश अंग्रेज़ी में शब्द **accomodation** अगणनीय है। 'I will help you find an accomodation' अशुद्ध प्रयोग है। इस प्रसंग में शुद्ध प्रयोग है—*'I will help you to find somewhere to live.'*

**2 accommodations** [*pl.*] (*AmE*) somewhere to live or stay, often also providing food or other services प्रायः भोजन और अन्य सुविधाएँ भी प्रदान करने वाला आवास **3** [U] (*technical*) the way in which part of your eye (**the lens**) automatically becomes flatter or thicker in order to create a clear image of the object that you want to look at वह रीति जिससे आँख का लेंस स्वयं ही उत्तल-अवतल हो जाता है ताकि देखी जाने वाली वस्तु का स्पष्ट बिंब बनाया जा सके ➪ **eye** पर चित्र देखिए।

**accompaniment** /ə'kʌmpənimənt अ'कम्पनिमन्ट्/ *noun* [C] something that goes together with another more important thing किसी अधिक महत्त्वपूर्ण वस्तु का संग करने वाली वस्तु; संलग्न

**accompanist** /ə'kʌmpənɪst अ'कम्पनिस्ट्/ *noun* [C] a person who plays the piano or another instrument, while sb else plays or sings the main part of the music (संगीत) मुख्य वादक या गायक के साथ संगत करने वाला वादक या संगीतकार

**accompany** /ə'kʌmpəni अ'कम्पनि/ *verb* [T] (*pres. part.* **accompanying**; *3rd person sing. pres.* **accompanies**; *pt, pp* **accompanied**) **1** to go together with sb/sth किसी के साथ-साथ जाना *Massive publicity accompanied the film's release.* **2 accompany sb** (**on sth**) to play music for a singer or another instrument स्वर संगत करना *She accompanied him on the guitar.*

**accomplice** /ə'kʌmplɪs अ'कम्प्लिस्/ *noun* [C] **an accomplice** (**to/in sth**) a person who helps sb to do sth bad, especially a crime अपराध करने में सहायक व्यक्ति

**accomplish** /ə'kʌmplɪʃ अ'कम्प्लिश्/ *verb* [T] to succeed in doing sth difficult that you planned to do किसी कठिन कार्य को करने में सफल होना *I managed to accomplish my goal of writing ten letters a day.*

**accomplished** /ə'kʌmplɪʃt अ'कम्प्लिश्ट्/ *adj.* highly skilled at sth किसी काम में अति निपुण *an accomplished actor*

**accomplishment** /ə'kʌmplɪʃmənt अ'कम्प्लिश्मन्ट्/ *noun* **1** [U] the act of completing sth successfully कोई काम सफलतापूर्वक पूरा करने की क्रिया *the accomplishment of a plan* **2** [C] something difficult that sb has succeeded in doing or learning सफलतापूर्वक किया या सीखा गया कठिन कार्य; उपलब्धि

**accord**[1] /ə'kɔ:d अ'कॉड्/ *noun* [C] an agreement, especially between countries औपचारिक समझौता या संधि (प्रायः देशों के बीच) *the Helsinki accords on human rights*

IDM **in accord** in agreement about sth किसी बात के अनुकूल होना

**of your own accord** without being forced or asked अपनी इच्छा से; बिना बाध्यता या आदेश के *He wasn't sacked from his job—he left of his own accord.*

**accord**[2] /ə'kɔ:d अ'कॉड्/ *verb* (*formal*) **1** [T] to give sth to sb किसी व्यक्ति को कुछ प्रदान करना (सम्मान, समर्थन आदि) **2** [I] **accord** (**with sth**) to match; to agree with किसी के साथ मेल खाना; संगति में होना; सहमत होना

**accordance** /ə'kɔ:dns अ'कॉड्न्स्/ *noun*

IDM **in accordance with sth** in a way that follows or obeys sth के अनुसार; अनुकूलतापूर्वक *to act in accordance with instructions*

**accordingly** /ə'kɔ:dɪŋli अ'कॉडिङ्लि/ *adv.* **1** in a way that is suitable तदनुसार; उपयुक्त रूप से *I realized that I was in danger and acted accordingly.* **2** (*formal*) therefore; for that reason अतः इसलिए; इस कारण से

**according to** /ə'kɔ:dɪŋ tə; *before vowels* tu अ'कॉडिइङ् ट; स्वर ध्वनियों के पूर्व टु/ *prep.* **1** as stated by sb; as shown by sth के अनुसार; के संदर्भ में *According to Madhuri, it's a brilliant film.* ○ *More people now have a high standard of living, according to the statistics.* **2** in a way that matches, follows or depends on sth के साथ मेल खाते हुए, के अनुसार चलते हुए *Everything went off **according to plan**.* ○ *The salary will be fixed according to age and experience.*

**accordion** /ə'kɔ:diən अ'कॉडिअन्/ *noun* [C] a musical instrument that you hold in both hands and play by pulling the two sides apart and then pushing them together, while pressing the keys and/or buttons with your fingers दोनों हाथों से पकड़कर बजाया जाने वाला एक वाद्य यंत्र ➪ पृष्ठ 789 पर चित्र देखिए।

**accost** /ə'kɒst अ'कॉस्ट्/ *verb* [T] to go up and talk to a stranger in a way that is rude or frightening किसी अपरिचित व्यक्ति के निकट जाना और उसके साथ अशिष्टता से पेश आना

**account¹** /əˈkaʊnt अˈकाउन्ट्/ *noun* [C] **1** somebody's report or description of sth that has happened घटित घटना का विवरण; लेखा-जोखा *She gave the police a full account of the robbery.* **2** (*abbr.* **a/c**) the arrangement by which a bank, post office, etc. looks after your money for you (बैंक, डाक-घर आदि में) जमा राशि का खाता *to open/close an account* ○ *I paid the cheque into my bank account.* **3** (*usually pl.*) a record of all the money that a person or business has received or paid out (ख़र्च या प्राप्त की गई राशि का) लेखा-जोखा, हिसाब-किताब *If you are self-employed you have to* ***keep*** *your own* ***accounts****.* **4** an arrangement with a shop, etc. that allows you to pay for goods or services at a later date उधार-खाता *Most customers* ***settle/pay*** *their* ***account*** *in full at the end of each month.*

IDM **by all accounts** according to what everyone says लोगों के अनुसार; आम धारणा में *By all accounts, she's a very good doctor.*

**by your own account** according to what you say yourself स्वयं अपनी दृष्टि से *By his own account, Mohit was not very good at his job.*

**on account of** because of के कारण *Our flight was delayed on account of bad weather.*

**on no account; not on any account** not for any reason कदापि नहीं; किसी भी दशा में नहीं *On no account should you walk home by yourself.*

**take account of sth; take sth into account** to consider sth, especially when deciding or judging sth सोच-विचार करते समय किसी बात को ध्यान में रखना या महत्त्व देना *We'll take account of your comments.* ○ *We'll take your comments into account.*

**account²** /əˈkaʊnt अˈकाउन्ट्/ *verb*

PHR V **account for sth** **1** to explain or give a reason for sth किसी बात को स्पष्ट करना या उसका कारण बताना *How can we account for these changes?* **2** to form the amount that is mentioned उल्लिखित मात्रा या अनुपात होना *Sales to Europe accounted for 80% of our total sales last year.*

**accountable** /əˈkaʊntəbl अˈकाउन्टबल्/ *adj.* expected to give an explanation of your actions, etc.; responsible उत्तरदायी, ज़िम्मेदार, जवाबदेह *She is too young to* ***be held accountable*** *for what she did.* ► **accountability** /əˌkaʊntəˈbɪləti अˌकाउन्टˈबिलटि/ *noun* [U] उत्तरदायित्व, जवाबदेही

**accountancy** /əˈkaʊntənsi अˈकाउन्टन्सि/ *noun* [U] the work or profession of an accountant लेखाकर्म, एकाउंटेंसी

**accountant** /əˈkaʊntənt अˈकाउन्टन्ट्/ *noun* [C] a person whose job is to keep or examine the financial accounts of a business, etc. लेखाकार, एकाउटेंट

**accreditation** /əˌkredɪˈteɪʃn अˌक्रेडिˈटेशन्/ *noun* [U] official approval given by an organization when sb/sth achieves a certain standard निर्धारित मानदंड को प्राप्त करने पर एक विशेष संस्था द्वारा दी गई अधिकृत मान्यता; प्रत्यायन

**accrue** /əˈkru: अˈक्रू/ *verb* (*formal*) **1** [I] **accrue (to sb) (from sth)** to increase over a period of time एक निर्धारित अवधि के दौरान बढ़ना; वृद्धि होना *interest accruing to savers from their bank accounts* **2** [T] to allow a sum of money or debts to grow over a period of time एक निर्धारित अवधि में राशि या ऋण में वृद्धि होना ✪ पर्याय **accumulate**

**accumulate** /əˈkju:mjəleɪt अˈक्यूम्यलेट्/ *verb* **1** to collect a number or quantity of sth over a period of time किसी कालावधि में किसी वस्तु को अच्छी मात्रा या संख्या में इकट्ठा कर लेना; संचय करना *Over the years, I've accumulated hundreds of books.* **2** [I] to increase over a period of time समय अवधि के दौरान बढ़ना ► **accumulation** /əˌkju:mjəˈleɪʃn अˌक्यूम्यˈलेशन्/ *noun* [C, U] संचय ► **accumulative** /əˈkju:mjələtɪv अˈक्यूम्यलटिव्/ *adj.* संचित

**accurate** /ˈækjərət ˈऐक्यरट्/ *adj.* exact and correct; without mistakes यथार्थ और सही; त्रुटिहीन *He managed to give the police an accurate description of the robbers.* ✪ विलोम **inaccurate** ► **accuracy** /ˈækjərəsi ˈऐक्यरसि/ *noun* [C] विशुद्धता, यथार्थता ✪ विलोम **inaccuracy** ► **accurately** ठीक ठाक *adv.* यथार्थ रूप से

**accusation** /ˌækjuˈzeɪʃn ˌऐक्युˈज़ेशन्/ *noun* [C, U] a statement saying that sb has done sth wrong दोषारोपण, आरोप

**accusative** /əˈkju:zətɪv अˈक्युज़टिव्/ *noun* [C] (*grammar*) the form of a noun, a pronoun, or an adjective in some languages when it is, or is connected with, the **direct object** of a verb (कुछ भाषाओं में) संज्ञा, सर्वनाम या विशेषण का वह रूप जो क्रिया का प्रत्यक्षकर्म होता है या उससे संबंधित होता है; कर्मकारक, द्वितीया विभक्ति *In the sentence 'I bought them.', 'them' is in the accusative.* ⇨ **dative, genitive, nominative** और **vocative** देखिए। ► **accusative** *adj* कर्मकारक

**accuse** /əˈkju:z अˈक्यूज़्/ *verb* [T] **accuse sb (of sth/doing sth)** to say that sb has done sth wrong or broken the law किसी व्यक्ति पर आरोप

लगाना; क़ानून तोड़ने का दोषी ठहराना *He was accused of murder and sent for trial.* ▶ **accuser** *noun* [C] आरोप लगाने वाला व्यक्ति

**the accused** /əˈkjuːzd अˈक्यूज़्ड् / *noun* [C] (*pl.* **the accused**) (used in a court of law) the person who is said to have broken the law (न्यायालय में) व्यक्ति जिस पर आरोप लगाया गया हो *The jury found the accused not guilty of murder.*

**accusing** /əˈkjuːzɪŋ अˈक्यूज़िङ् / *adj.* showing that you think sb has done sth wrong दोषारोपण का संकेत करते हुए *He gave me an accusing look.* ▶ **accusingly** *adv.* आरोप लगाते हुए

**accustom** /əˈkʌstəm अˈकस्टम् / *verb* [T] **accustom yourself/sb/sth to sth** to make yourself/sb/sth get used to sth आदी होना, आदत डालना, अभ्यस्त होना *It took me a while to accustom myself to working nights.*

**accustomed** /əˈkʌstəmd अˈकस्टम्ड् / *adj.* **1 accustomed to sth** if you are accustomed to sth, you are used to it and it is not strange for you किसी बात का आदी या अभ्यस्त *She's accustomed to travelling a lot in her job.* **2** (*formal*) usual; regular सामान्य; नियमित

**ace** /eɪs एस् / *noun* [C] **1** a playing card which has a single shape on it. An ace has either the lowest or the highest value in a game of cards (ताश के पत्तों में) इक्का *the ace of spades* ➪ **card** पर नोट देखिए। **2** (in tennis) a **service** that the person playing against you cannot hit back (टेनिस में) ऐसी सर्विस जिसे विरोधी खिलाड़ी लौटा न सके *to serve an ace*

**acetate** /ˈæsɪteɪt ˈऐसिटेट् / *noun* [U] **1** a chemical compound that is made from a type of acid (**acetic acid**) and that is used in making plastics एक रासायनिक यौगिक जो एक प्रकार के (ऐसीटिक अम्ल) से बनता है और प्लास्टिक बनाने में प्रयुक्त होता है; ऐसीटेट **2** a smooth type of artificial cloth रासायनिक पदार्थों से बना एक चिकना कपड़ा

**acetic acid** /əˌsiːtɪkˈæsɪd अˌसीटिक् ˈऐसिड् / *noun* [U] a type of acid that is in **vinegar** सिरके में पाया जाने वाला अम्ल

**acetone** /ˈæsɪtəʊn ˈऐसिटोन् / *noun* [U] a colourless liquid with a strong smell used for cleaning things, making paint thinner and producing various chemicals तीखी गंध वाला एक रंगहीन द्रव जिसे वस्तुएँ साफ करने, रंग को पतला करने व विभिन्न प्रकार के रासायनिक पदार्थों को बनाने के काम में लाया जाता है; ऐसीटोन

**acetylene** /əˈsetəliːn अˈसेटलीन् / *noun* [U] (*symbol* $C_2H_2$) a gas that burns with a very hot bright flame, used for cutting or joining metal चमकीली ज्वाला देने वाली एक गैस जो धातुओं को काटने के काम आती है

**ache**[1] /eɪk एक् / *noun* [C] a pain that lasts for a long time ऐसा दर्द जो देर तक रहे *to have toothache/earache/stomach-ache*

> NOTE **Ache** शब्द का प्रयोग प्रायः समासों में किया जाता है जैसे *toothache* और *earache*. ब्रिटिश अंग्रेज़ी में इन शब्दों के पूर्व 'a' या 'an' का प्रयोग नहीं किया जाता—*I've got toothache.* परंतु *headache* के पूर्व *a* का प्रयोग अनिवार्य है—*I've got a bad headache.* अमेरिकी अंग्रेज़ी में *ache* के पूर्व *'a'* या *'an'* लगाया जाता है, विशेषतः जब किसी विशेष दर्द की बात की जा रही हो—*I have an awful toothache.*

**ache**[2] /eɪk एक् / *verb* [I] to feel a continuous pain लगातार दर्द का अनुभव होना *His legs ached after playing football.*

**achieve** /əˈtʃiːv अˈचीव् / *verb* [T] **1** to complete sth by hard work and skill किसी कार्य को मेहनत व कौशल द्वारा संपन्न करना *They have achieved a lot in a short time.* **2** to gain sth, usually by effort or skill कुछ प्राप्त करना, प्रायः मेहनत और कौशल द्वारा *You have achieved the success you deserve.* ▶ **achievable** *adj.* प्राप्त करने योग्य; प्राप्य *Profits of Rs 100 lakh look achievable.* ○ *achievable goals*

**achievement** /əˈtʃiːvmənt अˈचीव्मन्ट् / *noun* [C, U] something that you have done successfully, especially through hard work or skill सफलतापूर्वक संपादित कार्य, विशेषतः परिश्रम और कौशल द्वारा प्राप्त उपलब्धि *He enjoys climbing mountains because it gives him **a sense of achievement**.*

**Achilles heel** /əˌkɪliːz ˈhiːl अˈकिलीज़् ˈहील्/ *noun* [C] a weak point or fault in sb/sth किसी वस्तु या व्यक्ति का कमज़ोर पक्ष

**Achilles tendon** /əˌkɪliːz ˈtendən अˈकिलीज़् ˈटेन्डन् / *noun* [C] the strong thin material inside your leg that connects the muscles at the back of the lower part of your leg (**calf**) to the back part of your foot (**heel**) टाँग के अंदर का मज़बूत और महीन पदार्थ जो पिंडली को एड़ी से जोड़ता है

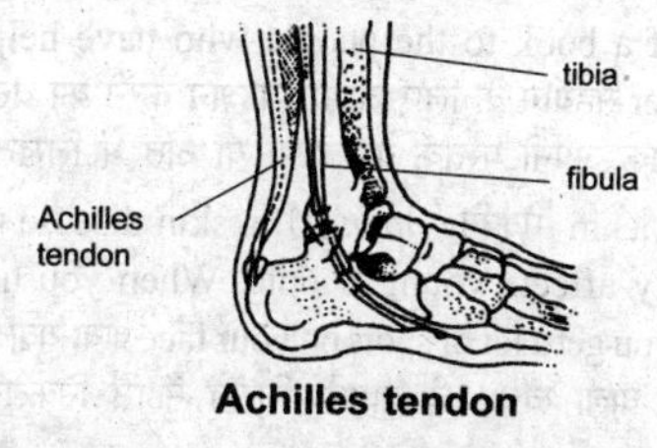

**Achilles tendon**

**acid**[1] /ˈæsɪd ˈऐसिड्/ *noun* [C, U] (in chemistry) a liquid substance that can dissolve metal and may burn your skin or clothes. Acids have a pH value of less than 7 (रसायन शास्त्र में) अम्ल, तेज़ाब, एसिड/ इस द्रव में धातुएँ घुल जाती हैं तथा इससे त्वचा और कपड़े जल सकते हैं। इसका pH मान 7 से कम होता है *sulphuric acid* ➪ **alkali** और **base** देखिए तथा **pH** पर चित्र देखिए।

**acid**[2] /ˈæsɪd ˈऐसिड्/ *adj.* **1** (used about a fruit, etc.) with a sour taste (फल आदि) खट्टे स्वाद का **2** (*also* **acidic** /əˈsɪdɪk अˈसिडिक्/) containing an acid अम्लीय, तेज़ाबी *an acid solution* ➪ **alkaline** देखिए तथा **pH** पर चित्र देखिए।

**acidity** /əˈsɪdəti अˈसिडटि/ *noun* [U] the quality of being acid खट्टापन, अम्लता *to measure the acidity of soil*

**acid rain** *noun* [U] rain that has chemicals in it from factories, etc. and that causes damage to trees, buildings and rivers वर्षा जिसमें कारख़ानों आदि के निकले रसायन होते हैं और जिससे पेड़ों, इमारतों और नदियों को नुक़सान पहुँचता है

**acknowledge** /əkˈnɒlɪdʒ अक्ˈनॉलिज्/ *verb* [T] **1** to accept or admit that sth is true or exists किसी बात की सचाई को स्वीकार करना; मान लेना, मान्यता देना *He **acknowledged (the fact) that** he had made a mistake.* ○ *He is acknowledged to be the country's greatest writer.* **2** to show that you have seen or noticed sb/sth or received sth कुछ देखने, जानने या प्राप्त करने का संकेत देना *The manager sent a card to all the staff to acknowledge their hard work.*

**acknowledgement** /əkˈnɒlɪdʒmənt अक्ˈनॉलिज्मन्ट्/ *noun* **1** [U] the act of showing that you have seen or noticed sb/sth किसी व्यक्ति या वस्तु की उपस्थिति को स्वीकार करने या मान्यता देने की क्रिया *The president gave a smile of acknowledgement to the photographers.* **2** [C, U] a letter, etc. that says that sth has been received or noticed किसी वस्तु की प्राप्ति की रसीद; पावती *I haven't received (an) acknowledgement of my job application yet.* **3** [C, *usually pl.*] a few words of thanks that an author writes at the beginning or end of a book to the people who have helped him/her सहयोग के लिए आभार प्रदर्शन करने का वक्तव्य जो लेखक अपनी पुस्तक के आरंभ या अंत में लिखता है

**acne** /ˌækni ˈऐक्नि/ *noun* [U] a skin disease that usually affects young people. When you have acne you get a lot of spots on your face प्रायः युवावस्था में होने वाली त्वचा की बीमारी जिसमें मुँहासे निकलते हैं

**acorn** /ˈeɪkɔːn ˈएकॉर्न्/ *noun* [C] the small nut of the **oak** tree, that grows in a base shaped like a cup बलूत के पेड़ का फल; बाँजफल, वंजुफल

**acoustic** /əˈkuːstɪk अˈकूस्टिक्/ *adj.* **1** connected with sound or the sense of hearing ध्वनि या सुनने की अनुभूति से संबंधित; ध्वानिक **2** (of a musical instrument) not electric (वाद्य-यंत्र) अविद्युतीय *an acoustic guitar* ➪ पृष्ठ 789 पर चित्र देखिए।

**acoustics** /əˈkuːstɪks अˈकूस्टिक्स्/ *noun* [*pl.*] the qualities of a room, etc. that make it good or bad for you to hear music, etc. in किसी कमरे आदि की वे विशेषताएँ जिनसे गीत की ध्वनि अच्छी या बुरी सुनाई देती है; श्रवणगुण *The theatre has excellent acoustics.*

**acquaint** /əˈkweɪnt अˈक्वेन्ट्/ *verb* [T] **acquaint sb/yourself with sth** (*formal*) to make sb or yourself become familiar with sth किसी वस्तु या बात से परिचित होना या करवाना *I spent several hours acquainting myself with the new computer system.*

**acquaintance** /əˈkweɪntəns अˈक्वेन्टन्स्/ *noun* **1** [C] a person that you know but who is not a close friend परिचित व्यक्ति परंतु घनिष्ठ मित्र नहीं **2** [U] **acquaintance with sb/sth** a slight knowledge of sb/sth किसी वस्तु या व्यक्ति के विषय में हलकी-फुलकी जानकारी

**acquainted** /əˈkweɪntɪd अˈक्वेन्टिड्/ *adj.* (*formal*) **1 acquainted with sth** knowing sth जानकार; परिचित *I went for a walk to **get acquainted** with my new neighbourhood.* **2 acquainted (with sb)** knowing sb, but usually not very closely किसी व्यक्ति से केवल परिचित (घनिष्ठ मित्रता नहीं)

**acquiesce** /ˌækwiˈes ˌऐक्विˈएस्/ *verb* [I] (*written*) **acquiesce in/to sth** to accept sth without argument, although you may not agree with it बिना विरोध किए कुछ भी मानने को सहमत होना ▶ **acquiescence** /ˌækwiˈesns ˌऐक्विˈएसन्स्/ *noun* [U] (*formal*) मौन स्वीकृति

**acquire** /əˈkwaɪə(r) अˈक्वाइअ(र्)/ *verb* [T] (*formal*) to obtain or buy sth कुछ अर्जित करना या ख़रीदना *The company has acquired shares in a rival business.*

**acquisition** /ˌækwiˈzɪʃn ˌऐक्विˈज़िश्न्/ *noun* **1** [U] the act of obtaining or buying sth कुछ अर्जित कर लेने या ख़रीद लेने की क्रिया *a study of language acquisition in children* **2** [C] something that you have obtained or bought अर्जित की गई या ख़रीदी गई वस्तु आदि *This sculpture is the museum's latest acquisition.*

**acquit** /əˈkwɪt अˈक्विट्/ *verb* [T] (**acquitting; acquitted**) **1 acquit sb (of sth)** to state formally that a person is not guilty of a crime किसी के निर्दोष होने की विधिवत घोषणा करना *The jury acquitted her of murder.* ✪ विलोम **convict** 2 (*formal*) **acquit yourself...** to behave in the way that is mentioned आशा या अपेक्षा के अनुसार व्यवहार करना; कर्तव्य निभाना *He **acquitted himself well** in his first match.* ▶ **acquittal** /əˈkwɪtl अˈक्विट्ल्/ *noun* [C, U] दोषमोचन, विमुक्ति

**acre** /ˈeɪkə(r) ˈऐक(र्)/ *noun* [C] a measure of land; 0·405 of a hectare एकड़; लगभग एक हेक्टेअर का 405 वाँ भाग का भूखंड *a farm of 20 acres/a 20-acre farm*

**acrid** /ˈækrɪd ˈऐक्रिड्/ *adj.* having a strong and bitter smell or taste that is unpleasant (गंध, स्वाद आदि) कड़वा, तीव्र और तीखा *acrid smoke from the factory*

**acrimony** /ˈækrɪməni ˈऐक्रिमनि/ *noun* [U] (*formal*) angry and bitter feelings or words क्रोधयुक्त और कटु भावनाएँ या शब्द *The dispute was settled without acrimony.* ▶ **acrimonious** /ˌækrɪˈməʊniəs ˌऐक्रिˈमोनिअस्/ *adj.* (*formal*) क्रोधपूर्ण और कटुतायुक्त *an acrimonious divorce*

**acrobat** /ˈækrəbæt ˈऐक्रबैट्/ *noun* [C] a person who performs difficult movements of the body, especially in a **circus** विशेषतः सर्कस में काम करने वाला नट; कलाबाज़

**acrobatic** /ˌækrəˈbætɪk ˌऐक्रˈबैटिक्/ *adj.* performing or involving difficult movements of the body कलाबाज़ी करते या दिखाते हुए *an acrobatic dancer* ○ *an acrobatic leap* ▶ **acrobatically** /ˌækrəˈbætɪkli ˌऐक्रˈबैटिक्लि/ *adv.* कलाबाज़ी करते या दिखाते हुए

**acrobatics** /ˌækrəˈbætɪks ˌऐक्रˈबैटिक्स्/ *noun* [U] (the art of performing) difficult movements of the body कलाबाज़ी

**acronym** /ˈækrənɪm ˈऐक्रनिम्/ *noun* [C] **an acronym (for sth)** a short word that is made from the first letters of a group of words किसी शब्द समूह के शब्दों के पहले अक्षरों से बना छोटा शब्द; आद्याक्षर शब्द *AIDS is an acronym for 'acquired immune deficiency syndrome'.*

**across** /əˈkrɒs अˈक्रॉस्/ *adv., prep.* **1** from one side of sth to the other एक ओर से दूसरी ओर; आर-पार *He walked across the field.* ○ *A smile spread across his face.* ○ *The river was about 20 metres across.* **2** on the other side of sth दूसरी तरफ़, उस ओर *There's a bank just across the road.*

**NOTE** 'On' और 'to the other side' अर्थों के लिए **across** या **over** का प्रयोग किया जाता है—*I ran across/over the road.* परंतु किसी ऊँची संरचना को पार करने के संदर्भ में सामान्यतः **over** का प्रयोग किया जाता है—*I can't climb over that wall.* 'Room' के संबंध में सामान्यतः **across** का प्रयोग किया जाता है—*I walked across the room to the door.*

**IDM** **across the board** involving or affecting all groups, members, cases, etc. सब (गुटों, सदस्यों, मामलों आदि) पर समान रूप से लागू या प्रभावकारी

**acrylic** /əˈkrɪlɪk अˈक्रिलिक्/ *noun* [C, U] an artificial material that is used in making clothes and paint एक कृत्रिम पदार्थ जो वस्त्र और पेंट बनाने में काम आता है; एक्रिलिक

**act¹** /ækt ऐक्ट्/ *verb* **1** [I] **act (on sth)** to do sth; to take action कुछ करना; कोई क्रिया करना, कार्रवाही करना *The doctor knew he had to act quickly to save the child.* **2 act as sth** to perform a particular function कोई विशेष काम करना; किसी विशेष उद्देश्य से काम करना, विशेष कर्तव्य निभाना *The man we met on the plane to Tokyo was kind enough to act as our guide.* **3** to behave in the way that is mentioned किसी विशेष तरीक़े से व्यवहार करना *Stop **acting like** a child!* ○ *Although she was trying to act cool, I could see she was really upset.* **4** [I, T] to perform in a play or film किसी नाटक या फ़िल्म में अभिनय करना *I acted in a play at school.*

**act²** /ækt ऐक्ट्/ *noun* [C] **1** a thing that you do काम, कार्य, कर्म *In a typical act of generosity they refused to accept any money.* ○ *to commit a violent act* **2** (*often* **Act**) one of the main divisions of a play or an opera नाटक या संगीत नाटक का अंक *How many scenes are there in Act 4 of* King Lear? **3** a short piece of entertainment, especially as part of a show एक छोटा मनोरंजक प्रदर्शन, जो विशेषतः एक बड़े प्रदर्शन का हिस्सा हो *Did you enjoy the clown's act?* **4** (*often* **Act**) a law made by a government सरकार द्वारा बनाया गया क़ानून; अधिनियम *The government **passed an act** forbidding the keeping of guns.* **5** behaviour that hides your true feelings असली भावनाओं को छिपाने वाला व्यवहार; स्वाँग, ढोंग *She seems very happy but she's just **putting on an act**.*

**IDM** **a hard act to follow** ⇨ **hard¹** देखिए।

**be/get in on the act** become involved in an activity that is becoming popular किसी ऐसी गतिविधि में लग जाना जो लोकप्रिय हो रही हो

**get your act together** to organize yourself so that you can do sth properly स्वयं को भली-भाँति सँभालना ताकि काम सही ढंग से हो सके *If he doesn't get his act together he's going to lose his job.*

**in the act (of doing sth)** while doing sth, especially sth wrong विशेषतः ग़लत काम करते समय *He was looking through the papers on her desk and she caught him in the act.*

**acting[1]** /ˈæktɪŋ ˈऐक्टिङ्/ *adj.* doing the job mentioned for a short time किसी अन्य का कार्यभार कुछ समय के लिए संभालना; कार्यकारी *Mr Kothari will be the acting director while Ms Gupta is away.*

**acting[2]** /ˈæktɪŋ ˈऐक्टिङ्/ *noun* [U] the art or profession of performing in plays or films नाटकों या फ़िल्मों में अभिनय की कला या व्यवसाय

**action** /ˈækʃn ˈऐक्श्न्/ *noun* **1** [U] doing things, often for a particular purpose सक्रियता, गतिविधि, क्रिया, कार्रवाही, प्रायः किसी विशेष उद्देश्य से *If we don't **take action** quickly it'll be too late!* ✪ विलोम **inaction** **2** something that you do किया गया कार्य *They should be judged by their actions, not by what they say.* **3** [*sing.*] the most important events in a story or play कहानी या नाटक की प्रमुखतम घटनाएँ *The action takes place in Jaipur.* **4** [U] exciting things that happen सक्रियता; उत्तेजक गतिविधियाँ *There's not much action in this boring town.* ○ *an **action-packed** film* **5** [U] fighting in a war युद्ध में लड़ाई; मुठभेड़ *Their son was **killed in action**.* **6** [*sing.*] the effect that one substance has on another एक पदार्थ का दूसरे पर पड़ने वाला प्रभाव *They're studying the **action of** alcohol **on** the brain.* **7** [C, U] the process of settling an argument in a court of law न्यायालय में कार्रवाई, मुक़दमा *He is going to **take legal action** against the hospital.*

IDM **in action** in operation; while working or doing sth सक्रियता की स्थिति में *We shall have a chance to see their new team in action next week.*

**into action** into operation सक्रिय स्थिति में; अमल में लाना, लागू करना *We'll put the plan into action immediately.*

**out of action** not able to do the usual things; not working सामान्य काम करने में असमर्थ (यंत्र आदि) ख़राब या बेकार *The coffee machine's out of action again.*

**activate** /ˈæktɪveɪt ˈऐक्टिव़ेट्/ *verb* [T] to make sth start working सक्रिय करना, क्रियाशील बना देना *A slight movement can activate the car alarm.*

**active** /ˈæktɪv ˈऐक्टिव़्/ *adj.* **1** involved in activity; lively सक्रिय, क्रियाशील; चुस्त, फुरतीला, जीवंत *My grandfather is very active for his age.* ✪ विलोम **inactive** **2** that produces an effect; that is in operation प्रभावशाली; सक्रिय *an active volcano* (= one that still erupts) **3** used about the form of a verb or a sentence when the subject of the sentence performs the action of the verb क्रिया का कर्मवाच्य रूप, इसमें क्रिया से सूचित गतिविधि को करने वाला कर्ता होता है *In the sentence 'The dog bit him', the verb is active.* NOTE 'The verb is in the active' भी कहा जा सकता है। ➪ **passive** देखिए।
▶ **actively** *adv.* सक्रियता से *She was actively looking for a job.*

**activist** /ˈæktɪvɪst ˈऐक्टिविस्ट्/ *noun* [C] a person who takes action to cause political or social change, usually as a member of a group किसी राजनैतिक या सामाजिक व्यवस्था में परिवर्तन लाने वाले दल का उत्साही कार्यकर्ता

**activity** /ækˈtɪvəti ऐक्ˈटिव़टि/ *noun* (*pl.* **activities**) **1** [U] a situation in which there is a lot of action or movement सक्रियता, क्रियाशीलता; गतिविधियों से पूर्ण स्थिति *The house was full of activity on the morning of the wedding.* ✪ विलोम **inactivity** **2** [C] something that you do, usually regularly and for enjoyment मनोरंजन के लिए नियमित रूप से की जाने वाली क्रिया *The hotel offers a range of leisure activities.*

**actor** /ˈæktə(r) ˈऐक्टर्(र्)/ *noun* [C] a man or woman whose job is to act in a play or film or on television अभिनेता या अभिनेत्री

**actress** /ˈæktrəs ˈऐक्ट्रस्/ *noun* [C] a woman whose job is to act in a play or film or on television अभिनेत्री

**actual** /ˈæktʃuəl ˈऐक्चुअल्/ *adj.* real; that happened असली; वास्तविक *The actual damage to the car was not as great as we had feared.*

**actually** /ˈæktʃuəli ˈऐक्चुअलि/ *adv.* **1** really; in fact वस्तुतः ; सचमुच *I can't believe that I'm actually going to America!* **2** although it may seem strange यद्यपि यह विचित्र लग सकता है *He actually expected me to cook his meal for him!*

NOTE बातचीत के प्रारंभ में **actually** शब्द का प्रयोग दूसरे का ध्यान आकृष्ट करने या नम्रता से किसी के वक्तव्य में सुधार करने के लिए किया जाता है—*Actually, I wanted to show you something. Do you have a minute?* ○ *I don't agree about the book. I think it's rather good, actually.* अंग्रेज़ी में **actually** का अर्थ 'at the present time' (वर्तमान समय में) नहीं होता। इस अर्थ के लिए **currently, at present** या **at the moment** का प्रयोग किया जाता है—*He's currently working on an article about China.* ○ *I'm studying for my exams at present.*

**actuary** /ˈæktʃuəri ˈऐक्चुअरि/ *noun* [C] (*pl.* **actuaries**) a person whose job involves calculating insurance risks and payments for insurance companies by studying how frequently accidents, fires, deaths, etc. happen बीमे के संदर्भ में, संभावित भुगतान की दृष्टि से ख़तरों का हिसाब लगाने वाला; बीमांकक

**acumen** /ˈækjəmən ˈऐक्यमन्/ *noun* [U] the ability to understand and judge things quickly and clearly स्थिति को तुरंत और स्पष्टता से समझ लेने की योग्यता; विदग्धता, कुशाग्रबुद्धि *business/financial acumen*

**acupuncture** /ˈækjupʌŋktʃə(r) ˈऐक्युपङ्क्च(र्)/ *noun* [U] a way of treating an illness or stopping pain by putting thin needles into parts of the body शरीर में बारीक सूइयों से छेद करके रोग ठीक करने की चिकित्सा प्रणाली; एक्युपंक्चर

**acupuncturist** /ˈækjupʌŋktʃərɪst ˈऐक्युपङ्क्चरिस्ट्/ *noun* [C] a person who is trained to perform acupuncture एक्युपंक्चर प्रणाली के प्रयोग में प्रशिक्षित व्यक्ति; एक्युपंक्चरिस्ट

**acute** /əˈkjuːt अˈक्यूट्/ *adj.* **1** very serious; very great बहुत गंभीर; बहुत अधिक *an acute shortage of food* ○ *acute pain* **2** (used about an illness) becoming dangerous very quickly (बीमारी) जो बहुत तेज़ी से ख़तरनाक बन जाए *acute appendicitis* ➪ **chronic** देखिए। **3** (used about feelings or the senses) very strong (भावनाएँ या इंद्रियाँ) तीक्ष्ण, प्रखर *Dogs have an acute sense of smell.* **4** showing that you are able to understand things easily (समझ, बुद्धि आदि) कुशाग्र, तेज़, होशियार *The report contains some acute observations on the situation.* ▶ **acutely** *adv.* तीव्रता से

**acute angle** *noun* [C] an angle of less than 90°, 90° से कम का कोण; न्यून कोण ➪ **obtuse angle, reflex angle** और **right angle** देखिए।

**AD** /ˌeɪˈdiː ˌएˈडी/ *abbr.* from the Latin 'anno domini'; used in dates for showing the number of years after the time when Jesus Christ was born लैटिन 'anno domini' का संक्षिप्त रूप; ईसा मसीह के जन्म के बाद के वर्षों का संकेत देने के लिए प्रयुक्त; ईसवी सन् ➪ **BC** देखिए।

**ad** /æd ऐड्/ *noun* (*informal*) = **advertisement** *I saw your ad in the local paper.*

**adage** /ˈædɪdʒ ˈऐडिज्/ *noun* [C] a well-known phrase expressing sth that is always true about people or the world कहावत, लोकोक्ति

**adamant** /ˈædəmənt ˈएडमन्ट्/ *adj.* (*formal*) very sure; refusing to change your mind अपने मत पर अटल, दृढ़; अड़ियल ▶ **adamantly** *adv.* अटल होकर, दृढ़ता के साथ

**Adam's apple** /ˌædəmzˈæpl ˌऐडम्ज़्ˈऐपल्/ *noun* [C] the part at the front of the throat which moves up and down when a man talks or swallows गले के सामने वाले भाग का वह हिस्सा जो बात करते समय या कुछ निगलते समया ऊपर-नीचे होता है; टेंटुआ

**adapt** /əˈdæpt अˈडैप्ट्/ *verb* **1** [I, T] **adapt (yourself) (to sth)** to become familiar with a new situation and to change your behaviour accordingly नई परिस्थिति से परिचित होकर असके अनुरूप अपने व्यवहार को बदलना *He was quick to adapt (himself) to the new system.* **2** [T] **adapt sth (for sth)** to change sth so that you can use it in a different situation किसी वस्तु को बदलना ताकि बदली हुई स्थिति में उसका उपयोग किया जा सके *The bus was adapted for disabled people.*

**adaptable** /əˈdæptəbl अˈडैप्टबल्/ *adj.* able to change to suit new situations नई परिस्थिति के अनुकूल परिवर्तनीय; अनुकूलनीय ▶ **adaptability** /əˌdæptəˈbɪləti अˌडैप्टˈबिलटि/ *noun* [U] अनुकूलनशीलता

**adaptation** /ˌædæpˈteɪʃn ˌऐडैप्ˈटेश्न्/ *noun* **1** [C] a play or film that is based on a novel, etc. किसी उपन्यास आदि पर आधारित कोई नाटक या फ़िल्म; रूपांतर **2** [U] the state or process of changing to suit a new situation नई परिस्थिति के अनुसार किसी वस्तु को बदलने की प्रक्रिया या स्थिति; अनुकूलन

**adaptor** (*also* **adapter**) /əˈdæptə(r) अˈडैप्ट(र्)/ *noun* [C] **1** a device that allows you to connect more than one piece of electrical equipment to an electricity supply point (**socket**) वह पुरज़ा जिससे विद्युत स्रोत बिंदु के साथ एकाधिक विद्युत उपकरणों को जोड़ा जा सकता है; एडाप्टर **2** a device for connecting pieces of electrical equipment that were not designed to be fitted together यंत्र जो विद्युत उपकरणों के उन अलग-अलग पुरज़ों को जोड़ता हो जो एक दूसरे के साथ जोड़े जाने के उद्देश्य से नहीं बनाए गए

**add** /æd ऐड्/ *verb* **1** [I, T] **add (sth) (to sth)** to put sth together with sth else, so that you increase the size, number, value, etc. किसी वस्तु को दूसरी वस्तु के साथ रखना या मिलाना जिससे उसका आकार, संख्या या मात्रा बढ़ जाए; जोड़ना, मिलाना *I added a couple more items to the list.* ○ *The juice contains no added sugar.* **2** [I, T] to put numbers or amounts together so that you get a total संख्याओं या राशियों का योग करना *If you **add 3 and 3 together** you get 6.* ✪ विलोम **subtract** **3** [T] to say sth more कुछ और कहना; आगे कहना *'By the way, please don't tell anyone I phoned you,' she added.*

**PHR V** **add sth on (to sth)** to include sth कुछ और शामिल करना *Ten per cent will be added on to your bill as a service charge.*

**add up** to seem to be a true explanation सत्य प्रतीत होना, सच्चा लगना *I'm sorry, but your story just doesn't add up.*
**add (sth) up** to find the total of several numbers एकाधिक संख्याओं का योग निकालना *The waiter hadn't added up the bill correctly.*
**add up to sth** to have as a total कुलयोग होना *How much does all the shopping add up to?*

**added to** *prep.* in addition to sth; as well as के अतिरिक्त; साथ ही

**addendum** /əˈdendəm अˈड्रेन्डम् / *noun* [C] (*pl.* **addenda** /-də -डा/) (*formal*) an item of extra information that is added to sth, especially to a book विशेषतः पुस्तक में जोड़ी गई अतिरिक्त जानकारी; परिशिष्ट

**adder** /ˈædə(r) ˈऐड(र्) / *noun* [C] a small poisonous snake एक छोटा जहरीला साँप; गेहुँअन

**addict** /ˈædɪkt ˈऐडिक्ट् / *noun* [C] a person who cannot stop taking or doing sth harmful व्यसनी व्यक्ति जिसे हानिकारक कार्य करने या हानिकारक वस्तुओं के सेवन की आदत हो *a drug addict* ▶ **addicted** /əˈdɪktɪd अˈडिक्टिड् / *adj.* **addicted (to sth)** व्यसनी, आसक्त आदि *He is addicted to heroin.* ✪ पर्याय **hooked on** ▶ **addiction** *noun* [C, U] व्यसन, लत, आसक्ति *the problem of teenage drug addiction*

**addictive** /əˈdɪktɪv अˈडिक्टिव् / *adj.* difficult to stop taking or doing जिसका सेवन छोड़ना कठिन हो जाए *a highly addictive drug* ○ *an addictive game*

**addition** /əˈdɪʃn अˈडिश्न् / *noun* **1** [U] adding sth, especially two or more numbers जोड़ने की क्रिया, विशेषतः संख्याओं को; संयोजन, योग ➪ **subtraction** देखिए। **2** [C] **an addition (to sth)** a person or thing that is added to sth किसी अन्य के साथ जोड़ा गया व्यक्ति या वस्तु
**IDM in addition (to sth)** as well as के अतिरिक्त, साथ ही *She speaks five foreign languages in addition to English.*

**additional** /əˈdɪʃənl अˈडिशनल् / *adj.* added; extra योजित; अतिरिक्त *a small additional charge for the use of the swimming pool* ▶ **additionally** /-ʃənəli -शनलि / *adv.* के अलावा

**additive** /ˈædətɪv ˈऐडटिव् / *noun* [C] a substance that is added to sth in small amounts for a special purpose पदार्थ जिसे अल्प मात्रा में और किसी विशेष उद्देश्य से किसी अन्य पदार्थ में मिलाया जाए; संयोजी *food additives* (= to add colour or flavour)

**address**[1] /əˈdres अˈड्रेस् / *noun* [C] **1** the number of the building and the name of the street and place where sb lives or works पता, ठिकाना *my home/business address* ***change of address*** **2** a series of words and/or numbers that tells you where you can find sb/sth using a computer शब्दों और/या संख्याओं की शृंखला जिससे कंप्यूटर की सहायता से किसी व्यक्ति या वस्तु का पता लगा सकते हैं *What's your email address?* **3** a formal speech that is given to an audience किसी श्रोतासमूह को दिया औपचारिक भाषण

**address**[2] /əˈdres अˈड्रेस् / *verb* [T] **1 address sth (to sb/sth)** to write the name and address of the person you are sending a letter, etc. to (पत्र आदि पर) पता लिखना *The parcel was returned because it had been wrongly addressed.* **2** to make an important speech to an audience किसी श्रोतासमूह को संबोधित करना; महत्त्वपूर्ण भाषण देना **3** (*formal*) **address (yourself to) sth** to try to deal with a problem, etc. समस्या के हल के लिए प्रयत्न करना *The government is finally addressing the question of corruption.* **4 address sb as sth** to talk or write to sb using a particular name or title किसी विशेष नाम या पदनाम से किसी व्यक्ति को संबोधित करना *She prefers to be addressed as 'Ms'.* **5** (*formal*) **address sth to sb** to make a comment, etc. to sb किसी विषय पर अपनी राय, आलोचना आदि देना या भेजना *Would you kindly address any complaints you have to the manager.*

**adenoids** /ˈædənɔɪdz ˈऐडनॉइड्ज़् / *noun* [*pl.*] soft areas at the back of the nose and throat that can swell up and cause breathing difficulties, especially in children (प्रायः बच्चों में) नाक और गले के पिछले भाग जो कभी-कभी सूज जाते हैं और साँस लेने-छोड़ने में कठिनाई पैदा कर सकते हैं; एडेनायड्स

**adept** /əˈdept अˈड्रेप्ट् / *adj.* **adept (at sth)** very good or skilful at sth कुशल, अति दक्ष, निपुण ✪ विलोम **inept**

**adequate** /ˈædɪkwət ˈऐडिक्वट् / *adj.* **1** enough for what you need आवश्यकता के अनुसार पर्याप्त *Make sure you take an adequate supply of water with you.* **2** just good enough; acceptable पर्याप्त, काफ़ी; ठीक, स्वीकार्य *Your work is adequate but I'm sure you could do better.* ✪ विलोम **inadequate** ▶ **adequacy** /ˈædɪkwəsi ˈऐडिक्वसि / *noun* [U] पर्याप्तता, उपयुक्तता ▶ **adequately** *adv.* पर्याप्त रूप से *The mystery has never been adequately explained.*

**adhere** /ədˈhɪə(r) अड्ˈहिअ(र्) / *verb* [I] (*formal*) **1 adhere (to sth)** to stick firmly to sth मज़बूती से चिपक जाना, जुड़ जाना, संसक्त होना *Make sure that the paper adheres firmly to the wall.* **2 adhere to sth** to continue to support an idea, etc.; to follow a rule किसी विचारधारा आदि को समर्थन देते रहना; किसी नियम का पालन करना

**adherent** /əd ˈhɪərənt अड् ˈहिअरन्ट् / *noun* [C] somebody who supports a particular idea किसी विचारधारा का समर्थक व्यक्ति ▸ **adherence** *noun* [U] निष्ठा, समर्थन

**adhesion** /əd ˈhi:ʒn अड् ˈहीश़्न् / *noun* [U] (*technical*) the process of sticking or the ability to stick to sth किसी के साथ चिपकने की प्रक्रिया; चिपकाव, आसंजन

**adhesive[1]** /əd ˈhi:sɪv अड् ˈहीसिव़् / *noun* [C] a substance that makes things stick together वस्तुओं को आपस में चिपकाने वाला पदार्थ (गोंद आदि); आसंजक

**adhesive[2]** /əd ˈhi:sɪv अड् ˈहीसिव़् / *adj.* that can stick, or can cause two things to stick together चिपकने वाला या दो वस्तुओं को चिपकाने वाला; आसंजनशील *He sealed the parcel with adhesive tape.* ✪ पर्याय **sticky**

**ad hoc** /ˌæd ˈhɒk ˌऐड् ˈहॉक् / *adj.* made or done suddenly for a particular purpose किसी विशेष उद्देश्य के लिए बनाया या किया गया; तदर्थ *They set up an ad hoc committee to discuss the matter.* ○ *Staff training takes place occasionally* ***on an ad hoc basis.***

**ad infinitum** /ˌæd ˌɪnfɪˈnaɪtəm ˌऐड् ˌइन्फ़ि ˈनाइटम् / *adv.* for ever; again and again सदा के लिए, अनंतकाल तक; बार-बार *We can't stay ad infinitum.* ○ *and so on, ad infinitum*

**adjacent** /əˈdʒeɪsnt अ ˈजेसन्ट् / *adj.* **adjacent (to sth)** situated next to or close to sth किसी के निकट या बग़ल में स्थित; आसन्न *She works in the office adjacent to mine.*

**adjectival** /ˌædʒek ˈtaɪvl ˌऐजे़क् ˈटाइव़्ल् / *adj.* that contains or is used like an adjective विशेषण-युक्त या विशेषण के समान प्रयुक्त; विशेषणात्मक *The adjectival form of 'smell' is 'smelly'.*

**adjective** /ˈædʒɪktɪv ˈऐजिक्टिव़् / *noun* [C] (*grammar*) a word that tells you more about a noun संज्ञा की विशेषता बताने वाला शब्द; विशेषण *The adjective 'reserved' is often applied to British people.* ○ *What adjective would you use to describe my sister?*

**adjoining** /əˈdʒɔɪnɪŋ अ ˈजॉइनिङ् / *adj.* next to, nearest to or joined to sth अगला, निकटतम या साथ लगा हुआ *A scream came from the adjoining room.*

**adjourn** /əˈdʒɜ:n अ ˈजॅन् / *verb* [I, T] to stop a meeting, a trial, etc. for a short time and start it again later किसी बैठक , न्यायिक कार्यवाही आदि को कुछ समय के लिए रोक देना, और बाद में पुनः आरंभ करना *The trial was adjourned until the following week.* ▸ **adjournment** *noun* [C] स्थगन

**adjudicate** /əˈdʒu:dɪkeɪt अ ˈजूडिकेट् / *verb* [I, T] (*written*) to act as an official judge in a competition or to decide who is right when two people or groups disagree about sth प्रतियोगिता या विवाद में अधिकृत रूप से निर्णय देना; फ़ैसला सुनाना

**adjudicator** /əˈdʒu:dɪkeɪtə(r) अ ˈजूडिकेट(र्) / *noun* [C] a person who acts as a judge, especially in a competition प्रतियोगिता आदि का निर्णायक; अधिनिर्णायक

**adjunct** /ˈædʒʌŋkt ˈऐजङ्क्ट् / *noun* [C] **1** (*grammar*) an adverb or a phrase that adds meaning to the verb in a sentence or part of a sentence क्रियाविशेषण या क्रिया या वाक्य के किसी अंश की विशेषता दर्शाने वाला वाक्यांश; अनुबंध *In the sentence 'He ran away in a panic', 'in a panic' is an adjunct.* **2** (*formal*) a thing that is added or joined to sth larger or more important अधिक महत्त्वपूर्ण या बड़ी वस्तु के साथ लगी कम महत्त्व की या छोटी वस्तु; अनुलग्नक

**adjust** /əˈdʒʌst अ ˈजस्ट् / *verb* **1** [T] to change sth slightly, especially because it is not in the right position थोड़े से परिवर्तन के साथ किसी वस्तु को ठीक स्थिति में लाना; मेल बैठना, समायोजित करना *The seat can be adjusted to different positions.* **2** [I] **adjust (to sth)** to get used to new conditions or a new situation नई परिस्थितियों के साथ समायोजन हो जाना; अनुकूल बनना *She found it hard to adjust to working at night.* ▸ **adjustment** *noun* [C, U] तालमेल, समायोजन, अनुकूलन *We'll just* ***make*** *a few* ***minor adjustments*** *and the room will look perfect.*

**adjustable** /əˈdʒʌstəbl अ ˈजस्टबल् / *adj.* that can be adjusted जिसे अनुकूल बनाया जा सके; जिसका समायोजन हो सके, समायोज्य *an adjustable mirror*

**adjustable spanner** (*BrE*) (*AmE* **monkey wrench**) *noun* [C] a tool that can be adjusted to hold and turn things of different widths पाना जिसे विभिन्न चौड़ाइयों की वस्तुएँ पकड़ने और घुमाने के लिए अनुकूल बनाया जा सके ➪ **spanner** और **wrench** देखिए तथा **tool** पर चित्र देखिए।

**ad lib** /ˌæd ˈlɪb ˌऐड् ˈलिब् / *adj., adv.* done or spoken without preparation बिना पूर्व तैयारी के किया गया या बोला गया *She had to speak ad lib because she couldn't find her notes.* ▸ **ad lib** *verb* [I] (**ad libbing; ad libbed**) बिना पूर्व तैयारी के करना या बोलना *He forgot his notes so he had to ad lib.*

**admin** = **administration**

**administer** /əd ˈmɪnɪstə(r) अड् ˈमिनिस्ट(र्) / *verb* [T] (*formal*) **1** to control or manage sth नियंत्रित करना; व्यवस्था करना, प्रशासन चलाना, देखभाल करना **2** to give sb sth, especially medicine किसी को कुछ देना, विशेषतः दवा

**administration** /əd͵mɪnɪˈstreɪʃn अड्͵मिनिˈस्ट्रेश्न्/ *noun* **1** (*also* **admin** /ˈædmɪn ˈऐड्मिन्/) [U] the control or the act of managing sth, for example a system, an organization or a business किसी व्यवस्था, संगठन या व्यापार को नियंत्रित या संचालित करने की क्रिया; प्रबंधन *The administration of a large project like this is very complicated.* ○ *A lot of the teachers' time is taken up by admin.* **2** (*also* **admin** /ˈædmɪn ˈऐड्मिन्/) [*sing.*] the group of people or part of a company that organizes or controls sth संचालन और नियंत्रण करने वाला व्यक्तिसमूह (अधिकारीगण), प्रशासन *the hospital administration* ○ *She works in admin, on the second floor.* **3 the Administration** [C] the government of a country, especially the US किसी देश की सरकार, विशेषतया संयुक्त राज्य अमेरिका की सरकार के लिए प्रयुक्त *the Bush Administration*

**administrative** /ədˈmɪnɪstrətɪv अड्ˈमिनिस्ट्रटिव्/ *adj.* connected with the organization of a country, business, etc., and the way in which it is managed (देश, व्यापार आदि का) प्रशासन-संबंधी, संचालन-संबंधी

**administrator** /ədˈmɪnɪstreɪtə(r) अड्ˈमिनिस्ट्रेट(र्)/ *noun* [C] a person whose job is to organize or manage a system, a business, etc. (प्रणाली, व्यापार का) प्रशासक, प्रबंधक

**admirable** /ˈædmərəbl ˈऐड्मरबल्/ *adj.* (*formal*) that you admire; excellent प्रशंसनीय; श्रेष्ठ ▶ **admirably** /ˈædmərəbli ˈऐड्मरब्लि/ *adv.* प्रशंसनीय रीति से या उत्तम *She dealt with the problem admirably.*

**admiral** /ˈædmərəl ˈऐड्मरल्/ *noun* [C] the most important officer in the navy नौसेना का सबसे उच्च अधिकारी; एडमिरल

**admiration** /͵ædməˈreɪʃn ͵ऐड्मˈरेश्न्/ *noun* [U] **admiration (for/of sb/sth)** a feeling of liking and respecting sb/sth very much किसी वस्तु या व्यक्ति के प्रति विशेष अनुराग और समादर की भावना *I have great admiration for what he's done.*

**admire** /ədˈmaɪə(r) अड्ˈमाइअ(र्)/ *verb* [T] **admire sb/sth (for sth/doing sth)** to respect or like sb/sth very much; to look at sb/sth with pleasure किसी के प्रति आदर व प्रशंसा का भाव रखना; किसी को प्रिय दृष्टि से देखना *I've always admired her for being such a wonderful mother.* ○ *We stopped at the top of the hill to admire the view.*

**admirer** /ədˈmaɪərə(r) अड्ˈमाइअर(र्)/ *noun* [C] a person who admires sb/sth प्रशंसक *I've always been a great admirer of her work.*

**admiring** /ədˈmaɪərɪŋ अड्ˈमाइअरिङ्/ *adj.* feeling or expressing admiration प्रशंसा का भाव रखना या उसे अभिव्यक्त करना ▶ **admiringly** *adv.* प्रशंसापूर्वक

**admissible** /ədˈmɪsəbl अड्ˈमिसबल्/ *adj.* that can be allowed or accepted, especially in a court of law विशेषतः किसी न्यायालय में स्वीकार करने या अनुमति देने योग्य; स्वीकृत *The judge ruled the tapes to be admissible as evidence.*

**admission** /ədˈmɪʃn अड्ˈमिश्न्/ *noun* **1** [C, U] **admission (to sth)** the act of allowing sb to enter a school, club, public place, etc. स्कूल, क्लब, सार्वजनिक स्थल आदि में प्रवेश देने या भरती करने की अनुमति *Admissions to British universities have increased by 15% this year.* ➪ **entrance** देखिए। **2** [U] the amount of money that you have to pay to enter a place प्रवेश शुल्क *The museum charges half-price admission on Mondays.* **3** [C] a statement that admits that sth is true स्वीकृत कथन; स्वीकरण

**admit** /ədˈmɪt अड्ˈमिट्/ *verb* (**admitting; admitted**) **1** [I, T] **admit sth; admit to sth/doing sth; admit (that...)** to agree that sth unpleasant is true or that you have done sth wrong किसी अप्रिय बात की सत्यता स्वीकारना या अपनी ग़लती मान लेना *He refused to admit to the theft.* ○ *I have to admit (that) I was wrong.* ○ *She admitted having broken the computer.* ✪ विलोम **deny** **2** [T] **admit sb/sth (into/to sth)** to allow sb/sth to enter; to take sb into a place प्रवेश करने देना; भरती करना *He was admitted to hospital with suspected appendicitis.*

**admittance** /ədˈmɪtns अड्ˈमिट्न्स्/ *noun* [U] (*formal*) being allowed to enter a place; the right to enter प्रवेश करने की अनुमति; भीतर जाने का अधिकार *The journalist tried to gain admittance to the minister's office.*

**admittedly** /ədˈmɪtɪdli अड्ˈमिटिड्लि/ *adv.* it must be admitted (that...) यह मानना होगा कि..., निस्संदेह *The work is very interesting. Admittedly, I do get rather tired.*

**admonish** /ədˈmɒnɪʃ अड्ˈमॉनिश्/ *verb* [T] (*formal*) **1 admonish sb (for sth/for doing sth)** to tell sb firmly that you do not approve of sth that he/she has done डाँटना, फटकारना *He was admonished for arriving late at work.* **2** to strongly advise sb to do sth कड़ी चेतावनी देना *She admonished the staff to call off the strike.*

**ad nauseam** /͵ædˈnɔːziæm ͵ऐड्ˈनॉज़िऐम्/ *adv.* if a person does or says sth **ad nauseam** he/she does or says it again and again until it becomes boring and annoying कुछ इतनी अधिक बार करना या कहना कि बेहद ऊबाऊ लगे या घृणा उत्पन्न करने लगे

**ado** /əˈduː अˈडू/ *noun*

IDM **without further/more ado** (*old-fashioned*) without delaying; immediately बिना देर किए, अविलंब; तुरंत

**adobe** /əˈdəʊbi अˈडोबि/ *noun* [U] mud that is dried in the sun and used as a building material कच्ची ईंट

**adolescence** /ˌædəˈlesns ˌऐडˈलेसन्स्/ *noun* [U] the period of a person's life between being a child and becoming an adult, between the ages of about 13 and 17 किशोरावस्था; 13 से 17 वर्ष के बीच की अवस्था

**adolescent** /ˌædəˈlesnt ˌऐडˈलेसन्ट्/ *noun* [C] a young person who is no longer a child and not yet an adult, between the ages of about 13 and 17; 13 से 17 की उम्र का लड़का या लड़की; किशोर, किशोरी *the problems of adolescents* ○ *an adolescent daughter* ➪ **teenager** देखिए।

**adopt** /əˈdɒpt अˈडॉप्ट्/ *verb* **1** [I, T] to take a child into your family and treat him/her as your own child by law किसी बच्चे को क़ानूनन गोद लेना *They couldn't have children so they adopted.* ○ *They're hoping to adopt a child.* **2** [T] to take and use sth किसी विधि को अपनाना *What approach did you adopt when dealing with the problem?* ▶ **adopted** *adj.* अंगीकृत, अपनाया हुआ; गोद लिया हुआ *an adopted child* ▶ **adoption** *noun* [C, U] दत्तक ग्रहण; अंगीकरण, अपने विचार या परिवार का अंग बनाना *The number of adoptions has risen in the past year* (= the number of children being adopted).

**adoptive** /əˈdɒptɪv अˈडॉप्टिव्/ *adj.* (used about parents) having legally taken a child to live with them as part of their family (माता-पिता) क़ानूनन गोद लेने वाले *the baby's adoptive parents*

**adorable** /əˈdɔːrəbl अˈडॉरबल्/ *adj.* (used about children or animals) very attractive and easy to feel love for (बच्चों या पशुओं के लिए प्रयुक्त) और स्नेह की भावना जगाने वाला; मनमोहक ✪ पर्याय **lovely**

**adore** /əˈdɔː(r) अˈडॉ(र्)/ *verb* [T] **1** to love and admire sb/sth very much स्नेह और आदर की भावना से देखना *Kirti adores her older sister.* **2** to like sth very much बहुत पसंद करना *She adores chocolates.* ▶ **adoration** /ˌædəˈreɪʃn ˌऐडˈरेशन्/ *noun* [U] अत्यधिक स्नेह व आदर की भावना; आराधना, श्रद्धा, प्यार ▶ **adoring** *adj.* चाहने वाले *his adoring fans*

**adorn** /əˈdɔːn अˈडॉन्/ *verb* [T] **adorn sth (with sth)** to add sth in order to make a thing or person more attractive or beautiful अधिक आकर्षक या मोहक बनाने के लिए सजाना ▶ **adornment** *noun* [C, U] सजावट, शृंगार, अलंकरण

**adrenal** /əˈdriːnl अˈड्रीनल्/ *adj.* connected with the production of **adrenalin** एड्रेनलिन के बनने से संबंधित

**adrenalin** /əˈdrenəlɪn अˈड्रेनलिन्/ *noun* [U] a substance that your body produces when you are very angry, frightened or excited and that makes your heart go faster क्रोधित, भयभीत या उत्तेजित आदि होने के कारण अधिवृक्क ग्रंथि द्वारा स्रावित पदार्थ

**adrift** /əˈdrɪft अˈड्रिफ़्ट्/ *adj.* (used about a boat) not tied to anything or controlled by anyone (नाव के लिए प्रयुक्त) ऐसी नाव जो न तो रस्सी से बँधी हो, न उस पर कोई अन्य नियंत्रण हो; मुक्तरूप से बहती (नाव)

**adroit** /əˈdrɔɪt अˈड्रॉइट्/ *adj.* (*written*) **adroit (at sth)** skilful and clever, especially in dealing with people दक्ष, चतुर, विशेषतः जनसंपर्क में *She is adroit at avoiding awkward questions.*

**adulation** /ˌædjuˈleɪʃn ˌऐड्युˈलेशन्/ *noun* [U] (*formal*) extreme admiration अत्यधिक प्रशंसा और आदर *The band learned to deal with the adulation of their fans.*

**adult** /ˈædʌlt; əˈdʌlt ˈऐडल्ट्; अˈडल्ट्/ *noun* [C] a person or an animal that is fully grown (व्यक्ति) वयस्क, बालिग़, (पशु) पूर्णतया विकसित *This film is suitable for both adults and children.* ▶ **adult** *adj.* वयस्क

**adult education** (*also* **continuing education**) *noun* [U] education for adults that is available outside the formal education system, for example at evening classes वयस्कों के लिए उपलब्ध ग़ैर-औपचारिक शिक्षा; प्रौढ़ शिक्षा

**adulterate** /əˈdʌltəreɪt अˈडल्टरेट्/ *verb* [T] (*often passive*) **adulterate sth (with sth)** to make food or drink less pure or of lower quality by adding sth to it किसी खाद्य पदार्थ में मिलावट करना; अपमिश्रण करना

**adulterer** /əˈdʌltərə(r) अˈडल्टर(र्)/ *noun* [C] (*formal*) a person who commits adultery परपुरुषगामी या परस्त्रीगामी; व्यभिचारी

**adultery** /əˈdʌltəri अˈडल्टरि/ *noun* [U] (*formal*) sex between a married person and sb who is not his/her wife/husband परपुरुष या परस्त्री के बीच यौन संबंध; परपुरुषगमन, परस्त्रीगमन, व्यभिचार *to commit adultery* ▶ **adulterous** /əˈdʌltərəs अˈडल्टरस् *adj.* व्यभिचारी *an adulterous relationship*

**adulthood** /ˈædʌlthʊd; əˈdʌlt- ˈऐडल्टहुड्; अˈडल्ट्-/ *noun* [U] the time in your life when you are an adult वयस्क होने की अवस्था

**Advaita** *noun* [U] (*IndE*) a branch of Hindu philosophy that emphasizes the unity of the individual and God मानव एवं ईश्वर के एकत्व को दर्शाने वाली हिंदू दार्शनिक शास्त्र की एक शाखा; अद्वैत *Advaita philosophy*

**advance**[1] /ədˈvɑːns अड्ˈव़ान्स्/ *verb* **1** to move forward आगे बढ़ना *The army advanced towards the city.* ✪ विलोम **retreat** **2** to make progress or help sth make progress प्रगति करना या प्रगति में सहायक होना *Our research has not advanced much recently.*

**advance**[2] /ədˈvɑːns अड्ˈव़ान्स्/ *noun* **1** [C, *usually sing.*] forward movement अग्रगति; आगे बढ़ने की क्रिया *the army's advance towards the border* ✪ विलोम **retreat** **2** [C, U] progress in sth किसी क्षेत्र में प्रगति *advances in computer technology* **3** [C] an amount of money that is paid to sb before the time when it is usually paid (राशी) पेशगी, अग्रिम, अगाऊ

IDM **in advance (of sth)** before a particular time or event किसी निश्चित समय या घटना से पहले *You should book tickets for the film well in advance.*

**advance**[3] /ədˈvɑːns अड्ˈव़ान्स्/ *adj.* (*not before a noun*) that happens before sth किसी होने वाली घटना से पहले की; अग्रिम *There was no advance warning of the earthquake.*

**advanced** /ədˈvɑːnst अड्ˈव़ान्स्ट्/ *adj.* **1** of a high level उच्चतर स्तर का *an advanced English class* **2** highly developed विकसित, उन्नत, अग्रवर्ती *a country that is not very advanced industrially*

**advancement** /ədˈvɑːnsmənt अड्ˈव़ान्स्मन्ट्/ *noun* (*formal*) **1** [U, C] the process of helping sth to make progress and succeed उन्नति, प्रगति *the advancement of knowledge/science* **2** [U] progress in a job, social class, etc. नौकरी में तरक़्क़ी सामाजिक स्तर में बढ़ोतरी, आदि *There is good opportunity for advancement if you have the right skills.*

**advantage** /ədˈvɑːntɪdʒ अड्ˈव़ान्टिज्/ *noun* **1** [C] **an advantage (over sb)** something that may help you to do better than other people लाभ या फ़ायदे की स्थिति *Her experience gave her a big advantage over the other people applying for the job.* ○ *Some runners try to gain an unfair advantage by taking drugs.* **2** [C, U] something that helps you or that will bring you a good result लाभ, फ़ायदा *the advantages and disadvantages of a plan* ✪ विलोम **disadvantage**

IDM **take advantage of sb/sth** **1** to make good or full use of sth किसी स्थिति का पूरा लाभ उठाना या उपयोग करना *We should take full advantage of these low prices while they last.* **2** to make unfair use of sb or of sb's kindness, etc. in order to get what you want अनुचित लाभ उठाना *Don't let him take advantage of you like this.*

**turn sth to your advantage** to use or change a bad situation so that it helps you प्रतिकूल स्थिति को अनुकूलता में बदलना

**advantageous** /ˌædvənˈteɪdʒəs, ऐड्व़न्ˈटेजस/ *adj.* that will help you or bring you a good result सहायक, उपयोगी, लाभदायक

**advent** /ˈædvent ˈऐड्वेन्ट्/ *noun* [*sing.*] **1** (*formal*) the fact of sb/sth arriving (किसी व्यक्ति या घटना का) आगमन **2 Advent** (in the Christian year) the four weeks before Christmas (ईसाई वर्ष में) क्रिसमस से पहले के चार सप्ताह

**adventure** /ədˈventʃə(r) अड्ˈवेन्च(र्)/ *noun* [C, U] an experience or event that is very unusual, exciting or dangerous असाधारण, उत्तेजक और संकटपूर्ण अनुभव या घटना *Our journey through the jungle was quite an adventure!*

**adventurer** /ədˈventʃərə(r) अड्ˈवेन्चर(र्)/ *noun* [C] **1** a person who enjoys exciting new experiences, especially going to unusual places व्यक्ति जिसे नए व उत्तेजक अनुभव प्राप्त करने का शौक़ हो **2** a person who is capable of taking risks and perhaps acting dishonestly in order to gain money or power जोख़िम उठाने को या बेईमानी से धन आदि कमाने को तैयार व्यक्ति

**adventurous** /ədˈventʃərəs अड्ˈवेन्चरस्/ *adj.* **1** (used about a person) liking to try new things or have adventures (व्यक्ति) ख़तरे उठाने और नए-नए साहसिक काम करने को तैयार **2** involving adventure साहस भरा, संकटपूर्ण *For a more adventurous holiday try mountain climbing.*

**adverb** /ˈædvɜːb ˈऐड्वब्/ *noun* [C] (*grammar*) a word that adds more information about place, time, manner, cause or degree to a verb, an adjective, a phrase or another adverb क्रियाविशेषण *In 'speak slowly', 'extremely funny', 'arrive late' and 'I know her well', 'slowly', 'extremely', 'late' and 'well' are adverbs.* ▶ **adverbial** /ædˈvɜːbiəl ऐड्ˈव़बिअल्/ *adj.* क्रियाविशेषणात्मक *'Very quickly indeed' is an adverbial phrase.*

**adversary** /ˈædvəsəri ˈऐड्व़सरि/ *noun* [C] (*pl.* **adversaries**) (*formal*) an enemy, or an opponent in a competition शत्रु; किसी स्पर्धा में विरोधी पक्ष

**adverse** /ˈædvɜːs ˈऐड्व़स्/ *adj.* (*formal*) making sth difficult for sb प्रतिकूल, विरुद्ध *Our flight was cancelled because of adverse weather conditions.* ✪ विलोम **favourable** ➪ **unfavourable** भी देखिए। ▶ **adversely** *adv.* प्रतिकूल रूप से

**adversity** /ədˈvɜːsəti अड्ˈवर्सटि/ *noun* [C, U] (*pl.* **adversities**) (*formal*) difficulties or problems कठिनाइयाँ, समस्याएँ, मुसीबतें; विपत्तियाँ

**advertise** /ˈædvətaɪz ˈऐड्वटाइज़्/ *verb* **1** [I, T] to put information in a newspaper, on television, on a picture on the wall, etc. in order to persuade people to buy sth, to interest them in a new job, etc. विज्ञापन करना, देना या लगाना *a poster advertising a new car* ○ *The job was advertised in the local newspapers.* **2** [I] **advertise for sb/sth** to say publicly in a newspaper, on a sign, etc. that you need sb to do a particular job, want to buy sth, etc. सार्वजनिक सूचना देना *The shop is advertising for a sales assistant.* ▶ **advertising** *noun* [U] विज्ञापन देने की क्रिया *The magazine gets a lot of money from advertising.* ○ *an advertising campaign*

**advertisement** /ədˈvɜːtɪsmənt अड्ˈवर्टिस्मन्ट्/ (*informal*) (*also* **ad**) *noun* [C] a piece of information in a newspaper, on television, a picture on a wall, etc. that tries to persuade people to buy sth, to interest them in a new job, etc. विज्ञापन, सार्वजनिक सूचना *an advertisement for a new brand of washing powder*

**advertiser** /ˈædvətaɪzə(r) ˈऐड्वटाइज़(र्)/ *noun* [C] a person or company that pays to put an advertisement in a newspaper, etc. विज्ञापनदाता, विज्ञापक

**advice** /ədˈvaɪs अड्ˈवाइस्/ *noun* [U] an opinion that you give sb about what he/she should do परामर्श, राय, सलाह *She **took** her doctor's **advice** and gave up smoking.*

> **NOTE** शब्द **advice** अगणनीय संज्ञा (uncountable noun) है। इसलिए 'an advice' या 'some advices' ग़लत प्रयोग हैं, परंतु *'a piece of advice'* और *'a lot of advice'* सही प्रयोग हैं।

**advisable** /ədˈvaɪzəbl अड्ˈवाइज़बल्/ *adj.* (*formal*) that is a good thing to do; sensible उचित, उपयुक्त; विवेकी *It is advisable to reserve a seat.* ✪ विलोम **inadvisable**

**advise** /ədˈvaɪz अड्ˈवाइज़्/ *verb* **1** [I, T] **advise sb (to do sth); advise (sb) (against sth/against doing sth); advise (sb) on sth** to tell sb what you think he/she should do सलाह या सुझाव देना *He did what the doctor advised.* ○ *She advises the Government on economic affairs.* **2** [T] (*formal*) **advise sb (of sth)** to officially tell sb sth; to inform sb आधिकारिक रूप से निर्देश देना या सूचित करना

**adviser** (*AmE* **advisor**) /ədˈvaɪzə(r) अड्ˈवाइज़(र्)/ *noun* [C] a person who gives advice to a company, government, etc. सलाहकार, परामर्शदाता *an adviser on economic affairs*

**advisory** /ədˈvaɪzəri अड्ˈवाइज़रि/ *adj.* giving advice only; not having the power to make decisions केवल सलाहकारी; निर्णय करने के अधिकार से वंचित

**advocacy** /ˈædvəkəsi ˈऐड्वकसि/ *noun* [U] **1 advocacy (of sth)** (*formal*) the giving of public support to an idea, a course of action or a belief समर्थन, हिमायत **2** (*technical*) the work of lawyers who speak about cases in courts of law वकालत

**advocate[1]** /ˈædvəkeɪt ˈऐड्वकेट्/ *verb* [T] (*formal*) to recommend or say that you support a particular plan or action (किसी योजना या कार्रवाही का) समर्थन करना; सिफ़ारिश करना

**advocate[2]** /ˈædvəkət ˈऐड्वकट्/ *noun* [C] **1 an advocate (of/for sth/sb)** a person who supports or speaks in favour of sb or of a public plan or action (किसी व्यक्ति, योजना या कार्रवाही का) समर्थक **2** a lawyer who defends sb in a court of law (न्यायालय में) वकील; एडवोकेट

**adze** (*AmE* **adz**) /ædz ˈऐड्ज़्/ *noun* [C] a heavy tool with a curved edge at 90° to the handle, used for cutting or shaping large pieces of wood लकड़ी काटने में प्रयुक्त भारी औज़ार; बसूला ➪ **tools** पर चित्र देखिए।

**aeolian** (*AmE* **eolian**) /iˈəʊliən इˈओलिअन्/ *adj.* (*technical*) connected with or caused by the action of the wind वायु की क्रिया से उत्पन्न या संबंधित; वातोढ़ (वायु द्वारा लाई गई)

**aeon** (*also* **eon**) /ˈiːən ˈईअन्/ *noun* [C] (*formal*) an extremely long period of time; thousands of years हज़ारों वर्षों का अत्यंत लंबा समय

**aerate** /ˈeəreɪt ˈएअरेट्/ *verb* [T] **1** to make it possible for air to become mixed with soil, water, etc. वायु को मिट्टी, पानी आदि में मिलाना **2** to add a gas to a liquid under pressure दबाव के साथ द्रव पदार्थ में गैस मिलाना *Soda is water that has been aerated.* ▶ **aerated** *adj.* वायुमिश्रित *aerated water*

**aerial[1]** /ˈeəriəl ˈएअरिअल्/ (*AmE* **antenna**) *noun* [C] a long metal stick on a building, car, etc. that receives radio or television signals कार या मकान पर लगी धातु की लंबी छड़ी जो रेडियो या टेलीविज़न तरंगें ग्रहण करती है; एरियल

**aerial[2]** /ˈeəriəl ˈएअरिअल्/ *adj.* from or in the air हवा से या हवा में; हवाई, आकाशीय *an aerial photograph of the town*

**aerobic** /eə'rəʊbɪk एअ'रोबिक्/ *adj.* **1** connected with or needing **oxygen** ऑक्सीजन से संबंधित या ऑक्सीजन पर आधारित ➪ **respiration** पर चित्र देखिए। **2** (used about physical exercise) that we do to improve the way our bodies use oxygen (शारीरिक व्यायाम के संदर्भ में) शरीर द्वारा ऑक्सीजन के प्रयोग में सुधार लाने वाला ➪ **anaerobic** देखिए।

**aerobics** /eə'rəʊbɪks एअ'रोबिक्स्/ *noun* [U] physical exercises that people do to music संगीत की लय पर किया जाने वाला शारीरिक व्यायाम *I do aerobics twice a week to keep fit.*

**aerodrome** /'eərədrəʊm 'एअरड्रोम्/ (*AmE* **airdrome**) *noun* [C] a small airport, used mainly by private planes छोटा हवाई अड्डा, प्रायः निजी विमानों द्वारा प्रयुक्त

**aerodynamics** /ˌeərəʊdaɪ'næmɪks ˌएअरोडाइ'नैमिक्स्/ *noun* [U] the scientific study of the way that things move through the air वायुगति विज्ञान; वायुगतिकि ▶ **aerodynamic** *adj.* वायुगतिक; वायुगतिविज्ञान से संबंधित *the aerodynamic design of a racing car* ▶ **aerodynamically** /-kli कलि/ *adv.* वायुगतिविज्ञान के अनुसार

**aeronautics** /ˌeərə'nɔ:tɪks ˌएअर'नॉटिक्स्/ *noun* [U] the science or practice of building and flying aircraft विमानों के निर्माण और उड़ाने का शास्त्र; विमानविज्ञान ▶ **aeronautical** /-'nɔ:tɪkl -'नॉटिक्ल्/ *adj.* विमानविज्ञान संबंधी, विमान संबंधी, विमान का *an aeronautical engineer*

**aeroplane** /'eərəpleɪn 'एअरप्लेन्/ (*also* **plane;** *AmE* **airplane**) *noun* [C] a vehicle that can fly through the air, with wings and one or more engines हवाई जहाज़, विमान, वायुयान ➪ **plane** पर चित्र देखिए।

**aerosol** /'eərəsɒl 'एअरसॉल्/ *noun* [C] a container in which a liquid substance is kept under pressure. When you press a button the liquid comes out in a fine spray द्रव पदार्थों को दाब में रखकर और बारीक़ धार का फ़व्वारे के रूप में छिड़कने वाला पात्र

**aerospace** /'eərəʊspeɪs 'एअरोस्पेस्/ *noun* [U] (*often used as an adjective*) the industry of building aircraft, and vehicles and equipment to be sent into space वायुयान, अंतरिक्ष यान बनाने का उद्योग

**aesthete** (*also AmE*) /'i:sθi:t 'ईस्थ़ीट्/ *noun* [C] (*formal*) a person who has a love and understanding of art and beautiful things कला और सुंदर वस्तुओं में रुचि तथा जानकारी रखने वाला व्यक्ति; सौंदर्यसंवेदी, सौंदर्यवादी

**aesthetic** /i:s'θetɪk ईस्'थ़ेटिक्/ (*AmE* **esthetic** /es'θetɪk एस्'थ़ेटिक्/) *adj.* concerned with beauty or art सुंदरता और कला से संबंधित; सौंदर्यपरक, सौंदर्यविषयक *The columns are there for purely aesthetic reasons* (= only to look beautiful). ▶ **aesthetically** (*AmE* **esthetically**) /-kli -क्लि/ *adv.* सौंदर्यकरण रीति से *The design is* ***aesthetically pleasing*** *as well as practical.*

**aesthetics** /i:s'θetɪks ईस्'थ़ेटिक्स्/ (*AmE* **esthetics**) *noun* [U] the study of beauty, especially in art कला सौंदर्य का शास्त्र; सौंदर्यशास्त्र

**aetiology** (*AmE* **etiology** /ˌi:ti'ɒlədʒi ˌईटि'ऑलजि/ *noun* [U] the scientific study of the causes of disease रोगों के कारणों का अध्ययन करने वाला शास्त्र; रोगहेतु विज्ञान

**afar** /ə'fɑ:(r) अ'फ़ा(र्)/ *adv.* (*written*)

IDM **from afar** from a long distance away बहुत दूर से

**affable** /'æfəbl 'ऐफ़ब्ल्/ *adj.* pleasant, friendly and easy to talk to मिलनसार, प्रियभाषी, सुशील ▶ **affability** /ˌæfə'bɪləti ˌऐफ़'बिलटि/ *noun* [U] मिलनसारिता, भद्रता ▶ **affably** /'æfəbli ˌऐफ़ब्लि/ मिलनसारिता से, भद्रता के साथ, सौजन्यपूर्वक

**affair** /ə'feə(r) अ'फ़ेअ(र्)/ *noun* **1** [C] an event or a situation मामला, प्रसंग, घटना, स्थिति *The whole affair has been extremely unpleasant.* **2 affairs** [*pl.*] important personal, business, national, etc. matters महत्त्वपूर्ण व्यक्तिगत, व्यवसायिक, राष्ट्रीय आदि मामले *the minister for foreign affairs* ○ *current affairs* (= the political and social events that are happening at the present time) **3** [*sing.*] something private that you do not want other people to know about नितांत निजी मामला *What happened between us is my affair. I don't want to discuss it.*

IDM **state of affairs** ➪ **state**[1] देखिए।

**affect** /ə'fekt अ'फ़ेक्ट्/ *verb* [T] **1** make sb/sth change in a particular way; to influence sb/sth किसी वस्तु या व्यक्ति के व्यवहार को प्रभावित करना; असर डालना *Her personal problems seem to be affecting her work.* ○ *This disease affects the brain.* ➪ **influence** पर नोट देखिए। **2** to make sb feel very sad, angry, etc. किसी को गहरा दुख, क्रोध आदि अनुभव कराना *The whole community was affected by the terrible tragedy.*

NOTE ध्यान दें! शब्द **affect** क्रिया है और शब्द **effect** संज्ञा है—*Smoking can affect your health.* ○ *Smoking can have a bad effect on your health.*

**affected** /ə'fektɪd अ'फ़ेक्टिड्/ *adj.* (used about a person or his/her behaviour) not natural or sincere (व्यक्ति या उसका व्यवहार) बनावटी, दिखावटी, कृत्रिम ✪ विलोम **unaffected** ▶ **affectation** /ˌæfek'teɪʃn ˌऐफ़ेक्'टेश्न्/ *noun* [C, U] बनावटी व्यवहार, दिखावा

**affection** /əˈfekʃn अˈफ़ेक्श्न्/ *noun* [C, U] **(an) affection (for/towards sb/sth)** a feeling of loving or liking sb/sth अनुराग, स्नेह

**affectionate** /əˈfekʃənət अˈफ़ेक्श्नट्/ *adj.* showing that you love or like sb very much स्नेही, स्नेहशील ▶ **affectionately** *adv.* स्नेहपूर्वक, सानुराग

**affidavit** /ˌæfəˈdeɪvɪt ˌऐफ़ˈडेविट्/ *noun* [C] (*technical*) a written statement that you say officially is true, and that can be used as evidence in a court of law शपथपत्र, हलफ़नामा *to make/swear/sign an affidavit*

**affiliate** /əˈfɪlieɪt अˈफ़िलिएट्/ *verb* [T] (*usually passive*) **affiliate sth (to sth)** to connect an organization to a larger organization किसी बड़ी संस्था से संबद्ध होना *Our local club is affiliated to the national association.* ▶ **affiliated** *adj.* संबद्ध ▶ **affiliation** /əˌfɪliˈeɪʃn अˌफ़िलिˈएशन्/ *noun* [C, U] संबद्धता, संबंधन

**affinity** /əˈfɪnəti अˈफ़िनटि/ *noun* [C, U] (*pl.* **affinities**) **1 (an) affinity (for/with sb/sth)** a strong feeling that you like and understand sb/sth, usually because you feel similar to him/her/it in some way सहज लगाव व पसंद की प्रबल भावना, प्रायः किसी से समानता अनुभव होने से उत्पन्न *He had always had an affinity for wild and lonely places.* **2 (an) affinity (with sb/sth); (an) affinity (between A and B)** a similar quality in two or more people or things दो या अधिक व्यक्तियों या वस्तुओं में समान गुण; समानता, सादृश्य

**affirm** /əˈfɜːm अˈफ़म्/ *verb* [T] (*formal*) to say formally or clearly that sth is true or that you support sth strongly दृढ़तापूर्वक किसी बात को सही कहना; निश्चयपूर्वक समर्थन करना ▶ **affirmation** /ˌæfəˈmeɪʃn ˌऐफ़ˈमेशन्/ *noun* [C, U] पुष्ट समर्थन, पुष्टि, दृढ़ कथन

**affirmative** /əˈfɜːmətɪv अˈफ़मटिव्/ *adj.* (*formal*) meaning 'yes' स्वीकृतिसूचक, सकारात्मक *an affirmative answer* NOTE इस वाक्यांश का प्रयोग भी किया जा सकता है ***an answer in the affirmative*** ✪ विलोम **negative**

**affix**[1] /əˈfɪks अˈफ़िक्स्/ *verb* [T] (*often passive*) (*formal*) **affix sth (to sth)** to stick or join sth to sth else चिपकाना, जोड़ना *The label should be firmly affixed to the package.*

**affix**[2] /ˈæfɪks ˈऐफ़िक्स्/ *noun* [C] (*grammar*) a letter or group of letters that are added to the beginning or end of a word and that change its meaning प्रत्यय या उपसर्ग *The 'un-' in 'unhappy' and the '-less' in 'painless' are affixes.* ➪ **prefix** और **suffix** देखिए।

**afflict** /əˈflɪkt अˈफ़्लिक्ट्/ *verb* [T] (*usually passive*) (*formal*) **afflict sb/sth (with sth)** to cause sb/sth to suffer pain, sadness, etc. दुख देना, सताना, पीड़ित करना ▶ **affliction** *noun* [C, U] दुख, वेदना, मनस्ताप

**affluent** /ˈæfluənt ˈऐफ़्लुअन्ट्/ *adj.* having a lot of money धनवान, समृद्ध ▶ **affluence** *noun* [U] समृद्धि, अमीरी *Increased exports have brought new affluence.*

**afford** /əˈfɔːd अˈफ़ॉड्/ *verb* [T] (*usually after can, could or be able to*) **afford sth/to do sth 1** to have enough money or time to be able to do sth कुछ करने या ख़रीद सकने के लिए पर्याप्त धन या समय निकाल सकना *We couldn't afford a television in those days.* ○ *I've spent more money than I can afford.* **2** to not be able to do sth or let sth happen because it would have a bad result for you हानि पहुँचाने की छूट न दे सकना, हानि न सह सकना *The other team was very good so we couldn't afford to make any mistakes.* ▶ **affordable** *adj.* आर्थिक पहुँच के भीतर *affordable prices*

**afforestation** /əˌfɒrɪˈsteɪʃn अˌफ़ॉरिˈस्टेशन्/ *noun* [U] planting trees on an area of land in order to form a forest वनरोपण ✪ विलोम **deforestation**

**affront** /əˈfrʌnt अˈफ़्रन्ट्/ *noun* [C] **an affront (to sb/sth)** something that you say or do that is insulting to sb/sth ऐसा कथन या व्यवहार जो दूसरे को अपमानजनक लगे; निरादर

**afloat** /əˈfləʊt अˈफ़्लोट्/ *adj.* (*not before a noun*) **1** on the surface of the water; not sinking पानी पर तिरता हुआ *A life jacket helps you **stay afloat** if you fall in the water.* **2** (used about a business, an economy, etc.) having enough money to survive (व्यापार, अर्थव्यवस्था आदि) अच्छी आर्थिक स्थिति में होना

**afoot** /əˈfʊt अˈफ़ुट्/ *adj.* (*not before a noun*) being planned or prepared तैयार या योजित किया जा रहा

**aforementioned** /əˌfɔːˈmenʃənd अˌफ़ॉˈमेन्शन्ड्/ (*also* **aforesaid** /əˈfɔːsed अˈफ़ॉसेड्/ *adj.* (*not before a noun*) (*formal*) or (*law*) mentioned before, in an earlier sentence पिछले वाक्य में कथित; पूर्वोल्लिखित *The aforementioned person was seen acting suspiciously.*

**aforethought** /əˈfɔːθɔːt अˈफ़ॉथ़ॉट्/ *adj.*

IDM **with malice aforethought** ➪ **malice** देखिए।

**afraid** /əˈfreɪd अˈफ़्रेड्/ *adj.* (*not before a noun*) **1 afraid (of sb/sth); afraid (of doing sth/to do sth)** having or showing fear; frightened डरा हुआ; भयभीत *Are you afraid of dogs?* ○ *I was too afraid to answer the door.* **2 afraid (that...); afraid (of doing sth)** worried about sth किसी बात को लेकर आशंकित *We were afraid that you* *would be angry.* ○ *to be afraid of offending sb* **3 afraid for sb/sth** worried that sb/sth will be harmed, lost, etc. संभावित हानि को लेकर चिंतित *When I saw the gun I was afraid for my life.*

> NOTE **Afraid** और **frightened** में तुलना कीजिए। **'Afraid'** का प्रयोग केवल संज्ञा के बाद किया जा सकता है, परंतु **frightened** का प्रयोग संज्ञा से पहले भी हो सकता है और बाद में भी—*a frightened animal* ○ *The animal was afraid/frightened.*

IDM **I'm afraid (that...)** used for saying politely that you are sorry about sth खेद जताने के लिए प्रयुक्त (नम्र अभिव्यक्ति) *I'm afraid I can't come on Sunday.* ○ *'Is this seat free?' 'I'm afraid not/it isn't.'*

**afresh** /əˈfreʃ अˈफ्रेश्/ *adv.* (*formal*) again, in a new way पुनः, नए सिरे से *to start afresh*

**aft** /ɑːft आफ़्ट्/ *adv., adj.* (*technical*) at, near or towards the back of a ship or an aircraft जलयान या वायुयान के पिछले हिस्से पर या के समीप ➪ **fore** देखिए।

**after** /ˈɑːftə(r) ˈआफ़्ट(र्)/ *prep., conj., adv.* **1** later than sth; at a later time पश्चात; बाद में *the week after next* ○ *I hope to arrive some time after lunch.* ○ *They arrived at the station after the train had left.* ○ *I went out yesterday morning, and **after that** I was at home all day.* ○ *That was in April. Soon after, I heard that he was ill.*

NOTE वाक्य के अंत में सामान्यतः **afterwards** का प्रयोग किया जाता है—*We played tennis and went to Charu's house afterwards.* **2 ... after...** repeated many times or continuing for a long time बारंबार, बार-बार, बहुत समय से जारी ***day after day*** *of hot weather* ○ *I've told them **time after time** not to do that.* **3** following or behind sb/sth किसी वस्तु या व्यक्ति के पीछे-पीछे; किसी के बाद *Shut the door after you.* ○ *C comes after B in the English alphabet.* **4** looking for or trying to catch or get sb/sth किसी के पीछे, किसी की तलाश में *The police were after him.* **5** because of sth किसी बात के कारण *After the way he behaved, I won't invite him here again.* **6** used when sb/sth is given the name of another person or thing किसी अन्य वस्तु या व्यक्ति के नाम पर नामकरण करने के लिए प्रयुक्त *We called our son Aryan after his grandfather.*

IDM **after all 1** used when sth is different in reality to what sb expected or thought अपेक्षा या धारणा से भिन्न वास्तविकता दर्शाने के लिए प्रयुक्त; आखिरकार, अंत में *So you decided to come after all* (= I thought you weren't going to come)! **2** used for reminding sb of a certain fact किसी को वास्तविकता याद दिलाने के लिए प्रयुक्त *She can't understand. After all, she's only two.*

**after-effect** *noun* [C] an unpleasant result of sth that comes some time later बाद का दुष्प्रभाव ➪ **effect** और **side effect** देखिए।

**afterlife** /ˈɑːftəlaɪf ˈआफ़्टलाइफ़्/ *noun* [*sing.*] a life that some people believe exists after death मृत्यु के बाद का कल्पित जीवन, परलोक का जीवन; मरणोत्तर जीवन

**aftermath** /ˈɑːftəmæθ ˈआफ़्टमैथ्/ *noun* [*sing.*] a situation that is the result of an important or unpleasant event किसी महत्त्वपूर्ण या अप्रिय घटना का परिणाम

**afternoon** /ˌɑːftəˈnuːn ˌआफ़्टˈनून्/ *noun* [C, U] the part of a day between midday and about six o'clock दिन का तीसरा पहर; अपराह्न *I studied all afternoon.* ○ *I usually go for a walk **in the afternoon**.* ○ *He goes swimming every afternoon.*

> NOTE किसी विशेष तीसरे पहर (afternoon) के संदर्भ में कहा जाता है **on Monday, Tuesday, Wednesday, etc. afternoon,** परंतु तीसरे पहर में की जाने वाली किसी क्रिया के विषय के संदर्भ में **in the afternoon** अभिव्यक्ति का प्रयोग किया जाता है।

**good afternoon** exclamation used when you see sb for the first time in the afternoon अपराह्न में पहली बार मिलने पर प्रयुक्त अभिवादन NOTE प्रायः केवल 'Afternoon' का प्रयोग किया जाता है *'Good afternoon, Mrs Mitra.' 'Afternoon, Raju.'* ➪ **morning** पर नोट देखिए।

**aftershave** /ˈɑːftəʃeɪv ˈआफ़्टशेव्/ *noun* [C, U] a liquid with a pleasant smell that men put on their faces after shaving हजामत बनाने के बाद चेहरे पर लगाया जाने वाला सुगंधित द्रव

**aftershock** /ˈɑːftəʃɒk ˈआफ़्टशॉक्/ *noun* [C] a smaller **earthquake** that happens after a bigger one किसी बड़े भूकंप के बाद का झटका

**aftertaste** /ˈɑːftəteɪst ˈआफ़्टटेस्ट्/ *noun* [*sing.*] a taste (usually an unpleasant one) that stays in your mouth after you have eaten or drunk sth कुछ खाने या पीने के बाद मुँह में रह जाने वाला (प्रायः अप्रिय) स्वाद

**afterthought** /ˈɑːftəθɔːt ˈआफ़्टथॉट्/ *noun* [C, *usually sing.*] something that you think of or add to sth else at a later time घटना घट जाने के बाद उत्पन्न विचार; अनुबोध

**afterwards** /ˈɑːftəwədz ˈआफ़्टवड्ज़्/ (*AmE* **afterward**) *adv.* at a later time बाद में, पश्चात *He was taken to hospital and died shortly afterwards.*

**again** /əˈgen; əˈgeɪn अˈगेन्; अˈगेन्/ *adv.* **1** once more; another time एक बार फिर, दुबारा; फिर कभी *Could you say that again, please?* ○ *Don't ever do that again!* **2** in the place or condition that sb/sth was in before पहले की तरह; पहले जैसे *I hope you'll soon be well again.* **3** in addition to sth

इसके अतिरिक्त, साथ ही *'Is that enough?' 'No, I'd like half as much again, please.'* (= one-and-a-half times the original amount)

IDM **again and again** many times अनेक बार; बारंबार *He said he was sorry again and again, but she wouldn't listen.*

**then/there again** used to say that sth you have just said may not happen or be true कथित के विपरीत संभावना का संकेत करने में प्रयुक्त *She might pass her test, but then again she might not.*

**yet again** ➪ **yet** देखिए।

**against** /əˈgenst; əˈgeɪnst अˈगेन्स्ट्; अˈगेन्स्ट्/ *prep.* **1** being an opponent to sb/sth in a game, competition, etc., or an enemy of sb/sth in a war or fight के विरुद्ध *We played football against a school from another district.* **2** not agreeing with or supporting sb/sth से असहमत, के पक्ष में न होना *Are you for or against the plan?* ○ *She felt that everybody was against her.* **3** what a law, rule, etc. says you must not do (क़ानून, नियम आदि) के विरुद्ध *It's **against the law** to buy cigarettes before you are sixteen.* **4** to protect yourself from sb/sth हानि या क्षति से बचने के लिए *Take these pills as a precaution against malaria.* **5** in the opposite direction to sth विपरीत दिशा में *We had to cycle against the wind.* **6** touching sb/sth for support सहारे के लिए किसी चीज़ के साथ टिकाना *I put the ladder against the wall.*

**agate** /ˈægət ˈऐगट्/ *noun* [U, C] a hard stone with bands or areas of colour, used in jewellery गोमेद (रत्न)

**age**[1] /eɪdʒ एज्/ *noun* **1** [C, U] the length of time that sb has lived or that sth has existed उम्र, आयु, वय, अवधि *Ali is 17 **years of age**.* ○ *Children of all ages will enjoy this film.*

> NOTE किसी व्यक्ति की उम्र जानने के लिए प्रश्न *How old is she?* का प्रयोग किया जाता है। इस प्रश्न का उत्तर हो सकता है—*She's eighteen.* या *She's eighteen years old.* परंतु अभिव्यक्ति *She's eighteen years.* सही नहीं है। उम्र के संदर्भ में प्रयुक्त वाक्य प्रयोग के निम्नलिखित उदाहरण हैं—*I'm nearly nineteen.* ○ *a girl of eighteen* ○ *an eighteen-year old girl*

**2** [C, U] a particular period in sb's life उम्र का एक ख़ास पड़ाव; विशेष अवस्था ***middle age/old age*** **3** [U] the state of being old वृद्धावस्था *a face lined with age* ○ *The doctor said she **died of old age**.* ➪ **youth** देखिए। **4** [C] a particular period of history इतिहास का कोई विशेष खंड; युग *the computer age* **5 ages** [*pl.*] (*informal*) a very long time काफ़ी लंबा समय *We had to wait (for) ages at the hospital.* ○ *It's ages since I've seen her.*

IDM **come of age** to become an adult in law वयस्क हो जाना, बालिग़ होना

**feel your age** ➪ **feel** देखिए।

**under age** not old enough by law to do sth (किसी कार्य के लिए क़ानून की दृष्टि से) अवयस्क, अल्पवयस्क, नाबालिग़

**age**[2] /eɪdʒ एज्/ *verb* [I, T] (*pres. part.* **ageing** or **aging**; *pt, pp* **aged** /eɪdʒd ऐज़्ड्/) to become or look old; to cause sb to look old वृद्धा होना या लगना; वृद्ध कर देना *I could see her illness had aged her.* ○ *an ageing aunt*

**aged** **1** /eɪdʒd एज़्ड्/ *adj.* (*not before a noun*) of the age mentioned अमुक आयु का *The woman, aged 26, was last seen at the New Delhi railway station.* **2 the aged** /ˈeɪdʒɪd ˈएजिड्/ *noun* [*pl.*] very old people अतिवृद्ध व्यक्ति NOTE **Senior citizen** अधिक प्रचलित और मान्य प्रयुक्ति है।

**age group** *noun* [C] people of about the same age or within a particular range of ages लगभग एक ही आयु या आयुवर्ग के लोग *This club is very popular with the 20–30 age group.*

**ageism** (*also* **agism**) /ˈeɪdʒɪzəm ˈएजिज़म्/ *noun* [U] unfair treatment of people because they are considered too old अतिवृद्ध मानकर उसके साथ किया गया अनुचित व्यवहार ▶ **ageist** /ˈeɪdʒɪst ˈएजिस्ट्/ *noun* इस प्रकार का व्यवहार करने वाला व्यक्ति ▶ **ageist** *adj.* (व्यवहार) इस तरह का

**ageless** /ˈeɪdʒləs ˈएज्लस्/ *adj.* (*written*) **1** never seeming to grow old जो कभी वृद्ध होता न लगे; चिरयुवा **2** existing for ever; impossible to give an age to चिरस्थायी; जिसकी उम्र आँकी न जा सके *the ageless mystery of the universe*

**age limit** *noun* [C] the oldest or youngest age at which you are allowed to do sth कुछ करने के लिए अधिकतम या न्यूनतम आयु सीमा *to be over/under the age limit*

**agency** /ˈeɪdʒənsi ˈएजन्सि/ *noun* [C] (*pl.* **agencies**) **1** a business that provides a particular service कोई विशेष सेवा प्रदान करने वाला व्यवसाय; एजेंसी *an advertising agency* **2** (*AmE*) a government department कोई सरकारी विभाग; सरकारी एजेंसी

**agenda** /əˈdʒendə अˈजेन्डा/ *noun* [C] a list of matters that need to be discussed or dealt with विचारणीय विषयों की सूची; एजेंडा, कार्यसूची *The first item **on the agenda** at the meeting will be security.* ○ *The government have **set an agenda** for reform over the next ten years.*

**agent** /ˈeɪdʒənt ˈएजन्ट्/ *noun* [C] **1** a person whose job is to do business for a company or for another person दूसरे की ओर से, उसका कारोबार करने वाला व्यक्ति; अभिकर्ता, एजेंट, प्रतिनिधि, आढ़तिया *a travel agent* ○ *an estate agent* **2** = **secret agent**

**age-old** *adj.* that has existed for a very long time युगों पुराना, चिरकाल से चला आ रहा *an age-old custom/problem*

**aggravate** /ˈægrəveɪt ˈऐग्रवेट्/ *verb* [T] **1** to make sth worse or more serious (स्थिति को) बिगाड़ देना; बदतर करना या होना, अधिक गंभीर बनाना **2** to make sb angry or annoyed (*informal*) किसी को क्रोधित कर देना ▶ **aggravation** /ˌægrəˈveɪʃn ˌऐग्रˈवेश्न्/ *noun* [C, U] (स्थिति को) बिगाड़ने या अधिक गंभीर बनाने की क्रिया

**aggregate** /ˈægrɪgət ˈऐग्रिगट्/ *noun*

IDM **on aggregate** in total कुल मिलाकर, कुल जोड़ *Our team won 3–1 on aggregate.*

**aggression** /əˈgreʃn अˈग्रेश्न्/ *noun* [U] **1** angry feelings or behaviour that make you want to attack other people आक्रामक भावनाएँ या व्यवहार *People often react to this kind of situation with fear or aggression.* **2** the act of starting a fight or war without reasonable cause बिना उचित कारण के लड़ाई या युद्ध आरंभ करने की कार्रवाही

**aggressive** /əˈgresɪv अˈग्रेसिव्/ *adj.* **1** ready or likely to fight or argue लड़ाका, हमलावर, झगड़ालू, आक्रामक *an aggressive dog* ○ *Some people get aggressive after drinking alcohol.* **2** using or showing force or pressure in order to succeed सफलता पाने के लिए आक्रामक रुख अपनाने वाला; आक्रामक रूप से क्रियाशील *an aggressive salesman* ▶ **aggressively** *adv.* आक्रामकता से *The boys responded aggressively when I asked them to make less noise.*

**aggressor** /əˈgresə(r) अˈग्रेस(र्)/ *noun* [C] a person or country that attacks sb/sth or starts fighting first आक्रमण में पहल करने वाला देश या व्यक्ति, हमलावर देश या व्यक्ति; आक्रमणकारी

**aggrieved** /əˈgriːvd अˈग्रीव्ड्/ *adj.* (*formal*) upset or angry at being treated unfairly अनुचित या अन्यायपूर्ण व्यवहार के कारण परेशान या क्रोधित; खिन्न

**aghast** /əˈgɑːst अˈगास्ट्/ *adj.* (*not before a noun*) (*written*) **aghast (at sth)** filled with horror and surprise when you see or hear sth भयचकित और विस्मित; भौचक्का *He stood aghast at the sight of so much blood.*

**agile** /ˈædʒaɪl ˈऐजाइल्/ *adj.* able to move quickly and easily फुरतीला, चपल ▶ **agility** /əˈdʒɪləti अˈजिलटि/ *noun* [U] फुरती, चपलता *This sport is a test of both physical and mental agility.*

**agitate** /ˈædʒɪteɪt ˈऐजिटेट्/ *verb* [I] **agitate (for/against sth)** to make other people feel very strongly about sth so that they want to help you achieve it (किसी विषय को लेकर) आंदोलन करना *to agitate for reform*

**agitated** /ˈædʒɪteɪtɪd ˈऐजिटेटिड्/ *adj.* worried or excited परेशान या उत्तेजित ▶ **agitation** /ˌædʒɪˈteɪʃn ˌऐजिˈटेश्न्/ *noun* [U] आंदोलन; उत्तेजना, अशांति

**agitator** /ˈædʒɪteɪtə(r) ˈऐजिटेट(र्)/ *noun* [C] a person who tries to persuade people to take part in political protest आंदोलनकर्ता, उत्पाती, उपद्रवी

**aglow** /əˈgləʊ अˈग्लो/ *adj.* (*written*) shining with warmth or happiness गरमी या प्रसन्नता से चमकता हुआ *The children's faces were aglow with excitement.*

**agnostic** /ægˈnɒstɪk ऐग्ˈनॉस्टिक्/ *noun* [C] a person who is not sure if God exists or not ईश्वर की सत्ता के विषय में संशय रखने वाला; संशयवादी, अज्ञेयवादी

**ago** /əˈgəʊ अˈगो/ *adv.* in the past; back in time from now अतीत में; वर्तमान से पहले, किसी निश्चित समय से पहले *Pawan left ten minutes ago* (= if it is twelve o'clock now, he left at ten to twelve). ○ ***a long time ago***. NOTE **Ago** का प्रयोग भूतकाल (simple past tense) के साथ किया जाता है, वर्तमान कृदंत रूप (present perfect tense) के साथ नहीं—*I arrived in Hyderabad three months ago.*

**agog** /əˈgɒg अˈगॉग्/ *adj.* (*not before a noun*) very excited while waiting to hear sth अति-उत्कंठित, अति-उत्सुक, अति-आतुर (समाचार के लिए) *We were all agog when she said she had good news.*

**agonize** (*also* **-ise**) /ˈægənaɪz ˈऐगनाइज़्/ *verb* [I] to worry or think for a long time about a difficult problem or situation किसी कठिन समस्या या परिस्थिति पर लंबे समय तक सोचना या चिंतित होना *to agonize over a difficult decision*

**agonized** (*also* **-ised**) /ˈægənaɪzd ˈऐगनाइज़्ड्/ *adj.* showing extreme pain or worry वेदनापूर्ण, पीड़ाग्रस्त, अति चिंतित या दुखी; व्यथित *an agonized cry*

**agonizing** (*also* **-ising**) /ˈægənaɪzɪŋ ˈऐगनाइज़िङ्/ *adj.* causing extreme worry or pain व्यथाकारक, पीड़ाजनक; चिंताजनक *an agonizing choice* ○ *an agonizing headache*

**agony** /ˈægəni ˈऐगनि/ *noun* [C, U] (*pl.* **agonies**) great pain or suffering तीव्र वेदना, तेज़ पीड़ा, व्यथा, कष्ट *to be/scream in agony*

**agoraphobia** /ˌægərəˈfəʊbiə ˌऐगरˈफ़ोबिआ/ *noun* [U] fear of being in public places where there are a lot of people सार्वजनिक या भीड़भाड़ वाली जगह में जाने से डर; विवृत-स्थान-भीति ▶ **agoraphobic** *adj.* विवृत-स्थान-भीति से संबंधित

**agrarian** /əˈgreəriən अˈग्रेअरिअन् / *adj.* (*formal*) connected with farming and the use of land for farming कृषि व कृषि भूमि से संबंधित

**agree** /əˈgriː अˈग्री / *verb* **1** [I] **agree (with sb/sth); agree (that...)** to have the same opinion as sb/sth किसी बात या व्यक्ति से सहमत होना; एकमत होना *'I think we should leave now.' 'Yes, I agree.'* ○ *I agree with Praveen.* ✪ विलोम **disagree** **2** [I] **agree (to sth/to do sth)** to say yes to sth किसी बात के लिए 'हाँ' करना; हामी भरना *I asked my boss if I could go home early and she agreed.* ✪ विलोम **refuse** **3** [I, T] **agree (to do sth); agree (on sth)** to make an arrangement or decide sth with sb किसी से सहमत होकर निर्णय लेना या प्रबंध करना *They agreed to meet again the following day.* ○ *Can we agree on a price?* **4** [I] **agree with sth** to think that sth is right किसी बात को सही या उचित मानना *I don't agree with experiments on animals.* **5** [I] to be the same as sth से मेल खाना, के अनुकूल होना *The two accounts of the accident do not agree.*

**agreeable** /əˈgriːəbl अˈग्रीअब्ल् / *adj.* **1** pleasant; nice रुचिकर, सुखद; मनोहर ✪ विलोम **disagreeable** **2** (*formal*) ready to agree राज़ी, सहमत; सहमत होने के लिए तैयार *If you are agreeable, we would like to visit your offices on 21 May.* ▶ **agreeably** /-əbli -अब्लि / *adv.* स्वीकार्यता से *I was agreeably surprised by the film.*

**agreement** /əˈgriːmənt अˈग्रीमन्ट् / *noun* **1** [U] the state of agreeing with sb/sth किसी बात या व्यक्ति से सहमति *We **are totally in agreement with** what you have said.* ✪ विलोम **disagreement** **2** [C] a contract or decision that two or more people have made together अनुबंध-पत्र, क़रारनामा *The leaders **reached an agreement** after five days of talks.*

**agriculture** /ˈægrɪkʌltʃə(r) ˈऐग्रिकल्च(र्) / *noun* [U] keeping animals and growing crops for food; farming खेती, कृषि *the Minister of Agriculture* ▶ **agricultural** /ˌægrɪˈkʌltʃərəl ˌऐग्रिˈकल्चरल् / *adj.* कृषि-संबंधी

**agrochemical** /ˈægrəʊkemɪkl, ऐग्रोकेमिकल् / *noun* [C] a chemical used in farming, especially for killing insects or for making plants grow better कृषि-रसायन; खेती में प्रयोग किए जाने वाले रसायन

**agronomist** /əˈgrɒnəmɪst अˈग्रॉनमिस्ट् / *noun* [C] a scientist who studies the relationship between the plants that farmers grow and the environment कृषिशास्त्री, सस्यविज्ञानी ▶ **agronomy** *noun* [U] कृषिशास्त्र, सस्यविज्ञान

**aground** /əˈgraʊnd अˈग्राउन्ड् / *adv.* if a ship **runs/goes aground,** it touches the ground in water that is not deep enough and it cannot move (जहाज़) छिछले पानी में फँसा *The oil tanker ran/went aground off the Spanish coast.* ▶ **aground** *adj.* छिछले पानी में फँसा हुआ; भूग्रस्त

**ah** /ɑː आ / *exclamation* used for expressing surprise, pleasure, understanding, etc. आश्चर्य, आनंद, बोध आदि दर्शाने के लिए प्रयुक्त *Ah, there you are.*

**aha** /ɑːˈhɑː आˈहा / *exclamation* used when you suddenly find or understand sth अचानक कोई जानकारी या सूचना मिलने पर आश्चर्य व्यक्त करने के लिए प्रयुक्त *Aha! Now I understand.*

**ahead** /əˈhed अˈहेड् / *adv., adj.* **ahead (of sb/sth)** **1** in front of sb/sth से आगे, आगे, सामने *The path ahead looked narrow and steep.* ○ *Look **straight ahead** and don't turn round!* **2** before or more advanced than sb/sth (किसी से) आगे, बढ़त में, अग्रसर *Jai arrived a few minutes ahead of us.* ○ *The Japanese are **way ahead** of us in their research.* **3** into the future आने वाले समय में, भविष्य में *We must **think ahead** and make a plan.* **4** winning in a game, competition, etc. किसी खेल में बढ़त *The goal put Italy 2–1 **ahead** at half-time.* ➪ **behind** देखिए।

IDM **ahead of your time** so modern that people do not understand you इतना आधुनिक कि समकालीन लोग समझ न पाएं

**streets ahead** ➪ **street** देखिए।

**ahimsa** *noun* [U] (*IndE*) the belief in non-violence अहिंसावाद

**aid¹** /eɪd एड् / *noun* **1** [U] help मदद, सहायता *to walk **with the aid of** a stick* ○ *He had to **go to the aid of** a child in the river.* ➪ **first aid** देखिए। **2** [C] a person or thing that helps you सहायक वस्तु, व्यक्ति या उपकरण *a hearing aid* ○ *dictionaries and other study aids* **3** [U] money, food, etc. that is sent to a country or to people in order to help them किसी देश या क्षेत्र को भेजी गई राहत सहायक सामग्री (राशी, खाद्य पदार्थ आदि) *We sent aid to the earthquake victims.* ○ *economic aid*

IDM **in aid of sb/sth** in order to collect money for sb/sth, especially for a charity की सहायता हेतु *a concert in aid of children in need*

**aid²** /eɪd एड् / *verb* [T] (*formal*) to help sb/sth सहायता करना, मदद पहुँचाना *Sleep aids recovery from illness.*

IDM **aid and abet** to help sb to do sth that is not allowed by law किसी व्यक्ति की ग़ैर-क़ानूनी काम में मदद करना

**aide** /eɪd एड्/ *noun* [C] a person who helps sb important in the government, etc.; an assistant वरिष्ठ अधिकारी का परिसहायक; सहायक

**AIDS** (*also* **Aids**) /eɪdz एड्ज़्/ *noun* [U] an illness which destroys the body's ability to fight infection शरीर की प्रतिरोधक क्षमता नष्ट करने वाला रोग; एड्स *to contract AIDS* ○ *the AIDS virus*

**NOTE** **AIDS** का विस्तृत रूप **Acquired Immune Deficiency Syndrome** है।

**ailing** /ˈeɪlɪŋ ˈएलिङ्/ *adj.* not in good health; weak बीमार; कमज़ोर *an ailing economy*

**ailment** /ˈeɪlmənt ˈएल्मन्ट्/ *noun* [C] (*formal*) any illness that is not very serious बीमारी जो बहुत गंभीर न हो

**aim**[1] /eɪm एम्/ *noun* **1** [C] something that you intend to do; a purpose लक्ष्य, उद्देश्य, अभिप्राय *Our aim is to open offices in India.* ○ *His only aim in life is to make money.* **2** [U] the act of pointing sth at sb/sth before trying to hit him/her/it with it निशाना बाँधने की क्रिया *She picked up the gun, **took aim** and fired.* ○ *Jyoti's aim was good and she hit the target.*

**aim**[2] /eɪm एम्/ *verb* **1** [I] **aim to do sth; aim at/for sth** to intend to do or achieve sth कोई काम करने या कुछ प्राप्त करने का इरादा रखना; लक्ष्य में रखना, उद्देश्य बनाना *The company is aiming at a 25% increase in profit.* ○ *to aim for perfection* **2** [T] **aim sth at sb/sth** to direct sth at a particular person or group किसी व्यक्ति या वर्ग को लक्ष्य बनाकर कुछ करना *The advertising campaign is aimed at young people.* **3** [I, T] **aim (sth) (at sb/sth)** to point sth at sb/sth before trying to hit him/her/it with it किसी पर निशाना साधना *She aimed (the gun) at the target and fired.*

**IDM** **be aimed at sth/doing sth** to be intended to achieve sth कुछ प्राप्त करने का इरादा रखना *The new laws are aimed at reducing heavy traffic in cities.*

**aimless** /ˈeɪmləs ˈएम्लस्/ *adj.* having no purpose निरुद्देश्य, लक्ष्यहीन *an aimless discussion* ▶ **aimlessly** *adv.* निरुद्देश्य भाव से

**ain't** /eɪnt एन्ट्/ (*informal*) ➪ **am not, is not, are not, has not, have not** का संक्षिप्त रूप

**NOTE** **Ain't** को सही प्रयोग नहीं माना जाता है।

**AIR** /ˌeɪaɪˈɑː(r) ˌएआई ˈआ(र्)/ *noun* [U] *abbr.* All India Radio. It is the radio broadcaster of India ऑल इंडिया रेडियो; भारत की रेडियो प्रसारण सेवा

**air**[1] /eə(r) एअ(र्)/ *noun* **1** [U] the mixture of gases that surrounds the earth and that people, animals and plants breathe वायु, हवा ***fresh air*** ○ *The air was polluted by smoke from the factory.* **2** [U] the space around and above things भूसतह के ऊपर ख़ाली स्थान *to throw a ball high **into the air*** ○ *in **the open air*** (= outside) **3** [U] travel or transport in an aircraft विमान द्वारा यात्रा या परिवहन *to travel **by air*** ○ *an air ticket* **4** [*sing.*] **an air (of sth)** the particular feeling or impression that is given by sb/sth किसी व्यक्ति या वस्तु द्वारा उत्पन्न विशेष भावना या प्रभाव *She has a confident air.*

**IDM** **a breath of fresh air** ➪ **breath** देखिए।

**clear the air** ➪ **clear**[3] देखिए।

**in the air** probably going to happen soon जिसके शीघ्र होने की संभावना हो; जो जल्द होने को हो *A feeling of change was in the air.*

**in the open air** ➪ **open**[1] देखिए।

**on (the) air** sending out programmes on the radio or television रेडियो या टेलीविज़न द्वारा कार्यक्रम का प्रसारण *This radio station is on the air 24 hours a day.*

**vanish, etc. into thin air** ➪ **thin**[1] देखिए।

**air**[2] /eə(r) एअ(र्)/ *verb* **1** [I, T] to put clothes, etc. in a warm place or outside in the fresh air to make sure they are completely dry; to become dry in this way कपड़े आदि को सुखाना; कपड़े आदि का सूखना **2** [I, T] to make a room, etc. fresh by letting air into it; to become fresh in this way कमरे के भीतर ताज़ी हवा आने देना; खुले में जाकर ताज़ी हवा खाना **3** [T] to tell people what you think about sth अपने विचार अभिव्यक्त करना, मन की बात कहना *The discussion gave people a chance to **air** their **views**.*

**airbase** /ˈeəbeɪs ˈएअबेस्/ *noun* [C] an airport for military aircraft सैनिक विमानों के लिए हवाई अड्डा

**airborne** /ˈeəbɔːn ˈएअबॉन्/ *adj.* **1** (used about a plane or passengers) flying in the air (विमान या विमानयात्रियों के लिए प्रयुक्त) आकाश में उड़ते हुए *Five minutes after getting on the plane we were airborne.* **2** (*only before a noun*) carried through the air वायुवाहित ➪ **water-borne** देखिए।

**airbrush**[1] /ˈeəbrʌʃ ˈएअब्रश्/ *noun* [C] an artist's tool for spraying paint onto a surface, that works by air pressure सतह पर रंग छिड़कने के लिए चित्रकारों द्वारा प्रयुक्त फुहारा जो दाब के सिद्धांत पर काम करता है; फुहाररंजित्र

**airbrush**[2] /ˈeəbrʌʃ ˈएअब्रश्/ *verb* [T] **airbrush sth (out)** to paint sth with an airbrush; to change a detail in a photograph using this tool एअरब्रश से किसी वस्तु पर रंग लगाना; एअरब्रश से किसी फ़ोटोचित्र में कुछ बदलाव लाना *Somebody had been airbrushed out of the picture.*

**air conditioner** *noun* [C] a machine that cools and dries air वातानुकूलित करने का यंत्र; एअर कंडीशनर

**air conditioning** *noun* [U] (*abbr.* **a/c**) the system that keeps the air in a room, building, etc. cool and dry वातानुकूलन ▶ **air-conditioned** *adj.* वातानुकूलित *air-conditioned offices*

**air-cooler** (*also* **room-cooler**) *noun* [C] (*IndE*) a device used for cooling and reducing the temperature inside buildings. It works on the principle of air being passed over water भवनों के अंदर का तापमान कम करने का उपकरण। इस प्रक्रिया में हवा पानी के ऊपर से गुज़रती है; कूलर

**aircraft** /ˈeəkrɑːft ˈएअक्राफ़्ट्/ *noun* [C] (*pl.* **aircraft**) any vehicle that can fly in the air, for example a plane वायु में उड़ने वाला किसी भी प्रकार का यान, जैसे विमान

**aircraft carrier** *noun* [C] a ship that carries military aircraft and that has a long flat area where they can take off and land सैनिक विमानों को ले जाने वाला जलपोत; विमान-वाहक

**aircrew** /ˈeəkruː ˈएअक्रू/ *noun* [C, *with sing. or pl. verb*] the pilot and other people who fly a plane, especially in the air force विमानकर्मी दल, विशेषतः वायु सेना में

**airdrome** /ˈeədrəʊm ˈएअड्रोम्/ (*AmE*) = **aerodrome**

**airdrop** /ˈeədrɒp ˈएअड्रॉप्/ *noun* [C] the act of dropping supplies, equipment, soldiers, etc. from an aircraft using a **parachute** पैराशूट की सहायता से विमान से सैनिकों, सामान आदि को ज़मीन पर उतारने की क्रिया

**airfield** /ˈeəfiːld ˈएअफ़ील्ड्/ *noun* [C] an area of land where aircraft can land or take off. An airfield is smaller than an airport हवाई पट्टी, यह हवाई अड्डे से छोटी होती है

**air force** *noun* [C, *with sing. or pl. verb*] the part of a country's military organization that fights in the air किसी देश की वायुसेना ➪ **army** और **navy** देखिए।

**air gun** (*also* **air rifle**) *noun* [C] a gun that uses air pressure to fire small metal balls (**pellets**) वायुदाब के प्रयोग से धातु की बनी छोटी गोलियाँ दाग़ने वाली बंदूक़

**air hostess** (*also* **hostess**) *noun* [C] a woman who looks after the passengers on a plane विमान परिचारिका ✪ पर्याय **stewardess** ➪ **steward** देखिए।

**airless** /ˈeələs ˈएअलस्/ *adj.* not having enough fresh air ताज़ी हवा से रहित; उमसदार, घुटनभरा *The room was hot and airless.*

**airlift** /ˈeəlɪft ˈएअलिफ़्ट्/ *noun* [C] an operation to take people, soldiers, food, etc. to or from an area by plane, especially in an emergency or when roads are closed or dangerous विशेषतः संकटकाल में किसी क्षेत्र से मनुष्यों, सैनिकों, खाद्य सामग्री आदि को विमान द्वारा दूसरे स्थान पर ले जाने की कार्रवाही; वायुवहन ▶ **airlift** *verb* [T] आपात स्थिति में विमान द्वारा वहन करना *Two casualties* ***were airlifted to safety***.

**airline** /ˈeəlaɪn ˈएअलाइन्/ *noun* [C] a company that provides regular flights for people or goods in aircraft नियमित विमान सेवा प्रदान करने वाली कंपनी

**airliner** /ˈeəlaɪnə(r) ˈएअलाइन(र्)/ *noun* [C] a large plane that carries passengers यात्रियों को ले जाने वाला बड़ा विमान

**airlock** /ˈeəlɒk ˈएअलॉक्/ *noun* [C] **1** a small room with a tightly closed door at each end, which you go through to reach another area at a different air pressure, for example on a spacecraft or **submarine** निर्वात कक्ष **2** a bubble of air that blocks the flow of liquid in a pipe or **pump** हवा का बुलबुला जिसके कारण किसी नली या पंप में से द्रव का प्रवाह रुक जाता है

**airmail** /ˈeəmeɪl ˈएअमेल्/ *noun* [U] the system for sending letters, packages, etc. by plane हवाई डाक सेवा *I sent the parcel (by) airmail.*

**airplane** /ˈeəpleɪn ˈएअप्लेन्/ (*AmE*) = **aeroplane**

**air pocket** *noun* [C] **1** a closed area that becomes filled with air एक बंद क्षेत्र जिसमें हवा भर जाए *Make sure there are no air pockets around the roots of the plant.* **2** an area of low air pressure that makes a plane suddenly drop while flying कम वायुदाब वाला क्षेत्र जहाँ उड़ता हुआ विमान एकाएक कुछ नीचे आ जाता है; हवाई गर्त

**airport** /ˈeəpɔːt ˈएअपॉट्/ *noun* [C] a place where aircraft can land and take off and that has buildings for passengers to wait in हवाई अड्डा, विमान पत्तन

**air raid** *noun* [C] an attack by military aircraft हवाई हमला

**air rifle** = **air gun**

**airship** /ˈeəʃɪp ˈएअशिप्/ *noun* [C] a large aircraft without wings, filled with gas that is lighter than air, and driven by engines गैस-भरा और इंजिनचालित बड़ा विमान जिसके पंख नहीं होते; वायु-पोत

**airsick** /ˈeəsɪk ˈएअसिक्/ *adj.* feeling sick or vomiting as a result of travelling on a plane विमान यात्रा के दौरान जी मिचलाना ▶ **airsickness** *noun* [U] उड्डयन अस्वस्थता ➪ **carsick, seasick** और **travel-sick** देखिए।

**airspace** /ˈeəspeɪs ˈएअस्पेस्/ *noun* [U] the part of the sky that is above a country and that belongs to that country by law वह आकाशीय क्षेत्र जो क़ानूनन उस देश का है जिसके ऊपर वह पड़ता है

**airstrip** /ˈeəstrɪp ˈएअस्ट्रिप्/ (*also* **landing strip**) *noun* [C] a narrow piece of land where aircraft can take off and land हवाई पट्टी

**airtight** /ˈeətaɪt ˈएअटाइट्/ *adj.* that air cannot get into or out of वायुरुद्ध

**airtime** /ˈeətaɪm ˈएअटाइम्/ *noun* [U] **1** the amount of time that is given to a subject on radio or television किसी कार्यक्रम की प्रसारण अवधि **2** the amount of time that is paid for when you use a **mobile phone** मोबाइल फ़ोन के प्रयोग के लिए निर्धारित समय जिसके लिए शुल्क अदा किया गया है *This deal gives you 90 minutes free airtime a week.*

**air-to-air** *adj.*(*usually before a noun*) from one aircraft to another while they are both flying हवा से हवा में *an air-to-air missile*

**air traffic controller** *noun* [C] a person whose job is to organize routes for aircraft, and to tell pilots by radio when they can land and take off हवाई यातायात नियंत्रक

**airwaves** /ˈeəweɪvz ˈएअवेव्ज़्/ *noun* [*pl.*] radio waves that are used in sending out radio and television programmes रेडियो तरंगें जिनके द्वारा रेडियो और टीवी कार्यक्रम प्रसारित किए जाते हैं *A well-known voice came **over the airwaves**.*

**airway** /ˈeəweɪ ˈएअवे/ *noun* [C] the passage from your nose and throat down into your lungs, through which you breathe श्वसन मार्ग

**airworthy** /ˈeəwɜːðɪ ˈएअवदि/ *adj.* (used about aircraft) safe to fly (विमान के लिए प्रयुक्त) उड़ान योग्य, उड़ने के लिए सुरक्षित ▶ **airworthiness** *noun* [U] उड़न योग्यता

**airy** /ˈeəri ˈएअरि/ *adj.* having a lot of fresh air inside हवादार

**aisle** /aɪl आइल्/ *noun* [C] a passage between the rows of seats in a church, theatre, etc. चर्च, थिएटर आदि में सीटों के बीच का रास्ता; पार्श्ववीथि, मध्यवीथि

**ajar** /əˈdʒɑː(r) अˈजा(र्)/ *adj.* (*not before a noun*) (used about a door) slightly open अधखुला (दरवाज़ा)

**akin** /əˈkɪn अˈकिन्/ *adj.* **akin to sth** similar to sth किसी के समान; सदृश

**à la carte** /ˌɑː lɑːˈkɑːt ˌआ लाˈकाट्/*adj., adv.* (used about a meal in a restaurant) where each dish on the list of available dishes (**menu**) has a separate price and there is not a fixed price for a complete meal (रेस्तराँ में मिलने वाला वह भोजन) जिसमें व्यजंन की क़ीमत अलग-अलग होती है और थाली का हिसाब नहीं होता

**alap** (*also* **alaap**) *noun* [U] (*IndE*) the improvised opening section of a Hindustani classical performance that starts at a low tempo उत्तर भारतीय शास्त्रीय संगीत के प्रदर्शन का प्रारंभिक अंश जो धीमी ताल से शुरू होता है (शास्त्रीय गायकी का पहला भाग)

**alarippu** *noun* [C, U] (*IndE*) a short opening prayer with which a **Bhartanatyam** performance usually begins. It is an introductory piece in which the dancer pays respect to the guru, the gods and the spectators देव वंदना जिससे भरतनाट्यम का प्रदर्शन प्रारंभ होता है। इस प्रारंभिक प्रस्तुति में नर्तक अपने गुरु, ईश्वर एवं दर्शकों का अभिवादन करता है

**alarm**[1] /əˈlɑːm अˈलाम्/ *noun* **1** [U] a sudden feeling of fear or worry एकाएक उत्पन्न डर या चिंता; घबराहट *She jumped up **in alarm*** **2** [*sing.*] a warning of danger ख़तरे की चेतावनी *A small boy saw the smoke and **raised the alarm**.* **3** [C] a machine that warns you of danger, for example by ringing a loud bell ख़तरे की चेतावनी देने वाला यंत्र (जैसे घंटी बजाकर) *The burglars **set off the alarm** when they broke the window.* ○ ***The fire/burglar alarm** went off in the middle of the night.* **4** [C] = **alarm clock**

IDM **a false alarm** ⇨ **false** देखिए।

**alarm**[2] /əˈlɑːm अˈलाम्/ *verb* [T] to make sb/sth feel suddenly frightened or worried किसी को एकाएक भयभीत या चिंतित कर देना

**alarm clock** (*also* **alarm**) *noun* [C] a clock that you can set to make a noise at a particular time to wake you up एलार्म घड़ी *She set the alarm clock for half past six.*

**alarmed** /əˈlɑːmd अˈलाम्ड्/ *adj.* **alarmed (at/by sth)** feeling frightened or worried भयभीत या चिंतित

**alarming** /əˈlɑːmɪŋ अˈलामिङ्/ *adj.* that makes you frightened or worried चिंताजनक, भयप्रद ▶ **alarmingly** *adv.* भयप्रद या चिंताजनक तरीक़े से

**alarmist** /əˈlɑːmɪst अˈलामिस्ट्/ *adj.* causing unnecessary fear and worry अनावश्यक डर या चिंता फैलाने वाला; भयप्रसारक *The reports of a flu epidemic were alarmist.* ▶ **alarmist** *noun* [C] अनावश्यक या अकारण भय उत्पन्न करने वाला व्यक्ति या वस्तु

**alas** /əˈlæs अˈलैस्/ *exclamation* (*formal*) used for expressing sadness about sth दुख या चिंता के उद्‌गार के लिए प्रयुक्त

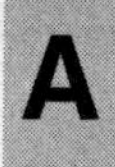



**albatross** /ˈælbətrɒs ˈएलुबट्रॉस्/ *noun* [C] **1** a very large white seabird with long wings that lives in the Pacific and Southern Oceans एक श्वेत रंग की बड़ी समुद्री चिड़िया जो प्रशांत महासागर और दक्षिणी समुद्री क्षेत्र में रहती है ➪ **seabird** पर चित्र देखिए। **2** [*usually sing.*] (*written*) a thing that causes problems or that prevents you from doing sth अवरोधक या समस्याजनक तत्व *The national debt is an albatross around the government's neck.*

**albeit** /ˌɔːlˈbiːɪt ˈऑल्ˈबीइट्/ *conj.* (*formal*) although यद्यपि, हालाँकि *He finally agreed to come, albeit unwillingly.*

**albino** /ælˈbiːnəʊ ऐल्ˈबीनो/ *noun* [C] (*pl.* **albinos**) a person or animal with very white skin, white hair and pink eyes सफ़ेद त्वचा, केश तथा गुलाबी आँखों वाला व्यक्ति या पशु

**album** /ˈælbəm ˈऐलुबम्/ *noun* [C] **1** a collection of songs on one CD, cassette, etc. एक सीडी या कैसेट में संग्रहीत गाने; एलबम् *The band are about to release their third album.* ➪ **single** देखिए। **2** a book in which you can keep stamps, photographs, etc. that you have collected ऐसी पुस्तक जिसमें डाक टिकट, फ़ोटोचित्र आदि संग्रहीत हों

**albumen** /ˈælbjumɪn ˈऐलुब्युमिन्/ *noun* [U] the clear inside part of an egg that turns white when you cook it (अंडे का) श्वेतक

**alchemist** /ˈælkəmɪst ˈऐलुकमिस्ट्/ *noun* [C] a person who studied alchemy प्राचीनकालिक रसायनशास्त्र का ज्ञाता; कीमियागर

**alchemy** /ˈælkəmi ˈऐलुकमि/ *noun* [U] **1** a form of chemistry in the Middle Ages which involved trying to discover how to change ordinary metals into gold प्राचीनकालिक रसायनशास्त्र जिसमें साधारण धातुओं को सोने में बदलने की विधि की खोज की जाती थी **2** (*written*) magic power that can change things वस्तुओं को बदल देने वाली जादुई शक्ति

**alcohol** /ˈælkəhɒl ˈऐलुकहॉल्/ *noun* **1** [U] drinks such as beer, wine, etc. that contain alcohol बिअर आदि मादक पेय **2** [U, C] the colourless liquid that is found in drinks such as beer, wine, etc. and is used in medicines, cleaning products, etc. बिअर, द्राक्षा आदि पेयों में पाए जाने वाला और दवाओं आदि में प्रयुक्त रंगहीन द्रव्य

**alcoholic¹** /ˌælkəˈhɒlɪk ˌऐलुकˈहॉलिक्/ *adj.* containing alcohol मादक *alcoholic drinks* ✪ विलोम **non-alcoholic** NOTE अलकोहलहीन पेय को **soft drinks** भी कहते हैं।

**alcoholic²** /ˌælkəˈhɒlɪk ˌऐलुकˈहॉलिक्/ *noun* [C] a person who cannot stop drinking large amounts of alcohol मादक पेय का आदी; शराबी, शराबख़ोर

**alcoholism** /ˈælkəhɒlɪzəm ˈऐलुकˈहॉलिज़म्/ *noun* [U] a medical condition that is caused by regularly drinking a large amount of alcohol and not being able to stop शराबख़ोरी के कारण उत्पन्न शरीरिक अक्षमता

**alcove** /ˈælkəʊv ˈऐलुकोव्/ *noun* [C] a small area in a room where one part of the wall is further back than the rest of the wall कमरे की दीवार में मेहराबदार ताख, आला

**ale** /eɪl एल्/ *noun* [U, C] a type of beer एक प्रकार की बिअर

**alert¹** /əˈlɜːt अˈलट्/ *adj.* **alert (to sth)** watching, listening, etc. for sth with all your attention सतर्क, चौकन्ना, चौकस *Security guards must be alert at all times.*

**alert²** /əˈlɜːt अˈलट्/ *noun* [C] a warning of possible danger संभावित ख़तरे की चेतावनी *a bomb alert*

IDM **on the alert (for sth)** ready or prepared for danger or an attack किसी ख़तरे या आक्रमण का सामना करने के लिए तैयार; सावधान

**alert³** /əˈlɜːt अˈलट्/ *verb* [T] **alert sb (to sth)** to warn sb of danger or a problem ख़तरे के प्रति सावधान करना

**alfalfa** /ælˈfælfə एल्ˈफ़ैल्फ़ा/ *noun* [U] a plant with small divided leaves and purple flowers, grown as food for farm animals and as a salad vegetable छोटे पत्तों और बैंगनी फूलों युक्त पौधा जो चारे और सलाद पत्ते के रूप में प्रयोग किया जाता है; लसुनघास

**algae** /ˈældʒiː; ˈælgiː ˈऐलुजी; ˈऐलुगी/ *noun* [*pl., with sing. or pl. verb*] very simple plants that grow mainly in water पानी में उगने वाली घास; शैवाल, सेवार

**algebra** /ˈældʒɪbrə ˈऐलुजिब्रा/ *noun* [U] (*mathematics*) a type of mathematics in which letters and symbols are used to represent numbers बीजगणित

▶ **algebraic** /ˌældʒɪˈbreɪɪk ˌऐलुजिˈब्रेइक्/ *adj.* बीजगणितीय *an algebraic equation*

**algorithm** /ˈælgərɪðəm ˈऐलुगरिद्म्/ *noun* [C] (*computing, mathematics*) a set of rules that must be followed when solving a particular problem गणितीय समस्याएँ हल करने के लिए कुछ निर्धारित नियम; प्रतीकगणित, ऐलगोरिद्म

**alias¹** /ˈeɪliəs ˈएलिअस्/ *noun* [C] a false name, for example one that is used by a criminal छद्मनाम, उर्फ़

**alias²** /ˈeɪliəs ˈएलिअस्/ *adv.* used for giving sb's false name किसी को उपनाम देने के लिए प्रयुक्त

**alibi** /ˈæləbaɪ ˈऐलबाइ/ *noun* [C] (*pl.* **alibis**) **an alibi (for sth)** a statement by sb that says you were in a different place at the time of a crime and so cannot be guilty of the crime अपराध के समय अन्यत्र उपस्थित होने का कथन; अन्यत्रता

**alien¹** /ˈeɪliən ˈएलिअन्/ *noun* [C] **1** a creature that comes from another planet अन्य लोकवासी, दूसरे ग्रह का वासी **2** (*formal*) a person who comes from another country विदेशी व्यक्ति

**alien²** /ˈeɪliən ˈएलिअन्/ *adj.* **1** of another country; foreign अन्यदेशीय; विदेशीय *an alien land* **2 alien (to sb)** very strange and completely different from your normal experience विचित्र व अनजान; सर्वथा अपरिचित

**alienate** /ˈeɪliəneɪt ˈएलिअनेट्/ *verb* [T] **1** to make people feel that they cannot share your opinions any more अपने से दूर कर देना, अपनों को दूर कर देना *The Prime Minister's new policies on defence have alienated many of his supporters.* **2 alienate sb (from sb/sth)** to make sb feel that he/she does not belong somewhere or is not part of sth लोगों से या समूह से किसी को भिन्न अनुभव कराना ▶ **alienation** /ˌeɪliəˈneɪʃn ˌएलिअˈनेश्न्/ *noun* [U] विलगाव, विमुखता

**alight¹** /əˈlaɪt अˈलाइट्/ *adj.* on fire; burning प्रदीप्त; जलता हुआ *A cigarette **set** the petrol **alight**.*

> **NOTE** **Alight** का प्रयोग संज्ञा के बाद ही किया जाता है, परंतु संज्ञा के पूर्व **burning** शब्द का प्रयोग किया जा सकता है—*The whole building was alight.* ○ *a burning building.*

**alight²** /əˈlaɪt अˈलाइट्/ *verb* [I] (*written*) **alight (from sth)** to get off a bus, train, etc. बस, रेलगाड़ी आदि से उतरना

**align** /əˈlaɪn अˈलाइन्/ *verb* [T] **1 align sth (with sth)** to arrange things in a straight line or so that they are parallel to sth else पंक्तिबद्ध करना, सीध मिलाना *to align the wheels of a car* **2 align yourself with sb** to say that you support the opinions of a particular group, country, etc. किसी दल, देश आदि के विचारों का समर्थन करना

**alignment** /əˈlaɪnmənt अˈलाइन्मन्ट्/ *noun* **1** [U] arrangement in a straight line or parallel to sth else सीध, संरेखण **2** [C, U] an agreement between political parties, countries, etc. to support the same thing सामान उद्देश्य से राजनीतिक दलों, राष्ट्रों आदि का सम्मिलन

**alike** /əˈlaɪk अˈलाइक्/ *adj., adv.* (*not before a noun*) **1** very similar बहुत समान, सर्वथा सदृश *The two boys are very alike.* **2** in the same way समान रूप से, समान रीति से *to treat women and men alike* ○ *The book is popular with adults and children alike.*

**alimentary canal** /ˌælɪmentəri kəˈnæl ˌऐलिमेन्टरि कˈनैल्/ *noun* [*sing.*] the long passage inside your body which food moves along, from the mouth to the opening where it leaves your body as waste आहार नाल, पोषण नाल

**alimony** /ˈælɪməni ˈऐलिमनि/ *noun* [U] money that you have to pay by law to your former wife or husband after getting divorced तलाक़ के बाद पूर्व पति या पत्नी को क़ानूनन दिया जाने वाला धन; गुजारा भत्ता

**alive** /əˈlaɪv अˈलाइव्/ *adj.* **1** not dead; living जीवित; ज़िंदा *The quick action of the doctors **kept** the child **alive**.*

> **NOTE** **Alive** का प्रयोग केवल संज्ञा के बाद ही हो सकता है, संज्ञा के पूर्व शब्द **living** का प्रयोग किया जाता है—*Are her parents still alive?* ○ *Does she have any living relatives?*

**2** continuing to exist जारी, विद्यमान, अमल में *Many old traditions are very much alive in this area of the country.* **3** full of life सजीव, फुरतीला, ज़िंदादिल *In the evening the town really **comes alive**.*

**alkali** /ˈælkəlaɪ ˈऐल्कलाइ/ *noun* [C, U] a chemical substance that reacts with acid to form a salt. An alkali has a pH value of more than 7 अम्ल के साथ अभिक्रिया होने पर एक रसायन जो लवण बनाता है; क्षार, क्षार का pH मान 7 से अधिक होता है ➪ **acid** और **base** देखिए तथा **pH** पर चित्र देखिए। ▶ **alkaline** *adj.* क्षारीय

**alkaloid** /ˈælkəlɔɪd ˈऐल्कलॉइड्/ *noun* [C] a poisonous substance that is found in some plants. Some alkaloids are used in drugs कुछ पौधों में पाया जाने वाला विषैला पदार्थ(औषधियों में प्रयुक्त)

**alkane** /ˈælkeɪn ˈऐल्केन्/ *noun* [C] any of a series of gases that contain **hydrogen** and **carbon** हाइड्रोजन और कार्बनयुक्त कोई भी गैस *Methane and propane are alkanes.*

**alkene** /ˈælkiːn ˈऐल्कीन्/ *noun* [C] any of a series of gases that contain **hydrogen** and **carbon** and that have a double **bond** हाइड्रोजन और कार्बन से युक्त कोई भी गैस जिसमें अणुओं को जोड़े रखने की सामान्य से दुगुनी शक्ति होती है

**all¹** /ɔːl ऑल्/ *det., pronoun* **1** the whole of a thing or of a period of time समस्त, समूचा, सारा *All (of) the food has gone.* ○ *all week/month/year* ○ *He worked hard all his life.* **2** every one of a group समूह या दल में सब; सभी *The people at the meeting all voted against the plan.* ○ *All of them voted against the plan.* **3** everything that; the only thing that सब का सब; केवल वही *I wrote down all I could remember.* ○ *All I've eaten today is one banana.*

**IDM above all** ➪ **above** देखिए।

**after all** ➪ **after** देखिए।

**for all** **1** in spite of के बावजूद, के होते हुए भी *For all her wealth and beauty, she was never very happy.* **2** used to show that sth is not important or of no interest or value to you उपेक्षा का भाव दिखाने के लिए प्रयुक्त ***For all I know** he's probably remarried by now.*

**in all** in total कुल मिलाकर *There were ten of us in all.*

**not all that...** not very बहुत अधिक नहीं *The film wasn't all that good.*

**(not) at all** (not) in any way किसी भी तरह (नहीं) *I didn't enjoy it at all.*

**not at all** used as a polite reply when sb thanks you for something धन्यवाद दिए जाने पर नम्र उत्तर देने के लिए प्रयुक्त

**all**[2] /ɔːl ऑल्/ *adv.* **1** completely; very पूरी तरह से; सब कुछ; बहुत अधिक *I didn't watch that programme—I forgot all about it.* ○ *They got all excited about it.* **2** (in sport) for each side (खेल में) बराबरी पर रहने पर *The score was two all.*

IDM **all along** from the beginning शुरू से ही *I knew you were joking all along.*

**all the better, harder, etc.** even better, harder, etc. than before पहले से अधिक अच्छा, कठिन आदि *It will be all the more difficult with two people missing.*

**all-** /ɔːl ऑल्/ *prefix* (*used in adjectives and adverbs*) **1** completely पूर्णतया; सब कुछ, संपूर्ण *an all-Indian show* ○ *an all-inclusive price* **2** in the highest degree सर्वाधिक, अधिकतम *all-important* ○ *all-powerful*

**Allah** the name for God in Islam अल्लाह

**allay** /əˈleɪ अˈले/ *verb* [T] (*formal*) to make sth less strong (पीड़ा, कष्ट, भय आदि की) तीव्रता या प्रबलता कम करना

**the all-clear** *noun* [*sing.*] a signal telling you that a situation is no longer dangerous ख़तरा टल जाने की स्थिति का संकेत

**allege** /əˈledʒ अˈलेज्/ *verb* [T] (*formal*) to say that sb has done sth wrong, but without having any proof that this is true बिना प्रमाण के आरोप लगाना *The woman alleged that Ranjit had attacked her with a knife.* ▶ **allegation** /ˌæləˈɡeɪʃn ˌऐलˈगेशन्/ *noun* [C] आरोप; प्रमाण रहित कथन *to **make allegations** of police corruption* ▶ **alleged** /əˈledʒd अˈलेज्ड्/ *adj.* (*only before a noun*) आरोपित ▶ **allegedly** /əˈledʒɪdli अˈलेजिड्लि/ *adv.* आरोपित रूप से *The man was allegedly shot while trying to escape.*

**allegiance** /əˈliːdʒəns अˈलीजन्स्/ *noun* [C, U] (*formal*) support for a leader, government, belief, etc. नेता, सरकार, विश्वास आदि के प्रति निष्ठा व समर्थन *Many people **switched allegiance** and voted against the government.*

**allegory** /ˈæləɡəri ˈऐलगरि/ *noun* [C, U] (*pl.* **allegories**) a story, play, picture, etc. in which each character or event is a symbol representing an idea or a quality, such as truth, evil, death, etc.; the use of such symbols प्रतीककथा, प्रतीकचित्र आदि जिसमें अमूर्तभाव, जैसे सत्य, प्रेम, धैर्य आदि सजीव पात्र के रूप में आते हैं या चित्रित होते हैं ▶ **allegorical** /ˌæləˈɡɒrɪkl ˌऐलˈगॉरिकल्/ *adj.* प्रतीकात्मक, लाक्षणिक, प्रतीक चित्रात्मक

**allele** /əˈliːl अˈलील्/ *noun* [C] (*technical*) one of two or more possible forms of a **gene** that are found at the same place on a **chromosome** किसी जीन के एक या अधिक संभावित रूप जो क्रोमोसोम में एक ही स्थान पर पाए जाते हैं

**allergen** /ˈælədʒən ˈऐलजन्/ *noun* [C] any substance that makes some people ill when they eat, touch or breathe it ऐसी कोई भी वस्तु जिसे खाने, छूने या साँस लेने पर कुछ लोग बीमार हो जाते हैं

**allergic** /əˈlɜːdʒɪk अˈलजिक्/ *adj.* **1 allergic (to sth)** having an allergy किसी वस्तु से एलर्जी होना; प्रत्यूर्ज *I'm allergic to pepper.* **2** caused by an allergy एलर्जी से उत्पन्न *an allergic reaction to dust*

**allergy** /ˈælədʒi ˈऐलजि/ *noun* [C] (*pl.* **allergies**) **an allergy (to sth)** a medical condition that makes you ill when you eat, touch or breathe sth that does not normally make other people ill किसी वस्तु या पदार्थ विशेष के प्रति असाधारण संवेदनशीलता से उत्पन्न बीमारी; प्रत्यूर्जता

**alleviate** /əˈliːvieɪt अˈलीव्रिएट्/ *verb* [T] to make sth less strong or bad (पीड़ा या कष्ट के) प्रभाव को कम करना *The doctor gave me an injection to alleviate the pain.* ▶ **alleviation** /əˌliːviˈeɪʃn अˌलीव्रिˈएशन्/ *noun* [U] उपशमन, कमी

**alley** /ˈæli ˈऐलि/ (*also* **alleyway** /ˈæliweɪ ˈऐलिवे/) *noun* [C] a narrow passage between buildings गली

**alliance** /əˈlaɪəns अˈलाइअन्स्/ *noun* [C] an agreement between groups, countries, etc. to work together and support each other मैत्री, संधि, समझौता, संबंध *The two parties **formed an alliance**.* ➪ **ally** देखिए।

**allied** /ˈælaɪd ˈऐलाइड्/ *adj.* **1** (used about organizations, countries, etc.) having an agreement to work together and support each other (संगठन, देश आदि) एक साथ काम करने और एक दूसरे का समर्थन करने के लिए संधिबद्ध **2** /əˈlaɪd अˈलाइड्/ **allied (to sth)** connected with; existing together with सहबद्ध; से संबंधित *The newspaper is closely allied to the government.*

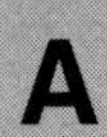

**alligator** /ˈælɪɡeɪtə(r) ˈएलिगेट(र्)/ *noun* [C] a large reptile with a long tail and a big mouth with sharp teeth. Alligators live in the lakes and rivers of America and China घड़ियाल, मगरमच्छ की एक जाति है जो अमेरिका और चीन की झीलों और नदियों में पाए जाते हैं ➪ **crocodile** देखिए।

**all-in** *adj.* including everything सब मिलाकर *an all-in price*

**alliteration** /əˌlɪtəˈreɪʃn अˌलिटˈरेश्न्/ *noun* [U] (*technical*) the use of the same letter or sound at the beginning of words that are close together, as in 'he built a big boat' किसी शब्द समूह में एक ही अक्षर या ध्वनि से आरंभ होने वाले शब्दों का प्रयोग; अनुप्रास अलंकार

**allocate** /ˈæləkeɪt ˈऐलकेट्/ *verb* [T] **allocate sth (to/for sb/sth)** to give sth to sb as his/her share or to decide to use sth for a particular purpose किसी कार्य के लिए धनराशि आदि निर्धारित करना; हिस्से के रूप में बाँटना *The government has allocated half the budget for education.* ▶ **allocation** /ˌæləˈkeɪʃn ˌऐलˈकेश्न्/ *noun* [C, U] आवंटन; धनराशि आदि का नियतन

**allot** /əˈlɒt अˈलॉट्/ *verb* [T] (**allotting; allotted**) **allot sth (to sb/sth)** to give a share of work, time, etc. to sb/sth किसी (व्यक्ति या काम) के लिए काम, समय आदि का हिस्सा नियत करना; अंश देना *Different tasks were allotted to each member of the class.* ○ *the allotted time*

**allotment** /əˈlɒtmənt अˈलॉट्मन्ट्/ *noun* [C, U] (*formal*) an amount of sth that sb is given or is allowed to have; the process of giving sth to sb बाँटा गया या निर्धारित हिस्सा; बाँटने की प्रक्रिया; आवंटन

**allotropy** /əˈlɒtrəpi अˈलॉट्रपि/ *noun* [U] (in chemistry) the ability that certain substances have to exist in more than one physical form (रसायन शास्त्र में) कुछ पदार्थों की, एक से अधिक रूपों में रहने की क्षमता; अपरूपता

**all out** *adj., adv.* using all your strength, etc. पूरी शक्ति आदि से *an all-out effort*

**allow** /əˈlaʊ अˈलाउ/ *verb* [T] **1 allow sb/sth to do sth; allow sth** to give permission for sb/sth to do sth or for sth to happen कुछ करने की अनुमति देना, कुछ होने देना *Photography is not allowed inside the temple.*

> **NOTE** **Allow, permit** और **let** में तुलना कीजिए। **Allow** का प्रयोग औपचारिक और अनौपचारिक अंग्रेज़ी दोनों में हो सकता है। इसका कर्मवाच्य (passive) रूप **be allowed to** अधिक प्रचलित है। **Permit** औपचारिक शब्द है और सामान्यतः केवल लिखित अंग्रेज़ी में प्रयुक्त होता है। **Let** अनौपचारिक शब्द है और बोलचाल की अंग्रेज़ी में अधिक प्रचलित है। **Let** का प्रयोग कर्मवाच्य (passive) में नहीं किया जाता है— *Visitors are not allowed/permitted to smoke in this area.* ○ *Smoking is not allowed/permitted.*

**2** to give permission for sb/sth to be or go somewhere किसी को कहीं आने या जाने की अनुमति देना *No dogs allowed.* ○ *I'm only allowed out on Friday and Saturday nights.* **3 allow sb/sth** to let sb have sth कुछ करने की अनुमति देना *My contract allows me four weeks' holiday a year.* **4 allow sb/sth to do sth** to make it possible for sb/sth to do sth किसी को कुछ करने की छूट देना *Working part-time would allow me to spend more time with my family.* **5 allow sth (for sb/sth)** to provide money, time, etc. for sb/sth किसी काम (या बात) के लिए या कुछ किए जाने के लिए धनराशि, समय आदि नियत करना *You should allow about 30 minutes for each question.*

**PHR V** **allow for sb/sth** to think about possible problems when you are planning sth and include extra time, money, etc. for them किसी बात की गुंजाइश रखना *The journey should take about two hours, allowing for heavy traffic.*

**allowable** /əˈlaʊəbl अˈलाउअब्ल्/ *adj.* that is allowed, especially by law or by the rules क़ानून या नियमों के अनुसार स्वीकार्य

**allowance** /əˈlaʊəns अˈलाउअन्स्/ *noun* [C] **1** an amount of sth that you are allowed वह मात्रा, राशि जिसे ले जाने आदि के लिए छूट मिली हो; छूट *Most flights have a 20 kg baggage allowance.* **2** an amount of money that you receive regularly to help you pay for sth that you need भत्ता

**IDM** **make allowances for sb/sth** to judge a person or his/her actions in a kinder way than usual because he/she has a particular problem or disadvantage निर्णय लेते समय किसी के लिए उसकी विशिष्ट समस्या या असुविधा के कारण नरमी बरतना

**alloy** /ˈælɔɪ ˈऐलॉइ/ *noun* [C, U] a metal made by mixing two types of metal together मिश्र धातु *Brass is an alloy of copper and zinc.*

**all right** (*informal* **alright**) *exclamation, adv., adj.* (*not used before a noun*) **1** good enough; OK ठीक, ठीक-ठाक *Is everything all right?* **2** safe; not hurt; well; OK सकुशल, ठीक, सुरक्षित *I hope the children are all right.* ○ *Do you feel all right?* **3** showing you agree to do what sb has asked; OK माँगी गई सहायता के लिए सहमति जताना—ज़रूर, अवश्य ही, क्यों नहीं? *'Can you get me some stamps?' 'Yes, all right.'*

**NOTE** स्थिति के अनुसार जब आपको कोई धन्यवाद देता है या माफ़ी माँगता है तो आप कहते हैं 'That's all right,'—*'Thanks for the lift home.' 'That's (quite) all right.'* ○ *'I'm so sorry I'm late.' 'That's all right. We haven't started yet anyway.'*

**all-round** *adj.* (*only before a noun*) able to do many different things well; good in many different ways अनेक कार्य करने में सक्षम *a superb all-round athlete* ○ *The school aims at the all-round development of the child.*

**all-rounder** *noun* [C] a person who can do many different things well हरफ़नमौला

**all-time** *adj.* (*only before a noun*) (used when you are comparing things or saying how good or bad sb/sth is) of any time (तुलना करते समय प्रयुक्त), सदैव का *It's my all-time favourite song.* ○ *an all-time great athlete.* ○ *Unemployment is at an all-time high.*

**allude** /əˈluːd अˈलूड्/ *verb* [I] (*formal*) **allude to sb/sth** to speak about sb/sth in an indirect way किसी व्यक्ति या वस्तु के बारे में अप्रत्यक्ष रूप से बात करना, संकेत मात्र देना ▶ **allusion** /əˈluːʒn अˈलूश़्न्/ *noun* [C, U] संकेत, इशारा *He likes to* ***make allusions to*** *the size of his salary.*

**allure** /əˈlʊə(r) अˈलुअ(र्)/ *noun* [U] (*written*) the quality of being attractive and exciting प्रलोभन, आकर्षण *the allure of the big city*

**alluring** /əˈlʊərɪŋ अˈलुअरिङ्/ *adj.* attractive and exciting in a way that is not easy to understand or explain रहस्यमय ढंग से लुभावना व मोहक *an alluring smile* ▶ **alluringly** *adv.* सम्मोहक रीति से

**alluvial** /əˈluːviəl अˈलूविअल्/ *adj.* (in geography) made of sand and earth that is left by rivers or floods (भूगोल में) नदियों से बहाकर लाई मिट्टी–रेती से बनी (भूमि), कछारी (भूमि), जलौढ़ (भूमि) *alluvial deposits/soil/plains*

**alluvium** /əˈluːviəm अˈलूविअम्/ *noun* [U] (in geography) sand and earth that is left by rivers or floods (भूगोल में) नदियों या बाढ़ों के घटने के बाद बची रेत और मिट्टी; कछार, कच्छ

**ally** /ˈælaɪ ˈऐलाइ/ *noun* [C] (*pl.* **allies**) **1** a country that has an agreement to support another country, especially in a war संधिबद्ध देश (विशेषतः युद्ध की स्थिति में) *India and its Asian allies* ➪ **alliance** देखिए। **2** a person who helps and supports you, especially when other people are against you साथ देने वाला व्यक्ति; पक्षधर *the Prime Minister's political allies*

**almighty** /ɔːlˈmaɪti ऑल्ˈमाइटि/ *adj.* **1** having the power to do anything सर्वशक्तिमान *Almighty God* **2** very great (*informal*) (*only before a noun*) बहुत बड़ा, अति विशाल *Suddenly we heard the most almighty crash.* **3 The Almighty** *noun* [*sing*] God ईश्वर, परमात्मा

**almirah** *noun* [C] (*IndE*) a cupboard, a wardrobe अलमारी *She keeps her jewellery locked up in the almirah.*

**almond** /ˈɑːmənd ˈआमन्ड्/ *noun* [C] a flat pale nut बादाम ➪ **nut** पर चित्र देखिए।

**almost** /ˈɔːlməʊst ˈऑल्मोस्ट्/ *adv.* *very* nearly; not quite लगभग; क़रीब-क़रीब *By nine o'clock almost everybody had arrived.* ○ *The film has almost finished.*

**alms** /ɑːmz आम्ज़्/ *noun* [*pl.*] money, food and clothes given to poor people निर्धनों को दिया गया दान (वस्त्र, भोजन, पैसा आदि) *She believes in giving alms regularly.*

**alone** /əˈləʊn अˈलोन्/ *adj., adv.* **1** without any other person अकेला; बिना किसी अन्य व्यक्ति के *The old man lives alone.*

**NOTE** **Alone** और **lonely** दोनों का अर्थ 'अकेले' या 'अकेला' है। **Lonely** (*AmE* **lonesome**) का अर्थ है कि कोई व्यक्ति साथियों के न होने से उदास या अप्रसन्न है, परंतु **alone** न तो प्रसन्नता और न ही अप्रसन्नता दर्शाता है। **Alone** का प्रयोग संज्ञा से पूर्व नहीं किया जाता। अर्थ 'अकेले' के लिए वाक्यांशों **on your own** और **by yourself** का प्रयोग भी किया जा सकता है।

**2** (*only after a noun or pronoun*) only केवल *You alone can help us.* ○ *The rent alone takes up most of my salary.*

**IDM** **go it alone** to start working on your own without the usual help सामान्यतः मिलने वाली सहायता के बिना कोई कार्य स्वयं ही करना शुरू करना

**leave sb/sth alone** ➪ **leave**[1] देखिए।

**let alone** ➪ **let** देखिए।

**along** /əˈlɒŋ अˈलॉङ्/ *prep., adv.* **1** from one end to or towards the other end of sth के साथ-साथ, एक सिरे से दूसरे सिरे तक या की ओर *I walked slowly along the road.* **2** on or beside sth long के समानांतर, के किनारे *Wild flowers grew along both sides of the river.* **3** forward आगे, के साथ-साथ *We moved along slowly with the crowd.* **4** (*informal*) with sb साथ *We're going for a walk. Why don't you* ***come along*** *too?*

**IDM** **all along** ➪ **all**[2] देखिए।

**along with sb/sth** together with sb/sth किसी व्यक्ति या वस्तु के साथ

**go along with sb/sth** to agree with sb's ideas or plans किसी के विचारों या योजनाओं से सहमत होना

**alongside** /əˌlɒŋˈsaɪd अˌलॉङ्ˈसाइड्/ *adv., prep.* **1** next to sb/sth or at the side of sth बग़ल में, बराबर में **2** together with sb/sth के साथ-साथ *the opportunity to work alongside experienced musicians*

**aloof** /əˈlu:f अˈलूफ़्/ *adj.* **1** not friendly to other people; distant मेल-जोल न बढ़ाने वाला; अलग, दूर, भावशून्य *Her shyness made her seem aloof.* **2 aloof (from sb/sth)** not involved in sth; apart अलग-थलग

**aloud** /əˈlaʊd अˈलाउड्/ (*also* **outloud**) *adv.* in a normal speaking voice that other people can hear; not silently ऊँचे स्वर में (जिसे दूसरे लोग आसानी से सुन सकें) *to read aloud from a book*

alpaca

**alpaca** /ælˈpækə ऐल्ˈपैका/ *noun* **1** a South American animal whose long hair makes good quality wool दक्षिण अमेरिका में पाया जाने वाला एक जानवर जिसके लंबे बाल बढ़िया ऊन बनाने के काम आते हैं; अल्पैका **2** the wool of the alpaca अल्पैका की ऊन

**alpha** /ˈælfə ˈएल्फ़ा/ *noun* [C] the first letter of the Greek alphabet (α) यूनानी वर्णमाला का पहला अक्षर; ऐल्फ़ा

**alphabet** /ˈælfəbet ˈएलुफ़बट्/ *noun* [C] a set of letters in a fixed order that you use when you are writing a language (किसी भाषा की) वर्णमाला *There are 26 letters in the English alphabet.*

**alphabetical** /ˌælfəˈbetɪkl ˌऐलुफ़ˈबेटिकल्/ *adj.* arranged in the same order as the letters of the alphabet वर्णानुक्रमिक से *The names are listed **in alphabetical order**.* ▸ **alphabetically** /-kli -क्लि/ *adv.* वर्णक्रम से

**alphanumeric** /ˌælfənju:ˈmerɪk ˈऐलुफ़न्यूˈमेरिक्/ *adj.* (*technical*) containing or using both numbers and letters जिसमें वर्ण और संख्याएँ दोनों का प्रयोग किया गया हो; वर्ण-संख्यात्मक *alphanumeric data*

**alpha particle** *noun* [C] a very small piece of matter with a positive electric charge passing through it, that is produced in a nuclear reaction नाभिकीय अभिक्रिया से उत्पन्न घनात्मक आवेश वाला कण; एल्फा कण

**alpine** /ˈælpaɪn ˈऐल्पाइन्/ *adj.* of or found in high mountains ऊँचे पहाड़ों का या ऊँचे पहाड़ों पर पाया जाने वाला *alpine flowers*

**already** /ɔ:lˈredi ऑल्ˈरेडि/ *adv.* **1** used for talking about sth that has happened before now or before a particular time in the past बीती घटना की चर्चा के लिए प्रयुक्त *'Would you like some lunch?' 'No, I've already eaten, thanks.'* ○ *Sita was already awake when I went into her room.* **2** (*used in negative sentences and questions for expressing surprise*) so early; as soon as this इतनी जल्दी *Have you finished already?* ○ *Surely you're not going already!*

**alright** /ɔ:lˈraɪt ऑल्ˈराइट्/ (*informal*) = **all right**

**Alsatian** /ælˈseɪʃn ऐल्ˈसेश्न्/ (*also* **German shepherd**) *noun* [C] a large dog, often trained to help the police or to guard buildings एक बड़ा कुत्ता जिसे प्रायः पुलिस की सहायता के लिए या घरों की रक्षा के लिए प्रशिक्षित किया जाता है; अलसेशन

**also** /ˈɔ:lsəʊ ˈऑल्सो/ *adv.* (*not with negative verbs*) in addition; too साथ ही; भी *He plays several instruments and also writes music.* ○ *The food is wonderful, and also very cheap.*

> NOTE **Also** की अपेक्षा **too** और **as well** कम औपचारिक हैं और बोलचाल की अंग्रेज़ी में काफ़ी प्रचलित हैं। **Also** का प्रयोग सामान्यतः मुख्य क्रिया से पहले या 'is', 'are', 'were' के बाद किया जाता है—*He also enjoys reading.* ○ *He has also been to Australia.* ○ *He is also intelligent.* **Too** और **as well** का प्रयोग सामान्यतः वाक्य या वाक्यांश के अंत में किया जाता है—*I really love this song, and I liked the first one too/as well.*

IDM **not only... but also** ➪ **only** देखिए।

**also-ran** *noun* [C] a person who is not successful, especially in a competition or an election चुनाव आदि स्पर्धा में असफल रहने वाला व्यक्ति

**altar** /ˈɔ:ltə(r) ˈऑल्टर(र्)/ *noun* [C] a high table that is the centre of a religious ceremony वेदी, वेदिका

**alter** /ˈɔ:ltə(r) ˈऑल्टर(र्)/ *verb* [I, T] to make sth different in some way, but without changing it completely; to become different आंशिक परिवर्तन करना; बदलना; परिवर्तित होना *We've altered our plan, and will now arrive at 7.00 p.m. instead of 8.00 a.m.* ○ *The village seems to have altered very little in the last twenty years.*

**alteration** /ˌɔ:ltəˈreɪʃn ˌऑल्टˈरेशन्/ *noun* [C, U] **(an) alteration (to/in sth)** a small change in sb/sth थोड़ा बदलाव, आंशिक परिवर्तन *We want to **make** a few **alterations** to the house before we move in.*

**altercation** /ˌɔːltəˈkeɪʃn ˌआल्टˈकेश्न्/ *noun* [C, U] (*formal*) a noisy argument or disagreement विवाद, झगड़ा, कहा-सुनी, अनबन

**alternate**[1] /ɔːlˈtɜːnət ऑल्ˈटनट्/ *adj.* **1** (used about two types of events, things, etc.) happening or following regularly one after the other (दो प्रकार की परिस्थितियों, वस्तुओं आदि के लिए प्रयुक्त) बारी-बारी से, पहले के बाद दूसरा और फिर पहला-ऐसा क्रम *alternate periods of sun and showers* **2** one of every two एक एक छोड़कर, हर दो में से एक *He works alternate weeks* (= he works the first week, he doesn't work the second week, he works again the third week, etc). ▶ **alternately** *adv.* बारी-बारी से *The bricks were painted alternately white and red.*

**alternate**[2] /ˈɔːltənəɪt ˈऑल्टनेट्/ *verb* **1** [I] **alternate with sth; alternate between A and B** (used about two types of events, things, etc.) to happen or follow regularly one after the other एक अवस्था से दूसरी अवस्था में जाना और पुनः पहली अवस्था में लौट आना और इस प्रकार क्रम चलते रहना *Busy periods at work alternate with times when there is not much to do.* **2 alternate A with B** to cause two types of events or things to happen or follow regularly one after the other बारी-बारी से रखना या करना *He alternated periods of work with periods of rest.* ▶ **alternation** /ˌɔːltəˈneɪʃn ˌआल्टˈनेश्न्/ *noun* [C, U] एकांतरण, प्रत्यावर्तन, क्रमांतरण

**alternate angles** *noun* [*pl.*] two angles, formed on opposite sides of a line that crosses two other lines. If the two lines that are crossed are **parallel** the alternate angles are equal एकांतर कोण, आसन्न कोण ➪ **angle** पर चित्र देखिए।

**alternating current** *noun* [C, U] (*abbr.* **AC**) a flow of electricity that changes direction regularly many times a second प्रति सेकंड नियमित रूप से अनेक बार दिशा परिवर्तन करने वाली विद्युत धारा; प्रत्यावर्ती विद्युत धारा ➪ **direct current** देखिए।

**alternative**[1] /ɔːlˈtɜːnətɪv ऑल्ˈटनटिव्/ *adj.* (*only before a noun*) **1** that you can use, do, etc. instead of sth else वैकल्पिक, विकल्पी, दूसरा *The highway was closed so we had to find an alternative route.* **2** different to what is usual or traditional वैकल्पिक, ग़ैर-पारंपरिक ▶ **alternatively** *adv.* विकल्पतः; वैकल्पिक रूप से *alternative medicine*

**alternative**[2] /ɔːlˈtɜːnətɪv ऑल्ˈटनटिव्/ *noun* [C] **an alternative (to sth)** one of two or more things that you can choose between विकल्प, दूसरी संभावना *What can I eat as an alternative to meat?*

**alternator** /ˈɔːltəneɪtə(r) ˈऑल्टनेट(र्)/ *noun* [C] a device, used especially in a car, that produces electrical current that moves in different directions कार में प्रयुक्त पुरज़ा जो विभिन्न दिशाओं में जाने वाली विद्युत धारा उत्पन्न करता है; आल्टरनेटर, प्रत्यावर्तित्र

**although** /ɔːlˈðəʊ ऑल्ˈद्रो/ *conj.* **1** in spite of the fact that यद्यपि, हालाँकि *Although she was tired, she stayed up late watching television.* **2** and yet; but तथापि; परंतु *I love dogs, although I wouldn't have one as a pet.*

> **NOTE** **Though** और **although** का एक ही अर्थ है परंतु **though** का प्रयोग केवल वाक्य के अंत में किया जाता है—*She knew all her friends would be at the party. She didn't want to go, though.* अवधारण (बल देने) के लिए **even though** का प्रयोग किया जा सकता है—*She didn't want to go, although/though/even though she knew all her friends would be there.*

**altimeter** /ˈæltɪmiːtə(r) ˈऐल्टिमीट(र्)/ *noun* [C] an instrument for showing height above sea level, used especially in an aircraft समुद्र तल से ऊँचाई मापने का यंत्र; तुंगतामापी, एल्टिमीटर ➪ **meter** पर चित्र देखिए।

**altitude** /ˈæltɪtjuːd ˈऐल्टिट्यूड्/ *noun* **1** [*sing.*] the height of sth above sea level समुद्र तल से ऊँचाई *The plane climbed to an altitude of 10,000 metres.* **2** [C] [*usually pl.*] a place that is high above sea level समुद्र तल से ऊँचा स्थान *You need to carry oxygen when you are climbing at high altitudes.*

**alto** /ˈæltəʊ ˈऐल्टो/ *noun* [C] (*pl.* **altos**) the lowest normal singing voice for a woman, the highest for a man; a woman or man with this voice स्त्री का निम्नतम और पुरुष का उच्चतम गानस्वर; इस प्रकार के गानस्वर से युक्त पुरुष या स्त्री

**altogether** /ˌɔːltəˈgeðə(r) ˌऑल्टˈगेद्र(र्)/ *adv.* **1** completely पूर्णतया, पूरे तौर पर, बिलकुल ही *I don't altogether agree with you.* **2** including everything; in total सब मिलाकर, कुल मिलाकर *Altogether there were six of us.* **3** when you consider everything; generally सब बातों को ध्यान में रखकर; सामान्य रूप से *Altogether, this town is a pleasant place to live.*

> **NOTE** **Altogether** और **all together** में अंतर है। **All together** का अर्थ है सब कुछ या सब एक साथ—*Put your books all together on the table.* ○ *Let's sing. All together now!*

**altostratus** /ˌæltəʊˈstrɑːtəs; -ˈstreɪtəs ˌऐल्टोˈस्ट्राटस्; -ˈस्ट्रेटस्/ *noun* [U] (*technical*) a layer of cloud of equal thickness that is formed at a height of between 2 and 7 kilometres बादल के समान मोटाई वाली परत जो 2 से 7 किलोमीटर की ऊँचाई पर बन जाती है; मध्यस्तरी मेघ

**altruism** /ˈæltruɪzəm ˈऐल्ट्रूइज़म्/ *noun* [U] (*formal*) the fact of caring about the needs and happiness of other people more than your own परोपकारिता, परहितवाद ▶ **altruistic** /ˌæltruˈɪstɪk ˌऐल्ट्रूˈइस्टिक्/ *adj.* परोपकारी, परहितवादी *altruistic behaviour*

**aluminium** /ˌæləˈmɪniəm ˌऐलˈमिनिअम्/ (*AmE* **aluminum** /əˈlu:mɪnəm अˈलूमिनम्/) (*symbol* **Al**) *noun* [U] a light silver-coloured metal that is used for making cooking equipment, etc. अल्यूमिनियम धातु *aluminium foil*

**alumna** /əˈlʌmnə अˈलम्ना/ *noun* [C] (*pl.* **alumnae** /-ni: -नी/) (*AmE formal*) a former female student of a school, college or university किसी शिक्षा संस्था की पूर्वछात्रा

**alumnus** /əˈlʌmnəs अˈलम्नस्/ *noun* [C] (*pl.* **alumni** /-naɪ -नाइ/) (*AmE formal*) a former male student of a school, college or university किसी शिक्षा संस्था का पूर्वछात्र

**alveolar** /ælˈvi:ələ; ælviˈəʊlə ऐल्ˈवीअला; ऐल्वीˈओला/ *noun* [C] a speech sound made with your tongue touching the part of your mouth behind your upper front teeth for example d̲ or t̲ वर्त्स्य ध्वनि; जिह्वा द्वारा ऊपर की दंतपंक्ति से स्पर्श करने पर उत्पन्न ध्वनि जैसे अंग्रेज़ी ध्वनि d̲ और t̲ ▶ **alveolar** *adj.* वर्त्स्य ध्वनि-संबंधित

**always** /ˈɔ:lweɪz ˈऑल्वेज़्/ *adv.* **1** at all times; regularly सदा, हमेशा; नियमित रूप से *I always get up at 6.30 a.m.* ○ *Why is the train always late when I'm in a hurry?* **2** all through the past until now हमेशा से, निरंतर *Tania has always been shy.* **3** for ever सर्वदा, हमेशा के लिए *I shall always remember this moment.* **4** (*only used with the continuous tenses*) again and again, usually in an annoying way बार-बार, लगातार, प्रायः खीझ उत्पन्न करने की स्थिति में *She's always complaining about something.* **5** used with 'can' or 'could' for suggesting sth that sb could do, especially if nothing else is possible 'can' या 'could' के साथ प्रयुक्त, जब यह बताना हो कि कुछ और न हो सकने पर, विकल्पतः क्या हो सकता है *If you haven't got enough money, I could always lend you some.*

> NOTE **Always** का प्रयोग सामान्यतः वाक्य के आरंभ में नहीं होता। इसका प्रयोग प्रायः मुख्य क्रिया के पहले या 'is', 'are', 'were' आदि के बाद में होता है—*He always wears those shoes.* ○ *Fauzia is always late.* **Always** वाक्य के आरंभ में तब आ सकता है, जब किसी को कुछ करने का निर्देश देना हो—*Always stop and look before you cross the road.*

**Alzheimer's disease** /ˈæltshaɪməz dɪzi:z ˈऐल्ट्साइमज़् डिज़ीज़्/ *noun* [*sing.*] a disease that affects the brain and makes some people become more and more confused as they get older मस्तिष्क को प्रभावित करने वाला एक रोग जिसमें आयु बढ़ने के साथ व्यक्ति की चिंतनशक्ति भी प्रभावित होती है; अल्झामीर रोग

**AM** /ˌeɪ ˈem ˌए ˈएम्/ *abbr.* amplitude modification; one of the systems of sending out radio signals आयाम आवर्धन; रेडियो संकेत भेजने की एक पद्धति

**am** ➪ **be**[1] देखिए।

**a.m.** /ˌeɪˈem ˌएˈएम्/ *abbr.* **1** (*AmE* **A.M.**) before midday दोपहर के 12 बजे से पहले; पूर्वाह्न *10 a.m.* (= 10 o'clock in the morning)

**amalgam** /əˈmælgəm अˈमैल्गम्/ *noun* **1** [C, *usually sing.*] (*formal*) a mixture or combination of things वस्तुओं का सम्मिश्रण या विलयन **2** [U] a mixture of **mercury** and another metal, used especially to fill holes in teeth पारे का अन्य धातु से मिश्रण विशेषतः दाँत में छिद्र भरने के लिए; पारद-मिश्रण

**amalgamate** /əˈmælgəmeɪt अˈमैल्गमेट्/ *verb* [I, T] (used especially about organizations, groups, etc.) to join together to form a single organization, group, etc. (संस्थाओं, संगठनों आदि को) मिलाकर एक कर देना; सम्मिश्रित करना; एकीकरण करना ▶ **amalgamation** /əˌmælgəˈmeɪʃn अˌमैल्गˈमेश्न्/ *noun* [C, U] एकीकरण; सम्मिश्रण

**amass** /əˈmæs अˈमैस्/ *verb* [T] to collect or put together a large quantity of sth किसी वस्तु को बड़ी मात्रा में एकत्रित या संचित कर देना *We've amassed a lot of information on the subject.*

**amateur**[1] /ˈæmətə(r) ˈऐमट(र्)/ *noun* [C] **1** a person who takes part in a sport or an activity for pleasure, not for money as a job शौक़िया, अव्यवसायी ✪ विलोम **professional** **2** (usually used when being critical) a person who does not have skill or experience when doing sth (प्रायः किसी व्यक्ति की आलोचना की दृष्टि से) आवश्यक कौशल या अनुभव के बिना काम करने वाला व्यक्ति

**amateur**[2] /ˈæmətə(r) ˈऐमट(र्)/ *adj.* **1** done, or doing sth, for pleasure (not for money as a job) शौक़ के रूप में (न कि आय के लिए) किया गया; शौक़िया तौर पर करने या होने वाला *an amateur production of a play* ○ *an amateur photographer* ✪ विलोम **professional** **2** (*also* **amateurish** /-rɪʃ -रिश्/) done without skill or experience आवश्यक कौशल या अनुभव के बिना किया गया *The painting was an amateurish fake.*

**amaze** /əˈmeɪz अˈमेज़्/ *verb* [T] to surprise sb very much; to be difficult for sb to believe अत्यधिक चकित कर देना; किसी बात का अविश्वसनीय हो जाना *Sometimes your behaviour amazes me!*

**amazed** /əˈmeɪzd अˈमेज़्ड्/ *adj.* **amazed (at/by sb/sth); amazed (to do sth/that...)** very surprised हक्का-बक्का, भौंचक्का, चकित *I was amazed by the change in his attitude.*

**amazement** /əˈmeɪzmənt अˈमेज़्मन्ट्/ *noun* [U] a feeling of great surprise बड़ा अचंभा, अधिक विस्मय या आश्चर्य *He looked at me* ***in amazement.*** ○ ***To my amazement****, I passed the test easily.*

**amazing** /əˈmeɪzɪŋ अˈमेज़िङ्/ *adj.* very surprising and difficult to believe; incredible आश्चर्यजनक और अविश्वसनीय; अतिविस्मयकारी *amazing courage* ▶ **amazingly** *adv.* आश्चर्यजनक रूप से

**ambassador** /æmˈbæsədə(r) ऐम्ˈबैसड(र्)/ *noun* [C] an important person who represents his/her country in a foreign country राजदूत; विदेश में किसी देश का आधिकारिक प्रतिनिधि *the Indian Ambassador to Britain* NOTE राजदूत का निवास और कार्यस्थल **embassy** होता है। ➪ **consul** भी देखिए।

**amber** /ˈæmbə(r) ˈऐम्ब(र्)/ *noun* [U] **1** a hard clear yellow-brown substance used for making jewellery or objects for decoration आभूषण या सजावटी चीजें बनाने में प्रयुक्त पीला-भूरा कठोर पदार्थ; कहरुबा, तृणमणि **2** a yellow-brown colour कहरुबा रंग *The three colours in traffic lights are red, amber and green.* ▶ **amber** *adj.* कहरुबा-संबंधित

**ambi-** /ˈæmbi ˈऐम्बि/ *prefix* (*in nouns, adjectives and adverbs*) referring to both of two दोनों पक्षों का सूचक; उभयात्मक, उभय- *ambivalent*

**ambidextrous** /ˌæmbiˈdekstrəs ˌऐम्बिˈडेक्स्ट्रस्/ *adj.* able to use the left hand and the right hand equally well उभयहस्तकुशल; दाएँ और बाएँ दोनों हाथों से समान रूप से काम कर सकने योग्य

**ambience** (*also* **ambiance**) /ˈæmbiəns ˈऐम्बिअन्स्/ *noun* [*sing.*] the character and atmosphere of a place किसी स्थान का वातावरण; परिवेश, माहौल

**ambient** /ˈæmbiənt ˈएम्बिअन्ट्/ *adj.* (*only before a noun*) **1** (*technical*) of the area around; on all sides परिवेशी; आसपास का *ambient temperature/conditions* **2** (used especially about music) creating a relaxed atmosphere (विशेषतः संगीत के लिए प्रयुक्त) सुखद, शिथिल व आरामदेह वातावरण उत्पन्न करते हुए *ambient music/lighting*

**ambiguity** /ˌæmbɪˈgjuːəti ˌऐम्बिˈग्यूअटि/ *noun* [C, U] (*pl.* **ambiguities**) the possibility of being understood in more than one way; sth that can be understood in more than one way अनेकार्थता की स्थिति; अस्पष्टता

**ambiguous** /æmˈbɪgjuəs ऐम्ˈबिग्युअस्/ *adj.* having more than one possible meaning जिसके एक से अधिक अर्थ निकाले जा सकें; अनेकार्थक ▶ **ambiguously** *adv.* अनेक अर्थ प्रकट करते हुए

**ambition** /æmˈbɪʃn ऐम्ˈबिश्न्/ *noun* **1** [C] **ambition (to do/be sth); ambition (of doing sth)** something that you very much want to have or do उच्च आकांक्षा, महत्त्वाकांक्षा *He finally* ***achieved*** *his* ***ambition*** *of becoming a doctor.* **2** [U] a strong desire to be successful, to have power, etc. महत्त्वाकांक्षा *One problem of young people today is their lack of ambition.*

**ambitious** /æmˈbɪʃəs ऐम्ˈबिशस्/ *adj.* **1 ambitious (to be/do sth)** having a strong desire to be successful, to have power, etc. महत्त्वाकांक्षी, उच्चाकांक्षी *We are ambitious to succeed.* **2** difficult to achieve or do because it takes a lot of work or effort प्रयत्नसाध्य *The company has announced ambitious plans for expansion.*

**ambivalent** /æmˈbɪvələnt ऐम्ˈबिव़लन्ट्/ *adj.* having or showing a mixture of feelings or opinions about sth or sb मिश्रित या मिली-जुली भावनाओं से युक्त; उभयमुख ▶ **ambivalence** *noun* [C, U] उभयमुखिता, द्वैधवृति मनोवृत्ति, दुतरफ़ापन

**amble** /ˈæmbl ˈऐम्बल्/ *verb* [I] to walk at a slow relaxed speed मंथर गति से चलना, टहलना, रहवाल चलना *We ambled down to the beach.*

**ambulance** /ˈæmbjələns ˈऐम्ब्यलन्स्/ *noun* [C] a special vehicle for taking ill or injured people to and from hospital बीमार या दुर्घटनाग्रस्त व्यक्तियों को ले जाने वाला वाहन; रोगी-वाहन, एम्बुलेंस

**ambush** /ˈæmbʊʃ ˈऐम्बुश्/ *noun* [C, U] a surprise attack from a hidden position घात लगाकर किया गया हमला *He was killed in an enemy ambush.* ○ *The robbers were waiting* ***in ambush.*** ▶ **ambush** *verb* [T] घात लगाना; छिपकर अचानक हमला करना

**ameba** (*AmE*) = **amoeba**

**ameliorate** /əˈmiːliəreɪt अˈमीलिअरेट्/ *verb* [T] (*formal*) to make sth better (स्थिति आदि) सुधारना, बेहतर करना *Steps have been taken to ameliorate the situation.*

**amen** /ɑːˈmen; eɪˈmen आˈमेन्; एˈमेन्/ *exclamation* a word used at the end of prayers by Christians and Jews ईसाइयों और यहूदियों की प्रार्थना के अंत में कहा गया शब्द; 'आमीन' ('ऐसा ही हो', 'तथास्तु')

**amenable** /əˈmiːnəbl अˈमीनबल्/ *adj.* happy to accept sth; willing to be influenced by sb/sth ख़ुशी से स्वीकार करने वाला; स्वेच्छा से प्रभावित होने वाला *I'm amenable to any suggestions you may have.*

**amend** /ə'mend अ'मेन्ड्/ *verb* [T] to change sth slightly in order to make it better बेहतर बनाने के लिए ज़रा-सा सुधारना; संशोधित करना

**amendment** /ə'mendmənt अ'मेन्ड्मन्ट्/ *noun* **1** [C] a part that is added or a small change that is made to a piece of writing, especially to a law किसी दस्तावेज़, क़ानून आदि में संशोधन **2** [U] an act of amending sth संशोधन प्रक्रिया

**amends** /ə'mendz अ'मेन्ड्ज़्/ *noun [pl.]*
IDM **make amends** to do sth for sb, that shows that you are sorry for sth bad that you have done before क्षतिपूर्ति करना, नुक़सान की भरपाई करना, हरजाना देना

**amenity** /ə'mi:nəti अ'मीनटि/ *noun* [C] (*pl.* **amenities**) something that makes a place pleasant or easy to live in किसी स्थान को अधिक आरामदेह बनाने के लिए सुख-साधन; सुविधाएँ *Among the town's amenities are two cinemas and a sports centre.*

**American** /ə'merɪkən अ'मेरिकन्/ *adj.* from or connected with the US संयुक्त राज्य अमेरिका का या उससे संबंधित *Have you met Bob? He's American.* ○ *an American accent* ▶ **American** *noun* [C] अमरीकी, अमेरिकी *American movie/tourists*

**American football** (*AmE* **football**) *noun* [U] a game played in the US by two teams of eleven players with a ball that is not round. The players wear hard hats (**helmets**) and other protective clothing and try to carry the ball to the end of the field अमेरिकन फुटबॉल—अंडाकार गेंद से 11-11 खिलाड़ियों की दो टीमें खेलती हैं सब खिलाड़ी सिर पर हेल्मेट और अन्य बचाव-उपकरण पहनते हैं और गेंद को हाथ, पैर से मारते-ढकेलते एक-दूसरे की लाइन के अंत तक ले जाते हैं

**Americanism** /ə'merɪkənɪzəm अ'मेरिकनिज़म्/ *noun* [C] a word, phrase or spelling that is typical of American English, used in another variety of English अमेरिकी इंगलिश में प्रयुक्त विशेष शब्द या शब्दों की वर्तनी

**Americanize** (*also* **-ise**) /ə'merɪkənaɪz अ'मेरिकनाइज़्/ *verb* [T] to make sb/sth American in character अमरीकीकरण करना या होना

**amethyst** /'æməθɪst 'ऐमथिस्ट्/ *noun* [C, U] a purple precious stone, used in making jewellery जामुनी रंग का क़ीमती पत्थर; जमुनिया, जंबुमणि, ऐमिथिस्ट

**amiable** /'eɪmiəbl 'एमिअबल्/ *adj.* friendly and pleasant मैत्रीपूर्ण और सौहार्दपूर्ण; मिलनसार ▶ **amiably** /-əbli अब्लि/ *adv.* मिलनसार भाव से, सौजन्य से

**amicable** /'æmɪkəbl 'ऐमिकब्ल्/ *adj.* made or done in a friendly way, without argument सौहार्दपूर्ण, स्नेही ▶ **amicably** /-əbli अब्लि/ *adv.* मित्रवत, मित्रभाव से

**amid** /ə'mɪd अ'मिड्/ (*also* **amidst** /ə'mɪdst अ'मिड्स्ट्/) *prep.* (*written*) in the middle of; among के बीच में; के मध्य

**amino acid** /ə,mi:nəʊ'æsɪd अ'मीनो 'ऐसिड्/ *noun* [C] any of the substances that are found in animals and plants and that combine to form a substance (**protein**) that is necessary for a healthy body and for growth पशुओं और पौधों में पाए जाने वाले उन तत्वों में से एक जो मिलकर प्रोटीन बनाते हैं। यह प्रोटीन शारीरिक स्वास्थ्य और विकास के लिए अनिवार्य होता है; अमीनो एसिड

**amir** = **emir**

**amiss** /ə'mɪs अ'मिस्/ *adj.*, *adv.* wrong; not as it should be ग़लत, ख़राब ढंग से *When I walked into the room I could sense that something was amiss.*
IDM **not come/go amiss** to be useful or pleasant उपयोगी या प्रियकर होना *Things are fine, although a bit more money wouldn't come amiss.*
**take sth amiss** to be upset by sth, perhaps because you have understood it in the wrong way बुरा मानना *Please don't take my remarks amiss.*

**ammeter** /'æmi:tə(r) 'ऐमीट(र्)/ *noun* [C] an instrument for measuring the strength of an electric current विद्युत धारा मापी यंत्र; ऐमीटर ➪ **meter** पर चित्र देखिए।

**ammonia** /ə'məʊniə अ'मोनिआ/ *noun* [U] (*symbol* **NH³**) a colourless gas with a strong smell; a clear liquid containing ammonia used for cleaning तेज़ गंध-युक्त रंगहीन गैस; अमोनिया; अमोनिया-युक्त तरल पदार्थ जो सफ़ाई के काम आता है

**ammonite** /'æmənaɪt 'ऐमनाइट्/ *noun* [C] a type of **fossil** एक प्रकार का जीवाश्म; अमोनाइट

**ammonium** /ə'məʊniəm अ'मोनिअम्/ *noun* [*sing.*] a chemical substance with a positive electrical charge that is found in liquids and salts that contain ammonia अमोनिया-युक्त पदार्थों में पाया जाने वाला एक विशेष रसायन जिसमें घनात्मक विद्युत आवेश होता है; अमोनियम

**ammunition** /,æmju'nɪʃn ,ऐम्यु'निश्न्/ *noun* [U] **1** the supply of bullets, etc. that you need to fire from a weapon गोला-बारूद, युद्ध सामग्री *The troops surrendered because they had run out of ammunition.* **2** facts or information that can be used against sb/sth ऐसे तथ्य जो किसी के विरोध में प्रयुक्त किए जा सकते हों

**amnesia** /æm'ni:ziə ऐम्'नीज़िआ/ *noun* [U] loss of memory याद्दाश्त खो बैठने की अवस्था; स्मृति-लोप

**amnesty** /'æmnəsti 'ऐम्नस्टि/ *noun* [C] (*pl.* **amnesties**) **1** a time when a government forgives political crimes सरकार द्वारा दिया गया क्षमादान; आम माफ़ी, सार्वजनिक क्षमादान **2** a time when people can give in illegal weapons without being arrested ग़ैर-क़ानूनी हथियारों के समर्पण के लिए लोगों को दी गई क्षमा-अवधि

**amniocentesis** /ˌæmniəʊsenˈtiːsɪs ˌऐम्निओसेन्ˈटीसिस्/ *noun* [U, *sing.*] a medical test in which some liquid is taken from a pregnant woman's **womb** to find out if the baby has particular illnesses or health problems एक डॉक्टरी परीक्षण जिसमें माता के गर्भाशय से तरल पदार्थ लेकर गर्भस्थ शिशु के स्वास्थ्य की जाँच की जाती है

**amniotic fluid** /ˌæmniɒtɪk ˈfluːɪd ˌऐम्निऑटिक् ˈफ़्लूइड्/ *noun* [U] the liquid that is around a baby when it is inside its mother's body गर्भस्थ शिशु के चारों ओर का तरल पदार्थ

**amoeba** (*AmE* **ameba**) /əˈmiːbə अˈमीबा/ *noun* [C] (*pl.* **amoebas** or **amoebae** /-biː -बी/) a very small living creature that consists of only one cell केवल एक कोशिका वाला अत्यंत सूक्ष्म जीव; अमीबा, जीवाणु

**amok** /əˈmɒk अˈमॉक्/ *adv.*

**IDM** **run amok** to suddenly start behaving violently, especially in a public place एकाएक हिंसक रीति से व्यवहार करने लगना, विशेषतः किसी सार्वजनिक स्थान पर *Football fans ran amok in Kolkata last night.*

**among** /əˈmʌŋ अˈमङ्/ (*also* **amongst** /əˈmʌŋst अˈमङ्स्ट्/) *prep.* **1** surrounded by; in the middle of से घिरा हुआ; के बीच में *I often feel nervous when I'm among strangers.* **2** in or concerning a particular group of people or things किसी विशेष वर्ग से संबंधित; किसी विशेष वर्ग में सम्मिलित *Discuss it* ***amongst yourselves*** *and let me know your decision.* ○ ***Among other things****, the drug can cause headaches and sweating.* **3** to each one (of a group) (वर्ग के प्रत्येक सदस्य को) आपस में *On his death, his money will be divided among his children.*

**amoral** /ˌeɪˈmɒrəl ˌएˈमॉरल्/ *adj.* (used about people or their behaviour) not following any moral rules; not caring about right or wrong (व्यक्ति व उनका आचरण) नैतिकता रहित; सदाचारविहीन ⇨ **moral** और **immoral** देखिए।

**amorous** /ˈæmərəs ˈऐमरस्/ *adj.* showing sexual desire and love for sb कामुकतापूर्ण, प्रेमातुर *She rejected his amorous advances.* ▶ **amorously** *adv.* कामुक रीति से

**amorphous** /əˈmɔːfəs अˈमॉफ़स्/ *adj.* (*technical*) having no definite shape, form or structure बिना किसी निश्चित आकृति, रूप या संरचना के; अनाकार

**amount¹** /əˈmaʊnt अˈमाउन्ट्/ *noun* [C] **1** the amount of sth is how much of it there is; a quantity of sth मात्रा; राशि; परिमाण *I spent an enormous amount of time preparing for the exam.* ○ ***a large amount of money*** **2** total or sum of money कुल धनराशि *You are requested to pay the full amount within seven days.*

**amount²** /əˈmaʊnt अˈमाउन्ट्/ *verb*

**PHR V** **amount to sth** **1** to add up to sth; to make sth as a total कुल योग होना *The cost of the repairs amounted to Rs 5000.* **2** to be equal to or the same as sth के बराबर होना *Whether I tell her today or tomorrow, it amounts to the same thing.*

**amp** /æmp ऐम्प्/ *noun* [C] **1** (*formal* **ampere** /ˈæmpeə(r) ˈऐम्पेअ(र्)/) a unit for measuring electric current विद्युत धारा मापने की इकाई; ऐम्पियर **2** (*informal*) = **amplifier**

**ampersand** /ˈæmpəsænd ˈऐम्पसैन्ड्/ *noun* [C] (*symbol* **&**) the symbol used to mean 'and' समुच्चय-चिह्न, '&' का चिह्न

**amphetamine** /æmˈfetəmiːn ऐम्ˈफ़ेटमीन्/ *noun* [C, U] an illegal drug that makes you feel excited and full of energy एक उत्तेजक परंतु ग़ैर-क़ानूनी दवा; एंफ़ेटामीन

**amphibian** /æmˈfɪbiən ऐम्ˈफ़िबिअन्/ *noun* [C] an animal that can live both on land and in water जल और थल दोनों में रह सकने वाला प्राणी; जलस्थलचर *frogs, toads and other amphibians*

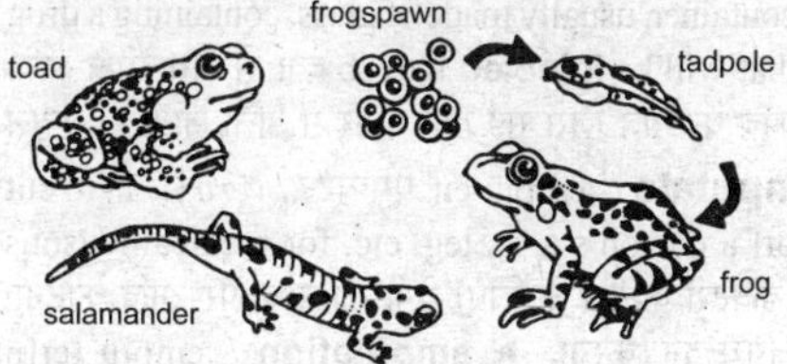


**amphibians**

**amphibious** /æmˈfɪbiəs ऐम्ˈफ़िबिअस्/ *adj.* able to live or be used both on land and in water जल और धरती दोनों में कार्यक्षम; उभयचर, जलस्थलचर *Frogs are amphibious.* ○ *amphibious vehicles*

**amphitheatre** (*AmE* **amphitheater**) /ˈæmfɪθɪətə(r) ऐम्ˈफ़िथिअट(र्)/ *noun* [C] a circular building without a roof and with rows of seats that rise in steps around an open space. Amphitheatres were used in ancient Greece and Rome गोलाकार या अंडाकार रंगमंडल जिसमें दीर्घाएँ बनी होती हैं। प्राचीन ग्रीस और रोम में ऐसे रंगमंडल होते थे

**ample** /ˈæmpl ˈऐम्पल्/ *adj.* **1** enough or more than enough पर्याप्त या पर्याप्त से अधिक; प्रचुर *We've got ample time to make a decision.* **2** large विशाल,

लंबा-चौड़ा, विस्तृत *There is space for an ample car park.* ▶ **amply** /ˈæmpli ˈऐम्प्लि/ *adv.* विस्तृता से

**amplifier** /ˈæmplɪfaɪə(r) ˈऐम्प्लिफ़ाइअ(र्)/ (*informal* **amp**) *noun* [C] a piece of electrical equipment for making sounds louder or signals stronger ध्वनि विस्तारक अथवा विद्युत शक्ति प्रवर्धक यंत्र

**amplify** /ˈæmplɪfaɪ ˈऐम्प्लिफ़ाइ/ *verb* (*pres. part.* **amplifying;** *3rd person sing. pres.* **amplifies;** *pt, pp* **amplified**) **1** to increase the strength of a sound, using electrical equipment विद्युत उपकरणों द्वारा ध्वनि-शक्ति में वृद्धि करना **2** to add details to sth in order to explain it more fully विस्तृत व्याख्या करना; विस्तार से कहना ▶ **amplification** /ˌæmplɪfɪˈkeɪʃn ˌऐम्प्लिफ़िˈकेश्न्/ *noun* [U] प्रवर्धन, विस्तारण, विस्तार

**amplitude** /ˈæmplɪtjuːd ˈऐम्प्लिट्यूड्/ *noun* [U, C] (*technical*) the greatest distance that a wave, especially a sound or radio wave, moves up and down तरंगों (विशेषतः ध्वनि या रेडियो तरंगों) के कंपन का अधिकतम आयाम; विस्तीर्णता

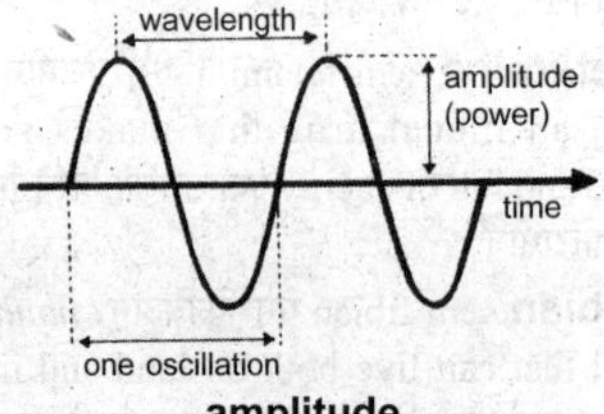


**amplitude**

**ampoule** /ˈæmpuːl ˈऐम्पूल्/ *noun* [C] a small container, usually made of glass, containing a drug that will be **injected** into sb दवा से भरा छोटा प्रायः काँच का पात्र जिसे सूई द्वारा शरीर में डाला जाता है; ऐंप्यूल

**amputate** /ˈæmpjuteɪt ˈऐम्प्युटेट्/ *verb* [I, T] to cut off a person's arm, leg, etc. for medical reasons (डॉक्टरी कारणों के लिए) रोगी का हाथ, पैर आदि काटना; अंगच्छेदन करना ▶ **amputation** /ˌæmpjuˈteɪʃn ˌऐम्प्युˈटेश्न्/ *noun* [C, U] अंगविच्छेदन

**amputee** /ˌæmpjuˈtiː ˌऐम्प्युˈटी/ *noun* [C] a person who has had an arm or a leg amputated व्यक्ति जिसका अंग कट चुका है; छिन्नांग

**amulet** /ˈæmjʊlət ˈऐम्युलट्/ *noun* [C] a piece of jewellery that some people wear because they think it protects them from bad luck, illness, etc. तावीज़

**amuse** /əˈmjuːz अˈम्यूज़्/ *verb* [T] **1** to make sb laugh or smile; to seem funny to sb किसी को हँसाना; किसी बात का मज़ेदार लगना *Everybody laughed but I couldn't understand what had amused them.* **2** to make time pass pleasantly for sb; to stop sb from getting bored किसी का जी बहलाना; मनोरंजन करना *I did some crosswords to amuse myself on the journey.*

**amused** /əˈmjuːzd अˈम्यूज़्ड्/ *adj.* thinking that sth is funny and wanting to laugh or smile किसी बात का मज़ेदार लगना *I was amused to hear his account of what happened.*

IDM **keep sb/yourself amused** to do sth in order to pass time pleasantly and stop sb/yourself getting bored किसी का या अपना जी बहलाना या मनोरंजन करना

**amusement** /əˈmjuːzmənt अˈम्यूज़्मन्ट्/ *noun* **1** [U] the feeling caused by sth that makes you laugh or smile, or by sth that entertains you मन-बहलाव, मनोविनोद *Much to the pupils' amusement, the teacher fell off his chair.* **2** [C] something that makes time pass pleasantly; an entertainment मनोरंजन का साधन *The holiday centre offers a wide range of amusements, including golf and tennis.*

**amusement arcade** = **arcade 2**

**amusing** /əˈmjuːzɪŋ अˈम्यूज़िङ्/ *adj.* causing you to laugh or smile हास्यकर, विनोदी, मनोरंजक *He's a very amusing person.* ○ *The story was quite amusing.*

**amylase** /ˈæmɪleɪz ˈऐमिलेज़्/ *noun* [U] an **enzyme** that allows the body to change some substances into simple sugars एक विशेष प्रकार का एंज़ाइम जिसके कारण शरीर में कुछ पदार्थ सरल शर्करा में बदल जाते हैं

**an** ➪ **a²** देखिए।

**anabolic steroid** /ˌænəbɒlɪk ˈsterɔɪd ˌऐनबॉलिक् ˈस्टेरॉइड्/ *noun* [C] a chemical substance that increases the size of the muscles. It is sometimes taken illegally by people who play sports एक रसायन जिसके सेवन से मांसपेशियों का आकार बढ़ता है; उपचयी स्टेरॉइड, खिलाड़ियों द्वारा इसका प्रयोग ग़ैर-क़ानूनी है

**anachronism** /əˈnækrənɪzəm अˈनैक्रनिज़म्/ *noun* [C] **1** a person, a custom, etc. that seems old-fashioned and does not belong in the present पुरातनपंथी व्यक्ति या व्यवहार जो वर्तमान में अजीब लगे **2** something that does not belong in the period of history in which it appears, for example in a book or a film कालदोषयुक्त प्रसंग *The movie, which is set in ancient Punjab, is full of anachronisms and inaccuracies.* ▶ **anachronistic** /əˌnækrəˈnɪstɪk अˌनैक्रˈनिस्टिक्/ *adj.* कालदोषपूर्ण

**anaemia** (*AmE* **anemia**) /əˈniːmiə अˈनीमिआ/ *noun* [U] a medical condition in which there are not enough red cells in the blood रक्त में लाल कणों की कमी; रक्ताल्पता, ख़ून की कमी, अरक्तता ▶ **anaemic** (*AmE* **anemic**) *adj.* अरक्तक

**anaerobic** /ˌæneəˈrəʊbɪk ˌऐनेअˈरोबिक्/ *adj.* **1** not needing **oxygen** जिसे ऑक्सीजन की ज़रूरत न हो;

ऑक्सीजन-निरपेक्ष *anaerobic bacteria* ➪ **respiration** पर चित्र देखिए। **2** (used about physical exercise) that is not intended to improve the way our bodies use **oxygen** ऐसे व्यायामों के लिए प्रयुक्त जिनमें ऑक्सीजन ग्रहण क्षमता बढ़ाना अभीष्ट नहीं होता ➪ **aerobic** देखिए।

**anaesthesia** (*AmE* **anesthesia**) /ˌænəsˈθiːziə ˌऐनस्ˈथ्रीज़िआ/ *noun* [U] the use of drugs that make you unable to feel pain during medical operations शल्य चिकित्सा से पूर्व दवा द्वारा संवेदनहीनता उत्पन्न करने की प्रक्रिया; संवेदनाहरण

**anaesthetic** (*AmE* **anesthetic**) /ˌænəsˈθetɪk ˌऐनस्ˈथ्रेटिक्/ *noun* [C, U] a substance that makes you unconscious or makes specific body parts numb so that you don't feel pain संवेदनहीनता उत्पन्न करने वाला पदार्थ; मूर्छक, संवेदनहारी *You'll need to be* ***under anaesthetic*** *for the operation.*

**anaesthetist** (*AmE* **anesthetist**) /əˈniːsθətɪst अˈनीसथ्रटिस्ट्/ *noun* [C] a person with the medical training necessary to give an **anaesthetic** to patients निश्चेतनाविज्ञानी, संवेदनाहरक

**anaesthetize** (*also* **-ise;** *AmE* **anesthetize**) /əˈniːsθətaɪz अˈनीसथ्रटाइज़्/ *verb* [T] to give an **anaesthetic** to sb किसी को निश्चेतन करना, बेहोशी की दवा देना

**anagram** /ˈænəgræm ˈऐनग्रैम्/ *noun* [C] a word or phrase that is made by arranging the letters of another word or phrase in a different order किसी शब्द या पदबंध के वर्णों के क्रम में परिवर्तन करने से बना अन्य शब्द या पदबंध; विपर्ययसिद्ध शब्द *'Worth' is an anagram of 'throw'.*

**anal** /ˈeɪnl ˈएनल्/ ➪ **anus** देखिए।

**analgesia** /ˌænəlˈdʒiːziə ˌएनल्ˈजीज़िआ/ *noun* [U] the loss of the ability to feel pain while still conscious; medicine that makes you unable to feel pain पीड़ाशून्यता; पीड़ाशून्य करने वाली दवा

**analgesic** /ˌænəlˈdʒiːzɪk ˌऐनल्ˈजीज़िक्/ *noun* [C] a substance that reduces pain पीड़ाहारी पदार्थ, पीड़ानाशक ▸ **analgesic** *adj.* पीड़ानाशक

**analogous** /əˈnæləgəs अˈनैलगस्/ *adj.* (*formal*) **analogous (to/with sth)** similar in some way; that you can compare आंशिक रूप से समरूप; अनुरूप; जिसकी तुलना की जा सके

**analogue** (*AmE* **analog**) /ˈænəlɒg ˈऐनलॉग्/ *adj.* (*technical*) **1** using an electronic system that uses continuously changing physical quantities to measure or store data आधार-सामग्री को मापने के लिए उसके निरंतर परिवर्तनशील गुणों का उपयोग करने वाली इलेक्ट्रानिक पद्धति से संबंधित; ऐनलॉग *an analogue circuit/computer/signal* **2** (used about a clock or watch) showing information using hands that move around a **dial** (घड़ी) जिसकी घूमती हुई सूइयों से अभीष्ट सूचना मिलती है ➪ **digital** देखिए।

**analogy** /əˈnælədʒi अˈनैलजि/ *noun* [C] (*pl.* **analogies**) **an analogy (between A and B)** a comparison between two things that shows a way in which they are similar दो वस्तुओं के बीच अधिक समानता या समरूपता दिखाती हुई तुलना *You could make an analogy between the human body and a car engine.*

IDM **by analogy** by comparing sth to sth else and showing how they are similar दो वस्तुओं की समानता की तुलना करते हुए

**analyse** (*AmE* **analyze**) /ˈænəlaɪz ˈऐनलाइज़्/ *verb* [T] to look at or think about the different parts or details of sth carefully in order to understand or explain it विश्लेषण करना; किसी तत्व के विभिन्न अंगों का अध्ययन एवं परीक्षण करना *The water samples are now being analysed in a laboratory.* ○ *to analyse statistics*

**analysis** /əˈnæləsɪs अˈनैलसिस्/ *noun* (*pl.* **analyses** /-siːz -सीज़्/) **1** [C, U] the careful examination of the different parts or details of sth विश्लेषण *Some samples of the water were sent to a laboratory* ***for analysis***. **2** [C] the result of a careful examination of sth विश्लेषण से प्राप्त परिणाम *Your analysis of the situation is different from mine.*

**analyst** /ˈænəlɪst ˈऐनलिस्ट्/ *noun* [C] a person whose job is to examine sth carefully as an expert विश्लेशण-कर्ता, विश्लेषण-विशेषज्ञ, विश्लेषक *a food analyst* ○ *a political analyst*

**analytical** /ˌænəˈlɪtɪkl ˌऐनˈलिटिक्ल्/ (*also* **analytic** /ˌænəˈlɪtɪk ˌऐनˈलिटिक्/) *adj.* using careful examination in order to understand or explain sth विश्लेषणात्मक

**anarchic** /əˈnɑːkɪk अˈनाकिक्/ *adj.* without rules or laws नियम और क़ानून से रहित; अराजक

**anarchism** /ˈænəkɪzəm ˈऐनकिज़म्/ *noun* [U] the political belief that there should be no government or laws in a country शासन को अनावश्यक मानने वाला राजनीतिक सिद्धांत; अराजकतावाद ▸ **anarchist** *noun* [C] अराजकतावादी

**anarchy** /ˈænəki ˈऐनकि/ *noun* [U] a situation in which people do not obey rules and laws; a situation in which there is no government in a country शासनहीनता की स्थिति; अराजकता

**anathema** /əˈnæθəmə अˈनैथ्रमा/ *noun* [U, C, *usually sing.*] (*formal*) a thing or an idea which you hate because it is the opposite of what you believe स्वयं के सिद्धांतों से नितांत भिन्न होने के कारण घृणा पैदा करने वाली वस्तु या विचार *Racial prejudice is (an) anathema to me.*

**anatomy** /əˈnætəmi अˈनैटमि / *noun* (*pl.* **anatomies**) **1** the scientific study of the structure of human or animal bodies शरीर-रचना-विज्ञान **2** [C] the structure of a living thing प्राणी की संरचना *the anatomy of the frog* ▶ **anatomical** /ˌænəˈtɒmɪkl ˌऐनˈटॉमिकल् / *adj.* शरीर-रचना-विज्ञान संबंधी ▶ **anatomist** /əˈnætəmɪst अˈनैटमिस्ट् / *noun* [C] शरीर-रचना-विज्ञानी

**ancestor** /ˈænsestə(r) ˈऐन्सेसट(र्) / *noun* [C] a person in your family who lived a long time before you पूर्वज, पुरखा, पूर्वपुरुष *My ancestors settled in this country a hundred years ago.* ➪ **descendant** देखिए। ✪ पर्याय **forebear** ▶ **ancestral** /ænˈsestrəl ऐन्ˈसेस्ट्रल् / *adj.* पैतृक, पुश्तैनी *her ancestral home* (= that had belonged to her ancestors)

**ancestry** /ˈænsestri ˈऐन्सेसट्रि / *noun* [C, U] (*pl.* **ancestries**) all of a person's ancestors वंशावली, वंशक्रम *He is **of** German **ancestry**.*

**anchor**[1] /ˈæŋkə(r) ˈऐङ्क(र्) / *noun* [C] **1** a heavy metal object at the end of a chain that you drop into the water from a boat in order to stop the boat moving लंगर **2 anchorman, anchorwoman**

**anchor**[2] /ˈæŋkə(r) ˈऐङ्क(र्) / *verb* **1** [I, T] to drop an anchor; to stop a boat moving by using an anchor लंगर डालना; लंगर डालकर नाव या पोत को एक स्थान पर रोके रखना **2** [T] to fix sth firmly so that it cannot move किसी वस्तु को कहीं पर मज़बूती से जमा देना

**anchorage** /ˈæŋkərɪdʒ ˈऐङ्करिज् / *noun* [C, U] **1** a place where boats or ships can **anchor** नावों और पोतों के रुकने का स्थान; लंगरगाह **2** a place where sth can be fastened to sth else स्थिरक, बाँधकर रखने की जगह *anchorage points for a baby's car seat*

**anchorman** /ˈæŋkəmæn ˈऐङ्कमैन् / *noun* [C] (*pl.* **-men** /-men -मेन् /) (*AmE* **anchor**) a man who presents a radio or television programme and introduces reports by other people रेडियो या टेलीविज़न कार्यक्रम का प्रस्तुतकर्ता; सूत्रधार

**anchorwoman** /ˈæŋkəwʊmən ˈऐङ्कवुमन् / *noun* [C] (*pl.* **-women** /-wɪmɪn -विमिन् /) (*AmE* **anchor**) a woman who presents a radio or television programme and introduces reports by other people रेडियो या टेलीविज़न कार्यक्रम की प्रस्तुतकर्त्री; महिला सूत्रधार

**anchovy** /ˈæntʃəvi ˈएन्चवि / *noun* [C, U] (*pl.* **anchovies**) a small fish with a strong salty flavour तीखे नमकीन स्वाद वाली एक छोटी मछली

**ancient** /ˈeɪnʃənt ˈएन्शन्ट् / *adj.* **1** belonging to a period of history that is thousands of years in the past प्राचीन, पुरातन, हज़ारों वर्ष पुराना *ancient history/civilization* ○ *the ancient world* **2** very old काफ़ी वृद्ध *I can't believe he's only 30—he looks ancient!*

**ancillary** /ænˈsɪləri एन्ˈसिलरि / *adj.* **ancillary (to sth) 1** providing necessary support to the main work or activities of an organization (मुख्य गतिविधियों में सहायक) *Ancillary hospital staff such as cleaners are often badly paid.* **2** in addition to sth else but not as important गौण, आनुषंगिक

**and** /ənd; ən; *strong form* ænd अन्ड्; अन्; प्रबल रूप ऐन्ड् / *conj.* **1** (*used to connect words or parts of sentences*) also; in addition to और; एवं, तथा, व *a boy and a girl* ○ *slowly and carefully* ○ *We were singing and dancing all evening.* **NOTE** जब दो वस्तुएँ निकटता से जुड़ी हों तो 'a' आदि को दोहराया नहीं जाता, जैसे *a knife and fork* ○ *my father and mother* **2** (used when you are saying numbers in sums) in addition to; plus और; युग *Twelve and six is eighteen.* **NOTE** बड़ी संख्याओं को बोलते समय 'hundred' शब्द के बाद *and* का प्रयोग किया जाता है *We say 2264 as two thousand, two hundred and sixty-four.* **3** used between repeated words to show that sth is increasing or continuing 'बढ़ते हुए' या 'ज़ारी' अर्थ दर्शाने के लिए प्रयुक्त *The situation is getting worse and worse.* ○ *I shouted and shouted but nobody answered.* **4** used instead of 'to' after certain verbs, for example 'go', 'come', 'try' क्रियाएँ 'go', 'come', 'try' आदि के साथ 'to' के स्थान पर प्रयुक्त *Go and answer the door for me, will you?* ○ *I'll try and find out what's going on.*

**androgynous** /ænˈdrɒdʒənəs ऐन्ˈड्रॉजनस् / *adj.* having both male and female characteristics; looking neither very male nor very female पुरुष और स्त्री दोनों के शारीरिक लक्षणों वाला; उभयलिंगी

**android** /ˈændrɔɪd ˈऐन्ड्रॉइड् / *noun* [C] a type of machine that looks like a real person मानवसदृश यंत्र ✪ पर्याय **robot**

**anecdotal** /ˌænɪkˈdəʊtl ˌऐनिक्ˈडोट्ल् / *adj.* based on **anecdotes** and possibly not true or accurate क़िस्सों पर आधारित जो ग़लत भी हो सकता है *The newspaper's 'monster shark' story was based on anecdotal evidence.*

**anecdote** /ˈænɪkdəʊt ˈऐनिक्डोट् / *noun* [C] a short interesting story about a real person or event किसी व्यक्ति या घटना के विषय में रोचक लघुकथा; क़िस्सा चुटकला, लतीफ़ा

**anemia, anemic** = **anaemia, anaemic**

**anemometer** /ænɪˈmɒmɪtə(r) ˈऐनिˈमॉमिट(र्)/ *noun* [C] (*technical*) an instrument for measuring the speed of wind पवनवेगमापी यंत्र ➪ **meter** पर चित्र देखिए।

**anemone** /əˈneməni अˈनेमनि/ *noun* [C] a small plant with white, red, blue or purple flowers that are shaped like cups and have dark centres एक छोटा पौधा जिसके प्यालेनुमा फूल सफ़ेद, लाल, नीले या बैंगनी रंग के होते हैं और मध्यबिंदु काले रंग का होता है ➪ **sea anemone** देखिए।

**anesthesia, anesthetic** = **anaesthesia, anaesthetic**

**anesthetist, anesthetize** = **anaesthetist, anaesthetize**

**anew** /əˈnjuː अˈन्यू/ *adv.* (*written*) again; in a new or different way फिर से; नए सिरे या भिन्न रीति से

**angel** /ˈeɪndʒl ˈएन्जल्/ *noun* [C] **1** a spirit who is believed to live in heaven with God. In pictures angels are usually dressed in white, with wings देवदूत, फ़रिश्ता **2** a person who is very kind अति दयावान

**angelic** /ænˈdʒelɪk ऐन्ˈजेलिक्/ *adj.* looking or acting like an angel देवदूत-समान ▶ **angelically** /-kli -क्लि/ *adv.* देवदूत की रीति से, देवदूत के समान आचरण करते हुए

**anger**[1] /ˈæŋgə(r) ˈऐङ्ग(र्)/ *noun* [U] the strong feeling that you have when sth has happened or sb has done sth that you do not like क्रोध, गुस्सा, रोष *He could not hide his anger at the news.* ○ *She was shaking with anger.*

**anger**[2] /ˈæŋgə(r) ˈऐङ्ग(र्)/ *verb* [T] to make sb become angry किसी को क्रोधित करना, गुस्सा दिलाना

**angina** /ænˈdʒaɪnə ऐन्ˈजाइना/ *noun* [U] very bad pain in the chest caused by not enough blood going to the heart during exercise हृदय तक पर्याप्त रक्त न पहुँचने के कारण उत्पन्न सीने में तीव्र दर्द; हृदयशूल

**angle**[1] /ˈæŋgl ˈऐङ्ग्ल्/ *noun* [C] **1** the space between two lines or surfaces that meet, measured in degrees (दो रेखाओं के बीच का) कोण *a right angle* (= an angle of 90°) ○ *The three angles of a triangle add up to 180°.* **2** the direction from which you look at sth किसी वस्तु को देखने की दिशा-विशेष *Viewed from this angle, the building looks bigger than it really is.* **3** a particular way of presenting or thinking about a situation etc. दृष्टिकोण, नज़रिया *looking at the issue from the financial angle*

**IDM at an angle** not straight कोण में, सीधा नहीं

**angle**[2] /ˈæŋgl ˈऐङ्ग्ल्/ *verb* **1** [I, T] to put sth in a position that is not straight; to be in this position

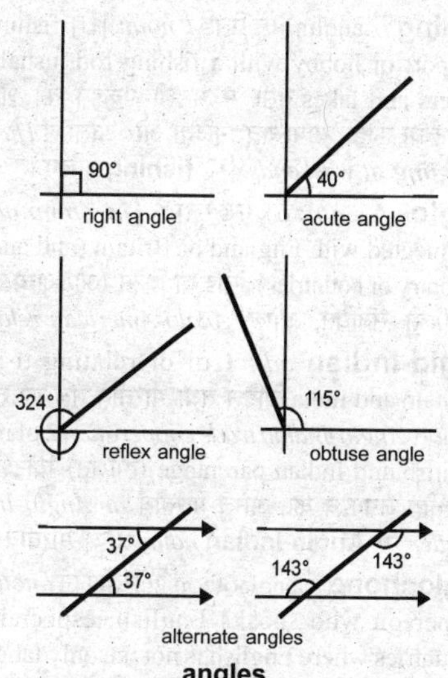

**angles**

(किसी वस्तु को) कुछ टेढ़े रखना; मोड़ देना, घुमाव देना *Angle the lamp towards the desk.* **2 angle sth (at/to/towards sb)** to show sth from a particular point of view; to aim sth at a particular person or group किसी वस्तु आदि को विशेष दृष्टिकोण से पेश करना; किसी विशिष्ट व्यक्ति या वर्ग को लक्ष्य में रखना *The new magazine is angled at young professional people.*

**PHR V angle for sth** to try to make sb give you sth, without asking for it in a direct way परोक्ष रीति से पाने का प्रयत्न करना *She was angling for an invitation to our party.*

**angler** /ˈæŋglə(r) ˈऐङ्ग्ल(र्)/ *noun* [C] a person who catches fish as a hobby शौक़िया मछली पकड़ने वाला व्यक्ति ➪ **fisherman** देखिए।

**Anglican** /ˈæŋglɪkən ˈऐङ्ग्लिकन्/ *noun* [C] a member of the Church of England or of a related church in another English-speaking country चर्च ऑफ़ इंग्लैंड या किसी अन्य अंग्रेज़ी भाषी देश के उससे जुड़े चर्च का सदस्य, आंग्ल या अंग्रेज़ी चर्च का सदस्य ▶ **Anglican** *adj.* आंग्लों का

**Anglicism** /ˈæŋglɪsɪzm ˈऐङ्ग्लिसिज़्म्/ *noun* a word, phrase or spelling that is typical of British English, used in another variety of English or another language ब्रिटिश अंग्रेज़ी का ऐसा प्रयोग (शब्द, वर्तनी आदि) जो अन्य भाषाओं या अंग्रेज़ी के अन्य भौगोलिक भेदों में प्रयुक्त होता हो, अन्य भाषाओं में प्रयुक्त अंग्रेज़ी शब्द

**anglicize** (*also* **-ise**) /ˈæŋglɪsaɪz ˈऐङ्ग्लिसाइज़्/ *verb* [T] to make sb/sth English in character अंग्रेज़ीकरण करना *Anjali anglicized her name to Angeline.*

**angling** /ˈæŋɡlɪŋ ˈऐङ्ग्लिङ्/ *noun* [U] fishing as a sport or hobby with a fishing rod, usually in rivers and lakes बंसी से मछली पकड़ने की शौक़िया क्रिया या क्रीड़ा, सामान्यतः नदियों और झीलों में *He goes angling at weekends.* ➪ **fishing** देखिए।

**Anglo-** /ˈæŋɡləʊ ˈऐङ्ग्लो/ (*in compounds*) connected with England or Britain (and another country or countries) इंग्लैंड या ब्रिटेन (और अन्य देश या देशों) से संबंधित; आंग्ल- *Anglo-American relations*

**Anglo-Indian** *adj.* **1** of or relating to both Britain and India ब्रिटिश तथा भारतीय मूल का तथा से संबंधित *Anglo-Indian trade cooperation* **2** of mixed British and Indian parentage (मिश्रित) ब्रिटिश तथा भारतीय जनकत्व का; आंग्ल-भारतीय *an Anglo-Indian writer* ▶ **Anglo-Indian** *noun* आंग्ल-भारतीय व्यक्ति

**anglophone** /ˈæŋɡləʊfəʊn ˈऐङ्ग्लोफ़ोन्/ *noun* [C] a person who speaks English, especially in countries where English is not the only language spoken अंग्रेज़ी भाषी, विशेषतः उन देशों में जहाँ केवल अंग्रेज़ी नहीं बोली जाती ▶ **anglophone** *adj.* अंग्रेज़ी भाषी-संबंधित *anglophone communities*

**angora** /æŋˈɡɔːrə ऐङ्ˈगॉरा/ *noun* [U] a type of soft wool or cloth एक प्रकार की नरम ऊन या कपड़ा; अंगोरा

**angry** /ˈæŋɡri ˈऐङ्ग्रि/ *adj.* (**angrier; angriest**) **angry (with sb) (at/about sth)** feeling or showing anger क्रोधित, गुस्सा, नाराज़ *Calm down, there's no need to get angry.* ○ *My parents will be angry with me if I get home late.* ▶ **angrily** *adv.* क्रोधपूर्वक, गुस्से से, क्रोध से

**angst** /æŋst ऐङ्स्ट्/ *noun* [U] a feeling of anxiety and worry about a situation or about your life स्थिति या जीवन के बारे में चिंता और व्याकुलता की भावना *songs full of teenage angst*

**anguish** /ˈæŋɡwɪʃ ˈऐङ्ग्विश्/ *noun* [U] (*written*) great mental pain or suffering गहरी वेदना या पीड़ा; मनोव्यथा ▶ **anguished** *adj.* अति व्यथित

**angular** /ˈæŋɡjələ(r) ˈऐङ्ग्यल(र्)/ *adj.* with sharp points or corners नुकीला, कोणवाला, कोणीय

**anicut** *noun* [C] (*IndE*) a dam built across a stream or river in order to supply water to the fields in the neighbouring area नदी पर बनाया गया बाँध जिसके पानी से आस-पास के खेतों की सिंचाई की जाती है

**animal** /ˈænɪml ˈऐनिमल्/ *noun* [C] **1** a creature that is not a bird, a fish, an insect or a human जानवर, पशु *the animal kingdom* **2** any living creature (including humans) that is not a plant पेड़-पौधों से भिन्न कोई भी जीवधारी; प्राणी *Humans are social animals.* ○ *farm animals* ○ *He studied the animals and birds of Southern Africa.* **3** a person who behaves in a cruel, violent or an unpleasant way or is very dirty निर्दयी, क्रूर या मैला व्यक्ति

**animate**[1] /ˈænɪmeɪt ˈऐनिमेट्/ *verb* [T] **1** to make sth have more life and energy अनुप्राणित करना; जान व स्फूर्ति डाल देना, प्राण का संचार करना *Her enthusiasm animated the whole room.* **2** (*usually passive*) to take a model, toy, etc. seem to move by taking a series of pictures of it in very slightly different positions and then showing the pictures as a continuous film किसी मॉडल, खिलौने आदि के चित्रों को एक-फ़िल्म के समान सजीव चलता हुआ दिखाना

**animate**[2] /ˈænɪmət ˈऐनिमट्/ *adj. informal* living; having life सजीव, जीवित-समान, जोशीला *animate beings* ✪ विलोम **inanimate**

**animated** /ˈænɪmeɪtɪd ˈऐनिमेटिड्/ *adj.* **1** interesting and full of energy रोचक और जोशीला *an animated discussion* **2** (used about films) using a process or method which makes pictures or models appear to move (चलचित्रों आदि) चित्रों को चलित रूप में दिखाने वाली प्रक्रिया का प्रयोग करते हुए *an animated cartoon*

**animation** /ˌænɪˈmeɪʃn ˌऐनिˈमेश्न्/ *noun* [U] **1** the state of being full of energy and enthusiasm भरपूर जोश और उत्साह **2** the method of making films, computer games, etc. with pictures or models that appear to move ऐसी फ़िल्में, कंप्यूटर-खेल आदि बनाने की तकनीक जिसमें चित्र आदि चलते हुए दिखाए जाते हैं *computer animation*

**animosity** /ˌænɪˈmɒsəti ˌऐनिˈमॉसटि/ *noun* [U, C] *pl.* **animosities animosity (toward(s) sb/sth) animosity (between A and B)** a strong feeling of anger and of not liking sb/sth शत्रुता, वैरभाव; द्वेष *There is still animosity between these two teams after last year's match.* ✪ पर्याय **hostility**

**anion** /ˈænaɪən ˈऐनाइअन्/ *noun* [C] (in chemistry) an **ion** with a negative electrical charge (रसायन शास्त्र में) ऋणात्मक आयन (विद्युतीकृत परमाणु) ऋणायन ➪ **cation** देखिए।

**aniseed** /ˈænəsiːd ˈऐनसीड्/ *noun* [U] the dried seeds of a plant that are used to give flavour to sweets and alcoholic drinks सौंफ

**ankle** /ˈæŋkl ˈऐङ्क्ल्/ *noun* [C] the part of your body where your foot joins your leg टखना *The water only came up to my ankles.* ➪ **body** पर चित्र देखिए।

**anklet** /ˈæŋklət ˈऐङ्क्लट्/ *noun* [C] a piece of jewellery worn around the top of your foot (**ankle**) पायल, पाज़ेब, नूपुर

**annals** /ˈænlz ˈऐन्ल्ज़्/ *noun* [*pl.*] an official record of events or activities year by year; historical records घटनाओं या गतिविधियों का आधिकारिक वार्षिक विवरण; ऐतिहासिक अभिलेख *The battle went down **in the annals** of British **history**.*

**annex** /əˈneks अˈनेक्स्/ *verb* [T] to take control of another country or region by force अन्य देश पर बलपूर्वक अधिकार कर लेना ▶ **annexation** /ˌænekseɪʃn ˌऐनेक्ˈसेश्न्/ *noun* [C, U] दूसरे देश को अपने देश में बलपूर्वक मिलाने की गतिविधि; समामेलन

**annexe** (*AmE* **annex**) /ˈæneks ˈऐनेक्स्/ *noun* [C] a building that is joined to a larger one किसी बड़े भवन से संलग्न छोटा भवन; उपभवन

**annihilate** /əˈnaɪəleɪt अˈनाइअलेट्/ *verb* [T] to destroy or defeat sb/sth completely पूरी तरह नष्ट या पराजित कर देना ▶ **annihilation** /əˌnaɪəˈleɪʃn अˌनाइअˈलेश्न्/ *noun* [U] संहार, विध्वंस

**anniversary** /ˌænɪˈvɜːsəri ˌऐनिˈव़सरि/ *noun* [C] (*pl.* **anniversaries**) a day that is exactly a year or a number of years after a special or important event वर्षगाँठ *the fiftieth anniversary of the country's independence* ○ *a wedding anniversary* ⇨ **birthday** देखिए।

**annotate** /ˈænəteɪt ˈऐनटेट्/ *verb* [T] to add notes to a book or text, giving explanations or comments व्याख्यात्मक टिप्पणियाँ देना ▶ **annotated** *adj.* सटिप्पण, नोट-युक्त ▶ **annotation** /ˌænəˈteɪʃn ˌऐन्ˈटेश्न्/ *noun* [C, U] व्याख्या, टीका, नोट

**announce** /əˈnaʊns अˈनाउन्स्/ *verb* [T] **1** to make sth known publicly and officially घोषणा करना, ऐलान करना *They announced that our train had been delayed.* ○ *The winners will be announced in next week's paper.* **2** to say sth in a firm or serious way गंभीरतापूर्वक या दृढ़ता के साथ कहना *She stormed into my office and announced that she was leaving.*

**announcement** /əˈnaʊnsmənt अˈनाउन्स्मन्ट्/ *noun* **1** [C] a statement that tells people about sth घोषणा, ऐलान, सूचना *Ladies and gentlemen, I'd like to **make an announcement**.* **2** [U] the act of telling people about sth घोषणा या सार्वजनिक तौर पर सूचना देने की क्रिया

**announcer** /əˈnaʊnsə(r) अˈनाउन्स(र्)/ *noun* [C] a person who introduces or gives information about programmes on radio or television उद्घोषक, घोषक, वाचक

**annoy** /əˈnɔɪ अˈनॉइ/ *verb* [T] to make sb angry or slightly angry किसी को क्रोधित या नाराज़ करना; परेशान या तंग करना; गुस्सा दिलाना *Close the door if the noise is annoying you.*

**annoyance** /əˈnɔɪəns अˈनॉइअन्स्/ *noun* **1** [U] the feeling of being annoyed नाराज़गी; खीझ, चिढ़ **2** [C] something that annoys sb परेशानी या खीझ पैदा करने वाली वस्तु

**annoyed** /əˈnɔɪd अˈनॉइड्/ *adj.* feeling angry or slightly angry नाराज़, खीझा हुआ *I shall be extremely annoyed if he turns up late again.* ○ *He's annoyed that nobody believes him.*

**annoying** /əˈnɔɪɪŋ अˈनॉइइङ्/ *adj.* making you feel angry or slightly angry कष्टकर, कष्टप्रद; खीझ पैदा करने वाला *It's so annoying that there's nobody here to answer questions.* ○ *annoying habit*

**annual**[1] /ˈænjuəl ˈऐन्युअल्/ *adj.* **1** happening or done once a year or every year वार्षिक, सालाना *the company's annual report* ○ *an annual festival* **2** for the period of one year वर्ष भर की अवधि का; वार्षिक *a person's annual salary* ○ *the annual sales figures* ▶ **annually** *adv.* प्रतिवर्ष

**annual**[2] /ˈænjuəl ˈऐन्युअल्/ *noun* [C] a book, especially one for children, that is published once each year वार्षिक प्रकाशन, वार्षिक अंक

**annuity** /əˈnjuːəti अˈन्यूअटि/ *noun* [C] (*pl.* **annuities**) a fixed amount of money that is paid to sb each year, usually for the rest of his/her life वार्षिकी, वार्षिक प्रतिभूति

**annul** /əˈnʌl अˈनल्/ *verb* [T] (*pres. part.* **annulling**; *pt, pp* **annulled**) (*usually passive*) to state officially that sth is no longer legally valid or recognized (किसी क़ानून, समझौते आदि को) रद्द करना, निरस्त करना *Their marriage was annulled after just six months.* ▶ **annulment** *noun* [C, U] निरस्तीकरण, निष्प्रभावन

**anode** /ˈænəʊd ˈऐनोड्/ *noun* [C] the place on a battery or other electrical device where the electric current enters बैटरी का वह भाग जिससे विद्युत प्रवेश करती है; धनाग्र ▶ **cathode** देखिए।

**anoint** /əˈnɔɪnt अˈनॉइन्ट्/ *verb* [T] **anoint sb (with sth)** to put oil or water on sb's head as part of a religious ceremony (धार्मिक संस्कार के रूप में) शरीर या सिर पर तेल या पानी लगाना

**anomalous** /əˈnɒmələs अˈनॉमलस्/ *adj.* different from what is normal सामान्य से भिन्न, असामान्य, बेमेल, असंगत

**anomaly** /əˈnɒməli अˈनॉमलि/ *noun* [C] (*pl.* **anomalies**) something that is different from what is normal or usual अपसामान्यता, असंगति *We discovered an anomaly in the sales figures for August.*

**anon** /əˈnɒn अˈनॉन्/ *abbr.* anonymous; used to show that the writer's name is not known अनाम; (लेखक) अज्ञात

**anonymity** /ˌænəˈnɪməti ˌऐनˈनिमटि / *noun* [U] the situation where a person's name is not known गुमनामी, अनामता

**anonymous** /əˈnɒnɪməs अˈनॉनिमस् / *adj.* **1** (used about a person) whose name is not known or made public (व्यक्ति) अनाम, अज्ञात *An anonymous caller told the police that a robbery was being planned.* **2** done, written, etc. by sb whose name is not known or made public गुमनाम व्यक्ति द्वारा किया या लिखा गया *He received an anonymous letter.* ▶ **anonymously** *adv.* नाम न बतलाते हुए; छुपे तौर पर

**anorak** /ˈænəræk ˈऐनरैक् / *noun* [C] (*BrE*) **1** a short coat with a covering for your head that protects you from rain, wind and cold वर्षा, हवा और ठंड आदि से बचाव करने वाला छोटा टोपीयुक्त कोट; ऐनोरक **2** (*slang*) a person who enjoys learning boring facts नीरस बातों में रस लेने वाला व्यक्ति

**anorexia** /ˌænəˈreksiə ˌऐनˈरेक्सिआ / (*also* **anorexia nervosa** /ˌænəˌreksiə nɜːˈvəʊsə ˌऐनˌरेक्सिआ नˈर्वोसा /) *noun* [U] an illness, especially affecting young women. It makes them afraid of being fat and so they do not eat विशेषतः युवतियों को होने वाला रोग जिसमें मोटे हो जाने का अस्वाभाविक डर पैदा हो जाता है और रोगी खाना-पीना बंद कर देती है; क्षुधा-नाश ➪ **bulimia** देखिए। ▶ **anorexic** *adj., noun* [C] क्षुधाअभाव का रोगी

**another** /əˈnʌðə(r) अˈनद़(र्) / *det., pronoun* **1** one more person or thing of the same kind अन्यतर, उसी प्रकार का दूसरा, एक और *Would you like another drink?* **2** a different thing or person दूसरी प्रकार का, कोई और *I'm afraid I can't see you tomorrow. Could we arrange another day?*

**IDM** **one after another/the other** ➪ **one**[1] देखिए। **yet another** ➪ **yet** देखिए।

**answer**[1] /ˈɑːnsə(r) ˈआन्स(र्) / *verb* [I, T] **1** to say or write sth back to sb who has asked you sth or written to you उत्तर देना; जवाब देना *I asked her what the matter was but she didn't answer.* ○ *Answer all the questions on the form.*

> **NOTE** **Answer** और **reply** उत्तर देने के अर्थ में सर्वाधिक प्रयुक्त क्रियाएँ हैं—*I asked him a question but he didn't answer.* ○ *I sent my application but they haven't replied yet.* ध्यान दें, व्यक्ति, प्रश्न या पत्र के संदर्भ में **answer** (बिना **to** के) का प्रयोग किया जाता है, परंतु पत्र के साथ **reply to** का प्रयोग किया जाता है। शब्द **respond** औपचारिक है और इसका प्रयोग अपेक्षाकृत कम किया जाता है—*Applicants must respond within seven days.* **Respond** का प्रयोग अपेक्षाकृत प्रतिक्रिया देखने के अर्थ में किया जाता हैं—*Despite all the doctor's efforts the patient did not respond to treatment.*

**2** to do sth as a reply प्रतिक्रिया दिखाना *Can you answer the phone for me, please?* ○ *I rang their doorbell but nobody answered.*

**PHR V** **answer back** to defend yourself against sth bad that has been written or said about you कटु आलोचना की प्रतिक्रिया में अपना बचाव करना

**answer (sb) back** to reply rudely to sb धृष्टतापूर्वक उत्तर देना

**answer for sb/sth** **1** to accept responsibility for sth/sb (किसी बात या व्यक्ति की) ज़िम्मेदारी स्वीकार करना; जवाबदेह होना *Somebody will have to answer for all the damage that has been caused.* **2** to speak in support of sb/sth (किसी बात या व्यक्ति के) समर्थन में बोलना

**answer**[2] /ˈɑːnsə(r) ˈआन्स(र्) / *noun* [C] **an answer (to sb/sth)** **1** something that you say, write or do as a reply उत्तर, जवाब *The answer to your question is that I don't know.* ○ *They've made me an offer and I have to* ***give*** *them* ***an answer*** *by Friday.* **2** a solution to a problem किसी समस्या का समाधान, हल *I didn't have any money so the only answer was to borrow some.* **3** a reply to a question in a test or exam (परीक्षा में) प्रश्न का उत्तर *My answer to question 5 was wrong.* **4** the correct reply to a question in a test or exam (परीक्षा में) प्रश्न का सही उत्तर; हल *What was the answer to question 4?*

**IDM** **in answer (to sth)** as a reply (to sth) (किसी बात के) उत्तर के रूप में; उत्तर स्वरूप

**answerable** /ˈɑːnsərəbl ˈआन्सरब्ल् / *adj* **answerable to sb (for sth)** having to explain and give good reasons for your actions to sb; responsible to sb जवाबदेह; उत्तरदायी

**answering machine** (*BrE* **answerphone** /ˈɑːnsəfəʊn ˈआन्सफ़ोन् /) *noun* [C] a machine that you connect to your telephone when you are away to answer the calls and record messages from the people who call टेलीफ़ोन से जुड़ा यंत्र जो मालिक की अनुपस्थिति में फ़ोन सुनता है और कॉल करने वाले व्यक्तियों का संदेश रिकॉर्ड कर लेता है; आंसरिंग मशीन *I rang him and left a message on his answering machine.*

**ant** /ænt ऐन्ट् / *noun* [C] a very small insect that lives in large groups and works very hard चींटी ➪ **insect** पर चित्र देखिए।

**antagonism** /ænˈtægənɪzəm ऐन्ˈटैगनिज़म् / *noun* [C, U] **antagonism (towards sb/sth); antagonism (between A and B)** a feeling of hate and of being against sb/sth घृणा व विरोध की भावना ▶ **antagonistic** /ænˌtægəˈnɪstɪk ऐन्ˌटैगˈनिस्टिक् / *adj.* विरुद्ध, प्रतिकूल

**antagonist** /æn'tægənɪst ऐन्'टैगनिस्ट्/ *noun* [C] (*formal*) a person who is strongly against sb/sth प्रबल विरोधी, प्रतिद्वंद्वी, शत्रु

**antagonize** (*also* **-ise**) /æn'tægənaɪz ऐन्'टैग्नाइज़्/ *verb* [T] to make sb angry or to annoy sb (किसी को अपना) विरोधी या दुश्मन बनाना; अत्यंत नाराज़ करना

**Antarctic** /æn'tɑ:ktɪk ऐन्'टाक्टिक्/ *adj.* connected with the coldest, most southern parts of the world दक्षिणी ध्रुव के प्रदेश से संबंधित; दक्षिण ध्रुवीय *an Antarctic expedition* ➪ **Arctic** देखिए।

**the Antarctic** /æn'tɑ:ktɪk ऐन्'टाक्टिक्/ *noun* [*sing.*] the most southern part of the world विश्व का धुर दक्षिणी प्रदेश; दक्षिण ध्रुव प्रदेश ➪ **earth** पर चित्र देखिए।

**Antarctic Circle** *noun* [*sing.*] the line of **latitude** 66° 30'S दक्षिणी ध्रुव वृत्त; अक्षांश 66° 30'S की रेखा ➪ **Arctic Circle** देखिए तथा **earth** पर चित्र देखिए।

**ante-** /'ænti 'एन्टि/ *prefix* (*in nouns adjectives and verbs*) before; in front of पूर्व, अग्र, पूर्ववर्ती *antenatal* ○ *ante-room* ➪ **post-** और **pre-** देखिए।

**anteater** /'ænti:tə(r) 'ऐन्टीट(र्)/ *noun* [C] an animal with a long nose and tongue that eats **ants** चींटियाँ खाने वाला एक जानवर जिसकी नाक और जीभ लंबी होती है; चींटीख़ोर

**antecedent** /ˌæntɪ'si:dnt ˌऐन्टि'सीड्न्ट्/ *noun* [C] **1** (*formal*) a thing or an event that exists or comes before another, and may have influenced it किसी अन्य घटना से पहले होने वाली घटना; पूर्ववृत्त, पूर्व-वृत्तांत **2 antecedents** [*pl.*] the people in sb's family who lived a long time ago पूर्वज, पुरखे ✪ पर्याय **ancestors** **3** (*grammar*) a word or phrase to which the following word, especially a pronoun, refers विशेषतः सर्वनाम द्वारा उल्लेखित शब्द या वाक्यांश *In 'He grabbed the ball and threw it in the air', 'ball' is the antecedent of 'it'.*

**antelope** /'æntɪləʊp 'ऐन्टिलोप्/ *noun* [C] (*pl.* **antelope** or **antelopes**) an African animal with horns and long, thin legs that can run very fast बारहसिंगा

**antenatal** /ˌænti'neɪtl ˌऐन्टि'नेट्ल्/ *adj.* connected with the care of pregnant women गर्भिणी महिलाओं की देखभाल से संबंधित; जन्मपूर्व, प्राक्प्रसव *an antenatal clinic* ○ *antenatal care* ➪ **post-natal** देखिए।

**antenna** /æn'tenə ऐन्'ट्रेना/ *noun* [C] **1** (*pl.* **antennae** /-ni: -नी/) one of the two long thin parts on the heads of insects and some animals that live in shells. Antennae are used for feeling things with कीड़ों और सीपियों में रहने वाले कुछ जानवरों के सिर पर निकले स्पर्शक ✪ पर्याय **feelers** ➪ **insect** पर चित्र देखिए। **2** (*pl.* **antennas**) (*AmE*) = **aerial**[1]

**anterior** /æn'tɪəriə(r) ऐन्'टिअरिअ(र्)/ *adj.* (*only before a noun*) (*technical*) (used about a part of the body) at or near the front (शरीर का कोई अंग) अग्रवर्ती या अगला

**anthem** /'ænθəm 'ऐन्थम्/ *noun* [C] a song, which has special importance for a country, organization, school, etc. and is sung on special occasions देश, संगठन, पाठशाला आदि द्वारा अपनाया गया विशेष गान जो विशेष अवसरों पर गाया जाता है *the national anthem*

**anther** /'ænθə(r) 'ऐन्थ(र्)/ *noun* [C] (*technical*) the part of a flower at the top of a **stamen** that produces **pollen** परागकोश ➪ **flower** पर चित्र देखिए।

**anthology** /æn'θɒlədʒi ऐन्'थॉलजि/ *noun* [C] (*pl.* **anthologies**) a book that contains pieces of writing or poems, often on the same subject, by different authors विभिन्न लेखकों की प्रायः एक ही विषय पर लिखी रचनाओं का संकलन; संग्रह

**anthracite** /'ænθrəsaɪt 'ऐन्थ्रसाइट्/ *noun* [U] a very hard type of coal that burns slowly without producing a lot of smoke or flames एक कठोर प्रकृति का कोयला जो धीरे-धीरे जलता है और जिसमें से न तो अधिक धुआँ निकलता है न लपटें

**anthrax** /'ænθræks 'ऐन्थ्रैक्स्/ *noun* [U] a serious disease that affects sheep and cattle and sometimes people, and can cause death गाय, बैलों और भेड़ों और कभी मनुष्यों को होने वाला गंभीर रोग जिसमें मृत्यु भी हो सकती है; ऐन्थ्रैक्स

**anthropo-** /'ænθrəpəʊ 'ऐन्थ्रपो/ *prefix* (*in nouns, adjectives and adverbs*) connected with human beings मानव-संबंधित, मानवीय *anthropology*

**anthropology** /ˌænθrə'pɒlədʒi ˌऐन्थ्र'पॉलजि/ *noun* [U] the study of human beings, especially of their origin, development, customs and beliefs मानव की उत्पत्ति, उसके विकास, प्रथाओं और विश्वासों का वैज्ञानिक अध्ययन; मानव-विज्ञान ▸ **anthropological** /ˌænθrəpə'lɒdʒɪkl ˌऐन्थ्रप'लॉजिक्ल्/ *adj.* मानव-शास्त्रीय ▸ **anthropologist** /ˌænθrə'pɒlədʒɪst ˌऐन्थ्र'पॉलजिस्ट्/ *noun* [C] मानव-विज्ञानी

**anti-** /'ænti 'ऐन्टि/ *prefix* (*in nouns, adjectives and adverbs*) **1** against विरोधी, रोधी; के विरुद्ध, के विपरीत का प्रतिरोधी *anti-war* ○ *antiperspirant* ○ *anticlockwise* **2** the opposite of प्रति, विपरीत *anticlimax*

**anti-aircraft** *adj.* (*only before a noun*) designed to destroy enemy aircraft विमान-भेदी *anti-aircraft fire/guns/missiles*

**antibacterial** /ˌæntibæk'tɪəriəl 'ऐन्टिबैक्'टिअरिअल्/ *adj.* that fights against bacteria that can cause disease प्रतिजीवाणु, जीवाणुनिरोधक

**antibiotic** /ˌæntibaɪˈɒtɪk ˈऐन्टिबाइˈऑटिक्/ *noun* [C] a medicine which is used for destroying bacteria and curing infections जीवाणुनाशक औषधि; प्रतिजैविक

**antibody** /ˈæntibɒdi ˈऐन्टिबॉडि/ *noun* [C] (*pl.* **antibodies**) a substance that the body produces in the blood to fight disease रक्त में उत्पन्न होने वाला रोगनिरोधी पदार्थ; प्रतिरक्षी, प्रतिपिंड

**anticipate** /ænˈtɪsɪpeɪt ऐन्ˈटिसिपेट्/ *verb* [T] to expect sth to happen (and prepare for it) (कुछ घटित होने की) प्रत्याशा करना (और उसके लिए तैयार रहना) *to anticipate a problem* ○ *I anticipate that the situation will get worse.*

**anticipation** /ænˌtɪsɪˈpeɪʃn ऐन्ˌटिसिˈपेश्न्/ *noun* [U] **1** the state of expecting sth to happen (and preparing for it) प्रत्याशा, पूर्वाभास *The government has reduced tax* ***in anticipation of*** *an early general election.* **2** excited feelings about sth that is going to happen कुछ अनुकूल घटित होने की प्रत्याशा में उत्तेजना-भरी भावनाएँ *They queued outside the stadium* ***in*** *excited* ***anticipation***.

**anticlimax** /ˌæntiˈklaɪmæks ˌऐन्टिˈक्लाइमैक्स्/ *noun* [C, U] an event, etc. that is less exciting than you had expected or than what has already happened उच्च प्रत्याशा के विपरीत घटित निराशाजनक घटना; प्रतिकर्ष

**anticline** /ˈæntiklaɪn ˌऐन्टिक्लाइन्/ *noun* [C] (*technical*) (in geology) an area of ground where layers of rock in the earth's surface have been folded into an arch (भूविज्ञान में) वह भूक्षेत्र जहाँ पृथ्वी की सतह पर स्थित चट्टान की परतें मेहराब की शकल में मुड़ी हों ➪ **syncline** देखिए।

**anticlockwise** /ˌæntiˈklɒkwaɪz ˌऐन्टिˈक्लॉक्वाइज़्/ (*AmE* **counter-clockwise**) *adv., adj.* in the opposite direction to the movement of the hands of a clock घड़ी की सूइयों के घूमने की विपरीत दिशा में *Turn the lid anticlockwise/in an anticlockwise direction.* ✪ विलोम **clockwise**

**anticoagulant** /ˌæntikəʊˈægjələnt ˌऐन्टिकोˈऐग्यलन्ट्/ *noun* [C] a substance that stops the blood from becoming thick and forming lumps (**clots**) रक्त को गाढ़ा होने और थक्का बनने से रोकने वाला पदार्थ; स्कंदरोधी

**antics** /ˈæntɪks ˈऐन्टिक्स्/ *noun* [*pl.*] funny, strange or silly ways of behaving अजीब और बेतुकी हरकतें; मसख़रापन

**anticyclone** /ˌæntiˈsaɪkləʊn ˌऐनटिˈसाइक्लोन्/ *noun* [C] an area of high air pressure that produces calm weather conditions with clear skies उच्च वायुमंडलीय दबाव वाला क्षेत्र जिसमें मौसम साफ़ और शांत हो जाता है; प्रतिचक्रवात ➪ **depression** देखिए।

**antidepressant** /ˌæntidɪˈpresnt ˌऐनटिडिˈप्रेसन्ट्/ *noun* (*medical*) a drug that is used to treat **depression** निराशा, उदासी, विषाद आदि दूर करने वाली दवा

**antidote** /ˈæntidəʊt ˈऐन्टिडोट्/ *noun* [C] **1** a medical substance that is used to prevent a poison or a disease from having an effect विषहर औषधि **2** anything that helps you to deal with sth unpleasant किसी भी अप्रिय प्रभाव से निपटने में सहायक कोई अन्य वस्तु; प्रतिकारक, प्रत्यौषध

**antifreeze** /ˈæntifri:z ˈऐन्टिफ़्रीज़्/ *noun* [U] a chemical that is added to the water in the **radiator** of cars and other vehicles to stop it from freezing कार आदि में रेडियेटर के पानी को जमने से रोकने वाला रसायन; जमाव-रोधी रसायन

**antigen** /ˈæntɪdʒən ˈऐन्टिजन्/ *noun* [C] a substance that enters the body and starts a process that can cause disease. The body then usually produces substances (**antibodies**) to fight the antigens शरीर में प्रवेश करने वाला रोगोत्पादक पदार्थ। इस पदार्थ के प्रतिरोध के लिए शरीर रोगनिरोधी पदार्थ उत्पन्न करता है; प्रतिजन

**anti-hero** *noun* [C] the main character in a film, story or play who does not have the qualities that a main character (**hero**) normally has, such as courage. An anti-hero is more like an ordinary person or is very unpleasant नायक के सामान्य गुणों से वंचित मुख्य पात्र; प्रतिनायक ➪ **hero** और **villain** देखिए।

**antihistamine** /ˌæntiˈhɪstəmi:n ˌएन्टिˈहिस्टमीन्/ *noun* [C, U] a drug used to treat an **allergy** एलर्जी दूर करने वाली दवा ➪ **histamine** देखिए।

**antimony** /ˈæntɪməni ˈऐन्टिमनि/ *noun* [U] a silver-white metal that breaks easily रुपहले-सफ़ेद रंग का धातु जो आसानी से टूट जाता है; अंजन, सुरमा

**antipathy** /ænˈtɪpəθi ऐन्ˈटिपथ्रि/ *noun* [C, U] **antipathy (to/towards sb/sth)** a strong feeling of not liking sb/sth; dislike प्रतिकूलता की प्रबल भावना; नापसंदगी, चिढ़, विद्वेष

**antiperspirant** /ˌæntiˈpɜ:spərənt ˌएन्टिˈपसपरन्ट्/ *noun* [C, U] a liquid that you use to reduce sweating, especially under your arms पसीना कम करने के लिए विशेषतः काँख में लगाया जाने वाला तरल पदार्थ

**the Antipodes** /ænˈtɪpədi:z ऐन्ˈटिपडीज़्/ *noun* [*pl.*] a way of referring to Australia and New Zealand ऑस्ट्रेलिया और न्यूज़ीलैंड के संबोधन के लिए प्रयुक्त शब्द ► **Antipodean** /ˌæntɪpəˈdi:ən ˌऐन्टिपˈडीअन्/ *adj.* ऑस्ट्रेलिया और न्यूजीलैंड से संबंधित

**antiquated** /ˈæntɪkweɪtɪd ˈऐन्टिक्वेटिड् / *adj.* old-fashioned and not suitable for the modern world पुरातन, अप्रचलित, गतप्रयोग

**antique** /ænˈtiːk ऐन्ˈटीक् / *adj.* very old and therefore unusual and valuable प्राचीनकाल की और अतएव असाधारण तथा मूल्यवान *an antique vase/table* ○ *antique furniture/jewellery* ▶ **antique** *noun* [C] पुरानी या प्राचीन काल की कोई वस्तु *an antique shop* ○ *That vase is an antique.*

**antiquity** /ænˈtɪkwəti ऐन्ˈटिक्वटि / *noun* (*pl.* **antiquities**) **1** [U] the ancient past, especially the times of the Ancient Greeks and Romans अति प्राचीनकाल **2** [C, *usually pl.*] a building or object from ancient times अति प्राचीन भवन या वस्तु *Greek/Roman antiquities* **3** [U] the state of being very old or ancient अतिप्राचीनता

**anti-Semitism** /ˌæntiˈsemətɪzəm ˌऐन्टिˈसेमटिज़्म् / *noun* [U] unfair treatment of Jewish people यहूदी समाज के प्रति भेदभाव ▶ **anti-Semitic** /ˌæntisəˈmɪtɪk ˌऐन्टि सˈमिटिक् / *adj.* यहूदी समाज के प्रति भेदभाव संबंधी

**antiseptic** /ˌæntiˈseptɪk ˌऐन्टिˈसेप्टिक् / *noun* [C, U] a liquid or cream that prevents a cut, etc. from becoming infected रोगाणु रोधक मरहम या कोई तरल पदार्थ *Put an antiseptic/some antiseptic on that scratch.* ▶ **antiseptic** *adj.* रोगाणु-रोधी; प्रतिरोधक *antiseptic cream*

**antisocial** /ˌæntiˈsəʊʃl ˌऐन्टिˈसोशल् / *adj.* **1** harmful or annoying to other people समाज-विरोधी *antisocial behaviour* **2** not liking to be with other people असामाजिक; जिसे सामाजिक मेलजोल पसंद न हो

**antithesis** /ænˈtɪθəsɪs ऐन्ˈटिथ़सिस् / *noun* [C, U] (*pl.* **antitheses** /ænˈtɪθəsiːz ऐन्ˈटिथ़सीज़् /) (*formal*) **1** the opposite of sth विपरीतता, उल्टा *Love is the antithesis of hate.* **2** a difference between two things दो वस्तुओं में अंतर

**antler** /ˈæntlə(r) ˈऐन्ट्ल(र्) / *noun* [C, *usually pl.*] a horn on the head of a **stag** हिरन का सींग; मृगश्रृंग *a pair of antlers*

**antonym** /ˈæntənɪm ˈऐन्टनिम् / *noun* [C] (*grammar*) a word that means the opposite of another word विलोम शब्द, विपर्याय, विपरीतार्थी ➪ **synonym** देखिए।

**anus** /ˈeɪnəs ˈएनस् / *noun* [C] the hole through which solid waste substances leave the body गुदा, मलद्वार ➪ **body** पर चित्र देखिए। ▶ **anal** /ˈeɪnl ˈएन्ल् / *adj.* गुदासंबंधी

**anvil** /ˈænvɪl ˈऐन्विल् / *noun* [C] **1** an iron block on which a **blacksmith** puts hot pieces of metal before shaping them with a hammer (लोहार की) निहाई **2** a very small bone inside the ear कान के अंदर की बहुत छोटी हड्डी

**anxiety** /æŋˈzaɪəti ऐङ्ˈज़ाइअटि / *noun* [C, U] (*pl.* **anxieties**) a feeling of worry or fear, especially about the future भय, चिंता या अनिश्चय की भावना विशेषतः भविष्य के प्रति *a feeling/state of anxiety* ○ *There are anxieties over the effects of unemployment.*

**anxious** /ˈæŋkʃəs ˈऐङ्क्शस् / *adj.* **1 anxious (about/for sb/sth)** worried and afraid चिंतित या डरा हुआ; व्याकुल *I began to get anxious when they still hadn't arrived at 9 o'clock.* ○ *an anxious look/expression* **2** causing worry and fear चिंताजनक *For a few anxious moments we thought we'd missed the train.* **3 anxious to do sth; anxious for sth** wanting sth very much अतिउत्सुक ▶ **anxiously** *adv.* चिंतित रूप से; अतिउत्सुकता से

**any** /ˈeni ˈएनि / *det., pronoun, adv.* **1** used instead of **some** in negative sentences and questions निषेधात्मक वाक्यों एवं प्रश्नों में 'some' के स्थान पर प्रयुक्त *We didn't have any lunch.* ○ *Do you have any questions?* ○ *I don't like any of his books.* ➪ **some** पर नोट देखिए। **2** used for saying that it does not matter which thing or person you choose जब किसी विशेष वस्तु का निर्देश न करना हो; कुछ, कोई भी, किसी भी *Take any book you want.* ○ *Come round any time—I'm usually in.* **3** (*used in negative sentences and questions*) at all; to any degree जब कम या अधिक का निर्देश करना हो *I can't run any faster.* ○ *Is your father any better?*

IDM **any moment/second/minute/day (now)** very soon बहुत शीघ्र, जल्दी ही *She should be home any minute now.*

**anybody** /ˈenibɒdi ˈएनिबॉडि / (*also* **anyone**) *pronoun* **1** (*usually in questions or negative statements*) any person कोई व्यक्ति, किसी व्यक्ति *I didn't know anybody at the party.* ○ *Would anybody else* (= any other person) *like to come with me?*

> NOTE **Somebody** और **anybody** में वही अंतर है जो **some** में तथा **any** में है। ➪ **some** और **somebody** पर नोट देखिए।

**2** any person, it does not matter who कोई भी व्यक्ति, चाहे कोई भी *Anybody can learn to swim.* ○ *Can anybody come, or are there special invitations?*

**anyhow** /ˈenihaʊ ˈएनिहाउ / *adv.* **1** = **anyway** **2** in a careless way; not arranged in any order बेतरतीब; लापरवाही से *She threw the clothes down onto the bed, just anyhow.*

**anyone** /ˈeniwʌn ˈएनिवन् / = **anybody**

**anyplace** /ˈenipleɪs ˈएनिप्लेस् / (*AmE*) = **anywhere**

**anything** /ˈeniθɪŋ ˈएनिथिङ्/ *pronoun* **1** (*usually in negative sentences and in questions*) one thing (of any kind) कुछ, कुछ भी *It was so dark that I couldn't see anything at all.* ○ *There isn't anything interesting in the newspaper today.* ○ *'I'd like a kilo of apples please.'* ***'Anything else'*** (= any other thing)*?*

> NOTE **Something** और **anything** में वही अंतर है जो **some** और **any** में है। ➪ **some** पर नोट देखिए।

**2** any thing or things: it does not matter what कोई भी वस्तु; कुछ भी *I'm very hungry—I'll eat anything!* ○ *I'll do anything you say.*

IDM **anything but** not at all बिलकुल भी नहीं; निश्चित रूप से नहीं *Their explanation was anything but clear.*
**anything like sb/sth** at all similar to sb/sth; nearly किसी भी रूप में समान नहीं; लगभग *She isn't anything like her sister, is she?* ○ *This car isn't anything like as fast as mine.*
**as happy, quick, etc. as anything** (*spoken*) very happy, quick, etc. बहुत (प्रसन्न, तेज़ आदि); अत्यधिक
**like anything** ➪ **like²** देखिए।
**not come to anything** ➪ **come** देखिए।

**anyway** /ˈeniweɪ ˈएनिवे/ (*also* **anyhow**) *adv.* **1** (used to add an extra point or reason) in any case (अतिरिक्त विचार जोड़ने के लिए) जो कुछ भी हो; हर हालत में *It's too late now, anyway.* ○ *I don't want to go out tonight, and anyway I haven't got any money.* ✪ पर्याय **besides** **2** in spite of sth; even so किसी बात के बावजूद भी; तथापि *I'm afraid I can't come to your party, but thanks anyway.* **3** used after a pause in order to change the subject or go back to a subject being discussed before जब बातचीत का रुख बदलना हो या पूर्वचर्चित विषय पर लौटना हो *Anyhow, that's enough about my problems. How are you?* **4** used to correct or slightly change what you have said जब कथन को थोड़ा बदलना या उसे सही करना हो *He works in a bank. He did when I last saw him, anyway.*

**anywhere** /ˈeniweə(r) ˈएनिवेअ(र्)/ (*AmE* **anyplace**) *adv.* **1** (*usually in negative sentences or in questions*) in, at or to any place कहीं भी, कहीं पर भी *I can't find my keys anywhere.* ○ *Is there a post office anywhere near here?*

> NOTE **Somewhere** और **anywhere** में वही अंतर है जो **some** और **any** में। ➪ **some** पर नोट देखिए।

**2** any place; it does not matter where किसी भी स्थान पर; चाहे कहीं भी *You can sit anywhere you like.*

**aorta** /eɪˈɔːtə एˈऑटा/ *noun* [C] the main **artery** that carries blood from the heart to the rest of the body हृदय से शरीर के अन्य भागों को रक्त पहुँचाने वाली धमनी; महाधमनी ➪ **heart** पर चित्र देखिए।

**apart** /əˈpɑːt अˈपाट्/ *adv.* **1** away from sb/sth or each other; not together दूर, अलग *The doors slowly slid apart.* ○ *Stand with your feet apart.* **2** into pieces टुकड़ों में, टुकड़े-टुकड़े *The material was so old that it just* ***fell/came apart*** *in my hands.*

IDM **take sth apart** to separate sth into pieces टुकड़े बनाकर *He took the whole bicycle apart.*
**tell A and B apart** to see the difference between A and B, A और B में अंतर बताना *It's very difficult to tell the twins apart.*

**apart from** (*AmE* **aside from**) *prep.* **1** except for को छोड़कर *I've answered all the questions apart from the last one.* ○ *There's nobody here apart from me.* **2** as well as; in addition to के अतिरिक्त; साथ ही *Apart from music, she also loves sport and reading.*

**apartheid** /əˈpɑːthaɪt अˈपाथाइट्/ *noun* [U] the former official government policy in South Africa of separating people of different races and making them live apart दक्षिण अफ़्रीका की पुरानी सरकारी नीति जिसके आधार पर श्वेत और काले-रंग वाले व्यक्तियों को अलग-अलग रखा जाता था; रंगभेद की नीति

**apartment** /əˈpɑːtmənt अˈपाट्मन्ट्/ *noun* [C] **1** (*AmE*) = **flat² 1** **2** a set of rooms rented for a holiday अवकाश मनाने के लिए किराए पर उपलब्ध कमरे *a self-catering apartment*

**apartment block** *noun* [C] a large building containing several apartments अनेक अपार्टमेंट वाला बड़ा भवन

**apathetic** /ˌæpəˈθetɪk ˌऐपˈथ़ेटिक्/ *adj.* lacking interest or desire to act उदासीन, अनिच्छुक

**apathy** /ˈæpəθi ˈऐपथि/ *noun* [U] the feeling of not being interested in or enthusiastic about anything उदासीनता, अनिच्छा

**ape¹** /eɪp एप्/ *noun* [C] a type of animal like a large monkey with no tail or only a very short tail एक प्रकार का बड़ा व पूँछहीन बंदर *Chimpanzees and gorillas are apes.*

**ape²** /eɪp एप्/ *verb* [T] to copy sb/else, especially in order to make fun of them किसी व्यक्ति की नक़ल उतारना, विशेषतः मज़ाक उड़ाने के लिए *The children were aping the teacher's way of walking.*

**aperitif** /əˌperəˈtiːf अˌपेरˈटीफ़्/ *noun* [C] an alcoholic drink that you have before a meal भोजन से पहले पिया जाने वाला एक प्रकार का मादक पेय

**aperture** /ˈæpətʃə(r) ˈऐपच(र्)/ *noun* [C] **1** (*formal*) a small opening in sth किसी वस्तु में छोटा छिद्र

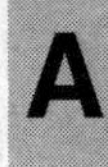



2 (*technical*) a small opening that allows light to reach a **lens** कैमरे के लैंस में प्रकाश जाने के लिए छोटा छिद्र ➪ **camera** पर चित्र देखिए।

**apex** /ˈeɪpeks ˈएपेक्स्/ *noun* [C, *usually sing.*] (*pl.* **apexes**) the top or highest part of sth शिखर या उच्चतम बिंदु *the apex of a roof/triangle*

**aphid** /ˈeɪfɪd ˈएफ़िड्/ *noun* [C] a very small insect that is harmful to plants. There are several different types of aphids पौधों के लिए हानिकर एक छोटा कीड़ा; माहूँ

**aphorism** /ˈæfərɪzəm ˈऐफ़रिज़म्/ *noun* [C] (*formal*) a short phrase that expresses in a clever way sth that is true सूक्ति

**apiary** /ˈeɪpiəri ˈएपिअरि/ *noun* (*pl.* **apiaries**) a place where bees are kept मधुवाटिका

**apiece** /əˈpi:s अˈपीस्/ *adv.* each प्रत्येक को/के लिए/के द्वारा *Zahir and Maninder scored a goal apiece.*

**apocalypse** /əˈpɒkəlɪps अˈपॉकलिप्स्/ *noun* 1 [*sing.*, U] the total destruction of the world संसार का पूर्ण विनाश 2 **the Apocalypse** [*sing.*] the end of the world, as described in the Bible बाइबिल में प्रतिपादित सृष्टि का अंत; प्रलय 3 [*sing.*] a situation causing very serious damage and destruction अति विनाशकारी स्थिति ▶ **apocalyptic** /əˌpɒkəˈlɪptɪk अˌपॉकˈलिप्टिक्/ *adj.* विनाशकारी

**apolitical** /ˌeɪpəˈlɪtɪkl ˌएपˈलिटिक्ल्/ *adj.* 1 (used about a person) किसी व्यक्ति के लिए प्रयुक्त not interested in politics; not thinking politics are important राजनीति से उदासीन; अराजनीतिक, राजनीति-विमुख 2 not connected with a political party किसी राजनीतिक दल से असंबद्ध; अराजनीतिक *an apolitical organization* 3 of no political significance, relevance or importance राजनीतिक सार्थकता, संगति या महत्ता विहीन

**apologetic** /əˌpɒləˈdʒetɪk अˌपॉलˈजेटिक्/ *adj.* feeling or showing that you are sorry for sth you have done खेदपूर्ण; क्षमा माँगते हुए *He was most apologetic about his son's bad behaviour.* ○ *I wrote him an apologetic letter.* ▶ **apologetically** /-li -लि/ *adv.* क्षमा माँगते हुए

**apologize** (*also* **-ise**) /əˈpɒlədʒaɪz अˈपॉलजाइज़्/ *verb* [I] **apologize (to sb) (for sth)** to say that you are sorry for sth that you have done (किसी से) (किसी बात के लिए) क्षमा याचना करना *You'll have to apologize to your teacher for being late.*

**apology** /əˈpɒlədʒi अˈपॉलजि/ *noun* [C, U] (*pl.* **apologies**) **(an) apology (to sb) (for sth)** a spoken or written statement that you are sorry for sth you have done, etc. क्षमापत्र, माफ़ीनामा *Please accept our apologies for the delay.* ○ *a letter of apology*

**apostle** /əˈpɒsl अˈपॉस्ल्/ *noun* [C] one of the twelve men chosen by Christ to spread his teaching ईसा मसीह द्वारा धर्मप्रचार के लिए नियुक्त बारह शिष्यों में से एक

**apostrophe** /əˈpɒstrəfi अˈपॉस्ट्रफ़ि/ *noun* [C] 1 the sign (') used for showing that you have left a letter or letters out of a word as in 'I'm', 'can't' or 'we'll' वर्णलोप का चिह्न 2 the sign (') used for showing who or what sth belongs to as in 'John's chair', 'the boys' room' or 'Russia's President' संबंधकारक का चिह्न

**appal** (*AmE* **appall**) /əˈpɔ:l अˈपॉल्/ *verb* [T] (**appalling; appalled**) (*usually passive*) to shock sb very much किसी को भयभीत या स्तब्ध कर देना; मानसिक आघात पहुँचाना ▶ **appalling** /əˈpɔ:lɪŋ अˈपॉलिङ्/ *adj.* भय और विस्मय उत्पन्न करने वाला ▶ **appallingly** *adv.* भय उत्पन्न करते हुए

**appalled** /əˈpɔ:ld अˈपॉल्ड्/ *adj.* **appalled (at sth)** feeling disgust at sth unpleasant or wrong जुगुप्सा अनुभव करना, बहुत बुरा लगना; स्तब्ध

**apparatus** /ˌæpəˈreɪtəs ˌऐपˈरेटस्/ *noun* [U] the set of tools, instruments or equipment used for doing a job or an activity किसी कार्य में प्रयुक्त उपकरणों आदि का सेट ➪ **laboratory** पर चित्र देखिए।

**apparent** /əˈpærənt अˈपैरन्ट्/ *adj.* 1 (*only before a noun*) that seems to be real or true but may not be वास्तविक जैसा, आभासी 2 **apparent (to sb)** clear; easy to see स्पष्ट; प्रकट, प्रत्यक्ष *It quickly became apparent to us that our teacher could not speak French.* ▶ **apparently** /əˈpærəntli अˈपैरन्ट्लि/ *adv.* according to what people say or to how sth appears, but perhaps not true ऊपरी तौर से; दृश्यमान रूप से *Apparently, he's already been married twice.* ○ *He was apparently undisturbed by the news.*

**apparition** /ˌæpəˈrɪʃn ˌऐपˈरिश्न्/ *noun* [C] a ghost or an image of a person who is dead भूत-प्रेत, मृत व्यक्ति की छाया

**appeal**[1] /əˈpi:l अˈपील्/ *verb* [I] 1 **appeal to sb (for sth); appeal for sth** to make a serious request for sth you need or want very much औपचारिक रूप से अनुरोध करना; निवेदन या याचना करना *Relief workers in the disaster area are appealing for more supplies.* ○ *She appealed to the kidnappers to let her son go.* 2 **appeal (to sb)** to be attractive or interesting to sb किसी के प्रति आकर्षित होना; (विचार आदि) पसंद आना, को अच्छा

लगना *The idea of living in the country doesn't appeal to me at all.* **3 appeal to sth** to influence sb's feelings or thoughts so that he/she will do sth you want अपने पक्ष में प्रभावित करना *We aim to appeal to people's generosity.* **4 appeal (against/for sth)** to ask sb in authority to make or change a decision निर्णय लेने या बदलने के लिए अनुरोध करना; याचना करना *He decided to appeal against his conviction.*

**appeal**[2] /əˈpiːl अˈपील्/ *noun* **1** [C] a serious request for sth you need or want very much प्रबल अनुरोध, गंभीर निवेदन *The police have made an urgent appeal for witnesses to come forward.* **2** [C] **an appeal to sth** a suggestion that tries to influence sb's feelings or thoughts so that he/she will do what you want अनुरोध, निवेदन **3** [C] a formal request to sb in authority to change a decision निर्णय पर पुनर्विचार के लिए अनुरोध; पुनरावेदन, प्रार्थना **4** [U] the attraction or interesting quality of sth/sb आकर्षण; मोहक गुण

**appealing** /əˈpiːlɪŋ अˈपीलिङ्/ *adj.* **1** attractive or interesting आकर्षण, रुचिकर *The idea of a lying on a beach sounds very appealing!* **2** showing that you need help, etc. संवेदना जगाने वाला; हृदयस्पर्शी *an appealing look* ▸ **appealingly** *adv.* संवेदनापूर्ण तरीक़े से

**appear** /əˈpɪə(r) अˈपिअ(र्)/ *verb* **1** *linking verb* **appear to be/do sth; appear (that)...** to seem प्रतीत होना, लगना *She appears to be very happy in her job.* ○ *It appears that you were given the wrong information.* ➪ **apparent** adjective देखिए। **2** [I] to suddenly be seen; to come into sight एकाएक दिखाई पड़ना; प्रकट होना *The bus appeared from round the corner.* ✪ विलोम **disappear** **3** [I] to begin to exist अस्तित्व में आना *The disease is thought to have appeared in Africa.* **4** [I] to be published or printed प्रकाशित होना *The article appeared in this morning's paper.* **5** [I] to perform or speak where you are seen by a lot of people (मंच आदि पर) उपस्थित होना, सामने आना *to appear on television/in a play*

**appearance** /əˈpɪərəns अˈपिअरन्स्/ *noun* **1** [U] the way that sb/sth looks or seems व्यक्ति या वस्तु का बाहरी रूप; रूप-रंग *A different hairstyle can completely change your appearance.* ○ *He gives the appearance of being extremely confident.* **2** [*sing.*] the coming of sb/sth आगमन *the appearance of television in the home in the 1950s* **3** [C] an act of appearing in public, especially on stage, television, etc. सार्वजनिक रूप से पेश होने की क्रिया; उपस्थिति, प्रकटन, प्रकाशन

**appease** /əˈpiːz अˈपीज़्/ *verb* [T] (*formal*) **1** to make sb calmer or less angry by agreeing to what he/she wants शांत करना या अभीष्ट वस्तु देकर संतुष्ट करना **2** to give a country what it wants in order to avoid war युद्ध से बचने के लिए किसी देश को उसकी अभीष्ट वस्तु देकर तुष्ट करना ▸ **appeasement** *noun* [U] तुष्टीकरण

**appendage** /əˈpendɪdʒ अˈपेन्डिज्/ *noun* [C] (*formal*) a smaller or less important part of sth larger बड़ी वस्तु का छोटा या कम महत्त्वपूर्ण अंग; उपांग, संलग्नक

**appendicitis** /əˌpendəˈsaɪtɪs अˌपेन्डˈसाइटिस्/ *noun* [U] an illness in which your appendix becomes extremely painful and usually has to be removed बीमारी जिसमें उदर के पास स्थित एक अंग में दर्द उत्पन्न होता है और इस अंग को निकालना पड़ता है

**appendix** /əˈpendɪks अˈपेन्डिक्स्/ *noun* [C] **1** (*pl.* **appendixes**) a small organ inside your body near your stomach. In humans, the appendix has no real function उदर के निकट एक छोटा अंग, उंडुक पुच्छ। मानव शरीर में इसका कोई वास्तविक उपयोग नहीं होता ➪ **body** पर चित्र देखिए। **2** (*pl.* **appendices** /-dɪsiːz -डिसीज़्/) a section at the end of a book, etc. that gives extra information पुस्तक आदि के अंत में अतिरिक्त जानकारी देने वाला परिशिष्ट

**appertain** /ˌæpəˈteɪn ˌऐप्ˈटेन्/ *verb*

**PHR V** **appertain to sb/sth** (*formal*) to belong or refer to sb/sth (से) संबंध रखना, (का) होना *These figures appertain to last year's sales.*

**appetite** /ˈæpɪtaɪt ˈऐपिटाइट्/ *noun* [C, U] a strong desire for sth, especially food भूख, क्षुधा, बुभुक्षा *Some fresh air and exercise should give you an appetite* ○ *He has a great **appetite for** work/life.* ○ *loss of appetite*

**IDM** **whet sb's appetite** ➪ **whet** देखिए।

**appetizer** (*also* **-iser**) /ˈæpɪtaɪzə(r) ˈऐपिटाइज़(र्)/ (*AmE*) = **starter**

**appetizing** (*also* **-ising**) /ˈæpɪtaɪzɪŋ ˈऐपिटाइज़िङ्/ *adj.* (used about food, etc.) that looks or smells attractive; making you feel hungry (खाद्य पदार्थ) क्षुधावर्धक

**applaud** /əˈplɔːd अˈप्लॉड्/ *verb* **1** [I, T] to hit your hands together noisily (**clap**) in order to show that you like sb/sth तालियाँ बजाकर अनुमोदन प्रकट करना *The audience applauded loudly.* **2** [T] (*usually passive*) to express approval of sth (का) अनुमोदन करना या स्वीकृति व्यक्त करना *The decision was applauded by everybody.*

**applause** /əˈplɔːz अˈप्लॉज़्/ *noun* [U] the noise made by a group of people hitting their hands together (**clapping**) to show their approval and enjoyment करतल-ध्वनि द्वारा शाबाशी, साधुवाद तालियाँ *Let's all give a big **round of applause** to the cook!*

**apple** /ˈæpl ˈऐपल्/ *noun* [C, U] a hard, round fruit with a smooth green, red or yellow skin सेब *apple juice* ➪ **fruit** पर चित्र देखिए।

**applet** /ˈæplət ˈऐप्लट्/ *noun* [C] (*computing*) a simple program that can make one thing or a few simple things happen, for example on a page on the Internet कंप्यूटर का एक सरल प्रोग्राम

**appliance** /əˈplaɪəns अˈप्लाइअन्स्/ *noun* [C] a piece of equipment for a particular purpose in the house (घरेलू उपयोग का) उपकरण *washing machines and other domestic appliances*

**applicable** /ˈæplɪkəbl; əˈplɪkəbl ˈऐप्लिकब्ल्; अˈप्लिकब्ल्/ *adj.* (*not before a noun*) **applicable (to sb/sth)** that concerns sb/sth; relevant to sb/sth संबंधित; उपयुक्त *This part of the form is only applicable to married women.*

**applicant** /ˈæplɪkənt ˈऐप्लिकन्ट्/ *noun* [C] a person who makes a formal request for sth (**applies for sth**), especially for a job, a place at a college, university, etc. आवेदक, अभ्यार्थी, उम्मीदवार *There were over 200 applicants for the job.*

**application** /ˌæplɪˈkeɪʃn ˌऐप्लिˈकेश्न्/ *noun* **1** [C, U] (**an**) **application (to sb) (for sth)** a formal written request, especially for a job or a place in a school, club, etc. किसी संस्था में प्रवेश या नौकरी के लिए आवेदन, औपचारिक अनुरोध *Applications for the job should be made to the Personnel Manager.* ○ *To become a member, fill in the **application form**.* **2** [C, U] the practical use (of sth) किसी वस्तु का व्यावहारिक उपयोग **3** [U] hard work; effort परिश्रम; प्रयत्न, मेहनत **4** [C] a program that is designed to do a particular job कंपयूटर में एक विशिष्ट कार्य हेतु निष्पादित प्रोग्राम *a database application*

**applied** /əˈplaɪd अˈप्लाइड्/ *adj.* (used about a subject) studied in a way that has a practical use प्रायोगिक, व्यावहारिक, अनुप्रयुक्त *You have to study applied mathematics as part of the engineering course.* ✪ विलोम **pure**

**apply** /əˈplaɪ अˈप्लाइ/ *verb* (*pres. part.* **applying;** *3rd person sing. pres.* **applies;** *pt, pp* **applied**) **1** [I] **apply (to sb) (for sth)** to ask for sth in writing लिखित माँग करना, आवेदन करना *I've applied to that company for a job.* ○ *She's applying for a place at university.* **2** [I] **apply (to sb/sth)** to concern or involve sb/sth (से) संबंधित होना, (पर) लागू करना *This information applies to all children born after 1997.* **3** [T] **apply sth (to sth)** to make practical use of sth किसी वस्तु का व्यावहारिक उपयोग करना; लागू करना *new technology which can be applied to solving problems in industry* **4** [T] to use a word, a name, etc. to describe sb/sth (*usually passive*) किसी शब्द, नाम आदि को वर्णन के लिए प्रयुक्त करना *I don't think the term 'music' can be applied to that awful noise.* **5** [T] **apply sth (to sth)** to put or spread sth onto sth किसी वस्तु का लेप लगाना *Apply the cream to the infected area twice a day.* **6** [T] **apply yourself/sth (to sth/doing sth)** to make yourself give all your attention to sth किसी पर पूरा ध्यान केंद्रित करना *to apply your mind to sth*

**appoint** /əˈpɔɪnt अˈपॉइन्ट्/ *verb* [T] **1 appoint sb (to sth)** to choose sb for a job or position किसी नौकरी या पद पर नियुक्त करना *The committee have appointed a new chairperson.* **2** (*formal*) **appoint sth (for sth)** to arrange or decide on sth निश्चित या नियत करना

**appointment** /əˈpɔɪntmənt अˈपॉइन्ट्मेन्ट्/ *noun* **1** [C, U] **an appointment (with sb)** an arrangement to see sb at a particular time पूर्वनियोजित भेंट *I have an appointment with Dr Dua at 3 o'clock.* ○ *I'd like to **make an appointment** to see the manager.* **2** [C] a job or a position of responsibility नियुक्ति, पद, नौकरी *a temporary/permanent appointment* **3** [C, U] **appointment (to sth)** the act of choosing sb for a job नियुक्तिकरण

**apportion** /əˈpɔːʃn अˈपॉश्न्/ *verb* [T] (*written*) **apportion sth (among/between/to sb)** to divide sth among people; to give a share of sth to sb हिस्सों में बाँट देना; वितरण करना *The land was apportioned between members of the family.* ○ *The programme gives the facts but does not **apportion blame**.*

**appraisal** /əˈpreɪzl अˈप्रेज़ल्/ *noun* [C, U] (*formal*) a judgement about the value or quality of sb/sth मूल्यांकन, मूल्यनिरूपण

**appraise** /əˈpreɪz अˈप्रेज़्/ *verb* [T] (*formal*) to judge the value or quality of sb/sth किसी वस्तु आदि का मूल्यांकन करना

**appreciable** /əˈpriːʃəbl अˈप्रीशब्ल्/ *adj.* large enough to be noticed or thought important इतना बड़ा कि सहज में ही दिखाई पड़े या महत्त्वपूर्ण लगे; पर्याप्त, अच्छा-ख़ासा, काफ़ी

**appreciate** /əˈpriːʃieɪt अˈप्रीशिएट्/ *verb* **1** [T] to enjoy sth or to understand the value of sb/sth किसी व्यक्ति या वस्तु के गुण पहचानना और उन्हें महत्त्व देना; रसास्वादन करना *My boss doesn't appreciate me.* ○ *I don't appreciate good coffee—it all tastes the same to me.* **2** [T] to understand a problem, situation, etc. समस्या, स्थिति आदि के महत्त्व या गंभीरता को समझना *I appreciate your problem but I'm afraid I can't help you.* **3** to be grateful for sth किसी बात के लिए आभारी होना *Thanks very much. I really appreciate your help.* **4** [I] to increase in value (ज़मीन, जायदाद आदि का) मूल्य बढ़ना या बढ़ाना

**appreciation** /əˌpriːʃiˈeɪʃn अˌप्रीशिˈएश्न्/ *noun* **1** [U] understanding and enjoyment of the value of sth गुण-ग्रहण; समालोचना, गुण-दोष विवेचन *I'm afraid I have little appreciation of modern architecture.* **2** [U] the feeling of being grateful for sth आभार, कृतज्ञता *We bought him a present to show our appreciation for all the work he had done.* **3** [U, *sing.*] understanding of a situation, problem, etc. किसी समस्या, स्थिति आदि का बोध, परिबोध, समझ **4** [U, *sing.*] an increase in value मूल्यवृद्धि

**appreciative** /əˈpriːʃətɪv अˈप्रीशटिव्/ *adj.* **1** feeling or showing pleasure or admiration प्रशंसात्मक, प्रशंसापूर्ण *an appreciative audience* **2 appreciative (of sth)** grateful for sth (किसी बात के लिए) आभारी *He was very appreciative of our efforts to help.*

**apprehend** /ˌæprɪˈhend ˌऐप्रिˈहेन्ड्/ *verb* [T] (*formal*) (used about the police) to catch sb and arrest him/her (पुलिस के संदर्भ में प्रयुक्त) पकड़कर गिरफ़्तार करना

**apprehensive** /ˌæprɪˈhensɪv ˌऐप्रिˈहेन्सिव्/ *adj.* worried or afraid that sth unpleasant may happen (भविष्य की किसी अप्रिय घटना के लिए) चिंतित, आशंकित, सशंक *I'm feeling apprehensive about tomorrow's exam.* ▶ **apprehension** /-ʃn -श्न्/ *noun* [C, U] संशय, भय, चिंता

**apprentice** /əˈprentɪs अˈप्रेन्टिस्/ *noun* [C] a person who works for low pay, in order to learn the skills needed in a particular job हुनर-विशेष सीखने के लिए कम वेतन पर काम करने को तैयार व्यक्ति; प्रशिक्षु, प्रशिक्षार्थी *an apprentice electrician/chef/plumber*

**apprenticeship** /əˈprentɪʃɪp अˈप्रेन्टिशिप्/ *noun* [C, U] the state or time of being an apprentice प्रशिक्षुता, प्रशिक्षार्थिता, प्रशिक्षु-अवस्था

**approach¹** /əˈprəʊtʃ अˈप्रोच्/ *verb* **1** [I, T] to come near or nearer to sb/sth पास आना या पहुँचना *The day of the exam approached.* **2** [T] to begin to deal with a problem, a situation, etc. किसी समस्या या स्थिति से निपटना, शुरू करना *What is the best way to approach this problem?* **3** [T] to speak to sb usually in order to ask for sth किसी व्यक्ति के पास अनुरोध या प्रस्ताव के साथ जाना; माँग पेश करना *I'm going to approach them about a loan.*

**approach²** /əˈprəʊtʃ अˈप्रोच्/ *noun* **1** [C] a way of dealing with sb/sth कुछ करने का तरीक़ा; दृष्टिकोण *Parents don't always know what approach to take with teenage children.* **2** [*sing.*] the act of coming nearer (to sb/sth) (किसी के) अधिक निकट आने की क्रिया *the approach of winter* **3** [C] a request for sth अनुरोध *The company has **made an approach to** us for financial assistance.* **4** [C] a road or path leading to sth व्यक्ति या वस्तु तक पहुँचने का मार्ग *the approach to the village*

**approachable** /əˈprəʊtʃəbl अˈप्रोचबल्/ *adj.* **1** friendly and easy to talk to मिलनसार **2** (*not before a noun*) that can be reached सुगम्य, अभिगम्य ✪ पर्याय **accessible**

**appropriate¹** /əˈprəʊpriət अˈप्रोप्रिअट्/ *adj.* **appropriate (for/to sth)** suitable or right for a particular situation, person, use, etc. किसी परिस्थिति, व्यक्ति या उपयोग आदि के लिए उपयुक्त या उचित *The matter will be dealt with by the appropriate authorities.* ○ *I don't think this film is appropriate for children.* ✪ विलोम **inappropriate** ▶ **appropriately** *adv.* उपयुक्त रीति से

**appropriate²** /əˈprəʊprieɪt अˈप्रोप्रिएट्/ *verb* [T] (*formal*) to take sth to use for yourself, usually without permission किसी वस्तु को बिना अनुमति अपने उपयोग के लिए ले जाना *He appropriated the money from the company's pension fund.* ▶ **appropriation** /əˌprəʊpriˈeɪʃn अˌप्रोप्रिˈएश्न्/ *noun* [U, *sing.*] विनियोग; अनुचित उपयोग

**approval** /əˈpruːvl अˈप्रूव्ल्/ *noun* [U] feeling, showing or saying that you think sth is good; agreement अनुमोदन, स्वीकृति *Everybody **gave** their **approval to** the proposal.*

**approve** /əˈpruːv अˈप्रूव्/ *verb* **1** [I] **approve (of sb/sth)** to be pleased about sth; to like sb/sth किसी को पसंद करना या उससे संतुष्ट होना; स्वीकार्य समझना *His father didn't approve of him becoming a dancer.* ✪ विलोम **disapprove** **2** [T] to agree formally to sth or to say that sth is correct औपचारिक रूप से सहमत होना या समर्थन करना *We need to get an accountant to approve these figures.*

**approving** /əˈpruːvɪŋ अˈप्रूविङ्/ *adj.* showing support or admiration for sth सहमति और प्रशंसा सूचक *'Good,' he said with an approving smile.* ▶ **approvingly** *adv.* सहमतिपूर्वक

**approx.** *abbr.* (*written*) approximate; approximately लगभग, क़रीब-क़रीब

**approximate** /əˈprɒksɪmət अˈप्रॉक्सिमट्/ *adj.* almost correct but not completely accurate लगभग सही *The approximate time of arrival is 3 o'clock.* ○ *I can only give you an approximate idea of the cost.*

**approximately** /əˈprɒksɪmətli अˈप्रॉक्सिमट्लि/ *adv.* about; roughly लगभग; क़रीब-क़रीब *It's approximately fifty kilometres from here.*

**approximation** /əˌprɒksɪˈmeɪʃn अˌप्रॉक्सिˈमेश्न्/ *noun* [C] a number, answer, etc. which is nearly, but not exactly, right लगभग सही गणना, उत्तर आदि

**Apr.** *abbr.* April अप्रैल *2 Apr. 2006*

**apricot** /ˈeɪprɪkɒt ˈएप्रिकॉट्/ *noun* [C] a small, round, yellow or orange fruit with a large seed (**stone**) inside ख़ूबानी

**April** /ˈeɪprəl ˈएप्रल्/ *noun* [U, C] (*abbr.* **Apr.**) the fourth month of the year, coming after March वर्ष का चौथा महीना, मार्च के बाद का महीना; अप्रैल

> **NOTE** वाक्यों में महीनों का प्रयोग कैसे करें यह जानने के लिए **January** पर नोट तथा उदाहरण देखिए।

**April Fool's Day** *noun* [*sing.*] 1 April पहली अप्रैल

> **NOTE** परंपरा-अनुसार, पहली अप्रैल को लोग हँसी-मज़ाक में प्रायः एक-दूसरे को झूठमूठ की कहानियाँ सुनाते हैं। जो इन कहानियों को सच मान ले, उसे **April Fool** कहा जाता है।

**apron** /ˈeɪprən ˈएप्रन्/ *noun* [C] a piece of clothing that you wear over the front of your usual clothes in order to keep them clean, especially when cooking (विशेषतः भोजन पकाते समय कपड़ों के ऊपर पहना जाने वाला एक ढीला वस्त्र ताकि अंदर के कपड़े ख़राब न हों; ऐप्रन

**apropos** /ˌæprəˈpəʊ ˈएप्रˈपो/ (*also* **apropos**) *prep.* on the subject of sth/sb किसी विषय पर *Apropos (of) what you were just saying he's the best man for job.*

**apt** /æpt ˈऐप्ट्/ *adj.* **1** suitable in a particular situation किसी स्थिति में उपयुक्त या संगत *I thought 'complex' was an apt description of the book.* **2 apt to do sth** often likely to do sth (किसी काम में) प्रवृत्त

**aptitude** /ˈæptɪtjuːd ˈऐप्टिट्यूड्/ *noun* [U,C] **aptitude (for sth/for doing sth)** natural ability or skill सहज अभिरुचि; रुझान, अभिक्षमता *She has an aptitude for learning languages.* ○ *an* ***aptitude test***

**aptly** /ˈæptli ˈऐप्टलि/ *adv.* in an appropriate way; suitably उपयुक्त रीति से; समुचित रूप से *The winner of the race was aptly named Suman Speedy.*

**aqualung** /ˈækwəlʌŋ ˈऐक्वलङ्/ *noun* [C] a container of air that a person carries on his or her back when swimming under the surface of the sea, a lake etc. (**diving**) and which provides air through a tube for the person to breathe गोताख़ोरों के पीठ से बंधी वायुभरी टंकी जो पानी की सतह के नीचे साँस लेने के लिए हवा पहुँचाती है

**aquamarine** /ˌækwəməˈriːn ˈऐक्वमˈरीन्/ *noun* **1** [C, U] a pale greenish-blue precious stone हलका हरापन लिए नीला रत्न; हरितनील, बेरूज **2** [U] a pale greenish-blue colour हलका हरापन लिया नीला रंग; हरितनील ▶ **aquamarine** *adj.* हरितनील, समुद्रवर्णी

**aquarium** /əˈkweəriəm अˈक्वेअरिअम्/ *noun* [C] (*pl.* **aquariums** or **aquaria** /-riə -रिआ/) **1** a glass container filled with water, in which fish and water animals are kept पानी से भरी शीशे की टंकी जिसमें मछली आदि जलजीवों को रखा जाता है; मछलीघर, जलजीवशाला **2** a building where people can go to see fish and other water animals जलजीवागार

**Aquarius** /əˈkweəriəs अˈक्वेअरिअस्/ *noun* [U] the eleventh sign of the **zodiac,** the Water Carrier कुंभ राशि

**aquatic** /əˈkwætɪk अˈक्वैटिक्/ *adj.* living or taking place in, on or near water जल में या जल के निकट रहने या होने वाला *aquatic plants* ○ *windsurfing and other aquatic sports*

**aqueduct** /ˈækwɪdʌkt ˈऐक्विडक्ट्/ *noun* [C] a structure like a bridge for carrying water across a valley or low ground पुल जैसा ढाँचा जिसके द्वारा पानी को घाटी के पार ले जाया जाता है; कृत्रिम जल-प्रणाल; जलसेतु

**aqueous** /ˈeɪkwiəs ˈएक्विअस्/ *adj.* (*technical*) containing water; like water जलयुक्त, जलीय; जल-सदृश

**aquifer** /ˈækwɪfə(r) ˈऐक्विफ़(र्)/ *noun* [C] (in geology) a layer of rock or soil that can take in and hold water (भूविज्ञान) चट्टान या मिट्टी की परत जिसमें पानी रुक सकता है

**Arab** /ˈærəb ˈऐरब्/ *noun* [C] a member of a people who lived originally in Arabia and who now live in many parts of the Middle East and North Africa अरब देश का वासी, अरब जाति का सदस्य ▶ **Arab** *adj.* अरब संबंधी *Arab countries*

**Arabic** /ˈærəbɪk ˈऐरबिक्/ *noun* [*sing.*] the language of Arab people अरबी भाषा

**arable** /ˈærəbl ˈऐरब्ल्/ *adj.* (in farming) connected with growing crops for sale, not keeping animals बिक्री के लिए खेती करने संबंधी *arable land/farmers*

**arachnid** /əˈræknɪd अˈरैक्निड्/ *noun* [C] any of the **class** of small creatures with eight legs that includes spiders मकड़ीवंशी

**arbitrage** /ˈɑːbɪtrɑːʒ; -trɪdʒ ˈआबिट्राश्; -ट्रिज्/ *noun* [U] (in business) the practice of buying sth, for example foreign money, in one place and selling it in another place where the price is higher (व्यापार में) विदेशी मुद्रा का लाभोन्मुख व्यापार; अंतरपणन

**arbitrageur** /ˌɑːbɪtrɑːˈʒɜː(r) ˈआबिट्राˈश़(र्)/ (*also* **arbitrager**) /ˈɑːbɪtrɪdʒə(r) ˈआर्बिट्रिज(र्)/ *noun* [C] a person whose job is to buy sth, for example foreign money, in one place and sell it in another place where the price is higher विदेशी मुद्रा का व्यापारी

**arbitrary** /ˈɑːbɪtrəri ˈआबिट्ररि/ *adj.* not seeming to be based on any reason or plan and sometimes seeming unfair बिना तर्क, नियम या योजना पर आधारित और कभी-कभी अनुचित; मनमाना, स्वेच्छाचारी ► **arbitrarily** *adv.* मनमाने ढंग से

**arbitrate** /ˈɑːbɪtreɪt ˈआबिट्रेट्/ *verb* [I, T] to settle an argument between two people or groups by finding a solution that both can accept किसी झगड़े में मध्यस्थता करना ► **arbitration** /ˌɑːbɪˈtreɪʃn ˈआबिˈट्रेश्न्/ *noun* [U] मध्यस्थता *The union and the management decided to* ***go to arbitration****.*

**arbitrator** /ˈɑːbɪtreɪtə(r) ˈआबिट्रेट(र्)/ *noun* [C] a person who is chosen to settle an argument between two people or two groups of people मध्यस्थ (व्यक्ति)

**arc** /ɑːk आक्/ *noun* [C] a curved line, part of a circle चाप, वृत्त का एक अंश, वृत्तांश ➪ **circle** पर चित्र देखिए।

**arcade** /ɑːˈkeɪd आˈकेड्/ *noun* [C] **1** a large covered passage or area with shops along one or both sides कोई बड़ा आच्छादित पथ या क्षेत्र जिसके एक या दोनों ओर दुकानें हों *a shopping arcade* **2** (*also* **amusement arcade**) a large room with machines and games that you put coins into to play एक बड़े कक्ष में मनोरंजन हेतु लगी मशीनें जिसमें सिक्का डालकर खेल खेले जाते हैं

**arcane** /ɑːˈkeɪn आˈकेन्/ *adj.* (*formal*) known to very few people and therefore difficult to understand बहुत कम लोगों को ज्ञात अतएव दुर्बोध *the arcane rules of cricket*

**arch¹** /ɑːtʃ आच्/ *noun* [C] **1** a curved structure that supports the weight of sth above it, such as a bridge or the upper part of a building चाप ➪ **archway** देखिए। **2** a structure with a curved top that is supported by straight sides, sometimes forming an entrance or built as a **monument** मेहराब, तोरण **3** the curved part of the bottom of your foot पैर के तलवे की चाप

**arch²** /ɑːtʃ आच्/ *verb* [I, T] to make a curve चाप बनाना

**arch-** /ɑːtʃ आच्/ *prefix* (*in nouns*) main, most important or most extreme सबसे महत्त्वपूर्ण, प्रधानतम, मुख्यतम *archbishop* ○ *arch-rival*

**archaeological** (*AmE* **archeological**) /ˌɑːkiəˈlɒdʒɪkl ˌआकिअˈलॉजिक्ल्/ *adj.* connected with archaeology पुरातत्त्वीय; पुरातत्व विज्ञान से संबंधित

**archaeologist** (*AmE* **archeologist**) /ˌɑːkiˈɒlədʒɪst ˌआकिˈऑलजिस्ट्/ *noun* [C] an expert in archaeology पुरातत्त्व विज्ञान मे विशेषज्ञ; पुरातत्त्वज्ञ

**archaeology** (*AmE* **archeology**) /ˌɑːkiˈɒlədʒi ˌआकिˈऑलजि/ *noun* [U] the study of the past, based on objects or parts of buildings that are found in the ground पुरातत्त्व विज्ञान

**archaic** /ɑːˈkeɪɪk आˈकेइक्/ *adj.* very old-fashioned; no longer used पुरातनपंथी; वर्तमान में अप्रचलित

**archbishop** /ˌɑːtʃˈbɪʃəp ˌआच्ˈबिशप्/ *noun* [C] a priest with a very high position, in some branches of the Christian Church, who is responsible for all the churches in a large area of a country (ईसाई धर्म में) महाधर्माध्यक्ष, आर्चबिशप *the Archbishop of Canterbury* (= the head of the Church of England) ➪ **bishop** देखिए।

**archer** /ˈɑːtʃə(r) ˈआच(र्)/ *noun* [C] a person who shoots **arrows** through the air by pulling back a tight string on a curved piece of wood **a bow** and letting go. In past times this was done in order to kill people, but it is now done as a sport धनुर्धर, तीरंदाज़; पुराने समय में युद्ध और शिकार में तीरंदाजी का प्रयोग किया जाता था, परंतु वर्तमान में यह क्रीड़ा के रूप में खेला जाता है

**archery** /ˈɑːtʃəri ˈआचरि/ *noun* [U] the sport of shooting arrows धनुर्विद्या, तीरंदाज़ी

**archetypal** /ˌɑːkiˈtaɪpl ˌआकिˈटाइप्ल्/ *adj.* (*written*) having all the qualities that make sb/sth a typical example of a particular kind of person or thing प्रतिनिधिक, प्रतिरूपी *He lived an archetypal rock star's lifestyle.*

**archetype** /ˈɑːkitaɪp ˈआकिटाइप्/ *noun* [C] (*written*) the most typical example of a particular kind of person or thing आदर्श, प्रतिनिधि, प्रतिरूप

**archipelago** /ˌɑːkɪˈpeləgəʊ ˌआकिˈपेलगो/ *noun* [C] (*pl.* **archipelagos** or **archipelagoes**) (in geography) a group of islands and the sea around them (भूगोल में) द्वीपसमूह

**architect** /ˌɑːkɪtekt ˌआकिटेक्ट्/ *noun* [C] a person whose job is to design buildings भवन-निर्माण की योजना बनाने वाला व्यक्ति; वास्तुशिल्पी, स्थापत्यविद

**architectural** /ˌɑːkɪˈtektʃərəl ˌआकि ˈटेक्चरल् / *adj.* connected with the design of buildings वास्तुसंबंधी

**architecture** /ˈɑːkɪtektʃə(r) ˈआकिट्टेक्च(र्) / *noun* **1** [U] the study of designing and making buildings भवन निर्माण का अध्ययन या विज्ञान; वास्तुकला, स्थापत्यकला **2** the style or design of a building or buildings वास्तुशैली, स्थापत्यशैली *modern architecture*

**archives** /ˈɑːkaɪvz ˈआकाइव्ज़् / *noun* [*pl.*] (*also* **archive**) [C] a collection of historical documents, etc. which show the history of a place or an organization; the place where they are kept ऐतिहासिक आलेखों का संग्रह; इस संग्रह को रखने का स्थान, पुरालेखागार *archive material on the First World War*

**archway** /ˈɑːtʃweɪ ˈआच्वे / *noun* [C] a passage or entrance with an arch over it तोरणपथ, तोरणद्वार, मेहराबदार पथ या द्वार

**Arctic** /ˈɑːktɪk ˈआक्टिक् / *adj.* **1** connected with the region around the **North Pole** उत्तरी धुव्रक्षेत्र का, उत्तरध्रवीय ➪ **Antarctic** देखिए। **2 arctic** extremely cold बहुत ठंडा

**the Arctic** /ˈɑːktɪk ˈआक्टिक् / *noun* [*sing.*] the area around the North Pole उत्तर ध्रुव प्रदेश ➪ **the Antarctic** देखिए।

**the Arctic Circle** *noun* [*sing.*] the line of **latitude** 66° 30'N, 66° 30'N की अक्षांश रेखा ➪ **the Antarctic Circle** देखिए और **earth** पर चित्र देखिए।

**ardent** /ˈɑːdnt ˈआड्न्ट् / *adj.* showing strong feelings, especially a strong liking for sb/sth उत्कट, जोशीला, उत्साही *He was an ardent supporter of Mohun Bagan.* ▶ **ardently** *adv.* उत्साहपूर्वक

**ardour** /ˈɑːdə(r) ˈआड(र्) / *noun* [U] very strong feelings of love; very strong feelings of admiration or excitement प्रबल प्रेम भावना; अत्यंत प्रशंसा तथा उत्तेजना की भावना *romantic ardour* ○ *revolutionary ardour*

**arduous** /ˈɑːdjuəs; -dʒu- ˈआड्युअस; -जुअस् / *adj.* full of difficulties; needing a lot of effort कठिनाइयों-भरा, दुष्कर; श्रमसाध्य *an arduous journey* ○ *arduous work*

**are** ➪ **be** देखिए।

**area** /ˈeəriə ˈएअरिआ / *noun* **1** [C] a part of a town, a country or the world क्षेत्र, इलाक़ा ○ *The wettest areas are in the East of the country.* ○ *Forests cover a large area of the country.* ➪ **district** पर नोट देखिए। **2** [C, U] the size of a surface, that you can calculate by multiplying the length by the width क्षेत्रफल *The area of the office is 35 square metres.* ○ *The office is 35 square metres **in area**.* ➪ **volume** देखिए। **3** [C] a space used for a particular activity किसी विशेष गतिविधि के लिए प्रयुक्त क्षेत्र, स्थान *The restaurant has a non-smoking area.* **4** [C] a particular part of a subject or activity विषय-क्षेत्र, कार्य-क्षेत्र *Training is one area of the business that we could improve.*

**areca** /ˈærɪkə ˈऐरिका / *noun* [C] a kind of palm tree that produces small hard nuts; betel nut ताड़ के वृक्ष की एक प्रकार जिससे काष्ठ फल की उपज होती है; सुपारी

**arena** /əˈriːnə अˈरीना / *noun* [C] **1** an area with seats around it where public entertainments (sporting events, concerts, etc.) are held रंगस्थली, क्रीडांगन **2** an area of activity that concerns the public आम जनता के किसी गतिविधि क्षेत्र-विशेष से संबंधित

**aren't** ➪ **are not** का संक्षिप्त रूप

**arête** /əˈret अˈरेट् / *noun* [C] (in geography) a long sharp piece of high land (**a ridge**) along the top of mountains (भूगोल में) तीक्ष्ण कटक (पर्वत श्रेणी); अरेत ➪ **glacial** पर चित्र देखिए।

**argon** /ˈɑːɡɒn ˈआगॉन् / *noun* [U] (*symbol* **Ar**) a colourless gas that does not react with chemicals and is used in electric lights विद्युत बल्बों में प्रयुक्त एक रंगहीन गैस जिसमें रासायनिक प्रतिक्रिया नहीं होती; आर्गन् **NOTE Argon** एक हानिरहित गैस है।

**argot** /ˈɑːɡəʊ ˈआगो / *noun* [U] informal words and phrases that are used by a particular group of people and that other people do not easily understand वर्ग विशेष द्वारा प्रयुक्त अनौपचारिक बोली जिसे अन्य लोग नहीं समझ पाते

**arguable** /ˈɑːɡjuəbl ˈआग्युअबल् / *adj.* **1** probably true; that you can give reasons for संभावित सत्य; तर्कणीय *It is arguable that all hospital treatment should be free.* **2** probably not true; that you can give reasons against विवादास्पद ▶ **arguably** /-əbli -अब्लि / *adv.* तार्किक रीति से *'King Lear' is arguably Shakespeare's best play.*

**argue** /ˈɑːɡjuː ˈआग्यू / *verb* **1** [I] **argue (with sb) (about/over sth)** to say things, often angrily, that show that you do not agree with sb about sth बहस करना *The children next door are always arguing.* ➪ **fight 1, 4** और **quarrel 2** देखिए। **2.** [I, T] **argue that...; argue (for/against sth)** to give reasons that support your opinion about sth पक्ष या विपक्ष में तर्क प्रस्तुत करना; तर्क-वितर्क करना *He argued against buying a new computer.*

**argument** /ˈɑːɡjumənt ˈआग्युमन्ट् / *noun* **1** [C, U] **an argument (with sb) (about/over sth)** an angry discussion between two or more people who disagree with each other विवाद, झगड़ा, बहस *Leela **had an argument** with her father about politics.* ○ *He accepted the decision without argument.* **2** [C] the reason(s) that you give to support your opinion about sth तर्क, दलील, युक्ति *What are the **arguments for/against** lower taxes?*

**argumentative** /ˌɑːgjuˈmentətɪv ˌआग्यु ˈमेन्टटिव़् / *adj.* often involved in or enjoying arguments विवादी, विवादप्रिय, झगड़ालू

**arid** /ˈærɪd ˈऐरिड् / *adj.* (used about land or climate) very dry; with little or no rain (भूमि या जलवायु) सूखा; निर्जल, वर्षाहीन

**Aries** /ˈeəriːz ˈएअरीज़् / *noun* [U] the first of the twelve signs of the **zodiac,** the Ram मेष, मेषराशि

**arise** /əˈraɪz अˈराइज़् / *verb* [I] (*pt* **arose** /əˈrəʊz अˈरोज़् /; *pp* **arisen** /əˈrɪzn अˈरिज़्न् /) to begin to exist; to appear अस्तित्व में आना; प्रकट होना *If any problems arise, let me know.*

**aristocracy** /ˌærɪˈstɒkrəsi ˌऐरिˈस्टॉक्रसि / *noun* [C] (*pl.* **aristocracies**) the people of the highest social class who often have special titles उच्चतम सामाजिक वर्ग के सदस्य, जिन्हें प्रायः विशेष उपाधियाँ मिली होती हैं; कुलीन वर्ग, उच्चवर्गीय समाज, अभिजात वर्ग ✪ पर्याय **nobility**

**aristocrat** /ˈærɪstəkræt ˈऐरिस्टक्रैट् / *noun* [C] a member of the highest social class, often with a special title उच्चतम सामाजिक वर्ग का प्रायः विशेष उपाधि प्राप्त सदस्य ▶ **aristocratic** /ˌærɪstəˈkrætɪk ˌऐरिस्टˈक्रैटिक् / *adj.* अभिजात वर्ग का; कुलीन

**arithmetic** /əˈrɪθmətɪk अˈरिथ्मटिक् / *noun* [U] (*mathematics*) the kind of mathematics which involves counting with numbers (adding, subtracting, multiplying and dividing) अंकगणित *I'm not very good at **mental arithmetic**.*

**arithmetic progression** (*also* **arithmetical progression**) *noun* [C] (*mathematics*) a series of numbers that decrease or increase by the same amount each time, for example 2, 4, 6, 8 समान अंतर से संख्याओं के बढ़ने या घटने की एक गणना विधि; समांतर श्रेढ़ी ➪ **geometric progression** देखिए।

**the ark** /ɑːk आक् / *noun* [*sing.*] (in the Bible) a large boat which Noah built to save his family and two of every type of animal from the flood (बाइबल में) नोह का जहाज़ जो उसने बाढ़ के प्रकोप से अपने परिवार और अन्य प्राणियों को बचाने के लिए बनाया था

**arm**[1] /ɑːm आम् / *noun* [C] **1** the long part at each side of your body connecting your shoulder to your hand बाँह, भुजा, बाहु *He was carrying a newspaper under his arm.* **2** the part of a piece of clothing that covers your arm; a sleeve कमीज़ आदि की आस्तीन **3** the part of a chair where you rest your arms कुरसी की बाँह

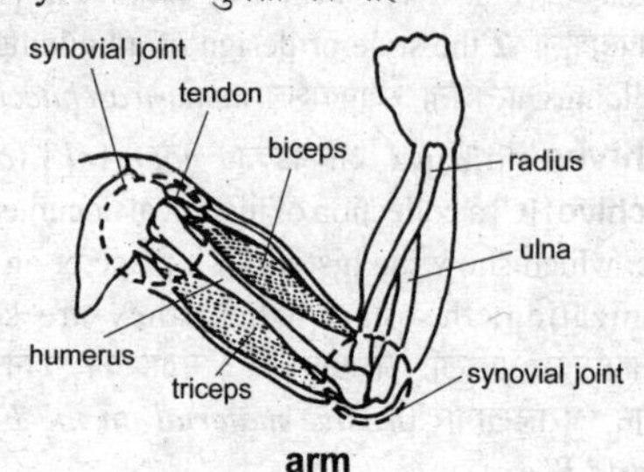

**arm**

IDM **arm in arm** with your arm folded around sb else's arm हाथ में हाथ डाले *The two friends walked arm in arm.*

**cross/fold your arms** to cross your arms in front of your chest हाथ पर हाथ रखना *She folded her arms and waited.* ○ *Jai was sitting with his arms crossed.*

**twist sb's arm** ➪ **twist**[1] देखिए।

**with open arms** ➪ **open**[1] देखिए।

**arm**[2] /ɑːm आम् / *verb* [I, T] to prepare sb/yourself to fight by supplying or getting weapons युद्ध के लिए हथियार प्राप्त करना या कराना ➪ **armed** और **arms** देखिए।

**armadillo** /ˌɑːməˈdɪləʊ ˌआमˈडिलो / *noun* [C] an American animal with a hard shell, that eats insects and rolls into a ball if sth attacks it कीड़े खाने वाला एक अमेरिकी प्राणी जिसका बाहरी आकार कठोर होता है, और जो हमला होने पर गेंदनुमा बन जाता है

**armament** /ˈɑːməmənt ˈआममन्ट् / *noun* [U] **1** (*also* **armaments**) [*pl.*] weapons, especially large guns, bombs, **tanks,** etc. युद्धसामग्री, विशेषतः तोप, बम, टैंक **2** the process of increasing the amount of weapons an army or a country has, especially to prepare for war युद्धसामग्री में वृद्धि करना (युद्ध की तैयारी के रूप में) ➪ **disarmament** देखिए।

**armaments** /ˈɑːməmənts ˈआममन्ट्स् / *noun* [*pl.*] weapons and military equipment हथियार और सैन्य उपकरण

**armband** /ˈɑːmbænd ˈआम्बैन्ड् / *noun* [C] **1** a piece of material that you wear around your arm भुजा पर बाँधी जाने वाली पट्टिका *The captain of the team* *wears an armband.* **2** a plastic ring filled with air which you can wear on each of your arms when you are learning to swim तैरना सीखने के लिए बाँहों में पहना जाने वाला, हवा से भरा प्लास्टिक का छल्ला; हवा भरा टायरनुमा रिंग

**armchair** /ˈɑːmtʃeə(r) ˈआम्चेअ(र्)/ *noun* [C] a soft comfortable chair with sides which support your arms हत्थेदार आरामदेह कुरसी

**armed** /ɑːmd आम्ड्/ *adj.* carrying a gun or other weapon; involving weapons हथियारबंद, सशस्त्र; जिसमें शस्त्रों का प्रयोग हो *All the terrorists were armed.* ○ *armed robbery* ✪ विलोम **unarmed**

**the armed forces** (*BrE* **the armed services**) *noun* [*pl.*] a country's army, navy and air force देश की थल सेना, नौ सेना और वायुसेना; देश की रक्षा सेनाएँ

**armful** /ˈɑːmfʊl ˈआम्फ़ुल्/ *noun* [C] the amount that you can carry in your arms दोनों हाथों से वहन की जा सकने वाली मात्रा

**armhole** /ˈɑːmhəʊl ˈआम्होल्/ *noun* [C] the opening in a piece of clothing where your arm goes through कोट, कमीज़ आदि का कंधे के पास का वह भाग जिसमें से हाथ डालकर पहनते हैं

**armistice** /ˈɑːmɪstɪs ˈआमिस्टिस्/ *noun* [C] an agreement between two countries who are at war that they will stop fighting युद्ध के बीच कुछ समय तक लड़ाई न करने की संधि; युद्ध विराम

**armour** (*AmE* **armor**) /ˈɑːmə(r) ˈआम(र्)/ *noun* [U] clothing, often made of metal, that soldiers wore in earlier times to protect themselves कवच, बख़्तर *a suit of armour*

**armoured** (*AmE* **armored**) /ˈɑːməd ˈआमड्/ *adj.* (used about a vehicle) covered with metal to protect it in an attack बख़्तरबंद गाड़ी

**armpit** /ˈɑːmpɪt ˈआम्पिट्/ *noun* [C] the part of the body under the arm at the point where it joins the shoulder काँख, बग़ल ➪ **body** पर चित्र देखिए।

**arms** /ɑːmz आम्ज़्/ *noun* [*pl.*] **1** weapons, especially those that are used in war युद्ध के हथियार **2** = **coat of arms**

IDM **up in arms** protesting angrily about sth कड़ा विरोध करते हुए *The workers were up in arms over the news that the factory was going to close.*

**army** /ˈɑːmi ˈआमि/ *noun* [C, *with sing. or pl. verb*] (*pl.* **armies**) **1** the military forces of a country which are trained to fight on land थलसेना, फ़ौज *the Indian Army* ○ *an army officer* ➪ **air force** और **navy** देखिए। **2** a large number of people, especially when involved in an activity together लोगों की बड़ी संख्या; दल, भीड़, समूह

**aroma** /əˈrəʊmə अˈरोमा/ *noun* [C] a smell, especially a pleasant one सुगंध, ख़ुशबू ▸ **aromatic** /ˌærəˈmætɪk ˌऐरˈमैटिक्/ *adj.* सुगंधित, ख़ुशबूदार

**aromatherapy** /əˌrəʊməˈθerəpi अˌरोमˈथ़ेरपि/ *noun* [U] the use of natural oils that smell pleasant for controlling pain or for **massage** सुगंधित प्राकृतिक तेलों द्वारा शरीर की मालिश की चिकित्साविधि

**aromatic** /ˌærəˈmætɪk ˌऐरˈमैटिक्/ *adj.* having a pleasant noticeable smell सुरभित, सुगंधित *aromatic oils/herbs* ✪ पर्याय **fragrant**

**arose** ➪ **arise** का past tense रूप

**around** /əˈraʊnd अˈराउन्ड्/ *adv., prep.* **1** (*also* **about**) in or to various places or directions विभिन्न दिशाओं में चारों ओर, इधर-उधर *They wandered around the town, looking at the shops.* **2** moving so as to face in the opposite direction विपरीत दिशा में घूम जाने के अर्थ में प्रयुक्त *Turn around and go back the way you came.* **3** on all sides; forming a circle चारों ओर; घेरा बनाते हुए *The park has a wall all around.* ○ *We sat down around the table.* NOTE अर्थ सं० **1, 2** और **3** में **around** के स्थान पर **round** का प्रयोग भी किया जा सकता है। **4** near a place (के) आस-पास *Is there a bank around here?* **5** (*also* **about**) present or available (पर) होना; उपस्थित या उपलब्ध *I went to the house but there was nobody around.* **6** (*also* **about**) approximately लगभग; क़रीब-क़रीब *I'll see you around seven* **7** (*also* **about**) used for activities with no real purpose निरर्थक गतिविधियों के संकेत के लिए प्रयुक्त *'What are you doing?' 'Nothing, just lazing around.'*

**arouse** /əˈraʊz अˈराउज़्/ *verb* [T] to cause a particular reaction in people दूसरे व्यक्तियों में कोई प्रतिक्रिया विशेष जागृत करना; जगाना, उत्तेजित करना *to arouse sb's curiosity/interest* ▸ **arousal** *noun* [C] उत्तेजन

**arraign** /əˈreɪn अˈरेन्/ *verb* [T] (*usually passive*) **arraign sb (for sth)** to bring a person to a court of law in order to formally accuse him/her of a crime औपचारिक रूप से अभियोग लगाने के लिए दोषी को कचहरी में लाना ▸ **arraignment** *noun* [C, U] दोषारोपण

**arrange** /əˈreɪndʒ अˈरेन्ज्/ *verb* **1** [T] to put sth in order or in a particular pattern व्यवस्थित करना, क्रम विशेष से सजाना *The books were arranged in alphabetical order.* ○ *Arrange the chairs in a circle.* **2 arrange (for) sth; arrange to do sth; arrange (sth) with sb** to make plans and preparations so that sth can happen in the future आयोजित करना; भविष्य में घटित होने वाली घटना के लिए प्रबंध या इंतज़ाम करना *We're arranging a surprise party for Mandira.*

**arranged marriage** *noun* [C] a marriage in which the parents choose the husband or wife for their child परिवारजनों द्वारा तय की गई शादी

**arrangement** /əˈreɪndʒmənt अˈरेन्ज़्मन्ट्/ *noun* 1 [C, *usually pl.*] plans or preparations for sth that will happen in the future (भविष्य की किसी घटना के लिए) व्यवस्था, प्रबंध या इंतज़ाम, बंदोबस्त *Come round this evening and we'll* ***make arrangements for*** *the party.* 2 [C, U] an agreement with sb to do sth समझौता *We both need to use the computer so we'll have to* ***come to*** *some* ***arrangement.*** 3 [C] a group of things that have been placed in a particular pattern वस्तुओं आदि की व्यवस्था का ढंग, सजावट; विन्यास *a flower arrangement*

**array** /əˈreɪ अˈरे/ *noun* [C] a large collection of things, especially one that is impressive and is seen by other people वस्तुओं का बड़ा संग्रह, विशेषतः प्रभावशाली प्रदर्शन के लिए

**arrears** /əˈrɪəz अˈरिअज़्/ *noun* [*pl.*] money that sb owes that he/she should have paid earlier बक़ाया राशि

IDM **be in arrears; fall/get into arrears** to be late in paying money that you owe भुगतान करने में देर होना; विलंब से भुगतान करना

**be paid in arrears** to be paid for work after you have done the work काम समाप्त होने के बाद भुगतान पाना

**arrest**[1] /əˈrest अˈरेस्ट्/ *verb* [T] when the police arrest sb, they take him/her prisoner in order to question him/her about a crime गिरफ़्तार करना; बंदी बनाना

**arrest**[2] /əˈrest अˈरेस्ट्/ *noun* [C, U] the act of arresting sb गिरफ़्तारी, बंदीकरण *The police* ***made*** *ten* ***arrests*** *after the riot.* ○ *The wanted man is now* ***under arrest.***

**arrival** /əˈraɪvl अˈराइव्ल्/ *noun* 1 [C, U] reaching the place to which you were travelling (किसी स्थान पर) आगमन, पहुँच *On our arrival we were told that our rooms had not been reserved.* 2 [C] people or things that have arrived पहुँचे हुए व्यक्ति, आगत वस्तुएँ *We brought in extra chairs for the late arrivals.*

**arrive** /əˈraɪv अˈराइव्/ *verb* [I] **1 arrive (at/in...)** to reach the place to which you were travelling (किसी स्थान पर) यात्रा करके पहुँचना *We arrived home at about midnight.* ○ *They arrived at the station ten minutes late.* 2 to come or happen आना, आ पहुँचना, होना *The day of the wedding had finally arrived.*

PHR V **arrive at** to reach sth (पर) पहुँचना *We finally arrived at a decision.*

**arrogant** /ˈærəgənt ˈऐरगन्ट्/ *adj.* thinking that you are better and more important than other people अक्खड़, घमंडी, अभिमानी ▶ **arrogance** *noun* [U] अक्खड़पन, घमंड ▶ **arrogantly** *adv.* घमंड से

**arrow** /ˈærəʊ ˈऐरो/ *noun* [C] 1 a thin piece of wood or metal, with one pointed end and feathers at the other end, that is shot by pulling back the string on a curved piece of wood (**a bow**) and letting go तीर, बाण ➪ **archer** देखिए। 2 the sign (→) which is used to show direction दिशानिर्देशक संकेत (→)

**arsenal** /ˈɑːsənl ˈआसन्ल्/ *noun* [C] 1 a collection of weapons such as guns and explosives युद्ध सामग्री का भंडार 2 a building where military weapons and explosives are made or stored स्थान जहाँ सैन्य सामग्री बनाई या जमा रखी जाती है; शस्त्रागार, आयुधनिर्माणशाला

**arsenic** /ˈɑːsnɪk ˈआस्निक्/ *noun* [U] (*symbol* **As**) a type of very strong poison संखिया नामक तीव्र विष

**arson** /ˈɑːsn ˈआसन्/ *noun* [U] the crime of setting fire to a building on purpose (दंगे-फ़साद आदि में) घरों और दुकानों में आग लगाने का अपराध; आगजनी

**arsonist** /ˈɑːsənɪst ˈआसनिस्ट्/ *noun* [C] a person who deliberately sets fire to a building आगजनी करने वाला व्यक्ति

**art** /ɑːt आट्/ *noun* 1 [U] the activity or skill of producing things such as paintings, designs, etc.; the objects that are produced कला; कलाकारी *an art class* ○ *modern art* ○ *I've never been good at art.* ➪ **work of art** देखिए। 2 [U] a skill or sth that needs skill कौशल या कौशलापेक्षी गतिविधि *There's an art* ***to*** *writing a good letter.* **3 the arts** [*pl.*] activities which involve creating things such as paintings, literature or music ललित कलाएँ जैसे चित्रकला, संगीतकला और साहित्य **4 arts** [*pl.*] subjects such as history or languages that you study at school or university भाषाएँ, साहित्य, सामाजिक-अध्ययन आदि पाठ्य विषय ➪ **sciences** देखिए।

**artefact** /ˈɑːtɪfækt ˈआटिफ़ैक्ट्/ *noun* [C] an object that is made by a person मानव-निर्मित कलाकृति; मानवीय कलाकृति

**arteriosclerosis** /ɑːˌtɪəriəʊskləˈrəʊsɪs आˌटिअरिओस्क्लेˈरोसिस्/ *noun* [U] (*medical*) a condition in which the walls of the **arteries** become thick and hard, making it difficult for blood to flow रक्तवाहिनी धमनियों के कड़ा पड़ जाने का रोग; धमनी काठिन्य

**artery** /ˈɑːtəri ˈआटरि/ *noun* [C] (*pl.* **arteries**) one of the tubes which take blood from the heart to other parts of the body हृदय से शरीर के अन्य भागों में रक्त ले जाने वाली नली; धमनी ➪ **carotid artery** और **vein** देखिए तथा **heart** पर चित्र देखिए। ▶**arterial** /ɑːˈtɪəriəl आˈटिअरिअल् / *adj.* धमनी-संबंधी, धमनीय *arterial blood/disease*

**artesian well** /ɑːˌtiːziən ˈwel आˌटीज़िअन् ˈवेल् / *noun* [C] a hole made in the ground through which water rises to the surface by natural pressure धरती में बनाया गया एक गड्ढा जिसमें से प्राकृतिक दाब के कारण भूमिगत पानी बाहर आ जाता है; आर्टीसियन कूप

**artful** /ˈɑːtfl ˈआट्फ़ल् / *adj.* clever at getting what you want, perhaps by not telling the truth चतुर, चालाक, संभवतः धूर्त तरीक़े अपनाने वाला

**arthritis** /ɑːˈθraɪtɪs आˈथ्राइटिस् / *noun* [U] a disease which causes swelling and pain in the places where your bones are connected (**joints**), where you bend your arms, fingers, etc. संधिवात, गठिया (रोग) ▶ **arthritic** /ɑːˈθrɪtɪk आˈथ्रिटिक् / *adj.* गठियाग्रस्त

**arthropod** /ˈɑːθrəpɒd ˈआथ्रपॉड् / *noun* [C] any of the **phylum** of animals that have a hard body without a **backbone** in it. Arthropods have legs that are made of more than one part and that can bend where the parts join together रीढ़ की हड्डी से रहित कठोर शरीर वाला कोई भी प्राणी; संधिपाद; इन प्राणियों की टाँगें कई भागों के जोड़ से बनी होती हैं और जोड़ों पर मुड़ सकती हैं *Spiders, insects and crustaceans are arthropods.*

**artichoke** /ˈɑːtɪtʃəʊk ˈआटिचोक् / *noun* [C] a green vegetable with a lot of thick pointed leaves. You can eat the bottom part of the leaves and its centre हाथीचक, वज्रांगी (एक वनस्पति)

**article** /ˈɑːtɪkl ˈआटिकल् / *noun* [C] **1** an object, especially one of a set वस्तु, सामान, विशेषतः किसी सेट का भाग *articles of clothing* **2** a piece of writing in a newspaper or magazine समाचार-पत्र या पत्रिका में कोई लेख **3** (*grammar*) the words 'a/an' (**the indefinite article**) or 'the' (**the definite article**) आर्टिकल

> **NOTE** **Articles** पर अधिक जानकारी के लिए **Quick Grammar Reference** खंड देखिए।

**articled** /ˈɑːtɪkld ˈआटिकल्ड् / *adj.* employed by a group of lawyers or other professional people while being trained in a job वेतनभोगी प्रशिक्षु *an articled clerk in a firm of lawyers*

**articulate**[1] /ɑːˈtɪkjələt आˈटिक्यलट् / *adj.* good at expressing your ideas clearly अपने विचारों को स्पष्ट रूप से व्यक्त करने में कुशल; अभिव्यक्ति-कुशल, वाग्मी ✪ विलोम **inarticulate**

**articulate**[2] /ɑːˈtɪkjuleɪt आˈटिक्यलट् / *verb* [I, T] to say sth clearly or to express your ideas or feelings विचारों या भावों को स्पष्टतया व्यक्त करना ▶ **articulation** /ɑːˌtɪkjuˈleɪʃn आटिक्युˈलेश्न् / *noun* [U] अभिव्यक्तिकरण

**artifice** /ˈɑːtɪfɪs ˈआटिफ़िस् / *noun* [U,C] (*formal*) the use of clever methods to trick sb चालबाज़ी

**artificial** /ˌɑːtɪˈfɪʃl ˌआटिˈफ़िश्ल् / *adj.* **1** not genuine or natural but made by people मानव द्वारा बनाया गया, न कि प्राकृतिक; कृत्रिम, नक़ली; अप्राकृतिक *artificial flowers* **2** not what it appears to be बनावटी, छद्म ▶ **artificially** /-ʃəli -शलि / *adv.* दिखावटी तौर पर, नक़ली

**artificial insemination** *noun* [U] the scientific process of making a woman or a female animal pregnant by putting male **sperm** inside her so that babies or young can be produced without sexual activity कृत्रिम गर्भाधान

**artificial intelligence** *noun* [U] (the study of) the way in which computers can be made to copy the way humans think युक्ति जिससे कंप्यूटर को मानव बुद्धि की नक़ल करने में सक्षम बनाया जा सके; यांत्रिक बुद्धि

**artificial respiration** *noun* [U] the process of helping a person who has stopped breathing begin to breathe again, usually by blowing into his/her mouth or nose कृत्रिम श्वसनक्रिया

**artillery** /ɑːˈtɪləri आˈटिलरि / *noun* [U] large, heavy guns that are moved on wheels; the part of the army that uses them तोपख़ाना; तोपची सैन्य दल

**artisan** /ˌɑːtɪˈzæn ˌआटिˈज़ैन् / *noun* [C] a person who makes things skilfully, especially with his/her hands कारीगर, शिल्पी ✪ पर्याय **craftsman**

**artist** /ˈɑːtɪst ˈआटिस्ट् / *noun* [C] somebody who produces art, especially paintings or drawings कलाकार, कलाकृति-निर्माता

**artiste** /ɑːˈtiːst आˈटिस्ट् / *noun* [C] a person whose job is to entertain people, by singing, dancing, etc. नर्तक, गायक आदि मनोरंजन करने वाला कलाकार

**artistic** /ɑːˈtɪstɪk आˈटिस्टिक् / *adj.* **1** connected with art कला संबंधी *the artistic director of the theatre* **2** showing a skill in art कलात्मक ▶ **artistically** /-kli -कलि / *adv.* कलात्मक रीति से

**artistry** /ˈɑːtɪstri ˈआटिस्ट्रि / *noun* [U] the skill of an artist कलाकार की कला, उसका कौशल

**artwork** /ˈɑːtwɜːk ˈआट्वक् / *noun* **1** [U] photographs, drawings, etc. that have been prepared for a book or magazine पुस्तक या पत्रिका के लिए बनाए गए चित्र, फ़ोटो आदि; कला-कार्य *a piece of artwork* **2** [C] a work of art, especially one in a museum or an **exhibition** विशेषतः संग्रहालय या प्रदर्शनी में रखी कलाकृति

**arty** /ˈɑːti ˈआटि/ *adj.* (*informal*) pretending or wanting to be very artistic or interested in the arts कलाढोंगी, कलाप्रेमी *He can't really like all those boring arty films.*

**Aryan[1]** *noun* [C] **1** a member of the group of people who spoke an Indo-European language and invaded northern India in the 2nd millennium BC आर्य समुदाय के सदस्य जो इंडो-यूरोपीय भाषा का प्रयोग करते थे तथा जिन्होंने द्वितीय सहस्राब्दि ईसा पूर्व में भारत पर आक्रमण किया था *Aryans came to India many centuries ago.* **2** a person who spoke any of the Indo-European languages इंडो-यूरोपीय भाषा बोलने वाला व्यक्ति **3** (according to the Nazi doctrine) a member of non-Jewish **Caucasian** race of people usually having **Nordic** features (नाटज़ी सिद्धांत के अनुसार) नॉर्डिक आकृति वाली कॉकेशियन मानव प्रजाति जो यहूदी वंश के नहीं

**Aryan[2]** *adjective* of or relating to the people of Indo-European origin इंडो-यूरोपीय मूल की प्रजाति से संबंधित

**Arya Samaj** *noun* [U] a Hindu reform movement of India that was founded by Swami Dayanand Saraswati in 1875 with the purpose of taking the Hindu religion back from superstitious beliefs to the teachings of Vedas स्वामी दयानन्द सरस्वती द्वारा सन् 1875 में संस्थापित हिंदू समाज सुधार आंदोलन जिसका उद्देश्य हिंदू धर्म में प्रचालित अंधविश्वास को दूर कर वैदिक शिक्षण का प्रचार करना था; आर्य-समाज

**as** /əz; *strong form* æz अज़्; प्रबल रूप ऐज़्/ *conj., prep., adv.* **1** while sth else is happening जिस समय *The phone rang just as I was leaving the house.* ○ *As she walked along the road, she thought about her father.* **2 as ... as** used for comparing people or things व्यक्तियों और वस्तुओं में तुलना करने के लिए प्रयुक्त; के बराबर, के जैसा, समान स्तर का, वैसा ही *Sheela's almost as tall as me.* ○ ***as soon as possible*** ○ ***twice as much as*** ○ *I haven't got as many books as you have.* **3** used for talking about sb/sth's job, role or function किसी के काम या उसकी भूमिका व्यक्त करने के लिए प्रयुक्त; के रूप में, के समान, के तौर पर *Think of me as your friend, not as your boss.* **4** in a particular way, state, etc.; like किसी विशेष तरीक़े से, जैसे *Please do as I tell you.* ○ *Leave the room **as it is**. Don't move anything.* **5** used at the beginning of a comment about what you are saying वक्तव्य की परिचायक टिप्पणी के आरंभ में प्रयुक्त ***As you know**, I've decided to leave at the end of the month.* **6** because क्योंकि *I didn't buy the dress, as I decided it was too expensive.*

IDM **as for** used when you are starting to talk about a different person or thing प्रसंग से भिन्न व्यक्ति या वस्तु के विषय में चर्चा आरंभ करने के लिए प्रयुक्त *Tara's upstairs. As for Ankit, I've no idea where he is.*

**as if; as though** used for saying how sb/sth appears जैसे मानो कि *She looks as if/though she's just got out of bed.*

**as it were** जैसी कि स्थिति है, वर्तमान स्थिति को देखते हुए used for saying that sth is only true in a certain way यह बताने के लिए प्रयुक्त कि कोई बात विशेष स्थिति में ही सच है *She felt, as it were, a stranger in her own house.*

**as of; as from** starting from a particular time एक विशेष समय-बिंदु से आरंभ होने वाला *As from next week, Abhishek Bhatt will be managing this department.*

**as to** about a particular thing; concerning एक विशेष वस्तु के विषय में; से संबंधित *I was given no instructions as to how to begin.*

**asana** *noun* [C] (*IndE*) a special way of sitting or standing while practising yoga योगाभ्यास करते समय, बैठने या खड़े होने की विशेष अवस्था; आसन

**asap** /ˌeɪ es eɪ ˈpiː ˌए एस् एˈपी/ *abbr.* as soon as possible यथाशीघ्र

**asbestos** /æsˈbestəs ऐस्ˈबेस्टस्/ *noun* [U] a soft grey material that does not burn and is used to protect against heat आसमानी रंग का और न जलने वाला कोमल पदार्थ जो ताप से बचाता है; ऐसबसटस

**ascend** /əˈsend अˈसेन्ड्/ *verb* [I, T] (*formal*) to go up ऊपर चढ़ना; बढ़ना ✪ विलोम **descend** ▶ **ascending** *adj.* बढ़ते हुए क्रम में *The questions are arranged **in ascending order** of difficulty.*

**Ascension Day** /əˈsenʃn deɪ अˈसेन्शन् डे/ *noun* the 40th day after Easter when Christians remember Christ leaving the earth and going to heaven (ईसाई धर्म में) ईस्टर के बाद का 40 वाँ दिन जिसे ईसाई लोग ईसा के स्वर्गारोहण के दिन के रूप में मनाते हैं

**ascent** /əˈsent अˈसेन्ट्/ *noun* [C] **1** the act of climbing or going up चढ़ाव, आरोहण *the ascent of Mt Everest* **2** a path or hill leading upwards चढ़ाई *There was a steep ascent before the path became flat again.* ✪ विलोम **descent**

**ascertain** /ˌæsəˈteɪn ˌऐसˈटेन्/ *verb* [T] (*formal*) to find sth out कुछ पता लगाना

**ascetic** /əˈsetɪk अˈसेटिक्/ *adj.* not allowing yourself physical pleasures, especially for religious reasons विशेषतः धार्मिक कारणों से भौतिक सुखों से विमुख ▶ **ascetic** *noun* [C] संन्यासी

**ascorbic acid** /əˌskɔːbɪk ˈæsɪd अˌस्कॉबिक् ऐसिड्/ (*also* **vitamin C**) *noun* [U] a natural substance that is found in fruit such as lemons and oranges and in green vegetables. Humans and animals need ascorbic acid in order to stay healthy नींबू, संतरे और हरी सब्ज़ियों में उपलब्ध एक प्राकृतिक पदार्थ जो मनुष्यों और प्राणियों के लिए स्वास्थ्यकर है

**ascribe** /əˈskraɪb अˈस्क्राइब्/ *verb* [T] **ascribe sth to sb/sth** to say that sth was written by or belonged to sb; to say what caused sth लेख लिखने या स्वामी होने का किसी को श्रेय देना; के लिए उत्तरदायी ठहराना *Many people ascribe this play to Kalidasa.*

**ASEAN** /ˈæsiæn ˈऐसिऐन्/ *abbr.* Association of South East Asian Nations ऐसिऐन; दक्षिण-पूर्वी एशियाई देशों का संगठन

**aseptic** /ˌeɪˈseptɪk ˌएˈसेप्टिक्/ *adj.* (*medical*) not having any harmful bacteria हानिकर जीवाणु से रहित

**asexual** /ˌeɪˈsekʃuəl ˌएˈसेक्शुअल्/ *adj.* **1** not involving sex; not having sexual organs यौन क्रिया से असंबद्ध, अयौन; जननेन्द्रियों से वंचित, अलिंगी *asexual reproduction* **2** not having sexual qualities; not interested in sex यौन लक्षणों से वंचित; यौन क्रिया का अनिच्छुक

**ash** /æʃ ऐश्/ *noun* **1** [U] (*also* **ashes** [*pl.*]) the grey or black powder which is left after sth has burned राख, भस्म *cigarette ash* ○ *the ashes of a fire* ➪ **volcano** पर चित्र देखिए। **2 ashes** [*pl.*] what is left after a dead person has been burned दाह-संस्कार के अवशेष; भस्मावशेष **3** [C] a type of forest tree that grows in cool countries ठंडे देशों में उगने वाला एक प्रकार का जंगली वृक्ष

**ashamed** /əˈʃeɪmd अˈशेम्ड्/ *adj.* (*not before a noun*) **ashamed (of sth/sb/yourself); ashamed (that...); ashamed (to do sth)** feeling guilty or embarrassed about sb/sth or because of sth you have done लज्जित, शर्मिंदा *She was ashamed of her old clothes.* ○ *She felt ashamed that she hadn't helped him.* ✪ विलोम **unashamed**

**ashen** /ˈæʃn ˈऐश्न्/ *adj.* (used about sb's face) very pale; without colour because of illness or fear (चेहरे के लिए प्रयुक्त) बहुत पीला; बीमारी या भय के कारण बेरंग

**Ashoka tree** *noun* [C] a small evergreen tree with orange or red flowers. It is sacred to the Buddhists and Hindus लाल या नारंगी फूलों वाला छोटा सदाबहार पेड़ जो हिंदुओं और बौद्ध धर्म में पूज्य है

**ashore** /əˈʃɔː(r) अˈशॉ(र्)/ *adv.* onto the land from the sea, a river, etc. तट पर, स्थल पर *The passengers went ashore for an hour while the ship was in port.* ➪ **shore** देखिए।

**ashram** *noun* [C] (*IndE*) **1** a place, often in a forest, where people who have withdrawn from society can live apart as a group; a religious retreat; a **hermitage** प्रायः वन में वह स्थान जहाँ समाज से निवर्तित लोग एक समूह में रहते हैं; धार्मिक निवर्तन; आश्रम **2** any of the four stages in the life of a person through which he/she will ideally pass according to Hindu philosophy (हिंदू धर्म में) जीवन के चार चरणों में से एक; आश्रम *grihastha ashram* ○ *vanaprastha ashram*

**ashtray** /ˈæʃtreɪ ˈऐश्ट्रे/ *noun* [C] a small dish for collecting the powder **ash** made when a cigarette burns सिगरेट की राख डालने के लिए छोटी तश्तरी; राखदानी, ऐशट्रे

**Asian** /ˈeɪʒn; ˈeɪʃn ˈएश़्न्; ˈएश्न्/ *noun* [C] a person from Asia or whose family was originally from Asia एशिया का मूल निवासी; एशियाई ▶ **Asian** *adj.* एशियाई

**aside**[1] /əˈsaɪd अˈसाइड्/ *adv.* **1** on or to one side; out of the way एक ओर; किनारे, दूर *We stood aside to let the man go past.* **2** to be kept separately, for a special purpose (विशेष उद्देश्य से) अलग रखा गया *I try to* ***set aside*** *a little money each month.*

**aside**[2] /əˈsaɪd अˈसाइड्/ *noun* [C] (in a play) **1** words spoken by an actor to the audience which the other characters on the stage are not intended to hear (नाटक में) कलाकार द्वारा दर्शकों को बोले गए शब्द जिन्हें रंगमंच पर अन्य कलाकारों को नहीं सुनना होता; स्वगत **2** a remark made in a low voice that is intended to be heard only by certain people दबी आवाज़ में बोले गए शब्द जो केवल कुछ लोगों के सुनने के लिए ही हों **3** a remark that is not directly connected with the main subject मुख्य विषय से हटकर कोई बात

**aside from** *prep.* = **apart from**

**ask** /ɑːsk आस्क्/ *verb* **1** [I, T] **ask (sb) (about sb/sth); ask sb sth** to put a question to sb in order to find out some information जानकारी के लिए प्रश्न पूछना *We need to ask about tickets.* ○ *'What's the time?' he asked.* **2** [I, T] **ask (sb) for sth; ask sth (of sb); ask sb to do sth** to request that sb gives you sth or does sth for you माँगना, निवेदन करना *She sat down and asked for a cup of coffee.* ○ *Ring this number and ask for Mrs Khan.* **3** [I, T] to request permission to do sth कुछ करने के लिए अनुमति माँगना *He asked to use our phone.* ○ *We asked if we could go home early.* **4** [T] **ask sb (to sth)** to invite sb बुलाना, निमंत्रण देना **5** [T] to say the price that you want for sth क़ीमत बताना *How much are they asking for their car?*

**IDM** **ask for trouble/it** to behave in a way that will almost certainly cause you problems मुसीबत मोल लेना *Driving when you're tired is just asking for trouble.*

**if you ask me** if you want my opinion अगर मेरी राय चाहिए

**PHR V** **ask after sb** to ask about sb's health or to ask for news of sb (किसी के स्वास्थ्य के संबंध में) पूछना, हालचाल जानना *Tina asked after you today.*

**askew** /əˈskjuː अˈस्क्यू/ *adv., adj.* (*not before a noun*) not in a straight or level position टेढ़ा, तिरछा

**asking price** *noun* [C] the price that sb wants to sell sth for बेचने के लिए बेचने वाले से माँगी क़ीमत ➪ **cost price** और **selling price** देखिए।

**asleep** /əˈsliːp अˈस्लीप्/ *adj.* (*not before a noun*) not awake; sleeping सोया हुआ, नींद में *The baby is fast/sound asleep.* ○ to ***fall asleep***

> **NOTE** ध्यान दें कि **asleep** का प्रयोग केवल संज्ञा के बाद और **sleeping** का प्रयोग केवल संज्ञा से पहले किया जाता है—*a sleeping child* ➪ **sleep**[2] देखिए।

**asp** /æsp ऐस्प्/ *noun* [C] a small poisonous snake found especially in North Africa विशेषतः उत्तरी अफ्रीक़ा में पाया जाने वाला एक छोटा विषैला साँप

**asparagus** /əˈspærəgəs अˈस्पैरगस्/ *noun* [U] a plant with long green or white **stems** that you can cook and eat as a vegetable शतावर, शतावरी, नागदौन

**aspect** /ˈæspekt ˈऐस्पेक्ट्/ *noun* [C] one of the qualities or parts of a situation, idea, problem, etc. किसी स्थिति, विचार, समस्या आदि का पहलू, पक्ष, दृष्टिकोण

**asphalt** /ˈæsfælt ˈऐस्फ़ैल्ट्/ *noun* [U] a thick black substance that is used for making the surface of roads एक काला गाढ़ा पदार्थ जिसे सड़कों की सतह बनाने में प्रयुक्त किया जाता है; डामर

**asphyxia** /æsˈfɪksiə ऐस्ˈफ़िक्सिआ/ *noun* [U] the state of being unable to breathe, which causes sb to die or to become unconscious साँस न ले पाने की स्थिति, जो बेहोशी या मृत्यु का कारण बन सकती है; श्वासरोध

**asphyxiate** /əsˈfɪksieɪt अस्ˈफ़िक्सिएट्/ *verb* [I, T] to make sb become unconscious or die by preventing him/her from breathing (किसी की) साँस रोक देना या साँस रुक जाना *He was asphyxiated by the smoke while he was asleep.* ▶ **asphyxiation** /əsˌfɪksiˈeɪʃn अस्ˌफ़िक्सिˈएश्न्/ *noun* [U] श्वासावरोध

**aspic** /ˈæspɪk ˈऐस्पिक्/ *noun* [U] clear **jelly** which food is sometimes put into when it is being served cold पारदर्शी जेली जिसमें किसी अन्य ठंडे खाद्य पदार्थ को डालकर परोसा जाता है

**aspire** /əˈspaɪə(r) अˈस्पाइअ(र्)/ *verb* [I] (*formal*) **aspire to sth/to do sth** to have a strong desire to have or do sth कुछ पाने की प्रबल अभिलाषा रखना; आकांक्षा करना *an aspiring actor* ▶ **aspiration** /ˌæspəˈreɪʃn ˌऐस्पˈरेश्न्/ *noun* [C, U] प्रबल अभिलाषा, आकांक्षा

**aspirin** /ˈæsprɪn; ˈæspərɪn ˈऐस्प्रिन्; ˈऐस्परिन्/ *noun* [C, U] a drug used to reduce pain and a high temperature ज्वर उतारने और दर्द कम करने की एक औषधि; ऐस्प्रिन

**ass** /æs ऐस्/ = **donkey**

**assailant** /əˈseɪlənt अˈसेलन्ट्/ *noun* [C] (*formal*) a person who attacks sb आक्रमणकारी, हमलावर व्यक्ति

**assassin** /əˈsæsɪn अˈसैसिन्/ *noun* [C] a person who kills a famous or important person for money or for political reasons किसी महत्त्वपूर्ण या लोकप्रिय व्यक्ति का हत्यारा; क़ातिल विशेषतः धन या राजनैतिक कारणों के लिए ▶ **assassinate** /əˈsæsɪneɪt अˈसैसिनेट्/ *verb* [T] धन के लालच या किन्हीं राजनैतिक कारणों से किसी लोकप्रिय या महत्त्वपूर्ण व्यक्ति की हत्या करना ➪ **kill** पर नोट देखिए। ▶ **assassination** /əˌsæsɪˈneɪʃn अˌसैसिˈनेश्न्/ *noun* [C, U] महत्त्वपूर्ण व्यक्ति की हत्या

**assault** /əˈsɔːlt अˈसॉल्ट्/ *noun* [C, U] **assault (on sb/sth)** a sudden attack on sb/sth अचानक हुआ हमला, प्रहार, धावा ▶ **assault** *verb* [T] अचानक हमला करना, धावा बोलना *He was charged with assaulting a police officer.*

**assault course** (*AmE* **obstacle course**) *noun* [C] an area of land with many objects that are difficult to climb, jump over or go through, which is used, especially by soldiers, for improving physical skills and strength ऐसा क्षेत्र जहाँ ऊँची या भांति-भांति के अवरोध होते हैं जिन्हें पार कर शारीरिक बल-कौशल बढ़ाया जा सकता है

**assemble** /əˈsembl अˈसेम्बल्/ *verb* **1** [I, T] to come together or bring sb/sth together in a group समूह के रूप में एकत्र करना या होना *I've assembled all the information I need for my essay.* **2** [T] to fit the parts of sth together किसी वस्तु के विभिन्न हिस्सों को जोड़ना *We spent hours trying to assemble our new bookshelves.*

**assembly** /əˈsembli अˈसेम्बलि/ *noun* (*pl.* **assemblies**) **1** [C, U] a large group of people who come together for a particular purpose समागम, सभा, जमावड़ा *school assembly* **2** [U] the action of fitting the parts of sth together किसी यंत्र के पुरज़े जोड़ने की क्रिया

**assembly line** *noun* [C] a line of people and machines in a factory that fit the parts of sth together in a fixed order कारख़ाने में कारीगरों और मशीनों की क्रमव्यवस्था जिसमें नियत क्रम में किसी चीज़ के पुरज़े जोड़े जाते हैं

**assent** /əˈsent अˈसेन्ट्/ *noun* [U] (*formal*) **assent (to sth)** official agreement to sth अधिकारिक स्वीकृति *The committee **gave** their **assent** to the proposed changes.* ▶ **assent** *verb* [I] **assent (to sth)** अधिकारिक स्वीकृति देना *Nobody would assent to the terms he proposed.*

**assert** /əˈsɜːt अˈसट्/ *verb* [T] **1** to say sth clearly and firmly स्पष्ट रूप से और बलपूर्वक कुछ कहना **2** to behave in a determined and confident way to make people listen to you or to get what you want दूसरों का ध्यान व आदर पाने के लिए आत्मविश्वासपूर्ण व्यवहार करना *You ought to assert yourself more.* ○ *to assert your authority*

**assertion** /əˈsɜːʃn अˈसशन्/ *noun* **1** [C] a statement that says you strongly believe that sth is true दृढ़ कथन, निश्चयपूर्वक कथन, दावा **2** [U] the action of showing, using or stating sth strongly दृढ़तापूर्ण व्यवहार

**assertive** /əˈsɜːtɪv अˈसटिव्/ *adj.* expressing your opinion clearly and firmly so that people listen to you or do what you want स्पष्ट और दृढ़ रीति से अपनी राय व्यक्त करते हुए, ताकि दूसरे उसे सुनें, समझें और करें ▶ **assertively** *adv.* आग्रहपूर्ण रीति से ▶ **assertiveness** *noun* [C] दृढ़ निश्चयात्मकता, हठधर्मिता

**assess** /əˈses अˈसेस्/ *verb* [T] **1** to judge or form an opinion about sth राय बनाना, आँकना *It's too early to assess the effects of the price rises.* **2 assess sth (at sth)** to guess or decide the amount or value of sth मूल्य या क़ीमत निर्धारित करना; मूल्यांकन करना *to assess the cost of repairs* ▶ **assessment** *noun* [C, U] सोचा-समझा अभिमत, मूल्यांकन, राय *I made a careful assessment of the risks involved.*

**assessor** /əˈsesə(r) अˈसेस(र्)/ *noun* [C] **1** an expert in a particular subject who is asked by a court of law or other official group to give advice न्यायालय या अन्य समिति को परामर्श देने वाला विशेषज्ञ; विधिपरामर्शदाता **2** a person who calculates the value or cost of sth or the amount of money to be paid मूल्य-निर्धारक, भुगतान-राशि *an insurance/a tax assessor* **3** a person who judges how well sb has done in an exam, a competition, etc. परीक्षक, निर्णायक *Marks are awarded by an external assessor.*

**asset** /ˈæset ˈऐसेट्/ *noun* [C] **1 an asset (to sb/sth)** a person or thing that is useful to sb/sth उपयोगी व्यक्ति या वस्तु *She's a great asset to the organization.* **2** (*usually pl.*) something of value that a person, company, etc. owns परिसंपत्ति, माल-मला, पूंजी

**assiduous** /əˈsɪdjuəs अˈसिड्युअस्/ *adj.* (*formal*) working very hard and taking great care that everything is done as well as it can be परिश्रमी, अध्यवसायी, मेहनती ✪ पर्याय **diligent** ▶ **assiduously** *adv.* पारिश्रमपूर्वक

**assign** /əˈsaɪn अˈसाइन्/ *verb* [T] **1 assign sth to sb/sth** to give sth to sb for a particular purpose विशेष उद्देश्य से कुछ देना *We have assigned 20% of our budget to the project.* **2 assign sb to sth** to give sb a particular job to do किसी को नियुक्त करना, कार्यभार सौंपना

**assignment** /əˈsaɪnmənt अˈसाइन्मन्ट्/ *noun* [C, U] a job or type of work that you are given to do कार्यभार, नियत कार्य, नियुक्ति *The reporter disappeared while on (an) assignment in the war zone.*

**assimilate** /əˈsɪməleɪt अˈसिमलेट्/ *verb* **1** [I, T] **assimilate (sb/sth) (into sth)** to become or allow sb/sth to become part of a country, a social group, etc. किसी देश या सामाजिक समूह में सम्मिलित हो जाना या किसी अन्य को सम्मिलित कर लेना **2** [T] to learn and understand sth जान लेना, आत्मसात कर लेना *to assimilate new facts/information/ideas* ▶ **assimilation** /əˌsɪməˈleɪʃn अˌसिमˈलेशन्/ *noun* [U] आत्मसात्करण

**assist** /əˈsɪst अˈसिस्ट्/ *verb* [I, T] (*formal*) **assist (sb) in/with sth; assist (sb) in doing sth** to help सहायता करना *Volunteers assisted in searching for the boy.*

**assistance** /əˈsɪstəns अˈसिस्टन्स्/ *noun* [U] (*formal*) help or support सहायता या समर्थन *financial assistance for poorer families* ○ *She shouted for help but nobody came to her assistance.*

**assistant** /əˈsɪstənt अˈसिस्टन्ट्/ *noun* [C] **1** a person who helps sb in a more important position सहायक, सहकार *the assistant manager* **2** (*AmE* **clerk**) a person who sells things to people in a shop दुकान में वस्तुएँ बेचने वाला व्यक्ति; बिक्री सहायक *a shop/sales assistant*

**Assoc.** *abbr.* = **association**

**associate¹** /əˈsəʊsiət अˈसोसिअट्/ *noun* [C] a person that you meet and get to know through your work व्यापार आदि कार्य में संगी; सहचर *a business associate*

**associate²** /əˈsəʊʃieɪt अˈसोशिएट्/ *verb* **1** [T] **associate sb/sth (with sb/sth)** to make a connection between people or things in your mind अपने मस्तिष्क में व्यक्तियों या वस्तुओं के बीच संबंध स्थापित करना; संबद्ध करना *I always associate the smell of the sea with my childhood.* **2** [I] **asso-**

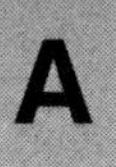

**ciate with sb** to spend time with sb किसी के साथ समय बिताना, संबंध या संपर्क रखना **3** [T] **associate yourself with sth** to say that you support sth or agree with sth किसी बात पर किसी का समर्थन करना ✪ पर्याय **disassociate**

**association** /əˌsəʊsiˈeɪʃn अˌसोसिˈएश्न्/ *noun* **1** [U] joining or working with another person or group किसी अन्य व्यक्ति या समूह के साथ काम करने की स्थिति सहकारिता; संयोग *We work **in association with** our New Delhi office.* **2** [C] a group of people or organizations who work together for a particular purpose संस्था, सभा, समाज, संघ *the National Association of Language Teachers* **3** [C, U] the act of connecting one person or thing with another in your mind अपने मस्तिष्क में वस्तुओं या व्यक्तियों को संबद्ध करने की क्रिया

**assonance** /ˈæsənəns ˈऐसनन्स्/ *noun* [U] (*technical*) the effect created when two syllables in words that are close together have the same vowel sound, but different consonants, or the same consonants but different vowels, for example, 'seen' and 'beat' or 'cold' and 'killed' शब्द के भीतर एक-सी स्वर ध्वनियों की उपस्थिति से उत्पन्न प्रभाव, उदाहरण के लिए 'seen' और 'beat' या 'cold' और 'killed'

**assorted** /əˈsɔːtɪd अˈसॉटिड्/ *adj.* of different types; mixed फुटकर, विविध, मिश्रित

**assortment** /əˈsɔːtmənt अˈसॉटमन्ट्/ *noun* [C] a group of different things or of different types of the same thing; a mixture विविध वस्तुओं का मिश्रण, एक ही वस्तु के विविध प्रकारों का मिश्रण

**Asst** (*also* **asst**) *abbr.* = **assistant**

**assuage** /əˈsweɪdʒ अˈस्वेज्/ *verb* [T] (*formal*) to make an unpleasant feeling less strong प्रतिकूल भावना आदि की तीक्ष्णता को कम करना *He hoped that by confessing he could assuage his guilt.*

**assume** /əˈsjuːm अˈस्यूम्/ *verb* [T] **1** to accept or believe that sth is true even though you have no proof; to expect sth to be true प्रमाण न होते हुए भी किसी बात को सत्य मान लेना; किसी बात के सत्य होने की आशा या अपेक्षा करना *I assume that you have the necessary documents.* ○ *Everyone assumed Ratan to be guilty.* **2** to pretend to have or be sb/sth कुछ होने का ढोंग करना ***to assume a false name*** **3** to begin to use power or to have a powerful position अधिकार प्रयोग करना या अधिकारपूर्ण पद का भार ग्रहण करना *to assume control of sth*

**assumption** /əˈsʌmpʃn अˈसम्प्श्न्/ *noun* **1** [C] something that you accept is true even though you have no proof कोई विचार, बात आदि जिसे प्रमाण न होते हुए भी सत्य माना जाए; पूर्वमान्यता, पूर्व धारणा *It's unfair to **make assumptions about** a person's character before you know them.* ○ *a reasonable/false assumption* **2** [U] **the assumption of sth** the act of taking power or of starting an important job सत्ता धारण करने या किसी महत्त्वपूर्ण कार्य को आरंभ करने की क्रिया

**assurance** /əˈʃɔːrəns अˈशॉरन्स्/ *noun* **1** [C] a promise that sth will certainly happen or be true पूर्ण आश्वासन *They **gave** me **an assurance that** the work would be finished by Friday.* **2** (*also* **self-assurance**) [U] the belief that you can do or succeed at sth; confidence आत्मविश्वास; अपने ऊपर पूरा भरोसा

**assure** /əˈʃɔː(r) अˈशॉ(र्)/ *verb* [T] **1** to promise sb that sth will certainly happen or be true, especially if he/she is worried आश्वासन देना, भरोसा दिलाना, ढाढ़स बाँधना या बँधाना *I assure you that it is perfectly safe.* **2** to make sth sure or certain निश्चित करना, सुनिश्चित करना *The success of the new product assured the survival of the company.*

**assured** /əˈʃɔːd अˈशॉड्/ (*also* **self-assured**) *adj.* believing that you can do sth or succeed at sth; confident आश्वासित; आत्मविश्वासी

**asterisk** /ˈæstərɪsk ˈऐस्टरिस्क्/ *noun* [C] the sign (*) that you use to make people notice sth in a piece of writing तारक; तारा चिह्न विशेषतः पाठक का ध्यान आकृष्ट करने के लिए प्रयुक्त

**asteroid** /ˈæstərɔɪd ˈऐस्टरॉइड्/ *noun* [C] any of The many small planets that go around the sun. They are also called minor planets सूर्य के चारों ओर घूमने वाले क्षुद्रग्रह, लघु ग्रह

**asthma** /ˈæsmə ˈऐस्मा/ *noun* [U] a medical condition that makes breathing difficult एक तरह का श्वास रोग; दमा

**asthmatic** /æsˈmætɪk ऐस्ˈमैटिक्/ *noun* [C] a person who has asthma दमे का रोगी ▶ **asthmatic** *adj.* दमा संबंधित

**astigmatism** /əˈstɪgmətɪzəm अˈस्टिग्मटिज़म्/ *noun* [C] a fault in the shape of a person's eye that prevents him/her from seeing clearly किसी व्यक्ति की आँख का ऐसा बेडौलपन जिसके कारण वह साफ़ नहीं देख पाता; अबिंदुकता, दृष्टिवैषम्य

**astonish** /əˈstɒnɪʃ अˈस्टॉनिश्/ *verb* [T] to surprise sb very much विस्मयचकित कर देना; अचंभे में डाल देना *She astonished everybody by announcing her engagement.* ▶ **astonished** *adj.* आश्चर्यचकित, भौंचक्का, विस्मित *I was astonished by the decision.*

**astonishing** /əˈstɒnɪʃɪŋ अˈस्टॉनिशिङ्/ *adj.* very surprising आश्चर्यजनक, विस्मयकारी ▶ **astonishingly** *adv.* आश्चर्यजनक रूप से

**astonishment** /əˈstɒnɪʃmənt अˈस्टॉनिशमन्ट्/ *noun* [U] very great surprise अति विस्मय, आश्चर्य, हैरानी *He dropped his book* ***in astonishment***.

**astound** /əˈstaʊnd अˈस्टाउन्ड्/ *verb* [T] (*usually passive*) to surprise sb very much भौचक्का या आश्चर्यचकित कर देना *We were astounded by how well he performed.*

**astounded** /əˈstaʊndɪd अˈस्टाउन्डिड्/ *adj. feeling or showing great surprise* एकदम भौंचक्का, हैरान

**astounding** /əˈstaʊndɪŋ अˈस्टाउन्डिङ्/ *adj.* causing sb to feel extremely surprised अतिविस्मयकारी

**astray** /əˈstreɪ अˈस्ट्रे/ *adv.*

IDM **go astray 1** to become lost or be stolen खो जाना या चोरी हो जाना **2** to go in the wrong direction सही रास्ते से भटक जाना

**lead sb astray** ⇨ **lead**[1] देखिए।

**astride** /əˈstraɪd अˈस्ट्राइड्/ *adv., prep.* with one leg on each side of sth टाँगें आर-पार फैला कर *to sit astride a horse*

**astringent** /əˈstrɪndʒənt अˈस्ट्रिन्जन्ट्/ *adj., noun* (*technical*) **1** (used about a liquid or a cream) able to stop a cut from bleeding, or to make the skin tighter so that it feels less **oily** (द्रव या क्रीम) रक्त प्रवाह रोधी या त्वचा संकोचक *an astringent cream* **2** (*formal*) critical in a harsh or clever way कठोर रूप से आलोचनात्मक *astringent comments* **3** slightly bitter but fresh in taste or smell हलका तीता परंतु ताज़ा

**astrologer** /əˈstrɒlədʒə(r) अˈस्ट्रॉलज(र्)/ *noun* [C] a person who is an expert in astrology ज्योतिषी

**astrology** /əˈstrɒlədʒi अˈस्ट्रॉलजि/ *noun* [U] the study of the positions and movements of the stars and planets and the way that some people believe they affect people and events सौर-ग्रहों तथा तारों की स्थितियों एवं गतियों और उनका मानव जीवन और घटनाओं पर प्रभाव का अध्ययन; फलित ज्योतिष ⇨ **horoscope** और **zodiac** देखिए।

**astronaut** /ˈæstrənɔːt ˈऐसट्रनॉट्/ *noun* [C] a person who travels in a spacecraft अंतरिक्ष यात्री

**astronomer** /əˈstrɒnəmə(r) अˈस्ट्रॉनम(र्)/ *noun* [C] a person who studies astronomy खगोलविद्, ज्योतिर्विद्

**astronomical** /ˌæstrəˈnɒmɪkl ˌऐस्ट्रˈनॉमिकल्/ *adj.* **1** connected with astronomy खगोल विद्या से संबंधित, खगोलीय **2** extremely high अत्यधिक, बहुत ज्यादा *astronomical house prices*

**astronomy** /əˈstrɒnəmi अˈस्ट्रॉनमि/ *noun* [U] the scientific study of the sun, moon, stars, etc. नक्षत्रों, सूर्य, ग्रहों तथा चंद्रमा का वैज्ञानिक अध्ययन; खगोलविज्ञान, गणित ज्योतिष

**astrophysics** /ˌæstrəʊˈfɪzɪks ˌऐस्ट्रोˈफ़िज़िक्स्/ *noun* [U] the scientific study of the physical and chemical structure of the stars, planets, etc. खगोल-भौतिकी

**astute** /əˈstjuːt अˈस्ट्यूट्/ *adj.* very clever; good at judging people or situations चतुर व होशियार, सयाना; व्यक्तियों या स्थितियों को परखने में कुशल

**asylum** /əˈsaɪləm अˈसाइलम्/ *noun* **1** [U] (*also* **political asylum**) protection that a government gives to people who have left their own country, usually because they were in danger for political reasons किसी राज्य या देश द्वारा अन्य देश के नागरिक को दी गई शरण (विशेषतः राजनैतिक कारणों से) *to seek/apply for/be granted asylum* ○ *the rights of* ***asylum seekers*** (= people asking for poitical asylum) **2** [C] (*old-fashioned*) a hospital where people who were mentally ill could be cared for, often for a long time मानसिक रोग चिकित्सालय

**asymmetric** /ˌeɪsɪˈmetrɪk ˌएसिˈमेट्रिक्/ (*also* **asymmetrical** /ˌeɪsɪˈmetrɪkl ˌएसिˈमेट्रिकल्/) *adj.* having two sides or parts that are not the same in size or shape जिसकी दो भुजाएँ या खंड आकार या आकृति में समान न हों; विषम, असममित ✪ विलोम **symmetrical** ▶ **asymmetrically** /-ɪkli -इकलि/ *adv.* असममित रूप से ▶ **asymmetry** /ˌeɪˈsɪmətri ˌएˈसिमट्रि/ *noun* [U] असममिति

**at** /ət; *strong form* æt अट्; प्रबल रूप ऐट्/ *prep.* **1** used to show where sb/sth is or where sth happens पर, में (स्थान का संदभ) *at the bottom/top of the page* ○ *He was standing at the door.* **2** used to show when sth happens में, पर (समय का संदभ) *I start work at 9 o'clock.* ○ *at the weekend* ○ *at night* **3** in the direction of sb/sth की ओर, पर (दिशा के संकेत का संदभ) *He pointed a gun at the policeman.* ○ *He shouted at me.* **4** because of sth पर (कारण बताने का संदभ) *I was surprised at her behaviour.* ○ *We laughed at his jokes.* **5** used to show what sb is doing or what is happening यह बताने के लिए प्रयुक्त कि कौन क्या कर रहा है या क्या हो रहा है *They were* ***hard at work***. ○ *The two countries were* ***at war***. **6** used to show the price, rate, speed, etc. of sth मूल्य, गति, दर आदि बताने के लिए प्रयुक्त *We were travelling at about 50 kilometers per hour.* **7** used with adjectives that show how well sb/sth does sth कोई क्या काम कितना अच्छा करता है, यह बताने के लिए विशेषण के साथ प्रयुक्त *She's not very* ***good at*** *French.*

**ate** ⇨ **eat** का past tense रूप

**atheism** /ˈeɪθiɪzəm ˈएथिइज़म्/ *noun* [U] the belief that there is no God नास्तिकवाद, निरीश्वरवाद ▸ **atheist** *noun* [C] नास्तिक, निरीश्वरवादी

**athlete** /ˈæθliːt ˈऐथ्लीट्/ *noun* [C] a person who can run, jump, etc. very well, especially one who takes part in sports competitions, etc. खेल-कूद प्रतियोगिताओं में भाग लेने वाला व्यक्ति

**athletic** /æθˈletɪk ऐथ्ˈलेटिक्/ *adj.* **1** connected with athletes or athletics खेल-कूद या खिलाड़ी से संबंधित *athletic ability* **2** (used about a person) having a fit, strong, and healthy body (व्यक्ति) बलिष्ठ, पुष्टकाय *athletic player*

**athletics** /æθˈletɪks ऐथ्ˈलेटिक्स्/ *noun* [U] sports such as running, jumping, throwing, etc. दौड़ना, कूदना, फेंकना आदि खेल

**atishoo** /əˈtɪʃuː अˈटिशू/ *exclamation* used to represent the sound that you make when you **sneeze** छींकने के समय मुख से निकलने वाली ध्वनि, अनुकरण मूलक शब्द 'छीं'

**atlas** /ˈætləs ˈऐट्लस्/ *noun* [C] (*pl.* **atlases**) a book of maps मानचित्रावली, एटलस *a road atlas of Delhi*

**ATM** /ˈei tiː ˌemˈ ऐ टी ˌएम्/ *abbr.* Automated Teller Machine—a machine in which you insert a special kind of plastic card to take out money from your bank account ऑटोमेटिड टैलर मशीन; एक ऐसी मशीन जिसमें एक विशेष प्लास्टिक कार्ड डालने पर धारक के बैंक खाते से पैसे की निकासी होती है

**atmosphere** /ˈætməsfɪə(r) ˈऐट्मस्फ़िअ(र्)/ *noun* **1** [C, *usually sing.*] the mixture of gases that surrounds the earth or any other star, planet, etc. पृथ्वी या किसी अन्य ग्रह आदि का वायुमंडल *the earth's atmosphere* **2** [*sing.*] the air in a place किसी स्थान का वातावरण *a smoky atmosphere* **3** [*sing.*] the mood or feeling of a place or situation (मानसिक) वातावरण, मनः स्थिति, मनोदशा; भावनाएँ *The atmosphere of the meeting was relaxed.* **4** [C] (*technical*) a measurement of pressure दाब की एक माप

**atmospheric** /ˌætməsˈferɪk ˌऐट्मस्ˈफ़ेरिक्/ *adj.* **1** connected with the earth's atmosphere वायुमंडलीय **2** creating a particular feeling or emotion विशिष्ट मनःस्थितिकारक *atmospheric music*

**atoll** /ˈætɒl ˈऐटॉल्/ *noun* [C] an island shaped like a ring with a lake of salt water **a lagoon** in the middle प्रवालद्वीप

**atom** /ˈætəm ˈऐटम्/ *noun* [C] the smallest part into which an element can be divided किसी तत्त्व का सबसे सूक्ष्म भाग; परमाणु ➪ **molecule** देखिए।

**atomic** /əˈtɒmɪk अˈटॉमिक्/ *adj.* of or concerning an atom or atoms परमाणु-विषयक, परमाण्विक *atomic physics* ➪ **nuclear** देखिए।

**atomic bomb** (*also* **atom bomb**) *noun* [C] a bomb that explodes using the energy that is produced when an atom or atoms are split परमाणु बम

**atomic energy** *noun* [U] the energy that is produced when an atom or atoms are split परमाणु ऊर्जा

**atomic mass** *noun* [C] the mass of an atom of a particular chemical substance परमाणु पिंड, पुंज या मात्रा, द्रव्यमान *Oxygen has an atomic mass of 16.*

**atomic number** *noun* [C] the number of **protons** that a chemical element has in its centre (**nucleus**) किसी रासायनिक तत्त्व के नाभि (केंद्र) में स्थित, घनात्मक विद्युत आवेश वाले प्रोटोनों की संख्या; परमाणु संख्या

**NOTE** मूल तत्त्वों को उनकी **atomic number** के अनुसार **periodic table** में संयोजित किया जाता है।

**atone** /əˈtəʊn अˈटोन्/ *verb* [I] (*formal*) **atone (for sth)** to show that you are sorry for doing sth wrong प्रायश्चित करना *to atone for your crimes* ▸ **atonement** *noun* [U] प्रायश्चित

**atrium** /ˈeɪtriəm ˈएट्रिअम्/ *noun* [C] **1** a large high open space in the centre of a modern building किसी आधुनिक इमारत के मध्य भाग में स्थित बड़ा या ऊँचा प्रांगण **2** either of the two upper spaces in the heart अलिंद, प्रकोष्ठ ➪ **heart** पर चित्र देखिए।

**atrocious** /əˈtrəʊʃəs अˈट्रोशस्/ *adj.* extremely bad or unpleasant बहुत ख़राब या अप्रिय *atrocious weather* **2** very cruel and shocking अति निर्दयी और दहलाने वाला ▸ **atrociously** *adv.* बहुत बुरी रीति से, क्रूरतापूर्वक

**atrocity** /əˈtrɒsəti अˈट्रॉसटि/ *noun* [C, U] (*pl.* **atrocities**) (an act of) very cruel treatment of sb/sth अति क्रूर व्यवहार, अत्याचार, पाशविक कृत्य *Both sides were accused of committing atrocities during the war.*

**atrophy** /ˈætrəfi ˈऐट्रफ़ि/ *noun* [U] (*medical*) the medical condition of losing flesh, muscle, strength, etc. in a part of the body because it does not have enough blood रक्त की कमी के कारण उत्पन्न शरीर के क्षीण होते जाने की स्थिति; अपुष्टि, क्षय

**attach** /əˈtætʃ अˈटैच्/ *verb* [T] **1 attach sth (to sth)** to fasten or join sth to sth जोड़ना, लगाना, बाँधना *I attached a label to each bag.* ✪ विलोम **detach** **2** (*usually passive*) **attach sb/sth to sb/sth** to make sb/sth join or belong to sb/sth (*usually passive*) से संबद्ध करना या होना *The research centre is attached to the university.* **3 attach sth to**

**sb/sth** to think that sth has a particular quality किसी वस्तु में कोई विशेषता या गुण देखना *Don't attach too much importance to what they say.*

**IDM** **(with) no strings attached; without strings** ⇨ **string** देखिए।

**attaché** /əˈtæʃeɪ अˈटैशे/ *noun* [C] a person who works in an **embassy** and who usually has special responsibility for a particular area of activity दूतावास का वह अधिकारी जिसे विशेष दायित्व सौंपा जाता है *a cultural/military attaché*

**attached** /əˈtætʃt अˈटैच्ट्/ *adj.* **attached to sb/sth** liking sb/sth very much अनुरक्त, लगाव-युक्त

**attachment** /əˈtætʃmənt अˈटैच्मन्ट्/ *noun* **1** [C] something that you can fit on sth else to make it do a different job संलग्न वस्तु *an electric drill with a range of attachments* **2** [C, U] **attachment (to/for sb/sth)** the feeling of liking sb/sth very much किसी व्यक्ति या वस्तु से लगाव; जुड़ाव *emotional attachment* **3** [C] (*computing*) a document that you send to sb using **email** ई-पत्र के साथ प्रेषित दस्तावेज़, फ़ोटो आदि सामग्री

**attack[1]** /əˈtæk अˈटैक्/ *noun* **1** [C, U] **(an) attack (on sb/sth)** trying to hurt or defeat sb/sth by using force आक्रमण, हमला *The town was* ***under attack from*** *all sides.* **2** [C, U] **(an) attack (on sb/sth)** an act of saying strongly that you do not like or agree with sb/sth कटु आलोचना *an outspoken attack on government policy* **3** [C] a short period when you suffer badly from a disease, medical condition, etc. (किसी रोग का) दौरा *an attack of asthma/flu/nerves* **4** [C] the act of trying to score a point in a game of sport (खेल में) धावा

**attack[2]** /əˈtæk अˈटैक्/ *verb* **1** [I, T] to try to hurt or defeat sb/sth by using force हमला या आक्रमण करना *The child was attacked by a dog.* **2** [T] to say strongly that you do not like or agree with sb/sth जोरदार ढंग से असहमति या अरुचि प्रकट करना **3** [T] to damage or harm sb/sth हानि पहुँचाना *a virus that attacks the nervous system* **4** [I, T] to try to score a point in a game of sport (खेल में) धावा बोलना *This team attacks better than it defends.*

**attacker** /əˈtækə(r) अˈटैक(र्)/ *noun* [C] a person who tries to hurt sb using force हमलावर, आक्रमणकारी *The victim of the assault didn't recognize his attackers.*

**attain** /əˈteɪn अˈटेन्/ *verb* [T] to succeed in getting or achieving sth, especially after a lot of effort (किसी कार्य या वस्तु को) करने या पाने में सफल होना, विशेषतः काफ़ी प्रयत्न के बाद

**attainable** /əˈteɪnəbl अˈटेनबल्/ *adj.* that can be achieved प्राप्य, साध्य *realistically attainable targets*

**attainment** /əˈteɪnmənt अˈटेन्मन्ट्/ *noun* **1** [U] the act of achieving sth प्राप्ति, सिद्धि *the attainment of the government's objectives* **2** [C] a skill or sth you have achieved कौशल आदि की सिद्धि

**attempt[1]** /əˈtempt अˈटेम्प्ट्/ *verb* [T] **attempt (to do) sth** to try to do sth that is difficult (कोई कठिन कार्य) करने का प्रयत्न करना *She was accused of attempted murder.* ○ *Don't attempt to make him change his mind.*

**attempt[2]** /əˈtempt अˈटेम्प्ट्/ *noun* [C] **1 an attempt (to do sth/at doing sth)** an act of trying to do sth प्रयत्न, प्रयास, कोशिश *The thief* ***made no attempt*** *to run away.* **2 an attempt (on sb/sth)** trying to attack or beat sb/sth किसी व्यक्ति या वस्तु पर हमला करने या उसे मारने की कोशिश *an attempt on sb's life*

**IDM** **a last-ditch attempt** ⇨ **last[1]** देखिए।

**attend** /əˈtend अˈटेन्ड्/ *verb* **1** [T] to go to or be present at a place (किसी स्थान पर) जाना या उपस्थित रहना *The children attend the local school.* **2** [I] (*formal*) **attend to sb/sth** to give your care, thought or attention to sb/sth or look after sb/sth किसी बात पर ध्यान देना या ग़ौर करना, किसी की देखभाल करना; किसी कार्य को निपटाना *Please attend to this matter immediately.*

**attendance** /əˈtendəns अˈटेन्डन्स्/ *noun* **1** [U] being present somewhere उपस्थिति, हाज़िरी *Attendance at lectures is compulsory.* **2** [C, U] the number of people who go to or are present at a place उपस्थित व्यक्तियों की संख्या; उपस्थिति *There was a poor attendance at the meeting.*

**attendant[1]** /əˈtendənt अˈटेन्डन्ट्/ *noun* [C] a person whose job is to serve or help people in a public place (सार्वजनिक स्थान पर) सेवक, परिचारक *a car park attendant*

**attendant[2]** /əˈtendənt अˈटेन्डन्ट्/ *adj.* (*only before a noun*) (*formal*) that goes together with or results from sth सहवर्ती, सहगामी, आनुषंगिक *unemployment and all its attendant social problems*

**attention[1]** /əˈtenʃn अˈटेन्शन्/ *noun* [U] **1** watching, listening to or thinking about sb/sth carefully ध्यान, मनोयोग *Shy people hate to be* ***the centre of attention****.* ○ *to hold sb's attention* **2** special care or action विशेष सावधानी या कार्रवाई *The hole in the roof needs urgent attention.* ○ *to require* ***medical attention*** **3** a position in which a soldier stands up straight and still (सैनिक की) सावधान मुद्रा *to stand/come to attention*

**IDM catch sb's attention/eye** ➪ **catch¹** देखिए। **draw (sb's) attention to sth** ➪ **draw¹** देखिए। **pay attention** ➪ **pay¹** देखिए।

**attention²** /əˈtenʃn अˈटेन्शन्/ *exclamation* used for asking people to listen to sth carefully 'ध्यान से सुनिए' के लिए प्रयुक्त शब्द

**attentive** /əˈtentɪv अˈटेन्टिव्/ *adj.* **attentive (to sb/sth)** watching, listening to or thinking about sb/sth carefully सावधान, सतर्क, चौकन्ना, एकाग्र ✪ विलोम **inattentive** ▶ **attentively** *adv.* सावधानी से *to listen attentively to sth*

**attest** /əˈtest अˈटेस्ट्/ *verb* [I, T] (*formal*) **1 attest (to sth)** to show that sth is true किसी बात की सत्यता को प्रमाणित करना; सत्यापित करना, तसदीक़ करना *Her long fight against cancer attested to her courage.* **2** to state that you believe that sth is true or genuine, for example in a court of law साक्ष्यांकित करना, किसी बात की गवाही देना, जैसे न्यायालय में *The signature was attested by two witnesses.*

**attic** /ˈætɪk ˈऐटिक्/ *noun* [C] the space or room just under the roof of a house often used for storing things अटारी ➪ **loft** देखिए।

**attire** /əˈtaɪə(r) अˈटाइअ(र्)/ *noun* [U] (*formal*) clothes वस्त्र, कपड़े, पोशाक

**attitude** /ˈætɪtjuːd ˈऐटिट्यूड्/ *noun* [C] **an attitude (to/towards sb/sth)** the way that you think, feel or behave सोचने, अनुभव करने का तरीक़ा विशेष; रुख, अभिवृत्ति, मनोवृत्ति, दृष्टिकोण *She has a very positive attitude to her work.*

**attn** *abbr.* (used in writing) 'for the attention of' (लेखन में प्रयुक्त) किसी के अवधान के लिए *Sales Dept, attn Rahul Garg*

**attorney** /əˈtɜːni अˈटनि/ (*AmE*) = **lawyer**

**attract** /əˈtrækt अˈट्रैक्ट्/ *verb* [T] **1** to cause sb/sth to go to sth or give attention to sth आकर्षित करना; आकृष्ट करना; लुभाना *Moths are attracted to light.* ○ *The new film has attracted a lot of publicity.* **2** (*usually passive*) to cause sb to like sb/sth आकृष्ट होना *Small children are attracted to bright colours.*

**attraction** /əˈtrækʃn अˈट्रैक्शन्/ *noun* **1** [U] a feeling of liking sb/sth आकर्षण *tourist attraction* **2** [C] sth that is interesting or enjoyable मोहक या आकर्षक वस्तु *The city offers all kinds of tourist attractions.* **3** [U] a force which pulls things towards each other खिंचाव, आकर्षणशक्ति *gravitational/magnetic attraction* ➪ **repulsion** देखिए तथा **magnet** पर चित्र देखिए।

**attractive** /əˈtræktɪv अˈट्रैक्टिव्/ *adj.* **1** that pleases or interests you; that you like दिलचस्प, मोहक; रुचिकर *an attractive part of the country* **2** (used about a person) beautiful or nice to look at (व्यक्ति) आकर्षक, मोहक ▶ **attractively** *adv.* आकर्षक रूप से ▶ **attractiveness** *noun* [U] आकर्षकता, मनोहारिता

**attributable** /əˈtrɪbjətəbl अˈट्रिब्यटबल्/ *adj.* (*not before a noun*) (*written*) **attributable to sb/sth** probably caused by the thing mentioned संभवतः उल्लिखित कारण से उत्पन्न; आरोप्य *Their illnesses are attributable to poor diet.*

**attribute¹** /əˈtrɪbjuːt अˈट्रिब्यूट्/ *verb* [T] **attribute sth to sb/sth** to believe that sth was caused or done by sb/sth कारण ठहरना, उत्तरदायी मानना, श्रेय देना *Kohli attributes his success to hard work.* ○ *a poem attributed to Shakespeare*

**attribute²** /ˈætrɪbjuːt ˈऐट्रिब्यूट्/ *noun* [C] a quality of sb/sth; a feature गुण; विशेषता, लक्षण *physical attributes*

**attributive** /əˈtrɪbjətɪv अˈट्रिब्यटिव्/ *adj.* (*grammar*) (*used about adjectives or nouns*) used before a noun to describe it संज्ञा के वर्णन के लिए संज्ञा से पहले प्रयुक्त; विशेषणात्मक *In 'the blue sky' and 'a family business', 'blue' and 'family' are attributive.* ➪ **predicative** देखिए। ▶ **attributively** *adv.* विशेषणात्मक तरीक़े से

**attrition** /əˈtrɪʃn अˈट्रिशन्/ *noun* [U] **1** (*formal*) a process of making sb/sth, especially your enemy, weaker by attacking him/her/it or causing problems for him/her/it over a period of time समय-समय पर आक्रमण करते रहकर या उलझनें पैदा कर शत्रु को दुर्बल बनाने की प्रक्रिया *It was a **war of attrition**.* **2** (*technical*) the gradual removal of material from a mass by moving against it over a long period of time किसी वस्तु के काफ़ी समय तक रगड़ खाने से क्रमिक क्षय की प्रक्रिया *The teeth show signs of attrition.* ➪ **erode** पर चित्र देखिए।

**atypical** /ˌeɪˈtɪpɪkl ˌएˈटिपिकल्/ *adj.* (*formal*) not typical of a particular type, group, etc. अपनी क़िस्म से अलग; अप्रतीकी, अप्रतिनिधिक ✪ विलोम **typical** ➪ **untypical** देखिए।

**aubergine** /ˈəʊbəʒiːn ˈओबश़ीन्/ (*AmE* **eggplant**) a round or long vegetable with dark purple skin बैंगन ➪ **vegetable** पर चित्र देखिए।

**auburn** /ˈɔːbən ˈऑबन्/ *adj.* (used about hair) reddish-brown (बालों का) लाल-भूरा रंग

**auction¹** /ˈɔːkʃn ˈऑक्शन्/ *noun* [C, U] a public sale at which items are sold to the person who

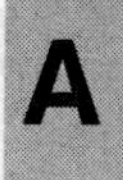



offers to pay the most money सार्वजनिक रूप से बेचने की प्रक्रिया जिस में सब से अधिक बोली लगाने वाले को माल मिलता है; नीलामी *The house was sold **at/by auction**.*

**auction**[2] /ˈɔːkʃn ˈऑक्शन्/ *verb* [T] **auction sth (off)** to sell sth at an auction नीलाम करना

**auctioneer** /ˌɔːkʃəˈnɪə(r) ˌऑक्शˈनिअ(र्)/ *noun* [C] a person who organizes the selling at an auction नीलामकर्ता

**audacious** /ɔːˈdeɪʃəs ऑˈडेशस्/ *adj.* (*written*) willing to take risks or do sth shocking ख़तरा उठाने या स्तब्धकारी कार्य करने को तैयार; निर्भीक, निडर *an audacious decision* ▶ **audaciously** *adv.* निडरता से, निर्भीकतापूर्वक

**audacity** /ɔːˈdæsəti ऑˈडैसटि/ *noun* [U] behaviour that risks being shocking स्तब्ध कर देने वाला आचरण या व्यवहार *He **had the audacity to** tell me I was rude!*

**audible** /ˈɔːdəbl ˈऑडब्ल्/ *adj.* that can be heard श्रव्य; सुनी जा सकने योग्य *Her speech was **barely audible**.* ✪ विलोम **inaudible** ▶ **audibly** /-əbli -अब्लि/ *adv.* सुनाई पड़ने लायक

**audience** /ˈɔːdiəns ˈऑडिअन्स्/ *noun* [C] **1** all the people who are watching or listening to a play, concert, speech, the television, etc. श्रोतागण, दर्शकगण *The audience was/were wild with excitement.* ○ *There were only about 200 people in the audience.* **2** a formal meeting with a very important person किसी अति महत्त्वपूर्ण व्यक्ति के साथ औपचारिक साक्षात्कार, दर्शन, भेंट *He was granted an audience with the President.*

**audio** /ˈɔːdiəʊ ˈऑडिओ/ *adj.* connected with the recording of sound ध्वनि को रिकार्ड करने से संबंधित *audio equipment* ○ *audio tape*

**audio-** /ˈɔːdiəʊ ˈऑडिओ/ *prefix* (*in nouns, adjectives and adverbs*) connected with hearing or sound श्रवणशक्ति या ध्वनि से संबंधित *audio-visual* ○ *an audio book* (= recording of a book that has been read aloud)

**audio-visual** *adj.* using both sound and pictures श्रव्य और दृश्य दोनों का प्रयोग करते हुए; दृश्य-श्रव्य

**audit** /ˈɔːdɪt ˈऑडिट्/ *noun* [C] an official examination of the present state of sth, especially of a company's financial records वर्तमान स्थिति की आधिकारिक जाँच, विशेषतः संस्था के हिसाब-किताब की; अंकेक्षण, लेखा-परीक्षण *to carry out an audit*

**audition**[1] /ɔːˈdɪʃn ऑˈडिश्न्/ *noun* [C] a short performance by a singer, actor, etc. to find out if he/she is good enough to be in a play, show, etc. परीक्षण हेतु गायक, अभिनेता आदि का लघु कला-प्रदर्शन

**audition**[2] /ɔːˈdɪʃn ऑˈडिश्न्/ *verb* [I, T] **audition (sb) (for sth)** to do or to watch sb do an audition परीक्षणात्मक कला-प्रदर्शन करना या देखना *I auditioned for a part in the play.*

**auditor** /ˈɔːdɪtə(r) ˈऑडिट(र्)/ *noun* [C] a person whose job is to examine a company's financial records किसी संस्था के हिसाब-किताब की आधिकारिक रूप से जाँच करने वाला व्यक्ति; अंकेक्षक, लेखा-परीक्षक

**auditorium** /ˌɔːdɪˈtɔːriəm ˌऑडिˈटॉरिअम्/ *noun* [C] (*pl.* **auditoriums** या **auditoria** /-riə -रिआ/) the part of a theatre, concert hall, etc. where the audience sits सिनेमा, रंगशाला आदि में दर्शकों के बैठने का स्थान; श्रोताकक्ष, प्रेक्षागृह

**au fait** /ˌəʊˈfeɪ ˌओˈफ़े/ *adj.* (*not before a noun*) completely familiar with sth किसी बात से पूर्णतः परिचित *Are you au fait with this type of computer system?*

**Aug.** *abbr.* August अगस्त *15 Aug. 1950*

**augment** /ɔːgˈment ऑग्ˈमेन्ट्/ *verb* [T] (*formal*) to increase the amount, value, size, etc. of sth किसी वस्तु का मूल्य, संख्या आकार आदि बढ़ाना

**augur** /ˈɔːgə(r) ˈऑग(र्)/ *verb*

IDM **augur well/ill for sb/sth** (*formal*) to be a good/bad sign of what will happen in the future भविष्य के लिए शुभ या अशुभ का संकेत होना

**August** /ˈɔːgəst ˈऑगस्ट्/ *noun* [U, C] (*abbr.* **Aug.**) the eighth month of the year, coming after July साल का आठवाँ महीना; अगस्त

NOTE महीनों का वाक्यों में प्रयोग कैसे होता है, यह जानने के लिए **January** पर नोट देखिए।

**aunt** /ɑːnt आन्ट्/ (*informal* **auntie; aunty** /ˈɑːnti; ˈआन्टि/) *noun* [C] the sister of your father or mother; the wife of your uncle माता या पिता की बहन; माता या पिता के भाई की पत्नी; बुआ, मौसी, चाची *Aunt Romilla*

**aura** /ˈɔːrə ˈऑरा/ *noun* [C] (*formal*) the distinct quality that seems to surround or come from somebody or something किसी व्यक्ति या वस्तु से जुड़ा विशेष गुण जो उसके भिन्न होने का आभास कराए; प्रभामंडल *These hills have a magical aura.*

**aural** /ˈɔːrəl ˈऑरल्/ *adj.* connected with hearing and listening श्रवण-संबंधी *an aural comprehension test* ⇨ **oral** देखिए। ▶ **aurally** *adj.* श्रवणगत रीति से

**auricle** /ˈɔːrɪkl ˈऑरिकल्/ *noun* [C] (*technical*) **1** either of the two upper spaces in the heart used to send blood around the body हृदय का उपरि-गह्वर जिसमें से रक्त प्रवाहित होकर सारे शरीर में जाता है **2** the outer part of the ear कान का बाहरी भाग; बहिकर्ण

**auspices** /ˈɔːspɪsɪz ˈऑस्पिसिज़्/ *noun* [*pl.*]
IDM **under the auspices of sb/sth** with the help and support of sb/sth किसी व्यक्ति या वस्तु की सहायता व समर्थन से; के तत्वाधान में

**auspicious** /ɔːˈspɪʃəs ऑˈस्पिशस्/ *adj.* that seems likely to be successful in the future भविष्य में सफल होने की संभावना लिए; सौभाग्यशाली, मांगलिक ✪ विलोम **inauspicious**

**austere** /ɒˈstɪə(r) ऑˈस्टिअ(र्)/ *adj.* **1** very simple; without decoration अति साधारण और सरल; आडंबरहीन, मितव्ययी **2** (used about a person) very strict and serious (व्यक्ति) अतिसंयमी और गंभीर **3** not having anything that makes your life more comfortable कठोर, सुख-सुविधा-रहित *The nuns lead simple and austere lives.* ▸ **austerity** /ɒˈsterəti ऑˈस्टेरटि/ *noun* [U] संयम, कठोरता, आडंबरहीनता

**Australasian** /ˌɒstrəˈleɪʒn; -ˈleɪʃn ˌऑस्ट्रˈलेश्न्; -ˈलेश्न्/ *adj.* of or from Australia and the islands of the south west Pacific ऑस्ट्रेलिया और उसके निकटवर्ती द्वीपों से संबंधित; ऑस्ट्रेलेशियाई

**authentic** /ɔːˈθentɪk ऑˈथ़ेन्टिक्/ *adj.* **1** that you know is real or genuine प्रामाणिक, असली *an authentic painting* **2** true or accurate सच्चा, सही *an authentic model of the building* ▸ **authenticity** /ˌɔːθenˈtɪsəti ˌऑथ़ेन्ˈटिसटि/ *noun* [U] प्रामाणिकता, असलियत, सच्चाई

**authenticate** /ɔːˈθentɪkeɪt ऑˈथ़ेन्टिकेट्/ *verb* [T] to produce evidence to show that sth is genuine, real or true (सच्चाई या असलियत को) प्रमाणित करना *The picture has been authenticated as a genuine Hussain.*

**author** /ˈɔːθə(r) ˈऑथ़(र्)/ *noun* [C] a person who writes a book, play, etc. लेखक, रचयिता *a well-known author of detective novels* ▸ **authorship** *noun* [U] कर्तृत्व, प्रवर्तकता, लेखक की पहचान

**authoritarian** /ɔːˌθɒrɪˈteəriən ऑˌथ़ॉरिˈटेअरिअन्/ *adj.* not allowing people the freedom to decide things for themselves सत्तावादी, अधिकारवादी *authoritarian parents*

**authoritative** /ɔːˈθɒrətətɪv ऑˈथ़ॉरटटिव़्/ *adj.* **1** having authority; demanding or expecting that people obey you अधिकारिक; आदेशात्मक, आज्ञासूचक *an authoritative tone of voice* **2** that you can trust because it/he/she has a lot of knowledge and information प्रमाणपुष्ट; प्रामाणिक तथा विश्वसनीय *They will be able to give you authoritative advice on the problem.*

**authority** /ɔːˈθɒrəti ऑˈथ़ॉरटि/ *noun* (*pl.* **authorities**) **1** [U] the power and right to give orders and make others obey आदेश देने और उसका पालन कराने का अधिकार *You must get this signed by a person **in authority*** (= who has the position of power). **2** [U] **authority (to do sth)** the right or permission to do sth कुछ करने का अधिकार या अनुमति *The police **have the authority** to question anyone they wish.* **3** [C] (*usually pl.*) a person, group or government department that has the power to give orders, make official decisions, etc. अधिकारी, अधिकारी वर्ग, सरकारी विभाग *I have to report this to the authorities.* **4** [U] a quality that sb has which makes it possible to influence and control other people अन्य व्यक्तियों पर प्रभाव डालने व उन्हें नियंत्रित करने का गुण *He spoke with authority and everybody listened.* **5** [C] **an authority (on sth)** a person with special knowledge (किसी विषय का) विशेषज्ञ *He's an authority on criminal law.*

**authorize** (*also* **-ise**) /ˈɔːθəraɪz ˈऑथ़राइज़्/ *verb* [T] to give official permission for sth or for sb to do sth कुछ करने का अधिकार देना; आधिकारिक रूप से अनुमति देना *He authorized his secretary to sign letters in his absence.* ▸ **authorization** (*also* **-isation**) /ˌɔːθəraɪˈzeɪʃn ˈऑथ़राइˈज़ेश्न्/ *noun* [U] प्राधिकार

**autism** /ˈɔːtɪzəm ˈऑटिज़म्/ *noun* [U] a mental condition in which a person finds it difficult to communicate or form relationships with other people मानसिक स्वास्थ्य की वह दशा जिसमें व्यक्ति अन्य व्यक्तियों से संबंध बनाने या उनसे विचारों का आदान-प्रदान करने में कठिनाई अनुभव करता है ▸ **autistic** /ɔːˈtɪstɪk ऑˈटिस्टिक/ *adj.* इस दशा से संबंधित *autistic behaviour/children*

**auto-** /ˈɔːtəʊ ˈऑटो/ (*also* **aut-**) *prefix* (*in nouns, adjectives and adverbs*) **1** about or by yourself अपने बारे में, स्वयं *an autobiography* **2** by itself without a person to operate it स्वयं-चालित, स्वचालित *automatic*

**autobiography** /ˌɔːtəbaɪˈɒgrəfi ˌऑटबाइˈऑग्रफ़ि/ *noun* [C, U] (*pl.* **autobiographies**) the story of a person's life written by that person आत्मकथा, आत्मचरित ➪ **biography** देखिए। ▸ **autobiographical** /ˌɔːtəˌbaɪəˈgræfɪkl ˌऑटˌबाइअˈग्रैफ़िक्ल्/ *adj.* आत्मकथात्मक, आत्मचरितात्मक

**autocracy** /ɔːˈtɒkrəsi ऑˈटॉक्रसि/ *noun* **1** [U] a system of government of a country in which one person has complete power एकतंत्र, निरंकुशता **2** [C] (*pl.* **autocracies**) a country that is ruled by one person who has complete power निरंकुश राज्य, एकतंत्रीय राष्ट्र

**autocrat** /ˈɔːtəkræt ˈऑटक्रैट्/ *noun* [C] **1** a ruler who has complete power पूर्णसत्ता संपन्न शासक, स्वेच्छाचारी शासक, निरंकुश शासक ➪ **despot** देखिए। **2** a person who expects to be obeyed by other people and does not care about their opinions or feelings अन्य व्यक्तियों से पूर्ण आज्ञाकारिता की अपेक्षा रखने वाला व्यक्ति; अधिनायक, तानाशाह ▶ **autocratic** /ˌɔːtəˈkrætɪk ˌऑटˈक्रैटिक्/ *adj.* निरंकुश, एकतंत्रीय

**autograph** /ˈɔːtəgrɑːf ˈऑटग्राफ़्/ *noun* [C] the signature of a famous person किसी प्रसिद्ध व्यक्ति के स्वाक्षर; हस्ताक्षर *The players stopped outside the stadium to **sign autographs**.* ▶ **autograph** *verb* [T] स्वाक्षर करना *The whole team have autographed the football.*

**autoimmune** /ˌɔːtəʊɪˈmjuːn ˌऑटोइˈम्यून्/ *adj.* (*only before a noun*) (*medical*) an **autoimmune** disease or medical condition is one which is caused by substances that usually prevent illness रोगप्रतिरोधी पदार्थों से उत्पन्न (रोग या स्वास्थ्य-दशा)

**automate** /ˈɔːtəmeɪt ˈऑटमेट्/ *verb* [T] (*usually passive*) to make sth operate by machine, without needing people मशीन द्वारा परिचालित होने योग्य बनाना

**automatic[1]** /ˌɔːtəˈmætɪk ˌऑटˈमैटिक्/ *adj.* **1** (used about a machine) that can work by itself without direct human control (मशीन) स्वयं-चालित *an automatic washing machine* **2** done without thinking बिना पहले सोचे किया (काम); अविचारित (कार्य) **3** always happening as a result of a particular action or situation स्वयंभू *All the staff have an automatic right to a space in the car park.* ▶ **automatically** /ˌɔːtəˈmætɪkli ˌऑटˈमैटिक्लि/ *adv.* यंत्रवत, अपने आप *The lights will come on automatically when it gets dark.*

**automatic[2]** /ˌɔːtəˈmætɪk ˌऑटˈमैटिक्/ *noun* [C] an automatic machine, gun or car स्वयं-चालित मशीन, बंदूक़ या कार *This car is an automatic.*

**automation** /ˌɔːtəˈmeɪʃn ˌऑटˈमेश्न्/ *noun* [U] the use of machines instead of people to do work मानव के स्थान पर मशीन का प्रयोग; मशीनी परिचालन

**automobile** /ˈɔːtəməbiːl ˈऑटमबील्/ (*AmE*) = **car[1]**

**autonomy** /ɔːˈtɒnəmi ऑˈटॉनमि/ *noun* [U] the right of a person, an organization, a region, etc. to govern or control his/her/its own affairs स्वायत्तता, स्वशासन ▶ **autonomous** /ɔːˈtɒnəməs ऑˈटॉनमस्/ *adj.* स्वायत्त; आंतरिक मामलों में स्वतंत्र

**autopsy** /ˈɔːtɒpsi ˈऑटॉप्सि/ *noun* [C] (*pl.* **autopsies**) an examination of a dead body to find out the cause of death मृत्यु का कारण जानने के लिए की गई शव-परीक्षा

**auto-rickshaw** (*also* **scooter**, **auto**) *noun* [C] (*IndE*) a covered motor vehicle that has three wheels, a driver's seat in front and a long seat for passengers at the back आवृत तिपहिया वाहन, जिसमें चालक आगे बैठता है और सवारियाँ लंबी सीट पर पीछे बैठती हैं; ऑटोरिक्शा

**autotroph** /ˈɔːtətrəʊf ˈऑटट्रोफ़्/ *noun* [C] (*technical*) a living thing that is able to feed itself using simple chemical substances such as **carbon dioxide** कार्बन डाइऑक्साइड जैसे रसायन से आत्म पोषण प्राप्त करने वाली सजीव वस्तु

**autumn** /ˈɔːtəm ˈऑटम्/ (*AmE* **fall**) *noun* [C, U] the season of the year that comes between summer and winter पतझड़ (मौसम) *In autumn the leaves on the trees begin to fall.* ➪ **season** पर चित्र देखिए। ▶ **autumnal** /ɔːˈtʌmnəl ऑˈटम्नल्/ *adj.* पतझड़कालीन

**auxiliary** /ɔːgˈzɪliəri ऑग्ˈज़िलिअरि/ *adj.* (*usually before a noun*) giving extra help अतिरिक्त सहायता देते हुए; सहायक, पूरक, अतिरिक्त *auxiliary nurses/troops/staff*

**auxiliary verb** *noun* [C] (*grammar*) a verb (for example *be, do* or *have*) that is used with a main verb to show tense, etc. or to form questions सहायक क्रिया जो मुख्य क्रिया के साथ प्रयुक्त होती है काल का संकेत, प्रश्न का अर्थ आदि देने के लिए

**auxin** /ˈɔːksɪn ˈऑक्सिन्/ *noun* [U] a chemical substance in plants that helps control their growth पौधों में पाया जाने वाला रसायन जो उनकी वृद्धि को नियंत्रित करने में सहायक होता है

**avail** /əˈveɪl अˈवेल्/ *noun* [U]

IDM **of little/no avail** not helpful; having little or no effect निरर्थक, बेकार

**to little/no avail** without success असफल *They searched everywhere, but to no avail.*

**availability** /əˌveɪləˈbɪləti अˌवेलˈबिलटि/ *noun* [U] the state of being available उपलब्ध होने की स्थिति; सुलभता, प्राप्यता *You will receive the colour you order, subject to availability* (= if it is available).

**available** /əˈveɪləbl अˈवेलबल्/ *adj.* **1 available (to sb)** (used about things) that you can get, buy, use, etc. उपलब्ध, (वस्तुएँ) *This information is easily available to everyone at the local library.* ○ *Refreshments are available at the snack bar.* **2** (used about people) free to be seen, talked to, etc. (व्यक्ति) बातचीत आदि के लिए उपलब्ध, सुलभ *The minister was not available for comment.*

**avalanche** /ˈævəlɑːnʃ ˈऐवलान्श् / *noun* [C] a very large amount of snow that slides quickly down the side of a mountain (पहाड़ों पर से) गिरती हुई बर्फ़ की चट्टानें; हिम-स्खलन

**the avant-garde** /ˌævɒ̃ ˈɡɑːd ˌऐवाँ ˈगाड् / *noun* [*sing.*] extremely modern works of art, music or literature, or the artists who create these अत्याधुनिक कलाकृति या कलाकार ▶ **avant-garde** *adj.* इस तरह की कला या कलाकार से संबंधित

**avarice** /ˈævərɪs ˈऐवरिस् / *noun* [U] (*formal*) extreme desire for money अत्यधिक धन-लोलुप ✪ पर्याय **greed** ▶ **avaricious** /ˌævəˈrɪʃəs ˌऐवˈरिशस् / *adj.* लालची, धन-लोलुप

**Ave.** *abbr.* Avenue पथ, मार्ग, वृक्ष-विधि *26 Central Ave.*

**avenge** /əˈvendʒ अˈव्रेन्ज् / *verb* [T] **avenge sth; avenge yourself on sb** to punish sb for hurting you, your family, etc. in some way बदला लेना, प्रतिशोध लेना *He wanted to avenge his father's murder.* ○ *He wanted to avenge himself on his father's murderer.* ➪ **revenge** देखिए।

**avenue** /ˈævənjuː ˈऐवन्यू / *noun* [C] **1** (*abbr.* **Ave.**) a wide street, especially one with trees or tall buildings on each side चौड़ी सड़क जिसके दोनों ओर पेड़ या ऊँची इमारतें हों *I live on Rashbehari Avenue.* ➪ **road** पर नोट देखिए। **2** a way of doing or getting sth कुछ करने या पाने का तरीक़ा, उपाय *We must explore every avenue open to us* (= try every possibility).

**average[1]** /ˈævərɪdʒ ˈऐवरिज् / *noun* **1** [C] the number you get when you add two or more figures together and then divide the total by the number of figures you added औसत संख्या *The average of 14, 3 and 1 is 6.* ○ *He has scored 93 goals at* ***an average of*** *1·55 per game.* **2** [*sing.*, U] the normal standard, amount or quality औसत या सामान्य मानक, मात्रा या गुण ***On average****, I buy a newspaper about twice a week.*

**average[2]** /ˈævərɪdʒ ˈऐवरिज् / *adj.* **1** (*only before a noun*) (used about a number) found by calculating the average (संख्या) औसत *What's the average age of your students?* **2** normal or typical सामान्य या प्रतिनिधिक ***above/below average*** *intelligence*

**average[3]** /ˈævərɪdʒ ˈऐवरिज् / *verb* [T] to do, get, etc. a certain amount as an average औसत निकालना *If we average 50 kilometre an hour we should arrive at about 4 o'clock.*

**PHR V** **average out (at sth)** to result in an average (of sth) औसत आना या निकलना

**averse** /əˈvɜːs अˈवस् / *adj.* (*formal*) **averse to sth** (*often with a negative*) against or not in favour of sth प्रतिकूल, असहमत, विरोधी *He is not averse to trying out new ideas.*

**aversion** /əˈvɜːʃn अˈवर्शन् / *noun* [C] **1** [*usually sing.*] **an aversion (to sb/sth)** a strong feeling of not liking sb/sth किसी व्यक्ति या वस्तु के प्रति विमुखता; विरुचि, विद्वेष *Most people* ***have an aversion*** *to spiders.* **2** a thing that you do not like अरुचिकर या नापसंद चीज़

**avert** /əˈvɜːt अˈवर्ट् / *verb* [T] to prevent sth unpleasant अप्रिय घटना को घटने से रोक लेना; अप्रिय स्थिति का निवारण करना, टालना *The accident could have been averted.*

**aviary** /ˈeɪviəri ˈएविअरि / *noun* [C] (*pl.* **aviaries**) a large cage or area in which birds are kept पक्षीशाला, दरबा

**aviation** /ˌeɪviˈeɪʃn ˌएविˈएशन् / *noun* [U] the designing, building and flying of aircraft विमान बनाने और उड़ाने की विद्या; वैमानिकी

**avid** /ˈævɪd ˈऐविड् / *adj.* **1** very enthusiastic about sth (usually a hobby) (किसी कार्य के प्रति) अत्युत्साही *an avid collector of antiques* **2 avid for sth** wanting to get sth very much कुछ पाने को अति-उत्सुक, अति-इच्छुक, उत्कंठित *Journalists crowded round the entrance, avid for news.* ▶ **avidly** *adv.* उत्कंठापूर्वक *He read avidly as a child.*

**avocado** /ˌævəˈkɑːdəʊ ˌऐवˈकाडो / *noun* [C] (*pl.* **avocados**) a tropical fruit that is wider at one end than the other, with a hard green skin and a large seed (**stone**) inside नाशपाती जैसा एक फल

**avoid** /əˈvɔɪd अˈव्रॉइड् / *verb* [T] **1 avoid sth/doing sth** to prevent sth happening or to try not to do sth कुछ होने से रोकना; कुछ करने से बचना *She has to avoid eating fatty food.* **2** to keep away from sb/sth किसी व्यक्ति, वस्तु या स्थिति से बच कर रहना *I leave home at 7 o'clock in order to avoid the rush hour.* ▶ **avoidance** *noun* [U] बचाव, परिहार

**avoidable** /əˈvɔɪdəbl अˈव्रॉइडबल् / *adj.* that can be prevented; unnecessary जिससे बचा जा सके; परिहार्य ✪ विलोम **unavoidable**

**avow** /əˈvaʊ अˈव्राउ / *verb* [I, T] (*formal*) to say firmly and often publicly what your opinion is, what you think is true, etc. दृढ़ता से कुछ खुले आम कहना, स्वीकार करना ▶ **avowal** /əˈvaʊəl अˈव्राउअल् / *noun* [C] (*formal*) स्वीकारोक्ति, स्पष्टोक्ति

**await** /əˈweɪt अˈवेट् / *verb* [T] (*formal*) to wait for sb/sth किसी की प्रतीक्षा करना *We sat down to await the arrival of the guests.*

**awake**[1] /ə'weɪk अ'वेक् / *verb* (*pt.* **awoke** /ə'wəʊk अ'वोक् /; *pp* **awoken** /ə'wəʊkən अ'वोकन् /) [I, T] to wake up; to make sb/sth wake up नींद से जागना; जगाना *I awoke to find that it was already 9 o'clock.* ○ *A sudden loud noise awoke us.* NOTE **Awake** की अपेक्षा **wake up** का प्रयोग अधिक किया जाता है।

**awake**[2] /ə'weɪk अ'वेक् / *adj.* (*not before a noun*) *not sleeping* जागा हुआ, जागृत *I was sleepy this morning but I'm* ***wide awake*** *now.* ○ *to* ***stay awake*** ○ *I hope our singing didn't* ***keep*** *you* ***awake*** *last night.* ✪ विलोम **asleep**

**awaken** /ə'weɪkən अ'वेकन् / *verb* **1** [I, T] (*written*) to wake up; to make sb/sth wake up नींद से जागना; जगाना *We were awakened by a loud knock at the door.* NOTE **Awaken** की अपेक्षा **wake up** का प्रयोग कहीं अधिक किया जाता है। **2** [T] (*formal*) to produce a particular feeling, attitude, etc. in sb (भावनाओं, मनोवृति आदि को) जगाना, जागृत करना *The film awakened memories of her childhood.*

PHR V **awaken sb to sth** to make sb notice or realize sth for the first time किसी को किसी बात के प्रति पहला अहसास दिलाना; जागरूक करना; सचेत करना, आगाह करना, सावधान करना

**awakening** /ə'weɪkənɪŋ अ'वेकनिङ् / *noun* [*sing.*] **1** the act of starting to feel or understand sth; the start of a feeling, etc. किसी भावना या समझ के सक्रिय होने की क्रिया; कुछ महसूस होने की क्रिया *the awakening of an interest in literature* **2** a moment when sb notices or realizes sth for the first time प्रथम बार कुछ अनुभव होने का क्षण *It was a rude* (= unpleasant) *awakening when I suddenly found myself unemployed.*

**award**[1] /ə'wɔːd अ'वॉड् / *noun* [C] **1** a prize, etc. that sb gets for doing sth well पुरस्कार, इनाम *This year the awards for best actor and actress went to two Americans.* **2** an amount of money given to sb as the result of a court decision न्यायालय के निर्णय के अनुसार किसी को दी गई धनराशि *She* ***received an award of*** *Rs 50,000 for damages.*

**award**[2] /ə'wɔːd अ'वॉड् / *verb* [T] **award sth (to sb)** to give sth to sb as a prize, payment, etc. पुरस्कार देना; धनराशि देना *She was awarded first prize in the gymnastics competition.*

**aware** /ə'weə(r) अ'वेअ(र्) / *adj.* **1 aware (of sb/sth); aware (that)** knowing about or realizing sth; conscious of sb/sth किसी बात का जानकार; किसी बात के विषय में सचेत *I am* ***well aware*** *of the problems you face.* ○ *There is no other entrance,* ***as far as I am aware.*** ✪ विलोम **unaware** **2** interested and informed इच्छुक और जानकार *Many young people are very politically aware.*

**awareness** /ə'weənəs अ'वेअनस् / *noun* [U] knowledge, consciousness or interest जानकारी, सतर्कता या दिलचस्पी *People's awareness of healthy eating has increased in recent years.*

**awash** /ə'wɒʃ अ'वॉश् / *adj.* (*not before a noun*) **awash (with sth)** covered with water; flooded जलप्लावित; परिपूर्ण *The city was awash with rumours.*

**away** /ə'weɪ अ'वे / *adv., adj.* **1 away (from sb/sth)** to a different place or in a different direction भिन्न स्थान या दिशा में; दूर *Go away! I'm busy!* ○ *I asked him a question, but he just looked away.* **2 away (from sth)** at a particular distance from a place एक स्थान से निश्चित दूरी पर; दूर *The village is two kilometres away from the sea.* ○ *My parents live five minutes away.* **3 away (from sth)** (used about people) not present; absent (व्यक्ति) अनुपस्थित, ग़ैर-हाज़िर *My neighbours are away on holiday at the moment.* **4** in the future भविष्य में *Our summer holiday is only three weeks away.* **5** into a place where sth is usually kept उस स्थान से जहाँ प्रायः कोई चीज़ रखी जाती है; से हटाकर *Put your books away now.* ➪ **throw sth away** देखिए। **6** continuously, without stopping लगातार, बिना रुके, निरंतर *They chatted away for hours.* **7** (used about a football, etc. match) on the other team's ground (फुटबॉल आदि मैच के संदर्भ में) दूसरी टीम के मैदान पर ○ *an away match/game* ✪ विलोम **(at) home** **8** until sth disappears किसी वस्तु, क्रिया आदि के लुप्त होने तक, निःशेष हो जाने तक *The crash of thunder slowly died away.* NOTE **give away, take away** भी देखिए।

IDM **do away with sb/sth** to get rid of sb/sth किसी व्यक्ति या वस्तु से छुटकारा पाना *The government are going to do away with the tax on fuel.*

**right/straight away** immediately; without any delay तुरंत, तत्काल; अविलंब *I'll phone the doctor right away.*

**awe** /ɔː ऑ/ *noun* [U] feelings of respect and either fear or admiration भय या प्रशंसा से प्रेरित आदर भाव *As a young boy he was very much in awe of his uncle.*

IDM **be in awe of sb/sth** to admire sb/sth and be slightly frightened of him/her/it कुछ डरते हुए से किसी के प्रति आदर भाव रखना

**awe-inspiring** *adj.* causing a feeling of respect and fear or admiration भय या प्रशंसा से प्रेरित आदर-भाव जगाने वाला

**awesome** /ˈɔːsəm ˈऑसम्/ *adj.* **1** impressive and sometimes frightening प्रभावशाली और कुछ डराने वाला-सा, अति विस्मयजनक *an awesome task* **2** (*AmE slang*) very good; excellent बहुत बढ़िया, शानदार; विस्मयकारी

**awful** /ˈɔːfl ˈऑफ़ल्/ *adj.* **1** very bad or unpleasant बहुत बुरा, अत्यधिक अरुचिकर *We had an awful holiday. It rained every day.* ○ *What an awful thing to say!* **2** terrible; very serious भयावह, भयंकर; बहुत गंभीर *I'm afraid there's been some awful news.* **3** (*only before a noun*) (*informal*) very great अत्यधिक *We've got* ***an awful lot*** *of work to do.*

**awfully** /ˈɔːfli ˈऑफ़लि/ *adv.* (*informal*) very; very much बहुत; बहुत अधिक *I'm awfully sorry.*

**awhile** /əˈwaɪl अˈवाइल्/ *adv.* for a short time लघु काल के लिए, कुछ समय के लिए *to wait awhile*

**awkward** /ˈɔːkwəd ˈऑक्वड्/ *adj.* **1** difficult to deal with निपटने में मुश्किल, कठिन, कष्टकर *an awkward position.* ○ *an awkward customer* ○ *The box isn't heavy but it's awkward to carry.* **2** not convenient, difficult असुविधाजनक, कष्टकर *My cousin always phones at an awkward time.* ○ *This tin-opener is very awkward to clean.* **3** embarrassed or embarrassing उलझनभरा, संकोच में डालने वाला *I often feel awkward in a group of people.* ○ *There was an awkward silence.* **4** not using the body in the best way; not elegant or comfortable शारीरिक अनुकूलता या शालीनता की चिंता न करते हुए; बेढंगेपन से या असुविधाजनक रूप से; भद्दा *I was sitting with my legs in an awkward position.* ▸ **awkwardly** *adv.* बेढंगे तरीक़े से ▸ **awkwardness** *noun* [U] बेढंगापन

**awning** /ˈɔːnɪŋ ˈऑनिङ्/ *noun* [C] a sheet of cloth or other material that stretches out from above a door or window to keep off the sun or rain सायबान, तिरपाल

**awoke** ➪ **awake**[1] का past tense रूप

**awoken** ➪ **awake**[1] का past participle रूप

**AWOL** /ˈeɪwɒl ˈऐवॉल्/ *abbr.* absent without leave (used especially when sb in the army, etc. has left his/her group without permission) 'absent without leave' का संक्षिप्त रूप (सेना के संदर्भ में) *He's gone AWOL from his base.*

**awry** /əˈraɪ अˈराइ/ *adv., adj.* (*not before a noun*) wrong, not in the way that was planned; untidy गलत, गडबड़; उलटा-पुलटा, अव्यवस्थित

**axe**[1] (*AmE* **ax**) /æks ˈएक्स्/ *noun* [C] a tool with a wooden handle and a heavy metal head with a sharp edge, used for cutting wood, etc. कुल्हाड़ी, कुल्हाड़ा, कुठार ➪ **gardening** पर चित्र देखिए।

**axe**[2] (*AmE* **ax**) /æks ˈएक्स्/ *verb* [T] **1** to remove sb/sth किसी वस्तु को हटा देना *Hundreds of jobs have been axed.* **2** to reduce sth by a great amount किसी वस्तु की मात्रा में अधिक कटौती कर देना *School budgets are to be axed.* **NOTE** समाचार-शीर्षकों में इस क्रिया का विशेष प्रयोग होता है।

**axiom** /ˈæksiəm ˈऐक्सिअम्/ *noun* [C] a rule or principle that most people believe to be true सब से स्वीकृत सिद्धांत या नियम; स्वयं सिद्ध कथन

**axiomatic** /ˌæksiəˈmætɪk ˈऐक्सिअˈमैटिक्/ *adj.* (*formal*) true in such an obvious way that you do not need evidence to show that it is true स्वतः सिद्ध (कथन आदि)

**axis** /ˈæksɪs ˈऐक्सिस्/ *noun* [C] (*pl.* **axes** /ˈæksiːz ˈऐक्सीज़्/) **1** a line we imagine through the middle of an object, around which the object turns किसी वस्तु के मध्य भाग में से जाती काल्पनिक रेखा जिसके चारों ओर वह वस्तु घूमती है; अक्ष *The earth rotates on its axis.* **2** a fixed line used for marking measurements on a **graph** ग्राफ़ पर माप अंकित करने के लिए प्रयुक्त स्थिर रेखा *the horizontal/vertical axis*

**axle** /ˈæksl ˈऐक्सल्/ *noun* [C] a bar that connects a pair of wheels on a vehicle धुरी; गाड़ी के दो पहियों को जोड़ने वाली कीली

**ayacut** *noun* [U] (*IndE*) the entire extent of land irrigated by a canal, dam or a tank नहर, बाँध या पोखर द्वारा सिंचित विस्तृत जमीन

**ayatollah** *noun* [C] a religious leader of Shiite Muslims in Iran ईरान के शिया मुसलमानों का धार्मिक नेता

**Ayurveda** *noun* [U] (*IndE*) the traditional Hindu system of medicine that uses a combination of diet, herbal treatment, and yogic breathing to treat illnesses आयुर्वेद

**azalea** /əˈzeɪliə अˈज़ेलिआ/ *noun* [C] a plant or bush with large flowers that may be pink, purple, white or yellow गुलाबी, बैंगनी, सफ़ेद या पीले रंग के बड़े फूलों वाला एक पौधा या झाड़ी

**azure** /ˈæʒə(r) ˈæzjʊə(r); ˈऐश़(र्) ˈऐज़ुअ(र्)/ *adj.* (*written*) bright blue in colour like the sky आसमानी रंग या रंग वाला; नभोनील ▸ **azure** *noun* [U] आसमानी रंग

# B b

**B, b** /biː बी / *noun* [C, U] (*pl.* **B's; b's** /biːz बीज़ /) the second letter of the English alphabet अंग्रेज़ी वर्णमाला का दूसरा अक्षर *'Bharat' begins with a 'B'.*

**b.** *abbr.* born जन्म *J S Bareja, b. 1928*

**BA** /ˌbiː ˈeɪ ˌबी ˈए / *abbr.* Bachelor of Arts; the degree that you receive when you complete a university or college course in an arts subject बी.ए., आर्ट्स विषय के कॉलेज या विश्वविद्यालय के पाठ्यक्रम की समाप्ति पर मिलने वाली उपाधि ➪ **BSc** और **MA** देखिए।

**baa** /bɑː बा / *noun* [*sing.*] the sound that a sheep makes भेड़ की आवाज़, मिमियाने की आवाज़

**babble¹** /ˈbæbl ˈबैब्ल् / *noun* [*sing.*] **1** the sound of many voices talking at the same time एक ही समय में सुनाई पड़ने वाली अलग-अलग बातों की आवाज़; अस्पष्ट बकबक **2** the sound of water running over stones पत्थरों पर से बहते पानी की आवाज़

**babble²** /ˈbæbl ˈबैब्ल् / *verb* [I] **1** to talk quickly or in a way that is difficult to understand तीव्र गति से या इस प्रकार बोलना कि बात समझ में न आए **2** to make the sound of water running over stones पत्थरों पर से बहते पानी की आवाज़ निकालना

**babe** /beɪb बेब् / *noun* [C] **1** (*AmE slang*) used when talking to sb, especially a girl or young woman लड़की या युवती से बात करते हुए उसके लिए प्रयुक्त *It's OK, babe.* **2** (*slang*) an attractive young woman कोई सुंदर युवती **3** (*old-fashioned*) a baby शिशु, छोटा बच्चा

**baboon** /bəˈbuːn बˈबून् / *noun* [C] a large African or Asian monkey with a long face like a dog's कुत्ते जैसे लंबे मुँह वाला अफ्रीक़ी या एशियाई बंदर; बैबून

**baby** /ˈbeɪbi ˈबेबि / *noun* [C] (*pl.* **babies**) **1** a very young child बहुत छोटा बच्चा; शिशु *She's* ***expecting a baby*** *early next year.* ○ *a baby boy/girl* **2** a very young animal or bird बहुत छोटा जानवर या पक्षी **3** (*slang*) a person, especially a girl or young woman, that you like or love प्यारी लगने वाली लड़की या युवती

**baby boom** *noun* [C, *usually sing.*] a time when more babies are born than usual, for example after a war शिशु जन्म में सहसा वृद्धि का समय (जैसे, युद्ध के बाद)

**baby boomer** *noun* [C] a person born during a baby boom 'बेबी बूम' के समय जन्मा व्यक्ति

**baby carriage** (*AmE*) = **pram**

**babyhood** /ˈbeɪbihʊd ˈबेबिहुड् / *noun* [U] the time of your life when you are a baby बचपन, शैशव

**babyish** /ˈbeɪbiɪʃ ˈबेबिइश् / *adj.* suitable for or behaving like a baby शिशु के लिए उपयुक्त या शिशु के समान आचरण करते हुए; शिशु-समान, शिशुजनोचित

**babysit** /ˈbeɪbisɪt ˈबेबिसिट् / *verb* [I] (**babysitting;** *pt, pp* **babysat**) to look after a child for a short time while the parents are out माता-पिता की अनुपस्थिति में बच्चे की अल्पकालिक देखभाल करना ▶ **babysitter** *noun* [C] इस तरह से देखभाल करने वाला व्यक्ति

**bachelor** /ˈbætʃələ(r) ˈबैचल(र्) / *noun* [C] **1** a man who has not yet married अविवाहित पुरुष, कुमार NOTE आजकल **single** शब्द का प्रयोग अधिक होता है। इसमें पुरुष और स्त्री दोनों आते हैं। **2** a person who has a first university degree विश्वविद्यालय की प्रथम स्नातक उपाधि पाने वाला व्यक्ति *a Bachelor of Arts/Science*

**bacillus** /bəˈsɪləs बˈसिलस् / *noun* [C] (*pl.* **bacilli** /bəˈsɪlaɪ बˈसिलाइ /) a type of very sall living creature (**bacterium**). There are several types of bacillus, some of which cause diseases बहुत छोटा जीवाणु, दंडाणु, ये जीवाणु बीमारी उत्पन्न कर सकते हैं

**back¹** /bæk बैक् / *noun* **1** [C] the part of a person's or animal's body between the neck and the bottom पीठ *She was standing* ***with her back to*** *me so I couldn't see her face.* ○ *A camel has a hump on its back.* **2** (*usually sing.*) the part or side of sth that is furthest from the front पीछे का भाग, पीछे की ओर *I sat* ***at the back of*** *the class.* ○ *Write your address* ***on the back of*** *the cheque.* **3** [C] the part of a chair that supports your upper body when you sit down कुरसी का वह भाग जो पीठ को सहारा देता है

IDM **at/in the back of your mind** if sth is at the back of your mind, it is in your thoughts but is not the main thing that you are thinking about अंतर्मन में

**back to front** with the back where the front should be (विशेषतः कपड़े का) आगे का भाग पीछे की ओर, और पीछे का भाग आगे *Wait a minute—you've got your jumper on back to front.* ➪ **way¹ 3** देखिए।

**behind sb's back** without sb's knowledge or agreement बिना किसी की जानकारी या सहमति के; किसी के पीठ पीछे *They criticized her behind her back.* ✪ विलोम **to sb's face**

**get off sb's back** (*informal*) to stop annoying sb, for example when you keep asking him/her to do sth परेशान करना बंद करना *I've told her I'll do the job by Monday, so I wish she'd get off my back!*

**know sth like the back of your hand** ➪ **know¹** देखिए।

**a pat on the back** ➪ **pat²** देखिए।

**turn your back on sb/sth** to refuse to be involved with sb/sth किसी का साथ देने से इनकार कर देना

**back²** /bæk बैक्/ *adj.* (*only before a noun*) **1** furthest from the front सबसे पीछे का *the back door* ○ *the back row of the theatre* ○ *back teeth* **2** owed from a time in the past पिछले समय का, अवशिष्ट *back pay/rent/taxes*

**IDM on the back burner** (*informal*) (used about an idea, a plan, etc.) left for the present time, to be done or considered later (किसी विचार, योजना आदि के लिए प्रयुक्त) वर्तमान में स्थगित; बाद में विचार हेतु

**take a back seat** to allow sb to play a more important or active role than you do in a particular situation स्वयं पीछे हट जाना ताकि कोई अन्य व्यक्ति अधिक महत्त्वपूर्ण या सक्रिय भूमिका निभा सके

**back³** /bæk बैक्/ *adv.* **1** in or to a place or state that sb/sth was in before पहले स्थान पर, जहाँ पहले थे वहीं *It started to rain so I **came back** home.* ○ ***Go back** to sleep.* ○ *Could I **have** my pen **back**, please?* ○ *I've got to **take** these books **back** to the library.* **2** away from the direction you are facing or moving in उलटी दिशा में; पीछे, पीछे की ओर *She walked away without **looking back**.* ○ *Could everyone **move back** a bit, please?* ✪ विलोम **forward** **3** away from sth; under control नियंत्रण में; रोके हुए *The police were unable to **keep** the crowds **back**.* ○ *She tried to **hold back** her tears.* **4** in return or in reply जवाब में, वापसी तौर पर *He said he'd **phone** me **back** in half an hour.* **5** in or into the past; ago पहले, पूर्व में *I met him a few years back, in Mumbai.* ○ ***Think back** to your first day at school.*

**IDM back and forth** from one place to another and back again, all the time बार-बार एक स्थान से दूसरे स्थान पर और पुनः वहीं *Travelling back and forth to work takes up quite a bit of time.*

**back⁴** /bæk बैक्/ *verb* **1** [I, T] to move backwards or to make sth move backwards स्वयं पीछे हटना, किसी वस्तु को पीछे हटाना *He backed the car into the garage.* **2** [I] to face sth at the back किसी चीज़ का ठीक पीछे होना; पीठ करना *Many of the colleges back onto the river.* **3** [T] to give help or support to sb/sth किसी को समर्थन करना, सहारा देना *We can go ahead with the scheme if the bank will agree to back us.* **4** [T] to bet money that a particular horse, team, etc. will win in a race or game (किसी घोड़े, टीम आदि पर) दाँव लगाना *Which team are you backing in the match?*

**back away (from sb/sth)** to move backwards because you are afraid, shocked, etc. डर, आघात आदि के मारे पीछे हटना

**PHR V back down** to stop saying that you are right दावा छोड़ देना, पीछे हट जाना *I think you are right to demand an apology. Don't back down now.*

**back out (of sth)** to decide not to do sth that you had promised to do वादे से मुकरना; अपनी बात से पीछे हट जाना *You promised you would come with me. You can't back out of it now!*

**back sb/sth up** to support sb; to say or show that sth is true किसी व्यक्ति या वस्तु को सच या सही मानते हुए उसका समर्थन करना *All the evidence backed up what the woman had said.*

**back (sth) up** to move backwards, especially in a vehicle पीछे हटना, विशेषतः वाहन में *Back up a little so that the other cars can get past.*

**back sth up** (*computing*) to make a copy of a computer program, etc. in case the original one is lost or damaged कंप्यूटर प्रोग्राम की सुरक्षा की दृष्टि से उस प्रोग्राम की अतिरिक्त प्रति बनाना

**backache** /ˈbækeɪk ˈबैक्एक्/ *noun* [U] a pain in your back पीठ या कमर का दर्द ➪ **ache** देखिए।

**backbone** /ˈbækbəʊn ˈबैक्बोन्/ *noun* **1** [C] the row of small bones that are connected together down the middle of your back रीढ़ की हड्डी ✪ पर्याय **spine** ➪ **body** पर चित्र देखिए। **2** [*sing.*] the most important part of sth किसी वस्तु का सबसे महत्त्वपूर्ण अंश *Agriculture is the backbone of the country's economy.*

**back-breaking** *adj.* (used about physical work) very hard and tiring (शरीरिक श्रम के लिए प्रयुक्त) कमर-तोड़, अति श्रमसाध्य

**backcloth** /ˈbækklɒθ ˈबैक्क्लॉथ्/ = **backdrop**

**backdate** /ˌbækˈdeɪt ˌबैक्ˈडेट्/ *verb* [T] to make a document, a cheque or a payment take effect from an earlier date चेक आदि दस्तावेज़ को पिछली तारीख़ से प्रभावी बनाना *The pay rise will be backdated to 1 April.*

**backdrop** /ˈbækdrɒp ˈबैक्ड्रॉप्/ (*also* **backcloth**) *noun* [C] a painted piece of material that is hung behind the stage in a theatre as part of the scenery पृष्ठपट

**backer** /ˈbækə(r) ˈबैक(र्)/ *noun* [C] a person, organization or company that gives support to sb, especially financial support सहायक या समर्थक व्यक्ति या संगठन, विशेषतः वित्तीय समर्थन देने वाला

**backfire** /ˌbækˈfaɪə(r) ˌबैक्ˈफ़ाइअ(र्)/ *verb* [I] to have an unexpected and unpleasant result, often the opposite of what was intended अप्रत्याशित, अप्रिय और प्रायः विपरीत परिणाम आना

**background** /ˈbækgraʊnd ˈबैक्ग्राउन्ड्/ *noun* **1** [*sing.*] the part of a view, scene, picture, etc. which is furthest away from the person looking at it पृष्ठभूमि, चित्रभूमि *You can see the mountains **in the background** of the photo.* ✪ विलोम **foreground** **2** [*sing.*] a position where sb/sth can be seen/heard, etc. but is not the centre of attention पृष्ठभूमि, नेपथ्य *The film star's husband prefers to stay in the background.* ○ *I like to have **background music** when I'm studying.* **3** [*sing.*] [U] the facts or events that are connected with a situation किसी परिस्थिति से संबद्ध तथ्य या घटनाएँ *The talks are taking place against a background of increasing tension.* **4** [C] the type of family and social class you come from and the education and experience you have (किसी व्यक्ति का) सामाजिक स्तर, शिक्षा एवं अनुभव *We get on very well together in spite of our different backgrounds.*

**backhand** /ˈbækhænd ˈबैक्हैन्ड्/ *noun* [*sing.*] a way of hitting the ball in tennis, etc. that is made with the back of your hand facing forward (टेनिस में) उलटे हाथ का प्रहार; हथेली को अंदर की तरफ़ रखकर किया गया प्रहार ✪ पर्याय **forehand**

**backing** /ˈbækɪŋ ˈबैकिङ्/ *noun* [U] help or support to do sth, especially financial support कुछ करने के लिए दी गई सहायता, समर्थन या प्रोत्साहन, विशेषतः वित्तीय समर्थन

**backlash** /ˈbæklæʃ ˈबैक्लैश्/ *noun* [*sing.*] a strong reaction against a political or social event or development किसी सामाजिक या राजनीतिक घटना की तीव्र प्रतिक्रिया

**backlog** /ˈbæklɒg ˈबैक्लॉग्/ *noun* [C] (*usually sing.*) an amount of work, etc. that has not yet been done and should have been done already कार्य जिसे अब तक कर लिया जाना चाहिए था; अवशिष्ट कार्य

**backpack**[1] /ˈbækpæk ˈबैक्पैक्/ *noun* [C] a large bag, often on a metal frame, that you carry on your back when travelling पीठ पर ले जाया जाने वाला बड़ा थैला ✪ पर्याय **rucksack**

**backpack**[2] /ˈbækpæk ˈबैक्पैक्/ *verb* [I] to go walking or travelling with your clothes, etc. in a backpack कपड़ों आदि से भरे बड़े थैले को पीठ पर ढोकर यात्रा करना *We went backpacking round Uttaranchal last summer.* ▶ **backpacker** *noun* [C] इस तरह का यात्री

**back-pedal** *verb* (*pres. part.* **back-pedalling;** *pt, pp* **back-pedalled** *AmE* **back-pedaling; back-pedaled**) **1 back-pedal (on sth)** to change an earlier statement or opinion; to not do sth that you promised to do पूर्व में दिए बयान या विचार को बदल देना; अपनी बात पर क़ायम न रहना *The protests have forced the government to back-pedal on plans to introduce a new tax.* **2** to move your feet backwards when you are riding a bicycle in order to go backwards or slow down (साइकिल चलाते हुए पीछे लौटने या चाल घटाने के लिए) उलटे पैडल मारना

**backside** /ˈbæksaɪd ˈबैक्साइड्/ *noun* [C] (*informal*) the part of your body that you sit on; your bottom नितंब

**backslash** /ˈbækslæʃ ˈबैक्स्लैश्/ *noun* [C] a mark ( \ ) used in computer **commands** कंप्यूटर आदेशों में प्रयुक्त एक चिह्न ( \ ) ➪ **slash**[2] देखिए।

**backstage** /ˌbækˈsteɪdʒ ˈबैक्ˈस्टेज्/ *adv.* in the part of a theatre where the actors get dressed, wait to perform, etc. रंगशाला के उस भाग में जहाँ अभिनेता तैयार आदि होते हैं; नेपथ्य में

**backstroke** /ˈbækstrəʊk ˈबैक्स्ट्रोक्/ *noun* [U] a style of swimming that you do on your back पीठ के बल तैरने की शैली *Can you **do backstroke**?* ➪ **swim** पर चित्र देखिए।

**backtrack** /ˈbæktræk ˈबैक्ट्रैक्/ *verb* [I] **1** to go back the same way you came जिस रास्ते आए उसी रास्ते लौट जाना **2 backtrack (on sth)** to change your mind about a plan, promise, etc. that you have made योजना, वादे आदि पर विचार बदल लेना *The union forced the company to backtrack on its plans to close the factory.*

**back-up** *noun* **1** [U] extra help or support that you can get if necessary आवश्यकता होने पर मिल सकने वाली अतिरिक्त सहायता **2** [C] (*computing*) a copy of a computer disk that you can use if the original one is lost or damaged कंप्यूटर डिस्क की वह स्थानापन्न या सुरक्षित प्रति जो मूल प्रति के खो या ख़राब हो जाने पर प्रयोग की जा सकती है *Always make a back-up of your files.*

**backward** /ˈbækwəd ˈबैक्वड्/ *adj.* **1** (*only before a noun*) directed towards the back उलटा, पश्चगामी *a backward step/glance* ✪ विलोम **forward** **2** slow to develop or learn विकसित होने या सीखने में पीछे; पिछड़ा *Our teaching methods are backward compared to some countries.*

**backwards** /ˈbækwədz ˈबैक्वड्ज़्/ (*also* **backward**) *adv.* **1** towards a place or a position that is behind पीछे की ओर *Could everybody take a step backwards?* **2** in the opposite direction to usual विपरीत दिशा में *Can you say the alphabet backwards?* ✪ विलोम **forwards**

IDM **backward(s) and forward(s)** first in one direction and then in the other, all the time बार-बार आगे-पीछे, इधर-उधर *The dog ran backwards and forwards, barking loudly.*

**backwash** /ˈbækwɒʃ ˈबैकवॉश्/ *noun* [U] (in geography) the movement of water back into the sea after a wave has hit the beach (भूगोल में) समुद्रतट से टकराने के बाद लहर का लौटकर समुद्र की ओर प्रवाह; प्रतिगामी धारा ➪ **swash** देखिए तथा **wave** पर चित्र देखिए।

**backwater** /ˈbækwɔːtə(r) ˈबैकवॉट(र्)/ *noun* [C] **1** a place that is away from where most things happen and so it is not affected by new ideas or outside events नए विचारों, घटनाओं, गतिविधियों और चहल-पहल से अप्रभावित स्थान **2** (*also* **backwaters**) a body of water or a part of a river pushed back by the currents of the sea and separated from it by large areas of sand समुद्री प्रवाह के कारण पीछे की ओर धकेला हुआ अप्रवाही जल जो विशाल रेतीले क्षेत्रों द्वारा नदी आदि से विभक्त हो जाता है *Kerala is famous for its backwaters.*

**backyard** /ˌbækˈjɑːd ˌबैकˈयाड्/ *noun* [C] **1** an area behind a house, usually with a hard surface made of stone or **concrete**, with a wall or fence around it घर का पिछला आँगन, प्रायः पत्थर से बना या दीवारों से घिरा हुआ **2** the whole area behind the house including the grass area and the garden घर के पीछे का सारा हिस्सा (घासवाली भूमि, बग़ीचा आदि भी), घर का पिछवाड़ा

**bacon** /ˈbeɪkən ˈबेकन्/ *noun* [U] thin pieces of salted or smoked meat from the back or sides of a pig सूअर की पीठ या बग़ल का नमक लगा या भुना हुआ मांस

**bacteria** /bækˈtɪəriə बैकˈटिअरिआ/ *noun* [*pl.*] (*sing. technical*) **bacterium** /-riəm रिअम्/) very small living things that can only be seen with special equipment (**a microscope**). Bacteria exist in large numbers in air, water, soil, plants and the bodies of people and animals. Some bacteria cause disease जीवाणु जो बड़ी संख्या में वायु, जल, मिट्टी और प्राणियों में पाए जाते हैं। कुछ जीवाणु बीमारी भी उत्पन्न कर सकते हैं ➪ **germ[1]** और **virus** देखिए। ▶ **bacterial** /-riəl -रिअल्/ *adj.* जीवाणु संबंधी *bacterial infections/growths*

**bad** /bæd बैड्/ *adj.* (**worse** /wɜːs वस्/, **worst** /wɜːst वस्ट्/) **1** not good; unpleasant बुरा, ख़राब, अप्रिय *Our family's had a bad time recently.* ○ *bad weather* **2** of poor quality; of a low standard घटिया, निम्नस्तरीय *Many accidents are caused by bad driving.* ○ *bad management* **3 bad (at sth/at doing sth)** not able to do sth well or easily; not skilful अयोग्य, अक्षम *a bad teacher/driver/cook* ○ *I've always been bad at sport.* **4** serious; severe बहुत ख़राब; गंभीर *The traffic was very bad on the way to work.* ○ *She went home with a bad headache.* ○ *That was a bad mistake!* **5** (used about food) not fresh or fit to eat; rotten (भोजन) बासी या खाने के अयोग्य; सड़ा हुआ *These eggs will **go bad** if we don't eat them soon.* **6** (used about parts of the body) not healthy; painful (शरीर के अंग) अस्वस्थ; पीड़ाक्रांत, दर्दीला *He's always had a bad heart.* ○ *bad back* **7** (used about a person or behaviour) not good; morally wrong (व्यक्ति या आचरण) बुरा, दुष्ट, अनैतिक *He was not a bad man, just rather weak.* **8** (*not before a noun*) **bad for sb/sth** likely to damage or hurt sb/sth नुक़सानदेह, हानिकर (संभावित रूप से) *Sugar is bad for your teeth.* **9 bad (for sth/to do sth)** difficult or not suitable मुश्किल या अनुपयुक्त, ग़लत *This is a bad time to phone, everyone's out to lunch.*

IDM **not bad** (*informal*) quite **good** बुरा या बुरी नहीं, ठीक-ठाक, अच्छा *'What was the film like?' 'Not bad.'*

**too bad** (*informal*) used to show that nothing can be done to change a situation स्थिति बदली नहीं जा सकती, यह बताने के लिए प्रयुक्त *'I'd much rather stay at home.' 'Well that's just too bad. We've said we'll go.'*

**badam** *noun* (*IndE*) almond बादाम, गिरिदार काष्ठ फल ➪ **nut** पर चित्र देखिए।

**baddy** (*also* **baddie**) /ˈbædi ˈबैडि/ *noun* [C] (*pl.* **baddies**) (*informal*) a bad person in a film, book, etc. फ़िल्म, कहानी आदि का दुष्ट पात्र ✪ विलोम **goody**

**badge** /bædʒ बैज्/ *noun* [C] a small piece of metal, cloth or plastic with a design or words on it that you wear on your clothing धातु, कपड़े या प्लास्टिक से बना बिल्ला जिस पर कुछ अंकित होता है और जो वस्त्र पर लगाया जाता है *The players all have jackets with the club badge on.*

**badger** /ˈbædʒə(r) ˈबैज(र्)/ *noun* [C] an animal with black and white lines on its head that lives in holes in the ground and comes out at night बिल में रहने वाला और रात में बाहर निकलने वाला एक छोटा जानवर जिसके सिर पर सफ़ेद व काली धारियाँ होती हैं; बिज्जू

**bad language** *noun* [U] words that are used for swearing अपशब्द, गाली

**badly** /ˈbædli ˈबैड्लि/ *adv.* (**worse** /wɜːs वस्/, **worst** /wɜːst वस्ट्/) **1** in a way that is not good enough; not well संतोषजनक रूप से; अच्छा नहीं *She did badly in the exams.* **2** seriously; severely गंभीर रूप से; बहुत अधिक *He was badly hurt in the accident.* **3** very much अत्यधिक *He badly needed a holiday.*

IDM **badly off** poor; not having enough of sth कंगाल, ग़रीब; पर्याप्त मात्रा से वंचित ✪ विलोम **well off**

**badminton** /ˈbædmɪntən ˈबैड्मिन्टन्/ *noun* [U] a game for two or four people in which players hit a type of light ball with feathers (**a shuttlecock**) over a high net, using a piece of equipment (**a racket**) which is held in the hand दो या चार खिलाड़ियों के बीच रैकेट और शटलकॉक से खेला जाने वाला खेल; बैडमिंटन

**badshah** (*also* **Badshah**) *noun* [C] the ruler of an empire; an emperor किसी साम्राज्य का शासक; बादशाह *the Mughal Badshah*

**bad-tempered** *adj.* often angry or impatient प्रायः चिड़चिड़ा, बदमिज़ाज या गुस्सेबाज़

**baffle** /ˈbæfl ˈबैफ़्ल्/ *verb* [T] to be impossible to understand; to confuse sb very much चकरा देना; उलझन में डाल देना *His illness baffled the doctors.* ▶ **baffled** *adj.* भ्रमित, उलझा हुआ *The instructions were so complicated that I was completely baffled.* ▶ **baffling** *adj.* चकरा देने वाला

**bag[1]** /bæg बैग्/ *noun* **1** [C] a strong container made of paper or thin plastic that opens at the top काग़ज़ या पतले प्लास्टिक से बना लिफ़ाफ़ा; थैली *She brought some sandwiches in a plastic bag.* **2** [C] a strong container made from cloth, plastic, leather, etc., usually with one or two handles, used to carry things in when travelling, shopping, etc. थैला, झोला *a shopping bag* ○ *Have you packed your bags yet?* **3** [C] the amount contained in a bag थैलाभर या झोलाभर मात्रा *She's eaten a whole bag of sweets!* ○ *a bag of crisps/sugar/flour* **4 bags** [*pl.*] folds of skin under the eyes, often caused by lack of sleep आँखों के नीचे की झुर्रीदार त्वचा, प्रायः अनिद्रा के कारण उत्पन्न **5 bags** [*pl.*] (*BrE informal*) **bags (of sth)** a lot (of sth); plenty (of sth) भरपूर, प्रचुर, काफ़ी *There's no hurry, we've got bags of time.*

**bag[2]** /bæg बैग्/ *verb* [T] (**bagging; bagged**) (*informal*) to try to get sth for yourself so that other people cannot have it हथिया लेना, झपट लेना *Somebody's bagged the seats by the pool!*

**bagel** /ˈbeɪgl ˈबेगल्/ *noun* [C] a type of bread roll in the shape of a ring बड़े छल्ले के आकार का एक ब्रेड रोल, बेगल

**baggage** /ˈbægɪdʒ ˈबैगिज्/ *noun* [U] bags, suit cases, etc. used for carrying a person's clothes and things on a journey यात्री का सामान (यात्रा के कपड़े और अन्य सामान हेतु सूटकेस, बक्सा आदि) *excess baggage* (= baggage weighing more than the airline's permitted limit) ✪ पर्याय **luggage**

**baggy** /ˈbægi ˈबैगि/ *adj.* (used about a piece of clothing) big; hanging loosely on the body (वस्त्र) ढीला-ढाला

**bagh** *noun* [C] (*IndE*) a large garden उद्यान, बग़ीचा, वाटिका *Shalimar Bagh in Srinagar is very well-planned.*

**bagpipes** /ˈbægpaɪps ˈबैग्पाइप्स्/ *noun* [*pl.*] a musical instrument, popular in Scotland, that is played by blowing air through a pipe into a bag and then pressing the bag so that the air comes out of other pipes स्काटलैंड में लोकप्रिय एक वाद्य यंत्र, मशकबीन ➪ **piano** पर नोट देखिए।

**bail[1]** /beɪl बेल्/ *noun* [U] money that sb agrees to pay if a person accused of a crime does not appear in front of the court on the day he/she is called. When bail has been arranged, the accused person can go free until that day ज़मानत, प्रतिभूति *She was* ***released on bail*** *of Rs 20,000.* ○ *The judge felt that he was a dangerous man and* ***refused*** *him* ***bail***.

**bail[2]** /beɪl बेल्/ *verb* [T] to let sb go free on bail ज़मानत पर छोड़ना

PHR V **bail sb out 1** to obtain sb's freedom by paying money to the court ज़मानत पर छुड़ाना *Her parents went to the police station and bailed her out.* **2** to rescue sb from a difficult situation (especially by providing money) किसी को परेशानी की हालत से निकालना (विशेषतः धन देकर)

**bailiff** /ˈbeɪlɪf ˈबेलिफ़्/ *noun* [C] an officer whose job is to take the possessions and property of people who cannot pay their debts एक न्यायिक अधिकारी जो उधार न चुकाने वालों की संपत्ति ज़ब्त करता है

**bait** /beɪt बेट्/ *noun* [U] **1** food or sth that looks like food that is put onto a hook to catch fish, animals or birds मछली आदि को फँसाने के लिए चारा, चुग्गा **2** something that is used for persuading or attracting sb किसी को लुभाने या मनाने के लिए प्रयोग में लाई गई वस्तु; प्रलोभन, लालच *Free offers are often used as bait to attract customers.*

**bajra** *noun* [U] **1** a type of millet commonly grown in north-western India which can be made into flour; pearl millet बाजरा; 'पर्ल मिलेट' **2** the plant which produces a type of millet called pearl millet बाजरे का पौधा *a field of bajra*

**bake** /beɪk बेक्/ *verb* [I, T] **1** to cook or be cooked in an oven in dry heat अँगीठी या चूल्हे में सूखे ताप से पकाना या पकना; सेंकना *I could smell bread baking* *in the oven.* ○ *On his birthday she baked him a cake.* ➪ **cook** देखिए। **2** to become or to make sth hard by heating it ताप से कड़ा हो जाना या कर देना *The hot sun baked the earth.*

**baked beans** *noun* [*pl.*] small white beans, usually cooked in a sauce and sold in cans चटनी में पकाई गई डिब्बाबंद सफ़ेद छोटी बीन (सेम)

**baker** /ˈbeɪkə(r) ˈबेक(र्)/ *noun* **1** [C] a person who bakes bread, cakes, etc. to sell in a shop नानबाई, बेचने के लिए केक, ब्रेड आदि बनाने वाला **2 the baker's** [*sing.*] a shop that sells bread, cakes, etc. नानबाई की दुकान *Get a loaf at the baker's.*

**bakery** /ˈbeɪkəri ˈबेकरि/ *noun* [C] (*pl.* **bakeries**) a place where bread, cakes, etc. are baked to be sold नानबाई की दुकान; बेकरी

**baking** /ˈbeɪkɪŋ ˈबेकिङ्/ *adj.* very hot बहुत गरम, तपाने वाला *The workers complained of the baking heat in the office in the summer.*

**baking powder** *noun* [U] a mixture of powders used to make cakes rise and become light as they are baked केक बनाते समय प्रयुक्त एक मिश्रण जिससे केक ऊपर उठता है और हलका हो जाता है; बेकिंग पाउडर

**baking soda** = **sodium bicarbonate**

**balance[1]** /ˈbæləns ˈबैलन्स्/ *noun* **1** [*sing.*] **(a) balance (between A and B)** a situation in which different or opposite things are of equal importance, size, etc. संतुलन, संतुलन की स्थिति *The course provides a good balance between academic and practical work.* ○ *Tourism has upset **the delicate balance of nature** on the island.* **2** [U] the ability to keep steady with an equal amount of weight on each side of the body दोनों तरफ भार उठाकर संतुलन बनाए रखने की क्षमता *to **lose balance*** ○ *You need a good **sense of balance** to ride a motorbike.* **3** [C, *sing.*] the amount that still has to be paid; the amount that is left after some has been used, taken, etc. बक़ाया; बाक़ी रक़म, बचा पैसा *You can pay a 10% deposit now, with **the balance** due in one month.* ○ *to check your **bank balance*** **4** [C] (*technical*) an instrument used for weighing things तराज़ू, तुला, काँटा

**IDM** **in the balance** uncertain अनिश्चित *Following poor results, the company's future hangs in the balance.*

**(catch/throw sb) off balance** (to find or put sb) in a position that is not safe and from which it is easy to fall असुरक्षित स्थिति में (होना या किसी को डालना) और गिरने की संभावना के साथ

**on balance** having considered all sides, facts, etc. कुल मिलाकर; सब पहलुओं को ध्यान में रखते हुए *On balance, I've had a pretty good year.*

**strike a balance (between A and B)** ➪ **strike[2]** देखिए।

**balance[2]** /ˈbæləns ˈबैलन्स्/ *verb* **1** [I, T] to be or to put sb/sth in a steady position so that the weight of him/her/it is not heavier on one side than on the other स्थिर या संतुलित स्थिति में करना या होना; संतुलन की स्थिति में रखना *I had to balance on the top step of the ladder to paint the ceiling.* ○ *Carefully, she balanced a glass on top of the pile of plates.* **2** [I, T] to have equal totals of money spent and money received आमद-ख़र्च का हिसाब सधना या साधना; आय-व्यय का संतुलित होना या को संतुलित करना *I must have made a mistake—the accounts don't balance.* **3** [I, T] **balance (sth) (out) (with sth)** to have or give sth equal value, importance, etc. in relation to other parts बराबर होना या करना; तुल्य होना या करना *The loss in the first half of the year was balanced out by the profit in the second half.* **4** [T] **balance sth against sth** to consider and compare one matter in relation to another तुलना द्वारा बराबरी पर लाना *In planning the new road, we have to balance the benefit to motorists against the damage to the environment.*

**balanced** /ˈbælənst ˈबैलन्स्ट्/ *adj.* keeping or showing a balance so that different things, or different parts of things exist in equal or correct amounts संतुलित, स्थिर *I like this newspaper because it gives a balanced view.* ○ *a **balanced diet*** ✪ विलोम **unbalanced**

**balance of payments** *noun* [*sing.*] the difference between the amount of money one country receives from other countries from exports, etc. and the amount it pays to them for imports and services in a particular period of time आयात-निर्यात के संदर्भ में अवधि-विशेष में प्राप्त राशि और भुगतान राशि के बीच का अंतर; भुगतान-शेष

**balance of power** *noun* [*sing.*] **1** a situation in which political power or military strength is divided between two countries or groups of countries दो देशों या गुटों की राजनैतिक या सैन्य शक्तियों में बराबरी की स्थिति; शक्ति सामंजस्य **2** the power that a smaller political party has when the larger parties need its support because they do not have enough votes on their own छोटे राजनैतिक पार्टी का शक्तिमान होना प्रायः जब बड़े राजनैतिक दलों को पर्याप्त मतों का अभाव हो और छोटे दलों का समर्थन वांछित हो

**balance of trade** (*also* **trade balance**) *noun* [*sing.*] the difference in value between the amount that a country buys from other countries (**imports**) and the amount that it sells to them (**exports**) आयात में व्यय मूल्य और निर्यात से प्राप्त मूल्य का अंतर; व्यापार-शेष

**balance sheet** *noun* [C] a written statement showing the amount of money and property that a company has, and how much has been received and paid out किसी संस्था की संपत्ति और आय-व्यय संबंधी ब्योरों का पक्का चिट्ठा, तुलन-पत्र, तलपट

**balcony** /ˈbælkəni ˈबैल्कनि / *noun* [C] (*pl.* **balconies**) **1** a platform built on an upstairs outside wall of a building, with a wall or rail around it छज्जा, बारजा ➪ **patio, terrace** और **veranda** देखिए। **2** an area of seats upstairs in a theatre सिनेमा हाल या रंगशाला में ऊपरी मंजिल पर लगी कुरसियाँ; बालकनी

**bald** /bɔ:ld बॉल्ड् / *adj.* **1** (used about people) having little or no hair on your head (व्यक्ति) गंजा *I hope I don't* ***go bald*** *like my father did.* ○ *He has a* ***bald patch*** *on the top of his head.* **2** (used about sth that is said) simple; without extra words (कथन) सीधा-सादा; शब्दांडबर-हीन, अनलंकृत *the bald truth*

**balding** /ˈbɔ:ldɪŋ ˈबॉल्डिङ् / *adj.* starting to lose the hair on your head गंजेपन की ओर बढ़ता हुआ, गंजा होता हुआ *a balding man in his fifties*

**baldly** /ˈbɔ:ldli ˈबॉल्ड्लि / *adv.* in a few words with nothing extra or unnecessary नपे-तुले शब्दों में *He told us baldly that he was leaving.*

**bale** /beɪl बेल् / *noun* [C] a large quantity of sth pressed tightly together and tied up गट्ठर *a bale of hay/cloth/paper/cotton*

**balk** = **baulk**

**ball** /bɔ:l बॉल् / *noun* [C] **1** a round object that you hit, kick, throw, etc. in games and sports गेंद *a tennis/golf/rugby ball* ○ *a football* **2** a round object or a thing that has been formed into a round shape गोला, गोल वस्तु, पिंड *a ball of wool* ○ *The children threw* ***snowballs*** *at each other.* ○ *We had meatballs and pasta for dinner.* **3** one throw, kick, etc. of the ball in some sports कुछ खेलों में गेंद की अकेली फेंक, ठोकर आदि *That was a great ball from the defender*. **4** a large formal party at which people dance एक बड़ी औपचारिक पार्टी जिसमें लोग नाचते हैं, बड़ी नृत्य-पार्टी

IDM **be on the ball** (*informal*) to always know what is happening and be able to react to or deal with it quickly स्थिति की हमेशा जानकारी रखना और तुरंत कार्रवाई करने की क्षमता रखना

**set/start the ball rolling** to start sth (an activity, conversation, etc.) that involves or is done by a group समूह द्वारा क्रिया-कलाप या बातचीत शुरू करना

**ballad** /ˈbæləd ˈबैलड् / *noun* [C] a long song or poem that tells a story, often about love प्रायः प्रेमविषयक गाथा, कथात्मक गीत अथवा कविता; गाथा गीत

**ballast** /ˈbæləst ˈबैलस्ट् / *noun* [U] heavy material placed in a ship or **hot-air balloon** to make it heavier and keep it steady हवा के गुब्बारे या जहाज़ को स्थिर रखने के लिए उसमें रखा गया भारी सामान; स्थिरक भार

**ball bearing** *noun* [C] one of a number of metal balls put between parts of a machine to make them move smoothly धातु-निर्मित गोली जो मशीन के पुरजों के बीच पड़ती है ताकि मशीन बराबर चलती रहे; बॉल बियरिंग

**ballerina** /ˌbæləˈri:nə ˌबैलˈरीना / *noun* [C] a woman who dances in ballets नृत्यांगना, बैले-नर्तकी

**ballet** /ˈbæleɪ ˈबैले / *noun* **1** [U] a style of dancing that tells a story with music but without words संगीतात्मक नृत्यनाटिका; बैले *a* ***ballet dancer*** **2** [C] a performance or work that consists of this type of dancing नृत्यनाटिका मंचन या प्रयोग; बैले-मंचन

**ballet dancer** *noun* [C] a person who dances in ballets बैले-नर्तक

**ball game** *noun* [C] **1** any game played with a ball गेंद का खेल, कंदुक-क्रीड़ा **2** a baseball match बेसबॉल का मैच

IDM **a (whole) new/different ball game** something completely new or different सर्वथा नूतन वस्तु या कार्य; एकदम भिन्न बात

**ballistics** /bəˈlɪstɪks बˈलिस्टिक्स् / *noun* [U] the scientific study of things that are shot or fired through the air, for example bullets वायु मे प्रक्षेपित होने वाली वस्तुओं (जैसे गोली) का वैज्ञानिक अध्ययन

**balloon** /bəˈlu:n बˈलून् / *noun* [C] **1** a small coloured object that you blow air into and use as a toy or for decoration गुब्बारा *to blow up/burst/pop a balloon* **2** (*also* **hot-air balloon**) a large balloon made of material that is filled with gas or hot air so that it can fly through the sky, carrying people in a basket underneath it (आकाश में उड़ाया जाने वाला) गैस का गुब्बारा जिसके नीचे लगी बड़ी टोकरी में लोग बैठते हैं

**ballot** /ˈbælət ˈबैलट् / *noun* **1** [U, C] a secret written vote गुप्त मतदान *The union will* ***hold a ballot*** *on the new pay offer.* ○ *The committee are elected by ballot every year.* **2** (*also* **ballot**

**paper**) [C] the piece of paper on which sb marks who he/she is voting for मतपत्र, मतपरची *What percentage of eligible voters **cast** their **ballots**?* ▶ **ballot** *verb* [T] **ballot sb (on sth)** मतदान कराना *The union is balloting its members on strike action.*

**ballot box** *noun* **1** [C] the box into which people put the piece of paper with their vote on मतपेटिका **2 the ballot box** [*sing.*] the system of voting in an election चुनाव में मतदान की पद्धति *People will express their opinion through the ballot box.* **2** (*also* **ballot paper**) [C] = **ballot²**

**ballpoint** /ˈbɔːlpɔɪnt ˈबॉल्पॉइन्ट्/ (*also* **ballpoint pen**) *noun* [C] a pen with a very small metal ball at the end that rolls ink onto paper एक तरह की क़लम जिसकी नोक पर एक बहुत छोटी धातु-निर्मित गोली होती है जिसके सहारे स्याही काग़ज़ पर उतरती है; बॉलप्वाइंट पेन ➪ **stationery** पर चित्र देखिए।

**ballroom** /ˈbɔːlruːm; -rʊm ˈबॉलरूम् -रुम्/ *noun* [C] a large room used for dancing on formal occasions औपचारिक अवसरों के लिए बड़ा नृत्य कक्ष; बॉलरूम

**ballroom dancing** *noun* [U] a formal type of dance in which couples dance together using particular steps and movements एक औपचारिक नृत्य जिसमें विशेष क़दमचाल के साथ जोड़े नृत्य करते हैं; बॉलरूम नृत्य

**balm** /bɑːm बाम्/ *noun* [U, C] cream that is used to make your skin feel better if you have hurt it or if it is very dry मरहम, मलहम

**balustrade** /ˌbæləˈstreɪd ˌबैलˈस्ट्रेड्/ *noun* [C] a row of posts, joined together at the top, built along the edge of a bridge, etc. जंगला, वेदिका

**balwadi** *noun* [C] (in India) a centre for looking after young children while their mothers are away on work. These centres are usually run by social workers (भारत में) समाज सेवकों द्वारा चालित नौकरीपेशा महिलाओं के शिशुओं की देखभाल का केंद्र; बालवाड़ी

**bamboo** /ˌbæmˈbuː ˌबैम्ˈबू/ *noun* [C] (*pl.* **bamboos**) a tall tropical plant of the grass family. Young bamboo plants can be eaten and the hard parts of the plant are used for making furniture, etc. बाँस का पेड़; बाँस के अंकुर खाने के काम आते हैं और उसके कठोर हिस्से फ़र्नीचर बनाने के *a bamboo chair* ➪ **plant** पर चित्र देखिए।

**ban** /bæn बैन्/ *verb* [T] (**ba<u>nn</u>ing; ba<u>nn</u>ed**) **ban sth; ban sb (from sth/from doing sth)** to officially say that sth is not allowed, often by law प्रायः क़ानूनी तौर पर प्रतिबंध या रोक लगाना; आधिकारिक *The government has banned the logging of trees.* ○ *He was fined Rs 10,000 and banned from driving for a year.* ▶ **ban** *noun* [C] **a ban (on sth)** रोक, प्रतिबंध *There is a ban on smoking in this office.* ○ *to impose/lift a ban*

**banal** /bəˈnɑːl बˈनाल्/ *adj.* not original or interesting मौलिक या दिलचस्प नहीं; अत्यंत साधारण, तुच्छ *a banal comment*

**banana** /bəˈnɑːnə बˈनाना/ *noun* [C] a curved fruit with yellow skin that grows in hot countries केला *a bunch of bananas* ➪ **fruit** पर चित्र देखिए।

**band** /bænd बैन्ड्/ *noun* [C] **1** (*with sing. or pl. verb*) a small group of musicians who play popular music together, often with a singer or singers हलका-फुलका लोकप्रिय संगीत बजाने वालों की टोली; बैंड *a rock/jazz band* ○ *He plays the drums in a band.* ○ *The band has/have released a new CD.* **2** (*with sing. or pl. verb*) a group of people who do sth together or have the same ideas संग काम करने वाले या समान विचारों वाले व्यक्तियों का दल, टोली, मंडली, समूह *A small band of rebels is/are hiding in the hills.* **3** a thin, flat, narrow piece of material used for fastening sth, or to put round sth पट्टी, पट्टा, फ़ीता, बंद, प्रायः कुछ बाँधने के लिए प्रयुक्त *She rolled up the papers and put an **elastic band** round them.* **4** a line of colour or material on sth that is different from what is around it धारी *She wore a red pullover with a green band across the middle.* **5** = **waveband**

**bandage** /ˈbændɪdʒ ˈबैन्डिज्/ *noun* [C] a long piece of soft white material that you tie round a wound or injury घाव पर बाँधने के लिए पट्टी ▶ **bandage** *verb* [T] **bandage sth (up)** पट्टी बाँधना *The nurse bandaged my hand up.*

**bandh** *noun* [C] (*IndE*) a general strike सार्वजनिक हड़ताल *Shopkeepers in Delhi declared a week's bandh to protest against VAT.*

**bandicoot rat** *noun* [C] a large Indian rat with a pointed nose and long tail, which is very destructive to crops लंबी पूंछ वाला बड़ी नसल का चूहा जो फ़सल के लिए अत्यंत हानिकारक होता है

**bandit** /ˈbændɪt ˈबैन्डिट्/ *noun* [C] a member of an armed group of thieves, who attack travellers यात्रियों पर हमला करने वाला सशस्त्र डाकू

**bandobast** = **bundobust**

**bandwagon** /ˈbændwægən ˈबैन्ड्वैगन्/ *noun*
**IDM** **climb/jump on the bandwagon** to copy what other people are doing because it is fashionable or successful दूसरों की देखा-देखी किसी कार्यक्रम में शामिल हो जाना क्योंकि वह प्रचलित है या उसे करने से सफलता मिलती है

**bandwidth** /ˈbændwɪdθ; -wɪtθ ˈबैन्ड्विड्थ् ; -विट्थ्/ *noun* [C, U] **1** (*technical*) a band of **frequencies** used for sending electronic signals इलेक्ट्रॉनिक संकेत भेजने में प्रयुक्त तरंग पट्टिका में आवृत्तियों का परास; बैंडचौड़ाई **2** (*computing*) a measurement of the amount of information that a particular computer **network** or Internet connection can send in a particular time. It is often measured in **bits** per second किसी कंप्यूटर नेटवर्क या इंटरनेट कनेक्शन द्वारा एक विशेष अवधि में भेजी जा सकने वाली सूचना का माप। इसे बिट्स प्रति सेकंड में मापा जाता है

**bandy¹** /ˈbændi ˈबैन्डि/ *adj.* (used about a person's legs) curving towards the outside so that the knees are wide apart (व्यक्ति की टाँगों के लिए प्रयुक्त) धनुषाकार टाँगों वाला; धनुजंघी, वक्रपाद

**bandy²** /ˈbændi ˈबैन्डि/ *verb* (*pres. part.* **bandying;** *3rd person sing. pres.* **bandies;** *pt, pp* **bandied**)

**PHR V bandy sth about/around** (*usually passive*) (used about a name, word, story, etc.) to mention sth frequently (किसी नाम, शब्द, कहानी आदि के लिए प्रयुक्त) बार-बार चर्चा करना

**bang¹** /bæŋ बैङ्/ *verb* [I, T] **1** to make a loud noise by hitting sth hard; to close sth or to be closed with a loud noise किसी पर ज़ोर से प्रहार करते हुए या किसी को बंद करते हुए *He banged his fist on the table and started shouting.* **2** to knock against sth by accident; to hit a part of the body against sth by accident अचानक किसी से टकरा जाना; शरीर के किसी अंग का टकरा जाना *As I was crossing the room in the dark I banged into a table.*

**bang²** /bæŋ बैङ्/ *noun* [C] **1** a sudden, short, very loud noise धमाका, धड़ाका *There was an enormous bang when the bomb exploded.* **2** a short, strong knock or hit, especially one that causes pain and injury टक्कर जिससे व्यक्ति को चोट पहुँचे *a nasty bang on the head*

**IDM with a bang** in a successful or exciting way सफलता प्राप्त करते हुए उत्तेजना के साथ *Our team's season started with a bang when we won our first five matches.*

**bang³** /bæŋ बैङ्/ *adv.* (*BrE informal*) exactly; directly; right बिलकुल सही; सीधे-सीधे; एकदम ठीक *Our computers are* ***bang up to date.*** ○ *The shot was bang on target.*

**IDM bang goes sth** (*informal*) used for expressing the idea that sth is now impossible यह बताने के लिए प्रयुक्त कि अमुक बात अब संभव नहीं *'It's raining!' 'Ah well, bang goes our picnic!'*

**bang⁴** /bæŋ बैङ्/ *exclamation* used to sound like the noise of a gun, etc. बंदूक़ के धमाके जैसी आवाज़ करने वाली

**bangle** /ˈbæŋgl ˈबैङ्ग्ल्/ *noun* [C] a circular metal band that is worn round the arm or wrist for decoration चूड़ी, कड़ा, कंगन

**bangs** /bæŋz बैङ्ज़्/ (*AmE*) = **fringe¹1**

**banish** /ˈbænɪʃ ˈबैनिश्/ *verb* [T] (*formal*) **1** to send sb away (especially out of the country), usually as a punishment दंडस्वरूप देश-निकाला देना, निर्वासित करना **2** to make sb/sth go away; to get rid of sb/sth किसी व्यक्ति या वस्तु को निकाल देना; (किसी व्यक्ति या वस्तु से) छुटकारा पाना *She banished all hope of winning from her mind.*

**banister** (*also* **bannister**) /ˈbænɪstə(r) ˈबैनिस्ट(र्)/ *noun* [C] (*usually plural*) the posts and rail at the side of a staircase जीने के पार्श्व में लगे स्तंभ और जंगले *The children loved sliding down the banister at the old house.*

**banjo** /ˈbændʒəʊ ˈबैन्जो/ *noun* [C] (*pl.* **banjos**) a musical instrument like a guitar, with a long thin neck, a round body and four or more strings चौड़े तथा गोल अधोभाग, लंबी गरदन और चार या अधिक तारों वाला गिटार जैसा एक वाद्य यंत्र; बैंजो ➪ **piano** पर नोट तथा पृष्ठ 789 पर चित्र देखिए।

**bank¹** /bæŋk बैङ्क्/ *noun* [C] **1** an organization which keeps money safely for its customers; the office or building of such an organization. You can take money out, save, borrow or exchange money at a bank बैंक *a bank account/loan* **2** a store of things, which you keep to use later भविष्य में प्रयोग के लिए रखा गया वस्तुओं आदि का संग्रह; कोष *a databank* ○ *a blood bank in a hospital* **3** the ground along the side of a river or canal नदी या नहर का किनारा, तट *People were fishing along the banks of the river.* **4** a higher area of ground that goes down or up at an angle, often at the edge of sth or dividing sth नदी-तट की भूमि; कछार *There were grassy banks on either side of the road.* **5** a mass of cloud, snow, etc. बादलों, हिम आदि का जमघट या जमाव *The sun disappeared behind a bank of clouds.*

**bank²** /bæŋk बैङ्क्/ *verb* [I] **bank (with/at)** to have an account with a particular bank खाता होना *I've banked with the State Bank of India for years.*

**PHR V bank on sb/sth** to expect and trust sb to do sth, or sth to happen (किसी पर) भरोसा रखना, आश्रित होना *Our boss might let you have the morning off but I wouldn't bank on it.*

**banker** /ˈbæŋkə(r) ˈबैङ्क(र्)/ *noun* [C] a person who owns or has an important job in a bank बैंक का स्वामी; बैंक-अधिकारी

**bank holiday** *noun* [C] (*BrE*) a public holiday (not a Saturday or Sunday) सार्वजनिक अवकाश का दिन (परंतु शनिवार और रविवार नहीं)

**banking** /ˈbæŋkɪŋ ˈबैङ्किङ्/ *noun* [U] the type of business done by banks बैंक-कर्म, बैकिंग *a career in banking*

**banknote** /ˈbæŋknəʊt ˈबैङ्क्नोट्/ = **note**[1] **4**

**bankrupt** /ˈbæŋkrʌpt ˈबैङ्क्रप्ट्/ *adj.* not having enough money to pay your debts ऋण न चुका पाने की स्थिति में; दिवालिया *The company must cut its costs or it will **go bankrupt**.* ▶ **bankrupt** *verb* [T] दिवाला निकलना *The failure of the new product almost bankrupted the firm.*

**bankruptcy** /ˈbæŋkrʌptsi ˈबैङ्क्रप्ट्सि/ *noun* [C, U] (*pl.* **bankruptcies**) the state of being bankrupt दिवालियापन, दिवाला *The company **filed for bankruptcy** in 2001.*

**bank statement** (*also* **statement**) *noun* [C] a printed list of all the money going into or out of your bank account during a certain period किसी खाते से विशेष अवधि के दौरान किया गया जमा या निकासी का मुद्रित विवरण

**banner** /ˈbænə(r) ˈबैन(र्)/ *noun* [C] a long piece of cloth with words or signs on it, which can be hung up or carried on two poles प्रायः दो डंडों पर लगा कपड़े का लंबा टुकड़ा जिस पर कुछ लिखा हो या प्रतीक चिह्न अंकित हो; बैनर *The demonstrators carried banners saying 'Stop the War'.*

**bannister** = **banister**

**banquet** /ˈbæŋkwɪt ˈबैङ्क्विट्/ *noun* [C] a formal dinner for a large number of people, usually as a special event at which speeches are made औपचारिक सामूहिक भोज जहाँ भाषण दिए जाते हैं

**banter** /ˈbæntə(r) ˈबैन्ट(र्)/ *noun* [U] friendly comments and jokes हँसी-दिल्लगी, परिहास, ठट्ठा ▶ **banter** *verb* [I] हँसी-मज़ाक करना

**banyan** /ˈbænjən ˈबैन्यन्/ (*also* **banyan tree**) *noun* [C] an Indian tree with branches that put out roots which grow downwards till they reach the ground. These then form new trunks that help to support the main trunk of the tree वट वृक्ष, बरगद का पेड़

**baptism** /ˈbæptɪzəm ˈबैप्टिज़म्/ *noun* [C, U] a ceremony in which a person becomes a member of the Christian Church by being held under water for a short time or having drops of water put onto his/her head. Often he/she is also formally given a name ईसाई चर्च का विधिवत सदस्य बनने का संस्कार जिसमें सदस्य बनने वाले व्यक्ति का जल से अभिषेक और प्रायः नामकरण भी किया जाता है; बपतिस्मा ➪ **christening** देखिए। ▶ **baptize** (*also* **-ise**) /bæpˈtaɪz बैप्ˈटाइज़्/ *verb* [T] बपतिस्मा करना ➪ **christen** देखिए।

**bar**[1] /bɑː(r) बा(र्)/ *noun* [C] **1** a place where you can buy and drink (especially alcoholic drinks) and sometimes have sth to eat जलपानगृह जहाँ पेय, विशेषतः मदिरा, और खाद्य पदार्थ उपलब्ध हों; बार *a coffee/snack bar* **2** a long, narrow, high surface where drinks are served लंबी-ऊँची पटरी जिस पर मदिरा आदि पेय परोसे जाते हैं; पानपटल *We sat on stools **at the bar**.* **3 a bar (of sth)** a small block of solid material, longer than it is wide सिल, सिल्ली, टिक्की, ठोस पदार्थ की छड़ *a bar of soap/chocolate* **4** a long, thin, straight piece of metal, often placed across a window or door, etc. to stop sb from getting through it दरवाज़े या खिड़की का अर्गला, अगरी **5 a bar (to sth)** a thing that prevents you from doing sth कुछ करने में बाधा, रुकावट *Lack of education is not always a bar to success in business.* **6** (in geography) a line of sand or mud that forms in the sea parallel to the beach (भूगोल में) समुद्रतट के समानांतर बनी रेत या मिट्टी पट्टी, रेखा **7** (*technical*) a measurement of pressure in the atmosphere वायुमंडल के दाब की एक माप

IDM **behind bars** (*informal*) in prison जेल में *The criminals are now safely behind bars.*

**bar**[2] /bɑː(r) बा(र्)/ *verb* [T] (**barring**; **barred**) **1** (*usually passive*) to close sth with a bar or **bars**[1] **4** अर्गला से दरवाज़ा आदि बंद करना *All the windows were barred.* **2** to block a road, path, etc. so that nobody can pass सड़क, पथ आदि पर रोक लगाना *A line of police officers barred the entrance to the embassy.* **3 bar sb from sth/from doing sth** to say officially that sb is not allowed to do, use or enter sth किसी क्रिया पर क़ानूनन रोक लगा देना, मनाही कर देना *He was barred from the club for fighting.*

**bar**[3] /bɑː(r) बा(र्)/ *prep.* except के सिवाय, के अलावा *All the seats were taken, bar one.*

**barb** /bɑːb बाब्/ *noun* [C] **1** the point of an arrow or a hook that is curved backwards to make it difficult to pull out तीर या हुक की पीछे मुड़ी नोक (ताकि उसे खींचकर निकाला न जा सके) **2** something that sb says that is intended to hurt another person's feelings ऐसी बात जो दूसरे की भावनाओं को आहत कर दे; चुभने वाली बात

**barbarian** /bɑːˈbeəriən बाˈबेअरिअन् / *noun* [C] a wild person with no culture, who behaves very badly बर्बर, असभ्य और कुसंस्कृत व्यक्ति

**barbaric** /bɑːˈbærɪk बाˈबेरिक् / *adj.* very cruel and violent बहुत क्रूर और नृशंस, अतिनिर्मम *barbaric treatment of prisoners* ▶ **barbarism** /ˈbɑːbərɪzəm ˈबाबरिज़म् / *noun* [U] अतिक्रूरता, अतिनृशंसता, अतिनिर्ममता *acts of barbarism committed in war*

**barbarity** /bɑːˈbærəti बाˈबैरटि / *noun* [U, C] (*pl.* **barbarities**) extremely cruel and violent behaviour अत्यंत क्रूर और उग्र व्यवहार, अतिनिर्मम व्यवहार

**barbecue** /ˈbɑːbɪkjuː ˈबाबिक्यू / (*abbr.* **BBQ**) *noun* [C] **1** a metal frame on which food is cooked outdoors over an open fire धातु का सीख़चा जिस पर खुले में आग पर भोजन पकाया जाता है; सीख **2** an outdoor party at which food is cooked in this way बाहर आयोजित प्रीतिभोज जिसमें इस प्रकार भोजन बनाया जाता है *Let's* ***have a barbecue*** *on the beach.* ➪ **roast² 2** देखिए। ▶ **barbecue** *verb* [T] इस तरह से भोजन पकाना *barbecued fish*

**barbed wire** /ˌbɑːbd ˈwaɪə(r) ˌबाब्ड् ˈवाइअ(र्) / *noun* [U] strong wire with sharp points on it मज़बूत कँटीला तार *a barbed wire fence*

**barber** /ˈbɑːbə(r) ˈबाब(र्) / *noun* **1** [C] a person whose job is to cut men's hair and sometimes to shave them नाई, हज्जाम ➪ **hairdresser** देखिए। **2 the barber's** [*sing.*] a shop where men go to have their hair cut नाई की दुकान

**barbiturate** /bɑːˈbɪtʃʊrət बाˈबिचुरट् / *noun* [C] a powerful drug that makes people sleep or become calmer शमनकारक या निद्राकारक औषधि

**bar chart** (*also* **bar graph**) *noun* [C] a diagram that uses narrow bands of different heights to show different amounts so that they can be compared दंड ग्राफ़; एक आरेख जो विभिन्न मात्रा-राशियों की तुलना के लिए उन्हें खड़ी पट्टियों द्वारा दिखाता है ➪ **chart** पर चित्र देखिए।

**bar code** *noun* [C] a pattern of thick and thin lines that is printed on things you buy. It contains information that a computer can read उपभोक्ता साम्रगी के पैकेट पर छपा मोटी और पतली रेखाओं का ख़ाका जिसमें निहित सूचना कंप्यूटर ही पढ़ता है

**bard** /bɑːd बाड् / *noun* [C] (*literary*) a person who writes poems; a poet कवि, शायर *Shakespeare is also known as the Bard of Avon.*

**bare** /beə(r) बेअ(र्) / *adj.* **1** (used about part of the body) not covered by clothing (शरीर का अंग) नग्न, खुला हुआ, वस्त्रहीन *bare arms/feet/shoulders* ➪ **naked** और **nude** देखिए। **2** without anything covering it or in it आवरणहीन, अनढका *They had taken the painting down, so the walls were all bare.* **3** just enough; the most basic or simple केवल, मात्र, निरा, सादा *You won't get good marks if you just do* ***the bare minimum***. ○ *I don't take much luggage when I travel, just* ***the bare essentials***.

IDM **with your bare hands** without weapons or tools बिना हथियार के *He killed the tiger with his bare hands.*

**bareback** /ˈbeəbæk ˈबेअबैक् / *adj.*, *adv.* riding a horse without a seat (**saddle**) घोड़े की पीठ पर बिना काठी के सवार *bareback riders in the circus*

**barefoot** /ˈbeəfʊt ˈबेअफ़ुट् / (*also* **barefooted**) *adj.*, *adv.* not wearing anything on your feet नंगे पाँव *We walked barefoot along the beach.*

**bareheaded** /ˌbeəˈhedɪd ˌबेअˈहेडिड् / *adj.*, *adv.* not wearing anything to cover your head नंगे सिर

**barely** /ˈbeəli ˈबेअलि / *adv.* (used especially after 'can' and 'could' to emphasize that sth is difficult to do) only just; almost not (विशेषतः 'can'और 'could' के बाद प्रयुक्त—इस बात पर बल देने के लिए कि अमुक काम कठिन है) मुश्किल से, कठिनाई से *I was so tired I could barely stand up.* ○ *I earn barely enough money to pay my rent.* ➪ **hardly** देखिए।

**bargain¹** /ˈbɑːɡən ˈबागन् / *noun* [C] **1** something that is cheaper or at a lower price than usual सस्ता सौदा *I found a lot of bargains in the sale.* **2** an agreement between people or groups about what each of them will do for the other or others समझौते का सौदा *I lent him the money but he didn't* ***keep*** *his* ***side of the bargain***.

IDM **into the bargain** (used for emphasizing sth) as well; in addition; also (किसी बात पर बल देने के लिए प्रयुक्त) साथ ही; के अतिरिक्त; भी *They gave me free tickets and a free meal into the bargain.*

**strike a bargain (with sb)** ➪ **strike²** देखिए।

**bargain²** /ˈbɑːɡən ˈबागन् / *verb* [I] **bargain (with sb) (about/over/for sth)** to discuss prices, conditions, etc. with sb in order to reach an agreement that suits each person सबके लाभ के सौदे पर समझौता करना *They bargained over the price.*

PHR V **bargain for/on sth** (*usually in negative sentences*) to expect sth to happen and be ready for it कुछ घटित होने की आशा करना और उसके लिए तैयार रहना *When I agreed to help him I didn't bargain for how much it would cost me.*

**barge**[1] /bɑːdʒ बाज़् / *noun* [C] a long narrow boat with a flat bottom that is used for carrying goods or people on a canal or river बोझा ढोने की लंबी सँकरी नौका; बजरा ➪ **boat** पर चित्र देखिए।

**barge**[2] /bɑːdʒ बाज़् / *verb* [I, T] to push people out of the way in order to get past them लोगों को इधर उधर ढकेलकर ज़बरदस्ती घुसना *He barged (his way) angrily through the crowd.*

**bar graph** = **bar chart**

**baritone** /ˈbærɪtəʊn ˈबैरिटोन् / *noun* [C] a male singing voice that is fairly low; a man with this voice पर्याप्त निम्न तान से गाने वाला पुरुष गायक; ऐसा पुरुष जिसकी आवाज़ ही पर्याप्त निम्न तान की हो **NOTE** यह स्वर **tenor** और **bass** के मध्य का है।

**barium** /ˈbeəriəm ˈबेअरिअम् / *noun* [U] (*symbol* **Ba**) a soft silver-white metal एक चाँदी जैसी सफ़ेद मुलायम धातु; बेरियम

**bark**[1] /bɑːk बाक् / *noun* **1** [U] the hard outer covering of a tree (पेड़ की) छाल, वल्कल **2** [C] the short, loud noise that a dog makes (कुत्ते की) भौंक

**bark**[2] /bɑːk बाक् / *verb* **1** [I] **bark (at sb/sth)** (used about dogs) to make a loud, short noise or noises (कुत्ते का) भौंकना **2** [T] **bark sth (out) (at sb)** to give orders, ask questions, etc. in a loud unfriendly way कड़वे शब्दों तथा ऊँचे स्वर में कुछ पूछना, आदेश देना आदि, चिड़चिड़ाकर कुछ कहना *The boss came in, barked out some orders and left again.*

**barley** /ˈbɑːli ˈबालि / *noun* [U] **1** a plant that produces grain that is used for food or for making beer and other drinks जौ या यव का पौधा **2** the grain produced by this plant जौ, यव ➪ **cereal** पर चित्र देखिए।

**barmaid** /ˈbɑːmeɪd ˈबामेड् / *noun* [C] (*AmE* **bartender**) a woman who serves drinks from behind a bar in a pub, etc. मदिरालय परिचारिका, मधुशाला परिचारिका

**barman** /ˈbɑːmən ˈबामन् / *noun* [C] (*pl.* **-men** /-mən -मन् /) (*AmE* **bartender**) a man who serves drinks from behind a bar in a pub, etc. मदिरालय परिचारक, मधुशाला परिचारक

**barn** /bɑːn बान् / *noun* [C] a large building on a farm in which crops or animals are kept खेत में बना बड़ा कमरा जिसमें फ़सल और पशुओं को रखा जाता है; खलियान, भुसौरा

**barometer** /bəˈrɒmɪtə(r) बˈरॉमिट(र्) / *noun* [C] **1** an instrument that measures air pressure and indicates changes in weather वायु का दाब मापने और मौसम में परिवर्तन का संकेत देने वाला यंत्र; वायुदाबमापी **2** something that indicates the state of sth (a situation, a feeling, etc.) (किसी स्थिति, भाव, आदि की) दशा का संकेतक *Results of local elections are often a barometer of the government's popularity.*

**baron** /ˈbærən ˈबैरन् / *noun* [C] **1** a man of a high social position in Britain; a nobleman (ब्रिटेन में) उच्च सामाजिक स्थिति का व्यक्ति; संभ्रांत व्यक्ति, सामंत **2** a person who controls a large part of a particular industry or type of business किसी उद्योग या व्यापार विशेष के बड़े हिस्से पर नियंत्रण रखने वाला व्यक्ति; बड़ा व शक्तिशाली उद्योगपति या व्यापारी *drug/oil barons*

**baroness** /ˈbærənəs ˈबैरनस् / *noun* [C] a woman of a high social position; the wife of a baron संभ्रांत महिला; संभ्रांत पुरुष (बैरन) की पत्नी

**baroque** (*also* **Baroque**) /bəˈrɒk बˈरॉक् / *adj.* used to describe a highly decorated style of European architecture, art and music of the 17th and early 18th centuries भवन-निर्माण, कला, और संगीत की 17वीं और 18वीं शताब्दी के यूरोप में प्रचलित अति-अलंकृत शैली संबंधित

**barracks** /ˈbærəks ˈबैरक्स् / *noun* [C, *with sing. or pl. verb*] (*pl.* **barracks**) a building or group of buildings in which soldiers live फ़ौजियों के रहने का भवन या भवन-शृंखला; बैरक *Guards were on duty at the gate of the barracks.*

**barrage** /ˈbærɑːʒ ˈबैराश़् / *noun* [C] **1** a continuous attack on a place with a large number of guns (किसी स्थान पर) बंदूक़ों से लगातार गोलियों की वर्षा **2** a large number of questions, comments, etc., directed at a person very quickly किसी व्यक्ति पर प्रश्नों, टिप्पणियों आदि की बौछार *The minister faced a barrage of questions from reporters.*

**barrel** /ˈbærəl ˈबैरल् / *noun* [C] **1** a large, round, wooden, plastic or metal container for liquids, that has a flat top and bottom and is wider in the middle द्रव पदार्थ रखने का प्लास्टिक, धातु या लकड़ी का ढोलनुमा बड़ा गोल पीपा जिसके सिरे चपटे और मध्य भाग चौड़ा होता है *a beer/wine/oil barrel* **2** a unit of measurement in the oil industry equal to approximately 159 litres तेल उद्योग में प्रचलित लगभग 159 लिटर की एक माप-इकाई *The price of oil is usually given per barrel.* **3** the long metal part of a gun like a tube through which the bullets are fired बंदूक़ की नाल, रिवॉल्वर की नली

**barren** /ˈbærən ˈबैरन् / *adj.* **1** (used about land or soil) not good enough for plants to grow on (भूमि या मिट्टी) ऊसर, बंजर **2** (used about trees or plants) not producing fruit or seeds (वृक्ष या पौधा) निष्फल

**barricade** /ˌbærɪˈkeɪd ˌबैरिˈकेड्/ *noun* [C] an object or line of objects that is placed across a road, entrance, etc. to stop people getting through सड़क, प्रवेश द्वार आदि पर वस्तुएँ जमा करने से बनी रोक या बाधा *The demonstrators **put up barricades** to keep the police away.* ▶ **barricade** *verb* [T] मोर्चाबंदी करना, अवरुद्ध करना

**PHR V barricade yourself in** to defend yourself by putting up a barricade रोक लगाकर अपनी रक्षा करना *Demonstrators took over the building and barricaded themselves in.*

**barrier** /ˈbæriə(r) ˈबैरिअ(र्)/ *noun* [C] **1** an object that keeps people or things separate or prevents them moving from one place to another लोगों या वस्तुओं के आने-जाने को रोकने या एक दूसरे से अलग करने वाली अवरोधक वस्तु *The crowd were all kept behind barriers.* ○ *The mountains form a natural barrier between the two countries.* ➪ **crash barrier** देखिए। **2 a barrier (to sth)** something that causes problems or makes it impossible for sth to happen उलझन या रुकावट पैदा करने वाली वस्तु; बाधा, व्यवधान *When you live in a foreign country, the **language barrier** is often the most difficult problem to overcome.*

**barring** /ˈbɑːrɪŋ ˈबारिङ्/ *prep.* except for; unless there is/are को छोड़कर, यदि कुछ न हुआ तो *Barring any unforeseen problems, we'll be moving house in a month.*

**barrister** /ˈbærɪstə(r) ˈबैरिस्ट(र्)/ *noun* [C] (in English law) a lawyer who is trained to speak for you in the higher courts (अंग्रेज़ी क़ानून में) उच्च न्यायालय में वकालत के लिए प्रशिक्षित वकील, बैरिस्टर ➪ **lawyer** पर नोट देखिए।

**barrow** /ˈbærəʊ ˈबैरो/ *noun* [C] **1** a small thing on two wheels on which fruit, vegetables, etc. are moved or sold in the street, especially in markets फल, सब्ज़ियाँ आदि बेचने के लिए प्रयुक्त दो पहियों का छोटा ठेला **2** = **wheelbarrow**

**bar staff** *noun* [U, *with pl. verb*] the people who serve drinks from behind a bar in a pub, etc. मधुशाला का परिचारक वर्ग *The bar staff are very friendly here.* ➪ **barmaid** और **barman** देखिए।

**bartender** /ˈbɑːtendə(r) ˈबाटेन्ड(र्)/ (*AmE*) = **barmaid** or **barman**

**barter** /ˈbɑːtə(r) ˈबाट(र्)/ *verb* [I, T] **barter sth (for sth); barter (with sb) (for sth)** to exchange goods, services, property, etc. for other goods, etc., without using money रुपये आदि मुद्रा के बिना वस्तुओं, सेवाओं आदि का लेन-देन करना *The farmer bartered his surplus grain for machinery.* ○ *The prisoners bartered with the guards for writing paper and books.* ▶ **barter** *noun* [U] मुद्रा के प्रयोग के बिना किया गया लेन-देन; वस्तु विनिमय

**basalt** /ˈbæsɔːlt ˈबैसॉल्ट्/ *noun* [U] (in geology) a type of dark rock that comes from **volcanoes** (भूविज्ञान में) ज्वालामुखियों से निकलने काला पत्थर, असिताश्म

**base**[1] /beɪs बेस्/ *noun* [C] **1** the lowest part of sth, especially the part on which it stands or at which it is fixed or connected to sth किसी वस्तु आदि का आधार, नींव; पेंदा, तल *the base of a column/glass/box* ○ *I felt a terrible pain **at the base of** my spine.* **2** an idea, fact, etc. from which sth develops or is made मूल विचार, पदार्थ, तथ्य आदि *The country needs a strong economic base.* **3** a place used as a centre from which activities are done or controlled आधार-स्थल, संचालन केंद्र, अड्डा *This hotel is an ideal base for touring the region.* **4** a military centre from which the armed forces operate सैनिक अड्डा *an army base* **5** (in baseball) one of the four points that a runner must touch (बेसबॉल में) चार आधार-बिंदुओं में से एक जिन्हें छूना खिलाड़ी के लिए आवश्यक है **6** a chemical substance with a pH value of more than 7, 7 से अधिक pH मूल्य का रसायन; क्षारक ➪ **acid** और **alkali** देखिए तथा **pH** पर चित्र देखिए।

**base**[2] /beɪs बेस्/ *verb* [T] (*usually passive*) **base sb/sth in** to make one place the centre from which sb/sth can work or move around एक स्थान को आधार-स्थल बनाना जहाँ से यात्रा आदि गतिविधियाँ की जा सकें *I'm based in Allahabad although my job involves a great deal of travel.* ○ *a Mumbai-based company*

**PHR V base sth on sth** to form or develop sth from a particular starting point or source एक विशिष्ट बिंदु या स्रोत से किसी वस्तु का विकास या निर्माण करना *This film is based on a true story.*

**baseball** /ˈbeɪsbɔːl ˈबेस्बॉल्/ *noun* [U] a team game that is popular in the US in which players hit the ball with a bat and run round four points (**bases**). They have to touch all four bases in order to score a point (**run**) अमेरिका में एक लोकप्रिय खेल जिसमें खिलाड़ी बल्ले द्वारा गेंद को मारते हैं और चार आधार-बिंदुओं के इर्द-गिर्द घूमते हैं। अंक पाने के लिए इन चारों बिंदुओं को छूना आवश्यक होता है; बेसबॉल

**baseboard** /ˈbeɪsbɔːd ˈबेस्बॉड्/ (*AmE*) = **skirting board**

**baseline** /ˈbeɪslaɪn ˈबेस्लाइन् / *noun* [*usually sing.*] **1** (*sport*) a line that marks each end of the court in games such as tennis or the edge of the area where a player can run in baseball टेनिस आदि खेल के मैदान की सीमाएँ अंकित करने वाली रेखा; सीमाद्योतक रेखा; बेसलाइन **2** (*technical*) a line or measurement that is used as a starting-point when comparing facts तथ्यों की तुलना के लिए आधार बिंदु के रूप में प्रयुक्त एक माप या रेखा

**basement** /ˈbeɪsmənt ˈबेस्मन्ट् / *noun* [C] a room or rooms in a building, partly or completely below ground level इमारत के वह कमरे जो अंशतः या पूर्णतः भूमि स्तर के नीचे हों; भूमिगत मंजिल *a basement flat* ➪ **cellar** देखिए।

**base metal** *noun* [C] a metal that is not a precious metal such as gold सस्ती धातु

**base rate** *noun* [C] a rate of interest, set by a central bank, that all banks in Britain use when calculating the amount of interest that they charge on the money they lend ब्याज-गणना की आधारभूत दर

**bases** ➪ **1 basis** का plural रूप **2 base[1]** का plural रूप

**bash[1]** /bæʃ बैश् / *verb* (*informal*) **1** [I, T] to hit sb/sth very hard (किसी से) ज़ोर से टकरा जाना *I didn't stop in time and bashed into the car in front.* **2** [T] to criticize sb/sth strongly (किसी की) तीखी आलोचना करना *The candidate continued to bash her opponent's policies.*

**bash[2]** /bæʃ बैश् / *noun* [C] (*informal*) **1** a hard hit ज़ोर से प्रहार *He gave Ali a bash on the nose.* **2** a large party or celebration समारोह या उत्सव

IDM **have a bash** (**at sth/at doing sth**) (*BrE spoken*) to try प्रयत्न करना, कोशिश करना *I'll get a screwdriver and have a bash at mending the light.*

**bashful** /ˈbæʃfl ˈबैश्फ़्ल् / *adj.* shy and embarrassed शरमीला और झेंपू

**basic** /ˈbeɪsɪk ˈबेसिक् / *adj.* **1** forming the part of sth that is most necessary and from which other things develop आधारभूत, बुनियादी *The basic question is, can we afford it?* ○ *basic information/facts/ideas* **2** of the simplest kind or level; including only what is necessary without anything extra मूल, मूलवर्ती; *This course teaches basic computer skills.* ○ *The* ***basic pay*** *is Rs 4000 a month—with extra for overtime.*

**basically** /ˈbeɪsɪkli ˈबेसिक्लि / *adv.* used to say what the most important or most basic aspect of sb/sth is मूल रूप से, बुनियादी तौर पर *The new design is basically the same as the old one.*

**basics** /ˈbeɪsɪks ˈबेसिक्स् / *noun* [*pl.*] the simplest or most important facts or aspects of sth; things that you need the most सबसे साधारण व महत्त्वपूर्ण तथ्य या पहलू; मूलभूत तथ्य; सर्वाधिक आवश्यक वस्तुएँ *So far, I've only learnt the basics of computing.*

**basil** /ˈbæzəl ˈबैज़ल् / *noun* [U] an aromatic annual plant native to tropical Asia with a strong pungent, sweet smell. It is used as a flavouring agent in cooking and is also considered sacred by Hindus तुलसी का पौधा; भारत में हिंदुओं द्वारा पवित्र मानी जाने वाली बूटी जिसका प्रयोग खाने में होता है

**basin** /ˈbeɪsn ˈबेस्न् / *noun* [C] **1** = **washbasin** **2** a round open bowl often used for mixing or cooking food भोजन बनाने आदि का कढ़ाहीनुमा पात्र **3** an area of land from which water flows into a river भूमि का वह क्षेत्र जिसमें से होकर पानी नदी में जाता है; द्रोणी, नदी-नाला *the Ganga River Basin*

**basis** /ˈbeɪsɪs ˈबेसिस् / *noun* (*pl.* **bases** /ˈbeɪsiːz ˈबेसीज़् /) **1** [*sing.*] the principle or reason which lies behind sth विचारधारा, विश्वास आदि का आधार *We made our decision* ***on the basis of*** *the reports which you sent us.* **2** [*sing.*] the way sth is done or organized (कुछ करने का) तरीक़ा या रीति-विशेष *They meet* ***on a regular basis***. ○ *to employ sb* ***on a*** *temporary/voluntary/part-time* ***basis*** **3** [C] a starting point, from which sth can develop आरंभिक बिंदु जहाँ से कुछ विकसित होता है; प्रवर्तन-बिंदु *She used her diaries as a basis for her book.*

**bask** /ˈbɑːsk; bæsk ˈबास्क्; बैस्क् / *verb* [I] **bask (in sth)** **1** to sit or lie in a place where you can enjoy the warmth किसी स्थान पर बैठकर या लेटकर गरमाहट का आनंद लेना *The children basked in the sunshine on the beach.* **2** to enjoy the good feelings you have when other people admire you, give you a lot of attention, etc. लोगों की प्रशंसा और शुभेच्छाओं से आनंदित होना *The team was still* ***basking in the glory*** *of winning the cup.*

**basket** /ˈbɑːskɪt ˈबास्किट् / *noun* [C] **1** a container for carrying or holding things, made of thin pieces of material such as wood, plastic or wire that bends easily डोलची, डलिया, टोकरी *a waste-paper basket* ○ *a shopping basket* ○ *a clothes/laundry basket* **2** a net that hangs from a metal ring high up at each end of a basketball court धातु-निर्मित छल्ले में लगा जाल **3** a score of one, two or three points in basketball, made by throwing the ball through one of the nets बास्केटबॉल में स्कोर (एक, दो, तीन, पाइंट) बताने के लिए प्रयुक्त

IDM **put all your eggs in one basket** ➪ **egg[1]** देखिए।

**basketball** /ˈbɑːskɪtbɔːl ˈबास्किट्बॉल् / *noun* [U] a game for two teams of five players. There is a net (**basket**) fixed to a metal ring high up at each end of the court and the players try to throw a ball through the other team's net in order to score points (**baskets**) बास्किटबॉल का खेल

**basmati** *noun* [U] a kind of long-grained rice grown in India and Pakistan. It is known for its delicate flavour बासमती चावल (खुशबूदार और लंबे दानों वाला)

**bass** /beɪs बेस् / *noun* **1** [U] the lowest part in music संगीत में निम्नतम स्वर; मंद स्वर **2** [C] the lowest male singing voice; a singer with this kind of voice निम्नतम तान का पुरुष स्वर; निम्नतम तान स्वर युक्त पुरुष ➪ **tenor** और **baritone** देखिए। **3** = **double bass** **4** [C] (*also* **bass guitar**) an electric guitar which plays very low notes एक प्रकार का विद्युत गिटार जिसमें से निम्न तान के स्वर निकलते हैं ➪ **piano** पर नोट देखिए। ▶ **bass** *adj.* (*only before a noun*) (संगीत में) निम्न तान संबंधित *a bass drum* ○ *Can you sing the bass part in this song?*

**bassoon** /bəˈsuːn बˈसून् / *noun* [C] a musical instrument that you blow which makes a very deep sound बहुत गहरा स्वर निकालने वाला एक वाद्य यंत्र; एक प्रकार की बाँसुरी, अलगोज़ा ➪ **piano** पर नोट देखिए।

**bastard** /ˈbɑːstəd; ˈbæs- ˈबास्टड्; ˈबैस्- / *noun* [C] (*old-fashioned*) a person whose parents were not married to each other when he/she was born अविवाहित माता-पिता की संतान; जारज, नाज़ायज़

**baste** /beɪst बेस्ट् / *verb* [T] to pour liquid fat or juices over meat, etc. while it is cooking पकते हुए मांस पर तेल, रस आदि द्रव पदार्थ उड़ेलना

**bat¹** /bæt बैट् / *noun* [C] **1** a piece of wood for hitting the ball in sports such as table tennis, cricket or baseball क्रिकेट, टेनिस या बेसबॉल का बल्ला *a cricket bat* ➪ **racket** और **stick** देखिए। **2** a small animal, like a mouse with wings, which flies and hunts at night चमगादड़

IDM **off your own bat** without anyone asking you or helping you बिना किसी की सहायता के

**bat²** /bæt बैट् / *verb* [I] (**batting; batted**) (used about one player or a whole team) to have a turn hitting the ball in sports such as cricket or baseball (एक खिलाड़ी या पूरी टीम का) बल्लेबाज़ी करना

IDM **not bat an eyelid;** (*AmE*) **not bat an eye** to show no surprise or embarrassment when sth unusual happens किसी विचित्र घटना पर ज़रा-सा भी आश्चर्य प्रकट न करना

**batch** /bætʃ बैच् / *noun* [C] **1** a number of things or people which belong together as a group टुकड़ी, दल, समूह *The bus returned to the airport for the next batch of tourists.* **2** (*computing*) a set of jobs that are done together on a computer कंप्यूटर पर एक साथ निष्पादित कार्य-समुच्चय *to process a batch job* ○ *a batch file/program*

**bated** /ˈbeɪtɪd ˈबेटिड् / *adj.*

IDM **with bated breath** excited or afraid, because you are waiting for sth to happen (किसी घटना की प्रतीक्षा में) उत्कंठित, आशंकित, साँस रोककर

**bath¹** /bɑːθ बाथ् / *noun* (*pl.* **baths** /bɑːðz बाद्ज़् /) **1** [C] (*also* **bathtub**) a large container for water in which you sit to wash your body स्नान का टब *Can you answer the phone? I'm in the bath!* **2** [*sing.*] an act of washing the whole of your body स्नान करने या नहाने की क्रिया *to **have a bath*** **3** [C, *usually pl.*] a public place where people went in past times to wash or have a bath प्राचीन समय में सार्वजनिक स्नानगृह *Roman baths*

**bath²** /bɑːθ बाथ् / *verb* **1** [T] to give sb a bath नहलाना, स्नान कराना *bath the baby* **2** [I] (*old-fashioned*) to have a bath नहाना, स्नान करना

**bathe** /beɪð बेद् / *verb* **1** [T] to wash or put part of the body in water, often for medical reasons शरीर के किसी अंग को जल से धोना या जल का स्पर्श देना (प्रायः चिकित्सा हेतु); शरीर-प्रक्षालन *She bathed the wound with antiseptic.* **2** [I] (*old-fashioned*) to swim in the sea or in a lake or river समुद्र, नदी, झील में तैरना ➪ **sunbathe** देखिए।

**bathed** /beɪðd बेद्ड् / *adj.* (*written*) **bathed in sth** (*not before a noun*) covered with sth किसी वस्तु से (मानो) ढक जाना या नहा जाना, ढका हुआ; आवरित *The room was bathed in moonlight.*

**bathing** /ˈbeɪðɪŋ ˈबेदिङ् / *noun* [U] the act of swimming in the sea, a river or a lake (not in a swimming pool) तैराक़ी (समुद्र, नदी, झील में, न कि तरणताल में) *Bathing is possible at a number of beaches along the coast.*

**bathos** /ˈbeɪθɒs ˈबेथॉस् / *noun* [U] (*formal*) (in literature) a sudden change, which is not usually deliberate, from a serious subject or feeling to sth ridiculous or unimportant (साहित्य में) उत्कर्ष से अपकर्ष स्थिति में सहसा परिवर्तन

**bathrobe** /ˈbɑːθrəʊb ˈबाथ्रोब् / = **dressing gown**

**bathroom** /ˈbɑːθruːm; -rʊm ˈबाथ्रूम्; -रुम् / *noun* [C] **1** a room where there is a bath, a place to wash your hands (**a washbasin**) and sometimes a toilet स्नानगृह, गुस्लख़ाना **2** a room with a toilet शौच सुविधायुक्त कमरा; शौचालय ➪ **toilet** पर नोट देखिए।

**bathtub** /ˈbɑːθtʌb ˈबाथ़्टब्/ = **bath**[1]

**batik** *noun* [U, C] a method of printing patterns on cloth by putting **wax** on the parts of the cloth that will not have any colour; a piece of cloth that is printed in this way कपड़े पर मोम के द्वारा विभिन्न डिज़ाइन बनाने की विधि; इस विधि से डिज़ाइन किया वस्त्र-खंड, छींट, बाटिक

**baton** /ˈbætɒn ˈबैटॉन्/ *noun* [C] **1** = **truncheon** **2** a short thin stick used by the leader of an orchestra आर्किस्ट्रा संचालक की छड़ी **3** a stick which a runner in a race (**a relay race**) passes to the next person in the team रिले-दौड़ की छड़ी जिसे एक धावक टीम के दूसरे धावक को थमाता है

**batsman** /ˈbætsmən ˈबैट्स्मन्/ *noun* [C] (**-men** /-mən -मन्/) (in cricket) one of the two players who hit the ball to score points (**runs**) (क्रिकेट में) बल्लेबाज़

**battalion** /bəˈtæliən बˈटैलिअन्/ *noun* [C] a large unit of soldiers that forms part of a larger unit in the army थल सेना के सैनिकों की बड़ी टुकड़ी जो एक बड़ी इकाई का हिस्सा हो; बटैलियन; पलटन

**batter**[1] /ˈbætə(r) ˈबैट(र्)/ *verb* [I, T] to hit sb/sth hard, many times बार-बार ज़ोर से प्रहार करना; कूटना, तोड़ना *The wind battered against the window.* ○ *He battered the door down.*

**batter**[2] /ˈbætə(r) ˈबैट(र्)/ *noun* [U] a mixture of flour, eggs and milk used to cover food such as fish, vegetables, etc. before frying them, or to make **pancakes** आटे, अंडे और दूध की लपसी जिसे मछली, सब्ज़ियों आदि पर (उन्हें पकाने से पहले) फैलाया जाता है या जिससे पैनकेक बनाया जाता है

**battered** /ˈbætəd ˈबैटड्/ *adj.* no longer looking new; damaged or out of shape घिसा-पिटा, जीर्ण-शीर्ण *a battered old hat*

**battery** *noun* (*pl.* **batteries**) **1** /ˈbætri ˈबैट्रि/[C] a device which provides electricity for a toy, radio, car, etc. खिलौने, कार, रेडियो को विद्युत उपलब्ध कराने वाला यंत्र; बैटरी *to recharge **a flat battery*** **2** /ˈbætri ˈबैट्रि/ [C] (*often used as an adjective*) a large number of very small cages in which chickens, etc. are kept on a farm चूज़े आदि रखने के बहुत-से छोटे-छोटे पिंजरे *a battery hen/farm* ➪ **free-range** देखिए। **3** /ˈbætəri ˈबैट्रि/ [U] the crime of attacking sb physically शारीरिक हमला करने का अपराध *He was charged with **assault and battery**.*

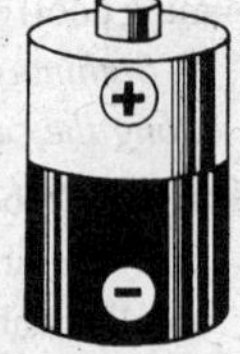

**battle**[1] /ˈbætl ˈबैट्ल्/ *noun* **1** [C, U] a fight, especially between armies in a war युद्ध में सेनाओं के बीच लड़ाई *the battle of Haldighati* ○ *to die/be killed **in battle*** **2** [C] **a battle (with sb) (for sth)** a competition, argument or fight between people or groups of people trying to win power or control संघर्ष, प्रतिस्पर्धा, लड़ाई *a legal battle for custody of the children* **3** [C *usually sing.*] **a battle (against/for sth)** a determined effort to solve a difficult problem or to succeed in a difficult situation कठिन समस्या या परिस्थिति का हल ढूँढ़ने का दृढ़ संकल्पयुक्त प्रयास, भरपूर कोशिश *After three years she lost her battle against cancer.*

IDM **a losing battle** ➪ **lose** देखिए।

**battle**[2] /ˈbætl ˈबैट्ल्/ *verb* [I] **battle (with/against sb/sth) (for sth); battle (on)** to try very hard to achieve sth difficult or to deal with sth unpleasant or dangerous किसी संकटपूर्ण अथवा अरुचिकर कार्य में सफलता के लिए संघर्ष करना, जी तोड़ कोशिश करना *The two brothers were battling for control of the family business.* ○ *Life is hard at the moment but we're battling on.*

**battlefield** /ˈbætlfiːld ˈबैट्ल्फ़ील्ड्/ (*also* **battleground** /ˈbætlgraʊnd ˈबैट्ल्ग्राउन्ड्/) *noun* [C] the place where a battle is fought युद्धक्षेत्र, रणभूमि

**battlements** /ˈbætlmənts ˈबैट्ल्मन्ट्स्/ *noun* [*pl.*] a low wall around the top of a castle with spaces in it that people inside could shoot through किले की छत पर बनी नीची दीवार जिसमें बंदूक़ चलाने की सुविधा के लिए छेद होते हैं; प्राचीर, परकोटा, फ़सील

**battleship** /ˈbætlʃɪp ˈबैट्ल्शिप्/ *noun* [C] the largest type of ship used in war बड़ा युद्धपोत

**bauble** /ˈbɔːbl ˈबॉबल्/ *noun* [C] **1** a piece of cheap jewellery भड़कीला व सस्ता गहना **2** a decoration in the shape of a ball that is hung on a Christmas tree क्रिसमस वृक्ष पर लटकाने की सजावटी गेंदनुमा वस्तु

**baulk** (*AmE* **balk**) /bɔːk बॉक्/ *verb* [I] **baulk (at sth)** to not want to do or agree to sth because it seems too difficult, dangerous or unpleasant (कठिन, ख़तरनाक या अरुचिकर होने के कारण) किसी बात का अनिच्छुक होना

**bauxite** /ˈbɔːksaɪt ˈबॉक्साइट्/ *noun* [U] a soft rock from which we get a light metal (**aluminium**) एक प्रकार की नरम चट्टान जिससे अल्यूमीनियम प्राप्त होता है; बॉक्साइट

**bawl** /bɔːl बॉल्/ *verb* [I, T] to shout or cry loudly चिल्लाना, चीख़ना

**bay** /beɪ बे/ *noun* [C] **1** a part of the coast where the land goes in to form a curve खाड़ी *the Bay of*

*Bengal* **2** a part of a building, aircraft or area which has a particular purpose (भवन, विमान या क्षेत्र का) कक्ष या खंड-विशेष *a parking/loading bay*
IDM **hold/keep sb/sth at bay** to stop sb/sth dangerous from getting near you; to prevent a situation or problem from getting worse (किसी ख़तरनाक व्यक्ति या परिस्थिति को) अपने से दूर रखना; (किसी परिस्थिति या समस्या को) बदतर होने से रोकना या बदतर न होने देना

**bayonet** /ˈbeɪənət ˈबेअनट्/ *noun* [C] a knife that can be fixed to the end of a gun बंदूक़ के सिरे पर लगा लंबा चाक़ू, संगीन, बेनट

**bay window** *noun* [C] a window in a part of a room that sticks out from the wall of a house कमरे की खिड़की जो मकान की दीवार से बाहर उभरती है

**bazaar** *noun* [C] **1** (in some eastern countries) a market बाज़ार **2** a sale where the money that is made goes to charity ऐसा विक्रय जिसमें अर्जित धन को दान में दिया जाता है *The school held a bazaar to raise money for the homeless.*

**bazooka** /bəˈzuːkə बˈज़ूका/ *noun* [C] a long gun, shaped like a tube, which is held on the shoulder and used to fire **rockets** नली के आकार की लंबी बंदूक़ जिसे कंधे पर रखकर राकेट दाग़े जाते हैं

**BBQ** *abbr.* = **barbecue**

**BC** /ˌbiːˈsiː ˌबी ˈसी/ *abbr.* before Christ; used in dates to show the number of years before the time when Christians believe Jesus Christ was born (ईसा पूर्व) ईसा मसीह का स्वीकृत जन्मतिथि से पहले की तारीख़ों का निर्देश करने के लिए प्रयुक्त *300 BC* ⇨ **AD** देखिए।

**BDO** /ˌbɪː dɪːˈəʊ ˌबी डी ˈओ/ *abbr.* Block Development Officer; (in India) a government official responsible for the local administration of a **block 6** ब्लॉक डिवैलपमन्ट ऑफ़िसर; किसी ब्लॉक के स्थानीय प्रशासन के लिए ज़िम्मेदार सरकारी अफ़सर

**be**[1] /bi; *strong form* biː बि; प्रबल रूप बी/ *verb* **1** *linking verb* **there is/are** to exist; to be present होना; उपस्थित रहना, विद्यमान होना *I tried phoning them but there was no answer.* ○ *There are a lot of trees in our garden.* **2** [I] used to give the position of sb/sth or the place where sb/sth is situated किसी व्यक्ति या वस्तु का स्थान या उसकी स्थिति बताने के लिए प्रयुक्त *Katrina's in her office.* ○ *Where are the scissors?* ○ *The bus stop is five minutes' walk from here.* ○ *Cochin is on the south coast.* **3** *linking verb* used to give the date or age of sb/sth or to talk about time तिथि, आयु या समय बताने के लिए प्रयुक्त *My birthday is on April 24th.* ○ *It was Tuesday yesterday.* ○ *He's older than Miranda.* **4** *linking verb* used when you are giving the name of people or things, describing them or giving more information about them व्यक्ति या वस्तु का परिचय देने, उसका वर्णन करने या उसके बारे में अधिक जानकारी देने के लिए प्रयुक्त *This is my friend, Anil.* ○ *I'm Amit.* **5** [I] (*used only in perfect tenses*) to go to a place (and return) कहीं जाना (और लौट आना) *Have you ever **been to** Japan?*

> NOTE **Has/have gone** में तुलना करें—*Gunjan's gone to the doctor's* (= she hasn't returned yet). ○ *Gunjan's been to the doctor's today* (= she has returned).

IDM **be yourself** to act naturally स्वाभाविक व्यवहार करना *Don't be nervous; just be yourself and the interview will be fine.*

**to-be** (*used to form compound nouns*) future भावी *his bride-to-be* ○ *mothers-to-be*

**be**[2] /bi; *strong form* biː बि; प्रबल रूप बी/ *auxiliary verb* **1** used with a past participle to form the passive; used with a present participle to form the continuous tenses (कर्मवाच्य बनाने के लिए) भूत कृदंत के साथ प्रयुक्त (निरंतरता बोधक काल रूप बनाने के लिए) वर्तमान कृदंत के साथ प्रयुक्त NOTE अतिरिक्त जानकारी के लिए **Quick Grammar Reference** खंड देखिए। **2 be to do sth** used to show that sth must happen or that sth has been arranged जब यह संकेत करना हो कि कोई बात अवश्य होनी है *You are to leave here at 10 'o'clock at the latest.* **3 if sb/sth were to do sth** used to show that sth is possible but not very likely हलकी संभावना के संकेत के लिए प्रयुक्त *If they were to offer me the job, I'd probably take it.*

**be-** /bi बि/ *prefix* **1** (*in verbs*) to make or treat sb/sth as किसी को कुछ मानना *They befriended him.* **2** wearing or covered with किसी वस्तु को धारण किए हुए, कुछ पहने हुए *bejewelled*

**beach** /biːtʃ बीच्/ *noun* [C] an area of sand or small stones beside the sea समुद्र तट, बालू-तट, किनारा, पुलिन *to sit **on the beach***

**beacon** /ˈbiːkən ˈबीकन्/ *noun* [C] a fire or light on a hill or tower, often near the coast, which is used as a signal प्रायः समुद्र तट के निकट पहाड़ी या मीनार पर स्थापित प्रकाश-शिखा जो स्थान और दिशा का संकेत देती है

**bead** /biːd बीड्/ *noun* [C] **1** a small round piece of wood, glass or plastic with a hole in the middle for putting a string through to make jewellery, etc. लकड़ी, शीशे या प्लास्टिक का बना माला का दाना, मनका **2 beads** [*pl.*] a circular piece of jewellery (**a necklace**) made of beads मनकों की माला **3** a drop of liquid (द्रव पदार्थ की) बूँद *There were **beads of sweat** on his forehead.*

**beady** /ˈbiːdi ˈबीडि / *adj.* (used about a person's eyes) small round and bright; watching everything closely or with suspicion (किसी व्यक्ति की आँखें) छोटी, गोल और चमकीली; पैनी या सब ओर या संदेह से देखने वाली

**beak** /ˈbiːk ˈबीक्/ *noun* [C] the hard pointed part of a bird's mouth पक्षी की चोंच

**beaker** /ˈbiːkə(r) ˈबीक(र्)/ *noun* [C] **1** a plastic or paper drinking cup, usually without a handle प्लास्टिक या काग़ज़ का प्रायः घुंडी रहित, चषक **2** a glass container used in scientific experiments, etc. for pouring liquids वैज्ञानिक प्रयोगों में द्रव पदार्थ उड़ेलने का शीशे का पात्र, बीकर ➪ **laboratory** पर चित्र देखिए।

**beam¹** /biːm बीम् / *noun* [C] **1** a line of light प्रकाश-रेखा, किरण; किरणपुंज *the beam of a torch* ○ *a laser beam* **2** a long piece of wood, metal, etc. that is used to support weight, for example in the floor or ceiling of a building लकड़ी, धातु आदि का लंबा मोटा, लट्ठा जो (फ़र्श या छत का) भार संभालने के प्रयोग में लाया जाता है; शहतीर, धरन **3** a happy smile प्रसन्नताभरी मुस्कराहट, मधुर मुस्कान

**beam²** /biːm बीम् / *verb* **1** [I] **beam (at sb)** to smile happily प्रसन्नता से मुस्कराना *I looked at Karan and he beamed back at me.* **2** [T] to send out radio or television signals रेडियो या टेलीविज़न के संकेत भेजना *The programme was beamed live by satellite to many different countries.* **3** [I] to send out light and warmth प्रकाश और ऊष्मा का प्रसार करना *The sun beamed down on them.*

**bean** /biːn बीन् / *noun* [C] **1** the seeds or seed containers (**pods**) from a climbing plant which are eaten as vegetables सेम, बीन *soya beans* ○ *a tin of baked beans* ○ *green beans* ➪ **vegetable** पर चित्र देखिए। **2** similar seeds from some other plants कुछ अन्य पौधों के इसी प्रकार के बीज *coffee beans*

**IDM full of beans/life** ➪ **full¹** देखिए।

**spill the beans** ➪ **spill** देखिए।

**bean sprouts** *noun* [*pl.*] bean seeds that are just beginning to grow, often eaten without being cooked मूँग या सेम के अँखुए जो प्रायः कच्चे ही खाए जाते हैं

**bear¹** /beə(r) बेअ(र्) / *noun* [C] **1** a large, heavy wild animal with thick fur and sharp teeth भालू, रीछ *a polar/grizzly/brown bear* ➪ **teddy** देखिए। **2** (in business) a person who sells shares in a company, hoping to buy them back later at a lower price ऐसा व्यक्ति जो अपने शेयर इस आशा में बेचता है कि मूल्य गिरेगा और वह उन्हें फिर ख़रीद लेगा; मंदडिया, मूल्यपाती (व्यापार में) *a bear market* ➪ **bull³** देखिए।

**bear²** /beə(r) बेअ(र्) / *verb* (*pt* **bore** /bɔː(r) बॉ(र्) /; *pp* **borne** /bɔːn बॉन् /) **1** [T] (*used with can/could in negative sentences and questions*) to be able to accept and deal with sth unpleasant अप्रिय वस्तु या स्थिति को सहने ओर उनसे निपटने की योग्यता रखना *The pain was almost more than he could bear.* ✪ पर्याय **stand** या **endure** **2** [T] **not bear sth/doing sth** to not be suitable for sth; to not allow sth (किसी स्थिति के लिए) सही या उपयुक्त न होना; किसी को अमान्य करना *What I would do if I lost my job **doesn't bear thinking about**.* **3** [T] (*formal*) to take responsibility for sth किसी बात की ज़िम्मेदारी लेना; दायित्व लेना *Customers will bear the full cost of the improvements.* **4** [T] to have a feeling, especially a negative feeling विचार (विशेषतः कटु भाव) मन में रखना *Despite what they did, she **bears** no **resentment** towards them.* ○ *He's not the type to **bear a grudge** against anyone.* **5** [T] to support the weight of sth किसी का भार वहन करना; संभालना *Twelve pillars bear the weight of the roof.* **6** [T] (*formal*) to show sth; to carry sth so that it can be seen किसी वस्तु को दिखाना या प्रदर्शित करना; किसी वस्तु को ऐसे ले जाना कि वह दिखाई दे *He still **bears the scars** of his accident.* **7** [T] (*written*) to give birth to children (संतान को) जन्म देना, उत्पन्न करना *She bore him two children, both sons.*

> **NOTE** अधिक प्रचलित प्रयोग है—*She had two children.* किसी व्यक्ति के पैदा होने का संकेत करने के लिए **be born** का प्रयोग किया जाता है—*Zahira was born in 1999.*

**8** [I] to turn or go in the direction that is mentioned निर्दिष्ट दिशा में जाना या मुड़ना *Where the road forks, bear left.*

**IDM bear the brunt of sth** to suffer the main force of sth किसी चीज़ का प्रभाव, झटका आदि झेलना, सहन करना *Her sons usually bore the brunt of her anger.*

**bear fruit** to be successful; to produce results सफल होना; सफल परिणाम निकलना

**bear in mind (that); bear/keep sb/sth in mind** ➪ **mind¹** देखिए।

**bear witness (to sth)** to show evidence of sth किसी बात का साक्ष्य प्रस्तुत करना; साक्षी होना *The burning buildings and empty streets bore witness to a recent attack.*

**PHR V bear down (on sb/sth)** **1** to move closer to sb/sth in a frightening way ख़तरनाक तरीक़े से (किसी के) पास आना *We could see the* *hurricane bearing down on the town.* **2** to push down hard on sb/sth किसी को ज़ोर से ढकेल देना; बलपूर्वक दबाना

**bear sb/sth out** to show that sb is correct or that sth is true सही सिद्ध करना या होना, सच निकलना

**bear up** to be strong enough to continue at a difficult time कठिन परिस्थिति या दृढ़तापूर्वक सामना कर लेना *How is he bearing up after his accident?*

**bear with sb/sth** to be patient with किसी (वस्तु या व्यक्ति) के प्रति सहनशील बने रहना *Bear with me I won't be much longer.*

**bearable** /ˈbeərəbl ˈबेअरबल्/ *adj.* that you can accept or deal with, although unpleasant सहन करने योग्य, सहनीय, सह्य *It was extremely hot but the breeze made it more bearable.* ✪ विलोम **unbearable**

**beard** /bɪəd बिअड्/ [C, U] the hair which grows on a man's cheeks and chin दाढ़ी *I'm going to **grow a beard**.* ➪ **goatee** और **moustache** देखिए।

**bearded** /ˈbɪədɪd ˈबिअडिड्/ *adj.* with a beard दाढ़ी वाला, दाढ़ीदार

**bearer** /ˈbeərə(r) ˈबेअर(र्)/ *noun* [C] a person who carries or brings sth (संदेश आदि का) वाहक *I'm sorry to be the bearer of bad news.*

**bearing** /ˈbeərɪŋ ˈबेअरिङ्/ *noun* **1** [U, *sing.*] (**a**) **bearing on sth** a relation or connection to the subject being discussed विचाराधीन विषय से संबंध; संबद्धता *Her comments **had** no **bearing** on our decision.* **2** [U, *sing.*] the way in which sb stands, moves or behaves (व्यक्ति का) बर्ताव करने, चलने या खड़े होने का तरीक़ा-विशेष *a man of dignified bearing* **3** [C] a direction measured from a fixed point using a special instrument (**a compass**) क़ुतुबनुमा की सहायता से जानी गई दिशा

IDM **get/find your bearings** to become familiar with where you are अपने परिवेश से परिचित होना

**lose your bearings** ➪ **lose** देखिए।

**beast** /biːst बीस्ट्/ *noun* [C] (*formal*) an animal, especially a large one बड़ा पशु या जानवर *a wild beast*

**beat**[1] /biːt बीट्/ *verb* (*pt* **beat;** *pp* **beaten** /ˈbiːtn ˈबीट्न्/) **1** [T] **beat sb (at sth); beat sth** to defeat sb; to be better than sth किसी को हरा देना; किसी से आगे निकल जाना; किसी से बेहतर होना *He always beats me at tennis.* ○ *If you want to keep fit, you can't beat swimming.* **2** [I, T] to hit sb/sth many times, usually very hard किसी को ज़ोर से पीटते जाना *The rain was beating on the roof of the car.* **3** [I, T] to make a regular sound or movement नियमित रूप से आवाज़ निकालना या हरकत करना *Her **heart beat** faster as she ran to pick up her child.* ○ *We could hear the drums beating in the distance.* **4** [T] to mix sth quickly with a fork, etc. काँटे, चम्मच आदि से तेज़ी से वस्तुओं को मिलाना *Beat the eggs and sugar together.*

IDM **beat about the bush** to talk about sth for a long time without mentioning the main point मुख्य मुद्दे पर न आकर घुमा-फिराकर बात करना

**(it) beats me** (*spoken*) I do not know जानकारी न होना; 'मुझे नहीं मालूम', 'मैं नहीं जानता' *It beats me where he's gone.* ○ *'Why is she angry?' 'Beats me!'*

**off the beaten track** in a place where people do not often go ऐसे स्थान पर जहाँ लोग प्रायः नहीं जाते

PHR V **beat sb/sth off** to fight until sb/sth goes away मारकर भगा देना *The thieves tried to take his wallet but he beat them off.*

**beat sb to sth** to get somewhere or do sth before sb else किसी अन्य से पहले पहुँचना या करना; पीछे धकेल देना, बाज़ी मार लेना *I wanted to get there first but Bani beat me to it.*

**beat sb up** to attack sb by hitting or kicking him/her many times (किसी की) बुरी तरह पिटाई करना

**beat**[2] /biːt बीट्/ *noun* **1** [C] a single hit on sth such as a drum or the movement of sth, such as your heart; the sound that this makes ढोल आदि वस्तुओं पर एक घात या ठोक; दिल की धड़कन जैसी चाल; इस तरह की चाल या ठोक से उत्पन्न ध्वनि *Her heart skipped a beat when she saw him.* **2** [*sing.*] a series of regular hits on sth such as a drum, or of movements of sth; the sound that this makes बहुत-सी घातों, ठोकों या धड़कनों की शृंखला; इस क्रिया की लगातार आवाज़; ताल *the beat of the drums* ➪ **heartbeat** देखिए। **3** [C] the strong rhythm that a piece of music has संगीत की उग्र लय, ताल **4** [*sing.*] the route along which a police officer regularly walks गश्त *Having more policemen **on the beat** helps reduce crime.*

**beating** /ˈbiːtɪŋ ˈबीटिङ्/ *noun* [C] **1** a punishment that you give to sb by hitting him/her विशेषतः दंडस्वरूप की गई पिटाई **2** (used in sport) a defeat (खेल में) हार, परास्तता

IDM **take a lot of/some beating** to be so good that it would be difficult to find sth better ऐसा होना कि कोई मुक़ाबला न कर सके, बेजोड़ होना, सबसे बेहतर होना *Madhuri's cooking takes some beating.*

**the Beaufort scale** /ˈbəʊfət skeɪl ˈबोफ़ट् स्केल्/ *noun* [*sing.*] a scale used to measure the speed of the wind, from **Force 0** (= calm) to **Force 12** (= a very strong wind) (**a hurricane**) वायु की गति मापने का पैमाना। इस पैमाने पर 'Force 0' शांत वातावरण और 'Force 12' तूफ़ान दर्शाते हैं

**beautician** /bjuːˈtɪʃn ब्यूˈटिश्न् / *noun* [C] a person whose job is to improve the way people look with beauty treatments, etc. सौंदर्यकार, सौंदर्य-विशेषज्ञ

**beautiful** /ˈbjuːtɪfl ˈब्यूटिफ़्ल् / *adj.* very pretty or attractive; giving pleasure to the senses सुंदर, ख़ूबसूरत, आकर्षक; रमणीय, प्रियकर *The view from the top of the hill was really beautiful.* ○ *A beautiful perfume filled the air.*

> **NOTE** **Beautiful** का प्रयोग प्रायः महिलाओं, लड़कियों और शिशुओं के लिए किया जाता है। यह शब्द **pretty** से अधिक प्रबल है; **pretty** का प्रयोग केवल उपर्युक्त तीनों के लिए किया जाता है। पुरुषों के लिए **handsome** या **good-looking** का प्रयोग किया जाता है।

▸ **beautifully** /-fli फ़्लि / *adv.* बढ़िया या सुंदर ढंग से *He plays the piano beautifully.* ○ *She was beautifully dressed.*

**beauty** /ˈbjuːti ˈब्यूटि/ *noun* (*pl.* **beauties**) **1** [U] the quality which gives pleasure to the senses; the state of being beautiful सुंदरता, ख़ूबसूरती, आकर्षण; सौंदर्य *I was amazed by the beauty of the mountains.* ○ *music of great beauty* **2** [C] a beautiful woman सुंदर महिला *She grew up to be a beauty.* **3** [C] a particularly good example of sth किसी वस्तु का श्रेष्ठ या उत्तम नमूना, उदाहरण *Look at this tomato—it's a beauty!*

**beauty contest** (*AmE* **pageant**) *noun* [C] a competition to choose the most beautiful from a group of women नारी सौंदर्य प्रतियोगिता

**beauty queen** *noun* [C] a woman who is judged to be the most beautiful in a competition (**a beauty contest**) नारी सौंदर्य प्रतियोगिता में श्रेष्ठ चुनी जाने वाली महिला; सौंदर्य साम्राज्ञी

**beauty shop** (*also* **beauty parlour**, *AmE* **beauty shop**) *noun* [C] a place where you can pay for treatment to your face, hair, nails, etc., which is intended to make you more beautiful सौंदर्यचर्या का व्यावसायिक केंद्र

**beauty spot** *noun* [C] **1** a place in the countryside which is famous for its attractive scenery सुरम्य स्थल **2** a small dark mark on a woman's face. It is considered to make her more attractive महिला के चेहरे का तिल जो सुंदरता का प्रतीक है

**beaver** /ˈbiːvə(r) ˈबीव़(र्) / *noun* [C] an animal with brown fur, a wide, flat tail and sharp teeth. It lives in water and on land and uses branches to build walls across rivers to hold back the water (**dams**) भूरे रंग की रोएँदार खाल, चौड़ी, चपटी पूँछ और नुकीले दाँतों वाला एक जानवर जो जल और थल दोनो में रह सकता है और पेड़ों की शाखाओं द्वारा नदी की धारा रोकने के लिए बाँध जैसी सरंचना बनाता है

**became** ⇨ **become** का past tense रूप

**because** /bɪˈkɒz बिˈकॉज़् / *conj.* for the reason that क्योंकि *They didn't go for a walk because it was raining.*

**because of** *prep.* as a result of; on account of के कारण, की वजह से, के परिणामस्वरूप; फलस्वरूप *They didn't go for a walk because of the rain.*

**beck** /bek बेक् / *noun*

**IDM** **at sb's beck and call** always ready to obey sb's orders (किसी के) आदेश के पालन के लिए सदा तैयार, आदेशार्थी

**beckon** /ˈbekən ˈबेकन् / *verb* [I, T] to show sb with a movement of your finger or hand that you want him/her to come closer इशारे से पास बुलाना *She beckoned me over to speak to her.*

**become** /bɪˈkʌm बिˈकम् / *linking verb* (*pt* **became** /bɪˈkeɪm बिˈकेम् /; *pp* **become**) to begin to be sth कुछ हो जाना, कुछ बन जाना *Mr Sinha became Chairman in 2005.* ○ *She wants to become a pilot.*

> **NOTE** इस अर्थ में विशेषणों के साथ **get** का प्रयोग भी किया जाता है—*She got nervous as the exam date came closer.* ○ *He's getting more like you every day.* **Get** का प्रयोग बातचीत में काफ़ी किया जाता है और यह **become** से कम औपचारिक है।

**PHR V** **become of sb/sth** to happen to sb/sth किसी को कुछ हो जाना; किसी के साथ कुछ होना *What became of Amina? I haven't seen her for years!*

**BEd** /ˌbiːˈed ˌबीˈएड् / *abbr.* Bachelor of Education; a degree in education for people who want to be teachers बी एड 'Bachelor of Education' का संक्षिप्त रूप है; शिक्षक बनने के लिए अपेक्षित उपाधि

**bed**[1] /bed बेड् / *noun* **1** [C, U] a piece of furniture that you lie on when you sleep पलंग, चारपाई, शय्या, खाट *to make the bed* (= to arrange the sheets etc. so that the bed is tidy and ready for sb to sleep in) ○ *What time do you usually **go to bed**?* ○ *to get into/out of bed* **2 -bedded** having the type or number of beds mentioned निर्दिष्ट प्रकार की शय्याओं वाला (कमरा, आदि) *a twin-bedded room* (= a room having two single beds next to each other) ○ *a bunk bed* (= two single beds built as a unit with one above the other used especially for children) **3** [C] the ground at the bottom of a river or the sea नदी, समुद्र आदि का तल *the seabed* **4** = **flower bed** **5** [C] a layer of rock in the earth's surface भूमि की सतह पर चट्टान की परत

**bed**[2] /bed बेड् / *verb* [T] (**bedding; bedded**) to fix sth firmly in sth (किसी वस्तु को किसी अन्य वस्तु में) मज़बूती से बैठाना या जमाना

**bedclothes** /ˈbedkləʊðz ˈबेड्क्लोद्ज़् / (*also* **bedcovers**) *noun* [*pl.*] the sheets, covers, etc. that you put on a bed पलंग पर बिछाए जाने वाली चादरें आदि

**bedding** /ˈbedɪŋ ˈबेडिङ् / *noun* [U] everything that you put on a bed and need for sleeping बिस्तर, बिछौना, बिछावन

**bedpan** /ˈbedpæn ˈबेड्पैन् / *noun* [C] a container used as a toilet by sb in hospital who is too ill to get out of bed रोगी द्वारा शौच आदि के लिए बिस्तर पर प्रयुक्त होने वाला पात्र; बेडपैन

**bedraggled** /bɪˈdrægld बिˈड्रैगल्ड् / *adj.* very wet and untidy or dirty बहुत गीला, मैला और बेढंगा *bedraggled hair*

**bedridden** /ˈbedrɪdn ˈबेड्रिड्न् / *adj.* being too old or ill to get out of bed रोग या वृद्धावस्था के कारण शय्याग्रस्त

**bedrock** /ˈbedrɒk ˈबेड्रॉक् / *noun* **1** [*sing.*] a strong base for sth, especially the facts or principles on which it is based सुदृढ़ आधार (प्रायः तथ्यों या सिद्धांतों का) *The poor suburbs traditionally **formed the bedrock of** the party's support.* **2** [U] the solid rock in the ground below the soil and sand तलवर्ती चट्टान, आधार-शैल ➪ **flood plain** पर चित्र देखिए।

**bedroom** /ˈbedru:m; -rʊm ˈबेड्रूम्; -रुम् / *noun* a room which is used for sleeping in सोने का कमरा, शयन कक्ष *You can sleep in the **spare bedroom**. ○ a three-bedroom house*

**bed-sheet** /ˈbedʃɪ:t ˈबेड्शीट् / *noun* [C] (*IndE*) = **sheet**[1]

**bedside** /ˈbedsaɪd ˈबेड्साइड् / *noun* [*sing.*] the area that is next to a bed शय्या के साथ की जगह *She sat **at his bedside** all night long. ○ **bedside table**.*

**bedsore** /ˈbedsɔ:(r) ˈबेड्सॉ(र्) / *noun* [C] a painful place on a person's skin that is caused by lying in bed for a long time काफ़ी समय तक शय्या पर लेटे रहने की बाध्यता के कारण रोगी की त्वचा पर उभरा पीड़ादायी स्थल (घाव); शय्या-व्रण

**bedspread** /ˈbedspred ˈबेड्स्प्रेड् / *noun* [C] an attractive cover for a bed that you put on top of the sheets and other covers पलंगपोश

**bed-tea** /ˈbedti: ˈबेड्टी / *noun* [U, C] (*IndE*) an early morning cup of tea usually taken in bed before breakfast सुबह की चाय जो नाश्ते से पहले पी जाती है *Some people can't get out of bed before having bed-tea.*

**bedtime** /ˈbedtaɪm ˈबेड्टाइम् / *noun* [U] the time that you normally go to bed सोने का समय

**bee** /bi: बी / *noun* [C] a black and yellow insect that lives in large groups and that makes a sweet substance that we eat (**honey**) मधुमक्खी

> **NOTE** मधुमक्खियों के झुंड को **swarm** कहते हैं। मधुमक्खियों की भिनभिनाहट के लिए **buzz** या **hum** शब्दों का प्रयोग किया जाता है। मधुमक्खियों के काटने को **sting** कहते हैं। **Beehive** और **bumblebee** भी देखिए।

**beedi** (*also* **bidi**) *noun* [C] (*IndE*) a type of cheap strong cigarette made from tobacco rolled in **tendu** leaf बीड़ी

**beef** /bi:f बीफ़् / *noun* [U] the meat from a cow गोमांस *a slice of **roast beef***

**beefy** /ˈbi:fi ˈबीफ़ि / *adj.* having a strong body with big muscles मांसल और सुदृढ़ शरीर वाला

**beehive** /ˈbi:haɪv ˈबीहाइव़् / (*also* **hive**) *noun* [C] a type of box that people use for keeping bees in मधुमक्खी-पेटिका, मधुमक्खी का छत्ता

**bee-keeper** *noun* [C] a person who owns and takes care of bees मधुमक्खी-पालक

**bee-keeping** *noun* [U] मधुमक्खी-पालन

**been** /bi:n बीन् / ➪ **be, go**[1] का past participle रूप

> **NOTE** **Been** वस्तुतः **be** और **go** दोनों का भूत कृदंत (past participle) रूप है—*I've never been seriously ill. ○ I've never been **to Lucknow**.* शब्द **gone** भी **go** का भूत कृदंत (past participle) रूप है। निम्नलिखित वाक्यों के अर्थ में अंतर पर ध्यान दीजिए—*I'm cold because I've just been outside* (= I am here now). ○ *Jim's not here, I'm afraid—he's just gone out* (= he is not here now).

**beep**[1] /bi:p बीप् / *noun* [C] a short high noise, for example made by the horn of a car लघु अवधि की और ऊँचे स्वर में उत्पन्न आवाज़, जैसे वाहन के भोंपू की

**beep**[2] /bi:p बीप् / *verb* **1** [I] (used about an electronic machine) to make a short high noise (इलेक्ट्रॉनिक यंत्र के लिए प्रयुक्त) लघु अवधि और ऊँचे स्वर में आवाज़ निकालना *The microwave beeps when the food is cooked.* **2** [I, T] when a car horn beeps, or when you beep it, it makes a short noise कार का भोंपू बजना या बजाना *I beeped my horn at the dog, but it wouldn't get off the road.* **3** [T] (*AmE*) = **bleep**[2] **2**

**beeper** /ˈbi:pə(r) ˈबीप(र्) / (*AmE*) = **bleeper**

**beer** /bɪə(r) बिअ(र्) / *noun* **1** [U] a type of alcoholic drink that is made from grain अनाज से बना एक प्रकार का मादक पेय; बियर **2** [C] a type or glass of beer एक प्रकार की बियर या बियर-भरा गिलास

**beeswax** /ˈbiːzwæks ˈबीज़्वैक्स्/ *noun* [U] a yellow sticky substance that is produced by bees. We use it to make candles and polish for wood मधुमक्खी का मोम, यह मोमबत्तियाँ और लकड़ी के पॉलिश बनाने में प्रयुक्त होता है

**beet** /biːt बीट्/ *noun* **1** (*BrE*) = **sugar beet** **2** (*AmE*) = **beetroot**

**beetle** /ˈbiːtl ˈबीट्ल्/ *noun* [C] an insect, often large, shiny and black, with a hard case on its back covering its wings. There are many different types of beetles एक प्रकार का बड़ा काला व चमकीला कीट जिसके पंखों पर कड़ा आवरण होता है; एक प्रकार का भौंरा, भृंग। यह कीट अनेक प्रकार का होता है ➪ **insect** पर चित्र देखिए।

**beetroot** /ˈbiːtruːt ˈबीट्रूट्/ (*AmE* **beet**) *noun* [C, U] a dark red vegetable which is the root of a plant. Beetroot is cooked and can be eaten hot or cold चुकंदर; लाल शलजम ➪ **vegetable** पर चित्र देखिए।

**befall** /bɪˈfɔːl बिˈफ़ॉल्/ *verb* [T] (*pt* **befell** /bɪˈfel बिˈफ़ेल्/; *pp* **befallen** /bɪˈfɔːlən बिˈफ़ॉलन्/) (*written*) (used about sth bad) to happen to sb (अशुभ के संदर्भ में) किसी को कुछ हो जाना, किसी पर कुछ आ पड़ना

**before[1]** /bɪˈfɔː(r) बिˈफ़ॉ(र्)/ *prep., conj.* **1** earlier than sb/sth; earlier than the time that किसी व्यक्ति या वस्तु से पहले; किसी समय-बिंदु से पहले *You can call me any time before 10 o'clock.* ○ *the week before last* **2** in front of sb/sth (in an order) किसी व्यक्ति या वस्तु से पहले या आगे (क्रम, महत्त्व, स्थान में) *A very difficult task lies before us.* ○ *a company that puts profit before safety* (= thinks profit is more important than safety) **3** (*formal*) in a position in front of sb/sth किसी व्यक्ति या वस्तु के सामने या आगे *You will appear before the judge tomorrow.* **4** rather than के बजाय, की अपेक्षा *I'd die before I apologized to him!*

**before[2]** /bɪˈfɔː(r) बिˈफ़ॉ(र्)/ *adv.* at an earlier time; already पूर्व में; अतीत में; किसी समय से पहले; पहले ही *It was fine yesterday but it rained the day before.*

**beforehand** /bɪˈfɔːhænd बिˈफ़ॉहैन्ड्/ *adv.* at an earlier time than sth किसी समय विशेष से पूर्व, पहले से *If you visit us, phone beforehand to make sure we're in.*

**befriend** /bɪˈfrend बिˈफ़्रेन्ड्/ *verb* [T] (*written*) to become sb's friend; to be kind to sb किसी का मित्र बन जाना; किसी के प्रति दयालु होना

**beg** /beg बेग्/ *verb* [I, T] (**begging; begged**) **1 beg (sb) for sth; beg sth (of/from sb); beg (sb) to do sth** to ask sb for sth strongly, or with great emotion बहुत भावुक होकर या दृढ़ता के साथ कुछ माँगना *He begged for forgiveness.* ✪ पर्याय **entreat** या **implore** **2 beg (for) sth (from sb)** to ask people for food, money, etc. because you are very poor भीख माँगना *There are people begging for food in the streets.*

**IDM I beg your pardon** (*formal*) **1** I am sorry मुझे खेद है *I beg your pardon. I picked up your bag by mistake.* **2** used for asking sb to repeat sth because you did not hear it properly किसी को कुछ दोहराने के लिए कहने के लिए प्रयुक्त

**began** ➪ **begin** का past tense रूप

**beggar** /ˈbegə(r) ˈबेगə(र्)/ *noun* [C] a person who lives by asking people for money, food, etc. on the streets भिखारी, भिक्षुक, भिखमंगा

**begin** /bɪˈgɪn बिˈगिन्/ *verb* (*pres. part.* **beginning;** *pt* **began** /bɪˈgæn बिˈगैन्/; *pp* **begun** /bɪˈgʌn बिˈगन्/) **1** [I, T] to start doing sth; to do the first part of sth (कोई काम) आरंभ करना, शुरू करना; पहले चरण का आरंभ करना *Shall I begin or will you?* ○ *I began reading this novel last month and I still haven't finished it.* **2** [I] to start to happen or exist, especially from a particular time कोई घटना शुरू होना, प्रारंभ होना, विशेषतः किसी ख़ास समय से *What time does the movie begin?* **3** [I] **begin (with sth)** to start in a particular way, with a particular event, or in a particular place किसी विशेष रीति से, किसी विशेष घटना से या किसी विशेष स्थान से शुरू होना *My name begins with 'W' not 'V'.* ○ *This is where the footpath begins.*

**NOTE** **Begin** या **start** के अर्थ बहुत मिलते-जुलते हैं, परंतु **start** काफ़ी अनौपचारिक प्रयोग है। इन दोनों के बाद क्रिया के 'to' या '-ing' रूप आ सकते हैं—*The baby began/started crying/to cry.* जब **begin** या **start** स्वयं '-ing' युक्त रूप में आएँ तो उनके बाद 'to' का प्रयोग अवश्य होता है—*The baby was just beginning/starting to cry.* कुछ अर्थों में केवल **start** का प्रयोग हो सकता है—*I couldn't start the car.* ○ *We'll have to start* (= leave) *early if we want to be in Dehradun by 2 o'clock.*

**IDM to begin with** **1** at first सर्वप्रथम, सबसे पहली बात *To begin with, they were very happy.* **2** used for giving your first reason for sth or to introduce your first point किसी विषय में अपने पहले तर्क देने का संकेत करने के लिए प्रयुक्त *We can't possibly go. To begin with, it's too far and we can't afford it either.* ▶ **beginner** *noun* [C] आरंभकर्ता, नौसिखिया

**beginning** /bɪˈgɪnɪŋ बिˈगिनिङ् / *noun* [C] the first part of sth; the time when or the place where sth starts किसी वस्तु का पहला भाग; किसी वस्तु का समय या स्थान संबंधी प्रारंभ-बिंदु; वह समय और स्थान जहाँ से कुछ आरंभ होता है; प्रारंभ, शुरुआत *I've read the article **from beginning to end**.* ○ *We're going away **at the beginning of** the school holidays.*

**begrudge** /bɪˈgrʌdʒ बिˈग्रज् / *verb* [T] **begrudge (sb) sth 1** to feel angry or upset because sb has sth that you think that he/she should not have किसी से ईर्ष्या या डाह करना *He's worked hard. I don't begrudge him his success.* **2** to be unhappy that you have to do sth कुछ करना पड़ रहा है, इस कारण नाख़ुश होना; कुढ़ना, बुरा लगना *I begrudge paying so much money in tax each month.*

**Begum** (*also* **begaum**) *noun* [C] **1** a Muslim queen or woman of high rank मुस्लिम साम्राज्ञी या उच्च पदवी वाली स्त्री **2** the title of a married Muslim woman, equivalent to Mrs विवाहित मुस्लिम स्त्री की पदवी, 'Mrs' के समतुल्य

**behalf** /bɪˈhɑːf बिˈहाफ़् / *noun*

**IDM on behalf of sb; on sb's behalf** for sb; as the representative of sb किसी के लिए; किसी की ओर से *I would like to thank you all on behalf of my colleagues and myself.*

**behave** /bɪˈheɪv बिˈहेव् / *verb* **1** [I] **behave well, badly, etc. (towards sb)** to act in a particular way विशिष्ट (अच्छा या बुरा) आचरण करना, व्यवहार करना *He **behaves as if/though** he was the boss.* **2** [I, T] **behave (yourself)** to act in the correct or appropriate way सही या उचित तरीक़े से पेश आना *I want you to behave yourselves while we're away.* ✪ विलोम **misbehave 3 -behaved** (*used to form compound adjectives*) behaving in the way mentioned उल्लेखित रीति से पेश आते हुए *a well-behaved child* ○ *a badly-behaved class*

**behaviour** (*AmE* **behavior**) /bɪˈheɪvjə(r) बिˈहेव्य(र्) / *noun* [U] the way that you act or behave आचरण, व्यवहार *He was sent out of the class for bad behaviour.*

**behead** /bɪˈhed बिˈहेड् / *verb* [T] to cut off sb's head, especially as a punishment किसी का सिर काट देना, विशेषतः दंडस्वरूप

**behind** /bɪˈhaɪnd बिˈहाइन्ड् / *prep., adv.* **1** in, at or to the back of sb/sth के पीछे, पीछे की ओर *The sun went behind a cloud.* ○ *He ran off but the police were close behind.* **2 behind (in/with) (sth)** later or less good than sb/sth; making less progress than sb/sth (किसी अन्य से) बाद में, कमतर; प्रगति में पीछे, पिछड़ा हुआ *The train is twenty minutes behind schedule.* ○ *We are a month behind with the rent.* ➪ **ahead** देखिए। **3** supporting or agreeing with sb/sth के पक्ष में, के समर्थन में *Whatever she decides, her family will be behind her.* **4** responsible for causing or starting sth के कारण *What is the reason behind his sudden change of opinion?* **5** used to say that sth is in sb's past जब यह संकेत करना हो कि यह अतीत की बात है, जब यह व्यक्त करना हो कि बात को भूल जाना ही ठीक है *It's time you **put** your problems **behind you*** (= forgot about them). **6** in the place where sb/sth is or was वापस उसी स्थान पर *Oh no! I've **left** the tickets **behind*** (= at home).

**beige** /beɪʒ बेश़् / *adj., noun* [U] (of) a light brown colour हलके भूरे रंग का, मटियाला

**being**[1] ➪ **be** देखिए।

**being**[2] /ˈbiːɪŋ ˈबीइङ् / *noun* **1** [U] the state of existing; existence अस्तित्व में होने की स्थिति; अस्तित्व, सत्ता *When did the organization **come into being**?* **2** [C] a living person or thing जीवधारी, प्राणी *a human being*

**belated** /bɪˈleɪtɪd बिˈलेटिड् / *adj.* coming late विलंबित, विलंब से किया हुआ *a belated apology* ▶ **belatedly** *adv.* विलंब से *They have realized, rather belatedly, that they have made a mistake.*

**belch** /beltʃ बेल्च् / *verb* **1** [I] to let gas out from your stomach through your mouth with a sudden noise डकार लेना **2** [T] to send out a lot of smoke, etc. (धुआँ आदि) वेग से बाहर फेंकना *The volcano belched smoke and ashes.* ▶ **belch** *noun* [C] डकार

**belie** /bɪˈlaɪ बिˈलाइ / *verb* [T] (*pres. part.* **belying;** *3rd person sing. pres.* **belies;** *pt, pp* **belied**) (*formal*) to give an idea of sth that is false or not true किसी स्थिति को असत्य रूप में प्रस्तुत करना; झुठलाना *His smiling face belied his true feelings.*

**belief** /bɪˈliːf बिˈलीफ़् / *noun* **1** [*sing.*, U] **belief in sb/sth** a feeling that sb/sth is true, morally good or right, or that sb/sth really exists विश्वास, आस्था *She has lost her belief in God.* ➪ **disbelief** देखिए। **2** [*sing.*, U] (*formal*) **belief (that)...** something you accept as true; what you believe धारणा; मंतव्य *It's my belief that people are basically good.* ○ ***Contrary to popular belief*** *the north of the town is not poorer than the south.* **3** [C] an idea about religion, politics, etc. धर्म, राजनीति, आदि के विषय में विचार, मत *Divorce is contrary to their religious beliefs.*

**IDM beyond belief** (in a way that is) too great, difficult, etc. to be believed अविश्वसनीय, जिस पर विश्वास करना बहुत कठिन है

**believable** /bɪˈliːvəbl बिˈलीव़बल्/ *adj.* that can be believed जिसका विश्वास किया जा सके; विश्वसनीय ✪ विलोम **unbelievable**

**believe** /bɪˈliːv बिˈलीव़्/ *verb* (*not used in the continuous tenses*) **1** [T] to feel sure that sth is true or that sb is telling the truth विश्वास करना, सही मान लेना *He said he hadn't taken any money but I didn't believe him.* ○ *Nobody believes a word she says.* ✪ विलोम **disbelieve 2** [T] **believe (that)...** to think that sth is true or possible, although you are not certain कुछ सही या संभव लगना यद्यपि निश्चित न होना *The escaped prisoner is believed to be in this area.* ○ *Four people are still missing, believed drowned.* **3 don't/can't believe sth** used to show anger or surprise at sth किसी बात पर क्रोध या आश्चर्य प्रकट करने के लिए प्रयुक्त *I can't believe (that) you're telling me to do it again!* **4** [I] to have religious beliefs धार्मिक विश्वास रखना, निष्ठा रखना

> NOTE क्रिया **believe** का प्रयोग निरंतरताबोधक कालों (continuous tenses) में नहीं किया जाता परंतु इसका -ing युक्त वर्तमान कृदंत (present participle) रूप काफ़ी प्रचलित है—*Believing the house to be empty, she quietly let herself in.*

IDM **believe it or not** it may be surprising but it is true बात आश्चर्यजनक है परंतु सच है *Believe it or not, this small restaurant often serves very good food.*

**give sb to believe/understand (that)** (*usually passive*) to give sb the impression or idea that sth is true किसी बात का विश्वास दिलाना *I was given to believe that I had got the job.*

PHR V **believe in sb/sth** to be sure that sb/sth exists (किसी की) सत्ता में विश्वास रखना *Do you believe in God?* ○ *Most young children believe in Santa Claus.*

**believe in sb/sth; believe in doing sth** to think that sb/sth is good or right किसी पर भरोसा रखना; किसी बात को सही या उपयुक्त मानना *They need a leader they can believe in.*

**believer** /bɪˈliːvə(r) बिˈलीव़(र्)/ *noun* [C] a person who has religious beliefs धार्मिक विश्वास रखने वाला व्यक्ति; विश्वासी, आस्तिक

IDM **be a (great/firm) believer in sth** to think that sth is good or right किसी में विश्वास करना, किसी को सही या उपयुक्त मानना *He is a great believer in getting things done on time.*

**belittle** /bɪˈlɪtl बिˈलिट्ल्/ *verb* [T] to make sb or the things he/she does, seem unimportant or not very good किसी व्यक्ति, कार्य आदि का महत्त्व घटाना; तुच्छ या छोटा समझना

**bell** /bel बेल्/ *noun* [C] **1** a metal object, often shaped like a cup, that makes a ringing sound when it is hit by a small piece of metal inside it घंटा, घंटी *the sound of church bells* ○ *Her voice came back* ***clear as a bell***. ➪ **bicycle** पर चित्र देखिए। **2** an electrical device that makes a ringing sound when the button on it is pushed; the sound that it makes बिजली की घंटी जो स्विच दबाने पर बजती है *Ring the doorbell and see if they're in.*

IDM **ring a bell** ➪ **ring²** देखिए।

**belligerent** /bəˈlɪdʒərənt बˈलिजरन्ट्/ *adj.* **1** unfriendly and aggressive शत्रुतापूर्ण और आक्रामक ✪ पर्याय **hostile 2** (*only before a noun*) (*formal*) (used about a country) fighting a war (देश) युद्धरत

**bellow** /ˈbeləʊ ˈबेलो/ *verb* **1** [I, T] to shout in a loud deep voice, especially because you are angry (गुस्से से) चीखना **2** [I] to make a deep low sound, like a **bull** साँड़ की तरह डकारना ► **bellow** *noun* [C] इस तरह की आवाज़, गरज, हुंकार

**belly** /ˈbeli ˈबेलि/ *noun* [C] (*pl.* **bellies**) the stomach or the front part of your body between your chest and your legs पेट, उदर

**belly button** (*informal*) = **navel**

**belong** /bɪˈlɒŋ बिˈलॉङ्/ *verb* [I] **1 belong to sb** to be owned by sb किसी की संपत्ति होना *Who does this pen belong to?* ○ *Don't take anything that doesn't belong to you.* **2 belong to sth** to be a member of a group or organization किसी वर्ग या संगठन का सदस्य होना *Do you belong to any political party?* **3** to have a right or usual place उचित या सामान्य स्थान होना *It took quite a long time before we felt we belonged in the village.*

**belongings** /bɪˈlɒŋɪŋz बिˈलॉङिङ्ज़्/ *noun* [*pl.*] the things that you own that can be moved, that is, not land and buildings किसी व्यक्ति का निजी सामान, चल संपत्ति

**beloved** /bɪˈlʌvd; bɪˈlʌvɪd बिˈलव्ड्; बिˈलविड्/ *adj.* (*formal*) much loved परम प्रिय *They had always intended to return to their beloved India.*

NOTE संज्ञा से पहले आने पर beloved का उच्चारण / bɪˈlʌvɪd बिˈलविड्/ होता है।

**below** /bɪˈləʊ बिˈलो/ *prep., adv.* at or to a lower position or level than sb/sth किसी वस्तु या व्यक्ति से नीचे या निचले स्तर पर *The temperature fell below freezing during the night.* ○ *Her marks in the exam were below average.* ➪ **under** पर नोट देखिए। ✪ विलोम **above**

**belt**[1] /belt बेल्ट्/ *noun* [C] **1** a thin piece of cloth, leather, etc. that you wear around your waist (कमर की) पेटी, कमरबंद, बेल्ट *I need a belt to keep these trousers up.* ➪ **seat belt** देखिए। **2** a long narrow piece of rubber, cloth, etc. in a circle, that is used for carrying things along or for making parts of a machine move (मशीन का) पट्टा *The suitcases were carried round on a **conveyor belt**.* **3** an area of land that has a particular quality or where a particular group of people live विशिष्ट गुणों वाला भूक्षेत्र या विशेष वर्ग के लोगों का निवास क्षेत्र ***the green belt*** in Delhi (= an area of countryside where you are not allowed to build houses, factories, etc.) ○ *the commuter belt*

IDM **below the belt** (*informal*) unfair or cruel अनुचित या निष्ठुर *That remark was rather below the belt.*

**tighten your belt** ➪ **tighten** देखिए।

**under your belt** (*informal*) that you have already done or achieved जो किया या पाया जा चुका हो; सफलता, उपलब्धि *She's already got four tournament wins under her belt.*

**belt**[2] /belt बेल्ट्/ *verb* (*informal*) **1** [T] to hit sb hard कसकर मारना **2** [I] to run or go somewhere very fast दौड़कर या तेज़ चाल से कहीं जाना *I was belting along on my bicycle.*

PHR V **belt sth out** to sing, shout or play sth loudly ऊँचे स्वर में गाना, बजाना या चीख़ना

**belt up** (*slang*) used to tell sb rudely to be quiet अशिष्टतापूर्वक चुप होने के लिए कहना, शांत रहने का रूखा आदेश देना *Belt up! I can't think with all this noise.*

**bemused** /bɪˈmjuːzd बिˈम्यूज़्ड्/ *adj.* confused and unable to think clearly उलझन में और स्पष्ट रूप से विचार करने में असमर्थ

**benami** *adj.* (*IndE*) a term used for those **transactions** (usually illegal) where the real owner or buyer remains **anonymous** and his place is taken by a **substitute** who doesn't actually make the payments but merely lends his name ऐसा लेन-देन का सौदा (सामान्यतः ग़ैर-क़ानूनी) जिसमें वास्तविक हितग्राही मालिक अज्ञात रहता है और उसकी जगह एक प्रतिस्थापी व्यक्ति जो पैसों का भुगतान नहीं करता अपना नाम दे देता है; बेनामी

**bench** /bentʃ बेन्च्/ *noun* [C] **1** a long wooden or metal seat for two or more people, often outdoors दो या अधिक व्यक्तियों के बैठने के लिए लकड़ी या लोहे की पट्टी, प्रायः बाहर खुले में स्थापित; बेंच *a park bench* **2** (in parliament) the seats where a particular group of politicians sit (संसद में) दल विशेष के सदस्यों की सीटें *the Opposition **benches*** **3 the bench** [*sing.*] (law) a judge in court or the seat where he/she sits; the position of being a judge or magistrate न्यायाधीश या न्यायाधीश की कुरसी; न्यायाधीश का पद

**benchmark** /ˈbentʃmɑːk ˈबेन्च्माक्/ *noun* [C] a standard that other things can be compared to तुलना के लिए निर्धारित मानक, कसौटी *These new safety features set a benchmark for other manufacturers to follow.*

**bend**[1] /bend बेन्ड्/ *verb* (*pt, pp* **bent** /bent बेन्ट्/) **1** [T] to make sth that was straight into a curved shape मोड़ना, झुकना, टेढ़ा करना *to bend a piece of wire into an S shape* ○ *It hurts when I bend my knee.* **2** [I] to be or become curved मोड़ खाना, घुमाव लेना *The road bends to the left here.* **3** [I] to move your body forwards and downwards शरीर को आगे और नीचे की ओर झुकाना *He **bent down** to tie up his shoelaces.*

IDM **bend the rules** to do sth that is not normally allowed by the rules नियम में छूट देना, लेना या ढील देना

**bend**[2] /bend बेन्ड्/ *noun* [C] a curve or turn, for example in a road मोड़ या घुमाव, झुकाव जैसे सड़क में *a sharp bend in the road*

IDM **round the bend** (*informal*) crazy; mad सनकी; पागल *His behaviour is **driving me round the bend*** (= annoying me very much).

**beneath** /bɪˈniːθ बिˈनीथ़/ *prep., adv.* **1** in, at or to a lower position than sb/sth; under किसी अन्य के नीचे, तले, नीचे की ओर *The ship disappeared beneath the waves.* ○ *He seemed a nice person but there was a lot of anger beneath the surface.* ➪ **under** पर नोट देखिए। **2** not good enough for sb उपयुक्त नहीं, लायक नहीं, अनुपयुक्त, अयोग्य, अशोभनीय *She felt that cleaning for other people was beneath her.*

**benefactor** /ˈbenɪfæktə(r) ˈबेनिफ़ैक्ट(र्)/ *noun* [C] a person who helps or gives money to a person or an organization किसी व्यक्ति या संस्था की सहायता, जैसे आर्थिक सहायता, प्रदान करने वाला व्यक्ति; दानी, उपकारी, परोपकारी

**beneficial** /ˈbenɪˈfɪʃl ˈबेनिˈफ़िश्ल्/ *adj.* **beneficial (to sb/sth)** having a good or useful effect लाभकारी, हितकर, फ़ायदेमंद

**beneficiary** /ˌbenɪˈfɪʃəri ˌबेनिˈफ़िशरि/ *noun* [C] (*pl.* **beneficiaries**) a person who gains as a result of sth, especially money or property when sb dies विशेषतः किसी की मृत्यु के बाद धन या संपत्ति प्राप्त करने वाला व्यक्ति; हिताधिकारी, लाभग्राही

**benefit[1]** /ˈbenɪfɪt ˈबेनिफ़िट्/ *noun* **1** [U, C] an advantage or useful effect that sth has लाभ, हित, फ़ायदा *A change in the law would be **to** everyone's **benefit**.* ○ *the benefits of modern technology* **2** [U] money that the government gives to people who are ill, poor, unemployed, etc. (रोगी, दरिद्र, बेरोज़गार व्यक्तियों आदि को) सरकारी आर्थिक सहायता ***below poverty line/housing benefit*** **3** [C, *usually pl.*] advantages that you get from your company in addition to the money you earn वेतन से अतिरिक्त लाभ तथा सुविधाएँ a company car and other benefits

IDM **for sb's benefit** especially to help, please, etc. sb के हित में, के सहायतार्थ *For the benefit of the newcomers, I will start again.*

**give sb the benefit of the doubt** to believe what sb says although there is no proof that it is true स्पष्ट प्रमाणों के अभाव में भी किसी की बात मान लेना, संदेह का लाभ देना

**benefit[2]** /ˈbenɪfɪt ˈबेनिफ़िट्/ *verb* (**benefiting; benefited** or **benefitting; benefitted**) **1** [T] to produce a good or useful effect लाभदायक या हितकारी प्रभाव होना; किसी का भला करना *The new tax laws will benefit people in the lower income group.* **2** [I] **benefit (from sth)** to receive an advantage from sth लाभान्वित होना, फ़ायदा पहुँचना *Small businesses have benefited from the changes in the law.*

**benevolent** /bəˈnevələnt बˈनेव़लन्ट्/ *adj.* (*formal*) kind, friendly and helpful to others दयालु, मित्रवत और परोपकारी ▶ **benevolence** *noun* [U] परोपकरी, हितकामना

**benign** /bɪˈnaɪn बिˈनाइन्/ *adj.* **1** (used about people) kind or gentle (व्यक्ति) उदार या सौम्य **2** (used about a disease, etc.) not dangerous (रोग या बीमारी) हलकी, सुसाध्य रोग *a benign tumour* ✪ विलोम **malignant**

**bent[1]** ⇨ **bend** का past tense और past participle रूप

**bent[2]** /bent बेन्ट्/ *adj.* **1** not straight मुड़ा, नत, टेढ़ा *It was so funny we were **bent double** with laughter.* **2** (*BrE informal*) (used about a person in authority) dishonest; corrupt (अधिकारी) बेईमान; भ्रष्ट *a bent policeman*

IDM **bent on sth/on doing sth** wanting to do sth very much; determined कुछ करने को अति-इच्छुक; कृतसंकल्प

**bent[3]** /bent बेन्ट्/ *noun* [*sing.*] **a bent for sth/for doing sth** a natural skill at sth or interest in sth रुझान, प्रवृत्ति, झुकाव *She has a bent for music.*

**benzene** /ˈbenziːn ˈबेन्ज़ीन्/ *noun* [U] a colourless liquid obtained from **petroleum** and used in making plastics and many chemical products पेट्रोलियम (खनिज तेल) से प्राप्त एक रंगहीन द्रव पदार्थ जिससे प्लास्टिक और दूसरे विभिन्न रासायनिक पदार्थ आदि बनते हैं; बेनज़ीन

**benzene ring** *noun* [C] a ring of six **carbon** atoms in benzene and many other compounds बेनज़ीन और अन्य यौगिकों आदि में उपलब्ध छह कार्बन अणुओं का वलय; बेनज़ीन-वलय

**bequeath** /bɪˈkwiːð बिˈक्वीद्/ *verb* [T] (*formal*) **bequeath sth (to sb)** to arrange for sth to be given to sb after you have died वसीयत करना, वसीयत में देना, उत्तरदान करना *He bequeathed one lakh rupees to charity.* NOTE इस अर्थ में **leave** का प्रयोग अधिक प्रचलित है।

**bequest** /bɪˈkwest बिˈक्वेस्ट्/ *noun* [C] (*formal*) something that you arrange to be given to sb after you have died वसीयत, उत्तरदान *He left a bequest to each of his grandchildren.*

**bereaved** /bɪˈriːvd बिˈरीव्ड्/ *adj.* (*formal*) **1** having lost a relative or close friend who has recently died शोकाकुल, शोकसंतप्त **2 the bereaved** *noun* [*pl.*] the people whose relative or close friend has died recently शोकाकुल व्यक्ति, शोकसंतप्त व्यक्ति

**bereavement** /bɪˈriːvmənt बिˈरीव्मन्ट्/ *noun* (*formal*) **1** [U] the state of having lost a relative or close friend who has recently died शोक, ग़मी, वियोग **2** [C] the death of a relative or close friend किसी संबंधी या निकट मित्र का निधन *There has been a bereavement in the family.*

**bereft** /bɪˈreft बिˈरेफ़्ट्/ *adj.* (*not before a noun*) (*formal*) **1 bereft of sth** completely lacking sth; having lost sth पूर्णतया रहित; से हीन या वंचित *bereft of ideas/hope* **2** (used about a person) sad and lonely because you have lost sb/sth (व्यक्ति) शोक से उदास और एकाकी *He was utterly bereft when his wife died.*

**beret** /ˈbereɪ ˈबेरे/ *noun* [C] a soft flat round hat नरम गोल टोपी

**berry** /ˈberi ˈबेरि/ *noun* [C] (*pl.* **berries**) a small soft fruit with seeds बेर जैसा सरस फल, बेरी *Those berries are poisonous.* ○ *a raspberry/strawberry/blueberry* ⇨ **fruit** पर चित्र देखिए।

**berserk** /bəˈzɜːk बˈज़क्/ *adj.* (*not before a noun*) very angry; crazy क्रोध से पागल; आपे से बाहर; सनकी, अत्यंत उत्तेजित *If the teacher finds out what you've done he'll **go berserk**.*

**berth** /bɜːθ बथ्/ *noun* [C] **1** a place for sleeping on a ship or train जहाज़ या रेलगाड़ी में बना शयन-स्थान,

शायिका, बर्थ *a cabin with four berths* **2** a place where a ship can stop and stay जहाज़ के रुकने का स्थान, गोदी, लंगरगाह

**beryllium** /bəˈrɪliəm बˈरिलिअम्/ *noun* [U] (*symbol* **Be**) a hard white metal that is used in making mixtures of other metals (**alloys**) एक सफ़ेद कठोर धातु जिससे अन्य मिश्र धातुएँ बनती है; बेरीलियम

**beseech** /bɪˈsiːtʃ बिˈसीच्/ *verb* [T] (*pt, pp* **besought** /bɪˈsɔːt बिˈसॉट्/ or *pt, pp* **beseeched**) (*formal*) to ask sb for sth in a worried way because you want or need it very much अनुनय करना, विनती करना

**beset** /bɪˈset बिˈसेट्/ *verb* [T] (*pres. part.* **besetting**; *pt, pp* **beset**) (*written*) to affect sb/sth in a bad way बुरा या हानिकारक प्रभाव डालना *The team has been beset by injuries all season.*

**beside** /bɪˈsaɪd बिˈसाइड्/ *prep.* at the side of, or next to sb/sth के बग़ल में, के पास *Come and sit beside me.* ○ *He kept his bag close beside him at all times.*

IDM **beside the point** not connected with the subject you are discussing विचारार्थ विषय से असंबद्ध, विषयेतर

**beside yourself** (**with sth**) not able to control yourself because of a very strong emotion भावुकता या क्रोध में आपे से बाहर *Shweta was almost beside herself with grief.*

**besides** /bɪˈsaɪdz बिˈसाइड्ज़्/ *prep., adv.* in addition to or as well as sb/sth; also के अतिरिक्त, के साथ; भी *There will be six people coming, besides you and Raj.*

**besiege** /bɪˈsiːdʒ बिˈसीज्/ *verb* [T] **1** to surround a place with an army सेना की सहायता से किसी स्थान को घेर लेना **2** (*usually passive*) (used about sth unpleasant or annoying) to surround sb/sth in large numbers घिर जाना (अप्रिय स्थिति का संदर्भ) *The actor was besieged by fans and reporters.*

**besotted** /bɪˈsɒtɪd बिˈसॉटिड्/ *adj.* (*not before a noun*) **besotted (with/by sb/sth)** so much in love with sb/sth that you cannot think or behave normally किसी की प्रीत में मतवाला पूर्णतया लीन, सम्मोहित

**besought** ⇨ **beseech** का past tense और past participle रूप

**bespectacled** /bɪˈspektəkld बिˈस्पेक्टक्ल्ड्/ *adj.* (*formal*) wearing **glasses** चश्माधारी

**best¹** /best बेस्ट्/ *adj.* (*superlative of* **good**) of the highest quality or level; most suitable सर्वोत्तम, श्रेष्ठ; अनुकूलतम *Who in the class is* ***best at*** *maths?* ○ ***It's best to*** *arrive early if you want a good seat.*

IDM **your best bet** (*informal*) the most sensible or appropriate thing for you to do in a particular situation सबसे अच्छी बात, सर्वाधिक उपयुक्त काम *There's nowhere to park in the city centre. Your best bet is to go in by bus.*

**the best/better part of sth** ⇨ **part¹** देखिए।

**best²** /best बेस्ट्/ *adv.* (*superlative of* **well**) to the greatest degree; most सबसे अच्छा; सबसे अधिक, सर्वाधिक *He works best in the morning.* ○ *Which of these dresses do you like best?* ○ *one of India's best-loved TV stars*

IDM **as best you can** as well as you can even if it is not perfectly यथासंभव, जितना अधिक हो सके उतना

**best³** /best बेस्ट्/ *noun* [*sing.*] **the best** the person or thing that is of the highest quality or level or better than all others सर्वोत्तम गुणों वाला व्यक्ति या वस्तु; सर्वश्रेष्ठ *Even the best of us make mistakes sometimes.* ○ *The best we can hope for is that the situation doesn't get any worse.* ⇨ **second-best** देखिए।

IDM **all the best** (*informal*) used when you are saying goodbye to sb and wishing him/her success किसी से विदा लेते समय शुभकामनाएँ देने के लिए प्रयुक्त *All the best! Keep in touch, won't you?*

**at best** if everything goes as well as possible; taking the most hopeful view, अधिक-से-अधिक अगर सब कुशल रहा तो; आशाप्रद दृष्टि से *We won't be able to deliver the goods before March, or, at best, the last week in February.*

**at its/your best** in its/your best state or condition सर्वोत्तम अवस्था में *This is an example of Raghu's work at its best.* ○ *No one is at their best first thing in the morning.*

**be (all) for the best** to be good in the end even if it does not seem good at first अंत में सब भला होना; 'सब ठीक हो जाएगा' की भावना *I didn't get the job, but I'm sure it's all for the best.*

**bring out the best/worst in sb** to show sb's best/worst qualities किसी की उत्कृष्ट या निकृष्ट विशेषताएँ सामने आना *The crisis really brought out the best in Tina.*

**do/try your best** to do all or the most that you can भरसक कोशिश करना

**look your best** to look as beautiful or attractive as possible यथासंभव सुंदर या आकर्षक दिखना

**make the best of sth/a bad job** to accept a difficult situation and try to be as happy as possible कठिन परिस्थिति को स्वीकार कर उसमें ख़ुश रहने की कोशिश करना

**best man** *noun* [*sing.*] a man who helps and supports the man who is getting married (**the bridegroom**) at a wedding विवाह के अवसर पर वर का सहायक साथी, सहबाला

**bestow** /bɪˈstəʊ बिˈस्टो/ *verb* [T] **bestow sth (on/upon sb)** to give sth to sb, especially to show how much he/she is respected कुछ प्रदान करना, विशेषतः आदर व्यक्त करने के लिए; अर्पित करना *The title was bestowed on him by the president.*

**best-seller** *noun* [C] a book or other product that is bought by large numbers of people बड़ी संख्या में बिकने वाली किताब या वस्तु ▶ **best-selling** *adj.* बड़ी संख्या में बिकने वाली *a best-selling novel*

**bet**[1] /bet बेट्/ *verb* [I, T] (*pres. part.* **betting;** *pt, pp* **bet** या **betted**) **1 bet (sth) (on sth)** to risk money on a race or an event by trying to predict the result. If you are right, you win money जुए, घुड़दौड़ या जुए जैसे अनिश्चित परिणाम के काम में बाज़ी लगाना, दाँव लगाना *I wouldn't bet on them winning the next election.* ✪ पर्याय **gamble** या **put money on sth** 2 (*spoken*) used to say that you are almost certain that sth is true or that sth will happen किसी बात के सत्य होने पर यक़ीन होने का भाव व्यक्त करने के लिए प्रयुक्त *I bet he arrives late—he always does.* ○ *I bet you're worried about your exam, aren't you?*

IDM **you bet** (*spoken*) a way of saying 'Yes, of course!' 'हाँ, निस्संदेह' कहने के लिए प्रयुक्त *'Are you coming too?' 'You bet (I am)!'*

**bet**[2] /bet बेट्/ *noun* [C] **1** an act of betting दाँव, बाज़ी, शर्त लगाने की क्रिया *to win/lose a bet* **2** an opinion कोई राय, मत *My bet is that he's missed the train.*

IDM **your best bet** ➪ **best**[1] देखिए।

**hedge your bets** ➪ **hedge**[2] देखिए।

**beta** /ˈbiːtə ˈबीटा/ *noun* the second letter of the Greek alphabet (β) ग्रीक वर्णमाला का दूसरा अक्षर (β)

**beta particle** *noun* [C] a fast-moving **electron** that is given off when an atom breaks up परमाणु के विखंडित होने पर उसमें से निकला द्रुतगामी इलेक्ट्रॉन

**betel** /ˈbɪːtl ˈबीट्ल्/ *noun* [C] (*also* **betel leaf**) the heart-shaped leaves of a climbing plant, commonly called **paan**, chewed by people in Asia पान लता के पत्ते, जिसे ऐशियाई मूल के लोग चबाते हैं

**betide** /bɪˈtaɪd बिˈटाइड्/ *verb*

IDM **woe betide sb** ➪ **woe** देखिए।

**betray** /bɪˈtreɪ बिˈट्रे/ *verb* [T] **1** to give information about sb/sth to an enemy; to make a secret known शत्रु को गोपनीय मामलों की जानकारी देना; रहस्य उजागर करना *She betrayed all the members of the group to the secret police.* ○ *to betray your country* ➪ **traitor** देखिए। **2** to hurt sb who trusts you, especially by not being loyal or faithful to him/her विश्वासघात करना *If you take the money you'll **betray** her **trust**.* ○ *When parents get divorced the children often **feel betrayed**.* **3** to show a feeling or quality that you would like to keep hidden भावना या गुण अनचाहे प्रकट करना, दिखना *Her steady voice did not betray the emotion she was feeling.* ▶ **betrayal** /bɪˈtreɪəl बिˈट्रेअल्/ *noun* [C, U] विश्वासघात

**better**[1] /ˈbetə(r) ˈबेट(र्)/ *adj.* **1** (*comparative of* **good**) **better than sb/sth** of a higher quality or level or more suitable than sb/sth किसी अन्य से बेहतर, अधिक अच्छा या उपयुक्त *I think her second novel was much better than her first.* ○ *He's far better at English than me.* **2** (*comparative of* **well**) less ill; fully recovered from an illness पहले से कम अस्वस्थ, बेहतर; बीमारी के बाद पूर्णतः स्वस्थ *You can't go swimming until you're better.*

**better**[2] /ˈbetə(r) ˈबेट(र्)/ *adv.* (*comparative of* **well**) in a better way; to a greater or higher degree बेहतर ढंग से; अधिक या बेहतर कोटि तक *I think you could have done this better.* ○ *Sangeeta speaks English better than I do.*

IDM **(be) better off 1** to be in a more pleasant or suitable situation अधिक सुखद या उपयुक्त स्थिति में होना *You look terrible. You'd be better off at home in bed.* **2** (*comparative of* **well off**) with more money बेहतर आर्थिक स्थिति में, अधिक संपन्न *We're much better off now I go out to work too.*

**the best/better part of sth** ➪ **part**[1] देखिए।

**you, etc. had better** you should; you ought to आप (ऐसा) करें; आपको (ऐसा) करना चाहिए *I think we'd better go before it gets dark.*

**know better (than that/than to do sth)** ➪ **know**[1] देखिए।

**think better of (doing) sth** ➪ **think** देखिए।

**better**[3] /ˈbetə(r) ˈबेट(र्)/ *noun* [*sing.*, U] something that is of higher quality बेहतर स्तर की वस्तु आदि; अधिक बढ़िया वस्तु *The hotel wasn't very good. I must say we'd expected better.*

IDM **get the better of sb/sth** to defeat or be stronger than sb/sth किसी को पराजित करना या किसी से अधिक सशक्त होना *When we have an argument she always gets the better of me.*

**between** /bɪˈtwiːn बिˈट्वीन्/ *prep., adv.* **1 between A and B; in between** in the space in the middle of two things, people, places etc. दो

वस्तुओं, व्यक्तियों, स्थानों आदि के बीच में; मध्य *I was sitting between Gagan and Charu.* ○ *a village between Delhi and Agra* **2 between A and B; in between** (used about two amounts, distances, ages, times, etc.) at a point that is greater or later than the first and smaller or earlier than the second; somewhere in the middle (दो दूरवर्ती स्थितियों मापों, फासलों, आयु, समय आदि के) मध्य में *They said they would arrive between 4 and 5 o'clock.* ○ *They've got this shirt in size 38 and size 42, but nothing in between.* **3** from one place to another and back again एक स्थान से दूसरे की ओर और पुनः वापस *There aren't any direct trains between here and Aligarh.* **4** involving or connecting two people, groups or things दो व्यक्तियों, दलों या वस्तुओं में सम्मिलित या साझा *There may be a connection between the two crimes.* **5** choosing one and not the other (of two things) दो में से एक को चुनते हुए *to choose between two jobs* ○ *What's the difference between 'some' and 'any'?* **6** by putting together the actions, efforts, etc. of two or more people दो या अधिक व्यक्तियों के कार्यों, प्रयासों आदि के सम्मिलन द्वारा *Between us we saved up enough money to buy a car.* **7** giving each person a share प्रत्येक व्यक्ति को हिस्सा देते हुए *We ate all the chocolates between us.*

NOTE **Between** का प्रयोग प्रायः दो व्यक्तियों या दो वस्तुओं के संदर्भ में होता है—*sitting between her mother and father* ○ *between the ages of 12 and 14.* तथापि **between** का प्रयोग कभी-कभी दो से अधिक व्यक्तियों या वस्तुओं के विषय में भी हो सकता है, यदि वे अलग-अलग माने गए हैं, जैसे परिभाषा सं. 7 में—*We drank a bottle of cold drink between the three of us.* **Among** का प्रयोग सदा दो से अधिक व्यक्तियों या वस्तुओं के समूहों के विषय में होता है—*You're among friends here.*

**bevel** /ˈbevl ˈबेव्‌ल्/ *noun* [C] **1** an edge or a surface that is cut at an angle, for example at the side of a picture frame or sheet of glass कोण पर कटा किनारा या सतह, जैसे चित्र के फ्रेम या शीशे की पत्तर का किनारा; कटाव **2** a tool for cutting edges or surfaces at an angle on wood or stone लकड़ी या पत्थर के किनारों या सतहों को किसी कोण पर काटने का औज़ार; गुनिया

**beverage** /ˈbevərɪdʒ ˈबेव्‌रिज्/ *noun* [C] (*written*) a drink कोई पेय पदार्थ

**beware** /bɪˈweə(r) बिˈवेअ(र्)/ *verb* [I] (*only in the imperative or infinitive form*) **beware (of sb/sth)** (used for giving a warning) to be careful (चेतावनी देने के लिए प्रयुक्त) सावधान रहना *Beware of the dog!* ○ *Beware of saying something that might hurt him.*

**bewilder** /bɪˈwɪldə(r) बिˈविल्ड(र्)/ *verb* [T] to confuse and surprise उलझन और अचरज में डालना *I was completely bewildered by his sudden change of mood.* ▶ **bewildered** *adj.* हक्का-बक्का, विस्मित और चकराया हुआ *a bewildered expression* ▶ **bewildering** *adj.* विस्मयकारी *a bewildering experience* ▶ **bewilderment** *noun* [U] घबराहट, संभ्रम, हैरानग़ी *to stare at sb* ***in bewilderment***

**bewitch** /bɪˈwɪtʃ बिˈविच्/ *verb* [T] to attract and interest sb very much जादू कर देना, मोहित कर लेना, लुभाना

**beyond** /bɪˈjɒnd बिˈयॉन्ड्/ *prep., adv.* **1** on or to the other side of की दूसरी ओर, के परे *beyond the distant mountains* ○ *We could see the mountains and the sea beyond.* **2** further than; later than से आगे; के बाद *Does the railway track continue beyond Guwahati?* ○ *Most people don't go on working beyond the age of 65.* **3** more than sth से अधिक, के अतिरिक्त *The house was* ***far beyond*** *what I could afford.* ○ *I haven't heard anything beyond a few rumours.* **4** used to say that sth is not possible किसी बात के संभव न होने का संकेत करने के लिए प्रयुक्त *The situation is* ***beyond*** *my* ***control****.* **5** too far or too advanced for sb/sth किसी के सामर्थ्य से बाहर *The activity was beyond the students' abilities.*

IDM **be beyond sb** (*informal*) to be impossible for sb to understand or imagine किसी की समझ या कल्पना से बाहर *Why she wants to go and live there is quite beyond me.*

**Bharatanatyam** *noun* [U] a classical dance form of southern India दक्षिण भारत की एक शास्त्रीय नृत्य शैली; भरतनाट्यम

**bhelpuri** *noun* [C] a popular Indian snack made with puffed rice, onions, spices, etc. and a hot, sweet and sour **chutney** भेलपुरी

**bi-** /baɪ बाइ/ *prefix* (*in nouns and adjectives*) two; twice; double दो; दो बार; दुगुना *bicentenary* ○ *bilingual*

**bias[1]** /ˈbaɪəs ˈबाइअस्/ *noun* (*pl.* **biases**) **1** [U, C, *usually sing.*] a strong feeling of favour towards or against one group of people, or on one side in an argument, often not based on fair judgement or facts प्रायः एकतरफ़ा, पूर्वाग्रह, विशेष झुकाव, पक्षपात *a bias against women drivers* **2** [C, *usually sing.*] an interest in one thing more than others; a special ability अपेक्षाकृत अधिक झुकाव; विशिष्टता *a course with a strong scientific bias*

**bias²** /ˈbaɪəs ˈबाइअस् / *verb* [T] (**biasing; biased** or **biassing; biassed**) to influence sb/sth, especially unfairly; to give an advantage to one group, etc. पक्षपात करना, तरफ़दारी करना; पक्षपात के लिए प्रेरित करना *Good newspapers should not be biased towards a particular political party.* ▶ **biased** *adj.* पक्षपातपूर्ण *a biased report*

**bib** /bɪb बिब् / *noun* [C] a piece of cloth or plastic that a baby or small child wears under the chin to protect its clothes while it is eating बच्चों के खाते या पीते समय गले में बाँधा जाने वाला कपड़ा या प्लास्टिक, गतिया; बिब

**the Bible** /ˈbaɪbl ˈबाइबल् / *noun* [*sing.*] **1** the book of great religious importance to Christian and Jewish people ईसाईयों और यहूदियों का धर्मग्रंथ, बाइबिल **2** a book, a magazine, etc. that gives important information on a particular subject विषय-विशेष पर महत्त्वपूर्ण जानकारी देने वाली पुस्तक, मैगज़ीन, आदि ▶ **biblical** /ˈbɪblɪkl ˈबिब्लिकल् / *adj.* बाइबिल-संबंधी

**bibliography** /ˌbɪbliˈɒɡrəfi ˌबिब्लिˈऑग्रफ़ि / *noun* [C] (*pl.* **bibliographies**) **1** a list of the books and articles that a writer used when he/she was writing a particular book or article संदर्भ ग्रंथ सूची; संदर्भिका **2** a book, a magazine etc. that gives important imformation on a particular subject विषय-विशेष पर महत्त्वपूर्ण जानकारी देने वाली पुस्तक, मैगज़ीन आदि **3** a list of books on a particular subject किसी विषय-विशेष पर पुस्तक सूची, ग्रंथ सूची

**bicarbonate** /ˌbaɪˈkɑːbənət ˌबाइˈकाबनट् / *noun* [U] a salt containing a double amount of **carbon dioxide** कार्बन डाइऑक्साइड की दुगुनी मात्रा वाला लवण; बाइकार्बोनेट ➪ **sodium bicarbonate** देखिए।

**bicarbonate of soda** = **sodium bicarbonate**

**bicentenary** /ˌbaɪsenˈtiːnəri ˌबाइसेन्ˈटीनरि / *noun* [C] (*pl.* **bicentenaries**) (*AmE* **bicentennial** /ˌbaɪsenˈteniəl ˌबाइसेन्ˈटेनिअल् /) the day or the year two hundred years after sth happened or began द्विशती, द्विशतवार्षिकी *the bicentenary of Tipu Sultan's death*

**bicentennial** /ˌbaɪsenˈteniəl ˌबाइसेन्ˈटेनिअल् / = **bicentenary**

**biceps** /ˈbaɪseps ˈबाइसेप्स् / *noun* [C] (*pl.* **biceps**) the large muscle at the front of the top part of your arm भुजा के शिखर पर आगे की बड़ी मांसपेशी; द्विशिर पेशी ➪ **triceps** देखिए तथा **arm** पर चित्र देखिए।

**bicker** /ˈbɪkə(r) ˈबिक(र्) / *verb* [I] to argue about unimportant things व्यर्थ की कलह करना, बेकार की बात पर झगड़ना *Ramesh is always bickering about pocket money with his parents.*

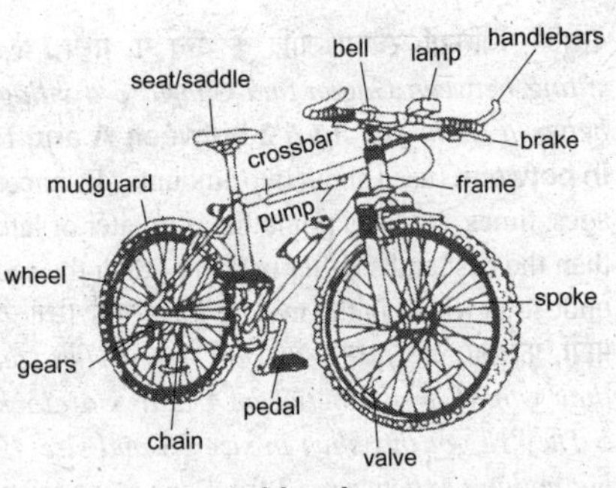


**bicycle**

**bicycle** /ˈbaɪsɪkl ˈबाइसिकल् / (*also* **bike**) a vehicle with two wheels, which you sit on and ride by moving your legs साइकिल NOTE साइकिल चलाने वाले व्यक्ति को **cyclist** कहते हैं।

**bid¹** /bɪd बिड् / *verb* (**bidding**; *pt, pp* **bid**) [I, T] **bid (sth) (for sth)** to offer to pay a particular price for sth, especially at a public sale where things are sold to the person who offers most money (**an auction**) नीलामी में बोली लगाना *I wanted to buy the vase but another man was* ***bidding against*** *me.*

**bid²** /bɪd बिड् / *noun* [C] **1 a bid (for sth); a bid (to do sth)** an effort to do, obtain, etc. sth; an attempt कुछ करने या पाने का प्रयास; उद्यम, उपक्रम *His bid for freedom had failed.* ○ *Tonight the Ethiopian athlete will* ***make a bid*** *to break the world record.* **2** an offer by a person or a business company to pay a certain amount of money for sth किसी वस्तु को ख़रीदने आदि के लिए कुछ धनराशि देने का प्रस्ताव, बोली ○ *At the auction we* ***made a bid*** *of Rs 5000 for the bed.* **3** (*AmE*) = **tender²** ▶ **bidder** *noun* [C] बोली लगाने वाला व्यक्ति *The house was sold to the highest bidder* (= the person who offered the most money).

**bide** /baɪd बाइड् / *verb*

IDM **bide your time** to wait for a good opportunity उपयुक्त अवसर की प्रतीक्षा करना *I'll bide my time until the situation improves.*

**bidi** = **beedi**

**biennial** /baɪˈeniəl बाइˈएनिअल् / *adj.* happening once every two years हर दो वर्षों में होने वाला; द्विवार्षिक, दोसाला

**bifocals** /ˌbaɪˈfəʊklz ˌबाइˈफ़ोकल्ज़् / *noun* [*pl.*] a pair of glasses with each piece of glass (**lens**) made in two parts. The top part is for looking at things at a distance, and the bottom part is for reading or for looking at things close to you दो हिस्सों वाले लेंस का चश्मा; इस लेंस से ऊपर के हिस्से से

दूर की और नीचे के हिस्से से पास की वस्तुएँ देखी जाती हैं ▶ **bifocal** *adj.* दो हिस्सों के लेंस वाला

**bifurcate** /ˈbaɪfəkeɪt ˈबाइफ़केट्/ *verb* [I] (of roads rivers, etc.) to divide into two separate parts (सड़कों, नदियों, आदि को) दो अलग भागों में विभाजित करना ▶ **bifurcation** /ˌbaɪfəˈkeɪʃn ˌबाइफ़ˈकेश्न्/ *noun* [C, U] द्विभाजन

**big** /bɪɡ बिग्/ *adj.* (**bigger; biggest**) **1** large; not small बड़ा, विशाल *a big house/town/salary* **2** great or important महत्त्वपूर्ण, प्रभावशाली *They had a big argument yesterday.* ○ *some of the big names in Bollywood* **3** (*only before a noun*) (*informal*) older आयु में बड़ा *a big brother/sister*

**NOTE** आकार या संख्या के संदर्भ में **big** और **large** दोनों का प्रयोग हो सकता है। **Large** अधिक औपचारिक प्रयोग है और व्यक्तियों के वर्णन में सामान्यतः प्रयुक्त नहीं किया जाता—*a big/large house* ○ *a big baby.* किसी व्यक्ति या वस्तु आदि का महत्त्व बताने के लिए अधिकतर **great** का प्रयोग किया जाता है—*a great occasion/musician.* 'ढेर सारा' के अर्थ में प्रयुक्त अगणनीय संज्ञाओं के साथ भी—**great** का प्रयोग किया जा सकता है—*great happiness/care/sorrow.* आकार, मात्रा आदि के वाचक विशेषण पर बल देने के लिए भी इसका प्रयोग किया जा सकता है। ➪ **great[1] 4** की प्रविष्टि देखिए।

**IDM Big deal** (*informal*) used to say that you think sth is not important or interesting किसी वस्तु के महत्त्वपूर्ण या रोचक न होने की स्थिति दर्शाने के लिए प्रयुक्त *'Look at my new bike!' 'Big deal! It's not as nice as mine.'*

**a big deal/no big deal** (*informal*) something that is (not) very important or exciting कुछ (अ) रोचक या (अ) महत्त्वपूर्ण बात, वस्तु आदि *Birthday celebrations are a big deal in our family.* ○ *We may lose, I suppose, but it's no big deal.*

**give sb a big hand** ➪ **hand[1]** देखिए।

**bigamy** /ˈbɪɡəmi ˈबिगमि/ *noun* [U] the state of being married to two people at the same time एक की समय में दो व्यक्तियों से विवाहित होने की स्थिति; द्विपतित्व या द्विपत्नीत्व ➪ **monogamy** और **polygamy** देखिए। ▶ **bigamist** *noun* [C] द्विविवाही, द्विपतिका स्त्री या द्विपत्नीक पुरुष

**the big bang** *noun* [*sing.*] the single large explosion that some scientists believe created the universe वह एकल बड़ा विस्फोट जिससे, कुछ वैज्ञानिकों के अनुसार, ब्रह्मांड की रचना हुई

**big-head** (*informal*) *noun* [C] a person who thinks he/she is very important or clever because of sth he/she has done स्वयं को बहुत चतुर या महत्त्वपूर्ण समझने वाला व्यक्ति; घमंडी *This is the role that could help her make it to the big time in Bollywood.*

**big toe** *noun* [C] the largest toe on a person's foot पैर का अँगूठा ➪ **body** पर चित्र देखिए।

**bike** /baɪk बाइक्/ *noun* [C] a bicycle or a motorbike साइकिल या मोटरसाइकिल *Hasan's just learnt to* ***ride a bike.*** ○ *We went* ***by bike.*** ○ *He came* ***on his bike.*** ➪ **bicycle** पर चित्र देखिए।

**bikini** /bɪˈkiːni बिˈकीनि/ *noun* [C] a piece of clothing, in two pieces, that women wear for swimming स्त्रियों के तैरने के लिए दो हिस्सों वाली पोशाक

**bilateral** /ˌbaɪˈlætərəl ˌबाइˈलैटरल्/ *adj.* **1** involving two groups of people or two countries द्विपक्षीय, दुतरफ़ा *bilateral trade/talks* **2** (*medical*) involving both sides of the body or brain द्विपार्शिवक ▶ **bilaterally** *adv.* दुतरफ़ा तौर पर, द्विपक्षीय स्तर पर

**bile** /baɪl बाइल्/ *noun* [U] the greenish-brown liquid with a bitter unpleasant taste that comes into your mouth when you vomit with an empty stomach पित्त

**bilge** /bɪldʒ बिल्ज्/ *noun* **1** [C] (*also* **bilges**) [*pl.*] the almost flat part of the bottom of a boat or a ship, inside or outside जहाज़ या नाव का पेंदा **2** (*also* **bilge water**) [U] dirty water that collects in a ship's bilge पेंदे का पानी

**bilingual** /ˌbaɪˈlɪŋɡwəl ˌबाइˈलिङ्ग्वल्/ *adj.* **1** having or using two languages द्वैभाषिक, दो भाषाओं से संबंधित *a bilingual dictionary* ➪ **monolingual** देखिए। **2** able to speak two languages equally well द्विभाषी, दो भाषाओं को अच्छी तरह बोलने में समर्थ *Our children are* ***bilingual in*** *English and Hindi.*

**bill[1]** /bɪl बिल्/ *noun* [C] **1** a piece of paper that shows how much money you owe sb for goods or services सामान या सेवा की क़ीमत के हिसाब का पर्चा, प्राप्यक, बिल *the electricity/gas/telephone bill* ○ *to pay a bill* **2** (*AmE* **check**) a piece of paper that shows how much you have to pay for the food and drinks that you have had in a restaurant रेस्तराँ में ख़रीदी वस्तुओं के लिए देय धनराशि का विवरण, बिल *Can I have the bill, please?* **3** = **note[1] 4** *a ten-rupee bill* **4** a plan for a possible new law विधेयक *The bill was passed/defeated.* **5** a programme of entertainment offered in a show, concert, etc. किसी प्रदर्शन आदि में मनोरंजक कार्यक्रम ***Topping the bill*** (= the most important performer) *is Hrithik Roshan.* **6** a bird's beak पक्षी की चोंच

**IDM foot the bill** ➪ **foot[2]** देखिए।

**bill²** /bɪl बिल् / *verb* [T] (*usually passive*) **bill sb/sth as sth** to describe sb/sth to the public in an advertisement, etc. किसी वस्तु या व्यक्ति को विज्ञापन में पेश करना *This young player is being billed as 'the new Sehwag'.*

**billboard** /ˈbɪlbɔːd ˈबिल्बॉड् / (*BrE* **hoarding**) *noun* [C] a large board near a road where advertisements are put विज्ञापन-बोर्ड

**billet** /ˈbɪlɪt ˈबिलिट् / *noun* [C] a place, often in a private house, where soldiers live temporarily निजी आवास का भाग जहाँ सैनिक अस्थायी रूप से टिकते हैं ▶ **billet** *verb* [T] (*usually passive*) सैनिकों को प्रायः निजी आवास में अस्थायी रूप से टिकाना *The troops were billeted in the town with local families.*

**billiards** /ˈbɪliədz ˈबिलिअड्ज़् / *noun* [U] a game played on a big table covered with cloth. You use a long stick (**a cue**) to hit three balls against each other and into pockets at the corners and sides of the table एक लंबी छड़ी द्वारा तीन गेंदों को एक विशेष मेज़ के कोनों में व किनारों में बने छेदों में डालने का खेल; बिलियर्डज़ *to have a game of/play billiards* **NOTE** किसी अन्य संज्ञा से पहले आने पर billiard ('s' रहित) रूप का प्रयोग किया जाता है—*a billiard table* ➪ **snooker** और **pool¹ 5** देखिए।

**billion** /ˈbɪljən ˈबिल्यन् / *number* 1,000,000,000 एक अरब

> **NOTE** गिनती करते समय **billion** ('s' रहित) का प्रयोग किया जाता है। शब्द **billions** का प्रयोग 'ढेर सारे' (रुपये आदि) के अर्थ में किया जाता है—*three billion rupees* ○ *billions of dollars*
> पूर्व में **billion** का प्रयोग one million million के अर्थ में किया जाता था परंतु इसके लिए अब **trillion** का प्रयोग किया जाता है। अंकों के विषय में अधिक जानकारी के लिए इस कोश के अंत में विशेष खंड देखिए।

**bill of exchange** *noun* [C] (*pl.* **bills of exchange**) a written order to pay a sum of money to a particular person on a particular date विनिमय-पत्र, हुंडी; व्यक्ति को निर्धारित तिथि पर निश्चित राशि देने विषयक लिखित आदेश

**bill of lading** /ˌbɪl əv ˈleɪdɪŋ ˌबिल् अव़् ˈलेडिङ् / *noun* [C] (*pl.* **bills of lading**) a list giving details of the goods that a ship, etc. is carrying जहाज़ आदि पर लादे गए माल की सूची; लदान-पत्र, लदान-बिल

**billow** /ˈbɪləʊ ˈबिलो / *verb* [I] **1** to fill with air and move in the wind लहराना *curtains billowing in the breeze* **2** to move in large clouds through the air बादलों की शकल में हवा में ऊपर उठना *Smoke billowed from the chimneys.*

**billy goat** /ˈbɪli ɡəʊt ˈबिलि गोट् / *noun* [C] a male goat बकरा ➪ **nanny goat** देखिए।

**bin** /bɪn बिन् / *noun* [C] **1** a container that you put rubbish in कूड़ा डालने का डिब्बा; कूड़ादान *to throw sth in the bin* ○ *a litter bin* **2** a container, usually with a lid, for storing bread, flour, etc. आटा आदि रखने का ढक्कनदार डिब्बा *a bread bin*

**binary** /ˈbaɪnəri ˈबाइनरि / *adj.* **1** (*computing, mathematics*) using only 0 and 1 as a system of numbers अंक-व्यवस्था के रूप में केवल 0 और 1 का प्रयोग करते हुए *the* ***binary system*** ○ *binary arithmetic* **2** (*technical*) based on only two numbers; consisting of two parts द्विचर, द्वि-अंकी; द्वि-अंगी ▶ **binary** *noun* [U] अंक व्यवस्था जिसमें केवल 0 और 1 का प्रयोग किया गया हो *The computer performs calculations* ***in binary*** *and converts the results to decimal.*

**bind¹** /baɪnd बाइन्ड् / *verb* [T] (*pt, pp* **bound** /baʊnd बाउन्ड् /) **1 bind sb/sth (to sb/sth); bind A and B (together)** to tie or fasten with string or rope रस्सी आदि से बाँधना *They bound the prisoner's hands behind his back.* **2 bind A to B; bind A and B (together)** to unite people, organizations, etc. so that they live or work together more happily or with better effect जनसमूहों, संगठनों, आदि के बीच पारस्परिक संबंध *The two countries are bound together by a common language.* **3 bind sb (to sth)** to force sb to do sth by making him/her promise to do it or by making it his/her duty to do it किसी कार्य के लिए किसी व्यक्ति को बाध्य करना, आवश्यक बनाना *to be bound by a law/an agreement* ○ *The contract binds you to completion of the work within two years.* **4** (*usually passive*) to fasten sheets of paper into a cover to form a book जिल्द बाँधना या चढ़ाना *The book was bound in leather.*

**binder** /ˈbaɪndə(r) ˈबाइन्ड(र्) / *noun* [C] a hard-cover for holding loose sheets of paper together खुले काग़ज़ों को संभालने के लिए सख़्त आवरण *a ring binder*

**binding¹** /ˈbaɪndɪŋ ˈबाइन्डिङ् / *adj.* making it necessary for sb to do sth he/she has promised or to obey a law, etc. बंधनकारी, बाध्यकारी *This contract is* ***legally binding***.

**binding²** /ˈbaɪndɪŋ ˈबाइन्डिङ् / *noun* **1** [C] a cover that holds the pages of a book together पुस्तक की जिल्द **2** [C, U] material that you fasten to the edge of sth to protect or decorate it सुरक्षा या अलंकरण के लिए प्रयुक्त किसी चीज़ को बाँधने वाली वस्तु **3 bindings** [*pl.*] (used in skiing) a device that fastens your boot to your **ski** (स्की-क्रीड़ा में) जूते से बाँधी जाने वाली लकड़ी या प्लास्टिक की पट्टी; स्की वस्तु

**binge**[1] /bɪndʒ बिन्ज़्/ *noun* [C] (*informal*) a period of eating or drinking too much अत्यधिक या बिना संयम के खाने या पीने का दौर *to go* ***on a binge***

**binge**[2] /bɪndʒ बिन्ज़्/ *verb* [I] (*pres. part.* **bingeing**) (*informal*) **binge (on sth)** to eat or drink too much, especially without being able to conrol yourself विशेषतः बिना संयम रखे अत्यधिक खाना या पीना

**bingo** /ˈbɪŋgəʊ ˈबिङ्गो/ *noun* [U] a game in which each player has a different card with numbers on it. The person in charge of the game calls numbers out and the winner is the first player to have all the numbers on their card called out कार्ड पर लिखी संख्याओं को मिलाने का एक खेल; बिंगो, जिस खिलाड़ी के कार्ड की सभी संख्याएँ बोली जा चुकी हो वह विजेता घोषित होता है

**binoculars** /bɪˈnɒkjələz बिˈनॉक्यलज़्/ *noun* [*pl.*] an instrument with two glass parts (**lenses**) which you look through in order to make objects in the distance seem nearer दो काँच-खंडों वाली दूरबीन ***pair of binoculars*** ➪ **telescope** देखिए।

**binomial** /baɪˈnəʊmiəl बाइˈनोमिअल्/ *noun* [C] an expression in mathematics that has two groups of numbers or letters, joined by the sign + or – गणित में + या – चिह्न से जुड़े दो पदों से बना व्यंजक; द्विपद ▶ **binomial** *adj.* द्विपदी, द्विपदयुक्त

**bio-** /ˈbaɪəʊ ˈबाइओ/ *prefix* (*in nouns, adjectives and adverbs*) connected with living things or human life जैविक; सजीवों से संबंधित *biology* ○ *biodegradable*

**biochemist** /ˌbaɪəʊˈkemɪst ˌबाइओˈकेमिस्ट्/ *noun* [C] a scientist who studies the chemistry of living things जीवरसायनविद्

**biochemistry** /ˌbaɪəʊˈkemɪstri ˌबाइओˈकेमिस्ट्रि/ *noun* **1** [U] the scientific study of the chemistry of living things सजीवों की रासायनिकी का वैज्ञानिक अध्ययन; जीवरसायन **2** [C, U] the chemical structure of a living thing किसी सजीव की रासायनिक संरचना ▶ **biochemical** /ˌbaɪəʊˈkemɪkl ˌबाइओˈकेमिकल्/ *adj.* जीवरसायन संबंधी

**biodegradable** /ˌbaɪəʊdɪˈgreɪdəbl ˌबाइओ-डिˈग्रेडबल्/ *adj.* that can be taken back into the earth naturally and so not harm the environment जो प्राकृतिक रूप से पुनः पृथ्वी में घुल-मिल जाए ताकि पर्यावरण को हानि न हो ✪ विलोम **non-biodegradable**

**biodiversity** /ˌbaɪəʊdaɪˈvɜːsəti ˌबाइओडाइˈव़सटि/ *noun* [U] the existence of a number of different kinds of animals and plants which together make a good and healthy environment जैव विविधता

**biogas** /ˈbaɪəʊgæs ˈबाइओगैस्/ *noun* [U] a mixture of **methane** and **carbon dioxide** produced by the decomposition of plant and animal waste, that is used as fuel पौधे एवं पशुओं के अपघटन से निर्मित मिथेन तथा कार्बन डाइऑक्साइड का मिश्रण (प्रायः ईंधन के रूप में प्रयुक्त); बायोगैस

**biographer** /baɪˈɒgrəfə(r) बाइˈऑग्रफ़(र्)/ *noun* [C] a person who writes the story of sb else's life जीवनी-लेखक, जीवनीकार, चरित लेखक

**biography** /baɪˈɒgrəfi बाइˈऑग्रफ़ि/ *noun* [C, U] (*pl.* **biographies**) the story of a person's life written by sb else (अन्य व्यक्ति द्वारा लिखित) किसी व्यक्ति का जीवनचरित; जीवनी *a biography of Mahatma Gandhi* ○ *I enjoy reading science fiction and biography.* ➪ **autobiography** देखिए। ▶ **biographical** /ˌbaɪəˈgræfɪkl ˌबाइअˈग्रैफ़िकल्/ *adj.* जीवन-संबंधी, जीवनीपरक

**biological** /ˌbaɪəˈlɒdʒɪkl ˌबाइअˈलॉजिकल्/ *adj.* **1** connected with the scientific study of animals, plants and other living things पशु-पौधों आदि सजीवों के वैज्ञानिक अध्ययन से संबंधित; प्राणिविज्ञान या जीवविज्ञान संबंधी *biological research* **2** involving the use of living things to destroy or damage other living things सजीवों की सहायता से अन्य सजीवों का विनाश करने वाला *biological weapons*

**biological warfare** (*also* **germ warfare**) *noun* [U] the use of harmful bacteria as weapons of war हानिकारक जीवाणुओं का युद्ध के अस्त्रों के रूप में प्रयोग; जैविक युद्ध

**biologist** /baɪˈɒlədʒɪst बाइˈऑलजिस्ट्/ *noun* [C] a scientist who studies biology जीवविज्ञानविद्, जीवविज्ञानी

**biology** /baɪˈɒlədʒi बाइˈऑलजि/ *noun* [U] the scientific study of living things सजीवों का वैज्ञानिक अध्ययन; जैविकी, जीवविज्ञान ➪ **botany** और **zoology** देखिए।

**biomass** /ˈbaɪəʊmæs ˈबाइओमैस्/ *noun* [U, *sing.*] (*technical*) the total quantity or weight of plants and animals in a particular area or volume एक विशिष्ट क्षेत्र में पौधों और प्राणियों का कुल भार या परिमाण; जैवपिंड

**biophysicist** /ˌbaɪəʊˈfɪzɪsɪst ˌबाइओˈफ़िज़िसिस्ट्/ *noun* [C] a scientist who uses the laws and methods of **physics** to study **biology** भौतिकी के नियमों और पद्धतियों द्वारा जीवविज्ञान का अध्ययन करने वाला वैज्ञानिक; जैवभौतिकी विज्ञानी

**biophysics** /ˌbaɪəʊˈfɪzɪks ˌबाइओˈफ़िज़िक्स्/ *noun* [U] the science which uses the laws and methods of **physics** to study **biology** भौतिकी के नियमों और पद्धतियों द्वारा जीवविज्ञान का अध्ययन; जैवभौतिकी ▶ **biophysical** /ˌbaɪəʊˈfɪzɪkl ˌबाइओˈफ़िज़िकल्/ *adj.* जैवभौतिकी-संबंधी

**biopsy** /ˈbaɪɒpsi ˈबाइऑप्सि / *noun* [C] (*pl.* **biopsies**) the removal of some tissues from sb's body in order to find out about a disease that he/she may have रोग की परख के लिए शरीर से किसी ऊतक को निकालने की क्रिया

**biorhythm** /ˈbaɪəʊrɪðəm ˈबाइओरिद्म् / *noun* [C, *usually pl.*] a regular series of changes in the life of a living creature, for example sleeping and waking सजीवों के जीवन में होने वाले परिवर्तनों की नियमित शृंखला; जैविक लय

**biosphere** /ˈbaɪəʊsfɪə(r) ˈबाइओस्फ़िअ(र्) / *noun* [*sing.*] (*technical*) the part of the earth's surface and atmosphere in which plants and animals can live पृथ्वी की सतह तथा वायुमंडल का वह क्षेत्र जहाँ सजीव सत्ताएँ रह सकती हैं; जीव-मंडल

**biped** /ˈbaɪped ˈबाइपेड् / *noun* [C] any creature with two feet दो पैरों वाला कोई भी प्राणी; द्विपाद ➪ **quadruped** देखिए।

**birch** /bɜːtʃ बर्च् / *noun* **1** (*also* **birch tree**) [C] a type of tree with smooth thin branches कोमल व पतली टहनियों वाला एक प्रकार का पेड़; भूर्ज, भोज (वृक्ष) **2** [U] the wood from this tree भूर्ज की लकड़ी

**bird** /bɜːd बड् / *noun* [C] a creature with feathers and wings which can (usually) fly पक्षी, चिड़िया *I could hear the birds singing outside.* ○ *There was a bird's nest in the hedge.*

IDM **kill two birds with one stone** ➪ **kill**[1] देखिए।

**bird of prey** *noun* [C] (*pl.* **birds of prey**) a bird that kills and eats other animals and birds शिकारी पक्षी

**birdwatcher** /ˈbɜːdwɒtʃə(r) ˈबड्वॉच(र्) / *noun* [C] a person who studies birds in their natural surroundings पक्षी-विशेषज्ञ, पक्षीविज्ञानी NOTE इसके लिए औपचारिक शब्द **ornithologist** है। ▶ **birdwatching** *noun* [U] पक्षी-अवलोकन

**birth** /bɜːθ बथ् / *noun* **1** [C, U] being born; coming out of a mother's body जन्म; माता के शरीर से बाहर आने की क्रिया *What's your **date of birth** (= the date on which you were born)?* **2** [U] the country you belong to किसी व्यक्ति का जन्म स्थान, कुल या वंश *She's lived in England since she was four but she's Indian **by birth**.* **3** [*sing.*] the beginning of sth किसी स्थिति का आरंभ; प्रवर्तन *the birth of an idea*

IDM **give birth (to sb)** to produce a baby शिशु को जन्म देना *She gave birth to her second child when she was 40.*

**birth certificate** *noun* [C] an official document that states the date and place of a person's birth and the names of his/her parents जन्म-प्रमाणपत्र

**birth control** *noun* [U] ways of limiting the number of children you have संतति-निग्रह ➪ **contraception** और **family planning** देखिए।

**birthday** /ˈbɜːθdeɪ ˈबथ्डे / *noun* [C] the day in each year which is the same date as the one when you were born जन्मदिन, जन्मदिवस *My birthday's on November 15th.* ○ *a birthday present/card/cake*

> NOTE शब्द **anniversary** और **birthday** के अर्थ अलग-अलग हैं। **Anniversary** हर साल पड़ने वाली वह तिथि है जिसपर अतीत में कोई महत्त्वपूर्ण घटना घटी थी—*our wedding anniversary* ○ *the anniversary of the end of the war.* जन्मदिवस के उपलक्ष्य में **Happy Birthday!** का प्रयोग होता है। अठाहरवीं सालगिरह महत्त्वपूर्ण माना जाता है क्योंकि तब क़ानूनन आप वयस्कता प्राप्त कर लेते हैं।

**birthmark** /ˈbɜːθmɑːk ˈबथ्माक् / *noun* [C] a red or brown mark on a person's body that has been there since he/she was born किसी व्यक्ति के शरीर पर जन्म से ही पाया जाने वाला लाल या भूरा चिह्न; जन्म चिह्न

**birthplace** /ˈbɜːθpleɪs ˈबथ्प्लेस् / *noun* **1** [C] the house or town where a person was born जन्मस्थल; जन्मस्थान **2** [*sing.*] the place where sth began प्रवर्तन-स्थल *India is the birthplace of yoga.*

**birth rate** *noun* [C] the number of babies born in a particular group of people during a particular period of time जन्म दर

**biryani** (*also* **biriyani, biriani**) *noun* [U, C] an Indian dish made with highly **seasoned** rice and meat or fish and vegetables बिरयानी

**biscuit** /ˈbɪskɪt ˈबिस्किट् / *noun* [C] **1** (*AmE* **cookie**) a type of small cake that is thin, hard and usually sweet बिस्कुट *a chocolate biscuit* ○ *a packet of biscuits* **2** (*AmE*) a type of small simple cake that is not sweet एक प्रकार का छोटा फीका सादा केक

**bisect** /baɪˈsekt बाइˈसेक्ट् / *verb* [T] (*technical*) to divide sth into two equal parts दो समान खंडों में विभक्त करना; द्विभाजन करना ▶ **bisection** /-ˈsekʃn -ˈसेक्श्न् / *noun* [C, U] द्वि-भाजन; अर्धन

**bishop** /ˈbɪʃəp ˈबिशप् / *noun* [C] **1** a priest with a high position in some branches of the Christian Church, who is responsible for all the churches in a city or a district चर्च-व्यवस्था में नगर या ज़िले की चर्चों का संरक्षक पादरी; बिशप ➪ **archbishop** देखिए। **2** a piece used in the game of **chess** that can move any number of squares in a **diagonal** line शतरंज का एक मोहरा, ऊँट

**bison** /ˈbaɪsn ˈबाइसन्/ *noun* [C] a large wild animal that looks like a cow with long curved horns. There are two types of bison, the North American (also called buffalo) and the European जंगली साँड; ये दो प्रकार के होते हैं—उत्तरी अमेरिकी और यूरोपियन

**bit**[1] /bɪt बिट्/ *noun* **1 a bit** [*sing.*] slightly, a little हलका-सा, थोड़ा *I was a bit annoyed with him.* ○ *Could you be a bit quieter, please?* **2 a bit** [*sing.*] a short time or distance थोड़ा-सा समय या ज़रा-सी दूरी *Could you move forward a bit?* ○ *I'm just going out for a bit.* **3 a bit** [*sing.*] (*informal*) a lot बहुत-सा, अत्यधिक *It must have rained **quite a bit** during the night.* **4** [C] **a bit of sth** a small piece, amount or part of sth किसी वस्तु आदि का छोटा टुकड़ा, मात्रा या अंश *There were bits of broken glass all over the floor.* ○ *Could you give me a bit of advice?* **5** [C] (*computing*) the smallest unit of information that is stored in a computer's memory कंप्यूटर-स्मृति में संचित सूचना की लघुतम इकाई **6** [C] a metal bar that you put in a horse's mouth when you ride it घोड़े की लगाम का मुँह में लगाया जाने वाला धातु का भाग; दहाना ➪ **horse** पर चित्र देखिए।

IDM **bit by bit** slowly or a little at a time थोड़ा-थोड़ा करके; धीरे-धीरे *Bit by bit we managed to get the information we needed.*

**a bit much** (*informal*) annoying or unpleasant कष्टप्रद या अप्रीतिकर *It's a bit much expecting me to work on Sundays.*

**a bit of a** (*informal*) rather a एक सीमा तक, अच्छा-ख़ासा या अच्छी-ख़ासी *I've got a bit of a problem.*

**bits and pieces** (*informal*) small things of different kinds तरह-तरह की छोटी वस्तुएँ, फुटकर चीज़ें *I've finished packing except for a few bits and pieces.*

**do your bit** (*informal*) to do your share of sth; to help with sth अपने हिस्से का काम करना; किसी कार्य में दूसरे की सहायता करना *It won't take long to finish if we all do our bit.*

**not a bit** not at all बिलकुल भी नहीं *The holiday was not a bit what we had expected.*

**to bits** **1** into small pieces छोटे टुकड़ों में *She angrily tore the letter to bits.* **2** very; very much अधिक; अत्यधिक *I was **thrilled to bits** when I won the competition.*

**bit**[2] ➪ **bite**[1] का past tense रूप

**bitch**[1] /bɪtʃ बिच्/ *verb* [I] (*informal*) **bitch (about sb/sth)** to say unkind and critical things about sb, especially when he/she is not there किसी की निंदा या आलोचना करना, विशेषतः पीठ पीछे

**bitch**[2] /bɪtʃ बिच्/ *noun* [C] a female dog कुत्ते की मादा; कुतिया

**bitchy** /ˈbɪtʃi ˈबिचि/ *adj.* (*informal*) talking about other people in an unkind way निंदात्मक, अपमानजनक *a bitchy remark*

**bite**[1] /baɪt बाइट्/ *verb* (*pt* **bit** /bɪt बिट्/; *pp* **bitten** /ˈbɪtn ˈबिटन्/) **1** [I, T] **bite (into sth); bite (sb/sth)** to cut or attack sb/sth with your teeth दाँतों से काटना; दाँतों से काटकर हमला करना *Don't worry about the dog—she never bites.* ○ *He picked up the bread and bit into it hungrily.* **2** [I, T] (used about some insects and animals) to push a sharp point into your skin and cause pain (किसी पतंगे या साँप आदि का) डंक मारना, डसना *He was bitten by a snake/mosquito/spider.* NOTE ततैया, मधुमक्खी, और छत्रिक (जेलीफ़िश) द्वारा डंक मारने को **bite** नहीं कहते; उसे **sting** कहते हैं। **3** [I] to begin to have an unpleasant effect अप्रिय प्रभाव होने लगना *In the South the failure of rains is starting to bite.*

IDM **bite sb's head off** to answer sb in a very angry way गुस्से से जवाब देना

**bite**[2] /baɪt बाइट्/ *noun* **1** [C] a piece of food that you can put into your mouth ग्रास *She took a big bite of the apple.* **2** [C] a painful place on the skin made by an insect, snake, dog, etc. (किसी कीड़े, साँप, कुत्ते आदि प्राणी के) डसने या काटने से बना घाव *I'm covered in mosquito bites.* **3** [*sing.*] (*informal*) a small meal; a snack अल्पाहार; हलका नाश्ता *Would you like **a bite to eat** before you go?*

**bitten** ➪ **bite**[1] का past participle रूप

**bitter**[1] /ˈbɪtə(r) ˈबिट(र्)/ *adj.* **1** caused by anger or hatred क्रोध या घृणा से प्रेरित, कड़वाहट-भरा *a bitter quarrel* **2 bitter (about sth)** (used about a person) very unhappy or angry about sth that has happened because you feel you have been treated unfairly (व्यक्ति) पक्षपाती व्यवहार भुगतने के कारण मर्माहत, दुखी व क्रोधित *She was very bitter about not getting the job.* **3** causing unhappiness or anger for a long time; difficult to accept दुखदायक; असह्य *Failing the exam was **a bitter disappointment** to him.* **4** having a sharp, unpleasant taste; not sweet कड़वा, तीखा, तिक्त *bitter coffee* **5** (used about the weather) very cold (मौसम) बहुत ठंडा *a bitter wind* ▶ **bitterness** *noun* [U] कटुता, कड़वापन *The pay cut caused bitterness among the staff.*

**bitter gourd** /ˈbɪtə(r) gʊəd ˈबिट(र्) गोड्/ (*also* **karela**) *noun* [C] (*IndE*) a vegetable with a rough green skin and which is bitter to taste करेला

**bitterly** /ˈbɪtəli ˈबिटलि/ *adv.* **1** (used for describing strong negative feelings or cold weather) extremely (कटु भावनाएँ या ठंडा मौसम) अत्यधिक *bitterly* *disappointed/resentful* ○ *a bitterly cold winter/wind* **2** in an angry and disappointed way क्रोध और निराशा से *'I've lost everything,' he said bitterly.*

**bitty** /ˈbɪti ˈबिटि/ *adj.* made up of lots of parts which do not seem to be connected अलग-अलग बहुत-से असंबंधित टुकड़ों से निर्मित; विश्रृंखलित *Your essay is rather bitty.*

**bitumen** /ˈbɪtʃəmən ˈबिचमन्/ *noun* [U] a black substance made from petrol, used for covering roads or roofs सड़कों पर या छतों पर डाला जाने वाला गाढ़ा तारकोल; डामर, बिटुमन

**bizarre** /bɪˈzɑ:(r) बिˈज़ा(र्)/ *adj.* very strange or unusual अत्यधिक अनोखा, विचित्र या असामान्य *The story had a most bizarre ending.*

**black¹** /blæk ब्लैक्/ *adj.* **1** of the darkest colour, like night or coal काला (रंग) **2** belonging to a race of people with dark skins अफ़्रीक़ा की श्याम वर्ण वाली जाति से संबंधित *the black population of Britain* ○ *black culture* **3** (used about coffee or tea) without milk or cream (कॉफ़ी या चाय) दूध या क्रीमरहित, काली *black coffee with sugar* **4** very angry बहुत क्रुद्ध *to give sb **a black look*** **5** (used about a situation) without hope; depressing (स्थिति) निराशापूर्ण; अवसादजनक *The economic outlook for the coming year is rather black.* **6** funny in a cruel or unpleasant way विचित्र या कष्टप्रद रीति से हास्यजनक *The film was a black comedy.*

IDM **black and blue** covered with blue, brown or purple marks on the body (**bruises**) because you have been hit by sb/sth बुरी तरह पिटने या चोट लगने के कारण बदरंग

**black and white** (used about television, photographs, etc.) showing no colours except black, white and grey (टेलीविज़न, फ़ोटोचित्र आदि) केवल श्याम-श्वेत रंग में

**black²** /blæk ब्लैक्/ *noun* **1** [U] the darkest colour, like night or coal सबसे गहरा रंग (रात या कोयले जैसा); काला, कृष्ण *People often **wear black** (= black clothes) at funerals.* **2** (*usually* **Black**) [C] a person who belongs to a race of people with dark skins काली त्वचा वालों की प्रजाति का व्यक्ति, ब्लैक ► **blackness** *noun* [U] कालापन, कालिमा

IDM **be in the black** to have some money in the bank बैंक में थोड़ा-बहुत पैसा होना ✪ विलोम **be in the red**

**in black and white** in writing or in print लिखित अथवा मुद्रित रूप में *I won't believe we've got the contract till I see it in black and white.*

**black³** /blæk ब्लैक्/ *verb*

PHRV **black out** to lose consciousness for a short time कुछ समय के लिए मूर्च्छित हो जाना; चारों तरफ अंधेरा छा जाना

**black belt** *noun* [C] **1** a belt that you can earn in some fighting sports such as **judo** or **karate** which shows that you have reached a very high standard जूडो या कराटे जैसे खेलों में अति उच्च उपलब्धि की प्राप्ति दर्शाने वाली बेल्ट; ब्लैक बेल्ट **2** a person who has gained a black belt ब्लैक बेल्ट प्राप्त व्यक्ति

**blackberry** /ˈblækbəri ˈब्लैकब़रि/ *noun* [C] (*pl.* **blackberries**) a small black fruit that grows wild on bushes जंगली झाड़ियों पर उगने वाला छोटा काला फल, काला जंगली बेर, काली अंची

**blackbird** /ˈblækbɜ:d ˈब्लैक्बड्/ *noun* [C] a common European bird. The male is black with a yellow beak and the female is brown एक आम यूरोपीय पक्षी; कस्तूरा, इस पक्षी के नर का रंग काला परंतु चोंच पीली और मादा का रंग भूरा होता है

**blackboard** /ˈblækbɔ:d ˈब्लैक्बॉड्/ (*AmE* **chalkboard**) *noun* [C] a piece of dark board used for writing on with chalk, which is used in a class श्याम पट्ट, ब्लैकबोर्ड

**black cotton soil** *noun* [U] (*also* **Regur**) a dark soil containing clay that is good for growing cotton. It is typical of the Deccan region in India गाढ़े रंग की मिट्टी जो कपास की खेती के लिए उपयुक्त होती है, भारत के दक्खिन इलाक़े की विशिष्ट प्ररुपी

**blackcurrant** /ˌblækˈkʌrənt ˌब्लैक्ˈकरन्ट्/ *noun* [C] a small round black fruit that grows on bushes झाड़ियों पर फलने वाला छोटा गोल काला फल

**blacken** /ˈblækən ˈब्लैकन्/ *verb* [T] **1** to make sth black काला करना **2** to make sth seem bad, by saying unpleasant things about it किसी की प्रतिष्ठा धूमिल करना; कलंक लगाना, कालिख पोतना *to blacken sb's name*

**black eye** *noun* [C] an area of dark-coloured skin around sb's eye where he/she has been hit चोटग्रस्त आँख के चारों ओर की काली पड़ गई त्वचा *He got a black eye in the fight.*

**blackhead** /ˈblækhed ˈब्लैक्हेड्/ *noun* [C] a small spot on the skin especially on the face with a black top विशेषतः चेहरे की त्वचा पर छोटा कील

**black hole** *noun* [C] (*technical*) an area in space that nothing, not even light, can escape from, because the force that pulls objects in space towards each other (**gravity**) is so strong there अंतरिक्ष का ऐसा क्षेत्र जहाँ भीतरी आकर्षण इतना प्रबल है कि कोई पदार्थ, यहाँ तक कि प्रकाश किरणें भी उससे बच नहीं सकती और उस में समा जाती हैं; कृषिणका-विवर

**black ice** *noun* [U] ice in a thin layer on the surface of a road सड़क पर बर्फ़ की पतली परत

**blacklist** /ˈblæklɪst ˈब्लैक्लिस्ट्/ *noun* [C] a list of people, companies, etc. that are considered unacceptable by some organization, country etc. ऐसे व्यक्तियों आदि की सूची जो किसी संस्था, देश आदि द्वारा अस्वीकार्य माने जाते हों और जिनसे संपर्क-व्यवहार नहीं बनाना चाहिए; काली सूची ▶ **blacklist** *verb* [T] काली सूची में डालना *She was blacklisted by all the major theatre groups.*

**black magic** *noun* [U] a type of magic that is used for evil purposes जादू-टोना, काला जादू

**blackmail** /ˈblækmeɪl ˈब्लैक्मेल्/ *noun* [U] the crime of forcing a person to give you money or do sth for you, usually by threatening to make known sth which he/she wants to keep secret कोई रहस्य खोलने की धमकी देकर धन ऐंठने का अपराध; भयादोहन ▶ **blackmail** *verb* [T] **blackmail sb (into doing sth)** भयादोहन करना ▶ **blackmailer** *noun* [C] भयादोहनकर्ता

**black mark** *noun* [C] a note, either in writing on an official record, or in sb's mind, of sth you have done or said that makes people think badly of you प्रतिकूल नोट *He earned a black mark for turning up late to the meeting.*

**black market** *noun* [C, *usually sing.*] the buying and selling of goods or foreign money in a way that is not legal मुद्रा या माल का अवैध क्रय विक्रय; काला बाज़ार, चोर बाज़ार *to buy/sell sth **on the black market***

**blackout** /ˈblækaʊt ˈब्लैक्आउट्/ *noun* [C] **1** a period of time during a war, when all lights must be turned off or covered so that the enemy cannot see them युद्ध के दौरान समय की वह अवधि जिसमें प्रकाश के स्रोत ढक या बुझा दिए जाते हैं ताकि दुश्मन को ठिकानों का पता न चले **2** a period when you lose consciousness for a short time अवधि जिसमें कुछ समय के लिए व्यक्ति मूर्च्छित हो जाता है *to have a blackout*

**blacksmith** /ˈblæksmɪθ ˈब्लैक्स्मिथ्/ *noun* [C] a person whose job is to make and repair things made of iron लोहार

**bladder** /ˈblædə(r) ˈब्लैड(र्)/ *noun* [C] the part of your body where waste liquid (**urine**) collects before leaving your body मूत्राशय; शरीर का वह अंग जहाँ मूत्र एकत्र होता है ➪ **body** पर चित्र देखिए।

**blade** /bleɪd ब्लेड्/ *noun* [C] **1** the flat, sharp part of a knife, etc. चाक़ू आदि का चपटा तेज़ धार वाला फ़लक; ब्लेड, धार ➪ **scythe** पर चित्र देखिए। **2** one of the flat, wide parts that turn round very quickly on an aircraft, etc. विमान आदि में तेज़ी से घूमने वाला एक चपटा, चौड़ा पुरज़ा **2** a long, thin leaf of grass घास का तिनका; पत्ती *a blade of grass*

**blame[1]** /bleɪm ब्लेम्/ *verb* [T] **1 blame sb (for sth); blame sth on sb/sth** to think or say that a certain person or thing is responsible for sth bad that has happened किसी व्यक्ति या वस्तु को ग़लती का ज़िम्मेदार या दोषी ठहराना *Some people blame the changes in the climate on pollution.* **2 not blame sb (for sth)** to think that sb is not wrong to do sth; to understand sb's reason for doing sth दोष न देना; किसी की विवशता को समझना *I don't blame you for feeling fed up.*

IDM **be to blame (for sth)** to be responsible for sth bad ग़लती के लिए उत्तरदायी होना *The police say that careless driving was to blame for the accident.*

**shift the blame/responsibility (for sth) (onto sb)** ➪ **shift[1]** देखिए।

**blame[2]** /bleɪm ब्लेम्/ *noun* [U] **blame (for sth)** responsibility for sth bad ग़लती का दायित्व *The government must **take the blame** for the economic crisis.* ○ *The report **put the blame on** rising prices.*

**blameless** /ˈbleɪmləs ˈब्लेम्लस्/ *adj.* (*written*) not guilty; that should not be blamed निर्दोष,बेक़सूर; अनिंद्य *He insisted that his wife was blameless and hadn't known about his crimes.*

**blanch** /blɑːntʃ ब्लान्च्/ *verb* **1** [I] (*written*) **blanch (at sth)** to become pale because you are shocked or frightened भय से पीला पड़ जाना **2** [T] to prepare food, especially vegetables, by putting it into boiling water for a short time सब्ज़ी बनाते समय थोड़ी देर के लिए उसे पानी में खौलाना

**bland** /blænd ब्लैन्ड्/ *adj.* **1** ordinary or not very interesting मामूली, अनाकर्षक, अरोचक *a rather bland style of writing* **2** (used about food) mild or lacking in taste (भोजन) फीका या बेस्वाद **3** not showing any emotion भावहीन ▶ **blandly** *adv.* भावहीनता से

**blank[1]** /blæŋk ब्लैङ्क्/ *adj.* **1** empty, with nothing written, printed or recorded on it ख़ाली, कोरा *a blank video/cassette/piece of paper/page* **2** without feelings, understanding or interest बिना भाव, समझ या रुचि के; भावशून्य *a blank expression on his face* ○ *My mind **went blank** when I saw the exam questions* ▶ **blankly** *adv.* भावशून्य रीति से *She stared at me blankly, obviously not recognizing me.*

**blank[2]** /blæŋk ब्लैङ्क्/ *noun* [C] an empty space रिक्त स्थान, ख़ाली जगह ***Fill in the blanks** in the following exercise.* ○ (*figurative*) *I couldn't remember his name—my mind was a complete blank.*

IDM **draw a blank** ➪ **draw[1]** देखिए।

**blank cheque** *noun* [C] a cheque that has been signed but that has an empty space so that the amount to be paid can be written in later ऐसा चेक जिस पर हस्ताक्षर हैं किंतु धनराशि निर्देश का स्थान ख़ाली है; कोरा चेक

**blanket[1]** /ˈblæŋkɪt ˈब्लैङ्किट्/ *noun* [C] **1** a cover made of wool, etc. that is put on beds to keep people warm कंबल, ऊनी चादर **2** a thick layer or covering of sth किसी वस्तु की मोटी परत; आवरण, चादर *a blanket of snow* ▶ **blanket** *verb* [T] **blanket sth (in/with sth)** मोटी परत से ढकना *The countryside was blanketed in snow.*

IDM **a wet blanket** ➪ **wet[1]** देखिए।

**blanket[2]** /ˈblæŋkɪt ˈब्लैङ्किट्/ *adj.* (*only before a noun*) affecting everyone or everything सब पर लागू; व्यापक *There is a **blanket ban** on journalists reporting the case.*

**blank verse** *noun* [U] (*technical*) poetry that has a regular rhythm but whose lines do not end with the same sound अतुकांत कविता

**blare** /bleə(r) ब्लेअ(र्)/ *verb* [I, T] **blare (sth) (out)** to make a loud, unpleasant noise ऊँची कर्कश ध्वनि उत्पन्न करना *Car horns were blaring in the street outside.* ○ *The loudspeaker blared out pop music.* ▶ **blare** *noun* [U, *sing.*] ऊँची कर्कश ध्वनि *the blare of a siren*

**blasphemy** /ˈblæsfəmi ˈब्लैस्फ़मि/ *noun* [U] writing or speaking about God in a way that shows a lack of respect ईश-निंदा ▶ **blasphemous** /ˈblæsfəməs ˈब्लैस्फ़मस्/ *adj.* ईश-निंदा-संबंधी, ईश-निंदापूर्ण

**blast[1]** /blɑːst ब्लास्ट्/ *noun* [C] **1** an explosion, especially one caused by a bomb विस्फोट, धमाका, विशेषतः बम का **2** a sudden strong current of air हवा का तेज़ झोंका; झकोरा *a blast of cold air* **3** a loud sound made by a musical instrument, etc. किसी वाद्य यंत्र द्वारा उत्पन्न ऊँची ध्वनि *The driver gave a few blasts on his horn.*

**blast[2]** /blɑːst ब्लास्ट्/ *verb* [T] **1** to make a hole, a tunnel, etc. in sth with an explosion विस्फोट द्वारा गड्ढा, सुरंग आदि बनाना *They blasted a tunnel through the mountainside.* **2** to criticize sth very strongly किसी की तीखी आलोचना करना

PHRV **blast off** (used about a spacecraft) to leave the ground; to take off (अंतरिक्ष यान का) ज़मीन छोड़ना; उड़ान भरना

**blast furnace** *noun* [C] a large structure like an oven in which rock containing iron (**iron ore**) is melted in order to take out the metal भट्टी जिसमें खनिज लौह को पिघलाकर धातु निकाली जाती है; वात्या-भट्टी, झोंका-भट्टी

**blast-off** *noun* [U] the time when a spacecraft leaves the ground वह समय जब अंतरिक्ष यान धरती से ऊपर उठता है, अंतरिक्ष यान के उड़ान भरने का समय

**blatant** /ˈbleɪtnt ˈब्लेटन्ट्/ *adj.* very clear or obvious साफ़, खुला या स्पष्ट *a blatant lie* NOTE इस शब्द का प्रयोग निंदात्मक अर्थ में किया जाता है। ▶ **blatantly** *adv.* खुले तौर पर, खुले आम

**blaze[1]** /bleɪz ब्लेज़्/ *noun* **1** [C] a large and often dangerous fire भयंकर आग *It took firefighters four hours to put out the blaze.* **2** [*sing.*] **a blaze of sth** a very bright show of light or colour ज्वाला की चमक; प्रदीप्ति *The garden was a blaze of colour.* ○ *The new theatre was opened **in a blaze of publicity**.*

**blaze[2]** /bleɪz ब्लेज़्/ *verb* [I] **1** to burn with bright strong flames चमकीली ज्वाला के साथ जलना **2 blaze (with sth)** to be extremely bright; to shine brightly बहुत चमकीला होना; प्रखर रूप से प्रदीप्त होना *I woke up to find that the room was blazing with sunshine.* ○ (*figurative*) *'Get out!' she shouted, her eyes blazing with anger.*

**blazer** /ˈbleɪzə(r) ˈब्लेज़(र्)/ *noun* [C] a jacket, especially one that has the colours or sign (**badge**) of a school, club or team on it रंगीन जाकेट जिस पर स्कूल आदि का बिल्ला लगा होता है *a school blazer*

**bleach[1]** /bliːtʃ ब्लीच्/ *verb* [T] to make sth white or lighter in colour by using a chemical or by leaving it in the sun रसायन के प्रयोग से या धूप के कारण रंग उड़ाना या सफ़ेद करना या होना; विरंजित करना

**bleach[2]** /bliːtʃ ब्लीच्/ *noun* [C, U] a strong chemical substance used for making clothes, etc. whiter or for cleaning things कपड़ों आदि को अधिक सफ़ेद या वस्तुओं को साफ़ करने वाला शक्तिशाली रासायनिक पदार्थ; विरंजक

**bleak** /bliːk ब्लीक्/ *adj.* **1** (used about a situation) bad; not encouraging or hopeful (स्थिति) ख़राब, बुरी; निराशापूर्ण *a bleak future for the next generation* **2** (used about a place) cold, empty and grey (स्थान) सर्द, उजाड़ और धूसर *the bleak Arctic landscape* **3** (used about the weather) cold and grey (मौसम) सर्द और धूलभरा *a bleak winter's day* ▶ **bleakly** *adv.* निराशपूर्ण तरह से ▶ **bleakness** *noun* [U] निराशापूर्णता, उत्साहहीनता

**bleary** /ˈblɪəri ˈब्लिअरि/ *adj.* (used about the eyes) red, tired and unable to see clearly (आँखें) लाल, थकी हुई और धुँधली दृष्टि वाली *We were all rather bleary-eyed after the journey.* ▶ **blearily** *adv.* धुँधलेपन से

**bleat** /bli:t ब्लीट्/ *verb* **1** [I] to make the sound of a sheep मिमियाना **2** [I, T] to speak in a weak or complaining voice क्षीण और शिकायत स्वर में कुछ कहना ▸ **bleat** *noun* [C] मिमियाने की आवाज़; मिमियाहट

**bleed** /bli:d ब्लीड्/ *verb* [I] (*pt, pp* **bled** /bled ब्लेड्/) to lose blood ख़ून बहना, रक्तस्राव होना ▸ **bleeding** *noun* [U] रक्तस्राव *He wrapped a scarf around his arm to stop the bleeding.*

**bleep¹** /bli:p ब्लीप्/ *noun* [C] a short, high sound made by a piece of electronic equipment किसी विद्युत यंत्र द्वारा उत्पन्न अल्पकालीन ऊँची ध्वनि

**bleep²** /bli:p ब्लीप्/ *verb* **1** [I] (used about machines) to make a short high sound (यंत्र) अल्पकालीन ऊँची ध्वनि निकालना **2** (*AmE* **beep**) [T] to attract a person's attention using an electronic machine विद्युत यंत्र की ध्वनि से किसी को बुलाना *Please bleep the doctor on duty immediately.*

**bleeper** /ˈbli:pə(r) ˈब्लीप(र्)/ (*AmE* **beeper**) *noun* [C] a small piece of electronic equipment that bleeps to let a person (for example a doctor) know when sb is trying to contact him/her ध्वनि उत्पन्न करने वाला एक प्रकार का छोटा विद्युतीय यंत्र जो मालिक को इस बात का संकेत देता है कि कोई संपर्क बनाने की कोशिश कर रहा है ✪ पर्याय **pager**

**blemish** /ˈblemɪʃ ˈब्लेमिश्/ *noun* [C] a mark that spoils the way sth looks दाग़ या धब्बा ▸ **blemish** *verb* [T] (*figurative*) दाग़ या धब्बा लगाना; कलंकित करना *The defeat has blemished the team's perfect record.*

**blend¹** /blend ब्लेन्ड्/ *verb* **1** [T] **blend A with B; blend A and B (together)** to mix मिश्रण बनाना *First blend the flour and the melted butter together.* **2** [I] **blend (in) with sth** to combine with sth in an attractive or suitable way उचित या आकर्षक नीति से (किसी के साथ) मिलना; मेल रखना *The new room is decorated to blend in with the rest of the house.* **3** [I] **blend (into sth)** to match or be similar to the surroundings sb/sth is in (किसी के) परिवेश से मेल खाना *These animals' ability to blend into their surroundings provides a natural form of defence.*

**blend²** /blend ब्लेन्ड्/ *noun* [C] a mixture मिश्रण *He had the right blend of enthusiasm and experience.*

**blender** /ˈblendə(r) ˈब्लेन्ड(र्)/ (*BrE* **liquidizer**) *noun* [C] an electric machine that is used for making food into liquid भोज्य पदार्थों को द्रव बनाने वाला विद्युतीय यंत्र; सम्मिश्रक ➪ **kitchen** पर चित्र देखिए।

**bless** /bles ब्लेस्/ *verb* [T] to ask for God's help and protection for sb/sth किसी के लिए ईश्वर की सुरक्षात्मक कृपा चाहना

IDM **be blessed with sth/sb** to be lucky enough to have sth/sb सौभाग्यशाली होना *Sri Lanka is an area blessed with many fine sandy beaches.*

**Bless you** what you say to a person who has a cold and has just **sneezed** (ज़ुकाम के कारण) छींकने पर अन्य व्यक्ति द्वारा कहा कथन

**blessed** /ˈblesɪd ˈब्लेसिड्/ *adj.* **1** having God's help and protection ईश्वरीय कृपा से मंडित, अभिमंत्रित **2** (in religious language) lucky; fortunate (धार्मिक भाषा में) सौभाग्यशाली, धन्य *Blessed are the pure in heart.* **3** (*formal*) giving great pleasure सुखद, आनंददायक *The cool breeze brought* ***blessed relief*** *from the heat.*

**blessing** /ˈblesɪŋ ˈब्लेसिङ्/ *noun* [C] **1** a thing that you are grateful for or that brings happiness सौभाग्य, वरदान *It's a great blessing that we have two healthy children.* ○ *Not getting that job was* ***a blessing in disguise*** (= something that seems to be unlucky but turns out to be a good thing). **2** [*usually sing.*] approval or support अनुमोदन या समर्थन *They got married without their parents' blessing.* **3** [*usually sing.*] (a prayer asking for) God's help and protection ईशकृपा के लिए प्रार्थना *The priest said a blessing.*

**blew** ➪ **blow¹** का past tense रूप

**blight¹** /blaɪt ब्लाइट्/ *verb* [T] to spoil or damage sth, especially by causing a lot of problems विशेषतः समस्याएँ उत्पन्न कर हानि पहुँचाना *an area blighted by unemployment*

**blight²** /blaɪt ब्लाइट्/ *noun* **1** [U, C] any disease that kills plants, especially crops that are grown for food फ़सलनाशक रोग *potato blight* **2** [*sing.*, U] **blight (on sb/sth)** something that has a bad effect on a situation, a person's life or the environment स्थिति, जीवन या पर्यावरण पर हानिकारक प्रभाव; अभिशाप

**blind¹** /blaɪnd ब्लाइन्ड्/ *adj.* **1** unable to see नेत्रहीन, नेत्र-विकलांग, अंधा *a blind person* ○ *to be completely/partially blind* NOTE नेत्रहीन व्यक्तियों को **blind** के स्थान पर **partially sighted** या **visually impaired** कहा जाता है। **2 blind (to sth)** not wanting to notice or understand sth ध्यान देने या समझाने में अनिच्छुक; उपेक्षाशील *He was completely blind to her faults.* **3** without reason or thought विवेकहीन, तर्कहीन *He drove down the highway in* ***a blind panic.*** **4** impossible to see round जिसके चारों ओर देखना संभव न हो *You should never overtake on* ***a blind corner.*** ▸ **blindly** *adv.* बिना सोचे-समझे ▸ **blindness** *noun* [U] अंधापन, विवेकशून्यता

**IDM** **turn a blind eye (to sth)** to pretend not to notice sth bad is happening so that you do not have to do anything about it जान-बूझकर अनदेखा करना ताकि कोई कार्रवाई न करनी पड़े

**blind²** /blaɪnd ब्लाइन्ड्/ *verb* [T] **1** to make sb unable to see देखने में असमर्थ बना देना, नेत्र ज्योतिहीन हो जाना या कर देना *Her grandfather had been blinded in an accident* (= permanently). ○ *Just for a second I was blinded by the sun* (= for a short while). **2 blind sb (to sth)** to make sb unable to think clearly or behave in a sensible way किसी को विवेकशून्य कर देना, स्पष्ट विचार-क्षमता से वंचित कर देना

**blind³** /blaɪnd ब्लाइन्ड्/ *noun* **1** [C] a piece of cloth or other material that you pull down to cover a window कपड़े या अन्य वस्तु से निर्मित खिड़की का पर्दा; झिलमिली **2 the blind** [*pl.*] people who are unable to see लोग जो नेत्रहीन हों

**blind date** *noun* [C] an arranged meeting between two people who have never met before to see if they like each other enough to begin a romantic relationship रूमानी रिश्तों के इच्छुक दो अपरिचितों के लिए तय की गई मुलाक़ात

**blinders** /ˈblaɪndəz ˈब्लाइन्डज़्/ (*AmE*) = **blinkers**

**blindfold** /ˈblaɪndfəʊld ˈब्लाइन्ड्फ़ोल्ड्/ *noun* [C] a piece of cloth, etc. that is used for covering sb's eyes आँखों पर बंधी पट्टी ▶ **blindfold** *verb* [T] आँखों पर पट्टी बाँधना

**blind spot** *noun* [C] **1** the part of the road just behind you that you cannot see when driving a car गाड़ी चलाते समय पीछे की सड़क का वह भाग जो चालक नहीं देख सकता; अंधस्थल **2** if you have a blind spot about sth, you cannot understand or accept it समझ से बाहर होने के कारण अस्वीकार्य

**blink** /blɪŋk ब्लिङ्क्/ *verb* **1** [I, T] to shut your eyes and open them again very quickly आँखें झपकाना या मिचकाना *Oh dear! You blinked just as I took the photograph!* ➪ **wink** देखिए। **2** [I] (used about a light) to come on and go off again quickly (रोशनी का) टिमटिमाना ▶ **blink** *noun* [C] झपकी, निमेष

**blinkers** /ˈblɪŋkəz ˈब्लिङ्कज़्/ (*AmE* **blinders**) *noun* [*pl.*] pieces of leather that are placed at the side of a horse's eyes to stop it from looking sideways घोड़े को इधर-उधर देखने से रोकने के लिए उसकी आँखों पर लगाए जाने वाले चमड़े के टुकड़े; अँधेरी, झापड़े

**blip** /blɪp ब्लिप्/ *noun* [C] **1** a light flashing on the screen of a piece of equipment, sometimes with a short high sound किसी यंत्र के परदे पर कौंधती रोशनी, कभी-कभी अल्पकालिक ऊँची आवाज़ के साथ **2** a small problem that does not last for long अस्थायी समस्या

**bliss** /blɪs ब्लिस्/ *noun* [U] perfect happiness परमानंद ▶ **blissful** /-fl -फ़्ल्/ *adj.* सुखद, आनंदमय ▶ **blissfully** /-fəli -फ़लि/ *adv.* सुखपूर्वक, सानंद

**blister¹** /ˈblɪstə(r) ˈब्लिसट(र्)/ *noun* [C] a small painful area of skin that looks like a bubble and contains clear liquid. Blisters are usually caused by rubbing or burning फ़फ़ोला, छाला

**blister²** /ˈblɪstə(r) ˈब्लिसट(र्)/ *verb* [I, T] **1** to get or cause blisters फ़फ़ोले होना या कर देना **2** to swell and crack or to cause sth to do this फूलना और दरकना या फुलाना और दरकाना *The paint is starting to blister.*

**blistering** /ˈblɪstərɪŋ ˈब्लिसटरिङ्/ *adj.* very strong or extreme बहुत तीव्र या अत्यधिक; चरम the *blistering midday heat* ○ *The runners set off at a blistering pace.*

**blitz** /blɪts ब्लिट्स्/ *noun* [C] **a blitz (on sth)** a sudden effort or attack on sb/sth एकाएक किया गया प्रयास या आक्रमण

**blizzard** /ˈblɪzəd ˈब्लिज़ड्/ *noun* [C] a very bad storm with strong winds and a lot of snow बर्फ़ानी तूफ़ान, हिम-झंझावात ➪ **storm** पर नोट देखिए।

**bloated** /ˈbləʊtɪd ˈब्लोटिड्/ *adj.* unusually large and uncomfortable because of liquid, food or gas inside (भोजन, द्रव या गैस अंदर होने के कारण) कष्टकर और फूला हुआ (पेट) *I felt a bit bloated after all that food.*

**blob** /blɒb ब्लॉब्/ *noun* [C] a small amount or drop of a thick liquid गाढ़े द्रव की बूँद *a blob of paint/cream/ink*

**bloc** /blɒk ब्लॉक्/ *noun* [C] a group of countries that work closely together because they have the same political interests समान राजनीतिक हित वाले देशों का गुट

**block¹** /blɒk ब्लॉक्/ *noun* [C] **1** a large, heavy piece of sth, usually with flat sides धातु या पत्थर का बड़ा और भारी खंड, प्रायः समतल पार्श्वों वाला; कुंदा *a block of wood* ○ *huge concrete blocks* **2** a large building that is divided into separate flats or offices अलग-अलग खंडों में बँटा एक बड़ा भवन *a block of flats* ➪ **apartment block** और **office block** देखिए। **3** a group of buildings in a town which has streets on all four sides भवन समूह जिसके चारों ओर सड़कें हों *The restaurant is three blocks away.* **4** a quantity of sth or an amount of time that is considered as a single unit परिमाण या समय की एकीभूत इकाई *The class is divided into two blocks of fifty minutes.* **5** [*usually sing.*] a thing that makes movement or progress difficult or impossible आवागमन या प्रगति में बाधा या अवरोध *a block to further progress in the talks* ➪ **road block** देखिए।

**6** (in India) a group of villages that form an administrative unit (भारत में) ग्राम समूहों की एक प्रशासनिक इकाई

**IDM** **have a block (about sth)** to be unable to think or understand sth properly कुछ सोचने-समझने में असमर्थ *I had a complete* ***mental block****. I just couldn't remember his name.*

**block²** /blɒk ब्लॉक्/ *verb* [T] **1 block sth (up)** to make it difficult or impossible for sb/sth to pass अवरोध या बाधा द्वारा आवागमन में रोक डालना *Many roads are completely blocked by snow.* **2** to prevent sth from being done किसी कार्य को पूरा होने से रोकना; रोड़े अटकाना *The management tried to block the deal.* **3** to prevent sth from being seen by sb किसी के दिखाई देने में बाधक होना *Get out of the way, you're blocking the view!*

**PHR V** **block sth off** to separate one area from another with sth solid किसी ठोस वस्तु से बाधा बनाकर एक क्षेत्र को दूसरे से अलग कर देना *This section of the road has been blocked off by the police.*

**block sth out** to try not to think about sth unpleasant किसी अप्रियकर घटना आदि के बारे में न सोचने की कोशिश करना; मन से निकाल देना *She tried to block out the memory of the crash.*

**block³** /blɒk ब्लॉक्/ *noun* [C] (in India) an administrative unit comprising a group of villages (भारत में) ग्राम समूह की एक प्रशासनिक इकाई

**blockade** /blɒˈkeɪd ब्लॉˈकेड्/ *noun* [C] a situation in which a place is surrounded by soldiers or ships in order to prevent goods or people from reaching it नाकेबंदी, नाकाबंदी, अवरोधन ▶ **blockade** *verb* [T] नाकेबंदी करना, अवरोधन लगाना

**blockage** /ˈblɒkɪdʒ ˈब्लॉकिज्/ *noun* [C] a thing that is preventing sth from passing; the state of being blocked अवरोधक, बाधक; अवरोध, बाधा, रुकावट *a blockage in the drainpipe* ○ *There are blockages on some major roads.*

**blockbuster** /ˈblɒkbʌstə(r) ˈब्लॉकबस्टर्(र्)/ *noun* [C] a book or film with an exciting story which is very successful and popular अति सफल व लोकप्रिय पुस्तक या फ़िल्म

**block capitals** *noun* [*pl.*] big letters such as 'A' (not 'a') बड़े अक्षर, जैसे A (न कि 'a') *Please write your name* ***in block capitals****.*

**bloke** /bləʊk ब्लोक्/ *noun* [C] (*slang*) a man आदमी, पुरुष *He's a really nice bloke.*

**blonde** (*also* **blond**) /blɒnd ब्लॉन्ड्/ *noun* [C] *adj.* (a person) with fair or yellow hair शुभ्र अथवा पीत वर्ण केशों वाला (व्यक्ति); शुभ्रकेशी *Most of our family have blonde hair.*

**NOTE** किसी महिला के वर्णन के संदर्भ में वर्तनी **blonde** का प्रयोग किया जाता है—*She's tall, slim and blonde.* संज्ञा के रूप में **blonde** केवल महिलाओं के लिए प्रयुक्त किया जाता है—*She's a blonde.* ➪ **brunette** भी देखिए।

**blood** /blʌd ब्लड्/ *noun* [U] the red liquid that flows through your body रक्त, ख़ून, रुधिर *The heart pumps blood around the body.* ➪ **bleed** देखिए।

**IDM** **in your blood** a strong part of your character व्यक्तित्व का अंतरंग भाग *Country side a love of the countryside was* ***in his blood***

**in cold blood** ➪ **cold¹** देखिए।

**shed blood** ➪ **shed²** देखिए।

**your (own) flesh and blood** ➪ **flesh** देखिए।

**bloodbath** /ˈblʌdbɑːθ ˈब्लड्बाथ्/ *noun* [*sing.*] an act of violently killing many people हत्याकांड

**blood count** *noun* [C] the number of red and white cells in your blood; a medical test to count these रक्त में लाल और श्वेत कोशिकाओं की संख्या; इनकी गणना करने वाला डॉक्टरी परीक्षण *to have a high/low/normal blood count*

**blood-curdling** *adj.* very frightening बहुत भयावह *a blood-curdling scream*

**blood donor** *noun* [C] a person who gives some of his/her blood for use in medical operations रक्तदाता

**blood group** (*also* **blood type**) *noun* [C] any of several different types of human blood मानव रक्त के अनेक प्रकारों में से एक; रुधिर-वर्ग *'What blood group are you?' 'O+'.*

**bloodless** /ˈblʌdləs ˈब्लड्लस्/ *adj.* **1** without killing or violence बिना हत्या या हिंसा के; बिना रक्त बहाए *a bloodless coup* **2** (used about a part of the body) very pale (शरीर का अंग) विवर्ण, बहुत पीला, रक्तहीन

**blood poisoning** *noun* [U] an illness in which the blood becomes infected with bacteria, especially because of a cut or an injury to the skin रक्त में जीवाणुओं के संक्रमण से उत्पन्न रोग; रक्त-विषाक्तता ✪ पर्याय **septicaemia**

**blood pressure** *noun* [U] the force with which the blood travels round the body रक्तचाप *to have* ***high/low blood pressure***

**bloodshed** /ˈblʌdʃed ˈब्लड्शेड्/ *noun* [U] the killing or harming of people रक्तपात, ख़ून-ख़राबा *Both sides in the war want to avoid further bloodshed.*

**bloodshot** /ˈblʌdʃɒt ˈब्लड्शॉट्/ *adj.* (used about the white part of the eyes) full of red lines, for example when sb is tired (आँखों) का सफ़ेद हिस्सा, थकने के कारण लाल डोरों से भरी, ख़ूनी (आँखें)

**bloodstain** /ˈblʌdsteɪn ˈब्लड्स्टेन् / *noun* [C] a mark or spot of blood on sth ख़ून का छींटा, रक्तबिंद ▶ **bloodstained** *adj.* रक्तरंजित

**bloodstream** /ˈblʌdstriːm ˈब्लड्स्ट्रीम् / *noun* [*sing.*] the blood as it flows through the body रक्तधारा *drugs injected straight into the bloodstream*

**bloodthirsty** /ˈblʌdθɜːsti ˈब्लड्थस्टि / *adj.* wanting to use violence or to watch scenes of violence रक्तपिपासु, ख़ूनख़्वार

**blood transfusion** *noun* [C] the process of putting new blood into a person's body किसी व्यक्ति के शरीर में नया रक्त डालना

**blood type** = **blood group**

**blood vessel** *noun* [C] any of the tubes in your body which blood flows through रक्तवाहिका, शिरा ➪ **vein, artery** और **capillary** देखिए।

**bloody** /ˈblʌdi ˈब्लडि / *adj.* (**bloodier; bloodiest**) **1** involving a lot of violence and killing हिंसा भरा, ख़ूनी, रक्तपातपूर्ण *a bloody war* **2** covered with blood ख़ून से सना, रुधिराक्त *a bloody knife*

**bloom**[1] /bluːm ब्लूम् / *noun* [C] a flower पुष्प, फूल
**IDM in bloom** with its flowers open खिले फूलों वाला (पौधा या बग़ीचा) *All the wild plants are in bloom.*

**bloom**[2] /bluːm ब्लूम् / *verb* [I] to produce flowers फूल खिलाना, बौराना, पुष्पित होना *This shrub blooms in March.*

**blossom**[1] /ˈblɒsəm ˈब्लॉसम् / *noun* [C, U] a flower or a mass of flowers, especially on a fruit tree in the spring फूल, बौर, मंजरी *The apple tree is **in blossom**.*

**blossom**[2] /ˈblɒsəm ˈब्लॉसम् / *verb* [I] **1** (used especially about trees) to produce flowers (पेड़ों का) पुष्पित होना **2 blossom (into sth)** to become more healthy, confident or successful अधिक स्वस्थ, आत्मविश्वासी या सफल होना *This young runner has blossomed into a top-class athlete.*

**blot**[1] /blɒt ब्लॉट् / *noun* [C] **1** a spot of sth, especially one made by ink on paper; a stain रोशनाई का धब्बा, दाग़, निशान **2 a blot on sth** a thing that spoils your happiness or other people's opinion of you (चरित्र पर) लांछन, कलंक

**blot**[2] /blɒt ब्लॉट् / *verb* [T] (**blotting; blotted**) **1** to make a spot or a mark on sth, especially ink on paper किसी सतह पर निशान, दाग़ या धब्बा लगाना **2** to remove liquid from a surface by pressing soft paper or cloth on it किसी सतह पर से द्रव सोखना
**PHR V blot sth out** to cover or hide sth छिपाना, मिटाना *Fog blotted out the view completely.* ○ *She tried to blot out the memory of what happened.*

**blotch** /blɒtʃ ब्लॉच् / *noun* [C] a temporary mark or an area of different colour on skin, plants, material, etc. त्वचा, पौधों आदि पर पड़ने वाला अस्थायी या कच्चा धब्बा *The blotches on her face showed that she had been crying.* ▶ **blotchy** (*also* **blotched**) *adj.* धब्बेदार

**blotting paper** *noun* [U] soft paper that you use for drying wet ink after you have written sth on paper स्याही-सोख़ता; सोख़ता काग़ज़

**blouse** /blaʊz ब्लाउज़् / *noun* [C] a piece of clothing like a shirt, worn by women महिलाओं का उपरिवस्त्र; ब्लाउज़, चोली

**blow**[1] /bləʊ ब्लो / *verb* (*pt* **blew** /bluː ब्लू /; *pp* **blown** /bləʊn ब्लोन् /) **1** [I, T] (used about wind, air, etc.) to be moving or to cause sth to move (हवा का) बहना, चलना *A gentle breeze was blowing.* **2** [I] to move because of the wind or a current of air (वस्तुओं का) हवा से उड़ना *The balloons blew away.* ○ *My papers blew all over the garden.* **3** [I] to send air out of the mouth फूँक मारना *The policeman asked me to blow into the breathalyser.* **4** [T] to make or shape sth by blowing air out of your mouth फूँक मारकर बुलबुले आदि बनाना *to blow bubbles/smoke rings* **5** [I, T] to produce sound from a musical instrument, etc. by blowing air into it फूँक मारकर सीटी; वाद्य यंत्र आदि बजाना *The referee's whistle blew for the end of the match.* ○ *He blew a few notes on the trumpet.* **6** [T] (*informal*) to waste an opportunity अवसर खो देना *I think I've blown my chances of promotion.* **7** [T] (*informal*) **blow sth (on sth)** to spend or waste a lot of money on sth किसी कार्य पर पैसा बरबाद करना *She blew all her savings on a trip to Egypt.* **8** [I, T] (used about a thin piece of wire (**a fuse**) in an electrical system) to stop working suddenly because the electric current is too strong; to make sth do this (फ़्यूज़ का) उड़ना *A fuse has blown.*
**IDM blow your nose** to clear your nose by blowing strongly through it into a piece of cloth (**handkerchief**) (रुमाल से) नाक साफ़ करना
**IDM blow over** to disappear without having a serious effect शांत हो जाना, बेअसर हो जाना *The scandal will soon blow over.*
**blow up 1** to explode or to be destroyed in an explosion विस्फोट हो जाना या विस्फोट में नष्ट हो जाना *The car blew up when the door was opened.* **2** to start suddenly and strongly कुछ प्रबल रूप से होने लगना *A storm blew up in the night.* ○ *A huge row blew up about money.* **3** (*informal*) to

become very angry बहुत क्रुद्ध हो जाना *The teacher blew up when I said I'd forgotten my homework.* **blow sth up** 1 to make sth explode or to destroy sth in an explosion विस्फोट करना या विस्फोट में नष्ट करना *The terrorists tried to blow up the plane.* 2 to fill sth with air or gas (किसी वस्तु में) हवा या गैस भरना *to blow up a balloon* 3 to make a photograph bigger फ़ोटो का आकार बढ़ाना; वर्धन करना

**blow[2]** /bləʊ ब्लो / *noun* [C] 1 a hard hit from sb's hand, a weapon, etc. घूँसा, प्रहार *She aimed a blow at me.* 2 **a blow (to sb/sth)** a sudden shock or disappointment आकस्मिक आघात या निराशा, हताशा *It was a blow when I didn't get the job.* 3 an act of blowing (नाक) छिनकने या सिनकने की क्रिया *Give your nose a blow!*

IDM **a blow-by-blow account, description, etc. (of sth)** an account, etc. of an event that gives all the exact details of it सारी घटना का ब्योरेवार विवरण

**come to blows (with sb) (over sth)** to start fighting or arguing (about sth) लड़ाई या बहस शुरू कर देना

**deal sb/sth a blow; deal a blow to sb/sth** ➪ **deal[1]** देखिए।

**blow-dry** *verb* [T] (*3rd person sing. pres.* **blowdries;** *pt, pp* **blow-dried**) to dry and shape sb's hair by holding a machine that produces hot air (**a hairdryer**) in your hand, and a brush बाल सुखाने वाली मशीन (हेअर ड्रायर) से बालों को सुखाना और सजाना

**blowhole** /ˈbləʊhəʊl ˈब्लोहोल् / *noun* [C] 1 a hole in the top of the head of a large sea animal (**whale**) through which it breathes श्वासक्रिया के लिए ह्वेल मछली के सिर पर का छिद्र 2 a hole in a large area of ice through which sea animals, for example **seals**, breathe बर्फ़ की फैली सतह में छेद जिसका उपयोग, सील आदि समुद्री जीव श्वास लेने के लिए करते हैं

**blowlamp** /ˈbləʊlæmp ˈब्लोलैम्प् / (*AmE* **torch; blowtorch**) *noun* [C] a tool with a very hot flame that you can point at a surface, for example to remove paint बहुत गरम हवा फेंकने वाला लैंपनुमा उपकरण; ब्लोलैंप, धमन-दीप

**blown** ➪ **blow[1]** का past participle रूप

**blowout** /ˈbləʊaʊt ˈब्लोआउट् / *noun* [C] (*informal*) 1 a burst tyre टायर का फटना, टायर फटना *We had a blowout on the way back home.* ✪ पर्याय **puncture** 2 a very large meal at which people eat too much; a large party or social event बड़े पैमाने पर आयोजित भोज, बृहद्भोज; बड़ी पार्टी, समारोह

**blowtorch** /ˈbləʊtɔːtʃ ˈब्लोटॉच् / = **blowlamp**

**blubber** /ˈblʌbə(r) ˈब्लब(र्) / *noun* [U] the fat of large sea animals (**whales**), from which we get oil ह्वेल मछली और अन्य स्थूल समुद्री प्राणियों की चरबी

**bludgeon** /ˈblʌdʒən ˈब्लजन् / *verb* [T] 1 to hit sb several times with a heavy object किसी भारी वस्तु से बार-बार बहुत कसकर मारना *He was bludgeoned to death with a hammer.* 2 **bludgeon sb (into sth/into doing sth)** to force sb to do sth, especially by arguing किसी को कुछ करने के लिए बाध्य करना विशेषत; युक्तियाँ देकर *They tried to bludgeon me into joining their protest.*

**blue[1]** /bluː ब्लू / *adj.* 1 having the colour of a clear sky when the sun shines नीला, आसमानी *His eyes were bright blue.* ○ *light/dark blue* 2 (*informal*) (often used in songs) sad उदास (प्राय: गानों में प्रयुक्त)

IDM **black and blue** ➪ **black[1]** देखिए।

**once in a blue moon** ➪ **once** देखिए।

**blue[2]** /bluː ब्लू / *noun* 1 [C, U] the colour of a clear sky when the sun shines नीला रंग, नील *a deep blue* ○ *dressed* ***in blue*** (= blue clothes) 2 **the blues** [*pl.,with sing. or pl. verb*] a type of slow sad music एक प्रकार का मंद विषादपूर्ण संगीत *a blues singer* 3 **the blues** [*pl.*] (*informal*) a feeling of great sadness; depression अत्यधिक उदास या निराशा; विषाद, खिन्नता *to have the blues*

IDM **out of the blue** suddenly; unexpectedly एकाएक; अप्रत्याशित रूप से *I didn't hear from him for years and then this letter came out of the blue.*

**blue-collar** *adj.* doing or involving physical work with the hands rather than office work शारीरिक श्रम-संबंधी (न कि कार्यालय में किया गया काम) ➪ **white-collar** देखिए।

**blueprint** /ˈbluːprɪnt ˈब्लूप्रिन्ट् / *noun* [C] a photographic plan or a description of how to make, build or achieve sth फ़ोटोचित्र खाका या कुछ बनाने, पाने आदि की कार्य योजना

**bluff[1]** /blʌf ब्लफ़् / *verb* [I, T] to try to make people believe that sth is true when it is not, usually by appearing very confident किसी को झाँसा देना

IDM **bluff your way in, out, through, etc. sth** to trick sb in order to get into, out of a place, etc. झाँसा देकर कुछ करना (चुपके से प्रवेश कर फिर निकल जाना आदि) *We managed to bluff our way into the stadium by saying we were journalists.*

**bluff[2]** /blʌf ब्लफ़् / *noun* 1 [U, C] making sb believe that you will do sth when you really have no intention of doing it, or that you know sth when, in fact, you do not know it झूठा विश्वास

दिलाना, झांसा देना **2** [C] a steep cliff, especially by the sea or a river ऊँची खड़ी चट्टान, विशेषतः समुद्र या नदी के किनारे ➪ **flood plain** पर चित्र देखिए।

IDM **call sb's bluff** ➪ **call**[1] देखिए।

**bluish** (*also* **blueish**) /ˈbluːɪʃ ˈब्लूइश्/ *adj.* (*informal*) slightly blue हलका नीला *bluish green*

**blunder**[1] /ˈblʌndə(r) ˈब्लन्ड(र्)/ *noun* [C] a stupid mistake भद्दी या मूर्खतापूर्ण भूल *I'm afraid I've **made a** terrible **blunder**.*

**blunder**[2] /ˈblʌndə(r) ˈब्लन्ड(र्)/ *verb* [I] to make a stupid mistake भद्दी भूल करना

PHR V **blunder about, around, etc.** to move in an uncertain or careless way, as if you cannot see where you are going इधर-उधर भटकना *We blundered about in the dark, trying to find the light switch.*

**blunt** /blʌnt ब्लन्ट्/ *adj.* **1** (used about a knife, pencil, tool, etc.) without a sharp edge or point (चाकू आदि) कुंद, भोथरा ✪ विलोम **sharp** **2** (used about a person, comment, etc.) very direct; saying what you think without trying to be polite (व्यक्ति, टिप्पणी आदि) मुँहफट, स्पष्टवादी, रूक्ष *I'm sorry to be so blunt, but I'm afraid you're just not good enough.* ▶ **blunt** *verb* [T] धार कम करना; कुंद या कुंठित करना ▶ **bluntly** *adv.* रूक्षता से ▶ **bluntness** *noun* [U] भोथरापन, रूखापन

**blur**[1] /blɜː(r) ब्ल(र्)/ *noun* [C, *usually sing.*] something that you cannot see clearly or remember well धुँधली या अस्पष्ट वस्तु *Without my glasses, their faces were just a blur.*

**blur**[2] /blɜː(r) ब्ल(र्)/ *verb* [I, T] (**blurring; blurred**) to become or to make sth less clear धुँधला हो जाना या कर देना *The words on the page blurred as tears filled her eyes.* ▶ **blurred** *adj.* धुँधला व अस्पष्ट

**blurt** /blɜːt ब्लट्/ *verb*

PHR V **blurt sth out** to say sth suddenly or without thinking बिना सोचे-समझे बोल उठना *We didn't want to tell Madhu but Seema blurted the whole thing out.*

**blush** /blʌʃ ब्लश्/ *verb* [I] to become red in the face, especially because you are embarrassed or feel guilty (लज्जा या झेंप से) मुख पर लाली छा जाना *She blushed with shame.* ▶ **blush** *noun* [C, *usually sing.*] (लज्जा या झेंप से) मुख पर लाली

**blusher** /ˈblʌʃə(r) ˈब्लश(र्)/ *noun* [U, C] a coloured cream or powder that some people put on their cheeks to give them more colour गालों पर लगाई जाने वाली अरुणिमा-वर्धक क्रीम या पाउडर

**blustery** /ˈblʌstəri ˈब्लसूटरि / *adj.* (used to describe the weather) with strong winds (मौसम) तूफ़ानी *The day was cold and blustery.*

**boa** /ˈbəʊə ˈबोआ / *noun* [C] a large snake, found in America, Africa and Asia, that kills animals for food by squeezing them अमेरिका, अफ़्रीक़ा तथा एशिया में पाए जाने वाला एक प्रकार का अजगर

**boa constrictor** /ˈbəʊə kənstrɪktə(r) ˈबोआ कन्स्ट्रिक्ट(र्)/ *noun* [C] a large South American snake that is a type of boa दक्षिण अमेरिका में पाया जाने वाला एक प्रकार का अजगर

**boar** /bɔː(r) बॉ(र्)/ *noun* [C] (*pl.* **boar** or **boars**) **1** a male pig नर सूअर **2** a wild pig जंगली या बनैला सूअर ➪ **pig** पर नोट देखिए।

**board**[1] /bɔːd बॉड्/ *noun* **1** [C] a long, thin, flat piece of wood used for making floors, walls, etc. फ़र्श, दीवार आदि के निर्माण में प्रयुक्त लकड़ी का तख़्ता, पटरा *The old house needed new **floorboards**.* **2** [C] a thin flat piece of wood, etc. used for a particular purpose किसी विशेष प्रयोजन के लिए निर्मित लकड़ी का पटल *an ironing board* ○ *a surfboard* ○ *a noticeboard* **3** [C, *with sing. or pl. verb*] a group of people who control an organization, company, etc. संस्था आदि का नियंत्रक मंडल, समिति, परिषद *The **board of directors** is/are meeting to discuss the firm's future.* ○ *a board meeting* **4** [U] the meals that are provided when you stay in a hotel, etc. होटल आदि में ठहरने पर वहां मिलने वाला भोजन *The prices are for a double room and **full board*** (= all the meals).

IDM **above board** ➪ **above** देखिए।

**across the board** ➪ **across** देखिए।

**on board** on a ship or an aircraft जलपोत या विमान पर सवार *All the passengers were safely on board.*

**board**[2] /bɔːd बॉड्/ *verb* [I, T] to get on a plane, ship, bus, etc. विमान, जहाज़, बस आदि में सवार होना *We said goodbye and boarded the train.* ○ *Air India flight 2210 to Mumbai is now boarding* (= ready to take passengers) *at Gate 4.*

PHR V **board sth up** to cover with **boards**[1] **1** फट्टों या तख़्तों से ढक देना *Nobody lives there now—it's all boarded up.*

**boarder** /ˈbɔːdə(r) बॉड(र्)/ *noun* [C] (*BrE*) **1** a child who lives at school and goes home for the holidays आवासी छात्र, अंतेवासी छात्र **2** a person who pays to live at sb's house किसी के मकान में शुल्क देकर ठहरने वाला, किरायेदार ➪ **lodger** देखिए।

**boarding card** (*also* **boarding pass**) *noun* [C] a card that you must show in order to get on a plane or ship विमान या जहाज़ में प्रवेश का अनुमति-पत्र

boats and ships

**boarding house** *noun* [C] a private house where you can pay to stay and have meals for a period of time निजी आवास जहाँ शुल्क देकर कुछ समय के लिए ठहरा जा सकता है; सराय

**boarding school** *noun* [C] a school that schoolchildren live at while they are studying, going home only in the holidays आवासीय विद्यालय, छात्रावास सहित विद्यालय

**boardroom** /ˈbɔːdruːm; -rʊm ˈबॉड्रूम्; रुम्/ *noun* [C] the room where the group of people in charge of a company or organization (**the board of directors**) meets निदेशक मंडल का परामर्श कक्ष; बोर्डरूम

**boast** /bəʊst बोस्ट्/ *verb* **1** [I] to talk with too much pride about sth that you have or can do शेख़ी बघारना, डींग हाँकना *I wish she wouldn't boast about her family so much.* **2** [T] (used about a place) to have sth that it can be proud of (स्थान) गौरव या प्रतिष्ठा लाने वाली वस्तु आदि से संपन्न होना *The town boasts over a dozen restaurants.*
▶ **boast** *noun* [C] शेख़ी, डींग, आत्मप्रशंसा, गर्व

**boastful** /ˈbəʊstfl ˈबोस्ट्फ़ल्/ *adj.* (used about a person or the things that he/she says) showing too much pride (व्यक्ति) शेख़ीबाज़, आत्मश्लाघी

**boat** /bəʊt बोट्/ *noun* [C] **1** a small vehicle that is used for travelling across water नाव, किश्ती *The cave can only be reached* ***by boat/in a*** *boat.* ○ *a rowing/fishing/motor boat* **2** any ship किसी भी प्रकार का जहाज़ *When does the next boat to Lakshadweep sail?*
IDM **rock the boat** ➪ **rock²** देखिए।

**bob** /bɒb बॉब्/ *verb* (**bo<u>bb</u>ing; bo<u>bb</u>ed**) [I, T] to move quickly up and down; to make sth do this जल्दी-जल्दी ऊपर-नीचे होना, डूबना-उतराना, ऊभ-चूभ हो जाना *The boats in the harbour were bobbing up and down in the water.* ○ *She bobbed her head down below the top of the wall.*
PHR V **bob up** to appear suddenly from behind or under sth अचानक उभर आना या प्रकट होना *He disappeared and then bobbed up again on the other side of the pool.*

**bobbin** /ˈbɒbɪn ˈबॉबिन्/ *noun* [C] a small circular device which you put thread round and that is used, for example, in a sewing machine फिरकी, बोबिन

**bobsleigh** /ˈbɒbsleɪ ˈबॉब्स्ले/ (*AmE* **bobsled** /ˈbɒbsled ˈबॉब्स्लेड्/) *noun* [C] a racing vehicle for two or more people that slides over snow along a track स्लेज; बर्फ़ की पट्टी पर फिसलती-दौड़ती गाड़ी ➪ **sleigh, sledge** और **toboggan** देखिए।

**bode** /bəʊd बोड्/ *verb*
IDM **bode well/ill (for sb/sth)** to be a sign that sb/sth will have a good/bad future अच्छा या बुरा शकुन होना

**bodice** /ˈbɒdɪs ˈबॉडिस्/ the top part of a woman's dress, above the waist (महिला की) चोली, अँगिया, कुरती

**bodily¹** /ˈbɒdɪli ˈबॉडिलि/ *adj.* of the human body; physical मानव शरीर-विषयक; शारीरिक, दैहिक *First we must attend to their bodily needs* (= make sure that they have a home, have enough to eat, etc.).

**bodily²** /ˈbɒdɪli ˈबॉडिलि/ *adv.* by taking hold of the body सशरीर, शरीर-समेत *She picked up the child and carried him bodily from the room.*

**body** /ˈbɒdi ˈबॉडि/ *noun* (*pl.* **bodies**) **1** [C] the whole physical form of a person or animal मानव या जानवर की सांगोपांग देह; सकल शरीर *the human body.* **2** [C] the part of a person that is not his/her legs, arms or head मानव शरीर का मध्यस्थित शरीरांग (सिर, टाँगों और भुजाओं को छोड़कर) *She had injuries to her head and body.* **3** [C] a dead person शव, लाश *The police have found a body in the canal.* **4** [C, *with sing. or pl. verb*] a group of people who work or act together, especially in an official way व्यक्ति-समूह जो आधिकारिक स्तर पर दल के रूप में काम करता है; निकाय *The governing body of the college meets/meet once a month.* **5** [*sing.*] the main part of sth किसी वस्तु का मुख्य भाग या अंश, ढाँचा *We agree with the body of the report, although not with certain details.* **6** [C] (*formal*) an object वस्तु, द्रव्य *The doctor removed a foreign body from the child's ear.*
IDM **in a body** all together सब मिलकर

**bodybuilding** /ˈbɒdibɪldɪŋ ˈबॉडिबिल्डिङ्/ *noun* [U] making the muscles of the body stronger and larger by exercise व्यायाम द्वारा शारीरिक पुष्टि
▶ **bodybuilder** *noun* [C] व्यायाम द्वारा शरीर की मांसपेशियाँ सुदृढ़ बनाने वाला व्यक्ति

**bodyguard** /ˈbɒdigɑːd ˈबॉडिगाड्/ *noun* [C] a person or group of people whose job is to protect sb अंगरक्षक

**body language** *noun* [U] showing how you feel by the way you move, stand, sit, etc., rather than by what you say (शब्दों के स्थान पर) शरीर की विभिन्न मुद्राओं द्वारा विचार अभिव्यक्ति; देह भाषा *I could tell by his body language that he was scared.*

**body odour** *noun* [U] (*abbr.* **BO**) the unpleasant smell from a person's body, especially of sweat शरीर की दुर्गंध, विशेषतः पसीने से उत्पन्न

**bodywork** /ˈbɒdiwɜːk ˈबॉडिवक्/ *noun* [U] the main outside structure of a vehicle, usually made of painted metal वाहन का मुख्य ढाँचा जो सामान्यतया रंगी हुई धातु का होता है

**bog** /bɒg बॉग्/ *noun* [C, U] an area of ground that is very soft and wet दलदल *a peat bog*

**bogey** /ˈbəʊgi ˈबोगि/ *noun* [C] **1** something that causes fear, often without reason भय उत्पन्न करने वाली वस्तु, प्रायः बिना किसी तर्क या अर्थ के; हौआ **2** (*informal*) a piece of the sticky substance (**mucus**) that forms inside your nose नाक का मल

**bogged down** *adj.* **1** (used about a vehicle) not able to move because it has sunk into soft ground (वाहन) दलदल में फँसा **2** (used about a person) not able to make any progress कार्य के किसी चरण में फँसा हुआ और प्रगति करने में असमर्थ (व्यक्ति)

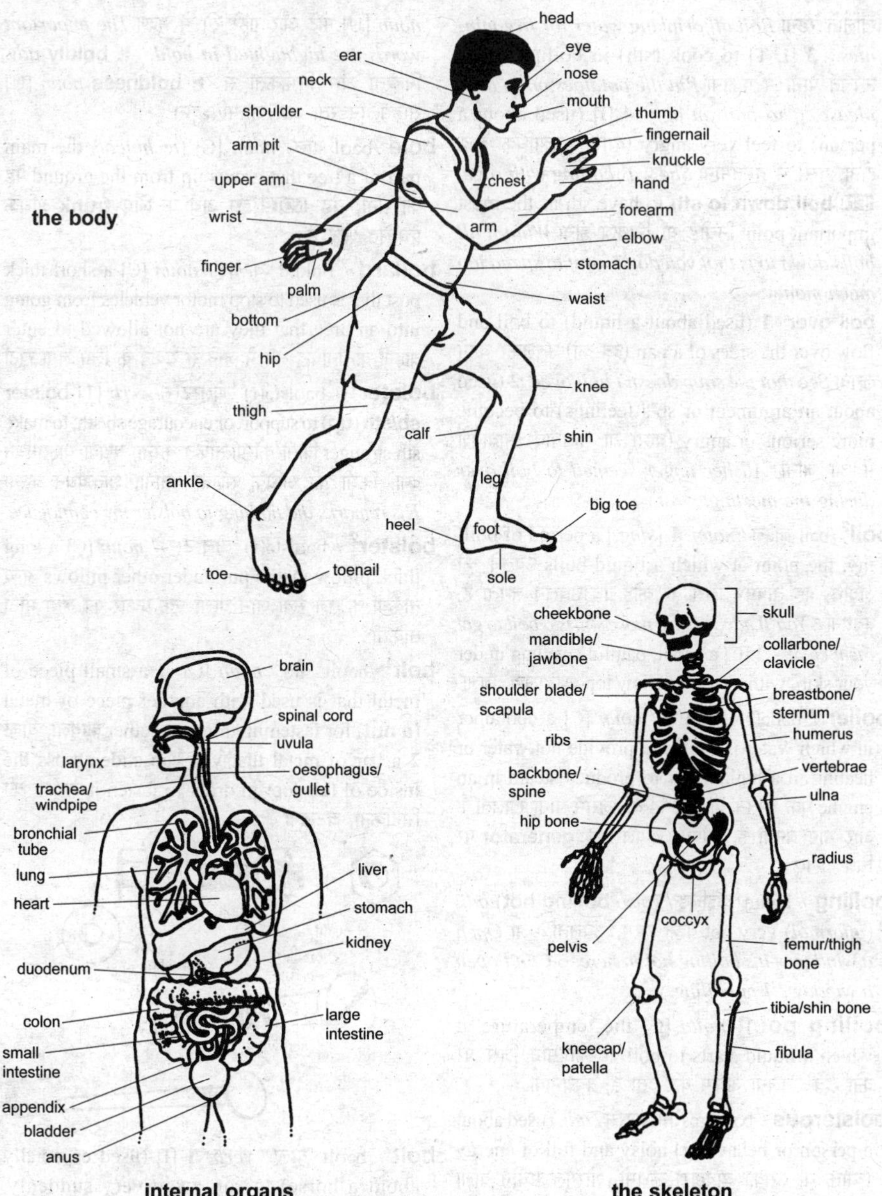


**boggle** /ˈbɒgl ˈबॉग्ल्/ *verb* [I] **boggle (at sth)** to be unable to imagine sth; to be impossible to imagine or believe स्तब्ध रह जाना, ठिठकना; विश्वास न कर पाना *'What will happen if his plan doesn't work?' 'The mind boggles!'* ⇨ **mind-boggling** भी देखिए।

**boggy** /ˈbɒgi ˈबॉगि/ *adj.* (used about land) soft and wet, so that your feet sink into it (भूमि) दलदली

**bogus** /ˈbəʊgəs ˈबोगस्/ *adj.* pretending to be real or genuine असली होने का ढोंग करते हुए; बनावटी, खोटा, जाली *a bogus policeman*

**boil[1]** /bɔɪl बॉइल्/ *verb* **1** [I] (used about a liquid) to reach a high temperature where bubbles rise to the surface and the liquid changes to a gas (द्रव का) उबलना, खौलना *Water boils at 100°C.* ○ *The kettle's boiling.* **2** [T] to heat a liquid until it boils and let it keep boiling द्रव को उबालते रहना,

खौलाते रहना *Boil all drinking water for five minutes.* **3** [I, T] to cook (sth) in boiling water उबलते पानी मे पकाना *Put the potatoes on to boil, please.* ○ *to boil an egg* **4** [I] (used about a person) to feel very angry (व्यक्ति) अत्यधिक क्रुद्ध होना, गुस्से में तमतमाना *She was boiling with rage.*
IDM **boil down to sth** to have sth as the most important point निचोड़ या निष्कर्ष होना *What it all boils down to is that you don't want to spend too much money.*
**boil over** **1** (used about a liquid) to boil and flow over the sides of a pan (द्रव का) उबलकर बहने लगना *See that the soup doesn't boil over.* **2** (used about an argument or sb's feelings) to become more serious or angry (बहस या भावनाएँ) भावावेश में आ जाना *All her anger seemed to boil over during the meeting.*

**boil²** /bɔɪl बॉइल्/ *noun* **1** [*sing.*] a period of boiling; the point at which a liquid boils उबलने की अवधि; वह तापमन जिस पर कोई द्रव उबलने लगता है; क्वथनांक *You'll have to give those shirts a boil to get them clean.* **2** [C] a small, painful swelling under your skin, with a red or yellow top व्रण, फ़ोड़ा, छाला

**boiler** /ˈbɔɪlə(r) ˈबॉइल(र्)/ *noun* [C] a container in which water is heated to provide hot water or heating in a building or to produce steam in an engine एक बरतन या बड़ा डिब्बा जिसमें पानी खौलता है और भाप बनती है, वाष्पित्र बॉयलर ➪ **generator** पर चित्र देखिए।

**boiling** /ˈbɔɪlɪŋ ˈबॉइलिङ्/ (*also* **boiling hot**) *adj.* (*informal*) very hot बहुत गरम; उबलता हुआ *Open a window—it's boiling hot in here.* ○ *Can I open a window? I'm boiling.*

**boiling point** *noun* [C] the temperature at which a liquid starts to boil वह तापमान जिस पर कोई द्रव उबलना आरंभ कर देता है; क्वथनांक

**boisterous** /ˈbɔɪstərəs ˈबॉइस्टरस्/ *adj.* (used about a person or behaviour) noisy and full of energy (व्यक्ति या उसका व्यवहार) ऊधमी, शोरगुल मचाने वाला किंतु प्रसन्नचित्त *Their children are very nice but they can get a bit too boisterous.*

**bold** /bəʊld बोल्ड्/ *adj.* **1** (used about a person or his/her behaviour) confident and not afraid (व्यक्ति या उसका व्यवहार) आत्मविश्वासी और निडर *Not many people are bold enough to say exactly what they think.* **2** that you can see clearly सुस्पष्ट, साफ़ *bold, bright colours* **3** (used about printed letters) in thick, dark type (मुद्रित अक्षर) मोटे और गहरे रंग में *Make the important text bold.* ▶ **bold** *noun* [U] मोटे और गहरे रंग में मुद्रण *The important words are highlighted* ***in bold****.* ▶ **boldly** *adv.* निडरता और निर्भीकता से ▶ **boldness** *noun* [U] साहस, निडरता और आत्मविश्वास

**bole** /bəʊl बोल्/ *noun* [C] (*technical*) the main part of a tree that grows up from the ground पेड़ का तना, धड़ NOTE इस अर्थ के लिए **trunk** अधिक प्रचलित शब्द है।

**bollard** /ˈbɒlɑːd ˈबॉलाड्/ *noun* [C] a short thick post that is used to stop motor vehicles from going into an area that they are not allowed to enter वाहनों को निषिद्ध क्षेत्र में जाने से रोकने के लिए लगा खूँटा

**bolster¹** /ˈbəʊlstə(r) ˈबोलस्ट(र्)/ *verb* [T] **bolster sb/sth (up)** to support or encourage sb/sth; to make sth stronger किसी को प्रोत्साहित करना, बढ़ावा या समर्थन देना; किसी को अधिक सशक्त बनाना; शक्तिवर्धन करना *His remarks did nothing to bolster my confidence.*

**bolster²** /ˈbəʊlstə(r) ˈबोलस्ट(र्)/ *noun* [C] a long thick pillow that is put under other pillows अन्य तकियों के तले रखा जाने वाला एक प्रकार का लंबा मोटा तकिया

**bolt¹** /bəʊlt बोल्ट्/ *noun* [C] **1** a small piece of metal that is used with another piece of metal (**a nut**) for fastening things together क़ाबला, बोल्ट **2** a bar of metal that you can slide across the inside of the door in order to fasten it दरवाज़े की सिटकिनी, चटखनी

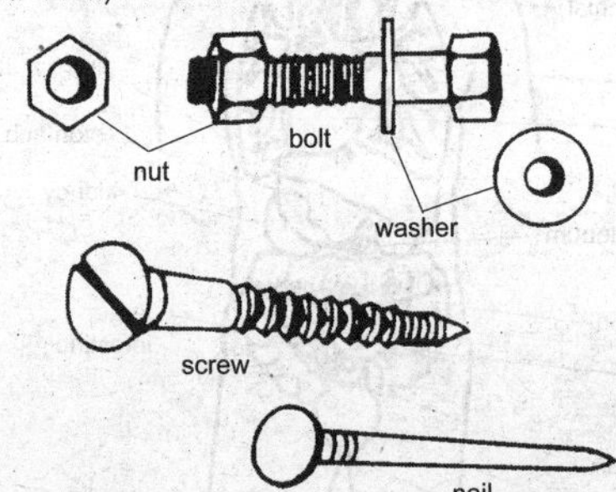


**bolt²** /bəʊlt बोल्ट्/ *verb* **1** [I] (used especially about a horse) to run away very suddenly, usually in fear (घोड़े का) अचानक डर के मारे भाग जाना, बगटुट भागना **2** [T] **bolt sth (down)** to eat sth very quickly जल्दी-जल्दी खाना; गटकना **3** [T] to fasten one thing to another using a **bolt¹ 1** एक वस्तु को दूसरी के साथ क़ाबलों से कसना या बाँधना *All the tables have been bolted to the floor so that nobody can steal them.* **4** [T] to fasten a door, etc. with a **bolt¹ 2** दरवाज़े को सिटकिनी द्वारा बंद करना; चटखनी लगाना *Make sure that the door is locked and bolted.*

**bolt**[3] /bəʊlt बोल्ट् / *adv.*

IDM **bolt upright** sitting or standing very straight एकदम सीधे बैठना या खड़े होना

**bomb**[1] /bɒm बॉम् / *noun* **1** [C] a container that is filled with material that will explode when it is thrown or dropped, or when a device inside it makes it explode बम, गोला, विस्फोटक पदार्थ से भरा पात्र *Fortunately, the car bomb failed to **go off**.* **2 the bomb** [*sing.*] nuclear weapons परमाणु बम, आणविक अस्त्र *How many countries have the bomb now?* **3 a bomb** [*sing.*] (*BrE informal*) a lot of money बहुत बड़ी राशि *That car must have cost you a bomb!*

**bomb**[2] /bɒm बॉम् / *verb* **1** [T] to attack a city, etc. with bombs (किसी शहर पर) बम गिराकर हमला करना *Enemy forces have bombed the bridge.* **2** (*informal*) **bomb along, down, up, etc.** to move along very fast in the direction mentioned, especially in a vehicle वाहन का दिशा-विशेष में बहुत तेज़ गति से जाना *He was bombing along at 100 kilometers an hour when the police stopped him.*

**bombard** /bɒmˈbɑːd बॉम्ˈबाड् / *verb* [T] to attack a place with bombs or guns (किसी स्थान पर) बमवर्षा करना, गोलाबारी करना *They bombarded the city until the enemy surrendered.* ○ (*figurative*) *The reporters bombarded the minister with questions.* ▸ **bombardment** *noun* [C, U] (किसी स्थान पर) गोलाबारी *The main radio station has **come under** enemy **bombardment**.*

**bomb disposal** *noun* [U] the job of dealing with bombs that have been found and have not yet exploded in order to make an area safe किसी क्षेत्र को सुरक्षित बनाए रखने के लिए वहाँ पाए गए बम को निष्क्रिय करना *a bomb disposal squad*

**bomber** /ˈbɒmə(r) ˈबॉम(र्) / *noun* [C] **1** a type of plane that drops bombs बमवर्षक विमान **2** a person who makes a bomb explode in a public place सार्वजनिक स्थल पर बम-विस्फ़ोट करने वाला व्यक्ति

**bombshell** /ˈbɒmʃel ˈबॉम्शेल् / *noun* [C, *usually sing.*] an unexpected and usually shocking event or a piece of news अप्रत्याशित और सामान्यतः मानसिक आघात पहुँचाने वाली घटना या समाचार *The chairman **dropped a bombshell** when he said he was resigning.*

**bona fide** /ˌbəʊnə ˈfaɪdi ˌबोना ˈफ़ाइडि / *adj.* real or genuine वास्तविक, प्रामाणिक, असली, सच्चा *This car park is for the use of bona fide customers only.*

**bond** /bɒnd बॉन्ड्/ *noun* [C] **1** something that joins two or more people or groups of people together, such as a feeling of friendship दो व्यक्तियों या जनसमूहों को बाँधने या जोड़ने वाली शक्ति, भावना आदि (जैसे मैत्री या बंधुत्व); बंधन, संबंध **2** a certificate that you can buy from a government or company that promises to pay you interest on the money you have given ऋणपत्र, बांड **2** (*technical*) (in chemistry) the way in which **atoms** are held together in a chemical compound (रसायन शास्त्र में) किसी रासायनिक मिश्रण में अणुओं के संयोजित होने की विधि; बंध

**bone**[1] /bəʊn बोन् / *noun* **1** [C] one of the hard parts inside the body of a person or animal that are covered with muscle, skin, etc. हड्डी, अस्थि *He's broken a bone in his hand.* ○ *This fish has got a lot of bones in it.* ➪ **body** पर चित्र देखिए। **2** [U] the substance that bones are made of द्रव्य जिससे हड्डी बनती है

IDM **have a bone to pick with sb** to be angry with sb about sth and want to talk about it with them किसी से किसी विषय पर नाराज़ होना और उसपर बातचीत करने की इच्छा करना

**make no bones about (doing) sth** to do sth in an open honest way without feeling nervous or worried about it बिना हिचकिचाहट के निष्कपट रूप से कोई कार्य करना *She made no bones about telling him exactly what she thought about him.*

**bone**[2] /bəʊn बोन् / *verb* [T] to take the bones out of sth हड्डियाँ निकालना *to bone a fish*

**bone-dry** *adj.* completely dry एकदम सूखा

**bone marrow** (*also* **marrow**) *noun* [U] the soft substance that is inside the bones of a person or animal मज्जा, अस्थि मज्जा

**bonemeal** /ˈbəʊnmiːl ˈबोन्मील् / *noun* [U] a substance made from animal bones which is used to make soil better for growing plants जानवरों की हड्डी से बना उर्वरक; अस्थिचूर्ण

**bonfire** /ˈbɒnfaɪə(r) ˈबॉन्फ़ाइअ(र) / *noun* [C] a large fire that you build outside to burn rubbish or as part of a festival, etc. कूड़े-करकट के ढेर को जलाने के लिए या किसी उत्सव में खुले में लगाई गई आग

**bonkers** /ˈbɒŋkəz ˈबॉङ्कज़् / *adj.* (*slang*) crazy; mad झक्की; विक्षिप्त *I'd **go bonkers** if I worked here full-time.*

**bonnet** /ˈbɒnɪt ˈबानिट् / *noun* [C] **1** (*AmE* **hood**) the front part of a car that covers the engine कार के इंजन को ढकने वाला ढक्कन; बोनेट **2** a type of hat which covers the sides of the face and is fastened with strings under the chin चेहरे के पार्श्वों को ढकने वाला छोटा गोल टोप जिसे ठुड्डी से बाँधा जाता है

**bonus** /ˈbəʊnəs ˈबोनस्/ *noun* [C] (*pl.* **bonuses**) **1** a payment that is added to what is usual अधिलाभांश, (नियमित के) अतिरिक्त राशि; बोनस *All our employees receive an annual bonus.* **2** something good that you get in addition to what you expect अतिरिक्त उपलब्धि या लाभ *I enjoy my job, and having my own office is* ***an added bonus****.*

**bony** /ˈbəʊni ˈबोनि/ *adj.* so thin that you can see the shape of the bones इतना दुबला-पतला कि हड्डियों की सरंचना दिखाई पड़े *long bony fingers*

**boo** /bu: बू/ *exclamation, noun* [C] (*pl.* **boos**) **1** a sound you make to show that you do not like sb/sth किसी वस्तु या वस्तु के प्रति अरुचि दर्शाने के लिए निकाली गई व्यंजक ध्वनि *The minister's speech was met with boos from the audience.* **2** a sound you make to frighten or surprise sb किसी को भयभीत या चकित करने के लिए प्रयुक्त ध्वनि *He jumped out from behind the door and said 'boo'.* ▶ **boo** *verb* [I, T] इस तरह की ध्वनि निकालना

**booby trap** /ˈbu:bi træp ˈबूबि ट्रैप्/ *noun* [C] a device that will kill, injure or surprise sb when he/she touches the object that it is connected to किसी वस्तु में छुपाया गया यंत्र जो वस्तु को छूने वाले व्यक्ति को मार, घायल या चौंका देता है ▶ **booby-trap** *verb* [T] (*pres. part.* **booby-trapping;** *pt, pp* **booby-trapped**) इस तरह से छल करना

**book¹** /bʊk बुक्/ *noun* **1** [C] a written work that is published as printed pages fastened together inside a cover, or in electronic form पुस्तक, किताब, ग्रंथ *I'm reading a book on astrology.* ○ *hardback/paperback books* **2** [C] a number of pieces of paper, fastened together inside a cover, for people to write or draw on लिखने या चित्र बनाने के लिए पुस्तिका; कापी, नोटबुक *Please write down all the new vocabulary in your exercise books.* ○ *a notebook* ○ *a sketch book* **3** [C] a number of things fastened together in the form of a book किताब की शकल में बँधे पन्ने *a book of stamps* ○ *a cheque book* **4 books** [*pl.*] the records that a company, etc., keeps of the amount of money it spends and receives किसी संस्था आदि के धन या लेन-देन का रिकार्ड, बही *We employ an accountant to* ***keep the books****.*

IDM **be in sb's good/bad books** (*informal*) to have sb pleased/angry with you किसी की कृपा या रोष का पात्र होना *He's been in his boss's bad books since he failed to complete the project on time.*

**by the book** exactly according to the rules कठोरता से नियमानुसार *A policeman must always do things by the book.*

(**be**) **on sb's books** (to be) on the list of an organization किसी संगठन की सूची में नाम शामिल होना *The employment agency has hundreds of qualified secretaries on its books.*

**book²** /bʊk बुक्/ *verb* **1** [I, T] to arrange to have or do sth at a particular time किसी विशिष्ट समय के लिए आरक्षण आदि की व्यवस्था करना *Have you booked a table, sir?* ○ *to book a seat on a plane/train/bus* **2** [T] (*informal*) to officially write down the name of a person who has done sth wrong अपराध के लिए नाम दर्ज करना *The player was booked for a foul and then sent off for arguing.*

PHR V **book in** to say that you have arrived at a hotel, etc., and sign your name on a list होटल आदि में पहुँचना और ठहरने वालों की सूची में नाम दर्ज करना

**book sb in** to arrange a room for sb at a hotel, etc. in advance अग्रिम तौर पर होटल में कमरे की व्यवस्था आदि करना, अग्रिम व्यवस्था करना *I've booked you in at the Taj.*

**bookcase** /ˈbʊkkeɪs ˈबुक्केस्/ *noun* [C] a piece of furniture with shelves to keep books on पुस्तकें रखने की टाँड़ों वाली अलमारी

**bookie** /ˈbʊki ˈबुकि/ (*informal*) = **bookmaker**

**booking** /ˈbʊkɪŋ ˈबुकिङ्/ *noun* [C, U] the arrangement you make in advance to have a hotel room, a seat on a plane, etc. होटल में कमरे, विमान में सीट आदि का अग्रिम आरक्षण *Did you manage to* ***make a booking****?* ○ *No advance booking is necessary.*

**booking office** *noun* [C] an office where you buy tickets टिकट घर

**bookkeeper** /ˈbʊkki:pə(r) ˈबुक्कीप(र्)/ *noun* [C] a person whose job is to keep an accurate record of the accounts of a business व्यापार में बहीखाता रखने वाला व्यक्ति; लेखाकार, मुनीम ▶ **bookkeeping** *noun* [U] बहीखाता रखने का कार्य; बहीखाता पद्धति

**booklet** /ˈbʊklət ˈबुक्लट्/ *noun* [C] a small thin book, usually with a soft cover, that gives information about sth किसी विषय पर जानकारी देने वाली पुस्तिका

**bookmaker** /ˈbʊkmeɪkə(r) ˈबुक्मेक(र्)/ (*also informal* **bookie**) *noun* **1** [C] a person whose job is to take bets on horse races, etc. घुड़दौड़ में लगे दाँवों का हिसाब रखने वाल व्यक्ति **2 bookmaker's** [*sing.*] a shop, etc. where you can bet money on a race or an event दुकान जहाँ घुड़दौड़ आदि पर दाँव लगाया जा सकता है

**bookmark** /ˈbʊkmɑ:k ˈबुक्माक्/ *noun* [C] **1** a narrow piece of card, etc. that you put between the pages of a book so that you can find the same place again easily किताब के पन्नों के बीच रखा

जाने वाला गत्ते आदि का पतला टुकड़ा जो इस बात का संकेत देता है कि पिछली बार किताब को कहाँ पढ़ना छोड़ा था; बुकमार्क **2** a file from the Internet that you have stored on your computer इंटरनेट से प्राप्त फ़ाइल जो कंप्यूटर में संचित की गई हो; बुकमार्क

**bookseller** /ˈbʊkselə(r) ˈबुकसेल(र्)/ *noun* [C] a person whose job is selling books पुस्तक-विक्रेता

**bookshop** /ˈbʊkʃɒp ˈबुकशॉप्/ (*AmE* **bookstore** /ˈbʊkstɔ:(r) ˈबुकस्टॉ(र्)/) *noun* [C] a shop that sells books पुस्तकों की दुकान ➪ **library** देखिए।

**bookstall** /ˈbʊkstɔ:l ˈबुकस्टॉल्/ (*AmE* **newsstand**) *noun* [C] a type of small shop, which is open at the front, selling newspapers, magazines and books, for example on a station स्टेशन आदि पर पुस्तकें, पत्रिकाएँ आदि बेचने वाली छोटी दुकान; बुकस्टाल

**bookworm** /ˈbʊkwɜ:m ˈबुकवम्/ *noun* [C] a person who likes reading books very much पढ़ने में बहुत रुचि रखने वाला व्यक्ति; किताबी कीड़ा

**boom[1]** /bu:m बूम्/ *noun* [C] **1** a period in which sth increases or develops very quickly समृद्धि और विकास की अवधि, गरम बाज़ारी या तेज़ी *There was a boom in car sales in the 1990s.* **2** [*usually sing.*] a loud deep sound गरज, धड़ाके की ध्वनि *the boom of distant guns* **3** a long pole to which the sail of a boat is fixed. You move the boom to change the position of the sail नाव की पाल को थामने वाला लंबा डंडा ➪ **boat** पर चित्र देखिए।

**boom[2]** /bu:m बूम्/ *verb* **1** [I, T] **boom (sth) (out)** to make a loud deep sound दनदनाना, गरजना *The loudspeaker boomed out instructions to the crowd.* **2** [I] to grow very quickly in size or value आकार या मूल्य में तेज़ी से वृद्धि होना *Business is booming in the IT industry.*

**boomerang** /ˈbu:məræŋ ˈबूमरैङ्/ *noun* [C] a curved piece of wood that returns to you when you throw it in a particular way एक प्रकार का टेढ़ा काष्ठखंड जो विशेष प्रकार से फेंकने पर फेंकने वाले के पास वापस आ जाता है

**boon** /bu:n बून्/ *noun* [C] a thing that is very helpful and that you are grateful for लाभ, वरदान

**boorish** /ˈbʊərɪʃ; ˈbɔ:r- ˈबुअरिश्; ˈबॉरि-/ *adj.* (used about people and their behaviour) very unpleasant and rude (व्यक्ति या उसका व्यवहार) असभ्य और अशिष्ट

**boost[1]** /bu:st बूस्ट्/ *verb* [T] to increase sth in number, value or strength संख्या, मूल्य या शक्ति में वृद्धि करना *If we lower the price, that should boost sales.* ○ *The good exam result boosted her confidence.*

**boost[2]** /bu:st बूस्ट्/ *noun* [C] something that encourages people; an increase प्रोत्साहन, बढ़ावा; वृद्धि *The fall in the value of the pound has led to a boost in exports.* ○ *The president's visit gave a boost to the soldiers' morale.*

**boot[1]** /bu:t बूट्/ *noun* [C] **1** a type of shoe that covers your foot completely and sometimes part of your leg टाँग तक ढकने वाला जूता, ऊँचा जूता, बूट *ski boots* ○ *walking/climbing boots* ○ *football boots* **2** (*AmE* **trunk**) the part of a car where you put luggage, usually at the back कार में सामान रखने का स्थान, प्रायः पीछे की तरफ़; डिक्की

**boot[2]** /bu:t बूट्/ *verb* (*informal*) **1** [T] to kick sth/sb hard ज़ोर से ठोकर मारना *He booted the ball over the fence.* **2** [I, T] to make a computer ready for use when it is first switched on कंप्यूटर को उपयोग के लिए तैयार करना

PHR V **boot sb/sth out** to force sb/sth to leave a place किसी को स्थान छोड़ने के लिए बाध्य करना

**booth** /bu:ð बूद्/ *noun* [C] a small enclosed place where one person can do sth privately, such as make a telephone call or vote टेलीफ़ोन करने, वोट डालने आदि जैसे विशेष प्रयोजनों के लिए बना छोटा-सा घिरा हुआ स्थान; प्रकोष्ठ, बूथ *a phone booth*

**booth capturing** *noun* [U] (*IndE*) the illegal action of gaining control of a **polling booth** in order to produce a result to a particular **candidate's** advantage ग़ैर-क़ानूनी तरीक़े से मतदान केंद्र पर कब्ज़ा करना ताकि परिणाम किसी विशेष उम्मीदवार के पक्ष में हो *Many instances of booth capturing have been reported during the recent elections.*

**booty** /ˈbu:ti ˈबूटि/ *noun* [U] things that are taken by thieves or captured by soldiers in a war लूट का माल, लूट

**booze[1]** /bu:z बूज़्/ *noun* [U] (*informal*) alcohol शराब, मादक द्रव

**booze[2]** /bu:z बूज़्/ *verb* [I] (*informal*) to drink a lot of alcohol अत्यधिक शराब पीना

**border[1]** /ˈbɔ:də(r) ˈबॉड(र्)/ *noun* [C] **1** a line that divides two countries, etc.; the land close to this line दो देशों की विभाजक सीमा; सीमांत प्रदेश *The refugees escaped **across/over the border**.*

NOTE दो देशों या राज्यों की विभाजक सीमा के संदर्भ में **border** और **frontier** दोनों शब्दों का प्रयोग किया जाता है। प्राकृतिक विभाजन के लिए सामान्यतः **border** शब्द का प्रयोग किया जाता है—*The river forms the border between the two countries.* छोटे क्षेत्रों के विभाजन के संदर्भ में **boundary** का प्रयोग किया जाता है—*the village boundary*

2 a band or narrow line around the edge of sth, often for decoration सजावटी किनारी *a white tablecloth with a blue border*

**border²** /ˈbɔːdə(r) ˈबॉड(र्)/ *verb* [T] to form a border to an area; to be on the border of an area किसी क्षेत्र की सीमाबंदी करना; किसी क्षेत्र के सीमांत पर होना *The road was bordered with trees.*

PHR V **border on sth** 1 to be almost the same as sth के लगभग होना; के समान होना *The dictator's ideas bordered on madness.* 2 to be next to sth के समीप होना *Our garden borders on the railway line.*

**borderline** /ˈbɔːdəlaɪn ˈबॉडलाइन्/ *noun* [*sing.*] the line that marks a division between two different cases, conditions, etc. दो भिन्न मामलों, परिस्थितियों आदि के बीच की सीमारेखा *He's **a borderline case**—he may pass the exam or he may fail.*

**bore¹** /bɔː(r) ˈबॉ(र्)/ *verb* 1 [T] to make sb feel bored, especially by talking too much किसी को ऊबा देना विशेषतः बहुत अधिक बोलकर *I hope I'm not boring you.* 2 [I, T] to make a long deep hole with a tool किसी औज़ार से लंबा गहरा छेद करना *This drill can bore (a hole) through solid rock.* 3 **bear²** का past tense रूप

**bore²** /bɔː(r) बॉ(र्)/ *noun* 1 [C] a person who talks a lot in a way that is not interesting बहुत अधिक और अरुचिकर बातें करने वाला व्यक्ति; कानखाऊ (व्यक्ति) 2 [*sing.*] (*informal*) something that you have to do that you do not find interesting अरुचिकर काम, उबाऊ काम *It's such a bore having to learn these lists of irregular verbs.*

**bored** /bɔːd बॉड्/ *adj.* **bored (with sth)** feeling tired and perhaps slightly annoyed because sth is not interesting or because you do not have anything to do ऊबा हुआ *The children **get bored** on long journeys.* ○ *He gave a bored yawn.* ○ *The play was awful—we were **bored stiff*** (= extremely bored).

**boredom** /ˈbɔːdəm ˈबॉडम्/ *noun* [U] the state of being bored ऊब, बोरियत, अरुचि, नीरसता

**boring** /ˈbɔːrɪŋ ˈबॉरिङ्/ *adj.* not at all interesting; dull उबाऊ, अरुचिकर, नीरस, शुष्क *a boring film/job/speech/man* ➪ **bored** देखिए।

**born¹** /bɔːn बॉन्/ *verb* **be born** to come into the world by birth; to start existing जन्म लेना, पैदा होना; अस्तित्व का आरंभ होना *I was born in Lucknow but I grew up in Varanasi.* ○ *The idea of free education for all was born in the nineteenth century.* ○ *His unhappiness was **born out of** a feeling of frustration.*

**born²** /bɔːn बॉन्/ *adj.* 1 (*only before a noun*) having a natural ability to do sth जन्मजात, प्राकृतिक गुण संपन्न *She's a born leader.* 2 **-born** (*used to from compound adjectives*) born in the place or state mentioned निर्दिष्ट स्थान पर या अवस्था में जन्मा *This India-born athlete now represents the US.*

**born-again** *adj.* (*only before a noun*) having found new, strong religious belief धार्मिक विश्वास की दृष्टि से पुनर्जात, द्विजात *a born-again Christian*

**borne** ➪ **bear²** का past participle रूप

**-borne** /bɔːn बॉन्/ *adj.* (*used to from compound adjectives*) carried by the thing mentioned -आनीत, -जात, से वाहित *water-borne diseases*

**boron** /ˈbɔːrɒn ˈबॉरॉन्/ *noun* [U] (*symbol* **B**) a brown or black substance that is used for making steel harder भूरा या काला पदार्थ जो इस्पात को अधिक कठोर बनाने के काम आता है; बोरॉन

**borough** /ˈbʌrə ˈबरा/ *noun* [C] a town, or an area inside a large town, that has some form of local government स्थानीय सरकार वाला लघु नगर या उपनगर

**borrow** /ˈbɒrəʊ ˈबॉरो/ *verb* [I, T] **borrow (sth) (from/off sb/sth)** 1 to take or receive sth from sb/sth that you intend to give back, usually after a short time उधार, कर्ज़ या ऋण लेना *I had to borrow from the bank to pay for my car.* NOTE **Borrow** और **lend** में अंतर पहचानिए। ये विलोम शब्द हैं। 2 to take words, ideas, etc. from another person and use them as your own; to copy sth किसी दूसरे के शब्दों, विचारों को अपना बना लेना; की नक़ल करना *That idea is borrowed from another book.*

**borrower** /ˈbɒrəʊə(r) ˈबॉरोअ(र्)/ *noun* [C] a person who borrows sth ऋणी, कर्ज़दार

**bosom** /ˈbʊzəm ˈबुज़म्/ *noun* 1 [*sing.*] (*formal*) a person's chest, especially a woman's breasts छाती, विशेषतः स्त्रियों का वक्षस्थल *She clutched the child to her bosom.* 2 [C] a woman's breast स्त्री का वक्षस्थल

IDM **in the bosom of sth** close to; with the protection of के निकट; की सुरक्षा में *He was glad to be back in the bosom of his family.*

**bosom friend** *noun* [C] a very close friend घनिष्ठ या अंतरंग मित्र, जिगरी दोस्त

**boss¹** /bɒs बॉस्/ *noun* [C] (*informal*) a person whose job is to give orders to others at work; an employer; a manager कर्मचारियों को आदेश देने वाला अधिकारी; मालिक; प्रबंधक *I'm going to ask the boss for a day off work.* ○ *OK. You're the boss* (= you make the decision).

**boss**[2] /bɒs बॉस्/ *verb* [T] **boss sb (about/around)** to give orders to sb, especially in an annoying way किसी पर हुक्म चलाना, रोब या धौंस जमाना *I wish you'd stop bossing me around.*

**bossy** /ˈbɒsi ˈबॉसि/ *adj.* liking to give orders to other people, often in an annoying way किसी पर धौंस जमाना पसंद होना *Don't be so bossy!* ▶ **bossily** *adv.* धौंस या रोब जमाते हुए ▶ **bossiness** *noun* [U] रोब, धौंस

**botanist** /ˈbɒtənɪst ˈबॉटनिस्ट्/ *noun* [C] a person who studies plants वनस्पतिशास्त्री

**botany** /ˈbɒtəni ˈबॉटनि/ *noun* [U] the scientific study of plants वनस्पति-शास्त्र ➪ **biology** और **zoology** देखिए। ▶ **botanical** /bəˈtænɪkl बˈटैनिक्ल्/ *adj.* वनस्पति-शास्त्र संबंधित *botanical gardens* (= a type of park where plants are grown for scientific study)

**botch** /bɒtʃ बॉच्/ *verb* [T] (*informal*) **botch sth (up)** to do sth badly; to make a mess of sth काम बिगाड़ देना; लापरवाही से काम करना *I've completely botched up this typing, I'm afraid.*

**both** /bəʊθ बोथ्/ *det., pronoun, adv.* **1** the two; the one as well as the other दोनों; एक के साथ दूसरा भी *I liked them both.* ○ *We were both very tired.* ○ *Both of us were tired.* NOTE 'The both women' या 'my both sisters' अशुद्ध प्रयोग हैं। **2 both... and...** केवल (यह) नहीं बल्कि (वह) भी—*Both he and his wife are vegetarian.*

**bother**[1] /ˈbɒðə(r) ˈबॉद्र(र्)/ *verb* **1** [T] to disturb, annoy or worry sb परेशान, तंग या चिंतित करना *I'm sorry to bother you, but could I speak to you for a moment?* ○ *Don't bother Geeta with that now—she's busy.* ✪ पर्याय **trouble** **2** [I] **bother (to do sth/doing sth); bother (about/with sth)** (*usually negative*) to make the effort to do sth; to spend time and/or energy doing something कुछ करने का प्रयास या कष्ट करना; किसी कार्य में समय और/या शक्ति लगाना *He didn't even bother to say thank you.* ○ *Don't bother waiting for me—I'll catch you up later.*

IDM **can't be bothered (to do sth)** used to say that you do not want to spend time or energy doing sth किसी काम में समय या शक्ति लगाने को तैयार न होना; कष्ट उठाने को तैयार न होना *I can't be bothered to do my homework now. I'll do it tomorrow.*

**not be bothered (about sth)** (*informal*) to think that sth is not important किसी कार्य को महत्त्वपूर्ण न समझना *'What would you like to do this evening?' 'I'm not bothered really.'*

**bother**[2] /ˈbɒðə(r) ˈबॉद्र(र्)/ *noun* [U] trouble or difficulty परेशानी, दुविधा, कष्ट *Thanks for all your help. It's saved me a lot of bother.*

**bothered** /ˈbɒðəd ˈबॉद्रड्/ *adj.* worried about sth परेशान, चिंतित *Sameer doesn't seem too bothered about losing his job.*

**bottle**[1] /ˈbɒtl ˈबॉट्ल्/ *noun* [C] **1** a glass or plastic container with a narrow neck for keeping liquids in (काँच या प्लास्टिक की) बोतल, शीशी *a perfume bottle* ○ *an empty bottle* **2** the amount of liquid that a bottle can hold बोतल में समा सकने वाले द्रव की मात्रा, बोतलभर द्रव *a bottle of cold drink*

**bottle**[2] /ˈbɒtl ˈबॉट्ल्/ *verb* [T] to put sth into bottles बोतल में कुछ भरना, बोतलबंद करना *After three or four months the wine is bottled.* ○ *bottled water* (= that you can buy in bottles)

PHR V **bottle sth up** to not allow yourself to express strong emotions भावनाओं को दबाए रखना *You'll make yourself ill if you keep your feelings bottled up.*

**bottle gourd** *noun* [C] a vegetable with a smooth light green skin and white flesh. It is also used, after drying, in the making of Indian musical instruments समतल हलके हरे छिलके और सफ़ेद गूदे वाली कद्दू वर्गीय सब्ज़ी। सामान्यतः इसे सुखाने के बाद, भारतीय संगीत वाद्य बनाने में भी प्रयुक्त किया जाता है

**bottleneck** /ˈbɒtlnek ˈबॉट्लनेक्/ *noun* [C] **1** a narrow piece of road that causes traffic to slow down or stop सड़क का वह तंग या संकरा भाग जिसके कारण यातायात मंद पड़ जाता है या रुक जाता है **2** something that slows down progress, especially in business or industry प्रगति को मंद करने वाले तत्व विशेषतः उद्योग या व्यापार में

**bottom**[1] /ˈbɒtəm ˈबॉटम्/ *noun* **1** [C, *usually sing.*] the lowest part of sth सबसे नीचे का हिस्सा, तल *The house is **at the bottom** of a hill.* ○ *The sea is so clear that you can see the bottom.* **2** [C] the flat surface on the outside of an object, on which it stands किसी वस्तु का आधार, तली *There's a label **on the bottom** of the box.* **3** [*sing.*] the far end of sth किसी वस्तु का अंतिम या दूरस्थ भाग *The bus stop is at **the bottom** of the road.* **4** [*sing.*] the lowest position in relation to other people, teams, etc. अन्यों की तुलना में सबसे निचला स्थान *She started **at the bottom** and now she's the Managing Director.* **5** [C] the part of your body that you sit on नितंब *He fell over and landed on his bottom.* ➪ **body** पर चित्र देखिए। **6 bottoms** [*pl.*] the lower part of a piece of clothing that is in two parts दो हिस्सों वाली पोशाक का निचला हिस्सा *track suit bottoms*

**IDM be at the bottom of sth** to be the cause of sth किसी बात का कारण होना
**from the (bottom of your) heart** ➪ **heart** देखिए।
**get to the bottom of sth** to find out the real cause of sth किसी बात के मूल कारण का पता लगना

**bottom**[2] /ˈbɒtəm ˈबॉटम्/ *adj.* (*only before a noun*) in the lowest position सबसे निचला *the bottom shelf* ○ *I live on the bottom floor.*

**bottomless** /ˈbɒtəmləs ˈबॉटम्लस्/ *adj.* very deep; without limit बहुत गहरा; अथाह *bottomless ocean*

**bottom line** *noun* [*sing.*] **1 the bottom line** the most important thing to consider when you are discussing or deciding sth, etc. चर्चा करते या निर्णय लेते समय विचारार्थ सबसे महत्त्वपूर्ण बात *A musical instrument should look and feel good, but the bottom line is how it sounds.* **2** the final profit or loss that a company has made in a particular period of time एक निश्चित अवधि में किसी कंपनी के लाभ या हानि की अंतिम स्थिति **3** the lowest price that sb will accept for sth किसी (कार्य या वस्तु) के लिए न्यूनतम मूल्य या भाव स्वीकार करना

**botulism** /ˈbɒtjulɪzəm ˈबॉट्युलिज़म्/ *noun* [U] a serious illness caused by **bacteria** in food that is old and has gone bad बाटुलस जीवाणु-युक्त सड़े भोजन के सेवन से उत्पन्न एक गंभीर रोग; बाटुलिज़म

**bough** /baʊ बाउ/ *noun* [C] one of the main branches of a tree शाखा, डाल

**bought** ➪ **buy**[1] का past tense और past participle रूप

**boulder** /ˈbəʊldə(r) ˈबोल्ड(र्)/ *noun* [C] a very large rock बड़ा शिलाखंड

**bounce** /baʊns बाउन्स्/ *verb* **1** [I, T] (used about a ball, etc.) to move away quickly after it has hit a hard surface; to make a ball do this (गेंद का) कठोर सतह से टकराकर उछलना; गेंद को इस प्रकार उछालना *A small boy came down the street, bouncing a ball.* **2** [I] to jump up and down continuously लगातार ऊपर-नीचे उछलना या कूदना *The children were bouncing on their beds.* **3** [I, T] (used about a cheque) to be returned by a bank without payment because there is not enough money in the account खाते में पर्याप्त राशी शेष न होने के कारण बैंक का चेक को बिना भुगतान के लौटाना ▶ **bounce** *noun* [C, U]
**PHRV bounce back** to become healthy, successful or happy again after an illness, a failure or a disappointment बीमारी, असफलता या निराशा के बाद पुनः स्वस्थ, सफल या प्रसन्न होना

**bouncy** /ˈbaʊnsi ˈबाउन्सि/ *adj.* **1** that bounces well or that can make things bounce उछलने वाला या उछालभरा *a bouncy ball/surface* **2** (used about a person) full of energy; lively (व्यक्ति) सजीव, ज़िंदादिल, प्रसन्नचित्त और उत्साही *She's a very bouncy person.*

**bound**[1] /baʊnd बाउन्ड्/ *adj.* (*not before a noun*) **1 bound to do sth** certain to do sth निश्चित रूप से होना या करना *You've done so much work that you're bound to pass the exam.* **2** having a legal or moral duty to do sth कुछ करने के लिए क़ानूनन या नैतिक रूप से बाध्य होना *The company is bound by employment laws.* ○ *She felt bound to refuse the offer.* **3 bound (for)** travelling to a particular place किसी स्थान की ओर यात्रा करना *a ship bound for Australia*
**IDM bound up with sth** very closely connected with sth बहुत निकटता से संबद्ध

**bound**[2] /baʊnd बाउन्ड्/ *verb* [I] to run quickly with long steps लंबे डग भरते हुए तेज़ दौड़ना *She bounded out of the house to meet us.* ▶ **bound** *noun* [C] लंबा डग *With a couple of bounds he had crossed the room.*

**bound**[3] ➪ **bind**[1] का past tense और past participle रूप

**boundary** /ˈbaʊndri ˈबाउन्ड्रि/ *noun* [C] (*pl.* **boundaries**) a real or imagined line that marks the limits of sth and divides it from other places or things (वास्तविक या काल्पनिक) विभाजक रेखा, सीमा रेखा *The main road is the boundary between the two districts.* ○ *Scientists continue to push back the boundaries of human knowledge.* ➪ **border** पर नोट देखिए।

**boundless** /ˈbaʊndləs ˈबाउन्ड्लस्/ *adj.* having no limit असीम, अंतहीन *boundless energy*

**bounds** /baʊndz बाउन्ड्ज़्/ *noun* [*pl.*] limits that cannot or should not be passed सीमाएँ *Price rises must be kept within reasonable bounds.*
**IDM out of bounds** not to be entered by sb (क्षेत्र) जहाँ प्रवेश निषिद्ध हो *This area is out of bounds to all staff.*

**bouquet** /buˈkeɪ बुˈके/ *noun* [C] a bunch of flowers that is arranged in an attractive way गुलदस्ता, पुष्पगुच्छ

**the bourgeoisie** /ˌbʊəʒwɑːˈziː ˌबुअश्वाˈज़ी/ *noun* (*sing., with sing. or pl. verb*) a class of people in society who are interested mainly in having more money and a higher social position वह वर्ग जिसके सदस्य मुख्यतः धन और उच्चतर सामाजिक स्थिति के आकांक्षी होते हैं; बुर्जुआ समाज, मध्यवर्गीय समाज ▶ **bourgeois** /ˈbʊəʒwɑː ˈबुअश्वा/ *adj.* बुर्जुआ, मध्यवर्गीय *bourgeois attitudes/ideas/values*

**bout** /baʊt बाउट्/ *noun* [C] **1** a short period of great activity उत्कट क्रियाशीलता का छोटा दौर *a bout of hard work* **2** a period of illness बीमारी का दौर *I'm just recovering from a bout of flu.*

**boutique** /buːˈtiːk बूˈटीक्/ *noun* [C] a small shop that sells fashionable clothes or expensive presents छोटी दुकान जहाँ लोकप्रिय कपड़े या महँगे उपहार बिकते हैं; बुटीक

**bovine** /ˈbəʊvaɪn ˈबोव़ाइन्/ *adj.* connected with cows गायों से संबंधित, गायों की, गोजातीय *bovine diseases*

**bow[1]** /baʊ बाउ/ *verb* **1** [I, T] **bow (sth) (to sb)** to bend your head or the upper part of your body forward and down, as a sign of respect आदर-प्रदर्शन के लिए झुकना; झुककर अभिवादन करना *The speaker bowed to the guests and left the stage.* ○ *He bowed his head respectfully.* **2** [I] **bow to sth** to accept sth (किसी बात को) मान लेना, स्वीकार करना *I do not think the unions should bow to pressure from the Government.*

**PHRV** **bow out (of sth/as sth)** to leave an important position or stop taking part in sth महत्त्वपूर्ण पद छोड़ देना या किसी काम से अलग हो जाना *After a long and successful career, she has decided to bow out of politics.* ○ *He finally bowed out as chairman after ten years.*

**bow[2]** /baʊ बाउ/ *noun* [C] **1** an act of **bowing[1] 1** आदर प्रदर्शन के लिए झुकने की क्रिया *The director of the play came on stage to* ***take a bow***. **2** the front part of a ship जहाज़ का अग्र भाग ➪ **stern** देखिए।

**bow[3]** /bəʊ बो/ *noun* [C] **1** a knot with two loose roundish parts and two loose ends that you use when you are tying shoes, etc. एक प्रकार की गाँठ जो जूतों के फ़ीतों में लगाई जाती है *He tied his laces in a bow.* **2** a weapon for shooting arrows. A bow is a curved piece of wood that is held in shape by a tight string धनुष **3** a long thin piece of wood with string stretched across it that you use for playing some musical instruments वायलिन आदि वाद्य यंत्र बजाने का चाप; गज *a violin bow* ➪ पृष्ठ 789 पर चित्र देखिए।

**bowel** /ˈbaʊəl ˈबाउअल्/ *noun* [C, *usually pl.*] one of the tubes that carries waste food away from your stomach to the place where it leaves your body बड़ी आँत, अँतड़ी

**bowel movement** *noun* [C] (*medical*) an act of emptying waste material from the bowels; the waste material that is emptied अँतड़ी साफ़ होने की क्रिया; मल, विष्ठा

**bowl[1]** /bəʊl बोल्/ *noun* [C] **1** a deep round dish without a lid that is used for holding food or liquid कटोरा, कटोरी *a soup bowl* **2** the amount of sth that is in a bowl कटोरा या कटोरी भर मात्रा *I usually have a bowl of cereal for breakfast.* **3** a large plastic container that is used for washing dishes, washing clothes, etc. बर्तन, कपड़े आदि धोने का प्लास्टिक आदि का खुला टब

**bowl[2]** /bəʊl बोल्/ *verb* [I, T] (in cricket) to throw the ball in the direction of the person with the bat (क्रिकेट में) बल्लेबाज़ को गेंद फेंकना, गेंदबाज़ी करना

**PHRV** **bowl sb over** **1** to knock sb down when you are moving quickly भागते हुए किसी को गिरा देना **2** to surprise sb very much in a pleasant way किसी को सुखद आश्चर्य में डालना

**bow legs** /ˌbəʊ ˈlegz ˌबोˈलेग्ज़्/ *noun* [*pl.*] legs that curve out at the knees धनुषाकार टाँगें, घुटने से मुड़ी टाँगें ▶ **bow-legged** /ˌbəʊ ˈlegɪd ˌबोˈलेगिड्/ *adj.* धनुषाकार टाँगों से संबंधित; धनुष्पदी

**bowler** /ˈbəʊlə(r) ˈबोल(र्)/ *noun* [C] **1** (*also* **bowler hat,** *AmE* **derby**) a round hard black hat, usually worn by men प्रायः पुरुषों द्वारा पहनी जाने वाली गोल कड़ी काली टोपी **2** (in cricket) the player who throws (**bowls**) the ball in the direction of the person with the bat (क्रिकेट में) गेंदबाज़

**bowling** /ˈbəʊlɪŋ ˈबोलिङ्/ *noun* [U] a game in which you roll a heavy ball down a special track (**a lane**) towards a group of wooden objects (**pins**) and try to knock them all down एक खेल जिसमें एक भारी गेंद को कुछ दूर रखे लकड़ी के छोटे मूसलों की ओर लुढ़काया जाता है और उन्हें गिराने की कोशिश की जाती है *to go bowling*

**bowls** /bəʊlz बोल्ज़्/ *noun* [U] a game in which you try to roll large wooden balls as near as possible to a smaller ball एक खेल जिसमें लकड़ी की बड़ी गेंदों को एक छोटी गेंद के पास से पास तक लुढ़काया जाता है *to play bowls*

**bow tie** /ˌbəʊ ˈtaɪ ˌबोˈटाइ/ *noun* [C] a tie in the shape of a **bow[3] 1**, that is worn by men, especially on formal occasions धनुष के आकार की टाई जिसे पुरुष औपचारिक अवसरों पर बाँधते हैं

**box[1]** /bɒks बॉक्स्/ *noun* **1** [C] a square or rectangular container for solid objects. A box often has a lid प्रायः ढक्कनदार बक्सा; संदूक *a cardboard box* ○ *a shoebox* **2** [C] a box and the things inside it बक्सा और उसमें भरा सामान, सामान से भरा बक्सा *a box of chocolates/matches/tissues* **3** [C] an empty square or rectangular space on a form in which you have to write sth प्रपत्र पर रिक्त चौकोर

या आयताकार स्थान जिसमें कोई सूचना भरनी होती है *Write your name in the box below.* **4** [C] a small enclosed area that is used for a particular purpose विशेष प्रयोजन के लिए निर्मित घेराबंद स्थान *a telephone box* ○ *the witness box* (= in a court of law) **5 the box** [*sing.*] (*informal*) television दूरदर्शन, टेलीविज़न *What's on the box tonight?*

**box²** /bɒks बॉक्स् / *verb* **1** [I, T] to fight in the sport of boxing मुक्केबाज़ी का खेल खेलना **2** [T] to put sth into a box बक्से के अंदर डालना *a boxed set of CDs* **PHR V** **box sb/sth in** to prevent sb/sth from getting out of a small space सीमित स्थान में अवरुद्ध कर देना *Someone parked behind us and boxed us in.*

**boxer** /ˈbɒksə(r) ˈबाक्स(र्) / *noun* [C] a person who does boxing as a sport मुक्केबाज़

**boxer shorts** (*also* **boxers**) *noun* [*pl.*] shorts that men use as underwear पुरुषों की जाँघिया

**boxing** /ˈbɒksɪŋ ˈबॉक्सिङ् / *noun* [U] a sport in which two people fight by hitting each other with their hands inside large gloves मुक्केबाज़ी *the world middleweight boxing champion* ○ *boxing gloves*

**Boxing Day** *noun* [C] the day after Christmas Day; 26 December क्रिसमस दिवस से अगला दिन; 26 दिसंबर

**box number** *noun* [C] a number used as an address, especially in newspaper advertisements पते के तौर पर प्रयुक्त संख्या, विशेषतः समाचार-पत्रों के विज्ञापनों में

**box office** *noun* **1** [C] the place in a cinema, theatre, etc. where the tickets are sold टिकट खिड़की **2** [*sing.*] used to describe how successful a film, play, actor etc. is by the number of people who buy tickets to see them टिकटों की बिक्री के आधार पर किसी फ़िल्म, नाटक, अभिनेता आदि की सफलता दर्शाने के लिए प्रयुक्त *The film flopped at the box office.*

**boy** /bɔɪ बॉइ / *noun* [C] a male child or a young man लड़का, पुत्र, युवक *They've got three children —two boys and a girl.* ○ *I used to play here when I was a boy.*

**boycott** /ˈbɔɪkɒt ˈबॉइकॉट् / *verb* [T] to refuse to take part in an event, buy things from a particular company, etc. because you strongly disapprove of it बहिष्कार करना *Several countries boycotted the Olympic Games in protest.* ▶ **boycott** *noun* [C] बहिष्कार *a boycott of the local elections*

**boyfriend** /ˈbɔɪfrend ˈबॉइफ्रेन्ड् / *noun* [C] a man or boy with whom a person has a romantic and/ or sexual relationship किसी व्यक्ति का पुरुष-प्रेमी

**boyhood** /ˈbɔɪhʊd ˈबॉइहुड् / *noun* [U] the time of being a boy लड़कपन, बालपन *My father told me some of his boyhood memories.*

**boyish** /ˈbɔɪɪʃ ˈबॉइइश् / *adj.* like a boy लड़के जैसा, बालकोचित *a boyish smile*

**Boy Scout** = **scout¹**

**bra** /brɑː ब्रा / *noun* [C] a piece of clothing that women wear under their other clothes to support their breasts अँगिया

**brace¹** /breɪs ब्रेस् / *noun* **1** [C] (*AmE* **braces**) [*pl.*] a metal frame that is fixed to a child's teeth in order to make them straight दाँत सीधे करने के लिए दाँतों पर पहनी जाने वाली धातु की तार **2 braces** (*AmE* **suspenders**) [*pl.*] a pair of straps that go over your shoulders to hold your trousers up पतलून को सहारा देने वाले फ़ीतों की जोड़ी (जो कंधों पर से आती है)

**brace²** /breɪs ब्रेस् / *verb* [T] **brace sth/yourself (for sth)** to prepare yourself for sth unpleasant स्वयं को अप्रिय स्थिति के लिए तैयार करना *You'd better brace yourself for some bad news.*

**bracelet** /ˈbreɪslət ˈब्रेसलट् / *noun* [C] a piece of jewellery, for example a metal chain or band, that you wear around your wrist or arm कलाई या बाँह पर पहना जाने वाला ज़ेवर; ब्रेसलेट

**bracing** /ˈbreɪsɪŋ ˈब्रेसिङ् / *adj.* making you feel healthy and full of energy स्फूर्तिदायक, पुष्टिकारक *bracing sea air*

**bracken** /ˈbrækən ˈब्रैकन् / *noun* [U] a type of plant (**fern**) that grows thickly on hills and in woods पहाड़ियों और जंगलो में उगने वाला एक पौधा ⇨ **fern** देखिए।

**bracket¹** /ˈbrækɪt ˈब्रैकिट् / *noun* [C] **1** [*usually pl.*] (*AmE* **parenthesis**) one of two marks, ( ) or [ ], that you put round extra information in a piece of writing कोष्ठक चिह्न *A translation of each word is given* ***in brackets***. **2 age, income, price, etc. bracket** prices, ages, etc. which are between two limits दो सीमाओं के भीतर की क़ीमतें, आय, उम्र आदि *to be in a high-income bracket* **3** a piece of metal or wood that is fixed to a wall and used as a support for a shelf, lamp, etc. सहारा देने के लिए दीवार पर लगा तख़्ता, लैंप आदि लगाने के लिए धातु या लकड़ी का टुकड़ा

**bracket²** /ˈbrækɪt ˈब्रैकिट् / *verb* [T] **1** to put **brackets¹ 1** round a word, number, etc. शब्द या संख्या आदि पर कोष्ठक लगाना **2 bracket A and B (together); bracket A with B** to think of two or more people or things as similar in some way समानता के आधार पर दो या अधिक व्यक्तियों या वस्तुओं को एक ही वर्ग में रखना

**brackish** /ˈbrækɪʃ ˈब्रैकिश्/ *adj.* (used about water) containing some salt but not as much as sea water (पानी) खारा, नमकीन, क्षारयुक्त

**brag** /bræg ब्रैग/ *verb* [I] (**bragging**; **bragged**) **brag (to sb) about/of sth**) to talk too proudly about sth डींग मारना, शेख़ी बघारना *She's always bragging to her friends about how clever she is.*

**braid** /breɪd ब्रेड्/ *noun* **1** [U] thin coloured rope that is used to decorate military uniforms, etc. सैनिक पोशाकों में प्रयुक्त सजावटी फ़ीता **2** [C] (*AmE*) = **plait**

**Braille** /breɪl ब्रेल्/ *noun* [U] a system of printing, using little round marks that are higher than the level of the paper they are on and which blind people can read by touching them नेत्रहीन व्यक्तियों के लिए उभरे अक्षरों की एक लिपि जिसे छू-छूकर पढ़ा जा सकता है; ब्रेल *The signs were written **in Braille**.*

**brain** /breɪn ब्रेन्/ *noun* **1** [C] the part of your body inside your head that controls your thoughts, feelings and movements मस्तिष्क, दिमाग़ *He suffered serious brain damage in a road accident.* ○ *a brain surgeon* ➪ **body** पर चित्र देखिए। **2** [C, U] the ability to think clearly; intelligence स्पष्ट चिंतन की क्षमता; प्रतिभा, बुद्धि *She has a very quick brain and learns fast.* **3** [C] (*informal*) a very clever person अति चतुर व्यक्ति *He's one of the best brains in the country.* **4 the brains** [*sing.*] the person who plans or organizes sth योजना निर्माण या आयोजन करने वाला व्यक्ति *She's the real brains in the organization.*

**IDM have sth on the brain** (*informal*) to think about sth all the time हमेशा कुछ सोचते रहना; की सनक या धुन होना

**rack your brains** ➪ **rack**[2] देखिए।

**brainchild** /ˈbreɪntʃaɪld ˈब्रेन्चाइल्ड्/ *noun* [*sing.*] the idea or invention of a particular person किसी व्यक्ति का स्वयं का आविष्कार या विचार

**brain-dead** *adj.* **1** having serious brain damage and needing a machine to stay alive (व्यक्ति) मृत मस्तिष्क; (व्यक्ति) जिसके मस्तिष्क को गंभीर आहत पहुँची हो और जिसे मशीनों के सहारे जिंदा रखने की ज़रूरत पड़े **2** (*informal*) unable to think clearly; stupid स्पष्ट सोचने में असमर्थ; मूर्ख

**brain drain** *noun* [*sing.*] (*informal*) the movement of highly skilled and educated people to a country where they can work in better conditions and earn more money सुशिक्षित और कार्य कुशल व्यक्तियों को बेहतर नौकरी और अधिक धन के लिए स्वदेश छोड़कर विदेश जाने की गतिविधि; मेधा पलायन, प्रतिभा प्रवास

**brainless** /ˈbreɪnləs ˈब्रेन्लस्/ *adj.* (*informal*) very silly; stupid अति मूर्ख; जड़मति

**brainstorm[1]** /ˈbreɪnstɔːm ˈब्रेन्स्टॉम्/ *noun* [C] **1** a moment of sudden confusion अचानक उत्पन्न उलझन या विक्षोभ की स्थिति *I **had a brainstorm** in the exam and couldn't answer any questions.* **2** (*AmE*) = **brainwave**

**brainstorm[2]** /ˈbreɪnstɔːm ˈब्रेन्स्टॉम्/ *verb* [I, T] to solve a problem or make a decision by thinking of as many ideas as possible in a short time अल्प अवधि में अनेक विकल्पों पर विचार करते हुए समस्या का समाधान खोजना या कोई निर्णय करना *We'll spend five minutes brainstorming ideas on how we can raise money.*

**brain-teaser** *noun* [C] a problem that is difficult but fun to solve समस्या जो कठिन है परंतु जिसका समाधान मनोरंजनकारी है

**brainwash** /ˈbreɪnwɒʃ ˈब्रेन्वॉश्/ *verb* [T] **brainwash sb (into doing sth)** to force sb to believe sth by using strong mental pressure प्रबल मानसिक दबाव बनाकर किसी व्यक्ति से किसी बात पर विश्वास दिलाना; मत-आरोपण करना *Television advertisements try to brainwash people into buying things that they don't need.* ▶ **brainwashing** *noun* [U] मत-आरोपण

**brainwave** /ˈbreɪnweɪv ˈब्रेन्वेव्/ (*AmE*) (*also* **brainstorm**) *noun* [C] (*informal*) a sudden clever idea अचानक पैदा हुई सूझ, विचार-तरंग *If I **have a brainwave**, I'll let you know.*

**brainy** /ˈbreɪni ˈब्रेनि/ *adj.* (*informal*) intelligent बुद्धिमान

**braise** /breɪz ब्रेज़्/ *verb* [T] to cook meat or vegetables slowly in a little liquid in a covered dish मांस या सब्ज़ी को बंद पात्र में थोड़े पानी में धीमे-धीमे पकाना

**brake[1]** /breɪk ब्रेक्/ *noun* [C] **1** the part of a vehicle that makes it go slower or stop वाहन की गति को मंद करने या रोकने वाला उपकरण; ब्रेक *She put her foot on the brake and just managed to stop in time.* ➪ **car** पर चित्र देखिए। **2** something that makes sth else slow down or stop अवरोधकारी या गतिरोधक उपाय *The Government must try to **put a brake on** inflation.*

**brake**[2] /breɪk ब्रेक्/ *verb* [I] to make a vehicle go slower or stop by using the brakes ब्रेक द्वारा गति मंद करना या रोक देना; ब्रेक लगाना *If the driver hadn't braked in time, the car would have hit me.*

**brake light** (*AmE* **stop light**) *noun* [C] a red light on the back of a vehicle that comes on when the **brakes** are used कार के पीछे की लाल बत्ती जो ब्रेक लगने पर जल उठती है

**bramble** /ˈbræmbl ˈब्रैम्बल्/ *noun* [C] a wild bush that has black or red berries काली या लाल बेरी वाली जंगली झाड़ी, झड़-बेरी

**bran** /bræn ब्रैन्/ *noun* [U] the brown outer covering of grains that is left when the grain is made into flour भूसी, चोकर

**branch**[1] /brɑːntʃ ब्रान्च्/ *noun* [C] **1** one of the main parts of a tree that grows out of the thick central part (**trunk**) शाखा, टहनी, डाल **2** an office, shop, etc. that is part of a larger organization कार्यालय, दुकान आदि जो स्वयं किसी बड़ी संस्था का अंग हैं; अंगभूत कार्यालय, शाखा *The company has branches in Kochi and Bangalore.* **3** a part of an academic subject शैक्षिक विषय का अंग; शाखा *Psychiatry is a branch of medicine.*

**branch**[2] /brɑːntʃ ब्रान्च्/ *verb*

**PHR V** **branch off** (used about a road) to leave a larger road and go off in another direction (किसी सड़क का) बड़ी सड़क से अलग होकर दूसरी ओर मुड़ना *A bit further on, the road branches off to the left.*

**branch out (into sth)** to start doing sth new and different from the things you usually do नई दिशा में सक्रिय होना

**brand**[1] /brænd ब्रैन्ड्/ *noun* [C] **1** the name of a product that is made by a particular company किसी कंपनी द्वारा निर्मित किसी उत्पाद का नाम, ब्रांड *a well-known brand of coffee* **2** a particular type of sth किसी वस्तु का विशेष प्रकार *a strange brand of humour*

**brand**[2] /brænd ब्रैन्ड्/ *verb* [T] **1** to mark an animal with a hot iron to show who owns it स्वामित्व के संकेत के लिए जानवर को गरम लोहे से दाग़ना **2 brand sb (as sth)** to say that sb has a bad character so that people have a bad opinion of him/her किसी पर कलंक लगाना *She was branded as a troublemaker after she complained about her long working hours.*

**branding iron** *noun* [C] a metal tool that is heated and used for marking farm animals to show who owns them स्वामित्व के संकेत के लिए पशुओं को दाग़ने का लोहा

**brandish** /ˈbrændɪʃ ˈब्रैन्डिश्/ *verb* [T] to wave sth in the air in an aggressive or excited way उत्तेजना में कोई वस्तु हवा में लहराना *The robber was brandishing a knife.*

**brand new** *adj.* completely new एकदम नया

**brandy** /ˈbrændi ˈब्रैन्डि/ *noun* [C, U] (*pl.* **brandies**) a strong alcoholic drink that is made from wine एक प्रकार की तेज़ शराब; ब्रांडी

**brash** /bræʃ ब्रैश्/ *adj.* too confident and direct धृष्ट, ढीठ और खरा *Her brash manner makes her unpopular with strangers.* ▶ **brashness** *noun* [U] धृष्टता, ढिठाई

**brass** /brɑːs ब्रास्/ *noun* **1** [U] a hard yellow metal that is a mixture of two other metals (**copper** and **zinc**) पीतल (ताँबे और जस्ता का मिश्रण) *brass buttons on a uniform* **2** [*sing.*] the group of musical instruments that are made of brass पीतल के वाद्य यंत्रों का शृंखला

**brat** /bræt ब्रैट्/ *noun* [C] a child who behaves badly and annoys you ढीठ बच्चा

**bravado** /brəˈvɑːdəʊ ब्रˈवाडो/ *noun* [U] a confident way of behaving that is intended to impress people, sometimes as a way of hiding a lack of confidence आत्मविश्वास की कमी को छुपाने के लिए कभी-कभी आत्मविश्वास का प्रदर्शन करना, प्रायः दूसरों को प्रभावित करने के लिए

**brave**[1] /breɪv ब्रेव्/ *adj.* **1** ready to do things that are dangerous or difficult without showing fear बहादुर, साहसी, वीर *the brave soldiers who fought in the war* ○ *'This may hurt a little, so try and be brave,' said the dentist.* **2** needing or showing courage साहसपूर्ण *a brave decision* ▶ **bravely** *adv.* साहसपूर्वक *The men bravely defended the town for three days.*

**IDM** **put on a brave face; put a brave face on sth** to pretend that you feel confident and happy when you do not निडरता का दिखावा करना

**brave**[2] /breɪv ब्रेव्/ *verb* [T] to face sth unpleasant, dangerous or difficult without showing fear कठिन स्थिति का निडरता से सामना करना

**bravery** /ˈbreɪvəri ˈब्रेवरि/ *noun* [U] actions that are brave वीरता, साहस, साहसी कार्य *After the war he received a medal for bravery.*

**bravo** /ˌbrɑːˈvəʊ ˌब्राˈव्रो/ *exclamation* a word that people shout to show that they have enjoyed sth that sb has done, for example a play शाबाश! वाह-वाह!

**brawl** /brɔːl ब्रॉल्/ *noun* [C] a noisy fight among a group of people, usually in a public place

झड़प, उपद्रव, प्रायः किसी सार्वजनिक स्थान पर ▶ **brawl** *verb* [I] झड़प होना *We saw some football fans brawling in the street.*

**brawn** /brɔːn ब्रॉन्/ *noun* [U] physical strength बाहुबल, शारीरिक शक्ति *To do this kind of job you need more brawn than brain* (= you need to be strong rather than clever). ▶ **brawny** *adj.* बाहुबल-संपन्न

**brazen** /ˈbreɪzn ˈब्रेज़्न्/ *adj.* without embarrassment, especially in a way which shocks people निर्लज्ज *Don't believe a word she says—she's a brazen liar!* ▶ **brazenly** *adv.* निर्लज्जता से

**breach[1]** /briːtʃ ब्रीच्/ *noun* **1** [C, U] **breach (of sth)** an act that breaks an agreement, a law, etc. नियम, समझौते की शर्तों आदि का उल्लंघन; नियम-भंग *a breach of confidence.* ○ *The company was found to be* ***in breach of*** *contract.* **2** [C] a break in friendly relations between people, groups, etc. मैत्री संबंधों में दरार, बाधा *The incident caused a breach between the two countries.* **3** [C] an opening in a wall, etc. that defends or protects sb/sth दीवार आदि में दरार (प्रायः सुरक्षा या संरक्षण के लिए) *The waves made a breach in the sea wall.*

**breach[2]** /briːtʃ ब्रीच्/ *verb* [T] **1** to break an agreement, a law, etc. समझौते, क़ानून आदि का उल्लंघन करना *He accused the Government of breaching international law.* **2** to make an opening in a wall, etc. that defends or protects sb/sth सुरक्षा या संरक्षण के लिए दीवार आदि में दरार बनाना

**bread** /bred ब्रेड्/ *noun* [U] a type of food made from flour and water mixed together and baked in an oven. **Yeast** is usually added to make the bread rise डबलरोटी, ब्रेड *a piece/slice of bread* ○ *a loaf of bread* ○ *white/brown/wholemeal bread*

**breadcrumbs** /ˈbredkrʌmz ˈब्रेड्क्रम्ज़्/ *noun* [*pl.*] very small bits of bread that are used in cooking ब्रेड के छोटे-छोटे टुकड़े

**breadth** /bredθ ब्रेड्थ्/ *noun* **1** [C, U] the distance between the two sides of sth चौड़ाई *We measured the length and breadth of the garden.* **2** [U] the wide variety of things, subjects, etc. that sth includes विस्तार और विविधता *I was amazed by the breadth of her knowledge.* ➪ **broad** adjective देखिए।

**IDM** **the length and breadth of sth** ➪ **length** देखिए।

**breadwinner** /ˈbredwɪnə(r) ˈब्रेड्विन(र्)/ *noun* [C, *usually sing.*] the person who earns most of the money that his/her family needs परिवार का वह व्यक्ति जिसकी कमाई से परिवार का पालन पोषण होता है *When his dad died, Sachin became the breadwinner.*

**break[1]** /breɪk ब्रेक्/ *verb* (*pt* **broke** /brəʊk ब्रोक्/; *pp* **broken** /ˈbrəʊkən ˈब्रोकन्/) **1** [I, T] to separate, or make sth separate, into two or more pieces टूटना या तोड़ना *She dropped the vase onto the floor and it broke.* ○ *He broke his leg in a car accident.* **2** [I, T] (used about a machine, etc.) to stop working; to stop a machine, etc. working (यंत्र आदि का) चलते-चलते रुक जाना या उसे रोक देना; ख़राब हो जाना *The photocopier has broken.* ○ *Be careful with my camera—I don't want you to break it.* **3** [T] to do sth that is against the law, or against what has been agreed or promised क़ानून, प्रतिज्ञा आदि का पालन न करना, क़ानून तोड़ना; वादा न निभाना *to break the law/rules/speed limit* ○ *Don't worry—I never break my promises.* **4** [I, T] to stop doing sth for a short time अल्प अवधि के लिए विराम देना या लेना *Let's break for coffee now.* ○ *We decided to break the journey and stop for lunch.* **5** [T] to make sth end समाप्त करना, छोड़ना *Once you start smoking it's very difficult to* ***break the habit****.* ○ *Suddenly, the silence was broken by the sound of a bird singing.* **6** [I] to begin प्रारंभ होना, प्रकट होना *The day was breaking as I left the house.* ○ *We ran indoors when the storm broke.* **7** [I] (used about a wave) to reach its highest point and begin to fall (लहर का) पूरा उठकर गिरने लगना *I watched the waves breaking on the rocks.* **8** [I] (used about the voice) to change suddenly (स्वर का) एकाएक बदलना *Most boys' voices break when they are 13 or 14 years old.* ○ *His voice was breaking with emotion as he spoke.*

> **NOTE** **Break** से बनने वाले मुहावरों के लिए **break** के साथ आने वाली संज्ञाओं, विशेषणों आदि की प्रविष्टियाँ देखिए। उदाहरण के लिए **break even** प्रविष्टि **even** में मिलेगी।

**PHR V** **break away (from sb/sth)** **1** to escape suddenly from sb who is holding you क़ैद या पकड़ से भाग जाना **2** to leave a political party, state, etc. in order to form a new one नया राजनीतिक दल, राज्य आदि बनाने के लिए पुराने से संबंध तोड़ना

**break down** **1** (used about a vehicle or machine) to stop working (वाहन या मशीन का) चलते-चलते बंद हो जाना *Akram's car broke down on the way to work this morning.* **2** (used about a system, discussion, etc.) to fail (व्यवस्था, बातचीत आदि का) टूट जाना, विफल हो जाना *Talks between* *the two countries have completely broken down.* **3** to lose control of your feelings and start crying भावनाओं पर नियंत्रण खोकर रोने लगना *He broke down in tears when he heard the news.*

**break sth down** **1** to destroy sth by using force बल प्रयोग कर तोड़ देना *The police had to break down the door to get into the house.* **2** to make a substance separate into parts or change into a different form in a chemical process रासायनिक प्रक्रिया में किसी पदार्थ को विभाजित करना या उसका रूप-परिवर्तन करना *Food is broken down in our bodies by the digestive system.*

**break in** to enter a building by force, usually in order to steal sth सामान्यतः चोरी के उद्देश्य से बलपूर्वक (घर में) प्रवेश करना

**break in (on sth)** to interrupt when sb else is speaking बोलते हुए व्यक्ति को बीच में टोकना; खलल डालना *The waiter broke in on our conversation to tell me I had a phone call.*

**break into sth** **1** to enter a place that is closed बलात प्रवेश करना *Thieves broke into his car and stole the radio.* ○ (*figurative*) *The company is trying to break into the Japanese market.* **2** to start doing sth suddenly एकाएक कुछ करने लगना *to break into song/a run*

**break off** to suddenly stop doing or saying sth (कुछ कहते-कहते या करते-करते) एकाएक रुक जाना *He started speaking and then broke off in the middle of a sentence.*

**break (sth) off** to remove a part of sth by force; to be removed in this way टुकड़ा तोड़ना, टुकड़ा टूटना *Could you break off another bit of chocolate for me?*

**break sth off** to end a relationship suddenly संबंध को एकाएक समाप्त कर देना *After a bad argument, they decided to* ***break off*** *their* ***engagement****.*

**break out** (used about fighting, wars, fires, etc.) to start suddenly युद्ध, आग आदि का भड़क उठना

**break out in sth** to suddenly have a skin problem त्वचा रोग का फूट पड़ना *to break out in spots/a rash*

**break out (of sth)** to escape from a prison, etc. जेल आदि से भाग निकलना

**break through (sth)** to manage to get past sth that is stopping you (पंक्ति आदि को) भेदकर रास्ता बनाना

**break up** **1** (used about events that involve a group of people) to end or finish (बैठक आदि का) समाप्त होना *The meeting broke up just before lunch.* **2** to start school holidays विद्यालय की छुट्टियों का शुरू होना *When do you break up for the summer holidays?*

**break up (with sb)** to end a relationship with a wife, husband, girlfriend or boyfriend किसी (के साथ) संबंध समाप्त करना

**break (sth) up** to separate into parts टुकड़ों में बँट जाना *The ship broke up on the rocks.*

**break sth up** to end an event by separating the people who are involved in it लोगों को अलग कर झगड़े को समाप्त करना *The police arrived and broke up the fight.*

**break with sth** to end a relationship or connection with sb/sth संबंध समाप्त करना या तोड़ना *to break with tradition/the past*

**break²** /breɪk ब्रेक् / *noun* [C] **1** a place where sth has been broken किसी वस्तु में दरार, छेद *a break in a pipe* **2** an opening or space in sth छिद्र, रास्ता या रिक्त स्थान *Wait for a break in the traffic before you cross the road.* **3** a short period of rest लघु विश्राम, अवकाश *We worked all day without a break.* ○ *to* ***take a break*** ⇨ **interval** देखिए। **4 break (in sth); break (with sb/sth)** a change from what usually happens or an end to sth सामान्य से विचलन, विच्छेद, समाप्ति *The incident led to a break in diplomatic relations.* ○ *She wanted to make a complete break with the past.* **5** (*informal*) a piece of good luck अनुकूल अवसर, सौभाग्य *to give sb a break* (= to help sb by giving him/her a chance to be successful)

**IDM** **break of day** the time when light first appears in the morning; dawn प्रभात

**give sb a break** **1** used to tell sb to stop saying things that are annoying or not true किसी को झूठी या बुरी लगने वाली बात कहने से रोकने के लिए प्रयुक्त *Give me a break and stop nagging, OK!* **2** to be fair to sb निष्पक्ष या न्यायोचित व्यवहार करना

**breakage** /ˈbreɪkɪdʒ ˈब्रेकिज् / *noun* [C, *usually pl.*] something that has been broken टूट-फूट *Customers must pay for any breakages.*

**breakaway** /ˈbreɪkəweɪ ˈब्रेकअवे / *adj.* (*only before a noun*) (used about a political group, an organization, or a part of a country) that has separated from a larger group or country राजनैतिक दल, संगठन या बड़े संगठन या देश का भाग) बड़े संगठन या देश से अलग हुआ पृथक्भूत (अंश) ▶ **breakaway** *noun* [C] पृथक्भूत अंश

**breakdown** /ˈbreɪkdaʊn ˈब्रेकडाउन् / *noun* [C] **1** a time when a vehicle, machine, etc. stops working वाहन, मशीन आदि में ख़राबी *I hope we don't* ***have a breakdown*** *on the highway.* **2** the failure or end of sth (किसी प्रक्रिया आदि की) असफलता, विफलता या समाप्ति *The breakdown of the talks* *means that a strike is likely.* **3** = **nervous breakdown** **4** a list of all the details of sth संपूर्ण व विस्तृत ब्योरे की सूची *I would like a full breakdown of how the money was spent.*

**breakdown truck** (*AmE* **tow truck**) *noun* [C] a lorry that is used to take away cars that need to be repaired सहायता-वाहन

**breaker** /ˈbreɪkə(r) ˈब्रेक(र्)/ *noun* [C] a large wave covered with white bubbles that is moving towards the beach तट की ओर बढ़ती बुलबुलेदार बड़ी लहर

**breakfast** /ˈbrekfəst ˈब्रेक्फ़स्ट्/ *noun* [C, U] the meal which you have when you get up in the morning सुबह का नाश्ता, कलेवा *to have **breakfast*** ○ *What do you usually have **for breakfast**?*

**break-in** *noun* [C] the act of entering a building by force, especially in order to steal sth सेंध लगाना, दीवार आदि तोड़ कर घुसना

**breakneck** /ˈbreɪknek ˈब्रेक्नेक्/ *adj.* (*only before a noun*) very fast and dangerous बहुत तेज़ और ख़तरनाक *He drove her to the hospital **at breakneck speed**.*

**breakthrough** /ˈbreɪkθruː ˈब्रेक्थ्रू/ *noun* [C] **a breakthrough (in sth)** an important discovery or development कोई महत्त्वपूर्ण खोज या विकास *Scientists are hoping to **make a breakthrough** in cancer research.*

**break-up** *noun* [C] **1** the end of a relationship between two people संबंध-विच्छेद *the break-up of a marriage* **2** the separation of a group or organization into smaller parts किसी बड़े संगठन का छोटे-छोटे हिस्सों में टूटने की क्रिया; विघटन

**breakwater** /ˈbreɪkwɔːtə(r) ˈब्रेक्वॉट(र्)/ *noun* [C] a wall built out into the sea to protect the land from the force of the waves लहरों के आघात से सुरक्षा के लिए समुद्र के पानी में बनाई गई दीवार; तरंग-रोधक दीवार

**bream** /briːm ब्रीम्/ *noun* [C, U] (*pl.* **bream**) a type of fish that can live in fresh or salt water and that you can eat खाने योग्य एक मछली जो ताज़े या लवण जल में रह सकती है; ब्रीम मछली

**breast** /brest ब्रेस्ट्/ *noun* [C] **1** one of the two soft round parts of a woman's body that can produce milk स्त्री का स्तन **2** a word used especially in literature for the top part of the front of your body, below the neck (साहित्य में) छाती के लिए प्रयुक्त शब्द **3** the front part of the body of a bird पक्षी के शरीर का सामने वाला भाग

**breastbone** /ˈbrestbəʊn ˈब्रेस्ट्बोन्/ *noun* [C] the long flat bone in the middle of your chest that the seven top pairs of curved bones (**ribs**) are connected to छाती के मध्य स्थित लंबी चपटी हड्डी जिससे पसलियाँ जुड़ी होती हैं; उरोस्थि **NOTE** इस अर्थ के लिए **sternum** अधिक औपचारिक शब्द है। ➪ **body** पर चित्र देखिए।

**breastfeed** /ˈbrestfiːd ˈब्रेस्ट्फ़ीड्/ *verb* [I, T] (*pt, pp* **breastfed**) to feed a baby with milk from the breast स्तनपान कराना, माँ का शिशु को दूध पिलाना

**breaststroke** /ˈbreststrəʊk ˈब्रेस्ट्स्ट्रोक्/ *noun* [U] a style of swimming on your front in which you start with your hands together, push both arms forward and then move them out and back through the water तैरने की एक शैली (आगे से दोनों हाथ बाँधकर दोनों बाँहों को आगे धकेलते हुए पानी में उन्हें बाहर और पीछे की ओर फैलाकर तैरना) *to do (the) breaststroke* ➪ **backstroke, butterfly** और **crawl** देखिए तथा **swim** पर चित्र देखिए।

**breath** /breθ ब्रेथ्/ *noun* **1** [U] the air that you take into and blow out of your lungs साँस, श्वास *to have bad breath* (= breath which smells unpleasant) **2** [C] an act of taking air into or blowing air out of your lungs श्वसन क्रिया *Take a few deep breaths before you start running.*

**IDM** **a breath of fresh air** the clean air which you breathe outside, especially when compared to the air inside a room or building बाहर खुले स्थान की ताज़ी हवा *Let's go for a walk. I need a breath of fresh air.* ○ (*figurative*) *Aslam's happy face is like a breath of fresh air in that miserable place.*

**catch your breath** ➪ **catch**[1] देखिए।

**get your breath (again/back)** to rest after physical exercise so that your breathing returns to normal व्यायाम के बाद विश्राम करना ताकि श्वसन क्रिया सामान्य हो जाए

**hold your breath** to stop breathing for a short time, for example when you are swimming or because of fear or excitement कुछ देर के लिए साँस रोकना (प्रायः तैरते समय, भय या उत्तेजनावश)

**(be/get) out of/short of breath** (to be/start) breathing very quickly, for example after physical exercise हाँफना

**say sth, speak, etc. under your breath** to say sth very quietly, usually because you do not want people to hear you फुसफुसाना

**take your breath away** to surprise sb very much किसी को आश्चर्य-चकित कर देना ➪ **breathtaking** adjective देखिए।

**take a deep breath** ➪ **deep**[1] देखिए।

**with bated breath** ➪ **bated** देखिए।

**breathalyse** (*AmE* **breathalyze**) /ˈbreθəlaɪz ˈब्रेथ़लाइज़् / *verb* [T] to test the breath of a driver with a special machine (**a breathalyser**) to measure how much alcohol he/she has drunk एक विशेष मशीन (ब्रिथलाइज़र) के द्वारा ड्राइवर के श्वास का परीक्षण करना ताकि यह पता चल सके कि उसने कितनी शराब पी रखी है

**breathe** /briːð ब्रीद् / *verb* [I, T] to take air, etc. into your lungs and blow it out again साँस लेना निकालना; श्वसन करना ***Breathe out*** *as you lift the weight and* ***breathe in*** *as you lower it.* ○ *I hate having to breathe (in) other people's cigarette smoke.* ▶ **breathing** *noun* [U] श्वसन *heavy/irregular breathing* ○ *breathing exercises*

**IDM** **not breathe a word (of/about sth) (to sb)** to not tell sb about sth that is secret रहस्य को गुप्त रखना

**breather** /ˈbriːðə(r) ˈब्रीद़(र्) / *noun* [C] (*informal*) a short rest अल्पकालिक विश्राम *to* ***have/take a breather***

**breathless** /ˈbreθləs ˈब्रेथ़्लस् / *adj.* **1** having difficulty breathing हाँफते हुए, साँस फूली हुई, बेदम *I was hot and breathless when I got to the top of the hill.* **2** not able to breathe because you are so excited, frightened, etc. उत्तेजना या घबराहट के कारण साँस न ले सकना *to be breathless with excitement* ▶ **breathlessly** *adv.* साँस फूलते हुए

**breathtaking** /ˈbreθteɪkɪŋ ˈब्रेथ़्टेकिङ् / *adj.* extremely surprising, beautiful, etc. अत्यंत आश्चर्यजनक, सुंदर आदि *breathtaking scenery*

**breath test** *noun* [C] a test by the police on the breath of a driver to measure how much alcohol he/she has drunk वाहन-चालक द्वारा पी गई शराब की मात्रा की जाँच के लिए श्वास-परीक्षण

**breed¹** /briːd ब्रीड् / *verb* (*pt, pp* **bred** /bred ब्रेड् /) **1** [I] (used about animals) to have sex and produce young animals (पशुओं का) प्रजनन करना *Many animals won't breed in zoos.* ✪ पर्याय **mate** **2** [T] to keep animals or plants in order to produce young from them पशुओं या पौधों को नसलें पैदा करने के लिए पालना *These cattle are bred to produce high yields of milk.* **3** [T] to cause sth का कारण होना या बनना *This kind of thinking breeds intolerance.* ▶ **breeding** *noun* [U] प्रजनन

**breed²** /briːd ब्रीड् / *noun* [C] a particular variety of an animal किसी पशु की विशेष नसल, क़िस्म *a breed of cattle/dog*

**breeder** /ˈbriːdə(r) ˈब्रीड(र्) / *noun* [C] a person who breeds animals or plants पशुओं या पौधों का प्रजनन की दृष्टि से पालन करने वाला व्यक्ति; प्रजनक *a dog breeder*

**breeding ground** *noun* [C] **1** a place where wild animals go to breed पशुओं का प्रजनन स्थल **2** a place where sth can develop फलने-फूलने का स्थान *a breeding ground for crime*

**breeze¹** /briːz ˈब्रीज़् / *noun* [C] a light wind मंद पवन, बयार, समीर *A warm breeze was blowing.*

**breeze²** /briːz ˈब्रीज़् / *verb* [I] **breeze along, in, out, etc.** to move in a confident and relaxed way मस्त व बेपरवाह रीति से घूमना *He just breezed in twenty minutes late without a word of apology.*

**breezy** /ˈbriːzi ˈब्रीज़ि / *adj.* **1** with a little wind मंद पवन के साथ **2** happy and relaxed प्रसन्न और निश्चित; प्रफुल्लित *You're bright and breezy this morning!*

**brevity** /ˈbrevəti ˈब्रेव़टि / *noun* [U] the state of being short or quick संक्षिप्तता या अल्पकालिकता ➪ **brief** adjective देखिए।

**brew** /bruː ब्रू / *verb* **1** [T] to make beer बिअर (एक प्रकार की मदिरा) बनाना **2** [T] to make a drink of tea or coffee by adding hot water गरम पानी डालकर चाय या क़ॉफी बनाना *to brew a pot of tea* **3** [I] (used about tea) to stand in hot water before it is ready to drink (चाय के लिए प्रयुक्त) गरम पानी में पकने देना पीने से पहले *Leave it to brew for a few minutes.*

**IDM** **be brewing** (used about sth bad) to develop or grow (किसी बुराई का) पैदा होना और बढ़ने लगना *There's* ***trouble brewing****.*

**brewery** /ˈbruːəri ˈब्रूअरि / *noun* [C] (*pl.* **breweries**) a place where beer is made बियर तैयार करने की फ़ैक्टरी

**bribe** /braɪb ब्राइब् / *noun* [C] money, etc. that is given to sb such as an official to persuade him/her to do sth to help you that is wrong or dishonest घूस, रिश्वत *to* ***accept/take bribes*** ▶ **bribe** *verb* [T] **bribe sb (with sth)** रिश्वत देना *They got a visa by bribing an official.* ▶ **bribery** /ˈbraɪbəri ब्राइबरि / *noun* [U] रिश्वत, रिश्वतख़ोरी, रिश्वत देने या लेने का अपराध

**bric-a-brac** /ˈbrɪk ə bræk ˈब्रिक् अ ब्रैक् / *noun* [U] small items of little value, for decoration in a house घर की छोटी व सस्ती सजावटी वस्तुएँ

**brick** /brɪk ब्रिक् / *noun* [C, U] a hard block of baked clay that is used for building houses, etc. ईंट *a lorry carrying bricks* ○ *a house built of red brick*

**bricklayer** /ˈbrɪkleɪə(r) ˈब्रिक्लेअ(र्) / *noun* [C] a person whose job is to build walls with bricks ईंटों की चिनाई करने वाला व्यक्ति; राज मिस्त्री

**brickwork** /ˈbrɪkwɜːk ˈब्रिक्वक् / *noun* [U] the part of a building that is made of bricks ईंट से बनी इमारत का अंश; ईंटों की चिनाई-प्रक्रिया

**bridal** /ˈbraɪdl ˈब्राइड्ल्/ *adj.* (*only before a noun*) connected with a bride वधू-विषयक

**bride** /braɪd ब्राइड्/ *noun* [C] a woman on or just before her wedding day वधू, दुल्हन *a* ***bride-to-be*** (= a woman whose wedding is soon) ➪ **wedding** पर नोट देखिए।

**bridegroom** /ˈbraɪdgruːm ˈब्राइड्ग्रूम्/ (*also* **groom**) *noun* [C] a man on or just before his wedding day दूल्हा, वर ➪ **wedding** पर नोट देखिए।

**bridesmaid** /ˈbraɪdzmeɪd ˈब्राइड्ज़्मेड्/ *noun* [C] a woman or girl who helps a woman on her wedding day (**the bride**) वधू-सखी ➪ **wedding** पर नोट देखिए।

**bridge**[1] /brɪdʒ ब्रिज्/ *noun* **1** [C] a structure that carries a road or railway across a river, valley, road or railway पुल, सेतु *a bridge over the River Yamuna* **2** [*sing.*] the high part of a ship where the captain and the people who control the ship stand जहाज़ का वह उठा हुआ भाग जहाँ कप्तान और चालक मंडल के सदस्य खड़े होते हैं **3** [U] a card game for four people ताश के पत्तों का एक खेल जिसे चार लोग खेलते हैं; ब्रिज

**bridge**[2] /brɪdʒ ब्रिज्/ *verb* [T] to build a bridge over sth पुल बनाना

IDM **bridge a/the gap** to fill a space between two people, groups or things or to bring them closer together दो व्यक्तियों, समूहों आदि के बीच का ख़ाली स्थान भरना ताकि वे निकट आ सकें, या उन्हें करीब लाना

**bridle** /ˈbraɪdl ˈब्राइड्ल्/ *noun* [C] the leather straps that you put on a horse's head so that you can control it when you are riding it घोड़े की लगाम, बाग ➪ **horse** पर चित्र देखिए।

**brief**[1] /briːf ब्रीफ़्/ *adj.* short or quick संक्षिप्त या अल्पकालिक *a brief description* ○ *Please be brief. We don't have much time.* ➪ **brevity** noun देखिए।

IDM **in brief** using only a few words संक्षेप में *In brief, the meeting was a disaster.*

**brief**[2] /briːf ब्रीफ़्/ *noun* [C] instructions or information about a job or task कार्य-संबंधी निर्देश या सूचनाएँ *He was given the brief of improving the image of the organization.*

**brief**[3] /briːf ब्रीफ़्/ *verb* [T] to give sb information or instructions about sth किसी को कुछ निर्देश या सूचना देना *The minister has been fully briefed on what questions to expect.*

**briefcase** /ˈbriːfkeɪs ˈब्रीफ़केस्/ *noun* [C] a flat case that you use for carrying papers, etc., especially when you go to work काग़ज़ आदि रखकर ले जाने का चपटा बक्सा; ब्रीफ़केस

**briefing** /ˈbriːfɪŋ ˈब्रीफ़िङ्/ *noun* [C, U] instructions or information that you are given before sth happens कार्य आरंभ होने से पहले दिए निर्देश या सूचनाएँ *a press/news briefing* (= where information is given to journalists)

**briefly** /ˈbriːfli ˈब्रीफ़्लि/ *adv.* **1** for a short time; quickly थोड़े समय के लिए; शीघ्रता से *She glanced briefly at the letter.* **2** using only a few words थोड़े शब्दों में; संक्षेप में *I'd like to comment very briefly on that last statement.*

**briefs** /briːfs ब्रीफ़्स्/ *noun* [*pl.*] underwear for men or women worn on the lower part of the body जाँघिया

**brigade** /brɪˈgeɪd ब्रिˈगेड्/ *noun* [C] **1** a unit of soldiers in the army सैनिकों की एक टुकड़ी या इकाई; ब्रिगेड **2** a group of people who work together for a particular purpose किसी एक विशेष कार्य के लिए गठित कार्य-दल *the fire brigade*

**brigadier** /ˌbrɪgəˈdɪə(r) ˌब्रिगˈडिअ(र्)/ *noun* [C] an important officer in the army सेना में एक उच्च अधिकारी; ब्रिगेडियर

**bright** /braɪt ब्राइट्/ *adj.* **1** having a lot of light प्रकाश-भरा, प्रदीप्त, उज्जवल, चमकीला *a bright, sunny day* ○ *eyes bright with happiness* **2** (used about a colour) strong and easy to see (रंग) चमकदार और सुस्पष्ट *a bright yellow jumper* **3** clever, or able to learn things quickly चतुर और बुद्धिमान; तेज़ *a bright child* ○ *a* ***bright idea*** **4** likely to be pleasant or successful उज्जवल, अनुकूल *The future looks bright.* **5** happy; cheerful प्रसन्नचित्त, प्रफुल्ल

▸ **brightly** *adv.* चमकीला *brightly coloured clothes*

▸ **brightness** *noun* [U] चमक, चमकीलापन, उज्जवलता, प्रभा

IDM **look on the bright side** ➪ **look**[1] देखिए।

**brighten** /ˈbraɪtn ˈब्राइट्न्/ *verb* [I, T] **brighten (sth) (up)** to become brighter or happier; to make sth brighter चमकना या चमकाना; प्रसन्न हो जाना या करना *His face brightened when he saw her.* ○ *to brighten up sb's day* (= make it happier)

**brilliant** /ˈbrɪliənt ˈब्रिलिअन्ट्/ *adj.* **1** having a lot of light; very bright अति प्रकाशमान; बहुत चमकीला *brilliant sunshine* **2** very clever, skilful or successful अति चतुर, कुशाग्र बुद्धि, प्रतिभाशाली या सफल *a brilliant young scientist* ○ *That's a brilliant idea!* **3** (*informal*) very good अत्यधिक अच्छा, रोचक *That was a brilliant film!* ▸ **brilliance** *noun* [U] चमक-दमक, दीप्ति, बुद्धिमत्ता ▸ **brilliantly** *adv.* चमकते हुए

**brim**[1] /brɪm ब्रिम्/ *noun* [C] **1** the top edge of a cup, glass, etc. प्याले, गिलास आदि का ऊपरी किनारा *The cup was full to the brim.* **2** the bottom part of a hat that is wider than the rest टोपी का सबसे निचला हिस्सा जो बाक़ी हिस्सों से अधिक चौड़ा होता है

**brim**[2] /brɪm ब्रिम्/ *verb* [I] (**brimming; brimmed**) **brim (with sth)** to be full of sth किसी वस्तु से भरा हुआ होना, लबालब होना *His eyes were brimming with tears.*

**PHR V** **brim over (with sth)** (used about a cup, glass, etc.) to have more liquid than it can hold (प्याला, गिलास आदि) इतना भरा होना कि किनारों से द्रव बहने लगे *The bowl was brimming over with water.* ○ (*figurative*) *to be brimming over with health/happiness*

**brine** /braɪn ब्राइन्/ *noun* [U] very salty water, used especially for keeping food fresh बहुत खारा या नमकीन पानी जो विशेषतः भोजन को ताज़ा रखने में प्रयुक्त होता है

**bring** /brɪŋ ब्रिङ्/ *verb* [T] (*pt, pp* **brought** /brɔːt ब्रॉट्/) **1** to carry or take sb/sth to a place with you साथ लाना *Could you bring us some water, please?* ○ (*figurative*) *He will bring valuable skills and experience to the team.* **2** to move sth somewhere ले आना *Raman brought a photo out of his wallet and showed it to us.* **3** to cause or result in sth कुछ होने का कारण बनना, के फलस्वरूप कुछ होना *The sight of her brought a smile to his face.* ○ *Money doesn't always bring happiness.* **4** to cause sb/sth to be in a certain place or condition किसी के स्थान पर होने या स्थिति में परिवर्तन का कारण बनना *Their screams brought people running from all directions.* ○ *An injury can easily **bring** an athlete's career **to an end**.* **5 bring yourself to do sth** to force yourself to do sth कुछ करने के लिए स्वयं को बाध्य करना *The film was so horrible that I couldn't bring myself to watch it.*

**NOTE** **Bring** से बनने वाले मुहावरों के लिए **bring** के साथ आने वाली संज्ञाओं, विशेषणों आदि की प्रविष्टियाँ देखिए। उदाहरण के लिए **bring up the rear** प्रविष्टि **rear** (संज्ञा/विशेषण) में मिलेगी।

**PHR V** **bring sth about** to cause sth to happen कुछ होने का कारण बनना, उत्पन्न करना *to bring about changes in people's lives*

**bring sth back** **1** to cause sth that existed before to be introduced again किसी स्थिति को पुनः वापस लाना *Nobody wants to bring back the days of child labour.* **2** to cause sb to remember sth कोई बात स्मरण दिलाना *The photographs brought back memories of his childhood.*

**bring sb/sth down** to defeat sb/sth; to make sb/sth lose a position of power किसी को पराजित करना; किसी को सत्ता से वंचित करना *to bring down the government*

**bring sth down** to make sth lower in level किसी वस्तु का स्तर घटाना, नीचे लाना (क़ीमतों में) कमी लाना *to bring down the price of sth*

**bring sth forward** **1** to move sth to an earlier time पूर्व दिनांक या पूर्व समय में आना *The date of the meeting has been brought forward by two weeks.* ✪ विलोम **put sth back** **2** to suggest sth for discussion चर्चा का प्रस्ताव रखना या सामने लाना

**bring sb in** to ask or employ sb to do a particular job किसी विशेष कार्य के लिए किसी को लाना या नियुक्त करना *A specialist was brought in to set up the new computer system.*

**bring sth in** to introduce sth प्रस्तुत करना; प्रयोग में लाना *The government have brought in a new law on dangerous drugs.*

**bring sth off** to manage to do sth difficult कोई कठिन काम कर दिखाना *The team brought off an amazing victory.*

**bring sth on** to cause sth किसी स्थिति का कारण बनना *Her headaches are brought on by stress.*

**bring sth out** to produce sth or cause sth to appear किसी वस्तु को सामने लाना, पेश करना *When is the company bringing out its next new model?*

**bring sb round** to make sb become conscious again होश में लाना *I splashed cold water on his face to try to bring him round.*

**bring sb round (to sth)** to persuade sb to agree with your opinion किसी को सहमत करा लेना; मना लेना *After a lot of discussion we finally brought them round to our point of view.*

**bring sth round to sth** to direct a conversation to a particular subject चर्चा का रुख विशेष विषय की ओर मोड़ना *I finally brought the conversation round to the subject of money.*

**bring sb up** to look after a child until he/she is adult and to teach him/her how to behave पालन-पोषण करना और अच्छा आचरण सिखाना *a well brought up child*

**bring sth up** **1** to be sick so that food that you have swallowed comes back out of your mouth; to vomit वमन या उल्टी करना **2** to introduce sth into a discussion or conversation किसी बात की चर्चा चलाना *I intend to bring the matter up at the next meeting.*

**brinjal** /ˈbrɪndʒl ˈब्रिन्ज़ल्/ *noun* [C] = **aubergine**

**brink** /brɪŋk ब्रिङ्क् / *noun* [*sing.*] **the brink (of sth)** if you are on the brink of sth, you are almost in a very new, exciting or dangerous situation नई, उत्तेजक या ख़तरनाक स्थिति के अति निकट होना *Just when the band were* ***on the brink*** *of becoming famous, they split up.*

**brisk** /brɪsk ब्रिस्क् / *adj.* **1** quick or using a lot of energy; busy फुरतीला, तेज़; व्यस्त *They set off* ***at a brisk pace***. ○ *Trading has been brisk this morning.* **2** confident and practical; wanting to get things done quickly आत्मविश्वासी और व्यावहारिक; फुरती से काम का निपटारा चाहने वाला ▶ **briskly** *adv.* तीव्रता से ▶ **briskness** *noun* [U] तीव्रता, फुरती, स्फूर्ति

**bristle[1]** /ˈbrɪsl ˈब्रिस्ल् / *noun* [C] **1** a short thick hair कड़ा छोटा बाल *The bristles on my chin hurt the baby's face.* **2** one of the short thick hairs of a brush ब्रश का एक छोटा कड़ा बाल

**bristle[2]** /ˈbrɪsl ˈब्रिस्ल् / *verb* [I] **1** (used about hair or an animal's fur) to stand up straight because of fear, anger, cold, etc. (बाल या पशु की रोएँदार खाल का) भय, क्रोध, ठंड आदि के कारण सीधे खड़ा होना **2 bristle (with sth) (at sb/sth)** to show that you are angry क्रोध प्रकट करना

PHR V **bristle with sth** to be full of sth किसी वस्तु से भरा हुआ होना; किसी बात की भरमार होना

**Britain** /ˈbrɪtn ˈब्रिट्न् / = **Great Britain** ➪ **United Kingdom** पर नोट देखिए।

**brittle** /ˈbrɪtl ˈब्रिट्ल् / *adj.* hard but easily broken कड़ा किंतु सरलता से टूटने वाला; भंगुर *The bones become brittle in old age.*

**broach** /brəʊtʃ ब्रोच् / *verb* [T] to start talking about a particular subject, especially one which is difficult or embarrassing चर्चा चलाना, ज़िक्र छेड़ना, विशेषतः किसी कठिन या उलझनदार विषय के संबंध में *How will you* ***broach the subject*** *of the money he owes us?*

**broad** /brɔːd ब्रॉड् / *adj.* **1** wide चौड़ा *a broad street/river* ○ *broad shoulders* ○ *a broad smile*

> NOTE चौड़ाई के लिए शब्द **wide** का प्रयोग अधिक किया जाता है—*The gate is four metres wide.*

✪ विलोम **narrow** ➪ **breadth** noun देखिए। **2** including many different people or things विस्तृत *We sell a* ***broad range*** *of products.* **3** without a lot of detail; general मोटा-मोटा; सामान्य (न कि विस्तृत) *I'll explain the new system* ***in broad terms***. **4** (used about the way sb speaks) very strong भारी (लहज़ा), कड़क आवाज़ में *She has a broad Somerset accent.*

IDM **(in) broad daylight** during the day, when it is easy to see दिनदहाड़े

**broad bean** *noun* [C] a type of large flat green bean that can be cooked and eaten बड़ी सेम, बांकला

**broadcast** /ˈbrɔːdkɑːst ˈब्रॉड्कास्ट् / *verb* [I, T] (*pt, pp* **broadcast**) to send out radio or television programmes रेडियो या टेलीविज़न कार्यक्रम प्रसारित करना *The Olympics are* ***broadcast live*** *around the world.* ▶ **broadcast** *noun* [C] रेडियो या टेलिविज़न कार्यक्रम *The next news broadcast is at 9 o'clock.*

**broadcaster** /ˈbrɔːdkɑːstə(r) ˈब्रॉड्कास्टर् / *noun* [C] a person who speaks on the radio or on television प्रसारक, प्रसारण-कर्ता

**broaden** /ˈbrɔːdn ˈब्रॉड्न् / *verb* [I, T] **broaden (sth) (out)** to become wider; to make sth wider चौड़ाई बढ़ना या बढ़ाना; अधिक चौड़ा होना या करना *The river broadens out beyond the bridge.* ○ (*figurative*) *Travel broadens the mind* (= it makes you understand other people better).

**broadly** /ˈbrɔːdli ˈब्रॉड्लि / *adv.* **1** (used to describe a way of smiling) with a big, wide smile (मुसकुराहट) खुलकर *He smiled broadly as he shook everyone's hand.* **2** generally मोटे तौर पर, सामान्यतया ***Broadly speaking****, the scheme will work as follows.*

**broad-minded** *adj.* happy to accept beliefs and ways of life that are different from your own उदार विचारों वाला ✪ विलोम **narrow-minded**

**broccoli** /ˈbrɒkəli ˈब्रॉकलि / *noun* [U] a thick green plant with green or purple flower heads that can be cooked and eaten फूलगोभी जैसी एक सब्ज़ी; ब्रॉकोलि ➪ **vegetable** पर चित्र देखिए।

**brochure** /ˈbrəʊʃə(r) ˈब्रोशर् / *noun* [C] a small book with pictures and information about sth विवरण-पुस्तिका, विवरणिका

**broil** /brɔɪl ब्रॉइल् / *verb* [T] (*AmE*) = **grill[2] 1**

**broke[1]** ➪ **break[1]** का past tense रूप

**broke[2]** /brəʊk ब्रोक् / *adj.* (*not before a noun*) (*informal*) having no money बिना धन के; कंगाल *I can't come out tonight—I'm absolutely broke.*

**broken[1]** ➪ **break[2]** का past tense रूप

**broken[2]** /ˈbrəʊkən ˈब्रोकन् / *adj.* **1** damaged or in pieces; not working टूटा हुआ, खंडित; बेकार, ख़राब, चालू हालत में न होना *a broken leg* ○ *How did the window* ***get broken***? **2** (used about a promise or an agreement) not kept (समझौता, वचन) भंग **3** not continuous; interrupted खंडित; बाधाग्रस्त *a broken line* ○ *a broken night's sleep* **4** (used about a foreign language) spoken slowly with a lot of mistakes (भाषा) टूटी-फूटी, अशुद्ध *to speak in broken English*

**broken-down** *adj.* **1** in a very bad condition बहुत बुरी हालत में, जर्जर *a broken-down old building* **2** (used about a vehicle) not working (मशीन, गाड़ी आदि) ख़राब, काम न करने वाली *A broken-down bus was blocking the road.*

**broken-hearted** = **heartbroken**

**broken home** *noun* [C] a family in which the parents do not live together, for example because they are divorced परिवार जिसमें माता-पिता संग नहीं रहते, जैसे तलाक़ होने के कारण; छिन्न-भिन्न परिवार *Many of the children came from broken homes.*

**broken marriage** *noun* [C] a marriage that has ended विच्छिन्न विवाह, खंडित विवाह

**broker** /ˈbrəʊkə(r) ˈब्रोक(र्)/ *noun* [C] a person who buys and sells things, for example shares in a business, for other people दलाल; आढ़तीया *an insurance broker*

**bromide** /ˈbrəʊmaɪd ˈब्रोमाइड्/ *noun* [U] a chemical compound used in medicine to make people feel calm औषधि में प्रयुक्त एक रासायनिक मिश्रण जो उपशामक होता है; ब्रोमाइड

**bromine** /ˈbrəʊmiːn ˈब्रोमीन्/ *noun* [U] (*symbol* **Br**) a dark red, poisonous gas with a strong smell गहरी लाल, विषैली और तेज़ गंध वाली गैस; ब्रोमाइन

**bronchial** /ˈbrɒŋkiəl ˈब्रॉङ्किअल्/ *adj.* connected with or affecting the two main branches of your **windpipe** (**bronchial tubes**) leading to your lungs श्वासनली की दो मुख्य शाखाओं से संबंधित; श्वसनी ➪ **body** पर चित्र देखिए।

**bronchitis** /brɒŋˈkaɪtɪs ˈब्रॉङ्ˈकाइटिस्/ *noun* [U] an illness of the tubes leading to the lungs (**bronchial tubes**) that causes a very bad cough श्वसनी-नलियों की एक बीमारी जिसके कारण बहुत बुरी तरह खाँसी होती है; श्वसनीशोथ

**bronchus** /ˈbrɒŋkəs ˈब्रॉङ्कस्/ *noun* [C] (*pl.* **bronchi** /ˈbrɒŋkaɪ ˈब्रॉङ्काइ/) one of the tubes that carry air to the lungs फेफड़ों तक हवा ले जाने वाली नलियों में से कोई एक; श्वसनी

**bronze** /brɒnz ब्रॉन्ज़्/ *noun* **1** [U] a reddish-brown metal that is made by mixing tin with another metal (**copper**) ताँबे और टिन के मिश्रण से बनी धातु; काँसा **2** [U] the colour of bronze काँसा रंग **3** [C] = **bronze medal** ▶ **bronze** *adj.* काँसे से संबंधित

**the Bronze Age** *noun* [*sing.*] the period in human history between the Stone Age and the Iron Age when people used tools and weapons made of bronze कांस्य युग

**bronzed** /brɒnzd ब्रॉन्ज़्ड्/ *adj.* having skin that has been turned brown, in an attractive way, by the sun सूर्यताप के फलस्वरूप काँसे की आभा वाली त्वचा

**bronze medal** *noun* [C] a round piece of bronze that you get as a prize for coming third in a race or a competition कांस्य पदक ➪ **gold** और **silver medal** देखिए।

**brooch** /brəʊtʃ ब्रोच्/ *noun* [C] a piece of jewellery with a pin at the back that women wear on their clothes जड़ाऊ पिन

**brood**[1] /bruːd ब्रूड्/ *verb* [I] **1 brood (on/over/about sth)** to worry, or to think a lot about sth that makes you worried or sad बहुत चिंता करना; किसी बात पर सोच-विचार कर परेशान या उदास होना *to brood on a failure* **2** (used about a female bird) to sit on her eggs (मादा पक्षी का) अंडों पर बैठना; अंडें सेना

**brood**[2] /bruːd ब्रूड्/ *noun* [C] all the young birds that belong to one mother एक ही मादा पक्षी के (एक ही बार में दिए) सब बच्चे

**brook** /brʊk ब्रुक्/ *noun* [C] a small flow of water छोटी जलधारा ✪ पर्याय **stream**

**broom** /bruːm ब्रूम्/ *noun* [C] a brush with a long handle that you use for removing (**sweeping**) dirt from the floor लंबे डंडे वाला झाड़ू, बुहारी, कूँचा

**broomstick** /ˈbruːmstɪk ब्रूमस्टिक्/ *noun* [C] the handle of a broom झाड़ू का डंडा

**Bros** (*AmE* **Bros.**) *abbr.* (used in the name of a company) Brothers (किसी कंपनी के नाम साथ प्रयुक्त) ब्रदर्स *Lalchand Bros Ltd*

**broth** /brɒθ ब्रॉथ्/ *noun* [U] soup सूप, शोरबा *chicken broth*

**brother** /ˈbrʌðə(r) ˈब्रद़(र्)/ *noun* [C] **1** a man or boy who has the same parents as another person भाई, सगा भाई *Sahil and Raghav are brothers.* ○ *a younger/older brother* ➪ **half-brother** और **step brother** देखिए।

> **NOTE** भाई और बहिन दोनों का अर्थ देने वाला कोई एक शब्द अंग्रेज़ी में लगभग नहीं है—*Have you got any brothers or sisters?* **Sibling** बहुत औपचारिक शब्द है इसलिए प्रायः अप्रयुक्त है।

**2** a man who is a member of a Christian religious community धार्मिक ईसाई समुदाय का सदस्य; ब्रदर **3** (*informal*) a man who you feel close to because he is a member of the same society, group, etc. as you उसी समाज, वर्ग आदि का पुरुष सदस्य; बंधु

**brotherhood** /ˈbrʌðəhʊd ˈब्रद़हुड्/ *noun* **1** [U] a feeling of great friendship and understanding between people भाई-चारा, मातृत्व, बंधुत्व *the brotherhood of man* (= a feeling of friendship between all the people in the world) **2** an organization which is formed for a particular, often religious, purpose प्रायः धार्मिक आधार पर बना भ्रातृसंघ

**brother-in-law** *noun* [C] (*pl.* **brothers-in-law**) **1** the brother of your husband or wife पति या पत्नी का भाई; जेठ या साला **2** the husband of your sister बहन का पति; बहनोई, जीजा

**brotherly** /ˈbrʌðəli ˈब्रद्लि/ *adj.* showing feelings of love and kindness that you would expect a brother to show भ्रातृवत, भाई जैसा (व्यवहार) *brotherly love/advice*

**brought** ➪ **bring** का past tense और past participle रूप

**brow** /braʊ ब्राउ/ *noun* **1** [C] = **eyebrow** **2** [C] = **forehead** **3** [*sing.*] the top part of a hill पहाड़ी का शिखर प्रदेश *Suddenly a car came over the brow of the hill.*

**browbeat** /ˈbraʊbiːt ˈब्राउब्रीट्/ *verb* [T] (*pt* **browbeat;** *pp* **browbeaten**) **browbeat sb (into doing sth)** to frighten or threaten sb in order to make him/her do sth धमकाकर कोई कार्य करवाना; धौंस जमाना *They were browbeaten into accepting the deal.*

**brown[1]** /braʊn ब्राउन्/ *noun, adj.* **1** [C, U] (of) the colour of earth or wood भूरा, धरती या लकड़ी के रंग का *brown eyes/hair* ○ *the yellows and browns of the trees in autumn* **2** having skin that the sun has made darker सूर्यताप के कारण भूरी त्वचा वाला *Although I often sunbathe, I never seem to* ***go brown.***

**brown[2]** /braʊn ब्राउन्/ *verb* [I, T] to become or make sth become brown भूरा हो जाना या कर देना *Brown the meat in a frying pan.*

**brownie** /ˈbraʊni ˈब्राउनि/ *noun* [C] a type of heavy chocolate cake that often contains nuts गिरीयुक्त बड़ा चॉकलेट केक

**brownish** /ˈbraʊnɪʃ ˈब्राउनिश्/ *adj.* fairly brown काफ़ी भूरा, भूरा-रती *She has brownish eyes.*

**browse** /braʊz ब्राउज़्/ *verb* **1** [I] to spend time pleasantly, looking round a shop, without a clear idea of what you are looking for क्या ख़रीदा जाए यह निश्चित न होने पर भी किसी दुकान में मस्ती से घूम कर समय बिताना *I spent hours browsing in the local bookshop.* **2** [I] **browse through sth** to look through a book or magazine without reading every part or studying it carefully पुस्तक या पत्रिका के पृष्ठों पर सरसरी नज़र डालना *I enjoyed browsing through the catalogue but I didn't order anything.* **3** [T] (*computing*) to look for and read information on a computer कंप्यूटर पर अभीष्ट जानकारी खोजना और उसे पढ़ना *I've just been browsing the Internet for information on Lakshadweep Islands.* ▶ **browse** *noun* [*sing.*] वस्तुओं पर सरसरी नज़र डालने की क्रिया, कंप्यूटर पर जानकारी खोजने और उसे पढ़ने की क्रिया; ग्रंथावलोकन; ग्रंथावलोकन

**browser** /ˈbraʊzə(r) ˈब्राउज़(र्)/ *noun* [C] (*computing*) a computer program that lets you look at words and pictures from other computer systems by receiving information through telephone wires एक कंप्यूटर प्रोग्राम जो टेलीफ़ोन तारों के जरिए अन्य कंप्यूटर तंत्रों के चित्र आदि दिखा सकता है *an Internet browser*

**bruise** /bruːz ब्रूज़्/ *noun* [C] a blue, brown or purple mark that appears on the skin after sb has fallen, been hit, etc. चोट के कारण त्वचा पर उभरा नीला-भूरा निशान; गुमटा, गुम्मट **NOTE** आँख पर हुए गुमटे को **black eye** कहते हैं। ▶ **bruise** *verb* [I, T] चोट लगने के कारण त्वचा पर नीला-भूरा निशान उभरना *I fell over and bruised my arm.* ○ *Handle the fruit carefully or you'll bruise it.*

**brunch** /brʌntʃ ब्रन्च्/ *noun* [C, U] (*informal*) a meal that you eat in the late morning as a combination of breakfast and lunch नाश्ते और दोपहर के खाने के मिश्रण के रूप में देर सुबह खाया जाने वाला भोजन; ब्रंच

**brunette** /bruːˈnet ब्रूˈनेट्/ *noun* [C] a white woman with dark brown hair गहरे भूरे बालों वाली श्वेत जाति की महिला ➪ **blonde** देखिए।

**brunt** /brʌnt ब्रन्ट्/ *noun*

**IDM** **bear the brunt of sth** ➪ **bear[2]** देखिए।

**brush[1]** /brʌʃ ब्रश्/ *noun* **1** [C] an object that is used for cleaning things, painting, tidying your hair, etc. ब्रश, ब्रुश, कूची, तूलिका *I took a brush and swept the dry leaves from the lawn.* ○ *a toothbrush* ○ *a paintbrush* ○ *a hairbrush* **2** [*sing.*] an act of cleaning, tidying the hair, etc. with a brush ब्रश से साफ़ करने, बाल बनाने आदि की क्रिया *The floor needs a brush.*

**IDM** **(have) a brush with sb/sth** (to have or almost have) an unpleasant meeting with sb/sth (किसी के साथ) भिंड़त होना

**brush[2]** /brʌʃ ब्रश्/ *verb* **1** [T] to clean, tidy, etc. sth with a brush ब्रश से साफ़ करना, सँवारना *Make sure you* ***brush*** *your* ***teeth*** *twice a day.* ○ ***Brush*** *your* ***hair*** *before you go out.* ➪ **clean[2]** पर नोट देखिए। **2** [I, T] to touch sb/sth lightly when passing चलते-चलते किसी को हलके-से स्पर्श करना *Leaves brushed against the car as we drove along the narrow road.*

**PHR V** **brush sb/sth aside** **1** to refuse to pay attention to sb/sth किसी की अपेक्षा करना; महत्त्व देने से इनकार करना *She brushed aside the protests and continued with the meeting.* **2** to push past sb/sth धक्का देते हुए निकल जाना *He hurried through the crowd, brushing aside the reporters who tried to stop him.*

**brush sth off (sth)/away** to remove sth with a brush or with the hand, as if using a brush ब्रश से या हाथ से कुछ (गंदगी आदि) हटाना *I brushed the dust off my jacket.*

**brush sth up/brush up on sth** to study or practise sth in order to get back knowledge or skill that you had before and have lost पूर्व में प्राप्त ज्ञान या कौशल को ताज़ा करना *She took a course to brush up her Spanish.*

**brush-off** *noun*

**IDM** **give sb the brush-off** to refuse to be friendly to sb मित्रतापूर्ण व्यवहार करने को तैयार न होना

**brusque** /bru:sk ब्रूस्क् / *adj.* using very few words and sounding rude कम शब्दों का प्रयोग करते हुए अशिष्ट व रूखा (व्यवहार, कथन आदि) *He gave a brusque 'No comment!' and walked off.* ▶ **brusquely** *adv.* अशिष्टता और रूखेपन से

**brutal** /ˈbru:tl ˈब्रूट्ल् / *adj.* very cruel and/or violent अति क्रूर और/या हिंसापूर्ण; पाशविक *a brutal murder* ○ *a brutal dictatorship* ▶ **brutally** /-təli -टलि/ *adv.* क्रूरता से; निर्दयता के साथ *He was brutally honest and told her that he didn't love her any more.*

**brutality** /bru:ˈtæləti ब्रूˈटैलटि / *noun* [C, U] (*pl.* **brutalities**) very cruel and violent behaviour क्रूर और हिंसापूर्ण व्यवहार, नृशंस आचरण, क्रूरता, बर्बरता

**brute**[1] /bru:t ब्रूट् / *noun* [C] **1** a cruel, violent man क्रूर, नृशंस व्यक्ति **2** a large strong animal बड़े आकार का शक्तिशाली पशु

**brute**[2] /bru:t ब्रूट् / *adj.* (*only before a noun*) using strength to do sth rather than thinking about it सीधे बल प्रयोग द्वारा न कि सोच-विचार के बाद *I think you'll have to use **brute force** to get this window open.*

**brutish** /ˈbru:tɪʃ ˈब्रूटिश् / *adj.* cruel and unpleasant क्रूरतापूर्ण और अप्रियकर; नृशंसतापूर्ण

**BSc** /ˌbi: es ˈsi: ˌबी एस् ˈसी / *abbr.* Bachelor of Science; the degree that you receive when you complete a university or college course in a science subject 'Bachelor of Science' का संक्षिप्त रूप; विज्ञान स्नातक ➪ **BA** और **MSc** देखिए।

**BSE** /ˌbi: es ˈi: ˌबी एस् ˈई / *abbr.* (*informal* **mad cow disease**) *noun* [U] bovine spongiform encephalopathy; a disease of cows which affects their brains and usually kills them, 'bovine spongiform encephalopathy' का संक्षिप्त रूप; गायों को होने वाला एक घातक मस्तिष्क-रोग ➪ **CJD** देखिए।

**bubble**[1] /ˈbʌbl बबल् / *noun* [C] a ball of air or gas, in liquid or floating in the air बुलबुला, बुदबुदा, बुल्ला *We knew where there were fish because of the bubbles on the surface.*

**bubble**[2] /ˈbʌbl बबल् / *verb* [I] **1** to produce bubbles or to rise with bubbles बुलबुलाना, बुदबुदाना, खदबदाना *Cook the pizza until the cheese starts to bubble.* ○ *The clear water bubbled up out of the ground.* **2 bubble (over) (with sth)** to be full of happy feelings ख़ुशी से फूला न समाना

**bubble bath** *noun* [U] a liquid that you can add to the water in a bath to produce a mass of white bubbles स्नान के जल में मिलाया जाने वाला द्रव जिससे जल में सफ़ेद बुलबुले बन जाते हैं

**bubblegum** /ˈbʌblgʌm ˈबब्लगम् / *noun* [U] a sticky sweet that you eat but do not swallow and that can be blown into bubbles out of the mouth चूसने की चिपचिपी गोली; बबलगम ➪ **chewing gum** देखिए।

**bubbly** /ˈbʌbli ˈबब्लि / *adj.* **1** full of bubbles बुलबुलेदार **2** (used about a person) happy and full of energy (व्यक्ति) ख़ुशी, उत्साह व चुस्ती से भरपूर

**buck**[1] /bʌk बक् / *noun* [C] **1** (*informal*) a US dollar एक अमेरिकी डालर *Could you lend me a few bucks?* **2** (*pl.* **buck** or **bucks**) the male of certain types of animal (**rabbits** and **deer**) कुछ पशुओं के नर प्राणी (नर-हिरण, नर-ख़रगोश) ➪ **deer** पर नोट देखिए।

**IDM** **pass the buck** ➪ **pass**[1] देखिए।

**buck**[2] /bʌk बक् / *verb* [I] (used about a horse) to jump into the air or to kick the back legs in the air (घोड़े या गधे का) दुलत्ती झाड़ना

**PHR V** **buck (sb/sth) up** (*informal*) to feel or to make sb feel better or happier आनंदित होना या करना; मनोदशा सुधारना *Drink this—it'll buck you up.* ○ *Unless you buck your ideas up* (= become more sensible and serious) *you'll never pass the exam.*

**bucket** /ˈbʌkɪt ˈबकिट् / *noun* [C] **1** a round, open container, usually made of metal or plastic, with a handle, that is used for carrying sth बालटी, डोर **2** (*also* **bucketful**) the amount that a bucket contains बालटीभर मात्रा *How many buckets of water do you think we'll need?*

**IDM** **a drop in the bucket** ➪ **drop**[2] देखिए।

**buckle[1]** /ˈbʌkl ˈबकल् / *noun* [C] a piece of metal or plastic at the end of a belt or strap that is used for fastening it बेल्ट पेटी पर बाँधने का बकलस; बकसुआ ➪ **button** पर चित्र देखिए।

**buckle[2]** /ˈbʌkl ˈबकल् / *verb* [I, T] **1** to fasten or be fastened with a buckle बकलस लगाना या बकलस से बाँधना **2** to become crushed or bent because of heat, force, weakness, etc. ताप, दबाव, कमज़ोरी आदि के कारण झुक जाना, क्षतिग्रस्त हो जाना *Some railway lines buckled in the heat.*

**buckwheat** /ˈbʌkwiːt ˈबक्वीट् / *noun* [U] a type of grain that is small and dark and that is grown as food for animals and for making flour एक प्रकार का अनाज जिसके दाने छोटे आकार और गहरे रंग के होते हैं और जिसका प्रयोग चारे और आटा बनाने के लिए किया जाता है; कूटू

**bud** /bʌd बड् / *noun* [C] a small lump on a tree or plant that opens and develops into a flower or leaf कली, अधखिला फूल *rosebuds* ➪ **flower** पर चित्र देखिए।

IDM **nip sth in the bud** ➪ **nip** देखिए।

**Buddhism** *noun* [U] an Asian religion that was started in India by Buddha बौद्ध धर्म

**Buddhist** *noun* [C] a person whose religion is Buddhism बौद्ध धर्म का अनुयायी ▶ **Buddhist** *adj.* बौद्ध *a Buddhist temple*

**budding** /ˈbʌdɪŋ ˈबडिङ् / *adj.* (*only before a noun*) wanting or starting to develop and be successful उभरता हुआ, उदीयमान *Have you got any tips for budding young photographers?*

**buddy** /ˈbʌdi ˈबडि / *noun* [C] (*pl.* **buddies**) (*informal*) a friend, especially a male friend of a man मित्र, विशेषतः किसी पुरुष का पुरुष मित्र

**budge** /bʌdʒ बज् / *verb* [I, T] **1** to move or make sth move a little किसी व्यक्ति या वस्तु का मामूली-सा हिलना; किसी व्यक्ति या वस्तु को हिलाना; सरकना; सरकाना *We just couldn't budge the car when it got stuck in the mud.* **2** to change or make sb change a firm opinion दृढ़ विचार को बदलना या बदलवाना *Neither side in the dispute is prepared to budge.*

**budgerigar** /ˈbʌdʒərigɑː(r) ˈबजरिगा(र्) / (*informal* **budgie**) *noun* [C] a small, brightly coloured bird that people often keep as a pet in a cage एक छोटा चमकीले रंग का पालतू पक्षी

**budget[1]** /ˈbʌdʒɪt ˈबजिट् / *noun* [C, U] **1** a plan of how to spend an amount of money over a particular period of time; the amount of money that is mentioned व्यवस्थाबद्ध ख़र्च की योजना; बजट, आय-व्यय पत्र; ख़र्च के लिए उल्लेखित या उपलब्ध राशि *The work was finished on time and* ***within budget.*** ○ *The builders are already 20%* ***over budget.*** **2** (*also* **Budget**) a statement by a government saying how much money it plans to spend on particular things in the next year and how it plans to collect money सरकार का वार्षिक बजट (प्रायः राशी संग्रह और व्यय के लिए) *Do you think taxes will go up in this year's budget?*

**budget[2]** /ˈbʌdʒɪt ˈबजिट् / *verb* [I, T] **budget (sth)** (**for sth**) to plan carefully how much money to spend on sth कार्य विशेष या प्रयोजन के लिए बजट बनाना *The government has budgeted Rs 100 crore for primary education.*

**budget[3]** /ˈbʌdʒɪt ˈबजिट् / *adj.* (*informal*) (used in advertisements) very cheap बहुत सस्ता (विज्ञापनों में प्रयुक्त) *budget holidays*

**budgetary** /ˈbʌdʒɪtəri ˈबजिटरि / *adj.* connected with plans for how to spend money during a particular period of time अवधि-विशेष के बजट से संबंधित

**budgie** /ˈbʌdʒi ˈबजि / (*informal*) = **budgerigar**

**buff** /bʌf बफ़् / *noun* [C] (*informal*) a person who knows a lot about a particular subject and is very interested in it किसी विषय का जानकार और शौक़ीन व्यक्ति *a film/computer buff*

**buffalo** /ˈbʌfələʊ ˈबफ़लो / *noun* [C] (*pl.* **buffalo** or **buffaloes**) **1** a large wild animal that lives in Africa and Asia that looks like a cow with long curved horns भैंस, भैंसा *a herd of buffalo* **2** = **bison** ➪ **water buffalo** देखिए।

**buffer** /ˈbʌfə(r) ˈबफ़(र्) / *noun* [C] **1** a thing or person that reduces the unpleasant effects of sth or prevents violent contact between two things, people, etc. किसी घटना आदि के दुष्प्रभाव को कम करने या दो व्यक्तियों, वस्तुओं के बीच टकराव को रोकने वाला व्यक्ति या वस्तु; प्रतिरोधक, बफ़र *UN forces are acting as a buffer between the two sides in the war.* **2** a flat round piece of metal with a spring behind it that is on the front or back of a train or at the end of a railway track. Buffers reduce the shock when sth hits them रेल के आगे, पीछे या रेलवे ट्रैक के अंत में लगा यंत्र जो टक्कर या झटकों के प्रभाव को कम करता है; बफ़र

**buffet[1]** /ˈbʊfeɪ ˈबुफ़े / *noun* [C] **1** a meal (usually at a party or a special occasion) at which food is placed on a long table and people serve themselves ऐसा भोजन जिसमें मेहमान स्वयं खाना परोसते हैं *Lunch was a cold buffet.* ○ *a buffet lunch* **2** part of a train where passengers can buy food and drinks; a cafe at a station रेलगाड़ी का वह भाग जहाँ भोज्य और पेय पदार्थ बिकते हैं; स्टेशन पर का छोटा रेस्तराँ या उपहार-कक्ष

**buffet[2]** /ˈbʌfɪt ˈबफ़िट्/ *verb* [T] to knock or push sth in a rough way from side to side दोनों ओर धक्का देना, धकेलना *The boat was buffeted by the rough sea.*

**bug[1]** /bʌg बग्/ *noun* **1** [C] any small insect कोई छोटा कीड़ा **2** [C] an illness that is not very serious and that people get from each other संक्रामक रोग जो गंभीर न हो *I don't feel very well—I think I've got the bug that's going round.* **3** [C] something wrong in a system or machine, especially a computer किसी यंत्र (विशेषतः कंप्यूटर) में आई ख़राबी *There's a bug in the software.* **4** [C] a very small device (**microphone**) that is hidden and secretly records people's conversations लोगों की बातचीत को चुपके-से रिकार्ड करने के लिए लगाया गया छोटा-सा गुप्त माइक्रोफ़ोन

**bug[2]** /bʌg बग्/ *verb* [T] (**bugging; bugged**) **1** to hide a very small device (**microphone**) somewhere so that people's conversations can be recorded secretly गुप्त माइक्रोफ़ोन को चोरी-छिपे लगा देना *Be careful what you say. This room is bugged.* **2** (*informal*) to annoy or worry sb किसी को परेशान या चिंतित करना

**build[1]** /bɪld बिल्ड्/ *verb* (*pt, pp* **built** /bɪlt बिल्ट्/) **1** [T] to make sth by putting pieces, materials, etc. together बनाना, निर्माण करना *They've built a new bridge across the river.* ○ *The house is built of stone.* **2** [I] to use land for building on निर्माण-कार्य के लिए भूमि का प्रयोग करना *There's plenty of land to build on around here.* **3** [T] to develop or increase sth विकास या वृद्धि करना *The government is trying to build a more modern society.* ○ *This book claims to help people to build their self-confidence.*

**PHR V build sth in/on; build sth into/onto sth** to make sth a part of sth else एक वस्तु को दूसरी वस्तु का अंग बनाना *We're planning to build two more rooms onto the back of the house.*

**build on sth** to use sth as a base from which you can make further progress उन्नति करने के लिए किसी को आधार के रूप में प्रयोग करना *Now that we're beginning to make a profit, we must build on this success.*

**build sth on sth** to base sth on sth किसी वस्तु को आधार बनाना *a society built on the principle of freedom and democracy*

**build up (to sth)** to become greater in amount or number; to increase मात्रा में बढ़ना; में बढ़ोतरी होना; की वृद्धि होना *The traffic starts to build up at this time of day.*

**build sth up 1** to make sth seem more important or greater than it really is वास्तविक से अधिक बड़ा या महत्त्वपूर्ण बना देना *I don't think it's a very serious matter, it's just been built up in the newspapers.* **2** to increase or develop sth over a period समयावधि में बढ़ना या विकसित होना *You'll need to build up your strength again slowly after the operation.*

**build[2]** /bɪld बिल्ड्/ *noun* [C, U] the shape and size of sb's body शरीर का आकार और आकृति; शरीर का गठन *She **has a** very athletic **build**.*

> **NOTE** शब्द **build** की तुलना शब्द **figure** से करिए। **Build** का प्रयोग सामान्यतः किसी व्यक्ति का आकार दर्शाने के लिए किया जाता है और इसका संबंध उस व्यक्ति के बल और मांसपेशी से होता है। इस शब्द का प्रयोग पुरुष और स्त्री दोनों के लिए किया जा सकता है। **Figure** सामान्यतः आकृति और उसकी आकर्षकता दर्शाता है और इस शब्द का प्रयोग सामान्यतया केवल स्त्रियों के लिए किया जाता है।

**builder** /ˈbɪldə(r) ˈबिल्ड(र्)/ *noun* [C] a person whose job is to build houses and other buildings भवन-निर्माता

**building** /ˈbɪldɪŋ ˈबिल्डिङ्/ *noun* **1** [C] a structure, such as a house, shop or school, that has a roof and walls भवन, इमारत *There are a lot of very old buildings in this town.* **2** [U] the process or business of making buildings भवन-निर्माण की प्रक्रिया या व्यवसाय *building materials* ○ *the building industry*

**building site** *noun* [C] an area of land on which a building is being built भवन-निर्माण का स्थल

**building society** *noun* [C] an organization like a bank with which people can save money and which lends money to people who want to buy a house भवन-निर्माण के लिए गठित संस्था (जो बचत खाता खोलने और ऋण की व्यवस्था करती है)

**build-up** *noun* [C, *usually sing.*] **1 a build-up (of sth)** an increase of sth over a period समयावधि में हुई वृद्धि *The build-up of tension in the area has made war seem more likely.* **2 a build-up (to sth)** a period of preparation or excitement before an event किसी घटना से पूर्व की तैयारी की अवधि या उत्तेजना भरी अवधि *The players started to get nervous in the build-up to the big game.*

**-built** /bɪlt -बिल्ट्/ (*used to form compound adjectives*) having a body with the shape and size mentioned किसी विशेष आकार और आकृति में ढला शरीर *a tall well-built man*

**built-in** *adj.* that is a part of sth and cannot be removed अंतरंग (भाग) जिसे निकाला या हटाया न जा सके *built-in cupboards*

**built-up** *adj.* covered with buildings निर्मित भवनों से आच्छादित *a built-up area*

**bulb** /bʌlb बल्ब्/ *noun* [C] **1** (*also* **light bulb**) the glass part of an electric lamp that gives out light बिजली के लैंप का शीशे वाला हिस्सा जिसमें से प्रकाश फैलता है *The bulb's gone* (= it no longer works) *in this lamp.* **2** the round root of certain plants कुछ पौधों की गोल जड़, कंद *a tulip bulb* ➪ **flower** पर चित्र देखिए।

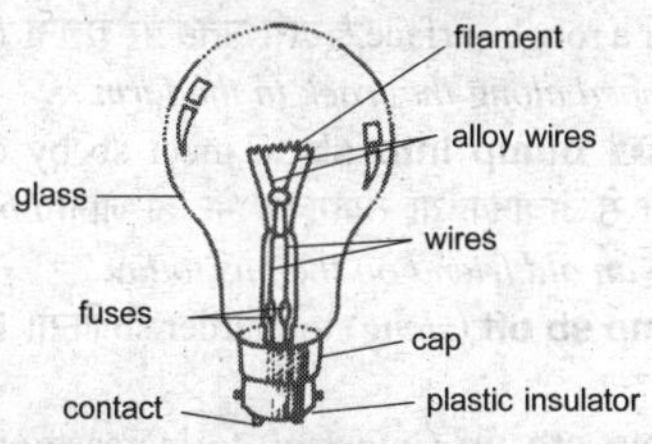

**light bulb**

**bulbous** /ˈbʌlbəs ˈबल्बस्/ *adj.* fat, round and ugly मोटा, गोल और भद्दा *a bulbous red nose*

**bulbul** *noun* [C] a small lively tropical songbird with a **crest** on its head that is usually found in Africa and Asia. It is also called the Indian Nightingale (अफ़्रीका तथा ऐशिया में पाए जाने वाला) कलगी वाला गायक पक्षी; बुलबुल

**bulge[1]** /bʌldʒ बल्ज्/ *noun* [C] a round lump that sticks out on sth बाहर की तरफ निकलता हुआ भाग, सूजन, उभार

**bulge[2]** /bʌldʒ बल्ज्/ *verb* [I] **1** to stick out in a lump from sth that is usually flat सामान्यतः चपटी वस्तु में उभार आना; उभारना, फूलना, सूजना *My stomach is starting to bulge. I must get more exercise.* **2 bulge (with sth)** to be full of sth किसी वस्तु से भर जाना *His bags were bulging with presents for the children.*

**bulging** /ˈbʌldʒɪŋ ˈबल्जिङ्/ *adj.* **1** sticking out बाहर को उभरता हुआ *He had a thin face and rather bulging eyes.* **2** very full ठसा-ठस भरा हुआ *She came home with bulging bags.*

**bulimia** /buˈlɪmiə; बुˈलिमिआ/ (*also* **bulimia nervosa** /buˌlɪmiə nɜːˈvəʊsə बुˌलिमिआ नˈव़ोसा/) *noun* [U] an illness in which a person keeps eating too much and then making himself/herself vomit in order to control his/her weight रोग जिसमें रोगी अपनी आहार मात्रा पर संयम नहीं रख पाता और फिर वज़न पर नियंत्रण रखने के लिए स्वयं को वमन कराता है; क्षुधातिशयता ➪ **anorexia** देखिए।
▶ **bulimic** /buˈlɪmɪk बुˈलिमिक्/ *adj., noun* [C] इस रोग से संबंधित या ग्रस्त

**bulk** /bʌlk बल्क्/ *noun* **1 the bulk (of sth)** [*sing.*] the main part of sth; most of sth किसी वस्तु का मुख्य भाग; अधिकांश या अधिकतर भाग *The bulk of the work has been done, so we should finish this week.* **2** [U] the size, quantity or weight of sth large किसी बड़ी वस्तु का आकार, मात्रा या भार *The cupboard isn't especially heavy—it's its bulk that makes it hard to move.* ○ *He slowly lifted his vast bulk out of the chair.*
IDM **in bulk** in large quantities बड़ी मात्रा में *If you buy in bulk, it's 10% cheaper.*

**bulky** /ˈbʌlki ˈबल्कि/ *adj.* large and heavy and therefore difficult to move or carry भारी-भरकम

**bull** /bʊl बुल्/ *noun* [C] **1** an adult male of the cow family साँड ➪ **cow** पर नोट देखिए। **2** the male of the elephant, **whale** and some other large animals हाथी, आदि बड़े प्राणियों का नर **3** (in business) a person who buys shares in a company, hoping to sell them soon afterwards at a higher price (व्यापार में) व्यक्ति जो किसी कंपनी के शेयर इस आशा से ख़रीदता है कि वह उन्हें जल्द ऊँचे दामों पर बेच देगा *a bull market* (= in which prices are rising) ➪ **bear[1] 2** देखिए।

**bulldog** /ˈbʊldɒg ˈबुलडॉग्/ *noun* [C] a strong dog with short legs, a large head and a short, thick neck छोटी टाँगों, बड़े सिर व मोटी गरदन वाला शक्तिशाली कुत्ता; बुलडॉग

**Bulldog clip™** *noun* [C] a metal device for holding papers together काग़ज़ों को साथ रखने में प्रयुक्त धातु से बना साधन ➪ **stationery** पर चित्र देखिए।

**bulldoze** /ˈbʊldəʊz ˈबुलडोज़्/ *verb* [T] to make ground flat or knock down a building with a bulldozer बुलडोजर द्वारा भूमि को समतल करना या इमारत को गिराना *The old buildings were bulldozed and new ones were built.*

**bulldozer** /ˈbʊldəʊzə(r) ˈबुलडोज़(र्)/ *noun* [C] a large, powerful vehicle with a broad piece of metal at the front, used for clearing ground or knocking down buildings भूमि को समतल बनाने या इमारतें गिराने वाली एक बड़ी शक्तिशाली मशीन जिसके अग्र भाग पर बड़ा चपटा धातु का उपकरण लगा होता है; बुलडोज़र

**bullet** /ˈbʊlɪt ˈबुलिट्/ *noun* [C] a small metal object that is fired from a gun (बंदूक़ की) गोली *The bullet hit her in the arm.* ○ *a bullet wound*

**bulletin** /ˈbʊlətɪn ˈबुलटिन्/ *noun* [C] **1** a short news report on television or radio; an official statement about a situation टेलीविज़न या रेडियो पर प्रसारित समाचार; किसी स्थिति पर आधिकारिक विवरण *The next **news bulletin** is at nine o'clock.* **2** a short newspaper that a club or an organization produces किसी क्लब या संस्था द्वारा प्रकाशित लघु समाचार-पत्रिका

**bulletin board** (*AmE*) = **noticeboard**

**bulletproof** /ˈbʊlɪtpruːf ˈबुलिट्प्रूफ़/ *adj.* made of a strong material that stops bullets from passing through it बंदूक़ की गोली पार न होने देने वाले मज़बूत पदार्थ से बना; बुलेटप्रूफ़

**bullfight** /ˈbʊlfaɪt ˈबुल्फ़ाइट्/ *noun* [C] a traditional public entertainment, especially in Spain, Portugal and Latin America, in which a man fights and kills a **bull** आदमी की साँड़ से लड़ाई का पारंपरिक खेल, स्पेन, पुर्तगाल और दक्षिण अमेरिकी देशों में लोकप्रिय है; बुलफ़ाइट ▶ **bullfighter** *noun* [C] इस खेल में भाग लेने वाला आदमी ▶ **bullfighting** *noun* [U] आदमी की साँड़ से लड़ाई का खेल

**bullion** /ˈbʊliən ˈबुलिअन्/ *noun* [U] bars of gold or silver सोने या चाँदी की छड़ें

**bullock** /ˈbʊlək ˈबुलक्/ *noun* [C] a young **bull** that has been **castrated** बैल

**bull's-eye** *noun* [C] the centre of a round object (**target**) that you shoot or throw things at in certain sports, or a shot that hits this एक गोल वस्तु का केंद्रबिंदु जहाँ निशाना लगाते हैं

**bully¹** /ˈbʊli ˈबुलि/ *noun* [C] (*pl.* **bullies**) a person who uses his/her strength or power to hurt or frighten people who are weaker अपने से कमज़ोर व्यक्ति पर धौंस या रोब जमाने वाला व्यक्ति; दबंग

**bully²** /ˈbʊli ˈबुलि/ *verb* [T] (*pres. part.* **bullying;** *3rd person sing. pres.* **bullies;** *pt, pp* **bullied**) **bully sb (into doing sth)** to use your strength or power to hurt or frighten sb who is weaker or to make him/her do sth अपने से कमज़ोर को धमकाकर कोई कार्य करवाना; उस पर रोब जमाना *Don't try to bully me into making a decision.* ▶ **bullying** *noun* [U] स्वयं से कमजोर व्यक्ति को डराने धमकाने की क्रिया *Bullying is a serious problem in many schools.*

**bum** /bʌm बम्/ *noun* [C] (*informal*) **1** (*BrE*) the part of your body on which you sit; bottom नितंब **2** an insulting word for a person who lives on the street सड़क पर रहने वाले व्यक्ति के लिए प्रयुक्त अपमानजनक शब्द **3** a lazy or useless person सुस्त या बेकार आदमी *a lazy bum*

**bumbag** /ˈbʌmbæg ˈबम्बैग्/ (*AmE* **fanny pack**) *noun* [C] (*informal*) a small bag worn around the waist to keep money, etc. in कमर पर बाँधा जाने वाला छोटा बैग जिसमें पैसे आदि रखे जाते हैं

**bumblebee** /ˈbʌmblbiː ˈबम्ब्ल्बी/ *noun* [C] a large hairy bee that makes a loud noise as it flies भौंरा ➪ **insect** पर चित्र देखिए।

**bump¹** /bʌmp बम्प्/ *verb* **1** [I] **bump against/into sb/sth to hit sb/sth** by accident when you are moving गति में रहते हुए किसी से टकराना *She bumped into a lamp post because she wasn't looking where she was going.* **2** [T] **bump sth (against/on sth)** to hit sth against or on sth by accident किसी से अचानक [illegible] जाना *I bumped my knee on the edge of the table.* **3** [I] to move along over a rough surface खुरदरी सतह पर चलना *The car bumped along the track to the farm.*

**PHR V** **bump into sb** to meet sb by chance किसी से अचानक या संयोगवश भेंट हो जाना *I bumped into an old friend on the bus today.*

**bump sb off** (*slang*) to murder sb किसी की हत्या कर देना

**bump sth up** (*informal*) to increase or make sth go up बढ़ना या बढ़ाना *All this publicity will bump up the sales of our new product.*

**bump²** /bʌmp बम्प्/ *noun* [C] **1** the action or sound of sth hitting a hard surface कड़ी सतह से टकराने की क्रिया या उससे उत्पन्न आवाज़ *She fell and hit the ground with a bump.* **2** a lump on the body, often caused by a hit चोट से बना गुमड़ा **3** a part of a surface that is higher than the rest of it किसी सतह का उभरा हुआ भाग *There are a lot of bumps in the road, so drive carefully.*

**bumper¹** /ˈbʌmpə(r) ˈबम्प(र्)/ *noun* [C] the bar fixed to the front and back of a motor vehicle to protect it if it hits sth टक्कर के प्रभाव से बचाव के लिए वाहन आदि के आगे-पीछे लगी पट्टी; बंपर, टक्कर-रोक

**bumper²** /ˈbʌmpə(r) ˈबम्प(र्)/ *adj.* larger than usual सामान्य से अधिक, भरा-पूरा *The unusually fine weather has produced a bumper harvest this year.*

**bumpy** /ˈbʌmpi ˈबम्पि/ *adj.* not flat or smooth ऊबड़-खाबड़ *a bumpy road* ○ *Because of the stormy weather, it was a very bumpy flight.* ✪ विलोम **smooth**

**bun** /bʌn बन्/ *noun* [C] **1** a small round sweet cake छोटा गोल मीठा केक; बन *a currant bun* **2** a small soft bread roll छोटा नरम ब्रेड रौल *a hamburger bun* **3** hair fastened tightly into a round shape at the back of the head बन के आकार का केशविन्यास; जूड़ा *She wears her hair **in a bun**.*

**bunch¹** /bʌntʃ बन्च्/ *noun* **1** [C] a number of things, usually of the same type, fastened or growing together एक ही प्रकार की वस्तुओं का गुच्छा

*a bunch of flowers* ○ *a bunch of bananas/grapes* ○ *a bunch of keys* **2 bunches** [*pl.*] long hair that is tied on each side of the head सिर के दोनों ओर बँधे लंबे बाल **3** [C, *with sing. or pl. verb*] (*informal*) a group of people व्यक्तियों का समूह, टोली *My colleagues are the best bunch of people I've ever worked with.*

**bunch**[2] /bʌntʃ बन्च्/ *verb* [I, T] **bunch (sth/sb) (up/together)** to stay together in a group; to form sth into a group or bunch दल या टोली बनकर जमे रहना; समूह या गुच्छा बनाना *The runners bunched up as they came round the final bend.* ○ *He kept his papers bunched together in his hand.*

**bund** *noun* [C] (*IndE*) any artificial embankment, dam or a barrier made of earth built across a river or stream to prevent flooding कोई भी कृत्रिम तटबंधन, बाँध या नदी पर बनी मिट्टी की रोधिका जिससे बाढ़ से बचाव होता है

**bundle**[1] /ˈbʌndl ˈबन्ड्ल्/ *noun* [C] a number of things tied or folded together पोटली, पुलिंदा, गठरी बंडल *a bundle of letters with an elastic band round them*

**bundle**[2] /ˈbʌndl ˈबन्ड्ल्/ *verb* [T] **1 bundle sth (up)** to make or tie a number of things together गठरी में एक साथ बाँधना, पुलिंदा बनाना *I bundled up the old newspapers and threw them away.* **2** to put or push sb or sth quickly and in a rough way in a particular direction दिशा-विशेष में झटके से डालना या ढकेलना *He was arrested and bundled into a police car.*

**bundobust** (*also* **bandobast**) *noun* [U] (*IndE*) arrangements or organization विस्तृत व्यवस्था या संगठन; बंदोबस्त

**bung**[1] /bʌŋ बङ्/ *noun* [C] a round piece of wood or rubber that is used for closing the hole in some types of container (**a barrel** or **a jar**) किसी पात्र के मुँह को बंद करने में प्रयुक्त रबड़ या कार्क का डाट

**bung**[2] /bʌŋ बङ्/ *verb* [T] (*informal*) to put or throw sth somewhere in a rough or careless way लापरवाही से वस्तुओं को फेंक देना

**bungalow** /ˈbʌŋgələʊ ˈबङ्गलो/ *noun* [C] a house that is all on one level, without stairs एक-मंजिला मकान; बंगला

**bungee jumping** /ˈbʌndʒi dʒʌmpɪŋ ˈबन्जि जम्पिङ्/ *noun* [U] a sport in which you jump from a high place, for example a bridge, with a thick elastic rope tied round your feet एक खेल जिसमें व्यक्ति मोटी लचीली रस्सी पैरों में बाँधकर पुल जैसी ऊँची जगह से छलाँग लगाता है; बंजी जम्पिंग

**bungle** /ˈbʌŋgl ˈबङ्गल्/ *verb* [I, T] to do sth badly or fail to do sth कोई कार्य भद्दे ढंग से करना; गड़बड़ कर देना, बिगाड़ देना; कुछ करने में असफल होना *a bungled robbery*

**bunk** /bʌŋk बङ्क्/ *noun* [C] **1** a bed that is fixed to a wall, for example on a ship or train जहाज़ या रेलगाड़ी में दीवार में लगी शय्या, शायिका **2 bunk bed** one of a pair of single beds built as a unit with one above the other एक-के-ऊपर एक लगी अकेली शय्याएँ

IDM **do a bunk** (*informal*) to run away or escape; to leave without telling anyone भाग निकलना; चुपके-से सरक जाना

**bunker** /ˈbʌŋkə(r) ˈबङ्क(र्)/ *noun* [C] **1** a strong underground building that gives protection in a war युद्ध में रक्षा के लिए ज़मीन के नीचे बनी मज़बूत इमारत; तलघर, बंकर **2** a hole filled with sand on a golf course गोल्फ़ के मैदान में बालू से भरा छेद

**bunny** /ˈbʌni ˈबनि/ *noun* [C] (*pl.* **bunnies**) (used by and to small children) a rabbit (बच्चों के लिए या बच्चों द्वारा प्रयुक्त शब्द) ख़रगोश

**Bunsen burner** /ˌbʌnsn ˈbɜːnə(r) ˌबन्सन् ˈबन(र्)/ *noun* [C] an instrument used in scientific work that produces a hot gas flame वैज्ञानिक प्रयोगों में प्रयुक्त उपकरण जिसमें से गरम गैस की लपट निकलती है; बन्सेन-ज्वलक ⇨ **laboratory** पर चित्र देखिए।

**buoy**[1] /bɔɪ बॉइ/ *noun* [C] a floating object, fastened to the bottom of the sea or a river, that shows the places where it is dangerous for boats to go ख़तरनाक स्थानों के बारे में नावों को चेतावनी देने वाली तैरती हुई वस्तु जो समुद्र या नदी के तल पर बँधी होती है

**buoy**[2] /bɔɪ बॉइ/ *verb* [T] **buoy sb/sth (up)** **1** to keep sb happy and confident किसी को प्रसन्न रखना और उसका आत्मविश्वास बढ़ाना *His encouragement buoyed her up during that difficult period.* **2** to keep sth at a high level ऊँचे स्तर पर रखना *Share prices were buoyed by the news of a takeover.*

**buoyant** /ˈbɔɪənt ˈबॉइअन्ट्/ *adj.* **1** (used about a material) floating or able to float or able to keep things floating (पदार्थ) उतराता हुआ या उतरा सकने वाला (वस्तु), तरणशील **2** happy and confident प्रसन्न तथा विश्वासपूर्ण *The team were in buoyant mood after their win.* **3** (used about prices, business activity, etc.) staying at a high level or increasing, so that people make more money क़ीमतों, व्यापारिक गतिविधियों आदि का निरंतर बढ़ती या ऊँचे स्तर पर रहना, ताकि सभी लोग धन अर्जित कर सकें

▶ **buoyancy** /-ənsi -अन्सि/ *noun* [U] उतराने की शक्ति; उत्प्लावन; क़ीमतों, व्यापार आदि में तेज़ी का रुख़-प्रफुल्लता *the buoyancy of the state's economy*

**burden**[1] /ˈbɜːdn ˈबड्न्/ *noun* [C] **1** something that is heavy and difficult to carry बोझा, वज़न **2** a responsibility or difficult task that causes a lot of work or worry अवांछित दायित्व या कार्य

**burden**[2] /ˈbɜːdn ˈबड्न्/ *verb* [T] **burden sb/yourself (with sth)** to give sb/yourself a res- ponsibility or task that causes a lot of work or worry अपने पर या किसी पर भारी ज़िम्मेदारी डालना

**bureau** /ˈbjʊərəʊ ˈब्युअरो/ *noun* [C] (*pl.* **bur eaux** or **bureaus** /-rəʊz -रोज़्/) **1** (*AmE*) one of certain government departments एक सरकारी विभाग *the Central Bureau of Investigation* **2** an organization that provides information सूचनाएँ उपलब्ध कराने वाली संस्था, सूचना-केंद्र *a tourist information bureau* **3** a writing desk with drawers and a lid दराज़ों वाली ढक्कनदार मेज़ जिस पर लेखनकार्य किया जाता है

**bureaucracy** /bjʊəˈrɒkrəsi ब्युअˈरॉक्रसि/ *noun* (*pl.* **bureaucracies**) **1** [U] (often used in a critical way) the system of official rules that an organization has for doing sth, that people often think is too complicated प्रायः निंदात्मक अर्थ में प्रयुक्त नौकरशाही, दफ़्तरशाही, लालफ़ीताशाही *Getting a visa involves a lot of unnecessary bureaucracy.* **2** [C, U] a system of government by a large number of officials who are not elected; a country with this system अनिर्वाचित अधिकारियों वाला प्रशासन तंत्र; ऐसे प्रशासन तंत्र वाला देश

**bureaucrat** /ˈbjʊərəkræt ˈब्युअरक्रैट्/ *noun* [C] (often used in a critical way) an official in an organization or government department (प्रायः निंदात्मक अर्थ में प्रयुक्त) नौकरशाह, अधिकारतंत्री, सरकारी अफ़सर

**bureaucratic** /ˌbjʊərəˈkrætɪk ˌब्युअरˈक्रैटिक्/ *adj.* connected with a **bureaucracy** or **bureaucrats**, and involving complicated official rules which may seem unnecessary नौकरशाही या लालफ़ीताशाही से संबंधित *You have to go through a complex bureaucratic procedure if you want to get your money back.*

**burette** (*AmE* **buret**) /bjuˈret ब्युˈरेट्/ *noun* [C] a glass tube with measurements marked on it and a tap at one end, used in chemistry रसायन शास्त्र में प्रयुक्त मापन-नलिका; ब्यूरेट ➪ **laboratory** पर चित्र देखिए।

**burger** /ˈbɜːgə(r) ˈबग(र्)/ *noun* [C] meat or vegetables cut into very small pieces and made into a flat round-shaped cutlet, that you eat between two pieces of bread डबलरोटी के बीच डाला हुआ मांस या सब्ज़ियों से बना गोल कटलट; बर्गर **2** = **hamburger**

**burglar** /ˈbɜːglə(r) ˈबगल(र्)/ *noun* [C] a person who enters a building illegally in order to steal चोरी करने के उद्देश्य से ग़ैर-क़ानूनी रूप से किसी इमारत में घुसने वाला व्यक्ति; सेंधमार ➪ **thief** देखिए। ▶ **burgle** /ˈbɜːgl ˈबगल्/ *verb* [T] सेंधमारी करना *Our flat was burgled while we were out.*

**burglar alarm** *noun* [C] a piece of equipment, usually fixed on a wall, that makes a loud noise when a burglar enters a building सेंधमार के इमारत में घुसने पर ज़ोर से बजने वाली घंटी

**burglary** /ˈbɜːgləri ˈबग्लरि/ *noun* [C, U] (*pl.* **burglaries**) the crime of entering a building illegally in order to steal सेंधमारी का अपराध *There was a burglary next door last week.* ○ *He is in prison for burglary.*

**burgundy** /ˈbɜːgəndi ˈबगन्डि/ *noun* **1 Burgundy** [U, C] (*pl.* **Burgundies**) a red or white wine from the Burgundy area of eastern France पूर्वी फ्रांस के बर्गंडि क्षेत्र की सफ़ेद या लाल मदिरा **2** [U] a dark red colour गहरा लाल रंग ▶ **burgundy** *adj.* गहरे लाल रंग से संबंधित

**burial** /ˈberiəl ˈबेरिअल्/ *noun* [C, U] the ceremony when a dead body is put in the ground (**buried**) दफ़न ➪ **funeral** पर नोट देखिए।

**burn**[1] /bɜːn बन्/ *verb* (*pt, pp* **burnt** /bɜːnt बन्ट्/ or **burned** /bɜːnd बन्ड्/) **1** [T] to destroy, damage or injure sb/sth with fire or heat आग या ताप से जलाना, हानि पहुँचाना या ज़ख़्मी करना *We took all the rubbish outside and burned it.* ○ *It was a terrible fire and the whole building was burnt to the ground* (= completely destroyed). **2** [I] to be destroyed, damaged or injured by fire or heat आग से जलना या ताप से नष्ट, क्षतिग्रस्त या ज़ख़्मी हो जाना *If you leave the cake in the oven for much longer, it will burn.* ○ *I can't spend too much time in the sun because I burn easily.* **3** [T] to produce a hole or mark in or on sth by burning जलाकर छेद करना *He dropped his cigarette and it burned a hole in the carpet.* **4** [I] to be on fire जलता हुआ *Firemen raced to the burning building.* **5** [T] to use sth as fuel किसी वस्तु का ईंधन के रूप में प्रयोग करना *an oil-burning lamp* **6** [I] to produce light प्रकाश करना, रोशनी फैलाना *I don't think he went to bed at all—I could see his light burning all night.* **7** [I] to feel very hot and painful गरमी और परेशानी महसूस करना *You have a temperature, your forehead's burning.* **8** [I] **burn (with sth)** to be filled with a very strong feeling भावनाएँ भड़कना *She was burning with indignation.*

**IDM sb's ears are burning** ➪ **ear** देखिए।

PHRV **burn down** (used about a building) to be completely destroyed by fire (भवन या इमारत) आग से जलकर पूर्णतया नष्ट हो जाना

**burn sth down** to completely destroy a building by fire भवन या इमारत को आग से जलाकर पूर्णतया नष्ट कर देना

**burn (sth) off** to remove sth or to be removed by burning किसी वस्तु का जल जाना या उसे जला डालना

**burn sth out** (*usually passive*) to completely destroy sth by burning (किसी वस्तु को) आग से जलाकर पूर्णतया नष्ट कर देना *the burnt-out wreck of a car*

**burn yourself out** (*usually passive*) to work, etc., until you have no more energy or strength पूरी तरह थक जाने तक काम करते रहना

**burn (sth) up** to destroy or to be destroyed by fire or strong heat आग या तेज़ ताप से किसी वस्तु को नष्ट कर देना या नष्ट हो जाना *The space capsule burnt up on its re-entry into the earth's atmosphere.*

**burn**[2] /bɜːn बर्न् / *noun* [C] damage or an injury caused by fire or heat आग या ताप से हुई क्षति *He was taken to hospital with* ***minor burns***. ○ *There's a cigarette burn on the carpet.*

**burner** /ˈbɜːnə(r) ˈबर्न(र्) / *noun* [C] the part of a cooker, etc. that produces a flame चूल्हे का वह भाग जिसमें से आँच निकलती है; बर्नर, ज्वालक ➪ **Bunsen burner** देखिए।

IDM **on the back burner** ➪ **back**[2] देखिए।

**burning** /ˈbɜːnɪŋ ˈबर्निङ् / *adj.* (*only before a noun*) **1** (used about a feeling) extremely strong (भावना) अत्यंत प्रबल *a burning ambition/desire* **2** very important or urgent अत्यधिक महत्त्वपूर्ण या तुरंत ध्यान देने योग्य *a burning issue/question* **3** feeling very hot बहुत गरम *the burning sun*

**burp** /bɜːp बर्प् / *verb* [I] to make a noise with the mouth when air rises from the stomach and is forced out डकार मारना या लेना *He sat back when he had finished his meal and burped loudly.*

▶ **burp** *noun* [C] डकार

**burrow**[1] /ˈbʌrəʊ ˈबरो / *noun* [C] a hole in the ground made by certain animals, for example rabbits, in which they live (ख़रगोश, लोमड़ी आदि का) बिल

**burrow**[2] /ˈbʌrəʊ ˈबरो / *verb* [I] to dig a hole in the ground, to make a tunnel or to look for sth (ख़रगोश आदि का) बिल खोदना; ज़मीन खोदना, कुछ ढूँढ़ना *These animals burrow for food.* ○ (*figurative*) *She burrowed in her handbag for her keys.*

**bursar** /ˈbɜːsə(r) ˈबस(र्) / *noun* [C] the person who manages the financial matters of a school, college or university विद्यालय, महाविद्यालय आदि का कोष-अधीक्षक

**bursary** /ˈbɜːsəri ˈबसरि / *noun* [C] (*pl.* **bursaries**) a sum of money given to a specially chosen student to pay for his/her studies at a college or university छात्रवृत्ति, अनुदान

**burst**[1] /bɜːst बर्स्ट् / *verb* (*pt, pp* **burst**) **1** [I, T] to break open suddenly and violently, usually because there is too much pressure inside; to cause this to happen भीतरी भारी दबाव से एकाएक फट जाना; एकाएक विस्फोटित कर देना *You'll burst that tyre if you blow it up any more.* ○ (*figurative*) *If I eat any more I'll burst!* **2** [I] **burst into, out of, through, etc.** to move suddenly in a particular direction, often using force किसी दिशा में ज़ोरों से अचानक बढ़ने लगना *She burst into the manager's office and demanded to speak to him.*

IDM **be bursting (with sth)** to be very full of sth किसी वस्तु से भरपूर होना *I packed so many clothes that my suitcase was bursting.* ○ *She was bursting with pride when she won the race.*

**be bursting to do sth** to want to do sth very much कुछ करने का अत्यधिक इच्छुक होना

**burst (sth) open** to open or make sth open suddenly or violently ज़ोर लगाकर अचानक खोल देना

**burst in on sb/sth** to interrupt sb/sth by arriving suddenly एकाएक पहुँचकर किसी कार्य में विघ्न डालना *The police burst in on the gang as they were counting the money.*

**burst into sth** to start doing sth suddenly एकाएक कुछ करने लगना *On hearing the news she* ***burst into tears*** (= started crying). ○ *The lorry hit a wall and* **burst into flames** (= started burning).

**burst out 1** to start doing sth suddenly कोई काम एकाएक करने लगना *He looked so ridiculous that I* ***burst out laughing***. **2** to say sth suddenly and with strong feeling एकाएक भावावेश में कुछ कहना *Finally she burst out, 'I can't stand it any more!'*

**burst**[2] /bɜːst बर्स्ट् / *noun* [C] **1** a short period of a particular activity, that often starts suddenly किसी गतिविधि की लहर, भभक या भड़क *a burst of energy/enthusiasm/speed* ○ *a burst of applause/gunfire* ○ *He prefers to work* ***in short bursts***. **2** an occasion when sth bursts or explodes; a crack or hole caused by this फटन, विस्फोट; फटने से बनी दरार *a burst in a water pipe*

**bury** /ˈberi ˈबेरि / *verb* [T] (*pres. part.* **burying**; *3rd person sing. pres.* **buries**; *pt, pp* **buried**) **1** to put a dead body in the ground (ज़मीन में) दफ़नाना *She wants to be buried in the village graveyard.* **2** to put sth in a hole in the ground and cover it किसी वस्तु को ज़मीन में गाड़ना *Our dog always buries its bones in the garden.* **3** (*usually passive*) to cover or hide sth/sb किसी वस्तु को ढकना या छिपाना *At last I found the photograph, buried at the bottom of a drawer.* ○ (*figurative*) *Sona buried in a book and didn't hear us come in.*

**bus** /bʌs बस्/ *noun* [C] (*pl.* **buses**) a big public vehicle which takes passengers along a fixed route and stops regularly to let people get on and off बस *We'll have to hurry up if we want to* ***catch the*** *9 o'clock bus.* ○ *We'd better run or we'll* ***miss the bus.***

**bush** /bʊʃ बुश्/ *noun* **1** [C] a plant like a small, thick tree with many low branches झाड़ी *a rose bush* ○ *The house was surrounded by thick bushes.* **2** (*often* **the bush**) [U] wild land that has not been cleared, especially in Africa and Australia जंगल जिसे साफ़ नहीं किया गया विशेषतः अफ़्रीक़ा और ऑस्ट्रेलिया में

IDM **beat about the bush** ➪ **beat**[1] देखिए।

**bushy** /bʊʃi बुशि/ *adj.* growing thickly घना *bushy hair/eyebrows*

**busier, busiest, busily** ➪ **busy**[1] देखिए।

**business** /ˈbɪznəs ˈबिज़्नस्/ *noun* **1** [U] buying and selling as a way of earning money; commerce व्यापार, कारोबार, धंधा, वाणिज्य *She's planning to* ***set up in business*** *as a hairdresser.* ○ *I'm going to* ***go into business*** *with my brother.* **2** [U] the work that you do as your job नौकरी से संबद्ध कार्य; काम, निर्धारित कार्य *The manager will be away* ***on business*** *next week.* ○ *a business trip* **3** [U] the number of customers that a person or company has had ग्राहकों की संख्या *Business has been good for the time of year.* **4** [C] a firm, a shop, a factory, etc. which produces or sells goods or provides a service वस्तुएँ बेचने या सेवाएँ प्रदान करने का प्रतिष्ठान *Small businesses are finding it hard to survive at the moment.* **5** [U] something that concerns a particular person किसी व्यक्ति-विशेष से संबंधित मामला, काम *The friends I choose are my business, not yours.* ○ *Our business is to collect the information, not to comment on it.* **6** [U] important matters that need to be dealt with or discussed चर्चा योग्य महत्त्वपूर्ण मुद्दे *First we have some unfinished business from the last meeting to deal with.* **7** [*sing.*] a situation or an event, especially one that is strange or unpleasant विशेषतः विचित्र, अपरिचित या अप्रिय स्थिति या घटना *The divorce was an awful business.* ○ *I found the whole business very depressing.*

IDM **get down to business** to start the work that has to be done निर्धारित कार्य शुरू करना

**go out of business** to have to close because there is no more money available धन के अभाव के कारण व्यापार करने की स्थिति में न होना; बंद हो जाना *The shop went out of business because it couldn't compete with the new supermarket.*

**have no business to do sth/doing sth** to have no right to do sth कुछ करने का अधिकार न होना *You have no business to read/reading my letters without asking me.*

**mind your own business** ➪ **mind**[2] देखिए।

**monkey business** ➪ **monkey** देखिए।

**businesslike** /ˈbɪznəslaɪk ˈबिज़्नसलाइक्/ *adj.* dealing with matters in an efficient and practical way, and not wasting time or thinking about personal things व्यावहारिक और कार्यकुशल रीति से बिना समय गँवाए और बिना व्यक्तिगत मामलों को बीच में लाते हुए *She has a very businesslike manner.*

**businessman** /ˈbɪznəsmæn; ˈbɪznəsmən ˈबिज़्नस्मैन्; ˈबिज़्नस्मन्/ *noun* [C] (*pl.* **-men** /-mən; -men -मन्; -मेन्/) **1** a man who works in business व्यापारी, व्यवसायी **2** a man who is skilful at dealing with money व्यापारकुशल व्यक्ति

**business studies** *noun* [U] the study of how to control and manage a company व्यवसाय-विद्या, व्यापार-शास्त्र *a course in business studies*

**businesswoman** /ˈbɪznəswʊmən ˈबिज़्नसवुमन्/ *noun* [C] (*pl.* **-women** /-wɪmɪn -विमिन्/) **1** a woman who works in business महिला व्यापारी, महिला व्यवसायी **2** a woman who is skilful at dealing with money व्यापारकुशल महिला

**busk** /bʌsk बस्क्/ *verb* [I] to sing or play music in the street so that people will give you money भीख माँगने के लिए सड़क पर गाना-बजाना

**busker** /ˈbʌskə(r) ˈबस्क(र्)/ *noun* [C] a street musician सड़कों पर घूमता गायक, भिक्षुक-गायक

**bust**[1] /bʌst बस्ट्/ *verb* [T] (*pt, pp* **bust** or **busted**) (*informal*) **1** to break or damage sth so that it cannot be used इस तरह तोड़ना या क्षति पहुँचाना कि पुनः प्रयोग न हो सके **2** to arrest sb (किसी को) बंदी बनाना *He was busted for possession of heroin.*

**bust**[2] /bʌst बस्ट्/ *adj.* (*not before a noun*) (*informal*) broken or not working टूटा हुआ या ख़राब *The zip on these trousers is bust.*

IDM **go bust** (*informal*) (used about a business) to close because it has lost so much money (व्यापार का) वित्तीय नुक़सान होने के कारण बंद हो जाना

**bust**[3] /bʌst बस्ट्/ *noun* [C] **1** a model in stone, etc. of a person's head, shoulders and chest पत्थर में बनी अर्ध प्रतिमा (ऊपरी धड़ मात्र) **2** a woman's breasts; the measurement round a woman's chest स्त्री का वक्षस्थल; स्त्री की छाती का नाप *This blouse is a bit too tight around the bust.* **3** (*informal*) an unexpected visit by the police in order to arrest people for doing sth illegal अपराधियों को गिरफ़्तार करने के लिए पुलिस का अकस्मात आ धमकना *a drugs bust*

**bustle**[1] /ˈbʌsl ˈबस्ल्/ *verb* **1** [I, T] to move in a busy, noisy or excited way; to make sb move somewhere quickly हलचल मचाना, शीघ्रता से कहीं ले जाना *He bustled about the kitchen making tea.* ○ *They bustled her out of the room before she could see the body.* **2** [I] **bustle (with sth)** to be full of people, noise or activity व्यक्तियों, शोर या गतिविधियों से भरा होना; हलचल होना *The streets were bustling with shoppers.*

**bustle**[2] /ˈbʌsl ˈबस्ल्/ *noun* [U] excited and noisy activity हलचल, शोर-शराबा *She loved the bustle of city life.*

**bust-up** *noun* [C] (*informal*) an argument विवाद, तकरार, बहस *He had a bust-up with his boss over working hours.*

**busy**[1] /ˈbɪzi ˈबिज़ि/ *adj.* (**busier; busiest**) **1 busy (at/with sth); busy (doing sth)** having a lot of work or tasks to do; not free; working on sth ख़ाली नहीं; काम में लगा हुआ; कार्यरत, व्यस्त *Mr Khan is busy until 4 o'clock but he could see you after that.* ○ *Don't disturb him. He's busy.* **2** (used about a period of time) full of activity and things to do (अवधि) सक्रियता-पूर्ण *I've had rather a busy week.* **3** (used about a place) full of people, movement and activity (स्थान) भीड़भाड़ वाला, हलचल भरा *The town centre was so busy that you could hardly move.* **4** (used about a telephone) being used (टेलीफ़ोन) व्यस्त, प्रयोग किया जा रहा *The line's busy at the moment. I'll try again later.* ▶ **busily** *adv.* व्यस्त रीति से *When I came in she was busily writing something at her desk.*

IDM **get busy** to start working सक्रिय होना; चालू होना; कार्य आरंभ करना *We'll have to get busy if we're going to be ready in time.*

**busy**[2] /ˈbɪzi ˈबिज़ि/ *verb* [T] (*pres. part.* **busying;** *3rd person sing. pres.* **busies;** *pt, pp* **busied**) **busy yourself with sth; busy yourself doing sth** to keep yourself busy; to find sth to do स्वयं को व्यस्त रखना; कुछ करते रहना

**busybody** /ˈbɪzibɒdi ˈबिज़िबॉडि/ *noun* [C] (*pl.* **busybodies**) a person who is too interested in other people's private lives दूसरों के निजी जीवन में अत्यधिक रुचि रखने वाला

**but**[1] /bət; *strong form* bʌt बट्; प्रबल रूप बट्/ *conj.* **1** used for introducing an idea which contrasts with or is different from what has just been said किंतु, परंतु, लेकिन *The weather will be sunny but cold.* ○ *Theirs is not the first but the second house on the left.* **2** however; and yet तथापि; मगर फिर भी ○ *I'd love to come but I can't make it till 8 o'clock.* **3** used when you are saying sorry for sth किसी बात के लिए माफ़ी माँगने के लिए प्रयुक्त *Excuse me, but is your name Asha Gupta?* ○ *I'm sorry, but I can't stay any longer.* **4** used for introducing a statement that shows that you are surprised or annoyed or that you disagree आश्चर्य, नाराज़गी या असहमति दर्शाने वाले कथन के आरंभ में प्रयुक्त *'Here's the book you lent me.' 'But it's all dirty and torn!'* ○ *'But that's not possible!'*

IDM **but then** however; on the other hand तथापि; इसके विपरीत *We could go swimming. But then perhaps it's too cold.*

**but**[2] /bət; *strong form* bʌt बट्; प्रबल रूप बट्/ *prep.* except के सिवाय, के अलावा *I've told no one but you about this.* ○ *We've had nothing but trouble with this washing machine!*

IDM **but for sb/sth** except for or without sb/sth को छोड़कर या किसी के बिना *We wouldn't have managed but for your help.*

**butane** /ˈbjuːteɪn ˈब्यूटेन्/ *noun* [U] a gas produced from petrol that is used in liquid form for cooking, heating, etc. पेट्रोल से बनी और द्रव रूप में प्रयुक्त गैस

**butcher**[1] /ˈbʊtʃə(r) ˈबुच(र्)/ *noun* **1** [C] a person who sells meat क़साई, मांस-विक्रेता *The butcher cut me four lamb chops.* **2 the butcher's** [*sing.*] a shop that sells meat क़साई की दुकान *She went to the butcher's for some chicken.* **3** [C] a person who kills a lot of people in a cruel way बहुत सारे व्यक्तियों की क्रूरता से हत्या करने वाला व्यक्ति

**butcher**[2] /ˈbʊtʃə(r) ˈबुच(र्)/ *verb* [T] to kill a lot of people in a cruel way निर्ममता से बहुत सारे व्यक्तियों की हत्या करना

**butchery** /ˈbʊtʃəri ˈबुचरि/ *noun* [U] cruel killing निर्मम हत्या **2** the work of preparing meat to be sold क़साई का काम

**butler** /ˈbʌtlə(r) ˈबट्ल(र्)/ *noun* [C] a man who works in a very large house, whose main duty is to organize and serve food and wine ख़ानसामाँ, भंडारी

**butt[1]** /bʌt बट्/ *verb* [T] to hit sb/sth with the head (किसी को) सिर से टक्कर मारना

**PHR V** **butt in (on sb/sth)** to interrupt sb/sth or to join in sth without being asked बाधा डालना; बिना आमंत्रण के शामिल हो जाना *I'm sorry to butt in but could I speak to you urgently for a minute?*

**butt[2]** /bʌt बट्/ *noun* [C] **1** the thicker, heavier end of a weapon or tool हथियार या औज़ार का मूठ वाला भाग; कुंदा या दस्ता *the butt of a rifle* **2** a short piece of a cigarette which is left when it has been smoked सिगरेट का अनबुझा टुकड़ा **3** (*informal*) the part of your body that you sit on; your bottom नितंब *Get up off your butt and do some work!* **4** a person who is often laughed at or talked about in an unkind way निर्मम हँसी का पात्र *Fat children are often the butt of other children's jokes.* **5** the act of hitting sb with your head किसी को सिर से टक्कर मारने की क्रिया

**butter[1]** /ˈbʌtə(r) ˈबट(र्)/ *noun* [U] a soft yellow or white fat that is made from cream and used for spreading on bread, etc. or in cooking मक्खन

**butter[2]** /ˈbʌtə(r) ˈबट(र्)/ *verb* [T] to spread butter on bread, etc. डबलरोटी आदि पर मक्खन लगाना *I'll cut the bread and you butter it.* ○ *hot buttered toast*

**buttercup** /ˈbʌtəkʌp ˈबटकप्/ *noun* [C] a wild plant with small shiny yellow flowers that look like cups एक जंगली पौधा जिसमें प्यालेनुमा चमकीले पीले छोटे-छोटे फूल खिलते हैं, बटरकप

**butterfly** /ˈbʌtəflaɪ ˈबटफ़्लाइ/ *noun* **1** [C] (*pl.* **butterflies**) an insect with a long, thin body and four brightly coloured wings तितली *Caterpillars develop into butterflies.* ➪ **insect** पर चित्र देखिए। **2** [U] a style of swimming in which both arms are brought over the head at the same time, and the legs move up and down together तैरने की एक शैली जिसमें तैराक दोनों बाँहों को सिर के ऊपर एक साथ ले जाता है और टाँगों को भी एक साथ ऊपर-नीचे चलाता है

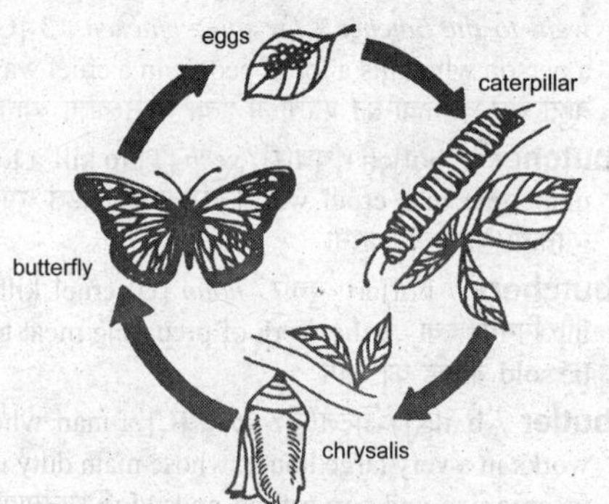

**the life cycle of a butterfly**

**IDM** **have butterflies (in your stomach)** (*informal*) to feel very nervous before doing sth कुछ करने से पहले घबराहट महसूस करना

**buttermilk** /ˈbʌtəmɪlk ˈबटमिल्क्/ *noun* [U] the liquid that is left when butter is separated from milk छाछ, मट्ठा

**buttock** /ˈbʌtək ˈबटक्/ *noun* [C, *usually pl.*] either of the two round soft parts at the top of your legs, which you sit on नितंब

**button** /ˈbʌtn ˈबट्न्/ *noun* [C] **1** a small, often round, piece of plastic, wood or metal that you use for fastening your clothes बटन *One of the buttons on my jacket has come off.* **2** a small part of a machine, etc. that you press in order to operate sth (मशीन आदि चलाने के लिए) घुंडी ***Press the button** to ring the bell.* ○ *To dial the same number again, **push the** 'redial' button.* ○ *Double click the right mouse button.*

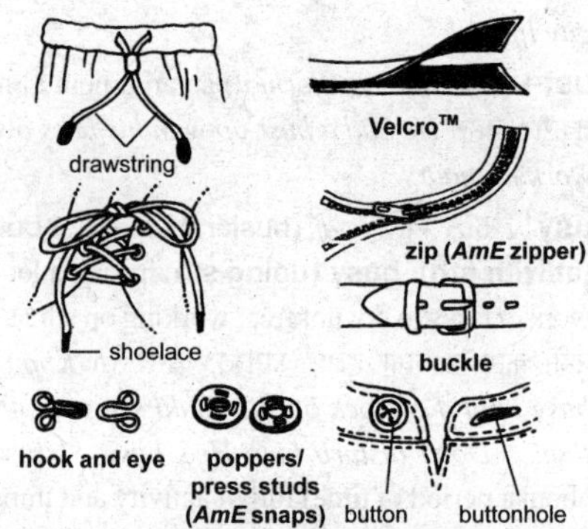

**buttons and fasteners**

**buttonhole** /ˈbʌtnhəʊl ˈबट्न्होल्/ *noun* [C] **1** a hole in a piece of clothing that you push a button through in order to fasten it काज जिसमें बटन फँसाते हैं **2** a flower worn in the buttonhole of a coat or jacket कोट के काज में लगाया गया फूल

**buttress** /ˈbʌtrəs ˈबट्रस्/ *noun* [C] a stone or brick structure that supports a wall or makes it stronger (दीवार के लिए) पुश्ता, टेक या सहारा, वप्र *Stone buttresses support the walls of the church.*

**buy[1]** /baɪ बाइ/ *verb* [T] (*pt, pp* **bought** /bɔːt बॉट्/) **buy sth (for sb); buy sb sth** to get sth by paying money for it ख़रीदना, मोल लेना *I'm going to buy a new dress for the party.* ○ *We bought this book for you in London.* ○ *Can I buy you a coffee?*

IDM **buy time** to do sth in order to delay an event, a decision, etc. किसी घटना, निर्णय आदि में विलंब करने के लिए कुछ करना

**buy sb off** (*informal*) to pay sb money, especially dishonestly, to stop him/her from doing sth you do not want him/her to do रिश्वत या घूस देना

PHR V **buy sb out** to pay sb for his/her share in a house, business, etc. in order to get full control of it yourself मकान, व्यापार आदि में हिस्सेदारी ख़रीदना ताकि उस पर पूरा अधिकार हो सके

**buy**[2] /baɪ बाइ/ *noun* [C] an act of buying sth or a thing that you can buy ख़रीदने की क्रिया या ख़रीदी जा सकने वाली वस्तु *I think your house was a very good buy* (= worth the money you paid).

**buyer** /ˈbaɪə(r) ˈबाइअ(र्)/ *noun* [C] **1** a person who is buying sth or may buy sth ख़रीदार *I think we've found a buyer for our house!* **2** a person whose job is to choose and buy goods to be sold in a large shop विक्रेता-ख़रीदार (दूसरी दुकान पर बेचने के लिए ख़रीदारी करने वाला)

**buyout** /ˈbaɪaʊt ˈबाइआउट्/ *noun* [C] the act of buying enough or all of the shares in a company in order to get control of it किसी कंपनी की सारी या लगभग सारी हिस्सेदारी ख़रीद लेना

**buzz**[1] /bʌz बज़्/ *verb* **1** [I] to make the sound that bees, etc. make when flying भिनभिनाना *A large fly was buzzing against the windowpane.* **2** [I] **buzz (with sth)** to be full of excitement, activity, thoughts, etc. किसी का उत्तेजना, विचार, सक्रियता आदि से भरपूर होना *Her head was buzzing with questions that she wanted to ask.* ○ *The room was buzzing with activity.* **3** [I, T] to call sb by using an electric bell, etc. बिजली की घंटी आदि बजाकर किसी को बुलाना *The doctor will buzz for you when he's ready.*

**buzz**[2] /bʌz बज़्/ *noun* **1** [C] the sound that a bee, etc. makes when flying भिनभिनाहट *the buzz of insects* **2** [*sing.*] the low sound made by many people talking at the same time फुसफुसाहट *I could hear the buzz of conversation in the next room.* **3** [*sing.*] (*informal*) a strong feeling of excitement or pleasure प्रबल उत्तेजना या ख़ुशी *a buzz of expectation* ○ *Flying first class* ***gave him a*** *real* ***buzz.*** ○ *She* ***gets a buzz out of*** *shopping for expensive clothes.*

**buzzard** /ˈbʌzəd ˈबज़ड्/ *noun* [C] a large **bird of prey** एक बड़ा शिकारी पक्षी

**buzzer** /ˈbʌzə(r) ˈबज़(र्)/ *noun* [C] a piece of equipment that makes a buzzing sound घंटी आदि की आवाज़ उत्पन्न करने वाला उपकरण; गुंजक, बज़र *Press your buzzer if you know the answer to a question.*

**buzzword** /ˈbʌzwɜːd ˈबज़्वड्/ *noun* [C] a word or phrase, especially one connected with a particular subject, that has become fashionable and popular किसी विषय से संबंधित लोकप्रिय व प्रचलित शब्द या वाक्यांश

**by** /baɪ बाइ/ *prep., adv.* **1** beside; very near बग़ल में; बहुत पास, समीप *Come and sit by me.* ○ *We stayed in a cottage by the sea.* ○ *The shops are close by.* **2** past किसी के पास से *He walked straight by me without speaking.* ○ *We stopped to let the ambulance get by.* **3** not later than; before तक; के पहले *I'll be home by 7 o'clock.* ○ *He should have telephoned by now/by this time.* **4** (*usually without* **the**) during a period of time; in a particular situation के दौरान; एक विशेष स्थिति में *By day we covered about thirty kilometres and by night we rested.* ○ *The electricity went off so we had to work by candlelight.* **5** used after a passive verb for showing who or what did or caused sth कर्त्ता या कारक दर्शाने के लिए कर्मवाच्य क्रिया के बाद प्रयुक्त *The event was organized by local people.* ○ *I was deeply shocked by the news.* ○ *Who was the book written by?/Who is the book by?* **6** through doing or using sth; by means of sth (के) द्वारा; के ज़रिये से *Will you be paying by cheque?* ○ *The house is heated by electricity.* ○ *by bus/car/plane/bicycle* ○ *We went in by the back door.* **7** as a result of sth; due to sth के फलस्वरूप; के कारण *I got on the wrong bus by mistake/accident.* ○ *I met an old friend by chance.* **8** according to sth; with regard to sth से, के अनुसार *It's 8 o'clock by my watch.* ○ *By law you have to attend school from the age of five.* ○ *She's French by birth.* ○ *He's a doctor by profession.* **9** used for multiplying or dividing गुणा या भाग दर्शाने के लिए प्रयुक्त *Four multiplied by five is twenty.* ○ *Six divided by two is three.* **10** used for showing the measurements of an area किसी क्षेत्र का माप दर्शाने के लिए प्रयुक्त *The table is six feet by three feet* (= six feet long and three feet wide). **11** (*often used with* **the**) in the quantity or period mentioned उल्लेखित मात्रा या अवधि के दौरान *You can rent a car by the day, the week or the month.* ○ *Copies of the book have sold by the million.* ○ *They came in one by one.* **12** to the amount mentioned उल्लेखित मात्रा में *Prices have gone up by 10%.* ○ *I missed the bus by a few minutes.* **13** (used with a part of the body or an article of clothing) holding (शरीर का अंग या वस्त्र) पकड़े हुए *He grabbed me by the arm.*

IDM **by and large** ➪ **large** देखिए।

**by the way** ➪ **way**[1] देखिए।

**by-** (*also* **bye-**) /baɪ बाइ/ *prefix* (*in nouns and verbs*) **1** less important कम महत्त्वपूर्ण, अपेक्षाकृत गौण, उप *a by-product* **2** near पासवाला, निकट का *a bystander*

**bye** /baɪ बाइ/ (*also* **bye- bye; bye-bye** *exclamation* (*informal*) goodbye अलविदा *Bye! See you tomorrow.*

**by-election** *noun* [C] an election to choose a new Member of Parliament for a particular town or area (**a constituency**). It is held when the former member has died or left suddenly नए संसद या विधायक के चुनाव के लिए उप-चुनाव (प्रायः किसी सदस्य की अकस्मात मृत्यु या पद छोड़ने के कारण); उप-चुनाव ➪ **general election** देखिए।

**bygone** /ˈbaɪgɒn ˈबाइगॉन्/ *adj.* (*only used before a noun*) that happened a long time ago बहुत समय पहले बीता हुआ; विगत *a bygone era*

**bygones** /ˈbaɪgɒnz ˈबाइगॉन्ज़्/ *noun* [*pl.*]

IDM **let bygones be bygones** to decide to forget disagreements or arguments that happened in the past पिछले झगड़े आदि भुला देने का निर्णय लेना

**by-law** (*also* **bye-law**) *noun* [C] a law that is made by a local authority and that has to be obeyed only in that area स्थानीय प्रशासन द्वारा बनाया गया नियम जो केवल उसी क्षेत्र में लागू होता है; उप-नियम, उप-विधि

**bypass[1]** /ˈbaɪpɑːs ˈबाइपास्/ *noun* [C] **1** a road which traffic can use to go round a town, instead of through it किसी शहर के भीतर जाने के बजाए बाहर-बाहर से ही पार करने का मार्ग; उप-मार्ग, बाह्य मार्ग ➪ **ring road** देखिए। **2** an operation on the heart to send blood along a different route so that it does not go through a part which is damaged or blocked हृदय की शल्य-क्रिया जिसमें रक्त प्रवाह के लिए भिन्न मार्ग बनाया जाता है *a triple bypass operation* ○ *heart bypass surgery*

**bypass[2]** /ˈbaɪpɑːs ˈबाइपास्/ *verb* [T] to go around or to avoid sth using a bypass उपमार्ग से निकलना *Let's try to bypass the town centre.* ○ (*figurative*) *It's no good trying to bypass the problem.*

**by-product** *noun* [C] **1** something that is formed during the making of sth else गौण उत्पाद; उपोत्पाद **2** something that happens as the result of sth else उपजात, उपोत्पाद

**bystander** /ˈbaɪstændə(r) ˈबाइस्टैन्ड(र्)/ *noun* [C] a person who is standing near and sees sth that happens, without being involved in it किसी घटना का मूक दर्शक *Several* ***innocent bystanders*** *were hurt when the two gangs attacked each other.*

**byte** /baɪt बाइट्/ *noun* [C] (*computing*) a unit of information that can represent one item, such as a letter or a number. A byte is usually made up of a series of eight smaller units (**bits**) किसी एक अक्षर, अंक आदि दर्शाने वाली सूचना की इकाई; बाइट, एक बाइट में आठ छोटी इकाइयों (**bits**) की शृंखला होती है

**byword** /ˈbaɪwɜːd ˈबाइवड्/ *noun* [C, *usually sing.*] **1 a byword for sth** a person or a thing that is a typical or well-known example of a particular quality व्यक्ति या वस्तु जो किसी विशेषता का प्रतिनिधिक माना जाता हो *A limousine is a byword for luxury.* **2** a word or phrase that is often used प्रायः प्रयुक्त शब्द या वाक्यांश; कहावत

# C c

**C, c**[1] /si: सी / *noun* [C, U] (*pl.* **C's; c's** /si:z सीज़् /) the third letter of the English alphabet अंग्रेज़ी वर्णमाला का तीसरा अक्षर *'Car' begins with a 'C'.*

**c**[2] /si: सी / *abbr.* **1 C** Celsius; centigrade सेल्सिअस; सेंटीग्रेड *Water freezes at 0°C.* **2 C** coulomb(s) विद्युत चार्ज की एक इकाई; कूलॉम **3** (before dates) about; approximately (तिथियों से पहले) लगभग; के आसपास *c 1770* ➪ **circa** देखिए।

**cab** /ˈkæb ˈकैब् / *noun* [C] **1** (*AmE*) = **taxi**[1] *Let's take a cab/go by cab.* **2** the part of a lorry, train, bus, etc. where the driver sits ट्रक, रेलगाड़ी आदि में चालक के बैठने का स्थान; चालक कक्ष

**cabaret** /ˈkæbəreɪ ˈकैबरे / *noun* [C, U] entertainment with singing, dancing, etc. in a restaurant or club रेस्तराँ या क्लब में गान, नृत्य आदि द्वारा मनोरंजन

**cabbage** /ˈkæbɪdʒ ˈकैबिज् / *noun* [C, U] a large round vegetable with thick green, dark red or white leaves बंदगोभी, करमकल्ला *Cabbages are easy to grow.* ○ *Do you like cabbage?* ➪ **vegetable** पर चित्र देखिए।

**cabin** /ˈkæbɪn ˈकैबिन् / *noun* [C] **1** a small room in a ship or boat, where a passenger sleeps जहाज़ या नाव में सोने के लिए छोटा कक्ष ➪ **boat** पर चित्र देखिए। **2** the part of a plane where the passengers sit विमान का वह भाग जहाँ यात्री बैठते हैं ➪ **plane** पर चित्र देखिए। **3** a small wooden house; a hut लकड़ी से बना छोटा मकान; कुटिर *a log cabin*

**cabin cruiser** *noun* [C] = **cruiser**[2]

**cabinet** /ˈkæbɪnət ˈकैबिनट् / *noun* [C] **1** a cupboard with shelves or drawers, used for storing things टाँड़ों या दराज़ों वाली अलमारी *a medicine cabinet* **2** (*also* **the Cabinet**) the most important ministers in a government, who have regular meetings with the Prime Minister मंत्रिमंडल, मंत्रिपरिषद, कैबिनेट *The Cabinet is/are meeting today to discuss the crisis.*

**cable** /ˈkeɪbl ˈकेबल् / *noun* **1** [C] a thick strong metal rope मोटा मज़बूत धातुनिर्मित तार; केबल **2** [C, U] a set of wires covered with plastic, etc., for carrying electricity or signals विद्युत या तरंगों के वहन के लिए प्लास्टिक से ढका तारों का समुच्चय *underground/overhead cables* ○ *a telephone cable* ○ *two metres of cable* **3** [U] = **cable television**

**cable car** *noun* [C] a vehicle like a box that hangs on a moving metal rope (**cable**) and carries passengers up and down a mountain पर्वतों पर आवागमन के लिए तार के मोटे रस्सों पर चलने वाली डब्बानुमा गाड़ी

**cable television** *noun* [U] a system of sending out television programmes along wires instead of by radio signals रेडियो तरंगों के स्थान पर केबलों द्वारा टेलीविज़न कार्यक्रम प्रसारित करने की पद्धति

**cache** /kæʃ कैश् / *noun* [C] **1** an amount of sth, especially drugs or weapons, that has been hidden गुप्त भण्डार विशेषतः नशीले पदार्थों या हथियारों का **2** (*computing*) a part of a computer's memory that stores copies of data so that the data can be found very quickly कंप्यूटर-स्मृति का वह भाग जहाँ सूचना-सामग्री की प्रतिलिपि संचित रहती है

**cackle** /ˈkækl ˈकैकल् / *verb* [I] to laugh in a loud, unpleasant way ज़ोर से व भद्दे तरीक़े से हँसना ▶ **cackle** *noun* [C] इस तरह की हँसी

**cactus** /ˈkæktəs ˈकैक्टस् / *noun* [C] (*pl.* **cactuses** or **cacti** /ˈkæktaɪ ˈकैक्टाइ /) a type of plant that grows in hot, dry areas, especially deserts. A cactus has a thick central part (**stem**) and sharp points (**prickles**) but no leaves नागफनी, सेहुँड़ ➪ **plant** पर चित्र देखिए।

**CAD** /kæd; ˌsi: eɪ ˈdi: कैड्; ˌसी ए ˈडी / *noun* [U] the abbreviation for 'computer aided design' (the use of computers to design machines, buildings, vehicles, etc.), 'computer aided design' का संक्षिप्त रूप (मशीनों, इमारतों, वाहनों आदि के निर्माण का ख़ाका बनाने के लिए कंप्यूटर का प्रयोग)

**cadaver** /kəˈdævə(r) कˈडैव़(र्) / *noun* [C] (*formal*) the body of a dead person शव, मृत शरीर

**cadence** /ˈkeɪdns ˈकेड्न्स् / *noun* [C] **1** (*formal*) the rise and fall of the voice in speaking बोलते समय स्वर का आरोह-अवरोह; लय **2** the end of a musical phrase संगीत-खंड का विराम बिंदु

**cadenza** /kəˈdenzə कˈडेन्ज़ा / *noun* [C] (in classical music) a short passage that is put into a piece of music to be played by one musician alone, and that shows the skill of that musician (शास्त्रीय संगीत में) किसी संगीत रचना का एक टुकड़ा जिसे एक संगीतज्ञ प्रस्तुत करता है (प्रायः संगीत कला में निपुणता दर्शाने के लिए)

**cadet** /kəˈdet कˈडेट् / *noun* [C] a young person who is training to be in the army, navy, air force or police (थल, जल या वायु सेना का) सैन्य छात्र, कैडेट

**cadge** /kædʒ कैज् / *verb* [I, T] (*informal*) **cadge (sth) (from/off sb)** to try to persuade sb to give or lend you sth दूसरे को ऐसे समझाना कि उससे कुछ मिल जाए *He's always trying to cadge money off me.*

**cadmium** /ˈkædmiəm ˈकैड्मिअम् / *noun* [U] (*symbol* **Cd**) a soft poisonous bluish-white metal that is used in batteries and in some industries बैटरी में तथा कुछ उद्योगों में इस्तेमाल होने वाली नरम विषैली नीली-सफ़ेद धातु; कैडमियम

**cadre** /ˈkaːdə(r) ˈकाड(र्) / *noun* [C] **1** (*with sing. or pl. verb*) a small group of people who are especially chosen and trained for a particular purpose किसी संगठन के कुछ सदस्य जो किसी विशेष उद्देश्य के लिए चुने एवं प्रशिक्षित किए जाते हैं *The Jammu and Kashmir cadre was specially trained to fight terrorism.* **2** a member of this kind of group इस प्रकार के संगठन का सदस्य *They were to become the cadres of the new Communist Party.*

**Caesarean** (*also* **-rian;** *AmE* **cesarean**) /siˈzeəriən सिˈज़ेअरिअन् / *noun* [C] a medical operation in which an opening is cut in a mother's body in order to take out the baby when a normal birth would be impossible or dangerous प्रसव कराने के लिए शल्य-क्रिया *to have a Caesarean* **NOTE** इस शल्य-क्रिया को **Caesarean section** या अमेरिकी अंग्रेज़ी में **C-section** कहते हैं।

**caesium** (*AmE* **cesium**) /ˈsiːziəm ˈसीज़िअम् / *noun* [U] (*symbol* **Cs**) a soft silver-white metal एक नरम चाँदी जैसी सफ़ेद धातु; सीज़िअम

**cafe** /ˈkæfeɪ ˈकैफ़े / *noun* [C] a small restaurant that serves drinks and light meals छोटा रेस्तराँ जहाँ नाश्ता व पेय मिलते हैं

**cafeteria** /ˌkæfəˈtɪəriə ˌकैफ़ˈटिअरिआ / *noun* [C] a restaurant, especially one for staff or workers, where people collect their meals themselves and carry them to their tables विशेषतः कर्मचारीगण के लिए रेस्तराँ जहाँ ग्राहक काउंटर से स्वयं जलपान लेते हैं ➪ **canteen** देखिए।

**cafetière** /ˌkæfəˈtjeə(r) ˌकैफ़ˈट्येअ(र्) / *noun* [C] a special glass container for making coffee with a metal part (**filter**) that you push down कॉफ़ी बनाने के लिए काँच का विशेष पात्र जिसे दबाया जाता है ➪ **percolator** देखिए।

**caffeine** /ˈkæfiːn ˈकैफ़ीन् / *noun* [U] the substance found in coffee and tea that makes you feel more awake and full of energy चाय और कॉफ़ी में पाए जाने वाला पदार्थ जो चुस्ती प्रदान करता है ➪ **decaffeinated** देखिए।

**cage** /keɪdʒ केज् / *noun* [C] a box made of bars or wire, or a space surrounded by wire or metal bars, in which a bird or animal is kept so that it cannot escape पशु या पक्षी का पिंजरा *a bird cage*
▶ **cage** *verb* [T] पिंजरे में बंद करना या रखना
▶ **caged** /keɪdʒd केज्ड् / *adj.* पिंजरे में बंद *He felt like a caged animal in the tiny office.*

**cagey** /ˈkeɪdʒi ˈकेजि / *adj.* (*informal*) **cagey (about sth)** not wanting to give information or to talk about sth दूसरों से जानकारी छिपाने वाला; गोपनशील

**cagoule** /kəˈguːl कˈगूल् / *noun* [C] a long jacket with a covering for the head (**hood**) that protects you from the rain or wind टोपी वाली लंबी जाकिट

**cajole** /kəˈdʒəʊl कˈजोल् / *verb* [I, T] **cajole (sb) (into sth/into doing sth); cajole sth out of sb** to persuade a person to do sth or give sth by being very nice to him/her ख़ुशामद से या उपहार देकर किसी से अपनी बात मनवाना *He cajoled me into agreeing to do the work.*

**cake**[1] /keɪk केक् / *noun* **1** [C, U] a sweet food made by mixing flour, eggs, butter, sugar, etc. together and baking the mixture in the oven आटे, अंडे, मक्खन, शक्कर आदि के मिश्रण को भट्टी में पकाकर बनाया गया मीठा पकवान; केक *to make/bake a cake* **2** [C] a mixture of other food, cooked in a round, flat shape केक के आकार में बना अन्य खाद्य पदार्थ *fish/potato cakes*

**IDM** **have your cake and eat it** to enjoy the advantages of sth without its disadvantages; to have both things that are available केवल लाभ का आनंद लेना; दोनों विकल्पों का लाभ प्राप्त करना
**a piece of cake** ➪ **piece**[1] देखिए।

**cake**[2] /keɪk केक् / *verb* [T] (*usually passive*) **cake sth (in/with sth)** to cover sth thickly with a substance that becomes hard when it dries किसी वस्तु पर किसी पदार्थ का मोटा लेप लगाना जो सूखकर कड़ा हो जाए *boots caked in mud*

**calamity** /kəˈlæməti कˈलैमटि / *noun* [C, U] (*pl.* **calamities**) a terrible event that causes a lot of damage or harm कठोर विपत्ति

**calcify** /ˈkælsɪfaɪ ˈकैल्सिफ़ाइ / *verb* [I, T] (*pres. part.* **calcifying** *3rd person sing. pres.* **calcifies;** *pt, pp* **calcified**) (*technical*) to become hard or make sth hard by adding **calcium** salts कैल्सियम के प्रयोग से किसी वस्तु का कड़ा हो जाना या कड़ा कर देना
▶ **calcification** /ˌkælsɪfɪˈkeɪʃn ˌकैल्सिफ़िˈकेशन् / *noun* [U] कैल्सियम के प्रयोग से किसी वस्तु को कड़ा करने की क्रिया

**calcium** /ˈkælsiəm ˈकैल्सिअम् / *noun* [U] (*symbol* **Ca**) a chemical element that is found in foods such as milk and cheese. It helps to make bones and teeth strong दूध व पनीर जैसे खाद्य पदार्थों में पाया जाने वाला एक रासायनिक तत्व जो हड्डियों व दाँतों को मज़बूत बनाने में सहायक होता है; कैल्सियम, चूना

**calcium carbonate** *noun* [U] (*symbol* **$CaCO_3$**) a white solid that exists naturally as chalk, **limestone** and **marble** खड़िया, चूने और संगमरमर में पाया जानेवाला सफ़ेद ठोस पदार्थ; कैल्सियम कार्बोनेट

**calculate** /ˈkælkjuleɪt ˈकैल्क्युलेट्/ *verb* [T] **1** to find sth out by using mathematics; to work sth out गणना करना, हिसाब लगाना, परिकलन करना *It's difficult to calculate how long the project will take.* **2** to consider or expect sth कुछ विचार करना, समझना या आशा करना *We calculated that the advantages would be greater than the disadvantages.*

IDM **be calculated to do sth** to be intended or designed to do sth अभिप्रेत या सुनियोजित होना *His remark was clearly calculated to annoy me.*

**calculating** /ˈkælkjuleɪtɪŋ ˈकैल्क्युलेटिङ्/ *adj.* planning things in a very careful way in order to achieve what you want, without considering other people स्वार्थपूर्ण अभीष्ट पाने के लिए सुनियोजित; चालाक *Her cold, calculating approach made her many enemies.*

**calculation**/ˌkælkjuˈleɪʃn ˌकैल्क्युˈलेश्न्/ *noun* **1** [C, U] finding an answer by using mathematics गणना, हिसाब, परिकलन *I'll have to **do** a few **calculations** before telling you how much I can afford.* ○ *Calculation of the exact cost is impossible.* **2** [U] (*formal*) careful planning in order to achieve what you want, without considering other people स्वार्थपूर्ण सुनियोजन; स्वहित को प्रधानता देते हुए बनाई गई योजना *His actions were clearly the result of deliberate calculation.*

**calculator** /ˈkælkjuleɪtə(r) कैल्क्युलेट(र्)/ *noun* [C] a small electronic machine used for calculating figures गणना करने वाला इलेक्ट्रॉनिक यंत्र; परिकलक, कैलकुलेटर *a pocket calculator*

**calculus** /ˈkælkjələs ˈकैल्क्यलस्/ *noun* [U] (*mathematics*) a type of mathematics that deals with rates of change, for example the speed of a falling object गणित की एक शाखा जिसका मूल विषय परिवर्तन मात्राएँ होती हैं; कलन

**calendar** /ˈkælɪndə(r) ˈकैलिन्ड(र्)/ *noun* [C] **1** a list that shows the days, weeks and months of a particular year कालदर्शक पंचांग; कैलेंडर **2** a system for dividing time into fixed periods and for marking the beginning and end of a year वर्ष आरंभ और अंत अंकित करने तथा सुनिश्चित अवधि खंडों में काल-विभाजन करने की पद्धति *the Muslim calendar* **3** a list of dates and events in a year that are important in a particular area of activity वर्ष भर में एक विशेष कार्यक्षेत्र में होने वाले आयोजनों और उनकी तिथियों की सूची *Wimbledon is a major event in the sporting calendar.*

**calendar month** = **month[1]** देखिए।

**calendar year** = **year[1]** देखिए।

**calf** /kɑːf काफ़्/ *noun* [C] (*pl.* **calves** /kɑːvz काव्ज़्/) **1** a young cow बछड़ा, बछिया **2** the young of some other animals, for example elephants हाथी आदि अन्य पशुओं का बच्चा **3** the back of your leg, below your knee टाँग की पिंडली *I've strained a calf muscle.* ➪ **body** पर चित्र देखिए।

**calibrate** /ˈkælɪbreɪt ˈकैलिब्रेट्/ *verb* [T] (*technical*) to mark units of measurement on an instrument so that it can be used for measuring sth accurately किसी उपकरण पर मापन इकाइयों का निर्धारण करना, ताकि किसी अन्य वस्तु या क्रिया का सही मापन किया जा सके; अंशांकन करना

**calibration**/ˌkælɪˈbreɪʃn ˌकैलिˈब्रेशन्/ *noun* (*technical*) **1** [U] the act of marking units of measurement on an instrument so that it can be used for measuring sth accurately किसी उपकरण पर मापन-इकाइयों के निर्धारण की क्रिया; अंशांकन **2** [C] the units marked on an instrument that is used for measuring such as a **thermometer** किसी उपकरण (जैसे थर्मामीटर) पर अंकित मापन-इकाइयाँ

**calibre** (*AmE* **caliber**) /ˈkælɪbə(r) ˈकैलिब(र्)/ *noun* [*sing.*] the quality or ability of a person or thing किसी व्यक्ति या वस्तु का गुण या योग्यता *The company's employees are of (a) high calibre.*

**caliper** (*AmE*) = **calliper**

**CALL** /kɔːl कॉल्/ *abbr.* 'computer assisted language learning' कंप्यूटर सहायता-युक्त भाषा विज्ञता

**call[1]** /kɔːl कॉल्/ *verb* **1** [I, T] **call (out) to sb; call (sth) (out)** to say sth loudly or to shout in order to attract attention ऊँची आवाज़ में बुलाना, पुकारना, चिल्लाना (प्रायः ध्यान आकर्षित करने के लिए) *'Hello, is anybody there?' she called.* ○ *He called out the names and the winners stepped forward.* **2** [I, T] to telephone sb किसी को फ़ोन करना *Who's calling, please?* ○ *I'll call you tomorrow.* **3** [T] to name or describe a person or thing in a certain way किसी को विशेष नाम देना या विशेष तरीक़े से वर्णन करना *They called the baby Shalu.* ○ *Are you calling me a liar?* **4** [T] to order or ask sb to come to a certain place किसी को स्थान-विशेष पर आने के लिए कहना *Can you call everybody in for lunch?* ○ *I think we had better call the doctor.* **5** [T] to arrange for sth to take place at a certain time समय विशेष पर कुछ करने की व्यवस्था करना *to* *call a meeting/an election/a strike* **6** [I] **call (in/round)** (**on sb/at**) to make a short visit to a person or place किसी से मिलने जाना *I called in on Mihir on my way home.* **7** [I] **call at** (used about a train, etc.) to stop at the places mentioned (रेलगाड़ी आदि का) निर्दिष्ट स्थानों पर रुकना *This is the express service to Agra, calling at Faridabad and Mathura.*

**IDM bring/call sb/sth to mind** ➪ **mind[1]** देखिए।
**call it a day** (*informal*) to decide to stop doing sth कार्य को विराम देने का निर्णय करना *Let's call it a day. I'm exhausted.*

**call sb's bluff** to tell sb to actually do what he/she is threatening to do (believing that he/she will not risk doing it) धमकाने वाले व्यक्ति को धमकी पूरा करने को कहना (इस आशा में कि वह ऐसा काम करने का ख़तरा नहीं उठाएगा)

**call sb names** to use insulting words about sb किसी को अपशब्द कहना

**call the shots/tune** (*informal*) to be in a position to control a situation and make decisions about what should be done किसी स्थिति पर नियंत्रण रखने और निर्णय लेने की स्थिति में होना

**PHR V call by** (*informal*) to make a short visit to a place or person as you pass राह चलते किसी से मिलना या कहीं जाना *I'll call by to pick up the book on my way to work.*

**call for sb** to collect sb in order to go somewhere together किसी को साथ चलने के लिए बुलाना *I'll call for you when it's time to go.*

**call for sth** to demand or need sth किसी वस्तु की माँग करना या उसकी ज़रूरत होना *The crisis calls for immediate action.*

**call sth off** to cancel sth (निर्णय आदि को) रद्द करना *The football match was called off because of the bad weather.*

**call sb out** to ask sb to come, especially to an emergency संकट के समय किसी को बुलाना *We had to call out the doctor in the middle of the night.*

**call sb up 1** to telephone sb किसी को फ़ोन करना *He called me up to tell me the good news.* **2** to order sb to join the army, navy or air force सेना में भरती होने का आदेश देना

**call sth up** to look at sth that is stored in a computer कंप्यूटर में संचित सूचना सामग्री को देखना *The bank clerk called up my account details on screen.*

**call[2]** /kɔːl कॉल्/ *noun* **1** (*also* **phone call**) [C] an act of telephoning or a conversation on the telephone फ़ोन करने या फ़ोन पर बात करने की क्रिया *I'll give you **a call** at the weekend.* ○ *to **make a** local call* **2** [C] a loud sound that is made to attract attention; a shout पुकार, आह्वान *a call for help* ○ *That bird's call is easy to recognize.* **3** [C] a short visit, especially to sb's house भेंट, मुलाक़ात (किसी के घर पर) *The doctor has several calls to make this morning.* **4** [C] a request, demand for sth अनुरोध, माँग *There have been calls for the minister to resign.* **5** [C, U] **call for sth** a need for sth किसी बात की आवश्यकता *The doctor said there was no call for concern.*

**IDM at sb's beck and call** ➪ **beck** देखिए।
(**be**) **on call** to be ready to work if necessary आवश्यकता होने पर किसी काम के लिए तैयार रहना *Dr Jindal will be on call this weekend.*

**call box** = **telephone box**

**called** /kɔːld कॉल्ड्/ *adj.* (*not before a noun*) to have a particular name कोई विशेष नाम होना *His wife is called Sandhya.*

**caller** /ˈkɔːlə(r) ˈकॉल(र्)/ *noun* [C] a person who telephones or visits sb फ़ोन करने वाला या किसी से मिलने आने वाला; फ़ोन-कर्त्ता या मुलाक़ाती

**calligraphy** /kəˈlɪgrəfi कˈलिग्रफ़ि/ *noun* [U] the art of writing beautifully with a special pen or brush एक विशेष क़लम या ब्रश से सुलेख की कला या सुंदर लिखावट; सुलेखन *I am learning calligraphy* ▶ **calligrapher** *noun* [C] इस तरह के सुलेख में कुशल व्यक्ति

**calliper** (*AmE* **caliper**) /ˈkælɪpə(r) ˈकैलिप(र्)/ *noun* **1 callipers** [*pl.*] (*mathematics*) an instrument with two long thin parts joined at one end, used for measuring the **diameter** of tubes and round objects व्यासमापी उपकरण, कैलिपर्स **2** (*AmE* **brace**) [C, *usually pl.*] a metal support for weak or injured legs दुर्बल या क्षतिग्रस्त टाँगों को सहारा देने वाला धातु निर्मित उपकरण; कैलिपर्स

**callous** /ˈkæləs ˈकैलस्/ *adj.* not caring about the feelings or suffering of other people दूसरों की भावनाओं या पीड़ा की उपेक्षा करते हुए; कठोर हृदय, बेदर्द

**callus** /ˈkæləs ˈकैलस्/ *noun* [C] an area of thick hard skin on a hand or foot, usually caused by rubbing रगड़ खाने से कड़ी पड़ गई हाथ या पैर की त्वचा; घट्टा

**calm[1]** /kɑːm काम्/ *adj.* **1** not excited, worried or angry; quiet शांत, चुपचाप *Try to **keep calm**—there's no need to panic.* ○ *She spoke in a calm voice.* **2** without big waves ऊँची लहरों से रहित; शांत तरंग *a calm sea* ✪ विलोम **rough** **3** without much wind तेज़ हवा से रहित; निर्वात *calm weather* ▶ **calmly** *adv.* शांत भाव से; शांतिपूर्वक ▶ **calmness** *noun* [U] शांति

**calm²** /kɑːm काम् / *verb* [I, T] **calm (sb/sth) (down)** to become or to make sb quiet or calm शांत हो जाना या (किसी को) शांत कर देना *Calm down! Shouting at everybody won't help.*

**calm³** /kɑːm काम् / *noun* [C, U] a period of time or a state when everything is peaceful शांति *After living in the city, I enjoyed the calm of country life.*

**calorie** /ˈkæləri ˈकैलरि / *noun* [C] **1** a unit for measuring how much energy food will produce भोजन से प्राप्त ऊर्जा की इकाई; कैलोरी *a low-calorie drink/ yoghurt/diet* **2** a unit for measuring a quantity of heat; the amount of heat needed to increase the temperature of a gram of water by one degree Celsius ऊष्मा की इकाई; ऊष्मा की उतनी मात्रा जिससे एक ग्राम जल का तापमान एक डिग्री सेल्सिअस बढ़ जाए

**calorific** /ˌkæləˈrɪfɪk ˌकैलˈरिफ़िक् / *adj.* (*technical*) connected with or producing heat ऊर्जा या ऊर्जा-उत्पादन से संबंधित *the calorific value of food* (= the amount of heat or energy produced by a particular amount of food)

**calve** /kɑːv काव् / *verb* **1** [I] (used about a cow) to give birth to a **calf** (गाय का) जनना, ब्याना **2** [I, T] (*technical*) (used about a large piece of ice) to break away from an **iceberg** or a **glacier** to lose a piece of ice in this way हिमखंड का हिमशैल या हिमनदी से टूट कर अलग होना; इस रीति से बर्फ़ के टुकड़े होना

**calves** ➪ **calf** का plural रूप

**calyx** /ˈkeɪlɪks ˈकेलिक्स् / *noun* [C] (*pl.* **calyxes** or **calyces** /ˈkeɪlɪsiːz ˈकेलिसीज़् /) (*technical*) the ring of small green leaves (**sepals**) that protect a flower before it opens खिलने से पहले फूल, कली की रक्षा करने वाले हरे पत्तों का दोना; बाह्यदलपुंज

**CAM** /kæm कैम् / *abbr.* 'computer aided manufacturing' कंप्यूटर सहायता-युक्त निर्माण

**camber** /ˈkæmbə(r) ˈकैम्ब(र्) / *noun* [C] a slight downward curve from the middle of a road to each side सड़क के मध्यभाग से दोनों ओर का हलका उतार

**camcorder** /ˈkæmkɔːdə(r) ˈकैम्कॉड(र्) / *noun* [C] a camera that you can carry around and use for recording pictures and sound on a video cassette सचल-वीडियो कैमरा जिससे ध्वनि भी रिकार्ड कर सकते हैं

**came** ➪ **come** का past tense रूप

**camel** /ˈkæml ˈकैम्ल् / *noun* [C] an animal that lives in the desert and has a long neck and either one or two large masses of fat (**humps**) on its back. It is used for carrying people and goods ऊँट ➪ **dromedary** देखिए।

**cameo** /ˈkæmiəʊ ˈकैमिओ / *noun* [C] (*pl.* **cameos**) **1** a small part in a film or play that is usually played by a famous actor किसी फ़िल्म या नाटक में वह छोटी भूमिका जिसे कोई प्रसिद्ध अभिनेता निभाता है *Aamir Khan plays a cameo role in the film.* **2** a piece of jewellery that has a design in one colour and a background in a different colour नक़्क़ाशीदार गहना जिसका पार्श्व और उस पर बनी आकृति अलग-अलग रंगों में हों

**camera** /ˈkæmərə ˈकैमरा / *noun* [C] a piece of equipment that you use for taking photographs or moving pictures फ़ोटोचित्र लेने या चलचित्र रिकार्ड करने का उपकरण; कैमरा *I need a new film for my camera.*

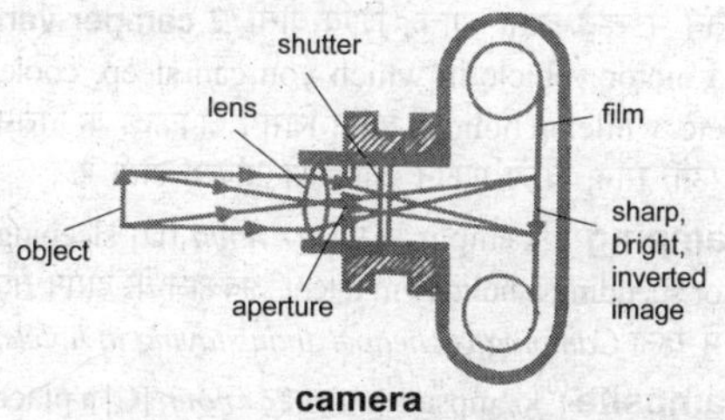

camera

**cameraman** /ˈkæmrəmən ˈकैम्रमन् / *noun* [C] (*pl.* **-men** /-mən -मन् /) a person whose job is to operate a camera for a film or a television company किसी फ़िल्म या टेलीविज़न कंपनी में कैमरा संचालित करने वाला व्यक्ति; कैमरामैन ➪ **photographer** देखिए।

**camouflage** /ˈkæməflɑːʒ ˈकैमफ़्लाश़् / *noun* [U] **1** materials or colours that soldiers use to make themselves and their equipment difficult to see युद्ध-सामग्री व सैनिकों को शत्रु से छिपाने के काम आने वाली वस्तुएँ या रंग; छद्मावरण **2** the way in which an animal's colour or shape matches its surroundings and makes it difficult to be spotted किसी पशु के रंग या आकृति का अपने परिवेश से मेल खाने का ऐसा तरीक़ा कि वह पहचान में न आए *The polar bear's white fur provides effective camouflage against the snow.* ▶ **camouflage** *verb* [T] छद्मावरण धारण करना

**camp¹** /kæmp कैम्प् / *noun* [C, U] a place where people live in tents or simple buildings away from their usual home शिविर, कैम्प *a refugee camp* ○ *The climbers set up camp at the foot of the mountain.*

**camp²** /kæmp कैम्प् / *verb* [I] **camp (out)** to sleep without a bed, especially outside in a tent बिना बिस्तर के सोना, विशेषतः घर से बाहर तंबू में *We camped next to a river.*

**campaign¹** /kæmˈpeɪn कैम्ˈपेन् / *noun* [C] **1** a plan to do a number of things in order to achieve a special aim किसी लक्ष्य को पाने के लिए योजना-निर्माण

*to launch an advertising/election campaign* **2** a planned series of attacks in a war युद्ध में अभियान-शृंखला

**campaign**[2] /kæmˈpeɪn कैम्ˈपेन्/ *verb* [I] **campaign (for/against sb/sth)** to take part in a planned series of activities in order to make sth happen or to prevent sth किसी विशेष उद्देश्य से नियोजित अभियान में भाग लेना; आंदोलन करना, आंदोलन में भाग लेना *Local people are campaigning for lower speed limits in the town.* ▶ **campaigner** *noun* [C] अभियान में भाग लेने वाला व्यक्ति *an animal rights campaigner*

**camper** /ˈkæmpə(r) ˈकैम्प(र्)/ *noun* [C] **1** a person who stays in a tent on holiday अवकाश के दौरान तंबू में रहने वाला व्यक्ति; शिविरवासी **2 camper van** a motor vehicle in which you can sleep, cook, etc. while on holiday वाहन जिसमें अवकाश के दौरान रहने, सोने, खाना पकाने आदि की सुविधा होती है

**camping** /ˈkæmpɪŋ ˈकैम्पिङ्/ *noun* [U] sleeping or spending a holiday in a tent अवकाश के दौरान तंबू में रहना *Camping is cheaper than staying in hotels.*

**campsite** /ˈkæmpsaɪt ˈकैम्प्साइट्/ *noun* [C] a place where you can stay in a tent तंबू लगाने का स्थान, कैंप-स्थल

**campus** /ˈkæmpəs ˈकैम्पस्/ *noun* [C, U] (*pl.* **campuses**) the area of land where the main buildings of a college or university are क्षेत्र जहाँ किसी महाविद्यालय या विश्वविद्यालय की मुख्य इमारतें स्थापित हों; महाविद्यालय या विश्वविद्यालय का अहाता या परिसर *the college campus*

**can**[1] /kən; *strong form* kæn कन्; प्रबल रूप कैन्/ *modal verb* (*negative* **cannot** /ˈkænɒt ˈकैनॉट्/ *short form* **can't** /kɑːnt कान्ट्/; *pt* **could** /kəd; *strong form* kʊd कड्; प्रबल रूप कुड्/; *negative* **could not** *short form* **couldn't** /ˈkʊdnt ˈकुड्न्ट्/) **1** used for showing that it is possible for sb/sth to do sth or that sb/sth has the ability to do sth क्षमता या सामर्थ्य दर्शाने के लिए प्रयुक्त *Can you ride a bike?* ○ *He can't speak French.*

**NOTE** **Can** के अनियतात्मक (infinitive) या कृदंत (participle) रूप नहीं होते हैं। भविष्य तथा पूर्णकाल (perfect) रूप बनाने के लिए **be able to** का प्रयोग किया जाता है—*He's been able to swim for almost a year.* **Could have** का प्रयोग यह बताने के लिए किया जाता है कि व्यक्ति में क्षमता तो थी परंतु उसने उसका उपयोग नहीं किया—*She could have passed the exam but she didn't really try.*

**2** used to ask for or give permission अनुमति माँगने या देने के लिए प्रयुक्त *Can I have a drink, please?* ○ *He asked if he could have a drink.*

**NOTE** जब विगत में माँगी या दी गई सामान्य अनुमति के बारे में बात करनी हो तब **could** का प्रयोग किया जाता है—*I could do anything I wanted when I stayed with my grandma.* परंतु जब हम विशेष अवसर के विषय में बात करते है तो **could** का प्रयोग नहीं किया जाता—*They were allowed to visit him in hospital yesterday.*

**3** used to ask sb to do sth आदेश देने या अनुरोध के लिए प्रयुक्त *Can you help me carry these books?* **4** used for offering to do sth प्रस्ताव रखने के लिए प्रयुक्त *Can I help at all?*

**NOTE** वृत्तिवाचक क्रियाओं (modal verbs) के विषय में अधिक जानकारी के लिए शब्दकोश के अंत में **Quick Grammar Reference** खंड देखिए।

**5** used to talk about sb's typical behaviour or of a typical effect किसी के सामान्य व्यवहार या सामान्य प्रभाव का संकेत करने में प्रयुक्त *You can be very annoying.* ○ *Wasp stings can be very painful.* **6** used in the negative for saying that you are sure sth is not true किसी बात के सत्य न होने का संकेत करने के लिए निषेधात्मक रूप में प्रयुक्त *That can't be Sonia—she's in Patna.* ○ *Surely you can't be hungry. You've only just had lunch.* **7** used with the verbs 'feel', 'hear', 'see', 'smell', 'taste' निम्नलिखित क्रियाओं के साथ प्रयुक्त 'feel', 'hear', 'see', 'smell', 'taste'

**NOTE** ये क्रियाएँ सातत्यबोधक कालों (continuous tenses) में प्रयुक्त नहीं की जाती हैं। 'Seeing' 'hearing' आदि के साथ **can** का प्रयोग किया जाता है—*I can smell something burning.* न कि *I'm smelling something burning.*

**can**[2] /kæn कैन्/ *noun* [C] **1** a metal or plastic container that is used for holding or carrying liquid (द्रव पदार्थ रखने के लिए) धातु या प्लास्टिक का डिब्बा *an oil can* **2** a metal container in which food or drink is kept without air so that it stays fresh भोज्य पदार्थों को निर्वात अवस्था में और ताज़ा बनाए रखने के लिए धातु का डिब्बा *a can of beans* ○ *a can of flavoured milk*

**NOTE** ब्रिटिश अंग्रेज़ी में खाद्य पदार्थों को रखने के डिब्बे को **tin** और पेय पदार्थों के डिब्बे को **can** कहते हैं।

**can**[3] /kæn कैन्/ *verb* [T] (**ca<u>nn</u>ing; ca<u>nn</u>ed**) to put food, drink, etc. into a can in order to keep it fresh for a long time लंबे समय तक ताज़ा बनाए रखने के लिए भोज्य पदार्थों को डिब्बे में बंद करना *canned fruit*

**canal** /kəˈnæl कˈनैल्/ *noun* [C] **1** a deep cut that is made through land so that boats or ships can travel along it or so that water can flow to an area where it is needed सिंचाई या यातायात के लिए

बनाई गई नहर *the Panama Canal* **2** one of the tubes in the body through which food, air, etc. passes शरीर में आहार तथा श्वास की नली

**canary** /kəˈneəri कˈनेअरि/ *noun* [C] (*pl.* **canaries**) a small yellow bird that sings and is often kept in a cage as a pet एक छोटी पीले रंग की चिड़िया जिसका स्वर मधुर होता है और जिसे प्रायः घरों में पाला जाता है; पीत चटकी, कनारी चिड़िया

**cancel** /ˈkænsl ˈकैन्सल्/ *verb* [T] (**cancelling; cancelled;** *AmE* **canceling; canceled**) **1** to decide that sth that has been planned or arranged will not happen पूर्वनियोजित कार्यक्रम, निर्णय आदि को रद्द करना, निरस्त करना *All flights have been cancelled because of the bad weather.* ➪ **postpone** देखिए। **2** to stop sth that you asked for or agreed to पूर्व कृत कार्य (आरक्षण, आदेश आदि) को रद्द करना *to cancel a reservation* ○ *I wish to cancel my order for these books.*

PHR V **cancel (sth) out** to be equal or have an equal effect बराबर होना या बराबर प्रभाव होना; समानता की स्थिति में आ जाना *What I owe you is the same as what you owe me, so our debts cancel each other out.*

**cancellation** /ˌkænsəˈleɪʃn ˌकैन्सˈलेशन्/ *noun* [C, U] the act of cancelling sth रद्द करने की क्रिया; निरसन *We had to make a last-minute cancellation of our air tickets to Mumbai*

**cancer** /ˈkænsə(r) ˈकैन्स(र्)/ *noun* **1** [U, C] a very serious disease in which cells in one part of the body start growing and form lumps in a way that is not normal एक ऐसा गंभीर रोग जिसमें शरीर के किसी भाग की कोशिकाओं की संख्या असामान्य रूप से बढ़ने लगती हैं; कैंसर *He died of cancer.* **2** [U] **Cancer** the fourth sign of the **zodiac,** the Crab कर्क राशि

**cancerous** /ˈkænsərəs ˈकैन्सरस्/ *adj.* (used especially about a part of the body or sth growing in the body) having cancer (शरीर का अंग) कैंसरग्रस्त *a cancerous growth* ○ *cancerous cells*

**candid** /ˈkændɪd ˈकैन्डिड्/ *adj.* saying exactly what you think स्पष्टवादी, तटस्थ, खरा ✪ पर्याय **frank** ➪ **candour** noun देखिए। ▶ **candidly** *adv.* स्पष्टता से; साफ़-साफ़

**candidacy** /ˈkændɪdəsi ˈकैन्डिडसि/ *noun* [U] being a candidate प्रत्याशी या उम्मीदवार होने की स्थिति; उम्मीदवारी

**candidate** /ˈkændɪdət ˈकैन्डिडट्/ *noun* [C] **1** a person who makes a formal request to be considered for a job or wants to be elected to a particular position (नौकरी, पद के लिए) प्रत्याशी, उम्मीदवार *We have some very good candidates for the post.* **2** a person who is taking an exam परीक्षार्थी

**candle** /ˈkændl ˈकैन्ड्ल्/ *noun* [C] a round stick of solid oil or fat with a piece of string (**a wick**) through the middle that you can burn to give light मोमबत्ती *to light/blow out a candle*

**candlelight** /ˈkændllaɪt ˈकैन्ड्ल्लाइट्/ *noun* [U] light that comes from a candle मोमबत्ती का प्रकाश *They had dinner **by candlelight**.*

**candlestick** /ˈkændlstɪk ˈकैन्ड्ल्स्टिक्/ *noun* [C] an object for holding a candle or candles मोमबत्तीदान

**candour** /ˈkændə(r) ˈकैन्ड(र्)/ *noun* [U] the quality of being honest; saying exactly what you think स्पष्टवादिता; निष्कपटता का गुण ➪ **candid** adjective देखिए।

**candy** /ˈkændi ˈकैन्डि/ *noun* [C, U] (*pl.* **candies**) (*AmE*) = **sweet²** **1** *Children love chocolate candy.*

**cane** /keɪn केन्/ *noun* **1** [C, U] the long and hard central part of certain plants (**bamboo** or **sugar**) that is like a tube and is used as a material for making furniture, etc. बाँस जैसे पौधों का सख़्त मध्यवर्ती तना जिसका प्रयोग फ़र्नीचर आदि बनाने में किया जाता है *sugarcane* ○ *a cane chair* **2** [C] a stick that is used to help sb walk बेंत, डंडी, छड़ी

**canine¹** /ˈkeɪnaɪn ˈकेनाइन्/ *adj.* connected with dogs कुत्तों से संबंधित

**canine²** /ˈkeɪnaɪn ˈकेनाइन्/ (*also* **canine tooth**) *noun* [C] one of the four pointed teeth in the front of a person's or an animal's mouth सामने के चार नुकीले दाँतों में से कोई एक; रदनक दाँत ➪ **incisor** और **molar** देखिए तथा **teeth** पर चित्र देखिए।

**canister** /ˈkænɪstə(r) ˈकैनिस्ट(र्)/ *noun* [C] a small round metal container टीन का पीपा, कनस्तर *a gas canister*

**cannabis** /ˈkænəbɪs ˈकैनबिस्/ *noun* [U] a drug made from a plant (**hemp**) that some people smoke for pleasure, but which is considered illegal भाँग जाति के एक पौधे से बनाया गया नशीला-पदार्थ जिसका सेवन कुछ लोग आनंद के लिए करते हैं किंतु जो ग़ैर-क़ानूनी है; चरस

**cannibal** /ˈkænɪbl ˈकैनिबल्/ *noun* [C] **1** a person who eats other people नरभक्षी मानव **2** an animal that eats the flesh of other animals of the same kind स्वजाति भक्षी ▶ **cannibalism** /ˈkænɪbəlɪzəm ˈकैनिबलिज़म्/ *noun* [U] स्वजाति भक्षण

**cannon** /ˈkænən ˈकैनन्/ *noun* [C] (*pl.* **cannon** or **cannons**) **1** a large gun on a ship, army vehicle, aircraft, etc. जहाज़, तोपगाड़ी, विमान आदि पर रखी बड़ी तोप **2** a large, simple gun that was used in past times for firing large stone or metal balls (**cannon balls**) विगत युग की भारी बड़ी तोप जो बड़े पत्थर और गोले बरसाती थी

**cannot** /ˈkænɒt ˈकैनॉट्/ ➪ **can**[1] देखिए।

**canoe** /kəˈnuː कˈनू/ *noun* [C] a light, narrow boat for one or two people that you can move through the water using a flat piece of wood (**a paddle**) दो व्यक्तियों के उपयोग की लंबी, संकरी और हलकी नाव जिसे चप्पू द्वारा चलाया जाता है; डोंगी ➪ **kayak** देखिए तथा **boat** पर चित्र देखिए। ▸ **canoe** *verb* [I] (*pres. part.* **canoeing;** *3rd person sing. pres.* **canoes;** *pt, pp* **canoed**) डोंगी चलाना *They canoed down the river.*

**canon** /ˈkænən ˈकैनन्/ *noun* [C] **1** (*formal*) a generally accepted rule, standard or principle by which sth is judged स्वीकृत नियम, मापदंड या सिद्धांत जिससे किसी वस्तु का मूल्यांकन होता है *the canons of good taste* **2** a list of books or other works that are generally accepted as the genuine work of a particular writer or as being important किसी लेखक की मान्यता दिलाने या महत्त्वपूर्ण पुस्तकों, लेखों आदि की प्रमाणित व सर्वस्वीकृत सूची *the Shakespeare canon* **3** a piece of music in which singers or instruments take it in turns to repeat the tune संगीत रचना जिसे गायक या वादक बारी-बारी से दुहराते हैं

**canopy** /ˈkænəpi ˈकैनपि/ *noun* [C] (*pl.* **canopies**) a cover that hangs or spreads above sth चँदवा, छत्र, वितान *The highest branches in the rainforest form a dense canopy.* ○ *a parachute canopy*

**can't** ➪ **cannot** का संक्षिप्त रूप

**canteen** /kænˈtiːn कैन्ˈटीन्/ *noun* [C] the place in a school, factory, office, etc. where the people who work there can get meals विद्यालय, कारख़ाने कार्यालय आदि में स्थित उपाहार-गृह; कैनटीन *the staff canteen* ➪ **cafeteria** देखिए।

**canter** /ˈkæntə(r) ˈकैन्टर्/ *verb* [I] (used about a horse and its rider) to run fairly fast but not very fast (घोड़े और घुड़सवार का) मध्यम गति से दौड़ना *We cantered along the beach.* ▸ **canter** *noun* [*sing.*] (घोड़े की) मध्यम गति की दौड़ ➪ **gallop** और **trot** देखिए।

**cantilever** /ˈkæntɪliːvə(r) ˈकैन्टिलीव़र्/ *noun* [C] a long piece of metal or wood that extends from a wall to support the end of a bridge or any other structure डाट; लकड़ी या धातु का लंबा टुकड़ा जो दीवार से बाहर की तरफ़ निकला होता है और पुल के छोर या किसी अन्य ढाँचे को बल देता है; बाहुधरण

**cantonment** /kænˈtɒnmənt कैन्ˈटॉन्मन्ट्/ *noun* [C] a military garrison or camp (especially in the Indian subcontinent) सैन्य छावनी, कैंटोनमन्ट (विशेषतः भारतीय उपमहाद्वीप में)

**canvas** /ˈkænvəs ˈकैन्व़स्/ *noun* **1** [U] a type of strong cloth that is used for making sails, bags, tents, etc. मोटा, भारी व मज़बूत कपड़ा जिसके पाल, बोरे, तंबू आदि बनते हैं; किरमिच **2** [C] a piece of strong cloth for painting a picture on चित्रकारी करने का मोटा मज़बूत कपड़ा; किरमिच, कैन्वस

**canvass** /ˈkænvəs ˈकैन्व़स्/ *verb* **1** [I, T] **canvass (sb) (for sth)** to try to persuade people to vote for a particular person or party in an election or to support sb/sth चुनाव आदि में प्रत्याशी विशेष या दल विशेष के पक्ष में समर्थन माँगना *He's canvassing for the Congress Party.* **2** [T] to find out what people's opinions are about sth किसी विषय पर लोगों की राय जानना

**canyon** /ˈkænjən ˈकैन्यन्/ *noun* [C] a deep valley with very steep sides तीखे ढाल वाली गहरी घाटी

**cap**[1] /kæp कैप्/ *noun* [C] **1** a soft hat that has a part sticking out at the front (**peak**) एक प्रकार की नरम टोपी जिसका सामने वाला भाग बाहर की तरफ़ निकला हुआ हो *a baseball cap* **2** a soft hat that is worn for a particular purpose विशेष उपयोग की नरम टोपी *a shower cap* **3** a covering for the end or top of sth ढक्कन *Please put the cap back on the bottle.* ➪ **top**[1] देखिए

**cap**[2] /kæp कैप्/ *verb* [T] (**capping; capped**) **1** to cover the top of sth ढकना, आच्छादित करना *mountains capped with snow* **2** to limit the amount of money that can be spent on sth ख़र्च की सीमा बाँधना; ख़र्च पर रोक लगाना **3** to follow sth with sth bigger or better बढ़ाकर या बेहतर ढंग से अनुसरण करना; से बढ़कर होना

**IDM** **to cap it all** as a final piece of bad luck दुर्भाग्यपूर्ण घटनाओं में अंतिम घटना *I had a row with my boss, my bike was stolen, and now to cap it all I've lost my keys!*

**capability** /ˌkeɪpəˈbɪləti ˌकेपˈबिलटि/ *noun* [C, U] (*pl.* **capabilities**) **capability (to do sth/of doing sth)** the quality of being able to do sth क्षमता, सामर्थ्य, योग्यता *I tried to fix the computer, but it was **beyond** my **capabilities**.*

**capable** /ˈkeɪpəbl ˈकेपब्ल्/ *adj.* **1 capable of (doing) sth** having the ability or qualities necessary to do sth कुछ करने में सक्षम या समर्थ *He's capable of passing the exam if he tries harder* ○ *I do not believe that she's capable of stealing*

2 having a lot of skill; good at doing sth अतिकुशल; सुयोग्य *She's a very capable teacher.* ✪ विलोम **incapable** ▶ **capably** *adv.* कुशलतापूर्वक

**capacitor** /kəˈpæsɪtə(r) कˈपैसिट(र्)/ *noun* [C] (*technical*) a device used to store an electric charge विद्युत चार्ज को संचित करने वाला उपकरण; संधारित्र

**capacity** /kəˈpæsəti कˈपैसटि/ *noun* (*pl.* **capacities**) 1 [*sing.*, U] the amount that a container or space can hold किसी पात्र या जगह की धारणशक्ति; धारिता *The tank has a capacity of 1000 litres.* ○ *The stadium was* ***filled to capacity***. 2 [*sing.*] **a capacity (for sth/for doing sth); a capacity (to do sth)** the ability to understand or do sth कुछ समझने या करने की क्षमता *That book is beyond the capacity of young children.* ○ *a capacity for hard work/for learning languages* 3 [C] the official position that sb has किसी व्यक्ति का पद *In his* ***capacity as*** *chairman of the council he could do a lot for the street children* 4 [*sing.*, U] the amount that a factory or machine can produce किसी कारख़ाने या मशीन की उत्पादन क्षमता *The power station is working* ***at full capacity***.

**cape** /keɪp केप्/ *noun* [C] 1 a piece of clothing with no sleeves that hangs from your shoulders बिना बाँहों का कंधों से लटकाने वाला ऊपरी वस्त्र; लबादा ➪ **cloak** देखिए। 2 a piece of high land that sticks out into the sea भूमि का नुकीला भाग जो समुद्र में दूर तक चला गया हो; अंतरीप *the Cape of Good Hope*

**capillary** /kəˈpɪləri कˈपिलरि/ *noun* [C] (*pl.* **capillaries**) 1 any of the smallest tubes in the body that carry blood शरीर की सबसे छोटी रुधिर-वाहिनियों में से एक; केशिका नली 2 a very small tube as thin as a hair बाल के समान पतली व बहुत छोटी नली

**capital[1]** /ˈkæpɪtl ˈकैपिट्ल्/ *noun* 1 (*also* **capital city**) [C] the town or city where the government of a country is राजधानी, मुख्य नगर *New Delhi is the capital of India.* 2 [U] an amount of money that you use to start a business or to put in a bank, etc. so that you earn more money (**interest**) on it मूलधन, पूँजी *When she had enough capital, she bought a shop.* 3 (*also* **capital letter**) [C] the large form of a letter of the alphabet वर्णमाला के अक्षर का बड़ा रूप (विशेषतः रोमन लिपि में) *Write your name in capitals.* 4 [C] a place that is well known for a particular thing प्रयोजन या वस्तु विशेष के लिए प्रसिद्ध स्थान *Niagara Falls is the honeymoon capital of the world.*

**capital[2]** /ˈkæpɪtl ˈकैपिट्ल्/ *adj.* 1 connected with punishment by death मृत्युदंड-संबंधी *a capital offence* (= a crime for which sb can be sentenced to death) 2 (used about letters of the alphabet) written in the large form (वर्णमाला के अक्षर) बड़े रूप में लिखे गए *'Dheeraj' begins with a capital 'D'.*

**capital gains** *noun* [*pl.*] profits that you make from selling sth, especially property विशेषतः संपत्ति बेचने से प्राप्त लाभ *to pay* ***capital gains tax***

**capital investment** *noun* [U] money that a business spends on buildings, equipment, etc. किसी कंपनी द्वारा भवन, उपकरण आदि पर ख़र्च की गई पूँजी

**capitalism** /ˈkæpɪtəlɪzəm ˈकैपिटलिज़म्/ *noun* [U] the economic system in which businesses are owned and run for profit by individuals and not by the state पूँजीवाद ➪ **communism, Marxism** और **socialism** देखिए। ▶ **capitalist** *noun* [C], *adj.* पूँजीवादी

**capitalize** (*also* **-ise**) /ˈkæpɪtəlaɪz ˈकैपिटलाइज़्/ *verb* [T] 1 to write or print a letter of the alphabet as a **capital;** to begin a word with a capital letter बड़ा अक्षर लिखना या मुद्रित करना; बड़े अक्षर से शब्द को शुरू करना 2 (*technical*) to sell possessions in order to change them into money संपत्ति बेचकर पूँजी बनाना 3 (*usually passive*) (*technical*) to provide a company etc. with the money it needs to function संस्थान आदि को क्रियाशील रहने के लिए पूंजी देना ▶ **capitalization** (*also* **-isation**) /ˌkæpɪtəlaɪˈzeɪʃn ˌकैपिटलाइˈज़ेश्न्/ *noun* [U] पूँजीकरण

**PHR V** **capitalize on sth** to use sth to your advantage अपने लाभ के लिए किसी वस्तु का प्रयोग करना *We can capitalize on the mistakes that our rivals have made.*

**capital punishment** *noun* [U] punishment by death for serious crimes गंभीर अपराध के लिए मृत्युदंड ➪ **death penalty** और **corporal punishment** देखिए।

**capitulate** /kəˈpɪtʃuleɪt कˈपिट्युलेट्/ *verb* [I] (*formal*) to stop fighting and accept that you have lost; to give in to sb हार मान लेना और झगड़ा समाप्त करना; झुक जाना ▶ **capitulation** /kəˌpɪtjuˈleɪʃn कˌपिट्युˈलेश्न्/ *noun* [C, U] हार मानने की क्रिया; आत्मसमर्पण

**capricious** /kəˈprɪʃəs कˈप्रिशस्/ *adj.* changing behaviour suddenly in a way that is difficult to predict आचरण या व्यवहार में ऐसा अचानक आए बदलाव से संबंधित जिसका पूर्वानुमान नहीं किया जा सके; सनकी, झक्की

**Capricorn** /ˈkæprɪkɔːn ˈकैप्रिकॉन्/ *noun* [U] the tenth sign of the **zodiac,** the Goat मकर राशि

**capsicum** /ˈkæpsɪkəm ˈकैप्सिकम्/ *noun* [C] a type of pepper which may be green, yellow or red and can be eaten cooked or not cooked पहाड़ी मिर्च (शिमला मिर्च)

**capsize** /kæpˈsaɪz कैप्ˈसाइज़् / *verb* [I, T] (used about boats) to turn over in the water (नाव का) पानी में पलट जाना *A big wave capsized the yacht.*

**capsule** /ˈkæpsjuːl ˈकैप्स्यूल् / *noun* [C] **1** a very small closed tube of medicine that you swallow दवा से भरी छोटी संपुटिका जिसे निगला जाता है; कैप्सूल **2** a container that is closed so that air, water, etc. cannot enter सीलबंद डिब्बा जिसमें वायु, जल आदि प्रवेश नहीं कर सकते

**Capt.** *abbr.* Captain; a position (**rank**) in the army कैप्टेन, कप्तान (सेना में)

**captain[1]** /ˈkæptɪn ˈकैप्टिन् / *noun* [C] **1** the person who is in command of a ship or an aircraft जलपोत या विमान का मुख्य संचालक; कप्तान **2** a person who is the leader of a group or team किसी समूह या दल का नेता; कप्तान *Who's (the) captain of the Indian team?* **3** an officer at a middle level in the army or navy सेना में मध्य स्तर का अधिकारी; कैप्टन

**captain[2]** /ˈkæptɪn ˈकैप्टिन् / *verb* [T] to be the captain of a group or team किसी समूह या दल का प्रमुख होना

**caption** /ˈkæpʃn ˈकैप्शन् / *noun* [C] the words that are written above or below a picture, photograph, etc. to explain what it is about चित्र, फ़ोटो आदि के ऊपर या नीचे दी लिखित सूचना; शीर्षक, अनुशीर्षक

**captivate** /ˈkæptɪveɪt ˈकैप्टिव़ेट् / *verb* [T] to attract and hold sb's attention किसी का ध्यान आकृष्ट रखना; मोहित कर देना ▶ **captivating** *adj.* मोहक, लुभावना

**captive[1]** /ˈkæptɪv ˈकैप्टिव़् / *adj.* kept as a prisoner; (used about animals) kept in a cage, etc. क़ैदी, बंदी; (पशुओं का) पिंजरे में बंद (*figurative*) *a **captive audience*** (= listening because they cannot leave)

IDM **hold sb captive** to keep sb as a prisoner and not allow him/her to escape किसी को बंदी बनाकर रखना

**take sb captive** to catch sb and hold him/her as your prisoner किसी को बंदी बना लेना NOTE उपर्युक्त अर्थ में **hold sb prisoner** और **take sb prisoner** अभिव्यक्तियों का भी प्रयोग किया जा सकता है।

**captive[2]** /ˈkæptɪv ˈकैप्टिव़् / *noun* [C] a prisoner क़ैदी, बंदी

**captivity** /kæpˈtɪvəti कैप्ˈटिव़टि / *noun* [U] the state of being kept in a place that you cannot escape from क़ैद, बंदी-स्थिति *Wild animals are often unhappy **in captivity**.*

**captor** /ˈkæptə(r) ˈकैप्ट(र्) / *noun* [C] a person who takes or keeps a person as a prisoner बंदी बनाने वाला व्यक्ति; बंदीकर्त्ता

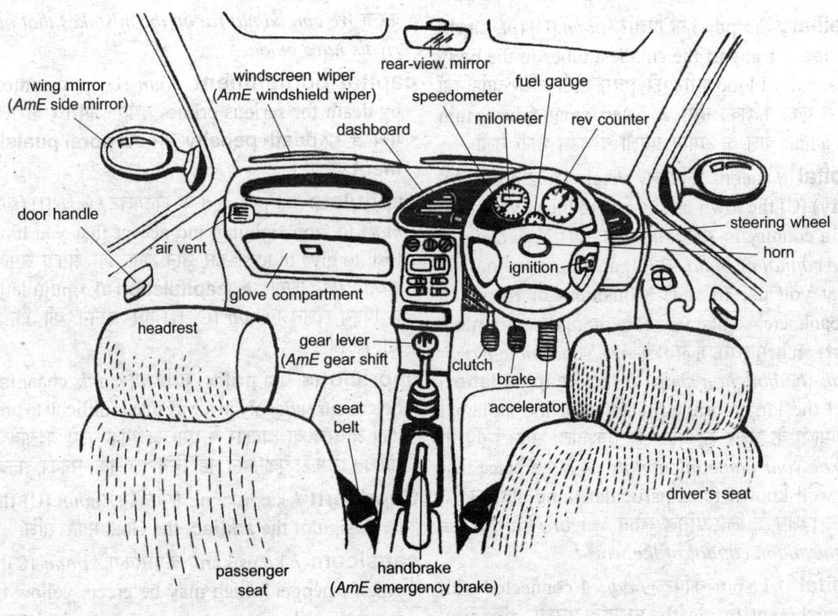


**car (*AmE* automobile)**

**capture**[1] /ˈkæptʃə(r) ˈकैप्च(र्)/ *verb* [T] **1** to take a person or animal prisoner किसी व्यक्ति या पशु को बंदी बनाना *The lion was captured and taken back to the zoo.* **2** to take control of sth किसी पर अधिकार या कब्ज़ा करना *The town has been captured by the rebels.* ○ *The company has captured 90% of the market.* **3** to make sb interested in sth किसी की रुचि प्रवृत्त करना *The story captured the children's imagination.* **4** to succeed in representing or recording sth in words, pictures, etc. शब्दों, चित्रों आदि में कुछ निरूपित करने में सफल होना *This poem captures the atmosphere of the carnival.* ○ *The robbery was captured on video.* **5** (*computing*) to put sth into a computer in a form that it can use किसी वस्तु को व्यवहार-योग्य रूप में कंप्यूटर में डालना

**capture**[2] /ˈkæptʃə(r) ˈकैप्च(र्)/ *noun* [U] the act of capturing sth or being captured बंदी बनाने या बनने की क्रिया; कब्ज़ा करने की क्रिया

**car** /kɑː(r) का(र्)/ *noun* [C] **1** (*also* **automobile**) a road vehicle with four wheels that can carry a small number of people मोटरकार *a new/second-hand car* ○ *Where can I park the car?*

> NOTE मोटरकार द्वारा यात्रा के लिए **go in the car** या **go by car** अभिव्यक्तियों का प्रयोग किया जाता है। इस अर्थ के लिए क्रिया **drive** का प्रयोग भी किया जा सकता है—*I come to work in the car/by car.* ○ *I drive to work.*

**2** a section of a train that is used for a particular purpose किसी विशेष प्रयोजन के लिए प्रयुक्त रेलगाड़ी का डिब्बा *a dining/sleeping car* **3** (*AmE*) = **carriage1**

**carafe** /kəˈræf कˈरैफ़्/ *noun* [C] a glass container like a bottle with a wide neck, in which wine or water is served (मदिरा या पानी पेश करने के लिए) चौड़ी गरदन वाला बोतलनुमा काँच का पात्र; काँच की सुराही

**caramel** /ˈkærəmel ˈकैरमेल्/ *noun* **1** [U] burnt sugar that is used to add flavour and colour to food जली हुई शक्कर (भोजन में रंग और स्वाद के लिए) **2** [C, U] a type of sticky sweet that is made from boiled sugar, butter and milk चाशनी, मक्खन और दूध से बनी एक प्रकार की चिपचिपी मिठाई

**carapace** /ˈkærəpeɪs ˈकैरपेस्/ *noun* [C] (*technical*) the hard shell on the back of some animals, for example **crabs** that protects them केकड़े आदि प्राणियों की पीठ पर का कड़ा आवरण; पृष्ठवर्म

**carat** (*AmE* **karat**) /ˈkærət ˈकैरट्/ *noun* [C] a unit for measuring how pure gold is or how heavy jewels are सोने की शुद्धता या रत्नों के तौल की इकाई; कैरट *a 20-carat gold diamond ring*

**caravan** /ˈkærəvæn ˈकैरवैन्/ *noun* [C] **1** (*AmE* **trailer**) a large vehicle that is pulled by a car. You can sleep, cook, etc. in a caravan when you are travelling or on holiday कारयुक्त बड़ा वाहन जिसमें आमोद यात्रा के दौरान रहने, सोने, खाना पकाने आदि का प्रबंध होता है; कारवाँ **2** a group of people and animals that travel together, for example across a desert यात्रियों और पशुओं का दल जो एक साथ मिलकर सफ़र करते हैं; कारवाँ, क़ाफ़िला

**carbohydrate**/ˌkɑːbəʊˈhaɪdreɪt ˌकाबोˈहाइड्रेट्/ *noun* [C, U] one of the substances in food, for example sugar, that gives your body energy भोजन में उपलब्ध एक तत्त्व, जैसे शक्कर, जो शरीर को ऊर्जा प्रदान करता हैं; कार्बोहाइड्रेट *Athletes need a diet that is high in carbohydrate.*

**carbon** /ˈkɑːbən ˈकाबन्/ *noun* [U] (*symbol* **C**) a chemical substance that is found in all living things, and also in diamonds, coal, petrol, etc. एक रासायनिक तत्त्व जो सभी सजीवों तथा हीरे, कोयले आदि में भी पाया जाता है; कार्बन

**carbonate** /ˈkɑːbəneɪt ˈकाबोनेट्/ *noun* [C] (*symbol* $CO_3$) a salt that is often formed by the reaction of **carbon dioxide** with another chemical substance सामान्यतः कार्बन डाइऑक्साइड और किसी अन्य रासायनिक तत्व की प्रतिक्रिया से निर्मित लवण

**carbon copy** *noun* [C] **1** a copy of a letter, etc. that was made using special paper (**carbon paper**) मसि-पत्र (कार्बन पेपर) लगाकर बनाई प्रति; कार्बन प्रति **2** an exact copy of sth किसी वस्तु आदि की एकदम सही प्रतिलिपि

**carbon dating** *noun* [U] a method of calculating the age of very old objects by measuring the amounts of different forms of **carbon** in them अति प्राचीन वस्तुओं की आयु जानने की एक विधि जिसमें उन वस्तुओं में विद्यमान कार्बन के विभिन्न रूपों की मात्रा को मापा जाता है; कार्बन तिथि-निर्धारण

**carbon dioxide** *noun* [U] (*symbol* $CO_2$) a gas that has no colour or smell that people and animals breathe out of their lungs रंगहीन और गंधहीन गैस जिसे मनुष्य और पशु श्वास में बाहर फेंकते हैं; कार्बन डाइऑक्साइड

**carbonic acid** /kɑːˌbɒnɪkˈæsɪd काˌबॉनिक्ˈऐसिड्/ *noun* [U] a very weak acid that is formed when **carbon dioxide** dissolves in water कार्बन डाइऑक्साइड के पानी में घुलने से बना क्षीण अम्ल; कार्बनिक एसिड

**carboniferous** /ˌkɑːbəˈnɪfərəs ˌकाबˈनिफ़रस्/ *adj.* (in geology) **1** producing or containing coal कोयला-उत्पादक या कोयला-युक्त **2 Carboniferous**

of the period in the earth's history when layers of coal were formed underground पृथ्वी के इतिहास के उस युग से संबंधित जब भूगर्भ में कोयले की तहें बनी थी

**carbon monoxide** /ˌkɑːbənməˈnɒksaɪd ˌकाबन्‌मˈनॉक्‌साइड्/ *noun* [U] (*symbol* **CO**) a poisonous gas formed when **carbon** burns partly but not completely. It is produced when petrol is burnt in car engines कार्बन के अंशतः (न कि पूर्णतः) जलने से बनी विषैली गैस (पेट्रोल जलने पर उत्पन्न)

**carbon paper** *noun* [U] thin paper with a dark substance on one side that you put between two sheets of paper to make a copy of what you are writing पतला काग़ज़ जिसके एक तरफ़ गहरे रंग के पदार्थ की परत होती है और जिसे दो पन्नों के बीच रखकर लिखी जा रही सामग्री की प्रतिलिपि बनाई जाती है; मसि-पत्र; कार्बन पेपर

**carburettor** (*AmE* **carburetor**) /ˌkɑːbəˈretə(r) ˌकाबˈरेटर्/ *noun* [C] the piece of equipment in a car's engine that mixes petrol and air कार के इंजिन का वह भाग जो पेट्रोल और हवा को मिश्रित करता है

**carcass** /ˈkɑːkəs ˈकाकस्/ *noun* [C] the dead body of an animal पशु का मृत शरीर ➪ **corpse** देखिए।

**carcinogen** /kɑːˈsɪnədʒən काˈसिनजन्/ *noun* [C] a substance that can cause **cancer** कैंसर पैदा कर सकने वाला एक तत्व

**carcinogenic** /ˌkɑːsɪnəˈdʒenɪk ˌकासिनˈजेनिक्/ *adj.* likely to cause **cancer** कैंसर पैदा करने की संभावना वाला; कार्सिनोजनक

**card** /kɑːd काड्/ *noun* **1** [U] thick rigid paper मोटा कड़ा काग़ज़; गत्ता; कार्ड **2** [C] a piece of card or plastic that has information on it गत्ते या प्लास्टिक का कार्ड जिस पर आवश्यक सूचना होती है *a membership/identity/credit/business card* **3** [C] a piece of card with a picture on it that you use for sending a special message to sb किसी को अभीष्ट संदेश भेजने के लिए सचित्र कार्ड *a New Year/birthday card* ○ *a get-well card* (= one that you send to sb who is ill) **4 playing card** [C] one of a set of 52 small pieces of card with shapes or pictures on them that are used for playing games ताश का पत्ता *a pack of cards* **5 cards** [*pl.*] games that are played with cards ताश; ताश के खेल *Let's play cards.* ○ *I never win at cards!*

> **NOTE** ताश की गड्डी **pack** में चार रंग **suits** होते हैं, दो लाल (**hearts** और **diamonds**) और दो काले (**clubs** और **spades**)। प्रत्येक **suit** में एक इक्का **ace**, एक राजा **king**, एक रानी **queen**, और एक गुलाम **jack** के अलावा 2 से 10 तक की संख्या के नौ अन्य पत्ते होते हैं। ताश खेलने से पहले हम पत्तों को **shuffle, cut** और **deal** करते हैं।

**IDM on the cards;** (*AmE*) **in the cards** (*informal*) likely to happen संभावित *Their marriage has been on the cards for some time now.*

**cardamom** /ˈkɑːdəməm ˈकाडमम्/ *noun* [U] the dried seeds of a plant belonging to South and South-East Asia, that is used as a spice in cooking इलायची

**cardboard** /ˈkɑːdbɔːd ˈकाड्‌बॉड्/ *noun* [U] very thick paper that is used for making boxes, etc. गत्ता, दफ़्ती जिससे डब्बे आदि बनाए जाते हैं *The goods were packed in cardboard boxes.*

**card catalog** (*AmE*) = **card index**

**cardholder** /ˈkɑːdhəʊldə(r) ˈकाड्‌होल्‌ड(र्)/ *noun* [C] a person who uses a card from a bank, etc. to pay for things बैंक आदि द्वारा प्रदत्त कार्ड का धारक; कार्डधारक

**cardiac** /ˈkɑːdiæk ˈकाडिऐक्/ *adj.* (*formal*) connected with the heart हृदय-विषयक; हृदय-संबंधी *cardiac surgery*

**cardiac arrest** *noun* [C] (*medical*) a serious medical condition when the heart stops working हृदय गति के रुक जाने की गंभीर स्थिति

**cardigan** /ˈkɑːdɪgən ˈकाडिगन्/ *noun* [C] a piece of clothing like a woollen jacket, that fastens at the front सामने से बंद होने वाली ऊनी जैकेट ➪ **sweater** पर नोट देखिए।

**cardinal** /ˈkɑːdɪnl ˈकाडिन्‌ल्/ *noun* [C] **1** a priest at a high level in the Roman Catholic church रोमन कैथॉलिक चर्च का उच्च स्तरीय पादरी **2 cardinal number** a whole number, for example 1, 2, 3, that shows quantity पूर्ण अंक जैसे 1, 2, 3, 4 जो मात्रा दर्शाता है ➪ **ordinal** देखिए।

**cardinal points** *noun* [*pl.*] (*technical*) the four main points (North, South, East and West) on an instrument that shows direction (**a compass**) दिशासूचक यंत्र के चार मुख्य बिंदु (उत्तर, दक्षिण, पूर्व और पश्चिम)

**card index** (*also* **index,** *AmE* **card catalog**) *noun* [C] a box of cards with information on them, arranged in the order of the alphabet वर्णमाला के क्रम में व्यवस्थित सूचना-अंकित कार्डों का डिब्बा ➪ **stationery** पर चित्र देखिए।

**cardio-** /ˈkɑːdiəʊ ˈकाडिओ/ *prefix* (*in nouns, adjectives and adverbs*) connected with the heart हृदय-संबंधी

**care[1]** /keə(r) केअ(र्)/ *noun* **1** [U] **care (for sb** ... looking after sb/sth so that he/she/it has what he/she/it needs for his/her/its health and protection किसी की देखभाल या देखरेख *All the children* ...

*their care were healthy and happy.* ○ *She's in intensive care* (= the part of the hospital for people who are very sesiously ill). **2** [U] **care (over sth/in doing sth)** thinking about what you are doing so that you do it well or do not make a mistake ध्यान, सावधानी *This box contains glasses—please handle it* ***with care***. **3** [C, U] something that makes you feel worried or unhappy चिंताजनक स्थिति; चिंता, परेशानी *Since Mr Mathur retired he* ***doesn't have a care in the world***.

IDM **in care** (used about children) living in a home which is organized by the government or the local council, and not with their parents (बच्चे) माता-पिता से अलग और किसी संस्था की देखरेख में *They were taken into care after their parents died.*

**take care (that.../to do sth)** to be careful ध्यान रखना या देना; सावधान रहना *Goodbye and take care!* ○ *Take care that you don't spill your tea.*

**take care of sb/sth** to deal with sb/sth; to organize or arrange sth कोई काम निबटाना; आयोजित या व्यवस्थाबद्ध करना *I'll take care of the food for the party.*

**take care of yourself/sb/sth** to keep yourself/ sb/sth safe from injury, illness, damage, etc.; to look after sb/sth किसी को, अपने को परेशानी या हानि से बचाना; किसी का ध्यान रखना या देखरेख करना *My mother took care of me when I was ill.*

**care**[2] /keə(r) केअ(र्)/ *verb* [I, T] **care (about sb/sth)** to be worried about or interested in sb/sth किसी व्यक्ति या वस्तु की चिंता करना या उसमें रुचि रखना *Money is the thing that she cares about most.* ○ *I don't care what you do.*

IDM **I, etc. couldn't care less** (*informal*) it does not matter to me, etc. at all मुझे ज़रा सी भी परवाह नहीं *I couldn't care less what Sanjay thinks.*

**who cares"** (*informal*) nobody is interested; it is not important to anyone किसी की भी दिलचस्पी नहीं, किसी के लिए भी महत्त्वपूर्ण नहीं *'I wonder who'll win the match.' 'Who cares?'*

**would you care for.../to do sth** (*formal*) a polite way to ask if sb would like sth or would like to do sth जब नम्रतापूर्वक पूछना हो क्या आप (कुछ) पसंद करेंगे? 'आप क्या लेंगें?

PHR V **care for sb** to look after sb किसी की देखभाल करना *Who cared for her while she was ill?*

**care for sb/sth** to like or love sb/sth किसी व्यक्ति या वस्तु को पसंद करना या चाहना *She still cares for Tony although he married someone else.*

**areer**[1] /kəˈrɪə(r) कˈरिअ(र्)/ *noun* [C] **1** a job or profesion that sb has been trained for and does for a long time; the series of jobs that sb has in a particular area of work नौकरी या पेशा जिसके लिए किसी व्यक्ति ने प्रशिक्षण लिया हो और जो वह काफ़ी समय तक करे; किसी विशेष कार्यक्षेत्र में जीविका हेतु नौकरियाँ *a successful career in politics* **2** the period of your life that you spend working जीविका और वृत्ति में बिताए समय की अवधि *She spent most of her career working in Singapore.*

**career**[2] /kəˈrɪə(r) कˈरिअ(र्)/ *verb* [I] to move quickly and in a dangerous way तेज़ और ख़तरनाक ढंग से गति करना *The car careered off the road and crashed into a wall.*

**carefree** /ˈkeəfri: ˈकेअफ़्री/ *adj.* with no problems or worries निश्चिंत, बेफ़िक्र, चिंतामुक्त

**careful** /ˈkeəfl ˈकेअफ़्ल्/ *adj.* **1 careful (of/with sth); careful (to do sth)** thinking about what you are doing so that you do not have an accident or make mistakes, etc. सावधान, ख़बरदार, सतर्क *That ladder doesn't look very safe. Be careful you don't fall.* ○ *a careful driver* **2** giving a lot of attention to details to be sure sth is right ध्यानपूर्ण, सावधानी से किया गया *I'll need to give this matter some careful thought.* ○ *a careful worker* ▶ **carefully** /ˈkeəfəli ˈकेअफ़लि/ *adv.* ध्यानपूर्वक, सावधानी से *Please listen carefully to the teacher's lecture.*

**careless** /ˈkeələs ˈकेअलस्/ *adj.* **1 careless (about/with sth)** not thinking enough about what you are doing so that you make mistakes असावधान, लापरवाह *The accident was caused by careless driving.* **2** resulting from a lack of thought or attention to detail असावधानी या लापरवाही के कारण उत्पन्न *a careless mistake* ▶ **carelessly** *adv.* असावधानी या लापरवाही से *She threw her coat carelessly on the chair.* ▶ **carelessness** *noun* [U] असावधानी, लापरवाही

**carer** /ˈkeərə(r) ˈकेअर(र्)/ (*AmE* **caregiver** /ˈkeəgɪvə(r) ˈकेअगिव़(र्)/) *noun* [C] a person who regularly looks after sb who is unable to look after himself/herself because of age, illness, etc. किसी बच्चे, बीमार आदि की नियमित रूप से देखभाल करने वाला व्यक्ति

**caress** /kəˈres कˈरेस्/ *verb* [T] to touch sb/sth in a gentle and loving way प्यार से स्पर्श करना; दुलराना ▶ **caress** *noun* [C] प्यार-दुलार से स्पर्श

**caretaker** /ˈkeəteɪkə(r) ˈकेअटेक(र्)/ (*AmE* **janitor**) *noun* [C] a person whose job is to look after a large building, for example a school or a block of flats किसी विशाल भवन की देखभाल की ज़िम्मेदारी वाला व्यक्ति; रखवाला

**cargo** /ˈkɑːgəʊ ˈकागो/ *noun* [C, U] (*pl.* **cargoes** *AmE* **cargos**) the goods that are carried in a ship or an aircraft विमान या जलपोत द्वारा ढोया जाने वाला माल; जहाज़ी माल, नौभार, कार्गो *a cargo ship*

**caricature** /ˈkærɪkətʃʊə(r) ˈकैरिकचुअ(र्)/ *noun* [C] a picture or description of sb that makes his/her appearance or behaviour funnier and more extreme than it really is किसी व्यक्ति का हास्यजनक चित्र या वर्णन जो उसके रूप-रंग या आचरण को उपहासात्मक रूप से बढ़ा-चढ़ा कर पेश करता है; विद्रूप, व्यंग्यचित्र, उपहासचित्र *Many of the people in the book are caricatures of the author's friends.*

**caring** /ˈkeərɪŋ ˈकेअरिङ्/ *adj.* showing that you care about other people दूसरों के प्रति चिंता और प्यार दिखानेवाला; परचिंतक *We must work towards a more caring society.*

**carnage** /ˈkɑːnɪdʒ ˈकानिज्/ *noun* [U] (*written*) the violent killing of a large number of people सामूहिक हत्याकांड, नरसंहार

**Carnatic music** *noun* [U] the main style of classical music of southern India as distinct from **Hindustani music** of the north दक्षिण भारतीय शास्त्रीय संगीत की प्रमुख शैली, यह उत्तर भारत के हिंदुस्तानी संगीत से भिन्न है

**carnation** /kɑːˈneɪʃn काˈनेश्न्/ *noun* [C] a white, pink or red flower with a pleasant smell सफ़ेद गुलाबी या लाल सुगंधित पुष्प; कार्नेशन

**carnival** /ˈkɑːnɪvl ˈकानिव्ल्/ *noun* [C] a public festival that takes place in the streets with music and dancing आनंदोत्सव, जनोत्सव, मनोरंजन मेला *the carnival in Goa*

**carnivore** /ˈkɑːnɪvɔː(r) ˈकानिव़ॉ(र्)/ *noun* [C] any animal that eats meat मांसाहारी या मांसभक्षी पशु ➪ **herbivore, insectivore** और **omnivore** देखिए। ▸ **carnivorous** /kɑːˈnɪvərəs काˈनिव़रस्/ *adj.* मांसभक्षी, मांसभक्षण विषयक *Lions are carnivorous animals.*

**carol** /ˈkærəl ˈकैरल्/ *noun* [C] a Christian religious song that people sing at Christmas ईसाईयों का धार्मिक भजन जो क्रिसमस पर गाया जाता है; क्रिसमस गीत

**carom** = **carrom**

**carousel** /ˌkærəˈsel ˌकैरˈसेल्/ *noun* [C] **1** (*AmE*) = **merry-go-round** **2** a moving belt at an airport that carries luggage for passengers to collect हवाई अड्डे पर लगा यात्रियों का सामान लाने वाला चलन-पट्टा

**carp** /kɑːp काप्/ *noun* [C, U] (*pl.* **carp**) a large fish that lives in lakes and rivers झीलों और नदियों में रहने वाली एक बड़ी मछली

**carpal** /ˈkɑːpl ˈकाप्ल्/ *noun* [C] any of the eight small bones in the wrist कलाई की कुल आठ छोटी हड्डियों में से कोई भी एक

**car park** (*AmE* **parking lot**) *noun* [C] an area or a building where you can leave your car कार खड़ी करने का स्थान *a multi-storey car park*

**carpel** /ˈkɑːpl ˈकाप्ल्/ *noun* [C] the female **reproductive** organ of a flower फूल का प्रजननकारी मादा अंश, अंडप ➪ **flower** पर चित्र देखिए।

**carpenter** /ˈkɑːpəntə(r) ˈकापन्ट(र्)/ *noun* [C] a person whose job is to make things from wood बढ़ई ➪ **joiner** देखिए।

**carpentry** /ˈkɑːpəntri ˈकापन्ट्रि/ *noun* [U] the skill or work of a carpenter बढ़ईगिरी

**carpet** /ˈkɑːpɪt ˈकापिट्/ *noun* **1** [C, U] (a piece of) thick material that is used for covering floors and stairs क़ालीन, ग़ालीचा *a fitted carpet* (= one that is cut to the exact shape of a room) ○ *a square metre of carpet* ➪ **rug** देखिए। **2** [C] a thick layer of sth that covers the ground ज़मीन पर किसी चीज़ को मोटी तह *The fields were under a carpet of snow.* ▸ **carpeted** *adj.* क़ालीन से ढका हुआ *All the rooms are carpeted.*

**car phone** *noun* [C] a telephone that you can use in a car कार में बैठे प्रयोग किया जा सकने वाला फ़ोन

**carriage** /ˈkærɪdʒ ˈकैरिज्/ *noun* [C] **1** (*also* **coach** *AmE* **car**) one of the separate parts of a train where people sit रेलगाड़ी का डिब्बा *a first-class carriage* **2** (*also* **coach**) a vehicle with wheels that is pulled by horses बग्घी, घोड़ा-गाड़ी

**carriageway** /ˈkærɪdʒweɪ ˈकैरिज्वे/ *noun* [C] one of the two sides of a highway or main road on which vehicles travel in one direction only मुख्य सड़क का एक पार्श्व जिस पर वाहन केवल एक दिशा में जाते हैं *the south-bound carriageway of the highway* ➪ **dual carriageway** देखिए।

**carrier** /ˈkæriə(r) ˈकैरिअ(र्)/ *noun* [C] **1** (in business) a company that transports people or goods (कारोबार में) यात्रियों या सामान को ढोने वाली कंपनी *the Dutch carrier, KLM* **2** a military vehicle or ship that is used for transporting soldiers, planes, weapons, etc. सैनिकों, विमानों, हथियारों आदि को ढो या वहन करने वाला सैन्य वाहन या जलपोत *an aircraft carrier* **3** a person or animal that can give an infectious disease to others but does not show the signs of the disease किसी संक्रामक रोग का मा वाहक व्यक्ति या पशु जो स्वयं आक्रांत नहीं होता; रो संवाहक *Some insects are carriers of tropical diseases.* **4** = **carrier bag**

**carrion** /ˈkæriən ˈकैरिअन्/ *noun* [U] the decaying dead flesh of an animal मृत पशु का सड़ता हुआ मांस

**carrom** (*also* **carom**) /kærˈəm कैरˈम्/ *noun* [C] a game played on a square board with coloured small discs also called coins. You use a larger flat disc called a **striker** to hit the small discs into the pockets at the corners of the board कैरम

**carrot** /ˈkærət ˈकैरट्/ *noun* **1** [C, U] a long thin orange vegetable that grows under the ground गाजर *grated carrot* ⇨ **vegetable** पर चित्र देखिए। **2** [C] something attractive that is offered to sb in order to persuade him/her to do sth किसी को कुछ करने को मनाने के लिए प्रस्तुत प्रलोभन

**carry** /ˈkæri ˈकैरि/ *verb* (*pres. part.* **carrying;** *3rd person sing. pres.* **carries** ) **1.**[T] to hold sb/sth in your hand, arms or on your back while you are moving from one place to another किसी वस्तु या व्यक्ति को हाथों, बाहों आदि में थामकर या पीठ पर लादकर एक स्थान से दूसरे स्थान तक ले जाना *She was carrying a rucksack on her back.* **NOTE** शरीर पर पहने हुए कपड़ों, गहनों आदि के लिए **wear** न कि **carry** का प्रयोग किया जाता है—*He was wearing a black jacket.* **2** [T] to have sth with you as you go some where साथ ले चलना *Do the police carry guns in your country?* **3** [T] to transport sb/sth from one place to another एक स्थान से दूसरे स्थान तक ले जाना; ढोना *A train carrying hundreds of passengers crashed yesterday.* **4** [T] to have an infectious disease that can be given to others, usually without showing any signs of the disease yourself संक्रामक रोग से आक्रांत होना परंतु सामान्यतः स्वयं रोग के लक्षणों से प्रभावित न होना; रोगवहन करना **5** [T] (*usually passive*) to officially approve of sth in a meeting, etc., because the largest number of people vote for it किसी प्रस्ताव आदि का पारित होना *The motion was carried by 12 votes to 9.* **6** [I] (used about a sound) to reach a long distance (ध्वनि का) दूर तक पहुँचना *You'll have to speak louder if you want your voice to carry to the back of the room.*

**IDM** **be/get carried away** to be so excited that you forget what you are doing इतना उत्तेजित हो जाना कि और बातों का ध्यान ही न रहे

**carry weight** to have influence on the opinion of sb else दूसरों के विचारों को प्रभावित करने की क्षमता होना *Saurabh's views carry a lot of weight with the boss.*

**PHR V** **carry it/sth off** to succeed in doing sth difficult कठिन काम करने में सफल होना *He felt nervous before he started his speech but he carried it off very well.*

**carry on (with sth/doing sth)** to continue जारी रखना *They ignored me and carried on with their conversation.*

**carry on sth** to do an activity किसी कार्य को करना; गतिविधि को आगे बढ़ाना *to carry on a conversation/a business*

**carry out sth** **1** to do sth that you have been ordered to do आदेशित कार्य को पूरा करना *The soldiers carried out their orders without question.* **2** to do a task, repair, etc. कार्य, मरम्मत आदि करना *to carry out tests/an investigation*

**carry-all** = **holdall**

**carrycot** /ˈkærikɒt ˈकैरिकॉट्/ *noun* [C] a small bed, like a box with handles, that you can carry a baby in शिशु को उठाकर ले जाने के लिए हत्थेदार बक्सेनुमा छोटा पलंग

**carry-on** *noun* [C] a small piece of luggage that you can take onto a plane with you विमान में साथ ले जाया जाने वाला छोटा सूटकेस या बैग

**carsick** /ˈkɑːsɪk ˈकासिक्/ *adj.* feeling sick or vomiting as a result of travelling in a car कार-यात्रा के कारण जी मतलाना *to get/feel/be carsick* ⇨ **airsick, seasick** और **travel-sick** देखिए।

**cart**[1] /kɑːt काट्/ *noun* [C] a vehicle with two or four wheels that is pulled by a horse and is used for transporting things घोड़ागाड़ी **2** (*also* **handcart**) a light vehicle with wheels that sb pushes or pulls by hand ठेला

**cart**[2] /kɑːt काट्/ *verb* [T] (*informal*) to take or carry sth/sb somewhere, often with difficulty प्रायः कठिनाई से सामान या व्यक्तियों का वहन करना *We left our luggage at the station because we didn't want to cart it around all day.*

**cartel** /kɑːˈtel काˈटेल्/ *noun* [C, *with sing. or pl. verb*] a group of separate companies that agree to increase profits by fixing prices and not competing with each other उत्पादों या कंपनियों का संघ जिसका मुख्य उद्देश्य क़ीमतें निश्चित कर लाभ बढ़ाना है और परस्पर स्पर्धा न करना है; उत्पादक संघ

**cartilage** /ˈkɑːtɪlɪdʒ ˈकाटिलिज्/ *noun* [C, U] a strong substance in the places where your bones join हड्डियों के जोड़ों पर सुदृढ़ पदार्थ; उपास्थि

**cartographer** /kɑːˈtɒgrəfə(r) काˈटॉग्रफ़(र्)/ *noun* [C] a person who draws or makes maps मानचित्रकार; नक़्शानवीस

**cartography** /kɑːˈtɒgrəfi काˈटॉग्रफ़ि/ *noun* [U] the art or process of drawing or making maps मानचित्र-निर्माण की कला या क्रिया; नक़्शानवीसी ▶ **cartographic** /ˌkɑːtəˈgræfɪk ˌकाटˈग्रैफ़िक्/ *adj.* मानचित्र-निर्माण से संबंधित

**carton** /ˈkɑːtn ˈकाटन्/ *noun* [C] a small container made of cardboard or plastic गत्ते या प्लास्टिक का डिब्बा, कार्टून *a carton of milk/orange juice*

**cartoon** /kɑːˈtuːn काˈटून्/ *noun* [C] **1** a funny drawing, especially in a newspaper or magazine विशेषतः समाचार पत्र या पत्रिका में प्रकाशित व्यंग्यचित्र, हास्यचित्र; कार्टून **2** a film that tells a story by using moving drawings instead of real people and places सचल चित्रों (न कि सजीवों) से बनी फ़िल्म

**cartoonist** /kɑːˈtuːnɪst काˈटूनिस्ट्/ *noun* [C] a person who draws cartoons हास्यचित्रकार; व्यंग्यचित्रकार, कार्टून-निर्माता या कार्टूनकार

**cartridge** /ˈkɑːtrɪdʒ ˈकाट्रिज्/ *noun* [C] **1** a small tube that contains explosive powder and a bullet. You put a cartridge into a gun when you want to fire it कारतूस **2** a closed container that holds sth that is used in a machine, for example film for a camera, ink for printing, etc. Cartridges can be removed and replaced when they are finished or empty किसी मशीन में प्रयुक्त सामग्री (जैसे कैमरे की फ़िल्म, मुद्रण के लिए स्याही) को रखने का बंद पात्र या पुरज़ा, इस पुरज़े को निकाला व पुनः भरा जा सकता है

**carve** /kɑːv काव्/ *verb* **1** [I, T] **carve (sth) (out of sth)** to cut wood or stone in order to make an object or to put a pattern or writing on it लकड़ी या पत्थर को काटकर कलाकृति बनाना या उस पर लिखना; नक़्क़ाशी करना; तराशना *The statue is carved out of marble.* **2** [T] to cut a piece of cooked meat into slices पके मांस के टुकड़े को कतलों में काटना *to carve a chicken*

**carving** /ˈkɑːvɪŋ ˈकाविङ्/ *noun* [C, U] an object or design that has been carved उत्कीर्ण वस्तु या कलाकृति *There are ancient carvings on the walls of the cave.*

**cascade**[1] /kæˈskeɪd कैˈस्केड्/ *noun* [C] **1** water that flows down the side of a mountain, etc. (**a waterfall**) झरना, जलप्रपात **2** a large quantity of sth that falls or hangs down प्रचुर मात्रा में नीचे को झूलती हुई कोई वस्तु (जैसे सिर के बाल) *a cascade of black hair*

**cascade**[2] /kæˈskeɪd कैˈस्केड्/ *verb* [I] to fall or hang down, especially in large amounts or in stages जलप्रपात की भांति गिरना *Water cascaded from the roof.*

**case** /keɪs केस्/ *noun* **1** [C] a particular situation or example of sth कोई विशेष स्थिति, घटना या उदाहरण; प्रकरण ***In some cases***, *people have had to wait two weeks for a doctor's appointment.* ○ *Cases of the disease are very unusual in this country.* **2 the case** [*sing.*] the true situation वास्तविक स्थिति, सचाई *The man said he worked in Mangalore, but we discovered later that this was not the case.* **3** [C] a crime or legal matter अपराध या क़ानूनी मामला *The police deal with hundreds of murder cases a year.* ○ *The case will come to court in a few months.* **4** [C, *usually sing.*] the facts and reasons that support one side in a discussion or legal matter किसी चर्चा या क़ानूनी मामले में एक पक्ष से संबंधित तथ्य और तर्क *She tried to* ***make a case for*** *shorter working hours, but the others disagreed.* **5** [C] (*especially in compounds*) a container or cover for sth किसी वस्तु के लिए पात्र, आवरण या ढक्कन *a bookcase* ○ *a pencil case.* **6** [C] = **suitcase** *Would you like me to carry your case?* **7** [C, U] (in the grammar of some languages) the form of a noun, an adjective or a pronoun that shows its relationship to another word (कुछ भाषाओं की व्याकरण में) कारक *The object of the verb is in the accusative case.*
➪ **accusative, dative, genitive, nominative** और **vocative** देखिए।

IDM **(be) a case of sth/doing sth** a situation in which sth is needed किसी स्थिति में अपेक्षित वस्तु; अपेक्षा, आवश्यकता *There's no secret to success in this business. It's just a case of hard work.*

**in any case** whatever happens or has happened; anyway जो कुछ भी हो या हुआ; जो कुछ भी हो *I don't know how much tickets for the match cost, but I'm going in any case.*

**in case** because sth might happen क्योंकि कुछ हो सकता है *I think I'll take an umbrella in case it rains.* ○ *I wasn't intending to buy anything but I took my credit card* ***just in case***.

**in case of sth** (*formal*) if sth happens अगर ऐसा हुआ तो *In case of fire, break this glass.*

**in that case** if that is the situation उस दशा में; यदि ऐसा हुआ तो *'I'm busy on Tuesday.' 'Oh well, in that case we'll have to meet another day.'*

**prove your/the case/point** ➪ **prove** देखिए।

**case history** *noun* [C] a record of a person's background, past illnesses, etc. व्यक्तिगत विवरण (व्यक्ति की पृष्ठभूमि, पहले हुई बीमारी आदि); व्यक्तिवृत्त

**case law** *noun* [U] (*technical*) law based on decisions made by judges in earlier legal processes (**cases**) न्यायधीशों के पिछले निर्णय पर आधारित क़ानून ➪ **statute law** देखिए।

**case study** *noun* [C] a detailed study of a person, group, situation, etc. over a period of time किसी व्यक्ति, समूह, परिस्थिति आदि का एक समयावधि में विस्तृत अध्ययन

**cash¹** /kæʃ कैश् / *noun* [U] **1** money in the form of coins or notes and not cheques, plastic cards, etc. रोकड़, नक़दी *Would you prefer me to pay* ***in cash*** *or by cheque?* **NOTE** सिक्कों और नोटों के संदर्भ में शब्द **cash** का प्रयोग किया जाता है, परंतु केवल सिक्कों के संदर्भ में शब्द **change** का प्रयोग किया जाता है। **2** (*informal*) money in any form पैसा (नक़द, रोकड़ आदि) *I'm a bit short of cash this month so I can't afford to go out for shopping.*

**cash²** /kæʃ कैश् / *verb* [T] to exchange a cheque, traveller's cheque, etc. for coins and notes चेक आदि नक़दी में भुनाना *I'm just going to the bank to cash a cheque.*

**PHR V** **cash in (on sth)** to take advantage of a situation, especially in a way that other people think is wrong किसी स्थिति का लाभ उठाना, विशेषतः अनुचित रीति से

**cashback** /ˈkæʃbæk ˈकैश्बैक् / *noun* [U] **1** an offer of money as a present that is made by some banks, companies selling cars, etc. in order to persuade customers to do business with them बैंकों, कंपनियों द्वारा ग्राहकों को धन वापसी का प्रलोभन ताकि ग्राहक उहीं से लेन-देन करे **2** a system in **supermarkets** which allows the customer to take money out of his/her bank account at the same time as paying for the goods with a **cash card** सुपर मार्केटों की ऐसी व्यवस्था कि कैशकार्ड का प्रयोग कर व्यक्ति ख़रीद का तुरंत भुगतान कर सकता है और साथ ही अपने बैंक खाते से धनराशि निकाल सकता है

**cash card** (*AmE* **ATM card**) *noun* [C] a plastic card given by a bank to its customers so that they can get money from a special machine (**cash machine**) in or outside a bank बैंक द्वारा ग्राहक को जारी प्लास्टिक कार्ड जिसे वे विशेष मशीनों से धन निकालने में प्रयुक्त करते हैं ➪ **cheque card** और **credit card** देखिए।

**cash crop** *noun* [C] plants that people grow to sell, and not to eat or use themselves बेचने (न कि अपने उपयोग) के लिए उगाई गई फ़सल; नक़दी फ़सल ➪ **subsistence crop** देखिए।

**cash desk** *noun* [C] the place in a large shop where you pay for things बड़ी दुकान में वह स्थान जहाँ भुगतान किया जाता है

**cashew** /ˈkæʃuː; kæˈʃuː ˈकैशू; कैˈशू / (*also* **cashew nut**) *noun* [C] a small kidney-shaped nut that we eat काजू ➪ **nut** पर चित्र देखिए।

**cash flow** *noun* [*sing.*] the movement of money into and out of a business as goods are bought and sold व्यापार में सामान के ख़रीदने और बेचने में धन का प्रवाह; नक़दी-प्रवाह *The company had cash-flow problems and could not pay its bills.*

**cashier** /kæˈʃɪə(r) कैˈशिअ(र्) / *noun* [C] the person in a bank, shop, etc. that customers pay money to or get money from ख़ज़ानची, रोकड़िया

**cash machine** (*also* **cash dispenser; cashpoint**, *AmE* **ATM** /ˌeɪ tiː ˈem ˌए टी ˈएम् /) *noun* [C] a machine inside or outside a bank that you can get money from at any time of day by putting in a special card (**cash card**) बैंक के अंदर या बाहर रखी मशीन जिसमें विशेष कार्ड डालकर किसी भी समय पैसा निकाला जा सकता है

**cashmere** /ˈkæʃmɪə(r) ˈकैश्मिअ(र्) / *noun* [U] a type of wool that is very fine and soft एक प्रकार की महीन और कोमल ऊन, कश्मीरी ऊन

**casing** /ˈkeɪsɪŋ ˈकेसिङ् / *noun* [C, U] a covering that protects sth सुरक्षा करने वाला आवरण *The keyboard has a black plastic casing.*

**casino** /kəˈsiːnəʊ कˈसीनो / *noun* [C] (*pl.* **casinos**) a place where people play games in which you can win or lose money, such as **roulette** ऐसा स्थान जहाँ खेल खेलकर पैसा जीता या हारा जा सकता है; जुआघर, कैसीनो

**cask** /kɑːsk कास्क् / *noun* [C] a large wooden container in which alcoholic drinks, etc. are stored मादक पेय आदि रखने के लिए लकड़ी का बड़ा पीपा

**casket** /ˈkɑːskɪt ˈकास्किट् / *noun* [C] **1** a small decorated box for holding jewels or other valuable things, especially in the past (गहने आदि रखने के लिए) सजावटी संदूकची जिसका विशेषतः पिछले ज़माने में प्रयोग किया जाता था **2** (*AmE*) = **coffin**

**cassava** /kəˈsɑːvə कˈसावा / *noun* [U] a tropical plant that has thick roots; a type of flour that is made from these roots मोटी जड़ों वाला उष्ण कटिबंधीय पौधा; इन जड़ों से बना आटा

**casserole** /ˈkæsərəʊl ˈकैसरोल् / *noun* **1** [C, U] a large dish of earthenware or glass with a lid for cooking and serving food मिट्टी या काँच का ढक्कनदार बड़ा बर्तन जिसमें खाना बनाया और परोसा जाता है; कैसरॉल **2** any food cooked in such a dish कैसरोल में बनाया गया व्यंजन

**cassette** /kəˈset कˈसेट् / *noun* [C] a small flat case with tape inside that you use for recording and playing music and other sounds ध्वनि को रिकॉर्ड करने और उसे बजाने के लिए टेप-युक्त छोटा चपटा डिब्बा; कैसेट *to put on/play/listen to a cassette*

**NOTE** **Cassette** के लिए दूसरा शब्द **tape** है। कैसेट के आरंभ-बिंदु पर जाने के लिए उसे **rewind** किया जाता है और आगे जाने के लिए **fast forward** ➪ **video** देखिए।

**cassette recorder** *noun* [C] a machine that you use for recording and playing cassettes कैसेट को रिकॉर्ड करने और बजाने की मशीन; कैसेट-रिकार्डर

**cast**[1] /kɑːst कास्ट्/ *verb* (*pt, pp* **cast**) **1** [T] (*usually passive*) to choose an actor for a particular role in a play, film, etc. नाटक, फ़िल्म आदि में किसी भूमिका के लिए अभिनय करने वाले व्यक्ति को चुनना *She always seems to be cast in the same sort of role.* **2** [I, T] to throw a fishing line or net into the water मछली पकड़ने का काँटा या जाल पानी में डालना **3** to make an object by pouring hot liquid metal into a shaped container (**a mould**) पिघली हुई धातु को साँचे में डालना या ढालना *a statue cast in bronze*

**IDM** **cast doubt on sth** to make people less sure about sth संदेह व्यक्त करना; संदेहजनक होना *The newspaper report casts doubt on the truth of the Prime Minister's statement.*

**cast an eye/your eye(s) over sb/sth** to look at sb/sth quickly शीघ्रता से निगाह डालना

**cast light on sth** to help to explain sth (को) समझने में सहायता देना; (पर) प्रकाश डालना *Can you cast any light on the problem?*

**cast your mind back** to make yourself remember sth स्मृति पर ज़ोर डालना; ज़ोर देकर कुछ याद करना *She cast her mind back to the day she met her husband.*

**cast a shadow (across/over sth)** to cause an area of shade to appear somewhere किसी क्षेत्र को छायांकित करना (*figurative*) *The accident cast a shadow over the rest of the holiday* (= stopped people enjoying it fully).

**cast a/your vote** to vote मतदान करना *The MPs will cast their votes in the leadership election tomorrow.*

**PHR V** **cast around/about for sth** to try to find sth कुछ ढूढ़ने या प्राप्त करने का प्रयास करना *The principal cast around desperately for a solution to the problem.*

**cast**[2] /kɑːst कास्ट्/ *noun* [C] all the actors in a play, film, etc. किसी नाटक, फ़िल्म आदि के समस्त कलाकार *The entire cast was/were excellent.*

**castaway** /ˈkɑːstəweɪ ˈकास्टवे/ *noun* [C] a person who is left alone somewhere after his/her ship has sunk डूबे हुए जहाज़ से बचकर अपरिचित भूमि पर अकेला पहुँचा हुआ व्यक्ति

**cast iron** *noun* [U] a hard type of iron ढला हुआ लोहा; ढलवाँ लोहा

**cast-iron** *adj.* made of cast iron ढलवें लोहे से बना (*figurative*) *a cast-iron alibi* (= one that people cannot doubt)

**castle** /ˈkɑːsl ˈकास्ल्/ *noun* [C] **1** a large building with high walls and towers that was built in the past to defend people against attack क़िला, दुर्ग *a medieval castle* **2** (in the game of **chess**) any of the four pieces placed in the corner squares of the board at the start of the game, usually made to look like a castle (शतरंज में) हाथी

**cast-off** *noun* [C, *usually pl.*] a piece of clothing that you no longer want and that you give to sb else or throw away वस्त्र जिसकी अब आवश्यकता नहीं है और जो किसी को दान दे दिया जाता है या फेंक दिया जाता है; पुराने उतरे हुए कपड़े; उतरन *When I was little I had to wear my sister's cast-offs.*

**castrate** /kæˈstreɪt कैˈस्ट्रेट्/ *verb* [T] to remove part of the sexual organs of a male animal or person so that it cannot produce young बधिया करना ➪ **neuter** देखिए। **2** ▶ **castration** /kæˈstreɪʃn कैˈस्ट्रेशन्/ *noun* [U] बधिया करने की क्रिया; जनदनाशन

**casual** /ˈkæʒuəl ˈकैशुअल्/ *adj.* **1** relaxed and not worried; without showing great effort or interest तनावमुक्त और अचिंतित; प्रयास, परवाह या रुचि से वंचित *I'm not happy about your casual attitude to your work.* **2** (used about clothes) not formal (पहनावा) अनौपचारिक *I always change into casual clothes as soon as I get home from work.* **3** (used about work) done only for a short period; not regular or permanent सीमित अवधि का (कार्य); अनियमित या अस्थायी *Most of the building work was done by casual labourers.* ▶ **casually** /ˈkæʒuəli ˈकैशुअलि/ *adv.* अनौपचारिक रूप से; लापरवाही से; अकस्मात *She walked in casually and said, 'I'm not late, am I?'* ○ *Dress casually, it won't be a formal party.* **4** (*only before a noun*) happening by chance; doing sth by chance आकस्मिक; संयोगवश *a casual meating* **5** (*usually before a noun*) (used about relationships) without deep affection बिना गहरे संबंध के *a casual friendship*

**casualty** /ˈkæʒuəlti ˈकैशुअल्टि/ *noun* (*pl.* **casualties**) **1** [C] a person who is killed or injured in a war or an accident दुर्घटना या युद्ध में घायल या मृत व्यक्ति *After the accident the casualties were taken to hospital.* **2** [C] a person or thing that suffers as a result of sth else किसी अन्य के कारण हानिग्रस्त

*Many small companies became casualties of the economic crisis.* 3 (*also* **casualty department,** *AmE* **emergency room**) [U] the part of a hospital where people who have been injured in accidents are taken for immediate treatment अस्पताल का वह विभाग जहाँ दुर्घटनाग्रस्त व्यक्तियों को तात्कालिक उपचार के लिए लाया जाता है; आपातकालीन विभाग

**cat** /kæt कैट्/ *noun* [C] 1 a small animal with soft fur that people often keep as a pet बिल्ली 2 a wild animal of the cat family बिल्ली जाति का कोई जंगली पशु *the big cats* (= lion, tiger, etc.)

**catalogue** (*AmE* **catalog**) /ˈkætəlɒg ˈकैटलॉग्/ *noun* [C] 1 a list of all the things that you can buy, see, etc. somewhere किसी स्थान पर, से ख़रीदी, देखी आदि जा सकने वाली वस्तुओं की सूची, सूचीपत्र 2 a series, especially of bad things एक शृंखला, विशेषतः अशुभ बातों की *a catalogue of disasters/errors/injuries* ▶ **catalogue** *verb* [T] सूची बनाना *She started to catalogue all the new library books.*

**catalyse** (*AmE* **catalyze**) /ˈkætəlaɪz ˈकैटलाइज़्/ *verb* [T] to make a chemical reaction happen faster रासायनिक प्रतिक्रिया को त्वरित या उत्प्रेरित करना ▶ **catalysis** /kəˈtæləsɪs कˈटैलसिस्/ *noun* [U] उत्प्रेरण

**catalyst** /ˈkætəlɪst ˈकैटलिस्ट्/ *noun* [C] 1 **a catalyst (for sth)** a person or a thing that causes change परिवर्तन लाने वाला व्यक्ति या वस्तु *The scandal was the catalyst for the candidate's election defeat.* 2 a substance that makes a chemical reaction happen faster उत्प्रेरक पदार्थ ▶ **catalytic** /ˌkætəˈlɪtɪk ˌकैटˈलिटिक्/ *adj.* उत्प्रेरक

**catalytic converter** *noun* [C] a device used in motor vehicles to reduce the damage caused to the environment by poisonous gases मोटरकारों में लगा उपकरण जो विषैली गैसों से पर्यावरण को हुई हानि को कम करता है

**catamaran**/ˌkætəməˈræn ˌकैटमˈरैन्/ *noun* [C] a fast sailing boat with two **hulls** दो पाटों वाली द्रुतगति नौका ➪ **boat** पर चित्र देखिए।

**catapult[1]** /ˈkætəpʌlt ˈकैटपल्ट्/ (*AmE* **slingshot**) *noun* [C] a Y-shaped stick with a piece of elastic tied to each side that is used by children for shooting stones गुलेल

**catapult[2]** /ˈkætəpʌlt ˈकैटपल्ट्/ *verb* [T] to throw sb/sth suddenly and with great force किसी वस्तु या व्यक्ति को एकाएक व बहुत ज़ोर से फेंकना *When the car crashed the driver was catapulted through the windscreen.* ○ (*figurative*) *The success of his first film catapulted him to fame.*

**cataract** /ˈkætərækt ˈकैटरैक्ट्/ *noun* [C] 1 a white area that grows over the eye as a result of disease मोतियाबिंद 2 a large **waterfall** बड़ा जलप्रपात

**catarrh** /kəˈtɑː(r) कˈटा(र्)/ *noun* [U] a thick liquid that forms in the nose and throat when you have a cold ज़ुकाम होने पर उत्पन्न बलगम; नज़ला; नाक

**catastrophe** /kəˈtæstrəfi कˈटैसट्रफ़ि/ *noun* [C] 1 a sudden disaster that causes great suffering or damage आकस्मिक महाविपत्ति या तबाही *major catastrophes such as floods and earthquakes* 2 an event that causes great difficulty, disappointment, etc. घोर परेशानी, निराशा आदि उत्पन्न करने वाली घटना *It'll be a catastrophe if I fail the exam again.* ▶ **catastrophic** /ˌkætəˈstrɒfɪk ˌकैटˈस्ट्रॉफ़िक्/ *adj.* संतापकारी, कष्टकारी *The war had a catastrophic effect on the whole country.*

**catch[1]** /kætʃ कैच्/ *verb* (*pt, pp* **caught** /kɔːt कॉट्/) 1 [T] to take hold of sth that is moving, usually with your hand or hands हाथों में लेना; पकड़ना; थामना *The dog caught the ball in its mouth.* 2 [T] to capture sb/sth that you have been following or looking for पीछाकर या ढूँढ़कर पकड़ना *Two policemen ran after the thief and caught him at the end of the street.* ○ *to catch a fish* 3 [T] to notice or see sb doing sth bad किसी को कोई ग़लत काम करते हुए देख लेना *I caught her taking money from my purse.* 4 [T] to get on a bus, train, plane, etc. बस, ट्रेन आदि पकड़ना *I caught the bus into town.* ✪ विलोम **miss** 5 [T] to be in time for sth; not to miss sb/sth किसी काम के लिए समय पर उपस्थित होना *We arrived just in time to catch the beginning of the film.* 6 [I, T] to become or cause sth to become accidentally connected to or stuck in sth अचानक कहीं पर अटक जाना या किसी को अटका देना *If we leave early we won't get caught in the traffic.* 7 [T] to hit sb/sth किसी को मारना; किसी पर प्रहार करना *The branch caught him on the head.* 8 [T] to get an illness बीमारी लगना *to catch a cold/flu/measles* 9 [T] to hear or understand sth that sb says किसी के कहे को सुनना या समझना *I'm sorry, I didn't quite catch what you said. Could you repeat it?*

IDM **catch sb's attention/eye** to make sb notice sth किसी का ध्यान आकर्षित करना *I tried to catch the waiter's eye so that I could get the bill.*

**catch your breath** 1 to rest after physical exercise so that your breathing returns to normal शारीरिक व्यायाम के बाद विश्राम करना ताकि श्वसन प्रक्रिया सामान्य हो जाए 2 to breathe in suddenly because you are surprised आश्चर्य के कारण अचानक लंबी साँस लेना

**catch fire** to start burning, often accidentally प्रायः दुर्घटनावश जलने लगना *Nobody knows how the building caught fire.*

**catch sb red-handed** to find sb just as he/she is doing sth wrong रँगे हाथों पकड़ना *The police caught the burglars red-handed with the stolen jewellery.*

**catch sight/a glimpse of sb/sth** to see sb/sth for a moment किसी को क्षण-भर के लिए देखना *We waited outside the theatre, hoping to catch a glimpse of the actress.*

**catch the sun 1** to shine brightly in the sunlight सूर्य के प्रकाश में ख़ूब चमकना *The panes of glass flashed as they caught the sun.* **2** to become burned or brown in the sun धूप की गरमी से झुलस जाना *Your face looks red. You've really caught the sun, haven't you?*

**PHRV catch on** (*informal*) **1** to become popular or fashionable लोकप्रिय या प्रचलित होना *The idea has never really caught on in this country.* **2** to understand or realize sth किसी बात को समझना या स्वीकार करना *She's sometimes a bit slow to catch on.*

**catch sb out** to cause sb to make a mistake by asking a clever question टेढ़ा सवाल पूछकर फँसाना *Ask me anything you like—you won't catch me out.*

**catch up (with sb); catch sb up** to reach sb who is in front of you जा पकड़ना; बराबरी के स्तर पर पहुँचना *Shamita has missed so much school she'll have to work hard to catch up with the rest of the class.* ○ *Go on ahead, I'll catch you up in a minute.*

**catch up on sth** to spend time doing sth that you have not been able to do for some time पहले न कर पाने की स्थिति में किसी कार्य में अधिक समय लगाना *I'll have to go into the office at the weekend to catch up on my work.*

**be/get caught up in sth** to be or get involved in sth, usually without intending to किसी स्थिति में उलझ या फँस जाना, प्रायः बिना इच्छा के *I seem to have got caught up in a rather complicated situation.*

**catch²** /kætʃ कैच्/ *noun* [C] **1** an act of catching sth, for example a ball पकड़ने या लपकने की क्रिया; पकड़ **2** the amount of fish that sb has caught पकड़ी हुई मछली की मात्रा *The fishermen brought their catch to the harbour.* **3** a device for fastening sth and keeping it closed जोड़ने या बाँधने और बंद रखने की युक्ति (जैसे दरवाज़े की चिटकनी) *I can't close my suitcase—the catch is broken.* ○ *a window catch* **4** a hidden disadvantage or difficulty in sth that seems attractive ऊपर से सरल या आकर्षक लगने वाली स्थिति या वस्तु में अंतर्निष्ट गुप्त असुविधा या कठिनाई *It looks like a good offer but I'm sure there must be a catch in it.*

**catching** /ˈkætʃɪŋ ˈकैचिङ्/ *adj.* (*not before a noun*) (*informal*) (used about a disease) that can easily be passed from one person to another (रोग) संक्रमणकारी **NOTE** इस अर्थ के लिए अधिक औपचारिक शब्द **infectious** है।

**catchment area** /ˈkætʃmənt eəriə ˈकैच्मन्ट् एअरिया/ *noun* [C] (*technical*) the area from which rain flows into a particular river or lake जलागम क्षेत्र, जलग्रहणक्षेत्र

**catchphrase** /ˈkætʃfreɪz ˈकैच्फ्रेज़्/ *noun* [C] a phrase that becomes famous for a while because it is used by a famous person उक्ति जो किसी प्रख्यात व्यक्ति द्वारा प्रयुक्त होने के कारण बहुप्रचलित हो जाती है

**catchy** /ˈkætʃi ˈकैचि/ *adj.* (used about a tune or song) easy to remember (धुन या गीत) जिसे याद रखना आसान हो

**catechism** /ˈkætəkɪzəm ˈकैटकिज़म्/ *noun* [*sing.*] a set of questions and answers that are used for teaching people about the beliefs of the Christian Church ईसाई चर्च की मान्यताओं को सिखाने की प्रश्नोत्तरी

**categorical** /ˌkætəˈgɒrɪkl ˌकैटˈगॉरिकल्/ *adj.* very definite सुनिश्चित, सुस्पष्ट *The answer was a categorical 'no'.* ▶ **categorically** /-kli -कृलि/ *adv.* सुनिश्चित रूप से, सुस्पष्ट रूप से *The Minister categorically denied the rumour.*

**categorize** (*also* **-ise**) /ˈkætəgəraɪz ˈकैटगराइज़्/ *verb* [T] to divide people or things into groups; to say that sb/sth belongs to a particular group वस्तुओं या व्यक्तियों का वर्गीकरण करना

**category** /ˈkætəgəri ˈकैटगरि/ *noun* [C] (*pl.* **categories**) a group of people or things that are similar to each other व्यक्तियों या वस्तुओं का वर्ग, संवर्ग, कोटि *This painting won first prize in the junior category.* ○ *These books are* ***divided into categories*** *according to subject.*

**cater** /ˈkeɪtə(r) ˈकेट(र्)/ *verb* [I] **1 cater for sb/sth; cater to sth** to provide what sb/sth needs or wants आवश्यकताओं की पूर्ति करना; आवश्यकतानुसार सेवाएँ या वस्तुएँ प्रदान करना *We need a hotel that caters for small children.* ○ *The menu caters to all tastes.* **2** to provide and serve food and drink at an event or in a place that a lot of people go to किसी समारोह या अन्य स्थान पर भोज्य पदार्थों की व्यवस्था करना

**caterer** /ˈkeɪtərə(r) ˈकेटर(र्)/ *noun* [C] a person or business that provides food and drink at events or in places that a lot of people go to खान-पान सेवा का प्रबंधकर्ता या व्यवसाय

**catering** /ˈkeɪtərɪŋ ˈकेटरिङ्/ *noun* [U] the activity or business of providing food and drink at events or in places that a lot of people go to खान-पान सेवाएँ प्रदान करने की गतिविधि या व्यवसाय; खानपान प्रबंध *the hotel and catering industry* ○ *Who's going to* ***do the catering*** *at the wedding?*

**caterpillar** /ˈkætəpɪlə(r) ˈकैटपिल(र्)/ *noun* [C] a small hairy animal with a long body and a lot of legs, which eats the leaves of plants. A caterpillar later becomes an insect with large, often colourful wings (**a butterfly** or **a moth**) सूँडी, इल्ली ➪ **insect** पर चित्र देखिए।

**catharsis** /kəˈθɑːsɪs कˈथ़ासिस्/ *noun* [U, C] (*pl.* **catharses** /kəˈθɑːsiːz कˈथ़ासीज़्/) (*technical*) the process of expressing strong feeling, for example through plays or other artistic activities, as a way of getting rid of anger, reducing suffering, etc. नाटक आदि कलाओं से अभिव्यक्ति द्वारा प्रबल भावनाओं का शमन; विरेचन, भावशांति ▶ **cathartic** /kəˈθɑːtɪk कˈथ़ाटिक्/ *adj.* विरेचनात्मक, भावशामक *It was a cathartic experience.*

**cathedral** /kəˈθiːdrəl कˈथ़ीड्रल्/ *noun* [C] a large church that is the most important one in a district किसी ज़िले का सर्वाधिक महत्त्वपूर्ण गिरजा

**catheter** /ˈkæθɪtə(r) ˈकैथ़िट(र)/ *noun* [C] a thin tube that is put into the body in order to remove liquids नाल-श्लाका (शरीर में से द्रव पदार्थ बाहर निकालने के लिए)

**cathode** /ˈkæθəʊd ˈकैथ़ोड्/ *noun* [C] the place on a battery or other electrical device where the electric current leaves बैटरी में वह बिंदु जहाँ से होकर विद्युत धारा बाहर निकलती है; कैथोड ➪ **anode** देखिए।

**cathode ray tube** *noun* [C] a tube inside a television, computer screen, etc. inside which **electrons** produce images on the screen टेलीविज़न, कंप्यूटर स्क्रीन आदि के अंदर की नली जिसमें निहित इलेक्ट्रॉन के कारण परदे पर चित्र बनते हैं; कैथोड किरण नलिका

**Catholic** /ˈkæθlɪk ˈकैथ़्लिक्/ = **Roman Catholic** ▶ **Catholicism** /kəˈθɒləsɪzəm कˈथ़ॉलसिज़म्/ = **Roman Catholicism**

**cation** /ˈkætaɪən ˈकैटाइअन्/ *noun* [C] (in chemistry) an **ion** with a positive electrical charge (रसायनशास्त्र में) धनात्मक विद्युत चार्ज वाला आयन; धनायन ➪ **anion** देखिए।

**catkin** /ˈkætkɪn ˈकैट्किन्/ *noun* [C] a group of very small soft flowers that grows on the branches of some trees. Some catkins are long and hang down like pieces of string; others are short and stand up कुछ वृक्षों की शाखाओं पर उगने वाले बहुत छोटे और कोमल फूलों का समूह; पुष्प मंजरी

**cattle** /ˈkætl ˈकैट्ल्/ *noun* [*pl.*] male and female cows, for example on a farm गाय-बैल, मवेशी, ढोर *a herd of cattle* ➪ **cow** पर नोट देखिए।

**Caucasian** /kɔːˈkeɪʒn कॉˈकेश़न्/ *noun* [C], *adj.* (of) a member of a race of people who have white or light-coloured skin गोरी जाति के सदस्य(का)

**caucus** /ˈkɔːkəs ˈकॉकस्/ *noun* [C] **1** a meeting of the members or leaders of a political party to choose representatives (**candidates**) or to decide policy; the members or leaders of a political party as a group सभा जिसमें राजनीतिक दल के सदस्य या नेतागण उम्मीदवार चुनते हैं या नीति-निर्धारण करते हैं; इन सदस्यों का दल **2** a group of people with similar interests, often within a larger organization or political party समान सोच वाले लोगों की टोली प्रायः किसी राजनीतिक दल या बड़े संगठन के भीतर; चौगुटा, चौकड़ी

**caught** ➪ **catch** का past tense और past participle रूप

**cauldron** (*AmE* **caldron**) /ˈkɔːldrən ˈकॉल्ड्रन्/ *noun* [C] a large, deep, metal pot that is used for cooking things over a fire कड़ाहा, बड़ी कड़ाही

**cauliflower** /ˈkɒliflaʊə(r) ˈकॉलिफ़्लाउअ(र्)/ *noun* [C, U] a large vegetable with green leaves and a round white centre that you eat when it is cooked फूलगोभी ➪ **vegetable** पर चित्र देखिए।

**cause[1]** /kɔːz कॉज़्/ *noun* **1** [C] a thing or person that makes sth happen कारण, हेतु, निमित *The police do not know the cause of the accident.* ○ *Smoking is one of the causes of heart disease.* **2** [U] **cause** (**for sth**) reason for feeling sth or behaving in a particular way भावना या आचरण-विशेष का कारण *The doctor assured us that there was no* ***cause for concern****.* ○ *I don't think you have any real* ***cause for complaint****.* **3** [C] an idea or organization that a group of people believe in and support व्यक्ति समूह विशेष द्वारा समर्पित विचार सिद्धांत या संगठन; उद्देश्य, आंदोलन *We are all committed to the cause of racial equality.*

IDM **a lost cause** ➪ **lost[2]** देखिए।

**be for/in a good cause** to be worth doing because it will help other people सहायतार्थ या हितकारी होने के कारण कोई कार्य करना सार्थक होना

**cause²** /kɔ:z कॉज़् / *verb* [T] to make sth happen कुछ होने का कारण बनना, उत्पन्न करना *The fire was caused by an electrical fault.* ○ *Is your leg causing you any pain?*

**causeway** /ˈkɔ:zweɪ ˈकॉज़्वे / *noun* [C] a road or path that is built higher than the area around it in order to cross water or wet ground गीली भूमि या जलमय क्षेत्र के आर-पार, ऊँचा उठा हुआ रास्ता; सेतुपथ *The island is connected to the mainland by a causeway.*

**caustic** /ˈkɔ:stɪk ˈकॉस्टिक् / *adj.* **1** (used about a substance) able to burn or destroy things by chemical action (पदार्थ) रासायनिक क्रिया द्वारा वस्तुओं को जला देने में सक्षम; दाहक **2** critical in a cruel way तीक्ष्ण, कटु रूप से निंदात्मक *a caustic remark*

**caustic soda** *noun* [U] a chemical used in making paper and soap काग़ज़ और साबुन बनाने के काम आने वाला रासायनिक पदार्थ; कॉस्टिक सोडा

**caution¹** /ˈkɔ:ʃn ˈकॉश्न् / *noun* **1** [U] great care, because of possible danger विशेष सावधानी, सतर्कता, चौकसी *Any advertisement that asks you to send money should be treated **with caution**.* **2** [C] a spoken warning that a judge or police officer gives to sb who has committed a small crime न्यायाधीश या पुलिस अधिकारी द्वारा दी गई मौखिक चेतावनी

**caution²** /ˈkɔ:ʃn ˈकॉश्न् / *verb* [I, T] **1 caution (sb) against sth** to warn sb not to do sth किसी बात के विरुद्ध सावधान करना *The Prime Minister's advisers have cautioned against calling an election too early.* **2** to give sb an official warning किसी को साधिकार चेतावनी देना *Akram was cautioned by the referee for wasting time.*

**cautionary** /ˈkɔ:ʃənəri ˈकॉशनरि / *adj.* giving a warning सतर्क या सचेत करने वाला; सचेतक *The teacher told us a **cautionary tale** about a girl who cheated in her exams.*

**cautious** /ˈkɔ:ʃəs ˈकॉशस् / *adj.* taking great care to avoid possible danger or problems सावधान, सतर्क, चौकस *I'm very cautious about expressing my opinions in public.* ▶ **cautiously** *adv.* सावधानी से

**cavalry** /ˈkævlri ˈकैव्ल्रि / *noun* [*sing., with sing. or pl. verb*] the part of the army that fought on horses in the past; the part of the modern army that uses heavily protected vehicles विगत युग की घुड़सवार सेना; आधुनिक युग की कड़ी सुरक्षा वाहनों का उपयोग करने वाली सेना

**cave¹** /keɪv केव् / *noun* [C] a large hole in the side of a cliff or hill, or under the ground गुफा, कंदरा, गुहा

**cave²** /keɪv केव् / *verb*

**PHR V cave in 1** to fall in अंदर गिर जाना या धँस जाना *The roof of the tunnel had caved in and we could go no further.* **2** to suddenly stop arguing or being against sth एकाएक बहस या विरोध समाप्त कर देना; हार मान लेना *He finally caved in and agreed to the plan.*

**caveman** /ˈkeɪvmæn ˈकेव्मैन् / *noun* [C] (*pl.* **-men** /-men -मेन् /) **1** a person who lived many thousands of years ago in **caves** (प्राचीनकाल का) गुहामानव, गुफावासी **2** (*informal*) a man who behaves in an aggressive way लड़ाका, झगड़ालू; आक्रामक प्रवृत्ति वाला व्यक्ति

**cavern** /ˈkævən ˈकैव़न् / *noun* [C] a large, deep hole in the side of a hill or under the ground; a big cave बड़ी अँधेरी गुफा ⇨ **limestone** पर चित्र देखिए।

**caviar** (*also* **caviare**) /ˈkæviɑ:(r) ˈकैविआ(र्) / *noun* [U] the eggs of a large fish (**a sturgeon**) that we eat. Caviar is usually very expensive एक प्रकार की बड़ी मछली (स्टर्जन) के अंडे जिन्हें व्यंजन के रूप में खाया जाता है

**cavity** /ˈkævəti ˈकैव़टि / *noun* [C] (*pl.* **cavities**) an empty space inside sth solid किसी ठोस पदार्थ में छिद्र, खाली स्थान *a cavity in a tooth* ○ *a wall cavity*

**cayenne** /keɪˈen केˈएन् / (*also* **cayenne pepper**) *noun* [U] a type of red pepper used in cooking to give a hot flavour to food एक प्रकार की लाल मिर्च

**cc** /ˌsi: ˈsi: ˌसी ˈसी/ *abbr.* 'cubic centimetre(s)' घनसेंटीमीटर *a 1200 cc engine*

**CCTV** /ˌsi: si: ti: ˈvi: ˌसी सी टी ˈव़ी / *abbr.* 'closed-circuit television' बंद परिपथ टेलीविज़न

**CD** /ˌsi:ˈdi: ˌसी ˈडी/ (*also* **compact disc**) *noun* [C] a small, round piece of hard plastic on which sound is recorded or information stored. सख़्त प्लास्टिक का छोटे गोल व चपटा टुकड़ा जिस पर ध्वनि रिकार्ड या सूचना सामग्री संचित की जाती है; सीडी, कॉम्पैक्ट डिस्क

**CD-ROM** /ˌsi: di: ˈrɒm ˌसी डी ˈरॉम् / *noun* [C, U] compact disc read-only memory; a CD for use on a computer, which has a lot of information recorded on it. The information cannot be changed or removed सी डी रॉम; कंप्यूटर में प्रयुक्त सी डी जिसमें प्रचुर सूचना सामग्री अंकित होती है परंतु इस सामग्री को न तो बदला और न ही मिटाया जा सकता है

**cease** /si:s सीस् / *verb* [I, T] (*formal*) to stop or end समाप्त होना या करना; रुकना या रोकना *Fighting in the area has now ceased.* ○ *That organization has ceased to exist.*

**ceasefire** /ˈsiːsfaɪə(r) ˈसीस्फ़ाइअ(र्)/ *noun* [C] an agreement between two groups to stop fighting each other युद्ध-विराम, लड़ाई-बंदी ➪ **truce** देखिए।

**ceaseless** /ˈsiːsləs ˈसीस्लस्/ *adj.* continuing for a long time without stopping लंबे समय तक जारी; निरंतर, लगातार ▶ **ceaselessly** *adv.* निरंतरतापूर्वक

**cedar** /ˈsiːdə(r) ˈसीड(र्)/ *noun* **1** [C] a type of large tree that never loses its leaves and has wide spreading branches देवदार वृक्ष; इस सदाबहार वृक्ष की शाखाएँ दूर तक फैलती हैं **2** (*also* **cedarwood** /ˈsiːdəwʊd ˈसीडवुड्/) [U] the hard red wood of the cedar tree देवदार की मज़बूत लाल लकड़ी

**cede** /siːd सीड्/ *verb* [T] (*written*) to give land or control of sth to another country or person किसी अन्य व्यक्ति या देश को भूमि या नियंत्रण सौंपना

**ceiling** /ˈsiːlɪŋ ˈसीलिङ्/ *noun* [C] **1** the top surface of the inside of a room कमरे के भीतर से ऊपर दिखने वाली छत भीतरी छत, सीलिंग *a room with a high/low ceiling* **2** a top limit ऊपरी सीमा *The Government has put a 10% ceiling on wage increases.*

**ceiling-fan** *noun* [C] (*IndE*) an electric fan that hangs from the ceiling of a room and is used to create a current of cool air विद्युत पंखा जो कमरे की भीतरी छत से लटकता है, बिजली से चलने वाला पंखा

**celebrate** /ˈselɪbreɪt ˈसेलिब्रेट्/ *verb* [I, T] to do sth to show that you are happy about sth that has happened or because it is a special day किसी विशेष अवसर पर उत्सव मनाना, समारोह करना *When I got the job we celebrated by going out for a meal.* ○ *My grandmother celebrated her 90th birthday yesterday.* ▶ **celebratory** /ˌseləˈbreɪtəri ˈसेलˈब्रेटरि/ *adj.* समारोहात्मक; समारोह या उत्सव से संबंधित *We went out for a celebratory meal after the match.*

**celebrated** /ˈselɪbreɪtɪd ˈसेलिब्रेटिड्/ *adj.* (*formal*) famous प्रसिद्ध, प्रख्यात *a celebrated poet*

**celebration** /ˌselɪˈbreɪʃn ˌसेलिˈब्रेशन्/ *noun* [C, U] the act or occasion of doing sth enjoyable because sth good has happened or because it is a special day उत्सव, समारोह *Diwali celebrations* ○ *I think this is an occasion for celebration!*

**celebrity**/səˈlebrəti सˈलेब्रटि/ *noun* [C] (*pl.* **celebrities**) a famous person कोई प्रख्यात व्यक्ति *a TV celebrity*

**celery** /ˈseləri ˈसेलरि/ *noun* [U] a vegetable with long green and white sticks that can be eaten without being cooked हरे और सफ़ेद डंठल वाली सब्ज़ी जो कच्ची भी खाई जा सकती है *a stick of celery*

**celestial** /səˈlestiəl सˈलेस्टिअल्/ *adj.* (*formal or literary*) (*usually before a noun*) of the sky or of heaven आकाश या स्वर्ग से संबंधित *celestial bodies* ○ *celestial light/music* ➪ **terrestrial** देखिए।

**celibate** /ˈselɪbət ˈसेलिबट्/ *adj.* (*formal*) not married and not never having sexual relations, often because of religious beliefs अविवाहित और शारीरिक संबंधों से परहेज रखने वाला प्रायः धार्मिक कारणों से; ब्रह्मचर्य, कौमार्यव्रत ▶ **celibacy** /ˈselɪbəsi ˈसेलिबसि/ *noun* [U] ब्रह्मचर्य, कौमार्यव्रत

**cell** /sel सेल्/ *noun* [C] **1** the smallest living part of an animal or a plant पशुओं या पौधे का लघुतम सजीव अंश; कोशिका *The human body consists of millions of cells.* ○ *red blood cells* **2** a small room in a prison or police station in which a prisoner is locked जेल या पुलिस थाने में क़ैदी को रखने की कोठरी **3** a device for producing an electric current, for example by the action of chemicals or light रसायनों की प्रक्रिया या प्रकाश आदि द्वारा विद्युत उत्पन्न करने वाला यंत्र; सेल *solar cells*

**cellar** /ˈselə(r) ˈसेल(र्)/ *noun* [C] an underground room that is used for storing things (सामग्री जमा करने के लिए) तहख़ाना ➪ **basement** देखिए।

**cellist** /ˈtʃelɪst ˈचेलिस्ट्/ *noun* [C] a person who plays the **cello** चेलो (वाद्य यंत्र) का वादक

**cello** /ˈtʃeləʊ ˈचेलो/ *noun* [C] (*pl.* **cellos**) a large musical instrument with strings. You sit down to play it and hold it between your knees तारों वाला एक बड़ा वाद्य यंत्र (इस वाद्य यंत्र को बैठकर व घुटनों के बीच थामकर बजाया जाता है)

**Cellophane™** /ˈseləfeɪn ˈसेलफ़ेन्/ *noun* [U] a transparent plastic material used for covering things प्लास्टिक-निर्मित पारदर्शी काग़ज़, सेलोफ़ेन; काचाभ काग़ज़

**cellphone** /ˈselfəʊn ˈसेल्फ़ोन्/ (*also* **cellular phone**) = **mobile phone**

**cellular** /ˈseljələ(r) ˈसेल्यल(र्)/ *adj.* consisting of **cells 1** कोशिका-निर्मित *cellular tissue*

**cellulose** /ˈseljuləʊs ˈसेल्युलोस्/ *noun* [U] a natural substance that forms the cell walls of all plants and trees and is used in making plastics, paper, etc. वनस्पतियों की कोशिका-भित्तियों को बनाने वाला एक प्राकृतिक पदार्थ; सेलुलोस, इस पदार्थ से प्लास्टिक, काग़ज़ आदि का निर्माण किया जाता है

**Celsius** /ˈselsiəs ˈसेलसिअस्/ (*also* **centigrade**) *adj.* (*abbr.* **C**) the name of a scale for measuring temperatures, in which water freezes at 0° and boils at 100° तापमान मापने की वह पद्धति जिसमें पानी का हिमांक 0° और क्वथनांक 100° पर होता है; सेल्सियस *The temperature tonight will fall to 7°C.*

**cement¹** /sɪˈment सिˈमेन्ट् / *noun* [U] a grey powder, that becomes hard after it is mixed with water and left to dry. It is used in building for sticking bricks or stones together or for making very hard surfaces ईंटों और पत्थरों को जोड़ने का मसाला; सीमेंट

**cement²** /sɪˈment सिˈमेन्ट् / *verb* [T] **1** to join two things together using cement, or a strong sticky substance सीमेंट या सीमेंट जैसे लसदार पदार्थ से दो वस्तुओं को जोड़ना **2** to make a relationship, agreement, etc. very strong किसी संबंध, समझौता आदि को सुदृढ़ करना *This agreement has cemented the relationship between our two countries.*

**cement mixer** (*also* **concrete mixer**) *noun* [C] a machine with a large round container (**a drum**) that holds sand, water and a grey powder (**cement**) and turns to mix them all together सीमेंट आदि को मिश्रित करने वाली मशीन

**cemetery** /ˈsemətri ˈसेमट्रि / *noun* [C] (*pl.* **cemeteries**) a place where dead people are buried, especially a place that does not belong to a church क़ब्रिस्तान, विशेषतः वह स्थान जो गिरजाघर की संपत्ति नहीं है ➪ **graveyard** और **churchyard** देखिए।

**censor¹** /ˈsensə(r) ˈसेन्स(र्) / *verb* [T] to remove the parts of a book, film, etc. that might offend people or that are considered politically dangerous पुस्तक, फ़िल्म आदि से उन आपत्तिजनक अंशों को हटाना जो किसी दल-विशेष की भावनाओं को ठेस पहुँचाने की संभावना रखते हों या जो राजनीतिक कारणों से हानिकारक माने जाते हों; अभिवेचन करना ▸ **censorship** *noun* [U] अभिवेचन व्यवस्था *state censorship of radio and television programmes*

**censor²** /ˈsensə(r) ˈसेन्स(र्) / *noun* [C] an official who censors books, films, etc. किताबों, फ़िल्मों आदि में से आपत्तिजनक अंशों को निकालने वाला अधिकारी

**censure** /ˈsenʃə(r) ˈसेन्श(र्) / *verb* [T] (*written*) to tell sb, in a strong and formal way, that he/she has done sth wrong अनुचित काम करने के लिए किसी की भर्त्सना करना *The attorney was censured for not revealing the information earlier.* ▸ **censure** *noun* [U] घोर निंदा, भर्त्सना

**census** /ˈsensəs ˈसेन्सस् / *noun* [C] (*pl.* **censuses**) an official count of the people who live in a country, including information about their ages, jobs, etc. जनगणना

**centenary** /senˈtiːnəri सेन्ˈटीनरि / *noun* [C] (*pl.* **centenaries**) (*AmE* **centennial** /senˈteniəl सेन्ˈटेनिअल् /) the year that comes exactly one hundred years after an important event or the beginning of sth शताब्दी, शतवार्षिकी *The year 2001 was the centenary of Disney's birth.*

**center** (*AmE*) = **centre**

**centi-** /ˈsentɪ- ˈसेन्टि / *prefix* (*in nouns*) **1** one hundred सौ *centipede* **2** (often used in units of measurement) one **hundredth** (प्रायः मापन की इकाइयों में प्रयुक्त) शतांश *centilitre*

**centigrade** /ˈsentɪgreɪd ˈसेन्टिग्रेड् / = **Celsius**

**centimetre** (*AmE* **centimeter**) /ˈsentɪmiːtə(r) ˈसेन्टिमीट(र्) / *noun* [C] (*abbr.* **cm**) a measure of length. There are 100 centimetres in a metre लंबाई मापने की इकाई; सेंटीमीटर, एक मीटर में 100 सेंटीमीटर होते हैं

**centipede** /ˈsentɪpiːd ˈसेन्टिपीड् / *noun* [C] a small animal like an insect, with a long thin body and very many legs बहुत-सारी टाँगों वाला छोटा कीड़ा जिसके शरीर का मध्य भाग पतला और लंबा होता है; कनखजूरा

**central** /ˈsentrəl ˈसेन्ट्रल् / *adj.* **1** in the centre of sth मध्यवर्ती, केंद्रीय *a map of central Europe* ○ *Our flat is very central* (= near the center of the city and therefore very convenient). **2** most important; main सर्वाधिक महत्त्वपूर्ण; मुख्य *The film's central character is a fifteen-year-old girl.* **3** (*only before a noun*) having control over all other parts अन्य सभी भागों पर नियंत्रण होते हुए; केंद्रीय *central government* (= the government of a whole country, not local government) ○ *the central nervous system*

**central heating** *noun* [U] a system for heating a building from one main point. Air or water is heated and carried by pipes to all parts of the building एक मुख्य बिंदु से सारे भवन को ताप देने की प्रणाली; केंद्रीय तापन-प्रणाली

**centralize** (*also* **-ise**) /ˈsentrəlaɪz ˈसेन्ट्रलाइज़् / *verb* [T] (*usually passive*) to give control of all the parts of a country or organization to a group of people in one place केंद्रीकरण करना *Our educational system is becoming increasingly centralized.* ▸ **centralization** (*also* **-isation**) /ˌsentrəlaɪˈzeɪʃn ˌसेन्ट्रलाइˈज़ेश्न् / *noun* [U] केंद्रीकरण

**centrally** /ˈsentrəli ˈसेन्ट्रलि / *adv.* in or from the centre केंद्रीय; केंद्र से *a centrally located hotel* (= near the centre of the town)

**central processing unit** *noun* [C] (*abbr.* **CPU**) (*computing*) the part of a computer that controls all the other parts of the system कंप्यूटर के विभिन्न भागों को नियंत्रित करने वाला केंद्रीय अंश; सेंट्रल प्रोसेसिंग युनिट

**central reservation** (*AmE* **median; median strip**) *noun* [C] a narrow piece of land with a barrier that separates the two sides of a highway बड़ी सड़क के आने ओर जाने वाले भागों को पृथक करने वाली संकरी अवरोधक पट्टी

**centre**[1] (*AmE* **center**) /ˈsentə(r) ˈसेन्‌ट(र्)/ *noun* **1** [C, *usually sing.*] the middle point or part of sth किसी वस्तु का मध्य बिंदु या भाग *I work in the centre of New Delhi.* ○ *She hit the target dead centre* (= exactly in the centre). ➪ **middle** पर नोट तथा **circle** पर चित्र देखिए। **2** [C] a building or place where a particular activity or service is based गतिविधि या सेवा-विशेष का आधार स्थल; केंद्र *a sports/health/shopping centre* ○ *This university is a centre of excellence for medical research.* **3** [C] a place where sb/sth is collected together; the point towards which sth is directed ऐसा स्थान जहाँ व्यक्ति या वस्तु आदि केंद्रित हों; वह बिंदु जिस ओर कोई क्रिया, वस्तु आदि निर्दिष्ट या प्रेरित हो *major urban/industrial centres* ○ *She always likes to be* ***the centre of attention***. ○ *You should bend your legs to keep a low* ***centre of gravity***. **4** [*sing.*] a political position that is not extreme मध्यम-मार्गी राजनीति *Her views are left of centre.*

**centre**[2] (*AmE* **center**) /ˈsentə(r) ˈसेन्‌ट(र्)/ *verb*
**PHR V** **centre on/around sb/sth** to have sb/sth as its centre किसी व्यक्ति या वस्तु का केंद्रबिंदु के रूप में होना *The life of the village centres on the school and the community centre.*

**centric** /ˈsentrɪk ˈसेन्‌ट्रिक्/ *suffix* (*used in compounds*) concerned with or interested in the thing mentioned निर्दिष्ट वस्तु से संबंधित; केंद्रित *Indocentric policies*

**centrifugal** /ˌsentrɪˈfjuːgl ˌसेन्‌ट्रिˈफ़्यूगल्/ *adj.* (*technical*) moving away from a centre point केंद्रबिंदु से दूर हटते हुए; अपकेंद्री *centrifugal force*

**centrifuge** /ˈsentrɪfjuːdʒ ˈसेन्‌ट्रिफ़्यूज्/ *noun* [C] (*technical*) a machine with a part that turns round very quickly to separate substances, for example liquids from solids, by forcing the heavier substance to the outer edge पदार्थों (जैसे द्रव और ठोस) को अलग-अलग करने वाली मशीन जो अति तीव्र गति से घूमती है और भारी पदार्थ को बाहर की तरफ़ धकेलती है; अपकेंद्रण यंत्र

**centripetal** /ˌsentrɪˈpiːtl ˌसेन्‌ट्रिˈपीट्‌ल्/ *adj.* (*technical*) moving towards a centre point केंद्र की ओर जाते हुए; अभिकेंद्री

**century** /ˈsentʃəri ˈसेन्‌चरि/ *noun* [C] (*pl.* **centuries**) **1** a particular period of 100 years that is used for giving dates शताब्दी या सदी-विशेष *We live in the 21st century* (= the period between the year 2000 and 2099). **2** any period of 100 years सौ साल की कोई भी अवधि *People have been making carpets in this area for centuries.*

**CEO** /ˌsiːiːˈəʊ ˌसी ई ˈओ/ *abbr.* the abbreviation for 'chief executive officer'; the person with the most powerful position in a company or business, 'chief executive officer' का संक्षिप्त रूप; किसी संस्था या कारोबार में सर्वाधिक महत्त्वपूर्ण पद वाला व्यक्ति; सी ई ओ

**cephalopod** /ˈsefələʊpɒd ˈसेफ़लोपॉड्/ *noun* [C] any of the **class** of sea animals that have a large soft head, large eyes and eight or ten long thin legs (**tentacles**) समुद्री प्राणियों का एक वर्ग जिनका सिर कोमल और बड़ा, आँखें भी बड़ी तथा 8 या 10 लंबी पतली टाँगें होती हैं; शीर्षपाद *Octopus and squid are cephalopods.*

**ceramic** /səˈræmɪk सˈरैमिक्/ *adj.* made of clay that has been baked मिट्टी से बनाकर आग में पकाया हुआ; मृत्तिका-संबंधित *ceramic tiles* ▶ **ceramic** *noun* [C, *usually pl.*] मृत्तिकाशिल्प *an exhibition of ceramics*

**cereal** /ˈsɪəriəl ˈसिअरिअल्/ *noun* [C, U] **1** any type of grain that can be eaten or made into flour, or the grass that the grain comes from अनाज, अन्न (गेहूँ, चावल आदि) *Wheat, barley and rye are cereals.* **2** a food that is made from grain, often eaten for breakfast with milk अन्न से बना खाद्य पदार्थ जिसे प्रायः नाश्ते में दूध के साथ लिया जाता है *a bowl of cereal*

**cerebellum** /ˌserɪˈbeləm ˌसेरिˈबेलम्/ *noun* [C] (*pl.* **cerebellums** or **cerebella** /-ˈbelə -ˈबेला/) the part of the brain at the back of the head that controls the movement of the muscles मस्तिष्क के पिछले हिस्से का भाग जो मांसपेशियों की गतिविधियों को नियंत्रित करता है; अनुमस्तिष्क

**cerebral** /ˈserəbrəl ˈसेरब्रल्/ *adj.* of the brain मस्तिष्क-विषयक; प्रमस्तिष्कीय

**cerebral palsy** *noun* [U] a medical condition, usually caused by brain damage before or at birth, that causes the loss of control of the arms and legs जन्म के समय या पहले हुई मस्तिष्क-क्षति जिसके कारण भुजाओं और टाँगों पर नियंत्रण भी क्षतिग्रस्त हो जाता है; प्रमस्तिष्कघात

**ceremonial** /ˌserɪˈməʊniəl ˌसेरिˈमोनिअल्/ *adj.* connected with a ceremony संस्कार या अनुष्ठान संबंधी; समारोहात्मक, उत्सवी *a ceremonial occasion* ▶ **ceremonially** /-niəli -निअलि/ *adv.* समारोहात्मक रूप से

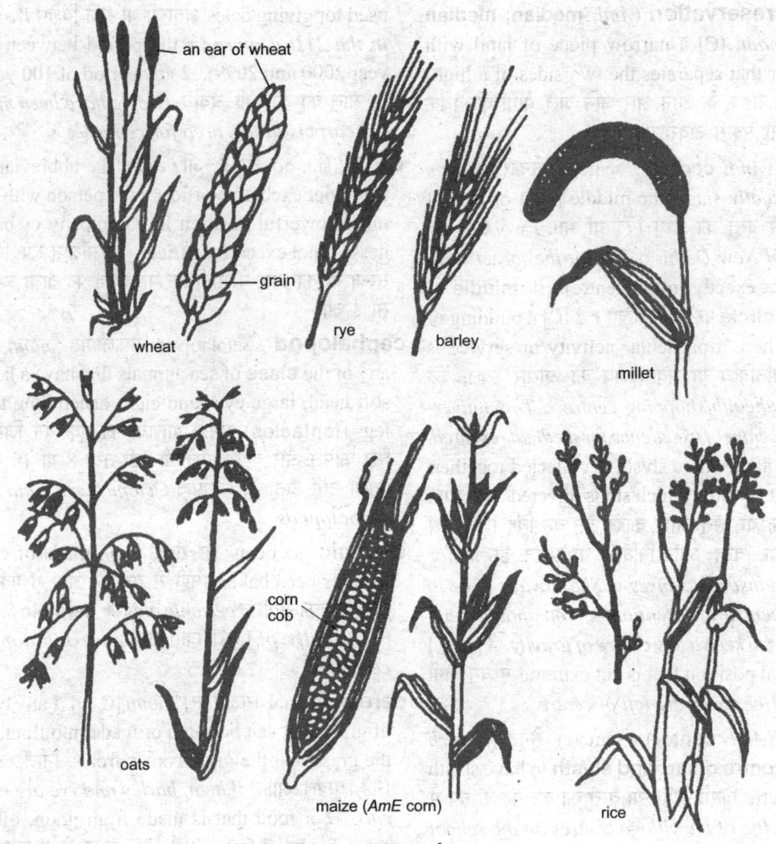


cereals

**ceremony** /ˈserəməni ˈसेरमनि/ *noun* (*pl.* **ceremonies**) **1** [C] a formal public or religious event औपचारिक सार्वजनिक समारोह अथवा धार्मिक अनुष्ठान *the opening ceremony of the Olympic Games* ○ *a wedding ceremony* **2** [U] formal behaviour, speech, actions, etc. that are expected on special occasions विशेष अवसरों पर प्रत्याशित औपचारिक आचरण, भाषण, व्यवहार आदि *The new hospital was opened* ***with great ceremony***.

**certain** /ˈsɜːtn ˈसट्न्/ *adj.* **1** (*not before a noun*) **certain (that...); certain (of sth)** completely sure; without any doubts पूर्णतया आश्वस्त; संदेह से मुक्त, असंदिग्ध *She's absolutely certain that there was somebody outside her window.* ○ *We're not quite certain what time the train leaves.* **2 certain (that...); certain (to do sth)** sure to happen or to do sth; definite अवश्यंभावी; सुस्पष्ट, निश्चित, पक्का *It is almost certain that unemployment will decrease this year.* ○ *The Director is certain to agree.* **3** (*only before a noun*) used for talking about a particular thing or person without naming him/her/it बिना नाम लिए किसी विशेष व्यक्ति या वस्तु के उल्लेख के लिए प्रयुक्त *There are certain reasons why I'd prefer not to meet him again.* **4** (*only before a noun*) some, but not very much कुछ, परंतु बहुत अधिक नहीं *I suppose I have* ***a certain amount of*** *respect for Mr Bhasin.* **5** noticeable but difficult to describe जिसका अनुभव तो हो परंतु वर्णन कठिन हो; अनुभवगम्य परंतु अवर्ण्य *There was a certain feeling of autumn in the air.* **6** (*formal*) used before a person's name to show that you do not know him/her किसी अज्ञात व्यक्ति के निर्देश के लिए उसके नाम से पहले प्रयुक्त; कोई; कोई एक *I received a letter from a certain Mrs Rao.*

IDM **for certain** without doubt निस्संदेह; पक्के तौर पर *I don't know for certain what time we'll arrive.*

**make certain (that...) 1** to do sth in order to be sure that sth else happens सुनिश्चित करना *They're doing everything they can to make certain that they win.* **2** to do sth in order to be sure that sth is true निश्चित होने के लिए पूछना, जानना आदि *We'd better phone Akram before we go to make certain he's expecting us.*

**certainly** /ˈsɜːtnli ˈसट्नलि / *adv.* **1** without doubt; definitely निस्संदेह; निश्चित रूप से *The number of students will certainly increase after 2010.* **2** (used in answer to questions) of course (प्रश्न के उत्तर में प्रयुक्त) अवश्य, बेशक *'Do you think I could borrow your notes?' 'Certainly.'*

**certainty** /ˈsɜːtnti ˈसट्नटि / *noun* (*pl.* **certainties**) **1** [U] the state of being completely sure about sth अवश्यंभाविता, निश्चितता *We can't say with certainty that there is life on other planets.* ✪ विलोम **uncertainty** **2** [C] something that is sure to happen घटना, परिणाम आदि जिसका होना निश्चित हो *It's now almost a certainty our team will win the league.*

**certificate** /səˈtɪfɪkət सˈटिफ़िकट् / *noun* [C] an official piece of paper that says that sth is true or correct औपचारिक या आधिकारिक प्रमाण-पत्र *a birth marriage/medical certificate*

**certify** /ˈsɜːtɪfaɪ ˈसटिफ़ाइ / *verb* [T] (*pres. part.* **certifying;** *3rd person sing. pres.* **certifies;** *pt, pp* **certified**) **1** to say formally that sth is true or correct प्रमाणित करना *We need someone to certify that this is her signature.* **2** to give sb a certificate to show that he/she has successfully completed a course of training for a particular profession किसी व्यक्ति को व्यवसाय-विशेष के लिए प्रशिक्षण पूरा करने पर प्रमाणपत्र देना *a certified accountant*

**certitude** /ˈsɜːtɪtjuːd ˈसटिट्यूड् / *noun* (*formal*) **1** [U] a feeling of being certain about sth निश्चित होने का भाव, निश्चय, विश्वास, भरोसा **2** [C] a thing about which you are certain वस्तु जिसपर विश्वास है

**cervix** /ˈsɜːvɪks ˈसर्विक्स् / *noun* [C] (*pl.* **cervices** / -vɪsiːz -व्रिसीज़् /) the narrow passage at the opening of the place where a baby grows inside a woman's body (**uterus**) गर्भाशय-ग्रीवा, गर्भाशय के विवर का संकीर्ण मार्ग (जहां माँ के पेट में बच्चा बढ़ता है) ▶ **cervical** /ˈseːvɪkl ˈसर्विकल् / *adj.* ग्रीवा-संबंधी

**cesarean** (*AmE*) = **Caesarean**

**cesium** (*AmE*) = **caesium**

**cessation** /səˈseɪʃn सˈसेश्न् / *noun* [U, C] (*formal*) the stopping of sth; a pause in sth समाप्ति; विराम *The UN have demanded an immediate cessation of hostilities.*

**cesspit** /ˈsespɪt ˈसेसपिट् / (*also* **cesspool** /ˈsespuːl ˈसेसपूल् /) *noun* [C] a covered hole or container in the ground for collecting waste from a building, especially from the toilets भूमि में गड़ा मलकुंड

**cf.** *abbr.* compare तुलना

**CFC** /ˌsiː efˈsiː ˌसी एफ़् ˈसी / *noun* [C, U] chlorofluorocarbon; a type of gas found, for example, in cans of spray which is harmful to the earth's atmosphere क्लोरोफ्लोरोकार्बन; परिवेश के लिए हानिप्रद एक गैस जो स्प्रेअर के डिब्बे आदि में पाई जाती है ➪ **ozone layer** देखिए।

**ch.** *abbr.* chapter अध्याय

**chaat** *noun* [U] a spicy north Indian snack made from pieces of raw fruit, boiled vegetables, etc. typically served from stalls or carts parked on the roadside चाट

**chain¹** /tʃeɪn चेन् / *noun* **1** [C, U] a line of metal rings that are joined together ज़ंजीर, चेन *a bicycle chain* ○ *She was wearing a silver chain round her neck.* ➪ **bicycle** पर चित्र देखिए। **2** [C] a series of connected things or people वस्तुओं या व्यक्तियों का सिलसिला; कड़ी *a chain of mountains/a mountain chain* ○ *The book examines the complex **chain of events** that led to the 1857 Mutiny.* **3** [C] a group of shops, hotels, etc. that are owned by the same company किसी एक कंपनी के स्वामित्व वाली दुकानों आदि की श्रृंखला *a chain of supermarkets* ○ *a fast-food chain*

**chain²** /tʃeɪn चेन् / *verb* [T] **chain sb/sth (to sth)**; **chain sb/sth(up)** to fasten sb/sth to sth else with a chain किसी वस्तु या व्यक्ति को ज़ंजीर से बाँधना *The dog is kept chained up outside.*

**chain reaction** *noun* [C] **1** (in chemistry) a chemical change that forms products which themselves cause more changes and new products (रसायनविज्ञान में) रासायनिक प्रतिक्रियाओं की श्रृंखला जिसमें उत्पादन स्वयं परिवर्तन और नए उत्पादन पैदा करते हैं; श्रृंखलाबद्ध प्रतिक्रिया **2** a series of events, each of which causes the next ऐसी घटनाओं का सिलसिला जिसमें हर घटना एक नई घटना को जन्म देती जाती है

**chain-smoke** *verb* [I] to smoke continuously, lighting one cigarette after another एक-के-बाद-एक लगातार सिगरेट पीना ▶ **chain-smoker** *noun* [C] इस तरह से सिगरेट पीने वाला व्यक्ति

**chain store** *noun* [C] one of a number of similar shops that are owned by the same company किसी एक ही कंपनी के स्वामित्व वाली दुकानों में से कोई एक दुकान

**chair¹** /tʃeə(r) चेअ(र्) / *noun* **1** [C] a piece of furniture for one person to sit on, with a seat, a back and four legs कुरसी *an armchair* **2** [*sing.*] the person who is controlling a meeting किसी सभा का सभापति या अध्यक्ष *Please address your questions to the chair.* **3** [C] the position of being in charge of a department in a university विश्वविद्यालय के किसी विभाग का प्रमुख *She holds the Chair of Economics at Delhi University.*

**chair²** /tʃeə(r) चेअ(र्)/ *verb* [T] to be the chairman or chairwoman of a meeting किसी बैठक की अध्यक्षता करना *Who's chairing the meeting this evening?*

**chairman** /ˈsʃeəmən ˈचेअमन्/ *noun* [C] (*pl.* **-men** /-men -मेन्/) **1** the head of a company or other organization किसी संगठन का प्रमुखतम व्यक्ति **2** a person who controls a meeting किसी सभा का अध्यक्षता करने वाला व्यक्ति ▶ **chairmanship** *noun* [*sing.*] अध्यक्षता

**chairperson** /ˈsʃeəpɜːsn ˈचेअपस्न्/ *noun* [C] (*pl.* **-persons**) a person who controls a meeting किसी सभा की अध्यक्षता करने वाला व्यक्ति; अध्यक्ष, सभापति

**chairwoman** /ˈsʃeəwʊmən ˈचेअवुमन्/ *noun* [C] (*pl.* **-women** /-wɪmɪn -विमिन्/) a woman who controls a meeting किसी सभा की महिला अध्यक्ष; अध्यक्षा

**chalet** /ˈʃæleɪ ˈशैले/ *noun* [C] (especially in Europe) a wooden house, usually one built in a mountain area or used by people on holiday (विशेषतः यूरोप में) सामान्यतः पहाड़ी क्षेत्र में या अवकाश के समय उपयोग के लिए बनाया गया लकड़ी का घर; शैले

**chalk¹** /tʃɔːk चॉक्/ *noun* **1** [U] a type of soft white rock एक प्रकार का नरम सफ़ेद पत्थर; खड़िया, चॉक मिट्टी *chalk cliffs* **2** [C, U] a small stick of soft white or coloured rock that is used for writing or drawing लिखने या आरेख बनाने की सफ़ेद या रंगीन खड़िया की सलाख; चॉक का टुकड़ा

**chalk²** /tʃɔːk चॉक्/ *verb* [I, T] to write or draw sth with chalk चॉक से लिखना या आरेख बनाना *Somebody had chalked a message on the wall.*

**PHR V** **chalk sth up** to succeed in getting sth कुछ पाने में सफल होना *The team has chalked up five wins this summer.*

**chalkboard** /ˈtʃɔːkbɔːd ˈचॉक्बॉड्/ = **blackboard**

**challan** *noun* [C] (*IndE*) **1** an official **receipt** for a payment; a form that is filled in order to pay cash or deposit a cheque in a bank, with the tax department, government office, etc. किसी भुगतान की आधिकारिक रसीद; कर विभाग, सरकारी दफ़्तर आदि को किया गया नक़द भुगतान या चेक जमा करने का प्रपत्र **2** a **fine** for breaking traffic rules यातायात नियम उल्लंघन पर किया गया जुरमाना; चालान

**challenge¹** /ˈtʃælɪndʒ ˈचैलिन्ज्/ *noun* [C] **1** something new and difficult that forces you to make a lot of effort चुनौती *The company will have to **face** many **challenges** in the coming months.* ○ *How will this government **meet the challenge** of rising unemployment?* **2 a challenge (to sb) (to do sth)** an invitation from sb to fight, play, argue, etc. against him/her मुक़ाबले की चुनौती; ललकार *The Prime Minister should accept our challenge and call a new election now.*

**challenge²** /ˈtʃælɪndʒ ˈचैलिन्ज्/ *verb* [T] **1 challenge sb (to sth/to do sth)** to invite sb to fight, play, argue, etc. against you मुक़ाबले की चुनौती देना; ललकारना *They've challenged us to a football match this Saturday.* **2** to question if sth is true, right, etc., or not किसी की सचाई, अधिकार, संपन्नता आदि पर प्रश्नचिह्न लगाना *She hates anyone challenging her authority.*

**challenger** /ˈtʃælɪndʒə(r) ˈचैलिन्ज(र्)/ *noun* [C] a person who invites you to take part in a competition, because he/she wants to win a title or position that you hold चुनौती देने या ललकारने वाला व्यक्ति

**challenging** /ˈtʃælɪndʒɪŋ ˈचैलिन्जिङ्/ *adj.* forcing you to make a lot of effort चुनौती-भरा *a challenging job*

**chamber** /ˈtʃeɪmbə(r) ˈचेम्ब(र्)/ *noun* [C] **1** an organization that makes important decisions, or the room or building where it meets महत्त्वपूर्ण निर्णय करने वाला संगठन; वह कक्ष या भवन जहाँ संगठन की बैठक होती है *a council chamber* **2** a closed space in the body, a machine, etc. शरीर, मशीन आदि में प्रकोष्ठ *the four chambers of the heart* **3** a room that is used for a particular purpose विशेष प्रयोजन के लिए कक्ष *a burial chamber*

**chambermaid** /ˈtʃeɪmbəmeɪd ˈचेम्बमेड्/ *noun* [C] a woman whose job is to clean and tidy hotel bedrooms होटल में परिचारिका

**chameleon** /kəˈmiːliən कˈमीलिअन्/ *noun* [C] a type of small reptile that can change the colour of its skin गिरगिट

**champagne** /ʃæmˈpeɪn शैम्ˈपेन्/ *noun* [U, C] a French white wine which has a lot of bubbles in it and is often very expensive सफ़ेद, बुलबुलों वाली और प्रायः बहुत महँगी फ्रेंच मदिरा; शैंपेन

**champion¹** /ˈtʃæmpiən ˈचैम्पिअन्/ *noun* [C] **1** a person, team, etc. that has won a competition विजेता (व्यक्ति, टीम आदि); चैंपियन *a world champion* ○ *a champion swimmer* **2** a person who speaks and fights for a particular group, idea, etc. किसी विचार या दल का प्रबल समर्थक; हिमायती *a champion of free speech*

**champion**[2] /ˈtʃæmpiən ˈचैम्पिअन्/ *verb* [T] to support or fight for a particular group or idea किसी दल या विचार का प्रबल समर्थन करना या उसके लिए संघर्ष करना *to champion the cause of human rights*

**championship** /ˈtʃæmpiənʃɪp ˈचैम्पिअन्शिप्/ *noun* [C, *usually pl.*] a competition or series of competitions to find the best player or team in a sport or game सर्वश्रेष्ठ खिलाड़ी या दल का निर्णय करने के लिए आयोजित स्पर्धा या स्पर्धाएँ *the World Hockey Championships*

**chance**[1] /tʃɑːns चान्स्/ *noun* **1** [C] **a chance of (doing) sth; a chance (that...)** a possibility संभावना *I think we* ***stand a*** *good* ***chance*** *of winning the competition.* ○ *Is there any chance of getting tickets for tonight's concert?* **2** [C] **chance (of doing sth/to do sth)** an opportunity अवसर *Be quiet and* ***give*** *her* ***a chance*** *to explain.* ○ *I think you should tell him now. You may not* ***get*** *another* ***chance****.* ➪ **occasion** पर नोट देखिए। **3** [C] a risk जोखिम, ख़तरा *We may lose some money but we'll just have to take that chance.* ○ *Fasten your seat belt—you shouldn't take (any) chances.* **4** [U] luck; the way that some things happen without any cause that you can see or understand भाग्य; संयोग *We met* ***by chance*** (= we had not planned to meet) *as I was walking down the street.*

IDM **by any chance** (used for asking sth politely) perhaps or possibly (नम्रता से पूछने में प्रयुक्त) संयोगवश *Are you, by any chance, going into town this afternoon?*

**the chances are (that)...** (*informal*) it is probable that संभावना है कि *The chances are that it will rain tomorrow.*

**no chance** (*informal*) there is no possibility of that happening कोई संभावना नहीं *'Perhaps your mother will give you the money.' 'No chance!'*

**on the off chance** in the hope that sth might happen, although it is not very likely इस आशा में कि शायद कुछ हो जाए, हालाँकि संभावना बहुत कम है *I didn't think you'd be at home, but I just called in on the off chance.*

**chance**[2] /tʃɑːns चान्स्/ *verb* **1** [T] (*informal*) **chance sth/doing sth** to risk sth जोखिम लेना; ख़तरा उठाना *It might be safe to leave the car here, but I'm not going to* ***chance it****.* **2** [I] (*formal*) **chance to do sth** to do sth without planning or trying to do it बिना योजना या इरादे के कुछ करना या कुछ हो जाना *I chanced to see the letter on his desk.*

**chance**[3] /tʃɑːns चान्स्/ *adj.* (*only before a noun*) not planned बिना किसी पूर्व योजना वाला; सांयोगिक, आकस्मिक *a chance meeting*

**chancellor** /ˈtʃɑːnsələ(r) ˈचान्सलर्/ *noun* [C] the head of the government or universities in some countries कुछ देशों में या विश्वविद्यालयों शासनाध्यक्ष *the German chancellor* ○ *the chancellor of Delhi University*

**chandelier** /ˌʃændəˈlɪə(r) ˌशैन्डˈलिअ(र्)/ *noun* [C] a large round frame with many branches for lights or candles, that hangs from the ceiling and is decorated with small pieces of glass छत से लटका झाड़-फानूस

**change**[1] /tʃeɪndʒ चेन्ज्/ *verb* **1** [I, T] to become different or to make sb/sth different बदलना, परिवर्तन करना *This town has changed a lot since I was young.* ○ *Our plans have changed—we leave in the morning.* ✪ पर्याय **alter** **2** [I, T] **change (sb/sth) to/into sth; change (from A) (to/into B)** to become a different thing; to make sb/sth take a different form बदल जाना; परिवर्तन कर देना *The traffic lights changed from green to red.* ○ *The new job changed him into a more confident person.* **3** [T] **change sth (for sth)** to take, have or use sth instead of sth else एक चीज़ छोड़कर दूसरी चीज़ लेना; बदलना *Could I change this blouse for a larger size?* ○ *to change a wheel on a car* **4** [T] **to change sth (with sb)** (*with plural noun*) to exchange sth with sb, so that you have what he/she had, and he/she has what you had अदला-बदली या विनिमय करना *The teams change ends at half-time.* ○ *If you want to sit by the window I'll change seats with you.* ✪ पर्याय **swap** **5** [I, T] **change (out of sth) (into sth)** to take off your clothes and put different ones on कपड़े बदलना *She changed out of her work clothes and into a clean dress.* **6** [T] to put clean things onto sb/sth किसी स्थान पर साफ़ वस्तुएँ रखना *The baby's nappy needs changing.* ○ *to change the bed* (= to put clean sheet on) **7** [T] **change sth (for/into sth)** to give sb money and receive the same amount back in money of a different type नोट भुनाना या तुड़ाना; दूसरी मुद्रा में विनिमय करना *Can you change a twenty-rupee note for two tens?* ○ *I'd like to change fifty dollars into Indian rupees.* **8** [I, T] to get out of one bus, train, etc. and get into another बस, ट्रेन बदलना; एक बस, ट्रेन आदि को छोड़कर दूसरी लेना *Can we get to Pune direct or do we have to change (trains)?*

IDM **change hands** to pass from one owner to another मालिक या स्वामित्व बदलना

**change your mind** to change your decision or opinion निर्णय या विचार बदलना *I'll have the green one. No, I've changed my mind—I want the red one.*
**change/swap places with sb** ➪ **place¹** देखिए।
**change the subject** to start talking about sth different चर्चा का विषय बदलना, प्रकरण बदलना
**change your tune** (*informal*) to change your opinion or feelings about sth किसी विषय पर अपनी राय या मनोभावों को बदलना
**change your ways** to start to live or behave in a different and better way from before अपना व्यवहार या जीवन शैली बदल लेना (बेहतरी के लिए)
**chop and change** ➪ **chop¹** देखिए।
**change over** (**from sth**) (**to sth**) to stop doing or using one thing and start doing or using sth else एक प्रणाली के स्थान पर दूसरी प्रणाली का उपयोग करना *The theatre has changed over to a computerized booking system.*

**change²** /tʃeɪndʒ चेन्ज् / *noun* **1** [C, U] **change** (**in/to sth**) the process of becoming or making sth different बदलाव, परिवर्तन *There was little change in the patient's condition overnight.* ○ *After two hot summers, people were talking about a change in the climate.* **2** [C] **a change** (**of sth**) something that you take, have or use instead of sth else एक वस्तु के स्थान पर प्रयुक्त दूसरी वस्तु *We must notify the bank of our change of address.* ○ *I packed my toothbrush and a change of clothes.* **3** [U] the money that you get back if you pay more than the amount sth costs छुट्टा, रेज़गारी; छोटे नोट या सिक्के *If a sheet of paper costs 50 paise and you pay with a rupee, you will get 50 paise change.* **4** [U] coins of low value छोटे सिक्के *He needs some change for the phone.* ○ *Have you got change for a hundred-rupee note* (= coins and notes of lower value that together make hundred rupees)*?*
IDM **a change for the better/worse** a person, thing or situation that is better/worse than the one before व्यक्ति, वस्तु या स्थिति में बदलाव
**a change of heart** a change in your opinion or the way that you feel मत-परिवर्तन, हृदय-परिवर्तन
**for a change** in order to do sth different from usual सामान्य से कुछ भिन्न करने के लिए *I usually cycle to work, but today I decided to walk for a change.*
**make a change** to be enjoyable or pleasant because it is different from what you usually do बदलाव के कारण आनंदप्रद या प्रीतिकर होना

**changeable** /ˈtʃeɪndʒəbl ˈचेन्जबल् / *adj.* likely to change; often changing जिसमें परिवर्तन संभावित है; प्रायः परिवर्तित होने वाला, परिवर्तनीय, परिवर्तन-योग्य

**changeover** /ˈtʃeɪndʒəʊvə(r) ˈचेन्जूओव़(र्) / *noun* [C] a change from one system to another एक प्रणाली को बदलकर दूसरी को अपनाने की क्रिया; प्रणाली परिवर्तन, परिवर्तन-क्रियाविधि

**changing room** *noun* [C] a room for changing clothes in, for example before or after playing sport पोशाक बदलने का कमरा

**channel¹** /ˈtʃænl ˈचैनल् / *noun* [C] **1** a television station कोई टेलीविज़न स्टेशन; चैनल *Which channel is the film on?* ➪ **station¹ 4** देखिए। **2** a band of radio waves used for sending out radio or television programmes रेडियो या टेलीविज़न कार्यक्रमों के प्रसारण के लिए प्रयुक्त तरंग; दैर्घ्य *terrestrial/satellite channels* **3** a way or route along which news, information, etc. is sent समाचार, सूचना आदि प्रेषित करने का मार्ग या माध्यम *a channel of communication* ○ *You have to order new equipment through the official channels.* **4** an open passage along which liquids can flow पानी आदि द्रवों के बहने के लिए खुली नाली *a drainage channel* **5** the part of a river, sea, etc. which is deep enough for boats to pass through नावों के आवागमन के योग्य किसी नदी, समुद्र आदि का गहरा भाग; जलमार्ग **6** a passage of water that connects two area of water, especially two seas विशेषतः दो समुद्रों को जोड़ने वाला जलमार्ग **7 the Channel** (*also* **the English Channel**) the sea between England and France इंग्लैंड और फ्रांस के मध्य का समुद्र

**channel²** /ˈtʃænl ˈचैनल् / *verb* [T] (**channelling; channelled** *AmE* **channeling; channeled**) to make sth move along a particular path or route पथ या मार्ग विशेष से कुछ ले जाना *Water is channelled from the river to the fields.* ○ (*figurative*) *You should channel your energies into something constructive.*

**chant¹** /tʃɑːnt चान्ट् / *noun* **1** [C] a word or phrase that is sung or shouted many times अनेक बार उच्चरित शब्द या वाक्यांश *A chant of 'we are the champions' went round the stadium.* **2** [C, U] a usually religious song with only a few notes that are repeated many times कोई संक्षिप्त व प्रायः धार्मिक गीत जिसे अनेक बार दुहराया जाता है

**chant²** /tʃɑːnt चान्ट् / *verb* [I, T] to sing or shout a word or phrase many times किसी शब्द या वाक्यांश को अनेक बार गाना या ऊँचे स्वर में बोलना *The protesters marched by, chanting slogans.*

**chaos** /ˈkeɪɒs ˈकेऑस् / *noun* [U] a state of great disorder; confusion घोर अव्यवस्था; गड़बड़ी, अस्तव्यस्तता *The country was* ***in chaos*** *after the war.* ○ *The heavy snow has* ***caused chaos*** *on the roads.*

**chaotic** /keɪˈɒtɪk केˈऑटिक्/ *adj.* in a state of chaos अव्यवस्थित, अस्तव्यस्त *With no one in charge the situation became chaotic.*

**chap** /tʃæp चैप्/ *noun* [C] (*informal*) a man or boy आदमी या लड़के के लिए प्रयुक्त शब्द

**chapatti** (*also* **chapati**) *noun* [C] a type of flat round Indian bread रोटी, चपाती

**chapel** /ˈtʃæpl ˈचैप्ल्/ *noun* [C, U] a small building or room that is used by some Christians as a church or for prayer गिरजाघर या प्रार्थना-कक्ष के रूप में प्रयुक्त छोटी इमारत या कमरा *a Methodist chapel*

**chaperone** /ˈʃæpərəʊn ˈशैपरोन्/ *noun* [C] in the past, an older person, usually a woman, who went to public places with a young woman who was not married, to look after her and to make sure that she behaved correctly (अतीत में) कुमारी की संरक्षिका वृद्ध महिला ▶ **chaperone** *verb* [T] कुमारी की संरक्षिका का काम करना

**chaplain** /ˈtʃæplɪn ˈचैप्लिन्/ *noun* [C] a priest who works in a hospital, school, prison, etc. अस्पताल, विद्यालय, कारागार आदि में कार्यरत ईसाई पुरोहित *an army chaplain*

**chapped** /tʃæpt चैप्ट्/ *adj.* (used about the lips or skin) rough, dry and sore, especially because of wind or cold weather (होंठ या त्वचा) ठंड या वायु के कारण खुरदरा, सूखा और दर्दीला

**chapter** /ˈtʃæptə(r) ˈचैप्ट(र्)/ *noun* [C] one of the parts into which a book is divided पुस्तक का अध्याय *Please read Chapter 2 for homework.* ○ (*figurative*) *The last few years have been a difficult chapter in the country's history.*

**character** /ˈkærəktə(r) ˈकैरक्ट(र्)/ *noun* **1** [C, *usually sing.*, U] the qualities that make sb/sth different from other people or things; the nature of sb/sth किसी व्यक्ति का चरित्र, विशिष्ट लक्षण; प्रकृति, स्वभाव *Although they are twins, their characters are quite different.* ○ *These two songs are very different* ***in character***. **2** [U] strong personal qualities प्रबल व्यक्तिगत गुण, व्यक्तित्व *The match developed into a test of character rather than just physical strength.* **3** [U] qualities that make sb/sth interesting रुचिकर बनाने वाले गुण *Modern houses often seem to lack character.* **4** [U] the opinion that people have of you किसी व्यक्ति के चरित्र, आचरण, चाल-चलन आदि के बारे में लोगों की राय *The article was a vicious attack on the actor's character.* **5** [C] (*informal*) an interesting, amusing, strange or unpleasant person रोचक, मज़ेदार, विचित्र या अप्रिय व्यक्ति *I saw a suspicious-looking character outside the bank, so I called the police.* **6** [C] a person in a book, story, etc. किसी किताब, कहानी आदि का पात्र *The main character in the film is a boy who meets an alien.* **7** [C] a letter or sign that you use when you are writing or printing लेखन या मुद्रण में प्रयुक्त अक्षर या चिह्न *Chinese characters*
IDM **in/out of character** typical/not typical of sb/sth प्रतिनिधिक या अप्रतिनिधिक *Tina's rude reply was completely out of character.*

**characteristic**[1] /ˌkærəktəˈrɪstɪk ˌकैरक्टˈरिस्टिक्/ *noun* [C] **a characteristic of (sb/sth)** a quality that is typical of sb/sth and that makes him/her/it different from other people or things किसी व्यक्ति या वस्तु का विशिष्ट लक्षण जिसके कारण वह अन्य व्यक्तियों से भिन्न लगता है; अभिलक्षण; विशेषता

**characteristic**[2] /ˌkærəktəˈrɪstɪk ˌकैरक्टˈरिस्टिक्/ *adj.* **characteristic of (sb/sth)** very typical of sb/sth किसी व्यक्ति या वस्तु का विशेष रूप से प्रतिनिधिक; लक्षणात्मक *The flat landscape is characteristic of this part of the country.* ✪ विलोम **uncharacteristic** ▶ **characteristically** /-kli -क्लि/ *adv.* विशिष्टतासूचक रूप से *'No' he said, in his characteristically direct manner.*

**characterization** (*also* **-isation**) /ˌkærəktəraɪˈzeɪʃn ˌकैरक्टराइˈज़ेश्न्/ *noun* [U, C] **1** the way that a writer makes the characters in a book or play seem real पात्र-वर्णन, चरित्र चित्रण **2** (*formal*) the way in which sb/sth is described (किसी व्यक्ति या वस्तु के) वर्णन का तरीक़ा

**characterize** (*also* **-ise**) /ˈkærəktəraɪz ˈकैरक्टराइज़्/ *verb* [T] (*formal*) **1** (*usually passive*) to be typical of sb/sth (किसी व्यक्ति या वस्तु) का प्रतिनिधिक या लक्षणात्मक होना *the tastes that characterize Gujarati cooking* **2 characterize sb/sth (as sth)** to describe what sb/sth is like किसी व्यक्ति या वस्तु के स्वभाव आदि का वर्णन करना *The President characterized the meeting as friendly and positive.*

**charade** /ʃəˈrɑːd शˈराड्/ *noun* **1** [C] a situation or event that is clearly false but in which people pretend to do or be sth झूठी स्थिति या घटना जिसमें लोग दिखावे का व्यवहार करते हैं *They pretend to be friends but it's all a charade. Everyone knows they hate each other.* **2 charades** [U] a party game in which people try to guess the title of a book, film, etc. that one person must represent using actions but not words एक खेल जिसमें एक व्यक्ति किसी फ़िल्म या पुस्तक के शीर्षक को मूक अभिनय द्वारा जतलाता है और दूसरे लोग उसका शब्दों में अनुमान लगाते हैं; अभिनय प्रहेलिका

**charcoal** /ˈtʃɑːkəʊl ˈचाकोल्/ *noun* [U] a black substance that is produced from burned wood. It can be used for drawing or as a fuel लकड़ी का कोयला; काठकोयला

**charge**[1] /tʃɑːdʒ चाज्/ *noun* **1** [C, U] the price that you must pay for goods or services ख़रीदी गई वस्तु या सेवा पर शुल्क, ख़र्च, व्यय *The hotel makes a small charge for changing currency.* ○ *We deliver **free of charge**.* ➪ **price** पर नोट देखिए। **2** [C, U] a statement that says that sb has done sth illegal or bad आरोप, अभियोग *He was arrested **on a charge of** murder.* **3** [U] a position of control over sb/sth; responsibility for sb/sth देखरेख या निगरानी का उत्तरदायित्व; कार्यभार, ज़िम्मेदारी *Who is **in charge of** the office while Varsha's away?* ○ *The assistant manager had to **take charge of** the team when the manager resigned.* **4** [C] a sudden attack where sb/sth runs straight at sb/sth else एकाएक धावा, हमला **5** [C] the amount of electricity that is put into a battery or carried by a substance बैटरी या अन्य पदार्थ में भरी गई विद्युत की मात्रा *a positive/negative charge*

IDM **bring/press charges (against sb)** to formally accuse sb of a crime so that there can be a trial in a court of law क़ानूनी कार्रवाई के लिए दोषारोपण करना

**reverse the charges** ➪ **reverse**[1] देखिए।

**charge**[2] /tʃɑːdʒ चाज्/ *verb* **1** [I, T] charge (sb/sth) for sth to ask sb to pay a particular amount of money दाम माँगना *We charge Rs 1100 per night for a single room.* ○ *They forgot to charge us for the dessert.* ➪ **overcharge** देखिए। **2** [T] **charge sb (with sth)** to accuse sb officially of doing sth which is against the law ग़ैर-क़ानूनी काम करने के लिए दोषारोपण करना *Six men have been charged with attempted robbery.* **3** [I, T] to run straight at sb/sth, or in a particular direction, in an aggressive or noisy way आक्रामक मुद्रा में आगे बढ़ना; धावा बोल देना *The bull put its head down ready to charge (us).* ○ *The children charged into the room.* **4** [T] to put electricity into sth किसी वस्तु में विद्युत-शक्ति भरना *to charge a battery* ➪ **recharge** देखिए।

**chariot** /ˈtʃæriət ˈचैरिअट्/ *noun* [C] an open vehicle with two wheels that was pulled by a horse or horses in ancient times दो पहियों वाला खुला वाहन जिसे प्राचीन काल में घोड़े खींचते थे; रथ

**charisma** /kəˈrɪzmə कˈरिज़्मा/ *noun* [U] a powerful personal quality that some people have to attract and influence other people कुछ व्यक्तियों में दूसरों को आकर्षित व प्रभावित करने का प्रबल व्यक्तिगत गुण, आकर्षण *The president of the students' union is not very clever, but he has great charisma.* ▶ **charismatic** /ˌkærɪzˈmætɪk ˌकैरिज़ˈमैटिक्/ *adj.* इस गुण से संबंधित; आकर्षक

**charitable** /ˈtʃærətəbl ˈचैरटबल्/ *adj.* **1** kind; generous दयालु; उदार *Some people accused him of lying, but a more charitable explanation was that he had made a mistake.* **2** connected with a charity परोपकारी, दानी

**charity** /ˈtʃærəti ˈचैरटि/ *noun* (*pl.* **charities**) **1** [C, U] an organization that collects money to help people who are poor, sick, etc. or to do work that is useful to society; the money or gifts collected or given to people who are poor, sick, etc. धन इकट्ठा कर दीनों-दुखियों की सहायता करने वाली संस्था; सहायतार्थ संस्था; दान की गई राशि, वस्तुएँ आदि *We went on a sponsored walk to **raise money for charity**.* **2** [U] kindness towards other people परोपकार, दयालुता *to act out of charity*

**charlatan** /ˈʃɑːlətən ˈशालटन्/ *noun* [C] a person who says that he/she has knowledge or skills that he/she does not really have जानकार होने या योग्यता रखने का पाखंड करने वाला व्यक्ति

**charm**[1] /tʃɑːm चाम्/ *noun* **1** [C, U] a quality that pleases and attracts people लोगों को प्रसन्नचित्त व आकृष्ट करने वाला गुण; आकर्षण, मनोहारिता *The charm of the island lies in its unspoilt beauty.* **2** [C] something that you wear because you believe it will bring you good luck मंत्र, तावीज़ *a necklace with a lucky charm on it*

**charm**[2] /tʃɑːm चाम्/ *verb* [T] **1** to please and attract sb किसी को मोहित या आकर्षित करना *Her drawings have charmed children all over the world.* **2** to protect sb/sth as if by magic किसी को मायाशक्ति या जादू जैसे प्रभाव से सुरक्षा प्रदान करना *He has led a charmed life, surviving serious illness and a plane crash.*

**charming** /ˈtʃɑːmɪŋ ˈचामिङ्/ *adj.* very pleasing or attractive बहुत सुखकर, रोचक या आकर्षक ▶ **charmingly** *adv.* आकर्षक या रोचक रूप से

**charred** /ˈtʃɑːd ˈचाड्/ *adj.* burnt black by fire आग से बुरी तरह से जला हुआ

**chart**[1] /tʃɑːt चाट्/ *noun* **1** [C] a drawing which shows information in the form of a diagram, etc. रेखाचित्र आदि के रूप में सूचना-सामग्री देने वाला चित्र; चार्ट *a temperature chart* ○ *This chart shows the company's sales for this year.* ➪ **pie chart** और **flow chart** देखिए। **2** [C] a map of the sea or the sky समुद्र या आकाश का मानचित्र *navigation charts* **3 the charts** [*pl.*] an official list of the songs or CDs, etc., that have sold the most in a particular week सप्ताह-विशेष में सर्वाधिक बिक्री वाले गानों या सीडीज़ की अधिकृत सूची

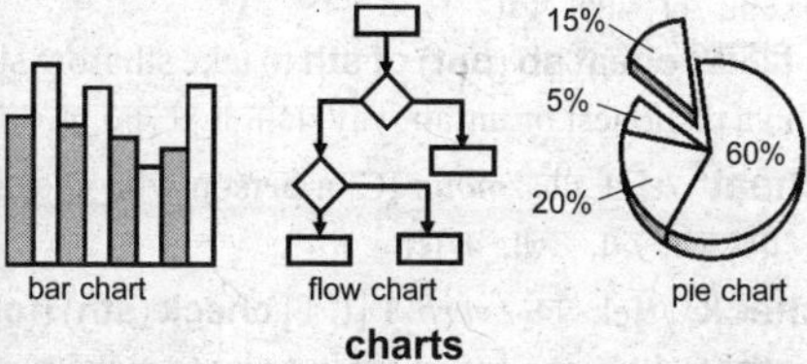


**charts**

**chart²** /tʃɑːt चाट्/ *verb* [T] **1** to follow or record the progress or development of sth carefully and in detail किसी घटना आदि की प्रगति या विकास को सावधानी से और विस्तारपूर्वक जानना या दर्ज करना *This television series charts the history of the country since independence.* **2** to make a map of one area of the sea or sky समुद्र या आकाश के एक भाग का मानचित्र बनाना *chart a coastline*

**charter¹** /ˈtʃɑːtə(r) ˈचाट(र्)/ *noun* [C, U] **1** a written statement of the rights, beliefs and purposes of an organization or a particular group of people किसी संगठन या व्यक्ति-समुदाय के अधिकारों, विश्वासों और उद्देश्यों का लिखित दस्तावेज़; अधिकारपत्र *The club's charter does not permit women to become members.* **2** the renting of a ship, plane, etc. for a particular purpose or for a particular group of people विमान, जहाज़ आदि को विशेष उद्देश्य से तथा विशेष व्यक्तियों के लिए भाड़े पर लेने की क्रिया, चार्टर करने की क्रिया *a charter airline*

**charter²** /ˈtʃɑːtə(r) ˈचाट(र्)/ *verb* [T] to rent a ship, plane, etc. for a particular purpose or for a particular group of people विमान, जहाज़ आदि को विशेष उद्देश्य से या विशेष व्यक्तियों के लिए भाड़े पर लेना; चार्टर करना *As there was no regular service to the island, we had to charter a boat.*

**chartered** /ˈtʃɑːtəd ˈचाटड्/ *adj.* (*only before a noun*) (used about people in certain professions) fully trained; having passed all the necessary exams (कुछ पेशों में व्यक्ति) पूर्णतया प्रशिक्षित; समस्त अपेक्षित परीक्षाओं में उत्तीर्ण *a chartered accountant*

**chase¹** /tʃeɪs चेस्/ *verb* **1** [I, T] **chase (after) sb/sth** to run after sb/sth in order to catch him/her/it पकड़ने के लिए किसी के पीछे-पीछे भागना; किसी का पीछा करना *The dog chased the cat up a tree.* ○ *The police car chased after the stolen van.* **2** [I] to run somewhere fast तेज़ी से किसी दिशा में भागना *The kids were chasing around the park.*

**chase²** /tʃeɪs चेस्/ *noun* [C] the act of following sb/sth in order to catch him/her/it किसी का पीछा करने की क्रिया *an exciting car chase*

IDM **give chase** to begin to run after sb/sth in order to try to catch him/her/it पकड़ने के लिए किसी के पीछे भागने लगना *The robber ran off and the policeman gave chase.*

**chasm** /ˈkæzəm ˈकैज़म्/ *noun* [C] **1** a deep hole in the ground जमीन में गहरा गड्ढा; गह्वर **2** a wide difference of feelings, interests, etc. between two people or groups दो व्यक्तियों या दलों की भावनाओं, रुचियों आदि में बड़ा अंतर

**chassis** /ˈʃæsi ˈशैसि/ *noun* [C] (*pl.* **chassis** /ˈʃæsi ˈशैसि/) the metal frame of a vehicle onto which the other parts fit किसी वाहन का धातु-निर्मित चौखटा जिस पर अन्य पुरज़े लगे होते हैं

**chaste** /tʃeɪst चेस्ट्/ *adj.* **1** (*formal*) never having had a sexual relationship, or only with the person sb is married to कभी यौन संबंध नही रखा या दंपत्ति तक सीमित यौन संबंध **2** (of language) pure; formal (भाषा) विशुद्ध; औपचारिक *She speaks chaste English.* ▶ **chastity** /ˈtʃæstəti ˈचैस्टटि/ *noun* [U] शुचिता

**chastise** /tʃæˈstaɪz चैˈस्टाइज़्/ *verb* [T] **1 chastise sb (for sth/for doing sth)** (*formal*) to criticize sb for doing sth wrong ग़लती के लिए आलोचना या निंदा करना; डाँटना **2** (*old-fashioned*) to punish sb physically किसी को शारीरिक दंड देना, ताड़ना देना ▶ **chastisement** *noun* [U] ताड़ना, दंड, सज़ा

**chat¹** /tʃæt चैट्/ *verb* [I] (**chatting; chatted**) **chat (with/to sb) (about sth)** to talk to sb in a friendly, informal way मैत्रीपूर्ण और अनौपचारिक रूप से बातचीत करना; गपशप करना

**chat²** /tʃæt चैट्/ *noun* [C, U] a friendly informal conversation मैत्रीपूर्ण अनौपचारिक बातचीत; गपशप

**chat room** *noun* [C] (*computing*) an area on the Internet where people can communicate with each other, usually about one particular topic इंटरनेट पर वह क्षेत्र जहाँ लोग एक-दूसरे से किसी विशेष विषय पर विचारों का आदान-प्रदान करते हैं

**chat show** *noun* [C] a television or radio programme on which well-known people are invited to talk about various issues टेलीविज़न या रेडियो कार्यक्रम जिसमें जाने-माने लोगों को विविध विषयों पर बातचीत के लिए आमंत्रित किया जाता है

**chatter** /ˈtʃætə(r) ˈचैट(र्)/ *verb* [I] **1** to talk quickly or for a long time about sth unimportant तेज़ गति से या देर तक किसी मामूली विषय पर बात करना; लगातार निरर्थक चर्चा करना; बकबक करना **2** (used about your teeth) to knock together because you are cold or frightened ठंड या डर के मारे (दाँतों का) कटकटाना, किटकिटाना ▶ **chatter** *noun* [U] लगातार की बकबक; (दाँतों की) किटकिट की आवाज़

**chatty** /ˈtʃæti ˈचैटि / *adj.* **1** talking a lot in a friendly way मित्र-भाव से देर तक बतियाते हुए; बातूनी **2** in an informal style अनौपचारिक रीति से *a chatty letter*

**chauffeur** /ˈʃəʊfə(r) ˈशोफ़(र्) / *noun* [C] a person whose job is to drive a car for sb else दूसरों के लिए उनकी कार चलाने की नौकरी करने वाला व्यक्ति; कार का वेतन भोगी ड्राइवर *a chauffeur-driven limousine* ▶ **chauffeur** *verb* [T] ड्राइवर की नौकरी करना

**chauvinism** /ˈʃəʊvɪnɪzəm ˈशोविनिज़म् / *noun* [U] **1** the belief that your country is better than all others अपने राष्ट्र को अन्य राष्ट्रों से श्रेष्ठ मानने की धारणा; उग्र राष्ट्रवाद **2** (*also* **male chauvinism**) the belief that men are better than women पुरुषों को महिलाओं से श्रेष्ठ मानने की धारणा ▶ **chauvinist** /ˈʃəʊvɪnɪst ˈशोविनिस्ट् / *noun* [C], *adj.* उग्र राष्ट्रवादी, पुरुष-श्रेष्ठतावादी

**cheap¹** /tʃiːp चीप् / *adj.* **1** low in price, costing little money सस्ता, कम क़ीमत का *Oranges are cheap at the moment.* ○ *Computers are getting cheaper all the time.* ✪ पर्याय **inexpensive** ✪ विलोम **expensive** **2** charging low prices सस्ते दाम का; कम क़ीमत लेने वाला *a cheap hotel/restaurant* **3** low in price and quality and therefore not attractive सस्ता, घटिया व अनाकर्षक *The clothes in that shop look cheap.*

**IDM** **dirt cheap** ⇨ **dirt** देखिए।

**cheap²** /tʃiːp चीप् / *adv.* (*informal*) for a low price सस्ते में, कम दाम में *I got this coat cheap in the sale.*

**IDM** **be going cheap** (*informal*) to be on sale at a lower price than usual नियमित रूप से कम दाम पर उपलब्ध

**cheapen** /ˈtʃiːpən ˈचीपन् / *verb* [T] **1** to make sb lose respect for himself or herself किसी का आत्मसम्मान घटाना *She felt cheapened by his treatment of her.* ✪ पर्याय **degrade** **2** to make sth lower in price किसी वस्तु का दाम घटा देना **3** to make sth seem to have less value किसी वस्तु आदि का महत्त्व या गुण कम कर देना *The movie was accused of cheapening human life.*

**cheaply** /ˈtʃiːpli ˈचीप्लि/ *adv.* for a low price सस्ते में

**cheat¹** /tʃiːt चीट् / *verb* **1** [T] to trick sb, especially when that person trusts you; to deceive sb किसी को ठगना, धोखा देना; छल करना *The shopkeeper cheated customers by giving them too little change.* **2** [I] **cheat (at sth)** to act in a dishonest or unfair way in order to get an advantage for yourself लाभ पाने के लिए बेईमानी या अनुचित व्यवहार करना *Praveen was caught cheating in the exam.* ○ *to cheat at cards* **3** [I] **cheat (on sb)** to not be faithful to your husband, wife or regular partner by having a secret sexual relationship with sb else किसी अन्य के साथ यौन-संबंध स्थापित करके जीवनसाथी के प्रति वफ़ादार न रहना; को धोखा देना

**PHR V** **cheat sb (out) of sth** to take sth from sb in a dishonest or unfair way बेईमानी से कुछ ले लेना

**cheat²** /tʃiːt चीट् / *noun* [C] a person who cheats धोखेबाज़, ठग, छली, कपटी

**check¹** /tʃek चेक् / *verb* **1** [I, T] **check (sth) (for sth)** to examine or test sth in order to make sure that it is safe or correct, in good condition, etc. किसी वस्तु के सुरक्षित या सही अवस्था में होने की जाँच करना *Check your work for mistakes before you hand it in.* ○ *The doctor X-rayed me to check for broken bones.* **2** [I, T] **check (sth) (with sb)** to make sure that sth is how you think it is कोई बात पक्के तौर पर मालूम करना; सुनिश्चित करना *You'd better check with Jai that it's OK to borrow his bike.* ○ *I'll phone and check what time the bus leaves.* **3** [T] to stop or make sb/sth stop or go more slowly रुकना या रोकना; गति और मंद करना *Rohit checked his pace as he didn't want to tire too early.* **4** [T] = **tick¹ 2**

**PHR V** **check in (at...); check into...** to go to a desk in a hotel or an airport and tell an official that you have arrived होटल या हवाई अड्डे पर पहुँचकर संबद्ध अधिकारी को अपने आगमन की सूचना देना

**check sth off** to mark names or items on a list सूची में नामों या मदों पर निशान लगाना; को चिह्नित करना; सूची से मिलान करना

**check (up) on sb/sth** to find out how sb/sth is किसी के हाल-चाल मालूम करना *We call my grandmother every evening to check up on her.*

**check out (of...)** to pay your bill and leave a hotel बिल का भुगतान कर होटल छोड़ना

**check sb/sth out** **1** to find out more information about sb/sth, especially to find out if sth is true or not कथन आदि की सत्यता या असत्यता की जांच करना *We need to check out these rumours of possible pay cuts.* **2** (*informal*) to look at sth, especially to find out if you like him/her/it किसी वस्तु आदि को परखना या आज़माना, विशेषतः यह जानने के लिए कि वह पसंद है कि नहीं *I'm going to check out that new club tonight.*

**check up on sb/sth** to make sure that sb/sth is working correctly, behaving well, etc., especially if you think he/she/it is not किसी के कार्य व्यवहार आदि के उचित होने या न होने को सुनिश्चित करना

**check**[2] /tʃek चेक् / *noun* **1** [C] **a check (on sth)** a close look at sth to make sure that it is safe, correct, in good condition, etc. किसी वस्तु के सुरक्षित या उचित अवस्था में होने को सुनिश्चित करने के लिए (वस्तु की) बारीकी से जाँच, परीक्षण *We **carry out/do** regular **checks** on our products to make sure that they are of high quality.* ○ *I don't go to games, but I like to **keep a check** on my team's results.* **2** [C] **a check (on/to sth)** (*formal*) sth that controls sth else and stops it from getting worse, etc. रोकथाम, रुकावट *a check on the spread of malaria* **3** [C, U] a pattern of squares, often of different colours वर्गों का पैटर्न (प्रायः अलग-अलग रंगों में), रंगबिरंगी वर्गाकृतियों का पैटर्न *a check jacket* ○ *a pattern of blue and red checks* **4** [U] the situation in a particular game (**chess**), in which a player must move to protect his/her king (शतरंज में) शह की ऐसी स्थिति जिसमें विपक्षी को अपने बादशाह को बचाने की चाल चलना अनिवार्य हो जाए ➪ **checkmate** देखिए। **5** [C] (*AmE*) = **cheque** **6** [C] (*AmE*) = **bill**[1] **7** [C] (*AmE*) = **tick**[2] **1**

**IDM** **hold /keep sth in check** to stop sth from advancing or increasing too quickly किसी की तेज़ बढ़त को रोकना

**checkbook** (*AmE*) = **chequebook**

**checkbox** *noun* [C] (*computing*) a square on a computer screen that allows you to choose sth by pressing (**clicking**) on it with your mouse button कंप्यूटर के परदे पर बना वर्गाकार चिह्न जिस पर माउस बटन से क्लिक किया जाता है; चेक बॉक्स

**checked** /tʃekt चेक्ट् / *adj.* with a pattern of squares चारख़ाने वाला *a red-and-white checked table cloth*

**checkers** /ˈtʃekəz ˈचेकज़् / (*AmE*) = **draught**[1] **2**

**check-in** *noun* [C] **1** the act of checking in at an airport हवाई अड्डे पर पहुँचकर अपने आगमन की सूचना देने की क्रिया *Our check-in time is 10.30 a.m.* **2** the place where you check in at an airport हवाई अड्डे पर अपने आगमन की सूचना देने का स्थान

**checking account** (*AmE*) = **current account**

**checklist** /ˈtʃeklɪst ˈचेक्लिस्ट् / *noun* [C] a list of things that you must do or have करणीय कार्यों या संग्रहणीय वस्तुओं की सूची; जाँचसूची

**checkmate** /ˌtʃekˈmeɪt ˌचेक्ˈमेट् / *noun* [U] the situation in a particular game (**chess**) in which you cannot protect your king and so have lost the game (शतरंज में) शहमात; ऐसी स्थिति जिसमें विपक्षी अपने बादशाह को बचा न सके और हार हो जाए ➪ **check**[2] **3** देखिए।

**checkout** /ˈtʃekaʊt ˈचेक्आउट् / *noun* [C] the place in a large food shop (**supermarket**) where you pay सुपर मार्केट में भुगतान करने का स्थान; भुगतान-स्थल, अदायगी काउन्टर

**checkpoint** /ˈtʃekpɔɪnt ˈचेक्पॉइन्ट् / *noun* [C] a place where all people and vehicles must stop and be checked जाँच चौकी *an army checkpoint*

**check-up** *noun* [C] a general medical examination to make sure that you are healthy स्वास्थ्य की स्थिति का सामान्य चिकित्सीय परीक्षण; डॉक्टरी जाँच

**cheddar** /ˈtʃedə(r) ˈचेड(र्) / *noun* [U] a type of hard yellow cheese एक प्रकार का ठोस पीला पनीर; चेडर

**cheek** /tʃiːk चीक् / *noun* **1** [C] either side of the face below your eyes गाल, कपोल ➪ **body** पर चित्र देखिए। **2** [C, U] rude behaviour; lack of respect अशिष्ट व्यवहार, आदरहीनता, निरादर *He's got a cheek, asking to borrow money again!*

**IDM** **(with) tongue in cheek** ➪ **tongue** देखिए।

**cheekbone** /ˈtʃiːkbəʊn ˈचीक्बोन् / *noun* [C] the bone below your eye आँख के नीचे की हड्डी; गंडास्थि ➪ **body** पर चित्र देखिए।

**cheeky** /ˈtʃiːki ˈचीकि / *adj.* (*BrE*) (**cheekier; cheekiest**) not showing respect; rude धृष्ट; अशिष्ट *Don't be so cheeky! Of course I'm not fat!*
▶ **cheekily** *adv.* अशिष्टतापूर्वक

**cheer**[1] /tʃɪə(r) चिअ(र्) / *verb* **1** [I, T] to shout to show that you like sth or to encourage sb who is taking part in competition, sport, etc. किसी को स्पर्धा, खेल आदि में प्रोत्साहित करने के लिए चिल्लाना आदि *Everyone cheered the winner as he crossed the finishing line.* **2** [T] to make sb happy or more hopeful किसी को प्रसन्न करना या उम्मीद बढ़ाना *They were all cheered by the good news.*

**PHR V** **cheer sb on** to shout in order to encourage sb in a race, competition, etc. दौड़ आदि स्पर्धा में प्रतियोगी को प्रोत्साहित करने के लिए शोर मचाना *As the runners started the last lap the crowd cheered them on.*

**cheer (sb/sth) up** to become or to make sb happier; to make sth look more attractive प्रसन्न होना या करना; किसी को अधिक आकर्षक बनाना *Cheer up! Things aren't that bad.* ○ *A few pictures would cheer this room up a bit.*

**cheer**[2] /tʃɪə(r) चिअ(र्) / *noun* [C] a loud shout to show that you like sth or to encourage sb who is taking part in a competition, sport, etc. वाहवाही, जयघोष *The crowd **gave a cheer** when the president appeared.*

**cheerful** /ˈtʃɪəfl ˈचिअफ़ल्/ *adj.* feeling happy; showing that you are happy प्रसन्न, प्रमुदित; हँसमुख *Bhavna is always very cheerful.* ○ *a cheerful smile* ▶ **cheerfully** /-fəli -फ़लि/ *adv.* प्रसन्नतापूर्वक ▶ **cheerfulness** *noun* [U] प्रसन्नता, प्रफुल्लता

**cheerleader** /ˈtʃɪəliːdə(r) ˈचिअलीड(र्)/ *noun* [C] (especially in the US) one of a group of girls or women at a sports match who wear special uniforms and shout, dance, etc. in order to encourage people to support the players (विशेषतः अमेरीका में) विशेष पोशाक पहने युवतियों की टोली की सदस्या जो दर्शकों को खिलाड़ियों के उत्साह-वर्धन के लिए प्रेरित करती है

**cheers** /tʃɪəz चिअज़्/ *exclamation* (*informal*) used to express good wishes before you have an alcoholic drink मदिरापान आरंभ करने से पहले शुभकामनाएँ व्यक्त करने के लिए प्रयुक्त *'Cheers,' she said, raising her wine glass.*

**cheery** /ˈtʃɪəri ˈचिअरि/ *adj.* happy and smiling प्रसन्न और मुस्कानयुक्त *a cheery remark/wave/smile* ▶ **cheerily** *adv.* प्रसन्नता से

**cheese** /tʃiːz चीज़्/ *noun* **1** [U] a type of food made from milk. Cheese is usually white or yellow in colour and can be soft or hard पनीर *a piece of cheese* ○ *a cheese sandwich* **2** [C] a type of cheese एक प्रकार का पनीर *a wide selection of cheeses*

**cheesecake** /ˈtʃiːzkeɪk ˈचीज़्केक्/ *noun* [C, U] a type of cake that is made from soft cheese and sugar on a pastry or biscuit base, often with fruit on top नरम पनीर और चीनी से बना केक जिसके नीचे बिस्कुट या पेस्ट्री होती है और ऊपर फल; चीज़ केक

**cheetah** *noun* [C] a large wild cat with black spots that can run very fast चीता

**chef** /ʃef शेफ़्/ *noun* [C] a professional cook, especially the head cook in a hotel, restaurant, etc. होटल या रेस्तराँ में मुख्य रसोइया

**chemical¹** /ˈkemɪkl ˈकेमिकल्/ *adj.* connected with chemistry; involving changes to the structure of a substance रसायनशास्त्र-विषयक; रासायनिक, किसी पदार्थ की बनावट में होने वाले या हुए परिवर्तन से संबंधित *a chemical reaction* ▶ **chemically** /-kli -क्लि/ *adv.* रासायनिक रूप से

**chemical²** /ˈkemɪkl ˈकेमिकल्/ *noun* [C] a substance that is used or produced in a chemical process रासायनिक प्रक्रिया से बना या उसमें प्रयुक्त पदार्थ; रसायन *Sulphuric acid is a dangerous chemical.* ○ *chemical weapons/warfare*

**chemist** /ˈkemɪst ˈकेमिस्ट्/ *noun* [C] **1** (*also* **pharmacist** *AmE* **druggist**) a person who prepares and sells medicines औषधि-निर्माता तथा विक्रेता **2 the chemist's** (*AmE* **drugstore**) a shop that sells medicines, soap, cosmetics, etc. औषधियाँ, साबुन, सौन्दर्य-वर्धन वस्तुएँ आदि बेचने की दुकान *I got my tablets from the chemist's.* **3** a person who is a specialist in chemistry रसायनशास्त्री, रसायनज्ञ

**chemistry** /ˈkemɪstri ˈकेमिस्ट्रि/ *noun* [U] **1** the scientific study of the structure of substances and what happens to them in different conditions or when mixed with each other रसायनशास्त्र **2** the structure of a particular substance पदार्थ-विशेष की संरचना या बनावट

**chemotherapy** /ˌkiːməʊˈθerəpi ˈकीमोˈथेरपि/ *noun* [U] the treatment of an illness using chemical substances रासायनिक पदार्थों द्वारा चिकित्सा; रसोचिकित्सा, कीमोथेरापी *She was suffering from leukaemia and is undergoing chemotherapy.*

**cheque** (*AmE* **check**) /tʃek चेक्/ *noun* [C, U] a piece of paper printed by a bank that you sign and use to pay for things बैंक द्वारा मुद्रित एवं जारी काग़ज़ प्रपत्र जिसे हस्ताक्षर कर भुगतान के लिए प्रयोग किया जा सकता है; चेक, दायक *She wrote out a cheque for Rs 5000.* ○ *I went to the bank to* ***cash a cheque***. ○ *Can I* ***pay by cheque***?

**chequebook** (*AmE* **checkbook**) /ˈtʃekbʊk ˈचेकबुक्/ *noun* [C] a book of cheques चेकों की पुस्तिका या गड्डी

**cherish** /ˈtʃerɪʃ ˈचेरिश्/ *verb* [T] **1** to love sb/sth and look after him/her/it carefully किसी से स्नेह करना और सावधानीपूर्वक देखरेख में रखना **2** to keep a thought, feeling, etc. in your mind and think about it often (विचार, भावना आदि) हृदय में सँजोए रखना और उसे प्रायः याद करना *a cherished memory*

**cherry** /ˈtʃeri ˈचेरि/ *noun* [C] (*pl.* **cherries**) **1** a small round black or red fruit that has a stone inside it (बेर जैसा) गुठली वाला छोटा काला या लाल फल; चेरी ➪ **fruit** पर चित्र देखिए। **2** (*also* **cherry tree**) the tree that produces cherries चेरी का वृक्ष

**cherub** /ˈtʃerəb ˈचेरब्/ *noun* [C] a type of **angel** that looks like a fat male child with wings कल्पित दिव्य प्राणी जो परों वाले स्थूलकाय नर बालक जैसा दिखता है; देवदूत, फ़रिश्ता

**chess** /tʃes ˈचेस्/ *noun* [U] a game for two people that is played on a board with 64 black and white squares (**a chessboard**). Each player has 16 pieces which can be moved according to fixed rules शतरंज का खेल, यह खेल दो व्यक्तियों के बीच 64 वर्गाकार काले व सफ़ेद ख़ानों वाले बोर्ड पर खेला जाता है प्रत्येक खिलाड़ी की 16–16 मोहरें होती हैं जिन्हें निश्चित नियमों के अनुसार चलाया जाता है *Can you* ***play chess***?

**chest** /tʃest ˈचेस्ट्/ *noun* [C] **1** the top part of the front of your body छाती, वक्षस्थल ➪ **body** पर चित्र देखिए। **2** a large strong box that is used for storing or carrying things लकड़ी की बड़ी पेटी

**IDM** **get sth off your chest** (*informal*) to talk about sth that you have been thinking or worrying about अपनी चिंता के विषय में बात करके दिल का बोझ हलका करना

**chestnut** /ˈtʃesnʌt ˈचेस्नट्/ *noun* [C] **1** (*also* **chestnut tree**) a tree with large leaves that produces smooth brown nuts in shells with sharp points on the outside चेस्टनट (एक फल) का वृक्ष **2** a smooth brown nut from the chestnut tree. You can eat some chestnuts चेस्टनट फल *roast chestnuts* ➪ **conker** देखिए तथा **nut** पर चित्र देखिए।

**chest of drawers** *noun* [C] a piece of furniture with drawers in it that is used for storing clothes, etc. दराज़ों वाली अलमारी

**chew** /tʃuː चू/ *verb* [I, T] **1** to break up food in your mouth with your teeth before you swallow it भोजन चबाना **2** **chew** (**on**) **sth** to bite sth continuously with the back teeth पिछले दाँतों से लगातार चबाते रहना *The dog was chewing on a bone.*

**chewing gum** (*also* **gum**) *noun* [U] a sweet sticky substance that you chew in your mouth but do not swallow एक प्रकार का मीठा चिपचिपा पदार्थ जिसे केवल चबाया (न कि निगला) जाता है; चूइंगगम; चर्वण गोंद ➪ **bubblegum** देखिए।

**chewy** /ˈtʃuːi ˈचूइ/ *adj.* (used about food) needing to be chewed a lot before it can be swallowed (खाद्य पदार्थ) जिसे निगलने लायक़ बनाने के लिए देर तक चबाने की आवश्यकता पड़े *chewy meat/toffee*

**chic** /ʃiːk शीक्/ *adj.* fashionable and elegant लोकप्रिय, आकर्षक और सुरुचि-संपन्न ▶ **chic** *noun* [U] लोकप्रिय और सुरुचि-संपन्न होने का गुण

**chick** /tʃɪk चिक्/ *noun* [C] a baby bird, especially a young chicken किसी भी पक्षी का बच्चा, विशेषतः मुरग़ी का बच्चा; चूज़ा

**chicken**[1] /ˈtʃɪkɪn ˈचिकिन्/ *noun* **1** [C] a bird that people often keep for its eggs and its meat मुरग़ी या मुरग़ा **2** [U] the meat of this bird मुरग़ा या मुरग़ी का मांस *chicken soup*

**NOTE** मुरग़ा-मुरग़ी और उसके मांस के लिए सामान्यतः शब्द **chicken** का प्रयोग किया जाता है। मुरग़े को **cock** (*AmE* **rooster**), मुरग़ी को **hen** और उनके बच्चे को **chick** कहते हैं।

**IDM** **Don't count your chickens** (**before they're hatched**) ➪ **count**[1] देखिए।

**chicken**[2] /ˈtʃɪkɪn ˈचिकिन्/ *verb*

**PHRV** **chicken out** (**of sth**) (*informal*) to decide not to do sth because you are afraid डर के मारे काम न करने का निर्णय लेना

**chickenpox** /ˈtʃɪkɪnpɒks ˈचिकिन्पॉक्स्/ *noun* [U] a disease, especially of children. When you have chickenpox you feel very hot and get red spots on your skin that make you want to scratch छोटी चेचक, जो विशेषतः बच्चों को निकलती हैं, इस रोग में रोगी को छोटे-छोटे लाल दाने निकलते हैं जिनमें खुजली उठती है

**chicory** /ˈtʃɪkəri ˈचिकरि/ (*AmE* **endive**) *noun* [U] a small pale green plant with bitter leaves that can be eaten cooked or not cooked खाने योग्य कड़वे पत्तों वाला एक छोटा पीला-हरा पौधा; चिकरी, कसनी

**chief**[1] /tʃiːf ˈचीफ़्/ *noun* [C] **1** the person who has command or control over an organization संगठन का प्रमुख; प्रधान *the chief of police* **2** the leader of a tribe क़बीले का सरदार

**chief**[2] /tʃiːf चीफ़्/ *adj.* (*only before a noun*) **1** most important; main सर्वाधिक महत्त्वपूर्ण; मुख्य *One of the chief reasons for his decision was money.* **2** of the highest level or position उच्चतम पद का, प्रमुखतम *the chief executive of a company*

**chiefly** /ˈtʃiːfli ˈचीफ़्लि/ *adv.* mainly; mostly मुख्य रूप से; अधिकांशतः *His success was due chiefly to hard work.*

**chieftain** /ˈtʃiːftən ˈचीफ़्टन्/ *noun* [C] the leader of a tribe क़बीले का सरदार

**chiffon** /ˈʃɪfɒn ˈशिफ़ॉन्/ *noun* [U] a very thin, transparent type of cloth used for making clothes, etc. एक प्रकार का बहुत महीन पारदर्शी कपड़ा जिससे पोशाकें आदि बनाई जाती हैं; शिफ़ॉन

**chiku** (*also* **chikoo**) *noun* [C] (*IndE*) **1** the sapodilla tree चीकू का वृक्ष **2** the edible fruit of this tree with black seeds; sapota. It is also known as the sapodilla plum चीकू का फल

**chilblain** /ˈtʃɪlbleɪn ˈचिल्ब्लेन्/ *noun* [C] a painful red area on your foot, hand, etc. that is caused by cold weather ठंड के कारण हाथ, पैर आदि पर बना दर्दीला चकत्ता

**child** /tʃaɪld चाइल्ड्/ *noun* [C] (*pl.* **children** /ˈtʃɪldrən ˈचिल्ड्रन्/) **1** a young boy or girl who is not yet an adult बालक या बालिका, बच्चा (जो अभी वयस्क नहीं हुआ है) *A group of children were playing in the park.* ○ *a six-year-old child* **2** a son or daughter of any age किसी भी आयु का पुत्र या पुत्री *She has two children but both are married and have moved away.*

**NOTE** वह बच्चा जिसके कोई भाई-बहिन नहीं हो, **only child** कहलाता है। क़ानूनी रूप से गोद लिए गए बच्चे को an **adopted child** कहते हैं। जिस बच्चे का पालन-पोषण किसी पराए परिवार द्वारा सीमित अवधि के लिए किया जाता है, उस बच्चे को उस परिवार का **foster child** कहा जाता है।

**childbirth** /ˈtʃaɪldbɜːθ ˈचाइल्ड्बथ्/ *noun* [U] the act of giving birth to a baby शिशुजन्म की प्रक्रिया *His wife died* ***in childbirth***.

**childcare** /ˈtʃaɪldkeə(r) ˈचाइल्ड्केअ(र्)/ *noun* [U] the job of looking after children, especially while the parents are at work विशेषतः काम-काजी दंपतियों के बच्चे की देखभाल; बाल देख-रेख *Some employers provide childcare facilities.*

**childhood** /ˈtʃaɪldhʊd ˈचाइल्ड्हुड्/ *noun* [C, U] the time when you are a child बाल्यावस्था, बचपन *Akanksha had a very unhappy childhood.*

**childish** /ˈtʃaɪldɪʃ ˈचाइल्डिश्/ *adj.* like a child बचकाना, नासमझी का *childish handwriting* ▶ **childishly** *adv.* बचकानी रीति से

**NOTE** अगर व्यक्तियों या उनके आचरण के संदर्भ में शब्द **childlike** का प्रयोग किया जाता है तो उसका अर्थ है कि अमुक व्यक्ति बच्चों के समान है—*His childlike enthusiasm delighted us all*. परंतु इसी संदर्भ में शब्द **childish** का अर्थ निंदात्मक होता है; यह शब्द दर्शाता है कि अमुक व्यक्ति या उसका आचरण बचकाना या मूर्खतापूर्ण है—*Don't be so childish! You can't always have everything you want.*

**childless** /ˈtʃaɪldləs ˈचाइल्ड्लस्/ *adj.* having no children निस्संतान

**childlike** /ˈtʃaɪldlaɪk ˈचाइल्ड्लाइक्/ *adj.* like a child बालक के समान, बालसुलभ ➪ **childish** देखिए।

**childminder** /ˈtʃaɪldmaɪndə(r) ˈचाइल्ड्माइन्ड(र्)/ *noun* [C] a person whose job is to look after a child while his/her parents are at work माता-पिता की अनुपस्थिति में उनके बच्चे की देखभाल करने वाला व्यक्ति

**childproof** /ˈtʃaɪldpruːf ˈचाइल्ड्प्रूफ़्/ *adj.* designed so that young children cannot open, use or damage it इस प्रकार निर्मित कि बच्चों की पहुँच से बाहर हो *childproof containers for medicine*

**children's home** *noun* [C] an institution where children live whose parents cannot look after them शिशु-सदन जहाँ ऐसे माता-पिता के बच्चे रहते हैं जो अपने बच्चे का पालन-पोषण करने में किसी कारण असमर्थ होते हैं

**chili** (*AmE*) = **chilli**

**chill**[1] /tʃɪl चिल्/ *noun* **1** [*sing.*] an unpleasant cold feeling सिहरन, कष्टकर ठंडक, सर्द *There's a chill in the air.* ○ (*figurative*) *A chill of fear went down my spine.* **2** [C] (*informal*) a common illness that affects your nose and throat; a cold सर्दी-ज़ुकाम *to catch a chill*

**chill**[2] /tʃɪl चिल्/ *verb* [I, T] **1** to become or to make sb/sth colder ठंडा होना या करना **2** (*also* **chill out**) (*informal*) to relax and not feel angry or nervous about anything तनाव, क्रोध या व्याकुलता से मुक्त होना; सहज होना *I work hard all week so on Sundays I just chill out.*

**chilli** (*AmE* **chili**) /ˈtʃɪli ˈचिलि/ *noun* [C, U] (*pl.* **chillies** or *AmE* **chilies**) a small green or red vegetable that has a very strong hot taste मिर्च (हरी या लाल) *chilli powder* ➪ **vegetable** पर चित्र देखिए।

**chilling** /ˈtʃɪlɪŋ ˈचिलिङ्/ *adj.* frightening भयानक, डरावना *a chilling ghost story*

**chilly** /ˈtʃɪli ˈचिलि/ *adj.* (**chillier; chilliest**) (used about the weather but also about people) too cold to be comfortable (मौसम) बहुत ठंडा और कष्टकर; (व्यक्ति) रूखा *It's a chilly morning. You need a coat on.* ○ *We got a very chilly reception* (= unfriendly).

**chime** /tʃaɪm चाइम्/ *verb* [I, T] (used about a bell or clock) to ring (घंटी या घड़ी का) बजना ▶ **chime** *noun* [C] घंटी या घड़ी के बजने की आवाज़

**PHR V** **chime in (with sth)** (*informal*) to interrupt a conversation and add your own comments किसी की बातचीत में दखल देकर अपनी टिप्पणी जोड़ना

**chimney** /ˈtʃɪmni ˈचिम्नि/ *noun* [C] a pipe through which smoke or steam is carried up and out through the roof of a building किसी भवन की छत के ऊपर निकला पाइप जिससे भवन का धुआँ आदि निकल जाता है; चिमनी; धुआँरा, धुआँकक्ष

**chimney sweep** *noun* [C] a person whose job is to clean the inside of chimneys with long brushes चिमनी को अंदर से साफ़ करने वाला व्यक्ति

**chimpanzee** /ˌtʃɪmpænˈziː ˌचिम्पैन्ˈज़ी/ (*informal* **chimp** /tʃɪmp चिम्प्/) *noun* [C] a small intelligent animal like a monkey but without a tail (**an ape**) which is found in Africa अफ़्रीक़ा में पाए जाने वाला एक प्रकार का पूंछहीन बंदर; चिंपांज़ी, वनमानुष ➪ **primate** पर चित्र देखिए।

**chin** /tʃɪn चिन्/ *noun* [C] the part of your face below your mouth ठोड़ी ➪ **body** पर चित्र देखिए

**china** /ˈtʃaɪnə ˈचाइना/ *noun* [U] **1** white clay of good quality that is used for making cups, plates, etc. चीनी मिट्टी, जिसके प्याले, प्लेट आदि बन

हैं *a china vase* **2** cups, plates, etc. that are made from china चीनी मिट्टी से बने बरतन आदि

**china clay** = **kaolin**

**chink** /tʃɪŋk चिङ्क्/ *noun* [C] a small narrow opening दरार *Daylight came in through a chink between the curtains.*

**chintz** /tʃɪnts चिन्ट्स्/ *noun* [U] a shiny cotton cloth with a printed design, usually of flowers, which is used for making curtains, covering furniture, etc. प्रायः फूलों के प्रिंट वाला चमकीला सूती कपड़ा जिसके परदे आदि बनाए जाते हैं; छींट

**chip**[1] /tʃɪp चिप्/ *noun* [C] **1** the place where a small piece of stone, glass, wood, etc. has broken off sth पत्थर, शीशे आदि का वह स्थान जहाँ से वह थोड़ा टूटा हुआ हो *This dish has a chip in it.* **2** a small piece of stone, glass, wood, etc. that has broken off sth चिप्पी, छिपटी, टुकड़ा, टूटन **3** (*AmE* **French fry**) (*usually pl.*) a thin piece of potato that is fried in hot fat or oil आलू का तला हुआ पतला लंबा टुकड़ा; आलू का चिप **4** (*also* **potato chip**) = **crisp**[2] **5** = **microchip** **6** a flat round piece of plastic that you use instead of money when you are playing some games कुछ खेलों में नक़द राशि के स्थान पर प्रयुक्त एक समतल गोल प्लास्टिक खंड

**IDM** **have a chip on your shoulder (about sth)** (*informal*) to feel angry about sth that happened a long time ago because you think it is unfair किसी पिछली अनुचित घटना, व्यवहार आदि को याद कर क्रोधित होना

**chip**[2] /tʃɪp चिप्/ *verb* [I, T] (**chipping; chipped**) **1** to break a small piece off the edge or surface of sth किसी वस्तु की सतह या किनारे से छोटा टुकड़ा तोड़ना *They chipped the paint trying to get the table through the door.* **2** (in sport) to kick or hit a ball a short distance through the air (खेल में) गेंद को मार कर थोड़ी दूर हवा में भेजना

**PHR V** **chip in (with sth)** (*informal*) **1** to interrupt when sb else is talking दूसरे की बात में हस्तक्षेप करना **2** to give some money as part of the cost of sth किसी वस्तु की लागत में हिस्सा बटाना *We all chipped in and bought him a present when he left.*

**chiropodist** /kɪˈrɒpədɪst किˈरॉपडिस्ट्/ (*AmE* **podiatrist**) *noun* [C, *with sing. or pl. verb*] a person whose job is to look after people's feet चरणरोग-चिकित्सक

**chiropody** /kɪˈrɒpədi किˈरॉपडि/ (*AmE* **podiatry**) *noun* [U] the care and treatment of people's feet चरणरोग-चिकित्सा

**chiropractor** /ˈkaɪərəʊpræktə(r) ˈकाइअरोप्रैक्ट(र्)/ *noun* [C] a person whose job involves treating some diseases and physical problems by pressing and moving the bones in a person's back (**spine**) रोगी की रीढ़ की हड्डी को दबाकर रोगों की चिकित्सा करने वाला चिकित्सक ➪ **osteopath** देखिए।

**chirp** /tʃɜːp चप्/ *verb* [I] (used about small birds and some insects) to make short high sounds (छोटे पक्षियों और कुछ कीड़ों का) चीं-चीं करना, चहचहाना, झंकारना

**chisel** /ˈtʃɪzl ˈचिज़्ल्/ *noun* [C] a tool with a sharp end that is used for cutting or shaping wood or stone लकड़ी या पत्थर काटने या गढ़ने की छेनी ➪ **tool** पर चित्र देखिए।

**chit** /tʃɪt चिट्/ *noun* **1** (*BrE*) [C] a short written note on a small piece of paper or a small document; a bill एक छोटे काग़ज़ के टुकड़े पर संक्षिप्त लिखित टिप्पणी या प्रलेख; परची **2** (*also* **chit fund**) a kind of savings scheme practised in India which involves small and regular contributions from individuals. These contributions are collected, invested and returned in a lump sum at a profit to the contributor भारत में प्रचलित एक प्रकार की बचत परियोजना जिसमें छोटे और नियमित रूप से योगदान होता है। इस धन संग्रह का निवेश योगदाताओं के पक्ष में होता है और मुनाफ़े के साथ एकमुश्त रक़म के तौर पर वापस की जाती है

**chivalry** /ˈʃɪvlri ˈशिव्लरि/ *noun* [U] polite and kind behaviour by men which shows respect towards women स्त्रियों के प्रति पुरुषों का सम्मानजनक, नम्र और सहृदयतापूर्ण आचरण ▶ **chivalrous** /ˈʃɪvlrəs ˈशिव्लरस्/ *adj.* स्त्रियों के प्रति सम्मानपूर्ण व्यवहार से संबंधित

**chive** /tʃaɪv चाइव्/ *noun* [C, *usually pl.*] a long thin green plant that tastes like onion and is used in cooking प्याज़ जैसे स्वाद वाला लंबा, पतला हरा पौधा जिसे भोजन पकाने में प्रयुक्त किया जाता है

**chloride** /ˈklɔːraɪd ˈक्लॉराइड्/ *noun* [U] a chemical compound of **chlorine** and another chemical क्लोरीन और अन्य रसायन के योग से बना रसायन; क्लोराइड

**chlorinate** /ˈklɔːrɪneɪt ˈक्लॉरिनेट्/ *verb* [T] to put chlorine in sth, especially water विशेषतः पानी में क्लोरीन मिलाना *a chlorinated swimming pool* ▶ **chlorination** /ˌklɔːrɪˈneɪʃn ˌक्लॉरिˈनेश्न्/ *noun* [U] क्लोरीनीकरण

**chlorine** /ˈklɔːriːn ˈक्लॉरीन्/ *noun* [U] a greenish-yellow gas with a strong smell, that is used for making water safe to drink or to swim in तीखी

गंध वाली हरी-पीली गैस जिसे पानी को पीने या तैरने योग्य बनाने के लिए प्रयुक्त किया जाता है; क्लोरीन

**chloroform** /ˈklɒrəfɔːm ˈक्लॉरफ़ॉम् / *noun* [U] (*symbol* **$CHCl_3$**) a colourless liquid with a strong smell used by doctors in the past to make people unconscious, for example before an operation तीखी गंध वाला रंगहीन द्रव पदार्थ जिसके प्रयोग से मरीज़ को शल्यचिकित्सा से पूर्व बेहोश किया जाता था; क्लोरोफ़ार्म

**chlorophyll** /ˈklɒrəfɪl ˈक्लॉरफ़िल् / *noun* [U] the green substance in plants that takes in light from the sun to help them grow पौधों में पाया जाने वाला हरा पदार्थ जो सूर्य की किरणों को आत्मसात कर पौधों की वृद्धि में सहायता करता है; पर्णहरित, क्लोरोफिल

**chloroplast** /ˈklɒrəplɑːst ˈक्लॉरप्लास्ट् / *noun* [C] (*technical*) the part of a green plant cell that contains chlorophyll and in which **photosynthesis** takes place हरे पौधों की कोशिका का क्लोराफ़िल वाला भाग जहाँ प्रकाश-संश्लेषण होता है

**chock-a-block** /ˌtʃɒk əˈblɒk ˌचॉक् अˈब्लॉक् / *adj.* (*not before a noun*) completely full पूर्णतया भरा हुआ, परिपूर्ण *The mall was chock-a-block with shoppers.*

**chocoholic** /ˌtʃɒkəˈhɒlɪk ˌचॉकˈहॉलिक् / *noun* [C] a person who loves chocolate and eats a lot of it चॉकलेट-प्रेमी

**chocolate**/ˈtʃɒklət ˈचॉक्लट् / *noun* **1** [U] a sweet brown substance made from seeds (**cocoa beans**) that you can eat as a sweet or use to give flavour to food and drinks कोको के बीजों से बनी मीठी भूरी मिठाई जिसे खाद्य पदार्थों को स्वाद-विशेष देने के लिए भी प्रयुक्त किया जाता है; चॉकलेट *a bar of **milk/plain chocolate*** ○ *a chocolate milkshake* **2** [C] a small sweet that is made from or covered with chocolate चॉकलेट से बनी या चॉकलेट की परत वाली मिठाई *a box of chocolates* **3** [C, U] a drink made from powdered chocolate with hot milk or water गरम दूध या पानी में चॉकलेट का चूरा मिलाने से बना पेय *a mug of **hot chocolate*** **4** [U] a dark brown colour गहरा भूरा रंग; कत्थई रंग

**choice**[1] /tʃɔɪs चॉइस् / *noun* **1** [C] **a choice (between A and B)** an act of choosing between two or more people or things दो या दो से अधिक व्यक्ति या वस्तु के मध्य चुनने की क्रिया; चयन, वरण *Vipul was forced to **make a choice** between moving house and losing his job.* **2** [U] the right or chance to choose चुनने का अधिकार या अवसर *There is a rail strike so we **have no choice** but to cancel our trip.* ○ *to have freedom of choice* ✪ पर्याय **option** **3** [C, U] two or more things from which you can or must choose विकल्प *This cinema offers a choice of six different films every night.* **4** [C] a person or thing that is chosen चुना हुआ व्यक्ति या वस्तु; पसंद *Rahul would be my choice as team captain.* ➪ **choose** verb देखिए।

IDM **out of/from choice** because you want to; of your own free will मनोवांछित रूप से; स्वेच्छा से *I wouldn't have gone to America out of choice. I was sent there on business.*

**choice**[2] /tʃɔɪs चॉइस् / *adj.* of very good quality बहुत बढ़िया, चुनिंदा *choice strawberries*

**choir** /ˈkwaɪə(r) ˈक्वाइअ(र्) / *noun* [C, *with sing. or pl. verb*] a group of people who sing together in churches, schools, etc. गायक-मंडली जो गिरजाघरों, विद्यालयों आदि में गायन प्रस्तुत करती है

**choke**[1] /tʃəʊk चोक् / *verb* **1** [I, T] **choke (on sth)** to be or to make sb unable to breathe because sth is stopping air getting into the lungs दम घुटना या घोटना *She was choking on a fish bone.* ○ *The smoke choked us.* ➪ **strangle** देखिए **2** [T] (*usually passive*) **choke sth (up) (with sth)** to fill a passage, space, etc., so that nothing can pass through मार्ग, स्थान आदि को भरकर बंद करना ताकि कुछ अन्य पार न कर सके *The roads to the coast were choked with traffic.* ○ *choked drains*

PHR V **choke sth back** to hide or control a strong emotion भावावेश को छिपाना या रोकना *to choke back tears/anger*

**choke**[2] /tʃəʊk चोक् / *noun* [C] **1** the device in a car, etc. that controls the amount of air going into the engine. If you pull out the choke it makes it easier to start the car कार का एक पुरज़ा जो इंज[न] में जाने वाली वायु की मात्रा को नियंत्रित करता है; चोक **2** an act or the sound of sb choking वायु या श्वास-अवरोध की क्रिया या आवाज़

**cholera** /ˈkɒlərə ˈकॉलरा / *noun* [U] a serious disease that causes stomach pains and vomiting and can cause death. Cholera is most common in hot countries and is carried by water हैज़ा, विशूचिका, हैज़ा गंदे पानी द्वारा फैलता है और इसका प्रभाव गरम प्रदेशों में अधिक होता है

**cholesterol** /kəˈlestərɒl कˈलेस्टरॉल् / *noun* [U] a substance that is found in the blood, etc. of people and animals. Too much cholesterol is thought to be a cause of heart disease मनुष्यों और पशुओं के रक्त में पाया जाने वाला एक पदार्थ विशेष जिसकी मात्रा में अत्यधिक वृद्धि होने से हृदय-रोग उत्पन्न हो सकते हैं; कोलेस्टेराल

**choose** /tʃuːz चूज़्/ *verb* [I, T] (*pt* **chose** /tʃəʊz चोज़्/; *pp* **chosen** /ˈtʃəʊzn ˈचोज़्न्/) **1 choose (between A and/or B); choose (A) (from B); choose sb/sth as sth** to decide which thing or person you want out of the ones that are available उपलब्ध वस्तुओं या व्यक्तियों में से चयन या चुनाव करना; चुनना *Choose carefully before you make a final decision.* ○ *Anjali had to choose between getting a job or going to college.* ○ *The viewers chose this programme as their favourite.* **2 choose (to do sth)** to decide or prefer to do sth कुछ करने का निर्णय करना; पसंद करना *You are free to leave whenever you choose.* ○ *They chose to resign rather than work for the new manager.* ➪ **choice** noun देखिए।

**IDM** **pick and choose** ➪ **pick**[1] देखिए।

**choosy** /ˈtʃuːzi ˈचूज़ि/ *adj.* (*informal*) (used about a person) difficult to please (व्यक्ति) जिसे संतुष्ट या प्रसन्न करना कठिन हो, जो आसानी से संतुष्ट न हो

**chop**[1] /tʃɒp चॉप्/ *verb* [T] (**chopping; chopped**) **chop sth (up) (into sth)** to cut sth into pieces with a knife, etc. चाकू आदि से टुकड़े-टुकड़े करना; सकर्तन करना *finely chopped herbs* ○ *Chop the onions up into small pieces.*

**IDM** **chop and change** to change your plans or opinions several times योजनाएँ या विचार अनेक बार बदलना

**PHR V** **chop sth down** to cut a tree, etc. at the bottom so that it falls down पेड़ आदि को नीचे से काटना ताकि वह गिर जाए

**chop sth off (sth)** to remove sth from sth by cutting it with a knife or a sharp tool किसी वस्तु का कोई भाग काटकर निकाल देना

**chop**[2] /tʃɒp चॉप्/ *noun* [C] **1** a thick slice of meat with a piece of bone in it हड्डीदार मांस का मोटा टुकड़ा या तिक्का ➪ **steak** देखिए। **2** an act of chopping sth काटने या चीरने की क्रिया *a karate chop*

**chopper** /ˈtʃɑpə(r) ˈचॉप(र्)/ *noun.* [C] (*informal*) = **helicopter**

**chopping board** *noun* [C] a piece of wood or plastic used for cutting meat or vegetables on लकड़ी या प्लास्टिक का टुकड़ा जिसपर मांस या सब्ज़ी काटी जाती है; संकर्तन पट्ट ➪ **kitchen** पर चित्र देखिए।

**choppy** /ˈtʃɒpi ˈचॉपि/ *adj.* (used about the sea) having a lot of small waves, slightly rough (समुद्र) लहरों भरा और कुछ अशांत

**chopstick** /ˈtʃɒpstɪk ˈचॉप्स्टिक्/ *noun* [C, *usually pl.*] one of the two thin pieces of wood used for eating with, especially in Asian countries बाँस आदि की लंबी तीलियाँ जिनसे विशेषतः कुछ एशियाई देशों के लोग खाना खाते हैं; चॉपस्टिक, चीनी काँटा

**choral** /ˈkɔːrəl ˈकॉरल्/ *adj.* (used about music) that is written for or involving a group of singers (**a choir**) (संगीत) गायक वृंद के लिए रचित या उससे संबंधित

**chord** /kɔːd कॉड्/ *noun* [C] **1** (*mathematics*) a straight line that joins two points on a curve वृत्त या वक्र रेखा के दो बिंदुओं को मिलाने वाली रेखा; जीवा ➪ **circle** पर चित्र देखिए।

**chore** /tʃɔː(r) चॉ(र्)/ *noun* [C] a job that is not interesting but that you must do अरुचिकर परंतु अनिवार्य कार्य *household chores*

**choreograph** /ˈkɒriəgrɑːf ˈकॉरिअग्राफ़्/ *verb* [T] to design and arrange the movements of a dance नृत्य-रचना का संयोजन करना ▶ **choreographer** /ˌkɒriˈɒgrəfə(r) ˌकॉरिˈऑग्रफ़(र्)/ *noun* [C] नृत्य-रचनाकार; नृत्य-निर्देशक

**choreography** /ˌkɒriˈɒgrəfi ˌकॉरिˈऑग्रफ़ि/ *noun* [U] the arrangement of movements for a dance performance नृत्य-रचना; नृत्य-प्रदर्शन के लिए गति-संयोजन; नृत्य निर्देशन

**chorus**[1] /ˈkɔːrəs ˈकॉरस्/ *noun* **1** [C] the part of a song that is repeated at the end of each verse पुनरावृत्त होने वाला गीतखंड, गीत की टेक या स्थायी ✪ पर्याय **refrain** **2** [C] a piece of music, usually part of a larger work, that is written for a large group of people (**a choir**) to sing गायक-वृंद के लिए रचित संगीत; वृंदगान, समवेत गान **3** [C, *with sing. or pl. verb*] a large group of people who sing together गायक-वृंद, गायक-मंडली **4** [C, *with sing. or pl. verb*] the singers and dancers in a musical show who do not play the main parts संगीत कार्यक्रम में गौण भागीदार गायक और नर्तक **5 a chorus of sth** [*sing.*] something that a lot of people say together अनेक व्यक्तियों द्वारा एक साथ कही गई बात, समवेत स्वर *a chorus of cheers/criticism/disapproval*

**chorus**[2] /ˈkɔːrəs ˈकॉरस्/ *verb* [T] (used about a group of people) to sing or say sth together (मंडली या दल का) एक साथ गीत गाना या कुछ कहना *'That's not fair!' the children chorused.*

**chose** ➪ **choose** का past tense रूप

**chosen** ➪ **choose** का past participle रूप

**Christ** /kraɪst क्राइस्ट्/ (*also* **Jesus; Jesus Christ** /ˌdʒiːzəsˈkraɪst ˌजीज़स्ˌक्राइस्ट्/) *noun* the man who Christians believe is the son of God and whose teachings the Christian religion is based on ईसा मसीह जिसे ईसाई लोग परमेश्वर का पुत्र मानते हैं, ईसा मसीह की शिक्षाओं पर ईसाई धर्म आधारित है

**christen** /ˈkrɪsn ˈक्रिसन्/ *verb* [T] **1** to give a person, usually a baby, a name during a Christian ceremony in which he/she is made a member of the Church ईसाई धर्म के अनुसार बालक का नामकरण करना और उसे चर्च का सदस्य बनाना *The baby was christened Leela Mary John.* ➪ **baptize** देखिए। **2** to give sb/sth a name किसी का नामकरण करना; किसी को नाम-विशेष देना *People drive so dangerously on this stretch of road that it has been christened it 'The Mad Mile'.*

**christening** /ˈkrɪsnɪŋ ˈक्रिस्निङ्/ *noun* [C] the church ceremony in the Christian religion in which a baby is given a name and welcomed into the Christian church (ईसाई धर्म में) गिरजाघर में आयोजित समारोह जिसमें शिशु का नामकरण किया जाता है और उसे ईसाई चर्च में सम्मिलित किया जाता है ➪ **baptism** देखिए।

**Christian** /ˈkrɪstʃən ˈक्रिस्चन्/ *noun* [C] a person whose religion is Christianity ईसाई, ईसाई धर्म का अनुयायी ▶ **Christian** *adj.* ईसाई धर्म से संबंधित

**Christianity** /ˌkrɪstiˈænəti ˌक्रिस्टिˈऐनटि/ *noun* [U] the religion that is based on the teachings of Jesus Christ ईसा मसीह की शिक्षाओं पर आधारित धर्म; ईसाई धर्म

**Christian name** (*AmE* **given name**) *noun* [C] the name given to a child when he/she is born; first name जन्म के समय शिशु को दिया गया नाम; प्रथम नाम; नाम का प्रथम भाग ➪ **name**[1] पर नोट देखिए।

**Christmas** /ˈkrɪsməs ˈक्रिस्मस्/ *noun* **1** [C, U] the period of time before and after 25 December, 25 दिसंबर से पहले और बाद की अवधि *Where are you spending Christmas this year?* **2 Christmas Day** [C] 25 December. It is the day on which the birth of Christ is celebrated each year, 25 दिसंबर यह दिन ईसा मसीह का जन्म दिवस के रूप में मनाया जाता है **NOTE** अनौपचारिक अंग्रेज़ी में क्रिसमस को कभी-कभी **Xmas** भी लिखा जाता है।

**Christmas carol** = **carol**

**Christmas Eve** *noun* [C] 24 December, the day before Christmas Day क्रिसमस दिवस से पूर्व का दिवस, 24 दिसंबर

**Christmas tree** *noun* [C] a real or artificial tree, which people bring into their homes and cover with coloured lights and decorations at Christmas एक वास्तविक या कृत्रिम वृक्ष जिसे क्रिसमस पर घर में लाकर रंग-बिरंगी रोशनियों तथा सजावटी सामान से सजाया जाता है; क्रिसमस वृक्ष

**chromatography** /ˌkrɒməˈtɒgrəfi ˌक्रॉमˈटॉग्रफ़ि/ *noun* [U] (*technical*) the separation of a liquid mixture by passing it through a material through which some parts of the mixture travel further than others द्रव-मिश्रण के द्रवों को एक-दूसरे से अलग करने की क्रिया। इस क्रिया में मिश्रण को एक ऐसे पदार्थ विशेष में से पार कराया जाता है जिसमें कुछ द्रव अन्यों से अधिक दूर चले जाते हैं; द्रव-मिश्रण का पृथक्करण

**chrome** /krəʊm क्रोम्/ (*also* **chromium** /ˈkrəʊmiəm ˈक्रोमिअम्/) *noun* [U] (*symbol* **Cr**) a hard shiny metal that is used for covering other metals अन्य धातुओं पर चढ़ाने के लिए प्रयुक्त एक कड़ी चमकदार धातु; क्रोम, क्रोमियम

**chromosome** /ˈkrəʊməsəʊm ˈक्रोमसोम्/ *noun* [C] a part of a cell in living things that decides the sex, character, shape, etc. that a person, an animal or a plant will have सजीवों की कोशिका का वह अंश जिससे मनुष्य, पशु या पौधे का लिंग, लक्षण, आकृति आदि निर्धारित होते हैं; गुणसूत्र, क्रोमोसोम ➪ **X chromosome** और **Y chromosome** देखिए।

**chronic** /ˈkrɒnɪk ˈक्रॉनिक्/ *adj.* (used about a disease or a problem) that continues for a long time (रोग या समस्या) पुरानी, चिरकालिक, दीर्घकालिक *There is a chronic shortage of housing in the city.* ➪ **acute** देखिए। ▶ **chronically** /-kli -क्लि/ *adv.* चिरकालिक रूप से

**chronicle** /ˈkrɒnɪkl ˈक्रॉनिकल्/ *noun* [C, *usually pl.*] a written record of historical events describing them in the order in which they happened ऐतिहासिक घटनाओं का कालानुक्रमित लिखित ब्योरा; इतिवृत्त

**chronological** /ˌkrɒnəˈlɒdʒɪkl ˌक्रॉनˈलॉजिकल्/ *adj.* arranged in the order in which the events happened घटित होने के क्रम में संयोजित (घटनाएँ); कालक्रमिक, कालानुक्रमिक *This book describes the main events in his life* ***in chronological order.*** ▶ **chronologically** /-kli -क्लि/ *adv.* कालक्रम से

**chronology** /krəˈnɒlədʒi क्रˈनॉलजि/ *noun* [U, C] (*pl.* **chronologies**) the order in which a series of events happened; a list of these events in order घटनाओं के घटित होने का क्रम; ऐसी घटनाओं की सूची *The exact chronology of these events is a subject for debate. ○ a chronology of Nehru's life*

**chrysalis** /ˈkrɪsəlɪs ˈक्रिसलिस्/ *noun* (*pl.* **chrysalises**) *noun* [C] the form of an insect, **a butterfly** or **a moth** while it is changing into an adult inside a hard case, also called a chrysalis तितली या फतिंगे की कोषावस्था जिसमें वह कोष में रहते हुए बड़ा होने लगता है; कोशस्थ ➪ **insect** पर चित्र देखिए।

**NOTE** इस स्थिति में रहने वाले अन्य कीटों को **pupa** कहते हैं।

**chrysanthemum** /krɪˈsænθəməm क्रिˈसैन्थमम्/ *noun* [C] a large garden flower which is brightly coloured and shaped like a ball बग़ीचे में उगने वाला बड़ा, रंगीन व गेंदाकार फूल; गुलदाउदी

**chubby** /ˈtʃʌbi ˈचबि/ *adj.* slightly fat in a pleasant way गोल-मटोल; प्रियकर रूप से मोटा *a baby with chubby cheeks*

**chuck** /tʃʌk चक्/ *verb* [T] (*informal*) to throw sth in a careless way लापरवाही से कुछ फेंक देना *You can chuck those old shoes in the bin.*

**PHR V chuck sth in** to give sth up छोड़ देना *He's chucked his job in because he was fed up.*

**chuck sb out (of sth)** to force sb to leave a place किसी को कोई स्थान को छोड़ने के लिए बाध्य करना; किसी को किसी स्थान से निकाल देना *They were chucked out of the cinema for making too much noise.*

**chuckle** /ˈtʃʌkl ˈचकल्/ *verb* [I] to laugh quietly मुँह बंद करके हँसना *Anirudh chuckled to himself as he read the letter.* ► **chuckle** *noun* [C] दबी हुई हँसी

**chug** /tʃʌg चग्/ *verb* [I] (**chugging; chugged**) **1** (used about a machine or engine) to make short repeated sounds while it is working or moving slowly (मशीन या इंजन का) घरघराना, घर-घर की आवाज़ उत्पन्न करना **2 chug along, down, up, etc.** to move in a particular direction making this sound घरघराते हुए किसी ओर जाना *The train chugged out of the station.*

**chunk** /tʃʌŋk चङ्क्/ *noun* [C] a large or thick piece of sth किसी वस्तु का मोटा बड़ा टुकड़ा *chunks of bread and cheese*

**chunky** /ˈtʃʌŋki ˈचङ्कि/ *adj.* **1** thick and heavy मोटा और भारी *chunky jewellery* **2** (used about a person) short and strong (व्यक्ति) नाटा व गठीला **3** (used about food) containing thick pieces (भोजन या व्यंजन) मोटे टुकड़ों वाला *chunky banana milkshake*

**church** /tʃɜːtʃ चर्च्/ *noun* **1** [C, U] a building where Christians go to pray, etc. गिरजाघर, चर्च, ईसाईयों का प्रार्थना-भवन *Do you go to church regularly?* **2 Church** [C] a particular group of Christians ईसाईयों का समुदाय-विशेष *the Anglican/Catholic/Methodist Church* **3 (the) Church** [*sing.*] the ministers or the institution of the Christian religion ईसाई पुरोहित वर्ग या ईसाई धर्म संस्था *the conflict between Church and State*

**churchyard** /ˈtʃɜːtʃjɑːd ˈचर्चयाड्/ *noun* [C] the area of land that is around a church चर्च-परिसर, चर्च-प्रांगण ➪ **cemetery** और **graveyard** देखिए।

**churn** /tʃɜːn चर्न्/ *verb* **1** [I, T] **churn (sth) (up)** to move, or to make water, mud, etc. move around violently पानी, मिट्टी आदि का तेज़ी या उग्रता से हिलना या हिलाना *The dark water churned beneath the huge ship.* ○ *Vast crowds had churned the field into a sea of mud.* **2** [I] if your stomach churns or sth makes it churn, you feel sick because you are disgusted or nervous जुगुप्सा या घबराहट से जी मिचलाना *Reading about the murder in the paper made my stomach churn.* **3** [T] to make butter from milk or cream मक्खन के लिए दूध या मलाई को बिलोना, मथना

**PHR V churn sth out** (*informal*) to produce large numbers of sth very quickly बड़ी संख्या में तेज़ी से उत्पादन करना *Modern factories can churn out cars at an amazing speed.*

**chute** /ʃuːt शूट्/ *noun* [C] a passage down which you can drop or slide things, so that you do not have to carry them ढालू प्रणाल जिसपर वस्तुओं को सरकाया जा सकता है और उन्हें उठाकर नहीं ले जाना पड़ता *a laundry/rubbish chute* (= from the upper floors of a high building) ○ *a water chute* (= at a swimming pool)

**chutney** /ˈtʃʌtni ˈचट्नि/ *noun* [U] a thick sweet sauce that is made from fruit or vegetables चटनी

**cicada** /sɪˈkɑːdə सिˈकाडा/ *noun* [C] a large insect that lives in many hot countries. It makes a continuous high sound by rubbing its legs together गरम प्रदेशों में पाया जाने वाला एक बड़ा कीट; फतिंगा, रइयाँ

**cider** /ˈsaɪdə(r) ˈसाइड(र्)/ *noun* [U] **1** an alcoholic drink made from apples सेब से बनी शराब *dry/sweet cider* **2** a drink made from apples that does not contain alcohol सेब से बना ऐलकोहल-रहित पेय

**cigar** /sɪˈgɑː(r) सिˈगा(र्)/ *noun* [C] a roll of dried tobacco leaves that people smoke. Cigars are larger than cigarettes सिगार, चुरुट

**cigarette** /ˌsɪgəˈret ˌसिगˈरेट्/ *noun* [C] tobacco in a tube of thin white paper that people smoke सिगरेट *a packet of cigarettes*

**cigarette lighter** (*also* **lighter**) *noun* [C] an object which produces a small flame for lighting cigarettes, etc. सिगरेट लाइटर, सिगरेट जलाने वाला उपकरण

**ciliary muscle** /ˈsɪliəri mʌsl ˈसिलिअरि मसल्/ *noun* [C] a muscle in the eye that controls how much the **lens** curves आँख की मांसपेशी जो आँख के लेंस के घुमाव को नियंत्रित करती है ➪ **eye** पर चित्र देखिए।

**cinder** /ˈsɪndə(r) ˈसिन्ड(र्)/ *noun* [C] a very small piece of burning coal, wood, etc. अंगारा

**cinema** /ˈsɪnəmə ˈसिनमा/ *noun* **1** [C] a place where you go to see a film स्थान जहाँ चलचित्र देखने जाते हैं; सिनेमा हॉल, सिनेमा घर *What's on at the cinema this week?* **2** [U] films in general; the film industry सामान्यतः फ़िल्में; फ़िल्म उद्योग *one of the great successes of India cinema*

**cinnamon** /ˈsɪnəmən ˈसिनमन्/ *noun* [U] the bark of a tropical tree or a brown powder made from this. It is used as a spice or to flavour food दालचीनी; दारचीनी

**circa** /ˈsɜːkə ˈसका/ *prep.* (*abbr.* **c**) (*written*) (used with dates) about; approximately (तिथियों के साथ प्रयुक्त) के आसपास; के लगभग *The vase was made circa 600 AD.*

**circle**[1] /ˈsɜːkl ˈसकल्/ *noun* **1** [C] a round shape like a ring गोल आकृति, वृत्त *The children were drawing circles and squares on a piece of paper.* ○ *We all stood in a circle and held hands.* **2** [C] a flat, round area गोला, घेरा *She cut out a circle of paper.* **3** [C] a group of people who are friends, or who have the same interest or profession समान रुचि या व्यवसाय वाले व्यक्तियों की मंडली, गुट *He has a large circle of friends.* ○ *Her name was well known in artistic circles.*

IDM **a vicious circle** ➪ **vicious** देखिए।

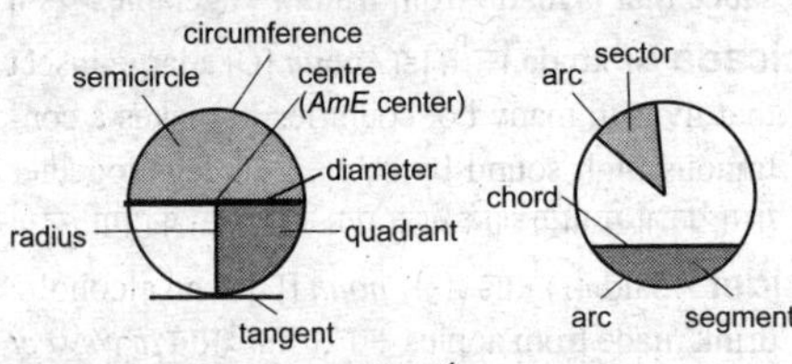

**circle**[1]

**circle**[2] /ˈsɜːkl ˈसकल्/ *verb* **1** [I, T] to move, or to move round sth, in a circle घेरे में चक्कर लगाना *The plane circled the town several times before it landed.* **2** [T] to draw a circle round sth गोला बनाना *There are three possible answers to each question. Please circle the correct one.*

**circuit** /ˈsɜːkɪt ˈसकिट्/ *noun* **1** [C] a circular journey or track round sth परिक्रमा, परिभ्रमण, वृत्ताकार यात्रा या पथ *The cars have to complete ten circuits of the track.* **2** [C] a complete circular path that an electric current can flow around विद्युत धारा का पूर्ण वृत्ताकार पथ या परिपथ सर्किट **3** [*sing.*] a series of sports competitions, meetings or other organized events that are regularly visited by the same people खेल-स्पर्धाओं, सभाओं या अन्य आयोजित घटनाओं की शृंखला जिसमें कुछ व्यक्ति नियमित रूप से सम्मिलित होते हैं *She's one of the best players on the tennis circuit.*

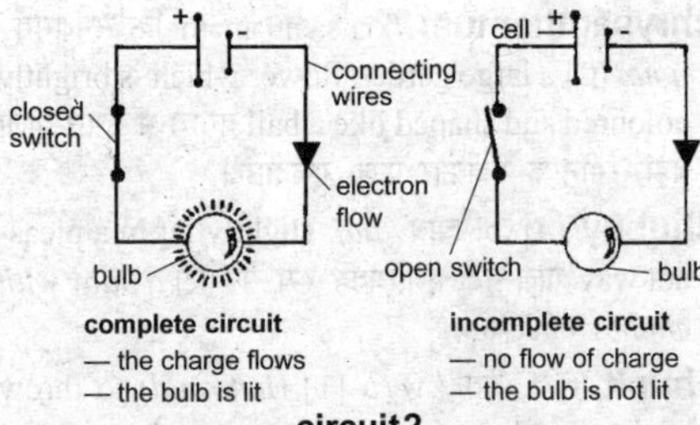

**circuit2**

**circuit board** *noun* [C] (*technical*) a board inside a piece of electrical equipment that holds circular paths (**circuits**) around which electric currents can flow विद्युत यंत्रों के अंदर का विद्युत परिपथ बोर्ड; सर्किट बोर्ड

**circuit-breaker** *noun* [C] (*technical*) a safety device that automatically stops the flow of electricity if there is danger ख़तरे की स्थिति में विद्युत प्रवाह को अवरुद्ध करने वाली स्वचालित सुरक्षा युक्ति; सर्किट ब्रेकर

**circular**[1] /ˈsɜːkjələ(r) ˈसक्यल(र्)/ *adj.* **1** round and flat; shaped like a circle गोल और समतल; वृत्ताकार, वृत्तीय, चक्रिल *a circular table* **2** (used about a journey, etc.) moving round in a circle (यात्रा आदि) चक्र के रूप में होने वाली *a circular tour of Delhi*

**circular**[2] /ˈsɜːkjələ(r) ˈसक्यल(र्)/ *noun* [C] a printed letter, notice or advertisement that is sent to a large number of people अनेक व्यक्तियों को प्रेषित एक मुद्रित पत्र, सूचना या विज्ञापन; गश्ती चिट्ठी, परिपत्र

**circulate** /ˈsɜːkjəleɪt ˈसक्यलेट्/ *verb* [I, T] **1** to go or be passed from one person to another एक व्यक्ति से दूसरे व्यक्ति के पास जाना या पहुँचाना; प्रचारित करना *We've circulated a copy of the report to each department.* **2** (used about a substance) to move or make sth move round continuously (पदार्थ का) निरंतर वृत्ताकार संचरण करते रहना *Blood circulates round the body.*

**circulation** /ˌsɜːkjəˈleɪʃn ˌसक्यˈलेशन्/ *noun* **1** [U] the movement of blood around the body शरीर में रक्त का संचरण **2** [U] the passing of sth from one person or place to another (किसी वस्तु का) एक व्यक्ति या स्थान से दूसरे तक पहुँचना; परिचालन *the circulation of news/information/rumours* ○ *Old twenty paise coins are no longer* ***in circulation*** (= being used by people). **3** [C] the number of copies of a newspaper, magazine, etc. that are sold each time it is produced समाचार पत्र आदि की पसार-संख्या

**circulatory** /ˌsɜːkjəˈleɪtəri ˌसक्यˈलेटरि/ *adj.* connected with the movement of blood around the body शरीर में रक्त के संचरण से संबंधित

**circum-** /ˈsɜːkəm ˈसकम्/ *prefix* (*in adjectives, nouns and verbs*) around चारों ओर, परि- *to circumnavigate* (= to sail around)

**circumcise** /ˈsɜːkəmsaɪz ˈसकम्साइज़्/ *verb* [T] to cut off the skin at the end of a man's sexual organ (**penis**) or to remove part of a woman's sexual organs (**clitoris**), for religious or sometimes (in the case of a man) medical reasons (धार्मिक या चिकित्सीय कारणों से) पुरुषों की शिश्न त्वचा और महिलाओं का भग-शिश्न काटकर निकाल देना; सुन्नत या ख़तना करना ▶ **circumcision** /ˌsɜːkəmˈsɪʒn ˌसकम्ˈसिश्न्/ *noun* [C, U] सुन्नत, ख़तना

**circumference** /səˈkʌmfərəns सˈकम्फ़रन्स्/ *noun* [C, U] the distance round a circle or sth circular परिधि की लंबाई; परिधि, घेरा, दायरा *The Earth is about 40,000 kilometres* ***in circumference***. ➪ **diameter** और **radius** देखिए तथा **circle** पर चित्र भी देखिए।

**circumnavigate** /ˌsɜːkəmˈnævɪɡeɪt ˌसकम्ˈनैविगेट्/ *verb* [T] to sail, fly or travel all around sth especially all the way around the world जहाज़, विमान या किसी वाहन में भूचक्रण करना ▶ **circumnavigation** /ˌsɜːkəmˌnævɪˈɡeɪʃn ˌसकम्ˌनैविˈगेश्न्/ *noun* [U] नौ-परिचालन; परिनौसंचालन, भूचक्रण

**circumspect** /ˈsɜːkəmspekt ˈसकम्स्पेक्ट्/ *adj.* (*formal*) thinking very carefully about sth before you do it because you think it may involve problems or dangers (परेशानियों या ख़तरे का पूर्वाभास होने के कारण) सावधान, सतर्क, चौकन्ना, होशियार

**circumstance** /ˈsɜːkəmstəns ˈसकम्स्टन्स्/ *noun* **1** [C, *usually pl.*] the facts and events that affect what happens in a particular situation परिस्थितियाँ; हालात *Police said there were no* ***suspicious circumstances*** *surrounding the boy's death.* **2 circumstances** [*pl.*] (*formal*) the amount of money that you have आर्थिक स्थिति *The company has promised to repay the money when its financial circumstances improve.*

IDM **in/under no circumstances** never; not for any reason कदापि नहीं; किसी भी कारण से नहीं

**in/under the circumstances** as the result of a particular situation (इन) परिस्थितियों में *My father was ill at that time, so under the circumstances I decided not to go on holiday.*

**circumstantial** /ˌsɜːkəmˈstænʃl ˌसकम्ˈस्टैन्शल्/ *adj.* (used in connection with the law) containing details and information that strongly suggest sth is true but are not actual proof of it (क़ानून में) परिस्थितियों द्वारा (न कि वास्तविक प्रमाण से) अनुमोदित; परिस्थितिगत (साक्ष्य) *circumstantial evidence*

**circumvent** /ˌsɜːkəmˈvent ˌसकम्ˈव्रेन्ट्/ *verb* [T] **1** to find a clever way of avoiding a difficulty or rule किसी परेशानी या नियम से बचने का उपाय खोजना **2** to go round sth that is in your way घूमकर या बाहर-बाहर से निकल जाना

**circus** /ˈsɜːkəs ˈसकस्/ *noun* [C] a show performed in a large tent by a company of people and animals सरकस

**cirque** /sɜːk सक्/ = **corrie** ➪ **glacial** पर चित्र देखिए।

**cirrhosis** /səˈrəʊsɪs सˈरोसिस्/ *noun* [U] a serious disease of the **liver** caused especially by drinking too much alcohol जिगर को प्रभावित करने वाला एक गंभीर रोग, जो विशेषतः अत्यधिक मदिरापान से उत्पन्न होता है; सिरोसिस

**cirrostratus** /ˌsɪrəʊˈstrɑːtəs; -ˈstreɪtəs ˌसिरोˈस्ट्राटस्; -स्ट्रेटस्/ *noun* [U] (*technical*) a type of cloud that forms a thin layer at a very high level बहुत ऊँचाई पर पतली परत वाला बादल; पक्षाभ-स्तरी मेघ

**cirrus** /ˈsɪrəs ˈसिरस्/ *noun* [U] (*technical*) a type of light cloud that forms high in the sky बहुत ऊँचाई पर बना हलका बादल; पक्षाभ मेघ

**cistern** /ˈsɪstən ˈसिस्टन्/ *noun* [C] a container for storing water, especially one that is connected to a toilet विशेषतः (शौचालय में) पानी भर कर रखने की टंकी

**citadel** /ˈsɪtədəl ˈसिटडल्/ *noun* [C] (in past times) a castle on high ground in or near a city where people could go when the city was being attacked (प्राचीन समय में) नगर-दुर्ग, गढ़, क़िला (*figurative*) *citadels of private economic power*

**cite** /saɪt साइट्/ *verb* [T] (*formal*) to mention sth or use sb's exact words as an example to support, or as proof of, what you are saying उदाहरण या प्रमाण-स्वरूप किसी बात का उल्लेख करना या किसी व्यक्ति के मूल शब्द उद्धृत करना *She cited a passage from the President's speech.* ▶ **citation** /saɪˈteɪʃn साइˈटेश्न्/ *noun* [C, U] उद्धरण, उद्धृत शब्द

**citizen** /ˈsɪtɪzn ˈसिटिज़्न्/ *noun* [C] **1** a person who is legally accepted as a member of a particular country किसी देश का विधिसम्मत निवासी, नागरिक *She was born in India, but became an American citizen in 1991.* **2** a person who lives in a town or city नगरवासी (न कि ग्रामवासी) *the citizens of Mumbai* ➪ **senior citizen** देखिए।

**citizenship** /ˈsɪtɪzənʃɪp ˈसिटिज़न्‌शिप्/ *noun* [U] the state of being a citizen of a particular country नागरिकता *After living in Spain for twenty years, he decided to apply for Spanish citizenship.*

**citric acid** /ˌsɪtrɪk ˈæsɪd ˌसिट्रिक् ˈऐसिड्/ *noun* [U] a weak acid that is found in the juice of oranges, lemons and other similar fruits संतरा, नींबू आदि के रस में पाया जाने वाला अम्ल

**citrus** /ˈsɪtrəs ˈसिट्रस्/ *adj.* used to describe fruit such as oranges and lemons संतरा, नींबू जैसे फलों आदि से संबंधित

**city** /ˈsɪti ˈसिटि/ *noun* **1** [C] (*pl.* **cities**) a large and important town नगर, शहर *Venice is one of the most beautiful cities in the world.* ○ *the city centre*

**civic** /ˈsɪvɪk ˈसिव़िक्/ *adj.* officially connected with a city or town नगर का या नगर से आधिकारिक रूप से संबंधित *civic pride* (= feeling proud because you belong to a particular town or city) ○ *civic duties* ○ *the civic centre* (= the area where the public buildings are in a town)

**civil** /ˈsɪvl ˈसिव़िल्/ *adj.* **1** (*only before a noun*) connected with the people who live in a country देश के नागरिकों से संबंधित *civil disorder* (= involving group of people within the same country) **2** (*only before a noun*) connected with the state, not with the army or any religion राज्य-विषयक (सेना या धर्मकेंद्र से असंबद्ध) *a civil wedding* (= not religious one) जो धार्मिक रीतियों पर आधारित न हो **3** (*only before a noun*) (in law) connected with the personal legal matters of ordinary people, and not criminal law (क़ानून में) सामान्य नागरिकों के निजी क़ानूनी मुद्दों से संबंधित *civil courts* **4** polite, but not very friendly विनम्र परंतु मित्रवत नहीं ► **civility** /səˈvɪləti सˈव़िलटि/ *noun* [U] विनम्रता, सभ्यता *Staff members are trained to treat customers with civility at all times.* ► **civilly** /ˈsɪvəli ˈसिव़लि/ *adv.* नम्रतापूर्वक, सभ्यता से

**civil engineering** *noun* [U] the design, building and repair of roads, bridges, etc; the study of this as a subject सड़क, पुल आदि की रूपरेखा, निर्माण और मरम्मत; इन सबका विषय के रूप में अध्ययन; सिविल अभियांत्रिकी

**civilian** /səˈvɪliən सˈव़िलिअन्/ *noun* [C] a person who is not in the army, navy, air force or police force व्यक्ति जो सेना या पुलिस बल में न हो; नागर *Two soldiers and one civilian were killed when the bomb exploded.*

**civilization** (*also* **-isation**) /ˌsɪvəlaɪˈzeɪʃn ˌसिव़लाइˈज़ेश्न्/ *noun* **1** [C, U] a society which has its own highly developed culture and way of life विकसित संस्कृति और जीवन-पद्धति वाला समाज; सभ्यता *the civilizations of ancient Greece and Rome* ○ *Western civilization* **2** [U] an advanced state of social and cultural development, or the process of reaching this state सामाजिक और सांस्कृतिक विकास की प्रगत अवस्था या इस अवस्था तक पहुँचने की प्रक्रिया *the civilization of the human race* **3** [U] all the people in the world and the societies they live in considered as a whole मानव जाति *Global warming poses a threat to the whole of civilization.*

**civilize** (*also* **-ise**) /ˈsɪvəlaɪz ˈसिव़लाइज़्/ *verb* [T] to make people or a society develop from a low social and cultural level to a more advanced one सभ्य करना या बनाना

**civilized** (*also* **-ised**) /ˈsɪvəlaɪzd ˈसिव़लाइज़्ड्/ *adj.* **1** (used about a society) well organized; having a high level of social and cultural development (समाज) सुसंगठित; सामाजिक और सांस्कृतिक दृष्टि से उन्नत **2** polite and reasonable नम्र और विवेकपूर्ण *a civilized conversation*

**civil rights** (*also* **civil liberties**) *noun* [*pl.*] a person's legal right to freedom and equal treatment in society, whatever his/her sex, race or religion समाज में किसी व्यक्ति को बिना भेदभाव मिलने वाले स्वतंत्रता और समानता के अधिकार; नागरिक अधिकार *the civil rights leader*

**civil servant** *noun* [C] an offcial who works for the government's or State's own organization (**the civil service**) लोक सेवा या प्रशासनिक सेवा में काम करने वाला अधिकारी

**the civil service** *noun* [*sing.*] the officials who work for the government, except those belonging to the armed forces सेना को छोड़कर सभी सरकारी विभागों में काम करने वाले अधिकारी

**civil war** *noun* [C, U] a war between groups of people who live in the same country एक ही देश के नागरिकों के दलों का आपस में युद्ध; गृहयुद्ध

**CJD** /ˌsiː dʒeɪˈdiː ˌसी जेˈडी/ *abbr.* creutzfeldt-jakob disease; a disease of the brain caused by eating infected meat क्रॉइटसफेल्ट-यैकब रोग; यह रोग दूषित या संक्रमित मांस खाने से उत्पन्न होता है और मस्तिष्क को प्रभावित करता है ➪ **BSE** देखिए।

**cl** *abbr.* centilitre(s) सेंटीलीटर

**clad** /klæd क्लैड्/ *adj.* (used before a noun) (*old-fashioned*) dressed (in); wearing a particular type of clothing वस्त्र पहने हुए, सवस्त्र या सपरिधान; विशेष प्रकार की पोशाक पहने हुए *The children were warmly clad in coats, hats and scarves.*

**claim**[1] /kleɪm क्लेम् / *verb* **1** [T] **claim (that); claim (to be sth)** to say that sth is true, without having any proof बिना प्रमाण प्रस्तुत किए सत्यता का दावा करना *Anirudh claims the book belongs to him.* ○ *This woman claims to be the oldest person in India.* **2** [I, T] **claim (for sth)** to ask for sth from the government, a company, etc. because you think it is your legal right to have it, or it belongs to you सरकार, कंपनी आदि से स्वामित्व या अधिकार का दावा करना *The police are keeping the necklace until somebody claims it.* ○ *(figurative) No one has claimed responsibility for the bomb attack.* **3** [T] to cause death मृत्यु का कारण बनना; के कारण मृत्यु होना *The earthquake claimed thousands of lives.*

**claim**[2] /kleɪm क्लेम् / *noun* [C] **1 a claim (that)** a statement that sth is true, which does not have any proof बिना प्रमाण के किसी बात के सच होने का दावा *I do not believe the Government's claim that they can reduce unemployment by the end of the year.* **2 a claim (to sth)** the right to have sth स्वामित्व का अधिकार *You will have to prove your claim to the property in a court of law.* **3 a claim (for sth)** a demand for money that you think you have a right to, especially from the government, a company, etc. धन की माँग रखने का अधिकर (विशेषतः सरकार, कंपनी आदि से) *to make an insurance claim* ○ *After the accident he decided to put in a claim for compensation.*
**IDM** **stake a/your claim** ➪ **stake**[2] देखिए।

**claimant** /ˈkleɪmənt ˈक्लेमन्ट् / *noun* [C] a person who believes he/she has the right to have sth दावेदार *The insurance company refused to pay the claimant any money.*

**clairvoyant** /kleəˈvɔɪənt क्लेअˈव़ॉइअन्ट् / *noun* [C] a person who some people believe has special mental powers and can see what will happen in the future भविष्यदर्शी व्यक्ति; अतीन्द्रियदर्शी व्यक्ति

**clam**[1] /klæm क्लैम् / *noun* [C] a type of shellfish that can be eaten एक प्रकार की खाने योग्य शंखमीन ➪ **shellfish** पर चित्र देखिए।

**clam**[2] /klæm क्लैम् / *verb* (**cla<u>mm</u>ing; cla<u>mm</u>ed**)
**PHR V** **clam up (on sb)** (*informal*) to stop talking and refuse to speak especially when sb asks you about sth चुप्पी साधना

**clamber** /ˈklæmbə(r) ˈक्लैम्ब(र्) / *verb* [I] **clamber up, down, out etc.** to move or climb with difficulty, usually using both your hands and feet हाथ-पैर के बल या कठिनाई से चढ़ना

**clammy** /ˈklæmi ˈक्लैमि / *adj.* cold, slightly wet and sticky in an unpleasant way ठंडा, नम और चिपचिपा *clammy hands*

**clamour** (*AmE* **clamor**) /ˈklæmə(r) ˈक्लैम(र्) / *verb* [I] **clamour for sth** to demand sth in a loud or angry way चिल्लाकर या क्रोध में कोई माँग करना *The public are clamouring for an answer to all these questions.* ► **clamour** (*AmE* **clamor**) *noun* [*sing.*] शोर-शराबे सहित की गई माँग *the clamour of angry voices*

**clamp**[1] /klæmp क्लैम्प् / *noun* [C] **1** a tool that you use for holding two things together very tightly दो वस्तुओं को इकट्ठे मज़बूती से पकड़े रखने के लिए उपकरण; शिकंजा, क्लेंप, बाँक ➪ **laboratory** और **vice** पर चित्र देखिए। **2** (*also* **wheel clamp**) a metal object that is fixed to the wheel of a car that has been parked illegally, so that it cannot drive away कार के पहिए का शिकंजा

**clamp**[2] /klæmp क्लैम्प् / *verb* [T] **1 clamp A and B (together); clamp A to B** to fasten two things together with a clamp शिकंजे से दो वस्तुओं को बाँधना *The metal rods were clamped together.* ○ *Clamp the wood to the table so that it doesn't move.* **2** to hold sth very firmly in a particular position कसकर वस्तुएँ पकड़ना या थामना *Her lips were clamped tightly together.*
**PHR V** **clamp down on sb/sth** (*informal*) to take strong action in order to stop or control sth गतिविधि आदि रोकने या नियंत्रित करने के लिए कड़ी कार्रवाई करना

**clampdown** /ˈklæmpdaʊn ˈक्लैम्प्डाउन् / *noun* [C] strong action to stop or control sth रोकथाम या नियंत्रण के लिए कड़ी कार्रवाई *a clampdown on tax evasion*

**clan** /klæn क्लैन् / *noun* [C, *with sing. or pl. verb*] a group of families who are related to each other परस्पर संबंधित परिवारों का समुदाय; गोत्र, कुल, वंश

**clandestine** /klænˈdestɪn क्लैन्ˈडेस्टिन् / *adj.* (*formal*) secret and often not legal गुप्त और प्रायः ग़ैर-क़ानूनी *a clandestine meeting*

**clang** /klæŋ क्लैङ् / *verb* [I, T] to make a loud ringing sound like that of metal being hit धातु से टकराने पर ध्वनि उत्पन्न होना; झनझनाना *The iron gates clanged shut.* ► **clang** *noun* [C] टनटनाहट, झनझनाहट

**clank** /klæŋk क्लैङ्क् / *verb* [I, T] to make a loud unpleasant sound like pieces of metal hitting each other (धातुओं का) खड़खड़ाना *The lift clanked its way up to the seventh floor.* ► **clank** *noun* [C] खड़खड़ाहट

**clap[1]** /klæp क्लैप्/ *verb* (**clapping; clapped**) **1** [I, T] to hit your hands together many times, usually to show that you like sth ताली बजाना *The audience clapped as soon as the singer walked onto the stage.* **2** [T] to put sth onto sth quickly and firmly शीघ्रता से और दृढ़तापूर्वक एक वस्तु पर दूसरी को रखना *'Oh no, I shouldn't have said that,' she said, clapping a hand over her mouth.*

**clap[2]** /klæp क्लैप्/ *noun* [C] **1** a sudden loud noise कड़क, कड़कड़ाहट *a clap of thunder* **2** an act of clapping ताली बजाने की क्रिया; ताली

**clarification** /ˌklærəfɪˈkeɪʃn ˈक्लैरफ़िˈकेश्न्/ *noun* [U] an act of making sth clear and easier to understand किसी प्रसंग को स्पष्ट और सुबोध बनाने की क्रिया; स्पष्टीकरण *We'd like some clarification of exactly what your company intends to do.* ➪ **clarity** देखिए।

**clarify** /ˈklærəfaɪ ˈक्लैरिफ़ाइ/ *verb* [T] (*pres. part.* **clarifying;** *3rd person sing. pres.* **clarifies;** *pt, pp* **clarified**) to make sth become clear and easier to understand किसी प्रसंग को स्पष्ट और सुबोध बनाना; स्पष्टीकरण करना *I hope that what I say will clarify the situation.* ➪ **clear** adjective देखिए।

**clarinet** /ˌklærəˈnet ˈक्लैरˈनेट्/ *noun* [C] a musical instrument that is made of wood. You play a clarinet by blowing through it बाँसुरी जैसा काष्ठनिर्मित वाद्य; क्लैरिनेट ➪ **piano** पर नोट देखिए।

**clarity** /ˈklærəti ˈक्लैरटि/ *noun* [U] the quality of being clear and easy to understand स्पष्टता और सुबोधता *clarity of expression* ➪ **clarification** देखिए।

**clash[1]** /klæʃ क्लैश्/ *verb* **1** [I] **clash (with sb)** (**over sth**) to fight or disagree seriously about sth किसी विषय पर (किसी से) झगड़ना या गंभीरता से असहमत होना *A group of demonstrators clashed with police outside the Parliament.* **2** [I] **clash (with sth)** (used about two events) to happen at the same time (दो घटनाओं का) एक ही समय में घटित होना *It's a pity the two concerts clash. I wanted to go to both of them.* **3 clash (with sth)** (used about colours, etc.) to not match or look nice together (रंगों का) मेल न खाना; संग भद्दा लगना *I don't think you should wear that tie—it clashes with your shirt.* **4** [I, T] (used about two metal objects) to hit together with a loud noise; to cause two metal objects to do this (दो धातु निर्मित पदार्थों का) ऊँची आवाज़ के साथ टकराना, खटखटाना *Their swords clashed.*

**clash[2]** /klæʃ क्लैश्/ *noun* [C] **1** a fight or serious disagreement झगड़ा या गंभीर मतभेद *a clash between police and demonstrators* **2** a big difference बड़ा अंतर, भारी मतभेद, संघर्ष *a clash of opinions* ○ *There was a personality clash between the two men* (= they did not get well on together or like each other). **3** a loud noise, made by two metal objects hitting each other टनक, टनकारने की आवाज़

**clasp[1]** /klɑːsp क्लास्प्/ *noun* [C] an object, usually of metal, which fastens or holds sth together बाँधने या मजबूती से पकड़ने की सामान्यतः धातु की वस्तु *the clasp on a necklace/brooch/handbag*

**clasp[2]** /klɑːsp क्लास्प्/ *verb* [T] to hold sb/sth tightly कसकर थामना *He clasped the child in his arms.*

**class[1]** /klɑːs क्लास्/ *noun* **1** [C, *with sing. or pl. verb*] a group of students who are taught together छात्रों की कक्षा *The whole class is/are going to the theatre tonight.* **2** [C, U] a lesson कक्षा-पाठ *Classes begin at 9 o'clock in the morning.* ○ *We watched an interesting video in class* (= during the lesson) *yesterday.* **3** [U, C] the way people are divided into social groups; one of these groups सामाजिक वर्गीकरण; सामाजिक वर्ग, श्रेणी *The idea of caste still divides Indian society.* ○ *class differences* **4** [C] (*technical*) a group of animals, plants, words, etc. of a similar type एक ही प्रकार के पशुओं, पौधों, शब्दों आदि का वर्ग *There are several different classes of insects.* **NOTE** श्रेणी के आधार पर **phylum** बड़ा है और **class** छोटा। **5** [U] (*informal*) high quality or style ऊँचा दर्जा, उच्च कोटि *Pele was a football player of great class.* **6** [C] (*especially in compounds*) each of several different levels of service that are available to travellers on a plane, train, etc. विमान, रेलगाड़ी आदि के विभिन्न दर्जों या श्रेणियों में से कोई एक *a first-class compartment on a train* ○ *He always travels business class.* **7** [C] (*used to form compound adjectives*) a mark that you are given when you pass your final university exam परीक्षा परिणाम में दर्जा, श्रेणी *a first-/second-/third-class degree*

**class[2]** /klɑːs क्लास्/ *verb* [T] **class sb/sth (as sth)** to put sb/sth in a particular group or type वस्तुओं को वर्गीकृत करना, विभिन्न वर्गों में रखना *Certain animals and plants are now classed as 'endangered species'.*

**classic[1]** /ˈklæsɪk ˈक्लैसिक्/ *adj.* (*usually before a noun*) **1** typical प्रतिनिधिक *It was a classic case of bad management.* **2** (used about a book, play, etc.) of high quality, important and having a value that will last (पुस्तक, नाटक आदि) उत्कृष्ट, महत्त्वपूर्ण और कालजयी *the classic film 'Gone With The Wind'* **3** attractive but simple and traditional in style; not affected by changes in fashion आकर्षक, परंतु शैली में सादा व पारंपरिक; प्रचलन से अप्रभावित

**classic²** /ˈklæsɪk ˈक्लैसिक्/ *noun* **1** [C] a famous book, play, etc. which is of high quality and has a value that will last उत्कृष्ट व कालजयी ग्रंथ; श्रेण्यग्रंथ *All of Charles Dickens' novels are classics.* **2 Classics** [U] the study of ancient Greek and Roman language and literature प्राचीन ग्रीक और रोमन वाङ्मय का अध्ययन

**classical** /ˈklæsɪkl ˈक्लैसिकल्/ *adj.* (*usually before a noun*) **1** (used about music) serious and having a value that lasts (संगीत) गंभीर व कालजयी; शास्त्रीय *I prefer classical music to pop.* ➪ **jazz, pop** और **rock** देखिए। **2** traditional, not modern पारंपरिक (न कि आधुनिक) *classical ballet* **3** connected with ancient Greece or Rome प्राचीन यूनान या रोम से संबंधित *classical architecture* ▶ **classically** /-kli -कलि/ *adv.* शास्त्रीय रूप से

**classified** /ˈklæsɪfaɪd ˈक्लैसिफ़ाइड्/ *adj.* officially secret अधिकृत रूप से गोपनीय *classified information*

**classified advertisement** (*informal* **classified ad**) *noun* [*usually pl.*] a small advertisement that you put in a newspaper if you want to buy or sell sth, employ sb, find a flat, etc. वर्गीकृत विज्ञापन, लघु विज्ञापन

**classify** /ˈklæsɪfaɪ ˈक्लैसिफ़ाइ/ *verb* [T] (*pres. part.* **classifying**; *3rd person sing. pres.* **classifies**; *pt, pp* **classified**) **classify sb/sth (as sth)** to put sb/sth into a group with other people or things of a similar type समान प्रकार की वस्तुओं या व्यक्तियों को एक वर्ग में रखना; वर्गीकृत करना *Would you classify it as an action film or a thriller?* ▶ **classification** /ˌklæsɪfɪˈkeɪʃn ˌक्लैसिफ़िˈकेशन्/ *noun* [C, U] वर्गीकरण *the classification of the different species of butterfly*

**classless** /ˈklɑːsləs ˈक्लासलस्/ *adj.* **1** with no division into social classes वर्गहीन (समाज) *It is hard to imagine a truly classless society.* **2** not clearly belonging to any particular social class सामाजिक वर्गभेद के प्रभाव से मुक्त *a classless accent*

**classmate** /ˈklɑːsmeɪt ˈक्लासमेट्/ *noun* [C] a person who is in the same class as you at school or college विद्यालय या महाविद्यालय का सहपाठी

**classroom** /ˈklɑːsruːm; -rʊm ˈक्लासरूम्; -रुम्/ *noun* [C] a room in a school, college, etc. where lessons are taught विद्यालय, महाविद्यालय आदि में अध्याय-कक्ष

**classy** /ˈklɑːsi ˈक्लासि/ *adj.* (**classier; classiest**) (*informal*) of high quality or style; expensive and fashionable (गुण या शैली में) बढ़िया या उत्कृष्ट; महँगा और लोकप्रिय व प्रचलित *a classy restaurant*

**clatter** /ˈklætə(r) ˈक्लैटर्/ *verb* [I, T] to make or cause sth hard to make a series of short loud repeated sounds खड़खड़ाना *The horses clattered down the street.* ▶ **clatter** *noun* [*usually sing.*] खड़खड़ाहट

**clause** /klɔːz क्लॉज़्/ *noun* [C] **1** one of the sections of a legal document that says that sth must or must not be done किसी क़ानूनी दस्तावेज़ का खंड, धारा, दफ़ा **2** (*grammar*) a group of words that includes a subject and a verb. A clause is usually only part of a sentence कर्ता और क्रिया युक्त वाक्यांश; उपवाक्य *The sentence 'After we had finished eating, we watched a film on the video' contains two clauses.*

**claustrophobia** /ˌklɔːstrəˈfəʊbiə ˌक्लॉस्ट्रˈफ़ोबिआ/ *noun* [U] fear of being in a small or enclosed space संकीर्ण या बंद स्थान में सीमित होने का भय; संवृत-स्थानभीति

**claustrophobic** /ˌklɔːstrəˈfəʊbɪk ˌक्लॉस्ट्रˈफ़ोबिक्/ *adj.* **1** extremely afraid of small, enclosed spaces छोटे, बंद स्थानों से अत्यधिक भयभीत *I always feel claustrophobic in lifts.* **2** used about sth that makes you feel afraid in this way इस प्रकार भयभीत करने वाले स्थान के लिए प्रयुक्त *a claustrophobic little room*

**clavicle** /ˈklævɪkl ˈक्लैविकल्/ (*medical*) = **collarbone**

**claw¹** /klɔː क्लॉ/ *noun* [C] **1** one of the long curved nails on the end of an animal's or a bird's foot किसी पशु या पक्षी का पंजा; नखर ➪ **shellfish** पर चित्र देखिए। **2** one of a pair of long, sharp fingers that certain types of shellfish and some insects have. They use them for holding or picking things up (कुछ कीटों और केकड़े आदि की) लंबी, नुकीली अंगुली जिससे वे वस्तुओं को पकड़ते हैं *the claws of a crab*

**claw²** /klɔː क्लॉ/ *verb* [I, T] **claw (at) sb/sth** to scratch or tear sb/sth with claws or with your fingernails पंजों या नाख़ूनों से खरोंचना या फाड़ना *The cat was clawing at the furniture.*

**clay** /kleɪ क्ले/ *noun* [U] heavy earth that is soft and sticky when it is wet and becomes hard when it is baked or dried चिकनी चिपकने वाली मिट्टी जो पकाने पर कड़ी हो जाती है *clay pots*

**clean¹** /kliːn क्लीन्/ *adj.* **1** not dirty साफ़, निर्मल, स्वच्छ *The whole house was beautifully clean.* ○ *Cats are very clean animals.* ✪ विलोम **dirty** **2** having no record of offences or crimes नियमभंग या अपराध के दोष से मुक्त *a clean driving licence* ➪ **cleanliness** noun देखिए।

**IDM** **a clean sweep** a complete victory in a sports competition, election, etc. that you get by winning all the different parts of it खेल प्रतियोगिता, चुनाव आदि में पूर्ण विजय

**clean²** /kli:n क्लीन्/ *verb* **1** [T] to remove dirt, dust and marks from sth किसी वस्तु से धूल और धब्बे हटाना; साफ़ करना *to clean the windows* ○ *Don't forget to clean your teeth!*

**NOTE** किसी चीज़ से गंदगी साफ़ करने के लिए सामान्य शब्द **clean** है। साबुन और पानी से सफ़ाई करने के लिए **wash**, गीले कपड़े से सतह को पोंछने के लिए **wipe**, सूखे कपड़े से सतह को साफ करने के लिए **dust** कूची या ब्रश से सफ़ाई करने के लिए **brush** और झाड़ू आदि से फ़र्श को साफ़ करने के लिए **sweep** शब्दों का प्रयोग किया जाता है।

**2** [I, T] to make the inside of a house, office, etc. free from dust and dirt घर, दफ़्तर आदि की अंदर से धूल और गंदगी साफ़ करना *Subhash comes in to clean after office hours.* **NOTE** इस अर्थ में **clean** के स्थान पर प्रायः **do the cleaning** का प्रयोग किया जाता है—*I do the cleaning once a week.*

**PHR V** **clean sth out** to clean the inside of sth किसी वस्तु को अंदर से साफ़ करना *I'm going to clean out all the cupboards next week.*

**clean (sth) up** to remove all the dirt from a place that is particularly dirty बहुत गंदे स्थान की पूरी तरह सफ़ाई करना *I'm going to clean up the kitchen before Mum and Dad get back.* ➪ **dry-clean** और **spring-clean** देखिए।

**clean³** /kli:n क्लीन्/ *adv.* (*informal*) completely पूरी तरह से *I clean forgot it was your birthday.*

**IDM** **come clean (with sb) (about sth)** (*informal*) to tell the truth about sth that you have been keeping secret सचाई को सामने लाना; सच्ची बात बताना

**go clean out of your mind** to be completely forgotten पूरी तरह से भुला दिया जाना

**clean-cut** *adj.* (used especially about a young man) having a clean, tidy appearance that is attractive and socially acceptable (विशेषतः युवक) साफ़-सुथरा और सुघड़ *The girls all go for Rahul's clean-cut good looks.*

**cleaner** /ˈkli:nə(r) ˈक्लीन(र्)/ *noun* **1** [C] a person whose job is to clean the rooms and furniture inside a house or other building घर या भवन के भीतर का सफ़ाई कर्मचारी *an office cleaner* **2** [C] a substance or a special machine that you use for cleaning sth सफ़ाई में प्रयुक्त पदार्थ या विशेष मशीन *liquid floor cleaners* ○ *a carpet cleaner* ➪ **vacuum cleaner** देखिए। **3 the cleaner's** = **dry-cleaner's**

**cleanliness** /ˈklenlinəs ˈक्लेन्लिनस्/ *noun* [U] being clean or keeping things clean स्वच्छता, सफ़ाई *High standards of cleanliness are important in a hotel kitchen.*

**cleanly** /ˈkli:nli ˈक्लीन्लि/ *adv.* easily or smoothly in one movement आसानी से या सफ़ाई से (किया गया) *The knife cut cleanly through the rope.*

**cleanse** /klenz क्लेन्ज़्/ *verb* [T] to clean your skin or a wound त्वचा या घाव को साफ़ करना ➪ **ethnic cleansing** देखिए।

**cleanser** /ˈklenzə(r) ˈक्लेन्ज़(र्)/ *noun* [C] a substance that you use for cleaning your skin, especially your face त्वचा, विशेषतः चेहरा, साफ़ करने के लिए पदार्थ

**clean-shaven** *adj.* (used about men) having recently shaved (पुरुष) सफ़ाचट दाढ़ी-मूँछ वाला

**clean-up** *noun* [C, *usually sing.*] the process of removing dirt or other bad things from a place किसी स्थान से गंदगी आदि साफ़ करने की प्रक्रिया *The clean-up of the town centre means that tourists can now go there safely at night.*

**clear¹** /klɪə(r) क्लिअ(र्)/ *adj.* **1** easy to see, hear or understand देखने, सुनने या समझने में स्पष्ट, साफ़ *His voice wasn't very clear on the telephone.* ○ *She gave me clear directions on how to get there.* **2 clear (about/on sth)** sure or definite; without any doubts or confusion सुनिश्चित; संदेह-मुक्त *I'm not quite clear about the arrangements for tomorrow.* ➪ **clarify** verb देखिए। **3 clear (to sb)** obvious सुस्पष्ट, प्रकट, प्रत्यक्ष *There are clear advantages to the second plan.* ○ *It was clear to me that he was not telling the truth.* **4** easy to see through पारदर्शी, साफ़ *The water was so clear that we could see the bottom of the lake.* **5 clear (of sth)** free from things that are blocking the way बाधामुक्त, साफ़ *The police say that most roads are now clear of snow.* **6** free from marks बेदाग़, चिह्न-रहित *a clear sky* (= without cloud) ○ *clear skin* (= without spot) **7** free from guilt निर्दोष, दोषरहित, दोषमुक्त *It wasn't your fault. You can have a completely clear conscience.*

**IDM** **make yourself clear; make sth clear/plain (to sb)** to speak so that there can be no doubt about what you mean साफ़-साफ़ कहना, साफ़ कर देना ○ *He made it quite clear that he was not happy with the decision.*

**clear²** /klɪə(r) क्लिअ(र्)/ *adv.* **1** = **clearly 1** *We can hear the telephone loud and clear from here.* **2 clear (of sth)** away from sth; not touching sth

से दूर; के पास नहीं, स्पर्श न करते हुए *stand clear of the doors* (= on a train)

IDM **keep/stay/steer clear (of sb/sth)** to avoid sb/sth because he/she/it may cause problems समस्या पैदा कर सकने वाले व्यक्ति या वस्तु से दूर रहना

**clear[3]** /klɪə(r) क्लिअ(र्)/ *verb* **1** [T] to remove sth that is not wanted or needed अवांछित या अनावश्यक वस्तु को हटाना *to clear the roads of snow/to clear snow from the roads* ○ *It's your turn to clear the table* (= to take away the dirty plates etc. after a meal). **2** [I] (used about smoke, etc.) to disappear (धुएँ आदि का) हट या दूर हो जाना, न रह जाना *The fog slowly cleared and the sun came out.* **3** [I] (used about the sky, the weather or water) to become free of clouds, rain, or mud (आकाश, मौसम या पानी का) साफ़ हो जाना *After a cloudy start, the weather will clear during the afternoon.* **4** [T] **clear sb (of sth)** to provide proof that sb is innocent of sth निर्दोष सिद्ध करना या होना *The man has finally been cleared of murder.* **5** [T] to jump over or get past sth without touching it लाँघना, फाँदना थोड़ा घूमकर बिना छुए निकल जाना **6** [T] to give official permission for a plane, ship, etc. to enter or leave a place विमान, जहाज़ आदि को प्रवेश या प्रस्थान की आधिकारिक अनुमति देना *At last the plane was cleared for take-off.* **7** [T] **clear sth (with sb)** to get official approval for sth to be done कुछ करने की आधिकारिक अनुमति लेना *I'll have to clear it with the manager before I can refund your money.* **8** [I] (used about a cheque) to go through the system that moves money from one account to another (चेक की) धनराशि का एक खाते में से दूसरे खाते में जाने की प्रक्रिया से गुज़रना

IDM **clear the air** to improve a difficult or uncomfortable situation by talking honestly about worries, doubts, etc. कठिन या असुविधाजनक स्थिति को निष्कपट बातचीत द्वारा सुधारना

**clear your throat** to cough slightly in order to make it easier to speak गला साफ़ करना; खँखारना

PHR V **clear off** (*informal*) used to tell sb to go away किसी को चले जाने का निर्देश देने के लिए प्रयुक्त

**clear sth out** to tidy sth and throw away things that you do not want अवांछित वस्तुएँ फेंककर या हटाकर स्थान आदि को सुव्यवस्थित करना

**clear up** (used about the weather or an illness) to get better (मौसम या बीमारी में) सुधार होना

**clear (sth) up** to make sth tidy (स्थान या वस्तु को) सुव्यवस्थित या ठीक-ठाक करना *Make sure you clear up properly before you leave.*

**clear sth up** to find the solution to a problem, cause of confusion, etc. समस्या का समाधान, परेशानी का कारण आदि ढूँढ़ लेना *There's been a slight misunderstanding but we've cleared it up now.*

**clearance** /ˈklɪərəns ˈक्लिअरन्स्/ *noun* [U] **1** the removing of sth that is old or not wanted अवांछित वस्तुएँ हटाने की क्रिया *The shop is having a clearance sale* (= selling things cheaply in order to get rid of them). **2** the distance between an object and something that is passing under or beside it, for example a ship or vehicle किसी जहाज़ या वाहन के बीच में से निकलने का स्थान *There was not enough clearance for the bus to pass under the bridge safely.* **3** official permission for sb/sth to do sth कुछ करने की अधिकारिक अनुमति

**clear-cut** *adj.* definite and easy to see or understand सुनिश्चित और स्पष्ट या सुबोध

**clear-headed** *adj.* able to think clearly, especially if there is a problem स्पष्ट सोचने में सक्षम

**clearing** /ˈklɪərɪŋ ˈक्लिअरिङ्/ *noun* [C] a small area without trees in the middle of a wood or forest जंगल के बीच में वृक्ष-रहित क्षेत्र

**clearly** /ˈklɪəli ˈक्लिअलि/ *adv.* **1** in a way that is easy to see, hear or understand साफ़, स्पष्ट या सुबोध रूप से *It was so foggy that we couldn't see the road clearly.* **2** in a way that is not confused स्पष्टतया, साफ़-साफ़, उलझनमुक्त रीति से *I'm so tired that I can't think clearly.* **3** without doubt; obviously निस्संदेह; प्रकट रूप से; स्पष्टतया *She clearly doesn't want to speak to you any more.*

**clear-sighted** *adj.* able to understand situations well and to see what might happen in the future समझदार और दूरदर्शिता संपन्न

**cleft** /kleft क्लेफ़्ट्/ *noun* [C] a natural opening or crack, especially in rock or in a person's chin चट्टान या किसी व्यक्ति की ठोड़ी में प्राकृतिक दरार

**clemency** /ˈklemənsi ˈक्लेमन्सि/ *noun* [U] (*formal*) kindness shown to sb when he/she is being punished (क़ानून में) दंड देते समय दिखाई गई दया, क्षमा

**clementine** /ˈkleməntiːn ˈक्लेमन्टीन्/ *noun* [C] a type of small orange एक प्रकार का छोटा संतरा

**clench** /klentʃ क्लेन्च्/ *verb* [T] to close or hold tightly बाँधना या जकड़ना, भींचना *She clenched her fists and looked as if she was going to hit him.*

**clergy** /ˈklɜːdʒi ˈक्लजि/ *noun* [*pl.*] the people who perform religious ceremonies in the Christian church ईसाई चर्च का पुरोहित-वर्ग *a member of the clergy*

**clergyman** /ˈklɜːdʒimən ˈक्लजिमन्/ *noun* [C] (*pl.* **-men** /-mən; -men -मन्; -मेन्/) a male member of the clergy ईसाई चर्च के पुरोहित-वर्ग का पुरुष सदस्य

**clergywoman** /ˈklɜːdʒiwʊmən ˈक्लजिवुमन् / *noun* [C] (*pl.* **-women** /-wɪmɪn -विमिन्/) a female member of the clergy ईसाई चर्च के पुरोहित-वर्ग की महिला सदस्य

**cleric** /ˈklerɪk ˈक्लेरिक् / *noun* [C] **1** a priest in the Christian church ईसाई चर्च का पादरी ✪ पर्याय **clergyman** **2** a religious leader in any religion (किसी भी धर्म में) धार्मिक नेता *Muslim clerics*

**clerical** /ˈklerɪkl ˈक्लेरिक्ल् / *adj.* **1** connected with the work of a clerk in an office लिपिक, क्लर्क के काम से संबंधित; लिपिकीय *clerical work* **2** connected with the clergy (ईसाई पुरोहित) के काम से संबंधित

**clerk** /klɑːk क्लाक् / *noun* [C] **1** a person whose job is to do written work or look after records or accounts in an office, bank, court of law, etc. क्लर्क, लिपिक **2** (*also* **sales clerk**) = **shop assistant**

**clever** /ˈklevə(r) ˈक्लेव़(र्) / *adj.* **1** able to learn, understand or do sth quickly and easily; intelligent चतुर, सयाना; बुद्धिमान *a clever student* ○ *How clever of you to mend my watch!* **2** (used about things, ideas, etc.) showing skill or intelligence (वस्तुएँ, विचार आदि) बुद्धि और चातुर्यपूर्ण *a clever device* ○ *a clever plan* ▶ **cleverly** *adv.* चतुराई से ▶ **cleverness** *noun* [U] चतुराई, बुद्धिमानी

**cliché** /ˈkliːʃeɪ ˈक्लीशे / *noun* [C] a phrase or idea that has been used so many times that it no longer has any real meaning or interest इतनी बार दोहराई जा चुकी उक्ति आदि जिसका अब कोई अर्थ या जिससे कोई रुचि नहीं रह गई है; घिसी-पिटी उक्ति

**click¹** /klɪk क्लिक् / *verb* **1** [I, T] to make a short sharp sound; to cause sth to do this 'खटाक' की आवाज़ करना; खटखट करवाना *The door clicked shut.* ○ *He clicked his fingers at the waiter.* **2** [I, T] **click (on sth)** (*computing*) to press one of the buttons on a mouse माउस का कोई बटन दबाना, क्लिक करना *To open a file, click on the menu.* ○ *Position the pointer and* ***double click*** *the left-hand mouse button* (= press it twice very quickly). **3** [I] (*informal*) (used about two people) to become friendly immediately (दो व्यक्तियों का) तुरंत मित्र बन जाना *We met at a party and just clicked.* **4** [I] (*informal*) (used about a problem, etc.) to become suddenly clear or understood (किसी समस्या आदि का) एकाएक समझ में आ जाना या स्पष्ट हो जाना *Once I'd found the missing letter, everything* ***clicked into place***.

**click²** /klɪk क्लिक् / *noun* [C] **1** a short sharp sound खटखट की ध्वनि *the click of a switch* **2** (*computing*) the act of pressing the button on a computer mouse माउस पर का बटन दबाने की क्रिया

**client** /ˈklaɪənt ˈक्लाइअन्ट् / *noun* [C] **1** somebody who receives a service from a professional person, for example a lawyer किसी व्यावसायिक व्यक्ति का सेवालाभी, जैसे वकील का मुवक्किल; सेवार्थी **2** (*computing*) one of a number of computers that is connected to a special computer (**server**) that stores shared information सभी के प्रयोग के लिए सार्वजनिक सूचना-सामग्री संचित करने वाले एक विशेष कंप्यूटर (सर्वर) से जुड़े बहुत सारे कंप्यूटरों में से कोई एक

> **NOTE** ध्यान दें! दुकानों या भोजनालयों के ग्राहकों के लिए **client** शब्द का प्रयोग नहीं किया जाता। इन व्यक्तियों को **customers** कहा जाता है। शब्द **clientele** औपचारिक शब्द है जो **clients** व **customers** दोनों के लिए प्रयुक्त किया जाता है।

**clientele** /ˌkliːənˈtel ˌक्लीअन्ˈटेल् / *noun* [U] all the customers, guests or clients who regularly go to a particular shop, hotel, organization, etc. ग्राहक-वर्ग, सेवार्थीवृंद **NOTE** शब्द **clientele** अन्य समान शब्दों, जैसे **customers** या **guests** से अधिक औपचारिक है।

**cliff** /klɪf क्लिफ़् / *noun* [C] a high, very steep area of rock, especially one next to the sea ऊँची खड़ी चट्टान, विशेषतः समुद्र के किनारे की; भृगु

**cliffhanger** /ˈklɪfhæŋə(r) ˈक्लिफ़्हैङ(र्) / *noun* [C] an exciting situation in a story, film, etc. when you cannot guess what is going to happen next and you have to wait until the next part in order to find out कहानी, फ़िल्म आदि में कुतूहलपूर्ण स्थितिं (जिसमें तुरंत यह पता न चले कि आगे क्या होगा)

**climactic** /klaɪˈmæktɪk क्लाइˈमैक्टिक् / *adj.* (*written*) (used about an event or a point in time) very exciting, most important (किसी घटना या समय-बिंदु के लिए प्रयुक्त) अति उत्तेजक, चरम, अति महत्त्वपूर्ण

**climate** /ˈklaɪmət ˈक्लाइमट् / *noun* [C] **1** the normal weather conditions of a particular region किसी क्षेत्र-विशेष की सामान्य जलवायु *a dry/humid/tropical climate* **2** the general opinions, etc. that people have at a particular time किसी समय-विशेष में सामान्य भाव; वातावरण, आबोहवा *What is the current* ***climate of opinion*** *regarding the death penalty?* ○ *the political climate*

**climatic** /klaɪˈmætɪk क्लाइˈमैटिक् / *adj.* connected with the **climate 1** जलवायु-संबंधी

**climatology** /ˌklaɪməˈtɒlədʒi ˌक्लाइमˈटॉलजि / *noun* [U] the scientific study of climate जलवायु-विज्ञान

**climax** /ˈklaɪmæks ˈक्लाइमैक्स् / *noun* [C] the most important and exciting part of a book, play, piece of music, event, etc. पुस्तक, नाटक, संगीत-रचना, घटना आदि का चरोमोत्कर्ष, पराकाष्ठा *The novel* ***reaches a dramatic climax*** *in the final chapter.* ▶ **climax** *verb* [I] चरमोत्कर्ष पर पहुँचना

**climb**[1] /klaɪm क्लाइम्/ *verb* **1** [I, T] **climb (up) (sth)** to move up towards the top of sth (पेड़, पहाड़ आदि पर) चढ़ना *to climb a tree/mountain/rope* ○ *to climb up a ladder* **2** [I] to move, with difficulty or effort, in the direction mentioned एक विशेष दिशा में प्रयास या कठिनाई से बढ़ना *I managed to climb out of the window.* **3** [I] to go up mountains, etc. as a sport पर्वतारोहण करना **4** [I] to rise to a higher position ऊपर की ओर उठना *The road climbed steeply up the side of the mountain.* ○ (*figurative*) *The value of the dollar climbed against the pound.*

IDM **climb/jump on the band wagon** ➪ **bandwagon** देखिए।

PHR V **climb down (over sth)** (*informal*) to admit that you have made a mistake; to change your opinion about sth in an argument अपनी ग़लती स्वीकारना; तर्क-वितर्क के बाद अपनी राय बदलना

**climb**[2] /klaɪm क्लाइम्/ *noun* [C] an act of climbing or a journey made by climbing चढ़ने की क्रिया या चढ़कर की गई यात्रा; चढ़ाई *The monastery could only be reached by a three-hour climb.*

**climbdown** /ˈklaɪmdaʊn ˈक्लाइम्डाउन्/ *noun* [C] an act of admitting you have been wrong; a change of opinion in an argument अपनी ग़लती स्वीकारने की क्रिया; तर्क-वितर्क के बाद अपनी राय बदलने की क्रिया

**climber** /ˈklaɪmə(r) ˈक्लाइम(र्)/ *noun* [C] a person who climbs mountains as a sport पर्वतारोही

**clinch** /klɪntʃ क्लिन्च्/ *verb* [T] (*informal*) to finally manage to get what you want in an argument or business agreement व्यापारिक सौदे या विवाद में फ़ैसला अंततः अपने पक्ष में निश्चित करने में सफल होना *to clinch a deal*

**cline** /klaɪn क्लाइन्/ *noun* [C] a continuous series of things, in which each one is only slightly different from the things next to it, but the last is very different from the first वस्तुओं की शृंखला जिसमें सन्निकट वस्तुएँ एक-दूसरे से बहुत मामूली रूप से भिन्न होती हैं परंतु पहली वस्तु और अंतिम वस्तु में बहुत अंतर होता है

**cling** /klɪŋ क्लिङ्/ *verb* [I] (*pt, pp* **clung** /klʌŋ क्लङ्/) **1 cling (on) to sb/sth; cling together** to hold on tightly to sb/sth चिपकना, लिपटना, जुड़े रहना *She clung to the rope with all her strength.* **2 cling (on) to sth** to continue to believe sth, often when it is not reasonable to do so प्रायः असंगत विश्वास या आस्था बनाए रखना *They were still clinging to the hope that the girl would be found alive.* **3 cling to sb/sth** to stick firmly to sth मज़बूती से चिपक या जुड़ जाना *His wet clothes clung to him.* ▸ **clingy** *adj.* चिपके हुए *a clingy child* (= that does not want to leave its parents) ○ *a clingy sweater*

**cling film** *noun* [U] thin transparent plastic used for covering food to keep it fresh महीन पारदर्शी प्लास्टिक जिस से भोज्य पदार्थों को ढका जाता है (उन्हें ताज़ा रखने के लिए)

**clinic** /ˈklɪnɪk ˈक्लिनिक्/ *noun* [C] **1** a small hospital or a part of a hospital where you go to receive special medical treatment विशेष चिकित्सा उपलब्ध करने वाला छोटा अस्पताल या बड़े अस्पताल का एक भाग; क्लीनिक *a private clinic* ○ *a dental clinic* **2** a time when a doctor sees patients and gives special treatment or advice विशेष चिकित्सा या चिकित्सीय परामर्श का समय

**clinical** /ˈklɪnɪkl ˈक्लिनिक्ल्/ *adj.* **1** connected with the examination and treatment of patients at a clinic or hospital किसी क्लीनिक या अस्पताल में रोगियों की परीक्षण और चिकित्सा से संबंधित; नैदानिक-उपचारात्मक *Clinical trials of the new drug have proved successful.* **2** (used about a person) cold and not emotional (व्यक्ति) शुष्क, रूखा और भावनाशून्य

**clinically** /ˈklɪnɪkli ˈक्लिनिक्लि/ *adv.* **1** according to medical examination चिकित्सीय परीक्षण के अनुसार; नैदानिक रूप से *to be clinically dead* **2** in a cold way; without showing any emotion रूखेपन से; भावशून्य होकर; भावुकता-रहित तरीक़े से

**clink** /klɪŋk क्लिङ्क्/ *noun* [*sing.*] the short sharp ringing sound that objects made of glass, metal, etc. make when they touch each other झनझनाहट *the clink of glasses* ▸ **clink** *verb* [I, T] झनझनाना

**clip**[1] /klɪp क्लिप्/ *noun* [C] **1** a small object, usually made of metal or plastic, used for holding things together वस्तुओं को एक साथ पकड़े रखने के लिए धातु या प्लास्टिक से बनी छोटी वस्तु; क्लिप *a paper clip* ○ *a hairclip* ➪ **stationery** पर चित्र देखिए। **2** a small section of a film that is shown so that people can see what the rest of the film is like (नमूने के तौर पर), पूरी फ़िल्म का छोटा अंश ➪ **trailer** देखिए। **3** (*informal*) a quick hit with the hand चपत, चुटकी या चिकोटी *She gave the boy a clip round the ear.* **4** the act of cutting sth to make it shorter किसी वस्तु को कतरने या काटकर छोटा करने की क्रिया *to cilp nails*

**clip**[2] /klɪp क्लिप्/ *verb* (**clipping; clipped**) **1** [I, T] to be fastened with a clip; to fasten sth to sth else with a clip क्लिप लगाना; क्लिप से बाँधना *Clip the photo to the letter, please.* **2** [T] to cut sth, especially by cutting small parts off काटना; छोटा करना (विशेषतः छोटे टुकड़ों को काटकर) *The hedge needs clipping.* **3** [T] to hit sb/sth quickly तेज़ी से टकराना *My wheel clipped the pavement and I fell off my bike.*

**clipboard** /ˈklɪpbɔːd ˈक्लिपबॉड्/ *noun* [C] **1** a small board with a part that holds papers at the top, used by sb who wants to write while standing or moving around क्लिपयुक्त बोर्ड जिसपर जमाकर रखे गए काग़ज़ों पर खड़ी अवस्था में या चलते हुए कुछ लिखा जा सकता है; क्लिपबोर्ड ➪ **stationery** पर चित्र देखिए। **2** (*computing*) a place where information from a computer file is stored for a short time until it is added to another file वह स्थान जहाँ एक कंप्यूटर फ़ाइल की सूचना अस्थायी रूप से, दूसरी फ़इल से जुड़ने तक, संचित रखी जाती है

**clippers** /ˈklɪpəz ˈक्लिपज़्/ *noun* [*pl.*] a small metal tool used for cutting things, for example hair or finger nails कतरनी, कैंची *a pair of nail clippers*

**clipping** /ˈklɪpɪŋ ˈक्लिपिङ्/ = **cutting**[1]

**clique** /kliːk क्लीक्/ *noun* [C] a small group of people with the same interests who do not want others to join their group समान रुचि वाले व्यक्तियों की छोटी मंडली जिसमें अन्य लोगों का प्रवेश अवांछनीय होता है; गुट

**clitoris** /ˈklɪtərɪs ˈक्लिटरिस्/ *noun* [C] the small part of the female sex organs which becomes larger when a woman is sexually excited स्त्री की योनि का एक अंश; भग-शिश्न

**cloak** /kləʊk क्लोक्/ *noun* **1** [C] a type of loose coat without sleeves that was more common in former times बिना बाहों का ढीला कोट जो पुराने समय में पहना जाता था; लबादा ➪ **cape** देखिए। **2** a thing that hides sth else छुपाने वाली वस्तु; आवरण *a cloak of mist*

**cloakroom** /ˈkləʊkruːm ˈक्लोक्रूम्/ *noun* [C] a room near the entrance to a building where you can leave your coat, bags, etc. अमानती सामानघर

**clobber** /ˈklɒbə(r) ˈक्लॉब(र्)/ *verb* [T] (*informal*) to hit sb hard बुरी तरह मारना या पीटना

**clock**[1] /klɒk क्लॉक्/ *noun* [C] **1** an instrument that shows you what time it is घड़ी *an alarm clock* ○ *a church clock* ➪ **watch** देखिए। **2** an instrument in a car that measures how far it has travelled यात्रा में तय की गई दूरी मापने का उपकरण *My car has got 10,000 kilometres on the clock.*

**IDM** **against the clock** if you do sth against the clock, you do it fast in order to finish before a certain time निर्धारित लक्ष्य को (समय रहते) अतिशीघ्र प्राप्त करना *It was a race against the clock to get the building work finished on time.*

**around/round the clock** all day and all night दिन-रात *They are working round the clock to repair the bridge.*

**put the clock/clocks forward/back** to change the time, usually by one hour, at the beginning/end of summer ऋतु के अनुसार समय आगे-पीछे करना

**clock**[2] /klɒk क्लॉक्/ *verb*

**PHR V** **clock in/on; clock off** to record the time that you arrive at or leave work, especially by putting a card into a type of clock कार्यालय आदि में लगी एक विशेष प्रकार की घड़ी में कार्ड डालकर आने-जाने का समय दर्ज करना

**clock sth up** to achieve a certain number or total कोई विशेष संख्या या योग प्राप्त करना; संख्यात्मक परिमाण दिखाना *Our car clocked up over 1000 kilometres while we were on holiday.*

**clockwise** /ˈklɒkwaɪz ˈक्लॉक्वाइज़्/ *adv., adj.* in the same direction as the hands of a clock घड़ी की सूइयों की अनुकूल दिशा में, दाहिनी परिक्रमा, दक्षिणावर्त *Turn the handle clockwise.* ○ *to move in a clockwise direction* ✪ विलोम (*BrE*) **anticlockwise**, (*AmE*) **counter-clockwise**

**clockwork** /ˈklɒkwɜːk ˈक्लॉक्वक्/ *noun* [U] a type of machinery found in certain toys, etc. that you operate by turning a key कुछ खिलौनों में लगी एक विशेष प्रकार की मशीन जिसे चाबी घुमाकर चलाते हैं *a clockwork toy* ○ *The plan went* ***like clockwork*** (= smoothly and without any problem).

**clog**[1] /klɒg क्लॉग्/ *noun* [C] a type of shoe made completely of wood or with a thick wooden base पूर्णतया लकड़ी से बना या लकड़ी से बने मोटे तले वाला एक प्रकार का जूता

**clog**[2] /klɒg क्लॉग्/ *verb* [I, T] (**clogging; clogged**) **clog** (**sth**) (**up**) (**with sth**) to block or become blocked अवरुद्ध हो जाना या कर देना *The drain is always clogging up.* ○ *The roads were clogged with traffic.*

**cloister** /ˈklɔɪstə(r) ˈक्लॉइस्ट(र्)/ *noun* [C, *usually pl.*] a covered passage with arches around a square garden, usually forming part of a large church (**cathedral**) or building where religious people live (**monastery** or **convent**) चौकोर उद्यान के चारों ओर का मेहराबदार आच्छादित पथ (प्रायः चर्च, मठ आदि धार्मिक स्थलों में)

**clone** /kləʊn क्लोन्/ *noun* [C] an exact copy of a plant or animal that is produced from one of its cells by scientific methods किसी पौधे या पशु की कोशिका से वैज्ञानिक पद्धति द्वारा बनी उसकी एकदम सही अनुकृति ▶ **clone** *verb* [T] वैज्ञानिक पद्धति के प्रयोग से किसी पौधे या पशु की सही अनुकृति बनाना *A team from the UK were the first to successfully clone an animal.*

**close**[1] /kləʊz क्लोज़्/ *verb* [I, T] **1** to shut बंद करना या होना *The door closed quietly. I've got a surprise.* **2** to be, or to make sth, not open to the public जनता के लिए बंद होना या करना *What time do the shops close? ○ The police have closed the road to traffic.* **3** to end or to bring sth to an end समाप्त करना, बंद करना *The meeting closed at 10 p.m. ○ Detectives have closed the case on the missing girl.* ✪ विलोम **open**

PHR V **close (sth) down** to stop all business or work permanently at a shop or factory दुकान या कारख़ाने को स्थायी रूप से बंद कर देना *The factory has had to close down. ○ Health inspectors have closed the restaurant down.*

**close in (on sb/sth)** to come nearer and gradually surround sb/sth, especially in order to attack किसी के निकट आकर क्रमशः उसे घेर लेना, विशेषतः उस पर हमला करने के लिए

**close sth off** to prevent people from entering a place or an area किसी स्थान में लोगों का प्रवेश अवरुद्ध करना *The police closed off the city centre because of a bomb alert.*

**close**[2] /kləʊz क्लोज़्/ *noun* [*sing.*] the end, especially of a period of time or an activity समाप्ति विशेषतः किसी विशिष्ट अवधि या गतिविधि की) *the close of trading on the stock market*

IDM **bring sth/come/draw to a close** to end समाप्त करना या होना *The chairman brought the meeting to a close. ○ The guests began to leave as the evening drew to a close.*

**close**[3] /kləʊs क्लोज़्/ *adj., adv.* **1** (*not before a noun*) **close (to sb/sth); close (together)** near के पास; निकट, समीप *to follow close behind someone ○ I held her close* (= tightly). **2** (used about a friend, etc.) known very well and liked (मित्र आदि) घनिष्ठ, चिर-परिचित और प्यारा *They invited only close friends to the wedding.* **3** near in a family relationship (संबंधी) निकट का *a close relative* **4** (used about a competition, etc.) only won by a small amount (किसी खेल, प्रतियोगिता आदि में) बहुत कम अंतर से जीता हुआ *a close match* ➪ **near**[1] पर नोट देखिए। **5** careful; thorough सावधान, सूक्ष्म; संपूर्ण *On close examination, you could see that the banknote was a forgery.* **6** (used about the weather, etc.) heavy and with little movement of air (मौसम आदि) घुटनभरा *It's so close today that there might be a storm.* ▶ **closely** *adv.* निकटता से *to watch sb closely ○ The insect closely resembles a stick.* ▶ **closeness** *noun* [U] निकटता

IDM **a close shave/thing** a bad thing that almost happened (ख़तरे से) बाल-बाल बचने की स्थिति *I wasn't injured, but it was a close shave.*

**at close quarters** at or from a position that is very near बहुत निकटता से

**close by (sb/sth)** at a short distance from sb/sth बहुत पास *She lives close by.*

**close/near/dear to sb's heart** ➪ **heart** देखिए।

**close on** nearly; almost के आस-पास; लगभग *He was born close on a hundred years ago.*

**close up (to sb/sth)** at or from a very short distance to sb/sth किसी के काफ़ी पास; काफ़ी पास से

**come close (to sth/to doing sth)** to almost do sth कोई काम लगभग कर डालना *We didn't win but we came close.*

**closed** /kləʊzd क्लोज़्ड्/ *adj.* not open; shut बंद *Keep your mouth closed. ○ The supermarket is closed.* ✪ विलोम **open**

**closed-circuit television** (*abbr.* **CCTV**) *noun* [U] a type of television system used inside a building, for example a shop, to protect it from crime अपराध पर नियंत्रण रखने के लिए किसी भवन में लगाई गई एक प्रकार की टेलीविज़न-व्यवस्था

**closet** /ˈklɒzɪt ˈक्लॉज़िट्/ *noun* [C] a large cupboard that is built into a room कमरे में लगी बड़ी अलमारी

**close-up** /ˈkləʊsʌp ˈक्लोस्अप्/ *noun* [C] a photograph or film of sb/sth that you take from a very short distance away बहुत पास से लिया गया फ़ोटोचित्र

**closing**[1] /ˈkləʊzɪŋ ˈक्लोज़िङ्/ *adj.* (*only before a noun*) coming at the end of a speech, a period of time or an activity किसी भाषण, अवधि या गतिविधि के अंत में; अंतिम *his closing remarks ○ The football season is now in its closing stages.* ✪ विलोम **opening**

**closing**[2] /ˈkləʊzɪŋ ˈक्लोज़िङ्/ *noun* [U] the act of permanently shutting sth such as a factory, hospital, school, etc. किसी कारख़ाने, अस्पताल, पाठशाला आदि को स्थायी रूप से बंद करने की क्रिया *the closing of the local school* ✪ विलोम **opening**

**closing time** *noun* [C] the time when a shop, etc. closes दुकान आदि के बंद होने का समय

**closure** /ˈkləʊʒə(r) ˈक्लोश़(र्)/ *noun* [C, U] the permanent closing, for example of a business स्थायी समाप्ति (जैसे किसी व्यापार की); समापन

**clot**[1] /klɒtm क्लॉट्/ *noun* [C] a lump formed by blood as it dries ख़ून का थक्का *They removed a blood clot from his brain.*

**clot**[2] /klɒt क्लॉट्/ *verb* [I, T] (**clotting; clotted**) to form or cause blood to form thick lumps ख़ून का थक्का बनना या बनाना *a drug that stops blood from clotting during operations*

**cloth** /klɒθ क्लॉथ़्/ *noun* **1** [U] a material made of cotton, wool, etc. that you use for making clothes, curtains, etc. (सूत, ऊन आदि से बना) कपड़ा जिससे वस्त्र, परदे आदि बनते हैं *a metre of cloth* **2** [C] (*pl.* **cloths** /klɒθs क्लॉथ़्स्/) a piece of material that you use for a particular purpose विशेष प्रयोजन के लिए प्रयुक्त कपड़े का टुकड़ा *a tablecloth* ○ *Where can I find a cloth to wipe this water up?*

**clothe** /kləʊð क्लोद्/ *verb* [T] to provide clothes for sb कपड़े पहनाना *to feed and clothe a child*

**clothed** /kləʊðd क्लोद्ड्/ *adj.* **clothed (in sth)** dressed; wearing sth कुछ पहने हुए *He was clothed in leather from head to foot.*

**clothes** /kləʊðz क्लोद्ज़्/ *noun* [*pl.*] the things that you wear, for example trousers, shirts, dresses, coats, etc. पोशाक, परिधान, पहनावा *Take off those wet clothes.* ○ *She was wearing new clothes.*

**NOTE** ध्यान दें! शब्द **clothes** हमेशा बहुवचन में प्रयुक्त होता है। यदि किसी एक पहनावे का संकेत करना हो तो **item/piece/article of clothing** का प्रयोग किया जाता है—*A kilt is an item of clothing worn in Scotland.* ➪ **garment** देखिए।

**clothes-hanger** = **hanger**

**clothes line** *noun* [C] a thin rope that you hang clothes on so that they can dry कपड़े सुखाने की डोरी, अलगनी

**clothes peg** (*AmE* **clothes pin**) = **peg**[1] **3**

**clothing** /ˈkləʊðɪŋ ˈक्लोदिङ्/ *noun* [U] the clothes that you wear, especially for a particular activity विशेष अवसर की पोशाक *waterproof/outdoor/winter clothing* **NOTE** **Clothes** की अपेक्षा **clothing** अधिक औपचारिक शब्द है।

**cloud**[1] /klaʊd क्लाउड्/ *noun* **1** [C, U] a mass of very small drops of water that floats in the sky and is usually white or grey बादल *The sun disappeared behind a cloud.* ○ *A band of thick cloud is spreading from the west.* **2** [C] a mass of smoke, dust, sand, etc. धुआँ, धूल, रेत आदि का गुबार *Clouds of smoke were pouring from the burning building.*

**IDM** **every cloud has a silver lining** even a very bad situation has a positive or hopeful side निराशापूर्ण स्थिति में भी आशा की किरण होती है

**under a cloud** with the disapproval of the people around you उपेक्षा या तिरस्कार की स्थिति में *She left her job under a cloud because she'd been accused of stealing.*

**cloud**[2] /klaʊd क्लाउड्/ *verb* **1** [I, T] to become or make sth difficult to see through धुँधला करना या हो जाना *His eyes clouded with tears.* **2** [T] to make sth less clear or easy to understand अस्पष्ट या दुर्बोध बनाना *Her personal involvement in the case was beginning to* ***cloud her judgement.*** **3** [T] to make sth less enjoyable; to spoil मज़ा कम कर देना; कम आनंददायक बना देना दूषित कर देना *Illness has clouded the last few years of his life.*

**PHRV** **cloud over** (used about the sky) to become full of clouds (आकाश का) मेघाच्छन्न हो जाना; बादलों से ढक जाना

**cloudburst** /ˈklaʊdbɜːst ˈक्लाउड्बस्ट्/ *noun* [C] a sudden heavy fall of rain एकाएक मूसलाधार वर्षा

**cloudless** /ˈklaʊdləs ˈक्लाउड्लस्/ *adj.* (used about the sky, etc.) clear; without any clouds (आकाश) साफ़, मेघहीन

**cloudy** /ˈklaʊdi ˈक्लाउडि/ *adj.* **1** (used about the sky, etc.) full of clouds (आकाश) मेघाच्छन्न; बादलों से ढका **2** (used about liquids, etc.) not clear (पानी या अन्य द्रव) गंदा, गँदला *cloudy water*

**clout** /klaʊt क्लाउट्/ *noun* (*informal*) **1** [C] a hard hit, usually with the hand ज़ोरदार प्रहार, सामान्यतः हाथों द्वारा *to give someone a clout* **2** [U] influence and power प्रभाव और शक्ति *He's an important man—he has a lot of clout in the company.*

**clove** /kləʊv क्लोव्/ *noun* [C] **1** the small dried flower of a tropical tree, used to give a special flavour in cooking लौंग (मसाला) **2** one of the small separate sections into which the root of the **garlic** plant is divided लहसुन की फाँक

**cloven hoof** *noun* [C] the foot of an animal such as a cow or a sheep, that is divided into two parts फटा खुर (जैसे गाय या भेड़ का); द्विशफ

**clover** /ˈkləʊvə(r) ˈक्लोव़(र्)/ *noun* [C] a small plant with pink or white flowers and leaves with three parts to them एक छोटा पौधा जिसके फूल गुलाबी या सफ़ेद होते हैं और पत्ते तीन भागों में विभक्त होते हैं; तिपतिया

**NOTE** कभी-कभी चार भागों में विभक्त पत्तों वाला तिपतिया भी मिल जाता है, ऐसे पौधे का मिलना अत्यंत सौभाग्य प्रद माना जाता है।

**clown**[1] /klaʊn क्लाउन्/ *noun* [C] **1** a person who wears funny clothes and a big red nose and does silly things to make people (especially children) laugh मसख़रा, जोकर **2** a person who makes jokes and does silly things to make the people around him/her laugh मसख़रा, विदूषक *At school, Amit was always the class clown.*

**clown[2]** /klaʊn क्लाउन् / *verb* [I] **clown (about/around)** to act in a funny or foolish way मसख़रापन या मूर्खता दिखाना *Stop clowning around and get some work done!*

**cloying** /ˈklɔɪɪŋ ˈक्लॉइइङ् / *adj.* (*formal*) **1** (used about food, a smell, etc.) so sweet that it is unpleasant बहुत अधिक मीठा और इस कारण अप्रिय (भोजन, गंध आदि) **2** using emotion in a very obvious way, so that the result is unpleasant भावनाओं का इस तरह स्पष्ट प्रदर्शन करते हुए कि परिणाम अप्रिय हो *Her novels are full of cloying sentimentality.*

**club[1]** /klʌb क्लब् / *noun* **1** [C] a group of people who meet regularly to share an interest, do sport, etc.; the place where they meet समान रुचि वाले व्यक्तियों की मंडली; इस मंडली का मिलन-स्थल; क्लब *to be a member of a club ○ a tennis/football/golf club* **2** (*also* **nightclub**) [C] a place where you can go to dance and drink late at night रात्रिकालीन मनोरंजन का स्थान; नाइट-क्लब **3** [C] a heavy stick, usually with one end that is thicker than the other, used as a weapon भारी डंडा जो सामान्यतः एक ओर से अधिक मोटा होता है; गदा, मुगदर **4** [C] a long stick that is specially shaped at one end and used for hitting a ball when playing golf गोल्फ़ के खेल में गेंद को मारने के लिए प्रयुक्त लंबी छड़ी ➪ **bat, racket** और **stick** देखिए। **5 clubs** [*pl.*] the group (**suit**) of playing cards with black shapes with three leaves on them ताश के पत्तों में चिड़ी के पत्ते *the two/ace/queen of clubs* ➪ **card** पर नोट देखिए। **6** [C] one of the cards from this suit चिड़ी के पत्तों में से कोई एक *I played a club.*

**club[2]** /klʌb क्लब् / *verb* (**clubbing; clubbed**) **1** [T] to hit sb/sth hard with a heavy object किसी पर भारी वस्तु से प्रहार करना **2** [I] **go clubbing** to go dancing and drinking in a club नृत्य और मदिरापान के लिए क्लब में जाना *She goes clubbing every Saturday.*

**PHR V** **club together (to do sth)** to share the cost of sth, for example a present किसी वस्तु (जैसे उपहार) की लागत में भागीदारी करना, हिस्सा बटाना *We clubbed together to buy him a leaving present.*

**cluck** /klʌk क्लक् / *noun* [C] the noise made by a chicken चूज़े की आवाज़, कुट-कुट, किड़-किड़ ▶ **cluck** *verb* [I] चूज़े जैसी आवाज़ निकालना, कुटकुटाना, किड़-किड़ करना

**clue** /kluː क्लू / *noun* [C] **a clue (to sth)** a piece of information that helps you solve a problem or a crime, answer a question, etc. अपराध या समस्या की गुत्थी सुलझने, प्रश्न का उत्तर पाने आदि का सूत्र, सुराग़ *The police were looking for clues to his disappearance. ○ the clues for solving a crossword puzzle*

**IDM** **not have a clue** (*informal*) to know nothing about sth किसी विषय आदि पर कोई जानकारी न होना; अता-पता न होना

**clued-up** /ˌkluːdˈʌp ˌक्लूड् ˈअप् / (*AmE* **clued-in**) *adj.* **clued-up (on sth)** knowing a lot about sth किसी विषय पर काफ़ी अधिक जानकारी होना *I'm not really clued-up on the technical details.*

**clueless** /ˈkluːləs ˈक्लूलस् / *adj.* (*informal*) not able to understand; stupid समझने में असफल; ग़ैर-जानकार; मूर्ख, अज्ञानी *I'm absolutely clueless about computers.*

**clump** /klʌmp क्लम्प् / *noun* [C] a small group of plants or trees growing together झुरमुट

**clumsy** /ˈklʌmzi ˈक्लम्ज़ि / *adj.* (**clumsier; clumsiest**) **1** (used about a person) careless and likely to knock into, drop or break things (व्यक्ति) लापरवाह और बेढंगे तरीक़े से काम करने वाला; फूहड़, भद्दा *She undid the parcel with clumsy fingers.* **2** (used about a comment, etc.) likely to upset or offend people (कथन, टिप्पणी आदि) किसी को नाराज़ या किसी की भावनाओं को ठेस पहुँचा सकने वाला; बेढंगा *He made a clumsy apology.* **3** large, difficult to use, and not attractive in design बड़ा, असुविधाजनक और बेढंगा *a clumsy piece of furniture* ▶ **clumsily** *adv.* बेढंगे से ▶ **clumsiness** *noun* [U] बेढंगापन

**clung** ➪ **cling** का past tense और past participle रूप

**clunk** /klʌŋk क्लङ्क् / *noun* [C] a short low sound made when two hard objects hit each other दो कड़ी वस्तुओं के टकराने से उत्पन्न खटखटाहट या झनझनाहट *The car door shut with a clunk.*

**cluster[1]** /ˈklʌstə(r) ˈक्लस्टर्(र्) / *noun* [C] a group of people, plants or things that stand or grow close together (व्यक्तियों, पौधों या वस्तुओं का) झुंड, समूह, गुच्छा

**cluster[2]** /ˈklʌstə(r) ˈक्लस्टर्(र्) / *verb*

**PHR V** **cluster around sb/sth** to form a group around sb/sth किसी के चारों ओर एकत्र होना; झुंड बनाना *The tourists clustered around their guide.*

**clutch[1]** /klʌtʃ क्लच् / *verb* [T] to hold sth tightly, especially because you are in pain, afraid or excited किसी वस्तु को मज़बूती से पकड़ लेना (विशेषतः दर्द, डर या उत्तेजना के कारण) *The child clutched his mother's hand in fear.*

**PHR V** **clutch at sth** to try to take hold of sth किसी वस्तु को पकड़े रखने की कोशिश करना *She clutched at the money but the wind blew it away.*

**clutch[2]** /klʌtʃ क्लच् / *noun* **1** [C] the part of a vehicle, etc. that you press with your foot when you are driving in order to change the **gear** the part of the engine that it is connected to वाहन का वह पुरज़ा जिसे गियर बदलने के लिए पैर से दबाया जाता है; क्लच; इंजिन का वह भाग जिससे क्लच जुड़ा रहता है *to press/release the clutch* ➪ **car** पर चित्र देखिए। **2 clutches** [*pl.*] power or control over sb किसी व्यक्ति पर अधिकार या नियंत्रण; शिकंजा, चंगुल, पकड़, काबू *He fell **into** the enemy's **clutches**.*

**clutter[1]** /ˈklʌtə(r) ˈक्लट(र्)/ *noun* [U] things that are where they are not wanted or needed and make a place untidy अस्तव्यस्त रूप से बिखरी वस्तुएँ *Who left all this clutter on the floor?* ▶ **cluttered** *adj.* अस्तव्यस्त, अव्यवस्थित *a cluttered desk*

**clutter[2]** /ˈklʌtə(r) ˈक्लट(र्)/ *verb* [T] **clutter sth (up)** to cover or fill sth with lots of objects in an untidy way बेढंगेपन से बहुत सारी वस्तुएँ फैला या डाल देना

**cm** *abbr.* centimetre(s) सेंटीमीटर

**Co.** *abbr.* company कंपनी

**c/o** *abbr.* care of, 'c/o' का प्रयोग किसी ऐसे व्यक्ति के पते में किया जाता है जो किसी अन्य व्यक्ति के घर पर निवास कर रहा है *Rita Khanna c/o Mrs Banerjee*

**co-** /kəʊ को/ *prefix* (*in adjectives, adverbs, nouns and verbs*) together with के साथ, सह- *co-pilot* ○ *coexist*

**coach[1]** /kəʊtʃ कोच्/ *noun* [C] **1** a person who trains people to compete in certain sports खेल प्रशिक्षक; कोच *a tennis coach* **2** a comfortable bus used for long journeys लंबी यात्रा के लिए प्रयुक्त आरामदेह बस *It's cheaper to travel **by coach** than by train.* **3** = **carriage1** **4** a large vehicle with four wheels pulled by horses, used in the past for carrying passengers पूर्व समय में यात्रियों के वहन के लिए प्रयुक्त चार पहियों वाली घोड़ा-गाड़ी, बग्घी ➪ **carriage** और **car** देखिए।

**coach[2]** /kəʊtʃ कोच्/ *verb* [I, T] **coach sb (in/for sth)** to train or teach sb, especially to compete in a sport or pass an exam विशेषतः खेल-स्पर्धा या परीक्षा के लिए किसी को प्रशिक्षण देना

**coaching** /ˈkəʊtʃɪŋ ˈकोचिङ्/ *noun* [U] **1** the process of training sb to play a sport, to do a job better or to improve a skill प्रशिक्षण देने की प्रक्रिया **2** the process of giving a student extra teaching in a particular subject किसी छात्र को विषय-विशेष के लिए अतिरिक्त प्रशिक्षण देने की क्रिया

**coagulate** /kəʊˈægjuleɪt कोˈऐग्युलेट्/ *verb* [I] (used about a liquid) to become thick and partly solid (द्रव पदार्थ का) गाढ़ा और कुछ ठोस हो जाना, जम जाना; स्कंदन होना *The blood was starting to coagulate inside the cut.* ▶ **coagulation** /kəʊˌægjuˈleɪʃn कोˌऐग्युˈलेश्न्/ *noun* [U] जमाव; स्कंदन

**coal** /kəʊl कोल्/ *noun* **1** [U] a type of black mineral that is dug (**mined**) from the ground and burned to give heat कोयला जिसे खान से निकाला जाता है *a lump of coal* ○ *a coal fire* **2 coals** [*pl.*] burning pieces of coal जलते हुए कोयले के टुकड़े

**coalesce** /ˌkəʊəˈles ˌकोअˈलेस्/ *verb* [I] **coalesce (into/with sth)** (*formal*) to come together to form one larger group, substance, etc. (अनेक इकाइयों का) एक बड़ी इकाई हो जाना; संलीन या सम्मिलित होना ▶ **coalescence** *noun* [U] सम्मिलन, संलयन

**coalface** /ˈkəʊlfeɪs ˈकोल्फ़ेस्/ *noun* [C] the place deep inside a mine where the coal is cut out of the rock कोयले की खान के अंदर खनन-स्थल; वह स्थान जहाँ पर चट्टान से कोयला काटकर निकाला जाता है

**coalition** /ˌkəʊəˈlɪʃn ˌकोअˈलिश्न्/ *noun* [C, *with sing. or pl. verb*] a government formed by two or more political parties working together गठबंधन सरकार *a coalition between the Congress and the Left parties*

**coal mine** (*also* **pit**) *noun* [C] a place, usually underground, where coal is dug from the ground कोयले की खान ➪ **colliery** देखिए।

**coal miner** (*also* **miner**) *noun* [C] a person whose job is to dig coal from the ground कोयला-खनिक, खान-मज़दूर

**coarse** /kɔːs कॉस्/ *adj.* **1** consisting of large pieces; rough, not smooth मोटे ढेलों वाला; खुरदुरा *coarse salt* ○ *coarse cloth* ✪ विलोम **fine** **2** (used about a person or his/her behaviour) rude, likely to offend people; having bad manners (व्यक्ति या उसका व्यवहार) रूखा; असभ्य ▶ **coarsely** *adv.* बड़े टुकड़ों में; रूखेपन से *Chop the onion coarsely* (= into pieces which are not too small). ○ *He laughed coarsely.*

**coarsen** /ˈkɔːsn ˈकॉस्न्/ *verb* [I, T] to become or to make sth coarse मोटा; खुरदुरा या रूखा हो जाना या बना देना

**coast[1]** /kəʊst कोस्ट्/ *noun* [C] the area of land that is next to or close to the sea समुद्रतट *After sailing for an hour we could finally see the coast.* ○ *Chennai is **on the** east **coast**.*

**coast[2]** /kəʊst कोस्ट्/ *verb* [I] **1** to travel in a car, on a bicycle, etc. (especially down a hill) without using power बिना इंजन की शक्ति के कार या साइकिल से लुढ़कते हुए जाना (विशेषतः पहाड़ी पर नीचे की ओर) **2** to achieve sth without much effort बिना अधिक प्रयास के प्राप्त कर लेना *They coasted to victory.*

**coastal** /ˈkəʊstl ˈकोस्ट्ल्/ *adj.* on or near a coast तटीय, तटवर्ती *coastal areas* ➪ **erode** पर चित्र देखिए।

**coastguard** /ˈkəʊstgɑːd ˈकोस्ट्गाड्/ *noun* [C] a person or group of people whose job is to watch the sea near the coast in order to help people or ships that are in danger or to stop illegal activities तटरक्षक

**coastline** /ˈkəʊstlaɪn ˈकोस्ट्लाइन्/ *noun* [C] the edge or shape of a coast तट-रेखा *a rocky coastline*

**coat**[1] /kəʊt कोट्/ *noun* [C] **1** a piece of clothing that you wear over your other clothes to keep warm when you are outside ठंड से बचने के लिए अन्य कपड़ों के ऊपर पहना जाने वाला वस्त्र; कोट *Put your coat on—it's cold outside.* ➪ **overcoat** और **raincoat** देखिए। **2** a piece of clothing that covers the top part of your body and is worn as part of suit; **jacket 1** सूट का वह भाग जो शरीर के ऊपरी भाग पर पहना जाता है; कोट **3** the fur or hair covering an animal's body पशु के शरीर पर के बाल; पशु की बालों वाली खाल *a dog with a smooth coat* **4** a layer of sth covering a surface सतह को ढकने वाली तह; अस्तर, विलेपन *The walls will probably need two coats of paint.*

**coat**[2] /kəʊt कोट्/ *verb* [T] **coat sth (with/in sth)** to cover sth with a layer of sth किसी वस्तु पर परत या तह चढ़ाना; लेपना, लेप लगाना *biscuits coated with milk chocolate*

**coat hanger** = **hanger**

**coating** /ˈkəʊtɪŋ ˈकोटिङ्/ *noun* [C] a thin layer of sth that covers sth else परत, लेप, आवरण *wire with a plastic coating*

**coat of arms** (*pl.* **coats of arms**) (*also* **arms**) *noun* [C] a design that is used as the symbol of a family, a town, a university, etc. कुल, नगर, विद्यापीठ आदि का प्रतीक चिह्न

**coax** /kəʊks कोक्स्/ *verb* [T] **coax sb (into/out of sth/doing sth); coax sth out of/from sb** to persuade sb gently ख़ुशामद, प्रेम आदि से राज़ी करवाना; फुसलाना *The child wasn't hungry, but his mother coaxed him into eating a little.* ○ *At last he coaxed a smile out of her.*

**cobalt** /ˈkəʊbɔːlt ˈकोबॉल्ट्/ *noun* [U] **1** (*symbol* **Co**) a hard silver-white metal that is often mixed with other metals and used to give a deep blue-green colour to glass कड़ी चाँदी जैसी सफ़ेद धातु जिसे अन्य धातुओं में मिलाकर शीशे को गहरा नीला-हरा रँगा जाता है; कोबाल्ट **2** (*also* **cobalt blue**) a deep blue-green colour गहरा नीला-हरा रंग

**cobble** /ˈkɒbl ˈकॉब्ल्/ *verb*

**PHR V** **cobble sth together** to make sth or put sth together quickly and without much care जल्दी में और बिना अधिक ध्यान दिए कुछ बनाना

**cobbler** /ˈkɒblə(r) ˈकॉब्ल(र्)/ *noun* [C] (*old-fashioned*) a person who repairs shoes मोची

**cobbles** /ˈkɒblz ˈकॉब्ल्ज़्/ (**cobblestones** /ˈkɒblstəʊnz ˈकॉब्ल्स्टोन्ज़्/) *noun* [*pl.*] small rounded stones used (in the past) for covering the surface of streets (पूर्व समय में) सड़क की सतह को ढकने के लिए प्रयुक्त छोटे गोल पत्थर ▶ **cobbled** *adj.* (सड़क आदि) छोटे गोल पत्थरों से ढकी

**cobra** /ˈkəʊbrə ˈकोब्रा/ *noun* [C] a poisonous snake that can spread out the skin at the back of its neck. Cobras live in Asia and Africa ऐशिया और अफ़्रीक़ा में पाया जाने वाला फनदार विषैला साँप; नाग, कोबरा ➪ **reptile** पर चित्र देखिए।

**cobweb** /ˈkɒbweb ˈकॉब्वेब्/ *noun* [C] a net of threads made by a spider in order to catch insects मकड़ी का जाला ➪ **web 1** देखिए।

**cocaine** /kəʊˈkeɪn कोˈकेन्/ (*informal* **coke**) *noun* [U] a dangerous drug that some people take for pleasure but which is **addictive** एक ख़तरनाक नशीला पदार्थ; कोकेन

**coccyx** /ˈkɒksɪks ˈकॉक्सिक्स्/ *noun* [C] the small bone at the bottom of the bones of your back (**spine**) रीढ़ की हड्डी के अधोभाग की छोटी हड्डी; अनुत्रिक ➪ **body** पर चित्र देखिए।

**cochineal** /ˌkɒtʃɪˈniːl ˌकॉचिˈनील्/ *noun* [U] a bright red substance used to give colour to food खाद्य पदार्थों में रंग के लिए डाला जाने वाला लाल चमकदार पदार्थ; क़िरमिज़

**cochlea** /ˈkɒkliə ˈकॉक्लिआ/ *noun* [C] the part of the inside of your ear (**inner ear**), which is shaped like a shell and is very important for hearing सीपी के आकार का कान के अंदर का भाग जो सुनने में विशेष सहायक होता है; कर्णावर्त

**cock**[1] /kɒk कॉक्/ *noun* [C] **1** (*AmE* **rooster**) an adult male chicken मुरग़ा ➪ **chicken** पर नोट देखिए। **2** an adult male bird of any type किसी भी जाति का वयस्क नर पक्षी

**cock**[2] /kɒk कॉक्/ *verb* [T] to hold up a part of the body शरीर के किसी भाग को ऊपर उठाना *The horse cocked its ears on hearing the noise.*

**PHR V** **cock sth up** (*slang*) to do sth very badly and spoil sth काम ख़राब कर देना ➪ **cock-up** देखिए।

**cock-a-doodle-doo** /ˌkɒk ə ˌduːdl ˈduː ˌकॉक् अˌडूड्ल् ˈडू/ *noun* [*sing.*] the noise made by an adult male chicken (**cock**) मुरग़े की आवाज़, कुकड़ूँ-कूँ

**cockatoo** /ˌkɒkəˈtuː ˌकॉकˈटू/ *noun* [C] (*pl.* **cockatoos**) a large brightly coloured bird with a lot of feathers standing up on top of its head एक कलग़ीदार रंग-बिरंगा बड़ा पक्षी; काकातुआ

**cockerel** /ˈkɒkərəl ˈकॉकरल्/ *noun* [C] a young male chicken नर चूज़ा

**cockle** /ˈkɒkl ˈकॉक्ल्/ *noun* [C] a small **shellfish** that can be eaten एक प्रकार की छोटी शंखमीन जिसे खाया जा सकता है

**cockpit** /ˈkɒkpɪt ˈकॉक्पिट्/ *noun* [C] **1** the part of a plane where the pilot sits विमान में चालक के बैठने का स्थान; कॉकपिट **2** the part of a racing car where the driver sits रेसिंग कार में चालक का स्थान

**cockroach** /ˈkɒkrəʊtʃ ˈकॉक्रोच्/ (*AmE* **roach**) *noun* [C] a large dark brown insect, usually found in dirty or slightly wet places एक बड़ा, गहरे भूरे रंग का कीड़ा जो प्रायः गंदी और गीली जगहों पर मिलता है; तिलचट्टा ➪ **insect** पर चित्र देखिए।

**cocktail** /ˈkɒkteɪl ˈकॉक्टेल्/ *noun* [C] **1** a drink made from a mixture of alcoholic drinks and fruit juices मादक पेय और फलों के रस के मिश्रण से बना पेय पदार्थ; मिश्रित पेय *a cocktail bar/party* **2** a mixture of small pieces of food that is served cold भोज्य पदार्थों के छोटे टुकड़ों का मिश्रण जो ठंडा परोसा जाता है *a prawn cocktail* **3** a mixture of different substances, usually ones that do not mix together well प्रायः उन विभिन्न पदार्थों का मिश्रण जो अच्छे से मिश्रित नहीं होते *a lethal cocktail of drugs*

**cock-up** *noun* [C] (*slang*) something that was badly done; a mistake that spoils sth बेढंगेपन से किया काम; काम बिगाड़ देने वाली ग़लती ➪ **cock**[2] देखिए।

**cocoa** /ˈkəʊkəʊ ˈकोको/ *noun* **1** [U] a dark brown powder made from the seeds of a tropical tree and used in making chocolate कोको वृक्ष के बीजों से बना एक गहरे भूरे रंग का चूरा जिससे चॉकलेट बनाई जाती है; कोको पाउडर **2** [C, U] a hot drink made from this powder mixed with milk or water; a cup of this drink दूध या पानी में कोको पाउडर को मिलाने से बना गरम पेय; प्याला-भर कोको *a cup of cocoa*

**coconut** /ˈkəʊkənʌt ˈकोकनट्/ *noun* [C, U] a large tropical fruit with a hard, hairy shell नारियल

**cocoon** /kəˈkuːn कˈकून्/ *noun* [C] a covering of thin threads that some insects make to protect themselves before becoming adults वयस्क होने से पहले कीटों द्वारा सुरक्षा के लिए बनाया गया महीन धागों का आवरण; कोया, कृमिकोश ➪ **chrysalis** देखिए।

**cod** /kɒd कॉड्/ *noun* [C, U] (*pl.* **cod**) a large sea fish that lives in the North Atlantic and that you can eat उत्तर अटलांटिक में रहने वाली और खाने योग्य बड़ी समुद्री मछली; कॉड, स्नेहमीन

**code**[1] /kəʊd कोड्/ *noun* **1** [C, U] a system of words, letters, numbers, etc. that are used instead of the real letters or words to make a message or information secret शब्दों, अक्षरों, संख्याओं आदि से बनी गुप्त संकेत-पद्धति; कूट-भाषा *They managed to break/crack the enemy code* (= find out what it means). ○ *They wrote letters to each other **in code**.* ➪ **decode** देखिए। **2** [C] a group of numbers, letters, etc. that is used for identifying sth संख्याओं, अक्षरों आदि की श्रेणी जिससे किसी की पहचान बनती है *What's the code* (= the telephone number) *for Agartala?* ➪ **bar code** देखिए। **3** [C] a set of rules for behaviour आचरण के नियम; आचार-संहिता, नियमावली *a code of practice* (= a set of standard agreed and accepted by a particular profession) **4** [U] (*computing*) instructions used to form computer programs कंप्यूटर-प्रोग्राम बनाने के निर्देश; कोड *segments of code*

**code**[2] /kəʊd कोड्/ *verb* [T] **1** (*also* **encode**) to put or write sth in **code**[1] **1** कूट-भाषा में लिखना या कहना *coded messages* ✪ विलोम **decode** **2** to use a particular system for identifying things वस्तुओं की पहचान के लिए प्रणाली-विशेष का प्रयोग करना *The files are colour-coded: blue for Asia, green for Africa.* **3** (*computing*) to write a computer program by putting one system of numbers, words and symbols into another system एक प्रणाली की संख्याओं, शब्दों, चिह्नों को दूसरी प्रणाली में डालकर कंप्यूटर-प्रोग्राम लिखना

**codeine** /ˈkəʊdiːn ˈकोडीन्/ *noun* [U] a drug that is used to reduce pain एक दर्द-निवारक औषधि; कोडीन

**codify** /ˈkəʊdɪfaɪ ˈकोडिफ़ाइ/ *verb* [T] (*pres. part.* **codifying**; *3rd person sing. pres.* **codifies**; *pt, pp* **codified**) (*technical*) to arrange laws, rules, etc. into a system क़ानूनों, नियमों आदि को व्यवस्थित करना; संहिता बनाना ▶ **codification** /ˌkəʊdɪfɪˈkeɪʃn ˌकोडिफ़िˈकेश्न्/ *noun* [U] संहिताकरण, कोडकरण

**co-educational** (*abbr.* **coed**) *adj.* (used about an educational institution) with both boys and girls together in the same classes (शिक्षा-संस्था) जिसमें उसी कक्षा में लड़के-लड़कियाँ इकट्ठे पढ़ रहे हों; सहशिक्षा-विषयक ✪ पर्याय **mixed** ▶ **co-education** *noun* [U] सहशिक्षा, सहशिक्षण

**coefficient** /ˌkəʊɪˈfɪʃnt ˌकोइˈफ़िश्न्ट्/ *noun* [C] **1** (*mathematics*) a number which is placed before another quantity and which multiplies it, for example 3 in the quantity 3x गुणांक, जैसे 3x में 3 **2** (*technical*) a number that measures a particular characteristic of a substance किसी पदार्थ की विशिष्टता का मापक गुणांक *the coefficient of friction/expansion*

**coerce** /kəʊˈɜːs कोˈअस्/ *verb* [T] (*formal*) **coerce sb (into sth/doing sth)** to force sb to do sth, for example by threatening him/her किसी से कोई कार्य ज़बरदस्ती कराना, जैसे धमकी द्वारा; कोई कार्य करने के लिए बाध्य करना ▶ **coercion** /kəʊˈɜːʃn कोˈअश्न्/ *noun* [U] बाध्यकारिता, ज़ोर-ज़बरदस्ती

**coexist** /ˌkəʊɪgˈzɪst ˌकोइग्ˈज़िस्ट्/ *verb* [I] to live or be together at the same time or in the same place as sb/sth (दो या अधिक व्यक्तियों या वस्तुओं का) एक ही समय या स्थान पर साथ-साथ रहना या होना ▶ **coexistence** *noun* [U] सह-अस्तित्व

**coffee** /ˈkɒfi ˈकॉफ़ि/ *noun* **1** [U] the cooked seeds (**coffee beans**) of a tropical tree, made into powder and used for making a drink कॉफ़ी के भूने दाने, जिन्हें पीसकर चूरा बनाया जाता है *Coffee is the country's biggest export.* ○ *decaffeinated/instant coffee* **2** [U] a drink made by adding hot water to this powder कॉफ़ी (पेय) *Would you prefer tea or coffee?* ○ *a cup of coffee* **3** [C] a cup of this drink प्याला-भर कॉफ़ी *Two coffees please.*

NOTE बिना दूध की कॉफ़ी को **black coffee** दूध वाली कॉफ़ी को **white coffee** और कैफ़ीन-रहित कॉफ़ी को **decaffeinated coffee** कहा जाता है। कॉफ़ी **weak** या **strong** हो सकती है। बाज़ार में बिकने वाले बने-बनाए क्रॉफ़ी पाउडर (जिसे गरम पानी या दूध में मिलाकर तुरंत कॉफ़ी पेय बनाया जा सकता है) को **instant coffee** कहते हैं। **Real coffee** ताज़ा पिसे कॉफ़ी पाउडर को उबालकर बनाई गई कॉफ़ी को कहते हैं।

**coffee bar** (*also* **coffee shop**) *noun* [C] a place in a hotel, a large shop, etc., where simple food, coffee, tea and other drinks without alcohol are served किसी होटल, बड़ी दुकान आदि में एक स्थान जहाँ सादा भोजन, कॉफ़ी, चाय आदि मदिरा-रहित पेय मिलते हैं

**coffee pot** *noun* [C] a container in which coffee is made and served कॉफ़ी बनाने और पेश करने का पात्र; कॉफ़ी-पात्र

**coffee table** *noun* [C] a small low table for putting magazines, cups, etc., on एक छोटी नीची मेज़ जिस पर पत्रिका, प्याले आदि रखे जाते हैं

**coffin** /ˈkɒfɪn ˈकॉफ़िन्/ (*AmE* **casket**) *noun* [C] a box in which a dead body is buried or burned (**cremated**) दफ़न या दाह-संस्कार के लिए मानव शव को रखने का संदूक; शवपेटिका, ताबूत ➪ **funeral** पर नोट देखिए।

**cog** /kɒg कॉग्/ *noun* [C] one of a series of teeth on the edge of a wheel that fit into the teeth on the next wheel and cause it to move पहिए के सिरे पर बने दाँत

**cogent** /ˈkəʊdʒənt ˈकोजन्ट्/ *adj.* (*formal*) strongly and clearly expressed in a way that influences what people believe प्रभावशाली और सुस्पष्ट तरीक़े से व्यक्त *a cogent argument/reason*

**cognac** /ˈkɒnjæk ˈकॉन्यैक्/ *noun* **1** [U] a type of **brandy** that is made in France फ्रांस में बनी एक तरह की ब्राँडी **2** [C] a glass of this drink गिलासभर फ्रेंच ब्राँडी

**cognition** /kɒgˈnɪʃn कॉग्ˈनिश्न्/ *noun* [U] the process by which knowledge and understanding is developed in the mind वह प्रक्रिया जिसके द्वारा मस्तिष्क में ज्ञान और बोध का विकास होता है; संज्ञान, अभिज्ञान

**cognitive** /ˈkɒgnətɪv ˈकॉग्नटिव्/ *adj.* (*usually before a noun*) connected with the processes of understanding बोध-प्रक्रिया से संबंधित, संज्ञानात्मक *cognitive abilities*

**cohabit** /kəʊˈhæbɪt कोˈहैबिट्/ *verb* [I] (*formal*) (used about a couple) to live together as if they are married (किसी महिला और पुरुष का) पति-पत्नी के समान संग रहना

**coherent** /kəʊˈhɪərənt कोˈहिअरन्ट्/ *adj.* (ideas, thoughts, etc.) clear and easy to understand; logical (विचार आदि) स्पष्ट और सुबोध; सुसंगत **2** (of a person) able to talk and express clearly स्पष्ट रूप में व्यक्त करने में सक्षम ✪ विलोम **incoherent** ▶ **coherence** *noun* [U] स्पष्टता और सुबोधता ▶ **coherently** *adv.* स्पष्ट और सुबोध रूप से

**cohesion** /kəʊˈhiːʒn कोˈहिश्न्/ *noun* [U] **1** the ability to stay or fit together well एक साथ जुड़े या जुटे रहने की योग्यता; सुसंगठन *What the team lacks is cohesion—all the players play as individuals.* **2** (*physics* or *chemistry*) the force causing molecules of a substance to stick together किसी पदार्थ के अणुओं को बाँधकर रखने वाला बल

**coil¹** /kɔɪl कॉइल्/ *verb* [I, T] to make sth into a round shape गोल आकार देना; कुंडल बनाना *a snake coiled under a rock*

**coil²** /kɔɪl कॉइल्/ *noun* [C] a length of rope, wire, etc. that has been made into a round shape (रस्सी, तार आदि की) पिंडी, छल्ला *a coil of rope*

**coin¹** /kɔɪn कॉइन्/ *noun* [C] a piece of money made of metal सिक्का *a five-rupee coin*

**coin²** /kɔɪn कॉइन्/ *verb* [T] to invent a new word or phrase नया शब्द या पद बनाना *Who was it who coined the phrase 'a week is a long time in politics'?*

**coinage** /ˈkɔɪnɪdʒ ˈकॉइनिज्/ *noun* [U] the system of coins used in a country देश-विशेष की सिक्का-प्रणाली *decimal coinage*

**coincide** /ˌkəʊɪnˈsaɪd ˌकोइन्ˈसाइड्/ *verb* [I] **coincide (with sth)** **1** (used about events) to happen at the same time as sth else (घटनाओं का) एक ही समय घटना *The President's visit is timed to coincide with the institution's centenary celebrations.* **2** to be exactly the same or very similar पूर्णतया या लगभग समान होना; पूर्णतया या लगभग मेल खाना *Our views coincide completely.* **3** (of objects to share the same space (वस्तुओं का) वही और उतनी ही जगह घेरे होना

**coincidence** /kəʊˈɪnsɪdəns कोˈइनूसिडन्स्/ *noun* [C, U] two or more similar things happening at the same time by chance, in a surprising way दो या अधिक समान घटनाओं का संयोगवश और आश्चर्यजनक रूप से एक साथ घटित होना; सपांत, संयोग *We hadn't planned to meet, it was just coincidence.*

**coincidental** /kəʊˌɪnsɪˈdentl को,इनूसिˈडेन्ट्ल्/ *adj.* resulting from two similar or related events happening at the same time by chance संयोगवश साथ होने वाली घटनाओं के परिणामस्वरूप; आकस्मिक ▶ **coincidentally** *adv.* संयोगवश, आकस्मिक रूप से

**coir** /ˈkɔɪə(r) ˈकॉइअ(र्)/ *noun* [U] coarse fibre derived from the outer husk of the coconut, used for making ropes, mats, mattresses etc. नारियल के बाहरी छिलके से प्राप्त खुरदरा रेशा, जिससे रस्सी आदि बनती है

**coke** /kəʊk कोक्/ *noun* [U] **1** a solid black substance produced from coal and used as a fuel कोयले से बना काला ठोस पदार्थ जो ईंधन के रूप में प्रयुक्त होता है; कोक **2** = **cocaine**

**Col.** *abbr.* Colonel कर्नल

**col** /kɒl कॉल्/ *noun* [C] a low point between two higher points in a line or group of mountains पर्वत शृखंला में दो शिखरों के बीच का नीचा स्थान

**cola** /ˈkəʊlə ˈकोला/ *noun* [C, U] a brown, sweet cold drink that does not contain alcohol; a glass or can of this अलकोहल-रहित भूरे रंग का मीठा शीतल पेय, कोला; गिलास-भर या डिब्बा-भर कोला

**colander** /ˈkʌləndə(r) ˈकलन्‌ड(र्)/ *noun* [C] a metal or plastic bowl with a lot of small holes in it that is used for removing water from food that has been boiled or washed (धातु या प्लास्टिक की कटोरीनुमा छलनी, छन्ना ➪ **kitchen** पर चित्र देखिए।

**cold¹** /kəʊld कोल्ड्/ *adj.* **1** having a low temperature; not hot or warm न्यून तापमान वाला; ठंडा, शीत *I'm not going into the sea, the water's too cold.* ○ *Shall I put the heating on? I'm cold.*

> **NOTE** **Cold, hot, cool** और **warm** में तुलना करें। **Cool** की अपेक्षा **cold** से अधिक और अप्रिय लगने वाली ठंडक का बोध होता है—*a terribly cold winter.* **Cool** का अर्थ है ख़ासा ठंडा जो सुहाए अर्थात शीतल हो—*It's terribly hot outside but it's nice and cool in here.* इसी प्रकार **warm** की अपेक्षा **hot** से अधिक और जलाने वाली गरमी का बोध होता है—*I can't drink this yet, it's too hot.* **Warm** का अर्थ है इतना गरम जो सुहाए अर्थात ऊष्म हो—*Come and sit by the fire, you'll soon get warm again.*

**2** (used about food or drink) not heated or cooked; having become cold after being heated or cooked (भोज्य पदार्थ) गरम न किया गया; ठंडा *Have your soup before it gets cold.* ○ *a cold drink* **3** (used about a person or sb's behaviour) very unfriendly; not showing kindness, understanding, etc. (व्यक्ति या उसका व्यवहार) रूखा; उदासहीन, तटस्थ *She gave him a cold, hard look.*

**IDM** **cold turkey** suddenly and completely, without getting used to sth gradually एकाएक और पूरी तरह से, न कि क्रमशः *I gave up smoking cold turkey.*

**get/have cold feet** (*informal*) to become/be afraid to do sth कुछ करने से डर जाना *She started to get cold feet as her wedding day approached.*

**in cold blood** in a cruel way and without pity क्रूरता या निर्ममता से *to kill sb in cold blood*

**cold²** /kəʊld कोल्ड्/ *noun* **1** [*sing.*, U] lack of heat; low temperature; cold weather ठंड; सर्दी; सर्द मौसम *We walked home in the snow, shivering with cold.* ○ *Come on, let's get out of the cold and go indoors.* **2** [C, U] a common illness of the nose and throat. When you have a cold you have a sore throat and often cannot breathe through your nose ज़ुकाम *I think I'm getting a cold.* ○ *Wear some warm clothes when you go out or you'll* ***catch cold.***

**cold-blooded** *adj.* **1** having a blood temperature that changes with the temperature of the surroundings (रक्त का तापमान) जो परिवेश के तापमान के अनुसार बदले *Reptiles are cold-blooded.* ✪ विलोम **warm-blooded** **2** cruel; having or showing no pity क्रूर, निर्मम; निर्दय, बेरहम *cold-blooded killers*

**cold cash** (*AmE*) = **hard cash**

**cold-hearted** *adj.* unkind; showing no kindness, understanding, etc. निर्दय; कठोर, उदासीन; दूसरों की भावनाओं या दृष्टिकोण को अनदेखा करते हुए

**coldly** /ˈkəʊldli ˈकोल्ड्लि/ *adv.* in an unfriendly way; in a way that shows no kindness or understanding रूखेपन या कठोरता से; निर्दयता से, उदासीनतापूर्वक

**coldness** /ˈkəʊldnəs ˈकोल्ड्नस्/ *noun* [U] the lack of warm feelings; unfriendly behaviour स्नेह-हीनता; अमित्रतापूर्ण या उदासीन व्यवहार

**cold snap** *noun* [C] a sudden short period of very cold weather छोटी अवधि की एकाएक आई शीत लहर

**cold sore** *noun* [C] a small painful area on the lips or inside the mouth that is caused by a **virus** विषाणु (वाइरस) द्वारा संक्रमण से होंठ या मुख के अंदर पड़ा दर्दीला छाला

**cold storage** *noun* [U] a place where food, etc. can be kept fresh or frozen until it is needed; the keeping of sth in a place like this स्थान जहाँ खाद्य पदार्थ को बहुत कम तापमान वाले वातावरण में ताज़ा रखा जा सकता है; ऐसी प्रक्रिया *to keep potatoes* ***in cold storage***

**colic** /ˈkɒlɪk ˈकॉलिक्/ *noun* [U] pain in the stomach area, which especially babies get पेटदर्द, उदरशूल, जो विशेषतः शिशुओं को होता है

**collaborate** /kəˈlæbəreɪt कˈलैबरेट्/ *verb* [I] **1 collaborate (with sb) (on sth)** to work together (with sb), especially to create or produce sth किसी के साथ काम करना; से सहयोग करना, विशेषतः सृजन या उत्पादन कार्य में *She collaborated with another author on the book.* **2 collaborate (with sb)** to help the enemy forces who have taken control of your country देश पर नियंत्रण कर चुकी शत्रुसेना का साथ देना; ग़द्दारी करना **NOTE** इस शब्द की व्यंजना निंदात्मक है। ▶ **collaboration** /kəˌlæbəˈreɪʃn कˌलैबˈरेश्न्/ *noun* [U, C] सहयोग ▶ **collaborator** *noun* [C] सहयोगी

**collage** /ˈkɒlɑːʒ ˈकॉलाश़्/ *noun* [C, U] a picture made by fixing pieces of paper, cloth, photographs, etc. onto a surface; the art of making a picture like this किसी सतह पर काग़ज़, कपड़े, फ़ोटोचित्रों आदि के टुकड़ों को साथ चिपकाकर बनाया चित्र; इस प्रकार से चित्र बनाने की कला; समुच्चित चित्र; कोलाज

**collagen** /ˈkɒlədʒən ˈकॉलज़न्/ *noun* [U] the main substance (**protein**) found in the parts of an animal's body that connect the organs and give them support पशुओं के शरीर में पाया जाने वाला मुख्य तत्त्व जो अंगों को जोड़ने और उन्हें आधार देने में सहायक होता है; कोलैजन

**collapse[1]** /kəˈlæps कˈलैप्स्/ *verb* **1** [I] to fall down or break into pieces suddenly अचानक ढह जाना या टुकड़े-टुकड़े हो जाना *A lot of buildings collapsed in the earthquake.* **2** [I] (used about a person) to fall down, usually because you are very ill, and perhaps become unconscious (व्यक्ति का) बहुत बीमार या बेहोश होने के कारण गिर पड़ना *The winner collapsed at the end of the race.* **3** [I] (used about a business, plan, etc.) to fail suddenly or completely (व्यापार, योजना आदि का) एकाएक या पूर्णतया बैठ जाना; असफल हो जाना या पतन होना *The company collapsed, leaving hundreds of people out of work.* **4** [I, T] to fold sth or be folded into a shape that uses less space किसी वस्तु को मोड़ना या तहाना; सिमटना

**collapse[2]** /kəˈlæps कˈलैप्स्/ *noun* **1** [C, U] the sudden or complete failure of sth, such as a business, plan, etc. (व्यापार, योजना आदि का) एकाएक या पूर्ण पतन; निपात *The peace talks were on the brink/verge of collapse.* **2** [*sing.*, U] (used about a building) a sudden fall (भवन का) एकाएक गिरने या ढहने की क्रिया *the collapse of the highway bridge* **3** [*sing.*,U] (used about a person) a medical condition when a person becomes very ill and suddenly falls down (व्यक्ति) शारीरिक शक्ति पूरी तरह से नष्ट होने की अवस्था

**collapsible** /kəˈlæpsəbl कˈलैप्सब्ल्/ *adj.* that can be folded into a shape that makes sth easy to store आसानी से छोटे आकार में मोड़ा या समेटा जा सकने वाला *a collapsible bed*

**collar[1]** /ˈkɒlə(r) ˈकॉल(र्)/ *noun* [C] **1** the part of a shirt, coat, dress, etc. that fits round the neck and is often folded over कमीज़, कोट, वस्त्र आदि का कॉलर *a coat with a fur collar* ➪ **dog collar, blue-collar** और **white-collar** देखिए। **2** a band of leather that is put round an animal's neck (especially a dog or cat) (कुत्तों या बिल्लियों आदि के) गले का पट्टा

**collar[2]** /ˈkɒlə(r) ˈकॉल(र्)/ *verb* [T] (*informal*) to catch hold of sb who does not want to be caught (भागते को) पकड़ लेना

**collarbone** /ˈkɒləbəʊn ˈकॉलबोन्/ (*formal* **clavicle**) *noun* [C] one of the two bones that connect your chest bones to your shoulder कंधे से छाती की हड्डियों को जोड़ने वाली हड्डी, जत्रुक-अस्थि, हँसली ➪ **body** पर चित्र देखिए।

**collate** /kəˈleɪt कˈलेट्/ *verb* [T] **1** to collect information from different places in order to put it together, examine and compare it जाँच, तुलना और मिलान के लिए विभिन्न स्थानों से सूचना एकत्र करना *to collate data/information/figures* **2** to collect pieces of paper or pages from a book and arrange them in the correct order अलग-अलग काग़ज़ों या पुस्तक के पृष्ठों को एकत्र कर उन्हें सही क्रम में रखना; व्यवस्थित करना ▶ **collation** *noun* [U] एकत्र सूचना की जाँच, तुलना और मिलान *the collation of data*

**collateral**[1] /kəˈlætərəl कˈलैटरल् / *noun* [U] property or sth valuable that you agree to give to sb if you cannot pay back money that you have borrowed उधार चुकाने में असमर्थता के कारण बदले में दी जाने वाली संपत्ति या मूल्यवान वस्तुएँ; समर्थक ऋणाधार या प्रतिभूति

**collateral**[2] /kəˈlætərəl कˈलैटरल् / *adj.* (*formal*) connected with sth else, but in addition to it and less important किसी अन्य से जुड़ी हुई या संबंधित किंतु कम महत्त्वपूर्ण; गौण, आनुषंगिक

**colleague** /ˈkɒliːg ˈकॉलीग् / *noun* [C] a person who works at the same place as you सहकर्मी

**collect**[1] /kəˈlekt कˈलेक्ट् / *verb* **1** [T] to bring a number of things together विभिन्न वस्तुओं को एकत्र करना, इकट्ठा करना *All the exam papers will be collected at the end.* **2** [T] to get and keep together a number of objects of a particular type over a period of time as a hobby रुचि की वस्तुओं का संग्रह करना *He used to collect stamps.* **3** [I, T] to ask for money from a number of people अलग-अलग लोगों से धन माँगना *to collect for charity* ○ *The landlord collects the rent at the end of each month.* **4** [I] to come together जमा होना, एकत्रित होना *A crowd collected to see what was going on.* ✪ पर्याय **gather** **5** [T] to go and get sb/sth from a particular place; to pick sb/sth up किसी स्थान पर जाकर किसी को लाना; किसी वस्तु या व्यक्ति को लेकर आना *to collect the children from school* **6** [T] **collect yourself/sth** to get control of yourself, your feelings, thoughts, etc. अपनी भावनाओं विचारों आदि को नियंत्रण में लाना; संयम में होना *She collected herself and went back into the room as if nothing had happened.* ○ *I tried to* ***collect my thoughts*** *before the exam.*

**collect**[2] /kəˈlekt कˈलेक्ट् / *adj., adv.* (*AmE*) (used about a telephone call) to be paid for by the person who receives the call (टेलीफ़ोन कॉल) जिसका ख़र्च कॉल पाने वाला उठाता है *a collect call* ○ *She called me collect.*

**collected** /kəˈlektɪd कˈलेक्टिड् / *adj.* calm and in control of yourself, your feelings, thoughts, etc. शांत और संयम में; भावनाओं, विचारों आदि पर नियंत्रण बनाए हुए *She felt cool, calm and collected before the interview.*

**collection** /kəˈlekʃn कˈलेक्शन् / *noun* **1** [C] a group of objects of a particular type that sb has collected as a hobby शौक़ की वस्तुओं का संग्रह *a stamp collection* **2** [C, U] the act of getting sth from a place or from people किसी वस्तु को किसी स्थान या व्यक्ति से प्राप्त करने की क्रिया; समाहरण, उगाही, उसूली, संग्रह क्रिया *cash collections for the show* **3** [C] a group of people or things व्यक्तियों या वस्तुओं का समूह; संचय *a large collection of papers on the desk* **4** [C] a number of poems, stories, letters, etc. published together in one book कविताओं, कहानियों, पत्रों आदि का संग्रह *a collection of modern poetry* **5** [C] the act of asking for money from a number of people (for charity, in church, etc.) लोगों से धर्मार्थ दान माँगने की क्रिया *a collection for the poor* **6** [C] a variety of new clothes or items for the home that are specially designed and sold at a particular time विशेष अवसर पर बिकने के लिए विशेष रूप से निर्मित विभिन्न प्रकार के नए वस्त्र, घर की वस्तुएँ आदि *Ritu Beri's stunning new autumn collection*

**collective**[1] /kəˈlektɪv कˈलेक्टिव् / *adj.* shared by a group of people together; not individual सामूहिक, न कि व्यक्तिगत *collective responsibility* ▶ **collectively** *adv.* सामूहिक रूप से *We took the decision collectively at a meeting.*

**collective**[2] /kəˈlektɪv कˈलेक्टिव् / *noun* [C, *with sing. or pl. verb*] an organization or business that is owned and controlled by the people who work in it ऐसा संगठन या व्यापार जिसपर उसके कर्मचारियों का ही नियंत्रण हो

**collective bargaining** *noun* [U] discussions between a **trade union** and an employer about the pay and working conditions of the union members मज़दूर संघ और मालिक के बीच वेतन आदि के विषयों पर सामूहिक सौदेबाज़ी

**collective noun** [C] (*grammar*) a **singular** noun, such as 'committee' or 'team', that refers to a group of people, animals or things and, in British English, can be used with either a **singular** or a plural verb अंग्रेज़ी व्याकरण में समूहवाचक संज्ञा (जैसे committee या team) जिसे ब्रिटिश अंग्रेज़ी में एकवचनांत या बहुवचनांत क्रिया के साथ प्रयुक्त किया जा सकता है

**collector** /kəˈlektə(r) कˈलेक्टर(र्) / *noun* [C] **1** (*usually in compounds*) a person who collects things as a hobby or as part of his/her job शौक़िया तौर पर या पेशे से वस्तुओं का संग्रहकर्त्ता *a stamp collector* ○ *a ticket/rent/tax collector* **2** (in India) the chief administrative government official in a district responsible for its general administration, development programmes, etc. (भारत में) जिलाधीश

**college** /ˈkɒlɪdʒ ˈकॉलिज् / *noun* **1** [C, U] an institution where you can study after you leave school महाविद्यालय *an art college.*

**NOTE** जब यह बताना हो कि कोई व्यक्ति छात्र के रूप में कॉलेज या विश्वविद्यालय में पढ़ने जाता है तो **college** शब्द से पहले **the** का प्रयोग नहीं किया जाता—*He's at college in Varanasi.* ○ *She's going to college in July.* परंतु यदि कोई व्यक्ति किसी और काम से महाविद्यालय जाता है तो शब्द college से पहले the का प्रयोग अनिवार्य है—*I went to an art exhibition at the college last night.*

**collide** /kəˈlaɪd कˈलाइड्/ *verb* [I] **collide (with sb/sth)** to crash; to hit sb/sth very hard while moving गतिमान वस्तुओं का टकराना; टकराव होना *He ran along the corridor and collided with his teacher.*

**colliery** /ˈkɒliəri ˈकॉलिअरि/ *noun* [C] (*pl.* **collieries**) a coal mine and its buildings कोयले की खान और उसकी इमारतें

**collision** /kəˈlɪʒn कˈलिश़्न्/ *noun* [C, U] a crash; an occasion when things or people collide भिड़ंत; वस्तुओं या व्यक्तियों के बीच टक्कर *It was a* ***head-on collision*** *and the driver was killed instantly.*

**IDM** **be on a collision course (with sb/sth)** **1** to be in a situation which is certain to end in a disagreement or argument ऐसी स्थिति में होना जिसमें असहमति या विवाद होना निश्चित है; टकराव के रास्ते पर होना **2** to be moving in a direction which is certain to cause a crash ऐसी दिशा में गति करना कि टक्कर होना निश्चित हो *The ship was on a collision course with an iceberg.*

**collocate** /ˈkɒləkeɪt ˈकॉलकेट्/ *verb* [I] **collocate (with sth)** (used about words) to be often used together in a language (शब्दों का) भाषा में एक साथ प्रयुक्त होना; सहप्रयुक्त होना *'Bitter' collocates with 'enemies' but 'sour' does not.* ▶ **collocate** /ˈkɒləkət ˈकॉलकट्/ *noun* [C] (भाषा में) सहप्रयुक्त शब्द *'Bitter' and 'enemies' are collocates.*

**collocation** /ˌkɒləˈkeɪʃn ˌकॉलˈकेश्न्/ *noun* [C] a combination of words in a language, that happens very often and more frequently than would happen by chance बहुधा और बारंबार एक साथ प्रयुक्त शब्दों का संयोजन; शब्दों का सहप्रयोग; शब्द विन्यास *A 'resounding success' and a 'crying shame' are English collocations.*

**colloquial** /kəˈləʊkwiəl कˈलोक्विअल्/ *adj.* (used about words, phrases, etc.) used in spoken conversation, not in formal situations (शब्द, वाक्यांश आदि) बोलचाल या बातचीत की भाषा में प्रयुक्त, न कि औपचारिक अवसरों पर ▶ **colloquially** /-kwiəli -क्विअलि/ *adv.* बोलचाल की भाषा के रूप में

**colloquialism** /kəˈləʊkwiəlɪzəm कˈलोक्विअलिज़म्/ *noun* [C] a word or phrase that is used in conversation but not in formal speech or writing अनौपचारिक बातचीत में प्रयुक्त शब्द या वाक्यांश; बोलचाल का प्रयोग

**collusion** /kəˈluːʒn कˈलूश़्न्/ *noun* [U] (*formal*) secret agreement, especially in order to do sth dishonest गुप्त समझौता, विशेषतः बेईमानी के कार्य में *The drugs were brought into the country with the collusion of customs officials.*

**cologne** /kəˈləʊn कˈलोन्/ = **eau de cologne**

**colon** /ˈkəʊlən ˈकोलन्/ *noun* [C] **1** the mark (:) used before a list, an explanation, an example, etc. अपूर्ण विराम (:) जिसे किसी सूची, स्पष्टीकरण, उदाहरण आदि के पूर्व लगाया जाता है; कोलन, द्विबिंदुक **2** the main and the longest part of the large **intestine**, not including the **rectum** बड़ी आँत का मुख्य और सबसे लंबा भाग; बृहदंत्र ➪ **body** पर चित्र देखिए।

**colonel** /ˈkɜːnl ˈकर्नल्/ *noun* [C] an officer of a high level in the army स्थल सेना में एक उच्च अधिकारी; कर्नल

**colonial** /kəˈləʊniəl कˈलोनिअल्/ *adj.* connected with or belonging to a country that controls another country (**colony**) किसी अन्य देश द्वारा नियंत्रित देश से संबंधित; औपनिवेशिक *Spain used to be a major colonial power.*

**colonialism** /kəˈləʊniəlɪzəm कˈलोनिअलिज़म्/ *noun* [U] the practice by which a powerful country controls another country or countries, in order to become richer उपनिवेशवाद

**colonist** /ˈkɒlənɪst ˈकॉलनिस्ट्/ *noun* [C] a person who goes to live in a country that has become a colony उपनिवेश का निवासी; उपनिवेश में जाकर बसा व्यक्ति

**colonize** (*also* **-ise**) /ˈkɒlənaɪz ˈकॉलनाइज़्/ *verb* [T] to take control of another country or place and make it a colony किसी देश या स्थान को उपनिवेश बनाना ▶ **colonization** (*also* **-isation**) /ˌkɒlənaɪˈzeɪʃn ˌकॉलनाइˈज़ेश्न्/ *noun* [U] उपनिवेशन, उपनिवेशीकरण

**colonnade** /ˌkɒləˈneɪd ˌकॉलˈनेड्/ *noun* [C] a row of stone columns with equal spaces between them, usually supporting a roof समदूरस्थ स्तंभों की पंक्ति, जो सामान्यतः किसी छत का आधार होती है; स्तंभावली, स्तंभ-श्रेणी

**colony** /ˈkɒləni ˈकॉलनि/ *noun* [C] (*pl.* **colonies**) **1** a country or area that is ruled by another, more powerful country उपनिवेश देश **2** (*with sing. or pl. verb*) a group of people who go to live permanently in another country but keep their own habits and traditions किसी अन्य देश में स्थायी रूप से बस जाने वाले व्यक्तियों का एक समुदाय जो यद्यपि अपनी ही परंपराओं का अनुसरण करता है **3** a group of the same type of animals, insects or plants living or growing in the same place एक ही स्थान पर रहने वाले एक ही प्रकार के प्राणियों, कीटों या पौधों की बस्ती *a colony of ants*

**color** (*AmE*) = **colour**

**colossal** /kəˈlɒsl कˈलॉसल्/ *adj.* extremely large अतिविशाल, वृहत्काय, बहुत बड़ा *a colossal building* ○ *a colossal amount of money*

**colour**[1] (*AmE* **color**) /ˈkʌlə(r) ˈकल(र्)/ *noun* **1** [C, U] the fact that sth is red, green, yellow, blue, etc. रंग (लाल, हरा, पीला आदि) *'What colour is your car?' 'Red.'* ○ *Those flowers certainly give the room a bit of colour.* **2** [U] the use of all the colours, not just black and white केवल श्याम और श्वेत ही नहीं बल्कि सब रंगों का प्रयोग; रंगीन *All the pictures in the book are* ***in colour***. ○ *a colour television* **3** [U] a red or pink colour in your face, particularly when it shows how healthy you are or that you are embarrassed चेहरे पर लाली या गुलाबीपन जो अच्छे स्वास्थ्य या झेंप का सूचक माना जाता है *You look much better now, you've got a bit more colour.* ○ *Colour flooded her face when she thought of what had happened.* **4** [U] interesting or exciting details रोचक और उत्तेजक बातें *It's a busy area, full of activity and colour.*

IDM **off colour** ill अस्वस्थ, बीमार

**with flying colours** ➪ **flying** देखिए।

**colour**[2] (*AmE* **color**) /ˈkʌlə(r) ˈकल(र्)/ *verb* [T] **1** to put colour on sth, for example by painting it (किसी वस्तु को) रँगना *Colour the picture with your crayons.* ○ *The area coloured yellow on the map is desert.* **2** to influence thoughts, opinions, etc. विचारों, मतों आदि को प्रभावित करना *You shouldn't let one bad experience colour your attitude to everything.*

PHR V **colour sth in** to fill a shape, a picture, etc. with colour using pencils, paint, etc. किसी आकृति, चित्र आदि में पेंसिल, पेंट आदि से रंग भरना *The children were colouring in pictures of animals.*

**colour-blind** *adj.* unable to see certain colours, especially red and green कुछ रंगों में (विशेषतः लाल और हरे में) भेद करने में असमर्थ; वर्णांध

**coloured** (*AmE* **colored**) /ˈkʌləd ˈकलड्/ *adj.* **1** having colour or a particular colour रंगीन; रंग-विशेष वाला *a coffee-coloured dress* ○ *brightly coloured lights* **2** (used about a person) belonging to a race that does not have white skin (व्यक्ति) श्वेत से भिन्न प्रजाति का; अश्वेत NOTE वर्तमान में शब्द **coloured** अर्थसंख्या **2** में अशोभन माना जाता है। प्रजाति विशेष के व्यक्ति का संकेत करने के लिए **Asian** आदि शब्द उपयुक्त हैं।

**colourful** (*AmE* **colorful**) /ˈkʌləfl ˈकलफ़्ल्/ *adj.* **1** with bright colours; full of colour चटकीले रंगों वाला; रंगबिरंगा *a colourful shirt* **2** full of interest or excitement रोचक या उत्तेजक *a colourful story* ○ *He has a rather colourful past.*

**colouring** (*AmE* **coloring**) /ˈkʌlərɪŋ ˈकलरिङ्/ *noun* **1** [U] the colour of a person's hair, skin, etc. किसी व्यक्ति के बालों, त्वचा आदि का रंग *to have fair/dark colouring* **2** [C, U] a substance that is used to give a particular colour to sth, especially food विशेषतः भोज्य पदार्थों को रंग-विशेष देने वाला पदार्थ; रंगने का पदार्थ

**colourless** (*AmE* **colorless**) /ˈkʌlələs ˈकललस्/ *adj.* **1** without any colour रंगहीन *a colourless liquid, like water* **2** not interesting or exciting; dull अरोचक, उबाऊ, नीरस

**colour scheme** *noun* [C] the way in which colours are arranged, especially in a room रंगों का संयोजन; वर्ण-योजना, विशेषतः कमरे में

**colt** /kəʊlt कोल्ट्/ *noun* [C] a young male horse घोड़े का नर बच्चा, बछेड़ा ➪ **filly** देखिए।

**column** /ˈkɒləm ˈकॉलम्/ *noun* [C] **1** a tall solid vertical post made of stone, supporting or decorating a building or standing alone पत्थर का बना खंभा, स्तंभ *Ashokan columns are famous for their Buddhist teachings.* **2** something that has the shape of a column खंभे की शकल का; स्तंभाकार *a column of smoke* (= smoke rising straight up) **3** one of the vertical sections into which a printed page, especially in a newspaper, is divided विशेषतः समाचार-पत्र के मुद्रित पृष्ठ का लंब रूप खंड कॉलम **4** a piece of writing in a newspaper or magazine that is part of a regular series or always written by the same writer समाचार-पत्र या पत्रिका में नियमित रूप से मुद्रित होने वाली शृंखला का एक भाग या एक ही लेखक द्वारा विभिन्न लेखों में से कोई एक *the travel/gossip column* **5** a series of numbers written one under the other एक के बाद दूसरे के नीचे लिखी संख्याओं की शृंखला *to add up a column of figures* **6** a long line of people, vehicles etc., one following behind another व्यक्तियों, वाहनों आदि की पंक्ति *a column of troops*

**columnist** /ˈkɒləmnɪst ˈकॉलम्निस्ट्/ *noun* [C] a journalist who writes regular articles in a newspaper or magazine समाचार-पत्र या पत्रिका में नियमित रूप से लिखने वाला पत्रकार; स्तंभकार *a gossip columnist*

**coma** /ˈkəʊmə ˈकोमा/ *noun* [C] a deep unconscious state, often lasting for a long time and caused by serious illness or injury (प्रायः गंभीर बीमारी या चोट से उत्पन्न) लंबी अवधि की अचेतन-अवस्था; गहरी मूर्छा

**comatose** /ˈkəʊmətəʊs ˈकोमटोस्/ *adj.* **1** (*informal*) deeply asleep गहरी नींद में बेसुध सोया हुआ *He had taken a sleeping pill and was comatose.* **2** (*medical*) deeply unconscious; in a coma प्रगाढ़ रूप से बेहोश; लंबी और गहरी बेहोशी में; सम्मूर्च्छित

**comb**[1] /kəʊm कोम्/ *noun* **1** [C] a flat piece of metal or plastic with teeth that you use for making your hair tidy कंघी, कंघा **2** [C, *usually sing.*] an act of combing the hair कंघी करने की क्रिया *Give your hair a comb before you go out.*

**comb**[2] /kəʊm कोम्/ *verb* [T] **1** to make your hair tidy using a comb कंघी से बाल सँवारना **2 comb sth (for sb/sth)** to search an area carefully किसी क्षेत्र में बारीकी से तलाश करना *Police are combing the woodland for the murder weapon.*

**combat**[1] /ˈkɒmbæt ˈकॉम्बैट्/ *noun* [C, U] a fight, especially in war लड़ाई, संघर्ष विशेषतः युद्ध में *unarmed combat* (= without weapons)

**combat**[2] /ˈkɒmbæt ˈकॉम्बैट्/ *verb* [T] to fight against sth; to try to stop or defeat sth किसी के विरुद्ध संघर्ष करना; किसी को रोकने या हराने का प्रयत्न करना *to combat terrorism* ○ *new medicines to combat heart disease*

**combatant** /ˈkɒmbətənt ˈकॉम्बटन्ट्/ *noun* [C] a person who takes part in fighting, especially in war योद्धा, युद्धरत सैनिक

**combination** /ˌkɒmbɪˈneɪʃn ˌकॉम्बिˈनेशन्/ *noun* [C, U] a number of people or things mixed or joined together; a mixture बहुसंख्यक वस्तुओं या व्यक्तियों का सम्मिश्रण या संयोजन; मिश्रण, मेल, योग *The team manager still hasn't found the right combination of players.*

**combine**[1] /kəmˈbaɪn कम्ˈबाइन्/ *verb* **1** [I, T] **combine (with sb/sth)** to join or mix two or more things together दो या अधिक वस्तुओं को जोड़ना या मिलाना *The two organizations combined to form one company.* ○ *Bad planning, combined with bad luck, led to the company's collapse.* **2** [T] **combine A and/with B** to do or have two or more things at the same time एक ही समय में दो या अधिक वस्तुओं का एक साथ होना *This car combines speed and reliability.*

**combine**[2] /ˈkɒmbaɪn ˈकॉम्बाइन्/ (*also* **combine harvester**) *noun* [C] a large farm machine that both cuts corn and separates the grain from the rest of the plant फ़सल काटने और अनाज छाँटने वाला बड़ा कृषि यंत्र ➪ **harvest** देखिए।

**combined** /kəmˈbaɪnd कम्ˈबाइन्ड्/ *adj.* done by a number of people joining together, resulting from the joining of two or more things सम्मिलित, संयुक्त *The* ***combined efforts*** *of the emergency services prevented a major disaster.*

**combustible** /kəmˈbʌstəbl कम्ˈबस्टबल्/ *adj.* able to begin burning easily सहज ज्वलनशील, सुदाह्य

**combustion** /kəmˈbʌstʃən कम्ˈबस्चन्/ *noun* [U] the process of burning आग से जलने की प्रक्रिया, दहन प्रक्रिया

**come** /kʌm कम्/ *verb* [I] (*pt* **came** /keɪm केम्/; *pp* **come**) **1** to move to or towards the person who is speaking or the place that sb is talking about (कहीं या किसी के पास) आना *Come here, please.* ○ *I hope you can come to my party.* **2 come (to...)** to arrive some where or reach a particular place or time (कहीं और किसी समय) पहुँचना, आ जाना **3** to be in a particular position in a series किसी क्रम में स्थान विशेष पर होना *March comes after February.* ○ *Seema came second in the exam.* **4 come in sth** to be available (वस्तुएँ आदि) उपलब्ध होना; गुण-विशेष में मिलना; आना *This blouse comes in a choice of four colours.* ○ *Do these trousers come in a larger size?* **5** to be produced by or from sth (किसी से के द्वारा ) पैदा होना, उत्पन्न होना *Wool comes from sheep.* **6** to become open or loose खुल जाना या ढीला हो जाना *Her hair has come untied.* **7 come to do sth** used for talking about how, why or when sth happened किसी घटना आदि के कारण तरीक़े या समय के वर्णन में प्रयुक्त *How did you come to lose your passport?* **8 come to/into sth** to reach a particular state दशा-विशेष में पहुँचना *We were all sorry when the holiday came to an end.* ○ *The present government came to power in 2005.*

IDM **come and go** to be present for a short time and then go away कुछ देर के लिए रुकना और फिर चले जाना *The pain in my ear comes and goes.*

**come easily /naturally to sb** to be easy for sb to do (किसी के लिए) कुछ करना आसान, स्वाभाविक होना *Apologizing does not come easily to her.*

**come to nothing; not come to anything** to fail; to not be successful विफल हो जाना; सफल न हो पाना *Unfortunately, all his efforts came to nothing.*

**how come...**" (*informal*) why or how क्यों या कैसे *How come you're back so early?*

**to come** (used after a noun) in the future भविष्य में आने वाले दिनों में *You'll regret it in years to come.*

**when it comes to sth/to doing sth** when it is a question of sth जब यह बात हो तो *When it comes to value for money, these prices are hard to beat.*

> **NOTE** **Come** से बनने वाले अन्य मुहावरों के लिए संबंधित संज्ञाओं, विशेषणों आदि की प्रविष्टियाँ देखिए। जैसे **come to a head** की व्याख्या **head** में मिलेगी।

**PHR V** **come about** to happen घटित होना; होना *How did this situation come about?*

**come across/over (as sth)** to make an impression of a particular type छाप या प्रभाव-विशेष छोड़ना *Divya comes across as being rather shy.*

**come across sb/sth** to meet or find sb/sth by chance संयोग से किसी से (किसी को) पाना या (किसी का) मिला जाना *I came across this book in a second-hand shop.*

**come along** 1 to arrive or appear सामने आना, प्रकट होना, पता चलना *When the right job comes along, I'll apply for it.* 2 = **come on**[2] 3 = **come on**[3]

**come apart** to break into pieces टुकड़े-टुकड़े हो जाना

**come away (from sth)** to become loose or separated from sth ढीला हो जाना या किसी से अलग होना *The wallpaper is coming away from the wall in the corner.*

**come away with sth** to leave a place with a particular opinion or feeling एक विशेष मत या मनोभाव के साथ किसी स्थान से प्रस्थान करना *We came away with a very favourable impression of Kanyakumari.*

**come back** 1 to return लौटना, वापस आना *I don't know what time I'll be coming back.* 2 to become popular or fashionable again पुन: लोकप्रिय या प्रचलित होना *Flared trousers are coming back again.*

**come back (to sb)** to be remembered स्मरण आना; याद आना *When I went to Kerala again, my Malayalam started to come back to me.*

**come before sb/sth** to be more important than sb/sth else किसी व्यक्ति या वस्तु का अन्य से अधिक महत्त्वपूर्ण होना *Raghav feels his family comes before his career.*

**come between sb and sb** to damage the relationship between two people दो व्यक्तियों के संबंध बिगाड़ना *Arguments over money came between the two brothers.*

**come by sth** to manage to get sth प्राप्त करने में सफल होना *Fresh oranges are hard to come by in the summer.*

**come down** 1 to fall down नीचे गिरना *The power lines came down in the storm.* 2 (used about an aircraft or spacecraft) to land (विमान या अंतरिक्ष-यान का) धरती पर उतरना *The helicopter came down in a field.* 3 (used about prices) to become lower (क़ीमतों का) कम होना *The price of electronic gadgets has come down in the past year.*

**come down to sth/to doing sth** (*informal*) to be able to be explained by a single important point मामले का केवल एक बिंदु पर केंद्रित हो जाना *It all comes down to having the right qualifications.*

**come down with sth** to become ill with sth रोग से ग्रस्त होना *I think I'm coming down with flu.*

**come forward** to offer help सहायता के लिए आगे आना *The police are asking witnesses to come forward.*

**come from...** to live in or have been born in a place स्थान-विशेष का निवासी होना या वहाँ की पैदाइश होना *Where do you come from originally?*

**come from (doing) sth** to be the result of sth (का) परिणाम होना *'I'm tired.' 'That comes from all the late nights you've had.'*

**come in** 1 to enter a place स्थान-विशेष में प्रवेश करना; घुसना *Come in and sit down.* 2 (used about the tides of the sea) to move towards the land and cover the beach (ज्वार-भाटा का) बाहर आकर समुद्रतट पर फैल जाना ➪ **tide**[1] देखिए। 3 to become popular or fashionable लोकप्रिय या फ़ैशनेबल हो जाना *Punk fashions came in in the seventies.* 4 (used about news or information) to be received (समाचार या सूचना का) प्राप्त होना या आना *Reports are coming in of fighting in Iraq.*

**come in for sth** to receive sth, especially sth unpleasant (अप्रीतिकर स्थिति आदि का) सामना करना *The government came in for a lot of criticism.*

**come of sth/of doing sth** to be the result of sth कुछ परिणाम निकलना; परिणामस्वरूप होना *We've written to several companies asking for help but nothing has come of it yet.*

**come off** 1 to be able to be removed अलग हो सकना, निकल सकना *Does the hood of the shirt come off?* 2 (*informal*) to be successful सफल होना *The deal seems unlikely to come off.* 3 (*informal*) (*used before an adverb*) to be in a good, bad, etc. situation as a result of sth किसी के परिणामस्वरूप अच्छी, बुरी आदि स्थिति में होना *Unfortunately, Maya came off worst in the fight.*

**come off (sth)** 1 to fall off sth गिर पड़ना *Kim came off her bicycle and broke her leg.* 2 to become removed from sth किसी वस्तु से टूटकर अलग हो जाना *One of the legs has come off this table.*

**come off it** (*spoken*) used to say that you do not believe sb/sth or that you strongly disagree with sb किसी पर अविश्वास या किसी से प्रबल असहमति

जताने के लिए प्रयुक्त *'I thought it was quite a good performance.' 'Oh, come off it—it was awful!'*

**come on** 1 to start to act, play in a game of sport, etc. खेल, मंच आदि में सामने आना या पेश होना *The audience jeered every time the villain came on.* ○ *The substitute came on in the second half.* 2 (*also* **come along**) to make progress or to improve प्रगति करना या सुधरना *Your English is coming on nicely.* 3 (*also* **come along**) used to tell sb to hurry up, try harder, etc. किसी को जल्दी करने, अधिक प्रयास करने आदि कहने के लिए प्रयुक्त *Come on or we'll be late!* 4 to begin शुद्ध होना या करना *I think I've got a cold coming on.*

**come out** 1 to appear; to be published प्रकट होना; प्रकाशित होना *The rain stopped and the sun came out.* ○ *The report came out in 2006.* 2 to become known पता चलना *It was only after his death that the truth came out.* 3 (used about a photograph, etc.) to be produced successfully (फ़ोटो चित्र आदि का) उत्पन्न होने में सफल होना

**come out (of sth)** to be removed from sth (किसी वस्तु से) निकालना; दूर होना, छूटना *Turmeric stains don't come out easily.*

**come out against sth** to say in public that you do not like or agree with sth सार्वजनिक रूप से असहमति या नापसंदगी प्रकट करना

**come out in sth** to become covered in spots, etc. धब्बे पड़ जाना; दाने हो जाना *Heat makes him come out in a rash.*

**come out with sth** to say sth unexpectedly अप्रत्याशित रूप से कुछ कहने लगना *The children came out with all kinds of excuses for not doing their homework.*

**come over** = **come across/over**

**come over (to...) (from...)** to visit people or a place a long way away दूर स्थित व्यक्ति के पास या प्रदेश में जाना *They've invited us to come over to Australia for a holiday.*

**come over sb** (used about a feeling) to affect sb (किसी भाव से) अभिभूत हो जाना *A feeling of despair came over me.*

**come round** 1 (used about an event that happens regularly) to happen (घटना का यथासमय) घटित होना *The end of the holidays always comes round very quickly.* 2 (*also* **come to**) to become conscious again पुनः होश में आना ✪ विलोम **pass out**

**come round (to...)** to visit a person or place not far away किसी निकट-स्थित व्यक्ति के पास या स्थान पर जाना

**come round (to sth)** to change your opinion so that you agree with sb/sth दूसरे की बात मानते हुए अपने विचार बदल लेना *They finally came round to our way of thinking.*

**come through** (used about news, information, etc.) to arrive (समाचार, सूचना आदि का) आना, मिलना *The football results are just coming through.*

**come through (sth)** to escape injury or death in a dangerous situation, illness, etc. ख़तरनाक परिस्थिति, बीमारी आदि से बच निकलना *to come through an enemy attack*

**come to** = **come round 2**

**come to sth** 1 to equal or total a particular amount धनराशि-विशेष या कुलयोग-विशेष होना *The bill for the meal came to Rs 225.* 2 to result in a bad situation दुर्दशा हो जाना *We will sell the house to pay our debts if we have to but we hope it won't come to that.*

**come under** to be included in a particular section, department, etc. विशेष खंड, विभाग आदि के अंतर्गत होना; वर्ग या श्रेणी में आना *Garages that sell cars come under 'car dealers' in the telephone book.*

**come up** 1 to happen or be going to happen in the future घटित होना या भविष्य में संभवतः घटित होना *Something's come up at work so I won't be home until late tonight.* 2 to be discussed or mentioned चर्चित या उल्लिखित होना *The subject of religion came up.* 3 (used about the sun and moon) to rise (सूर्य और चंद्रमा का) निकलना, उदय होना 4 (used about a plant) to appear above the soil (पौधे का) उग आना

**come up against sb/sth** to find a problem or difficulty that you have to deal with समस्या या मुश्किल का उत्पन्न होना

**come up to sth** to be as good as usual or as necessary सामान्यतया या आवश्यकतानुसार संतोषजनक होना; अपेक्षित स्तर तक पहुँचना *This piece of work does not come up to your usual standard.*

**come up with sth** to find an answer or solution to sth समस्या का समाधान पा लेना *Engineers have come up with new ways of saving energy.*

**comeback** /ˈkʌmbæk ˈकम्बैक् / *noun* [C] a return to a position of strength or importance that you had before पहले के समान शक्तिशाली और महत्त्वपूर्ण स्थिति, पद आदि पर वापसी *The former world champion is hoping to make a comeback.*

**comedian** /kəˈmiːdiən कˈमीडिअन् / (*also* **comic**) *noun* [C] a person whose job is to entertain people and make them laugh, for example by telling jokes व्यक्ति जिसका पेशा लोगों का मनोरंजन करना और उन्हें हँसाना है; पेशेवर मसख़रा, विदूषक, हास्य-अभिनेता NOTE हास्य अभिनेत्री (महिला) को कभी-कभी **comedienne** कहा जाता है।

**comedown** /ˈkʌmdaʊn ˈकम्‌डाउन्/ *noun* [C, *usually sing.*] (*informal*) a loss of importance or social position महत्त्व या सामाजिक प्रतिष्ठा में गिरावट *It's **a bit of a comedown** for her having to move to a smaller house.*

**comedy** /ˈkɒmədi ˈकॉमडि/ *noun* **1** [C] (*pl.* **comedies**) an amusing play, film, etc. that has a happy ending सुखांत और मनोरंजन-प्रधान नाटक, फ़िल्म आदि; प्रहसन ➪ **tragedy** देखिए। **2** [U] the quality of being amusing or making people laugh मनोरंजकता

**comet** /ˈkɒmɪt ˈकॉमट्/ *noun* [C] an object in space that looks like a bright star with a tail and that moves around the sun धूमकेतु, पुच्छल तारा

**comfort**[1] /ˈkʌmfət ˈकम्‌फ़ट्/ *noun* **1** [U] the state of having everything your body needs, or of having a pleasant life शारीरिक आवश्यकताओं की पूर्ति की स्थिति; आराम, आनंद, सुख-सुविधा *Most people expect to live **in comfort** in their old age.* ○ *to travel in comfort* **2** [U] the feeling of being physically relaxed and in no pain शारीरिक आराम, चैन व सुविधा *This car has been specially designed for extra comfort.* ✪ विलोम **discomfort**. **3** [U] help or kindness to sb who is suffering सांत्वना, दिलासा *I tried to offer a few words of comfort.* **4 a comfort (to sb)** [*sing.*] a person or thing that helps you when you are very sad or worried सांत्वना या दिलासे का स्रोत, व्यक्ति या वस्तु *You've been a real comfort to me.* **5** [C] something that makes your life easier or more pleasant जीवन को आरामदेह बनाने वाला सुख-साधन *the comforts of home*

**comfort**[2] /ˈkʌmfət ˈकम्‌फ़ट्/ *verb* [T] to try to make sb feel less worried or unhappy चैन या सुख पहुँचाना; दिलासा देना *to comfort a crying child*

**comfortable** /ˈkʌmftəbl ˈकम्‌फ़्टबल्/ *adj.* **1** (*also informal*) that makes you feel physically relaxed and in no pain; that provides you with everything your body needs आरामदेह, सुखद *a comfortable temperature* (= not too hot or too cold) ○ *Sit down and make yourselves comfortable.* ○ *a comfortable pair of shoes* ✪ विलोम **uncomfortable** **2** not having or causing worry, difficulty, etc. तनावमुक्त, निश्चिंत *He did not feel comfortable in the presence of so many women.* **3** having or providing enough money for all your needs आर्थिक दृष्टि से सुखी *They are not wealthy but they're quite comfortable.* ▶ **comfortably** *adv.* आरंभ के साथ, सुखपूर्वक *Jeena was sitting comfortably in the armchair.* ○ *You can't live comfortably on such low wages.*

**comic**[1] /ˈkɒmɪk ˈकॉमिक्/ *adj.* that makes you laugh; connected with comedy हास्यजनक, हँसनेवाला; सुखांत-रचना से संबंधित *a comic scene in a play*

**comic**[2] /ˈkɒmɪk ˈकॉमिक्/ *noun* [C] **1** = **comedian** **2** (*also* **comic book**) a magazine for children that tells stories through pictures बच्चों के लिए चित्रकथा पत्रिका; मनोरंजक चित्र पुस्तिका

**comical** /ˈkɒmɪkl ˈकॉमिकल्/ *adj.* that makes you laugh; funny हास्यकर; विनोदक ▶ **comically** /-kli -कलि/ *adv.* हास्यास्पद रीति से

**comic strip** (*also* **strip cartoon**) *noun* [C] a short series of pictures that tell a funny story, for example in a newspaper छोटी हास्य-चित्रकथा, जैसे समाचार-पत्र में प्रकाशित

**coming** /ˈkʌmɪŋ ˈकमिङ्/ *noun* [C] the moment when sth new arrives or begins वह क्षण जब कोई नई वस्तु आती है या आरंभ होती है; आगमन, प्रारंभ *The coming of the computer meant the loss of many jobs.* ▶ **coming** *adj.* आगामी, आने वाला *We've got a lot of plans for the coming year.*

**comma** /ˈkɒmə ˈकॉमा/ *noun* [C] the mark (,) used for dividing parts of a sentence or items in a list (सूची की मदों को) अलग-अलग करने की छपाई या लेखन की युक्ति; अल्पविराम का चिह्न (,)

**command**[1] /kəˈmɑːnd कˈमान्ड्/ *noun* **1** [C] an order आदेश, आज्ञा, हुक्म *The captain's commands must be obeyed without question.* **2** [C] (*computing*) an instruction given to a computer कंप्यूटर को दिया गया निर्देश **3** [U] control over sb/sth किसी पर नियंत्रण, अधिकार या क़ाबू *Who is **in command of** the expedition?* ○ *to **take command of** a situation* **4** [*sing.*] the state of being able to do or use sth well किसी कार्य में कुशलता या योग्यता *She has a good command of French.*

IDM **at/by sb's command** (*formal*) because you were ordered by sb किसी के आदेश पर *At the command of their officer the troops opened fire.*

**be at sb's command** to be ready to obey sb आदेश-पालन के लिए तैयार रहना *I'm completely at your command.*

**command**[2] /kəˈmɑːnd कˈमान्ड्/ *verb* **1** [I, T] (*formal*) **command (sb to do sth)** to tell or order sb to do sth किसी को कुछ करने का आदेश देना *I command you to leave now!* **2 command sb/sth** [T] to control or be in charge of sb/sth किसी पर नियंत्रण रखना; देखरेख का दायित्व होना *to command a ship/regiment/army* **3** [T] to deserve and get sth कुछ पाने का पात्र होना *The old man commanded great respect.*

**commandant** /ˈkɒməndænt ˈकॉमन्डैन्ट् / *noun* [C] the officer in charge of a particular military group or institution विशेष सैनिक दल या संस्था का प्रमुख अधिकारी; सैनिक छावनी का सर्वोच्च अधिकारी; कमांडेंट

**commandeer** /ˌkɒmənˈdɪə(r) ˌकॉमन्ˈडिअ(र्) / *verb* [T] to take control or possession of sth for military or police use किसी वस्तु का सैनिक या पुलिसकर्म के उद्देश्य से अधिग्रहण करना

**commander** /kəˈmɑːndə(r) कˈमान्ड(र्) / *noun* [C] a person who controls or is in charge of a military organization or group सैन्य संस्था या दल का प्रधान या प्रमुख अधिकारी; कमान्डर

**commander-in-chief** *noun* [C] (*abbr.* **C-in-C**) (*pl.* **commanders-in-chief**) the officer who commands all the armed forces of a country or all its forces in a particular area किसी देश या क्षेत्र विशेष की सेना का प्रधान सेनापति

**commanding** /kəˈmɑːndɪŋ कˈमान्डिङ् / *adj.* **1** in charge or having control of sb/sth नियंत्रक या अधिकार-प्राप्त *Who is your commanding officer?* **2** strong or powerful दृढ़ या प्रभावशाली *to speak in a commanding tone of voice*

**commandment** (*also* **Commandment**) /kəˈmɑːndmənt कˈमान्ड्मन्ट् / *noun* [C] (*formal*) one of the ten important laws that Christian people should obey ईसाईयों के लिए निर्धारित दस ईश्वरीय आदेशों में से एक

**commando** /kəˈmɑːndəʊ कˈमान्डो / *noun* [C] (*pl.* **commandos**) one of a group of soldiers who is trained to make sudden attacks in enemy areas विशेष सैनिक टुकड़ी का सदस्य जिसे शत्रु क्षेत्रों में अचानक और अप्रत्याशित रूप से आक्रमण करने का प्रशिक्षण दिया गया हो; छापामार सैनिक; कमांडो

**commemorate** /kəˈmeməreɪt कˈमेमरेट् / *verb* [T] to exist or take place in order to make people remember a special event पूर्व की किसी घटना-विशेष की स्मृति ताज़ा करने के लिए होना; घटना-विशेष के सम्मान में स्मरणोत्सव मनाना *a statue commemorating all the soldiers who died in the last war* ▸ **commemoration** /kəˌmeməˈreɪʃn कˌमेमˈरेश्न् / *noun* [C, U] स्मरणोत्सव *The concerts were held* ***in commemoration*** *of the 50th anniversary of Indian independance.*

**commence** /kəˈmens कˈमेन्स् / *verb* [I, T] (*formal*) **commence sth/doing sth** to start or begin आरंभ होना ▸ **commencement** *noun* [C, U] आरंभ, शुरुआत

**commend** /kəˈmend कˈमेन्ड् / *verb* [T] (*formal*) to say officially that sb/sth is very good अधिकृत रूप से प्रशंसा करना; सराहना करना *Saurabh was commended for his excellent work.*

**commendable** /kəˈmendəbl कˈमेन्डब्ल् / *adj.* (*formal*) that people think is good सराहनीय, प्रशंसनीय, प्रशंसा योग्य *She acted with commendable honesty and fairness.*

**commensurate** /kəˈmenʃərət कˈमेन्शरट् / *adj.* (*formal*) **commensurate with sth** corresponding in size, importance, quality, etc. आकार, महत्त्व, योग्यता आदि के अनुरूप *His boss informed him that his salary would be commensurate with his experience.* ▸ **commensurately** /kəˈmenʃərətli कˈमेन्शरटलि / *adj* adequately; with equal measure or extent पर्याप्त रूप से; समान मात्रा या परिमाण में

**comment**[1] /ˈkɒment ˈकॉमेन्ट् / *noun* [C, U] **comment (about/on sth)** something that you say or write that gives your opinion or feeling about sth टिप्पणी, सम्मति; राय जताने वाला कथन *The chancellor was not available for comment.* ○ *I heard someone* ***make a*** *rude* ***comment*** *about my clothes.* ➪ **observation** और **remark** देखिए।

IDM **no comment** used in reply to a question when you do not want to say anything at all किसी विषय पर टिप्पणी देने से इनकार करने के लिए प्रयुक्त *'Mr President, how do you feel about these latest developments?' 'No comment.'*

**comment**[2] /ˈkɒment ˈकॉमेन्ट् / *verb* [I] **comment (on sth)** to say what you think or feel about sth किसी विषय पर अपनी राय देना; टिप्पणी करना, सम्मति देना *Several people commented on how ill Sheila looked.*

**commentary** /ˈkɒməntri ˈकॉमन्ट्रि / *noun* (*pl.* **commentaries**) **1** [C, U] a spoken description on the radio or television of sth as it is happening रेडियो या टेलीविज़न पर किसी घटित होते खेल, उत्सव आदि का मौखिक विवरण; आँखों-देखा हाल *a sports commentary* **2** [C] a written explanation or discussion of sth such as a book or play किसी पुस्तक आदि की लिखित व्याख्या; विवरण या चर्चा टीका-टिप्पणी **3** [C] something that shows what sth is like; a criticism or discussion of sth स्थिति आदि का वर्णन; समीक्षा, आलोचना या चर्चा *This drug scandal is a sad commentary on the state of the sport.*

**commentate** /ˈkɒmənteɪt ˈकॉमन्टेट् / *verb* [I] **commentate (on sth)** to give a spoken description on the radio or television of sth as it is happening रेडियों या टेलीविज़न पर किसी घटित होती हुई घटना (खेल, उत्सव) का मौखिक विवरण देना; आँखों-देखा हाल बताना

**commentator** /ˈkɒmənteɪtə(r) ˈकॉमन्टेटर(र्) / *noun* [C] **1** a person who commentates on sth वर्णन या समीक्षा करने वाला; विवरणकार *a sports commentator*

**2** a person who gives his/her opinion about sth on the radio, on television or in a newspaper रेडियो, टेलीविज़न या समाचार-पत्र समीक्षक या टिप्पणीकार *a political commentator*

**commerce** /ˈkɒmɜːs ˈकॉमस्/ *noun* [U] the business of buying and selling things वस्तुओं की क्रय-विक्रय की गतिविधि; वाणिज्य

**commercial**[1] /kəˈmɜːʃl कˈमशल्/ *adj.* **1** connected with buying and selling goods and services वस्तुएँ और सेवाएँ ख़रीदने और बेचने से संबंधित; वाणिज्यिक *commercial law* **2** making or trying to make money धनार्जन-संबंधी, व्यावसायिक, व्यापारिक *Although it won a lot of awards, the film was not a commercial success.* **3** selling sth or sold in large quantities to the public बड़ी संख्या या मात्रा में उपभोक्ताओं को सामग्री या सेवा बेचने से संबंधित; व्यापारिक *commercial airlines ○ commercial products*
▶ **commercially** /-ʃəli -शलि/ *adv.* व्यावसायिक रूप से, लाभ-हानि के संतुलन की दृष्टि से *The factory was closed down because it was no longer commercially viable.*

**commercial**[2] /kəˈmɜːʃl कˈमशल्/ *noun* [C] an advertisement on television or the radio टेलीविज़न या रेडियो पर प्रसारित विज्ञापन

**commercialism** /kəˈmɜːʃəlɪzəm कˈमशलिज़म्/ *noun* [U] the attitude that making money is more important than anything else धन कमाने को सर्वोपरि मानने की मनोवृत्ति; वाणिज्यवाद

**commercialize** (*also* **-ise**) /kəˈmɜːʃəlaɪz कˈमशलाइज़्/ *verb* [T] to try to make money out of sth, even if it means spoiling it पैसा बनाने को प्रधानता देना; व्यापारीकरण करना *Festivals have become very commercialized over recent years.*
▶ **commercialization** (*also* **-isation**) /kəˌmɜːʃəlaɪˈzeɪʃn कˌमशलाइˈज़ेशन्/ *noun* [U] व्यापारीकरण, वाणिज्यीकरण

**commiserate** /kəˈmɪzəreɪt कˈमिज़रेट्/ *verb* [I] (*formal*) **commiserate (with sb) (on/over/for sth)** to feel sorry for and show understanding towards sb who is unhappy or in difficulty पीड़ित या दुखी व्यक्ति के प्रति सहानुभूति व्यक्त करना *I commiserated with Ratna over losing her job.*

**commission**[1] /kəˈmɪʃn कˈमिशन्/ *noun* **1** (*often* **Commission**) [C, *with sing or pl. verb*] an official group of people who are asked to find out about sth आयोग *A Commission was appointed to investigate the causes of the accident.* **2** [C, U] money that you get for selling sth दलाली, आढ़त, कमीशन *The company's agents get 10% commission on everything they sell.* **3** [C, U] money that a bank, etc. charges for providing a particular service बैंक आदि द्वारा प्रदत्त सेवा के लिए शुल्क; आढ़त **4** [C] a formal request to an artist, writer, etc. to produce a piece of work चित्रकार, लेखक आदि से विशिष्ट कार्य आदि का, औपचारिक अनुरोध *He received a commission to write a play for the festival.*

**commission**[2] /kəˈmɪʃn कˈमिशन्/ *verb* [T] **commission sb (to do sth); commission sth (from sb)** to ask an artist, writer, etc. to do a piece of work लेखक आदि से विशिष्ट कार्य हेतु अनुरोध करना *to commission an architect to design a building*

**commissioner** /kəˈmɪʃənə(r) कˈमिशन(र्)/ *noun* [C] the head of the police or of a government department in some countries पुलिस या किसी सरकारी विभाग का आयुक्त ➪ **High Commissioner** देखिए।

**commit** /kəˈmɪt कˈमिट्/ *verb* [T] (**committing; committed**) **1** to do sth bad or illegal कोई ग़लत या ग़ैर-क़ानूनी कार्य करना *to commit a crime ○ to commit suicide* **2 commit sb/yourself (to sth/to doing sth)** to make a definite agreement or promise to do sth निश्चित और सुस्पष्ट समझौता करना या वचन देना *I can't commit myself to helping you tomorrow.* **3 commit yourself (on sth)** to make a decision or give an opinion publicly so that it is then difficult to change it सार्वजनिक रूप से कोई निर्णय घोषित करना या सम्मति प्रकट करना, ताकि उसे आसानी से बदला न जा सके *I'm not going to commit myself on who will win the election.* ➪ **non committal** देखिए। **4** (*formal*) to decide to use money or time in a certain way किसी रीति-विशेष में धन व्यय करने का निर्णय करना *The government has committed Rs 100 crore to primary education.* **5** (*formal*) **commit sb to sth** to send sb to a prison, mental hospital, etc. किसी को कारागार, मानसिक चिकित्सालय आदि में भेजना; के सुपुर्द करना

**commitment** /kəˈmɪtmənt कˈमिट्मन्ट्/ *noun* **1** [U] **commitment (to sth)** being prepared to give a lot of your time and attention to sth because you believe it is right or important किसी उचित या महत्त्वपूर्ण लगने वाले कार्य के प्रति संलग्नता; प्रतिबद्धता *I admire the brother's commitment to protecting the environment.* **2** [C, U] a promise or agreement to do sth; a responsibility वचन, वायदा; वचनबद्धता, दायित्व *When I* ***make a commitment*** *I always stick to it. ○ Shyamlee now works fewer hours because of family commitments.*

**committed** /kəˈmɪtɪd कˈमिटिड्/ *adj.* **committed (to sth)** prepared to give a lot of your time and attention to sth because you believe it is right or important (किसी उचित या महत्त्वपूर्ण लगने वाले कार्य में) संलग्न, प्रतिबद्ध *The company is committed to providing quality products.*

**committee** /kəˈmɪti कˈमिटि/ *noun* [C, *with sing. or pl. verb*] a group of people who have been chosen to discuss sth or decide sth समिति, कमेटी *to be/sit on a committee* ○ *The planning committee meets/meet twice a week.*

**commodity** /kəˈmɒdəti कˈमॉडटि/ *noun* [C] (*pl.* **commodities**) a product or material that can be bought and sold व्यापार की वस्तु; माल, सामान *Salt was once a very valuable commodity.*

**commodore** /ˈkɒmədɔ:(r) ˈकॉमडॉ(र्)/ *noun* [C] an officer at a high level in the navy नौसेना में उच्च पदाधिकारी

**common**[1] /ˈkɒmən ˈकॉमन्/ *adj.* **1** happening or found often or in many places; usual प्रायः या बहुत सारे स्थानों पर पाया जाने या होने वाला; सामान्य, आम *Drinking and driving is one of the most common causes of road accidents.* ○ *The daisy is a common wild flower.* ✪ विलोम **uncommon** **2 common (to sb/sth)** shared by or belonging to two or more people or groups; shared by most or all people सर्व-सामान्य; सार्वजनिक *This type of behaviour is common to most children of that age.* ○ *We have a common interest in gardening.* **3** (*only before a noun*) not special; ordinary अविशेष; साधारण, मामूली, आम *The officers had much better living conditions than the common soldiers.* **4** (*informal*) having or showing a lack of education अशिक्षित, गँवारू *Don't speak like that. It's common!*

**IDM** **be common/public knowledge** ➪ **knowledge** देखिए।

**common**[2] /ˈkɒmən ˈकॉमन्/ *noun* [C] an area of open land that anyone can use (किसी भी व्यक्ति द्वारा प्रयुक्त किया जा सकने वाला) सार्वजनिक क्षेत्र

**IDM** **have sth in common (with sb/sth)** to share sth with sb/sth else समान होना, एक जैसा होना *to have a lot in common with sb*

**in common with sb/sth** (*formal*) in the same way as sb/sth else; like sb/sth किसी अन्य की भाँति; औरों के समान, समान रूप से *This company, in common with many others, is losing a lot of money.*

**common denominator** *noun* [C] (*mathematics*) a number that can be divided exactly by all the numbers below the line in a set of **fractions** for example one of the common denominators of the fractions ½, ⅓ and ¼ is 12 वह संख्या जो भिन्नों के समुच्चय में सभी हरों से पूर्णतया विभाजित हो जाती है; सार्वहर, उदाहरण के लिए ½, ⅓, ¼ में संख्या 12 एक सार्वहर है ➪ **denominator** देखिए।

**common ground** *noun* [U] beliefs, interests, etc. that two or more people or groups share व्यक्तियों या वर्गों के समान, विश्वास हित आदि; समान आधार; सामान्य आधार

**commonly** /ˈkɒmənli ˈकॉमन्लि/ *adv.* normally; usually सामान्यतः, प्रायः

**common noun** *noun* [C] (*grammar*) a word, such as *book* or *town* that refers to an object or a thing but is not the name of a particular person, place or thing (अंग्रेज़ी व्याकरण में) जातिवाचक संज्ञा

**commonplace** /ˈkɒmənpleɪs ˈकॉमन्प्लेस्/ *adj.* not exciting or unusual; ordinary घिसा-पिटा; साधारण, मामूली

**common room** *noun* [C] a room in a school, university, etc. where students or teachers can go to relax when they are not in class शिक्षा संस्थाओं आदि में वह कमरा जहाँ छात्र या अध्यापक अपने ख़ाली समय में विश्राम कर सकते हैं; कॉमन रूम

**common sense** *noun* [U] the ability to make good sensible decisions or to behave in a sensible way सहज बुद्धि, सूझ-बूझ, व्यवहार-बुद्धि

**commotion** /kəˈməʊʃn कˈमोशन्/ *noun* [*sing.*, U] great noise or excitement शोरगुल, उत्तेजना, हुल्लड़, गड़बड़ी

**communal** /kəˈmju:nl; ˈkɒmjənl कˈम्यूनल्; ˈकॉम्यनल्/ *adj.* **1** shared by a group of people सामूहिक, सामुदायिक, पंचायती *a communal kitchen* **2** involving different groups of people in a community साम्प्रदायिक, समुदाय-संबंधी *communal tension in the city*

**communalism** /kəˈmju:nəlɪzəm कˈम्यूनलिज़म्/ *noun* [U] a strong sense of loyalty to the interests of one particular group (religious, ethnic, etc.) rather than to society as a whole which can lead to extreme behaviour or violence towards others सांप्रदायिकता ▸ **communalist** /kəˈmju:nəlɪst कˈम्यूनलिस्ट्/ *adj* सांप्रदायवादी ▸ **communalistic** /kəˈmju:nəlɪstic कˈम्यूनलिस्टिक/ *adj* सांप्रदायकतावादी

**commune** /ˈkɒmju:n ˈकॉम्यून्/ *noun* [C, *with sing. or pl. verb*] a group of people, not from the same family, who live together and share their property and responsibilities एक साथ रह रहे (न कि एक ही परिवार के) ऐसे लोगों का समुदाय जिनकी संपत्ति और दायित्वों में समान भागीदारी है; समुदाय, कम्यून

**communicable** /kəˈmju:nɪkəbl कˈम्यूनिकबूल्/ *adj* that can spread from one person or animal to another संक्रामक *communicable diseases*

**communicate** /kəˈmju:nɪkeɪt कˈम्यूनिकेट्/ *verb* **1** [I, T] to share and exchange information, ideas with sb सूचनाओं, विचारों और भावनाओं का आदान-प्रदान या संचार करना *Parents often have difficulty communicating with their teenage children.* ○ *Our boss is good at communicating her ideas to the team.* **2** [T] (*formal*) (*usually passive*) to pass a disease from one person or animal to another एक व्यक्ति या पशु का दूसरे को रोग संचारित करना **3** [I] to lead from one place to another एक स्थान से दूसरे स्थान पर ले जाना *two rooms with a communicating door*

**communication** /kəˌmju:nɪˈkeɪʃn कˌम्यूनिˈकेशन्/ *noun* **1** [U] the act of sharing or exchanging information, ideas or feelings सूचनाओं, विचारों और भावनाओं के आदान-प्रदान की क्रिया; संपर्क, संचार *Radio is the only means of communication in remote areas.* ○ *We are* ***in*** *regular* ***communication with*** *our head office in Mumbai.* **2 communications** [*pl.*] the methods that are used for travelling to and from a place or for sending messages between places यातायात और संदेश-प्रेषण की व्यवस्था; संचार-व्यवस्था *The telephone lines are down so communications are very difficult.* **3** [C] (*formal*) a message संदेश, संवाद, सूचना *a communication from head office*

**communicative** /kəˈmju:nɪkətɪv कˈम्यूनिकटिव़्/ *adj.* willing and able to talk and share ideas, etc. बातचीत या विचारों के आदान-प्रदान का इच्छुक व इसमें सक्षम *Sangeeta has excellent communicative skills.*

**communion** /kəˈmju:niən कˈम्यूनिअन्/ *noun* [U] **1** (*formal*) the sharing of thoughts or feelings विचारों या भावनाओं का आदान-प्रदान **2 Communion** a Christian church ceremony in which people share bread and wine ईसाई चर्च में समारोह जिसमें लोग ब्रेड और मदिरा का सेवन मिल-बाँटकर करते हैं

**communiqué** /kəˈmju:nɪkeɪ कˈम्यूनिके/ *noun* [C] (*written*) an official statement, especially from a government, a political group, etc. विशेषत: सरकार, राजनीतिक दल आदि के द्वारा जारी विज्ञप्ति; आधिकारिक वक्तव्य

**communism** /ˈkɒmjunɪzəm ˈकॉम्युनिज़म्/ *noun* [U] the political system in which the state owns and controls all factories, farms, services etc. and aims to treat everyone equally राजनीतिक व्यवस्था जिसमें राज्य सभी कारख़ानों, खेतों, सेवाओं आदि का स्वामी व नियंत्रक होता है और प्रजा के सभी सदस्यों को समानता प्रदान करने का उद्देश्य रखता है; साम्यवाद, कम्यूनिज़्म ➪ **Marxism, socialism** और **capitalism** देखिए।

**communist** (*also* **Communist**) /ˈkɒmjənɪst ˈकॉम्यनिस्ट्/ *noun* [C] a person who believes in or supports communism; a member of the Communist Party साम्यवादी, कम्युनिस्ट; साम्यवादी दल का सदस्य ▶ **communist** (*also* **Communist**) *adj.* साम्यवाद-संबंधी *communist sympathies*

**community** /kəˈmju:nəti कˈम्यूनटि/ *noun* (*pl.* **communities**) **1 the community** [*sing.*] all the people who live in a particular place, area, etc. when considered as a group एक समूह के रूप में संगठित स्थान-विशेष के समस्त निवासी; समुदाय *Recent increases in crime have disturbed the whole community.* **2** [C, *with sing. or pl. verb*] a group of people who have sth in common समानता-युक्त व्यक्तियों का वर्ग *the Indian community in Britain* ○ *the business community* **3** [U] the feeling of belonging to a group in the place where you live एक स्थान के निवासियों में एक समुदाय के रूप में संगठित होने की भावना; समुदाय-भावना *There is a strong sense of community in the neighbourhood.*

**community centre** *noun* [C] a building that local people can use for meetings, classes, sports, etc. वह भवन जहाँ समुदाय के सदस्य बैठक केंद्र आयोजित कर सकते है; सामुदायिक

**community service** *noun* [U] work helping people in the local community that sb does without being paid, sometimes because he/she has been ordered to do it by a court of law as punishment स्थान विशेष के लोगों की निःशुल्क या दंड स्वरूप सेवा; समुदाय-सेवा

**commutator** /ˈkɒmjuteɪtə(r) ˈकॉम्युटेट(र्)/ *noun* [C] (*technical*) **1** a device that connects a motor to the electricity supply मोटर को विद्युत स्रोत से जोड़ने वाला उपकरण **2** a device for changing the direction in which electricity flows विद्युत प्रवाह की दिशा को बदलने वाला उपकरण; दिक्-परिवर्तक

**commute** /kəˈmju:t कˈम्यूट्/ *verb* [I] to travel a long distance from home to work every day प्रतिदिन निवास स्थान से कार्य-स्थान तक यात्रा करना *A lot of people commute between Delhi and Ghaziabad.* ▶ **commuter** *noun* [C] दैनिक यात्री

**compact** /kəmˈpækt कम्ˈपैक्ट्/ *adj.* small and easy to carry छोटा और उठाकर ले जाने में सुविधाजनक *a compact camera*

**compact disc** = **CD**

**companion** /kəmˈpæniən कम्ˈपैनिअन् / *noun* [C] a person or animal with whom you spend a lot of time or go somewhere साथी, सखा, सहचर (मनुष्य या पशु) *a travelling companion*

**companionship** /kəmˈpæniənʃɪp कम्ˈपैनिअ-नशिप् / *noun* [U] the pleasant feeling of having a friendly relationship with sb and not being alone साहचर्य, मैत्री, साथ

**company** /ˈkʌmpəni ˈकम्पनि / *noun* (*pl.* **companies**) **1** [C, *with sing. or pl. verb*] a business organization selling goods or services व्यापारिक संस्था या संगठन; कंपनी *The company is/are planning to build a new factory.* NOTE नामों में प्रयुक्त शब्द **company** बड़े अक्षर से प्रारंभ किया जाता है। इस अर्थ में **company** का संक्षिप्त **Co.** है—*the Walt Disney Company ○ Milton & Co.* **2** [C, *with sing. or pl. verb*] a group of actors, singers, dancers, etc. अभिनेताओं, गायकों, नर्तकों आदि का दल, मंडली, टोली *a ballet company ○ the Royal Shakespeare Company* **3** [U] being with a person किसी व्यक्ति का साथ; सहचर्य *I always enjoy my Uncle's company. ○ Jeff is very good company* (= pleasant to be with). **4** [U] a visitor or visitors अतिथि (एक या अनेक) *Sorry, I wouldn't have called if I'd known you had company.*

IDM **keep sb company** to go or be with sb so that he/she is not alone किसी के साथ जाना या होना *She was nervous so I went with her to keep her company.*

**part company** ➪ **part**[2] देखिए।

**comparable** /ˈkɒmpərəbl ˈकॉम्परबल् / *adj.* **comparable (to/with sb/sth)** of a similar standard or size; that can be compared with sth समान स्तर या आकार का, तुलना करने योग्य; तुलनीय *A comparable flat in my city would be a lot cheaper.*

**comparative**[1] /kəmˈpærətɪv कम्ˈपैरटिव् / *adj.* **1** that compares things of the same kind तुलनात्मक *a comparative study of systems of government* **2** compared with sth else or with what is usual or normal सामान्य या किसी अन्य से तुलना करते हुए, सापेक्ष, अपेक्षाकृत *He had problems with the written exam but passed the practical exam with comparative ease.* **3** (*grammar*) (*used about the form of an adjective or adverb*) expressing a greater amount, quality, size, etc. (विशेषण या क्रियाविशेषण के) अपेक्षाकृत अधिकता प्रकट करने वाले रूप का संकेत करने के लिए प्रयुक्त; उत्तरावस्था *'Hotter' and 'more quickly' are the comparative forms of 'hot' and 'quickly'.*

**comparative**[2] /kəmˈpærətɪv कम्ˈपैरटिव् / *noun* [C] (*grammar*) the form of an adjective or adverb that expresses a greater amount, quality, size, etc. विशेषण या क्रियाविशेषण का अपेक्षाकृत अधिकता का सूचक रूप, उत्तरावस्था का रूप *'Bigger' is the comparative of 'big'.*

**comparatively** /kəmˈpærətɪvli कम्ˈपैरटिव्लि / *adv.* when compared with sth else or with what is usual; fairly अपेक्षाकृत, अपेक्षया *The disease is comparatively rare nowadays.*

**compare** /kəmˈpeə(r) कम्ˈपेअ(र्) / *verb* **1** [T] **compare A and B; compare A with/to B** to consider people or things in order to see how similar or how different they are वस्तुओं या व्यक्तियों में समानता और असमानता पर विचार करना; तुलना करना *I'm quite a patient person, **compared with** him. ○ **Compared to** the place where I grew up, this town is exciting.* **2** [T] **compare A to B** to say that sb/sth is similar to sb/sth else व्यक्तियों या वस्तुओं में समानता दिखाना; तुलना करना *When it was built, people compared the stadium to a spaceship.* **3** [I] **compare (with/to sb/sth)** to be as good as sb/sth व्यक्तियों या वस्तुओं का बराबर होना *Her last film was brilliant but this one simply doesn't compare.*

IDM **compare notes (with sb)** to discuss your opinions, ideas, experiences, etc. with sb else अपने विचारों, अनुभवों आदि पर किसी अन्य के साथ चर्चा करना

**comparison** /kəmˈpærɪsn कम्ˈपैरिसन् / *noun* [C, U] an act of comparing; a statement in which people or things are compared तुलना, तुलना-विषयक कथन; तुलनात्मक मूल्यांकन *Put the new one and the old one side by side, **for comparison**. ○ It's hard to **make comparisons** between two athletes from different sports.*

IDM **by/in comparison (with sb/sth)** when compared की तुलना में *In comparison with many other people, they're quite well off.*

**compartment** /kəmˈpɑːtmənt कम्ˈपाट्मन्ट् / *noun* [C] **1** one of the separate sections into which some larger parts of a train (**carriages**) are divided रेलगाड़ी का डिब्बा *a first-class compartment* **2** one of the separate sections into which certain containers are divided कुछ पात्रों का ख़ाना; खंड *The drugs were discovered in a secret compartment in his suitcase.*

**compass** /ˈkʌmpəs ˈकम्पस् / *noun* [C] **1** an instrument for finding direction, with a needle that always points north क़ुतुबनुमा, दिक्सूचक *They had to find their way back to the camp using a map and a compass.* **2 compasses** [*pl.*] a V-shaped instrument that is used for drawing circles (गोला खींचने का) परकार *a pair of compasses* ➪ पृष्ठ 234 पर चित्र देखिए।

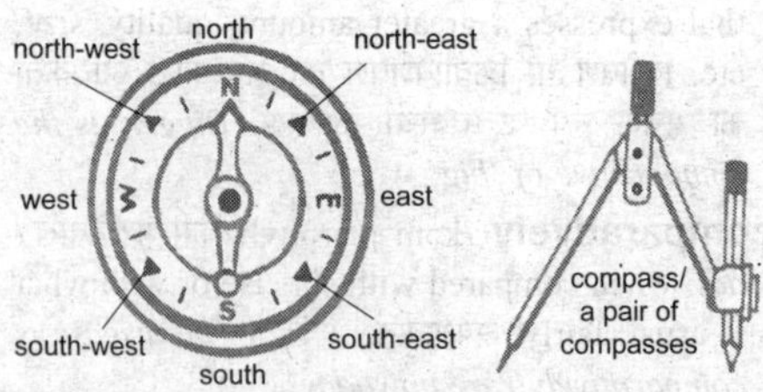


**compass**

**compassion** /kəmˈpæʃn कम्ˈपैश्न्/ *noun* [U] **compassion (for sb)** understanding or pity for sb who is suffering दयाभाव, करुणा, सहानुभूति, संवेदना *to have/feel/show compassion* ▶ **compassionate** /-ʃənət -शनट्/ *adj.* दयालू, संवेदनासूचक

**compatible** /kəmˈpætəbl कम्ˈपैटबल्/ *adj.* **compatible (with sb/sth)** suitable to be used together, or to live or exist together एक-दूसरे के साथ संगत; एक-दूसरे के अनुकूल (प्रयोग करने में या साथ रहने में) *These two computer systems are not compatible.* ○ *Arun's diet is not compatible with his active lifestyle.* ✪ विलोम **incompatible** ▶ **compatibility** /kəmˌpætəˈbɪləti कम्ˌपैटˈबिलटि/ *noun* [U] संगति, अनुकूलता

**compatriot** /kəmˈpætriət कम्ˈपैट्रिअट्/ *noun* [C] a person who comes from the same country as you देशभाई, समदेश, हमवतन

**compel** /kəmˈpel कम्ˈपेल्/ *verb* [T] (**compelling; compelled**) (*formal*) **compel sb to do sth** to force sb to do sth कुछ करने के लिए किसी को बाध्य या विवश करना *I felt compelled to tell her what I really thought of her.*

**compelling** /kəmˈpelɪŋ कम्ˈपेलिङ्/ *adj.* that forces or persuades you to do or to believe sth बाध्यकर, प्रबल प्रेरक; विवश करने वाला *compelling evidence* ➪ **compulsion** *noun* देखिए।

**compensate** /ˈkɒmpenseɪt ˈकॉम्पेन्सेट्/ *verb* **1** [I] **compensate (for sth)** to remove or reduce the bad effect of sth बुरे प्रभाव को दूर या कम करना; क्षति की पूर्ति करना, कमी को पूरा करना *His willingness to work hard compensates for his lack of skill.* **2** [I, T] **compensate (sb) (for sth)** to pay sb money because you have injured him/her or lost or damaged his/her property क्षति की पूर्ति के रूप में धन देना, हर्जाना देना *The airline sent me a cheque to compensate for losing my luggage.*

**compensation** /ˌkɒmpenˈseɪʃn ˌकॉम्पेन्ˈसेश्न्/ *noun* **1** [U] **compensation (for sth)** money that you pay to sb because you have injured him/her or lost or damaged his/her property मुआवज़ा, क्षतिपूर्ति (राशि) *I got Rs 10,000 (in) compensation for my injuries.* **2** [C, U] a fact or action that removes or reduces the bad effect of sth दुष्प्रभावनाशक स्थिति या क्रिया *City life can be very tiring but there are compensations* (= good things about it).

**compère** /ˈkɒmpeə(r) ˈकॉम्पेअ(र्)/ *noun* [C] a person who entertains the audience and introduces the different performers in a show किसी कार्यक्रम का प्रस्तुतकर्ता; सूत्रधार ▶ **compère** *verb* [T] कार्यक्रम प्रस्तुत करना; का सूत्रधार होना *Who compèred the show?*

**compete** /kəmˈpiːt कम्ˈपीट्/ *verb* [I] **compete (in sth) (against/with sb) (for sth)** to try to win or achieve sth, or to try to be better than sb else; to take part in a competition दूसरे से जीतने या उससे आगे निकलने का प्रयत्न करना, मुक़ाबला करना; स्पर्धा में भाग लेना *The world's best athletes compete in the Olympic Games.* ○ *Supermarkets have such low prices that small shops just can't compete.*

**competence** /ˈkɒmpɪtəns ˈकॉम्पिटन्स्/ *noun* [U] the fact of having the ability or skill that is needed for sth कुछ करने की क्षमता, विशिष्ट योग्यता सामर्थ्य, सक्षमता *She quickly proved her competence in her new position.* ✪ विलोम **incompetence**

**competent** /ˈkɒmpɪtənt ˈकॉम्पिटन्ट्/ *adj.* **1** having the ability or skill needed for sth सक्षम, योग्य *a highly competent player* ○ *She is competent at her job.* ✪ विलोम **incompetent** **2** good enough, but not excellent अच्छा (परंतु बहुत अच्छा या उत्कृष्ट नहीं) *The singer gave a competent, but not particularly exciting, performance.* ▶ **competently** *adv.* सक्षम रूप से, क्षमतापूर्वक, काफ़ी अच्छे ढंग से

**competition** /ˌkɒmpəˈtɪʃn ˌकॉम्पˈटिश्न्/ *noun* **1** [C] an organized event in which people try to win sth प्रतियोगिता, प्रतिस्पर्धा *to **go in for/enter a competition*** ○ *They **hold a competition** every year to find the best young artist.* **2** [U] a situation where two or more people or organizations are trying to achieve, obtain, etc. the same thing or to be better than sb else मुक़ाबला, होड़ *He is **in competition with** three other people for promotion.* ○ *There was **fierce competition** among the players for places in the team.* **3 the competition** [*sing., with sing. or pl. verb*] the other people, companies, etc. who are trying to achieve the same as you प्रतियोगी व्यक्ति, कंपनियाँ आदि; प्रतिस्पर्धी *If we are going to succeed, we must offer a better product than the competition.*

**competitive** /kəmˈpetətɪv कम्ˈपेटटिव़् / *adj.* **1** involving people or organizations competing against each other प्रतिस्पर्धात्मक *The travel industry is a highly competitive business.* ○ *competitive sports* **2** able to be as successful as or more successful than others अन्यों के समान या अन्यों से अधिक सफल; प्रतिस्पर्धा में सक्षम, मुक़ाबले में ठहरने वाला *They are trying to make the company competitive in the international market.* ○ *Our prices are highly competitive* (= as low as or lower then those of the others). **3** (used about people) wanting very much to win or to be more successful than others (व्यक्ति) प्रतिस्पर्धा में विजय या सफलता का अभिलाषी *She's a very competitive player.* ▶ **competitively** *adv.* प्रतिस्पर्धात्मक रीति से *Their products are competitively priced.* ▶ **competitiveness** *noun* [U] प्रतिस्पर्धात्मकता

**competitor** /kəmˈpetɪtə(r) कम्ˈपेटिट(र्) / *noun* [C] a person or organization that is competing against others प्रतिस्पर्धी, प्रतियोगी व्यक्ति या संस्था *There are ten competitors in the first race.* ○ *Two local companies are our main competitors.*

**compilation** /ˌkɒmpɪˈleɪʃn ˌकॉम्पिˈलेश्न् / *noun* **1** [C] a collection of pieces of music, writing, film, etc. that are taken from different places and put together अलग-अलग गीतों, लेखों, फ़िल्मों आदि के अंशों का संग्रह; संकलन *a compilation CD of the band's greatest hits* **2** [U] the act of compiling sth संग्रह-कार्य, संकलन-कार्य

**compile** /kəmˈpaɪl कम्ˈपाइल् / *verb* **1** [I] to collect information and arrange it in a list, book, etc. सूचना का संग्रह कर उसे संयोजित करना (सूची, पुस्तक आदि में) *to compile a dictionary/a report/a list* **2** [I, T] (*computing*) to translate instructions from one computer language into another for a computer to understand निर्देशों का एक कंप्यूटर भाषा से दूसरी कंप्यूटर भाषा में अनुवाद करना (कंप्यूटर द्वारा समझने के लिए)

**complacent** /kəmˈpleɪsnt कम्ˈप्लेसन्ट् / *adj.* feeling too satisfied with yourself or with a situation, so that you think that there is no need to worry अपनी उन्नति से अति-संतुष्ट व निश्चिंत *He had won his matches so easily that he was in danger of becoming complacent.* ▶ **complacency** /kəmˈpleɪsnsi कम्ˈप्लेसन्सि / *noun* [U] आत्मसंतोष, अति-संतोष ▶ **complacently** *adv.* आत्मसंतोषपूर्वक, अति संतुष्ट होकर

**complain** /kəmˈpleɪn कम्ˈप्लेन् / *verb* [I] **1 complain (to sb) (about sth/that...)** to say that you are not satisfied with or happy about sth किसी बात से असंतोष व्यक्त करना; शिकायत करना *People are always complaining about the weather.* ○ *We complained to the hotel manager that the room was too noisy.* ➪ **grumble** और **protest** पर नोट देखिए। **2** (*formal*) **complain of sth** to say that you have a pain or illness दर्द या बीमारी के बारे में बताना *He went to the doctor, complaining of chest pains.*

**complaint** /kəmˈpleɪnt कम्ˈप्लेन्ट् / *noun* **complaint (about sth); complaint (that...)** **1** [C] a statement that you are not satisfied with sth शिकायत, असंतोष का कारण *You should **make a complaint** to the company that made the machine.* **2** [U] the act of complaining शिकायत करने की क्रिया *I wrote a **letter of complaint** to the manager about the terrible service I had received.* ○ *Ashutosh's behaviour never gave the teachers **cause for complaint**.* **3** [C] an illness or disease बीमारी, रोग *a heart complaint*

**complement[1]** /ˈkɒmplɪmənt ˈकॉम्प्लिमन्ट् / *noun* [C] **1** (*formal*) a thing that goes together well with sth else पूरक या अनुकूल वस्तु; संपूरक *Ice cream is the perfect complement to this dessert.* **2** the total number that makes a group complete मदों, सदस्यों की पूर्ण संख्या; किसी दल, वर्ग के कुल सदस्य, मदें *Without a full complement of players, the team will not be able to take part in the match.* **3** (*grammar*) a word or words, especially a noun or adjective, used after a verb such as 'be' or 'become' and describing the subject of that verb अंग्रेज़ी व्याकरण में क्रियाएँ 'be' या 'become' के बाद प्रयुक्त पूरक शब्द (विशेषतः संज्ञा या विशेषण) *In 'He's friendly' and 'He's a fool', 'friendly' and 'fool' are complements.*

**complement[2]** /ˈkɒmplɪment ˈकॉम्प्लिमन्ट् / *verb* [T] to go together well with पूरक या अनुकूल होना *The colours of the furniture and the carpet complement each other.*

**complementary** /ˌkɒmplɪˈmentri ˌकॉम्-प्लिˈमेन्ट्रि / *adj.* going together well with sb/sth; adding sth which the other person or thing does not have संगत, अनुकूल; पूरक *They work well together because their skills are complementary—he's practical and she's creative.*

**complete[1]** /kəmˈpliːt कम्ˈप्लीट् / *adj.* **1** having or including all parts; with nothing missing संपूर्ण; सर्वांशपूर्ण, सारा *I gave a complete list of the stolen items to the police.* ○ *The book explains the complete history of the place.* **2** (*not before a noun*) finished or ended समाप्त, संपन्न *The repair work should be completed by Wednesday.*

✪ विलोम **incomplete** (अर्थ संख्याओं **1** और **2** के लिए) **3 complete (with sth)** including sth extra, in addition to what is expected अतिरिक्त अंश समेत *The computer **comes complete with** instruction manual and printer.* **4** (*only before a noun*) as great as possible; total; in every way अधिकतम सीमा तक; पूरा-का-पूरा; सब तरह से *It was a complete waste of time.* ○ *The room is a complete mess.* ▶ **completeness** *noun* [U] पूर्णता

**complete²** /kəmˈpliːt कम्ˈप्लीट्/ *verb* [T] **1** to make sth whole किसी को पूरा करना *We need two more players to complete the team.* **2** to finish sth; to bring sth to an end समाप्त करना; पूरा करना; संपन्न करना *She completed her teacher training course in June 2004.* **3** to write all the necessary information on sth (for example a form) किसी विषय पर सारी आवश्यक जानकारी लिखना, जैसे प्रपत्र पर *Please complete the following in capital letters.*

**completely** /kəmˈpliːtli कम्ˈप्लीट्लि/ *adv.* in every way; fully; totally सब तरह से; पूरे तौर पर; संपूर्ण रूप से *The building was completely destroyed by fire.*

**completion** /kəmˈpliːʃn कम्ˈप्लीश्न्/ *noun* [U] (*formal*) the act of finishing sth or the state of being finished काम पूरा करने की क्रिया या काम के पूरा हो जाने की स्थिति; समाप्ति; संपन्नता *You will be paid on completion of the work.* ○ *The new highway is due for completion within two years.*

**complex¹** /ˈkɒmpleks ˈकॉम्प्लेक्स्/ *adj.* made up of several connected parts and often difficult to understand; complicated अनेक परस्पर संबद्ध अंशों से निर्मित और प्रायः दुर्बोध; पेचीदा; जटिल *a complex problem/subject*

**complex²** /ˈkɒmpleks ˈकॉम्प्लेक्स्/ *noun* [C] **1** a group of connected things, especially buildings परस्पर संयुक्त या शृंखलाबद्ध वस्तुओं की श्रेणी, विशेषतः भवनों की *a shopping/sports complex* **2 a complex (about sth)** an emotional problem that makes sb worry too much about sth in a way that is not normal एक मनोवैज्ञानिक दशा जिसमें व्यक्ति किसी विषय पर अस्वाभाविक ढंग से अत्यधिक चिंता करने लगता है; मनोग्रंथि *He's got a complex about his height.* ○ *an inferiority complex*

**complexion** /kəmˈplekʃn कम्ˈप्लेक्श्न्/ *noun* [C] **1** the natural colour and quality of the skin on your face चेहरे की त्वचा का प्राकृतिक रंग और गुण, रूप-रंग *a dark/fair complexion* ○ *a healthy complexion* **2** [*usually sing.*] the general nature or character of sth (किसी वस्तु या स्थिति का) सामान्य स्वरूप *These announcements **put a different complexion on** our situation.*

**complexity** /kəmˈpleksəti कम्ˈप्लेक्सटि/ *noun* (*pl.* **complexities**) **1** [U] the state of being complex and difficult to understand जटिलता और दुर्बोधता *an issue of great complexity* **2** [C] one of the many details that make sth complicated जटिलता का कोई पहलू *I haven't time to explain the complexities of the situation now.*

**compliant** /kəmˈplaɪənt कम्ˈप्लाइअन्ट्/ *adj.* (*formal*) **compliant (with sth)** working or done in agreement with particular rules, orders, etc. नियम, आदेश आदि के अनुसार, के अनुरूप *All new products must be compliant with 150 specifications.* ▶ **compliance** *noun* [U] अनुपालन, अनुरूपता *A hard hat must be worn at all times **in compliance with** safety regulations.*

**complicate** /ˈkɒmplɪkeɪt ˈकॉमप्लिकेट्/ *verb* [T] to make sth difficult to understand or deal with समझने या व्यवहार में दुर्बोध बना देना, उलझा देना *Let's not complicate things by adding too many details.* ▶ **complicated** *adj.* जटिल, पेचीदा, दुर्बोध *a novel with a very complicated plot*

**complication** /ˌkɒmplɪˈkeɪʃn ˌकॉम्प्लिˈकेश्न्/ *noun* [C] **1** something that makes a situation hard to understand or to deal with उलझन, परेशानी, जटिलता, पेचीदगी *Unless there are any unexpected complications, I'll be arriving next month.* **2** a new illness that you get when you are already ill रोगी को लगने वाला एक और रोग, नया रोग *Unless he develops complications, he'll be out of hospital in a week.*

**complicity** /kəmˈplɪsəti कम्ˈप्लिसटि/ *noun* [U] (*formal*) the fact of being involved with sb else in a crime अपराध में सहयोग, साँठ-गाँठ, मिली भगत

**compliment¹** /ˈkɒmplɪmənt ˈकॉम्प्लिमन्ट्/ *noun* **1** [C] **a compliment (on sth)** a statement or action that shows admiration for sb प्रशंसा, तारीफ़ *People often **pay** her **compliments** on her piano playing.* **2 compliments** [*pl.*] (*formal*) used to say that you like sth or to thank sb for sth प्रशंसा या आभार प्रदर्शन की अभिव्यक्ति के लिए प्रयुक्त *Tea and coffee are provided with the compliments of the hotel management* (= without charge).

**compliment²** /ˈkɒmplɪment ˈकॉम्प्लिमन्ट्/ *verb* [T] **compliment sb (on sth)** to say that you think sb/sth is very good किसी की अच्छाई, गुण आदि के लिए प्रशंसा करना या बधाई देना *She complimented them on their smart appearance.*

**complimentary** /ˌkɒmplɪˈmentri ˌकॉम्प्लिˈमेन्ट्रि/ *adj.* **1** showing that you think sb/sth is very good प्रशंसात्मक, सम्मानसूचक *He made several complimentary remarks about her work.* **2** given free of charge सम्मानार्थ, निःशुल्क *a complimentary theatre ticket*

**comply** /kəmˈplaɪ कम्ˈप्लाइ/ *verb* [I] (*pres. part.* **complying**; *3rd person sing. pres.* **complies;** *pt, pp* **complied**) (*formal*) **comply (with sth)** to obey an order or request आदेश या अनुरोध को मानना *All office buildings must comply with the safety regulations.*

**component** /kəmˈpəʊnənt कम्ˈपोनन्ट्/ *noun* [C] one of several parts of which sth is made किसी संपूर्ण वस्तु का भाग; अवयव, घटक *the components of a machine/system* ▶ **component** *adj.* घटक *the component parts of an engine*

**compose** /kəmˈpəʊz कम्ˈपोज़्/ *verb* **1** [T] to be the parts that together form sth घटकों का अपने से बड़ी वस्तु को बनाना *the parties that compose the coalition government* **2** [I, T] to write music संगीत-रचना करना *to compose beautiful melodies* **3** [T] to produce a piece of writing, using careful thought विचारपूर्वक कुछ लिखना *I sat down and composed a letter of reply.* **4** [T] to make yourself, your feelings, etc. become calm and under control स्वयं को नियंत्रित या संयत करना; शांत होना *The news came as such a shock that it took me a while to **compose myself**.*

**composed** /kəmˈpəʊzd कम्ˈपोज़्ड्/ *adj.* **1 composed of sth** made or formed from several different parts, people, etc. विभिन्न घटकों, व्यक्तियों आदि से निर्मित *The committee is composed of politicians from all parties.* **2** calm, in control of your feelings शांत, आत्म-नियंत्रित, संयत *Although he felt very nervous, he managed to appear composed.*

**composer** /kəmˈpəʊzə(r) कम्ˈपोज़(र्)/ *noun* [C] a person who writes music संगीत का रचनाकार

**composite** /ˈkɒmpəzɪt ˈकॉम्पज़िट्/ *adj.* consisting of different parts or materials विभिन्न घटकों या प्रदार्थों से बना; विभिन्न घटकों से निर्मित; संग्रथित; मिश्रित ▶ **composite** *noun* [C] यौगिक, संघटित

**composition** /ˌkɒmpəˈzɪʃn ˌकॉम्पˈज़िश्न्/ *noun* **1** [U] the parts that form sth; the way in which the parts of sth are arranged घटक; घटकों के संयोजन की रीति *the chemical composition of a substance* ○ *the composition of the population* **2** [C] a piece of music that has been written by sb किसी के द्वारा रचित संगीत *R D Burman's best-known compositions* **3** [U] the act or skill of writing a piece of music or text गीत या संगीत रचने की क्रिया या कौशल *She studied both musical theory and composition.* **4** [C] a short piece of writing done at school, in an exam, etc. शिक्षण कार्य, परीक्षा आदि में लघु लेख *Write a composition of about 300 words on one of the following subjects.*

**compost** /ˈkɒmpɒst ˈकॉम्पॉस्ट्/ *noun* [U] a mixture of dead plants, old food, etc. that is added to soil to help plants grow कूड़ा-खाद, वानस्पतिक खाद

**composure** /kəmˈpəʊʒə(r) कम्ˈपोश़(र्)/ *noun* [U] the state of being calm and having your feelings under control शांत और आत्म-नियंत्रित होने की अवस्था; संयम

**compound[1]** /ˈkɒmpaʊnd ˈकॉम्पाउन्ड्/ *noun* [C] **1** something that consists of two or more things or substances combined together यौगिक पदार्थ *a chemical compound* **2** (*grammar*) a noun, an adjective or a verb made of two or more words or parts of words, written as one or more words, or joined by a **hyphen** (अंग्रेज़ी व्याकरण में) दो या अधिक शब्दों या शब्दांशों से बना शब्द; यौगिक संज्ञा, विशेषण या क्रिया; समस्त पद *'Car park', 'bad-tempered' and 'bathroom' are all compounds.* **3** an area of land with a group of buildings on it, surrounded by a wall or fence दीवार या बाढ़े से घेरा गया भूक्षेत्र जिस पर अनेक भवन बने हों

**compound[2]** /kəmˈpaʊnd कम्ˈपाउन्ड्/ *verb* [T] to make sth such as a problem worse समस्या आदि को और बिगाड़ देना; स्थिति को बदतर कर देना

**comprehend** /ˌkɒmprɪˈhend ˌकॉम्प्रिˈहेन्ड्/ *verb* [T] (*formal*) to understand sth completely (किसी बात को) पूरी तरह समझना *She's too young to comprehend what has happened.*

**comprehensible** /ˌkɒmprɪˈhensəbl ˌकॉम्प्रिˈहेन्सब्ल्/ *adj.* easy to understand समझने में आसान, सरल-सुबोध *The book is written in clear, comprehensible language.* ✪ विलोम **incomprehensible**

**comprehension** /ˌkɒmprɪˈhenʃn ˌकॉम्प्रिˈहेन्श्न्/ *noun* **1** [U] (*formal*) the ability to understand समझने की योग्यता, बोधन-क्षमता *The horror of war is **beyond comprehension**.* ✪ विलोम **incomprehension** **2** [C, U] an exercise that tests how well you understand spoken or written language लिखित या मौखिक अभिव्यक्ति के बोधन को परखने के लिए अभ्यास *a listening comprehension*

**comprehensive[1]** /ˌkɒmprɪˈhensɪv ˌकॉम्प्रिˈहेन्सिव्/ *adj.* **1** including everything or nearly everything that is connected with a particular subject व्यापक, विस्तृत *a guidebook giving comprehensive information on the area* **2** (used about education) educating children of all levels of ability in the same school एक ही स्कूल में विविध योग्यता-स्तरों के बच्चों की शिक्षा व्यवस्था से संबंधित *a comprehensive education system*

**comprehensive²** /ˌkɒmprɪˈhensɪv ˌकॉम्प्रि ˈहेन्सिव़् / (*also* **comprehensive school**) (*BrE*) *noun* [C] a secondary school in which children of all levels of ability are educated ऐसा माध्यमिक विद्यालय जहाँ विविध योग्यता-स्तरों के बच्चे एक साथ पढ़ते हैं *I went to the local comprehensive.*

**comprehensively** /ˌkɒmprɪˈhensɪvli ˌकॉम्प्रि ˈहेन्सिव़्लि / *adv.* completely; thoroughly पूरी तरह से; भली-भांति

**compress** /kəmˈpres कम् ˈप्रेस् / *verb* [T] **1 compress sth (into sth)** to make sth fill less space than usual दबाकर भरना, संपीडित करना, संक्षिप्त करना *Divers breathe compressed air from tanks.* ○ *He found it hard to compress his ideas into a single page.* **2** (*computing*) to make computer files, etc. smaller so that they use less space on a disk, etc. कंप्यूटर फ़ाइलों को संपीडित कर छोटा बनाना ताकि वे डिस्क आदि पर कम स्थान घेरे या डिस्क में समा सके ✪ विलोम **decompress** ▶ **compression** /kəmˈpreʃn कम् ˈप्रेश्न् / *noun* [U] दबाव, संपीडन

**comprise** /kəmˈpraɪz कम् ˈप्राइज़् / *verb* [T] **1** to consist of; to have as parts or members मिलकर बना होना; सदस्यों या अंशों से युक्त होना; के अंतर्गत होना *a house comprising three bedrooms, kitchen, bathroom and a living room* **2** to form or be part of sth किसी को बनाना या उसका अंग होना *Women comprise 62% of the staff.*

**compromise¹** /ˈkɒmprəmaɪz ˈकॉम्प्रमाइज़् / *noun* [C, U] **a compromise (on sth)** an agreement that is reached when each person gets part, but not all, of what he/she wanted सुलह आदि के लिए किया गया समझौता जिसमें हर व्यक्ति की केवल कुछ ही माँगें पूरी होती हैं; मध्य रास्ता *to **reach a compromise*** ○ *Both sides will have to be prepared to **make compromises**.*

**compromise²** /ˈkɒmprəmaɪz ˈकॉम्प्रमाइज़् / *verb* **1** [I] **compromise (with sb) (on sth)** to accept less than you want or are aiming for, especially in order to reach an agreement अभीष्ट से कुछ कम पर मान जाना, विशेषतः सुलह या समझौते के लिए *Unless both sides are prepared to compromise, there will be no peace agreement.* ○ *The company never compromises on the quality of its products.* **2** [T] **compromise sb/sth/yourself** to put sb/sth/yourself in a bad or dangerous position, especially by doing sth that is not very sensible ग़लत काम करके अपने को या किसी अन्य को संकट की स्थिति में डालना *He compromised himself by accepting money from them.*

**compulsion** /kəmˈpʌlʃn कम् ˈपल्शन् / *noun* **1** [U] the act of forcing sb to do sth or being forced to do sth किसी बात के लिए स्वयं या किसी को बाध्य करने की या बाध्य होने की क्रिया; विवशता, दबाव *There is no compulsion to take part. You can decide yourself.* ⇨ **compel** verb देखिए। **2** [C] a strong desire that you cannot control, often to do sth that you should not do अनियंत्रित व प्रायः अनुचित मनोवेग ✪ पर्याय **urge**

**compulsive** /kəmˈpʌlsɪv कम् ˈपल्सिव़् / *adj.* **1** (used about a bad or harmful habit) caused by a strong desire that you cannot control (बुरी आदत) अनियंत्रित इच्छा के अधीन; (आदतन) मजबूर, विवश, बाध्यकारी *compulsive eating* **2** (used about a person) having a bad habit that he/she cannot control (व्यक्ति) अनियंत्रित बुरी आदत वाला *a compulsive gambler/shoplifter* **3** so interesting or exciting that you cannot take your attention away from it इतना रुचिकर या उत्तेजक कि ध्यान हटाना मुश्किल हो *This book makes compulsive reading.* ▶ **compulsively** *adv.* विवशतापूर्वक

**compulsory** /kəmˈpʌlsəri कम् ˈपल्सरि / *adj.* that must be done, by law, rules, etc. (क़ानून-नियम आदि से) अनिवार्य, बाध्यकर *Maths and English are compulsory subjects on this course.* ○ *It is compulsory to wear a hard hat on the building site.* ✪ पर्याय **obligatory** NOTE जो करना अनिवार्य न हो उसके लिए **non-compulsory, voluntary** या **optional** शब्द प्रयुक्त होते हैं।

**compute** /kəmˈpjuːt कम् ˈप्यूट् / *verb* [T] (*formal*) to calculate sth हिसाब लगाना; परिकलन या संगणन करना

**computer** /kəmˈpjuːtə(r) कम् ˈप्यूट(र्) / *noun* [C] an electronic machine that can store, find and arrange information, calculate amounts and control other machines जानकारी संचित करने, ढूँढ़ने व व्यवस्थित करने, परिकलन करने व अन्य मशीनों पर नियंत्रण रख पाने वाली एक इलेक्ट्रॉनिक मशीन; कंप्यूटर *The bills are all done **by computer**.* ○ *a computer program*

**computerize** (*also* **-ise**) /kəmˈpjuːtəraɪz कम् ˈप्यूटराइज़् / *verb* [T] to use computers to do a job or to store information (सूचना-संग्रह या किसी कार्य के लिए) कंप्यूटर का प्रयोग करना *The whole factory has been computerized.* ○ *We have now computerized the library catalogue.* ▶ **computerization** (*also* **-isation**) /kəmˌpjuːtəraɪˈzeɪʃn कम्ˌप्यूटराइˈज़ेश्न् / *noun* [U] कंप्यूटरीकरण

**computer-literate** *adj.* able to use a computer कंप्यूटर-प्रयोग का जानकार; कंप्यूटर-दक्ष

**computing** /kəmˈpjuːtɪŋ कम्ˈप्यूटिङ्/ *noun* [U] the use of computers कंप्यूटर का प्रयोग *She did a course in computing.*

**comrade** /ˈkɒmreɪd ˈकॉम्रेड्/ *noun* [C] **1** (*formal*) a person who fights on the same side as you in a war सहयोद्धा, साथी सैनिक *He saw many of his comrades die in battle.* **2** (*old-fashioned*) a person who is a member of the same **socialist** political party or group as the speaker वक्ता के राजनीतिक दल का या समाजवादी दल का साथी सदस्य; कामरेड *Comrades, we will fight against injustice!* ▶ **comradeship** /ˈkɒmreɪdʃɪp ˈकॉम्रेड्शिप्/ *noun* [U] मैत्री, बंधुता, भाईचारा *He enjoys the comradeship of the army.*

**con**[1] /kɒn कॉन्/ *verb* [T] (**conning; conned**) (*informal*) **con sb (into doing sth/out of sth)** to cheat sb, especially in order to get money किसी से धोखा करना, विशेषतः धन ऐंठने के लिए *He conned her into investing in a company that didn't really exist.* ○ *The old lady was conned out of her life savings.*

**con**[2] /kɒn कॉन्/ *noun* [C] (*informal*) a trick, especially in order to cheat sb out of some money धोखा, चालाकी, ठगी, विशेषतः धन ऐंठने के लिए

IDM **the pros and cons** ➪ **pro** देखिए।

**con-** /kɒn कॉन्/ *prefix* (*used in adjectives, adverbs, nouns and verbs*) with; together साथ; एक साथ *concurrent* ○ *convene*

**concave** /kɒnˈkeɪv कॉन्ˈकेव्/ *adj.* having a surface that curves towards the inside of sth, like the inside of a bowl (सतह) अंदर की तरफ़ मुड़ती हुई; अवतल, नतोदर ➪ **convex** देखिए तथा **lens** पर चित्र देखिए।

**conceal** /kənˈsiːl कन्ˈसील्/ *verb* [T] (*formal*) **conceal sth/sb (from sb/sth)** to hide sth/sb; to prevent sth/sb from being seen or discovered (किसी से कुछ) छिपाना; गुप्त रखना *She tried to conceal her anger from her friend.* ▶ **concealment** *noun* [U] छिपाव, संगोपन *the concealment of the facts of the case*

**concede** /kənˈsiːd कन्ˈसीड्/ *verb* [T] (*formal*) **1** to admit that sth is true although you do not want to किसी सचाई को न चाहते हुए भी मान लेना; स्वीकार करना *When it was clear that he would lose the election, he conceded defeat.* **2 concede sth (to sb)** to allow sb to take sth although you do not want to दूसरे को अनिच्छा से कुछ ले जाने का अधिकार प्रदान करना *They lost the war and had to concede territory to their enemy.* ➪ **concession** noun देखिए।

**conceit** /kənˈsiːt कन्ˈसीट्/ *noun* [U] too much pride in yourself and your abilities and importance अहंकार, घमंड ▶ **conceited** *adj.* अहंकारी, घमंडी *He's so conceited—he thinks he's the best at everything!*

**conceivable** /kənˈsiːvəbl कन्ˈसीवबल्/ *adj.* possible to imagine or believe कल्पनीय, विश्वास योग्य *I made every conceivable effort to succeed.* ✪ विलोम **inconceivable** ▶ **conceivably** /-əbli -बलि/ *adv.* विश्वास योग्य रीति से *She might just conceivably be telling the truth.*

**conceive** /kənˈsiːv कन्ˈसीव्/ *verb* **1** [T] (*formal*) to think of a new idea or plan नया विचार आना या नई योजना के बारे में सोचना *He conceived the idea for the novel during his journey through India.* **2** [I, T] (*formal*) **conceive (of) sb/sth (as sth)** to think about sb/sth in a particular way; to imagine किसी के विषय में विशेष प्रकार से सोचना; कल्पना करना *He started to conceive of the world as a dangerous place.* **3** [I, T] to become pregnant गर्भ धारण करना ➪ **conception** noun देखिए।

**concentrate** /ˈkɒnsntreɪt ˈकॉन्सन्ट्रेट्/ *verb* [I, T] **1 concentrate (sth) (on sth/doing sth)** to give all your attention or effort to sth (किसी कार्य आदि पर) ध्यान या प्रयास केंद्रित करना *I need to concentrate on passing this exam.* ○ *I tried to concentrate my thoughts on the problem.* **2** to come together or to bring people or things together in one place वस्तुओं या व्यक्ति का केंद्रीभूत होना या केंद्रित करना *Most factories are concentrated in one small area of the town.*

**concentrated** /ˈkɒnsntreɪtɪd ˈकॉन्सन्ट्रेटिड्/ *adj.* **1** showing determination सुदृढ़, पक्के इरादे वाला *With one concentrated effort we can finish the work by tonight.* **2** made stronger by the removal of some liquid सांद्रित; (द्रव को निकालकर) गाढ़ा बनाया हुआ *This is concentrated orange juice. You have to add water before you drink it.* ✪ विलोम **dilute**

**concentration** /ˌkɒnsnˈtreɪʃn ˌकॉन्सन्ˈट्रेशन्/ *noun* **1** [U] **concentration (on sth)** the ability to give all your attention or effort to sth (ध्यान या प्रयास की) एकाग्रता; केंद्रीकरण *This type of work requires total concentration.* ○ *Don't* ***lose your concentration*** *or you might make a mistake.* **2** [C] **concentration (of sth)** a large amount of people or things in one place बड़ी संख्या या मात्रा में व्यक्तियों या वस्तुओं

का एक स्थान पर केंद्रीकरण *There is a high concentration of chemicals in the drinking water here.*

**concentration camp** *noun* [C] a prison (usually a number of buildings inside a high fence) where civilians political prisoners and sometimes prisoners of war are kept, usually under very harsh conditions आम नागरिकों, राजनीतिक बंदियों और कभी-कभी युद्ध बंदियों को प्रायः कठोर परिस्थितियों में क़ैद रखने के लिए कारागार; नज़रबंदी शिविर

**concentric** /kənˈsentrɪk कन्ˈसेन्ट्रिक् / *adj.* (used about circles of different sizes) having the same centre point (विभिन्न आकारों के वृत्त) एक ही केंद्र वाले; संकेंद्रिक

**concept** /ˈkɒnsept ˈकॉन्सेप्ट् / *noun* [C] **the concept (of sth/that...)** an idea; a basic principle विचार; मूल सिद्धांत *It is difficult to* ***grasp the concept*** *of eternity.* ► **conceptual** /kənˈseptʃuəl कन्ˈसेप्चुअल् / *adj.* विचारात्मक, धारणात्मक

**conception** /kənˈsepʃn कन्ˈसेप्शन् / *noun* **1** [C, U] **(a) conception (of sth)** an understanding of how or what sth is समझ, बोध *We have no real conception of what people suffered during the war.* **2** [U] the process of forming an idea or a plan विचार या योजना बनाने की प्रक्रिया **3** [U, C] the moment when a woman or female animal becomes pregnant स्त्री, मादा पशु के गर्भधारण करने का क्षण ➪ **conceive** verb देखिए।

**concern¹** /kənˈsɜːn कन्ˈसन् / *verb* [T] **1** to affect or involve sb/sth किसी को प्रभावित या शामिल करना; किसी से संबंधित होना *This does not concern you. Please go away.* ○ *It is important that no risks are taken* ***where*** *safety* ***is concerned.*** **2** to be about sth किसी के विषय में होना; से संबंधित होना *The main problem concerns the huge cost of the project.* **3** to worry sb किसी को चिंतित करना *What concerns me is that we have no long-term plan.* **4 concern yourself with sth** to give your attention to sth किसी बात पर ध्यान देना *You needn't concern yourself with the hotel booking. The travel agent will take care of it.*

**IDM be concerned in sth** to have a connection with or be involved in sth किसी बात से संबद्ध होना *She was concerned in a drugs case some years ago.*

**be concerned with sth** to be about sth किसी के विषय में होना *Tonight's programme is concerned with the effects of the law on ordinary people.*

**concern²** /kənˈsɜːn कन्ˈसन् / *noun* **1** [C, U] concern **(for/about/over sb/sth); concern (that...)** a feeling of worry; sth that causes worry चिंता; परवाह; चिंताजनक बात *The safety officer assured us that there was no* ***cause for concern.*** ○ *My main concern is that we'll run out of money.* **2** [C] something that is important to you or that involves you किसी के लिए कोई महत्त्वपूर्ण या संबंधित बात *Financial matters are not my concern.* **3** [C] a company or business कंपनी या व्यापार; व्यापारिक संस्था *a large industrial concern*

**IDM a going concern** ➪ **going²** देखिए।

**concerned** /kənˈsɜːnd कन्ˈसन्ड् / *adj.* **concerned (about/for sth); concerned (that...)** worried and feeling concern about sth किसी के लिए चिंतित और परेशान *If you are concerned about your baby's health you should consult a doctor immediately.* ✪ विलोम **unconcerned**

**concerning** /kənˈsɜːnɪŋ कन्ˈसनिङ् / *prep.* about; on the subject of के विषय में; के विषय पर *She refused to answer questions concerning her private life.*

**concert** /ˈkɒnsət ˈकॉन्सट् / *noun* [C] a performance of music संगीत का सार्वजनिक प्रदर्शन; संगीत समारोह *The band is on tour doing concerts all over the country.* ➪ **recital** देखिए।

**IDM in concert (with sb/sth)** (*formal*) working together with sb/sth किसी के साथ मिलकर काम करते हुए

**concerted** /kənˈsɜːtɪd कन्ˈसटिड् / *adj.* done by a group of people working together अनेक व्यक्तियों द्वारा मिल-जुलकर किया हुआ; समन्वित, संगठित *We must all* ***make a concerted effort*** *to finish the work on time.*

**concertina** /ˌkɒnsəˈtiːnə ˌकॉन्सˈटीना / *noun* [C] a musical instrument that you hold in your hands and play by pressing the ends together and pulling them apart हारमोनियम की तरह का एक वाद्य यंत्र ➪ **piano** पर नोट देखिए।

**concession** /kənˈseʃn कन्ˈसेश्न् / *noun* **1** [C, U] **(a) concession (to sb/sth)** something that you agree to do in order to end an argument सुलह के लिए दी गई रियायत; छूट *Employers have been forced to* ***make concessions*** *to the union.* ➪ **concede** verb देखिए। **2** [C] a lower price for certain groups of people वर्ग-विशेष के लोगों के लिए क़ीमत में कटौती; रियायत *Concessions are available for students.*

**concessionary** /kənˈseʃənəri कन्ˈसेशनरि / *adj.* having a lower price for certain groups of people वर्ग-विशेष के लोगों के लिए कम क़ीमत; रियायती *a concessionary fare*

**conch** /kɒntʃ कॉन्च् / *noun* [C] (*pl.* **conches**) (*IndE*) the shell of a sea creature. In India certain kind of conches are played by blowing into them on **auspicious** occasions like marriages शंख; एक प्रकार की समुद्री जीव की सीपी को शंख कहते हैं। भारत में कुछ प्रकार के शंखों को उनमें फूंक मारकर विवाह जैसे मंगलमय अवसरों पर बजाया जाता है

**conciliate** /kənˈsɪlieɪt कन्ˈसिलिएट् / *verb* [I, T] to try to make a group of people less angry, especially in order to end a dispute विवाद समाप्ति के लिए लोगों को शांत करने का प्रयत्न करना; सुलह या समझौते पर पहुँचने की कोशिश करना

**conciliation** /kənˌsɪliˈeɪʃn कन्ˌसिलिˈएशन् / *noun* [U] the process of ending an argument or a disagreement विवाद या असहमति को समाप्त करने की प्रक्रिया; सुलह, समझौता *All attempts at conciliation have failed and civil war seems inevitable.*

**conciliatory** /kənˈsɪliətəri कन्ˈसिलिअटरि / *adj.* that tries to end an argument or a disagreement सुलह करने वाली, समझौताकारी, मेल-मिलाप का *a conciliatory speech/gesture*

**concise** /kənˈsaɪs कन्ˈसाइस् / *adj.* giving a lot of information in a few words; brief थोड़े शब्दों में काफ़ी सूचना देते हुए; संक्षिप्त *He gave a clear and concise summary of what had happened.* ▶ **concisely** *adv.* संक्षेप से ▶ **conciseness** *noun* [U] संक्षिप्तता

**conclude** /kənˈkluːd कन्ˈक्लूड् / *verb* **1** [T] **conclude sth from sth** to form an opinion as the result of thought or study सोच-विचार या अध्ययन के बाद निष्कर्ष या नतीजे पर पहुँचना *From the man's strange behaviour I concluded that he was drunk.* **2** [I, T] (*formal*) to end or to bring sth to an end समाप्त करना या होना *The President concluded his tour with a visit to a charity concert.* **3** [T] **conclude sth (with sb)** to formally arrange or agree to sth औपचारिक रूप से आयोजित या स्वीकार करना *conclude a business deal/treaty*

**conclusion** /kənˈkluːʒn कन्ˈक्लूश़न् / *noun* **1** [C] **the conclusion (that...)** an opinion that you reach after thinking about sth carefully निष्कर्ष, निर्णय, परिणाम, नतीजा *After trying to phone Uday for days, I* ***came to the conclusion*** *that he was on holiday.* ○ *Have you* ***reached*** *any* ***conclusions*** *from your studies?* **2** [C, *usually sing.*] (*formal*) an end to sth समाप्ति, समापन *Let us hope the peace talks* ***reach a*** *successful* ***conclusion****.* **3** [U] an act of arranging or agreeing to sth formally औपचारिक रूप से आयोजित या स्वीकार करने की क्रिया *The summit ended with the conclusion of an arms-reduction treaty.*

IDM **a foregone conclusion** ➪ **foregone** देखिए।

**in conclusion** finally; lastly सारांश रूप में; अंत में

**jump to conclusions** ➪ **jump**¹ देखिए।

**conclusive** /kənˈkluːsɪv कन्ˈक्लूसिव् / *adj.* that shows sth is definitely true or real निर्णायक, निश्चायक *The blood tests gave conclusive proof of the disease.* ✪ विलोम **inconclusive** ▶ **conclusively** *adv.* निर्णायक या निश्चायक रूप से

**concoct** /kənˈkɒkt कन्ˈकॉक्ट् / *verb* [T] **1** to make sth unusual by mixing different things together विभिन्न वस्तुओं को मिलाकर कुछ विचित्र तैयार करना **2** to make up or invent sth (an excuse, a story, etc.) बहाना बनाना, (कपट) जाल रचना ▶ **concoction** /kənˈkɒkʃn कन्ˈकॉक्शन् / *noun* [C] मिश्रण, काढ़ा; मनगढ़ंत क़िस्सा

**concord** /ˈkɒŋkɔːd ˈकॉङ्कॉड् / *noun* [U] **1 concord (with sth)** (*formal*) peace and agreement शांति और सामंजस्य; मेल व सहमति *The two countries now live in concord.* ✪ पर्याय **harmony 2** (*grammar*) **concord (with sth)** (used about words in a phrase) the fact of having to have a particular form according to other words in the phrase (वाक्यांश में शब्दों का) एक-दूसरे के अनुसार निर्धारित होना; शब्द रूपों की अन्विति

**concordance** /kənˈkɔːdəns कन्ˈकॉडन्स् / *noun* **1** [C] a list in A to Z order of the words used in a book, etc. showing where and how often they are used पुस्तक में प्रयुक्त शब्दों की वर्णाक्रम में सूची; शब्दानुक्रमणिका **2** [C] a list produced by a computer that shows all the examples of an individual word in a book, etc. किसी पुस्तक में प्रयुक्त शब्द-विशेष के उदाहरणों की कंप्यूटर-निर्मित सूची **3** [U] (*technical*) the state of being similar to or agreeing with sth सामंजस्य, सादृश्य, समानता, मेल *There is reasonable concordance between the results.*

**concourse** /ˈkɒŋkɔːs ˈकॉङ्कॉस् / *noun* [C] a large hall or space inside a building such as a station or an airport रेलवे स्टेशन या हवाई अड्डे के भवन में विशाल कक्ष या खुला स्थान

**concrete**¹ /ˈkɒŋkriːt ˈकॉङ्क्रीट् / *adj.* real or definite; not only existing in the imagination यथार्थ प्रत्यक्ष, ठोस; मूर्त (काल्पनिक नहीं) *Can you give me a concrete example of what you mean?* ✪ विलोम **abstract** ▶ **concretely** *adv.* मूर्त रूप से

**concrete**² /ˈkɒŋkriːt ˈकॉङ्क्रीट् / *noun* [U] a hard substance made from cement mixed with sand, water, small stones (**gravel**), etc., that is used in building भवन-निर्माण में प्रयुक्त सीमेंट-रेत-पानी-रोड़ी का मिश्रण; कंकरीट *a modern office building of glass and concrete* ○ *a concrete floor/bridge*

**concrete³** /ˈkɒŋkriːt ˈकॉङ्क्रीट्/ *verb* [T] **concrete sth (over)** to cover sth with concrete किसी वस्तु पर कंकरीट का लेप करना

**concrete mixer** = **cement mixer**

**concur** /kənˈkɜː(r) कन्ˈक(र्)/ *verb* [I] (**concurring; concurred**) (*formal*) to agree सहमत होना

**concurrence** /kənˈkʌrəns कन्ˈकरन्स्/ *noun* (*formal*) **1** [U, *sing.*] agreement सहमति, स्वीकृति *The doctor must seek the concurrence of a relative before carrying out the procedure.* **2** [*sing.*] an example of two or more things happening at the same time दो या अधिक वस्तुओं/घटनाओं के एक साथ होने या घटित होने की स्थिति *an unfortunate concurrence of events*

**concurrent** /kənˈkʌrənt कन्ˈकरन्ट्/ *adj.* existing or happening at the same time as sth else समकालिक ▶ **concurrently** *adv.* समकालिक रूप से *The semi-finals are played concurrently, so it is impossible to watch both.*

**concuss** /kənˈkʌs कन्ˈकस्/ *verb* [T] (*usually passive*) to injure sb's brain by hitting his/her head सिर पर प्रहार द्वारा मस्तिष्क को आघात पहुँचाना *I was slightly concussed when I fell off my bicycle.* ▶ **concussion** /kənˈkʌʃn कन्ˈकशन्/ *noun* [U] सिर पर प्रहार से मस्तिष्क आघात; मस्तिष्क-संघट्टन *He was rushed to hospital, but only suffered mild concussion*

**condemn** /kənˈdem कन्ˈडेम्/ *verb* [T] **1 condemn sb/sth (for/as sth)** to say strongly that you think sb/sth is very bad or wrong किसी की तीव्र निंदा करना; दोषी या अपराधी ठहराना *A government spokesman condemned the bombing as a cowardly act of terrorism.* **2 condemn sb (to sth/to do sth)** to say what sb's punishment will be; to sentence sb किसी के लिए दंड की घोषणा करना; किसी को दंडित करना *The murderer was condemned to death.* ○ (*figurative*) *Their poor education condemns them to a series of low-paid jobs.* **3 condemn sth (as sth)** to say officially that sth is not safe enough to use किसी वस्तु को औपचारिक रूप से प्रयोग के लिए असुरक्षित ठहराना *The building was condemned as unsafe and was demolished.*

**condemnation** /ˌkɒndemˈneɪʃn ˌकॉन्डेम्ˈनेशन्/ *noun* [C, U] the act of comdemning sth; a statement that condemns किसी को दोषी या अपराधी ठहराने की क्रिया; निंदा-प्रस्ताव *The bombing brought condemantion from all around the world.*

**condensation** /ˌkɒndenˈseɪʃn ˌकॉन्डेन्ˈसेशन्/ *noun* [U] **1** small drops of liquid that are formed when warm air touches a cold surface ठंडी सतह पर गरम हवा के स्पर्श के कारण सतह पर बनी छोटी बूँदें **2** the process of a gas changing to a liquid गैस के द्रवीकरण की प्रक्रिया

**condense** /kənˈdens कन्ˈडेन्स्/ *verb* **1** [I, T] to change or make sth change from gas to liquid गैस का द्रव बनना या बनाना *Steam condenses into water when it touches a cold surface.* ➪ **evaporate** देखिए। **2** [T] to make a liquid thicker by removing some of its water content द्रव को गाढ़ा करना; संघनन करना *condensed milk* **3** [T] **condense sth (into sth)** to make smaller or shorter so that it fills less space छोटा या संक्षिप्त करना *We'll have to condense these three chapters into one.*

**condenser** /kənˈdensə(r) कन्ˈडेन्स(र्)/ *noun* **1** a piece of equipment that cools gas in order to turn it into liquid गैस को ठंडा कर द्रव बनाने वाला उपकरण; कंडेंसर ➪ **generator** पर चित्र देखिए। **2** a device that stores electricity, especially in a car engine विद्युत को संचालित करने वाला उपकरण, विशेषतः कार इंजिन में

**condescend** /ˌkɒndɪˈsend ˌकॉन्डिˈसेन्ड्/ *verb* [I] **1 condescend (to sb)** to behave towards sb in a way that shows that you think you are better or more important than him/her; to patronize sb दूसरों पर स्वयं की वरिष्ठता दिखाते हुए व्यवहार करना; संरक्षक की भाँति (दूसरों से) व्यवहार करना **2 condescend (to do sth)** to do sth that you believe is below your level of importance कोई ऐसा कार्य करना जो अपनी दृष्टि में तुच्छ हो *Priyanka only condescends to speak to me when she wants me to do something for her.* ▶ **condescending** *adj.* स्वयं की वरिष्ता दिखाने वाला व्यवहार करते हुए *a con descending smile* ▶ **condescension** /ˌkɒndɪˈsenʃn ˌकॉन्डिˈसेन्शन्/ *noun* [U] इस तरह का व्यवहार

**condiment** /ˈkɒndɪmənt ˈकॉन्डिमन्ट्/ *noun* [C, *usually pl.*] **1** a substance such as salt or pepper that is used to give flavour to food भोजन को स्वाद देने वाला पदार्थ, जैसे नमक व मिर्च **2** a sauce, etc. that is used to give flavour to food, or that is eaten with food चटनी, अचार आदि स्वादवर्धक पदार्थ

**condition¹** /kənˈdɪʃn कन्ˈडिशन्/ *noun* **1** [U, *sing.*] the state that sb/sth is in अवस्था, दशा, स्थिति, हालत *to be in poor/good/excellent condition* ○ *He looks really ill. He is certainly not in a condition to* *drive home.* **2** [C] something that must happen so that sth else can happen or be possible शर्त, प्रतिबंध *One of the conditions of the job is that you agree to work on Sundays.* ○ *He said I could borrow his bike* ***on one condition****—that I didn't let anyone else ride it.* **3 conditions** [*pl.*] the situation or surroundings in which people live, work or do things लोगों के रहने, काम करने आदि की परिस्थितियाँ, हालात *The prisoners were kept* ***in*** *terrible* ***conditions****.* ○ *poor living/housing/working conditions* **4** [C] a medical problem that you have for a long time पुरानी बीमारी *to have a heart/lung condition*

IDM **on condition (that...)** only if इस शर्त पर कि; केवल तभी *I agreed to help on condition that I got half the profit.*

**on no condition** (*formal*) not for any reason किसी भी दशा में नहीं *On no condition must the press find out about this.*

**out of condition** not physically fit शारीरिक रूप से अस्वस्थ

**condition²** /kən'dɪʃn कन्'डिशन्/ *verb* [T] to affect or control the way that sb/sth behaves किसी के व्यवहार को प्रभावित या नियंत्रित करना; रीति-विशेष से अनुकूलित करना *Boys are conditioned to feel that they are stronger than girls.*

**conditional** /kən'dɪʃənl कन्'डिशनल्/ *adj.* **1 conditional (on/upon sth)** that only happens if sth else is done or happens first शर्त पर निर्भर, सशर्त; किसी अन्य घटना आदि पर निर्भर *My college admission is conditional on my getting good marks in the exams.* ✪ विलोम **unconditional** **2** (*grammar*) describing a situation that must exist before sth else can happen. A conditional sentence often contains the word 'if' (अंग्रेज़ी व्याकरण में) शर्तयुक्त स्थिति को व्यक्त करने वाला (वाक्य); हेतुमद वाक्य, ऐसे वाक्यों में प्रायः 'if' शब्द प्रयुक्त होता है *if you don't study, you won't pass the exam' is a conditional sentence.* ▶ **conditionally** /-ʃənəli -शनलि/ *adv.* शर्त के साथ, सशर्त रीति से

**conditioner** /kən'dɪʃənə(r) कन्'डिशन(र्)/ *noun* [C, U] a substance that keeps sth in a good condition किसी वस्तु को अच्छी दशा में रखने वाला पदार्थ; कंडीशनर *Do you use conditioner on your hair?*

**condolence** /kən'dəʊləns कन्'डोलन्स्/ *noun* [*pl.*, U] an expression of how sorry you feel for sb whose relative or close friend has just died शोक की अभिव्यक्ति; संवेदना *offer your condolences* ○ *a message of condolence*

**condominium** /ˌkɒndə'mɪniəm 'कॉन्ड'मिनिअम्/ (*informal* **condo** /'kɒndəʊ 'कॉन्डो/) *noun* [C] a flat or block of flats owned by the people who live in them एक फ़्लैट या फ़्लैट-शृंखला जिनमें उनके स्वामी रहते हैं

**condone** /kən'dəʊn कन्'डोन्/ *verb* [T] to accept or agree with sth that most people think is wrong अधिकांश लोगों द्वारा ग़लत मानी जाने वाली बात की अनदेखी करना *I can never condone violence—no matter what the circumstances are.*

**conducive** /kən'dju:sɪv कन्'ड्यूसिव्/ *adj.* (*formal*) **conducive (to sth)** helping or making sth happen सहायक या किसी का कारण बनना *This hot weather is not conducive to hard work.*

**conduct¹** /kən'dʌkt कन्'डक्ट्/ *verb* [T] **1** (*formal*) to organize and do sth, especially research व्यवस्थित रूप से कुछ करना, विशेषतः अनुसंधान-कार्य *to conduct tests/a survey/an inquiry* **2** to stand in front of an orchestra and direct the musicians मंच पर वाद्यवृंद का संचालन करना **3** (*formal*) **conduct yourself well, badly, etc.** to behave in a particular way विशेष प्रकार से अच्छा, बुरा आदि आचरण करना **4** to allow heat or electricity to pass along or through sth (पदार्थ का) अपने अंदर से ताप या विद्युत को गुज़रने देना; संवाहन का माध्यम बनाना *Rubber does not conduct electricity.*

**conduct²** /'kɒndʌkt 'कॉन्डक्ट्/ *noun* [U] **1** a person's behaviour किसी व्यक्ति का आचरण *His conduct has always been of the highest standard.* ○ *a code of conduct* (= a set of rules of behaviour) **2** (*formal*) **conduct of sth** the act of controlling or organizing sth प्रबंधन, परिचालन की क्रिया *She was criticized for her conduct of the bank's affairs.*

**conduction** /kən'dʌkʃn कन्'डक्शन्/ *noun* [U] (*technical*) the process by which heat or electricity passes through a material किसी पदार्थ में से ताप या विद्युत के गुज़रने की प्रक्रिया; चालन, संवाहन

**conductive** /kən'dʌktɪv कन्'डक्टिव्/ *adj.* able to conduct electricity, heat, etc. अपने में से ताप, विद्युत आदि को गुज़रने देने में समर्थ; संवाहन-क्षम, चालक ▶ **conductivity** /ˌkɒndʌk'tɪvəti ˌकॉन्डक्'टिविटि/ *noun* [U] संवाहकता, चालकता

**conductor** /kən'dʌktə(r) कन्'डक्ट(र्)/ *noun* [C] **1** a person who stands in front of an orchestra and directs the musicians वाद्यवृंद का संचालक **2** (*BrE*) a person whose job is to collect money from passengers on a bus or to check their tickets बस-कंडक्टर, बस का टिकट-बाबू **3** (*AmE*) = **guard¹ 5** **4** a substance that allows heat or electricity to pass through or along it वह पदार्थ जो ताप या विद्युत को अपने में से गुज़रने दे; संवाहक पदार्थ, चालक ➪ **semiconductor** देखिए।

**cone** /kəʊn कोन्/ *noun* [C] **1** a shape or object that has a round base and a point at the top गोल तल और नुकीले शीर्ष वाली आकृति या वस्तु; शंकु *traffic cones* ○ *an ice cream cone* ➪ **conical** adjective तथा **solid** पर चित्र देखिए। **2** the hard fruit of some trees (**pine** and **fir**) चीड़ आदि वृक्षों का कठोर फल ➪ **conifer** देखिए।

**confectionery** /kənˈfekʃənəri कन्ˈफ़ेक्शनरि/ *noun* [U] (*pl.* **confectioneries**) sweets, cakes, chocolates, etc. मिठाइयाँ, केक, चॉकलेट आदि मिष्ठान **2** [C] a shop that sells sweets, cakes, chocolates etc. मिष्ठान बेचने वाली दुकान

**confederacy** /kənˈfedərəsi कन्ˈफ़ेडरसि/ *noun* [*sing.*] a union of states, groups of people or political parties with the same aim समान उद्देश्य वाले राज्यों, राजनैतिक दलों या व्यक्तियों की मंडलियों का गुट या संघ; राज्यसंघ, महासंघ, राज्यमंडल

**confederate**[1] /kənˈfedərət कन्ˈफ़ेडरट्/ *noun* [C] a person who helps sb, especially to do sth illegal or secret किसी का सहायक या सहभागी, विशेषतः ग़ैर-क़ानूनी या गुप्त कार्य में

**confederate**[2] /kənˈfedərət कन्ˈफ़ेडरट्/ *adj.* belonging to a union of states, groups of people or political parties with the same aim (**a confederacy**) राज्य संघ विषयक

**confederation** /kənˌfedəˈreɪʃn कन्ˌफ़ेडˈरेशन्/ *noun* [C, U] an organization of smaller groups which have joined together छोटे वर्गों, राज्यों आदि का संगठन; परिसंघ *a confederation of independent republics*

**confer** /kənˈfɜː(r) कन्ˈफ़(र्)/ *verb* (**conferring; conferred**) **1** [I] **confer (with sb) (on/about sth)** to discuss sth with sb before making a decision निर्णय लेने से पहले विचार-विमर्श करना *The Prime Minister is conferring with his advisers.* **2** [T] (*written*) **confer sth (on sb)** to give sb a special right or advantage किसी को विशेष अधिकार या लाभ प्रदान करना

**conference** /ˈkɒnfərəns ˈकॉन्फ़रन्स्/ *noun* [C] a large official meeting, often lasting several days, at which members of an organization, profession, etc. meet to discuss important matters महत्त्वपूर्ण मामलों पर चर्चा के लिए आयोजित सभा; सम्मेलन *international conference on global warming*

**confess** /kənˈfes कन्ˈफ़ेस्/ *verb* [I, T] **confess (to sth/to doing sth); confess (sth) (to sb)** to admit that you have done sth bad or wrong अपराध या दोष स्वीकार करना *The young woman confessed to stealing the money.* ○ *They confessed to their mother that they had spent all the money.* ➪ **own up (to)** देखिए।

**confession** /kənˈfeʃn कन्ˈफ़ेशन्/ *noun* [C, U] an act of admitting that you have done sth bad or wrong अपराध-स्वीकरण, दोष-स्वीकृति *The police persuaded the man to make a full confession.*

**confetti** /kənˈfeti कन्ˈफ़ेटि/ *noun* [U] small pieces of coloured paper that people throw over a man and woman who have just got married रंगीन काग़ज़ के छोटे टुकड़े जिन्हें लोग (अभिनंदन स्वरूप) नवदंपति पर डालते हैं

**confide** /kənˈfaɪd कन्ˈफ़ाइड्/ *verb* [T] **confide sth to sb** to tell sb sth that is secret किसी को कोई गोपनीय बात या रहस्य बताना *She did not confide her love to anyone—not even to her best friend.*

**PHR V confide in sb** to talk to sb that you trust about sth secret or private विश्वासपात्र व्यक्ति को गोपनीय या निजी बात बताना

**confidence** /ˈkɒnfɪdəns ˈकॉन्फ़िडन्स्/ *noun* [U] **1 confidence (in sb/sth)** trust or strong belief in sb/sth (किसी पर) भरोसा या पक्का विश्वास *The public is losing confidence in the present government.* ○ *I have every confidence in Sangeeta's ability to do the job.* **2** the feeling that you are sure about your own abilities, opinion, etc. आत्मविश्वास *I didn't* ***have the confidence*** *to tell her I thought she was wrong.* ○ *to be* ***full of confidence*** ➪ **self-confidence** देखिए। **3** a feeling of trust in sb to keep sth a secret किसी पर भरोसा या विश्वास कि वह गोपनीय बात को बाहर नहीं जाने देगा *The information was given to me* ***in strict confidence****.* ○ *It took a while to* ***win/gain*** *her confidence.*

**confident** /ˈkɒnfɪdənt ˈकॉन्फ़िडन्ट्/ *adj.* **confident (of sth/that...); confident (about sth)** feeling or showing that you are sure about your own abilities, opinions, etc. स्वयं की योग्यताओं, विचारों पर विश्वस्त; आत्मविश्वासी *Surabhi feels confident of passing/that she can pass the exam.* ○ *to be confident of success* ○ *You should feel confident about your own abilities.* ○ *Shiv has a very confident manner.* ➪ **self-confident** देखिए। ► **confidently** *adv.* आत्मविश्वासपूर्वक *She stepped confidently onto the stage and began to sing.*

**confidential** /ˌkɒnfɪˈdenʃl ˌकॉनफ़िˈडेन्श्ल्/ *adj.* secret; not to be shown or told to other people

गोपनीय *The letter was marked 'private and confidential'.* ▶ **confidentiality** /ˌkɒnfɪˌdenʃiˈæləti ˌकॉन्फ़िˌडेन्शिˈऐलटि / *noun* [U] गोपनीयता ▶ **confidentially** /-ʃəli -शलि / *adv.* गोपनीय रूप से

**configuration** /kənˌfɪgəˈreɪʃn कन्ˌफ़िगˈरेश्न् / *noun* [C] **1** (*formal*) the way in which the parts of sth, or a group of things, are arranged किसी वस्तु के विभिन्न भागों की विन्यास-व्यवस्था; संविन्यास, संरूपण, रचना, बनावट **2** (*computing*) the equipment and programs that form a computer system and the particular way that these are arranged किसी कंप्यूटर-पद्धति का निर्माण करने वाले उपकरण और प्रोग्राम और उनकी विशिष्ट संयोजन व्यवस्था

**configure** /kənˈfɪgə(r) कन्ˈफ़िग(र्) / *verb* [T] **1** (*formal*) to arrange parts of sth, or a group of things, in a particular way किसी वस्तु के विभिन्न भागों का विशिष्ट रीति से संयोजन करना **2** (*computing*) to arrange computer equipment for a particular task कार्य-विशेष के लिए कंप्यूटर भागों को व्यवस्थित करना

**confine** /kənˈfaɪn कन्ˈफ़ाइन् / *verb* [T] **1 confine sb/sth (in/to sth)** to keep a person or animal in a particular, usually small, place किसी व्यक्ति या वस्तु को किसी (छोटे) स्थान के भीतर रोके रखना; परिरुद्ध करना *The prisoners are confined to their cells for long periods at a time.* **2 confine sb/sth/ yourself to sth** to stay within the limits of sth सीमित रखना; सीमा-विशेष में रखना *Please confine your questions to the topic we are discussing.*

**confined** /kənˈfaɪnd कन्ˈफ़ाइन्ड् / *adj.* (used about a space) very small (स्थान) बहुत छोटा

**confinement** /kənˈfaɪnmənt कन्ˈफ़ाइन्मन्ट् / *noun* [U] being kept in a small space छोटी जगह या सीमा के भीतर रखे जाने की स्थिति; क़ैद *to be kept **in solitary confinement*** (= in a prison)

**confines** /ˈkɒnfaɪnz ˈकॉन्फ़ाइन्ज़् / *noun* [*pl.*] (*formal*) the limits of sth सीमाएँ *Patients are not allowed beyond the confines of the hospital grounds.*

**confirm** /kənˈfɜːm कन्ˈफ़म् / *verb* [T] **1** to say or show that sth is true or correct, especially by giving evidence विशेषतः प्रमाण देकर किसी बात की पुष्टि करना *Seeing the two of them together confirmed our suspicions.* ○ *Can you confirm that you will be able to attend the survivor?* **2** to make a position, an agreement etc. more definite or official; to establish sb/sth firmly पद, समझौता आदि पक्का करना; सुदृढ़ करना *Her position in the company has been confirmed.* ▶ **confirmation** /ˌkɒnfəˈmeɪʃn ˌकॉन्फ़ˈमेश्न् / *noun* [C, U] पुष्टि, अनुमोदन *We are waiting for confirmation of the report.*

**confirmed** /kənˈfɜːmd कन्ˈफ़म्ड् / *adj.* (*only before a noun*) fixed in a particular habit or way of life (आदत या जीवन-शैली) न बदली जा सकने वाली; पक्की, स्थायी *a confirmed bachelor*

**confiscate** /ˈkɒnfɪskeɪt ˈकॉन्फ़िस्केट् / *verb* [T] to take sth away from sb as a punishment दंडस्वरूप कोई वस्तु ज़ब्त कर लेना *Any cigarettes found in school will be confiscated.* ▶ **confiscation** /ˌkɒnfɪˈskeɪʃn ˌकॉन्फ़िˈस्केश्न् / *noun* [C, U] ज़ब्ती, कुरकी

**conflict¹** /ˈkɒnflɪkt ˈकॉन्फ़्लिक्ट् / *noun* [C, U] **1 (a) conflict with sb/sth (over sth)** a fight or an argument (किसी बात पर) झगड़ा, संघर्ष या विवाद *an armed conflict* ○ *The new laws have brought the Government **into conflict** with the unions over pay increases.* **2** a difference between two or more ideas, wishes, etc. दो या अधिक विचारों, इच्छाओं आदि में परस्पर विरोध, अंतर, प्रतिकूलता *Many women have to cope with the conflict between their career and their family.* ○ *a conflict of interests*

**conflict²** /kənˈflɪkt कन्ˈफ़्लिक्ट् / *verb* [I] **A and B conflict; A conflicts with B** to disagree with or be different from sb/sth किसी अन्य से असहमत या भिन्न होना; प्रतिकूल या विरोधी होना, मेल न खाना *The statements of the two witnesses conflict.* ○ *conflicting results*

**conform** /kənˈfɔːm कन्ˈफ़ॉम् / *verb* [I] **conform (to sth) 1** to obey a rule or law नियम या क़ानून का अनुपालन करना; के अनुसार होना; संगत होना *This building does not conform to fire regulations.* **2** to behave in the same way as most other people in a group or society किसी दल या समाज के अधिकांश सदस्यों की तरह ही आचरण करना *Children are under a lot of pressure to conform when they first start school.* ▶ **conformity** /kənˈfɔːməti कन्ˈफ़ॉमटि / *noun* [U] अनुरूपता, अनुकूलता

**conformist** /kənˈfɔːmɪst कन्ˈफ़ॉमिस्ट् / *noun* [C] a person who behaves in the same way as most other people and who does not want to be different अधिकांश लोगों की तरह ही आचरण करने वाला व्यक्ति जो भिन्न होने की इच्छा भी नहीं रखता है ✪ विलोम **nonconformist**

**conformity** /kənˈfɔːməti कन्ˈफ़ॉमटि / *noun* [U] (*formal*) behaviour which conforms to rules and customs नियमों, रिवाजों और व्यवहार-रूढ़ियों के अनुरूप आचरण

**confront** /kənˈfrʌnt कन्ˈफ्रन्ट्/ *verb* [T] **1 confront sth; confront sb with sb/sth** to think about, or to make sb think about, sth that is difficult or unpleasant किसी मुसीबत का या अप्रिय स्थिति समाना करना या सामना करवाना; के आमने-सामने होना *to confront a problem/difficulty/issue* ○ *When the police confronted him with the evidence, he confessed.* **2** to stand in front of sb, for example because you want to fight him/her (झगड़े या सामना करने के लिए) किसी के सामने खड़ा होना *The unarmed demonstrators were confronted by a row of soldiers.*

**confrontation** /ˌkɒnfrʌnˈteɪʃn ˌकॉन्फ्रन्ˈटेश्न्/ *noun* [C, U] a fight or an argument संघर्ष या विवाद

**confuse** /kənˈfjuːz कन्ˈफ़्यूज़्/ *verb* [T] **1** (*usually passive*) to make sb unable to think clearly or to know what to do उलझन में डाल देना; गड़बड़ा या चकरा देना; सोच-विचार में दुविधा पैदा करना *He confused everybody with his pages of facts and figures.* **2 confuse A and/with B** to mistake sb/sth for sb/sth else एक को दूसरा समझ लेना *I often confuse Nikhil with his brother. They look very much alike.* **3** to make sth complicated किसी बात को जटिल या पेचीदा बना देना *The situation is confused by the fact that so many organizations are involved.*

**confused** /kənˈfjuːzd कन्ˈफ़्यूज़्ड्/ *adj.* **1** not able to think clearly स्पष्ट रूप से सोच-विचार करने में असमर्थ; चकराया या उलझा हुआ, भ्रमित *When he regained consciousness he was dazed and confused.* **2** difficult to understand दुर्बोध, उलझाव-भरा, अस्पष्ट *The workers presented a confused stand—the management couldn't understand what the main point was.* ▶ **confusedly** /-zədli -ज़ड्लि/ *adv.* अस्त-व्यस्त भाव से

**confusing** /kənˈfjuːzɪŋ कन्ˈफ़्यूज़िङ्/ *adj.* difficult to understand समझने में मुश्किल; चकरा देने वाला उलझन में डालने वाला *Her instructions were contradictory and confusing.* ▶ **confusingly** *adv.* चकरा देने के ढंग से

**confusion** /kənˈfjuːʒn कन्ˈफ़्यूश़्न्/ *noun* [U] **1** the state of not being able to think clearly or not understanding sth उलझन, घबराहट, भ्रम, किंकर्तव्यविमूढ़ता *He stared in confusion at the exam paper.* ○ *There is still a great deal of confusion as to the true facts.* **2** a state of disorder अव्यवस्था या अस्त-व्यस्तता की स्थिति *Their unexpected visit threw all our plans into confusion.* **3** the act of mistaking sb/sth for sb/sth else पहचानने में ग़लती करने की क्रिया; भ्रम *To avoid confusion, all luggage should be labelled with your name and destination.*

**congeal** /kənˈdʒiːl कन्ˈजील्/ *verb* [I, T] (used about a liquid) to become solid; to make a liquid solid (द्रव का) ठोस हो जाना; द्रव को ठोस बनाना; जमना, जमाना *congealed blood*

**congenial** /kənˈdʒiːniəl कन्ˈजीनिअल्/ *adj.* (*formal*) pleasant प्रीति कर, सौहार्दपूर्ण *We spent an evening in congenial company.*

**congenital** /kənˈdʒenɪtl कन्ˈजेनिट्ल्/ *adj.* (used about a disease) beginning at and continuing since birth (रोग) जन्म से तक विद्यमान; जन्मजात

**congested** /kənˈdʒestɪd कन्ˈजेस्टिड्/ *adj.* **1 congested (with sth)** crowded; full of traffic भीड़-भाड़ वाला; वाहनों से खचाखच भरा *The streets of Mumbai are congested with traffic.* ▶ **congestion** /kənˈdʒestʃən कन्ˈजेस्चन्/ *noun* [U] the state of being very full of people or traffic खचाखच भरे होने या जमाव की स्थिति; संकुलन **2** the state of a part of the body being blocked with blood or mucus शरीर के किसी भाग में रक्त या बलगम का जमाव *chest congestion*

**conglomerate** /kənˈglɒmərət कन्ˈग्लॉमरट्/ *noun* [C] a large firm made up of several different companies विभिन्न कंपनियों से मिलकर बनी एक बड़ी कंपनी

**conglomeration** /kənˌglɒməˈreɪʃn कन्ˌग्लॉमˈरेश्न्/ *noun* [C] a group of many different things that have been brought together बहुत-सी अलग-अलग वस्तुओं का ढेर या समूह; सपिंडित, गुच्छित

**congratulate** /kənˈgrætʃuleɪt कन्ˈग्रैचुलेट्/ *verb* [T] **congratulate sb (on sth)** to tell sb that you are pleased about sth he/she has done; to praise sb किसी को किसी बात की बधाई देना; किसी की प्रशंसा करना *I congratulated Preeti on passing her driving test.*

**congratulations** /kənˌgrætʃuˈleɪʃnz कन्ˌग्रैचुˈलेश्न्ज़्/ *noun* [*pl.*] used for telling sb that you are happy with his/her good luck or success किसी को बधाई देने में प्रयुक्त *Congratulations on the birth of your baby boy!*

**congregate** /ˈkɒŋgrɪgeɪt ˈकॉङ्ग्रिगेट्/ *verb* [I] to come together in a crowd or group भीड़ या समूह के रूप में इकट्ठा होना; एकत्रित होना

**congregation** /ˌkɒŋgrɪˈgeɪʃn ˌकॉङ्ग्रिˈगेश्न्/ *noun* [C, *sing. or pl. verb*] **1** the act of coming together in a crowd or group; a gathering एकत्रित होने की क्रिया; सभा, जमाव **2** the group of people who attend a particular church चर्च-विशेष में जाने वाले व्यक्तियों का समूह

**congress** /ˈkɒŋgres ˈकॉङ्ग्रेस् / *noun* [C, *with sing. or pl. verb*] **1** a large formal meeting or series of meetings बड़ा व औपचारिक सम्मेलन या अनेक छोटे सम्मेलन *a medical congress* **2 Congress** the name in some countries (for example the US) for the group of people who are elected to make the laws कुछ देशों (जैसे संयुक्त राज्य अमेरिका) में विधान-मंडल

**congressional** /kənˈgreʃənl कन्ˈग्रेशनल् / *adj.* connected with a congress or Congress सम्मेलन या कांग्रेस (जैसे अमेरिका का) से संबंधित

**congruent** /ˈkɒŋgruənt ˈकॉङ्ग्रुअन्ट् / *adj.* **1** (*mathematics*) having exactly the same size and shape एक ही आकार और आकृति वाले *congruent triangles* **2** (*formal*) congruent (**with sth**) suitable for sth (किसी के) उपयुक्त

**conic** /ˈkɒnɪk ˈकॉनिक् / *adj.* connected with **cones** शंकु-विषयक

**conical** /ˈkɒnɪkl ˈकॉनिकल् / *adj.* having a round base and getting narrower towards a point at the top शंकु के आकार का, शंक्वाकार ➪ **cone** noun देखिए।

**conifer** /ˈkɒnɪfə(r); ˈkəʊn- ˈकॉनिफ़(र्); कोनि- / *noun* [C] a tree with short, very thin leaves (**needles**) that stay green all through the year and that has hard brown fruit (**cones**) एक सदा बहार वृक्ष जिसके फल शंक्वाकार होते हैं; शंकुवृक्ष ▶ **coniferous** /kəˈnɪfərəs कˈनिफ़रस् / *adj.* शंकुधारी

**conjecture** /kənˈdʒektʃə(r) कन्ˈजेक्च(र्) / *verb* [I,T] (*formal*) to guess about sth without real proof or evidence वास्तविक प्रमाण या साक्ष्य के बिना अनुमान लगाना; अटकल लगाना ▶ **conjecture** *noun* [C, U] प्रमाण-रहित अनुमान

**conjoined** /kənˈdʒɔɪnd कन्ˈजॉइन्ड् / *adj.* (*technical*) joined together परस्पर संयुक्त

**conjoined twin** = **Siamese twin**

**conjugal** /ˈkɒndʒəgl ˈकॉन्जगल् / *adj.* (*formal*) connected with marriage and the relationship between husband and wife विवाह तथा दांपत्य संबंधों से संबंधित

**conjugate** /ˈkɒndʒəgeɪt ˈकॉन्जगेट् / *verb* [T] to give the different forms of a verb क्रिया पद के विभिन्न रूप देना ▶ **conjugation** /ˌkɒndʒuˈgeɪʃn ˌकॉन्जुˈगेशन् / *noun* [C, U] क्रिया रूप

**conjunction** /kənˈdʒʌŋkʃn कन्ˈजङ्कशन् / *noun* [C] a word that is used for joining other words, phrases or sentences संयोजक शब्द; समुच्चयबोधक शब्द *'And', 'but' and 'or' are conjunctions.*

**IDM in conjunction with sb/sth** together with sb/sth किसी के साथ मिलकर; के साथ-साथ

**conjunctivitis** /kənˌdʒʌŋktɪˈvaɪtɪs कन्ˌजङ्कटिˈवाइटिस् / *noun* [U] an eye disease that causes pain and swelling in part of the eye, and that can be passed from one person to another एक संक्रामक नेत्र रोग जिसमें आँखों में दर्द और सूजन होती है; नेत्रश्लेष्मला शोथ

**conjure** /ˈkʌndʒə(r) ˈकन्ज(र्) / *verb* [I] to do tricks by clever, quick hand movements, that appear to be magic जादू करने जैसी हाथ की सफ़ाई दिखाना; बाज़ीगरी दिखाना ▶ **conjuring** *noun* [U] हाथ की सफ़ाई दिखाने की क्रिया *a conjuring trick*

**PHRV Conjure sth up 1** to cause an image to appear in your mind मन में चित्र बनना *Goan music conjures up images of sunshine, flowers and sandy beaches.* **2** to make sth appear quickly or suddenly किसी वस्तु का तुरंत और एकाएक प्रकट हो जाना *Mum can conjure up a meal out of almost anything.*

**conjuror** (*also* **conjurer**) /ˈkʌndʒərə(r) ˈकन्जर(र्) / *noun* [C] a person who does clever tricks that appear to be magic बाज़ीगर, जादूगर ➪ **magician** देखिए।

**connect** /kəˈnekt कˈनेक्ट् / *verb* **1** [I, T] **connect (sth) (up) (to/with sth)** to be joined to sth; to join sth to sth else किसी के साथ जुड़ना; दो वस्तुओं को जोड़ना, मिलाना *The printer is connected to the computer.* ○ *This highway connects New Delhi with Mathura.* ➪ **disconnect** देखिए। **2** [T] **connect sb/sth (with sb/sth)** to have an association with sb/sth else; to realize or show that sb/sth is involved with sb/sth else किसी के साथ संबंध होना; किसी के साथ संबंधित या सम्मिलित होने की जानकारी होना *There was no evidence that she was connected with the crime.* **3** [I] **connect (with sth)** (used about a bus, train, plane, etc.) to arrive at a particular time so that passengers can change to another bus, train, plane, etc. (बस, रेलगाड़ी आदि का) ऐसे समय पर पहुँचना कि यात्री अन्य बस, ट्रेन आदि ले सकें; एक बस या रेलगाड़ी का दूसरी बस या रेलगाड़ी से मेल होना *a connecting flight*

**connection** /kəˈnekʃn कˈनेक्शन् / *noun* [C] **1 a connection between A and B; a connection with/to sth** an association or relationship between two or more people or things दो या अधिक व्यक्तियों या वस्तुओं में संबंध; संयोजन, मेल *Is there any connection between the two organizations?* ○ *What's your connection with Malaysia? Have you worked there?* **2** a place where two wires, pipes, etc. join together दो तारों, नलियों आदि का योजन-बिंदु *The radio doesn't work. There must be* *a loose connection somewhere.* **3** a bus, train, plane, etc. that leaves soon after another arrives पहली बस, रेलगाड़ी आदि के पहुँचने के तुरंत बाद जाने वाली बस आदि; पहली बस या रेलगाड़ी से मेल होने वाली बस या रेलगाड़ी *Our bus was late so we missed our connection.*

IDM **in connection with sb/sth** (*formal*) about or concerning के विषय में या के संबंध में *I am writing to you in connection with your application.*

**in this/that connection** (*formal*) about or concerning this/that इस या उस संबंध में

**connive** /kəˈnaɪv कˈनाइव़् / *verb* [I] **connive at sth; connive (with sb) (to do sth)** to work secretly with sb to do sth that is wrong; to do nothing to stop sb doing sth wrong गुप्त रीति से कोई ग़लत काम करना; किसी को ग़लत काम करने से न रोकना; ग़लत काम की अनदेखी करना *The two parties connived to get rid of the president.*

**connoisseur** /ˌkɒnəˈsɜː(r) ˌकॉनˈस(र्) / *noun* [C] a person who knows a lot about art, good food, music, etc. कला, स्वादिष्ट भोजन, संगीत आदि का विशेष जानकार; गुणग्राहक, गुणज्ञ, पारखी

**connotation** /ˌkɒnəˈteɪʃn ˌकॉनˈटेश्न् / *noun* [C] an idea expressed by a word in addition to its main meaning शब्द के मुख्य अर्थ के अलावा अन्य आशय; संकेतार्थ *'Spinster' means a single woman but it has negative connotations.*

**conquer** /ˈkɒŋkə(r) ˈकॉङ्क(र्) / *verb* [T] **1** to take control of a country or city and its people by force, especially in a war युद्ध में किसी देश को जीतना; उस पर अधिकार करना *Napoleon's ambition was to conquer Europe.* ○ (*figurative*) *The young singer conquered the hearts of audiences all over the world.* **2** to succeed in controlling or dealing with a strong feeling, problem, etc. भावावेश; समस्या आदि पर सफलतापूर्वक नियंत्रण पाना *She's trying to conquer her fear of flying.*

**conqueror** /ˈkɒŋkərə(r) ˈकॉङ्कर(र्) / *noun* [C] a person who has conquered sth (विशेषतः युद्ध में) विजेता

**conquest** /ˈkɒŋkwest ˈकॉङ्क्वेस्ट् / *noun* **1** [C, U] an act of conquering sth जीत, विजय *the Norman conquest* (= of England in1066 AD) ○ *the conquest of Mount Everest* **2** [C] an area of land that has been taken in a war युद्ध में जीता गया भूक्षेत्र

**conscience** /ˈkɒnʃəns ˈकॉन्शन्स् / *noun* [C, U] the part of your mind that tells you if what you are doing is right or wrong स्वयं के कर्म के अच्छे या बुरे होने का ज्ञान; अंतःकरण, अंतश्चेतना *a clear/a guilty conscience*

IDM **have sth on your conscience** to feel guilty because you have done sth wrong ग़लत काम के लिए दोषी महसूस करना; अपराध-बोध

**conscientious** /ˌkɒnʃiˈenʃəs ˌकान्शिˈएन्शस् / *adj.* **1** (used about people) careful to do sth correctly and well (व्यक्ति) ईमानदार, कर्तव्यनिष्ठ *He's a conscientious worker.* **2** (used about actions) done with great care and attention (कर्म या कार्य) सावधानी से किया गया *conscientious work* ▶ **conscientiously** *adv.* ईमानदारी से; शुद्ध अंतःकरण से

**conscious** /ˈkɒnʃəs ˈकॉन्शस् / *adj.* **1** able to see, hear, feel, etc. things; awake सजग, सचेत; होश में, जगा हुआ *The injured driver was still conscious when the ambulance arrived.* ✪ विलोम **unconscious** **2 conscious (of sth/that...)** noticing or realizing that sth exists; aware of sth किसी वस्तु के अस्तित्व के प्रति सचेत; किसी के प्रति जागरुक या जानकार *She didn't seem conscious of the danger.* ○ *Vikas suddenly became conscious that someone was following him.* **3** that you do on purpose or for a particular reason जान-बूझकर, सोद्देश्य या सकारण *We made a conscious effort to treat both children equally.* ➪ **deliberate** देखिए। ▶ **consciously** *adv.* पूरी चेतना के साथ

**consciousness** /ˈkɒnʃəsnəs ˈकॉन्शसनस् / *noun* **1** [U] the state of being able to see, hear, feel, etc. सजगता, चेतना होश *As he fell, he hit his head and **lost consciousness**.* ○ *She **regained consciousness** after two weeks in a coma.* **2** [U, *sing.*] **consciousness (of sth)** the state of realizing or noticing that sth exists किसी बात के अस्तित्व के प्रति सजगता *There is (a) growing consciousness of the need to save energy.*

**conscript**[1] /kənˈskrɪpt कन्ˈस्क्रिप्ट् / *verb* [T] to make sb join the army, navy or air force सेना में अनिवार्य भरती करना ▶ **conscription** *noun* [U] अनिवार्य सैन्य भरती

**conscript**[2] /ˈkɒnskrɪpt ˈकॉन्स्क्रिप्ट् / *noun* [C] a person who has been conscripted अनिवार्यतः सेना में भरती व्यक्ति ➪ **volunteer**[1] **2** देखिए।

**conscription** /kənˈskrɪptʃn कन्ˈस्क्रिप्शन् / *noun* [U] the system of making sb join the army, etc. अनिवार्य सैन्य भरती

**consecrate** /ˈkɒnsɪkreɪt ˈकॉन्सिक्रेट् / *verb* [T] to state formally in a special ceremony that a place or an object can be used for religious purposes धार्मिक उद्देश्य से किसी स्थान या वस्तु को औपचारिक रूप से संस्कारित करना ▶ **consecration** /ˌkɒnsɪˈkreɪʃn ˌकॉन्सिˈक्रेश्न् / *noun* [C, U] संस्कारीकरण, पवित्रीकरण

**consecutive** /kən'sekjətɪv कन्'सेक्यटिव़् / *adj.* coming or happening one after the other एक के बाद लगातार आते या होते हुए; क्रमिक *This is the team's fourth consecutive win.* ▶ **consecutively** *adv.* निरंतर, क्रमिक रूप से

**consensus** /kən'sensəs कन्'सेन्सस् / *noun* [*sing.*, U] (a) **consensus (among/between sb) (on/about sth)** agreement among a group of people (लोगों के बीच) आम सहमति; सर्वसम्मति *to* ***reach a consensus*** ○ *There is no consensus among experts about the causes of global warming.*

**consent**[1] /kən'sent कन्'सेन्ट् / *verb* [I] **consent (to sth)** to agree to sth; to allow sth to happen किसी बात से सहमत होना; किसी बात के लिए स्वीकृति या अनुमति देना

**consent**[2] /kən'sent कन्'सेन्ट् / *noun* [U] agreement; permission सहमति, स्वीकृति, अनुमति *The child's parents had to give their consent to the operation.*

**consequence** /'kɒnsɪkwəns 'कॉन्सिक्वन्स् / *noun* **1** [C] something that happens or follows as a result of sth else परिणाम, नतीजा, फल, प्रभाव *Many people may lose their jobs* ***as a consequence of*** *recent poor sales.* **2** [U] (*formal*) importance महत्त्व *It is of no consequence.*

**consequent** /'kɒnsɪkwənt 'कॉन्सिक्वन्ट् / *adj.* (*formal*) (*only before a noun*) following as the result of sth else फलस्वरूप, परिणाम-स्वरूप *The lack of rain and consequent poor harvests have led to food shortages.* ▶ **consequently** *adv.* फलस्वरूप *She didn't work hard enough, and consequently failed the exam.*

**conservation** /ˌkɒnsə'veɪʃn ˌकॉन्स'वेशन् / *noun* [U] **1** the protection of the natural world प्राकृतिक वातावरण का संरक्षण *Conservation groups are protesting against the plan to build a road through the forest.* **2** not allowing sth to be wasted, damaged or destroyed क्षति से बचाव; बचाव का उपाय *the conservation of energy* ➪ **conserve** verb देखिए।

**conservationist** /ˌkɒnsə'veɪʃənɪst ˌकॉन्स'वेशनिस्ट् / *noun* [C] a person who believes in protecting the natural world, old buildings etc. and works for it प्रकृति, पुरानी इमारतें आदि के संरक्षण का समर्थक और उसके लिए काम करने वाला व्यक्ति

**conservatism** /kən'sɜːvətɪzəm कन्'सव़टिज़म् / *noun* [U] the disapproval of new ideas and change नए विचारों और परिवर्तन का निरुमोदन, विरोध, रूढ़िवादिता

**conservative**[1] /kən'sɜːvətɪv कन्'सव़टिव़् / *adj.* **1** not liking change; traditional परिवर्तन का विरोधी; पारंपरिक, रूढ़िवादी **2** (used when you are guessing how much sth costs) lower than the real figure or amount (लागत या मूल्य का अनुमान) वास्तविक मूल्य से कम *Even* ***a conservative estimate*** *would put the damage at about Rs 40,000 to repair.* ▶ **conservatively** *adv.* रूढ़िवादी रूप से

**conservative**[2] /kən'sɜːvətɪv कन्'सव़टिव़् / *noun* [C] a person who does not like change परिवर्तन-विमुख व्यक्ति, रूढ़िवादी

**conservatory** /kən'sɜːvətri कन्'सव़ट्रि / *noun* [C] (*pl.* **conservatories**) a room with a glass roof and walls often built onto the outside of a house मकान के बाहर की ओर बना काँच-निर्मित कक्ष

**conserve** /kən'sɜːv कन्'सव़् / *verb* [T] to avoid wasting sth बरबाद होने से बचाना *to conserve water* ➪ **conservation** noun देखिए।

**consider** /kən'sɪdə(r) कन्'सिड(र्) / *verb* [T] **1 consider sb/sth (for/as sth); consider doing sth** to think about sth carefully, often before making a decision (निर्णय लेने से पहले) किसी बात पर सावधानी से विचार करना; सोचना *She had never considered nursing as a career.* ○ *We're considering going to Kerala for our holidays.* **2 consider sb/sth (as/to be) sth; consider that...** to think about sb/sth in a particular way किसी विषय पर विशेष रीति से विचार करना; समझना, मानना *He considered that the risk was too great.* ○ *Jayeeta considers herself an expert on the subject.* **3** to remember or pay attention to sth, especially sb's feelings किसी पर (विशेषतः किसी की भावनाओं पर) ध्यान देना; ध्यान में रखना *I can't just move abroad. I have to consider my family.*

**considerable** /kən'sɪdərəbl कन्'सिडरबल् / *adj.* great in amount or size परिणाम या आकार में बड़ा *A considerable number of people preferred the old building to the new one.* ▶ **considerably** /-rəbli -रबलि / *adv.* काफ़ी अधिक *This flat is considerably larger than our last one.*

**considerate** /kən'sɪdərət कन्'सिडरट् / *adj.* **considerate (towards sb); considerate (of sb) (to do sth)** careful not to upset people; always thinking of other people's wishes and feelings दूसरों की भावनाओं या आवश्यकताओं का ध्यान रखने वाला; संवेदनशील *It was very considerate of you to offer to drive me home.* ✪ विलोम **inconsiderate**

**consideration** /kənˌsɪdə'reɪʃn कन्ˌसिड'रेशन् / *noun* **1** [U] (*formal*) an act of thinking about sth carefully or for a long time किसी बात पर देर तक सावधानी से विचार करने की क्रिया *I have given some consideration to the idea but I don't think it would work.* **2** [C] something that you think about when you are making a decision निर्णय लेते समय विचार करने योग्य मुद्दा *If he changes his job, the salary will be an important consideration.* **3** [U] **consideration (for sb/sth)** the quality of thinking about what other people need or feel दूसरों की आवश्यकताओं या भावनाओं का लिहाज़ *Most drivers show little consideration for cyclists.*

IDM **take sth into consideration** to think about sth when you are forming an opinion or making a decision निर्णय लेते समय किसी विशेष बात को ध्यान में रखना

**considering** /kənˈsɪdərɪŋ कन्ˈसिडरिङ् / *prep., conj.* (used for introducing a surprising fact) when you think about or remember sth (किसी आश्चर्यजनक तथ्य को प्रस्तुत करने के लिए प्रयुक्त) (इस बात को) ध्यान में रखते हुए *Considering you've only been studying for a year, you speak English very well.*

**consign** /kənˈsaɪn कन्ˈसाइन् / *verb* [T] (*formal*) **consign sb/sth to sth** to put or send sb/sth somewhere, especially in order to get rid of him/her/it पीछा छुड़ाने के लिए किसी को कहीं रख या भेज देना; के सुपुर्द करना *I think I can consign this junk mail straight to the bin.*

**consignment** /kənˈsaɪnmənt कन्ˈसाइन्मन्ट् / *noun* [C] goods that are being sent to sb/sth भेजा गया माल, प्रेषित माल *a new consignment of books*

**consist** /kənˈsɪst कन्ˈसिस्ट् / *verb* (*not used in the continuous tenses*)

PHR V **consist in sth** to have sth as its main point किसी में कोई बात मुख्य होना *Her job consisted in welcoming the guests as they arrived.*

**consist of sth** to be formed or made up of sth (से, का) बना होना *The band consists of a singer, two guitarists and a drummer.*

NOTE यद्यपि इस क्रिया का प्रयोग सातत्यबोधक कालों (continuous tenses) में नहीं होता तथापि इससे बनने वाला -ing युक्त वर्तमान कृदंत (present participle) रूप काफ़ी दिखाई पड़ता है—*It's a full-time course consisting of six different modules.*

**consistency** /kənˈsɪstənsi कन्ˈसिस्टन्सि / *noun* (*pl.* **consistencies**) **1** [U] the quality of always having the same standard, opinions, behaviour, etc. किसी मापदंड, सम्मति, आचरण आदि के स्तर का समान रूप से बनें रहने का गुण; संगति, सामंजस्य *Your work lacks consistency. Sometimes it's excellent but at other times it's full of mistakes.* ✪ विलोम **inconsistency** **2** [C, U] how thick or smooth a liquid substance is (द्रव का) घनापन या गाढ़ापन; गाढ़ेपन का माप *The mixture should have a thick, sticky consistency.*

**consistent** /kənˈsɪstənt कन्ˈसिस्टन्ट् / *adj.* **1** always having the same opinions, standard, behaviour, etc.; not changing विचार, मापदंड आचरण आदि का सदैव एक सा होना; अपरिवर्तनीय **2 consistent (with sth)** agreeing with or similar to sth संगत, अनुकूल *I'm afraid your statement is not consistent with what the other witnesses said.* ✪ विलोम **inconsistent** ▶ **consistently** *adv.* संगत रीति से *We must try to maintain a consistently high standard.*

**consolation** /ˌkɒnsəˈleɪʃn ˌकॉन्सˈलेश्न् / *noun* [C, U] a thing or person that makes you feel better when you are sad दिलासा देने या धैर्य बँधाने वाली वस्तु या व्यक्ति; सांत्वना *It was some consolation to me to know that I wasn't the only one who had failed the exam.* ✪ पर्याय **comfort**

**console**[1] /kənˈsəʊl कन्ˈसोल् / *verb* [T] to make sb happier when he/she is very sad or disappointed; दुःख या निराशा में धैर्य बाँधना, दिलासा या सांत्वना देना ✪ पर्याय **comfort**

**console**[2] /ˈkɒnsəʊl ˈकॉन्सोल् / *noun* [C] a flat surface which contains all the controls and switches for a machine, a piece of electronic equipment, etc. वह समतल सतह जिस पर किसी मशीन के सभी नियंत्रक उपकरण स्थापित होते हैं

**consolidate** /kənˈsɒlɪdeɪt कन्ˈसॉलिडेट् / *verb* [I, T] to become or to make your position of power firmer or stronger so that is likely to continue अपनी स्थिति को अधिक दृढ़ या मज़बूत बनाना ताकि ऐसी स्थिति जारी रह सके; पक्का करना *We're going to consolidate what we've learnt so far by doing some revision exercises today.* **2** to join things together into one; to be joined into one वस्तुओं को जोड़कर एक बनाना; संघटित करना ▶ **consolidation** /kənˌsɒlɪˈdeɪʃn कन्ˌसॉलिˈडेश्न् / *noun* [U] दृढ़ीकरण

**consonant** /ˈkɒnsənənt ˈकॉन्सनन्ट् / *noun* [C] any of the letters of the English alphabet except a, e, i, o, and u अंग्रेज़ी वर्णमाला में a, e, i, o और u को छोड़कर अन्य सभी अक्षर; व्यंजन ➪ **vowel** देखिए।

**consortium** /kənˈsɔːtiəm कन्ˈसॉटिअम् / *noun* [C] (*pl.* **consortiums** or **consortia** /-tiə -टिआ /) a group of companies that work closely together for a particular purpose कंपनियों का समूह जो विशेष उद्देश्य से एक साथ काम करती हैं; संघ, संगठन

**conspicuous** /kən'spɪkjuəs कन्'स्पिक्युअस् / *adj.* easily seen or noticed सुस्पष्ट, प्रकट, साफ़, प्रत्यक्ष ✪ विलोम **inconspicuous** ► **conspicuously** *adv.* प्रकट रूप से

**conspiracy** /kən'spɪrəsi कन्'स्पिरसि / *noun* [C, U] (*pl.* **conspiracies**) a secret plan by a group of people to do sth bad or illegal अनुचित या ग़ैर-क़ानूनी काम की गुप्त योजना; षड्यंत्र, साजिश

**conspirator** /kən'spɪrətə(r) कन्'स्पिरट(र्) / *noun* [C] a member of a group of people who are planning to do sth bad or illegal षड्यंत्र में भागीदार; षड्यंत्रकारी

**conspire** /kən'spaɪə(r) कन्'स्पाइअ(र्) / *verb* [I] **1 conspire (with sb) (to do sth)** to plan to do sth bad or illegal with a group of people कुछ लोगों के साथ षड्यंत्र की योजना बनाना *A group of terrorists were conspiring to blow up the plane.* **2 conspire (against sb/sth)** (used about events) to seem to work together to make sth bad happen (घटनाओं का) मिलकर प्रतिकूल हो जाना *When we both lost our jobs in the same week, we felt that everything was conspiring against us.*

**constable** /'kʌnstəbl 'कनस्टबल् / = **police constable**

**constabulary** /kən'stæbjələri कन्'स्टैबयलरि / *noun* [C] (*pl.* **constabularies**) the police force of a particular area क्षेत्र-विशेष का पुलिसबल

**constant** /'kɒnstənt 'कॉनस्टन्ट् / *adj.* **1** happening or existing all the time or again and again निरंतर, लगातार *The constant noise gave me a headache.* **2** that does not change एक समान; स्थिर, अपरिवर्तनीय *You use less petrol if you drive at a constant speed.*

**constantly** /'kɒnstəntli 'कॉनस्टन्टलि / *adv.* always; again and again सदा; बराबर, बार-बार, लगातार *The situation is constantly changing.*

**constellation** /,kɒnstə'leɪʃn ,कॉनस्ट'लेशन् / *noun* [C] a group of stars that forms a pattern and has a name तारामंडल, नक्षत्र

**consternation** /,kɒnstə'neɪʃn ,कॉनस्ट'नेशन् / *noun* [U] a feeling of shock or worry भयाकुलता या चिंता *We stared at each other **in consternation**.*

**constipated** /'kɒnstɪpeɪtɪd 'कॉनस्टिपेटिड् / *adj.* not able to empty waste from your body क़ब्ज़ का शिकार ► **constipation** /,kɒnstɪ'peɪʃn ,कॉनस्टि'पेशन् / *noun* [U] क़ब्ज़ *to suffer from/have constipation*

**constituency** /kən'stɪtjuənsi कन्'स्टिट्युअन्सि / *noun* [C] (*pl.* **constituencies**) the district and the residents of a district who elect a legislator or an official चुनाव-क्षेत्र; एक निश्चित भूक्षेत्र और उसके निवासी जो किसी विधायक या अफ़सर का चुनाव करते हैं

**constituent** /kən'stɪtjuənt कन्'स्टिट्युअन्ट् / *noun* [C] **1** one of the parts that form sth किसी वस्तु का घटक *Hydrogen and oxygen are the constituents of water.* **2** a person who lives in the district that a politician represents किसी चुनाव-क्षेत्र का निवासी

**constitute** /'kɒnstɪtjuːt 'कॉनस्टिट्यूट् / *verb, linking verb* (*formal*) (*not used in the continuous tenses*) **1** to be one of the parts that form sth किसी का घटक या अंश होना *Women constitute a high proportion of part-time workers.* **2** to be considered as sth; to be equal to sth कुछ विशेष माना या समझा जाना; किसी के बराबर होना *The presence of the troops constitutes a threat to peace.*

> **NOTE** यद्यपि इस क्रिया का प्रयोग सातत्यबोधक कालों (continuous tenses) में नहीं होता तथापि इसका -ing युक्त वर्तमान कृदांत (present participle) रूप आम दिखाई पड़ता है—*Management has to fix a maximum number of hours as constituting a day's work.*

**constitution** /,kɒnstɪ'tjuːʃn ,कॉनस्टि'ट्यूशन् / *noun* **1** [C] the basic laws or rules of a country or organization किसी देश या संगठन के आधारभूत विधि-विधान; संविधान *the Indian constitution* **2** [U] the way the parts of sth are put together; the structure of sth किसी वस्तु की बनावट-संरचना या गठन *the constitution of DNA*

**constitutional** /,kɒnstɪ'tjuːʃənl ,कॉनस्टि'ट्यूशनल् / *adj.* connected with or allowed by the constitution of a country, etc. देश आदि के संविधान से संबंधित; संवैधानिक *It is not constitutional to imprison a person without trial.*

**constrain** /kən'streɪn कन्'स्ट्रेन् / *verb* [T] (*formal*) **constrain sb/sth (to do sth)** to limit sb/sth; to force sb/sth to do sth किसी व्यक्ति या वस्तु को सीमित करना; अवरुद्ध करना; कुछ करने के लिए बाध्य करना *The company's growth has been constrained by high taxes.*

**constraint** /kən'streɪnt कन्'स्ट्रेन्ट् / *noun* [C, U] something that limits you अवरोधकारी तत्व; प्रतिबंध; सीमित करने वाले नियंत्रण *There are always some financial constraints on a project like this.* ✪ पर्याय **restriction**

**constrict** /kən'strɪkt कन्'स्ट्रिक्ट् / *verb* [I, T] **1** to become or make sth tighter, narrower or less संकुचित होना या करना; सिकुड़ना, कसना *She felt her throat constrict with fear.* ○ *The valve constricts* *the flow of air.* **2** to limit a person's freedom to do sth किसी व्यक्ति की स्वतंत्रता को सीमाबद्ध करना ▸ **constriction** *noun* [C, U] संकुचन, दबाव

**construct** /kənˈstrʌkt कन्ˈस्ट्रक्ट् / *verb* [T] to build or make sth किसी वस्तु का निर्माण करना, बनाना; रचना *Early houses were constructed out of mud and sticks.* **NOTE** **Build** की अपेक्षा **construct** प्रयोग अधिक औपचारिक है।

**construction** /kənˈstrʌkʃn कन्ˈस्ट्रक्शन् / *noun* **1** [U] the act or method of building or making sth निर्माण कार्य या पद्धति *A new bridge is now* ***under construction.*** ○ *He works in the construction industry.* **2** [C] (*formal*) something that has been built or made; a building निर्मित वस्तु; संरचना, भवन, इमारत *The new pyramid was a construction of glass and steel.* **3** [C] the way that words are used together in a phrase or sentence वाक्य-रचना *a grammatical construction*

**constructive** /kənˈstrʌktɪv कन्ˈस्ट्रक्टिव् / *adj.* useful or helpful उपयोगी या सहायक *constructive suggestions/criticisms/advice* ▸ **constructively** *adv.* रचनात्मक या उपयोगी रूप से

**construe** /kənˈstruː कन्ˈस्ट्रू / *verb* [T] (*formal*) **construe sth (as sth)** to understand the meaning of sth in a particular way किसी बात का विशेष अर्थ लगाना, किसी बात का विशेष ढंग से समझा जाना *Her confident manner is often construed as arrogance.* ➪ **misconstrue** देखिए।

**consul** /ˈkɒnsl ˈकॉन्सल् / *noun* [C] an official appointed by a goverment in a foreign city helping people from his/her own country who are living or visiting there विदेशी नगर में पदस्थ किसी देश का प्रतिनिधि अधिकारी जो अपने देश से आए देशवासियों की सहायता करता है; दूत ▸ **consular** /ˈkɒnsjələ(r) ˈकॉन्स्यल(र्) / *adj.* दूत-विषयक

**consulate** /ˈkɒnsjələt ˈकॉन्स्यलट् / *noun* [C] the building where a consul works दूत का कार्यालय ➪ **embassy** देखिए।

**consult** /kənˈsʌlt कन्ˈसल्ट् / *verb* **1** [T] **consult sb/sth (about sth)** to ask sb for some information or advice, or to look for it in a book, etc. (किसी के विषय में) किसी से जानकारी या सलाह माँगना पुस्तक आदि में जानकारी ढूँढ़ना *If the symptoms continue, consult your doctor.* **2** [I] **consult with sb** to discuss sth with sb विचार-विमर्श या किसी से बातचीत करना *Vivek consulted with his brothers before selling the family business.*

**consultancy** /kənˈsʌltənsi कन्ˈसलटन्सि / *noun* (*pl.* **consultancies**) **1** [C] a company that gives expert advice on a particular subject सलाह या परामर्श देने वाली कंपनी **2** [U] expert advice that sb is paid to provide on a particular subject विशेषज्ञ की परामर्श-सेवा

**consultant** /kənˈsʌltənt कन्ˈसल्टन्ट् / *noun* [C] **1** a person who gives advice to people on business, law, etc. परामर्शदाता, सलाहकार *a firm of management consultants* **2** a hospital doctor who is a specialist in a particular area of medicine अस्पताल में विशेषज्ञ चिकित्सक *a consultant psychiatrist*

**consultation** /ˌkɒnslˈteɪʃn ˌकॉन्सल्ˈटेशन् / *noun* [C, U] **1** a discussion between people before a decision is taken निर्णय लेने से पहले लोगों में विचार-विमर्श *Diplomats met for consultations on the hostage crisis.* ○ *The measures were introduced without consultation.* **2** (*formal*) meeting sb to get information or advice, or looking for it in a book जानकारी लेने या परामर्श करने की क्रिया *a consultation with a doctor*

**consume** /kənˈsjuːm कन्ˈस्यूम् / *verb* [T] (*formal*) **1** to use sth such as fuel, energy or time ईंधन, ऊर्जा, समय आदि का प्रयोग करना; उपयोग करना **2** to eat or drink sth कुछ खाना या पीना *Wrestlers can consume up to 10,000 calories in a day.* ➪ **consumption** noun देखिए। **3** (used about fire) to destroy sth (आग का) किसी वस्तु को जला डालना; नष्ट करना **4** (used about an emotion) to affect sb very strongly (भावना-विशेष से) बहुत अधिक प्रभावित हो जाना *She was consumed by grief when her son was killed.*

**consumer** /kənˈsjuːmə(r) कन्ˈस्यूम(र्) / *noun* [C] **1** a person who buys things or uses services उपभोक्ता **2** a person or an animal that eats or uses sth कुछ खाने या प्रयोग करने वाला व्यक्ति या पशु ➪ **food chain** पर चित्र देखिए।

**consuming** /kənˈsjuːmɪŋ कन्ˈस्यूमिङ् / *adj.* (*only before a noun*) that takes up a lot of your time and attention जिसमें बहुत समय और ध्यान लगता हो; ग्रसित करने वाला *Sport is her consuming passion.*

**consummate**[1] /ˈkɒnsəmət ˈकॉन्समट् / *adj.* (*only before a noun*) (*formal*) extremely skilled; a perfect example of sth अतिदक्ष; किसी कार्य में पूर्ण रूप से कुशल *a consummate performer/professional*

**consummate**[2] /ˈkɒnsəmeɪt ˈकॉन्समट् / *verb* [T] (*formal*) to make a marriage or relationship complete by having sex यौन क्रिया करके विवाह या संबंध को पूर्ण बनाना ▸ **consummation** /ˌkɒnsəˈmeɪʃn ˌकॉन्सˈमेशन् / *noun* [C, U] संपूर्ण करने की क्रिया

**consumption** /kən'sʌmpʃn कन्'सम्प्श्न्/ *noun* [U] **1** the amount of fuel, etc. that sth uses प्रयुक्त ईंधन आदि की मात्रा *a car with low fuel consumption* **2** the act of using, eating, etc. sth किसी को प्रयोग करने, उपयोग करने आदि की क्रिया *The meat was declared unfit for human consumption* (= for people to eat). ➪ **consume** verb देखिए।

**cont.** (*also* **contd**) *abbr.* continued सतत, जारी, सतंत *cont. on p 91*

**contact[1]** /'kɒntækt 'कॉन्टैक्ट्/ *noun* **1** [U] **contact (with sb/sth)** meeting, talking to or writing to sb else भेंट, चर्चा या पत्र द्वारा संपर्क; संचार संपर्क *They are trying to* ***make contact*** *with the kidnappers.* ○ *We* ***keep in contact*** *with our office in Kolkata.* **2** [U] **contact (with sb/sth)** the state of touching sb/sth स्पर्श *This product should not* ***come into contact*** *with food.* **3** [C] a person that you know who may be able to help you किसी काम में सहायक व्यक्ति; परिचित व्यक्ति जो सहायता पहुँचाने की स्थिति में हो *business contacts* **4** [C] an electrical connection विद्युत संपर्क की युक्ति *The switches close the contacts and complete the circuit.* ➪ **bulb** पर चित्र देखिए।

**contact[2]** /'kɒntækt कॉन्टैक्ट्/ *verb* [T] to telephone or write to sb किसी को फ़ोन करना या पत्र लिखना *Is there a phone number where I can contact you?*

**contact lens** *noun* [C] a small thin piece of plastic that fits onto your eye to help you to see better दृष्टि में सुधार लाने के लिए आँख पर लगाया जाने वाला प्लास्टिक का छोटा पतला टुकड़ा; संस्पर्श लेन्स; कॉनटेक्ट लेन्स

**contagious** /kən'teɪdʒəs कन्'टेजस्/ *adj.* (used about a disease) that you can get by touching sb/sth (रोग) संपर्क या स्पर्श द्वारा फैलने वाला; संसर्गज *Measles is a highly contagious disease.* ○ (*figurative*) *Her laugh is contagious.* ➪ **infectious** पर नोट देखिए। ▶ **contagion** /kən'teɪdʒən कन्'टेजन्/ *noun* [U] स्पर्श या संपर्क से फैलने वाला रोग, रोग का संक्रमण

**contain** /kən'teɪn कन्'टेन्/ *verb* [T] (*not used in the continuous tenses*) **1** to have sth inside or as part of itself अपने अंदर कुछ होना या अपना अंग होना; समावेशित होना *Each box contains 24 tins.* **2** to keep sth within limits; to control sth सीमा के भीतर रखना; नियंत्रित करना *efforts to contain inflation* ○ *She found it hard to contain her anger.*

**NOTE** यद्यपि इस क्रिया का प्रयोग सातत्यबोधक कालों (continuous tenses) में नहीं होता तथापि इसका -ing युक्त वर्तमान कृदंत (present participle) रूप आम दिखाई पड़ता है—*petrol containing lead*

**Contain** या **include**" जब यह बताना हो कि एक वस्तु के भीतर अन्य वस्तुएँ हैं तो **contain** का प्रयोग किया जाता है—*a jar containing olives* ○ *This film contains violent scenes.* जब यह बताना हो कि कोई वस्तु (अंश) अपने से बड़े (पूर्ण) का हिस्सा है तो **include** का प्रयोग किया जाता है—*a team of seven people inluding a cameraman and a doctor* ○ *The price of the holiday includes accommodation.*

**container** /kən'teɪnə(r) कन्'टेन(र्)/ *noun* [C] **1** a box, bottle, packet, etc. in which sth is kept डिब्बा, बोतल, पैकेट आदि जिसमें कुछ रखा जाता है; पात्र *a plastic container* **2** a large metal box that is used for transporting goods by sea, road or rail धातु-निर्मित बड़ा बक्सा जिससे समुद्र, सड़क या रेलमार्ग से माल ढोया जाता है; कंटेनर *a container lorry/ship*

**contaminant** /kən'tæmɪnənt कन्'टैमिनन्ट्/ *noun* [C] any substance that makes sth dirty or not pure किसी वस्तु को मैला या दूषित कर देने वाला पदार्थ; प्रदूषक

**contaminate** /kən'tæmɪneɪt कन्'टैमिनेट्/ *verb* [T] to add a substance which will make sth dirty or harmful कोई पदार्थ डालकर किसी वस्तु को दूषित कर देना; संदूषित करना *The town's drinking water was contaminated with poisonous chemicals.* ▶ **contamination** /kən,tæmɪ'neɪʃn कन्,टैमि'नेशन्/ *noun* [U] संदूषण

**contemplate** /'kɒntəmpleɪt 'कॉन्टम्प्लेट्/ *verb* [T] **1** to think carefully about sth or the possibility of doing sth किसी विषय या संभावना पर सावधानी से विचार करना चिंतन करना *Before her illness she had never contemplated retiring.* **2** to look at sb/sth, often quietly or for a long time किसी व्यक्ति या वस्तु को शांत भाव से और देर तक देखना ▶ **contemplation** /,kɒntəm'pleɪʃn ,कॉन्टम्'प्लेशन्/ *noun* [U] चिंतन, अवलोकन

**contemporary[1]** /kən'temprəri कन्'टेम्प्ररि/ *adj.* **1** belonging to the same time as sb/sth else समकालीन, समकालिक *The programme includes contemporary film footage of the First World War.* **2** of the present time; modern इसी समय का; वर्तमान-कालिक; आधुनिक *contemporary music/art/society*

**contemporary[2]** /kən'temprəri कन्'टेम्प्ररि/ *noun* [C] (*pl.* **contemporaries**) a person who lives or does sth at the same time as sb else समकालीन व्यक्ति

**contempt** /kən'tempt कन्'टेम्प्ट्/ *noun* [U] **contempt (for sb/sth)** the feeling that sb/sth does not deserve any respect or is without value

तिरस्कार, अवज्ञा *The teacher treated my question **with contempt**.* ▶ **contemptuous** /kən'temptʃuəs कन्'टेम्प्चुअस्/ *adj.* तिरस्कारपूर्ण *The boy just gave a contemptuous laugh when I asked him to be quiet.*

**contemptible** /kən'temptəbl कन्'टेम्प्टबल्/ *adj.* (*formal*) not deserving any respect at all तिरस्करणीय; तिरस्कार के योग्य *contemptible behaviour*

**contend** /kən'tend कन्'टेन्ड्/ *verb* **1** [I] **contend with/against sb/sth** to have to deal with a problem or a difficult situation समस्या या मुश्किल परिस्थिति का सामना करना *She's had a lot of problems to contend with.* **2** [T] (*formal*) to say or argue that sth is true कोई बात दावे से कहना; विवाद करना *The young man contended that he was innocent.* **3** [I] **contend (for sth)** to compete against sb to win or gain sth स्पर्धा करना, मुक़ाबला करना *Two athletes are contending for first place.*

**contender** /kən'tendə(r) कन्'टेन्ड(र्)/ *noun* [C] a person who may win a competition प्रतिस्पर्धी *There are only two serious contenders for the leadership.*

**content**[1] /kən'tent कन्'टेन्ट्/ *adj.* (*not before a noun*) **content (with sth); content to do sth** happy or satisfied with what you have or do संतुष्ट *I don't need a new car—I'm perfectly content with the one I've got.*

**content**[2] /'kɒntent 'कॉन्ट्रेन्ट्/ *noun* **1 contents** [*pl.*] the thing or things that are inside sth भीतर या अंदर रखी वस्तु या वस्तुएँ *Add the contents of this packet to a litre of cold milk and mix well.* **2** [*sing.*] the main subject, ideas, etc. of a book, article, television programme, etc. पुस्तक, लेख, टेलीविज़न कार्यक्रम आदि की विषय-वस्तु का मूल विषय, विचार आदि *The content of the essay is good, but there are too many grammatical mistakes.* **3** the amount of a particular substance that sth contains अंतर्निहित वस्तु की मात्रा *Many processed foods have a high sugar content.*

**content**[3] /kən'tent कन्'टेन्ट्/ *noun* [*sing.*]

**IDM to your heart's content** ➪ **heart** देखिए।

**content**[4] /kən'tent कन्'टेन्ट्/ *verb* [T] **content yourself with sth** to accept sth even though it was not exactly what you wanted जो मिले उसी से संतोष करना (चाहे वह अपेक्षा से कम हो) *The restaurant was closed, so we had to content ourselves with a sandwich.*

**contented** /kən'tentɪd कन्'टेन्टिड्/ *adj.* happy or satisfied प्रसन्न या संतुष्ट *The baby gave a contented chuckle.* ▶ **contentedly** *adv.* संतोषपूर्वक

**contention** /kən'tenʃn कन्'टेन्शन्/ *noun* (*formal*) **1** [U] arguing; disagreement विवाद; झगड़ा, असहमति **2** [C] your opinion; sth that you say is true दृष्टिकोण; कथन, मत *The government's contention is that unemployment will start to fall next year.*

**IDM in contention (for sth)** having a chance of winning a competition प्रतियोगिता में जीतने की संभावना होना; स्पर्धा करना *Four teams are still in contention for the cup.*

**contentious** /kən'tenʃəs कन्'टेन्शस्/ *adj.* likely to cause argument विवादग्रस्त, विवादास्पद *a contentious issue*

**contentment** /kən'tentmənt कन्'टेन्ट्मन्ट्/ *noun* [U] a feeling of happy satisfaction मधुर संतुष्टि, संतोष

**contest**[1] /'kɒntest 'कॉन्ट्टेस्ट्/ *noun* [C] a competition to find out who is the best, strongest, most beautiful, etc. प्रतिस्पर्धा, मुक़ाबला, प्रतियोगिता *I've decided to **enter** that writing **contest**.* ○ *The by-election will be a contest between the two main parties.*

**contest**[2] /kən'test कन्'टेस्ट्/ *verb* [T] **1** to take part in a competition or try to win sth स्पर्धा में भाग लेना *Twenty-four teams will contest next year's World Cup.* **2** to say that sth is wrong or that it was not done properly प्रतिवाद करना, चुनौती देना *They contested the decision, saying that the judges had not been fair.*

**contestant** /kən'testənt कन्'टेस्टन्ट्/ *noun* [C] a person who takes part in a contest प्रतिस्पर्धी, प्रतियोगी *Four contestants appear on the quiz show each week.*

**context** /'kɒntekst 'कॉन्ट्टेक्स्ट्/ *noun* [C, U] **1** the situation in which sth happens or that caused sth to happen संदर्भ, प्रसंग *To **put** our company **in context**, we are now the third largest in the country.* **2** the words that come before or after a word, phrase or sentence that help you to understand its meaning किसी शब्द, वाक्यांश या वाक्य से पहले या बाद के शब्द जो अर्थ समझने में सहायक होते हैं *You can often guess the meaning of a word from its context.* ○ *Taken **out of context**, his comment made no sense.*

**continent** /'kɒntɪnənt 'कॉन्टिनन्ट्/ *noun* **1** [C] one of the seven main areas of land on the Earth महाद्वीप *Asia, Africa and Antarctica are continents.* **2 the Continent** [*sing.*] the main part of Europe not including the British Isles ब्रिटिश द्वीपसमूह को छोड़कर यूरोप का मुख्य भाग

**continental** /ˌkɒntɪˈnentl ˌकॉन्टिˈनेन्ट्ल् / *adj.* **1** connected with or typical of a continent महाद्वीप से संबंधित या महाद्वीप की विशिष्टता वाला *Moscow has a continental climate—hot summers and cold winters.* **2** connected with the main part of Europe not including the British Isles ब्रिटिश द्वीपसमूह को छोड़कर यूरोप के मुख्य भाग से संबंधित *continental food*

**continental breakfast** *noun* [C] a cold breakfast of bread and jam with coffee ब्रैड, जैम और कॉफ़ी का प्रातःकालीन जलपान

**continental drift** *noun* [U] (in geology) the slow movement of the continents towards and away from each other during the history of the earth (भूविज्ञान में) पृथ्वी के इतिहास के दौरान महाद्वीपों का मंदगति से निकट आने और एक-दूसरे से दूर जाने की क्रिया; महाद्वीपीय विस्थापन ➪ **plate tectonics** देखिए।

**continental shelf** *noun* [*sing.*] (in geology) the area of land under the sea on the edge of a continent (भूविज्ञान में) महाद्वीप के छोर पर समुद की सतह के नीचे जलमग्न भूक्षेत्र; महाद्वीपीय शेल्फ़

**continental slope** *noun* [*sing.*] (in geology) the steep surface that goes down from the outer edge of the **continental shelf** to the ocean floor (भूविज्ञान में) महाद्वीप जलमग्नसीमा के बाहरी छोर से समुद्र तल की ओर जाने वाली ढालू पट्टी; महाद्वीपीय ढाल

**contingency** /kənˈtɪndʒənsi कन्ˈटिन्जन्सि / *noun* [C] (*pl.* **contingencies**) a possible future situation or event भविष्य में संभावित स्थिति या घटना *We'd better make* ***contingency plans*** *just in case something goes wrong.* ○ *We've tried to prepare for every possible contingency.*

**contingent** /kənˈtɪndʒənt कन्ˈटिन्जन्ट् / *noun* [C, *with sing. or pl. verb*] **1** a group of people from the same country, organization, etc. who are attending an event किसी सम्मेलन आदि में उपस्थित एक ही देश या संगठन के व्यक्तियों का दल *the Indian contingent at the conference* **2** a group of armed forces forming part of a larger force सैन्य दल जो किसी वृहत्तर सैन्यदल का भाग हो

**continual** /kənˈtɪnjuəl कन्ˈटिन्युअल् / *adj.* happening again and again बारंबार होने वाला, लगातार, निरंतर *His continual phone calls started to annoy her.* ➪ **incessant** देखिए। ▶ **continually** *adv.* बारंबार

**continuation** /kənˌtɪnjuˈeɪʃn कन्ˌटिन्युˈएशन् / *noun* [*sing.*, U] something that continues or follows sth else; the act of making sth continue क्रम आदि में अगली या जारी रहने वाली वस्तु आदि; निरंतरता; जारी रहने की स्थिति; जारी रखने की क्रिया *The team are hoping for a continuation of their recent good form.* ○ *Continuation of the current system will be impossible.*

**continue** /kənˈtɪnjuː कन्ˈटिन्यू / *verb* **1** [I] to keep happening or existing without stopping होते रहना; जारी रहना; लगातार बने रहना *If the pain continues, see your doctor.* **2** [I, T] **continue (doing/to do sth); continue (with sth)** to keep doing sth without stopping कोई काम लगातार करते रहना *They ignored me and continued their conversation.* ○ *He continued working/to work late into the night.* **3** [I, T] to begin to do or say sth again after you had stopped (रुकने के बाद) फिर से शुरू करना *The meeting will continue after lunch.* **4** [I, T] to go further in the same direction (उसी दिशा में) आगे बढ़ना *The next day we continued our journey.*

**continued** /kənˈtɪnjuːd कन्ˈटिन्यूड् / *adj.* going on without stopping लगातार जारी, निरंतर *There are reports of continued fighting near the border.*

**continuity** /ˌkɒntɪˈnjuːəti ˌकॉन्टिˈन्यूअटि / *noun* [U] the fact of continuing without stopping or of staying the same निरंतरता, अविच्छिन्नता *The students will have the same teacher for two years to ensure continuity.*

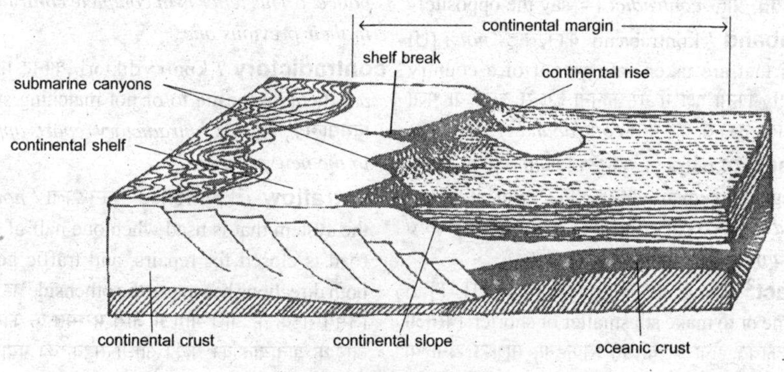


continental shelf/slope

**continuous** /kənˈtɪnjuəs कन्ˈटिन्युअस्/ *adj.* happening or existing without stopping बिना रुके होने वाला; लगातार *There was a continuous line of cars stretching for miles.* ▸ **continuously** *adv.* निरंतर *It has rained continuously here for three days.*

**the continuous tense** (*also* **the progressive tense**) *noun* [C] (*grammar*) the form of a verb such as 'I am waiting', 'I was waiting' or 'have been waiting' which is made from a part of 'be' and a verb ending in '-ing' and is used to describe an action that continues for a period of time (अंग्रेज़ी व्याकरण में) कुछ समय तक जारी रहने वाली क्रिया का वर्णन करने के लिए 'be' के रूप और '-ing' से बनने वाला क्रियापद; सातत्यबोधक काल

**continuum** /kənˈtɪnjuəm कन्ˈटिन्युअम्/ *noun* [C] (*pl.* **continua** /-juə -युआ/) a continuous series of things, in which each one is only slightly different from the things next to it, but the last is very different from the first शृंखला जिसमें हर अगली वस्तु पिछली से थोड़ी ही भिन्न होती है परंतु अंतिम और प्रथम में बहुत अंतर होता है; सतत वस्तु शृंखला

**contort** /kənˈtɔːt कन्ˈटॉट्/ *verb* [I, T] to move or to make sth move into a strange or unusual shape मरोड़कर आकृति बिगड़ना या बिगाड़ना *His face contorted/was contorted with pain.* ▸ **contortion** *noun* [C] विकृति, कुंचन, ऐंठन

**contour** /ˈkɒntʊə(r) ˈकॉन्टुअ(र्)/ *noun* [C] **1** the shape of the outer surface of sth किसी वस्तु की बाह्य आकृति; रूपरेखा *I could just make out the contours of the house in the dark.* **2** (*also* **contour line**) a line on a map joining places of equal height मानचित्र पर समान ऊँचाई के स्थानों को मिलाने वाली रेखा; कंटूर, परिरेखा

**contra-** /ˈkɒntrə ˈकॉन्ट्रा/ *prefix* (*used in nouns, verbs and adjectives*) against; opposite के विरुद्ध; के विपरीत; प्रति- *contradict* (= say the opposite)

**contraband** /ˈkɒntrəbænd ˈकॉन्ट्रबैन्ड्/ *noun* [U] goods that are taken into or out of a country illegally किसी देश में ग़ैर-क़ानूनी ढंग से लाया या भेजा गया माल; तस्करी का माल *contraband cigarettes*

**contract¹** /ˈkɒntrækt ˈकॉन्ट्रैक्ट्/ *noun* [C] a written legal agreement इक़रारनामा, अनुबंध-पत्र *They **signed a** three-year **contract with** a major record company.* ○ *a temporary contract*

**contract²** /kənˈtrækt कन्ˈट्रैक्ट्/ *verb* **1** [I, T] to become or to make sth smaller or shorter (वस्तुओं का) संकुचित होना या करना; सिकुड़ना, संक्षिप्त होना या करना *Metals contract as they cool.* ✪ विलोम **expand** **2** [T] to get an illness or disease, especially a serious one विशेषतः गंभीर बीमारी या रोग से ग्रस्त होना *to contract pneumonia* **3** [I, T] to make a written legal agreement with sb to do sth किसी के साथ कुछ करने का लिखित क़ानूनी समझौता करना; इक़रारनामा करना *His firm has been contracted to supply all the furniture for the new building.*

**PHRV** **contract sth out (to sb)** to arrange for work to be done by sb outside your own company (बाहर से) काम करने का ठेका देना

**contraction** /kənˈtrækʃn कन्ˈट्रैक्श्न्/ *noun* **1** [U] the process of becoming or of making sth become smaller or shorter संकुचन या संकोचन की प्रक्रिया; सिकुड़न, संक्षिप्तीकरण *the expansion and contraction of a muscle* **2** [C] a shorter form of a word or words शब्दों या किसी शब्द का छोटा या संक्षिप्त रूप *'Mustn't' is a contraction of 'must not'.*

**contractor** /kənˈtræktə(r) कन्ˈट्रैक्ट(र्)/ *noun* [C] a person or company that has a contract to do work or provide goods or services for another company (सामान या सेवा देने वाला) ठेकेदार व्यक्ति या कंपनी

**contractual** /kənˈtræktʃuəl कन्ˈट्रैक्चुअल्/ *adj.* connected with or included in a contract ठेके या अनुबंध से संबंधित या उसमें शामिल

**contradict** /ˌkɒntrəˈdɪkt ˌकॉन्ट्रˈडिक्ट्/ *verb* [T] to say that sth is wrong or not true; to say the opposite of sth (किसी बात को) ग़लत ठहराना; (किसी बात का) खंडन करना; विरोध में बोलना *These instructions seem to contradict previous ones.*

**contradiction** /ˌkɒntrəˈdɪkʃn ˌकॉन्ट्रˈडिक्श्न्/ *noun* [C, U] a statement, fact or action that is opposite to or different from another one खंडन या विरोध (कथन, तथ्य या कार्य के रूप में) *There were a number of contradictions in what he told the police.* ○ *This letter is **in** complete **contradiction to** their previous one.*

**contradictory** /ˌkɒntrəˈdɪktəri ˌकॉन्ट्रˈडिक्टरि/ *adj.* being opposite to or not matching sth else विरोधात्मक, असंगत *Contradictory reports appeared in the newspapers.*

**contraflow** /ˈkɒntrəfləʊ ˈकॉन्ट्रफ़्लो/ *noun* [C] the system that is used when one half of a wide road is closed for repairs, and traffic going in both directions has to use the other side वह व्यवस्था जिसमें सड़क के आधे भाग में जारी मरम्मत के कारण दोनों ओर के यातायात को बाक़ी आधी सड़क का प्रयोग करना पड़ता है

**contraption** /kənˈtræpʃn कन्ˈट्रैप्शन्/ *noun* [C] a strange or complicated piece of equipment विचित्र, असामान्य या जटिल उपकरण *The first aeroplanes were dangerous contraptions.*

**contrary[1]** /ˈkɒntrəri ˈकॉन्ट्रिर/ *adj.* **1** (*only before a noun*) completely different; opposite पूर्णतया भिन्न; विपरीत *I thought it was possible, but she took the contrary view.* **2 contrary to** completely different from; opposite to; against किसी से पूर्णतया भिन्न; के विपरीत; के विरुद्ध ***Contrary to popular belief*** (= to what many people think) *not all politicians are corrupt.*

**contrary[2]** /ˈkɒntrəri ˈकॉन्ट्रिर/ *noun*

IDM **on the contrary** the opposite is true; certainly not इसके विपरीत; बिलकुल नहीं *'You look as if you're not enjoying yourself.' 'On the contrary, I'm having a great time.'*

**to the contrary** (*formal*) saying the opposite विपरीत बात कहना *Unless I hear anything to the contrary, I shall assume that the arrangements haven't changed.*

**contrast[1]** /ˈkɒntrɑːst ˈकॉन्ट्रास्ट्/ *noun* **1** [U] comparison between two people or things that shows the differences between them दो व्यक्तियों या वस्तुओं में तुलना जो उनमें अंतर स्पष्ट करती है ***In contrast to*** *previous years, we've had a very successful summer.* **2** [C, U] **(a) contrast (to/with sb/sth); (a) contrast (between A and B)** a clear difference between two things or people that is seen when they are compared दो व्यक्तियों या वस्तुओं में तुलना से उभरकर आया स्पष्ट अंतर *There is a tremendous contrast between the climate in the valley and the climate in the hills.* **3** [C] something that is clearly different from sth else when the two things are compared स्पष्टतया भिन्न अलग वस्तु (तुलना करने पर) *This house is quite a contrast to your old one!*

**contrast[2]** /kənˈtrɑːst कन्ˈट्रास्ट्/ *verb* **1** [T] **contrast (A and/with B)** to compare people or things in order to show the differences between them दो व्यक्तियों या वस्तुओं के बीच अंतर दिखाने के लिए तुलना करना *The film contrasts his poor childhood with his later life as a millionaire.* **2** [I] **contrast with sb/sth** to be clearly different when compared तुलना करने पर स्पष्टतया भिन्न होनां *This comment contrasts sharply with his previous remarks.*

**contravene** /ˌkɒntrəˈviːn ˌकॉन्ट्रˈवीन्/ *verb* [T] (*formal*) to break a law or a rule क़ानून या नियम तोड़ना; उल्लंघन करना ▶ **contravention** /ˌkɒntrəˈvenʃn ˌकॉन्ट्रˈव्रेन्शन्/ *noun* [C, U] नियम या क़ानून का भंग; उल्लंघन

**contribute** /ˈkɒntrɪbjuːt; kənˈtrɪbjuːt ˈकॉन्ट्रिब्यूट्; कन्ˈट्रिब्यूट्/ *verb* **contribute (sth) (to/towards sth) 1** [I, T] to give a part of the total, together with others योगदान करना, अंशदान करना *Would you like to contribute towards our collection for famine relief?* ○ *The research has contributed a great deal to our knowledge of cancer.* **2** [I] to be one of the causes of sth किसी स्थिति का एक या अन्यतम कारण होना *It is not known whether the bad weather contributed to the accident.* **3** [I, T] to write articles for a magazine or newspaper किसी पत्रिका या समाचार-पत्र के लिए लेख आदि लिखना

**contribution** /ˌkɒntrɪˈbjuːʃn ˌकॉन्ट्रिˈब्यूशन्/ *noun* [C] **a contribution (to/toward sth)** something that you give, especially money or help, or do together with other people धन या सहायता के रूप में अंशदान *If we all* ***make a*** *small* ***contribution****, we'll be able to buy Rani a good farewell present.*

**contributor** /kənˈtrɪbjətə(r) कन्ˈट्रिब्यट(र्)/ *noun* [C] a person who contributes to sth योगदान करने वाला व्यक्ति; अंशदाता, सहयोगकर्ता

**contributory** /kənˈtrɪbjətəri कन्ˈट्रिब्यटरि/ *adj.* helping to cause or produce sth उत्पन्न करने मे सहायक *Alcohol was a contributory factor in her death.*

**contrive** /kənˈtraɪv कन्ˈट्राइव्/ *verb* [T] **1** to manage to do sth, although there are difficulties कठिनाइयों के बावजूद कुछ करने में सफल होना *If I can contrive to get off work early, I'll see you later.* **2** to plan or invent sth in a clever and/or dishonest way चतुराई या और बेईमानी से कुछ करने की योजना बनाना *He contrived a scheme to cheat insurance companies.*

**contrived** /kənˈtraɪvd कन्ˈट्राइव्ड्/ *adj.* hard to believe; not natural or realistic अविश्वसनीय; अस्वाभाविक या अयथार्थ *The ending of the film seemed rather contrived.*

**control[1]** /kənˈtrəʊl कन्ˈट्रोल्/ *noun* **1** [U] **control (of/over sb/sth)** power and ability to make sb/sth do what you want किसी व्यक्ति या वस्तु पर नियंत्रण, संचालन, क़ाबू में रखने की क्षमता *Rebels managed to* ***take control*** *of the radio station.* ○ *Some teachers find it difficult to* ***keep control*** *of their class.* ○ *He* ***lost control*** *of the car and crashed.* ○ *I was late because of circumstances* ***beyond my control****.* **2** [C, U] (a) **control (on/over sth)** a limit on sth; a way of keeping sb/sth within certain limits (किसी पर) नियंत्रण, सीमा; निर्धारित सीमा के भीतर रखने का तरीक़ा *price controls* ○ *The* *faults forced the company to review its* ***quality control*** *procedures.* **3** [C] one of the parts of a machine that is used for operating it मशीन के परिचालन के लिए एक पुरज़ा, कंट्रोल *the controls of an aeroplane/a TV* ○ *a control panel* **4** [*sing.*] the place from which sth is operated or where sth is checked किसी कार्य के संचालन या निरीक्षण का केंद्र *We went through passport control and then got onto the plane.*

IDM **be in control (of sth)** to have the power or ability to deal with sth किसी स्थिति से निबटने की ताक़त या क्षमता होना *The police are again in control of the area following last night's violence.*

**be/get out of control** to be/become impossible to deal with किसी स्थिति से निबटना असंभव हो जाना; नियंत्रण से बाहर हो जाना *The demonstration got out of control and fighting broke out.*

**under control** being dealt with successfully सफलतापूर्वक निपटाया गया; नियंत्रित *It took several hours to bring the fire under control.*

**control²** /kənˈtrəʊl कन्ˈट्रोल/ *verb* [T] (**controlling; controlled**) **1** to have power and ability to make sb/sth do what you want (किसी पर) नियंत्रण रखना *Police struggled to control the crowd.* ○ *I couldn't control myself any longer and burst out laughing.* **2** to keep sth within certain limits (किसी को) सीमित या नियंत्रण में रखना *measures to control price rises* ▶ **controller** *noun* [C] नियंत्रक, नियंत्रणकर्ता *air traffic controllers*

**control tower** *noun* [C] a building at an airport from which the movements of aircraft are controlled हवाई अड्डे की वह इमारत जहाँ से विमानों के आवागमन को नियंत्रित किया जाता है; नियंत्रक-मीनार

**controversial** /ˌkɒntrəˈvɜːʃl ˌकॉन्ट्रˈवशुल्/ *adj.* causing public discussion and disagreement विवादास्पद *a controversial issue/decision/plan*

**controversy** /ˈkɒntrəvɜːsi; kənˈtrɒvəsi ˈकॉन्ट्रवसि; कन्ˈट्रॉवसि/ *noun* [C, U] (*pl.* **controversies**) public discussion and disagreement about sth (किसी विषय पर) सार्वजनिक चर्चा और विवाद *The plans for changing the town centre caused a great deal of controversy.*

**convalesce** /ˌkɒnvəˈles ˌकॉन्वˈलेस्/ *verb* [I] to rest and get better over a period of time after an illness बीमारी के बाद स्वास्थ्य-लाभ करना ▶ **convalescence** /ˌkɒnvəˈlesns ˌकॉन्वˈलेसन्स्/ *noun* [*sing.*, U] स्वास्थ्य-लाभ ▶ **convalescent** /ˌkɒnvəˈlesnt ˌकॉन्वˈलेसन्ट्/ *adj.* स्वास्थ्यलाभ-संबंधित

**convection** /kənˈvekʃn कन्ˈवेक्शन्/ *noun* [U] the process in which heat moves through a gas or a liquid as the hotter part rises and the cooler, heavier part sinks गैस या द्रव में ताप फैलने की प्रक्रिया जिसमें गरम भाग ऊपर उठता है और ठंडा भाग नीचे आता है; संवहन *convection currents*

**convene** /kənˈviːn कन्ˈवीन्/ *verb* [I, T] (*formal*) to come together or to bring people together for a meeting, etc. किसी बैठक आदि के लिए लोगों का एकत्र होना या लोगों को एकत्र करना; बैठक आदि बुलाना, आयोजित करना

**convenience** /kənˈviːniəns कन्ˈवीनिअन्स्/ *noun* **1** [U] the quality of being easy, useful or suitable for sb आसानी, सुविधा, उपयुक्तता *a building designed* ***for the convenience of*** *disabled people* ○ ***For convenience****, you can pay for everything at once.* **2** [C] something that makes things easier, quicker or more comfortable सुविधाजनक उपकरण, सुख-सुविधा *houses with all the modern conveniences* **3** [C] a public toilet सार्वजनिक शौचालय

**convenient** /kənˈviːniənt कन्ˈवीनिअन्ट्/ *adj.* **1** suitable or practical for a particular purpose; not causing difficulty विशेष उद्देश्य की दृष्टि से उपयुक्त या व्यावहारिक; आसान, सुविधाजनक *I'm willing to meet you on any day that's convenient for you.* ○ *It isn't convenient to talk at the moment, I'm in the middle of a meeting.* ✪ विलोम **inconvenient** **2** close to sth; in a useful position किसी के निकट; उपयोगी या सुविधाजनक स्थिति में *Our house is convenient for the shops.* ▶ **conveniently** *adv.* सुविधापूर्वक

**convent** /ˈkɒnvənt ˈकॉन्वन्ट्/ *noun* [C] a place where **nuns** live together विशेषतः ईसाई साध्वियों का आश्रम; कॉन्वेंट ➪ **monastery** देखिए।

**convention** /kənˈvenʃn कन्ˈवेन्शन्/ *noun* **1** [C, U] a traditional way of behaving or of doing sth प्रथा, परिपाटी, परंपरा, रिवाज़ *It is an Indian convention to touch the feet of the elders when you meet them.* ○ *The film shows no respect for convention.* **2** [C] a large meeting of the members of a profession, political party, etc. सम्मेलन *the Congress Party Convention* ✪ पर्याय **conference** **3** [C] a formal agreement, especially between different countries औपचारिक समझौता, विशेषतः देशों के बीच *the Lahore Convention*

**conventional** /kənˈvenʃənl कन्ˈवेन्शनल्/ *adj.* always behaving in a traditional or normal way परंपरागत, पारंपरिक, रूढ़िगत, निरंतर, सामान्य *conventional attitudes* ○ *I quite like him but he's so conventional* (= boring because of this). ✪ विलोम **unconventional** ▶ **conventionally** /-ʃənəli -शनलि/ *adv.* पारंपरिक रूप से

**converge** /kənˈvɜːdʒ कन्ˈवृज् / *verb* [I] **converge (on sb/sth)** (used about two or more people or things) to move towards each other or meet at the same point from different directions (दो व्यक्तियों या वस्तुओं का) विभिन्न दिशाओं से आकर एक बिंदु पर मिलना; अभिसरित होना *Fans from all over the country converge on the village during the annual music festival.* ➪ **short-sighted** पर चित्र देखिए। ▶ **convergence** *noun* [U] केंद्राभिमुखता, अभिसरन ▶ **convergent** *adj.* केंद्राभिमुखी, अभिसारी

**conversant** /kənˈvɜːsnt कन्ˈवृसन्ट् / *adj.* (*formal*) **conversant with sth** knowing about sth; familiar with sth जानकार या परिचित (होना) *All employees should be conversant with basic accounting.*

**conversation** /ˌkɒnvəˈseɪʃn ˌकॉनुव़ˈसेशन् / *noun* [C, U] a talk between two or more people बातचीत, वार्तालाप, वार्ता *I **had a** long **conversation** with her about her plans for the future.* ○ *His job is his only **topic of conversation**.*
IDM **deep in thought/conversation** ➪ **deep**[1] देखिए।

**conversational** /ˌkɒnvəˈseɪʃənl ˌकॉनुव़ˈसेशनल् / *adj.* **1** not formal; as used in conversation अनौपचारिक; बातचीत या बोलचाल की भाषा में प्रयुक्त **2** (*only before a noun*) connected with conversation बातचीत से संबंधित ▶ **conversationally** /nəli -नलि / *adv.* बातचीत की रीति से

**converse** /kənˈvɜːs कन्ˈवृस् / *verb* [I] (*formal*) to talk to sb; to have a conversation किसी से बातचीत करना; वार्तालाप करना

**conversely** /ˈkɒnvɜːsli ˈकॉनुवृसलि / *adv.* (*formal*) in a way that is opposite to sth विपरीत रीति से; इसके विपरीत *People who earn a lot of money have little time to spend it. Conversely, many people with limitless time do not have enough money to do what they want.*

**conversion** /kənˈvɜːʃn कन्ˈवृशन् / *noun* [C, U] (a) **conversion (from sth) (into/to sth) 1** the act or process of changing from one form, system or use to another एक रूप, पद्धति या उपयोग-प्रकार से दूसरे में परिवर्तन की क्रिया या प्रक्रिया *a conversion table for miles and kilometres* **2** becoming a member of a different religion धर्म-परिवर्तन

**convert**[1] /kənˈvɜːt कन्ˈवृट् / *verb* [I, T] **1 convert (sth) (from sth) (into/to sth)** to change from one form, system or use to another एक रूप, पद्धति या उपयोग-प्रकार से दूसरे में परिवर्तन करना, बदलना *a sofa that converts into a double bed* ○ *How do you convert pounds into kilograms?* **2 convert (sb) (from sth) (to sth)** to change or to persuade sb to change to a different religion किसी का धर्म-परिवर्तन करना; धर्म परिवर्तन के लिए किसी को तैयार करना *As a young man he converted to Christianity.*

**convert**[2] /ˈkɒnvɜːt ˈकॉनुवृट् / *noun* [C] **a convert (to sth)** a person who has changed his/her religion धर्मांतरित व्यक्ति

**convertible**[1] /kənˈvɜːtəbl कन्ˈवृटबल् / *adj.* able to be changed into another form रूपांतरित हो सकने योग्य *convertible currencies* (= that can be exchanged for other currencies)

**convertible**[2] /kənˈvɜːtəbl कन्ˈवृटबल् / *noun* [C] a car with a roof that can be folded down or taken off ऐसी कार जिसकी छत की तह बनाकर उसे लपेटा जा सकता है

**convex** /ˈkɒnveks ˈकॉनुवेक्स् / *adj.* having a surface that curves towards the outside of sth, like an eye (सतह) बाहर की ओर मुड़ती हुई (जैसे आँख); उन्नतोतर, उत्तल *a convex lens* ➪ **concave** देखिए तथा **lens** पर चित्र देखिए।

**convey** /kənˈveɪ कन्ˈवे / *verb* [T] **1 convey sth (to sb)** to make ideas, thoughts, feelings, etc. known to sb विचारों, भावनाओं आदि को किसी अन्य तक पहुँचाना *The film conveys a lot of information but in an entertaining way.* ○ *Please convey my sympathy to her at this sad time.* **2** (*formal*) to take sb/sth from one place to another, especially in a vehicle विशेषतः वाहन द्वारा एक स्थान से दूसरे स्थान पर पहुँचाना

**conveyor belt** *noun* [C] a moving belt that carries objects from one place to another, for example in a factory (कारख़ानों जैसे स्थानों में) सामान ढोने की और लगातार चलने वाली पट्टी; संवाहक पट्टी

**convict**[1] /kənˈvɪkt कन्ˈविक्ट् / *verb* [T] **convict sb (of sth)** to say officially in a court of law that sb is guilty of a crime न्यायालय द्वारा अपराधी या दोषी ठहराया जाना *He was convicted of armed robbery and sent to prison.* ✪ विलोम **acquit**

**convict**[2] /ˈkɒnvɪkt ˈकॉनुविक्ट् / *noun* [C] a person who has been found guilty of a crime and put in prison व्यक्ति जिसका दोष सिद्ध हो चुका हो और जिसे कारावास में डाल दिया गया हों; दोषी, अपराधी, क़ैदी

**conviction** /kənˈvɪkʃn कन्ˈविक्शन् / *noun* **1** [C, U] the action of finding sb guilty of a crime in a court of law न्यायालय द्वारा अपराधी ठहराए जाने की क्रिया; दोषसिद्धि *He has several previous convictions for burglary.* **2** [C] a very strong opinion or belief प्रबल मत या आस्था *religious convictions*

3 [U] the feeling of being certain about what you are doing किसी काम के विषय में पक्का विश्वास होने की अनुभूति *He played without conviction and lost easily.*

**convince** /kənˈvɪns कन्ˈविन्स् / *verb* [T] **1 convince sb (of sth/that...)** to succeed in making sb believe sth किसी को विश्वास दिलाना; आश्वस्त करना *She convinced him of the need to go back.* ○ *I couldn't convince her that I was right.* **2 convince sb (to do sth)** to persuade sb to do sth किसी को कोई काम करने के लिए तैयार कर लेना, मना लेना; राज़ी करना *The salesman convinced them to buy a new microwave oven.*

**convinced** /kənˈvɪnst कन्ˈविन्स्ट् / *adj.* (*not before a noun*) completely sure about sth किसी विषय में पूर्णतया आश्वस्त *He's convinced of his ability to win.*

**convincing** /kənˈvɪnsɪŋ कन्ˈविन्सिङ् / *adj.* **1** able to make sb believe sth आश्वस्त करने वाला, यक़ीन दिलाने वाला *Her explanation for her absence wasn't very convincing.* **2** (used about a victory) complete; clear (जीत) पूर्ण; स्पष्ट *a convincing win* ▸ **convincingly** *adv.* आश्वासनकारी रीति से

**convivial** /kənˈvɪviəl कन्ˈविविअल् / *adj.* (*formal*) happy and friendly in atmosphere or character प्रसन्नचित्त, ख़ुशनुमा, मिलनसार ▸ **conviviality** /kənˌvɪviˈæləti कन्ˌविविˈऐलटि / *noun* [U] मिलनसारी

**convocation** /ˌkɒnvəˈkeɪʃn ˌकॉन्वˈकेश्न् / *noun* [C] **1** the action of calling together a group of people formally usually for a special purpose एक जन समूह का किसी विशेष उद्देश्य के लिए औपचारिक रूप से एकत्रीकरण की प्रक्रिया **2** a ceremony held at a university or college when students receive their degrees etc. on sucessful completion of a course दीक्षांत समारोह

**convoluted** /ˈkɒnvəluːtɪd ˈकान्वलूटिड / *adj.* (an argument, story or sentence) extremely complicated and difficult to follow (तर्क, कहानी या वाक्य)अत्यंत जटिल तथा अबोध्य *a convoluted explanation*

**convoy** /ˈkɒnvɔɪ ˈकॉन्वॉइ / *noun* [C, U] a group of vehicles or ships travelling together एक साथ जा रहे वाहनों या जहाज़ों का क़ाफ़िला *a convoy of lorries* ○ *warships travelling **in convoy***

**convulse** /kənˈvʌls कन्ˈवल्स् / *verb* [I, T] to make a sudden violent movement in sb's body; to make this movement (शरीर का) अनियंत्रित रूप से अचानक ज़ोर से हिलना-डुलना; दौरा पड़ना; किसी को इस प्रकार से हिलाना-डुलाना; मरोड़ना *He was convulsed with pain.*

**convulsion** /kənˈvʌlʃn कन्ˈवल्श्न् / *noun* [C, *usually pl.*] a sudden violent movement of the body that you cannot control ज़ोरदार ऐंठन, मरोड़, दौरा *Children sometimes have convulsions when they are ill.*

**convulsive** /kənˈvʌlsɪv कन्ˈवल्सिव् / *adj.* (used about movements or actions) sudden and impossible to control (क्रिया, गतिविधि आदि) आकस्मिक और अनियंत्रित; अत्यंत खलबली पूर्ण

**coo** /kuː कू / *verb* [I] **1** to make a soft low sound like a bird (**a dove**) कूकना, कबूतर जैसे गुटरगूं करना **2** to speak in a soft, gentle voice कोमल और मंद स्वर में बोलना *He went to the cot and cooed over the baby.*

**cook¹** /kʊk कुक् / *verb* **1** [I, T] to prepare food for eating by heating it भोजन बनाना; पकाना *My mother taught me how to cook.* ○ *The sauce should be cooked on a low heat for twenty minutes.* **2** [I] (used about food) to be prepared for eating by being heated भोजन का पकना *I could smell something cooking in the kitchen.* ➪ **bake, boil, fry, grill, toast** और **roast** देखिए।

**PHRV cook sth up** (*informal*) to invent sth that is not true कहानी गढ़ना, नक़ली हिसाब-किताब आदि बनाना *She cooked up an excuse for not arriving on time.*

**cook²** /kʊk कुक् / *noun* [C] a person who cooks खाना पकाने वाला व्यक्ति; रसोइया, बावरची *My sister is an excellent cook.*

**cookbook** /ˈkʊkbʊk ˈकुक्बुक् / (*BrE* **cookery book**) *noun* [C] a book that gives instructions on cooking and how to cook individual dishes (**recipes**) पाक-विधि सिखाने की पुस्तिका; पाक-पुस्तिका

**cooker** /ˈkʊkə(r) ˈकुक(र्) / *noun* [C] (*BrE*) a large piece of kitchen equipment for cooking using gas or electricity. It consists of an oven, a flat top on which pans can be placed and often a device which heats the food from above (**a grill**) रसोईघर में प्रयुक्त गैस या बिजली से चलने वाला और खाना पकाने के लिए प्रयुक्त उपकरण ➪ **pressure cooker** भी देखिए।

**cookery** /ˈkʊkəri ˈकुकरि / *noun* [U] the skill or activity of preparing and cooking food भोजन बनाने की क्रिया या कुशलता; पाकक्रिया, पाकशास्त्र *Chinese/French/Italian cookery*

**cookie** /ˈkʊki ˈकुकि / *noun* [C] **1** = **biscuit** **2** (*computing*) a computer file with information in it that is sent to the central **server** each time a particular person uses a **network** or the Internet सूचना-पूरित कंप्यूटर-फ़ाइल जिसे किसी विशेष कंप्यूटर प्रयोगकर्ता द्वारा इंटरनेट का प्रयोग करने पर केंद्रीय सर्वर को भेजा जाता है; कंप्यूटर-कुकी

**cooking** /ˈkʊkɪŋ ˈकुकिङ्/ *noun* [U] **1** the preparation of food for eating भोजन पकाने की क्रिया; पाकक्रिया *Cooking is one of her hobbies.* ○ *I do **the cooking** in our house.* **2** food produced by cooking पकाकर बनाया भोजन *He missed his mother's cooking when he left home.*

**cool[1]** /ku:l कूल्/ *adj.* **1** fairly cold; not hot or warm शीतल; गर्म या उष्ण नहीं *It was a cool evening so I put on a pullover.* ○ *What I'd like is a long cool drink.* ➪ **cold[1]** पर नोट देखिए। **2** calm; not excited or angry शांत; उत्तेजित या क्रोधित नहीं *She always manages to remain cool under pressure.* **3** unfriendly; not showing interest रूखा, उदासीन; उत्साहहीन, रुचिहीन *When we first met, she was rather cool towards me, but later she became friendlier.* **4** (*slang*) very good or fashionable बहुत अच्छा या लोकप्रिय *Those are cool shoes you're wearing!*

**cool[2]** /ku:l कूल्/ *verb* **1** [I, T] **cool (sth/sb) (down/off)** to lower the temperature of sth; to become **cool[1] 1** शीतल या ठंडा करना या होना *Let the soup cool (down).* ○ *After the game we needed to cool off.* ○ *A nice cold drink will soon cool you down.* **2** [I] (used about feelings) to become less strong (भावनाओं का) शांत होना

**PHRV** **cool (sb) down/off** to become or make sb calmer शांत होना या करना

**cool[3]** /ku:l कूल्/ *noun* [*sing.*] **the cool** a cool temperature or place; the quality of being cool ठंडा स्थान; ठंडक *We sat in the cool of a cafe, out of the sun.*

**IDM** **keep/lose your cool** (*informal*) to stay calm/to stop being calm and become angry, nervous, etc. शांतचित्त रहना क्रोधित या उत्तेजित हो जाना; धैर्य बनाए रखना या धैर्य खो देना

**coolant** /ˈku:lənt ˈकूलन्ट्/ *noun* [C, U] a liquid that is used for cooling an engine, a nuclear **reactor,** etc. इंजन, परमाणु भट्टी आदि को शीतल करने के लिए प्रयुक्त द्रव

**cooler** /ˈku:lə(r) ˈकूल(र्)/ *noun* [C] a container or machine that cools things or keeps them cool एक पात्र या उपकरण जो वस्तुओं को ठंडा करता या रखता है *The office has a new water-cooler.* ○ *We always take a cooler full of drinks to the beach.* ➪ **air-cooler** भी देखिए।

**cooling-off period** *noun* [C] a period of time when sb can think again about a decision that he/she has made समय की वह अवधि जिसके दौरान किसी निर्णय पर पुनर्विचार किया जा सकता है; पुनर्विचार-अवधि

**coolly** /ˈku:lli ˈकूल्लि/ *adv.* in a calm way; without showing much interest or excitement शांतभाव से बिना उत्तेजित हुए या बिना विशेष दिलचस्पी के

**coolness** /ˈku:lnəs ˈकूल्नस्/ *noun* [U] the quality or state of being cool शीतलता, ठंडक; शांतचित्तता, उदासीनता *his coolness under stress* ○ *their coolness towards strangers*

**coop[1]** /ku:p कूप्/ *noun* [C] a cage for chickens, etc. मुरग़ियों का दरबा

**coop[2]** /ku:p कूप्/ *verb*

**PHRV** **coop sb/sth up (in sth)** to keep sb/sth inside a small space किसी वस्तु को सीमित स्थान में बंद रखना *The children were cooped up indoors all day because the weather was so bad.*

**cooperate** (*also* **co-operate**) /kəʊˈɒpəreɪt कोˈऑपरेट्/ *verb* [I] **cooperate (with sb/sth)** **1** to work with sb else to achieve sth (किसी से) सहयोग करना; मिलकर काम करना *Our company is cooperating with a Danish firm on this project.* **2** to be helpful by doing what sb asks you to do अपने हिस्से का काम करके सहायता करना; सहयोग करना *If everyone cooperates by following the instructions, there will be no problem.*

**cooperation** (*also* **co-operation**) /kəʊˌɒpəˈreɪʃn को,ऑपˈरेश्न्/ *noun* [U] **1 cooperation (with sb)** working together with sb else to achieve sth (किसी से) सहयोग, सहकारिता *Schools are working in close cooperation with parents to improve standards.* **2** help that you give by doing what sb asks you to do किसी के माँगने पर दी सहायता, सहयोग *The police asked the public for their cooperation in the investigation.*

**cooperative[1]** (*also* **co-operative**) /kəʊˈɒpərətɪv कोˈऑपरटिव्/ *adj.* **1** done by people working together मिलकर किया गया; सहकारिता पर आधारित, सहकारी *a cooperative business venture* **2** helpful; doing what sb asks you to do सहयोगी सहायताकारी; अपेक्षा पूरी करने वाला *My firm were very cooperative and allowed me to have time off.* ✪ विलोम **uncooperative**

**cooperative[2]** (*BrE* **co-operative**) /kəʊˈɒpərətɪv कोˈऑपरटिव्/ *noun* [C] a business or organization that is owned and run by all of the people who work for it सहकारिता पर आधारित व्यापार या संगठन; सहकारी संस्था *a workers' cooperative*

**coordinate[1]** (*BrE* **co-ordinate**) /kəʊˈɔ:dɪneɪt कोˈऑडिनेट्/ *verb* [T] to organize different things or people so that they work together वस्तुओं या व्यक्तियों के बीच समन्वय स्थापित करना ताकि वे

मिल-जुलकर काम कर सकें; तालमेल बनाना *It is her job to coordinate the various departments.*

**coordinate²** (*BrE* **co-ordinate**) /kəʊˈɔːdɪnət कोˈऑडिनट्/ *noun* [C] one of the two sets of numbers and/or letters that are used for finding the position of a point on a map, graph, computer screen, etc. ग्राफ़, नक़्शे आदि पर किसी बिंदु की स्थिति नियत करने के लिए प्रयुक्त दो में से कोई भी एक अंक या/और अक्षर; निर्देशांक

**coordination** (*BrE* **co-ordination**) /kəʊˌɒːdɪˈneɪʃn कोˌऑडिˈनेश्न्/ *noun* [U] **1** the organization of different things or people so that they work together विभिन्न वस्तुओं या व्यक्तियों का समन्वित संगठन; तालमेल, समन्वय **2** the ability to control the movements of your body properly शरीर की विभिन्न क्रियाओं को सम्यक रूप से नियंत्रित करने की क्षमता

**coordinator** (*BrE* **co-ordinator**) /kəʊˈɔːdɪneɪtə(r) कोˈऑडिनेट(र्)/ *noun* [C] a person who is responsible for organizing different things or people so that they work together संयोजक, समन्वयकर्ता

**cop¹** /kɒp कॉप्/ (*also* **copper**) *noun* [C] (*informal*) a police officer पुलिस अधिकारी

**cop²** /kɒp कॉप्/ *verb* (**copping; copped**) (*informal*)

**PHR V** **cop out (of sth)** (*informal*) to avoid sth that you should do, because you are afraid or lazy अपना काम करने से बचना (आशंका या सुस्ती के कारण) *She was going to help me with the cooking but she copped out at the last minute.*

**cope** /kəʊp कोप्/ *verb* [I] **cope (with sb/sth)** to deal successfully with a difficult matter or situation कठिन स्थिति से सफलतापूर्वक निपटना *She sometimes finds it difficult to cope with all the pressure at work.*

**copier** /ˈkɒpiə(r) ˈकॉपिअ(र्)/ = **photocopier**

**copious** /ˈkəʊpiəs ˈकोपिअस्/ *adj.* in large amounts बड़ी मात्रा में; प्रचुर, भरपूर *She made copious notes at the lecture.* ✪ पर्याय **plentiful** ▶ **copiously** *adv.* प्रचुरतापूर्वक, प्रचुरता से

**cop-out** *noun* [C] (*informal*) a way of avoiding sth that you should do अपने काम से बच निकलने का तरीक़ा

**copper** /ˈkɒpə(r) ˈकॉप(र्)/ *noun* [U] (*symbol* **Cu**) a common reddish-brown metal तांबा, ताम्र *electric wires made of copper*

**copra** /ˈkɒprə ˈकॉपरा/ *noun* [U] the dried white part of a **coconut** नारियल का सूखा-सफ़ेद अंश; खोपरा, गरी

**copse** /kɒps कॉप्स्/ *noun* [C] a small area of trees or bushes वृक्षों या झाड़ियों वाला छोटा भूक्षेत्र

**copulate** /ˈkɒpjuleɪt ˈकॉप्युलेट्/ *verb* [I] (*formal*) (used especially about animals) to have sex (विशेषतः जानवरों का) संभोग करना ▶ **copulation** /ˌkɒpjuˈleɪʃn ˌकॉप्युˈलेश्न्/ *noun* [U] (विशेषतः जानवरों की) संभोग क्रिया

**copy¹** /ˈkɒpi ˈकॉपि/ *noun* [C] (*pl.* **copies**) **1** something that is made to look exactly like sth else प्रतिलिपि, नक़ल *I kept a copy of the letter I wrote.* ○ *the master copy* (= the original piece of paper from which copies are made) ○ *to make a copy of a computer file* ⇨ **hard copy** और **photocopy** देखिए। **2** one book, newspaper, record, etc. of which many have been printed or produced मुद्रित पुस्तक, समाचारपत्र आदि की एक प्रति *I managed to buy the last copy of the book left in the shop.*

**copy²** /ˈkɒpi ˈकॉपि/ *verb* (*pres. part.* **copying;** *3rd person sing. pres.* **copies;** *pt, pp* **copied**) **1** [T] to make sth exactly the same as sth else कोई वस्तु किसी अन्य वस्तु के पूर्णतया समान कोई वस्तु बनाना; (किसी की) हूबहू नक़ल करना *The children copied pictures from a book.* ○ *It is illegal to copy videos.* **2 copy sth (down/out)** to write down sth exactly as it is written somewhere else लेख आदि उतारना; लिखकर प्रतिलिपि बनाना *I copied down the address on the brochure.* ○ *I copied out the letter more neatly.* **3** [T] = **photocopy** **4** [T] to do or try to do the same as sb else अनुकरण करना *She copies everything her friends do.* ✪ पर्याय **imitate** **5** [I] **copy (from sb)** to cheat in an exam or test by writing what sb else has written परीक्षा में नक़ल लगाना

**copyright** /ˈkɒpiraɪt ˈकॉपिराइट्/ *noun* [C, U] the legal right to be the only person who may print, copy, perform, etc. a piece of original work, such as a book, a song or a computer program किसी पुस्तक, गीत, कंप्यूटर प्रोग्राम आदि को छापने, प्रतिलिपि बनाने, प्रसारित करने आदि का क़ानूनी अधिकार जो केवल उस रचना के रचयिता को प्राप्त होता है; स्वत्वाधिकार प्रकाशनाधिकार; कॉपीराइट

**coral** /ˈkɒrəl ˈकॉरल्/ *noun* [U] a hard red, pink or white substance that forms in the sea from the bones of very small sea animals मूंगा *a coral reef* (= a line of rock in the sea formed by coral)

**cord** /kɔːd कॉड्/ *noun* **1** [C, U] (a piece of) strong thick string मज़बूत डोरी, रस्सी **2** [C, U] (a piece of) wire covered with plastic; flex प्लास्टिक चढ़ी तार

**3 cords** [*pl.*] trousers made of a thick soft cotton cloth **corduroy** कॉर्डराय नामक मोटे परंतु नरम सूती कपड़े से बनी पतलून ➪ **vocal cords** देखिए।

**cordial** /ˈkɔːdiəl ˈकॉडिअल् / *adj.* pleasant and friendly ख़ुशनुमा और मैत्रीपूर्ण *a cordial greeting/smile* ▶ **cordially** /-diəli -डिअलि / *adv.* मित्रभाव से

**cordless** /ˈkɔːdləs ˈकॉड्लस् / *adj.* without a **cord 2** बिना तार का *a cordless phone/kettle/iron*

**cordon[1]** /ˈkɔːdn ˈकॉड्न् / *noun* [C] a line or ring of police or soldiers that prevents people from entering an area पुलिस या सेना द्वारा सुरक्षा के लिए डाला गया घेरा

**cordon[2]** /ˈkɔːdn ˈकॉड्न् / *verb*

PHR V **cordon sth off** to stop people entering an area by surrounding it with a ring of police or soldiers सिपाहियों द्वारा किसी स्थान पर सुरक्षा घेरा बनाकर वहाँ पर लोगों का प्रवेश अवरुद्ध करना *The street where the bomb was discovered was quickly cordoned off.*

**corduroy** /ˈkɔːdərɔɪ ˈकॉडरॉइ / *noun* [U] a thick soft cotton cloth with lines on it, used for making clothes धारीदार मोटा नरम कपड़ा जिससे कपड़े बनाए जाते हैं; कॉर्डराय *a corduroy jacket*

**core** /kɔː(r) कॉ(र्) / *noun* **1** [C] the hard centre of certain fruits, containing seeds कुछ फलों का बीच का बीज वाला कड़ा भाग *an apple core* **2** [*sing.*] the central or most important part of sth किसी का केंद्रीय या सबसे महत्त्वपूर्ण अंश *the core curriculum* (= the subjects that all the pupils have to study) ○ *What's the core issue here?* **3** [C] the central part of a planet किसी ग्रह का केंद्रीय भाग *the earth's core* ➪ **seismic** पर चित्र देखिए।

IDM **to the core** completely; in every way पूर्णतया; हर प्रकार से, सब प्रकार से *The news shook him to the core* (= shocked him very much).

**coriander** /ˌkɒriˈændə(r) ˌकॉरिˈऐन्ड(र्) / *noun* [U] a plant whose leaves and seeds are used in cooking to flavour food धनिया (पौधा)

**cork** /kɔːk कॉक् / *noun* **1** [U] a light soft material which comes from the outside of a type of tree हलका नरम पदार्थ जो एक प्रकार के पेड़ की छाल होती है; कॉर्क *cork floor tiles* **2** [C] a round piece of cork that you push into the end of a bottle to close it, especially a bottle of wine कार्क से बनी डाट जो बोतल के ऊपर लगाई जाती है

**corkscrew** /ˈkɔːkskruː ˈकॉक्स्क्रू / *noun* [C] a tool that you use for pulling **cork 2** out of bottles बोतलों पर लगी डाट को खोलने का उपकरण ➪ **kitchen** पर चित्र देखिए।

**corn** /kɔːn कॉन् / *noun* **1** [U] any plant that is grown for its grain, such as wheat; the seeds from these plants अनाज वाला पौधा (जैसे गेहूँ, जौ, मक्का आदि); इन पौधों के बीज या दाने *a field of corn* ○ *a corn field* **2** [U] = **maize** ➪ **cereal** पर चित्र देखिए। **3** [U] = **sweetcorn** **4** [C] a small, painful area of hard skin on the toe पैर की उँगली पर कड़ी खाल का घट्टा जिसमें पीड़ा होती है

**cornea** /ˈkɔːniə ˈकॉनिआ / *noun* [C] the transparent part that covers and protects the outer part of your eye आँख का बाहरी पारदर्शी रक्षक आवरण; कार्निया ➪ **eye** पर चित्र देखिए। ▶ **corneal** /ˈkɔːniəl ˈकॉनिअल् / *adj.* कार्निया-विषयक

**corner[1]** /ˈkɔːnə(r) ˈकॉन(र्) / *noun* [C] **1** a place where two lines, edges, surfaces or roads meet कोना, नुक्कड़ *The shop is* ***on the corner*** *of Shashtri Road and Palam Road.* ○ *He went* ***round the corner*** *at top speed.* **2** a quiet or secret place or area शांत या गुप्त स्थल *a remote corner of Tamil Nadu* **3** a difficult situation from which you cannot escape कठिन स्थिति जिससे बच निकलना असंभव हो *to get yourself into a corner* **4** (used in football) a free kick from the corner of the field (फ़ुटबॉल में) मैदान के कोने से रक्षक टीम के गोल की ओर मारी गई सीधी किक

IDM **cut corners** to do sth quickly and not as well as you should तेज़ी से कोई काम जैसे-तैसे कर डालना

**(just) round the corner** very near बहुत निकट *There's a phone booth just round the corner.*

**corner[2]** /ˈkɔːnə(r) ˈकॉन(र्) / *verb* [T] **1** to get a person or an animal into a position from which he/she/it cannot escape (किसी व्यक्ति या जानवर को) घेर लेना; फँसाना; विषम परिस्थिति में डाल देना जहाँ से निकलने या बचने का कोई रास्ता न हो *He cornered me at the party and started telling me all his problems.* **2** to get control in a particular area of business so that nobody else can have any success in it व्यापार के एक क्षेत्र को ऐसे हथिया लेना कि दूसरा उसमें प्रवेश न कर सके; एकाधिकार जमा लेना *That company's really* ***cornered the market*** *in health foods.*

**cornerstone** /ˈkɔːnəstəʊn ˈकॉनस्टोन् / *noun* [C] **1** a stone at the corner of the base of a building, often put there in a special ceremony (भवन की) आधारशिला **2** the most important part of sth that the rest depends on किसी बात का सर्वाधिक महत्त्वपूर्ण अंश जिस पर वह आधारित है; आधार

**cornflakes** /ˈkɔ:nfleɪks ˈकॉनृफ़्लेक्स्/ *noun* [*pl.*] food made of small pieces of dried corn and eaten with milk for breakfast सूखे मक्के के छोटे टुकड़ों से बनाया गया भोज्य पदार्थ जिसे दूध में डालकर खाया जाता है; मकई का चिवड़ा; कॉर्नफ़्लेक्स

**cornflour** /ˈkɔ:nflaʊə(r) ˈकॉनृफ़्लाउअ(र्)/ *AmE* **cornstarch** /ˈkɔ:nstɑ:tʃ ˈकॉनृस्टाच्/) *noun* [U] very fine flour often used to make sauces, etc. thicker अनाज (मकई) का बहुत महीन आटा जिसे प्रायः चटनी, रसे आदि को गाढ़ा करने में प्रयुक्त किया जाता है

**corny** /ˈkɔ:ni ˈकॉनि/ *adj.* (*informal*) too ordinary or familiar to be interesting or amusing घिसा-पिटा, पिटा-पिटाया, बहुत मामूली *a corny joke*

**corollary** /kəˈrɒləri कˈरॉलरि/ *noun* [C] (*pl.* **corollaries**) a situation, a statement or a fact that is the natural and direct result of another one ऐसी स्थिति या कथन जो अन्य स्थिति या कथन का स्वाभाविक और प्रत्यक्ष परिणाम है; निष्कर्ष, अनुमिति

**coronary**[1] /ˈkɒrənri ˈकॉरन्रि/ *adj.* connected with the heart हृदय की या हृदय से संबंधित

**coronary**[2] /ˈkɒrənri ˈकॉरन्रि/ *noun* [C] (*pl.* **coronaries**) a type of heart attack एक प्रकार का दिल का दौरा

**coronation** /ˌkɒrəˈneɪʃn ˌकॉरˈनेश्न्/ *noun* [C] an official ceremony at which sb is made a king or queen राज्याभिषेक

**coroner** /ˈkɒrənə(r) ˈकॉरन(र्)/ *noun* [C] a person whose job is to find out the causes of death of people who have died in violent or unusual ways हिंसा या अस्वाभाविक कारणों से होने वाली मृत्यु की जाँच करने वाला अधिकारी; अपमृत्यु अधिकारी

**Corp.** *abbr.* Corporation निगम, संस्थान *West Coast Motor Corp.*

**corporal** /ˈkɔ:pərəl ˈकॉपरल्/ *noun* [C] a person at a low level in the army or air force थल सेना या वायु सेना का एक छोटा अधिकारी

**corporal punishment** *noun* [U] the punishment of people by hitting them, especially the punishment of children by parents or teachers शारीरिक दंड, विशेषतः माता-पिता या अध्यापक द्वारा बच्चों को दिया गया ➪ **capital punishment** देखिए।

**corporate** /ˈkɔ:pərət ˈकॉपरट्/ *adj.* of or shared by all the members of a group or organization सामूहिक रूप से किसी समूह या संगठन की *corporate responsibility*

**corporation** /ˌkɔ:pəˈreɪʃn ˌकॉपˈरेश्न्/ *noun* [C, *with sing. or pl. verb*] **1** a large business company कोई बड़ी व्यापारिक कंपनी; कारपोरेशन *multinational corporations* ○ *the British Broadcasting Corporation* **2** a group of people elected to govern a particular town or city किसी नगर के प्रशासन के लिए निर्वाचित व्यक्ति-समुदाय; नगर-निगम

**corps** /kɔ:(r) कॉ(र्)/ *noun* [C, *with sing. or pl. verb*] (*pl.* **corps** /kɔ:(r) कॉ(र्)/) **1** a part of an army with special duties विशेष कार्यभार वाली सैनिक टुकड़ी *the medical corps* **2** a group of people involved in a special activity किसी विशेष गतिविधि में संलग्न व्यक्तियों का समूह *the diplomatic corps*

**corpse** /kɔ:ps कॉप्स्/ *noun* [C] a dead body, especially of a person शव, लाश (विशेषतः किसी व्यक्ति का) ➪ **carcass** देखिए।

**corpus** /ˈkɔ:pəs ˈकॉपस्/ *noun* [C] (*pl.* **corpora** /ˈkɔ:pərə ˈकॉपरा/ or **corpuses** /-sɪz सिज़्/) a collection of written or spoken texts लिखित या मौखिक रचनाओं या अभिव्यक्तियों का संग्रह

**corpuscle** /ˈkɔ:pʌsl ˈकॉपसल्/ *noun* [C] any of the red or white cells found in blood लाल या सफ़ेद रक्त-कणिका *red/white corpuscles*

**correct**[1] /kəˈrekt कˈरेक्ट्/ *adj.* **1** with no mistakes; right or true शुद्ध, त्रुटिहीन; सही या सत्य *Well done! All your answers were correct.* ○ *Have you got the correct time, please?* **2** (used about behaviour, manners, dress, etc.) suitable, proper or right (व्यवहार, आचरण, वस्त्र आदि) उपयुक्त या सही *What's the correct form of address for a vicar?* ✪ विलोम **incorrect** ▸ **correctly** *adv.* सही तौर पर ▸ **correctness** *noun* शुद्धता

**correct**[2] /kəˈrekt कˈरेक्ट्/ *verb* [T] **1** to make a mistake, fault, etc. right or better ग़लती को शुद्ध करना; सुधारना, सही करना *to correct a spelling mistake* ○ *to correct a test* (= make the mistake in it) **2** to tell sb what mistakes he/she is making or what faults he/she has (किसी की) ग़लती बताना *He's always correcting me when I'm talking to people.* ▸ **correction** *noun* [C, U] त्रुटि-शोधन, सुधार कार्य *Some parts of the report needed correction.*

**correction fluid** *noun* [U] a white liquid that you use to cover mistakes that you make when you are writing or typing, and that you can write on top of सफ़ेद द्रव जिसे ग़लत लिखे या टंकित अंश पर लगाकर उस पर फिर कुछ लिखा जाता है; करेक्शन फ़्ल्यूड ➪ **stationery** पर चित्र देखिए।

**corrective** /kəˈrektɪv कˈरेक्टिव्/ *adj.* intended to make sth right that is wrong सुधारात्मक *to take corrective action*

**correlate** /ˈkɒrəleɪt ˈकॉरलेट्/ *verb* [I, T] to have or to show a relationship or connection between two or more things दो या अधिक वस्तुओं के बीच संबंध स्थापित या प्रदर्शित करना ▶ **correlation** /ˌkɒrəˈleɪʃn ˌकॉरˈलेश्न्/ *noun* [C, U] पारस्परिक सहसंबंध *There is a correlation between a person's diet and height.*

**correspond** /ˌkɒrəˈspɒnd ˌकॉरˈस्पॉन्ड्/ *verb* [I] **1 correspond (to/with sth)** to be the same as or equal to sth; to match किसी के समान या बराबर होना; मेल खाना *Does the name on the envelope correspond with the name inside the letter?* **2** (*formal*) **correspond (with sb)** to write letters to and receive them from sb पत्रों का आदान-प्रदान करना; पत्र-व्यवहार या पत्राचार करना *They corresponded for a year before they met.*

**correspondence** /ˌkɒrəˈspɒndəns ˌकॉरˈस्पॉन्डन्स्/ *noun* **1** [U] (*formal*) the act of writing letters; the letters themselves पत्र-व्यवहार, पत्राचार; भेजे या प्राप्त किए गए पत्र *There hasn't been any correspondence between them for years.* **2** [C, U] a close connection or relationship between two or more things दो या अधिक वस्तुओं के बीच निकट संपर्क या संबंध; मेल, अनुकूलता *There is no correspondence between the two sets of figures.*

**correspondent** /ˌkɒrəˈspɒndənt ˌकॉरˈस्पॉन्डन्ट्/ *noun* [C] **1** a person who provides news or writes articles for a newspaper, etc., especially from a foreign country किसी समाचार-पत्र आदि का संवाददाता या लेखक जो विशेषतः विदेश में स्थित हो *our Middle East correspondent, Rahul Bhargav* **2** a person who writes letters to sb पत्र-लेखक

**corresponding** /ˌkɒrəˈspɒndɪŋ ˌकॉरˈस्पॉन्डिङ्/ *adj.* (*only before a noun*) related or similar to sth किसी से संबंधित या उसके समान; मेल खाता हुआ *Sales are up 10% compared with the corresponding period last year.* ▶ **correspondingly** *adv.* किसी के समान होकर, समानतापूर्वक, तदनुसार

**corridor** /ˈkɒrɪdɔː(r) ˈकॉरिडॉ(र्)/ *noun* [C] a long narrow passage in a building or train, with doors that open into rooms, etc. (भवन या रेलगाड़ी में) गलियारा

**corrie** /ˈkɒri ˈकॉरि/ (*also* **cirque; cwm**) *noun* [C] (in geography) a round area shaped like a bowl in the side of a mountain (भूगोल में) पर्वत के ढाल में प्याले के आकार का गोल भूक्षेत्र

**corroborate** /kəˈrɒbəreɪt कˈरॉबरेट्/ *verb* [T] (*formal*) to support a statement, idea, etc. by providing new evidence नए प्रमाण द्वारा किसी विचार आदि की संपुष्टि या समर्थन करना *The data corroborated Mr Prasad's claim about the company doing well.* ▶ **corroboration** /kəˌrɒbəˈreɪʃn कˌरॉबˈरेश्न्/ *noun* [U] संपुष्टिकरण, समर्थन

**corrode** /kəˈrəʊd कˈरोड्/ *verb* [I, T] (used about metals) to become weak or to be destroyed by chemical action; to cause a metal to do this (धातुओं का) रासायनिक क्रिया द्वारा क्षीण या नष्ट हो जाना या कर देना *Parts of the car were corroded by rust.* ▶ **corrosion** /kəˈrəʊʒn कˈरोश्न्/ *noun* [U] क्षय, छीजन ▶ **corrosive** /kəˈrəʊsɪv कˈरोसिव्/ *adj.* क्षयकारी, छीजने वाला

**corrugated** /ˈkɒrəgeɪtɪd ˈकॉरगेटिड्/ *adj.* (used about metal or cardboard) shaped into folds (धातु या गत्ता) लपेटा, तह किया

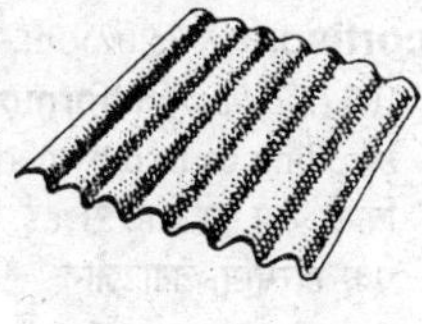

**corrupt[1]** /kəˈrʌpt कˈरप्ट्/ *adj.* **1** doing or involving illegal or dishonest things in exchange for money, etc. भ्रष्ट *corrupt officials who accept bribes* ○ *corrupt business practices* **2** (*computing*) containing changes or faults and no longer in the original state (कंप्यूटर) दोष आ जाने के कारण मूलरूप में न रह पाना; सदोष *corrupt software* ○ *The text on the disk seems to be corrupt.*

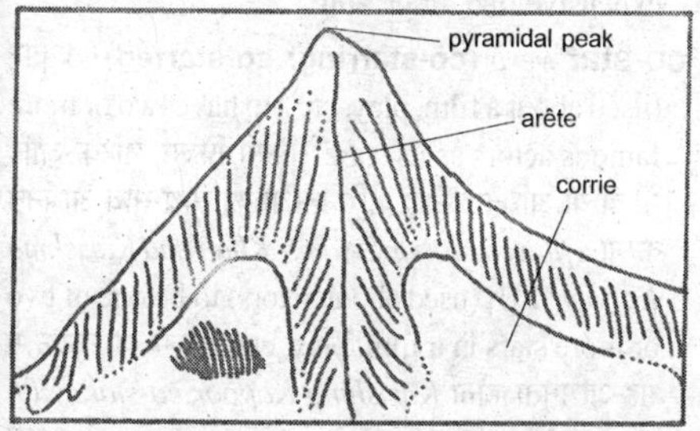


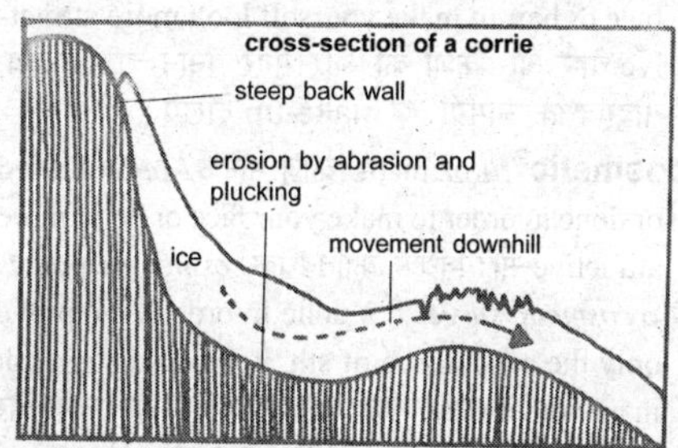


corrie

**corrupt²** /kəˈrʌpt कˈरप्ट्/ *verb* **1** [T] to cause sb/sth to start behaving in a dishonest or immoral way भ्रष्ट करना *Too many people are corrupted by power.* **2** [I, T] (*computing*) to cause mistakes to appear in a computer file, etc. with the result that the information in it is no longer correct कंप्यूटर फ़ाइल आदि का सदोष हो जाना *The program has somehow corrupted the system files.* ○ *corrupted data*

**corruption** /kəˈrʌpʃn कˈरप्शन्/ *noun* [U] **1** dishonest or immoral behaviour or activities भ्रष्टाचार *There were accusations of corruption among senior police officers.* **2** the process of making sb/sth corrupt किसी को भ्रष्ट करने की प्रकिया

**corset** /ˈkɔːsɪt ˈकॉसिट्/ *noun* [C] a piece of clothing that some women wear pulled tight around their middle to make them look thinner महिलाओं द्वारा शरीर के मध्य भाग में पहना जाने वाला तंग वस्त्र जिससे वे कुछ अधिक पतली दिखती हैं

**cortex** /ˈkɔːteks ˈकॉट्टेक्स्/ *noun* [C] (*pl.* **cortices** /ˈkɔːtɪsiːz ˈकॉटिसीज़्/) (*technical*) the outer layer of an organ in the body, especially the brain शरीर के किसी अंग, विशेषतः मस्तिष्क, का बाह्य आवरण, झिल्ली *the cerebral cortex* (= around the brain)

**cortisone** /ˈkɔːtɪzəʊn; -səʊn ˈकॉटिज़ोन्; -सोन्/ *noun* [U] (*medical*) a **hormone** that is used to reduce swelling caused by certain diseases and injuries किसी रोग या चोट से हुई सूजन को कम करने में प्रयुक्त एक हॉरमोन; कोर्टिज़ोन

**cosine** /ˈkəʊsaɪn ˈकोसाइन्/ *noun* [C] (*mathematics*) (*abbr.* **cos**) the **ratio** of the length of the side next to an **acute angle** to the length of the longest side (**the hypotenuse**) in a **right-angled** triangle किसी समकोण त्रिभुज में न्यून कोण के साथ की भुजा का सबसे लंबी भुजा से अनुपात; कोटिज्या, कोज्या ➪ **sine** और **tangent** देखिए।

**cosmetic¹** /kɒzˈmetɪk कॉज़् ˈमेटिक्/ *noun* [C, *usually pl.*] a substance that you put on your face or hair to make yourself look more attractive चेहरे और केशों को और सुंदर बनाने वाला पदार्थ; सौंदर्यवर्धक सामग्री ➪ **make-up** देखिए।

**cosmetic²** /kɒzˈmetɪk कॉज़्ˈमेटिक्/ *adj.* **1** used or done in order to make your face or body more attractive सौंदर्यवर्धक, कांतिवर्धक *cosmetic products* ○ *cosmetic surgery* **2** done in order to improve only the appearance of sth, without changing it in any other way केवल दिखावे के लिए या ऊपरी तौर पर किया गया (न कि मूलभूत रूप से) *changes in government policy which are purely cosmetic*

**cosmic** /ˈkɒzmɪk ˈकॉज़्मिक्/ *adj.* connected with space or the universe अंतरिक्ष या ब्रह्मांड से संबंधित

**cosmopolitan** /ˌkɒzməˈpɒlɪtən ˌकॉज़्मˈपॉलिटन्/ *adj.* **1** containing people from all over the world विश्व के विभिन्न भागों से आए व्यक्तियों वाला; सर्वदेशीय *a cosmopolitan city* **2** influenced by the culture of other countries अन्य देशों की संस्कृति से प्रभावित *a cosmopolitan and sophisticated young woman*

**the cosmos** /ˈkɒzmɒs ˈकॉज़्मॉस्/ *noun* [*sing.*] the universe ब्रह्मांड

**cost¹** /kɒst कॉस्ट्/ *noun* **1** [C, U] the money that you have to pay for sth क़ीमत, मूल्य *The hospital was built **at a cost of** Rs 10 million.* ○ *The damage will have to be repaired regardless of cost.* ➪ **price** पर नोट देखिए। **2** [*sing.*, U] what you have to give or lose in order to obtain sth else कुछ पाने के लिए दिया गया कुछ धन आदि; किसी चीज़ के लिए चुकाई गई क़ीमत *He achieved great success but only **at the cost of** a happy family life.* **3 costs** [*pl.*] the total amount of money that needs to be spent in a business किसी कारोबार में लागत, ख़र्च

IDM **at all costs/at any cost** using whatever means are necessary to achieve sth हर क़ीमत पर; कुछ पाने के लिए हर प्रकार के साधन का प्रयोग *We must win at all costs.*

**cover the cost** (**of sth**) ➪ **cover¹** देखिए।

**to your cost** in a way that is unpleasant or bad for you परेशानी उठाकर *Life can be lonely at university, as I found out to my cost.*

**cost²** /kɒst कॉस्ट्/ *verb* [T] (*pt, pp* **cost**) **1** to have the price of क़ीमत या दाम होना *How much does a return ticket to Pune cost?* ○ *We'll take the bus—it won't cost much.* ○ (*informal*) *How much did your car cost you?* **2** to make you lose sth हानि उठाना, हाथ की चीज़ गँवाना *That one mistake cost him his job.*

IDM **cost the earth/a fortune** to be very expensive बहुत मँहगा होना

**co-star** *verb* (**co-starring; co-starred**) **1** [T] (used about a film, play, etc.) to have two or more famous actors as its stars (किसी फ़िल्म, नाटक आदि में) दो या अधिक प्रसिद्ध अभिनेताओं का साथ-साथ अभिनय करना *a film co-starring Aamir Khan and Karishma Kapoor* **2** [I] (used about actors) to be one of two or more stars in a film, play, etc. फ़िल्म या नाटक में सह-अभिनेता होना *Karishma Kapoor co-stars with Aamir Khan in the film.* ▸ **co-star** *noun* [C] सह-अभिनेता *His co-star was Rani Mukherjee.*

**cost-effective** *adj.* giving the best possible profit or results in comparison with the money that is spent लागत मूल्य का अधिकतम लाभ देने वाला *This alarm system is the most cost-effective way of protecting your property.*

**costly** /ˈkɒstli ˈकॉस्ट्लि/ *adj.* (**costlier; costliest**) **1** costing a lot of money; expensive बड़ी लागत वाला; महँगा, क़ीमती *a costly repair bill* **2** involving great loss of time, effort, etc. जिसमें बहुत समय और शक्ति लगे हों *a costly mistake*

**cost price** *noun* [U] the cost of producing sth or the price at which it is sold without making any money लागत, मूल्य ➪ **asking price** और **selling price** देखिए।

**costume** /ˈkɒstjuːm ˈकॉस्ट्यूम्/ *noun* **1** [C, U] a set or style of clothes worn by people in a particular country or in a particular historical period किसी विशेष देश या काल में लोगों की विशेष पोशाक *17th century costume* ○ *tribal costume* **2** [C, U] clothes that an actor, etc. wears in order to look like sth else अभिनय में पहनी गई पोशाक विशेष *One of the children was dressed in a pirate's costume.* **3** [C] = **swimsuit**

**cosy** /ˈkəʊzi कोज़ि/ *adj.* (**cosier; cosiest**) (*AmE* **cozy**) warm and comfortable गरम और आरामदेह *The room looked cosy and inviting in the fire light.*

**cot** /kɒt कॉट्/ (*AmE* **crib**) *noun* [C] **1** a bed with high sides for a baby बच्चों की शय्या जिसके पार्श्व उठे हुए हों **2** = **camp bed**

**cottage** /ˈkɒtɪdʒ ˈकॉटिज्/ *noun* [C] a small and usually old house, especially in the country (देहाती इलाक़े में बना) छोटा और प्रायः पुराना घर; कुटिया

**cottage cheese** *noun* [U] a type of soft white cheese in small wet lumps पनीर

**cotton** /ˈkɒtn ˈकॉट्न्/ *noun* [U] **1** a natural cloth or thread made from the thin white hairs of the cotton plant रूई, सूत या कपास का कपड़ा या धागा *a cotton shirt* **2** = **cotton wool**

**cotton wool** *noun* [U] a soft mass of cotton, used for cleaning the skin, cuts, etc. मरहम-पट्टी आदि के लिए प्रयुक्त रूई

**cotyledon** /ˌkɒtɪˈliːdn ˌकॉटिˈलीड्न्/ *noun* [C] a part inside a seed that looks like a small leaf, which the developing plant uses as a store of food. Cotyledons are the first parts of the seed to appear above the ground when it begins to grow बीज का पत्तेनुमा अंदरी भाग जो विकसित होते पौधे के लिए अन्नभंडार का काम करता है; बीजपत्र

**couch**[1] /kaʊtʃ काउच्/ *noun* [C] a long seat, often with a back and arms, for sitting or lying on टेक और बाजुओं वाली आरामदेह लंबी कुरसी; काउच *They were sitting on the couch in the living room.*

**couch**[2] /kaʊtʃ काउच्/ *verb* [T] (*usually passive*) (*formal*) to express a thought, idea, etc. in the way mentioned विचारों, भावनाओं को अभीष्ट रूप में व्यक्त करना *His reply was couched in very polite terms.*

**cougar** /ˈkuːgə(r) ˈकूग(र)/ = **puma**

**cough**[1] /kɒf कॉफ़्/ *verb* **1** to send air out of your throat and mouth with a sudden loud noise, especially when you have a cold, have sth in your throat, etc. खाँसना **2** [T] **cough (up) sth** to send sth out of your throat and mouth with a sudden loud noise खखारना; खाँसते हुए मुँह से कुछ बाहर निकालना *When he started coughing (up) blood he called the doctor.*

**PHRV** **cough (sth) up** (*informal*) to give money when you do not want to अनिच्छापूर्वक धन देना *Come on, cough up what you owe me!*

**cough**[2] /kɒf कॉफ़्/ *noun* [C] **1** an act or the sound of coughing खाँसने की क्रिया या आवाज़ *He gave a nervous cough before he started to speak.* **2** an illness or infection that makes you cough a lot खाँसी की बीमारी *Santosh's got a bad cough.*

**could** /kəd; *strong form* kʊd कड्; प्रबल रूप कुड्/ *modal verb* (*negative* **could not**; *short form* **couldn't** /ˈkʊdnt ˈकुड्न्ट्/) **1** used for saying that sb had the ability or was allowed to do sth पूर्व समय में योग्यता या अनुमति दर्शाने के लिए प्रयुक्त *I could run three kilometres without stopping when I was younger.*

> **NOTE** पूर्व समय में अवसर-विशेष पर संभावना व्यक्त करने के लिए **could** के स्थान पर **was/were able to** या **managed to** का प्रयोग किया जाता है—*The firemen were able to/managed to rescue the children.* परंतु इस संदर्भ के निषेधात्मक वाक्यों में **couldn't** का प्रयोग किया जा सकता है—*The firemen couldn't rescue the children.*

**2** used for saying that sth may be or may have been possible संभावना व्यक्त करने के लिए प्रयुक्त *She could be famous one day.* ○ *You could have said you were going to be late* (= I'm annoyed that you didn't)*!* **3** used for asking permission politely नम्रतापूर्वक अनुमति माँगने के लिए प्रयुक्त *Could I possibly borrow your car?* **4** used for asking sb politely to do sth for you कुछ करने के लिए विनम्रता से अनुरोध करने के लिए प्रयुक्त *Could you open the door? My hands are full.*

NOTE वृत्तिवाचक क्रियाओं (modal verbs) पर अधिक जानकारी के लिए शब्दकोश के अंत में **Quick Grammar Reference** खंड देखिए।

**5** used for making a suggestion सुझाव देने के लिए प्रयुक्त *'What do you want to do tonight?' 'We could go to the cinema or we could just stay in.'* **6** used with the verbs 'feel', 'hear', 'see', 'smell', 'taste' निम्नलिखित क्रियाओं के साथ प्रयुक्त 'feel', 'hear', 'see', 'smell', 'taste'

NOTE इन क्रियाओं का प्रयोग सातत्यबोधक कालों (continuous tenses) में नहीं होता। यदि अतीत काल के किसी क्षण विशेष के लिए seeing, hearing आदि का अर्थ व्यक्त करना हो तो **could** का प्रयोग किया जाता है—*We could hear/see children playing outside.* (न कि *We were hearing children playing outside.*)

**coulomb** /ˈku:lɒm ˈकूलॉम्/ *noun* [C] (*abbr.* **C**) a unit of electric charge, equal to the quantity of electricity carried in one second by one **ampere** विद्युत चार्ज की इकाई (एक सेकंड में एक एम्पीयर द्वारा ले जाई गई विद्युत मात्रा के बराबर)

**council** (*also* **Council**) /ˈkaʊnsl ˈकाउनुसल्/ *noun* [C, *with sing. or pl. verb*] **1** a group of people who are elected to govern an area such as a town or county नगर या जिले के प्रशासन के लिए निर्वाचित व्यक्तियों का समूह; परिषद *The city council has/have decided to build a new road.* ○ *My dad's on the local council.* **2** a group of people chosen to give advice, manage affairs, etc. for a particular organization or activity विशिष्ट संगठन या कार्यक्रम के संचालन हेतु परामर्शदाता व्यक्तियों का समूह; सलाहकार परिषद *the Arts Council*

**councillor** /ˈkaʊnsələ(r) ˈकाउनुसल(र्)/ *noun* [C] a member of a council परिषद सदस्य; पार्षद *to elect new councillors*

**counsel**[1] /ˈkaʊnsl ˈकाउनुसल्/ *verb* [T] (**counselling; counselled** *AmE* **counseling; counseled**) **1** to give professional advice and help to sb with a problem किसी समस्या के विषय में व्यावसायिक रूप से सलाह देना **2** (*written*) to tell sb what you think he/she should do; to advise सलाह, परामर्श देना *The company's lawyers counselled the managing director against making public statements.*

**counsel**[2] /ˈkaʊnsl ˈकाउनुसल्/ *noun* [U] **1** (*written*) advice सलाह, परामर्श **2** a lawyer who speaks in a court of law न्यायालय में मुक़दमा लड़ने वाला वकील *the counsel for the defence/prosecution*

**counselling** (*AmE* **counseling**) /ˈkaʊnsəlɪŋ ˈकाउनुसलिङ्/ *noun* [U] professional advice and help given to people with problems समस्याओं के विषय में दी गई औपचारिक सलाह और सहायता *Many students come to us for counselling.*

**counsellor** (*AmE* **counselor**) /ˈkaʊnsələ(r) ˈकाउनुसल(र्)/ *noun* [C] a person whose job is to give advice परामर्शदाता, सलाहकार *a marriage counsellor*

**count**[1] /kaʊnt काउन्ट्/ *verb* **1** [I] to say numbers one after another in order गिनती करना, गिनना *Close your eyes and count (up) to 20.* **2** [T] **count sth** to calculate the total number or amount of sth गिनती करना, गिन कर हिसाब लगाना *The teacher counted the children as they got on the bus.* **3** [T] to include sb/sth when you are calculating an amount or number गिनती में शामिल करना; हिसाब में जोड़ना *There were thirty people on the bus, not counting the driver.* **4** [I] **count (for sth)** to be important or valuable महत्त्वपूर्ण या मूल्यवान होना *I sometimes think my opinion counts for nothing at work.* **5** [I] **count (as sth)** to be valid or accepted मान्य होना, स्वीकार होना *The referee had already blown his whistle so the goal didn't count.* ○ *Will my driving licence count as identification?* **6** [I, T] to consider sb/sth in a particular way रीति-विशेष में मानना, समझना *You should count yourself lucky to have a good job.* ○ *On this airline, children over 12 count/are counted as adults.*

IDM **Don't count your chickens (before they're hatched)** used to say that you should not be too confident that sth will be successful because sth might still go wrong यह कहने के लिए प्रयुक्त कि सफलता के प्रति अतिविश्वास ठीक नहीं

PHR V **count against sb** to be considered as a disadvantage असुविधा या घाटे की बात समझा जाना *Do you think my age will count against me?*

**count on sb/sth** to expect sth with confidence; to depend on sb/sth किसी से विश्वास के साथ आशा करना; किसी पर निर्भर होना *Can I count on you to help me?*

**count sb/sth out** **1** to count things slowly, one by one एक-एक करके धीरे-धीरे गिनना *She carefully counted out the money into my hand.* **2** (*informal*) to not include sb/sth किसी को शामिल न करना *If you're going swimming, you can count me out!*

**count**[2] /kaʊnt काउन्ट्/ *noun* [C] **1** [*usually sing.*] an act of counting or a number that you get after counting गिनती की प्रक्रिया; गिनी गई संख्या; गिनती में आया कुल जोड़ ***At the last count**, there* *were nearly two million unemployed.* ○ *On the count of three, all lift together.* **2** [*usually pl.*] a point that is made in a discussion, argument, etc. विवाद आदि के दौरान प्रस्तुत कोई विचार बिंदु *I proved her wrong* ***on all counts.***

IDM **keep/lose count (of sth)** to know/not know how many there are of sth हिसाब रखना या हिसाब न रखना *I've lost count of the number of times he's told that joke!*

**countable** /ˈkaʊntəbl ˈकाउन्टबल्/ *adj.* (*grammar*) that can be counted गणनीय; जिसकी गणना की जा सके *'Chair' is a countable noun, but 'sugar' isn't.* ○ *Countable nouns are marked* [C] *in this dictionary.* ✪ विलोम **uncountable**

**countdown** /ˈkaʊntdaʊn ˈकाउन्टडाउन्/ *noun* [C] the act of saying numbers backwards to zero just before sth important happens शून्य तक उलटी गिनती गिनना (किसी महत्त्वपूर्ण घटना के घटित होने से पहले) *the countdown to the lift-off of a rocket* ○ (*figurative*) *The countdown to this summer's Olympic Games has started.*

**countenance** /ˈkaʊntənəns ˈकाउन्टनन्स्/ *noun* [C] (*written*) a person's face or his/her expression किसी व्यक्ति का चेहरा या उसकी भावाभिव्यक्ति

**counter-** /ˈkaʊntə(r) ˈकाउन्ट(र्)/ *prefix* (*in nouns, verbs, adjectives and adverbs*) against; opposite के विरुद्ध; के विपरीत, प्रति- *a counter-argument* ○ *counterproductive*

**counter**[1] /ˈkaʊntə(r) ˈकाउन्ट(र्)/ *noun* [C] **1** a long, flat surface in a shop, bank, etc., where customers are served किसी दुकान, बैंक आदि में एक लंबा समतल फट्टा जहाँ ग्राहकों से व्यवहार होता है; काउंटर, पटल *The man* ***behind the counter*** *in the bank was very helpful.* **2** a small object (usually round and made of plastic) that is used in some games to show where a player is on the board टोकन या छोटी गोल टिक्की जो बोर्ड पर खेले जाने वाले खेलों में खिलाड़ी की स्थिति का संकेत करती है **3** an electronic device for counting sth गणना करने वाला इलेक्ट्रॉनिक उपकरण *The rev counter is next to the speedometer.* ➪ **Geiger counter** देखिए।

**counter**[2] /ˈkaʊntə(r) ˈकाउन्ट(र्)/ *verb* [I, T] **1** to reply or react to criticism आलोचना का जवाब देना; प्रतिक्रिया या विरोध करना *He countered our objections with a powerful defence of his plan.* **2** to try to reduce or prevent the bad effects of sth प्रतिकार करना; निष्प्रभावी करने का प्रयास करना *The shop has installed security cameras to counter theft.*

**counter**[3] /ˈkaʊntə(r) ˈकाउन्ट(र्)/ *adv.* **counter to sth** in the opposite direction to sth किसी के विपरीत दिशा आदि में *The results of these experiments* ***run counter to*** *previous findings.*

**counteract** /ˌkaʊntərˈækt ˌकाउन्टर्ˈऐक्ट्/ *verb* [T] to reduce the effect of sth by acting against it आवश्यक कदम उठाकर किसी क्रिया या स्थिति को निष्प्रभावी करना *measures to counteract traffic congestion*

**counter-attack** *noun* [C] an attack made in reaction to an enemy or opponent's attack जवाबी हमला; प्रत्याक्रमण ▶ **counter-attack** *verb* [I, T] जवाबी हमला करना

**counter-clockwise** = **anticlockwise**

**counterfeit** /ˈkaʊntəfɪt ˈकाउन्टफ़िट्/ *adj.* not genuine, but copied so that it looks like the real thing जाली, नक़ली, प्रतिलिपि के रूप में *counterfeit money*

**counterfoil** /ˈkaʊntəfɔɪl ˈकाउन्टफ़ॉइल्/ *noun* [C] the part of a cheque, receipt, ticket, etc. that is kept by the giver as a record चेक, रसीद, टिकट आदि का वह हिस्सा जो देने वाला रिकार्ड हेतु अपने पास रखता है; प्रतिपर्ण, मुसन्ना

**counterpart** /ˈkaʊntəpɑːt ˈकाउन्टपाट्/ *noun* [C] a person or thing that has a similar position or function in a different country or organization वह व्यक्ति या वस्तु जो अन्य देश या संगठन में समान पद पर है; प्रतिरूप, प्रतिस्थानी *the Indian President and his Italian counterpart* (= the Italian President)

**counterproductive** *adj.* having the opposite effect to the one you want विपरीत-प्रभावकारी; लाभप्रद होने के बजाय हानिकर

**countersign** /ˈkaʊntəsaɪn ˈकाउन्टसाइन्/ *verb* [T] (*technical*) to sign a document that has already been signed by another person, especially in order to show that it is valid किसी अन्य व्यक्ति द्वारा हस्ताक्षरित दस्तावेज़ पर पुनः हस्ताक्षर करना (विशेषतः यह दिखाने के लिए यह क़ानूनन मान्य है); प्रतिहस्ताक्षर करना

**countless** /ˈkaʊntləs ˈकाउन्ट्लस्/ *adj.* (*only before a noun*) very many अनगिनत, असंख्य *I've tried to phone him countless times but he's not there.*

**country** /ˈkʌntri ˈकन्ट्रि/ *noun* (*pl.* **countries**) **1** [C] an area of land with its own people, government, etc. देश *India, Sri Lanka and other Asian countries* ○ *There was rain over much of the country during the monsoons.*

NOTE **State** का अर्थ है ऐसा देश जो अपने में सुसंगठित राजनीतिक समुदाय है और जिस पर एक विधिक सरकार का नियंत्रण है। **State** शब्द स्वयं

सरकार के अर्थ में भी प्रयुक्त होता है—*the member states of SAARC*. भारत में तथा कुछ अन्य देशों में **state** शब्द राज्य के लिए भी प्रयुक्त किया जाता है—*The states of Bihar, Orissa and West Bengal.* **Land** शब्द अपेक्षया अधिक और औपचारिक या साहित्यिक है—*Explorers who set out to discover new lands.*

**2 the country** [*sing.*] the people who live in a country देश के निवासी *a survey to find out what the country really thinks* **3 the country** [*sing.*] land which is away from towns and cities देहात, ग्रामीण क्षेत्र (शहरों और क़स्बों से दूर) *Do you live in a town or* ***in the country****?*

**NOTE** देहात या ग्रामीण क्षेत्र के अर्थ में **countryside** शब्द का भी प्रयोग होता है परंतु इस शब्द से ग्रामीण क्षेत्र के प्राकृतिक तत्वों जैसे पहाड़ियों, नदियों, पेड़ आदि को प्रमुखता देना अभीष्ट होता है—*beautiful countryside* ○ *the destruction of the country-side by new roads.* ➪ **scenery** पर भी नोट देखिए।

**4** [U] an area of land ज़मीन का इलाक़ा; भूक्षेत्र *We looked down over miles of open country.* ○ *hilly country* ✪ पर्याय **terrain**

**country house** *noun* [C] a large house in the country, usually owned by an important family and often with a lot of land देहात में बना बड़ा मकान जो सामान्यतः किसी महत्त्वपूर्ण या बड़े घराने की संपत्ति हो और जिसके साथ काफ़ी सारी ज़मीन भी हो

**countryman** /ˈkʌntrimən ˈकन्ट्रिमन् / *noun* [C] (*pl.* **-men** /-mən -मन् /) a person from your own **country 1** समदेशवासी, हमवतन *Bhupati beat his* ***fellow countryman*** *Paes in the final.*

**the countryside** /ˈkʌntrisaɪd ˈकन्ट्रिसाइड् / *noun* [U, *sing.*] land which is away from towns and cities, where there are fields, woods, etc. क़स्बों और शहरों से दूर खेतों, जंगलों आदि वाला भूक्षेत्र *From the hill there is a magnificent view of the surrounding countryside.* ➪ **country** पर नोट देखिए।

**county** /ˈkaʊnti ˈकाउन्टि / *noun* [C] (*pl.* **counties**) an area in Britain, Ireland or the US which has its own local government ब्रिटेन, आयरलैंड और संयुक्त राज्य अमेरिका में स्थानीय स्वशासन वाला क्षेत्र; काउंटी *the county of Nottinghamshire* ○ *Orange County, California* ➪ **province** और **state 4** भी देखिए।

**coup** /kuː कू / *noun* [C] **1** (*also* **coup d'état**) /ˌkuːdeɪˈtɑː ˌकुडेˈटा / a sudden, illegal and often violent change of government शासन-व्यवस्था में एकाएक, ग़ैर-क़ानूनी और प्रायः हिंसक रीति से परिवर्तन; बलात सत्ता-परिवर्तन; सरकार का तख़्ता-पलट *a coup to overthrow the President* ○ *an attempted coup* (= one which did not succeed) **2** a clever and successful thing to do चतुराई भरी सफलता, चतुराई से प्राप्त सफलता *Getting that promotion was a real coup.*

**couple**[1] /ˈkʌpl ˈकपल् / *noun* [C, *with sing. or pl. verb*] two people who are together because they are married or in a relationship दंपत्ति, पति-पत्नी *a married couple* ○ *Is/Are that couple over there part of our group?* ➪ **pair** देखिए।

**IDM a couple of people/things 1** two people/things दो व्यक्ति या वस्तुएँ, जोड़ा, युग्म *I need a couple of glasses.* **2** a few कुछेक (व्यक्ति या वस्तुएँ) *I last saw her a couple of months ago.*

**couple**[2] /ˈkʌpl ˈकपल् / *verb* [T] (*usually passive*) to join or connect sb/sth to sb/sth else दो वस्तुओं को जोड़ना; दो वस्तुओं का जुड़ना *The fog, coupled with the amount of traffic on the roads, made driving very difficult.*

**couplet** /ˈkʌplət ˈकपलट् / *noun* [C] two lines of poetry of equal length one after the other कविता की समान रूप से लंबी दो पंक्तियाँ; द्विपदी

**coupon** /ˈkuːpɒn ˈकूपॉन् / *noun* [C] **1** a small piece of paper which you can use to buy goods at a lower price, or which you can collect and then exchange for goods काग़ज़ की विशेष छोटी परची जिसे दिखाकर कम दाम पर वस्तुएँ ख़रीदी जा सकती हैं या विनिमय में प्राप्त की जा सकती हैं; कूपन *a coupon worth 10% off your next purchase* **2** a printed form in a newspaper or magazine which you use to order goods, enter a competition, etc. समाचार-पत्र, पत्रिका में छपी परची जिसे वस्तुओं को ख़रीदने का आदेश देने, किसी स्पर्धा में प्रवेश के लिए आवेदन करने आदि के लिए प्रयोग में लाया जाता है; कूपन

**courage** /ˈkʌrɪdʒ ˈकरिज् / *noun* [U] the ability to control fear in a situation that may be dangerous or unpleasant साहस, हिम्मत, बहादुरी *It took real courage to go back into the burning building.* ○ *She* ***showed*** *great* ***courage*** *all through her long illness.* ✪ पर्याय **bravery** ▸ **courageous** /kəˈreɪdʒəs कˈरेजस् / *adj.* साहसी, हिम्मती

**IDM pluck up courage** ➪ **pluck** देखिए।

**courier** /ˈkʊriə(r) ˈकुरिअ(र्) / *noun* [C] **1** a person whose job is to carry letters, important papers, etc., especially when they are urgent अत्यावश्यक पत्रादि ले जाने वाला व्यक्ति; तुरंती पत्रों का वाहक व्यक्ति *The package was delivered by the overnight courier.* **2** a person whose job is to look after a group of tourists पर्यटक-दल का प्रबधंक या सहायक

**course** /kɔːs कॉस्/ *noun* **1** [C] **a course (in/on sth)** a complete series of lessons or studies पाठ्यक्रम, पाठ्यविवरण *I've decided to* ***enrol on a*** *computer* ***course***. ○ *I'm going to* ***take/do a course*** *in self-defence.* **2** [C, U] the route or direction that sth, especially an aircraft, ship or river, takes विमान, जलपोत या नदी का मार्ग या उसकी दिशा *to be* ***on/off course*** (= going in the right/wrong direction) ○ (*figurative*) *I'm on course* (= making the right amount of progress) *to finish this work by the end of the week.* **3** (*also* **course of action**) [C] a way of dealing with a particular situation स्थिति-विशेष का सामना करने, से निबटने का तरीक़ा *In that situation resignation was the only course open to him.* **4** [*sing.*] the development of sth over a period of time अवधि-विशेष में हुआ विकास *events that changed* ***the course of history*** ○ *In the normal course of events* (= the way things normally happen) *such problems do not arise.* **5** [C] the first, second, third, etc. separate part of a meal भोजन में अलग-अलग दौर (पहला, दूसरा आदि) *a three-course lunch* ○ *I had chicken for the* ***main course***. **6** [C] an area where golf is played or where certain types of race take place वह मैदान जहाँ गोल्फ़ खेला जाता है या विशेष प्रकार की दौड़ें आयोजित की जाती हैं *a golf course* ○ *a race-course* **7** [C] **a course (of sth)** a series of medical treatments डॉक्टरी इलाजों का सिलसिला *The doctor put her on a course of tablets.*

IDM **be on a collision course (with sb/sth)** ➪ **collision** देखिए।

**in the course of sth** during sth के दौरान *He mentioned it in the course of conversation.*

**in the course of time** when enough time has passed; eventually काफ़ी समय बीत जाने पर; अंततोगत्वा

**in due course** ➪ **due**[1] देखिए।

**a matter of course** ➪ **matter**[1] देखिए।

**of course** naturally; certainly स्वाभाविक रूप से; निश्चित रूप से *Of course, having children has changed their lives a lot.* ○ *'Can I use your phone?' 'Of course (you can).'*

**coursebook** /ˈkɔːsbʊk ˈकॉस्बुक्/ *noun* [C] a book for studying from that is used regularly in class पाठ्यपुस्तक

**coursework** /ˈkɔːswɜːk ˈकॉस्वक्/ *noun* [U] work that students do during a course of study, not in exams, that is included in their final mark छात्र का अध्ययनकालीन अभ्यास कार्य (जिसे अंतिम मूल्यांकन में शामिल किया जाता है *Coursework accounts for 50% of the final marks.*

**court**[1] /kɔːt कॉट्/ *noun* **1** [C, U] a place where legal trials take place and crimes, etc. are judged न्यायालय, कचहरी *A man has been charged and will* ***appear in court*** *tomorrow.* ○ *Bharat's company are refusing to pay him so he's decided to* ***take them to court***. **2 the court** [*sing.*] the people in a court, especially those taking part in the trial न्यायालय में उपस्थित व्यक्ति, विशेषतः वे जो मुक़दमे का हिस्सा हैं *Please tell the court exactly what you saw.* **3** [C, U] an area where certain ball games are played टेनिस आदि गेंद वाले खेलों का मैदान *a tennis/squash/badminton court* ➪ **pitch**[1] देखिए। **4** [C] a king or queen, their family and all the people who look after them राजदरबार *the court of Emperor Akbar*

**court**[2] /kɔːt कॉट्/ *verb* [T] **1** to try to gain sb's support by paying special attention to him/her किसी पर विशेष ध्यान देकर या ख़ुशामद कर उसका समर्थन प्राप्त करने की कोशिश करना *Politicians from all parties will be courting voters this week.* **2** to do sth that might have a very bad effect संकट को आमंत्रित करने वाला काम करना *India is courting ecological disaster if it continues to dump waste in its rivers.*

**courteous** /ˈkɜːtiəs ˈकटिअस्/ *adj.* polite and pleasant, showing respect for other people शिष्ट, भद्र, विनम्र और प्रीतिकर ✪ विलोम **discourteous**

▸ **courteously** *adv.* शिष्टतापूर्वक

**courtesy** /ˈkɜːtəsi ˈकटसि/ *noun* (*pl.* **courtesies**) **1** [U] polite and pleasant behaviour that shows respect for other people शिष्ट व्यवहार, सौजन्य *She didn't even* ***have the courtesy*** *to say that she was sorry.* **2** [C] (*formal*) a polite thing that you say or do when you meet people in formal situations शिष्टाचार के शब्द, अभिवादन *The two presidents exchanged courtesies before their meeting.*

IDM **(by) courtesy of sb** (*formal*) with the permission or because of the kindness of sb के सौजन्य से *These pictures are being shown by courtesy of NDTV.*

**court martial** *noun* [C] a military court that deals with matters of military law; a trial that takes place in such a court सैन्य क़ानून के मामले देखने वाला सैन्य न्यायालय; सैन्य अदालत; कोर्ट मार्शल *His case will be heard by a court martial.*

▸ **court-martial** *verb* [T] (**court-martialling; court-martialled;** *AmE* **court-martialing; court-martialed**) सैन्य न्यायालय में मुक़दमा चलाना

**court of law** = **court**[1] **1**

**courtroom** /ˈkɔːtruːm ˈकॉट्रूम्/ *noun* [C] the place or room where a court of law meets न्याय-भवन, अदालत-कक्ष

**courtship** /ˈkɔːtʃɪp ˈकॉट्शिप्/ *noun* [C, U] (*old-fashioned*) the relationship between a man and a woman before they get married विवाह-पूर्व प्रेम-निवेदन; प्रेम-संबंध

**courtyard** /ˈkɔːtjɑːd ˈकॉट्याड्/ *noun* [C] an area of ground, without a roof, that has walls or buildings around it, for example in a castle or between houses or flats आँगन, प्रांगण, मैदान

**cousin** /ˈkʌzn ˈकज़्न्/ (*also* **first cousin**) *noun* [C] the child of your aunt or uncle चाचा-चाची/मामा-मामी/मौसी-मौसा/बुआ-फूफा की संतान *Seema and I are cousins.* **NOTE** शब्द **cousin** चचेरे, फुफेरे ममेरे, मौसेरे भाई और बहिन दोनों के लिए प्रयुक्त होता है। ➪ **second cousin** देखिए।

**covalent** /ˌkəʊˈveɪlənt ˌको ˈव़ेलन्ट्/ *adj.* (*technical*) (used about the way atoms are joined together) sharing an **electron** सहसंयुक्त, अणुओं का सहसंयोजन-प्रकार; सहसंयोजक

**cove** /kəʊv कोव़्/ *noun* [C] a small area of the coast where the land curves round so that it is protected from the wind, etc. छोटी खाड़ी *a sandy cove*

**covenant** /ˈkʌvənənt ˈकव़नन्ट्/ *noun* [C] a promise to sb, or a legal agreement, especially one to pay a regular amount of money to sb/sth प्रतिज्ञापत्र या क़ानूनी समझौता, वचन पत्र (विशेषत: किसी को नियमित रूप से धनराशि देने के विषय में) ► **covenant** *verb* [T] लिखित वचन देना *All profits are covenanted to local charities.*

**cover[1]** /ˈkʌvə(r) ˈकव़(र्)/ *verb* [T] **1 cover sb/sth (up/over) (with sth)** to put sth on or in front of sth to hide or protect it छिपाने या बचाने के लिए ढकना *I covered the floor with newspaper before I started painting.* ○ (*figurative*) *Prachi laughed to cover* (= hide) *her embarrassment.* ✪ विलोम **uncover 2 cover sb/sth in/with sth** to be on the surface of sth; to make sth do this सतह पर फैलना या फैलाना *Porters covered the walls.* ○ *The eruption of the volcano covered the town in a layer of ash.* **3** to fill or spread over a certain area क्षेत्र-विशेष में फैल जाना *The floods cover an area of about 15,000 square kilometres.* **4** to include or to deal with sth शामिल करना या निपटना *All the papers covered the election in depth.* ○ *The course covered both American and European history.* **5** to travel a certain distance कोई दूरी विशेष तय करना *We covered about 500 kilometres that day.* **6** to be enough money for sth (किसी आवश्यकता के लिए) पर्याप्त धन होना *We'll give you some money to cover your expenses.* **7 cover sb/sth against/for sth** to protect sb/sth by insurance बीमा द्वारा सुरक्षित करना *The insurance policy covers us for any damage to our property.* **8 cover (for sb)** to do sb's job while he/she is away from work किसी की अनुपस्थिति में उसका काम करना *Mr Mehta's phoned in sick so we'll have to find someone to cover (for him).*

**IDM cover the cost (of sth)** to have or make enough money to pay for sth भुगतान करने के लिए पर्याप्त धनराशि होना

**PHR V cover sth up** to prevent people hearing about a mistake or sth bad ग़लतियों की जानकारी जनता को न होने देना *The police have been accused of trying to cover up the facts of the case.*

**cover up for sb** to hide a person's mistakes or crimes in order to protect him/her किसी की ग़लतियों और दोषों को छिपाना (उसके बचाव के लिए)

**cover[2]** /ˈkʌvə(r) ˈकव़(र्)/ *noun* **1** [C] something that is put on or over sth, especially in order to protect it (सुरक्षा के लिए) आवरण, ढक्कन *a plastic cover for a computer* ○ *a duvet cover* **2** [C] the outside part of a book or magazine पुस्तक या पत्रिका का आवरण-पृष्ठ *I read the magazine from cover to cover* (= from beginning to end). **3** [U] **cover (against sth)** insurance against sth, so that if sth bad happens you get money or help in return सुरक्षा के लिए बीमा, सुरक्षा-कवच, बीमा-कवर *The policy **provides cover** against theft.* **4** [U] protection from the weather, damage, etc. ख़राब मौसम, हानि आदि से बचाव; बचाव का उपाय *When the storm started we had to **take cover** in a shop doorway.* ○ *When the gunfire started everyone **ran for cover**.* ✪ पर्याय **shelter 5 the covers** [*pl.*] the sheets, etc. on a bed पलंग की चादरें **6** [C, U] **a cover (for sth)** something that hides what sb is really doing असलियत को छिपाने का साधन *The whole company was just a cover for all kinds of criminal activities.* ○ *police officers working **under cover*** **7** [U] doing sb's job for him/her while he/she is away from work किसी की अनुपस्थिति में उसका काम करने वाला व्यक्ति; स्थानापन्न व्यक्ति *Manisha's off next week so we'll have to arrange cover.*

**IDM under (the) cover of sth** hidden by sth की आड़ में, की ओट में *They attacked under cover of darkness.*

**coverage** /ˈkʌvərɪdʒ ˈकव़रिज्/ *noun* [U] **1** the act or amount of reporting on an event in newspapers, on television, etc. समाचार पत्र या टेलीविज़न पर प्रस्तुत घटना-विवरण *TV coverage of the Olympic Games was excellent.* **2** the amount or quality of information included in a book, magazine, etc. पुस्तक आदि में संगृहीत सूचना या जानकारी की मात्रा या गुणवत्ता *The grammar section provides coverage of all the most problematic areas.*

**coveralls** /ˈkʌvərɔːlz ˈकव़रॉल्ज़्/ (*AmE*) = **overall[2]**

**covering** /ˈkʌvərɪŋ ˈकव़रिङ्/ *noun* [C] something that cover the surface of sth आवरण, चादर, जिल्द *there was a thick covering of dust over everything.*

**covering letter** *noun* [C] a letter that you send with other documents, a package, etc. that gives more information about it किसी दस्तावेज़ आदि के साथ जाने वाला पत्र जिसमें उसके विषय में आवश्यक जानकारी होती है; सहपत्र

**covert** /ˈkʌvət ˈकव़ट्/ *adj.* done secretly गुप्त, छिपकर किया गया *a covert police operation* ▶ **covertly** *adv.* गुप्त रूप से; छिपाकर

**cover-up** *noun* [C] an act of preventing sth bad or dishonest from becoming known बेईमानी का छिपाव *Several newspapers claimed that there had been a government cover-up.*

**covet** /ˈkʌvət ˈकव़ट्/ *verb* [T] (*formal*) to want to have sth very much (especially sth that belongs to sb else) लालच, लोभ करना, ललचाना (विशेषतः किसी दूसरे की वस्तु के लिए)

**covetous** /ˈkʌvətəs ˈकव़टस्/ *adj.* (*formal*) having a strong desire for the things that other people have, especially wealth धनलोलुप ▶ **covetousness** *noun* [U] धनलोलुपता

**cow** /kaʊ काउ/ *noun* [C] **1** a large female animal that is kept on farms to produce milk गाय *to milk a cow* ○ *a herd of cows*

> **NOTE** नर और मादा जानवर दोनों को प्रायः **cow** कह देते हैं। नर पशु के लिए विशेष शब्द **bull** है। प्रजनन में असमर्थ और भार ढोने वाले नर पशु को **ox** कहते हैं। गाय के बच्चे को **calf** कहते हैं। बहुत सारी गायों के लिए सामूहिक शब्द **cattle** है।

**2** the adult female of certain large animals, for example elephants हाथी आदि जैसे कुछ बड़े आकार के पशुओं की वयस्क मादा

**coward** /ˈkaʊəd ˈकाउअड्/ *noun* [C] a person who has no courage and is afraid in dangerous or unpleasant situations कायर, डरपोक ▶ **cowardly** *adj.* कायरता से

**cowardice** /ˈkaʊədɪs ˈकाउअडिस्/ *noun* [U] a lack of courage; behaviour that shows that you are afraid कायरता

**cowboy** /ˈkaʊbɔɪ ˈकाउबॉइ/ *noun* [C] a man whose job is to look after cows (usually on a horse) in certain parts of the US घोड़े पर सवार चरवाहा (अमेरिका के कुछ भागों में)

**cower** /ˈkaʊə(r) ˈकाउअ(र्)/ *verb* [I] to move back or into a low position because of fear डर के मारे पीछे हटना या दुबक कर बैठ जाना *The dog cowered under the table when the storm started.*

**cowl** /kaʊl काउल्/ *noun* [C] a covering for the head that is worn especially by a man belonging to a religious group (**a monk**) महंतों, साधुओं की टोपी

**coy** /kɔɪ कॉइ/ *adj.* pretending to be shy or innocent दिखावटी तौर पर लज्जालु या भोला *She lifted her head a little and gave him a coy smile.* ▶ **coyly** *adv.* संकोचपूर्वक

**cozy** = **cosy**

**CPU**/ˌsiːpiːˈjuː ˌसी पी ˈयू/ *abbr.* = central processing unit सैंट्रल प्रॉसेसिंग युनिट

**crab** /kræb क्रैब्/ *noun* **1** [C] a sea animal with a flat shell and ten legs. The front two legs have long curved points (**pincers**) on them. Crabs move sideways केकड़ा **2** [U] the meat from a crab केकड़े का मांस ➪ **shellfish** पर चित्र देखिए।

**crack[1]** /kræk क्रैक्/ *verb* **1** [I, T] to break or to make sth break so that a line appears on the surface, but without breaking into pieces चटकना, दरकना; दरार पड़ना *Don't put boiling water into that glass—it'll crack.* ○ *The stone cracked the window but didn't break it.* **2** [T] to break sth open फ़ोड़ना, चटकाना, तोड़ना *Crack two eggs into a bowl.* **3** [I, T] to make a sudden loud, sharp sound; to cause sth to make this sound कड़क की आवाज़ करना, कड़कना; कड़काना *to crack a whip/your knuckles* **4** [T] to hit a part of your body against sth; to hit sb with sth शरीर के अंग का किसी से टकराना; किसी पर चोट करना *She stood up and cracked her head on the cupboard door.* ○ *She cracked the thief over the head with her umbrella.* **5** [I] to no longer be able to deal with pressure and so lose control दबाव को झेल न पाना और नियंत्रण खो बैठना *He cracked under the strain of all his problems.* **6** [I] (used about sb's voice) to suddenly change in a way that is not controlled आवाज़ का एकाएक बदल जाना (कि उस पर नियंत्रण न रहे) *Her voice cracked as she spoke about her* *parents' death.* **7** [T] (*informal*) to solve a problem समस्या का हल निकाल लेना *to crack a code* ○ *The police have cracked an international drug-smuggling ring.* **8** [T] to tell or make a joke चुटकुला सुनाना *Stop cracking jokes and do some work!*

IDM **get cracking** (*informal*) to start doing sth immediately तुरंत कोई काम करने लगना *I have to finish this job today so I'd better get cracking.*

PHRV **crack down (on sb/sth)** (used about people in authority) to start dealing strictly with bad or illegal behaviour अधिकारियों का अपराधों से निपटने की कड़ी कार्रवाई में लग जाना *The police have started to crack down on drug dealers.*

**crack up 1** (*informal*) to be unable to deal with pressure and so lose control and become mentally ill तनाव को न झेल पाने के कारण मानसिक संतुलन खो बैठना *He cracked up when his wife left him.* **2** (*slang*) to suddenly start laughing, especially when you should be serious एकाएक हँसने लगना, विशेषतः जब गंभीरता की आवश्यकता हो

**crack²** /kræk क्रैक्/ *noun* **1** [C] a line on the surface of sth where it has broken, but not into separate pieces दरार, दरक *a pane of glass with a crack in it* ○ (*figurative*) *They had always seemed happy together, but then cracks began to appear in their relationship.* **2** [C] a narrow opening बारीक दरार या छेद *a crack in the curtains* **3** [C] a sudden loud, sharp sound अचानक उत्पन्न कड़क ध्वनि *There was a loud crack as the gun went off.* **4** [C] a hard hit on a part of the body शरीर पर कड़ी चोट; चटक *Suddenly a golf ball gave him a nasty crack on the head.* **5** [C] (*informal*) an amusing, often critical, comment; a joke व्यंग्यपूर्ण टिप्पणी; परिहास चुटकुला *She **made a crack** about his bald head and he got angry.* **6** [U] a dangerous and illegal drug that some people take for pleasure and cannot then stop taking ख़तरनाक व ग़ैर-क़ानूनी नशीला पदार्थ

IDM **the crack of dawn** very early in the morning बहुत सवेरे

**have a crack (at sth/at doing sth)** (*informal*) to try to do sth कुछ करने का प्रयत्न करना *I'm not sure how to play but I'll have a crack at it.*

**crack³** /kræk क्रैक्/ *adj.* (used about soldiers or sports players) very well trained and skilful सुप्रशिक्षित (सैनिक या खिलाड़ी) *crack troops* ○ *He's a crack shot* (= very accurate at shooting) *with a rifle.*

**crackdown** /ˈkrækdaʊn ˈक्रैक्डाउन्/ *noun* [C] action to stop bad or illegal behaviour अपराध रोकने की कार्रवाई, कड़ाई *Fifty people have been arrested in a police crackdown on street crime.*

**cracker** /ˈkrækə(r) ˈक्रैक(र्)/ *noun* [C] a thin dry biscuit that is often eaten with cheese पनीर के साथ खाया जाने वाला पतला कुरकुरा बिस्कुट

**crackle** /ˈkrækl ˈक्रैक्ल्/ *verb* [I] to make a series of short, sharp sounds चट-चट की लगातार आवाज़ करना *The radio started to crackle and then it stopped working.* ▶ **crackle** *noun* [*sing.*] चट-चट की लगातार आवाज़ *the crackle of dry wood burning*

**cradle¹** /ˈkreɪdl ˈक्रेड्ल्/ *noun* [C] a small bed for a baby. Cradles can often be moved from side to side बच्चे का पालना

**cradle²** /ˈkreɪdl ˈक्रेड्ल्/ *verb* [T] to hold sb/sth carefully and gently in your arms सावधानी और कोमलता से किसी को हाथों में सँभालना

**craft** /krɑːft क्राफ़्ट्/ *noun* **1** [C, U] a job or activity for which you need skill with your hands हस्तशिल्पी, दस्तकारी *an arts and crafts exhibition* ○ *I studied craft and design at school.* ➪ **handicraft** देखिए। **2** [C] any job or activity for which you need skill कोई भी कार्य जिसमें कौशल की आवश्यकता हो *He regards acting as a craft.* **3** [C] (*pl.* **craft**) a boat, aircraft or spacecraft नाव, विमान या अंतरिक्षयान

**craftsman** /ˈkrɑːftsmən ˈक्राफ़्ट्स्मन्/ *noun* [C] (*pl.* **-men** /-men -मेन्/) a person who makes things skilfully, especially with his/her hands हस्तशिल्पी, दस्तकार ✪ पर्याय **artisan**

**craftsmanship** /ˈkrɑːftsmənʃɪp ˈक्राफ़्ट्स्मन्शिप्/ *noun* [U] the skill used by sb to make sth of high quality with his/her hands शिल्पकारिता, कारीगरी

**crafty** /ˈkrɑːfti ˈक्राफ़्टि/ *adj.* clever at getting or achieving things by using unfair or dishonest methods धूर्त, चालाक, चालबाज़ ▶ **craftily** *adv.* धूर्तता से

**crag** /kræg क्रैग्/ *noun* [C] a steep, rough rock on a hill or mountain किसी पर्वत या पहाड़ी पर खड़ी चट्टान

**craggy** /krægi क्रैगि/ *adj.* **1** having a lot of steep rough rock चट्टानी, पथरीला **2** (used about a man's face) strong and with deep lines, especially in an attractive way पुरुष का रोबीला पर आकर्षक (चेहरा)

**cram** /kræm क्रैम्/ *verb* (**cra<u>mm</u>ing; cra<u>mm</u>ed**) **1** [T] to push people or things into a small space (वस्तुओं या व्यक्तियों को तंग स्थान में) ठूँसना *I managed to cram all my clothes into the bag but*

*I couldn't close it.* ○ *We only spent two days in Shimla but we managed to cram a lot of sight-seeing in.* **2** [I] to move, with a lot of other people, into a small space अनेक व्यक्तियों के साथ तंग स्थान में घुस जाना; ठसाठस भर जाना *He only had a small car but they all managed to cram in.* **3** [I] to study very hard and learn a lot in a short time before an exam परीक्षा से पूर्व बहुत कम समय में बहुत पढ़ाई करना; रटना, रट्टा मारना

**crammed** /kræmd क्रैम्ड्/ *adj.* very or too full ठसाठस भरा हुआ; भरपूर *That book is crammed with useful information.*

**cramp** /kræmp क्रैम्प्/ *noun* [U] a sudden pain that you get in a muscle, that makes it difficult to move मांसपेशी में अचानक हुई दर्दभरी ऐंठन

**cramped** /kræmpt क्रैम्प्ट्/ *adj.* not having enough space सँकरा और सीमित; तंग *The flat was terribly cramped with so many of us living there.*

**cranberry** /ˈkrænbəri ˈक्रैन्बरि/ *noun* [C] (*pl.* **cranberries**) a small red berry with a sour taste, that can be made into sauce or juice खट्टी छोटी लाल बेरी (रस या चटनी बनाने में प्रयुक्त)

**crane[1]** /kreɪn क्रेन्/ *noun* [C] **1** a large machine with a long metal arm that is used for moving or lifting heavy objects भारी वज़न उठाने की बड़ी मशीन; क्रेन **2** a large water bird with long legs and a long neck सारस

**crane[2]** /kreɪn क्रेन्/ *verb* [I, T] to stretch your neck forward in order to see or hear sth कुछ देखने या सुनने के लिए गरदन बाहर को निकालना *We all craned forward to get a better view.*

**crane fly** *noun* [C] a small flying insect with very long legs उड़ सकने वाला छोटा कीड़ा जिसकी टाँगें बहुत लंबी होती हैं

**cranium** /ˈkreɪniəm ˈक्रेनिअम्/ *noun* [*sing.*] (*formal*) the bone inside your head ✪ पर्याय **skull** कपाल, खोपड़ी ▸ **cranial** *adj.* कपाल-संबंधी

**crank** /kræŋk क्रैङ्क्/ *noun* [C] a person with strange ideas or who behaves in a strange way झक्की; सनकी व्यक्ति

**cranny** /ˈkræni ˈक्रैनि/ *noun* [C] (*pl.* **crannies**) a small opening in a wall, rock, etc. दीवार, चट्टान आदि में छोटा-सा छेद

**IDM every nook and cranny** ➪ **nook** देखिए।

**crash[1]** /kræʃ क्रैश्/ *verb* **1** [I, T] to have an accident in a vehicle; to drive a vehicle into sth (गाड़ी आदि का) टकराना; गाड़ी को किसी जगह पर मार देना *He braked too late and crashed into the car in front.* **2** [I] to hit sth hard, making a loud noise धमाके के साथ किसी से टकरा जाना *The tree crashed to the ground.* **3** [I] to make a loud noise धमाका करना *I could hear thunder crashing outside.* **4** [I] (used about money or business) to suddenly lose value or fail (व्यापार, क़ीमतें आदि) अचानक गिर जाना **5** [I] (used about a computer) to suddenly stop working (कंप्यूटर का) काम करना एकाएक बंद हो जाना *We lost the data when the computer crashed.*

**crash[2]** /kræʃ क्रैश्/ *noun* [C] **1** a sudden loud noise made by sth breaking, hitting sth, etc. किसी वस्तु के गिरने या टूटने से उत्पन्न धमाका, ज़ोर की आवाज़ *I heard a crash and ran outside.* **2** an accident when a car or other vehicle hits sth and is damaged वाहन की टक्कर से हुई दुर्घटना *a car/plane crash* **3** (used about money or business) a sudden fall in the value or price of sth व्यापार या मूल्य में अचानक गिरावट *the Stock Market crash* **4** a sudden failure of a machine, especially a computer कंप्यूटर आदि किसी मशीन में एकाएक आई ख़राबी

**crash[3]** /kræʃ क्रैश्/ *adj.* done in a very short period of time लघु अवधि में किया गया; अल्पकालिक, गहन *She did a* ***crash course*** *in French before going to work in France.*

**crash barrier** *noun* [C] a fence that keeps people or vehicles apart, for example when there are large crowds or between the two sides of the road लोगों और वाहनों की भिड़ंत रोकने के लिए लगा अवरोध

**crash helmet** *noun* [C] a hard hat worn by motorbike riders, racing drivers, etc. मोटर-साइकिल, स्कूटर सवारों आदि द्वारा पहना जाने वाला सख़्त टोप

**crash-land** *verb* [I] to land a plane in a dangerous way in an emergency संकटकाल में विमान का ख़तरनाक तरीक़े से उतरना ▸ **crash-landing** *noun* [C] ख़तरनाक तरीक़े से उतरना, ध्वंस-अवतारण *to make a crash-landing*

**crass** /kræs क्रैस्/ *adj.* stupid, showing that you do not understand sth अत्यंत मूर्ख, ठस दिमाग *It was a crass comment to make when he knew how upset she was.*

**crate** /kreɪt क्रेट्/ *noun* [C] a large box in which goods are carried or stored सामान को इकट्ठा कर ले जाने का बड़ा बक़्सा

**crater** /ˈkreɪtə(r) ˈक्रेट(र्)/ *noun* [C] **1** a large hole in the ground ज़मीन में बड़ा गड्ढा *The bomb left a large crater.* ○ *craters on the moon* **2** the hole in the top of a mountain through which hot gases and liquid rock are forced (**a volcano**) ज्वालामुखी का मुँह जिसमें से गरम गैसें और लावा निकलता है ➪ **volcano** पर चित्र देखिए।

**cravat** /krəˈvæt क्रˈवैट्/ *noun* [C] a wide piece of cloth that some men tie around their neck and wear inside the collar of their shirt गुलूबंद

**crave** /kreɪv क्रेव्/ *verb* [I, T] **crave (for) sth** to want and need to have sth very much किसी वस्तु के लिए अत्यधिक लालायित होना, ज़ोरदार तलब उठना; तरसना

**craving** /ˈkreɪvɪŋ ˈक्रेविङ्/ *noun* [C] a strong desire for sth किसी वस्तु के लिए तीव्र लालसा, गहरी ललक, ज़ोरदार तलब *When she was pregnant she used to **have cravings for** all sorts of peculiar food.*

**crawl[1]** /krɔːl क्रॉल्/ *verb* [I] **1** to move slowly with your body on or close to the ground, or on your hands and knees हाथों और घुटनों के बल चलना; रेंगना *Their baby has just started to crawl.* ○ *An insect crawled across the floor.* **2** (used about vehicles) to move very slowly (वाहनों का) बहुत धीरे-धीरे चलना, रेंगना *The traffic crawls through the centre of town in the rush-hour.* **3** (*informal*) **crawl (to sb)** to be very polite or pleasant to sb in order to be liked or to gain sth किसी की खुशामद करना

**IDM be crawling with sth** to be completely full of or covered with unpleasant animals (किसी स्थान का) कीड़ों-मकोड़ों से भर जाना; (किसी स्थान पर) कीड़े-मकोड़े भर जाना *The kitchen was crawling with insects.* ○ (*figurative*) *The village is always crawling with tourists at this time of year.*

**crawl[2]** /krɔːl क्रॉल्/ *noun* **1** [*sing.*] a very slow speed बहुत धीमी गति, रेंग *The traffic slowed to a crawl.* **2** (*often* **the crawl**) [*sing.*, U] a style of swimming which you do on your front. When you do the crawl, you move first one arm and then the other over your head, turn your face to one side so that you can breathe and kick up and down with your legs एक प्रकार की तैराक़ी

**crayfish** /ˈkreɪfɪʃ ˈक्रेफ़िश्/ (*AmE* **crawfish** /ˈkrɔːfɪʃ ˈक्रॉफ़िश्/) *noun* [C, U] a shellfish that lives in rivers, lakes or the sea and can be eaten. A crayfish is similar to, but smaller than a **lobster** समुद्र, नदी या झील में रहने वाली एक प्रकार की शंखमीन, चिंगट

**crayon** /ˈkreɪən ˈक्रेइअन्/ *noun* [C, U] a soft, thick, coloured pencil that is used for drawing or writing, especially by children नरम, मोटी रंगीन खड़िया या पेंसिल जिससे बच्चे चित्र बनाते हैं या लिखते हैं ▶ **crayon** *verb* [I, T] रंगीन खड़िया से चित्र बनाना या लिखना

**craze** /kreɪz क्रेज़्/ *noun* [C] **a craze (for sth) 1** a strong interest in sth, that usually only lasts for a short time किसी बात में प्रायः अस्थायी या अल्पकालिक परंतु गहरी दिलचस्पी; सनक, धुन, पागलपन *There was a craze for that kind of music last year.* **2** something that a lot of people are very interested in बहुत-से लोगों को अत्यधिक पसंद वस्तु; दीवाना बना देने वाली चीज़ *cellphones are the latest craze among teenagers.*

**crazy** /ˈkreɪzi ˈक्रेज़ि/ *adj.* (**crazier; craziest**) (*informal*) **1** very silly or foolish सनकी, पागल, मूर्ख *You must be crazy to turn down such a wonderful offer.* **2** very angry बहुत क्रोधित *She **goes crazy** when people criticize her.* **3 crazy about sb/sth** liking sb/sth very much किसी वस्तु के लिए अत्यंत उत्साही; दीवाना, बावला *He's always been crazy about horses.* **4** showing great excitement अति उत्तेजित, पागल *The fans **went crazy** when their team scored the first goal.* ▶ **crazily** *adv.* पागलपन से ▶ **craziness** *noun* [U] पागलपन

**creak** /kriːk क्रीक्/ *verb* [I] to make the noise of wood bending or of sth not moving smoothly लकड़ी के मुड़ने से या ऐसी आवाज़ होना; चरचराना, चरमराना *The floorboards creaked when I walked across the room.* ▶ **creak** *noun* [C] चरचराहट, चरमराहट ▶ **creaky** *adj.* चरमराता, चरचराता हुआ *creaky stairs*

**cream[1]** /kriːm क्रीम्/ *noun* **1** [U] the thick yellowish-white liquid that rises to the top of milk मलाई, क्रीम *coffee with cream* ○ *whipped cream* (= cream that has been beaten) **2** [C, U] a substance that you rub into your skin to keep it soft or as a medical treatment मलहम *(an) antiseptic cream* **3 the cream** [*sing.*] the best part of sth or the best people in a group किसी वस्तु का सर्वोत्तम अंश या किसी समुदाय के सर्वश्रेष्ठ व्यक्ति

**cream[2]** /kriːm क्रीम्/ *adj. noun* [U] (of) a yellowish-white colour हलका पीला; (लगभग) सफेद रंग का

**cream[3]** /kriːm क्रीम्/ *verb*

**PHR V cream sb/sth off** to take away the best people or part from sth for a particular purpose उद्देश्य-विशेष से किसी वस्तु का सर्वोत्तम अंश या किसी वर्ग के सर्वश्रेष्ठ व्यक्तियों को ले जाना *The big clubs cream off the country's best young players.*

**creamy** /ˈkriːmi ˈक्रीमी/ *adj.* (**creamier; creamiest**) **1** containing cream; thick and smooth like cream मलाईदार; क्रीम के समान गाढ़ा और चिकना *a creamy sauce* **2** having a light colour like cream क्रीम जैसे हलके रंग का *creamy skin*

**crease[1]** /kri:s क्रीस्/ *noun* [C] **1** an untidy line on paper, material, a piece of clothing, etc. that should not be there काग़ज़ आदि पर बनी टेढ़ी-मेढ़ी रेखा या कपड़े पर बनी सिलवट *Your shirt needs ironing, it's full of creases.* ○ *When I unrolled the poster, there was a crease in it.* **2** a tidy straight line that you make in sth, for example when you fold it तह लगाते समय बनी साफ़-सुथरी सीधी रेखा *He had a sharp crease in his trousers.*

**crease[2]** /kri:s क्रीस्/ *verb* [I, T] to get creases; to make sth get creases सिलवटें पड़ना; सिलवटें डालना *Hang up your jacket or it will crease.* ○ *Crease the paper carefully down the middle.*

**create** /kriˈeɪt क्रिˈएट्/ *verb* [T] to cause sth new to happen or exist कुछ नया उत्पन्न, रचना, बनाना, करना; अस्तित्व में लाना *a plan to create new jobs in the company* ○ *He created a bad impression at the interview.*

**creation** /kriˈeɪʃn क्रिˈएश्न्/ *noun* **1** [U] the act of causing sth new to happen or exist कोई नई वस्तु बनाने या अस्तित्व में लाने की क्रिया; नवनिर्माण *the creation of new independent states* ➪ **job creation** देखिए। **2** (*usually* **the Creation**) [*sing.*] the act of making the whole universe, as described in the Bible सृष्टि या ब्रह्मांड की रचना, विशेषतः जैसे बाइबल में वर्णित है **3** [C] something new that sb has made or produced नई रचना, नवनिर्माण

**creative** /kriˈeɪtɪv क्रिˈएटिव्/ *adj.* (*only before a noun*) **1** involving the use skill or imagination to make or do new things कौशल या कल्पना के प्रयोग से रचना करते हुए; रचनात्मक, सृजनात्मक *She's a fantastic designer—she's so creative.* **2** connected with producing new things सृजनात्मक, सृजनकारी *His creative life went on until he was well over 80 years.* ► **creatively** *adv.* सृजनात्मक रीति से

**creativity** /ˌkri:eiˈtɪvəti ˌक्रीएˈटिव़टि/ *noun* [U] the ability to make or produce new things using skill or imagination सृजन-क्षमता *We want teaching that encourages children's creativity.*

**creator** /kriˈeɪtə(r) क्रिˈएट(र्)/ *noun* [C] a person who makes or produces sth new सृजनकर्ता

**creature** /ˈkri:tʃə(r) ˈक्रीच(र्)/ *noun* [C] a living thing such as an animal, a bird, a fish or an insect, but not a plant पशु, पक्षी आदि प्राणी (परंतु पौधे नहीं); जीव *sea creatures*

**crèche** /kreʃ क्रेश्/ *noun* [C] a place where small children are looked after while their parents are working, shopping, etc. माता-पिता की अनुपस्थिति में शिशुओं की देखभाल का स्थान; शिशुसदन, शिशुगृह

**credentials** /krəˈdenʃlz क्रˈडेन्श्ल्ज़्/ *noun* [*pl.*] **1** the qualities, experience, etc. that make sb suitable for sth व्यक्ति के गुण, अनुभव आदि जिनसे वह कार्य-विशेष के लिए उपयुक्त माना जाता है *He has the perfect credentials for the job.* **2** a document that is proof that you have the training, education, etc. necessary to do sth, or proof that you are who you say you are व्यक्ति की शिक्षा, ट्रेनिंग आदि की सत्यता को प्रभावित करने वाला दस्तावेज़; प्रत्यय-पत्र

**credibility** /ˌkredəˈbɪləti ˌक्रेडˈबिलटि/ *noun* [U] the quality that sb has that makes people believe or trust him/her विश्वास योग्य होने का गुण; विश्वसनीयता, विश्वास्यता *The Prime Minister had lost all credibility and had to resign.*

**credible** /ˈkredəbl ˈक्रेडब्ल्/ *adj.* **1** that you can believe विश्वसनीय; विश्वास करने योग्य *It's hardly credible that such a thing could happen without him knowing it.* ✪ विलोम **incredible** **2** that seems possible संभव होने योग्य; संभाव्य *We need to think of a credible alternative to nuclear energy.*

**credit[1]** /ˈkredɪt ˈक्रेडिट्/ *noun* **1** [U] a way of buying goods or services and not paying for them until later उधार *I bought the television **on credit**.* **2** [C, U] a sum of money that a bank, etc. lends to sb बैंक आदि द्वारा प्रदत्त ऋण *The company was not able to get any further credit and went bankrupt.* **3** [U] having money in an account at a bank बैंक के खाते में धनराशि की स्थिति *No bank charges are made if your account remains **in credit**.* **4** [C] a payment made into an account at a bank बैंक खाते में जमा की गई धनराशि *There have been several credits to her account over the last month.* ✪ विलोम **debit[1]** **5** [U] an act of saying that sb has done sth well श्रेय, प्रतिष्ठा *He **got all the credit** for the success of the project.* ○ *I can't **take** any **credit**; the others did all the work.* ○ *She didn't do very well but at least **give** her **credit for** trying.* **6** [*sing.*] **a credit to sb/sth** a person or thing that you should be proud of गर्व करने योग्य व्यक्ति या वस्तु; गौरव *She is a credit to her school.* **7 the credits** [*pl.*] the list of the names of the people who made a film or television programme, shown at the beginning or end of the film फ़िल्म आदि के आरंभ या अंत में प्रदर्शित उन व्यक्तियों की नामावली जिन्होंने फ़िल्म या कार्यक्रम निर्माण में सहयोग दिया **8** [C] a part of a course at a college or university, that a student has completed successfully महाविद्यालय या विश्वविद्यालय में छात्र द्वारा सफलतापूर्वक पूरा किया गया अध्ययन; पाठ्यक्रमांश

IDM **do sb credit** (used about sb's qualities or achievements) to be so good that people should be proud of him/her (गुणों और उपलब्धियों के आधार पर) लोगों के आदर और प्रशंसा का पात्र बनना *His courage and optimism do him credit.*

**(be) to sb's credit** used for showing that you approve of sth that sb has done, although you have criticized him/her for sth else किसी को किसी बात का श्रेय देना (यद्यपि उसका कोई अन्य आचरण उपयुक्त न था) *The company, to its credit, apologized and refunded my money.*

**have sth to your credit** to have finished sth that is successful सफलता के लिए यशस्वी होना *He has three best-selling novels to his credit.*

**credit²** /ˈkredɪt ˈक्रेडिट्/ *verb* [T] **1** to add money to a bank account बैंक खाते के जमापक्ष में धनराशि जोड़ना; खाते में जमा करना *Has the cheque been credited to my account yet?* **2 credit sb/sth with sth; credit sth to sb/sth** to believe or say that sb/sth has a particular quality or has done something well किसी व्यक्ति या वस्तु में कुछ विशिष्ट गुण मानना; श्रेय देना *Of course I wouldn't do such a stupid thing—credit me with a bit more sense than that!* **3** (*especially in negative sentences and questions*) to believe sth (कुछ) विश्वास करना, मानना *I simply cannot credit that he has made the same mistake again!*

**creditable** /ˈkredɪtəbl ˈक्रेडिटबल्/ *adj.* of a quite good standard that cannot be criticized, though not excellent अनिंदनीय गुणवत्ता का (हालाँकि श्रेष्ठ नहीं); प्रशंसनीय, श्रेयस्कर

**credit card** *noun* [C] a small plastic card that allows sb to get goods or services without using money. You usually receive a bill once a month for what you have bought एक प्लास्टिक निर्मित कार्ड जिस पर उधार ले सकते हैं और निश्चित अवधि के बाद भुगतान कर सकते हैं; क्रेडिट कार्ड *Can I pay by credit card?* ⇨ **cash card, cheque card** और **debit card** देखिए।

**credit note** *noun* [C] a letter that a shop gives you when you have returned sth and that allows you to have goods of the same value in exchange यह दिखाने वाला पत्र कि आपने कुछ सामान लौटाया है और उसके बदले उतनी क़ीमत का कुछ और ले सकते हैं; साख-पत्र, जमा-पत्र

**creditor** /ˈkredɪtə(r) ˈक्रेडिट(र्)/ *noun* [C] a person or company from whom you have borrowed money ऋणदाता, लेनदार (व्यक्ति या कंपनी)

**creed** /kriːd क्रीड्/ *noun* [C] a set of beliefs or principles (especially religious ones) that strongly influence sb's life धार्मिक मान्यताएँ और सिद्धांत जिनका किसी व्यक्ति पर विशेष प्रभाव होता है; मत, पथ, संप्रदाय

**creek** /kriːk क्रीक्/ *noun* [C] **1** a narrow piece of water where the sea flows into the land समुद्र की संकरी खाड़ी **2** a small river; a stream छोटी नदी; धारा

**creep¹** /kriːp क्रीप्/ *verb* [I] (*pt, pp* **crept** /krept क्रेप्ट्/) **1** to move very quietly and carefully so that nobody will notice you चुपचाप और सावधानी से चलना ताकि और कोई देख न सके, चुपके-से खिसकना *She crept into the room so as not to wake him up.* **2** to move forward slowly धीरे-धीरे आगे बढ़ना *The traffic was only creeping along.*

IDM **make your flesh creep** ⇨ **flesh** देखिए।

**creep in** to begin to appear प्रकट होने लगना *All sorts of changes are beginning to creep into the education system.*

**creep²** /kriːp क्रीप्/ *noun* [C] (*informal*) a person that you do not like because he/she tries too hard to be liked by people in authority अति खुशामदी व्यक्ति

IDM **give sb the creeps** (*informal*) to make sb feel frightened or nervous किसी को डरा देना या घबराहट में डाल देना

**creeper** /ˈkriːpə(r) ˈक्रीप(र्)/ *noun* [C] a plant that grows up trees or walls or along the ground वृक्षों, दीवारों के सहारे चढ़ने वाला या ज़मीन पर फैलने वाला पौधा

**creepy** /ˈkriːpi ˈक्रीपि/ *adj.* (*informal*) that makes you feel nervous or frightened सशंकित या भयभीत करने वाला

**cremate** /krəˈmeɪt क्रˈमेट्/ *verb* [T] to burn the body of a dead person as part of a funeral service दाह-कर्म करना, शवदाह करना ► **cremation** /krəˈmeɪʃn क्रˈमेश्न्/ *noun* [C, U] दाह-कर्म, शवदाह, दाह-संस्कार ⇨ **funeral** पर नोट देखिए।

**crematorium** /ˌkreməˈtɔːriəm ˌक्रमˈटॉरिअम्/ *noun* [C] a building in which the bodies of dead people are burned शवदाहगृह

**creosote** /ˈkriːəsəʊt ˈक्रीअसोट्/ *noun* [U] a thick brown liquid that is painted onto wood to protect it from rain, etc. लकड़ी पर लेपने का एक गाढ़ा भूरा द्रव (तेल)(जो लकड़ी को वर्षा के प्रभाव से बचाता है), क्रिओसोट तेल ► **creosote** *verb* [T] क्रिओसोट का लेप करना

**crêpe** (*also* **crepe**) /ˈkreɪp ˈक्रेप्/ *noun* **1** [U] a light thin material, made especially from cotton or another natural material (**silk**), with a surface that is covered in lines as if it has been folded सूत और रेशम के मिश्रण से बना धारीदार सतह वाला महीन कपड़ा; क्रेप *a crêpe bandage* **2** [U] a type of strong rubber with a rough surface, used for making the bottoms of shoes खुरदरी सतह वाला एक प्रकार का मज़बूत रबर (जिससे जूते की तली बनती है) *crêpe-soled shoes* **3** [C] a very thin type of round cake (**pancake**) एक प्रकार का पतला गोल केक (पैनकेक), मैदे और अंडे से बना मीठा पूआ

**crept** ➪ **creep**[1] का past tense और past participle रूप

**crescendo** /krəˈʃendəʊ क्रˈशेन्डो / *noun* [C, U] (*pl.* **crescendos**) a noise or piece of music that gets louder and louder (संगीत या ध्वनि) आरोह या उत्कर्ष स्वर ✪ विलोम **diminuendo**

**crescent** /ˈkresnt ˈक्रेसन्ट् / *noun* [C] **1** a curved shape that is pointed at both ends, like the moon in its first and last stages अर्धचंद्र या चाप जैसी आकृति (जैसी द्वितीया और अंतिम तिथियों में चंद्रमा की होती है) ➪ **shape** पर चित्र देखिए। **2** a street that is curved चाप के आकार की सड़क

**cress** /kres क्रेस् / *noun* [U] a small plant with very small green leaves that does not need to be cooked and is eaten raw in salads and sandwiches छोटा और बहुत छोटी हरी पत्तियों वाला चनसर नाम का पौधा जिसकी पत्तियों का सलाद बनता है

**crest** /krest क्रेस्ट् / *noun* [C] **1** a group of feathers on the top of a bird's head पक्षी के सिर पर की कलगी; शिखा **2** a design used as the symbol of a particular family, organization, etc., especially one that has a long history किसी प्राचीन कुल या संगठन का चिह्न विशेष; कुलचिह्न *the family/school crest* **3** the top part of a hill or wave किसी पहाड़ी या तरंग का शिखर *surfers riding the crest of the wave* ➪ **wave** पर चित्र देखिए।

**crestfallen** /ˈkrestfɔːlən ˈक्रेस्ट्फ़ॉलन् / *adj.* sad or disappointed दुखी या निराश

**crevasse** /krəˈvæs क्रˈवैस् / *noun* [C] a deep crack in a very thick layer of ice हिम की ख़ासी मोटी परत में गहरी दरार

**crevice** /ˈkrevɪs ˈक्रेविस् / *noun* [C] a narrow crack in a rock, wall, etc. चट्टान, दीवार आदि में सँकरी दरार

**crew** /kruː क्रू / *noun* [C, *with sing. or pl. verb*] **1** all the people who work on a ship, aircraft, etc. जहाज़, विमान आदि के सभी कर्मचारी **2** a group of people who work together एक साथ काम करने वालों का दस्ता *a camera crew* (= people who film things for television, etc.)

**crew cut** *noun* [C] a very short style of hair for men पुरुषों की छोटे बाल रखने की शैली; पुरुषों का लघु केश विन्यास

**crib**[1] /krɪb क्रिब् / = **cot**

**crib**[2] /krɪb क्रिब् / *verb* [I, T] (**cri<u>bb</u>ing; cri<u>bb</u>ed**) **crib (sth) (from/off sb)** to copy sb else's work and pretend it is your own दूसरे के काम की नक़ल कर उसे अपना बताना

**crick** /krɪk क्रिक् / *noun* [*sing.*] a pain in your neck, back, etc. that makes it difficult for you to move easily गरदन, पीठ आदि का दर्द जिससे आपका हिलना कठिन हो जाए ▶ **crick** *verb* [T] गरदन आदि में दर्द हो जाना *I've cricked my neck.*

**cricket** /ˈkrɪkɪt ˈक्रिकिट् / *noun* **1** [U] a game that is played with a bat and ball on a large area of grass by two teams of eleven players क्रिकेट का खेल, क्रिकेट **2** [C] an insect that makes a loud noise by rubbing its wings together झींगुर

**cricketer** /ˈkrɪkɪtə(r) ˈक्रिकिट(र्) / *noun* [C] a person who plays cricket क्रिकेट खिलाड़ी

**crime** /kraɪm क्राइम् / *noun* **1** [C] something which is illegal and which people are punished for, for example, by being sent to prison अपराध, जुर्म *to* ***commit a crime*** **2** [U] illegal behaviour or activities ग़ैर-क़ानूनी आचरण या गतिविधियाँ *There has been an increase in car crime recently.* ○ *to fight crime* **3** (*usually* **a crime**) [*sing.*] something that is morally wrong अनैतिक या अनुचित काम *It is a crime to waste food when people are starving.*

**crime wave** *noun* [*sing.*] a sudden increase in the number of crimes that are committed अपराधों में एकाएक वृद्धि

**criminal**[1] /ˈkrɪmɪnl ˈक्रिमिनल् / *noun* [C] a person who has done something illegal अपराधी, मुजरिम

**criminal**[2] /ˈkrɪmɪnl ˈक्रिमिनल् / *adj.* **1** (*only before a noun*) connected with crime अपराध से संबंधित; आपराधिक *Deliberate damage to public property is a* ***criminal offence***. ○ *criminal law* **2** morally wrong अनैतिक, अनुचित *a criminal waste of taxpayers' money*

**criminally** /ˈkrɪmɪnəli ˈक्रिमिनलि / *adv.* according to the laws that deal with crime अपराध-संबंधी क़ानूनों के अनुसार *criminally insane*

**criminology** /ˌkrɪmɪˈnɒlədʒi ˌक्रिमिˈनॉलजि / *noun* [U] the scientific study of crimes and criminals अपराध विज्ञान, अपराध और अपराधियों का वैज्ञानिक अध्ययन ▶ **criminologist** /-dʒɪst -जिस्ट् / *noun* [C] अपराध विज्ञानी ▶ **criminological** /ˌkrɪmɪnəˈlɒdʒɪkl ˌक्रिमिनˈलॉजिकल् / *adj.* अपराधविज्ञान-विषयक

**crimson** /ˈkrɪmzn ˈक्रिम्ज़्न् / *adj., noun* [U] (of) a dark red colour गहरे लाल रंग का; किरमिज़ी

**cringe** /krɪndʒ क्रिन्ज़् / *verb* [I] **1** to feel embarrassed झेंप जाना *awful family photographs which* ***make you cringe*** **2** to move away from sb/sth because you are frightened डर के मारे पीछे हट जाना *The dog cringed in terror when the man raised his arm.*

**crinkle** /ˈkrɪŋkl ˈक्रिङ्कल् / *verb* [I, T] **crinkle (sth) (up)** to have, or to make sth have, thin folds or lines in it सिलवटों से भरा होना या किसी में सिलवटें डालना *He crinkled the silver paper up into a ball.* ▶ **crinkly** /ˈkrɪŋkli ˈक्रिङ्कलि / *adj.* सिलवटें-भरा *crinkly material*

**cripple** /ˈkrɪpl ˈक्रिपल् / *verb* [T] (*usually passive*) **1** to damage sb's body so that he/she is no longer able to walk or move normally शरीर को अपंग बना देना *to be crippled with arthritis* **2** to seriously damage or harm sb/sth (किसी को) गंभीर रूप से क्षतिग्रस्त कर देना *The recession has crippled the motor industry.* ▶ **crippling** *adj.* अपंग बना देने वाला; बुरी तरह क्षतिग्रस्त करने वाला *They had crippling debts and had to sell their house.*

**crisis** /ˈkraɪsɪs ˈक्राइसिस् / *noun* [C, U] (*pl.* **crises** /-siːz -सीज़् /) a time of great danger or difficulty; the moment when things change and either improve or get worse घोर संकट या कठिनाई की घड़ी; वस्तुओं में परिवर्तन (सुधार या बिगाड़) का क्षण *the international crisis caused by the invasion* ○ *a friend you can rely on in times of crisis*

**crisp**[1] /krɪsp क्रिस्प् / *adj.* **1** pleasantly hard and dry कुरकुरा, खस्ता, करारा *Store the biscuits in a tin to keep them crisp.* **2** firm and fresh or new सख़्त और ताज़ा *a crisp salad/apple* ○ *a crisp cotton dress* **3** (used about the air or weather) cold and dry (मौसम या हवा) ठंडा और खुश्क *a crisp winter morning* **4** (used about the way sb speaks) quick, clear but not very friendly (बोलने की शैली) तुरंत, स्पष्ट पर कुछ रूखी *a crisp reply* ▶ **crisply** *adv.* तुरंत और रूखेपन से *'I disagree,' she said crisply.* ▶ **crispy** *adj.* (*informal*) = **crisp**[1] **1, 2**

**crisp**[2] /krɪsp क्रिस्प् / (*AmE* **chip; potato chip**) *noun* [C] a very thin piece of potato that is fried in oil, dried and then sold in packets. Crisps usually have salt or another flavouring on them तले हुए आलू के कतले जिन्हें बंद लिफ़ाफ़ों में बेचा जाता है *a packet of crisps*

**criss-cross** /ˈkrɪskrɒs ˈक्रिस् क्रॉस् / *adj.* (*only before a noun*) with many straight lines that cross over each other एक-दूसरे को काटती बहुत-सी सीधी रेखाओं वाला; ख़ानेदार *a criss-cross pattern* ▶ **criss-cross** *verb* [I, T] ख़ानेदार बनाना *Many footpaths crisscross the countryside.*

**criterion** /kraɪˈtɪəriən क्राइˈटिअरिअन् / *noun* [C] (*pl.* **criteria** /-riə -रिआ /) the standard that you use when you make a decision or form an opinion about sb/sth कसौटी, मानक, मापदंड *What are the criteria for deciding who gets a place on the course?*

**critic** /ˈkrɪtɪk ˈक्रिटिक् / *noun* [C] **1** a person who says what is bad or wrong with sb/sth दोष बताने वाला व्यक्ति; आलोचक, समीक्षक *He is a long-standing critic of the council's transport policy.* **2** a person whose job is to give his/her opinion about a play, film, book, work of art, etc. नाटक, फ़िल्म, पुस्तक आदि का समीक्षक *a film/restaurant/art critic*

**critical** /ˈkrɪtɪkl ˈक्रिटिकल् / *adj.* **1 critical (of sb/sth)** saying what is wrong with sb/sth दोषदर्शी, आलोचनात्मक *The report was very critical of safety standards on the railways.* **2** (*only before a noun*) describing the good and bad points of a play, film, book, work of art, etc. नाटक, फ़िल्म आदि के गुण-दोष बताते हुए *a critical guide to this month's new films* **3** dangerous or serious ख़तरनाक या गंभीर; नाज़ुक *The patient is* ***in a critical condition***. **4** very important; at a time when things can suddenly become better or worse अति महत्त्वपूर्ण; नाज़ुक दौर में *The talks between the two leaders have reached a critical stage.* ▶ **critically** /-ɪkli -टिक्लि/ *adv.* नाज़ुक तौर पर, संकटग्रस्त रूप से *a critically ill patient* ○ *a critically important decision*

**criticism** /ˈkrɪtɪsɪzəm ˈक्रिटिसिज़म् / *noun* **1** [C, U] (an expression of) what you think is bad about sb/sth आलोचना, निंदा, दोषन्वेषण *The council has* ***come in for*** *severe* ***criticism*** *over the plans.* **2** [U] the act of describing the good and bad points of a play, film, book, work of art, etc. नाटक, फ़िल्म आदि के गुण-दोष बताने का कार्य; समीक्षा *literary criticism*

**criticize** (*also* **-ise**) /ˈkrɪtɪsaɪz ˈक्रिटिसाइज़् / *verb* [I, T] **criticize (sb/sth) (for sth)** to say what is bad or wrong with sb/sth किसी की निंदा या आलोचना करना *The doctor was criticized for not sending the patient to the hospital.*

**critique** /krɪˈtiːk क्रिˈटीक्/ *noun* [C] a piece of writing that describes the good and bad points of sb/sth विवेचनात्मक टीका, समालोचना, समीक्षा

**croak** /krəʊk क्रोक् / *verb* [I] to make a harsh low noise like a particular animal (**a frog**) मेंढक का टर्र-टर्र करना ▶ **croak** *noun* [C] टर्र-टर्र की आवाज़

**crochet** /ˈkrəʊʃeɪ ˈक्रोशे / *noun* [U] a way of making clothes, cloth, etc. by using wool or cotton and a needle with a hook at one end क्रोशिए या काँटे से कपड़ों की बुनाई-कढ़ाई ▶ **crochet** *verb* [I, T] (*pt*, *pp* **crocheted** /-ʃeɪd -शेड्/) क्रोशिए से बुनाई-कढ़ाई करना ➪ **knit** देखिए।

**crockery** /ˈkrɒkəri ˈक्रॉकरि/ *noun* [U] cups, plates and dishes प्याले, प्लेटें और तश्तरियाँ; बर्तन

**crocodile** /ˈkrɒkədaɪl ˈक्रॉकडाइल्/ *noun* [C] a large reptile with a long tail and a big mouth with sharp teeth. Crocodiles live in rivers and lakes in hot countries मगरमच्छ, घड़ियाल ➪ **alligator** देखिए।

**crocus** /ˈkrəʊkəs ˈक्रोकस्/ *noun* [C] a small yellow, purple or white flower that grows in early spring वसंत के आरंभ में खिलने वाला छोटा पीला-बैंगनी या सफ़ेद फूल; केसर, क्रोकस

**croissant** /ˈkrwæsɒ̃ ˈक्रवैसाँ/ *noun* [C] a type of bread roll, shaped in a curve, that is often eaten with butter for breakfast प्रायः प्रातःकालीन जलपान में मक्खन के साथ खाया जाने वाला चंद्राकार ब्रेड रौल या लपेटवाँ डबलरोटी

**crony** /ˈkrəʊni ˈक्रोनि/ *noun* [C] (*pl.* **cronies**) (*informal*) (often used in a critical way) a friend यार, लंगोटिया दोस्त

**crook** /krʊk क्रुक्/ *noun* [C] **1** (*informal*) a dishonest person; a criminal बेईमान व्यक्ति; अपराधी **2** a bend or curve in sth (किसी वस्तु में) मोड़ या घुमाव *the crook of your arm* (= the inside of your elbow)

**crooked** /ˈkrʊkɪd ˈक्रुकिड्/ *adj.* **1** not straight or even मुड़ा-तुड़ा, टेढ़ा-मेढ़ा *That picture is crooked.* ○ *crooked teeth* **2** (*informal*) not honest बेईमान, कपटी *a crooked accountant*

**crop¹** /krɒp क्रॉप्/ *noun* **1** [C] all the grain, fruit, vegetables, etc. of one type that a farmer grows at one time फ़सल, पैदावार, उपज *a crop of apples* **2** [C, *usually pl.*] plants that are grown on farms for food अन्न के पौधे *Rice and soya beans are the main crops here.* **3** [*sing.*] a number of people or things which have appeared at the same time एक ही समय में प्रकट होने वाली अनेक वस्तुएँ या उपस्थित व्यक्ति *the recent crop of movies about aliens*

**crop²** /krɒp क्रॉप्/ *verb* (**cropping; cropped**) **1** [T] to cut sth very short काटकर बहुत छोटा करना *cropped hair* **2** [I] to produce a **crop¹ 1** फ़सल उगाना

**PHR V** **crop up** to appear suddenly, when you are not expecting it अप्रत्याशित रूप से एकाएक प्रकट होना *We should have finished this work yesterday but some problems cropped up.*

**cropper** /ˈkrɒpə(r) ˈक्रॉपर्/ *noun*

**IDM** **come a cropper** (*informal*) **1** to fall over or have an accident गिर पड़ना या दुर्घटनाग्रस्त हो जाना **2** to fail विफल हो जाना

**croquet** /ˈkrəʊkeɪ ˈक्रोके/ *noun* [U] a game that you play on grass. When you play croquet you use long wooden hammers (**mallets**) to hit balls through metal arches (**hoops**) घास के मैदान पर खेले जाने वाला खेल जिसमें लकड़ी के सोटों से गेंद को मार कर धातु-निर्मित मेहराबों में से निकाला जाता है

**crore** /krɔː(r) क्रॉ(र्)/ *noun* ten million; one hundred lakhs सौ लाख; एक करोड़

**cross¹** /krɒs क्रॉस्/ *noun* [C] **1** a mark that you make by drawing one line across another (×). The sign is used for showing the position of sth, for showing that sth is not correct, etc. काटा, काटे का चिह्न *I drew a cross on the map to show where our house is.* ○ *An incorrect answer is marked with a cross.* **2** (*also* **the Cross**) the two pieces of wood in the shape of a cross on which people were killed as a punishment in former times, or something in this shape (Ç) that is used as a symbol of the Christian religion क्रॉस, सूली, सलीब (इसे ईसाई धर्म का चिह्न माना जाता है) *She wore a gold cross round her neck.* ➪ **crucifix** देखिए। **3** [*usually sing.*] **a cross (between A and B)** something (especially a plant or an animal) that is a mixture of two different types of thing विभिन्न प्रकार के दो पशुओं या पौधों की संकर प्रजाति *a fruit which is a cross between a peach and an apple* **4** (in sports such as football) a kick or hit of the ball that goes across the front of the goal फ़ुटबॉल को मारा गया ऐसा किक जो गोल के सामने से आर-पार चला जाए

**IDM** **noughts and crosses** ➪ **nought** देखिए।

**cross²** /krɒs क्रॉस्/ *verb* **1** [I, T] **cross (over) (from sth/to sth)** to go from one side of sth to the other एक पार्श्व या पक्ष से दूसरे पार्श्व या पक्ष में जाना; पार करना *to cross the road* ○ *Which of the runners crossed the finishing line first?* **2** [I] (used about lines, roads, etc.) to pass across each other सड़कों, रेखाओं आदि का एक-दूसरे को काटना *The two roads cross just north of the village.* **3** [T] to put sth across or over sth else एक वस्तु के ऊपर दूसरी वस्तु को आर-पार या तिरछे रखना *to cross your arms* **4** [T] to make sb angry by refusing to do what he/she wants you to do किसी की बात न मानकर उसे क्रोधित कर देना *He's an important man. It could be dangerous to cross him.* **5** [T] **cross sth with sth** to produce a new type of plant or animal by mixing two different types पौधों या पशुओं के विभिन्न प्रकारों के मिश्रण से नई प्रजाति तैयार करना *If you cross a horse with a donkey, you get a mule.* **6** [I, T] (in sports such as football and hockey) to pass the ball across the front of the goal (फ़ुटबॉल, हॉकी आदि खेलों में) गेंद को गोल के सामने से आर-पार मारना

IDM **cross my heart (and hope to die)** (*spoken*) use for emphasizing that what you are saying is true जब इस बात पर बल देना हो कि जो कहा जा रहा है वह सच है

**cross your fingers; keep your fingers crossed** ➪ **finger**[1] देखिए।

**cross your mind** (used about a thought, idea, etc.) to come into your mind (विचार आदि) मन में आना; सूझना *It never once crossed my mind that she was lying.*

PHR V **cross sth off (sth)** to remove sth from a list, etc. by drawing a line through it आर-पार रेखा खींचकर सूची में से नाम काट देना *Cross Patel's name off the guest list—he can't come.*

**cross sth out** to draw a line through sth that you have written because you have made a mistake, etc. लिखे हुए को आर-पार रेखा खींचकर काट देना (क्योंकि वह ग़लत था)

**cross**[3] /krɒs क्रॉस्/ *adj.* (*informal*) **cross (with sb) (about sth)** angry or annoyed क्रोधित या परेशान *I was really cross with her for leaving me with all the work.* NOTE **Angry** की अपेक्षा **cross** कम औपचारिक शब्द है। ▶ **crossly** *adv.* गुस्से से *'Be quiet,' Dad said crossly.*

**crossbar** /ˈkrɒsbɑː(r) ˈक्रॉस्बा(र्)/ *noun* [C] **1** the piece of wood over the top of a goal in football, etc. फ़ुटबॉल आदि खेलों में गोल क्षेत्र के ऊपर लगा लकड़ी का डंडा **2** the metal bar that joins the front and back of a bicycle साइकिल के अगले और पिछले हिस्से को जोड़ने वाला धातु-निर्मित डंडा ➪ **bicycle** पर चित्र देखिए।

**cross-breed**[1] *verb* [I, T] (*pt, pp* **cross-bred**) to make an animal or a plant breed with a different type of animal or plant; to breed with an animal or plant of a different type भिन्न प्रजाति के पौधों या पशु के समागम से नया पौधा या पशु बनाना; संकर नसल उत्पन्न करना *a cross-bred puppy* ▶ **cross-breeding** *noun* [U] संकर पशु या पौधा उत्पन्न करने की प्रक्रिया; संकरण

**cross-breed**[2] *noun* [C] an animal or a plant that has been produced by breeding two different types of animal or plant संकर पशु या पौधा

**cross-check** *verb* [T] **cross-check sth (against sth)** to make sure that information, figures, etc. are correct by using a different method or system to check them जाँच करने की भिन्न पद्धति का प्रयोग कर सूचना आदि के सही होने को सुनिश्चित करना *Cross-check your measurements against those suggested in the manual.*

**cross-country** *adj., adv.* across fields and natural land; not using roads or tracks खेतों के आर-पार; सड़कों का प्रयोग न कर खुले मैदान में होकर *We walked about 10 kilometres cross-country before we saw a village.*

**cross-examine** *verb* [T] to ask sb questions in a court of law, etc. in order to find out the truth about sth कचहरी में बारीकी से सवाल पूछना ताकि सचाई का पता चल सके; प्रतिपरीक्षा या जिरह करना ▶ **cross-examination** *noun* [C, U] जिरह, प्रतिपरीक्षा

**cross-eyed** *adj.* having one or both your eyes looking towards your nose भेंगा

**cross-fertilize** (*also* **-ise**) *verb* [T] to make a plant develop and grow fruit or seeds using a type of powder (**pollen**) from a different kind of plant भिन्न प्रकार के पौधे के पराग का प्रयोग कर किसी पौधे के फल या बीज की उपज को बढ़ाना; पर-संसेचन करना ▶ **cross-fertilization** (*also* **-isation**) *noun* [U, *sing.*] पर-संसेचन; पर-निषेचन

**crossfire** /ˈkrɒsfaɪə(r) ˈक्रॉस्फ़ाइअ(र्)/ *noun* [U] a situation in which guns are being fired from two or more different directions दो या अधिक दिशाओं से जवाबी गोलीबारी *The journalist was killed in crossfire.* ○ (*figurative*) *When my cousins argued, I sometimes got* ***caught in the crossfire****.*

**crossing** /ˈkrɒsɪŋ ˈक्रॉसिङ्/ *noun* [C] **1** a place where you can cross over sth वह स्थान जहाँ से दूसरी ओर जा सकते हैं; पारपथ *You should cross the road at the pedestrian crossing.* ○ *a border crossing* **2** (*BrE* **level crossing**) a place where a road and a railway line cross each other स्थान जहाँ सड़क और रेल की पटरी एक दूसरे को काटती है **3** a journey from one side of a sea or river to the other समुद्र या नदी के एक किनारे से दूसरे किनारे पर जाना *We had a rough crossing.*

**cross-legged** /ˌkrɒsˈlegd ˈक्रॉस्ˈलेगड्/ *adj., adv.* sitting on the floor with your legs pulled up in front of you and with one leg or foot over the other पालथी मारकर बैठे हुए; एक टाँग के ऊपर दूसरी टाँग रखकर बैठे हुए *to sit cross-legged*

**cross purposes** *noun*

IDM **at cross purposes** if two people are at cross purposes, they do not understand each other because they are talking about different things without realizing it अनजाने में अलग-अलग विषयों पर बात कर रहे होने के कारण ग़लतफ़हमी का शिकार होना

**cross-reference** *noun* [C] a note in a book that tells you to look in another place in the book for more information पुस्तक के अन्यत्र भाग में अधिक सूचना का संदर्भ कथन

**crossroads** /ˈkrɒsrəʊdz ˈक्रॉस्रोड्ज़् / *noun* [C] (*pl.* **crossroads**) a place where two or more roads cross each other चौराहा, चौक *When you come to the next crossroads turn right.*

IDM **at a/the crossroads** at an important point in sb's life or development किसी व्यक्ति के जीवन का एक महत्त्वपूर्ण समय या किसी कार्य के विकास में एक महत्त्वपूर्ण क्षण; निर्णायक अवस्था

**cross-section** *noun* [C] **1** a picture of what the inside of sth would look like if you cut through it अनुप्रस्थ काट का चित्र; किसी वस्तु की आंतरिक स्थिति दर्शाने वाला चित्र *a cross-section of the human brain* ➪ **flower** पर चित्र देखिए। **2** a number of people, etc. that come from the different parts of a group, and so can be considered to represent the whole group किसी बड़े समुदाय केंद्र का प्रतिनिधि व्यक्ति *The families we studied were chosen to represent a cross-section of society.* ▶ **cross-sectional** *adj.* प्रतिनिधिक अंश से संबंधित

**crosswalk** /ˈkrɒswɔːk ˈक्रॉस्वॉक् / = **pedestrian crossing**

**crosswind** /ˈkrɒswɪnd ˈक्रॉस्विन्ड् / *noun* [C] a wind that is blowing across the direction that you are moving in तिरछी हवा

**crossword** /ˈkrɒswɜːd ˈक्रॉस्वड् / (*also* **crossword puzzle**) *noun* [C] a word game in which you have to write the answers to questions (**clues**) in square spaces, which are arranged in a pattern वर्ग पहेली *Every morning I try to* ***do the crossword*** *in the newspaper.*

**crotch** /krɒtʃ क्रॉच् / (*also* **crutch**) *noun* [C] the place where your legs, or a pair of trousers, join at the top ऊरूसंधि, जहाँ जाँघें मिलती है; काँटा, जहाँ पजामे या पैंट की टाँगें मिलती हैं

**crouch** /kraʊtʃ क्राउच् / *verb* [I] **crouch (down)** to bend your legs and body so that you are close to the ground टाँगों और शरीर को ऐसे झुकाना कि ज़मीन तक पहुँच जाए; सिकुड़ कर बैठना *He crouched down behind the sofa.*

**crow[1]** /krəʊ क्रो / *noun* [C] a large black bird that makes a loud noise कौआ

IDM **as the crow flies** (used for describing distances) in a straight line एकदम सीध में पड़ने वाली (दूरी) *It's a kilometre as the crow flies but three kilometres by road.*

**crow[2]** /krəʊ क्रो / *verb* [I] **1** to make a loud noise like a male chicken (**cock**) makes मुरग़े की तरह बाँग देना **2** (*informal*) to speak very proudly about sth; to boast डींग हाँकना

**crowbar** /ˈkrəʊbɑː(r) ˈक्रोबा(र्) / *noun* [C] a long iron bar that is used for forcing sth open किसी वस्तु को तोड़कर खोलने के लिए प्रयुक्त लोहे का लंबा डंडा; सब्बल, रंभा

**crowd[1]** /kraʊd क्राउड् / *noun* **1** [C, *with sing. or pl. verb*] a large number of people in one place भीड़, जनसमूह *The crowd was/were extremely noisy.* ○ *He pushed his way through the crowd.* **2 the crowd** [*sing.*] ordinary people जन साधारण; आम जनता *He wears weird clothes because he wants to* ***stand out from the crowd.*** **3** [C, *with sing. or pl. verb*] (*informal*) a group of people who know each other परस्पर परिचित लोग *Jagat, Lata and Sonam will be there—all the usual crowd.*

**crowd[2]** /kraʊd क्राउड् / *verb* **1** [I] **crowd around/round (sb)** (used about a lot of people) to stand in a large group around sb/sth किसी के चारों ओर भीड़ का जमा हो जाना *Fans crowded round the singer hoping to get his autograph.* **2** [T] (used about a lot of people) to fill an area किसी स्थान पर भीड़ हो जाना *Groups of tourists crowded the main streets.* ○ (*figurative*) *Memories crowded her mind.*

PHR V **crowd into sth; crowd in** to go into a small place and make it very full किसी तंग स्थान पर लोगों का भर जाना *Somehow we all crowded into their small living room.*

**crowd sb/sth into sth; crowd sb/sth in** to put a lot of people into a small place किसी तंग स्थान पर बहुत-से लोगों को भर देना *Ten prisoners were crowded into one small cell.*

**crowd sth out; crowd sb out (of sth)** to completely fill a place so that nobody else can enter किसी स्थान को ऐसे पूरा भर देना कि कोई अन्य न समा सके *Students crowd out the cafe at lunchtimes.* ○ *Smaller companies are being crowded out of the market.*

**crowded** /ˈkraʊdɪd ˈक्राउडिड् / *adj.* full of people भीड़-भरा, भीड़-भाड़ वाला *a crowded bus* ○ *people living in poor and crowded conditions*

**crown[1]** /kraʊn क्राउन् / *noun* **1** [C] a circle made of gold and jewels, that a king or queen wears on his/her head on official occasions औपचारिक अवसरों पर राजा या रानी द्वारा धारण किया जाने वाला स्वर्ण-रत्न निर्मित मुकुट, ताज **2 the Crown** [*sing.*] the state as represented by a king or queen राज्य जिसका प्रतिनिधित्व राजा या रानी द्वारा होता है; साम्राज्य *an area of land belonging to the Crown* **3** [*sing.*] the top of your head or of a hat सिर या टोपी का शिखर **4** [*sing.*] the top of a hill पहाड़ी या टोपी का शिखर

**crown[2]** /kraʊn क्राउन्/ *verb* [T] **1** to put a crown on the head of a new king or queen in an official ceremony औपचारिक समारोह में नए राजा या रानी को ताज पहनाना *Shah Jahan was crowned in 1628 AD.* ○ (*figurative*) *the newly crowned world champion* **2** (*usually passive*) **crown sth (with sth)** to have or put sth on the top of sth किसी के शिखर पर कुछ होना या रख देना *The mountain was crowned with snow.* ○ (*figurative*) *Her years of hard work were finally crowned with success.*

**crowning** /ˈkraʊnɪŋ ˈक्राउनिङ्/ *adj.* (*only before a noun*) the best or most important सर्वोत्तम या सर्वश्रेष्ठ *Winning the World Championship was the crowning moment of her career.*

**Crown prince** *noun* [C] (*feminine* **Crown princess**) the person who has the right to become the next king or queen अगला राजा या रानी बनने का अधिकारी व्यक्ति, युवराज या युवराज्ञी

**crucial** /ˈkruːʃl ˈक्रूश्ल्/ *adj.* **crucial (to/for sth)** extremely important अत्यधिक महत्त्वपूर्ण, निर्णायक *Early diagnosis of the illness is crucial for successful treatment.* ✪ पर्याय **vital** ▶ **crucially** /-ʃəli -शलि/ *adv.* निर्णायक रूप से

**crucible** /ˈkruːsɪbl ˈक्रूसिबल्/ *noun* [C] **1** a pot in which substances are heated to high temperatures, metals are melted, etc. पात्र जिसमें धातु को गलाते हैं; कुठाली, कुल्हिया, घरिया ⇨ **laboratory** पर चित्र देखिए। **2** (*formal*) a place or situation in which people or ideas are tested, often creating sth new or exciting in the process व्यक्तियों या विचारों की कड़ी परीक्षा, जिसमें से प्रायः नई बातें भी सामने आती हैं

**crucifix** /ˈkruːsəfɪks ˈक्रूसफ़िक्स्/ *noun* [C] a small model of a cross with a figure of Jesus on it सूली पर चढ़े ईसा की मूर्ति

**crucifixion** /ˌkruːsəˈfɪkʃn ˌक्रूसˈफ़िक्श्न्/ *noun* [C, U] the act of crucifying sb किसी को सूली पर चढ़ाने की क्रिया *the Crucifixion of Christ*

**crucify** /ˈkruːsɪfaɪ ˈक्रूसिफ़ाइ/ *verb* [T] (*pres. part.* **crucifying**; *3rd person sing. pres.* **crucifies;** *pt, pp* **crucified**) to kill sb by nailing or tying him/her to a cross किसी को सूली पर चढ़ाकर मारना

**crude** /kruːd क्रूड्/ *adj.* **1** simple and basic, without much detail, skill, etc. सरल और बुनियादी; अपरिष्कृत *The method was crude but very effective.* ○ *She explained how the system worked* ***in crude terms*** **2** in its natural state, before it has been treated with chemicals अपने प्रकृत रूप में; अशोधित *crude oil* ▶ **crudely** *adv.* अशिष्ट या अपरिकृष्ट रूप से *a crudely drawn face*

**cruel** /kruːəl क्रूअल्/ *adj.* (**crue<u>l</u>ler; crue<u>l</u>lest**) causing physical or mental pain or suffering to sb/sth निर्मम, क्रूर *I think it's cruel to keep animals in cages.* ○ *a cruel punishment* ▶ **cruelly** /ˈkruːəli ˈक्रूअलि/ *adv.* निर्ममता से

**cruelty** /ˈkruːəlti ˈक्रूअल्टि/ *noun* (*pl.* **cruelties**) **1** [U] **cruelty (to sb/sth)** cruel behaviour निर्मम आचरण; निर्ममता, क्रूरता *cruelty to children* **2** [C, *usually pl.*] a cruel act क्रूर कार्य *the cruelties of war*

**cruise[1]** /kruːz क्रूज़्/ *verb* [I] **1** to travel by boat, visiting a number of places, as a holiday अवकाश मनाने के लिए समुद्र-विहार करना *to cruise around the Caribbean* **2** to stay at the same speed in a car, plane, etc. कार, विमान आदि का एक ही गति पर चलते रहना *cruising at 80 kilometres an hour*

**cruise[2]** /kruːz क्रूज़्/ *noun* [C] a holiday in which you travel on a ship and visit a number of different places समुद्री पर्यटन, समुद्र-विहार *They're planning to* ***go on a cruise****.*

**cruiser** /ˈkruːzə(r) ˈक्रूज़(र्)/ *noun* [C] **1** a large fast ship used in a war बड़ा व तीव्रगामी युद्धपोत **2** a motorboat which has room for people to sleep in it शयन कक्ष की सुविधा वाली मोटर बोट = **cabin cruiser** ⇨ **boat** पर चित्र देखिए।

**crumb** /krʌm क्रम्/ *noun* [C] a very small dry piece of bread, cake or biscuit डबल रोटी, केक या बिस्कुट का बहुत छोटा सूखा हुआ टुकड़ा

**crumble** /ˈkrʌmbl ˈक्रम्बल्/ *verb* [I, T] **crumble (sth) (up)** to break or make sth break into very small pieces टुकड़े-टुकड़े हो जाना या कर देना *The walls of the church are beginning to crumble.* ○ *Support for the government is beginning to crumble.* ▶ **crumbly** /-bli -ब्लि/ *adj.* भुरभुरा *This cheese has a crumbly texture.*

**crumpet** /ˈkrʌmpɪt ˈक्रम्पिट्/ *noun* [C] a flat round bread-like cake with holes in the top that you eat hot with butter एक प्रकार का समतल, गोल, छिद्रिल, ब्रेड जैसा केक जिसे मक्खन के साथ गरमागरम खाते हैं

**crumple** /ˈkrʌmpl ˈक्रम्पल्/ *verb* [I, T] **crumple (sth) (into sth); crumple (sth) (up)** to be pressed or to press sth into an untidy shape दबकर सिलवट पड़ना या मुड़-तुड़ जाना; दबाकर मोड़-तोड़ देना *The front of the car crumpled when it hit the wall.* ○ *She crumpled the letter into a ball*

**crunch[1]** /krʌntʃ क्रन्च्/ *verb* **1** [T] **crunch sth (up)** to make a loud noise when you are eating sth hard कड़ी चीज़ खाते हुए कचर-कचर आवाज़ करना *to crunch an apple* **2** [I] to make a loud noise like the sound of sth being crushed किसी वस्तु के कुचले जाने की ऊँची आवाज़ होना *We crunched through the snow.* ▶ **crunchy** /ˈkrʌntʃi ˈक्रन्चि / *adj.* कचर-कचर की आवाज़ देने वाला; कुरकुरा *a crunchy apple*

**crunch[2]** /krʌntʃ क्रन्च् / *noun* [*sing.*] an act or noise of crunching कुरकुरे पदार्थ को चबाने की क्रिया; कुरकुरे पदार्थ को चबाने पर होने वाली आवाज़ *There was a loud crunch as he sat on the box of eggs.*
IDM **if/when it comes to the crunch** if/when you are in a difficult situation and must make a difficult decision कठिन परिस्थिति में कठिन निर्णय लेने की आवश्यकता पड़ना *If it comes to the crunch, I'll stay and fight.*

**crusade** /kru:ˈseɪd क्रूˈसेड् / *noun* [C] **1** a fight for sth that you believe to be good or against sth that you believe to be bad नैतिक मूल्यों के संरक्षण के लिए या अनीति के विरोध के लिए संघर्ष *Mr Khan is leading a crusade against drugs in his neighbourhood.* **2 Crusade** one of the wars fought in Palestine by European Christians against Muslims in the Middle Ages मध्य युग में यूरोपीय ईसाइयों द्वारा मुसलमानों के विरुद्ध फिलस्तीन में लड़ा गया युद्ध; धर्मयुद्ध, जिहाद ▶ **crusader** *noun* [C] धर्मयोद्धा; (अनीति के विरोध के लिए) संघर्षकर्ता, आंदोलनकर्ता

**crush[1]** /krʌʃ क्रश् / *verb* [T] **1** to press sb/sth hard so that he/she/it is broken, damaged or injured कुचलना, रौंदना, मसलना *Most of the eggs got crushed when she sat on them.* **2 crush sth (up)** to break sth into very small pieces or a powder किसी वस्तु के छोटे-छोटे टुकड़े कर देना; पीस देना *Crush the garlic and fry in oil.* **3** to defeat sb/sth completely किसी को पूर्णतया पराजित कर देना *The army was sent in to crush the rebellion.*

**crush[2]** /krʌʃ क्रश् / *noun* **1** [*sing.*] a large group of people in a small space तंग स्थान में भीड़ *There was such a crush that I couldn't get near the bar.* **2** [C] (*informal*) **a crush (on sb)** a strong feeling of love for sb that only usually lasts for a short time प्यार का अल्पकालिक आवेश *Maria **had a huge crush** on her neighbour.*

**crushing** /ˈkrʌʃɪŋ ˈक्रशिङ् / *adj.* (*only before a noun*) that defeats sb/sth completely; very bad पूर्णतया या बुरी तरह हराने वाला; बहुत बुरा *a crushing defeat*

**crust** /krʌst क्रस्ट् / *noun* [C, U] **1** the hard part on the outside of a piece of bread, a pie, etc. डबलरोटी आदि की बाहरी कड़ी सतह, पपड़ी **2** a hard layer on the outside of sth किसी वस्तु की बाहरी कठोर परत *the earth's crust*

**crustacean** /krʌˈsteɪʃn क्रˈस्टेश्न् / *noun* [C] (*technical*) any creature with a soft body in several sections and covered with a hard outer shell. Crustaceans usually live in water अंदर से नरम शरीर और बाहर से कड़ी खाल वाला कोई भी जीव; ये जीव सामान्यतः पानी में रहते हैं *Crabs, lobsters, shrimps and prawns are crustaceans.*

**crusty** /ˈkrʌsti ˈक्रस्टि / *adj.* **1** having a hard **crust 1** कड़ी परत वाला, पपड़ीदार *crusty bread* **2** (*informal*) bad-tempered and impatient बदमिज़ाज और अधीर *a crusty old man*

**crutch** /krʌtʃ क्रच् / *noun* [C] **1** a type of stick that you put under your arm to help you walk when you have hurt your leg or foot बैसाखी *She was **on crutches** for two months after she broke her ankle.* ➪ **walking stick** देखिए। **2** = **crotch**

**crux** /krʌks क्रक्स् / *noun* [*sing.*] the most important or difficult part of a problem किसी समस्या का सबसे कठिन या महत्त्वपूर्ण अंश *The **crux of the matter** is how to stop this from happening again.*

**cry[1]** /kraɪ क्राइ / *verb* (*pres. part.* **crying;** *3rd person sing. pres.* **cries;** *pt, pp* **cried**) **1** [I] to make a noise and produce tears in your eyes, for example, because you are unhappy or have hurt yourself रोना, विलाप करना *The baby never stops crying.* **2** [I, T] **cry (out)** to shout or make a loud noise चिल्लाना या चीख़ना *We could hear someone crying for help.* ○ *'Look!' he cried, 'There they are.'*
IDM **a shoulder to cry on** ➪ **shoulder[1]** देखिए।
**cry your eyes out** to cry a lot for a long time देर तक बहुत अधिक रोना
**cry out for sth** to need sth very much किसी वस्तु की अत्यधिक आवश्यकता होना *The city is crying out for a new transport system.*

**cry[2]** /kraɪ क्राइ / *noun* (*pl.* **cries**) **1** [C] a shout or loud high noise चीख़ या चिल्लाहट *the cries of the children in the playground* ○ (*figurative*) *Her suicide attempt was really **a cry for help**.* **2** [*sing.*] an act of **crying[1] 1** रोने की क्रिया *After a good cry I felt much better.*
IDM **a far cry from sth/from doing sth** ➪ **far[1]** देखिए।

**crying** /ˈkraɪɪŋ ˈक्राइइङ् / *adj.* (*only before a noun*) (used to talk about a bad situation) very great (ख़राब परिस्थिति) घोर, अत्यधिक *There's a crying need for more doctors.* ○ *It's **a crying shame** that so many young people can't find jobs.*

**cryptic** /ˈkrɪptɪk ˈक्रिप्टिक् / *adj.* having a hidden meaning that is not easy to understand; mysterious गुप्त अर्थ वाला; रहस्यमय ▶ **cryptically** /-kli -क्लि / *adv.* रहस्यात्मक रीति से

**crypto-** /ˈkrɪptəʊ ˈक्रिप्टो / *prefix (used in nouns)* hidden; secret छिपा हुआ; गोपनीय

**crystal** /ˈkrɪstl ˈक्रिस्ट्ल् / *noun* **1** [C] a regular shape that some mineral substances form when they become solid ठोस हो जाने पर बनी धातुओं की सुनिश्चित आकृति; रवा *salt crystals* **2** [U] a clear mineral that can be used in making jewellery एक पारदर्शी धातु जो आभूषण बनाने के काम आती है, स्फटिक, बिल्लौर **3** [U] very high-quality glass उत्तम कोटि का काँच *a crystal vase*

**crystal ball** *noun* [C] a glass ball used by people who claim they can predict what will happen in the future by looking into it काँच की गेंद जिसमें कुछ लोग देखकर भविष्यवाणी कर सकते हैं

**crystal clear** *adj.* **1** (used about water, glass, etc.) that you can see through perfectly (जल, काँच आदि) पूर्णतया पारदर्शी **2** very easy to understand सुबोध, सुगम *The meaning is crystal clear.*

**crystalline** /ˈkrɪstəlaɪn ˈक्रिस्टलाइन् / *adj.* made of or similar to **crystals** रवे जैसा, रवेदार, क्रिस्टल-सदृश, क्रिस्टलीय

**crystallize** (*also* **-ise**) /ˈkrɪstəlaɪz ˈक्रिस्टलाइज़् / *verb* [I, T] **1** (used about thoughts, beliefs, plans, etc.) to become clear and fixed; to make thoughts, etc. become clear and fixed (विचार, विश्वास आदि) स्पष्ट और सुनिश्चित होना; (विचार, विश्वास आदि को) स्पष्ट और सुनिश्चित कर देना *Our ideas gradually began to crystallize into a definite strategy.* **2** to form or make sth form into **crystals** किसी वस्तु का स्फटिक बन जाना या उसे स्फटिक बना देना ▶ **crystallization** (*also* **-isation**) /ˌkrɪstəlaɪˈzeɪʃn ˌक्रिस्टलाइˈज़ेश्न् / *noun* [U] क्रिस्टलीकरण

**cu.** *abbr.* cubic घनीय *a volume of 3 cu. ft*

**cub** /kʌb कब् / *noun* [C] a young bear, lion, etc. शेर, भालू आदि का बच्चा ➪ **lion** पर चित्र देखिए।

**cube[1]** /kju:b क्यूब् / *noun* [C] **1** a solid shape that has six equal square sides छह समान पार्श्वों वाला ठोस पिंड; घनाकृति ➪ **solid** पर चित्र देखिए। **2** (in mathematics) the number that you get if you multiply a number by itself twice (गणित में) घनफल *the cube of 5 ($5^3$) is 125 (= 5×5×5).* ➪ **square[1]** देखिए।

**cube[2]** /kju:b क्यूब् / *verb* [T] (in mathematics) (*usually passive*) to multiply a number by itself twice (गणित में) घनफल निकालना *Four cubed ($4^3$) is 64 (= 4×4×4).* ➪ **square[1]** और **cube root** देखिए।

**cube root** *noun* [C] (in mathematics) a number which, when multiplied by itself twice, produces a particular number (गणित में) घनमूल *The cube root of 64 ($\sqrt[3]{64}$) is 4.* ➪ **square root** देखिए।

**cubic** /ˈkju:bɪk ˈक्यूबिक् / *adj.* connected with a measurement of volume expressed as a **cube[1] 2** घन में व्यक्त माप से संबंधित; घनीय *The lake holds more than a million cubic metres of water.*

**cubicle** /ˈkju:bɪkl ˈक्यूबिकल् / *noun* [C] a small room that is made by separating off part of a larger room बड़े कमरे में विभाजन कर बनाया छोटा कमरा; कक्षक *There are cubicles at the swimming pool for changing your clothes.*

**cuckoo** /ˈkʊku: ˈकुकू / *noun* [C] a bird which makes a sound like its name. Cuckoos put their eggs into the **nests** of other birds कोयल

**cucumber** /ˈkju:kʌmbə(r) ˈक्यूकम्ब(र्) / *noun* [C, U] a long, thin vegetable with a dark green skin that does not need to be cooked ककड़ी, खीरा ➪ **vegetable** पर चित्र देखिए।

**cud** /kʌd कड् / *noun* [U] the food that cows and similar animals bring back from the stomach into the mouth to eat again गाय-बैल की जुगाली *cows chewing the cud*

**cuddle** /ˈkʌdl ˈकड्ल् / *verb* [I, T] to hold sb/sth closely in your arms प्यार से बाँहों में थामना *The little girl was cuddling her favourite doll.* ▶ **cuddle** *noun* [C] गलबहियाँ *He **gave** the child **a cuddle** and kissed her goodnight.*

**PHRV** **cuddle up (to/against sb/sth); cuddle up (together)** to move close to sb and sit or lie in a comfortable position पास-पास आराम से बैठना या लेटना *They cuddled up together for warmth.*

**cuddly** /ˈkʌdli ˈकड्लि / *adj.* soft and pleasant to hold close to you नरम, प्रियकर व आरामदेह; आलिंगन-योग्य, प्यार से कोमलतापूर्वक साथ सटा हुआ *a cuddly toy*

**cue** /kju: क्यू / *noun* [C] **1** a word or movement that is the signal for sb else to say or do sth, especially in a play विशेषतः नाटक में वह शब्द या क्रिया-व्यापार जो संकेत करता है कि क्या कहा जाए या किया जाए; संकेत इशारा *When Mala puts the tray on the table, that's your cue to come on stage.* **2** an example of how to behave उचित आचरण या व्यवहार का उदाहरण, कैसा व्यवहार किया जाए-इसका उदाहरण *I'm not sure how to behave at a Japanese wedding, so I'll **take my cue from** the hosts.* **3** a long, thin wooden stick used to hit the ball in some games that are played on a special table (snooker and billiards) बिलियर्ड्स और स्नूकर खेलों में प्रयुक्त लंबी व पतली छड़ी

**IDM** **(right) on cue** at exactly the moment expected एकदम ठीक समय पर *Just as I was starting to worry about Sagar, he phoned right on cue.*

**cuff** /kʌf कफ़्/ *noun* [C] **1** the end part of a sleeve, which often fastens at the wrist (कमीज़ की बाँह का) कफ़ **2 cuffs** [*pl.*] = **handcuffs** **3** a light hit with the open hand हलका तमाचा

**IDM** **off the cuff** (used about sth you say) without thought or preparation before that moment बिना तैयारी के *I haven't got the figures here, but, off the cuff, I'd say the rise is about 10%.*

**cufflink** /ˈkʌflɪŋk ˈकफ़्लिङ्क्/ *noun* [C, *usually pl.*] one of a pair of small objects used instead of a button to fasten a shirt sleeve together at the wrist (कमीज़ की बाँहों के) कफ़ों को जोड़ने वाली सजावटी वस्तु जो बटन के स्थान पर प्रयुक्त होती है

**cuisine** /kwɪˈziːn क्वि ˈज़ीन्/ *noun* [U] (*formal*) the style of cooking of a particular country, restaurant, etc. किसी विशेष देश, रेस्तराँ आदि की भोजन बनाने की शैली; पाक शैली *Italian cuisine*

**NOTE** **Cuisine** की अपेक्षा **cooking** कम औपचारिक शब्द है।

**cul-de-sac** /ˈkʌl də sæk ˈकल् ड सैक्/ *noun* [C] (*pl.* **cul-de-sacs**) a street that is closed at one end एक सिरे पर बंद सड़क

**culinary** /ˈkʌlɪnəri ˈकलिनरि/ *adj.* (*formal*) connected with cooking भोजन पकाने संबंधी, पाक-कला विषयक

**cull** /kʌl कल्/ *verb* [T] **1** to kill a number of animals in a group to prevent the group from becoming too large कुछ पशुओं को मार देना ताकि उनका झुंड बहुत बड़ा न हो जाए; छँटाई करना **2** to collect information, ideas, etc., from different places विभिन्न सूत्रों से जानकारी, विचार आदि एकत्र करना *I managed to cull some useful addresses from the Internet.* ▶ **cull** *noun* [C] छँटाई *a deer cull*

**culminate** /ˈkʌlmɪneɪt ˈकलमिनेट्/ *verb* [I] (*formal*) **culminate in sth** to reach a final result अंतिम परिणाम पर पहुँचना; चरम सीमा तक पहुँचना *The team's efforts culminated in victory in the championships.* ▶ **culmination** /ˌkʌlmɪˈneɪʃn ˌकलमिˈनेश्न्/ *noun* [*sing.*] अंतिम परिणति, पराकाष्ठा *The joint space mission was the culmination of years of research.*

**culottes** /kjuːˈlɒts क्यूˈलॉट्स्/ *noun* [*pl.*] women's wide short trousers that are made to look like a skirt महिलाओं का चौड़ा छोटा पाजामा जो स्कर्ट जैसा लगता है; क्यूलाटस *a pair of culottes*

**culpable** /ˈkʌlpəbl ˈकल्पबल्/ *adj.* (*formal*) responsible for sth bad that has happened ग़लती के लिए ज़िम्मेदार; दोषी

**culprit** /ˈkʌlprɪt ˈकल्प्रिट्/ *noun* [C] a person who has done sth wrong अपराधी, दोषी

**cult** /kʌlt कल्ट्/ *noun* [C] **1** a type of religion or religious group, especially one that is considered unusual विशेषतः विचित्र या सामान्य से भिन्न धर्म या धार्मिक समुदाय; पंथ, संप्रदाय **2** a person or thing that has become popular with a particular group of people वर्ग-विशेष में लोकप्रिय व्यक्ति या वस्तु *cult movies*

**cultivar** /ˈkʌltɪvɑː(r) ˈकल्टिवा(र्)/ *noun* [C] (*technical*) a particular variety of a plant whose characteristics have been controlled by people in the way it has been bred किसी पौधे की विशेष प्रजाति जिसे विशिष्ट गुणों की दृष्टि से विकसित किया गया हो

**cultivate** /ˈkʌltɪveɪt ˈकल्टिवेट्/ *verb* [T] **1** to prepare and use land for growing plants for food or to sell फ़सल उगाने के लिए खेत जोतना *to cultivate the soil* **2** to grow plants for food or to sell फ़सल उगाना; खेती करना *Olives have been cultivated for centuries in the Mediterranean countries.* **3** to try hard to develop a friendship with sb किसी से दोस्ती के लिए विशेष प्रयास करना *He cultivated links with colleagues abroad.* ▶ **cultivation** /ˌkʌltɪˈveɪʃn ˌकल्टिˈवेश्न्/ *noun* [U] खेती, जुताई ➪ **shifting cultivation** देखिए।

**cultivated** /ˈkʌltɪveɪtɪd ˈकल्टिवेटिड्/ *adj.* **1** well educated, with good manners (व्यक्ति) शिक्षित और भद्र **2** (used about land) used for growing plants for food or to sell (ज़मीन) फ़सल उगाने के लिए प्रयोग में लाई गई **3** (used about plants) grown on a farm, not wild (पौधे) खेत में उगाए गए (जंगल में नहीं)

**cultural** /ˈkʌltʃərəl ˈकल्चरल्/ *adj.* **1** connected with the customs, ideas, beliefs, etc. of a society or country किसी समाज या देश की प्रथाओं, विचारधाराओं, विश्वासों आदि से संबंधित; सांस्कृतिक *The country's cultural diversity is a result of taking in immigrants from all over the world.* ➪ **multicultural** देखिए। **2** connected with art, music, literature, etc. कला, संगीत, साहित्य आदि से संबंधित; सांस्कृतिक *The city has a rich cultural life, with many theatres, concert halls and art galleries.* ▶ **culturally** /-rəli -रलि/ *adv.* सांस्कृतिक दृष्टि से

**culture** /ˈkʌltʃə(r) ˈकल्च(र्)/ *noun* **1** [C, U] the customs, ideas, beliefs, etc. of a particular society, country, etc. किसी समाज, देश आदि की प्रथाएँ, विचारधाराएँ, विश्वास आदि; संस्कृति *people from many different cultures* **2** [U] art, literature, music, etc. कला; साहित्य, संगीत आदि; संस्कृति *Kolkata has always been a centre of culture.* **3** [C] (*medical*) a group of cells or bacteria, especially taken from a person or an animal and grown for medical or scientific study चिकित्सीय या वैज्ञानिक अध्ययन के लिए संवर्धित कोशिका-जीवाणु-समूह, विशेषतः किसी व्यक्ति या पशु से लिया गया; संवर्धन *Yoghurt is made from active cultures.*

**cultured** /ˈkʌltʃəd ˈकल्चड्/ *adj.* well educated, showing a good knowledge of art, music, literature, etc. सुशिक्षित तथा कला-संगीत आदि का मर्मज्ञ; सुसंस्कृत

**culture shock** *noun* [U] a feeling of confusion, etc. that you may have when you go to live in or visit a country that is very different from your own अतिभिन्न संस्कृति वाले समाज से संपर्क के परिणामस्वरूप उत्पन्न भ्रम और परेशानी

**culvert** /ˈkʌlvət ˈकल्वट्/ *noun* [C] a pipe for water that goes under a road, etc. सड़क आदि के नीचे से जाने वाला पानी का नाला या नाली; पुलिया

**cum** /kʌm कम्/ *prep.* (*used for joining two nouns together*) also used as; as well as और यह भी; साथ में; -सह- (दो संज्ञाओं को जोड़ने के लिए प्रयुक्त) *a bedroom-cum-study*

**cumbersome** /ˈkʌmbəsəm ˈकम्बसम्/ *adj.* **1** heavy and difficult to carry, use, wear, etc. भारी-भरकम; भारी होने के कारण ले जाने, प्रयोग में लाने, पहनने आदि में मुश्किल; बोझिल **2** (used about a system, etc.) slow and complicated (पद्धति आदि) मंद गति वाली और पेचीदा *cumbersome legal procedures*

**cumin** /ˈkjumɪŋ ˈक्युमिन्/ the dried seeds of the **cumin** plant used as a spice especially in Indian cooking ज़ीरा

**cumulative** /ˈkju:mjələtɪv ˈक्यूम्यलटिव्/ *adj.* increasing steadily in amount, degree, etc. परिमाण आदि की दृष्टि से निरंतर बढ़ने वाला; संचयी *a cumulative effect*

**cumulonimbus** /ˌkju:mjʊləʊˈnɪmbəs ˌक्यूम्यूलोˈनिम्बस्/ *noun* [U] (*technical*) a type of cloud that forms a large very high mass, with a flat base at a fairly low level, and often a flat top. It is seen, for example, during **thunderstorms** प्रायः गरज भरे तूफ़ान के समय आकाश में बने घने बादल जो शीर्ष और तले पर समतल होते हैं; कपासी वर्षी मेघ

**cumulus** /ˈkju:mjələs ˈक्यूम्यलस्/ *noun* [U] (*technical*) a type of thick white cloud एक प्रकार का घना सफ़ेद बादल; कपासी मेघ

**cunning** /ˈkʌnɪŋ ˈकनिङ्/ *adj.* clever in a dishonest or bad way चालाक, धूर्त *He was as cunning as a fox.* ○ *a cunning trick* ✪ पर्याय **sly** या **wily** ▶ **cunning** *noun* [U] धूर्त, चालाकी ▶ **cunningly** *adv.* चालाकी या धूर्तता से

**cup**[1] /kʌp कप्/ *noun* [C] **1** a small container usually with a handle, used for drinking liquids प्याला, कप *a teacup* ○ *a cup of coffee* **2** (in sport) a large metal cup given as a prize; the competition for such a cup (खेल में) पुरस्कार स्वरूप दिया गया बड़ा धातु-निर्मित कप; इस कप के लिए स्पर्धा *Our team won the cup in the basketball tournament.* ○ *the World Cup* **3** an object shaped like a cup कप के आकार की कोई वस्तु *an eggcup*

IDM **not sb's cup of tea** not what sb likes or is interested in रुचि का विषय न होना, पसंद न होना *Horror films aren't my cup of tea.*

**cup**[2] /kʌp कप्/ *verb* [T] (**cupping; cupped**) to form sth, especially your hands, into the shape of a cup; to hold sth with your hands shaped like a cup हाथों से कप की आकृति बनाना; देना; कप की आकृति में ढले हाथों में कुछ सँभालना *I cupped my hands to take a drink from the stream.*

**cupboard** /ˈkʌbəd ˈकबड्/ *noun* [C] a piece of furniture, usually with shelves inside and a door or doors at the front, used for storing food, clothes, etc. भोजन, वस्त्रों आदि को संभालकर रखने की दरवाज़ों वाली अलमारी

**cup final** *noun* [C] (especially in football) the last match in a series of matches in a competition that gives a cup as a prize to the winner स्पर्धा का अंतिम खेल जिसमें विजेता को पुरस्कार स्वरूप कप मिलता है (विशेषतः फ़ुटबॉल में)

**cupful** /ˈkʌpfʊl ˈकप्फ़ुल्/ *noun* [C] the amount that a cup will hold (किसी वस्तु की) कप में आने वाली मात्रा; कपभर *two cupfuls of water*

**cup tie** *noun* [C] (especially in football) a match between two teams in a competition that gives a cup as a prize to the winner (विशेषत; फ़ुटबॉल में) दो टीमों के बीच स्पर्धा का वह मैच जिसमें विजेता को पुरस्कार स्वरूप मिलता है

**curable** /ˈkjʊərəbl ˈक्युअरबल्/ *adj.* (used about a disease) that can be made better (रोग) जिसका इलाज हो सके; सुसाध्य ✪ विलोम **incurable**

**curate** /ˈkjʊərət ˈक्युअरट्/ *noun* [C] a priest at a low level in the Church of England, who helps the priest in charge (**vicar**) of a church district चर्च आफ़ इंग्लैंड में मुख्य पुरोहित का सहायक

**curator** /kjʊəˈreɪtə(r) क्युअˈरेट(र्)/ *noun* [C] a person whose job is to look after the things that are kept in a museum संग्रहालय का अध्यक्ष

**curb[1]** /kɜːb कब्/ *verb* [T] to limit or control sth, especially sth bad किसी बात (विशेषतः) बुरी स्थिति पर रोक लगाना; नियंत्रण में लाना *He needs to learn to curb his anger.*

**curb[2]** /kɜːb कब्/ *noun* [C] **1 a curb (on sth)** a control or limit on sth नियंत्रण, रोक, अंकुश *a curb on local government spending* **2** = **kerb**

**curd** /kɜːd कड्/ *noun* [U] (*also* **curds**) [*pl.*] a thick soft substance that forms when milk turns sour दही

**curdle** /ˈkɜːdl ˈकड्ल्/ *verb* [I, T] (used about liquids) to turn sour or to separate into different parts; to make something do this (द्रव पदार्थों का) खट्टा हो जाना या फट जाना; (द्रव पदार्थों को) खट्टा कर देना या फाड़ देना *I've curdled the sauce.* ➪ **blood-curdling** देखिए।

**cure[1]** /kjʊə(r) क्युअ(र्)/ *verb* [T] **1 cure sb (of sth)** to make sb healthy again after an illness (रोगी को) पुनः स्वस्थ कर देना; रोगमुक्त करना *The treatment cured him of cancer.* **2** to make an illness, injury, etc. end or disappear रोग का उपचार करना; इलाज करना *It is still not possible to cure the common cold.* ○ (*figurative*) *The plumber cured the problem with the central heating.* **3** to make certain types of food last longer by drying, smoking or salting them खाद्य पदार्थों को सुखाकर, धुआँ देकर या नमक लगाकर लंबे समय के लिए सुरक्षित रखना *cured chicken*

**cure[2]** /kjʊə(r) क्युअ(र्)/ *noun* [C] **a cure (for sth) 1** a medicine or treatment that can cure an illness, etc. रोग का उपचार करने वाली औषधि या चिकित्सा *There is no cure for this illness.* **2** a return to good health; the process of being cured पुनः स्वास्थ्य लाभ; रोग से मुक्ति की प्रक्रिया *The new drug brought about a miraculous cure.*

**curfew** /ˈkɜːfjuː ˈकफ़्यू/ *noun* [C] a time after which people are not allowed to go outside their homes, for example, during a war समयविशेष के बाद घर से बाहर निकलने पर पाबंदी का आदेश; कफ़्र्यू *The government imposed a dusk-to-dawn curfew.* ○ *She has a ten o'clock curfew.*

**curiosity** /ˌkjʊəriˈɒsəti ˌक्युअरिˈऑसटि/ *noun* (*pl.* **curiosities**) **1** [U] a desire to know or learn जिज्ञासा, कुतूहल, उत्सुकता ***Out of curiosity****, he opened her letter.* **2** [C] an unusual and interesting person or thing विचित्र व रुचिकर व्यक्ति या वस्तु *The museum was full of historical curiosities.*

**curious** /ˈkjʊəriəs ˈक्युअरिअस्/ *adj.* **1 curious (about sth); curious (to do sth)** wanting to know or learn sth कुछ जानने या सीखने का इच्छुक; उत्सुक, जिज्ञासु *He was curious to know how the machine worked.* **2** unusual or strange असाधारण या विचित्र *It was curious that she didn't tell anyone about the incident.* ► **curiously** *adv.* उत्सुकता से

**curl[1]** /kɜːl कल्/ *verb* **1** [I, T] to form or to make sth form into a curved or round shape किसी वस्तु को मोड़ना या गोलाई देना; घुँघराला बनाना; छल्ला या कुंडलाकार बनाना *Does your hair curl naturally?* **2** [I] to move round in a curve गोलाई में घूमना *Smoke curled up into the sky.*

PHR V **curl up** to pull your arms, legs and head close to your body सिकुड़कर बैठना *The cat curled up in front of the fire.*

**curl[2]** /kɜːl कल्/ *noun* [C] **1** a piece of hair that curves round घुँघराले बाल *Her hair fell in curls round her face.* **2** a thing that has a curved round shape कुण्डलाकार वस्तु, छल्ला *a curl of blue smoke*

**curler** /ˈkɜːlə(r) ˈकल(र्)/ *noun* [C] a small plastic or metal tube that you roll your hair around in order to make it curly बालों को छल्लेदार बनाने की प्लास्टिक या धातु की नली

**curly** /ˈkɜːli ˈकलि/ *adj.* full of curls; shaped like a curl छल्लेदार, घुँघराला; छल्लेनुमा, छल्ले के आकार का *curly hair* ✪ विलोम **straight**

**currant** /ˈkʌrənt ˈकरन्ट्/ *noun* [C] **1** a very small dried grape used to make cakes, etc. किशमिश **2** (*often in compounds*) one of several types of small soft fruit किसी प्रकार का छोटा-नरम फल (जैसे मुनक्का) *blackcurrants*

**currency** /ˈkʌrənsi ˈकरन्सि/ *noun* (*pl.* **currencies**) **1** [C, U] the system or type of money that a particular country uses देश विशेष में प्रचलित धन-व्यवस्था या प्रकार मुद्रा *foreign currency* ○ *a weak/strong/stable currency* **2** [U] the state of being believed, accepted or used by many people लोगों द्वारा स्वीकार्य या विश्वसनीय होने की स्थिति, स्वीकार्यता या विश्वसनीयता *The new ideas soon **gained currency**.*

**current[1]** /ˈkʌrənt ˈकरन्ट्/ *adj.* **1** of the present time; happening now वर्तमानकालीन; इस समय प्रचलित *current fashions/events* **2** generally accepted; in common use सामान्यतः स्वीकार्य; सामान्यतः प्रचलित *Is this word still current?*

**current[2]** /ˈkʌrənt ˈकरन्ट्/ *noun* **1** [C] a continuous flowing movement of water, air, etc. निरंतर बहती जलधारा, वायु आदि; धारा, प्रवाह *to swim **against/with the current*** ○ (*figurative*) *a current of anti-government feeling* **2** [U] the flow of electricity through a wire, etc. तार आदि में से गुज़रती विद्युत धारा

**current account** (*AmE* **checking account**) *noun* [C] a bank account from which you can take out your money when you want, with a cheque book or cash card चालू खाता, बैंक जिसमें से आवश्यकतानुसार चेक या कैश कार्ड से पैसा निकाला जा सकता है

**current affairs** *noun* [*pl.*] important political or social events that are happening at the present time वर्तमान में घटित महत्त्वपूर्ण राजनीतिक या सामाजिक घटनाएँ; सामयिक विषय

**currently** /ˈkʌrəntli ˈकरन्ट्लि/ *adv.* at present; at the moment वर्तमान में; आजकल *He is currently working in Spain.* ➪ **actually** पर नोट देखिए।

**curriculum** /kəˈrɪkjələm कˈरिक्यलम्/ *noun* [C] (*pl.* **curriculums** or **curricula** /-lə -ला/) all the subjects that are taught in a school, college or university; the contents of a particular course of study विद्यालय, महाविद्यालय या विश्वविद्यालय में पढ़ाए जाने वाले समस्त विषय; पाठ्यचर्या, पाठ्यक्रम; पाठ्यक्रम विशेष का पाठ्यविवरण *Sanskrit is not **on the curriculum** at our school.* ➪ **syllabus** देखिए।

**curriculum vitae** /kəˌrɪkjələm ˈviːtaɪ कˌरिक्यलम् व़ीटाइ/ = **CV**

**curry** /ˈkʌri ˈकरि/ *noun* [C, U] (*pl.* **curries**) a gravy-based liquid dish of meat, vegetables, etc. containing a lot of spices usually served with rice मसालेदार, मांसाहारी या शाकाहारी रसेदार व्यंजन *a hot/mild curry* ▶ **curried** *adj.* मसालेदार व रसेदार *curried chicken*

**curry leaf** *noun* [C] the leaf of a shrub or small tree native to India and Sri Lanka which is used to give a special flavour to cooking कड़ी पत्ता

**curry powder** *noun* [U] a fine mixture of strongly flavoured spices that is used to make curry व्यंजन बनाने के ज़ायकेदार मसालों का मिश्रण

**curse¹** /kɜːs कस्/ *noun* [C] **1** a word used for expressing anger; a swear word क्रोधव्यंजक शब्द; अपशब्द, गाली **2** a word or words expressing a wish that sth terrible will happen to sb अभिशाप, शाप, बददुआ *The family seemed to be under a curse* **3** something that causes great harm विनाशकारी प्रभाव, अभिशाप *the curse of drug addiction*

**curse²** /kɜːs कस्/ *verb* **1** [I, T] **curse (sb/sth) (for sth)** to swear at sb/sth; to use rude language to express your anger किसी को गाली देना; क्रोध व्यंजक दुर्वचन बोलना *He dropped the box, cursing himself for his clumsiness.* **2** [T] to use a magic word or phrase against sb because you wish him/her harm शाप देना *She cursed his family.*

**cursor** /ˈkɜːsə(r) ˈकस(र्)/ *noun* [C] (*computing*) a small sign on a computer screen that shows the position you are at कंप्यूटर स्क्रीन पर एक लघु चिह्न जो दर्शाता है कि प्रयोगकर्ता किस स्थानबिंदु पर है; कर्सर

**cursory** /ˈkɜːsəri ˈकसरि/ *adj.* quick and short; done in a hurry तुरंत और संक्षिप्त, सरसरी; जल्दबाज़ी में किया गया *a cursory glance*

**curt** /kɜːt कट्/ *adj.* short and not polite संक्षिप्त और रूखा *She gave him a curt reply and slammed the phone down.* ▶ **curtly** *adv.* रूखेपन से ▶ **curtness** *noun* [U] रूखापन

**curtail** /kɜːˈteɪl कˈटेल्/ *verb* [T] (*formal*) to make sth shorter or smaller; to reduce छोटा या संक्षिप्त करना; कम करना; घटाना *I had to curtail my answer as I was running out of time.* ▶ **curtailment** *noun* [C, U] काट-छाँट, संक्षेपण

**curtain** /ˈkɜːtn ˈकट्न्/ *noun* [C] **1** (*AmE* **drape**) a piece of material that you can move to cover a window, etc. (खिड़की आदि का) परदा *Could you **draw the curtains**, please* (= could you open/close the curtains)? **2** a thing that covers or hides sth कोई भी ढकने या छिपाने वाली वस्तु *a curtain of mist*

**curtsy** (*also* **curtsey**) /ˈkɜːtsi ˈकट्सि/ *noun* [C] (*pl.* **curtsies** or **curtseys**) a movement made by a woman as a sign of respect, done by bending the knees, with one foot behind the other आदर की अभिव्यक्ति के लिए किसी महिला की विशेष क्रिया जिसमें वह एक पैर के पीछे दूसरे को रखते हुए घुटने को मोड़ती है ▶ **curtsy** (*also* **curtsey**) *verb* [I] किसी स्त्री का इस तरह अभिवादन करना

**curve¹** /kɜːv कव़्/ *noun* [C] a line that bends round वक्र रेखा *a curve on a graph*

**curve²** /kɜːv कव़्/ *verb* [I, T] to bend or to make sth bend in a curve वक्राकार मुड़ना या मोड़ना *The bay curved round to the south.* ○ *a curved line*

**cushion¹** /ˈkʊʃn ˈकुश्न्/ *noun* [C] **1** a bag filled with soft material, for example, feathers, which you put on a chair, etc. to make it more comfortable गद्दी, गद्दा, कुशन NOTE पलंग पर रखी गद्दी को **pillow** कहते हैं। **2** something that acts or is shaped like a cushion गद्दे जैसी (काम करने वाली) या गद्दे के आकार की वस्तु *A hovercraft rides on a cushion of air.*

**cushion²** /ˈkʊʃn ˈकुश्न्/ *verb* [T] **1** to make a fall, hit, etc. less painful गिरने या चोट खाने की क्रिया को सहनीय बनाना *The snow cushioned his fall.* **2** to reduce the unpleasant effect of sth

किसी के अप्रिय प्रभाव को कम करना *She spent her childhood on a farm, cushioned from the effects of the war.*

**cushy** /ˈkʊʃi ˈकुशि/ *adj.* (*informal*) too easy, needing little effort (in a way that seems unfair to others) बहुत आसान, आराम वाला (इस रीति से कि दूसरों को अनुचित लगे) *a cushy job*

**custard** /ˈkʌstəd ˈकस्टड्/ *noun* [U] a sweet yellow sauce made from milk, eggs and sugar दूध-अंडा-चीनी मिलाकर बनी मीठी पीली खीर; कस्टर्ड

**custard apple** *noun* [C] (*pl.* **custard apples**) a large fleshy tropical fruit with a dark rough skin and sweet yellow pulp शरीफ़ा

**custodian** /kʌˈstəʊdiən कˈस्टोडिअन्/ *noun* [C] **1** (*formal*) a person who looks after sth, especially a museum, library, etc. (संग्रहालय, पुस्तकालय आदि का) अभिरक्षक-प्रबंधक, देखभाल करनेवाला व्यक्ति **2** = **caretaker**

**custody** /ˈkʌstədi ˈकस्टडि/ *noun* [U] **1** the legal right or duty to take care of sb/sth किसी की देखभाल का क़ानूनी अधिकार; अभिरक्षा *After the divorce, the mother **had custody of** the children.* **2** the state of being guarded, or kept in prison temporarily, especially by the police पुलिस की हिरासत, पुलिस की देख-रेख में सुरक्षा *The man was **kept in custody** until his trial.*

**custom** /ˈkʌstəm ˈकस्टम्/ *noun* **1** [C, U] a way of behaving which a particular group or society has had for a long time प्रथा, रिवाज़, चलन *according to **local custom*** ➪ **habit** पर नोट देखिए। **2** [*sing.*] (*formal*) something that a person does regularly आदत *It's my custom to drink tea in the afternoon.* **3** [U] commercial activity; the practice of people buying things regularly from a particular shop, etc. व्यापारिक गतिविधि, व्यापार ग्राहकी; किसी विशेष दुकान से ही लोगों द्वारा ख़रीदारी *The local shop lost a lot of custom when the new supermarket opened.* ➪ **customs** देखिए।

**customary** /ˈkʌstəməri ˈकस्टमरि/ *adj.* according to custom; usual प्रथानुसार, रूढ़िगत, रिवाजी; सामान्य *It is customary to exchange sweets at Diwali in our country.*

**customer** /ˈkʌstəmə(r) ˈकस्टम(र्)/ *noun* [C] a person who buys goods or services in a shop, restaurant, etc. ग्राहक, ख़रीदार *The shop assistant was serving a customer.* ➪ **client** देखिए।

**customs** (*also* **Customs**) /ˈkʌstəmz ˈकस्टम्ज़्/ *noun* [*pl.*] **1** (**Excise and Customs**) the government department that collects taxes on goods bought and sold, and/or goods brought into the country and that checks what is being brought in चुंगी विभाग; सीमाशुल्क विभाग *a customs officer* **2** the place at an airport, etc. where government officials check your luggage to make sure you are not bringing goods into the country illegally हवाई अड्डे आदि पर वह स्थान जहाँ सरकारी अधिकारी लाए गए सामान की जाँच करते हैं **3** the taxes that must to paid to the government when goods are brought in from another country सीमाशुल्क, चुंगी *custom duty/duties* ➪ **excise** देखिए।

**cut¹** /kʌt कट्/ *verb* (*pres. part.* **cutting;** *pt, pp* **cut**) **1** [I, T] to make an opening, wound or mark in sth using a sharp tool, for example, a pair of scissors or a knife (चाकू, कैंची आदि से) काटना, कतरना *Be careful not to cut yourself on that broken glass!* **2** [T] **cut sth (from sth)** to remove sth or a part of sth, using a knife, etc. (चाकू आदि से) काटकर अलग करना *She cut two slices of bread* (= from the loaf). **3** [T] **cut sth (in/into sth)** to divide sth into pieces with a knife, etc. (चाकू आदि से) किसी वस्तु के हिस्से करना *She cut the cake into eight (pieces).* ○ *He cut the rope in two.* **4** [T] to make sth shorter by using scissors, etc. (कैंची आदि से) काटकर छोटा करना *I cut my own hair.* **5** [T] to make or form sth by removing material with a sharp tool तेज़ धार के औज़ार से काटकर कुछ बनाना *She cut a hole in the card and pushed the string through.* ○ *They cut a path through the jungle.* **6** [T] to reduce sth or make it shorter; to remove sth काट कर निकाल देना; घटाना या संक्षिप्त करना; हटा देना *to cut taxes/costs/spending* ○ *Several violent scenes in the film were cut.* **7** [T] (computing) to remove a piece of text from the screen कंप्यूटर स्क्रीन से लिखित सामग्री को हटा देना *Use the **cut and paste** buttons to change the order of the paragraphs.* **8** [I] **cut across, along, through, etc. (sth)** to go across, etc. sth, in order to make your route shorter रास्ते को छोटा करने के लिए मैदान के बीच में से निकलना; छोटे रास्ते से जाना *It's much quicker if we cut across the field.* **9** [T] (*spoken*) to stop sth (बीच में) रोकना *Cut the chat and get on with your work!* **10** [T] to deeply offend sb or hurt his/her feelings किसी को बहुत रुष्ट कर देना या भावनाओं को चोट पहुँचाना *His cruel remarks cut her deeply.*

> **NOTE** **Cut** से बनने वाले मुहावरों के लिए संबंधित संज्ञाओं, विशेषणों आदि की प्रविष्टियाँ देखिए। उदाहरण के लिए **cut corners** की व्याख्या **corner** में मिलेगी।

**PHR V** **cut across sth** to affect or be true for different groups that usually stay separate प्रायः अलग रहनेवाले समूहों, देशों आदि को समान रूप से प्रभावित करना, सबके लिए समान होना *The question of aid for the earthquake victims cuts across national boundaries.*

**cut sth back; cut back (on sth)** to reduce sth (किसी में) कटौती करना *to cut back on public spending*

**cut sth down** **1** to make sth fall down by cutting it काटकर गिराना *to cut down a tree* **2** to make sth shorter संक्षिप्त करना; छोटा करना *I have to cut my essay down to 2000 words.*

**cut sth down; cut down (on sth)** to reduce the quantity or amount of sth; to do sth less often मात्रा या राशि में कमी करना; किसी के प्रयोग में कमी लाना *You should cut down on fatty foods.*

**cut in (on sb/sth)** to interrupt sb/sth बाधा पहुँचाना; बीच में बोलना *She kept cutting in on our conversation.*

**cut sb off** to stop or interrupt sb's telephone conversation फ़ोन-वार्ता को बीच में रोक देना या उसमें बाधा पहुँचाना *We were cut off before I could give her my message.*

**cut sb/sth off** (*usually passive*) to stop the supply of sth to sb किसी वस्तु की आपूर्ति रोकना

**cut sth off** to block a road, etc. so that nothing can pass (सड़क आदि को) बंद करना *We must cut off all possible escape routes.*

**cut sth off (sth)** to remove sth from sth larger by cutting काटकर अलग करना *Be careful you don't cut your fingers off using that electric saw.*

**cut sb/sth off (from sb/sth)** (*usually passive*) to prevent sb/sth from moving from a place or contacting people outside कहीं जाने या किसी से मिलने पर रोक लगाना *The farm was cut off from the village by heavy snow.*

**cut sth open** to open sth by cutting काटकर खोलना या कटकर खुलना *She fell and cut her head open.*

**cut sth out** **1** to remove sth or to form sth into a particular shape by cutting काटकर निकालना या काटकर विशेष रूप देना *He cut the job advertisement out of the newspaper.* **2** to not include sth शामिल न करना; निकाल देना *Cut out the boring details!* **3** (*informal*) to stop saying or doing sth that annoys sb किसी को ऐसा कहने या करने से रोकना जो दूसरें को बुरा लगे *Cut that out and leave me alone!* **4** (*informal*) to stop doing or using sth किसी को कुछ करने या किसी को प्रयोग करने से रोकना *You'll only lose weight if you cut out sweet things from your diet.*

**be cut out for sth; be cut out to be sth** to have the qualities needed to do sth; to be suitable for sth/sb कुछ करने के लिए अपेक्षित गुणों से संपन्न होना; किसी काम के उपयुक्त होना *You're not cut out to be a soldier.*

**cut sth up** to cut sth into small pieces with a knife, etc. (चाक़ू आदि से) किसी चीज़ के छोटे टुकड़े करना

**cut²** /kʌt कट्/ *noun* [C] **1** an injury or opening in the skin made with a knife, etc. (चाक़ू आदि से हुआ) घाव *He had a deep cut on his forehead.* **2** an act of cutting काटने की प्रक्रिया *to have a cut and blow-dry* (= at the hairdresser's) **3 a cut (in sth)** a reduction in size, amount, etc. आकार, राशि आदि में कटौती *a cut in government spending* ○ *a power cut* (= when the electric current is stopped temporarily) **4** a piece of meat from a particular part of an animal किसी प्राणी के अंग विशेष के मांस का टुकड़ा *cheap cuts of lamb* **5** (*informal*) a share of the profits from sth, especially sth dishonest बेईमानी से हुए लाभ में हिस्सा ➪ **short cut** देखिए।

**cutback** /ˈkʌtbæk ˈकट्बैक्/ *noun* [C] a reduction in amount or number मात्रा या संख्या में कटौती *The management were forced to make cutbacks in staff.*

**cute** /kju:t क्यूट्/ *adj.* attractive; pretty आकर्षक; सुंदर *Your little girl is so cute!* ○ *a cute smile*

**cuticle** /ˈkju:tɪkl ˈक्यूटिक्ल्/ *noun* [C] **1** an area of hard skin at the base of the nails on your fingers and toes अंगुलियों और अँगूठों के नाख़ूनों के जड़ की कठोर त्वचा; उपचर्म, उपत्वचा **2** a hard outer layer that covers and protects a plant पौधे को ढकने और बचाने वाली बाहरी कठोर परत

**cutlery** /ˈkʌtləri ˈकट्लरि/ *noun* [U] the knives, forks and spoons that you use for eating food भोजन खाने के छुरी-काँटे-चम्मच; कटलरी

**cutlet** /ˈkʌtlət ˈकट्लट्/ *noun* [C] **1** a mixture of chopped meat, fish, vegetables or other foods, made into a flat shape, covered with breadcrumbs, and fried मांस, मछली, सब्ज़ियों या अन्य खाद्य पदार्थों के टुकड़ों के मिश्रण को समतल आकृति में ढालकर डबलरोटी के चूरे में लपेटकर तला गया व्यंजन; कटलेट **2** a small, thick piece of meat, often with bone in it, that is cooked हड्डीदार माँस का पकाया गया टुकड़ा

**cut-off** *noun* [C] the level or time at which sth stops सीमांत स्तर या समय, व्यवच्छेदन-तिथि, स्तर और समय जहाँ किसी का विराम-बिंदु हो *The cut-off date is 12 May. After that we'll end the offer.*

**cut-price** (*also* **cut-rate**) *adj.* sold at a reduced price; selling goods at low prices घटाए गए दाम पर बिकाऊ; कम क़ीमत पर बिकने वाला *cut-price offers* ○ *a cut-price store*

**cutters** /ˈkʌtəz ˈकटज़्/ *noun* [*pl.*] a tool that you use for cutting through sth, for example, metal काटने का उपकरण *a pair of wire cutters*

**cut-throat** *adj.* caring only about success and not worried about hurting any one केवल सफलता की चिंता करते हुए और दूसरों की भावनाओं की उपेक्षा करते हुए; निर्मम, गलाकाट *cut-throat business practices*

**cutting**[1] /ˈkʌtɪŋ ˈकटिङ्/ *noun* [C] **1** (*AmE* **clipping**) a piece cut out from a newspaper, etc. (समाचार पत्रों आदि से) काटा गया लेख; कतरना *press cuttings* **2** a piece cut off from a plant that you use for growing a new plant (पौधे की) क़लम

**cutting**[2] /ˈkʌtɪŋ ˈकटिङ्/ *adj.* (used about sth you say) unkind; meant to hurt sb's feelings (कथन) निर्मम; भावनाओं को चोट पहुँचाने वाला *a cutting remark*

**CV** /ˌsiː ˈviː ˌसी ˈव्ही/ (*AmE* **resumé**) *noun* [*sing.*] curriculum vitae; a formal list of your education and work experience, often used when you are trying to get a new job व्यक्ति की शिक्षा और कार्य-अनुभव का विवरण (जो नौकरी ढूँढ़ने में प्रायः काम आता है) करिक्युलम वीटाइ, व्यक्तिगत विवरण

**cwm** /kʊm कुम्/ = **corrie**

**cwt.** *abbr.* a hundred weight; a measure of weight, about 50.8 kg, 50.8 भार मापन की इकाई, किलोग्राम के बराबर इकाई

**cyanide** /ˈsaɪənaɪd ˈसाइअनाइड्/ *noun* [U] a poisonous chemical एक विषैला रसायन; सायनाइड

**cybercafe** /ˈsaɪbəkæfeɪ ˈसाइबकैफ़े/ *noun* [C] a cafe with computers where customers can pay to use the Internet निर्धारित दर से भुगतान कर कंप्यूटर-प्रयोग की सुविधा देने वाली दुकान

**cybernetics** /ˌsaɪbəˈnetɪks ˌसाइबˈनेटिक्स्/ *noun* [U] the scientific study of communication and control, in which, for example, human and animal brains are compared with machines and electronic devices संप्रेषण और नियंत्रण की प्रक्रियाओं का वैज्ञानिक अध्ययन जिसमें उदाहरण के लिए पशु के मस्तिष्क का मशीन और इलेक्ट्रॉनिक उपकरण से तुलना की जाती है; साइबरनेटिक्स

**cyberspace** /ˈsaɪbəspeɪs ˈसाइबस्पेस्/ *noun* [U] a place that is not real, where electronic messages exist while they are being sent from one computer to another एक अ-भौतिक स्थल जहाँ एक से दूसरे कंप्यूटर को जा रहे इलेक्ट्रॉनिक संदेश स्थित होते हैं

**cycle**[1] /ˈsaɪkl ˈसाइक्ल्/ *noun* [C] **1** the fact of a series of events being repeated many times, always in the same order घटना-शृंखलाओं या प्रक्रियाओं की उसी क्रम में अनेक बार पुनरावृत्ति होना; चक्र घटनाचक्र, प्रक्रियाचक्र *the carbon/nitrogen cycle* ➪ **rock** और **water** पर चित्र देखिए। **2** a bicycle or motor cycle साइकिल या मोटर-साइकिल *a cycle shop* ✪ पर्याय **bike**

**cycle**[2] /ˈsaɪkl ˈसाइक्ल्/ *verb* [I] to ride a bicycle साइकिल पर सवार होना *He usually cycles to school.*

**cycle rickshaw** *noun* [C] a small light vehicle with three wheels that is used in some Asian countries to carry people over short distances रिक्शा

**cyclic** /ˈsaɪklɪk; sɪk- ˈसाइक्लिक्; -ˈसिक्/ (*also* **cyclical** /ˈsaɪklɪkl; sɪk- ˈसाइक्लिकल्; -ˈसिक्/) *adj.* following a repeated pattern पुनरावृत होने वाला चक्रीय, चक्राकार

**cyclist** /ˈsaɪklɪst ˈसाइक्लिस्ट्/ *noun* [C] a person who rides a bicycle साइकिल-सवार

**cyclone** /ˈsaɪkləʊn ˈसाइक्लोन्/ *noun* [C] a violent wind that moves in a circle causing a storm चक्रवात, बवंडर ➪ **storm** पर नोट देखिए। ▶ **cyclonic** /saɪˈklɒnɪk साइˈक्लॉनिक्/ *adj.* चक्रवाती

**cygnet** /ˈsɪgnət ˈसिग्नट्/ *noun* [C] the young of **a swan** हंस का बच्चा, हंस-शावक

**cylinder** /ˈsɪlɪndə(r) ˈसिलिन्ड(र्)/ *noun* [C] **1** an object shaped like a tube बेलन के आकार की वस्तु, सिलिंडर ➪ **solid** पर चित्र देखिए। **2** a tube-shaped part of an engine, for example, in a car कार आदि में इंजिन का बेलनाकार पुरज़ा, सिलिंडर ▶ **cylindrical** /səˈlɪndrɪkl सˈलिन्ड्रिकल्/ *adj.* बेलनाकार

**cymbal** /ˈsɪmbl ˈसिम्बल्/ *noun* [C, *usually pl.*] one of a pair of round metal plates used as a musical instrument. Cymbals make a loud ringing sound when you hit them together or with a stick झाँझ, मंजीरा ➪ पृष्ठ 789 पर चित्र देखिए।

**cynic** /ˈsɪnɪk ˈसिनिक्/ *noun* [C] a person who believes that people only do things for themselves, rather than to help others व्यक्ति जो सबको स्वार्थी समझता हो, दोषदर्शी *Don't be such a cynic. He did it to help us, not for the money.* ▶ **cynical** /ˈsɪnɪkl ˈसिनिकल्/ *adj.* हरेक को स्वार्थी समझने वाला *a cynical remark* ▶ **cynically** /-kli -क्लि/ *adv.* दोषदर्शिता से ▶ **cynicism** /ˈsɪnɪsɪzem ˈसिनिसिज़म्/ *noun* [U] दोषदर्शिता

**cypress** /ˈsaɪprəs ˈसाइप्रस्/ *noun* [C] a tall straight tree of the kind that does not lose its leaves in winter (**an evergreen**) एक सदाबहार ऊँचा वृक्ष

**Cyrillic** /səˈrɪlɪk सˈरिलिक्/ *noun* [U] the alphabet that is used in languages such as Russian रूसी जैसी भाषाओं की लिपि

**cyst** /sɪst सिस्ट्/ *noun* [C] a swelling or a lump filled with liquid in the body or under the skin शरीर के अंदर बन जाने वाली एक खोखली गाँठ जिसमें द्रव पदार्थ जमा हो जाता है

**cystic fibrosis** /ˌsɪstɪk faɪˈbrəʊsɪs ˌसिस्टिक् फ़ाइˈब्रोसिस्/ *noun* [U] a serious medical condition that some people are born with, in which some organs do not work correctly. It can cause death एक गंभीर जन्मजात रोग जिसमें रोगी के कुछ अंग ठीक तरह काम नहीं करते, जिसमें रोग से मृत्यु भी हो सकती है

**cystitis** /sɪˈstaɪtɪs सिˈस्टाइटिस्/ *noun* [U] an infection, especially in women, of the organ in which liquid waste collects before leaving the body (**the bladder**) that makes it painful to go to the toilet मूत्रालय की सूजन (विशेषतः महिलाओं में)

**cytology** /saɪˈtɒlədʒi साइˈटॉलजि/ *noun* [U] the study of the structure and function of plant and animal cells पौधों और पशुओं की कोशिकाओं का वैज्ञानिक अध्ययन; कोशिकाविज्ञान

**cytoplasm** /ˈsaɪtəʊplæzəm ˈसाइटोप्लैज़म्/ *noun* [U] the material that a cell is made of, except for the **nucleus** द्रव्य या पदार्थ जिससे कोशिका का निर्माण होता है (उसके मध्य भाग को छोड़कर), कोशिका द्रव्य

**czar, czarina** = **tsar, tsarina**

# D d

**D, d** /diː डी/ *noun* [C, U] (*pl.* **D's; d's** /diːz डीज़्/) the fourth letter of the English alphabet अंग्रेज़ी वर्णमाला का चौथा अक्षर *'Delhi' begins with a 'D'.*

**d.** *abbr.* died निधन *J L Nehru, d. 1964*

**dab[1]** /dæb डैब्/ *verb* [I, T] (**dabbing; dabbed**) to touch sth lightly, usually several times हलके हाथ से लगाना (प्रायः अनेक बार), थपथपाना, थपकना *He dabbed the cut with some cotton wool.*
PHRV **dab sth on/off (sth)** to put sth on or to remove sth lightly थपथपाकर कुछ लगाना जैसे पाउडर आदि *to dab some antiseptic on a wound*

**dab[2]** /dæb डैब्/ *noun* [C] **1** a light touch थपकी, हलका स्पर्श *She gave her eyes a dab with a handkerchief.* **2** a small quantity of sth that is put on a surface (पाउडर आदि की) थोड़ी-सी मात्रा जो कहीं पर लगा दी जाए *a dab of paint/perfume*

**dabble** /ˈdæbl ˈडैब्ल्/ *verb* **1** [I] to become involved in sth in a way that is not very serious किसी काम में हलकी-फुलकी रुचि रखना *to dabble in politics* **2** [T] to put your hands, feet, etc. in water and move them around पानी में हाथ-पैर डालकर थप-थप करना *We sat on the bank and dabbled our toes in the river.*

**dacoit** *noun* [C] (*IndE*) a member of an armed gang of robbers डकैत

**dacoity** *noun* [C, U] (*pl.* **dacoities**) (*IndE*) armed robbery carried out by a gang of **dacoits** डकैती

**dad** /dæd डैड्/ *noun* [C] (*informal*) father पिता *Is that your dad? ○ Come on, Dad!*

**daddy** /ˈdædi ˈडैडि/ *noun* [C] (*pl.* **daddies** / डैडीज़्/) (*informal*) (used by children) father (बच्चों द्वारा पिता के लिए प्रयुक्त शब्द) डैडी *I want my daddy!*

**daffodil** /ˈdæfədɪl ˈडैफ़डिल्/ *noun* [C] a tall yellow flower that grows in the spring वसंत ऋतु का लंबी डंडी वाला पीला फूल; डैफ़ोडिल, नरगिस

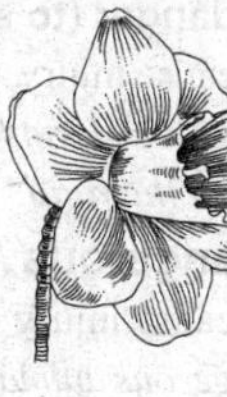

**daft** /dɑːft डाफ़्ट्/ *adj.* (*informal*) silly; foolish बेवकूफ़; मूर्ख *Don't be daft. ○ a daft idea*

**dagger** /ˈdægə(r) ˈडैग(र्)/ *noun* [C] a type of knife used as a weapon, especially in past times कटार, दुधारी छुरा, विशेषतः अतीत काल में प्रयुक्त

**daily[1]** /ˈdeɪli ˈडेलि/ *adj., adv.* done, made or happening every day प्रतिदिन, प्रतिदिन का, दैनिक *a daily routine/delivery/newspaper*

**daily[2]** /ˈdeɪli ˈडेलि/ *noun* [C] (*pl.* **dailies**) (*informal*) a newspaper that is published every day except Sunday रविवार को छोड़कर प्रतिदिन निकलने वाला अख़बार

**dainty** /ˈdeɪnti ˈडेन्टि/ *adj.* **1** small and pretty छोटा और सुंदर *a dainty lace handkerchief* **2** (used about a person's movements) very careful in a way that tries to show good manners नज़ाकत भरी (हरकत, चाल आदि), सुरुचिपूर्ण *Vedika took a dainty bite of the giant hot dog.* ▶ **daintily** *adv.* नज़ाकत से

**dairy[1]** /ˈdeəri ˈडेअरि/ *noun* [C] (*pl.* **dairies**) **1** a place on a farm where milk is kept and butter, cheese, etc. are made डेरी, दुग्धशाला **2** a company which sells milk, butter, eggs, etc. दूध, मक्खन आदि बेचने वाली कंपनी

**dairy[2]** /ˈdeəri ˈडेअरि/ *adj.* (*only before a noun*) **1** made from milk दुग्ध-निर्मित *dairy products/produce* (= milk, butter, cheese, etc.) **2** connected with the production of milk दुग्ध-उत्पादन से संबंधित *dairy cattle ○ a dairy farm*

**dais** /ˈdeɪɪs ˈडेइस्/ *noun* [C] a raised platform, usually at end of a room for speakers or guests of honour (वक्ताओं या माननीय अतिथियों के लिए) मंच

**daisy** /ˈdeɪzi ˈडेज़ि/ *noun* [C] (*pl.* **daisies**) a small white flower with a yellow centre, which usually grows wild in grass एक छोटा-सा सफ़ेद जंगली फूल जो बीच में पीला होता है; डेज़ी

**dam** /dæm डैम्/ *noun* [C] a wall built across a river to hold back the water and form a lake (**reservoir**) behind it बाँध (पानी रोकने के लिए नदी पर बनाया गया) ▶ **dam** *verb* [T] (*pres. part.* **damming;** *pt, pp* **dammed**) बाँध बनाकर पानी को रोकना

**damage[1]** /ˈdæmɪdʒ ˈडैमिज़्/ *noun* **1** [U] **damage (to sth)** harm or injury caused when sth is broken or spoiled किसी चीज़ के टूटने से होने वाली हानि या क्षति *Earthquakes can **cause** terrible **damage** ○ to **repair the damage*** **2** **damages** [*pl.*] money that you can ask for if sb damages sth of yours or hurts you हरजाना, क्षतिपूर्ति के रूप में दिया गया धन, मुआवज़ा *Mrs Roy, who lost a leg in the crash, was awarded damages of Rs 100,000.*

**damage[2]** /ˈdæmɪdʒ ˈडैमिज़्/ *verb* [T] to spoil or harm sth, for example by breaking it हानि पहुँचाना, नुक़सान करना (जैसे कुछ तोड़ देना) *The roof was dam-*

*aged by the storm.* ▶ **damaging** *adj.* हानिकारक, नुक़सानदेह *These rumours could be damaging to her reputation.*

**dame** /deɪm डेम्/ *noun* [C] **Dame** (*BrE*) a title given to a woman as an honour because of sth special that she has done विशेष उपलब्धि पर किसी महिला को दी गई सम्मान-पदवी *Dame Agatha Christie*

**damn¹** /dæm डैम्/ *verb* [I, T] (*slang*) a swear word that people use to show that they are angry झुँझलाहट व्यंजक शब्द *Damn (it)! I've left my money behind.*

**damn²** /dæm डैम्/ (*also* **damned**) *adj., adv.* (*slang*) **1** (a swear word that people use for emphasizing what they are saying) very अतिशय के भाव को बलपूर्वक व्यक्त करने के लिए प्रयुक्त *Read it! It's a damn good book.* **2** a swear word that people use to show that they are angry क्रोध व्यजंक शब्द के रूप में प्रयुक्त *Some damn fool has parked too close to me.*

**damn³** /dæm डैम्/ *noun*

**IDM not give a damn (about sb/sth)** not care at all कोई परवाह नहीं करना *I don't give a damn what he thinks about me.*

**damning** /ˈdæmɪŋ ˈडैमिङ्/ *adj.* that criticizes sth very much कटु आलोचना से पूर्ण, निंदात्मक *There was a damning article about the book in the newspaper.*

**damp¹** /dæmp डैम्प्/ *adj.* a little wet सीलनभरा *The house had been empty and felt rather damp.* ▶ **damp** *noun* [U] सीलन, नमी *She hated the damp and the cold of the English climate.* ➪ **wet** पर नोट देखिए।

**damp²** /dæmp डैम्प्/ *verb* [T] **damp sth (down)** **1** to make a fire burn less strongly or stop burning आग की रोक-थाम करना या उसे बुझा देना *He tried to damp (down) the flames.* **2** to make sth less strong or urgent किसी की शक्ति क्षीण करना, (जोश) ठंडा करना *He tried to damp down their expectations in case they failed.*

**dampen** /ˈdæmpən ˈडैम्पन्/ *verb* [T] **1** to make sth less strong or urgent किसी की शक्ति क्षीण करना, (जोश) ठंडा करना *Even the awful weather did not dampen their enthusiasm for the trip.* **2** to make sth a little wet नम करना, हलका गीला करना *He dampened his hair to try to stop it sticking up.*

**damson** /ˈdæmzn ˈडैम्ज़्न्/ *noun* a type of small dark purple fruit (**plum**) आलू बुख़ारा

**dance¹** /dɑːns डान्स्/ *noun* **1** [C] a series of steps and movements which you do to music नाच, नृत्य **2** [U] dancing as a form of art or entertainment नृत्य-कला *She's very interested in modern dance.* **3** [C] (*old-fashioned*) a social meeting at which people dance with each other नृत्य-गोष्ठी, सामाजिक प्रसंग जिसमें लोग एक-दूसरे के साथ नाचते हैं *My parents met at a dance.*

**dance²** /dɑːns डान्स्/ *verb* **1** [I, T] to move around to the rhythm of music by making a series of steps नाचना, नृत्य करना *I can't dance very well.* ○ *to dance the samba* **2** [I] to jump and move around with energy उछल-कूद करते हुए नाचना, उछल-कूद करना *She was dancing up and down with excitement.*

**dancer** /ˈdɑːnsə(r) ˈडान्स(र्)/ *noun* [C] a person who dances, often as a job नर्तक *a ballet dancer* ○ *She's a good dancer.*

**dancing** /ˈdɑːnsɪŋ ˈडान्सिङ्/ *noun* [U] the action of moving to music संगीत की धुन पर नाचना *Will there be dancing at the party?*

**dandelion** /ˈdændɪlaɪən ˈडैन्डिलाइअन्/ *noun* [C] a small wild plant with a bright yellow flower चमकीले पीले फूल वाला एक छोटा जंगली पौधा; डैन्डिलायन

**dandruff** /ˈdændrʌf ˈडैन्ड्रफ़्/ *noun* [U] small pieces of dead skin in the hair, that look like white powder बालों में रूसी

**danger** /ˈdeɪndʒə(r) ˈडेन्ज(र्)/ *noun* **1** [U, C] the chance that sb/sth may be hurt, killed or damaged or that sth bad may happen ख़तरा, संकट, भय *When he saw the men had knives, he realized his life was* ***in danger****. The men kept on running until they thought they were* ***out of danger****.* **2** [C] **a danger (to sb/sth)** a person or thing that can cause injury, pain or damage to sb ख़तरनाक व्यक्ति या वस्तु *Drunk drivers are a danger to everyone on the road.*

**dangerous** /ˈdeɪndʒərəs ˈडेन्जरस्/ *adj.* likely to cause injury or damage ख़तरनाक, भयंकर *a dangerous animal/road/illness* ▶ **dangerously** *adv.* ख़तरनाक ढंग से *He was standing dangerously close to the cliff edge.*

**dangle** /ˈdæŋgl ˈडैङ्गल्/ *verb* [I, T] to hang freely; to hold sth so that it hangs down in this way झूलना, लटकना; झुलाना, लटकाना *She sat on the fence with her legs dangling.* ○ *The police dangled a rope from the bridge and the man grabbed it.*

**dank** /dæŋk डैङ्क् / *adj.* wet, cold and unpleasant गीला, ठंडा और बुरा लगने वाला

**dare[1]** /deə(r) डेअर(र्) / *verb* **1** [I] *(usually in negative sentences)* **dare (to) do sth** to have enough courage to do sth साहस करना *Nobody dared (to) speak.* ○ *I daren't ask her to lend me any more money.*

> **NOTE** **Dare** का निषेधवाचक रूप है **dare not** (प्रायः **daren't**) या **do not/does not (don't/doesn't) dare** तथा भूतकाल रूप है **did not (didn't) dare** ।

**2** [T] **dare sb (to do sth)** to ask or tell sb to do sth in order to see if he/she has the courage to do it (किसी व्यक्ति को किसी बात की) चुनौती देना, ललकारना *Can you jump off that wall? Go on, I dare you!*
**IDM** **don't you dare** used for telling sb very strongly not to do sth जब किसी को कोई काम करने से रोकना हो *Don't you dare tell my parents about this!*
**how dare you** used when you are angry about sth that sb has done जब किसी के ग़लत किए पर रोष व्यक्त करना हो *How dare you speak to me like that!*
**I dare say** used when you are saying sth is probable जब यह बताना हो कि कोई बात संभव है *'I think you should accept the offer.' 'I dare say you're right.'*

**dare[2]** /deə(r) डेअ(र्) / *noun* [C, *usually sing.*] something dangerous that sb asks you to do, to see if you have the courage to do it किसी के साहस की परीक्षा के लिए उसे ख़तरनाक काम की चुनौती देना *'Why did you try to swim across the river?' '**For a dare**.'*

**daredevil** /ˈdeədevl ˈडेअडेव्ल् / *noun* [C] a person who likes to do dangerous things दुस्साहसी व्यक्ति

**daring** /ˈdeərɪŋ ˈडेअरिङ् / *adj.* involving or taking risks; brave साहसी; बहादुर, निर्भीक ▶ **daring** *noun* [U] साहस, निर्भीकता *The climb required skill and daring.*

**dark[1]** /dɑːk डाक् / *adj.* **1** with no light or very little light अँधेरा *It was a dark night, with no moon.* ○ *What time does it **get dark** in winter?* **2** (used about a colour) not light; nearer black than white (रंग) गहरा, गाढ़ा; काला-सा, साँवला *dark blue* ✪ विलोम **light** या **pale** **3** *(usually BrE)* (used about a person's hair, skin or eyes) brown or black; not fair (व्यक्ति के बाल, त्वचा या आँखों का रंग) भूरा या काला; गोरा नहीं *She was small and dark with brown eyes.* **4** *(only before a noun)* hidden and frightening; mysterious छुपा हुआ या डरावना; रहस्यमय *He seemed friendly, but there was a dark side to his character.* **5** *(only before a noun)* sad; without hope दुखी; निराश, निराशापूर्ण *the dark days of the recession*

**dark[2]** /dɑːk डाक् / *noun* [*sing.*] **the dark** the state of having no light अँधेरा *He's afraid of the dark.* ○ *Why are you sitting alone **in the dark**?*
**IDM** **before/after dark** before/after the sun goes down in the evening सूर्यास्त से कुछ पहले या बाद; संध्या या रात्रि
**(be/keep sb) in the dark (about sth)** (be/keep sb) in a position of not knowing about sth अंधेरे में होना या रखना, जानकारी न होना या न देना *Don't keep me in the dark. Tell me!*

**the dark ages** *noun* [*pl.*] **1 the Dark Ages** the period in western Europe between the end of the Roman Empire (about 500 AD) and the end of the 10th century AD अंधकार-युग, पश्चिमी यूरोप के इतिहास में रोमन साम्राज्य के अंत (लगभग 500 ईसवी सन्) से दसवीं शताब्दी ईसवी के बीच का समय **2** a period of history or a time when sth was not developed or modern इतिहास में निकास या आधुनिकता के अभाव का समय *Back in the dark ages of computing, in about 1980, they started a software company.*

**darken** /ˈdɑːkən ˈडाकन् / *verb* [I, T] to become or to make sth darker अँधेरा (काला) होना या कर देना *The sky suddenly darkened and it started to rain.*

**dark glasses** = **sunglasses**

**darkly** /ˈdɑːkli डाकली / *adv.* *(written)* **1** in a frightening or unpleasant way भयभीत करने या बुरा लगने वाले ढंग से *He hinted darkly that someone would soon be going to hospital.* **2** showing a dark colour कालिमा बिखेरते हुए, काला लगते हुए

**darkness** /ˈdɑːknəs ˈडाक्नस् / *noun* [U] the state of being dark अँधेरा, कालापन *We sat **in total darkness**, waiting for the lights to come back on.*

**darkroom** /ˈdɑːkruːm; -rʊm ˈडाक्रूम्; -रुम् / *noun* [C] a room that can be made completely dark so that film can be taken out of a camera and photographs can be produced there पूरी तरह अँधेरा कमरा, डार्करूम (जहाँ कैमरे से फ़िल्म निकालकर उसे धोने और बनाने का काम किया जाता है)

**darling** /ˈdɑːlɪŋ ˈडालिङ् / *noun* [C] a word that you say to sb you love प्रिय व्यक्ति के लिए संबोधन के रूप में प्रयुक्त

**darn** /dɑːn डान् / *verb* [I, T] to repair a hole in clothes by sewing across it in one direction and then in the other (कपड़े में हुए छेदों को) रफ़ू करना *I hate darning socks.*

**dart[1]** /dɑːt डाट् / *noun* **1** an object like a small arrow. It is thrown in a game or shot as a weapon एक छोटा तीर जिसे खेल में फेंका जाता है या अस्त्र के रूप

में चलाया जाता है *The keeper fired a tranquillizer dart into the tiger to send it to sleep.* **2 darts** [U] a game in which you throw darts at a round board with numbers on it **(a dartboard)** एक खेल जिसमें तीर एक लक्ष्यपटल (एक गोल तख़्ता जिस पर संख्याएँ अंकित होती हैं) पर फेंके जाते हैं

**dart²** /dɑːt डाट्/ *verb* [I, T] to move or make sth move suddenly and quickly in a certain direction अचानक और तेज़ी से एक ओर जाना या भेजना *A rabbit darted across the field.* ○ *She darted an angry glance at me.*

**dash¹** /dæʃ डैश्/ *noun* **1** [*sing.*] an act of going somewhere suddenly and quickly अचानक और तेज़ी से कहीं जाने की क्रिया *Suddenly the prisoner made a dash for the door.* **2** [C, *usually sing.*] a small amount of sth that you add to sth else चुटकी भर कोई वस्तु (किसी अन्य वस्तु में मिलाने के लिए) *a dash of lemon juice* **3** [C] a small horizontal line (–) used in writing, especially for adding extra information लेखन में प्रयुक्त रेखा (–) (विशेषतः जब कोई बात जोड़नी हो, सूचना में वृद्धि करनी हो) ➪ **hyphen** देखिए।

**dash²** /dæʃ डैश्/ *verb* **1** [I] to go somewhere suddenly and quickly अचानक और तेज़ी से कहीं चले जाना *We all dashed for shelter when it started to rain.* ○ *I must dash—I'm late.* **2** [I, T] to hit sth with great force; to throw sth so that it hits sth else very hard (किसी वस्तु पर) कसकर चोट करना; (किसी वस्तु को) कसकर ऐसे फेंकना कि वह दूसरी वस्तु पर ज़ोरदार चोट करे *She dashed her racket to the ground.*

IDM **dash sb's hopes (of sth/of doing sth)** to completely destroy sb's hopes of doing sth (किसी की) आशाओं को पूरी तरह छिन्न-भिन्न कर देना

PHR V **dash sth off** to write or draw sth very quickly बहुत तेज़ी से कुछ लिखना *I dashed off a note to my boss and left.*

**dashboard** /ˈdæʃbɔːd ˈडैश्बॉड्/ *noun* [C] the part in a car in front of the driver where most of the switches, etc. are डैशबोर्ड, ड्राइवर के सामने लगा बोर्ड जिस पर कार के अधिकतर स्विच लगे होते हैं ➪ **car** पर चित्र देखिए।

**data** /ˈdeɪtə; ˈdɑːtə ˈडेटा; ˈडाटा/ *noun* [U, *pl.*] (used as a plural noun in technical English, when the singular is **datum**) facts or information (तकनीकी अंग्रेज़ी में बहुवचन संज्ञा के रूप में प्रयुक्त जबकि एकवचन रूप datum है) तथ्य समूह या सूचना-संग्रह, डाटा *to gather/collect data* ○ *data capture/retrieval* (= ways of storing and looking at information on a computer) ○ *data processing*

**database** /ˈdeɪtəbeɪs ˈडेटबेस्/ *noun* [C] a large amount of data that is stored in a computer and can easily be used, added to, etc. कंप्यूटर में संचित विपुल सूचना-सामग्री; डाटाबेस

**date¹** /deɪt डेट्/ *noun* **1** [C] a particular day of the month or year महीने या वर्ष का विशेष दिन, तिथि, दिनांक, तारीख़ *What's the date today?* ○ *What's your date of birth?* ○ *We'd better **fix a date** for the next meeting.* **2** [*sing.*] a particular time एक विशेष समय *We can discuss this **at a later date**.* **3** [C] an arrangement to meet sb, especially a boyfriend or girlfriend किसी से भेंट करने की व्यवस्था (विशेषतः पुरुष-मित्र या महिला-मित्र) *Shall we **make a date** to have lunch together?* ➪ **blind date** देखिए। **4** [C] a small, sweet, dark brown fruit that comes from a tree which grows in hot countries खजूर, छुआरा

IDM **out of date 1** not fashionable; no longer useful अप्रचलित, पुराना; बेकार *out-of-date methods/machinery* **2** no longer able to be used जिसकी प्रयोग करने की निर्धारित अवधि समाप्त हो चुकी है *I must renew my passport. It's out of date.*

**to date** (*formal*) until now अब तक *We've had very few complaints to date.*

**up to date 1** completely modern अद्यतन, पूर्णतया आधुनिक *The new kitchen will be right up to date, with all the latest gadgets.* **2** with all the latest information; having done everything that you should नवीनतम सूचनाओं से युक्त; समस्त अपेक्षाओं को पूर्ण किया हुआ *In this report we'll bring you up to date with the latest news from the area.*

**date²** /deɪt डेट्/ *verb* **1** [T] to discover or guess how old sth is (किसी का) काल निर्धारित करना *The skeleton has been dated at about 3000 BC.* **2** [T] to write the day's date on sth (किसी पर) तारीख़ डालना *The letter is dated 24 March 2000.* **3** [I, T] to seem, or to make sb/sth seem, old-fashioned पुरानी चाल का लगना या लगवाना *We chose a simple style so that it wouldn't date as quickly.*

PHR V **date back to...; date from...** to have existed since... अमुक तिथि से चला आ रहा है *The house dates back to the seventeenth century.*

**dated** /ˈdeɪtɪd ˈडेटिड्/ *adj.* old-fashioned; belonging to a time in the past पुरानी चाल का, अप्रचलित; पुराने ज़माने का *This sort of jacket looks rather dated now.*

**the date line** = **the International Date Line**

**dative** /ˈdeɪtɪv ˈडेटिव्/ *noun* [C] (*grammar*) the form of a noun, a pronoun, or an adjective in some languages when it is, or is connected with, the **indirect object** of a verb (कुछ भाषाओं में) संज्ञा, सर्वनाम या विशेषण का गौण कर्म संबंधी रूप *In the sentence 'Give me the book', 'me' is in the dative.* ➪ **accusative, genitive, nominative** और **vocative** देखिए।

**datum** /ˈdeɪtəm ˈडेटम्/ = **data**

**daub** /dɔ:b डॉब्/ *verb* [T] **daub A on B; daub B with A** to spread a substance such as paint, mud, etc. thickly and/or carelessly onto sth (दीवार आदि पर रंग आदि को) पोतना, लीपना *The walls had been daubed with graffiti.*

**daughter** /ˈdɔ:tə(r) ˈडॉट(र्)/ *noun* [C] a female child पुत्री, लड़की *I have two sons and one daughter.*

**daughter-in-law** *noun* [C] (*pl.* **daughters-in-law**) the wife of your son पुत्रवधू

**daunt** /dɔ:nt डॉन्ट्/ *verb* [T] (*usually passive*) to frighten or to worry sb by being too big or difficult डराना या निरुत्साहित करना *Don't be daunted by all the controls—in fact it's a simple machine to use.* ▶ **daunting** *adj.* निरुत्साहित करने वाला *a daunting task*

**dawdle** /ˈdɔ:dl ˈडॉड्ल्/ *verb* [I] to go somewhere very slowly सुस्ती से चलना *Stop dawdling! We've got to be there by two.*

**dawn**[1] /dɔ:n डॉन्/ *noun* **1** [U, C] the early morning, when light first appears in the sky ऊषा-काल, बड़े सवेरे *before/at dawn* ○ *Dawn was breaking* (= it was starting to get light) *as I set off to work.* **2** [*sing.*] **the beginning** प्रारंभ *the dawn of civilization*

**IDM the crack of dawn** ➪ **crack**[2] देखिए।

**dawn**[2] /dɔ:n डॉन्/ *verb* [I] **1** (*formal*) to begin to grow light, after the night दिन निकलना *The day dawned bright and cold.* ○ (*figurative*) *A new era of peace is dawning.* **2 dawn (on sb)** to become clear (to sb) कोई बात सूझना *Suddenly it dawned on her. 'Of course!' she said. 'You're Mohan's brother!'*

**day** /deɪ डे/ *noun* **1** [C] a period of 24 hours. Seven days make up a week दिन, 24 घंटों की अवधि *'What day is it today?' 'Tuesday.'* ○ *I'd already spoken to him the day before/the previous day.* ○ *I work six days a week. Sunday's my day off (when I do not work).* **2** [C, U] the time when the sky is light; not night दिन का समय *It's been raining all day (long).* ○ *Owls sleep* **by day** (= during the day) *and hunt at night.* **3** [C] the hours of the day when you work दिन में काम करने के घंटे *She's expected to work a seven-hour day.* **4** [C] (*also* **days**) a particular period of time in the past पिछले जमाने की कोई विशेष काल-अवधि *in Raj Kapoor's days* ○ *There weren't so many cars in those days.*

**IDM at the end of the day** ➪ **end**[1] देखिए।

**break of day** ➪ **break**[2] देखिए।

**call it a day** ➪ **call**[1] देखिए।

**day by day** every day; as time passes प्रतिदिन; समय बीतने के साथ *Day by day, she was getting a little bit stronger.*

**day in, day out** every day, without any change प्रतिदिन, बिना किसी परिवर्तन के *He sits at his desk working, day in, day out.*

**day-to-day** happening as a normal part of each day; usual दिन-प्रतिदिन का; रिवाज़ी, रोज़मर्रा का

**from day to day; from one day to the next** within a short period of time थोड़े समय के अंदर, अगले दिन, आज के बाद *Things change so quickly that we never know what will happen from one day to the next.*

**have a field day** ➪ **field day** देखिए।

**it's early days (yet)** ➪ **early** देखिए।

**make sb's day** (*informal*) to make sb very happy (किसी को) बहुत प्रसन्न करना

**one day; some day** at some time in the future किसी दिन, भविष्य में कभी *Some day we'll go back and see all our old friends.*

**the other day** a few days ago; recently कुछ दिन पहले; हाल में *I bumped into him in town the other day.*

**the present day** ➪ **present**[1] देखिए।

**these days** in the present age; nowadays वर्तमान में; आजकल

**daybreak** /ˈdeɪbreɪk डेब्रेक/ *noun* [U] the time in the early morning when light first appears सूर्योदय ✪ पर्याय **dawn**

**daydream** /ˈdeɪdri:m ˈडेड्रीम्/ *noun* [C] thoughts that are not connected with what you are doing; often pleasant scenes in your imagination दिवास्वप्न, वास्तविकता से कटे हुए विचार; काल्पनिक आनंद *The child stared out of the window, lost in a daydream.* ▶ **daydream** *verb* [I] काल्पनिक आनंद में मग्न होना, दिवास्वप्न देखना, मन के लड्डू खाना *Don't just sit there daydreaming—do some work!*

**daylight** /ˈdeɪlaɪt ˈडेलाइट्/ *noun* [U] the light that there is during the day दिन की रोशनी, सूर्य का प्रकाश *The colours look quite different* ***in daylight.*** ○ *daylight hours*

**IDM broad daylight** ➪ **broad** देखिए।

**day return** *noun* [C] (*BrE*) a train or bus ticket for going somewhere and coming back on the same day. It is cheaper than a normal return ticket दैनिक वापसी यात्रा के लिए बस या रेल का टिकट, सामान्य वापसी टिकट से कम यात्रा-व्यय

**daytime** /ˈdeɪtaɪm ˈडेटाइम्/ *noun* [U] the time when it is light; not night दिन के समय *These flowers open **in the daytime** and close again at night.* ○ *daytime TV*

**daze** /deɪz डेज़्/ *noun*

IDM **in a daze** unable to think or react normally; confused कुछ सोचने या करने में असमर्थ, जड़; चकित-भ्रमित

**dazed** /deɪzd डेज़्ड्/ *adj.* unable to think or react normally; confused जड़; किंकर्तव्यविमूढ़ *He had a dazed expression on his face.*

**dazzle** /ˈdæzl ˈडैज़्ल्/ *verb* [T] (*usually passive*) **1** (used about a bright light) to make sb unable to see for a short time (तेज़ रोशनी में) चौंधिया देना, चौंध उत्पन्न कर देना *She was dazzled by the other car's headlights.* **2** to impress sb very much किसी को अत्यंत प्रभावित कर देना *He had been dazzled by her beauty.* ▶ **dazzling** *adj.* चौंधिया देने वाला *a dazzling light*

**DC** /ˌdiː ˈsiː ˌडी ˈसी / *abbr.* = **direct current**

**DDT** /ˌdiː diː ˈtiː ˌडी डी ˈटी / *abbr., noun* [U] a poisonous chemical substance that farmers use to kill insects डीडीटी, एक विषैला रसायन जिसे किसान कीटों को मारने में इस्तेमाल करते हैं

**de-** /diː डी / *prefix* (*in nouns, verbs, adjectives and adverbs*) **1** the opposite of किसी के विपरीत, विपरीत प्रभावकारी *decompress* **2 taking sth away** किसी से रहित *decaffeinated coffee*

**deacon** /ˈdiːkən ˈडीकन्/ *noun* [C] (*feminine* **deaconess**) an official in some Christian churches ईसाई चर्चों में एक अधिकारी

**dead¹** /ded डेड्/ *adj.* **1** no longer alive मृत, निर्जीव *Police found a dead body under the bridge.* ○ *The man was shot dead by a masked gunman.* ○ *dead leaves* ➪ **death** noun देखिए। **2** no longer used; finished जो अब प्रयोग में नहीं है; अप्रयोग के कारण समाप्त, मृत *Latin is a dead language.* ✪ विलोम **living** **3** (*not before a noun*) (used about a part of the body) no longer able to feel any thing (शरीर का कोई अंग) चेतनाहीन, निस्संज्ञ *Oh no, my foot's **gone dead**. I was sitting on it for too long.* **4** (*not before a noun*) (used about a piece of equipment) no longer working (कोई उपकरण) निष्क्रिय *I picked up the telephone but the line was dead.* ○ *This battery's dead.* **5** without movement, activity or interest निष्प्राण, एकदम शांत *This town is completely dead after 11 o'clock at night.* **6** (*only before a noun*) complete or exact पूर्ण या एकदम ठीक, यथार्थ *a dead silence/calm* ○ *The arrow hit the dead centre of the target.*

IDM **drop dead** ➪ **drop¹** देखिए।

**dead²** /ded डेड्/ **the dead** *noun* [*pl.*] people who have died मृत व्यक्ति, मृतक *A church service was held in memory of the dead.*

IDM **in the dead of night** in the middle of the night, when it is very dark and quiet आधी रात के सन्नाटे में

**dead³** /ded डेड्/ *adv.* completely, exactly or very पूरी तरह, अत्यधिक *The car made a strange noise and then stopped dead.* ○ *He's dead keen to start work.*

**deaden** /ˈdedn ˈडेड्न्/ *verb* [T] to make sth less strong, painful, etc. (किसी को) मंद कर देना, पीड़ा कम कर देना *They gave her drugs to try and deaden the pain.*

**dead end** *noun* [C] **1** a road, passage, etc. that is closed at one end एक ओर से बंद सड़क, गली आदि *We came to a dead end and had to turn back.* **2** a point, situation, etc. from which you can make no further progress अंतिम बिंदु (जहाँ से आगे आप नहीं जा सकते), चरमांत *The police had reached a dead end in their investigations.* ○ *He felt he was in **a dead-end job*** (= one with low wages and no hope of promotion), *so he left.*

**dead heat** *noun* [C] the result of a race when two people, etc. finish at exactly the same time दो प्रतियोगियों का एक साथ दौड़ समाप्त करना

**deadline** /ˈdedlaɪn ˈडेड्लाइन्/ *noun* [C] a time or date before which sth must be done or finished किसी कार्य का पूरा करने के लिए निर्धारित अंतिम तिथि *I usually **set** myself **a deadline** when I have a project to do.* ○ *A journalist is used to having to **meet deadlines**.*

**deadlock** /ˈdedlɒk ˈडेड्लॉक्/ *noun* [*sing.*, U] a situation in which two sides cannot reach an agreement स्थिति जिसमें दोनों पक्ष समझौते पर न पहुँच सकें, गतिरोध *Talks have reached (a) deadlock.* ○ *to try to break the deadlock*

**dead loss** *noun* [C, *usually sing.*] (*informal*) a person or thing that is not helpful or useful बेकार व्यक्ति या वस्तु

**deadly** /ˈdedli ˈडेड्लि / *adj., adv.* (**deadlier; deadliest**) **1** causing or likely to cause death घातक, जानलेवा *a deadly poison/weapon/disease* **2** very great; complete अत्यधिक; पूर्ण *They're deadly enemies.* **3** completely; extremely पूर्णतया; अत्यधिक *I'm not joking. In fact I'm deadly serious.* **4** extremely accurate, so that no defence is possible अचूक (निशानेबाज़) *That player is deadly when he gets in front of the goal.*

**deadpan** /ˈdedpæn ˈडेड्पैन्/ *adj.* without any expression on your face or in your voice भावशून्य, कोरा *He told the joke with a completely deadpan face.*

**deadweight** /ˌdedˈweɪt ˌडेड्ˈवेट्/ *noun* [C, *usually sing.*] **1** a thing that is very heavy and difficult to lift or move अत्यधिक भारी वस्तु **2** a person or thing that makes it difficult to make progress or succeed प्रगति या सफलता में बाधक व्यक्ति या वस्तु

**dead wood** *noun* [U] people or things that have become use less or unnecessary in an organization बेकार हो चुका व्यक्ति या वस्तु

**deaf** /def डेफ़्/ *adj.* **1** unable to hear anything or unable to hear very well बहरा, बधिर, श्रवण-विकलांग *You'll have to speak louder. My father's a bit deaf.* ○ *to go deaf* **2 the deaf** *noun* [*pl.*] people who cannot hear बधिर या बहरे व्यक्ति **3 deaf to sth** not wanting to listen to sth (कोई बात) सुनने का अनिच्छुक *I've told her what I think but she's deaf to my advice.* ▶ **deafness** *noun* [U] बहरापन

**deafen** /ˈdefn ˈडेफ़्न्/ *verb* [T] (*usually passive*) to make sb unable to hear by making a very loud noise (ज़ोरदार आवाज़ कर किसी को) बहरा बना देना *We were deafened by the loud music.* ▶ **deafening** *adj.* बहरा बना देने वाला *deafening music*

**deal**[1] /diːl डील्/ *verb* (*pt, pp* **dealt** /delt डेल्ट्/) **1** [I, T] **deal (sth) (out); deal (sth) (to sb)** to give cards to players in a game of cards (ताश के खेल में) पत्ते बाँटना *Start by dealing seven cards to each player.* **2** [I] **deal (in sth); deal (with sb)** to do business, especially buying and selling goods (किसी चीज़ का) व्यापार करना, (किसी से) लेन-देन करना *He deals in second-hand cars.* ○ *Our firm deals with customers all over the world.* **3** [I, T] (*informal*) to buy and sell illegal drugs ग़ैर-क़ानूनी दवाएँ ख़रीदना और बेचना

**IDM deal sb/sth a blow; deal a blow to sb/sth** **1** to hit sb/sth किसी पर प्रहार करना *He was dealt a nasty blow to the head in the accident.* **2** to give sb a shock, etc. किसी को आघात पहुँचाना *This news dealt a terrible blow to my father.*

**PHRV deal sth out** to give sth to a number of people (व्यक्तियों के बीच) बाँटना *The profits will be dealt out among us.*

**deal with sb** to treat sb in a particular way; to handle sb किसी से विशेष प्रकार का व्यवहार करना; किसी से निपटना *He's a difficult man. Nobody quite knows how to deal with him.*

**deal with sth** **1** to take suitable action in a particular situation in order to solve a problem, complete a task, etc.; to handle sth (किसी काम को) निपटाना *My secretary will deal with my correspondence while I'm away.* **2** to have sth as its subject चर्चा या विचार का विषय होना *This chapter deals with letter writing.*

**deal**[2] /diːl डील्/ *noun* [C] **1** an agreement or arrangement, especially in business व्यापारिक समझौता, सौदा *We're hoping to **do a deal** with an Italian company.* ○ *Let's **make a deal** not to criticize each other's work.* ○ *I'll help you with your essay if you'll fix my bike.' 'OK, **it's a deal!**'* **2** the way that sb is treated बरताव, व्यवहार *With high fares and unreliable services, rail users are **getting a raw deal**.* ○ *The new law aims to give pensioners **a fair deal**.* **3** the action of giving cards to players in a card game ताश के खेल में पत्तों की बँटाई

**IDM a big deal/no big deal** ➪ **big** देखिए।

**a good/great deal (of sth)** a lot (of sth) अत्यधिक *I've spent a great deal of time on this report.*

**dealer** /ˈdiːlə(r) ˈडील(र्)/ *noun* [C] **1** a person whose business is buying and selling things व्यापारी *a dealer in gold and silver* ○ *a drug dealer* **2** the person who gives the cards to the players in a game of cards ताश के पत्ते बाँटने वाला

**dealing** /ˈdiːlɪŋ ˈडीलिंग्/ *noun* **1 dealings** [*pl.*] relations, especially in business संबंध (विशेषतः व्यापार में), लेन-देन *We had some dealings with that firm several years ago.* **2** [U] buying and selling क्रय-विक्रय, ख़रीद-फ़रोख़्त, व्यापार *share dealing*

**dealt** ➪ **deal**[1] का past tense और past participle रूप

**dean** /diːn डीन्/ *noun* [C] **1** a priest who is responsible for a large church or a number of small churches बड़े चर्च या अनेक छोटे चर्चों का अध्यक्ष पादरी **2** an important official at some universities or colleges विश्वविद्यालय या कॉलेज में एक प्रमुख अधिकारी (विभाग या संकाय का अध्यक्ष)

**dear**[1] /dɪə(r) डिअ(र्)/ *adj.* **1** used at the beginning of a letter before the name or title of the person you are writing to प्रिय (पत्राचार में शिष्ट संबोधन के रूप में प्रयुक्त) *Dear Sarah,...* ○ *Dear Sir or Madam,...* **2 dear (to sb)** loved by or important to sb किसी का पसंदीदा, प्रिय या किसी के लिए मूल्यवान *It was a subject that was very dear to him.* ○ *She's one of my dearest friends.* **3** expensive महँगा, क़ीमती *How can people afford to smoke when cigarettes are so dear?*

**IDM close/dear/near to sb's heart** ➪ **heart** देखिए।

**dear²** /dɪə(r) डिअ(र्)/ **1** used for expressing disappointment, sadness, surprise, etc. निराशा, दुख, आश्चर्य आदि व्यक्त करने के लिए प्रयुक्त *Dear me! Aren't you ready?* **2** (*old-fashioned*) used when speaking to sb you know well घनिष्ठ व्यक्ति के लिए प्रयुक्त संबोधन *Would you like a cup of tea, dear?*

**dearly** /ˈdɪəli ˈडिअलि/ *adv.* **1** very much अत्यधिक *I'd dearly like to go there again.* **2** (*formal*) in a way that causes damage or suffering, or costs a lot of money हानिकारक, कष्टप्रद या पैसे की बरबादी वाला *I've already paid dearly for that mistake.*

**dearth** /dɜːθ डथ़्/ *noun* [*sing.*] **a dearth (of sb/sth)** a lack of sth; not enough of sth किसी वस्तु की कमी; अपर्याप्तता *There's a dearth of young people in the village.*

**death** /deθ डेथ़्/ *noun* **1** [C, U] the end of sb/sth's life; dying जीवन की समाप्ति; मृत्यु *The police do not know the* ***cause of death.*** ○ *There was no food and people were* ***starving to death.*** ➪ **dead** adjective देखिए। **2** [U] the end (of sth) किसी वस्तु का अंत, अवसान *the death of communism*

IDM **catch your death** ➪ **catch¹** देखिए।

**a matter of life and/or death** ➪ **matter¹** देखिए।

**put sb to death** (*usually passive*) (*formal*) to kill sb as a punishment, in past times दंड स्वरूप (किसी की) हत्या करना

**sick to death of sb/sth** ➪ **sick¹** देखिए।

**sudden death** ➪ **sudden** देखिए।

**deathbed** /ˈdeθbed ˈडेथ़्बेड्/ *noun* [C] the bed in which sb is dying or dies मृत्युशय्या

**death certificate** *noun* an official document signed by a doctor that states the time and cause of sb's death मृत्यु-प्रमाणपत्र

**deathly** /ˈdeθli ˈडेथ़्लि/ *adj., adv.* like death मृत्यु-सदृश, मृत्युवश, मृत्युसमान *There was a deathly silence.*

**death penalty** *noun* [*sing.*] the legal punishment of being killed for a crime मृत्युदंड ➪ **capital punishment** देखिए।

**death row** *noun* [U] (especially in the US) the cells in a prison for prisoners who are waiting to be killed as punishment for a serious crime (विशेषतः अमेरिका में) जेल में काल कोठरियाँ (जिनमें मृत्युदंड प्राप्त कैदी रखे जाते हैं) *prisoners* ***on death row***

**death toll** *noun* [C] the number of people killed in a disaster, war, accident, etc. (विपदा, युद्ध, दुर्घटना आदि में) मरने वालों की संख्या

**death trap** *noun* [C] a building, road, vehicle, etc. that is dangerous and could cause sb's death ख़तरनाक स्थान या वस्तु (इमारत, सड़क, वाहन आदि) जो किसी की मृत्यु का कारण बन सकता है

**debase** /dɪˈbeɪs डिˈबेस्/ *verb* [T] (*usually passive*) (*formal*) to reduce the quality or value of sth गुणवत्ता या महत्त्व कम कर देना

**debatable** /dɪˈbeɪtəbl डिˈबेटब्ल्/ *adj.* not certain; that you could argue about अनिश्चित; विवाद योग्य, मतभेदग्रस्त *It's debatable whether people have a better lifestyle these days.*

**debate¹** /dɪˈbeɪt डिˈबेट्/ *noun* **1** [C] a formal argument or discussion of a question at a public meeting or in Parliament वाद-विवाद, बहस (सार्वजनिक सभा, संसद आदि में) **2** [U] general discussion about sth expressing different opinions सामान्य चर्चा (जिसमें भिन्न-भिन्न विचारों की अभिव्यक्ति होती है) *There's been a lot of debate about the cause of acid rain.*

**debate²** /dɪˈbeɪt डिˈबेट्/ *verb* **1** [I, T] to discuss sth in a formal way or at a public meeting बहस या वाद-विवाद में भाग लेना **2** [T] to think about or discuss sth before deciding what to do सोच-विचार करना *They debated whether to go or not.*

**debauched** /dɪˈbɔːtʃt डिˈबॉच्ट्/ *adj.* behaving in a way that is immoral or unacceptable to most people अनैतिक, ऐसा व्यवहार करने वाला जिसे अधिकांश व्यक्ति स्वीकार नहीं करते हैं *debauched way of life*

**debilitate** /dɪˈbɪlɪteɪt डिˈबिलिटेट्/ *verb* [T] (*formal*) **1** to make sb's body or mind weaker (शरीर या मन को) निर्बल कर देना *a debilitating disease* **2** to make a country, an organization, etc. weaker (किसी देश, संगठन आदि को) दुर्बल या अशक्त कर देना

**debit¹** /ˈdebɪt ˈडेबिट्/ *noun* [C] an amount of money paid out of a bank account बैंक खाते से निकाली गई रक़म ✪ विलोम **credit** ➪ **direct debit** देखिए।

**debit²** /ˈdebɪt ˈडेबिट्/ *verb* [T] to take an amount of money out of a bank account, etc. usually as a payment; to record this बैंक के खाते से पैसे की निकासी करना; निकासी दर्ज करना

**debit card** *noun* [C] a plastic card that can be used to take money directly from your bank account when you pay for sth बैंक खाते में से पैसा निकालने के लिए प्रयुक्त प्लास्टिक का कार्ड; निकासी कार्ड, डेबिट कार्ड ➪ **credit card** देखिए।

**debris** /ˈdebriː ˈडेब्री/ *noun* [U] pieces from sth that has been destroyed, especially in an accident मलबा, दुर्घटना आदि में विनष्ट वस्तु के टुकड़े

**debt** /det डेट्/ *noun* **1** [C] an amount of money that you owe to sb कर्ज़, ऋण *She borrowed a lot of money and she's still paying off the debt.* **2** [U] the state of owing money कर्ज़दार या ऋणी

होने की स्थिति *After he lost his job, he **got into debt**.* 3 [C, *usually sing.*] (*formal*) something that you owe sb, for example because he/she has helped or been kind to you सहायता, दया आदि के लिए कृतज्ञता, एहसान *In his speech he acknowledged his debt to his family and friends for their support.*

IDM **be in/out of debt** to owe/not owe money ऋणी होना या न होना

**be in sb's debt** (*formal*) to feel grateful to sb for sth that he/she has done for you किसी का कृतज्ञ या एहसानमंद होना

**debtor** /ˈdetə(r) ˈडेट(र्)/ *noun* [C] a person who owes money कर्ज़दार, ऋणी

**début** (*also* **debut**) /ˈdeɪbjuː ˈडेब्यू/ *noun* [C] a first appearance in public of an actor, sportsperson etc. किसी अभिनेता, खिलाड़ी आदि का जनता के सामने प्रथम प्रदर्शन *She **made** her **début** in Mumbai in 1959.*

**Dec.** *abbr.* December दिसंबर *5 Dec. 2001*

**deca-** /ˈdekə ˈडेका/ *prefix* (*in nouns, verbs, adjectives and adverbs*) ten; having ten दस; दस वाला *decathlon* (= a competition in which people do ten different sports)

**decade** /ˈdekeɪd; dɪˈkeɪd ˈडेकेड्; डिˈकेड्/ *noun* [C] a period of ten years दस वर्ष की अवधि; दशक

**decadence** /ˈdekədəns ˈडेकडन्स्/ *noun* [U] behaviour, attitudes, etc. that show low moral standards आचरण, सोच आदि में नैतिक पतन ▶ **decadent** /ˈdekədənt ˈडेकडन्ट्/ *adj.* पतनोन्मुख, ह्रासोन्मुख *a decadent society*

**decaffeinated** /ˌdiːˈkæfɪneɪtɪd ˌडीˈकैफ़िनेटिड्/ *adj.* (used about coffee or tea) with most or all of the substance that makes you feel awake and gives you energy (**caffeine**) removed कैफ़ीन-रहित (चाय, कॉफ़ी)

**decant** /dɪˈkænt डिˈकैन्ट्/ *verb* [T] **decant sth (into sth)** to gradually pour a liquid from one container into another, for example to separate solid material from the liquid द्रव पदार्थ को एक बोतल से दूसरी बोतल में धीरे-धीरे ऐसे डालना कि ठोस पदार्थ द्रव से अलग हो जाए, निथारना, निस्तारण करना

**decapitate** /dɪˈkæpɪteɪt डिˈकैपिटेट्/ *verb* [T] (*formal*) to cut off a person's head (किसी व्यक्ति का) सिर धड़ से अलग कर देना, शिरच्छेद करना

**decathlon** /dɪˈkæθlən डिˈकैथ्लन्/ *noun* [C] a sports event in which people compete in ten different sports एक खेल स्पर्धा जिसमें प्रत्येक खिलाड़ी दस अलग-अलग खेलों में भाग लेता है

**decay**[1] /dɪˈkeɪ डिˈके/ *verb* [I] **1** to become bad or be slowly destroyed ख़राब होना या धीरे-धीरे नष्ट हो जाना *the decaying carcass of a dead sheep* ✪ पर्याय **rot 2** to become weaker or less powerful दुर्बल या क्षीण हो जाना *His business empire began to decay.* ▶ **decayed** *adj.* क्षीण *a decayed tooth*

**decay**[2] /dɪˈkeɪ डिˈके/ *noun* [U] the process or state of being slowly destroyed धीरे-धीरे, क्रमशः नष्ट होने की प्रक्रिया या स्थिति; क्षय *tooth decay* ○ *The old farm was in a terrible state of decay.*

**Deccan** *noun* [C] **1** a vast peninsula in India, south of the river Narmada भारत में नर्मदा नदी के दक्षिण में स्थित एक विशाल प्रायद्वीप **2** the entire plateau region of south-central India between the Eastern and Western Ghats दक्षिण-मध्य भारत में पूर्वी और पश्चिमी घाटों के बीच का समस्त पठार क्षेत्र; दक्खिन

**the deceased** /dɪˈsiːst डिˈसीस्ट्/ *noun* [*sing.*] (*formal*) a person who has died, especially one who has died recently दिवंगत व्यक्ति (विशेषतः जिसका अभी देहांत हुआ हो) *Many friends of the deceased were present at the funeral.* ▶ **deceased** *adj.* दिवंगत

**deceit** /dɪˈsiːt डिˈसीट्/ *noun* [U] dishonest behaviour; trying to make sb believe sth that is not true धोखाधड़ी, चालबाज़ी; बहकाने का प्रयास, बहकावा, फ़र्ज़ीवाड़ा *Their marriage eventually broke up because she was tired of his lies and deceit.*

**deceitful** /dɪˈsiːtfl डिˈसीट्फ़्ल्/ *adj.* dishonest; trying to make sb believe sth that is not true कपटी; बहकाने वाला ▶ **deceitfully** /-fəli -फ़लि/ *adv.* कपटपूर्वक, धूर्तता से ▶ **deceitfulness** *noun* [U] कपटपूर्णता, धूर्तता

**deceive** /dɪˈsiːv डिˈसीव्/ *verb* [T] **deceive sb/yourself (into doing sth)** to try to make sb believe sth that is not true बहकाना, भ्रमित करना *He deceived his mother into believing that he had earned the money, not stolen it.* ➪ **deception** या **deceit** noun देखिए।

**December** /dɪˈsembə(r) डिˈसेम्ब(र्)/ *noun* [U, C] (*abbr.* **Dec.**) the twelfth month of the year, coming after November वर्ष का बारहवाँ महीना (नवंबर के बाद का मास); दिसंबर

NOTE महीना बताने वाले शब्दों का वाक्यों में कैसे प्रयोग होता है, इसके लिए **January** पर नोट देखिए।

**decency** /ˈdiːsnsi ˈडीसन्सि/ *noun* [U] moral or correct behaviour शालीनता, शिष्ट आचरण *She **had the decency to** admit that it was her fault.*

**decent** /ˈdiːsnt ˈडीसन्ट्/ *adj.* **1** being of an acceptable standard; satisfactory शालीन; उचित, उपयुक्त *All she wants is a decent job with decent wages.* **2** (used about people or behaviour) honest and fair; treating people with respect (व्यक्ति या व्यवहार) ईमानदार और उचित; सम्मानपूर्ण **3** not likely to offend or shock sb मर्यादित, मर्यादा के भीतर जो किसी को बुरा न लगे *I can't come to the door, I'm not decent* (= I'm not dressed). ✪ विलोम **indecent** ▶ **decently** *adv.* शालीनता से

**deception** /dɪˈsepʃn डिˈसेप्शन्/ *noun* [C, U] making sb believe or being made to believe sth that is not true धोखा देने की क्रिया *He had obtained the secret papers* ***by deception.*** ➪ **deceive** verb देखिए।

**deceptive** /dɪˈseptɪv डिˈसेप्टिव्/ *adj.* likely to give a false impression or to make sb believe sth that is not true छलपूर्ण, भ्रमक, धोखा देने वाला *The water is deceptive. It's much deeper than it looks.* ▶ **deceptively** *adv.* छलपूर्वक *She made the task sound deceptively easy.*

**deci-** /ˈdesɪ- ˈडेसि/ *prefix* (*used in nouns*) one-tenth दसवाँ हिस्सा *a decilitre*

**decibel** /ˈdesɪbel ˈडेसिबेल्/ *noun* [C] a measurement of how loud a sound is ध्वनि-तीव्रता की मापन इकाई, डेसिबल

**decide** /dɪˈsaɪd डिˈसाइड्/ *verb* **1** [I, T] **decide (to do sth); decide against (doing) sth; decide about/on sth; decide that...** to think about two or more possibilities and choose one of them दो या अधिक विकल्पों पर विचार कर एक का चयन करना *There are so many to choose from—I can't decide!* ○ *She decided against borrowing the money.* **2** [T] to influence sth so that it produces a particular result निर्णय करना, विनिश्चय करना *Your votes will decide the winner.* **3** [T] to cause sb to make a decision निश्चय पर पहुँचना *What finally decided you to leave?* ➪ **decision** noun और **decisive** adjective देखिए।

**decided** /dɪˈsaɪdɪd डिˈसाइडिड्/ *adj.* clear; definite स्पष्ट; निश्चित *There has been a decided improvement in his work.* ➪ **undecided** देखिए। ▶ **decidedly** *adv.* निश्चित रूप से

**deciduous** /dɪˈsɪdʒuəs डिˈसिजुअस्/ *adj.* (used about a tree) of a type that loses its leaves every autumn (वृक्ष) जिसमें प्रतिवर्ष पतझड़ आता है जिसके पत्ते प्रतिवर्ष झड़ते हैं ➪ **evergreen** देखिए।

**decimal**[1] /ˈdesɪml ˈडेसिमल्/ *adj.* based on or counted in units of ten or **tenths** दशमलव पद्धति से संबद्ध, दस या दसवें अंशों की इकाइयों में परिगणित *The figure is accurate to two* ***decimal places*** (= shows two figures after the decimal point).

**decimal**[2] /ˈdesɪml ˈडेसिमल्/ (*also* **decimal fraction**) *noun* [C] (*mathematics*) a **fraction** that is shown as a decimal point followed by the number of **tenths, hundredths,** etc. दशमलव भिन्न *Three quarters expressed as a decimal is 0.75.* ➪ **vulgar fraction** देखिए।

**decimal point** *noun* [C] a mark like a full stop used to separate the whole number from the **tenths, hundredths,** etc. of a decimal, for example in 0.61 दशमलव बिंदु

**decimate** /ˈdesɪmeɪt ˈडेसिमेट्/ *verb* [T] (*usually passive*) to kill large numbers of animals, plants or people in a particular area क्षेत्र विशेष के पशुओं, पौधों या मनुष्यों को बड़ी संख्या में मार डालना *The rabbit population was decimated by the disease.* **2** to badly damage sth or make sth weaker किसी को अत्यधिक नुक़सान पहुँचाना या अशक्त कर देना

**decimetre** (*AmE* **decimeter**) /ˈdesɪmiːtə(r) ˈडेसिमीट(र्)/ *noun* [C] a unit for measuring length. There are ten decimetres in a metre लंबाई मापने की इकाई, एक मीटर का दसवाँ हिस्सा; डेसीमीटर

**decipher** /dɪˈsaɪfə(r) डिˈसाइफ़(र्)/ *verb* [T] to succeed in reading or understanding sth that is not clear कूट (गूढ़) लेखन को पढ़ लेना या समझ लेना; कूटवाचन करना *It's impossible to decipher his handwriting.*

**decision** /dɪˈsɪʒn डिˈसिश़न्/ *noun* **1** [C, U] **a decision (to do sth); a decision on/about sth; a decision that...** a choice or judgement that you make after thinking about various possibilities निर्णय, निश्चय *Have you* ***made a decision*** *yet?* ○ *I* ***took the decision*** *that I believed to be right.* **2** [U] being able to decide clearly and quickly स्पष्टता और शीघ्रता से निर्णय या निश्चय करने में समर्थ व्यक्ति *We are looking for someone with decision for this job.* ➪ **decide** verb देखिए।

**decisive** /dɪˈsaɪsɪv डिˈसाइसिव् / *adj.* **1** making sth certain or final निर्णायक या अंतिम *the decisive battle of the war* **2** having the ability to make clear decisions quickly स्पष्टता और शीघ्रता से निर्णय या निश्चय करने में सक्षम *It's no good hesitating. Be decisive.* ✪ विलोम **indecisive** ➪ **decide** verb देखिए। ▶ **decisively** *adv.* निर्णायक तरह से ▶ **decisiveness** *noun* [U] निर्णय-क्षमता

**deck** /dek डेक्/ *noun* [C] **1** one of the floors of a ship or bus जलपोत या बस की कोई भी मंज़िल, डेक ➪ **plane** पर चित्र देखिए। **2** (*AmE*) = **pack**[1] **6** *a deck of cards*

**IDM** **on deck** on the part of a ship which you can walk on outside जलपोत के डेक पर (जहाँ बाहर टहल सकते हैं) *I'm going out on deck for some fresh air.*

**deckchair** /ˈdektʃeə(r) ˈडेक्चेअ(र्)/ *noun* [C] a chair that you use outside, especially on the beach. You can fold it up and carry it लकड़ी के ढांचे में कैनवास लगी आराम कुरसी जो इकट्ठी हो जाती है; फ़ोल्डिंग चेअर

**declamation** /ˌdekləˈmeɪʃn ˌडेक्लˈमेश्न्/ *noun* **1** [U] the act of speaking to an audience about something in a formal way वक्तृता **2** [C] a speech or a piece of writing expressing strong feelings and opinions प्रबल भावनाओं और विचारों वाला जोशिला भाषण *Declamations against the government are common enough.*

**declaration** /ˌdekləˈreɪʃn ˌडेक्लˈरेश्न्/ *noun* **1** [C, U] an official statement about sth (किसी के विषय में) घोषणा *In his speech he made a strong declaration of support for the rebels.* ○ *a declaration of war* **2** [C] a written statement giving information on goods or money you have earned, on which you have to pay tax आय पर देय कर की दृष्टि से दिया गया घोषणा-पत्र, आय पर देय कर के विषय में आवश्यक सूचना देने वाली लिखित घोषणा *a customs declaration*

**declare** /dɪˈkleə(r) डिˈक्लेअ(र्)/ *verb* [T] **1** to state sth publicly and officially or to make sth known in a firm, clear way (कोई बात) सार्वजनिक और आधिकारिक रूप से घोषित करना, (किसी बात की) घोषणा करना *to* ***declare war*** *on another country* ○ *I declare that the winner of the award is Mahendra Singh Dhoni.* **2** to give information about goods or money you have earned, on which you have to pay tax कर-भुगतान की दृष्टि से अपनी आय का विवरण देना *You must declare all your income on this form.*

**declension** /dɪˈklenʃn डिˈक्लेन्श्न्/ *noun* [C] (*grammar*) **1** the forms of a word that change in some languages according to the number, **case** and **gender** of the word (कुछ भाषाओं में) एक शब्द के विभिन्न रूप जो उस शब्द के वचन, कारक और लिंग के अनुसार (परिवर्तित) होते हैं **2** the set of forms of a particular word in some languages (कुछ भाषाओं में) एक शब्द की रूपावली *Latin nouns of the second declension*

**decline**[1] /dɪˈklaɪn डिˈक्लाइन्/ *verb* **1** [I] to become weaker, smaller or less good (किसी का) ह्रास होना, क्षीण होना *declining profits* ○ *The standard of education has declined in this country.* **2** [I, T] (*formal*) to refuse, usually politely (नम्रता से) अस्वीकार करना *Thank you for the invitation but I'm afraid I have to decline.* **3** [I, T] (*grammar*) if a noun, an adjective or a pronoun declines, it has different forms according to whether it is the subject or the object of a verb, whether it is in the singular or plural, etc. When you decline a noun, etc., you list these forms संज्ञा, विशेषण या सर्वनाम शब्दों के विविध रूप प्रस्तुत करना, कारक विभक्तियाँ लगाना

**decline**[2] /dɪˈklaɪn डिˈक्लाइन्/ *noun* [C, U] **(a) decline (in sth)** a process or period of becoming weaker, smaller अशक्त और क्षीण होने की प्रक्रिया या अवधि *a decline in sales* ○ *As an industrial power, the country is* ***in decline.***

**decode** /ˌdiːˈkəʊd ˌडिˈकोड्/ *verb* [T] to find the meaning of a secret message (**code**) गुप्त संदेश (कोड) का अर्थ निकालना ✪ विलोम **encode**

**decoder** /ˌdiːˈkəʊdə(r) ˌडिˈकोड(र्)/ *noun* [C] a device that changes electronic signals into a form that can be understood एक उपकरण जो इलेक्ट्रॉनिक संकेतों को ऐसे रूप में बदल देता है कि हम उन्हें समझ सकें *a satellite/video decoder*

**decompose** /ˌdiːkəmˈpəʊz ˌडीकम्ˈपोज़्/ *verb* [I, T] to slowly be destroyed by natural chemical processes प्राकृतिक रासायनिक प्रक्रियाओं द्वारा क्रमशः नष्ट हो जाना, विघटित होना *The body was so badly decomposed that it couldn't be identified.* ▶ **decomposition** /ˌdiːkɒmpəˈzɪʃn ˌडीकॉम्पˈज़िश्न्/ *noun* [U] विघटन *the decomposition of organic waste* ➪ **food chain** पर चित्र देखिए।

**decompress** /ˌdiːkəmˈpres ˌडीकम्ˈप्रेस्/ *verb* **1** [I, T] to have the air pressure in sth reduced to a normal level or to reduce it to its normal level किसी वस्तु के दबाव को सामान्य स्तर तक करना या दबाव को उसके सामान्य स्तर पर लाना **2** [T] (*computing*) to give files their original size again after they have been made smaller to fit into less space on a disk, etc. (कंप्यूटर) डिस्क पर संकोचित या संपीडित फ़ाइलों को पुनः उनके मूल आकार में लाना

**decompression** /ˌdiːkəmˈpreʃn ˌडीकम्ˈप्रेश्न्/ *noun* [U] **1** a reduction in air pressure वायु दाब में घटाव *decompression sickness* (= the problems that people experience when they come up to the surface after swimming very deep in the sea) **2** the act of reducing the pressure of the air वायु दाब को घटाने की प्रक्रिया **3** (*technical*) the process of allowing sth that has been made smaller to fill the space that it originally needed संकर्षित या संकोचित वस्तु को पुनः अपने मूल आकार में लौटने की प्रक्रिया

**deconstruct** /dɪːkənˈstrʌkt डीकन्ˈस्ट्रक्ट्/ *verb* [T] (in Philosophy and Literary Criticism) to analyse a text in order to show that there is no single explanation of the meaning of a piece of writing but that a different meaning emerges each time in the act of reading (दर्शनशास्त्र और साहित्यिक समालोचना में) विश्लेषण द्वारा यह प्रकट करना कि किसी आलेख के अर्थ की कोई एक व्याख्या नहीं होती और प्रत्येक अध्ययन प्रयास में भिन्न-भिन्न अर्थ उभरते हैं

**decor** /ˈdeɪkɔ:(r) ˈडेकॉ(र्)/ *noun* [U, *sing*.] the style in which the inside of a building is decorated भवन की आंतरिक सजावट की शैली

**decorate** /ˈdekəreɪt ˈडेकरेट्/ *verb* **1** [T] **decorate sth (with sth)** to add sth in order to make a thing more attractive to look at (किसी वस्तु को किसी अन्य वस्तु से) सजाना-सँवारना *Decorate the cake with cherries and nuts.* **2** [I, T] (*BrE*) to put paint and/or coloured paper onto walls, ceilings and doors in a room or building किसी इमारत या कमरे को अंदर से सँवारना (दीवार आदि पर पेंट करके या वाल पेपर लगाकर)

**decoration** /ˌdekəˈreɪʃn ˌडेकˈरेश्न्/ *noun* **1** [C, U] something that is added to sth in order to make it look more attractive सजावट का सामान **2** [U] the process of decorating a room or building; the style in which sth is decorated सजावट की प्रक्रिया; सजावट की शैली या का ढंग *The house is in need of decoration.*

**decorative** /ˈdekərətɪv ˈडेकरटिव्/ *adj.* attractive or pretty to look at आकर्षक या देखने में सुंदर *The cloth had a decorative lace edge.*

**decorator** /ˈdekəreɪtə(r) ˈडेकरेटर(र्)/ *noun* [C] a person whose job is to paint and decorate houses and buildings रंगाई एवं सजावट करने वाला व्यक्ति; सज्जाकार

**decoy** /ˈdi:kɔɪ ˈडिकॉइ/ *noun* [C] a person or object that is used in order to trick sb/sth into doing what you want, going where you want, etc. किसी व्यक्ति या वस्तु द्वारा किसी को लुभाना या कुछ मनचाहा करने या कही जाने के लिए फाँसना ▶ **decoy** *verb* [T] किसी को मनचाहे ढंग से फँसाना

**decrease**[1] /dɪˈkri:s डिˈक्रीस्/ *verb* [I, T] to become or to make sth smaller or less घटना या घटाना *Profits have decreased by 15%.* ✪ विलोम **increase**

**decrease**[2] /ˈdi:kri:s ˈडीक्रीस्/ *noun* [C, U] **(a) decrease (in sth)** the process of becoming or making sth smaller or less; the amount that sth is reduced by घटने या घटाने की प्रक्रिया; घटने की मात्रा *a 10% decrease in sales*

**decree** /dɪˈkri: डिˈक्री/ *noun* [C] an official order given by a government, a ruler, etc. सरकार, शासक आदि द्वारा जारी आदेश ▶ **decree** *verb* [T] आधिकारिक आदेश जारी करना *The government decreed a state of emergency.*

**decrepit** /dɪˈkrepɪt डिˈक्रेपिट्/ *adj.* (used about a thing or person) old and in very bad condition or poor health (व्यक्ति या वस्तु) जीर्ण-शीर्ण या दुर्बल

**dedicate** /ˈdedɪkeɪt ˈडेडिकेट्/ *verb* [T] **1 dedicate sth to sth** to give all your energy, time, efforts, etc. to sth किसी काम में अपनी शक्ति, समय आदि लगाना *He dedicated his life to helping the poor.* **2 dedicate sth to sb** to say that sth is specially for sb (किसी को कुछ) विशेष रूप से अर्पित करना *He dedicated the book he had written to his brother.*

**dedicated** /ˈdedɪkeɪtɪd ˈडेडिकेटिड्/ *adj.* giving a lot of your energy, time, efforts, etc. to sth that you believe to be important अभीष्ट लक्ष्य के प्रति समर्पित *dedicated nurses and doctors*

**dedication** /ˌdedɪˈkeɪʃn ˌडेडिˈकेश्न्/ *noun* **1** [U] wanting to give your time and energy to sth because you feel it is important अभीष्ट के प्रति समर्पण *I admire her dedication to her career.* **2** [C] a message at the beginning of a book or piece of music saying that it is for a particular person किसी पुस्तक या संगीत-रचना के आरंभ में अंकित संदेश कि रचना किसे समर्पित है

**deduce** /dɪˈdju:s डिˈड्यूस्/ *verb* [T] to form an opinion using the facts that you already know ज्ञात तथ्यों के आधार पर निष्कर्ष निकालना *From his name I deduced that he was an Indian.* ➪ **deduction** noun देखिए।

**deduct** /dɪˈdʌkt डिˈडक्ट्/ *verb* [T] **deduct sth (from sth)** to take sth such as money or points away from a total amount कुल राशि में से कुछ अंश (पैसा, अंक आदि) घटाना या काटना *Marks will be deducted for untidy work.*

**deduction** /dɪˈdʌkʃn डिˈडक्श्न्/ *noun* [C, U] **1** something that you work out from facts that you already know; the ability to think in this way ज्ञात तथ्यों के आधार पर प्राप्त निष्कर्ष; निष्कर्ष निकालने की क्षमता *It was a brilliant piece of deduction by the detective.* ➪ **deduce** verb तथा **induction 2** देखिए। **2 deduction (from sth)** taking away an amount or number from a total; the amount or number taken away from the total कुल में से कुछ राशि या संख्या की कटौती; कुल में से काटी गई राशि या संख्या *What is your total income after deductions* (= when tax, insurance, etc. are taken away)? ➪ **deduct** verb देखिए।

**deductive** /dɪˈdʌktɪv डिˈडक्टिव्/ *adj.* using knowledge about things that are generally true in order to think about and understand particular situations or problems तर्क से प्राप्त निष्कर्ष से संबंधित; निगमनात्मक ➪ **inductive** देखिए।

**deed** /di:d डीड्/ *noun* [C] **1** (*formal*) something that you do; an action जो किया जाए; कार्य, क्रिया *a brave/good/evil deed* **2** a legal document that shows that you own a house or building भवन के स्वामित्व से संबंधित क़ानूनी दस्तावेज़

**deem** /di:m डीम्/ *verb* [T] (*formal*) to have a particular opinion about sth किसी बात को विशेष रूप में समझना या मानना *He did not even deem it necessary to apologize.*

**deep[1]** /di:p डीप्/ *adj.* **1** going a long way down from the surface गहरा, सतह से नीचे की ओर लंबाई में जाने वाला *to dig a deep hole* ○ *a deep cut* ○ *a coat with deep pockets* ➪ **depth** noun देखिए। **2** going a long way from front to back गहरा, आगे से पीछे की ओर लंबाई में जाने वाला *deep shelves* **3** measuring a particular amount from top to bottom or from front to back ऊपर से नीचे या आगे से पीछे तक की मात्रा को मापने वाला *The water is only a metre deep at this end of the pool.* ○ *shelves 40 centimetres deep* **4** (used about sounds) low (ध्वनि, आवाज) नीची, मंद *a deep voice* **5** (used about colours) dark; strong (रंग) गहरा; तीखा *a deep red* **6** (used about an emotion) strongly felt (प्रेम भावना आदि) प्रगाढ़ *He felt a very deep love for the child.* **7** (used about sleep) not easy to wake from (निद्रा) गहरी, गाढ़ी *I was in a deep sleep and didn't hear the phone ringing.* **8** dealing with difficult subjects or details; thorough गंभीर, कठिन विषयों और ब्योरे से संबंधित या पूर्ण; परिपूर्ण *His books show a deep understanding of human nature.* ▸ **the deep** *noun* [U] मध्य *in the deep of the night* (= in the middle of the night) ▸ **deeply** *adv.* गहराई से *a deeply unhappy person* ○ *to breathe deeply*

**IDM** **deep in thought/conversation** thinking very hard or giving sb/sth your full attention चिंतन में मग्न या पूरा ध्यान देते हुए

**take a deep breath** to breathe in a lot of air, especially in preparation for doing something difficult गहरी साँस लेना (विशेषतः किसी कठिन काम की तैयारी के रूप में) *He took a deep breath then walked onto the stage.*

**deep[2]** /di:p डीप्/ *adv.* a long way down or inside sth किसी गहराई विशेष तक, गहन *He dug his hands deep into his pockets.*

**IDM** **deep down** in what you really think or feel मन-ही-मन *I tried to appear optimistic but deep down I knew there was no hope.*

**dig deep** ➪ **dig[1]** देखिए।

**Deepavali** (*also* **Diwali**) *noun* [C] (*IndE*) the Hindu festival of lights held in October/November, celebrated by the lighting of **clay** lamps, **candles**, and with **fireworks** दीपावली; दीवाली

**deepen** /ˈdi:pən ˈडीपन्/ *verb* [I, T] to become or to make sth deep or deeper अधिक गहरा होना या किसी को अधिक गहरा करना *The river deepens here.*

**deep-freeze** = **freezer**

**deep-fried** *adj.* cooked in oil that covers the food completely तेल में डूबोकर तला हुआ

**deep-rooted** (*also* **deep-seated**) *adj.* strongly felt or believed and therefore difficult to change सुदृढ़, प्रगाढ़ *deep-rooted fears*

**deep-sea** *adj.* of or in the deeper parts of the sea सागर के अपेक्षाकृत गहरे भागों में होने वाला, गंभीर सागर में स्थित *deep-sea fishing/diving*

**deer** /dɪə(r) डिअ(र्)/ *noun* [C] (*pl.* **deer**) a large wild grass-eating animal. The male has large horns shaped like branches (**antlers**) हिरन

> **NOTE** नर हरिण को **buck** कहते हैं और यदि उसके भरे-पूरे सींग हो तो उसे **stag** कहते हैं। मादा हरिण को **doe** कहते हैं और मृग-शावक को **fawn** कहते हैं।

**deface** /dɪˈfeɪs डिˈफ़ेस्/ *verb* [T] to spoil the way sth looks by writing on or marking its surface किसी चीज़ के ऊपर लिखकर या उस पर निशान लगाकर उसका रंग-रूप बिगाड़ देना, किसी को विरूपित करना

**de facto** /ˌdeɪˈfæktəʊ ˌडेˈफ़ैक्टो/ *adj.* (*formal*) a Latin expression used to say that sth exists even though it may not be legally accepted as existing एक लैटिन शब्द जिसका अर्थ है भौतिक रूप से वास्तविक (भले ही वह क़ानूनन सम्मत न हो) *The general took de facto control of the country.* ▸ **defacto** *adv.* वास्तव में, वस्तुतः

**defamatory** /dɪˈfæmətri डिˈफ़ैमट्रि/ *adj.* (*formal*) (used about speech or writing) intended to harm sb by saying or writing bad or false things about him/her (भाषण या लेखन) मानहानिकारक, निंदात्मक

**defame** /dɪˈfeɪm डिˈफ़ेम्/ *verb* [T] (*formal*) to harm sb by saying or writing bad or false things about him/her मानहानि करना, निंदा करना ▸ **defamation** /ˌdefəˈmeɪʃn ˌडेफ़ˈमेशन्/ [U, C] मानहानि, निंदा *The company sued the paper for defamation.*

**default[1]** /dɪˈfɔ:lt डिˈफ़ॉल्ट्/ *noun* [*sing.*] (*computing*) a course of action taken by a computer when it is not given any other instruction कंप्यूटर में पड़ा पहले का कार्यक्रम जो इसलिए सक्रिय है कि उसे निर्देश देकर बदला नहीं गया

**IDM** **by default** because nothing happened, not because of successful effort किसी की अनुपस्थिति के कारण (न कि प्रयास से) *They won by default, because the other team didn't turn up.*

**default²** /dɪˈfɔːlt डिˈफ़ॉल्ट्/ *verb* [I] **1 default (on sth)** to not do sth that you should do by law क़ानून के अनुसार काम न करना *If you default on the credit payments* (= you don't pay them), *the car will be taken back.* **2** (*computing*) **default (to sth)** to take a particular course of action when no other command is given नए निर्देश के अभाव में कंप्यूटर का पहले के कार्यक्रम के अनुसार सक्रिय बने रहना

**defeat¹** /dɪˈfiːt डिˈफ़ीट्/ *verb* [T] **1** to win a game, a fight, a vote, etc. against sb; to beat sb किसी पर विजय प्राप्त करना; किसी को हराना *The army defeated the rebels after three days of fighting.* **2** to be too difficult for sb to do or understand कुछ करने या समझने में अत्यंत कठिन होना *I've tried to work out what's wrong with the car but it defeats me.* **3** to prevent sth from succeeding कोई प्रयास सफल न होने देना *The local residents are determined to defeat the council's building plans.*

**defeat²** /dɪˈfiːt डिˈफ़ीट्/ *noun* **1** [C] an occasion when sb fails to win or be successful against sb else (किसी से) हार, पराजय *This season they have had two victories and three defeats.* **2** [U] the act of losing or not being successful हारने या पराजित होने की क्रिया *She refused to* ***admit defeat*** *and kept on trying.*

**defeatism** /dɪˈfiːtɪzəm डिˈफ़ीटिज़्म्/ *noun* [U] the attitude of expecting sth to end in failure निराशावादी सोच (असफल रहने की आशंका)

**defeatist** /dɪˈfiːtɪst डिˈफ़ीटिस्ट्/ *adj.* expecting not to succeed असफलता की आशंका वाला, पराजयवादी *a defeatist attitude/view* ▶ **defeatist** *noun* [C] सहज ही पराजय को स्वीकार करने वाला व्यक्ति *Don't be such a defeatist, we haven't lost yet!*

**defecate** /ˈdefəkeɪt ˈडेफ़केट्/ *verb* [I] (*formal*) to get rid of waste from the body; to go to the toilet मलत्याग करना

**defect¹** /ˈdiːfekt ˈडीफ़ेक्ट्/ *noun* [C] sth that is wrong with or missing from sb/sth दोष, ख़राबी या त्रुटि *a speech defect* ○ *defects in the education system* ▶ **defective** /dɪˈfektɪv डिˈफ़ेक्टिव्/ *adj.* दोषपूर्ण, त्रुटिपूर्ण

**defect²** /dɪˈfekt डिˈफ़ेक्ट्/ *verb* [I] to leave your country, a political party, etc. and join one that is considered to be the enemy अपना देश, राजनीतिक दल आदि को छोड़कर शत्रुदेश, विरोधी दल आदि में शामिल होना ▶ **defection** *noun* [C, U] दल-बदल ▶ **defector** *noun* [C] दल-बदलू

**defence** (*AmE* **defense**) /dɪˈfens डिˈफ़ेन्स्/ *noun* **1** [U] something that you do or say to protect sb/sth from attack, bad treatment, criticism, etc. (आक्रमण से) प्रतिरक्षा, बचाव करना *Would you fight* ***in defence of*** *your country?* ○ *I must say* ***in*** *her* ***defence*** *that I have always found her very reliable.* ➪ **self-defence** देखिए। **2** [C] **a defence (against sth)** something that protects sb/sth from sth, or that is used to fight against attack आक्रमण के विरुद्ध मोर्चाबंदी *the body's defences against disease* **3** [U] the military equipment, forces, etc. for protecting a country देश के रक्षा के लिए सैन्य उपकरण, सेनाएँ आदि *Spending on defence needs to be reduced.* **4** [C] (in law) an argument in support of the accused person in a court of law (क़ानून में) न्यायालय में अभियुक्त की ओर से प्रस्तुत तर्क *His defence was that he was only carrying out orders.* **5 the defence** [*sing., with sing. or pl. verb*] (in law) the lawyer or lawyers who are acting for the accused person in a court of law (क़ानून में) अभियुक्त का या के वकील, बचाव पक्ष *The defence claims/claim that many of the witnesses were lying.* ➪ **the prosecution** देखिए। **6** (*usually* **the defence**) [*sing.*, U] (in sport) action to prevent the other team scoring; the players who try to do this (खेल में) गोल बचाने की क्रिया क्षेत्ररक्षण; क्षेत्ररक्षक खिलाड़ी, रक्षा पंक्ति के खिलाड़ी *She plays in defence.*

**defenceless** /dɪˈfensləs डिˈफ़ेन्सलस्/ *adj.* unable to defend yourself against attack जो आक्रमण से अपनी रक्षा न कर सके; अरक्षित

**defend** /dɪˈfend डिˈफ़ेन्ड्/ *verb* **1** [T] **defend sb/sth/yourself (against/from sb/sth)** to protect sb/sth from harm or danger (संकट से किसी की) रक्षा करना *Would you be able to defend yourself if someone attacked you in the street?* **2** [T] **defend sb/sth/yourself (against/from sb/sth)** to say or write sth to support sb/sth that has been criticized किसी की आलोचना होने पर उसके समर्थन में बोलना या लिखना *The minister went on television to defend the government's policy.* **3** [T] (in law) to speak for sb who is accused of a crime in a court of law (क़ानून में) अभियुक्त के बचाव में बोलना **4** [I, T] (in sport) to try to stop the other team or player scoring (खेल में) गोल बचाना *They defended well and managed to hold onto their lead.* **5** [T] to take part in a competition that you won before and try to win it again (पूर्व विजेता द्वारा) पुनः विजय प्राप्ति के लिए स्पर्धा में भाग लेना *She successfully defended her title.* ○ *He is the defending champion.*

**defendant** /dɪˈfendənt डिˈफ़ेन्डन्ट्/ *noun* [C] a person who is accused of a crime in a court of law प्रतिवादी, अभियुक्त

**defender** /dɪˈfendə(r) डिˈफ़ेन्ड(र्)/ *noun* [C] a person who defends sb/sth, especially in sport किसी की रक्षा करने वाला, रक्षक (विशेषतः खेल में, जैसे गोल रक्षक)

**defense** (*AmE*) = **defence**

**defensible** /dɪˈfensəbl डिˈफ़ेन्सबल्/ *adj.* **1** that can be supported by reasons or arguments that show that it is right or should be allowed जिसे तर्कों और युक्तियों से उचित ठहराया जा सके; न्यायसंगत *morally defensible* **2** (used about a place) that can be defended against an attack (स्थान) जिसकी आक्रमण से रक्षा की जा सके; रक्षणीय

**defensive**[1] /dɪˈfensɪv डिˈफ़ेन्सिव़्/ *adj.* **1** that protects sb/sth from attack आक्रमण से रक्षा करने वाला, रक्षात्मक *The troops took up a defensive position.* ✪ विलोम **offensive** **2** showing that you feel that sb is criticizing you आलोचना के प्रति संवेदनशील या असहनशील *When I asked him about his new job, he became very defensive and tried to change the subject.*

**defensive**[2] /dɪˈfensɪv डिˈफ़ेन्सिव़्/ *noun*

**IDM** **on the defensive** acting in a way that shows that you expect sb to attack or criticize you बचाव की मुद्रा में होना *My questions about her past immediately put her on the defensive.*

**defer** /dɪˈfɜː(r) डिˈफ़(र्)/ *verb* [T] (**deferring; deferred**) (*formal*) to leave sth until a later time (किसी काम को) स्थागित करना *She deferred her place at university for a year.*

**deference** /ˈdefərəns ˈडेफ़रन्स्/ *noun* [U] polite behaviour that you show towards sb/sth, usually because you respect him/her (किसी के प्रति) आदर भाव

**IDM** **in deference to sb/sth** because you respect and do not wish to upset sb (किसी का) आदर करते हुए (किसी के) सम्मान में *In deference to her father's wishes, she didn't mention the subject again.*

**defiance** /dɪˈfaɪəns डिˈफ़ाइअन्स्/ *noun* [U] open refusal to obey sb/sth (किसी का) आदेश मानने से साफ़ इनकार, खुली अवज्ञा *an **act of defiance*** ○ *He continued smoking **in defiance of** the doctor's orders.*

**defiant** /dɪˈfaɪənt डिˈफ़ाइअन्ट्/ *adj.* showing open refusal to obey sb/sth खुल्लम-खुल्ला अवज्ञा करने वाला ➪ **defy** verb देखिए। ▶ **defiantly** *adv.* अवज्ञापूर्वक

**defibrillator** /dɪˈfɪbrɪleɪtə(r) डिˈफ़िब्रिलेट(र्)/ *noun* [C] a piece of equipment used in hospitals to control the movements of the heart muscles by giving the heart a controlled electric shock हृदय की मांसपेशियों की हरकत को बिजली के झटके देकर नियंत्रित करने वाली मशीन

**deficiency** /dɪˈfɪʃnsi डिˈफ़िश्न्सि/ *noun* (*pl.* **deficiencies**) **deficiency (in/of sth)** **1** [C, U] the state of not having enough of sth; a lack अपर्याप्तता; न्यूनता, कमी *a deficiency of vitamin C* **2** [C] a fault or a weakness in sb/sth दोष या दुर्बलता *The problems were caused by deficiencies in the design.*

**deficient** /dɪˈfɪʃnt डिˈफ़िश्न्ट्/ *adj.* **1 deficient (in sth)** not having enough of sth हीन, किसी वस्तु का अभाव होना *food that is deficient in minerals* **2** not good enough or not complete बहुत अच्छा नहीं, अपर्याप्त या अपूर्ण

**deficit** /ˈdefɪsɪt ˈडेफ़िसिट्/ *noun* [C] the amount by which the money you receive is less than the money you have spent घाटा, कमी, अभाव *a trade deficit*

**define** /dɪˈfaɪn डिˈफ़ाइन्/ *verb* [T] **1** to say exactly what a word or idea means किसी शब्द या भाव को ठीक से समझना *How would you define 'happiness'?* **2** to explain the exact nature of sth clearly किसी के सही स्वरूप की व्याख्या करना *We need to define the problem before we can attempt to solve it.*

**definite** /ˈdefɪnət ˈडेफ़िनट्/ *adj.* **1** fixed and unlikely to change; certain सुनिश्चित और अपरिवर्तनीय; संदेहरहित, निश्चित, अवश्यंभावी *I'll give you a definite decision in a couple of days.* ✪ विलोम **indefinite** **2** clear; easy to see or notice स्पष्ट; निश्चयात्मक, प्रत्यक्ष *There has been a definite change in her attitude recently.*

**the definite article** *noun* [C] (*grammar*) the name used for the word 'the' शब्द 'the' के लिए प्रयुक्त पद, निश्चायक आर्टिकल ➪ **the indefinite article** देखिए।

**NOTE** निश्चायक आर्टिकल (definite article) के बारे में अधिक जानकारी के लिए इस शब्दकोश के अंत में **Quick Grammar Reference** देखिए।

**definitely** /ˈdefɪnətli ˈडेफ़िनट्लि/ *adv.* certainly; without doubt पक्के तौर पर; निस्संदेह *I'll definitely consider your advice.*

**definition** /ˌdefɪˈnɪʃn ˌडेफ़िˈनिश्न्/ *noun* [C, U] a description of the exact meaning of a word or idea किसी शब्द या भाव के सही अर्थ का विवरण, परिभाषा

**definitive** /dɪˈfɪnətɪv डिˈफ़िनटिव़् / *adj.* in a form that cannot be changed or that cannot be improved जिसमें परिवर्तन या सुधार संभव नहीं, निर्णायक *This is the definitive version.* ▸ **definitively** *adv.* निर्णायक रूप से

**deflate** /dɪˈfleɪt; diː- डिˈफ़्लेट्; डी-/ *verb* **1** [I, T] to become or to make sth smaller by letting the air or gas out of it (किसी की) हवा निकलना या निकालना *The balloon slowly deflated.* ✪ विलोम **inflate** **2** [T] to make sb feel less confident, proud or excited आत्म-विश्वास या गौरवभाव को चोट पहुँचना, आत्मविश्वास-न्यूनता का शिकार होना *I felt really deflated when I got my exam results.*

**deflect** /dɪˈflekt डिˈफ़्लेक्ट्/ *verb* **1** [C] to change direction after hitting sb/sth; to make sth change direction in this way (किसी से) टकरा कर दिशा बदलना; टक्कर देकर किसी की दिशा बदलना *The ball deflected off a defender and into the goal.* **2** to turn sb's attention away from sth (किसी के) ध्यान को (कहीं से) हटाना *Nothing could deflect her from her aim.*

**deflection** /dɪˈflekʃn डिˈफ़्लेक्शन्/ *noun* a change of direction after hitting sb/sth (किसी से टकरा कर) दिशा-परिवर्तन

**defoliate** /ˌdiːˈfəʊlieɪt ˌडीˈफ़ोलिएट्/ *verb* [T] (*technical*) to destroy the leaves of trees or plants, especially with chemicals वृक्षों या पौधों के पत्तों को नष्ट करना (विशेषतः रसायनों के द्वारा), निष्पत्रण करना ▸ **defoliation** /ˌdiːˌfəʊliˈeɪʃn ˌडीˌफ़ोलिˈएशन्/ *noun* [U] वृक्षों का निष्पत्रण

**deforestation** /ˌdiːˌfɒrɪˈsteɪʃn ˌडीˌफ़ॉरिˈस्टेशन्/ *noun* [U] cutting down trees over a large area वृक्षों की कटाई, जंगल की कटाई ✪ विलोम **afforestation**

**deform** /dɪˈfɔːm डिˈफ़ॉम्/ *verb* [T] to change or spoil the natural shape of sth किसी के प्रकृत रूप को बिगाड़ देना, विरूपित करना; विकृत करना

**deformed** /dɪˈfɔːmd डिˈफ़ॉम्ड्/ *adj.* having a shape that is not normal because it has grown wrongly भद्दी शकल का, विरूपित

**deformity** /dɪˈfɔːməti डिˈफ़ॉमटि/ *noun* (*pl.* **deformities**) [C, U] the condition of having a part of the body that is an unusual shape because of disease, injury, etc. रोग या चोट के कारण रूप का विकृत हो जाना, विरूपता *The drug caused women to give birth to babies with severe deformities.*

**defraud** /dɪˈfrɔːd डिˈफ़्रॉड्/ *verb* [T] **defraud sb (of sth)** to get sth from sb in a dishonest way (किसी को) धोखा देना, ठग लेना *He defrauded the company of millions.*

**defrost** /ˌdiːˈfrɒst डिˈफ़्रॉस्ट्/ *verb* **1** [T] to remove the ice from sth बर्फ़ गला कर हटाना *to defrost a fridge* **2** [I, T] (used about frozen food) to return to a normal temperature; to make food do this (बर्फ़ में रक्षित भोजन का) सामान्य तापमान पर लौटना या लौटाना; ठंडे किए गए खाद्य पदार्थों का सामान्य होना या करना *Defrost the chicken thoroughly before cooking.*

**deft** /deft डेफ़्ट्/ *adj.* (used especially about movements) skilful and quick (गतिविधि) दक्ष और त्वरित ▸ **deftly** *adv.* दक्षतापूर्वक

**defunct** /dɪˈfʌŋkt डिˈफ़ङ्क्ट्/ *adj.* no longer existing or in use जो न अस्तित्व में हो और न प्रयोग में; अप्रचलित

**defuse** /ˌdiːˈfjuːz ˌडीˈफ़्यूज़्/ *verb* [T] **1** to remove part of a bomb so that it cannot explode बम को निष्क्रिय करने के लिए उसका पिन आदि निकालना *Army experts defused the bomb safely.* **2** to make a situation calmer or less dangerous (तनावभरी) स्थिति को शांत करना *She defused the tension by changing the subject.*

**defy** /dɪˈfaɪ डिˈफ़ाइ/ *verb* [T] (*pres. part.* **defying**; *3rd person sing. pres.* **defies;** *pt, pp* **defied**) **1** to refuse to obey sb/sth (किसी का) कहा न मानना, अवज्ञा करना *She defied her parents and went abroad.* ➪ **defiant** adjective तथा **defiance** noun देखिए। **2 defy sb to do sth** to ask sb to do sth that you believe to be impossible किसी को ऐसा काम करने के लिए कहना जो असंभव हो *I defy you to prove me wrong.* **3** to make sth impossible or very difficult किसी बात को असंभव या बहुत कठिन बना देना *It's such a beautiful place that it defies description.*

**degenerate**[1] /dɪˈdʒenəreɪt डिˈजुनरेट्/ *verb* [I] to become worse, lower in quality, etc. किसी स्थिति में गिरावट आना *The calm discussion degenerated into a nasty argument.* ▸ **degeneration** /dɪˌdʒenəˈreɪʃn डिˌजेनˈरेशन्/ *noun* [U] गिरावट, अपकर्ष

**degenerate**[2] /dɪˈdʒenərət डिˈजुनरट्/ *adj.* having moral standards that have fallen to a very low level चरित्रहीन, भ्रष्ट, पतित

**degradation** /ˌdegrəˈdeɪʃn ˌडेग्रˈडेशन्/ *noun* [U] **1** the action of making sb be less respected; the state of being less respected अपमानित होने की क्रिया; अपमानित होने की अवस्था *the degradation of being in prison* **2** causing the condition of sth to become worse (किसी की) स्थिति को बिगाड़ना, विकृत करना *environmental degradation*

**degrade** /dɪˈgreɪd डिˈग्रेड्/ *verb* [T] to make people respect sb less किसी के सम्मान को घटाना *It's the sort of film that really degrades women.* ▸ **degrading** *adj.* अपयशकारी

**degree** /dɪˈgriː डिˈग्री/ *noun* **1** [C] a measurement of temperature तापमान को मापने की इकाई *Water boils at 100 degrees Celsius (100°C).* ○ *three degrees below zero/minus three degrees (–3°)* **2** [C] a measurement of angles कोणों को मापने की इकाई *a forty-five degree (45°) angle* ○ *An angle of 90 degrees is called a right angle.* **3** [C, U] (used about feelings or qualities) a certain amount or level (भावनाओं या विशेषताओं की) एक विशेष मात्रा या स्तर *There is always **a degree of** risk involved in mountaineering.* ○ *I sympathize with her **to some degree**.* **4** [C] an official document gained by successfully completing a course at university or college विश्वविद्यालय की उपाधि (जो पाठ्यक्रम को सफलता से पूरा करने पर विद्यार्थी को मिलती है) *She's got **a degree in** Philosophy.* ○ *to **do a** Chemistry **degree***

**dehumanize** (*also* **-ise**) /ˌdiːˈhjuːmənaɪz ˌडीˈह्यूमनाइज़्/ *verb* [T] to make sb lose his/her human qualities such as kindness, pity, etc. किसी को मानवीय गुणों से वंचित करना ▸ **dehumanization** (*also* **-isation**) /ˌdiːˌhjuːmənaɪˈzeɪʃn ˌडीˈह्यूमनाइˈज़ेश्न्/ *noun* [U] अपमानवीकरण

**dehydrate** /diːˈhaɪdreɪt डीˈहाइड्रेट्/ *verb* **1** [T] (*usually passive*) to remove all the water from sth (किसी में से) जलीय अंश निकाल देना, (किसी को) सुखाना *Dehydrated vegetables can be stored for months.* **2** [I, T] to lose too much water from your body (शरीर का) अधिक मात्रा में पानी खो देना *If you run for a long time in the heat, you start to dehydrate.* ▸ **dehydration** /ˌdiːhaɪˈdreɪʃn ˌडीहाइˈड्रेश्न्/ *noun* [U] निर्जलीकरण *Several of the runners were suffering from severe dehydration.*

**de-ice** /ˌdiːˈaɪs ˌडीˈआइस्/ *verb* [T] to remove the ice from sth कहीं से बर्फ़ हटाना *The car windows need de-icing.* ➪ **defrost** देखिए।

**deign** /deɪn डेन्/ *verb* [T] **deign to do sth** to do sth although you think you are too important to do it कोई ऐसा काम करना जो आपको छोटा लगे या ऐसा काम करना कि लगे आप दूसरे पर विशेष कृपा कर रहे हैं *He didn't even deign to look up when I entered the room.*

**deity** /ˈdeɪəti ˈडेअटि/ *noun* [C] (*pl.* **deities**) (*formal*) a god देवता

**dejected** /dɪˈdʒektɪd डिˈजेक्टिड्/ *adj.* very unhappy, especially because you are disappointed हताश, अत्यंत खिन्न, हतोत्साहित *The fans went home dejected after watching their team lose.* ▸ **dejectedly** *adv.* हताशा से ▸ **dejection** *noun* [U] हताशा, निराशा

**delay[1]** /dɪˈleɪ डिˈले/ *verb* **1** [T] to make sb/sth slow or late किसी को देर करवा देना *The plane was delayed for several hours because of bad weather.* **2** [I, T] **delay (sth/doing sth)** to decide not to do sth until a later time किसी काम में देर लगा देना, किसी काम को बाद में करने का निर्णय करना *I was forced to delay the trip until the following week.*

**delay[2]** /dɪˈleɪ डिˈले/ *noun* [C, U] a situation or period of time where you have to wait विलंब या देरी *Delays are likely on the roads because of heavy traffic.* ○ *If you smell gas, report it without delay* (= immediately).

**delegate[1]** /ˈdelɪgət ˈडेलिगेट्/ *noun* [C, U] a person who has been chosen to speak or take decisions for a group of people, especially at a meeting प्रतिनिधि

**delegate[2]** /ˈdelɪgeɪt ˈडेलिगेट्/ *verb* [I, T] to give sb with a lower job or position a particular task to do अपने से छोटे पद के व्यक्ति को अपने काम का दायित्व सौंपना *You can't do everything yourself. You must learn how to delegate.*

**delegation** /ˌdelɪˈgeɪʃn ˌडेलिˈगेश्न्/ *noun* **1** [C, *with sing. or pl. verb*] a group of people who have been chosen to speak or take decisions for a larger group of people, especially at a meeting प्रतिनिधि मंडल *The British delegation walked out of the meeting in protest.* **2** [U] giving sb with a lower job or position a particular task to do अपने से छोटे पद के व्यक्ति को अपने काम का दायित्व सौंपने की क्रिया

**delete** /dɪˈliːt डिˈलीट्/ *verb* [T] to remove sth that is written लिखित अंश को हटाना ▸ **deletion** /dɪˈliːʃn डिˈलीशन्/ *noun* [C, U] लिखित अंश को हटाने की क्रिया; अपमार्जन

**deliberate[1]** /dɪˈlɪbərət डिˈलिबरट्/ *adj.* **1** done on purpose; planned जान-बूझ कर किया हुआ; योजनानुसार *Was it an accident or was it deliberate?* ✪ पर्याय **intentional** **2** done slowly and carefully, without hurrying धीरे-धीरे सावधानी से बिना जल्दबाज़ी के किया हुआ *She spoke in a calm, deliberate voice.*

**deliberate[2]** /dɪˈlɪbəreɪt डिˈलिबरेट्/ *verb* [I, T] (*formal*) to think about or discuss sth fully before making a decision निर्णय करने से पहले किसी

बात को पूरी तरह सोचना-समझना, भलि-भाँति सोचना *The judges deliberated for an hour before announcing the winner.*

**deliberately** /dɪˈlɪbərətli डिˈलिबरट्लि/ *adv.* **1** on purpose विशेष उद्देश्य से, जान-बूझ कर *I didn't break it deliberately, it was an accident.* ✪ पर्याय **intentionally** या **purposely** **2** slowly and carefully, without hurrying धीरे-धीरे और सावधानी से बिना जल्दबाज़ी के

**deliberation** /dɪˌlɪbəˈreɪʃn डिˌलिबˈरेश्न्/ *noun* (*formal*) **1** [C, U] discussion or thinking about sth in detail विस्तृत विचार-विमर्श *After much deliberation I decided to reject the offer.* **2** [U] the quality of being very slow and careful in what you say and do सावधानी, सतर्कता, धैर्यपूर्वक सोच-विचार करना *He spoke with great deliberation.*

**delicacy** /ˈdelɪkəsi ˈडेलिकसि/ *noun* (*pl.* **delicacies**) **1** [U] the quality of being easy to damage or break कोमलता, नज़ाकत **2** [U] the fact that a situation is difficult and sb may be easily offended कठिन स्थिति जिसमें व्यक्ति जल्दी रुष्ट हो सकता है; संवेदनशीलता *Be tactful! It's a matter of some delicacy.* **3** [C] a type of food that is considered particularly good स्वादिष्ट व्यंजन *Try this dish, it's a local delicacy.*

**delicate** /ˈdelɪkət ˈडेलिकट्/ *adj.* **1** easy to damage or break नाज़ुक, आसानी से टूट जाने वाला *delicate skin* ○ *the delicate mechanisms of a watch* **2** frequently ill or hurt सुकुमार, बार-बार रोगी हो जाने वाला *He was a delicate child and often in hospital.* **3** (used about colours, flavours, etc.) light and pleasant; not strong (रंग, स्वाद आदि) हलका और प्रीतिकर; तीखी नहीं *a delicate shade of pale blue* **4** needing skilful treatment and care कुशलता और सावधानी की अपेक्षा वाला *Repairing this is going to be a very delicate operation.* ▶ **delicately** *adv.* नज़ाकत से, कोमलता से *She stepped delicately over the broken glass.*

**delicious** /dɪˈlɪʃəs डिˈलिशस्/ *adj.* having a very pleasant taste or smell स्वादिष्ट या सुगंधित *This soup is absolutely delicious.*

**delight**[1] /dɪˈlaɪt डिˈलाइट्/ *noun* **1** [U] great pleasure; joy अत्यंत प्रसन्नता; आनंद *She laughed with delight as she opened the present.* **2** [C] something that gives sb great pleasure आनंददायक वस्तु *The story is a delight to read.* ▶ **delightful** /-fl -फ़ल्/ *adj.* आनंदप्रद *a delightful view* ▶ **delightfully** /-fəli -फ़लि/ *adv.* आनंदपूर्वक

**delight**[2] /dɪˈlaɪt डिˈलाइट्/ *verb* [T] to give sb great pleasure (किसी को) अत्यधिक आनंदित कर देना *She delighted the audience by singing all her old songs.*

PHR V **delight in sth/in doing sth** to get great pleasure from sth (किसी बात से) अत्यधिक आनंदित होना *He delights in playing tricks on people.*

**delighted** /dɪˈlaɪtɪd डिˈलाइटिड्/ *adj.* **delighted (at/with/about sth); delighted to do sth/that...** extremely pleased अति प्रसन्न, बहुत ख़ुश *She was delighted at getting the job/that she got the job.*

**delinquency** /dɪˈlɪŋkwənsi डिˈलिङ्क्वन्सि/ *noun* [U] (*formal*) bad or criminal behaviour, especially among young people अपराधी आचरण (विशेषतः किशोरों का); किशोर-अपचारिता अपराधवृत्ति

**delinquent** /dɪˈlɪŋkwənt डिˈलिङ्क्वन्ट्/ *adj.* (*formal*) (usually used about a young person) behaving badly and often breaking the law किशोर-अपराधी, अल्पवयस्क द्वारा किया गया अपराध ▶ **delinquent** *noun* [C] बाल अपराधी *a juvenile delinquent*

**delirious** /dɪˈlɪriəs; -ˈlɪəriəs डिˈलिरिअस्; -ˈलिअरिअस्/ *adj.* **1** speaking or thinking in a crazy way, often because of illness उन्मादग्रस्त, प्रलापी, अंडबंड बोलने वाला (प्रायः रोगी होने के कारण) **2** extremely happy अत्यधिक प्रसन्न, ख़ुशी से पागल, उन्मत ▶ **deliriously** *adv.* उन्मादपूर्वक

**delirium** /dɪˈlɪriəm डिˈलिरिअम्/ *noun* [U] a mental state where sb becomes **delirious 1** ज्वर में उत्पन्न मस्तिष्क विभ्रम *fever accompanied by delirium*

**deliver** /dɪˈlɪvə(r) डिˈलिव़ (र्)/ *verb* **1** [I, T] to take sth (goods, letters, etc.) to the place requested or to the address on it निर्दिष्ट या बताए गए ठिकाने या पते पर सामान, पत्र आदि पहुँचाना, वितरण करना *Your order will be delivered within five days.* **2** [T] to help a mother to give birth to her baby शिशु को जन्म देने में माता की सहायता करना *to deliver a baby* **3** [T] (*formal*) to say sth formally भाषण देना *to deliver a speech/lecture/warning* **4** [I] **deliver (on sth)** (*informal*) to do or give sth that you have promised वादे के अनुसार काम करना या कुछ देना *The new leader has made a lot of promises, but can he deliver on them?*

IDM **come up with/deliver the goods** ➪ **goods** देखिए।

**delivery** /dɪˈlɪvəri डिˈलिव़रि/ *noun* (*pl.* **deliveries**) **1** [U] the act of taking sth (goods, letters, etc.) to the place or person who has ordered it or whose address is on it निर्दिष्ट स्थान, व्यक्ति या पते पर सामान, पत्र आदि पहुँचाने का कार्य; वितरण *Please allow 28 days for delivery.* ○ *a delivery van* **2** [C] an occasion when sth is delivered वितरण की व्यवस्था, वितरण कब-कब होता है—इसका संकेत *Is there a delivery here on Sundays?* **3** [C] something (goods, letters, etc.) that is delivered वितरित सामान, पत्र आदि *The shop is waiting for a new delivery of apples.* **4** [C] the process of giving birth to a baby शिशु-जन्म की प्रक्रिया *an easy delivery*

**delta** /ˈdeltə ˈडेल्टा/ *noun* [C] an area of flat land shaped like a triangle where a river divides into smaller rivers as it goes into the sea नदी का मुहाना, त्रिभुज के आकार का समतल क्षेत्र जहाँ पहुँचकर नदी अनेक छोटी धाराओं में बँट जाती है और समुद्र में समा जाती है

**delude** /dɪˈlu:d डिˈलूड्/ *verb* [T] to make sb believe sth that is not true किसी को भ्रमित करना या भ्रम में रखना *If he thinks he's going to get rich quickly, he's deluding himself.* ➪ **delusion** noun देखिए।

**deluge[1]** /ˈdelju:dʒ ˈडेल्यूज्/ *noun* [C] **1** a sudden very heavy fall of rain; a flood एकाएक मूसलाधार वर्षा; बाढ़ **2 a deluge (of sth)** a very large number of things that happen or arrive at the same time एक ही समय में एक साथ होने वाली बहुत-सी बातें, एक साथ घटित होने वाली बातों की भरमार *The programme was followed by a deluge of complaints from the public.*

**deluge[2]** /ˈdelju:dʒ ˈडेल्यूज्/ *verb* [T] (*usually passive*) to send or give sb/sth a very large quantity of sth, all at the same time किसी को एक ही समय में बहुत-सी सामग्री भेजना या देना *They were deluged with applications for the job.*

**delusion** /dɪˈlu:ʒn डिˈलूश़्न्/ *noun* [C, U] a false belief भ्रम, भ्रांति *He seems to be **under the delusion** that he's popular.* ➪ **delude** verb देखिए।

**deluxe** /ˌdəˈlʌks ˌडˈलक्स्/ *adj.* of extremely high quality and more expensive than usual उच्च कोटि का और सामान्य से अधिक महँगा, अति विशिष्ट *a deluxe hotel*

**delve** /delv डेल्व्/ *verb* [I] **delve into sth** to search inside sth (किसी की) गहरी ख़ोज करना *She delved into the bag and brought out a tiny box.* ○ (*figurative*) *We must delve into the past to find the origins of the custom.*

**demand[1]** /dɪˈmɑ:nd डिˈमान्ड्/ *noun* **1** [C] **a demand (for sth/that...)** a strong request or order that must be obeyed प्रबल अनुरोध या आदेश (जिसका पालन अवश्य हो) *a demand for changes in the law* **2 demands** [*pl.*] something that sb makes you do, especially sth that is difficult or tiring किसी बात की अपेक्षा होना (विशेषतः उसकी जो कठिन और श्रमसाध्य हो) *Running a marathon **makes** huge **demands** on the body.* **3** [U] **demand (for sth/sb)** the desire or need for sth among a group of people किसी वस्तु की इच्छा या आवश्यकता *We no longer sell that product because there is no demand for it.*

**IDM in demand** wanted by a lot of people बहुत-से लोगों द्वारा वांछित, जिसकी बहुत माँग हो, बहुत माँग में होना *I'm in demand this weekend—I've had three invitations!*

**on demand** whenever you ask for it माँग या अनुरोध पर, जब भी माँग करें तभी *This treatment is available from your doctor on demand.*

**demand[2]** /dɪˈmɑ:nd डिˈमान्ड्/ *verb* [T] **1 demand to do sth/that... ; demand sth** to ask for sth in an extremely firm or aggressive way अत्यंत दृढ़ता और आक्रामकता, ज़ोर-शोर से कोई वस्तु माँगना *I walked into the office and demanded to see the manager.* ○ *Your behaviour was disgraceful and I demand an apology.* **2** to need sth (किसी बात की) अपेक्षा होना *a sport that demands skill as well as strength*

**demanding** /dɪˈmɑ:ndɪŋ डिˈमान्डिङ्/ *adj.* **1** (used about a job, task, etc.) needing a lot of effort, care, skill, etc. (कार्य) प्रचुर प्रयास, सावधानी, दक्षता आदि की अपेक्षा वाला *It will be a demanding schedule—I have to go to six cities in six days.* **2** (used about a person) always wanting attention or expecting very high standards of people (व्यक्ति) दूसरों से सदा कठिन श्रम की अपेक्षा रखने वाला *Young children are very demanding.* ○ *a demanding boss*

**demarcate** /ˈdi:ma:keit ˈडीमाकेट्/ *verb* [T] to show or mark the limits of sth सीमांकन करना

**demarcation** /ˌdi:mɑ:ˈkeɪʃn ˌडीमाˈकेश्न्/ *noun* [U, C] a border or line that separates two things, such as types of work, groups of people or areas of land किन्हीं दो वस्तुओं (जैसे कार्य के प्रकारों, व्यक्ति-समूहों, भूक्षेत्रों) को पृथक करने वाली सीमा या रेखा

**demeanour** (*AmE* **demeanor**) /dɪˈmi:nə(r) डिˈमीन(र्)/ *noun* [U] (*formal*) the way a person behaves, dresses, speaks, looks, etc. that show what their character is like व्यवहार, आचरण *reserved demeanour*

**dementia** /dɪˈmenʃə डिˈमेन्शा/ *noun* [U] a serious mental problem caused by brain disease or injury, that affects the ability to think, remember and behave normally मस्तिष्क रोग या आघात से उत्पन्न एक गंभीर मानसिक विकार जो व्यक्ति की सोचने, याद रखने और सामान्य व्यवहार की क्षमता पर प्रतिकूल प्रभाव डालता है

**demi-** /ˈdemi ˈडेमि/ *prefix* (*used in nouns*) half; partly आधा, अर्ध; आंशिक

**demise** /dɪˈmaɪz डिˈमाइज़्/ *noun* [*sing.*] **1** the end or failure of sth (किसी की) समाप्ति या विफलता *Poor business decisions led to the company's demise.* **2** (*written*) the death of a person व्यक्ति का निधन

**demo** /ˈdeməʊ ˈडेमो/ *noun* [C] (*pl.* **demos**) = **demonstration 2, 3**

**demo-** *prefix* (*used in nouns, adjectives and verbs*) connected with people or population जनता या जनसंख्या से संबंधित *democracy*

**democracy** /dɪˈmɒkrəsi डिˈमॉक्रसि/ *noun* (*pl.* **democracies**) **1** [U] a system in which the government of a country is elected by the people लोकतंत्र, जनतंत्र **2** [C] a country that has this system लोकतांत्रिक देश **3** [U] the right of everyone in an organization, etc. to be treated equally and to vote on matters that affect them संगठन के समस्त सदस्यों को प्राप्त समानता का और अपने से संबंधित मामलों पर मत व्यक्त करने का अधिकार *There is a need for more democracy in the company.*

**democrat** /ˈdeməkræt ˈडेमक्रैट्/ *noun* [C] **1** a person who believes in and supports democracy लोकतंत्रवादी व्यक्ति

**democratic** /ˌdeməˈkrætɪk ˌडेमˈक्रैटिक्/ *adj.* **1** based on the system of democracy लोकतंत्र पर आधारित, लोकतांत्रिक *democratic elections* ○ *a democratic government* **2** having or supporting equal rights for all people सबसे लिए समान अधिकारों वाला या उन का समर्थन करने वाला लोकतांत्रिक निर्णय *a democratic decision* (= made by all the people involved) ✪ विलोम **undemocratic** ▶ **democratically** /-kli -क्लि/ *adv.* लोकतांत्रिक पद्धति से *a democratically elected government*

**demography** /dɪˈmɒgrəfi डिˈमॉग्रफ़ि/ *noun* [U] the changing number of births, deaths, diseases, etc. in a community over a period of time; the scientific study of these changes एक अवधि में जन्म, मृत्यु आदि के कारण किसी जन-समुदाय की संख्या में परिवर्तन; इन परिवर्तनों का वैज्ञानिक अध्ययन, जनसांख्यिकी *the social demography of Africa* ▶ **demographic** /ˌdeməˈgræfɪk ˈडेमˈग्रैफ़िक्/ *adj.* जनसंख्या-विषयक *demographic changes/trends/factors*

**demolish** /dɪˈmɒlɪʃ डिˈमॉलिश्/ *verb* [T] to destroy sth, for example a building (भवन आदि को) गिरा देना, तोड़ देना, ध्वस्त कर देना *The old shops were demolished and a supermarket was built in their place.* ○ (*figurative*) *She demolished his argument in one sentence.* ▶ **demolition** /ˌdeməˈlɪʃn ˌडेमˈलिश्न्/ *noun* [C, U] ध्वंस, विनाश, तोड़-फोड़

**demon** /ˈdiːmən ˈडीमन्/ *noun* [C] an evil spirit दुष्टात्मा, भूत, पिशाच

**demonic** /dɪˈmɒnɪk डिˈमॉनिक्/ *adj.* connected with, or like, a demon दुष्टात्मा-विषयक, पैशाचिक

**demonstrate** /ˈdemənstreɪt ˈडेमन्स्ट्रेट्/ *verb* **1** [T] **demonstrate sth (to sb)** to show sth clearly by giving proof प्रमाण देकर सिद्ध करना *Using this chart, I'd like to demonstrate to you what has happened to our sales.* **2** [I, T] **demonstrate sth (to sb)** to show and explain to sb how to do sth or how sth works किसी वस्तु की कार्यविधि या कार्यपद्धति को प्रदर्शित करना और समझाना *The crew demonstrated the use of life jackets just after take-off.* **3** [I] **demonstrate (against/for sb/sth)** to take part in a public protest for or against sb/sth किसी के विरोध अथवा समर्थन में जुलूस, सार्वजनिक प्रदर्शन आदि में भाग लेना *Enormous crowds have been demonstrating against the government.*

**demonstration** /ˌdemənˈstreɪʃn ˌडेमन्ˈस्ट्रेश्न्/ *noun* **1** [C, U] something that shows clearly that sth exists or is true किसी बात के सत्य होने का संकेत *This accident is a clear demonstration of the system's faults.* **2** [C, U] an act of showing or explaining to sb how to do sth or how sth works किसी वस्तु की कार्यविधि या कार्यपद्धति को प्रदर्शित करने या समझाने की क्रिया *The salesman gave me a demonstration of what the computer could do.* **3** [C] **a demonstration (against/for sb/sth)** a public protest for or against sb/sth किसी बात के समर्थन या विरोध में जुलूस या सार्वजनकि प्रदर्शन *demonstrations against a new law*

**demonstrative** /dɪˈmɒnstrətɪv डिˈमॉन्स्ट्रटिव़्/ *adj.* **1** (used about a person) showing feelings, especially loving feelings, in front of other people (व्यक्ति) अपनी भावनाओं (विशेषतः प्यार की भावनाओं को) अन्य व्यक्तियों के सामने प्रदर्शित करने वाला, सार्वजनिक भाव-प्रदर्शक **2** (*grammar*) used to identify the person or thing that is being referred to संकेतवाचक सर्वनाम *'This' and 'that' are demonstrative pronouns.*

**demonstrator** /ˈdemənstreɪtə(r) ˈडेमन्स्ट्रेट(र्)/ *noun* [C] a person who takes part in a public protest प्रदर्शनकारी, सार्वजनिक प्रदर्शन में भाग लेने वाला व्यक्ति

**demoralize** (*also* **-ise**) /dɪˈmɒrəlaɪz डिˈमॉरलाइज़्/ *verb* [T] to make sb lose confidence or the courage to continue doing sth किसी का मनोबल गिराना या उत्साहभंग करना (कि वह काम करना बंद कर दे) *Repeated defeats demoralized the team.* ▶ **demoralization** (*also* **-isation**) /dɪˌmɒrəlaɪˈzeɪʃn

डि,मॉरलाइ'ज़ेश्न् / *noun* [U] मनोबल-ह्रास ▶ **demoralizing** (*also* **-ising**) *adj.* मनोबल गिराने वाला *Constant criticism can be extremely demoralizing.*

**demote** /ˌdiːˈməʊt ˌडि'मोट् / *verb* [T] (*usually passive*) **demote sb (from sth) (to sth)** to move sb to a lower position or level, often as a punishment व्यक्ति के निचले पद या स्तर पर भेजना (प्रायः दंड स्वरूप), पदावनति करना ✪ विलोम **promote** ▶ **demotion** /ˌdiːˈməʊʃn ˌडि'मोश्न् / *noun* [C, U] पदावनति

**demure** /dɪˈmjʊə(r) डि'म्युअ(र्) / *adj.* (used especially about a girl or young woman) shy, quiet and polite (लड़की या युवती) शरमीली, शांत और विनीत

**den** /den डेन् / *noun* [C] **1** the place where certain wild animals live, for example lions (शेर आदि की) माँद, गुफ़ा **2** a secret place, especially for illegal activities गुप्त स्थान (विशेषतः ग़ैर-क़ानूनी कामों के लिए) *a gambling den*

**denial** /dɪˈnaɪəl डि'नाइअल् / *noun* **1** [C] a statement that sth is not true खंडन, वंचन *The minister issued a denial that he was involved in the scandal.* **2** [C, U] **(a) denial (of sth)** refusing to allow sb to have or do sth (किसी के अधिकार आदि को) नकारना, अस्वीकारना *a denial of personal freedom* **3** [U] a refusal to accept that sth unpleasant or painful has happened प्रतिवाद, कष्टप्रद मानने से इनकार करना *He's been **in denial** ever since the accident.* ➪ **deny** verb देखिए।

**denim** /ˈdenɪm 'डेनिम् / *noun* [U] a thick cotton material (often blue) that is used for making clothes, especially trousers (**jeans**) मोटी सूती कपड़ा (प्रायः नीला) जिससे पैंट, जींस आदि बनती हैं; डेनिम *a denim jacket*

**denitrify** /ˌdiːˈnaɪtrɪfaɪ ˌडी'नाइट्रिफ़ाइ / *verb* [T] (*pres. part.* **denitrifying;** *3rd person sing. pres.* **denitrifies;** *pt, pp* **denitrified**) (*technical*) to remove **nitrates** or **nitrites** from sth, especially from soil, air or water मिट्टी, वायु या पानी में से नाइट्रेट निकालना, विनाइट्रीकरण करना ▶ **denitrification** /diːˌnaɪtrɪfɪˈkeɪʃn डी,नाइट्रिफ़ि'केश्न् / *noun* [U] विनाइट्रीकरण

**denomination** /dɪˌnɒmɪˈneɪʃn डि,नॉमि'नेश्न् / *noun* [C] one of the different religious groups that you can belong to पंथ विशेष जिससे आप जुड़े हों

**denominator** /dɪˈnɒmɪneɪtə(r) डि'नॉमिनेट(र्) / *noun* [C] (*mathematics*) the number below the line in a **fraction** showing how many parts the whole is divided into, for example the 4 in ¾ भिन्न वाली संख्या में हर (जैसे ¾ में 4) ➪ **numerator** और **common denominator** देखिए।

**denote** /dɪˈnəʊt डि'नोट् / *verb* [T] to mean or be a sign of sth किसी बात का द्योतक होना या उसे द्योतित करना *In algebra the sign 'x' always denotes an unknown quantity.*

**denouement** (*also* **dénouement**) /ˌdeɪˈnuːmɒ ˌडे'नूमॉ / *noun* [C] the end of a play, book, etc., where everything is explained or settled; the end result of a situation किसी साहित्यिक रचना की समाप्ति जहाँ (द्वंद्व का) समाधान होता है; किसी प्रसंग का अंतिम परिणाम; निर्वहण, समाप्ति *an exciting/unexpected denouement*

**denounce** /dɪˈnaʊns डि'नाउन्स् / *verb* [T] to say publicly that sth is wrong; to be very critical of a person in public सार्वजनिक रूप से किसी बात को ग़लत ठहराना; सार्वजनिक रूप से किसी की तीव्र निंदा करना *The actor has been denounced as a bad influence on young people.* ▶ **denunciation** *noun* सार्वजनिक निंदा

**dense** /dens डेन्स् / *adj.* **1** containing a lot of things or people close together घनीभूत, बहुत-सी वस्तुओं या व्यक्तियों के जुटाव वाला *dense forests* ○ *areas of dense population* **2** difficult to see through घना, सघन *dense fog* **3** (*informal*) not intelligent; stupid प्रतिमाहीन; मंदबुद्धि ▶ **densely** *adv.* घने रूप में *densely populated areas*

**density** /ˈdensəti 'डेन्सटि / *noun* (*pl.* **densities**) **1** [U] the number of things or people in a place in relation to its area घनत्व, किसी स्थान के क्षेत्रफल का, वहाँ की वस्तुओं या व्यक्तियों की संख्या का आनुपातिक संबंध *There is a high density of wildlife in this area.* **2** [C, U] (*technical*) the relation of the weight of a substance to its size किसी वस्तु के आकार का उसके भार से आनुपातिक संबंध; सघनता *Lead has a high density.*

**dent¹** /dent डेन्ट् / *noun* [C] a place where a flat surface, especially metal, has been hit and damaged but not broken किसी की (विशेषतः धातु की) समतल सतह पर चोट के कारण पिचका हुआ स्थान

**dent²** /dent डेन्ट् / *verb* [T] to damage a flat surface by hitting it but not breaking it किसी वस्तु की समतल सतह को चोट मारकर पिचका देना *I hit a wall and dented the front of the car.*

**dental** /ˈdentl 'डेन्ट्ल् / *adj.* connected with teeth दाँतों का, दाँत-संबंधी, दंत्य *dental care/treatment*

**dentist** /ˈdentɪst 'डेन्टिस्ट् / *noun* **1** [C] a person whose job is to look after people's teeth दाँत का डॉक्टर, दंत-चिकित्सक **2 the dentist's** [*sing.*] the place where a dentist works दंत-चिकित्सालय *I have to go to the dentist's today.*

**dentistry** /ˈdentɪstri ˈडेन्टिस्ट्रि/ *noun* [U] **1** the medical study of the teeth and mouth दाँत और मुख का डॉक्टरी अध्ययन **2** the care and treatment of people's teeth दंत-चिकित्सा

**dentures** /ˈdentʃəz ˈडेन्चर्ज़्/ = **false teeth**

**denunciation** /dɪˌnʌnsiˈeɪʃn डि,नन्सिˈएश्न्/ *noun* [C, U] an expression of strong disapproval of sb/sth in public किसी की तीखी सार्वजनिक भर्त्सना ➪ **denounce** verb देखिए।

**deny** /dɪˈnaɪ डिˈनाइ/ *verb* [T] (*pres. part.* **denying;** *3rd person sing. pres.* **denies;** *pt, pp* **denied**) **1 deny sth/doing sth; deny that...** to state that sth is not true; to refuse to admit or accept sth किसी बात से इनकार करना; किसी बात को नकारना *In court he denied all the charges.* ○ *She denied telling lies/that she had told lies.* ✪ विलोम **admit 2** (*formal*) **deny sb sth; deny sth** (to sb) to refuse to allow sb to have sth किसी को कुछ करने से इनकार करना *She was denied permission to remain in the country.* ➪ **denial** noun देखिए।

**deodar** *noun* [C] the Himalayan Cedar; a large evergreen coniferous tree commonly found in the Himalayas देवदार वृक्ष; हिमालय में सामान्यतः पाए जाने वाले सदाबहार शंकुवृक्ष

**deodorant** /diˈəʊdərənt डिˈओडरन्ट्/ *noun* [C, U] a chemical substance that you put onto your body to prevent bad smells दुर्गंध को रोकने वाला रासायनिक पदार्थ, दुर्गंध-निवारक पदार्थ, दुर्गंध-नाशक पदार्थ

**dep.** *abbr.* departs प्रस्थान *dep. Kolkata 15.32*

**depart** /dɪˈpɑːt डिˈपाट्/ *verb* [I] (*formal*) to leave a place, usually at the beginning of a journey (कहीं से, कहीं के लिए) प्रस्थान करना, रवाना होना *The next train to the airport departs from platform number 2.* ➪ **departure** noun देखिए तथा **leave**[1] पर नोट भी देखिए।

**department** /dɪˈpɑːtmənt डिˈपाट्मन्ट्/ *noun* **1** one of the sections into which an organization, for example a school or a business, is divided (विद्यालय या व्यापारिक संगठन का) विभाग *the Modern Languages department* ○ *She works in the accounts department.* **2** a division of the government responsible for a particular subject; a ministry सरकार में विषय विशेष का विभाग; मंत्रालय *the Department of Health*

**departmental** /ˌdiːpɑːtˈmentl ˌडीपाट्ˈमेन्ट्ल्/ *adj.* concerning a department विभाग से संबंधित, विभागीय *There is a departmental meeting once a month.*

**departmental store** *noun* [C] a large shop that is divided into sections selling different types of goods बड़ी दुकान जिसमें अलग-अलग वस्तुओं के अलग-अलग विभाग होते हैं, डिपार्टमेंट स्टोर, बहुविभागीय भंडार

**departure** /dɪˈpɑːtʃə(r) डिˈपाच(र्)/ *noun* [C, U] **1** leaving or going away from a place प्रस्थान क्रिया, रवानगी *Passengers should check in at least one hour before departure.* ➪ **depart** verb देखिए। **2 a departure (from sth)** an action which is different from what is usual or expected सामान्य से हटने की क्रिया (सामान्य व्यवहार से) विचलन *a departure from normal practice*

**depend** /dɪˈpend डिˈपेन्ड्/ *verb*

**IDM that depends; it (all) depends** (used alone or at the beginning of a sentence) used to say that you are not certain of sth until other things have been considered अन्य पर निर्भर होना; अन्य द्वारा निश्चित होना (अकेले या वाक्य के आरंभ में प्रयुक्त) कुछ कहा नहीं जा सकता, कह नहीं सकता के अर्थ में प्रयुक्त; यह इस बात पर निर्भर है *'Can you lend me some money?' 'That depends. How much do you want?'* ○ *I don't know whether I'll see him. It depends what time he gets here.*

**PHR V depend on sb/sth** to be able to trust sb/sth to do sth; to rely on sb/sth किसी बात के लिए किसी पर भरोसा या विश्वास रखना; किसी के भरोसे रहना *If you ever need any help, you know you can depend on me.* ○ *You can't depend on the trains. They're always late.* ○ *I was depending on getting the money today.*

**depend on sb/sth (for sth)** to need sb/sth to provide sth किसी बात के लिए (किसी अन्य पर) निर्भर होना *Our organization depends on donations from the public.*

**depend on sth** to be decided or influenced by sb/sth किसी बात का अन्य द्वारा निश्चित होना या निर्धारित होना *His whole future depends on these exams.*

**dependable** /dɪˈpendəbl डिˈपेन्डबल्/ *adj.* that can be trusted भरोसेमंद, विश्वसनीय, भरोसे लायक़ *The bus service is very dependable.* ✪ पर्याय **reliable**

**dependant** (*AmE* **dependent**) /dɪˈpendənt डिˈपेन्डन्ट्/ *noun* [C] a person who depends on sb else for money, a home, food, etc. (किसी पर) आश्रित व्यक्ति *insurance cover for you and all your dependants*

**dependence** /dɪˈpendəns डिˈपेन्डन्स्/ *noun* [U] **dependence on sb/sth** the state of needing sb/sth आश्रित रहने की स्थिति, निर्भरता *The country wants to reduce its dependence on imported oil.*

**dependency** /dɪˈpendənsi डिˈपेन्डनसि / *noun* [U] the state of being dependent on sb/sth; the state of being unable to live without sth, especially a drug किसी अन्य पर निर्भरता; किसी वस्तु (विशेषतः नशीली पदार्थ) की विवशतापूर्ण आवश्यकता

**dependent** /dɪˈpendənt डिˈपेन्डन्ट् / *adj.* **1 dependent (on sb/sth)** needing sb/sth to support you किसी पर निर्भर, पराश्रित *The industry is heavily dependent on government funding.* ○ *Do you have any dependent children?* **2 dependent on sb/sth** influenced or decided by sth किसी के द्वारा निश्चित या निर्धारित *The price you pay is dependent on the number in your group.* ✪ विलोम **independent**

**depict** /dɪˈpɪkt डिˈपिक्ट् / *verb* [T] **1** to show sb/sth in a painting or drawing किसी वस्तु को चित्र या आरेख बनाकर दिखाना, चित्रांकन करना, चित्रित करना *a painting depicting a country scene* **2** to describe sb/sth in words किसी व्यक्ति या वस्तु का शब्दों में वर्णन करना *The novel depicts rural life a century ago.*

**deplete** /dɪˈpliːt डिˈप्लीट् / *verb* [T] to reduce the amount of sth so that there is not much left किसी वस्तु की मात्रा को घटाना (कि वह बहुत कम बचे), किसी वस्तु को निःशेष करना *We are depleting the world's natural resources.* ▶ **depletion** /dɪˈpliːʃn डिˈप्लीशन् / *noun* [U] निःशेषण

**deplorable** /dɪˈplɔːrəbl डिˈप्लॉरब्ल् / *adj.* (*formal*) morally bad and deserving disapproval शोचनीय, निंदनीय *They are living in deplorable conditions.* ▶ **deplorably** /-əbli -अब्लि / *adv.* शोचनीय रूप से

**deplore** /dɪˈplɔː(r) डिˈप्लॉ(र्) / *verb* [T] (*formal*) to feel or say that sth is morally bad किसी ग़लत बात के लिए खेद प्रकट करना, ग़लत बात की निंदा करना *I deplore such dishonest behaviour.*

**deploy** /dɪˈplɔɪ डिˈप्लॉइ / *verb* [T] **1** to put soldiers or weapons in a position where they are ready to fight सेना या हथियारों को संभावित लड़ाई के लिए तैयार करना; तैनात करना **2** to use sth in a useful and successful way किसी वस्तु का प्रभावी ढंग से इस्तेमाल करना ▶ **deployment** *noun* [U] तैनाती *the deployment of troops*

**depopulate** /ˌdiːˈpɒpjuleɪt ˌडीˈपाप्युलेट् / *verb* [T] (*formal*) (*usually passive*) to reduce the number of people living in a place किसी स्थान के निवासियों की संख्या को कम करना ▶ **depopulation** /ˌdiːpɒpjuˈleɪʃn ˌडीपॉप्युˈलेशन् / *noun* [U] जनसंख्या-ह्रास

**deport** /dɪˈpɔːt डिˈपॉट् / *verb* [T] to force sb to leave a country because he/she has no legal right to be there किसी को देश छोड़ने के लिए बाध्य करना निर्वासित करना (क्योंकि उसे वहाँ रहने का क़ानूनी अधिकार नहीं) *A number of illegal immigrants have been deported.* ▶ **deportation** /ˌdiːpɔːˈteɪʃn ˌडीपॉˈट्रेशन् / *noun* [C, U] देशनिकाला, निर्वासन

**depose** /dɪˈpəʊz डिˈपोज़् / *verb* [T] to remove a ruler or leader from power शासक या नेता को सत्ता से च्युत करना *There was a revolution and the dictator was deposed.*

**deposit**[1] /dɪˈpɒzɪt डिˈपॉज़िट् / *verb* [T] **1** to put sth down somewhere किसी निर्धारित स्थान पर कुछ रखना *He deposited his bags on the floor and sat down.* **2** (used about liquid or a river) to leave sth lying on a surface, as the result of a natural or chemical process (किसी द्रव या नदी का) प्राकृतिक या रासायनिक प्रक्रिया के फलस्वरूप तले पर (किसी वस्तु की) परतें जमाना *mud deposited by a flood* **3** to put money into an account at a bank बैंक के खाते में पैसा डालना *He deposited Rs 200 a week into his savings account.* **4 deposit sth (in sth); deposit sth (with sb/sth)** to put sth valuable in an official place where it is safe until needed again किसी अधिकृत स्थान पर कुछ समय के लिए मूल्यवान वस्तुएँ रखना (सुरक्षा के लिए) *Valuables can be deposited in the hotel safe.*

**deposit**[2] /dɪˈpɒzɪt डिˈपॉज़िट् / *noun* [C] **1 a deposit (on sth)** a sum of money which is the first payment for sth, with the rest of the money to be paid later (किसी को देय) बड़ी राशि के छोटे अंश का भुगतान करना *Once you have paid a deposit, the booking will be confirmed.* **2 a deposit (on sth)** [*usually sing.*] a sum of money that you pay when you rent sth and get back when you return it without damage किसी वस्तु को किराये पर लेते समय जमा कराई गई राशि (जो बाद में वापिस मिल जाती है), अमानती रकम, प्रतिभूति धनराशि *Boats can be hired for Rs 50 an hour, plus Rs 20 as deposit.* **3** a sum of money paid into a bank account बैंक के खाते में जमा की गई धनराशि **4** a substance that has been left on a surface or in the ground as the result of a natural or chemical process प्राकृतिक या रासायनिक प्रक्रिया के फलस्वरूप (किसी द्रव या नदी के) तल पर जमा पदार्थ *mineral deposits*

**deposit account** *noun* [C] (*BrE*) a type of bank account where your money earns interest. You cannot take money out of a deposit account without arranging it first with the bank निश्चित अवधि का जमा-खाता (जिस पर ब्याज मिलता है और जिसे बैंक की सहमति से ही समयपूर्व निकाला जा सकता है)

**deposition** /ˌdepəˈzɪʃn ˌडेपˈज़िश्न् / *noun* **1** [U, C] (*technical*) the natural process of leaving a layer of a substance on rocks or soil; a substance left in this way एक प्राकृतिक प्रक्रिया जिसमें चट्टान या मिट्टी पर किसी वस्तु की तह जम जाती है; तह के रूप में जमी वस्तु *marine/river deposition* **2** [U, C] the act of removing sb, especially a ruler, from power किसी को (विशेषत: शासक को) सत्ता से हटाने की क्रिया *the deposition of the king* **3** [C] (*law*) a formal statement, taken from sb and used in a court of law कचहरी में दिया गया बयान

**depot** /ˈdepəʊ ˈड्रेपो / *noun* [C] **1** a place where large numbers of vehicles (buses, lorries, etc.) are kept when not in use (बस आदि वाहनों को रखने का) स्थल, डेपो **2** a place where large amounts of food, goods or equipment are stored गोदाम **3** (*AmE*) a small bus or railway station छोटा बस अड्डा या रेलवे स्टेशन

**depraved** /dɪˈpreɪvd डिˈप्रेव्ड् / *adj.* morally bad चरित्रहीन, भ्रष्ट, दुष्ट

**depravity** /dɪˈprævəti डिˈप्रैव़टि / *noun* [U] (*formal*) the state of being morally bad चरित्रहीनता, दुष्टता *a life of depravity*

**depreciate** /dɪˈpriːʃieɪt डिˈप्रीशिएट् / *verb* [I] to become less valuable over a period of time एक अवधि के बाद (किसी वस्तु का) मूल्य घट जाना, मूल्य ह्रास होना *New cars start to depreciate the moment they are on the road.* ▶ **depreciation** /dɪˌpriːʃiˈeɪʃn डिˌप्रीशिˈएशन् / *noun* [C, U] मूल्य-ह्रास

**depress** /dɪˈpres डिˈप्रेस् / *verb* [T] **1** to make sb unhappy and without hope or enthusiasm (किसी को) उदास करना, निराश करना, हताश करना *The thought of going to work tomorrow really depresses me.* **2** (used about business) to cause sth to become less successful (व्यापार में) किसी प्रवृत्ति को हतोत्साहित करना *The reduction in the number of tourists has depressed local trade.* **3** (*formal*) to press sth down on a machine, etc. मशीन आदि में किसी वस्तु को दबाना *To switch off the machine, depress the lever.* ▶ **depressing** *adj.* उदास करने वाला, विषादकारी, निराशाजनक *The thought of growing old alone is very depressing.* ▶ **depressingly** *adv.* निराशाजनक रूप से

**depressed** /dɪˈprest डिˈप्रेस्ट् / *adj.* **1** very unhappy, often for a long period of time बहुत उदास (प्राय: लंबे समय तक) *He's been very depressed since he lost his job.* **2** (used about a place or an industry) without enough businesses or jobs (कोई स्थान या उद्योग) मंदी से ग्रस्त

**depression** /dɪˈpreʃn डिˈप्रेश्न् / *noun* **1** [U] a feeling of unhappiness that lasts for a long time. Depression can be a medical condition and may have physical signs, for example being unable to sleep, etc. विषाद का भाव, अवसाद (यह देर तक रहता है और कभी-कभी अनिद्रा आदि के रूप में प्रकट होता है) *clinical/post-natal depression* **2** [C, U] a period when the economic situation is bad, with little business activity and many people without a job व्यापार में मंदी का दौर *The country was in the grip of (an) economic depression.* **3** [C] a part of a surface that is lower than the parts around it घसकन, गर्त, अपने चारों और के हिस्सों की तुलना में किसी वस्तु का धँसा हुआ हिस्सा *Rain water collects in shallow depressions in the ground.* **4** [C] (*technical*) a weather condition in which the pressure of the air becomes lower, often causing rain मौसम की स्थिति जिसमें वायुदाब कम हो जाता है और फलस्वरूप प्राय: वर्षा होती है ➪ **anticyclone** देखिए।

**deprive** /dɪˈpraɪv डिˈप्राइव़् / *verb* [T] **deprive sb/sth of sth** to prevent sb/sth from having sth; to take away sth from sb किसी को किसी से वंचित करना; किसी से कोई वस्तु छीन लेना *The prisoners were deprived of food.* ▶ **deprivation** /ˌdeprɪˈveɪʃn ˌडेप्रिˈव़ेश्न् / *noun* [U] वंचन

**deprived** /dɪˈpraɪvd डिˈप्राइव्ड् / *adj.* not having enough of the basic things in life, such as food, money, etc. जीवन की मूलभूत सुविधाओं से वंचित *He came from a deprived background.*

**Dept** *abbr.* department विभाग *the Sales Dept*

**depth** /depθ ड्रेप्थ् / *noun* **1** [C, U] the distance down from the top to the bottom of sth गहराई, किसी वस्तु के ऊपर से नीचे तक की दूरी *The hole should be 3 cm in depth.* **2** [C, U] the distance from the front to the back of sth गहराई, किसी वस्तु के आगे से पीछे तक की दूरी *the depth of a shelf* **3** [U] the amount of emotion, knowledge, etc. that a person has किसी व्यक्ति की भावना, ज्ञान आदि की मात्रा, थाह, गंभीरता *He tried to convince her of the depth of his feelings for her.* **4** [C, *usually pl.*] the deepest, most extreme or serious part of sth किसी वस्तु का सबसे चरम और अतिशयपूर्ण पक्ष, घोर ***in the depths of*** *winter* (= when it is coldest) ➪ **deep** adjective देखिए।

**IDM** **in depth** looking at all the details; in a thorough way विस्तारपूर्वक; पूर्णतया *to discuss a problem in depth*

**out of your depth** **1** (*BrE*) in water that is too deep for you to stand up in अपनी ऊँचाई से भी अधिक गहरे पानी में होना **2** in a situation that is too difficult for you स्थिति का अत्यंत कठिन होना या अपने सामर्थ्य से बाहर की कठिनाई में पड़ जाना, बूते से बाहर की बात होना

**deputation** /ˌdepjuˈteɪʃn ˌडेप्यु ˈटेश्न् / *noun* [C, *with sing. or pl. verb*] a group of people sent to sb to act or speak for others प्रतिनिधि मंडल, शिष्ट मंडल

**deputize** (*also* **-ise**) / ˈdepjutaɪz ˈडेप्यूटाइज़् / *verb* [I] **deputize (for sb)** to act for sb in a higher position, who is away or unable to do sth उच्चतर पद पर नियुक्त व्यक्ति की अनुपस्थिति में उसके स्थान पर काम करना

**deputy** / ˈdepjuti ˈडेप्यूटि / *noun* [C] (*pl.* **deputies**) the second most important person in a particular organization, who does the work of his/her manager if the manager is away किसी संगठन में द्वितीय स्थान का अधिकारी संगठन का उप-प्रमुख या प्रमुख का स्थानापन्न *the deputy head of a school*

**derail** /dɪˈreɪl डि ˈरेल् / *verb* [T] to cause a train to come off a railway track रेलगाड़ी को पटरी से उतार देना

**derailment** /dɪˈreɪlmənt डि ˈरेल्मन्ट् / *noun* [C, U] an occasion when sth causes a train to come off a railway track रेलगाड़ी का पटरी से उतर जाने की घटना

**deranged** /dɪˈreɪndʒd डि ˈरेन्ज्ड् / *adj.* thinking and behaving in a way that is not normal, especially because of mental illness सामान्य रूप से काम करने में असमर्थ (विशेषतः मानसिक रोग के कारण)

**derby** / ˈdɑːbi ˈडाबि / *noun* [C] (*pl.* **derbies**) **1** (*BrE*) a race or sports competition दौड़ या खेल-प्रतियोगिता *a motorcycle derby* **2** (*BrE*) **the Derby** a horse race which takes place every year at Epsom (England) प्रतिवर्ष एप्सम (इंग्लैंड) में होने वाली घुड़दौड़ का नाम, डर्बी, एप्सम डर्बी **3** (*AmE*) = **bowler 1**

**deregulate** / ˌdiːˈregjuleɪt ˌडी ˈरेग्युलेट् / *verb* [T] (*usually passive*) to free a commercial or business activity from rules and controls वाणिज्यिक या व्यापारिक गतिविधि को नियमों और नियंत्रणों के बंधन से मुक्त करना *deregulated financial markets* ▶ **deregulation** / ˌdiːˌregjuˈleɪʃn ˌडी ˌरेग्यु ˈलेश्न् / *noun* [U] विनियंत्रण

**derelict** / ˈderəlɪkt ˈडेरलिक्ट् / *adj.* no longer used and in bad condition अप्रयुक्त और दुर्दशाग्रस्त, वीरान, उजड़ा हुआ *a derelict house*

**deride** /dɪˈraɪd डि ˈराइड् / *verb* [T] to say that sb/ sth is ridiculous; to laugh at sth in a cruel way किसी को हास्यास्पद बताना; किसी का कठोरता से उपहास करना ▶ **derision** /dɪˈrɪʒn डि ˈरिश़्न् / *noun* [U] उपहास *Her comments were met with derision.* ▶ **derisive** /dɪˈraɪsɪv डि ˈराइसिव़् / *adj.* उपहासपूर्ण '*What rubbish!' he said with a derisive laugh.*

**derisory** /dɪˈraɪsəri डि ˈराइसरि / *adj.* too small or of too little value to be considered seriously अत्यंत तुच्छ होने के कारण अविचारणीय, उपहास के योग्य, उपेक्षणीय *Union leaders rejected the derisory pay offer.*

**derivation** / ˌderɪˈveɪʃn ˌडेरि ˈव़ेश्न् / *noun* [C, U] the origin from which a word or phrase has developed मूल शब्द जिससे संबंधित शब्द या पदबंध विकसित या व्युत्पन्न हों

**derivative** /dɪˈrɪvətɪv डि ˈरिव़टिव़् / *noun* [C] a form of sth (especially a word) that has developed from the original form मूल शब्द से विकसित या व्युत्पन्न शब्द *'Sadness' is a derivative of 'sad.'*

**derive** /dɪˈraɪv डि ˈराइव़् / *verb* **1** [T] (*formal*) **derive sth from sth** to get sth (especially a feeling or an advantage) from sth किसी से कुछ (विशेषतः कोई भावना या भौतिक लाभ) प्राप्त करना *I derive great satisfaction from my work.* **2** [I, T] (used about a name or word) to come from sth; to have sth as its origin (किसी नाम या शब्द का) किसी से व्युत्पन्न होना *The town derives its name from the river on which it was built.*

**dermatitis** / ˌdɜːməˈtaɪtɪs ˌडम ˈटाइटिस् / *noun* [U] a skin condition in which the skin becomes red, swollen and sore एक त्वचा-रोग जिसमें त्वचा लाल, सूजनयुक्त और दर्दीली हो जाती है

**dermatologist** / ˌdɜːməˈtɒlədʒɪst ˌडम ˈटॉलजिस्ट् / *noun* [C] a doctor who studies and treats skin diseases चर्म-रोग चिकित्सक, त्वचा-विशेषज्ञ

**dermatology** / ˌdɜːməˈtɒlədʒi ˌडम ˈटॉलजि / *noun* [U] the scientific study of skin diseases चर्म-रोग-विज्ञान, त्वचा-विज्ञान ▶ **dermatological** / ˌdɜːmətəˈlɒdʒɪkl ˌडमट ˈलॉजिकल् / *adj.* चर्म या त्वचा-रोग विषयक

**derogatory** /dɪˈrɒgətri डि ˈरॉगट्रि / *adj.* expressing a lack of respect for, or a low opinion of sth अनादरपूर्ण *derogatory comments about the standard of my work*

**desalination** / ˌdiːˌsælɪˈneɪʃn ˌडी ˌसैलि ˈनेश्न् / *noun* [U] the process of removing salt from sea water समुद्र-जल को नमक रहित करने की प्रक्रिया, समुद्र-जल का खारापन दूर करने की क्रिया; विलवणीकरण

**descant** / ˈdeskænt ˈडेस्कैन्ट् / *noun* [C] (in music) a tune that is sung or played at the same time as, and usually higher than, the main tune (संगीत में) मुख्य राग के साथ, प्रायः मुख्य से उच्चतर स्वर में बजाया जाने वाला राग

**descend** /dɪˈsend डि ˈसैन्ड् / *verb* [I, T] (*formal*) to go down to a lower place; to go down sth नीचे

आना; उतरना *The plane started to descend and a few minutes later we landed.* ○ *She descended the stairs slowly.* ✪ विलोम **ascend**

IDM **be descended from sb** to have sb as a relative in past times किसी का वंशज होना *He says he's descended from an Indian prince.*

**descendant** /dɪˈsendənt डिˈसेन्डन्ट्/ *noun* [C] a person who belongs to the same family as sb who lived a long time ago वंशज *Her family are descendants of one of the first Englishmen to arrive in India.* ➪ **ancestor** देखिए।

**descent** /dɪˈsent डिˈसेन्ट्/ *noun* **1** [C] a movement down to a lower place उतार, अवरोहण *The pilot informed us that we were about to begin our descent.* **2** [U] a person's family origins वंशक्रम *He is* ***of Indian descent.***

**describe** /dɪˈskraɪb डिˈस्क्राइब्/ *verb* [T] **describe sb/sth (to/for sb); describe sb/sth (as sth)** to say what sb/sth is like, or what happened किसी व्यक्ति या वस्तु या घटना का वर्णन करना *Can you describe the bag you lost?* ○ *The thief was described as tall, thin, and aged about twenty.*

**description** /dɪˈskrɪpʃn डिˈस्क्रिप्श्न्/ *noun* **1** [C, U] a picture in words of sb/sth or of sth that happened किसी व्यक्ति, वस्तु या घटना का शब्दचित्र *The man gave the police a detailed description of the burglar.* **2** [C] a type or kind of sth (किसी का प्रकार) या क़िस्म *It must be a tool* ***of some description,*** *but I don't know what it's for.*

**descriptive** /dɪˈskrɪptɪv डिˈस्क्रिप्टिव्/ *adj.* that describes sb/sth, especially in a skilful or interesting way वर्णनात्मक, वर्णनप्रधान *a piece of descriptive writing* ○ *She gave a highly descriptive account of the journey.*

**desecrate** /ˈdesɪkreɪt ˈडेसिक्रेट्/ *verb* [T] to damage a place of religious importance or treat it without respect धार्मिक स्थल को हानि पहुँचाना या उसका अनादर करना या उसे अपवित्र करना *desecrated graves* ► **desecration** /ˌdesɪˈkreɪʃn ˌडेसिˈक्रेश्न्/ *noun* [U] अपवित्रीकरण *the desecration of a cemetery*

**desert¹** /ˈdezət ˈडेज़ट्/ *noun* [C, U] a large area of land, usually covered with sand, that is hot and has very little water and very few plants रेगिस्तान, मरूस्थल

**desert²** /dɪˈzɜːt डिˈज़ट्/ *verb* **1** [T] to leave sb/sth, usually for ever किसी को (प्रायः सदा के लिए) छोड़ जाना *Many people have deserted the countryside and moved to the towns.* **2** [I, T] (used especially about sb in the armed forces) to leave without permission बिना अनुमति के छोड़ भागना (विशेषतः किसी सशस्त्र सैनिक का) *He deserted because he didn't want to fight.* ► **desertion** *noun* [C, U] अवैध पलायन

**deserted** /dɪˈzɜːtɪd डिˈज़टिड्/ *adj.* empty, because all the people have left वीरान, परित्यक्त *a deserted house*

**deserter** /dɪˈzɜːtə(r) डिˈज़ट(र्)/ *noun* [C] a person who leaves the armed forces without permission बिना अनुमति के सशस्त्र सेना की सेवा छोड़ने वाला व्यक्ति, भगोड़ा

**desertification** /dɪˌzɜːtɪfɪˈkeɪʃn डिˌज़टिफ़िˈकेश्न्/ *noun* [U] (*technical*) the process of becoming a desert or of making an area of land into a desert किसी क्षेत्र के मरूस्थल बनने या बनाने की प्रक्रिया; मरूस्थलीकरण

**desert island** *noun* [C] an island, especially a tropical one, where nobody lives उजाड़ या सुनसान द्वीप (विशेषतः बहुत गरम क्षेत्र का)

**deserve** /dɪˈzɜːv डिˈज़व्/ *verb* [T] (*not used in the continuous tenses*) to earn sth, either good or bad, because of sth that you have done अच्छे या बुरे कर्म के अनुसार अच्छ या बुरे फल का पात्र होना *We've done a lot of work and we deserve a break.* ○ *He deserves to be punished severely for such a crime.*

> NOTE यद्यपि यह क्रिया सातत्यबोधक कालों (continuous tenses) में प्रयुक्त नहीं होती, परंतु इसका -ing से बनने वाला वर्तमान कृदंत (present participle) रूप पर्याप्त मात्रा में दिखाई पड़ता है—*There are other aspects of the case deserving attention.*

**deservedly** /dɪˈzɜːvɪdli डिˈज़विड्लि/ *adv.* in a way that is right because of what sb has done उचित रूप से, योग्यता के अनुकूल *He deservedly won the Best Actor award.*

**deserving** /dɪˈzɜːvɪŋ डिˈज़विङ्/ *adj.* **deserving (of sth)** that you should give help, money, etc. to योग्य, सुपात्र *This charity is a most deserving cause.*

**desiccated** /ˈdesɪkeɪtɪd ˈडेसिकेटिड्/ *adj.* **1** used about food dried in order to keep it for a long time (भोज्य पदार्थ) सुखाया हुआ, निर्जलीकृत *desiccated coconut* **2** (*technical*) completely dry पूर्णतया निर्जलीकृत *desiccated soil*

**desiccation** /ˌdesɪˈkeɪʃn ˌडेसिˈकेश्न्/ *noun* [U] the process of becoming completely dry पूर्ण निर्जलीकरण की प्रक्रिया

**design¹** /dɪˈzaɪn डिˈज़ाइन्/ *noun* **1** [U] the way in which sth is planned and made or arranged डिज़ाइन, ख़ाका *Design faults have been discovered* *in the car.* **2** [U] the process and skill of making drawings that show how sth should be made, how it will work, etc. किसी वस्तु के निर्माण, कार्य आदि की रूपरेखा बनाने की प्रक्रिया और दक्षता *to study industrial design* ○ *graphic design* **3** [C] **a design (for sth)** a drawing or plan that shows how sth should be made, built, etc. किसी वस्तु के निर्माण की रूपरेखा या योजना *The architect showed us her design for the new theatre.* **4** [C] a pattern of lines, shapes, etc. that decorate sth सजावट के लिए रेखाओं, आकृतियों आदि का पैटर्न *a T-shirt with a geometric design on it* ✪ पर्याय **pattern**

**design²** /dɪˈzaɪn डिˈज़ाइन्/ *verb* **1** [I, T] to plan and make a drawing of how sth will be made किसी वस्तु की निर्माण की योजना और रूपरेखा बनाना *to design cars/dresses/houses* **2** [T] to invent, plan and develop sth for a particular purpose उद्देश्य विशेष से किसी वस्तु की योजना बनाना और निर्माण करना *The bridge wasn't designed for such heavy traffic.*

**designate** /ˈdezɪɡneɪt ˈडेज़िग्नेट्/ *verb* [T] (*usually passive*) (*formal*) **1 designate sth (as) sth** to give sth a name to show that it has a particular purpose किसी को उद्देश्य विशेष से नाम देकर निर्दिष्ट करना *This has been designated (as) a conservation area.* **2 designate sb (as) sth** to choose sb to do a particular job or task किसी व्यक्ति को कार्य विशेष के लिए नामित करना *Who has she designated (as) her deputy?* **3** to show or mark sth किसी बात का संकेत करना *These arrows designate the emergency exits.*

**designer** /dɪˈzaɪnə(r) डिˈज़ाइन(र्) / *noun* [C] a person whose job is to make drawings or plans showing how sth will be made डिज़ाइनर; किसी वस्तु के निर्माण की रूपरेखा बनाने वाला वेशभूषाकार *a fashion/jewellery designer* ○ *designer jeans* (= made by a famous designer)

**desirable** /dɪˈzaɪərəbl डिˈज़ाइअरब्ल् / *adj.* **1** wanted, often by many people; worth having वांछनीय; अपेक्षित *Experience is desirable but not essential for this job.* **2** sexually attractive रूपरंग से आकर्षक, मोहक ✪ विलोम **undesirable**

**desire¹** /dɪˈzaɪə(r) डिˈज़ाइअ(र्)/ *noun* [C, U] **(a) desire (for sth/to do sth)** **1** the feeling of wanting sth very much; a strong wish अत्यधिक चाह; तीव्र इच्छा *the desire for a peaceful solution to the crisis* ○ *I have no desire to visit that place again.* **2** the wish for a sexual relationship with sb कामेच्छा, कामवासना

**desire²** /dɪˈzaɪə(r) डिˈज़ाइअ(र्)/ *verb* [T] **1** (*formal*) (*not used in the continuous tenses*) to want; to wish for अभिलाषा रखना; इच्छा करना *The service in the restaurant left a lot to be desired* (= was very bad). **2** to find sb/sth sexually attractive किसी के प्रति कामेच्छा से आकृष्ट होना

> **NOTE** यद्यपि इस क्रिया का सातत्यबोधक कालों (continuous tenses) में प्रयोग नहीं होता तथापि इसका -ing से बनने वाले वर्तमान कृदंत (present participle) रूप पर्याप्त मात्रा में दिखाई पड़ता है—*Not desiring another argument, she turned away.*

**desk** /desk डेस्क्/ *noun* [C] **1** a type of table, often with drawers, that you sit at to write or work डेस्क, मेज़ (प्रायः दराजों वाली) *The pupils took their books out of their desks.* ○ *He used to be a pilot but now he has **a desk job*** (= he works in an office). **2** a table or place in a building where a particular service is provided मेज़ या वह स्थान जहाँ कोई विशेष सेवा पेश की जाती है *an information desk*

**desktop** /ˈdesktɒp ˈडेस्क्टॉप्/ *noun* [C] **1** the top of a desk मेज़ का ऊपरी भाग **2** a computer screen on which you can see symbols (**icons**) showing the programs, etc. that are available to be used कंप्यूटर स्क्रीन जिस पर कंप्यूटर में उपलब्ध प्रोग्रामों के संकेतचित्र होते हैं **3** (*also* **desktop computer**) a computer that can fit on a desk मेज़ पर रखा जाने वाला कंप्यूटर ➪ **laptop** और **palmtop** देखिए।

**desktop publishing** (*abbr.* **DTP**) *noun* [U] the use of a small computer and a machine for printing, to produce books, magazines and other printed material पुस्तक आदि मुद्रित करने के लिए कंप्यूटर और प्रिंटर का प्रयोग

**desolate** /ˈdesələt ˈडेसलट्/ *adj.* **1** (used about a place) empty in a way that seems very sad (स्थान) निर्जन और अवसादपूर्ण *desolate wasteland* **2** (used about a person) lonely, very unhappy and without hope (व्यक्ति) एकाकी, उदास और निराश ▶ **desolation** /ˌdesəˈleɪʃn ˌडेसˈलेश्न्/ *noun* [U] अवसाद, निराशा *a scene of desolation.* ○ *He felt utter desolation when his wife died.*

**despair¹** /dɪˈspeə(r) डिˈस्पेअ(र्)/ *noun* [U] the state of having lost all hope पूर्ण निराशा *I felt like giving up **in despair**.* ▶ **despairing** *adj.* निराशापूर्ण *a despairing cry* ➪ **desperate** देखिए।

**despair²** /dɪˈspeə(r) डिˈस्पेअ(र्) / *verb* [I] **despair (of sb/sth)** to lose all hope that sth will happen (अनुकूल बात होने की) आशा छोड़ बैठना *We began to despair of ever finding somewhere to live.*

**despatch** /dɪˈspætʃ डिˈस्पैच्/ = **dispatch**

**desperate** /ˈdespərət ˈडेस्परट् / *adj.* **1** out of control and ready to do anything to change the situation you are in because it is so terrible अत्यधिक निराशा के कारण दुस्साहसी, निराशोन्मत *She became desperate when her money ran out.* **2** done with little hope of success, as a last thing to try when everything else has failed निराशा की अवस्था में अंतिम उपाय के रूप में किया गया *I made a desperate attempt to persuade her to change her mind.* **3 desperate (for sth/to do sth)** wanting or needing sth very much किसी वस्तु के लिए अत्यधिक व्यग्र *Let's go into a cafe. I'm desperate for a drink.* **4** terrible, very serious भयावह, अति गंभीर, घोर *There is a desperate shortage of skilled workers.* ▶ **desperately** *adv.* निराशाजन्य दुस्साहस के साथ, अत्यधिक *She was desperately* (= extremely) *unlucky not to win.* ▶ **desperation** /ˌdespəˈreɪʃn ˌडेस्पˈरेश्न् / *noun* [U] नैराश्य, दुस्साहस

**despicable** /dɪˈspɪkəbl डिˈस्पिकबल् / *adj.* very unpleasant or evil निंदनीय, जघन्य *a despicable act of terrorism*

**despise** /dɪˈspaɪz डिˈस्पाइज़् / *verb* [T] to hate sb/sth very much (किसी से) अत्यधिक घृणा करना *I despise him for lying to me.*

**despite** /dɪˈspaɪt डिˈस्पाइट् / *prep.* without being affected by the thing mentioned के बावजूद *Despite having very little money, they enjoy life.* ○ *The scheme went ahead despite public opposition.* ✪ पर्याय **in spite of**

**despondent** /dɪˈspɒndənt डिˈस्पॉन्डन्ट् / *adj.* **despondent (about/over sth)** without hope; expecting no improvement निराश; सुधार के प्रति आशा रहित *She was becoming increasingly despondent about finding a job.* ▶ **despondency** /dɪˈspɒndənsi डिˈस्पॉन्डन्सि / *noun* [U] निराशा, खिन्नता

**despot** /ˈdespɒt ˈडेस्पॉट् / *noun* [C] a ruler with great power, especially one who uses it in a cruel way निरंकुश शासक ➪ **autocrat** देखिए। ▶ **despotic** /dɪˈspɒtɪk डिˈस्पॉटिक् / *adj.* निरंकुश, स्वेच्छाकारी *despotic power/rule*

**dessert** /dɪˈzɜːt डिˈज़ट् / *noun* [C, U] something sweet that is eaten after the main part of a meal भोजन के अंत में परोसा जाने वाला मधुर व्यंजन *What would you like **for dessert**—ice cream or fresh fruit?* ➪ **pudding** और **sweet** देखिए।

**dessertspoon** /dɪˈzɜːtspuːn डिˈज़ट्स्पून् / *noun* [C] a spoon used for eating sweet food after the main part of a meal भोजनपरांत मधुर व्यंजन खाने में प्रयुक्त चम्मच

**destabilize** (*also* **-ise**) /ˌdiːˈsteɪbəlaɪz ˌडीˈस्टेबलाइज़् / *verb* [T] to make a system, government, country, etc. become less safe and successful किसी सरकार, व्यवस्था आदि को अस्थिर करना *Terrorist attacks were threatening to destabilize the government.* ➪ **stabilize** देखिए।

**destination** /ˌdestɪˈneɪʃn ˌडेस्टिˈनेश्न् / *noun* [C] the place where sb/sth is going गंतव्य स्थान, मंज़िल *I finally reached my destination two hours late.* ○ *popular holiday destinations like the Bahamas*

**destined** /ˈdestɪnd ˈडेस्टिन्ड् / *adj.* **1 destined for sth/to do sth** having a future that has been decided or planned at an earlier time पहले से नियत परिणाम वाला *I think she is destined for success.* ○ *He was destined to become one of the country's leading politicians.* **2 destined for...** travelling towards a particular place स्थान विशेष को जाने के लिए निर्धारित *I boarded a bus destined for Kanpur.*

**destiny** /ˈdestəni ˈडेस्टनि / *noun* (*pl.* **destinies**) **1** [C] the things that happen to you in your life, especially things that you cannot control नियति, भवितव्यता, जीवन में घटित होने वाली घटनाएँ (जो नियंत्रित नहीं की जा सकती) *She felt that it was her destiny to be a great singer.* **2** [U] a power that people believe controls their lives भाग्य, क़िस्मत, दैव ✪ पर्याय **fate**

**destitute** /ˈdestɪtjuːt ˈडेस्टिट्यूट् / *adj.* without any money, food or a home धन, भोजन या घर की सुविधा से वंचित, दीन-हीन, निराश्रय, बेसहारा ▶ **destitution** /ˌdestɪˈtjuːʃn ˌडेस्टिˈट्यूश्न् / *noun* [U] निराश्रयता

**destroy** /dɪˈstrɔɪ डिˈस्ट्रॉइ / *verb* [T] **1** to damage sth so badly that it can no longer be used or no longer exists किसी वस्तु को इस तरह हानि पहुँचाना कि वह इस्तेमाल न हो सके या समाप्त हो जाए, नष्ट करना *The building was destroyed by fire.* ○ *The defeat destroyed his confidence.* **2** to kill an animal, especially because it is injured or dangerous (चोट लगने या ख़तरनाक होने के कारण) किसी पशु को मार देना *The horse broke its leg and had to be destroyed.*

**destroyer** /dɪˈstrɔɪə(r) डिˈस्ट्रॉइअ(र्) / *noun* [C] **1** a small ship that is used when there is a war युद्ध में काम आने वाला छोटा जहाज़ **2** a person or thing that destroys sth विनाशकारी व्यक्ति या वस्तु

**destruction** /dɪˈstrʌkʃn डिˈस्ट्रक्श्न् / *noun* [U] the action of destroying sth विनाश-क्रिया *The war brought death and destruction to the city.* ○ *the destruction of the rainforests*

**destructive** /dɪˈstrʌktɪv डिˈस्ट्रक्टिव् / *adj.* causing a lot of harm or damage विनाशकारी

**detach** /dɪˈtætʃ डिˈटैच् / *verb* [T] **detach sth (from sth)** to separate sth from sth it is connected to किसी वस्तु को उससे अलग करना जिससे वह जुड़ी है, वियोजित करना *Detach the form at the bottom of the page and send it to the head office address* ✪ विलोम **attach**

**detachable** /dɪˈtætʃəbl डिˈटैचबल् / *adj.* that can be separated from sth it is connected to जो जिससे जुड़ा है, उससे अलग किया जा सके; वियोज्य *a coat with a detachable hood*

**detached** /dɪˈtætʃt डिˈटैच्ट् / *adj.* **1** (used about a house) not joined to any other house जो किसी अन्य मकान से लगा हुआ नहीं, असंबद्ध, अलग-अलग **2** not being or not feeling personally involved in sth; without emotion निर्लिप्त; भावना शून्य, विरक्त (व्यक्ति)

**detachment** /dɪˈtætʃmənt डिˈटैच्मन्ट् / *noun* **1** [U] the fact or feeling of not being personally involved in sth निर्लिप्तता **2** [C] a group of soldiers who have been given a particular task away from the main group मुख्य दल से अलग उद्देश्य विशेष से नियुक्त सैनिक टुकड़ी

**detail**[1] /ˈdiːteɪl ˈडीटेल् / *noun* [C, U] one fact or piece of information एक तथ्य या सूचना, ब्योरा *On the application form you should give details of your education and experience.* ○ *The work involves close attention to detail.* ▶ **detailed** *adj.* विस्तृत *a detailed description*

IDM **go into detail(s)** to talk or write about the details of sth; to explain sth fully किस प्रसंग के ब्योरे देना; किसी बात का विस्तारपूर्वक वर्णन करना *I can't go into detail now because it would take too long.*

**in detail** including the details; thoroughly विस्तार से; पूरी तरह, पूर्णतया *We haven't discussed the matter in detail yet.*

**detail**[2] /ˈdiːteɪl ˈडीटेल् / *noun* [T] to give a full list of sth; to describe sth completely (किसी बात का) विवरण देना; पूरी तरह वर्णन करना *He detailed all the equipment he needed for the job.*

**detain** /dɪˈteɪn डिˈटेन् / *verb* [T] to stop sb from leaving a place; to delay sb किसी व्यक्ति को किसी स्थान से जाने न देना; किसी को देरी कराना *A man has been detained by the police for questioning* (= kept at the police station). ○ *Don't let me detain you if you're busy.* ➪ **detention** देखिए।

**detainee** /ˌdiːteɪˈniː ˌडीटेˈनी / *noun* [C] a person who is kept in prison, usually because of his or her political opinions जेल में नज़रबंद (प्रायः राजनीतिक कारणों से)

**detect** /dɪˈtekt डिˈटेक्ट् / *verb* [T] to notice or discover sth that is difficult to see, feel, etc. ऐसी बात को देख लेना या खोज लेना जिसे सामान्यतः जानना कठिन हो *I detected a slight change in his attitude.* ○ *Traces of blood were detected on his clothes.* ▶ **detectable** *adj.* जिसका पता लगाया जा सके ▶ **detection** *noun* [U] पता लगाने की क्रिया; अभिज्ञान *The crime escaped detection* (= was not discovered) *for many years.*

**detective** /dɪˈtektɪv डिˈटेक्टिव् / *noun* [C] a person, especially a police officer, who tries to solve crimes जासूस, गुप्तचर (विशेषतः पुलिस अफ़सर)

**detective story** *noun* [C] a story about a crime in which sb tries to find out who the guilty person is जासूसी कहानी

**detector** /dɪˈtektə(r) डिˈटेक्टर(र्) / *noun* [C] a machine that is used for finding or noticing sth किसी वस्तु (धातु, विस्फ़ोटक आदि) का पता लगाने वाली मशीन *a smoke/metal/lie detector*

**détente** (*AmE* **detente**) /ˌdeɪˈtɑːnt ˌडेˈटॉन्ट् / *noun* [U] (*formal*) an improvement in the relationship between two or more countries which have been unfriendly towards each other in the past पहले विरोधी रहे दो या अधिक देशों के बीच संबंध-सुधार

**detention** /dɪˈtenʃn डिˈटेन्श्न् / *noun* [U, C] **1** the act of stopping a person leaving a place, especially by keeping him/her in prison किसी व्यक्ति को निरुद्ध करने की प्रक्रिया (विशेषतः उसे जेल में बंद कर) निवारक नज़रबंदी *They were kept* ***in detention*** *for ten days.* **2** the punishment of being kept at school after the other schoolchildren have gone home स्कूल की छुट्टी के बाद स्कूल में रोके रखने का दंड ➪ **detain** verb देखिए।

**detention centre** (*AmE* **detention center**) *noun* [C] **1** a place like a prison where young people who have broken the law are kept युवा अपराधियों के लिए नज़रबंदी शिविर **2** a place like a prison where people, especially people who have entered a country illegally, are kept for a short time गैर-क़ानूनी आवजकों के लिए नज़रबंदी शिविर

**deter** /dɪˈtɜː(r) डिˈटर(र्) / *verb* [T] (**deterring; deterred**) **deter sb (from doing sth)** to make sb decide not to do sth, especially by telling him/her that it would have bad results किसी को कोई काम करने से रोकना (उसके संभावित दुष्परिणामों को देखते हुए) ➪ **deterrent** noun देखिए।

**detergent** /dɪˈtɜːdʒənt डिˈटजन्ट् / *noun* [C, U] a chemical liquid or powder that is used for cleaning things वस्तुओं को साफ़ करने के लिए प्रयुक्त रासायनिक द्रव पदार्थ या पाउडर

**deteriorate** /dɪˈtɪəriəreɪt डिˈटिअरिअरेट्/ *verb* [I] to become worse (स्थिति का) बिगड़ना, बदतर होना *The political tension is deteriorating into civil war.* ▶ **deterioration** /dɪˌtɪəriəˈreɪʃn डिˌटिअरिअˈरेश्न्/ *noun* [C, U] स्थिति में गिरावट, पतन, ह्रास

**determination** /dɪˌtɜːmɪˈneɪʃn डिˌटमिˈनेश्न्/ *noun* [U] **1 determination (to do sth)** the quality of having firmly decided to do sth, even if it is very difficult दृढ़ निश्चय *You need great determination to succeed in business.* **2** (*formal*) the process of deciding sth officially किसी बात के औपचारिक या अधिकृत रूप से निर्धारित होने की प्रक्रिया *the determination of future government policy*

**determine** /dɪˈtɜːmɪn डिˈटमिन्/ *verb* [T] **1** (*formal*) to discover the facts about sth किसी प्रसंग के तथ्यों का पता लगाना *We need to determine what happened immediately before the accident.* **2** to make sth happen in a particular way or be of a particular type निर्धारित करना *The results of the tests will determine what treatment you need.* ○ *Age and experience will be* ***determining factors*** *in our choice of candidate.* **3** (*formal*) to decide sth officially अधिकृत रूप से निर्णय करना *A date for the meeting has yet to be determined.*

**determined** /dɪˈtɜːmɪnd डिˈटमिन्ड्/ *adj.* **determined (to do sth)** having firmly decided to do sth or to succeed, even if it is difficult कृतसंकल्प, दृढ़निश्चयी *She's a very determined athlete.*

**determiner** /dɪˈtɜːmɪnə(r) डिˈटमिन(र्)/ *noun* [C] (*grammar*) a word that comes before a noun to show how the noun is being used निर्धारक शब्द, संज्ञा से पहले प्रयुक्त शब्द जो संज्ञा की प्रयोग विधि को निर्धारित करता है *'Her', 'most' and 'those' are all determiners.*

**deterrent** /dɪˈterənt डिˈटेरन्ट्/ *noun* [C] something that should stop you doing sth निरोधक, कुछ (अनुचित) करने से रोकने वाला, निवारक *Their punishment will be a deterrent to others.* ➪ **deter** verb देखिए। ▶ **deterrent** *adj.* निरोधकारी

**detest** /dɪˈtest डिˈटेस्ट्/ *verb* [T] to hate or not like sb/sth at all किसी से घृणा करना या किसी को बिलकुल पसंद न करना *They absolutely detest each other.*

**detonate** /ˈdetəneɪt ˈडेटनेट्/ *verb* [I, T] to explode or to make a bomb, etc. explode बम आदि का विस्फोट होना या करना

**detonator** /ˈdetəneɪtə(r) ˈडेटनेट(र्)/ *noun* [C] a device for making sth, especially a bomb, explode किसी वस्तु (विशेषतः बम का) विस्फोट करने वाला उपकरण विस्फोटकारी उपकरण

**detour** /ˈdiːtʊə(r) ˈडीटुअ(र्)/ *noun* [C] **1** a longer route from one place to another that you take in order to avoid sth/sb or in order to see or do sth घुमावदार या चक्करदार रास्ता *Because of the accident we had to make a five-kilometre detour.* **2** (*AmE*) = **diversion 2**

**detract** /dɪˈtrækt डिˈट्रैक्ट्/ *verb* [I] detract from sth to make sth seem less good or important किसी की साख घटाना *These criticisms in no way detract from the team's achievements.*

**detriment** /ˈdetrɪmənt ˈडेट्रिमन्ट्/ *noun*
**IDM to the detriment of sb/sth** harming or damaging sb/sth हानिकारक, नुक़सानदेह *Doctors claim that the changes will be to the detriment of patients.* ▶ **detrimental** /ˌdetrɪˈmentl ˌडेट्रिˈमेन्ट्ल्/ *adj.* हानिकारक *Too much alcohol is* ***detrimental to*** *your health.*

**detritus** /dɪˈtraɪtəs डिˈट्राइटस्/ *noun* [U] (*technical*) natural waste material that is left after sth has been used or broken up किसी वस्तु के उपयोग में आने या टूटने के बाद प्राकृतिक प्रक्रिया से बना मलबा

**deuce** /djuːs ड्यूस्/ *noun* [U] a score of 40 points to each player in a game of tennis टेनिस में 40–40 अंको की बराबरी; ड्यूस

**deus ex machina** /ˌdeɪʊs eks ˈmækɪnə ˌडेउस् एक्स्ˈमैकिना/ *noun* [*sing.*] (in literature) an unexpected power or event that saves a situation that seems without hope, especially in a play or novel साहित्यिक कृति में प्रदर्शित किसी कठिन परिस्थिति का दैवी समाधान

**deuterium** /djuˈtɪəriəm ड्युˈटिअरिअम्/ *noun* [U] (*symbol* **D**) a type of **hydrogen** that is twice as heavy as the usual type एक प्रकार की हाइड्रोजन जो सामान्य हाइड्रोजन से दुगुनी भारी होती है

**devalue** /ˌdiːˈvæljuː ˌडीˈवैल्यू/ *verb* [T] **1** to reduce the value of the money of one country in relation to the value of the money of other countries एक देश की मुद्रा का, दूसरे देश की मुद्रा के मुकाबले, मूल्य घटाया जाना *The rupee has been devalued against the dollar.* **2** to reduce the value or importance of sth किसी वस्तु के महत्त्व को कम करना *The refusal of the top players to take part devalues this competition.* ▶ **devaluation** /ˌdiːˌvæljuˈeɪʃn ˌडीˌवैल्यूˈएश्न्/ *noun* [U] अवमूल्यन

**devastate** /ˈdevəsteɪt ˈडेवस्टेट्/ *verb* [T] **1** to destroy sth or damage it badly सर्वनाश करना, तबाह करना *a land devastated by war* **2** to make sb extremely upset and shocked किसी को बहुत परेशान करना और सदमा पहुँचाना *This tragedy has dev-*

*astated the community.* ▶ **devastation** /ˌdevəˈsteɪʃn ˌडेव़ˈस्टेश्न्/ *noun* [U] सर्वनाश, तबाही *a scene of total devastation*

**devastated** /ˈdevəsteɪtɪd ˈडेव़स्टेटिड्/ *adj.* extremely shocked and upset अतिस्तब्ध और परेशान *They were devastated when their baby died.*

**devastating** /ˈdevəsteɪtɪŋ ˈडेव़स्टेटिङ्/ *adj.* **1** that destroys sth completely पूर्णतया विनाशकारी *a devastating explosion* **2** that shocks or upsets sb very much अत्यधिक दुखद और स्तब्धकारी *The closure of the factory was a devastating blow to the workers.*

**develop** /dɪˈveləp डिˈवेलप्/ *verb* **1** [I, T] to grow slowly, increase, or change into sth else; to make sb/sth do this विकसित होना; विकास करना *Scientists have developed a drug against this disease.* ○ *Over the years, she's developed her own unique singing style.* **2** [I, T] to begin to have a problem or disease; to start to affect sth समस्या या रोग से आक्रांत होने की शुरुआत होना; किसी स्थिति का पनपना शुरू होना *to develop cancer/AIDS* ○ *Trouble is developing along the border.* **3** [T] to make an idea, a story, etc. clearer or more detailed by writing or talking about it more किसी विचार आदि का विकास करना, उसे अधिक स्पष्ट करना और विस्तार देना *She went on to develop this theme later in the lecture.* **4** [T] to make pictures or negatives from a piece of film by using special chemicals फ़िल्म को धोना, डेवलप करना *to develop a film* **5** [T] to build houses, shops, factories, etc. on a piece of land किसी भूखंड पर मकान आदि बनाना, भूखंड को विकसित करना *This site is being developed for offices.*

**developed** /dɪˈveləpt डिˈवेलप्ट्/ *adj.* of a good level or standard विकसित, उन्नत *a highly developed economy*

**developer** /dɪˈveləpə(r) डिˈवेलप(र्)/ (*also* **property developer**) *noun* [C] a person or company that builds houses, shops, etc. on a piece of land किसी भूखंड पर निर्माण-कार्य में संलग्न व्यक्ति या कंपनी

**developing** /dɪˈveləpɪŋ डिˈवेलपिङ्/ *adj.* (used about a poor country) that is trying to develop or improve its economy आर्थिक दृष्टि से विकास करता हुआ, विकासशील (निर्धन देश) *a developing country* ○ *the developing world*

**development** /dɪˈveləpmənt डिˈवेलप्मन्ट्/ *noun* **1** [U] the process of becoming bigger, stronger, better etc., or of making sb/sth do this अधिक विस्तृत, सुदृढ़, बेहतर आदि होने या बनाने की प्रक्रिया, विकसित होने या करने की प्रक्रिया *the development of tourism in Goa* ○ *a child's intellectual development* **2** [U, C] the process of creating sth more advanced; a more advanced product किसी वस्तु को अधिक उन्नत और प्रगत बनाने की प्रक्रिया; अधिक उन्नत और प्रगत वस्तु या उत्पाद *She works in* ***research and development*** *for a drug company.* ○ *the latest developments in space technology* **3** [C] a new event that changes a situation नई घटना जो परिस्थिति को बदल दे, परिवर्तनकारी घटना *This week has seen a number of new developments in the crisis.* **4** [C, U] a piece of land with new buildings on it; the process of building on a piece of land भूखंड जिस पर नया निर्माण हुआ हो; भूखंड पर नया निर्माण करने की प्रक्रिया *a new housing development* ○ *The land has been bought for development.*

**deviant** /ˈdiːviənt ˈडीविअन्ट्/ *adj.* different from what most people consider to be normal and acceptable उचित और सामान्य व्यवहार से अलग या हटा हुआ, असामान्य *deviant behaviour* ▶ **deviant** *noun* [C] असामान्य व्यक्ति *sexual deviants* ▶ **deviance** /ˈdiːviəns ˈडीविअन्स्/ *noun* असामान्यता **deviancy** /ˈdiːviənsi ˈडीविअन्सि/ *noun* [U] असामान्यता *a study of social deviance and crime*

**deviate** /ˈdiːvieɪt ˈडीविएट्/ *verb* [I] **deviate (from sth)** to change or become different from what is normal or expected सामान्य या स्वीकृति व्यवहार को बदलना या उससे हट कर आचरण करना, लीक से हटना या हटाना, उपयुक्त व्यवहार से हटना *He never once deviated from his original plan.*

**deviation** /ˌdiːviˈeɪʃn ˌडीविˈएश्न्/ *noun* [C, U] a difference from what is normal or expected, or from what is approved of by society समाज में स्वीकृत व्यवहार से भिन्नता या परिवर्तन, मर्यादा भंग, विचलन, नव रूढ़ि निर्माण *a deviation from our usual way of doing things*

**device** /dɪˈvaɪs डिˈवाइस्/ *noun* [C] **1** a tool or piece of equipment made for a particular purpose युक्ति, उपकरण, मशीन *a security device* ○ *labour-saving devices such as washing machines and vacuum cleaners* ➪ **tool** पर चित्र देखिए। **2** a clever method for getting the result you want चाल, योजना, युक्ति *Critics dismissed the speech as a political device for winning support.*

**devil** /ˈdevl ˈडेव्ल्/ *noun* [C] **1 the Devil** the most powerful evil being, according to the Christian, Jewish and Muslim religions शैतान (ईसा, यहूदी और इस्लाम धर्मों में) ➪ **Satan** देखिए। **2** an evil being; a spirit दुष्ट आत्मा; भूत, प्रेत **3** (*spoken*) a word used to show pity, anger, etc. when you are talking about a person किसी व्यक्ति के लिए दया, क्रोध आदि व्यक्त करने के लिए प्रयुक्त शब्द *The poor devil died in hospital two days later.* ○ *Those kids can be little devils sometimes.*

IDM **be a devil** used to encourage sb to do sth that he/she is not sure about doing किसी को प्रोत्साहित करने के लिए प्रयुक्त शब्द *Go on, be a devil—buy both of them.*

**speak/talk of the devil** used when the person who is being talked about appears unexpectedly चर्चित व्यक्ति के एकाएक सामने आ जाने पर प्रयुक्त शब्द

**devious** /ˈdiːviəs ˈडीविअस्/ *adj.* clever but not honest or direct चालबाज़, छली *a devious trick/plan* ▶ **deviously** *adv.* छलपूर्वक

**devise** /dɪˈvaɪz डिˈव़ाइज़्/ *verb* [T] to invent a new way of doing sth कुछ करने का नया तरीक़ा निकालना *They've devised a plan for keeping traffic out of the city centre.*

**devoid** /dɪˈvɔɪd डिˈव़ॉइड्/ *adj.* (*formal*) **devoid of sth** not having a particular quality; without sth से विहीन; से रहित *devoid of hope/ambition/imagination*

**devolution** /ˌdiːvəˈluːʃn ˌडीव़ˈलूशन्/ *noun* [U] the act of giving political power from central to local government राजनीतिक सत्ता का केंद्रीय सरकार से राज्य या स्थानीय सरकारों को हस्तांतरण, सत्ता का विकेंद्रीकरण ⇨ **devolve** verb देखिए।

**devolve** /dɪˈvɒlv डिˈव़ॉल्व़्/ *verb*

PHR V **devolve on/upon sb/sth** (*written*) **1** if property, money, etc. devolves on/upon you, you receive it after sb dies किसी के देहांत के बाद उसकी संपत्ति को उत्तराधिकारी को सौंपा जाना **2** if a duty, responsibility, etc. devolves on/upon you, it is given to you by sb at a higher level of authority उच्चतर स्तर से कार्य, दायित्व आदि का हस्तांतरण होना

**devolve sth to/on/upon sb** to give a duty, responsibility, power, etc. to sb who has less authority than you दायित्व, शक्ति आदि का निचले स्तर पर हस्तांतरण होना *The central government devolved most tax-raising powers to the regional authorities.* ⇨ **devolution** noun देखिए।

**devote** /dɪˈvəʊt डिˈव़ोट्/ *verb* [T] **devote yourself/sth to sb/sth** to give a lot of time, energy, etc. to sb/sth किसी काम में बहुत-सा समय और शक्ति लगाना *She gave up work to devote herself full-time to her music.*

**devoted** /dɪˈvəʊtɪd डिˈव़ोटिड्/ *adj.* **devoted (to sb/sth)** loving sb/sth very much; completely loyal to sb/sth किसी से प्रेम करने वाला; किसी के प्रति पूर्णतया समर्पित *Nakul's absolutely devoted to his wife.*

**devotee** /ˌdevəˈtiː ˌडेवोˈटी/ *noun* [C] **a devotee (of sb/sth)** a person who likes sb/sth very much किसी का बहुत शौक़ीन या प्रेमी *Devotees of science fiction will enjoy this new film.*

**devotion** /dɪˈvəʊʃn डिˈव़ोशन्/ *noun* [U] **devotion (to sb/sth)** **1** great love for sb/sth किसी से बहुत प्रेम *a mother's devotion to her children* **2** the act of giving a lot of your time, energy, etc. to sb/sth किसी काम में बहुत-सा समय और शक्ति लगाने की क्रिया; समर्पणभाव *devotion to duty* **3** very strong religious feeling गहरी धार्मिक आस्था

**devour** /dɪˈvaʊə(r) डिˈव़ाउअ(र्)/ *verb* [T] **1** to eat sth quickly because you are very hungry भूख के मारे जल्दी-जल्दी खाना, भकोसना, भक्षण करना **2** to do or use sth quickly and completely तेज़ी से और पूरी तरह कोई काम कर डालना

**devout** /dɪˈvaʊt डिˈव़ाउट्/ *adj.* very religious अत्यधिक धर्मनिष्ठ *a devout Muslim family* ▶ **devoutly** *adv.* निष्ठापूर्वक

**dew** /djuː ड्यू/ *noun* [U] small drops of water that form on plants, leaves, etc. during the night ओस, शबनम

**dew point** *noun* [U] (in geography) the temperature at which air can hold no more water. Below this temperature the water comes out of the air in the form of drops ओसांक, तापमान का वह बिंदु जहाँ वायु में जल का अंश नहीं रहता। इस तापमान से नीचे के बिंदु पर जल ओस बन कर वायु में से निकल जाता है या जल ओस बन जाता है

**dexterity** /dekˈsterəti डेक्ˈस्टेरटि/ *noun* [U] skill at doing things, especially with your hands दक्षता, निपुणता (विशेषतः हाथ के काम में)

**dextrose** /ˈdekstrəʊz ˈडेक्स्ट्रोज़्/ *noun* [U] a form of a natural type of sugar (**glucose**) एक प्रकार के प्राकृतिक मीठे (ग्लूकोज) का रूप, एक प्रकार का ग्लूकोज़ ⇨ **fructose, glucose, lactose** और **sucrose** देखिए।

**dharma** *noun* [U] the basic principle of divine law in Hinduism, Buddhism and Jainism; a code of proper conduct **conforming** to one's duty and nature हिंदू, बौद्ध तथा जैन धर्मों में दिव्य विधान का मूल सिद्धांत; अपने कर्तव्य और स्वरूप के अनुकूल उचित आचार संहिता

**dhol** *noun* [C] a large double-sided drum, played with a stick held in each hand. It is often played as an **accompaniment** with Indian folk dances ढोल; भारतीय लोक नृत्य में संगत के लिए ढोल का प्रयोग होता है

**dholak** *noun* [C] a medium-sized two-sided drum, traditionally played during wedding ceremonies across the Indian subcontinent ढोलक; भारतीय उपमहाद्वीप में विवाह समारोह में ढोलक का पारंपरिक प्रयोग होता है

**dhoti** *noun* [C] the traditional Indian dress consisting of a long piece of unstitched cloth for the lower part of the body worn by men of the Indian subcontinent धोती

**di-** /daɪ डाई / *prefix* (*used in nouns*) used in chemistry to refer to substances that contain two atoms of the type mentioned रसायन शास्त्र में दो वर्गों या अंशों से बने पदार्थों का संकेत करने वाले शब्दों में प्रयुक्त *dioxide*

**diabetes** /ˌdaɪəˈbiːtiːz ˌडाइअˈबीटीज़् / *noun* [U] a serious disease in which a person's body cannot control the level of sugar in the blood मधुमेह (का रोग)

**diabetic[1]** /ˌdaɪəˈbetɪk ˌडाइअˈबेटिक् / *noun* [C] a person who suffers from diabetes मधुमेह का रोगी

**diabetic[2]** /ˌdaɪəˈbetɪk ˌडाइअˈबेटिक् / *adj.* connected with diabetes or diabetics मधुमेह या मधुमेह के रोगी से संबंधित *diabetic chocolate* (= safe for diabetics)

**diagnose** /ˈdaɪəgnəʊz ˈडाइअग्नोज़् / *verb* [T] **diagnose sth (as sth); diagnose sb as/with sth** to find out and say exactly what illness a person has or what the cause of a problem is समस्या या रोग की पहचान करना या का निदान करना *His illness was diagnosed as bronchitis.*

**diagnosis** /ˌdaɪəgˈnəʊsɪs ˌडाइअग्ˈनोसिस् / *noun* [C, U] (*pl.* **diagnoses** /-siːz सीज़् /) the act of saying exactly what illness a person has or what the cause of a problem is रोगी के रोग और समस्या के कारण को पहचानने की क्रिया, निदान-क्रिया *to make a diagnosis*

**diagnostic** /ˌdaɪəgˈnɒstɪk ˌडाइअग्ˈनॉस्टिक् / *adj.* connected with finding out exactly what a problem is and what caused it, especially an illness समस्या (विशेषतः रोग) को पहचानने से संबंधित; निदान-विषयक *to carry out diagnostic tests*

**diagonal** /daɪˈægənl डाइˈऐगनल् / *adj.* (used about a straight line) at an angle; joining two opposite sides of sth at an angle वर्ग के सम्मुख कोणों को मिलाने वाली सीधी रेखा या वर्ग के एक कोण से दूसरे कोण तक खींची गई सीधी रेखा; विकर्ण रेखा *Draw a diagonal line from one corner of the square to the opposite corner.* ▶ **diagonal** *noun* [C] विकर्ण रेखा ▶ **diagonally** /-nəli -नलि / *adv.* विकर्णतः

**diagram** /ˈdaɪəgræm ˈडाइअग्रैम् / *noun* [C] a simple picture that is used to explain how sth works or what sth looks like आरेख, रेखाचित्र, रेखा-लेख जो किसी की कार्यविधि या आकृति दर्शाता है या का वर्णन करता है *a diagram of the body's digestive system* ▶ **diagrammatic** /ˌdaɪəgrəˈmætɪk ˌडाइअग्रˈमैटिक् / *adj.* आरेखीय, आरेखपरक

**dial[1]** /ˈdaɪəl ˈडाइअल् / *noun* [C] **1** the round part of a clock, watch, control on a machine, etc. that shows a measurement of time, amount, temperature, etc. घड़ी आदि का गोलाकार भाग जिस पर समय, मात्रा आदि की इकाइयाँ अंकित होती है; डायल, अंकपट्ट *a dial for showing air pressure* **2** the round control on a radio, cooker, etc. that you turn to change sth रेडियो आदि पर लगा गोलाकार पुरज़ा जिसे प्रोग्राम आदि बदलने के लिए घुमाते हैं, रेडियो का डायल **3** the round part with holes in it on some older telephones that you turn to call a number पुराने टेलीफ़ोन-यंत्रों में लगा छेदों वाला गोल डायल, टेलीफ़ोन का डायल

**dial[2]** /ˈdaɪəl ˈडाइअल् / *verb* [I, T] (**dialling; dialled** *AmE* **dialing; dialed**) to push the buttons or move the dial on a telephone in order to call a telephone number टेलीफ़ोन का नंबर मिलाने के लिए डायल घुमाना या बटन दबाना *You can now dial direct to Singapore.* ○ *to dial the wrong number*

**dialect** /ˈdaɪəlekt ˈडाइअलेक्ट् / *noun* [C, U] a form of a language that is spoken in one area of a country किसी प्रदेश विशेष की बोली; उपभाषा *a local dialect*

**dialling code** *noun* [C] the numbers that you must dial on a telephone for a particular area or country क्षेत्र विशेष के लिए निर्धारित संख्याएँ जिन्हें फ़ोन लगाने के लिए डायल करना आवश्यक है *international dialling codes*

**dialling tone** *noun* [C, U] the sound that you hear when you pick up a telephone to make a call टेलीफ़ोन रिसीवर उठाने पर सुनाई देने वाला स्वर

**dialogue** (*AmE* **dialog**) /ˈdaɪəlɒg ˈडाइअलॉग् / *noun* [C, U] **1** (a) conversation between people in a book, play, etc. नाटक आदि में संवाद, लोगों के बीच वार्तालाप *On the tape you will hear a short dialogue between a shop assistant and a customer.* **2** (a) discussion between people who have different opinions अलग-अलग विचारों वाले लोगों के बीच वार्तालाप या विचार-विमर्श *(a) dialogue between the major political parties*

**dialogue box** (*AmE* **dialog box**) *noun* [C] (*computing*) a box that appears on a computer screen asking you to choose what you want to do next कंप्यूटर स्क्रीन पर उभरने वाला बॉक्स जो आपको अगली क्रिया संपादित करने का आधार प्रदान करता है

**dialysis** /ˌdaɪˈæləsɪs ˌडाइˈऐलसिस् / *noun* [U] a process for separating substances from a liquid, especially for taking waste substances out of the blood of people with damaged **kidneys** डायलसिस; क्षतिग्रस्त गुर्दों के रोगियों के लिए रक्तशोधन की प्रक्रिया

**diameter** /daɪˈæmɪtə(r) डाइˈऐमिट(र्)/ *noun* [C] a straight line that goes from one side to the other of a circle, passing through the centre वृत के केंद्र से गुज़रते हुए एक छोर से दूसरे छोर तक जाने वाली सीधी रेखा, व्यास ➪ **radius** और **circumference** देखिए तथा **circle** पर चित्र देखिए।

**diamond** /ˈdaɪəmənd ˈडाइअमन्ड्/ *noun* **1** [C, U] a hard, bright precious stone which is very expensive and is used for making jewellery. A diamond usually has no colour हीरा (एक महँगा रत्न) **2** [C] a flat shape that has four sides of equal length and points at two ends समचतुर्भुज, सपाट आकृति ➪ **shape** पर चित्र देखिए। **3 diamonds** [*pl.*] the group (**suit**) of playing cards with red shapes like **diamonds 2** on them ताश में ईंट के पत्तों का सेट *the seven of diamonds* **4** [C] one of the cards from this suit ईंट का एक पत्ता या ईंट के सेट से एक पत्ता *I haven't got any diamonds.*

**diamond wedding** *noun* [C] the 60th anniversary of a wedding विवाह की साठवीं वर्षगाँठ, विवाह की हीरक-जयंती ➪ **golden wedding, ruby wedding** और **silver wedding** देखिए।

**diaper** /ˈdaɪəpə(r) ˈडाइअप(र्)/ (*AmE*) = **nappy**

**diaphragm** /ˈdaɪəfræm ˈडाइअफ़्रैम्/ *noun* [C] the muscle between your lungs and your stomach that helps you to breathe फेफड़ों और पेट के बीच की मांसपेशी (जो श्वसन में सहायक है); मध्यपट

**diarrhoea** (*AmE* **diarrhea**) /ˌdaɪəˈrɪə ˌडाइअˈरिआ/ *noun* [U] an illness that causes you to get rid of waste material (**faeces**) from your body very often and in a more liquid form than usual दस्त की बीमारी, अतिसार रोग

**diary** /ˈdaɪəri ˈडाइअरि/ *noun* [C] (*pl.* **diaries**) **1** a book in which you write down things that you have to do, remember, etc. डायरी *I'll just check in my diary to see if I'm free that weekend.* ➪ **calendar** पर नोट देखिए। **2** a book in which you write down what happens to you each day डायरी, दैनिकी, रोज़नामचा *Do you **keep a diary**?*

**diatomic** /ˌdaɪəˈtɒmɪk ˌडाइअˈटॉमिक्/ *adj.* (*technical*) (in chemistry) consisting of two atoms (रसायनशास्त्र में) द्वि-अंशी, दो अंशों वाला

**dice** /daɪs डाइस्/ *noun* [C] (*pl.* **dice**) a small square object with a different number of spots (from one to six) on each side, used in certain games पासा खेलने का छह पहलों वाला वर्गाकार दाना जिस पर एक से छह तक बिंदियाँ बनी होती हैं ***Throw the dice** to see who goes first.*

**dichotomy** /daɪˈkɒtəmi डाइˈकॉटमि/ *noun* [C, *usually sing.*] (**dichotomies**) **a dichotomy (between A and B)** (*formal*) the separation that exists between two groups or things that are completely opposite to and different from each other एक दूसरे से सर्वथा विपरीत और भिन्न दो वर्गों या वस्तुओं की पृथक्ता; द्वि-विभाजन

**dictate** /dɪkˈteɪt डिक्ˈटेट्/ *verb* **1** [I, T] **dictate (sth) (to sb)** to say sth aloud so that sb else can write or type it बोलकर लिखाना, लिखाने के लिए बोलना *to dictate a letter to a secretary* **2** [I, T] **dictate (sth) (to sb)** to tell sb what to do in a way that seems unfair हुक्म देना, अपनी मनवाना *Parents can't dictate to their children how they should run their lives.* **3** [T] to control or influence sth किसी बात से नियंत्रित या निश्चित होना *The kind of house people live in is usually dictated by how much they earn.*

**dictation** /dɪkˈteɪʃn डिक्ˈटेशन्/ *noun* [C, U] spoken words that sb else must write or type लिखने के लिए बोले गए शब्द; श्रुतलेख *We had a dictation in English today* (= a test in which we had to write down what the teacher said).

**dictator** /dɪkˈteɪtə(r) डिक्ˈटेट(र्)/ *noun* [C] a ruler who has total power in a country, especially one who rules the country by force तानाशाह, अधिनायक, पूर्णशक्ति संपन्न शासक ► **dictatorship** *noun* [C, U] तानाशाही, अधिनायकतंत्र *a military dictatorship*

**dictatorial** /ˌdɪktəˈtɔːriəl ˌडिक्टˈटॉरिअल्/ *adj.* **1** connected with or controlled by a ruler who has total power, especially one who rules by force (**a dictator**) तानाशाह से संबंधित, तानाशाही, अधिनायकीय *a dictatorial regime* **2** using power in an unreasonable way by telling people what to do and not listening to their views or wishes आततायी, स्वेच्छाचारी व्यक्ति, दूसरों की बात को अनसुना कर देने वाला व्यक्ति

**diction** /ˈdɪkʃən ˈडिक्शन्/ *noun* [U] **1** the way and manner in which sb pronounces words शब्दोच्चारण *clear diction* **2** (*technical*) the choice and use of words and phrases in speech or writing शब्द एवं शब्द समूह का भाषण और लेख में सही चुनाव और प्रयोग

**dictionary** /ˈdɪkʃənri ˈडिक्शनरि/ *noun* [C] (*pl.* **dictionaries**) **1** a book that contains a list of the words in a language in the order of the alphabet and that tells you what they mean, in the same or another language कोश, एक पुस्तक जिस में अकारादि क्रम में किसी भाषा के शब्द दिए होते हैं और

उन के उसी भाषा में या किसी अन्य भाषा में उस शब्द के अर्थ दिए जाते हैं, शब्दकोश *to look up a word in a dictionary ○ a bilingual/monolingual dictionary* **2** a book that lists the words connected with a particular subject and tells you what they mean विशिष्ट शब्दकोश (जैसे मुहावरा कोश, सहप्रयोग कोश), द्विभाषी शब्दकोश, विश्वकोशीय शब्दकोश *a dictionary of idioms ○ a medical dictionary*

**did** ➪ **do** का past tense रूप

**didactic** /daɪˈdæktɪk डाइˈडैक्‌टिक्/ *adj.* (*formal*) **1** designed to teach people sth, especially a moral lesson शिक्षात्मक (विशेषतः नैतिक शिक्षा से संबंधित) *didactic art/ poetry* **2** telling people things rather than letting them find out for themselves उपदेशप्रधान *Her way of teaching literature is too didactic.* ▶ **didactically** /-kli -क्लि/ *adv.* उपदेशपूर्वक

**didn't** ➪ **did not** का संक्षिप्त रूप

**die** /daɪ डाइ/ *verb* (*pres. part.* **dying;** *3rd person sing. pres.* **dies;** *pt, pp* **died**) **1** [I, T] **die (from/ of sth)** to stop living मरना, प्राण त्याग करना *to die of hunger ○ to die for what you believe in ○ to die a natural/violent death* ➪ **dead** adjective तथा **death** noun देखिए। **2** [I] to stop existing; to disappear अस्तित्व में न रहना; समाप्त हो जाना; लुप्त हो जाना *The old customs are dying.*

**IDM** **be dying for sth/to do sth** (*spoken*) to want sth/to do sth very much किसी वस्तु की बहुत लालसा होना, किसी चीज़ की तलब उठना *I'm dying for a cup of coffee.*

**die hard** to change or disappear only slowly or with difficulty मंदगति से या कठिनाई से बदलना या समाप्त होना या ग़ायब हो जाना *Old attitudes towards women die hard.*

**to die for** (*informal*) if you think that sth is to die for, you really want it and would do anything to get it किसी वस्तु को पाने की अत्यधिक लालसा रखना, किसी वस्तु को पाने के लिए कुछ भी करने को तैयार हो जाना *They have a house in town that's to die for.*

**die laughing** to find sth very funny जब कोई बात बहुत मज़ेदार या हँसाने वाली लगे *I thought I'd die laughing when he told that joke.*

**PHRV** **die away** to slowly become weaker before stopping or disappearing क्रमशः क्षीण होते हुए समाप्त हो जाना *The sound of the engine died away as the car drove into the distance.*

**die down** to slowly become less strong क्रमशः क्षीण होना *Let's wait until the storm dies down before we go out.*

**die off** to die one by one until there are none left एक-एक करके सबका समाप्त हो जाना

**die out** to stop happening or disappear प्रचलन में न रहना या लुप्त हो जाना *The use of horses on farms has almost died out in this country.*

**diesel** /ˈdiːzl ˈडीज़ल्/ *noun* **1** [U] a type of heavy oil used in some engines instead of petrol डीज़ल, एक प्रकार का भारी तेल *a diesel engine ○ a taxi that runs on diesel* **2** [C] a vehicle that uses diesel डीज़ल चालित वाहन *My new car's a diesel.* ➪ **petrol** देखिए।

**diet¹** /ˈdaɪət ˈडाइअट्/ *noun* **1** [C, U] the food that a person or animal usually eats सामान्य भोजन, आहार, खुराक *They **live on a diet of** rice and vegetables. ○ I always try to have a healthy, balanced diet* (= including all the different types of food that our body needs). **2** [C] certain foods that a person who is ill, or who wants to lose weight is allowed to eat रोगी या वज़न कम करने के इच्छुक व्यक्ति के लिए निर्धारित भोजन, पथ्य, परहेज़ी खुराक *a low-fat diet ○ a sugar-free diet* ▶ **dietary** /ˈdaɪətəri ˈडाइअटरि/ *adj.* पथ्य-विषयक, भोजन-विषयक *dietary habits/requirements*

**IDM** **be/go on a diet** to eat only certain foods or a small amount of food because you want to lose weight वज़न कम करने के लिए निर्धारित प्रकार का या थोड़ी मात्रा में भोजन लेना

**diet²** /ˈdaɪət ˈडाइअट्/ *verb* [I] to try to lose weight by eating less food or only certain kinds of food निधारित प्रकार के या अल्प मात्रा में भोजन से वज़न कम करने का प्रयास करना

**dietetics** /ˌdaɪəˈtetɪks ˌडाइअˈटेटिक्स्/ *noun* [U] the scientific study of the food we eat and its effect on our health आहार-शास्त्र, भोजन और स्वास्थ्य पर उसके प्रभाव का वैज्ञानिक अध्ययन

**differ** /ˈdɪfə(r) ˈडिफ़(र्)/ *verb* [I] **1 differ (from sb/sth)** to be different भिन्न या अलग होना *How does this car differ from the more expensive model?* **2 differ (with sb) (about/on sth)** to have a different opinion मतभेद होना, अलग राय रखना या राय न मिलना *I'm afraid I differ with you on that question.*

**difference** /ˈdɪfrəns ˈडिफ़्रन्स्/ *noun* **1** [C] **a difference (between A and B)** the way that people or things are not the same or the way that sb/sth has changed अंतर, भेद, फ़र्क *What's the difference between this computer and that cheaper one? ○ From a distance it's hard to **tell the difference** between the twins.* **2** [C, U] **dif-**

ference (in sth) (between A and B) the amount by which people or things are not the same or by which sb/sth has changed अंतर, शेष, बाक़ी *There's an age difference of three years between the two children.* ○ *We gave a 30% deposit and must* ***pay the difference*** *when the work is finished* (= the rest of the money) **3** [C] a disagreement that is not very serious मामूली मतभेद या असहमति *There was* ***a difference of opinion*** *over how much we owed.*

**IDM make a, some, etc. difference (to sb/sth)** to have an effect (on sb/sth) (किसी पर या किसी बात का) प्रभाव होना *Marriage made a big difference to her life.*

**make no difference (to sb/sth); not make any difference** to not be important (to sb/sth); to have no effect (किसी के लिए या कोई बात) बेमानी या बेमतलब होना; प्रभावहीन होना

**split the difference** ⇨ **split**[1] देखिए।

**different** /ˈdɪfrənt ˈडिफ़्रन्ट्/ *adj.* **1 different (from/to sb/sth)** not the same भिन्न, अलग प्रकार का, एक जैसा नहीं *The two houses are very different in style.* ○ *You'd look completely different with short hair.* ✪ विलोम **similar** NOTE अमेरिकी अंग्रेज़ी में **different than** का प्रयोग भी होता है। **2** separate; individual अलग-अलग; विशिष्ट, अपनी तरह का *This coat is available in three different colours.* ▶ **differently** *adv.* अलग तरह से *I think you'll feel differently about it tomorrow.*

**differential**[1] /ˌdɪfəˈrenʃl ˌडिफ़ˈरेन्शल्/ *noun* [C] **1 a differential (between A and B)** a difference in the amount, value or size of sth, especially the difference in rates of pay for people doing different work in the same industry or profession (दो वस्तुओं में) परिमाण, महत्त्व या आकार की दृष्टि से होने वाले अंतर या भेद (विशेषतः एक ही व्यवसाय या उद्योग में भिन्न-भिन्न कामों के लिए निर्धारित भुगतान-दरों में अंतर) **2** (*also* **differential gear**) a **gear** that makes it possible for a vehicle's back wheels to turn around at different speeds when going around corners वाहन के पिछले पहियों को नियंत्रित करने वाला गियर (जिसके कारण मोड़ों पर घूमते हुए उनकी स्पीड अलग-अलग होती है); गियर विभेदक

**differential**[2] /ˌdɪfəˈrenʃl ˌडिफ़ˈरेन्शल्/ *adj.* (*only before a noun*) (*formal*) showing or depending on a difference; not equal भिन्नता प्रदर्शक या भिन्नता पर आधारित; असमान

**differentiate** /ˌdɪfəˈrenʃieɪt ˌडिफ़ˈरेन्शिएट्/ *verb* **1** [I, T] **differentiate between A and B; differentiate A (from B)** to see or show how things are different वस्तुओं के बीच अंतर पहचानना और उसे स्पष्ट करना *It is hard to differentiate between these two types of seed.* **2** [T] **differentiate sth (from sth)** to make one thing different from another एक चीज़ को दूसरी से अलग दिखाना *The coloured feathers differentiate the male bird from the plain brown female.* ✪ पर्याय **distinguish 3** [I] to treat one person or group differently from another किसी व्यक्ति या व्यक्ति समूह को दूसरे से अलग मानना *We don't differentiate between the two groups—we treat everybody alike.* ✪ पर्याय **discriminate** ▶ **differentiation** /ˌdɪfəˌrenʃiˈeɪʃn ˌडिफ़ˌरेन्शिˈएशन्/ *noun* [U] अंतर, भेद, फ़र्क

**difficult** /ˈdɪfɪkəlt ˈडिफ़िकल्ट्/ *adj.* **1 difficult (for sb) (to do sth)** not easy to do or understand (कार्य आदि) कठिन, मुश्किल *a difficult test/problem* ○ *I* ***find it difficult to*** *get up early in the morning.* **2** (used about a person) not friendly, reasonable or helpful (व्यक्ति) टेढ़ा, अविवेकी या सहायता न करने वाला *a difficult customer*

**difficulty** /ˈdɪfɪkəlti ˈडिफ़िकलटि/ *noun* (*pl.* **difficulties**) **1** [U, C] **difficulty (in sth/in doing sth)** a problem; a situation that is hard to deal with समस्या; कष्टकर स्थिति *I'm sure you won't* ***have*** *any* ***difficulty*** *getting a visa for America.* ○ *We* ***had no difficulty*** *selling our car.* ○ *We found a hotel* ***without difficulty****.* ○ *If you borrow too much money you may* ***get into*** *financial* ***difficulties****.* **2** [U] how hard sth is to do or to deal with कठिनाई, कठिनता, दुःसाध्यता *The questions start easy and then increase in difficulty.*

**diffident** /ˈdɪfɪdənt ˈडिफ़िडन्ट्/ *adj.* not having confidence in your own strengths or abilities आत्मसंशयी, अपनी शक्ति या योग्यता में विश्वास न रखने वाला; आत्मविश्वासहीन ▶ **diffidence** *noun* [U] आत्मसंशय, आत्मविश्वासहीनता

**diffract** /dɪˈfrækt डिˈफ़्रैक्ट्/ *verb* [T] (*technical*) (in physics) to break up a ray of light or a system of waves by passing them through a narrow opening or across an edge, causing patterns to form between the waves produced (**interfer-**

wavelength

path of wave

narrow opening similar in size to wavelength = greater diffraction

wide opening much larger than wavelength = less diffraction

**diffraction**

**ence**) (भौतिकशास्त्र में) तंग सुराख में से या किनारे के आरपार जाते हुए प्रकाश-किरणों या लहर शृंखला का बहुरंगी पैटर्न में विभाजन करना; व्यतिकरण ▶ **diffraction** /dɪˈfrækʃn डिˈफ्रैक्शन् / *noun* [U] बहुरंगी पैटर्न में विभाजन, विवर्तन

**diffuse**[1] /dɪˈfju:z डिˈफ़्यूज़् / *verb* **1** [I, T] (*formal*) to spread sth or become spread widely in all directions सब दिशाओं में दूर-दूर तक फैलना या (किसी वस्तु को) फैलाना, चारों ओर बिखरना या बिखराना, छितरना या छितराना; विसरण **2** [I, T] (*technical*) if a gas or liquid diffuses or is diffused in a substance, it becomes slowly mixed with that substance (किसी गैस या द्रव का) धीरे-धीरे अन्य वस्तु में मिल जाना या मिलकर एक हो जाना **3** [T] (*formal*) to make light shine less brightly by spreading it in many directions प्रकाश को बिखरा या छितराकर महिम कर देना; विसरण ▶ **diffusion** /dɪˈfju:ʒn डिˈफ़्यूश़न् / *noun* [C] बिखराव, छितराव, विसरण

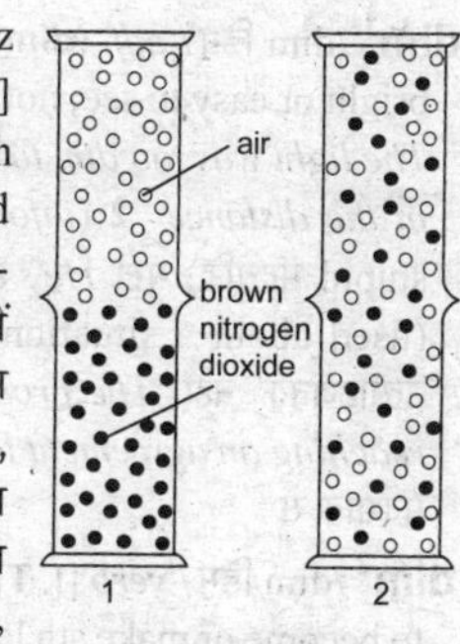


**diffuse**[2] /dɪˈfju:s डिˈफ़्यूज़् / *adj.* spread over a wide area दूर-दूर तक बिखरा या छितरा हुआ; विसरित

**dig**[1] /dɪg डिग् / *verb* [I, T] (*pres. part.* **digging**; *pt, pp* **dug** /dʌg डग /) to move earth and make a hole in the ground खोदना, गड्ढा करना *The children are busy digging in the sand.* ○ *to dig a hole*

**IDM** **dig deep** to try harder, give more, go further, etc. than is usually necessary सामान्य से अधिक प्रयत्न करना, दान करना, आगे बढ़ना आदि *Charities for the homeless are asking people to dig deep into their pockets in this cold weather.*

**dig your heels in** to refuse to do sth or to change your mind about sth किसी काम को करने से इनकार कर देना या विचार बदल लेना

**PHRV** **dig (sth) in; dig sth into sth** to push or press (sth) into sb/sth किसी चीज़ को धकेलना या दबाना *My neck is all red where my collar is digging in.* ○ *He dug his hands deep into his pockets.*

**dig sb/sth out (of sth)** **1** to get sb/sth out of sth by moving the earth, etc. that covers him/her/it खोदकर या मिट्टी हटा कर (किसी को) बाहर निकालना *Rescue workers dug the survivors out of the rubble.* **2** to get or find sb/sth by searching किसी वस्तु को खोज निकालना *Leela went into the attic and dug out some old photos.*

**dig sth up** **1** to remove sth from the earth by digging किसी वस्तु को ज़मीन खोदकर निकालना *to dig up potatoes* **2** to make a hole or take away soil by digging खोदकर गड्ढा करना या मिट्टी हटाना *Workmen are digging up the road in front of our house.* **3** to find information by searching or studying पढ़कर या खोजकर जानकारी एकत्र करना *Newspapers have dug up some embarrassing facts about his private life.*

**dig**[2] /dɪg डिग् / *noun* **1** [C] a hard push ज़ोरदार झटका *to give sb a dig in the ribs* (= with your elbow) **2** [C] something that you say to upset sb ताना, फ़ब्ती *The others kept **making digs** at him because of the way he spoke.* **3** [C] an occasion or place where a group of people try to find things of historical or scientific interest in the ground in order to study them पुरातत्त्व-संबंधी खुदाई *an archaeological dig*

**digest** /daɪˈdʒest डाइˈजेस्ट् / *verb* [T] **1** to change food in your stomach so that it can be used by the body (आहार को) पचाना **2** to think about new information so that you understand it fully नई बात को अच्छी तरह समझना *The lecture was interesting, but too much to digest all at once.*

**digestible** /daɪˈdʒestəbl डाइˈजेसटबल् / *adj.* (used about food) easy for your body to deal with (**digest**) (भोजन) सुपाच्य ✪ विलोम **indigestible**

**digestion** /daɪ dʒestʃən डाइˈजेसचन् / *noun* [C, U] the process of changing food in your stomach so that it can be used by the body पाचन-क्रिया ▶ **digestive** /daɪˈdʒestɪv डाइˈजेस्टिव् / *adj.* पाचन-संबंधी *the digestive system*

**digger** /ˈdɪgə(r) ˈडिग(र्)/ *noun* [C] **1** a large machine that is used for digging up the ground खुदाई करने वाली मशीन **2** a person or an animal that digs खुदाई करने वाला व्यक्ति या पशु

**digit** /ˈdɪdʒɪt ˈडिजिट् / *noun* [C] any of the numbers from 0 to 9, 0 से 9 तक कोई अंक *a six-digit telephone number*

**digital** /ˈdɪdʒɪtl ˈडिजिट्ल् / *adj.* **1** using an electronic system that uses the numbers 1 and 0 to record sound or store information, and that gives high-quality results ध्वनि-रिकार्डिंग या सूचना-संग्रहण के लिए 1 और 0 अंक का प्रयोग करने वाली इलेक्ट्रॉनिक पद्धति *a digital recording* **2** showing information by using numbers अंकों से सूचना देने वाला, अंकीय, अंकों में दर्शाने वाला; अंकदर्शी *a digital watch*

**digitize** (*also* **-ise**) /ˈdidʒɪtaɪzˈडिजिटाइज़् / *verb* [T] to change data into a **digital** form that can be easily read and processed by a computer (कंप्यूटर) सूचना-सामग्री को अंकीय रूप में परिवर्तित करना (इसे कंप्यूटर सरलता से पढ़ सकता है और विविध रूपों में परिवर्तित कर सकता है) *a digitized map*

**dignified** /ˈdɪgnɪfaɪd ˈडिग्निफ़ाइड् / *adj.* behaving in a calm, serious way that makes other people respect you गरिमामय, मान-मर्यादा-पूर्ण, शालीन *dignified behaviour* ✪ विलोम **undignified**

**dignitary** /ˈdɪgnɪtəri ˈडिग्निटरि / *noun* (*pl.* **dignitaries**) a person who is influential or has an important official position महानुभाव, उच्च पदस्थ

**dignity** /ˈdɪgnəti ˈडिग्नटि / *noun* [U] **1** calm, serious behaviour that makes other people respect you शांत और गंभीर आचरण *to behave* ***with dignity*** **2** the quality of being serious and formal गरिमा, मर्यादा *the quiet dignity of the funeral service*

**digress** /daɪˈgres डाइˈग्रेस् / *verb* [I] (*formal*) to stop talking or writing about the main subject under discussion and start talking or writing about another less important one मुख्य विषय से हटकर अन्य विषय (अपेक्षाकृत गौण) की चर्चा करने लगना या में संलग्न हो जाना ▶ **digression** /daɪˈgreʃn डाइˈग्रेशन् / *noun* [C, U] विषयांतर

**dike** ➪ **dyke** देखिए।

**dilapidated** /dɪˈlæpɪdeɪtɪd डिˈलैपिडेटिड् / *adj.* (used about buildings, furniture, etc.) old and broken (भवन, फ़र्नीचर आदि) जीर्ण-शीर्ण, टूटा-फूटा ▶ **dilapidation** /dɪˌlæpɪˈdeɪʃn डि,लैपिˈडेशन् / *noun* [U] जीर्ण-शीर्ण स्थिति

**dilate** /daɪˈleɪt डाइˈलेट् / *verb* [I, T] to become or to make sth larger, wider or more open बढ़ना या बढ़ाना, बड़ा होना या करना, फैलना या फैलाना *Her eyes dilated with fear.* ○ *dilated pupils/nostrils* ▶ **dilation** *noun* [U] विस्तार, फैलाव, विस्फारण

**dilemma** /dɪˈlemə डाइˈलेमा / *noun* [C] a situation in which you have to make a difficult choice between two or more things दुविधा, असमंजस *Doctors* ***face a*** *moral* ***dilemma*** *of when to keep patients alive artificially and when to let them die.* ○ *to be* ***in a dilemma***

**diligence** /ˈdɪlɪdʒəns ˈडिलिजन्स् / *noun* [U] (*formal*) the quality of doing work carefully and thoroughly परिश्रम, कर्मठता, अध्यवसाय

**diligent** /ˈdɪlɪdʒənt ˈडिलिजन्ट् / *adj.* (*formal*) showing care and effort in your work or duties परिश्रमी, सावधान और कर्मठ *a diligent student/worker* ▶ **diligently** *adv.* परिश्रमपूर्वक

**dilute** /daɪˈluːt डाइˈलूट् / *verb* [T] **dilute sth (with sth)** to make a liquid weaker by adding water or another liquid (पानी या कोई अन्य द्रव मिलाकर) किसी द्रव को पतला करना ▶ **dilute** *adj.* तनुकृत, विरल, पतला

**dim**[1] /dɪm डिम् / *adj.* (**dimmer; dimmest**) **1** not bright or easy to see; not clear मंद, धुँधला, अस्पष्ट *The light was too dim to read by.* ○ *a dim shape in the distance* **2** (*informal*) not very clever; stupid मंदबुद्धि; मूर्ख *He's a bit dim.* **3** (*informal*) (used about a situation) not hopeful (स्थिति) उत्साहजनक नहीं *The prospects of the two sides reaching an agreement look dim.* ▶ **dimly** *adv.* मंदभाव से

**dim**[2] /dɪm डिम् / *verb* [I, T] (**dimming; dimmed**) to become or make sth less bright or clear धुँधला या अस्पष्ट हो जाना या कर देना *The lights dimmed.* ○ *to dim the lights*

**dimension** /daɪˈmenʃn डाइˈमेन्शन् / *noun* **1** [C, U] a measurement of the length, width or height of sth लंबाई, चौड़ाई या ऊँचाई का मापन, आयाम **2 dimensions** [*pl.*] the size of sth including its length, width and height लंबाई, चौड़ाई और ऊँचाई से मिलकर निर्धारित (किसी वस्तु का) आकार *to measure the dimensions of a room* ○ (*figurative*) *The full dimensions of this problem are only now being recognized.* **3** [C] something that affects the way you think about a problem or situation किसी समस्या या स्थिति का पहलू; आयाम *to add a new dimension to a problem/situation* **4 -dimensional** /-ʃnəl -शनल् / (*used to form compound adjectives*) having the number of dimensions mentioned आयामों की निर्दिष्ट संख्या से युक्त *a three-dimensional object*

**diminish** /dɪˈmɪnɪʃ डिˈमिनिश् / *verb* [I, T] (*formal*) to become or to make sth smaller or less important; decrease छोटा होना या छोटा करना, महत्त्व घटाना; कम होना या करना *The world's rainforests are diminishing fast.* ○ *The bad news did nothing to diminish her enthusiasm for the plan.*

**diminutive** /dɪˈmɪnjətɪv डिˈमिन्यटिव् / *adj.* (*formal*) much smaller than usual सामान्य से काफ़ी छोटा, नन्हा

**dimple** /ˈdɪmpl ˈडिम्पल् / *noun* [C] a round area in the skin on your cheek, etc., which often only appears when you smile मुसकराते गाल या ठुड्डी पर पड़ने वाला गड्ढा

**din** /dɪn डिन् / *noun* [*sing.*] a lot of unpleasant noise that continues for some time शोर-शराबा, हल्ला-गुल्ला

**dine** /daɪn डाइन्/ *verb* to eat a meal, especially in the evening भोजन करना (विशेषतः सायंकाल में) *We dined at an exclusive French restaurant.*

PHRV **dine out** to eat in a restaurant रेस्तराँ में भोजन करना

**diner** /ˈdaɪnə(r) ˈडाइन(र्)/ *noun* [C] **1** a person who is eating at a restaurant रेस्तराँ में भोजन करने वाला **2** (*AmE*) a restaurant that serves simple, cheap food सस्ते भोजन का रेस्तराँ

**dinghy** /ˈdɪŋgi ˈडिङ्गि/ *noun* [C] (*pl.* **dinghies**) **1** a small boat that you sail छोटी नाव, डोंगी ➪ **yacht** देखिए। **2** a small open boat, often used to take people to land from a larger boat छोटी खुली नाव; डोंगी ➪ **boat** पर चित्र देखिए।

**dingy** /ˈdɪndʒi ˈडिन्जि/ *adj.* dirty and dark गंदा और अँधेरा *a dingy room/hotel*

**dining room** *noun* [C] a room where you eat meals भोजन-कक्ष

**dinner** /ˈdɪnə(r) ˈडिन(र्)/ *noun* **1** [C, U] the main meal of the day, eaten either at midday or in the evening दिन का मुख्य भोजन (दोपहर को या शाम को) *Would you like to **go out for/to dinner** one evening?* **2** [C] a formal occasion in the evening during which a meal is served रात्रिभोज *The club is holding its annual dinner next week.*

**dinner jacket** (*AmE* **tuxedo**) *noun* [C] a black or white jacket that a man wears on formal occasions. A dinner jacket is usually worn with a special tie (**a bow tie**) औपचारिक भोज के समय पहना जाने वाला जाकेट, डिनर के समय का जाकेट, डिनर-जाकेट, भोज-कोट

**dinosaur** /ˈdaɪnəsɔː(r) ˈडाइनसॉ(र्)/ *noun* [C] one of a number of very large animals that disappeared from the earth (**became extinct**) millions of years ago बहुत पहले विलुप्त एक विशालकाय जानवर; डायनासोर

**diocese** /ˈdaɪəsɪs ˈडाइअसीस्/ *noun* [C] an area containing a number of churches, for which a **bishop** is responsible एक बिशप (वरिष्ठ ईसाई धर्मगुरु) के अधीन क्षेत्र जहाँ अनेक चर्च हों; बिशपक्षेत्र, धर्मप्रांत

**diode** /ˈdaɪəʊd ˈडाइओड्/ *noun* [C] (*technical*) an electronic device in which the electric current flows in one direction only एक इलेक्ट्रॉनिक उपकरण जिसमें विद्युत धारा केवल एक दिशा में प्रवाहित होती है; डायोड

**dioxide** /daɪˈɒksaɪd डाइˈऑक्साइड्/ *noun* [C, U] (*technical*) a compound formed by combining two atoms of **oxygen** and one atom of another chemical element ऑक्सीजन के दो अंश के साथ अन्य रासायनिक तत्व के एक अंश से मिलकर बना यौगिक; डाइऑक्साइड

**Dip.** *abbr.* diploma डिप्लोमा

**dip[1]** /dɪp डिप्/ *verb* (**dipping; dipped**) **1** [T] **dip sth (into sth); dip sth (in)** to put sth into liquid and immediately take it out again किसी वस्तु को द्रव में डुबोकर एकदम निकालना *Reena dipped her toe into the pool to see how cold it was.* **2** [I, T] to go down or make sth go down to a lower level नीचे की ओर जाना या किसी वस्तु को नीचे की ओर धकेलना, ढलान की ओर जाना या धकेलना, घटना या घटाना *The road suddenly dipped down to the river.* ○ *The company's sales have dipped disastrously this year.*

PHRV **dip into sth** **1** to use part of an amount of sth that you have अपने स्वामित्व की वस्तु के एक अंश का उपयोग करना *Tushar had to dip into his savings to pay for his new suit.* **2** to read parts, but not all, of sth (पुस्तक के) कुछ अंशों को पढ़ना, यहाँ-वहाँ से पुस्तक पढ़ लेना *I've only dipped into the book. I haven't read it all the way through.*

**dip[2]** /dɪp डिप्/ *noun* **1** [C] a fall to a lower level, especially for a short time अस्थायी रूप से घट जाना, कम हो जाना *a dip in sales/temperature* **2** [C] an area of lower ground ढाल, उतार *The cottage was in a dip in the hills.* **3** [C] (*informal*) a short swim (नदी या समुद्र में) डुबकी *We went for a dip before breakfast.* **4** [C, U] a thick sauce into which you dip biscuits, vegetables, etc. before eating them गाढ़ी चटनी (जिसमें बिस्कुट आदि डुबोकर खाते हैं) *a cheese/chilli dip*

**diphtheria** /dɪfˈθɪəriə डिफ़्ˈथिअरिआ/ *noun* [U] a serious disease of the throat that makes it difficult to breathe गले का गंभीर रोग जिसमें साँस लेने में कठिनाई होती है

**diphthong** /ˈdɪfθɒŋ ˈडिफ़्थॉङ्/ *noun* [C] two vowel sounds that are pronounced together to make one sound, for example the /aɪ/ sound in 'fine' एक साथ उच्चरित दो स्वरों से बनी एकल ध्वनि; द्विस्वर, संधि-स्वर, संयुक्त स्वर जैसे शब्द 'fine' में /आइ/ की ध्वनि

**diploid** /ˈdɪplɔɪd ˈडिप्लॉइड्/ *adj.* (*technical*) (used about a cell) containing two complete sets of **chromosomes** one from each parent दो पूर्ण गुणसूत्र सेटों वाली कोशिका, द्विगुणित ➪ **haploid** देखिए।

**diploma** /dɪˈpləʊmə डिˈप्लोमा/ *noun* [C] **a diploma (in sth)** a certificate that you receive when you complete a course of study, often at a college डिप्लोमा, शैक्षिक प्रमाण-पत्र *I'm studying for a diploma in hotel management.*

**diplomacy** /dɪˈpləʊməsi डिˈप्लोमसि/ *noun* [U] **1** the activity of managing relations between different countries राजनय, अंतर्राष्ट्रीय कूटनीति *If diplomacy fails, there is a danger of war.* **2** skill in dealing with people without upsetting or offending them व्यवहार-कुशलता *He handled the tricky situation with tact and diplomacy.*

**diplomat** /ˈdɪpləmæt ˈडिप्‌लमैट्/ *noun* [C] an official who represents his/her country in a foreign country विदेश में नियुक्त किसी देश का प्रतिनिधित्व करने वाला अधिकारी, राजनयज्ञ, कूटनीतिज्ञ, राजनयिक (व्यक्ति) *a diplomat at the embassy in Rome*

**diplomatic** /ˌdɪpləˈmætɪk ˌडिप्‌लˈमैटिक्/ *adj.* **1** connected with **diplomacy 1** कूटनीतिक, कूटनीति-विषयक *to break off diplomatic relations* **2** skilful at dealing with people व्यवहार-कुशल, चतुर, चातुर्य-पूर्ण *He searched for a diplomatic reply so as not to offend her.* ▶ **diplomatically** /-kli -क्लि/ *adv.* कूटनीतिक रीति से, चतुराई से

**dire** /ˈdaɪə(r) ˈडाइअ(र्)/ *adj.* (*formal*) very bad or serious; terrible भयानक, गंभीर; दारुण *dire consequences/poverty*

IDM **be in dire straits** to be in a very difficult situation अत्यंत कठिनाई में होना *The business is in dire straits financially.*

**direct¹** /dəˈrekt; डˈरेक्ट्; dɪ-; डि-; daɪ- डाइ-/ *adj., adv.* **1** with nobody/nothing in between; not involving anyone/anything else सीधा, प्रत्यक्ष, मध्यस्थ-रहित; साक्षात, सीधा *The Indian Prime Minister is **in direct contact with** the US President.* **2** going from one place to another without turning or stopping; straight सीधे, बिना मुड़े, बिना घूमे जाने वाला *a direct flight to Hong Kong* ○ *This bus goes direct to Ladakh.* **3** saying what you mean; clear ईमानदारी का, ईमानदार; स्पष्ट *Politicians never give a **direct answer** to a **direct question**.* ○ *She sometimes offends people with her direct way of speaking.* ✪ विलोम **indirect** (संख्या 1, 2 और 3 के लिए) **4** (*only before a noun*) complete; exact पूरा; ठीक *What she did was in direct opposition to my orders.*

**direct²** /dəˈrekt; डˈरेक्ट; dɪ-; डि-; daɪ- डाइ-/ *verb* [T] **1 direct sth to/towards sb/sth; direct sth at sb/sth** to point or send sth towards sb/sth or in a particular direction किसी दिशा विशेष की ओर किसी बात का संकेत करना या लक्ष्य करना *In recent weeks the media's attention has been directed towards events abroad.* ○ *The advert is directed at young people.* ○ *The actor directed some angry words at a photographer.* **2** to manage or control sb/sth (किसी व्यक्ति या वस्तु को) निर्देशित करना, नियंत्रित करना *A policeman was in the middle of the road, directing the traffic.* ○ *to direct a play/film* **3 direct sb (to...)** to tell or show sb how to get somewhere (किसी को कहीं पहुँचने का) रास्ता बताना *I was directed to an office at the end of the corridor.* ➪ **lead¹ 1** पर नोट देखिए। **4** (*formal*) to tell or order sb to do sth निर्देश या आदेश देना *Take the tablets as directed by your doctor.*

**direct action** *noun* [U, C] the use of strikes, protests, etc. instead of discussion in order to get what you want सीधी कार्रवाई, उद्देश्य-प्राप्ति के लिए बातचीत के स्थान पर हड़ताल आदि का सहारा लेना

**direct current** *noun* [C, U] a flow of electricity that goes in one direction only केवल एक दिशा में जाने वाला विद्युत प्रवाह, सीधी विद्युत धारा, डायरेक्ट करेंट, दिष्ट धारा ➪ **alternating current** देखिए।

**direct debit** *noun* [C, U] an order to your bank that allows sb else to take a particular amount of money out of your account on certain dates बैंक को दिया निर्देश जिसके अनुसार खाते से निर्दिष्ट तिथियों में निर्धारित राशि निकाली जा सकती हो, बैंक को सीधी निकासी हेतु निर्देश

**direction** /dəˈrekʃn; डˈरेक्श्न्; dɪ-; डि-; daɪ- डाइ-/ *noun* **1** [C, U] the path, line or way along which a person or thing is moving, looking, pointing, developing, etc. (गति की) दिशा, रास्ता *A woman was seen running **in the direction of** the station.* ○ *We met him coming **in the opposite direction**.* ○ ***a step in the right direction*** ○ *I've got such a hopeless **sense of direction**—I'm always getting lost.* **2** [C, U] a purpose; an aim सार्थकता; लक्ष्य *I want a career that gives me a (sense of) direction in life.* **3** [C] (*usually pl.*) information or instructions about how to do sth or how to get to a place (कुछ करने या कहीं जाने के विषय में) सूचना, निर्देश या कोई काम कैसे किया जाए या किसी ठिकाने पर कैसे पहुँचा जाए, इस विषय में निर्देश, जानकारी *I'll give you **directions** to my house.* **4** [U] the act of managing or controlling sth प्रबंधन या मार्गदर्शन *This department is under the direction of Mrs Walia*

**directive** /dəˈrektɪv; डˈरेक्टिव्; dɪ-; daɪ- डि-; डाइ-/ *noun* [C] an official order to do sth (कुछ करने का) आधिकारिक आदेश, निदेश *a directive on safety at work*

**directly¹** /dəˈrektli; डˈरेक्ट्लि; dɪ-; daɪ- डि- डाइ-/ *adv.* **1** in a direct line or way सीधी दिशा में; सीधे तरीक़े से *He refused to answer my question directly.* ○ *Lung cancer is directly related to smoking.* ✪ विलोम **indirectly** **2** immediately; very soon तुरंत; बहुत जल्दी *Wait where you are. I'll be back directly.*

**directly**[2] /də'rektli; ड'रेक्ट्लि dɪ-; daɪ- डि- डाइ- / *conj.* as soon as ज्यों ही *I phoned him directly I heard the news.*

**direct mail** *noun* [U] advertisements that are sent to people through the post डाक के माध्यम से लोगों को भेजे जाने वाले विज्ञापन

**direct object** *noun* [C] a noun or phrase that is affected by the action of a verb प्रत्यक्ष कर्म, क्रियापद से उक्त संज्ञा *In the sentence 'Anu bought a record', 'a record' is the direct object.* ➪ **indirect object** देखिए।

> **NOTE** प्रत्यक्ष कर्म (direct object) के विषय में अधिक जानकारी के लिए इस शब्दकोश के अंत में **Quick Grammar Reference** खंड देखिए।

**director** /də'rektə(r); ड'रेक्ट(र्) / dɪ-; daɪ- डि- डाइ- / *noun* [C] **1** a person who manages or controls a company or organization संचालक, निदेशक, निर्देशक *the managing director of Reliance* ○ *She's on the board of directors* (= group of directors) *of a large computer company.* **2** a person who is responsible for a particular activity or department in a company, a college, etc. किसी कंपनी या शिक्षा संस्था में विभाग का प्रमुख या अध्यक्ष *the director of studies of a language school* **3** a person who tells the actors, etc. what to do in a film, play, etc. फ़िल्म या नाटक का निर्देशक *a film/theatre director*

**directory** /də'rektəri; ड'रेक्टरि; dɪ-; daɪ- डि-; डाइ- / *noun* [C] (*pl.* **directories**) **1** a list of names, addresses and telephone numbers in the order of the alphabet वर्णक्रम में नामों, पतों और टेलीफ़ोन नंबरों की सूची; (टेलीफ़ोन) निर्देशिका *the telephone directory* ○ *I tried to look up Jai's number but he's ex-directory* (= he has chosen not to be listed in the telephone directory). **2** (*computing*) a file containing a group of other files or programs in a computer कंप्यूटर की फ़ाइल जिसमें अन्य फ़ाइलें और प्रोग्राम समाविष्ट हों

**direct speech** *noun* [U] (*grammar*) the actual words that a person said साक्षात या प्रत्यक्ष कथन, किसी व्यक्ति के कहे मूल शब्द ➪ **indirect speech** देखिए।

> **NOTE** साक्षात या प्रत्यक्ष कथन (direct speech) के विषय में अधिक जानकारी के लिए इस शब्दकोश के अंत में **Quick Grammar Reference** खंड देखिए।

**dirt** /dɜ:t डट् / *noun* [U] **1** a substance that is not clean, such as dust or mud मैल, गंदगी *His face and hands were covered in dirt.* **2** earth or soil मिट्टी, धूल *a dirt track* **3** damaging information about sb नीचतापूर्ण बात *The press are always trying to **dig up dirt** on the President's love life.*

**IDM dirt cheap** extremely cheap बहुत सस्ता, मिट्टी के भाव

**dirty**[1] /'dɜ:ti 'डटि / *adj.* (**dirtier; dirtiest**) **1** not clean मैला, गंदा *Your hands are dirty. Go and wash them!* ○ *Gardening is dirty work* (= it makes you dirty). ✪ विलोम **clean** **2** unpleasant or dishonest अप्रिय या बेईमान, कुत्सित, घृणित *He's a dirty player.* ○ *He doesn't sell the drugs himself—he gets kids to **do** his **dirty work** for him.*

**IDM a dirty word** an idea or thing that you do not like or agree with नापसंद या अस्वीकार्य वस्तु या विचार *Work is a dirty word to Fardeen.*

**dirty**[2] /'dɜ:ti 'डटि / *verb* [I, T] (*pres. part.* **dirtying;** *3rd person sing.* **dirties;** *pt, pp* **dirtied**) to become or to make sth dirty गंदा, मैला होना या कर देना ✪ विलोम **clean**

**dirty**[3] /'dɜ:ti 'डटि / *adv.*

**IDM play dirty** (*informal*) to behave or play a game in an unfair way अनुचित आचरण करना (सामान्यतः खेल में)

**dis-** /dɪs डिस् / *prefix* (*in adjectives, adverbs, nouns and verbs*) not; the opposite of नहीं; के विपरीत *discontinue* ○ *disarmament*

**disability** /ˌdɪsə'bɪləti ˌडिस'बिलटि / *noun* (*pl.* **disabilities**) **1** [U] the state of being unable to use a part of your body properly, usually because of injury or disease शारीरिक रूप से अशक्त होने की स्थिति, विकलांगता (प्रायः चोट या रोग के कारण) *physical disability* **2** [C] something that makes you unable to use a part of your body properly शरीर को अशक्त बनाने वाला गुण-धर्म, विकलांगता *Because of his disability, he needs constant care.*

**disable** /dɪs'eɪbl डिस्'एबल् / *verb* [T] (*usually passive*) to make sb unable to use part of his/her body properly, usually because of injury or disease (प्रायः चोट या रोग के कारण) किसी को विकलांग कर देना या किसी का विकलांग हो जाना *Many soldiers were disabled in the war.*

**disabled** /dɪs'eɪbld डिस्'एब्ल्ड् / *adj.* **1** unable to use a part of your body properly विकलांग, अपंग *A car accident left her permanently disabled.* **2 the disabled** *noun* [*pl.*] people who are disabled विकलांग या अपंग व्यक्ति *The hotel has improved facilities for the disabled.*

**disadvantage** /ˌdɪsəd'vɑ:ntɪdʒ ˌडिसड्'व़ान्टिज् / *noun* [C] **1** something that may make you less successful than other people प्रतिकूल बात, घाटे की

बात, सफलता या उन्नति में बाधक *Your qualifications are good but your main disadvantage is your lack of experience.* **2** something that is not good or that causes problems परेशानी की बात या हानि ○ *What are the advantages and disadvantages of nuclear power?* ✪ विलोम **advantage**

IDM **put sb/be at a disadvantage** to put sb/be in a situation where he/she/you may be less successful than other people किसी बात के विषय में, अन्य व्यक्तियों की तुलना में घाटे में रहना या प्रतिकूल स्थिति में होना *The fact that you don't speak the language will put you at a disadvantage in France.*
**to sb's disadvantage** (*formal*) not good or helpful for sb हानिकर, असुविधापूर्ण, अलाभकारी *The agreement will be to your disadvantage—don't accept it.*

**disadvantaged** /ˌdɪsədˈvɑːntɪdʒd ˌडिसड्ˈवान्टिज्ड्/ *adj.* in a bad social or economic situation; poor सामाजिक या आर्थिक दृष्टि से दुर्बल; ग़रीब *extra help for the most disadvantaged members of society*

**disadvantageous** /ˌdɪsædvænˈteɪdʒəs ˌडिसैड्वैन्ˈटेजस्/ *adj.* causing sb to be in a worse situation compared to other people अन्य व्यक्तियों की तुलना में अधिक प्रतिकूलताग्रस्त

**disagree** /ˌdɪsəˈɡriː ˌडिसˈग्री/ *verb* [I] **1 disagree (with sb/sth) (about/on sth)** to have a different opinion from sb/sth; to not agree (किसी से) अलग राय रखना या होना; सहमत न होना *They strongly disagreed with my idea.* **2** to be different मेल न खाना *These two sets of statistics disagree.* ✪ विलोम **agree**

PHR V **disagree with sb** (used about sth you have eaten or drunk) to make you feel ill; to have a bad effect on you (खाने या पीने की चीज़ का) हज़म न होना; बुरा असर होना

**disagreeable** /ˌdɪsəˈɡriːəbl ˌडिसˈग्रीअबल्/ *adj.* (*formal*) unpleasant अप्रिय, अरुचिकर ✪ विलोम **agreeable** ▶ **disagreeably** /-əbli -अब्लि/ *adv.* अप्रिय रूप से, असहमत होते हुए

**disagreement** /ˌdɪsəˈɡriːmənt ˌडिसˈग्रीमन्ट्/ *noun* [C, U] **disagreement (with sb) (about/on/over sth)** a situation in which people have a different opinion about sth and often also argue किसी विषय में लोगों की राय का अलग-अलग होना, मतभेद या मतभिन्नता, असहमति *It's normal for couples to* ***have disagreements****.* ○ *Meena resigned after a disagreement with her boss.* ✪ विलोम **agreement**

**disallow** /ˌdɪsəˈlaʊ ˌडिसˈलाउ/ *verb* [T] to not allow or accept sth न मानना या स्वीकार करना, स्वीकृति न देना *The goal was disallowed because the player was offside.*

**disappear** /ˌdɪsəˈpɪə(r) ˌडिसˈपिअ(र्)/ *verb* [I] **1** to become impossible to see or to find अदृश्य हो जाना, गायब हो जाना, खो जाना, मिल न पाना *He walked away and disappeared into a crowd of people.* **2** to stop existing लुप्त हो जाना *Plant and animal species are disappearing at an alarming rate.* ✪ पर्याय **vanish** ✪ विलोम **appear** ▶ **disappearance** *noun* [C, U] अदृश्यता, अंतर्धान होना *The mystery of her disappearance was never solved.*

**disappoint** /ˌdɪsəˈpɔɪnt ˌडिसˈपॉइन्ट्/ *verb* [T] to make sb sad because what he/she had hoped for has not happened or is less good, interesting, etc. then he/she had hoped (किसी को) निराश करना, हताश करना *I'm sorry to disappoint you but I'm afraid you haven't won the prize.*

**disappointed** /ˌdɪsəˈpɔɪntɪd ˌडिसˈपॉइन्टिड्/ *adj.* **disappointed (about/at sth); disappointed (in/with sb/sth); disappointed that...** sad because you/sb/sth did not succeed or because sth was not as good, interesting, etc. as you had hoped (विफलता या आशा के अनुरूप न होने के कारण) निराश *Sourav was deeply disappointed at not being chosen for the team.* ○ *We were disappointed with our hotel.*

**disappointing** /ˌdɪsəˈpɔɪntɪŋ ˌडिसˈपॉइन्टिङ्/ *adj.* making you feel sad because sth was not as good, interesting, etc. as you had hoped निराशाजनक, निराशापूर्ण *It has been a disappointing year for the company.* ▶ **disappointingly** *adv.* निराशाजनक रीति से

**disappointment** /ˌdɪsəˈpɔɪntmənt ˌडिसˈपॉइन्ट्मन्ट्/ *noun* **1** [U] the state of being disappointed निराशा ***To his great disappointment*** *he failed to get the job.* **2** [C] **a disappointment (to sb)** a person or thing that disappoints you निराश करने वाला व्यक्ति या वस्तु *She has suffered many disappointments in her career.*

**disapproval** /ˌdɪsəˈpruːvl ˌडिसˈप्रूवल्/ *noun* [U] a feeling that sth is bad or that sb is behaving badly अस्वीकृति (बुरा होने के कारण) *She shook her head* ***in disapproval****.*

**disapprove** /ˌdɪsəˈpruːv ˌडिसˈप्रूव्/ *verb* [I] **disapprove (of sb/sth)** to think that sb/sth is bad, foolish, etc. (किसी बात को) अनुचित समझना, नापसंद करना *His parents strongly disapproved of him leaving college before he had finished his course.* ▶ **disapproving** *adj.* अस्वीकृतिसूचक, नापसंदगी वाला *After he had told the joke there was a disapproving silence.* ▶ **disapprovingly** *adv.* नापसंद करते हुए *Dinesh frowned disapprovingly when I lit a cigarette.*

**disarm** /dɪsˈɑːm डिस्ˈआम्/ *verb* **1** [T] to take weapons away from sb किसी से हथियार ले लेना, किसी को निहत्था (या निःशस्त्र) कर देना *The police caught and disarmed the terrorists.* **2** [I] (used about a country) to reduce the number of weapons it has (देश) हथियारों की संख्या में कमी करना **3** [T] to make sb feel less angry (किसी का) क्रोध शांत करना *Jyoti could always disarm the teachers with a smile.*

**disarmament** /dɪsˈɑːməmənt डिस्ˈआममन्ट्/ *noun* [U] reducing the number of weapons that a country has निःशस्त्रीकरण *nuclear disarmament*

**disassociate** = **dissociate**

**disaster** /dɪˈzɑːstə(r) डिˈज़ास्ट(र्)/ *noun* **1** [C] an event that causes a lot of harm or damage महाविनाश, तबाही *earthquakes, floods and other natural disasters* **2** [C, U] a terrible situation or event घोर विपत्ति, महाविपदा *This year's lack of rain could **spell disaster** for the region.* **3** [C, U] (*informal*) a complete failure पूर्णतया विफल प्रयास *The school play was an absolute disaster. Everything went wrong.* ▶ **disastrously** *adv.* पूर्ण विफलता के साथ, पूर्णतया विफल होते हुए *the plan went disastrously wrong.*

**disastrous** /dɪˈzɑːstrəs डिˈज़ास्ट्रस्/ *adj.* terrible, harmful or failing completely अनर्थकारी *Our mistake had disastrous results.*

**disband** /dɪsˈbænd डिस्ˈबैन्ड्/ *verb* [I, T] to stop existing as a group; to separate विघटित हो जाना या कर देना; अलग-अलग हो जाना या कर देना

**disbelief** /ˌdɪsbɪˈliːf ˌडिस्बिˈलीफ़्/ *noun* [U] the feeling of not believing sb/sth अविश्वास, शंका *'It can't be true!' he shouted **in disbelief**.*

**disbelieve** /ˌdɪsbɪˈliːv ˌडिस्बिˈलीव़्/ *verb* [T] to think that sth is not true or that sb is not telling the truth (किसी बात या व्यक्ति में) विश्वास न करना, अविश्वास करना *I have no reason to disbelieve her.* ✪ विलोम **believe**

**disc** (*AmE* **disk**) /dɪsk डिस्क्/ *noun* [C] **1** a round flat object तश्तरी, तवा, गोल सपाट वस्तु **2** = **disk** **3** one of the pieces of thin strong material (**cartilage**) between the bones in your back रीढ़ की हड्डियों के बीच का पतला मज़बूत पदार्थ

**discard** /dɪsˈkɑːd डिस्ˈकाड्/ *verb* [T] (*formal*) to throw sth away because it is not useful (बेकार समझकर) फेंक देना

**discern** /dɪˈsɜːn डिˈसन्/ *verb* [T] to see or notice sth with difficulty कठिनाई से किसी वस्तु को देख या पहचान पाना *I discerned a note of anger in his voice.* ▶ **discernible** *adj.* दृश्य, दृष्टिगोचर *The shape of a house was just discernible through the mist.*

**discerning** /dɪˈsɜːnɪŋ डिˈसनिङ्/ *adj.* able to recognize the quality of sb/sth विवेकशील, गुणवत्ता ग्राही *The discerning music lover will appreciate the excellence of this recording.*

**discharge**[1] /dɪsˈtʃɑːdʒ डिस्ˈचाज्/ *verb* [T] **1** to send sth out (a liquid, gas, etc.) (द्रव, गैस आदि को) छोड़ना *Smoke and fumes are discharged from the factory.* **2** to allow sb officially to leave; to send sb away (अस्पताल आदि से) छुट्टी देना; (किसी को) बाहर या दूर भेज देना या मुक्त कर देना *to discharge sb from hospital* **3** to do sth that you have to do निर्धारित काम करना *to discharge a duty/task*

**discharge**[2] /ˈdɪstʃɑːdʒ ˈडिस्चाज्/ *noun* [C, U] **1** the action of sending sb/sth out or away बाहर या दूर भेजने की क्रिया, निकास या बहाव, मुक्ति या छुट्टी *The discharge of oil from the leaking tanker could not be prevented.* **2** a substance that has come out of somewhere स्राव, (कहीं से) निकला हुआ पदार्थ *yellowish discharge from a wound*

**disciple** /dɪˈsaɪpl डिˈसाइप्ल्/ *noun* [C] a person who follows a teacher, especially a religious one शिष्य, चेला, अनुयायी

**disciplinary** /ˌdɪsəˈplɪnəri ˌडिसˈप्लिनरि/ *adj.* connected with punishment for breaking rules नियमभंग के लिए दंडित करने से संबंधित; अनुशासनिक

**discipline**[1] /ˈdɪsəplɪn ˈडिसप्लिन्/ *noun* **1** [U] the practice of training people to obey rules and behave well नियम-पालन और सदाचरण की शिक्षा, अनुशासन *A good teacher must be able to **maintain discipline** in the classroom.* **2** [U] the practice of training your mind and body so that you control your actions and obey rules; a way of doing this अनुशासन, मर्यादा, मन या स्वभाव पर नियंत्रण *It takes a lot of **self-discipline** to study for ten hours a day.* **3** [C] a subject of study; a type of sporting event अध्ययन का विषय; ज्ञान-विज्ञान की शाखा; एक प्रकार की खेल-प्रतियोगिता *Hemant's a good all-round athlete, but the long jump is his strongest discipline.*

**discipline**[2] /ˈdɪsəplɪn ˈडिसप्लिन्/ *verb* [T] **1** to train sb to obey and to behave in a controlled way (किसी को) अनुशासित करना, नियंत्रित आचरण का प्रशिक्षण देना *You should discipline yourself to practise the piano every morning.* **2** to punish sb दंड देना

**disc jockey** = **DJ**

**disclaim** /dɪsˈkleɪm डिस्ˈक्लेम्/ *verb* [T] to say that you do not have sth किसी वस्तु को रखने या कोई काम करने से इनकार करना या किसी बात को मानने से इनकार करना *to disclaim responsibility/knowledge* ✪ पर्याय **deny**

**disclose** /dɪsˈkləʊz डिस्ˈक्लोज़्/ *verb* [T] (*formal*) to tell sth to sb or to make sth known publicly किसी को कोई बात बताना या सार्वजनिक रूप से प्रकट करना *The newspapers did not disclose the victim's name.*

**disclosure** /dɪsˈkləʊʒə(r) डिस्ˈक्लोश(र्)/ *noun* [C, U] making sth known; the facts that are made known प्रकटीकरण; प्रकट की गई बात *the disclosure of secret information* ○ *He resigned following disclosures about his private life.*

**disco** /ˈdɪskəʊ ˈडिस्को/ *noun* [C] (*pl.* **discos**) (*old-fashioned*) a place, party, etc. where people dance to pop music स्थान, पार्टी आदि जहाँ पॉप संगीत पर लोग नाचते हैं; डिस्को *Are you going to the college disco?* ➪ **club[1] 2** देखिए।

**discolour** (*AmE* **discolor**) /dɪsˈkʌlə(r) डिस्ˈकल(र्)/ *verb* [I, T] to change or to make sth change colour (often by the effect of light, age or dirt) रंग बिगड़ना या बिगाड़ना (प्रायः प्रकाश पड़ने से, बढ़ती आयु या गंदगी के कारण)

**discomfort** /dɪsˈkʌmfət डिस्ˈकम्फ़ट्/ *noun* [U] **1** a slight feeling of pain बे-आरामी, परेशानी *There may be some discomfort after the operation.* ✪ विलोम **comfort** **2** a feeling of embarrassment उलझन, शर्म *I could sense Jatin's discomfort when I asked him about his job.*

**disconcert** /ˌdɪskənˈsɜːt ˌडिस्कन्ˈसट्/ *verb* [T] (*usually passive*) to make sb feel confused or worried (किसी के) चित को विक्षुब्ध कर देना *She was disconcerted when everyone stopped talking and looked at her.* ▸ **disconcerting** *adj.* विक्षोभकारी ▸ **disconcertingly** *adv.* विक्षोभकारी रीति से

**disconnect** /ˌdɪskəˈnekt ˌडिसक्ˈनेक्ट्/ *verb* [T] **1** to stop a supply of water, gas or electricity going to a piece of equipment or a building (किसी भवन या उपकरण की) पानी, गैस या बिजली की आपूर्ति काटना **2** to separate sth from sth (किसी को किसी से) अलग करना *The brake doesn't work because the cable has become disconnected from the lever.*

**disconsolate** /dɪsˈkɒnsələt डिस्ˈकॉन्सलट्/ *adj.* extremely unhappy, disappointed and sad beyond comforting मायूस, निराश *The disconsolate players left for home without a trophy.* ✪ पर्याय **dejected** ▸ **disconsolately** /-tli -ट्लि/ *adv.* मायूसी से

**discontent** /ˌdɪskənˈtent ˌडिस्कन्ˈटेन्ट्/ (*also* **discontentment** /ˌdɪskənˈtentmənt ˌडिस्कन्ˈटेन्ट्मन्ट्/) *noun* [U] the state of being unhappy with sth असंतोष *The management could sense growing discontent among the staff.* ▸ **discontented** *adj.* असंतुष्ट *to be/feel discontented*

**discontinue** /ˌdɪskənˈtɪnjuː ˌडिस्कन्ˈटिन्यू/ *verb* [T] (*formal*) to stop sth or stop producing sth (किसी को) रोक देना या (किसी वस्तु का) उत्पादन बंद कर देना

**discord** /ˈdɪskɔːd ˈडिस्कॉड्/ *noun* (*formal*) [U] disagreement or argument असहमति, अवज्ञा या विवाद, झगड़ा

**discordant** /dɪsˈkɔːdənt डिस्ˈकॉडन्ट्/ *adj.* that spoils a general feeling of agreement बेमेल, असंगत *Her criticism was the only discordant note in the discussion.*

**discount[1]** /ˈdɪskaʊnt ˈडिस्काउन्ट्/ *noun* [C, U] a lower price than usual; reduction सामान्य से कम दाम; छूट *Staff get 20% discount on all goods.*

**discount[2]** /dɪsˈkaʊnt डिस्ˈकाउन्ट्/ *verb* [T] to consider sth not true or not important (किसी बात को) असत्य या महत्त्वहीन मानना, नगण्य समझना (किसी बात पर) ध्यान न देना *I think we can discount that idea. It's just not practical.*

**discourage** /dɪsˈkʌrɪdʒ डिस्ˈकरिज्/ *verb* [T] **discourage sb (from doing sth)** to stop sb doing sth, especially by making him/her realize that it would not be successful or a good idea (किसी व्यक्ति को) निरुत्साहित करना (यह समझाते हुए कि सफलता नहीं मिलेगी) *I tried to discourage Jai from giving up his job.* ○ *Don't let these little problems discourage you.* ✪ विलोम **encourage** ▸ **discouraged** *adj.* निरुत्साहित *After failing the exam again Pavan felt very discouraged.* ▸ **discouraging** *adj.* निरुत्साहित करते हुए *Constant criticism can be very discouraging.*

**discouragement** /dɪsˈkʌrɪdʒmənt डिस्ˈकरिज्मन्ट्/ *noun* [C, U] a thing that makes you not want to do sth; the action of trying to stop sb from doing sth निराशाजनक बात; निरुत्साहित करने की क्रिया; निरुत्साहन

**discourse** /ˈdɪskɔːs ˈडिस्कॉस्/ *noun* [C, U] (*formal*) **1** a long and serious discussion of a subject in speech or writing किसी विषय पर गंभीर चर्चा (भाषण या लेख) **2** the use of language in speech and writing in order to produce meaning; language that is studied, usually in order to see how the different parts of a text are connected लिखित और मौखिक माध्यम में भाषा का सार्थक प्रयोग; किसी पाठ (अनुच्छेद) के विभिन्न अंशों की संबद्धता का अध्ययन *discourse analysis*

**discover** /dɪˈskʌvə(r) डि'स्कव़(र्)/ *verb* [T] **1** to find or learn sth that nobody had found or knew before किसी नई बात का पता लगाना या उसे जानना *Scientists are hoping to discover the cause of the epidemic.* **2** to find or learn sth without expecting to or that sb does not want you to find (किसी अज्ञात बात या वस्तु को) अप्रत्याशित रूप से खोज निकालना या उसे जान लेना *The police discovered drugs hidden under the floor.* ▶ **discoverer** *noun* [C] खोजकर्ता *Parkinson's disease was named after its discoverer.*

**discovery** /dɪˈskʌvəri डि'स्कव़रि/ *noun* (*pl.* **discoveries**) **1** [U] the act of finding sth खोज *The discovery of X-rays changed the history of medicine.* **2** [C] something that has been found खोजी गई वस्तु *scientific discoveries*

**discredit** /dɪsˈkredɪt डिस्'क्रेडिट्/ *verb* [T] to make people stop respecting or believing sb/sth (किसी को) बदनाम करना, (किसी की) प्रतिष्ठा घटाना *Journalists are trying to discredit the President by inventing stories about his past life.* ▶ **discredit** *noun* [U] बदनामी, अपयश

**discreet** /dɪˈskriːt डि'स्क्रीट्/ *adj.* careful in what you say and do so as not to cause embarrassment or difficulty for sb सावधान, सतर्क (कि दूसरे को परेशानी न हो) *I don't want anyone to find out about our agreement, so please be discreet.* ▶ **discreetly** *adv.* सावधानी से ➪ **discretion** noun देखिए। ✪ विलोम **indiscreet**

**discrepancy** /dɪsˈkrepənsi डिस'क्रेपन्सि/ *noun* [C, U] (*pl.* **discrepancies**) a difference between two things that should be the same (दो बातों में) असंगति, अंतर *Something is wrong here. There is a discrepancy between these two sets of figures.*

**discretion** /dɪˈskreʃn डि'स्क्रेश्न्/ *noun* [U] **1** the freedom and power to make decisions by yourself विवेक, समझ-बूझ, स्वनिर्णय *You must decide what is best. Use your discretion.* **2** care in what you say and do so as not to cause embarrassment or difficulty for sb समझदारी, बुद्धिमानी *This is confidential but I know I can rely on your discretion.* ➪ **discreet** adjective देखिए।

**IDM at sb's discretion** depending on what sb thinks or decides किसी के विवेकानुसार या इच्छानुसार *Pay increases are awarded at the discretion of the director.*

**discriminate** /dɪˈskrɪmɪneɪt डि'स्क्रिमिनेट्/ *verb* **1** [I] **discriminate (against sb)** to treat one person or group worse than others (किसी के प्रति) भेदभाव करना या रखना *It is illegal to discriminate against any ethnic or religious group.* **2** [I, T] **discriminate (between A and B)** to see or make a difference between two people or things (किन्हीं दो के बीच) भेदभाव करना, (किन्हीं दो वस्तुओं या वर्गों को) अलग-अलग समझना *The immigration law discriminates between political and economic refugees.*

**discriminating** /dɪˈskrɪmɪneɪtɪŋ डि'स्क्रिमिनेटिङ्/ *adj.* able to judge that the quality of sth is good विवेकशील, समझदार *discriminating listeners*

**discrimination** /dɪˌskrɪmɪˈneɪʃn डि,स्क्रिमि'नेश्न्/ *noun* [U] **1 discrimination (against sb)** treating one person or group worse than others भेदभाव करने की क्रिया, भेदभाव का व्यवहार *sexual/racial/religious discrimination* **2** (*formal*) the state of being able to see a difference between two people or things विवेकशीलता, समझदार, अच्छे-बुरे में अंतर करने की योग्यता *discrimination between right and wrong*

**discriminatory** /dɪˈskrɪmɪnətəri डि'स्क्रिमिनट्रि/ *adj.* unfair; treating one person or a group of people worse than others अनुचित; भेदभावपूर्ण *discriminatory practices*

**discursive** /dɪsˈkɜːsɪv डिस्'कसिव़्/ *adj.* (used about a style of writing or speaking) moving from one point to another without any strict structure (भाषण या लेखन) असंबद्ध, विशृंखल, अगठित

**discus** /ˈdɪskəs 'डिस्कस्/ *noun* **1** [C] a heavy round flat object that is thrown as a sport खेल में इस्तेमाल होने वाला चक्का, डिस्कस **2 the discus** [*sing.*] the sport or event of throwing a discus as far as possible चक्का फेंकने का खेल, डिस्कस-थ्रो, चक्का-फेंक

**discuss** /dɪˈskʌs डि'स्कस् / *verb* [T] **discuss sth (with sb)** to talk or write about sth seriously or formally (लेख या भाषण के रूप में) गंभीर विचार-विमर्श करना *I must discuss the matter with my parents before I make a decision.*

**discussion** /dɪˈskʌʃn डि'स्कश्न्/ *noun* [C, U] the process of talking about sth seriously or deeply चर्चा-परिचर्चा, विचार-विमर्श *After much discussion we all agreed to share the cost.* ○ *We had a long discussion about art.*

**IDM under discussion** being talked about चर्चाधीन, परिचर्चा का विषय *Plans to reform the health services are under discussion in Parliament.*

**disdain** /dɪsˈdeɪn डिस्'डेन्/ *noun* [U] the feeling that sb/sth is not good enough to be respected तिरस्कार, अवज्ञा *Monica felt that her boss always* *treated* her ideas *with disdain*. ▶ **disdainful** /-fl -फ़ुल् / *adj.* तिरस्कारपूर्ण ▶ **disdainfully** /-fəli -फ़लि / *adv.* तिरस्कारपूर्वक

**disease** /dɪˈziːz डिˈज़ीज़् / *noun* [C, U] an illness of the body in humans, animals or plants (मनुष्यों, पशुओं या पौधों को) रोग *an infectious/contagious disease* ○ *These children* ***suffer from a*** *rare* ***disease.*** ○ *Rats and flies* ***spread disease.*** ▶ **diseased** *adj.* रोगी, रोगाक्रांत, रुग्ण *His diseased kidney had to be removed.*

NOTE **Illness** और **disease** का समान रूप से प्रयोग हो सकता है। तथापि **disease** उस रोग को कहते हैं जिसका निश्चित नाम हो और निश्चित लक्षण हों। **Diseases** बैक्टीरिया, वायरस आदि के कारण होते हैं तथा प्रायः छूत से फैलते हैं (संक्रामक होते हैं)। **Illness** का तात्पर्य है साधारण रोग या वह अवधि जिसमें कोई व्यक्ति बीमार रहा हो।

**disembark** /ˌdɪsɪmˈbɑːk ˌडिसिम्ˈबाक् / *verb* [I] (*formal*) to get off a ship or an aircraft जलपोत या विमान से नीचे आना या उतरना ✪ विलोम **embark** ▶ **disembarkation** /ˌdɪsˌembɑːˈkeɪʃn ˌडिस्ˌएम्बाˈकेश्न् / *noun* [U] उतार, अवरोहण

**disenchanted** /ˌdɪsɪnˈtʃɑːntɪd ˌडिसिन्ˈचान्टिड् / *adj.* having lost your good opinion of sb/sth किसी व्यक्ति या वस्तु के विषय में अपनी अच्छी धारणा खो देना, मोहभंग होना *Fans are already becoming disenchanted with the new team manager.* ▶ **disenchantment** *noun* [U] मोहभंग

**disenfranchise** /ˌdɪsɪnˈfræntʃaɪz ˌडिसिन्ˈफ़्रैन्चाइज़् / *verb* [T] to take away sb's rights, especially their right to vote किसी को अधिकार से, विशेषतः मताधिकार से वंचित कर देना ✪ विलोम **enfranchise**

**disentangle** /ˌdɪsɪnˈtæŋgl ˌडिसिन्ˈटैङ्गल् / *verb* [T] to free sb/sth that had become connected to sb/sth else in a confused and complicated way किसी लिपटी हुई वस्तु से किसी व्यक्ति या वस्तु को मुक्त करना *My coat got caught up in some bushes and I couldn't disentangle it.* ○ (*figurative*) *Listening to the woman's story, I found it hard to disentangle the truth from the lies.*

**disfigure** /dɪsˈfɪgə(r) डिस्ˈफ़िग(र्) / *verb* [T] to spoil the appearance of sb/sth किसी की शकल को बिगाड़ना, किसी को विरूपित करना *His face was permanently disfigured by the fire.*

**disgrace**[1] /dɪsˈgreɪs डिस्ˈग्रेस् / *noun* **1** [U] the state of not being respected by other people, usually because you have behaved badly सार्वजनिक बदनामी, अपयश *She left the company* ***in disgrace*** *after admitting stealing from colleagues.* **2** [*sing.*] **a disgrace (to sb/sth)** a person or thing that gives a very bad impression and makes you feel sorry and embarrassed (व्यक्ति या वस्तु) कलंक, अपयश की बात *The streets are covered in litter. It's a disgrace!*

**disgrace**[2] /dɪsˈgreɪs डिस्ˈग्रेस् / *verb* [T] to behave badly in a way that makes you or other people feel sorry and embarrassed बदनामी कराना, कलंकित कराना *My brother disgraced himself by starting a fight at the wedding.*

**disgraceful** /dɪsˈgreɪsfl डिस्ˈग्रेस्फ़्ल् / *adj.* very bad, making other people feel sorry and embarrassed लज्जाजनक, शर्मनाक *The behaviour of the team's fans was absolutely disgraceful.* ▶ **disgracefully** /-fəli -फ़लि/ *adv.* लज्जाजनक तरीक़े से

**disgruntled** /dɪsˈgrʌntld डिस्ˈग्रन्ट्ल्ड् / *adj.* disappointed and annoyed निराश और रुष्ट

**disguise**[1] /dɪsˈgaɪz डिस्ˈगाइज़् / *verb* [T] **disguise sb/sth (as sb/sth)** to change the appearance, sound, etc. of sb/sth so that people cannot recognize him/her/it आकृति, आवाज़ आदि को ऐसे बदल लेना या बदल देना कि पहचाना न जा सके *They disguised themselves as fishermen and escaped in a boat.* ○ (*figurative*) *His smile disguised his anger.*

**disguise**[2] /dɪsˈgaɪz डिस्ˈगाइज़् / *noun* [C, U] a thing that you wear or use to change your appearance so that nobody recognizes you छद्मवेश, स्वाँग *She is so famous that she has to go shopping* ***in disguise.*** ○ *The robbers were wearing heavy disguises so that they could not be identified.*

**disgust**[1] /dɪsˈgʌst डिस्ˈगस्ट् / *noun* [U] **disgust (at sth)** a strong feeling of not liking or approving of sth/sb that you feel is unacceptable, or sth/sb that looks, smells, etc. unpleasant प्रबल अनिच्छा, जुगुप्सा *The film was so bad that we walked out* ***in disgust.*** ○ ***Much to my disgust,*** *I found a hair in my soup.*

**disgust**[2] /dɪsˈgʌst डिस्ˈगस्ट्/ *verb* [T] **1** to cause a strong feeling of not liking or approving of sb/sth जुगुप्सा उत्पन्न करना *Cruelty towards animals absolutely disgusts me.* **2** to make sb feel sick विरुचि उत्पन्न करना, घिन पैदा करना *The way he eats with his mouth open completely disgusts me.*

**disgusted** /dɪsˈgʌstɪd डिस्ˈगस्टिड् / *adj.* **disgusted (at/with sb/sth)** not liking or approving of sb/sth at all खीझ होना, झल्लाहट होना *We were disgusted at the standard of service we received.*

**disgusting** /dɪsˈgʌstɪŋ डिस्ˈगस्टिङ् / *adj.* very unpleasant बहुत बुरा, घृणित *What a disgusting smell!*

**disgustingly** /dɪsˈɡʌstɪŋli डिस्ˈगस्टिङ्लि/ *adv.* **1** (often used to show you are jealous of sb/sth) extremely अत्यधिक (प्रायः ईर्ष्यासूचक) *Our neighbours are disgustingly rich.* **2** in a way that you do not like or approve of or that makes you feel sick बुरी तरह से *The kitchen was disgustingly dirty.*

**dish**[1] /dɪʃ डिश्/ *noun* **1** [C] a round container for food that is deeper than a plate रकाबी, तश्तरी, गहरी प्लेट **2** [C] a type of food prepared in a particular way व्यंजन, विशेष प्रकार से बनाया गया पकवान *The **main dish** was curry.* ○ *It was served with a selection of **side dishes**.* **3 the dishes** [*pl.*] all the plates, cups, etc. that you use during a meal भोजन में प्रयुक्त सब तश्तरियाँ, प्याले आदि बर्तन *I'll cook and you can wash the dishes.* **4** = **satellite dish**

**dish**[2] /dɪʃ डिश्/ *verb*

**PHRV dish sth out** (*informal*) to give away a lot of sth भरपूर मात्रा में (कोई वस्तु) देना *to dish out advice*

**dish sth up** (*informal*) to serve food भोजन परोसना

**disheartened** /dɪsˈhɑːtnd डिस्ˈहाट्न्ड्/ *adj.* sad or disappointed दुखी या निराश

**disheartening** /dɪsˈhɑːtnɪŋ डिस्ˈहाट्निङ्/ *adj.* making you lose hope and confidence; causing disappointment आशा और विश्वास को डिगाने वाला; निराशाजनक ✪ विलोम **heartening**

**dishevelled** (*AmE* **disheveled**) /dɪˈʃevld डिˈशेव्ल्ड्/ *adj.* (used about a person's appearance) very untidy (व्यक्ति की शकल, कपड़े, बाल आदि) अस्त-व्यस्त, मैला-कुचैला

**dishonest** /dɪsˈɒnɪst डिस्ˈऑनिस्ट्/ *adj.* that you cannot trust; likely to lie, steal or cheat बेईमान; धोखेबाज़ ✪ विलोम **honest** ▶ **dishonestly** *adv.* बेईमानी से, धोखे से ▶ **dishonesty** *noun* [U] बेईमानी, धोखा

**dishonour**[1] (*AmE* **dishonor**) /dɪsˈɒnə(r) डिस्ˈऑनर्(र्)/ *noun* [U, *sing.*] (*formal*) the state of no longer being respected, especially because you have done sth bad बेइज़्ज़ती, अपयश *Her illegal trading has **brought dishonour on** the company.* ✪ विलोम **honour** ▶ **dishonourable** /-nərəbl -नरबल्/ *adj.* यशोहीन, अपकीर्तिकर ✪ विलोम **honourable**

**dishonour**[2] (*AmE* **dishonor**) /dɪsˈɒnə(r) डिस्ˈऑनर्(र्)/ *verb* [T] (*formal*) to do sth bad that makes people stop respecting you or sb/sth close to you बदनामी लाना, लांछित होना, ग़लत काम करना

**dishwasher** /ˈdɪʃwɒʃə(r) ˈडिश्वॉश(र्)/ *noun* [C] a machine that washes plates, cups, knives, forks, etc. तश्तरियाँ, प्याले आदि धोने की मशीन; डिशवॉशर

**disillusion** /ˌdɪsɪˈluːʒn ˌडिसिˈलूश़न्/ *verb* [T] to destroy sb's belief in or good opinion of sb/sth किसी के विश्वास को तोड़ना, विश्वास-भंग करना ▶ **disillusion** (*also* **disillusionment**) *noun* [U] विश्वास-भंग *I feel increasing disillusion with the government.*

**disillusioned** /ˌdɪsɪˈluːʒnd ˌडिसिˈलूश़्न्ड्/ *adj.* disappointed because sb/sth is not as good as you first thought किसी में प्रतिष्ठित विश्वास के टूटने से निराशाग्रस्त *She's disillusioned with nursing.*

**disinfect** /ˌdɪsɪnˈfekt ˌडिसिन्ˈफ़ैक्ट्/ *verb* [T] to clean sth with a liquid that destroys bacteria किसी वस्तु को द्रव के प्रयोग से रोगाणु-विहीन करना *to disinfect a wound* ▶ **disinfection** *noun* [U] रोगाणुनाशन

**disinfectant** /ˌdɪsɪnˈfektənt ˌडिसिन्ˈफ़ेक्टन्ट्/ *noun* [C, U] a substance that destroys bacteria and is used for cleaning (किसी वस्तु को साफ़ करने के लिए प्रयुक्त) रोगाणुनाशक पदार्थ

**disinherit** /ˌdɪsɪnˈherɪt ˌडिसिन्ˈहेरिट्/ *verb* [T] to prevent sb, especially your son or daughter, from receiving your money or property after your death (किसी को) उत्तराधिकार से वंचित करना ➪ **inherit** देखिए।

**disintegrate** /dɪsˈɪntɪɡreɪt डिस्ˈइन्टिग्रेट्/ *verb* [I] to break into many small pieces टुकड़े-टुकड़े हो जाना, विखंडित होना, विघटित होना *The spacecraft exploded and disintegrated.* ▶ **disintegration** /ˌdɪsˌɪntɪˈɡreɪʃn ˌडिस्ˌइन्टिˈग्रेशन्/ *noun* [U] विखंडन, विघटन *the disintegration of the empire*

**disinterest** /dɪsˈɪntrəst डिस्ˈइन्ट्रस्ट्/ *noun* [U] **1** lack of interest अरुचि, विरुचि, अनिच्छा **2** the fact of not being involved in sth and therefore able to be fair निष्पक्ष, बेलाग, निःस्वार्थ

**disinterested** /dɪsˈɪntrəstɪd डिस्ˈइन्ट्रस्टिड्/ *adj.* fair, not influenced by personal feelings निष्पक्ष, तटस्थ, व्यक्तिगत भावनाओं से अप्रभावित *disinterested advice* ➪ **uninterested** देखिए।

**disjointed** /dɪsˈdʒɔɪntɪd डिस्ˈजॉइन्टिड्/ *adj.* (used especially about ideas, writing or speech) not clearly connected and therefore difficult to follow विश्रृंखलित और इसलिए समझने में कठिन ▶ **disjointedly** *adv.* विश्रृंखलित रूप से

**disk** /dɪsk डिस्क्/ *noun* [C] **1** (*AmE*) = **disc** **2** (*computing*) a flat piece of plastic that stores information for use by a computer कंप्यूटर में प्रयोग के लिए सूचना संचित करने वाली प्लास्टिक निर्मित वस्तु, डिस्क ➪ **floppy disk** और **hard disk** देखिए।

**disk drive** *noun* [C] (*computing*) a piece of electrical equipment that passes information to or from a computer disk एक विद्युत उपकरण जो कंप्यूटर डिस्क में या डिस्क से सूचना हस्तांतरित करता है; डिस्क ड्राइव

**diskette** /dɪsˈket डिस्ˈकेट्/ = **floppy disk**

**dislike**[1] /dɪsˈlaɪk डिस्ˈलाइक्/ *verb* [T] **dislike (doing) sth** to think that sb/sth is unpleasant (किसी व्यक्ति या वस्तु को) नापसंद करना *I really dislike flying.* ○ *What is it that you dislike about living here?* ✪ विलोम **like**

**dislike**[2] /dɪsˈlaɪk डिस्ˈलाइक्/ *noun* [C, U, *sing.*] **(a) dislike (of/for sb/sth)** the feeling of not liking sb/sth नापसंदगी, नफ़रत *He seems to have a strong dislike of hard work.*

IDM **take a dislike to sb/sth** to start disliking sb/sth (किसी व्यक्ति या वस्तु को) नापसंद करने लगना, नापसंदगी की शुरुआत होना *He took an instant dislike to his boss.*

**dislocate** /ˈdɪsləkeɪt ˈडिस्लकेट्/ *verb* [T] to put sth (usually a bone) out of its correct position (किसी वस्तु, प्रायः हड्डी का) अपने स्थान से हट जाना, हटा दिया जाना, जोड़ उखड़ना, उखाड़ना *He dislocated his shoulder during the game.* ▶ **dislocation** /ˌdɪsləˈkeɪʃn ˌडिस्लˈकेश्न्/ *noun* [C, U] विस्थापन, स्थान-भ्रंश, उखड़ा जोड़

**dislodge** /dɪsˈlɒdʒ डिस्ˈलॉज्/ *verb* [T] **dislodge sth (from sth)** to make sb/sth move from its correct fixed position (किसी व्यक्ति या वस्तु को) अपनी सही जगह या पद से निकाल बाहर करना *The strong wind dislodged several tiles from the roof.*

**disloyal** /dɪsˈlɔɪəl डिस्ˈलॉइअल्/ *adj.* **disloyal (to sb/sth)** not supporting your friends, family, country etc.; doing sth that will harm them (मित्र, परिवार, देश आदि के प्रति) निष्ठाहीन, बेवफ़ा; बेवफ़ाई करने वाला *It was disloyal to your friends to repeat their conversation to Prem.* ✪ विलोम **loyal** ▶ **disloyalty** /-ˈlɔɪəlti -ˈलॉइअल्टि/ *noun* [C, U] (*pl.* **disloyalties**) बेवफ़ाई, अनिष्ठा

**dismal** /ˈdɪzməl ˈडिज़्मल्/ *adj.* **1** causing or showing sadness; depressing दुखद या दुखभरा; निराशाजनक *dismal surroundings* ✪ पर्याय **miserable** **2** (*informal*) of low quality; poor निम्नस्तरीय; घटिया *a dismal standard of work*

**dismantle** /dɪsˈmæntl डिस्ˈमैन्ट्ल्/ *verb* [T] to take sth to pieces; to separate sth into the parts it is made from (किसी वस्तु) को विखंडित या टुकड़े-टुकड़े कर देना; (किसी मशीन आदि के) पुरज़े खोलना *The photographer dismantled his equipment and packed it away.*

**dismay** /dɪsˈmeɪ डिस्ˈमे/ *noun* [U] a strong feeling of disappointment and sadness प्रबल निराशा और व्याकुलता *I realized **to my dismay** that I was going to miss the plane.* ▶ **dismay** *verb* [T] (*usually passive*) हतोत्साह करना *I was dismayed to hear that my old school had been knocked down.*

**dismember** /dɪsˈmembə(r) डिस्ˈमेम्ब(र्)/ *verb* [T] to cut a dead body into pieces शव के टुकड़े करना

**dismiss** /dɪsˈmɪs डिस्ˈमिस्/ *verb* [T] **1 dismiss sb/sth (as sth)** to decide not to think about sth/sb किसी बात को ख़ारिज कर देना, सोच-विचार के लायक़ न मानना *He dismissed the idea as nonsense.* **2 dismiss sb (from sth)** to order an employee to leave his/her job (किसी व्यक्ति को) नौकरी से निकाल देना, बरख़ास्त कर देना *He was dismissed for refusing to obey orders.* NOTE **Dismiss** की तुलना में **fire** और **sack** कम औपचारिक हैं। **3** to send sb away विसर्जित कर देना, छुट्टी दे देना, जाने देना *The lesson ended and the teacher dismissed the class.* **4** (used in law) to say that a trial or court case should not continue, usually because there is not enough evidence (क़ानून में) मामला ख़ारिज कर देना, पर्याप्त सबूत के अभाव में मामले को समाप्त कर देना *The case was dismissed.* ▶ **dismissal** /dɪsˈmɪsl डिस्ˈमिसल्/ *noun* [C, U] बरख़ास्तगी, ख़ारिजी, सेवानिवृत्ति, अस्वीकृति, सेवामुक्ति *She was hurt at their dismissal of her offer of help.* ○ *a case of unfair dismissal*

**dismissive** /dɪsˈmɪsɪv डिस्ˈमिसिव्/ *adj.* **dismissive (of sb/sth)** saying or showing that you think that sb/sth is not worth considering seriously (किसी व्यक्ति या वस्तु के प्रति) उपेक्षाशील, उपेक्षाकारी, अगंभीर, (किसी व्यक्ति, वस्तु को) सोच-विचार के लायक न मानने वाला *The boss was dismissive of all the efforts I had made.* ▶ **dismissively** *adv.* उपेक्षापूर्वक

**dismount** /dɪsˈmaʊnt डिस्ˈमाउन्ट्/ *verb* [I] to get off sth that you ride (a horse, a bicycle, etc.) (घोड़े, साइकिल आदि से) नीचे उतरना ✪ विलोम **mount**

**disobedient** /ˌdɪsəˈbiːdiənt ˌडिसˈबीडिअन्ट्/ *adj.* refusing or failing to obey आदेश को मानने से इनकार करने वाला या आदेश का पालन न कर सकने वाला, अवज्ञाकारी ✪ विलोम **obedient** ▶ **disobedience** *noun* [U] अवज्ञा

**disobey** /ˌdɪsəˈbeɪ ˌडिसˈबे/ *verb* [I, T] to refuse to do what you are told to do आदेश के पालन से इनकार करना, आदेश को न मानना *He was punished for disobeying orders.* ✪ विलोम **obey**

**disorder** /dɪsˈɔːdə(r) डिस्ˈऑड(र्)/ *noun* **1** [U] an untidy, confused or badly organized state अव्यवस्था, गड़बड़ी *His financial affairs are **in** complete **disorder**.* ✪ विलोम **order** **2** [U] violent behaviour by a large number of people उपद्रव,

दंगा *Disorder broke out on the streets of the capital.* **3** [C, U] an illness in which the mind or part of the body is not working properly मन या शरीर का विकार, रोग *treatment for **eating disorders** such as anorexia* ○ *a kind of **mental disorder***

**disordered** /dɪsˈɔːdəd डिस्ˈऑडड्/ *adj.* untidy, confused or badly organized अव्यवस्थित, गड़बड़

**disorderly** /dɪsˈɔːdəli डिस्ˈऑडलि/ *adj.* **1** (used about people or behaviour) out of control and violent; causing trouble in public (व्यक्ति या आचरण) अनियंत्रित और हिंसक; उपद्रवी, दंगाई *They were arrested for being **drunk and disorderly**.* **2** untidy अस्त-व्यस्त, फूहड़ ✪ विलोम **orderly**

**disorganization** (*also* **-isation**) /dɪsˌɔːɡənaɪˈzeɪʃn डिस्ˌऑगनाइˈज़ेश्न्/ *noun* [U] a lack of careful planning and order योजनाबद्धता और व्यवस्था का अभाव, कुव्यवस्था, बदइंतज़ामी ✪ विलोम **organization**

**disorganized** (*also* **-ised**) /dɪsˈɔːɡənaɪzd डिस्ˈऑगनाइज़्ड्/ *adj.* badly planned; not able to plan well कुव्यवस्थित; योजना निर्माण या सुनियोजन में असमर्थ ✪ विलोम **organized**

**disorientate** /dɪsˈɔːriənteɪt डिस्ˈऑरिअन्टेट्/ (*AmE* **disorient** /dɪsˈɔːrient डिस्ˈऑरिअन्ट्/) *verb* [T] to make sb become confused about where he/she is दिशा के विषय में भ्रमित हो जाना, कर देना *The road signs were very confusing and I soon became disorientated.* ▶ **disorientation** /dɪsˌɔːriənˈteɪʃn डिस्ˌऑरिअन्ˈटेशन्/ *noun* [U] दिग्-भ्रांति, स्थिति भ्रांति (भौतिकी में) अपन्यास

**disown** /dɪsˈəʊn डिस्ˈओन्/ *verb* [T] to say that you no longer want to be connected with or responsible for sb/sth (किसी को) अपनाने से इनकार कर देना *When he was arrested, his family disowned him.*

**disparage** /dɪˈspærɪdʒ डिˈस्पैरिज्/ *verb* [T] (*formal*) to talk about sb/sth in a critical way; to say that sb/sth is of little value or importance (किसी की) निंदा करना; (किसी को) तुच्छ समझना ▶ **disparaging** *adj.* निंदात्मक, अपमानजनक *disparaging remarks*

**disparate** /ˈdɪspərət ˈडिस्परट्/ *adj.* (*formal*) **1** consisting of people or things that are very different from each other in character or quality व्यक्ति या वस्तु जो आचरण और गुण में बेहद भिन्न हों *disparate groups of people/individuals* **2** (of two or more things) so markedly different/dissimilar from each other that they cannot be compared (दो या अधिक वस्तु) एक दूसरे से अतुल्य रूप से भिन्न या असमान *disparate ideas*

**disparity** /dɪˈspærəti डिˈस्पैरटि/ *noun* [U, C] (*pl.* **disparities**) (*formal*) a difference, especially one that is caused by unfair treatment असमानता, विषमता (विशेषतः अनुचित व्यवहार के फलस्वरूप)

**dispatch** (*BrE* **despatch**) /dɪˈspætʃ डिˈस्पैच्/ *verb* [T] (*formal*) to send sb/sth to a place (किसी व्यक्ति या वस्तु को कहीं) भेजना *Your order will be dispatched within seven days.*

**dispel** /dɪˈspel डिˈस्पेल्/ *verb* [T] (**dispelling**; **dispelled**) to make sth, especially a feeling or a belief, disappear (शंका आदि को) दूर कर देना *His reassuring words dispelled all her fears.*

**dispensable** /dɪˈspensəbl डिˈस्पेन्सबल्/ *adj.* not necessary जो सर्वथा आवश्यक या अपरिहार्य न हो, परिहार्य *I suppose I'm dispensable. Anybody could do my job.* ✪ विलोम **indispensable**

**dispensary** /dɪˈspensəri डिˈस्पेन्सरि/ *noun* [C] (*pl.* **dispensaries**) **1** a place in a hospital, shop, etc. where medicines are prepared for patients अस्पताल का वह स्थान जहाँ रोगियों के लिए दवाएँ तैयार की जाती हैं; डिस्पेंसरी, दवाघर **2** (*old-fashioned*) a place where patients are treated, especially one run by a charity हस्पताल, औषद्यालय (विशेषतः धर्मार्थ)

**dispense** /dɪˈspens डिˈस्पेन्स्/ *verb* [T] (*formal*) to give or provide people with sth किसी को कोई वस्तु मुहैया या उपलब्ध कराना *a machine that dispenses hot and cold drinks*

**PHRV** **dispense with sb/sth** to get rid of sb/sth that is not necessary अनपेक्षित व्यक्ति या वस्तु का परित्याग करना, से पीछा छुड़ाना *They decided to dispense with luxuries and live a simple life.*

**dispenser** /dɪˈspensə(r) डिˈस्पेन्स(र्)/ *noun* [C] a machine or container from which you can get sth मशीन या डिब्बा जिससे आपको अभीष्ट वस्तु मिलती है; डिस्पेंसर *a cash dispenser at a bank* ○ *a soap/tape dispenser* ➪ **stationery** पर चित्र देखिए।

**dispersal** /dɪˈspɜːsl डिˈस्पसल्/ *noun* [U, C] (*written*) the process of sending sb/sth in different directions; the process of spreading sth over a wide area व्यक्तियों या वस्तुओं को तितर-बितर कर देने की प्रक्रिया; छितराने या बिखेरने की प्रक्रिया, छितराव, बिखराव *police trained in crowd dispersal* ○ *the dispersal of seeds*

**disperse** /dɪˈspɜːs डिˈस्पस्/ *verb* [I, T] to separate and go in different directions; to make sb/sth do this बिखर जाना, विसर्जित हो जाना; बिखरा देना, विसर्जित कर देना *When the meeting was over, the group dispersed.* ○ *The police arrived and quickly dispersed the crowd.*

**dispersion** /dɪˈspɜːʃn डिˈस्पश्न्/ *noun* [U] (*technical*) the process by which people or things are spread over a wide area आबादी या चीज़ों के दूर-दूर तक फैलने या विकीर्ण होने की प्रक्रिया, बिखराव, प्रकीर्णन, विकीर्णन, परिक्षेपण *population dispersion* ○ *the dispersion of light*

**dispirited** /dɪˈspɪrɪtɪd डिˈस्पिरिटिड्/ *adj.* having lost confidence or hope; depressed निरुत्साहित; विषण्ण, खिन्न

**displace** /dɪsˈpleɪs डिस्ˈप्लेस्/ *verb* [T] **1** to remove and take the place of sb/sth किसी का स्थान ले लेना या छीन लेना *Sampras was finally displaced as the top tennis player in the world.* **2** to force sb/sth to move from the usual or correct place किसी को अपनी जगह छोड़ने के लिए बाध्य करना; विस्थापित करना *refugees displaced by the war* ▶ **displacement** *noun* [U] विस्थापन

**display[1]** /dɪˈspleɪ डिˈस्प्ले/ *verb* [T] **1** to put sth in a place where people will see it or where it will attract attention किसी वस्तु को ऐसे स्थान पर रखना कि लोग उसे देख सकें या उस ओर उनका ध्यान आकृष्ट हो, किसी वस्तु को प्रदर्शित करना *Posters for the concert were displayed throughout the city.* **2** to show signs of sth (for example a feeling or a quality) गुण या भाव का प्रदर्शन करना *She displayed no interest in the discussion.*

**display[2]** /dɪˈspleɪ डिˈस्प्ले/ *noun* [C] **1** an arrangement of things in a public place for people to see सार्वजनिक स्थान पर वस्तुओं का व्यवस्थित प्रदर्शन *a window display in a shop* **2** a public event in which sth is shown in action किसी वस्तु की क्रियाशीलता का सार्वजनिक प्रदर्शन *a firework display* **3** behaviour that shows a particular feeling or quality विशिष्ट भाव या गुण का प्रदर्शन *a sudden display of aggression* **4** (*computing*) words, pictures, etc. that can be seen on a computer screen कंप्यूटर स्क्रीन पर दिखाई पड़ने वाला शब्द, चित्र आदि

IDM **on display** in a place where people will see it and where it will attract attention (वस्तुएँ) प्रदर्शनार्थ (कि लोग उन्हें देखें) *Treasures from the sunken ship were put on display at the museum.*

**displease** /dɪsˈpliːz डिस्ˈप्लीज़्/ *verb* [T] (*formal*) to annoy sb or to make sb angry or upset किसी को रुष्ट या नाराज़ करना ▶ **displeased** *adj.* अप्रसन्न, रुष्ट ✪ विलोम **pleased**

**displeasure** /dɪsˈpleʒə(r) डिस्ˈप्लेश(र्)/ *noun* [U] (*formal*) the feeling of being annoyed or not satisfied रोष, नाराज़गी *I wrote to express my displeasure at not having been informed sooner.*

**disposable** /dɪˈspəʊzəbl डिˈस्पोज़ब्ल्/ *adj.* made to be thrown away after being used once or for a short time एक बार प्रयोग के बाद फेंकने योग्य *a disposable razor/syringe*

**disposal** /dɪˈspəʊzl डिˈस्पोज़्ल्/ *noun* [U] the act of getting rid of sth or throwing sth away किसी वस्तु से मुक्ति पाने या उसे फेंक देने की क्रिया; निपटान *the disposal of dangerous chemical waste* ○ *bomb disposal*

IDM **at sb's disposal** available for sb to use at any time सुविधानुसार उपयोगार्थ

**dispose** /dɪˈspəʊz डिˈस्पोज़्/ *verb*

PHR V **dispose of sb/sth** to throw away or sell sth; to get rid of sb/sth that you do not want किसी वस्तु को फेंक या बेच देना, निपटाना; अनचाही वस्तु से छुटकारा पाना

**disposition** /ˌdɪspəˈzɪʃn ˌडिस्पˈज़िश्न्/ *noun* **1** [C] (*usually sing.*) the natural qualities of a person's character किसी व्यक्ति के स्वभाव की प्रकृत विशेषताएँ, स्ववृत्ति, स्वभाव, मिज़ाज *to have a cheerful disposition* ○ *people of a nervous disposition* **2** [C] (*usually sing.*) **a disposition to/towards sth; a disposition to do sth** (*formal*) a usual way of behaving प्रवृत्ति, रुख *to have/show a disposition towards acts of violence* **3** [C] (*usually sing.*) (*formal*) the way sth is put or arranged in a place व्यवस्था **4** [C, U] (*law*) a formal act of giving property or money to sb (किसी को) संपत्ति या धन की सुपुर्दगी

**disproportionate** /ˌdɪsprəˈpɔːʃənət ˌडिस्प्रˈपॉशनट्/ *adj.* **disproportionate (to sth)** too large or too small when compared to sth else अन्य वस्तु की तुलना में बहुत बड़ा या बहुत छोटा; असंगत, अनुपातहीन, बेमेल ▶ **disproportionately** *adv.* बेमेलपन से, असंगत रूप से

**disprove** /ˌdɪsˈpruːv ˌडिस्ˈप्रूव्/ *verb* [T] to show that sth is not true किसी बात को असत्य सिद्ध करना

**dispute[1]** /ˈdɪspjuːt; dɪˈspjuːt ˈडिस्प्यूट्; डिˈस्प्यूट्/ *noun* [C, U] **(a) dispute (between A and B) (over/about sth)** a disagreement or argument between two people, groups or countries (दो व्यक्तियों, समूहों या देशों के बीच) विवाद, झगड़ा *There was some dispute between Sameer and his boss about whose fault it was.* ○ *a pay dispute*

IDM **in dispute** in a situation of arguing or being argued about विवादी या विवादग्रस्त होने की स्थिति *He is in dispute with the tax office about how much he should pay.*

**dispute²** /dɪˈspjuːt डिˈस्प्यूट्/ *verb* [T] to argue about sth and to question if it is true or right विवाद या बहस करना, झगड़ा करना *The player disputed the referee's decision.*

**disqualify** /dɪsˈkwɒlɪfaɪ डिस्ˈक्वॉलिफ़ाइ/ *verb* [T] (*pres. part.* **disqualifying;** *3rd person sing. pres.* **disqualifies;** *pt, pp* **disqualified**) **disqualify sb (from sth/doing sth); disqualify sb (for sth)** to officially prevent sb from doing sth or taking part in sth, usually because he/she has broken a rule or law किसी को कोई विशेष काम करने से क़ानूनन रोकना, अयोग्य ठहराना (प्रायः क़ानून भंग का दोषी होने के कारण) *He was disqualified from driving for two years.* ○ *The team were disqualified for cheating.* ▶ **disqualification** /dɪsˌkwɒlɪfɪˈkeɪʃn डिस्ˌक्वॉलिफ़िˈकेश्न्/ *noun* [C, U] अनर्हता, अयोग्यता

**disregard** /ˌdɪsrɪˈgɑːd ˌडिस्रिˈगाड्/ *verb* [T] to take no notice of sb/sth; to treat sth as unimportant किसी की उपेक्षा करना, किसी बात पर ध्यान न देना; किसी बात को महत्त्वहीन या उपेक्षणीय समझना *These are the latest instructions. Please disregard any you received before.* ▶ **disregard** *noun* [U, *sing.*] उपेक्षा **disregard (for sb/sth)** बिना परवाह किए *He rushed into the burning building with complete disregard for his own safety.*

**disrepair** /ˌdɪsrɪˈpeə(r) ˌडिस्रिˈपेअ(र्)/ *noun* [U] the state of being in bad condition because repairs have not been made जीर्ण-शीर्ण अवस्था (मरम्मत के अभाव में) *Over the years the building* ***fell into disrepair****.*

**disreputable** /dɪsˈrepjətəbl डिस्ˈरेप्यटब्ल्/ *adj.* not to be trusted; well known for being bad or dishonest ग़ैर-भरोसेमंद; कुत्सित, बदनाम, कुख्यात, अशोभनीय *disreputable business methods* ✪ विलोम **reputable**

**disrepute** /ˌdɪsrɪˈpjuːt ˌडिस्रिˈप्यूट्/ *noun* [U] the situation when people no longer respect sb/sth बदनामी, कुख्याती *Such unfair decisions* ***bring*** *the legal system* ***into disrepute****.*

**disrespect** /ˌdɪsrɪˈspekt ˌडिस्रिˈस्पेक्ट्/ *noun* [U] **disrespect (for/to sb/sth)** a lack of respect for sb/sth that is shown in what you do or say (किसी के लिए प्रदर्शित) अनादर, अशिष्टता ✪ विलोम **respect** ▶ **disrespectful** /-fl -फ़्ल्/ *adj.* अशिष्ट ✪ विलोम **respectful** ▶ **disrespectfully** /-fəli -फ़लि/ *adv.* अशिष्टतापूर्वक

**disrupt** /dɪsˈrʌpt डिस्ˈरप्ट्/ *verb* [T] to stop sth happening as or when it should (किसी क्रिया को) विच्छिन्न कर देना, विघ्न पैदा करना, विघटन करना *The strike severely disrupted flights to New Delhi.* ▶ **disruption** *noun* [C, U] विच्छिन्नता, बाधा, विदारण, (भूगर्भशास्त्र में) विघटन ▶ **disruptive** /dɪsˈrʌptɪv डिस्ˈरप्टिव्/ *adj.* विच्छेदकारी, बाधक

**dissatisfaction** /ˌdɪsˌsætɪsˈfækʃn ˌडिस्ˌसैटिस्ˈफ़ैक्श्न्/ *noun* [U] **dissatisfaction (with/at sb/sth)** the feeling of not being satisfied or pleased असंतोष, नाराज़गी *There is some dissatisfaction among teachers with the plans for the new exam.* ✪ विलोम **satisfaction**

**dissatisfied** /dɪsˈsætɪsfaɪd डिस्ˈसैटिस्फ़ाइड्/ *adj.* **dissatisfied (with sb/sth)** not satisfied or pleased असंतुष्ट, नाराज़ *complaints from dissatisfied customers* ✪ विलोम **satisfied**

**dissect** /dɪˈsekt डिˈसेक्ट्/ *verb* [T] to cut up a dead body, a plant, etc. in order to study it अध्ययनार्थ शव, पौधे आदि के टुकड़े करना, चीर-फाड़ करना ▶ **dissection** *noun* [C, U] चीर-फाड़

**dissent¹** /dɪˈsent डिˈसेन्ट्/ *noun* [U] (*formal*) disagreement with official or generally agreed ideas or opinions सामान्य धारणा से असहमति *There is some dissent within the Congress Labour Party on these policies.*

**dissent²** /dɪˈsent डिˈसेन्ट्/ *verb* [I] (*formal*) **dissent (from sth)** to have opinions that are different to those that are officially held सामान्य धारणाओं से असहमति प्रकट करना, विसम्मति प्रकट करना, विसम्मत होना ▶ **dissenting** *adj.* असहमति का, विसम्मत

**dissertation** /ˌdɪsəˈteɪʃn ˌडिसˈटेश्न्/ *noun* [C] a long piece of writing on sth that you have studied, especially as part of a university degree पढ़े हुए विषय पर लंबा निबंध, प्रबंध (विशेषतः विश्वविद्यालीय शिक्षा के अंतर्गत) ➪ **thesis** देखिए।

**disservice** /dɪsˈsɜːvɪs डिस्ˈसर्विस्/ *noun* [U, *sing.*] **do (a) disservice to sb/sth** to do sth that harms sb and the opinion other people have of him/her (किसी के लिए) अनिष्टकारक होना, (किसी को) हानि पहुँचाना

**dissident** /ˈdɪsɪdənt ˈडिसिडन्ट्/ *noun* [C] a person who strongly disagrees with and criticizes his/her government, especially in a country where it is dangerous to do this अपनी सरकार की नीतियों का कठोर आलोचक (विशेषतः जहाँ आलोचना करना जोखिम भरा हो) ▶ **dissidence** *noun* [U] विमति, विसम्मति

**dissimilar** /dɪˈsɪmɪlə(r) डिˈसिमिल(र्)/ *adj.* **dissimilar (from/to sb/sth)** not the same; different असदृश; विसदृश, भिन्न *The situation you're in is not dissimilar to mine.* ✪ विलोम **similar**

**dissociate** /dɪˈsəʊʃieɪt डिˈसोशिएट्; -ˈsəʊs-ˈसोस्-/ (*also* **disassociate** /ˌdɪsəˈsəʊʃieɪt ˌडिसˈसोशिएट्; -ˈsəʊs-ˈसोस्/) *verb* [T] **dissociate sb/sth/your self (from sth)** to show that you are not connected with or do not support sb/sth; to show that two things are not connected with each other संबंध-विच्छेद करना या समर्थन न देना; दो वस्तुओं के अलग हो जाने की बात को प्रतिपादित करना *She dissociated herself from the views of the extremists in her party.* ✪ विलोम **associate**

**dissolution** /ˌdɪsəˈluːʃn ˌडिसˈलूश्न् / *noun* [U] the official act of ending a marriage, a business agreement or a parliament वैवाहिक संबंध, व्यापारिक समझौता या संसद का आधिकारिक तौर पर रद्द या भंग होना

**dissolve** /dɪˈzɒlv डिˈज़ॉल्व् / *verb* [I, T] (used about a solid) to become or to make sth become liquid घुलना या घोलना *Sugar dissolves in water.* ○ *Dissolve two tablets in cold water.*

**dissuade** /dɪˈsweɪd डिˈस्वेड् / *verb* [T] **dissuade sb (from doing sth)** to persuade sb not to do sth (किसी को कोई काम करने से) मना करना, रोकना *I tried to dissuade her from spending the money, but she insisted.* ✪ विलोम **persuade**

**distance**[1] /ˈdɪstəns ˈडिसटन्स् / *noun* **1** [C, U] the amount of space between two places or things (दो स्थानों या वस्तुओं के बीच) दूरी *The map tells you the distances between the major cities.* ○ *The house is **within walking distance** of the shops.* **2** [*sing.*] a point that is a long way from sb/sth (किसी से) काफ़ी दूर का स्थान *At this distance I can't read the number on the bus.* ○ *From a distance the village looks quite attractive.*

IDM **in the distance** far away बहुत दूर *I could just see Padma in the distance.*

**keep your distance** to stay away from sb/sth (किसी व्यक्ति या वस्तु से) दूर रहना

**within striking distance** ➪ **strike**[2] देखिए।

**distance**[2] /ˈdɪstəns ˈडिसटन्स् / *verb* [T] **distance yourself from sb/sth** to become less involved or connected with sb/sth (किसी व्यक्ति या वस्तु से) अधिक मेल-जोल न रखना *She was keen to distance herself from the views of her colleagues.*

**distant** /ˈdɪstənt ˈडिसटन्ट् / *adj.* **1** a long way away in space or time स्थान या समय की दृष्टि से काफ़ी दूर *travel to distant parts of the world* ○ *in the not-too-distant future* (= quite soon) **2** (used about a relative) not closely related (संबंधी) दूर का *a distant cousin* **3** not very friendly रूखा, प्रगाढ़तारहित *He has a rather distant manner and it's hard to get to know him well.* **4** seeming to be thinking about sth else प्रकटतः कुछ और सोचते हुए, सूनापन लिए हुए *She had a distant look in her eyes and clearly wasn't listening to me.*

**distaste** /dɪsˈteɪst डिस्ˈटेस्ट् / *noun* [U, *sing.*] not liking sth; the feeling that sb/sth is unpleasant or offends you अरुचि; नाक-भौं सिकोड़ते हुए, नापसंदगी *She looked around the dirty kitchen with distaste.*

**distasteful** /dɪsˈteɪstfl डिस्ˈटेस्टफ़्ल् / *adj.* unpleasant or causing offence अरुचिकर या बुरा लगने वाला *a distasteful remark*

**distend** /dɪˈstend डिˈस्टेन्ड् / *verb* [I, T] (*formal*) या (*medical*) to swell or make sth swell because of pressure from inside अंदरूनी दबाव के कारण फूलना या फुलाना, अफरना या अफराना *starving children with distended bellies* ► **distension** /dɪˈstenʃn डिˈस्टेन्शन् / *noun* [U] अफरन, अफराव, फुलाव

**distil** (*AmE* **distill**) /dɪˈstɪl डिˈस्टिल् / *verb* [T] (**distilling; distilled**) to make a liquid pure by heating it until it becomes a gas and then collecting the liquid that forms when the gas cools द्रव को शुद्ध करने के लिए उसे भाप बनाना और फिर ठंडा करके पुनः द्रव बनाना ► **distillation** /ˌdɪstɪˈleɪʃn ˌडिस्टिˈलेशन् / *noun* [C, U] द्रवशोधन, आसवन

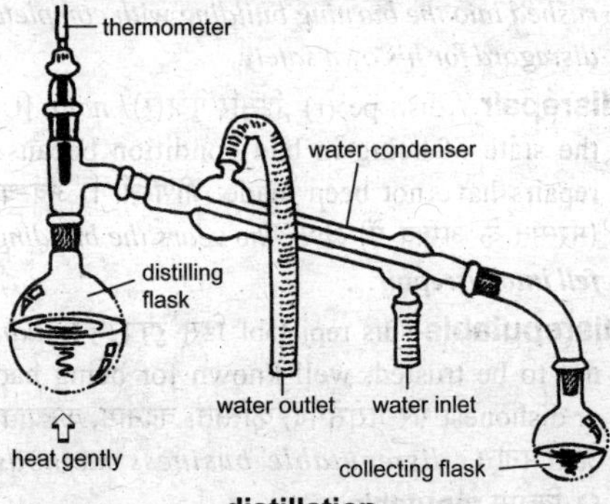


**distillation**

**distillery** /dɪˈstɪləri डिˈस्टिलरि / *noun* [C] (*pl.* **distilleries**) a factory where strong alcoholic drink is made by the process of distilling मद्य-निर्माणशाला, शराब बनाने का कारख़ाना

**distinct** /dɪˈstɪŋkt डिˈस्टिङ्क्ट् / *adj.* **1** clear; easily seen, heard or understood स्पष्ट; सुव्यक्त *There has been a distinct improvement in your work recently.* ○ *I had **the distinct impression** that she was lying.* **2 distinct (from sth)** clearly different स्पष्टतया भिन्न *Her books fall into two distinct groups: the novels and the travel stories.* ○ *This region, as distinct from other parts of the country, relies heavily on tourism.* ✪ विलोम **indistinct**

**distinction** /dɪˈstɪŋkʃn डिˈस्टिङ्क्श्न्/ *noun* **1** [C, U] (a) **distinction (between A and B)** a clear or important difference between things or people व्यक्तियों या वस्तुओं के बीच में स्पष्ट या सार्थक अंतर *We must **make a distinction** between classical and popular music here.* **2** [C, U] the quality of being excellent; fame for what you have achieved उत्कृष्टता; यश, यशस्विता, विशिष्टता *a violinist **of distinction*** **3** [C] the highest mark that is given to students in some exam for excellent work परीक्षा में उत्कृष्ट कार्य के लिए परीक्षार्थी को प्राप्त उच्चतम अंक *Hemant got a distinction in maths.*
IDM **draw a distinction between sth and sth** ➪ **draw** देखिए।

**distinctive** /dɪˈstɪŋktɪv डिˈस्टिङ्क्टिव्/ *adj.* clearly different from others and therefore easy to recognize सबसे स्पष्टतया अलग और सरलता से पहचान में आने वाला, भेदकारी *The soldiers were wearing their distinctive red berets.* ▶ **distinctively** *adv.* विशिष्ट रूप से

**distinctly** /dɪˈstɪŋktli डिˈस्टिङ्क्ट्लि/ *adv.* **1** clearly साफ़-साफ़ *I distinctly heard her say that she would be here on time.* **2** very; particularly बहुत; विशेषत: *His behaviour has been distinctly odd recently.*

**distinguish** /dɪˈstɪŋgwɪʃ डिˈस्टिङ्ग्विश्/ *verb* **1** [I, T] **distinguish between A and B; distinguish A from B** to recognize the difference between two things or people दो वस्तुओं या व्यक्तियों में अंतर पहचानना *He doesn't seem able to distinguish between what's important and what isn't.* ✪ पर्याय **differentiate** **2** [T] **distinguish A (from B)** to make sb/sth different from others (किसी व्यक्ति या वस्तु को) दूसरों से अलग करना (जिससे उसकी अपनी पहचान बने) *distinguishing features* (= things by which sb/sth can be recognized) ○ *The power of speech distinguishes humans from animals.* **3** [T] to see, hear or recognize with effort प्रयत्न करके ही देख, सुन या पहचान पाना *I listened carefully but they were too far away for me to distinguish what they were saying.* **4** [T] **distinguish yourself** to do sth which causes you to be noticed and admired विशिष्टता प्रदर्शित करना *She distinguished herself in the exams.*

**distinguishable** /dɪˈstɪŋgwɪʃəbl डिˈस्टिङ्ग्विशबल्/ *adj.* **1** possible to recognize as different from sb/sth else जो अन्य व्यक्ति या वस्तु से अलग पहचाना जा सके, प्रभेद्य *The male bird is distinguishable from the female by the colour of its beak.* **2** possible to see, hear or recognize with effort जिसे प्रयत्न करके ही देखा, सुना या पहचाना जा सके *The letter is so old that the signature is barely distinguishable.* ✪ विलोम **indistinguishable**

**distinguished** /dɪˈstɪŋgwɪʃt डिˈस्टिङ्ग्विश्ट्/ *adj.* important, successful and respected by other people सम्मानित

**distort** /dɪˈstɔ:t डिˈस्टॉट्/ *verb* [T] **1** to change the shape or sound of sth so that it seems strange or is not clear शकल या आवाज़ को बिगाड़ देना *Her face was distorted with grief.* **2** to change sth and show it falsely तोड़-मरोड़कर पेश करना *Foreigners are often given a distorted view of this country.* ▶ **distortion** *noun* [C, U] विरूपण

**distract** /dɪˈstrækt डिˈस्ट्रैक्ट्/ *verb* [T] **distract sb (from sth)** to take sb's attention away from sth किसी व्यक्ति का किसी वस्तु से ध्यान हटाना

**distracted** /dɪˈstræktɪd डिˈस्ट्रैक्टिड्/ *adj.* unable to give your full attention to sth because you are worried or thinking about sth else व्याकुल या अनमना, चिंता के कारण जिसका ध्यान अन्यत्र हो

**distraction** /dɪˈstrækʃn डिˈस्ट्रैक्श्न्/ *noun* [C, U] something that takes your attention away from what you were doing or thinking about काम से ध्यान बँटाने वाली वस्तु, एकाग्रता भंग होना
IDM **to distraction** with the result that you become upset, excited, or angry and unable to think clearly ध्यान बँटने के कारण परेशान हो जाना *The noise of the traffic outside at night is driving me to distraction.*

**distraught** /dɪˈstrɔ:t डिˈस्ट्रॉट्/ *adj.* extremely sad and upset बहुत व्याकुल, विक्षिप्त

**distress**[1] /dɪˈstres डिˈस्ट्रेस्/ *noun* [U] **1** the state of being very upset or of suffering great pain or difficulty अत्यधिक पीड़ा और कष्ट *She was **in** such **distress** that I didn't want to leave her on her own.* **2** the state of being in great danger and needing immediate help गंभीर संकट में, अतएव सहायता का अपेक्षी होना *The ship's captain radioed that it was **in distress**.*

**distress**[2] /dɪˈstres डिˈस्ट्रेस्/ *verb* [T] to make sb very upset or unhappy किसी को परेशान या नाराज़ कर देना *Try not to say anything to distress the patient further.* ▶ **distressed** *adj.* परेशान, दुखी *She was too distressed to talk.* ▶ **distressing** *adj.* परेशान करने वाला, विक्षोभकारी *a distressing experience/illness*

**distribute** /dɪˈstrɪbju:t; डिˈस्ट्रिब्यूट्; ˈdɪstrɪbju:t ˈडिस्ट्रिब्यूट्/ *verb* [T] **1 distribute sth (to/among sb/sth)** to give things to a number of people वितरण करना, बाँट देना *Tickets will be distributed* *to all club members.* ○ *They distributed emergency food supplies to the areas that were most in need.* **2** to transport and supply goods to shops, companies, etc. दुकानों आदि तक माल पहुँचाना *Which company distributes this product in your country?* **3** to spread sth equally over an area किसी इलाक़े में या सतह पर किसी वस्तु को (बराबर) फैलाना *Make sure that the weight is* ***evenly distributed.***

**distribution** /ˌdɪstrɪˈbjuːʃn ˌडिस्ट्रि'ब्यूशन्/ *noun* **1** [U, C] the act of giving or transporting sth to a number of people or places कुछ वितरित करने या कहीं सामान पहुँचाने की क्रिया, वितरण *the distribution of food parcels to the refugees* **2** [U] the way sth is shared out; the pattern in which sth is found जिस रूप में कोई वस्तु बँटी हो, बाँट, वितरण; जिस रूप में कोई वस्तु पाई जाए, फैलाव, वितरण *a map to show the distribution of rainfall in India*

**distributor** /dɪˈstrɪbjətə(r) डि'स्ट्रिब्यट(र्)/ *noun* [C] a person or company that transports and supplies goods to a number of shops and companies वितरक (व्यक्ति या कंपनी)

**district** /ˈdɪstrɪkt 'डिस्ट्रिक्ट्/ *noun* [C] **1** a part of a town or country that is special for a particular reason or is of a particular type किसी नगर या देश का विशिष्टता वाला क्षेत्र *rural districts* ○ *the financial district of the city* **2** an official division of a town or country किसी नगर या देश का आधिकारिक खंड या प्रभाग *the district council* ○ *postal districts*

> NOTE **District** प्रायः किसी नगर या देश का भाग होता है और इसकी सीमाएँ निश्चित होती है—*the district controlled by a council.* **Region** अपेक्षाकृत बड़ा होता है और प्रायः केवल देश का भाग होता है और इसकी सीमाएँ भी निश्चित नहीं होतीं—*the industrial regions of the country.* **Area** सर्वाधिक सामान्य शब्द है और यह **district** के लिए भी प्रयुक्त हो सकता है, **region** के लिए भी—*the poorer areas of a town* ○ *an agricultural area of the country.* एक नगर के किसी भाग का संकेत करने के लिए हम अधिकतर **part** का प्रयोग करते है—*Which part of Delhi do you live in?*

**distrust** /dɪsˈtrʌst डिस्'ट्रस्ट्/ *noun* [U, *sing.*] **(a) dis trust (of sb/sth)** the feeling that you cannot believe sb/sth; a lack of trust किसी पर भरोसा न कर सकने का भाव; अविश्वास ▶ **distrust** *verb* [T] अविश्वास करना *She distrusts him because he lied to her once before.* ➪ **mistrust** देखिए। ▶ **distrustful** *adj.* अविश्वासी

**disturb** /dɪˈstɜːb डि'स्टब्/ *verb* [T] **1** to interrupt sb while he/she is doing sth or sleeping; to spoil a peaceful situation किसी के कुछ काम करते समय उसमें बाधा पहुँचाना; शांति भंग करना *I'm sorry to disturb you but there's a phone call for you.* ○ *Their sleep was disturbed by a loud crash.* **2** to cause sb to worry किसी को चिंता में डाल देना *It disturbed her to think that he might be unhappy.* **3** to move sth or change its position किसी को अपने सामान्य स्थान से हटा देना या उसे बदल देना *I noticed a number of things had been disturbed and realized that there had been a burglary.*

**disturbance** /dɪˈstɜːbəns डि'स्टबन्स्/ *noun* [C, U] something that makes you stop what you are doing, or that upsets the normal condition of sth बाधा, गड़बड़ी *They were arrested for causing a disturbance* (= fighting) *in the town centre.* ○ *emotional disturbance*

**disturbed** /dɪˈstɜːbd डि'स्टब्ड्/ *adj.* having mental or emotional problems मानसिक समस्याओं से ग्रस्त

**disturbing** /dɪˈstɜːbɪŋ डि'स्टबिङ्/ *adj.* making you worried or upset चिंतित या परेशान

**disuse** /dɪsˈjuːs डिस्'यूस्/ *noun* [U] the state of not being used any more प्रयोग या उपयोग में न रहना, अनुपयोग, अप्रयोग *The farm buildings had been allowed to* ***fall into disuse.***

**disused** /ˌdɪsˈjuːzd डिस्'यूज़्ड्/ *adj.* not used any more अप्रयुक्त, जिसका प्रयोग अब नहीं हो रहा *a disused railway line*

**ditch**[1] /dɪtʃ डिच्/ *noun* [C] a long narrow hole that has been dug into the ground, especially along the side of a road or field for water to flow along सड़क या खेत के साथ-साथ बनाई गई खाई (पानी के बहने के लिए) खंदक, खात

IDM **a last-ditch attempt** ➪ **last**[1] देखिए।

**ditch**[2] /dɪtʃ डिच्/ *verb* [T] (*informal*) to get rid of or leave sb/sth किसी से छुटकारा पाना या किसी को छोड़ देना *She ditched her old friends when she became famous.*

**dither** /ˈdɪðə(r) 'डिद्र(र्)/ *verb* [I] to be unable to decide sth; to hesitate निश्चय करने में असमर्थ होना या निश्चय न कर सकना; हिचकना *Stop dithering and make up your mind!*

**ditto** /ˈdɪtəʊ 'डिटो/ *noun* [C] (represented by the mark (") and used instead of repeating the thing written above it) the same, (") चिह्न से सूचित और पूर्वोक्त को न दुहराकर उसके स्थान पर प्रयुक्त ▶ **ditto** *adv.* तदेव *'I'm starving.' 'Ditto (= me too).'*

**diurnal** /daɪˈɜːnl डाइˈअनूल्/ *adj.* **1** used about animals and birds active during the day (पशु और पक्षी) दिन में सक्रिय रहने वाला; दिनचर ✪ विलोम **nocturnal 2** (in astronomy) taking one day जिसमें एक दिन लगे, एकदिवसीय या एक दिनी *the diurnal rotation of the earth*

**divan** /dɪˈvæn डिˈवैन्/ *noun* [C] a type of bed with only a thick base to lie on but no frame at either end दीवान, एक प्रकार का पलंग जिसका तख़्ता सख़्त और दोनों सिरे खुले होते हैं

**dive[1]** /daɪv डाइव्/ *verb* [I] (*pt* **dived;** *AmE* **dove**/dəʊv डोव्/; *pp* **dived**) **1 dive (off/from sth) (into sth); dive in** to jump into water with your arms and head first बाँहों और सिर के बल पानी में गोता लगाना *A passer-by dived in and saved the drowning man.* **2** to swim under the surface of the sea, a lake, etc. समुद्र, झील आदि में गहराई में तैरना *people diving for pearls* ○ *I'm hoping to* ***go diving*** *on holiday.* **3** to move quickly and suddenly downwards तेज़ी से और एकाएक झपटकर (किसी चीज़ के) नीचे जाना *He dived under the table and hid there.* ○ *The goalkeeper dived to save the penalty.*

PHRV **dive into sth** to put your hand quickly into a pocket or bag in order to find or get sth जेब या थैले में तेज़ी से हाथ डालना (कुछ निकालने के लिए)

**dive[2]** /daɪv डाइव्/ *noun* [C] **1** the act of diving into water पानी में गोता लगाने की क्रिया, गोता **2** a quick and sudden downwards movement नीचे की ओर झपट्टेदार गति

**diver** /ˈdaɪvə(r) ˈडाइव़(र्)/ *noun* [C] **1** a person who swims under the surface of water using special equipment विशेष उपकरण से सज्जित गोताख़ोर **2** a person who jumps into water with his/her arms and head first बाँहों और सिर के बल पानी में छलाँग लगाने वाला व्यक्ति ➪ **swim** पर चित्र देखिए।

**diverge** /daɪˈvɜːdʒ डाइˈव़ज़्/ *verb* [I] **diverge (from sth) 1** (used about roads, lines, etc.) to separate and go in different directions (सड़कों, रेखाओं आदि का) एक दूसरे से अलग होकर विभिन्न दिशाओं में जाना *The paths suddenly diverged and I didn't know which one to take.* ➪ **short-sighted 2** to be or become different (विचारों का) भिन्न होना या हो जाना *Attitudes among teachers diverge on this question.*

**diverse** /daɪˈvɜːs डाइˈव़स्/ *adj.* very different from each other एक दूसरे से अलग; विविध *people from diverse social backgrounds* ○ *My interests are very diverse.* ➪ **diversity** noun देखिए।

**diversify** /daɪˈvɜːsɪfaɪ डाइˈव़सिफ़ाइ/ *verb* [I, T] (*pres. part.* **diversifying;** *3rd person sing. pres.* **diversifies;** *pt, pp* **diversified**) **diversify (sth) (into sth)** to increase or develop the number or types of sth विविधता लाना, उत्पन्न करना, विविध रूपों में विकसित, विभक्त होना या करना *To remain successful in the future, the company will have to diversify.* ▶ **diversification** /daɪˌvɜːsɪfɪˈkeɪʃn डाइˌव़सिफ़िˈकेश्न्/ *noun* [C, U] विविधीकरण, वैविध्यीकरण

**diversion** /daɪˈvɜːʃn डाइˈव़श्न्/ *noun* **1** [C, U] the act of changing the direction or purpose of sth, especially in order to solve or avoid a problem (किसी का) दिशा-परिवर्तन या उद्देश्य-परिवर्तन (विशेषतः समस्या के समाधान के लिए) *the diversion of a river to prevent flooding* ○ *the diversion of government funds to areas of greatest need* **2** [C] (*AmE* **detour**) a different route which traffic can take when a road is closed मुख्य मार्ग बंद होने पर यातायात के लिए बना अन्य मार्ग, दूसरा रास्ता, सहपथ *For Chandigarh follow the diversion.* **3** [C] something that takes your attention away from sth ध्यान बाँटने वाली बात *Some prisoners created a diversion while others escaped.*

**diversity** /daɪˈvɜːsəti डाइˈव़सिटि/ *noun* [U] the wide variety of sth विविधता *cultural and ethnic diversity*

**divert** /daɪˈvɜːt डाइˈव़ट्/ *verb* [T] **divert sb/sth (from sth) (to sth); divert sth (away from sth)** to change the direction or purpose of sb/sth, especially to avoid a problem (किसी का) दिशा-परिवर्तन या उद्देश्य-परिवर्तन करना (विशेषतः समस्या के समाधान के लिए) *Government money was diverted from defence to education.* ○ *Politicians often criticize each other to divert attention away from their own mistakes.*

**divide[1]** /dɪˈvaɪd डिˈव़ाइड्/ *verb* **1** [I, T] **divide (sth) (up) (into sth)** to separate into different parts विभाजित करना *The egg divides into two cells.* ○ *The house was divided up into flats.* **2** [T] **divide sth (out/up) (between/among sb)** to separate sth into parts and give a part to each of a number of people (किसी वस्तु को) विभाजित कर उसके खंडों को अनेक लोगों में बाँटना *The robbers divided the money out between themselves.* **3** [T] **divide sth (between A and B)** to use different parts or amounts of sth for different purposes किसी वस्तु के विभिन्न अंशों (या मात्राओं) को विभिन्न उद्देश्यों से प्रयोग में लाना या विभिन्न उद्देश्यों के लिए किसी वस्तु को बाँटना *They divide their time* *between their two homes.* **4** [T] to separate two places or things दो स्थानों या वस्तुओं को अलग करना *The river divides the old part of the city from the new.* **5** [T] to cause people to disagree लोगों में फूट डालना या लोगों को विभक्त करना *The question of immigration has divided the country.* **6** [T] **divide sth by sth** to calculate how many times a number will go into another number (गणित में) एक संख्या को दूसरी संख्या से भाग देना *Ten divided by five is two.* ✪ विलोम **multiply**

**divide²** /dɪˈvaɪd डि'वाइड्/ *noun* [C] **a divide (between and B)** a difference between two groups of people that separates them from each other अलगाव, अंतर, मतभेद *a divide between the rich and the poor*

**divided highway** (*AmE*) = **dual carriageway**

**dividend** /ˈdɪvɪdend 'डिविडेन्ड्/ *noun* [C] a part of a company's profits that is paid to the people who own shares in it (**shareholders**) कंपनी के शेयरधारकों को मिलने वाला लाभांश

**divine** /dɪˈvaɪn डि'वाइन्/ *adj.* connected with God or a god दिव्य, दैवी, ईश्वरीय

**diving** /ˈdaɪvɪŋ 'डाइविङ्/ *noun* [U] the activity or sport of jumping into water or swimming under the surface of the sea, a lake, etc. गोताख़ोरी, समुद्र, झील आदि में गोता लगाने या तैरने का खेल

**diving board** *noun* [C] a board at the side of a swimming pool from which people can jump into the water गोता लगाने का मंच या तख़्ता

**divisible** /dɪˈvɪzəbl डि'विज़बल्/ *adj.* that can be divided विभाज्य, जो विभाजित हो सके *Twelve is divisible by three.*

**division** /dɪˈvɪʒn डि'विश़न्/ *noun* **1** [U, *sing.*] **division (of sth) (into sth); division (of sth) (between A and B)** the separation of sth into different parts; the sharing of sth between different people, groups, places, etc. विभाजन; बँटवारा, वितरण *There is a growing economic division between the north and south of the country.* ○ *an unfair division of the profits* **2** [U] dividing one number by another (गणित में) भाग, एक संख्या का दूसरी संख्या से विभाजन *the teaching of multiplication and division* **3** [C] **a division (in/within sth); a division (between and B)** a disagreement or difference of opinion between sb/sth मतभेद, मतांतर *deep divisions within the Samajvadi Party* **4** [C] a part or section of an organization किसी संगठन का भाग, खंड या प्रभाग *the company's sales division* ○ *the First Division* (= of the football league) **5** [C] a line that separates sth; a border विभाजक रेखा; सीमा *the river marks the division between the two counties.*

**divisive** /dɪˈvaɪsɪv डि'वाइसिव्/ *adj.* (*formal*) likely to cause disagreements or arguments between people मतभेदकारी, लोगों को विभाजित करने वाला, विभाजक, विभाजनकारी *a divisive policy*

**divorce¹** /dɪˈvɔːs डि'वॉस्/ *noun* [C, U] the legal end of a marriage क़ानूनन विवाह-विच्छेद या तलाक़ *to **get a divorce***

**divorce²** /dɪˈvɔːs डि'वॉस्/ *verb* [T] **1** to legally end your marriage to sb (क़ानून के अनुसार) तलाक़ देना, लेना या होना *My parents **got divorced** when I was three.* ○ *She divorced him a year after their marriage.* **2 divorce sb/sth from sth** to separate sb/sth from sth एक वस्तु को दूसरी वस्तु से पृथक करना *Sometimes these modern novels seem completely divorced from everyday life.* ▶ **divorced** *adj.* असंबद्ध, पृथक्कृत या पृथग्भूत

**divorcee** /dɪˌvɔːˈsiː डि,वॉ'सी/ *noun* [C] a person who is divorced तलाक़शुदा व्यक्ति

**divulge** /daɪˈvʌldʒ डाइ'वल्ज्/ *verb* [T] (*formal*) to tell sth that is secret गुप्त बात बताना, (रहस्य) प्रकट करना *The phone companies refused to divulge details of their costs.*

**Diwali** = **Deepawali**

**DIY** /ˌdiː aɪ ˈwaɪ ,डी आइ 'वाइ/ *abbr.* do it yourself; the activity of making and repairing things yourself around your home स्वयं करें; घर में मरम्मत आदि ख़ुद करने की क्रिया *a DIY expert*

**dizzy** /ˈdɪzi 'डिज़ि/ *adj.* **1** feeling as if everything is turning round and that you might fall (व्यक्ति) जिसे चक्कर आ रहा हो, चक्कर से आक्रांत *I **feel/get dizzy** at high altitudes.* **2** very great; extreme बहुत अधिक; अत्यंत, चरम *the dizzy pace of life in Mumbai* ○ *The following year, the band's popularity reached **dizzy heights**.* ▶ **dizziness** *noun* [U] चक्कर

**DJ** /ˌdiː ˈdʒeɪ ,डी 'जे/ (*also* **disc jockey**) *noun* [C] a person who plays records and talks about music on the radio or in a club रेडियो पर या क्लब में संगीत कार्यक्रम का प्रस्तुतकर्ता (व्यक्ति); डीजे

**DNA** /ˌdiː en ˈeɪ ,डी एन 'ए/ *noun* [U] the chemical in the cells of an animal or a plant that controls what characteristics that animal or plant will have किसी सजीव प्राणी या पौधे की कोशिकाओं में विद्यमान रसायन जो उसके गुणधर्म को निर्धारित करता है

**do¹** /də; *strong form* du: ड; प्रबल रूप डू / *auxiliary verb* **1** used with other verbs to form questions and negative sentences, also in short answers and short questions at the end of a sentence (**question tags**) मुख्य क्रिया के साथ प्रयुक्त (सहायक) क्रिया-प्रश्नवाचक, निषेधवाचक तथा वाक्यांत में लघु-प्रश्न तथा लघु-उत्तर वाक्यों में NOTE इस शब्दकोश के अंत में **Quick Grammar Reference** देखिए। **2** used for emphasizing the main verb मुख्य क्रिया पर बल देने के लिए प्रयुक्त *I can't find the receipt now but I'm sure I did pay the phone bill.* **3** used to avoid repeating the main verb मुख्य क्रिया को दोहराने से बचने के लिए प्रयुक्त *He earns a lot more than I do.* ○ *She's feeling much better than she did last week.*

**do²** /du: डू / *verb* **1** [T] to perform an action, activity or job (कुछ कार्य) करना *What is the government doing about pollution* (= what action are they taking)? ○ *What do you do* (= what is your job)? ○ *to do the cooking/ironing/aerobics/windsurfing* ○ *What did you* ***do with*** *the keys* (= where did you put them)? **2** [I] to make progress or develop; to improve sth प्रगति या विकास करना; किसी बात में सुधार करना *'How's your daughter doing at school'* ○ *'She's doing well.'* ○ *Last week's win has* ***done wonders for*** *the team's confidence.* ○ *This latest scandal will* ***do nothing for*** (= will harm) *this government's reputation.* **3** [T] to make or produce sth कोई चीज़ तैयार करना *The photocopier does 60 copies a minute.* ○ *to do a painting/drawing* **4** [T] to provide a service कोई सेवा उपलब्ध कराना *Do you do eye tests here?* **5** [T] to study sth or find the answer to sth किसी विषय का अध्ययन करना या किसी प्रश्न का उत्तर खोजना या को हल करना *to do French/a course/a degree* ○ *I can't do question three.* **6** [T] to travel a certain distance or at a certain speed एक निश्चित दूरी तय करना या निश्चित रफ़्तार से जाना *This car does 120 kilometres per hour.* ○ *I normally do about five kilometres when I go running.* **7** [T] to have a particular effect कोई विशेष प्रभाव होना *A holiday will do you good.* ○ *The storm did a lot of damage.* **8** [I, T] to be enough or suitable पर्याप्त या उपयुक्त होना *If you haven't got a pen, a pencil will do.*

IDM **be/have to do with sb/sth** to be connected with sb/sth किसी कार्य से संबद्ध होना *I'm not sure what Payal's job is, but I think it's something to do with animals.*

**could do with sth** to want or need sth किसी बात की इच्छा या आवश्यकता होना *I could do with a holiday.*

**how do you do?** ⇨ **how** देखिए।

**make do with sth** ⇨ **make¹** देखिए।

PHRV **do away with sth** to get rid of sth किसी वस्तु या व्यक्ति से छुटकारा पाना *Most European countries have done away with their royal families.*

**do sb out of sth** to prevent sb having sth in an unfair way; to cheat sb किसी को कुछ प्राप्त करने से अनुचित तरीक़े से रोकना या किसी को उसका प्राप्य जबरन न लेने देना; किसी को ठगना *They've done me out of my share of the money!*

**do sth up** **1** to fasten a piece of clothing कोई पोशाक या वस्त्र पहनना *Hurry up. Do up your jacket and we can go!* **2** to repair a building and make it more modern किसी भवन की मरम्मत कर उसे अधिक आधुनिक या सुंदर बनाना

**do without** to manage without having sth किसी वस्तु के बिना काम चलाना *If there isn't any coffee left, we'll just have to do without.*

**do³** /du: डू / *noun* [C] (*pl.* **dos** /du:z डूज़् /) (*BrE informal*) a party or other social event पार्टी या अन्य सामाजिक कार्यक्रम

IDM **dos and don'ts** things that you should and should not do विधि-निषेध, नियम *the dos and don'ts of mountain climbing*

**doab** *noun* (*IndE*) the area of land between two rivers that meet, such as the one between the Ganges and the Yamuna in India दो संगामी नदियों के बीच की ज़मीन, जैसे भारत में गंगा, यमुना दोआब

**docile** /ˈdəʊsaɪl ˈडोसाइल् / *adj.* (used about a person or animal) quiet and easy to control (व्यक्ति या पशु) शांत और सरलता से नियंत्रण में आने वाला या सधने वाला; शांत और विनीत

**dock¹** /dɒk डॉक् / *noun* **1** an area of a port where ships stop to be loaded, repaired, etc. गोदी, बंदरगाह का हिस्सा जहाँ जहाज़ का माल उतारा-चढ़ाया जाता है, जहाज़ की मरम्मत होती है आदि **2 docks** [*pl.*] a group of docks with all the buildings, offices, etc. that are around them भवनों, दफ़्तरों आदि से घिरा गोदी-समूह *He works down at the docks.* **3** [C, *usually sing.*] the place in a court of law where the person who is accused sits or stands कचहरी में अभियुक्त के लिए बना कठघरा **4** (*AmE*) = **landing stage**

**dock²** /dɒk डॉक् / *verb* **1** [I, T] if a ship docks or you dock a ship, it sails into a port and stops at the dock जहाज़ का गोदी में आना, जहाज़ को गोदी में लाना *The ship had docked/was docked at Mumbai.* **2** [T] to take away part of the money sb earns, especially as a punishment किसी की कमाई में से कुछ अंश काट लेना (विशेषतः दंडस्वरूप) *They've docked Rs 200 off my wages because I was late.*

**docker** /ˈdɒkə(r) ˈडॉक(र्)/ *noun* [C] a person whose job is moving goods on and off ships गोदी-मज़दूर, बंदरगाह-मज़दूर

**doctor¹** /ˈdɒktə(r) ˈडॉक्‌ट(र्)/ *noun* **1** [C] a person who has been trained in medicine and who treats people who are ill डॉक्टर, चिकित्सक *Our family doctor is Dr Verma.* ○ *I've got a doctor's appointment at 10 o'clock.*

> **NOTE** एक डॉक्टर अपने **patients** से जैसे बरतता है उसके लिए **sees** या **treats** कहते हैं। वह उनके लिए इलाज या **medicine prescribe** करता है जिसे **prescription** पर लिखा जाता है।

**2 the doctor's** [*sing.*] the place where a doctor sees his/her patients; a doctor's surgery डॉक्टर की दुकान या क्लिनिक *I'm going to the doctor's today.* **3** [C] a person who has got the highest degree from a university (**doctorate**) विश्वविद्यालय की सर्वोच्च उपाधि-डॉक्टरेट-प्राप्त व्यक्ति, डॉक्टर *a Doctor of Philosophy*

**doctor²** /ˈdɒktə(r) ˈडॉक्‌ट(र्)/ *verb* [T] **1** to change sth that should not be changed in order to gain an advantage अनुचित रूप से किसी वस्तु में कुछ बदलना या किसी वस्तु से छेड़छाड़ करना *The results of the survey had been doctored.* **2** to add sth harmful to food or drink खाने या पीने की चीज़ में हानिकर वस्तु मिला देना

**doctorate** /ˈdɒktərət ˈडॉक्‌टरट्/ *noun* [C] the highest university degree विश्वविद्यालय की सर्वोच्च उपाधि; डॉक्टरेट

**doctrine** /ˈdɒktrɪn ˈडॉक्‌ट्रिन्/ *noun* [C, U] a set of beliefs that is taught by a church, political party, etc. चर्च, राजनीतिक दल आदि द्वारा प्रतिपादित मत, सिद्धांत

**document** /ˈdɒkjumənt ˈडॉक्युमन्ट्/ *noun* [C] **1** an official piece of writing which gives information, proof or evidence दस्तावेज़, लिखित सूचना, साक्ष्य या प्रमाण *Her solicitor asked her to read and sign a number of documents.* **2** (*computing*) a computer file that contains text that has a name that identifies it नाम विशेष से अंकित टेक्स्ट-युक्त कंप्यूटर फ़ाइल *Save the document before closing.*

**documentary** /ˌdɒkjuˈmentri ˌडॉक्युˈमेन्ट्रि/ *noun* [C] (*pl.* **documentaries**) a film, television or radio programme that gives facts or information about a particular subject किसी विषय विशेष का परिचय देने वाला फ़िल्म, टेलिविज़न या रेडियो का प्रोग्राम; वृत्तचित्र

**dodge¹** /dɒdʒ डॉज्/ *verb* **1** [I, T] to move quickly in order to avoid sb/sth किसी से बचने के लिए तेज़ी से निकल जाना, कतरा कर निकल जाना *I had to dodge between the cars to cross the road.* **2** [T] to avoid doing sth that you should do दिए गए काम को करने से बचना *Don't try to dodge your responsibilities!*

**dodge²** /dɒdʒ डॉज्/ *noun* [C] (*informal*) a clever way of avoiding sth चकमा, झाँसा देना *The man had been involved in a massive tax dodge.*

**dodgy** /ˈdɒdʒi ˈडॉजि/ *adj.* (**dodgier; dodgiest**) (*BrE informal*) involving risk; not honest or not to be trusted जिसमें धोखा खाने का ख़तरा हो; ईमानदारी-रहित या ग़ैर-भरोसेमंद *a dodgy business deal*

**doe** /dəʊ डो/ *noun* [C] a female rabbit, **deer** or **hare** मादा ख़रगोश, मादा हरिण या हरिणी ➪ **deer** पर नोट देखिए।

**does** /dʌz डज़्/ ➪ **do** देखिए।

**doesn't** /ˈdʌznt ˈडज़न्ट्/ ➪ **does not** का संक्षिप्त रूप

**dog¹** /dɒg डॉग्/ *noun* [C] **1** an animal that many people keep as a pet, or for working on farms, hunting, etc. कुत्ता प्रजाति

> **NOTE** कुत्ते की विभिन्न क्रियाओं के लिए शब्द **bark, growl** या **whine** प्रयुक्त होते हैं। प्रसन्न होने पर कुत्ते के पूँछ हिलाने को **wag** कहते हैं।

**2** a male dog or other animal (**fox**)

**dog²** /dɒg डॉग्/ *verb* [T] (**dogging; dogged**) to follow sb closely क़रीब से पीछा करना *A shadowy figure was dogging their every move.* ○ (*figurative*) *Bad luck and illness have dogged her career from the start.*

**dog-eared** *adj.* (used about a book or piece of paper) in bad condition with untidy corners and edges because it has been used a lot (पुस्तक या काग़ज़ के लिए प्रयुक्त) अधिक प्रयोग के कारण (पृष्ठ का मुड़ा कोना)

**dogged** /ˈdɒgɪd ˈडॉगिड्/ *adj.* refusing to give up even when sth is difficult दृढ़ निश्चयी, पक्का *I was impressed by his **dogged determination** to succeed.* ▶ **doggedly** *adv.* दृढ़तापूर्वक *She doggedly refused all offers of help.*

**dogma** /ˈdɒgmə ˈडॉग्मा/ *noun* [C, U] a belief or set of beliefs that people are expected to accept as true without questioning निर्धारित सिद्धांत जिन्हें प्रश्न किए बिना स्वीकारना होता है

**dogmatic** /dɒgˈmætɪk डॉग्ˈमैटिक्/ *adj.* being certain that your beliefs are right and that others should accept them, without considering other opinions or evidence हठधर्मी, हठधर्मिता पर आधारित मत ▶ **dogmatically** /-kli -क्लि/ *adv.* हठपूर्वक

**dogsbody** /ˈdɒgzbɒdi ˈडॉग्ज़्बॉडि/ *noun* [C] (*pl.* **dogsbodies**) (*BrE informal*) a person who has to do the boring or unpleasant jobs that no one else wants to do and who is considered less important than other people महत्त्वहीन व्यक्ति जिसे बेकार के काम सौंपे जाएँ

**do it yourself** (especially *BrE*) = **DIY**

**the doldrums** /ˈdɒldrəmz ˈडॉलड्रम्ज़्/ *noun* [*pl.*] an area of the Atlantic Ocean near the line around the middle of the earth (**the equator**) where the weather can be calm for long periods of time or there can be sudden storms भूमध्य रेखा के पास अटलांटिक महासागर का इलाक़ा जहाँ मौसम लंबे समय तक शांत रहता है या एकाएक आँधियाँ आती हैं; विषुव प्रशांत मंडल

**PHRV** **in the doldrums** **1** not active or busy निष्क्रियता, (व्यापार आदि का) मंदा होना *Business has been in the doldrums recently.* **2** sad or unhappy खिन्न या उदास

**dole[1]** /dəʊl डोल्/ *verb* (*informal*)

**PHRV** **dole sth out** to give sth, especially food, money, etc. in small amounts to a number of people लोगों में थोड़ा-थोड़ा कुछ बाँटना

**the dole[2]** /dəʊl डोल्/ *noun* [*sing.*] (*BrE informal*) money that the State gives every week to people who are unemployed सरकार की ओर से दिया जाने वाला बेरोज़गारी भत्ता *I lost my job and had to go* ***on the dole****.*

**doleful** /ˈdəʊlfl ˈडोल्फ़्ल्/ *adj.* sad or unhappy खिन्न या उदास *She looked at him with doleful eyes.* ▶ **dolefully** /-fəli फ़लि/ *adv.* उदासी के साथ, खिन्नतापूर्वक

**doll** /dɒl डॉल्/ *noun* [C] a child's toy that looks like a small person or a baby गुड़िया (बच्चों का खिलौना)

**dollar** /ˈdɒlə(r) ˈडॉल(र्)/ *noun* **1** [C] (*symbol* $) a unit of money in some countries, for example the US, Canada and Australia अमेरिका, कनाडा आदि देशों की मुद्रा; डॉलर **NOTE** एक डॉलर में 100 **cents** होते हैं। **2** [C] a note or coin that is worth one dollar एक डॉलर के बराबर का नोट या सिक्का **3 the dollar** [*sing.*] the value of the US dollar on international money markets अंतर्राष्ट्रीय मुद्रा बाज़ार में अमेरिकी डॉलर का मूल्य

**dollop** /ˈdɒləp ˈडॉलप्/ *noun* [C] (*informal*) a lump of sth soft, especially food कोमल वस्तु (विशेषतः खाद्य पदार्थ) का डला या छोटा गोला *a dollop of ice cream*

**dolphin** /ˈdɒlfɪn ˈडॉल्फ़िन्/ *noun* [C] an intelligent animal that lives in the sea and looks like a large fish. Dolphins usually swim in large groups प्रचेत, अक़्लमंद प्रज्ञावान मछली जैसा एक समुद्री जीव; डॉल्फ़िन; ये समूह बनाकर तैरते हैं

**domain** /dəˈmeɪn; डˈमेन्; dəʊ- डो-/ *noun* [C] **1** an area of knowledge or activity (ज्ञान या कार्य का) क्षेत्र *I don't know—that's outside my domain.* ○ *This issue is now* ***in the public domain*** (= the public knows about it). **2** (*computing*) a set of Internet addresses that end with the same group of letters इंटरनेट पतों का सेट जिसके अंत में एक ही समूह के अक्षर आते हैं

**dome** /dəʊm डोम्/ *noun* [C] a round roof on a building गुंबद, इमारत की गोल छत, बुर्जी, कलश *the dome of Taj Mahal* ▶ **domed** *adj.* गुंबद वाला *a domed roof*

**domestic** /dəˈmestɪk डˈमेस्टिक्/ *adj.* **1** not international; only within one country अंतरराष्ट्रीय नहीं, घरेलू; अंतर्देशीय *domestic flights* ○ *domestic affairs/politics* **2** (*only before a noun*) connected with the home or family घर या परिवार से संबंधित, घरेलू या पारिवारिक, निजी, आंतरिक *domestic chores/tasks* ○ *the growing problem of* ***domestic violence*** (= violence between members of the same family) **3** (used about animals) kept as pets or on farms; not wild (जीव-जंतु) पालतू; जंगली नहीं *domestic animals such as cats, dogs and horses* **4** (used about a person) enjoying doing things in the home, such as cooking and cleaning (व्यक्ति) घर के कामों (भोजन बनाना, सफ़ाई करना आदि) में रुचि रखने वाला

**domesticate** /dəˈmestɪkeɪt डˈमेस्टिकेट्/ *verb* [T] to tame animals and cultivate plants for food (पौधों, पशुओं आदि को) घरेलू बनाना; पालतू बनाना

**domesticated** /dəˈmestɪkeɪtɪd डˈमेस्टिकेटिड्/ *adj.* **1** (used about animals) happy being near people and being controlled by them (जीव-जंतु) पालतू (बनाया हुआ) **2** (used about people) good at cleaning the house, cooking, etc. (व्यक्ति) घरेलू कार्य में रुचि रखने वाला *Men are expected to be much more domesticated nowadays.*

**domicile** /ˈdɒmɪsaɪl ˈडॉमिसाइल्/ *noun* [C] (*formal* or *law*) the place or country of residence, which is legally or officially recognized (क़ानून में) अधिवास, निवास स्थान

**dominance** /ˈdɒmɪnəns ˈडॉमिनन्स्/ *noun* [U] control or power प्रभुत्व या प्राबल्य, प्राधान्य, प्रमुखता *Japan's dominance of the car industry*

**dominant** /ˈdɒmɪnənt ˈडॉमिनन्ट्/ *adj.* **1** more powerful, important or noticeable than others अन्यों की अपेक्षा अधिक सशक्त और प्रभावशाली, अभिभावी *His mother was the dominant influence in his life.* **2** (*technical*) a **dominant** physical characteristic, for example brown eyes, appears in a child even if it has only one **gene** किसी शिशु का विशिष्ट शारीरिक लक्षण (जैसे भूरी आँखें) (भले ही जो माता या पिता में से किसी एक का 'जीन' हो) ➪ **recessive** देखिए।

**dominate** /ˈdɒmɪneɪt ˈडॉमिनेट्/ *verb* **1** [I, T] to be more powerful, important or noticeable than others अन्यों की अपेक्षा अधिक सशक्त और प्रभावशाली होना *The Italian team dominated throughout the second half of the game.* ○ *She always tends to dominate the conversation.* **2** [T] (used about a building or place) to be much higher than everything else (किसी भवन या स्थान का) अन्य सब वस्तुओं से बहुत ऊँचा होना *The palace dominates the area for miles around.* ▶ **domination** /ˌdɒmɪˈneɪʃn ˌडॉमिˈनेश्न्/ *noun* [U] प्रभुत्व, प्राबल्य

**domineering** /ˌdɒmɪˈnɪərɪŋ ˌडॉमिˈनिअरिङ्/ *adj.* having a very strong character and wanting to control other people सशक्त व्यक्तित्व का स्वामी और लोगों पर हुक्म चलाने वाला; निरंकुश

**dominion** /dəˈmɪniən डˈमिनिअन्/ *noun* (*formal*) **1** [U] the power to rule and control शासनाधिकार, प्रभुसत्ता *to have dominion over an area* **2** [C] an area controlled by one government or ruler एक सरकार या शासक द्वारा शासित क्षेत्र, प्रभुत्व, आधिपत्य *the dominions of the Mughal empire*

**domino** /ˈdɒmɪnəʊ ˈडॉमिनो/ *noun* [C] (*pl.* **dominoes**) one of a set of small flat pieces of wood or plastic, marked on one side with two groups of spots representing numbers, that are used for playing a game (**dominoes**) एक तरफ अंकित चपटी आयातकार गोटियाँ जिनसे एक प्रकार का खेल खेला जाता है

**donate** /dəʊˈneɪt डोˈनेट्/ *verb* [T] **donate sth (to sb/sth)** to give money or goods to an organization, especially one for people or animals who need help दान करना (विशेषतः ज़रूरतमंद को) *She donated a large sum of money to cancer research.*

**donation** /dəʊˈneɪʃn डोˈनेश्न्/ *noun* [C] money, etc. that is given to a person or an organization such as a charity, in order to help people or animals in need (ज़रूरतमंदों को धन आदि का) दान

**done[1]** ➪ **do** का past participle रूप

**done[2]** /dʌn डन्/ *adj.* (*not before a noun*) **1** finished समाप्त, पूर्ण, संपन्न *I've got to go out as soon as this job is done.* **2** (used about food) cooked enough (भोजन) अच्छी तरह पकाया हुआ *The meat's ready but the vegetables still aren't done.*

IDM **over and done with** completely finished; in the past पूर्णतया समाप्त; अतीत में

**done[3]** /dʌn डन्/ *exclamation* used for saying that you accept an offer जब प्रस्ताव की स्वीकृति देनी हो या जब किसी प्रस्ताव के लिए हाँ करनी हो *'I'll give you twenty ruppes for it.' 'Done!'*

**donkey** /ˈdɒŋki ˈडॉङ्कि/ *noun* [C] (*also* **ass**) an animal like a small horse, with long ears गधा

IDM **donkey's years** (*informal*) a very long time बहुत लंबा समय, दीर्घकाल *They've known each other for donkey's years.*

**donor** /ˈdəʊnə(r) ˈडोन(र्)/ *noun* [C] **1** a person who gives blood or a part of his/her own body for medical use डॉक्टरी चिकित्सा के लिए अपने अंग का दान करने वाला व्यक्ति; शरीरांगदाता *a blood/kidney donor* **2** somebody who gives money or goods to an organization that helps people or animals दानी, दाता

**don't** ➪ **do** देखिए।

**donut** (*AmE*) = **doughnut**

**doodle** /ˈduːdl ˈडूड्ल्/ *verb* [I] to draw lines, patterns, etc. without thinking, especially when you are bored यों ही बिना अधिक ध्यान दिए रेखाएँ खींचना या चित्र बनाना (विशेषतः बोर होने पर) ▶ **doodle** *noun* [C] यों ही बिना अधिक ध्यान दिए रेखाएँ खींचने या चित्र बनाने का काम

**doom** /duːm डूम्/ *noun* [U] death or a terrible event in the future which you cannot avoid निश्चित सर्वनाश, क़यामत, विनाश *a sense of impending doom* (= that something bad is going to happen) ▶ **doomed** *adj.* जिसका नाश होना निश्चित है *The plan was doomed from the start.*

**door** /dɔː(r) डॉ(र्)/ *noun* [C] **1** a piece of wood, glass, etc. that you open and close to get in or out of a room, building, car, etc. दरवाज़ा, द्वार, किवाड़ *to open/shut/close the door* ○ *to answer the door* (= to open the door when sb knocks or rings the bell) **2** the entrance to a building, room, car, etc. इमारत, कमरे, कार आदि का प्रवेश बिंदु, दरवाज़ा *I looked through the door and saw her sitting there.*

IDM **(from) door to door** (from) house to house एक मकान से दूसरे मकान तक, घर-घर *The journey takes about five hours, door to door.* ○ *a door-to-door salesman* (= a person who visits people in their homes to try and sell them things)

**next door (to sb/sth)** in the next house, room, etc. अगले, मकान, कमरे आदि में *Do you know the people who live next door?*

**out of doors** outside (घर से) बाहर *Shall we eat out of doors today?* ✪ पर्याय **outdoors** ✪ विलोम **indoors**

**doorbell** /ˈdɔːbel ˈडॉबेल्/ *noun* [C] a bell on the outside of a house which you ring when you want to go in दरवाज़े की घंटी

**doorman** /ˈdɔːmən ˈडॉमन्/ *noun* [C] (*pl.* **-men** /-mən -मन्/) a man, often in uniform, whose job is to stand at the entrance to a large building such as a hotel or a theatre, and open the door for visitors, find them taxis, etc. दरबान, ड्योढ़ीदार, द्वारपाल, प्रतिहार

**doormat** /ˈdɔːmæt ˈडॉमैट्/ *noun* [C] **1** a piece of material on the floor in front of a door which you can clean your shoes on before going inside पायदान, पाँवपोंछ, पायंदाज **2** (*informal*) a person who allows other people to treat him/her badly without complaining लोगों के दुर्व्यवहार का शिकार व्यक्ति (जो शिकायत नहीं करता)

**doorstep** /ˈdɔːstep ˈडॉस्टैप्/ *noun* [C] a step in front of a door outside a building दहलीज़ या मुख्य द्वार के पहले वाली सीढ़ी; देहली, देहरी

IDM **on your/the doorstep** very near to you बहुत निकट *The sea was right on our doorstep.*

**doorway** /ˈdɔːweɪ ˈडॉवे/ *noun* [C] an opening filled by a door leading into a building, room, etc. दीवार में दरवाज़े की जगह, द्वारमार्ग, दरवाज़ा जो भवन या कक्ष में जाने का मार्ग है *She was standing in the doorway.*

**dope**[1] /dəʊp डोप्/ *noun* (*informal*) **1** [U] an illegal drug, especially **cannabis** or **marijuana** (ग़ैर-क़ानूनी) मादक द्रव्य (विशेषतः चरस, भाँग) **2** [C] a stupid person मूर्ख व्यक्ति *What a dope!*

**dope**[2] /dəʊp डोप्/ *verb* [T] to give a drug secretly to a person or an animal, especially to make him/her/it sleep व्यक्ति या पशु को चुपके से मादक द्रव्य देना (विशेषतः उसे बेहोश करने या सुलाने के लिए)

**dopey** /ˈdəʊpi ˈडोपि/ *adj.* **1** tired and not able to think clearly, especially because of drugs, alcohol or lack of sleep अलसाया और बेसुध (विशेषतः नशीला पदार्थ, मदिरा या नींद पूरी न होने के कारण) **2** (*informal*) stupid; not intelligent मूर्ख; प्रतिभाहीन

**dormant** /ˈdɔːmənt ˈडॉमन्ट्/ *adj.* not active for some time कुछ समय के लिए निष्क्रिय *a dormant volcano*

**dormitory** /ˈdɔːmətri ˈडॉमट्रि/ *noun* [C] (*pl.* **dormitories**) (*also* **dorm**) **1** a large bedroom with a number of beds in it, especially in a school, etc. अनेक पलंगों वाला बड़ा शयनकक्ष (विशेषतः स्कूल आदि में) **2** (*AmE*) a building at a college or university where students live कॉलेज या विश्वविद्यालय का छात्रावास

**dorsal** /ˈdɔːsl ˈडॉसल्/ *adj.* (*only before a noun*) on or connected with the back of a fish or an animal किसी पशु या मछली की पीठ का, पृष्ठीय *a shark's dorsal fin* ➪ **pectoral** और **ventral** देखिए तथा **fish** पर चित्र देखिए।

**dosa** *noun* [C] a south Indian pancake made form finely ground rice and lentils. It is sometimes stuffed with spiced vegetables and is usually eaten with **chutney** डोसा, डोसा चटनी के साथ परोसा जाता है

**dosage** /ˈdəʊsɪdʒ ˈडोसिज्/ *noun* [C, *usually sing.*] the amount of a medicine you should take over a period of time दवा की निर्धारित मात्रा, ख़ुराक *The recommended dosage is one tablet every four hours.*

**dose** /dəʊs डोस्/ *verb* [T] to give sb/yourself a medicine or drug दवा की ख़ुराक देना या लेना *She dosed herself with aspirin and went to work.*

**dossier** /ˈdɒsieɪ ˈडॉसिए/ *noun* [C] a collection of papers containing detailed information about a person, an event or a subject जिसमें किसी व्यक्ति, घटना या विषय पर विस्तृत जानकारी हो *The police probably have a dossier on him.*

**dot**[1] /dɒt डॉट्/ *noun* [C] **1** a small, round mark, like a full stop बिंदु, बिंदी *a white dress with black dots* ○ *The letters 'i' and 'j' have dots above them.*

> NOTE (व्यक्ति के) **email** पते पर **dot** का प्रयोग होता है। जैसे **anil@yahoo.com** को पढ़ेंगे 'Anil **at** yahoo **dot** com.

**2** something that looks like a dot बिंदु जैसी दिखने वाली वस्तु *He watched until the aeroplane was just a dot in the sky.*

IDM **on the dot** (*informal*) at exactly the right time or at exactly the time mentioned एकदम ठीक समय पर

**dot**[2] /dɒt डॉट्/ *verb* [T] (**dotting; dotted**) (*usually passive*) to mark with a dot बिंदु लगाना

IDM **be dotted about/around** to be spread over an area किसी क्षेत्र में फैले होना *There are restaurants dotted about all over the centre of town.*

**be dotted with** to have several things or people in or on it किसी (स्थान) में या पर अनेक वस्तुओं का (बिंदुओं की भाँति) बिखरे होना *a hillside dotted with sheep*

**dot-com** /dɒtˈkɒm डॉट्ˈकॉम्/ *noun* [C] (*computing*) a company that sells goods and services on the Internet इंटरनेट पर सामान और सेवाएँ उपलब्ध कराने वाली कंपनी; डॉट-कॉम

**dote** /dəʊt डोट्/ *verb* [I] **dote on sb/sth** to have or show a lot of love for sb/sth and think he/she/it is perfect किसी पर लट्टू हो जाना, किसी को बहुत प्यार देना, किसी से अतिशय स्नेह करना *He's always doted on his eldest son.* ▶ **doting** *adj.* अतिस्नेही *doting parents*

**dotted line** *noun* [C] a line of small round marks (**dots**) which show where sth is to be written on a form, etc. (फ़ार्म पर) बिंदुओं से बनी रेखा (जिस पर कुछ लिखा जाए) *Sign on the dotted line.*

**double**[1] /ˈdʌbl ˈडबल्/ *adj., det.* **1** twice as much or as many (as usual) दुगुना, दूना *His income is double hers.* ○ *We'll need double the amount of juice.* **2** having two equal or similar parts दो समान या एक जैसे अंशों वाला, दुहरा *double doors* ○ *My phone number is two four double three four* (= 24334). **3** made for or used by two people or things दो व्यक्तियों के लिए या के द्वारा प्रयुक्त, वस्तु *a double garage*

**double**[2] /ˈdʌbl ˈडबल्/ *adv.* in twos or two parts युग्म, युगल, दो एक साथ या इकट्ठे *When I saw her with her twin sister I thought I was* ***seeing double****.*

**double**[3] /ˈdʌblˈडबल्/ *noun* **1** [U] twice the (usual) number or amount दुगुनी संख्या या मात्रा *When you work overtime, you get paid double.* **2** [C] a person who looks very much like another बिलकुल दूसरे जैसा दिखने वाला व्यक्ति *I thought it was you I saw in the supermarket. You must have a double.* **3** [C] an actor who replaces another actor in a film to do dangerous or other special things फ़िल्म में मूल अभिनेता का स्थानापन्न (जो उसके बदले ख़तरनाक या अन्य भूमिकाएँ निभाता है) **4** [C] a bedroom for two people in a hotel, etc. दो व्यक्तियों के लिए होटल का कमरा, डबल रूम **5 doubles** [*pl.*] (in some sports, for example tennis) with two pairs playing (टेनिस आदि में) युगल मैच, डबल्स मैच, मैच जिसमें दोनों ओर से दो-दो खिलाड़ी खेलते हैं *the Men's Doubles final*

**double**[4] /ˈdʌblˈडबल्/ *verb* **1** [I, T] to become or to make sth twice as much or as many; to multiply by two दुगुना होना या करना; दो से गुणा करना *The price of houses has almost doubled.* ○ *Think of a number and double it.* **2** [I] **double (up) as sth** to have a second use or function किसी वस्तु का एक और ढंग से भी प्रयोग होना, दूसरा या गौण कार्य भी करना *The small room doubles (up) as a study.*

**PHRV** **double (sb) up/over** (to cause sb) to bend the body (दर्द या हँसी से) दुहरा हो जाना *to be doubled up with pain/laughter*

**double-barrelled** (*AmE* **double-barreled**) *adj.* **1** (used about a gun) having two long metal tubes through which bullets are fired (**barrels**) दुनाली (बंदूक़) **2** (used about a family name) having two parts, sometimes joined by the mark (-) (**a hyphen**) दो अंशों वाले (हाइफ़न से संयुक्त) कुलनाम के लिए प्रयुक्त *Mr Day-Lewis*

**double bass** (*also* **bass**) *noun* [C] the largest musical instrument with strings, that you can play either standing up or sitting down एक प्रकार का बड़ा वायलिन ➪ **piano** पर नोट देखिए।

**double-breasted** *adj.* (used about a coat or jacket) having two rows of buttons down the front सामने से दो जोड़ी बटनों की पंक्ति (ऊपर से नीचे) वाला (कोट) ➪ **single-breasted** देखिए।

**double-check** *verb* [I, T] to check sth again, or with great care दुबारा या सावधानी से जाँच करना

**double chin** *noun* [C] fat under a person's chin that looks like another chin दुहरी ठुड्डी, भारी ठुड्डी के नीचे की मांसपेशी (जो एक और ठुड्डी जैसी दिखती है)

**double-cross** *verb* [T] to cheat sb who believes that he/she can trust you after you have agreed to do sth dishonest together (ग़लत काम में किसी का साथ देने और उस पर विश्वास करने वाले) व्यक्ति को धोखा देना

**double-decker** *noun* [C] a bus with two floors दुमंजिली बस, डबलडेकर

**double Dutch** *noun* [U] conversation or writing that you cannot understand at all अस्पष्ट भाषण या लेखन (जिसे समझना असंभव हो)

**double figures** *noun* [U] a number that is more than nine (नौ से अधिक) दो अंकों वाली कोई संख्या *Inflation is now* ***in double figures****.*

**double glazing** *noun* [U] two layers of glass in a window to keep a building warm or quiet दोहरे काँच वाली खिड़की (जो इमारत को गरम और शोर से मुक्त रखती है) ▶ **double-glazed** *adj.* दोहरे काँच वाला

**doubly** /ˈdʌbliˈडब्लि/ *adv.* **1** in two ways दो तरह से *He was doubly blessed with both good looks and talent.* **2** more than usually पक्के तौर पर *I made doubly sure that the door was locked.*

**doubt**[1] /daʊt डाउट्/ *noun* [C, U] **doubt (about sth); doubt that... ; doubt as to sth** (a feeling of) uncertainty संदेह का भाव, अनिश्चय *If you have any doubts about the job, feel free to ring me and discuss them.* ○ *There's some doubt that Jassi will pass the exam.*

**IDM** **cast doubt on sth** ➪ **cast**[1] देखिए।

**give sb the benefit of the doubt** ➪ **benefit**[1] देखिए।

**in doubt** not sure or definite संदिग्ध, अनिश्चित
**no doubt** (used when you expect sth to happen but you are not sure that it will) probably संभवतः, शायद *No doubt she'll write when she has time.*
**without (a) doubt** निस्संदेह, निश्चित रूप से *It was, without doubt, the coldest winter for many years.*

**doubt[2]** /daʊt डाउट्/ *verb* [T] to think sth is unlikely or to feel uncertain (about sth) संदेह की स्थिति में होना या संदेह करना *She never doubted that he was telling the truth.* ○ *He had never doubted her support.*

**doubtful** /ˈdaʊtfl ˈडाउट्फ़्ल्/ *adj.* **1** unlikely or uncertain संदिग्ध या अनिश्चित *It's doubtful whether/if we'll finish in time.* ○ *It was doubtful that he was still alive.* **2 doubtful (about sth/about doing sth)** (used about a person) not sure (व्यक्ति) अनिश्चित, संदेहाकुल, सशंक, संशयी *He still felt doubtful about his decision.* ▶ **doubtfully** /-fəli -फ़लि/ *adv.* संदेहपूर्वक *'I suppose it'll be all right,' she said doubtfully.*

**doubtless** /ˈdaʊtləs ˈडाउट्लस्/ *adv.* almost certainly निस्संदेह, लगभग निश्चित रूप से *Doubtless she'll have a good excuse for being late!*

**dough** /dəʊ डो/ *noun* [U] **1** a mixture of flour, water, etc. used for baking into bread, etc. गुँथा आटा, लोई **2** (*informal*) money पैसा, धन

**doughnut** (*AmE* **donut**) /ˈdəʊnʌt ˈडोनट्/ *noun* [C] a small cake in the shape of a ball or a ring, made from a sweet dough cooked in very hot oil गेंद या छल्ले के आकार का छोटा केक; डोनट

**dour** /dʊə(r) डुअ(र्)/ *adj.* (used about a person's manner or expression) cold and unfriendly (व्यक्ति का रंग-ढंग या हाव-भाव) रूखा और कर्कश

**douse** (*also* **dowse**) /daʊs डाउस्/ *verb* [T] **1 douse sth (with sth)** to stop a fire from burning by pouring liquid over it आग को बुझाना *The firefighters managed to douse the flames.* **2 douse sb/sth (in/with sth)** to cover sb/sth with liquid द्रव पदार्थ से सराबोर या तरबतर कर देना *to douse yourself in perfume* (= wear too much of it)

**dove[1]** /dʌv डव्/ *noun* [C] a type of white bird, often used as a sign of peace सफ़ेद कबूतर, फ़ाख़्ता, पेंडुकी, पंडुक

**dove[2]** /dəʊv डोव्/ ⇨ (*AmE*) **dive[1]** का past tense रूप

**dowdy** /ˈdaʊdi ˈडाउडि/ *adj.* (used about a person or the clothes he/she wears) not attractive or fashionable (व्यक्ति या उसकी पोशाक) अनाकर्षक या पुरानी चाल का, की

**down[1]** /daʊn डाउन्/ *adv., prep.* **1** to or at a lower level or place; from the top towards the bottom of sth नीचे; ऊँचाई से नीचे की ओर *Can you get that book down from the top shelf?* ○ *Her hair hung down her back.* ○ *The rain was running down the window.* **2** along के साथ-साथ *We sailed down the river towards the sea.* ○ *'Where's the nearest garage?' 'Go down this road and take the first turning on the right.'* **3** from a standing or vertical position to a sitting or horizontal one ज़मीन पर खड़े से लेटने की गति *I think I'll sit/lie down.* **4** to or in the south दक्षिण की ओर या दक्षिण में *We went down to Chennai for our holiday.* **5** used for showing that the level, amount, strength, etc. of sth is less or lower जब किसी का स्तर, मात्रा, शक्ति आदि के कम होने या करने का संकेत करना हो, कम होने या घटने का सूचक *Do you mind if I turn the heating down a bit?* **6** (*written*) on paper काग़ज़ पर (लिखित), लिखित रूप में *Put these dates down in your diary.* **7 down to sb/sth** even including तक, को भी शामिल करते हुए *We had everything planned down to the last detail.*

IDM **be down to sb** to be sb's responsibility पर दायित्व होना, के लिए ज़िम्मेदार होना *When my father died it was down to me to look after the family's affairs.*
**be down to sth** to have only the amount mentioned left एक प्रक्रिया में किसी वस्तु का अंतिम होना *I need to do some washing—I'm down to my last shirt.*
**down and out** having no money, job or home दुर्दशाग्रस्त या दुर्दशा का शिकार, न घर-न नौकरी-न पैसा
**down under** (*informal*) (in) Australia ऑस्ट्रेलिया (में)

**down[2]** /daʊn डाउन्/ *verb* [T] (*informal*) to finish a drink quickly पेय को तेज़ी से पी जाना या समाप्त कर देना *She **downed** her drink **in one*** (= she drank the whole glass without stopping).

**down[3]** /daʊn डाउन्/ *adj.* **1** sad उदास, खिन्न, अवनत *You're looking a bit down today.* **2** lower than before पहले से कम *Unemployment figures are down again this month.* **3** (used about computers) not working (कंप्यूटर) बंद, रुका हुआ, निष्क्रिय *I can't access the file as our computers have been down all morning.*

**down[4]** /daʊn डाउन्/ *noun* [U] very soft feathers बहुत कोमल पंख *a duvet filled with duck down*

IDM **ups and downs** ⇨ **up[2]** देखिए।

**down-and-out** *noun* [C] a person who has got no money, job or home पैसा-नौकरी-घर गँवा चुका व्यक्ति, साधनहीन हो चुका व्यक्ति, फटेहाल

**downcast** /ˈdaʊnkɑːst ˈडाउन्कास्ट्/ *adj.* **1** (used about a person) sad and without hope (व्यक्ति) खिन्न और निराश **2** (used about eyes) looking down (आँखें) नीचे झुकी हुई

**downfall** /ˈdaʊnfɔːl ˈडाउन्फ़ॉल्/ *noun* [*sing.*] a loss of a person's money, power, social position, etc.; the thing that causes this धन, सत्ता, समाज में आदर आदि की हानि, अधःपतन; अधःपतनकारी वस्तु *The government's downfall seemed inevitable.* ○ *Greed was her downfall.*

**downgrade** /ˌdaʊnˈɡreɪd ˌडाउन्ˈग्रेड्/ *verb* [T] **downgrade sb/sth (from sth) (to sth)** to reduce sb/sth to a lower level or position of importance किसी के पद या महत्त्व को घटा देना *Shamim's been downgraded from manager to assistant manager.*

**downhearted** /ˌdaʊnˈhɑːtɪd ˌडाउन्ˈहाटिड्/ *adj.* sad विषण्ण, दुखी

**downhill** /ˌdaʊnˈhɪl ˌडाउन्ˈहिल्/ *adj., adv.* (going) in a downward direction; towards the bottom of a hill नीचे की ओर जाने वाला; पहाड़ी के तल की ओर *It's an easy walk. The road runs downhill most of the way.* ✪ विलोम **uphill**

**IDM go down hill** to get worse बदतर हो जाना *Their relationship has been going downhill for some time now.*

**download¹** /ˌdaʊnˈləʊd ˌडाउन्ˈलोड्/ *verb* [T] (*computing*) to copy a computer file, etc. from a large computer system to a smaller one बृहत कंप्यूटर तंत्र से अपने कंप्यूटर में फ़ाइल आदि उतार लेना ✪ विलोम **upload¹** ▶ **downloadable** /-əbl -अबल्/ *adj.* उतार लेने योग्य

**download²** /ˈdaʊnləʊd ˌडाउन्लोड्/ *noun* (*computing*) **1** [U] the act or process of copying data from a large computer system to a smaller one बड़े कंप्यूटर तंत्र से छोटे कंप्यूटर में फ़ाइल उतारने का कार्य या प्रक्रिया **2** [C] a computer file that is copied from a large computer system to a smaller one बड़े कंप्यूटर से छोटे कंप्यूटर में उतारी गई फ़ाइल *It's one of the most popular free software downloads.* ➪ **upload²** देखिए।

**downmarket** /ˌdaʊnˈmɑːkɪt ˌडाउन्ˈमाकिट्/ *adj., adv.* cheap and of low quality सस्ता और घटिया क़िसम का

**downpour** /ˈdaʊnpɔː(r) ˈडाउन्पॉ(र्)/ *noun* [C] a heavy, sudden fall of rain मूसलाधार वर्षा, एकाएक भारी वर्षा, घनघोर वर्षा

**downright** /ˈdaʊnraɪt ˈडाउन्राइट्/ *adj.* (*only before a noun*) (used about sth bad or unpleasant) complete (अरुचिकर या बुरी स्थिति) पूर्णतया, पूरी तरह *The holiday was a downright disaster.* ▶ **downright** *adv.* पूर्णतया *The way he spoke to me was downright rude!*

**downside** /ˈdaʊnsaɪd ˈडाउन्साइड्/ *noun* [C, *usually sing.*] the disadvantages or negative aspects of sth नकारात्मक या अलाभकारी पक्ष *All good ideas have a downside.*

**downsize** /ˈdaʊnsaɪz ˈडाअन्साइज़्/ *verb* [I, T] to reduce the number of people who work in a company, business, etc. in order to reduce costs (ख़र्चे में कमी के लिए) किसी संगठन के कर्मचारियों की संख्या घटाना

**Down's syndrome** /ˈdaʊnz sɪndrəʊm ˈडाउन्ज़् सिन्ड्रोम्/ *noun* [U] a condition that some people are born with. People with this condition have a flat, wide face and lower than average intelligence एक जन्मजात विकृति (इस विकृति से ग्रस्त व्यक्ति का चेहरा सपाट और चौड़ा और बुद्धि मंद होती है)

**downstairs** /ˌdaʊnˈsteəz ˌडाउन्ˈस्टेअज़्/ *adv., adj.* towards or on a lower floor of a house or building निचली मंजिल पर *He fell downstairs and broke his arm.* ✪ विलोम **upstairs**

**downstream** /ˌdaʊnˈstriːm ˌडाउन्ˈस्ट्रीम्/ *adv., adj.* in the direction in which a river flows नदी प्रवाह के साथ-साथ, बहाव या प्रवाह की ओर; अनुप्रवाहगामी *We were rowing downstream.* ✪ विलोम **upstream**

**down-to-earth** *adj.* (used about a person) sensible, realistic and practical (व्यक्ति) बुद्धिमान, यथार्थवादी और व्यवहारकुशल

**downtrodden** /ˈdaʊntrɒdn ˈडाउन्ट्रॉड्न्/ *adj.* (used about a person) made to suffer bad treatment or living conditions by people in power, but being too tired, poor, ill, etc. to change this (व्यक्ति) पददलित और पीड़ित, शोषित

**downturn** /ˈdaʊntɜːn ˈडाउन्टन्/ *noun* (*usually sing.*) **a downturn (in sth)** a drop in the amount of business that is done; a time when the economy becomes weaker व्यापार में मंदी; अर्थव्यवस्था में मंदी का समय *a downturn in sales/trade/business* ✪ विलोम **upturn**

**downward** /ˈdaʊnwəd ˈडाउन्वड्/ *adj., adv.* (*only before a noun*) towards the ground or a lower level नीचे की ओर जाने वाला, अधोमुखी *a downward movement* ▶ **downwards** /ˈdaʊnwədz ˈडाउन्वड्ज़्/ *adv.* नीचे की ओर *She laid the picture face downwards on the table.* ✪ विलोम **upward(s)**

**dowry** /ˈdaʊri ˈडाउरि/ *noun* [C] (*pl.* **dowries**) an amount of money or property which, in some countries, a woman's family gives to the man she is marrying दहेज, वरदक्षिणा

**dowse** = **douse**

**doz.** *abbr.* dozen दर्जन

**doze** /dəʊz डोज़्/ *verb* [I] to sleep lightly and/or for a short time झपकी लेना, ऊँघना *He was dozing in front of the television.* ▶ **doze** *noun* [*sing.*]

**PHR V** **doze off** to go to sleep, especially during the day झपकी लेना (विशेषतः दिन के समय) *I'm sorry—I must have dozed off for a minute.*

**dozen** /ˈdʌzn ˈडज़्न्/ (*abbr.* **doz.**) *noun* [C] (*pl.* **dozen**) twelve or a group of twelve दर्जन, बारह या बारह का समुच्चय *A dozen eggs, please.* ○ *half a dozen* (= six) ○ *two dozen sheep*

**IDM** **dozens (of sth)** (*informal*) very many दर्जनों, बीसियों, अनेकानेक *I've tried phoning her dozens of times.*

**dozy** /ˈdəʊzi ˈडोज़ि/ *adj.* **1** wanting to sleep; not feeling awake ऊँघने का इच्छुक; अर्धनिद्रालु **2** (*BrE informal*) stupid: not intelligent बेवकूफ़; मंदबुद्धि *You dozy thing—look what you've done!*

**DPhil** /ˌdiː ˈfɪl ˌडी ˈफ़िल्/ *abbr.* Doctor of Philosophy; an advanced university degree that you receive when you complete a piece of research into a special subject विषय विशेष में अध्ययन पूर्ण करने पर विश्वविद्यालय से प्राप्त डिग्री; डी फिल ✪ पर्याय **PhD**

**Dr** *abbr.* doctor डॉक्टर *Dr Kamal Malik*

**drab** /dræb ड्रैब्/ *adj.* not interesting or attractive अनाकर्षक, फीका, बेचमक, नीरस *a drab grey office building*

**draft[1]** /drɑːft ड्राफ़्ट्/ *noun* [C] **1** a piece of writing, etc. which will probably be changed and improved; not the final version प्रारूप, मसौदा, पहली प्रति, ख़ाका, आरेख, रूपरेखा *the first draft of a speech/essay* **2** a written order to a bank to pay money to sb बैंक का ड्राफ़्ट, बैंक के लिए धनादेश *Payment must be made **by bank draft**.* **3** (*AmE*) = **draught[1] 1**

**draft[2]** /drɑːft ड्राफ़्ट्/ *verb* [T] **1** to make a first or early copy of a piece of writing लेख का प्रारूप, मसौदा या पहली प्रति तैयार करना *I'll draft a letter and show it to you before I type it.* **2** (*AmE*) (*usually passive*) to force sb to join the armed forces सेना में भरती के लिए किसी को बाध्य करना *He was drafted into the army.*

**draftsman** (*AmE*) = **draughtsman**

**drafty** (*AmE*) = **draughty**

**drag[1]** /dræg ड्रैग्/ *verb* (**dragging; dragged**) **1** [T] to pull sb/sth along with difficulty किसी वस्तु को ज़ोर लगाकर घसीटना *The box was so heavy we had to drag it along the floor.* **2** [T] to make sb come or go somewhere (किसी को) उसकी अनिच्छा से साथ आने या कहीं और जाने के लिए विवश या तैयार करना *She's always trying to drag me along to museums and galleries, but I'm not interested.* **3** [I] **drag (on)** to be boring or to seem to last a long time (किसी गतिविधि का) उबाऊ होना या देर तक चलना, नीरस होना *The speeches dragged on for hours.* **4** [T] (*computing*) to move sth across the screen of the computer using the mouse कंप्यूटर स्क्रीन पर किसी वस्तु को, माउस की सहायता से घुमाना, एक स्थल से दूसरे स्थल तक ले जाना *Click on the file and drag it into the new folder.*

**PHR V** **drag sth out** to make sth last longer than necessary किसी बात को ज़रूरत से ज्यादा खींचना या लंबा करना *Let's not drag this decision out—shall we go or not?*

**drag sth out (of sb)** to force or persuade sb to give you information आवश्यक जानकारी देने के लिए किसी को बाध्य या तैयार करना

**drag[2]** /dræg ड्रैग्/ *noun* **1** [*sing.*] (*informal*) a person or thing that is boring or annoying उबाऊ या बुरा लगने वाला व्यक्ति या काम *'The car's broken down.' 'Oh no! What a drag!'* **2** [C] an act of breathing in cigarette smoke सिगरेट का कश खींचने की क्रिया *He took a long drag on his cigarette.*

**dragon** /ˈdrægən ˈड्रैगन्/ *noun* [C] (in stories) a large animal with wings, which can breathe fire (कहानियों में) आग उगलने वाला एक बड़ा पंखदार छिपकली जैसा जीव; ड्रैगन, परदार साँप

**dragonfly** /ˈdrægənflaɪ ˈड्रैगन्फ़्लाइ/ *noun* [C] (*pl.* **dragonflies**) an insect with a long thin body, often brightly coloured, and two pairs of large wings. Dragon flies often live near water एक लंबा पतला परदार चमकीला कीड़ा; चिउरा ➪ **insect** पर चित्र देखिए।

**drain[1]** /dreɪn ड्रेन्/ *noun* [C] a pipe or hole in the ground that dirty water, etc. goes down to be carried away गंदे पानी की नाली

**IDM** **a drain on sb/sth** something that uses up time, money, strength, etc. कोई वस्तु जिसमें समय, धन, शक्ति आदि व्यय हो *The cost of travelling is a great drain on our budget.*

**(go) down the drain** (*informal*) (to be) wasted बरबाद हो जाना, अपव्यय हो जाना *All that hard work has gone down the drain.*

**drain²** /dreɪn ड्रेन्/ *verb* **1** [I, T] to become empty or dry as liquid flows away and disappears; to make sth dry or empty in this way द्रव निकल जाने से सूखा हो जाना; सूखा कर देना *The whole area will have to be drained before it can be used for farming.* **2** [I, T] **drain (sth) (from/out of sth); drain (sth) (away/off)** to flow away; to make a liquid flow away बह जाना; द्रव को बहने देना *The sink's blocked—the water won't drain away at all.* ○ (*figurative*) *He felt all his anger begin to drain away.* **3** [T] to drink all the liquid in a glass, cup, etc. सारा द्रव पदार्थ पीकर गिलास, प्याले आदि को खाली कर देना, गिलास, प्याले आदि में रखे समूचे द्रव पदार्थ को पी जाना *He drained his glass in one gulp.* **4** [T] **drain sb/sth (of sth)** to make sb/sth weaker, poorer, etc. by slowly using all the strength, money, etc. available किसी व्यक्ति को धीरे-धीरे धन, शक्ति आदि से क्षीण कर देना *My mother's hospital expenses were slowly draining my funds.* ○ *The experience left her* ***emotionally drained***.

**drainage** /ˈdreɪnɪdʒ ˈड्रेनिज्/ *noun* [U] a system used for making water, etc. flow away from a place पानी आदि के निकासी की प्रणाली

**draining board** *noun* [C] the place in the kitchen where you put plates, cups, knives, etc. to dry after washing them रसोई में वह स्थान जहाँ प्लेटें आदि धोकर सूखने के लिए रखी जाती हैं

**drainpipe** /ˈdreɪnpaɪp ˈड्रेन्पाइप्/ *noun* [C] a pipe which goes down the side of a building and carries water from the roof into a hole in the ground (**drain**) परनाला, छत के पानी को नीचे लाने वाला पाइप

**drama** /ˈdrɑːmə ˈड्रामा/ *noun* **1** [C] a play for the theatre, radio or television नाटक (थियेटर, रेडियो या टेलीविज़न के लिए) **2** [U] plays as a form of writing; the performance of plays नाटक (एक लिखित रचना के रूप में); नाटक का मंचन *He wrote some drama as well as poetry.* **3** [C, U] an exciting event; exciting things that happen उत्तेजक या नाटकीय घटना; उत्तेजक या नाटकीय घटनाओं की शृंखला *a real-life courtroom drama*

**dramatic** /drəˈmætɪk ड्रˈमैटिक्/ *adj.* **1** noticeable or sudden and often surprising अकस्मात होने वाली और प्रायः आश्चर्यकारी (बात), नाटकीय *a dramatic change/increase/fall/improvement* **2** exciting or impressive उत्तेजक या असरदार, नाटकीय *the film's dramatic opening scene* **3** connected with plays or the theatre नाटक या रंगमंच से संबंधित, नाटकीय या रंगमंचीय, नाट्य विषयक *Shakespeare's dramatic works* **4** (used about a person, a person's behaviour, etc.) showing feelings, etc. in a very obvious way because you want other people to notice you प्रदर्शन या दिखावा करने वाला (व्यक्ति), दिखाने का (आचरण) *Calm down. There's no need to be so dramatic about everything!* ▶ **dramatically** /-kli -क्लि/ *adv.* प्रदर्शनात्मक रीति से, दिखावा करते हुए

**dramatist** /ˈdræmətɪst ˈड्रैमटिस्ट्/ *noun* [C] a person who writes plays for the theatre, radio or television नाटककार, नाटक-लेखक

**dramatize** (*also* **-ise**) /ˈdræmətaɪz ˈड्रैमटाइज़्/ *verb* **1** [T] to make a book, an event, etc. into a play (किसी कहानी आदि को) नाटक की विधा में प्रस्तुत करना *The novel has been dramatized for television.* **2** [I, T] to make sth seem more exciting or important than it really is किसी घटना को वास्तविकता से अधिक उत्तेजक या बड़ा बना देना *The newspaper was accused of dramatizing the situation.* ▶ **dramatization** (*also* **-isation**) /ˌdræmətaɪˈzeɪʃn ˌड्रैमटाइˈज़ेश्न्/ *noun* [C, U] नाटकीकरण, नाट्य-रूपांतरण

**drank** ⇨ **drink** का past tense रूप

**drape** /dreɪp ड्रेप्/ *verb* [T] **1 drape sth round/over sth** to put a piece of material, clothing, etc. loosely on sth किसी वस्तु पर कोई पोशाक या अन्य वस्तु यों ही डाल देना *He draped his coat over the back of his chair.* **2 drape sb/sth (in/with sth)** (*usually passive*) to cover sb/sth (with cloth, etc.) किसी वस्तु को कपड़े से लपेटना *The furniture was draped in dust sheets.* ▶ **drape** *noun* [C] (*AmE*) = **curtain**

**drastic** /ˈdræstɪk ˈड्रास्टिक्/ *adj.* extreme, and having a sudden very strong effect अत्यधिक और भरपूर असरदार, उग्र, प्रचंड *There has been a drastic rise in crime in the area.* ▶ **drastically** /-kli -क्लि/ *adv.* अत्यधिक

**draught¹** /drɑːft ड्राफ़्ट्/ *noun* **1** (*AmE* **draft**) [C] a flow of cold air that comes into a room कमरे में आने वाला ठंडी हवा का झोंका *Can you shut the door? There's a draught in here.* **2 draughts** (*AmE* **checkers**) [U] a game for two players that you play on a black and white board using round black and white pieces ड्राफ़्ट्स या चेकर्स का खेल जिसे दो खिलाड़ी सफ़ेद और काले खानों वाले बोर्ड पर सफ़ेद और काली गोटियों से खेलते हैं ▶ **draughty** *adj.* झोंकेदार, हवादार

**draught²** /drɑːft ड्राफ़्ट्/ *adj.* (used about beer, etc.) served from a large container (**a barrel**) rather than in a bottle बड़े डिब्बे से (न कि बोतल से) परोसी गई (बियर) *draught beer*

**draughtsman** (*AmE* **draftsman** /ˈdrɑːftsmən ˈड्राफ़्ट्स्मन्/) *noun* [C] (*pl.* **-men** /-mən -मन्/) a person whose job is to do technical drawings तकनीकी आरेख या नक़्शे बनाने वाला, नक़्शा-नवीस

**Dravidian** *adj.* connected with a group of languages spoken in southern India and Sri Lanka दक्षिण भारत और श्रीलंका में प्रचलित द्रविड़ भाषाओं से संबंधित

**draw**[1] /drɔː ड्रॉ/ *verb* (*pt* **drew** /druː ड्रू/; *pp* **drawn** /drɔːn ड्रॉन्/) **1** [I, T] to do a picture or diagram of sth with a pencil, pen, etc. but not paint (पेंट को छोड़कर पेंसिल, पेन आदि से) किसी का चित्र या आरेख बनाना *Shall I draw you a map of how to get there?* ○ *I'm good at painting but I can't draw.* **2** [I] to move in the direction mentioned निर्दिष्ट दिशा में (आगे, समीप) बढ़ना, आना *The train drew into the station.* ○ *I became more anxious as my exams drew nearer.* **3** [T] to pull sth/sb into a new position or in the direction mentioned किसी वस्तु को खींचकर नई स्थिति या दिशा में लाना, खींचना, खींचकर ले जाना; निकालना या बढ़ाना *She drew the letter out of her pocket and handed it to me.* ○ *to draw* (= open or close) *the curtains* **4** [T] **draw sth (from sth)** to learn or decide sth as a result of study, research or experience अध्ययन के फलस्वरूप कोई नई बात जानना या निष्कर्ष निकालना या निर्णय पर पहुँचना *Can we* ***draw*** *any* conclusions *from this survey?* ○ *There are important* ***lessons to be drawn*** *from this tragedy.* **5** [T] **draw sth (from sb/sth)** to get or take sth from sb/sth (किसी से कुछ) प्राप्त करना या लेना *He draws the inspiration for his stories from his family.* **6** [T] **draw sth (from sb); draw sb (to sb/sth)** to make sb react to or be interested in sb/sth प्रतिक्रियास्वरूप कुछ प्राप्त करना या आकृष्ट करना *The advertisement has drawn criticism from people all over the country.* ○ *The musicians drew quite a large crowd.* **7** [I, T] to finish a game, competition, etc. with equal scores so that neither person or team wins किसी स्पर्धा में प्रतियोगियों का बराबरी पर छूटना *The two teams drew.* ○ *The match was drawn.*

**IDM** **bring sth/come/draw to an end** ➪ **end**[1] देखिए।

**draw (sb's) attention to sth** to make sb notice sth किसी बात की ओर ध्यान खींचना *The article draws attention to the problem of unemployment.*

**draw a blank** to get no result or response किसी परिणाम पर न पहुँचना, कोई उत्तर न पाना *Detectives investigating the case have drawn a blank so far.*

**draw a distinction between sth and sth** to show how two things are different दो वस्तुओं के बीच अंतर दिखाना

**draw the line at sth** to say 'no' to sth even though you are happy to help in other ways किसी काम के लिए ना कहना *I do most of the cooking but I draw the line at washing up as well!*

**draw lots** to decide sth by chance लाटरी से तय करना, परची निकालकर फ़ैसला करना *They drew lots to see who should stay behind.*

**PHRV** **draw in** to get dark earlier as winter arrives सर्दी आने पर जल्दी अँधेरा होना *The days/nights are drawing in.*

**draw out** (used about days) to get longer in the spring वसंत आने पर (दिनों का) लंबा हो जाना

**draw sth out** to take money out of a bank account बैंक के खाते से पैसा निकालना

**draw up** (used about a car, etc.) to drive up and stop in front of or near sth (कार आदि का) किसी के सामने या पास आकर रुकना *A police car drew up outside the building.*

**draw sth up** to prepare and write a document, list, etc. कोई दस्तावेज़, सूची आदि तैयार करना *Our solicitor is going to draw up the contract.*

**draw**[2] /drɔː ड्रॉ/ *noun* [C] **1** a result of a game or competition in which both players or teams get the same score so that neither of them wins खेल में बराबरी या बराबरी का खेल *The match* ***ended in a draw.*** **2** an act of deciding sth by chance by pulling out names or numbers from a bag, etc. परची निकालकर मामला तय करने का कार्य *She won her bike in a prize draw.*

**drawback** /ˈdrɔːbæk ˈड्रॉबैक्/ *noun* [C] a disadvantage or problem कमी, न्यूनता, त्रुटि, असुविधा *His lack of experience is a major drawback.*

**drawer** /drɔː(r) ड्रॉ(र्)/ *noun* [C] a container which forms part of a piece of furniture such as a desk, that you can pull out to put things in दराज़ *There's some paper in the top drawer of my desk.*

**drawing** /ˈdrɔːɪŋ ˈड्रॉइङ्/ *noun* **1** [C] a picture made with a pencil, pen, etc. but not paint (पेंट को छोड़कर पेंसिल, पेन आदि से बना) चित्र, आरेख, ड्राइंग ➪ **painting** पर नोट देखिए। **2** [U] the art of drawing pictures आरेखन कला *She's good at drawing and painting.*

**drawing pin** (*AmE* **thumbtack**) *noun* [C] a short pin with a flat top, used for fastening paper, etc. to a board or wall दीवार या बोर्ड पर काग़ज़ को जमाने के लिए प्रयुक्त पिन; ड्राइंग पिन ➪ **stationery** पर चित्र देखिए।

**drawing room** *noun* [C] (*old-fashioned*) a living room, especially in a large house बैठक, ड्रॉइंग रूम

**drawl** /drɔːl ड्रॉल्/ *verb* [I, T] to speak slowly, making the vowel sounds very long लंबी स्वर-ध्वनियों में धीरे-धीरे बोलना, मंद उच्चारण करना ▶ **drawl** *noun* [*sing.*] लंबी स्वर-ध्वनियों में मंद-मंद बोलने की शैली, मंद उच्चारण *to speak with a drawl*

**drawn**[1] ➪ **draw** का past participle रूप

**drawn**[2] /drɔːn ड्रॉन्/ *adj.* (used about a person or his/her face) looking tired, worried or ill (व्यक्ति का चेहरा) थका, चिंतित या बीमार-सा, लटका हुआ

**drawn-out** *adj.* lasting longer than necessary आवश्यकता से अधिक लंबा चलने वाला *long drawn-out negotiations*

**drawstring** /ˈdrɔːstrɪŋ ˈड्रॉस्ट्रिङ् / *noun* [C] a piece of string that is sewn inside the material at the top of a bag, pair of trousers, etc. that can be pulled tighter in order to make the opening smaller थैले, पाजामे आदि का नाड़ा या इज़ारबंद जिसे खींच कर थैला, पाजामा आदि बंद किया जाता है *The trousers fasten with a drawstring.* ➪ **button** पर चित्र देखिए।

**dread**[1] /dred ड्रेड्/ *verb* [T] to be very afraid of or worried about sth (किसी बात को लेकर) बहुत भयभीत या चिंतित होना, आशंकित होना *I'm dreading the exams.* ○ *I **dread to think** what my father will say.* ▶ **dreaded** *adj.* भयभीत, चिंतित

**dread**[2] /dred ड्रेड्/ *noun* [U, *sing.*] great fear अत्यधिक भय *He lived **in dread of** the same thing happening to him one day.*

**dreadful** /ˈdredfl ˈड्रेड्फ़्ल्/ *adj.* very bad or unpleasant बहुत घटिया या नीरस, अरुचिकर *We had a dreadful journey—traffic jams all the way!* ○ *I'm afraid there's been a dreadful* (= very serious) *mistake.*

**dreadfully** /ˈdredfəli ˈड्रेड्फ़लि/ *adv.* **1** very; extremely बहुत; अत्यधिक *I'm dreadfully sorry, I didn't mean to upset you.* **2** very badly बहुत बुरी तरह से, अरुचिकर ढंग से *The party went dreadfully and everyone left early.*

**dreadlocks** /ˈdredlɒks ˈड्रेड्लॉक्स्/ *noun* [*pl.*] hair worn in long thick pieces, especially by people of African origin लंबी मोटी चोटियों में गुँथे बाल (विशेषतः अफ़्रीकी मूल के लोगों में)

**dream**[1] /driːm ड्रीम्/ *noun* **1** [C] a series of events or pictures which happen in your mind while you are asleep सपना, स्वप्न *I had a strange **dream** last night.* ○ *That horror film has given me **bad dreams**.* ➪ **nightmare** देखिए। **2** [C] something that you want very much to happen, although it is not likely कोई अवास्तविक-सी महत्त्वाकांक्षा *Becoming a professional dancer was **a dream come true**.* **3** [*sing.*] a state of mind in which you are not thinking about what you are doing कल्पनाओं में मग्न रहने की मानसिक स्थिति, कल्पनामग्नता की मनोदशा *You've been in a dream all morning!*

**dream**[2] /driːm ड्रीम्/ *verb* (*pt, pp* **dreamed** /driːmd ड्रीम्ड्/ or **dreamt** /dremt ड्रेम्ट्/) **1** [I, T] **dream (about sb/sth)** to see or experience pictures and events in your mind while you are asleep स्वप्न या सपना देखना *I dreamt about the house that I lived in as a child.* ○ *I dreamed that I was running but I couldn't get away.* ➪ **daydream** देखिए। **2** [I] **dream (about/of sth/doing sth)** to imagine sth that you would like to happen मनचाहा होने की कल्पना करना *I've always dreamt about winning lots of money.* **3** [I] **dream (of doing sth/that...)** to imagine that sth might happen किसी बात की कल्पना करना *When I watched the Olympics on TV, I **never dreamt** that one day I'd be here competing!*

PHR V **dream sth up** (*informal*) to think of a plan, an idea, etc., especially sth strange अजीबोग़रीब बातें सोचना

**dreamer** /ˈdriːmə(r) ˈड्रीम(र्)/ *noun* [C] a person who thinks a lot about ideas, plans, etc. which may never happen instead of thinking about real life अवास्तविक योजनाओं और विचारों वाला व्यक्ति, ख्याली पुलाव पकाने वाला व्यक्ति; स्वप्नद्रष्टा

**dreamy** /ˈdriːmi ˈड्रीमि/ *adj.* looking as though you are not paying attention to what you are doing because you are thinking about sth else (व्यक्ति) विचारों में खोया हुआ, कल्पनामग्न *a dreamy look/expression* ▶ **dreamily** *adv.* विचारमग्नता के साथ

**dreary** /ˈdrɪəri ˈड्रिअरि/ *adj.* (**drearier; dreariest**) not at all interesting or attractive; boring नीरस या अनाकर्षक; उबाऊ

**dredge** /dredʒ ड्रेज्/ *verb* [T] to clear the mud, etc. from the bottom of a river, canal, etc. using a special machine नदी, नहर आदि के तले पर जमा कीचड़ को विशेष मशीन से साफ़ करना

PHR V **dredge sth up** to mention sth unpleasant from the past that sb would like to forget गड़े मुर्दे उखाड़ना; अतीत की अप्रिय बात का स्मरण करना *The newspaper had dredged up all sorts of embarrassing details about her private life.*

**dredger** /ˈdredʒə(r) ˈड्रेज(र्)/ *noun* [C] a boat or machine that is used to clear mud, etc. from the bottom of a river, or to make the river wider एक प्रकार की नाव या मशीन जो नदी के तल का कीचड़ साफ करने या नदी को चौड़ा करने के लिए प्रयोग में लाई जाती है; ड्रेजर

**dregs** /dregz ड्रेग्ज़् / *noun* [*pl.*] **1** the last drops in a container of liquid, containing small pieces of solid waste तलछट; डिब्बे में रखे द्रव पदार्थ की अंतिम बूँदें जिसमें कूड़ा-करकट होता है **2** the worst and most useless part of sth किसी वस्तु का सबसे घटिया और बेकार अंश *These people were regarded as the dregs of society.*

**drench** /drentʃ ड्रेन्च् / *verb* [T] (*usually passive*) to make sb/sth completely wet तर-बतर कर देना पूरी तरह भिगो देना, सराबोर कर देना *Don't go out while it's raining so hard or you'll* ***get drenched****.*

**dress**[1] /dres ड्रेस् / *noun* **1** [C] a piece of clothing worn by a girl or a woman. It covers the body from the shoulders to the knees or below लड़की या स्त्री की कंधों से घुटनो तक लंबी पोशाक, प्रसाधन **2** [U] clothes for either men or women (पुरुषों या स्त्रियों के) कपड़े, पहनावा, परिधान *formal/casual dress* ○ *He was wearing Bulgarian national dress.*

**dress**[2] /dres ड्रेस् / *verb* **1** [I, T] to put clothes on sb or yourself कपड़े पहनना या पहनाना *He dressed quickly and left the house.* ○ *My husband dressed the children while I got breakfast ready.* ✪ विलोम **undress** NOTE **Dress** की अपेक्षा **get dressed** अधिक प्रचलित है। **2** to wear a particular style of clothes विशिष्ट प्रकार के कपड़े पहनना *to dress well/badly/casually* ○ *to be well dressed/badly dressed/casually dressed* **3** [T] to clean, treat and cover a wound घाव की मरहम-पट्टी करना *to dress a wound*

IDM **(be) dressed in sth** wearing sth (कुछ विशेष) पहने हुए *The people at the funeral were all dressed in white.*

PHRV **dress up** **1** to put on special clothes, especially in order to look like sb/sth else विशेष पोशाक पहनना (विशेषतः किसी की तरह दिखने के लिए) *The children decided to dress up* ***as*** *pirates.* **2** to put on formal clothes, usually for a special occasion किसी विशेष अवसर के लिए औपचारिक पोशाक पहनना *You don't need to dress up for the party.*

**dresser** /ˈdresə(r) ˈड्रेस(र्) / *noun* [C] a piece of furniture with cupboards at the bottom and shelves above. It is used for holding dishes, cups, etc. एक विशेष तरह का फ़र्नीचर जिसमें नीचे अलमारी और ऊपर ख़ाने होते है (प्लेटें, प्याले आदि रखने के लिए)

**dressing** /ˈdresɪŋ ˈड्रेसिङ् / *noun* **1** [C] a covering that you put on a wound to protect it and keep it clean घाव को ढके रखने वाली पट्टी जो उसे सुरक्षित और साफ बनाए रखती है **2** [C, U] a sauce for food, especially for salads चटनी (विशेषतः सलाद के साथ)

**dressing gown** (*also* **bathrobe** *AmE* **robe**) *noun* [C] a piece of clothing like a loose coat with a belt, which you wear before or after a bath, before you get dressed in the morning, etc. पेटीदार ढीला कोट (जिसे स्नान से पहले या बाद में पहना जाता है); ड्रेसिंग गाउन

**dressing room** *noun* [C] a room for changing your clothes in, especially one for actors or for sports players पोशाक बदलने का कमरा (विशेषतः अभिनेताओं या खिलाड़ियों के लिए); प्रसाधन कक्ष

**dressing table** *noun* [C] a piece of furniture in a bedroom, which has drawers and a mirror शृंगार-मेज़, शयनकक्ष में रखी दराज़ों और दर्पण वाली मेज

**drew** ⇨ **draw**[1] का past tense रूप

**dribble** /ˈdrɪbl ˈड्रिबल् / *verb* **1** [I, T] (used about a liquid) to move downwards in a thin flow; to make a liquid move in this way (द्रव पदार्थ का) बूँद-बूँद टपकना या टपकाना *The paint dribbled down the side of the pot.* **2** [I] to allow liquid (**saliva**) to run out of the mouth मुँह से लार टपकाना *Small children often dribble.* **3** [I] (used in ball games) to make a ball move forward by using many short kicks or hits (गेंद वाले खेलों में) गेंद पर बार-बार हलका प्रहार करते हुए उसे आगे ले जाना *He dribbled round the goalkeeper and scored.*

**dried**[1] ⇨ **dry**[2] का past tense, past participle रूप

**dried**[2] /draɪd ड्राइड् / *adj.* (used about food) with all the liquid removed from it (भोज्य पदार्थ) सुखाया हुआ *dried milk* ○ *dried fruit*

**drier**[1] *adj.* ⇨ **dry**[1] देखिए।

**drier**[2] (*also* **dryer**) /ˈdraɪə(r) ˈड्राइअ(र्) / *noun* [C] a machine that you use for drying sth किसी वस्तु को सुखाने वाली मशीन; ड्रायर *a hairdrier*

**drift**[1] /drɪft ड्रिफ़्ट् / *verb* [I] **1** to be carried or moved along by wind or water वायु या जल की धारा या प्रवाह से बह जाना *The boat drifted out to sea.* **2** to move slowly or without any particular purpose धीरे-धीरे या उद्देश्यविहीन भटकना; इधर-उधर व्यर्थ घूमना *He drifted from room to room.* ○ *She drifted into acting almost by accident.* **3** (used about snow or sand) to be moved into piles by wind or water (बर्फ़ या रेत का) वायु या जलके प्रवाह से ढेर लग जाना *The snow drifted up to two metres deep in some places.*

PHRV **drift apart** to slowly become less close or friendly with sb किसी व्यक्ति से घनिष्ठता कम हो जाना, व्यक्तियों के बीच दूरी पैदा हो जाना

**drift**[2] /drɪft ड्रिफ़्ट् / *noun* **1** [C] a slow movement towards sth किसी ओर मंद गति *the country's drift into economic decline* **2** [*sing.*] the general meaning of sth किसी बात का सामान्य अर्थ *I don't understand all the details of the plan but* ***I get the drift***. 3 [C] a pile of snow or sand that was made by wind or water वायु या जल द्वारा निर्मित बर्फ़ या रेत का ढेर

**drill**[1] /drɪl ड्रिल्/ *noun* 1 [C] a tool or machine that is used for making holes in things वस्तुओं में छेद करने की मशीन; बरमा, ड्रिल मशीन *a dentist's drill* ➪ **tool** पर चित्र देखिए। 2 [U] exercise in marching, etc. that soldiers do सैनिकों की क़वायद, ड्रिल 3 [C] something that you repeat many times in order to learn sth सीखने के लिए अनेक बार दुहराई गई वस्तु, (शिक्षण में) अभ्यास की वस्तु 4 [C, U] practice for what you should do in an emergency संकट के निवारण का अभ्यास, संकट में बचाव के उपायों का अभ्यास *a fire drill*

**drill**[2] /drɪl ड्रिल्/ *verb* 1 [I, T] to make a hole in sth with a drill (किसी वस्तु में) बरमे से छेद करना *to drill a hole in sth* ○ *to drill for oil* 2 [T] to teach sb by making him/her repeat sth many times अभ्यास के द्वारा कुछ सिखाना

**drily** (*also* **dryly**) /ˈdraɪli ˈड्राइलि/ *adv.* (used about the way sb says sth) in an amusing way that sounds serious गंभीरता का अभिनय करते हुए *'I can hardly contain my excitement,' Peter said drily* (= he was not excited at all).

**drink**[1] /drɪŋk ड्रिङ्क्/ *verb* (*pt* **drank** /dræŋk ड्रैङ्क्/; *pp* **drunk** /drʌŋk ड्रङ्क्/) 1 [I, T] to take liquid into your body through your mouth द्रव पदार्थ पीना *Would you like anything to drink?* ○ *We sat drinking coffee and chatting for hours.* 2 [I, T] to drink alcohol शराब पीना *I never* ***drink and drive*** *so I'll have an orange juice.* ○ *Her brother used to* ***drink heavily*** *but he's teetotal now.*

**PHR V** **drink to sb/sth** to wish sb/sth good luck by holding your glass up in the air before you drink पीने से पहले गिलास को उठाकर किसी के लिए शुभकामनाएँ प्रकट करना *We all drank to the future of the bride and groom.* ➪ **toast**[2] देखिए।

**drink (sth) up** to finish drinking sth (चाय आदि) पीकर ख़त्म करना *Drink up your tea—it's getting cold.*

**drink**[2] /drɪŋk ड्रिङ्क्/ *noun* [C, U] 1 liquid for drinking पेय पदार्थ *Can I* ***have a drink*** *please?* ○ *a drink of milk* ○ *soft drinks* (= cold drinks without alcohol) 2 alcoholic drink एलकोहल युक्त या नशीला पेय; शराब, मदिरा *He's got a drink problem.* ○ *Shall we* ***go for a drink***?

**drink-driver** (*AmE* **drunk-driver**) *noun* [C] a person who drives after drinking too much alcohol ▶ **drink-driving** *noun* [U] शराब के नशे में गाड़ी चलाना *He was convicted of drink-driving and was fined.*

**drinker** /ˈdrɪŋkə(r) ˈड्रिङ्क(र्)/ *noun* [C] a person who drinks a lot of sth, especially alcohol कोई पेय (विशेषतः शराब) का आदी; शराबी *a heavy drinker* ○ *I'm not a big coffee drinker.*

**drinking** /ˈdrɪŋkɪŋ ˈड्रिङ्किङ्/ *noun* [U] drinking alcohol शराब पीना, मदिरापान करना *Her drinking became a problem.*

**drinking water** *noun* [U] water that is safe to drink पीने का साफ़ पानी

**drip**[1] /drɪp ड्रिप्/ *verb* (**dri<u>p</u>ping; dri<u>p</u>ped**) 1 [I] (used about a liquid) to fall in small drops (द्रव का) बूँद-बूँद टपकना *Water was dripping down through the roof.* 2 [I, T] to produce drops of liquid द्रव की बूँदें टपकाना *The tap is dripping.* ○ *Her finger was dripping blood.*

**drip**[2] /drɪp ड्रिप्/ *noun* 1 [*sing.*] the act or sound of water dripping पानी टपकने की क्रिया या ध्वनि 2 [C] a drop of water that falls down from sb/sth कहीं से टपकती बूँद *We put a bucket under the hole in the roof to catch the drips.* 3 (*AmE* **IV**) [C] a piece of medical equipment, like a tube, that is used for putting liquid food or medicine straight into a person's blood एक डॉक्टरी उपकरण (ट्यूब जैसा) जिससे पेय पदार्थ या औषधि को सीधे व्यक्ति के रक्त में पहुँचाया जाता है; ड्रिप *She's* ***on a drip***.

**drive**[1] /draɪv ड्राइव्/ *verb* (*pt* **drove** /drəʊv ड्रोव्/; *pp* **driven** /ˈdrɪvn ˈड्रिव्न्/) 1 [I, T] to control or operate a car, train, bus, etc. कार, ट्रेन, बस आदि को नियंत्रित करना या चलाना, ड्राइव करना *Can you drive?* ○ *to drive a car/train/bus/lorry* 2 [I, T] to go or take sb somewhere in a car, etc. मोटर कार में कहीं जाना या किसी को ले जाना *I usually drive to work.* ○ *We drove Leela to the airport.* 3 [T] to force people or animals to move in a particular direction (पशु, व्यक्ति आदि को) एक विशेष दिशा में हाँकना *The dogs drove the sheep into the field.* 4 [T] to force sth into a particular position by hitting it किसी वस्तु पर प्रहार करके उसे स्थिति विशेष में पहुँचाना *to drive a post into the ground* 5 [T] to cause sb to be in a particular state or to do sth किसी व्यक्ति को विशिष्ट मानसिक स्थिति में पहुँचाना *His constant stupid questions* ***drive me mad***. ○ *to drive sb to despair* 6 [T] to make sb/sth work very hard बहुत परिश्रम करवाना *You shouldn't drive yourself so hard.* 7 [T] to make a machine work by giving it power ऊर्जा के द्वारा किसी मशीन को चलाना *What drives the wheels in this engine?*

**IDM be driving at** (*informal*) to want to say sth; to mean कुछ कहने की चाहत होना; कुछ आशय होना *I'm afraid I don't understand what you are driving at.*

**drive sth home (to sb)** to make sth clear so that people understand it स्पष्ट करना ताकि बात समझ में आ सके

**drive off** (used about a car, driver, etc.) to leave प्रस्थान करना

**drive sb/sth off** to make sb/sth go away (किसी व्यक्ति या वस्तु को) भगा देना

**drive**[2] /draɪv ड्राइव़् / *noun* **1** [C] a journey in a car कार द्वारा यात्रा *The supermarket is only a five-minute drive away.* ○ *Let's* ***go for a drive***. **2** [C] a wide path or short road that leads to the door of a house घर के दरवाज़े तक का चौड़ा रास्ता या छोटी सड़क *We keep our car on the drive.* **3** [C] a street, usually where people live एक सड़क जिस पर प्रायः आवास होते हैं या लोग रहते हैं *They live at 23 Marine Drive.* **4** [C] a big effort by a group of people in order to achieve sth लक्ष्य प्राप्ति के लिए किसी संगठन का सशक्त प्रयास *The company is launching a big sales drive.* **5** [U] the energy and determination you need to succeed in doing sth सफलता के लिए अपेक्षित शक्ति और दृढ़ निश्चय *You need lots of drive to run your own company.* **6** [C, U] a strong natural need or desire प्रबल प्राकृतिक आवश्यकता या इच्छा **7** [C] (in sport) a long hard hit *This player has the longest drive in golf.* **8** [C] (*computing*) the part of a computer that reads and stores information कंप्यूटर का वह अंश जो सूचना का ग्रहण और संचय करता है *a 224MB hard drive* ○ *a CD drive* ⇨ **disk drive** देखिए। **9** [U] the equipment in a vehicle that takes power from the engine to the wheels वाहन का उपकरण जो शक्ति को इंजिन से पहियों तक पहुँचाता है *a car with four-wheel drive*

**drive-by** *adj.* (*AmE*) (*only before a noun*) (used about a shooting) done from a moving car चलती कार से किया गया (शिकार) *drive-by killings*

**drive-in** *noun* [C] (*AmE*) a place where you can eat, watch a film, etc. in your car एक ऐसा स्थान जहाँ आप कार में बैठे-बैठे भोजन, फ़िल्म देखना आदि कर सकते हैं

**driven** ⇨ **drive**[1] का past participle देखिए।

**driver** /ˈdraɪvə(r) ˈड्राइव़(र्) / *noun* [C] a person who drives a vehicle वाहन चालक, ड्राइवर *a bus/train driver*

**drive-through** *noun* [C] a restaurant, bank, etc. where you can be served without getting out of your car ऐसा रेस्तराँ, बैंक आदि जहाँ कार में बैठे-बैठे आप सेवाएँ प्राप्त कर सकते हैं

**driving**[1] /ˈdraɪvɪŋ ˈड्राइव़िङ् / *noun* [U] the action or skill of controlling a car, etc. वाहन चलाने या ड्राइव करने का कार्य *a* ***driving school*** ○ *Did you pass your* ***driving test*** *first time?* ○ *How long have you had a* ***driving licence*** (= an official piece of paper that says you are allowed to drive a car, etc.)?

**IDM be in the driving seat** ⇨ **seat**[1] देखिए।

**driving**[2] /ˈdraɪvɪŋ ˈड्राइव़िङ् / *adj.* very strong बहुत सशक्त, ज़ोरदार, प्रबल *driving rain* ○ *driving ambition* ○ *Who's the driving force behind this plan?*

**drizzle** /ˈdrɪzl ˈड्रिज़्ल् / *noun* [U] light rain with very small drops बूँदाबाँदी होना ▸ **drizzle** verb [I] बूँदाबाँदी, फुहार ⇨ **weather** पर नोट देखिए।

**dromedary** /ˈdrɒmədəri ˈड्रॉमडरि / *noun* [C] (*pl.* **dromedaries**) an animal that lives in the desert and has a long neck and a large mass of fat (**hump**) on its back. A dromedary is a type of **camel** एक कूबड़ वाला ऊँट

**drone** /drəʊn ड्रोन् / *verb* [I] to make a continuous low sound लगातार धीमी आवाज़ करना, भिनभिनाहट *the sound of the tractors droning away in the fields*

**PHRV drone on** to talk in a flat or boring voice सपाट, फीके या उबाऊ स्वर में बोलना *We had to listen to the chairman drone on about sales for hours.*

▸ **drone** *noun* [*sing.*] धीमी आवाज़

**drongo** /ˈdrɒːŋgəʊ ˈड्रॉङ्गो / *noun* [C] a long fork-tailed bird with glossy black **plumage**, usually found in Asia, Africa and Australia एशिया, अफ़्रीक़ा और ऑस्ट्रेलिया में सामान्यतः पाए जाने वाला, लंबी द्विशाखी पूँछ और चमकीले पंख वाला पक्षी

**drool** /druːl ड्रूल् / *verb* [I] **1** to let liquid (**saliva**) come out from the mouth, usually at the sight or smell of sth good to eat मुँह से लार टपकना (प्रायः स्वादिष्ट भोजन को देखकर या उसकी गंध से) **2 drool (over sb/sth)** to show in a silly or exaggerated way that you want or admire sb/sth very much किसी वस्तु के प्रति अपनी तीव्र पसंद को बेतुकेपन से दिखाना या प्रदर्शित करना *teenagers drooling over photographs of their favourite pop stars*

**droop** /druːp ड्रूप् / *verb* [I] to bend or hang downwards, especially because of weakness or because you are tired नीचे झुकना (विशेषतः दुर्बलता या थकान से) *The flowers were drooping without water.* ▸ **drooping** *adj.* नीचे झुकती हुई *a drooping moustache*

**drop**[1] /drɒp ड्रॉप् / *verb* (**dropping; dropped**) **1** [T] to let sth fall गिराना, गिरने देना *That vase was very expensive. Whatever you do, don't drop it!* **2** [I] to fall गिरना *The parachutist dropped* *safely to the ground.* ○ *At the end of the race she dropped to her knees exhausted.* **3** [I, T] to become lower; to make sth lower नीचे के बिंदु पर आ जाना, कम हो जाना; नीचा करना, कम करना *The temperature will drop to minus three overnight.* ○ *They ought to drop their prices.* ○ *to drop your voice* (= speak more quietly) **4** [T] **drop sb/sth (off)** to stop your car, etc. so that sb can get out, or in order to take sth out (नीचे उतरने या उतारने के लिए) कार को रोकना *Drop me off at the traffic lights, please.* ○ *I'll drop the parcel at your house.* **5** [T] **drop sb/sth (from sth)** to no longer include sb/sth in sth हटा देना *Rahul has been dropped from the team.* **6** [T] to stop doing sth (किसी काम को) बंद कर देना, छोड़ देना *I'm going to drop geography next term* (= stop studying it).

IDM **drop dead** (*informal*) to die suddenly सहसा मृत्यु हो जाना या एकाएक मर जाना

**drop sb a line** (*informal*) to write a letter to sb किसी को पत्र लिखना

**drop back; drop behind (sb)** to move into a position behind sb else, because you are moving more slowly किसी से पीछे रह जाना (मंदगति के कारण) *Towards the end of the race she dropped behind the other runners.*

**drop by; drop in (on sb)** to go to sb's house on an informal visit or without having told him/her you were coming बिना पूर्व सूचना के किसी के घर जा पहुँचना, अनौपचारिक प्रवास

**drop off** (*informal*) to fall into a light sleep हलकी नींद में सो जाना *I dropped off in front of the television.*

**drop out (of sth)** to leave or stop doing sth before you have finished किसी काम को बीच में छोड़ देना *His injury forced him to drop out of the competition.*

**drop²** /drɒp ड्रॉप्/ *noun* **1** [C] a very small amount of liquid that forms a round shape (द्रव पदार्थ की) बूँद *a drop of blood/rain* **2** [C, *usually sing.*] a small amount of liquid द्रव की ज़रा-सी मात्रा *I just have a drop of milk in my coffee.* **3** [*sing.*] a fall to a smaller amount or level गिरावट, कमी *The job is much more interesting but it will mean a drop in salary.* ○ *a drop in prices/temperature* **4** [*sing.*] a distance down from a high point to a lower point ऊँचाई से सीधे नीचे की दूरी, ऊपर से नीचे तक की दूरी *a sheer drop of 40 metres to the sea* **5 drops** [*pl.*] liquid medicine that you put into your eyes, ears or nose बूँद वाली दवा, औषधि *The doctor prescribed me drops to take twice a day.*

IDM **a drop in the ocean;** (*AmE*) **a drop in the bucket** an amount of sth that is too small or unimportant to make any real difference to a situation समुद्र में एक बूँद के समान महत्त्वहीन, ऊँट के मुँह में जीरा

**at the drop of a hat** immediately; without having to stop and think about it तुरंत; एकदम

**drop-dead** *adv.* (*informal*) used before an adjective to emphasize how attractive sb/sth is किसी के अति सुंदर होने पर बल देने के लिए विशेषण से पहले प्रयुक्त, अत्यधिक *She's drop-dead gorgeous.*

**droplet** /ˈdrɒplət ˈड्रॉप्लट्/ *noun* [C] a small amount of a liquid that forms a round shape नन्हीं बूँद

**drop-out** *noun* [C] **1** a person who leaves school, university, etc. before finishing his/her studies बीच में पढ़ाई छोड़ देने वाला व्यक्ति **2** a person who does not accept the ideas and ways of behaving of the rest of society सबसे अलग तरह का व्यक्ति

**dropper** /ˈdrɒpə(r) ˈड्रॉप(र्)/ *noun* [C] a short glass tube that has a rubber end with air in it. A dropper is used for measuring drops of liquids, especially medicines बूँद टपकाने वाली नली; ड्रॉपर, बिंदुपाति ⇨ **laboratory** पर चित्र देखिए।

**droppings** /ˈdrɒpɪŋz ˈड्रॉपिङ्ज़्/ *noun* waste material from the bodies of small animals or birds पक्षियों की बीट

**drought** /draʊt ड्राउट्/ *noun* [C, U] a long period without rain सूखा, अनावृष्टि

**drove** ⇨ **drive¹** का past tense रूप

**drown** /draʊn ड्राउन्/ *verb* **1** [I, T] to die in water because it is not possible to breathe; to make sb die in this way डूबकर मरना; डुबोकर मारना *The girl fell into the river and drowned.* ○ *Twenty people were drowned in the floods.* **2** [T] **drown sb/sth (out)** (used about a sound) to be so loud that you cannot hear sb/sth else आवाज़ का इतना ऊँचा होना कि कुछ और सुनाई न पड़े *His answer was drowned out by the loud music.*

**drowse** /draʊz ड्राउज़्/ *verb* [I] to be in a light sleep or to be almost asleep ऊँघना या लगभग सो जाना

**drowsy** /ˈdraʊzi ˈड्राउज़ि/ *adj.* not completely awake उनींदु, निद्रालु ✪ पर्याय **sleepy** ▶ **drowsily** *adv.* ऊँघते हुए ▶ **drowsiness** *noun* [U] उनींदापन, ऊँघ

**drudgery** /ˈdrʌdʒəri ˈड्रजरि/ *noun* [U] hard and boring work कठोर और उबाऊ काम

**drug¹** /drʌg ड्रग्/ *noun* [C] **1** a chemical which people use to give them pleasant or exciting feelings. It is illegal in many countries to use drugs

नशीला पदार्थ *He doesn't drink or **take drugs**.* ○ *She suspected her son was **on drugs**.* **2** a chemical which is used as a medicine औषधि, औषधि के रूप में प्रयुक्त रसायन *drug companies* ○ *Some drugs can only be obtained with a prescription from a doctor.*

**drug[2]** /drʌg ड्रग्/ *verb* [T] (**drugging; drugged**) **1** to give a person or animal a chemical to make him/her/it fall asleep or unconscious नींद या बेहोशी लाने वाली दवा *The lion was drugged before the start of the journey.* **2** to put a drug into food or drink खाने या पीने की वस्तु में नशीली दवा डालना *I think his drink was drugged.*

**drug addict** *noun* [C] a person who cannot stop taking drugs नशीली दवा का आदी, नशेबाज़, नशाख़ोर ▸ **drug addiction** *noun* [U] नशेबाज़ी, नशाख़ोरी

**druggist** /ˈdrʌgɪst ˈड्रगिस्ट्/ (*AmE*) = **chemist 1**

**drugstore** /ˈdrʌgstɔ:(r) ˈड्रगस्टॉ(र्)/ (*AmE*) = **chemist 2**

**drum[1]** /drʌm ड्रम्/ *noun* [C] **1** a musical instrument like an empty container with plastic or skin stretched across the ends. You play a drum by hitting it with your hands or with sticks ढोल, नगाड़ा *She plays the drums in a band.* ⇨ **piano** पर नोट देखिए तथा पृष्ठ 789 पर चित्र देखिए। **2** a round container ढोलनुमा पीपा, ड्रम *an oil drum*

**drum[2]** /drʌm ड्रम्/ *verb* (**drumming; drummed**) **1** [I] to play a drum ढोल बजाना **2** [I, T] to make a noise like a drum by hitting sth many times किसी वस्तु को थपथपाना (कि उसमें से ढोल जैसी आवाज़ निकले) *to drum your fingers on the table* (= because you are annoyed, impatient, etc.)

PHRV **drum sth into sb** to make sb remember sth by repeating it many times बार-बार कहकर याद दिलाना

**drum sth up** to try to get support or business समर्थन पाने या व्यापार बढ़ाने का प्रयास करना *to drum up more custom*

**drumlin** /ˈdrʌmlɪn ˈड्रम्लिन्/ *noun* [C] (in geography) a very small hill formed by the movement of a large mass of ice (**a glacier**) (भूगोल में) बड़े हिमनद के खिसकने से बनी छोटी पहाड़ी, हिमनदोढ़

**drummer** /ˈdrʌmə(r) ˈड्रम(र्)/ *noun* [C] a person who plays a drum or drums ढोल बजाने वाला व्यक्ति, ढोलकिया

**drumstick** /ˈdrʌmstɪk ˈड्रम्स्टिक्/ *noun* [C] **1** a stick used for playing the drums ढोल बजाने की लकड़ी, चोब **2** the lower leg of a chicken or similar bird that we cook and eat मुरग़ी आदि की टाँग का निचला हिस्सा (जो पकाकर खाया जाता है) **3** the long thin edible fruit of the drumstick tree सहिजन की फली

**drunk[1]** /drʌŋk ड्रङ्क्/ *adj.* (*not before a noun*) having drunk too much alcohol शराब के नशे में चूर, बहुत शराब पिए हुए *to get drunk* ▸ **drunk** (*old-fashioned* **drunkard**) *noun* [C] शराबी *There were two drunks asleep under the bridge.*

**drunk[2]** ⇨ **drink** का past participle रूप

**drunk-driver** (*usually AmE*) = **drink-driver**

**drunken** /ˈdrʌŋkən ˈड्रङ्कन्/ *adj.* (*only before a noun*) **1** having drunk too much alcohol शराब के नशे में चूर, बहुत शराब पिए हुए **2** showing the effects of too much alcohol अत्यधिक मदिरापन से प्रभावित, अति मदिरापान के प्रभाव को दर्शाने वाला *drunken singing* ▸ **drunkenly** *adv.* नशे में धुत्त होकर ▸ **drunkenness** *noun* [U] मदोन्मत्तता

**dry[1]** /draɪ ड्राइ/ *adj.* (**drier; driest**) **1** without liquid in it or on it; not wet सूखा, शुष्क *The paint is dry now.* ○ *Rub your hair dry with a towel.* **2** having little or no rain वर्षान्यून या वर्षाहीन (मौसम), कम वर्षा वाला या वर्षारहित (मौसम), सूखा *a hot, dry summer* ○ *a dry climate* ✪ विलोम **wet** (संख्या **1** और **2** लिए) **3** (used about hair or skin) not having enough natural oil (बाल या त्वचा) रुखा या रुखी, प्राकृतिक चिकनाई की कमी वाला **4** (used about wine) not sweet (मदिरा) हलकी कड़वी **5** (used about what sb says, or sb's way of speaking) amusing, although it sounds serious (कहने का ढंग) ऊपर से गंभीर परंतु वस्तुतः विनोदपूर्ण, हलका-फुलका *a dry sense of humour* **6** boring उबाऊ *dry legal documents* **7** without alcohol; where no alcohol is allowed एलकोहल या मादकता रहित; नशाबंदी वाला क्षेत्र या समय *Saudi Arabia is a dry country.* ▸ **dryness** *noun* [U] सूखापन, शुष्कता

IDM **be left high and dry** ⇨ **high[1]** देखिए।

**dry[2]** /draɪ ड्राइ/ *verb* [I, T] (*pres. part.* **drying;** *3rd person sing. pres.* **dries;** *pt, pp* **dried**) to become dry; to make sth dry (किसी वस्तु का) सूखना; (किसी वस्तु को) सुखाना *I hung my shirt in the sun to dry.* ○ *to dry your hands on a towel*

PHRV **dry (sth) out** to become or make sth become completely dry पूरी तरह सूख जाना या (किसी वस्तु को) सुखा देना *Don't allow the soil to dry out.*

**dry up 1** (used about a river, etc.) to have no more water in it (नदी आदि का) सूख जाना **2** to stop being available काम आदि मिलना बंद हो जाना, अभाव की स्थिति होना *Because of the recession a lot of building work has dried up.* **3** to forget what you were going to say, for example because you are very nervous (घबराहट के कारण) बात भूल जाना

**dry (sth) up** to dry plates, knives, forks, etc. with a towel after they have been washed धोने के बाद बर्तनों को तौलिये से पोंछना

**dry-clean** *verb* [T] to clean clothes using special chemicals, without using water बिना पानी के विशेष रसायनों द्वारा कपड़े साफ़ करना, सूखी धुलाई करना, ड्राइक्लीन करना, निर्जल धुलाई करना

**dry-cleaner's** (*also* **cleaner's**) *noun* [C] the shop where you take your clothes to be cleaned ड्राइक्लीनर की दुकान

**dry land** *noun* [U] land, not the sea (सूखी) धरती, ज़मीन (न कि समुद्र), शुष्क भूमि *I was glad to be back on dry land again.*

**DTP** /ˌdiː tiː ˈpiː ˌडी टी ˈपी/ *abbr.* = **desktop publishing**

**dual** /ˈdjuːəl ˈड्यूअल्/ *adj.* (*only before a noun*) having two parts; double दो अंशों वाला; दोहरा, द्वैत *to have dual nationality*

**dual carriageway** (*AmE* **divided highway**) *noun* [C] a wide road that has an area of grass or a fence in the middle to separate the traffic going in one direction from the traffic going in the other direction (हरित पट्टी या बाड़ की सहायता से) बीच में से विभाजित चौड़ी सड़क (जो आने और जाने वाले वाहनों को अलग रखती है)

**dub** /dʌb डब्/ *verb* [T] (**du**__**bb**__**ing; du**__**bb**__**ed**) **1** to give sb/sth a new or amusing name (**a nickname**) (किसी को) नया या रोचक नाम देना *Bill Clinton was dubbed 'Slick Willy'.* **2 dub sth (into sth)** to change the sound in a film so that what the actors said originally is spoken by actors using a different language एक भाषा की फ़िल्म के संवाद का दूसरी भाषा में अनुवाद करना, डब करना *I don't like foreign films when they're dubbed into English. I prefer subtitles.* ➪ **subtitle** देखिए। **3** to make a piece of music by mixing different pieces of recorded music together पहले रिकार्ड किए गए अलग-अलग गानों के अंशों को मिलाकर नया गाना तैयार करना या पुराने गानों के टुकड़ों को मिलाकर नया गाना बनाना

**dubious** /ˈdjuːbiəs ˈड्यूबिअस्/ *adj.* **1 dubious (about sth/about doing sth)** not sure or certain अनिश्चित, शंकालु, सशंक, संदिग्ध *I'm very dubious about whether we're doing the right thing.* **2** that may not be honest or safe बेईमानी वाला या असुरक्षित, संदेहास्पद, साफ़-सुथरा या पारदर्शी नहीं *dubious financial dealings* ▶ **dubiously** *adv.* संदेहास्पद रीति से

**duchess** /ˈdʌtʃəs ˈडचस्/ *noun* [C] a woman who has the same position as a **duke,** or who is the wife of a **duke** ड्यूक की पत्नी या ड्यूक के अधिकार रखने वाली महिला

**duck**[1] /dʌk डक्/ *noun* (*pl.* **ducks** or **duck**) **1** [C] a common bird that lives on or near water. Ducks have short legs, special (**webbed**) feet for swimming and a wide beak बतख़ **2** [C] a female duck मादा बतख़

> **NOTE** नर बतख़ को **drake** कहते हैं और शिशु बतख़ को **duckling** कहते हैं। बतख़ की आवाज़ के लिए **quack** शब्द प्रयुक्त होता है।

**3** [U] the meat of a duck बतख़ का गोश्त *roast duck with orange sauce*

**duck**[2] /dʌk डक्/ *verb* **1** [I, T] to move your head down quickly so that you are not seen or hit by sb/sth (आक्रमण से या देखे जाने से बचने के लिए) तुरंत सिर झुका लेना *The boys ducked out of sight behind a hedge.* ○ *I had to duck my head down to avoid the low doorway.* **2** [I, T] (*informal*) **duck (out of) sth** to try to avoid sth difficult or unpleasant कठिन या अप्रिय स्थिति से बचने का प्रयत्न करना; कन्नी काटना *She tried to duck out of apologizing.* **3** [T] to push sb's head under water for a short time, especially when playing पानी में खेलते हुए (किसी के) सिर को क्षणभर के लिए डुबोना *The kids were ducking each other in the pool.*

**duct** /dʌkt डक्ट्/ *noun* [C] a tube that carries liquid, gas, etc. द्रव गैस आदि को ले जाने वाली नली *They got into the building through the air duct.* ○ *tear ducts* (= in the eye)

**dud** /dʌd डड्/ *noun* [C] (*informal*) a thing that cannot be used because it is not real or does not work properly नक़ली होने के कारण या ठीक से काम न करने के कारण प्रयोग में न आने वाली वस्तु

**dude** /duːd ड्यूड्/ *noun* [C] (*AmE slang*) a man व्यक्ति, आदमी

**due**[1] /djuː ड्यू/ *adj.* **1** (*not before a noun*) expected or planned to happen or arrive जिसका होना या पहुँचना प्रत्याशित हो या योजना के अनुसार हो, जिसके घटित होने या पहुँचने की आशा हो या वह योजनानुसार हो *The conference is due to start in four weeks' time.* ○ *What time is the next train due (in)?* ○ *The baby is due in May.* **2** (*not before a noun*) having to be paid जो दिया जाना है, देय *The rent is due on the fifteenth of each month.* **3 due (to sb)** that is owed to you because it is your right to have it जो प्राप्त करना है, प्राप्य *Make sure you claim all the benefits that are due to you.* **4 due to sb/sth** caused by or because of sb/sth के कारण, के फलस्वरूप *His illness is probably due to stress.* **5 due for sth** expecting sth or having the right to sth प्रत्याशित या हक़दार *I think that I'm due for a pay rise.*

**IDM in due course** at some time in the future, quite soon भविष्य में किसी समय (काफ़ी जल्दी), उचित समय पर; यथासमय *All applicants will be informed of our decision in due course.*

**due**[2] /dju: ड्यू / *adv.* (used before 'north', 'south', 'east' and 'west') exactly ('उत्तर', 'दक्षिण', 'पूर्व', और 'पश्चिम' से पहले प्रयुक्त) ठीक, एकदम, बिल्कुल *The aeroplane was flying due east.*

**due**[3] /dju: ड्यू / *noun*

**IDM give sb his/her due** to be fair to a person किसी को उसका प्राप्य श्रेय देना, किसी के प्रति निष्पक्ष होना *She doesn't work very quickly, but to give Sudha her due, she is very accurate.*

**duel** /ˈdju:əl ˈड्यूअल् / *noun* [C] a formal type of fight with guns or other weapons which was used in the past to decide an argument between two men किसी प्रसंग पर आयोजित दो व्यक्तियों के बीच सशस्त्र युद्ध (अतीत में प्रचलित); द्वंद्वयुद्ध

**duet** /djuˈet ड्युˈएट् / (*also* **duo**) *noun* [C] a piece of music for two people to sing or play युगलगान या वादन, जुगलबंदी ➪ **solo** देखिए।

**dug** ➪ **dig** का past tense और past participle रूप

**duke** /dju:k ड्यूक् / (*also* **Duke**) *noun* [C] a man of the highest hereditary rank, a nobleman सर्वोच्च वंशानुगत पद का व्यक्ति, अतिसंभ्रांत व्यक्ति, ड्यूक ➪ **duchess** देखिए।

**dull** /dʌl डल् / *adj.* **1** not interesting or exciting; boring अरुचिकर या अनुत्तेजक; उबाऊ *Miss Sharma's lessons are always so dull.* **2** धुँधला, फीका, निष्प्रभ, मेघाच्छादित *a dull and cloudy day* **3** not loud, sharp or strong धीमा-धीमा, मंद, हलका *Her head hit the floor with a dull thud.* ✪ विलोम **sharp** ▶ **dullness** *noun* [U] मंदता ▶ **dully** *adv.* मंद भाव से

**duly** /ˈdju:li ˈड्यूलि / *adv.* (*formal*) in the correct or expected way उचित या अपेक्षित रीति से; यथोचित *We all duly assembled at 7.30 a.m. as agreed.*

**dumb** /dʌm डम् / *adj.* **1** not able to speak गूँगा, मूक *to be deaf and dumb* ○ (*figurative*) *They were* ***struck dumb*** *with amazement.* **2** (*informal*) stupid मूर्ख *What a dumb thing to do!* ▶ **dumbly** *adv.* गूँगा होकर *Kanchan did all the talking, and I just nodded dumbly.*

**dumbfounded** /dʌmˈfaʊndɪd डम्ˈफ़ाउन्डिड् / *adj.* very surprised भौंचक्का, हक्का-बक्का

**dummy** /ˈdʌmi ˈडमि / *noun* [C] (*pl.* **dummies**) **1** a model of the human body used for putting clothes on in a shop window or while you are making clothes मानव शरीर का मॉडल, डमी (दुकान में पोशाक पहनाकर रखने या दर्ज़ी द्वारा पोशाक बनाने के लिए प्रयुक्त) *a tailor's dummy* **2** (*informal*) a stupid person मूर्ख व्यक्ति **3** (*AmE* **pacifier**) a rubber object that you put in a baby's mouth to keep him/her quiet and happy चूसनी **4** something that is made to look like sth else but that is not the real thing वास्तविक प्रतीत होने वाली नक़ली वस्तु *The robbers used dummy hand guns in the raid.*

**dump**[1] /dʌmp डम्प् / *verb* [T] **1** to get rid of sth that you do not want, especially in a place which is not suitable अवांछित वस्तु से पिंड छुड़ाना (विशेषतः अनुपयुक्त स्थान पर डालकर) *Nuclear waste should not be dumped in the sea.* ○ (*figurative*) *I wish you wouldn't keep dumping the extra work on me.* **2** to put sth down quickly or in a careless way किसी वस्तु को लापरवाही से तुरत-फुरत डाल देना *The children dumped their bags in the hall and ran off to play.* **3** (*informal*) to get rid of sb, especially a boyfriend or girlfriend किसी से पीछा छुड़ाना (विशेषतः पुरुष या महिला मित्र से) *Did you hear that Latika dumped Chandan last night?*

**dump**[2] /dʌmp डम्प् / *noun* [C] **1** a place where rubbish or waste material from factories, etc. is left कूड़ा-करकट डालने का स्थान *a rubbish dump* **2** (*informal*) a place that is very dirty, untidy or unpleasant गंदा, मैला या अरुचिकर स्थान *The flat is cheap but it's a real dump.*

**IDM down in the dumps** unhappy or sad उदास या दुखी

**dumper truck** (*BrE*) (*AmE* **dump truck**) *noun* [C] a lorry that carries material such as stones or earth in a special container which can be lifted up so that the load can fall out कूड़ा ढोने वाला विशेष प्रकार का ट्रक

**dumpling** /ˈdʌmplɪŋ ˈडम्प्लिङ् / *noun* [C] a small ball of flour and fat (**dough**) that is steamed and usually eaten with meat and soup आटे की छोटी लोई जिसे भाप से पकाकर प्रायः मांस और सूप के साथ खाया जाता है

**dune** /dju:n ड्यून् / (*also* **sand dune**) *noun* [C] a low hill of sand by the sea or in the desert बालू का टीला (समुद्र के पास या रेगिस्तान में बना), बालूटिब्बा

**dung** /dʌŋ डंङ् / *noun* [U] waste material from the bodies of large animals गोबर, लीद *cow dung*

**dungarees** /ˌdʌŋgəˈri:z ˌडङ्गˈरीज़् / (*AmE* **overalls**) *noun* [*pl.*] a piece of clothing, similar to trousers, but covering your chest as well as your legs and with straps that go over the shoulders

पतलून की तरह की पोशाक जो कंधों के ऊपर से नीचे छाती और टाँगों तक आती है; डँगरी *a pair of dungarees*

dungarees

**dungeon** /ˈdʌndʒən ˈडनूजन्/ *noun* [C] an old underground prison, especially in a castle ज़मीन के नीचे बना क़ैदख़ाना (विशेषतः किले में), भूमिगत कैदख़ाना

**duo** /ˈdjuːəʊ ˈड्यूओ/ *noun* [C] (*pl.* **duos**) **1** two people playing music or singing together एक साथ प्रदर्शन करने वाले गायकों या वादकों की जोड़ी; युगलगान, युगलवादन **2** = **duet**

**duodenum** /ˌdjuːəˈdiːnəm ˌड्यूअˈडीनम्/ *noun* [C] the first part of the small **intestine** छोटी आँत का अगला भाग, ग्रहणी ➪ **body** पर चित्र देखिए।

**dupe** /djuːp ड्यूप्/ *verb* [T] to lie to sb in order to make him/her believe sth or do sth किसी से कुछ मनवाने या करवाने के लिए झूठ बोलना; झाँसा देना *The woman was duped into carrying the drugs.*

**duplex** /ˈdjuːpleks ˈड्यूप्लेक्स्/ *noun* [C] **1** a flat having rooms on two floors connected by a staircase फ़्लैट या मकान जिसकी दोनों मंजिलों पर कमरे ज़ीने या सीढ़ियों द्वारा जुड़े हों **2** a house with two separate units sharing a wall सामान्य दीवार वाला द्विखंडीय मकान

**duplicate¹** /ˈdjuːplɪkeɪt ˈड्यूप्लिकेट्/ *verb* [T] **1** to make an exact copy of sth किसी वस्तु की सही नक़ल बना लेना; अनुलिपि बनाना **2** to do sth that has already been done किसी काम को दोबारा करना *We don't want to duplicate the work of other departments.* ▶ **duplication** /ˌdjuːplɪˈkeɪʃn ˌड्यूप्लिˈकेशन्/ *noun* [U] पुनरावृत्ति, अनुलिपिकरण

**duplicate²** /ˈdjuːplɪkət ˈड्यूप्लिकट्/ *noun* [C] something that is exactly the same as sth else (किसी की) हूबहू नक़ल ▶ **duplicate** *adj.* (*only before a noun*) समरूप, प्रतिरूप *a duplicate key*

IDM **in duplicate** with two copies (for example of an official piece of paper) that are exactly the same (काग़ज़ात आदि) दो प्रतियाँ *The contract must be in duplicate.* ➪ **triplicate** देखिए।

**durable** /ˈdjʊərəbl ˈड्युअरब्ल्/ *adj.* likely to last for a long time without breaking or getting weaker टिकाऊ, स्थायी *a durable fabric* ▶ **durability** /ˌdjʊərəˈbɪləti ˌड्युअरˈबिलटि/ *noun* [U] टिकाऊपन

**duration** /djuˈreɪʃn ड्युˈरेश़न्/ *noun* [U] the time that sth lasts अवधि, मियाद *Please remain seated for the duration of the flight.*

**duress** /djuˈres ड्युˈरेस्/ *noun* [U] threats or force that are used to make sb do sth धमकी या दबाव (कुछ करवाने या मनवाने के लिए) *He signed the confession **under duress**.*

**during** /ˈdjʊərɪŋ ˈड्युअरिङ्/ *prep.* within the period of time mentioned के दौरान, की अवधि तक, निर्दिष्ट कालावधि में *During the summer holidays we went swimming every day.* ○ *Grandpa was taken very ill during the night.*

NOTE ध्यान दिया जाए कि जब कुछ घटित होने के समय की बात करनी हो तो **during** का प्रयोग होता है और वह (घटना या बात) कितनी देर तक रही यह बताना हो तो **for** का—*I went shopping during my lunch break. I was out for about 25 minutes.*

**dusk** /dʌsk डस्क्/ *noun* [U] the time in the evening when the sun has already gone down and it is nearly dark साँझ, शाम का झुटपुटा, गोधूलि वेला ➪ **dawn** और **twilight** देखिए।

**dusky** /ˈdʌski ˈडस्कि/ *adj.* **1** (*literary*) dim; having little light; not very bright; dark धुंधला; कम रोशनी वाला; मद्धिम; श्यामल *dusky night* **2** (*literary*) sad and gloomy उदास और निराशाजनक *dusky shadows from his past* **3** naturally having dark skin श्यामल वर्ण वाला *a dusky beauty* **4** of a dark colour गहरे रंग का *a shade of dusky blue*

**Dusserah** *noun* [C] a festival that celebrates the victory of good over evil. It is celebrated across India in October/November and is the grand culmination of a ten-day festival दशहरा; दस दिनों के त्यौहार की शानदार समाप्ति जो भारत में अक्टूबर या नवंबर में मनाया जाता है

**dust¹** /dʌst डस्ट्/ *noun* [U] very small pieces of dry dirt, sand, etc. in the form of a powder धूल, मिट्टी, गर्द *a thick layer of dust* ○ *chalk/coal dust* ○ *The tractor came up the track in a cloud of dust.* ○ *a speck* (= small piece of dust) ▶ **dusty** *adj.* धूलभरा *This shelf has got very dusty.*

**dust²** /dʌst डस्ट्/ *verb* [I, T] to clean a room, furniture, etc. by removing dust with a cloth कपड़े से कमरा, फ़र्नीचर आदि की धूल झाड़ना *Let me dust those shelves before you put the books on them.* ➪ **clean²** पर नोट देखिए।

**dustbin** /ˈdʌstbɪn ˈडस्ट्बिन्/ (*AmE* **garbage can; trash can**) *noun* [C] a large container for rubbish that you keep outside your house कूड़ादान, कचरा-पेटी

**dust bowl** *noun* [C] (in geography) an area of land that has become desert because there has been too little rain or too much farming (भूगोल में) मरुभूमि में परिवर्तित भूक्षेत्र (अनावृष्टि या अति कृषि के कारण)

**duster** /ˈdʌstə(r) ˈडस्टर्(र्)/ *noun* [C] a soft dry cloth that you use for cleaning furniture, etc. झाड़न (कपड़ा)

**dustpan** /ˈdʌstpæn ˈडस्ट्पैन्/ *noun* [C] a flat container with a handle into which you brush dirt from the floor कूड़ा बटोरने का पात्र *Where do you keep your* ***dustpan and brush****?*

**Dutch** /dʌtʃ डच्/ *adj.* from the Netherlands नीदरलैंड्स (हॉलैंड) का निवासी, डच

**Dutch courage** *noun* [U] (*BrE*) a feeling of courage or confidence that a person gets from drinking alcohol मदिरापान से उत्पन्न हिम्मत या विश्वास का भाव, शराबी जोश

**dutiful** /ˈdju:tɪfl ˈड्यूटिफ़्ल्/ *adj.* happy to respect and obey sb कर्तव्यपरायण, कर्तव्यशील *a dutiful son* ▶ **dutifully** /-fəli -फ़लि/ *adv.* कर्तव्य भाव से

**duty** /ˈdju:ti ˈड्यूटि/ *noun* [C, U] (*pl.* **duties**) **1** something that you have to do because people expect you to do it or because you think it is right कर्तव्य, फ़र्ज़ *A soldier must* ***do*** *his* ***duty****.* ○ *a sense of moral duty* **2** the tasks that you do when you are at work काम, कार्य *the duties of a policeman* ○ *Which nurses are on night duty this week?* **3 duty (on sth)** a tax that you pay, especially on goods that you bring into a country शुल्क, कर (विशेषतः आयातित वस्तुओं पर)

**IDM on/off duty** (used about doctors, nurses, police officers, etc.) to be working/not working (डॉक्टर, नर्स, पुलिस अधिकारी आदि) काम पर, ड्यूटी पर/ड्यूटी से मुक्त *The porter's on duty from 8 a.m. till 4 a.m.* ○ *What time does she go off duty?*

**duty-free** *adj., adv.* (used about goods) that you can bring into a country without paying tax (आयातित वस्तुएँ) शुल्क-मुक्त, शुल्क से छूट प्राप्त *an airport duty-free shop* ○ *How much wine can you bring into India duty-free?* ➪ **tax-free** देखिए।

**duvet** /ˈdu:veɪ ˈडूवे/ *noun* [C] a thick cover filled with feathers or another soft material that you sleep under to keep warm in bed भारी रज़ाई, लिहाफ़ ➪ **quilt** देखिए।

**Dvaita** *noun* [U] a branch of Hindu philosophy that states that the individual and God have separate existences; the doctrine of duality ईश्वर और आत्मा को भिन्न मानने वाली हिंदू सैद्धांतिक धारणा; द्वैत सिद्धांत ➪ **Advaita** देखिए।

**DVD** /ˌdi: vi: ˈdi: ˌडी वी ˈडी/ *noun* [C] a disc with different types of information on it, especially photographs and video, that can be used on a computer (short for 'digital videodisc' or 'digital versatile disc') डीवीडी (digital video-versatile disc का संक्षिप्त रूप) कंप्यूटर में प्रयुक्त एक प्रकार की डिस्क जिसमें फ़ोटो वीडियो आदि संगृहीत होते हैं *a DVD-ROM* drive

**dwarf**[1] /dwɔ:f ड्वॉफ़्/ *noun* [C] (*pl.* **dwarfs** or **dwarves** /dwɔ:vz ड्वॉव्ज़्/) **1** a person, animal or plant that is much smaller than the usual size (व्यक्ति, पशु या पौधा) बौना, ठिगना, नाटा **2** (in children's stories) a very small person (बालकथाओं में) ठिगना, नाटा आदमी

**dwarf**[2] /dwɔ:f ड्वॉफ़्/ *verb* [T] (used about a large object) to make sth seem very small in comparison (बृहदाकार वस्तु का) (अपनी तुलना में) अन्य वस्तुओं को बौना बना देना *The skyscraper dwarfs all the other buildings around.*

**dwell** /dwel ड्वेल्/ *verb* [I] (*pt, pp* **dwelt** /dwelt ड्वेल्ट् or **dwelled**) (*old-fashioned, formal*) to live or stay in a place एक स्थान पर रहना या रुकना

**PHRV dwell on/upon sth** to think or talk a lot about sth that it would be better to forget (भूल जाने योग्य) विषय पर बहुत सोचना या बात करना या ऐसे विषय पर बहुत सोचना या बात करना जिसे भूल जाना बेहतर है *I don't want to dwell on the past. Let's think about the future.*

**dweller** /ˈdwelə(r) ˈड्वेल(र्)/ *noun* [C] (*often in compounds*) a person or animal that lives in the place mentioned निर्दिष्ट स्थान पर रहने वाला व्यक्ति या पशु *city-dwellers*

**dwelling** /ˈdwelɪŋ ˈड्वेलिङ्/ *noun* [C] (*formal*) the place where a person lives; a house निवास-स्थान; आवास गृह

**dwindle** /ˈdwɪndl ˈड्विन्ड्ल्/ *verb* [I] **dwindle (away)** to become smaller or weaker कम होना, घट जाना, क्रमिक रूप से कम या क्षीण होते जाना *Their savings dwindled away to nothing.*

**dye**[1] /daɪ डाइ/ *verb* [T] (*pres. part.* **dyeing;** *3rd person sing. pres.* **dyes;** *pt, pp* **dyed**) to make sth a different colour (किसी वस्तु को) रँगना *Does she dye her hair?* ○ *I'm going to dye this blouse black.*

**dye**[2] /daɪ डाइ/ *noun* [C, U] a substance that is used to change the colour of sth किसी वस्तु को रँगने वाला रंग

**dying** ➪ **die** का present participle रूप

**dying** /ˈdaɪɪŋ ˈडाइइङ्/ *adj.* **1** during the last few minutes, seconds, etc. before something ends समाप्ति से पूर्व के कुछ आख़िरी क्षण *They managed to win the game in the dying minutes.* **2** happening at the time of somebody's death मृत्युकालीन

**dyke** (*also* **dike**) /daɪk डाइक्/ *noun* [C] **1** a long thick wall that is built to prevent the sea or a river from flooding low land बाँध, तटबंध **2** a long narrow space dug in the ground and used for taking water away from land नहर

**dynamic** /daɪˈnæmɪk डाइˈनैमिक्/ *adj.* **1** (used about a person) full of energy and ideas; active (व्यक्ति) ऊर्जा तथा नाना प्रकार के विचारों से पूर्ण; सक्रिय, गतिशील **2** (used about a force or power) that causes movement गति उत्पन्न करने वाली (शक्ति) ▶ **dynamism** /ˈdaɪnəmɪzəm ˈडाइनमिज़म्/ *noun* [U] गतिशीलता

**dynamics** /daɪˈnæmɪks डाइˈनैमिक्स्/ *noun* **1** [*pl.*] the way in which people or things behave and react to each other in a particular situation एक विशिष्ट स्थिति में व्यक्तियों या वस्तुओं के परस्पर व्यवहार का तरीक़ा **2** [U] the scientific study of the forces involved in movement गति से संबंधित शक्तियों का वैज्ञानिक अध्ययन; गतिविज्ञान *fluid dynamics*

**dynamite** /ˈdaɪnəmaɪt ˈडाइनमाइट्/ *noun* [U] **1** a powerful explosive substance एक प्रकार का शक्तिशाली विस्फोटक पदार्थ; डाइनामाइट **2** a thing or person that causes great excitement, shock, etc. अत्यधिक उत्तेजना या दहशत फैलाने वाली वस्तु या व्यक्ति *His news was dynamite.*

**dynamo** /ˈdaɪnəməʊ ˈडाइनमो/ *noun* [C] (*pl.* **dynamos**) a device that changes energy from the movement of sth such as wind or water into electricity वायु या जल आदि की गति से उत्पन्न ऊर्जा को विद्युत में बदलने वाली मशीन

**dynasty** /ˈdɪnəsti ˈडिनस्टि/ *noun* [C] (*pl.* **dynasties**) a series of rulers who are from the same family एक ही परिवार में जन्मे शासकों की श्रेणी, वंश परंपरा, राजवंश *the Gupta dynasty in India.*

**dysentery** /ˈdɪsəntri ˈडिसन्ट्रि/ *noun* [U] a serious disease which causes you to get rid of waste material from your body very often in liquid form (**to have diarrhoea**), and to lose blood पेचिश (का रोग); यह गंभीर रोग होता है जिसमें दस्त द्वारा शरीर से अवांछित तत्त्व बाहर निकल जाते हैं और रक्त की भी कमी होती है; अतिसार

**dyslexia** /dɪsˈleksiə डिस्ˈलेक्सिआ/ *noun* [U] a difficulty that some people have with reading and spelling शब्दों के उच्चारण करने में या वर्तनी स्पष्ट करने में होने वाली कठिनाई, अप-पठन ▶ **dyslexic** *noun* [C], *adj.* व्यक्ति की वाचन एवं वर्तनी निर्देशन संबंधी कठिनाई से संबंधित

# E e

**E, e**[1] /iː ई / *noun* [C, U] (*pl.* **E's; e's** /iːz ईज़् /) the fifth letter of the English alphabet अंग्रेज़ी वर्णमाला का पाँचवाँ अक्षर *'Egg' begins with an 'E'.*

**E**[2] *abbr.* east(ern) पूर्वी *E Asia*

**e-** /iː ई / *prefix* (*computing*) (*in nouns and verbs*) connected with the use of electronic communication, especially the Internet, for sending information, doing business, etc. इलेक्ट्रॉनिक संचार, विशेषत: इंटरनेट के प्रयोग से संबंधित गतिविधियों के निर्देशक शब्दों (संज्ञाओं और क्रियाओं) में प्रयुक्त पूर्वपद; ई *e-business/ e-commerce* ➪ **email** देखिए।

**ea.** *abbr.* each प्रत्येक

**each** /iːtʃ ईच् / *det., pronoun* every individual person or thing प्रत्येक व्यक्ति या वस्तु *Each lesson lasts an hour.* ○ *Each of the lessons lasts an hour.* ○ *The lessons each last an hour.*

**each other** *pronoun* used for saying that A does the same thing to B as B does to A एक दूसरे को/से, परस्पर *Zeenat and Zaheer love each other very much* (= Zeenat loves Zaheer and Zaheer loves Zeenat). ○ *We looked at each other.*

**eager** /ˈiːɡə(r) ˈईग(र्) / *adj.* **eager (to do sth); eager (for sth)** full of desire or interest आतुर, उत्सुक *We're all eager to start work on the new project.* ○ *eager for success* ✪ पर्याय **keen** ▶ **eagerly** *adv.* उत्सुकता से ▶ **eagerness** *noun* [U] उत्सुकता

**eagle** /ˈiːɡl ˈईगल् / *noun* [C] a very large bird that can see very well. It eats small birds and animals तीखी नज़र वाला एक बड़ा पक्षी (जो छोटे पशु-पक्षी खाता है); बाज़, उकाब

**ear** /ɪə(r) इअ(र्) / *noun* **1** [C] one of the two parts of the body of a person or animal that are used for hearing कान, श्रवणेंद्रिय ➪ **body** पर चित्र देखिए। **2** [*sing.*] **an ear (for sth)** an ability to recognize and repeat sounds, especially in music or language संगीत या भाषा में स्वर को पहचानने और दोहराने की क्षमता *Yukta has a good ear for languages.* **3** [C] the top part of a plant that produces grain अनाज की बाली (जिसमें दाने लगते हैं) *an ear of corn* ➪ **cereal** पर चित्र देखिए।

**IDM sb's ears are burning** used when a person thinks that other people are talking about him/ her, especially in an unkind way किसी व्यक्ति का यह सोचना कि दूसरे उसकी निंदा कर रहे हैं—यह बताने के लिए प्रयुक्त

**play (sth) by ear** to play a piece of music that you have heard without using written notes अपनी स्मृति से (न कि चिह्नबद्ध स्वर-माला से) संगीत-रचना का गायन या वादन करना

**go in one ear and out the other** (used about information, etc.) to be forgotten quickly किसी बात आदि को) जल्दी ही भूल जाना *Everything I tell him seems to go in one ear and out the other.*

**play it by ear** to decide what to do as things happen, instead of planning in advance घटनाओं के घटने के दौरान ही कारवाई पर निर्णय लेना (बजाय पहले से ही विचार करने के) *We don't know what Amit's reaction will be, so we'll just have to play it by ear.*

**prick up your ears** ➪ **prick**[1] देखिए।

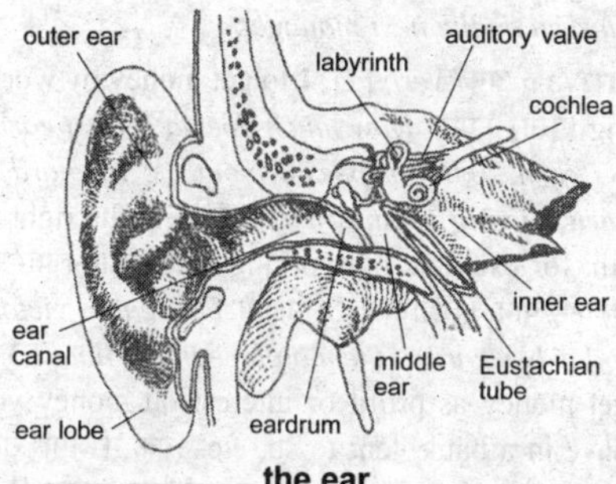


**the ear**

**earache** /ˈɪəreɪk ˈइअएक् / *noun* [U] a pain in your ear कान में दर्द, कर्णशूल *I've got earache.* ➪ **ache** पर नोट देखिए।

**eardrum** /ˈɪədrʌm ˈइअड्रम् / *noun* [C] a thin piece of skin inside the ear that is tightly stretched and that allows you to hear sound कान का परदा, कर्ण पटह ➪ **ear** पर चित्र देखिए।

**earl** /ɜːl अल् / *noun* [C] a British man of a high social position उच्च सामाजिक पद का ब्रिटिश पुरुष; अर्ल

**ear lobe** *noun* [C] the round soft part at the bottom of your ear कान के नीचे का गोल कोमल भाग; ललरी, कर्णपालि ➪ **ear** पर चित्र देखिए।

**early** /ˈɜːli ˈअलि / *adj., adv.* (**earlier; earliest**) **1** near the beginning of a period of time, a piece of work, a series, etc. किसी कालावधि, कार्य आदि के प्रारंभ में; जल्दी, प्रारंभिक *I think Vipin's in his early twenties.* ○ *The project is still in its early stages.* **2** before the usual or expected time सामान्य या प्रत्याशित समय से पहले; जल्दी, शीघ्र *She arrived five minutes early for her interview.*

**IDM at the earliest** not before the date or time mentioned निर्दिष्ट तारीख़ या समय से पहले नहीं; यथासंभव शीघ्र, यथाशीघ्र *I can repair it by Friday at the earliest.*

**it's early days (yet)** used to say that it is too soon to know how a situation will develop यह बताने के लिए प्रयुक्त कि स्थिति के विषय में कुछ भी कहना जल्दबाज़ी होगी

**the early hours** very early in the morning in the hours after midnight बहुत सवेरे (अर्धरात्रि के बाद)

**an early/a late night** ➪ **night** देखिए।

**early on** soon after the beginning शुरू होते ही, प्रारंभ में ही *He achieved fame early on in his career.*

**an early riser** a person who usually gets up early in the morning सुबह जल्दी नींद से जागने वाला व्यक्ति

**earmark** /ˈɪəmɑːk ˈइअमाक्/ *verb* [T] **earmark sb/sth (for sth/sb)** to choose sb/sth to do sth in the future भविष्य में किसी काम के लिए किसी व्यक्ति या वस्तु को चुन लेना *Everybody says Anu has been earmarked as the next manager.*

**earn** /ɜːn अन्/ *verb* [T] **1** to get money by working (पैसा) कमाना *How much does a dentist earn?* ○ *I earn 20,000 rupees a month.* ○ *It's hard to **earn a living** as an artist.* **2** to win the right to sth, for example by working hard (कठिन परिश्रम से) कुछ पाने का अधिकारी हो जाना *The team's victory today has earned them a place in the final.* **3** to get money as profit or interest on money you have in a bank, lent to sb, etc. (बैंक में जमा राशि आदि पर) लाभ या ब्याज के रूप में धन प्राप्त करना *How much interest will my savings earn in this account?*

**earnest** /ˈɜːnɪst ˈअनिस्ट्/ *adj.* serious or determined गंभीर या दृढ़निश्चय वाला *He's such an earnest young man—he never makes a joke.* ○ *They were having a very earnest discussion.* ▶ **earnestly** *adv.* दृढ़निश्चय के साथ

**IDM in earnest** **1** serious and sincere about what you are going to do (अपने कार्य के प्रति) गंभीर और निष्ठावान *He was in earnest about wanting to leave the university.* **2** happening more seriously or with more force than before पूर्व की अपेक्षा अधिक गंभीरता या शक्ति के साथ *After two weeks work began in earnest on the project.*

**earnings** /ˈɜːnɪŋz ˈअनिङ्ज़्/ *noun* [*pl.*] the money that a person earns by working कमाया हुआ धन; कमाई, अर्जन *Average earnings have increased by 5%.*

**earphones** /ˈɪəfəʊnz ˈइअफ़ोनज़्/ *noun* [*pl.*] a piece of equipment that fits over or in the ears and is used for listening to music, the radio, etc. संगीत आदि सुनने के लिए कान पर लगाया जाने वाला उपकरण; इयरफ़ोन

**earring** /ˈɪərɪŋ ˈइअरिङ्/ *noun* [C] a piece of jewellery that is worn in or on the lower part of the ear कान का छल्ला (आभूषण) *Do these earrings clip on or are they for pierced ears?*

**earshot** /ˈɪəʃɒt ˈइअशॉट्/ *noun* [U]

**IDM (be) out of/within earshot** where a person cannot/can hear श्रवण-सीमा के बाहर या अंदर (होना) *Wait until he's out of earshot before you say anything about him.*

**earth**[1] /ɜːθ अथ्/ *noun* **1** (*also* **the earth; the Earth**) [*sing.*] the world; the planet on which we live संसार; पृथ्वी, ग्रह जिस पर हम रहते हैं *life on earth* ○ *The earth goes round the sun.* ➪ **the solar system** देखिए। **2** [*sing.*] the surface of the world; land विश्व का ऊपरी तल; भूमि, ज़मीन *The spaceship fell towards earth.* ○ *I could feel the earth shake when the earthquake started.* **3** [U] the substance that plants grow in; soil खेती की ज़मीन; मिट्टी, मृदा *The earth around here is very fertile.* ➪ **ground** पर नोट देखिए। **4** [C, *usually sing.*] (*AmE* **ground**) a wire that makes a piece of electrical equipment safer by connecting it to the ground तार जिसे ज़मीन में गाड़ने से विद्युत उपकरण सुरक्षित हो जाता है

**IDM charge/pay the earth** (*informal*) to charge/pay a very large amount of money बहुत बड़ी मात्रा में पैसा वसूल या अदा करना

**cost the earth/a fortune** ➪ **cost**[2] देखिए।

**how/why/where/who etc. on earth** (*informal*) used for emphasizing sth or expressing surprise किसी बात पर बल देने या आश्चर्य व्यक्त करने के लिए प्रयुक्त *Where on earth have you been?*

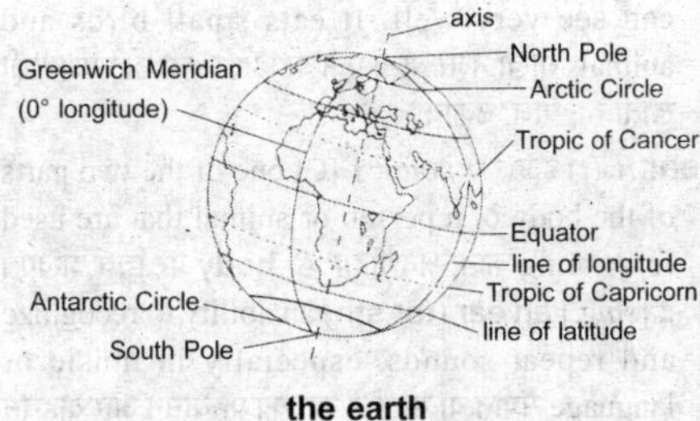


**the earth**

**earth**[2] /ɜːθ अथ्/ (*AmE* **ground**) *verb* [T] to make a piece of electrical equipment safer by connecting it to the ground with a wire ज़मीन में तार गाड़कर विद्युत उपकरण की सुरक्षा की व्यवस्था करना

**earthenware** /ˈɜːθnweə(r) ˈअथ्नवेअ(र्)/ *adj.* made of very hard baked clay ख़ूब सिकी मिट्टी से बना *an earthenware bowl* ▶ **earthenware** *noun* [U] ख़ूब सिकी मिट्टी का बरतन

**earthly** /ˈɜːθli ˈअथ्लि / *adj.* (*often in questions or negatives*) possible संभव *What earthly use is a gardening book to me? I haven't got a garden!*

**earthquake** /ˈɜːθkweɪk ˈअथ्क्वेक् / (*informal* **quake**) *noun* [C] violent movement of the earth's surface भूकंप, भूचाल

**earthworm** /ˈɜːθwɜːm ˈअथ्वम् / *noun* [C] a small, long, thin animal with no legs or eyes that lives in the soil केंचुआ

**earwig** /ˈɪəwɪg ˈइअविग् / *noun* [C] a small brown insect with a long body and two curved pointed parts (**pincers**) that stick out at the back end of its body कनखजूरा, कनगोजर, कर्णकीट

**ease¹** /iːz ईज़् / *noun* [U] a lack of difficulty आसानी, सरलता, सुगमता *She answered the questions* ***with ease.*** ➪ **easy** adjective देखिए। ✪ विलोम **unease**

IDM **(be/feel) at (your) ease** to be/feel comfortable, relaxed, etc. कोई घबराहट न होना, तनावमुक्त महसूस करना *They were all so kind and friendly that I felt completely at ease.*

**ease²** /iːz ईज़् / *verb* **1** [I, T] to become or make sth less painful or serious राहत महसूस करना या पहुँचाना *The pain should ease by this evening.* ○ *This money will ease their financial problems a little.* ➪ **easy** adjective देखिए। **2** [T] to move sth slowly and gently धीमे-धीमे और कोमलता से (किसी वस्तु को) घुमाना *He eased the key into the lock.*

IDM **ease sb's mind** to make sb feel less worried किसी के मन का बोझ हलका करना

PHR V **ease off** to become less strong or unpleasant ढीला पड़ जाना

**ease up** to work less hard मेहनत कम करना

**easel** /ˈɪːzl ˈईज़्ल् / *noun* [C] a wooden frame that holds a picture while it is being painted लकड़ी का चौखटा जिसके सहारे उस चित्र-फ़लक को रखते हैं जिस पर चित्र बनाया जा रहा है

**easily** /ˈɪːzəli ˈईज़लि / *adv.* **1** without difficulty आसानी से, सरलता से *I can easily ring up and check the time.* **2 easily the best, worst, nicest, etc.** without doubt निस्संदेह, निश्चित रूप से *It's easily his best novel.*

**east¹** /iːst ईस्ट् / *noun* [*sing.*] (*abbr.* **E**) **1** (*also* **the east**) the direction you look towards in order to see the sun rise; one of the four main directions that we give names to (**the points of the compass**) पूर्व दिशा, पूरब ➪ **compass** पर चित्र देखिए। *Which way is east?* ○ *a cold wind from the east* ○ *Which state is* ***to the east of*** *Sikkim?* **2 the east** the part of any country, city, etc. that is further to the east than the other parts किसी देश या नगर का पूरब की ओर का भाग (अन्य भागों की अपेक्षा अधिक पूर्वाभिमुख) *Norwich is in the east of England.* **3 the East** the countries of Asia, for example China and Japan एशिया के देश (जैसे चीन और जापान) ➪ **the Far East** और **the Middle East** देखिए। ➪ **north, south** और **west** भी देखिए।

**east²** /iːst ईस्ट् / (*also* **East**) *adj., adv.* in or towards the east or from the east पूर्व दिशा में या की ओर या पूर्व दिशा से *They headed east.* ○ *the East Coast of America* ○ *We live east of the city.* ○ *an east wind*

**eastbound** /ˈɪːstbaʊnd ˈईस्ट्बाउन्ड् / *adj.* travelling or leading towards the east पूर्व दिशा की ओर जाने वाला *The eastbound carriageway of the highway is blocked.*

**Easter** /ˈiːstə(r) ˈईस्टर(र्) / *noun* [U] a festival on a Sunday in March or April when Christians celebrate Christ's return to life; the time before and after Easter Sunday मार्च या अप्रैल के किसी रविवार को आने वाला पर्व जिसमें ईसाई लोग ईसा का पुनरुत्थान मनाते हैं; ईस्टर के रविवार से पहले और बाद का समय; ईस्टर पर्व *the Easter holidays* ○ *Are you going away* ***at Easter****?*

**easterly** /ˈiːstəli ˈईस्टलि / *adj.* **1** towards or in the east पूर्व दिशा में या की ओर *They travelled in an easterly direction.* **2** (used about winds) coming from the east (हवाएँ) पूर्व की ओर से आने वाली, पुरवाई या पुरवैया *cold easterly winds*

**eastern** (*also* **Eastern**) /ˈiːstən ˈईस्टन् / *adj.* **1** of, in or from the east of a place पूर्व का/में/से, पूर्वी *Eastern India* ○ *the eastern shore of the lake* **2** from or connected with the countries of the East एशिया के देशों से संबंधित *Eastern cookery* (= that comes from Asia)

**eastward** /ˈiːstwəd ˈईस्ट्वड् / *adj.* (*also* **eastwards**) *adj., adv.* towards the east पूर्व दिशा की ओर *to travel in an eastward direction* ○ *The Ganga flows eastwards.*

**easy¹** /ˈiːzi ˈईज़ि / *adj.* (**easier; easiest**) **1** not difficult आसान, सरल *an easy question* ○ *It isn't easy to explain the system.* ○ *The system isn't easy to explain.* ✪ विलोम **hard** **2** comfortable, relaxed and not worried सुविधा-संपन्न, तनावरहित और निश्चिंत *an easy life* ○ *My mind's easier now.* ➪ **uneasy** देखिए। ➪ **ease** noun, verb भी देखिए।

IDM **free and easy** ➪ **free¹** देखिए।

**easy²** /ˈiːzi ˈईज़ि / *adv.* (**easier; easiest**)

IDM **easier said than done** (*spoken*) more difficult to do than to talk about कहना आसान है, करना कठिन *'You should get her to help you.' 'That's easier said than done.'*

**go easy on sb/on/with sth** (*informal*) **1** to be gentle or less strict with sb (किसी के साथ) नरमी का बरताव करना या नरमी बरतना *Go easy on him; he's just a child.* **2** to avoid using too much of sth (किसी वस्तु की) अति से बचना *Go easy on the salt; it's bad for your heart.*

**take it/things easy** to relax and not work too hard or worry too much (अधिक चिंता या परिश्रम के बिना) आराम से काम करना

**easy chair** *noun* [C] a large comfortable chair with arms आराम कुरसी

**easy-going** *adj.* (used about a person) calm, relaxed and not easily worried or upset by what other people do (व्यक्ति) शांत, तनावमुक्त व आसानी से चिंतित न होने वाला

**eat** /iːt ईट्/ *verb* (*pt* **ate** /et एट्/; *pp* **eaten** /ˈiːtn ˈईट्न्/) **1** [I, T] to put food into your mouth, then bite and swallow it (खाद्य पदार्थों को मुँह में लेकर चबाना और निगल जाना या खाना) *Who ate all the biscuits?* ○ *Eat your dinner up, Rahul* (= finish it all). **2** [I] to have a meal *What time shall we eat?*

IDM **have sb eating out of your hand** to have control and power over sb (किसी व्यक्ति पर) नियंत्रण और अधिकार होना

**have your cake and eat it** ➪ **cake**[1] देखिए।

PHR V **eat sth away/eat away at sth** to damage or destroy sth slowly over a period of time धीमे-धीमे कुछ लंबे समय तक किसी वस्तु को नुक़सान पहुँचाते रहना या नष्ट कर देना *The sea had eaten away at the cliff.*

**eat out** to have a meal in a restaurant किसी रेस्तराँ में भोजन करना

**eatable** /ˈiːtəbl ˈईटब्ल्/ *adj.* = **edible** ▶ **eatable** (*usually* **eatables**) /ˈiːtəblz ˈईटब्ल्ज़्/ *noun* articles of food or substances that can be used as food खाद्य पदार्थ

**eater** /ˈiːtə(r) ˈईट(र्)/ *noun* [C] a person who eats in a particular way किसी विशेष तरीक़े से खाने वाला *My uncle's a big eater* (= he eats a lot). ○ *We're not great meat eaters in our family.*

**eatery** /ˈiːtəri ˈईटरि/ *noun* (*pl.* **eateries**) (*informal*) a café or restaurant जलपान गृह; रेस्तराँ *A new eatery has opened in that mall.*

**eau de Cologne** /ˌəʊ də kəˈləʊn ˌओ ड कˈलोन्/ (*also* **cologne**) *noun* [U] a type of pleasant smelling liquid (**perfume**) that is not very strong हलकी और सुहानी ख़ुशबू वाला एक इत्र; यू-डि-कोलोन

**eaves** /iːvz ईव्ज़्/ *noun* [*pl.*] the edges of a roof that stick out over the walls छज्जा, ओलती

**eavesdrop** /ˈiːvzdrɒp ˈईव्ज़्ड्रॉप्/ *verb* [I] (**eavesdropping; eavesdropped**) **eavesdrop (on sb/sth)** to listen secretly to other people talking दूसरों की बातों को छिपकर सुनना, कनसुई लेना *They caught her eavesdropping on their conversation.*

**ebb**[1] /eb एब्/ *verb* [I] **1** (used about sea water) to flow away from the land, which happens twice a day समुद्र जल का उतरना, (समुद्र में) भाटा आना (यह दिन में दो बार होता है) ✪ पर्याय **go out** **2 ebb (away)** (used about a feeling, etc.) to become weaker (भावना आदि) प्रबलता कम हो जाना *The crowd's enthusiasm began to ebb.*

**ebb**[2] /eb एब्/ *noun* [*sing.*] **the ebb** the time when sea water flows away from the land भाटा आने का समय

NOTE समुद्र जल की दिन में दो बार होने वाली हलचल को **tide** कहते हैं। ➪ **high tide** देखिए।

IDM **the ebb and flow (of sth)** (used about a situation, noise, feeling, etc.) a regular increase and decrease in the progress or strength of sth (किसी स्थिति, शोर, भावना आदि की) प्रगति या शक्ति में क्रमिक व नियमित वृद्धि और ह्रास

**ebony** /ˈebəni ˈएबनि/ *noun* [U] a hard black wood आबनूस की लकड़ी (जो सख़्त और काली होती है)

**eccentric** /ɪkˈsentrɪk इक्ˈसेन्ट्रिक्/ *adj.* (used about people or their behaviour) strange or unusual (व्यक्ति या व्यवहार) सनकी, ख़ब्ती, झक्की *People said he was mad but I think he was just slightly eccentric.* ▶ **eccentric** *noun* [C] सनकी, ख़ब्ती, झक्की *She's just an old eccentric.* ▶ **eccentricity** /ˌeksenˈtrɪsəti ˌएकसेन्ˈट्रिसटि/ *noun* [C, U] (*pl.* **eccentricities**) सनक, ख़ब्त, झक

**ecclesiastical** /ɪˌkliːziˈæstɪkl इˌक्लीज़िˈऐस्टिक्ल्/ *adj.* connected with or belonging to the Christian Church ईसाई चर्च-विषयक *ecclesiastical law*

**echo**[1] /ˈekəʊ ˈएको/ *noun* [C] (*pl.* **echoes**) a sound that is repeated as it is sent back off a surface such as the wall of a tunnel गूँज, प्रतिध्वनि *I could hear the echo of footsteps somewhere in the distance.*

**echo**[2] /ˈekəʊ ˈएको/ *verb* **1** [I] (used about a sound) to be repeated; to come back as an echo (ध्वनि का) दोहराया जाना, प्रतिध्वनित होना; (ध्वनि का) गूँज के रूप में लौटना *Their footsteps echoed in the empty hall.* **2** [I, T] **echo sth (back); echo (with/to sth)** to repeat or send back a sound; to be full of a particular sound आवाज़ को दोहराना या लौटाना; ध्वनि-विशेष का व्याप्त हो जाना *The tunnel echoed back their calls.* ○ *The hall echoed with their laughter.* **3** [T] to repeat what sb has said, done or thought किसी

के कहे, किए या सोचे को दोहराना *The child echoed everything his mother said.* ○ *The newspaper article echoed my views completely.*

**echo sounder** *noun* [C] a device for finding how deep the sea is or where objects are in the water by measuring the time it takes for sound to return to the person listening (सुनने वाले के पास आवाज़ के लौटने का समय मापते हुए) समुद्र की गहराई, या समुद्र में पड़ी वस्तुओं का ठिकाना जानने का उपकरण ▶ **echo-sounding** *noun* [C, U] प्रतिध्वनिक मापन ➪ **sonar** पर चित्र देखिए।

**eclair** /ɪˈkleə(r) इˈक्लेअ(र्)/ *noun* [C] a type of long thin cake, usually filled with cream and covered with chocolate एक प्रकार का लंबा पतला केक (जिसके अंदर क्रीम होती है और ऊपर चॉकलेट की परत)

**eclipse**[1] /ɪˈklɪps इˈक्लिप्स्/ *noun* [C] an occasion when the moon or the sun seems to completely or partly disappear, because one of them is passing between the other and the earth चंद्रमा या सूर्य का कुछ देरी के लिए, पूर्ण रूप से, या आंशिक रूप से पृथ्वी वासियों को दिखाई न पड़ना; ग्रहण *a total/partial eclipse of the sun* ➪ **shadow** पर चित्र देखिए।

**eclipse**[2] /ɪˈklɪps इˈक्लिप्स्/ *verb* [T] (used about the moon, etc.) to cause an eclipse of the sun, etc. सूर्य या चंद्र का ग्रहण लगना

**eco-friendly** /ˌiːkəʊˈfrendli ˌईकोˈफ्रेन्ड्लि/ *adj.* not harmful to the environment पर्यावरण के अनुकूल *eco-friendly products/fuel*

**ecologist** /ɪˈkɒlədʒɪst इˈकॉलजिस्ट्/ *noun* [C] a person who studies or is an expert in ecology पर्यावरण-विशेषज्ञ

**ecology** /ɪˈkɒlədʒi इˈकॉलजि/ *noun* [U] the relationship between living things and their surroundings; the study of this subject सजीवों का अपने परिवेश से संबंध; पर्यावरण का अध्ययन; पर्यावरण-विज्ञान ▶ **ecological** /ˌiːkəˈlɒdʒɪkl ˌईकˈलॉजिकल्/ *adj.* पर्यावरण-विषयक *an ecological disaster* ▶ **ecologically** /-kli -क्लि/ *adv.* पर्यावरण की दृष्टि से

**economic** /ˌiːkəˈnɒmɪk ˌईकˈनॉमिक्; ˌekə- ˌएक-/ *adj.* **1** (*only before a noun*) connected with the supply of money, business, industry, etc. आर्थिक; धन के लेन-देन, व्यापार, उद्योग आदि से संबंधित *The country is facing growing economic problems.* **2** producing a profit लाभकारी *The mine was closed because it was not economic.* ➪ **economical** देखिए। ✪ विलोम **uneconomic** ▶ **economically** /ˌiːkəˈnɒmɪkli ˌईकˈनॉमिक्लि; ˌekə- ˌएक-/ *adv.* आर्थिक दृष्टि से *The country was economically very underdeveloped.*

**economical** /ˌiːkəˈnɒmɪkl ˌईकˈनॉमिकल्; ˌekə- ˌएक-/ *adj.* that costs or uses less time, money, fuel, etc. than usual किफ़ायती, मितव्ययी *an economical car to run* ➪ **economic** देखिए। ✪ विलोम **uneconomical** ▶ **economically** /-kli -क्लि/ *adv.* किफ़ायती ढंग से *The train service could be run more economically.*

**economics** /ˌiːkəˈnɒmɪks ˌईकˈनॉमिक्स्; ˌekə- ˌएक-/ *noun* [U] the study or principles of the way money, business and industry are organized मुद्रा, व्यवसाय और उद्योग की संगठन रीतियों के सिद्धांतों का अध्ययन; अर्थशास्त्र *a degree in economics* ○ *the economics of a company*

**economist** /ɪˈkɒnəmɪst इˈकॉनमिस्ट्/ *noun* [C] a person who studies or is an expert in economics अर्थशास्त्री

**economize** (*also* **-ise**) /ɪˈkɒnəmaɪz इˈकॉनमाइज़्/ *verb* [I] **economize (on sth)** to save money, time, fuel, etc.; to use less of sth धन, समय, ईंधन आदि बचाना; किसी चीज़ की किफ़ायत करना

**economy** /ɪˈkɒnəmi इˈकॉनमि/ *noun* (*pl.* **economies**) **1** (*also* **the economy**) [C] the operation of a country's money supply, commercial activities and industry अर्थ-व्यवस्था *There are signs of improvement in the economy.* ○ *the economies of America and Japan* **2** [C, U] careful spending of money, time, fuel, etc.; trying to save, not waste sth धन, समय आदि की किफ़ायत; बचत *Our department is **making economies** in the amount of paper it uses.* ○ *economy class* (= the cheapest class of air travel)

**ecosystem** /ˈiːkəʊsɪstəm ˈईकोसिस्टम्/ *noun* [C] all the plants and animals in a particular area considered together with their surroundings क्षेत्र-विशेष में पाए जाने वाले व अपने परिवेष से संबंधित सभी पौधे व पशु; पारिस्थितिकी तंत्र

**ecotourism** /ˌiːkəʊˈtʊərɪzəm ˌईकोˈटुअरिज़म्/ *noun* [U] **tourism** to places that not many people have the chance to see, especially when some of the money paid by the tourists is used to protect the local environment and animals क्षेत्र विशेष के पर्यावरण के संरक्षण को ध्यान में रखकर आयोजित पारिस्थितिक पर्यटन

**ecstasy** /ˈekstəsi ˈएकस्टसि/ *noun* [C, U] (*pl.* **ecstasies**) a feeling or state of great happiness आह्लाद और आनंद की भावना *to be **in ecstasy*** ○ *She **went into ecstasies** about the ring he had bought her.*

**ecstatic** /ɪkˈstætɪk इक्ˈस्टैटिक्/ *adj.* extremely happy अति प्रसन्न

**eczema** /ˈeksɪmə एक्सिमा/ *noun* [U] a disease which makes your skin red and dry so that you want to scratch it एक प्रकार का चर्मरोग जिसमें त्वचा लाल व शुष्क हो जाती है और उसमें खारिश होती है; पामा, छाजन

**ed.** *abbr.* edited by; edition; editor (द्वारा) संपादित, संस्करण, संपादक

**eddy** /ˈedi ˈएडि/ *noun* [C] (*pl.* **eddies**) a circular movement of water, wind, dust, etc. (पानी का) भँवर, (जल, वायु, धूल आदि का) बवंडर; वायु, जल आदि का चक्राकार घूमना

**edge**[1] /edʒ एज्/ *noun* [C] **1** the place where sth, especially a surface, ends किसी समतल वस्तु का किनारा, छोर *the edge of a table* ○ *The leaves were brown and curling at the edges.* ○ *I stood at the water's edge.* **2** the sharp cutting part of a knife, etc. (चाकू आदि की) धार

IDM **an/the edge on/over sb/sth** a small advantage over sb/sth अन्यों की अपेक्षा कुछ बेहतर स्थिति में *She knew she had the edge over the other candidates.*

**(be) on edge** to be nervous, worried or quick to become upset or angry परेशान, चिंतित या तुरंत क्रोधित हो जाना *I'm a bit on edge because I am going to get my exam results today.*

**edge**[2] /edʒ एज्/ *verb* **1** [T] (*usually passive*) **edge sth (with sth)** to put sth along the edge of sth else किसी वस्तु से किसी अन्य वस्तु का किनारा बनाना *The cloth was edged with lace.* **2** [I, T] **edge (your way/sth) across, along, away, back, etc.** to move yourself/sth somewhere slowly and carefully धीरे-धीरे, सावधानी से आगे बढ़ना या बढ़ाना; सरकना या सरकाना *We edged closer to get a better view.* ○ *She edged her chair up to the window.*

**edgeways** /ˈedʒweɪz ˈएज्वेज़्/ (*also* **edgewise** /-waɪz वाइज़्/) *adv.*

IDM **not get a word in edgeways** ⇨ **word**[1] देखिए।

**edgy** /ˈedʒi ˈएजि/ *adj.* (*informal*) nervous, worried or quick to become upset or angry परेशान, चिंतित या तुरंत क्रोधित होने वाला; चिड़चिड़ा

**edible** /ˈedəbl ˈएडबल्/ *adj.* good or safe to eat खाने योग्य, खाने में स्वादिष्ट और सुरक्षित; खाद्य *Are these mushrooms edible?* ✪ विलोम **inedible**

**edict** /ˈiːdɪkt ˈईडिक्ट्/ *noun* [C] (*formal*) an offical order or statement issued by sb in a position of power राजविज्ञप्ति, फ़रमान

**edifice** /ˈedɪfɪs ˈएडिफ़िस्/ *noun* [C] (*informal*) a large impressive building भव्य भवन, बड़ी शानदार इमारत

**edit** /ˈedɪt ˈएडिट्/ *verb* [T] **1** to prepare a piece of writing to be published, making sure that it is correct, the right length, etc. (लेख आदि का) संपादन करना (भाषाशोधन, सामग्री का आकार नियंत्रण आदि करना) **2** to prepare a film, television or radio programme by cutting and arranging filmed material in a particular order फ़िल्म, टीवी, रेडियो प्रोग्राम तथा फ़िल्माई सामग्री को आवश्यकतानुसार काटकर व्यवस्थित करना **3** to be in charge of a newspaper, magazine, etc. समाचार पत्र, पत्रिका आदि का प्रमुख होना

**edition** /ɪˈdɪʃn इˈडिशन्/ *noun* [C] **1** the form in which a book is published; all the books, newspapers, etc. published in the same form at the same time पुस्तक का प्रकाशित रूप, संस्करण; एक ही समय और रूपाकार में प्रकाशित समस्त पुस्तकें, समाचारपत्र आदि *a paperback/hardback edition* ○ *the morning edition of a newspaper* **2** one of a series of newspapers, magazines, television or radio programmes समाचारपत्रों, पत्रिकाओं, दूरदर्शन या रेडियो कार्यक्रमों की शृंखला में से कोई एक *And now for this week's edition of 'Panorama'...*

**editor** /ˈedɪtə(r) ˈएडिटर्(र्)/ *noun* [C] **1** the person who is in charge of all or part of a newspaper, magazine, etc. and who decides what should be included संपादक *the financial editor* ○ *Who is the editor of 'The Times of India'?* **2** a person whose job is to prepare a book to be published by checking for mistakes and correcting the text पांडुलिपि को परिष्कृत करके प्रकाशन योग्य बनाने वाला; संपादक **3** a person whose job is to prepare a film, television programme, etc. for showing to the public by cutting and putting the filmed material in the correct order चित्रित दृश्यों को समुचित क्रम में व्यस्थित कर उन्हें फ़िल्म, दूरदर्शन कार्यक्रम आदि के लिए तैयार करने वाला व्यक्ति; संपादक

**editorial** /ˌedɪˈtɔːriəl ˌएडिˈटॉरिअल्/ *noun* [C] an article in a newspaper, usually written by the head of the newspaper (**editor**), giving an opinion on an important subject संपादकीय लेख

**educate** /ˈedʒukeɪt ˈएजुकेट्/ *verb* [T] to teach or train sb, especially in school शिक्षा देना, शिक्षित करना (विशेषतः विद्यालय आदि में) *Young people should be educated to care for their environment.* ○ *All their children were educated at private schools.*

**educated** /ˈedʒukeɪtɪd ˈएजुकेटिड्/ *adj.* having studied and learnt a lot of things to a high standard शिक्षित, उच्च शिक्षा प्राप्त *a highly educated woman*

**education** /ˌedʒuˈkeɪʃn ˌएजुˈकेशन्/ *noun* [C, *usually sing.*, U] the teaching or training of people, especially in schools शिक्षा, तालीम, पढ़ाई *primary, secondary, higher, adult education* ○ *She received an excellent education.* ▶ **educational** /-ʃənl -शनल्/ *adj.* शिक्षा-संबंधी, शैक्षिक *an educational toy/visit/experience*

**eel** /iːl ईल्/ *noun* [C] a long fish that looks like a snake साँपनुमा लंबी मछली, सर्पमीन

**eerie** (*also* **eery**) /ˈɪəri ˈइअरि/ *adj.* strange and frightening विचित्र और भयानक; भयोत्पादक *an eerie noise* ▶ **eerily** *adv.* विचित्र और भयानक रूप से ▶ **eeriness** *noun* [U] विचित्रता और भयोत्पादकता

**efface** /ɪˈfeɪs इˈफ़ेस्/ *verb* [T] (*formal*) to make sth disappear; to remove sth (किसी वस्तु को) विलुप्त कर देना; मिटा देना या हटा देना

**effect** /ɪˈfekt इˈफ़ेक्ट्/ *noun* **1** [C, U] (**an**) **effect** (**on sb/sth**) a change that is caused by sth; a result प्रभाव; परिणाम *the effects of acid rain on the lakes and forests* ○ *Her shouting* ***had little or no effect*** *on him.* ○ *Despite her terrible experience, she seems to have suffered no* ***ill effects****.* ➪ **after-effect** और **side effect** देखिए तथा **affect** पर नोट देखिए। **2** [C, U] a particular look, sound or impression that an artist, writer, etc. wants to create कलाकार, लेखक आदि द्वारा सृजित विशिष्ट रूप-रंग, ध्वनि या प्रभाव *How does the artist* ***create the effect of*** *moonlight?* ○ *He likes to say things just for effect* (= to impress people). **3 effects** [*pl.*] (*formal*) your personal possessions व्यक्तिगत चल संपत्ति, सामान

IDM **come into effect** (used especially about laws or rules) to begin to be used (विशेषतः क़ानूनों या नियमों पर) अमल होने लगना, लागू हो जाना

**in effect 1** in fact; for all practical purposes वस्तुतः, असल में; लगभग सभी कार्यों के लिए *Though they haven't made an official announcement, she is, in effect, the new director.* **2** (used about a rule, a law, etc.) in operation; in use (नियम, क़ानून आदि) प्रचलन में; व्यवहार में *The new rules will be in effect from next month.*

**take effect 1** (used about a drug, etc.) to begin to work; to produce the result you want (दवा का) काम करने लगना; अभीष्ट प्रभाव होना *The anaesthetic took effect immediately.* **2** (used about a law, etc.) to come into operation (क़ानून आदि का) लागू हो जाना, प्रभावी हो जाना *The ceasefire takes effect from midnight.*

**to this/that effect** with this/that meaning ऐसा या वैसा अर्थ देने वाला; इस या उस अर्थ में *I told him to leave her alone, or words to that effect.*

**effective** /ɪˈfektɪv इˈफ़ेक्टिव़्/ *adj.* **1** successfully producing the result that you want अभीष्ट प्रभाव उत्पन्न करने वाला; प्रभावोत्पादक *a medicine that is effective against the common cold* ○ *That picture would look more effective on a dark background.* ✪ विलोम **ineffective** **2** real or actual, although perhaps not official वास्तविक (भले ही वह आधिकारिक न हो) *The soldiers gained effective control of the town.* ▶ **effectiveness** *noun* [U] प्रभावोत्पादकता

**effectively** /ɪˈfektɪvli इˈफ़ेक्टिव़्लि/ *adv.* **1** in a way that successfully produces the result you wanted प्रभावोत्पादक रीति से *She dealt with the situation effectively.* **2** in fact; in reality वास्तव में; यथार्थतः *It meant that, effectively, they had lost.*

**effector** /ɪˈfektə(r) इˈफ़ेक्ट(र्)/ *noun* [C] an organ or a cell in the body that is made to react by sth outside the body शरीर का अंग या कोशिका जिसमें (शरीर-बाह्य क्रिया की) प्रतिक्रिया होती है

**effeminate** /ɪˈfemɪnət इˈफ़ेमिनट्/ *adj.* (used about a man or his behaviour) like a woman (पुरुष या पुरुष का आचरण) स्त्रियों जैसा, स्त्रियोचित, स्त्रैण

**effervescent** /ˌefəˈvesnt ˌएफ़ˈव़ेसन्ट्/ *adj.* **1** (used about people and their behaviour) excited, enthusiastic and full of energy (जन समूह और उनका आचरण) उत्तेजनापूर्ण, उत्साहपूर्ण और ऊर्जान्वित **2** (used about a liquid) having or producing small bubbles of gas (द्रव) गैस के बुलबुले वाला या बुलबुले उत्पन्न करने वाला ▶ **effervescence** /ˌefəˈvesns ˌएफ़ˈव़ेसन्स्/ *noun* [U] उत्तेजना, बुदबुदाहट

**efficacious** /ˌefɪˈkeɪʃəs ˌएफ़िˈकेशस्/ *adj.* (*formal*) (of things) producing the desired result (वस्तु) प्रभावोत्पादक, अमोघ, फलदायक *They hope that the new drug will prove especially efficacious in relieving pain.* ✪ पर्याय **effective**

**efficacy** /ˈefɪkəsi ˌएफ़िकसि/ *noun* [U] (*formal*) the ability of sth like a drug or a medical treatment to bring about the results that are wanted किसी औषधि या चिकित्सीय उपचार की प्रभावोत्पादकता *The efficacy of the drug should be evaluated before launching it in the market.*

**efficient** /ɪˈfɪʃnt इˈफ़िश्न्ट्/ *adj.* able to work well without making mistakes or wasting time and energy कार्य-कुशल *Our secretary is very efficient.* ○ *You must find a more efficient way of organizing your time.* ✪ विलोम **inefficient** ▶ **efficiency** /ɪˈfɪʃnsi इˈफ़िश्न्सि/ *noun* [U] कार्यकुशलता दक्षता, क्षमता ▶ **efficiently** *adv.* कार्यकुशलतापूर्वक

**effigy** /ˈefɪdʒi ˈएफ़िजि/ *noun* [C] (*pl.* **effigies**) **1** a statue of a famous or religious person or a god

(प्रसिद्ध या धार्मिक व्यक्ति या ईश्वर की) मूर्ति **2** a model of a person that makes him/her look ugly (किसी व्यक्ति का भद्दा लगने वाला) पुतला *The demonstrators burned a crude effigy of the president.*

**effluent** /ˈefluənt ˈएफ़्लुअन्ट् / *noun* [U] liquid waste, especially chemicals produced by factories बहिष्प्रवाही; विशेषतः कारख़ानों में बना रसायन

**effort** /ˈefət ˈएफ़ट् / *noun* **1** [U] the physical or mental strength or energy that you need to do sth; sth that takes a lot of energy मानसिक या शारीरिक प्रयास (कोई काम करने के लिए अपेक्षित); ऐसा कार्य जिसमें बहुत शक्ति या प्रयास लगे *They have* ***put a lot of effort into*** *their studies this year.* ○ *He* ***made no effort*** *to contact his parents.* **2** [C] **an effort (to do sth)** something that is done with difficulty or that takes a lot of energy कठिनाई से या बहुत शक्ति लगाकर किया जाने वाला काम *It was a real effort to stay awake during the lecture.*

**effortless** /ˈefətləs ˈएफ़टलस् / *adj.* needing little or no effort so that sth seems easy आसान, सरल, सहज, निश्चेष्ट ▸ **effortlessly** *adv.* आसानी से

**e.g.** /ˌiːˈdʒiː ˌईˈजी / *abbr.* for example उदाहरण स्वरूप *popular sports, e.g. football, tennis, swimming*

**egalitarian** /iˌɡælɪˈteəriən इˌगैलिˈटेअरिअन् / *adj.* (used about a person, system, society, etc.) following the principle that everyone should have equal rights (व्यक्ति, प्रणाली, समाज आदि) सबके लिए समान अधिकारों को मान्यता देने वाला; समानतावादी

**egg**[1] /eg एग् / *noun* **1** [C] an almost round object with a hard shell that contains a young bird, reptile or insect (पक्षी, साँप या कीड़े का) अंडा ➪ **insect** पर चित्र देखिए। **2** [C, U] a bird's egg, especially one from a chicken, etc. that we eat पक्षी का अंडा (विशेषतः मुरग़ी का) जो खाया जाता है

> NOTE अंडे **boiled, fried, poached** या **scrambled** किए जा सकते हैं।

**3** [C] (in women and female animals) the small cell that can join with a male seed (**sperm**) to make a baby (स्त्रियों और मादा पशुओं में) अंडकोशिका जो पुरुष शुक्राणु के साथ मिलकर संतानोत्पत्ति करती है; डिंब

IDM **put all your eggs in one basket** to risk everything by depending completely on one thing, plan, etc. instead of giving yourself several possibilities केवल एक ही विकल्प पर पूर्णतया निर्भर रहना

**egg**[2] /eg एग् / *verb* **egg sb on (to do sth)** to encourage sb to do sth that he/she should not do न करने योग्य काम के लिए किसी को उकसाना

**egg cup** *noun* [C] a small cup for holding a boiled egg उबला अंडा रखने का छोटा कप

**eggplant** /ˈeɡplɑːnt ˈएग्प्लान्ट् / (*AmE*) = **aubergine**

**eggshell** /ˈeɡʃel ˈएग्शेल् / *noun* [C, U] the hard outside part of an egg अंडे का छिलका, अंडकवच

**ego** /ˈiːɡəʊ ˈईगो / *noun* [C] (*pl.* **egos**) the (good) opinion that you have of yourself व्यक्ति का स्वयं के बारे में (उच्च) विचार; अहंकार, घमंड *It was a blow to her ego when she lost her job.*

**egocentric** /ˌiːɡəʊˈsentrɪk ˌईगोˈसेन्ट्रिक् / *adj.* thinking only about yourself and not what other people need or want अहंकारी, घमंडी ✪ पर्याय **selfish**

**egoism** /ˈiːɡəʊɪzəm ˈईगोइज़म्; ˈeg- ˈएग्- / (*also* **egotism** /ˈiːɡəʊtɪzəm ˈईगोटिज़म्; ˈeg- ˈएग्- /) *noun* [U] thinking about yourself too much; thinking that you are better or more important than anyone else अहंकार भाव; अहम्मन्यता, अन्यों की अपेक्षा अपने को बड़ा समझना ▸ **egoist** /ˈiːɡəʊɪst ˈईगोइस्ट्; ˈeg- ˈएग्- / (*also* **egotist** /ˈiːɡəʊtɪst ˈईगोटिस्ट्; ˈeg- ˈएग्- /) *noun* [C] अहंकारी व्यक्ति *I hate people who are egoists.* ▸ **egoistic** /iːɡəʊˈɪstɪk ईगोˈइसटिक् / (*also* **egotistical** /iːɡəʊˈtɪstɪkl ईगोˈटिसटिकल् ; ˈeg- ˈएग्- /) *adj.* आत्मश्लाघा से

**eh** /eɪ ए / *exclamation* (*BrE informal*) **1** used for asking sb to agree with you दूसरे को अपने से सहमत कराने के लिए प्रयुक्त *'Good party, eh?'* **2** used for asking sb to repeat sth दूसरे का यह कहने के लिए प्रयुक्त कि वह अपनी बात दोहराए *'Did you like the film?' 'Eh?' 'I asked if you liked the film!'*

**Eid** (*also* **Id**) *noun* [C, U] any of several Muslim festivals, especially one that celebrates the end of a month when people **fast** during the day (**Ramadan**) ईद का त्यौहार

**eight** /eɪt एट् / *number* **1** 8 आठ (अंक)

> NOTE संख्याओं के वाक्य-प्रयोग के उदाहरणों के लिए **six** की प्रविष्टि देखिए।

**2 eight-** (*used to form compounds*) having eight of sth आठ (टुकड़े, पहलू आदि) वाला, अठ-/अष्ट- *an eight-sided shape*

**eighteen** /ˌeɪˈtiːn ˌएˈटीन् / *number* 18 अट्ठारह (का अंक)

> NOTE संख्याओं के वाक्य-प्रयोग के उदाहरणों के लिए **six** की प्रविष्टि देखिए।

**eighteenth** /ˌeɪˈtiːnθ ˌएˈटीन्थ़ / *pronoun, det., adv.* 18th अट्ठारहवाँ/वीं ➪ **sixth** पर उदाहरण देखिए।

**eighth**[1] /eɪtθ एट्थ़ / *noun* [C] the fraction ⅛ one of eight equal parts of sth भिन्न ⅛, आठवाँ अंश

**eighth**[2] /eɪtθ एट्थ़ / *pronoun, det., adv.* 8th आठवाँ/वीं ➪ **sixth** पर उदाहरण देखिए।

**eightieth** /ˈeɪtiəθ ˈएटिअथ़्/ *pronoun, det., adv.* 80th अस्सीवाँ/वीं ➪ **sixth** पर उदाहरण देखिए।

**eighty** /ˈeɪti ˈएटि/ *number* 80 अस्सी की संख्या

**NOTE** संख्याओं के वाक्य-प्रयोग के उदाहरणों के लिए **sixty** की प्रविष्टि देखिए।

**either¹** /ˈaɪðə(r) ˈआइद़र(र्) ˈi:ðə(r) ˈईद़र(र्)/ *det., pronoun* **1** one or the other of two; it does not matter which दो में से कोई एक; दो में से कोई भी *You can choose either soup or salad, but not both.* ○ *You can ask either of us for advice.* ○ *Either of us is willing to help.* **2** both दोनों *It is a pleasant road, with trees on either side.*

**either²** /ˈaɪðə(r) ˈआइद़र (र्); ˈi:ðə(r) ˈईद़र (र्)/ *adv.* **1** (*used after two negative statements*) also भी *I don't like Paras and I don't like Neetu much either.* ○ *'I can't remember his name.' 'I can't either.'* **NOTE** इस अर्थ में **neither can I** का प्रयोग भी किया जा सकता है। स्वीकारात्मक कथनों के साथ अनुबंध के लिए **too** की प्रविष्टि देखिए। **2** used for emphasizing a negative statement निषेधात्मक कथन या निषेध पर बल देने के लिए प्रयुक्त *The restaurant is quite good. And it's not expensive either.*

**either³** /ˈaɪðə(r) ˈआइद़र (र्); ˈi:ðə(r) ˈईद़र (र्)/ *conj.* **either... or...** used when you are giving a choice, usually of two things जब (प्रायः दो) विकल्प दिए जाएँ, जब (प्रायः दो) विकल्पों में से चुनने के लिए कहना हो *I can meet you either on Thursday or Friday.* ○ *You can either write or phone.*

**ejaculate** /iˈdʒækjuleɪt इˈजैक्युलेट्/ *verb* **1** [I] to send out liquid (**semen**) from the male sexual organ (**penis**) पुरुष वीर्य का स्खलन होना **2** [I, T] (*old fashioned*) to say sth suddenly कोई बात सहसा कह उठना, अचानक बोल पड़ना; उद्‌गार करना ▸ **ejaculation** /iˌdʒækjuˈleɪʃn इˌजैक्युˈलेशन्/ *noun* [C, U] वीर्यस्खलन, उद्‌गार

**eject** /iˈdʒekt इˈजेक्ट्/ *verb* **1** [T] (*formal*) (*usually passive*) **eject sb (from sth)** to push or send sb/sth out of a place (usually with force) किसी व्यक्ति या वस्तु को निकाल बाहर करना (प्रायः ज़बरदस्ती) *The protesters were ejected from the building.* **2** [I, T] to remove a tape, disk etc. from a machine, usually by pressing a button किसी मशीन से टेप, डिस्क आदि को बाहर निकाल लेना (प्रायः बटन दबाकर) *To eject the CD, press this button.* ○ *After recording for three hours the video will eject automatically.* **3** [I] to escape from an aircraft that is going to crash संकटग्रस्त विमान में से बाहर आ जाना

**eke** /i:k ईक्/ *verb*

**PHR V** **eke sth out** to make a small amount of sth last a long time थोड़ी-सी चीज़ से देर तक काम चलाना

**elaborate¹** /ɪˈlæbərət इˈलैबरट्/ *adj.* very complicated; done or made very carefully विस्तारपूर्वक प्रस्तुत; बहुत सावधानी से निर्मित; परिष्कृत *an elaborate pattern* ○ *elaborate plans*

**elaborate²** /ɪˈlæbəreɪt इˈलैबरेट्/ *verb* [I] (*formal*) **elaborate (on sth)** to give more details about sth विस्तार से वर्णन करना *Could you elaborate on that idea?*

**elaichi** *noun* = **cardamom**

**elapse** /ɪˈlæps इˈलैप्स्/ *verb* [I] (*formal*) (used about time) to pass (समय का) बीतना, व्यतीत होना

**elastic¹** /ɪˈlæstɪk इˈलैस्टिक्/ *noun* [U] material with rubber in it which can stretch रबर वाला और इसलिए लचीला फ़ीता आदि

**elastic²** /ɪˈlæstɪk इˈलैस्टिक्/ *adj.* **1** (used about material, etc.) that returns to its original size and shape after being stretched (पदार्थ) लचीला; खींचने के बाद छोड़ने पर पूर्व अवस्था में लौट आने वाला **2** that can be changed; not fixed लचकदार, जिसे बदला जा सके; कठोर नहीं *Our rules are quite elastic.*

**elastic band** = **rubber band**

**elasticity** /ˌi:læˈstɪsəti ˌईलैˈस्टिसटि/ *noun* [U] the quality that sth has of being able to stretch and return to its original size and shape लचीलापन, प्रत्यास्थता

**elated** /ɪˈleɪtɪd इˈलेटिड्/ *adj.* very happy and excited अति प्रसन्न और उत्तेजित; प्रफुल्लित, उल्लसित ▸ **elation** /iˈleɪʃn इˈलेशन्/ *noun* [U] अति प्रसन्नता, उल्लास, हर्ष

**elbow¹** /ˈelbəʊ ˈएल्बो/ *noun* [C] **1** the place where the bones of your arm join and your arm bends कोहनी ➪ **body** पर चित्र देखिए। **2** the part of the sleeve of a coat, jacket, etc. that covers the elbow कोट आदि की आस्तीन में कोहनी को ढकने वाला भाग

**elbow²** /ˈelbəʊ ˈएल्बो/ *verb* [T] to push sb with your elbow कोहनी से धकेलना *She elbowed me out of the way.*

**elbow room** *noun* [U] enough space to move freely पर्याप्त स्थान (खुलकर चलने-फिरने के लिए)

**elder¹** /ˈeldə(r) ˈएल्ड(र्)/ *adj.* (*only before a noun*) older (of two members of a family) (परिवार के दो सदस्यों में) आयु में बड़ा *My elder daughter is at university now but the other one is still at school.* ○ *an elder brother/sister*

**elder²** /ˈeldə(r) ˈएल्ड(र्)/ *noun* **1** [*sing.*] **the elder** the older of two people दो व्यक्तियों में (आयु में) बड़ा *Who is the elder of the two?* **2** **my, etc. elder** [*sing.*] a person who is older than me, etc. (मुझसे

या किसी अन्य से) बड़ा व्यक्ति *He is her elder by several years.* **3 elders** [*pl.*] older people वयोवृद्ध लोग *Do children still respect the opinions of their elders?*

**elderly** /ˈeldəli ˈएल्डलि/ *adj.* **1** (used about a person) old (व्यक्ति) वयोवृद्ध **NOTE** वयोवृद्धों के लिए यह आदरसूचक शब्द है। **2 the elderly** *noun* [*pl.*] old people in general वयोवृद्ध लोगों का समाज *The elderly need special care in winter.* ➪ **old** देखिए।

**eldest** /ˈeldɪst ˈएल्डिस्ट्/ *adj., noun* [C] (the) oldest (of three or more members of a family) (परिवार के तीन या अधिक सदस्यों में) आयु में सबसे बड़ा *Their eldest child is a boy.* ○ *Ashok's got four boys. The eldest has just gone to university.*

**elect** /ɪˈlekt इˈलेक्ट्/ *verb* [T] **1 elect sb (to sth); elect sb (as sth)** to choose sb to have a particular job or position by voting for him/her मतदान के द्वारा (किसी को) निर्वाचित करना या चुनना *He was elected to the Parliament in 2000.* ○ *The committee elected her as their representative.* **2** (*formal*) **elect to do sth** to decide to do sth कुछ करने का निर्णय करना

**election** /ɪˈlekʃn इˈलेक्श्न्/ *noun* [C, U] (the time of) choosing a Member of Parliament, President, etc. by voting मतदान द्वारा संसद सदस्य, राष्ट्रपति आदि का निर्वाचन *In India presidential elections are held every five years.* ○ *If you're interested in politics why not **stand for election** yourself?*

**NOTE** भारत में लगभग हर पाँचवें वर्ष **general elections** होते हैं। कभी-कभी बीच में **by-elections** भी होते हैं। प्रत्येक **constituency** में मतदाताओं को **candidates** की सूची में से एक व्यक्ति को चुनना अनिवार्य होता है।

**elective** /ɪˈlektɪv इˈलेक्टिव्/ *adj.* (*usually before a noun*) (*formal*) **1** using or chosen by election निर्वाचन करने वाला या निर्वाचित *an elective democracy* ○ *an elective member* **2** having the power to elect निर्वाचन अधिकार रखने वाला या वाली *an elective body* **3** (used about medical treatment) that you choose to have; that is not urgent (चिकित्सा प्रणाली), मनचाही जो आप कराना चाहते है; जो अत्यावश्यक नहीं *elective surgery* **4** (used about a course or subject) that a student can choose (पाठ्यक्रम या विषय) वैकल्पिक

**elector** /ɪˈlektə(r) इˈलेक्ट(र्)/ *noun* [C] a person who has the right to vote in an election मतदाता, निर्वाचन या चुनाव में मतदान करने का अधिकारी व्यक्ति **NOTE** इस अर्थ में **voter** अधिक प्रचलित शब्द है।

▶ **electoral** /ɪˈlektərəl इˈलेक्टरल्/ *adj.* चुनाव संबंधी *the electoral register/roll* (= the list of electors in an area)

**electorate** /ɪˈlektərət इˈलेक्टरट्/ *noun* [C, *with sing. or pl.verb*] all the people who can vote in a region, country, etc. एक क्षेत्र, देश आदि के सभी मतदाता

**electric** /ɪˈlektrɪk इˈलेक्ट्रिक्/ *adj.* **1** producing or using electricity विद्युत उत्पन्न करने वाला या उससे चलने वाला *an electric current* ○ *an electric kettle* **2** very exciting बहुत उत्तेजक या उत्तेजनापूर्ण *The atmosphere in the room was electric.*

**electrical** /ɪˈlektrɪkl इˈलेक्ट्रिकल्/ *adj.* of or about electricity विद्युत से संबंधित *an electrical appliance* (= a machine that uses electricity)

**the electric chair** *noun* [*sing.*] a chair used in some countries for killing criminals with a very strong electric current एक विशेष कुरसी जिसे कुछ देशों में अपराधियों को विद्युत प्रवाह द्वारा मृत्युदंड देने के लिए इस्तेमाल किया जाता है

**electrician** /ɪˌlekˈtrɪʃn इˌलेक्ˈट्रिश्न्/ *noun* [C] a person whose job is to make and repair electrical systems and equipment बिजली के उपकरणों की मरम्मत करने वाला; बिजली मिस्त्री

**electricity** /ɪˌlekˈtrɪsəti इˌलेक्ˈट्रिसटि/ *noun* [U] a type of energy that we use to make heat, light and power to work machines, etc. विद्युत, बिजली, विद्युतधारा *Turn that light off. We don't want to waste electricity.*

**NOTE** सामान्यतः बिजली **power stations** में **generate(d)** (उत्पादित) होती है। इसे **generators** या **batteries** से भी बनाया जा सकता है।

**electric razor** = **shaver**

**electric shock** (*also* **shock**) *noun* [C] a sudden painful feeling that you get if electricity goes through your body बिजली से लगने वाला झटका

**electrify** /ɪˈlektrɪfaɪ इˈलेक्ट्रिफ़ाइ/ *verb* [T] (*pres. part.* **electrifying;** *3rd person sing. pres.* **electrifies;** *pt, pp* **electrified**) **1** to supply sth with electricity (किसी का) विद्युतीकरण करना *The railways are being electrified.* **2** to make sb very excited (किसी को) बहुत उत्तेजित कर देना *Ronaldo electrified the crowd with his pace and skill.*

**electro-** /ɪˈlektrəʊ इˈलेक्ट्रो/ *prefix* (*used in nouns, adjectives, verbs and adverbs*) connected with electricity विद्युत (विषयम), विद्युतयुक्त, वैद्युत *electromagnetism*

**electrocute** /ɪˈlektrəkjuːt इˈलेक्ट्रक्यूट्/ *verb* [T] to kill sb with electricity that goes through the body बिजली के झटके से (किसी को) मारना ▶ **electrocution** /ɪˌlektrəˈkjuːʃn इˌलेक्ट्रˈक्यूश्न्/ *noun* [U] बिजली से मौत, विद्युत-आघात से मृत्यु

**electrode** /ɪˈlektrəʊd इˈलेक्ट्रोड् / *noun* [C] one of two points (**terminals**) where an electric current enters or leaves a battery, etc. बैटरी का बिंदु जहाँ से विद्युत धारा आती या जाती है, इलेक्ट्रोड, विद्युदग्र

**electrolysis** /ɪˌlekˈtrɒləsɪs इˌलेक्ˈट्रॉलसिस् / *noun* [U] **1** a way of permanently getting rid of hairs on the body by using an electric current विद्युत के प्रयोग से शरीर के बालों को स्थायी रूप से साफ़ करने की विधि **2** (*technical*) a way of separating a liquid into its different chemical parts by passing an electric current through it विद्युत के प्रयोग से द्रव के विभिन्न रासायनिक अंशों को पृथक करने की विधि; विद्युत द्वारा अपघटन, वैद्युत अपघटन

**electrolyte** /ɪˈlektrəlaɪt इˈलेक्ट्रलाइट् / *noun* [C] (*technical*) a liquid that an electric current can pass through, especially in an electric cell or battery एक द्रव जिसमें से विद्युत धारा गुज़र सकती है (विशेषतः बिजली के सेल या बैटरी में); इलेक्ट्रोलाइट ▸ **electrolytic** /ɪˌlektrəˈlɪtɪk इˌलेक्ट्रˈलिटिक् / *adj.* इलेक्ट्रोलाइट-विषयक

**electromagnetic** /ɪˌlektrəʊmægˈnetɪk इˌलेकट्रोमैग्ˈनेटिक् / *adj.* (in physics) having both electrical characteristics and the ability to attract metal objects विद्युत के लक्षणों के साथ चुंबकीय क्षमता से भी युक्त; विद्युतचुंबकीय ▸ **electromagnetism** /ɪˌlektrəʊˈmægnətɪzəm इˌलेक्ट्रोˈमैग्नटिज़म् / *noun* [U] विद्युतचुंबकत्व

**electron** /ɪˈlektrɒn इˈलेक्ट्रॉन् / *noun* [C] one of the three types of **particles** that form all atoms. Electrons have a negative electric charge तीन प्रकार के मूल कणों में से एक जिनसे सब परमाणु बनते हैं, परमाणु का घटक मूल कण, इलेक्ट्रॉन में ऋणात्मक विद्युत चार्ज होता है ➪ **neutron** और **proton** देखिए।

**electronic** /ɪˌlekˈtrɒnɪk इˌलेक्ˈट्रॉनिक् / *adj.* **1** using electronics इलेक्ट्रॉनिक्स-प्रयोगी, इलेक्ट्रॉनिक्स के प्रयोग से पुष्ट, इलेक्ट्रॉनिक्स-आधारित *electronic equipment* ○ *That dictionary is available in electronic form* (= on a computer disk). **2** done using a computer कंप्यूटर के प्रयोग से निष्पादित *electronic banking/shopping* ▸ **electronically** /-kli -क्लि / *adv.* कंप्यूटर का प्रयोग करते हुए

**electronics** /ɪˌlekˈtrɒnɪks इˌलेक्ˈट्रॉनिक्स् / *noun* [U] the technology used to produce computers, radios, etc. कंप्यूटर, रेडियो आदि के निर्माण में प्रयुक्त प्रौद्योगिकी इलेक्ट्रॉनिक्स *the electronics industry*

**electrostatic** /ɪˌlektrəʊˈstætɪk इˌलेक्ट्रोˈस्टैटिक् / *adj.* (*technical*) used to talk about electric charges that are not moving, rather than electric currents (गतिशील के स्थान पर) स्थिर विद्युत चार्जों से संबंधित

**elegant** /ˈelɪgənt ˈएलिगन्ट् / *adj.* having a good or attractive style आकर्षक, रमणीक *She looked very elegant in her new dress.* ○ *an elegant coat* ▸ **elegance** /ˈelɪgəns ˈएलिगन्स् / *noun* [U] रमणीकता ▸ **elegantly** *adv.* रमणीक भाव से

**elegy** /ˈelədʒi ˈएलजि / *noun* [C] (*pl.* **elegies**) a poem or song that expresses sadness, especially for sb who has died शोक-कविता, शोक-गीत (विशेषतः दिवंगत हेतु)

**element** /ˈelɪmənt ˈएलिमन्ट् / *noun* **1** [C] one important part of sth (किसी का) प्रमुख घटक, अंश, तत्व *Cost is an important element when we're thinking about holidays.* **2** [C, *usually sing.*] **an element of sth** a small amount of sth (किसी वस्तु की) अल्प मात्रा *There was an element of truth in what he said.* **3** [C] people of a certain type विशेष प्रकार के लोग *The criminal element at football matches causes a lot of trouble.* **4** [C] one of the simple chemical substances, for example iron, gold, etc. कोई मूल रसायन (जैसे लोहा, सोना), मूल तत्व **5** [C] the metal part of a piece of electrical equipment that produces heat किसी विद्युत उपकरण का ताप-उत्पादक धातु-निर्मित अंश; एलिमेंट **6 the elements** [*pl.*] (bad) weather (ख़राब) मौसम *to be exposed to the elements*

IDM **in/out of your element** in a situation where you feel comfortable/uncomfortable अनुकूल या प्रतिकूल स्थिति में *Balu's in his element speaking to a large group of people, but I hate it.*

**elementary** /ˌelɪˈmentri ˌएलिˈमेन्ट्रि /*adj.* **1** connected with the first stages of learning sth शिक्षा की प्रारंभिक चरणों से संबंधित *an elementary course in English* ○ *a book for elementary students* **2** basic; not difficult मूलभूत; सरल *elementary physics*

**elephant** /ˈelɪfənt ˈएलिफ़न्ट् / *noun* [C] a very large grey animal with big ears, two long curved teeth (**tusks**) and a long nose (**trunk**) हाथी

**elevate** /ˈelɪveɪt ˈएलिव़ेट् / *verb* [T] (*formal*) to move sb/sth to a higher place or more important position किसी व्यक्ति या वस्तु को ऊँचा उठाना या उच्चतर पद पर पहुँचाना *an elevated platform* ○ *He was elevated to the Board of Directors.*

**elevation** /ˌelɪˈveɪʃn ˌएलिˈव़ेश्न् / *noun* **1** [C, U] (*formal*) the process of moving to a higher place or more important position ऊपर उठने या उच्चतर पद पर पहुँचने की प्रक्रिया *his elevation to the presidency* **2** [C] the height of a place (above sea-level) किसी स्थान की ऊँचाई (समुद्र तल से) *The city is at an elevation of 2000 metres.*

**elevator** /ˈelɪveɪtə(r) ˈएलिव़ेट(र्) / (*AmE*) = **lift**[2] **1**

**eleven** /ɪˈlevn इˈलेव्न्/ *number* 11 ग्यारह (का अंक)

**NOTE** संख्याओं के वाक्य-प्रयोग के उदाहरणों के लिए **six** की प्रविष्टि देखिए।

**eleventh** /ɪˈlevnθ इˈलेव्न्थ्/ *pronoun, det., adv.* 11th ग्यारहवाँ/वीं ➪ **sixth** पर उदाहरण देखिए।

**elf** /elf एल्फ़्/ *noun* [C] (*pl.* **elves** /elvz एल्व्ज़्/) (in stories) a small creature with pointed ears who has magic powers (कहानियों में) नुकीले कानों और जादुई शक्तियों वाला एक छोटा प्राणी

**elicit** /ɪˈlɪsɪt इˈलिसिट्/ *verb* [T] (*formal*) **elicit sth (from sb)** to manage to get information, facts, a reaction, etc. from sb किसी से सूचना, तथ्य आदि निकलवाना

**eligibility** /ˌelɪdʒəˈbɪləti ˌएलिजˈबिलटि/ *noun* [U] the quality of having the necessary qualifications or requirements योग्यता, वांछनीयता

**eligible** /ˈelɪdʒəbl ˈएलिजबल्/ *adj.* **eligible (for sth/to do sth)** having the right to do or have sth कुछ करने या कुछ पाने का अधिकार रखने वाला; उपयुक्त *In India you are eligible to vote when you are eighteen.* ✪ विलोम **ineligible**

**eliminate** /ɪˈlɪmɪneɪt इˈलिमिनेट्/ *verb* [T] **1** to remove sb/sth that is not wanted or needed अवांछित या अनावश्यक व्यक्ति या वस्तु को हटा देना *We must try and eliminate the problem.* **2** (*usually passive*) to stop sb going further in a competition, etc. स्पर्धा आदि में आगे बढ़ने से रोकना *The school team was eliminated in the first round of the competition.* ▶ **elimination** /ɪˌlɪmɪˈneɪʃn इˌलिमिˈनेशन्/ *noun* [U] बहिष्करण

**elite** /eɪˈliːt एˈलीट्/ *noun* [C, *with sing. or pl. verb*] a social group that is thought to be the best or most important because of its power, money, intelligence, etc. शक्ति, धन, बुद्धि आदि की दृष्टि से श्रेष्ठ समझा जाने वाला वर्ग, संभ्रांत वर्ग; अभिजात वर्ग *an intellectual elite* ○ *an elite group of artists*

**elitism** /eɪˈliːtɪzəm एˈलीटिज़म्/ *noun* [U] the belief that some people should be treated in a special way संभ्रांतभाव, आभिजात्य, संभ्रांतता ▶ **elitist** /-tɪst -टिस्ट्/ *noun* [C], *adj.* अभिजात्यवादी

**elk** /elk एल्क्/ (*AmE* **moose**) *noun* [C] a very large wild animal (**deer**) with large flat horns (**antlers**) बड़े चपटे सींगों वाला बृहदाकार जंगली जानवर

**ellipse** /ɪˈlɪps इˈलिप्स्/ *noun* [C] (*technical*) a regular **oval** like a circle that has been pressed in from two sides दो पार्श्वों से दबी हुई अंडाकार आकृति

**elliptical** /ɪˈlɪptɪkl इˈलिप्टिकल्/ *adj.* **1** having a word or words left out of a sentence deliberately जिस वाक्य में से एक या अधिक शब्द लुप्त हों; लुप्तपद *an elliptical remark* (= one that suggests more than is actually said) **2** (*also* **elliptic** /ɪˈlɪptɪk इˈलिप्टिक्/) (*technical*) connected with or in the form of an ellipse लंबा और गोल आकृति का; लंबवर्तुलाकार, अंडाकार आकृति से संबंधित ▶ **elliptically** /-kli -क्लि/ *adj.* अंडाकार आकृति में *to speak/write elliptically*

**elm** /elm एल्म्/ (*also* **elm tree**) *noun* [C] a tall tree with broad leaves चौड़े पत्तों वाला एक ऊँचा पेड़

**elocution** /ˌeləˈkjuːʃn ˈएलˈक्यूशन्/ *noun* [U] the ability to speak clearly, correctly and without a strong **accent** श्रेष्ठ वक्तृत्व कला

**elongate** /ˈiːlɒŋgeɪt ˈईलॉङ्गेट्/ *verb* [I, T] to become longer; to make sth longer लंबा हो जाना; लंबा कर देना *The seal pup's body elongates as it gets older.* ▶ **elongation** /ˌiːlɒŋˈgeɪʃn ˌईलॉङ्ˈगेशन्/ *noun* [U] लंबा करने की क्रिया *the elongation of vowel sounds*

**elongated** /ˈiːlɒŋgeɪtɪd ˈईलॉङ्गेटिड्/ *adj.* long and thin लंबा और पतला

**elope** /ɪˈləʊp इˈलोप्/ *verb* [I] **elope (with sb)** to run away secretly to get married विवाह करने के लिए चुपचाप भाग जाना

**eloquent** /ˈeləkwənt ˈएलक्वन्ट्/ *adj.* (*formal*) able to use language and express your opinions well, especially when you speak in public सार्वजनिक प्रसंग में वाणी का प्रयोग करने में दक्ष; वाक्चतुर ▶ **eloquence** *noun* [U] वाक्चातुर्य ▶ **eloquently** *adv.* वाक्चातुर्यपूर्वक

**else** /els एल्स्/ *adv.* (*used after words formed with only -, no-, some-, and after question words*) another, different person, thing or place अन्य और भिन्न व्यक्ति, वस्तु या स्थान *This isn't mine. It must be **someone else's**.* ○ ***Everybody else** is allowed to stay up late.* ○ *You'll have to pay. **Nobody else** will.* ○ ***What else** would you like?*

**IDM** **or else** otherwise; if not अन्यथा; नहीं तो *You'd better go to bed now or else you'll be tired in the morning.* ○ *He's either forgotten or else he's decided not to come.*

**elsewhere** /ˌelsˈweə(r) ˌएल्सˈवेअ(र्)/ *adv.* in or to another place अन्यत्र, कहीं और *He's travelled a lot —in Europe and elsewhere.*

**elucidate** /ɪˈluːsɪdeɪt इˈलूसिडेट्/ *verb* [T] (*formal*) to make sth clearer by explaining it स्पष्ट करना, व्याख्या करना *I will try to elucidate what I think are the problems.* ▶ **elucidation** /ɪˌluːsɪˈdeɪʃn इˌलूसिˈडेशन्/ *noun* [U, C] व्याख्या, स्पष्टीकरण *These grammar notes need elucidation.*

**elude** /ɪˈluːd इˈलूड्/ *verb* [T] (*formal*) **1** to manage to avoid being caught पकड़े जाने से बच जाना, बच निकलना *The escaped prisoner eluded the police for three days.* **2** to be difficult or impossible to remember याद न रह पाना *I remember his face but his name eludes me.*

**elusive** /ɪˈluːsɪv इˈलूसिव्/ *adj.* not easy to catch, find or remember जिसे पकड़ना, ढूँढ़ना या याद रखना आसान न हो

**elves** ⇨ **elf** का plural रूप

**emaciated** /ɪˈmeɪʃieɪtɪd इˈमेशिएटिड्/ *adj.* extremely thin and weak because of illness, lack of food, etc. बीमारी, अपर्याप्त भोजन आदि के कारण बहुत दुबला-पतला; क्षीणकाय ▶ **emaciation** /ɪˌmeɪsiˈeɪʃn इˌमेसिˈएश्न्/ *noun* [U] क्षीणता, दुबलापन

**email** /ˈiːmeɪl ˈईमेल्/ *noun* **1** [U] a way of sending electronic messages or data from one computer to another एक कंप्यूटर से दूसरे कंप्यूटर को इलेक्ट्रॉनिक संदेश या सूचना सामग्री भेजने की विधि; ई-मेल, ई-पत्र *to send a message **by email*** **2** [C, U] a message or messages sent by email ई-मेल से प्रेषित संदेश *I'll **send** you **an email** tomorrow.* ▶ **email** *verb* [T] ई-मेल पद्धति द्वारा संदेश आदि भेजना *I'll email the information to you.*

**emanate** /ˈeməneɪt ˈएमनेट्/ *verb* [T] (*formal*) to produce or show sth उत्पन्न करना या प्रदर्शित करना *He emanates power and confidence.*

PHR V **emanate from sth** to come from sth or somewhere (किसी से या कहीं से) कुछ निकलना, आना *The sound of loud music emanated from the building.*

**emancipate** /ɪˈmænsɪpeɪt इˈमैन्सिपेट्/ *verb* [T] (*formal*) to give sb the same legal, social and political rights as other people किसी व्यक्ति को वही क़ानूनी, सामाजिक और राजनीतिक अधिकार देना जो अन्य लोगों को प्राप्त है ▶ **emancipation** /ɪˌmænsɪˈpeɪʃn इˌमैन्सिˈपेश्न्/ *noun* [U] अधिकार-संपन्नता

**embalm** /ɪmˈbɑːm इम्ˈबाम्/ *verb* [T] to treat a dead body with special substances in order to keep it in good condition शव को सुरक्षित रखने के लिए उस पर रसायनों का लेप करना

**embankment** /ɪmˈbæŋkmənt इम्ˈबैङ्क्मन्ट्/ *noun* [C] a wall of stone or earth that is built to stop a river from flooding or to carry a road or railway बाँध, तटबंध

**embargo** /ɪmˈbɑːɡəʊ इम्ˈबागो/ *noun* [C] (*pl.* **embargoes**) an official order to stop doing business with another country दूसरे देश से व्यापार पर रोक लगाने का शासनादेश *to impose an embargo on sth* ○ *to lift/remove an embargo*

**embark** /ɪmˈbɑːk इम्ˈबाक्/ *verb* [I] to get on a ship जलपोत पर सवार होना *Passengers with cars must embark first.* ✪ विलोम **disembark** ▶ **embarkation** /ˌembɑːˈkeɪʃn ˌएमबाˈकेश्न्/ *noun* [C, U] जलपोत-आरोहण

PHR V **embark on sth** (*formal*) to start sth (new) कोई (नया) काम शुरू करना *I'm embarking on a completely new career.*

**embarrass** /ɪmˈbærəs इम्ˈबैरस्/ *verb* [T] to make sb feel uncomfortable or shy (किसी को) लज्जित करना, झेंपाना *Don't ever embarrass me in front of my friends again!* ○ *The Minister's mistake embarrassed the government.*

**embarrassed** /ɪmˈbærəst इम्ˈबैरस्ट्/ *adj.* feeling uncomfortable or shy because of sth silly you have done, because people are looking at you, etc. सबके सामने लज्जित अनुभव करना *I felt so embarrassed when I dropped my glass.*

**embarrassing** /ɪmˈbærəsɪŋ इम्ˈबैरसिङ्/ *adj.* making you feel uncomfortable or shy परेशानी में डालने वाला या झेंपाने वाला *an embarrassing question/mistake/situation* ▶ **embarrassingly** *adv.* परेशानी में डालते हुए

**embarrassment** /ɪmˈbærəsmənt इम्ˈबैरस्मन्ट्/ *noun* **1** [U] the feeling you have when you are embarrassed लज्जित होने का भाव **2** [C] a person or thing that makes you embarrassed दूसरे को लज्जित करने वाला व्यक्ति या वस्तु

**embassy** /ˈembəsi ˈएमबसि/ *noun* [C] (*pl.* **embassies**) (the official building of) a group of officials (**diplomats**) and their head (**ambassador**), who represent their government in a foreign country दूतावास ⇨ **consulate** देखिए।

**embed** /ɪmˈbed इमˈबेड्/ *verb* [T] (**embe<u>dd</u>ing; embe<u>dd</u>ed**) (*usually passive*) to fix sth firmly and deeply (in sth else) किसी वस्तु को (अन्य वस्तु में) मज़बूती से बैठाना, जड़ना *The axe was embedded in the piece of wood.*

**embellish** /ɪmˈbelɪʃ इमˈबेलिश्/ *verb* [T] (*written*) **1** to make sth more beautiful by adding decoration to it सजाना, सँवारना, अलंकृत करना, शोभा में वृद्धि करना **2** to make a story more interesting by adding details that are not always true नई (न कि हमेशा सच) बातें जोड़कर कहानी की रोचकता बढ़ाना ▶ **embellishment** *noun* [U, C] सजावट, अलंकरण

**ember** /ˈembə(r) ˈएम्ब(र्)/ *noun* [C, *usually pl.*] a piece of wood or coal that is not burning, but is still red and hot after a fire has died अंगारा; बुझ चुकी आग में दहकता कोयले का टुकड़ा

**embezzle** /ɪmˈbezl इम्ˈबेज़्ल्/ *verb* [T] to steal money that you are responsible for or that belongs to your employer ग़बन करना ▶ **embezzlement** *noun* [U] ग़बन

**embitter** /ɪmˈbɪtə(r) इम्ˈबिट(र्)/ *verb* [T] to make sb feel angry or disappointed about sth over a long period of time किसी को कड़वाहट से भर देना, या क्रोधित या निराश कर देना ▶ **embittered** *adj.* कड़वाहट-भरा *a sick and embittered old man*

**emblem** /ˈembləm ˈएम्ब्लम्/ *noun* [C] an object or symbol that represents sth प्रतीक वस्तु या चिह्न *The dove is the emblem of peace.*

**embody** /ɪmˈbɒdi इम्ˈबॉडि/ *verb* [T] (*pres. part.* **embodying**; *3rd person sing. pres.* **embodies**; *pp, pt* **embodied**) (*formal*) **1** to be a very good example of sth किसी बात का श्रेष्ठ उदाहरण होना *To me she embodies all the best qualities of a teacher.* **2** to include or contain sth (किसी वस्तु को) समाविष्ट करना या (कोई वस्तु) समाए होना *This latest model embodies many new features.* ▶ **embodiment** *noun* [C] जीता-जागता नमूना, मूर्त रूप *She is the embodiment of a caring mother.*

**embrace** /ɪmˈbreɪs इम्ˈब्रेस्/ *verb* **1** [I, T] to put your arms around sb as a sign of love, happiness, etc. (प्रेम, प्रसन्नता आदि से) आलिंगन करना, गले लगाना **2** [T] (*formal*) to include समाविष्ट करना *His report embraced all the main points.* **3** [T] (*formal*) to accept sth with enthusiasm स्वेच्छा से स्वीकार करना *She embraced Christianity in her later years.* ▶ **embrace** *noun* [C] आलिंगन *He held her in a warm embrace.*

**embroider** /ɪmˈbrɔɪdə(r) इम्ˈब्रॉइड(र्)/ *verb* **1** [I, T] to decorate cloth by sewing a pattern or picture on it कपड़े पर कढ़ाई करना, कपड़े पर नमूना या चित्र टाँककर उसे सजाना **2** [T] to add details that are not true to a story to make it more interesting कहानी की रोचकता बढ़ाने के लिए उसमें नई और काल्पनिक बातें जोड़ना ▶ **embroidery** /-dəri -डरि/ *noun* [U] कढ़ाई

**embryo** /ˈembriəʊ ˈएम्ब्रिओ/ *noun* [C] (*pl.* **embryos** /-əʊz -ओज़्/) a baby, an animal or a plant in the early stages of development before birth जन्म से पहले की आरंभिक अवस्थाओं में शिशु, पशु, पौधा; भ्रूण ➪ **foetus** देखिए। ▶ **embryonic** /ˌembriˈɒnɪk ˌएम्ब्रिˈऑनिक्/ *adj.* भ्रूणीय

**emerald** /ˈemərəld ˈएमरल्ड्/ *noun* [C] a bright green precious stone चमकीले हरे रंग का रत्न, मरकत, पन्ना ▶ **emerald** (*also* **emerald green**) *adj.* मरकत के समान *an emerald green dress*

**emerge** /iˈmɜːdʒ इˈमज्/ *verb* [I] **emerge (from sth) 1** to appear or come out from somewhere कहीं से प्रकट होना या निकलना *A man emerged from the shadows.* ○ (*figurative*) *The country emerged from the war in ruins.* **2** to become known पता चलना, मालूम होना, जानकारी मिलना *During investigations **it emerged that** she was lying about her age.* ▶ **emergence** /-dʒəns -जन्स्/ *noun* [U] आविर्भाव, प्रकटन *the emergence of AIDS in the 1980s*

**emergency** /iˈmɜːdʒənsi इˈमजनसि/ *noun* [C, U] (*pl.* **emergencies**) a serious event that needs immediate action संकटकाल, आपातस्थिति, आपातकाल *In an emergency phone 100 for help.* ○ *The government has declared **a state of emergency**.* ○ *an emergency exit*

**emergency room** (*AmE*) = **casualty 3**

**emigrant** /ˈemɪɡrənt ˈएमिग्रन्ट्/ *noun* [C] a person who has gone to live in another country उत्प्रवासी व्यक्ति, विदेश में जा बसा व्यक्ति ➪ **immigrant** देखिए।

**emigrate** /ˈemɪɡreɪt ˈएमिग्रेट्/ *verb* [I] **emigrate (from...) (to...)** to leave your own country to go and live in another उत्प्रवास करना, स्वदेश छोड़कर विदेश में जा बसना *They emigrated from India to Australia twenty years ago.* ▶ **emigration** /ˌemɪˈɡreɪʃn ˌएमिˈग्रेश्न्/ *noun* [C, U] उत्प्रवासन ➪ **immigrant, immigration** और **migrate** देखिए।

**eminent** /ˈemɪnənt ˈएमिनन्ट्/ *adj.* (*formal*) (used about a person) famous and important (व्यक्ति) प्रख्यात और महत्त्वपूर्ण; प्रतिष्ठित *an eminent scientist*

**eminently** /ˈemɪnəntli ˈएमिनन्ट्लि/ *adv.* (*formal*) very; extremely बहुत; अत्यधिक *She is eminently suitable for the job.*

**emir** (*also* **amir**) /eˈmɪə(r) एˈमिअ(र्); ˈeɪmɪə(r) ˈएमिअ(र्)/ *noun* [C] the title given to some Muslim rulers अमीर; कुछ मुस्लिम शासकों को दी गई पदवी *the Emir of Kuwait*

**emirate** /ˈemɪərət ˈएमिअरट्; ˈemɪrət ˈएमिरट्/ *noun* [C] **1** the position held by an emir; the period of time that he is in power अमीर की पदवी; अमीर के सत्ता में रहने की अवधि **2** an area of land that is ruled over by an emir अमीर की रियासत *the United Arab Emirates*

**emissary** /ˈemɪsəri ˈएमिसरि/ *noun* [C] (*pl.* **emissaries**) (*formal*) a person who is sent somewhere, especially to another country, in order to give sb an official message or to perform a special task आधकारिक प्रतिनिधि, दूत

**emit** /iˈmɪt इˈमिट्/ *verb* [T] (**emitting; emitted**) (*formal*) to send out sth, for example, a smell, a sound, smoke, heat or light (गंध, आवाज़, धुआँ, गरमी या प्रकाश को) प्रसारित करना या छोड़ना *The animal emits a powerful smell when scared.* ▶ **emission** /iˈmɪʃn इˈमिश्न् / *noun* [C, U] निस्सरण, उत्सर्जन *sulphur dioxide emissions from power stations*

**emolument** /ɪˈmɒljumənt इˈमॉल्युमन्ट् / *noun* [*usually pl.*] (*formal*) a payment that is made, especially in money or any other form, for your services पारिश्रमिक

**emotion** /ɪˈməʊʃn इˈमोश्न् / *noun* [C, U] a strong feeling such as love, anger, fear, etc. (प्रेम, क्रोध, भय आदि) मनोभाव, भावना, भावावेश *to control/express your emotions* ○ *His voice was filled with emotion.*

**emotional** /ɪˈməʊʃənl इˈमोशनल् / *adj.* **1** connected with people's feelings भावनात्मक *emotional problems* **2** causing strong feelings भावुक, भावावेशपूर्ण *He gave an emotional speech.* **3** having strong emotions and showing them in front of people प्रकट रूप से भावुक *She always* ***gets*** *very* ***emotional*** *when I leave.* ▶ **emotionally** /-ʃənəli -शनलि / *adv.* भावुकतापूर्वक *She felt physically and emotionally drained after giving birth.*

**emotive** /ɪˈməʊtɪv इˈमोटिव् / *adj.* causing strong feelings भावात्मक, भावप्रधान, भावनापूर्ण *emotive language* ○ *an emotive issue*

**empathy** /ˈempəθi ˈएम्पथि / *noun* [C, U] **empathy (with/for sb/sth); empathy (between A and B)** the ability to imagine how another person is feeling and so understand his/her mood समानुभूति, अन्य व्यक्ति की भावनाओं को समझने की क्षमता; तादात्म्य *Some adults* ***have*** *great* ***empathy*** *with children.* ▶ **empathize** (*also* **-ise**) /ˈempəθaɪz ˈएम्पथाइज़् / *verb* [I] **empathize (with sb/sth)** (के साथ) तादात्म्य या समानुभूति होना *He's a popular teacher because he empathizes with his students.*

**emperor** /ˈempərə(r) ˈएम्पर(र्) / *noun* [C] the ruler of an empire एक साम्राज्य का प्रमुख; सम्राट

**emphasis** /ˈemfəsɪs ˈएम्फ़सिस् / *noun* [C, U] (*pl.* **emphases** /-si:z -सीज़् /) **1 emphasis (on sth)** (giving) special importance or attention (to sth) (किसी पर) विशेष ध्यान, बल या महत्त्व *There's a lot of emphasis on science at our school.* ○ *You should* ***put*** *a greater* ***emphasis*** *on quality rather than quantity when you write.* **2** the force that you give to a word or phrase when you are speaking; a way of writing a word to show that it is important बोलते समय किसी शब्द पर बलाघात या विशेष ज़ोर; लिखते समय विशेष महत्त्व के शब्द का विशिष्ट रूप से अंकन *In the word 'photographer' the emphasis is on the second syllable.* ○ *I underlined the key phrases of my letter for emphasis.* ✪ पर्याय **stress**[1]

**emphasize** (*also* **-ise**) /ˈemfəsaɪz ˈएम्फ़साइज़् / *verb* [T] **emphasize (that...)** to put emphasis on sth किसी पर विशेष बल देना *They emphasized that healthy eating is important.* ○ *They emphasized the importance of healthy eating.* ✪ पर्याय **stress**[2]

**emphatic** /ɪmˈfætɪk इम्ˈफ़ैटिक् / *adj.* said or expressed in a strong way (कथन, अभिव्यक्ति आदि) सशक्त, ज़ोरदार, बलपूर्ण, बलयुक्त *an emphatic refusal* ▶ **emphatically** /-kli -क्लि / *adv.* बलपूर्वक

**empire** /ˈempaɪə(r) ˈएम्पाइअ(र्) / *noun* [C] **1** a group of countries that is governed by one country साम्राज्य; एक देश द्वारा शासित देशों का समूह *the Roman Empire* ➪ **emperor** और **empress** देखिए। **2** a very large company or group of companies बहुत बड़ी कंपनियों का समूह

**empirical** /ɪmˈpɪrɪkl इम्ˈपिरिक्ल् / *adj.* (*formal*) based on experiments and practical experience, not on ideas (विचारों के स्थान पर) प्रयोगों और व्यावहारिक अनुभव पर आधारित *empirical evidence* ▶ **empirically** /-kli -क्लि / *adv.* अनुभव और प्रयोग के आधार पर या की दृष्टि से

**empiricism** /ɪmˈpɪrɪsɪzəm इम्ˈपिरिसिज़म् / *noun* [U] (*formal*) the use of experiments or experience as the basis for your ideas; the belief in these methods ज्ञान की प्रतिष्ठा के लिए अनुभव या प्रयोग का व्यवहार; अनुभववाद, प्रयोगवाद ▶ **empiricist** *noun* [C] अनुभववादी, प्रयोगवादी *the English empiricist, John Locke*

**employ** /ɪmˈplɔɪ इमˈप्लॉइ / *verb* [T] **1 employ sb (in/on sth); employ sb (as sth)** to pay sb to work for you काम में लगाना, नौकरी पर रखना, नियुक्त करना, काम के लिए वेतन देना *He is employed as a lorry driver.* ○ *They employ 600 workers.* ○ *Three people are employed on the task of designing a new computer system.* ➪ **unemployed** देखिए। **2** (*formal*) **employ sth (as sth)** to use का प्रयोग करना *In an emergency, an umbrella can be employed as a weapon.*

**employee** /ɪmˈplɔɪi: इम्ˈप्लॉई / *noun* [C] a person who works for sb कर्मचारी *The factory has 500 employees.*

**employer** /ɪmˈplɔɪə(r) इम्ˈप्लॉइअ(र्) / *noun* [C] a person or company that employs other people नौकरी देने वाला व्यक्ति या कंपनी; मालिक

**employment** /ɪmˈplɔɪmənt इम्ˈप्लॉइमन्ट्/ *noun* [U] **1** the state of having a paid job वेतन पर नौकरी; रोज़गार *to be in/out of employment* ○ *This bank can **give employment to** ten extra staff.* ○ *It is difficult to **find employment** in the north of the country.* ➪ **unemployment** देखिए और **work**[1] पर नोट देखिए। **2** (*formal*) the use of sth (किसी का) प्रयोग *the employment of force*

**employment agency** *noun* [C] a company that helps people to find work and other companies to find workers लोगों को नौकरी दिलाने वाली और कंपनियों के लिए कर्मचारी जुटाने वाली कंपनी

**empower** /ɪmˈpaʊə(r) इमˈपाउअ(र्)/ *verb* [T] (*formal*) (*usually passive*) to give sb power or authority (to do sth) कार्यविशेष के लिए किसी को अधिकार देना या अधिकृत करना ▸ **empowerment** *noun* [U] अधिकृतीकरण

**empress** /ˈemprəs ˈएम्प्रस्/ *noun* [C] **1** a woman who rules an empire साम्राज्ञी **2** the wife of a man who rules an empire (**emperor**) सम्राट की पत्नी

**empty**[1] /ˈempti ˈएम्प्टि/ *adj.* **1** having nothing or nobody inside it ख़ाली *an empty box* ○ *The bus was half empty.* **2** without meaning or value निरर्थक, खोखला *It was an empty threat* (= it was not meant seriously). ○ *My life feels empty now the children have left home.* ▸ **emptiness** /ˈemptinəs ˈएम्प्टिनस्/ *noun* [U] ख़ालीपन

**empty**[2] /ˈempti ˈएम्प्टि/ *verb* (*pres. part.* **emptying;** *3rd person sing. pres.* **empties;** *pt, pp* **emptied**) **1** [T] **empty sth (out/out of sth)** to remove everything that is inside a container, etc. (वस्तुएँ निकालकर डिब्बे आदि को) ख़ाली करना, (डिब्बे आदि में भरी वस्तुओं को) बाहर निकलना *I've emptied a wardrobe for you to use.* ○ *Lalit emptied everything out of his desk and left.* **2** [I] to become empty ख़ाली हो जाना *The cinema emptied very quickly once the film was finished.*

**empty-handed** *adj.* without getting what you wanted; without taking sth to sb ख़ाली हाथ, मनचाही वस्तु बिना पाए; बिना कुछ साथ में लिए *The robbers fled empty-handed.*

**emu** /ˈiːmjuː ˈईम्यू/ *noun* [C] a large Australian bird with long legs that can run very fast but cannot fly लंबी टांगों से तेज़ भागने वाला ऑस्ट्रेलियाई पक्षी जो उड़ नहीं सकता; इम्यु

**emulate** /ˈemjuleɪt ˈएम्युलेट्/ *verb* [T] (*formal*) to try to do sth as well as, or better than, sb किसी के बराबर होने या उससे आगे बढ़ने की चेष्टा करना ▸ **emulation**/ˈemjuleɪʃn ˈएम्युˈलेशन्/ *noun* [C, U] अनुकरण NOTE इस अर्थ में कम औपचारिक शब्द **copy** है।

**emulsifier** /ɪˈmʌlsɪfaɪə(r) इˈमल्सिफ़ाइअ(र्)/ *noun* [C] a substance that is added to mixtures of food to make the different liquids or substances in them combine to form a smooth mixture भोज्य पदार्थों के मिश्रण में मिलाया जाने वाला पदार्थ जिससे द्रव तथा अन्य पदार्थों का मिश्रण (इमल्शन) तैयार हो जाता है; पायसीकारक

**emulsify** /ɪˈmʌlsɪfaɪ इˈमल्सिफ़ाइ/ *verb* [I, T] (*pres. part.* **emulsifying;** *3rd person sing. pres.* **emulsifies;** *pt, pp* **emulsified**) if two liquids of different thicknesses emulsify or are emulsified, they combine to form a smooth mixture भिन्न स्तरों का गाढ़ापन लिए दो मिश्रणों से मिश्रण बनना या बनाना, इमल्शन बनना या बनाना; पायस बनाना

**emulsion** /ɪˈmʌlʃn इˈमल्शन्/ *noun* [C, U] **1** any mixture of liquids that do not normally mix together, such as oil and water प्रायः मिश्रित न होने वाले (जैसे तेल और पानी) द्रवों का मिश्रण; पायस, इमल्शन **2** (*also* **emulsion paint**) a type of paint used on walls and ceilings that dries without leaving a shiny surface दीवारों आदि पर लगने वाला एक प्रकार का रंग जो बिना चमकदार सतह छोड़े सूख जाता है **3** (*technical*) a substance on the surface of film used for photographs that makes it sensitive to light फ़ोटोग्राफ़िक फ़िल्म पर लगा पदार्थ जिससे फ़िल्म प्रकाश के प्रति संवेदनशील हो जाती है

**en-** /ɪn इन्-/ (*also* **em-** /ɪm इम्/ *before* b, m or p) *prefix* (*in verbs*) **1** to put into the thing or condition mentioned (क्रियाओं में) यथानिर्दिष्ट रीति से काम करने का अर्थ देने के लिए प्रयुक्त *encase* ○ *endanger* ○ *empower* **2** to cause to be कुछ होने का कारण बनना, करवाना *enlarge* ○ *embolden*

**enable** /ɪˈneɪbl इˈनेबल्/ *verb* [T] **enable sb/sth to do sth** to make it possible for sb/sth to do sth (किसी कार्य को) करने के योग्य बनाना *The new law has enabled more women to return to work.*

**enact** /ɪˈnækt इˈनैक्ट्/ *verb* [T] **1** (*law*) to pass a law क़ानून बनाना *legislation enacted by parliament* **2** (*formal*) to perform a play or act a part in a play नाटक का प्रदर्शन, मंचन करना या नाटक में कोई भूमिका निभाना *scenes from history enacted by local residents* **3 be enacted** (*formal*) to take place घटित होना, कोई बात होना *They were unaware of the drama being enacted a few feet away from them.*

**enamel** /ɪˈnæml इˈनैमल्/ *noun* [U] **1** a hard, shiny substance used for protecting or decorating metal, etc. एक कड़ा और चमकीला पदार्थ जो धातु को सुरक्षित रखने और सुरक्षित बनाने में काम आता है; इनैमल, तामचीनी *enamel paint* **2** the hard white outer covering of a tooth दाँतों का सख़्त सफ़ेद बाहरी आवरण; इनैमल, दंतवल्क

**enc.** (*also* **encl.**) *abbr.* (used at the end of a business letter to show that there is sth else in the envelope with the letter) enclosed यह संक्षिप्ति व्यवहारिक पत्र के अंत में यह दर्शाने के लिए प्रयुक्त की जाती है कि लिफ़ाफ़े में पत्र के अतिरिक्त कुछ और भी संलग्न है

**encephalitis** /enˌsefəˈlaɪtəs एन्ˌसेफ़ˈलाइटस्; -ˌkefə-ˌकेफ़-/ *noun* [U] (*medical*) a condition in which the brain becomes swollen, caused by an infection or **allergic** reaction दिमाग़ में सूजन का रोग (संक्रमण या किसी शारीरिक प्रतिक्रिया से उत्पन्न); दिमाग़ी सूजन, मस्तिष्क-शोथ

**enchanted** /ɪnˈtʃɑːntɪd इन्ˈचान्टिड्/ *adj.* **1** (in stories) affected by magic powers (कहानियों में) जादुई शक्तियों से प्रभावित **2** (*formal*) pleased or very interested मंत्रमुग्ध, आनंदविभोर *The audience was enchanted by her singing.*

**enchanting** /ɪnˈtʃɑːntɪŋ इन्ˈचान्टिङ्/ *adj.* very nice or pleasant; attractive मुग्ध करने वाला; मोहक, आकर्षक

**encircle** /ɪnˈsɜːkl इन्ˈसक्ल्/ *verb* [T] (*formal*) to make a circle round sth; to surround चारों ओर घेरा बनाना; चारों ओर से घेर लेना *The police encircled the robbers.*

**enclose** /ɪnˈkləʊz इन्ˈक्लोज़्/ *verb* [T] **1 enclose sth (in sth)** (*usually passive*) to surround sth with a wall, fence, etc.; to put one thing inside another चारों ओर से घेरना (दीवार आदि बनाकर); एक वस्तु के भीतर दूसरी को रखना *The jewels were enclosed in a strong box.* ○ *He gets very nervous in enclosed spaces.* **2** to put sth in an envelope, package, etc. with sth else किसी वस्तु को लिफ़ाफे आदि में किसी अन्य वस्तु के साथ रखना; संलग्न करना *Can I enclose a letter with this parcel?* ○ ***Please find enclosed** a cheque for Rs 1000.*

**enclosure** /ɪnˈkləʊʒə(r) इन्ˈक्लोश़(र्)/ *noun* [C] **1** a piece of land inside a wall, fence, etc. that is used for a particular purpose दीवार या बाड़े से घिरी जमीन, घेरा आदि जिसका प्रयोग किसी विशेष उद्देश्य के लिए होता है *a wildlife enclosure* **2** something that is placed inside an envelope together with the letter लिफ़ाफे में पत्र के साथ रखी वस्तु; संलग्नक या अनुलग्नक

**encode** /ɪnˈkəʊd इन्ˈकोड्/ *verb* [T] **1** = **code² 1** **2** (*computing*) to change information into a form that a computer can deal with सूचना को ऐसा रूप देना कि कंप्यूटर उसका उपयोग कर सके

**encore¹** /ˈɒŋkɔː(r) ˈऑङ्कॉ(र्)/ *exclamation* called out by an audience that wants the performers in a concert, etc. to sing or play sth extra श्रोताओं, दर्शकों की कलाकारों से कुछ और भी सुनने-दिखाने की फ़रमाइश के लिए प्रयुक्त शब्द

**encore²** /ˈɒŋkɔː(r) ˈऑङ्कॉ(र्)/ *noun* [C] a short, extra performance at the end of a concert, etc. संगीत सभा आदि के अंत में दर्शकों की फ़रमाइश पर प्रस्तुत छोटा, अतिरिक्त कार्यक्रम

**encounter¹** /ɪnˈkaʊntə(r) इन्ˈकाउन्ट(र्)/ *verb* [T] **1** to experience sth (a danger, difficulty, etc.) (ख़तरा; कठिनाई आदि का) सामना करना *I've never encountered any discrimination at work.* ✪ पर्याय **meet with** **2** (*formal*) to meet sb unexpectedly; to experience or find sth unusual or new अकस्मात किसी से भेंट होना; कुछ असाधारण तथा नया अनुभव होना ✪ पर्याय **come across**

**encounter²** /ɪnˈkaʊntə(r) इन्ˈकाउन्ट(र्)/ *noun* [C] **an encounter (with sb/sth); an encounter (between A and B)** an unexpected (often unpleasant) meeting or event आकस्मिक (प्रायः अप्रिय) भेंट या कोई घटना, आमना-सामना, मुठभेड़ *I've had a number of **close encounters*** (= situations which could have been dangerous) *with bad drivers.*

**encourage** /ɪnˈkʌrɪdʒ इन्ˈकरिज्/ *verb* [T] **1 encourage sb/sth (in sth/to do sth)** to give hope, support or confidence to sb (किसी को) प्रोत्साहित करना; (किसी की) हिम्मत बढ़ाना *The teacher encouraged her students to ask questions.* **2** to make sth happen more easily (किसी को) बढ़ावा देना *The government wants to encourage new businesses.* ✪ विलोम **discourage** ▶ **encouragement** *noun* [C, U] प्रोत्साहन, बढ़ावा ▶ **encouraging** *adj.* प्रोत्साहनकारी

**encroach** /ɪnˈkrəʊtʃ इन्ˈक्रोच्/ *verb* [I] (*formal*) **encroach (on/upon sth)** to use more of sth than you should जितना चाहिए उससे अधिक लेना, अपनी सीमा को लाँघना *I do hope that I am not encroaching too much upon your free time.*

**encrypt** /ɪnˈkrɪpt इन्ˈक्रिप्ट्/ *verb* [T] (*computing*) to put information into a special form (**code**) especially in order to stop people being able to look at or understand it सूचना-सामग्री को विशिष्ट कोड में रूपांतरित करना (ताकि वह लोगों की पहुँच से बाहर रहे); सूचना का कूटांकित करना ▶ **encryption** /ɪnˈkrɪpʃn इन्ˈक्रिप्शन्/ *noun* [U] सूचना-कूटांकन

**encyclopedia** (*also* **encyclopaedia**) /ɪnˌsaɪkləˈpiːdiə इन्ˌसाइक्लˈपीडिआ/ *noun* [C] (*pl.* **encyclopedias**) a book or set of books that gives information about very many subjects, arranged in the order of the alphabet (= from A to Z) विश्वकोश

**end**[1] /end एन्ड्/ *noun* [C] **1** the furthest or last part of sth; the place or time where sth stops अंत; समाप्ति *My house is* ***at the end of*** *the street.* ○ *There are some seats* ***at the far end of*** *the room.*

NOTE **In the end** समय का संकेत देता है और इसका अर्थ है अंत में—*We were too tired to cook, so in the end we decided to eat out.* **At the end of sth** द्वारा हम किसी पुस्तक, फ़िल्म आदि के उस बिंदु का संकेत करते है जहाँ वह समाप्त होने को होती है—*At the end of the meal we had a row about who should pay for it.*
**End** का प्रयोग कभी-कभी अन्य संज्ञा से पहले (भी) होता है—*the end house* ○ *the end seat*

NOTE केवल दौड़ों और स्पर्धाओं के संदर्भ में **finish** का प्रयोग **end** के अर्थ में होता है।

**2** (*formal*) an aim or purpose उद्देश्य, लक्ष्य, प्रयोजन *They were prepared to do anything to achieve their ends.* **3** a little piece of sth that is left after the rest has been used किसी वस्तु के अधिकांश भाग के प्रयोग के बाद बचा छोटा टुकड़ा *a cigarette end*

IDM **at an end** (*formal*) finished or used up (लगभग) पूर्णतया समाप्त *Her career is at an end.*

**at the end of your tether** having no more patience or strength बिना अतिरिक्त धैर्य या शक्ति के

**at the end of the day** (*spoken*) used to say the most important fact in a situation प्रसंग की सबसे महत्त्वपूर्ण बात कहने के लिए प्रयुक्त *At the end of the day, you have to make the decision yourself.*

**at a loose end** ➪ **loose**[1] देखिए।

**at your wits' end** ➪ **wit** देखिए।

**bring sth/come/draw to an end** (to cause sth) to finish किसी बात या स्थिति का समाप्त होना या करना *His stay in Sri Lanka was coming to an end.*

**a dead end** ➪ **dead**[1] देखिए।

**end to end** in a line with the ends touching सिरों से जुड़े हुए और पंक्ति बनाते हुए *They put the tables end to end.*

**in the end** finally; after a long period of time or series of events अंत में; लंबी अवधि के बाद या अनेक घटनाओं के बाद *He wanted to get home early but in the end it was midnight before he left.*

**make ends meet** to have enough money for your needs गुज़ारे लायक धन होना *It's hard for us to make ends meet.*

**make sb's hair stand on end** ➪ **hair** देखिए।

**a means to an end** ➪ **means** देखिए।

**no end of sth** (*spoken*) too many or much; a lot of sth बहुत अधिक; अत्यधिक *She has given us no end of trouble.*

**odds and ends** ➪ **odds** देखिए।

**on end** (used about time) continuously (समय-निर्देश के लिए प्रयुक्त) निरंतर, लगातार *He sits and reads for hours on end.*

**put an end to sth** to stop sth from happening any more किसी बात को आगे न चलने देना, किसी बात को समाप्त कर देना

**end**[2] /end एन्ड्/ *verb* [I, T] **end (in/with sth)** (to cause sth) to finish समाप्त होना या करना *The road ends here.* ○ *How does this story end?* ○ *The match ended in a draw.* ○ *I think we'd better end this conversation now.*

PHRV **end up (as sth); end up (doing sth)** to find yourself in a place/situation that you did not plan or expect अनियोजित या अप्रत्याशित स्थान या स्थिति में पहुँच जाना *We got lost and ended up in the centre of town.* ○ *She had always wanted to be a writer but ended up as a teacher.* ○ *There was nothing to eat at home so we ended up getting a takeaway.*

**endanger** /ɪnˈdeɪndʒə(r) इन्ˈडेन्ज(र्)/ *verb* [T] to cause danger to sb/sth (व्यक्ति या वस्तु को) ख़तरे में डालना *Smoking endangers your health.*

**endangered** /ɪnˈdeɪndʒəd इन्ˈडेन्जड्/ *adj.* (used about animals, plants, etc.) in danger of disappearing from the world (**becoming extinct**) (पशु, पौधे आदि) जिनका अस्तित्व ख़तरे में है; संकटग्रस्त *The giant panda is* ***an endangered species.***

**endear** /ɪnˈdɪə(r) इन्ˈडिअ(र्)/ *verb* [T] (*formal*) **endear sb/yourself to sb** to make sb/yourself liked by sb दूसरे का प्रिय हो जाना, स्वयं को औरों का प्रिय बना लेना *She managed to endear herself to everybody by her kindness.* ▶ **endearing** *adj.* प्रिय लगने वाला, प्रीतिकर ▶ **endearingly** *adv.* प्रीतिकर रीति से

**endeavour** (*AmE* **endeavor**) /ɪnˈdevə(r) इन्ˈडेव़(र्)/ *verb* [I] (*formal*) **endeavour (to do sth)** to try hard कठोर परिश्रम करना; भरसक प्रयास करना *She endeavoured to finish her work on time.* ▶ **endeavour** *noun* [C, U] कठोर परिश्रम, उद्यम, परिश्रम

**endemic** /enˈdemɪk एन्ˈडेमिक्/ *adj.* (often used about a disease or problem) regularly found in a particular place or among a particular group of people and difficult to get rid of (प्रायः किसी रोग या समस्या के लिए प्रयुक्त) किसी विशेष स्थान या व्यक्ति वर्ग में नियमित रूप से पाया जाने वाला और जिससे छुटकारा मुश्किल है; जातीय, स्थानिक *Malaria is endemic in many hot countries.* ➪ **epidemic** और **pandemic** देखिए।

**ending** /ˈendɪŋ ˈएन्डिङ्/ *noun* [C] **1** the end (of a story, play, film, etc.) कहानी, नाटक, सिनेमा आदि की समाप्ति *That film made me cry but I was pleased that it had **a happy ending**.* **2** (*grammar*) the last part of a word, which can change शब्द का अंतिम अंश जो परिवर्तित हो सकता है *When nouns end in -ch or -sh or -x, the plural ending is -es not -s.*

**endless** /ˈendləs ˈएन्ड्लस्/ *adj.* **1** very large in size or amount and seeming to have no end आकार या मात्रा में बहुत अधिक; अनंत *The possibilities are endless.* **2** lasting for a long time and seeming to have no end बहुत लंबा, अंतहीन-सा, मानो अंतहीन *Our plane was delayed for hours and the wait seemed endless.* ✪ पर्याय **interminable** ▶ **endlessly** *adv.* अंतहीन रूप से

**endorse** /ɪnˈdɔːs इन्ˈडॉस्/ *verb* [T] **1** to say publicly that you give official support or agreement to a plan, statement, decision, etc. किसी योजना घोषणा, निर्णय आदि का सार्वजनिक तौर पर या अधिकृत रूप से समर्थन करना *Members of all parties endorsed a ban on firearms.* **2** (*BrE*) (*usually passive*) to add a note to the document which allows you to drive a vehicle (**driving licence**) to say that the driver has broken the law ड्राइविंग लाइसेंस पर नियम-भंग की नोट अंकित करना ▶ **endorsement** *noun* [C, U] समर्थन, पृष्ठांकन, अनुमोदन

**endoscope** /ˈendəskəʊp ˈएनुडस्कोप्/ *noun* [C] (*medical*) an instrument for looking at the inside of the body शरीर के अंदरूनी भाग को देखने का यंत्र

**endoskeleton** /ˈendəʊskelɪtn ˈएनुडोस्केलिट्न्/ *noun* [C] the bones inside the body of animals that give it shape and support पशुओं के अंदर हड्डी का ढाँचा जो उसे एक आकृति में थामे रखता है, पशुओं का अंतःकंकाल ➪ **exoskeleton** देखिए।

**endosperm** /ˈendəʊspɜːm ˈएनुडोस्पम्/ *noun* [U] (*technical*) the part of a seed that stores food for the development of a plant पौधे के बीज का वह भाग जो पौधे के विकास के लिए भोजन को संचित रखता है; भ्रूणपोष

**endothermic** /ˌendəʊˈθɜːmɪk ˌएनुडोˈथ्रमिक्/ *adj.* (*technical*) (used about a chemical reaction or process) needing heat in order to take place (रासायनिक प्रतिक्रिया या प्रक्रिया) ताप से निष्पन्न होने वाली

**endow** /ɪnˈdaʊ इन्ˈडाउ/ *verb* [T] to give a large sum of money to a school, a college or another institution किसी विद्यालय, महाविद्यालय या संस्था को बड़ी धनराशि दान में देना

PHR V **be endowed with sth** to naturally have a particular characteristic, quality, etc. स्वाभाविक अथवा सहजात प्रतिभा से युक्त होना *She was endowed with courage and common sense.*

**endow sb/sth with sth** **1** to believe or imagine that sb/sth has a particular quality ऐसा मानना या कल्पना करना कि किसी व्यक्ति या वस्तु में गुणविशेष विद्यमान है *He had endowed the girl with the personality he wanted her to have.* **2** (*formal*) to give sth to sb/sth किसी को कुछ देना; दान करना

**endowment** /ɪnˈdaʊmənt इन्ˈडाउमन्ट्/ *noun* [C, U] money that sb gives to a school, a college or another institution; the act of giving this money किसी संस्था को दिया गया दान, स्थायी निधि; ऐसे दान देने की क्रिया; अक्षयनिधि

**end product** *noun* [C] something that is produced by a particular process or activity विशिष्ट प्रक्रिया या गतिविधि से उत्पन्न वस्तु, अंतिम परिणाम

**endurance** /ɪnˈdjʊərəns इन्ˈड्युअरन्स्/ *noun* [U] the ability to continue doing sth painful or difficult for a long period of time without complaining सहनशक्ति, सहिष्णुता

**endure** /ɪnˈdjʊə(r) इन्ˈड्युअ(र्)/ *verb* (*formal*) **1** [T] to suffer sth painful or uncomfortable, usually without complaining विशेषतः बिना शिकायत किए सहन करना, चुपचाप पीड़ा झेलना *She endured ten years of loneliness.* ✪ पर्याय **bear** **2** [I] to continue टिकना, बने रहना ✪ पर्याय **last** ▶ **enduring** *adj.* स्थायी, टिकाऊ

**enemy** /ˈenəmi ˈएनमि/ *noun* (*pl.* **enemies**) **1** [C] a person who hates and tries to harm you शत्रु, दुश्मन, विरोधी *They used to be friends but became **bitter enemies**.* ○ *He has **made** several enemies during his career.* ➪ **enmity** noun देखिए। **2 the enemy** [*with sing. or pl. verb*] the army or country that your country is fighting against शत्रु-सेना या शत्रु-देश *The enemy is/are approaching.* ○ *enemy forces*

**energetic** /ˌenəˈdʒetɪk ˌएनˈज़ेटिक्/ *adj.* full of or needing energy and enthusiasm शक्ति व उमंग संपन्न, ऊर्जायुक्त, कर्मठ *Jogging is a very energetic form of exercise.* ▶ **energetically** /-kli -क्लि/ *adv.* कर्मठतापूर्वक

**energize** (*BrE* **-ise**) /ˈenədʒaɪz ˈएनजाइज़्/ *verb* [T] (*pres. part* **energizing;** *3rd person sing. pres.* **energizes;** *pp, pt* **energized**) **1** to make sb enthusiastic and alert about sth किसी व्यक्ति को उत्साहित और सतर्क करना **2** to give sb more energy, strength, etc. and to raise to a higher energy level बल अर्जित करना, ताक़त देना और उर्जा स्तर को बढ़ाना *an energizing drink* **3** (*technical*) to supply power or energy विद्युत या ऊर्जा की आपूर्ति करना

**energy** /ˈenədʒi ˈएनजि/ *noun* (*pl.* **energies**) **1** [U] the ability to be very active or do a lot of work without getting tired बहुत सक्रिय रहने की या बिना थके अत्यधिक श्रम करने की क्षमता; ऊर्जा *Children are usually* ***full of energy***. **2** [U] the power that comes from coal, electricity, gas, etc. that is used for producing heat, driving machines, etc. कोयला, विद्युत, गैस आदि से उत्पन्न शक्ति (जिससे ताप उत्पन्न होता है, मशीनें चलती हैं), ऊर्जा *nuclear energy* **3 energies** [*pl.*] the effort and attention that you give to doing sth किसी काम में लगने वाला प्रयत्न और ध्यान *She devoted all her energies to helping the blind.* **4** [U] (*technical*) the ability of a substance or system to produce movement किसी वस्तु या प्रणाली में निहित गति उत्पन्न करने की क्षमता *kinetic/potential energy*

**enforce** /ɪnˈfɔːs इन्ˈफ़ॉस्/ *verb* [T] to make people obey a law or rule or do sth that they do not want to लोगों को क़ानून या नियम या उनकी अनचाही बात मानने के लिए बाध्य करना *How will they enforce the new law?* ▶ **enforced** *adj.* बाध्य *enforced redundancies* ▶ **enforcement** *noun* [U] बाध्यता

**enfranchise** /ɪnˈfræntʃaɪz इन्ˈफ़्रैन्चाइज़्/ *verb* [T] (*formal*) (*usually passive*) to give sb the right to vote in an election चुनाव में (किसी को) मतदान का अधिकार देना ✪ विलोम **disenfranchise** ▶ **enfranchisement** /ɪnˈfræntʃaɪzmənt इन्ˈफ़्रैन्चाइज़्मन्ट्/ *noun* [U] मताधिकार-संपन्नता

**engage** /ɪnˈɡeɪdʒ इन्ˈगेज्/ *verb* (*formal*) **1** [T] to interest or attract sb (किसी को) आकृष्ट करना या (काम में) लगाना *You need to engage the students' attention right from the start.* **2** [T] **engage sb (as sth)** to give work to sb (किसी को) कुछ काम देना *They engaged him as a cook.* **3** [I, T] **engage (sth) (with sth)** to make parts of a machine fit together मशीन के पुरज़ों को ठीक से बैठाना *Engage the clutch before selecting a gear.*

**PHRV** **engage in sth** to take part in sth किसी काम में भाग लेना *I don't engage in that kind of gossip!*

**engaged** /ɪnˈɡeɪdʒd इन्ˈगेज्ड्/ *adj.* **1** (*formal*) **engaged (in/on sth)** (used about a person) busy doing sth (व्यक्ति) कार्य में व्यस्त, रत *They are engaged in talks with the trade unions.* **2 engaged (to be)** having agreed to get married (किसी के साथ) सगाई होना *We've just* ***got engaged***. ○ *Sheela is engaged to Sahil.* **3** (*AmE* **busy**) (used about a telephone) in use (टेलीफ़ोन) प्रयोग में; व्यस्त *I can't get through—the line is engaged.* **4** (used about a toilet) in use (शौचालय) उपयोग में ✪ विलोम **vacant**

**engagement** /ɪnˈɡeɪdʒmənt इन्ˈगेज्मन्ट्/ *noun* [C] **1** an agreement to get married; the time when you are engaged सगाई; सगाई की रस्म *He broke off their engagement.* **2** (*formal*) an arrangement to go somewhere or do sth at a fixed time; an appointment निर्धारित समय पर कुछ करने या कहीं जाने का निश्चय; पूर्व नियोजित भेंट *I can't come on Tuesday as I have a* ***prior engagement***.

**engine** /ˈendʒɪn ˈएन्जिन्/ *noun* [C] **1** the part of a vehicle that produces power to make the vehicle move इंजन; वाहन का गति-उत्पादक भाग *This engine runs on diesel.* ○ *a car/jet engine* ➪ **motor** पर नोट देखिए। **2** (*also* **locomotive**) a vehicle that pulls a railway train रेल का इंजन

**engine driver** (*also* **train driver**, *AmE* **engineer**) *noun* [C] a person whose job is to drive a railway engine रेल-इंजन का ड्राइवर (व्यक्ति), इंजन चालक

**engineer[1]** /ˌendʒɪˈnɪə(r) ˌएन्जिˈनिअ(र्)/ *noun* [C] **1** a person whose job is to design, build or repair engines, machines, etc. अभियंता, इंजीनियर *a civil/chemical/electrical/mechanical engineer* **2** (*AmE*) = **engine driver**

**engineer[2]** /ˌendʒɪˈnɪə(r) ˌएन्जिˈनिअ(र्)/ *verb* [T] (*formal*) to arrange for sth to happen by careful secret planning सुविचारित और गुप्त रीति से किसी काम को अंजाम देना *Her promotion was engineered by her father.*

**engineering** /ˌendʒɪˈnɪərɪŋ ˌएन्जिˈनिअरिङ्/ *noun* [U] (the study of) the work that is done by an engineer इंजीनियरी (विद्या), इंजीनियरिंग, अभियांत्रिकी *mechanical/civil/chemical engineering*

**English** /ˈɪŋɡlɪʃ ˈइङ्ग्लिश्/ *noun* **1** [U] the language that is spoken in Britain, the US, Australia, etc. अंग्रेज़ी भाषा *Do you speak English?* ○ *I've been learning English for five years.* **2 the English** [*pl.*] the people of England इंग्लैंड देश के लोग

**English breakfast** *noun* [C] a meal that is eaten in the morning and consists of a lot of cooked food, **toast**, eggs, meat, tea, coffee, etc. टोस्ट, अंडे, मीट, चाय, कॉफ़ी आदि वाला प्रातःकालीन नाश्ता ➪ **continental breakfast** देखिए।

**engrave** /ɪnˈɡreɪv इन्ˈग्रेव्/ *verb* [T] **engrave B on A; engrave A with B** to cut words or designs on metal, stone, etc. धातु, पत्थर आदि पर शब्द या आकृति उकेरना *His name is engraved on the cup.* ○ *The cup is engraved with his name.*

**engraving** /ɪnˈɡreɪvɪŋ इन्ˈग्रेविङ्/ *noun* [C, U] a design that is cut into a piece of metal or stone; a picture made from this किसी धातु या पत्थर पर उकेरी गई आकृति; ऐसा किया गया चित्र

**engrossed** /ɪnˈɡrəʊst इन्ˈग्रोस्ट्/ *adj.* **engrossed (in/with sth)** so interested in sth that you give it all your attention किसी काम में तल्लीन *She was completely engrossed in her book.*

**engulf** /ɪnˈɡʌlf इन्ˈगल्फ़्/ *verb* [T] **1** (*written*) to cover or surround sb/sth completely परिग्रहण करना; किसी व्यक्ति या वस्तु को पूरा घेर या ढक लेना *Within a few minutes the factory was engulfed in flames.* **2** to strongly affect sb/sth किसी व्यक्ति या वस्तु को बहुत प्रभावित करना *She was engulfed in tears when she heard the news*

**enhance** /ɪnˈhɑːns इन्ˈहान्स्/ *verb* [T] (*formal*) to improve sth or to make sth look better बेहतर दिखने के लिए, किसी वस्तु में सुधार लाना

**enigma** /ɪˈnɪɡmə इˈनिग्मा/ *noun* [C] (*pl.* **enigmas**) a person, thing or situation that is difficult to understand (व्यक्ति, वस्तु या परिस्थिति) जिसे समझना कठिन हो; पेचीदा ▶ **enigmatic** /ˌenɪɡˈmætɪk ˌएनिग्ˈमैटिक्/ *adj.* पहेलीनुमा, रहस्यमय, पेचीदा

**enjoy** /ɪnˈdʒɔɪ इन्ˈजॉइ/ *verb* [T] **1 enjoy sth/enjoy doing sth** to get pleasure from sth (किसी वस्तु का) आनंद लेना *I really enjoyed that meal.* ○ *He enjoys listening to music while he's driving.* **2 enjoy yourself** to be happy; to have a good time आनंदित होना; आनंद का समय गुज़ारना *I enjoyed myself at the party last night.*

**enjoyable** /ɪnˈdʒɔɪəbl इन्ˈजॉइअबल्/ *adj.* giving pleasure आनंदप्रद

**enjoyment** /ɪnˈdʒɔɪmənt इन्ˈजॉइमन्ट्/ *noun* [U, C] pleasure or a thing which gives pleasure आनंद या आनंदित करने वाली वस्तु *She gets a lot of enjoyment from teaching.* ○ *One of her main enjoyments is foreign travel.*

**enlarge** /ɪnˈlɑːdʒ इन्ˈलाज्/ *verb* [I, T] to make sth or to become bigger (आकार में) बड़ा होना या करना *I'm going to have this photo enlarged.*
**PHR V** **enlarge on sth** to say or write more about sth (किसी बात को) विस्तार के साथ कहना या लिखना

**enlargement** /ɪnˈlɑːdʒmənt इन्ˈलाज्मन्ट्/ *noun* [C, U] making sth bigger or sth that has been made bigger किसी वस्तु को आकार में बड़ा करने की क्रिया या इस प्रकार बड़ी बनी वस्तु *an enlargement of a photo*

**enlighten** /ɪnˈlaɪtn इन्ˈलाइट्न्/ *verb* [T] (*formal*) to give sb information so that he/she understands sth better अपेक्षित जानकारी देते हुए किसी बात की समझ को बढ़ाना

**enlightened** /ɪnˈlaɪtnd इन्ˈलाइट्न्ड्/ *adj.* having an understanding of people's needs, a situation, etc. that shows a modern attitude to life प्रबुद्ध; समाज की आधुनिकतावादी अपेक्षाओं का बेहतर जानकार

**enlightenment** /ɪnˈlaɪtnmənt इन्ˈलाइट्न्मन्ट्/ *noun* **1** [U] the process of gaining knowledge and understanding sth or making sb understand sth clearly ज्ञानोदय *Gautam Buddha renounced the world after gaining enlightenment.* **2** the final stage reached in Buddhist and Hindu religions when you are at peace with the universe and no longer feel desire बौद्ध एवं हिंदू धर्मों में वह अंतिम अवस्था जब संसार से इच्छा रहित शांति का आभास हो *spiritual enlightenment* **3** (*also* **the Enlightenment**) [*sing.*] the period in the eighteenth century when many writers and scientists began to emphasize the importance of science and reason rather than religion अट्ठारहवीं सदी का वह युग जब कई लेखकों एवं वैज्ञानिकों ने विज्ञान और तर्क को धर्म से अधिक महत्त्वपूर्ण दर्शाया

**enlist** /ɪnˈlɪst इन्ˈलिस्ट्/ *verb* **1** [T] to get help, support, etc. सहायता, समर्थन आदि प्राप्त करना *We need to enlist your support.* **2** [I, T] to join the army, navy or air force; to make sb a member of the army, etc. सेना में भरती होना या (किसी को) भरती करना *They enlisted as soon as war was declared.*

**en masse** /ˌɒ̃nˈmæs ˌऑन्ˈमैस्/ *adv.* all together and in large numbers सामूहिक रूप से, एक साथ बड़ी संख्या में *The young people of the village decided to emigrate en masse.*

**enmity** /ˈenməti ˈएनमटि/ *noun* [U] the feeling of hatred towards an enemy शत्रुता, वैर, दुश्मनी

**enormity** /ɪˈnɔːməti इˈनॉमटि/ *noun* [*sing.*] (*formal*) the very great size, effect, etc. of sth; the fact that sth is very serious किसी वस्तु की विशालता; प्रभाव की गंभीरता; अति गंभीरता की स्थिति *the enormity of a task/decision/problem*

**enormous** /ɪˈnɔːməs इˈनॉमस्/ *adj.* very big or very great विशाल या अत्यधिक *an enormous building* ○ *enormous pleasure* ▶ **enormously** *adv.* अत्यधिक

**enough[1]** /ɪˈnʌf इˈनफ़्/ *det., pronoun* **1** as much or as many of sth as necessary पर्याप्त, काफ़ी, जितना (मात्रा या संख्या) आवश्यक हो उतना *We've saved enough money to buy a computer.* ○ *Not everybody can have a book—there aren't enough.* **2** as much or as many as you want मनचाही मात्रा या संख्या में; काफ़ी *I've had enough of living in a city* (= I don't want to live in a city any more). ○ *Don't give me any more work. I've got quite enough already.*

**enough[2]** /ɪˈnʌf इˈनफ़्/ *adv.* (*used after verbs, adjectives and adverbs*) **1** to the necessary amount or degree; sufficiently अपेक्षित मात्रा में या सीमा तक; पर्याप्त रूप से *You don't practise enough.*

○ *He's not old enough to travel alone.* **2** quite, but not very किसी हद तक (परंतु अधिक नहीं), ठीक-ठाक *She plays well enough, for a beginner.*

IDM **fair enough** ➪ **fair**[1] देखिए।

**funnily, strangely, etc. enough** it is funny, etc. that... मज़े की बात है कि... के अर्थ में प्रयुक्त *Funnily enough, I thought exactly the same myself.*

**sure enough** ➪ **sure** देखिए।

**enquire** (*also* **inquire**) /ɪnˈkwaɪə(r) इन्ˈक्वाइअ(र्)/ *verb* (*formal*) [I, T] **enquire (about sb/sth)** to ask for information about sth (किसी के विषय में) पूछताछ करना *Could you enquire when the trains to Delhi leave?* ○ *We need to enquire about hotels in Mumbai.*

PHR V **enquire after sb** to ask about sb's health कुशल-क्षेम पूछना

**enquire into sth** to study sth in order to find out all the facts तथ्यों के लिए जाँच-पड़ताल करना, छानबीन करना *The journalist enquired into the politician's financial affairs.*

**enquirer** /ɪnˈkwaɪərə(r) इन्ˈक्वाइअर(र्)/ *noun* [C] (*formal*) a person who asks for information पूछताछ करने वाला व्यक्ति

**enquiring** /ɪnˈkwaɪərɪŋ इन्ˈक्वाइअरिङ्/ *adj.* **1** interested in learning new things जिज्ञासु; नई बातें जानने का इच्छुक *We should encourage children to have an enquiring mind.* **2** asking for information जिज्ञासापूर्ण *He gave me an enquiring look.* ▶ **enquiringly** *adv.* जिज्ञासा भाव से

**enquiry** (*also* **inquiry**) /ɪnˈkwaɪəri इन्ˈक्वाइअरि/ *noun* (*pl.* **enquiries**) **1** [C] (*formal*) **an enquiry (about/concerning/into sb/sth)** a question that you ask about sth किसी के विषय में पूछताछ के लिए किया गया प्रश्न *I'll **make** some **enquiries** into English language courses at the university.* **2** [U] the act of asking about sth (किसी के विषय में) पूछताछ का काम *After weeks of enquiry he finally found what he was looking for.* **3** [C] an official process to find out the cause of sth किसी स्थिति का कारण जानने की आधिकारिक प्रक्रिया; आधिकारिक जाँच *After the accident there was an enquiry into safety procedures.*

**enrage** /ɪnˈreɪdʒ इन्ˈरेज़्/ *verb* [T] (*formal*) to make sb very angry (किसी व्यक्ति को) बहुत गुस्सा दिलाना, अत्यधिक क्रोधित कर देना

**enrich** /ɪnˈrɪtʃ इन्ˈरिच्/ *verb* [T] **1** to improve the quality, flavour, etc. of sth किसी वस्तु की गुणवत्ता आदि बढ़ाना *These cornflakes are enriched with vitamins/are vitamin-enriched.* **2** to make sb/sth rich or richer (किसी व्यक्ति या वस्तु को) संपन्न या अधिक संपन्न बनाना ✪ विलोम **impoverish** ▶ **enrichment** *noun* [U] संवर्धन

**enrol** (*AmE* **enroll**) /ɪnˈrəʊl इन्ˈरोल्/ *verb* [I, T] (**enrolling; enrolled**) to become or to make sb a member of a club, school, etc. संस्था आदि का सदस्य बनना या बनाना, स्कूल आदि में भरती होना या करना *They enrolled 100 new students last year.* ○ *I've enrolled on an Italian course.* ▶ **enrolment** (*AmE* **enrollment**) *noun* [C, U] स्कूल में भरती, क्लब की सदस्यता *Enrolment for the course will take place next week.*

**en route** /ˌɒ̃ˈruːt; ˌɒŋ-, आँˈरूट्; ˌऑन्-/ *adv.* **en route (from...) (to...); en route (for...)** on the way; while travelling from/to a place रास्ते में; को जाते हुए या से आते हुए *The car broke down when we were en route for Agra.*

**ensemble** /ɒnˈsɒmbl ऑन्ˈसॉम्ब्ल्/ *noun* [C] **1** [*with sing. or pl. verb*] a small group of musicians, dancers or actors who perform together एक साथ कार्यक्रम प्रस्तुत करने वाले संगीतज्ञों, नर्तकों या अभिनेताओं की मंडली; कलाकार-मंडली *a brass/wind/string ensemble* ○ *The ensemble is/are based in Delhi.* **2** [*usually sing.*] (*formal*) a number of things considered as a group a set of clothes that are worn together कुछ वस्तुएँ जिनका एक समूह बनता है जैसे मेल खाने वाले कपड़ों का सेट

**ensue** /ɪnˈsjuː इन्ˈस्यू/ *verb* [I] (*formal*) to happen after (and often as a result of) sth else (किसी के बाद या फलस्वरूप) कुछ घटित होना

**en suite** /ˌɑ̃ˈswiːt; ˌɒn- आँˈस्वीट्; ˌऑन्-/ *adj., adv.* (used about a bedroom and bathroom) forming one unit (शयनकक्ष और स्नानगृह से मिलकर बनी) एक इकाई *The bedroom has a bathroom en suite.*

**ensure** (*AmE* **insure**) /ɪnˈʃɔː(r) इन्ˈशॉ(र्)/ *verb* [T] to make sure that sth happens or is definite किसी बात को सुनिश्चित करना, किसी बात का सुनिश्चित होना *Please ensure that the door is locked before you leave.*

**entail** /ɪnˈteɪl इन्ˈटेल्/ *verb* [T] (*formal*) to make sth necessary; to involve sth किसी चीज़ को आवश्यक बनाना; किसी वस्तु का साथ लगा होना, अनुक्रम बंधन करना *The job sounds interesting but I'm not sure what it entails.*

**entangled** /ɪnˈtæŋgld इन्ˈटैङ्ग्ल्ड्/ *adj.* caught in sth else (किसी में) उलझा या फँसा हुआ *The bird was entangled in the net.* ○ (*figurative*) *I've got myself entangled in some financial problems.*

**enter** /ˈentə(r) ˌएन्ट(र्)/ *verb* 1 [I, T] (*formal*) to come or go into a place (किसी स्थान में) प्रवेश करना, प्रवेश पाना *Don't enter without knocking.* ○ *They all stood up when he entered the room.* ⇨ **entrance** और **entry** nouns देखिए।

NOTE **Enter** के साथ कोई पूर्वसर्ग (preposition) नहीं लगता। **Come into** और **go into** अधिक प्रचलित प्रयोग हैं।

2 [T] to become a member of sth, especially a profession or an institution सदस्य बनना, विशेषतः किसी व्यवसाय या संस्था का *She entered the legal profession in the year 2000.* ○ *to enter school/college/university* ⇨ **entrant** noun देखिए। 3 [T] to begin or become involved in an activity, a situation, etc. किसी गतिविधि या परिस्थिति में पड़ जाना या उलझ जाना *When she entered the relationship, she had no idea he was planing to settle abroad.* ○ *We have just entered a new phase in international relations.* 4 [I, T] **enter (for) sth; enter sb (in/for sth)** to put your name or sb's name on the list for an exam, race, competition, etc. परीक्षा, स्पर्धा आदि में प्रत्याशी या प्रतियोगी के रूप में नाम दर्ज़ करना या करवाना *I entered a competition in the Sunday paper and I won Rs 2000!* 5 [T] **enter sth (in/into/on/onto sth)** to put names, numbers, details, etc. in a list, book, computer, etc. किसी सूची, पुस्तक, कंप्यूटर आदि में नाम, संख्याएँ, विवरण आदि दर्ज़ करना *I've entered all the data onto the computer.* ○ *Enter your password and press return.*

PHRV **enter into sth** 1 to start to think or talk about sth किसी के विषय में सोचने या बात करने की शुरुआत करना *I don't want to enter into details now.* 2 to be part of sth; to be involved in sth किसी बात का हिस्सा होना; किसी बात में पड़ना *This is a business matter. Friendship doesn't enter into it.*

**enter into sth (with sb)** to begin sth कोई काम शुरू करना *The government has entered into negotiations with the unions.*

**enterprise** /ˈentəpraɪz ˈएन्टप्राइज़्/ *noun* 1 [C] a new plan, project, business, etc. नई योजना, व्यापार आदि; उपक्रम, उद्यम *It's a very exciting new enterprise.* ○ *a new industrial enterprise* 2 [U] the ability to think of new projects or create new businesses and make them successful नई योजनाएँ बनाने या नए उद्यमों को शुरू करने की क्षमता; उद्यमिता *We need men and women of enterprise and energy.*

**enterprising** /ˈentəpraɪzɪŋ ˈएन्टप्राइज़िङ्/ *adj.* having or showing the ability to think of new projects or new ways of doing things and make them successful नई योजनाएँ बनाने या नए उद्यमों को शुरू करने की क्षमता से संपन्न; उद्यमी *Our enterprising landlord opened up his vacant plot as a car park and charged people to park there.*

**entertain** /ˌentəˈteɪn ˌएन्टˈटेन्/ *verb* 1 [T] **entertain (sb) (with sth)** to interest and amuse sb in order to please him/her किसी का जी बहलाना (ताकि वह ख़ुश रहे) *I find it very hard to keep my class entertained on a Friday afternoon.* 2 [I, T] to welcome sb as a guest, especially to your home; to give sb food and drink लोगों का अतिथि के रूप में सत्कार करना (विशेषतः घर में); भोजन आदि से सत्कार करना *They entertain a lot.* ○ *They do a lot of entertaining.*

**entertainer** /ˌentəˈteɪnə(r) ˌएन्टˈटेन(र्)/ *noun* [C] a person whose job is to amuse people, for example, by singing, dancing or telling jokes गाने, नाच आदि के द्वारा लोगों का मनोरंजन करने वाला व्यक्ति

**entertaining** /ˌentəˈteɪnɪŋ ˌएन्टˈटेनिङ्/ *adj.* interesting and amusing रोचक और मनोरंजक

**entertainment** /ˌentəˈteɪnmənt ˌएन्टˈटेनृमन्ट्/ *noun* [U, C] film, music, etc. used to interest and amuse people लोगों के मनोरंजन के लिए चलचित्र, संगीत आदि *There's a full programme of entertainments every evening.*

**enthral** (*AmE* **enthrall**) /ɪnˈθrɔːl इन्ˈथ्रॉल्/ *verb* [T] (**enthra<u>l</u>ling; enthra<u>l</u>led**) to hold sb's interest and attention completely पूरा-पूरा ध्यान खींच लेना, मंत्रमुग्ध कर देना, मोहित करना *He was enthralled by her story.* ▶ **enthralling** *adj.* मंत्रमुग्धकारी

**enthrone** /ɪnˈθrəʊn इन्ˈथ्रोन्/ *verb* (*usually passive*) to perform a ceremony in which a king or a queen is crowned when they start to rule राज्याभिषेक करना

**enthusiasm** /ɪnˈθjuːziæzəm इन्ˈथ्यूज़िऐज़म्/ *noun* [U] **enthusiasm (for/about sth/doing sth)** a strong feeling of excitement or interest in sth and a desire to become involved in it उमंग, उत्साह; किसी स्थिति के साथ जुड़ जाने की तीव्र इच्छा *Karan showed great enthusiasm for the new project.*

**enthusiast** /ɪnˈθjuːziæst इन्ˈथ्यूज़िऐस्ट्/ *noun* [C] a person who is very interested in an activity or subject उमंगी, उत्साही व्यक्ति

**enthusiastic** /ɪnˌθjuːziˈæstɪk इन्ˌथ्यूज़िˈएस्टिक्/ *adj.* **enthusiastic (about sth/doing sth)** full of excitement and interest in sth (किसी वस्तु या कार्य के विषय में) उत्साहपूर्ण; उत्तेजना और रुचि से पूर्ण ▶ **enthusiastically** /-kli -क्लि/ *adv.* उत्साहपूर्वक

**entice** /ɪnˈtaɪs इन्ˈटाइस्/ *verb* [T] **entice sb (into sth/doing sth)** to persuade sb to do sth or to go somewhere by offering him/her something nice कुछ इनाम या लालच देकर किसी को कुछ करने के लिए मनाना; लुभाना, फुसलाना *Advertisements try to entice people into buying more things than they need.* ▶ **enticement** *noun* [C, U] प्रलोभन, फुसलाहट

**enticing** /ɪnˈtaɪsɪŋ इन्ˈटाइसिङ्/ *adj.* attractive and interesting लुभाने वाला, सम्मोहक

**entire** /ɪnˈtaɪə(r) इन्ˈटाइअ(र्)/ *adj.* (*only before a noun*) whole or complete पूरा, समूचा, संपूर्ण *He managed to read the entire book in two days.* **NOTE** **Entire** में **whole** की अपेक्षा अर्थबल अधिक है। ▶ **entirely** *adv.* पूर्णतया *I entirely agree with you.* ▶ **entirety** /ɪnˈtaɪərəti इन्ˈटाइअरटि/ *noun* [U] पूर्णता *We must consider the problem in its entirety* (= as a whole).

**entitle** /ɪnˈtaɪtl इन्ˈटाइट्ल्/ *verb* [T] **entitle sb (to sth)** (*usually passive*) to give sb the right to have or do sth (कुछ पाने या करने का) अधिकारी होना *I think I'm entitled to a day's holiday—I've worked hard enough.*

**entitled** /ɪnˈtaɪtld इन्ˈटाइट्ल्ड्/ *adj.* (used about books, plays, etc.) with the title (पुस्तक, नाटक आदि) शीर्षकयुक्त *Deepa's first book was entitled 'Aquarium'.*

**entitlement** /ɪnˈtaɪtlmənt इन्ˈटाइट्ल्मन्ट्/ *noun* (*formal*) **1** [U] **entitlement (to sth)** the official right to have or do sth (कुछ पाने या करने का) वैधानिक या नियम सम्मत अधिकार *This may affect your entitlement to compensation.* **2** [C] something that you have the official right to; the amount that you have the right to receive वस्तु जिस पर आपका वैधानिक अधिकार है; धनराशि जिसे पाना आपका अधिकार है *The contributions will affect your pension entitlements.*

**entity** /ˈentəti ˈएन्टटि/ *noun* [C] (*pl.* **entities**) something that exists separately from sth else and has its own identity अलग और स्वतंत्र अस्तित्व वाली वस्तु *The kindergarten and the school are in the same building but they're really **separate entities**.*

**entomology** /ˌentəˈmɒlədʒi ˌएन्टˈमॉलजि/ *noun* [U] the scientific study of insects कीटविज्ञान

**entrails** /ˈentreɪlz ˈएन्ट्रेल्ज़्/ *noun* [*pl.*] the organs inside the body of a person or an animal, especially the tubes that carry food away from the stomach (**intestines**) आँतें, अँतड़ियाँ

**entrance** /ˈentrəns ˈएन्ट्रन्स्/ *noun* **1** [C] **the entrance (to/of sth)** the door, gate or opening where you go into a place प्रवेश द्वार *I'll meet you at the entrance to the theatre.* **2** [C] **entrance (into/onto sth)** the act of coming or going into a place, especially in a way that attracts attention प्रवेश क्रिया (विशेषतः जो ध्यान आकृष्ट करे) *He made a dramatic entrance onto the stage.* ✪ पर्याय **entry** ✪ विलोम **exit** (अर्थ संख्या **1** और **2** का) **3** [U] **entrance (to sth)** the right to enter a place (किसी स्थान में) प्रवेश का अधिकार *They were refused entrance to the club because they were wearing shorts.* ○ *an entrance fee* ✪ पर्याय **entry** ➪ **admission** और **admittance** देखिए। **4** [U] **entrance (into/to sth)** permission to join a club, society, university, etc. (किसी क्लब, समाज, विश्वविद्यालय आदि में) प्रवेश या सदस्यता की अनुमति *You don't need to take an entrance exam to get into university.* ➪ **admission** देखिए।

**entrant** /ˈentrənt ˈएन्ट्रन्ट्/ *noun* [C] a person who enters a profession, competition, exam, university, etc. किसी व्यवसाय, स्पर्धा आदि में प्रवेश करने वाला व्यक्ति

**entreat** /ɪnˈtriːt इन्ˈट्रीट्/ *verb* [T] (*formal*) to ask sb to do sth, often in an emotional way विनती करना (प्रायः भावुकता या नम्रतापूर्वक) ✪ पर्याय **beg**

**entrepreneur** /ˌɒntrəprəˈnɜː(r) ˌऑन्ट्रप्रˈन(र्)/ *noun* [C] a person who makes money by starting or running businesses, especially when this involves taking financial risks व्यावसायिक उद्यम (विशेषतः जिसमें वित्तीय ख़तरा हो) आरंभ करने वाला या उसमें संलग्न व्यक्ति; उद्यमी, उद्यमकर्ता ▶ **entrepreneurial** /-ˈnɜːriəl -ˈनरिअल्/ *adj.* उद्यमकर्ता विषयक ▶ **entrepreneurship** *noun* [U] उद्यमिता

**entrust** /ɪnˈtrʌst इन्ˈट्रस्ट्/ *verb* [T] (*formal*) **entrust A with B/entrust B to A** to make sb responsible for sth (किसी को किसी काम का) दायित्व सौंपना *I entrusted Minu with the arrangements for the party.* ○ *I entrusted the arrangements for the party to Minu.*

**entry** /ˈentri ˈएन्ट्रि/ *noun* (*pl.* **entries**) **1** [C] the act of coming or going into a place किसी स्थान में जाने या प्रवेश करने की क्रिया; प्रवेश *The thieves forced an entry into the building.* ✪ पर्याय **entrance** **2** [U] **entry (to/into sth)** the right to enter a place किसी स्थान में प्रवेश का अधिकार *The immigrants were refused entry at the airport.* ○ *The sign says 'No Entry'.* ○ *an entry visa* ✪ पर्याय **entrance** ➪ **admission** और **admittance** देखिए। **3** [U] the right to take part in sth or become a member of a group किसी गतिविधि में भाग लेने या किसी संगठन की सदस्यता का अधिकार *countries seeking entry into the organization* **4** [C] a person or thing that is entered for a competition, etc. स्पर्धा आदि में प्रविष्ट व्यक्ति या वस्तु; प्रविष्टि *There were thousands of entries for the Indian Idol contest.* ○ *The winning entry is number 45!* **5** [C] one item that is written down in a list, account book, dictionary, etc. सूची, लेखा बही, शब्दकोश आदि में प्रविष्ट मद, प्रविष्टि *an entry in a diary ○ You'll find 'ice-skate' after the entry for 'ice'.* **6** [C] a door, gate, passage, etc. where you enter a building, etc. (भवन आदि का) प्रवेश-द्वार ✪ पर्याय **entrance**

**enumerate** /ɪˈnjuːməreɪt इˈन्यूमरेट्/ *verb* [T] (*formal*) to name a list of things separately, one by one गणन करना, एक-एक कर वस्तुओं का नाम बताना *The teacher asked the students to enumerate the various after-effects of Industrial Revolution.*

**enunciate** /ɪˈnʌnsieɪt इˈनन्सिएट्/ *verb* [I, T] **1** to say or pronounce words or part of words clearly शब्दों या शब्दों के भागों का स्पष्ट उच्चारण करना **2** [T] (*formal*) to express an idea clearly विचार को स्पष्ट रूप से अभिव्यक्त करना, प्रतिज्ञापन करना

**envelop** /ɪnˈveləp इन्ˈवेलप्/ *verb* [T] (*formal*) to cover or surround sb/sth completely (in sth) किसी व्यक्ति या वस्तु का (किसी अन्य वस्तु को) ढकना, लपेटना या आवृत करना *The hills were enveloped in mist.*

**envelope** /ˈenvələʊp; ˈɒn- ˈएन्वलोप्; ˈऑन्-/ *noun* [C] the paper cover for a letter पत्र का लिफ़ाफ़ा

> **NOTE** पत्र लिखने के बाद लिफ़ाफ़े पर **address** (पता) लिखा जाता है, लिफ़ाफ़े को **seal** (बंद) किया जाता है और लिफ़ाफ़े के दाईं ओर कोने पर **stamp** (टिकट) चिपकाया जाता है। ➪ **stamped/self-addressed envelope** देखिए।

**enviable** /ˈenviəbl ˈएन्विअबल्/ *adj.* (used about sth that sb else has and that you would like) attractive दूसरे के पास होने से अपने लिए भी स्पृहणीय ✪ विलोम **unenviable** ➪ **envy** verb और noun देखिए।

**envious** /ˈenviəs ˈएन्विअस्/ *adj.* **envious (of sb/sth)** wanting sth that sb else has दूसरे के पास जो वस्तु है उसका इच्छुक *She was envious of her sister's success.* ✪ पर्याय **jealous** ➪ **envy** verb और noun देखिए। ▸ **enviously** *adv.* ईर्ष्यापूर्ण स्पृहा के साथ

**environment** /ɪnˈvaɪrənmənt इन्ˈव़ाइरन्मन्ट्/ *noun* **1** [C, U] the conditions in which you live, work, etc. रहने, काम करने आदि की परिस्थितियाँ; वातावरण *a pleasant working environment* **2 the environment** [*sing.*] the natural world, for example the land, air and water, in which people, animals and plants live वह प्राकृतिक संसार (जैसे भूमि, वायु और जल) जिसमें लोग, पशु और पौधे रहते हैं; पर्यावरण *We need stronger laws to protect the environment.* ➪ **surroundings** देखिए। ▸ **environmental** /ɪnˌvaɪrənˈmentl इन्ˌव़ाइरन्ˈमेन्ट्ल्/ *adj.* पर्यावरण-विषयक *environmental science* ▸ **environmentally** /-təli -टलि/ *adv.* पर्यावरण की दृष्टि से *These products are **environmentally friendly**.*

**environmentalist** /ɪnˌvaɪrənˈmentəlɪst इन्ˌव़ाइरन्ˈमेन्टलिस्ट्/ *noun* [C] a person who wants to protect the environment पर्यावरण की रक्षा का इच्छुक व्यक्ति, पर्यावरण-प्रेमी **2** a person who is expert on environmental problems पर्यावरण संबंधी समस्याओं का विशेषज्ञ

**envisage** /ɪnˈvɪzɪdʒ इन्ˈव़िज़िज्/ *verb* [T] (*formal*) to think of sth as being possible in the future; to imagine भविष्य में संभावित स्थिति के विषय में सोचना; कल्पना करना *I don't envisage any problems with this.*

**envoy** /ˈenvɔɪ ˈएन्व़ॉइ/ *noun* [C] a person who is sent by a government with a message to another country अन्य देश में सरकार द्वारा संदेशवाहक दूत, राजकीय दूत, राजदूत

**envy**[1] /ˈenvi ˈएन्व़ि/ *noun* [U] **envy (of sb); envy (at/of sth)** the feeling that you have when sb else has sth that you want किसी वस्तु के लिए ईर्ष्या *It was difficult for her to hide her envy of her friend's success.*

**IDM be the envy of sb** to be the thing that causes sb to feel envy ईर्ष्या की वस्तु होना, स्पृहणीय होना *The city's transport system is the envy of many of its neighbours.* ➪ **enviable** और **envious** देखिए।

**envy**[2] /ˈenvi ˈएन्व़ि/ *verb* [T] (*pres. part.* **envying;** *3rd person sing. pres.* **envies;** *pt, pp* **envied**) **envy (sb) (sth)** to want sth that sb else has; to feel envy दूसरे की वस्तु को अपने लिए भी चाहना; ईर्ष्या अनुभव करना *I've always envied your good luck.* ○ *I don't envy you that job* (= I'm glad that I don't have it).

**enzyme** /ˈenzaɪm ˈएन्ज़ाइम्/ *noun* [C] (*technical*) a substance, usually produced by plants and animals, which helps a chemical change to happen more quickly, without being changed itself (प्रायः पौधों और पशुओं द्वारा उत्पादित) एक प्रकार का पदार्थ जो रासायनिक परिवर्तन के घटित होने में सहायता करता है परंतु स्वयं परिवर्तित नहीं होता; एन्ज़ाइम

**eolian** (*AmE*) = **aeolian**

**eon** = **aeon**

**epaulette** (*AmE* **epaulet**) /ˈepəlet ˈएपलेट्/ *noun* [C] a decoration on the shoulder of a coat, jacket, etc., especially when part of a military uniform कंधे पर लगाया जाने वलाा सजावटी चिह्न (विशेषतः सैनिक वरदी के साथ)

**ephemeral** /ɪˈfemərəl इˈफ़ेमरल्/ *adj.* (*formal*) lasting or used for only a short period of time क्षणिक, अल्पकालिक *ephemeral pleasures*

**epic** /ˈepɪk ˈएपिक्/ *adj.* very long and exciting बहुत लंबा और उत्तेजना भरा *an epic struggle/journey* ▶ **epic** *noun* [C] वीरगाथा, महान कथा *The 'Mahabharata' is a well-known Indian epic.*

**epicentre** (*AmE* **epicenter**) /ˈepɪsentə(r) ˈएपिसेन्ट(र्)/ *noun* [C] the point on the earth's surface where the effects of a sudden movement (**earthquake**) are felt most strongly पृथ्वी का वह भाग जहाँ भूकंप का झटका सबसे अधिक महसूस किया जाता है; अधिकेंद्र ➪ **seismic** पर चित्र देखिए।

**epidemic** /ˌepɪˈdemɪk ˌएपिˈडेमिक्/ *noun* [C] a large number of people or animals suffering from the same disease at the same time एक ही समय में एक ही रोग से बड़ी संख्या में पीड़ित मनुष्य और पशु; महामारी ➪ **endemic** और **pandemic** देखिए।

**epidemiology** /ˌepɪˌdiːmiˈɒlədʒi ˌएपिˈडीमिˈऑलजि/ *noun* [U] the scientific study of the spread and control of diseases रोगों के फैलने और उन पर नियंत्रण का वैज्ञानिक अध्ययन; महामारी का वैज्ञानिक अध्ययन; महामारी-विज्ञान ▶ **epidemiological** /ˌepɪˌdiːmiəˈlɒdʒɪkl ˌएपिˌडीमिअˈलॉजिकल्/ *adj.* महामारी-अध्ययन संबंधी ▶ **epidemiologist** /ˌepɪˌdiːmiˈɒlədʒɪst ˌएपिˈडीमिˈऑलजिस्ट्/ *noun* [C] महामारी-विज्ञानी

**epidermis** /ˌepɪˈdɜːmɪs ˌएपिˈडमिस्/ *noun* [*sing.*, U] the outer layer of the skin बाहरी त्वचा ➪ **flower** पर चित्र देखिए। ▶ **epidermal** *adj.* बाहरी त्वचा से संबंधित

**epiglottis** /ˌepɪˈglɒtɪs ˌएपिˈग्लॉटिस्/ *noun* [C] a small thin thing at the back of your tongue that moves to prevent food or drink from entering your lungs when you swallow गले की घंटी, कौआ, उपजिह्वा

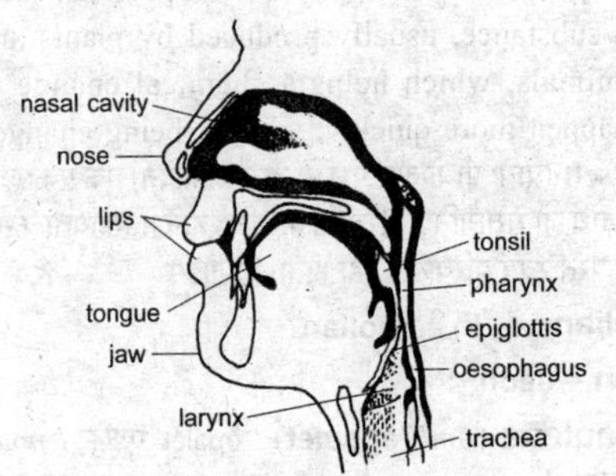


**epigram** /ˈepɪgræm ˈएपिग्रैम्/ *noun* [C] a short poem or phrase that expresses an idea in a clever or amusing way सुभाषित, सूक्ति ▶ **epigrammatic** /ˌepɪgrəˈmætɪk ˌएपिग्रˈमैटिक्/ *adj.* सूक्तिपरक

**epigraph** /ˈepɪgrɑːf ˈएपिग्राफ़्/ *noun* [C] a short phrase or sentence, etc. on a building or statue, or as an introduction to a book or a part of it भवन या प्रतिमा पर शिलालेख या किसी पुस्तक का प्रस्तावना अभिलेख

**epilepsy** /ˈepɪlepsi ˈएपिलेप्सि/ *noun* [U] a disease of the brain that can cause a person to become unconscious (sometimes with violent movements that he/she cannot control) मिरगी का रोग

**epileptic** /ˌepɪˈleptɪk ˌएपिˈलेप्टिक्/ *noun* [C] a person who suffers from epilepsy मिरगी का रोगी ▶ **epileptic** *adj.* मिरगी रोग से संबंधित *an epileptic fit*

**epilogue** /ˈepɪlɒg ˈएपिलॉग्/ *noun* [C] a short piece that is added at the end of a book, play, etc. and that comments on what has gone before किसी पुस्तक, नाटक आदि का अंतवचन, उपसंहार, भरत वाक्य ➪ **prologue** देखिए।

**episode** /ˈepɪsəʊd ˈएपिसोड्/ *noun* [C] **1** one separate event in sb's life, a novel, etc. किसी के जीवन, उपन्यास आदि की एक घटना *That's an episode in my life I'd rather forget.* **2** one part of a television or radio story that is shown in several parts (**a serial**) टीवी या रेडियो के धारावाहिक का एक भाग

**epitaph** /ˈepɪtɑːf ˈएपिटाफ़्/ *noun* [C] words that are written or said about a dead person, especially words written on a stone where he/she is buried दिवंगत व्यक्ति के लिए कहे गए शब्द, विशेषतः उसकी समाधि पर अंकित; समाधिलेख

**epithet** /ˈepɪθet ˈएपिथ्रेट्/ *noun* [C] **1** an adjective or phrase that is used to describe sb/sth's character or most important quality, especially in order to say something good or bad about sb/sth (किसी व्यक्ति या वस्तु की) किसी विशेषता या गुण का वर्णन करने वाला विशेषण या पद *The novel is neither old enough nor good enough to deserve the epithet 'classic'.* **2** an insulting word or phrase that is used about a person or group of people किसी व्यक्ति या व्यक्तिसमूह के लिए प्रयुक्त अपमानजनक शब्द *Racial epithets were written all over the wall.*

**epitome** /ɪˈpɪtəmi इˈपिटमि/ *noun* [*sing.*] **the epitome (of sth)** a perfect example of sth किसी बात का आदर्श उदाहरण *Her clothes are the epitome of good taste.*

**epitomize** (*also* **-ise**) /ɪˈpɪtəmaɪz इˈपिटमाइज़्/ *verb* [T] to be typical of sth किसी बात का आदर्श नमूना होना *This building epitomizes modern trends in architecture.*

**epoch** /ˈiːpɒk ˈईपॉक्/ *noun* [C] a period of time in history (that is important because of special events, characteristics, etc.) इतिहास का विशिष्ट युग या काल

**equable** /ˈekwəbl ˈएक्वब्ल् / *adj (formal)* **1** calm and not easily irritated or annoyed धीर, शांत *an equable temperament* **2** (of weather) keeping a steady temperature with no sudden changes (मौसम) एकरूप या समान तापमान बनाए हुए *an equable climate* ▸ **equably** /ˈekwəbli ˈएक्वब्लि / *adj* एकरूपता से, धीरतापूर्वक *She deals with problems equably, without losing her temper.*

**equal**[1] /ˈi:kwəl ˈईक्वल् / *adj.* **1 equal (to sb/sth)** the same in size, amount, value, number, level, etc. (आकार, मात्रा, मोल संख्या आदि की दृष्टि से) बराबर, समान *They are equal in weight.* ○ *They are of equal weight.* ○ *Divide it into two equal parts.* ✪ विलोम **unequal** **2** having the same rights or being treated the same as other people समान अधिकारों वाला या समानता के दर्जे वाला *This company has an equal opportunities policy* (= gives the same chance of employment to everyone). **3** *(formal)* **equal to sth** having the strength, ability etc. to do sth (अपेक्षित शक्ति, क्षमता आदि की दृष्टि से) योग्य, उपयुक्त *I'm afraid Varun just isn't equal to the job.* **IDM be on equal terms (with sb)** to have the same advantages and disadvantages as sb else लाभ और हानि दोनों दृष्टियों से बराबरी की स्थिति में होना

**equal**[2] /ˈi:kwəl ˈईक्वल् / *verb* (**equalling; equalled** *AmE* **equaling; equaled**) **1** *(linking verb)* (used about numbers, etc.) to be the same as sth संख्याएँ आदि के बराबर होना *44 plus 17 equals 61 is written as 44 + 17 = 61.* **2** [T] to be as good as sb/sth किसी व्यक्ति या स्थिति की बराबरी करना *He ran an excellent race, equalling the world record.*

**equal**[3] /ˈi:kwəl ˈईक्वल् / *noun* [C] a person who has the same ability, rights, etc. as you do समान क्षमता और अधिकार वाला व्यक्ति *to treat sb as an equal*

**equality** /iˈkwɒləti इˈक्वॉलटि / *noun* [U] the situation in which everyone has the same rights and advantages समानता, बराबरी *racial equality* (= between people of different races) ✪ विलोम **inequality**

**equalize** (*also* **-ise**) /ˈi:kwəlaɪz ˈईक्वलाइज़् / *verb* [I] *(sport)* to reach the same number of points as your opponent (खेल) की बराबरी पर आना

**equally** /ˈi:kwəli ˈईक्वलि / *adv.* **1** to the same degree or amount समान रूप, मात्रा आदि से *They both worked equally hard.* **2** in equal parts बराबर भागों में *His money was divided equally between his children.* **3** *(formal)* (used when you are comparing two ideas or commenting on what you have just said) at the same time; but/and also (तुलना या टिप्पणी करते समय प्रयुक्त) समतुल्य रूप से; परंतु, और साथ ही *I do not think what he did was right. Equally, I can understand why he did it.*

**equate** /iˈkweɪt इˈक्वेट् / *verb* [T] **equate sth (with sth)** to consider one thing as being the same as sth else एक वस्तु को दूसरी के बराबर मानना *You can't always equate money with happiness.*

**equation** /iˈkweɪʒn इˈक्वेश़्न् / *noun* [C] (in mathematics) a statement that two quantities are equal (गणित में) दो मात्राओं या संख्याओं का समीकरण *2x + 5 = 11 is an equation.*

**the equator** (*also* **the Equator**) /iˈkweɪtə(r) इˈक्वेट(र्) / *noun* [*sing.*] the imagined line around the earth at an equal distance from the North and South Poles भूमध्य रेखा *north/south of the Equator* ○ *The island is on the equator.* ➪ **earth** पर चित्र देखिए।

**equatorial** /ˌekwəˈtɔ:riəl ˌएक्वˈटॉरिअल् / *adj.* near the imagined line round the centre of the earth **(the equator)** भूमध्य रेखा के निकट का *equatorial rainforests*

**equestrian** /iˈkwestriən इˈक्वेस्ट्रिअन् / *adj.* *(formal)* connected with horse riding घुड़सवारी से संबंधित

**equidistant** /ˌi:kwɪˈdɪstənt; ˌek- ˌईक्विˈडिस्टन्ट्; ˌएक- / *adj.* **equidistant (from sth)** *(formal)* equally far from two or more places दो या अधिक स्थानों से समान दूरी पर स्थित

**equilateral** /ˌi:kwɪˈlætərəl; ˌek- ˌईक्विˈलैटरल्; ˌएक- / *adj.* (used about a triangle) having all sides the same length (त्रिभुज) समान लंबाई की भुजाओं वाला; समभुज ➪ **triangle** पर चित्र देखिए।

**equilibrium** /ˌi:kwɪˈlɪbriəm; ˌek- ˌईक्विˈलिब्रिअम्; ˌएक- / *noun* [U, *sing.*] **1** a state of balance, especially between forces or influences that are working in opposite ways संतुलन की स्थिति (विशेषतः विरोधी शक्तियों या प्रभावों के बीच) *The point at which the solid and the liquid are* ***in equilibrium*** *is called the freezing point.* **2** a calm state of mind and a balance of emotions मानसिक शांति और भाव-संतुलन

**equine** /ˈekwaɪn ˈएक्वाइन् / *adj.* connected with horses; like a horse अश्व-संबंधी; अश्व के समान

**equinox** /ˈi:kwɪnɒks; ˈek- ˈईक्विनॉक्स्; ˌएक- / *noun* [C] one of the two times in the year (around 20 March and 22 September) when the sun is above the imagined line round the centre of the earth **(equator)** and day and night are of equal length वर्ष के वे दो अवसर (20 मार्च और 22 सितंबर के आसपास)

जब सूर्य भूमध्य रेखा के ऊपर होता है और दिन और रात बराबर होते हैं; विषुवत *the spring/autumn equinox* ➪ **solstice** देखिए तथा **season** पर चित्र देखिए।

**equip** /iˈkwɪp इˈक्विप् / *verb* [T] (**equipping; equipped**) **equip sb/sth (with sth)** **1** (*usually passive*) to supply sb/sth with what is needed for a particular purpose किसी को विशेष उद्देश्य की पूर्ति करने वाला सामान पहुँचाना *We shall equip all schools with new computers over the next year.* ○ *The flat has a **fully-equipped** kitchen.* **2** to prepare sb for a particular task किसी को विशेष कार्य के लिए तैयार करना *The course equips students with all the skills necessary to become a chef.*

**equipment** /iˈkwɪpmənt इˈक्विप्मन्ट् / *noun* [U] the things that are needed to do a particular activity विशेष कार्य-संपादन के लिए अपेक्षित वस्तुएँ; साधन *office/sports/computer equipment*

> **NOTE** **Equipment** शब्द अगणनीय है। यदि एक नग की बात करनी हो तो **a piece of equipment** पद का प्रयोग किया जाता है—*a very useful piece of kitchen equipment.*

**equitable** /ˈekwɪtəbl ˈएक्विटब्ल् / *adj.* (*formal*) fair and reasonable; treating everyone in an equal way सही और उचित; सबके साथ समान व्यवहार करते हुए; निष्पक्ष *an equitable distribution of resources* ✪ विलोम **inequitable**

**equivalent** /iˈkwɪvələnt इˈक्विवलन्ट् / *adj.* **equivalent (to sth)** equal in value, amount, meaning, importance, etc. मूल्य, मात्रा, अर्थ, महत्त्व आदि की दृष्टि से समान; समकक्ष *The Indian Lok Sabha is roughly equivalent to the American House of Representatives.* ▶ **equivalent** *noun* [C] समानार्थक *There is no English equivalent to the French 'bon appétit'.*

**er** /ɜː(r) अ(र्) / *exclamation* used in writing to show the sound that sb makes when he/she cannot decide what to say next असमंजस की द्योतक ध्वनि का लिखित रूप

**era** /ˈɪərə ˈइअरा / *noun* [C] a period of time in history (that is special for some reason) इतिहास का एक कालखंड, या युग (किसी कारण से विशिष्ट); संवत् *We are living in the era of the computer.*

**eradicate** /ɪˈrædɪkeɪt इˈरैडिकेट् / *verb* [T] (*formal*) to destroy or get rid of sth completely (रोग आदि) को जड़ से उखाड़ देना, पूर्णतया उन्मूलित कर देना *Scientists have completely eradicated some diseases, such as smallpox.* ▶ **eradication** /ɪˌrædɪˈkeɪʃn इˌरैडिˈकेश्न् / *noun* [U] उन्मूलन

**erase** /ɪˈreɪz इˈरेज़् / *verb* [T] (*formal*) to remove sth completely (a pencil mark, a recording on tape, a computer file, etc.) (पेंसिल का निशान, टेप अभिलेखन, कंप्यूटर फ़ाइल आदि को) पूरी तरह मिटा देना (*figurative*) *He tried to erase the memory of those terrible years from his mind.* **NOTE** सामान्यतः हम कहते हैं—***rub out*** *a pencil mark* ▶ **eraser** *noun* [C] (*AmE*) = **rubber 2**

**erect[1]** /ɪˈrekt इˈरेक्ट् / *adj.* standing straight up सीधा खड़ा *He stood with his head erect.* ✪ पर्याय **upright**

**erect[2]** /ɪˈrekt इˈरेक्ट् / *verb* [T] (*formal*) to build sth or to stand sth straight up (किसी वस्तु का) निर्माण करना या सीधा खड़ा करना *to erect a statue* ○ *Huge TV screens were erected above the stage.*

**erection** /ɪˈrekʃn इˈरेक्श्न् / *noun* [U] (*formal*) the act of building sth or standing sth straight up किसी वस्तु का निर्माण करने या उसे सीधा खड़ा करने की क्रिया

**erode** /ɪˈrəʊd इˈरोड् / *verb* [T] (*usually passive*) (used about the sea, the weather, etc.) to destroy sth slowly (समुद्र, मौसम आदि का) किसी वस्तु को धीरे-धीरे क्षीण करना; अपक्षरित करना *The cliff has been eroded by the sea.* ▶ **erosion** /ɪˈrəʊʒn इˈरोश़्न् / *noun* [U] क्षरण *the erosion of rocks by the sea*

**erotic** /ɪˈrɒtɪk इˈरॉटिक् / *adj.* causing sexual excitement कामोत्तेजक *an erotic film/poem/dream*

**err** /ɜː(r) अ(र्) / *verb* [I] (*formal*) to be or do wrong; to make mistakes ग़लत होना या ग़लती करना; ग़लतियाँ करना

**IDM** **err on the side of sth** to do more of sth than is necessary in order to avoid the opposite happening प्रतिकूल परिणाम से बचने के लिए आवश्यकता से अधिक बचाव आदि कर जाना *It is better to err on the side of caution* (= it is better to be too careful rather than not careful enough).

**errand** /ˈerənd ˈएरन्ड् / *noun* [C] (*old-fashioned*) a short journey to take or get sth for sb, for example to buy sth from a shop किसी को कुछ देने या किसी के लिए कुछ लाने के लिए की गई छोटी यात्रा, जैसे ख़रीदारी के लिए

**errant** /ˈerənt ˈएरन्ट् / *adj.* (*only before a noun*) (*formal* or *humorous*) behaving badly in some way, especially by disobeying your parents or leaving home; not behaving in an acceptable way अनुचित व्यवहार वाला, विशेषतः माता-पिता की अवज्ञा करने वाला या घर छोड़ने वाला; अस्वीकार्य आचरण शैली में व्यवहार करते हुए *an errant husband*

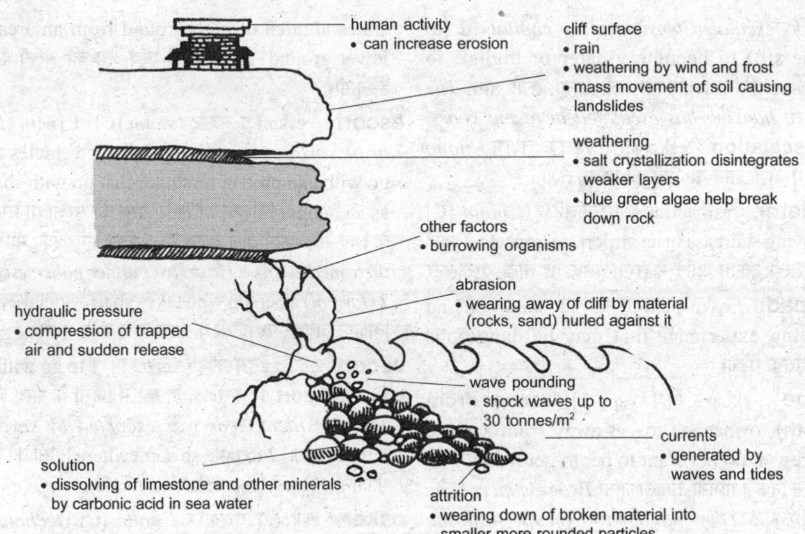
human activity
• can increase erosion
cliff surface
• rain
• weathering by wind and frost
• mass movement of soil causing landslides
weathering
• salt crystallization disintegrates weaker layers
• blue green algae help break down rock
other factors
• burrowing organisms
abrasion
• wearing away of cliff by material (rocks, sand) hurled against it
hydraulic pressure
• compression of trapped air and sudden release
wave pounding
• shock waves up to 30 tonnes/m²
currents
• generated by waves and tides
solution
• dissolving of limestone and other minerals by carbonic acid in sea water
attrition
• wearing down of broken material into smaller more rounded particles

**coastal erosion**

**erratic**[1] /ɪˈrætɪk इˈरैटिक् / *adj.* (used about a person's behaviour, or about the quality of sth) changing without reason; that you can never be sure of (व्यक्ति का व्यवहार) अनिश्चित, सनकी, मनमौजी, अनियत *Ravi is a talented player but he's very erratic* (= sometimes he plays well, sometimes badly). ▶ **erratically** /-kli -क्लि / *adv.* अनिश्चित ढंग से

**erratic**[2] /ɪˈrætɪk इˈरैटिक् / *noun* [C] (in geography) a large rock than has been carried by a moving mass of ice **(a glacier)** and left far away from where it was formed when the ice melted (भूगोल में) हिमनद के दबाव के कारण अपने स्थान से हटी हुई चट्टान

**erratum** /eˈrɑːtəm एˈराटम् / *noun* [C] (*pl.* **errata**) (*technical*) a mistake in a book or any printed or written document (shown in a list at the back or front of it) added after the book is printed लिखाई या छपाई की भूलचूक जो किसी पुस्तक, मुद्रित या लिखित काग़ज़ात की अशुद्धि सूची में दृश्य होती है (प्रायः छपाई के बाद)

**erroneous** /ɪˈrəʊniəs इˈरोनिअस् / *adj.* (*formal*) not correct; based on wrong information अशुद्ध; ग़लत सूचना पर आधारित *erroneous conclusions/assumptions* ▶ **erroneously** *adv.* ग़लती से

**error** /ˈerə(r) ˈएर(र्) / *noun* **1** [C] (*formal*) a mistake भूल, ग़लती, त्रुटि *The telephone bill was far too high due to a* ***computer error****.* ○ *an* ***error of judgement*** ○ *to* ***make an error*** **NOTE** **Error** शब्द **mistake** की अपेक्षा अधिक औपचारिक है। कुछ अभिव्यक्तियों में केवल **error** का ही प्रयोग हो सकता है, जैसे ***error of judgement, human error****.* **2** [U] the state of being wrong ग़लती, चूक *The letter was sent to you* ***in error****.* ○ *The accident was the result of* ***human error****.*

**IDM** **trial and error** ➪ **trial** देखिए।

**erstwhile** /ˈɜːstwaɪl ˈअस्ट्वाइल् / *adj.* (*only before a noun*) (*formal*) former; in the past भूतपूर्व; पूर्वकाल में *an erstwhile ruler.* ○ *Her erstwhile friends turned against her.*

**erudite** /ˈerudaɪt ˈएरुडाइट् / *adj* (*formal*) having or showing great knowledge that is based on careful study विद्वत्तापूर्ण, विद्वान *an erudite professor* ▶ **erudition** /ˌeruˈdɪʃn ˌएरुˈडिशन् / *noun* [U] विद्वत्ता

**erupt** /ɪˈrʌpt इˈरप्ट् / *verb* [I] **1** (used about a volcano) to explode and throw out fire, rock that has melted **(lava)**, smoke, etc. (ज्वालामुखी का) फूट उठना या पड़ना (और आग, लावा आदि उगलना) **2** (used about violence, shouting, etc.) to start suddenly (हिंसा आदि का) एकाएक आरंभ हो जाना, भड़क उठना *The demonstration erupted into violence.* **3** (used about a person) to suddenly become very angry (व्यक्ति का) अचानक बहुत क्रुद्ध हो जाना, गुस्से से फट पड़ना ▶ **eruption** *noun* [C, U] विस्फोट *a volcanic eruption*

**erythrocyte** /ɪˈrɪθrəsaɪt इˈरिथ्रसाइट् / *noun* [C] (*technical*) a red blood cell लाल रक्त कोशिका

**escalate** /ˈeskəleɪt ˈएसकलेट् / *verb* [I, T] **1 escalate (sth) (into sth)** (to cause sth) to become stronger or more serious (किसी स्थिति का) अधिक तीव्र होना या करना या अधिक गंभीर बनना या बनाना *The demonstrations are escalating into violent protests in all the major cities.* ○ *The terrorist* *attacks escalated tension in the capital.* **2** (to cause sth) to become greater or higher; to increase (किसी स्थिति में) तेज़ी आना, तेज़ी लाना *The cost of housing has escalated in recent years.* ▶ **escalation** /ˌeskəˈleɪʃn ˌएस्कˈलेश्न्/ *noun* [C, U] तेज़ी लाने या आने की क्रिया; तेज़ी

**escalator** /ˈeskəleɪtə(r) ˈएस्कलेटर्(र्)/ *noun* [C] a moving staircase in an airport, a shop, etc. (हवाई अड्डे, बड़ी दुकान आदि में लगी) चलती हुई सीढ़ी; एस्केलेटर

**escapade** /ˌeskəˈpeɪd ˈएस्कˈपेड्/ *noun* [C] an exciting experience that may be dangerous दुःसाहसिक घटना

**escape[1]** /ɪˈskeɪp इˈस्केप्/ *verb* **1** [I] **escape (from sb/sth)** to manage to get away from a place where you do not want to be; to get free अनचाहे स्थान से निकल भागना; निकल जाना *Two prisoners have escaped.* ○ *They managed to escape from the burning building.* **2** [I, T] to manage to avoid sth dangerous or unpleasant किसी संकटपूर्ण या अप्रिय स्थिति से बच निकलना *The two men in the other car escaped unhurt in the accident.* ○ *Piyush Jain escaped injury when his car skidded off the road.* ○ *to escape criticism/punishment* **3** [T] to be forgotten or not noticed by sb किसी बात को भूल जाना या किसी बात पर ध्यान न जाना *His name escapes me.* ○ *to escape sb's notice* **4** [I] (used about gases or liquids) to come or get out of a container, etc. (गैस या द्रव का) पात्र से रिसना *There's gas escaping somewhere.* ▶ **escaped** *adj.* भागा हुआ, भगोड़ा *an escaped prisoner*

**escape[2]** /ɪˈskeɪp इˈस्केप्/ *noun* **1** [C, U] **escape (from sth)** the act of **escaping 1, 2** पलायन; भागने की क्रिया *There have been twelve escapes from the prison this year.* ○ *She had **a narrow/lucky escape** when a lorry crashed into her car.* ○ *When the guard fell asleep they were able to **make** their **escape**.* ➪ **fire escape** भी देखिए। **2** [U, *sing.*] something that helps you forget your normal life सामान्य जीवन को भुलाने का सहायक; साधन; बचाव, मुक्ति, निस्तार *For him, listening to music is a means of escape.* ○ *an escape from reality*

**escapism** /ɪˈskeɪpɪzəm इˈस्केपिज़म्/ *noun* [U] an activity, a form of entertainment, etc. that helps you to avoid or forget unpleasant or boring things अप्रिय स्थिति से बचने या उसे भूलने में सहायक कोई गतिविधि; पलायनवाद *For Nina reading is a **form of** escapism.* ▶ **escapist** /-pɪst -पिस्ट्/ *adj.* पलायनवादी

**escarpment** /ɪˈskɑːpmənt इˈस्कापमन्ट्/ *noun* [C] (*technical*) a very steep piece of ground that separates an area of high ground from an area of lower ground तेज़ ढाल जो ऊँचे क्षेत्र को अलग करती है; कग़ार

**escort[1]** /ˈeskɔːt इˈस्कॉट्/ *noun* [C] **1** [*with sing. or pl. verb*] one or more people or vehicles that go with and protect sb/sth, or that go with sb/sth as an honour विशिष्ट व्यक्ति या वस्तु की सुरक्षा या सम्मान के लिए साथ जाने वाले वाहन या व्यक्ति; अनुरक्षक, मार्गरक्षी *an armed escort* ○ *He arrived **under police escort**.* **2** (*formal*) a person who takes sb to a social event विशिष्ट अवसर पर किसी के साथ जाने वाला व्यक्ति

**escort[2]** /ɪsˈkɔːt इस्ˈकाट्/ *verb* [T] **1** to go with sb as an **escort 1** अनुरक्षक के रूप में किसी के साथ जाना *The President's car was escorted by several police cars.* **2** to take sb somewhere किसी को कहीं ले जाना *Pranay escorted her to the door.*

**esker** /ˈeskə(r) ˈएस्क(र्)/ *noun* [C] (*technical*) a long line of small stones and earth that has been left by a large mass of ice that has melted बर्फ़ पिघलने के बाद पीछे बचे रह गए कंकड़ और मिट्टी; हिमनद

**Eskimo** /ˈeskɪməʊ ˈएस्किमो/ (*old-fashioned*) = **Inuit** NOTE **Inuits** अपने को **Eskimos** कहलाना पसंद नहीं करते हैं।

**esophagus** (*AmE*) = **oesophagus**

**especial** /ɪˈspeʃl इˈस्पेश्ल्/ *adj.* (*only before a noun*) (*formal*) not usual; special साधारण नहीं; विशेष *This will be of especial interest to you.*

**especially** /ɪˈspeʃəli इˈस्पेशलि/ *adv.* **1** more than other things, people, situations, etc.; particularly विशेषतया, ख़ास तौर पर, विशेषकर, सर्वप्रधान *She loves animals, especially dogs.* ○ *Teenage boys especially can be very competitive.* **2** for a particular purpose or person विशेष प्रयोजन से या व्यक्ति के लिए *I made this especially for you.* ✪ पर्याय **specially** **3** very (much) विशेष अधिक *It's not an especially difficult exam.* ○ *'Do you like jazz?' 'Not especially.'*

**espionage** /ˈespiənɑːʒ ˈएस्पिअनाश़्/ *noun* [U] the act of finding out secret information about another country or organization जासूसी, गुप्तचरी ➪ **spy** verb देखिए।

**essay** /ˈeseɪ ˈएसे/ *noun* [C] **an essay (on/about sth)** a short piece of writing on one subject (किसी विषय पर) निबंध *We have to write a 1000-word essay on tourism for homework.*

**essence** /ˈesns ˈएसन्स्/ *noun* **1** [U] the basic or most important quality of sth सारतत्व; किसी वस्तु की मूलभूत और सर्वाधिक महत्त्वपूर्ण विशेषता *Although both* *parties agree **in essence**, some minor differences remain.* **2** [C, U] a substance (usually a liquid) that is taken from a plant or food and that has a strong smell or taste of that plant or food तीखी गंध या स्वाद वाले पौधों या खाद्य पदार्थों से निकाला गया अरक *coffee/vanilla essence*

**essential** /ɪˈsenʃl इ ˈसेन्शल् / *adj.* completely necessary; that you must have or do परमावश्यक; सर्वथा अपेक्षित *essential medical supplies* ○ *Maths is essential for a career in computers.* ○ *It is essential that all school-leavers should have a qualification.* ▶ **essential** *noun* [C, *usually pl.*] मूलभूत वस्तु *food, and other essentials such as clothing and heating*

**essentially** /ɪˈsenʃəli इ ˈसेन्शलि / *adv.* when you consider the basic or most important part of sth मूल रूप से, मूलतः *The problem is essentially one of money.* ✪ पर्याय **basically**

**establish** /ɪˈstæblɪʃ इ ˈस्टैब्लिश् / *verb* [T] **1** to start or create an organization, a system, etc. संस्था, व्यवस्था आदि स्थापित करना, निर्धारित करना *The school was established in 1875.* ○ *Before we start on the project we should establish some rules.* **2** to start a formal relationship with sb/sth किसी व्यक्ति या वस्तु के साथ औपचारिक संबंध बनाना *The government is trying to establish closer links between the two countries.* **3 establish sb/sth (as sth)** to become accepted and recognized as sth किसी विशेष रूप में मान्य होना; प्रतिष्ठित होना *She has been trying to establish herself as a novelist for years.* **4** to discover or find proof of the facts of a situation स्थिति-विशेष के तथ्यों का पता लगाना *The police have not been able to establish the cause of the crash.*

**establishment** /ɪˈstæblɪʃmənt इ ˈस्टैब्लिश्मन्ट् / *noun* **1** [C] (*formal*) an organization, a large institution or a hotel संगठन, बड़ी संस्था, प्रतिष्ठान *an educational establishment* **2 the Establishment** [*sing.*] the people in positions of power in a country, who usually do not support change किसी देश का सत्ताधारी वर्ग जो प्रायः परिवर्तन का विरोधी होता है **3** [U] the act of creating or starting a new organization, system, etc. किसी नए संगठन की स्थापना या किसी नई पद्धति आदि की शुरुआत *the establishment of new laws on taxes*

**estate** /ɪˈsteɪt इ ˈस्टेट् / *noun* [C] **1** a large area of land in the countryside that is owned by one person or family एक व्यक्ति या परिवार के स्वामित्व वाली देहात में स्थित भूसंपत्ति; जागीर *He owns a large estate in Haryana.* **2** an area of land that has a lot of houses or factories of the same type on it ऐसा भूक्षेत्र जहाँ एक ही प्रकार के बहुत-से मकान या कारख़ाने हों *an industrial estate* (= where there are a lot of factories) ○ *a housing estate* **3** all the money and property that sb leaves when he/she dies मृतक द्वारा छोड़ी हुई संपदा (धन, भूखंड)

**estate agent** (*AmE* **Realtor™**; **real estate agent**) *noun* [C] a person whose job is to buy and sell houses and land for other people जायदाद का दलाल

**estate car** (*AmE* **station wagon**) *noun* [C] a car with a door at the back and a long area for luggage behind the back seat पीछे दरवाज़ा लगी ऐसी कार जिसमें पिछली सीट के बाद सामान रखने की जगह होती है

**esteem** /ɪˈstiːm इ ˈस्टीम् / *noun* [U] (*formal*) great respect; a good opinion of sb सम्मान; किसी के प्रति आदरभाव

**ester** /ˈestə(r) ˈएस्टर्(र्) / *noun* [C] (in chemistry) a type of natural substance (**organic compound**) that is formed by combining an acid and an alcohol (रसायन शास्त्र में) अम्ल और एलकोहल के मिश्रण से बना प्राकृतिक पदार्थ (जैव यौगिक)

**esthetic** (*AmE*) = **aesthetic**

**estimate[1]** /ˈestɪmət ˈएस्टिमट् / *noun* [C] **1** an estimate (of sth) a guess or judgement about the size, cost, etc. of sth, before you have all the facts and figures सभी तथ्यों के बिना किसी वस्तु के आकार, क़ीमत आदि का अनुमान या आकलन *Can you give me **a rough estimate** of how many people will be at the meeting?* ○ ***At a conservative estimate*** (= the real figure will probably be higher), *the job will take six months to complete.* **2 an estimate (for sth/doing sth)** a written statement from a person who is going to do a job for you, for example a **builder** or a painter, telling you how much it will cost आकलन का विवरण *They gave me an estimate for repairing the roof.* ➪ **quotation** देखिए।
IDM **a ballpark figure/estimate** ➪ **ballpark** देखिए।

**estimate[2]** /ˈestɪmeɪt ˈएस्टिमेट् / *verb* [T] **estimate sth (at sth); estimate that...** to calculate the size, cost, etc. of sth approximately, before you have all the facts and figures किसी काम का आकलन करना, मूल्यांकन करना, अनुमान लगाना *The police estimated the crowd at 10,000.* ○ *She estimated that the work would take three months.*

**estimation** /ˌestɪˈmeɪʃn ˌएस्टिˈमेश्न् / *noun* [U] (*formal*) opinion or judgement मत, विचार या परख *Who is to blame, **in your estimation**?*

**estranged** /ɪˈstreɪndʒd इˈस्ट्रेन्ज़्ड् / *adj.* **1** no longer living with your husband/wife (पति या पत्नी) एक दूसरे से अलग रहते हुए *her estranged husband* **2 estranged (from sb)** no longer friendly or in contact with sb who was close to you किसी समय में रहे घनिष्ठ संबंध से अब विमुख *He became estranged from his family following an argument.*

**estrogen** (*AmE*) = **oestrogen**

**estuary** /ˈestʃuəri ˈएस्चुअरि / *noun* [C] (*pl.* **estuaries**) the wide part (**mouth**) of a river where it joins the sea नदी का मुहाना

**ETA** /ˌiːtiːˈeɪ ˌई टी ˈए / *abbr.* estimated time of arrival; the time at which an aircraft, ship, etc. is expected to arrive अनुमानित आगमन समय; किसी विमान, जहाज़ आदि का अनुमानित आगमन समय

**etc.** *abbr.* etcetera; and so on, and other thing of a similar kind 'आदि' या 'इत्यादि'; समतुल्य प्रकार की अन्य वस्तुएँ या व्यक्ति *sandwiches, biscuits, cakes, etc.*

**eternal** /ɪˈtɜːnl इˈटर्नल् / *adj.* **1** without beginning or end; existing or continuing for ever अनादि या अनंत; चिरंतन, शाश्वत, अमर *Some people believe in eternal life* (= after death). **2** happening too often; seeming to last for ever बार-बार का या की; अंतहीन-सा *I'm tired of these eternal arguments!* ▶ **eternally** /-nəli -नलि / *adv.* शाश्वत भाव से, सदा-सर्वदा *I'll be **eternally grateful** if you could help me.*

**eternity** /ɪˈtɜːnəti इˈटनटि / *noun* **1** [U] time that has no end; the state or time after death अनंत काल; पारलौकिक जीवन **2 an eternity** [*sing.*] a period of time that never seems to end अनंत लगने वाला समय *It seemed like an eternity before the ambulance arrived.*

**ethane** /ˈiːθeɪn ˈइथेन् / *noun* [U] (*symbol* $C_2H_6$) (in chemistry) a gas that has no colour or smell and that can burn. Ethane is found in natural gas and in **petroleum** (रसायनशास्त्र में) एक गंध-रंग-रहित ज्वलनशील गैस जो नैचुरल गैस और पेट्रोलियम में पाई जाती है; इथेन

**ethanol** /ˈeθənɒl ˈएथ़नॉल् / (*also* **ethyl alcohol**) *noun* [U] the type of alcohol in alcoholic drinks, also used as a fuel or as a **solvent** मादक द्रव्यों में पाया जाने वाला एक प्रकार का एलकोहल जो ईंधन और विलायक का काम करता है

**ethereal** /ɪˈθɪəriəl इˈथ़िअरिअल् / *adj.* (*formal*) extremely delicate and light, in a way that seems unreal; of heaven or the spirit अत्यंत कोमल और हलका, अवास्तविक जैसा; पारलौकिक *ethereal music/beauty*

**ethical** /ˈeθɪkl ˈएथ़िकल् / *adj.* **1** connected with beliefs of what is right or wrong उचित-अनुचित के विचार से संबंधित; नैतिक *That is an ethical problem.* **2** morally correct नैतिक दृष्टि से उचित, नैतिकतापूर्ण *Although she didn't break the law, her behaviour was certainly not ethical.* ▶ **ethically** /-kli -क्लि / *adv.* नैतिकतापूर्वक

**ethics** /ˈeθɪks ˈएथ़िक्स् / *noun* **1** [U] the study of what is right and wrong in human behaviour नीतिशास्त्र; मानवीय व्यवहार में उचित-अनुचित की मीमांसा **2** [*pl.*] beliefs about what is morally correct or acceptable उचित-अनुचित का विचार *The medical profession has its own **code of ethics**.*

**ethnic** /ˈeθnɪk ˈएथ़्निक् / *adj.* connected with or typical of a particular race or religion विशेष जाति या धर्म से संबंधित या उसका प्रतिनिधिक *ethnic minorities* ○ *ethnic food/music/clothes*

**ethnic cleansing** *noun* [U] the policy of forcing people of a certain race or religion to leave an area or country विशेष जाति या धर्म के लोगों को किसी इलाक़े या देश को छोड़ने के लिए बाध्य करने की नीति

**ethnography** /eθˈnɒgrəfi एथ़्ˈनॉग्रफ़ि / *noun* [U] the scientific description of different races and cultures विभिन्न जातियों और संस्कृतियों का वैज्ञानिक विवरण; नृजाति वर्णन ▶ **ethnographic** /ˌeθnəˈgræfɪk एथ़्ˈनॉग्रैफ़िक् / *adj.* नृजाति वर्णन विषयक *ethnographic research/studies*

**ethnology** /eθˈnɒlədʒi एथ़्ˈनॉलजि / *noun* [U] the scientific study and comparison of human races मानव जातियों का वैज्ञानिक अध्ययन; नृजाति विज्ञान ▶ **ethnological** /ˌeθnəˈlɒdʒɪkl ˌएथ़्नˈलॉजिकल् / *adj.* नृजाति विज्ञान विषयक ▶ **ethnologist** /eθˈnɒlədʒɪst एथ़्ˈनॉलजिस्ट् / *noun* [C] नृजातिविज्ञानी

**ethyl alcohol** /ˌeθɪl 'ælkəhɒl; ˌiːθaɪl ˌएथ़िल्ˈऐल्क-हॉल्; ˌईथ़ाइल् / = **ethanol**

**etiology** (*AmE*) = **aetiology**

**etiquette** /ˈetɪket ˌएटिकेट् / *noun* [U] the rules of polite and correct behaviour शिष्टाचार *social/professional etiquette*

**etymology** /ˌetɪˈmɒlədʒi ˌएटिˈमॉलजि / *noun* (*pl.* **etymologies**) **1** [U] the study of the origins and history of words and their meanings शब्दों और उनके अर्थों के उद्‌भव और विकास का अध्ययन; व्युत्पत्तिशास्त्र **2** [C] an explanation of the origin and history of a particular word शब्द-विशेष की उत्पत्ति एवं इतिहास की व्याख्या

**eucalyptus** /ˌjuːkəˈlɪptəs ˌयूकˈलिप्टस्/ *noun* [C] (*pl.* **eucalyptuses** or **eucalypti** /-taɪ -टाइ/) a tall straight tree that grows especially in Australia and Asia. Its leaves produce an oil with a strong smell, that is used in medicine गंधसफ़ेदा, यूकेलिप्टस का वृक्ष ➪ **marsupial** पर चित्र देखिए।

**eulogize** (*BrE* **-ise**) /ˈjuːlədʒaɪz ˈयूलजाइज़्/ *verb* [I, T] (*formal*) to praise sb/sth very highly किसी व्यक्ति या वस्तु की उच्च प्रशंसा करना *All the critics eulogized her style of writing.* ▶ **eulogistic** /ˌjuːləˈdʒɪstɪk ˌयूलˈजिस्टिक्/ *adj.* प्रशंसात्मक

**eulogy** /ˈjuːlədʒi ˈयूलजि/ *noun* (*pl.* **eulogies**) **1** [C, U] **(a) eulogy (of/to sb/sth)** a speech or piece of writing that says good things about sb/sth प्रशस्ति, प्रशंसाभरा भाषण या लेख *a eulogy to marriage* **2** [C] **a eulogy (for/to sb)** a speech given at a funeral saying good things about the person who has died मृतक के अंतिम संस्कार पर उसकी प्रशंसा में दिया गया भाषण

**eunuch** /ˈjuːnək ˈयूनक्/ *noun* [C] **1** a man whose **testicles** have been removed (**castrated**), epecially one who guarded the **harem** in some Asian countries in the past बधिया किया गया पुरुष, विशेषतः जो कुछ एशियाई देशों में पूर्व काल में हरम की रखवाली किया करता था; नपुंसक, हिजड़ा **2** a person without power or influence शक्तिहीन या प्रभावहीन व्यक्ति *a political eunuch*

**euphemism** /ˈjuːfəmɪzəm ˈयूफ़मिज़म्/ *noun* [C, U] an indirect word or expression that you use instead of a more direct one when you are talking about sth that is unpleasant or embarrassing; the use of such expressions कटु प्रसंग को परोक्ष और कम अप्रिय रीति से व्यक्त करने वाला शब्द; मंगलभाषित, मंगलभाषित का व्यवहार *'Pass away' is a euphemism for 'die'.* ▶ **euphemistic** /ˌjuːfəˈmɪstɪk ˈयूफ़ˈमिस्टिक/ *adj.* मंगलभाषित *euphemistic language* ▶ **euphemistically** /-kli -क्लि/ *adv.* मंगल भाषण की रीति से

**euphoria** /juːˈfɔːriə यूˈफ़ॉरिआ/ *noun* [U] (*formal*) an extremely strong feeling of happiness प्रसन्नता का अतिरेक; उल्लासोन्माद ▶ **euphoric** /juːˈfɒrɪk यूˈफ़ॉरिक्/ *adj.* उल्लासोन्मादपूर्ण *My euphoric mood could not last.*

**Euro-** /ˈjʊərəʊ ˈयुअरो/ *prefix* (*in nouns and adjectives*) connected with Europe or the European Union यूरोप या यूरोपीय संघ से संबंधित *a Euro-MP* ○ *Euro-elections*

**European**[1] /ˌjʊərəˈpiːən ˌयुअरˈपीअन्/ *adj.* of or from Europe यूरोप का/से, यूरोपीय *European languages*

**European**[2] /ˌjʊərəˈpiːən ˌयुअरˈपीअन्/ *noun* [C] a person from a European country यूरोपीय व्यक्ति

**the European Union** *noun* [*sing.*] (*abbr.* **EU**) an economic and political association of certain European countries यूरोपीय देशों का आर्थिक-राजनीतिक संघ

**Eustachian tube** /juːˈsteɪʃn tjuːb युˈस्टेश्न् ट्यूब्/ *noun* [C] a thin tube that connects the middle ear with the upper **pharynx** and equalizes air pressure on either side of the **eardrum** यूटेशी नलीका, कंठकर्णनली ➪ **ear** पर चित्र देखिए।

**euthanasia** /ˌjuːθəˈneɪziə ˌयुथˈनेज़िआ/ *noun* [U] the practice (illegal in most countries) of killing sb without pain who wants to die because he/she is suffering from a disease that cannot be cured असाध्य रोग से पीड़ित होने के कारण मृत्यु के इच्छुक व्यक्ति का प्राणहरण; आत्ममरण-स्वीकृति

**eutrophication** /ˌjuːtrəfɪˈkeɪʃn ˌयूट्रफ़िˈकेश्न्/ *noun* [U] (*technical*) the process of too many plants growing on the surface of a river, lake, etc., often because chemicals that are used to help crops grow have been carried there by rain नदी, झील आदि में बड़ी संख्या में पौधे उग आने की प्रक्रिया

**evacuate** /ɪˈvækjueɪt इˈवैक्युएट्/ *verb* [T] to move people from a dangerous place to somewhere safer; to leave a place because it is dangerous लोगों को ख़तरानाक स्थान से हटाकर सुरक्षित स्थान पर ले जाना; ख़तरनाक होने के कारण किसी स्थान को छोड़ना; निष्क्रमण करना *Thousands of people were evacuated from the war zone.* ○ *The village had to be evacuated when the river burst its banks.* ▶ **evacuation** /ɪˌvækjuˈeɪʃn इˌवैक्युˈएश्न्/ *noun* [C, U] निष्क्रमण

**evacuee** /ɪˌvækjuˈiː इˌवैक्युˈई/ *noun* [C] a person who is sent away from a place because it is dangerous, especially during a war ख़तरे की संभावना वाले स्थान से हटाया गया व्यक्ति; निष्क्रमणार्थी

**evade** /ɪˈveɪd इˈवेड्/ *verb* [T] **1** to manage to escape from or to avoid meeting sb/sth बच निकलना (ताकि सामना न करना पड़े) *They managed to evade capture and escaped to France.* **2** to avoid dealing with or doing sth से किनाराकशी करना, से कन्नी काटना *to evade responsibility* ○ *I asked her directly, but she evaded the question.* ➪ **evasion** noun देखिए।

**evaluate** /ɪvæljueɪt इवैल्युएट्/ *verb* [T] (*formal*) to study the facts and then form an opinion about sth तथ्यों के आधार पर मूल्यांकन करना *We evaluated the situation very carefully before we made our decision.* ▶ **evaluation** /ɪˌvæljuˈeɪʃn इˌवैल्युˈएश्न्/ *noun* [C, U] मूल्यांकन

**evangelical** /ˌiːvænˈdʒelɪkl ˌईवैन्ˈजेलिक्ल् / *adj.* (of certain Protestant churches) believing that religious ceremony is not as important as belief in Jesus Christ and study of the Bible धार्मिक कर्मकांड की अपेक्षा ईसा और बाइबल, पर अधिक विश्वास करने वाले (कतिपय प्रोटेस्टैंट गिराज़घरों से संबंधित)

**evaporate** /ɪˈvæpəreɪt इˈवैपरेट् / *verb* [I] **1** (used about a liquid) to change into steam or gas and disappear (द्रव का) भाप बन जाना *The water evaporated in the sunshine.* ➪ **condense** देखिए। **2** to disappear completely छू-मंतर हो जाना, ग़ायब हो जाना *All her confidence evaporated when she saw the exam paper.* ► **evaporation** /ɪˌvæpəˈreɪʃn इˌवैपˈरेश्न् / *noun* [U] वाष्पीकरण

**evasion** /ɪˈveɪʒn इˈव़ेश्न् / *noun* [C, U] **1** the act of avoiding sth that you should do किनाराकशी, करणीय से बचने का काम; अपवंचन *He has been sentenced to two years' imprisonment for* ***tax evasion***. ○ *an evasion of responsibility* **2** a statement that avoids dealing with a question or subject in a direct way बहानों भरा बयान, टालमटोल वाला बयान *The President's reply was full of evasions.* ➪ **evade** verb देखिए।

**evasive** /ɪˈveɪsɪv इˈव़ेसिव़् / *adj.* trying to avoid sth; not direct टालमटोल वाला; घुमा-फिरा कर कहा गया *Anu gave an evasive answer.*

**eve** /iːv ईव़् / *noun* [C] the day or evening before a religious festival, important event, etc. किसी महत्त्वपूर्ण अवसर की पूर्व संध्या *Christmas eve* ○ *He injured himself on the eve of the final match.*

**even[1]** /ˈiːvn ˈईव़्न् / *adj.* **1** flat, level or smooth समतल, सपाट *The game must be played on an even surface.* **2** not changing; regular स्थिर, संयत; नियमित *He's very* ***even-tempered***, *in fact I've never seen him angry.* **3** (used about a competition, etc.) equal, with one side being as good as the other (स्पर्धा आदि) बराबरी का *The contest was very even until the last few minutes of the game.* ✪ विलोम **uneven** (अर्थ सं. **1, 2, 3** का) **4** (used about numbers) that can be divided by two (संख्याएँ) दो से विभाज्य, सम *2, 4, 6, 8, 10, etc. are even numbers.* ✪ विलोम **odd**

IDM **be/get even (with sb)** (*informal*) to hurt or harm sb who has hurt or harmed you बदला लेना, हिसाब चुकता करना

**break even** to make neither a loss nor a profit न हानि और न ही लाभ होना

**even[2]** /ˈiːvn ˈईव़्न् / *adv.* **1** used for emphasizing sth that is surprising भी; चकित करने वाली बात पर बल देने के लिए प्रयुक्त *It isn't very warm here even in summer.* ○ *He didn't even open the letter.* **2 even more, less, bigger, nicer, etc.** used when you are comparing things, to make the comparison stronger भी; वस्तुओं की तुलना के लिए प्रयुक्त (तुलना को असरदार बनाने के लिए) *You know even less about it than I do.* ○ *It is even more difficult than I expected.*

IDM **even if** used for saying that what follows 'if' makes no difference भले ही, यह बताने के लिए प्रयुक्त कि **'if'** के बाद कही बात का कोई असर नहीं *I wouldn't ride a horse, even if you paid me.*

**even so** (used for introducing a new idea, fact, etc. that is surprising) in spite of that; nevertheless के बावजूद; तथापि, फिर भी (नया विचार, तथ्य आदि जो आश्चर्यजनक हो, के परिचय के लिए प्रयुक्त) *There are a lot of spelling mistakes; even so it's quite a good essay.*

**even though** although यद्यपि, हालाँकि *I like her very much even though she can be very annoying.* ➪ **although** पर नोट देखिए।

**evening** /ˈiːvnɪŋ ˈईव़्निङ् / *noun* [C, U] the part of the day between the afternoon and the time that you go to bed सायंकाल, शाम *Most people watch television* ***in the evening***. ○ *an evening class* (= a course of lessons for adults that takes place in the evening)

> NOTE शाम के समय पहली बार मिलने पर **'Good evening'** प्रयुक्त किया जाता है। कई बार हम केवल **evening** कह देते हैं—*'Good evening, Mrs Walia.' 'Evening, Mr Mehta.'*

**evenly** /ˈiːvnli ˈईव़्नलि / *adv.* in a smooth, regular or equal way सुव्यवस्थित या समान रूप से *The match was very evenly balanced.* ○ *Spread the cake mixture evenly in the tin.*

**event** /ɪˈvent इˈव़ेन्ट् / *noun* [C] **1** something that happens, especially sth important or unusual घटना (विशेषतः महत्त्वपूर्ण या असाधारण) *a historic event* ○ *The events of the past few days have made things very difficult for the Government.* **2** a planned public or social occasion आयोजित सार्वजनिक कार्यक्रम *a fund-raising event* **3** one of the races, competitions, etc. in a sports programme खेलों में होने वाली कोई एक प्रतियोगिता *The next event is the 800 metres.*

IDM **at all events/in any event** whatever happens चाहे कुछ भी हो जाए *I hope to see you soon, but in any event I'll phone you on Sunday.*

**in the event of sth** (*formal*) if sth happens ऐसी स्थिति में, अगर ऐसा हुआ तो *In the event of fire leave the building as quickly as possible.*

**eventful** /ɪˈventfl इˈव़ेन्ट्फ़्ल् / *adj.* full of important, dangerous, or exciting things happening महत्त्वपूर्ण, ख़तरनाक या उत्तेजक स्थितियों से भरा हुआ घटनापूर्ण

**eventual** /ɪˈventʃuəl इˈवेन्चुअल्/ *adj.* (*only before a noun*) happening as a result at the end of a period of time or of a process अवधि या प्रक्रिया के अंत में परिणामस्वरूप होने वाला; अंततोगत्वा होने वाला *It is impossible to say what the eventual cost will be.*

**eventually** /ɪˈventʃuəli इˈवेन्चुअलि/ *adv.* in the end; finally अंत में; अंततोगत्वा *He eventually managed to persuade his parents to let him buy a motorbike.* ✪ पर्याय **finally**

**ever**[1] /ˈevə(r) ˈएव़(र्)/ *adv.* **1** (*used in questions and negative sentences, when you are comparing things, and in sentences with 'if'*) at any time किसी भी समय *She **hardly ever** (= almost never) goes out.* ○ *Today is hotter **than ever**.* ○ *This is the best meal I have ever had.* **2** (*used in questions with verbs in the perfect tenses*) at any time up to now अब तक कभी भी *Have you ever been to Spain?* **3** used with a question that begins with 'when', 'where', 'who', 'how', etc., to show that you are surprised or shocked प्रश्नात्मक शब्दों 'when', 'where' आदि वाले ऐसे वाक्यों में प्रयुक्त जिनसे आश्चर्य की अभिव्यक्ति हो ***How ever** did he get back so quickly?* ○ ***Whatever** were you thinking about when you wrote this?* ➪ **whatever, whenever, however** इत्यादि देखिए।

IDM **(as) bad, good, etc. as ever** (as) bad, good, etc. as usual or as always हमेशा की तरह बुरा, अच्छा आदि *In spite of his problems, Ankur is as cheerful as ever.*

**ever after** (used especially at the end of stories) from that moment on for always (प्राय: कहानियों के अंत में प्रयुक्त) तब से हमेशा के लिए, उसके बाद हमेशा *The prince married the princess and they lived happily ever after.*

**ever since...** all the time from... until now जब से... तब से या तब से... जब से *She has had a car ever since she was at university.*

**ever so/ever such (a)** very (*informal*) अत्यंत *He's ever so kind.* ○ *He's ever such a kind man.*

**for ever** ➪ **forever 1** देखिए।

**ever-**[2] /ˈevə(r) ˈएव़(र्)/ (*in compounds*) always; continuously हमेशा; लगातार *the ever-growing problem of pollution*

**evergreen** /ˈevəgriːn ˈएव़ग्रीन्/ *noun* [C], *adj.* (a tree or bush) with green leaves all through the year (वृक्ष या झाड़ी) सदाबहार, जिसके पत्ते साल भर हरे रहते हैं ➪ **deciduous** देखिए।

**everlasting** /ˌevəˈlɑːstɪŋ ˌएव़ˈलास्टिङ्/ *adj.* (*formal*) continuing for ever; never changing शाश्वत; स्थायी *everlasting life/love*

**every** /ˈevri ˈएव़्रि/ *det.* **1** (*used with singular nouns*) all of the people or things in a group of three or more तीन या अधिक व्यक्तियों या वस्तुओं के समूह में सभी; प्रत्येक *I've read every book in this house.* ○ *You were out every time I phoned.* ➪ **everybody** पर नोट देखिए। **2** all that is possible सभी संभव, हर संभव *You have every chance of success.* ○ *She had every reason to be angry.* **3** used for saying how often sth happens (यह बताने के लिए प्रयुक्त कि कोई बात कितनी बार होती है); हर, प्रति *We see each other **every day**.* ○ *Take the medicine every four hours* (= at 8, 12, 4 o'clock, etc.) ○ *I work **every other day*** (= on Monday, Wednesday, Friday, etc.)

**everybody** /ˈevribɒdi ˈएव़्रिबॉडि/ (*also* **everyone** /ˈevriwʌn ˈएव्रिवन्/) *pronoun* [*with sing. verb*] every person; all people प्रत्येक व्यक्ति; सभी लोग *Is everybody here?* ○ *The police questioned everyone who was at the party.*

> NOTE **Everyone** केवल मनुष्यों के लिए प्रयुक्त होता है और इसके बाद शब्द 'of' नहीं आता। **Every one** का अर्थ है प्रत्येक व्यक्ति या वस्तु और इसके बाद प्राय: शब्द 'of' आता है। ***Every one of** his records has been successful.* ➪ **somebody** पर नोट भी देखिए।

**everyday** /ˈevrideɪ ˈएव़्रिडे/ *adj.* (*only before a noun*) normal or usual सामान्य, रोज़मर्रा का *The computer is now part of everyday life.*

**everyplace** /ˈevripleɪs ˈएव़्रिप्लेस्/ (*AmE*) = **everywhere**

**everything** /ˈevriθɪŋ ˈएव़्रिथिङ्/ *pronoun* [*with sing. verb*] **1** each thing; all things प्रति वस्तु; सभी वस्तुएँ *Everything is very expensive in this shop.* ○ *We can leave **everything else** (= all the other things) until tomorrow.* **2** the most important thing सबसे महत्त्वपूर्ण चीज़ *Money isn't everything.*

**everywhere** /ˈevriweə(r) ˈएव़्रिवेअ(र्)/ *adv.* in or to every place सब जगह, सर्वत्र *I've looked everywhere, but I still can't find it.*

**eve-teasing** /ˌiːvˈtiːzɪŋ ˌईव़्ˈटीज़िङ्/ *noun* [U] the act of publicly troubling and annoying women by using offensive language and behaviour महिलाओं से सार्वजनिक दुराचार (प्राय: अपमानजनक भाषा एवं व्यवहार द्वारा) *Women must stand up against eve-teasing.* ▶ **eve-teaser** /ˌiːvˈtiːzə(r) ˌईव़्ˈटीज़(र्)/ *noun* [C] महिलाओं से सार्वजनिक रूप से दुराचार करने वाला पुरुष

**evict** /ɪˈvɪkt इˈव़िक्ट्/ *verb* [T] to force sb (officially) to leave the house or land which he/she is renting मकान या ज़मीन से किसी (किराएदार) को (क़ानूनन)

बेदख़ल करना *They were evicted for not paying the rent.* ▶ **eviction** *noun* [C, U] बेदख़ली, निष्कासन

**evidence** /ˈevɪdəns ˈएविडन्स् / *noun* [U] **evidence (of/for sth); evidence that...** the facts, signs, etc. that make you believe that sth is true सबूत, साक्ष्य, गवाही *There was not enough evidence to prove him guilty.* ○ *Her statement to the police was **used in evidence** against him.* ○ *The witnesses to the accident will be asked to **give evidence** in court.*

NOTE **Evidence** अगणनीय है। यदि एक अदद गवाही या सबूत की बात करनी हो तो **piece** का (भी) प्रयोग होता है—*One **piece of evidence** is not enough to prove somebody guilty.*

IDM **(to be) in evidence** that you can see; present in a place जो दिखाई पड़े, दृष्टिगोचर; (किसी स्थान पर) उपस्थित *When we arrived there was no ambulance in evidence.*

**evident** /ˈevɪdənt ˈएविडन्ट् / *adj.* clear (to the eye or mind); obvious स्पष्ट (दीखने में या सोच में); सुस्पष्ट, प्रकट *It was evident that the damage was very serious.*

**evidently** /ˈevɪdəntli ˈएविडन्ट्लि / *adv.* **1** clearly; that can be easily seen or understood स्पष्ट रूप से; जो आसानी से दिखाई दे या समझ में आए *She was evidently extremely shocked at the news.* **2** according to what people say आम मत के अनुसार स्पष्ट रूप से *Evidently he has decided to leave.*

**evil**[1] /ˈiːvl ˈईव्ल् / *adj.* morally bad; causing trouble or harming people बुरा, दुष्ट, पापी; लोगों को दुखी करने वाला *In the play Duryodhan is portrayed as an evil king.*

**evil**[2] /ˈiːvl ˈईव्ल् / *noun* [C, U] a force that causes bad or harmful things to happen बुराई, दुष्टता *The play is about the good and evil in all of us.* ○ *Drugs and alcohol are two of the evils of modern society.*

IDM **the lesser of two evils** ➪ **lesser** देखिए।

**evocative** /ɪˈvɒkətɪv इˈव़ॉकटिव् / *adj.* **evocative (of sth)** making you think of or remember a strong image or feeling, in a pleasant way प्रिय रूप से प्रबल छवि या अनुभव का स्मरण कराते हुए *evocative smells/sounds/music* ○ *Her book is wonderfully evocative of village life.*

**evoke** /ɪˈvəʊk इˈव़ोक् / *verb* [T] (*formal*) to produce a memory, feeling, etc. in sb (किसी में) स्मृति, अनुभूति आदि को जगाना *For me, that music always evokes hot summer evenings.* ○ *Her novel evoked a lot of interest.*

**evolution** /ˌiːvəˈluːʃn; ˌev- ˌईव़ˈलूशन्; ˌएव- / *noun* [U] **1** the development of plants, animals, etc. over many thousands of years from simple early forms to more advanced ones कालक्रम से सजीवों का विकास *Darwin's Theory of Evolution* **2** the gradual process of change and development of sth परिवर्तन और विकास की क्रमिक प्रक्रिया *Political evolution is a slow process.*

**evolve** /iˈvɒlv इˈव़ॉल्व़् / *verb* **1** [I, T] (*formal*) to develop or to make sth develop gradually, from a simple to a more advanced form सरल-साधारण से उच्चतर-जटिल रूपों में क्रमशः विकसित होना या करना *His style of painting has evolved gradually over the past 20 years.* **2 evolve (from sth)** (used about plants, animals, etc.) to develop over many thousands of years from simple forms to more advanced ones (पौधे, पशु आदि का) हज़ारों वर्षों के दौरान सरल से जटिल और उच्चतर रूपों में विकसित होना

**ewe** /juː यू / *noun* [C] a female sheep मादा भेड़ ➪ **sheep** पर नोट तथा चित्र देखिए।

**ex-** /eks एक्स् / *prefix* (*in nouns*) former भूतपूर्व, पूर्व *ex-wife* ○ *ex-president*

**exacerbate** /ɪgˈzæsəbeɪt इग्ˈज़ैसबेट् / *verb* [T] (*formal*) to make sth worse, especially a disease or problem बिगाड़ देना (विशेषतः रोग या समस्या को) ✪ पर्याय **aggravate** ▶ **exacerbation** /ɪgˌzæsəˈbeɪʃn इग्ˌज़ैसˈबेशन् / *noun* [U, C] बिगाड़, उग्रता

**exact**[1] /ɪgˈzækt इग्ˈज़ैक्ट् / *adj.* **1** (completely) correct; accurate (बिलकुल) सही; यथार्थ, त्रुटिहीन *He's in his mid-fifties. Well, 56 **to be exact**.* ○ *She's **the exact opposite** of her sister.* **2** able to work in a way that is completely accurate एकदम सही रूप से कार्य करने में सक्षम *You need to be very exact when you calculate the costs.* ▶ **exactness** *noun* [U] विशुद्धता

**exact**[2] /ɪgˈzækt इग्ˈज़ैक्ट् / *verb* [T] (*formal*) **exact sth (from sb)** to demand and get sth from sb (किसी से) कुछ माँगना और उसे पा लेना; वसूल करना

**exacting** /ɪgˈzæktɪŋ इग्ˈज़ैक्टिङ् / *adj.* needing a lot of care and attention; difficult बहुत सावधानी और ध्यान की अपेक्षा वाला; कठिन, श्रमसाध्य *exacting work*

**exactly** /ɪgˈzæktli इग्ˈज़ैक्ट्लि / *adv.* **1** (used to emphasize that sth is correct in every way) just (किसी बात के सही होने पर बल देने के लिए प्रयुक्त) एकदम, बिलकुल *You've arrived at exactly the right moment.* ○ *I found exactly what I wanted.* **2** used to ask for, or give, completely correct information एकदम ठीक जानकारी माँगने या देने के लिए प्रयुक्त *He took exactly one hour to finish.* ✪ पर्याय **precisely 3** (*spoken*) (used for agreeing with a statement) yes; you are right (किसी बात से सहमत होने

के लिए प्रयुक्त) हाँ; आप ठीक कहते हैं *'I don't think she's old enough to travel on her own.' 'Exactly.'*

IDM **not exactly** (*spoken*) **1** (used when you are saying the opposite of what you really mean) not really; not at all (जब आप अपनी मंशा से उलटी बात कह बैठें) नहीं, ऐसी बात नहीं; बिलकुल नहीं *He's not exactly the most careful driver I know.* **2** (used when you are correcting sth that sb has said) जब दूसरे की (ग़लत) बात को काटकर सही बात कहनी हो *'So you think I'm wrong?' 'No, not exactly, but....'*

**exaggerate** /ɪgˈzædʒəreɪt इग्ˈज़ैजरेट्/ *verb* [I, T] to make sth seem larger, better, worse, etc. than it really is (किसी बात को) बढ़ा-चढ़ा कर कहना *Don't exaggerate. I was only two minutes late, not twenty.* ○ *The problems have been greatly exaggerated.* ▶ **exaggeration** /ɪgˌzædʒəˈreɪʃn इग्ˌज़ैजˈरेश्न्/ *noun* [C, U] अतिशयोक्ति *It's rather an exaggeration to say that all the students are lazy.*

**exalt** /ɪgˈzɔːlt इग्ˈज़ॉल्ट्/ *verb* [T] (*formal*) **1** to make somebody rise to a higher rank or position पद या स्तर में ऊँचा करना; उन्नत करना *He was exalted to the post of a general.* ○ *His influence helped him get an exalted position in the ministry of defense.* **2** to praise sb/sth a lot व्यक्ति या वस्तु की अत्यधिक प्रशंसा करना

**exam** /ɪgˈ zæm इग्ˈजैम्/ (*formal* **examination**) *noun* [C] a written, spoken or practical test of what you know or can do परीक्षा (लिखित, मौखिक या प्रायोगिक) *an English exam* ○ *the exam results* ○ ***to/take/sit an exam*** ○ ***to pass/fail an exam***

NOTE शब्द **test, exam** से कम औपचारिक है। **Test** का स्तर **exam** के स्तर से प्रायः कम होता है।

**examination** /ɪgˌzæmɪˈneɪʃn इग्ˌज़ैमिˈनेश्न्/ *noun* **1** [C, U] the act of looking at sth carefully, especially to see if there is anything wrong or to find the cause of a problem सावधानीपूर्वक जाँच, बारीक छानबीन, तहक़ीक़ात *On close examination, it was found that the passport was false.* ○ *a medical examination* **2** [C] (*formal*) = **exam**

**examine** /ɪgˈzæmɪn इग्ˈज़ैमिन्/ *verb* [T] **1** to consider or study an idea, a subject, etc. very carefully बहुत सावधानी से किसी विषय, धारणा आदि पर विचार करना *These theories will be examined in more detail later on in the lecture.* **2 examine sb/sth (for sth)** to look at sb/sth carefully in order to find out sth (किसी वस्तु की खोज में) किसी की सावधानी से छानबीन करना *The detective examined the room for clues.* **3** (*formal*) **examine sb (in/on sth)** to test what sb knows or can do किसी के ज्ञान या योग्यता की परीक्षा लेना *You will be examined on everything that has been studied in the course.*

**examiner** /ɪgˈzæmɪnə(r) इग्ˈज़ैमिन(र्)/ *noun* [C] a person who tests sb in an exam परीक्षक

**example** /ɪgˈzɑːmpl इग्ˈज़ाम्प्ल्/ *noun* [C] **1 an example (of sth)** something such as an object, a fact or a situation which shows, explains or supports what you say उदाहरण, मिसाल *This is **a typical example of** a Mughal house.* **2 an example (to sb)** a person or thing or a type of behaviour that is good and should be copied आदर्श व अनुकरणीय (व्यक्ति, वस्तु या आचरण) *Raju's bravery should be an example to us all.*

IDM **follow sb's example/lead** ➪ **follow** देखिए।

**for example; e.g.** used for giving a fact, situation, etc., which explains or supports what you are talking about उदाहरणार्थ, मिसाल के तौर पर *In many countries, India, for example, family life is much more important than in Europe.*

**set a(n) (good/bad) example (to sb)** to behave in a way that should/should not be copied अच्छा या बुरा उदाहरण पेश करना *Parents should always take care when crossing roads in order to set a good example to their children.*

**exasperate** /ɪgˈzæspəreɪt इग्ˈज़ैस्परेट्/ *verb* [T] to make sb angry; to annoy sb very much (किसी को) क्रोधित करना; बहुत अधिक परेशान करना *She was exasperated by the lack of progress.* ▶ **exasperating** *adj.* क्रोधजनक, आवेशकर, क्षोभकारी *an exasperating problem* ▶ **exasperation** /ɪgˌzæspəˈreɪʃn इग्ˌज़ैस्पˈरेश्न्/ *noun* [U] आवेश, उत्तेजना, क्षोभ *She finally threw the book across the room **in exasperation**.*

**excavate** /ˈekskəveɪt ˈएक्स्कवेट्/ *verb* [I, T] to dig in the ground to look for old objects or buildings that have been buried for a long time; to find sth by digging in this way ज़मीन में चिरकाल से दबी वस्तुओं के लिए खुदाई करना; खुदाई से कुछ प्राप्त करना *An ancient building has been excavated in a valley near the village.* ▶ **excavation** /ˌekskəˈveɪʃn ˌएक्सकˈव़ेश्न्/ *noun* [C, U] खुदाई, खनन, उत्खनन *Excavations on the site have revealed Harappan artefacts.*

**excavator** /ˈekskəveɪtə(r) ˈएक्स्कव़ेट(र्)/ *noun* [C] **1** a large machine that is used for digging and moving earth खुदाई करने और मिट्टी हटाने की मशीन **2** a person who digs in the ground to look for old buildings and objects खुदाई करने वाला व्यक्ति; खनक, उत्खनक

**exceed** /ɪkˈsiːd इक्ˈसीड्/ *verb* [T] **1** to be more than a particular number or amount संख्या या मात्रा विशेष से अधिक हो जाना *The weight of the bag should not exceed 20 kilos.* **2** to do more than the law, a rule, an order, etc. allows you to do क़ानूनी मर्यादा, नियम, आज्ञा आदि का उल्लंघन करना *He was stopped by the police for exceeding the speed limit* (= driving faster than is allowed). ➪ **excess** और **excessive** देखिए।

**exceedingly** /ɪkˈsiːdɪŋli इक्ˈसीडिङ्लि/ *adv.* (*formal*) very अत्यधिक *an exceedingly difficult problem*

**excel** /ɪkˈsel इक्ˈसेल्/ *verb* (**excelling; excelled**) (*formal*) **1** [I] **excel (in/at sth/doing sth)** to be very good at doing sth किसी काम में विशेष कुशल होना *Sonia excels at sports.* **2** [T] **excel yourself** to do sth even better than you usually do किसी काम को सामान्य की अपेक्षा बेहतर ढंग से करना *Tarun's cooking is always good but this time he really excelled himself.*

**excellence** /ˈeksələns ˈएक्सलन्स्/ *noun* [U] the quality of being very good श्रेष्ठता, उत्कृष्टता *The head teacher said that she wanted the school to be a centre of academic excellence.*

**Excellency** /ˈeksələnsi ˈएक्सलन्सि/ *noun* [C] (*pl.* **Excellencies**) **(His/Her/Your) Excellency** a title used when talking to or about sb who has a very important official position as the representative of his or her own country in another country **(an ambassador)** अन्य देश के प्रतिनिधि (राजदूत आदि) के लिए प्रयुक्त सम्मानसूचक शब्द; महामहिम

**excellent** /ˈeksələnt ˈएक्सलन्ट्/ *adj.* very good; of high quality बहुत बढ़िया; उच्च स्तर का, उत्कृष्ट *He speaks excellent French.* ▸ **excellently** *adv.* बढ़िया ढंग से, उत्कृष्ट रीति से

**except¹** /ɪkˈsept इक्ˈसेप्ट्/ *prep.* **except (for) sb/sth; except that...** not including sb/sth; apart from the fact that को छोड़कर; सिवा इसके *The museum is open every day except Mondays.* ○ *It was a good hotel except that it was rather noisy.*

**except²** /ɪkˈsept इक्ˈसेप्ट्/ *verb* [T] (*formal*) **except sb/sth (from sth)** (*usually passive*) to leave sb/sth out; to not include sb/sth को छूट मिलना; को छोड़ देना (शामिल न करना) *Nobody is excepted from helping with the housework.* ▸ **excepting** *prep.* सिवा, को छोड़कर *I swim every day excepting Sundays.*

**exception** /ɪkˈsepʃn इक्ˈसेप्शन्/ *noun* [C] a person or thing that is not included in a general statement (व्यक्ति या वस्तु) अपवाद *Everybody was poor as a student and I was* ***no exception***.

IDM **make an exception (of sb/sth)** to treat sb/sth differently किसी को विशेष छूट देना, का ख़ास ख़्याल रखना *We don't usually allow children under 14 but we'll make an exception in your case.*

**with the exception of** except for; apart from के सिवा; के अतिरिक्त *He has won every major tennis championship with the exception of Wimbledon.*

**without exception** in every case; including everyone/everything हर हालत में; बिना किसी अपवाद के *Everybody without exception must take the test.*

**exceptional** /ɪkˈsepʃənl इक्ˈसेप्शनल्/ *adj.* very unusual; unusually good बहुत असाधारण; असामान्य रूप से अच्छा *You will only be allowed to leave early in exceptional circumstances.* ➪ **unexceptional** देखिए। ▸ **exceptionally** /-ʃənəli -शनलि/ *adv.* असाधारण रूप से *The past year has been exceptionally difficult for us.*

**excerpt** /ˈeksɜːpt ˈएक्सर्प्ट्/ *noun* [C] a short piece taken from a book, film, piece of music, etc. किसी पुस्तक, फ़िल्म आदि से लिया गया कोई अंश; उद्धरण

**excess¹** /ɪkˈses इक्ˈसेस्/ *noun* [*sing.*] **an excess (of sth)** more of sth than is necessary or usual; too much of sth ज़रूरत या सामान्य से अधिक; अत्यधिक *An excess of fat in your diet can lead to heart disease.*

IDM **in excess of** more than (किसी से) अधिक (मात्रा या संख्या में) *Her debts are in excess of Rs 10,000.* ➪ **exceed** verb देखिए।

**excess²** /ˈekses ˈएक्सेस्/ *adj.* (*only before a noun*) more than is usual or allowed; extra सामान्य या नियमानुकूल से अधिक; अतिरिक्त *Cut any excess fat off the meat.* ➪ **exceed** verb देखिए।

**excessive** /ɪkˈsesɪv इक्ˈसेसिव्/ *adj.* too much; too great or extreme अत्यधिक; बहुत अधिक *He was driving at excessive speed when he crashed.* ▸ **excessively** *adv.* अत्यधिक

**exchange¹** /ɪksˈtʃeɪndʒ इक्सˈचेन्ज्/ *noun* **1** [C, U] giving or receiving sth in return for sth else विनिमय, अदला-बदली *a useful exchange of information* ○ *We can offer free accommodation* ***in exchange for*** *some help in the house.* **2** [U] the relation in value between kinds of money used in different countries एक देश की मुद्रा का दूसरे देश की मुद्रा से मूल्यगत संबंध; विनिमय-संबंध *What's the* ***exchange rate*** *for dollars?* ○ *Most of the country's* ***foreign exchange*** *comes from oil.* ➪ **Stock Exchange** देखिए। **3** [C] a visit by a group of students or teachers to another country and a return visit by a similar group from that country दो देशों के छात्रों और अध्यापकों का एक दूसरे के देश में जाना *She went on an exchange to Germany when she was sixteen.* **4** [C] an angry conversation or argument क्रोधपूर्ण बातचीत या बहस; झड़प *She ended up having a* ***heated exchange*** *with her neighbours about the noise the night before.*

**exchange**[2] /ɪksˈtʃeɪndʒ इक्स्ˈचेन्ज् / *verb* [T] **exchange A for B; exchange sth (with sb)** to give or receive sth in return for sth else की अदला-बदली करना *I would like to exchange this skirt for a bigger size.* ○ *They exchanged glances* (= they looked at each other).

**exchequer** /ɪksˈtʃekə(r) इक्स्ˈचेक(र्) / *noun* [*sing.*] (*usually* **the Exchequer**) the government department that controls public money in Britain and some countries ब्रिटेन तथा कुछ अन्य देशों में राजस्व विभाग ➪ **Treasury** देखिए। **2** the public or national supply of money धन की राष्ट्रीय या सार्वजनिक आपूर्ति *The indefinite strike by the transporters caused a massive loss to the exchequer.*

**excise** /ˈeksaɪz ˈएक्साइज़् / *noun* [U] a government tax on certain goods that are produced or sold inside a country, for example, tobacco, alcohol, etc. सरकार द्वारा देश के भीतर कुछ वस्तुओं के उत्पादन और बिक्री पर लगाया गया कर ➪ **customs** देखिए।

**excitable** /ɪkˈsaɪtəbl इक्ˈसाइटब्ल् / *adj.* easily excited सहज उत्तेजित होने वाला; उत्तेजनशील

**excite** /ɪkˈsaɪt इक्ˈसाइट् / *verb* [T] **1** to make sb feel happy and enthusiastic or nervous किसी की भावनाओं (प्रसन्नता या अधीरता) को उभारना, किसी का भावोत्तेजन करना *Don't excite the baby too much or we'll never get him off to sleep.* **2** to make sb react in a particular way विशेष प्रकार की प्रतिक्रिया उत्पन्न करना *The programme excited great interest.*

**excited** /ɪkˈsaɪtɪd इक्ˈसाइटिड् / *adj.* **excited (about/at/by sth)** feeling or showing happiness and enthusiasm; not calm उत्तेजित, व्यग्र; अधीर *Are you getting excited about your holiday?* ○ *We're all very excited at the thought of moving house.* ▶ **excitedly** *adv.* उत्तेजित होकर

**excitement** /ɪkˈsaɪtmənt इक्ˈसाइट्मन्ट् / *noun* [U] the state of being excited, especially because sth interesting is happening or will happen उत्तेजना, उत्साहमयी प्रसन्नता *There was **great excitement** as the winner's name was announced.* ○ *The match was **full of excitement**.*

**exciting** /ɪkˈsaɪtɪŋ इक्ˈसाइटिङ् / *adj.* causing strong feelings of pleasure and interest उत्तेजक *That's very exciting news.* ○ *Bangalore is one of the most exciting cities in India.*

**exclaim** /ɪkˈskleɪm इक्ˈस्क्लेम् / *verb* [I, T] to say sth suddenly and loudly because you are surprised, angry, etc. भावावेश में अचानक चिल्लाकर कुछ कहना *'I just don't believe it!' he exclaimed.*

**exclamation** /ˌekskləˈmeɪʃn ˌएक्स्क्लˈमेश्न् / *noun* [C] a short sound, word or phrase that you say suddenly because of a strong emotion, pain, etc. भावावेश में प्रकट उद्‌गार, चिल्ला पड़ना, चीत्कार *'Ouch!' is an exclamation.* ✪ पर्याय **interjection**

**exclamation mark** (*AmE* **exclamation point**) *noun* [C] a mark (!) that is written after an exclamation विस्मयादिबोधक चिह्न (!)

**exclude** /ɪkˈskluːd इक्ˈस्क्लूड् / *verb* [T] (*not used in the continuous tenses*) **1** to leave out; not include छोड़ देना; शामिल न करना *The price excludes all extras such as drinks or excursions.* **2 exclude sb/sth (from sth)** to prevent sb/sth from entering a place or taking part in sth किसी का किसी स्थान पर प्रवेश या किसी गतिविधि में भाग लेने पर प्रतिबंध होना *Women are excluded from the temple.* ○ *Mohan was excluded from the game for cheating.* ✪ विलोम **include** **3** to decide that sth is not possible किसी बात की संभावना को नकारना *The police had **excluded the possibility** that the child had run away.*

**excluding** /ɪkˈskluːdɪŋ इक्ˈस्क्लूडिङ् / *prep.* leaving out; without को छोड़कर; के बिना *Lunch costs Rs 50 per person excluding drinks.* ✪ विलोम **including**

**exclusion** /ɪkˈskluːʒn इक्ˈस्क्लूश़न् / *noun* [U] keeping or leaving sb/sth out व्यक्ति या वस्तु को छोड़ देना या बाहर रखना; अलहदमी

**exclusive**[1] /ɪkˈskluːsɪv इक्ˈस्क्लूसिव् / *adj.* **1** (*only before a noun*) only to be used by or given to one person, group, etc.; not to be shared केवल एक व्यक्ति, समूह आदि के उपयोग के लिए; अन्य के लिए नहीं, अनन्य *This car is for the Director's exclusive use.* **2** expensive and not welcoming people who are thought to be of a lower social class महँगा और निम्नतर वर्ग के लोगों की पहुँच से बाहर *an exclusive restaurant* ○ *a flat in an exclusive part of the city* **3 exclusive of sb/sth** not including sb/sth; without बिना शामिल किए; के बिना *Lunch costs Rs 70 per person exclusive of drinks.*

**exclusive**[2] /ɪkˈskluːsɪv इक्ˈस्क्लूसिव् / *noun* [C] a newspaper story that is given to and published by only one newspaper केवल किसी एक समाचारपत्र को उपलब्ध कराया गया और उसी में छपने वाला लेख आदि

**exclusively** /ɪkˈskluːsɪvli इक्ˈस्क्लूसिव्लि / *adv.* only; not involving anyone/anything else केवल; किसी अन्य को सम्मिलित न करते हुए *The swimming pool is reserved exclusively for members of the club.*

**excommunicate** /ˌekskəˈmju:nɪkeɪt ˌएक्सक ˈम्यूनिकेट् / *verb* [T] **excommunicate sb (for sth)** to punish sb by officially not allowing them to remain a member of a Christian Church, especially the Roman Catholic Church प्रायः दंडस्वरुप ईसाई चर्च (विशेषतः रोमन कैथोलिक चर्च) की सदस्यता से बहिष्कृत करना *The Church excommunicated him for blasphemy.* ▶ **excommunication** /ˌekskəˌmju:nɪˈkeɪʃn ˌएक्सक ˌम्यूनि ˈकेशन् / *noun* [C, U] चर्च से बहिष्करण

**excrement** /ˈekskrɪmənt ˈएक्स्क्रिमन्ट् / *noun* [U] (*formal*) the solid waste material that you get rid of when you go to the toilet मल, विष्ठा ✪ पर्याय **faeces**

**excrete** /ɪkˈskri:t इक् ˈस्क्रीट् / *verb* [T] (*formal*) to get rid of solid waste material from the body मल त्याग करना ▶ **excretion** /ɪkˈskri:ʃn इक् ˈस्क्रीशन् / *noun* [U] मलत्याग

**excruciating** /ɪkˈskru:ʃieɪtɪŋ इक् ˈस्क्रूशिएटिङ् / *adj.* extremely painful बहुत अधिक दर्द करने वाला

**excursion** /ɪkˈskɜ:ʃn इक् ˈस्कशन् / *noun* [C] a short journey or trip that a group of people make for pleasure सैर-सपाटा *to **go on an excursion** to the seaside* ➪ **travel** पर नोट देखिए।

**excusable** /ɪkˈskju:zəbl इक् ˈस्क्यूज़बल् / *adj.* that you can forgive क्षमा करने योग्य, माफ़ी के लायक, क्षम्य *an excusable mistake* ✪ विलोम **inexcusable**

**excuse**[1] /ɪkˈskju:s इक् ˈस्क्यूस् / *noun* [C] **an excuse (for sth/doing sth)** a reason (that may or may not be true) that you give in order to explain your behaviour सफ़ाई, बहाना *There's **no excuse for** rudeness.* ○ *to **make an excuse***

**excuse**[2] /ɪkˈskju:z इक् ˈस्क्यूज़् / *verb* [T] **1 excuse sb/sth (for sth/for doing sth)** to forgive sb for sth he/she has done wrong that is not very serious छोटी-मोटी ग़लती माफ़ करना *Please excuse the interruption but I need to talk to you.* **2** to explain sb's bad behaviour and make it seem less bad अशिष्ट आचरण की सफ़ाई देना, आचरण की अशिष्टता को कम कर के बताना *Nothing can excuse such behaviour.* **3 excuse sb (from sth)** to free sb from a duty, responsibility, etc. किसी को ज़िम्मेदारी से मुक्त करना *She excused herself* (= asked if she could leave) *and left the meeting early.*

> **NOTE** **Excuse me** का प्रयोग किसी को टोकने या किसी अपरिचित व्यक्ति से बातचीत शुरु करने के लिए किया जाता है—*Excuse me, can you tell me the way to the station?* अमेरिकी अंग्रेज़ी और कभी-कभी ब्रिटिश अंग्रेज़ी में किसी बात पर माफ़ी माँगने के लिए **excuse me** का प्रयोग किया जाता है—*Did I tread on your toe? Excuse me.*

**execute** /ˈeksɪkju:t ˈएक्सिक्यूट् / *verb* [T] **1 execute sb (for sth)** (*usually passive*) to kill sb as an official punishment क़ानूनन मृत्युदंड देना *He was executed for murder.* **2** (*formal*) to perform a task, etc. or to put a plan into action किसी कार्य को संपादित करना या योजना को क्रियान्वित करना ▶ **execution** /ˌeksɪˈkju:ʃn ˌएक्सि ˈक्यूशन् / *noun* [C, U] मृत्युदंड, फाँसी; अमल, लागूकरण

**executioner** /ˌeksɪˈkju:ʃənə(r) ˌएक्सि ˈक्यूशन(र्) / *noun* [C] a person whose job is to execute criminals फाँसी देने वाला; जल्लाद

**executive**[1] /ɪgˈzekjətɪv इग् ˈज़ेक्यटिव् / *adj.* **1** (used in connection with people in business, government, etc.) concerned with managing, making plans, decisions, etc. (व्यापार, शासन आदि से जुड़े व्यक्तियों के लिए प्रयुक्त) प्रबंध-कार्य, योजना-निर्माण आदि से संबंधित; कार्यकारी, कार्यनिष्पादनपरक *an executive director of the company* ○ *executive decisions/jobs/duties* **2** (used about goods, buildings, etc.) designed to be used by important business people महत्त्वपूर्ण व्यापारियों या अधिकारियों द्वारा प्रयुक्त (वस्तुसामग्री, भवन आदि) *an executive briefcase*

**executive**[2] /ɪgˈzekjətɪv इग् ˈज़ेक्यटिव् / *noun* **1** [C] a person who has an important position as a manager of a business or organization कार्यकारी अधिकारी, प्रबंधक *She's a senior executive in a computer company.* **2** [*sing.*] the group of people who are in charge of an organization or a company किसी संस्था का प्रबंधक वर्ग

**exemplary** /ɪgˈzempləri इग् ˈज़ेम्प्लरि / *adj.* very good; that can be an example to other people श्रेष्ठ, बहुत अच्छा; औरों के लिए आदर्श *exemplary behaviour*

**exemplify** /ɪgˈzemplɪfaɪ इग् ˈज़ेम्प्लिफ़ाइ / *verb* [T] (*pres. part.* **exemplifying;** *3rd person sing. pres.* **exemplifies;** *pt, pp* **exemplified**) to be a typical example of sth किसी का विशिष्ट उदाहरण होना

**exempt**[1] /ɪgˈzempt इग् ˈज़ेम्प्ट् / *adj.* (*not before a noun*) **exempt (from sth)** free from having to do sth or pay for sth किसी बाध्यता से मुक्त *Children under 16 are exempt from dental charges.* ▶ **exemption** /ɪgˈzempʃn इग् ˈज़ेम्प्शन् / *noun* [C, U] मुक्ति, छूट

**exempt**[2] /ɪgˈzempt इग् ˈज़ेम्प्ट् / *verb* [T] (*formal*) **exempt sb/sth (from sth)** to say officially that sb does not have to do sth or pay for sth आधिकारिक रूप से छूट देना

**exercise**[1] /ˈeksəsaɪz ˈएक्ससाइज़् / *noun* **1** [U] physical or mental activity that keeps you healthy and strong व्यायाम, कसरत *The doctor advised him to **take regular exercise**.* 2 [C] (*usually pl.*) a movement or activity that you do in order to stay healthy or to become skilled at sth व्यायाम क्रिया *breathing/stretching/relaxation exercises* 3 [C] a piece of work that is intended to help you learn or practise sth अभ्यास *an exercise on phrasal verbs* 4 [C] **an exercise in sth** an activity or a series of actions that have a particular aim उद्देश्य विशेष से किया गया प्रयोग *The project is an exercise in getting the best results at a low cost.* 5 [U] (*formal*) **exercise of sth** the use of sth, for example a power, right, etc. (किसी का) व्यवहार, इस्तेमाल *the exercise of patience/judgement/discretion* 6 [C, *usually pl.*] a series of activities by soldiers to practise fighting युद्धाभ्यास *military exercises*

**exercise**[2] /ˈeksəsaɪz ˈएक्ससाइज़् / *verb* 1 [I] to do some form of physical activity in order to stay fit and healthy शारीरिक व्यायाम करना *It is important to exercise regularly.* 2 [T] to make use of sth, for example a power, right, etc. (सत्ता, अधिकार आदि का) इस्तेमाल करना *You should exercise your right to vote.*

**exert** /ɪɡˈzɜːt इग्ˈज़ट् / *verb* [T] 1 to make use of sth, for example influence, strength, etc., to affect sb/sth किसी वस्तु को प्रयोग में लाना (जैसे प्रभाव, ताक़त आदि) *Parents exert a powerful influence on their children's opinions.* 2 **exert yourself** to make a big effort सामान्य से अधिक प्रयत्न करना *You won't make any progress if you don't exert yourself a bit more.*

**exertion** /ɪɡˈzɜːʃn इग्ˈज़श्न् / *noun* [U, C] using your body in a way that takes a lot of effort; sth that you do that makes you tired अत्यधिक शारीरिक प्रयास; थकाने वाला काम *At his age physical exertion was dangerous.*

**exhale** /eksˈheɪl एक्स्ˈहेल् / *verb* [I, T] (*formal*) to breathe out the air, smoke, etc. in your lungs साँस, धुआँ, को फेफड़ों से बाहर निकालना ✪ विलोम **inhale** ▸ **exhalation** /ˌekshəˈleɪʃn ˈएक्स्हˈलेश्न् / *noun* [U] बाहर साँस निकालना उत्-श्वसन

**exhaust**[1] /ɪɡˈzɔːst इग्ˈज़ॉस्ट् / *noun* 1 [U] the waste gas that comes out of a vehicle, an engine or a machine किसी वाहन, इंजन या मशीन से निकलने वाली अकृष्य या व्यर्थ गैस *car exhaust fumes/emissions* 2 [C] (*also* **exhaust pipe** *AmE* **tailpipe**) a pipe (particularly at the back of a car) through which waste gas escapes from an engine or machine कार में पीछे लगे इंजन की अकृष्य हवा निकालने वाला पाइप

**exhaust**[2] /ɪɡˈzɔːst इग्ˈज़ॉस्ट् / *verb* [T] 1 to make sb very tired बहुत थका देना *The long journey to work every morning exhausted him.* 2 to use sth up completely; to finish sth (किसी वस्तु को) पूरा-का-पूरा इस्तेमाल कर लेना; समाप्त कर देना *All the supplies of food have been exhausted.* 3 to say everything you can about a subject, etc. किसी विषय पर सब बातें कह देना *Well, I think we've exhausted that topic.*

**exhausted** /ɪɡˈzɔːstɪd इग्ˈज़ॉस्टिड् / *adj.* very tired बहुत थका हुआ; चकनाचूर

**exhausting** /ɪɡˈzɔːstɪŋ इग्ˈज़ॉस्टिङ् / *adj.* making sb very tired बहुत थकाने वाला; थकाऊ *Teaching young children is exhausting work.*

**exhaustion** /ɪɡˈzɔːstʃən इग्ˈज़ॉस्चन् / *noun* [U] the state of being extremely tired अत्यंत थक जाने की स्थिति, गहरी थकान

**exhaustive** /ɪɡˈzɔːstɪv इग्ˈज़ॉस्टिव् / *adj.* including everything possible संपूर्ण, सर्वांगीण *This list is certainly not exhaustive.*

**exhibit**[1] /ɪɡˈzɪbɪt इग्ˈज़िबिट् / *noun* [C] an object that is shown in a museum, etc. or as a piece of evidence in a court of law संग्रहालय में प्रदर्शित या कचहरी में प्रमाण के रूप में दी गई वस्तु

**exhibit**[2] /ɪɡˈzɪbɪt इग्ˈज़िबिट् / *verb* [T] 1 to show sth in a public place for people to enjoy or to give them information किसी वस्तु का सार्वजनिक प्रदर्शन करना *His paintings have been exhibited in the local art gallery.* 2 (*formal*) to show clearly that you have a particular quality, feeling. etc. किसी भाव आदि को प्रकट करना *The refugees are exhibiting signs of exhaustion and stress.*

**exhibition** /ˌeksɪˈbɪʃn ˌएक्सिˈबिश्न् / *noun* 1 [C] a collection of objects, for example works of art, that are shown to the public प्रदर्शनी, नुमाइश *an exhibition of photographs* ○ *Her paintings will be **on exhibition** in Mumbai for the whole of April.* 2 [C] an occasion when a particular skill is shown to the public किसी कला या कौशल का सार्वजनिक प्रदर्शन *We saw an exhibition of folk dancing last night.* 3 [*sing.*] (*formal*) the act of showing a quality, feeling, etc. किसी गुण या भाव का प्रदर्शन *The game was a superb exhibition of football at its best.*

**exhibitor** /ɪɡˈzɪbɪtə(r) इग्ˈज़िबिट(र्) / *noun* [C] a person, for example, an artist, a photographer, etc., who shows his/her work to the public कलाकार, फ़ोटोग्राफ़र आदि जो अपनी कला का सार्वजनिक प्रदर्शन करता है; प्रदर्शक

**exhilarate** /ɪɡˈzɪləreɪt इग् ˈज़िलरेट् / *verb* [T] (*usually passive*) to make sb feel very excited and happy रोमांचित और प्रसन्न करना *We felt exhilarated by our walk along the beach.* ▶ **exhilarating** *adj.* रोमांचक, आह्लादकारी ▶ **exhilaration** /ɪɡˌzɪləˈreɪʃn इग्ˌज़िलˈरेश्न् / *noun* [U] रोमांच, आह्लाद

**exhume** /eksˈhjuːm एक्स्ˈह्यूम् / *verb* [T] (*usually passive*) (*formal*) to remove a dead body from the ground especially in order to examine how the person died क़ब्र से शव को खोदकर निकालना (विशेषतः मृतक की मृत्यु का कारण पता लगाने के लिए); शवोत्खनन करना ▶ **exhumation** /ˌekshjuːˈmeɪʃn ˌएक्स्ह्यूˈमेश्न् / *noun* [U] शवोत्खनन

**exile** /ˈeksaɪl ˈएक्साइल् / *noun* **1** [U] the state of being forced to live outside your own country (especially for political reasons) देशनिकाला, निर्वासन (विशेषतः राजनीतिक आधार पर); स्वदेश छोड़कर अन्यत्र रहने की बाध्यता *They lived* ***in exile*** *in London for many years.* **2** [C] a person who is forced to live outside his/her own country (especially for political reasons) निर्वासित व्यक्ति ➪ **refugee** देखिए। ▶ **exile** *verb* [T] (*usually passive*) *After the revolution the king was exiled.*

**exist** /ɪɡˈzɪst इग्ˈज़िस्ट् / *verb* [I] **1** (*not used in the continuous tenses*) to be real; to be found in the real world; to live अस्तित्व होना; जीवित रहना *Dreams only exist in our imagination.* ○ *Fish cannot exist out of water.* **2 exist (on sth)** to manage to live जीवित रह पाना, गुज़र-बसर करना *I don't know how she exists on the wage she earns.*

**existence** /ɪɡˈzɪstəns इग्ˈज़िस्टन्स् / *noun* **1** [U] the state of existing अस्तित्व *This is the oldest human skeleton* ***in existence***. ○ *How did the universe* ***come into existence?*** **2** [*sing.*] a way of living, especially when it is difficult (कठिनाई से) गुज़ारा, जीवित रहने की स्थिति *They lead a miserable existence in a tiny flat in Mumbai.*

**existing** /ɪɡˈzɪstɪŋ इग्ˈज़िस्टिङ् / *adj.* (*only before a noun*) that is already there or being used; present प्रचलित; वर्तमान *Under the existing law you are not allowed to work in this country.*

**exit¹** /ˈeksɪt; ˈegzɪt ˈएक्सिट्; ˈएग्ज़िट् / *noun* [C] **1** a door or way out of a public building or vehicle सार्वजनिक भवन या वाहन से बाहर निकलने का दरवाज़ा या मार्ग; निकास द्वार या निकास-मार्ग *The emergency exit is at the back of the bus.* **2** the act of leaving sth चले जाना, निर्गम *If I see her coming I'll make a quick exit.* ○ *an exit visa* (= one that allows you to leave a country) ✪ विलोम **entrance** (अर्थ सं. **1** और **2** का) **3** a place where traffic can leave a road or a highway to join another road सड़क पर वह स्थान जहाँ वाहन एक सड़क या मोटरमार्ग छोड़कर अन्य पर जा सकते हैं *At the round about take the third exit.*

**exit²** /ˈeksɪt; ˈegzɪt ˈएक्सिट्; ˈएग्ज़िट् / *verb* [I, T] (*formal*) to leave a place प्रस्थान करना, विलोपन करना *He exited through the back door.* ○ *I exited the database and switched off the computer.*

**exodus** /ˈeksədəs ˈइक्सडस् / *noun* a situation in which many people leave a place at the same time एक ही समय में बहुत-से लोगों का एक स्थान को छोड़ना; सामूहिक प्रस्थान; निर्गमन

**exonerate** /ɪɡˈzɒnəreɪt इग्ˈज़ॉनरेट् / *verb* [T] (*formal*) (*usually passive*) to say officially that sb was not responsible for sth bad that happened आधिकारिक रूप से दोषमुक्त घोषित करना

**exorbitant** /ɪɡˈzɔːbɪtənt इग्ˈज़ॉबिटन्ट् / *adj.* (*formal*) (used about the cost of sth) much more expensive than it should be असाधारण रूप से महँगा

**exorcise** (*AmE* **-ize**) /ˈeksɔːsaɪz ˈएक्सॉसाइज़् / *verb* [T] **1 exorcise sth (from sth)** to make an evil spirit leave a place by special prayers or ceremonies प्रार्थना या झाड़-फूँक द्वारा भूत उतारना या भगाना *The priest was called to exorcise the ghost.* ○ *The ghost was exorcised from the bungalow.* **2** (*written*) to remove sth that is bad or painful from your mind दर्द या बुरी यादों को भूलना *She helped him in exorcising the unhappy memories from his mind.*

**exorcism** /ˈeksɔːsɪzəm ˈएक्सॉसिज़म् / *noun* [C, U] the act of forcing an evil spirit to leave a place by prayers or ceremonies भूत-प्रेत निवारण की क्रिया *There was peace in the house after the exorcism.*

**exorcist** /ˈeksɔːsɪst ˈएक्सॉसिस्ट् / *noun* [C] a person who makes spirits leave a place by prayers or ceremonies भूत-निवारक

**exoskeleton** /ˈeksəʊskelɪtn ˈएक्सोस्केलिट्न् / *noun* [C] a hard outer covering that protects the bodies of certain animals, such as insects कीट आदि सजीवों का कड़ा सुरक्षा आवरण ➪ **endoskeleton** देखिए।

**exothermic** /ˌeksəʊˈθɜːmɪk ˌएक्सोˈथमिक् / *adj.* (*technical*) (used about a chemical reaction or process) producing heat ताप उत्पादक प्रक्रिया से संबंधित ➪ **water** पर चित्र देखिए।

**exotic** /ɪɡˈzɒtɪk इग्ˈज़ॉटिक् / *adj.* unusual or interesting because it comes from a different country or culture अन्य देश या संस्कृति का होने के कारण असामान्य या आकर्षक; अन्यस्थानिक *exotic plants/animals/fruits*

**expand** /ɪkˈspænd इक्ˈस्पैन्ड् / *verb* [I, T] to become or to make sth bigger फैलना या फैलाना *Metals expand when they are heated.* ○ *We hope to expand our business this year.* ✪ विलोम **contract**

PHR V **expand on sth** to give more details of a story, plan, idea, etc. किसी कथा, योजना, विचार आदि का विस्तार करना

**expanse** /ɪkˈspæns इक्ˈस्पैन्स् / *noun* [C] a large open area (of land, sea, sky, etc.) (ज़मीन, समुद्र, आकाश का) बड़ा और खुला इलाक़ा

**expansion** /ɪkˈspænʃn इक्ˈस्पैन्शन् / *noun* [U] the action of becoming bigger or the state of being bigger than before फैलाव, विस्तार *The rapid expansion of the university has caused a lot of problems.*

**expansive** /ɪkˈspænsɪv इक्ˈस्पैन्सिव् / *adj.* (*formal*) (used about a person) talking a lot in an interesting way; friendly (व्यक्ति) खुले दिल वाला, खुशमिज़ाज, मैत्रीपूर्ण

**expatriate** /ˌeksˈpætriət ˌएक्स्ˈपैट्रिअट् / (*informal* **expat**) *noun* [C] a person who lives outside his/her own country अपने देश से बाहर रहने वाला व्यक्ति; निर्वासित व्यक्ति *Indian expatriates in America.*

**expect** /ɪkˈspekt इक्ˈस्पेक्ट् / *verb* [T] **1** to think or believe that sb/sth will come or that sth will happen (किसी की) आशा करना, प्रत्याशा करना *She was expecting a letter from the bank this morning but it didn't come.* ○ *I expect that it will rain this afternoon.* ➪ **wait**[1] पर नोट देखिए। **2 expect sth (from sb); expect sb to do sth** to feel confident that you will get sth from sb or that he/she will do what you want किसी से कुछ पाने या आपना मनचाहा करने की आशा करना *He expects a high standard of work from everyone.* ○ *Factory workers are often expected to work at nights.* **3** (*not used in the continuous tenses*) to think that sth is true or correct; to suppose किसी बात को सच या सही मानना; कल्पना करना *'Whose is this suitcase?' 'Oh it's Surya's, I expect.* ○ *'Will you be able to help me later on?'* ***'I expect so.'***

NOTE यद्यपि यह क्रिया सातत्यबोधक कालों (continuous tenses) में प्रयुक्त नहीं होती तथापि इसका (-ing) वाला वर्तमानकालिक कृदंत रूप (present participle) प्रायः दिखाई देता है—*She flung the door open, expecting to see Raghav standing there.*

**expectancy** /ɪkˈspektənsi इक्ˈस्पेक्टन्सि / *noun* [U] the state of expecting sth to happen; hope कुछ घटित होने की आशा, प्रत्याशा; अपेक्षा, उम्मीद *a look/feeling of expectancy* ➪ **life expectancy** देखिए।

**expectant** /ɪkˈspektənt इक्ˈस्पेक्टन्ट् / *adj.* **1** thinking that sth good will happen; hopeful अनुकूल घटने की आशा से युक्त; आशापूर्ण *an expectant audience* ○ *expectant faces* **2** pregnant गर्भवती *Expectant mothers need a lot of rest.* ▶ **expectantly** *adv.* आशा के साथ, आशापूर्वक

**expectation** /ˌekspekˈteɪʃn ˌएक्स्पेक्ˈटेशन् / *noun* (*formal*) **1** [U] **expectation (of sth)** the belief that sth will happen or come किसी बात की आशा *The dog was sitting under the table* ***in expectation*** *of food.* **2** [C, *usually pl.*] hope for the future भविष्य में कुछ होने की आशा या विश्वास *They had great expectations for their daughter, but she didn't really live up to them.*

IDM **against/contrary to (all) expectation(s)** very different to what was expected आशा के विपरीत

**not come up to (sb's) expectations** to not be as good as expected उम्मीद पर खरा न उतरना

**expedient** /ɪkˈspiːdiənt इक्ˈस्पीडिअन्ट् / *adj.* (*formal*) (used about an action) convenient or helpful for a purpose, but possibly not completely honest or moral (कार्य) उद्देश्यसिद्धि की दृष्टि से सुविधापूर्ण, परंतु पूर्णतया उचित या नैतिक नहीं; स्वार्थ साधक *The government decided that it was expedient not to increase taxes until after the election.* ▶ **expediency** /-ənsi -अन्सि / *noun* [U] उपयुक्तता, समयोचितता

**expedition** /ˌekspəˈdɪʃn ˌएक्स्पˈडिशन् / *noun* [C] **1** a long journey for a special purpose उद्देश्य विशेष से की गई लंबी यात्रा, अभियान; खोजयात्रा *a scientific expedition to Antarctica* **2** a short journey that you make for pleasure सैर-सपाटे का छोटा कार्यक्रम *a fishing expedition*

**expel** /ɪkˈspel इक्ˈस्पेल् / *verb* [T] (**expelling; expelled**) **1** to force sb to leave a country, school, club, etc. देश, स्कूल आदि से निकाल बाहर करना; निष्कासित करना *The government has expelled all foreign journalists.* ○ *The boy was expelled from school for smoking.* **2** to send sth out by force बलपूर्वक बाहर निकालना *to expel air from the lungs* ➪ **expulsion** noun देखिए।

**expend** /ɪkˈspend इक्ˈस्पेन्ड् / *verb* [T] (*formal*) **expend sth (on sth)** to spend or use money, time, care, etc. in doing sth किसी कार्य में धन, समय, ध्यान आदि लगाना

**expendable** /ɪkˈspendəbl इक्ˈस्पेन्डब्ल् / *adj.* (*formal*) not considered important enough to be saved जिसे बचाना महत्त्वपूर्ण न समझा जाए; उत्सर्जनीय *In a war human life is expendable.*

**expenditure** /ɪkˈspendɪtʃə(r) इक्ˈस्पेन्डिच(र्)/ *noun* [U, *sing.*] (*formal*) the act of spending money; the amount of money that is spent धन व्यय करना; व्यय की गई राशि की मात्रा *Government expenditure on education is very low.*

**expense** /ɪkˈspens इक्ˈस्पेन्स्/ *noun* **1** [C, U] the cost of sth in time or money ख़र्च, क़ीमत (समय या धन का) *Running a car is a great expense.* ○ *The movie was filmed in Kashmir **at great expense**.* **2 expenses** [*pl.*] money that is spent for a particular purpose उद्देश्य विशेष से किया गया ख़र्च *You can claim back your travelling expenses.*

IDM **at sb's expense 1** with sb paying; at sb's cost किसी अन्य के ख़र्च पर *My trip is at the company's expense.* **2** against sb, so that he/she looks silly किसी को नीचा दिखाते हुए *They were always making jokes at Raghav's expense.*

**at the expense of sth** harming or damaging sth हानि या नुक़सान पहुँचाते हुए; को खोकर या गँवाकर *He was a successful businessman, but it was at the expense of his family life.*

**expensive** /ɪkˈspensɪv इक्ˈस्पेन्सिव्/ *adj.* costing a lot of money ख़र्चीला, बहुत महँगा, क़ीमती ✪ विलोम **inexpensive** या **cheap** ▶ **expensively** *adv.* बहुत महँगे ढंग से

**experience[1]** /ɪkˈspɪəriəns इक्ˈस्पिअरिअन्स्/ *noun* **1** [U] the things that you have done in your life; the knowledge or skill that you get from seeing or doing sth जीवन में किए गए काम; अनुभव, तजुरबा *We all learn **by experience**.* ○ *She has five years' teaching experience.* ○ *I know **from experience** what will happen.* **2** [C] something that has happened to you (often something unusual or exciting) घटना जो आपके साथ घटी है (प्रायः असाधारण या रोमांचक); अनुभव *She wrote a book about her experiences in Africa.*

**experience[2]** /ɪkˈspɪəriəns इक्ˈस्पिअरिअन्स्/ *verb* [T] to have sth happen to you; to feel का अनुभव होना; को महसूस करना *to experience pleasure/pain/difficulty*

**experienced** /ɪkˈspɪəriənst इक्ˈस्पिअरिअन्स्ट्/ *adj.* having the knowledge or skill that is necessary for sth अनुभवी, तजुरबेकार *He's an experienced diver.* ✪ विलोम **inexperienced**

**experiment[1]** /ɪkˈsperɪmənt इक्ˈस्पेरिमन्ट्/ *noun* [C, U] a scientific test that is done in order to get proof of sth or new knowledge नई जानकारी या प्रमाण के लिए किया गया वैज्ञानिक प्रयोग *to carry out/perform/conduct/do an experiment* ○ *We need to prove this theory **by experiment**.* ▶ **experimentally** /-təli -टलि/ *adv.* प्रयोग द्वारा

**experiment[2]** /ɪkˈsperɪmənt इक्ˈस्पेरिमन्ट्/ *verb* [I] **experiment (on/with sth)** to do tests to see if sth works or to try to improve it किसी पर प्रयोग करना *Is it really necessary to experiment on animals?* ○ *We're experimenting with a new timetable this month.*

**experimental** /ɪkˌsperɪˈmentl इक्ˌस्पेरिˈमेन्ट्ल्/ *adj.* connected with experiments or trying new ideas प्रयोग का या की, प्रयोगशील या प्रयोगात्मक *We're still at the experimental stage with the new product.* ○ *experimental schools*

**expert** /ˈekspɜːt ˈएक्स्पट्/ *noun* [C] **an expert (at/in/on sth)** a person who has a lot of special knowledge or skill विषय का विशेषज्ञ *She's a leading expert in the field of genetics.* ○ *a computer expert* ○ *Let me try—I'm an expert at parking cars in small spaces.* ▶ **expert** *adj.* कुशल, प्रवीण, सुविज्ञ *He's an expert cook.* ○ *I think we should get expert advice on the problem.* ▶ **expertly** *adv.* विशेषज्ञतापूर्ण

**expertise** /ˌekspɜːˈtiːz ˌएक्स्पˈटीज़्/ *noun* [U] a high level of special knowledge or skill विषय की विशेषज्ञता

**expire** /ɪkˈspaɪə(r) इक्ˈस्पाइअ(र्)/ *verb* [I] (*formal*) (used about an official document, agreement, etc.) to come to the end of the time when you can use it or in which it has effect (सरकारी दस्तावेज़, करार आदि) प्रयोग की निर्धारित समयावधि का समाप्त हो जाना *My passport's expired. I'll have to renew it.* ✪ पर्याय **run out**

**expiry** /ɪkˈspaɪəri इक्ˈस्पाइअरि/ *noun* [U] the end of a period when you can use sth प्रयोग की अवधि की समाप्ति *The expiry date on this yoghurt was 20 November.*

**explain** /ɪkˈspleɪn इक्ˈस्प्लेन्/ *verb* [I, T] **explain (sth) (to sb) 1** to make sth clear or easy to understand समझना, स्पष्ट करना *She explained how I should fill in the form.* ○ *I don't understand this. Can you explain it to me?* **2** to give a reason for sth किसी बात का कारण बताना *The manager explained to the customers why the goods were late.*

IDM **explain yourself 1** to give reasons for your behaviour, especially when it has upset sb अपने आचरण की सफ़ाई देना (विशेषतः जब दूसरे को बुरा लगा हो) **2** to say what you mean in a clear way अपनी मंशा को स्पष्ट रूप से बताना

PHR V **explain sth away** to give reasons why sth is not your fault or is not important कारण बताते हुए अपनी निर्दोषता या प्रसंग के मामूलीपन को स्पष्ट करना

**explanation** /ˌekspləˈneɪʃn ˌएक्स्प्लˈनेश्न् / *noun* **1** [C, U] **an explanation (for sth)** a statement, fact or situation that gives a reason for sth किसी बात के कारण की व्याख्या; स्पष्टीकरण *He could not* ***give an explanation*** *for his behaviour.* **2** [C] a statement or a piece of writing that makes sth easier to understand व्याख्या, विवेचना, ख़ुलासा *That idea needs some explanation.*

**explanatory** /ɪkˈsplænətri इक्ˈस्प्लैनट्रि / *adj.* giving an explanation व्याख्या-युक्त, व्याख्यात्मक, स्पष्टीकरणात्मक *There are some explanatory notes at the back of the book.* ○ *Those instructions are self-explanatory* (= they don't need explaining).

**expletive** /ɪkˈspliːtɪv इक्ˈस्प्लीटिव् / *noun* [C] (*formal*) a word, especially a rude word, that you use when you are angry or in pain अपशब्द, गाली ✪ पर्याय **swear word**

**explicable** /ɪkˈsplɪkəbl; ˈeksplɪkəbl इक्ˈस्प्लिकब्ल्; ˈएक्स्प्लिकब्ल् / *adj.* that can be explained जिसे स्पष्ट किया जा सके *Manoj's strange behaviour is only explicable in terms of the stress he is under.* ✪ विलोम **inexplicable**

**explicit** /ɪkˈsplɪsɪt इक्ˈस्प्लिसिट् / *adj.* **1** clear, making sth easy to understand सुव्यक्त, समझने में सरल *I gave you explicit instructions not to touch any thing.* ○ *She was quite explicit about her feelings on the subject.* ➪ **implicit** देखिए। **2** not hiding anything एकदम प्रकट, जिसमें कुछ भी गुप्त नहीं ▶ **explicitly** *adv.* स्पष्ट रूप से *He was explicitly forbidden to stay out later than midnight.*

**explode** /ɪkˈspləʊd इक्ˈस्प्लोड् / *verb* [I, T] to burst with a loud noise धमाके से फूटना, विस्फोट होना *The army exploded the bomb at a safe distance from the houses.* ○ (*figurative*) *My father exploded* (= became very angry) *when I told him how much the car would cost to repair.* ➪ **explosion** noun देखिए।

**exploit¹** /ɪkˈsplɔɪt इक्ˈस्प्लॉइट् / *verb* [T] **1** to use sth or to treat sb unfairly for your own advantage (किसी का) शोषण करना *Some employers exploit foreign workers, making them work long hours for low pay.* **2** to develop sth or make the best use of sth किसी वस्तु को बनाना या बेहतरीन उपयोग करना *This region has been exploited for oil for fifty years.* ○ *Solar energy is a source of power that needs to be exploited more fully.* ▶ **exploitation** /ˌeksplɔɪˈteɪʃn ˌएक्स्प्लॉइˈटेश्न् / *noun* [U] शोषण, दोहन *They're making you work seven days a week? That's exploitation!*

**exploit²** /ˈeksplɔɪt ˈएक्स्प्लॉइट् / *noun* [C] something exciting or interesting that sb has done साहसिक कार्य, कारनामा

**exploration** /ˌekspləˈreɪʃn ˌएक्स्प्लˈरेश्न् / *noun* [C, U] the act of travelling around a place in order to learn about it खोजयात्रा *space exploration*

**exploratory** /ɪkˈsplɒrətri इक्ˈस्प्लॉरट्रि / *adj.* done in order to find sth out खोजपरक *The doctors are doing some exploratory tests to try and find out what's wrong.*

**explore** /ɪkˈsplɔː(r) इक्ˈस्प्लॉ(र्) / *verb* [I, T] to travel around a place, etc. in order to learn about it खोजयात्रा करना *They went on an expedition to explore the River Brahmaputra* ○ (*figurative*) *We need to explore* (= look carefully at) *all the possibilities before we decide.*

**explorer** /ɪkˈsplɔːrə(r) इक्ˈस्प्लॉर(र्) / *noun* [C] a person who travels around a place in order to learn about it खोजयात्री (व्यक्ति)

**explosion** /ɪkˈspləʊʒn इक्ˈस्प्लोश्न् / *noun* [C] **1** a sudden and extremely violent bursting विस्फोट, धमाका *Two people were killed in the explosion.* **2** a sudden dramatic increase in sth एकाएक वृद्धि *the population explosion* ➪ **explode** verb देखिए।

**explosive¹** /ɪkˈspləʊsɪv इक्ˈस्प्लोसिव् / *adj.* **1** capable of exploding and therefore dangerous विस्फोटात्मक, धमाकेदार *Hydrogen is highly explosive.* **2** causing strong feelings or having dangerous effects भावोत्तेजक या ख़तरनाक प्रभाव छोड़ने वाला

**explosive²** /ɪkˈspləʊsɪv इक्ˈस्प्लोसिव् / *noun* [C] a substance that is used for causing explosions विस्फोटक पदार्थ

**exponent** /ɪkˈspəʊnənt इक्ˈस्पोनन्ट् / *noun* [C] **1** a person who supports an idea, a **theory,** etc. and persuades others that it is good मत, वाद आदि का समर्थ और प्रचारक *She was* ***a leading exponent*** *of free trade during her political career.* **2** a person who is able to perform a particular activity with skill कला विशेष में अति निपुण व्यक्ति *the most famous exponent of the Kathak dance form* **3** (in mathematics) a small number or symbol that shows how many times a quantity must be multiplied by itself (गणितशास्त्र में) घातांक

**export¹** /ɪkˈspɔːt इक्ˈस्पॉट् / *verb* [I, T] **1** to send goods, etc. to another country, usually for sale

वस्तुओं का निर्यात करना (प्रायः बिक्री के लिए) *India exports tea and cotton.* ✪ विलोम **import** 2 (*computing*) to move information from one program to another सूचना-सामग्री का एक प्रोग्राम से दूसरे में स्थानांतरण करना

**export²** /ˈekspɔːt ˈएक्स्पॉट्/ *noun* **1** [U] sending goods to another country for sale वस्तुओं का निर्यात *Most of our goods are produced for export.* ○ *the export trade* **2** [C, *usually pl.*] something that is sent to another country for sale निर्यातित माल *What are India's main exports?* ✪ विलोम **import** ▶ **exporter** *noun* [C] निर्यातक *Japan is the largest exporter of electronic goods.* ✪ विलोम **importer**

**expose** /ɪkˈspəʊz इक्ˈस्पोज़्/ *verb* [T] **1 expose sth (to sb); expose sb/sth (as sth)** to show sth that is usually hidden; to tell sth that has been kept secret प्रायः गुप्त रहने वाली वस्तु को बाहर लाना; रहस्य खोल देना, भंडा फोड़ देना *She didn't want to expose her true feelings to her family.* ○ *The politician was exposed as a liar on TV.* **2 expose sb/sth to sth** to put sb/sth or yourself in a situation that could be difficult or dangerous किसी को या अपने को ख़तरनाक स्थिति में डालना *to be exposed to radiation/danger* **3 expose sb to sth** to give sb the chance to experience sth कुछ सीखने या अनुभव करने का अवसर पाना या देना *I like Kathak because I was exposed to it as a child.* **4** (in photography) to allow light onto the film inside a camera when taking a photograph (फ़ोटोग्राफ़ी में) फ़ोटो लेते समय कैमरे के अंदर फ़िल्म में प्रकाश का प्रवेश होने देना

**exposed** /ɪkˈspəʊzd इक्ˈस्पोज़्ड्/ *adj.* (used about a place) not protected from the wind and bad weather (स्थान) खुला, अरक्षित

**exposure** /ɪkˈspəʊʒə(r) इक्ˈस्पोश़(र्)/ *noun* **1** [U, C] the act of making sth public; the thing that is made public किसी वस्तु को प्रदर्शित करने की क्रिया; प्रदर्शित की गई वस्तु, रहस्योद्घाटन, प्रदर्शन *The new movie has been given a lot of exposure in the media.* ○ *The politician resigned because of the exposures about his private life.* **2** [U] being allowed or forced to experience sth किसी स्थिति या वस्तु के संपर्क में आने के लिए अनुमति या दबाव *Exposure to radiation is almost always harmful.* ○ *Television can give children exposure to other cultures from an early age.* **3** [U] a harmful condition when a person becomes very cold because he/she has been outside in very bad weather ख़राब मौसम में बाहर रहने के कारण रोगग्रस्त; अनाश्रयता *The climbers all died of exposure.* **4** [C] the amount of film that is used when you take one photograph एक फ़ोटो खींचने में इस्तेमाल हुई फ़िल्म *How many exposures are there on this film?*

**express¹** /ɪkˈspres इक्ˈस्प्रेस्/ *verb* [T] **1** to show sth such as a feeling or an opinion by words or actions भाव या विचार को शब्दों या कार्यों द्वारा व्यक्त करना; अभिव्यक्त करना *I found it very hard to express what I felt about her.* ○ *to express fears/concern about sth* **2 express yourself** to say or write your feelings, opinions, etc. अपने भावों, विचारों आदि को बोलकर या लिखकर व्यक्त करना *I don't think she expresses herself very well in that article.*

**express²** /ɪkˈspres इक्ˈस्प्रेस्/ *adj., adv.* **1** going or sent quickly तीव्रगामी, एक्सप्रेस *an express coach* ○ *We'd better send the parcel express if we want it to get there on time.* **2** (used about a wish, command, etc.) clearly and definitely stated (इच्छा, आदेश आदि) स्पष्ट और सुनिश्चित *It was her express wish that he should have the picture after her death.*

**express³** /ɪkˈspres इक्ˈस्प्रेस्/ (*also* **express train**) *noun* [C] a fast train that does not stop at all stations तेज़ रफ़्तार की रेलगाड़ी जो सब स्टेशनों पर नहीं रुकती; एक्सप्रेस ट्रेन

**expression** /ɪkˈspreʃn इक्ˈस्प्रेश्न्/ *noun* **1** [C, U] something that you say that shows your opinions or feelings विचारों या भावनाओं की अभिव्यक्ति *Freedom of expression is a basic human right.* ○ *an expression of gratitude/sympathy/anger* **2** [C] the look on a person's face that shows what he/she is thinking or feeling चेहरे की मुद्रा, चेहरे का भाव *He had a puzzled expression on his face.* **3** [C] a word or phrase with a particular meaning विशेष अर्थ वाला शब्द *'I'm starving' is an expression meaning 'I'm very hungry'.* ○ *a slang/an idiomatic expression*

**expressive** /ɪkˈspresɪv इक्ˈस्प्रेसिव़्/ *adj.* showing feelings or thoughts भावभरा, भावाभिव्यंजक *That is a very expressive piece of music.* ○ *Abhay has a very expressive face.* ▶ **expressively** *adv.* भावाभिव्यंजक रूप से

**expressly** /ɪkˈspresli इक्ˈस्प्रेसलि/ *adv.* **1** clearly; definitely स्पष्ट रूप से; सुनिश्चित रूप से *I expressly told you not to do that.* **2** for a special purpose; specially विशेष उद्देश्य से; विशेषकर *These scissors are expressly designed for left-handed people.*

**expressway** /ɪkˈspresweɪ इक्ˈस्प्रेस्वे/ (*AmE*) = **motorway**

**expulsion** /ɪkˈspʌlʃn इक्ˈस्पल्श्न्/ *noun* [C, U] the act of making sb leave a place or an institution किसी स्थान या संस्था से निष्कासन *There have been three expulsions from school this year.* ➪ **expel** verb देखिए।

**exquisite** /ˈekskwɪzɪt; ɪkˈskwɪzɪt ˈएक्स्क्विज़िट्; इक्ˈस्क्विज़िट्/ *adj.* extremely beautiful and pleasing अत्यंत सुंदर और प्रीतिकर *She has an exquisite face.* ○ *I think that ring is exquisite.* ▶ **exquisitely** *adv.* बहुत ख़ूबसूरती से

**ext.** *abbr.* extension number of a telephone टेलीफ़ोन की विस्तार संख्या *ext. 3492*

**extend** /ɪkˈstend इक्ˈस्टेन्ड्/ *verb* **1** [T] to make sth longer or larger (in space or time) (स्थान और समय की दृष्टि से) किसी का विस्तार करना *Could you extend your visit for a few days?* ○ *Since my injury I can't extend this leg fully* (= make it completely straight). **2** [I, T] to cover the area or period of time mentioned क्षेत्र का विस्तार होना, समयावधि में वृद्धि होना *The desert extends over a huge area of the country.* ○ *The company is planning to extend its operations into Asia.* **3** [T] (*formal*) to offer sth to sb किसी को कुछ पेश करना *to extend hospitality/a warm welcome/an invitation to sb*

**extension** /ɪkˈstenʃn इक्ˈस्टेन्श्न्/ *noun* [C] **1** an extra period of time that you are allowed for sth विशेष प्रयोजन से समयवृद्धि *I've applied for an extension to my work permit.* **2** a part that is added to a building भवन में बढ़ाया या जोड़ा गया अंश; विस्तरण *They're building an extension on the hospital.* **3** a telephone that is connected to a central telephone in a house or to a central point (**switchboard**) in a large office building मुख्य टेलीफ़ोन का एक्सटेंशन(फ़ोन) *What's your extension number?* ○ *Can I have extension 4342, please?*

**extensive** /ɪkˈstensɪv इक्ˈस्टेन्सिव्/ *adj.* **1** large in area or amount आकार या विस्तार में व्यापक, लंबा-चौड़ा या मात्रा में अधिक; विस्तृत *The house has extensive grounds.* ○ *Most of the buildings suffered extensive damage.* **2** (used about methods of farming) producing a small amount of food from a large area of land with a small amount of money and effort (कृषि के तरीक़े) जिनसे बड़े खेत में थोड़ी मेहनत और लागत से थोड़ी पैदावार होती है *extensive agriculture* ➪ **intensive** देखिए। ▶ **extensively** *adv.* बहुत अधिक

**extent** /ɪkˈstent इक्ˈस्टेन्ट्/ *noun* [U] **the extent of sth** the length, area, size or importance of sth किसी वस्तु की लंबाई, विस्तार, आकार या महत्त्व *I was amazed at the extent of his knowledge.* ○ *The* ***full extent of*** *the damage is not yet known.*

IDM **to a certain/to some extent** used to show that sth is only partly true एक सीमा तक, कुछ हद तक *I agree with you to a certain extent but there are still a lot of points I disagree with.*

**to what extent** how far; how much कहाँ तक; कितना; किस हद तक *I'm not sure to what extent I believe her.*

**exterior¹** /ɪkˈstɪəriə(r) इक्ˈस्टिअरिअ(र्)/ *adj.* on the outside बाहर का या की; बाहरी *the exterior walls of a house* ✪ विलोम **interior**

**exterior²** /ɪkˈstɪəriə(r) इक्ˈस्टिअरिअ(र्)/ *noun* [C] the outside of sth; the appearance of sb/sth बाहरी हिस्सा; चेहरा, बाहरी रूप *The exterior of the house is fine but inside it isn't in very good condition.* ○ *Despite his calm exterior, Reena suffers badly from stress.*

**exterminate** /ɪkˈstɜːmɪneɪt इक्ˈस्टमिनेट्/ *verb* [T] to kill a large group of people or animals बड़ी संख्या में लोगों और पशुओं को मार देना; संहार करना ▶ **extermination** /ɪkˌstɜːmɪˈneɪʃn इक्ˌस्टमिˈनेश्न्/ *noun* [U] विध्वंस, संहार

**external** /ɪkˈstɜːnl इक्ˈस्टन्ल्/ *adj.* **1** connected with the outside of sth बाहरी हिस्से का, बाहर स्थित, बाह्य *The cream is for external use only* (= to be used on the skin). **2** coming from another place बाहर से आने वाला; बाह्य *You will be tested by an external examiner.* ✪ विलोम **internal** ▶ **externally** /-nəli -नलि/ *adv.* बाह्य रूप से

**extinct** /ɪkˈstɪŋkt इक्ˈस्टिङ्क्ट्/ *adj.* **1** (used about a type of animal, plant, etc.) no longer existing (पशु, पौधे आदि की जाति) विलुप्त, अविद्यमान *Tigers are nearly extinct in the wild.* **2** (used about a volcano) no longer active (ज्वालामुखी) निष्क्रिय ▶ **extinction** /ɪkˈstɪŋkʃn इक्ˈस्टिङ्क्श्न्/ *noun* [U] विलोप *The giant panda is in danger of extinction.*

**extinguish** /ɪkˈstɪŋgwɪʃ इक्ˈस्टिङ्ग्विश्/ *verb* [T] (*formal*) to cause sth to stop burning (आग) बुझाना *The fire was extinguished very quickly.* ✪ पर्याय **put out** ▶ **extinguisher** = **fire extinguisher**

**extort** /ɪkˈstɔːt इक्ˈस्टॉट्/ *verb* [T] (*formal*) **extort sth (from sb)** to get sth by using threats or violence धमकियों या हिंसा द्वारा ज़बरदस्ती वसूल करना *The gang were found guilty of extorting money from small businesses.* ▶ **extortion** *noun* [U] ज़बरन वसूली

**extortionate** /ɪkˈstɔːʃənət इक्ˈस्टॉशनट्/ *adj.* (used especially about prices) much too high (क़ीमतें) बहुत ही ज़्यादा, आसमान छूती हुई; अतिशय

**extra**[1] /ˈekstrə ˈएक्स्ट्रा/ *adj., adv.* more than is usual, expected, or than exists already सामान्य, अपेक्षित या अब तक उपलब्ध से अधिक; अतिरिक्त *I'll need some extra money for the holidays.* ○ *'What size is this sweater?' 'Extra large.'* ○ *Is dessert included in the price of the meal or is it extra?* ○ *I tried to be extra nice to him yesterday because it was his birthday.*

**extra**[2] /ˈekstrə ˈएक्स्ट्रा/ *noun* [C] **1** something that costs more, or that is not normally included वस्तु जिसका दाम अलग से देना होता है *Optional extras such as colour printer, scanner and modem are available on top of the basic package.* **2** a person in a film, etc. who has a small unimportant part, for example in a crowd फ़िल्म आदि में बहुत छोटी व महत्त्वहीन भूमिका करने वाला व्यक्ति

**extra-** /ˈekstrə ˈएक्स्ट्रा/ *prefix* (*in adjectives*) **1** outside; beyond निर्धारित ढाँचे से बाहर; इतर, अलग तरह का *extramarital affair* ○ *extraterrestrial beings* **2** very; more than usual बहुत; सामान्य से अधिक, अति *extra-thin* ○ *extra-special*

**extract**[1] /ɪkˈstrækt इक्ˈस्ट्रैक्ट्/ *verb* [T] (*formal*) to take sth out, especially with difficulty किसी वस्तु को बाहर निकालना (विशेषतः कठिनाई से) *I think this tooth will have to be extracted.* ○ *I wasn't able to extract an apology from her.*

**extract**[2] /ˈekstrækt ˈएक्स्ट्रैक्ट्/ *noun* [C] a part of a book, piece of music, etc., that has often been specially chosen to show sth पुस्तक आदि से विशेष प्रयोजन से लिया गया अंश; उद्धरण *The newspaper published extracts from the controversial novel.*

**extraction** /ɪkˈstrækʃn इक्ˈस्ट्रैक्श्न्/ *noun* (*formal*) **1** [C, U] the act of taking sth out (किसी वस्तु को) बाहर निकालने की क्रिया *extraction of salt from sea water* ○ *Dentists report that children are requiring fewer extractions.* **2** [U] family origin परिवार का मूल, कुल *He's an American but he's of Italian extraction.*

**extra-curricular** /ˌekstrə kəˈrɪkjələ(r) ˌएक्स्ट्रा कˈरिक्यल(र्)/ *adj.* not part of the normal course of studies (**curriculum**) in a school or college (स्कूल, कॉलेज में) नियमित पाठ्यक्रम से अलग कोटि का; पाठ्यक्रमेतर *The school offers many extra-curricular activities such as sport, music, drama, etc.*

**extradite** /ˈekstrədaɪt ˈएक्स्ट्रडाइट्/ *verb* [T] to send a person who may be guilty of a crime from the country in which he/she is living to the country which wants to put him/her on trial for the crime भगोड़े अभियुक्त को न्याय प्रक्रिया के लिए उसके देश को सौंपना; प्रत्यर्पण करना *The suspected terrorists were captured in Belgium and extradited to India.* ▶ **extradition** /ˌekstrəˈdɪʃn ˌएक्स्ट्रˈडिश्न्/ *noun* [C, U] प्रत्यर्पण

**extraordinary** /ɪkˈstrɔːdnri इक्ˈस्ट्रॉड्न्रि/ *adj.* **1** very unusual असाधारण, अद्भुत *She has an extraordinary ability to whistle and sing at the same time.* **2** not what you would expect in a particular situation; very strange स्थिति-विशेष में अप्रत्याशित; बहुत विचित्र *That was extraordinary behaviour for a teacher!* ✪ विलोम **ordinary** ▶ **extraordinarily** /ɪkˈstrɔːdnrəli इक्ˈस्ट्रॉड्न्रलि/ *adv.* असाधारण रूप से *He was an extraordinarily talented musician.*

**extrapolate** /ɪkˈstræpəleɪt इक्ˈस्ट्रैपलेट्/ *verb* [I, T] **extrapolate (sth) (from/to sth)** (*formal*) to form an opinion or make a judgement about a situation by using facts that you know from a different situation अन्य स्थिति से संबंधित तथ्यों के आधार पर स्थिति विशेष का मूल्यांकन करना *The figures were obtained by extrapolating from past trends.* ○ *We have extrapolated the results from research done in other countries.* ▶ **extrapolation** /ɪkˌstræpəˈleɪʃn इक्ˌस्ट्रैपˈलेश्न्/ *noun* [U, C] बाह्यकलन, निष्कर्ष *Their age can be determined by extrapolation from their growth rate.*

**extraterrestrial** /ˌekstrətəˈrestriəl ˌएक्स्ट्रटˈरेस्ट्रिअल्/ *noun* [C] (in stories) a creature that comes from another planet; a creature that may exist on another planet (कहानियों में) अन्य ग्रह से आने वाला प्राणी; अन्य ग्रह पर रहने की संभावना रखने वाला प्राणी ▶ **extraterrestrial** *adj.* अन्य ग्रह से संबंधित; अलौकिक

**extravagant** /ɪkˈstrævəgənt इक्ˈस्ट्रैवगन्ट्/ *adj.* **1** spending or costing too much money फ़िज़ूलख़र्च या बेहद महँगा *He's terribly extravagant—he travels everywhere by taxi.* ○ *an extravagant present* **2** exaggerated; more than is usual, true or necessary अतिशयोक्तिपूर्ण; सामान्य, यथार्थ या आवश्यकता से अधिक *The advertisements made extravagant claims for the new medicine.* ▶ **extravagance** *noun* [C, U] फ़िज़ूलख़र्ची ▶ **extravagantly** *adv.* बढ़ा-चढ़ा कर

**extreme** /ɪkˈstriːm इक्ˈस्ट्रीम्/ *adj.* **1** the greatest or strongest possible यथासंभव अधिकतम, चरम *You must take extreme care when driving at night.* ○ *extreme heat/difficulty/poverty* **2** much stronger than is considered usual, acceptable, etc. अतिवादी *Her extreme views on immigration are shocking to most people.* **3** (*only before a noun*) as far away as possible from the centre in the direction mentioned केंद्र बिंदु से किसी दिशा में अधिकतम दूर; चरम बिंदु *There could be snow in the extreme north of the country.* ○ *politicians on the extreme left of the party* ➪ **moderate** और **radical** देखिए। ▶ **extreme** *noun* [C] चरम सीमा, पराकाष्ठा *Shikha used to be very shy but now she's gone to the opposite extreme.*

**extremely** /ɪkˈstriːmli इक्ˈस्ट्रीम्लि/ *adv.* very अत्यधिक *Listen carefully because this is extremely important.*

**extreme sport** *noun* [C] a very dangerous sport or activity which some people do for fun बहुत ख़तरे वाला खेल या कोई काम जिसे लोग शौक़िया करते हैं

**extremist** /ɪkˈstriːmɪst इक्ˈस्ट्रीमिस्ट्/ *noun* [C] a person who has extreme political opinions उग्र राजनीतिक विचारों वाला व्यक्ति; अतिवादी, चरमपंथी ➪ **moderate** और **radical** देखिए। ▶ **extremism** *noun* [U] अतिवाद, उग्रवाद

**extremity** /ɪkˈstreməti इक्ˈस्ट्रेमटि/ *noun* [C] (*pl.* **extremities**) the part of sth that is furthest from the centre किसी वस्तु के केंद्र से सबसे दूर का अंश; पराकाष्ठा

**extricate** /ˈekstrɪkeɪt ˈएक्स्ट्रिकेट्/ *verb* [T] to manage to free sb/sth from a difficult situation or position कठिन परिस्थिति से (किसी को) मुक्त करने में सफल होना

**extrovert** /ˈekstrəvɜːt ˈएक्स्ट्रवट्/ *noun* [C] a person who is confident and full of life and who prefers being with other people to being alone आत्मविश्वासी व उत्साह से परिपूर्ण व्यक्ति जिसे अकेलेपन के बजाए साथियों के बीच रहना अधिक पसंद होता है; बहिर्मुखी ✪ विलोम **introvert**

**extrusive** /ɪkˈstruːsɪv इक्ˈस्ट्रूसिव्/ *adj.* (*technical*) (used about rock) that has been pushed out of the earth by a **volcano** ज्वालामुखी द्वारा पृथ्वी में से बाहर फेंके गए (पत्थर)

**exuberant** /ɪgˈzjuːbərənt इग्ˈज़्यूबरन्ट्/ *adj.* (used about a person or his/her behaviour) full of energy and excitement (व्यक्ति या उसका आचरण) उल्लासपूर्ण, जानदार, जीवंत ▶ **exuberance** *noun* [U] उल्लास, जीवंतता

**eye¹** /aɪ आइ/ *noun* [C] **1** one of the two organs of your body that you use to see with आँख, नेत्र *She opened/closed her eyes.* ○ *He's got blue eyes.* ➪ **black eye** देखिए। **2** the ability to see sth देखने की शक्ति *He has **sharp eyes*** (= he can see very well). ○ *She has an eye for detail* (= she notices small details). **3** the hole at one end of a needle that the thread goes through सूई की आँख; सूई के एक सिरे पर बना छेद जिसमें से धागा जाता है

IDM **an eye for an eye** used to say that you should punish sb by doing to him/her what he/she has done to sb else ईंट का जवाब पत्थर से देने के अर्थ में प्रयुक्त

**as far as the eye can see** ➪ **far²** देखिए।

**be up to your eyes in sth** (*informal*) to have more of sth than you can easily do or manage अपने उपभोग या अपने सामर्थ्य से अधिक पा जाना

**before sb's very eyes** in front of sb so that he/she can clearly see what is happening ठीक आँखों के सामने

**cast an eye/your eye(s) over sb/sth** ➪ **cast¹** देखिए।

**catch sb's attention/eye** ➪ **catch¹** देखिए।

**cry your eyes out** ➪ **cry¹** देखिए।

**have (got) your eye on sb** to watch sb carefully to make sure that he/she does nothing wrong किसी पर कड़ी नज़र रखना

**have (got) your eye on sth** to be thinking about buying sth किसी वस्तु के ख़रीदने के बारे में सोचना

**in the eyes of sb/in sb's eyes** in the opinion of sb किसी की राय में *She was still a child in her mother's eyes.*

**in the public eye** ➪ **public¹** देखिए।

**keep an eye on sb/sth** to make sure that sb/sth is safe; to look after sb/sth किसी की सुरक्षा को सुनिश्चित करना; किसी का ध्यान रखना *Please could you keep an eye on the house while we're away?*

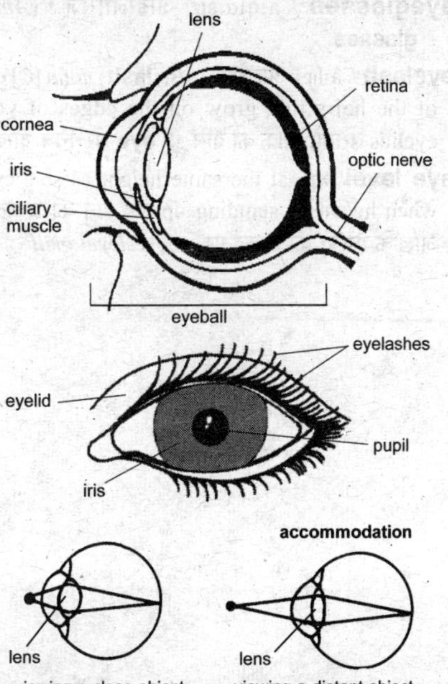

the eye

**keep an eye open/out (for sb/sth)** to watch or look out for sb/sth किसी के विषय में सावधान रहना

**keep your eyes peeled/skinned (for sb/sth)** to watch carefully for sb/sth किसी पर आँख गड़ाए रखना

**look sb in the eye** ➪ **look¹** देखिए।

**the naked eye** ➪ **naked** देखिए।

**not bat an eye** ➪ **bat²** देखिए।

**see eye to eye (with sb)** ➪ **see** देखिए।

**set eyes on sb/sth** ➪ **set¹** देखिए।

**turn a blind eye** ➪ **blind¹** देखिए।

**with your eyes open** knowing what you are doing यह जानते हुए कि आप क्या कर रहे हैं, सब कुछ जानते हुए *You went into the new job with your eyes open, so you can't complain now.*

**eye²** /aɪ आइ/ *verb* [T] (*pres. part.* **eyeing** or **eying;** *pt, pp* **eyed**) to look at sb/sth closely किसी को सूक्ष्मता से देखना *She eyed him with suspicion.*

**eyeball** /ˈaɪbɔːl ˈआइबॉल्/ *noun* [C] the whole of your eye (including the part which is hidden inside the head) पूरी आँख, आँख का डेला, नेत्र-गोलक

**eyebrow** /ˈaɪbraʊ ˈआइब्राउ/ *noun* [C] the line of hair that is above your eye भौंहें ➪ **body** पर चित्र देखिए।

IDM **raise your eyebrows** ➪ **raise** देखिए।

**eye-catching** *adj.* (used about a thing) attracting your attention immediately because it is interesting, bright or pretty सुंदर होने के कारण तुरंत ध्यान आकृष्ट करने वाली (वस्तु)

**eyeglasses** /ˈaɪɡlɑːsɪz ˈआइग्लासिज़्/ (*AmE*) = **glasses**

**eyelash** /ˈaɪlæʃ ˈआइलैश्/ (*also* **lash**) *noun* [C] one of the hairs that grow on the edges of your eyelids बरौनी; पलक का बाल ➪ **eye** पर चित्र देखिए।

**eye level** *adj.* at the same height as sb's eyes when he/she is standing up खड़े होने की स्थिति में आँख के बराबर की ऊँचाई पर *an eye-level grill*

**eyelid** /ˈaɪlɪd ˈआइलिड्/ (*also* **lid**) *noun* [C] the piece of skin that can move to cover your eye पलक, नेत्रच्छद ➪ **eye** पर चित्र देखिए।

IDM **not bat an eyelid** ➪ **bat²** देखिए।

**eyeliner** /ˈaɪlaɪnə(r) ˈआइलाइनर्/ *noun* [U] colour that is put around the edge of the eyes with a type of pencil to make them look more attractive आँखों की कोर पर सब ओर विशेष पेंसिल से लगाया जाने वाला रंग (ताकि व्यक्ति अधिक सुंदर लगे); काजल

**eye-opener** *noun* [C] something that makes you realize the truth about sth सचाई का अहसास कराने वाली बात; आँखें खोल देने वाली बात

**eyepiece** /ˈaɪpiːs ˈआइपीस्/ *noun* [C] the piece of glass (**lens**) at the end of a **telescope** or **microscope** that you look through दूर-वीक्षण यंत्र (टेलीस्कोप) या अणु-वीक्षण यंत्र (माइक्रोस्कोप) में लगा ताल (लेंस) ➪ **laboratory** पर चित्र देखिए।

**eyeshadow** /ˈaɪʃædəʊ ˈआइशैडो/ *noun* [U] colour that is put on the skin above the eyes to make them look more attractive आँखों के ऊपर की त्वचा पर लगाने का रंग (जिससे आँखें अधिक सुंदर दिखें)

**eyesight** /ˈaɪsaɪt ˈआइसाइट्/ *noun* [U] the ability to see देखने की शक्ति, दृष्टि, नज़र *good/poor eyesight*

**eyesore** /ˈaɪsɔː(r) ˈआइसॉर्/ *noun* [C] something that is ugly and unpleasant to look at देखने में भद्दी वस्तु *All this litter in the streets is a real eyesore.*

**eyewitness** /ˈaɪwɪtnəs ˈआइविट्नस्/ = **witness¹ 1**

**e-zine** /ˈiːziːn ˈईज़ीन्/ *noun* [C] a magazine that you can pay to read in electronic form on your computer कंप्यूटर पर इलेक्ट्रॉनिक रूप में उपलब्ध पढ़ने योग्य पत्रिका

# F f

**F, f**[1] /ef एफ़्/ *noun* [C, U] (*pl.* **F's; f's** /efs एफ़्स्/) the sixth letter of the English alphabet अंग्रेज़ी वर्णमाला का छठा अक्षर, *'Father' begins with an 'F'.*

**F**[2] *abbr.* **1** Fahrenheit फ़ैरनहाइट *Water freezes at 32°F.* **2** (*also* **fem**) female or feminine स्त्री या मादा; स्त्री-विषयक

**fable** /ˈfeɪbl ˈफ़ेबल्/ *noun* [C] a short story that teaches a lesson (**a moral**) and that often has animals as the main characters नीति का उपदेश देने वाली कथा (जिसके पात्र प्रायः पशु होते हैं); नीति कथा *Aesop's fables*

**fabric** /ˈfæbrɪk ˈफ़ैब्रिक्/ *noun* **1** [C, U] (a type of) cloth or soft material that is used for making clothes, curtains, etc. पोशाकें, परदे आदि बनाने का कपड़ा *cotton fabrics* **2** [*sing.*] the basic structure of a building or system किसी भवन या प्रणाली का मूल ढाँचा *The Industrial Revolution changed the fabric of society.*

**fabricate** /ˈfæbrɪkeɪt ˈफ़ैब्रिकेट्/ *verb* [T] (*usually passive*) **1** to invent sth false in order to deceive people मनगढ़ंत बातें करना, झूठी बातें गढ़ना, विरचना करना *According to the newspapers the evidence was totally fabricated.* **2** (*technical*) to make or produce goods, equipment, etc. from various different materials संविरचन करना ➪ **manufacture** देखिए। ▶ **fabrication** /ˌfæbrɪˈkeɪʃn ˌफ़ैब्रिˈकेश्न्/ *noun* [C, U] संविरचन *According to the police, the evidence presented in court was a complete fabrication.*

**fabulous** /ˈfæbjələs ˈफ़ैब्यलस्/ *adj.* **1** very good; excellent बहुत अच्छा; उच्च कोटि का *It was a fabulous concert.* **2** very great अत्यधिक *fabulous wealth/riches/beauty*

**façade** (*also* **facade**) /fəˈsɑːd फ़ˈसाड्/ *noun* [C] **1** the front wall of a large building that you see from the outside बड़ी इमारत की सामने से दिखाई देने वाली दीवार; अग्रभित्ति **2** the way sb/sth appears to be, which is not the way he/she/it really is बाहरी दिखावा (जो वास्तविकता से भिन्न होता है) *His good humour was just a façade.*

**face**[1] /feɪs फ़ेस्/ *noun* [C] **1** the front part of your head; the expression that is shown on it चेहरा; चेहरे का भाव *He came in with a smile on his face.* ○ *Her face lit up* (= showed happiness) *when Jai came into the room.* ➪ **body** पर चित्र देखिए। **2** the front or one side of sth किसी का सामने या एक ओर का हिस्सा; सम्मुख भाग *the north face of the mountain* ○ *He put the cards* ***face up/down*** *on the table.* ○ *a clock face* **3 -faced** (*used to form compound adjectives*) having the type of face or expression mentioned निर्दिष्ट प्रकार के चेहरे या भाव वाला *red/round/sour-faced*

IDM **face to face (with sb/sth)** close to and looking at sb/sth आमने-सामने

**keep a straight face** ➪ **straight**[1] देखिए।

**lose face** ➪ **lose** देखिए।

**make/pull faces/a face (at sb/sth)** to make an expression that shows that you do not like sb/sth (नापसंदगी दिखाने के लिए) मुँह बिचकाना

**make/pull faces** to make rude expressions with your face चेहरे पर अशिष्टता का भाव लाना *The children made faces behind the teacher's back.*

**put on a brave face; put a brave face on sth** ➪ **brave**[1] देखिए।

**save face** ➪ **save**[1] देखिए।

**to sb's face** if you say sth to sb's face, you do it when that person is with you किसी के मुँह पर कुछ कहने के लिए प्रयुक्त ✪ विलोम **behind sb's back**

**face** /feɪs फ़ेस्/ *verb* [T] **1** to have your face or front pointing towards sb/sth or in a particular direction (किसी के) सामने होना *The garden faces south.* ○ *Can you all face the front, please* **2** to have to deal with sth unpleasant; to deal with sb in a difficult situation अप्रिय स्थिति का सामना करना; कठिन परिस्थिति में किसी व्यक्ति से निबटना *I can't face another argument.* ○ *He couldn't face going to work yesterday—he felt too ill.* **3** to need attention or action from sb आवश्यक ध्यान या कार्रवाई की अपेक्षा होना *There are several problems facing the government.* ○ *We are faced with a difficult decision.*

IDM **let's face it** (*informal*) we must accept it as true हमें मानना होगा कि यह सच है *Let's face it, we can't afford a holiday this year.*

PHR V **face up to sth** to accept a difficult or unpleasant situation and do sth about it स्थिति कठिन या अप्रिय है, ऐसा मानते हुए उसका सामना करना

**facecloth** /ˈfeɪsklɒθ ˈफ़ेस्क्लॉथ्/ (*also* **flannel**) *noun* [C] (*BrE*) a small square towel that is used for washing the face, hands, etc. हाथ-मुँह धोने का छोटा तौलिया

**faceless** /ˈfeɪsləs ˈफ़ेस्लस्/ *adj.* without individual character or identity जिसका निजी व्यक्तित्व या पहचान न हो *faceless civil servants*

**facelift** /ˈfeɪslɪft ˈफ़ेस्लिफ़्ट्/ *noun* [C] a medical operation that makes your face look younger अधिक युवा दिखने के लिए चेहरे की सर्जरी ➪ **plastic surgery** देखिए।

**face-saving** *adj.* (*only before a noun*) said or done in order to avoid looking silly or losing other people's respect अपने सम्मान की रक्षा के लिए की गई या कही गई (बात); लाज-बचाऊ *In his interview, the captain made face-saving excuses for his team's defeat.*

**facet** /ˈfæsɪt ˈफ़ैसिट्/ *noun* [C] **1** one part or particular aspect of sth (किसी वस्तु का) एक अंश या विशेष पहलू **2** one side of a precious stone नग या रत्न का एक फलक

**facetious** /fəˈsiːʃəs फ़ˈसीशस्/ *adj.* trying to be amusing about a subject at a time that is not appropriate so that other people become annoyed अनुपयुक्त समय पर अनुचित रूप से हँसी-मज़ाक़ वाला; हँसोड़ *He kept making facetious remarks during the lecture.* ▸ **facetiously** *adv.* मज़ाक़िया तौर पर

**face value** *noun* [U, *sing.*] the cost or value that is shown on the front of stamps, coins, etc. टिकटों, सिक्कों आदि पर अंकित मूल्य

**IDM** **take sb/sth at (its, his, etc.) face value** to accept sb/sth as it, he, etc. appears to be व्यक्ति या वस्तु जैसा सामने से लगे वैसा ही उसे मान लेना *Don't take his story at face value. There's something he hasn't told us yet.*

**facial** /ˈfeɪʃl ˈफ़ेश्ल्/ *adj.* connected with a person's face व्यक्ति के चेहरे से संबंधित; चेहरे का *a facial expression* ○ *facial hair*

**facile** /ˈfæsaɪl ˈफ़ैसाइल्/ *adj.* (used about a comment, argument, etc.) not carefully thought out (टिप्पणी, युक्ति आदि) बिना भली-भाँति सोचा हुआ; लचर

**facilitate** /fəˈsɪlɪteɪt फ़ˈसिलिटेट्/ *verb* [T] (*formal*) to make sth possible or easier किसी बात को संभव या आसान बनाना

**facility** /fəˈsɪləti फ़ˈसिलटि/ *noun* (*pl.* **facilities**) **1 facilities** [*pl.*] a service, building, piece of equipment, etc. that makes it possible to do sth कोई सेवा, इमारत, मशीन आदि जिसकी सहायता से हम कोई काम कर पाते हैं; सुविधा *Our town has excellent sports facilities* (= a stadium, swimming pool, etc.). **2** [C] an extra function or ability that a machine, etc. may have किसी मशीन आदि का अतिरिक्त गुण, सुविधा *This word processor has a facility for checking spelling.*

**facsimile** /fækˈsɪməli फ़ैक्ˈसिमलि/ *noun* [C, U] an exact copy of a picture, piece of writing, etc. किसी चित्र आदि की हूबहू प्रतिलिपि; नक़ल ➪ **fax** देखिए।

**fact** /fækt फ़ैक्ट्/ *noun* **1** [C] something that you know has happened or is true तथ्य, सचाई *I know for a fact that Pawan wasn't ill yesterday.* ○ ***The fact that*** *I am older than you makes no difference at all.* ○ *You must* ***face facts*** *and accept that he has gone.* **2** [U] true things; reality सच्ची बातें; असलियत, वास्तविकता *The film is based on fact.*
✪ विलोम **fiction**

**IDM** **as a matter of fact** ➪ **matter**[1] देखिए।

**the fact (of the matter) is (that)...** the truth is that... यह तो सच है कि..., किसी चर्चा के प्रसंग में वास्तविकता पर बल देने के लिए प्रयुक्त *I would love a car, but the fact is that I just can't afford one.*

**facts and figures** detailed information विस्तृत जानकारी *Before we make a decision, we need some more facts and figures.*

**a fact of life** something unpleasant that you must accept because you cannot change it जीवन की (कोई) अप्रिय वास्तविकता जिसे बदला नहीं जा सकता

**the facts of life** the details of sexual behaviour and how babies are born शिशु जन्म से संबंधित तथा यौन आचरण का विवरण

**hard facts** ➪ **hard**[1] देखिए।

**in (actual) fact** **1** (used for emphasizing that sth is true) really; actually (किसी सचाई पर बल देने के लिए प्रयुक्त) सचमुच; असल में *I thought the lecture would be boring but in actual fact it was rather interesting.* **2** used for introducing more detailed information विस्तृत जानकारी देने के लिए प्रयुक्त *It was cold. In fact it was freezing.*

**faction** /ˈfækʃn ˈफ़ैक्श्न्/ *noun* [C] a small group of people within a larger one whose members have some different aims and beliefs to those of the larger group बड़े दल के भीतर छोटा दल जिसके उद्देश्य और विचार बड़े दल से कुछ अलग होते हैं; गुट *rival factions within the organization* ▸ **factional** *adj.* गुटीय, गुट-संबंधी *factional rivalries/disputes*

**factor** /ˈfæktə(r) ˈफ़ैक्ट(र्)/ *noun* [C] **1** one of the things that influences a decision, situation, etc. किसी निर्णय, स्थिति आदि को प्रभावित करने वाला तत्व; कारक *His unhappiness at home was a major factor in his decision to go abroad.* **2** (*technical*) (in mathematics) a whole number (except 1) by which a larger number can be divided (गणित में) गुणक; (1 को छोड़कर) वह पूर्ण संख्या जिससे उससे बड़ी संख्या विभाजित हो सके *2, 3, 4 and 6 are factors of 12.*

**factory** /ˈfæktri; -təri ˈफ़ैक्ट्रि; ˈफ़ैक्टरि/ *noun* [C] (*pl.* **factories**) a building or group of buildings where goods are made in large quantities by machine फ़ैक्टरी, कारख़ाना

**factual** /ˈfæktʃuəl ˈफ़ैक्चुअल् / *adj.* based on or containing things that are true or real तथ्यों पर आधारित *a factual account of the events* ➪ **fictional** देखिए।

**faculty** /ˈfæklti ˈफ़ैक्लटि / *noun* [C] (*pl.* **faculties**) **1** one of the natural abilities of a person's body or mind शरीर या मन की नैसर्गिक क्षमता *the faculty of hearing/sight/speech* **2** (*also* **Faculty**) one department in a university, college, etc. विश्वविद्यालय या कॉलेज में कोई विभाग या संकाय *the Faculty of Law/Arts*

> **NOTE** **The Faculty** विश्वविद्यालय या कॉलेज के शिक्षक वर्ग के संदर्भ में प्रयुक्त किया जा सकता है और इस प्रयोग के साथ क्रिया एकवचन या बहुवचन में आ सकती है—*The Faculty has/have been invited to the meeting.*

**fad** /fæd फ़ैड् / *noun* [C] (*informal*) a fashion, interest, etc. that will probably not last long चलन, फ़ैशन, रुचि आदि जो ज़्यादा समय तक प्रचलित रहने की संभावना नहीं रखता

**fade** /feɪd फ़ेड् / *verb* **1** [I, T] to become or make sth become lighter in colour or less strong or fresh किसी वस्तु का रंग फीका पड़ जाना या क्षीण होना *Jeans fade when you wash them.* ○ *Look how the sunlight has faded these curtains.* **2** [I] **fade (away)** to disappear slowly (from sight, hearing, memory, etc.) (याददाश्त, दृष्टि, श्रवण आदि से) धीरे-धीरे लुप्त हो जाना *The cheering of the crowd faded away.* ○ *The smile faded from his face.*

**faeces** (*AmE* **feces**) /ˈfiːsiːz ˈफ़ीसीज़् / *noun* [*pl.*] (*technical*) the solid waste material that you get rid of when you go to the toilet विष्ठा, मल

**fag** /fæg फ़ैग् / *noun* (*BrE*) **1** [C] (*slang*) a cigarette सिगरेट **2** [*sing.*] (*informal*) a piece of work that you do not want to do अनचाहा काम

**Fahrenheit** /ˈfærənhaɪt ˈफ़ैरन्हाइट् / *noun* [U] (*abbr.* **F**) the name of a scale which measures temperatures ताप या गरमी के एक पैमाने का नाम *Water freezes at 32° Fahrenheit (32°F).* ➪ **Celsius** देखिए।

**fail[1]** /feɪl फ़ेल् / *verb* **1** [I, T] to not be successful in sth असफल होना *She failed her driving test.* ○ *I feel that I've failed—I'm 35 and I still haven't got a steady job.* ➪ **pass** और **succeed** देखिए। **2** [T] to decide that sb is not successful in a test, exam, etc. परीक्षा आदि में अनुत्तीर्ण करना *The examiners failed half of the candidates.* ✪ विलोम **pass** **3** [I] **fail to do sth** to not do sth कुछ करना भूल जाना *She never fails to do her homework.* **4** [I, T] to not be enough or not do what people are expecting or wanting आवश्यकता से कम होना या लोगों की अपेक्षा पर खरा न उतरना *If the crops fail, people will starve.* ○ *I think the government has failed us.* **5** [I] (used about health, eye sight, etc.) to become weak (स्वास्थ्य, नज़र आदि का) कमज़ोर हो जाना *His health is failing.* **6** [I] to stop working काम करना बंद कर देना *My brakes failed on the hill but I managed to stop the car.*

**fail[2]** /feɪl फ़ेल् / *noun* [C] the act of not being successful in an exam परीक्षा में असफलता ✪ विलोम **pass**

**IDM** **without fail** always, even if there are difficulties हमेशा, बिना चूके (भले ही कठिनाइयाँ हों) *The postman always comes at 8 o'clock without fail.*

**failing[1]** /ˈfeɪlɪŋ ˈफ़ेलिङ् / *noun* [C] a weakness or fault दुर्बलता या दोष *She's not very patient—that's her only failing.*

**failing[2]** /ˈfeɪlɪŋ ˈफ़ेलिङ् / *prep.* if sth is not possible के न होने पर; अगर कुछ संभव न हो तो *Ask Manav to go with you, or failing that, try Anu.*

**failure** /ˈfeɪljə(r) ˈफ़ेल्य(र्) / *noun* **1** [U] lack of success असफलता, नाक़ामयाबी *All my efforts ended in failure.* **2** [C] a person or thing that is not successful असफल व्यक्ति या प्रयास *His first attempt at skating was a miserable failure.* ✪ विलोम **success** (अर्थ सं. **1** और **2** के लिए) **3** [C, U] **failure to do sth** not doing sth that people expect you to do अपेक्षित कार्य कर पाने में असमर्थता; चूक *I was very disappointed at his failure to come to the meeting.* **4** [C, U] an example of sth not working properly उचित या उपयुक्त रूप से कार्य न कर पाने की स्थिति *She died of heart failure.* ○ *There's been a failure in the power supply.*

**faint[1]** /feɪnt फ़ेन्ट् / *adj.* **1** (used about things that you can see, hear, feel, etc.) not strong or clear (देखने, सुनने आदि में) अस्पष्ट *a faint light/sound* ○ *There is still a faint hope that they will find more people alive.* **2** (used about people) almost losing consciousness; very weak (व्यक्ति) लगभग मूर्छित; बहुत दुर्बल *I **feel faint**—I'd better sit down.* **3** (used about actions, etc.) done without much effort (काम) आधे मन से किया; अधूरा *He made a faint protest.* ▶ **faintly** *adv.* अस्पष्ट रूप से

**IDM** **not have the faintest/foggiest (idea)** to not know at all कुछ भी मालूम न होना *I haven't the faintest idea where they've gone.*

**faint[2]** /feɪnt फ़ेन्ट् / *verb* [I] to lose consciousness मूर्छित हो जाना

**fair[1]** /feə(r) फ़ेअ(र्) / *adj., adv.* **1** appropriate and acceptable in a particular situation उचित, सही *That's a fair price for that house.* ○ *I think **it's***

***fair to say that*** *the number of homeless people is increasing.* **2 fair (to/on sb)** treating each person or side equally, according to the law, the rules, etc. प्रत्येक व्यक्ति या पक्ष से समानता का व्यवहार करते हुए *That's not fair—he got the same number of mistakes as I did and he's got a better mark.* ○ *It wasn't fair on her to ask her to stay so late.* ○ *a fair trial* ✪ विलोम **unfair** (अर्थ सं. **1** और **2** के लिए) **3** quite good, large, etc. काफ़ी अच्छा, अधिक आदि *They have a fair chance of success.* **4** (used about the skin or hair) light in colour (त्वचा या केश) हलके रंग का *Laila has fair hair and blue eyes.* **5** (used about the weather) good, without rain (मौसम) अच्छा, साफ़

IDM **fair enough** (*spoken*) used to show that you agree with what sb has suggested किसी के सुझाव से सहमति जताने के लिए प्रयुक्त

**fair play** equal treatment of both/all sides according to the rules दोनों या सभी पक्षों से नियमानुकूल समानता का व्यवहार *The referee is there to ensure fair play during the match.*

**(more than) your fair share of sth** (more than) the usual or expected amount of sth सामान्यतः या अपेक्षित मात्रा (से अधिक)

**fair²** /feə(r) फ़ेअ(र्)/ *noun* [C] **1** (*also* **funfair**) a type of entertainment in a field or park. At a fair you can ride on machines or try and win prizes at games. Fairs usually travel from town to town मैदान या पार्क में विविध प्रकार के मनोरंजन का आयोजन; मेला **2** a large event where people, businesses, etc. show and sell their goods बड़ी प्रदर्शनी *a trade fair* ○ *the Delhi book fair*

**fairground** /ˈfeəgraʊnd ˈफ़ेअग्राउन्ड्/ *noun* [C] a large outdoor area where fairs are held प्रदर्शनी का मैदान

**fair-haired** *adj.* with light-coloured hair हलके रंग के बालों वाला ✪ पर्याय **blond**

**fairly** /ˈfeəli ˈफ़ेअलि/ *adv.* **1** in an acceptable way; in a way that treats people equally or according to the law, rules, etc. उचित रीति से; निष्पक्षतापूर्वक *I felt that the teacher didn't treat us fairly.* ✪ पर्याय **unfairly** **2** quite, not very काफ़ी, बहुत ज़्यादा नहीं, ठीक-ठाक *He is fairly tall.* ➪ **rather** पर नोट देखिए।

**fairness** /ˈfeənəs ˈफ़ेअनस्/ *noun* [U] treating people equally or according to the law, rules, etc. औचित्य, निष्पक्षता

**fairy** /ˈfeəri ˈफ़ेअरि/ *noun* [C] (*pl.* **fairies**) (in stories) a small creature with wings and magic powers (कहानियों में) परी

**fairy tale** (*also* **fairy story**) *noun* [C] a story that is about fairies, magic, etc. परी कथा

**faith** /feɪθ फ़ेथ्/ *noun* **1** [U] **faith (in sb/sth)** strong belief (in sb/sth); trust (पूर्ण) विश्वास; भरोसा *I've got great/little faith in his ability to do the job.* ○ *I have **lost faith** in him.* **2** [U] strong religious belief दृढ़ धार्मिक विश्वास; आस्था *I've lost my faith.* **3** [C] a particular religion विशेष धर्म या मत *the Jewish faith*

IDM **in good faith** with honest reasons for doing sth अच्छी या नेक नीयत से *I bought the car in good faith. I didn't know it was stolen.*

**faithful** /ˈfeɪθfl ˈफ़ेथ्फ़्ल्/ *adj.* **faithful (to sb/sth)** **1** always staying with and supporting a person, organization or belief (व्यक्ति, संस्था, मत आदि के प्रति) सच्चा और निष्ठावान *He was always faithful to his wife* (= he didn't have sexual relations with anyone else). ✪ पर्याय **loyal** ✪ विलोम **unfaithful** **2** true to the facts; accurate तथ्यानुकूल; बिलकुल सही *a faithful description* ► **faithfully** /-fəli -फ़लि/ *adv.* निष्ठापूर्वक, वफ़ादारी से ► **faithfulness** *noun* [U] वफ़ादारी ➪ **fidelity** भी देखिए।

**fake¹** /feɪk फ़ेक्/ *noun* [C] **1** a work of art, etc. that seems to be real or genuine but is not (कलाकृति) जो लगे असली पर हो नक़ली **2** a person who is not really what he/she appears to be अपनी असलियत से भिन्न व्यक्ति; जालसाज़ ► **fake** *adj.* नक़ली *a fake passport*

**fake²** /feɪk फ़ेक्/ *verb* [T] **1** to copy sth and try to make people believe it is the real thing किसी वस्तु की ऐसी नक़ल बनाना कि लोगों को वह असली लगे *He faked his father's signature.* **2** to make people believe that you are feeling sth that you are not कुछ अनुभव करने का ढोंग करना *I faked surprise when he told me the news.*

**falcon** /ˈfɔːlkən ˈफ़ॉल्कन्/ *noun* [C] a bird with long pointed wings that kills and eats other animals, a type of **bird of prey**. Falcons can be trained to hunt शिकारी पक्षी जैसे बाज़, जिसे पालकर शिकार करने का प्रशिक्षण दिया जा सकता है

**fall¹** /fɔːl फ़ॉल्/ *verb* [I] (*pt* **fell** /fel फ़ेल्/; *pp* **fallen** /ˈfɔːlən ˈफ़ॉलन्/) **1** to drop down towards the ground ज़मीन पर गिरना *He fell off the ladder onto the grass.* ○ *The rain was falling steadily.* **2 fall (down/over)** to suddenly stop standing and drop to the ground नीचे गिर जाना *She slipped on the ice and fell.* ○ *The little boy fell over and hurt his knee.* **3** to hang down नीचे लटकना *Her hair fell down over her shoulders.* **4** to become lower or less कम होना, घटना *The temperature is falling.* ○ *The price of coffee has fallen again.* ✪ विलोम **rise** 5 to be defeated पराजित हो जाना; हार जाना *The Government fell because of the scandal.* 6 (*written*) to be killed (in battle) (युद्ध में) मारा जाना *Millions of soldiers fell in the war.* 7 to change into a different state; to become बदलकर कुछ और हो जाना; कुछ हो जाना *He **fell asleep** on the sofa.* ○ *I must get some new shoes—these ones are **falling to pieces**.* 8 (*formal*) to come or happen होना, पड़ना *My birthday falls on a Sunday this year.* 9 to belong to a particular group, type, etc. किसी वर्ग विशेष के अंतर्गत होना *Animals fall into two groups, those with backbones and those without.*

**IDM fall flat** ➪ **flat**[1] देखिए।

**fall/slot into place** ➪ **place**[1] देखिए।

**fall short (of sth)** ➪ **short**[1] देखिए।

**PHR V fall apart** to break (into pieces) (किसी वस्तु के) टुकड़े हो जाना *My bookcase is falling apart.*

**fall back on sb/sth** to use sb/sth when you are in difficulty कठिनाई होने पर किसी वस्तु या व्यक्ति का प्रयोग करना *When the electricity was cut off we fell back on candles.*

**fall for sb** (*informal*) to be strongly attracted to sb; to fall in love with sb किसी व्यक्ति के प्रति अत्यधिक आकृष्ट होना; किसी व्यक्ति से प्रेम हो जाना

**fall for sth** (*informal*) to be tricked into believing sth that is not true किसी के झाँसे में आ जाना *He makes excuses and she falls for them every time.*

**fall out (with sb)** to argue and stop being friendly (with sb) झगड़ा होना और मित्रता समाप्त हो जाना

**fall through** to fail or not happen रद्द हो जाना, न हो सकना *Our trip to Japan has fallen through.*

**fall**[2] /fɔːl फ़ॉल्/ *noun* 1 [C] an act of falling down or off sth नीचे या कहीं से गिरने की क्रिया *She **had a** nasty **fall** from her horse.* 2 [C] **a fall (of sth)** the amount of sth that has fallen or the distance that sth has fallen गिरी हुई वस्तु (जैसे बर्फ़) की मात्रा या दूरी जहाँ से वस्तु (जैसे गेंद) गिरती है *We have had a heavy fall of snow.* ○ *a fall of four metres* 3 [C] **a fall (in sth)** a decrease (in value, quantity, etc.) गिरावट, कमी (क़ीमत, गुणवत्ता आदि में) *There has been a sharp fall in the price of oil.* ✪ पर्याय **drop** ✪ विलोम **rise** 4 [*sing.*] **the fall of sth** a (political) defeat; a failure (राजनीतिक) पराजय; विफलता *the fall of the Mughal Empire* 5 **falls** [*pl.*] a large amount of water that falls from a height down the side of a mountain, etc. झरना, निर्झर, प्रपात *Niagara Falls* ✪ पर्याय **waterfall** 6 [C] (*AmE*) = **autumn**

**fallacy** /ˈfæləsi ˈफ़ैलसि/ *noun* (*pl.* **fallacies**) [C, U] (*formal*) a false belief or a wrong idea झूठा विश्वास या भ्रांत धारणा *It's a fallacy to believe that money brings happiness* (= it's not true).

**fallen** ➪ **fall**[1] का past participle रूप

**fallible** /ˈfæləbl ˈफ़ैलबल्/ *adj.* able or likely to make mistakes जिसमें या जिसके द्वारा ग़लतियों की गुंजाइश हो; दोषक्षम *Even our new computerized system is fallible.* ✪ विलोम **infallible**

**Fallopian tubes** /fəˈləʊpiən tjuːbz फ़ˈलोपिअन् ट्यूब्ज़्/ *noun* [C, *usually pl.*] the two tubes in the body of a woman or a female animal along which eggs travel from the place where they are produced (**the ovaries**) to the place where a baby is formed (**the uterus**) स्त्री या मादा पशु के शरीर में दो नलियाँ जिनमें से होकर डिंब अंडाशय से गर्भाशय तक पहुँचता है; डिंबवाही नलियाँ

**fallout** /ˈfɔːlaʊt ˈफ़ॉलआउट्/ *noun* [U] 1 dangerous waste that is carried in the air after a nuclear explosion आणविक विस्फोट के बाद वायु द्वारा फैलाया गया ख़तरनाक कचरा; नाभिकीय विस्फोट का मलबा 2 the effect or result of sth प्रभाव या परिणाम

**fallow** /ˈfæləʊ ˈफ़ैलो/ *adj.* (used about land) not used for growing plants, especially so that the quality of the land will improve (भूमि) जिस पर खेती इसलिए नहीं की जाती कि उसकी उत्पादन क्षमता में वृद्धि हो; परती (भूमि); उर्वरता बढ़ाने के उद्देश्य से ख़ाली छोड़ दी गई (धरती) *The farmer let the field **lie fallow** for two years.*

**false** /fɔːls फ़ॉल्स्/ *adj.* 1 not true; not correct असत्य, ग़लत *I think the information you have been given is false.* ○ *I got a completely false impression of him from our first meeting.* ✪ विलोम **true** 2 not real; artificial असली नहीं; नक़ली, बनावटी; कृत्रिम *false hair/eyelashes/teeth* ✪ विलोम **real** या **natural** 3 not genuine, but made to look real in order to trick people दिखावटी, आभासी, नक़ली *This suitcase has a false bottom.* ○ *a false name/passport* 4 (used about sb's behaviour or expression) not sincere or honest (व्यक्ति का आचरण या भावाभिव्यक्ति) छद्म, दिखावटी *a false smile* ○ *false modesty* ▶ **falsely** *adv.* असत्य रूप से *She was falsely accused of stealing a wallet.*

**IDM a false alarm** a warning about a danger that does not happen घटित न होने वाले ख़तरे की चेतावनी; झूठी चेतावनी

**a false friend** a word in another language that looks similar to a word in your own but has a different meaning किसी अन्य भाषा का शब्द जो अपनी भाषा के किसी शब्द से रुपाकृति (वर्तनी) में समान परंतु अर्थ में भिन्न होता है; भ्रामक शब्द

**under false pretences** pretending to be or to have sth in order to trick people झाँसा देते हुए, कपटपूर्वक *She got into the club under false pretences—she isn't a member at all!*

**false teeth** (*also* **dentures**) *noun* [*pl.*] artificial teeth that are worn by sb who has lost his/her natural teeth नक़ली दाँत

**falsify** /ˈfɔːlsɪfaɪ ˈफ़ॉल्सिफ़ाइ / *verb* [T] (*pres. part.* **falsifying;** *3rd person sing. pres.* **falsifies;** *pt, pp* **falsified**) (*formal*) to change a document, information, etc. so that it is no longer true in order to trick sb दस्तावेज़ आदि बदलना (ताकि सचाई छिपाई जा सके); जालसाज़ी करना

**falter** /ˈfɔːltə(r) ˈफ़ॉल्ट(र्) / *verb* [I] **1** to become weak or move in a way that is not steady अशक्त होना या अस्थिर होना; लड़खड़ाना *The engine faltered and stopped.* **2** to lose confidence and determination विश्वास और दृढ़ता खो देना; डगमगाना *Sampras faltered and missed the ball.*

**fame** /feɪm फ़ेम् / *noun* [U] being known or talked about by many people because of what you have achieved यश, प्रसिद्धि *Pop stars achieve fame at a young age.* ○ *The town's only* ***claim to fame*** *is that there was a riot there.*

**famed** /feɪmd फ़ेम्ड् / *adj.* **famed (for sth)** well known (for sth) प्रख्यात, प्रसिद्ध *Goans are famed for their singing.* ➪ **famous** देखिए।

**familiar** /fəˈmɪliə(r) फ़ˈमिलिअ(र्) / *adj.* **1 familiar (to sb)** well known to you; often seen or heard and therefore easy to recognize सुपरिचित; जाना-पहचाना *to look/sound familiar* ○ *Chinese music isn't very familiar to people in Europe.* ○ *It was a relief to see a familiar face in the crowd.* **2 familiar with sth** having a good knowledge of sth (किसी का) अच्छा जानकार *People in Europe aren't very familiar with Chinese music.* ✪ विलोम **unfamiliar** (अर्थ सं **1** और **2** के लिए) **3 familiar (with sb)** (used about a person's behaviour) too friendly and informal (व्यक्ति का आचरण) घनिष्ठतापूर्ण, अंतरंग और अनौपचारिक *I was annoyed by the waiter's familiar behaviour.*

**familiarity** /fəˌmɪliˈærəti फ़ˌमिलिˈऐरटि / *noun* [U] **1 familiarity (with sth)** having a good knowledge of sth (किसी की) अच्छी जानकारी *His familiarity with the area was an advantage.* **2** being too friendly and informal बहुत अधिक घनिष्ठता, अंतरंगता और अनौपचारिकता या व्यवहार

**familiarize** (*also* **-ise**) /fəˈmɪliəraɪz फ़ˈमिलिअराइज़् / *verb* [T] **familiarize sb/yourself (with sth)** to teach sb about sth or learn about sth until you know it well किसी चीज़ की पूरी जानकारी पाना या देना *I want to familiarize myself with the plans before the meeting.*

**family** /ˈfæməli ˈफ़ैमलि / *noun* (*pl.* **families**) **1** [C, *with sing. or pl. verb*] a group of people who are related to each other एक दूसरे से संबंधित लोग; परिवार *I have quite a large family.*

> NOTE शब्द **family** के दो अभिप्राय हैं: (i) केवल माता-पिता और उनके बच्चे (**a nuclear family**), (ii) अन्य रिश्तेदार दादा-दादी, चाचा-चाची आदि भी (**an extended family**).
> शब्द **family** का प्रयोग एक इकाई के अर्थ में किया जाए तो क्रिया एकवचन में आती है—*Almost every family in the village owns a television.* जब परिवार के अलग-अलग सदस्यों के अर्थ में इसका प्रयोग हो तो क्रिया बहुवचन में रहती है—*My family are all very tall.* जब समूचे परिवार को लेकर कुछ कहना हो तो शब्द **family** का प्रयोग एक अन्य संज्ञा के साथ भी हो सकता है—*family entertainment* ○ *the family car*

**2** [C, U] children बच्चे, संतान *Do you have any family?* ○ *We are planning to* ***start a family*** *next year* (= to have our first baby). ○ *to bring up/raise a family* **3** [C] a group of animals, plants, etc. that are of a similar type एक ही प्रकार के पशुओं, पौधों आदि का वर्ग *Lions belong to the cat family.*

IDM **run in the family** to be found very often in a family किसी परिवार में किसी बात की प्रवृत्ति होना *Red hair runs in the family.*

**family doctor** (*BrE*) = **GP**

**family name** *noun* [C] the name that is shared by members of a family कुल-नाम, वंश-नाम ✪ पर्याय **surname** ➪ **name** पर नोट देखिए।

**family planning** *noun* [U] controlling the number of children you have by using birth control संतति-निरोध के द्वारा बच्चों की संख्या को सीमित रखना; परिवार-नियोजन ➪ **contraception** देखिए।

**family tree** *noun* [C] a diagram that shows the relationship between different members of a family over a long period of time परिवार के सदस्यों के बीच लंबे समय से चले आ रहे रिश्ते दिखाने वाला आरेख; वंश-वृक्ष, वंशावली

**famine** /ˈfæmɪn ˈफ़ैमिन् / *noun* [C, U] a lack of food over a long period of time in a large area that can cause the death of many people दुर्भिक्ष, अकाल *There is a severe famine in many parts of Africa.* ○ *The long drought* (= a lack of rain or water) *was followed by famine.*

**famished** /ˈfæmɪʃt ˈफ़ैमिश्ट् / *adj.* (*informal*) (*not before a noun*) very hungry बहुत भूखा

**famous** /ˈfeɪməs ˈफ़ेमस्/ *adj.* **famous (for sth)** well known to many people प्रख्यात; जिन्हें लोग अच्छे कार्यों के लिए जानें *a famous singer* ○ *Banaras is famous for its saris.* ➪ **infamous** और **notorious** देखिए।

**famously** /ˈfeɪməsli ˈफ़ेमस्लि/ *adv.* in a way that is famous ऐसे कि कोई (व्यक्ति या वस्तु) प्रसिद्ध हो जाए *the words he famously uttered just before he died*

**IDM** **get on/along famously** to have a very good relationship with sb किसी व्यक्ति के साथ अच्छे संबंध होना

**fan¹** /fæn फ़ैन्/ *noun* [C] **1** somebody who admires and is very enthusiastic about a sport, a film star, a singer, etc. किसी खिलाड़ी, अभिनेता, गायक आदि का उत्साही प्रशंसक *football fans* ○ *He's a Hrithik Roshan fan.* ○ *fan mail* (= letters from fans to the person they admire) **2** a machine with parts that turn around very quickly to create a current of cool or warm air बिजली का पंखा *an electric fan* ○ *a fan heater* **3** an object in the shape of a half-circle made of paper, feathers, etc. that you wave in your hand to create a current of cool air काग़ज़ आदि से बना हाथ का पंखा

**fan²** /fæn फ़ैन्/ *verb* [T] (**fanning; fanned**) **1** to make air blow on sb/sth by waving a **fan¹ 3**, your hand, etc. in the air पंखा करना *She used a newspaper to fan her face.* **2** to make a fire burn more strongly by blowing on it हवा करके आग को भड़काना *The strong wind really fanned the flames.*

**PHR V** **fan out** to spread out फैल जाना *The police fanned out across the field.*

**fanatic** /fəˈnætɪk फ़ˈनैटिक्/ *noun* [C] a person who is very enthusiastic about sth and may have extreme or dangerous opinions (especially about religion or politics) कट्टर व्यक्ति (विशेषतः धर्म या राजनीति के विषय में) *a religious fanatic* ○ *She's a health-food fanatic.* ✪ पर्याय **fiend** या **freak** ▶ **fanatical** /-kli -कलि/ *adj.* कट्टर *He's fanatical about keeping things tidy.* ▶ **fanatically** /-kli -क्लि/ *adv.* कट्टरतापूर्वक ▶ **fanaticism** /-tɪsɪzəm -टिसिज़म्/ *noun* [U] कट्टरता

**fan belt** *noun* [C] the belt that operates the machinery that cools a car engine पट्टा जो कार के इंजन को ठंडा करने वाली मशीन को चलाता है

**fancy¹** /ˈfænsi ˈफ़ैन्सि/ *verb* [T] (*pres. part.* **fancying;** *3rd person sing. pres.* **fancies;** *pt, pp* **fancied**) **1** (*BrE informal*) to like the idea of having or doing sth; to want sth or to want to do sth किसी बात की मनोनुकूल कल्पना करना; किसी (वस्तु या काम) की चाह रखना *What do you fancy to eat?* ○ *I don't fancy going out in this rain.* **2** (*BrE informal*) to be sexually attracted to sb किसी के प्रति यौनाकर्षित होना *Prem keeps looking at you. I think he fancies you.* **3** **fancy yourself (as) sth** to think that you would be good at sth; to think that you are sth (although this may not be true) अपने को कुछ मानना या समझना (भले ही ऐसा सच न हो) *He fancied himself (as) a poet.*

**fancy²** /ˈfænsi ˈफ़ैन्सि/ *adj.* not simple or ordinary जो सीधा-सादा या साधारण न हो; विशिष्ट *My father doesn't like fancy food.* ○ *I just want a pair of black shoes—nothing fancy.*

**fancy³** /ˈfænsi ˈफ़ैन्सि/ *noun*

**IDM** **take sb's fancy** to attract or please sb किसी व्यक्ति को कुछ अच्छा लगना *If you see something that takes your fancy I'll buy it for you.*

**take a fancy to sb/sth** to start liking sb/sth किसी व्यक्ति या वस्तु को पसंद करने लगना *I think that Leena's really taken a fancy to you.*

**fancy dress** *noun* [U] special clothes that you wear to a party at which people dress up to look like a different person (for example from history or a story) पार्टी में पहने जाने वाली विशेष पोशाक जिनमें व्यक्ति किसी अन्य पात्र की तरह दीखता है; फैंसी ड्रेस *It was Children's Day and everyone went* ***in fancy dress****.*

**fanfare** /ˈfænfeə(r) ˈफ़ैन्फ़ेअ(र्)/ *noun* [C] a short loud piece of music that is used for introducing sb important, for example a king or queen राजा या रानी जैसे विशिष्ट व्यक्ति के आगमन को सूचित करने वाली मंगल ध्वनि; तुरही नाद

**fang** /fæŋ फ़ैङ्/ *noun* [C] a long sharp tooth of a dog, snake, etc. कुत्ते, सांप आदि का लंबा दाँत

**fantasize** (*also* **-ise**) /ˈfæntəsaɪz ˈफ़ैन्टसाइज़्/ *verb* [I, T] to imagine sth that you would like to happen मनचाही बात होने की कल्पना करना *He liked to fantasize that he had won a gold medal at the Olympics.*

**fantastic** /fænˈtæstɪk फ़ैन्ˈटैस्टिक्/ *adj.* **1** (*informal*) very good; excellent बहुत अच्छा; उत्कृष्ट *She's a fantastic swimmer.* **2** strange and difficult to believe विचित्र और अविश्वसनीय *a story full of fantastic creatures from other worlds* **3** (*informal*) very large or great बहुत बड़ा या अधिक *A Rolls Royce costs a fantastic amount of money.* ▶ **fantastically** /-kli -क्लि/ *adv.* विचित्र और अविश्वसनीय रूप से

**fantasy** /ˈfæntəsi ˈफ़ैन्टसि/ *noun* [C, U] (*pl.* **fantasies**) situations that are not true, that you just imagine काल्पनिक परिस्थितियाँ, वास्तविकता से दूर की बात *I have a fantasy about going to live in the Bahamas.* ○ *They live in a world of fantasy.*

**fanzine** /ˈfænzi:n ˈफ़ैन्ज़ीन् / *noun* [C] a magazine that is written by and for people **(fans)** who like a particular sports team, singer, etc. किसी विशेष टीम, गायक आदि के प्रशंसकों की निजी पत्रिका या उनके लिए प्रकाशित पत्रिका

**FAQ** /ˌef eɪ ˈkju: ˌएफ़् ऐ ˈक्यू / *noun* [C] a document on the Internet that contains the most *frequently asked questions* about a subject and the answers to these questions इंटरनेट पर डाला गया विवरण-पत्र जिसमें किसी विषय पर बहुधा पूछे जाने वाले प्रश्न (*frequently asked questions* FAQ) और उनके उत्तर दिए होते हैं

**far[1]** /fɑ:(r) फ़ा(र्)/ *adj.* (**farther** /ˈfɑ:ðə(r) ˈफ़ाद़(र्)/ or **further** /ˈfɜ:ðə(r) ˈफ़द्र(र्)/, **farthest** /ˈfɑ:ðɪst ˈफ़ाद्रिस्ट् / or **furthest** /ˈfɜ:ðɪst ˈफ़द्रिस्ट् /) **1** a long way away; distant बहुत दूर; दूरस्थ *Let's walk—it's not far.* **2** (*only before a noun*) the largest distance away of two or more things दो या अधिक वस्तुओं की अधिकतम दूरी *the far side of the river* **3** (*only before a noun*) a long way from the centre in the direction mentioned (निर्दिष्ट दिशा में) केंद्र से बहुत दूर *politicians from the far left of the party*

IDM **a far cry from sth/from doing sth** an experience that is very different from sth/doing sth किसी असल वस्तु या काम से बहुत अधिक भिन्न अनुभव

**far[2]** /fɑ:(r) फ़ा(र्)/ *adv.* (**farther** /ˈfɑ:ðə(r) ˈफ़ाद्र(र्)/ or **further** /ˈfɜ:ðə(r) ˈफ़द्र(र्)/, **farthest** /ˈfɑ:ðɪst ˈफ़ाद्रिस्ट् / or **furthest** /ˈfɜ:ðɪst ˈफ़दिस्ट् /) **1** (at) a distance दूर *Jaipur's not far from here.* ○ *How far did we walk yesterday?* ○ *If we sit too far away from the screen I won't be able to see the film.* ○ *I can't swim as far as you.* ○ *How much further is it?*

NOTE इस अर्थ में **far** का प्रयोग निषेधवाचक और प्रश्नवाचक वाक्यों में होता है। वाक्य स्वीकारात्मक हो तो **a long way** का प्रयोग होता है—*It's a long way from here to the sea.* कुछ वाक्यों में ध्वनित अर्थ निषेध का होता है परंतु बाह्य रूप स्वीकारात्मक होता है। **Far** का प्रयोग उनमें हो सकता है—*Let's get a bus. It's much too far to walk.*

**2** very much बहुत अधिक *She's far more intelligent than I thought.* ○ *There's far too much salt in this soup.* **3** (to) a certain degree एक सीमा (तक) *How far have you got with your homework?* ○ *The company employs local people as far as possible.* **4** a long time बहुत देर तक *We danced far into the night.*

IDM **as far as** to the place mentioned but not further निर्दिष्ट स्थान तक पर आगे नहीं *We walked as far as the river and then turned back.*

**as/so far as** used for giving your opinion or judgement of a situation किसी स्थिति के विषय में अपनी राय देने के लिए प्रयुक्त; जहाँ तक... ***As far as I know**, she's not coming, but I may be wrong.* ○ ***So far as** school work **is concerned**, he's hopeless.* ○ ***As far as I'm concerned**, this is the most important point.* ○ ***As far as I can see**, the accident was Raju's fault, not Radha's.*

**as far as the eye can see** to the furthest place you can see जितनी अधिक दूर तक नज़र जा सके

**by far** (*used for emphasizing comparative or superlative words*) by a large amount बड़े पैमाने पर *Kamran is by far the best student in the class.*

**far from doing sth** instead of doing sth (कुछ करने) के बजाय, के स्थान पर *Far from enjoying the film, he fell asleep in the middle.*

**far from sth** almost the opposite of sth; not at all किसी बात से लगभग उलटा; बिलकुल भी नहीं *He's far from happy* (= he's very sad or angry).

**far from it** (*informal*) certainly not; just the opposite यक़ीनन नहीं; इसके एकदम विपरीत *'Did you enjoy your holiday?' 'No, far from it. It was awful.'*

**few and far between** ➪ **few** देखिए।

**go far 1** to be enough काफ़ी होना *This food won't go very far between three of us.* **2** to be successful in life ज़ीवन में सफल होना *Dinesh is very talented and should go far.*

**go too far** to behave in a way that causes trouble or upsets other people ऐसा आचरण करना कि लोग परेशान हो जाएँ; सीमा से बाहर जाना *He's always been naughty but this time he's gone too far.*

**so far** until now अभी तक *So far the weather has been good but it might change.*

**so far so good** (*spoken*) everything has gone well until now अब तक तो सब ठीक रहा

**faraway** /ˈfɑ:rəweɪ ˈफ़ारअवे / *adj.* (*only before a noun*) **1** (*written*) a great distance away बहुत दूर का *He told us stories of faraway countries.* **2** (used about a look in a person's eyes) as if you are thinking of sth else (व्यक्ति की आँखों का भाव) किसी अन्य सोच में मग्न; अन्यमनस्क, दुचित्ता *She stared out of the window with a faraway look in her eyes.*

**farce** /fɑ:s फ़ास् / *noun* [C] **1** something important or serious that is not organized well or treated with respect ढोंग, तमाशा; चलताऊ ढंग से आयोजित कोई गंभीर या महत्त्वपूर्ण कार्यक्रम *The meeting was a farce—everyone was shouting at the same time.* **2** a funny play for the theatre full of ridiculous situations बेतुकी परिस्थितियों से पूर्ण हास्यजनक नाटक ▶ **farcical** /ˈfɑ:sɪkl ˈफ़ासिक्ल् / *adj.* हास्यास्पद, बेतुका

**fare**[1] /feə(r) फ़ेअ(र्)/ *noun* [C] the amount of money you pay to travel by bus, train, taxi, etc. किसी वाहन में यात्रा करने का भाड़ा; किराया *What's the fare to Bangalore?* ○ *Adults pay* ***full fare****, children pay* ***half fare****.*

**fare**[2] /feə(r) फ़ेअ(र्)/ *verb* [I] (*formal*) to be successful or not successful in a particular situation किसी काम में सफल या विफल होना *How did you fare in your examination* (= did you do well or badly)*?*

**the Far East** *noun* [*sing.*] China, Japan and other countries in E and SE Asia सुदूर पूर्व (के देश); पूर्व और दक्षिण-पूर्व एशिया के देश—चीन, जापान आदि ➪ **the Middle East** देखिए।

**farewell** /ˌfeəˈwel ˌफ़ेअˈवेल्/ *noun* [C, U] the act of saying goodbye to sb अलविदा कहने की क्रिया *He said his farewells and left.* ○ *a farewell party/drink* ▶ **farewell** *exclamation* (*old-fashioned*) विदाई

**far-fetched** *adj.* not easy to believe अस्वाभाविक-सा, सहज विश्वसनीय नहीं, कष्ट-कल्पित *It's a good book but the story's too far-fetched.*

**farm**[1] /fɑːm फ़ाम्/ *noun* [C] an area of land with fields and buildings that is used for growing crops and keeping animals कृषिक्षेत्र (जहाँ खेती की भूमि, इमारतें और पशुशालाएँ हों); फ़ार्म *to work* ***on a farm*** ○ *farm buildings/workers/animals*

**farm**[2] /fɑːm फ़ाम्/ *verb* [I, T] to use land for growing crops or keeping animals भूमि पर खेती करना या पशु पालना *She farms 200 acres.*

**farmer** /ˈfɑːmə(r) ˈफ़ाम(र्)/ *noun* [C] a person who owns or manages a farm किसी कृषि क्षेत्र का मालिक या प्रबंधक

**farmhouse** /ˈfɑːmhaʊs ˈफ़ाम्हाउस्/ *noun* [C] the house on a farm where the farmer lives फ़ार्म पर बना निवास; फ़ार्म हाउस

**farming** /ˈfɑːmɪŋ ˈफ़ामिङ्/ *noun* [U] managing a farm or working on it कृषि; कृषि का संचालन *farming methods/areas*

**farmyard** /ˈfɑːmjɑːd ˈफ़ाम्याड्/ *noun* [C] an outside area near a farmhouse surrounded by buildings or walls फ़ार्म हाउस का अहाता

**far-reaching** *adj.* having a great influence on a lot of other things अन्य अनेक वस्तुओं को अत्यधिक प्रभावित करने वाला; दूरगामी *far-reaching changes*

**far-sighted** *adj.* **1** being able to see what will be necessary in the future and making plans for it भविष्य के लिए आवश्यकतानुसार योजनाएँ बनाने में समर्थ; दूरदर्शी **2** (*AmE*) = **long-sighted**

**fart** /fɑːt फ़ाट्/ *verb* [I] (*informal*) to suddenly let gas from the stomach escape from your bottom अपान वायु छोड़ना; पादना ▶ **fart** *noun* [C] अपान वायु, पाद

**farther** /ˈfɑːðə(r) ˈफ़ाद्र(र्)/ ➪ **far** का comparative रूप ➪ **further** पर नोट देखिए।

**farthest** /ˈfɑːðɪst ˈफ़ाद्रिस्ट्/ ➪ **far** का superlative रूप

**fascinate** /ˈfæsɪneɪt ˈफ़ैसिनेट्/ *verb* [T] to attract or interest sb very much आकृष्ट करना या रुचि जगाना; मोहित करना *Chinese culture has always fascinated me.* ▶ **fascinating** *adj.* आकर्षक, मोहक ▶ **fascination** /ˌfæsɪˈneɪʃn ˌफ़ैसिˈनेश्न्/ *noun* [C, U] आकर्षण, सम्मोहन

**fascism** (*also* **Fascism**) /ˈfæʃɪzəm ˈफ़ैशिज़म्/ *noun* [U] an extreme (**right-wing**) political system धुर दक्षिणीपंथी राजनीतिक विचारधारा; फ़ासीवाद या फ़ासिस्टवाद ▶ **fascist** (*also* **Fascist**) /ˈfæʃɪst ˈफ़ैशिस्ट्/ *noun* [C], *adj.* फ़ासीवादी

**fashion** /ˈfæʃn ˈफ़ैश्न्/ *noun* **1** [C, U] the style of dressing or behaving that is the most popular at a particular time समय-विशेष में सर्वाधिक लोकप्रिय व्यवहार या वस्त्रधारण की शैली; फ़ैशन, प्रचलन *What is* ***the latest fashion*** *in hairtyles?* ○ *a fashion show/model/magazine* ○ *Jeans are always* ***in fashion****.* ○ *That colour is* ***out of fashion*** *this year.* **2** [*sing.*] the way you do sth कुछ करने का तरीक़ा, विधि या शैली *Watch him. He's been behaving* ***in a*** very strange ***fashion****.*

**fashionable** /ˈfæʃnəbl ˈफ़ैश्नब्ल्/ *adj.* **1** popular or in a popular style at the time समय-विशेष में लोकप्रिय; फ़ैशनेबल, प्रचलित *a fashionable area/dress/opinion* **2** considering fashion to be important शौक़ीन, फ़ैशन-पसंद *fashionable society* ✪ विलोम **unfashionable** या **old-fashioned** ▶ **fashionably** /-nəbli -नब्लि/ *adv.* प्रचलित तरीक़े से

**fast**[1] /fɑːst फ़ास्ट्/ *adj.* **1** able to move or act at great speed तेज़, तीव्रगामी *a fast car/worker/runner/reader* ➪ **quick** पर नोट देखिए। **2** (used about a clock or watch) showing a time that is later than the real time (घड़ी) सही से अधिक समय दिखाते हुए; तेज़ *The clock is five minutes fast.* ✪ विलोम **slow** **3** (used about camera film) very sensitive to light, and therefore good for taking photographs in poor light or of things that are moving quickly (कैमरा फ़िल्म) प्रकाश के प्रति अति संवेदनशील और इसलिए कम प्रकाश में तथा तीव्रगामी पदार्थों के फ़ोटो लेने में समर्थ **4** (*not before a noun*) firmly fixed कसकर बँधा हुआ, गहरा या पक्का *He made the boat fast* (= he tied it to something) *before he got out.* ○ *Do you think the colour in this T-shirt is fast* (= will not come out when washed)*?*

IDM **fast and furious** very fast and exciting तेज़ और उत्तेजक

**hard and fast** ➪ **hard**[1] देखिए।

**fast²** /fɑ:st फ़ास्ट्/ *adv.* **1** quickly तेज़, तेज़ गति से *She ran very fast.* **2** firmly or deeply गहराई से, गहरे *Sameer was **fast asleep** by ten o'clock.* ○ *Our car was stuck fast in the mud.*

**fast³** /fɑ:st फ़ास्ट्/ *verb* [I] to eat no food for a certain time, usually for religious reasons उपवास रखना *Muslims fast during Ramadan.* ▶ **fast** *noun* [C] उपवास

**fasten** /ˈfɑ:sn ˈफ़ासन्/ *verb* **1** [I, T] **fasten (sth) (up)** to close or join the two parts of sth; to become closed or joined किसी वस्तु के दो भागों को बाँधना या बंद करना; बँध जाना या बंद हो जाना *Please fasten your seat belts.* ○ *Fasten your coat up—it's cold outside.* ○ *My dress fastens at the back.* **2** [T] **fasten sth (on/to sth); fasten A and B (together)** to fix or tie sth to sth, or two things together किसी पर किसी वस्तु को लगाना या दो वस्तुओं को मज़बूती से जोड़ना *Fasten this badge on your jacket.* ○ *How can I fasten these pieces of wood together?* **3** [T] to close or lock sth firmly so that it will not open किसी वस्तु को मज़बूती से बंद कर देना (ताकि वह खुले नहीं) *Close the window and fasten it securely.*

**fastener** /ˈfɑ:snə(r) ˈफ़ासन(र्)/ (*also* **fastening**) /ˈfɑ:snɪŋ ˈफ़ासनिङ्/ *noun* [C] something that fastens things together वस्तुओं को बाँधने या कसने वाली वस्तु

**fast food** *noun* [U] food that can be served very quickly in special restaurants and is often taken away to be eaten in the street कुछ भोजनालयों में मिलने वाला ऐसा भोजन जिसे तुरंत परोसा जा सकता है और प्रायः बाहर ले जाकर खाया जाता है *a fast food restaurant*

**fast forward** *verb* [T] to make a videotape or a cassette go forward quickly without playing it वीडियो टेप या कैसेट को बिना बजाए आगे बढ़ाना; फास्ट फ़ॉर्वड करना ▶ **fast forward** *noun* [U] फ़ास्ट फ़ॉर्वर्ड बटन *Press fast forward to advance the tape.* ○ *the fast-forward button* ➪ **rewind** देखिए।

**fastidious** /fæˈstɪdiəs फ़ैˈस्टिडिअस्/ *adj.* difficult to please; wanting everything to be perfect तुनकमिज़ाज, कठिनाई से संतुष्ट होने वाला; हर बात को उत्कृष्टतम रूप में देखने का इच्छुक; पूर्णतावादी

**fat¹** /fæt फ़ैट्/ *adj.* (**fatter; fattest**) **1** (used about people's or animal's bodies) weighing too much; covered with too much flesh (मनुष्यों और पशुओं का शरीर) बहुत भारी; मोटा, मांसल शरीर वाला *You'll get fat if you eat too much.* ✪ विलोम **thin**

> **NOTE** किसी व्यक्ति को **fat** कहना अच्छा नहीं समझा जाता। इसके लिए **plump, stout** या **overweight** अधिक शिष्ट शब्द हैं।

**2** (used about a thing) thick or full (वस्तु) मोटी या भरी हुई *a fat wallet/book*

**fat²** /fæt फ़ैट्/ *noun* **1** [U] the soft white substance under the skins of animals and people पशुओं और मनुष्यों की त्वचा के नीचे का कोमल, श्वेत, पदार्थ; चरबी *I don't like meat with fat on it.* ➪ **fatty** adjective देखिए। **2** [C, U] the substance containing oil that we obtain from animals, plants or seeds and use for cooking खाने का तेल जो पशुओं, पौधों या बीजों से मिलता है *Cook the onions in a little fat.*

**fatal** /ˈfeɪtl ˈफ़ेट्ल्/ *adj.* **1** causing or ending in death घातक; जिससे अंत में मृत्यु हो जाए, जानलेवा *a fatal accident/disease* ➪ **mortal** देखिए। **2** causing trouble or a bad result परिणाम में दुखदायी, अनिष्टकर *She made the fatal mistake of trusting him.* ▶ **fatally** /-təli -टलि/ *adv.* घातक रूप से *fatally injured*

**fatality** /fəˈtæləti फ़ˈटैलटि/ *noun* [C] (*pl.* **fatalities**) a person's death caused by an accident, in war, etc. दुर्घटना, युद्ध आदि में किसी की मृत्यु *There were no fatalities in the fire.*

**fate** /feɪt फ़ेट्/ *noun* **1** [U] the power that some people believe controls everything that happens वह शक्ति जिसे लोग सब घटनाओं का नियामक मानते हैं; नियति *It was fate that brought them together again after twenty years.* **2** [C] your future; something that happens to you (किसी व्यक्ति का) भविष्य; घटित होने वाली घटनाएँ *Both men suffered the same fate—they both lost their jobs.* ✪ विलोम **fortune**

**fateful** /ˈfeɪtfl ˈफ़ेट्फ़्ल्/ *adj.* having an important effect on the future भविष्य को गहराई से प्रभावित करने वाला *a fateful decision*

**father¹** /ˈfɑ:ðə(r) ˈफ़ाद(र्)/ *noun* [C] **1** a person's male parent पिता *Vijay looks exactly like his father.* **2 Father** the title of certain priests (ईसाई) पुरोहितों की उपाधि; फ़ादर *Father O'Reilly*

**father²** /ˈfɑ:ðə(r) ˈफ़ाद(र्)/ *verb* [T] to become a father (का) पिता बनना *to father a child*

**Father Christmas** (*also* **Santa Claus**) *noun* [C] an old man with a red coat and a long white beard who, children believe, brings presents at Christmas लाल कोट और लंबी सफ़ेद दाढ़ी वाला एक वृद्ध व्यक्ति जिसे बच्चे ऐसा मानते हैं कि वह क्रिसमस पर उनके लिए उपहार लाता है

**fatherhood** /ˈfɑ:ðəhʊd ˈफ़ादहुड्/ *noun* [U] the state of being a father पिता होने या बनने की स्थिति; पितृत्व

**father-in-law** *noun* [C] (*pl.* **fathers-in-law**) the father of your husband or wife श्वसुर; ससुर

**fatherly** /ˈfɑːðəli ˈफ़ादलि/ *adj.* like or typical of a father पिता के समान, पितृवत, पितृतुल्य *Would you like a piece of fatherly advice?*

**fathom[1]** /ˈfæðəm ˈफ़ैदम्/ *verb* [T] (*usually in the negative*) to understand sth किसी बात को समझना *I can't fathom what he means.*

**fathom[2]** /ˈfæðəm ˈफ़ैदम्/ *noun* [C] a measure of the depth of water; 6 feet (1.8 metres) पानी की गहराई की एक माप; छह फ़ीट (1.8 मीटर)

**fatigue** /fəˈtiːg फ़ˈटीग्/ *noun* [U] **1** the feeling of being extremely tired गहरी थकान *He was suffering from mental and physical fatigue.* **2** weakness in metals caused by a lot of use अधिक प्रयोग में आने से धातु में उत्पन्न कमज़ोरी *The plane crash was caused by metal fatigue in a wing.*

**fatten** /ˈfætn ˈफ़ैट्न्/ *verb* [T] **fatten sb/sth (up)** to make sb/sth fatter अधिक मोटा करना *He's fattening the pigs up for the market.*

**fattening** /ˈfætnɪŋ ˈफ़ैट्निङ्/ *adj.* (used about food) that makes people fat (भोजन) मोटापा बढ़ाने वाला *Chocolate is very fattening.*

**fatty** /ˈfæti ˈफ़ैटि/ *adj.* (**fattier; fattiest**) (used about food) having a lot of fat in or on it (भोजन) तेल या चरबी वाला

**fatty acid** *noun* [C] an acid that is found in fats and oils चरबियों और तेल में पाया जाने वाला अम्ल

**faucet** /ˈfɔːsɪt ˈफ़ॉसिट्/ (*AmE*) = **tap[2] 2**

**fault[1]** /fɔːlt फ़ॉल्ट्/ *noun* **1** [C] something wrong or not perfect in a person's character or in a thing (व्यक्ति के चरित्र या किसी वस्तु में), दोष *One of my faults is that I'm always late.* ➪ **mistake** पर नोट देखिए। **2** [U] responsibility for a mistake ग़लती की ज़िम्मेदारी *It will be your **own fault** if you don't pass your exams.* **3** [C] (*technical*) a place where there is a break in the layers of rock in the earth's surface and the rocks on either side have moved in opposite directions पृथ्वी की सतह पर वह स्थान जहाँ चट्टान की परतों में दरार आ जाती है और फलस्वरूप दोनों ओर की चट्टानें विपरीत दिशाओं में खिसक जाती हैं; भ्रंश ➪ **limestone** पर चित्र देखिए।

**IDM be at fault** to be wrong or responsible for a mistake ग़लती पर होना या ग़लती के लिए ज़िम्मेदार होना *The other driver was at fault—he didn't stop at the traffic lights.*

**find fault (with sb/sth)** ➪ **find[1]** देखिए।

**fault[2]** /fɔːlt फ़ॉल्ट्/ *verb* [T] to find sth wrong with sb/sth (किसी व्यक्ति या वस्तु की) ग़लती निकालना *It was impossible to fault her English.*

**faultless** /ˈfɔːltləs ˈफ़ॉल्ट्लस्/ *adj.* without any mistakes; perfect निर्दोष, त्रुटिहीन; श्रेष्ठ, उत्कृष्ट *The pianist gave a faultless performance.*

**faulty** /ˈfɔːlti ˈफ़ॉल्टि/ *adj.* (used especially about electricity or machinery) not working properly (बिजली या मशीन) जिसमें ख़राबी आ जाए *a faulty switch*

**fauna** /ˈfɔːnə ˈफ़ॉना/ *noun* [U] all the animals of an area or a period of time काल-विशेष या क्षेत्र विशेष के जीव-जंतु *the flora and fauna of the Sunderbans* ➪ **flora** देखिए।

**faux pas** /ˌfəʊˈpɑː, फ़ोˈपा/ *noun* [C] (*pl.* **faux pas** /ˌfəʊ ˈpɑːz ,फ़ोˈपाज़्/) something you say or do that is embarrassing or offends people स्वयं को शरमिंदा या लोगों को रुष्ट करने वाली बात या काम *to **make a faux pas***

**favour[1]** (*AmE* **favor**) /ˈfeɪvə(r) ˈफ़ेव(र्)/ *noun* **1** [C] something that helps sb (किसी की) सहायता; अनुग्रह *Would you **do me a favour** and post this letter for me?* ○ *Could I **ask you a favour**?* ○ *Are they paying you for the work, or are you doing it **as a favour**?* **2** [U] **favour (with sb)** liking or approval (किसी पर) कृपादृष्टि या (किसी का) समर्थन *I'm afraid I'm **out of favour** with my neighbour since our last argument.* ○ *The new boss's methods didn't **find favour** with the staff.*

**IDM in favour of sb/sth** in agreement with से सहमत *Are you in favour of private education?*

**in sb's favour** to the advantage of sb किसी के पक्ष में *The committee decided in their favour.*

**favour[2]** (*AmE* **favor**) /ˈfeɪvə(r) ˈफ़ेव(र्)/ *verb* [T] **1** to support sb/sth; to prefer को समर्थन देना; अधिक पसंद करना *Which suggestion do you favour?* **2** to treat one person very well and so be unfair to others किसी एक व्यक्ति के साथ अधिक अच्छा बरताव करना और अन्यों के साथ पक्षपात करना *Parents must try not to favour one of their children.*

**favourable** (*AmE* **favorable**) /ˈfeɪvərəbl ˈफ़ेवरबल्/ *adj.* **1** showing liking or approval अनुकूल *He made a favourable impression on the interviewers.* **2** (often used about the weather) suitable or helpful (मौसम) उपयुक्त या सहायक *Conditions are favourable for skiing today.* ✪ विलोम **unfavourable** या **adverse** ▶ **favourably** (*AmE* **favorably**) /-rəbli -रब्लि/ *adv.* अनुकूलतापूर्वक

**favourite[1]** (*AmE* **favorite**) /ˈfeɪvərɪt ˈफ़ेवरिट्/ *noun* **1** liked more than any other किसी भी अन्य से अधिक प्रिय; पसंदीदा *What is your favourite colour?* ○ *Who is your favourite singer?*

**favourite[2]** (*AmE* **favorite**) /ˈfeɪvərɪt ˈफ़ेव़रिट्/ *noun* [C] **1** a person or thing that you like more than any others (व्यक्ति या वस्तु) स्नेहभाजन या विशेष प्रिय *The other kids were jealous of Rashmi because she was the teacher's favourite.* **2 favourite (for sth/to do sth)** the horse, team, competitor, etc. who is expected to win (घोड़ा, टीम, प्रतियोगी आदि) प्रत्याशित विजेता; जिसकी विजय सर्वाधिक संभावित है *Saurabh is the hot favourite for the leadership of the party.* ✪ विलोम **outsider**

**favouritism** (*AmE* **favoritism**) /ˈfeɪvərɪtɪzəm ˈफ़ेव़रिटिज़म्/ *noun* [U] giving unfair advantages to the person or people that you like best पक्षपात, तरफ़दारी *The referee was accused of* ***showing favouritism*** *to the home side.*

**fawn[1]** /fɔːn फ़ॉन्/ *adj., noun* [U] (of) a light yellowish-brown colour हलके पीले-भूरे रंग का

**fawn[2]** /fɔːn फ़ॉन्/ *noun* [C] a young animal **(deer)** मृगछौना, शिशु हरिण ➪ **deer** पर नोट देखिए।

**fax[1]** /fæks फ़ैक्स्/ *noun* **1** [C, U] a copy of a letter, etc. that you can send by telephone lines using a special machine टेलीफ़ोन द्वारा विशेष मशीन के माध्यम से भेजा पत्र (प्रतिलिपि), फ़ैक्स; दूरपत्र *They need an answer today so I'll* ***send a fax***. ○ *They contacted us* ***by fax***. **2** [C] (*also* **fax machine**) the machine that you use for sending faxes फ़ैक्स भेजने की मशीन *Have you got a fax?* ○ *What's your fax number?*

**fax[2]** /fæks फ़ैक्स्/ *verb* [T] **fax sth (to sb); fax sb (sth)** to send sb a fax फ़ैक्स के द्वारा भेजना *We will fax our order to you tomorrow.* ○ *I've faxed her a copy of the letter.*

**faze** /feɪz फ़ेज़्/ *verb* [T] (*informal*) to make sb worried or nervous किसी को चिंतित या परेशान कर देना

**fear[1]** /fɪə(r) फ़िअ(र्)/ *noun* [C, U] the feeling that you have when sth dangerous, painful or frightening might happen भय, डर *He was shaking* ***with fear*** *after the accident.* ○ *People in this area live* ***in constant fear*** *of crime.*

IDM **no fear** (*spoken*) (used when answering a suggestion) certainly not (सुझाव के उत्तर में प्रयुक्त) कदापि नहीं

**fear[2]** /fɪə(r) फ़िअ(र्)/ *verb* [T] **1** to be afraid of sb/sth or of doing sth किसी बात या काम से डरना *We all fear illness and death.* **2** to feel that sth bad might happen or might have happened ऐसा लगना कि कुछ बुरा हो सकता है या हो चुका होगा; आशंका होना या करना *The government fears that it will lose the next election.* ○ *Thousands of people are feared dead in the earthquake.*

PHR V **fear for sb/sth** to be worried about sb/sth किसी व्यक्ति या वस्तु के विषय में चिंतित होना *Parents often fear for the safety of their children.*

**fearful** /ˈfɪəfl ˈफ़िअफ़्ल्/ *adj.* (*formal*) **1 fearful (of sth/doing sth); fearful that...** afraid or worried about sth भयभीत या चिंतित *You should never be fearful of starting something new.* ○ *They were fearful that they would miss the plane.* ➪ **frightened** और **scared** देखिए तथा **afraid** पर नोट देखिए। **2** terrible भयानक, भयंकर, भीषण *the fearful consequences of war* ▶ **fearfully** /-fəli -फ़लि/ *adv.* भयपूर्वक, डरते हुए ▶ **fearfulness** *noun* [U] भयंकरता, भयानकता

**fearless** /ˈfɪələs ˈफ़िअलस्/ *adj.* never afraid सर्वथा निडर, निर्भय, बेख़ौफ़ ▶ **fearlessly** *adv.* निर्भय भाव से, बिना डरे ▶ **fearlessness** *noun* [U] निर्भयता

**feasible** /ˈfiːzəbl ˈफ़ीज़ब्ल्/ *adj.* possible to do जिसे किया जा सके; व्यवहार-साध्य *a feasible plan* ▶ **feasibility** /ˌfiːzəˈbɪləti ˌफ़ीज़ˈबिलटि/ *noun* [U] व्यवहार-साध्यता

**feast** /fiːst फ़ीस्ट्/ *noun* [C] a large, special meal, especially to celebrate sth प्रीतिभोज, दावत ▶ **feast** *verb* [I] **feast (on sth)** (किसी वस्तु को) छककर खाना *They feasted on exotic dishes.*

**feat** /fiːt फ़ीट्/ *noun* [C] something you do that shows great strength, skill or courage शक्ति और कुशलता या साहस से पूर्ण कार्य; उल्लेखनीय उपलब्धि *That new bridge is a remarkable feat of engineering.* ○ *Persuading Harish to give you a pay rise was* ***no mean feat*** (= difficult to do).

**feather** /ˈfeðə(r) ˈफ़ेद़(र्)/ *noun* [C] one of the light, soft things that grow in a bird's skin and cover its body पंख, पर

**feature[1]** /ˈfiːtʃə(r) ˈफ़ीच(र्)/ *noun* [C] **1** an important or noticeable part of sth (किसी का) महत्त्वपूर्ण या उल्लेखनीय भाग *Mountains and lakes are the main features of the landscape of Kashmir.* ○ *Noise is a feature of city life.* **2** a part of the face चेहरे का कोई अंग (आँख, नाक आदि) *Her eyes are her best feature.* **3 a feature (on sth)** a newspaper or magazine article or television programme about sth पत्र-पत्रिका में विशिष्ट लेख या विशिष्ट टीवी कार्यक्रम; रूपक लेख *There's a feature on kangaroos in this magazine.* **4** (*also* **feature film**) a long film that tells a story कथा-प्रधान लंबी फ़िल्म; कथा-चित्र, फ़ीचर फ़िल्म ▶ **featureless** *adj.* विशिष्टताविहीन, नीरस *dull, featureless landscape*

**feature[2]** /ˈfiːtʃə(r) ˈफ़ीच(र्)/ *verb* **1** [T] to include sb/sth as an important part किसी को मुख्य अंश के रूप

में शामिल करना *The film features many well-known actors.* **2** [I] **feature in sth** to have a part in sth किसी का अंश बनना, किसी को किसी में शामिल करना *Does marriage feature in your future plans?* ✪ पर्याय **figure**

**Feb.** February फ़रवरी

**February** /ˈfebruəri ˈफ़ेब्रुअरि/ *noun* [U, C] (*abbr.* **Feb.**) the second month of the year, coming after January वर्ष का दूसरा महीना; फ़रवरी

NOTE महीनों के नामों के वाक्य-प्रयोग के लिए **January** की प्रविष्टि में नोट और उदाहरण देखिए।

**feces** (*AmE*) = **faeces**

**fed** ⇨ **feed[1]** का past tense और past participle रूप

**federal** /ˈfedərəl ˈफ़ेडरल्/ *adj.* **1** organized as a federation संघ के रूप में संगठित; संघात्मक *a federal system of rule* **2** connected with the central government of a federation संघ के केंद्रीय शासन से संबंधित; संघीय *That is a federal, not a state law.*

**federalist** /ˈfedərəlɪst ˈफ़ेडरलिस्ट्/ *noun* [C] a supporter of a system of government in which the individual states of a country have control of their own affairs, but are controlled by a central government for national decisions ऐसी शासन-प्रणाली का समर्थक जिसमें देश के अलग-अलग राज्य निजी मामले ख़ुद तय करते हैं परंतु राष्ट्रीय स्तर के मामलों पर केंद्रीय शासन का नियंत्रण होता है; संघवादी ▶ **federalist** *adj.* संघात्मक, संघपरक *a federalist future for Europe* ▶ **federalism** /ˈfedərəlɪzəm ˈफ़ेडरलिज़म्/ *noun* [U] संघवाद *European federalism*

**federate** /ˈfedəreɪt ˈफ़ेडरेट्/ *verb* [I] (*technical*) (used about states, organizations, etc.) to unite under a central government or organization while keeping some local control (राज्यों, संगठनों आदि के लिए प्रयुक्त) आंशिक रूप में स्थानीय नियंत्रण रखते हुए कुल मिलाकर एक केंद्रीय शासन के अंतर्गत संगठित होना

**federation** /ˌfedəˈreɪʃn ˌफ़ेडˈरेश्न्/ *noun* [C] a group of states, etc. that have joined together to form a single group राज्यों आदि के मिलने से बना एक शीर्ष संगठन; फ़ेडरेशन

**fed up** *adj.* (*informal*) (*not before a noun*) **fed up (with/of sb/sth/doing sth)** bored or unhappy; tired of sth ऊबा हुआ, परेशान; थका हुआ *What's the matter? You look really fed up.* ○ *I'm fed up with waiting for the phone to ring.*

**fee** /fi: फ़ी/ *noun* [C] **1** (*usually pl.*) the money you pay for professional advice or service from doctors, lawyers, schools, universities, etc. शुल्क, फ़ीस; डॉक्टर आदि को उनसे परामर्श के लिए किया गया भुगतान *We can't afford private school fees.* ○ *Most ticket agencies will **charge a** small **fee**.* **2** the cost of an exam, the cost of becoming a member of a club, the amount you pay to go into certain buildings, etc. परीक्षा आदि में प्रवेश, क्लब की सदस्यता आदि के लिए किया गया भुगतान; शुल्क *How much is the entrance fee?* ⇨ **pay[2]** पर नोट देखिए।

**feeble** /ˈfi:bl ˈफ़ीबल्/ *adj.* **1** with no energy or power; weak शक्तिहीन; दुर्बल, कमज़ोर *a feeble old man* ○ *a feeble cry* **2** not able to make sb believe sth पूर्णतया विश्वास योग्य नहीं; अशक्त, बेदम *a feeble argument/excuse* ▶ **feebly** *adv.* हलके से, अशक्त भाव से *He shook his head feebly.*

**feed[1]** /fi:d फ़ीड्/ *verb* (*pt, pp* **fed** /fed फ़ेड्/) **1** [T] **feed sb/sth (on) (sth)** to give food to a person or an animal (मनुष्य या पशु को) खिलाना, भोजन देना *Don't forget to feed the dog.* ○ *Some of the snakes in the zoo are fed (on) rats.* **2** [I] **feed (on sth)** (used about animals or babies) to eat (पशुओं या शिशुओं के लिए प्रयुक्त) भोजन खाना *What do horses feed on in the winter?* ○ *Bats feed at night.* **3** [T] **feed A (with B); feed B into/to/through A** to supply sb/sth with sth; to put sth into sth else किसी को कोई वस्तु पहुँचाना; एक वस्तु में अन्य वस्तु को डालना *This channel feeds us with news and information 24 hours a day.* ○ *Metal sheets are fed through the machine one at a time.*

**feed[2]** /fi:d फ़ीड्/ *noun* **1** [C] a meal for an animal or a baby पशु या शिशु की ख़ुराक *When's the baby's next feed due?* **2** [U] food for animals पशुओं का चारा *cattle feed*

**feedback** /ˈfi:dbæk ˈफ़ीड्बैक्/ *noun* [U] information or comments about sth that you have done which tells you how good or bad it is काम की गुणवत्ता के विषय में दी गई सूचना या टिप्पणी; कर्त्ता को प्रतिसूचना, प्रतिपुष्टि *The teacher spent five minutes with each of us to **give** us **feedback on** our homework.*

**feel[1]** /fi:l फ़ील्/ *verb* (*pt, pp* **felt** /felt फ़ेल्ट्/) **1** *linking verb* (*usually with an adjective*) to be in the state that is mentioned कुछ महसूस होना, कुछ लगना *to feel cold/sick/tired/happy* ○ *How are you feeling today?* ○ *You'll feel better in the morning.* **2** *linking verb* used to say how sth seems to you when you touch, see, smell, experience, etc. it स्पर्श, दृष्टि, गंध आदि के अनुभव बताने के लिए प्रयुक्त *He **felt as if** he had been there before.* ○ *My head **feels as though** it will burst.* **3** [T] to notice or experience sth physical or emotional भौतिक या भावानात्मक स्तर पर महसूस करना *I damaged the nerves and now I can't feel anything in this hand.*

○ *I felt something crawling up my back.* **4** [T] to touch sth in order to find out what it is like किसी को स्पर्श करना (यह देखने के लिए कि कैसा लगता है) *Feel this material. Is it cotton or silk?* ○ *I felt her forehead to see if she had a temperature.* **5** [I] **feel (about) (for sb/sth)** to try to find sth with your hands instead of your eyes देखने के बजाय छूकर पता लगाना *She felt about in the dark for the light switch.* **6** [T] to be affected by sth किसी चीज़ के असर में आना (किसी को) कुछ लगना *Do you feel the cold in winter?* ○ *She felt it badly when her mother died.*

**IDM feel free (to do sth)** (*informal*) used to tell sb he/she is allowed to do sth किसी को मनचाहा करने की छूट है, यह बताने के लिए प्रयुक्त *Feel free to use the phone.*

**feel like sth/doing sth** to want sth or to want to do sth किसी वस्तु को पाने या कोई काम करने का इच्छुक होना *Do you feel like going out?*

**feel your age** to realize that you are getting old, especially compared to other younger people around you बढ़ती उम्र का असर महसूस करना (विशेषतः साथ के युवाओं के मुक़ाबले)

**not feel yourself** to not feel healthy or well स्वस्थ या नीरोग महसूस न करना

**PHR V feel for sb** to understand sb's feelings and situation and feel sorry for him/her किसी के साथ सहानुभूति होना *I really felt for him when his wife died.*

**feel up to sth/to doing sth** to have the strength and the energy to do or deal with sth कुछ करने या निपटाने की कार्य शक्ति होना *I really don't feel up to eating a huge meal.*

**feel[2]** /fiːl फ़ील्/ *noun* [*sing.*] **1** the impression sth gives you when you touch it; the impression that a place or situation gives you स्पर्श का अनुभव; स्पर्शज्ञान; स्थान या परिस्थिति का अनुभव या उससे उत्पन्न प्रभाव *You can tell it's wool by the feel.* ○ *The town has a friendly feel.* **2** an act of touching sth in order to learn about it किसी वस्तु के विषय में जानने के लिए उसे स्पर्श करने की क्रिया; स्पर्श *Let me have a feel of that material.*

**feeler** /ˈfiːlə(r) ˈफ़ील(र्)/ *noun* [C, *usually pl.*] either of the two long thin parts on the heads of some insects and of some animals that live in shells that they use to feel and touch things with कुछ कीटों और सीपी में रहने वाले कुछ प्राणियों के सिर पर लगे बारीक अंग जो स्पर्श द्वारा वस्तुओं की टोह लेते हैं; शृंगिका, स्पर्शक ✪ पर्याय **antenna**

**feeling** /ˈfiːlɪŋ ˈफ़ीलिङ्/ *noun* **1** [C] **a feeling (of sth)** something that you feel in your mind or body शरीर या मन की अनुभूति; अहसास, भावना *a feeling of hunger/happiness/fear/helplessness* ○ *I've got a funny feeling in my leg.* **2** [*sing.*] a belief or idea that sth is true or is likely to happen किसी बात के सच होने या कुछ घटित होने की संभावना का अहसास; प्रतीति *I **get the feeling** that Aryan doesn't like me much.* ○ *I **have a** nasty **feeling** that Parag didn't get our message.* **3** [C, U] **feeling(s) (about/on sth)** an attitude or opinion about sth किसी बात पर अभिवृत्ति, सोच या राय *What are your feelings on this matter?* ○ *My own feeling is that we should postpone the meeting.* ○ *Public feeling seems to be against the new dam.* **4** [U, C, *usually pl.*] a person's emotions; strong emotion किसी व्यक्ति के मनोभाव; भावावेश, प्रबल भावना *I have to tell Udit his work's not good enough but I don't want to **hurt** his **feelings**.* ○ *Let's practise that song again, this time **with feeling**.* **5** [C, U] **(a) feeling/feelings (for sb/sth)** love or understanding for sb/sth किसी के प्रति लगाव या हमदर्दी *She doesn't have much (of a) feeling for music.* ○ *He still has feelings for his first job.* **6** [U] the ability to feel in your body भौतिक संवेदना की क्षमता *After the accident he lost all feeling in his legs.*

**IDM bad/ill feeling** unhappy relations between people लोगों के बीच दुर्भावना, वैरपूर्ण या कष्टकर परस्पर संबंध *The decision caused a lot of bad feeling at the factory.*

**no hard feelings** ➪ **hard[1]** देखिए।

**feet** ➪ **foot[1]** का plural रूप

**feign** /feɪn फ़ेन्/ *verb* [T] (*formal*) to pretend that you have a particular feeling or that you are tired or ill, etc. किसी विशिष्ट भावना होने का या थकान, बीमारी आदि का स्वाँग रचना *He feigned illness to avoid going to the party.* ○ *He feigned innocence.*

**feldspar** /ˈfeldspɑː(r) ˈफ़ेल्ड्स्पा(र्)/ *noun* [U, C] (in geology) a type of white or red rock (भूविज्ञान में) एक प्रकार का सफ़ेद या लाल चट्टान

**feline** /ˈfiːlaɪn ˈफ़ीलाइन्/ *adj.* connected with an animal of the cat family; like a cat बिल्ली प्रजाति से संबंधित; बिल्ली के समान

**fell[1]** ➪ शब्द **fall[1]** का past tense रूप

**fell[2]** /fel फ़ेल्/ *verb* [T] to cut down a tree किसी पेड़ को काट डालना

**fellow[1]** /ˈfeləʊ ˈफ़ेलो/ *noun* [C] **1** a member of an academic or professional organization, or of certain universities किसी शैक्षिक या व्यावसायिक संगठन या किसी विशेष विश्वविद्यालय का सदस्य; फ़ेलो, रत्न सदस्य *a fellow of the Institute of Chartered Accountants* **2** a person who is paid to study a particular thing at a university किसी विश्वविद्यालय में वेतन पर अध्ययनरत व्यक्ति; फ़ेलो, अध्येता *Tanushree is a research fellow in the biology department.* **3** (*old-fashioned*) a man कोई पुरुष; इनसान, एक जना

**fellow²** /ˈfeləʊ ˈफ़ेलो/ *adj.* (*only before a noun*) another or others like yourself in the same situation सहभागी, साथी; उसी स्थिति में अन्य लोग *Her fellow students were all older than her.* ○ *fellow workers/passengers/citizens*

**fellowship** /ˈfeləʊʃɪp ˈफ़ेलोशिप्/ *noun* **1** [U] a feeling of friendship between people who share an interest समान रुचि के लोगों के बीच मैत्री की भावना **2** [C] a group or society of people who share the same interest or belief समान रुचि या विश्वास वाले लोगों का समूह, समाज या संघ **3** [C] the position of a college or university fellow किसी महाविद्यालय या विश्वविद्यालय में अध्येतावृति; छात्रवृति

**felon** /ˈfelən ˈफ़ेलन्/ *noun* [C] a person who commits a serious crime such as murder घोर अपराधी, जैसे हत्यारा; आततायी

**felony** /ˈfeləni ˈफ़ेलनि/ *noun* [C, U] (*pl.* **felonies**) the act of committing a serious crime such as murder; a crime of this type हत्या जैसा घोर अपराध करने की क्रिया; कोई भी घोर अपराध ➪ **misdemeanour** देखिए।

**felt¹** ➪ **feel¹** का past tense और past participle रूप

**felt²** /felt ˈफ़ेल्ट्/ *noun* [U] a type of soft cloth made from wool, etc. which has been pressed tightly together ऊन आदि को दबाकर बनाया गया मुलायम कपड़ा; नमदा, फ़ेल्ट *a felt hat*

**felt-tip pen** (*also* **felt tip**) *noun* [C] a type of pen with a point made of felt फ़ेल्ट की नोक वाला क़लम ➪ **stationery** पर चित्र देखिए।

**female¹** /ˈfiːmeɪl ˈफ़ीमेल्/ *adj.* **1** being a woman or a girl स्त्री या लड़की *a female artist/employer/student* **2** being of the sex that produces eggs or gives birth to babies अंडा देने या शिशुओं को जन्म देने वाली; मादा *a female cat* **3** (used about plants and flowers) that can produce fruit फल देने वाले पौधे और फूलों के लिए प्रयुक्त

**female²** /ˈfiːmeɪl ˈफ़ीमेल्/ *noun* [C] **1** an animal that can produce eggs or give birth to babies; a plant that can produce fruit मादा पशु; मादा पौधा **2** a woman or a girl स्त्री या लड़की

> **NOTE** **Female** और **male** शब्दों का प्रयोग प्राणियों के प्राकृतिक लिंग का निर्देश करने के लिए होता है। स्त्रियोचित गुणों का निर्देश करने वाला शब्द **feminine** है और पुरुषोचित गुणों का **masculine** है।

**feminine** /ˈfemənɪn ˈफ़ेमनिन्/ *adj.* **1** typical of or looking like a woman; connected with women स्त्रियोचित, स्त्री-सदृश; स्त्री-विषयक *My daughter always dresses like a boy. She hates looking feminine.* ➪ **female** पर नोट और **masculine** देखिए। **2** (*abbr.* **fem**) (*grammar*) (in English) of the forms of words used to describe females (अंग्रेज़ी में) शब्दों के स्त्रीलिंग रूप से संबंधित *'Lioness' is the feminine form of 'lion'.* **3** (*abbr.* **fem**) (in the grammar of some languages) belonging to a certain class of nouns, adjectives or pronouns (कुछ भाषाओं के व्याकरण में) निश्चित कोटि की संज्ञाओं, विशेषणों और सर्वनामों से संबंधित (जो केवल स्त्रीलिंग होते हैं) *The German word for a flower is feminine.* ➪ **masculine** और **neuter** देखिए। ▶ **femininity** /ˌfeməˈnɪnəti ˌफ़ेमˈनिनटि/ *noun* [U] स्त्रियोचित गुण, नारीत्व

**feminism** /ˈfemənɪzəm ˈफ़ेमनिज़म्/ *noun* [U] the belief that women should have the same rights and opportunities as men ऐसा विश्वास या सिद्धांत कि स्त्रियों को पुरुषों के समान अधिकार और अवसर प्राप्त होने चाहिए; नारीवाद ▶ **feminist** /ˈfemənɪst ˈफ़ेमनिस्ट्/ *noun* [C], *adj.* नारीवादी, नारी समान अधिकारवाद; नारीवाद से संबंधित

**femur** /ˈfiːmə(r) ˈफ़ीम(र्)/ *noun* [C] the large thick bone in the top part of your leg above the knee जाँघ की हड्डी; उर्विका ✪ पर्याय **thigh bone** ➪ **body** पर चित्र देखिए।

**fence¹** /fens फ़ेन्स्/ *noun* [C] a line of wooden or metal posts joined by wood, wire, metal, etc. to divide land or to keep in animals लकड़ी या धातु के लट्ठों से बनी बाड़ या घेरा (भूखंड को विभाजित करने या पशुओं की सुरक्षा के लिए)

**IDM** **sit on the fence** ➪ **sit** देखिए।

**fence²** /fens फ़ेन्स्/ *verb* **1** [T] to surround land with a fence ज़मीन को बाड़ से घेरना; बाड़ा लगाना **2** [I] to fight with a long thin pointed weapon (**a foil**) as a sport तलवार से लड़ाई का खेल खेलना; पटेबाज़ी करना

**PHR V** **fence sb/sth in 1** to surround sb/sth with a fence व्यक्ति या वस्तु को बाड़ से घेरना *They fenced in their garden to make it more private.* **2** to limit sb's freedom किसी व्यक्ति की स्वतंत्रता को सीमित कर देना *She felt fenced in by so many responsibilities.*

**fence sth off** to separate one area from another with a fence बाड़ लगाकर एक भूखंड को दूसरे से अलग करना

**fencing** /ˈfensɪŋ ˈफ़ेन्सिङ्/ *noun* [U] the sport of fighting with long thin pointed weapons (**foils**) तलवार-क्रीड़ा; पटेबाज़ी

**fend** /fend फ़ेन्ड् / *verb*

PHR V **fend for yourself** to look after yourself without help from anyone else बिना किसी की सहायता के अपनी देखभाल स्वयं करना *It's time Bakul left home and learned to fend for himself.*

**fend sb/sth off** to defend yourself from sb/sth that is attacking you किसी के हमले से अपने को बचाना *Politicians usually manage to fend off awkward questions.*

**fender** /ˈfendə(r) ˈफ़ेन्डर्(र्)/ *noun* [C] **1** (*AmE*) = **wing 4** **2** a low metal frame in front of an open fire that stops coal or wood from falling out चूल्हे या भट्टी के आगे बना लोहे का जँगला जो जलते हुए कोयले या लकड़ी को बाहर नहीं गिरने देता

**fennel** /ˈfenl ˈफ़ेनल्/ *noun* [U] a plant that has a thick round stem and leaves with a strong taste. The base is used as a vegetable and the seeds and leaves are used in cooking to give a special flavour to food सौंफ (पौधा)

**fenugreek** /ˈfenjugriːk ˈफ़ेनुग्रीक्/ *noun* [U] a leguminous herb with yellowish-brown seeds used as a spice मेथी

**feral** /ˈferəl ˈफ़ेरल्/ *adj.* (used about animals) living wild, especially after escaping from life as a pet or on a farm (पशु) वन में जाकर रहने वाला, विशेषतः खेत या पालतू जीवन की क़ैद से भाग निकलने के बाद

**ferment¹** /fəˈment फ़ˈमेन्ट्/ *verb* [I, T] to change or bring a chemical change in sth due to yeast or bacterial action, especially changing sugar to alcohol ख़मीर उठना या उठाना *The wine is starting to ferment.* ▶ **fermentation** /ˌfɜːmenˈteɪʃn ˌफ़मेन्ˈटेश्न्/ *noun* [U] ख़मीर उठाने की प्रक्रिया

**ferment²** /ˈfɜːment ˈफ़मेन्ट्/ *noun* [U] a state of political or social excitement and change राजनीतिक या सामाजिक उत्तेजना, अनिश्चय और परिवर्तन की स्थिति *The country is **in ferment** and nobody's sure what will happen next.*

**fern** /fɜːn फ़न्/ *noun* [C] a green plant with no flowers and a lot of long thin leaves लंबी पतली पत्तियों वाला पौधा जिसमें फूल नहीं लगते; पर्णांग ➪ **plant** पर चित्र देखिए।

**ferocious** /fəˈrəʊʃəs फ़ˈरोशस्/ *adj.* very aggressive and violent अति आक्रामक और हिंसक; उग्र व ख़ूनख़्वार *a ferocious beast/attack/storm/war* ▶ **ferociously** *adv.* उग्र व हिंसात्मक ढंग से

**ferocity** /fəˈrɒsəti फ़ˈरॉसटि/ *noun* [U] violence; cruel and aggressive behaviour हिंसा, उग्रता; निर्मम और आक्रामक आचरण ➪ **fierce** adjective देखिए।

**ferret** /ˈferɪt ˈफ़ेरिट्/ *noun* [C] a small aggressive animal used for hunting rats and rabbits छोटा हिंसक जंतु जिसे चूहों और ख़रगोशों के शिकार के लिए प्रयुक्त किया जाता है

**ferrous** /ˈferəs ˈफ़ेरस्/ *adj.* (*technical*) containing iron लौहयुक्त

**ferry¹** /ˈferi ˈफ़ेरि/ *noun* [C] (*pl.* **ferries**) a boat that carries people, vehicles or goods across a river or across a narrow part of the sea सवारियों, वाहनों आदि को नदी या समुद्र के संकरे भाग के पार पहुँचाने के काम में आने वाली नौका *a car ferry*

**ferry²** /ˈferi ˈफ़ेरि/ *verb* [T] (*pres. part.* **ferrying;** *3rd person sing. pres.* **ferries;** *pt, pp* **ferried**) to carry people or goods in a boat or other vehicle from one place to another, usually for a short distance नाव या अन्य वाहन से सवारियों या माल को, प्रायः छोटी दूरी तक ढोना *Could you ferry us across to the island?*

**fertile** /ˈfɜːtaɪl ˈफ़टाइल्/ *adj.* **1** (used about land or soil) that plants grow well in (ज़मीन या मिट्टी) उपजाऊ **2** (used about people, animals or plants) that can produce babies, fruit or new plants (मनुष्य, पशु या पौधे) संतान-उत्पत्ति या फल, नए पौधों आदि के उत्पादन में सक्षम; उर्वर **3** (used about a person's mind) full of ideas (व्यक्ति की कल्पनाशक्ति) विचारों से भरपूर उर्वर *a fertile imagination* ✪ विलोम **infertile** ➪ **sterile** देखिए। ▶ **fertility** /fəˈtɪləti फ़ˈटिलटि/ *noun* [U] उर्वरता, उत्पादन-क्षमता *Nowadays farmers can use chemicals to increase their soil's fertility* ✪ विलोम **infertility**

**fertilize** (*also* **-ise**) /ˈfɜːtəlaɪz ˈफ़टलाइज़्/ *verb* [T] **1** (*technical*) to put a male seed into an egg, a plant or a female animal so that a baby, fruit or a young animal starts to develop गर्भाधान करना; शुक्राणु या पुष्प-पराग प्रदान करना **2** to put natural or artificial substances on soil in order to make plants grow better पौधों की उत्पत्ति बढ़ाने के लिए मिट्टी में प्राकृतिक या कृत्रिम पदार्थ मिलाना ▶ **fertilization** (*also* **-isation**) /ˌfɜːtəlaɪˈzeɪʃn ˌफ़टलाइˈज़ेश्न्/ *noun* [U] गर्भाधान

**fertilizer** (*also* **-iser**) /ˈfɜːtɪlaɪzə(r) ˈफ़टिलाइज़र्(र्)/ *noun* [C, U] a natural or chemical substance that is put on land or soil to make plants grow better उत्पादन-क्षमता बढ़ाने के लिए ज़मीन या मिट्टी में डाला जाने वाला प्राकृतिक या कृत्रिम पदार्थ; उर्वरक, खाद ➪ **manure** देखिए।

**fervent** /ˈfɜːvənt ˈफ़वन्ट्/ *adj.* having or showing very strong feelings about sth जोशीला, उत्साही *She's a fervent believer in women's rights.* ○ *a fervent belief/hope/desire* ▶ **fervently** *adv.* जोशीलेपन से

**fervour** (*AmE* **fervor**) /ˈfɜːvə(r) ˈफ़व़(र्)/ *noun* [U] very strong feelings about sth; enthusiasm किसी विषय पर गहरी व प्रबल भावनाएँ; जोश, उत्साह

**fester** /ˈfestə(r) ˈफ़ेस्टर्/ *verb* [I] **1** (used about a cut or an injury) to become infected (घाव या चोट का) कीटाणुओं से संक्रमित हो जाना, मवाद से भर जाना *a festering sore/wound* **2** (used about an unpleasant situation, feeling or thought) to become more unpleasant because you do not deal with it successfully (अप्रिय स्थिति आदि का) सफलतापूर्वक न निपटाए जाने के कारण और अधिक कटु हो जाना, कटुता में वृद्धि हो जाना

**festival** /ˈfestɪvl ˈफ़ेस्टिव्ल्/ *noun* [C] **1** a day or time when people celebrate sth (especially a religious event) (धार्मिक आदि) त्योहार, पर्व *Christmas is an important Christian festival.* **2** a series of plays, films, musical performances, etc. often held regularly in one place नाटक, फ़िल्म आदि कलाओं का शृंखलाबद्ध व एक ही स्थान पर नियमित रूप से होने वाला आयोजन; उत्सव, समारोह *the Cannes Film Festival* ○ *a dance festival*

**festive** /ˈfestɪv ˈफ़ेस्टिव्/ *adj.* happy, because people are enjoying themselves celebrating sth आनंदमय, ख़ुशियों भरा, उल्लासपूर्ण, उत्सव-संबंधित *the festive season*

**festivity** /fəˈstɪvəti फ़ेˈस्टिवटि/ *noun* **1** (*pl.* **festivities**) [*pl.*] happy events when people celebrate sth आमोद-प्रमोद; ख़ुशियाँ मनाने से संबंधित गतिविधियाँ *The festivities went on until dawn.* **2** [U] being happy and celebrating sth ख़ुशियाँ मनाने की स्थिति; आनंदोत्सव *The wedding was followed by three days of festivity.*

**fetal** (*AmE*) = **foetal**

**fetch** /fetʃ फ़ेच्/ *verb* [T] **1** to go to a place and bring back sb/sth कहीं जाकर कुछ लाना *Shall I fetch you your coat?* ○ *Shall I fetch your coat for you?* **2** (used about goods) to be sold for the price mentioned (सामान) निर्दिष्ट मूल्य पर बिकना *'How much will your car fetch?' 'It should fetch about Rs 75,000.'*

**fête** /feɪt फ़ेट्/ *noun* [C] an outdoor event with competitions, entertainment and things to buy, often organized to make money for a particular purpose (प्रायः किसी विशिष्ट प्रयोजन के लिए पैसे इकट्ठे करने हेतु) खुले मैदान में लगने वाला आनंद-मेला जिसमें स्पर्धाओं, मनोरंजन, समान की बिक्री का आयोजन होता है *the school/village/church fête*

**fetus** (*AmE*) = **foetus**

**feud** /fju:d फ़्यूड्/ *noun* [C] **a feud (between A and B); a feud (with sb) (over sb/sth)** an angry and serious argument between two people or groups that continues over a long period of time दो व्यक्तियों या व्यक्ति-समूहों के बीच लंबे समय तक चलने वाला झगड़ा; पुश्तैनी रंजिश *a family feud* (= within a family or between two families) ► **feud** *verb* [I] पुश्तैनी रंजिश का चलते रहना

**feudal** /ˈfju:dl ˈफ़्यूड्ल्/ *adj.* connected with the system of feudalism सामंतवाद से संबंधित *the feudal system*

**feudalism** /ˈfju:dəlɪzəm ˈफ़्यूडलिज़म्/ *noun* [U] the social system which existed in the Middle Ages in Europe, in which people worked and fought for a person who owned land and received land and protection from him in return यूरोप की मध्ययुगीन सामाजिक प्रथा जिसमें लोग अपने मालिक की चाकरी करते थे और मालिक उनकी रक्षा; सामंतवाद

**fever** /ˈfi:və(r) ˈफ़ीव़र्/ *noun* **1** [C, U] a condition of the body when it is too hot because of illness ज्वर; बुख़ार *A high fever can be dangerous, especially in small children.*

> NOTE किसी व्यक्ति को बुख़ार होने की स्थिति व्यक्त करने के लिए ***has a temperature*** वाक्यांश का प्रयोग किया जाता है।

**2** [*sing.*] **a fever (of sth)** a state of nervous excitement आशंकाभरी उत्तेजना की स्थिति

**feverish** /ˈfi:vərɪʃ ˈफ़ीव़रिश्/ *adj.* **1** suffering from or caused by a fever ज्वर से आक्रांत या उत्पन्न *a feverish cold/dream* **2** (*usually before a noun*) showing great excitement अत्यधिक उत्तेजित ► **feverishly** *adv.* अत्यधिक उत्तेजना में/से

**few** /fju: फ़्यू/ *det. adj. noun* (*used with a plural countable noun and a plural verb*) **1** not many थोड़े-से, गिने-चुने; बहुत-से नहीं *Few people live to be 100.* ○ *There are fewer cars here today than yesterday.* ○ *Few of the players played really well.* **2 a few** a small number of; some (किसी की) थोड़ी-सी संख्या; कुछ *a few people* ○ *a few hours/days/years* ○ *I'll meet you later. I've got a few things to do first.* ○ *I knew a few of the people there.* ➪ **less** पर नोट देखिए।

IDM **few and far between** not happening very often; not common लंबे अंतराल पर, कभी-कभी या बहुत कम; जब-तब

**a good few; quite a few** quite a lot बहुत-से, बहुतेरे *It's been a good few years since I saw him last.*

**ff.** *abbr.* used to show that sth starts on a particular page or line and continues for several pages or lines more यह बताने के लिए प्रयुक्त कि प्रसंग विशेष अमुक पृष्ठ या पंक्ति से शुरू होकर अनेक पंक्तियों या पृष्ठों तक जाता है *British Politics, p 10 ff.*

**fiancé** (*feminine* **fiancée**) /fiˈɒnseɪ फ़िˈऑन्से/ *noun* [C] a person who has promised to marry sb मँगेर या मँगेतर, वाग्दत्त या वाग्दत्ता *This is my fiancé Prem. We got engaged a few weeks ago.*

**fiasco** /fiˈæskəʊ फ़िˈऐस्को/ *noun* (*pl.* **fiascos** *AmE* **fiascoes**) an event that does not succeed, often in a way that causes embarrassment विफलता, प्रायः ऐसी जो शरमिंदगी लाए; बंटाढार *Our last party was a complete fiasco.*

**fib** /fɪb फ़िब्/ *noun* [C] (*informal*) something you say that is not true असत्य कथन, झूठ, झूठी बात, गप *Please don't tell fibs.* ✪ पर्याय **lie** ▶ **fib** *verb* [I] (**fibbing; fibbed**) झूठ बोलना NOTE **Fib** का प्रयोग हलके-फुलके झूठ के लिए किया जाता है।

**fibre** (*AmE* **fiber**) /ˈfaɪbə(r) ˈफ़ाइब(र्)/ *noun* **1** [U] parts of plants that you eat which are good for you because they help to move food quickly through your body रेशा, तंतु *Wholemeal bread is **high in fibre**.* **2** [C, U] a material or a substance that is made from natural or artificial threads प्राकृतिक या कृत्रिम तंतु से बना पदार्थ ***natural fibres*** (= for example cotton and wool) ○ ***man-made/synthetic fibres*** (= for example, nylon, polyester, etc.) **3** [C] one of the thin threads which form a natural or artificial substance बारीक तंतु जिससे कोई प्राकृतिक या कृत्रिम पदार्थ बनता है *cotton/wool/nerve/muscle fibres*

**fibreglass** (*AmE* **fiberglass**) /ˈfaɪbəglɑːs ˈफ़ाइबग्लास्/ (*also* **glass fibre**) *noun* [U] a material made from small threads of plastic or glass, used for making small boats, parts of cars, etc. प्लास्टिक या शीशे के महीन तंतुओं से बनी पदार्थ जिससे छोटी नावें, कार के पुरज़े आदि बनते हैं; फ़ाइबरग्लास

**fibre optics** (*AmE* **fiber optics**) *noun* [U] the use of very thin pieces of glass, etc. (**fibres**) for sending information in the form of light signals प्रकाश संकेतों के रूप में सूचना-संप्रेषण के लिए फ़ाइबर का प्रयोग; तंतु प्रकाशिकी ▶ **fibre-optic** *adj.* फ़ाइबर के प्रयोग द्वारा सूचना को प्रकाश संकेतों के रूप में भेजने की पद्धति से संबंधित *fibre-optic cables*

**fibrin** /ˈfaɪbrɪn; ˈfɪbrɪn ˈफ़ाइब्रिन्; ˈफ़िब्रिन्/ *noun* [U] a substance that forms in the blood to help stop the blood from flowing, for example when there is a cut रक्त में बनने वाला पदार्थ जो चोट लगने आदि की स्थिति में रक्त के प्रवाह को रोकने में सहायक होता है; फ़ाइब्रिन

**fibrinogen** /faɪˈbrɪnədʒən फ़ाइˈब्रिनजन्/ *noun* [U] a substance in the blood from which **fibrin** is made रक्त में पाया जाने वाला पदार्थ जिससे फ़ाइब्रिन बनता है

**fibula** /ˈfɪbjələ ˈफ़िब्यला/ *noun* [C] (*technical*) the outer bone of the two bones in the lower part of your leg, between your knee and your foot घुटने से टखने के बीच की दो हड्डियों में से बाहरी हड्डी; बहिर्जंघिका ➪ **tibia** देखिए तथा **body** पर चित्र देखिए।

**fickle** /ˈfɪkl ˈफ़िकल्/ *adj.* always changing your mind or your feelings so you cannot be trusted मत, भावनाएँ आदि निरंतर बदलते हुए और इसलिए अविश्वसनीय; अस्थिरमति, चंचल *a fickle friend*

**fiction** /ˈfɪkʃn ˈफ़िक्शन्/ *noun* [U] stories, novels, etc. which describe events and people that are not real कहानियाँ, उपन्यास, कथाएँ आदि जो काल्पनिक घटनाओं और व्यक्तियों का वर्णन करते हैं; कथा-साहित्य *I don't read much fiction.* ✪ विलोम **non-fiction** ➪ **fact** देखिए।

**fictional** /ˈfɪkʃənl ˈफ़िक्शनल्/ *adj.* not real or true; only existing in stories, novels, etc. कल्पित, काल्पनिक; केवल कथालोक में *The book gave a fictional account of a doctor's life.* ➪ **factual** देखिए।

**fictitious** /fɪkˈtɪʃəs फ़िक्ˈटिशस्/ *adj.* invented; not real मनगढ़ंत; बनावटी *The novel is set in a fictitious village called Gangapur.*

**fiddle[1]** /ˈfɪdl ˈफ़िडल्/ *noun* [C] (*informal*) **1** = **violin** **2** (*BrE*) a dishonest action, especially one connected with money बेईमानी, विशेषतः पैसे के मामले में *a tax fiddle*

**fiddle[2]** /ˈfɪdl ˈफ़िड्ल्/ *verb* **1** [I] **fiddle (about/around) (with sth)** to play with sth carelessly, because you are nervous or not thinking आशंका में या निरुद्देश्य किसी वस्तु से खिलवाड़ करना *He sat nervously, fiddling with a pencil.* **2** [T] (*informal*) to change the details or facts of sth (business accounts, etc.) in order to get money dishonestly बेईमानी से लाभ पाने के लिए तथ्यों, हिसाब आदि में हेरा-फेरी करना *She fiddled her expenses form.*

**fiddler** /ˈfɪdlə(r) ˈफ़िड्ल(र्)/ *noun* [C] a person who plays a musical instrument with strings (**a violin**), especially to play a certain kind of music (**folk music**) वायलिन-वादक

**fiddly** /ˈfɪdli ˈफ़िड्लि/ *adj.* (*informal*) difficult to do or manage with your hands (because small or complicated parts are involved) हाथों से करने या सँभालने में कठिन (क्योंकि पुरज़े छोटे या पेचीदा हैं)

**fidelity** /fɪˈdeləti फ़िˈडेलटि/ *noun* [U] **1** (*formal*) **fidelity (to sb/sth)** the quality of being faithful, especially to a wife or husband by not having a sexual relationship with anyone else आपसी संबंधों में एकनिष्ठता, विशेषतः पति-पत्नी के बीच NOTE इस अर्थ के लिए कम औपचारिक शब्द **faithfulness** है। ✪ विलोम **infidelity** **2** (used about translations, the reproduction of music, etc.) the quality of being accurate or close to the original (अनुवाद आदि पुनरुक्तिपरक क्रियाओं की) विशुद्धता या मूलनिष्ठता ➪ **hi-fi** देखिए।

**fidget** /ˈfɪdʒɪt ˈफ़िजिट्/ *verb* [I] **fidget (with sth)** to keep moving your body, hands or feet because you are nervous, bored, excited, etc. बेचैनी, ऊब, उत्तेजना आदि के कारण हिलते-डुलते रहना *She fidgeted nervously with her keys.* ▶ **fidgety** *adj.* अधीर, बेचैन

**field**[1] /fiːld फ़ील्ड्/ *noun* [C] **1** an area of land on a farm, usually surrounded by fences or walls, used for growing crops or keeping animals in कृषिभूमि का वह अंश जहाँ फ़सलें उगाई जाती हैं या पशुओं को अंदर आने से रोकने के लिए दीवार या बाड़ लगाई जाती है; खेत **2** an area of study or knowledge अध्ययन या ज्ञान का क्षेत्र *He's an expert in the field of economics.* ○ *That question is outside my field* (= not one of the subjects that I know about). **3** an area of land used for sports, games or some other activity वह भूक्षेत्र जहाँ खेल-कूद या खुले में की जाने वाली गतिविधि की जाती है; मैदान *a football field* ○ *an airfield* (= where aeroplanes land and take off) ○ *a battlefield* ➪ **pitch** देखिए। **4** an area affected by or included in sth किसी से प्रभावित या किसी में समाविष्ट क्षेत्र *a magnetic field* ○ *It's outside my field of vision* (= I can't see it). ➪ **magnet** पर चित्र देखिए। **5** an area of land where oil, coal or other minerals are found क्षेत्र जहाँ तेल, कोयला और अन्य खनिज मिलते हैं *a coalfield* ○ *a North Sea oilfield*

**field**[2] /fiːld फ़ील्ड्/ *verb* **1** [I, T] (in cricket, baseball, etc.) to (be ready to) catch and throw back the ball after sb has hit it (क्रिकेट, बेसबॉल आदि में) बल्लेबाज़ द्वारा मारी गेंद को लपकना और वापस फेंकना; फील्डिंग या क्षेत्ररक्षण करना **NOTE** जब एक टीम **fielding** करती है तो दूसरी **batting** करती है। **2** [T] to choose a team for a game of football, cricket, etc. (फ़ुटबॉल, क्रिकेट आदि के लिए) टीम का चयन करना *New Zealand is fielding an excellent team for the next match.*

**field day** *noun*

**IDM have a field day** to get the opportunity to do sth you enjoy, especially sth other people disapprove of मनचाही मौजमस्ती करने का मौका मिलना *The newspapers always have a field day when there's a political scandal.*

**fielder** /ˈfiːldə(r) ˈफ़ील्ड(र्)/ *noun* [C] (in cricket and baseball) a member of the team that is trying to catch the ball rather than hit it (क्रिकेट और बेसबॉल में) क्षेत्ररक्षक (न कि बल्लेबाज़) टीम का सदस्य; फील्डर

**field event** *noun* [C] a sport, such as jumping and throwing, that is not a race and does not involve running छलाँग लगाना, चक्का फेंकना आदि खेल क्रीड़ा जिसमें दौड़ न लगानी हो ➪ **track event** देखिए।

**fieldwork** /ˈfiːldwɜːk ˈफ़ील्ड्वक्/ *noun* [U] practical research work done outside school, college, etc. विद्यालय, महाविद्यालय आदि से बाहर जाकर किया गया क्रियात्मक अनुसंधान कार्य; फ़ील्डवर्क

**fiend** /fiːnd फ़ीन्ड्/ *noun* [C] **1** a very cruel person अति निर्मम व्यक्ति **2** (*informal*) a person who is very interested in one particular thing किसी बात-विशेष में अत्यधिक रुचि रखने वाला व्यक्ति *a health fiend* ✪ पर्याय **fanatic**

**fiendish** /ˈfiːndɪʃ ˈफ़ीन्डिश्/ *adj.* **1** very unpleasant or cruel अति अप्रिय या दुष्ट; पैशाचिक **2** (*informal*) clever and complicated चालाकी या चतुराई भरा और पेचीदा *a fiendish plan* ▶ **fiendishly** *adv.* निर्ममता से

**fierce** /fɪəs फ़िअस्/ *adj.* **1** angry, aggressive and frightening क्रुद्ध, आक्रामक और डरावना; बर्बर *The house was guarded by fierce dogs.* **2** very strong; violent बहुत कड़ा; ज़बरदस्त, उग्र, प्रचंड, भीषण *fierce competition for jobs* ○ *a fierce attack* ➪ **ferocity** noun देखिए। ▶ **fiercely** *adv.* उग्रतापूर्वक, प्रचंड भाव से

**fiery** /ˈfaɪəri ˈफ़ाइअरि/ *adj.* **1** looking like fire दीखने में आग जैसा; आग्नेय *She has fiery red hair.* **2** quick to become angry गुस्सैल; तुरंत क्रोधित हो जाने वाला *a fiery temper*

**FIFA** /ˈfiːfə ˈफ़ीफ़ा/ *abbr.* the organization that is in charge of international football अंतरराष्ट्रीय फ़ुटबॉल संगठन

**fifteen** /ˌfɪfˈtiːn ˌफ़िफ़्ˈटीन्/ *number* 15 पंद्रह (का अंक)

> **NOTE** संख्यावाची शब्दों के वाक्य-प्रयोग के उदाहरणों के लिए **six** की प्रविष्टि देखिए।

**fifteenth** /ˌfɪfˈtiːnθ ˌफ़िफ़्ˈटीन्थ्/ *pronoun, det. adv.* 15th पंद्रहवाँ ➪ **sixth**[1] की प्रविष्टि में दिए उदाहरण देखिए।

**fifth**[1] /fɪfθ फ़िफ़्थ्/ *pronoun, det. adv.* 5th पाँचवाँ ➪ **sixth**[1] की प्रविष्टि में दिए उदाहरण देखिए।

**fifth**[2] /fɪfθ फ़िफ़्थ्/ *noun* [C] the fraction $\frac{1}{5}$ ; one of five equal parts of sth भिन्न $\frac{1}{5}$ ; पाँचवाँ हिस्सा

**fiftieth** /ˈfɪftiəθ ˈफ़िफ़्टिअथ्/ *pronoun, det. adv.* 50th पचासवाँ, 50 वाँ **NOTE sixth**[1] की प्रविष्टि में दिए उदाहरण देखिए।

**fifty** /ˈfɪfti ˈफ़िफ़्टि/ *number* 50 पचास (का अंक)

> **NOTE** संख्यावाची शब्दों के वाक्य-प्रयोग के उदाहरणों के लिए **six** की प्रविष्टि देखिए।

**fifty-fifty** *adj., adv.* equal or equally (between two people, groups, etc.) (दो व्यक्तियों, समूहों आदि में) बराबर, बराबर का *You've got **a fifty-fifty chance** of winning.* ○ *We'll divide the money fifty-fifty.*

**fig** /fɪg फ़िग्/ *noun* [C] (a type of tree with) a soft sweet fruit full of small seeds that grows in warm countries and is often eaten dried अंजीर (का पेड़)

**fig.** *abbr.* **1** figure, illustration आरेख या चित्र *See diagram at fig. 2.* **2** figurative(ly) आलंकारिक रूप (से)

**fight**[1] /faɪt फ़ाइट्/ *verb* (*pt, pp* **fought** /fɔːt फ़ॉट्/) **1** [I, T] **fight (against sb)** to use physical strength, guns, weapons, etc. against sb/sth शारीरिक शक्ति, हथियारों आदि से किसी के विरुद्ध लड़ना *They gathered soldiers to fight the invading army.* ○ *My younger brothers were always fighting.* **2** [I, T] **fight (against sth)** to try very hard to stop or prevent sth कुछ रोकने का ज़ोरदार प्रयास करना *to fight a fire/a decision/prejudice* ○ *to fight against crime/disease* **3** [I] **fight (for sth/to do sth)** to try very hard to get or keep sth कुछ पाने या कुछ प्राप्त कर उसे सुरक्षित रखने के लिए कठिन प्रयत्न करना *to fight for your rights* **4** [I] **fight (with sb) (about/over sth)** to argue किसी बात पर किसी से झगड़ना; बहस करना *It's not worth fighting about money.* ➪ **argue** और **quarrel**[2] देखिए।

**PHR V** **fight back** to protect yourself with actions or words by attacking sb who has attacked you (किसी पर) जवाबी हमला करना, पलटवार करना *If he hits you again, fight back!*

**fight**[2] /faɪt फ़ाइट्/ *noun* **1** [C] **a fight (with sb/sth); a fight (between A and B)** the act of using physical force against sb/sth किसी के विरुद्ध शारीरिक शक्ति के प्रयोग द्वारा लड़ाई; हाथापाई *Don't **get into a fight** at school, will you?* ○ *Fights broke out between rival groups of fans.* **2** [sing.] **a fight (against/for sth) (to do sth)** the work done trying to destroy, prevent or achieve sth कुछ पाने, रोकने या नष्ट करने के लिए संघर्ष, लड़ाई *Workers won their fight against the management to stop the factory from closing down.* **3** [C] **a fight (with sb/sth) (about/over sth)** an argument about sth बहस, झगड़ा *I **had a fight** with my father over what time I had to be home.* **4** [U] the desire to continue trying or fighting संघर्षशक्ति *I've had some bad luck but I've still got plenty of fight in me.*

**IDM** **pick a fight** ➪ **pick**[1] देखिए।

**fighter** /ˈfaɪtə(r) ˈफ़ाइट(र्)/ *noun* [C] **1** (*also* **fighter plane**) a small fast military aircraft used for attacking enemy aircraft एक प्रकार का छोटा युद्धक विमान; लड़ाकू हवाई जहाज़ *a fighter pilot* ○ *a jet fighter* **2** a person who fights in a war or in sport (**a boxer**) योद्धा, मुक्केबाज़

**fighting** /ˈfaɪtɪŋ ˈफ़ाइटिङ्/ *noun* [U] an occasion when people fight लड़ाई-झगड़ा *There has been street fighting in many parts of the city today.*

**figurative** /ˈfɪɡərətɪv ˈफ़िगरटिव्/ *adj.* (*abbr.* **fig.**) (used about a word or an expression) not used with its exact meaning but used for giving an imaginative description or a special effect (शब्द या शब्दावली) साधारण अर्थ के स्थान पर विशिष्ट प्रभाव को उत्पन्न करने वाला; आलंकारिक *'He exploded with rage' is a figurative use of the verb 'to explode'.* ➪ **literal** और **metaphor** देखिए। ▶ **figuratively** *adv.* आलंकारिक रूप से

**figure**[1] /ˈfɪɡə(r) ˈफ़िग(र्)/ *noun* [C] **1** an amount (in numbers) or a price राशि (संख्या में) या मूल्य *The unemployment figures are lower this month.* **2** a written sign for a number (0 to 9) संख्या (0 से 9) का लिखित रूप *Write the numbers in figures, not words.* ○ *He has a six-figure income/an income in six figures* (= Rs 100,000 or more). ○ *Interest rates are now down to single figures* (= less than 10%). ○ *double figures* (= 10 to 99) **3 figures** [*pl.*] (*informal*) mathematics अंकगणित *I don't **have a head for figures*** (= I'm not very good with numbers). **4** a well-known or important person सुप्रसिद्ध या महत्त्वपूर्ण व्यक्ति *an important political figure* **5** the shape of the human body, especially a woman's body that is attractive मानव शरीर (विशेषतः स्त्री-शरीर) की आकृति *She's got a beautiful slim figure.* ➪ **build**[2] पर नोट देखिए। **6** a person that you cannot see very clearly or do not know व्यक्ति या चेहरा जो साफ़ दिखाई नहीं देता या पहचान में नहीं आता *Two figures were coming towards us in the dark.* **7** (*abbr.* **fig.**) a diagram or picture used in a book to explain sth पुस्तक में प्रयुक्त आरेख या चित्र *Figure 3 shows the major cities of India.*

**IDM** **a ballpark figure/estimate** ➪ **ballpark** देखिए।

**facts and figures** ➪ **fact** देखिए।

**in round figures/numbers** ➪ **round**[1] देखिए।

**figure**[2] /ˈfɪɡə(r) ˈफ़िग(र्)/ *verb* **1** [I] **figure (as sth) (in/among sth)** to be included in sth; to be an important part of sth किसी में शामिल या उल्लेख किया जाना; किसी का महत्त्वपूर्ण अंश होना *Women don't figure much in his novels.* ✪ पर्याय **feature** **2** [T] **figure (that)** to think or guess sth सोचना या अनुमान लगाना *I figured he was here because I saw his car outside.*

**IDM** **it/that figures** (*informal*) that is what I expected जैसा कि मैने अनुमान लगाया था

**PHR V** **figure on sth/on doing sth** to include sth in your plans योजना में सम्मिलित करना *I figure on arriving in Ujjain on Wednesday.*

**figure sb/sth out** to find an answer to sth or to understand sb किसी बात का पता होना या उसे समझना *I can't figure out why she married him in the first place.*

**figurehead** /ˈfɪɡəhed ˈफ़िगहेड्/ *noun* [C] **1** a person who has the position of a head in a country or organization but who has no real power or authority नाम मात्र का अध्यक्ष या नेता *In the parliamentary system of government, the president is merely a figurehead.* **2** a statue made of wood and usually representing a woman that used to be fixed to the front of a ship लकड़ी की पुतली जिसे जहाज़ के सामने वाले हिस्से पर स्थापित किया जाता था

**figure of speech** *noun* [C] (*pl.* **figures of speech**) a word or expression used not with its original meaning but in an imaginative way to make a special effect अलंकार; आलंकारिक शब्द या शब्दावली

**filament** /ˈfɪləmənt ˈफ़िलमन्ट्/ *noun* [C] **1** a thin wire in a **light bulb** that produces light when electricity is passed through it विद्युत धारा पार होने पर बल्ब में प्रकाश उत्पन्न करने वाली महीन तार; फ़िलामेंट ➪ **bulb** पर चित्र देखिए। **2** a long thin piece of sth that looks like a thread किसी वस्तु का धागे जैसा दीखने वाला लंबा महीन टुकड़ा; तंतु *glass/metal filaments* **3** a long thin part of the male part of a flower (**stamen**) that supports the part where **pollen** is produced (**anther**) फूल के बीच का रेशा पुतंतु ➪ **flower** पर चित्र देखिए।

**file[1]** /faɪl फ़ाइल्/ *noun* [C] **1** a box or a cover that is used for keeping papers together (काग़ज़-पत्र रखने का) बक्सा या आवरण ➪ **stationery** पर चित्र देखिए। **2** a collection of information or material on one subject that is stored together in a computer or on a disk, with a particular name कंप्यूटर की फ़ाइल जिसमें किसी एक विषय पर कंप्यूटर या डिस्क में सूचना-राशि एक विशिष्ट नाम से संचित रहती है *to open/close a file* ○ *to create/delete/save/copy a file* **3 a file (on sb/sth)** a collection of papers or information about sb/sth kept inside a file किसी व्यक्ति या वस्तु के विषय में एकत्रित काग़ज़ात या जानकारी *The police are now keeping a file on all known traffic offenders.* **4** a metal tool with a rough surface used for shaping hard substances or for making surfaces smooth खुरदरे सतह वाला धातु का औज़ार जिससे किसी कड़े पदार्थ को आकृति देते हैं या सतह को चिकना करते हैं; रेती, फाइल *a nail file* ➪ **tool** पर चित्र देखिए।

**IDM** **on file** kept in a file फ़ाइल में सँभालकर रखे गए *We have all the information you need on file.*

**in single file** in a line, one behind the other एक पंक्ति में, एक के पीछे दूसरी

**the rank and file** ➪ **rank[1]** देखिए।

**file[2]** /faɪl फ़ाइल्/ *verb* **1** [T] **file sth (away)** to put and keep documents, etc. in a particular place so that you can find them easily; to put sth into a file काग़ज़ात आदि को किसी एक स्थान पर सँभाल कर रखना ताकि उन्हे ढूँढ़ने में कोई परेशानी न हो; किसी वस्तु को फ़ाइल में रखना *I filed the letters away in a drawer.* **2** [I] **file in, out, past, etc.** to walk or march in a line पंक्तिबद्ध होकर चलना *The children filed out of the classroom.* **3** [T] **file sth (away, down, etc.)** to shape sth hard or make sth smooth with a file रेती से किसी वस्तु को काटकर शकल देना या चिकना करना *to file your nails* **4 file a case** to make an official complaint in a court of law मुक़दमा दायर करना, न्यायालय के समक्ष लाना

**filial** /ˈfɪliəl ˈफ़िलिअल्/ *adj* (*only before a noun*) (*formal*) connected to or related with the relationship between children and their parents संतानीय, संतानविषयक *filial affection*

**fill** /fɪl फ़िल्/ *verb* **1** [I, T] **fill (sth/sb) (with sth)** to make sth full or to become full किसी में कुछ पूरी तरह से भरना या किसी वस्तु का पूरा भर जाना *The news filled him with excitement.* ○ *The room filled with smoke within minutes.* **2** [T] to take a position or to use up your time doing sth कोई पद प्राप्त करना या किसी काम में समय का अधिकतम उपयोग करना *I'm afraid that the teaching post has just been filled* (= somebody has got the job).

**PHR V** **fill sth in** (*AmE* **fill sth out**) **1** to complete a form, etc. by writing information on it आवेदन पत्र आदि में आवश्यक सूचना अंकित कर उसे भरना *Could you fill in the application form, please?* **2** to fill a hole or space completely to make a surface flat छेद या दरार को भरकर बंद कर देना ताकि सतह समतल हो जाए *You had better fill in the cracks in the wall before you paint it.*

**fill (sth) up** to become or to make sth completely full पूरी तरह भर जाना या भर देना *There weren't many people at first but then the room filled up.*

**filler cap** *noun* [C] a lid for covering the end of the pipe through which petrol is put into a motor vehicle पेट्रोल डालने के लिए प्रयुक्त नली के सिरे पर लगने वाला ढक्कन; फ़िलर कैप

**fillet** (*AmE* **filet**) /ˈfɪlɪt ˈफ़िलिट्/ *noun* [C, U] a piece of meat or fish with the bones taken out मांस या मछली का टुकड़ा जिसमें से हड्डी निकाल ली गई हो; कतला

**filling[1]** /ˈfɪlɪŋ ˈफ़िलिङ्/ *noun* **1** [C] the material that a dentist uses to fill a hole in a tooth दाँतों के छेद में भरी जाने वाली वस्तु; भराव, भरता, फ़िलिंग *a gold filling* **2** [C, U] the food inside a sandwich, pie, cake, etc. सैंडविच, केक आदि के अंदर भरा भोज्य पदार्थ

**filling²** /ˈfɪlɪŋ ˈफ़िलिङ्/ *adj.* (used about food) that makes you feel full (भोजन) जिससे पेट भर जाए *Pasta is very filling.*

**filly** /ˈfɪli ˈफ़िलि/ *noun* [C] (*pl.* **fillies**) a young female horse घोड़े की मादा जवान बच्ची; बछेड़ी ➪ **colt** देखिए।

**film¹** /fɪlm फ़िल्म्/ *noun* **1** (*AmE* **movie**) [C] a story, play, etc. shown in moving pictures at the cinema or on television सिनेमाघर या टेलीविज़न पर दिखाया जाने वाला चलचित्र (कथा, नाटक आदि को प्रस्तुत करने वाला); फ़िल्म *Let's go to the cinema—there's a good film on this week.* ○ *to* ***watch a film*** *on TV* ○ *to* ***see a film*** *at the cinema* ○ *a horror/documentary/feature film* ○ *a film director/producer/critic* **2** [U] the art or business of making films चलचित्र-निर्माण की कला या व्यवसाय *She's studying film and theatre.* ○ *the film industry* **3** [U] moving pictures of real events वास्तविक घटनाओं के चलचित्र *The programme included a film of the town one hundred years ago.* **4** [C] a roll of thin plastic that you use in a camera to take photographs फ़ोटोचित्र खींचने के लिए कैमरे में डाली जाने वाली फ़िल्म *to have a film developed* ○ *Fast film is better if there's not much light.* ➪ **camera** पर चित्र देखिए। **5** [C, *usually sing.*] a thin layer of a substance or material किसी वस्तु या पदार्थ की पतली परत *Oil forms a film on the surface of the water.*

**film²** /fɪlm फ़िल्म्/ *verb* [I, T] to record moving pictures of an event, story, etc. with a camera कैमरे से कहानी आदि का चलचित्र या फ़िल्म बनाना; घटना, कहानी आदि को फ़िल्माना *A lot of Hindi films are now being filmed abroad.* ○ *The man was filmed stealing from the shop.*

**film star** *noun* [C] a person who is a well-known actor in films फ़िल्मों का सुप्रसिद्ध अभिनेता; फ़िल्म स्टार

**filter¹** /ˈfɪltə(r) ˈफ़िल्ट(र्)/ *noun* [C] **1** a device for holding back solid substances from a liquid or gas that passes through it द्रव या गैस को छानने का उपकरण; छन्ना, छन्नी, फ़िल्टर *a coffee filter* ○ *an oil filter* **2** a piece of coloured glass used with a camera to hold back some types of light कैमरे के साथ प्रयुक्त एक छोटा रंगीन शीशा जो कुछ प्रकार की प्रकाश रेखाओं को पार नहीं होने देता

**filter²** /ˈfɪltə(r) ˈफ़िल्ट(र्)/ *verb* **1** [T] to pass a liquid through a filter छन्नी में से द्रव को पार करना *Do you filter your water?* **2** [I] **filter in, out, through, etc.** to move slowly and/or in small amounts मंद गति से और/या अल्प मात्राखंडों में गति करना *Sunlight filtered into the room through the curtains.* ○ (*figurative*) *News of her illness filtered through to her friends.*

PHR V **filter sth out (of sth)** to remove sth that you do not want from a liquid, light, etc. using a special device or substance किसी विशेष उपकरण या पदार्थ द्वारा छानकर अनचाही वस्तुओं को निकाल देना *This chemical filters impurities out of the water.* ○ (*figurative*) *This test is designed to filter out weaker candidates before the interview stage.*

**filter paper** *noun* [U, C] a type of paper used in chemistry for separating solids from liquids; a piece of this paper used, for example in making coffee रासायनिक प्रयोग में प्रयुक्त एक प्रकार का काग़ज़ जो छन्नी का काम करता है; कॉफी आदि बनाने में प्रयुक्त छन्नी काग़ज़ ➪ **laboratory** पर चित्र देखिए।

**filth** /fɪlθ फ़िल्थ्/ *noun* [U] **1** unpleasant dirt मैल, गंदी धूल, गंदगी *The room was covered in filth.* **2** sexual words or pictures that cause offence अश्लील शब्द या चित्र जो भावनाओं को ठेस पहुँचा सकते हैं

**filthy** /ˈfɪlθi ˈफ़िल्थि/ *adj.* (**filthier; filthiest**) **1** very dirty बहुत गंदा **2** (used about language, books, films, etc.) connected with sex, and causing offence (भाषा, पुस्तक, फ़िल्म आदि) अत्यंत अश्लील और भावनाओं को ठेस पहुँचाने वाला

**filtrate** /ˈfɪltreɪt ˈफ़िल्ट्रेट्/ *noun* [C] a liquid that has passed through a **filter** फ़िल्टर से छना हुआ द्रव

**filtration** /fɪlˈtreɪʃn फ़िल्ˈट्रेश्न्/ *noun* [U] the process of passing a liquid or gas through a **filter** फ़िल्टर में से द्रव या गैस छनने की प्रक्रिया

**fin** /fɪn फ़िन्/ *noun* [C] **1** paired or unpaired expansions of the skin of a fish which are helpful in swimming मछली का एक अंग जिससे वह तैरती है, मछली का सुफना ➪ **fish** पर चित्र देखिए। **2** a flat, thin part that sticks out of an aircraft, a vehicle, etc. to improve its balance and movement through the air or water विमान, वाहन आदि में पंखनुमा वस्तु जो विमान, आदि का संतुलन और गति साधती है

**final¹** /ˈfaɪnl ˈफ़ाइनल्/ *adj.* **1** (*only before a noun*) last (in a series) अंतिम (क्रम की दृष्टि से) *This will be the final lesson of our course.* ○ *I don't want to miss the final episode of that serial.* **2** not to be changed जिसे बदला नहीं जा सकता; अंतिम, निर्णायक *The judge's decision is always final.* ○ *I'm not lending you the money, and that's final!*

IDM **the last/final straw** ➪ **straw** देखिए।

**final²** /ˈfaɪnl ˈफ़ाइनल्/ *noun* **1** [C] the last game or match in a series of competitions or sporting events खेल-स्पर्धाओं की शृंखला में अंतिम खेल या मैच *The first two runners in this race go through to the final.* ➪ **semi-final** देखिए। **2 finals** [*pl.*] the exams you take in your last year at university विश्वविद्यालय शिक्षा के अंतिम वर्ष में अंतिम परीक्षाएँ

**finale** /fɪˈnɑːli फ़िˈनालि/ *noun* [C] the last part of a piece of music, an opera, a show, etc. संगीत रचना, कार्यक्रम आदि का अंतिम अंश

**finalist** /ˈfaɪnəlɪst ˈफ़ाइनलिस्ट्/ *noun* [C] a person who is in the **final² 1** of a competition खेल-स्पर्धा के अंतिम चरण (फ़ाइनल) में पहुँचा खिलाड़ी ➪ **semifinalist** देखिए।

**finalize** (*also* **-ise**) /ˈfaɪnəlaɪz ˈफ़ाइनलाइज़्/ *verb* [T] to make firm decisions about plans, dates, etc. योजनाओं, तारीख़ों आदि को अंतिम रूप देना *Have you finalized your holiday arrangements yet?*

**finally** /ˈfaɪnəli ˈफ़ाइनलि/ *adv.* **1** after a long time or delay अंततोगत्वा, आख़िरकार, अंत में *It was getting dark when the plane finally took off.* ✪ पर्याय **eventually** **2** used to introduce the last in a list of things सूची, शृंखला आदि के अंतिम अंश को प्रस्तुत करने के लिए प्रयुक्त *Finally, I would like to say how much we have all enjoyed this evening.* ✪ पर्याय **lastly** **3** in a definite way so that sth will not be changed अंतिम रूप से; पक्के तौर पर; निर्णायक रूप से *We haven't decided finally who will get the job yet.*

**finance¹** /ˈfaɪnæns ˈफ़ाइनैन्स्/ *noun* **1** [U] the money you need to start or support a business, etc. व्यवसाय, व्यापार आदि को शुरू करने या बढ़ाने के लिए आपेक्षित धन *How will you raise the finance to start the project?* **2** [U] the activity of managing money धन-व्यवस्था की प्रक्रिया; वित्तीय प्रबंध-संचालन *Who is the new Minister of Finance?* ○ *an expert in finance* **3 finances** [*pl.*] the money a person, company, country, etc. has to spend व्यक्ति, संस्था, देश आदि द्वारा व्यय की जाने वाली धनराशि *What are our finances like at the moment* (= how much money have we got)?

**finance²** /ˈfaɪnæns; fəˈnæns ˈफ़ाइनैन्स्; फ़ˈनैन्स्/ *verb* [T] to provide the money to pay for sth भुगतान के लिए धन की व्यवस्था करना *Your trip will be financed by the company.*

**financial** /faɪˈnænʃl; fəˈnæ- फ़ाइˈनैन्श्ल्; फ़ˈनै-/ *adj.* connected with money धन-विषयक, वित्तीय *The business got into financial difficulties.* ▶ **financially** *adv.* /-ʃəli -शलि/ वित्तीय दृष्टि से

**finch** /fɪntʃ फ़िन्च्/ *noun* [C] a small bird with a short strong beak छोटी व मज़बूत चोंच वाली एक छोटी चिड़िया; कुलिंग

**find¹** /faɪnd फ़ाइन्ड्/ *verb* [T] (*pt, pp* **found** /faʊnd फ़ाउन्ड्/) **1** to discover sth that you want or that you have lost after searching for it खोज या ढूँढ़ निकालना; का पता लगाना; पा लेना *Did you find the pen you lost?* ○ *After six months she finally found a job.* ○ *Scientists haven't yet found a cure for AIDS.* ○ *I hope you find an answer to your problem.*

> NOTE निम्नलिखित अभिव्यक्तियों पर ध्यान दें **find the time, find the money**—*I never seem to find the time to write letters these days.* ○ *We'd like to go on holiday but we can't find the money.*

**2** to discover sth by chance अचानक या संयोग से कुछ पता लगा लेना *I've found a piece of glass in this milk.* ○ *We went into the house and found her lying on the floor.* ○ *This animal can be found* (= exists) *all over the world.* **3** to have an opinion about sth because of your own experience अपने अनुभव के आधार पर किसी के विषय में कुछ राय बनाना; किसी को कुछ लगना *I find that book very difficult to understand.* ○ *We didn't find the film at all funny.* ○ *How are you finding life as a student?* **4** to suddenly realize or see sth एकाएक कुछ पता लगना या देखना *I got home to find that I'd left the tap on all day.* ○ *Sahil turned a corner and suddenly found himself in the park.* **5** to arrive at sth naturally; to reach sth नैसर्गिक रूप से कुछ पा लेना; कहीं पहुँच जाना *Water always finds its own level.* ○ *These birds find their way to Africa every winter.*

IDM **find fault (with sb/sth)** to look for things that are wrong with sb/sth and complain about them किसी की ग़लती निकालने की दृष्टि से कार्य आदि करना और शिकायत करना

**find your feet** to become confident and independent in a new situation नई स्थिति में विश्वासपूर्वक जम जाना; आत्मनिर्भर हो जाना

PHRV **find (sth) out** to get some information; to discover a fact जानकारी लेना; कुछ पता लगाना *Have you found out how much the tickets cost?* ○ *I later found out that Madhu had been lying to me.*

**find sb out** to discover that sb has done sth wrong किसी के ग़लत किए को खोज निकालना *He had used a false name for years before they found him out.*

**find²** /faɪnd फ़ाइन्ड्/ *noun* [C] a thing or a person that has been found, especially one that is valuable or useful महत्त्वपूर्ण या उपयोगी वस्तु या व्यक्ति के रूप में नई खोज *Archaeologists made some interesting finds when they dug up the field.* ○ *This new young player is quite a find!*

**finder** /ˈfaɪndə(r) ˈफ़ाइन्ड(र्)/ *noun* [C] a person or thing that finds sth खोज करने वाला व्यक्ति या वस्तु

**finding** /ˈfaɪndɪŋ ˈफ़ाइन्डिङ्/ *noun* [C, *usually pl.*] information that is discovered as a result of research into sth अनुसंधान से प्राप्त जानकारी या निष्कर्ष *the findings of a survey/report/committee*

**fine[1]** /faɪn फ़ाइन्/ *adj.* **1** in good health, or happy and comfortable सुस्वस्थ या ख़ुश और आराम से *'How are you?' '**Fine thanks.**'* ○ *'Do you want to change places?' 'No I'm fine here, thanks.'* **2** all right; acceptable काफ़ी ठीक; संतोषजनक, स्वीकार्य *'Do you want some more milk in your coffee?' 'No **that's fine**, thanks.'* ○ *Don't cook anything special—a sandwich will be fine.* ○ *The hotel rooms were fine but the food was awful.*

> NOTE अर्थ संख्या **1** और **2** का प्रयोग प्रश्नवाचक और निषेधवाचक वाक्यों में नहीं किया जाता अर्थात *'Are you fine?'* या *'This isn't fine'*. मान्य नहीं हैं।

**3** (used about weather) bright with sunlight; not raining (मौसम) साफ़, सूर्य चमकता हुआ; वर्षा नहीं *Let's hope it stays fine for the match tomorrow.* **4** (*only before a noun*) of very good quality, beautiful, well made उच्च कोटि का, सुंदर, सुडौल; श्रेष्ठ, बढ़िया *a fine piece of work* ○ *fine detail/carving/china* **5** very thin or narrow बहुत पतला या तंग; बारीक *That hairstyle's no good for me—my hair's too fine.* ○ *You must use a fine pencil for the diagrams.* ✪ विलोम **thick** **6** made of very small pieces, grains, etc. बहुत महीन टुकड़ों, कणों आदि से बना हुआ *Salt is finer than sugar.* ✪ विलोम **coarse** **7** difficult to notice or understand दिखाई पड़ने या समझ आने में कठिन; सूक्ष्म, बारीक, नाज़ुक *I couldn't understand **the finer points** of his argument.* ○ *There's **a fine line between** being reserved and being unfriendly.*

**fine[2]** /faɪn फ़ाइन्/ *noun* [C] a sum of money that you have to pay for breaking a law or rule अर्थदंड, जुरमाना *a parking fine* ○ *You'll **get a fine** if you park your car there.* ▶ **fine** *verb* [T] **fine sb (for sth/doing sth)** अर्थदंड या जुरमाना लगाना *He was fined Rs 500 for driving without a licence.*

**finely** /ˈfaɪnli ˈफ़ाइन्लि/ *adv.* **1** into small pieces सूक्ष्म या बारीक टुकड़ों में; बारीक-बारीक *The onions must be finely chopped for this recipe.* **2** very accurately अति बढ़िया व सही ढंग से; बारीकी से *a finely tuned instrument*

**finery** /ˈfaɪnəri ˈफ़ाइनरि/ *noun* [U] (*literary*) elegant and beautiful clothes and jewellery, especially those that are worn for a special occasion सुंदर व सुरुचिपूर्ण कपड़े व गहने, विशेषतः किसी विशेष अवसर पर पहने जाने वाले; अलंकार *Most of the guests at the party were dressed in all their finery.*

**finger[1]** /ˈfɪŋɡə(r) ˈफ़िङ्ग(र्)/ *noun* [C] one of the five parts at the end of each hand अंगुलि, उँगली *little finger, ring finger, middle finger, forefinger (or index finger), thumb*

> NOTE कभी-कभी अँगूठे को अंगुलियों में शमिल कर लिया जाता है, परंतु कभी-कभी इनमें भिन्नता भी दर्शाई जाती है—*Hold the pen between your finger and thumb.* पैर की पाँच अँगुलियों को **toes** कहते हैं। ➪ **body** पर चित्र देखिए।

IDM **cross your fingers; keep your fingers crossed** to hope that sb/sth will be successful or lucky किसी की सफलता के लिए कामना करना या आशावान होना *I'll keep my fingers crossed for you in your exams.* ○ *There's nothing more we can do now—just cross our fingers and hope for the best.*

**have green fingers** ➪ **green[1]** देखिए।

**snap your fingers** ➪ **snap[1]** देखिए।

**finger[2]** /ˈfɪŋɡə(r) ˈफ़िङ्ग(र्)/ *verb* [T] to touch or feel sth with your fingers अंगुलियों से किसी वस्तु को छूना या महसूस करना

**fingermark** /ˈfɪŋɡəmɑːk ˈफ़िङ्गमाक्/ *noun* [C] a mark on sth made by a dirty finger किसी वस्तु पर पड़ा गंदी अंगुलि का निशान

**fingernail** /ˈfɪŋɡəneɪl ˈफ़िङ्गनेल्/ (*also* **nail**) *noun* [C] the thin hard layer that covers the outer end of each finger (अंगुली का) नाख़ून ➪ **body** पर चित्र देखिए।

**fingerprint** /ˈfɪŋɡəprɪnt ˈफ़िङ्गप्रिन्ट्/ *noun* [C] the mark made by the skin of a finger, used for identifying people अंगुलि की छाप (लोगों की पहचान के लिए) *The burglar left his fingerprints all over the house.*

**fingertip** /ˈfɪŋɡətɪp ˈफ़िङ्गटिप्/ *noun* [C] the end of a finger अंगुलि का सिरा या अग्रभाग

IDM **have sth at your fingertips** to have sth ready for quick and easy use किसी वस्तु का तुरंत सुलभ होना किसी बात की पूरी जानकारी होना *They asked some difficult questions but luckily I had all the facts at my fingertips.*

**finish[1]** /ˈfɪnɪʃ ˈफ़िनिश्/ *verb* **1** [I, T] **finish (sth/doing sth)** to complete sth or reach the end of sth किसी काम को पूरा या समाप्त करना *What time does the film finish?* ○ *Haven't you finished yet? You've taken ages!* ○ *The Ethiopian runner won and the Kenyans finished second and third.* ○ *Finish your work quickly!* ○ *Have you finished typing that letter?* **2** [T] **finish sth (off/up)** to eat, drink or use the last part of sth अंतिम बचा भाग को खाना, पीना या प्रयोग में लाना *Finish up your milk, Tina!* ○ *Who finished off all the bread?* **3** [T] **finish sth (off)** to complete the last details of sth or make sth perfect बचा-खुचा काम पूरा करना या (किसी को) परिष्कृत करना *He stayed up all night to finish off the article he was writing.* ○ *He's just **putting the finishing touches to** his painting.*

**PHRV** **finish sb/sth off** (*informal*) to kill sb/sth; to be the thing that makes sb unable to continue किसी को मार डालना; पूरी तरह थका देना *The cat played with the mouse before finishing it off.* ○ *I was very tired towards the end of the race, and that last hill finished me off.*

**finish with sb** (*informal*) to end a relationship with sb किसी के साथ संबंध समाप्त कर देना *Reena's not going out with Tarun any more—she finished with him last week.*

**finish with sth** to stop needing or using sth किसी वस्तु की और आवश्यकता न रहना; उपयोग करना समाप्त कर देना; पूरा उपयोग कर लेना *I'll borrow that book when you've finished with it.*

**finish**[2] /ˈfɪnɪʃ ˈफ़िनिश् / *noun* [C] **1** the last part or end of sth किसी वस्तु का अंतिम अंश; अंत, समाप्ति *There was a dramatic finish to the race when two runners fell.* ○ *I enjoyed the film* ***from start to finish***. **2** the last covering of paint, polish, etc. that is put on a surface to make it look good रंग-रोगन की आख़िरी परत जिससे सतह में चमक आ जाती है

**finished** /ˈfɪnɪʃt ˈफ़िनिश्ट् / *adj.* **1** (*not before a noun*) **finished (with sb/sth)** having stopped doing sth, using sth or dealing with sb/sth किसी वस्तु का उपयोग पूरा कर लेना *'Are you using the computer?' 'Yes, I won't be finished with it for another hour or so.'* **2** (*not before a noun*) not able to continue जो जारी न रह पाए; ख़त्म *The business is finished—there's no more money.* **3** made; completed तैयार; पूरा, पूर्ण *the finished product/article*

**finite** /ˈfaɪnaɪt ˈफ़ाइनाइट् / *adj.* having a definite limit or a fixed size सीमित, परिमित *The world's resources are finite.* ✪ विलोम **infinite**

**fir** /fɜː(r) फ़(र्) / (*also* **fir tree**) *noun* [C] a tree with thin leaves (**needles**) that do not fall off in winter देवदार (का वृक्ष)

**fir cone** *noum* [C] the fruit of the fir tree देवदार का फल

**fire**[1] /ˈfaɪə(r) ˈफ़ाइअ(र्) / *noun* **1** [C, U] burning and flames, especially when it destroys and is out of control आग व उसकी लपटें जो विशेषतः विनाशकारी और अनियंत्रित हो *Firemen struggled for three hours to* ***put out the fire***. ○ *In very hot weather, dry grass can* ***catch fire*** (= start burning). ○ *Did someone* ***set fire to*** *that pile of wood?* **2** [C] burning wood or coal used for warming people or cooking food (सेंक देने वाली) आग, अग्नि *They tried to* ***light a fire*** *to keep warm.* ○ *It's cold—don't let the fire go out!* **3** [C] a machine for heating a room, etc. कमरा गरम करने आदि की मशीन *a gas/an electric fire* **4** [U] shooting from guns बंदूक़ की गोलाबारी *The soldiers came* ***under fire*** *from all sides.* ○ *I could hear gun fire in the distance.*

**IDM** **get on/along like a house on fire** ➪ **house**[1] देखिए।

**open fire** ➪ **open**[2] देखिए।

**come/be under fire** be strongly criticized कटु आलोचना का विषय होना या का पात्र होना *The government has come under fire from all sides for its foreign policy.*

**fire**[2] /ˈfaɪə(r) ˈफ़ाइअ(र्) / *verb* **1** [I, T] **fire (sth) (at sb/sth); fire (sth) (on/into sb/sth)** to shoot bullets, etc. from a gun or other weapon बंदूक़ आदि से गोली दाग़ना; तीर छोड़ना, शस्त्र या हथियार द्वारा युद्धोपकरण छोड़ना *Can you hear the guns firing?* ○ *The soldiers fired on the crowd, killing twenty people.* ○ *She fired an arrow at the target.* ○ (*figurative*) *If you stop firing questions at me I might be able to answer!* **2** [T] (*informal*) to remove an employee from a job कर्मचारी को नौकरी से निकाल देना *He was fired for always being late.* **3** [T] **fire sb with sth** to produce a strong feeling in sb प्रबल भावनाएँ जगाना; अनुप्राणित करना; (की भावना) भड़काना *Her speech fired me with determination.*

**fire alarm** *noun* [C] a bell or other signal to warn people that there is a fire आग लगने की सूचना या चेतावनी देने वाला घंटा या अन्य संकेत

**firearm** /ˈfaɪərɑːm ˈफ़ाइअर्आम् / *noun* [C] a gun that you can carry आग्नेय अस्त्र (रिवॉल्वर, राइफ़ल आदि)

**firebrand** /ˈfaɪəbrænd ˈफ़ाइअब्रैन्ड् / *noun* [C] a person who encourages other people to take strong political action, often causing trouble (कठोर राजनीतिक कार्रवाई के लिए) अत्यंत उत्साही व्यक्ति जो दूसरों को प्रोत्साहित करता है, प्रायः जिससे उपद्रव फैलता है

**fire brigade** (*AmE* **fire department**) *noun* [C, *with sing. or pl. verb*] an organization of people trained to deal with fires प्रशिक्षित अग्निशामक दल

**-fired** /ˈfaɪəd ˈफ़ाइअड् / (*used in compounds*) using the fuel mentioned निर्दिष्ट ईंधन से युक्त *gas-fired central heating*

**fire engine** *noun* [C] a special vehicle that carries equipment for dealing with large fires भंयकर आग बुझाने वाले उपकरणों का वहन करने वाला विशेष वाहन; दमकल

**fire escape** *noun* [C] a special staircase on the outside of a building that people can go down if there is a fire भवन के बाहर लगी विशेष सीढ़ी जो भवन में आग लगने पर बाहर निकलने के लिए इस्तेमाल की जा सकती है

**fire extinguisher** (*also* **extinguisher**) *noun* [C] a metal container with water or chemicals inside that you use for stopping small fires अग्निशामक यंत्र

**firefighter** /ˈfaɪəfaɪtə(r) ˈफ़ाइअफ़ाइट(र्)/ *noun* [C] a person whose job is to stop fires आग बुझाने के लिए प्रशिक्षित व्यक्ति

**firelight** /ˈfaɪəlaɪt ˈफ़ाइअलाइट्/ *noun* [U] the light that comes from a fire आग से उत्पन्न प्रकाश

**fireman** /ˈfaɪəmən ˈफ़ाइअमन्/ (*pl.* **-men** /-mən -मन्/) = **firefighter**

**fireplace** /ˈfaɪəpleɪs ˈफ़ाइअप्लेस्/ *noun* [C] the open place in a room where you light a fire कमरे में वह स्थान जहाँ सेंक के लिए आग जलाई जाती है; अँगीठी

**fireproof** /ˈfaɪəpru:f ˈफ़ाइअप्रूफ़्/ *adj.* able to take great heat without burning or being badly damaged आग के तीव्र ताप को सहन करने में सक्षम *a fireproof door*

**fireside** /ˈfaɪəsaɪd ˈफ़ाइअसाइड्/ *noun* [*sing.*] the part of a room beside the fire कमरे में अग्निस्थल के आस-पास का स्थान *Come and sit by the fireside.*

**fire station** *noun* [C] a building where **firefighters** wait to be called, and where the vehicles that they use are kept अग्निशमन-केंद्र, दमकल केंद्र

**fire temple** /ˈfaɪə(r), templ ˈफ़ाइअ(र्), टेम्पल्/ *noun* [C] a place of worship for **Zoroastrians**, where the sacred fire is housed पारसी (ज़रदुश्त) धर्म का अनुकरण करने वालों का पूजा स्थल जहाँ पावन अग्नि प्रज्वलित रहती है

**firewall** /ˈfaɪəwɔ:l ˈफ़ाइअवॉल्/ *noun* [C] (*computing*) a part of a computer system that is designed to prevent people from getting information without authority but still allows them to receive information that is sent to them कंप्यूटर प्रणाली का वह भाग जो उपयोगकर्ता को अनधिकृत रूप से सूचना प्राप्त करने से रोकता है परंतु उस सूचना को नहीं रोकता जो उन्हें भेजी जाती है

**firewood** /ˈfaɪəwʊd ˈफ़ाइअवुड्/ *noun* [U] wood used for burning on fires जलाने की लकड़ी

**firework** /ˈfaɪəwɜ:k ˈफ़ाइअवक्/ *noun* [C] a small object that burns or explodes with coloured lights and loud sounds, used for entertainment फुलझड़ी आदि आतिशबाज़ी

**firing line** *noun*

IDM **be in the firing line** **1** to be in a position where you can be shot at गोली लगने की स्थिति में होना **2** to be in a position where people can criticize you or say that sth is your fault आलोचना का शिकार बनने या दोषारोपित होने की स्थिति में होना

**firing squad** *noun* [C] a group of soldiers who have been ordered to shoot and kill a prisoner सैनिकों का दस्ता जिसे क़ैदी को गोली से मार देने का आदेश दिया गया है

**firm**[1] /fɜ:m फ़म्/ *adj.* **1** able to stay the same shape when pressed; quite hard सख़्त; सुदृढ़, काफ़ी कड़ा *a firm mattress* ○ *firm muscles* **2** strong and steady or not likely to change मज़बूत और स्थिर या जिसमें परिवर्तन संभावित न हो *She kept a firm grip on her mother's hand.* ○ *a firm commitment/decision/offer* **3 firm (with sb)** strong and in control दृढ़ व नियंत्रण में; सख़्त व कठोर; अडिग *You have to show the examiner that you have a firm grasp* (= good knowledge) *of grammar.* ▶ **firmly** *adv.* दृढ़तापूर्वक ▶ **firmness** *noun* [U] कठोरता; दृढ़ता

IDM **a firm hand** strong control or discipline कठोर नियंत्रण या अनुशासन

**firm**[2] /fɜ:m फ़म्/ *noun* [C, *with sing. or pl. verb*] a business company व्यापारिक प्रतिष्ठान *Which firm do you work for?*

**firni** *noun* [U] (*IndE*) a sweet dish made of milk, nuts, **raisins** and rice; a variation of rice pudding फ़िरनी

**first**[1] /fɜ:st फ़स्ट्/ *det.* coming before all others; that has not happened before सबसे पहला; पहली बार होने वाला; प्रथम *She's expecting her first baby.* ○ *the first half of the game* ○ *You've won the first prize!* ○ *What were your first impressions of this country when you arrived?* ➪ **one** देखिए।

IDM **at first glance/sight** when first seen or examined पहली नज़र में *The task seemed impossible at first glance, but it turned out to be quite easy.*

**first/last thing** ➪ **thing** देखिए।

**first**[2] /fɜ:st फ़स्ट्/ *adv.* **1** before any others सबसे पहले *Rahul arrived first at the party.* ○ *Binny's very competitive—he always wants to* ***come first*** *when he plays a game.* **2** before doing anything else कुछ भी अन्य करने से पहले *I'll come out later. I've got to finish my homework first.* **3** for the first time पहली बार *Where did you first meet your husband?* **4** at the beginning पहले-पहले; शुरुआत में *When I first started my job I hated it.* **5** used for introducing the first thing in a list क्रम में पहली वस्तु के प्रस्तुतीकरण में प्रयुक्त; सबसे पहले *There are several people I would like to thank: First, my mother.* ✪ पर्याय **firstly**

IDM **at first** at the beginning शुरू में *At first I thought he was joking, but then I realized he was serious.*

**come first** to be more important to sb than anything else किसी बात का अन्यों की अपेक्षा अधिक महत्त्वपूर्ण होना

**first and foremost** more than anything else; most importantly सर्वाधिक महत्त्वपूर्ण

**first come, first served** (*informal*) people will be dealt with, served, seen, etc. strictly in the order in which they arrive पहले आओ, पहले पाओ *Tickets can be bought here on a first come, first served basis.*

**first of all** as the first thing (to be done or said) सबसे पहले *In a moment I'll introduce our guest speaker, but first of all, let me thank you all for coming.*

**first off** (*informal*) before anything else किसी और बात से पहले *First off, let's decide who does what.*

**head first** ➪ **head**[1] देखिए।

**first**[3] /fɜːst फ़र्स्ट्/ *noun, pronoun* **1 the first** [C] (*pl.* **the first**) the first person or thing, people or things पहला व्यक्ति या वस्तु, लोग या वस्तुएँ *Are we the first to arrive?* ○ *I'd be* ***the first to admit*** (= I will most willingly admit) *I might be wrong.* **2 a first** [*sing.*] an important event that is happening for the first time पहली बार घटी कोई महत्त्वपूर्ण घटना *This operation is a first in medical history.* IDM **from the (very) first** from the beginning आरंभ से

**first aid** *noun* [U] medical help that you give to sb who is hurt or ill before the doctor arrives चिकित्सक के पहुँचने से पहले रोगी को दी गई चिकित्सा; प्राथमिक चिकित्सा *a first aid kit/course* ○ *to give sb first aid*

**firstborn** /ˈfɜːstbɔːn ˈफ़र्स्टबॉन्/ *noun* [C] (*old-fashioned*) a person's first child किसी व्यक्ति की पहली संतान ▶ **firstborn** *adj.* (*only before a noun*) जेठा, पहलौठा

**first class** *noun* [U] **1** the best and most expensive seats or accommodation on a train, ship, etc. रेलगाड़ी, जहाज़ आदि में प्रथम श्रेणी जिसमें श्रेष्ठ सेवाएँ उपलब्ध होती हैं **2** (in Britain) the quickest form of mail (ब्रिटेन में) द्रुतगामी डाकसेवा *First class costs more.* **3** the highest standard of degree given by a university विश्वविद्यालय द्वारा प्रदत्त उच्चतम श्रेणी ▶ **first class** *adv.* प्रथम श्रेणी में, द्रुतगामी डाकसेवा से *to travel first class* ○ *I sent the letter first class on Tuesday.*

**first-class** *adj.* **1** in the best group; of the highest standard सर्वश्रेष्ठ कोटिका; सर्वोत्कृष्ट *a first-class player* ✪ पर्याय **excellent** **2** giving or using the best and most expensive type of service सर्वोत्कृष्ट और सबसे महँगी सेवा से संबंधित *first-class rail travel* **3** (*only before a noun*) used to describe a university degree of the highest class from a British university विश्वविद्यालय की सर्वोच्च उपाधि का निर्देश करने के लिए प्रयुक्त *She was awarded a first-class degree in French.*

**first-degree** *adj.* (*only before a noun*) **1** (used about murder) of the most serious kind (हत्या के विषय में प्रयुक्त) अति गंभीर, जघन्य, संगीन **2** (used about burns) of the least serious of three kinds, affecting only the surface of the skin (जल जाने के विषय में प्रयुक्त) शुरुआती दौर का, जो केवल त्वचा की सतह को प्रभावित करता है ➪ **second-degree** और **third-degree** देखिए।

**the first floor** *noun* [C] **1** (*BrE*) the floor of a building above the one on street level (**the ground floor**) भूमि की समतल मंजिल के ठीक ऊपर वाली मंजिल *I live in a flat* ***on the first floor.*** ○ *a first-floor flat* **2** (*AmE*) the floor of a building on street level किसी भवन की वह मंजिल जो भूमि के समतल है

**first gear** *noun* [C] the lowest **gear** on a car, bicycle, etc. कार, साइकिल आदि का सबसे नीचे का गियर *To move off,* ***put*** *the car* ***into first gear*** *and slowly release the clutch.*

**first generation** *noun* [*sing.*] people who have left their country to go and live in a new country स्वदेश छोड़कर विदेश में बस जाने वाले लोग ▶ **first-generation** *adj.* सबसे पहले आकर बसे, पहली पीढ़ी के *first-generation Indians in the UK*

**first-hand** *adj., adv.* (used about information, experience, a story, etc.) heard, seen or learnt by yourself, not from other people (सूचना, अनुभव, कथा आदि) स्वयं को व सीधे प्राप्त; प्रत्यक्ष, न कि किसी स्रोत से *He gave me a first-hand account of the accident* (= he had seen it). ○ *I've experienced the problem first-hand, so I know how you feel.*

**first lady** *noun* [C, *usually sing.*] **the First Lady** the wife of the President or the leader of a state राष्ट्रपति या किसी राज्य के अध्यक्ष की पत्नी

**firstly** /ˈfɜːstli ˈफ़र्स्ट्लि/ *adv.* used to introduce the first point in a list किसी सूची में पहली बात को प्रस्तुत करने के लिए प्रयुक्त; प्रथमतः, पहली बात, पहले *They were angry firstly because they had to pay extra, and secondly because no one had told them about it.* ✪ पर्याय **first**

**first name** *noun* [C] the first of your names that come before your family name किसी व्यक्ति का निजी नाम (जो कुल नाम से पहले आता है) *'What's Mr Desai's first name?' 'Raghav, I think.'* ➪ **name**[1] देखिए।

**the first person** *noun* [*sing.*] **1** (*grammar*) the set of pronouns and verb forms used by a speaker to refer to himself or herself, or to a group including himself or herself वक्ता या वक्ता समूह द्वारा अपने आपको निर्दिष्ट करने के लिए प्रयुक्त सर्वनाम तथा क्रिया पद;

उत्तम पुरुष *'I am' is the first person singular of the verb 'to be'.* ○ *'I', 'me', 'we' and 'us' are first person pronouns.* **2** the style of writing a novel, telling a story, etc. as if it happened to you उपन्यास लिखने, कहानी सुनाने आदि की वह शैली जिसमें यह लगे कि लेखक या विवरण देने वाले आदि के साथ ही सब घटा हो; उत्तम पुरुष शैली *The author writes in the first person.* ➪ **the second person** और **the third person** देखिए।

**first-rate** *adj.* excellent; of the best quality उत्कृष्ट; सर्वश्रेष्ठ, अति उत्तम

**the First World** *noun* [*sing.*] the rich industrial countries of the world संसार के धनी औद्योगिक देश ➪ **the Third World** देखिए।

**fiscal** /ˈfɪskl ˈफ़िस्क्ल्/ *adj.* connected with government or public money, especially taxes सरकार या सार्वजनिक धन (विशेषतः करों) से संबंधित; राजवित्तीय

**fish**[1] /fɪʃ फ़िश्/ *noun* (*pl.* **fish** or **fishes**) **1** [C] an animal that lives and breathes in water and swims मछली *How many fish have you caught?* ○ *The list of endangered species includes nearly 600 fishes.*

> **NOTE** शब्द **fish** का बहुवचन रूप **fish** अधिक प्रचलित है। मछली के विभिन्न प्रकारों का निर्देश करने के लिए **fishes** का प्रयोग किया जा सकता है।

**2** [U] fish as food मछली का मांस; भोज्य पदार्थ के रूप में मछली *We're having fish for dinner.*

**fish**[2] /fɪʃ फ़िश्/ *verb* [I] **1 fish (for sth)** to try to catch fish मछली पकड़ने की कोशिश करना *He's fishing for trout.* ○ *They often **go fishing** at weekends.* **2 fish (around) (in sth) (for sth)** to search for sth in water or in a deep or hidden place पानी या किसी गहरे या गुप्त स्थान में कुछ खोजना *She fished (around) for her keys in the bottom of her bag.*

**PHRV fish for sth** to try to get sth you want in an indirect way अभीष्ट वस्तु को घुमावदार तरीक़े से पाने की कोशिश करना *to fish for an invitation*

**fish sth out (of sth)** to take or pull sth out (of sth) especially after searching for it किसी वस्तु को (किसी अन्य वस्तु में से) खींचकर बाहर निकालना, विशेषतः उसे ढूँढ़ लेने के बाद *After the accident they fished the car out of the canal.*

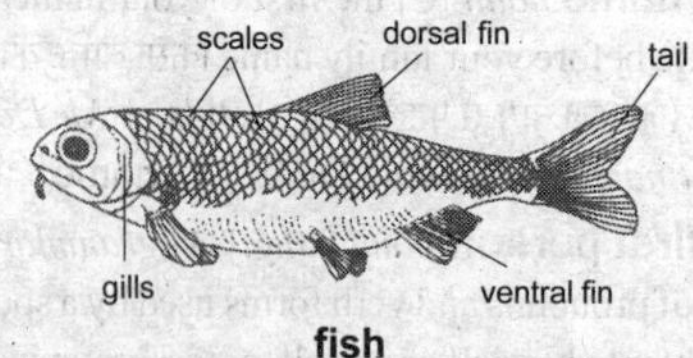

**fish**

**fisherman** /ˈfɪʃəmən ˈफ़िशमन्/ *noun* [C] (*pl.* **-men** /-men -मेन्/) a person who catches fish either as a job or as a sport मछली पकड़ने वाला व्यक्ति (व्यावसायिक या शौक़िया तौर पर); मछुआरा ➪ **angler** देखिए।

**fishing** /ˈfɪʃɪŋ ˈफ़िशिङ्/ *noun* [U] catching fish as a job, sport or hobby मछली पकड़ना, व्यावसायिक या शौक़िया तौर पर *Fishing is a major industry in Iceland.* ➪ **angling** देखिए।

**fishing rod** *noun* [C] a long thin stick with a long thread (**line**) and a hook on it for catching fish मछली पकड़ने की लंबे धागे और काँटे वाली छड़; लग्गी

**fishmeal** /ˈfɪʃmiːl ˈफ़िश्मील्/ *noun* [U] dried fish made into powder and used as animal food or used by farmers to make plants grow well मछली को सुखाकर बनाया गया चूर्ण जो पशुओं के चारे या पौधों की खाद के रूप में प्रयुक्त होता है; मत्स्यचूर्ण

**fishmonger** /ˈfɪʃmʌŋɡə(r) ˈफ़िश्मङ्ग(र्)/ *noun* (*BrE*) **1** [C] a person whose job is to sell fish मछली बेचने वाला व्यक्ति; मछली-विक्रेता **2 the fishmonger's** [*sing.*] a shop that sells fish मछली की बिक्री की दुकान

**fishy** /ˈfɪʃi ˈफ़िशि/ *adj.* **1** tasting or smelling like a fish मछली के स्वाद या गंध वाला *a fishy smell* **2** (*informal*) seeming suspicious or dishonest संदिग्ध या असत्य लगने वाला *The police thought the man's story sounded extremely fishy.*

**fission** /ˈfɪʃn ˈफ़िशन्/ *noun* [U] **1** (*also* **nuclear fission**) (in physics) the action or process of dividing the central part (**nucleus**) of an atom, when a large amount of energy is created (भौतिकी विज्ञान में) परमाणु के केंद्रीय अंश को विखंडित करने की क्रिया या प्रक्रिया, जिसमें बड़ी मात्रा में ऊर्जा बनती है; परमाणु-विखंडन ➪ **fusion** देखिए। **2** (in biology) the division of cells into new cells as a method of creating more cells (जीव विज्ञान में) कोशिकाओं का विभाजन और नवकोशिका निर्माण

**fissure** /ˈfɪʃə(r) ˈफ़िश(र्)/ *noun* [C] (*technical*) a long deep crack in sth, especially in rock or in the earth लंबी गहरी दरार विशेषतः चट्टान या धरती में

**fist** /fɪst फ़िस्ट्/ *noun* [C] a hand with the fingers closed together tightly कसकर बंद अंगुलियों वाला हाथ; मुट्ठी *She **clenched** her **fists** in anger.*

**fit**[1] /fɪt फ़िट्/ *verb* (**fitting; fitted**) (*AmE pt, pp usually* **fit**) **1** [I, T] to be the right size or shape for sb/sth किसी व्यक्ति या वस्तु के लिए आकार या बनावट में एकदम सही होना; उचित होना *These jeans fit very well.* ○ *This dress doesn't fit me any more.* ○ *This key doesn't fit in the lock.* **2** [T] **fit (sb/sth) in/into/on/onto sth** to find or have enough space for sb/sth किसी व्यक्ति या वस्तु के लिए पर्याप्त जगह निकालना

या होना *I can't fit into these trousers any more.* ○ *Can you fit one more person in the car?* ○ *I can't fit all these books onto the shelf.* **3** [T] to put or fix sth in the right place किसी वस्तु को सही जगह पर रखना या जमाना *The builders are fitting new windows today.* ○ *I can't fit these pieces of the model together.* **4** [T] to be or make sb/sth right or suitable सही या उपयुक्त होना, करना या बनाना *I don't think Kartik's fitted for such a demanding job.* ○ *That description fits Anuradha perfectly.*

PHR V **fit sb/sth in; fit sb/sth in/into sth** to find time to see sb or to do sth किसी व्यक्ति या कार्य के लिए समय निकालना *The doctor managed to fit me in this morning.*

**fit in (with sb/sth)** to be able to live, work, etc. in an easy and natural way (with sb/sth) सहज भाव से किसी के साथ काम कर सकना *The new girl found it difficult to fit in (with the other children) at school.*

**fit²** /fɪt फ़िट्/ *adj.* (**fitter; fittest**) **1 fit (for sth/to do sth)** strong and in good physical health (especially because of exercise) हृष्ट-पुष्ट और सुस्वस्थ विशेषतः व्यायाम के कारण *Swimming is a good way to **keep fit**.* ○ *My dad's almost recovered from his illness, but he's still not fit enough for work.* ○ *She goes to keep-fit classes.* ✪ विलोम **unfit** **2 fit (for sb/sth); fit to do sth** good enough; suitable एकदम सही; उपयुक्त *Do you think she is fit for the job?* ○ *These houses are not fit (for people) to live in.*

**fit³** /fɪt फ़िट्/ *noun* **1** [C] a sudden attack of an illness, in which sb loses consciousness and his/her body may make violent movements किसी बीमारी का दौरा जिसमें रोगी अचेत हो जाता है और उसके शरीर में तीव्र ऐंठन होती है *to have fits* **2** [C] a sudden short period of coughing, laughter, etc. that you cannot control खाँसी, हँसी आदि का दौरा जो क़ाबू से बाहर हो; लहर, मौज *a fit of laughter/anger* **3** [*sing.*] (*usually after an adjective*) the way in which sth (for example a piece of clothing) fits (वस्तु आदि) सही बैठने या अनुकूल होने का ढंग *a good/bad/tight/loose fit*

**fitness** /ˈfɪtnəs ˈफ़िट्नस्/ *noun* [U] **1** the condition of being strong and healthy पूर्ण स्वस्थता, पूरी तंदुरुस्ती *Fitness is important in most sports.* **2 fitness for sth/to do sth** the quality of being suitable उपयुक्तता *The directors were not sure about his fitness for the job.*

**fitted** /ˈfɪtɪd ˈफ़िटिड्/ *adj.* made or cut to fit a particular space and fixed there स्थान-विशेष में जमाने के लिए बनाया या काटा-पीटा गया *a fitted carpet* ○ *a fitted kitchen* (= one with fitted cupboards)

**fitting¹** /ˈfɪtɪŋ ˈफ़िटिङ्/ *adj.* **1** (*formal*) right; suitable सही, ठीक; उपयुक्त *It would be fitting for the Olympics to be held in Greece, as that is where they originated.* **2 -fitting** used in compounds to describe how clothes, etc. fit कपड़ों आदि की फिटिंग के संकेत के लिए यौगिक शब्दों में प्रयुक्त उत्तर पद *a tight-fitting dress* ○ *loose-fitting trousers*

**fitting²** /ˈfɪtɪŋ ˈफ़िटिङ्/ *noun* [C, *usually pl.*] the things that are fixed in a building or on a piece of furniture but that can be changed or moved if necessary भवन में या फ़र्नीचर में स्थायी रूप से जड़ा सामान जिसे बदला या अन्यत्र ले जाया जा सके; फ़िटिंग ➪ **fixture** देखिए।

**five** /faɪv फ़ाइव्/ *number* **1** 5 पाँच (का अंक) ➪ **fifth** की प्रविष्टि देखिए।

NOTE संख्याओं के वाक्य-प्रयोग के लिए **six** की प्रविष्टि देखिए।

**2 five-** (*used in compounds*) having five of the thing mentioned पाँच से युक्त (कोई चीज़) *a five-day week* ○ *a five-hour flight*

**fiver** /ˈfaɪvə(r) ˈफ़ाइव़(र्)/ *noun* [C] (*BrE informal*) a five-rupee note; Rs 5 पाँच रुपये का नोट

**fix¹** /fɪks फ़िक्स्/ *verb* [T] **1** to put sth firmly in place so that it will not move किसी वस्तु को किसी पर दृढ़ता से जमाना; बैठाना, जड़ना *Can you fix this new handle to the door?* ○ (*figurative*) *I found it difficult to keep my mind fixed on my work.* **2** to repair sth किसी वस्तु की मरम्मत करना *The electrician's coming to fix the ceiling fan.* ✪ पर्याय **repair** **3 fix sth (up)** to decide or arrange sth किसी बात पर निर्णय लेना; व्यवस्था या प्रबंध करना *We need to fix the price.* ○ *Have you fixed (up) a date for the party?* **4 fix sth (up)** to get sth ready किसी वस्तु को तैयार करना *They're fixing up their spare room for the new baby.* **5** (*usually passive*) (*informal*) to arrange the result of sth in a way that is not honest or fair किसी काम के नतीजे को बेईमानी से तय करना *Fans of the losing team suspected that the match had been fixed.* **6 fix sth (for sb)** to prepare sth (especially food or drink) कुछ तैयार करना (विशेषतः खाद्य या पेय पदार्थ) *Can I fix you a drink/a drink for you?*

PHR V **fix sb up (with sth)** (*informal*) to arrange for sb to have sth किसी के लिए किसी बात की व्यवस्था या प्रबंध करना *I can fix you up with a place to stay.*

**fix²** /fɪks फ़िक्स्/ *noun* [C] **1** a solution to a problem, especially one that is easy or temporary समस्या का विशेषतः सरल या अस्थायी समाधान *There's no **quick fix** to this problem.* **2** [*usually sing.*] (*informal*) a difficult situation कोई कठिन स्थिति; समस्या *I was **in a real fix**—I'd locked the car keys inside* *the car.* **3** [*usually sing.*] (*informal*) a result that is dishonestly arranged बेईमानी से तय किया नतीजा

**fixation** /fɪkˈseɪʃn फ़िक्ˈसेशन्/ *noun* [C] **a fixation (with sth)** an interest in sth that is too strong and not normal किसी बात में अत्यधिक व अस्वभाविक रुचि; बहुत गहरा व असामान्य लगाव

**fixed** /fɪkst फ़िक्स्ट्/ *adj.* **1** already decided पहले से निश्चित *a fixed date/price/rent* **2** not changing अपरिवर्तनीय; स्थायी *He has such fixed ideas that you can't discuss anything with him.*

IDM **(of) no fixed abode/address** (*formal*) (with) no permanent place to live बिना किसी स्थायी निवास के *The poor man, of no fixed abode, was found guilty of robbery.*

**fixture** /ˈfɪkstʃə(r) ˈफ़िक्स्च(र्)/ *noun* [C] **1** a sporting event arranged for a particular day विशेष दिन के लिए नियत कोई खेल-स्पर्धा *to arrange/cancel/play a fixture* **2** [*usually pl.*] a piece of furniture or equipment that is fixed in a house or building and sold with it किसी मकान या भवन में लगा सामान या फ़र्नीचर जो मकान के साथ ही बिकता है *Does the price of the house include fixtures and fittings?* ➪ **fitting** देखिए।

**fizz** /fɪz फ़िज़्/ *noun* [U] the bubbles in a liquid and the sound they make द्रव पदार्थ में उत्पन्न बुलबुले और उनकी (सी-सी की) आवाज़; बुदबुदाहट *This lemonade's lost its fizz.* ▶ **fizz** *verb* [I] बुदबुदाना

**fizzle** /ˈfɪzl ˈफ़िज़्ल्/ *verb*

PHR V **fizzle out** to end in a weak or disappointing way निम्न स्तरीय या निराशाजनक ढंग से समाप्त होना *The game started well but it fizzled out in the second half.*

**fizzy** /ˈfɪzi ˈफ़िज़ि/ *adj.* (used about a drink) containing many small bubbles of gas (पेय पदार्थ) गैस के छोटे बुलबुलों से भरपूर; बुलबुलेदार

NOTE बुलबुलों वाली शराब को **sparkling** कहते हैं (**fizzy** नहीं)। ➪ **still** देखिए।

**fizzy drink** (*AmE* **soda**) *noun* [C] a sweet drink without alcohol that contains many small bubbles एलकोहल रहित मीठा व बुलबुलेदार पेय

**fjord** /ˈfjɔːd ˈफ़्यॉड्/ *noun* [C] a long narrow piece of sea between cliffs, especially in Norway खड़ी चट्टानों के बीच का लंबा सँकरा समुद्री मार्ग, विशेषतः नार्वे में

**flabbergasted** /ˈflæbəgɑːstɪd ˈफ़्लैबगास्टिड्/ *adj.* (*informal*) extremely surprised and/or shocked अत्यधिक चकित या/और स्तब्ध; हक्का-बक्का, भौंचक्का

**flabby** /ˈflæbi ˈफ़्लैबि/ *adj.* having too much soft fat instead of muscle बहुत अधिक कोमल चरबी वाला; थुलथुल *a flabby stomach*

**flaccid** /ˈflæsɪd ˈफ़्लैसिड्/ *adj.* **1** (*formal*) soft and weak कोमल और दुर्बल; शिथिल *flaccid muscles* **2** (*technical*) (used about parts of plants) not containing enough water (पौधों के भाग) जिनमें जल की मात्रा पर्याप्त नहीं

**flag¹** /flæg फ़्लैग्/ *noun* [C] a piece of cloth with a pattern or picture on it, often tied to a pole (**flagpole**) or rope and used as a symbol of a country, club, etc. or as a signal झंडा, ध्वजा, पताका

**flag²** /flæg ˈफ़्लैग्/ *verb* [I] (**flagging; flagged**) to become tired or less strong थक जाना, कमज़ोर होना, ढीला पड़ जाना

PHR V **flag sb/sth down** to wave to sb in a car to make him/her stop वाहन चालक को रोकने के लिए हाथ हिला कर इशारा करना

**flagrant** /ˈfleɪgrənt ˈफ़्लेग्रन्ट्/ *adj.* (*only before a noun*) (used about an action) shocking because it is done in a very obvious way and shows no respect for people, laws, etc. (कर्म) स्तब्धकारी, शर्मनाक, प्रत्यक्ष रूप से अपमानजनक

**flail** /fleɪl फ़्लेल्/ *verb* [I, T] to wave or move about without control बिना सँभाले इधर-उधर घुमाना, हाथ-पैर मारना, लहराना *The insect's legs were flailing in the air.* ○ *Don't flail your arms about like that—you might hurt someone.*

**flair** /fleə(r) फ़्लेअ(र्)/ *noun* **1 (a) flair for sth** [*sing.*] a natural ability to do sth well किसी काम को अच्छे तरीक़े से करने की नैसर्गिक योग्यता; जन्मजात प्रवृत्ति या कौशल *She has a flair for languages.* **2** [U] the quality of being interesting or having style रुचिकर, आकर्षक या सुरुचिपूर्ण होने का गुण *That poster is designed with her usual flair.*

**flak** /flæk फ़्लैक्/ *noun* [U] (*informal*) criticism कटु आलोचना *He'll get some flak for missing that goal.*

**flake¹** /fleɪk फ़्लेक्/ *noun* [C] a small thin piece of sth किसी वस्तु का छोटा पतला टुकड़ा, पपड़ी, कण *snowflakes* ○ *flakes of paint*

**flake²** /fleɪk फ़्लेक्/ *verb* [I] **flake (off)** to come off in flakes पपड़ी बनकर उतरना *This paint is very old—it's beginning to flake (off).*

**flamboyant** /flæmˈbɔɪənt फ़्लैम्ˈबॉइअन्ट्/ *adj.* **1** (used about a person) acting in a loud, confident way that attracts attention (व्यक्ति या उसका आचरण) भड़कीला व आत्मविश्वासी और इस कारण ध्यानाकर्षक *a flamboyant gesture/style/personality* **2** bright and easily noticed चटकीला और चमकदार, भड़कीला *flamboyant colours* ▶ **flamboyance** *noun* [U] भड़कीलापन व दिखावा; चटकीलापन ▶ **flamboyantly** *adv.* चटकीलेपन से

**flame** /fleɪm फ़्लेम्/ *noun* [C, U] an area of bright burning gas that comes from sth that is on fire लपट, ज्वाला *The house was* ***in flames*** *when the fire engine arrived.* ○ *The piece of paper* ***burst into flames*** *in the fire* (= suddenly began to burn strongly).

**Flame of the Forest** *noun* [C] a common name used to refer to a tree native to southern Asia. It has brilliant red flowers सुर्ख लाल फूलों वाले पेड़; पलाश का वृक्ष

**flaming** /ˈfleɪmɪŋ ˈफ़्लेमिङ्/ *adj.* (*only before a noun*) **1** (used about anger, an argument, etc.) violent (क्रोध, विवाद आदि) ज़ोरदार, उग्र *We had a flaming argument over the telephone bills.* **2** burning brightly अति प्रज्वलित, चमकदार **3** (*slang*) used as a mild swear word हलकी गाली के तौर पर प्रयुक्त *I can't get in—I've lost the flaming key.* **4** (used about colours, especially red) very bright (रंग, विशेषतः लाल) चमकदार, भड़कीला, प्रदीप्त *flaming red hair* ○ *a flaming sunset*

**flamingo** /fləˈmɪŋɡəʊ फ़्लˈमिङ्गो/ *noun* [C] (*pl.* **flamingoes** or **flamingos**) a large pink and red bird that has long legs and lives near water लंबी टाँगों वाला बड़ा गुलाबी रंग का पक्षी जो पानी के पास रहता है; हंसावर

**flammable** /ˈflæməbl ˈफ़्लैमबल्/ *adj.* able to burn easily जिसमें आग आसानी से लग सके; प्रज्वलनशील ✪ पर्याय **inflammable** ✪ विलोम **non-flammable**

**flan** /flæn फ़्लैन्/ *noun* [C, U] a round open pie that is filled with fruit, cheese, vegetables, etc. गोल खुली कचौड़ी जैसा खाद्य पदार्थ जिसके अंदर फल, पनीर, सब्ज़ियाँ आदि भरे जाते हैं

**flank¹** /flæŋk फ़्लैङ्क्/ *noun* [C] **1** the side of an animal's body पशु के शरीर का पार्श्व भाग **2** the parts of an army at the sides in a battle युद्धरत सेना के पार्श्व भाग

**flank²** /flæŋk फ़्लैङ्क्/ *verb* [T] (*usually passive*) to be placed at the side or sides of पार्श्व या पार्श्वों में स्थित *The road was flanked by trees.*

**flannel** /ˈflænl ˈफ़्लैनल्/ *noun* **1** [U] a type of soft woollen cloth एक प्रकार का कोमल ऊनी कपड़ा; फलालैन **2** = **facecloth**

**flap¹** /flæp फ़्लैप्/ *noun* [C] a piece of material, paper, etc. that is fixed to sth at one side only, often covering an opening किसी वस्तु में खुली जगह को ढकने के लिए केवल एक पार्श्व से जुड़ा हुआ काग़ज़, कपड़ा पल्ला (जेब आदि का) *the flap of an envelope*

IDM **be in/get into a flap** (*informal*) to be in/get into a state of worry or excitement चिंता या उत्तेजना से ग्रस्त हो जाना

**flap²** /flæp फ़्लैप्/ *verb* (**flapping; flapped**) **1** [I, T] to move (sth) up and down or from side to side, especially in the wind (पंखों आदि का) फड़फड़ाना (विशेषतः हवा में) *The sails were flapping in the wind.* ○ *The bird flapped its wings and flew away.* **2** [I] (*informal*) to become worried or excited चिंतित या उत्तेजित हो जाना *Stop flapping—it's all organized!*

**flare¹** /fleə(r) फ़्लेअ(र्)/ *verb* [I] to burn for a short time with a sudden bright flame एकाएक चमकभरी लपट के साथ जल उठना; भभकना

PHR V **flare up** **1** (used about a fire) to suddenly burn more strongly (आग का) एकाएक भड़कना **2** (used about violence, anger, etc.) to start suddenly or to become suddenly worse (हिंसा, क्रोध आदि का) एकाएक भड़क उठना या बदतर हो जाना

**flare²** /fleə(r) फ़्लेअ(र्)/ *noun* **1** [*sing.*] a sudden bright light or flame एकाएक चमकी रोशनी या उठी लपट; धधक, प्रदीप्ति, लौ **2** [C] a thing that produces a bright light or flame, used especially as a signal चमकदार रोशनी या लपट उत्पन्न करने वाली वस्तु, विशेषतः संकेत के रूप में प्रयुक्त

**flared** /fleəd फ़्लेअड्/ *adj.* (used about trousers and skirts) becoming wider towards the bottom (पतलून और स्कर्ट) नीचे क्रमशः चौड़े होते हुए

**flash¹** /flæʃ फ़्लैश्/ *verb* **1** [I, T] to produce or make sth produce a sudden bright light for a short time क्षण भर के लिए चमकदार रोशनी करना या करवाना; कौंधना *The neon sign above the door flashed on and off all night.* ○ *That lorry driver's flashing his lights at us.* **2** [I] to move very fast बहुत तेज़ी से गुज़र जाना *I saw something flash past the window.* ○ *Thoughts kept flashing through my mind and I couldn't sleep.* **3** [T] to show sth quickly फुरती से कुछ दिखाना *The detective flashed his card and went straight in.* **4** [T] to send sth by radio, television, etc. रेडियो, टेलिविज़न आदि द्वारा प्रसारित करना *The news of the disaster was flashed across the world.*

PHR V **flash back** (used about a person's thoughts) to return suddenly to a time in the past (व्यक्ति के विचारों का) एकाएक अतीत में लौट जाना; किसी व्यक्ति का सहसा अतीत की स्मृति में डूब जाना *Something he said made my mind flash back to my childhood.*

**flash²** /flæʃ फ़्लैश्/ *noun* **1** [C] a sudden bright light that comes and goes quickly तेज़ी से जलने-बुझने वाली चमकदार रोशनी, कौंध, क्षणिक तेज़ प्रकाश *a flash of lightning* **2** [C] **a flash (of sth)** a sudden strong feeling or idea एकाएक उभरा सशक्त

भाव या विचार *a flash of inspiration* ○ *The idea came to me in a flash.* **3** [C, U] a bright light that you use with a camera for taking photographs when it is dark; the device for producing this light कैमरे में लगी चमकदार रोशनी (अँधेरे में फ़ोटो लेते समय प्रयुक्त); ऐसी रोशनी उत्पन्न करने वाला उपकरण

IDM **in/like a flash** very quickly बहुत तेज़ी से

**(as) quick as a flash** ➪ **quick**[1] देखिए।

**flashback** /ˈflæʃbæk ˈफ़्लैश्बैक् / *noun* [C, U] a part of a film, play, etc. that shows sth that happened before the main story फ़िल्म, नाटक आदि का वह अंश जिसमें मुख्य कथा से पहले की घटना का वर्णन होता है; अतीतावलोकन, पूर्वदृश्य, पूर्व घटना प्रसंग

**flash flood** *noun* [C] a sudden flood of water caused by heavy rain भारी वर्षा से आई आकस्मिक बाढ़

**flashlight** /ˈflæʃlaɪt ˈफ़्लैश्लाइट् / (*AmE*) = **torch 1**

**flashy** /ˈflæʃi ˈफ़्लैशि / *adj.* (**flashier; flashiest**) attracting attention by being very big, bright and expensive बहुत बड़ा, चमकदार और महँगा होने के कारण ध्यान आकृष्ट करने वाला; तड़क-भड़क वाला *a flashy sports car*

**flask** /flɑːsk फ़्लास्क् / *noun* [C] **1** (*also* **Thermos**™) a type of container for keeping a liquid hot or cold द्रव पदार्थ के गरम या ठंडा बनाए रखने वाली एक प्रकार की बड़ी बोतल; फ़्लास्क, थर्मस **2** a bottle with a narrow neck that is used for storing and mixing chemicals in scientific work वैज्ञानिक प्रयोगों में रसायनों को संचित और मिश्रित करने के लिए प्रयुक्त एक प्रकार की पतली गरदन वाली बोतल ➪ **laboratory** पर चित्र देखिए।

**flat**[1] /flæt फ़्लैट् / *adj., adv.* (**flatter; flattest**) **1** smooth and level, with no parts that are higher than the rest (सतह आदि) सपाट, समतल *He **fell flat on his face** in the mud.* **2** not high or deep जो ऊँचा या गहरा न हो, चपटा *You need flat shoes for walking.* ○ *a flat dish* **3** without much interest or energy नीरस, स्फूर्तिहीन, फीका *Things have been a bit flat since their son left.* **4** (*only before a noun*) (used about sth that you say or decide) that will not change; firm (कथन या निर्णय) अपरिवर्तनीय; पक्का, दृढ़ *He answered our request with a flat 'No!'* **5** (in music) lower than the correct note (संगीत में) बेसुरा *That last note was flat. Can you sing it again?* ○ *You're singing flat.* ➪ **sharp** देखिए। **6** (used about a drink) not fresh because it has lost its bubbles (पेय पदार्थ) बासी क्योंकि उसमें बुलबुले नहीं रहे; जिसका स्वाद ख़त्म हो चुका हो *Open a new bottle. That lemonade has **gone flat**.* **7** (*BrE*) (used about a battery) no longer producing electricity; not working (बैटरी) जो अब बिजली पैदा नहीं कर रही; चुकी हुई; विद्युतविहीन *We couldn't start the car because the battery was completely flat.* **8** (used about a tyre) without enough air in it (टायर) जिसकी हवा निकल चुकी है, चपटा, चिपका हुआ *This tyre looks flat—has it got a puncture?* **9** (used about the cost of sth) that is the same for everyone; that is fixed (किसी वस्तु की क़ीमत) सबके लिए समान; निश्चित *We charge a flat fee of Rs 500, however long you stay.* **10** (used for emphasizing how quickly sth is done) in exactly the time mentioned and no longer (काम में शीघ्रता पर बल देने के लिए प्रयुक्त) एकदम उल्लेखनीय समय में न, कि उससे अधिक *She can get up and go out of the house in ten minutes flat.*

IDM **fall flat** (used about a joke, a story, an event, etc.) to fail to produce the effect that you wanted (कोई मज़ाक़, कहानी, घटना आदि) वांछित प्रभाव उत्पन्न करने में विफल

**flat out** as fast as possible; without stopping यथाशीघ्र; बिना रुके *He's been working flat out for two weeks and he needs a break.*

**flat**[2] /flæt फ़्लैट् / *noun* **1** [C] (*AmE* **apartment**) a set of rooms that is used as a home (usually in a large building) (प्रायः बड़े भवन में) रहने के लिए प्रयुक्त कमरों का सेट; फ़्लैट, अपार्टमेंट *Do you rent your flat or have you bought it?*

> NOTE अमेरिकी अंग्रेज़ी में शब्द **apartment** ही सामान्य प्रयोग है। ब्रिटिश अंग्रेज़ी में अवकाश आदि में ठहरने के लिए (न कि बाकायदा रहने के लिए) भाड़े पर लिए फ़्लैट को **apartment** कहते हैं—*We're renting an apartment in London.*
>
> मकान मालिक को **landlord**, मकान मालकिन को **landlady** व किराएदार को **tenant** कहते हैं। मकान मालिक/मकान मालकिन का अपने घर को किराए पर देने को **rent** क्रिया द्वारा व्यक्त किया जाता है। फ़्लैट **furnished** (पहले से साज-सामानयुक्त) या **unfurnished** हो सकता है। एक ऊँची आधुनिक इमारत जिसमें बहुत सारे फ़्लैट होते हैं **block of flats** कहलाती है। फ़्लैट में संग रहने वाले व्यक्ति को **flatmate** कहते हैं।

**2** [C] (*symbol* #) (in music) a note which is half a note lower than the note with the same letter (संगीत में) कोमल स्वर, सुर से नीचे ➪ **sharp** देखिए। **3** [*sing.*] **the flat (of sth)** the flat part or side of sth किसी वस्तु का चपटा भाग या पार्श्व *the flat of your hand* **4** [C] a tyre on a vehicle that has no air in it वायुरहित टायर

**flatfish** /ˈflætfɪʃ ˈफ़्लैट्फ़िश् / *noun* [C] (*pl.* **flatfish**) any sea fish with a flat body चपटे शरीर वाली कोई भी समुद्री मछली *Plaice and turbot are flatfish.*

**flatly** /ˈflætli ˈफ़्लैट्लि / *adv.* **1** in a direct way; absolutely एकदम सीधे; साफ़-साफ़, पूर्णतः *He flatly denied the allegations.* **2** in a way that shows no interest or emotion रुचिहीन या नीरस भाव से

**flatten** /ˈflætn ˈफ़्लैट्न् / *verb* [I, T] **flatten (sth) (out)** to become or make sth flat समतल हो जाना या कर देना *The countryside flattens out as you get nearer the sea.* ○ *The storms have flattened crops all over the country.*

**flatter** /ˈflætə(r) ˈफ़्लैट(र्) / *verb* [T] **1** to say nice things to sb, often in a way that is not sincere, because you want to please him/her or because you want to get an advantage for yourself ख़ुशामद या चापलूसी करना; लाभ के इरादे से किसी की दिखावटी प्रशंसा करना **2 flatter yourself (that)** to choose to believe sth good about yourself although other people may not think the same अपने विषय में बहुत अच्छा सोचना (भले ही दूसरे लोग ऐसा न सोचें) *He flatters himself that he speaks fluent French.* **3** (*usually passive*) to give pleasure or honour to sb किसी को ख़ुशी या सम्मान देना *I felt very flattered when they gave me the job.*

**flattering** /ˈflætərɪŋ ˈफ़्लैटरिङ् / *adj.* making sb look or sound more attractive or important than he/she really is (किसी को) वास्तविकता से अधिक आकर्षक या महत्त्वपूर्ण दर्शाते हुए

**flattery** /ˈflætəri ˈफ़्लैटरि / *noun* [U] saying good things about sb/sth that you do not really mean ख़ुशामद, चापलूसी, चाटुकारिता

**flaunt** /flɔːnt फ़्लॉन्ट् / *verb* [T] to show sth that you are proud of so that other people will admire it किसी बात पर इतराना (ताकि दूसरे लोग भी तारीफ़ करें)

**flautist** /ˈflɔːtɪst ˈफ़्लॉटिस्ट् / *noun* [C] a person who plays a musical instrument that you blow into (**a flute**) बांसुरी-वादक

**flavour**[1] (*AmE* **flavor**) /ˈfleɪvə(r) ˈफ़्लेव़(र्) / *noun* [C, U] **1** the taste (of food) (भोजन का) स्वाद; लज़्ज़त *Do you think a little salt would improve the flavour?* ○ *ten different flavours of yoghurt* **2** [*sing.*] an idea of the particular quality or character of sth किसी वस्तु के विशेष गुण या वैशिष्ट्य का अनुमान *This video will give you a flavour of what the city is like.*

**flavour**[2] (*AmE* **flavor**) /ˈfleɪvə(r) ˈफ़्लेव़(र्) / *verb* [T] to give flavour to sth किसी वस्तु को ज़ायक़ेदार बनाना *Add a little tamarind to flavour the sauce.* ○ *strawberry-flavoured milkshake*

**flavouring** (*AmE* **flavoring**) /ˈfleɪvərɪŋ ˈफ़्लेव़रिङ् / *noun* [C, U] something that you add to food or drink to give it a particular taste खाद्य या पेय पदार्थ को विशेष स्वाद देने के लिए उसमें डाली गई वस्तु *no artificial flavourings*

**flaw** /flɔː फ़्लॉ / *noun* [C] **1 a flaw (in sth)** a mistake in sth that makes it not good enough, or means that it does not function as it should दोष, त्रुटि, कमी, अभाव *There are some flaws in her argument.* **2** a mark or crack in an object that means that it is not perfect किसी वस्तु पर कोई निशान या दरार (जिससे वह अधूरी लगे) **3 a flaw (in sb/sth)** a bad quality in sb's character किसी के चरित्र में कमी; चरित्र-दोष ▶ **flawed** *adj.* सदोष *I think your plan is flawed.*

**flawless** /ˈflɔːləs ˈफ़्लॉलस् / *adj.* perfect; with no faults or mistakes परिपूर्ण; निर्दोष *a flawless diamond*

**flax** /flæks फ़्लैक्स् / *noun* [U] **1** a plant with blue flowers that is cultivated for its seed (**linseed**) and for the thread made from its stalk सन का पौधा **2** the thread made from the stalks of the plant, used to make linen सन के रेशे

**flea** /fliː फ़्ली / *noun* [C] a very small jumping insect without wings that lives on animals, for example cats and dogs. Fleas bite people and animals and make them scratch एक पंखहीन कीट जो पशुओं और मनुष्य के शरीर में बसेरा बना लेता है; पिस्सू ➪ **insect** पर चित्र देखिए।

**flea market** *noun* [C] a market, often in a street, where old and used goods are sold ऐसा बाज़ार जहाँ पुराना सामान बिकता है; कबाड़ी बाज़ार

**fleck** /flek फ़्लेक् / *noun* [C, *usually pl.*] a very small mark on sth; a very small piece of sth (किसी वस्तु पर) बहुत छोटा निशान; (किसी वस्तु का) बहुत छोटा टुकड़ा *After painting the ceiling, her hair was covered with flecks of white paint.*

**fledgling** (*BrE* **fledgeling**) /ˈfledʒlɪŋ ˈफ़्लेजलिङ् / *noun* [C] **1** a young bird that has just learnt to fly चिड़िया का बच्चा जिसने अभी-अभी उड़ना सीखा है **2** (*usually before another noun*) a person, an organization or a system that is new and without experience अनुभवहीन व्यक्ति, संगठन या प्रणाली *fledgling democracies*

**flee** /fliː फ़्ली / *verb* [I, T] (*pt, pp* **fled** /fled फ़्लेड् /) **flee (to.../into...); flee (from) sb/sth** to run away or escape from sth कहीं से फ़रार हो जाना या निकल भागना *The robbers fled the town with Rs 200,000.*

**fleece** /fliːs फ़्लीस् / *noun* [C] **1** the wool coat of a sheep भेड़ के शरीर पर ऊन की चादर, कच्ची ऊन ➪ **sheep** पर चित्र देखिए। **2** a piece of clothing like a jacket, made of warm artificial material गरमी देने वाली कृत्रिम सामग्री से बना वस्त्र (जाकेट आदि)

**fleet** /fliːt फ़्लीट् / *noun* [C, *with sing. or pl. verb*] **1** a group of ships or boats that sail together संग यात्रा करने वाले जहाज़ों या नावों का बेड़ा *a fishing fleet* **2 a fleet (of sth)** a group of vehicles (especially taxis, buses or aircraft) that are travelling together or owned by one person एक साथ जा रहे या एक ही व्यक्ति के स्वामित्व वाले वाहनों का समूह

**flesh** /fleʃ फ़्लेश् / *noun* [U] **1** the soft part of a human or animal body (between the bones and under the skin) मानव या पशु के शरीर का कोमल अंश (जो त्वचा और अस्थियों के बीच में होता है); मांस **NOTE** पशुओं के उस मांस को **meat** कहते है जिसे मनुष्य खाते हैं। **2** the part of a fruit or vegetable that is soft and can be eaten फल या वनस्पति का खाने योग्य कोमल अंश; गूदा

**IDM** **your (own) flesh and blood** a member of your family अपने परिवार का सदस्य

**in the flesh** in person, not on television, in a photograph, etc. शरीरतः साक्षात सामने खड़ा न कि किसी चित्र में

**make your flesh creep** to make you feel disgusted and/or nervous खिझाना और/या आशंकित और उत्तेजित करना *The way he smiled made her flesh creep.*

**flew** ➪ **fly**[1] का past tense रूप

**flex**[1] /fleks फ़्लेक्स् / (*AmE* **cord**) *noun* [C, U] (a piece of) wire inside a plastic tube, used for carrying electricity to electrical equipment प्लास्टिक नली के अंदर की तार जो विद्युत उपकरण तक बिजली पहुँचाती है; फ़्लेक्स

**NOTE** **Flex** के अंत में **plug** होता है जिसे **socket** या **power point** में लगाया जाता है।

**flex**[2] /fleks फ़्लेक्स् / *verb* [T] to bend or move a leg, arm, muscle, etc. in order to exercise it टाँग, बाँह, मांसपेशी आदि की व्यायाम के लिए उन्हें मोड़ना या चलाना

**flexible** /ˈfleksəbl ˈफ़्लेक्सबल् / *adj.* **1** able to bend or move easily without breaking लचकीला, लचकदार **2** that can be changed easily जिसे आसानी से बदला जा सके; परिवर्तनीय *flexible working hours* ✪ विलोम **inflexible** ▶ **flexibility** /ˌfleksəˈbɪləti ˌफ़्लेक्सˈबिलटि / *noun* [U] लचकीलापन

**flexitime** /ˈfleksitaɪm ˈफ़्लेक्सिटाइम् / (*AmE* **flextime** /ˈflekstaɪm ˈफ़्लेक्स्टाइम् /) *noun* [U] a system in which employees work a particular number of hours each week or month but can choose when they start and finish work each day एक कार्य-प्रणाली जिसमें कर्मचारी स्वयं प्रतिदिन के काम के घंटे निर्धारित करता है यद्यपि प्रति सप्ताह या प्रतिमास के लिए उसके काम के कुल घंटें निश्चित होते हैं; लचकीली कार्य-निष्पादन प्रणाली *She works flexitime.*

**flick** /flɪk फ़्लिक् / *verb* **1** [T] **flick sth (away, off, onto, etc.)** to hit sth lightly and quickly with your finger or hand in order to move it अंगुली या हाथ से किसी वस्तु को हलके से और तेज़ी के साथ ठोकना या झाड़ना *She flicked the dust off her jacket.* ○ *Please don't flick ash on the carpet.* **2** [I, T] **flick (sth) (away, off, out, etc.)** to move, or to make sth move, with a quick sudden movement अचानक तेज़ी के साथ किसी वस्तु का हिलना या उसे हिलाना *She flicked the switch and the light came on.* ▶ **flick** *noun* [C] हलका प्रहार; अंगुलियों या हाथ से हलकी ठोक

**PHR V** **flick/flip through sth** to turn over the pages of a book, magazine, etc. quickly without reading everything पुस्तक, पत्रिका आदि के पृष्ठों को बिना पूरी तरह पढ़ते हुए जल्दी-जल्दी पलटना

**flicker**[1] /ˈflɪkə(r) ˈफ़्लिक(र्) / *verb* [I] **1** (used about a light or a flame) to keep going on and off as it burns or shines (रोशनी या लपट का) जलते समय लुपलुपाना, कँपकँपाना, टिमटिमाना *The candle flickered and went out.* **2** (used about a feeling, thought, etc.) to appear for a short time (किसी भावना, विचार आदि का) क्षणभर के लिए प्रकट होना *A smile flickered across her face.* **3** to move lightly and quickly up and down कोमलता से और तेज़ी के साथ ऊपर-नीचे गति करना *His eyelids flickered for a second and then he lay still.*

**flicker**[2] /ˈflɪkə(r) ˈफ़्लिक(र्) / *noun* [C, *usually sing.*] **1** a light that shines on and off quickly टिमटिमाती रोशनी **2** a small, sudden movement of part of the body शरीर के किसी अंग की हलकी थरथराहट **3** a feeling of sth that only lasts for a short time किसी भावना की क्षणिक अनुभूति *a flicker of hope/interest/doubt*

**flier** = **flyer**

**flies** ➪ **fly** देखिए।

**flight** /flaɪt फ़्लाइट् / *noun* **1** [C] a journey by air विमान यात्रा; उड़ान *to book a flight* ○ *a direct/scheduled/charter flight* ○ *They met **on a flight** to Australia.* ○ *a manned space flight to Mars* **2** [C] an aircraft that takes you on a particular journey यात्रा-विशेष पर जाने वाला विमान *Flight number 281 from New Delhi to Chennai is boarding now* (= is ready for passengers to get on it). **3** [U] the action of flying उड़ने की क्रिया; उड़ान *It's unusual to see swans **in flight*** (= when they are flying). **4** [C] a number of stairs or steps going up or down सीढ़ियों की कतार; ज़ीना *a flight of stairs* **5** [C, U] the action of running away or escaping from a dangerous or difficult situation किसी ख़तरनाक या कठिन स्थिति से दूर भागने या बच निकलने की क्रिया; पलायन *the refugees' flight from the war zone*

**flight attendant** *noun* [C] a person whose job is to serve and take care of passengers on an aircraft विमान यात्रा में यात्रियों की देखभाल करने वाला व्यक्ति; विमान-परिचारक या परिचारिका ✪ पर्याय **air hostess, steward, stewardess**

**flight deck** *noun* [C] **1** an area at the front of a large plane where the pilot sits to use the controls and fly the plane बड़े विमान के आगे वाले हिस्से में पायलट का कक्ष जहाँ बैठकर वह विमान की उड़ान को नियंत्रित करता है ➪ **plane** पर चित्र देखिए। **2** a long flat surface on top of an **aircraft carrier** where they take off and land विमानवाही जलपोत में सबसे ऊपर लंबा समतल क्षेत्र जहाँ से विमान उड़ान भरते व उतरते हैं

**flightless** /ˈflaɪtləs ˈफ़्लाइट्लस्/ *adj.* (used about birds and insects) not able to fly (पक्षी और कीड़े) उड़ने में असमर्थ

**flight path** *noun* [C] the route taken by an aircraft through the air विमान के उड़ने का निर्धारित मार्ग; उड़ानपथ

**flimsy** /ˈflɪmzi ˈफ़्लिम्ज़ि/ *adj.* **1** not strong; easily broken or torn कमज़ोर; आसानी से टूटने या फटने वाला *a flimsy bookcase* ○ *a flimsy blouse* **2** weak; not making you believe that sth is true दुर्बल; अविश्वसनीय *He gave a* ***flimsy excuse*** *for his absence.*

**flinch** /flɪntʃ फ़्लिन्च्/ *verb* [I] **1 flinch (at sth); flinch (away)** to make a sudden movement backwards because of sth painful or frightening दर्द या डर के मारे एकाएक पीछे हटना **2 flinch from sth/doing sth** to avoid doing sth because it is unpleasant किसी अप्रिय बात से कतराना *She didn't flinch from telling him the whole truth.*

**fling[1]** /flɪŋ फ़्लिङ्/ *verb* [T] (*pt, pp* **flung** /flʌŋ फ़्लङ्/) to throw sb/sth suddenly and carelessly or with great force एकाएक और लापरवाही से या ज़ोर से कोई वस्तु फेंकना; पटकना, दे मारना *He flung his coat on the floor.*

**fling[2]** /flɪŋ फ़्लिङ्/ *noun* [C, *usually sing.*] a short period of fun and pleasure मौज़-मस्ती की लघु अवधि; थोड़े समय की रंगरलियाँ

**flint** /flɪnt फ़्लिन्ट्/ *noun* **1** [U] very hard grey stone that produces small flames (**sparks**) when you hit it against steel चक़मक़ पत्थर जिसे लोहे पर रगड़ने से चिनगारियाँ निकलती हैं **2** [C] a small piece of flint or metal that is used to produce sparks (for example in a cigarette lighter) सिगरेट-लाइटर आदि में लगा चक़मक़ पत्थर या धातु

**flip** /flɪp फ़्लिप्/ *verb* (**flipping; flipped**) **1** [I, T] to turn (sth) over with a quick movement झटके से (कुछ) पलटना *She flipped the book open and started to read.* **2** [T] to throw sth into the air and make it turn over हवा में उछालना; उछालकर फेंकना *Let's flip a coin to see who starts.* **3** [I] **flip (out)** (*spoken*) to become very angry or excited अत्यधिक क्रोधित या उत्तेजित हो जाना; उबल पड़ना *When his father saw the damage to the car he flipped.*

**PHR V flick/flip through sth** ➪ **flick** देखिए।

**flip-flop** (*AmE* **thong**) *noun* [C, *usually pl.*] a simple open shoe with a thin strap that goes between your big toe and the toe next to it अँगूठेदार चप्पल या सैंडल

**flippant** /ˈflɪpənt ˈफ़्लिपन्ट्/ (*informal* **flip**) *adj.* not serious enough about things that are important महत्त्वपूर्ण बातों के प्रति बेपरवाह; छिछोरा, चंचल

**flipper** /ˈflɪpə(r) ˈफ़्लिप(र्)/ *noun* [C, *usually pl.*] **1** a flat arm that is part of the body of some sea animals which they use for swimming कुछ समुद्री जंतुओं का चपटी बाँह जैसा अंग (पंख) जो तैरने में सहायक होता है *Seals have flippers.* **2** a rubber shoe shaped like an animal's flipper that people wear so that they can swim better, especially under water समुद्री जंतुओं के पंख जैसा रबर का जूता जिसे ग़ोताख़ोर गहरे पानी में तैरते समय पहनते हैं

**flipping** /ˈflɪpɪŋ ˈफ़्लिपिङ्/ *adj., adv.* (*slang*) used as a mild way of swearing किसी को कोसने के लिए प्रयुक्त शब्द *When's the flipping bus coming?*

**flirt[1]** /flɜːt फ़्लट्/ *verb* [I] **flirt (with sb)** to behave in a way that suggests you find sb attractive though you are not serious about a relationship बिना गंभीरता के हलके ढंग से प्रेम-प्रदर्शित करना; इश्कबाज़ी करना *Who was that man Jaya was flirting with at the party?* ○ (*figurative*) *to flirt with death/danger/disaster*

**PHR V flirt with sth** to think about doing sth (but not very seriously) कुछ करने के बारे में सोचना (परंतु गंभीरता से नहीं) *She had flirted with the idea of becoming a model for a while.*

**flirt[2]** /flɜːt फ़्लट्/ *noun* [C] a person who behaves in a way that suggests he/she finds sb attactive and is trying to attract him/her, but not in a very serious way इश्कबाज़, दिखावटी प्रेमी

**flit** /flɪt फ़्लिट्/ *verb* [I] (**flitting; flitted**) **flit (from A to B); flit (between A and B)** to fly or move quickly from one place to another without staying anywhere for long फुदकना; जल्दी-जल्दी स्थान बदलना

**float[1]** /fləʊt फ़्लोट्/ *verb* **1** [I] to move slowly through air or water हवा या पानी में तिरना, बहना, उतराना *The boats were floating gently down the river.* ○ *The smell of freshly baked bread floated in through the window.* **2** [I] **float (in/on sth)** to stay on the surface of a liquid and not sink पानी

आदि द्रव की सतह पर बने रहना; उतराना *Wood floats in water.* **3** [T] to sell shares in a company or business to the public for the first time किसी कंपनी के शेयरों को पहली बार आम जनता को बेचना *The company was floated on the stock market in 2005.* **4** [I, T] (used in economics) if a government **floats** its country's money, or allows it to **float,** it allows its value to change freely according to the value of the money of other countries (अर्थशास्त्र में) सरकार द्वारा अपने देश की मुद्रा को खुला छोड़ना ताकि वह अपने बूते अन्य देशों की मुद्रा से विनिमय करे *The Indian government floated the rupee on the foreign exchange market.* **5** [I, T] to suggest an idea or a plan, especially in order to find out what people think about it मत, योजना आदि विचारार्थ प्रस्तुत करना, विशेषतः अन्य लोगों का दृष्टिकोण जानने के लिए *float the idea of barring smoking in public places*

**float²** /fləʊt फ़्लोट्/ *noun* [C] **1** a lorry or other vehicle that is decorated and used in a celebration that travels through the streets जुलूस में समारोहपूर्वक चलने वाला सजावटी वाहन (ट्रक आदि); शोभायान *a carnival float* **2** a light object used in fishing that moves on the water when a fish has been caught मछली पकड़ने में प्रयुक्त एक हलकी वस्तु जो मछली पकड़ी जाने पर पानी में तैरने लगती है **3** a light object used for helping people to learn to swim तैरना सीखने में सहायक एक हलकी वस्तु

**floating** /ˈfləʊtɪŋ ˈफ़्लोटिङ्/ *adj.* not fixed; not living permanently in one place अस्थायी; जिसका किसी एक स्थान पर स्थायी निवास नहीं; चलायमान *the city's floating population*

**flock¹** /flɒk फ़्लॉक्/ *noun* [C] **1** a group of sheep or birds भेड़ों या पक्षियों का झुंड ➪ **herd** देखिए। **2** a large number of people बड़ी संख्या में लोग; लोगों के झुंड *Flocks of tourists visit Nainital every summer.*

**flock²** /flɒk फ़्लॉक्/ *verb* [I] (used about people) to go or meet somewhere in large numbers (लोगों का) बड़ी संख्या में कहीं पहुँचना *People are flocking to her latest exhibition.*

**floe** /fləʊ फ़्लो/ = **ice floe**

**flog** /flɒg फ़्लॉग्/ *verb* [T] (**flogging; flogged**) **1** (*usually passive*) to hit sb hard several times with a stick or a long thin piece of leather (**whip**) as a punishment दंडस्वरूप किसी को चाबुक या छड़ी से पीटना; कोड़े बरसाना **2** (*informal*) to sell sth कुछ बेचना

**flogging** /ˈflɒgɪŋ ˈफ़्लॉगिङ्/ *noun* [C, U] the act of hitting sb several times with a long thin piece of leather (**whip**) or a stick as a punishment दंडस्वरूप किसी को छड़ी या चाबुक से मारने की क्रिया; कोड़े बरसाने की क्रिया

**flood¹** /flʌd फ़्लड्/ *verb* **1** [I, T] to fill a place with water; to be filled or covered with water किसी स्थान पर पानी भर देना; किसी में पानी भर जाना; बाढ़ आना *I left the taps on and it flooded the bathroom.* ○ *The River Brahmaputra floods almost every year.* **2** [I] **flood in/into/out of sth** to go somewhere in large numbers किसी स्थान पर बड़ी संख्या में जाना/आना; की भरमार होना *Since the television programme was shown, phone calls have been flooding into the studio.* **3** [I, T] (used about a thought, feeling, etc.) to fill sb's mind suddenly मन में एकाएक (विचार, भाव आदि) भर जाना *At the end of the day all his worries came flooding back.*

**flood²** /flʌd फ़्लड्/ *noun* [C] **1** a large amount of water that has spread from a river, the sea, etc. that covers an area which should be dry बाढ़, जल प्रवाह, सैलाब *Many people have been forced to leave their homes because of the floods.* **2 a flood (of sth)** a large number or amount बड़ी संख्या या मात्रा *She received a flood of letters after the accident.*

**floodlight** /ˈflʌdlaɪt ˈफ़्लड्लाइट्/ *noun* [C] a powerful light that is used for lighting places where sports are played, the outside of public buildings, etc. सार्वजनिक भवन के बाहर, समारोह-स्थल आदि पर प्रयुक्त तीव्र प्रकाश देने वाली बत्ती; पूर-प्रकाश

**floodlit** /ˈflʌdlɪt ˈफ़्लड्लिट्/ *adj.* lit by powerful lights (**floodlights**) तीव्र प्रकाश देने वाली बत्तियों से सुप्रकाशित; पूर-प्रकाशित *a floodlit hockey match*

**flood plain** *noun* [C] an area of flat land beside a river that regularly becomes flooded when there is too much water in the river नदी के साथ का समतल भूक्षेत्र जहाँ नदी में जलस्तर बढ़ने पर नियमित रूप से पानी भर जाता है; कछार, बाढ़कृत मैदान

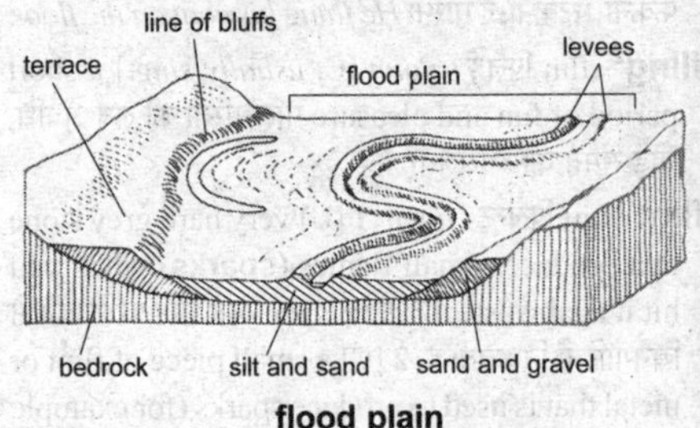


**flood plain**

**floor¹** /flɔː(r) फ़्लॉ(र्)/ *noun* **1** [C, *usually sing.*] the flat surface that you walk on indoors फ़र्श *Don't come in—there's broken glass **on the floor**!* ○ *a wooden/concrete/marble floor* ➪ **ground** पर नोट देखिए। **2** [C] all the rooms that are on the same level of a building भवन के एक ही तल के सब कमरे; मंज़िल *My office is **on the second floor**.*

> **NOTE** ब्रिटिश अंग्रेज़ी में **ground floor** का अर्थ है सड़क के स्तर की मंजिल (भूतल) और **first floor** उससे ऊपर की मंजिल है। अमेरिकी अंग्रेज़ी में सड़क के स्तर की मंजिल (भूतल) को **first floor** कहते हैं।

**3** [C, *usually sing.*] the ground or surface at the bottom of the sea, a forest, etc. समुद्र, जंगल आदि की गहरी सतह या ज़मीन; तल *the ocean/valley/cave/forest floor* **4 the floor** [*sing.*] the part of the parliament, public meeting place etc. where people sit संसद, सार्वजनिक गोष्ठी आदि का सभाकक्ष

**floor**[2] /flɔ:(r) फ़्लॉ(र्)/ *verb* [T] (*informal*) to surprise or confuse sb completely with a question or a problem प्रश्न या समस्या द्वारा किसी को पूरी तरह चौंका या घबरा देना *Some of the questions I was asked in the interview completely floored me.*

**floorboard** /ˈflɔ:bɔ:d ˈफ़्लॉबॉड्/ *noun* [C] one of the long wooden boards used to make a floor फ़र्श बनाने के लिए प्रयुक्त लकड़ी का तख़्ता ➪ **joist** पर चित्र देखिए।

**flop**[1] /flɒp फ़्लॉप्/ *verb* [I] (**flopping; flopped**) **1 flop into, onto sth; flop (down/back)** to sit or lie down in a sudden and careless way because you are very tired बहुत थक जाने के कारण धड़ाम-से बैठ या लेट जाना *I was so tired that all I could do was flop onto the sofa and watch TV.* **2 flop around, back, down, etc.** to move, hang or fall in a careless way without control लापरवाही से बगैर सँभले सरकना, लटकना या गिरना *I can't bear my hair flopping in my eyes.* **3** (used about a book, film, record, etc.) to be a complete failure with the public (पुस्तक, फ़िल्म आदि) जनता के बीच पूर्णतया विफल हो जाना

**flop**[2] /flɒp फ़्लॉप्/ *noun* [C] (used about a film, play, party, etc.) something that is not a success; a failure असफल पुस्तक, फ़िल्म आदि; विफलता *a box-office flop*

**floppy** /ˈflɒpi ˈफ़्लॉपि/ *adj.* soft and hanging downwards; not rigid कोमल और नीचे लटकता हुआ; ढीला-ढाला *a floppy hat*

**floppy disk** (*also* **floppy**, *pl.* **floppies**) (*also* **diskette**) *noun* [C] a square piece of plastic that can store information from a computer कंप्यूटर से सूचना संचित करने वाली प्लास्टिक की चौकोर तश्तरी; फ़्लॉपी डिस्क *Don't forget to back up your files onto a floppy disk.*

**flora** /ˈflɔ:rə ˈफ़्लॉरा/ *noun* [*pl.*] all the plants growing in a particular area क्षेत्र-विशेष में उगने वाले सब पेड़-पौधे *He's studying the **flora and fauna** (= the plants and animals) of the Andaman and Nicobar Islands.* ➪ **fauna** देखिए।

**floral** /ˈflɔ:rəl ˈफ़्लॉरल्/ *adj.* decorated with a pattern of flowers, or made with flowers पुष्प-रचना से सज्जित या पुष्प-निर्मित

**florist** /ˈflɒrɪst ˈफ़्लॉरिस्ट्/ *noun* **1** [C] a person who has or works in a shop where flowers are sold फूल बेचने वाला व्यक्ति; पुष्प विक्रेता **2 the florist's** [*sing.*] a shop that sells flowers फूलों की दुकान

**flotation** /fləʊˈteɪʃn फ़्लोˈटेश्न्/ *noun* **1** (*also* **float**) [C, U] (*technical*) the process of selling shares in a company to the public for the first time in order to obtain money किसी कंपनी द्वारा पूँजी-संग्रह के लिए जनता को पहली बार शेयर बेचने की प्रक्रिया *plans for (a) flotation on the stock exchange* **2** [U] the act of floating on or in water पानी पर या में तिरने की क्रिया

**flounder** /ˈflaʊndə(r) ˈफ़्लाउन्ड(र्)/ *verb* [I] **1** to find it difficult to speak or act (usually in a difficult or embarrassing situation) कुछ कहने या करने में कठिनाई अनुभव करना (प्रायः कठिन या घबराहट पैदा करने वाली स्थिति में); लड़खड़ाना *The questions they asked her at the interview had her floundering helplessly.* **2** to have a lot of problems and be in danger of failing completely समस्याग्रस्त होना या विफलता के कगार पर पहुँचना *By the end of the year the business was floundering.* **3** to move with difficulty, for example when trying to get out of some water, wet earth, etc. कठिनाई से चल पाना (जैसे पानी, दलदल आदि में से निकलने की कोशिश करते हुए)

**flour** /ˈflaʊə(r) ˈफ़्लाउअ(र्)/ *noun* [U] a very thin powder made from wheat or other grain and used for making bread, cakes, biscuits, etc. आटा

**flourish**[1] /ˈflʌrɪʃ ˈफ़्लरिश्/ *verb* **1** [I] to be strong and healthy; to develop in a successful way सशक्त होते जाना; फलना-फूलना; सफलता की ओर अग्रसर होना; उन्नति करना *a flourishing business* **2** [T] to wave sth in the air so that people will notice it (किसी वस्तु को हवा में लहराना ताकि लोग उसे देख पाएँ) *He proudly flourished two tickets for the concert.*

**flourish**[2] /ˈflʌrɪʃ ˈफ़्लरिश्/ *noun* [C] an exaggerated movement प्रभावशाली ढंग से ध्यान आकर्षित करने के लिए की गई क्रिया *He opened the door for her with a flourish.*

**flout** /flaʊt फ़्लाउट्/ *verb* [T] to refuse to obey or accept sth (क़ानून, नियम आदि) अवहेलना करना, न मानना, उल्लंघन करना *to flout the rules of the organization* ○ *to flout sb's advice*

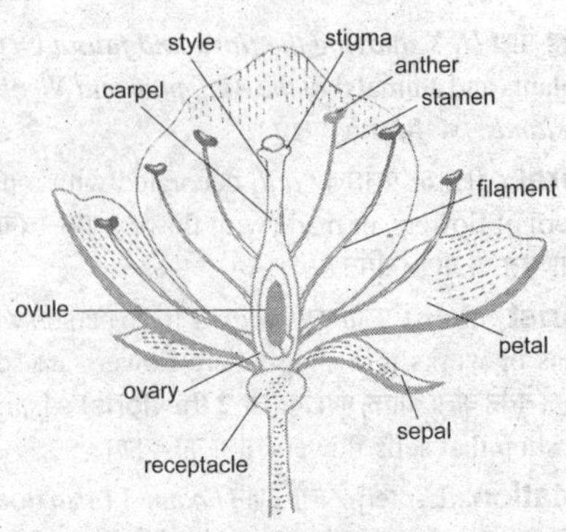


cross-section of a flower

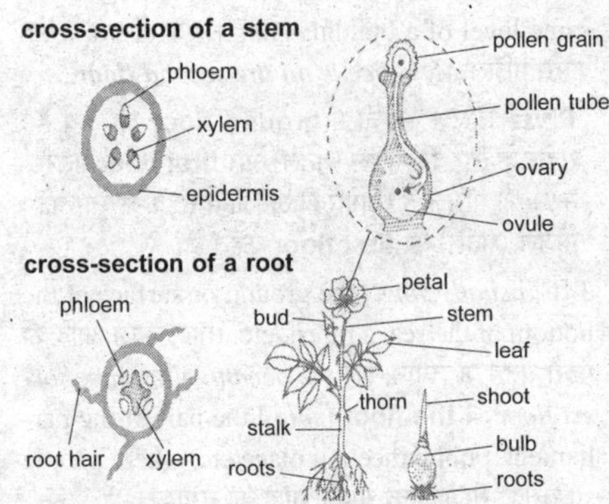


**flow[1]** /fləʊ फ़्लो / *noun* [*sing.*] **a flow (of sth/sb)** **1** a steady, continuous movement of sth/sb लगातार बहने की क्रिया; बहाव, प्रवाह *Press hard on the wound to stop the flow of blood.* **2** a supply of sth आपूर्ति; प्राप्त कराने की क्रिया *the flow of information between the school and the parents* **3** the way in which words, ideas, etc. are joined together smoothly शब्दों, विचारों आदि का सामंजस्यपूर्ण समायोजन, विचारों की सतत अभिव्यक्ति *Once Charlie's* ***in full flow****, it's hard to stop him talking.*

IDM **the ebb and flow (of sth)** ➪ **ebb[2]** देखिए।

**flow[2]** /fləʊ फ़्लो / *verb* [I] **1** to move in a smooth and continuous way (like water) बिना बाधा के निरंतर गति करना, बहना, प्रवाहित होना *This river flows south into the Arabian sea.* ○ *a fast-flowing stream* ○ *Traffic began to flow normally again after the accident.* **2** (used about words, ideas, actions, etc.) to be joined together smoothly (शब्दों, विचारों, क्रियाओं आदि का) सुगठित रूप में अभिव्यक्त होना *As soon as we sat down at the table, the conversation began to flow.* **3** (used about hair and clothes) to hang down in a loose way (बालों और कपड़ों का) ढीले-ढाले तौर पर लटकना *a long flowing dress.*

**flow chart** (*also* **flow diagram**) *noun* [C] a diagram that shows the connections between different stages of a process or parts of a system क्रमदर्शी आरेख, प्रवाह चार्ट ➪ **chart[1]** पर चित्र देखिए।

**flower[1]** /ˈflaʊə(r) ˈफ़्लाउअ(र्) / *noun* [C] **1** the coloured part of a plant or tree from which seeds or fruit grow पुष्प, फूल, सुमन **2** a plant that is grown for its flowers पुष्प-पादप, फूलों वाला पौधा *to grow flowers*

**flower[2]** /ˈflaʊə(r) ˈफ़्लाउअ(र्) / *verb* [I] to produce flowers फूलों से भर जाना, में फूल लगना *This plant flowers in late summer.*

**flower bed** *noun* [C] a piece of ground in a garden or park where flowers are grown फूलों की क्यारी

**flowerpot** /ˈflaʊəpɒt ˈफ़्लाउअपॉट् / *noun* [C] a pot in which a plant can be grown गमला

**flowery** /ˈflaʊəri ˈफ़्लाउअरि / *adj.* **1** covered or decorated with flowers फूलों या फूलों के चित्रों से ढका हुआ या सजाया हुआ *a flowery dress/hat/pattern* **2** (used about a style of speaking or writing) using long, difficult words when they are not necessary (मौखिक या लिखित शैली) जिसमें अनावश्यक रूप से लंबे और कठिन शब्दों का प्रयोग हो; आडंबरपूर्ण, लच्छेदार

**flown** ➪ **fly[1]** का past participle रूप

**fl oz** *abbr.* = **fluid ounce(s)**

**flu** /flu: फ़्लू / (*formal* **influenza**) *noun* [U] an illness that is like a bad cold but more serious. You usually feel very hot and your arms and legs hurt ज़ुकाम के साथ बुख़ार और बदन दर्द; (रोग) फ़्लू

**fluctuate** /ˈflʌktʃueɪt ˈफ़्लकचुएट् / *verb* [I] **fluctuate (between A and B)** (used about prices and numbers, or people's feelings) to change frequently from one thing to another (क़ीमतों और संख्याओं या जनभावनाओं में) बार-बार उतार-चढ़ाव होना *The number of students fluctuates between 100 and 150.*
► **fluctuation** /ˌflʌktʃuˈeɪʃn ˌफ़्लकचुˈएश्न् / *noun* [C, U] उतार-चढ़ाव, घट-बढ़

**flue** /flu: फ़्लू / *noun* [C] a pipe or tube, especially in a chimney, that takes smoke, gas or hot air away from a fire or an oven धुआँ, गैस या गरम हवा बाहर निकालने के लिए नली जो विशेषतः चिमनी या धुआँकश में लगी होती है

**fluent** /ˈflu:ənt ˈफ़्लूअन्ट् / *adj.* **1 fluent (in sth)** able to speak or write a language easily and accurately किसी भाषा को सरलतापूर्वक और शुद्ध रीति से बोलने या लिखने में समर्थ; धाराप्रवाह अभिव्यक्ति में समर्थ *After a year in France she was fluent in French.* **2** (used about speaking, reading or writing) expressed in a smooth and accurate way (बोलने पढ़ने या लिखने की क्रिया) सरलतापूर्वक और शुद्ध रीति से

संपन्न; सप्रवाह *He speaks fluent German.* ▶ **fluency** /ˈfluːənsi ˈफ़्लूअन्सि/ *noun* [U] सरल और विशुद्धता, धाराप्रवाह का गुण *My knowledge of Japanese grammar is good but I need to work on my fluency.* ▶ **fluently** *adv.* प्रवाह के साथ, सरलता और विशुद्धता के साथ

**fluff** /flʌf फ़्लफ़्/ *noun* [U] **1** very small pieces of wool, cotton, etc. that form into balls and collect on clothes and other surfaces (ऊनी और सूती कपड़ों पर) बन जाने वाले रोएँ **2** the soft new fur on young animals or birds पशुओं या पक्षियों के शिशुओं के शरीर पर कोमल नई रोएँदार खाल

**fluffy** /ˈflʌfi ˈफ़्लफ़ि/ *adj.* **1** covered in soft fur रोएँदार; कोमल फ़र वाला *a fluffy kitten* **2** that looks or feels very soft and light देखने या छूने में बहुत कोमल और हलका *fluffy clouds/towels*

**fluid[1]** /ˈfluːɪd ˈफ़्लूइड्/ *noun* [C, U] a substance that can flow; a liquid बह सकने वाला पदार्थ; द्रव; तरल पदार्थ *The doctor told her to drink plenty of fluids.* ○ *cleaning fluid*

**fluid[2]** /ˈfluːɪd ˈफ़्लूइड्/ *adj.* **1** able to flow smoothly like a liquid द्रव के समान सरलता से बहने वाला (*figurative*) *I like her fluid style of dancing.* **2** (used about plans, etc.) able to change or likely to be changed (योजनाएँ आदि) जो बदल सकती हैं या (संभावित रूप से) जिन्हें बदला जा सकता है; सुपरिवर्तनीय

**fluid ounce** *noun* [C] (*abbr.* **fl oz**) a measure of liquid; in Britain, 0.0284 of a litre; in the US, 0.0295 of a litre द्रव पदार्थ की माप; ब्रिटेन में एक लिटर का 0.0284 तथा अमेरिका में 0.0295 भाग

**fluke** /fluːk फ़्लूक्/ *noun* [C, *usually sing.*] (*informal*) a surprising and lucky result that happens by accident, not because you have been clever or skilful आश्चर्यजनक और सुखद संयोग से प्राप्त परिणाम (न कि कौशलपूर्वक अर्जित)

**flung** ➪ **fling[1]** का past tense, और past participle रूप

**fluorescent** /ˌflɔːˈresnt; ˌflʊəˈre- ˌफ़्लॉˈरेसन्ट्; ˌफ़्लुअˈरे-/ *adj.* **1** producing a bright white light by radiation चमकदार सफ़ेद रोशनी देने वाला; प्रतिदीप्त *fluorescent lighting* **2** very bright and easy to see even in the dark; seeming to shine बहुत चमकदार और अंधकार में भी दिखाई पड़ने वाला; चमकीला-सा *fluorescent pink paint*

**fluoride** /ˈflɔːraɪd ˈफ़्लॉराइड्/ *noun* [U] a chemical substance that can be added to water or toothpaste to help prevent bad teeth एक रासायनिक पदार्थ जिसे दाँतों की रक्षा के लिए पानी या टूथपेस्ट में मिलाया जा सकता है; फ़्लोराइड

**fluorine** /ˈflɔːriːn ˈफ़्लॉरीन्/ *noun* [U] (*symbol* **F**) a poisonous pale yellow gas एक विषैली हलकी पीली गैस; फ़्लोरीन

**flurry** /ˈflʌri ˈफ़्लरि/ *noun* [C] (*pl.* **flurries**) **1** a short time in which there is suddenly a lot of activity एकाएक उत्पन्न हलचल की सीमित कालावधि *a flurry of excitement/activity* **2** a sudden short fall of snow or rain बर्फ़ या वर्षा का आकस्मिक झोंका

**flush[1]** /flʌʃ ˈफ़्लश्/ *verb* **1** [I] (used about a person or his/her face) to go red (व्यक्ति का चेहरा) लाल हो जाना *Reena flushed and could not hide her embarrassment.* **NOTE** इस अर्थ के लिए **blush** अधिक प्रचलित शब्द है। **2** [T] to clean a toilet by pressing or pulling a handle that sends water into the toilet पानी की टंकी चलाकर शौचालय साफ़ करना **3** [I] (used about a toilet) to be cleaned with a short flow of water (शौचस्थल का) पानी के बहाव से साफ़ होना *The toilet won't flush.* **4** [T] **flush sth away, down, etc.** to get rid of sth in a flow of water पानी के बहाव से नष्ट या साफ़ करना *You can't flush tea leaves down the sink—they'll block it.*

**flush[2]** /flʌʃ ˈफ़्लश्/ *noun* [C, *usually sing.*] **1** a hot feeling or red colour that you have in your face when you are embarrassed, excited, angry, etc. लज्जा, उत्तेजना, क्रोध आदि के कारण चेहरे के गरम या लाल हो जाने की क्रिया; चेहरे पर झलकता भावावेग या लालिमा *The harsh words brought a flush to her cheeks.* ○ *a flush of anger* **2** the act of cleaning a toilet with a quick flow of water; the system for doing this पानी को तेज़ चलाकर शौचस्थल साफ़ करने की क्रिया; पानी के प्रवाह द्वारा शौचस्थल साफ़ करने की प्रणाली

**flushed** /flʌʃt फ़्लश्ट्/ *adj.* with a hot red face गरम लाल चेहरे वाला *You look very flushed. Are you sure you're all right?*

**fluster** /ˈflʌstə(r) ˈफ़्लस्टर्/ *verb* [T] (*usually passive*) to make sb feel nervous and confused (because there is too much to do or not enough time) किसी को बहुत काम देकर या हड़बड़ी मचाकर घबराहट, परेशानी या उलझन में डालना *Don't get flustered—there's plenty of time.* ▶ **fluster** *noun* [*sing.*] घबराहट, परेशानी व उलझन *I always get* ***in a fluster*** *before exams.*

**flute** /fluːt फ़्लूट्/ *noun* [C] a musical instrument like a pipe that you hold sideways and play by blowing over a hole at one side बाँसुरी, मुरली ➪ पृष्ठ 789 पर चित्र देखिए।

**flutist** /ˈfluːtɪst ˈफ़्लूटिस्ट्/ (*AmE*) = **flautist**

**flutter[1]** /ˈflʌtə(r) ˈफ़्लटर्/ *verb* **1** [I, T] to move or make sth move quickly and lightly, especially through the air तेज़ गति से और कोमलता के साथ हिलना या किसी वस्तु को हिलाना, विशेषतः हवा में; फड़फड़ाना, फरफराना, लहराना *The flags were fluttering in the wind.* ○ *The bird fluttered its wings and tried to fly.* **2** [I] your heart or stomach flutters when you feel nervous and excited घबराहट, परेशानी और उत्तेजना के कारण हृदय या पेट में हलचल होना

**flutter²** /ˈflʌtə(r) ˈफ़्लटर्(र्)/ *noun* [C, *usually sing.*] **1** the state of being confused, nervous or excited घबराहट, उलझन या उत्तेजना की अवस्था **2** a quick, light movement त्वरित, कोमल गति; फड़फड़ाहट *the flutter of wings/eyelids* **3** (*slang*) a bet on a race, etc. घुड़दौड़ आदि में बाज़ी *I sometimes **have a flutter** on the horses.*

**fluvial** /ˈfluːviəl ˈफ़्लूविअल् / *adj.* (*technical*) connected with rivers नदियों से संबंधित

**flux** /flʌks फ़्लक्स् / *noun* [C, *usually sing.*, U] (*technical*) a continuous movement निरंतर होने वाली गति *a flux of neutrons* ○ *magnetic flux*

**fly¹** /flaɪ फ़्लाइ / *verb* (*pres. part.* **flying;** *3rd person sing. pres.* **flies;** *pt* **flew** /fluː फ़्लू /; *pp* **flown** /fləʊn फ़्लोन् /) **1** [I] (used about a bird, insect, aircraft, etc.) to move through the air (पक्षी, कीट, विमान आदि का) हवा में गति करना, उड़ना *This bird has a broken wing and can't fly.* ○ *I can hear a plane flying overhead.* **2** [I, T] to travel or carry sth in an aircraft, etc. विमान में यात्रा करना या कुछ ले जाना *My daughter is flying (out) to Singapore next week.* ○ *Supplies of food were flown (in) to the starving people.* **3** [I, T] (used about a pilot) to control an aircraft (पायलट का) विमान को उड़ाना *You have to have special training to fly a jumbo jet.* **4** [I] to move quickly or suddenly, especially through the air तीव्र गति से या एकाएक गति करना विशेषतः वायु में *A large stone **came flying** through the window.* ○ *I slipped and my shopping **went flying** everywhere.* ○ *Suddenly the door **flew open** and Ravi came running in.* ○ (*figurative*) *The weekend has just **flown by** and now it's Monday again.* **5** [I, T] to move about in the air; to make sth move about in the air हवा में इधर-उधर हिलना या किसी वस्तु को हिलाना; फहरना या फहराना, उड़ाना *The flags are flying.* ○ *to fly a flag/kite* ⇨ **flight** noun देखिए।

IDM **as the crow flies** ⇨ **crow¹** देखिए।

**fly off the handle** (*informal*) to become very angry in an unreasonable way अनुचित रूप से बहुत क्रुद्ध हो जाना

**let fly (at sb/sth)** **1** to shout angrily at sb गुस्से से किसी पर चिल्लाना **2** to hit sb in anger गुस्से में किसी पर चोट करना *She let fly at him with her fists.*

**fly²** /flaɪ फ़्लाइ / *noun* [C] **1** (*pl.* **flies**) a small insect with two wings मक्खी *Flies buzzed round the dead cow.* ⇨ **insect** पर चित्र देखिए। **2** (*also* **flies**) [*pl.*] an opening down the front of a pair of trousers that fastens with buttons or another device (**a zip**) and is covered with a narrow piece of material पतलून का सामने का खुला भाग जो बटन या जिप से बंद होता है

**flyer** (*also* **flier**) /ˈflaɪə(r) ˈफ़्लाइअ(र्)/ *noun* [C] **1** (*informal*) a person who flies a plane (usually a small one, not a passenger plane) सामान्यतः छोटा विमान उड़ाने वाला व्यक्ति; उड़ाका, वैमानिक, विमानचालक **2** a person who travels in a plane as a passenger विमान का यात्री *frequent flyers* **3** a thing, especially a bird or an insect, that flies in a particular way विशेष ढंग से उड़ने वाली कोई वस्तु, विशेषतः पक्षी या कीट *Ducks are strong flyers.* **4** a small sheet of paper that advertises a product or an event and is given to a large number of people किसी वस्तु या कार्यक्रम का विज्ञापन करने वाला छोटा काग़ज़ जिसे बड़ी संख्या में लोगों में बाँटा जाता है **5** (*informal*) a person, an animal or a vehicle that moves very quickly बहुत तेज़ चलने वाला व्यक्ति, पशु या वाहन

**flying** /ˈflaɪɪŋ ˈफ़्लाइइङ् / *adj.* able to fly उड़ने में सक्षम, उड़ने वाला *flying insects*

IDM **with flying colours** with great success; very well उल्लेखनीय सफलता के साथ; बहुत अच्छी तरह *Manoj passed the exam with flying colours.*

**get off to a flying start** to begin sth well; to make a good start किसी काम को अच्छे ढंग से शुरू करना; अच्छी शुरुआत करना

**flying saucer** *noun* [C] a round spacecraft that some people say they have seen and that they believe comes from another planet गोलाकार अंतरिक्ष यान जिसे कुछ लोग देखने का दावा करते हैं और मानते है कि वह यान किसी अन्य ग्रह से आया है; उड़नतश्तरी

**flying visit** *noun* [C] a very quick visit कुछ पलों की भेंट, तूफ़ानी सफ़र *I can't stop. This is just a flying visit.*

**flyover** /ˈflaɪəʊvə(r) ˈफ़्लाइओव़(र्)/ (*AmE* **overpass**) *noun* [C] a type of bridge that carries a road over another road एक सड़क के ऊपर से दूसरी सड़क को ले जाने वाला पुल; उड़ान पुल, उपरिसेतु, फ़्लाइओवर

**FM** /ˌefˈem ˌएफ़्ˈएम् / *abbr.* frequency modulation; one of the systems of sending out radio signals रेडियो संकेत भेजने की एक प्रणाली; आवृत्ति माडुलन

**foal** /fəʊl फ़ोल् / *noun* [C] a young horse बछेड़ा, घोड़े का शावक ⇨ **horse** पर नोट देखिए।

**foam[1]** /fəʊm फ़ोम् / *noun* [U] **1** (*also* **foam rubber**) a soft light rubber material that is used inside seats, cushions, etc. गद्दियों आदि में डाला जाने वाला कोमल हलका रबर; फ़ोम *a foam mattress* **2** a mass of small air bubbles that form on the surface of a liquid द्रव की सतह पर बनने वाले हवा के बुलबुलों का ढेर; झाग *white foam on the tops of the waves* **3** an artificial substance that is between a solid and a liquid and is made from very small bubbles द्रव और ठोस के बीच का और बहुत छोटे बुलबुलों से बना कृत्रिम पदार्थ *shaving foam*

**foam[2]** /fəʊm फ़ोम् / *verb* [I] to produce foam झाग पैदा करना *We watched the foaming river below.*

**fob** /fɒb फ़ॉब् / *verb* (**fo<u>bb</u>ing; fo<u>bb</u>ed**)

**PHR V** **fob sb off (with sth)** **1** to try to stop sb asking questions or complaining by telling him/her sth that is not true किसी को प्रश्न पूछने, आपत्ती प्रकट करने से यह कहकर रोकना कि वह बात असत्य है *Don't let them fob you off with any more excuses.* **2** to try to give sb sth that he/she does not want किसी को उसकी अनचाही वस्तु देने की कोशिश करना *Don't try to fob me off with that old car—I want a new one.*

**focal** /ˈfəʊkl ˈफ़ोकल् / *adj.* (*only before a noun*) central; very important; connected with or providing a focus केंद्रीय; बहुत महत्त्वपूर्ण; किरणकेंद्र देने से संबंधित, संनाभि

**focal length** *noun* [C] (*technical*) the distance between the centre of a mirror or a **lens** and its **focus** एक दर्पण या लेंस के केंद्रबिंदु से उसके फ़ोकस की दूरी; नाभीय दूरी ➪ **lens** पर चित्र देखिए।

**focal point** *noun* **1** [*sing.*] the centre of interest or activity अभिरुचि या क्रिया-कलाप का केंद्रबिंदु **2** [C] (*technical*) = **focus[2] 2** ➪ **lens** पर चित्र देखिए।

**focus[1]** /ˈfəʊkəs ˈफ़ोकस् / *verb* [I, T] (**focu<u>s</u>ing; focu<u>s</u>ed** or **focu<u>ss</u>ing; focu<u>ss</u>ed**) **focus (sth) (on sth)** **1** to give all your attention to sth किसी बात पर सारा ध्यान लगाना *to focus on a problem* **2** (used about your eyes or a camera) to change or be changed so that things can be seen clearly आँखों या कैमरे का वस्तुओं से ऐसा मेल होना या बैठना कि वस्तुएँ साफ दिखें; आँखों या कैमरे का फ़ोकस बनना या बनाना *Gradually his eyes focused.* ○ *I focussed (the camera) on the person in the middle of the group.*

**focus[2]** /ˈfəʊkəs ˈफ़ोकस् / *noun* [C] (*pl.* **focuses** or **foci** /ˈfəʊsaɪ ˈफ़ोसाइ /) **1** [*usually sing.*] the centre of interest or attention; special attention that is given to sb/sth रुचि या ध्यान का केंद्र; व्यक्ति या वस्तु पर दिया गया विशेष ध्यान *The school used to be the focus of village life.* **2** (*also* **focal point**) (*technical*) a point at which rays or waves of light, sound, etc. meet after **reflection** or **refraction;** the point from which rays or waves of light, sound, etc. seem to come वह बिंदु जहाँ किरणें या प्रकाश, ध्वनि आदि की तरंगें परावर्तन या अनुवर्तन के बाद मिलती हैं; वह बिंदु जहाँ से किरणें या प्रकाश, ध्वनि आदि की तरंगें आती हुई प्रतीत होती हैं

**IDM** **in focus/out of focus** (used about a photograph or sth in a photograph) clear/not clear (फ़ोटो या फ़ोटो में अंकित वस्तु या व्यक्ति) स्पष्ट या अस्पष्ट *This picture is so badly out of focus that I can't recognize anyone.*

**fodder** /ˈfɒdə(r) ˈफ़ॉड(र्) / *noun* [U] food that is given to farm animals पशुओं का भोजन, चारा

**foe** /fəʊ फ़ो / *noun* [C] (*written*) an enemy शत्रु, दुश्मन

**foetal** (*AmE* **fetal**) /ˈfiːtl ˈफ़ीट्ल् / *adj.* (*technical*) connected with or typical of a baby that is still developing in its mother's body माँ के शरीर में बढ़ते बच्चे से संबंधित; भ्रूण-विषयक

**foetus** (*AmE* **fetus**) /ˈfiːtəs ˈफ़ीटस् / *noun* [C] (*pl.* **foetuses; fetuses**) a young human or animal that is still developing in its mother's body स्त्री या मादा पशु के शरीर में बढ़ता बच्चा; भ्रूण **NOTE** गर्भ में भूर्ण के विकास के आरंभिक चरण को **embryo** कहते हैं।

**fog** /fɒg फ़ॉग् / *noun* [U, C] thick white cloud that forms close to the land or sea. Fog makes it difficult for us to see ज़मीन या समुद्र पर बनने वाला घना सफ़ेद बादल; धुँध, कोहरा कोहरे में कुछ देखना कठिन होता है *Patches of dense fog are making driving dangerous.* ○ *Bad fogs are common in late December.*

**NOTE** **Mist** की अपेक्षा **fog** अधिक घना होता है। **Haze** गरमी का परिणाम होता है और प्रदूषण के कारण होता है। ➪ **weather** पर नोट देखिए।

**foggy** /ˈfɒgi ˈफ़ॉगि / *adj.* (**foggier; foggiest**) used to describe the weather when there is fog (मौसम) कोहरे वाला

**IDM** **not have the faintest/foggiest (idea)** ➪ **faint[1]** देखिए।

**foil[1]** /fɔɪl फ़ॉइल् / *noun* **1** [U] (*also* **tinfoil**) metal that has been made into very thin sheets, used for putting around food धातु को पीटकर बनाई हुई काग़ज़ जैसी पतली पन्नी जिसे भोज्य पदार्थ को लपेटने के लिए प्रयुक्त किया जाता है; वर्क *aluminium foil* **2** [C] a long, thin, pointed weapon used in a type of fighting sport (**fencing**) लड़ाई के खेल में प्रयुक्त (भोथरी या खुट्टल) तलवार

**foil**[2] /fɔɪl फ़ॉइल् / *verb* [T] to prevent sb from succeeding, especially with a plan; to prevent a plan from succeeding किसी को सफल न होने देना, विशेषतः योजना बनाकर; योजना को विफल कर देना *The prisoners were foiled in their attempt to escape.*

**foist** /fɔɪst फ़ॉइस्ट् / *verb*

**PHRV** **foist sth on/upon sb** to force sb to accept sth that he/she does not want किसी को उसकी अनचाही बात मानने के लिए विवश कर देना; किसी पर उसकी इच्छा के विरुद्ध कुछ लाद देना

**fold**[1] /fəʊld फ़ोल्ड् / *verb* **1** [T] **fold sth (up)** to bend one part of sth over another part in order to make it smaller, tidier, etc. किसी वस्तु के एक भाग को मोड़कर दूसरे पर जमाना (उसे छोटा करने, सँभालने आदि के लिए); तह लगाना, तहाना, मोड़ना *He folded the letter into three before putting it into the envelope.* ○ *Fold up your clothes neatly, please.* ✪ विलोम **unfold** **2** [I] **fold (up)** to be able to be made smaller in order to be carried or stored more easily किसी वस्तु का मुड़ सकना ताकि उसे आसानी से उठाया या रखा जा सके *This table folds up flat.* ○ *a folding bed* **3** [T] **fold A in B; fold B round/over A** to put sth around sth else किसी वस्तु को दूसरी में लपेटना *I folded the photos in a sheet of paper and put them away.* **4** [I] (used about a business, a play in the theatre, etc.) to close because it is a failure (व्यापार, नाटक आदि का) विफल हो जाने के कारण बंद या समाप्त हो जाना; सिमट जाना

**IDM** **cross/fold your arms** ➪ **arm**[1] देखिए।

**fold**[2] /fəʊld फ़ोल्ड् / *noun* [C] **1** the mark or line where sth has been folded तहाने से बनी रेखा या निशान **2** a curved shape that is made when there is more material, etc. than is necessary to cover sth चुन्नट, शिकन *the folds of a dress/curtain* **3** a small area inside a fence where sheep are kept together in a field खेत में बना भेड़ों का बाड़ा

**folder** /ˈfəʊldə(r) ˈफ़ोल्ड(र्) / *noun* [C] **1** a cardboard or plastic cover that is used for holding papers, etc. काग़ज़ात आदि सँभालने के लिए प्रयुक्त गत्ते या प्लास्टिक का आवरण; फ़ोल्डर ➪ **stationery** पर चित्र देखिए। **2** a collection of information or files on one subject that is stored in a computer or on a disk किसी विषय पर कंप्यूटर या डिस्क में सूचना-राशि या फ़ाइलों का संग्रह

**foliage** /ˈfəʊliɪdʒ ˈफ़ोलिइज् / *noun* [U] (*formal*) all the leaves of a tree or plant किसी पेड़ या पौधे के सब पत्ते-पत्तियाँ

**folic acid** /ˌfɒlɪk ˈæsɪd ˌफ़ॉलिक् ˈएसिड् / *noun* [U] a natural substance that is found in green vegetables, and certain types of meat, for example **liver** and **kidneys**. We must eat this substance so that our bodies can produce red blood cells हरी सब्ज़ियों और मांस (विशेषतः जिगर और गुरदे) में पाया जाने वाला एक प्राकृतिक पदार्थ; फ़ोलिक अम्ल, यह पदार्थ हमारे शरीर में रक्त कोशिकाएँ उत्पन्न करता है

**folio** /ˈfəʊliəʊ ˈफ़ोलिओ / *noun* [C] (*pl.* **folios**) **1** a book made with large sheets of paper, especially as used in early printing बड़े आकार के पन्नों या काग़ज़ों से बनी पुस्तक (विशेषतः पहले की छपाई में) **2** (*technical*) a single sheet of paper from a book numbered on one side किसी पुस्तक का अकेला अंकित पन्ना; पर्ण, एकभंज, फोलिओ **3** printing a page number on the pages of a book पृष्ठों पर पृष्ठ संख्या अंकित होना; पन्ना इंदराज

**folk**[1] /fəʊk फ़ोक् / *noun* **1** (*AmE* **folks**) [*pl.*] (*informal*) people in general लोग, जनसाधारण, लोगबाग *Some folk are never satisfied.* **2** [*pl.*] a particular type of people विशेष प्रकार के लोग *Old folk often don't like change.* ○ *country folk* **3** **folks** [*pl.*] (*informal*) used as a friendly way of addressing more than one person एक से अधिक व्यक्तियों को मैत्री भाव से संबोधित करने के लिए प्रयुक्त *What shall we do today, folks?* **4** **folks** [*pl.*] (*informal*) your parents or close relatives माता-पिता या निकट संबंधी *How are your folks?* **5** [U] (*also* **folk music**) music in the traditional style of a country or community किसी देश या जनसमुदाय का पारंपरिक संगीत; लोक संगीत *Do you like Irish folk?*

**folk**[2] /fəʊk फ़ोक् / *adj.* traditional in a community; of a traditional style किसी जनसमुदाय की परंपरा में मान्य; पारंपरिक शैली का *Bihu is a folk dance of Assam.* ○ *folk music* ○ *a folk song*

**folklore** /ˈfəʊklɔː(r) ˈफ़ोक्लॉ(र्) / *noun* [U] traditional stories and beliefs परंपरागत कथाएँ और विश्वास; लोक कथाएँ

**follicle** /ˈfɒlɪkl ˈफ़ॉलिक्ल् / *noun* [C] one of the very small holes in the skin which hairs grow from त्वचा में अति सूक्ष्म छिद्र जहाँ से बाल उगते हैं; रोमकूप

**follow** /ˈfɒləʊ ˈफ़ॉलो / *verb* **1** [I, T] to come, go or happen after sb/sth किसी व्यक्ति या वस्तु के पीछे आना, जाना या होना *You go first and I'll follow (on) later.* ○ *The dog followed her (around) wherever she went.* ○ *I'll have soup followed by spaghetti.* **2** [T] to go along a road, etc.; to go in the same direction as sth (सड़क के साथ-साथ) जाना; किसी अन्य दिशा में चलते जाना *Follow this road for a mile and then turn right at the post office.* ○ *The road follows the river for a few kilometres.* **3** [T] to do sth or to happen according to instructions, an example, what is usual, etc. निर्देशों के अनुसार काम

करना या होना; पालन या अनुसरण करना *When lighting fireworks, it is important to **follow the instructions** carefully.* ○ *The day's events followed the usual pattern.* **4** [I, T] to understand the meaning of sth किसी (शब्द, कहानी आदि) के अर्थ को समझना *The children couldn't follow the plot of that film.* **5** [T] to keep watching or listening to sth as it happens or develops गतिविधियों या विकास के चरणों को घटित होते देखते-सुनते रहना; के बारे में निरंतर ज्ञान रखना *The film follows the career of a young dancer.* ○ *Have you been following the tennis championships?* **6** [I] **follow (on) (from sth)** to be the logical result of sth; to be the next logical step after sth किसी बात का तर्कसंगत परिणाम होना; किसी स्थिति का अगला तर्कसंगत क़दम होना *It doesn't follow that old people can't lead active lives.* ○ *Intermediate Book One follows on from Elementary Book Two.*

**IDM a hard act to follow** ➪ **hard**[1] देखिए।

**as follows** used for introducing a list सूची को प्रस्तुत करने के लिए प्रयुक्त; निम्नलिखित *The names of the successful candidates are as follows...*

**follow in sb's footsteps** to do the same job as sb else who did it before you वही करना जो पहले किसी ने किया है; किसी के नक़्शेक़दम पर चलना *He followed in his father's footsteps and joined the army.*

**follow sb's example/lead** to do what sb else has done or decided to do किसी के किए काम को आदर्श मानकर उसका अनुसरण करना

**follow suit** to do the same thing that sb else has just done वही करना जो किसी ने अभी-अभी किया है

**follow your nose** to go straight forward सीधे आगे चलना

**PHRV follow sth through** to continue doing sth until it is finished किसी काम को उसके पूरा होने तक करते रहना

**follow sth up** **1** to take further action about sth किसी बात के विषय में आगे की कार्रवाई करना *You should follow up your letter with a phone call.* **2** to find out more about sth किसी बात के विषय में और अधिक जानकारी प्राप्त करना *We need to follow up the story about the school.*

**follower** /ˈfɒləʊə(r) ˈफ़ॉलोअ(र्)/ *noun* [C] a person who follows or supports a person, belief, etc. किसी व्यक्ति, विश्वास आदि का अनुसरण या समर्थन करने वाला व्यक्ति; किसी का अनुयायी या समर्थक

**following**[1] /ˈfɒləʊɪŋ ˈफ़ॉलोइङ्/ *adj.* **1** next (in time) अगला (समय की दृष्टि से) *He became ill on Sunday and was hospitalized the following day.* **2** that are going to be mentioned next जिन्हें आगे बताया गया है; निम्नलिखित *Please could you bring the following items to the meeting...*

**following**[2] /ˈfɒləʊɪŋ ˈफ़ॉलोइङ्/ *noun* **1** [*sing.*] a group of people who support or admire sth किसी के समर्थक या प्रशंसक व्यक्ति; अनुयायीगण *The Brazilian soccer team has a large following all over the world.* **2 the following** [*pl.*] the people or things that are going to be mentioned next आगे वर्णित व्यक्ति या वस्तुएँ *The following are the winners of the competition...*

**following**[3] /ˈfɒləʊɪŋ ˈफ़ॉलोइङ्/ *prep.* after; as a result of के बाद; के परिणामस्वरूप *Following the riots many students have been arrested.*

**follow-up** *noun* [C] something that is done as a second stage to continue or develop sth किसी काम को जारी रखने के तौर पर किया गया काम; अनुवर्ती कार्रवाई *As a follow-up to the television series, the BBC is publishing a book.*

**folly** /ˈfɒli ˈफ़ॉलि/ *noun* [C, U] (*pl.* **follies**) (*formal*) an act that is not sensible and may have a bad result विवेकहीन कार्य या क्रिया जिसका दुष्परिणाम हो सकता है; मूर्खता का काम; नासमझी *It would be folly to ignore their warnings.*

**foment** /fəʊˈment फ़ोˈमेन्ट्/ *verb* [T] (*formal*) to cause trouble or violence and make people fight each other or the government हिंसा या उपद्रव करना या उसे बढ़ावा देना *They were accused of fomenting political unrest.* ✪ पर्याय **incite**

**fond** /fɒnd फ़ॉन्ड्/ *adj.* **1** (*not before a noun*) **fond of sb/sth; fond of doing sth** liking a person or thing, or liking doing sth किसी व्यक्ति, वस्तु या काम को पसंद करना; का शौक़ीन होना *Elephants are very fond of bananas.* ○ *I'm not very fond of getting up early.* ○ *Teachers often **grow fond** of their students.* **2** (*only before a noun*) kind and loving करुण और स्नेहमय *I have **fond memories** of my grandmother.*

**fondle** /ˈfɒndl ˈफ़ॉन्ड्ल्/ *verb* [T] to touch sb/sth gently in a loving or sexual way प्यार से या कामुक भाव से किसी को छूना या सहलाना

**fondly** /ˈfɒndli ˈफ़ॉन्ड्लि/ *adv.* in a loving way स्नेहपूर्वक, प्यार के साथ *Mrs Datta will be fondly remembered by all her former students.*

**fondness** /ˈfɒndnəs ˈफ़ॉन्ड्नस्/ *noun* [U, *sing.*] **(a) fondness (for sb/sth)** a liking for sb/sth किसी व्यक्ति या वस्तु के प्रति स्नेह, अनुराग *I've always had a fondness for cats.* ○ *My grandmother talks about her schooldays **with fondness**.*

**font** /fɒnt फ़ॉन्ट्/ *noun* [C] (*computing*) the particular shape and style of a set of letters that are used in printing, on a computer screen, etc. छपाई के अक्षरों की विशेष आकृति और बनावट; फ़ांट

**food** /fu:d फ़ूड् / *noun* **1** [U] something that people or animals eat (मनुष्यों और पशुओं के खाने का) भोजन; आहार *Food and drink will be provided after the meeting.* ○ *There is a shortage of food in some areas.* **2** [C, U] a particular type of food that you eat विशेष प्रकार का खाद्य पदार्थ *My favourite food is pasta.* ○ *Have you ever had Japanese food?* ○ *baby food* ○ *dog food* ○ *health foods*

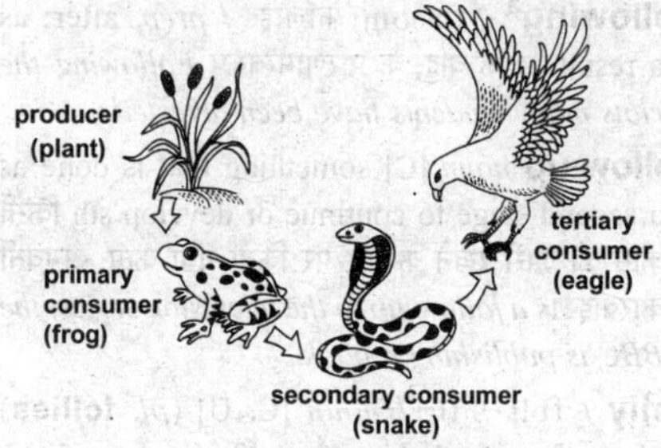

**food chain**

**food chain** *noun* [C] a series of organisms in which each creature eats the one below it in the series and becomes a source of food for the organisms above it सजीव प्राणियों की ऐसी शृंखला जिसमें अगला प्राणी पिछले को अपना भोजन बनाता है; आहार शृंखला

**food poisoning** *noun* [U] an illness that is caused by eating food that is bad खाद्य विषाक्तता

**food processor** *noun* [C] an electric machine that can mix food and also cut food into small pieces भोज्य पदार्थों को काटने और मिश्रित करने वाली बिजली चालित मशीन; फ़ूड प्रोसेसर ➪ **kitchen** पर चित्र देखिए।

**foodstuff** /ˈfu:dstʌf ˈफ़ूड्स्टफ़् / *noun* [C, *usually pl.*] a substance that is used as food खाद्य पदार्थ *There has been a sharp rise in the cost of basic foodstuffs.*

**food web** *noun* [C] a system of **food chains** that are related to and dependent on each other आहार-शृखंला से बना खाद्य जाल

**fool¹** /fu:l फ़ूल् / *noun* [C] a person who is silly or who acts in a silly way मूर्ख या मूर्खता का आचरण करने वाला व्यक्ति; बेवकूफ़ *I felt such a fool when I realized my mistake.* ➪ **April Fool** देखिए।

IDM **make a fool of sb/yourself** to make sb/yourself look foolish or silly मूर्ख या बेवकूफ़ बन जाना या (किसी को) बना देना *Akhil got caught while lying and made a complete fool of himself.*

**fool²** /fu:l फ़ूल् / *verb* **1** [T] **fool sb (into doing sth)** to trick sb मूर्ख बनाना, झाँसा देना *Don't be fooled into believing everything that the salesman says.* **2** [I] to speak without being serious मज़ाक़ में कहना *You didn't really believe me when I said I was going to America, did you? I was only fooling.*

PHR V **fool about/around** to behave in a silly way बेवकूफ़ी का काम करना *Stop fooling around with that knife or someone will get hurt!*

**foolhardy** /ˈfu:lhɑ:di ˈफ़ूलहाडि / *adj.* taking unnecessary risks अनावश्यक ख़तरे मोल लेने वाला; दुस्साहसी

**foolish** /ˈfu:lɪʃ ˈफ़ूलिश् / *adj.* **1** silly; not sensible बेवकूफ़; बेअकल, बुद्धिहीन, विवेकहीन *I was foolish enough to trust him.* **2** looking silly or feeling embarrassed बेवकूफ़-सा, शरमिंदा *I felt a bit foolish when I couldn't remember the man's name.* ▶ **foolishly** *adv.* मूर्खतापूर्वक *I foolishly agreed to lend him money.* ▶ **foolishness** *noun* [U] मूर्खता, विवेकहीनता, नासमझी

**foolproof** /ˈfu:lpru:f ˈफ़ूलप्रूफ़ / *adj.* not capable of going wrong or being wrongly used जिसे ग़लत तरीक़े से इस्तेमाल नहीं किया जा सकता है; ग़लत इस्तेमाल की संभावना से परे *Our security system is absolutely foolproof.*

**foot¹** /fʊt फ़ुट् / *noun* (*pl.* **feet** /fi:t फ़ीट् /) **1** [C] the lowest part of the body, at the end of the leg, on which a person or animal stands पैर, पाँव *to get/rise **to your feet*** (= stand up) ○ *I usually go to school **on foot*** (= walking). ○ *a foot brake/pedal/pump* (= one that is operated by your foot) **2 -footed** (*used to form compound adjectives and adverbs*) having or using the type of foot or number of feet mentioned निर्दिष्ट प्रकार के (बायाँ या दायाँ) पैर वाला या निर्दिष्ट संख्या (चार, छह आदि) पैरों वाला *There are no left-footed players in the team.* ○ *a four-footed creature* **3** [C] the part of a sock, etc. that covers the foot ज़ुराब आदि का वह हिस्सा जो पैर को ढकता है (ज़ुराब का पैर) **4** [*sing.*] **the foot of sth** the bottom of sth किसी वस्तु का तला *There's a note at the foot of the page.* ○ *the foot of the stairs* ○ *the foot of the bed* ✪ विलोम **top** **5** [C] (*abbr.* **ft**) measurement of length; 30.48 centimetres लंबाई की एक माप; 30.48 सेंटीमीटर *'How tall are you?' 'Five foot six (inches).'* ○ *a six-foot high wall*

IDM **back on your feet** completely healthy again after an illness or a time of difficulty बीमारी या कठिनाई में से गुज़रने के बाद पुनः पूर्ण स्वस्थ होना

**be rushed/run off your feet** to be extremely busy; to have too many things to do बहुत व्यस्त होना; हाथ में बहुत सारे काम होना *Over the end of the year we were rushed off our feet at work.*

**fall/land on your feet** to be lucky in finding yourself in a good situation, or in getting out of a difficult situation भाग्यशाली होना या कठिन स्थिति में से निकल आना

**find your feet** ➪ **find[1]** देखिए।

**get/have cold feet** ➪ **cold[1]** देखिए।

**get/start off on the right/wrong foot (with sb)** (*informal*) to start a relationship well/badly संबंध की अच्छी या ख़राब शुरुआत होना

**have one foot in the grave** (*informal*) to be so old or ill that you are not likely to live much longer मौत के नज़दीक होना; मरणासन्न होना

**put your foot down** (*informal*) to say firmly that sth must (not) happen दृढ़तापूर्वक अपनी बात कहना (प्रायः मना करना) *I put my foot down and told Amit he couldn't use our car any more.*

**put your foot in it** (*informal*) to say or do sth that makes sb embarrassed or upset दूसरे को परेशानी में डालने वाली या शरमिंदा करने वाली बात कहना या काम करना

**put your feet up** to sit down and relax, especially with your feet off the floor and supported बैठ जाना और आराम करना, विशेषतः पाँव ऊपर रखकर *I'm so tired that I just want to go home and put my feet up.*

**set foot in/on sth** ➪ **set[1]** देखिए।

**stand on your own (two) feet** to take care of yourself without help; to be independent अपनी देख-रेख स्वयं करना; आत्मनिर्भर होना

**under your feet** in the way; stopping you from working, etc. किसी की राह में रोड़े अटकाते हुए *Would somebody get these children out from under my feet and take them to the park?*

**foot[2]** /fʊt फ़ुट्/ *verb*

**IDM foot the bill (for sth)** to pay (for sth) किसी बात के लिए भुगतान करना

**footage** /ˈfʊtɪdʒ ˈफ़ुटिज्/ *noun* [U] part of a film showing a particular event फ़िल्म का अंश जिसमें विशेष घटना दिखाई गई हो *The documentary included footage of the assassination of Kennedy.*

**football** /ˈfʊtbɔːl ˈफ़ुट्बॉल्/ *noun* **1** (*also* **soccer**) [U] a game that is played by two teams of eleven players who try to kick a round ball into a goal फ़ुटबॉल का खेल *a football pitch/match* **NOTE** अमेरिका में इस खेल के लिए प्रचलित शब्द **soccer** है। अमेरिकी लोग **football** शब्द का प्रयोग **American football** के लिए करते हैं। **2** [C] the large round ball that is used in this game फ़ुटबॉल खेल में प्रयुक्त गेंद; फ़ुटबॉल

**footballer** /ˈfʊtbɔːlə(r) ˈफ़ुट्बॉल(र्)/ *noun* [C] a person who plays football फ़ुटबॉल का खिलाड़ी *a talented footballer*

**footbridge** /ˈfʊtbrɪdʒ ˈफ़ुट्ब्रिज्/ *noun* [C] a narrow bridge used only by people who are walking पैदल चलने वालों के लिए बना तंग पुल; पैदल-पुल

**foothills** /ˈfʊthɪlz ˈफ़ुट्हिल्ज़्/ *noun* [*pl.*] hills or low mountains at the base of a higher mountain or line of mountains ऊँचे पहाड़ या पहाड़ों के नीचे की छोटी पहाड़ियाँ

**foothold** /ˈfʊthəʊld ˈफ़ुट्होल्ड्/ *noun* [C] a place where you can safely put your foot when you are climbing चढ़ाई करते समय पैर जमाने की जगह (*figurative*) *We need to get a foothold in the soap market.*

**footing** /ˈfʊtɪŋ ˈफ़ुटिङ्/ *noun* [*sing.*] **1** being able to stand firmly on a surface पाँव की मज़बूत पकड़ *Climbers usually attach themselves to a rope in case they* ***lose their footing.*** ○ (*figurative*) *The company is now* ***on a firm footing*** *and should soon show a profit.* **2** the level or position of sb/sth (in relation to sb/sth else) किसी व्यक्ति या वस्तु का स्तर या पद (अन्य व्यक्ति या वस्तु की तुलना में) *to be* ***on an equal footing*** *with sb*

**footnote** /ˈfʊtnəʊt ˈफ़ुट्नोट्/ *noun* [C] an extra piece of information that is added at the bottom of a page in a book पुस्तक के पृष्ठ पर नीचे दी गई अतिरिक्त टिप्पणी; पाद-टिप्पणी

**footpath** /ˈfʊtpɑːθ ˈफ़ुट्पाथ़्/ *noun* [C] a path for people to walk on लोगों के चलने का रास्ता, पटरी, फ़ुटपाथ *a public footpath*

**footprint** /ˈfʊtprɪnt ˈफ़ुट्प्रिन्ट्/ *noun* [C] a mark that is left on the ground by a foot or a shoe ज़मीन पर बना पैर या जूते का निशान; पद चिह्न ➪ **track** देखिए।

**footstep** /ˈfʊtstep ˈफ़ुट्स्टेप्/ *noun* [C] the sound of sb walking चलने की आहट, पगध्वनि, पदचाप *I heard his footsteps in the hall.*

**IDM follow in sb's foot steps** ➪ **follow** देखिए।

**footwear** /ˈfʊtweə(r) ˈफ़ुट्वेअ(र्)/ *noun* [U] boots or shoes बूट या जूते

**for[1]** /fə(r); *strong form* fɔː(r) फ़(र्); प्रबल रूप फ़ॉ(र्)/ *prep.* **1** showing the person that will use or have sth किसी वस्तु को प्रयोग में लाने वाले व्यक्ति का निर्देश करने वाला शब्द; के लिए, के वास्ते *Here is a letter for you.* ○ *He made lunch for them.* ○ *It's a book for children.* **2** in order to do, have or get sth किसी वस्तु का उपयोग बताने वाला शब्द; के निमित्त, के हेतु *What did you do that for* (= why did you do that)? ○ *Do you learn English for your job or for fun?* ○ *to go for a walk/swim/drink* **3** in order to help sb/sth व्यक्ति या वस्तु की सहायता का सूचक *What can I do for you?* ○ *You should take some medicine for your cold.* ○ *Doctors are fighting for his life.* **4** in support of (sb/sth) (व्यक्ति या वस्तु) के पक्ष में; के

समर्थन में *Are you for or against shops opening on Sundays?* **5** meaning sth or representing sb/sth किसी का अर्थ बताने या प्रतिनिधित्व करने का सूचक *What's the 'C' for in 'BBC'?* ○ *What's the Russian for 'window'?* **6** showing the place that sb/sth will go to यात्रा के लक्ष्यभूत स्थान का सूचक, (पर पहुँचने के लिए) *Is this the train for Kanpur?* ○ *They set off for the shops.* **7** (showing a reason) as a result of कारण बताने का सूचक; के कारण *Sheila didn't want to come for some reason.* ○ *He was sent to prison for robbery.* **8** (showing the price or value of sth); in exchange for (किसी वस्तु की क़ीमत का सूचक); के बदले में *You get one point for each correct answer.* ○ *The officer was accused of giving secret information for cash.* **9** showing a length of time समय के विस्तार का सूचक *I'm going away for a few days.* ○ *for a while/a long time/ages* ○ *They have left the town for good* (= they will not return).

**NOTE** कोई बात समय के किस निश्चित बिंदु से आरंभ हुई, यह बताने के लिए शब्द **since** का प्रयोग किया जाता है—*He has been in hospital since Monday.* इस अर्थ में शब्द **ago** का भी प्रयोग किया जाता है—*He went to hospital five days ago.*

**10** showing how many times sth has happened कोई बात कितनी बार हुई है, इसका सूचक शब्द *I'm warning you for the last time.* ○ *I met him for the second time yesterday.* **11** at a particular, fixed time किसी विशेष, निश्चित समय पर, के अवसर पर, पर *What did they give you for your birthday?* ○ *Shall we have eggs for breakfast?* **12** showing a distance दूरी का सूचक *He walked for five kilometers.* **13** (*after an adjective*) showing how usual, suitable, difficult, etc. sb/sth is in relation to sb/sth else दूसरे की तुलना में कोई व्यक्ति या वस्तु कितनी सामान्य, उपयुक्त आदि है इसका सूचक; की दृष्टि से *She's tall for her age.* ○ *It's quite warm for January.*

**IDM be (in) for it** (*informal*) to be going to get into trouble or be punished परेशानी में पड़ने के क़रीब होना *If you arrive late again you'll be in for it.*

**for all** in spite of के होते हुए भी, के बराबर *For all his money, he's a very lonely man.*

**forever** ➪ **forever[1]** देखिए।

**for[2]** /fə(r); *strong form* fɔ:(r) फ़(र्); प्रबल रूप फ़ॉ(र्) / *conj.* (*formal*) because क्योंकि *The children soon lost their way, for they had never been in the forest alone before.*

**forage[1]** /ˈfɒrɪdʒ ˈफ़ॉरिज् / *verb* [I] **forage (for sth)** (used about animals) to search for food (पशुओं के लिए प्रयुक्त) चारा या भोजन खोजना

**forage[2]** /ˈfɒrɪdʒ ˈफ़ॉरिज् / *noun* [U] plants that are grown as food for horses and cows पौधे जो घोड़ों और गौओं का चारा बनाने में प्रयोग में लाए जाते हैं; चारा

**forbid** /fəˈbɪd फ़ˈबिड् / *verb* [T] (*pres. part.* **forbidding;** *pt* **forbade** /fəˈbæd फ़ˈबैड् /; *pp* **forbidden** /fəˈbɪdn फ़ˈबिड्न् /) **1** (*usually passive*) to not allow sth किसी बात की मनाही होना; निषिद्ध, वर्जित होना *Smoking is forbidden inside the building.* **2 forbid sb to do sth** to order sb not to do sth किसी को कोई काम करने से मना करना *My parents forbade me to see Jeena again.*

**forbidding** /fəˈbɪdɪŋ फ़ˈबिडिङ् / *adj.* looking unfriendly or frightening अप्रिय, बुरा या भयानक

**force[1]** /fɔ:s फ़ॉस् / *noun* **1** [U] physical strength or power शारीरिक या भौतिक शक्ति या बल *The force of the explosion knocked them to the ground.* ○ *The police **used force** to break up the demonstration.* **2** [U] power and influence शक्ति और प्रभाव *the force of public opinion* **3** [C] a person or thing that has power or influence शक्तिशाली या प्रभावशाली व्यक्ति या वस्तु *Britain is no longer a major force in international affairs.* ○ *The president has been **the driving force** behind the company's success.* **4** [C] a group of people who are trained for a particular purpose विशेष प्रयोजन से प्रशिक्षित व्यक्ति-समूह; बल *a highly trained workforce* ○ *the police force* **5** (*usually pl.*) the soldiers and weapons that an army, etc. has सेना के सैनिक और शस्त्र, सशस्त्र सेना *the armed forces* **6** [C, U] (*technical*) a power that can cause change or movement परिवर्तनकारी या गति उत्पन्न करने वाली शक्ति *the force of gravity* ○ *magnetic/centrifugal force* ➪ **hydraulic** पर चित्र देखिए। **7** [C, *usually sing.*] a measure of wind strength वायु-शक्ति का एक माप *a force 9 gale*

**IDM bring sth/come into force** to start using a new law, etc.; to start being used नए क़ानून आदि को लागू करना; का लागू होना, प्रभावी होना *The government want to bring new anti-pollution legislation into force next year.*

**force of habit** if you do sth from or out of force of habit, you do it in a particular way because you have always done it that way in the past आदतन, अभ्यासवश

**in force 1** (used about people) in large numbers (व्यक्ति) बड़ी संख्या में *The police were present in force at the football match.* **2** (used about a law, rule, etc.) being used (क़ानून, नियम आदि) लागू, प्रभावी, जारी *The new speed limit is now in force.*

**join forces (with sb)** to work together in order to achieve a shared goal समान लक्ष्य को प्राप्त करने के लिए एक साथ काम करना

**force**[2] /fɔːs फ़ॉस्/ *verb* [T] **1 force sb (to do sth); force sb (into sth/doing sth)** to make sb do sth that he/she does not want to do किसी को उसका अनचाहा काम करने के लिए विवश करना; बाध्य करना *She forced herself to speak to him.* ○ *The President was forced into resigning.* **2** to use physical strength to do sth or to move sth कुछ करने या चलाने-हिलाने के लिए शारीरिक शक्ति का प्रयोग करना *The window had been forced (open).* ○ *We had to force our way through the crowd.* **3** to make sth happen when it will not happen naturally अस्वाभाविक रूप से जबरन कुछ करना *to force a smile/laugh* ○ *To force the issue, I gave him until midday to decide.*

IDM **force sb's hand** to make sb do sth that he/she does not want to do, or make him/her do it sooner than intended किसी को उसकी इच्छा के विपरीत या अभीष्ट समय से पहले कुछ करने के लिए बाध्य करना

**forceful** /ˈfɔːsfl ˈफ़ॉस्फ़्ल्/ *adj.* having the power to persuade people लोगों को प्रेरित करने की शक्ति से युक्त; शक्तिशाली, प्रभावशाली *He has a very forceful personality.* ○ *a forceful speech*

**forceps** /ˈfɔːseps ˈफ़ॉसेप्स्/ *noun* [*pl.*] a special instrument that looks like a pair of scissors but is not sharp. Forceps are used by doctors for holding things firmly कैंची की शकल का विशेष उपकरण जो पैना नहीं होता; सर्जन की चिमटी, सँड़सी *a pair of forceps*

**forcible** /ˈfɔːsəbl ˈफ़ॉसबल्/ *adj.* (*only before a noun*) done using (physical) force बलपूर्वक किया जाने वाला *The police made a forcible entry into the building.* ▶ **forcibly** /ˈfɔːsəbli ˈफ़ॉसब्लि/ *adv.* बलपूर्वक, बलप्रयोग करते हुए *The hawkers were forcibly removed by the police.*

**ford** /fɔːd फ़ॉड्/ *noun* [C] a place in a river where you can walk or drive across because the water is not deep नदी में वह उथला स्थान जहाँ से होकर नदी पार की जा सकती है; उथला या छिछला पाट

**fore**[1] /fɔː(r) फ़ॉ(र्)/ *noun*

IDM **be/come to the fore** to be in or get into an important position so that you are noticed by people प्रमुखता की या महत्त्वपूर्ण स्थिति आदि पर आसीन होना ताकि सबकी दृष्टि में आ सके

**fore**[2] /fɔː(r) फ़ॉ(र्)/ *adj.* (*only before a noun*) *adv.* (*technical*) at, near or towards the front of a ship or an aircraft जलपोत या विमान के अग्रभाग पर, निकट या की ओर ➪ **aft** देखिए।

**fore-** /fɔː फ़ॉ-/ *prefix* (*in nouns and verbs*) **1** before; in advance पूर्ववर्ती, अग्रिम रूप में किया गया; भविष्यात्मक *foreword* ○ *foretell* **2** in front of सामने वाला, अग्रवर्ती *the foreground of the picture*

**forearm** /ˈfɔːrɑːm ˈफ़ॉरआम्/ *noun* [C] the lower part of your arm बाँह का निचला हिस्सा ➪ **body** पर चित्र देखिए।

**forebear** (*also* **forbear**) /ˈfɔːbeə(r) ˈफ़ॉबेअ(र्)/ *noun* [C, *usually pl.*] (*formal*) a person in your family who lived a long time before you परिवार का पूर्वज; पुरखा ✪ पर्याय **ancestor**

**foreboding** /fɔːˈbəʊdɪŋ फ़ॉˈबोडिङ्/ *noun* [U, *sing.*] a strong feeling that danger or trouble is coming अनिष्ट का प्रबल पूर्वाभास *She was suddenly filled with **a sense of foreboding**.*

**forecast** /ˈfɔːkɑːst ˈफ़ॉकास्ट्/ *verb* [T] (*pt, pp* **forecast**) to say (with the help of information) what will probably happen in the future (सूचना के आधार पर) भविष्य में संभावित स्थिति की बात करना; पूर्वानुमान या भविष्यवाणी करना *The government did not forecast the sudden rise in inflation.* ○ *Rain has been forecast for tomorrow.* ▶ **forecast** *noun* [C] पूर्वानुमान *a sales forecast for the coming year* ➪ **weather forecast** देखिए।

**forecourt** /ˈfɔːkɔːt ˈफ़ॉकॉट्/ *noun* [C] a large open area in front of a building such as a hotel or petrol station किसी इमारत के सामने का बड़ा खुला क्षेत्र; बड़ा प्रांगण

**forefinger** /ˈfɔːfɪŋɡə(r) ˈफ़ॉफ़िङ्ग(र्)/ (*also* **index finger**) *noun* [C] the finger next to the thumb अँगूठे से अगली अंगुलि; तर्जनी

**forefront** /ˈfɔːfrʌnt ˈफ़ॉफ़्रन्ट्/ *noun* [*sing.*] the leading position; the position at the front महत्त्वपूर्ण स्थिति, नेतृत्व का पद; सबसे आगे की स्थिति *Our department is right at **the forefront of** scientific research.*

**forego** = **forgo**

**foregone** /ˈfɔːɡɒn ˈफ़ॉगॉन्/ *adj.*

IDM **a foregone conclusion** a result that is or was certain to happen अवश्यंभावी परिणाम; परिणाम जो निश्चित है या था

**foreground** /ˈfɔːgraʊnd ˈफ़ॉग्राउन्ड्/ *noun* [*sing.*] **1** the part of a view, picture, photograph, etc. that appears closest to the person looking at it किसी दृश्य, चित्र, फ़ोटो आदि में आगे का हिस्सा (जो देखने वाले को अपने सबसे निकट लगता है); पुरोभाग *Notice the artist's use of colour **in the foreground** of the picture.* **2** a position where you will be noticed most सबसे आगे का स्थान, सर्वप्रमुख स्थान जो सबकी दृष्टि में आएगा *He likes to be in the foreground at every meeting.* ✪ विलोम **background**

**forehand** /ˈfɔːhænd ˈफ़ॉहैन्ड् *noun* [C] a way of hitting the ball in tennis, etc. that is made with the inside of your hand facing forward टेनिस के खेल में लगाया गया सीधे हाथ (खब्बू खिलाड़ी के लिए बाँए हाथ) का शॉट; फोरहैन्ड ✪ विलोम **backhand**

**forehead** /ˈfɔːhed; ˈfɒrɪd ˈफ़ॉहेड्; ˈफ़ॉरिड् / (*also* **brow**) *noun* [C] the part of a person's face above the eyes and below the hair ललाट, मस्तक, माथा ➪ **body** पर चित्र देखिए।

**foreign** /ˈfɒrən फ़ॉरन् / *adj.* **1** belonging to or connected with a country that is not your own स्वदेश से भिन्न देश का या उससे संबंधित; विदेशी *a foreign country/coin/accent* ○ *to learn a foreign language* **2** (*only before a noun*) dealing with or involving other countries अन्य देशों के साथ व्यवहार से संबंधित; विदेशी *foreign policy* (= government decisions concerning other countries) ○ *foreign affairs/news/trade* ○ *the Indian Foreign Minister* **3** (used about an object or a substance) not being where it should be (कोई वस्तु या पदार्थ) विजातीय, जो अपने स्थान से हट गया है, बाहरी *The X-ray showed up a foreign body* (= object) *in her stomach.*

**foreigner** /ˈfɒrənə(r) ˈफ़ॉरन(र्) / *noun* [C] a person who belongs to a country that is not your own आपने देश से भिन्न देश का निवासी; विदेशी व्यक्ति

**foreign exchange** *noun* [C, U] the system of buying and selling money from a different country; the place where it is bought and sold विदेशी मुद्रा के विनिमय की प्रणाली; इस विनिमय प्रक्रिया का स्थल

**foreleg** /ˈfɔːleg ˈफ़ॉलेग् / (*also* **front leg**) *noun* [C] either of the two legs at the front of an animal that has four legs चौपाये प्राणियों के आगे की दो टाँगों में से कोई भी एक; अग्रपाद ➪ **hind** देखिए।

**foremost** /ˈfɔːməʊst ˈफ़ॉमोस्ट् / *adj.* most famous or important; best सबसे प्रसिद्ध या महत्त्वपूर्ण; सर्वोत्तम *Ajay Devgan is among the foremost actors of our times.*

**IDM first and foremost** ➪ **first**[2] देखिए।

**forename** /ˈfɔːneɪm ˈफ़ॉनेम् / *noun* [C] (*formal*) your first name, that is given to you when you are born किसी व्यक्ति का निजी नाम; प्रथम नाम जो जन्म के समय रखा जाता है ➪ **name** पर नोट देखिए।

**forensic** / fəˈrensɪk; -ˈrenzɪk फ़ˈरेनसिक् ; रेनज़िक् / *adj.* (*only before a noun*) using scientific tests to find out about a crime अपराध-संबंधी खोजबीन के लिए वैज्ञानिक परीक्षणों का प्रयोग करने वाला; फोरेंसिक *The police are carrying out forensic tests to try and find out the cause of death.*

**forerunner** /ˈfɔːrʌnə(r) ˈफ़ॉरन(र्) / *noun* [C] **a forerunner (of sb/sth)** a person or thing that is an early example or a sign of sth that appears or develops later व्यक्ति या वस्तु जो बाद मे होने वाली घटना का पूर्व संकेत हो; अग्रदूत, पूर्वगामी *Country music was undoubtedly one of the forerunners of rock and roll.*

**foresee** / fɔːˈsiː फ़ॉˈसी / *verb* [T] (*pt* **foresaw** / fɔːˈsɔː फ़ॉˈसॉ / ; *pp* **foreseen** /fɔːˈsiːn फ़ॉˈसीन्/) to know or guess that sth is going to happen in the future भविष्य में होने वाली घटना को पहले से जान लेना या उसका अनुमान लगाना *Nobody could have foreseen the result of the election.* ➪ **unforeseen** देखिए।

**foreseeable** /ˈfɔːˈsiːəbl ˈफ़ॉˈसीअबल् / *adj.* that can be expected; that you can guess will happen प्रत्याशित; जिसका अनुमान लगाया जा सके *These problems were foreseeable.* ○ *The weather won't change **in the foreseeable future*** (= as far ahead as we can see).

**foreshadow** /fɔːˈʃædəʊ फॉˈशैडो / *verb* [T] (*formal*) to show or act as a sign of sth that will happen in the future पूर्वाभास देना, पूर्व संकेत करना *Political unrest foreshadowed the fall of the government.*

**foreshore** /ˈfɔːʃɔː(r) ˈफ़ॉशॉ(र्) / *noun* [C, *usually sing.*,U] **1** (on a beach or by a river) the part of the **shore** between the highest and lowest levels reached by the water अग्रतट, तटाग्र **2** the part of the **shore** between the highest level reached by the water and the area of land that has buildings, plants, etc. on it अग्रतट और भूक्षेत्र जिस पर भवन, पौधे आदि हैं

**foresight** /ˈfɔːsaɪt ˈफ़ॉसाइट् / *noun* [U] the ability to see what will probably happen in the future and to use this knowledge to make careful plans भविष्य में घटित होने वाली बातों को जान लेने तथा उस जानकारी का समुचित उपयोग करने की क्षमता; दूरदर्शिता *My neighbour had the foresight to move house before the new flyover was built.* ➪ **hindsight** देखिए।

**foreskin** /ˈfɔːskɪn ˈफ़ॉस्किन् / *noun* [C] the piece of skin that covers the end of the male sexual organ पुरुष जननेंद्रिय के अग्रभाग को ढकने वाली त्वचा; शिश्न का आवरण

**forest** /ˈfɒrɪst ˈफ़ॉरिस्ट् / *noun* [C, U] a large area of land covered with trees जंगल, वन *the **tropical rainforests** of South America* ○ *a forest fire*

**NOTE** **Wood** से **forest** बड़ा होता है। बहुत गरम इलाक़े के वन प्रदेश को **jungle** कहते हैं।

**forestall** /fɔːˈstɔːl फ़ॉˈस्टॉल् / *verb* [T] (*written*) to take action to prevent sb from doing sth or sth from happening किसी को कुछ करने से या किसी घटना को घटित होने से पहले ही रोकने की कार्रवाई करना; पहले से ही रोक-थाम करना

**forestry** /ˈfɒrɪstri ˈफ़ॉरिस्ट्रि / *noun* [U] the science of planting and taking care of trees in forests वन संपदा के विकास और देखभाल का विज्ञान; वनविज्ञान

**foretell** /fɔːˈtel फ़ॉˈटेल् / *verb* [T] (*pt, pp* **foretold** /fɔːˈtəʊld फ़ॉˈटोल्ड् / (*formal*) to say what will happen in the future पूर्वकथन करना, भविष्यवाणी करना *The lady foretold that a bright and happy future lay ahead for him.* ➪ **predict** देखिए।

**forethought** /ˈfɔːθɔːt ˈफ़ॉथॉट् / *noun* [U] careful thought about, or preparation for, the future भविष्य के विषय में सावधानी से सोच-विचार या अपेक्षित तैयारी; पूर्वचिंतन

**forever** /fərˈevə(r) फ़र्ˈएव़(र्)/ *adv.* **1** (*also* **for ever**) for all time; permanently हमेशा के लिए; स्थायी रूप से *I wish the holidays would last forever!* ○ *I realized that our relationship had finished forever.* **2** (*only used with the continuous tenses*) very often; in a way which is annoying बहुत बार; ऐसे कि बुरा लगे *Our neighbours are forever having noisy parties.*

**foreword** /ˈfɔːwɜːd ˈफ़ॉवड् / *noun* [C] a piece of writing at the beginning of a book that introduces the book and/or its author पुस्तक के आरंभ में एक छोटा लेख जो पुस्तक और/या लेखक का सामान्य परिचय देता है; आमुख

**forfeit** /ˈfɔːfɪt ˈफ़ॉफ़िट् / *verb* [T] to lose sth or have sth taken away from you, usually because you have done sth wrong ग़लती के फलस्वरूप कुछ गँवाना या किसी वस्तु से वंचित हो जाना *Because of his violent behaviour he forfeited the right to visit his children.* ▸ **forfeit** *noun* [C] ज़ब्ती, दंड-भराई

**forgave** ➪ **forgive** का past tense रूप

**forge[1]** /fɔːdʒ फ़ॉज् / *verb* [T] **1** to make an illegal copy of sth ग़ैर-क़ानूनी तरीक़े से किसी वस्तु की नक़ल बनाना; जालसाज़ी करना *to forge a signature/bank note/passport/cheque* ➪ **counterfeit** देखिए। **2** to put a lot of effort into making sth strong and successful किसी वस्तु को सशक्त और उन्नत बनाने के लिए विशेष प्रयास करना *Our school has forged links with a school in Japan.*

**PHRV** **forge ahead** to go forward or make progress quickly आगे बढ़ना या तेज़ी से प्रगति करना

**forge[2]** /fɔːdʒ फ़ॉज् / *noun* [C] a place where objects are made by heating and shaping metal स्थान जहाँ धातु को तपाकर और ढालकर वस्तुएँ बनाई जाती हैं; लोहारख़ाना, ढलाईघर

**forgery** /ˈfɔːdʒəri ˈफ़ॉजरि / *noun* (*pl.* **forgeries**) **1** [U] the crime of illegally copying a document, signature, painting, etc. ग़ैर-क़ानूनी ढंग से दस्तावेज़, हस्ताक्षर आदि की नक़ल करने का अपराध; जालसाज़ी **2** [C] a document, signature, picture, etc. that is a copy of the real one ऐसा दस्तावेज़, चित्र आदि जो मूल की ग़ैर-क़ानूनी प्रतिलिपि है

**forget** /fəˈget फ़ˈगेट् / *verb* (*pt* **forgot** /fəˈgɒt फ़ˈगॉट् ; *pp* **forgotten** /fəˈgɒtn फ़ˈगॉट्न् /) **1** [T] **forget (doing) sth** to not be able to remember sth याद न रहना, भूल जाना *I've forgotten her telephone number.* ○ *He forgot that he had invited her to the party.* **2** [I, T] **forget (about) sth; forget to do sth** to fail to remember to do sth that you ought to have done कुछ करना याद न रहना *'Why didn't you come to the party?' 'Oh dear! I completely forgot about it!'* ○ *Don't forget to do your homework!* **3** [T] to fail to bring sth with you किसी वस्तु को साथ लाना याद न रहना, कहीं कुछ छुट जाना *When my father got to the airport he realized he'd forgotten his passport.* **4** [I, T] **forget (about) sb/sth; forget about doing sth** to make an effort to stop thinking about sb/sth; to stop thinking that sth is possible प्रयासपूर्वक किसी बात को सोचना बंद करना; बात को दिमाग़ से निकाल देना *Forget about your work and enjoy yourself!* ○ *'I'm sorry I shouted at you.' 'Forget it* (= don't worry about it).*'*

**forgetful** /fəˈgetfl फ़ˈगेट्फ़्ल् / *adj.* often forgetting things प्रायः बातें भूल जाने वाला; भुलक्कड़ *My grandmother's nearly 80 and she's starting to get a bit forgetful.* ✪ पर्याय **absent-minded**

**forgivable** /fəˈgɪvəbl फ़ˈगिव़ब्ल् / *adj.* that can be forgiven क्षमा के योग्य

**forgive** /fəˈgɪv फ़ˈगिव़् / *verb* [T] (*pt* **forgave** /fəˈgeɪv फ़ˈगेव़् /; *pp* **forgiven** /fəˈgɪvn फ़ˈगिव़्न् /) **1 forgive sb/yourself (for sth/for doing sth)** to stop being angry towards sb for sth that he/she has done wrong किसी को क्षमा या माफ़ करना *I can't forgive him for his behaviour last night.* ○ *I can't forgive him for behaving like that last night.* **2 forgive me (for doing sth)** used for politely saying sorry नम्रता के साथ माफ़ी व्यक्त करने के लिए प्रयुक्त *Forgive me for asking, but where did you get that dress?* ▸ **forgiveness** *noun* [U] क्षमा, माफ़ी *He **begged for forgiveness** for what he had done.*

**forgiving** /fəˈgɪvɪŋ फ़ˈगिविङ् / *adj.* ready and able to forgive क्षमा करने के लिए उद्यत और समर्थ; क्षमाशील

**forgo** (*also* **forego**) /fɔːˈgəʊ फ़ॉˈगो / *verb* [T] (*pt* **forwent** /fɔːˈwent फ़ॉˈवेन्ट् /; *pp* **forgone** /fɔːˈgɒn फ़ॉˈगॉन् /) (*formal*) to decide not to have or do sth that you want अभीष्ट काम को जान-बूझकर न करना; स्वेच्छा से परित्याग करना

**forgot** ➪ **forget** का past tense रूप

**forgotten** ➪ **forget** का past participle रूप

**fork[1]** /fɔːk फ़ॉक् / *noun* [C] **1** a small metal object with a handle and two or more points (**prongs**) that you use for lifting food to your mouth when eating भोजन खाने के लिए प्रयुक्त काँटा; फ़ोर्क *a knife and fork* **2** a large tool with a handle and three or more points (**prongs**) that you use for digging the ground ज़मीन खोदने का बड़ा औज़ार; पाँचा *a garden fork* ➪ **gardening** पर चित्र देखिए। **3** a place where a road, river, etc. divides into two parts; one of these parts सड़क, नदी आदि का वह स्थान जहाँ वह दो शाखाओं में विभक्त होती है; इन दो में से कोई एक शाखा *After about two kilometres you'll come to a fork in the road.*

**fork²** /fɔ:k फ़ॉक्/ *verb* [I] **1** (used about a road, river, etc.) to divide into two parts (सड़क, नदी आदि का) दो शाखाओं में विभक्त होना *Bear right where the road forks at the top of the hill.* **2** to go along the left or right fork of a road सड़क के दाएँ या बाएँ छोर के साथ-साथ जाना *Fork right up the hill.*

**PHR V** **fork out (for sth)** (*informal*) to pay for sth when you do not want to न चाहते हुए भी किसी वस्तु के लिए भुगतान करना *I forked out over Rs 300 for that book.*

**forked** /fɔ:kt फ़ॉक्ट्/ *adj.* with one end divided into two parts, like the shape of the letter Y जिसका एक सिरा दो शाखाओं में विभक्त हो; द्विशाखित (जैसे Y की आकृति) *a bird with a forked tail* ○ *the forked tongue of the snake*

**forked lightning** *noun* [U] the type of **lightning** that is like a line that divides into smaller lines near the ground शाखित तड़ित ➪ **sheet lightning** देखिए।

**fork-lift truck** (*also* **fork-lift**) *noun* [C] a vehicle with special equipment on the front for moving and lifting heavy objects ऐसा वाहन जिसमें आगे की ओर सामान ढोने या उठाने वाली मशीन (क्रेन) लगी होती है

**forlorn** /fəˈlɔ:n फ़ˈलॉन्/ *adj.* lonely and unhappy; not cared for अकेला और उदास; उपेक्षित

**form¹** /fɔ:m फ़ॉम्/ *noun* **1** [C] a particular type or variety of sth or a way of doing sth किसी वस्तु या कार्यप्रणाली का विशेष रूप; प्रकार *Swimming is an excellent form of exercise.* ○ *We never eat meat **in any form**.* **2** [C, U] the shape of sb/sth किसी व्यक्ति या वस्तु की आकृति या आकार *The articles will be published **in** book **form**.* **3** [C] an official document with questions on it and spaces where you give answers and personal information व्यक्तिगत सूचना आदि देने के लिए प्रयुक्त प्रपत्र; फ़ॉर्म *an **entry form** for a competition* ○ *to fill in an **application form*** **4** [C] (*grammar*) a way of spelling or changing a word in a sentence शब्द की विशेष वर्तनी देने या उसमें परिवर्तन का एक प्रकार; रूप *the irregular forms of the verbs* ○ *The plural form of mouse is mice.* **5** [U] the state of being fit and strong for a sports player, team, etc. खिलाड़ी, टीम आदि की स्वस्थ होने की स्थिति *to be **in/out of form*** **6** [U] how well sb/sth is performing at a particular time, for example in sport or business समय विशेष में किसी की दक्षता का स्तर (विशेषतः खेल या व्यापार में) *to be **on/off form*** ○ *On present form the Italian team should win easily.*

**IDM** **true to form** ➪ **true** देखिए।

**form²** /fɔ:m फ़ॉम्/ *verb* **1** [I, T] to begin to exist or to make sth exist कुछ होने की शुरुआत होना; अस्तित्व में आना *A pattern was beginning to form in the monthly sales figures.* ○ *These tracks were formed by rabbits.* **2** [T] to make or organize sth कुछ बनाना या संगठित करना *to form a government* ○ *In English we usually form the past tense by adding '-ed'.* **3** [T] to become or make a particular shape विशेष आकार धारण करना या बनाना; विशिष्ट संरचना बनाना *The police formed a circle around the house.* ○ *to form a line/queue* **4** to be the thing mentioned निर्दिष्ट वस्तु होना, जैसा बताया गया है वैसा होना *Seminars form the main part of the course.* ○ *The survey **formed part of** a larger programme of market research.* **5** [T] to begin to have or think sth कुछ बनाने या सोचने लगना *I haven't formed an opinion about the new boss yet.* ○ *to form a friendship*

**formal** /ˈfɔ:ml ˈफ़ॉम्ल्/ *adj.* **1** (used about language or behaviour) used when you want to appear serious or official and in situations in which you do not know the other people very well (भाषण या आचरण) औपचारिक, गंभीरतापूर्ण और ऐसी स्थिति में उपयुक्त जिसमें अन्य व्यक्ति आपके सुपरिचित न हों *'Yours faithfully' is a formal way of ending a letter.* ○ *She has a very formal manner—she doesn't seem to be able to relax.* ○ *a formal occasion* (= one where you behave politely and wear the clothes that people think are suitable)

> **NOTE** इस शब्दकोश में कुछ शब्दों के साथ (*formal*) औपचारिक या (*informal*) अनौपचारिक का लेबल लगा है—इससे स्थिति विशेष में सही शब्द चुनने में आपको सुविधा होगी। प्रत्येक औपचारिक शब्द के लिए उसका समानार्थक एक अनौपचारिक शब्द भी प्रायः भाषा में होता है।

**2** official औपचारिक, विधि-अनुकूल, आधिकारिक रूप से *I shall make **a formal complaint** to the hospital about the way I was treated.* ✪ विलोम **informal**

▶ **formally** /-məli -मलि/ *adv.* औपचारिक रूप से

**formaldehyde** /fɔːˈmældɪhaɪd फ़ॉˈमैल्डिहाइड् / *noun* [U] **1** (*symbol* $CH_2O$) a colourless gas with a strong smell तीखी गंध वाली एक रंगहीन गैस; फ़ॉर्मलडिहाइड **2** (*also* **formalin** /ˈfɔːməlɪn ˈफ़ॉमलिन्/) a liquid made by mixing formaldehyde and water, used especially for keeping examples of animals, plants, etc. (**specimens**) in a good condition for a long time so that they can be studied by experts or scientists फ़ार्मलडिहाइड और पानी के मिश्रण से बना एक द्रव पदार्थ जिसे पशुओं और पौधों के नमूनों को लंबे समय तक सुरक्षित रखने के लिए प्रयुक्त किया जाता है; फ़ार्मलिन

**formality** /fɔːˈmæləti फ़ॉˈमैलटि / *noun* (*pl.* **formalities**) **1** [C] an action that is necessary according to custom or law प्रथा या क़ानून के अनुसार आवश्यक कार्रवाई; औपचारिकता *There are certain formalities to attend to before we can give you a visa.*

> **NOTE** किसी कार्रवाई को **just a formality** कहने का तात्पर्य है कि उसे प्रथा या क़ानून के अनुसार आवश्यक तो माना जाता है, परंतु इसके इलावा उसका ख़ास महत्त्व नहीं है।

**2** [U] careful attention to rules of language and behaviour भाषा और सामान्य आचरण के नियमों पर पूरा ध्यान; शिष्टाचार, औपचारिकता

**format¹** /ˈfɔːmæt ˈफ़ॉमैट्/ *noun* [C] the shape of sth or the way it is arranged or produced किसी वस्तु की आकृति या प्रकार जिसमें वह संयोजित अथवा निर्मित है *It's the same book but in a different format.*

**format²** /ˈfɔːmæt ˈफ़ॉमैट्/ *verb* [T] (**formatting; formatted**) **1** (*computing*) to prepare a computer disk so that data can be recorded on it कंप्यूटर डिस्क तैयार करना ताकि उसमें सूचना संचित की जा सके **2** to arrange text on a page or a screen किसी पृष्ठ या परदे पर लिखित सामग्री को सँजोना *to format a letter*

**formation** /fɔːˈmeɪʃn फ़ॉˈमेश्न् / *noun* **1** [U] the act of making or developing sth किसी वस्तु को बनाने या विकसित करने की क्रिया; निर्माण *the formation of a new government* **2** [C, U] a number of people or things in a particular shape or pattern विशेष आकृति या पैटर्न में संयोजित लोग या वस्तुएँ; संरचना, विन्यास *rock formations* ○ *A number of planes flew over* ***in formation***. ○ *formation dancing*

**formative** /ˈfɔːmətɪv ˈफ़ॉमटिव़् / *adj.* having an important and lasting influence (on sb's character and opinions) (किसी के चरित्र और विचारों को) गंभीर और स्थायी रूप से प्रभावित करने वाला *A child's early years are thought to be the most formative ones.*

**former** /ˈfɔːmə(r) ˈफ़ॉम(र्) / *adj.* (*only before a noun*) of an earlier time; belonging to the past पूर्वकाल का; अतीतकालीन *Rajiv Gandhi, the former Indian Prime Minister* ○ *In former times people often had larger families.*

**the former** /ˈfɔːmə(r) ˈफ़ॉम(र्) / *noun* [*sing.*] the first (of two people or things just mentioned) (दो निर्दिष्ट व्यक्तियों या वस्तुओं से) पहला, पहले का या वाला *Of the two hospitals in the town—the General and the Royal—the former* (= the General) *has the better reputation.* ➪ **the latter** देखिए।

**formerly** /ˈfɔːməli ˈफ़ॉमलि / *adv.* in the past; before now अतीत में; अब से पहले *the country of Myanmar (formerly Burma)* ○ *The hotel was formerly a palace.*

> **NOTE** **Was formerly** के अर्थ में **used to be** पदबंध अधिक प्रचलित प्रयोग है।

**formidable** /ˈfɔːmɪdəbl ˈफ़ॉमिडब्ल् / *adj.* **1** inspiring fear डर पैदा करने वाला *His mother is a rather formidable lady.* **2** difficult to deal with; needing a lot of effort जिससे निपटना मुश्किल है, विकट; प्रयत्नसाध्य

**formula** /ˈfɔːmjələ ˈफ़ॉम्यला / *noun* [C] (*pl.* **formulas** or **formulae** /-liː -ली /) **1** (*technical*) a group of signs, letters or numbers used in science or mathematics to express a general law or fact विज्ञान या गणितशास्त्र में सामान्य नियम और तथ्य को प्रस्तुत करने के लिए प्रयुक्त चिह्नों, अक्षरों, संख्याओं का समूह; सूत्र, फ़ार्मूला *What is the formula for converting miles to kilometres?* **2** a list of (often chemical) substances used for making sth; the instructions for making sth किसी वस्तु को बनाने में प्रयुक्त पदार्थों (प्रायः रसायनों) की सूची; किसी वस्तु को बनाने के निर्देश **3 a formula for (doing) sth** a plan of how to get or do sth कुछ प्राप्त करने या काम करने की योजना; तरीक़ा, नुस्ख़ा *What is her formula for success?* ○ *Unfortunately, there's no* ***magic formula*** *for a perfect marriage.*

**formulate** /ˈfɔːmjuleɪt ˈफ़ॉम्युलेट् / *verb* [T] **1** to prepare and organize a plan or ideas for doing sth कुछ करने की योजना बनाना या उसके लिए विचारों को व्यवस्थित करना; सूत्रित करना *to formulate a plan* **2** to express sth (clearly and exactly) (सुव्यवस्थित रूप से) अभिव्यक्त करना *She struggled to formulate a simple answer to his question.*

**forsake** /fəˈseɪk फ़ˈसेक् / *verb* [T] (*pt* **forsook** /fəˈsʊk फ़ˈसुक् /; *pp* **forsaken** /fəˈseɪkən फ़ˈसेकन् ) (*old-fashioned*) to leave a person or a place for ever (especially when you should stay) किसी व्यक्ति या स्थान का सदा के लिए परित्याग करना (विशेषतः अनपेक्षित रूप से)

**fort** /fɔːt फ़ॉट्/ *noun* [C] a strong building that is used for military defence सैनिक सुरक्षा के लिए निर्मित मज़बूत इमारत; क़िला, दुर्ग

**forth** /fɔːθ फ़ॉथ्/ *adv.*

**IDM** **and so forth** and other things like those just mentioned और ऐसी अन्य बातें *The sort of job that you'll be doing is taking messages, making tea and so forth.*

**back and forth** ➪ **back³** देखिए।

**forthcoming** /ˌfɔːθˈkʌmɪŋ ˌफ़ॉथ्ˈकमिङ्/ *adj.* **1** that will happen or appear in the near future निकट भविष्य में होने वाला; आगामी *Look in the local paper for a list of **forthcoming events**.* **2** (*not before a noun*) offered or given प्रदान किया या दिया गया; सुलभ *If no money is forthcoming, we shall not be able to continue the project.* **3** (*not before a noun*) (used about a person) ready to be helpful, give information, etc. (व्यक्ति) सहायता करने, जानकारी देने आदि के लिए तैयार या तत्पर

**forthright** /ˈfɔːθraɪt ˈफ़ॉथ्राइट्/ *adj.* saying exactly what you think in a clear and direct way अपनी सोच की सही अभिव्यक्ति में समर्थ; खरा-खरा कहने वाला, स्पष्टवादी

**forthwith** /ˌfɔːθˈwɪθ ˌफ़ॉथ्ˈविथ्/ *adv.* (*old-fashioned*) immediately तुरंत, तत्काल

**fortieth** /ˈfɔːtiəθ ˈफ़ॉटिअथ्/ *pronoun, det., adv.* 40th चालीसवाँ ➪ **sixth¹** की प्रविष्टि में दिए गए उदाहरण देखिए।

**fortification** /ˌfɔːtɪfɪˈkeɪʃn ˌफ़ॉटिफ़िˈकेश्न्/ *noun* [C, *usually pl.*] walls, towers, etc., built especially in the past to protect a place against attack (विशेषतः पहले के युग में) आक्रमण से बचाव के लिए निर्मित दीवारें, बुर्ज आदि; क़िलाबंदी

**fortify** /ˈfɔːtɪfaɪ ˈफ़ॉटिफ़ाइ/ *verb* [T] (*pres. part.* **fortifying**; *3rd person sing. pres.* **fortifies;** *pt, pp* **fortified**) **1** to make a place stronger and ready for an attack हमले का सामना करने के लिए किसी स्थान को मज़बूत और तैयार करना; क़िलाबंदी करना *to fortify a city* **2** to add sth (nutrients, alcohol etc.) to improve the quality and strength of food or drink अधिक पौष्टिक बनाना *Health drinks are fortified with vitamins and proteins.*

**fortnight** /ˈfɔːtnaɪt ˈफ़ॉट्नाइट्/ *noun* [C, *usually sing.*] two weeks दो सप्ताह की अवधि, पखवाड़ा, पक्ष *We're going on holiday for a fortnight.* ○ *School finishes in a fortnight/in a fortnight's time* (= two weeks from now).

**fortnightly** /ˈfɔːtnaɪtli ˈफ़ॉट्नाइट्लि/ *adj., adv.* (happening or appearing) once every two weeks प्रत्येक पखवाड़े में एक बार (प्रकट या घटित होने वाला); पाक्षिक *This magazine is published fortnightly.*

**fortress** /ˈfɔːtrəs ˈफ़ॉट्रस्/ *noun* [C] a castle or other large strong building that it is not easy to attack कोई क़िला या अन्य बड़ी मज़बूत इमारत जिसपर हमला करना कठिन हो

**fortunate** /ˈfɔːtʃənət ˈफ़ॉचनट्/ *adj.* lucky भाग्यशाली *It was fortunate that he was at home when you phoned.* ✪ विलोम **unfortunate**

**fortunately** /ˈfɔːtʃənətli ˈफ़ॉचनट्लि/ *adv.* by good luck सौभाग्य से *Fortunately the traffic wasn't too bad so I managed to get to the meeting on time.* ✪ पर्याय **luckily**

**fortune** /ˈfɔːtʃuːn ˈफ़ॉचून्/ *noun* **1** [C, U] a very large amount of money बहुत बड़ी धनराशि; विशाल संपत्ति, भरपूर पैसा *I always **spend a fortune** on presents at Christmas.* ○ *She went to Bollywood in search of **fame and fortune**.* **2** [U] chance or the power that affects what happens in a person's life; luck संयोग या शक्ति जो किसी व्यक्ति के जीवन की घटनाओं को प्रभावित करे; भाग्य, क़िस्मत *Fortune was not on our side that day* (= we were unlucky). ✪ पर्याय **fate** **3** [C, *usually pl.*] the things (both good and bad) that happen to a person, family, country, etc. किसी व्यक्ति, परिवार, देश आदि के साथ घटित होने वाली बातें (शुभ और अशुभ दोनों) *The country's fortunes depend on its industry being successful.* **4** [C] what is going to happen to a person in the future किसी व्यक्ति का भविष्य *Show me your hand and I'll try to **tell your fortune**.* ✪ पर्याय **fate** या **destiny**

**IDM** **cost the earth/a fortune** ➪ **cost²** देखिए।

**fortune teller** *noun* [C] a person who tells people what will happen to them in the future लोगों का भविष्य बताने वाला व्यक्ति; ज्योतिषी

**forty** /ˈfɔːti ˈफ़ॉटि/ *number* 40 चालीस (का अंक)

> **NOTE** संख्याओं के वाक्य-प्रयोग के उदाहरणों के लिए **sixty** की प्रविष्टि देखिए।

**IDM** **forty winks** (*informal*) a short sleep, especially during the day हलकी नींद, झपकी (विशेषतः दिन के समय)

**forum** /ˈfɔːrəm ˈफ़ॉरम्/ *noun* [C] **a forum (for sth)** a place or meeting where people can exchange and discuss ideas स्थान या सभा जहाँ लोग विचार-विमर्श करते हैं; मंच, फ़ोरम

**forward¹** /ˈfɔːwəd ˈफ़ॉवड्/ *adv.* **1** (*also* **forwards**) in the direction that is in front of you; towards the front, end or future सामने की दिशा में; आगे, अंत या भविष्य की ओर *Keep going forward and try not to look back.* ✪ विलोम **back** या **backward(s)** **2** in the direction of progress; ahead प्रगति की दिशा में; आगे *The new form of treatment is a big step forward in the fight against AIDS.*

**NOTE** **Forward** का प्रयोग अनेक क्रियाओं के बाद होता है, जैसे **bring, come, look, put.** इनसे बनने वाले शब्दों के अर्थ के लिए उक्त verb प्रविष्टियों को देखिए।

**IDM** **backward(s) and forward(s)** ➪ **backwards** देखिए।

**put the clock/clocks forward/back** ➪ **clock**¹ देखिए।

**forward**² /ˈfɔːwəd ˈफ़ॉवड्/ *adj.* **1** (*only before a noun*) towards the front or future आगे की ओर का; अग्रवर्ती या भविष्योन्मुख *forward planning* **2** having developed earlier than is normal or expected; advanced सामान्य या अपेक्षित अवधि से पहले प्रौढ़ता प्राप्त; अपने समय से आगे; प्रगत, प्रगतिशील ✪ विलोम **backward** **3** behaving towards sb in a way that is too confident or too informal दूसरों से बहुत अधिक आत्मविश्वास या घनिष्ठता से पूर्ण व्यवहार करने वाला; प्रगल्भ, बेतकल्लुफ़ *I hope you don't think I'm being too forward, asking you so many questions.*

**forward**³ /ˈfɔːwəd ˈफ़ॉवड्/ *verb* [T] **1** to send a letter, etc. received at one address to a new address एक पते पर प्राप्त पत्र को नए पते पर भेजना; अग्रसारित, अग्रेषित करना **2** to help to improve sth or to make sth progress किसी स्थिति के सुधार या प्रगति में सहायक होना

**forward**⁴ /ˈfɔːwəd ˈफ़ॉवड्/ *noun* [C] an attacking player in a sport such as football फ़ुटबॉल आदि खेलों में अगली पंक्ति का खिलाड़ी; फ़ारवर्ड

**forwarding address** *noun* [C] a new address to which letters, etc. should be sent नया पता जिस पर पत्र आदि भेजे जाएँ *The previous owners didn't leave a forwarding address.*

**forward-looking** *adj.* thinking about or planning for the future; having modern ideas भविष्य के लिए योजनाएँ बनाने वाला; भविष्योन्मुख; विचारों में आधुनिक

**forwent** ➪ **forgo** का past tense रूप

**fossil** /ˈfɒsl ˈफ़ॉस्ल्/ *noun* [C] (part of) an animal or plant that lived thousands of years ago which has turned into rock हज़ारों वर्ष पहले का पशु या पौधे (का अंश) जो अब पत्थर बन चुका है; जीवाश्म

**fossil fuel** *noun* [C, U] a natural fuel such as coal or oil, that was formed millions of years ago from dead animals or plants in the ground कोयला या तेल जैसा प्राकृतिक ईंधन जिसका निर्माण लाखों वर्ष पहले ज़मीन में दबे मृत पशुओं या पौधों से हुआ; पुराकालीन ईंधन

**fossilize** (*also* **-ise**) /ˈfɒsəlaɪz ˈफ़ॉसलाइज़्/ *verb* [I, T] (*usually passive*) to turn into rock or to make (part of) an animal or plant turn into rock over thousands of years पशु या पौधे (के अंश) का हज़ारों वर्षों के दौरान पत्थर बन जाना या पत्थर बना देना; जीवाश्म बन जाना या बना देना *fossilized bones*

**foster** /ˈfɒstə(r) ˈफ़ॉस्ट(र्)/ *verb* [T] **1** to take a child who needs a home into your family and to care for him/her without becoming the legal parent किसी ग़ैर बच्चे को अपनाकर अपने परिवार में पालन-पोषण करना परंतु गोद लेने की क़ानूनी कार्रवाई किए बिना *to foster a homeless child*

**NOTE** इस प्रकार से अपनाए गए बच्चे को **foster-child** तथा ऐसा करने वाले दंपति को **foster-parents** कहते हैं ➪ **adopt** देखिए।

**2** to help or encourage the development of sth (especially feelings or ideas) (विशेषतः भावों या विचारों के) विकास को प्रोत्साहित करना; संवर्धित करना

**fought** ➪ **fight**¹ का past tense, और past participle रूप

**foul**¹ /faʊl फ़ाउल्/ *adj.* **1** that smells or tastes disgusting बदबूदार, ख़राब गंध या स्वाद वाला *a foul-smelling cigar* ○ *This coffee tastes foul!* **2** very bad or unpleasant बहुत ख़राब या अप्रिय *Careful what you say—he's* ***in a foul temper/mood***. ○ *The* ***foul weather*** *prevented our plane from taking off.* **3** (used about language) very rude; full of swearing (भाषा) धृष्टता-पूर्ण, अशिष्ट; अपशब्द-पूर्ण *foul language*

**IDM** **fall foul of sb/sth** to get in trouble with sb/sth because you have done sth wrong अपनी ग़लती के कारण किसी परेशानी में पड़ जाना *At twenty-two she fell foul of the law for the first time.*

**foul**² /faʊl फ़ाउल्/ *verb* **1** [I, T] (used in sports) to break the rules of the game (खेल में) नियम का उल्लंघन करना **2** [T] to make sth dirty (with rubbish, waste, etc.) (कूड़े आदि से) किसी स्थान को गंदा करना *Dogs must not foul the pavement.*

**PHR V** **foul sth up** (*spoken*) to spoil sth बिगाड़ देना; अव्यवस्थित कर देना *The delay on the train fouled up my plans for the evening.*

**foul**³ /faʊl फ़ाउल्/ *noun* [C] (used in sports) an action that is against the rules (खेल में) नियम का उल्लंघन *He was sent off for a foul on the goalkeeper.*

**foul play** *noun* [U] **1** violence or crime that causes sb's death हिंसा या अपराध जिसमें किसी की मृत्यु हो जाए *The police suspect foul play.* **2** action that is against the rules of a sport किसी खेल के नियम का उल्लंघन

**found**¹ ➪ **find**¹ का past tense और past participle रूप

**found**² /faʊnd फ़ाउन्ड्/ *verb* [T] **1** to start an organization, institution, etc. किसी संगठन, संस्था आदि की स्थापना करना *This museum was founded in 1921.* **2** to be the first to start building and living in a town or country किसी नगर या देश का निर्माण कर वहाँ बसने में सर्वप्रथम होना; सबसे पहले पहुँच कर किसी नगर या देश को स्थापित करना *Liberia was founded by freed American slaves.* **3 found sth (on sth)** (*usually passive*) to base sth on sth किसी वस्तु को किसी अन्य पर आधारित करना; एक वस्तु को दूसरी वस्तु का आधार बनाना *The book was founded on real life.*

**foundation** /faʊnˈdeɪʃn फ़ाउन्ˈडेश्न्/ *noun* **1 foundations** [*pl.*] a layer of bricks, etc. under the surface of the ground that forms the solid base of a building भवन की नींव; बुनियाद **2** [C, U] the idea, principle, or fact on which sth is based आधारभूत विचार, सिद्धांत या तथ्य *This coursebook aims to give students a solid foundation in grammar.* ○ *That rumour is completely without foundation* (= it is not true). **3** [C] an organization that provides money for a special purpose किसी विशेष उद्देश्य से धन उपलब्ध कराने वाला संगठन; निधि *The British Heart Foundation* **4** [U] the act of starting a new institution or organization नई संस्था या संगठन का प्रवर्तन, स्थापना

**foundation stone** *noun* [C] a large block of stone that is put at the base of an important new public building in a special ceremony विशेष आयोजन के साथ किसी नए महत्त्वपूर्ण सार्वजनिक भवन की नींव में रखा गया बड़ा पत्थर; आधारशिला

**founder** /ˈfaʊndə(r) ˈफ़ाउन्ड(र्)/ *noun* [C] a person who starts a new institution or organization नई संस्था या संगठन का प्रवर्तन करने वाला व्यक्ति; संस्थापक

**founder member** *noun* [C] one of the original members of a club, organization, etc. किसी क्लब, संगठन आदि का मूल सदस्य; संस्थापक सदस्य

**foundry** /ˈfaʊndri ˈफ़ाउन्ड्रि/ *noun* [C] (*pl.* **foundries**) a place where metal or glass is melted and shaped into objects धातु या शीशे को गलाकर विभिन्न वस्तुएँ गढ़ने का कारख़ाना; ढलाई-घर, फ़ाउंड्री

**fountain** /ˈfaʊntən ˈफ़ाउन्टन्/ *noun* [C] **1** a decoration (in a garden or in a square in a town) that sends a flow of water into the air; the water that comes out of a fountain (कृत्रिम या सजावटी) जलयंत्र, फ़व्वारा; फ़व्वारे से निकलने वाला पानी **2** a strong flow of liquid or another substance that is forced into the air द्रव या अन्य पदार्थ की हवा में छोड़ी गई तेज़ धार *a fountain of blood/sparks*

**fountain pen** *noun* [C] a type of pen that you fill with ink फ़ाउंटेन पेन, ऐसी क़लम जिसमें रोशनाई भरी जाती है ➪ **stationery** पर चित्र देखिए।

**four** /fɔː(r) फ़ॉ(र्)/ *number* **1** 4 चार (अंक)

> **NOTE** संख्याओं के वाक्य-प्रयोग के उदाहरणों के लिए **six** की प्रविष्टि देखिए।

**2 four-** (*in compounds*) having four of the thing mentioned चार-वाला *four-legged animals*

**IDM on all fours** with your hands and knees on the ground; crawling हाथों और घुटनों के बल; रेंगते हुए *The children went through the tunnel on all fours.*

**four-letter word** *noun* [C] a swear word that shocks or offends people (often with four letters) अंग्रेज़ी भाषा में अश्लील शब्द (प्रायः अंग्रेज़ी के चार अक्षरों से बना)

**fourteen** /ˌfɔːˈtiːn ˌफ़ॉˈटीन्/ *number* 14 चौदह (का अंक)

> **NOTE** संख्याओं के वाक्य-प्रयोग के उदाहरणों के लिए **six** की प्रविष्टि देखिए।

**fourteenth** /ˌfɔːˈtiːnθ,फ़ॉˈटीन्थ्/ *pronoun, det., adv.* 14th चौदहवाँ

**fourth** /fɔːθ फ़ॉथ्/ *pronoun, det., adv.* 4th चौथा

> **NOTE** भिन्न ¼ के लिए शब्द **quarter** का प्रयोग किया जाता है—*a quarter of an hour* (= fifteen minutes)

**four-wheel drive** *noun* [C, U] a system which provides power to all four wheels of a vehicle, making it easier to control; a vehicle with this system वाहन के चारों पहियों को गति-शक्ति देने वाली प्रणाली जिससे वाहन पर नियंत्रण रखना आसान रहता है; ऐसी प्रणाली से युक्त वाहन *a car with four-wheel drive* ○ *We rented a four-wheel drive to get around the island.*

**fowl** /faʊl फ़ाउल्/ *noun* [C] (*pl.* **fowl** or **fowls**) a bird, especially a chicken, that is kept on a farm पालतू पक्षी, विशेषतः मुरग़ा या मुरग़ी

**fox** /fɒks फ़ॉक्स्/ *noun* [C] a wild animal like a small dog with reddish fur, a pointed nose and a thick tail लोमड़ी

> **NOTE** लोमड़ी के लिए प्रायः **sly** या **cunning** विशेषणों का प्रयोग किया जाता है। मादा लोमड़ी को **vixen** कहते हैं और लोमड़ी के बच्चे को **cub** कहते हैं।

**foyer** /ˈfɔɪeɪ ˈफ़ॉइए/ *noun* [C] an entrance hall in a cimema, theatre, hotel, etc. where people meet or wait सिनेमा, होटल आदि में प्रवेश करते ही बना खुला क्षेत्र जहाँ लोग मिल सकते हैं या प्रतीक्षा कर सकते है; अग्रदीर्घा

**fraction** /ˈfrækʃn ˈफ्रैक्श्न्/ *noun* [C] **1** a small part or amount छोटा अंश या छोटी मात्रा *For a fraction of a second I thought the car was going to crash.* **2** a division of a number भिन्न *½ and ¼ are fractions.* ➪ **vulgar fraction** और **integer** देखिए।

**fractional distillation** /ˌfrækʃənl dɪstɪˈleɪʃn ˌफ्रैक्शनल् डिस्टिˈलेश्न्/ *noun* [U] (*technical*) the process of separating the parts of a liquid mixture by heating it. As the temperature goes up, each part in turn becomes a gas, which then cools as it moves up a tube and can be collected as a liquid द्रव-मिश्रण को तपा कर उसके अंश-विभाजन की प्रक्रिया, ताप बढ़ने के साथ प्रत्येक अंश गैस में बदल जाता है और फिर ठंडा होकर नली में से गुज़रते हुए द्रव बन जाता है

**fractionally** /ˈfrækʃənəli ˈफ्रैक्शनलि / *adv.* to a very small degree; slightly बहुत छोटे अंश या मात्रा में; बहुत थोड़ा; ज़रा-सा *fractionally faster/taller/heavier*

**fracture** /ˈfræktʃə(r) ˈफ्रैक्च(र्) / *noun* [C, U] a break in a bone or other hard material हड्डी या अन्य किसी कठोर वस्तु में टूट; अस्थि-भंग ▶ **fracture** *verb* [I, T] हड्डी, कठोर वस्तु आदि टूटना, तोड़ बैठना *She fell and fractured her ankle.* ○ *A water pipe fractured and flooded the bathroom.*

**fragile** /ˈfrædʒaɪl ˈफ्रैजाइल् / *adj.* easily damaged or broken सहज क्षतिग्रस्त होने या टूट जाने वाला; भंगुर

**fragment[1]** /ˈfrægmənt ˈफ्रैग्मन्ट् / *noun* [C] a small piece that has broken off or that comes from sth larger किसी वस्तु का टूटा हुआ टुकड़ा या बड़ी वस्तु का अंश *The archaeologists found fragments of Harappan pottery on the site.* ○ *I heard only a fragment of their conversation.*

**fragment[2]** /frægˈment फ्रैग्ˈमेन्ट् / *verb* [I, T] (*formal*) to break (sth) into small pieces (किसी वस्तु को), खंडों में तोड़ना या खंडित करना *The country is becoming increasingly fragmented by civil war.*

**fragrance** /ˈfreɪgrəns ˈफ्रेग्रन्स् / *noun* [C, U] a pleasant smell ख़ुशबू, सुगंध

**fragrant** /ˈfreɪgrənt ˈफ्रेग्रन्ट् / *adj.* having a pleasant smell ख़ुशबूदार, सुगंधित

**frail** /freɪl ˈफ्रेल् / *adj.* weak or not healthy दुर्बल या अस्वस्थ *My aunt is still very frail after her accident.*

**frailty** /ˈfreɪlti ˈफ्रेल्टि / *noun* [C, U] (*pl.* **frailties**) weakness of a person's body or character व्यक्ति के शरीर या चरित्र की दुर्बलता

**frame[1]** /freɪm फ्रेम् / *noun* [C] **1** a border of wood or metal that goes around the outside of a door, picture, window, etc. लकड़ी या धातु का चौखटा जो दरवाज़े, खिड़की आदि पर लगाया जाता है *a window frame* **2** the basic strong structure of a piece of furniture, building, vehicle, etc. which gives it its shape फ़र्नीचर, इमारत, वाहन आदि को उसका आकार-विशेष देने के लिए बुनियादी मज़बूत ढाँचा *the frame of a bicycle/an aircraft* ➪ **bicycle** पर चित्र देखिए। **3** [*usually pl.*] a structure made of plastic or metal that holds the two pieces of glass (**lenses**) in a pair of glasses प्लास्टिक या धातु से बना ऐनक का फ्रेम **4** [*usually sing.*] the basic shape of a human or animal body मानव या पशु के शरीर का आधारभूत ढाँचा *He has a large frame but he's not fat.*

IDM **frame of mind** a particular state or condition of your feelings; the mood भावनाओं की विशेष स्थिति; मनोदशा, मनःस्थिति *I'm not in the right frame of mind for a party. I'd prefer to be on my own.*

**frame[2]** /freɪm फ्रेम् / *verb* [T] **1** to put a border around sth (especially a picture or photograph) (विशेषतः चित्र या फ़ोटो पर) फ्रेम चढ़ाना *Let's have this photograph framed.* **2** (*usually passive*) to give false evidence against sb in order to make him/her seem guilty of a crime किसी के विरुद्ध झूठी गवाही देना (ताकि वह अपराधी लगे) *The man claimed that he had been framed by the police.* **3** (*formal*) to express sth in a particular way किसी बात को विशेष प्रकार से व्यक्त करना *The question was very carefully framed.*

**framework** /ˈfreɪmwɜːk ˈफ्रेम्वक् / *noun* [C] **1** the basic structure of sth that gives it shape and strength किसी वस्तु का बुनियादी ढाँचा जिससे वस्तु को एक शकल और मज़बूती मिलती है *A greenhouse is made of glass panels fixed in a metal framework.* ○ (*figurative*) *the basic framework of society* **2** a system of rules or ideas which help you decide what to do निर्णय के आधारभूत सिद्धांत, सैद्धांतिक आधार या रूपरेखा *The plan may be changed but it will provide a framework on which we can build.*

**franc** /fræŋk फ्रैङ्क् / *noun* [C] the unit of money that is used in France, Belgium, Switzerland and several other countries फ्रांस, बेलिजयम, स्विट्ज़रलैंड आदि कुछ देशों की मुद्रा की इकाई; फ्रैंक

**franchise** /ˈfræntʃaɪz ˈफ्रैन्चाइज़् / *noun* **1** [C, U] official permission to sell a company's goods or services in a particular area किसी विशेष क्षेत्र में कंपनी की वस्तुएँ बेचने या सेवाएँ उपलब्ध कराने की औपचारिक अनुमति *They have the franchise to sell this product in the southern region.* ○ *Most fast-food restaurants are operated* ***under franchise***. **2** [U] (*formal*) the right to vote in elections मताधिकार

**frank** /fræŋk फ्रैङ्क् / *adj.* showing your thoughts and feelings clearly; saying what you mean विचारों और भावों को स्पष्टता से व्यक्त करते हुए; अभीष्ट का अभिव्यंजक; स्पष्टकारी *To be perfectly frank with you, I don't think you'll pass your driving test.* ▶ **frankly** *adv.* स्पष्टता से *Please tell me frankly what you think about my idea.* ▶ **frankness** *noun* [U] स्पष्टता

**frantic** /ˈfræntɪk ˈफ़ैन्टिक् / *adj.* **1** extremely worried or frightened अत्यधिक चिंतित या भयभीत *The women went frantic when she couldn't find her purse.* ○ *frantic cries for help* **2** very busy or done in a hurry बहुत व्यस्त या जल्दबाज़ी में किया गया *a frantic search for the keys* ○ *We're not busy at work now, but things get frantic at Christmas.* ▸ **frantically** /-kli -कृलि / *adv.* व्यस्ततापूर्वक, चिंता व जल्दबाज़ी में

**fraternal** /frəˈtɜːnl फ्रˈटन्ल् / *adj.* (*formal*) connected with the relationship that exists between brothers; like a brother भाइयों का; भाइयों के बीच का; भाई जैसा *fraternal love/rivalry*

**fraternity** /frəˈtɜːnəti फ्रˈटनटि / *noun* (*pl.* **fraternities**) **1** [U] the feeling of friendship and support between people in the same group एक ही वर्ग के लोगों के बीच परस्पर मैत्री और सहायता की भावना; भाईचारा, भ्रातृभाव, बंधुता **2** [C] a group of people who share the same work or interests एक ही काम से जुड़े या अभिरुचि वाले लोगों का समुदाय; भ्रातृसंघ, बिरादरी *the medical fraternity*

**fraud** /frɔːd फ्रॉड् / *noun* **1** [C, U] (an act of) cheating sb in order to get money, etc. illegally ग़ैर-क़ानूनी ढंग से धन आदि ठगने की क्रिया; धोखाधड़ी *The accountant was sent to prison for fraud.* ○ *Massive amounts of money are lost every year in credit card frauds.* **2** [C] a person who tricks sb by pretending to be sb else कोई और होने का ढोंग करके ठगने वाला व्यक्ति; धोखेबाज़, चालबाज़, कपटी

**fraudulent** /ˈfrɔːdjələnt ˈफ्रॉड्यलन्ट् / *adj.* (*formal*) done in order to cheat sb; dishonest किसी को धोखा देने के लिए किया गया; कपटपूर्ण *the fraudulent use of stolen cheques*

**fraught** /frɔːt फ्रॉट् / *adj.* **1 fraught with sth** filled with sth unpleasant अरुचिकर बातों से परिपूर्ण *a situation fraught with danger/difficulty* **2** (used about people) worried and nervous; (used about a situation) very busy so that people become nervous (व्यक्ति) चिंतित और परेशान; (स्थिति) इतनी व्यस्ततापूर्ण कि लोग परेशान हो जाएँ *Things are usually fraught at work on Mondays.*

**fray¹** /freɪ फ्रे / *verb* [I, T] **1** if cloth, etc. frays or becomes frayed, some of the threads at the end start to come apart अत्यधिक प्रयोग से घिस जाने के कारण कपड़े आदि में से तार निकलने लगना; जीर्ण हो जाना *This shirt is beginning to fray at the cuffs.* ○ *a frayed rope* **2** if a person's nerves, etc. fray or become frayed, he/she starts to get annoyed थकान आदि से खीझ कर व्यक्ति का क्रोध में आने लगना *Tempers began to fray towards the end of the match.*

**fray²** /freɪ फ्रे / *noun* [*sing*] a fight, an argument or any lively action scene झगड़ा, बहस या कोई सक्रिय घटना-क्षेत्र *join the fray* ○ *The minister was forced to join the political fray.*

**freak¹** /friːk फ्रीक् / *noun* [C] **1** (*informal*) a person who has a very strong interest in sth किसी बात में अत्यधिक रुचि रखने वाला व्यक्ति; किसी रुचि के वशीभूत व्यक्ति; सनकी, कट्टर *a fitness/computer freak* ✪ पर्याय **fanatic** **2** a very unusual and strange event, person, animal, etc. अत्यंत असाधारण और विचित्र घटना, व्यक्ति, पशु आदि *a freak accident/storm/result* ○ *The other kids think Anshu's a freak because she doesn't watch TV.*

**freak²** /friːk फ्रीक् / *verb* [I, T] (*informal*) **freak (sb) (out)** to react very strongly to sth that makes you feel shocked, frightened, upset, etc.; to make sb react strongly स्तब्ध, भयभीत या बहुत परेशान करने वाली बात पर कठोर प्रतिक्रिया व्यक्त करना; किसी के द्वारा कठोर प्रतिक्रिया का कारण बनना *She freaked out when she heard the news.* ○ *The film 'Psycho' really freaked me out.*

**freckle** /ˈfrekl ˈफ्रेकल् / *noun* [C, *usually pl.*] a small brown spot on your skin त्वचा पर छोटा भूरा दाग़; चकत्ता *A lot of people with red hair have got freckles.* ➪ **mole** देखिए। ▸ **freckled** *adj.* चकत्तेदार

**free¹** /friː फ्री / *adj.* **1** not in prison, in a cage, etc.; not held or controlled बंधन-मुक्त; स्वतंत्र, आज़ाद *The government* **set** *Mandela* **free** *in 1989.* ○ *There is nowhere around here where dogs can run free.* **2 free (to do sth)** not controlled by the government, rules, etc. शासन, नियम आदि के अधीन नहीं; मुक्त, स्वतंत्र *There is free movement of people across the border.* ○ *free speech/press* **3** costing nothing निःशुल्क, मुफ़्त *Admission to the museum is free/free of charge.* ○ *Children under five usually travel free on trains.* **4** not busy or being used ख़ाली; व्यस्त या प्रयोग में नहीं *I'm afraid Mr Kapur is not free this afternoon.* ○ *I don't get much* **free time**. ○ *Is this seat free?* **5 free from/of sth** not having sth dangerous, unpleasant, etc. भय, चिंता, अरुचिकर आदि के प्रभाव से मुक्त *free of worries/responsibility* ○ *free from pain*

**IDM feel free** ➪ **feel 1** देखिए।

**free and easy** informal or relaxed अनौपचारिक या तनाव-मुक्त *The atmosphere in our office is very free and easy.*

**get, have, etc. a free hand** to get, have, etc. permission to make your own decisions about sth किसी को किसी बात पर निर्णय लेने में खुली छूट होना

**of your own free will** because you want to, not because sb forces you स्वेच्छा से; न कि किसी के दबाव में आकर

**free**[2] /friː फ्री / *verb* [T] **1 free sb/sth (from sth)** to let sb/sth leave or escape from a place where he/she/it is held बंदीगृह से छोड़ना; क़ैद से आज़ाद करना; बंधनमुक्त करना *to free a prisoner* ○ *The protesters freed the animals from their cages.* **2 free sb/sth of/from sth** to take away sth that is unpleasant from sb प्रतिकूल परिस्थिति से छुटकारा दिलाना *The medicine freed her from pain for a few hours.* **3 free sb/sth (up) for sth; free sb/sth (up) to do sth** to make sth available so that it can be used; to put sb in a position in which he/she can do sth उपयोग के लिए उपलब्ध कराना; किसी को कुछ करने की छूट देना

**free agent** *noun* [C] a person who can do what he/she wants because nobody else has the right to tell him/her what to do स्वेच्छा से काम करने के लिए स्वतंत्र व्यक्ति

**freedom** /ˈfriːdəm ˈफ्रीडम् / *noun* **1** [U] the state of not being held prisoner or controlled by sb else स्वतंत्रता, आज़ादी; दूसरे की क़ैद या नियंत्रण से मुक्ति *The opposition leader was given his freedom after 25 years.* **2** [C, U] the right or ability to do or say what you want स्वेच्छा से कुछ करने या कहने का अधिकार या योग्यता *You have the freedom to come and go as you please.* ○ *freedom of speech* ○ *the rights and freedoms of the individual* ➪ **liberty** देखिए। **3** [U] **freedom from sth** the state of not being affected by sth unpleasant प्रतिकूल परिस्थिति से मुक्ति *freedom from fear/hunger/pain* **4** [U] **the freedom of sth** the right to use sth with nothing to limit you किसी वस्तु के उपयोग की पूरी स्वतंत्रता *You can have the freedom of the whole house while we're away.*

**freedom fighter** *noun* [C] a person who belongs to a group that takes part in a movement to liberate a country from an unpopular government सत्ता परिवर्तन के लिए सक्रिय समुदाय का सदस्य; स्वतंत्रता सेनानी

**free enterprise** [U] the operation of private business without government control सरकारी नियंत्रण से मुक्त निजी आधार पर व्यापारिक गतिविधि; स्वतंत्र उद्यम

**freehand** /ˈfriːhænd ˈफ्रीहैन्ड् / *adj., adv.* (used about a drawing) done by hand, without the help of any instruments (चित्र) केवल हाथ से बनाया गया (उपकरणों के बिना) *a freehand sketch* ○ *to draw freehand*

**freehold** /ˈfriːhəʊld ˈफ्रीहोल्ड् / *noun* [C, U] the fact of owning a building or piece of land for a period of time that is not limited असीमित समय के लिए भवन या भूसंपति पर स्वामित्व; फ्रीहोल्ड, पूर्ण स्वामित्तव, मालिकाना हक़ *Do you own the freehold of this house?* ▶ **freehold** *adj., adv.* भवन या भूक्षेत्र पर पूर्ण स्वामित्व वाला, पूर्ण स्वामित्व की रीति से, मालिकाना हक़ के तौर पर *a freehold property* ○ *to buy a house freehold* ➪ **leasehold** देखिए।

**freekick** *noun* [C] (in football, rugby etc.) a situation in which a player of one team is allowed to kick the ball because a member of the other team has broken a rule (फ़ुटबॉल, रगबी आदि में) एक टीम के खिलाड़ी द्वारा नियम भंग पर दूसरी टीम के खिलाड़ी को गेंद को किक मारने का अवसर; फ्री किक

**freelance** /ˈfriːlɑːns ˈफ्रीलान्स् / *adj., adv.* earning money by selling your services or work to different organizations rather than being employed by a single company किसी एक संगठन का कर्मचारी न होकर विभिन्न संगठनों को शुल्क पर अपनी सेवाएँ देने से संबंधित; स्वच्छंद कार्य से संबंधित *a freelance journalist* ○ *She works freelance.* ▶ **freelance** (*also* **freelancer**) *noun* [C] स्वतंत्र रूप से (कर्मचारी न होकर) विभिन्न संस्थाओं को शुल्क पर अपनी सेवाएँ देने वाला व्यक्ति; स्वच्छंद कार्यकर्त्ता ▶ **freelance** *verb* [I] इस तरह से कार्य करना

**freely** /ˈfriːli ˈफ्रीलि / *adv.* **1** in a way that is not controlled or limited अनियंत्रित या असीमित रीति से; स्वतंत्रतापूर्वक *He is the country's first freely elected president for 40 years.* **2** without trying to avoid the truth even though it might be embarrassing; in an honest way सचाई को न छिपाते हुए (भले ही शरमिंदगी उठानी पड़े); सचाई से; ईमानदारी से *I freely admit that I made a mistake.*

**free market** *noun* [C] an economic system in which the price of goods and services is affected by supply and demand rather than controlled by the government सरकारी नियत्रंण के स्थान पर माँग और आपूर्ति के अनुसार वस्तुओं और सेवाओं के मूल्य-निर्धारण की अर्थिक प्रणाली; निर्बोध या मुक्त बाज़ार

**free port** *noun* [C] a port at which tax is not paid on goods that have been brought there for a short time before being sent to a different country निःशुल्क बंदरगाह

**free-range** *adj.* (used about farm birds or their eggs) kept or produced in a place where birds can move around freely (पक्षी या अंडे) निबाध गतिविधि की सुविधा वाले स्थान पर रखे हुए *free-range hens/eggs* ➪ **battery** देखिए।

**free speech** *noun* [U] the right to express any opinion in public जनता के सामने अपने विचार रखने का अधिकार; स्वतंत्र अभिव्यक्ति

**free trade** *noun* [U] a system of international commercial activity in which there are no limits or taxes on imports and exports अंतरराष्ट्रीय व्यापार-प्रणाली जिसमें आयात-निर्यात पर न कर लगता है न उसकी मात्रा पर नियंत्रण; मुक्त व्यापार *a free-trade agreement/area*

**freeway** /ˈfriːweɪ ˈफ्रीवे / (*AmE*) = **motorway**

**freeze[1]** /fri:z ˈफ्रीज़्/ *verb* (*pt* **froze** /frəʊz फ्रोज़्/; *pp* **frozen** /ˈfrəʊzn ˈफ्रोज़्न्/) **1** [I, T] to become hard (and often change into ice) because of extreme cold; to make sth do this अत्यधिक सर्दी के कारण जम जाना (और प्रायः बर्फ़ बन जाना); किसी वस्तु को इस प्रकार जमा देना *Water freezes at 0° Celsius.* ○ *The ground was **frozen solid** for most of the winter.* ○ *frozen peas/fish/food* **2** [I] used with 'it' to describe extremely cold weather when water turns into ice अत्यधिक ठंडे मौसम को दर्शाने के लिए (वाक्य में 'it' के साथ प्रयुक्त) *I think it's going to freeze tonight.* **3** [I, T] to be very cold or to die from cold बहुत सर्दी होना या सर्दी के कारण मर जाना *It was so cold on the mountain that we thought we would **freeze to death**.* ○ *Turn the heater up a bit—I'm **frozen stiff**.* **4** [I] to stop moving suddenly and completely because you are frightened or in danger डर के मारे या ख़तरे के कारण गति का एकाएक और पूर्णतया अवरुद्ध हो जाना *The terrible scream made her freeze with terror.* ○ *Suddenly the man pulled out a gun and shouted 'Freeze!'* **5** [T] to keep the money you earn, prices, etc. at a fixed level for a certain period of time विशेष अवधि के लिए आय, मूल्य, ख़र्च आदि को स्थिर रखना *Spending on defence has been frozen for one year.*

**freeze[2]** /fri:z ˈफ्रीज़्/ *noun* [C] **1** a period of weather when the temperature stays below 0°C (**freezing point**) शीत लहर जब तापमान 0°C (हिमांक) से भी कम रहता है **2** the fixing of the money you earn, prices, etc. at one level for a certain period of time विशेष अवधि के लिए आय, मूल्य आदि को स्थिर रखने की क्रिया *a wage/pay/price freeze*

**freeze-dried** *adj.* (used about food or drink) frozen and then dried very quickly, so that it can be kept for a long time (खाद्य और पेय पदार्थ) ठंडा कर जमाए गए और फिर बहुत शीघ्र सुखाए गए (ताकि लंबे समय तक वे सुरक्षित रहें); प्रशीतित और निर्जलीकृत

**freezer** /ˈfri:zə(r) ˈफ्रीज़(र्)/ (*also* **deep freeze**) *noun* [C] a large box or cupboard in which you can store food for a long time at a temperature below 0° Celsius (**freezing point**) so that it stays frozen एक बड़ा बक्सा या अलमारी जिसमें खाद्य पदार्थों को हिमांक से नीचे के तापमान पर रखा जाता है ताकि वे सुरक्षित रहें; फ्रीज़र ➪ **fridge** देखिए।

**freezing[1]** /ˈfri:zɪŋ ˈफ्रीज़िङ्/ *adj.* (*informal*) very cold बहुत ठंडा *Can we turn the central heating on? I'm freezing.* ○ *Put a coat on, it's absolutely freezing outside.*

**freezing[2]** /ˈfri:zɪŋ ˈफ्रीज़िङ्/ (*also* **freezing point**) *noun* [U] the temperature at which water freezes तापमान जिस पर पानी जम जाता है; हिमांक *Last night the temperature fell to six degrees below freezing.*

**freight** /freɪt फ्रेट्/ *noun* [U] goods that are carried from one place to another by ship, lorry, etc. the system for carrying goods in this way जहाज़, ट्रक आदि द्वारा ढोया जाने वाला माल; इस प्रकार माल ढोने की प्रणाली *Your order will be sent by air freight.* ○ *a freight train*

**freight car** (*AmE*) = **wagon**

**freighter** /ˈfreɪtə(r) ˈफ्रेट(र्)/ *noun* [C] a ship or an aircraft that carries only goods and not passengers केवल माल (यात्री नहीं) ढोने वाला जहाज़ या विमान

**French horn** *noun* [C] a metal (**brass**) musical instrument that consists of a long tube curved around in a circle with a wide opening at the end सींगनुमा लंबी नली वाला पीतल से बना एक वाद्य जिसके अंत में बड़ा छेद होता है; फ्रेंच हॉर्न

**French window** (*AmE* **French door**) *noun* [C] one of a pair of glass doors that open onto a garden or **balcony** छज्जे या बग़ीचे में खुलने वाला शीशे का दरवाज़ा

**frenzied** /ˈfrenzid ˈफ्रेन्ज़िड्/ *adj.* that is wild and out of control उत्तेजित और बेक़ाबू *a frenzied attack* ○ *frenzied activity*

**frenzy** /ˈfrenzi ˈफ्रेन्ज़ि/ *noun* [*sing.*,U] a state of great emotion or activity that is not under control नियंत्रण-विहीन अत्यधिक उत्तेजना या हलचल; उन्माद, पागलपन

**frequency** /ˈfri:kwənsi ˈफ्रीक्वन्सि/ *noun* (*pl.* **frequencies**) **1** [U] the number of times sth happens in a particular period विशेष अवधि में होने वाली किसी क्रिया की आवृत्ति संख्या; बारंबारता *Fatal accidents have decreased in frequency in recent years.* **2** [U] the fact that sth happens often बार-बार कुछ घटित होने का तथ्य *The frequency of child deaths from cancer near the nuclear power station is being investigated.* **3** [C, U] the rate at which a sound wave or radio wave moves up and down (**vibrates**) ध्वनि-तरंगों या रेडियो तरंगों के कंपन की दर *high-frequency/low-frequency sounds* ➪ **wavelength** देखिए।

**frequent[1]** /ˈfri:kwənt ˈफ्रीक्वन्ट्/ *adj.* happening often प्रायः घटित होने वाला, बार-बार होने वाला; बहुल *His visits became less frequent.* ✪ विलोम **infrequent** ▶ **frequently** *adv.* बार-बार

**frequent[2]** /friˈkwent फ्रिˈक्वेन्ट्/ *verb* [T] (*formal*) to go to a place often किसी स्थान पर बार-बार जाना *He spent most of his evenings in Paris frequenting bars and clubs.*

**fresh** /freʃ फ्रेश् / *adj.* **1** (used especially about food) produced or picked very recently; not frozen or in a tin (विशेषतः खाद्य पदार्थ) ताज़ा; जो ठंडा किया हुआ या डिब्बाबंद न हो *fresh bread/fruit/flowers* ➪ **stale** देखिए। **2** left somewhere or experienced recently हाल ही में कहीं पर छूटा हुआ या अनुभव किया गया *fresh blood/footprints* ○ *Write a few notes while the lecture is still* ***fresh in*** *your* ***mind***. **3** new and different नया और भिन्न *They have decided to* ***make a fresh start*** *in a different town.* ○ *I'm sure he'll have some fresh ideas on the subject.* **4** (used about water) without salt; not sea water (पानी) जो खारा न हो; मीठा; समुद्री जल नहीं **5** pleasantly clean or bright एकदम साफ़, चमकदार या रोशनीदार *Open the window and let some* ***fresh air*** *in.* **6** not tired तरोताज़ा, न कि थका हुआ *I'll think about the problem again in the morning when I'm fresh.* **7 fresh from/out of sth** having just finished sth हाल ही में कुछ प्राप्त या समाप्त किया गया *Life isn't easy for a young teacher fresh from university.* ▶ **freshly** *adv.* तरोताज़ा; कुछ ही देर पहले *freshly baked bread* ▶ **freshness** *noun* [U] ताज़ापन, नयापन

IDM **break fresh/new ground** ➪ **ground**[1] देखिए।

**freshen** /ˈfreʃn ˈफ्रेश्न् / *verb* [T] **freshen sth (up)** to make sth cleaner or brighter किसी वस्तु को अधिक साफ़, शुद्ध या चमकदार बनाना

PHR V **freshen up** to wash and make yourself clean and tidy नहा-धोकर स्वच्छ और चुस्त होना

**fresher** /ˈfreʃə(r) ˈफ्रेश(र्) / *noun* [C] (*BrE*) a student who is in his/her first year at university, college, etc. विश्वविद्यालय, कॉलेज आदि में प्रथम वर्ष का छात्र

**freshman** /ˈfreʃmən ˈफ्रेश्मन् / *noun* [C] (*pl.* **-men** /-mən -मन् /) (*AmE*) a student who is in his/her first year at college, high school, university, etc. विश्वविद्यालय, कॉलेज आदि में प्रथम वर्ष का छात्र; नवागंतुक

**freshwater** /ˈfreʃwɔːtə(r) ˈफ्रेश्वॉट(र्) / *adj.* (*only before a noun*) **1** living in water that is not the sea and is not salty मीठे पानी में रहने वाला; तालाब या नदी का, न कि समुद्र का *freshwater fish* **2** having water that is not salty मीठे पानी वाला, न कि खारे पानी वाला *freshwater lakes/pools* ➪ **saltwater** देखिए।

**fret**[1] /fret फ्रेट् / *verb* [I] (**fretting; fretted**) **fret (about/at/over sth)** to be worried and unhappy about sth किसी विषय में चिंतित और दुखी होना

**fret**[2] /fret फ्रेट् / *noun* [C] one of the bars across the long thin part of a guitar, etc. that show you where to put your fingers to produce a particular sound गिटार आदि के लंबे संकरे भाग के आर-पार लगी छड़ जो विशेष ध्वनि को उत्पन्न करने के लिए अंगुली रखने के लिए प्रयुक्त होती है ➪ पृष्ठ 789 पर चित्र देखिए।

**fretsaw** /ˈfretsɔː ˈफ्रेट्सॉ / *noun* [C] a tool with a narrow blade, used for cutting patterns into wood for decoration पतली टेढ़ी आरी

**fretwork** /ˈfretwɜːk ˈफ्रेट्वक् / *noun* [U] patterns cut into wood, metal, etc. to decorate it; the process of making these patterns लकड़ी आदि में बनाए गए जाली आदि सजावटी पैटर्न; पैटर्न बनाने की प्रक्रिया; जाली का काम; लकड़ी आदि की नक़्क़ाशी

**Fri.** *abbr.* Friday शुक्रवार

**friction** /ˈfrɪkʃn ˈफ्रिक्श्न् / *noun* [U] **1** the rubbing of one surface or thing against another एक वस्तु की सतह का दूसरी से रगड़ खाना; रगड़, घर्षण *You have to put oil in the engine to reduce friction between the moving parts.* **2 friction (between A and B)** disagreement between people or groups लोगों या समूहों में मतभेद *There is a lot of friction between the older and younger members of staff.*

**Friday** /ˈfraɪdeɪ; -di ˈफ्राइडे; -डि / *noun* [C, U] (*abbr.* **Fri.**) the day of the week after Thursday शुक्रवार

> NOTE दिनों के नामों का पहला अक्षर बड़ा होता है। दिनों के वाक्य-प्रयोग के उदाहरणों के लिए **Monday** की प्रविष्टि देखिए।

**fridge** /frɪdʒ फ्रिज् / (*formal* **refrigerator,** *AmE* **icebox**) *noun* [C] a metal container with a door in which food, etc. is kept cold (but not frozen) so that it stays fresh दरवाज़ायुक्त धातु का पात्र जिसमें खाद्य पदार्थ को ठंडा बनाए रखा जाता है (परंतु जमाकर नहीं) ताकि वह खराब न हो; रेफ्रिजरेटर, फ्रिज ➪ **freezer** देखिए।

**fried**[1] ➪ **fry**[1] का past tense और past participle रूप

**fried**[2] /fraɪd फ्राइड् / *adj.* (used about food) cooked in hot fat or oil (भोजन) तेल में पकाया गया *a fried egg*

**friend** /frend फ्रेन्ड् / *noun* [C] **1** a person that you know and like (not a member of your family), and who likes you मित्र, दोस्त (जो परिवार का सदस्य नहीं है) *Seema and I are* ***old friends***. *We were at school together.* ○ *We're only inviting* ***close friends*** *and relatives to the wedding.* ○ *One of my friends told me about this restaurant.* ➪ **boyfriend, girlfriend** और **penfriend** देखिए। **2 a friend of/to sth** a person who supports an organization, a charity, etc., especially by giving money; a person who supports a particular idea, etc. किसी संगठन आदि का समर्थक (विशेषतः धन आदि द्वारा सहायता करने वाला); विशेष विचारधारा का समर्थक *the Friends of the Churchill Hospital*

IDM **be/make friends (with sb)** to be/become a friend (of sb) (किसी का) मित्र बनना या बनाना *Sachin is rather shy and finds it hard to make friends.*

**a false friend** ➪ **false** देखिए।

**friendly**[1] /ˈfrendli ˈफ़्रेन्ड्लि/ *adj.* (**friendlier; friendliest**) **1 friendly to/toward(s) sb** behaving in a kind and open way (व्यवहार) जिसमें आत्मीयता और खुलापन हो; मैत्रीपूर्ण, दोस्ताना *Everyone here has been very friendly towards us.* **2** showing kindness in a way that makes people feel happy and relaxed प्रसन्नता और शांति देने वाली आत्मीयता से युक्त; सुखद और प्रीतिकर *a friendly smile/atmosphere* ✪ विलोम **unfriendly** (अर्थ संख्या **1** और **2** के लिए) **3 friendly with sb** treating sb as a friend किसी के साथ मैत्रीपूर्ण व्यवहार करते हुए *Udhav* ***become*** *quite* ***friendly*** *with the boy next door.* ○ *Are you* ***on friendly terms*** *with your neighbours?* **4** (*in compounds*) helpful to sb/sth; not harmful to sth किसी व्यक्ति या वस्तु के अनुकूल; जो किसी के लिए हानिकर न हो *Our computer is extremely* ***user-friendly.*** ○ *ozone-friendly sprays* **5** in which the people, teams, etc. taking part are not competing seriously जिसमें लोग, टीमें आदि केवल मनोरंजन हेतु भाग लें (गंभीर स्पर्धाभाव से नहीं) *a friendly argument* ○ *I've organized a friendly match against my brother's team.* ▶ **friendliness** *noun* [U] मैत्रीपूर्णता, दोस्तानापन

**friendly**[2] /ˈfrendli ˈफ़्रेन्ड्लि/ *noun* [C] (*pl.* **friendlies**) a sports match that is not part of a serious competition औपचारिक स्पर्धा का भाग न होकर मैत्रीभाव वाला खेल; फ्रेंडली मैच

**friendship** /ˈfrendʃɪp ˈफ़्रेन्ड्शिप्/ *noun* **1** [C] **a friendship (with sb); a friendship (between A and B)** a relationship between people who are friends मित्रता; दोस्ती *a close/lasting/lifelong friendship* **2** [U] the state of being friends मित्र होने का भाव; मित्र-भावना *Our relationship is based on friendship, not love.*

**frigate** /ˈfrɪgət ˈफ़्रिगट्/ *noun* [C] a small fast ship in the navy that travels with other ships in order to protect them नौसेना में द्रुतगामी छोटा जहाज़ जो अन्य जहाज़ों की सुरक्षा के लिए उनके साथ जाता है

**fright** /fraɪt फ़्राइट्/ *noun* [C, U] a sudden feeling of fear or shock सहसा उत्पन्न भय या सदमा *I hope I didn't* ***give you a fright*** *when I shouted.* ○ *The child cried out* ***in fright.***

**frighten** /ˈfraɪtn ˈफ़्राइट्न्/ *verb* [T] to make sb/sth afraid or shocked व्यक्ति या वस्तु को भयभीत कर देना या सदमा पहुँचाना *That programme about crime really frightened me.*

PHRV **frighten sb/sth away off** to cause a person or animal to go away by frightening him/her/it मनुष्य या पशु को डराकर भगा देना *Walk quietly so that you don't frighten the birds away.*

**frightened** /ˈfraɪtnd ˈफ़्राइट्न्ड्/ *adj.* **1** full of fear or worry बहुत भयभीत या चिंतित *Frightened children were calling for their mothers.* ○ *I was frightened that they would think that I was rude.* **2 frightened of sb/sth** afraid of a particular person, thing or situation किसी विशेष व्यक्ति, वस्तु या स्थिति से डरने वाला *When I was young I was frightened of spiders.* ➪ **afraid** पर नोट देखिए।

**frightening** /ˈfraɪtnɪŋ ˈफ़्राइट्निङ्/ *adj.* making you feel afraid or shocked डराने या सदमा पहुँचाने वाला *a frightening experience* ○ *It's frightening that time passes so quickly.*

**frightful** /ˈfraɪtfl ˈफ़्राइट्फ़्ल्/ *adj.* (*old-fashioned*) **1** very bad or unpleasant बहुत बुरा या अप्रिय *The weather this summer has been frightful.* **2** (used for emphasizing sth) very bad or great (किसी बात पर बल देने के लिए प्रयुक्त) बहुत ख़राब या अत्यधिक *We're in a frightful rush.*

**frightfully** /ˈfraɪtfəli ˈफ़्राइट्फ़लि/ *adv.* (*old-fashioned*) very बहुत, अत्यधिक *I'm frightfully sorry.*

**frigid** /ˈfrɪdʒɪd ˈफ़्रिजिड्/ *adj.* **1** (usually used about a woman) unable to enjoy sex (स्त्री) यौन-आनंद के अनुभव में असमर्थ; मंदकामी **2** not showing any emotion भावशून्य, उमंग-रहित

**frill** /ˈfrɪl ˈफ़्रिल्/ *noun* [C] **1** a decoration for the edge of a dress, shirt, etc. which is made by forming many folds in a narrow piece of cloth किसी पोशाक के सिरे पर कपड़े की पट्टी की अनेक तहों से बनाई गई सजावटी किनारी; झालर **2** [*usually pl.*] something that is added for decoration that you feel is not necessary अनावश्यक व दिखावटी सजावट *We just want a plain simple meal—no frills.* ▶ **frilly** *adj.* सजावटदार *a frilly dress*

**fringe**[1] /frɪndʒ ˈफ़्रिन्ज्/ *noun* [C] **1** (*AmE* **bangs** [*pl.*]) the part of your hair that is cut so that it hangs over your forehead इस प्रकार काटे गए बाल कि माथे पर लटकें *Your hair looks better with a fringe.* **2** a border for decoration on a piece of clothing, etc. that is made of lots of hanging threads बहुत सारे लटकते धागों से पोशाक पर बनाया गया सजावटी किनारा **3** the outer edge of an area or a group that is a long way from the centre or from what is usual किसी क्षेत्र या व्यक्ति-समूह का बाहरी किनारा जो केंद्रबिंदु से काफ़ी दूर है; सीमांत, अंतिम छोर *Some people* ***on the fringes of*** *the coalition government are opposed to the policy on disinvestment.*

**fringe**[2] /frɪndʒ ˈफ़्रिन्ज्/ *verb*

IDM **be fringed with sth** to have sth as a border or around the edge किसी वस्तु का (किसी अन्य वस्तु का) झालर की तरह किनारा बन जाना *The lake was fringed with pine trees.*

**fringe benefit** *noun* [C, *usually pl.*] an extra thing that is given to an employee in addition to the money he/she earns कर्मचारी को नियमित वेतन के अतिरिक्त मिलने वाली सुविधाएँ; अतिरिक्त सुविधा

**NOTE** इस अर्थ में **perk** अधिक अनौपचारिक शब्द है।

**frisk** /frɪsk फ़्रिस्क् / *verb* **1** [T] to pass your hands over sb's body in order to search for hidden weapons, drugs, etc. गुप्त हथियारों आदि का पता लगाने के लिए किसी के शरीर को हाथों से टटोलना, तलाशी लेना **2** [I] (used about an animal or child) to play and jump about happily and with a lot of energy (पशु या शिशु का) ख़ुशी के मारे ख़ूब उछल-कूद करना

**frisky** /ˈfrɪski ˈफ़्रिस्कि / *adj.* full of life and wanting to play ज़िंदादिल और उछल-कूद मचाने वाला

**fritter** /ˈfrɪtə(r) ˈफ़्रिट(र्) / *verb*

**PHRV** **fritter sth away (on sth)** to waste time or money on things that are not important बेकार की चीज़ों या बातों पर समय और धन बर्बाद करना

**frivolity** /frɪˈvɒləti फ़्रिˈव़ॉलटि / *noun* [U] silly behaviour (especially when you should be serious) ओछा या हलकेपन का व्यवहार (विशेषतः जब गंभीरता अपेक्षित हो)

**frivolous** /ˈfrɪvələs ˈफ़्रिव़लस् / *adj.* not serious; silly अगंभीर; मूर्खतापूर्ण

**frizzy** /ˈfrɪzi ˈफ़्रिज़ि / *adj.* (used about hair) very curly (बाल) बहुत घुंघराले

**fro** /frəʊ फ़्रो / *adv.*

**IDM** **to and fro** ➪ **to** देखिए।

**frock** /frɒk फ़्रॉक् / *noun* [C] (*old-fashioned*) (*especially BrE*) a dress एक पोशाक, फ़्रॉक *a party frock*

**frog** /frɒg फ़्रॉग् / *noun* [C] a small animal with smooth skin and long back legs that it uses for jumping. Frogs live in or near water मेंढक ➪ **amphibian** पर चित्र देखिए।

**frogman** /ˈfrɒgmən ˈफ़्रॉगमन् / *noun* [C] (*pl.* **-men** /-mən -मन् /) a person whose job is to work under the surface of water wearing special rubber clothes and using breathing equipment विशेष प्रकार की रबर की पोशाक पहने और सांस लेने में सहायक उपकरण के साथ गहरे पानी में काम करने वाला व्यक्ति; गोताख़ोर *Police frogmen searched the river.*

**frogspawn** /ˈfrɒgspɔːn ˈफ़्रॉगस्पॉन् / *noun* [U] an almost transparent substance that is between a liquid and a solid and contains the eggs of a **frog** मेंढ़क के अंडों की थैली जो लगभग पारदर्शी, और द्रव तथा ठोस अंशों के बीच में स्थित होती है ➪ **ambhibian** पर चित्र देखिए।

**frolic** /ˈfrɒlɪk ˈफ़्रॉलिक् / *verb* [I] to behave in a playful way विनोदी व्यवहार करना, खेलकूद करना *A group of happy children were frolicking in the park.*

▶ **frolic** *noun* [C, *usually pl.*] विनोदी व्यवहार, उल्लास

**from** /frəm; *strong form* frɒm फ़्रम्; प्रबल रूप फ़्रॉम् / *prep.* **1** showing the place, direction or time that sb/sth starts or started स्थान, दिशा या समय की दृष्टि से किसी व्यक्ति या वस्तु के कुछ आरंभ करने या होने का सूचक; से *a cold wind from the east* ○ *Water was dripping from the tap.* ○ *Sanjay's on holiday from next Friday.* ○ *The supermarket is open* ***from*** *8 a.m.* ***till*** *8 p.m. every day.* **2** showing the person who sent or gave sth उस व्यक्ति का सूचक जो किसी को कुछ देता या भेजता है; से *I borrowed this jacket from my sister.* ○ *a phone call from my father* **3** showing the origin of sb/sth व्यक्ति या वस्तु के मूल स्थान या स्रोत का सूचक; का/से *'Where do you come from?' 'I'm from Kerala.'* ○ *cheeses from France and Italy* ○ *quotations from Shakespeare* **4** showing the material which is used to make sth उस वस्तु का सूचक जिससे कोई वस्तु बनाई जाती है; से *Paper is* ***made from*** *wood.* ○ *This sauce is made from mint and tamarind.*

**NOTE** **Made of** से उस सामग्री का संकेत होता है जो किसी निर्मित वस्तु का रूप धारण करती है—*a table made of wood* ○ *a house made of bricks*

**5** showing the distance between two places दो स्थानों के बीच दूरी का सूचक; से *The house is five kilometres from the town centre.* ○ *I work not far from here.* **6** showing the point at which a series of prices, figures, etc., start उस बिंदु का सूचक जहाँ से क़ीमतों, अंकों आदि की शृंखला आरंभ होती है; से *Our prices start from Rs 250 a bottle.* ○ *Tickets cost from Rs 25 to Rs 125.* **7** showing the state of sb/sth before a change व्यक्ति या वस्तु की उस स्थिति का सूचक जहाँ किसी बात में बदलाव आया; से *The time of the meeting has been changed* ***from*** *7* ***to*** *8 o'clock.* ○ *The article was translated* ***from*** *Malayalam* ***into*** *English.* ○ *Things have gone* ***from bad to worse.*** **8** showing that sb/sth is taken away, removed or separated from sb/sth else किसी व्यक्ति या वस्तु का किसी अन्य व्यक्ति या वस्तु से अलग होने या किए जाने का सूचक; से *Children don't like being separated from their parents for a long period.* ○ *(in mathematics) 8 from 12 leaves 4.* **9** showing sth that you want to avoid उस स्थिति का सूचक जिससे कोई बचना चाहता है; से *There was no shelter from the wind.* ○ *This game will stop you from getting bored.* **10** showing the cause of sth किसी स्थिति के कारण का सूचक; से *People in the camps are suffering from* *hunger and cold.* **11** showing the reason for making a judgement or forming an opinion कोई निर्णय करने या राय बताने के कारण का सूचक; से *You can tell quite a lot from a person's handwriting.* **12** showing the difference between two people, places or things दो व्यक्तियों, स्थानों या वस्तुओं के बीच अंतर का सूचक *Can you tell margarine from butter? ○ Is Bengali very different from Oriya?*

**IDM from... on** starting at a particular time and continuing for ever विशिष्ट समय-बिंदु से आरंभ होकर हमेशा के लिए रहने वाला *She never spoke to him again* ***from that day on.*** *○* ***From now on*** *you must earn your own living.*

**frond** /frɒnd फ्रॉन्ड्/ *noun* [C] **1** a long leaf, often divided into parts along the edge, of some plants or trees कुछ पौधों या वृक्षों का लंबा पत्ता जो किनारे से प्रायः विभाजित होता है *the fronds of a palm tree* **2** a long piece of **seaweed** that looks like one of these leaves पत्ते जैसी लंबी समुद्री घास

**front¹** /frʌnt फ्रन्ट्/ *noun* **1 the front** [C, *usually sing.*] the side or surface of sth/sb that faces forward किसी व्यक्ति या वस्तु का सामने दीखने वाला हिस्सा *a dress with buttons down the front ○ the front of a building* (= the front wall) *○ a card with flowers* ***on the front*** *○ She slipped on the stairs and spilt coffee all down her front.* **2 the front** [C, *usually sing.*] the most forward part of sth; the area that is just outside of or before sb/sth किसी वस्तु का सबसे अगला हिस्सा; सामने का या बाहर का इलाक़ा *Young children should not travel* ***in the front of*** *the car. ○ There is a small garden* ***at the front of*** *the house.*

> **NOTE On the front of** का अर्थ है 'किसी वस्तु की सामने वाली सतह पर'—*The number is shown on the front of the bus.*
> **In front (of sth)** का अर्थ है, किसी अन्य व्यक्ति या वस्तु से अधिक आगे; किसी अन्य व्यक्ति या वस्तु के सामने—*There were three people in front of me in the queue. ○ A car has stopped in front of the bus.*
> **At/In the front (of sth)** का अर्थ है 'किसी वस्तु के अंदर के सबसे अगले हिस्से में,'—*The driver sits at the front of the bus.*
> इन वाक्यों को भी देखिए—*The teacher usually stands in* ***front*** *of the class. ○ The noisy children were asked to sit at the front of the class* (= in the front seats).

**3** [C] a particular area of activity किसी गतिविधि विशेष का कार्यक्षेत्र *Things are difficult* ***on the*** *domestic/political/economic* ***front*** *at the moment. ○ Progress has been made* ***on all fronts.*** **4 the front** [*sing.*] the line or area where fighting takes place in a war वह क्षेत्र जहाँ युद्ध लड़ाई होती है; लड़ाई का मोर्चा, युद्धक्षेत्र *to be sent to the front* **5** [*sing.*] a way of behaving that hides your true feelings ऐसा व्यवहार जो सच्ची भावनाओं को व्यक्त न होने दे; छद्म आचरण; बाहरी दिखावा *His brave words were just a front. He was really feeling very nervous.* **6** [C] a line or area where warm air and cold air meet ऐसी रेखा या क्षेत्र जहाँ गरम और ठंडी हवा मिलती है ***A cold front*** *is moving in from the north.*

**IDM back to front** ➪ **back¹** देखिए।

**in front** further forward than sb/sth; ahead किसी से और आगे; आगे *Some of the children ran on in front. ○ After three laps the Kenyan runner was in front.*

**in front of sb/sth 1** in a position further forward than but close to sb/sth किसी व्यक्ति या वस्तु से और आगे परंतु उसके पास की स्थिति *The bus stops right in front of our house. ○ Don't stand in front of the television. ○ The book was open in front of her on the desk.* **2** if you do sth in front of sb, you do it when that person is there in the same room or place as you एक ही स्थान पर किसी अन्य व्यक्ति की उपस्थिति में; के सामने *I couldn't talk about that in front of my parents.*

**up front** (*informal*) as payment before sth is done काम शुरू करने से पहले भुगतान के रूप में *I want half the money up front and half when the job is finished.*

**front²** /frʌnt फ्रन्ट्/ *adj.* (*only before a noun*) of or at the **front¹ 2** सामने या सामने का *the front door/garden/room ○ sit in the front row ○ front teeth*

**frontage** /ˈfrʌntɪdʒ ˈफ्रन्टिज्/ *noun* [C, U] the front of a building, especially when this faces a road or river भवन का सामने का हिस्सा, विशेषतः जब वह सड़क या नदी के सामने हो

**frontal** /ˈfrʌntl ˈफ्रन्ट्ल्/ *adj.* (*not before a noun*) from the front आगे से *a frontal attack*

**frontier** /ˈfrʌntɪə(r) ˈफ्रन्टिअ(र्)/ *noun* **1** [C] **the frontier (between A and B)** the line where one country joins another; border वह रेखा जहाँ एक देश की सीमा दूसरे देश की सीमा से लगती है; सीमारेखा *the end of frontier controls in Europe* ➪ **border** पर नोट देखिए। **2 the frontiers** [*pl.*] the limit between what we do and do not know हमारे ज्ञान और अज्ञान के बीच की सीमा रेखा *Scientific research is constantly* ***pushing back the frontiers of*** *our knowledge about the world.*

**front-page** *adj.* interesting or important enough to appear on the front page of a newspaper रोचकता और महत्त्व की दृष्टि से समाचार-पत्र के पहले पन्ने पर छपने लायक; मुख पृष्ठ का *front-page news/headlines*

**frost**[1] /frɒst फ्रॉस्ट्/ *noun* [C, U] the weather condition when the temperature falls below 0° Celsius (**freezing point**) and a thin layer of ice forms on the ground and other surfaces, especially at night हिमांक से नीचे के तापमान वाला मौसम जिसमें (विशेषतः रात के समय) ज़मीन पर बर्फ़ की हलकी परत जम जाती है; पाला *There was a* ***hard frost*** *last night.* ○ *It will be a chilly night with some* ***ground frost****.*

**frost**[2] /frɒst फ्रॉस्ट्/ *verb* [T] = **ice 2**

PHR V **frost over/up** to become covered with a thin layer of ice बर्फ़ की पतली परत से ढक जाना *The window has frosted over/up.* ➪ **defrost** देखिए।

**frostbite** /ˈfrɒstbaɪt ˈफ्रॉस्ट्बाइट्/ *noun* [U] a serious medical condition of the fingers, toes, etc. that is caused by very low temperatures बहुत ठंड के कारण अंगुलियों आदि का गल जाना; शीतक्षत

**frosted** /ˈfrɒstɪd ˈफ्रॉस्टिड्/ *adj.* (used about glass or a window) with a special surface so you can not see through it (शीशा या खिड़की) अपारदर्शी

**frosting** /ˈfrɒstɪŋ ˈफ्रॉस्टिङ्/ = **icing**

**frosty** /ˈfrɒsti ˈफ्रास्टि/ *adj.* **1** very cold, with frost बहुत ठंडा, पाले वाला *a cold and frosty morning* **2** cold and unfriendly रूखा और अमैत्रीपूर्ण *a frosty welcome*

**froth**[1] /frɒθ फ्रॉथ्/ *noun* [U] a mass of small white bubbles on the top of a liquid, etc. द्रव आदि पर छोटे सफ़ेद बुलबुलों का ढेर; झाग ▶ **frothy** *adj.* झागदार *frothy beer* ○ *a frothy cappuccino*

**froth**[2] /frɒθ फ्रॉथ्/ *verb* [I] to have or produce a mass of white bubbles झाग होना या झाग पैदा करना *The mad dog was frothing at the mouth.*

**frown** /fraʊn फ्राउन्/ *verb* [I] to show you are angry, serious, etc. by making lines appear on your forehead above your nose ऐसे क्रोध प्रदर्शित करना कि माथे पर रेखाएँ दिखाई देने लगें; भौंहें तन जाना, त्योरी चढ़ना ▶ **frown** *noun* [C] त्योरी

PHR V **frown on/upon sth** to disapprove of sth किसी बात से नाराज़गी दिखाना *Smoking is very much frowned upon these days.*

**froze** ➪ **freeze**[1] का past tense रूप

**frozen**[1] ➪ **freeze**[1] का past participle रूप

**frozen**[2] /ˈfrəʊzn ˈफ्रोज़न्/ *adj.* **1** (used about food) stored at a low temperature in order to keep it for a long time (खाद्य पदार्थ) सुरक्षित रखने के लिए कम तापमान पर भंडारण *frozen meat/vegetables* **2** (*informal*) (used about people and parts of the body) very cold (मनुष्य और शरीर के अंग) बहुत ठंडा *My feet are frozen!* ○ *I was* ***frozen stiff****.* ✪ पर्याय **freezing** **3** (used about water) with a layer of ice on the surface (पानी) जिसकी सतह पर बर्फ़ की परत हो *The pond is frozen. Let's go skating.*

**fructose** /ˈfrʌktəʊs; -təʊz ˈफ्रक्टोस्; -टोज़्/ *noun* [U] a type of natural sugar that is found in fruit juice फलों के रस में विद्यमान एक प्रकार की प्राकृतिक शक्कर ➪ **dextrose, glucose, lactose** और **sucrose** देखिए।

**frugal** /ˈfruːgl ˈफ्रूगल्/ *adj.* **1** using only as much money or food as is necessary केवल उतना ही धन या भोजन का इस्तेमाल करते हुए जितना आवश्यक हो; क़िफ़ायती, मितव्ययी *a frugal existence/life* **2** (used about meals) small, simple and not costing very much (भोजन) थोड़ा, सादा और सस्ता ▶ **frugality** /fruˈgæləti फ्रुˈगैलटि/ *noun* [U] किफ़ायतशारी, मितव्ययिता ▶ **frugally** /ˈfruːgəli ˈफ्रूगलि/ *adv.* किफ़ायत से *to live/eat frugally*

**fruit** /fruːt फ्रूट्/ *noun* **1** [C, U] the part of a plant or tree that contains seeds and that we eat फल *Try and eat more* ***fresh fruit*** *and vegetables.* ○ *Marmalade is made with* ***citrus fruit*** (= oranges, lemons, grapefruit, etc.). ○ *fruit juice* ➪ पृष्ठ 486 पर चित्र देखिए।

> NOTE **'A fruit'** कहने का तात्पर्य है **'a type of fruit'** (एक प्रकार का फल)—*Most big supermarkets sell all sorts of tropical fruits.*
> जब किसी एक विशेष फल की बात करनी हो तो हम उसका नाम लेते हैं—*Would you like an apple?* या उसके अगणनीय रूप का प्रयोग करते हैं—*Would you like some fruit?*

**2** [C] the part of any plant in which the seed is formed पौधे का वह भाग जिसमें बीज बनता है **3** [*pl.*] **the fruits (of sth)** a good result or success from work that you have done किसी काम का अच्छा परिणाम; लाभ, फल

IDM **bear fruit** ➪ **bear**[2] देखिए।

**fruit fly** *noun* [C] (*pl.* **fruitflies**) a small flying insect that eats plants that have died, and fruit मरे हुए पौधों और फलों को खाने वाला छोटा उड़न कीट

**fruitful** /ˈfruːtfl ˈफ्रूटफ़ल्/ *adj.* producing good results; useful अच्छे परिणाम देने वाला; उपयोगी, लाभदायक, सफल *fruitful discussions*

**fruition** /fruˈɪʃn फ्रुˈइश्न्/ *noun* [U] (*formal*) the time when a plan, etc. starts to be successful वह समय जब किसी योजना के सुपरिणाम आने लगें; सिद्धि *After months of hard work, our efforts were* ***coming to fruition****.*

**fruitless** /ˈfruːtləs ˈफ्रूटलस्/ *adj.* producing poor or no results; not successful अपर्याप्त अथवा शून्य परिणाम देने वाला, निष्फल; विफल, असफल *a fruitless search*

**frustrate** /frʌˈstreɪt फ्रˈस्ट्रेट्/ *verb* [T] **1** to cause a person to feel annoyed or impatient because he/she cannot do or achieve what he/she wants किसी व्यक्ति में खीझ और निराशा उत्पन्न होना या करना (क्योंकि

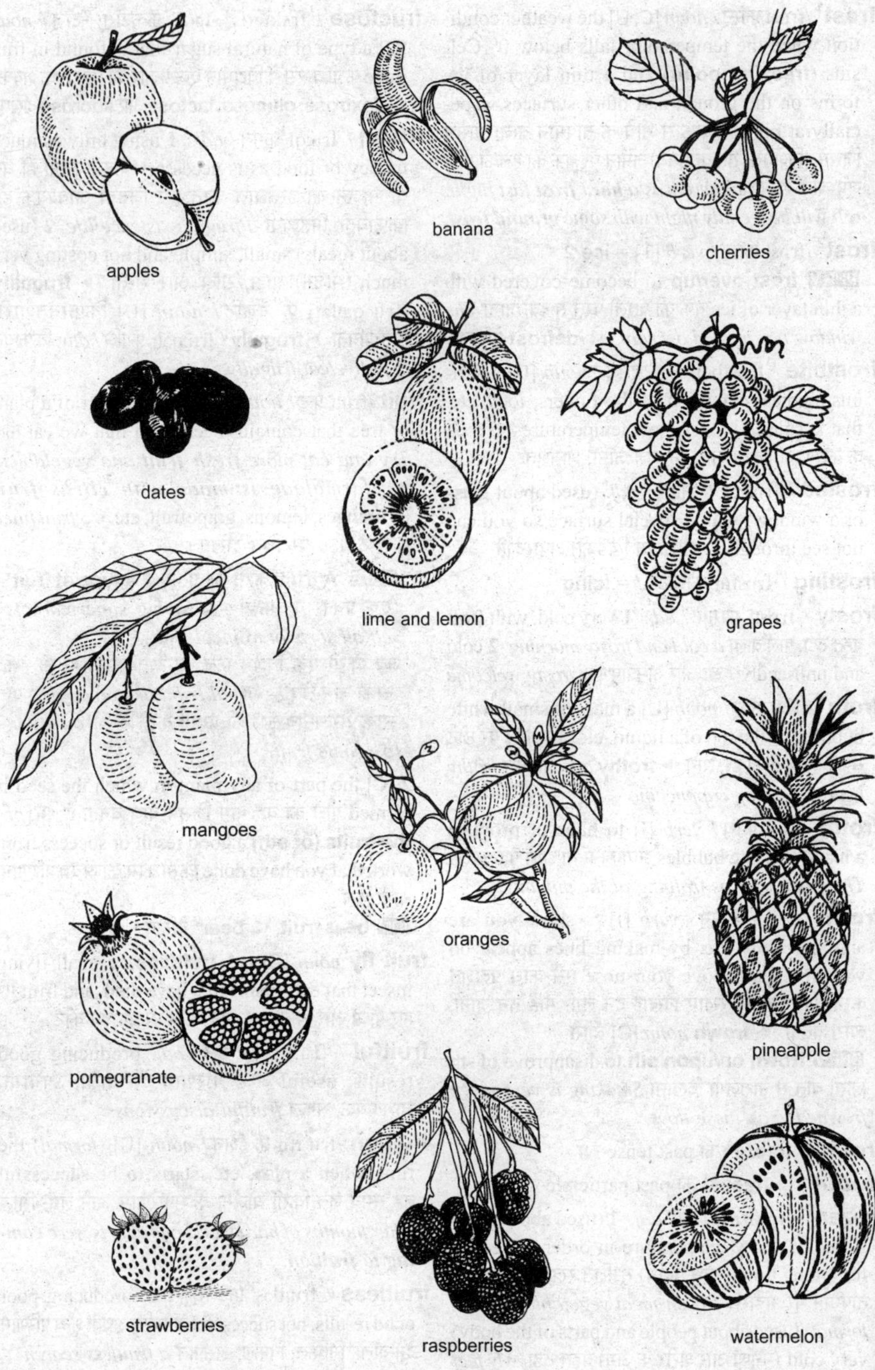
apples
banana
cherries
dates
lime and lemon
grapes
mangoes
oranges
pineapple
pomegranate
strawberries
raspberries
watermelon

fruit

उसे अभीष्ट फल प्राप्त नहीं हुआ); व्यक्ति को हतोत्साहित या निरुत्साहित करना *It's the lack of money that really frustrates him.* **2** (*formal*) to prevent sb from doing sth or sth from happening किसी को कुछ करने देना या कुछ होने न देना; विफल या निष्फल करना *The rescue work has been frustrated by bad weather conditions.* ▶ **frustrated** *adj.* हताश, कुंठित *He felt very frustrated at his lack of progress in learning Chinese.* ▶ **frustrating** *adj.* हताशकारी, कुंठा उत्पन्न करने वाली

**frustration** /frʌˈstreɪʃn फ्रˈस्ट्रेश्न् / *noun* [C, U] a feeling of anger because you cannot get what you want; sth that causes you to feel like this अभीष्ट काम न कर पाने से हुई खीझ, कुंठा, हताशा; खीझ पैदा करने वाली स्थिति *He felt anger and frustration at no longer being able to see very well.* ○ *Every job has its frustrations.*

**fry[1]** /fraɪ फ्राइ / *verb* [I, T] (*pres. part.* **frying;** *3rd person sing. pres.* **fries**; *pt, pp* **fried** /fraɪd फ्राइड् /) to cook sth or to be cooked in hot fat or oil तेल में कुछ पकाना या पकना; तलना *to fry an egg* ○ *I could smell fish frying in the kitchen.*

**fry[2]** /fraɪ फ्राइ / (*AmE* **French fry**) *noun* [C] (*pl.* **fries**) a long thin piece of potato fried in oil तेल में तला आलू का लंबा टुकड़ा

**frying pan** (*AmE* **frypan; skillet**) *noun* [C] a flat pan with a long handle that is used for frying food लंबे हत्थे वाला व समतल कढ़ाही या तसला जिसमें खाद्य पदार्थ तले जाते हैं; फ्राइंग पैन ➪ **pan** पर चित्र देखिए।

**ft** *abbr.* foot, feet; a measure of length, about 30.5 cm फुट, फीट; लंबाई का एक माप, लगभग 30.5 से.मी. *a room 10 ft by 6 ft*

**fuel[1]** /ˈfjuːəl ˈफ़्यूअल् / *noun* **1** [U] material that is burned to produce heat or power ईंधन **2** [C] a type of fuel ईंधन का एक प्रकार *I think gas is the best fuel for central heating.*

**fuel[2]** /ˈfjuːəl ˈफ़्यूअल् / *verb* [T] (**fuelling; fuelled** *AmE* **fueling; fueled**) to make sb feel an emotion more strongly मनोभाव को उद्दीप्त कर देना *Her interest in the Spanish language was fuelled by a visit to Spain.*

**fugitive** /ˈfjuːdʒətɪv ˈफ़्यूजटिव् / *noun* [C] a person who is running away or escaping (for example from the police) (पुलिस आदि के) नियंत्रण से पहले भागने वाला; भगोड़ा ➪ **refugee** देखिए।

**fulcrum** /ˈfʊlkrəm ˈफ़ुल्क्रम् / *noun* [C, *usually sing.*] (*technical*) the point on which sth turns or is

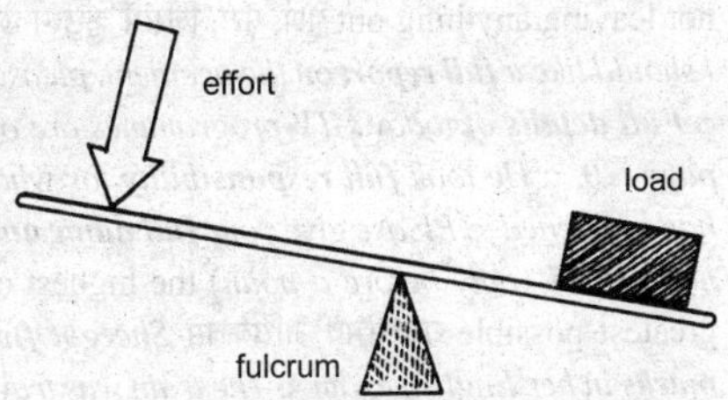


supported वह आधार-बिंदु जिस पर कोई वस्तु घूमती है या जिस पर किसी वस्तु को टिकाया जाता है; टेक, आधार, आलंब

**fulfil** (*AmE* **fulfill**) /fʊlˈfɪl फ़ुलˈफ़िल् / *verb* [T] (**fulfilling; fulfilled**) **1** to make sth that you wish for happen; to achieve a goal अभीष्ट काम को पूरा करना; लक्ष्य की प्राप्ति करना *He finally fulfilled his childhood dream of becoming a doctor.* ○ *to fulfil your ambition/potential* **2** to do or have everything that you should or that is necessary अपेक्षित या आवश्यक कार्रवाई करना या अपेक्षाओं को पूरा करना *to fulfil a duty/obligation/promise/need* ○ *The conditions of entry to university in this country are quite difficult to fulfil.* **3** to have a particular role or purpose कोई विशेष भूमिका अदा करना या कोई विशेष उद्देश्य होना *India fulfils a very important role within the United Nations.* **4** to make sb feel completely happy and satisfied भरपूर प्रसन्नता और संतोष देना *I need a job that really fulfils me.* ▶ **fulfilled** *adj.* प्रसन्न व संतुष्ट *When I had my baby I felt totally fulfilled.* ▶ **fulfilling** *adj.* संतुष्टिकर *I found working abroad a very fulfilling experience.*

**fulfilment** /fʊlˈfɪlmənt फ़ुलˈफ़िल्मन्ट् / (*AmE* **fulfillment**) *noun* [U] the act of achieving a goal; the feeling of satisfaction that you have when you have done sth लक्ष्य की प्राप्ति; काम पूरा कर लेने से उत्पन्न संतोष-भावना *the fulfilment of your dreams/hopes/ambitions* ○ *to find personal/emotional fulfilment*

**full[1]** /fʊl फ़ुल् / *adj.* **1** holding or containing as much or as many as possible जितना भरा जा सके उतना भरा हुआ, पूरा भरा *The bin needs emptying. It's **full up*** (= completely full). ○ *a full bottle* ○ *The bus was full so we had to wait for the next one.* ○ (*figurative*) *We need a good night's sleep because we've got a full* (= busy) *day tomorrow.* **2 full of sb/sth** containing a lot of sb/sth जिसमें बहुत सामान या व्यक्ति भरे हों; परिपूर्ण *The room was full of people.* ○ *His work was full of mistakes.* ○ *The children are full of energy.* **3 full (up)** having had enough to eat and drink भरपूर खाया-पिया *No more, thank you. I'm full (up).* **4** (*only before a noun*) complete;

not leaving anything out पूर्ण, पूरा; जिसमें कुछ न छूटे *I should like **a full report** on the accident, please.* ○ ***Full details** of today's TV programmes are on page 20.* ○ *He took **full responsibility** for what had happened.* ○ *Please give your **full name and address**.* **5** (*only before a noun*) the highest or greatest possible यथासंभव अधिकतम *She got **full marks** in her English exam.* ○ *The train was travelling **at full speed**.* **6 full of sb/sth/yourself** thinking or talking a lot about sb/sth/yourself अपने या किसी के बारे में बहुत अधिक बातें सोचने या कहने वाला *When she got back from holiday she was full of everything they had seen.* ○ *He's **full of himself*** (= thinks that he is very important) *since he got that new job.* **7** round in shape शकल में गोल, गोलाकार *She's got quite **a full figure**.* ○ *He's quite **full in the face**.* **8** (used about clothes) made with plenty of material (पोशाक) अपेक्षाकृत अधिक कपड़े से बनी *a full skirt*

IDM **at full stretch** working as hard as possible भरपूर मेहनत के साथ काम करते हुए

**full of beans/life** with a lot of energy and enthusiasm प्रचुर शक्ति और उत्साह के साथ

**have your hands full** ➪ **hand¹** देखिए।

**in full** with nothing missing; completely पूरा-का-पूरा; पूरा, पूर्ण रूप से *Your money will be refunded in full* (= you will get all your money back). ○ *Please write your name in full.*

**in full swing** at the stage when there is the most activity पूरे ज़ोरों पर *When we arrived the party was already in full swing.*

**in full view (of sb/sth)** in a place where you can easily be seen ऐसे स्थान पर जहाँ पर सबकी नज़र पड़ सके *In full view of the guards, he tried to escape over the prison wall.*

**to the full** as much as possible यथासंभव अधिकतम *to enjoy life to the full*

**full²** /fʊl फुल्/ *adv.* **full in/on (sth)** straight; directly एकदम सीधे; आमने-सामने *Rahul hit him full in the face.* ○ *The two cars crashed full on.*

**full-blown** *adj.* fully developed पूर्णतया विकसित *to have full-blown chicken pox*

**full board** *noun* [U] (in a hotel, etc.) including all meals (होटल आदि में) जिसमें समूचा भोजन व्यय शामिल है ➪ **half board** और **bed and breakfast** देखिए।

**full-fledged** = **fully-fledged**

**full-length** *adj.* **1** (used about a picture, mirror, etc.) showing a person from head to foot (चित्र, दर्पण आदि) जिसमें व्यक्ति सिर से पैर तक दिखाई दे **2** not made shorter जिसे संक्षिप्त नहीं किया गया *a full-length film* **3** (used about a dress, skirt, etc.) reaching the feet (पोशाक, स्कर्ट आदि) पैरों तक पहुँचने वाली; पूरी लंबाई की

**full moon** *noun* [*sing.*] the moon when it appears as a complete circle पूर्ण चंद्र, पूर्णिमा का चंद्रमा ➪ **new moon** देखिए।

**full-scale** *adj.* (*only before a noun*) **1** using every thing or person that is available जिसमें सभी उपलब्ध वस्तुओं या व्यक्तियों का उपयोग किया जाए; सुविस्तृत *The police have started a full-scale murder investigation.* **2** (used about a plan, drawing, etc.) of the same size as the original object (योजना, आरेखित चित्र आदि) मूल वस्तु के समान आकार वाला *a full-scale plan/model*

**full stop** (*AmE* **period**) *noun* [C] a mark (.) that is used in writing to show the end of a sentence वाक्य की समाप्ति को दर्शाने वाला चिह्न (.)

**full-time** *adj.*, *adv.* for a whole of the normal period of work पूर्ण सामान्य कार्य अवधि के लिए; पूर्णकालिक *He has a full-time job.* ○ *He works full time.* ○ *We employ 800 full-time staff.* ➪ **part-time** देखिए।

**fully** /ˈfʊli ˈफ़ुलि/ *adv.* completely; to the highest possible degree पूर्णतया; यथासंभव अधिकतम *I'm fully aware of the problem.* ○ *All our engineers are fully trained.*

**fully-fledged** /ˌfʊli fledʒd ˌफ़ुलि ˈफ़्लेजड्/ (*AmE* **full-fledged**) *adj.* completely trained or completely developed पूर्णतया प्रशिक्षित या पूर्णतया विकसित *Computer science is now a fully-fledged academic subject.*

**fumble** /ˈfʌmbl ˈफ़म्बल्/ *verb* [I] to try to find or take hold of sth with your hands in a nervous or careless way परेशानी की हालत में या लापरवाही से कुछ ढूँढ़ने या पकड़ने की कोशिश करना; टटोलना *'It must be here somewhere', she said, fumbling in her pocket for her key.*

**fume** /fju:m फ़्यूम्/ *verb* [I] to be very angry about sth किसी बात पर बहुत क्रुद्ध होना

**fumes** /fju:mz फ़्यूम्ज़्/ *noun* [*pl.*] smoke or gases that smell unpleasant and that can be dangerous to breathe in धुआँ या बदबूदार गैस जिसका साँस के साथ अंदर जाना ख़तरनाक हो सकता है *diesel/petrol/exhaust fumes*

**fumigate** /ˈfju:mɪgeɪt ˈफ़्यूमिगेट्/ *verb* [T] to use special chemicals, smoke or gas to destroy the harmful insects or bacteria in a place किसी स्थान के हानिकारक कीटों को नष्ट करने के लिए विशेष रसायनों, धुआँ या गैस का प्रयोग करना; किसी स्थान को धुआँरना *to fumigate a room* ▶ **fumigation** /ˌfju:mɪˈgeɪʃn ˌफ़्यूमिˈगेशन्/ *noun* [U] धूमीकरण

**fun**[1] /fʌn फ़न् / *noun* [U] pleasure and enjoyment; an activity or a person that gives you pleasure and enjoyment मौज-मस्ती; ऐसी क्रिया या व्यक्ति जो लोगों को प्रसन्नता और आनंद दे *We **had** a lot of **fun** at the party last night.* ○ *The party was **great fun**.* ○ *Have fun* (= enjoy yourself)! ○ ***It's no fun** having to get up at 4 o'clock every day.*

IDM **(just) for fun/for the fun of it** (just) for amusement or pleasure; not seriously (केवल) मौज मस्ती के लिए; हलके-फुलके ढंग से, बिना गंभीरता के *I don't need French for my work. I'm just learning it for fun.*

**in fun** as a joke मज़ाक़ के रूप में *It was said in fun. They didn't mean to upset you.*

**make fun of sb/sth** to laugh at sb/sth in an unkind way; to make other people do this निर्दयता से किसी का मज़ाक़ उड़ाना; लोगों से किसी का मज़ाक़ उड़वाना *The older children are always making fun of him because of his accent.*

**poke fun at sb/sth** ⇨ **poke** देखिए।

**fun**[2] /fʌn फ़न् / *adj.* amusing or enjoyable जी बहलाने वाला या आनंदपूर्ण *to have a fun time/day out* ○ *Prateek's a fun guy.*

**function**[1] /ˈfʌŋkʃn ˈफ़ङ्क्श्न् / *noun* [C] **1** the purpose or special duty of a person or thing किसी व्यक्ति या वस्तु का उद्देश्य, विशेष कार्य या दायित्व *The function of the heart is to pump blood through the body.* ○ *to perform/fulfil a function* **2** an important social event, ceremony, etc. कोई महत्त्वपूर्ण सामाजिक कार्यक्रम, उत्सव आदि *The president attends hundreds of official functions every year.* **3** (*mathematics*) a quantity whose value depends on the varying values of others. In the statement $2x = y$, $y$ is a function of $x$ एक ऐसी मात्रा जिसका मूल्य अन्यों के परिवर्तित होते हुए मूल्यों पर निर्भर है (जैसे $2x = y$, में $y$, $x$ का फलन है); प्रकार्य

**function**[2] /ˈfʌŋkʃn ˈफ़ङ्क्श्न् / *verb* [I] to work correctly; to be in action ठीक से काम करना; चालू हालत में होना *Only one engine was still functioning.* ✪ पर्याय **operate**

**functional** /ˈfʌŋkʃənl ˈफ़ङ्क्शन्ल् / *adj.* **1** practical and useful rather than attractive व्यवहारोपयोगी (न कि आकर्षक); जो काम अच्छा करे (न कि देखने में अच्छा हो) *cheap functional furniture* **2** working; being used कार्यशील; प्रयोग में आता हुआ *The system is now fully functional.*

**functionality** /ˌfʌŋkʃəˈnæləti ˌफ़ङ्क्श ˈनैलटि / *noun* [C, U] (*pl.* **functionalities**) (*computing*) the set of functions that a computer or other electronic system can perform कंप्यूटर या अन्य किसी इलेक्ट्रॉनिक उपकरण के द्वारा संपन्न किए जाने वाले प्रकार्य; प्रकार्यात्मकता *new software with additional functionality*

**function key** *noun* [C] (*computing*) one of the **keys** on a computer which are used to perform a particular operation कंप्यूटर के कुंजीपटल पर एक कुंजी जिससे विशेष प्रकिया संपादित की जाए

**fund**[1] /fʌnd फ़न्ड् / *noun* **1** [C] a sum of money that is collected for a particular purpose विशेष उद्देश्य से संगृहीत धनराशि; कोष, फंड *They contributed Rs 500 to the flood relief fund.* **2 funds** [*pl.*] money that is available and can be spent व्यय के लिए उपलब्ध धनराशि; कोष, निधि *The hospital is trying to **raise funds** for a new X-ray machine.*

**fund**[2] /fʌnd फ़न्ड् / *verb* [T] to provide a project, school, charity etc. with money किसी परियोजना, विद्यालय आदि को धन उपलब्ध कराना *The school is not funded by government money.*

**fundamental** /ˌfʌndəˈmentl ˌफ़न्डˈमेन्ट्ल् / *adj.* basic and important; from which everything else develops बुनियादी और महत्त्वपूर्ण; मूल स्रोत से संबंधित *There will be fundamental changes in the way the school is run.* ○ *There is a fundamental difference between your opinion and mine.* ► **fundamentally** /-təli -टलि / *adv.* बुनियादी तौर पर *The government's policy has changed fundamentally.*

**fundamentalist** /ˌfʌndəˈmentəlɪst ˌफ़न्डˈमेन्टलिस्ट् / *noun* [C] a person who strictly follows the rules and teachings of any religion किसी धर्म के मूल सिद्धांतों का प्रगाढ़ अनुयायी; मूलतत्ववादी, मूलप्रमाणवादी *religious fundamentalist* ► **fundamentalism** *noun* [U] मूलतत्ववाद, मूलप्रमाणवाद

**fundamentals** /ˌfʌndəˈmentlz ˌफ़न्डˈमेन्ट्ल्ज़् / *noun* [*pl.*] basic facts or principles मौलिक तथ्य अथवा सिद्धांत

**fund-raiser** *noun* [C] a person whose job is to find ways of collecting money for a charity or an organization धर्मार्थ कार्य अथवा संगठन के लिए धनराशि एकत्रित करने वाला व्यक्ति ► **fund-raising** *noun* [U] फंड एकत्रित करने की क्रिया *fund-raising events*

**funeral** /ˈfjuːnərəl ˈफ़्यूनरल् / *noun* [C] a ceremony (usually religious) for burying or burning a dead person मृतक का अंतिम संस्कार

**funeral director** = **undertaker**

**funfair** /ˈfʌnfeə(r) ˈफ़न्फ़ेअ(र्) / = **fair**[2] **1**

**fungicide** /ˈfʌŋgɪsaɪd ˈफ़ङ्गिसाइड् / *noun* [C, U] a substance that kills a type of plant with no leaves or flowers (**fungus**) that grows on other plants or animals and harms them फफूँदनाशक पदार्थ

**fungus** /ˈfʌŋɡəs ˈफ़ङ्गस्/ *noun* [C, U] (*pl.* **fungi** /ˈfʌŋɡiː; -ɡaɪ ˈफ़ङ्गी; -गाइ/ or **funguses**) a plant that is not green and does not have leaves or flowers (for example a **mushroom**), or that is like a wet powder and grows on old wood or food, walls, etc. Some fungi can be harmful ऐसा पौधा जो न हरा होता है या जिसमें फूल और पत्ते नहीं होते हैं (जैसे कुकुरमुत्ता)। यह गीले चूर्ण जैसा होता है और पुरानी लकड़ी, दीवार आदि पर उग आता है; फफूँद, फूई, भुकड़ी; कुछ फफूँद हानिकर होती हैं ➪ **mould** और **toadstool** देखिए ▶ **fungal** *adj.* फफूँद-विषयक *a fungal disease/infection/growth*

**funnel** /ˈfʌnl ˈफ़नल्/ *noun* [C] **1** an object that is wide at the top and narrow at the bottom, used for pouring liquid, powder, etc. into a small opening मुँह पर चौड़ी और नीचे से तंग एक वस्तु जिससे द्रव पदार्थ, पाउडर आदि को छोटे मुँह वाले पात्रों आदि में डाला जाता है; कीप, फ़नल ➪ **laboratory** पर चित्र देखिए। **2** the metal chimney of a ship, engine, etc. जहाज़, इंजन आदि की धातु-निर्मित चिमनी

**funnily** /ˈfʌnɪli; -əli ˈफ़निलि; -अलि/ *adv.* in a strange or unusual way विचित्र या असाधारण तरीक़े से *She's walking very funnily.*

IDM **funnily enough** used for expressing surprise at sth strange that has happened किसी बात के विचित्र लगने पर आश्चर्य व्यक्त करने के लिए प्रयुक्त *Funnily enough, my parents weren't at all cross about it.*

**funny** /ˈfʌni ˈफ़नि/ *adj.* (**funnier; funniest**) **1** that makes you smile or laugh जो मुसकराने या हँसने के लिए प्रेरित करे *a funny story* ○ *He's an extremely funny person.* ○ *That's the funniest thing I've heard in ages!* **2** strange or unusual; difficult to explain or understand विचित्र या असाधारण; जिसे समझाना या समझना कठिन हो *Oh dear, the engine is making a funny noise.* ○ *It's funny that they didn't phone to let us know they couldn't come.* ○ ***That's funny***—*he was here a moment ago and now he's gone.* ○ *Can I sit down for a minute? I feel a bit* ***funny*** (= a bit ill usually).

**funny bone** *noun* [C, *usually sing.*] (*informal*) the bone at your elbow कोहनी की हड्डी

**fur** /fɜː(r) फ़(र्)/ *noun* **1** [U] the soft thick hair that covers the bodies of some animals कुछ पशुओं के शरीर को ढकने वाले कोमल घने बाल; लोम, फ़र **2** [C, U] the skin and hair of an animal that is used for making clothes, etc.; a piece of clothing that is made from this पोशाक आदि बनाने में प्रयुक्त पशु की खाल और बाल; पशु की खाल और बाल से बनी पोशाक; फ़र, लोमचर्म *a fur coat*

**furious** /ˈfjʊəriəs ˈफ़्युअरिअस्/ *adj.* **1 furious (with sb); furious (at sth)** very angry बहुत क्रुद्ध *He was furious with her for losing the car keys.* ○ *He was furious at having to catch the train home.* ➪ **fury** देखिए। **2** very strong; violent ज़ोरदार; उग्र, प्रचंड *A furious row has broken out over the closure of the school.* ▶ **furiously** *adv.* उग्रतापूर्वक

IDM **fast and furious** ➪ **fast**[1] देखिए।

**furnace** /ˈfɜːnɪs ˈफ़निस्/ *noun* [C] a large, very hot, enclosed fire that is used for melting metal, burning rubbish, etc. भट्ठी

**furnish** /ˈfɜːnɪʃ ˈफ़निश्/ *verb* [T] to put furniture in a room, house, etc. किसी कमरे या भवन में मेज़-कुरसी आदि फ़र्नीचर लगाना *The room was comfortably furnished.* ▶ **furnished** *adj.* फ़र्नीचरयुक्त *She's renting a furnished room in Pune.*

**furnishings** /ˈfɜːnɪʃɪŋz ˈफ़निशिङ्ज़्/ *noun* [*pl.*] the furniture, carpets, curtains, etc. in a room, house, etc. कमरे या भवन में लगा फ़र्नीचर, कालीन, परदे आदि सामान

**furniture** /ˈfɜːnɪtʃə(r) ˈफ़निच(र्)/ *noun* [U] the things that can be moved, for example, tables, chairs, beds, etc. in a room, house or office फ़र्नीचर, जैसे मेज़ें, कुरसियाँ, पलंग आदि जिन्हें एक जगह से हटाकर दूसरी जगह रखा जा सकता है *modern/antique/second-hand furniture* ○ *garden/office furniture*

> NOTE ध्यान दीजिए **'furniture'** अगणनीय संज्ञा है—*They only got married recently and they haven't got much furniture.*
> यदि हम किसी एक नग की बात करें तो कहेंगे ***'a piece of furniture'***—*The only nice piece of furniture in the room was an antique desk.*

**furrow** /ˈfʌrəʊ ˈफ़रो/ *noun* [C] **1** a line in a field that is made for planting seeds in by a farming machine that turns the earth (**plough**) बीज बोने के लिए हल या मशीन से खेत में बनाई गई रेखा; कूँड़, सीता, हलरेखा **2** a deep line in the skin on a person's face, especially on the forehead व्यक्ति के चेहरे पर (विशेषत: माथे पर) बनी गहरी रेखा, गहरी झुर्री, शिकन ➪ **wrinkle** देखिए।

**furry** /ˈfɜːri ˈफ़रि/ *adj.* having fur फ़रवाला, फ़रदार *a small furry animal.*

**further**[1] /ˈfɜːðə(r) ˈफ़द(र्)/ *adj.*, *adv.* **1** more; to a greater degree कुछ या कोई और, और कोई; इससे अधिक *Are there* ***any further questions****?* ○ *Please let us know if you require any* ***further information****.* ○ *I have* ***nothing further to say*** *on the subject.* ○ *The museum is closed* ***until further notice*** (= until another announcement is made).

○ *Can I have time to consider the matter further?* **2** (*also* **farther**) (*the comparative of* **far**) at or to a greater distance in time or space समय या स्थान की दृष्टि से कुछ दूर या आगे *It's not safe to go any further.* ○ *I can't remember any further back than 1975.*

NOTE दूरी के संदर्भ में **further** और **farther** दानों शब्दों का प्रयोग किया जा सकता है—*Agra is further/farther from Delhi than Mathura is.* ○ *I jumped further/farther than you did.* अन्य अर्थों में केवल **further** का प्रयोग किया जा सकता है—*We need a **further** week to finish the job.*

IDM **further afield** ➪ **far**[2] देखिए।

**further**[2] /ˈfɜːðə(r) ˈफ़द्र(र्) / *verb* [T] (*formal*) to help sth to develop or be successful किसी के विकास या सफल होने में सहायक होना; आगे बढ़ाना *to further the cause of peace.*

**furthermore** /ˌfɜːðəˈmɔː(r)ˌफ़द्रˈमॉ(र्) / *adv.* also; in addition भी; के अतिरिक्त

**furthest** ➪ **far** का superlative रूप

**furtive** /ˈfɜːtɪv ˈफ़टिव़् / *adj.* secret, acting as though you are trying to hide sth because you feel guilty गुप्त; छिपाने के प्रयत्न का आभास देते हुए (अपराधबोध के कारण) ▶**furtively** *adv.* छिपाते हुए, लुके-छिपे, चुपचाप

**fury** /ˈfjʊəri ˈफ़्युअरि / *noun* [U] very great anger अत्यधिक क्रोध; उन्माद *She was speechless with fury.* ➪ **furious** adjective देखिए।

**fuse**[1] /fjuːz फ़्यूज़् / *noun* [C] **1** a small piece of wire in an electrical system, machine, etc. that melts and breaks if there is too much power. This stops the flow of electricity and prevents fire or damage विद्युत प्रणाली, मशीन आदि में एक छोटा तार जो बिजली प्रवाह बढ़ जाने पर पिघल या टूट जाता है फलतः विद्युतधारा बंद हो जाती है और आग या नुक़सान का ख़तरा टल जाता है; फ़्यूज़ *A fuse has blown—that's why the house is in darkness.* ○ *That plug needs a 15 amp fuse.* **2** a piece of rope, string, etc. or a device that is used to make a bomb, etc. explode at a particular time बम में लगाई गई रस्सी, डोरी आदि या कोई युक्ति ताकि वह पूर्वनिर्धारित समय पर फट जाए; पलीता, फ़्यूज़

**fuse**[2] /fjuːz फ़्यूज़् / *verb* [I, T] **1** (used about two things) to join together to become one; to make two things do this (दो वस्तुओं का) परस्पर जुड़कर एक हो जाना; दो वस्तुओं को इस प्रकार जोड़ना *As they heal, the bones will fuse together.* ○ *The two companies have been fused into one large organization.* **2** to stop working because a **fuse**[1] **1** has melted; to make a piece of electrical equipment do this फ़्यूज़ पिघल जाने के कारण (मशीन आदि का) बंद हो जाना; किसी विद्युत उपकरण को (फ़्यूज़ पिघल जाने के कारण) बंद कर देना *The lights have fused.* ○ *I've fused the lights.*

**fuselage** /ˈfjuːzəlɑːʒ ˈफ़्यूज़लाश़् / *noun* [C] the main part of a plane (not the engines, wings or tail) विमान का मुख्य भाग (इंजन, पंख या अंतिम अंश इसमें शामिल नहीं) ➪ **plane** पर चित्र देखिए।

**fusion** /ˈfjuːʒn ˈफ़्यूश़्न् / *noun* **1** [U, *sing.*] the process or the result of joining different things together to form one विभिन्न वस्तुओं के जुड़कर एक हो जाने की प्रक्रिया या उसका परिणाम *the fusion of two political systems* **2** (*also* **nuclear fusion**) [U] (in physics) the action or process of combining the central parts (**nuclei**) of atoms to form a heavier central part (**nucleus**), with energy being created (भौतिक विज्ञान में) परमाणुओं के केंद्रीय अंशों के संयुक्त होने का कार्य या प्रक्रिया जिससे एक अधिक भारी केंद्रीय अंश का निर्माण होता है और ऊर्जा भी बनती है, परमाणु-संलयन ➪ **fission** देखिए।

**fuss**[1] /fʌs फ़स् / *noun* [*sing.*, U] a time when people behave in an excited, a nervous or an angry way, especially about sth unimportant बेकार किसी बात पर उत्तेजित या क्रोधित हो जाने की क्रिया; हो-हल्ला *The waiter didn't **make a fuss** when I spilt my drink.* ○ *What's all the fuss about?*

IDM **make/kick up a fuss (about/over sth)** to complain strongly ज़ोरदार शिकायत करना

**make a fuss of/over sb/sth** to pay a lot of attention to sb/sth किसी व्यक्ति या वस्तु पर काफ़ी अधिक ध्यान देना *My grandmother used to make a big fuss of me when she visited.*

**fuss**[2] /fʌs फ़स् / *verb* [I] **1** to be worried or excited about small things छोटी-छोटी बातों पर चिंतित या उत्तेजित हो जाना *Stop fussing. We're not going to be late.* **2 fuss (over sb/sth)** to pay too much attention to sb/sth किसी व्यक्ति या वस्तु पर बहुत अधिक ध्यान देना (अनावश्यक रूप से) *Stop fussing over all the details.*

IDM **not be fussed (about sb/sth)** (*BrE* **spoken**) to not care very much अधिक परवाह न करना *'Where do you want to go for lunch' 'I'm not fussed.'*

**fussy** /ˈfʌsi ˈफ़सि / *adj.* **1 fussy (about sth)** (used about people) giving too much attention to small details and therefore difficult to please (व्यक्ति) छोटी-छोटी बातों पर बहुत अधिक ध्यान देने वाला अतएव प्रायः असंतुष्ट *He is very fussy about food* (= there are many things that he does not eat). ➪ **particular** और **picky** देखिए। **2** having too much detail or decoration बहुत अधिक भरा-भरा या भड़कीला *I don't like that pattern. It's too fussy.*

**futile** /ˈfjuːtaɪl ˈफ़्यूटाइल् / *adj.* (used about an action) having no success; useless (कार्रवाई) असफल; व्यर्थ *They made a last futile attempt to make him change his mind.* ▶ **futility** *noun* [U] व्यर्थता

**future** /ˈfjuːtʃə(r) ˈफ़्यूच(र्)/ *noun* **1 the future** [*sing.*] the time that will come after the present वर्तमान के बाद का समय; भविष्य *Who knows what will happen in the future?* ○ *in the near/distant future* (= soon/not soon) **2** [C] what will happen to sb/sth in the time after the present किसी व्यक्ति या वस्तु के साथ वर्तमान के बाद जो घटित हो; भविष्य *Our children's futures depend on a good education.* ○ *The company's future does not look very hopeful.* **3** [U] the possibility of being successful सफल होने की संभावना; भविष्य *I could see no future in this country so I left to work abroad.* **4 the future** [*sing.*] = **the future tense** ▶ **future** *adj.* (*only before a noun*) भावी *She met her future husband when she was still at college.* ○ *You can keep that book **for future reference*** (= to look at again later).

IDM **in future** from now on आगे से, भविष्य में *Please try to be more careful in future.*

**the future perfect** *noun* [*sing.*] (*grammar*) the form of a verb which expresses an action in the future that will be finished before the time mentioned. The future perfect is formed with the future tense of 'have' and the past participle of the verb (अंग्रेज़ी व्याकरण में) क्रिया का वह रूप जो निर्दिष्ट समय से पहले, भविष्य में होने वाले कार्यों के समाप्त हो जाने की सूचना देता है; पूर्ण भविष्यत। पूर्ण भविष्यत क्रिया रूप 'have' के भविष्यतकाल और मुख्य क्रिया के भूत कृदंत को मिलाकर बनता है *'We'll have been married for ten years next month' is **in the future perfect**.*

**the future tense** (*also* **the future**) *noun* [*sing.*] (*grammar*) the form of a verb that expresses what will happen after the present (अंग्रेज़ी व्याकरण में) वर्तमान के बाद होने वाली स्थिति का वर्णन करने वाला क्रिया रूप; भविष्यत काल

NOTE भविष्यत कालों (future tenses) के विषय में अधिक जानकारी के लिए इस शब्दकोश के अंत में **Quick Grammar Reference** देखिए।

**fuzzy** /ˈfʌzi ˈफ़ज़ि / *adj.* not clear जो साफ़ न हो, धुँधला, अस्पष्ट *The photo was a bit fuzzy but I could just make out my mother on it.*

# G g

**G, g¹** /dʒiː जी / *noun* [C, U] (*pl.* **G's; g's** /dʒiːz जीज़् / the seventh letter of the English alphabet अंग्रेज़ी वर्णमाला का सातवाँ अक्षर *'Girl' begins with a 'G'.*

**g²** *abbr.* gram(s) ग्राम

**gable** /ˈgeɪbl ˈगेबल् /*noun* [C] the pointed part at the top of an outside wall of a house between two parts of the roof मकान की छत के दो हिस्सों के बीच बाहरी दीवार के सिर का नुकीला हिस्सा; तिकोना

**gadget** /ˈgædʒɪt ˈगैजिट् / *noun* [C] (*informal*) a small device, tool or machine that has a particular but usually unimportant purpose एक छोटा उपकरण या मशीन जो एक विशेष परंतु प्रायः महत्त्वहीन कार्य करती है; छोटा-मोटा औज़ार

**gag¹** /gæg गैग् / *noun* [C] **1** a piece of cloth, etc. that is put in or over sb's mouth in order to stop him/her from talking किसी को बोलने से रोकने के लिए उसके मुँह में या मुँह पर रखा गया कपड़े का टुकड़ा आदि **2** a joke चुटकुला

**gag²** /gæg गैग् / *verb* [T] (**gagging; gagged**) to put a gag in or over sb's mouth किसी के मुँह में कपड़ा आदि ठूँसना (उसे बोलने से रोकने के लिए)

**gage** (*AmE*) = **gauge¹**

**gaiety** /ˈgeɪəti ˈगेअटि / *noun* [U] a feeling of happiness and fun ख़ुशी और मौज-मस्ती की भावना

**gaily** /ˈgeɪli ˈगेलि / *adj.* happily; cheerfully प्रसन्नता से; ख़ुशी-ख़ुशी

**gain¹** /geɪn गेन् / *verb* **1** [T] to obtain or win sth, especially sth that you need or want वस्तु तक पहुँचना या प्राप्त करना, विशेषतः अपेक्षित या अभीष्ट वस्तु; पाना *They managed to gain access to secret information.* ○ *The country gained its independence ten years ago.* **2** [T] to gradually get more of sth किसी वस्तु का क्रमशः बढ़ना *The train was gaining speed.* ○ *to gain weight/confidence* ✪ विलोम **lose** **3** [I,T] **gain (sth) (by/from sth/doing sth)** to get an advantage कुछ लाभ होना या पाना *I've got nothing to gain by staying in this job.* ✪ विलोम **lose**

IDM **gain ground** to make progress; to become stronger or more popular आगे बढ़ना, उन्नति करना; अधिक सशक्त या लोकप्रिय होना

PHR V **gain in sth** to gradually get more of sth क्रमशः प्राप्ति में वृद्धि होना *He's gained in confidence in the past year.*

**gain on sb/sth** to get closer to sb/sth that you are trying to catch जिसे पकड़ना अभीष्ट हो उसके क्रमशः पास पहुँचना *I saw the other runners were gaining on me so I increased my pace.*

**gain²** /geɪn गेन् / *noun* [C, U] an increase, improvment or advantage in sth किसी वस्तु में वृद्धि, सुधार या लाभ *We hope to make a gain* (= more money) *when we sell our house.* ○ *a **gain in weight** of one kilo*

**gait** /geɪt गेट् / *noun* [*sing.*] the way that sb/sth walks किसी व्यक्ति, पशु आदि के चलने का तरीक़ा; चाल

**gala** /ˈgɑːlə ˈगाला / *noun* [C] a special social or sporting occasion कोई विशेष सामाजिक कार्यक्रम; किसी खेल का विशेष कार्यक्रम *a swimming gala*

**galaxy** /ˈgæləksi ˈगैलक्सि / *noun* (*pl.* **galaxies**) **1** [C] any of the large systems of stars, etc. in outer space बाह्य अंतरिक्ष में तारों का समूह **2 the Galaxy** (*also* **the Milky Way**) [*sing.*] the system of stars that contains our sun and its planets, seen as a bright band in the night sky सूर्य और ग्रहों का तारापथ जो रात्रिकालीन आकाश में सुप्रकाशित पट्टी जैसा दीखता हैं; आकाशगंगा, मंदाकिनी

**gale** /geɪl गेल् / *noun* [C] a very strong wind बहुत तेज़ हवा, आँधी, झंझा *Several trees blew down in the gale.* ➪ **storm** पर नोट देखिए।

**gall¹** /gɔːl गॉल् / *noun* **1** [U] rude behaviour showing a lack of respect that is surprising because the person doing it is not embarrassed निर्लज्ज, अप्रत्याशित, अशिष्टता व दुस्साहसपूर्ण *He arrived two hours late then **had the gall** to complain about the food.* **2** [U] (*formal*) a bitter feeling full of hatred घृणाभरी कटुता ✪ पर्याय **resentment** **3** [C] a swelling on plants and trees caused by insects, disease, etc. कीट आदि से पौधों और वृक्षों पर उभरी सूजन, वृक्षव्रण **4** (*old-fashioned*) = **bile**

**gall²** /gɔːl गॉल् / *verb* [T] to make sb feel upset and angry, especially because sth is unfair ग़लत बात पर किसी को परेशान और क्रोधित कर देना *It galls me to have to apologize to her.*

**gall.** *abbr.* gallon(s) गैलन

**gallant** /ˈgælənt ˈगैलन्ट् / *adj.* (*formal*) **1** showing courage in a difficult situation साहसी, पराक्रमी, बहादुर *gallant men/soldiers/heroes* ✪ पर्याय **brave** **2** (used about men) polite to and showing respect for women (पुरुष) महिलाओं के प्रति विनम्र एवं सम्मान प्रदर्शित करने वाला

**gallantry** /ˈgæləntri ˈगैलन्ट्रि/ *noun* [C, U] (*pl.* **gallantries**) **1** courage, especially in battle साहस, विशेषतः युद्ध में **2** polite behaviour towards women by men महिलाओं के प्रति पुरुषों का सम्मानजनक आचरण

**gall bladder** *noun* [C] an organ that is connected to your **liver** where **bile** is stored, which helps your body to deal with fats जिगर से जुड़ा पित्त को संचित करने वाला अंग जिससे शरीर को चरबी से निपटने में सहायता मिलती है; पित्ताशय

**gallery** /ˈgæləri ˈगैलरि/ *noun* [C] (*pl.* **galleries**) **1** a building or room where works of art are shown to the public कला के सार्वजनिक प्रदर्शन के लिए भवन या कक्ष; कलादीर्घा, गैलरी *an art gallery* **2** an upstairs area at the back or sides of a large hall or theatre where people can sit किसी बड़े भवन या नाट्यगृह में ऊपरवाली मंजिल पर पीछे या बग़ल में दर्शकों के बैठने का स्थान; दर्शकदीर्घा

**galley** /ˈgæli ˈगैलि/ *noun* [C] **1** a long flat ship with sails, especially one used by the ancient Greeks or Romans in war, which was usually rowed by criminals or **slaves** विशेषतः प्राचीन ग्रीक या रोमन योद्धाओं द्वारा युद्ध में प्रयुक्त पालों वाला लंबा चौरस जलपोत जिसे अपराधी या दास चप्पुओं से चलाते थे **2** the kitchen on a ship or plane जलपोत या विमान की रसोई

**gallon** /ˈgælən ˈगैलन्/ *noun* [C] (*abbr.* **gall.**) a measure of liquid; 4.5 litres (or 3.8 litres in an American gallon) द्रव की एक माप, गैलन; 4.5 लिटर (या अमेरिकी गैलन में 3.8 लिटर) **NOTE** एक गैलन में आठ **pints** होते हैं।

**gallop** /ˈgæləp ˈगैलप्/ *verb* [I] (used about a horse or a rider) to go at the fastest speed (घोड़ा या घुड़सवार के बारे में प्रयुक्त) अधिक गति से दौड़ना; घोड़े का चौकड़ियाँ भरना ➪ **canter** और **trot** देखिए। ▶ **gallop** *noun* [*sing.*] (चौकड़ी) घोड़े की अधिकतम गति

**gallows** /ˈgæləʊz ˈगैलोज़्/ *noun* [C] (*pl.* **gallows**) a wooden frame used in the past for killing people by hanging पुराने ज़माने में लोगों को फाँसी पर लटकाने के लिए प्रयुक्त लकड़ी का बड़ा चौखटा

**gallstone** /ˈgɔ:lstəʊn ˈगॉल्स्टोन्/ *noun* [C] a hard painful mass that can form in the **gall bladder** पित्ताशय में बन जाने वाली कष्टदायक कठोर वस्तु; पथरी

**galore** /gəˈlɔ:(r) गˈलॉ(र्)/ *adv.* (*only before a noun*) in large numbers or amounts बड़ी संख्या या मात्रा में

**galvanize** (*also* **-ise**) /ˈgælvənaɪz ˈगैल्व़नाइज़्/ *verb* [T] to cover iron or steel in a whitish metal (**zinc**) to protect it from being damaged by water (**rusting**) लोहे या इस्पात पर जस्ता चढ़ाना ताकि ज़ंग न लगे

**gamble¹** /ˈgæmbl ˈगैम्बल्/ *verb* [I,T] **gamble (sth) (on sth)** to bet money on the result of a card game, horse race, etc. ताश का खेल, घुड़दौड़ आदि के परिणामों पर बाज़ी लगाना; जुआ खेलना *She gambled all her money on the last race.* ✪ पर्याय **bet** ▶ **gambler** *noun* [C] जुआरी *He's a compulsive gambler.* ▶ **gambling** *noun* [U] जुआ

**PHR V** **gamble on sth/on doing sth** to act in the hope that sth will happen although it may not किसी बात पर बाज़ी लगाना *I wouldn't gamble on the weather staying fine.*

**gamble²** /ˈgæmbl ˈगैम्बल्/ *noun* [C] something you do that is a risk जोखिम का काम *Setting up this business was a bit of a gamble, but it paid off* (= was successful) *in the end.*

**game¹** /geɪm गेम्/ *noun* **1** [C] **a game (of sth)** a form of play or sport with rules; a time when you play it नियमानुसार खेले जाने वाला खेल; खेल खेलने का अवसर *Shall we **play a game**? ○ Let's **have a game** of chess.* **2** [C] an activity that you do to have fun मौज-मस्ती के लिए किया गया काम *Some children were playing a game of robbers and police.* **3** [C] how well sb plays a sport खेलने का ढंग या स्तर *My new racket has really improved my game.* **4 games** [*pl.*] an important sports competition बड़ी व महत्त्वपूर्ण खेल स्पर्धा *Where were the last Olympic Games held?* **5** [C] (*informal*) a secret plan or trick कोई गुप्त योजना या चाल *Stop **playing games** with me and tell me where you've hidden my bag.* **6** [U] wild animals or birds that are killed for sport or food खेल-खेल में या खाने के लिए मारे गए वन्यपशु या पक्षी; शिकार *big game* (= lion, tiger, etc.)

**IDM** **give the game away** to tell a person sth that you are trying to keep secret किसी को यह बताना कि कोई बात गुप्त रखी जा रही है *It was the expression on her face that gave the game away.*

**game²** /geɪm गेम्/ *adj.* (used about a person) ready to try sth new, unusual, difficult, etc. (व्यक्ति) नया, असाधारण, कठिन काम करने के लिए तैयार *I've never been sailing before but I'm game to try.*

**gamekeeper** /ˈgeɪmki:pə(r) ˈगेम्कीप(र्)/ *noun* [C] a person who is responsible for private land where people hunt animals and birds निजी शिकारगाह का प्रबंधक; आखेटपाल

**gamete** /ˈgæmi:t ˈगैमीट्/ *noun* [C] a male or female cell that joins with a cell of the opposite sex to form a **zygote** नर या मादा कोशिका जो विपरीत लिंग के साथ मिलकर शिशु का निर्माण करने वाली कोशिका बनाती है; युग्मक कोशिका

**gamma** /ˈgæmə ˈगैमा/ *noun* [C] the third letter of the Greek alphabet [Γ, γ] ग्रीक वर्णमाला का तीसरा अक्षर

**gamma radiation** *noun* [U] (*also* **gamma rays**) [*pl.*] rays that are sent out by some dangerous (**radioactive**) substances कुछ ख़तरनाक रेडियो-सक्रिय पदार्थों से निकलने वाली किरणें ➪ **wavelength** पर चित्र देखिए।

**gammon** /ˈgæmən ˈगैमन्/ *noun* [U] meat from the back leg or side of a pig that has been **cured**. Gammon is usually served in thick slices मसालेदार या भुना हुआ सूअर के पुट्ठे का मांस, इस भोजन को मोटी कतलियों के रूप में परोसा जाता है

**gander** /ˈgændə(r) ˈगैन्ड (र्)/ *noun* [C] a male bird (goose) नरहंस

**Gandhian** *adj.* connected with or related to the way of life of Mahatma Gandhi or his teachings महात्मा गाँधी की जीवन शैली या उनकी शिक्षा से जुड़ी या संबंधित

**gang[1]** /gæŋ गैङ्/ *noun* [C, *with sing. or pl. verb*] **1** an organized group of criminals अपराधियों का संगठित गिरोह **2** a group of young people who cause trouble, fight other groups, etc. तोड़-फोड़ करने, उपद्रव मचाने वाले युवकों का दल; जवान गुंडों की टोली *The woman was robbed by a gang of youths.* ○ *gang warfare/violence* **3** (*informal*) a group of friends who meet regularly मित्र-मंडली

**gang[2]** /gæŋ गैंग्/ *verb*

**gang up on sb** (*informal*) to join together with other people in order to act against sb किसी के खिलाफ़ औरों के साथ एकजुट हो जाना *She's upset because she says the other kids are ganging up on her.*

**gangrene** /ˈgæŋgriːn ˈगैंङ्ग्रीन्/ *noun* [U] the death of a part of the body because the blood supply to it has been stopped as a result of disease or injury रोग या चोट के कारण रक्त आपूर्ति रुक जाने के फलस्वरूप शरीर के किसी अंग का निष्प्राण हो जाना; गलन, विगलन, गैंग्रीन ▶ **gangrenous** /ˈgæŋgrɪnəs गैङ्ग्रिनस्/ *adj.* गैंग्रीन-संबंधी, गैंग्रीन से पीड़ित

**gangster** /ˈgæŋstə(r) ˈगैंङ्स्ट(र्)/ *noun* [C] a member of a group of criminals अपराधियों के गिरोह का सदस्य; डाकू

**gangway** /ˈgæŋweɪ ˈगैङ्वे/ *noun* [C] **1** a passage between rows of seats in a cinema, an aircraft, etc. सिनेमाघर, विमान आदि में कुरसियों की कतारों के बीच का गलियारा **2** a bridge that people use for getting on or off a ship जलपोत पर सवार होने या उससे उतरने के लिए प्रयुक्त पुल

**gantry** /ˈgæntri ˈगैन्ट्रि/ *noun* [C] (*pl.* **gantries**) a tall metal frame like a bridge that is used to support signs over a road, lights over a stage, etc. लंबा पुल-नुमा धातुनिर्मित चौखटा जो सड़क पर संकेत पट्टियों को, मंच पर रोशनी को थामने आदि के लिए प्रयुक्त होता है

**gaol, gaoler** (*BrE*) = **jail, jailer**

**gap** /gæp गैप्/ *noun* [C] **1 a gap (in/between sth)** an empty space in sth or between two things दो वस्तुओं के बीच ख़ाली जगह; किसी वस्तु में छेद या दरार *The sheep got out through a gap in the fence.* **2** a period of time when sth stops, or between two events किसी प्रक्रिया के विराम या दो घटनाओं के बीच विराम का समय; अंतराल *I returned to teaching after a gap of about five years.* ○ *a gap in the conversation* **3** a difference between people or their ideas व्यक्तियों या विचारों के बीच अंतर, विषमता, मतभेद *The gap between the rich and the poor is getting wider.* **4** a part of sth that is missing ख़ाली स्थान, रिक्त, टूटा हुआ भाग *In this exercise you have to fill (in) the gaps in the sentences.* ○ *I think our new product should fill* ***a gap in the market***.

IDM **bridge a/the gap** ➪ **bridge[2]** देखिए।

**gape** /geɪp गेप्/ *verb* [I] **1 gape (at sb/sth)** to stare at sb/sth with your mouth open मुँह खोले किसी व्यक्ति या वस्तु को एकटक देखना *We gaped in astonishment when we saw what Anita was wearing.* **2 gape (open)** to be or become wide open पूरी तरह खुल जाना या खुला हुआ होना *a gaping hole/wound.*

**garage** /ˈgærɑːʒ; ˈgærɪdʒ ˈगैराश़्; ˈगैरिज्/ *noun* [C] **1** a small building where a car, etc. is kept कार आदि रखने का कमरा; गराज़ *The house has a double garage.* **2** a place where vehicles are repaired and/or petrol is sold वाहनों की मरम्मत और/या पेट्रोल की बिक्री का स्थान *a garage mechanic* ➪ **petrol station** देखिए।

**garam masala** *noun* [U] a mixture of spices like **cloves, cardamom, black pepper**, etc. that is used in Indian cookery भारतीय पाक कला में प्रयुक्त लौंग, इलायची, काली मिर्च आदि जैसे मसालों का मिश्रण; गरम मसाला

**Garba** *noun* [U] a folk dance from Gujarat in which the dancers move in circles in a clockwise and an anticlockwise direction गरबा; गुजरात का एक लोक नृत्य जिसमें घेरे बनाकर दाएँ ओर और फिर बाएँ ओर नर्तक नृत्य करते हैं

**garbage** /ˈgɑːbɪdʒ ˈगाबिज्/ (*AmE*) = **rubbish**

**garbage can** (*AmE*) = **dustbin**

**garbled** /ˈgɑːbld ˈगाबल्ड्/ *adj.* (used about a message, story, etc.) difficult to understand because it is not clear (संदेश, कहानी, आदि) अस्पष्टता के कारण दुर्बोध

**garden[1]** /ˈgɑːdn ˈगाड्न्/ *noun* [C] **1** (*AmE* **yard**) a piece of land next to a house where flowers and vegetables can be grown, usually with a piece of grass (**lawn**) घर से लगी प्रायः घास वाली ज़मीन जहाँ फूल और सब्ज़ियाँ उगाई जा सकती हैं; बग़ीचा *the back/front garden* ○ *garden flowers* ○ *garden chairs* ➪ **yard** पर नोट देखिए। **2 gardens** [*pl.*] a public park सार्वजनिक उद्यान

**garden²** /ˈgɑːdn ˈगाड्न्/ *verb* [I] to work in a garden बग़ीचे में काम करना; बाग़वानी करना *She's been gardening all afternoon.*

**garden centre** *noun* [C] a place where plants, seeds, garden equipment, etc. are sold पौधे, बीज, बग़ीचे के औज़ार आदि बेचने का स्थान

**gardener** /ˈgɑːdnə(r) ˈगाड्न(र्)/ *noun* [C] a person who works in a garden as a job or for pleasure शौक़िया या नौकरी के तौर पर बग़ीचे में काम करने वाला; माली, बाग़वान

**gardening** /ˈgɑːdnɪŋ ˈगाड्निङ्/ *noun* [U] looking after a garden बग़ीचे की देखभाल; बाग़वानी *I'm going to **do some gardening** this afternoon.* ○ *gardening tools/gloves*

**garden party** *noun* [C] a formal social event that takes place outside, usually in a large garden in summer प्रायः ग्रीष्म ऋतु में बड़े बग़ीचे में आयोजित औपचारिक समारोह; उद्यान-भोज, गार्डन पार्टी

**gargle** /ˈgɑːgl ˈगाग्ल्/ *verb* [I] to wash your throat with a liquid (which you do not swallow) किसी द्रव पदार्थ से ग़रारे करना

**garish** /ˈgeərɪʃ ˈगेअरिश्/ *adj.* very bright or decorated and therefore unpleasant बहुत चमकीला या भड़कीला और इसलिए अरुचिकर ✪ पर्याय **gaudy**

**garland** /ˈgɑːlənd ˈगालन्ड्/ *noun* [C] a circle of flowers and leaves that is worn on the head or around the neck or is hung in a room, etc. as decoration (फूलों की) माला, हार *a garland of*

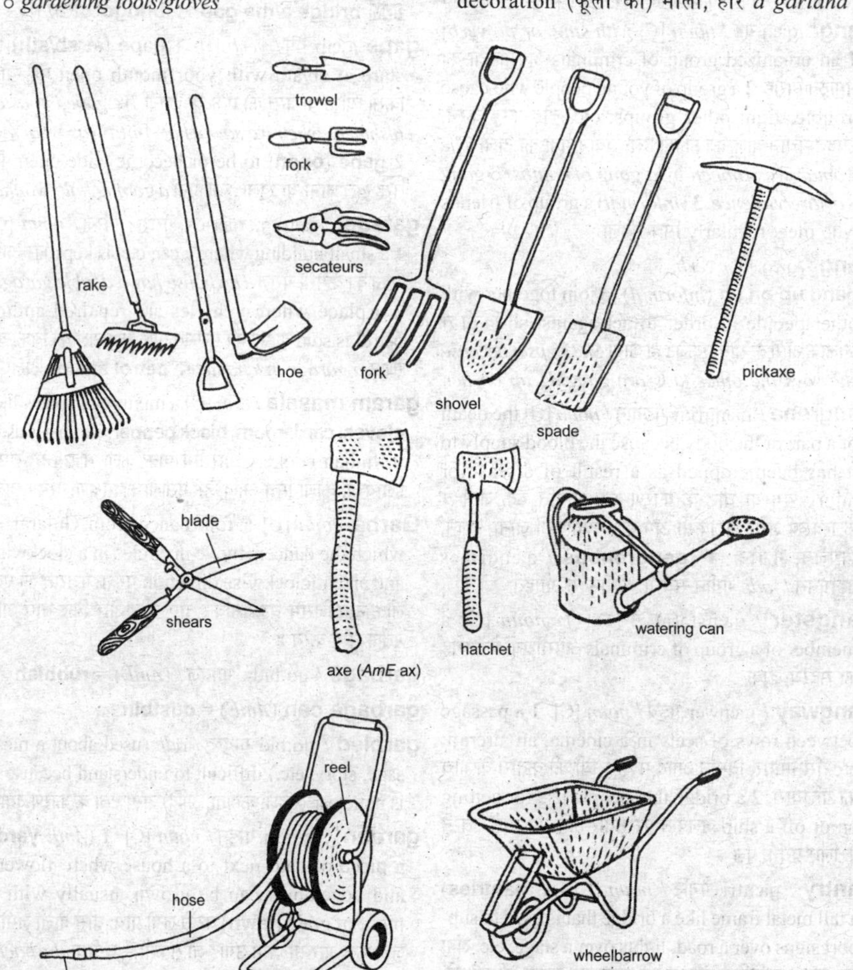


**gardening equipment**

*flowers* ▶ **garland** *verb* [T] माला से किसी व्यक्ति या वस्तु को सुसज्जित करना *The chief guest was garlanded on his arrival.*

**garlic** /ˈgɑːlɪk ˈगालिक्/ *noun* [U] a plant with a strong taste and smell that looks like a small onion and is used in cooking लहसुन *Chop two* ***cloves of garlic*** *and fry in oil.*

**garment** /ˈgɑːmənt ˈगामन्ट्/ *noun* [C] (*formal*) one piece of clothing पहनने का वस्त्र ➪ **clothes** देखिए।

**garnish** /ˈgɑːnɪʃ ˈगानिश्/ *verb* [T] to decorate a dish of food with a small amount of another food भोजन को अन्य खाद्य पदार्थ की अल्प मात्रा से सजाना ▶ **garnish** *noun* [U, C] भोजन की सजावट के लिए प्रयुक्त खाद्य पदार्थ

**garrison** /ˈgærɪsn ˈगैरिसन्/ *noun* [C] a group of soldiers who are living in and guarding a town or building नगर या भवन में उसकी रक्षा के लिए रह रही सेना; दुर्ग सेना, रक्षक सेना

**gas**[1] /gæs गैस्/ *noun* (*pl.* **gases;** *AmE* **gasses**) **1** [C, U] a substance like air that is not a solid or a liquid वायु के समान पदार्थ जो न ठोस है न द्रव; गैस *Hydrogen and oxygen are gases.* **2** [U] a particular type of gas or mixture of gases that is used for heating or cooking तपाने या भोजन बनाने के लिए प्रयुक्त एक विशेष प्रकार की गैस या गैसों का मिश्रण *a gas cylinder* **3** [U] (*AmE*) = **petrol**

**gas**[2] /gæs गैस्/ *verb* [T] (**gassing; gassed**) to poison or kill sb with gas ज़हरीली गैस सुँघाकर किसी को मार देना

**gas chamber** *noun* [C] a room that can be filled with poisonous gas in order to kill animals or people ऐसा कमरा जिसमें विषैली गैस छोड़कर पशुओं या मनुष्यों को मार दिया जाता है; गैस चैंबर

**gaseous** /ˈgæsiəs ˈगैसिअस्/ *adj.* like gas or containing gas गैस जैसा या गैस-युक्त

**gash** /gæʃ गैश्/ *noun* [C] a long deep cut or wound लंबा गहरा कटाव या घाव *He had a nasty gash in his arm.* ▶ **gash** *verb* [T] गहरा घाव करना

**gasket** /ˈgæskɪt ˈगैस्किट्/ *noun* [C] a flat piece of rubber, etc. placed between two metal surfaces in a pipe or an engine to prevent steam, gas or oil from escaping रबर आदि का समतल टुकड़ा जिसे पाइप या इंजन की दो धातुई सतहों के बीच में रख देते हैं ताकि भाप या तेल बाहर न निकले; गैसकिट *The engine had* ***blown a gasket*** (= had allowed steam, etc. to escape). ○ (*figurative*) *He* ***blew a gasket*** (= became very angry) *at the news.*

**gas mask** *noun* [C] a piece of equipment that is worn over the face to protect against poisonous gas विषैली गैस से बचाव के लिए मुँह पर पहना उपकरण; गैस मास्क

**gas meter** *noun* [C] an instrument that measures the amount of gas that you use in your home घर में इस्तेमाल गैस की मात्रा को मापने वाला उपकरण; गैस मीटर

**gasoline** /ˈgæsəliːn ˈगैसलीन्/ (*also* **gas**) (*AmE*) = **petrol**

**gasp** /gɑːsp गास्प्/ *verb* [I] **1 gasp (at sth)** to take a sudden loud breath with your mouth open, usually because you are surprised or in pain (प्रायः हैरानी या परेशानी में) खुले मुँह से अचानक ज़ोर-ज़ोर से साँस लेना; हाँफना, तेजी से साँस लेना **2** to have difficulty breathing साँस लेने में कठिनाई अनुभव करना; हाँफना, रुक-रुक कर साँस लेना *I pulled the boy out of the pool and he lay there* ***gasping for breath.*** ▶ **gasp** *noun* [C] हँफनी *to give a gasp of surprise/pain/horror.*

**gas station** (*AmE*) = **petrol station**

**gastric** /ˈgæstrɪk ˈगैस्ट्रिक्/ *adj.* (*medical*) (*only before a noun*) connected with the stomach पेट से संबंधित, आमाशय-संबंधी *a gastric ulcer* ○ *gastric juices* (= the acids in your stomach that deal with the food you eat)

**gastritis** /gæˈstraɪtɪs गैˈस्ट्राइटिस्/ *noun* [U] an illness in which the inside of the stomach becomes swollen and painful आमाशय में सूजन और दर्द की बीमारी

**gastro-enteritis** /ˌgæstrəʊ ˌentəˈraɪtɪs ˈगैस्ट्रो,एन्टˈराइटिस्/ *noun* [U] an illness in which the inside of the stomach and the tube that carries food out of the stomach (**intestine**) become swollen and painful आमाशय और आँतों में सूजन और दर्द की बीमारी

**gastronomic** /ˌgæstrəˈnɒmɪk ˌगैस्ट्रˈनॉमिक्/ *adj.* connected with good food अच्छे भोजन से संबंधित

**gastropod** /ˈgæstrəpɒd ˈगैस्ट्रपॉड्/ *noun* [C] any of a **class** of animals with a soft body and usually a shell, that can live either on land or in water कोमल शरीर और कड़े आवरण वाला प्राणी जो भूमि और जल दोनों में रह सकता है; जठरपाद *Snails and slugs are gastropods.* ➪ **mollusc** पर चित्र देखिए।

**gate** /geɪt गेट्/ *noun* [C] **1** the part of a fence, wall, etc. like a door that can be opened to let people or vehicles through द्वार, फाटक, गेट *Please keep the garden gate closed.* **2** (*also* **gateway**) the space in a wall, fence, etc. where the gate is दीवार, बाड़ आदि में बना द्वार का स्थान *Drive through the gates and you'll find the car park on the right.*

3 the place at an airport where you go to get on or off a plane हवाई अड्डे में बना द्वार जहाँ से विमान पर चढ़ते और उतरते हैं *Air Deccan Flight 201 to Bangalore is now boarding at Gate 16.*

**gateau** /ˈgætəʊ ˈगैटो / *noun* [C] (*pl.* **gateaux**) a large cake that is usually decorated with cream, fruit, etc. प्रायः क्रीम, फल आदि से सजा एक बड़ा केक; गाटो (केक)

**gatecrash** /ˈgeɪtkræʃ ˈगेट्क्रैश् / *verb* [I, T] to go to a private party without being invited बिना निमंत्रण किसी निजी पार्टी में आना ► **gatecrasher** *noun* [C] बिना निमंत्रण पार्टी में जाने वाला; अनिमंत्रित मेहमान

**gatepost** /ˈgeɪtpəʊst ˈगेट्पोस्ट् / *noun* [C] either of the posts at the end of a gate which it is supported by or fastened to when it is closed मुख्य द्वार या फाटक का स्तंभ; द्वार स्तंभ

**gateway** /ˈgeɪtweɪ ˈगेट्वे / *noun* [C] **1**= **gate 2** **2** [*sing.*] **the gate way to sth** the place which you must go through in order to get to somewhere else वह स्थान जहाँ से गुज़रना अनिवार्य है, अन्यत्र पहुँचने के लिए द्वार मार्ग; तोरण

**gather** /ˈgæðə(r) ˈगैद़(र्) / *verb* **1** [I,T] **gather (round) (sb/ sth); gather sb/sth (round) (sb/ sth)** (used about people) to come or be brought together in a group (व्यक्तियों का) इकट्ठा या एकत्र होना *A crowd soon gathered at the scene of the accident.* ○ *We all gathered round and listened to what the guide was saying.* **2** [T] **gather sth (together/up)** to bring many things together बहुत-सी वस्तुओं को इकट्ठा करना *He gathered up all his papers and put them away.* ○ *They have gathered together a lot of information on the subject.* **3** [T] (*formal*) to pick wild flowers, fruit, etc. from a wide area बड़े इलाक़े में से जंगली फल-फूल चुनना *to gather mushrooms* **4** [T] to understand or find out sth (from sb/sth) समझना या (किसी व्यक्ति या वस्तु से) कुछ पता लगाना *I gather from your letter that you have several years' experience of this kind of work.* **5** [I, T] to gradually become greater; to increase क्रमशः अधिक होना; बढ़ना *I gathered speed as I cycled down the hill.*

**gathering** /ˈgæðərɪŋ ˈगैद़रिङ् / *noun* [C] a time when people come together; a meeting लोगों का जमाव, मिलन; सभा *a family gathering*

**gaudy** /ˈgɔːdi ˈगॉडि / *adj.* very bright or decorated and therefore unpleasant भड़कीला, शोख़, चटकीला और इसलिए अप्रिय ✪ पर्याय **garish**

**gauge**[1] (*AmE* **gage**) /geɪdʒ गेज् / *noun* [C] **1** an instrument for measuring the amount of sth किसी वस्तु की मात्रा मापने का उपकरण; पैमाना *a fuel/temperature/pressure gauge* ➪ **car** पर चित्र देखिए। **2** (*technical*) a measurement of the width of sth or of the distance between two things किसी वस्तु की चौड़ाई या दो वस्तुओं के बीच की दूरी का माप; गेज *a narrow-gauge railway* **3 a gauge (of sth)** a fact that you can use to judge a situation, sb's feelings, etc. किसी स्थिति या किसी के मनोभाव को समझने में सहायक तथ्य

**gauge**[2] /geɪdʒ गेज् / *verb* [T] **1** to make a judgement or to calculate sth by guessing किसी स्थिति का मूल्यांकन करना या अनुमान से हिसाब लगाना *It was difficult to gauge the mood of the audience.* **2** to measure sth accurately using a special instrument विशेष उपकरण द्वारा किसी वस्तु का सही माप करना

**gaunt** /gɔːnt गॉन्ट् / *adj.* (used about a person) very thin because of hunger, illness, etc. (व्यक्ति) भूख, रोग आदि के कारण बहुत दुबला

**gaur** *noun* [C] a wild ox found in the mountainous areas of eastern India and Southeast Asia पूर्वी भारत और दक्षिण-पूर्वी एशिया के पर्वतीय इलाक़ों में पाए जाने वाला जंगली भैंसा; गौर

**gauze** /gɔːz गॉज़् / *noun* **1** [U] light transparent material, usually made of cotton or **silk** हलका पारदर्शी पदार्थ (प्रायः सूती या रेशमी); सूती या रेशमी जाली **2** [U] a thin material like a net, that is used for covering an area of skin that you have hurt or cut महीन तार की जाली (घाव को ढकने में प्रयुक्त); गॉज़ **3** [U, C] material made from a **network** of wire; a piece of this तार से बनी जाली का सामान; एक अदद ऐसा सामान *a wire gauze* ➪ **laboratory** पर चित्र देखिए।

**gave** ➪ **give** का past tense रूप

**gawp** /gɔːp गॉप्/ *verb* [I] (*informal*) **gawp (at sb/ sth)** to look or stare in a stupid way मूर्खों की तरह देखना या घूमना *Lots of drivers slowed down to gawp at the accident.*

**gay**[1] /geɪ गे/ *adj.* **1** sexually attracted to people of the same sex; homosexual समान लिंग के व्यक्ति के प्रति कामुक भाव से आकृष्ट; समलिंगी *the gay community* ○ *a gay bar/club* (= for gay people) ➪ **lesbian** देखिए। **2** (*old-fashioned*) happy and full of fun ख़ुशमिज़ाज और मौज-मस्ती भरा ➪ **gaiety** noun देखिए।

**gay**[2] /geɪ गे/ *noun* [C] a person, especially a man, who is sexually attracted to people of the same sex; a homosexual समान लिंग के व्यक्ति के प्रति कामुक भाव से अकृष्ट व्यक्ति, विशेषतः पुरुष; समलिंगी पुरुष ➪ **lesbian** देखिए।

**gaze** /geɪz गेज़् / *verb* [I] to look steadily for a long time देर तक स्थिर दृष्टि से देखना; टकटकी लगा कर देखना; एकटक देखना *She sat at the window gazing dreamily into space.* ▶ **gaze** *noun* [*sing.*] एकटक दृष्टि

**gazette** /gəˈzet गˈज़ेट् / *noun* [C] **1** an official newspaper containing important information about decisions that have been made, people who have been employed, etc. published by an organization राजपत्र, सूचनापत्र, गज़ेट **2** a word used in the titles of some newspapers कुछ समाचार पत्रों के शीर्षकों में प्रयुक्त शब्द *The Morning Gazette*

**GDP** /ˌdʒiː diːˈpiː ˌजी डी ˈपी / *abbr.* gross domestic product; the total value of all the goods and services produced in a country in one year सकल घरेलू उत्पाद; किसी देश में एक वर्ष के भीतर निर्मित वस्तुओं तथा उपलब्ध सेवाओं का कुल मूल्य ➪ **GNP** देखिए।

**gear[1]** /gɪə(r) गिअ(र्)/ *noun* **1** [C] the machinery in a vehicle that turns engine power into a movement forwards or backwards वाहन का वह पुरज़ा जिससे इंजन वाहन को आगे या पीछें धकेलता है; गियर *Most cars have four or five forward gears and a reverse.* ➪ **bicycle** पर चित्र देखिए। **2** [U] a particular position of the gears in a vehicle वाहन में गियरों की विशेष स्थिति *first/second/top/reverse gear ○ to change gear* **3** [U] equipment or clothing that you need for a particular activity, etc. किसी विशेष काम के लिए अपेक्षित उपकरण या वस्त्र *camping/fishing/sports gear* **4** [*sing.*] an instrument or part of a machine that is used for a particular purpose विशेष उद्देश्य से प्रयुक्त मशीनी उपकरण या पुरज़ा *the landing gear of an aeroplane*

**gear[2]** /gɪə(r) गिअ(र्)/ *verb*

**PHR V** **gear sth to/towards sb/sth** (*usually passive*) to make sth suitable for a particular purpose or person किसी वस्तु को व्यक्ति विशेष या उद्देश्य विशेष के अनुकूल बनाना *There is a special course geared towards the older learner.*

**gear up (for sb/sth); gear sb/sth up (for sb/sth)** to get ready or to make sb/sth ready व्यक्ति या वस्तु का तैयार होना या को तैयार करना

**gearbox** /ˈgɪəbɒks ˈगिअबॉक्स् / *noun* [C] the metal case that contains the **gears[1]** **1** of a car, etc. कार आदि का गियरबॉक्स

**gear lever** (*AmE* **gear shift**) *noun* [C] a stick that is used for changing **gear[1]** in a car, etc. कार का गियर बदलने वाली छड़ ➪ **car** पर चित्र देखिए।

**gee** /dʒiː जी / *exclamation* (*AmE*) used for expressing surprise, pleasure, etc. आश्चर्य, प्रसन्नता आदि व्यक्त करने के लिए प्रयुक्त

**geese** ➪ **goose** का plural रूप

**Geiger counter** /ˈgaɪgə kaʊntə(r) ˈगाइगा काउन्ट(र्) *noun* [C] a machine used for finding and measuring the rays that are sent out by dangerous **radioactive** substances रेडियो-सक्रिय पदार्थों से निकली किरणों का पता लगाने तथा मापने की मशीन

**gel** /dʒel जेल् / *noun* [C, U] (*usually compounds*) a thick substance that is between a liquid and a solid एक गाढ़ा पदार्थ (द्रव और ठोस के बीच का), जैल, जेली *hair gel ○ shower gel*

**gelatin** /ˈdʒelətɪn ˈजेलटिन् / (*also* **gelatine** /ˈdʒelətiːn ˈजेलटीन् /) *noun* [U] a clear substance without any taste that is made from boiling animal bones and is used to make liquid food **set** पशुओं की हड्डियों को उबालकर बनाया गया एक पारदर्शी पदार्थ जिसे तरल भोज्य पदार्थ को जमाने के लिए प्रयुक्त किया जाता है; सरेस, जिलेटिन

**gelignite** /ˈdʒelɪgnaɪt ˈजेलिग्नाइट् / *noun* [U] a substance that is used for making explosions विस्फोटकों को बनाने के लिए प्रयुक्त पदार्थ; जेलिग्नाइट

**gem** /dʒem जेम् / *noun* [C] **1** a jewel or precious stone रत्न, हीरा **2** a person or thing that is especially good उत्कृष्ट व्यक्ति या वस्तु

**Gemini** /ˈdʒemɪnaɪ ˈजेमिनाइ / *noun* [U] the third sign of the **zodiac**; the Twins राशिचक्र में तीसरी राशि; मिथुन राशि

**Gen.** *abbr.* General; an officer in the army जनरल; सेना में एक पदाधिकारी

**gender** /ˈdʒendə(r) ˈजेन्ड(र्) / *noun* [C, U] **1** (*formal*) the fact of being male or female पुरुष या स्त्री होना, लिंग ✪ पर्याय **sex** **2** (*grammar*) (in some languages) the division of nouns, pronouns, etc. into different classes (**masculine, feminine** and **neuter**); one of these three types (कुछ भाषाओं में) संज्ञाओं, सर्वनामों आदि का (पुल्लिंग, स्त्रीलिंग, नपुंसकलिंग) में वर्गीकरण; इनमें से कोई एक लिंग

**gene** /dʒiːn जीन् / *noun* [C] a unit of information inside a cell which controls what a living thing will be like. Genes are passed from parents to children कोशिका के अंदर एक ज्ञानतंतु जो किसी सजीव के रूप-व्यवहार को नियंत्रित करता है; जीन, जीन माता-पिता से उनकी संतानों तक पहुँचते हैं ➪ **genetics** देखिए।

**general[1]** /ˈdʒenrəl ˈजेन्रल् / *adj.* **1** affecting all or most people, places, things, etc. सभी या अधिकतम लोगों, स्थानों, वस्तुओं आदि से संबंधित; सामान्य, सर्वसामान्य *Fridges were once a luxury, but now they are in general use. ○ the general public* (= most ordinary people) **2** (*only before a noun*) referring to or describing the main part of sth, not the details किसी वस्तु के मुख्य अंश (न कि विस्तार) का निर्देश करने

वाला *Your general health is very good.* ○ ***As a general rule*** *the most common verbs in English tend to be irregular.* **3** not limited to one subject or area of study; not specialized किसी एक विषय या अध्ययन-क्षेत्र तक सीमित नहीं; जिसमें विशिष्टता की बात न हो *Children need a good general education.* ○ *The quiz tests your* ***general knowledge***. ○ *a general hospital* **4** (*usually in compounds*) with responsibility for the whole of an organization संपूर्ण संगठन के दायित्व वाला *a general manager*

IDM **in general** **1** in most cases; usually अधिकांशतः; सामान्यतया *In general, standards of hygiene are good.* **2** as a whole कुल मिलाकर *I'm interested in American history in general, and the civil war in particular.*

**general²** /ˈdʒenrəl ˈजेन्‌रल्/ *noun* [C] (*abbr.* **Gen.**) an army officer in a very high position सेना का उच्च पदाधिकारी; जनरल

**general election** *noun* [C] an election in which all the people of a country vote to choose a government वह चुनाव जिसमें सरकार चुनने के लिए सभी लोग मतदान करें; आम चुनाव ➪ **by-election** देखिए।

**generalization** (*also* **-isation**) /ˌdʒenrəlaɪˈzeɪʃn ˌजेन्‌रलाइ ˈज़ेश्न्/ *noun* [C, U] a general statement that is based on only a few facts or examples; the act of making such a statement केवल कुछ तथ्यों और उदाहरणों पर आधारित सामान्य वक्तव्य, निष्कर्ष; सामान्य वक्तव्य देने का काम *You can't* ***make*** *sweeping* ***generalizations about*** *French people if you've only been there for a day!*

**generalize** /ˈdʒenrəlaɪz ˈजे़न्‌रलाइज़्/ *verb* [I] **generalize (about sth)** to form an opinion or make a statement using only a small amount of information instead of looking at the details सीमित सूचना के आधार पर (न कि विस्तार में जाकर) राय बनाना या वक्तव्य देना

**generally** /ˈdʒenrəli ˈजेन्‌रलि/ *adv.* **1** by or to most people अधिकतम व्यक्तियों द्वारा या के लिए *He is generally considered to be a good doctor.* **2** usually सामान्यतया *She generally cycles to work.* **3** without discussing the details of sth किसी वस्तु के ब्योरों पर चर्चा किए बिना *Generally speaking, houses in America are bigger than houses in this country.*

**general practitioner** = **GP**

**generate** /ˈdʒenəreɪt ˈजेनरेट्/ *verb* [T] to produce or create sth किसी वस्तु का उत्पादन या निर्माण करना *to generate heat/power/electricity*

**generation** /ˌdʒenəˈreɪʃn ˌजेनˈरेश्न्/ *noun* **1** [C] all the people in a family, group or country who were born at about the same time किसी परिवार, समूह या देश के वे लोग जो एक ही समय में पैदा हुए; पीढ़ी *We should look after the planet for future generations.* ○ *This photograph shows three generations of my family* (= children, parents and grandparents). ➪ **first generation** देखिए।

> NOTE **Generation** शब्द एकवचनांत है जो एकवचन या बहुवचन क्रिया के साथ प्रयुक्त किया जाता है—*The younger generation only seem/seems to be interested in money.*

**2** [C] the average time that children take to grow up and have children of their own, usually considered to be about 25–30 years वह औसत अवधि जिसमें बच्चे बड़े हो जाते हैं और स्वयं माता-पिता बन जाते हैं, यह अवधि सामान्यतया 25–30 वर्ष की मानी जाती है *A generation ago foreign travel was still only possible for a few people.* **3** [U] the production of sth, especially heat, power, etc. किसी वस्तु (विशेषतया ताप, विद्युत आदि) का उत्पादन

**the generation gap** *noun* [*sing.*] the difference in behaviour, and the lack of understanding, between young people and older people युवाओं और वृद्धों के आचरण में अंतर और आपसी समझ में कमी

**generator** /ˈdʒenəreɪtə(r) ˈजेनरेट(र्)/ *noun* [C] a machine that produces electricity विद्युत उत्पन्न करने वाली मशीन; जेनरेटर

**generic** /dʒəˈnerɪk जˈनेरिक्/ *adj.* **1** shared by, including or typical of a whole group of things; not specific जो किसी समूह की सभी वस्तुओं में समान हो या उनका प्रातिनिधिक हो; अविशिष्ट **2** (used about a product, especially a drug) not using the name of the company that made it (कोई उत्पादित वस्तु, विशेषतः औषधि) जिस पर निर्माता कंपनी के नाम का उल्लेख नहीं ▶ **generically** /dʒəˈnerɪkli जˈनेरिक्‌लि/ *adv.* प्रातिनिधिक रूप से

**generosity** /ˌdʒenəˈrɒsəti ˌजेनˈरॉसटि/ *noun* [U] the quality of being generous उदारता

**generous** /ˈdʒenərəs ˈजेनरस्/ *adj.* **1** happy to give more money, help, etc. than is usual or expected असामान्य या अप्रत्याशित रूप से धन, सहायता आदि देने में प्रसन्नता अनुभव करने वाला; उदार *It was very generous of your parents to lend us all that money.* **2** larger than usual सामान्य से अधिक; प्रचुर *a generous helping of pasta* ▶ **generously** *adv.* उदारतापूर्वक *People gave very generously to our appeal for the homeless.*

**genesis** /ˈdʒenəsɪs ˈजेनसिस्/ *noun* [*sing.*] (*formal*) the beginning or origin of sth (किसी का) उद्‌भव, प्रारंभ

**genetic** /dʒəˈnetɪk जˈनेटिक्/ *adj.* connected with **genes** or with **genetics** आनुवंशिक विज्ञान, अनुवंशिकी

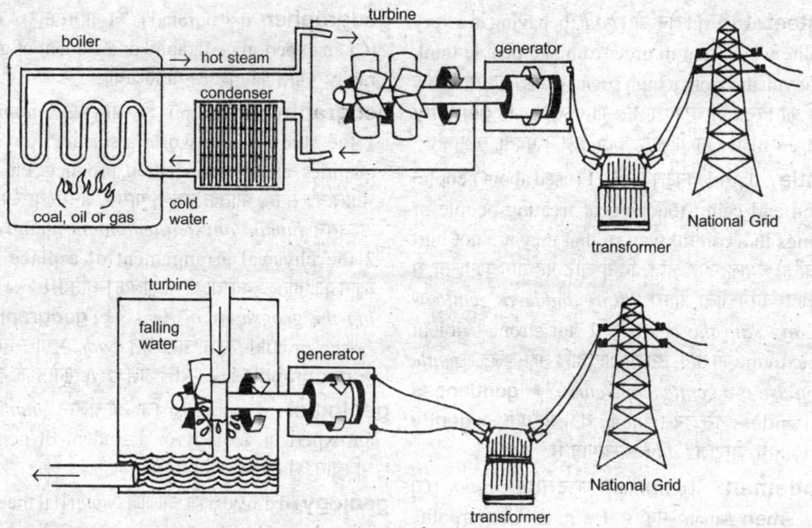


generator

जनन विज्ञान *The disease is caused by a genetic defect.* ▶ **genetically** /-kli -कलि /*adv.*जीन-विज्ञान या जनन-विज्ञान की दृष्टि से

**genetically modified** *adj.* (*abbr.* **GM**) (used about food, plants, etc.) that has been grown from cells whose **genes** have been changed artificially (खाद्य पदार्थ, पौधे आदि) कृत्रिम रूप से परिवर्तित जीन की कोशिकाओं से उत्पादित

**genetic engineering** *noun* [U] the science of changing the way a human, an animal or a plant develops by changing the information in its **genes** जीन-परिवर्तन के द्वारा मनुष्य, पशु या पौधे के विकास में परिवर्तन का वैज्ञानिक अध्ययन

**genetics** /dʒəˈnetɪks जˈनेटिक्स् / *noun* [U] the scientific study of the way that the development of living things is controlled by qualities that have been passed on from parents to children सजीवों में विभिन्न लक्षणों का माता-पिता से उनकी संतान तक पहुँचाने की विकास-प्रक्रिया का वैज्ञानिक अध्ययन; आनुवंशिकता विज्ञान, जनन-विज्ञान ➪ **gene** देखिए।

**genial** /ˈdʒiːniəl ˈजीनिअल् / *adj.* (used about a person) pleasant and friendly (व्यक्ति) प्रसन्नचित्त और मित्रवत

**genie** /ˈdʒiːni ˈजीनि / *noun* [C] a spirit with magic powers, especially one that lives in a bottle or a lamp जादुई शक्ति संपन्न प्रेतात्मा, विशेषतः बोतल या लैंप में रहने वाली; जिन, जिन्न

**genitals** /ˈdʒenɪtlz ˈजेनिट्ल्ज़् / (*also* **genitalia** /ˌdʒenɪˈteɪliə ˌजेनिˈटेलिआ /) *noun* [*pl.*] (*formal*) the parts of a person's sex organs that are outside the body व्यक्ति के जननांग ▶ **genital** /ˈdʒenɪtl ˈजेनिट्ल् / *adj.*जनन-संबंधी

**genitive** /ˈdʒenətɪv ˈजेनटिव् / *noun* [C] (*grammar*) (in some languages) the special form of a noun, a pronoun or an adjective that is used to show possession or close connection between two things (कुछ भाषाओं में) संज्ञा, सर्वमान या विशेषण का विशिष्ट रूप जो दो वस्तुओं के बीच संबंध प्रदर्शित करता हैं; संबंधकारक रूप, षष्ठी विभक्ति रूप ➪ **accusative**, **dative**, **nominative** और **vocative** भी देखिए। ▶ **genitive** *adj* संबंधकारक या षष्ठी विभक्ति का

**genius** /ˈdʒiːniəs जीनिअस् / *noun* **1** [U] very great and unusual ability अति महान और असाधारण क्षमता *Her idea was **a stroke of genius**.* **2** [C] a person who has very great and unusual ability, especially in a particular subject असाधारण क्षमता संपन्न व्यक्ति, विशेषतः किसी विषय विशेष में *Ramanujan was a mathematical genius.* ➪ **prodigy** देखिए। **3** [*sing.*] **a genius for(doing) sth** a very good natural skill or ability उच्च कोटि की नैसर्गिक कुशलता या योग्यता

**genocide** /ˈdʒenəsaɪd जेनसाइड् / *noun* [U] the murder of all the people of a particular race, religion, etc. विशेष प्रजाति, धर्म आदि के लोगों की सामूहिक हत्या; नरसंहार

**genome** /ˈdʒiːnəʊm ˈजीनोम् / *noun* [C] the complete set of **genes** in a cell or living thing एक कोशिका या सजीव में स्थित पूर्ण जीन-समुच्चय *the decoding of the human genome*

**genre** /ˈʒɑːnrə ˈशानृ / *noun* [C] (*formal*) a particular type or style of literature, art, film or music that you can recognize because of its special characteristics साहित्य, कला, फ़िल्म या संगीत का विशेष प्रकार जिसकी पहचान के विशिष्ट लक्षण होते हैं; रूप विधा

**gent** /ˈdʒent ˈजेन्ट् / (*informal*) = **gentleman**

**genteel** /dʒen'ti:l जेन्'टील् / *adj.* behaving in a very polite way, often in order to make people think that you are from a high social class उच्च सामाजिक वर्ग का विनम्र आचरण वाला; भद्र, कुलीन ▶ **gentility** /ˌdʒen'tɪləti ˌजेन्'टिलटि / *noun* [U] भद्रता, कुलीनता

**gentle** /'dʒentl 'जेन्ट्ल् / *adj.* **1** (used about people) kind and calm; touching or treating people or things in a careful way so that they are not hurt (व्यक्ति) दयालु और शांत; बिना चोट पहुँचाए कोमलता से व्यवहार करने वाला, सौम्य *'I'll try and be as gentle as I can,' said the dentist.* **2** not strong, violent or extreme जो तीव्र, उग्र या अतिवादि नहीं; हलका *gentle exercise* ○ *a gentle slope/curve* ▶ **gentleness** /'dʒentlnəs 'जेन्ट्लूनस् / *noun* [U] सौम्यता ▶ **gently** /'dʒentli 'जेन्ट्लि / *adv.* सौम्यभाव से

**gentleman** /'dʒentlmən 'जेन्ट्लूमन् / *noun* [C] (*pl.* **-men** /-mən -मन् /) **1** a man who is polite and who behaves well towards other people भद्र या सौम्य व्यक्ति, दयालु और शांत व्यक्ति; सज्जन **2** (*formal*) used when speaking to or about a man or men in a polite way किसी पुरुष या पुरुषों के बारे में विनम्रता से निर्देश करने के लिए प्रयुक्त ***Ladies and gentlemen*** (= at the beginning of a speech) ○ *Mrs Gupta, there is a gentleman here to see you.* **3** (*old-fashioned*) a rich man with a high social position धनी संभ्रांत व्यक्ति

**gentry** /'dʒentri 'जेन्ट्रि / *noun* [*pl.*] (*usually* **the gentry**) (*old-fashioned*) people belonging to a high social class अमीर वर्ग, भद्र वर्ग

**the Gents** *noun* [*sing.*] (*informal*) a public toilet for men पुरुषों के लिए सार्वजनिक शौचालयं ➪ **toilet** पर नोट देखिए।

**genuine** /'dʒenjuɪn 'जेन्युइन् / *adj.* **1** real; true वास्तविक; असली *He thought that he had bought a genuine Rolex watch but it was a cheap fake.* ➪ **imitation** देखिए। **2** sincere and honest; that can be trusted सच्चा और ईमानदार; विश्वास के योग्य ▶ **genuinely** *adv.* ईमानदारी से

**genus** /'dʒi:nəs 'जीनस् / *noun* [C] (*pl.* **genera** /'dʒenərə 'जेनरा /) (*technical*) a group into which animals, plants, etc. that have similar characteristics are divided, smaller than a **family** and larger than a **species** समान लक्षणों वाले पशुओं, पौधों आदि का वर्ग जो 'family' (परिवार) से छोटा और 'species' (जाति) से बड़ा होता है; जीनस, वंश, प्रजाति

**geo-** *prefix* (*in nouns, adjectives and adverbs*) of the earth पृथ्वी-विषयक, पृथ्वी का *geophysical* ○ *geoscience*

**geographer** /dʒi'ɒgrəfə(r) जि'ऑग्रफ़(र्) / *noun* [C] an expert in geography or a student of geography भूगोल का विशेषज्ञ या विद्यार्थी

**geography** /dʒi'ɒgrəfi जि'ऑग्रफ़ि / *noun* [U] **1** the study of the world's surface, physical qualities, climate, population, products, etc. विश्व भूगोल की सतह, भौतिक लक्षण, मौसम, जनसंख्या आदि का अध्ययन *human/physical/economic geography* **2** the physical arrangement of a place किसी स्थान की भौतिक व्यवस्था या भौगोलिक स्थिति *We're studying the geography of Asia.* ▶ **geographical** /ˌdʒi:ə'græfɪkl ˌजीअ'ग्रैफ़िकल् / *adj.* भूगोल-विषयक ▶ **geographically** /-kli -क्लि / *adv.* भूगोल की दृष्टि से

**geologist** /dʒi'ɒlədʒɪst जि'ऑलजिस्ट् / *noun* [C] an expert in geology or a student of geology भूविज्ञान का विशेषज्ञ या विद्यार्थी

**geology** /dʒi'ɒlədʒi जि'ऑलजि / *noun* [U] the study of rocks, and of the way they are formed चट्टानों और उनके निर्माण-प्रकार का अध्ययन; भूविज्ञान

**geological** /ˌdʒi:ə'lɒdʒɪkl ˌजीअ'लॉजिकल् / *adj.* भूविज्ञान-विषयक

**geometric** /ˌdʒi:ə'metrɪk ˌजीअ'मेट्रिक् / (*also* **geometrical** /-kl -क्ल् /) *adj.* **1** of geometry ज्यामिति का, ज्यामिति-विषयक, रेखागणित **2** consisting of regular shapes and lines सुडौल, नियत आकृतियों और रेखाओं वाला *a geometric design/pattern* ▶ **geometrically** /-kli -क्लि / *adv.* सुडौलता से; ज्यामिति की दृष्टि से

**geometric progression** / *noun* [C] (*mathematics*) a series of numbers in which each is multiplied or divided by a fixed number to produce the next, for example 1, 3, 9, 27, 81 संख्याओं की शृंखला जिसमें प्रत्येक को एक निश्चित संख्या से गुणा या भाग किया जाता है और फलतः अगली संख्या आती है जैसे 1, 3, 9, 27, 81; गुणोत्तर वृद्धि ➪ **arithmetic progression** देखिए।

**geometry** /dʒi'ɒmətri जि'ऑमट्रि / *noun* [U] the study in mathematics of lines, shapes, curves, etc. गणित के अंतर्गत रेखाओं, आकृतियों, वक्रताओं आदि का अध्ययन; ज्यामिति, रेखागणित

**geothermal** /ˌdʒi:əʊ'θɜ:ml ˌजीओ'थ़मल् / *adj.* connected with the natural heat of rock deep in the ground ज़मीन की गहराई में चट्टान के नैसर्गिक ताप से संबंधित *geothermal energy*

**geriatrics** /ˌdʒeri'ætrɪks ˌजेरि'ऐट्रिक्स् / *noun* [U] the medical care of old people बुज़ुर्गों के स्वास्थ्य की देखभाल; ज़रा-चिकित्सा, वृद्ध-परिचर्या ▶ **geriatric** *adj.* वृद्ध-परिचर्या से संबंधित

**germ** /dʒɜ:m जम् / *noun* **1** [C] a very small living thing that causes disease रोग उत्पन्न करने वाला बहुत

छोटा जीव; रोगाणु ➪ **bacteria** और **virus** देखिए। **2** [*sing.*] **the germ of sth** the beginning of sth that may develop बाद में विकसित होने वाली वस्तु का आरंभ बिंदु; स्रोत *the germ of an idea*

**German measles** /ˌdʒɜːmən ˈmiːzlz ˌजमन् ˈमीज़ल्ज़् / (*also* **rubella**) *noun* [U] a mild disease that causes red spots all over the body. It may damage a baby if the mother catches it when she is pregnant एक हलका रोग जिसमें शरीर पर लाल चकत्ते हो जाते हैं; खसरा, यदि गर्भवती को खसरा हो जाए तो उससे गर्भस्थ शिशु को नुक़सान हो सकता है

**German shepherd** = **Alsatian**

**germinate** /ˈdʒɜːmɪneɪt ˈजमिनेट् / *verb* [I, T] (used about a seed) to start growing; to cause a seed to do this (बीज का) बढ़ने लगना, अंकुरित होना, बीज को बढ़ाने लगना, अंकुरित करना ▶ **germination** /ˌdʒɜːmɪˈneɪʃn ˌजमिˈनेश्न् / *noun* [U] अंकुरण

**gerrymander** /ˈdʒerimændə(r) ˈजेरिमैन्ड(र्) / *verb* [I,T] to change the size and borders of an area for voting in order to give an unfair advantage to one party in an election चुनाव-क्षेत्रों की सीमाओं को इस प्रकार बदलना कि दल-विशेष को अनुचित लाभ हो ▶ **gerrymandering** *noun* [U] चुनाव-क्षेत्र का सीमा-परिवर्तन

**gerund** /ˈdʒerənd ˈजेरन्ड् / *noun* [C] (*grammar*) a noun, ending in -ing, that has been made from a verb क्रिया से बनने वाला संज्ञा रूप जो '-ing' से अंत होता है *In the sentence 'His hobby is collecting stamps', 'collecting' is a gerund.*

**gestation** /dʒeˈsteɪʃn जेˈस्टेश्न् / *noun* [U, *sing.*] the period of time that a baby (human or animal) develops inside its mother's body; the process of developing inside the mother's body माँ के गर्भ में मानव या पशु-शिशु के विकसित होने की कालावधि या प्रक्रिया; गर्भकाल *The **gestation period** of a horse is about eleven months.*

**gesticulate** /dʒeˈstɪkjuleɪt ˈजेˈस्टिक्युलेट् / *verb* [I] to make movements with your hands and arms in order to express sth अपनी बात कहने के लिए हाथों और बाँहों से संकेत करना

**gesture**[1] /ˈdʒestʃə(r) ˈजेस्चर(र्) / *noun* [C] **1** a movement of the hand, head, etc. that expresses sth कुछ कहने के लिए हाथ, सिर आदि को हिलाने की क्रिया; अंग-संकेत *I saw the boy **make a** rude **gesture** at the policeman before running off.* **2** something that you do that shows other people what you think or feel विचार या भाव के प्रदर्शन हेतु कोई क्रिया

**gesture**[2] /ˈdʒestʃə(r) ˈजेस्चर(र्) / *verb* [I, T] to point at sth, to make a sign to sb किसी वस्तु की ओर संकेत करना; किसी व्यक्ति को संकेत से कुछ कहना *She asked them to leave and gestured towards the door.*

**get** /get गेट् / *verb* (*pres. part.* **getting**; *pt* **got** /gɒt गॉट् /; *pp* **got**: *AmE* **gotten** /ˈgɒtn ˈगॉट्न् /) **1** [T] (*no passive*) to receive, obtain or buy sth: किसी वस्तु को पाना, लेना या ख़रीदना *I got a letter from my sister.* ○ *Did you get a present for your mother?* ○ *How much did you get for your old car* (= when you sold it)? ○ *to get a shock/surprise* **2** [T] **have/has got sth** to have sth किसी वस्तु को पास रखना *I've got a lot to do today.* ○ *My daughter's got brown hair.* ○ *Have you got a spare pen?* **3** [T] (*no passive*) to go to a place and bring sth back; fetch कहीं जाकर कुछ लेकर आना; लाना ***Go and get** me a pen, please.* ○ *Sam's gone to get his mother from the station.* **4** [I] to become; to reach a particular state or condition; to make sb/sth be in a particular state or condition हो जाना; किसी भावना से ग्रस्त होना; व्यक्ति या वस्तु का किसी विशेष अवस्था को प्राप्त करना *It's getting dark.* ○ *to get angry/bored/hungry/fat* ○ *He's always **getting into trouble** with the police.* **5** [I] to arrive at or reach a place कहीं पहुँचना या कहीं तक आ जाना *We should get to Delhi at about ten.* ○ *What time do you usually **get home**?* ➪ **get in, on, etc.** देखिए। **6** [I, T] to move or go somewhere; to move or put sth somewhere कहीं चलना या जाना; खिसकना या किसी वस्तु को कहीं खिसकाना *I can't swim so I couldn't get across the river.* ○ *My grandmother's 92 and and she doesn't get out of the house much.* **7** [I] used instead of 'be' in passive 'be' के स्थान पर कर्मवाच्य में प्रयुक्त *She got bitten by a dog.* ○ *Don't leave your wallet on the table or it'll get stolen.* **8** [T] **get sth done, mended, etc.** to cause sth to be done, mended, etc. कोई काम करवाना; मरम्मत, सुधार आदि करवाना *Let's get this work done, then we can go out.* ○ *I'm going to **get my hair cut**.* **9** [T] **get sb/sth to do sth** to make or persuade sb/sth to do sth किसी व्यक्ति या वस्तु से कुछ करवाना या मनवाना *I got him to agree to the plan.* ○ *I can't get the television to work.* **10** [T] to catch or have an illness, pain, etc. बीमार पड़ना, दर्द होना इत्यादि *I think I'm getting a cold.* ○ *He gets really bad headaches.* **11** [T] to use a form of transport किसी यातायात-साधन का प्रयोग करना *Shall we walk or get the bus?* **12** [I] to hit, hold or catch sb/sth किसी व्यक्ति या वस्तु को चोट पहुँचाना; कब्ज़े में लेना या पकड़ना *A boy threw a stone at me but he didn't get me.* **13** [T] to hear or understand sth कुछ सुनना या समझना *I'm sorry, I didn't get that. Could you repeat it?* ○ *Did you **get** that **joke** that Kiran told?* **14** [T]

**get (sb) sth; get sth (for sb)** to prepare food भोजन तैयार करना *Can I get you anything to eat?* ○ *Joe's in the kitchen getting breakfast for everyone.* **15** [I] **get to do sth** to have the chance to do sth कुछ करने का मौका मिलना *Did you get to try the new computer?* **16** [I] (*used with verbs in the -ing form*) to start doing sth कुछ करने लगना *We don't have much time so we'd better get working.* ○ *We'd better **get going** if we don't want to be late.*

IDM **get somewhere/nowhere (with sb/sth)** to make/not make progress प्रगति करना या न करना *I'm getting nowhere with my research.*

NOTE **Get** से बनने वाले मुहावरों के लिए संबंधित संज्ञा और विशेषण पदों की प्रविष्टियाँ देखिए। उदाहरण के लिए **get rid of** के लिए **rid** की प्रविष्टि देखिए।

PHR V **Get about/around** to move or travel from place to place एक जगह से दूसरी जगह जाना या सफ़र करना *My grandmother needs a stick to get around these days.*

**get about/around/round** (used about news, a story, etc.) to become known by many people (समाचार, कहानी आदि) अनेक लोगों को पता चल जाना

**get sth across (to sb)** to succeed in making people understand sth लोगों को कुछ समझाने में सफल होना *The party failed to get its policies across to the voters.*

**get ahead** to progress and be successful in sth, especially a career किसी काम में प्रगति कर सफल होना, विशेषत: जीविका या पेशे में

**get along 1** (*spoken*) (*usually in the continuous tenses*) to leave a place किसी स्थान से चले जाना *I'd love to stay, but I should be getting along now.* **2** ➪ **get on** देखिए।

**get around 1** ➪ **get about/around** देखिए। **2** ➪ **get about/ around/round** देखिए।

**get around sb** ➪ **get round/around sb** देखिए।

**get around sth** ➪ **get round/around sth** देखिए।

**get around to sth/doing sth** ➪ **get round/ around to sth/doing sth** देखिए।

**get at sb** to criticize sb a lot किसी की बहुत अधिक आलोचना करना *The teacher's always getting at me about my spelling.*

**get at sb/sth** to be able to reach sth; to have sth available for immediate use किसी वस्तु तक पहुँच पाना; तुरंत उपयोग के लिए किसी वस्तु का उपलब्ध होना *The files are locked away and I can't get at them.*

**get at sth** (*only used in the continuous tenses*) to try to say sth without saying it in a direct way; to suggest प्रत्यक्ष के स्थान पर परोक्ष रीति से कुछ कहना; कुछ जताना, व्यंजित करना *I'm not quite sure what you're getting at—am I doing something wrong?*

**get away (from)** to succeed in leaving or escaping from sb or a place किसी व्यक्ति या स्थान से चले जाने या निकल जाने में सफल होना *He kept talking to me and I couldn't get away from him.* ○ *The thieves got away in a stolen car.*

**get away with sth/doing sth** to do sth bad and not be punished for it कोई ग़लत काम करना और उसके लिए दंडित होने से बच जाना *He lied but he got away with it.*

**get back** to return to the place where you live or work अपने निवास या कार्य-स्थल पर लौट आना

**get sth back** to be given sth that you had lost or lent खोई हुई या उधार दी गई वस्तु वापस पाना *Can I borrow this book? You'll get it back next week, I promise.*

**get back to sb** to speak to, write to or telephone sb later, especially in order to give an answer जवाबी तौर पर बात करना, पत्र आदि लिखना या फ़ोन करना *I'll get back to you on prices when I've got some more information.*

**get back to sth** to return to doing sth or talking about sth फिर लौटकर कुछ काम करना या कोई बात कहना, कुछ करने या कहने पर लौट आना *I woke up early and couldn't get back to sleep.* ○ *Let's get back to the point you raised earlier.*

**get behind (with sth)** to fail to do, pay sth, etc. on time, and so have more to do, pay, etc. the next time समय पर काम का भुगतान आदि न कर पाने के कारण अगली बार अधिक काम, भुगतान आदि करना; काम भुगतान आदि में पिछली चूक की भरपाई करना *to get behind with your work/rent.*

**get by (on/in/with sth)** to manage to live or do sth with difficulty गुज़ारा चल पाना या कोई काम मुश्किल से कर पाना *It's very hard to get by on such a low income.* ○ *My Marathi is good and I can get by in Gujarati.*

**get sb down** to make sb unhappy किसी को नाराज़ कर देना

**get down to sth/doing sth** to start working on sth किसी काम में लग जाना *We'd better stop chatting and get down to work.* ○ *I must get down to answering these letters.*

**get in** to reach a place किसी स्थान पर पहुँचना *What time does your train get in?*

**get in; get into sth 1** to climb into a car कार में बैठना *We all got in and Raj drove off.* **2** to be elected to a political position किसी राजनीतिक पद के लिए निर्वाचित होना *She got into Parliament in 2004.*

**get sb in** to call sb to your house to do a job किसी को काम करने के लिए घर पर बुलाना

**get sth in 1** to collect or bring sth inside; to buy a supply of sth इकट्ठा करना या अंदर ले आना; कोई सामान

ख़रीदना *It's going to rain—I'd better get the washing in from outside.* **2** to manage to find an opportunity to say or do sth कुछ कहने या करने का मौका निकाल लेना *He talked all the time and I couldn't get a word in.*

**get in on sth** to become involved in an activity किसी गतिविधि का हिस्सा बन जाना

**get into sb** (*informal*) (used about a feeling or attitude) to start affecting sb strongly, causing him/her to behave in an unusual way (कोई भावना या रुझान) बहुत अधिक प्रभावित होकर असाधारण रीति से व्यवहार करना *I wonder what's got into him—he isn't usually unfriendly.*

**get into sth** **1** to put on a piece of clothing with difficulty मुश्किल से कोई वस्त्र पहन पाना *I've put on so much weight I can't get into my trousers.* **2** to start a particular activity; to become involved in sth विशेष काम की शुरुआत करना; किसी बात में उलझ जाना *How did you first get into the music business?* ○ *We got into an argument about politics.* **3** to become more interested in or familiar with sth किसी काम में अधिक रुचि लेना या उससे परिचित होना *I've been getting into yoga recently.*

**get off (sb/sth)** used especially to tell sb to stop touching you/sb/sth से दूर रहो या परे हटो कहने के लिए प्रयुक्त *Get off (me) or I'll call the police!* ○ *Get off that money, it's mine!*

**get off (sth)** **1** to leave a bus, train, etc.; to climb down from a bicycle, horse, etc. बस, ट्रेन आदि से उतरना; साइकिल, घोड़ा आदि से नीचे आना या उतरना **2** to leave work with permission at a particular time अनुमति के साथ विशेष समय पर काम से चले जाना *I might be able to get off early today.*

**get off (with sth)** to be lucky to receive no serious injuries or punishment गंभीर चोट या दंड से बच जाना *to get off with just a warning*

**get on** **1** to progress or become successful in life, in a career, etc. जीवन, पेशा आदि में आगे बढ़ना और सफल होना **2** (*only used in the continuous tenses*) to be getting old उम्र बढ़ना; वृद्ध होना *He's getting on—he's over 70, I'm sure.* **3** (*only used in the continuous tenses*) to be getting late देर होते जाना *Time's getting on—we don't want to be late.*

**get on/along** to have a particular amount of success विशेष मात्रा में सफलता प्राप्त करना *How are you getting on in your course?* ○ *'How did you get on at your interview?' 'I got the job!'*

**get on/along with sb; get on/along (together)** to have a friendly relationship with sb किसी के साथ मित्रवत संबंध होना *Do you get on well with your colleagues?*

**get on/along with sth** to make progress with sth that you are doing चालू या जारी काम में प्रगति करना *How are you getting on with that essay?*

**get on/onto sth** to climb onto a bus, train, bicycle, horse, etc. बस, रेलगाड़ी, साइकिल आदि पर चढ़ना या सवार होना *I got on just as the train was about to leave.*

**get on for** (*only used in the continuous tenses*) to be getting near to a certain time or age किसी विशेष समय या आयु के निकट पहुँचना *I'm not sure how old he is but he must be getting on for 50.*

**get on to sb (about sth)** to speak or write to sb about a particular matter विशेष प्रसंग में किसी से बात करना या पत्र आदि लिखना

**get on with sth** to continue doing sth, especially after an interruption कोई काम जारी रखना, विशेषतः किसी रुकावट के बाद *Stop talking and get on with your work!*

**get out** (used about a piece of information) to become known, after being secret until now (किसी बात का) देर तक गुप्त रहने के बाद सबको पता चल जाना

**get sth out (of sth)** to take sth from its container किसी वस्तु को उसे रखने की जगह से बाहर निकालना *I got my keys out of my bag.*

**get out of sth/doing sth** to avoid a duty or doing sth that you have said you will do कुछ करने के वादे से मुकरना

**get sth out of sb** to persuade or force sb to give you sth किसी को कुछ देने के लिए मनाना या विवश करना

**get sth out of sb/sth** to gain sth from sb/sth किसी व्यक्ति या वस्तु से कुछ प्राप्त करना *I get a lot of pleasure out of music.*

**get over sth** **1** to deal with a problem successfully समस्या से सफलतापूर्वक निपटना *We'll have to get over the problem of finding somewhere to live first.* **2** to feel normal again after being ill or having an unpleasant experience बीमार रहने या दुखद अनुभव में से गुज़रने के बाद पुनः सामान्य स्थिति में आ जाना *He still hasn't got over his wife's death.*

**get sth over with** (*informal*) to do and complete sth unpleasant that has to be done अप्रिय परंतु अपेक्षित काम को पूरा कर लेना *I'll be glad to get my visit to the dentist's over with.*

**get round** ➪ **get about/around/round** देखिए।

**get round/around sb** (*informal*) to persuade sb to do sth or agree with sth किसी को कुछ करने के लिए मना लेना या कोई बात मान लेना *My father says he won't lend me the money but I think I can get round him.*

**get round/around sth** to find a way of avoiding or dealing with a problem किसी समस्या से बचने या निपटने का रास्ता ढूँढ़ लेना

**get round/around to sth/doing sth** to find the time to do sth, after a delay (कुछ विलंब के बाद) कुछ करने का समय निकाल लेना *I've been meaning to reply to that letter for ages but I haven't got round to it yet.*

**get through sth** to use or complete a certain amount or number of sth किसी वस्तु को, निश्चित मात्रा या संख्या की दृष्टि से, प्रयोग में ले आना या पूरा कर लेना *I got through a lot of money at the weekend.* ○ *I got through an enormous amount of work today.*

**get (sb) through (sth)** to manage to complete sth difficult or unpleasant; to help sb to do this किसी अप्रिय या कठिन कार्य को पूरा कर लेना, या करवा देना *She got through her final exams easily.*

**get through (to sb)** **1** to succeed in making sb understand sth किसी को कुछ समझाने में सफल हो जाना *They couldn't get through to him that he was completely wrong.* **2** to succeed in speaking to sb on the telephone किसी से फ़ोन पर बात कर पाने में सफल होना *I couldn't get through to them because their phone was engaged all day.*

**get to sb** (*informal*) to affect sb in a bad way किसी पर किसी बात का दुष्प्रभाव होना *Public criticism is beginning to get to the team manager.*

**get sb/sth together** to collect people or things in one place व्यक्तियों या वस्तुओं को एक स्थान पर इकट्ठा कर लेना *I'll just get my things together and then we'll go.*

**get together (with sb)** to meet socially or in order to discuss or do sth किसी बात पर चर्चा के लिए एक साथ मिल बैठना *Let's get together and talk about it.*

**get up** to stand up खड़ा हो जाना *He got up to let an elderly woman sit down.*

**get (sb) up** to get out of bed or make sb get out of bed सुबह जाग जाना या किसी को जगा देना *What time do you have to get up in the morning?* ○ *Could you get me up at 6 a.m. tomorrow?*

**get up to sth** **1** to reach a particular point or stage in sth किसी काम के एक विशेष बिंदु या चरण तक पहुँच जाना *We've got up to the last section of our grammar book.* **2** to be busy with sth, especially sth secret or bad किसी काम में लगे रहना, विशेषतः गुप्त या अनुचित काम में *I wonder what the children are getting up to?*

**getaway** /ˈgetəweɪ ˈगेटवे़/ *noun* [C] an escape (after a crime) (अपराध के बाद) बच निकलने की क्रिया; रफ़ू-चक्कर *to **make a getaway*** ○ *a getaway car/driver*

**get-together** *noun* [C] (*informal*) an informal social meeting or party अनौपचारिक सामाजिक कार्यक्रम या पार्टी

**geyser** /ˈgiːzə(r) ˈगीज़(र्)/ *noun* [C] (in geography) a place where naturally hot water comes out of the ground. Sometimes hot water or steam goes up into the air (भूगोल में) गरम पानी का प्राकृतिक स्रोत, उष्णोत्स (कभी-कभी गरम जल या वाष्प वायु में विलीन हो जाता है) ➪ **volcano** पर चित्र देखिए।

**gharana** *noun* [U, C] (*IndE*) (in music, dance, etc.) a style or method used by a particular teacher or group of teachers who pass it on to their next generation or to their pupils (संगीत, नृत्य आदि में) विशिष्ट गुरु या गुरुओं के गायन एवं नृत्य की विशेष शैली का घराना जो अगली पीढ़ी के शिष्यों को पारित होता है; घराना *The Kirana Gharana*

**ghastly** /ˈgɑːstli ˈगास्ट्लि/ *adj.* extremely unpleasant or bad अत्यंत अप्रिय या हानिकर *a ghastly accident*

**ghat** *noun* [C] **1** a broad flight of steps leading down to a river नदी तक नीचे पहुँचने वाली चौड़ी सीढ़ी; घाट *Varanasi has many ghats.* **2 Ghats** [*pl.*] the mountains near the eastern and western coasts of India भारत के पूर्वी एवं पश्चिमी तट के समीप स्थित पर्वत; घाट *Western Ghats* ○ *Eastern Ghats.* **3** a place where dead bodies are cremated after a ceremony श्मशान घाट

**ghatam** *noun* [C] a South Indian classical percussion instrument shaped like a pot दक्षिण भारतीय शास्त्रीय ताल वाद्य; घटम

**ghazal** *noun* [C] a traditional form of poetry in Persian or Urdu. It has a fixed number of verses and is usually set to music फ़ारसी एवं उर्दू कविता कि पारंपरिक शैली जिसमें नियत छंदो को प्रायः संगीतबद्ध किया जाता है; ग़ज़ल *Jagjit Singh is a famous ghazal singer.*

**ghee** *noun* [U] clarified butter used in Indian and south Asian cooking घी

**gherao** *noun* [C] a way of protesting in South Asia in which a group of people surround a place of work, etc. preventing those in authority from leaving until their demands are heard or met दक्षिण एशिया में प्रचलित एक विरोध प्रक्रिया जिसमें लोग अपनी माँगों की सुनवाई या पूर्ति होने तक कार्य-स्थल आदि को तथा आधिकारिक गण को घेरकर रखते हैं; घेराव ▶ **gherao** *verb* [T] घेराव करना *The employees gheraoed the manager to press for an increment.*

**gherkin** /ˈgɜːkɪn ˈगकिन्/ (*AmE* **pickle**) *noun* [C] a small green vegetable (**cucumber**) that is stored in salt water or **vinegar** before being eaten सिरके में पड़ा खीरा या ककड़ी

**ghetto** /ˈgetəʊ ˈगेटो/ *noun* [C] (*pl.* **ghettoes**) a part of a town where many people of the same race, religion, etc. live in poor conditions शहर का एक भाग जहाँ एक ही जाति, धर्म आदि के लोग गरीबी की अवस्था में रहते हैं; घेटो

**ghost** /gəʊst गोस्ट्/ *noun* [C] the spirit of a dead person that is seen or heard by sb who is still living जीवित व्यक्ति को दिखाई या सुनाई पड़ने वाली मृतक की आत्मा; प्रेतात्मा, भूत *I don't believe in ghosts.* ○ *a ghost story* ➪ **spectre** देखिए।

**ghostly** /ˈgəʊstli ˈगोस्ट्लि/ *adj.* looking or sounding like a ghost; full of ghosts देखने या सुनने में प्रेतात्मा जैसा, प्रेतात्माओं से भरा हुआ; भुतहा *ghostly noises*

**ghost town** *noun* [C] a town whose inhabitants have all left वीरान हो चुका शहर; भुतहा शहर

**ghostwriter** /ˈgəʊstraɪtə(r) ˈगोस्ट्राइट(र्)/ *noun* [C] a person who writes a book, etc. for a famous person (whose name appears as the author) प्रसिद्ध व्यक्ति के लिए उसी के नाम से पुस्तक लिखने वाला व्यक्ति; अन्यार्थ लेखक

**giant** /ˈdʒaɪənt ˈजाइअन्ट्/ *noun* [C] **1** (in stories) an extremely large, strong person (कहानियों में) बृहदाकार शक्तिशाली व्यक्ति; दैत्य **2** something that is very large बहुत बड़े आकार की कोई वस्तु; भीमकाय *the multinational oil giants* (= very large companies) ▶ **giant** *adj.* असामान्य रूप से विशाल *a giant new shopping centre*

**gibberish** /ˈdʒɪbərɪʃ ˈजिबरिश्/ *noun* [U] words that have no meaning or that are impossible to understand अर्थहीन शब्द जिन्हें समझना असंभव है; अनाप-शनाप, बड़बड़

**gibbon** /ˈgɪbən ˈगिबन्/ *noun* [C] a small **ape** with long arms, which is found in South East Asia दक्षिण-पूर्व एशिया में पाया जाने वाला पुच्छविहीन लंबी बाँहों वाला बंदरनुमा छोटा प्राणी; गिबन

**giblets** /ˈdʒɪbləts ˈजिब्लट्स्/ *noun* [*pl.*] the inside parts of a chicken or other bird, including the heart and liver, that are usually removed before it is cooked मुरग़े या अन्य पक्षी के आंतरिक अंग (दिल और जिगर भी) जिन्हें पकाने से पहले प्रायः निकाल देते हैं

**giddy** /ˈgɪdi ˈगिडि/ *adj.* having the feeling that everything is going round and that you are going to fall जिसे चक्कर आ रहा हो, चक्कर से आक्रांत *I feel giddy. I must sit down.* ✪ पर्याय **dizzy**

**gift** /gɪft गिफ़्ट्/ *noun* [C] **1** something that you give to sb; a present ऐसी कोई भी वस्तु जो आप ख़ुशी से दूसरे को देते हैं; उपहार, भेंट *This watch was a gift from my mother.* ○ *The company **made a gift of** a computer to a local school.* ➪ **present** पर नोट देखिए। **2 a gift (for sth/doing sth)** natural ability नैसर्गिक क्षमता

**gifted** /ˈgɪftɪd ˈगिफ़्टिड्/ *adj.* having natural ability or great intelligence नैसर्गिक क्षमता या विशेष प्रतिभा से संपन्न, अत्यंत प्रतिभाशाली

**gig** /gɪg गिग्/ *noun* [C] (*informal*) an event where a musician or band is paid to perform कार्यक्रम जिसमें संगीतज्ञ या बैंड पैसा लेकर प्रदर्शन करते हैं

**gigantic** /dʒaɪˈgæntɪk जाइˈगैन्टिक्/ *adj.* extremely big अत्यधिक बड़ा; विशाल, विराट

**giggle** /ˈgɪgl ˈगिग्ल्/ *verb* [I] to laugh in a silly way that you cannot control, because you are amused or nervous प्रसन्नता या अधीरता के कारण बेक़ाबू होकर हँसना, ही-ही करना, हें-हें करना ▶ **giggle** *noun* [C] इस प्रकार की हँसी *I've got the giggles* (= I can't stop laughing).

**gill** /gɪl गिल्/ *noun* [C, *usually pl.*] one of the parts on the side of a fish's head that it breathes through मछली के सिर की तरफ़ का अंग जिससे वह साँस लेती है; मछली का गलफड़ा ➪ **fish** पर चित्र देखिए।

**gilt** /gɪlt गिल्ट्/ *noun* [U] a thin covering of gold सोने की पतली परत; मुलम्मा

**gimmick** /ˈgɪmɪk ˈगिमिक्/ *noun* [C] an idea for attracting customers or persuading people to buy sth ग्राहकों को आकृष्ट करने या ख़रीदारी के लिए उकसाने की चाल *New magazines often use free gifts or other gimmicks to get people to buy them.*

**gin** /dʒɪn जिन्/ *noun* [C, U] a strong, colourless alcoholic drink एक प्रकार की तेज़ रंगहीन शराब; जिन

**ginger** /ˈgɪndʒə(r) ˈजिन्ज(र्)/ *noun* [U], *adj.* **1** a root that tastes hot and is used in cooking अदरक *ground ginger* ○ *ginger biscuits* **2** (of) a light brownish-orange colour हलके भूरे-नारंगी रंग का *ginger hair*

**ginger ale** (*also* **ginger beer**) *noun* [U] a drink that does not contain alcohol and is flavoured with a spice (**ginger**) एलकोहल-रहित अदरक के स्वाद वाला पेय पदार्थ

**gingerly** /ˈdʒɪndʒəli ˈजिन्जलि/ *adv.* very slowly and carefully so as not to cause harm, make a noise, etc. बहुत धीमे और सावधानी से (कि न कुछ नुक़सान हो न आवाज़)

**gipsy** = **gypsy**

**giraffe** /dʒəˈrɑːf जˈराफ़्/ *noun* [C] (*pl.* **giraffe** or **giraffes**) a large African animal with a very long neck and legs and big dark spots on its skin बड़े आकार का एक अफ़्रीक़ी पशु जिसकी गरदन और टाँगें लंबी और खाल पर काले गहरे बड़े चकत्ते होते हैं; जिराफ़

**girder** /ˈgɜːdə(r) ˈगड(र्)/ *noun* [C] a long, heavy piece of iron or steel that is used in the building of bridges, large buildings, etc. पुल, बड़ी इमारतें आदि बनाने में प्रयुक्त लोहे या इस्पात के लंबे, भारी टुकड़े; गर्डर, लोहे का गाडर

**girl** /gɜːl गर्ल्/ *noun* [C] **1** a female child कन्या, लड़की, मादा शिशु *There are more boys than girls in the class.* **2** a daughter बेटी, पुत्री *They have two boys and a girl.* **3** a young woman नवयुवती *The girl at the cash desk was very helpful.* **4 girls** [*pl.*] a woman's female friends of any age लड़की की सहेलियाँ *a night out with the girls*

**girlfriend** /ˈgɜːlfrend ˈगर्ल्फ्रेन्ड्/ *noun* [C] **1** a girl or woman with whom sb has a romantic and/or sexual relationship महिला-मित्र जिसके साथ किसी के यौन-आकर्षण वाले संबंध हों *Have you got a girlfriend?* **2** a girl or woman's female friend सहेली

**Girl Guide** (*BrE old-fashioned*) = **guide[1] 5**

**girlhood** /ˈgɜːlhʊd ˈगर्लहुड्/ *noun* [U] the time when sb is a **girl 1** कन्यावस्था

**girlish** /ˈgɜːlɪʃ ˈगर्लिश्/ *adj.* looking, sounding or behaving like a girl लड़की जैसा दीखने, लगने या आचरणवाला; कन्यासुलभ *a girlish figure/giggle*

**giro** /ˈdʒaɪrəʊ ˈजाइरो/ *noun* (*pl.* **giros**) (*BrE*) **1** [U] a system for moving money from one bank, etc. to another एक बैंक से दूसरे बैंक में पैसा स्थानांतरित करने की प्रणाली **2** [C] a cheque that the government pays to people who are unemployed or cannot work बेरोज़गार और बेकार लोगों को सरकार से मिलने वाला चेक या धन

**girth** /gɜːθ गर्थ्/ *noun* **1** [U, C] the measurement around sth, especially a person's waist किसी वस्तु के घेरे का (विशेषतः व्यक्ति के कमर की) माप, घेरा **2** [C] a leather or cloth strap that is fastened around the middle of a horse to keep the seat (**saddle**) or a load in place घोड़े की काठी कसने की (चमड़े या कपड़े से बनी) पेटी; कसन

**gist** /dʒɪst जिस्ट्/ *noun* **the gist (of sth)** [*sing.*] the general meaning of sth rather than all the details सारांश (न कि सारा विवरण) *I know a little Spanish so I was able to **get the gist** of what he said.*

**give[1]** /gɪv गिव्/ *verb* (*pt* **gave** /geɪv गेव्/; *pp* **given** /gɪvn/ गिव्न्) **1** [T] **give sb sth, give sth to sb** to let sb have sth, especially sth that he/she wants or needs किसी को कुछ देना (विशेषतः जिसकी इच्छा या ज़रूरत हो) *I gave Jaspreet a book for her birthday.* ○ *Give me that book a minute—I just want to check something.* **2** [T] **give sb sth; give sth to sb** to make sb have sth, especially sth he/she does not want किसी को कुछ लेने के लिए बाध्य करना, किसी को उसकी इच्छा के विरुद्ध कुछ देना *Mr Ahuja gives us too much homework.* ○ *Playing chess gives me a headache.* **3** [T] to make sb have a particular feeling, idea, etc. किसी के मन में कोई भाव, विचार आदि उत्पन्न करना *Swimming always gives me a good appetite.* ○ *to give sb a surprise/shock/fright* ○ *What gives you the idea that he was lying?* **4** [T] **give (sb) sth; give sth to sb** to let sb have your opinion, decision, judgement, etc. किसी को अपनी राय, अनुमति, निर्णय आदि देना *Can you give me some advice?* ○ *My boss has given me permission to leave early.* ○ *The judge gave him five years in prison.* **5** [T] **give sb sth; give sth to sb** to speak to people in a formal situation औपचारिक अवसर पर कुछ कहना या बताना *to give a speech/talk/lecture* ○ *The officer was called to give evidence in court.* **6** [T] **give (sb) sth for sth; give (sb) sth (to do sth)** to pay in order to have sth बदले में कुछ लेने के लिए देना *How much did you give him for fixing the car?* ○ (*figurative*) *I'd give anything* (= I would love) *to be able to sing like that.* **7** [T] to spend time dealing with sb/sth व्यक्ति या वस्तु के विषय में विचार करते हुए समय व्यतीत करना *We need to give some thought to this matter urgently.* **8** [T] **give (sb/sth) sth** to do sth to sb/sth; to make a particular sound or movement व्यक्ति या वस्तु के साथ कुछ करना; ख़ास तरह की आवाज़ निकालना या हरकत करना *to give sth a clean/wash/polish* ○ ***Give** me **a call** when you get home.* ○ *She opened the door and gave a shout of horror.* **9** [T] to perform or organize sth for people लोगों के लिए कोई कार्यक्रम करना *The company gave a party to celebrate its 50th anniversary.* **10** [I] to bend or stretch under pressure दबाव से झुकना या फैलना *The branch began to give under my weight.*

IDM **not care/give a damn (about sb/sth)** ➪ **damn[3]** देखिए।

**give or take** more or less the number mentioned निर्दिष्ट संख्या कम या अधिक *It took us two hours to get here, give or take five minutes.*

> NOTE **Give** शब्द वाले मुहावरों के लिए संज्ञाओं, विशेषणों आदि की प्रविष्टियाँ देखिए। उदाहरण के लिए **give way** की प्रविष्टि **way** पर प्रविष्ट है।

PHR V **give sth away** to give sth to sb without wanting money in return बदले में धन की इच्छा न करते हुए किसी को कुछ देना *When she got older she gave all her toys away.* ○ *We are giving away a free CD with this month's issue.*

**give sth/sb away** to show or tell the truth about sth/sb which was secret वस्तु या व्यक्ति के विषय में सचाई (जो अब तक छिपी थी) उजागर कर देना *He smiled politely and didn't give away his real feelings.*

**give (sth) back** to return sth to the person that you took or borrowed it from किसी से उधार ली वस्तु

को उसे लौटाना *I lent him some books months ago and he still hasn't given them back to me.*

**give sth in** to give sth to the person who is collecting it जो व्यक्ति वस्तु विशेष सबसे ले रहा है उसे वह वस्तु देना *I've got to give this essay in to my teacher by Friday.*

**give in (to sb/sth)** to stop fighting against sb/sth; to accept that you have been defeated व्यक्ति या वस्तु से संघर्ष रोक देना; अपनी हार मान लेना

**give sth off** to send sth (for example smoke, a smell, heat, etc.) out into the air (धुआँ, गंध, गरमी आदि को) बाहर हवा में धकेलना *Cars give off poisonous fumes.*

**give out** (used about a machine, etc.) to stop working (मशीन आदि का) बंद हो जाना *His heart gave out and he died.*

**give sth out** to give one of sth to each person प्रत्येक व्यक्ति को किसी वस्तु की एक-एक प्रति बाँटना *Could you give out these books to the class, please?*

**give up** to stop trying to do sth; to accept that you cannot do sth कुछ करने की कोशिश को रोक देना; किसी काम को करने में अपनी असमर्थता को मान लेना *They gave up once the other team had scored their third goal.* ○ *I give up. What's the answer?*

**give sb up; give up on sb** to stop expecting sb to arrive, succeed, improve, etc. किसी के कहीं पहुँचने, किसी बात में सफल या सुधार होने आदि की आशा छोड़ बैठना *Her work was so poor that all her teachers gave up on her.*

**give sth up; give up doing sth** to stop doing or having sth that you did or had regularly before पिछली आदत, सोच आदि को छोड़ देना *I've tried many times to give up smoking.* ○ *Don't give up hope. Things are bound to improve.*

**give yourself/sb up (to sb)** to go to the police when they are trying to catch you; to tell the police where sb is पकड़ने में लगी पुलिस को आत्मसमर्पण कर देना; पुलिस को किसी के ठिकाने के बारे में बताना

**give sth up (to sb)** to give sth to sb who needs or asks for it किसी को उसकी ज़रूरत की या माँगी हुई वस्तु देना *He gave up his seat on the bus to an elderly woman.*

**give²** /gɪv गिव् / *noun* [U] the quality of being able to bend or stretch a little कुछ झुक या फैल सकने का गुण

IDM **give and take** a situation in which two people, groups, etc. respect each others' rights and needs दो व्यक्तियों, समूहों आदि के बीच एक दूसरे के अधिकार और आवश्यकताओं के लिए आदर भाव, समझौता, एक दूसरे की मानना *There has to be some give and take for a marriage to succeed.*

**giveaway** /ˈgɪvəweɪ ˈगिव्अवे / *noun* [C] (*informal*) **1** a thing that is included free when you buy sth ख़रीदी वस्तु के साथ मुफ़्त मिली चीज़ **2** something that makes you guess the truth about sb/sth व्यक्ति या वस्तु के विषय में सचाई को बता देने वाली वस्तु, स्थिति, रहस्य का प्रकटीकरण या विश्वासघात *She said she didn't know about the money but her face was **a dead giveaway**.*

**given¹** /ˈgɪvn ˈगिव्न् / *adj.* (*only before a noun*) already stated or decided पूर्वतः कथित या निश्चित *At any given time, up to 200 people are using the library.*

**given²** /ˈgɪvn ˈगिव्न् / *prep.* considering sth मानते हुए कि *Given that you had very little help, I think you did very well.*

**given name** (*AmE*) = **first name** ➪ **name** पर नोट देखिए।

**gizzard** /ˈgɪzəd ˈगिज़ड् / *noun* [C] the part of a bird's stomach in which food is changed into smaller pieces before it can be **digested** पक्षी के आमाशय का वह अंश जिसमें पचने से पहले खाद्य पदार्थ खंड-खंड हो जाता है, पक्षी का पेडू या दूसरा उदर, मांसपेशीय उदर; पेषणी

**glacial** /gleɪʃl; ˈgleɪsiəl ˈग्लेश्ल्; ˈग्लेसिअल्/ *adj.* **1** caused by ice or a glacier बर्फ़ या हिमनदी से बना *a glacial valley* **2** extremely cold अत्यधिक ठंडा *glacial winds*

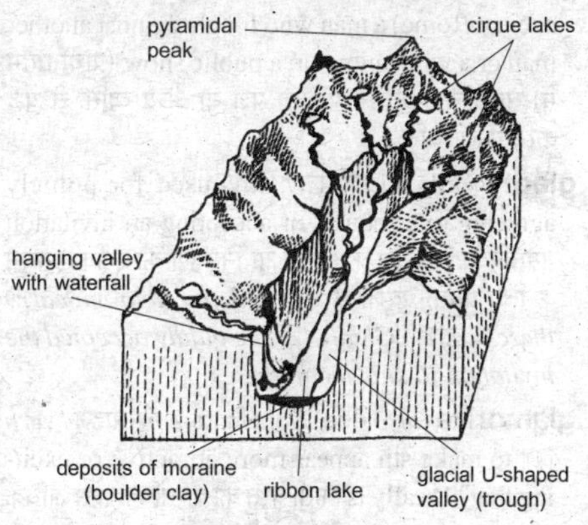

**glacial features**

**glaciation** /ˌgleɪsiˈeɪʃn ˌग्लेसिˈएश्न् / *noun* [U] (in geography) the movement of a mass of ice over an area of land, and the things that are caused or created by this (भूगोल में) बड़े भूक्षेत्र पर हिमराशि का चलना और उसके प्रभाव; हिमनदन

**glacier** /ˈglæsiə(r); ˈgleɪs- ˈग्लैसिअ(र्); ˈग्लेस्- / *noun* [C] a mass of ice that moves slowly down a valley घाटी में धीरे-धीरे चलती हिमराशि; हिमनदी

**glad** /glæd ग्लैड्/ *adj.* **1** (*not before a noun*) **glad (about sth); glad to do sth/that** happy; pleased प्रसन्न; सुखी, संतुष्ट *Are you glad about your new job?* ○ *I'm glad to hear he's feeling better.* ○ *I'm glad (that) he's feeling better.* ○ *I'll be glad when these exams are over.*

NOTE किसी विशेष घटना या परिस्थिति के बारे में प्रसन्न होने पर शब्द **glad** या **pleased** को प्रयुक्त किया जाता है। किसी बात या मन की दशा आदि के वर्णन के लिए **happy** का प्रयोग होता है और यह उस संज्ञा से पहले भी प्रयुक्त किया जाता है जिसका वह वर्णन करता है—*This kind of music always makes me feel happy.* ○ *She's such a happy child—she's always laughing.*

**2 glad (of sth); glad (if...)** grateful for sth किसी बात के लिए कृतज्ञ *If you are free, I'd be glad of some help.* ○ *I'd be glad if you could help me.* **3** (*only before a noun*) (*old-fashioned*) bringing happiness प्रसन्नतादायक *I want to be the first to tell her the glad news.* ▶ **gladness** *noun* [U] प्रसन्नता

**gladden** /ˈglædn ˈग्लैड्न्/ *verb* [T] to make sb glad or happy किसी को प्रसन्न या हर्षित करना

**glade** /gleɪd ग्लेड्/ *noun* [C] (*written*) an open space in a forest or wood where there are no trees वनप्रदेश का वृक्ष-रहित खुला इलाक़ा ✪ पर्याय **clearing**

**gladiator** /ˈglædieɪtə(r) ˈग्लैडिएट(र्)/ *noun* [C] (in ancient Rome) a man who fought against another man or a wild animal in a public show (प्राचीन रोम में) सार्वजनिक प्रदर्शन में वन्य पशु या अन्य व्यक्ति से युद्ध करने वाला व्यक्ति

**gladly** /ˈglædli ˈग्लैड्लि/ *adv.* used for politely agreeing to a request or accepting an invitation नम्रतापूर्वक अनुरोध को मानने या निमंत्रण को स्वीकार करने के लिए प्रयुक्त; ख़ुशी से *'Could you help me carry these bags?' 'Gladly.'* ○ *She gladly accepted the invitation to stay the night.*

**glamorize** (*also* **-ise**) /ˈglæməraɪz ˈग्लैमराइज़्/ *verb* [T] to make sth appear more attractive or exciting than it really is किसी वस्तु को वास्तविकता से अधिक आकर्षक या उत्तेजक लगने वाली बना देना, लुभावना बना देना *Television tends to glamorize violence.*

**glamour** (*AmE* **glamor**) /ˈglæmə(r) ˈग्लैम(र्)/ *noun* [U] the quality of seeming to be more exciting or attractive than ordinary things or people साधारण वस्तुओं या व्यक्तियों से अधिक उत्तेजक लगने का गुण; लुभावनापन *Young people are attracted by the glamour of city life.* ▶ **glamorous** /-mərəs -मरस्/ *adj.* लुभावना *the glamorous world of show business* ▶ **glamorously** *adv.* लुभावनेपन से

**glance**[1] /glɑːns ग्लान्स्/ *verb* [I] to look quickly at sb/sth किसी व्यक्ति या वस्तु पर उड़ती नज़र डालना *She glanced round the room to see if they were there.* ○ *The receptionist glanced down the list of names.*

PHR V **glance off (sth)** to hit sth at an angle and move off again in another direction किसी वस्तु के कोने से टकराकर फिर दूसरी दिशा में मुड़ जाना *The ball glanced off his knee and into the net.*

**glance**[2] /glɑːns ग्लान्स्/ *noun* [C] a quick look उड़ती नज़र *to take/have a glance at the newspaper headlines*

IDM **at a (single) glance** with one look एक नज़र में, एक बार देखकर *I could tell at a glance that something was wrong.*

**at first glance/sight** ➪ **first**[1] देखिए।

**gland** /glænd ग्लैन्ड्/ *noun* [C] any of the small parts (**organs**) inside your body that produce chemical substances for your body to use शरीर के द्वारा उपयोग हेतु रसायनों को उत्पन्न करने वाला शरीर के अंदर का कोई अंग; ग्रंथी *sweat glands* ▶ **glandular** /ˈglændjʊlə(r) ˈग्लैन्ड्युल(र्)/ *adj.* ग्रंथि-विषयक

**glare**[1] /gleə(r) ग्लेअ(र्)/ *verb* [I] **1 glare (at sb/sth)** to look at sb in a very angry way किसी को क्रोध से देखना, आँखें तरेरना **2** to shine with strong light that hurts your eyes आँखों को चुभने वाले तेज़ प्रकाश के साथ चमकना, चकाचौंध उत्पन्न करना

**glare**[2] /gleə(r) ग्लेअ(र्)/ *noun* **1** [U] strong light that hurts your eyes आँखों को चुभने वाली तेज़ रोशनी; चकाचौंध *the glare of the sun/a car's headlights* **2** [C] a very angry look अत्यंत क्रोधभरी दृष्टि

**glaring** /ˈgleərɪŋ ˈग्लेअरिङ्/ *adj.* **1** very easy to see; shocking सहज दिखाई पड़ने वाली; स्तब्धकारी, क्षोभजनक *a glaring mistake/injustice* **2** (used about a light) too strong and bright (प्रकाश) बहुत तीखा और चटकीला **3** angry क्रुद्ध *glaring eyes* ▶ **glaringly** *adv.* क्षोभजनक रूप से *a **glaringly obvious** mistake*

**glass** /glɑːs ग्लास्/ *noun* **1** [U] a hard substance that you can usually see through that is used for making windows, bottles, etc. पारदर्शी शीशा, काँच *He cut himself on broken glass.* ○ *a sheet/pane of glass* ○ *a glass jar/dish/vase* **2** [C] a drinking container made of glass; the amount of liquid it contains शीशे का गिलास; गिलास में भरे द्रव की मात्रा *a wine glass* ○ *He drank three glasses of milk.*

**glasses** /ˈglɑːsɪz ˈग्लासिज़्/ [*formal* **spectacles** (*informal* **specs**, *AmE* **eyeglasses**)] *noun* [*pl.*] **two lenses** in a frame that rests on the nose and ears. People wear glasses in order to be able to see better or to protect their eyes from bright sunlight ऐनक, चश्मा *My sister has to* ***wear glasses****.* ○ *reading glasses* ○ *dark glasses/sunglasses*

**glass fibre** = **fibreglass**

**glassful** /ˈglɑːsfʊl ˈग्लास्फ़ुल् / *noun* [C] the amount of liquid that one glass holds एक गिलास में समाने वाले द्रव की मात्रा; गिलासभर

**glasshouse** /ˈglɑːshaʊs ˈग्लास्हाउस् / = **greenhouse**

**glassy** /ˈglɑːsi ˈग्लासि / *adj.* **1** looking like glass शीशे जैसा, काँच-सा **2** (used about the eyes) showing no interest or expression (आँखें) भावशून्य, क्रियाशून्य

**glaucoma** /glɔːˈkəʊmə ग्लॉˈकोमा / *noun* [U] an eye disease that causes gradual loss of sight एक नेत्र रोग जिसमें क्रमशः दृष्टि क्षीण होती जाती है; ग्लॉकोमा, काला मोतिया

**glaze[1]** /gleɪz ग्लेज़् / *verb* [T] **1** to fit a sheet of glass into a window, etc. खिड़की आदि में शीशे की चादर लगाना ➪ **double-glazing** देखिए। **2 glaze sth (with sth)** to cover a pot, brick, pie, etc. with a shiny transparent substance (before it is put into an oven) (अवन, तंदूर या भट्ठी में रखने से पहले) बरतन, ईंट, केक आदि पर चमकीली पारदर्शी पन्नी चढ़ाना **PHR V glaze over** (used about the eyes) to show no interest or expression (आँखों का) न कोई भाव व्यक्त करना न हरकत करना, जड़-सा हो जाना

**glaze[2]** /gleɪz ग्लेज़् / *noun* [C, U] (a substance that gives) a shiny transparent surface on a pot, brick, pie, etc. किसी बरतन, ईंट आदि को चमकदार पारदर्शी आभा देने वाला (पदार्थ)

**glazed** /gleɪzd ग्लेज़्ड् / *adj.* (used about the eyes, etc.) showing no interest or expression (आँखें) जड़प्रायः या भावशून्य

**glazier** /ˈgleɪziə(r) ˈग्लेज़िअ(र्) / *noun* [C] a person whose job is to fit glass into windows, etc. खिड़की आदि पर शीशा लगाने वाला कारीगर

**gleam** /gliːm ग्लीम् / *noun* [C, *usually sing.*] **1** a soft light that shines for a short time क्षणस्थायी कोमल प्रकाश *the gleam of moonlight on the water* **2** a sudden expression of an emotion in sb's eyes किसी की आँखों में भाव का एकाएक चमकना *I saw a gleam of amusement in his eyes.* **3** a small amount of sth (किसी वस्तु की) अल्प मात्रा *a faint gleam of hope* ► **gleam** *verb* [I] चमकना *gleaming white teeth* ○ *Their eyes gleamed with enthusiasm.*

**glean** /gliːn ग्लीन् / *verb* [T] **glean sth (from sb/sth)** to obtain information, knowledge, etc., sometimes with difficulty and often from various different places प्रयासपूर्वक और प्रायः विभिन्न स्रोतों से सूचना, ज्ञान आदि का संग्रह *These figures have been gleaned from a number of studies.*

**glee** /gliː ग्ली / *noun* [U] a feeling of happiness, usually because sth good has happened to you or sth bad has happened to sb else उल्लास का भाव (क्योंकि आपके साथ अच्छा हुआ या दूसरे के साथ बुरा हुआ) *She couldn't hide her glee when her rival came last in the race.* ► **gleeful** /-fl -फ़्ल् / *adj.* उल्लसित ► **gleefully** /-fəli फ़लि / *adv.* उल्लसित होकर

**glen** /glen ग्लेन् / *noun* [C] a deep, narrow valley, especially in Scotland or Ireland गहरी, तंग घाटी (विशेषतः स्कॉटलैंड या आयरलैंड में)

**glib** /glɪb ग्लिब् / *adj.* using words in a way that is clever and quick, but not sincere चतुराई और फुरती से (मगर सचाई से नहीं) अपनी बात कहने वाला; वाक्पटु *a glib salesman/politician* ○ *a glib answer/excuse* ► **glibly** *adv.* वाक्पटुता से ► **glibness** *noun* [U] वाक्पटुता

**glide** /glaɪd ग्लाइड् / *verb* [I] **1** to move smoothly without noise or effort बिना बोले या प्रयास किए कोमलता से सरकना या फिसलना *The dancers glided across the floor.* **2** to fly in a glider ग्लाइडर में उड़ना *I've always wanted to* ***go gliding****.*

**glider** /ˈglaɪdə(r) ˈग्लाइड(र्) / *noun* [C] a light aircraft without an engine that flies using air currents वायु-तरंगों के सहारे उड़ने वाला इंजन-रहित हलका विमान, ग्लाइडर ➪ **hang-glider** देखिए। ► **gliding** *noun* [U] ग्लाइडर में उड़ने की क्रिया

**glimmer** /ˈglɪmə(r) ˈग्लिम(र्) / *noun* [C] **1** a weak light that is not steady अस्थिर मद्धिम प्रकाश, टिमटिमाहट, झिलमिलाहट *I could see a faint glimmer of light in one of the windows.* **2** a small sign of sth (किसी बात का) हलका संकेत *a glimmer of hope* ► **glimmer** *verb* [I] झिलमिलाना, टिमटिमाना

**glimpse** /glɪmps ग्लिम्प्स / *noun* [C] **1 a glimpse (at/of sth)** a very quick and not complete view of sb/sth व्यक्ति या वस्तु का संक्षिप्त और अधूरा दृश्य; झाँकी, झलक *I just managed to* ***catch a glimpse*** *of the fox's tail as it ran down a hole.* **2 a glimpse (into/of sth)** a short experience of sth that helps you understand it किसी वस्तु का संक्षिप्त अनुभव (जो उसे समझने में सहायक है); झलक *The programme gives us an interesting glimpse into the life of the cheetah.* ► **glimpse** *verb* [T] झलक दिखाना

**glint** /glɪnt ग्लिन्ट् / *verb* [I] to shine with small bright flashes of light प्रकाश की संक्षिप्त चमकीली कौंध के साथ चमकना, झिलमिलाना *His eyes glinted at the thought of all that money.* ► **glint** *noun* [C] झिलमिल, चमक

**glisten** /ˈglɪsn ˈग्लिसन् / *verb* [I] (used about wet surfaces) to shine (भीगी सतह का) चमकना *Her eyes glistened with tears.* ○ *Tears glistened in her eyes.*

**glitter** /ˈglɪtə(r)ˈग्लिट(र्)/ *noun* [U] **1** a shiny appearance consisting of many small flashes of light चमक-दमक; जगमगाना *the glitter of jewellery* **2** the exciting quality that sth appears to have किसी वस्तु का आकर्षण और रोमांच *the glitter of a career in show business* **3** very small, shiny pieces of thin metal or paper, used as a decoration सजावट के लिए प्रयुक्त धातु या काग़ज़ की पन्नियाँ *The children decorated their pictures with glitter.* ▶ **glitter** *verb* [I] चमचमाना

**glittering** /ˈglɪtərɪŋˈग्लिटरिङ्/ *adj.* **1** very impressive or successful बहुत प्रभावशाली या सफल *a glittering career/performance* **2** shining brightly with many small flashes of light चमचमाता, जगमगाता

**gloat** /gləʊt ग्लोट्/ *verb* [I] **gloat (about/over sth)** to feel or express happiness in an unpleasant way because sth good has happened to you or sth bad has happened to sb else काँइयापन दिखाते हुए ख़ुश होना (क्योंकि आपके साथ अच्छा हुआ या दूसरे के साथ बुरा)

**global** /ˈgləʊblˈग्लोबल्/ *adj.* **1** affecting the whole world संपूर्ण विश्व को प्रभावित करने वाला; विश्वव्यापी *the global effects of pollution* **2** considering or including all parts सब अंशों को ध्यान में रखते हुए या समाविष्ट करते हुए; वैश्विक, सार्वभौम, व्यापक *We must take a global view of the problem.* ▶ **globally** /-bəli -बलि/ *adv.* विश्वव्यापी प्रकार से

**globalize** (*also* **-ise**) /ˈgləʊbəlaɪzˈग्लोबलाइज़्/ *verb* [I, T] (*technical*) if sth, for example a business company, globalizes or is globalized, it operates all around the world व्यापारिक कंपनी आदि का विश्वस्तर पर काम करना; भूमंडलीकरण या वैश्वीकरण होना या करना ▶ **globalization** (*also* **-isation**) /ˌgləʊbəlaɪˈzeɪʃn ˌग्लोबलाइˈज़ेशन्/ *noun* [U] भूमंडलीकरण, वैश्वीकरण *the globalization of world trade*

**the global village** *noun* [*sing.*] the world considered as a single community connected by computers, telephones, etc. विश्व को ऐसा एक समुदाय समझने की दृष्टि जो कंप्यूटर आदि संचार-साधनों से परस्पर संयुक्त है; वैश्विक समाज, विश्व ग्राम

**global warming** *noun* [*sing.*] the increase in the temperature of the earth's atmosphere, caused by the increase of certain gases कुछ गैसों में वृद्धि के कारण पृथ्वी के वायुमंडल के तापमान में वृद्धि ⇨ **greenhouse effect** देखिए।

**globe** /gləʊb ग्लोब्/ *noun* **1 the globe** [*sing.*] the earth पृथ्वी, विश्व *to travel all over the globe* **2** [C] a round object with a map of the world on it संसार के मानचित्र वाली एक गोल वस्तु; ग्लोब, पृथ्वी का गोलाकार मानचित्र **3** [C] any object shaped like a ball गेंद के आकार की कोई वस्तु; गोला, गोलक

**globe artichoke** = **artichoke**

**globetrotter** /ˈgləʊbtrɒtə(r)ˈग्लोब्ट्रॉट(र्)/ *noun* [C] (*informal*) a person who travels to many countries विश्वयात्री; भूपर्यटक

**globule** /ˈglɒbju:l ˈग्लॉब्यूल्/ *noun* [C] a small drop or ball of a liquid द्रव की छोटी बूँद *There were globules of fat in the soup.*

**gloom** /glu:m ग्लूम्/ *noun* [U] **1** a feeling of being sad and without hope निराशापूर्ण उदासी *The news brought deep gloom to the village.* **2** a state when it is almost completely dark पूर्ण अंधकार, घना अँधेरा

**gloomy** /ˈglu:miˈग्लूमि/ *adj.* (**gloomier; gloomiest**) **1** dark in way that makes you feel sad ऐसा गहरा कि उदास कर दे *This dark paint makes the room very gloomy.* **2** sad and without much hope उदास और निराश *Don't be so gloomy—cheer up!* ▶ **gloomily** *adv.* उदासीभरी निराशा के साथ

**glorified** /ˈglɔ:rɪfaɪdˈग्लॉरिफ़ाइड्/ *adj.* (*only before a noun*) described in a way that makes sb/sth seem better, bigger, more important, etc. than he/she/it really is बढ़ा-चढ़ा कर कहा गया

**glorify** /ˈglɔ:rɪfaɪ ˈग्लोरिफ़ाइ/ *verb* [T] (*pres. part.* **glorifying;** *3rd person sing. pres.* **glorifies;** *pt, pp* **glorified**) to make sb/sth appear better or more important than he/she/it really is बढ़ा-चढ़ाकर कहना *His biography does not attempt to glorify his early career.*

**glorious** /ˈglɔ:riəs ˈग्लॉरिअस्/ *adj.* **1** having or deserving fame or success प्रसिद्धि या सफलता को प्राप्त करने वाला या उसका अधिकारी; गौरवपूर्ण, शानदार *a glorious victory* **2** wonderful; splendid आश्चर्यजनक; भव्य *a glorious day/view* ▶ **gloriously** *adv.* भव्यतापूर्वक

**glory¹** /ˈglɔ:ri ˈग्लॉरि/ *noun* [U] **1** fame or honour that you get for achieving sth उपलब्धि से प्राप्त यश या सम्मान *The winning team was welcomed home **in a blaze of glory**.* **2** great beauty महान सौंदर्य

**glory²** /ˈglɔ:ri ˈग्लॉरि/ *verb* (*pres. part.* **glorying;** *3rd person sing. pres.* **glories;** *pt, pp* **gloried**)

**PHR V** **glory in sth** to take (too much) pleasure or pride in sth किसी बात में (अत्यधिक) आनंद या गौरव अनुभव करना *He gloried in his sporting successes.*

**gloss¹** /glɒs ग्लॉस्/ *noun* [U, *sing.*] (a substance that gives sth) a smooth, shiny surface सतह को चिकना और चमकदार बनानेवाला (पदार्थ) *gloss paint* ○ *gloss photographs* ⇨ **matt** देखिए।

**gloss²** /glɒs ग्लॉस्/ *verb*

**PHR V** **gloss over sth** to avoid talking about a problem, mistake, etc. in detail किसी समस्या, भूल आदि के विषय में विस्तार से बात करने से बचना, समस्या आदि की अनदेखी करना

**glossary** /ˈglɒsəri ˈग्लॉसरि / *noun* [C] (*pl.* **glossaries**) a list of special or unusual words and their meanings, usually at the end of a text or book विशेष या असामान्य शब्दों की अर्थयुक्त सूची (प्रायः लेख या पुस्तक के अंत में); शब्दार्थ सूची, शब्दावली

**glossy** /ˈglɒsi ˈग्लॉसि / *adj.* (**glossier; glossiest**) smooth and shiny चिकना और चमकदार *glossy hair* ○ *a glossy magazine* (= printed on shiny paper)

**glottal stop** /ˌglɒtl ˈstɒp ˌग्लॉट्ल् ˈस्टॉप् / *noun* [C] (*technical*) a speech sound made by closing and opening the **glottis**, which in English sometimes takes the place of a /t/, for example in *butter* स्वरयंत्रमुख या श्वास द्वार को बंद करने और खोलने से उत्पन्न ध्वनि (जैसे अंग्रेज़ी 'butter' में /t/); श्वासद्वारीय स्वर

**glottis** /ˈglɒtɪs ˈग्लॉटिस् / *noun* [C] the part of the **larynx** in the throat that contains the muscles that move to produce the voice (**vocal cords**) and the narrow opening between them श्वासद्वार, स्वरयंत्रमुख

**glove** /glʌv ग्लव् / *noun* [C] a piece of clothing that covers your hand and has five separate parts for the fingers दस्ताना *I need a new pair of gloves for the winter.* ○ *leather/woollen/rubber gloves* ➪ **mitten** पर चित्र देखिए।

**glove compartment** (*also* **glove box**) *noun* [C] a small enclosed space or shelf facing the front seats of a car, used for keeping small things in कार की आगे की सीटों के सामने बना आला या ख़ाना (छोटी-छोटी चीजें रखने के लिए) ➪ **car** पर चित्र देखिए।

**glow** /gləʊ ग्लो / *verb* [I] **1** to produce light and/or heat without smoke or flames बिना धुएँ या लपटों के प्रकाश और या ताप उत्पन्न करना *A cigarette glowed in the dark.* **2 glow (with sth)** to be warm or red because of excitement, exercise, etc. उत्तेजना, व्यायाम आदि के कारण शरीर का गरमा जाना, चेहरे पर लाली छा जाना *to glow with health/enthusiasm/pride* ▶ **glow** *noun* [*sing.*] लाली, लालिमा, चमक, सुर्खी *the glow of the sky at sunset*

**glower** /ˈglaʊə(r) ˈग्लाउअ(र्) / *verb* [I] **glower (at sb/sth)** to look angrily (at sb/sth) (व्यक्ति या वस्तु को) क्रोध से देखना

**glowing** /ˈgləʊɪŋ ˈग्लोइङ् / *adj.* saying that sb/sth is very good व्यक्ति या वस्तु के लिए प्रशंसापूर्ण *His teacher wrote a glowing report about his work.* ▶ **glowingly** *adv.* प्रशंसापूर्ण रीति से

**glow-worm** *noun* [C] a type of insect. The female has no wings and produces a green light at the end of her tail जुगनू (मादा के पंख नहीं होते और उसकी पूँछ के अंतिम सिरे पर हरा प्रकाश होता है)

**glucose** /ˈgluːkəʊs ˈग्लूकोस् / *noun* [U] a type of sugar that is found in fruit फल में पाई जाने वाली शक्कर; ग्लूकोज़ ➪ **dextrose, fructose, lactose** और **sucrose** भी देखिए।

**glue**[1] /gluː ग्लू / *noun* [U] a thick sticky liquid that is used for joining things together सरेस, लेई, गोंद *Stick the photo in with glue.*

**glue**[2] /gluː ग्लू / *verb* [T] (*pres. part.* **gluing**) **glue A (to/onto B); glue A and B (together)** to join a thing or things together with glue सरेस से चीज़ों को जोड़ना *Do you think you can glue the handle back onto the teapot?*

**IDM glued to sth** (*informal*) giving all your attention to sth and not wanting to leave it किसी वस्तु पर पूरा ध्यान देना और उसे छोड़कर जाने का अनिच्छुक होना या किसी वस्तु से चिपके रहना *He just sits there every evening glued to the television.*

**glum** /glʌm ग्लम् / *adj.* sad and quiet उदास और चुपचाप ▶ **glumly** *adv.* उदासी के साथ

**glut** /glʌt ग्लट् / *noun* [C, *usually* sing.] more of sth than is needed आवश्यकता से अधिक; भरमार *The glut of coffee has forced down the price.*

**gluten** /ˈgluːtn ˈग्लूट्न् / *noun* [U] a sticky substance that is found in grains that we make into flour, for example wheat गेहूँ आदि में पाया जाने वाला लसलसा पदार्थ जिसका आटा बन जाता है; लासा

**glutton** /ˈglʌtn ˈग्लट्न् / *noun* [C] **1** a person who eats too much बहुत अधिक खाने वाला व्यक्ति; पेटू, खाऊ **2** (*informal*) **a glutton for sth** a person who enjoys having or doing sth difficult, unpleasant, etc. कठिन, अप्रिय आदि काम करने में आनंद लेने वाला *She's a glutton for hard work —she never stops.*

**gluttony** /ˈglʌtəni ˈग्लटनि / *noun* [U] the habit of eating and drinking too much बहुत अधिक खाने और पीने की आदत; पेटूपन, खाऊपन

**glycerine** (*AmE* **glycerin**) /ˈglɪsəriːn ˈग्लिसरीन् / *noun* [U] a thick sweet colourless liquid made from fats and oils and used in medicines, beauty products and explosive substances ग्लिसरीन; चरबी और तेलों से बना एक गाढ़ा मीठा रंगहीन द्रव पदार्थ जो सौंदर्य प्रसाधनों और विस्फोटकों में डाला जाता है

**GM** /ˌdʒiː ˈem ˌजी ˈएम् / *abbr.* genetically modified जीन की दृष्टि से संशोधित

**GMT** /ˌdʒiː em ˈtiː ˌजी एम् ˈटी/ *abbr.* Greenwich Mean Time; the time system that is used in Britain during the winter and for calculating the time in other parts of the world ग्रीनिच मीन टाईम; ब्रिटेन में प्रचलित मानक समय प्रणाली (भारत में IST, इंडियन स्टैंडर्ड टाईम से तुलनीय)

**gnarled** /nɑ:ld नाल्ड्/ *adj.* rough and having grown into a strange shape, because of old age or hard work (अधिक आयु या परिश्रम के कारण) खुरदुरा और टेढ़ा-मेढ़ा; ग्रंथित *The old man had gnarled fingers.* ○ *a gnarled oak tree*

**gnash** /næʃ नैश्/ *verb*

**IDM gnash your teeth** to feel very angry and upset about sth गुस्से में दाँत पीसना

**gnat** /næt नैट्/ *noun* [C] a type of very small fly that bites मच्छर, डाँस ✪ पर्याय **midge**

**gnaw** /nɔ: नॉ/ *verb* **1** [I, T] **gnaw (away) (at/on) sth** to bite a bone, etc. many times with your back teeth पिछले दाँतों से हड्डी आदि को अनेक बार काटना या कड़ी वस्तु को कुतरना **2** [I] **gnaw (away) at sb** to make sb feel worried or frightened over a long period of time लंबे समय तक किसी को चिंता या डर में रखना या किसी को लगातार सताना *Fear of the future gnawed away at her all the time.*

**gneiss** /naɪs नाइस्/ *noun* [U] (*technical*) a type of **metamorphic** rock formed at high pressure and temperature deep in the ground ज़मीन की गहराई में उच्च दाब और तापमान से बनी चट्टान; पट्टिताश्म

**gnome** /nəʊm नोम्/ *noun* [C] (in children's stories, etc.) a little old man with a beard and a pointed hat who lives under the ground (बाल कथाओं में) पाताल में रहने वाला एक दढ़ियल और नुकीली टोपी पहने बूढ़ा बौना

**GNP** /ˌdʒi: enˈpi: ˌजी एनˈपी/ *abbr.* gross national product; the total value of all the goods and services produced by a country in one year, including the total amount of money that comes from foreign countries सकल राष्ट्रीय उत्पाद; एक वर्ष में सब स्रोतों से एक देश की कुल प्राप्ति **NOTE GNP** = **GDP** + net foreign income (नगद विदेशी आय) ➪ **GDP** देखिए।

**go[1]** /gəʊ गो/ *verb* (*pres. part.* **going**; *3rd person sing. pres.* **goes** /gəʊz गोज़्/; *pt* **went** /went वेन्ट्/; *pp* **gone** /gɒn गॉन्/) **1** [I] to move or travel from one place to another एक स्थान से दूसरे स्थान को जाना *She always goes home by bus.* ○ *We're going to Lucknow tomorrow.* ○ *We've still got fifty kilometres to go.*

> **NOTE** जब कोई व्यक्ति कहीं जाकर लौट आए तो उसके निर्देश के लिए शब्द **go** के भूत कृदंत (past participle) रूप **been** का प्रयोग होता है। **Gone** का प्रयोग तब करते हैं जब यह बताना हो कि कोई व्यक्ति कहीं गया था परंतु अभी लौटा नहीं है—*I've just been to Mumbai. I got back this morning.* ○ *Sreekant's gone to Delhi. He'll be back in two weeks.*

**2** [I] to travel to a place to take part in an activity or do sth कुछ करने या किसी कार्य में शामिल होने के लिए कहीं जाना *Are you going to Dinesh's party?* ○ *to go for a swim/drive/drink/walk/meal* ○ *They've gone on holiday.* **3** [I] to belong to or stay in an institution किसी संस्था से संबद्ध होना या वहाँ रुकना *Which school do you go to?* ○ *to go to hospital/prison/college/university* **4** [I] to leave a place किसी स्थान से जाना; प्रस्थान करना *I have to go now. It's nearly 4 o'clock.* ○ *What time does the train go?* **5** [I] to lead to or reach a place or time कहीं या कभी पहुँचाना या पहुँचना *Where does this road go to?* **6** [I] to be put or to fit in a particular place स्थान विशेष पर रखा जाना या अटना *Where does this vase go?* ○ *My clothes won't all go in one suitcase.* **7** [I] to happen in a particular way; to develop ख़ास ढंग से कुछ होना; विकसित होना *How's the new job going?* **8** *linking verb* to become; to reach a particular state हो जाना; दशा विशेष को प्राप्त होना *Her hair is going grey.* ○ *to go blind/deaf/bald/senile/mad* **9** [I] to stay in the state mentioned (ध्यान आदि में आने से) रह जाना *Many mistakes go unnoticed.* **10** [I] to be removed, lost, used, etc.; to disappear हटा दिया जाना, गुम हो जाना, इस्तेमाल हो जाना, आदि; ग़ायब हो जाना *Has your headache gone yet?* ○ *I like the furniture, but that carpet will have to go.* ○ *About half my salary goes on rent.* **11** [I] to work correctly ठीक से काम करना *This clock doesn't go.* ○ *Is your car going at the moment?* **12** [I] to become worse or stop working correctly बदतर हो जाना या ठीक से काम करना बंद कर देना *The brakes on the car have gone.* ○ *His sight/voice/mind has gone.* **13 go (with sth); go (together)** [I] to look or taste good with sth else किसी अन्य वस्तु के साथ स्वाद में या दीखने में मेल खाना *This sauce goes well with rice or pasta.* ○ *These two colours don't really go.* **14** [I] to have certain words or a certain tune विशेष शब्दों का प्रयुक्त होना या विशेष धुन में निबद्ध होना *How does that song go?* **15** [I] (used about time) to pass (समय का) गुज़रना *The last hour went very slowly.* **16** [I] to start an activity कोई गतिविधि आरंभ करना *Everybody ready to sing? Let's go!* **17** [I] to make a sound आवाज़ पैदा करना *The bell went early today.* ○ *Cats go 'miaow'.* **18** [I] (*spoken, informal*) used in the present tense for saying what a person said किसी के कहे को उद्धृत करने के लिए वर्तमान काल में प्रयुक्त *I said, 'How are you, Imran?' and he goes, 'It's none of your business!'* **19** [I] (*informal*) (*only used in the continuous tenses*) to be available उपलब्ध होना *Are there any jobs going* *in your department?* **20** [I] (*informal*) used for saying that you do not want sb to do sth bad or stupid यह कहने के लिए प्रयुक्त कि लोग ग़लत काम न करें *You can borrow my bike again, but don't go breaking it this time!* ○ *I hope Jatin doesn't go and tell everyone about our plan.*

IDM **as people, things, etc. go** compared to the average person or thing औसत व्यक्ति या वस्तु की तुलना में (प्रयुक्त) *As Chinese restaurants go, it wasn't bad.*

**be going to do sth** **1** used for showing what you plan to do in the future भविष्य की योजना की बात करने के लिए प्रयुक्त या यह बताने के लिए प्रयुक्त कि भविष्य में आप क्या करने वाले हैं *We're going to sell our car.* **2** used for saying that you think sth will happen कुछ होने वाला है यह आशंका जताने के लिए प्रयुक्त *It's going to rain soon.* ○ *Oh no! He's going to fall!*

**go all out for sth, go all out to do sth** to make a great effort to do sth कुछ करने का भरसक प्रयास करना

**go for it** (*informal*) to do sth after not being sure about it अनिश्चय भाव से कुछ करना *'Do you think we should buy it?' 'Yeah, let's go for it!'*

**have a lot going for you** to have many advantages अनेक लाभ होना

**Here goes!** said just before you start to do sth difficult or exciting कोई चुनौतीभरा काम शुरू करने से पहले ये शब्द कहे जाते हैं

**to go** that is/are left before sth ends शेष रह जाना *How long (is there) to go before the end of the lesson?*

> NOTE **Go** से बनने वाली अन्य प्रविष्टियों के लिए संबधित संज्ञा, विशेषण आदि की प्रविष्टियाँ देखिए। जैसे **go astray** आपको **astray** में मिलेगा।

PHR V **go about** ➪ **go round/around/about**

**go about sth/doing sth** to start trying to do sth difficult किसी कठिन काम को करने का प्रयास आरंभ करना *I wouldn't have any idea how to go about building a house.*

**go about with sb** ➪ **go round/around/about with sb**

**go after sb/sth** to try to catch or get sb/sth किसी वस्तु को पाने का प्रयास करना

**go against sb** to not be in sb's favour or not be to sb's advantage किसी के अनुकूल या लाभ की बात न होना *The referee's decision went against him.*

**go against sb/sth** to do sth that sb/sth says you should not do मना किए गए काम को करना *She went against her parents' wishes and married him.*

**go ahead** **1** to take place after being delayed or in doubt विलंब या अनिश्चय के बाद होना *Although several members were missing, the meeting went ahead without them.* **2** to travel in front of other people in your group and arrive before them अपने दल के लोगों से आगे चलकर ठिकाने पर पहले पहुँच जाना

**go ahead (with sth)** to do sth after not being sure that it was possible अनिश्चय के बावजूद कुछ करना *We decided to go ahead with the match in spite of the heavy rain.* ○ *'Can I take this chair?' 'Sure, go ahead.'*

**go along** to continue; to progress चलते रहना; प्रगति करना या आगे बढ़ना *The course gets more difficult as you go along.*

**go along with sb/sth** to agree with sb/sth; to do what sb else has decided व्यक्ति या वस्तु से सहमत होना; अन्य व्यक्ति द्वारा निश्चित काम को करना *I'm happy to go along with whatever you suggest.*

**go around** ➪ **go round/around/about with** देखिए।

**go around with sb** ➪ **go round/around/about with sb** देखिए।

**go away** **1** to disappear or leave ग़ायब हो जाना या चले जाना *I've got a headache that just won't go away.* ○ *Just go away and leave me alone!* **2** to leave the place where you live for at least one night कम से कम एक रात के लिए अपने निवास से चले जाना *We're going away to the coast this weekend.*

**go back (to sth)** **1** to return to a place कहीं पर लौटना *It's a wonderful city and I'd like to go back there one day.* **2** to return to an earlier matter or situation पिछले प्रसंग पर लौटना *Let's go back to the subject we were discussing a few minutes ago.* **3** to have its origins in an earlier period of time मूल की दृष्टि से प्राचीन कालखंड से जुड़े होना *A lot of the buildings in the village go back to the fifteenth century.*

**go back on sth** to break a promise, an agreement, etc. वादे से मुकर जाना, दिए वचन को तोड़ देना *I promised to help them and I can't go back on my word.*

**go back to sth/doing sth** to start doing again sth that you had stopped doing पहले रोके काम को पुनः आरंभ करना *When the children got a bit older she went back to full-time work.*

**go by** **1** (used about time) to pass (समय का) गुज़रना *As time went by, her confidence grew.* **2** to pass a place किसी स्थान से गुज़रना *She stood at the window watching people go by.*

**go by sth** to use particular information, rules, etc. to help you decide your actions or opinions अपनी कार्यविधि या राय तय करने के लिए विशेष जानकारी नियम आदि का इस्तेमाल करना

**go down** **1** (used about a ship, etc.) to sink (जहाज़ आदि का) डूबना **2** (used about the sun) to disappear from the sky (सूर्य का) आकाश से लुप्त हो जाना **3** to become lower in price, level, etc.; to fall किसी वस्तु के मूल्य, स्तर आदि का घट जाना; कम हो जाना *The number of people out of work went down last month.*

**go down (with sb)** (*used with adverbs, especially 'well' or 'badly' or in questions beginning with 'how'*) to be received in a particular way by sb (कुछ क्रियाविशेषणों, विशेषतः well या badly, या how से आरंभ होने वाले प्रश्नवाचक वाक्यों के साथ प्रयुक्त) किसी वस्तु को किसी व्यक्ति द्वारा एक विशेष रूप में ग्रहण किया जाना *The film went down well with the critics.*

**go down with sth** to catch an illness; to become ill with sth बीमारी लग जाना; किसी रोग से आक्रांत हो जाना

**go for sb** to attack sb किसी व्यक्ति पर आक्रमण करना

**go for sb/sth** **1** to be true for a particular person or thing व्यक्ति या वस्तु विशेष के लिए सच होना *We've got financial problems but I suppose the same goes for a great many people.* **2** to choose sb/sth किसी व्यक्ति या वस्तु को चुनना *I think I'll go for the roast chicken.*

**go in** (used about the sun) to disappear behind a cloud (सूर्य का) बादल के पीछे छिप जाना

**go in for sth** to enter or take part in an exam or competition किसी परीक्षा में बैठना या प्रतियोगिता में भाग लेना

**go in for sth/doing sth** to do or have sth as a hobby or interest किसी बात का शौक़ या उसमें रुचि होना

**go into sth** **1** to hit sth while travelling in/on a vehicle कार में सफ़र करते हुए किसी से टकरा जाना *I couldn't stop in time and went into the back of the car in front.* **2** to start working in a certain type of job विशेष प्रकार का काम शुरू करना *When she left school she went into nursing.* **3** to look at or describe sth in detail किसी वस्तु को गहराई से देखना या विस्तार से वर्णन करना *I haven't got time to go into all the details now.*

**go off** **1** to explode फूटना, विस्फोट होना *A bomb has gone off in the city centre.* **2** to make a sudden loud noise ऊँची आवाज करना या में बजना *I woke up when my alarm clock went off.* **3** (used about lights, heating, etc.) to stop working (बत्ती आदि का) गुल हो जाना *There was a power cut and all the lights went off.* **4** (used about food and drink) to become too old to eat or drink; to go bad (खाद्य और पेय का) बासी हो जाना; ख़राब हो जाना **5** to become worse in quality गुणवत्ता कम हो जाना *I used to like that band but they've gone off recently.*

**go off sb/sth** to stop liking or being interested in sb/sth किसी व्यक्ति या वस्तु में रुचि समाप्त हो जाना *I went off spicy food after I was ill last year.*

**go off (with sb)** to leave with sb किसी के साथ चले जाना *I don't know where Sidharth is—he went off with friends an hour ago.*

**go off with sth** to take sth that belongs to sb else किसी दूसरे की चीज़ ले जाना

**go on** **1** (used about lights, heating, etc.) to start working (बत्ती आदि का) जल उठना *I saw the lights go on in the house opposite.* **2** (used about time) to pass (समय) गुज़रना *As time went on, she became more and more successful.* **3** (*used especially in the continuous tenses*) to happen or take place कुछ घटित होना या कोई बात होना *Can anybody tell me what's going on here?* **4** (used about a situation) to continue without changing (स्थिति) बिना बदले चलते रहना *This is a difficult period but it won't go on forever.* **5** to continue speaking after stopping for a moment क्षण भर रुककर बोलना जारी रखना *Go on. What happened next?* **6** used for encouraging sb to do sth किसी का हौसला बढ़ाने के लिए प्रयुक्त *Oh go on, let me borrow your car. I'll bring it back in an hour.*

**go on sth** to use sth as information so that you can understand a situation किसी स्थिति को समझने के लिए किसी बात को सूत्र के समान प्रयुक्त करना *There were no witnesses to the crime, so the police had very little to go on.*

**go on (about sb/sth)** to talk about sb/sth for a long time in a boring or annoying way उबाऊ ढंग से व्यक्ति या वस्तु के विषय में बात करते जाना *She went on and on about work.*

**go/be on (at sb) (about sth)** to keep complaining about sth किसी की शिकायत करते रहना *She's always (going) on at me to mend the roof.*

**go on (doing sth)** to continue doing sth without stopping or changing बिना रुके या स्थिति बदले अविराम भाव से कुछ करते रहना *We don't want to go on living here for the rest of our lives.*

**go on (with sth)** to continue doing sth, perhaps after a pause or break कोई काम करते जाना (संभवतः विराम के बाद) *She ignored me and went on with her meal.*

**go on to do sth** to do sth after completing sth else दूसरा काम समाप्त कर कोई नया काम करना

**go out** **1** to leave the place where you live or work for a short time, returning on the same day घर या कार्य स्थल से कहीं जाना और उसी दिन लौट आना *Let's go out for a meal tonight* (= to a restaurant). **2** to stop shining or burning बुझ जाना *Suddenly all the lights went out.* **3** to stop being fashionable or in use फ़ैशन या चलन में न रहना *That kind of music went out in the seventies.* **4** (used about the sea) to move away from the land (समुद्र) जमीन से दूर हो जाना, भाटा आना *Is the tide coming in or going out?* ✪ पर्याय **ebb** ➪ **tide[1]** देखिए।

**go out (with sb); go out (together)** to spend time regularly with sb, having a romantic and/or sexual relationship प्रेमी या प्रेमिका के साथ नियमित रूप से समय गुज़ारना *Is Madhu going out with anyone?* ○ *They went out together for five years before they got married.*

**go over sth** to look at, think about or discuss sth carefully from beginning to end किसी बात को पूरे तौर पर देखना, सोचना और उस पर विचार करना *Go over your work before you hand it in.*

**go over to sth** to change to a different side, system, habit, etc. पाला, प्रणाली, आदत आदि बदलना

**go round** (used especially after 'enough') to be shared among all the people (विशेषतः 'enough' के बाद प्रयुक्त) सब लोगों को कुछ मिल जाना, किसी में सब लोगों का हिस्सा होना *In this area, there aren't enough jobs to go round.*

**go round/around/about** (used about a story, an illness, etc.) to pass from person to person (कहानी, बीमारी, आदि) एक से दूसरे तक पहुँचना *There's a rumour going round that he's going to resign.*

**go round (to...)** to visit sb's home, usually a short distance away कुछ दूरी पर किसी के घर जाना *I'm going round to Gupta's for dinner tonight.*

**go round/around/about with sb** to spend time and go to places regularly with sb किसी के साथ नियमित रूप से रहना और जगह-जगह जाना *Her parents don't like the people she has started going round with.*

**go through** to be completed successfully सफलतापूर्वक पूरा होना *The deal went through as agreed.*

**go through sth 1** to look in or at sth carefully, especially in order to find sth किसी को बारीकी से देखना या टटोलना (विशेषतः इसलिए कि खोई हुई चीज़ मिल जाए) *I went through all my pockets but I couldn't find my wallet.* **2** to look at, think about or discuss sth carefully from beginning to end शुरू से अंत तक किसी बात पर ग़ौर करना, सोचना और विचार करना *We'll start the lesson by going through your homework.* **3** to have an unpleasant experience प्रतिकूल अनुभव में से गुजरना *I'd hate to go through such a terrible ordeal again.*

**go through with sth** to do sth unpleasant or difficult that you have decided, agreed or threatened to do निश्चय के अनुसार कोई अप्रिय या कठिन काम करना *Do you think she'll go through with her threat to leave him?*

**go together** used about two or more things **1** to belong to the same set or group (दो या अधिक वस्तुओं के लिए प्रयुक्त) एक ही समूह से जुड़े होना **2** to look or taste good together मिल कर अच्छा लगना (देखने में या स्वाद में)

**go towards sth** to be used as part of the payment for sth किसी वस्तु के भुगतान के अंश के रूप में प्रयुक्त *The money I was given for my birthday went towards my new bike.*

**go under 1** to sink below the surface of some water थोड़े पानी में डूबना 2 (*informal*) (used about a company) to fail and close (कंपनी) विफल होकर बंद हो जाना *A lot of firms are going under in the recession.*

**go up 1** to become higher in price, level, amount, etc.; to rise मूल्य, स्तर, मात्रा आदि का बढ़ जाना; ऊपर की ओर जाना, उठना *The birth rate has gone up by 10%.* **2** to start burning suddenly and strongly एकाएक तेज़ी से जलने लगना *The car crashed into a wall and went up in flames.* **3** to be built बन कर तैयार हो जाना

**go with sth 1** to be included with sth; to happen as a result of sth किन्ही बातों का संग-संग चलना; किसी बात के परिणामस्वरूप कुछ घटित होना *Pressure goes with the job.* **2** to look or taste good with sth else किसी अन्य वस्तु के साथ मेल खाना (दीखने में या स्वाद में) *What colour carpet would go with the walls?*

**go without (sth)** to choose or be forced to not have sth कुछ गँवाने को विवश होना *They went without sleep night after night while the baby was ill.*

**go**[2] /gəʊ गो/ *noun* (*pl.* **goes** /gəʊz गोज़्/) [C] **1** a turn to play in a game, etc. खेल आदि में बारी *Whose go is it?* ○ *Hurry up—it's your go.* ✪ पर्याय **turn** **2** (*informal*) **a go (at sth/doing sth)** an occasion when you try to do sth; an attempt कुछ करने के प्रयास का अवसर; प्रयास, कोशिश *I've never played this game before, but I'll* ***give it a go***. ○ *Anand passed his driving test* ***first go***.

IDM **be on the go** (*informal*) to be very active or busy बहुत सक्रिय या व्यस्त होना *I'm exhausted. I've been on the go all day.*

**have a go at sb** (*informal*) to criticize sb/sth व्यक्ति या वस्तु की आलोचना करना

**make a go of sth** (*informal*) to be successful at sth किसी बात में सफल होना

**goad** /gəʊd गोड्/ *verb* [T] **goad sb/sth (into sth/doing sth)** to cause sb to do sth by making him/her angry किसी को क्रोधित कर उससे कुछ करवा लेना

**go-ahead**[1] *noun* [*sing.*] **the go-ahead (for sth)** permission to do sth कुछ करने की अनुमति *It looks like the council are going to* ***give us the go-ahead*** *for the new building.*

**go-ahead**[2] *adj.* enthusiastic to try new ways of doing things नए ढंग से काम करने के लिए उत्साही

**goal** /gəʊl गोल्/ *noun* [C] **1** (in football, rugby, hockey, etc.) the area between two posts into which the ball must be kicked, hit, etc. for a point or points to be scored (फ़ुटबॉल रगबी, हॉकी आदि में) गोल *He crossed the ball in front of the goal.* **2** a point that is scored when the ball goes into the goal गोल होने के बाद अर्जित अंक *Mohun Bagan won by three goals to two.* ○ *to score a goal* **3** your purpose or aim उद्देश्य या लक्ष्य *This year I should **achieve** my **goal** of visiting all the capital cities of India.*

**goalkeeper** /ˈgəʊlkiːpə(r) ˈगोल्कीप(र्)/ (*informal* **goalie** /ˈgəʊli ˈगोलि/ or **keeper**) *noun* [C] (in football, hockey, etc.) the player who stands in front of the **goal 1** and tries to stop the other team from scoring (फ़ुटबॉल, हॉकी आदि में) गोलरक्षक, गोलकीपर *The goalkeeper made a magnificent save.*

**goalless** /ˈgəʊlləs ˈगोल्लस्/ *adj.* with no goals scored बिना कोई गोल बनाए *a goalless draw* ○ *The match finished goalless.*

**goalpost** /ˈgəʊlpəʊst ˈगोल्पोस्ट्/ *noun* [C] (in football, hockey, etc.) one of the two posts that form the sides of a goal. They are joined together by a bar (**the crossbar**) (फ़ुटबॉल, हॉकी आदि में) गोल का खंभा

**goat** /gəʊt गोट्/ *noun* [C] a small animal with horns which lives in mountain areas or is kept on farms for its milk and meat बकरी, बकरा

> NOTE बकरे को **billy goat** कहते हैं और बकरी को **nanny goat**।

**goatee** /gəʊˈtiː गोˈटी/ *noun* [C] a small pointed beard on a man's chin पुरुष की ठुड्डी पर छोटी नुकीली दाढ़ी, बकर दाढ़ी, बुच्ची दाढ़ी

**gobar gas** *noun* [U] a gas produced from cow dung which is used as fuel गोबर गैस ➪ **biogas** देखिए।

**gobble** /ˈgɒbl ˈगॉब्ल्/ *verb* [I, T] (*informal*) **gobble sth (up down)** to eat quickly and noisily तेज़ी से आवाज़ करते हुए खाना; भकोसना, शीघ्रता से गटक जाना

**gobbledegook** (*also* **gobbledygbook**) /ˈgɒbldiguːk ˈगॉब्लडिगूक्/ *noun* [U] (*informal*) complicated language that is hard to understand समझने में कठिन, पेचीदा भाषा; शब्दजाल

**go-between** *noun* [C] a person who takes messages between two people or groups दो व्यक्तियों या समूहों के बीच संदेश वहन करने वाला व्यक्ति; बिचौलिया, दलाल, मध्यस्थ

**goblin** /ˈgɒblɪn ˈगॉब्लिन्/ *noun* [C] (in stories) a small ugly creature who tricks people (कहानियों में) लोगों को धोखा देने वाला छोटा भद्दा प्राणी; बैताल, पिशाच

**gobsmacked** /ˈgɒbsmækt ˈगॉब्स्मैक्ट्/ *adj.* (*informal*) so surprised that you cannot speak अति विस्मय से अवाक ✪ पर्याय **speechless**

**god** /gɒd गॉड्/ *noun* **1** [*sing.*] **God** (not used with *the*) the being or spirit in Christianity, Islam and Judaism who people pray to and who people believe created the universe परमेश्वर, परमात्मा, सृष्टिकर्ता *Do you believe in God?* ○ *Muslims worship God in a mosque.* **2** (*feminine* **goddess**) a being or spirit that people believe has power over a particular part of nature or that represents a particular quality दिव्य शक्ति संपन्न सत्ता, देवी-देवता *Indra is the Indian god of rain and Lakshmi is the goddess of wealth.*

> NOTE **'God'** शब्द का प्रयोग अनेक अभिव्यक्तियों में होता है। आश्चर्य या स्तब्धता व्यक्त करने के लिए *'Oh my God'* कहा जाता है—*'Oh my God I have won the lottery!'* ख़ुशी और राहत का भाव व्यक्त करने के लिए हम *'thank God'* कहते हैं—*Thank God you've arrived—I was beginning to think you'd had an accident.* जब हम किसी से कुछ करने के लिए कहते हैं और बताना चाहते हैं कि वह अत्यावश्यक है या जब हम किसी से नाराज़ होते हैं तो *For God's sake* कहते हैं—*For God's sake, shut up!*

**godchild** /ˈgɒdtʃaɪld ˈगॉड्चाइल्ड्/ (**goddaughter** or **godson**) *noun* [C] a child that a chosen friend of the family (**godmother** or **godfather**) promises to help and to make sure is educated as a Christian परिवार के मित्र द्वारा पाल-पोस कर शिक्षित किया गया बालक या बालिका; धर्मपुत्र, धर्मपुत्री

**goddess** /ˈgɒdes ˈगॉडेस्/ *noun* [C] a female god देवी, पूजित नारी

**godfather** /ˈgɒdfɑːðə(r) ˈगॉड्फ़ाद(र्)/ (*also* **godmother** or **godparent**) *noun* [C] a person chosen by a child's family who promises to help the child and to make sure he/she is educated as a Christian बच्चे के परिवार द्वारा चुना गया व्यक्ति जो उसे पाल-पोसकर शिक्षित करने का व्रत लेता है; धर्मपिता

**godforsaken** /ˈgɒdfəseɪkən ˈगॉड्फ़सेकन्/ *adj.* (used about a place) not interesting or attractive in any way (स्थान) रोचकता और आकर्षण से रहित, वीरान और उदास

**godown** /ˈgeʊdaʊn ˈगोडाउन्/ = **warehouse**

**godsend** /ˈgɒdsend ˈगॉड्सेन्ड्/ *noun* [C] something unexpected that is very useful because it comes just when it is needed अचानक मिली अभीष्ट वस्तु (जो आवश्यकता के क्षणों में मिली), ईश्वरीय वरदान, सौभाग्य

**goggles** /ˈgɒglz ˈगॉग्ल्ज़्/ *noun* [*pl.*] special glasses that you wear to protect your eyes from water, wind, dust, etc. धूप, पानी, हवा, धूल आदि से बचाव का विशेष चश्मा ➪ **mask** देखिए।

**going[1]** /ˈgəʊɪŋ ˈगोइङ्/ *noun* **1** [*sing.*] (*formal*) the act of leaving a place किसी स्थान को छोड़ जाने की क्रिया; प्रस्थान *We were all saddened by his going.* ✪ पर्याय **departure** **2** [U] the rate or speed of travel, progress, etc. यात्रा, प्रगति आदि की दर या चाल *Three children in four years? That's not bad going!* **3** [U] how difficult it is to make progress प्रगति में बाधा, आगे बढ़ने में कठिनाई, ऊबड़-खाबड़ रास्ता *The path up the mountain was* ***rough going***. ○ *It'll be* ***hard going*** *if we need to finish this by Friday!*

IDM **get out, go, leave, etc. while the going is good** to leave a place or stop doing sth while it is still easy to do so अनुकूलता के बावजूद भी किसी स्थान को छोड़ देना या काम को बंद कर देना

**going[2]** /ˈgəʊɪŋ ˈगोइङ्/ *adj.*

IDM **a going concern** a successful business सफल व्यापार, फलता-फूलता व्यापार

**the going rate (for sth)** the usual cost (of sth) किसी वस्तु का आम भाव, चालू दर *What's the going rate for an office cleaner?*

**going-over** *noun* [*sing.*] (*informal*) **1** a very careful examination of sth किसी वस्तु की बारीक जाँच-पड़ताल *Give the car* ***a good going-over*** *before deciding whether to buy it.* **2** a serious physical attack on sb किसी पर गंभीर आक्रमण, संगीन हमला

**goings-on** *noun* [*pl.*] (*informal*) unusual things that are happening असामान्य घटनाएँ

**goitre** (*AmE* **goiter**) /ˈgɔɪtə(r) ˈगॉइट(र्)/ *noun* [U] a swelling in the front of the throat caused by an increase in the size of the thyroid gland घेघा, गलगंड

**go-kart** /ˈgəʊ kɑːt ˈगो काट्/ *noun* [C] a vehicle like a very small car with no roof or doors, used for racing छोटी कार जैसा बिना छत और दरवाज़ों का वाहन (दौड़-स्पर्धा में प्रयुक्त)

**gold** /gəʊld गोल्ड्/ *noun* **1** [U] (*symbol* **Au**) a precious yellow metal that is used for making coins, jewellery, etc. सोना, स्वर्ण *Is your bracelet made of solid gold?* ○ *22 carat gold* **2** [C] = **gold medal** ▶ **gold** *adj.* सोने का, स्वर्णिम *The invitation was written in gold letters.* ➪ **golden** देखिए।

IDM **(as) good as gold** ➪ **good[1]** देखिए।

**have a heart of gold** ➪ **heart** देखिए।

**golden** /ˈgəʊldən ˈगोल्डन्/ *adj.* **1** made of gold or bright yellow in colour like gold सोने का बना या सोने के रंग का *a golden crown* ○ *golden hair/sand* **2** best, most important, favourite, etc. सर्वोत्तम, सबसे मनपसंद *The golden rule is 'Keep your eye on the ball'.* ○ *a golden opportunity*

IDM **the golden rule (of sth)** ➪ **rule[1] 2** देखिए।

**golden-wedding** *noun* [C] the 50th anniversary of a wedding विवाह की स्वर्ण जयंती या पचासवीं वर्षगाँठ *The couple celebrated their golden wedding in August.* ➪ **diamond wedding, ruby wedding** और **silver wedding** देखिए।

**goldfish** /ˈgəʊldfɪʃ ˈगोल्ड्फ़िश्/ *noun* [C] (*pl.* **goldfish**) a small orange fish, often kept as a pet in a bowl or a small pool in the garden (**pond**) नारंगी रंग की छोटी पालतू मछली; गोल्डफ़िश

**gold medal** (*also* **gold**) *noun* [C] the prize for first place in a sports competition खेल-स्पर्धा में प्रथम स्थान का पुरस्कार; स्वर्ण पदक ➪ **silver medal** और **bronze medal** देखिए।

**gold mine** *noun* [C] **1** a place where gold is taken from the ground सोने की खान **2 a gold mine (of sth)** a place, person or thing that provides a lot of sth किसी वस्तु को प्रचुरता से उपलब्ध कराने वाला स्थान, व्यक्ति या वस्तु *This website is a gold mine of information.*

**goldsmith** /ˈgəʊldsmɪθ ˈगोल्ड्स्मिथ़्/ *noun* [C] a person who makes, repairs or sells articles made of gold सुनार, स्वर्णकार

**golf** /gɒlf गॉल्फ़्/ *noun* [U] a game that is played outdoors on a large area of grass (**golf course**) and in which you use a stick (**golf club**) to hit a small hard ball (**golf ball**) into a series of holes (usually 18) घास वाले बड़े मैदान (गोल्फ़ कोर्स) में खेला जाने वाला एक खेल जिसमें एक छड़ी (गोल्फ़ क्लब) से एक छोटी सख़्त गेंद (गोल्फ़ बॉल) को मार कर (प्रायः 18) छेदों में डाला जाता है; गोल्फ़ का खेल *to play a round of golf*

**golfer** /ˈgɒlfə(r) ˈगॉल्फ़(र्)/ *noun* [C] a person who plays golf गोल्फ़ का खिलाड़ी

**golly** /ˈgɒli ˈगॉलि/ *exclamation* (*informal*) used for expressing surprise आश्चर्य की अभिव्यक्ति के लिए प्रयुक्त

**gone[1]** ➪ **go[1]** का past participle of रूप

**gone[2]** /gɒn गॉन्/ *adj.* (*not before a noun*) not present any longer; completely used or finished अब मौजूद नहीं; पूर्णतया समाप्त *He stood at the door for a moment, and then he was gone.*

NOTE 'लुप्त' या 'समाप्त' के अर्थ में शब्द **'gone'** का प्रयोग क्रिया **'be'** के साथ होता है (देखिए ऊपर दिया उदाहरण), जब हमें बताना हो कि कोई वस्तु लुप्त होकर कहाँ गई तो हम शब्द **'have'** का प्रयोग करते हैं— *Nobody knows where they have gone.*

**gone**[3] /gɒn गॉन्/ *prep.* later than बीता हुआ, हो चुका *Hurry up! It's gone six already!*

**gong** /gɒŋ गॉङ्/ *noun* [C] a round and flat metal disc that gives a **resonant** sound when struck with a stick. It is also used to give signals, for example in schools it is sounded at the end of each period घंटा; तालवाद्य का एक प्रकार

**gonna** /ˈgɒnə ˈगॉना/ (*informal*) a way of writing 'going to' to show that sb is speaking in an informal way, 'going to' लिखने का एक ढंग जो अनौपचारिकता दर्शाता है

> **NOTE** आप स्वयं **'gonna'** को प्रयोग न करें (यदि किसी के बोलने की नक़ल न उतार रहे हों), इसे अशुद्ध माना जा सकता है। यही बात **wanna** (= want to) और **gotta** (= got to) के साथ है।

**gonorrhoea** (*AmE* **gonorrhea**) /ˌgɒnəˈrɪə ˌगॉनˈरिआ/ *noun* [U] a disease of the sexual organs, caught by having sex with a person who has it यौन संसर्ग से उत्पन्न एक यौन रोग; सूज़ाक

**goo** /gu: गू/ *noun* [U] (*informal*) a sticky wet substance चिपचिपा गीला पदार्थ ➪ **gooey** adjective देखिए।

**good**[1] /gʊd गुड्/ *adj.* (**better** /ˈbetə(r) ˈबेट(र्)/, **best** /best बेस्ट्/) **1** of a high quality or standard उच्च गुणवत्ता या स्तर का, अच्छा *a good book/film/actor* ○ *That's a really good idea!* **2 good at sth; good with sb/sth** able to do sth or deal with sb/sth well किसी काम को अच्छे ढंग से करने में समर्थ; सक्षम *Nisha's really good at science subjects but she's* ***no good at*** *languages.* ○ *He's very good with children.* **3** pleasant or enjoyable प्रीतिकर या आनंदप्रद *It's good to be home again.* ○ *good news/weather* ○ ***Have a good time*** *at the party!* **4** morally right or well behaved सच्चरित्र या शालीन *She was a very good person—she spent her whole life trying to help other people.* ○ *Were the children good while we were out?* **5 good (to sb); good of sb** kind; helpful दयालु; सहायक *They were good to me when I was ill.* ○ *It was good of you to come.* **6 good (for sb/sth)** having a positive effect on sb/sth's health or condition स्वास्थ्य के लिए हितकर *Green vegetables are very good for you.* **7 good (for sb/sth)** suitable or convenient उपयुक्त या सुविधापूर्ण *This beach is very good for surfing.* ○ *I think Puneet would be a good person for the job.* **8** (used about a reason, etc.) acceptable and easy to understand (तर्क आदि) स्वीकार्य और सरलता से बोधगम्य *a good excuse/explanation/reason* ○ *She has good reason to be pleased—she's just been promoted.* **9 good (for sth)** that can be used or can provide sth उपयोगी या प्रयोग के योग्य, इस्तेमाल हो सकने वाला *I've only got one good pair of shoes.* ○ *This ticket's good for another three days.* **10 a good...** more, larger, etc. than is usual or expected सामान्य या प्रत्याशित से अधिक ***a good many/a good few*** *people* (= a lot of people) ○ *a good distance* (= a long way) **11** used when you are pleased about sth अपनी संतुष्टि व्यक्त करने के लिए प्रयुक्त *'Leena's invited us to dinner next week.' 'Oh, good!'*

**IDM a good/great many** ➪ **many** देखिए।

**as good as** almost; virtually लगभग; वस्तुतः *The project is as good as finished.*

**(as) good as gold** very well behaved शिष्ट, सुशील

**be in/for a good cause** ➪ **cause**[1] देखिए।

**in good faith** ➪ **faith** देखिए।

**good for you, him, her, etc.** (*informal*) used to show that you are pleased that sb has done sth clever किसी की सफलता पर संतुष्टि व्यक्त करने के लिए प्रयुक्त *'I passed my driving test!' 'Well done! Good for you!'*

**for good measure** ➪ **measure**[2] देखिए।

**so far so good** ➪ **far**[2] देखिए।

**good**[2] /gʊd गुड्/ *noun* [U] **1** behaviour that is morally right or acceptable नैतिक दृष्टि से उचित या स्वीकार्य आचरण *the difference between good and evil* ○ *I'm sure there's some good in everybody.* **2** something that will help sb/sth; advantage व्यक्ति या वस्तु के लिए सहायक; लाभ *She did it* ***for the good*** *of her country.* ○ *I know you don't want to go into hospital, but it's* ***for your own good.*** ➪ **goods** की प्रविष्टि भी देखिए।

**IDM be no good (doing sth)** to be of no use or value बेकार, व्यर्थ *It's no good standing here in the cold. Let's go home.* ○ *This sweater isn't any good. It's too small.*

**do you good** to help or be useful to you आपकी मदद करना या आपके काम आना *It'll do you good to meet some new people.*

**for good** for ever सदा के लिए *I hope they've gone for good this time!*

**not much good** (*informal*) bad or not useful ज़्यादा अच्छा नहीं, ठीक-ठीक *'How was the party?' 'Not much good.'*

**a/the world of good** ➪ **world** देखिए।

**goodbye** /ˌgʊdˈbaɪ ˌगुड्ˈबाइ/ *exclamation* said when sb goes or you go विदा लेते या देते समय प्रयुक्त *We said goodbye to Sachin at the airport.* ▶ **goodbye** *noun* [C] अलविदा *We said our goodbyes and left.*

**Good Friday** [C] the Friday before Easter when Christians remember the death of Christ ईस्टर पर्व से पहले का शुक्रवार, इस दिन ईसाई लोग ईसा मसीह की मृत्यु को याद करते हैं; गुड फ्राइडे

**good-humoured** *adj.* pleasant and friendly ख़ुशमिज़ाज, प्रसन्नचित्त

**goodies** /ˈgʊdiz ˈगुडिज़्/ *noun* [*pl.*] (*informal*) exciting things that are provided or given परोसी गई सुहानी-स्वादिष्ट वस्तुएँ *There were lots of cakes and other goodies on the table.*

**good-looking** *adj.* (usually used about a person) attractive (व्यक्ति) देखने में आकर्षक, सुदर्शन ➪ **beautiful** पर नोट देखिए।

**good looks** *noun* [*pl.*] an attractive appearance (of a person) (व्यक्ति का) आकर्षक चेहरा-मोहरा

**good-natured** *adj.* friendly or kind मित्रवत या करुणाशील

**goodness** /ˈgʊdnəs ˈगुड्नस्/ *noun* [U] **1** the quality of being good अच्छाई, नैतिकता ✪ पर्याय **virtue** **2** the part of sth that has a good effect, especially on sb/sth's health अच्छा प्रभाव, अच्छाई (विशेषतः व्यक्ति या वस्तु के स्वास्थ्य पर) *Wholemeal bread has more goodness in it than white.*

> NOTE **Goodness** का प्रयोग अनेक अभिव्यक्तियों में होता है। आश्चर्य व्यक्त करने के लिए जैसे *Goodness (me)!* का प्रयोग होता है। ख़ुशी एवं राहत व्यक्त करने के लिए *Thank goodness* प्रयुक्त होता है—*Thank goodness it's stopped raining!* किसी कार्य की अत्यावश्यकता व्यक्त करने के लिए या किसी पर अप्रसन्नता प्रकट करने के लिए अभिव्यक्ति *For goodness' sake* प्रयुक्त होती है—*For goodness' sake, hurry up!*

**goods** /gʊdz गुड्ज़्/ *noun* [*pl.*] **1** things that are for sale बिकने का सामान, बिकाऊ माल *a wide range of consumer goods* ○ *electrical goods* ○ *stolen goods* **2** (*AmE* **freight**) things that are carried by train or lorry रेलगाड़ी या ट्रक से ढोया जाने वाला माल *a goods train* ○ *a heavy goods vehicle* (= HGV)
IDM **come up with/deliver the goods** (*informal*) to do what you have promised to do वादा निभाना

**good sense** *noun* [U] good judgement or intelligence अच्छी निर्णय शक्ति या बुद्धि, समझदारी *He had the good sense to refuse the offer.*

**goodwill** /ˌgʊdˈwɪl ˌगुड्ˈविल्/ *noun* [U] friendly, helpful feelings towards other people दूसरों के प्रति सद्भाव *The visit was designed to promote friendship and goodwill.*

**goody** (*also* **goodie**) /ˈgʊdi ˈगुडि/ *noun* [C] (*pl.* **goodies**) (*informal*) a good person in a film, book, etc. फ़िल्म, पुस्तक आदि में प्रदर्शित सच्चरित्र व्यक्ति ✪ विलोम **baddy**

**goody-goody** *noun* [C] a person who always behaves well so that other people have a good opinion of him/her सदा शिष्ट व्यवहार करने वाला व्यक्ति (ताकि लोग उसकी तारीफ़ करें), शिष्टता का दिखावा करने वाला व्यक्ति

**gooey** /ˈguːi ˈगूइ/ *adj.* (*informal*) soft and sticky नरम और चिपचिपा *gooey cakes*

**goof** /guːf गूफ़्/ *verb* [I] (*informal*) to make a silly mistake बेवकूफ़ीभरी ग़लतियाँ करना

**goose** /guːs गूस्/ *noun* [C] (*pl.* **geese** /giːs गीस्/) a large white bird that is like a duck, but bigger. Geese are kept on farms for their meat बतख़ जैसा बड़ा सफ़ेद पक्षी जिसे माँस के लिए पाला जाता है; गीज़

**gooseberry** /ˈgʊzbəri ˈगुज़्बरि/ *noun* [C] (*pl.* **gooseberries**) a small green fruit that is covered in small hairs and has a sour taste एक हरा रोएँदार छोटा खट्टा फल; काकबदरी
IDM **play gooseberry** to be present when two lovers want to be alone प्रेमियों के एकांत मिलन में बाधक होना

**goose pimples** (*also* **goose bumps**) *noun* [*pl.*] small points or lumps which appear on your skin because you are cold or frightened ठंड या डर के मारे त्वचा पर होने वाले दाने; चर्मांकुरण

**gore**[1] /gɔː(r) गॉ(र्)/ *noun* [U] thick blood that comes from a wound घाव से बहने वाला गाढ़ा ख़ून, ख़ून का थक्का ➪ **gory** adjective देखिए।

**gore**[2] /gɔː(r) गॉ(र्)/ *verb* [T] (used about an animal) to wound sb with a horn, etc. (पशु का) किसी को सींग मार कर घायल कर देना *She was gored to death by a bull.*

**gorge**[1] /gɔːdʒ गॉज्/ *noun* [C] a narrow valley with steep sides and a river running through it तीखी ढालों वाली तंग घाटी जिस के बीच में से नदी बहती है ➪ **limestone** पर चित्र देखिए।

**gorge**[2] /gɔːdʒ गोज्/ *verb* [I,T] **gorge (yourself) (on/with sth)** to eat a lot of food खूब भोजन खाना; भकोसना

**gorgeous** /ˈgɔːdʒəs ˈगॉजस्/ *adj.* (*informal*) extremely pleasant or attractive अत्यंत प्रीतिकर या आकर्षक, भव्य, शानदार *You look gorgeous in that dress.*
▶ **gorgeously** *adv.* भव्यता के साथ, शानदार ढंग से

**gorilla** /gəˈrɪlə गˈरिला/ *noun* [C] a large very powerful African **ape** with a black or brown hairy body काले या भूरे बालों से ढका एक बहुत बड़ा ताक़तवर अफ्रीक़ी बंदर, गुरिल्ला या गोरिला, वनमानुष

**gory** /ˈgɔːri ˈगॉरि / *adj.* full of violence and blood हिंसा और रक्तपात से पूर्ण *a gory film*

**gosh** /gɒʃ गॉश् / *exclamation* (*informal*) used for expressing surprise, shock, etc. आश्चर्य, सदमा आदि व्यक्त करने के लिए प्रयुक्त

**gosling** /ˈgɒzlɪŋ ˈगॉज़्लिङ् / *noun* [C] a young **goose** हंसशावक

**gospel** /ˈgɒspl ˈगॉस्प्ल् / *noun* **1 Gospel** [*sing.*] one of the four books in the Bible that describe the life and teachings of Jesus Christ बाइबिल की चार पुस्तकों में से कोई एक जिसमें ईसा के जीवन और शिक्षाओं का वर्णन है; इसोपदेश *St Matthew's/Mark's/Luke's/John's Gospel* **2** (*also* **gospel truth**) [U] the truth अकाट्य सत्य, वेदवाक्य *You can't take what he says as gospel.* **3** (*also* **gospel music**) [U] a style of religious music that is especially popular among black American Christians श्याम वर्ण अमेरिकी ईसाईयों में लोकप्रिय एक प्रकार का धार्मिक संगीत

**gossip** /ˈgɒsɪp ˈगॉसिप् / *noun* **1** [U] informal talk about other people and their private lives, that is often unkind or not true इधर-उधर की बात, दूसरों के बारे में हलकी-फुलकी (और प्रायः झूठी) बात; गप *Mahesh phoned me up to tell me the latest gossip.* **2** [C] an informal conversation about other people and their private lives दूसरों के निजी जीवन के बारे में हलकेपन से बातचीत *The two neighbours were having a good gossip over the fence.* **3** [C] a person who enjoys talking about other people's private lives दूसरों के बारे में बातें करने में मज़ा लेने वाला व्यक्ति; गप्पी ▶ **gossip** *verb* [I] गप लगाना

**gossip column** *noun* [C] a part of a newspaper or magazine where you can read about the private lives of famous people अख़बार की पत्रिका का स्तंभ जिसमें प्रसिद्ध व्यक्तियों के निजी जीवन के बारे में मज़ेदार बातें छपती हैं

**got** ➪ **get** का past tense और past participle रूप

**gotta** /ˈgɒtə ˈगॉटा / (*AmE informal*) a way of writing 'got to' or 'got a' to show that sb is speaking in an informal way अनौपचारिक रूप से 'got to' या 'got a' लिखने या बोलने का तरीक़ा

> NOTE आप स्वयं **'gotta'** का प्रयोग न करें यदि किसी के बोलने की नक़ल न उतार रहे हों, इसे अशुद्ध माना जा सकता है; यही बात **'gonna'** और **'wanna'** के साथ भी है—*I gotta go* (= I have to go). ○ *Gotta* (= have you got a) *minute?*

**gotten** (*AmE*) ➪ **get** का past participle रूप

**gouge** /gaʊdʒ गाउज् / *verb* [T] to make a hole in a surface using a sharp object in a rough way नुकीले औज़ार से ज़ोर लगाकर छेद करना

PHR V **gouge sth out** to remove or form sth by digging into a surface खोद कर किसी वस्तु को बाहर निकालना

**goulash** /ˈguːlæʃ ˈगूलैश् / *noun* [C, U] a hot Hungarian dish of meat that is cooked slowly in liquid with **paprika** द्रव में तीखे मसाले डाल कर धीमी आँच पर बनाया मांस (जो हंगरी में लोकप्रिय है)

**gourd** /gʊəd; gɔːd गुअड्; गॉड् / *noun* [C] a type of large fruit, not normally eaten, with hard skin and a soft inside. Gourds are often dried and used as containers सख़्त आवरण और मुलायम गूदे वाला कद्दू वर्गीय फल; तूंबा, प्रायः इन्हें सुखाकर पात्र बनाए जाते हैं

**gourmand** /ˈgʊəmənd ˈगुअमन्ड् / *noun* [C] a person who enjoys eating and eats large amounts of food खाने में और ख़ूब खाने में रुचि रखने वाला व्यक्ति; भोजनभट्ट, पेटू

**gourmet** /ˈgʊəmeɪ ˈगुअमे / *noun* [C] a person who enjoys food and knows a lot about it भोजनप्रेमी तथा भोजन-विशेषज्ञ व्यक्ति

**gout** /gaʊt गाउट् / *noun* [U] a disease that causes painful swelling in the places where two bones fit together (**joints**), especially of the toes, knees and fingers गठिया, जोड़ों का दर्द

**govern** /ˈgʌvn ˈगव्न् / *verb* **1** [I, T] to rule or control the public affairs of a country, city, etc. किसी देश या नगर पर शासन-प्रशासन करना *Britain is governed by the Prime Minister and the Cabinet.* **2** [T] (*usually passive*) to influence or control sb/sth व्यक्ति या वस्तु को प्रभावित या नियंत्रित करना *Our decision will be governed by the amount of money we have to spend.*

**governess** /ˈgʌvənəs ˈगवनस् / *noun* [C] (especially in the past) a woman employed to teach the children of a rich family in their home and to live with them अमीर बच्चों के घर में रह कर उन्हें शिक्षा प्रदान करने वाली धात्री, शिक्षिका

**government** /ˈgʌvənmənt ˈगवनृमन्ट् / *noun* **1** [C] (*often* **the Government**) (*abbr.* **govt**) the group of people who rule or control a country सरकार, शासन *He has resigned from the Government.* ○ *government policy/money/ministers.*

> NOTE एक वचन रूप में **'government'** के साथ एकवचनांत या बहुवचनांत क्रिया प्रयुक्त हो सकती है। यदि सरकार को एक अकेली इकाई मानें तो एकवचनांत क्रिया ही प्रयुक्त होती है—*The Government welcomes the proposal.* यदि सरकार के सभी व्यक्तिगत

सदस्यों के बारे में बात करें तो बहुवचनांत क्रिया प्रयुक्त होगी—*The Government are still discussing the problem.* सरकार या शासन के विभिन्न प्रकार हैं: *communist* (साम्यवादी), *conservative* (अनुदार), *democratic* (लोकतांत्रिक), *liberal* (उदार), *reactionary* (प्रतिक्रियावादी), *socialist* (समाजवादी) आदि। किसी देश में सरकार/शासन के अन्य रूप भी हो सकते हैं: *military* (सैनिक), *provisional* (अस्थायी या अंतरिम), *central* (केंद्रीय), *federal* (संघीय), *coalition* (गठबंधनात्मक) आदि। ➪ **local government** और **opposition** देखिए।

**2** [U] the activity or method of controlling a country देश पर नियंत्रण की क्रिया या पद्धति *weak/strong/corrupt government* ○ *Which party is **in government**?*

**governmental** /ˌɡʌvənˈmentl ˌगव़न्ˈमेन्ट्ल् / *adj.* सरकारी, शासन-संबंधी *a governmental department* ○ *different government systems*

**governor** /ˈɡʌvənə(r) ˈगवन(र्)/ *noun* [C] **1** a person who rules or controls a region or state (especially in the US) किसी राज्य का प्रमुख शासनाधिकारी; राज्यपाल, गवर्नर *the Governor of West Bengal* **2** the leader or member of a group of people who control an organization किसी संगठन का संचालक या संचालक-मंडल का सदस्य *the Governor of the Reserve Bank of India* ○ *school governors*

**govt** *abbr.* (*written*) = **government**

**gown** /ɡaʊn गाउन्/ *noun* [C] **1** a long formal dress for a special occasion विशेष अवसर के लिए एक औपचारिक पोशाक; गाउन *a ball gown* **2** a long loose piece of clothing that is worn over clothes by judges, doctors performing operations, etc. एक लंबा ढीला वस्त्र जो जज लोग और आपरेशन करते समय डॉक्टर लोग अपने कपड़ों के ऊपर पहन लेते हैं, जजों और डॉक्टरों का गाउन; चोगा, लबादा

**GP** /ˌdʒiːˈpiː ˌजीˈपी/ *abbr.* general practitioner; a doctor who treats all types of illnesses and works in the local community in a **practice**, not in a hospital निजी तौर पर कार्यरत तथा सब प्रकार के रोगों का इलाज करने वाला डॉक्टर, जनरल या प्राइवेट प्रैक्टीशनर

**grab** /ɡræb ग्रैब्/ *verb* (**grabbing; grabbed**) **1** [I, T] **grab sth (from sb)** to take sth with a sudden movement झपटकर किसी चीज़ को पकड़ना; छीनना ***Grab hold of** his arm in case he tries to run!* ○ *(figurative) He grabbed the opportunity of a free trip to America.* ➪ **snatch** देखिए। **2** [I] **grab at/for sth** to try to get or catch sb/sth व्यक्ति या वस्तु को पकड़ने की कोशिश करना *Suhail grabbed at the ball but missed.* **3** [T] to do sth quickly because you are in a hurry जल्दी के कारण किसी काम को तेज़ी से करना *I'll just grab something to eat and then we'll go.* ▶ **grab** /ɡræb ग्रैब्/ *noun* [C] झपट्टा *She made a grab for the boy but she couldn't stop him from falling.*

**grace** /ɡreɪs ग्रेस्/ *noun* [U] **1** the ability to move in a smooth and controlled way सुकोमल तथा अनुशासित चेष्टा-क्षमता; लालित्य **2** extra time that is allowed for sth दिया गया अतिरिक्त समय; मोहलत **3** a short prayer of thanks to God before or after a meal भोजन के पूर्व और पश्चात संक्षिप्त ईश-वंदना

IDM **sb's fall from grace** a situation in which sb loses the respect that people had for him/her by doing sth wrong or immoral अनुचित या अनैतिक काम के फलस्वरूप दूसरों का सम्मान खो बैठना, ग़लत काम के कारण लोगों की नज़र में गिर जाना

**have the grace to do sth** to be polite enough to do sth विनीत भाव से कोई काम करना

**with good grace** in a pleasant and reasonable way, without complaining शालीनता के साथ *He accepted the refusal with good grace.*

**graceful** /ˈɡreɪsfl ˈग्रेस्फ़्ल्/ *adj.* having a smooth, attractive movement or form लालित्यपूर्ण, मनोहारी *a graceful dancer* ○ *graceful curves* ➪ **gracious** देखिए। ▶ **gracefully** /-fəli -फ़लि/ *adv.* लालित्यपूर्वक, चारु भाव से *The goalkeeper rose gracefully to catch the ball.* ○ *She accepted the decision gracefully* (= without showing her disappointment). ▶ **gracefulness** *noun* [U] लालित्यमयता, चारुता

**graceless** /ˈɡreɪsləs ˈग्रेस्लस्/ *adj.* **1** not knowing how to be polite to people अशिष्ट **2** (used about a movement or a shape) ugly and not elegant (चेष्टा या रूप) भद्दा, भोंडा ▶ **gracelessly** *adv.* भद्देपन से, अशिष्ट भाव से

**gracious** /ˈɡreɪʃəs ˈग्रेशस्/ *adj.* **1** (used about a person or his/her behaviour) kind, polite and generous (व्यक्ति या उसका आचरण) दयालु, नम्र और उदार *a gracious smile* **2** (*only before a noun*) showing the easy comfortable way of life that rich people can have वैभवपूर्ण, सुख-सुविधापूर्ण *gracious living* ➪ **graceful** देखिए। ▶ **graciously** *adv.* नम्रता से, शालीनता से ▶ **graciousness** *noun* [U] शालीनता, नम्रता

IDM **good gracious!** used for expressing surprise आश्चर्य व्यक्त करने के लिए प्रयुक्त *Good gracious! Is that the time?*

**grade[1]** /ɡreɪd ग्रेड्/ *noun* [C] **1** the quality or the level of ability, importance, etc. that sb/sth has किसी व्यक्ति या वस्तु की योग्यता, महत्ता आदि का स्तर या गुणवत्ता; श्रेणी *Which grade of petrol do you need?* ○ *We need to use high-grade materials for this job.* **2** a mark that is given for school work, etc.

or in an exam परीक्षा में स्कूल कार्य के लिए दिए गए अंक *He got good/poor grades this term.* **3** (*AmE*) a class or classes in a school in which all the children are the same age स्कूल में एक ही उम्र के बच्चों की कक्षा या कक्षाएँ *My daughter is in the third grade.* IDM **make the grade** (*informal*) to reach the expected standard; to succeed उच्च स्तर को प्राप्त करना; सफल होना

**grade[2]** /greɪd ग्रेड्/ *verb* [T] (*usually passive*) to put things or people into groups according to their quality, ability, size, etc. गुणवत्ता, योग्यता, आकार आदि के अनुसार वस्तुओं या व्यक्तियों का वर्गीकरण; श्रेणीकरण *I've graded their work from 1 to 10.* ○ *Eggs are graded by size.*

**gradient** /ˈgreɪdiənt ˈग्रेडिअन्ट्/ *noun* [C] the degree at which a road, etc. goes up or down सड़क आदि की ढलान या चढ़ाव की मात्रा *The hill has a gradient of 1 in 4* (= 25%). ○ *a steep gradient*

**gradual** /ˈgrædʒuəl ˈग्रैजुअल्/ *adj.* happening slowly or over a long period of time; not sudden मंद गति से लंबी कालावधि में संपन्न; एकाएक नहीं, क्रमिक *a gradual increase* ► **gradually** *adv.* क्रमशः *After the war life gradually got back to normal.*

**graduate[1]** /ˈgrædʒuət ˈग्रैजुअट्/ *noun* [C] **1 a graduate (in sth)** a person who has a first degree from a university, etc. विश्वविद्यालय की प्रथम उपाधि प्राप्त व्यक्ति, विश्वविद्यालय का स्नातक *a law graduate/a graduate in law* ○ *a graduate of Delhi University/a Delhi University graduate* ➪ **post-graduate, undergraduate, bachelor** और **student** देखिए। **2** (*AmE*) a person who has completed a course at a school, college, etc. स्कूल, कॉलेज आदि का निर्धारित पाठ्यक्रम पूरा करने वाला व्यक्ति; स्नातक *a high-school graduate*

**graduate[2]** /ˈgrædʒueɪt ˈग्रैजुएट्/ *verb* [I] **1 graduate (in sth) (from sth)** to get a (first) degree from a university, etc. विश्वविद्यालय आदि से (प्रथम) उपाधि प्राप्त करना, स्नातक बनना *She graduated in History from Delhi University.* **2** (*AmE*) **graduate (from sth)** to complete a course at a school, college, etc. स्कूल, कॉलेज आदि में निर्धारित पाठ्यक्रम पूरा करना **3 graduate (from sth) to sth** to change (from sth) to sth more difficult, important, expensive, etc. किसी एक स्थिति से दूसरी उच्चतर (कठिन, महत्त्वपूर्ण, बहुमूल्य) स्थिति में जाना

**graduation** /ˌgrædʒuˈeɪʃn ˌग्रैजुˈएशन्/ *noun* **1** [U] the act of successfully completing a university degree or (in the US) studies at a high school विश्वविद्यालय या (अमेरिका में) स्कूल के अध्ययन-क्रम को सफलतापूर्वक पूरा करना, विश्वविद्यालय या स्कूल का स्नातक बनना **2** [*sing.*] a ceremony in which certificates are given to people who have graduated उपाधि-वितरण समारोह; दीक्षांत समारोह

**graffiti** /grəˈfi:ti ग्रˈफ़ीटि/ *noun* [U, *pl.*] pictures or writing on a wall, etc. in a public place किसी सार्वजनिक स्थान में दीवार पर बना चित्र या की गई लिखावट *Vandals had covered the walls in graffiti.*

**graft** /grɑ:ft ग्राफ़्ट्/ *noun* [C] **1** a piece of a living plant that is fixed onto another plant so that it will grow पौधे की क़लम **2** a piece of living skin, bone, etc. that is fixed onto a damaged part of a body in an operation सजीव त्वचा, हड्डी आदि का टुकड़ा जिसे शल्य-क्रिया द्वारा शरीर के क्षतिग्रस्त भाग पर लगा दिया जाता है; रोपण *a skin graft* ► **graft** *verb* [T] **graft sth onto sth** प्रत्यारोपण करना *Skin from his leg was grafted onto the burnt area of his face.* ➪ **transplant** देखिए।

**grain** /greɪn ग्रेन्/ *noun* **1** [U,C] the seeds of wheat, rice, etc. गेहूँ, चावल आदि के दाने *The US is a major producer of grain.* ○ *grain exports* ○ *a few grains of rice* ➪ **cereal** पर चित्र देखिए। **2** [C] **a grain of sth** a very small piece of sth किसी वस्तु का कण *a grain of sand/salt/sugar* ○ (*figurative*) *There isn't **a grain of truth** in the rumour.* **3** [U] the natural pattern of lines that can be seen or felt in wood, rock, stone, etc. लकड़ी, चट्टान, पत्थर आदि में नैसर्गिक तंतु-रचना

IDM **(be/go) against the grain** to be different from what is usual or natural सामान्य या प्राकृतिक स्थिति से भिन्न, निजी प्रकृति से भिन्न

**gram** (*also* **gramme**) /græm ग्रैम्/ *noun* [C] (*abbr.* **g**) a measure of weight. There are 1000 grams in a kilogram भार की इकाई, एक किलोग्राम में 1000 ग्राम होते हैं

**grammar** /ˈgræmə(r) ˈग्रैम(र्)/ *noun* **1** [U] the rules of a language, for example for forming words or joining words together in sentences भाषा में शब्दरचना और वाक्यरचना के विषय; व्याकरण *Russian grammar can be difficult for foreign learners.* **2** [U] the way in which sb uses the rules of a language भाषा के नियमों के प्रयोग की रीति *You have a good vocabulary, but your grammar needs improvement.* **3** [C] a book that describes and explains the rules of a language व्याकरण का ग्रंथ *a French grammar*

**grammatical** /grəˈmætɪkl ग्रˈमैटिकल्/ *adj.* **1** connected with grammar व्याकरण विषयक *the grammatical rules for forming plurals* **2** following the rules of a language व्याकरण के अनुकूल *The sentence is not grammatical.* ▶ **grammatically** /-kli -क्लि / *adv.* व्याकरण की दृष्टि से

**gramme** = **gram**

**gramophone** /ˈɡræməfəʊn ˈग्रैमफ़ोन् / (*AmE old-fashioned*) = **record player**

**gran** /ɡræn ग्रैन् / (*BrE informal*) = **grandmother**

**granary** /ˈɡrænəri ˈग्रैनरि / *noun* [C] (*pl.* **granaries**) a large building for storing grains अन्नागार, धान्यागार

**granary bread** /ˈɡrænəri bred ˈग्रैनरि ब्रेड् / *noun* [U] a type of brown bread containing whole grains of wheat गेहूँ के साबुत कणों से बनी एक प्रकार की भूरी डबलरोटी; ब्राउन ब्रेड

**grand[1]** /ɡrænd ग्रैन्ड् / *adj.* **1** impressive and large or important (also used in names) प्रभावशाली और बड़ा या महत्त्वपूर्ण (नामों के साथ भी प्रयुक्त), शानदार *Our house isn't very grand, but it has a big garden.* ○ *the Grand Canyon* ○ *the Grand Hotel* ⇨ **grandeur** noun देखिए। **2** used in compounds before a noun to show a family relationship पारिवारिक संबंध दिखाने के लिए यौगिक शब्दों में संज्ञा के साथ प्रयुक्त *grandson* **3** (*informal*) very good or pleasant बहुत अच्छा या सुखद *You've done a grand job!* ▶ **grandly** *adv.* शान से, भव्यतापूर्वक ▶ **grandness** *noun* [U] वैभव, भव्यता

**grand[2]** /ɡrænd ग्रैन्ड् / *noun* [C] (*pl.* **grand**) (*slang*) 1000 pounds or dollars, 1000 पाउंड या डालर

**grandad** /ˈɡrændæd ˈग्रैन्डैड् / (*BrE informal*) = **grandfather**

**grandchild** /ˈɡræntʃaɪld ˈग्रैन्चाइल्ड् / (*pl.* **grandchildren**) (*also* **granddaughter** and **grandson**) *noun* [C] the daughter or son of your child आपके बेटे या बेटी की पुत्री, पोती या नातिन; धेवती

**grandeur** /ˈɡrændʒə(r) ˈग्रैन्ज(र्) / *noun* [U] (*formal*) **1** the quality of being large and impressive भव्यता, महिमा *the grandeur of the Himalayas* **2** the feeling of being important बड़प्पन का अहसास

**grandfather** /ˈɡrænfa:ðə(r) ˈग्रैन्फ़ाद्र(र्) / *noun* [C] the father of one of your parents माता या पिता के पिता, दादा या नाना *My grandfather is very active.*

**grandfather clock** *noun* [C] a clock that stands on the floor in a tall wooden case लंबे लकड़ी के बक्से में जड़ी फ़र्श पर खड़ी बड़ी घड़ी

**grandiose** /ˈɡrændiəʊs ˈग्रैन्डिओस् / *adj.* bigger or more complicated than necessary अनावश्यक रूप से बड़ा और पेचीदा

**grandma** /ˈɡrænmɑ: ˈग्रैन्मा / (*informal*) = **grandmother**

**grandmaster** /ˈɡræn,ma:stə(r) ˈग्रैन्,मास्ट(र्) / *noun* [C] a title awarded to a chess player who is regarded as having the highest level of skill शतरंज के खिलाड़ी को अव्वल दर्जे की दक्षता के लिए दी गई पदवी; ग्रैंड मास्टर

**grandmother** /ˈɡrænmʌðə(r) ˈग्रैन्मद्र(र्) / *noun* [C] the mother of one of your parents माता या पिता की माता; दादी या नानी

**grandpa** /ˈɡrænpɑ: ˈग्रैन्पा / (*informal*) = **grandfather**

**grandparent** /ˈɡrænpeərənt ˈग्रैन्पेअरन्ट् / (*also* **grandmother** and **grandfather**) *noun* [C] the mother or father of one of your parents माता या पिता के माता या पिता, दादा-दादी या नाना-नानी *This is a picture of two of my great-grandparents* (= the parents of one of my grandparents).

> **NOTE** यदि यह स्पष्ट करना हो कि नाना की बात की जा रही है या दादा की तो कहेंगे—*My maternal/paternal grandfather* या *my mother's/father's father.*

**grand piano** *noun* [C] a large flat piano (with horizontal strings) बड़ा चौरस पियानो (जिसके तार क्षैतिज स्थिति में होते हैं)

**Grand Prix** /,ɡrɑ̃:ˈpri:, ग्राँ ˈप्री / *noun* [C] (*pl.* **Grands Prix** /,ɡrɑ̃:ˈpri:, ग्राँ ˈप्री /) one of a series of important international races for racing cars or motorbikes कारों या मोटर साइकिलों की दौड़ की प्रसिद्ध अंतरराष्ट्रीय शृंखला में से एक; ग्राँ प्री

**grand slam** *noun* [C] winning all the important matches or competitions in a particular sport, for example tennis or **rugby** किसी विशेष खेल (जैसे टेनिस या रगबी) में सभी महत्त्वपूर्ण मैचों या स्पर्धाओं में विजय प्राप्ति; ग्रैंड स्लैम

**grandstand** /ˈɡrænstænd ˈग्रैन्स्टैन्ड् / *noun* [C] rows of seats, usually covered by a roof, from which you get a good view of a sports competition, etc. सीटों की पंक्ति (प्रायः छत से ढकी) जहाँ बैठकर आप खेल स्पर्धा को अच्छी तरह देख सकते हैं; महादीर्घा, ग्रैंडस्टैंड

**grand total** *noun* [C] the amount that you get when you add several totals together अनेक योगों को मिलाकर आया योग; महायोग

**granite** /ˈɡrænɪt ˈग्रैनिट् / *noun* [U] a hard grey rock कड़ी भूरी या सलेटी चट्टान; ग्रेनाइट

**granny** /ˈɡræni ˈग्रैनि / (*pl.* **grannies**) (*informal*) = **grandmother**

**grant[1]** /ɡrɑ:nt ग्रान्ट् / *verb* [T] **1** (*formal*) to (officially) give sb what he/she has asked for (आधिकारिक तौर पर) किसी को कुछ प्रदान करना *He was* *granted permission to leave early.* **2** to agree (that sth is true) मानना (कि कोई बात सच है) *I grant you that New York is an interesting place but I still wouldn't want to live there.*

IDM **take sb/sth for granted** to be so used to sb/sth that you forget his/her/its true value and are not grateful अति परिचय के कारण दूसरे के असली महत्व को न मानना और उसकी उपेक्षा करना *In developed countries we take running water for granted.*

**take sth for granted** to accept sth as being true किसी बात को सच मान कर चलना *We can take it for granted that the new students will have at least an elementary knowledge of English.*

**grant**[2] /grɑ:nt ग्रान्ट्/ *noun* [C] money that is given by the government, etc. for a particular purpose सरकार द्वारा उद्देश्य विशेष से दिया गया धन; अनुदान *a student grant* (= to help pay for university education) ○ *to apply for/be awarded a grant*

**granted** /ˈgrɑ:ntɪd ˈग्रान्टिड्/ *adv.* used for saying that sth is true, before you make a comment about it किसी बात पर टिप्पणी करने से पहले उसे सच मानने की मानसिकता को व्यक्त करने के लिए प्रयुक्त *'We've never had any problems before.' 'Granted, but this year there are 200 more people coming.'*

**grantha** *noun* [U] an ancient script that was once prevalent in South India दक्षिण भारत में प्रचलित प्राचीन लिपि; ग्रंथ

**granular** /ˈgrænjələ(r) ˈग्रैन्यल(र्)/ *adj.* (*technical*) made of a mass of small hard pieces; looking or feeling like a mass of small hard pieces दानेदार; दानेदार-सा दीखने या लगने वाला

**granulated sugar** /ˌgrænjuleɪtɪd ˈʃʊgə(r) ˌग्रैन्युलेटिड् ˈशुग(र्)/ *noun* [U] white sugar in the form of small grains दानेदार चीनी

**granule** /ˈgrænju:l ˈग्रैन्यूल्/ *noun* [C] a small hard piece of sth सख़्त दाना *instant coffee granules*

**grape** /greɪp ग्रेप्/ *noun* [C] a green or purple berry that grows in bunches on a climbing plant (**a vine**) and that is used for making wine अंगूर *a bunch of grapes* ➪ **fruit** पर चित्र देखिए।

NOTE हरे अंगूरों को सामान्यतया **'white'** और बैंगनी रंग के अंगूरों को **'black'** कहा जाता है। सुखाए हुए अंगूरों को **raisins, currants** या **sultanas** कहते हैं।

IDM **sour grapes** ➪ **sour** देखिए।

**grapefruit** /ˈgreɪpfru:t ˈग्रेप्फ्रूट्/ *noun* [C] (*pl.* **grapefruit** or **grapefruits**) a large round yellow fruit with a thick skin and a sour taste चकोतरा

**the grapevine** /ˈgreɪpvaɪn ˈग्रेप्वाइन्/ *noun* [*sing.*] the way that news is passed from one person to another एक से दूसरे तक ख़बर *I heard **on/through the grapevine** that you're moving.*

**graph** /grɑ:f ग्राफ़्/ *noun* [C] a diagram in which a line or a curve shows the relationship between two quantities, measurements, etc. एक आरेख जिसमें दो मात्राओं, मापों आदि के बीच संबंध को सीधी या वक्र रेखा से दिखाया जाता है, लेखाचित्र; ग्राफ़ *a graph showing/to show the number of cars sold each month*

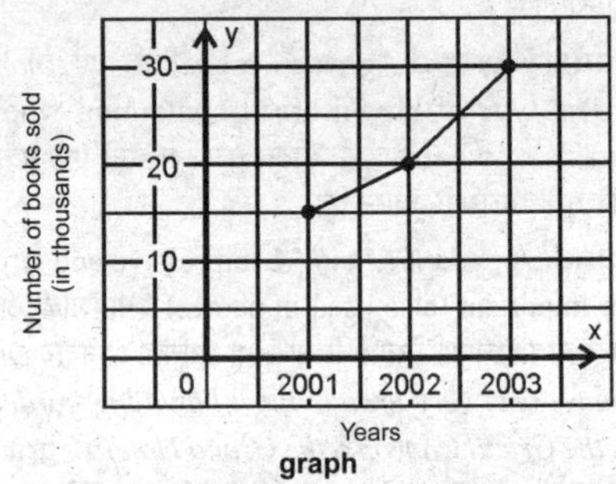


**graph**

**graphic** /ˈgræfɪk ˈग्रैफ़िक्/ *adj.* **1** (*only before a noun*) connected with drawings, diagrams, etc. आरेखन, आरेख आदि से संबंधित *graphic design* ○ *a graphic artist* **2** (used about descriptions) clear and giving a lot of detail, especially about sth unpleasant (वर्णन) स्पष्ट और सुविस्तृत (विशेषतः किसी अप्रिय स्थिति का) *She described the accident in graphic detail.* ▶ **graphically** /-kli -क्लि/ *adv.* स्पष्टता और विस्तार के साथ

**graphics** /ˈgræfɪks ˈग्रैफ़िक्स्/ *noun* [*pl.*] the production of drawings, diagrams, etc. आरेखन चित्रों, आरेखों आदि का निर्माण *computer graphics*

**graphite** /ˈgræfaɪt ˈग्रैफ़ाइट्/ *noun* [U] a soft black substance (a form of **carbon**) that is used in pencils पेंसिलों में प्रयुक्त कोमल काला पदार्थ; ग्रैफ़ाइट्, काला सीसा, सुरमा

**graph paper** *noun* [U] paper with small squares of equal size printed on it, used for drawing **graphs** and other diagrams आरेखन-चित्रों और अन्य आरेखों के बनाने के लिए प्रयुक्त वर्गांकित काग़ज़; ग्राफ़ पेपर

**grapple** /ˈgræpl ˈग्रैप्ल्/ *verb* [I] **grapple (with sb)** to get hold of sb/sth and fight with or try to control him/her/it व्यक्ति या वस्तु को पकड़कर उससे लड़ना या उसे क़ाबू में करने की कोशिश करना

**grasp**[1] /grɑ:sp ग्रास्प्/ *verb* [T] **1** to take hold of sb/sth suddenly and firmly व्यक्ति या वस्तु को एकाएक कसकर पकड़ लेना *Lalita grasped the child firmly by the hand before crossing the road.* ○ *(fig-*

*urative) to grasp an opportunity/a chance* **2** to understand sth completely किसी बात को पूरी तरह समझ लेना *I don't think you've grasped how serious the situation is.*

PHR V **grasp at sth** to try to take hold of sth किसी वस्तु को पकड़ने की कोशिश करना

**grasp²** /grɑːsp ग्रास्प् / *noun* [*sing.*,U] **1** a firm hold of sb/sth व्यक्ति या वस्तु पर मज़बूत पकड़ *Get a good grasp on the rope before pulling yourself up.* ○ *I grabbed the boy, but he slipped from my grasp.* **2** a person's understanding of a subject or of difficult facts व्यक्ति का किसी विषय या कठिन तथ्यों का ज्ञान He has ***a good grasp of*** *English grammar.* **3** the ability to get or achieve sth कुछ पाने या पा लेने की क्षमता *Finally their dream was **within** their **grasp**.*

**grasping** /ˈgrɑːspɪŋ ˈग्रास्पिङ् / *adj.* wanting very much to have a lot more money, power, etc. अधिकाधिक धन, शक्ति आदि का प्रबल आकांक्षी

**grass** /grɑːs ग्रास् / *noun* **1** [U] the common green plant with thin leaves which covers fields and parts of gardens. Cows, sheep, horses, etc. eat grass घास *Don't walk on the grass.* ○ *I must cut the grass at the weekend.* ○ *a blade* (= one leaf) *of grass* NOTE बग़ीचे में घास वाले क्षेत्र को **lawn** कहते हैं। **2** [C] one type of grass घास का एक प्रकार *an arrangement of dried flowers and grasses*

**grasshopper** /ˈgrɑːshɒpə(r) ˈग्रास्हॉप(र्) / *noun* [C] an insect that lives in long grass or trees and that can jump high in the air. Grasshoppers make loud noises टिड्डा ➩ **insect** पर चित्र देखिए।

**grassland** /ˈgrɑːslænd ˈग्रास्लैन्ड् / *noun* [U] (*also* **grasslands**) [*pl.*] a large area of open land covered with wild grass जंगली घास वाला खुला बड़ा मैदान

**grassroots** *noun* [*pl.*] the ordinary people in an organization, not those who make decisions किसी संगठन के साधारण लोग (जो निर्णय-प्रक्रिया में भाग नहीं लेते); जन साधारण

**grassy** /ˈgrɑːsi ˈग्रासि / *adj.* covered with grass घसियाला, घास से ढका

**grate¹** /greɪt ग्रेट् / *verb* **1** [T] to rub food into small pieces using a metal tool **(grater)** खाद्य पदार्थों को कद्दूकस पर घिसना या कसना *grated cheese/carrot* **2** [I] **grate (on sb)** to annoy or irritate किसी को नाराज़ या तंग करना **3** [I] **grate (against/on sth)** to make a sharp unpleasant sound (when two metal surfaces rub against each other) (दो धातु निर्मित पदार्थों के टकराने पर) किर-किर की आवाज़ करना; किरकिराना

**grate²** /greɪt ग्रेट् / *noun* [C] the metal frame that holds the wood, coal, etc. in a **fireplace** अँगीठी की जाली

**grateful** /ˈgreɪtfl ˈग्रेट्फ़्ल् / *adj.* **grateful (to sb) (for sth); grateful (that...)** feeling or showing thanks (to sb) (किसी का) कृतज्ञ *We are very grateful to you for all the help you have given us.* ○ *He was very grateful that you did as he asked.* ✪ विलोम **ungrateful** ➩ **gratitude** noun देखिए।
▶ **gratefully** /-fəli -फ़लि / *adv.* कृतज्ञतापूर्वक

**grater** /ˈgreɪtə(r) ˈग्रेट(र्) / *noun* [C] a kitchen tool that is used for cutting food (for example cheese) into small pieces by rubbing it across its rough surface खाद्य पदार्थों को घिसने का उपकरण; कद्दूकस ➩ **kitchen** पर चित्र देखिए।

**gratify** /ˈgrætɪfaɪ ˈग्रैटिफ़ाइ / *verb* [T] (*pres. part.* **gratifying;** *3rd person sing. pres.* **gratifies;** *pt, pp* **gratified**) (*usually passive*) (*formal*) to give sb pleasure and satisfaction प्रसन्नता और संतोष देना
▶ **gratifying** *adj.* प्रसन्नतादायक और संतुष्टिकारक; सुखद

**grating** /ˈgreɪtɪŋ ˈग्रेटिङ् / *noun* [C] a flat frame made of metal bars that is fixed over a hole in the road, a window, etc. खिड़की आदि की धातुनिर्मित जाली

**gratitude** /ˈgrætɪtjuːd ˈग्रैटिट्यूड् / *noun* [U] **gratitude (to sb) (for sth)** the feeling of being grateful or of wanting to give your thanks to sb कृतज्ञता या किसी को धन्यवाद देने की इच्छा ✪ विलोम **ingratitude**

**gratuity** /grəˈtjuːəti ग्रˈट्यूअटि / *noun* [C] (*pl.* **gratuities**) (*formal*) a small amount of extra money that you give to sb who serves you, for example in a restaurant (रेस्तराँ आदि में) सेवा देने वाले व्यक्ति को ग्राहक द्वारा दिया गया कुछ अतिरिक्त पैसा या इनाम ✪ पर्याय **tip**

**grave¹** /greɪv ग्रेव् / *noun* [C] the place where a dead body is buried क़ब्र *I put some flowers on my grandmother's grave.* ➩ **tomb** देखिए।

IDM **have one foot in the grave** ➩ **foot¹** देखिए।

**grave²** /greɪv ग्रेव् / *adj.* (*formal*) **1** bad or serious प्रतिकूल या गंभीर *These events could have **grave consequences** for us all.* ○ *The children were **in grave danger**.* **2** (used about people) sad or serious (व्यक्ति) उदास या गंभीर ➩ **gravity** noun देखिए।
NOTE दोनो अर्थों में **serious** अधिक प्रचलित है।
▶ **gravely** *adv.* गंभीरता से *gravely ill*

**gravel** /ˈgrævl ˈग्रैव्ल् / *noun* [U] very small stones that are used for making roads, paths, etc. कंकड़, बजरी, रोड़ी (सड़क, पथ आदि निर्माण में प्रयुक्त)

**gravestone** /ˈɡreɪvstəʊn ˈग्रेव्स्टोन् / *noun* [C] a stone in the ground that shows the name, dates, etc. of the dead person who is buried there क़ब्र का पत्थर जिस पर मृतक का नाम आदि लिखा होता है ➪ **headstone** और **tombstone** देखिए।

**graveyard** /ˈɡreɪvjɑːd ˈग्रेव्याड् / *noun* [C] an area of land next to a church where dead people are buried क़ब्रिस्तान ➪ **cemetery** और **churchyard** देखिए।

**gravitational** /ˌɡrævɪˈteɪʃənl ˌग्रैवि ˈटेशन्ल् / *adj.* connected with or caused by the force of **gravity** गुरुत्वाकर्षण बल से संबंधित या उत्पन्न *a gravitational field ○ the gravitational pull of the moon* ▸ **gravitationally** /-ʃənəli -शनलि / *adv.* गुरुत्वाकर्षण की दृष्टि से

**gravity** /ˈɡrævəti ˈग्रैवटि / *noun* [U] **1** the natural force that makes things fall to the ground when you drop them गुरुत्वाकर्षक बल *the force of gravity* **2** (*formal*) importance महत्त्व **NOTE** **Seriousness** अधिक प्रचलित शब्द है। ➪ **grave** adjective देखिए।

**gravy** /ˈɡreɪvi ˈग्रेवि / *noun* [U] a thin sauce that is made from the juices that come out of meat while it is cooking शोरबा; मांस के पकने पर उसमें से निकला रस ➪ **sauce** देखिए।

**gray** (*AmE*) = **grey**

**graze¹** /ɡreɪz ग्रेज़् / *verb* **1** [I] (used about cows, sheep, etc.) to eat grass (that is growing in a field) गायों, भेड़ों आदि पशुओं का मैदान में उगी घास खाना *There were cows grazing by the river.* **2** [T] to break the surface of your skin by rubbing it against sth rough रगड़ खाकर छिल जाना *The child fell and grazed her knee.* **3** [T] to pass sth and touch it lightly हलके से छूते हुए निकल जाना *The bullet grazed his shoulder.*

**graze²** /ɡreɪz ग्रेज़् / *noun* [C] a slight injury where the surface of the skin has been broken by rubbing it against sth rough रगड़ से लगी खरोंच

**grease¹** /ɡriːs ग्रीस् / *noun* [U] **1** a thick substance containing oil and used, for example, to make engines run smoothly ग्रीज़; तेल वाला गाढ़ा पदार्थ जिससे इंजन आसानी से चलता है *engine grease* **2** animal fat that has been made soft by cooking पकने से नरम हुई पशु की चरबी *You'll need very hot water to get all the grease off those pans.*

**grease²** /ɡriːs ग्रीस् / *verb* [T] to rub grease or fat on or in sth किसी चीज़ पर ग्रीज़ या तेल लगाना *Grease the tin thoroughly to stop the cake from sticking.*

**greaseproof paper** /ˌɡriːspruːf ˈpeɪpə(r) ˌग्रीस्प्रूफ़् ˈपेप(र्) / (*AmE* **wax paper**) *noun* [U] paper that does not let fat, oil etc. pass through it, used in cooking and for putting round food ग्रीज़, तेल आदि को अंदर जाने से रोकने वाला काग़ज़ (भोजन बनाने में और भोज्य पदार्थों को लपेटने में प्रयुक्त)

**greasy** /ˈɡriːsi ˈग्रीसि / *adj.* (**greasier; greasiest**) covered with or containing a lot of grease ग्रीज़ से भरा या सना हुआ *greasy skin/hair ○ greasy food*

**great¹** /ɡreɪt ग्रेट् / *adj.* **1** large in amount, degree, size, etc.; a lot of मात्रा, आकार आदि में बड़ा; बहुत अधिक *The party was a great success. ○ We had great difficulty in solving the problem.* **2** particularly important; of unusually high quality विशेष रूप से महत्त्वपूर्ण; असामान्य रूप से उच्च स्तर का *Einstein was perhaps the greatest scientist of the century.* ➪ **big** पर नोट देखिए। **3** (*informal*) good; wonderful अच्छा; आश्चर्यजनक *We had **a great time** in Paris. ○ **It's great** to see you again.* **4** (*informal*) (used to emphasize adjectives of size, quantity, etc.) very; very good(आकार, मात्रा आदि के विशेषणों पर बल देने के लिए प्रयुक्त) बहुत, बहुत अच्छा *There was a **great big** dog in the garden. ○ They were great friends.* **5 great-** used before a noun to show a family relationship पारिवारिक रिश्ता बताने के लिए संज्ञा से पहले प्रयुक्त (पूर्वपद)

> **NOTE** पारिवारिक रिश्ते के सूचक शब्दों से पहले **great-** लगाने से बुज़ुर्ग पीढ़ी का बोध होता है। आपके माता या पिता की चाची आदि आपकी **great-aunt** हैं। आपके नाती-नातिन की बेटी या बेटा आपका **great-grandchild** है। आपके दादा-दादी या नाना-नानी के माता-पिता आपके **great-grandparents** हैं। आपके दादा-दादी या नाना-नानी के दादा या नाना **great-great-grandfather** हैं।

▸ **greatness** *noun* [U] महानता, महत्ता, विशालता

**IDM** **go to great lengths** ➪ **length** देखिए।

**a good/great deal** ➪ **deal²** देखिए।

**a good/great many** ➪ **many** देखिए।

**great²** /ɡreɪt ग्रेट् / *noun* [C, *usually pl.*] (*informal*) a person or thing of special ability or importance विशेष रूप से महत्त्वपूर्ण या योग्य व्यक्ति या वस्तु *That film is one of the all-time greats.*

**Great Britain** (*also* **Britain**) (*abbr.* **GB**) England, Wales and Scotland इंग्लैंड, वेल्स और स्कॉटलैंड ➪ **United Kingdom** पर नोट देखिए।

**greatly** /ˈɡreɪtli ˈग्रेट्लि / *adv.* very much अत्यधिक

**greed** / ɡriːd ग्रीड् / *noun* [U] **greed (for sth)** a desire for more food, money, power, etc. than you really need आवश्यकता से अधिक पाने की इच्छा; लोभ, लालच

**greedy** /ˈgri:di ग्रीडि / *adj.* **(greedier; greediest) greedy (for sth)** wanting more food, money, power, etc. than you really need लोभी, लालची *Don't be so greedy you've had three pieces of cake already.* ▶ **greedily** *adv.* लोभ से ▶ **greediness** *noun* [U] लालचीपन

**green**[1] /gri:n ग्रीन् / *adj.* **1** having the colour of grass or leaves हरा *dark/light/pale green* **2** connected with protecting the environment or the natural world प्रकृति के पर्यावरण की सुरक्षा से संबंधित *the Green party* ○ *green products* (= that do not damage the environment) **3** (*informal*) (used about a person) with little experience of life or a particular job (व्यक्ति) जीवन या किसी काम के विषय में लगभग अनुभवहीन *The new batsmen got out early as he was still very green.* **4** jealous (wanting to have what sb else has got) ईर्ष्यालु *He was **green with envy** when he saw his neighbour's new car.* **5** (used about the skin) a strange, pale colour (because you feel sick) (त्वचा) विचित्र, पीला रंग (बीमारी के कारण) *At the sight of all the blood he **turned green** and fainted.*

IDM **give sb/get the green light** (*informal*) to give sb/get permission to do sth किसी को कोई काम करने की अनुमति देना

**have green fingers;** (*AmE*) **have a green thumb** (*informal*) to have the ability to make plants grow well पौधों को बढ़ाने की शक्ति

**green**[2] /gri:n ग्रीन् / *noun* **1** [C, U] the colour of grass or leaves हरा रंग *They were all dressed in green.* ○ *The room was decorated in greens and blues.* **2 greens** [*pl.*] green vegetables that are usually eaten cooked हरी सब्ज़ियाँ *To have a healthy complexion you should eat more greens.* **3** [C] (*BrE*) an area of grass in the centre of a village गाँव के बीच घास का मैदान **4** [C] a flat area of very short grass used in games such as golf गोल्फ़ आदि खेलों का बहुत छोटी घास वाला चौरस मैदान

**green belt** *noun* [C, U] (*BrE*) an area of open land around a city where building is not allowed शहर के चारों ओर का खुला इलाक़ा जहाँ भवन नहीं बनाए जा सकते; हरित क्षेत्र

**green card** *noun* [C] a document that allows sb from another country to live and work in the US एक अमेरिकी दस्तावेज़ जो विदेशियों को वहाँ रहने और काम करने की अनुमति देता है; ग्रीन कार्ड

**greenery** /ˈgri:nəri ग्रीनरि / *noun* [U] attractive green leaves and plants आकर्षक हरे पत्ते और पौधे; हरियाली

**greenfield** /ˈgri:nfi:ld ˈग्रीन्फ़ील्ड् / *adj.* (*only before a noun*) used to describe an area of land that has not yet had buildings on it, but for which building development may be planned वह इलाक़ा जिस पर अभी भवन नहीं हैं परंतु भवन बनाए जा सकते हैं *a greenfield site*

**greenfly** /ˈgri:nflaɪ ˈग्रीन्फ़्लाइ / *noun* [C] (*pl.* **greenflies** or **greenfly**) a small flying insect that is harmful to plants पौधों के लिए हानिकारक एक छोटा उड़न कीट

**greengage** /ˈgri:ngeɪdʒ ˈग्रीन्गेज् / *noun* [C] a small round yellowish-green fruit like a **plum** आलूबुख़ारे जैसा छोटा गोल पीला-हरा फल

**greengrocer** /ˈgri:ngrəʊsə(r) ˈग्रीन्ग्रोस(र्) / *noun* (*BrE*) **1** [C] a person who has a shop that sells fruit and vegetables सब्ज़ी और फल का विक्रेता ➪ **grocer** देखिए। **2 the green grocer's** [*sing.*] a shop that sells fruit and vegetables सब्ज़ी और फल की दुकान

**greenhouse** /ˈgri:nhaʊs ˈग्रीन्हाउस् / (*also* **glasshouse**) *noun* [C] a building made of glass in which plants are grown पौधा घर, पादप गृह ➪ **hothouse** देखिए।

**the greenhouse effect** *noun* [*sing.*] the warming of the earth's atmosphere as a result of harmful gases, etc. in the air हानिकर गैस आदि के कारण पृथ्वी के वातावरण के गरमा जाने की क्रिया ➪ **global warming** देखिए।

**greenish** /ˈgri:nɪʃ ˈग्रीनिश् / *adj.* slightly green हलका हरा

**green pepper** *noun* [C] = **pepper**[1] **2**

**green room** /ˈgri:nˌrum ˈग्रीन्ˌरुम् / *noun* [C] a room in a theatre, television studio, etc. where the performers can get ready for the show or wait and relax when they are not performing नेपथ्यशाला; ग्रीन रूम

**green tea** *noun* [U] a pale tea made from leaves that have been dried but that have not gone through a chemical process (**fermentation**) ऐसे पत्तों से बनी चाय जो सुखाए हुए हैं और ख़मीर उठने की प्रक्रिया में से नहीं गुज़रे; ग्रीन टी

**Greenwich Mean Time** /ˌgrenɪtʃˈmi:n taɪm ˌग्रेनिचˈमीन् टाइम् / = **GMT**

**greet** /gri:t ग्रीट् / *verb* [T] **1 greet sb (with sth)** to welcome sb when you meet him/her; to say hello to sb किसी से मिलने पर उसका अभिवादन करना; स्वागत करना *He greeted me with a friendly smile.* ○ (*figurative*) *As we entered the house we were greeted by the smell of cooking.* **2 greet sb/sth**

(**as/with**) **sth** (*usually passive*) to react to sb or receive sth in a particular way प्रतिक्रिया प्रकट करना या ख़ास ढंग से किसी बात को लेना *The news was greeted with a loud cheer.*

**greeting** /ˈgriːtɪŋ ˈग्रीटिङ् / *noun* [C] the first words you say when you meet sb or write to him/her किसी से मिलने या किसी को पत्र आदि लिखने पर कहे या लिखे प्रथम शब्द, अभिवादन शब्द या संबोधन शब्द *'Hello' and 'Hi' are informal greetings.*

**gregarious** /grɪˈgeəriəs ग्रिˈगेअरिअस् / *adj.* liking to be with other people लोगों से मिलना-जुलना पंसद करने वाला; मिलनसार, सुसामाजिक ✪ पर्याय **sociable**

**grenade** /grəˈneɪd ग्रˈनेड् / *noun* [C] a small bomb that is thrown by hand or fired from a gun हथगोला, ग्रेनेड; हाथ से फेंका या बंदूक़ से दाग़ा गया छोटा बम

**grew** ➪ **grow** का past tense रूप

**grey[1]** (*AmE* **gray**) /greɪ ग्रे / *adj.* **1** having the colour between black and white काले और सफ़ेद के बीच के रंग वाला, स्लेटी, राख जैसे रंग वाला *dark/light/pale grey* ○ *He was wearing a grey suit.* **2** having grey hair खिचड़ी बालों वाला, पलित केशी *He's **going grey**.* **3** (used about the weather) full of cloud; not bright (मौसम) बादलों वाला; धुँधला *grey skies* ○ *a grey day* **4** boring and sad; without interest or variety उबाऊ और उदास; रोचकता या विविधता से रहित

**grey[2]** /greɪ ग्रे/ (*AmE* **gray**) *noun* [C, U] the colour between black and white काले और सफ़ेद के बीच का रंग, राख जैसा रंग, स्लेटी रंग *dressed in grey*

**greyhound** /ˈgreɪhaʊnd ˈग्रेहाउन्ड् / *noun* [C] a large thin dog that can run very fast and that is used for racing बहुत तेज़ दौड़ने वाला बड़े आकार का छरहरा कुत्ता (जिसे दौड़-प्रतियोगिता में इस्तेमाल किया जाता है) *greyhound racing*

**greyish** /ˈgreɪɪʃ ˈग्रेइश् / (*AmE* **grayish**) *adj.* slightly grey हलका स्लेटी

**grid** /grɪd ग्रिड् / *noun* [C] **1** a pattern of straight lines that cross each other to form squares एक दूसरे को काटती वर्ग बनाती सीधी रेखाओं का पैटर्न; ग्रिड *She drew a grid to show how the students had scored in each part of the test.* **2** a frame of parallel metal or wooden bars, usually covering a hole in sth धातु या लकड़ी की समानांतर छड़ों की चौखट (प्रायः छेद ढकने के लिए), जाली या जंगला **3** a system of squares that are drawn on a map so that the position of any place can be described or found मानचित्र पर बनी वर्ग-प्रणाली जिस पर किसी स्थान की स्थिति अंकित की जा सकती है या पता लगाया जा सकता है *a grid reference* **4** the system of electricity wires, etc. taking power to all parts of a country विद्युत-वितरण के लिए बिजली की तारों की व्यवस्था; ग्रिड *the National Grid* ➪ **generator** पर चित्र देखिए।

**griddle** /ˈgrɪdl ˈग्रिड्ल् / *noun* [C] a circular iron plate that is heated on a cooker or over a fire and used for cooking तवा

**gridlock** /ˈgrɪdlɒk ˈग्रिड्लॉक् / *noun* [U, C] a situation in which there are so many cars in the streets of a town that the traffic cannot move at all सड़क पर ढेर सारी कारों का जमघट कि यातायात रुक जाए ▸ **gridlocked** *adj.* जमघट में फँसा

**grief** /griːf ग्रीफ़् / *noun* [U] great sadness (especially because of the death of sb you love) गहरा शोक (विशेषतः किसी प्रिय के निधन से उत्पन्न)

IDM **good grief** (*spoken*) used for expressing surprise or shock आश्चर्य या मानसिक आघात व्यक्त करने के लिए प्रयुक्त *Good grief! Whatever happened to you?*

**grievance** /ˈgriːvəns ˈग्रीव़न्स् / *noun* [C] **a grievance (against sb)** something that you think is unfair and that you want to complain or protest about शिकायत; व्यथा

**grieve** /griːv ग्रीव़् / *verb* **1** [I] **grieve (for sb)** to feel great sadness (especially about the death of sb you love) (प्रियजन के निधन पर) गहरी उदासी होना **2** [T] (*formal*) to cause unhappiness विषाद उत्पन्न करना

**grill[1]** /grɪl ग्रिल् / *noun* [C] **1** a part of a cooker where the food is cooked by heat from above कुकर का वह भाग जिस पर ऊपर से आते ताप से भोजन पकता है **2** a metal frame that you put food on to cook over an open fire जाली **3** = **grille**

**grill[2]** /grɪl ग्रिल् / *verb* **1** (*AmE* **broil**) [I, T] to cook under a grill ग्रिल के नीचे पकाना *grilled steak/chicken/fish* **2** [T] (*informal*) **grill sb (about sth)** to question sb for a long time किसी से देर तक पूछताछ करना

**grille** /grɪl ग्रिल् / (*also* **grill**) *noun* [C] a metal frame that is placed over a window, a piece of machinery, etc. किसी मशीन, खिड़की आदि पर रखी जाली

**grim** /grɪm ग्रिम् / *adj.* (**grimmer; grimmest**) **1** (used about a person) very serious; not smiling (व्यक्ति) गंभीर; अप्रफुल्लित **2** (used about a situation, news, etc.) unpleasant or worrying (स्थिति, समाचार आदि) अप्रिय या चिंताजनक *The news is grim, I'm afraid.* **3** (used about a place) unpleasant to look at; not attractive (स्थान) देखने में अप्रिय, कुदर्शन; अनाकर्षक *a grim block of flats* **4** (*BrE informal*) feeling ill अनमना, विषण्ण *I was feeling grim yesterday but I managed to get to work.* ▸ **grimly** *adv.* अनमनेपन से, विषादपूर्वक

**grimace** /ˈgrɪməs; grɪˈmeɪs ˈग्रिमस्; ग्रिˈमेस्/ *noun* [C] an ugly expression on your face that shows that you are angry, disgusted or that sth is hurting you क्रोध, घृणा, पीड़ा आदि को दर्शाने वाली चेहरे पर ऐंठन, खिंचाव आदि *a grimace of pain* ▸ **grimace** *verb* [I] चेहरा विकृत हो जाना *She grimaced with pain.*

**grime** /graɪm ग्राइम्/ *noun* [U] a thick layer of dirt मैल की मोटी परत; कालिख़

**grimy** /ˈgraɪmi ˈग्राइमि/ *adj.* very dirty बहुत मैला

**grin** /grɪn ग्रिन्/ *verb* [I] (**grinning; grinned**) **grin (at sb)** to give a broad smile (so that you show your teeth) खुलकर मुसकराना (कि दाँत दीखें); खीसें निपोरना *She grinned at me as she came into the room.* ▸ **grin** *noun* [C]

**grind**[1] /graɪnd ग्राइन्ड्/ *verb* [T] (*pt, pp* **ground** /graʊnd ग्राउन्ड्/) **1 grind sth (down/up); grind sth (to/into sth)** to press and break sth into very small pieces or into a powder between two hard surfaces or in a special machine मशीन में पीसना; दलना *Wheat is ground into flour.* ○ *ground pepper/coffee* **2** to make sth sharp or smooth by rubbing it on a rough hard surface किसी वस्तु को खुरदुरी कड़ी सतह पर घिस कर चिकना बनाना या उसकी धार तेज़ करना *to grind a knife on a stone* **3 grind sth in/into sth** to press or rub sth into a surface किसी जगह पर कोई चीज़ दबाना या रगड़ना *He ground his cigarette into the ashtray.* **4** to rub sth together or make sth rub together, often producing an unpleasant noise किरकिराना *Some people **grind** their **teeth** while they're asleep.*

IDM **grind to a halt/standstill** to stop slowly धीमा होकर रुक जाना

**grind**[2] /graɪnd ग्राइन्ड्/ *noun* [*sing.*] (*informal*) an activity that is tiring and boring and that takes a lot of time थकाऊ, उबाऊ और लंबी चलने वाली क्रिया *the **daily grind** of working life*

**grinder** /ˈgraɪndə(r) ˈग्राइन्ड(र्)/ *noun* [C] a machine for grinding पीसने की मशीन *a coffee grinder*

**grip**[1] /grɪp ग्रिप्/ *verb* [I, T] (**gripping; gripped**) **1** to hold sb/sth tightly व्यक्ति या वस्तु को कसकर पकड़ना *She gripped my arm in fear.* **2** to interest sb very much; to hold sb's attention किसी की अत्यधिक रुचि जगाना; किसी के ध्यान को बाँधे रहना *The book grips you from start to finish.* ➪ **gripping** adjective देखिए।

**grip**[2] /grɪp ग्रिप्/ *noun* **1** [*sing.*] **a grip (on sb/sth)** a firm hold (on sb/sth) (व्यक्ति या वस्तु पर) मज़बूत पकड़ *I relaxed my grip and he ran away.* ○ *The climber slipped and lost her grip.* ○ (*figurative*) *The teacher kept a firm grip on the class.* **2** [*sing.*] **a grip (on sth)** an understanding of sth किसी वस्तु की समझ **3** [C] the person whose job it is to move the cameras while a film is being made फ़िल्म की शूटिंग के समय कैमरों को सरकाने वाला व्यक्ति

IDM **come/get to grips with sth** to start to understand and deal with a problem समस्या को समझकर उसका हल निकालने में लगना

**get/keep/take a grip/hold (on yourself)** (*informal*) to try to behave in a calmer or more sensible way; to control yourself शांत भाव और समझदारी से व्यवहार करना; अपने ऊपर संयम रखना

**in the grip of sth** experiencing sth unpleasant that cannot be stopped प्रतिकूल और बेक़ाबू स्थिति में आ जाना *a country in the grip of recession*

**gripe** /graɪp ग्राइप्/ *noun* [C] (*informal*) a complaint about sb/sth व्यक्ति या वस्तु की शिकायत ▸ **gripe** *verb* [I] शिकायत करना

**gripping** /ˈgrɪpɪŋ ˈग्रिपिङ्/ *adj.* exciting; holding your attention उत्तेजक, रोमांचक; ध्यान को बाँध लेने वाली *a gripping film/book*

**grisly** /ˈgrɪzli ˈग्रिज़्लि/ *adj.* (used for describing sth that is concerned with death or violence) terrible; horrible (मृत्यु या हिंसा के घटना के वर्णन के लिए प्रयुक्त) भयानक, ख़ौफ़नाक़ बीभत्स, दिल-दहलाऊ *a grisly crime/death/murder* ➪ **gruesome** देखिए।

**gristle** /ˈgrɪsl ˈग्रिसल्/ *noun* [U] a hard substance in a piece of meat that is unpleasant to eat मांस खाते समय मुँह में अटकता हड्डी का टुकड़ा ▸ **gristly** *adv.* हड्डी के टुकड़े वाला

**grit**[1] /grɪt ग्रिट्/ *noun* [U] **1** small pieces of stone or sand रोड़ी या बजरी *I've got some grit/a piece of grit in my shoe.* **2** (*informal*) courage; determination that makes it possible for sb to continue doing sth difficult or unpleasant साहस; कठिन काम को जारी रखने का दृढ़ निश्चय

**grit**[2] /grɪt ग्रिट्/ *verb* [T] (**gritting; gritted**) to spread small pieces of stone and sand on a road that is covered with ice बर्फ़ से ढकी सड़क पर रोड़ी और बजरी फैलाना

IDM **grit your teeth** **1** to bite your teeth tightly together दाँतों को ज़ोर से भींचना *She gritted her teeth against the pain as the doctor examined her injured foot.* **2** to use your courage or determination in a difficult situation कठिन परिस्थिति में साहस या दृढ़ निश्चय दिखाना

**groan** /grəʊn ग्रोन्/ *verb* [I] **groan (at/with sth)** to make a deep sad sound because you are in pain, or to show that you are unhappy about sth दर्द में

कराहना या किसी बात पर रोष प्रकट करना *He groaned with pain.* ○ *All the students were* ***moaning and groaning*** (= complaining) *about the amount of work they had to do.* ▶ **groan** *noun* [C] कराहट, रोष

**grocer** /ˈgrəʊsə(r) ˈग्रोस(र्)/ *noun* **1** [C] a person who has a shop that sells food and other things for the home घरेलू उपयोग की चीज़ें बेचने वाला व्यक्ति; पंसारी ➪ **greengrocer** देखिए। **2 the grocer's** [*sing.*] a shop that sells food and other things for the home पंसारी की दुकान

**groceries** /ˈgrəʊsəriz ˈग्रोसरिज़्/ *noun* [*pl.*] food, etc. that is sold by a grocer or in a larger food shop (**supermarket**) सुपरमार्केट में बिकने वाली खाद्य वस्तुएँ आदि

**groggy** /ˈgrɒgi ˈग्रॉगि/ *adj.* (*informal*) weak and unable to walk steadily because you feel ill, have not had enough sleep, etc. नींद में बाधा आदि के कारण बीमार-सा महसूस करना

**groin** /grɔɪn ग्रॉइन्/ *noun* [C] **1** the front part of your body where it joins your legs शरीर का वह भाग जहाँ टाँगें मिलती हैं; ऊरूमूल **2** (*AmE*) = **groyne**

**groom¹** /gruːm ग्रूम्/ *noun* [C] **1** = **bridegroom** **2** a person who looks after horses, especially by cleaning and brushing them घोड़ों की देखभाल करने वाला व्यक्ति; सईस

**groom²** /gruːm ग्रूम्/ *verb* [T] **1** to clean or look after an animal by brushing, etc. पशु की देखभाल करना (सफ़ाई करना आदि) *to groom a horse/dog/cat* **2 groom sb (for/as sth)** (*usually passive*) to choose and prepare sb for a particular career or job किसी को विशेष व्यवसाय या नौकरी के लिए चुनना और तैयार करना

**groove** /gruːv ग्रूव्/ *noun* [C] a long deep line that is cut in the surface of sth किसी सतह पर गहराई में की गई रेखा के आकार की काट; खाँचा, नाली

**grope** /grəʊp ग्रोप्/ *verb* **1** [I] **grope (about/around) (for sth)** to search for sth or find your way using your hands because you cannot see दिखाई न पड़ने के कारण हाथों से रास्ता खोजना; टटोलना *He groped around for the light switch.* **2** [T] (*informal*) to touch sb sexually, especially when he/she does not want you to कामुकता से किसी का स्पर्श करना (विशेषतः उसकी इच्छा के विरुद्ध)

**gross** /grəʊs ग्रोस्/ *adj.* **1** (*only before a noun*) being the total amount before anything is taken away कुल राशि (जिसमें से कुछ घटाया नहीं गया) *gross income* (= before tax, etc. is taken away) ✪ विलोम **net** **2** (*formal*) (*only before a noun*) very great or serious बहुत बड़ा या गंभीर *gross indecency/negligence/misconduct* **3** very rude and unpleasant बहुत अशिष्ट **4** very fat and ugly बहुत मोटा और भद्दा

**gross domestic product** *noun* [*sing.*, U] = **GDP**

**grossly** /ˈgrəʊsli ˈग्रोस्लि/ *adv.* very अत्यधिक *That is grossly unfair.*

**gross national product** *noun* [*sing.*, U] = **GNP**

**grotesque** /grəʊˈtesk ग्रोˈटेस्क्/ *adj.* strange or ugly in a way that is not natural बेतुका, अजीबोग़रीब, भद्दा, विकृत

**grotty** /ˈgrɒti ˈग्रॉटि/ *adj.* (*informal*) (**grottier; grottiest**) unpleasant; of poor quality असुखद; घटिया क़िस्म का *She lives in a grotty flat.*

**ground¹** /graʊnd ग्राउन्ड्/ *noun* **1 the ground** [*sing.*] the solid surface of the earth पृथ्वी की कठोर सतह *He slipped off the ladder and fell to the ground.* ○ *waste ground* (= that is not being used) **2** [U] an area or type of soil कोई क्षेत्र या एक प्रकार की मिट्टी *solid/marshy/stony ground*

> **NOTE** जिस ग्रह पर हम रहते हैं उसे **Earth** कहते हैं। जो समुद्र नहीं है उसे **land** कहते हैं—*The sailors sighted land.* ○ *The astronauts returned to Earth.* भूमि जिसे ख़रीदते या बेचते हैं उसे भी **land** कहते हैं—*The price of land in Tokyo is extremely high.* घर से बाहर आप के पैर के नीचे की सतह को **the ground** कहते हैं। घर के अंदर की सतह को **the floor** कहते हैं—*Don't sit on the ground. You'll get wet.* ○ *Don't sit on the floor. I'll get another chair.* पौधे **earth** या **soil** में उगते हैं।

**3** [C] a piece of land that is used for a particular purpose विशेष प्रयोजन से काम में आने वाला भूखंड *a sports ground* ○ *a playground* **4 grounds** [*pl.*] land or gardens surrounding a large building बड़े भवन के चारों ओर की भूमि या बग़ीचे *the grounds of the palace* **5** [U] an area of interest, study, discussion, etc. रुचि, अध्ययन, चर्चा आदि का विषय या क्षेत्र *The lecture went over* ***the same old ground****/covered a lot of* ***new ground****.* ○ *to be on dangerous ground* (= saying sth likely to cause anger) **6** [C, *usually pl.*] **grounds (for sth/doing sth)** a reason for sth किसी बात का कारण या आधार *She retired* ***on*** *medical* ***grounds****.* ○ *grounds for divorce* **7** (*AmE*) = **earth¹ 4**

**IDM** **above/below ground** above/below the surface of the earth पृथ्वी की सतह के ऊपर या नीचे

**break fresh/new ground** to make a discovery or introduce a new method or activity कोई नई बात खोजना या नई पद्धति या प्रक्रिया को पेश करना

**gain ground** ➪ **gain¹** देखिए।

**get off the ground** (used about a business, project, etc.) to make a successful start (व्यापार, परियोजना आदि की) सफल शुरुआत करना

**give/lose ground (to sb/sth)** to allow sb to have an advantage; to lose an advantage for yourself किसी को लाभ लेने देना; अपनी लाभ की स्थिति गँवा देना, किसी का फ़ायदा कर देना; अपना नुक़सान कर लेना *Labour lost a lot of ground to the Liberal Democrats at the elections.*

**hold/keep/stand your ground** to refuse to change your opinion or to be influenced by pressure from other people अपनी बात पर डटे रहना या क़ायम रहना

**thin on the ground** difficult to find; not common जिसका पता लगाना कठिन हो; आम नहीं

**ground**[2] /graʊnd ग्राउन्ड्/ *verb* [T] **1** (*usually passive*) to force an aircraft, etc. to stay on the ground विमान आदि का भूग्रस्त रहने या उड़ान न भरने के लिए बाध्य होना *to be grounded by fog* **2** (*usually passive*) to punish a child by not allowing them to go out with their friends for a period of time (प्रायः दंड के रूप में) बच्चों को कुछ समय तक मित्रों के साथ खेलने या बाहर जाने से रोक देना **3** (*AmE*) = **earth**[2]

**ground**[3] ➪ **grind**[1] का past tense, past participle रूप *ground almonds*

**ground beef** (*AmE*) = **mince**

**ground crew** (*also* **ground staff**) *noun* [C, U] the people in an airport whose job it is to look after an aircraft while it is on the ground हवाई अड्डे पर खड़े विमान की देखभाल करने वाले कर्मचारी; ग्राउंड स्टाफ़

**ground floor** (*AmE* **first floor**) *noun* [C] the floor of a building that is at ground level भवन की भूतल स्थित मंज़िल *a ground-floor flat* ➪ **floor** पर नोट देखिए।

**grounding** /ˈgraʊndɪŋ ˈग्राउन्डिङ्/ *noun* [*sing.*] **a grounding (in sth)** the teaching of the basic facts or principles of a subject किसी विषय के मौलिक तथ्यों या सिद्धांतों का अध्ययन

**groundless** /ˈgraʊndləs ˈग्राउन्ड्लस्/ *adj.* having no reason or cause निराधार, बेबुनियाद, बिना वजह *Our fears were groundless*

**groundnut** /ˈgraʊndnʌt ˈगाउन्ड्नट्/ = **peanut**

**groundsheet** /ˈgraʊndʃiːt ˈग्राउन्ड्शीट्/ *noun* [C] a large piece of material that does not let water through, that is placed on the ground inside a tent टेंट के अंदर ज़मीन पर रखने की बड़ी चादर जिसमें से पानी रिस नहीं सकता

**groundwater** /ˈgraʊndwɔːtə(r) ˈग्राउन्ड्वॉट(र्)/ *noun* [U] water that is found under the ground in soil, rocks, etc. भूगर्भ में पाया जाने वाला जल

**groundwork** /ˈgraʊndwɜːk ˈग्राउन्ड्वक्/ *noun* [U] work that is done in preparation for further work or study उच्चतर अध्ययन के लिए की गई आरंभिक तैयारी

**group**[1] /gruːp ग्रूप्/ *noun* [C] **1** [*with sing. or pl. verb*] a number of people or things that are together in the same place or that are connected in some way समूह, दल, किसी प्रकार से परस्पर संबंधित या एक ही स्थान पर स्थित लोग या वस्तुएँ *Students were standing **in groups** waiting for their exam results.* ○ *people of many different social groups* ○ ***a pressure group*** (= a political group that tries to influence the government) ○ ***blood group***

> **NOTE** **Group** का एकवचन में प्रयोग एकवचनांत या बहुवचनांत क्रिया (singular or plural verb) के साथ भी हो सकता है। यदि समूह में सदस्यों को इस दृष्टि से देखा जाए कि वे अनेक व्यक्तियों का एक समुदाय है तो बहुवचनांत क्रिया (plural verb) का प्रयोग अधिक प्रचलित है।

**2** (used in business) a number of companies that are owned by the same person or organization (व्यापार) एक ही व्यक्ति या संगठन के स्वामित्व वाली अनेक कंपनियाँ **3** (*old-fashioned*) a number of people who play music together एक साथ संगीत कार्यक्रम पेश करने वाले अनेक लोग, शायरों-वादकों की टोली *a pop group* ➪ **band** देखिए।

**group**[2] /gruːp ग्रूप्/ *verb* [I, T] **group (sb/sth) (around/round sb/sth); group (sb/sth) (together)** to put sb/sth or to form into one or more groups व्यक्ति या वस्तु को एक या अधिक वर्गों में रखना या उनका एक या अधिक वर्ग बनाना *Group these words according to their meaning.*

**grouping** /ˈgruːpɪŋ ˈग्रूपिङ्/ *noun* **1** [C] a number of people or organizations that have the same interests, aims or characteristics and are often part of a larger group समान हितों, ध्येयों या लक्षणों वाले व्यक्ति या संगठन जो प्रायः किसी बड़े समूह का अंग होते हैं *These small nations constitute an important grouping within the SAARC nations.* **2** [U] the act of forming sth into a group किसी वस्तु को किसी वर्ग में रखने की क्रिया; वर्गीकरण

**grouse** /graʊs ग्राउस्/ *noun* [C] (*pl.* **grouse**) a fat brown bird with feathers on its legs that is shot for sport in some countries तीतर जैसा एक बड़ा पक्षी जिसका शिकार किया जाता है (कुछ देशों में)

**grove** /grəʊv ग्रोव्/ *noun* [C] a small group of trees, especially of one particular type वृक्षों का छोटा समूह (विशेषतः एक ही प्रकार के), वृक्षावली, कुंज, बग़ीचा, उपवन *an olive grove*

**grovel** /ˈgrɒvl ˈग्रॉव्ल्/ *verb* [I] (**grovelling; grovelled** *AmE* **groveling; groveled**) **1 grovel (to sb) (for sth)** to try too hard to please sb who is more important than you or who can give you sth that you want अपने से बड़े (अधिकारी) को ख़ुश करने का भरपूर प्रयास करना, किसी के आगे नाक रगड़ना; घिघियाना *to grovel for forgiveness* **2 grovel (around/about) (for sth)** to move around on your hands and knees (usually when you are looking for sth) रेंगते हुए या हाथों और घुटनों के बल चलना (प्रायः कुछ खोजते समय) ▶ **grovelling** *adj.* घिघियाने वाला *He wrote a grovelling letter to my bank manager.*

**grow** /grəʊ ग्रो/ *verb* (*pt* **grew** /gru: ग्रू/; *pp* **grown** /grəʊn ग्रोन्/) **1** [I] **grow (in sth)** to increase in size or number; to develop into an adult form आकार या संख्या की दृष्टि से बढ़ना; बड़ा होना *a growing child* ○ *She's growing in confidence all the time.* ○ *You must invest if you want your business to grow.* **2** [I, T] (used about plants) to exist and develop in a particular place; to make plants grow by giving them water, etc. (पौधों का) एक विशेष स्थान पर होना और बढ़ना; पौधों को बड़ा करना *Palm trees don't grow in cold climates.* ○ *We grow vegetables in our garden.* **3** [T] to allow your hair or nails to grow बालों या नाख़ूनों को बढ़ने देना *to grow a beard/moustache* **4** *linking verb* to gradually change from one state to another; to become क्रमशः दशा-परिवर्तन होना; हो जाना *It began to grow dark.* ○ *to grow older/wiser/taller/bigger* ○ *The teacher was growing more and more impatient.*

**NOTE** इस अर्थ में **get** कम औपचारिक शब्द है।

**PHR V grow into sth 1** to gradually develop into a particular type of person बड़ा होकर कुछ ख़ास बनना *She has grown into a very attractive young woman.* **2** to become big enough to fit into clothes, etc. पोशाक आदि के लिहाज़ से बड़ा हो जाना, बड़ा हो जाने के कारण पोशाक आदि का फ़िट न होना *The coat is too big for him, but he will soon grow into it.*

**grow on sb** to become more pleasing अधिक रुचिकर हो जाना, अधिक पसंद आने लगना *I didn't like ginger at first, but it's a taste that grows on you.*

**grow out of sth** to become too big or too old for sth किसी वस्तु का उपयोग की दृष्टि से आकार या आयु में बड़ा हो जाना, आकार या आयु बढ़ जाने के कारण किसी चीज़ का छोटा पड़ जाना *She's grown out of that dress I made her last year.*

**grow (sth) out** (used about hairstyles, etc.) to disappear gradually as your hair grows; to allow your hair to grow in order to change the style (विशिष्ट केशविन्यास शैली आदि का) केशवृद्धि के साथ लुप्त हो जाना; केशवृद्धि के साथ केशविन्यास शैली का बदल जाना

**grow up 1** to develop into an adult; to mature बड़े होकर युवा हो जाना; परिपक्व होना, प्रौढ़ता को प्राप्त होना *What do you want to be when you grow up* (= what job do you want to do later)? ○ *She grew up* (= spent her childhood) *in Spain.* **2** (used about a feeling, etc.) to develop or become strong (भावनाओं आदि में) वृद्धि होना या उनका अधिक मुख्य हो जाना *A close friendship has grown up between them.*

**growing** /ˈgrəʊɪŋ ˈग्रोइङ्/ *adj.* increasing अधिकाधिक, बढ़ता हुआ *A growing number of people are becoming vegetarian these days.*

**growl** /graʊl ग्राउल्/ *verb* [I] **growl (at sb/sth)** (used about dogs and other animals) to make a low noise in the throat to show anger or to give a warning (कुत्ते या अन्य जानवरों का) दूसरों पर गुर्राना (गुस्सा व्यक्त करने या चेतावनी देने के लिए) ▶ **growl** *noun* [C] गुर्राहट, धमकी

**grown** /grəʊn ग्रोन्/ *adj.* physically an adult शरीर से व्यस्क या जवान *a fully grown elephant*

**grown-up**[1] *adj.* physically or mentally adult शरीर या मन से *She's very grown-up for her age.* ✪ पर्याय **mature**

**grown-up**[2] *noun* [C] an adult person वयस्क

**growth** /grəʊθ ग्रोथ्/ *noun* **1** [U] the process of growing and developing वृद्धि और विकास *A good diet is very important for children's growth.* ○ *a growth industry* (= one that is growing) **2** [U, *sing.*] an increase (in sth) (किसी में ) वृद्धि, बढ़त *population growth* **3** [C] a lump caused by a disease that grows in a person's or an animal's body रोग के कारण मनुष्य या पशु के शरीर में बनी गाँठ *a cancerous growth* **4** [U] something that has grown बढ़ने वाली वस्तु *several days' growth of beard*

**groyne** (*AmE* **groin**) /grɔɪn ग्रॉइन्/ *noun* [C] a low wall built out into the sea to prevent it from washing away sand and stones from the beach समुद्र तट से बालू और पत्थरों को बहाकर ले जाने से बचाने के लिए समुद्र में जाकर बनाई गई छोटी दीवार, समुद्रजल में बनी तटरक्षक दीवार

**grub** /grʌb ग्रब्/ *noun* **1** [C] the first form that an insect takes when it comes out of the egg. Grubs are short, fat and white अंडे से बाहर आने पर कीट की प्रथम स्थिति; लार्वा, सूँड़ी **2** [U] (*informal*) food भोजन

**grubby** /ˈgrʌbi ˈग्रबि/ *adj.* (**grubbier; grubbiest**) (*informal*) dirty after being used and not washed मैला-कुचैला, गंदा

**grudge**[1] /grʌdʒ ग्रज्/ *noun* [C] **a grudge (against sb)** unfriendly feelings towards sb, because you are angry about what has happened in the past

अतीत की घटनाओं से क्रोधित होने के कारण मन में उत्पन्न प्रतिकूल भावनाएँ, किसी से घृणा, वैमनस्य, ईर्ष्या या दुर्भावना *to **bear a grudge** against sb*

**grudge[2]** /grʌdʒ ग्रज्/ *verb* [T] **grudge sb sth**; **grudge doing sth** to be unhappy that sb has sth or that you have to do sth किसी की उपलब्धि पर या कुछ करने के लिए विवश होने पर बुरा लगना *I don't grudge him his success—he deserves it.* ○ *I grudge having to pay so much tax.* ➪ **begrudge** देखिए।

**grudging** /ˈgrʌdʒɪŋ ˈग्रजिङ्/ *adj.* given or done although you do not want to अनिच्छापूर्ण दिया गया या किया गया कार्य *grudging thanks* ▶ **grudgingly** *adv.* अनिच्छापूर्वक

**gruel** /ˈgru:əl ˈग्रूअल्/ *noun* [U] a simple dish made by boiling cereals like oats in water or milk, eaten, especially in the past, by poor people दलिया

**gruelling** (*AmE* **grueling**) /ˈgru:əlɪŋ ˈग्रूअलिङ्/ *adj.* very tiring and long बहुत थकाने वाला और लंबा *a gruelling nine-hour march*

**gruesome** /ˈgru:səm ˈग्रूसम्/ *adj.* (used about sth concerned with death or injury) very unpleasant or shocking (मृत्यु या चोट से संबंधित स्थिति) बहुत दुखद या स्तब्ध कर देने वाला; बीभत्स ➪ **grisly** देखिए।

**gruff** /grʌf ग्रफ़्/ *adj.* (used about a person or a voice) rough and unfriendly (व्यक्ति या स्वर) रूखा और कठोर ▶ **gruffly** *adv.* रूखेपन से

**grumble** /ˈgrʌmbl ˈग्रम्बल्/ *verb* [I] to complain in a bad-tempered way; to keep saying that you do not like sth खीझते हुए शिकायत करना; नापसंद होने की रट लगाए रखना; बुड़बुड़ाना *The students were always grumbling about the standard of the food.*

> **NOTE** जब कोई बात आशा के अनुसार न हो तो सामान्यतः **grumble** या **moan** शब्दों का व्यवहार किया जाता है। यदि इसके विरोध में कोई क़दम उठाना हो तो आधिकारिक अफ़सर के पास जाकर शिकायत करने को **complain** कहते हैं।

▶ **grumble** *noun* [C] बुड़बुड़ाना

**grumpy** /ˈgrʌmpi ˈग्रम्पि/ *adj.* (*informal*) bad-tempered बदमिज़ाज, चिड़चिड़ा ▶ **grumpily** *adv.* चिड़चिड़ेपन से

**grunt** /grʌnt ग्रन्ट्/ *verb* [I, T] to make a short low sound in the throat. People grunt when they do not like sth or are not interested and do not want to talk (अरुचि व्यक्त करते हुए) बुड़बुड़ाना *I tried to find out her opinion but she just grunted when I asked her.* ▶ **grunt** *noun* [C] अरुचि व्यंजक बुड़बुड़ाहट

**guano** /ˈgwɑ:nəʊ ˈग्वानो/ *noun* [U] the waste substance passed from the bodies of seabirds, that is used by farmers to make plants grow well समुद्री जंतुओं की विष्ठा जो खाद का काम करती है

**guarantee[1]** /ˌgærənˈti:ˌ गैरन्ˈटी/ *noun* [C, U] **1** a firm promise that sth will be done or that sth will happen पक्का वादा कि कुछ किया जाएगा या कुछ होगा; गारंटी, आश्वासन *The refugees are demanding guarantees about their safety before they return home.* **2** a written promise by a company that it will repair or replace a product if it breaks in a certain period of time निश्चित अवधि में क्षतिग्रस्त होने पर सुधार करने का कंपनी का लिखित या औपचारिक आश्वासन; गारंटी *The watch comes with a year's guarantee.* ○ *Is the computer still **under guarantee**?* ➪ **warranty** देखिए। **3** something that makes sth else certain to happen किसी अन्य बात के होने को निश्चित करने वाली बात; गारंटी, पक्की बात *Without a reservation there's no guarantee that you'll get a seat on the train.*

**guarantee[2]** /ˌgærənˈti:ˌ गैरन्ˈटी/ *verb* [T] **1** to promise that sth will be done or will happen कुछ करने या घटित होने का वादा करना; गारंटी देना *They have guaranteed delivery within one week.* **2** to give a written promise to repair or replace a product if anything is wrong with it ख़राबी पाए जाने पर माल की मरम्मत करने या उसे बदलने का लिखित वादा करना *This washing machine is guaranteed for three years.* **3** to make sth certain to happen किसी बात के घटित होने को निश्चित करना *Tonight's win guarantees the team a place in the final.*

**guarantor** /ˌgærəntɔ:(r)ˌ गैरन्ट(र्)/ *noun* [C] **1** (*formal*) a person who agrees to be responsible for making sure that sth happens or is done प्रतिभू *The United Nations will act as a guarantor of the peace settlement.* **2** (*legal*) a person who formally agrees to pay a debt if you cannot औपचारिक रूप से किसी का ऋण चुकाने वाला व्यक्ति; प्रतिभू *You must have a guarantor in order to take a loan.*

**guard[1]** /gɑ:d गाड्/ *noun* **1** [C] a person who protects a place or people, or who stops prisoners from escaping सुरक्षा कर्मचारी *a security guard* ➪ **warder** और **bodyguard** देखिए। **2** [U] the state of being ready to prevent attack or danger आक्रमण या संकट का सामना करने की तैयारी *Soldiers **keep guard** at the gate.* ○ *The prisoner arrived **under** armed **guard**.* **3** [*sing., with sing. or pl. verb*] a group of soldiers, police officers, etc. who protect sb/sth किसी की सुरक्षा के लिए तैनात सैनिकों, पुलिस अधिकारियों आदि का समूह *The president always travels with* *an armed guard.* **4** [C] (*often in compounds*) something that covers sth dangerous or protects sth सुरक्षा करने वाली कोई वस्तु *a fireguard* ○ *a mudguard* (= over the wheel of a bicycle) **5** (*AmE* **conductor**) [C] a person who is in charge of a train but does not drive it रेलगाड़ी का प्रभारी-अधिकारी (जो उसका चालक नहीं होता); गार्ड **6** [U] a position that you take to defend yourself, especially in sports such as boxing (मुक्केबाज़ी आदि स्पर्धा में) बचाव की स्थिति

IDM **off/on (your) guard** not ready/ready for an attack, surprise, mistake, etc. आकस्मिक आक्रमण, अचंभा या भूल आदि का सामना करने के लिए तैयार नहीं *The question caught me off (my) guard and I didn't know what to say.*

**guard[2]** /gɑːd गाड्/ *verb* [T] **1** to keep sb/sth safe from other people; protect व्यक्ति या वस्तु को दूसरे लोगों से बचाकर रखना; रक्षा करना *The building was guarded by men with dogs.* ○ (*figurative*) *a closely guarded secret* **2** to be ready to stop prisoners from escaping कैदियों को भागने से रोकने को तैयार होना

PHRV **guard against sth** to try to prevent sth or stop sth happening किसी बात को घटित न होने देना या इसकी कोशिश करना

**guarded** /ˈgɑːdɪd ˈगाडिड्/ *adj.* (used about an answer, statement, etc.) careful; not giving much information or showing what you feel (उत्तर, वक्तव्य आदि) सतर्क; जिसमें अधिक जानकारी नहीं या भावनाओं की खुली अभिव्यक्ति नहीं ✪ विलोम **unguarded** ▶ **guardedly** *adv.* सतर्कतापूर्वक

**guardian** /ˈgɑːdiən ˈगाडिअन्/ *noun* [C] **1** a person or institution that guards or protects sth किसी की रक्षा या बचाव करने वाला व्यक्ति या संगठन; संरक्षक *The police are the guardians of law and order.* **2** a person who is legally responsible for the care of another person, especially of a child whose parents are dead किसी अन्य (विशेषतः अनाथ बच्चा) की देखभाल के लिए क़ानूनी तौर पर उत्तरदायी व्यक्ति

**guava** /ˈgwɑːvə ˈग्वावा/ *noun* [C] the fruit of a tropical American tree, with yellow skin and a pink inside अमरूद

**guerrilla** (*also* **guerilla**) /gəˈrɪlə गˈरिला/ *noun* [C] a member of a small military group who are not part of an official army and who make surprise attacks on the enemy अधिकृत सेना से अलग एक छोटे सैन्य दल का सदस्य जो शत्रु पर अचानक आक्रमण करता है; गुरिल्ला

**guess[1]** /ges गेस्/ *verb* **1** [I, T] **guess (at sth)** to try to give an answer or make a judgement about sth without being sure of all the facts (किसी बात का) अनुमान करना *I'd guess that he's about 45.* ○ *If you're not sure of an answer, guess.* ○ *We can only guess at her reasons for leaving.* **2** [I, T] to give the correct answer when you are not sure about it; to guess correctly निश्चित न होने पर भी सही उत्तर देना; सही अनुमान लगाना *Can you guess my age?* ○ *You'll never guess what Ankur just told me!* ○ *Did I guess right?* **3** [T] (*AmE informal*) to imagine that sth is probably true or likely किसी बात को संभावित रूप से सच या संभव मानना *I guess you're tired after your long journey.* ✪ पर्याय **suppose** **4** [T] used to show that you are going to say sth surprising or exciting आश्चर्यकारी या उत्तेजनापूर्ण बात कहे जाने की तैयारी या भाव व्यक्त करने के लिए प्रयुक्त *Guess what! I'm getting married!*

**guess[2]** /ges गेस्/ *noun* [C] an effort you make to imagine a possible answer or give an opinion when you cannot be sure if you are right सही होने के निश्चय के बिना संभावित उत्तर की कल्पना या अपनी सम्मति देने का प्रयास, (किसी बात का) अंदाज़ा, अनुमान *I don't know how far it is, but* ***at a guess*** *I'd say about 50 kilometres.* ○ *I'd say it'll take about four hours, but that's just* ***a rough guess****.*

IDM **anybody's/anyone's guess** something that nobody can be certain about जिसके विषय में कोई भी निश्चित नहीं हो सकता *What's going to happen next is anybody's guess.*

**your guess is as good as mine** I do not know मालूम नहीं होना *'Where's Raj?' 'Your guess is as good as mine.'*

**guesswork** /ˈgeswɜːk गेस्वक्/ *noun* [U] an act of guessing अंदाज़ा या अनुमान लगाना; अटकलबाज़ी *I arrived at the answer* ***by pure guesswork****.*

**guest** /gest गेस्ट्/ *noun* [C] **1** a person who is invited to a place or to a special event विशेष स्थान या अवसर पर आमंत्रित व्यक्ति; अतिथि, मेहमान *wedding guests* ○ *Who is the guest speaker at the conference?* **2** a person who is staying at a hotel, etc. होटल आदि में ठहरा व्यक्ति *This hotel has accommodation for 500 guests.*

IDM **be my guest** (*informal*) used to give sb permission to do sth that he/she has asked to do किसी को उसकी माँगी हुई वस्तु देते समय प्रयुक्त अभिव्यक्ति *'Do you mind if I have a look at your newspaper?' 'Be my guest!'* अतिथि-गृह

**guest house** *noun* [C] a small hotel, sometimes in a private house अतिथि-गृह

**guidance** /ˈgaɪdns ˈगाइड्न्स्/ *noun* [U] **guidance (on sth)** help or advice सहायता या परामर्श *The centre offers guidance for unemployed people on how to find work.*

**guide**[1] /gaɪd गाइड्/ *noun* [C] **1** a book, magazine, etc. that gives information or help on a subject किसी विषय पर जानकारी या मदद देने वाली पुस्तक, पत्रिका आदि; गाइड *Your Guide to Using the Internet* **2** (*also* **guidebook**) a book that gives information about a place for travellers and tourists यात्रियों और पर्यटकों को किसी स्थान के विषय में जानकारी देने वाली पुस्तक; गाइड, संदर्शिका, कुंजी **3** a person who shows tourists or travellers where to go पर्यटकों या यात्रियों को बताने वाला व्यक्ति, गाइड; मार्गदर्शक *She works as a tour guide in Goa.* **4** something that helps you to judge or plan sth कुछ निश्चय करने या योजना बनाने में मददगार वस्तु ***As a rough guide**, use twice as much water as rice.* **5 Guide** a member of an organization **(the Guides)** that teaches girls practical skills and organizes activities such as camping शिविर लगाना आदि गतिविधियों को आयोजित करने वाली तथा लड़कियों को व्यावहारिक कौशलों का अभ्यास कराने वाली संस्था **the guides** की सदस्य NOTE लड़कों के लिए बने इसी प्रकार के संगठन को **the Scouts** कहते हैं।

**guide**[2] /gaɪd गाइड्/ *verb* [T] **1** to help a person or a group of people to find the way to a place; to show sb a place that you know well व्यक्ति या व्यक्ति समूह को कहीं जाने का रास्ता बताना; किसी को वह स्थान दिखाना जिसे आप जानते हैं *He guided us through the busy streets to our hotel.* ➪ **lead** पर नोट देखिए। **2** to have an influence on sb/sth व्यक्ति या वस्तु पर असर होना *I was guided by your advice.* **3** to help sb deal with sth difficult or complicated कठिन या पेचीदा स्थिति से निपटने में किसी की सहायता करना; मार्गदर्शन करना *The manual will guide you through every step of the procedure.* **4** to carefully move sb/sth or to help sb/sth to move in a particular direction विशेष दिशा में व्यक्ति या वस्तु को सावधानी से चलाना या हिलाना या उसमें मदद करना *A crane lifted the piano and two men carefully guided it through the window.*

**guided** /ˈgaɪdɪdˈगाइडिड्/ *adj.* led by a guide गाइड की अगुवाई में संपन्न, गाइड-निर्देशित *a guided tour/ walk*

**guideline** /ˈgaɪdlaɪnˈगाइड्लाइन्/ *noun* [C] **1** [*usually pl.*] official advice or rules on how to do sth कार्य करने संबंधी नियम या आधिकारिक परामर्श **2** something that can be used to help you make a decision or form an opinion निर्णय करने या राय स्थिर करने में सहायक वस्तु *These figures are a useful guideline when buying a house.*

**guild** /gɪld गिल्ड्/ *noun* [C, *with sing. or pl. verb*] **1** an organization of people who do the same job or who have the same interests or aims समान व्यवसाय, अभिरुचि या लक्ष्य वाले व्यक्तियों का संगठन; गिल्ड *the Screen Actors' Guild* **2** an association of skilled workers in the Middle Ages मध्यकाल में कुशल कारीगरों का संघ

**guile** /gʌɪl गाइल्/ *noun* [U] (*formal*) the ability to be clever but by using dishonest means छल-कपट, फ़रेब

**guillotine** /ˈgɪləti:nˈगिलटीन्/ *noun* [C] **1** a machine used for cutting paper काग़ज़ काटने की मशीन **2** a machine that was used in France in the past for cutting people's heads off विगत युग में फ्रांस में लोगों के सिर काटने के लिए व्यवहार में लाई गई मशीन; गिलोटिन ▶ **guillotine** *verb* [T] सिर या काग़ज़ काटना

**guilt** /gɪlt गिल्ट्/ *noun* [U] **1 guilt (about/at sth)** the bad feeling that you have when you know that you have done sth wrong ग़लत काम करने से उपजी प्रतिकूल भावना; दोष-भावना, अपराध-बोध *He sometimes had a sense of guilt about not spending more time with his children.* **2** the fact of having broken a law नियम-भंग; अपराध *We took his refusal to answer questions as an admission of guilt.* ✪ विलोम **innocence** **3** the responsibility for doing sth wrong or for sth bad that has happened; the blame for sth अनुचित काम करने या होने का दायित्व; दोषारोपण *It's difficult to say whether the guilt lies with the parents or the children.*

**guilty** /ˈgɪltiˈगिल्टि/ *adj.* **1 guilty (of sth)** having broken a law; being responsible for doing sth wrong क़ानून तोड़ने वाला; ग़लत काम करने वाला *She **pleaded guilty/not guilty** to the crime.* ○ *The jury **found** him **guilty** of fraud.* ✪ विलोम **innocent** **2 guilty (about sth)** having an unpleasant feeling because you have done sth bad अपराध-बोध से ग्रस्त *I **feel** really **guilty** about lying to Sameer.* ○ *It's hard to sleep with **a guilty conscience**.* ▶ **guiltily** *adv.* अपराध-बोध के साथ

**guinea pig** /ˈgɪni pɪgˈगिनि पिग्/ *noun* [C] **1** a small animal with no tail that is often kept as a pet बिना पूँछ का छोटा पालतू जानवर **2** a person who is used in an experiment व्यक्ति जिसे परीक्षण के लिए इस्तेमाल किया जाए *I volunteered to act as a guinea pig in their research.*

**guise** /gaɪz गाइज़्/ *noun* [C] a way in which sb/sth appears, which is often different from usual or hides the truth वास्तविक से भिन्न रूप; छद्म *The President was at the meeting **in his guise as** chairman of the charity.* ○ *His speech presented racist ideas **under the guise of** nationalism.*

**guitar** /gɪˈtɑ:(r) गिˈटा(र्)/*noun* [C] a type of musical instrument with strings that you play with your fingers or with a piece of plastic (**a plectrum**) गिटार, तारों वाला एक संगीत वाद्य जिसे अंगुलियों या प्लास्टिक खंड से बजाते हैं ➪ **piano** पर नोट देखिए तथा पृष्ठ 789 पर चित्र देखिए।

**guitarist** /gɪˈtɑːrɪst गिˈटारिस्ट्/ *noun* [C] a person who plays the guitar गिटार-वादक

**gulab jamun** *noun* [C] an Indian sweet that consists of deep fried balls of **dough** and milk soaked in rose-flavoured sugar syrup गुलाब जामुन

**gulf** /gʌlf गल्फ़्/ *noun* **1** [C] a part of the sea that is almost surrounded by land खाड़ी, अधिकांशतः भूमि से घिरा समुद्र का भाग *the Gulf of Mexico* **2 the Gulf** [*sing.*] (*informal*) a way of referring to the Persian Gulf फ़ारस की खाड़ी का एक और नाम **3** [C] an important or serious difference between people in the way they live, think or feel लोगों की सोच और रहन-सहन में मूलभूत अंतर, विचारों की खाई *the gulf between rich and poor*

**the Gulf Stream** *noun* [*sing.*] a warm current of water flowing across the Atlantic Ocean from the Gulf of Mexico towards Europe मेक्सिको की खाड़ी से अटलांटिक महासागर होते हुए यूरोप को जाने वाली उष्ण जलधारा; खाड़ीधारा, गल्फ़ स्ट्रीम

**gull** /gʌl गल्/ (*also* **seagull**) *noun* [C] a white or grey sea bird that makes a loud noise ऊँचा बोलने वाला एक सफ़ेद या स्लेटी समुद्री पक्षी; सामुद्रिक पक्षी ➪ **seabird** पर चित्र देखिए।

**gullet** /ˈgʌlɪt ˈगलिट्/ *noun* [C] the tube through which food passes from your mouth to your stomach मुख से आमाशय को जाने वाली आहार-नली **NOTE** इस अर्थ में अधिक औपचारिक शब्द **oesophagus** है। ➪ **body** पर चित्र देखिए।

**gullible** /ˈgʌləbl ˈगलबल्/ *adj.* (used about a person) believing and trusting people too easily, and therefore easily tricked (व्यक्ति) दूसरों पर शीघ्र विश्वास करने और अतएव धोखा खाने वाला; भोला-भाला

**gully** /ˈgʌli ˈगलि/ *noun* [C] (*pl.* **gullies**) a small, narrow passage or valley, usually formed by a **stream** or by rain छोटा सँकरा रास्ता या घाटी (जो प्रायः जलधारा या वर्षाजल से बन जाता है), बरसाती नाला

**gulmohar** *noun* [C] an exotic deciduous tree bearing masses of reddish-orange flowers गुलमोहर वृक्ष

**gulp¹** /gʌlp गल्प्/ *verb* **1** [I, T] **gulp sth (down); gulp (for) sth** to swallow large amounts of food, drink, etc. quickly बड़ी मात्रा में खाने-पीने की चीजों को निगल जाना; गटगटाना *He gulped down his breakfast and went out.* ○ *She finally came to the surface, desperately gulping (for) air.* **2** [I] to make a swallowing movement because you are afraid, surprised, etc. भय या आश्चर्य के कारण गटागट निगल जाना

**gulp²** /gʌlp गल्प्/ *noun* [C] **1** the action of breathing in or swallowing sth साँस लेने या निगलने की क्रिया *I drank my coffee **in one gulp** and ran out of the door.* **2 a gulp (of sth)** the amount that you swallow when you gulp वह मात्रा जो निगली जाए; कौर, ग्रास, घूँट

**gum** /gʌm गम्/ *noun* **1** [C] either of the firm pink parts of your mouth that hold your teeth मसूड़ा **2** [U] a substance that you use to stick things together (especially pieces of paper) गोंद, वस्तुओं (विशेषतः काग़ज़ों) को परस्पर चिपकाने वाला पदार्थ **3** = **chewing gum** ➪ **bubblegum** देखिए।

**gun¹** /gʌn गन्/ *noun* [C] **1** a weapon that is used for shooting बंदूक़ *The robber held a gun to the bank manager's head.*

> **NOTE** **'Gun'** के साथ प्रायः प्रयुक्त क्रियाएँ हैं **load, unload, point, aim, fire.** विभिन्न प्रकार की बंदूक़ों के नाम हैं **machine gun, pistol, revolver, rifle, shotgun.**

**2** a tool that uses pressure to send out a substance or an object पिचकारी *a grease gun* ○ *a staple gun*
**IDM** **jump the gun** ➪ **jump¹** देखिए।

**gun²** /gʌn गन्/ *verb* [T] (**gu<u>n</u>ning; gu<u>n</u>ned**)
**PHR V** **gun sb down** (*informal*) to shoot and kill or seriously injure sb किसी को गोली मारना या गंभीर रूप से घायल करना

**gunboat** /ˈgʌnbəʊt ˈगन्बोट्/ *noun* [C] a small ship used in war that carries heavy guns तोपों वाला युद्धपोत; तोपनाव

**gunfire** /ˈgʌnfaɪə(r) ˈगन्फ़ाइअ(र्)/ *noun* [U] the repeated firing of guns गोलीबारी, या गोलियों की बौछार *We could hear gunfire in the streets.*

**gunman** /ˈgʌnmən ˈगन्मन्/ *noun* [C] (*pl.* **-men** /-mən -मन्/) a man who uses a gun to rob or kill people बंदूक़ की नोक पर लोगों को लूटने या मारने वाला; सशस्त्र डाकू

**gunnysack** /ˈgʌnisæk ˈगनिसैक्/ *noun* [C] a big strong bag made of rough material such as jute fibre and used for carrying or storing things like grains, potatoes, sand, etc. टाट, बोरा

**gunpoint** /ˈgʌnpɔɪnt ˈगन्पॉइन्ट्/ *noun*
**IDM** **at gunpoint** threatening to shoot sb बंदूक़ का भय दिखाना *He held the hostages at gunpoint.*

**gunpowder** /ˈgʌnpaʊdə(r) ˈगन्पाउड(र्)/ *noun* [U] an explosive powder that is used in guns, etc. तोपों या बंदूक़ों में प्रयुक्त विस्फोटक; बारूद

**gunshot** /ˈgʌnʃɒt ˈगन्‌शॉट्/ *noun* [C] the firing of a gun or the sound that it makes तोप या बंदूक़ की मार की सीमा या आवाज़

**gurdwara** *noun* [C] a Sikh place of worship गुरुद्वारा

**gurgle** /ˈgɜːgl ˈगगूल्/ *verb* [I] **1** to make a sound like water flowing quickly through a narrow space गड़गड़ की ध्वनि (मानो पानी तेज़ी से सँकरे मार्ग से बह रहा है) *a gurgling stream* **2** if a baby gurgles, it makes a noise in its throat because it is happy बच्चे का गले से गरगर की आवाज़ निकालना (बच्चे की प्रसन्नता का द्योतक) ▶ **gurgle** *noun* [C] गड़गड़, गरगर, गरारा

**guru** /ˈgʊruː ˈगुरू/ *noun* [C] **1** a spiritual leader or teacher in the Hindu religion गुरु, हिंदू धर्म में आध्यात्मिक नेता या शिक्षक **2** somebody whose opinions you admire and respect, and whose ideas you follow आदरणीय और अनुकरणीय व्यक्ति *a management/fashion guru*

**Guru Granth Sahib** (*also* **the Granth Sahib**) *noun* the sacred book of the Sikhs ग्रंथ साहिब, सिक्खों का धार्मिक ग्रंथ

**gush** /gʌʃ गश्/ *verb* **1** [I] **gush (out of/from/into sth); gush out/in** (used about a liquid) to flow out suddenly and in great quantities (द्रव का) बड़ी मात्रा में एकाएक बाहर निकलना *Blood gushed from the wound.* ○ *I turned the tap on and water gushed out.* **2** [T] (used about a container/vehicle, etc.) to produce large amounts of a liquid (किसी डिब्बे या वाहन में से) बड़ी मात्रा में द्रव पदार्थ का बहना *The broken pipe was gushing water all over the road.* **3** [I, T] to express pleasure or admiration too much so that it does not sound sincere अत्यधिक (प्रायः झूठी) प्रसन्नता या प्रशंसा व्यक्त करना ▶ **gush** *noun* [C] धार; सहसा तेज़ बहाव *a sudden gush of water*

**gust** /gʌst गस्ट्/ *noun* [C] a sudden strong wind तेज़ हवा का झकोरा ▶ **gust** *verb* [I] वायु का (झोंकों में) बहना

**gusto** /ˈgʌstəʊ ˈगस्टो/ *noun*

IDM **with gusto** with great enthusiasm भरपूर उत्साह के साथ

**gut¹** /gʌt गट्/ *noun* **1** [C] the tube in your body that food passes through when it leaves your stomach आँत, अँतड़ी ➪ **intestine** देखिए। **2 guts** [*pl.*] the organs in and around the stomach, especially of an animal उदर के चारों ओर के अंग (विशेषतः पशु में) **3 guts** [*pl.*] (*informal*) courage and determination साहस और दृढ़ निश्चय ***takes guts*** *to admit that you are wrong.* ○ *I don't* ***have the guts*** *to tell my boss what he's doing wrong.* **4** [C] a person's fat stomach व्यक्ति का फूला हुआ पेट, व्यक्ति की भारी तोंद *a beer gut* (= caused by drinking beer)

IDM **work/sweat your guts out** to work extremely hard अत्यधिक परिश्रम करना

**gut²** /gʌt गट्/ *verb* [T] (**gutting; gutted**) **1** to remove the organs from inside an animal, fish, etc. किसी पशु के अंदर के अंग या अँतड़ियाँ निकाल देना **2** to destroy the inside of a building भवन का अंदरूनी भाग नष्ट कर देना *The warehouse was gutted by fire.*

**gut³** /gʌt गट्/ *adj.* (*only before a noun*) based on emotion or feeling rather than on reason (तर्क के स्थान पर) भावनाओं पर आधारित *a gut feeling/reaction*

**gutter** /ˈgʌtə(r) ˈगट(र्)/ *noun* [C] **1** a long piece of metal or plastic with a curved bottom that is fixed to the edge of a roof to carry away the water when it rains वर्षा का पानी निकालने वाला धातु या प्लास्टिक का पाइप; परनाला, मोरी **2** a lower part at the edge of a road along which the water flows away when it rains सड़क के साथ बनी बरसाती पानी की नाली **3** the very lowest level of society समाज का दरिद्रतम स्तर *She rose from the gutter to become a great star.*

**guy** /gaɪ गाइ/ *noun* **1** [C] (*informal*) a man or a boy व्यक्ति या लड़का *He's a nice guy.* **2 guys** [*pl.*] (*informal*) used when speaking to a group of men and women लोगों का समूह *What do you guys want to eat?* **3** [*sing.*] (*BrE*) a model of a man that is burned on 5 November in memory of Guy Fawkes गाई फ़ॉक्स की स्मृति में 5 नवंबर को जलाया जाने वाला मानव-पुतला

**guzzle** /ˈgʌzl ˈगज़ल्/ *verb* [I, T] (*informal*) to eat or drink too fast and too much बहुत तेज़ी से बहुत मात्रा में खाना या पीना

**gym** /dʒɪm जिम्/ *noun* **1** (*formal* **gymnasium**) [C] a large room or a building with equipment for doing physical exercise शारीरिक व्यायाम करने के लिए उपकरण-युक्त कमरा या भवन; जिम, व्यायामशाला *I work out at the gym twice a week.* **2** [U] = **gymnastics** *gym shoes*

**gymkhana** *noun* [C] **1** a sports event in which people (especially on horses) compete in races and jumping competitions जिमखाना; एक खेल जिसमें प्रतियोगी (विशेषकर घोड़ों पर सवार होकर) दौड़ या घुड़दौड़ प्रतियोगिताओं में स्पर्धा करते हैं **2** (*IndE*) a public place with facilities for sports खेलकूद के लिए सार्वजनिक सुविधा स्थल; जिम

**gymnasium** /dʒɪmˈneɪziəm जिम्ˈनेज़िअम्/ *noun* [C] (*pl.* **gymnasiums** or **gymnasia** /-zɪə -ज़िआ/) = **gym 1**

**gymnast** /ˈdʒɪmnæst ˈजिमनैस्ट्/ *noun* [C] a person who does gymnastics व्यायाम करने वाला व्यक्ति; व्यायामी

**gymnastics** /dʒɪmˈnæstɪks जिमˈनैस्टिक्स्/ (*also* **gym**) *noun* [U] physical exercises that are done indoors, often using special equipment such as bars and ropes घर के अंदर प्रायः उपकरणों का प्रयोग करते हुए किया गया व्यायाम; जिमनास्टिक्स

**gynaecology** (*AmE* **gynecology**) /ˌgaɪnəˈkɒlədʒi ˌगाइनˈकॉलजि/ *noun* [U] the study and treatment of the diseases and medical problems of women स्त्री-रोग विज्ञान ▶ **gynaecological** (*AmE* **gyne-**) /ˌgaɪnəkəˈlɒdʒɪkl ˌगाइनकˈलॉजिकल्/ *adj.* स्त्री-रोग संबंधी ▶ **gynaecologist** (*AmE* **gyne-**) /ˌgaɪnəˈkɒlədʒɪst ˌगाइनˈकॉलजिस्ट्/ *noun* [C] स्त्री-रोग विशेषज्ञ

**gypsum** /ˈdʒɪpsəm ˈजिप्सम्/ *noun* [U] a soft white rock like chalk that is used in the building industry भवन-निर्माण के लिए प्रयुक्त खड़ियाँ जैसा सफ़ेद मुलायम खनिज; जिप्सम, चिरोड़ी

**gypsy** (*also* **gipsy**) /ˈdʒɪpsi ˈजिप्सि/ *noun* [C] (*pl.* **gypsies**) a member of a race of people who traditionally spend their lives travelling around from place to place, living in **caravans** पहिएदार घरों के साथ स्थान-स्थान पर घूमने वाली जाति का सदस्य; जिप्सी, घुमंतू, ख़ानाबदोश, बनजारा ➪ **traveller** देखिए।

**gyroscope** /ˈdʒaɪrəskəʊp ˈजाइरस्कोप्/ (*informal* **gyro**) /ˈdʒaɪrəʊ ˈजाइरो/ *noun* [C] a device consisting of a wheel that turns very quickly inside a frame and does not change position when the frame is moved चौखटे में जड़ा तेज़ी से घूमने वाला पहिएदार उपकरण (जो चौखटे के घूमने पर भी स्थिर रहता है), जाइरोस्कोप, घूर्णाक्षदर्शी

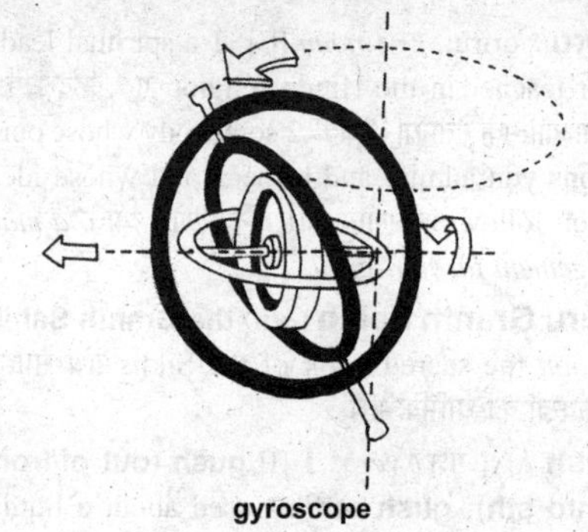
gyroscope

# H h

**H, h** /eɪtʃ एच्/ *noun* [C, U] (*pl.* **H's; h's** /ˈeɪtʃɪz एचिज़्/) the eighth letter of the English alphabet अंग्रेज़ी वर्णमाला का आठवाँ अक्षर *'Hat' begins with an 'H'*

**ha**[1] /hɑː हा/ *exclamation* **1** used for showing that you are surprised or pleased आश्चर्य या ख़ुशी प्रकट करने के लिए प्रयुक्त *Ha! I knew he was hiding something!* **2 ha! ha!** used in written language to show that sb is laughing हँसते समय मुँह से निकलने वाली ध्वनि का लिखित रूप, हा-हा

**ha**[2] *abbr.* hectare(s) हेक्टेअर

**habit** /ˈhæbɪt ˈहैबिट्/ *noun* **1** [C] **a/the habit (of doing sth)** something that you do often and almost without thinking, especially sth that is hard to stop doing आदत, अभ्यास, ऐसी बात जिसे हम प्रायः बिना पूर्व विचार के करें और जिसे रोकना कठिन हो *I'm trying to **get into the habit** of hanging up my clothes every night.* ○ *Once you start smoking it's hard to break the habit.* ➪ **habitual** adjective देखिए।

NOTE किसी एक व्यक्ति की आदत को **habit** कहते हैं और किसी एक समूह, समुदाय के आदतों के विषय में बात करें तो शब्द **custom** प्रयुक्त होता है—*the custom of giving presents at Christmas*

**2** [U] usual behaviour सामान्य व्यवहार *I think I only smoke **out of habit** now I don't really enjoy it.*

IDM **force of habit** ➪ **force**[1] देखिए।

**kick the habit** ➪ **kick**[1] देखिए।

**habitable** /ˈhæbɪtəbl ˈहैबिटबल्/ *adj.* (used about buildings) suitable to be lived in (भवन) रहने लायक ✪ विलोम **uninhabitable**

**habitat** /ˈhæbɪtæt ˈहैबिटैट्/ *noun* [C] the natural home of a plant or an animal किसी पौधे या पशु का प्राकृतिक आवास *I've seen wolves in the zoo, but not in their natural habitat.*

**habitation** /ˌhæbɪˈteɪʃn ˌहैबिˈटेशन्/ *noun* [U] (*formal*) living in a place किसी स्थान पर रहने की क्रिया; निवास, रिहाइश

**habitual** /həˈbɪtʃuəl हˈबिचुअल्/ *adj.* **1** doing sth very often आदतन कुछ करने वाला, आदी, अभ्यस्त *a habitual liar* **2** which you always have or do; usual जिसे करने के आप आदी या अभ्यस्त हैं; नियमित *He had his habitual cigarette after lunch.* ▶ **habitually** /-tʃuəli -चुअलि/ *adv.* नियमित रूप से; आदतन, अभ्यासवश

**hack** /hæk हैक्/ *verb* [I, T] **1 hack (away) (at) sth** to cut sth in a rough way with a tool such as a large knife चाक़ू आदि से किसी वस्तु को काट डालना *He hacked at the branch of the tree until it fell.* **2** (*informal*) **hack (into) (sth)** to use a computer to look at and/or change information that is stored on another computer without permission बिना अनुमति के एक कंप्यूटर में संचित सूचना की दूसरे कंप्यूटर द्वारा चोरी करना

**hacker** /ˈhækə(r) ˈहैक(र्)/ *noun* [C] (*informal*) a person who uses a computer to look at and/or change information on another computer without permission कंप्यूटर संचित सूचना की चोरी करने वाला व्यक्ति; हैकर

**hacksaw** /ˈhæksɔː ˈहैक्सॉ/ *noun* [C] a tool with a narrow cutting edge in a frame, used for cutting metal धातुओं को काटने वाली आरी

**had**[1] /hæd; हैड्;/ ➪ **have** का past tense और past participle रूप

**had**[2] /hæd हैड्/ *adj.*

IDM **be had** (*informal*) to be tricked धोखा खाना *I've been had. This watch I bought doesn't work.*

**haddock** /ˈhædək ˈहैडक्/ *noun* [C, U] (*pl.* **haddock**) a sea fish that you can eat and that lives in the North Atlantic उत्तर अटलांटिक में पाई जाने वाली खाने की समुद्री मछली; हैडक

**hadn't** ➪ **had not** का संक्षिप्त रूप

**haematite** (*AmE* **hematite**) /ˈhiːmətaɪt ˈहीमटाइट्/ *noun* [U] a dark red rock from which we get iron गहरी लाल चट्टान जिससे लोहा मिलता है

**haemo-** (*AmE* **hemo-**) /ˈhiːməʊ ˈहीमो/ *prefix* (*in nouns and adjectives*) connected with blood रक्तविषयक *haemophilia*

**haemoglobin** (*AmE* **hemoglobin**) /ˌhiːməˈɡləʊbɪn ˌहीमˈग्लोबिन्/ *noun* [U] a red substance in the blood that carries the gas we need to live (**oxygen**) and contains iron रक्त में उपलब्ध लाल कण जिनमें लोहा होता है और जो ऑक्सीजन का वहन करते हैं

**haemophilia** (*AmE* **hemophilia**) /ˌhiːməˈfɪliə ˌहीमˈफ़िलिआ/ *noun* [U] a disease that causes a person to bleed a lot even from very small injuries because the blood does not **clot** अधिक रक्तस्राव का रोग (क्योंकि ख़ून का थक्का नहीं बनता)

**haemophiliac** (*AmE* **hemophiliac**) /ˌhiːməˈfɪliæk ˌहीमˈफ़िलिऐक्/ *noun* [C] a person who suffers from haemophilia अधिक रक्तस्राव का रोगी

**haemorrhage** (*AmE* **hemorrhage**) /ˈhemərɪdʒ ˈहेमरिज्/ *noun* [C, U] a lot of bleeding inside the body शरीर के अंदर अत्यधिक रक्त बहना; आंतरिक रक्तस्राव ▶ **haemorrhage** *verb* [I] शरीर के अंदर रक्तस्राव होना

**haemorrhoids** (*AmE* **hemorrhoids**) /ˈhemərɔɪdz ˈहेमरॉइड्ज़्/ (*also* **piles**) *noun* [*pl.*] a medical condition in which the tubes that carry blood (**veins**) to the opening where waste food leaves the body (**the anus**) swell and become painful बवासीर; अर्श; गुदा द्वार तक रक्त ले जाने वाली नलिकाओं में सूजन और दर्द

**haggard** /ˈhægəd ˈहैगड्/ *adj.* (used about a person) looking tired or worried (व्यक्ति) देखने में थका हुआ और चिंतित

**haggle** /ˈhægl ˈहैग्ल्/ *verb* [I] **haggle (with sb) (over/about sth)** to argue with sb until you reach an agreement, especially about the price of sth मोल-भाव करना (विशेषतः किसी वस्तु के दाम के विषय में) *In the market, some tourists were haggling over the price of a carpet.*

**haiku** /ˈhaɪkuː ˈहाइकू/ *noun* [C] (*pl.* **haiku** or **haikus**) a Japanese poem with three lines of five, seven and five syllables तीन पंक्तियों और प्रायः पाँच, सात और पाँच मात्राओं वाली विशेष प्रकार की जापानी कविता; हाइकू

**hail¹** /heɪl हेल्/ *verb* **1** [T] **hail sb/sth as sth** to proclaim that sb/sth is very good or very special व्यक्ति या वस्तु की सार्वजनिक रूप से प्रशंसा करना *The book was hailed as a masterpiece.* **2** [T] to call or wave to sb/sth किसी व्यक्ति या वस्तु को पुकारकर या हाथ के इशारे से बुलाना *to hail a taxi* **3** [I] when it hails, small balls of ice fall from the sky like rain आकाश से ओले गिरना ➪ **weather** पर नोट देखिए।

**hail²** /heɪl हेल्/ *noun* **1** [U] small balls of ice (**hailstones**) that fall from the sky like rain ओले **2** [*sing.*] **a hail of sth** a large amount of sth that is aimed at sb in order to harm him/her किसी व्यक्ति को हानि पहुँचाने के लिए उसे लक्ष्य बना कर किसी वस्तु की भारी बौछार *a hail of bullets/stones/abuse*

**hair** /heə(r) हेअ(र्)/ *noun* **1** [U, C] the mass of long thin strands that grow on the head and body of people and animals; one such strand बाल, केश *He has got short black hair.* ○ *Dinesh's losing his hair* (= going bald). ○ *The dog left hairs all over the furniture.* ➪ **body** पर चित्र देखिए। **2 -haired** *adj.* (*used in compounds*) having the type of hair mentioned निर्दिष्ट प्रकार के बालों वाला *a dark-haired woman* ○ *a long-haired dog*

**NOTE** बालों के रंगों के लिए कुछ विशेष शब्द **auburn, blonde, dark, fair, ginger** और **red** हैं। बालों की देखरेख और सजावट (केशचर्या और केश रचना) की क्रमशः कई क्रियाएँ प्रयुक्त की जाती हैं **brush, comb, wash** या **shampoo** और इसके बाद **blow-dry**। आप बालों को बीच में से या किनारे से **part** (या बालों की **parting**) कर सकते हैं। केश प्रसाधक (**hairdresser**) से आप बालों को **cut** या **perm** करवा सकते हैं।

**3** a very thin thread-like structure that grows on the surface of some plants कुछ पौधों पर उगने वाले रोएँ *The leaves and stem are covered in fine hairs.*

**IDM keep your hair on** (*spoken*) (used to tell sb to stop shouting and become less angry) calm down किसी को चुप होने के लिए या शांत हो जाने के लिए कहने हेतु प्रयुक्त

**let your hair down** (*informal*) to relax and enjoy yourself after being formal आराम फ़रमाना

**make sb's hair stand on end** to frighten or shock sb किसी को डरा देना, स्तब्ध कर देना या सदमा पहुँचाना

**not turn a hair** to not show any reaction to sth that many people would find surprising or shocking आश्चर्यजनक और स्तब्धकारी मानी जाने वाली बात पर कोई प्रतिक्रिया न दिखाना

**split hairs** ➪ **split¹** देखिए।

**hairbrush** /ˈheəbrʌʃ ˈहेअब्रश्/ *noun* [C] a brush that you use on your hair बालों का ब्रश

**haircut** /ˈheəkʌt ˈहेअकट्/ *noun* [C] **1** the act of sb cutting your hair बालकटाई, हजामत, केशकर्त्तन *You need (to have) a haircut.* **2** the style in which your hair has been cut केश-रचना, केश-विन्यास *That haircut really suits you.*

**hairdo** /ˈheədu: ˈहेअडू/ (*informal*) = **hairstyle**

**hairdresser** /ˈheədresə(r) ˈहेअड्रेस(र्)/ *noun* **1** [C] a person whose job is to cut, shape, colour, etc. hair केश-प्रसाधक, नाई, हज्जाम, केशकर्मी, हेअरड्रेसर

**NOTE** पुरुषों का और स्वयं पुरुष नाई **barber** कहलाता है।

**2 (the hairdresser's)** [*sing.*] the place where you go to have your hair cut केश-प्रसाधन केंद्र, नाई की दुकान

**hairdryer** (*also* **hairdrier**) /ˈheədraɪə(r) ˈहेअड्राइअ(र्)/ *noun* [C] a machine that dries hair by blowing hot air through it बाल सुखाने वाली मशीन

**hairgrip** /ˈheəgrɪp ˈहेअग्रिप्/ *noun* [C] a U-shaped pin that is used for holding the hair in place बालों को सँभालने की U-आकृति की पिन

**hairless** /ˈheələs ˈहेअलस् / *adj.* without hair केशहीन ➪ **bald** देखिए।

**hairline¹** /ˈheəlaɪn ˈहेअलाइन् / *noun* [C] the place on a person's forehead where his/her hair begins to grow वह रेखा जहाँ से व्यक्ति के बाल शुरू होते हैं

**hairline²** /ˈheəlaɪn ˈहेअलाइन् / *adj.* (used about a crack in sth) very thin (दरार) बहुत बारीक *a hairline fracture of the bone*

**hairpin bend** /ˌheəpɪn ˈbend ˌहेअपिन् ˈबेन्ड् / *noun* [C] (*BrE*) a very sharp bend in a road, especially a mountain road सड़क पर तीखा या तीव्र मोड़ (विशेषत: पहाड़ी सड़क पर)

**hair-raising** *adj.* sth that makes you very frightened बहुत डरावना, रोमांचकारी, रोंगटे खड़े करने वाला *a hair-raising experience*

**hairspray** /ˈheəspreɪ ˈहेअस्प्रे / *noun* [U, C] a substance you spray onto your hair to hold it in place वह पदार्थ जिसे बालों को बाँधकर रखने के लिए उन पर छिड़का जाता है; हेअरस्प्रे ✪ पर्याय **lacquer**

**hairstyle** /ˈheəstaɪl ˈहेअस्टाइल् / (*informal* **hairdo**) *noun* [C] the style in which your hair has been cut or arranged बालों को काटने और सजाने का ढंग; केश-विन्यास शैली

**hairstylist** /ˈheəstaɪlɪst ˈहेअस्टाइलिस्ट् / (*also* **stylist**) *noun* [C] a person whose job is to cut and shape sb's hair बालों को काटने तथा सजाने वाला व्यक्ति; केश-प्रसाधक

**hairy** /ˈheəri ˈहेअरि / *adj.* (**hairier; hairiest**) **1** having a lot of hair बालों से भरा; रोमिल, रोएँदार **2** (*slang*) dangerous or worrying ख़तरनाक या चिंताजनक

**hajj** (*also* **haj**) *noun* [*sing.*] the religious journey (**pilgrimage**) to Mecca that many Muslims make मक्का की तीर्थयात्रा; हज

**half¹** /hɑːf हाफ़् / *det., noun* [C] (*pl.* **halves** /hɑːvz हाव़्ज़् /) one of two equal parts of sth आधा, किसी वस्तु के दो समान भागों में से एक *Beckham scored in the first half* (= of a match). ○ *Half the people in the office leave at 5 p.m.* ➪ **halve** verb देखिए।

IDM **break, cut, etc. sth in half** to break, etc. sth into two parts किसी वस्तु को दो टुकड़ों में बाँटना

**do nothing/not do anything by halves** to do whatever you do completely and properly किसी काम को पूर्ण तथा उचित रूप से करना

**go half and half/go halves with sb** to share the cost of sth with sb किसी वस्तु की लागत को आधा-आधा कर लेना

**half²** /hɑːf हाफ़् / *adv.* not completely; to the amount of half पूरा नहीं; आधी मात्रा में ***half full*** ○ *The hotel was only **half finished**.* ○ *He's half German* (= one of his parents is German).

IDM **half past** (in time) 30 minutes past an hour (समय) पूरे घंटे के बाद 30 मिनट, साढ़े (चार, पाँच, छह आदि) *half past six* (= 6.30)

**not half as much, many, good, bad, etc.** much less बहुत कम *This episode wasn't half as good as the last.*

**half-baked** *adj.* (*informal*) not well planned or considered अधपका, अधकचरा, सुनियोजित या सुविचारित नहीं *a half-baked idea/scheme*

**half board** *noun* [U] (*BrE*) a price for a room in a hotel, etc. which includes breakfast and an evening meal होटल आदि के कमरे का किराया जिसमें नाश्ता और एक सायंकालीन भोजन शामिल होता है ➪ **full board** और **bed and breakfast** देखिए।

**half-brother** *noun* [C] a brother with whom you share one parent सौतेला भाई ➪ **stepbrother** देखिए।

**half-hearted** *adj.* without interest or enthusiasm बेमन से किया गया; उत्साहहीन ▶**half-heartedly** *adv.* बेमन से

**half-life** *noun* [C] (*technical*) the time taken for the **radioactivity** of a substance to fall to half its original value किसी वस्तु की रेडियो-सक्रियता के आधा रह जाने में लगने वाला समय; अर्ध आयु

**half note** (*AmE*) = **minim**

**half-sister** *noun* [C] a sister with whom you share one parent सौतेली बहन ➪ **stepsister** देखिए।

**half-term** *noun* [C] (*BrE*) a holiday of one week in the middle of a three-month period of school (**term**) स्कूल के तीन महीने के सत्र के मध्य में एक सप्ताह का अवकाश

**half-time** *noun* [U] (in sport) the period of time between the two halves of a match (खेल में) एक मैच के दो अर्धांशों के बीच का समय, हाफ़-टाइम; मध्यकाल, अर्धकाल

**halfway** /ˌhɑːfˈweɪ ˌहाफ़् ˈवे / *adj., adv.* at an equal distance between two places; in the middle of a period of time दो स्थानों के बीच बराबर की दूरी पर, आधे रास्ते में; एक समयावधि के मध्य में, बीचोंबीच *They have a break halfway through the morning.* ✪ पर्याय **midway**

**hall** /hɔːl हॉल् / *noun* [C] **1** (*also* **hallway**) a room or passage that is just inside the front entrance of a house or public building किसी मकान या सार्वजनिक भवन के मुख्य द्वार से अंदर आने पर मिलने

वाला कमरा या गलियारा *There is a public telephone in the **entrance hall** of this building.* **2** a building or large room in which meetings, concerts, dances, etc. can be held एक भवन या बड़ा कमरा जहाँ सभा आदि हो सकती है; हॉल *a concert hall* ➪ **town hall** देखिए।

**hallmark** /ˈhɔːlmɑːk ˈहॉल्‌माक्/ *noun* [C] **1** a characteristic that is typical of sb किसी का प्रातिनिधिक लक्षण *The ability to motivate students is the hallmark of a good teacher.* **2** a mark that is put on objects made of valuable metals, giving information about the quality of the metal and when and where the object was made मूल्यवान धातुओं से बनी वस्तुओं पर अंकित चिह्न जिसमें धातु की गुणवत्ता तथा वस्तु के निर्माण केंद्र की सूचना होती है

**hallo** = **hello**

**hall of residence** *noun* [C] (*pl.* **halls of residence**) (*AmE* **dormitory**) (in colleges, universities, etc.) a building where students live (कॉलेज, विश्वविद्यालय आदि का) छात्रावास

**Hallowe'en** /ˌhæləʊˈiːn ˌहैलोˈईन्/ *noun* [*sing.*] (especially in the US) (*also* **Halloween**) the night of October 31st (before All Saints' Day) (ऑल सेंट्स डे से पहले) 31 अक्तूबर की रात्रि

**NOTE** लोगों का मानना है कि हैलोवीन के समय ही जादूगरनियाँ और भूत प्रकट होते हैं। बच्चे भूत आदि बनकर लोगों को ठगने का मज़ाक करते हैं। अमेरिका में बच्चे घर-घर जाकर **'trick or treat'** कहते हैं और लोग उन्हें मिठाई देते हैं।

**hallucination** /həˌluːsɪˈneɪʃn हˌलूसिˈनेश्‌न्/ *noun* [C, U] seeing or hearing sth that is not really there (because you are ill or have taken a drug) (बीमारी या नशे में होने वाला) दृष्टिभ्रम या मतिभ्रम, (ऐसी बातें देखना या सुनना जो वस्तुतः हैं नहीं); निर्मूलभ्रम

**hallucinogen** /ˌhæˈluːsɪnədʒən ˌहैˈलूसिनजन्/ *noun* [C] a drug that affects people's minds and makes them see and hear things that are not really there दृष्टिभ्रम या मतिभ्रम कराने वाली दवाई ▶ **hallucinogenic** /həˌluːsɪnəˈdʒenɪk हैˌलूसिनˈजनिक्/ *adj.* दृष्टिभ्रमकारी *hallucinogenic drugs*

**hallway** /ˈhɔːlweɪ ˈहॉल्‌वे/ = **hall**

**halo** /ˈheɪləʊ ˈहेलो/ *noun* [C] (*pl.* **halos** or **haloes**) the circle of light shown around the head of an important religious person in a painting or the ring of light around heavenly bodies चित्रों में महापुरुषों के सिर के चारों ओर बना प्रकाशवृत्त, प्रभामंडल या आकाशीय पिंड (सूर्य, चंद्रमा, तारे आदि) के चारों ओर का परिवेश

**halogen** /ˈhælədʒən ˈहैलजन्/ *noun* [C] any of five chemical substances that are not metals and that combine with **hydrogen** to form strong acid compounds from which simple salts can be made (धातुओं से भिन्न) पाँच रसायनों में से कोई एक जिसके हाइड्रोजन के साथ मिलने से शक्तिशाली अम्ल बनते हैं जिनसे अकृत्रिम नमक बनाया जा सकता है *The halogens are fluorine, chlorine, bromine, iodine and astatine.*

**halt** /hɔːlt हॉल्ट्/ *noun* [*sing.*] a short stop in some activity, movement or growth (कार्य, गतिविधि या विकास प्रक्रिया में) लघु विराम या रुकाव *Work **came to a halt** when the machine broke down.* ▶ **halt** *verb* [I, T] (*formal*) रोकना *An accident halted the traffic in the town centre for half an hour.*

**IDM** **grind to a halt/standstill** ➪ **grind**[1] देखिए।

**halter** /ˈhɔːltə(r) ˈहॉल्‌ट(र्)/ *noun* [C] **1** a rope or leather strap put around the head of a horse for leading it with घोड़े की गरदन में बाँधी जाने वाली रस्सी या चमड़े की पट्टी **2** (*usually used as an adjective*) a strap around the neck that holds a woman's dress or shirt in position without the back and shoulders being covered महिला की पोशाक या कमीज़ को थामने वाली पट्टी जो पीठ या कंधे को नहीं ढकती

**halve** /hɑːv हाव्/ *verb* **1** [I, T] to reduce by a half; to make sth reduce by a half आधा कम हो जाना; किसी चीज़ को आधा कम कर देना, अधियाना *Shares in the company have halved in value.* ○ *We aim to halve the number of people on our waiting list in the next six months.* **2** to divide sth into two equal parts किसी चीज़ को आधा-आधा बाँटना *First halve the peach and then remove the stone.*

**ham** /hæm हैम्/ *noun* [U] meat from a pig's back leg that has been smoked, etc. (**cured**) to keep it fresh सूअर की पिछली टाँग का मांस जिसे ताज़ा रखने के लिए धुँआरा जाता है

**hamburger** /ˈhæmbɜːɡə(r) ˈहैम्‌बग(र्)/ *noun* **1** (*also* **burger**) [C] meat that has been cut up small and pressed into a flat round shape. Hamburgers are often eaten in a bread roll मांस के टुकड़ों को दबाकर बनाई गई चपटी गोल टिक्की (इसे डबलरोटी में लपेट कर खाया जाता है); हैमबर्गर **2** [U] (*AmE*) = **mince**

**hamlet** /ˈhæmlət ˈहैम्‌लट्/ *noun* [C] a very small village बहुत छोटा गाँव; पुरवा, उपग्राम

**hammer**[1] /ˈhæmə(r) ˈहैम(र्)/ *noun* [C] a tool with a heavy metal head that is used for hitting nails, etc. हथौड़ा ➪ **tool** पर चित्र देखिए।

**hammer**[2] /ˈhæmə(r) ˈहैम(र्)/ *verb* **1** [I, T] **hammer sth (in/into/onto sth)** to hit with a hammer

हथौड़े से ठोकना *She hammered the nail into the wall.* **2** [I] to hit sth several times, making a loud noise ऊँची आवाज़ पैदा करते हुए बार-बार प्रहार करना

IDM **hammer sth into sb** to force sb to remember sth by repeating it many times किसी बात को बार-बार कहकर उसे याद कराना

**hammer sth out** to succeed in making a plan or agreement after a lot of discussion काफ़ी चर्चा के बाद कोई योजना या सहमति बनाने में सफल होना

**hammering** /ˈhæmərɪŋ ˈहैमरिङ्/ *noun* **1** [U] the noise that is made by sb using a hammer or by sb hitting sth many times हथौड़े से या अन्य किसी चीज़ के अनेक प्रहार से तेज़ आवाज़ करना **2** [C] (*BrE informal*) a very bad defeat करारी हार

**hammock** /ˈhæmək ˈहैमक्/ *noun* [C] a bed, made of strong cloth (**canvas**) or rope, which is hung up between two trees or poles मज़बूत कपड़े से बना पलंग जिसे दो पेड़ों या खंभों के बीच लटकाया जाता है; दलारा, दोला

**hamper[1]** /ˈhæmpə(r) ˈहैम्प(र्)/ *verb* [T] (*usually passive*) to make sth difficult अवरुद्ध होना, रुकना *The building work was hampered by bad weather.*

**hamper[2]** /ˈhæmpə(r) ˈहैम्प(र्)/ *noun* [C] a large basket with a lid that is used for carrying food भोजन ले जाने की बड़ी ढक्कनदार टोकरी

**hamster** /ˈhæmstə(r) ˈहैम्स्ट(र्)/ *noun* [C] a small animal that is kept as a pet. Hamsters are like small rats but are fatter and do not have a tail. They store food in the sides of their mouths एक छोटा पालतू जानवर, हैमस्टर। ये चूहों जैसे होते हैं मगर अधिक मोटे और बिना पूँछ के। ये मुँह के पार्श्वों में भोजन जमा कर के रखते हैं

**hamstring** /ˈhæmstrɪŋ ˈहैमस्ट्रिङ्/ *noun* [C] one of the five strong thin tissues (**tendons**) behind your knee that connect the muscles of your upper leg to the bones of your lower leg घुटने के पीछे की नस जो टाँग के ऊपर के हिस्से की मांसपेशियों को नीचे की हड्डियों से जोड़ती है; घुटनस

**hand[1]** /hænd हैन्ड्/ *noun* **1** [C] the part of your body at the end of your arm which has a thumb, four fingers and a palm हाथ *He* ***took*** *the child* ***by the hand***. ○ *She was on her hands and knees* (= crawling on the floor) *looking for an earring.* ➪ **body** पर चित्र देखिए। **2 a hand** [*sing.*] (*informal*) some help थोड़ी मदद, कुछ सहायता *I'll give you a hand with the washing up.* ○ *Do you want/need a hand?* **3** [C] the part of a clock or watch that points to the numbers घड़ी की सूई *the hour/minute/second hand* **4** [C] a person who does physical work on a farm, in a factory etc. खेत, कारख़ाने आदि का मज़दूर *farmhands* **5** [C] the set of playing cards that sb has been given in a game of cards (ताश के खेल में) दिए गए हाथ के पत्ते; ताश का हाथ, बारी *have a good/bad hand* **6 -handed** *adj.* (*used in compounds*) having, using or made for the type of hand(s) mentioned निर्दिष्ट प्रकार के हाथ(ों) वाला *heavy-handed* (= clumsy and careless) ○ *right-handed/left-handed*

IDM **(close/near) at hand** (*formal*) near in space or time स्थान या समय की दृष्टि से निकट *Help is close at hand.*

**be an old hand (at sth)** ➪ **old** देखिए।

**by hand** **1** done by a person and not by machine हाथ से या व्यक्ति द्वारा (न कि मशीन से) *I had to do all the sewing by hand.* **2** not by post डाक द्वारा नहीं, किसी के हाथों, दस्ती तौर पर *The letter was delivered by hand.*

**catch sb red-handed** ➪ **catch[1]** देखिए।

**change hands** ➪ **change[1]** देखिए।

**a firm hand** ➪ **firm[1]** देखिए।

**(at) first hand** (used about information that you have received) from sb who was closely involved (सूचना, जानकारी प्राप्त) पूरी तरह से जानकार व्यक्ति से, मूल से या सीधे, प्रत्यक्ष रूप से *Did you get this information first hand?* ➪ **second-hand** देखिए।

**force sb's hand** ➪ **force[2]** देखिए।

**get, have, etc. a free hand** ➪ **free[1]** देखिए।

**get, etc. the upper hand** ➪ **upper** देखिए।

**get/lay your hands on sb/sth** **1** to find or obtain sth कुछ पता लगाना या प्राप्त करना *I need to get my hands on a good computer.* **2** (*informal*) to catch sb किसी को पकड़ना *Just wait till I get my hands on that boy!*

**give sb a big hand** to hit your hands together to show approval, enthusiasm, etc. प्रशंसा, उत्साहवर्धन में ताली बजाना *The audience gave the girl a big hand when she finished her song.*

**hand in hand** **1** holding each other's hands एक-दूसरे का हाथ थामे *The couple walked hand in hand along the beach.* **2** usually happening together; closely connected प्रायः एक साथ होने वाले; निकटता से संयुक्त *Drought and famine usually go hand in hand.*

**your hands are tied** to not be in a position to do as you would like because of rules, promises, etc. नियम आदि के कारण मनमानी न कर पाना, हाथ बँधे होना

**hands off (sb/sth)** (*informal*) used for ordering sb not to touch sth किसी व्यक्ति या वस्तु से दूर रहने को कहने के लिए प्रयुक्त

**hands up** 1 used in a school, etc. for asking people to lift one hand and give an answer स्कूल की कक्षा में प्रश्न का उत्तर देने के लिए छात्रों से हाथ खड़े करने को कहने के लिए प्रयुक्त *Hands up, who'd like to go on the trip this afternoon?* 2 used by a person with a gun to tell other people to put their hands in the air बंदूक़धारी का लोगों से हाथ खड़े करने का आदेश देना

**have a hand in sth** to take part in or share sth किसी बात में हिस्सा बँटाना

**have sb eating out of your hand** ➪ **eat** देखिए।

**have your hands full** to be very busy so that you cannot do anything else अत्यधिक व्यस्त होना (कि कोई और काम न हो सके)

**a helping hand** ➪ **help**[1] देखिए।

**hold sb's hand** to give sb support in a difficult situation कठिनाई में किसी की सहायता करना *I'll come to the dentist's with you to hold your hand.*

**hold hands (with sb)** (used about two people) to hold each other's hands (दो व्यक्तियों का) एक-दूसरे का हाथ थामना

**in hand** 1 being dealt with at the moment; under control वर्तमान में व्यवस्थापित होना; नियंत्रण में होना *The situation is in hand.* ✪ विलोम **out of hand** 2 (used about money, etc.) not yet used (धन आदि) जो बच गया है; जो व्यय न हुआ हो *If you have time in hand at the end of the exam, check what you have written.*

**in safe hands** ➪ **safe**[1] देखिए।

**in your hands** in your possession, control or care किसी के आधिपत्य, नियंत्रण या देखरेख में *The matter is in the hands of a solicitor.*

**keep your hand in** to do an activity from time to time so that you do not forget how to do it or lose the skill समय-समय पर कोई कार्यविशेष करते रहना ताकि आप उसे करना भूल न जाएँ, अभ्यास करते रहना

**lend (sb) a hand/lend a hand (to sb)** ➪ **lend** देखिए।

**off your hands** not your responsibility any more भार मुक्त होना, दायित्व न होना

**on hand** available to help or to be used सहायता या उपयोग के लिए उपलब्ध *There is always an adult on hand to help when the children are playing outside.*

**on your hands** being your responsibility की ज़िम्मेदारी या का दायित्व होना *We seem to have a problem on our hands.*

**on the one hand... on the other (hand)** used for showing opposite points of view विपरीत दृष्टिकोण का संकेत करने के लिए प्रयुक्त *On the one hand, of course, cars are very useful. On the other hand, they cause a huge amount of pollution.*

**(get/be) out of hand** not under control बेक़ाबू, नियंत्रण से बाहर *Violence at football matches is getting out of hand.* ✪ विलोम **in hand**

**out of your hands** not in your control; not your responsibility के बस की न होना; की ज़िम्मेदारी न होना *I can't help you, I'm afraid. The matter is out of my hands.*

**shake sb's hand/shake hands (with sb)/ shake sb by the hand** ➪ **shake**[1] देखिए।

**to hand** near or close to you के निकट या पास, के हाथ में *I'm afraid I haven't got my diary to hand.*

**try your hand at sth** ➪ **try**[1] देखिए।

**turn your hand to sth** to have the ability to do sth कुछ करने की योग्यता होना *She can turn her hand to all sorts of jobs.*

**wash your hands of sb/sth** ➪ **wash**[1] देखिए।

**with your bare hands** ➪ **bare** देखिए।

**hand²** /hænd हैन्ड्/ *verb* [T] **hand sb sth; hand sth to sb** to give or pass sth to sb किसी को कुछ देना या आगे बढ़ाना

**have (got) to hand it to sb** used to show admiration and approval of sb's work or efforts किसी के काम या प्रयत्न की सराहना करने के लिए प्रयुक्त *You've got to hand it to Rita—she's a great cook.*

**PHR V** **hand sth back (to sb)** to give or return sth to the person who owns it or to where it belongs किसी वस्तु को उसके मालिक या मूल स्रोत को लौटाना

**hand sth down (to sb)** 1 to pass customs, traditions, etc. from older people to younger ones बुज़ुर्ग पीढ़ी द्वारा युवा पीढ़ी को प्रथा, परंपरा आदि सौंपना 2 to pass clothes, toys, etc. from older children to younger ones in the family परिवार के बड़े बच्चों से छोटे बच्चों को कपड़े, खिलौने, आदि सौंपना, देना

**hand sth in (to sb)** to give sth to sb in authority किसी अधिकारी को कुछ सौंपना *I found a wallet and handed it in to the police.*

**hand sth on (to sb)** to send or give sth to another person किसी अन्य व्यक्ति को दे देना *When you have read the article, please hand it on to another student.*

**hand sth out (to sb)** to give sth to many people in a group लोगों में बाँटना *Food was handed out to the starving people.*

**hand (sth) over (to sb)** to give sb else your position of power or the responsibility for sth अपनी सत्ता, अधिकार या दायित्व किसी को सौंपना

**hand (sb) over to sb** (used at a meeting or on the television, radio, telephone, etc.) to let sb speak or listen to another person (किसी सभा, टेलीविज़न कार्यक्रम आदि में) किसी दूसरे को कहने देना या दूसरे की बात सुनने देना

**hand sb/sth over (to sb)** to give sb/sth (to sb) व्यक्ति या वस्तु को कुछ देना *People were tricked into handing over large sums of money.*

**hand sth round** to offer to pass sth, especially food and drinks, to all the people in a group समूह के सभी सदस्यों को खाद्य और पेय पदार्थ आगे बढ़ाने के लिए सामने आना

**handbag** /ˈhændbæg ˈहैन्ड्बैग् / (*AmE* **purse**) *noun* [C] a small bag in which women carry money, keys, etc. (महिलाओं द्वारा पैसे, चाबियाँ आदि ले जाने का) हैंडबैग, पर्स

**handbook** /ˈhændbʊk ˈहैन्ड्बुक् / *noun* [C] a small book that gives instructions on how to use sth or advice and information about a particular subject लघु निर्देश पुस्तिका; हैंडबुक

**handbrake** /ˈhændbreɪk ˈहैन्ड्ब्रेक् / (*AmE* **emergency brake; parking brake**) *noun* [C] a device that is operated by hand to stop a car from moving when it is parked हस्त चालित युक्ति जो पार्क की हुई कार को चलने से रोकती है; हैंडब्रेक, कार में हाथ से लगने वाला ब्रेक ➪ **car** पर चित्र देखिए।

**handcuffs** /ˈhændkʌfs ˈहैन्ड्कफ़्स् / (*also* **cuffs**) *noun* [*pl.*] a pair of metal rings that are joined together by a chain and put around the wrists of prisoners हथकड़ी

**handful** /ˈhændfʊl ˈहैन्ड्फ़ुल् / *noun* **1** [C] **a handful (of sth)** as much or as many of sth as you can hold in one hand मुट्ठीभर (चीज़) *a handful of sand* **2** [*sing.*] a small number (of sb/sth) (व्यक्ति या वस्तु) थोड़ी संख्या में *Only a handful of people came to the meeting.* **3 a handful** [*sing.*] (*informal*) a person or an animal that is difficult to control बेक़ाबू व्यक्ति या पशु

**handgun** /ˈhændgʌn ˈहैंड्गन् / *noun* [C] a small gun that you can hold and fire with one hand एक हाथ से चलने वाली छोटी बंदूक़; हैंडगन

**handicap**[1] /ˈhændikæp ˈहैन्डिकैप् / *noun* [C] **1** some thing that makes doing sth more difficult; a disadvantage बाधा, रुकावट; प्रतिकूलता *Not speaking French is going to be a bit of a handicap in my new job.* **2** a disadvantage that is given to a strong competitor in a sports event, etc. so that the other competitors have more chance किसी खेल में प्रबल खिलाड़ी के लिए निर्धारित प्रतिकूलता की स्थिति ताकि दूसरे खिलाड़ी को अधिक अवसर मिलें **3** (*old-fashioned*) = **disability** NOTE अब इस शब्द को अपमानजनक समझा जाता है।

**handicap**[2] /ˈhændikæp ˈहैन्डिकैप् / *verb* [T] (**handicapping; handicapped**) (*usually passive*) to give or be a disadvantage to sb किसी के लिए कोई बात प्रतिकूल होना या प्रतिकूलता पैदा करना *They were handicapped by their lack of education.*

**handicapped** /ˈhændikæpt ˈहैन्डिकैप्ट् / *adj.* (*old-fashioned*) = **disabled** NOTE अब यह शब्द अपमानजनक समझा जाता है।

**handicraft** /ˈhændikrɑːft ˈहैन्डिक्राफ़्ट् / *noun* **1** [C] an activity that needs skill with the hands as well as artistic ability, for example sewing हस्तकौशल तथा कलात्मक क्षमता वाली गतिविधि (जैसे सीना-पिरोना); हस्तशिल्प **2 handicrafts** [*pl.*] the objects that are produced by this activity हस्तशिल्प से बना सामान

**handiwork** /ˈhændiwɜːk ˈहैन्डिवक् / *noun* [U] **1** a thing that you have made or done, especially using your artistic skill कलात्मक कौशल से बनाई वस्तु *She put the dress on and stood back to admire her handiwork.* **2** a thing done by a particular person or group, especially sth bad विशेष व्यक्ति या वर्ग का किया काम (विशेषत: बुरा काम); कारनामा

**handkerchief** /ˈhæŋkətʃɪf; -tʃiːf ˈहैङ्कचिफ़्; -चीफ़् / *noun* [C] (*pl.* **handkerchiefs** or **handkerchieves** /-tʃiːvz -चीव़्ज़् /) a square piece of cloth or soft thin paper that you use for clearing your nose (कपड़े या काग़ज़ का) रूमाल NOTE अधिक अनौपचारिक शब्द है **hanky** या **hankie** कोमल पतले काग़ज़ के रूमाल को **paper handkerchief** या **tissue** भी कहते हैं।

**handle**[1] /ˈhændl ˈहैन्ड्ल् / *verb* [T] **1** to touch or hold sth with your hand(s) हाथ से छूना या सँभालना *Wash your hands before you handle food.* **2** to deal with or to control sb/sth किसी काम को निपटाना या नियंत्रित करना *This port handles 100 million tons of cargo each year.* ○ *I have a problem at work and I don't really know how to handle it.*

▶ **handler** *noun* [C] सँभालने वाला *baggage/dog/food handlers*

**handle**[2] /ˈhændl ˈहैन्ड्ल् / *noun* [C] a part of sth that is used for holding or opening it मूठ, हत्था, हैंडल, किसी वस्तु का अंश जो उसे थामने या खोलने में प्रयुक्त होता है *She turned the handle and opened the door.* ➪ **scythe** पर चित्र देखिए।

IDM **fly off the handle** ➪ **fly**[1] देखिए।

**handlebar** /ˈhændlbɑː(r) ˈहैन्ड्लबा(र्) / *noun* [C, *usually pl.*] the metal bar at the front of a bicycle that you hold when you are riding it

साइकिल के सामने का डंडा (सवार होते समय इसे पकड़ा जाता है); हैंडलबार ➪ **bicycle** पर चित्र देखिए।

**handloom** *noun* [C] a machine for weaving cloth, operated by hand सूत या धागे से वस्त्र बनाने का यंत्र जिसे हाथ से चलाया जाता है; करघा *a handloom sari*

**hand luggage** (*AmE* **carry-on bag**) *noun* [U] a small bag, etc. that you can keep with you on a plane विमान यात्रा में साथ रखने का छोटा थैला

**handmade** /ˌhændˈmeɪd ˌहैन्ड्ˈमेड्/ *adj.* made by hand and of very good quality, not by machine हाथ से (न कि मशीन से) बना और बढ़िया; हस्तनिर्मित

**handout** /ˈhændaʊt ˈहैन्ड्आउट्/ *noun* [C] **1** food, money, etc. given to people who need it badly ज़रूरतमंदों को दिया गया भोजन, धन आदि सामान **2** a free document that is given to a lot of people, to advertise sth or explain sth, for example in a class विज्ञापन की दृष्टि से या समझाने के लिए बहुत-से लोगों में (जैसे कक्षा में) निःशुल्क बाँटा गया लिखित काग़ज़, पर्चा, इश्तहार

**hand-picked** *adj.* chosen carefully or personally सावधानी से या स्वयं चुना गया

**handrail** /ˈhændreɪl ˈहैन्ड्रेल्/ *noun* [C] a long narrow wooden or metal bar at the side of some steps, a bath, etc. that you hold for support or balance सीढ़ियों या स्नानगृह में किनारे पर लगी लंबी सँकरी लकड़ी या धातु का डंडा (सहारे या संतुलन के लिए), रेलिंग

**handset** = **receiver**[1]

**handshake** /ˈhændʃeɪk ˈहैन्ड्शेक्/ *noun* [C] the action of shaking sb's right hand with your own when you meet him/her मिलने पर दूसरे व्यक्ति से दायाँ हाथ मिलाना

**handsome** /ˈhænsəm ˈहैन्सम्/ *adj.* **1** (used about a man) attractive (पुरुष) आकर्षक, सुंदर ➪ **beautiful** पर नोट देखिए। **2** (used about money, an offer, etc.) large or generous (धनराशि, भेंट आदि) बड़ी या प्रचुर *a handsome profit* ▸ **handsomely** *adv.* यथोचित रूप से *Her efforts were handsomely rewarded.*

**hands-on** *adj.* learnt by doing sth yourself, not watching sb else do it; practical स्वयं करके (न कि दूसरे को देखकर) सीखा हुआ; व्यावहारिक *She needs some hands-on computer experience.*

**handstand** /ˈhændstænd ˈहैन्ड्स्टैन्ड्/ *noun* [C] a movement in which you put your hands on the ground and lift your legs straight up in the air हाथों को ज़मीन पर रखकर टाँगों को सीधे ऊपर उठाने की क्रिया, हाथों के बल उलटे खड़े होने की क्रिया

**handwriting** /ˈhændraɪtɪŋ ˈहैन्ड्राइटिङ्/ *noun* [U] a person's style of writing by hand व्यक्ति की हस्तलेखन शैली, लिखावट, हस्तलिपि

**handwritten** /ˌhændˈrɪtn ˌहैन्ड्ˈरिट्न्/ *adj.* written by hand, not typed or printed हाथ से लिखा (न कि टंकित या मुद्रित)

**handy** /ˈhændi ˈहैन्डि/ *adj.* (**handier; handiest**) **1** useful; easy to use उपयोगी; उपयोग में आसान, सुविधानजक *a handy tip* ○ *a handy gadget* **2 handy (for sth/doing sth)** within easy reach of sth; nearby पहुँच के भीतर; निकट *Always keep a first-aid kit handy for emergencies.* **3** skilful in using your hands or tools to make or repair things हाथ से वस्तुएँ बनाने या सुधारने में कुशल *is very handy around the house.*

**IDM** **come in handy** to be useful at some time मौका पड़ने पर उपयोगी होना *Don't throw that box away. It may come in handy.*

**handyman** /ˈhændimæn ˈहैन्डिमैन्/ *noun* [*sing.*] a person who is clever at making or repairing things, especially around the house चीज़ों को (विशेषतः घर के आसपास की) बनाने या सुधारने में कुशल

**hang**[1] /hæŋ हैन्ङ्/ *verb* (*pt, pp* **hung** /hʌŋ हङ्/)

> **NOTE** भूतकाल (past tense) और भूत कृदंत (past participle) **hanged** का प्रयोग केवल अर्थ संख्या 2 में होता है।

**1** [I, T] to fasten sth or be fastened at the top so that the lower part is free or loose किसी वस्तु का लटकना, टँगना या उसे लटकाना या टाँगना *I left the washing hanging on the line all day.* ○ *A cigarette hung from his lips.* **2** [T] to kill sb/yourself by putting a rope around the neck and allowing the body to drop downwards किसी को फाँसी देना या स्वयं को फाँसी लगाना *He was hanged for murder.* **3** [I] **hang (above/over sb/sth)** to stay in the air in a way that is unpleasant or threatening हवा में इस प्रकार टँग जाना जिससे परेशानी या नुक़सान हो *Smog hung in the air over the city.*

**IDM** **be/get hung up (about/on sb/sth) to think about sb/sth** all the time in a way that is not healthy or good किसी बात को या किसी के विषय में लगातार सोचते जाना (जो ठीक या अच्छी बात नहीं) *She's really hung up about her parents' divorce.*

**hang (on) in there** (*spoken*) to have courage and keep trying, even though a situation is difficult कठिनाई के बावजूद भी साहसपूर्ण प्रयत्न करते रहना, जमे रहना *The worst part is over now. Just hang on in there and be patient.*

**PHR V** **hang about/around** (*informal*) to stay in or near a place not doing very much आस-पास आवारा फिरना

**hang back** **1** to not want to do or say sth, often because you are shy or not sure of yourself (शर्म या अनिश्चय के मारे) कुछ करने या कहने की चाह न होना;

झिझकना **2** to stay in a place after other people have left it दूसरों के जाने के बाद भी उसी स्थान पर रुके रहना

**hang on 1** to wait for a short time थोड़ी प्रतीक्षा करना *Hang on a minute. I'm nearly ready.* **2** to hold sth tightly किसी चीज़ को कसकर पकड़ना *Hang on, don't let go!*

**hang on sth** to depend on sth किसी बात पर निर्भर रहना

**hang on to sth 1** (*informal*) to keep sth किसी वस्तु को रखे रहना *Let's hang on to the car for another year.* **2** to hold sth tightly किसी वस्तु को मज़बूती से थामना *He hung on to the child's hand as they crossed the street.*

**hang sth out** to put washing, etc. on a clothes line so that it can dry कपड़ों को रस्सी पर सूखने के लिए डालना

**hang over sb** to be present or about to happen in a way which is unpleasant or threatening इस ढंग से दिमाग़ में घूमते रहना कि परेशानी हो *This essay has been hanging over me for days.*

**hang sth up** to put sth on a nail, hook, etc. अलगनी, खूँटी आदि पर टाँगना *Hang your coat up over there.*

**hang up** to end a telephone conversation and put the telephone down फ़ोन संवाद समाप्त कर फ़ोन को नीचे रख देना

**hang up on sb** (*informal*) to end a telephone conversation without saying goodbye because you are angry नाराज़गी के कारण फ़ोन संवाद को एकाएक काट देना

**hang**[2] /hæŋ हैन्ङ्/ *noun*

**IDM get the hang of (doing) sth** (*informal*) to learn how to use or do sth किसी वस्तु का उपयोग सीखना *It took me a long time to get the hang of my new computer.*

**hangar** /ˈhæŋə(r) ˈहैङ(र्)/ *noun* [C] a big building where planes are kept विमान को रखने की इमारत; हैंगर

**hanger** /ˈhæŋə(r) ˈहैङ(र्)/ (*also* **coat hanger, clothes-hanger**) *noun* [C] a metal, plastic or wooden object with a hook that is used for hanging up clothes in a cupboard अलमारी में कपड़े टाँगने के लिए प्रयुक्त धातु, प्लास्टिक या लकड़ी का बना घुंडीदार छड़ी-नुमा वस्तु; हैंगर

**hanger-on** /ˌhæŋər ˈɒn ˌहैङर् ˈऑन्/ *noun* [C] (*pl.* **hangers-on**) a person who tries to be friendly with sb who is rich or important धनी या प्रख्यात व्यक्ति से मैत्री का इच्छुक व्यक्ति

**hang-glider** *noun* [C] a type of frame covered with cloth, which a person holds and flies through the air with as a sport कपड़ा लगा चौखटा जिसे पकड़कर व्यक्ति हवा में तैरता है (एक खेल के रूप में); हैंग-ग्लाइडर ▶ **hang-gliding** *noun* [U] हैंग-ग्लाइडर से हवा में तैरना

**hanging** /ˈhæŋɪŋ ˈहैङिङ्/ *noun* [C, U] death as a form of punishment for a crime, caused by putting rope around a person's neck and letting the body drop downwards फाँसी द्वारा मौत

**hanging valley** *noun* [C] (in geography) a valley which has been cut across by a deeper valley or cliff (भूगोल में) एक घाटी जिसे दूसरी अधिक गहरी घाटी या ऊँची खड़ी चट्टान काटती है ➪ **glacial** पर चित्र देखिए।

**hangman** /ˈhæŋmən ˈहैङ्मन्/ *noun* [*sing.*] **1** a person whose job is to kill criminals as a form of punishment by hanging them with a rope क़ैदी को फाँसी लगाने वाला; जल्लाद **2** a word game where the aim is to guess all the letters of a word before a stick picture of a person hanging is completed एक शब्द क्रीड़ा जिसमें सभी अक्षरों का अनुमान लगाना होता है, इससे पहले कि फाँसी चढ़ते व्यक्ति का कठ चित्र पूरा हो जाए

**hangover** /ˈhæŋəʊvə(r) ˈहैङ्ओव़(र्)/ *noun* [C] pain in your head and a sick feeling that you have if you have drunk too much alcohol the night before पिछली रात को अधिक मदिरापान के कारण सुबह होने वाला सिरदर्द और बेचैनी

**hang-up** *noun* [C] (*slang*) **a hang-up (about sb/sth)** an emotional problem about sth that makes you embarrassed or worried आपको परेशान करने वाली भावनात्मक समस्या *He has a real hang-up about his height.*

**hanker** /ˈhæŋkə(r) ˈहैङ्क(र्)/ *verb* [I] **hanker after/for sth** to want sth very much (often sth that you cannot easily have) किसी (प्रायः दुर्लभ) वस्तु को बहुत अधिक चाहना

**hanky** (*also* **hankie**) /ˈhæŋki ˈहैङ्कि/ *noun* [C] (*pl.* **hankies**) (*informal*) = **handkerchief**

**haphazard** /hæpˈhæzəd हैप्ˈहैज़ड्/ *adj.* with no particular order or plan; badly organized सुनियोजित नहीं; बेतरतीब, अव्यवस्थित ▶ **haphazardly** *adv.* अव्यवस्थित रूप से

**haploid** /ˈhæplɔɪd ˈहैप्लॉइड्/ *adj.* (*technical*) (used about a cell) containing only the set of **chromosomes** from one parent (कोशिका) जिसमें केवल माता का या पिता का गुणसूत्र-समुच्चय होता है; अगुणित, मूलसंख्यक ➪ **diploid** देखिए।

**happen** /ˈhæpən ˈहैपन्/ *verb* [I] **1** (of an event or situation) to take place, usually without being planned first (किसी घटना या स्थिति का) घटित हो जाना (बिना किसी पूर्व योजना के) *Can you describe to the police what happened after you left the party?* ○ *How did the accident happen?*

> NOTE **Happen** और **occur** का प्रयोग अनियोजित घटनाओं के लिए होता है। **Occur** अधिक औपचारिक है। **Take place** से घटना के पूर्व-नियोजित होने का संकेत मिलता है—*The wedding took place on Sunday July 25th.*

**2 happen to sb/sth** to be what sb/sth experiences किसी को कुछ अनुभव होना *What do you think has happened to Ritu? She should have been here an hour ago.* ○ *What will happen to the business when your father retires?* **3 happen to do sth** to do sth by chance अचानक कर देना या हो जाना *I happened to meet him in Chennai yesterday.*

IDM **as it happens/happened** (used when you are adding to what you have said) actually (कह दी गई बात के साथ कुछ और कहने के लिए प्रयुक्त) वस्तुतः *As it happens, I did remember to bring the book you wanted.*

**it (just) so happens** ➪ **so**[1] देखिए।

**happening** /ˈhæpənɪŋ ˈहैपनिङ्/ *noun* [C, *usually pl.*] a thing that happens; an event (that is usually strange or difficult to explain) जो घटित होता है; घटना (प्रायः विचित्र और पेचीदा) *Strange happenings have been reported in that old hotel.*

**happily** /ˈhæpɪli ˈहैपिलि/ *adv.* **1** in a happy way प्रसन्नतापूर्वक *I would happily give up my job if I didn't need the money.* **2** it is lucky that; fortunately भाग्य अच्छा था कि; सौभाग्य या ख़ुशक़िस्मती से *The police found my handbag and, happily, nothing had been stolen.*

**happy** /ˈhæpi ˈहैपि/ *adj.* (**happier; happiest**) **1 happy (to do sth); happy for sb; happy that...** feeling or showing pleasure; pleased आनंद का अनुभव करने या उसे व्यक्त करने वाला; प्रसन्न, प्रफुल्ल *I was really happy to see Prakash again yesterday.* ○ *You look very happy today.* ○ *Congratulations! I'm very happy for you.* ✪ विलोम **unhappy** या **sad** ➪ **glad** पर नोट देखिए। **2** giving or causing pleasure प्रसन्नतादायक या प्रसन्नताकारक *a happy marriage/memory/childhood* ○ *The film is sad but it has **a happy ending**.* **3 happy (with/about sb/sth)** satisfied that sth is good and right; not worried किसी बात के ठीक और उचित होने के विषय में संतुष्ट; चिंतित नहीं *I'm not very happy with what you've done.* ○ *She doesn't feel happy about the salary she's been offered.* **3 happy to do sth** (*not before a noun*) ready to do sth; pleased कुछ करने के लिए उद्यत; ख़ुश *I'll be happy to see you any day next week.* **4 Happy** used to wish sb an enjoyable time उल्लास के क्षणों में अभिवादन के लिए प्रयुक्त *Happy Birthday!* **5** (*before a noun*) lucky; fortunate ख़ुशक़िस्मत; भाग्यशाली *a happy coincidence.* ✪ विलोम **unhappy** ▸ **happiness** *noun* [U] प्रसन्नता, ख़ुशी

**happy-go-lucky** *adj.* not caring or worried about life and the future जीवन और भविष्य के विषय में निश्चित; बेपरवाह

**happy hour** *noun* [C, *usually sing.*] a time when a pub or bar sells alcoholic drinks at lower prices than usual वह समय जब मदिरा कुछ सस्ती मिलती है

**harass** /ˈhærəs; həˈræs ˈहैरस्; हˈरैस्/ *verb* [T] to annoy or worry sb by doing unpleasant things to him/her, especially over a long time किसी को (विशेषतः लंबे समय तक) बुरी लगने वाली बातें करके नाराज़ या चिंतित कर देना; सताना, तंग करना, उत्पीड़ित करना *The court ordered him to stop harassing his ex-wife.* ▸ **harassment** *noun* [U] परेशानी, उत्पीड़न *She accused her boss of **sexual harassment**.*

**harassed** /ˈhærəst; həˈræst ˈहैरस्ट्; हˈरैस्ट्/ *adj.* tired and worried because you have too much to do काम के बोझ से थका और परेशान; उत्पीड़ित

**harbour**[1] (*AmE* **harbor**) /ˈhɑːbə(r) ˈहाब(र्)/ *noun* [C, U] a place on the coast where ships can be tied up (**moored**) and protected from the sea and bad weather बंदरगाह

**harbour**[2] (*AmE* **harbor**) /ˈhɑːbə(r) ˈहाब(र्)/ *verb* [T] **1** to keep feelings or thoughts secret in your mind for a long time लंबे समय तक अपनी भावनाओं और विचारों को छिपा कर रखना *She began to **harbour doubts** about the decision.* **2** to hide or protect sb/sth that is bad बुरे को छिपा कर रखना या बचाना, शरण देना, आश्रय देना *They were accused of harbouring terrorists.*

**hard**[1] /hɑːd हाड्/ *adj.* **1** not soft to touch; not easy to break or bend कड़ा; जिसे तोड़ना या मोड़ना आसान न हो, कठोर, सख़्त *The bed was so hard that I couldn't sleep.* ○ *Diamonds are the hardest known mineral.* ✪ विलोम **soft** **2 hard (for sb) (to do sth)** difficult to do or understand; not easy जिसे करना या समझना कठिन हो, दुष्कर और दुर्बोध; कठिन *The first question in the exam was very hard.* ○ *It's hard for young people to find good jobs nowadays.* ○ *I find his attitude very hard to take* (= difficult to accept). ✪ विलोम **easy**

3 needing or using a lot of physical strength or mental effort अत्यधिक शारीरिक या बौद्धिक श्रम की अपेक्षा वाला; श्रमसाध्य *Hard work is said to be good for you.* 4 (used about a person) not feeling or showing kindness or pity; not gentle (व्यक्ति) निष्करुण, दयाहीन, कठोर हृदय *You have to be hard to succeed in business.* ✪ विलोम **soft** या **lenient** 5 (used about conditions) unpleasant or unhappy; full of difficulty (परिस्थितियाँ) परेशानी भरी; कठिनाई भरी *He had a hard time when his parents died.* ○ *to have a hard day/life/childhood* 6 (used about the weather) very cold (मौसम) बहुत ठंडा *The forecast is for a hard winter/frost.* ✪ विलोम **mild** 7 (used about water) containing particular minerals so that soap does not make many bubbles (पानी) जिसमें ऐसे खनिज हों कि साबुन के बुलबुले नहीं बनें *We live in a **hard water** area.* ✪ विलोम **soft** ▸ **hardness** *noun* [U] कड़ापन, कठोरता

IDM **a hard act to follow** a person or a thing that it is difficult to do better than व्यक्ति या वस्तु जिससे बेहतर होना कठिन हो

**be hard at it** to be working very hard किसी बात के लिए बहुत परिश्रम करना

**be hard on sb/sth** 1 to treat sb/sth in a harsh way or to make things difficult किसी पर कड़ाई करना या उसके लिए मुश्किलें पैदा करना *Don't be too hard on her—she's only a child.* 2 to be unfair to sb किसी के साथ अन्याय करना *Moving the office to the country is a bit hard on the people who haven't got a car.*

**give sb a hard time** (*informal*) to make a situation unpleasant, embarrassing or difficult for sb किसी को परेशानी में डाल देना

**hard and fast** (used about rules, etc.) that cannot be changed (नियम आदि) कठोर, अनुल्लंघनीय, दृढ़बद्ध *There are no hard and fast rules about this.*

**hard facts** information that is true, not just people's opinions जानकारी, जनमत मात्र नहीं

**hard luck** ➪ **luck** देखिए।

**hard of hearing** unable to hear well कुछ-कुछ बहरा, ऊँचा सुनने वाला

**hard to swallow** difficult to believe जिस पर विश्वास करना कठिन हो; अविश्वसनीय

**have a hard job doing/to do sth; have a hard time doing sth** to do sth with great difficulty बहुत कठिनाई से कुछ कर पाना

**no hard feelings** (*spoken*) used to tell sb you do not feel angry after an argument, etc. विवाद के बाद शिष्टाचार में कहने के लिए प्रयुक्त कि नाराज़गी नहीं है *'No hard feelings, I hope,' he said, offering me his hand.*

**the hard way** through having unpleasant or difficult experiences, rather than learning from what you are told अप्रिय या कठिन अनुभवों में से स्वयं गुज़रकर (न कि दूसरे के बताए से सीखना) *She won't listen to my advice so she'll just have to **learn the hard way**.*

**take a hard line (on sth)** to deal with sth in a very serious way that you will not allow anyone to change कठोर रुख अपनाते हुए काम करना *The government has taken a hard line on people who drink and drive.*

**hard**[2] /hɑːd हाड्/ *adv.* 1 with great effort, energy or attention बहुत प्रयास, शक्ति या ध्यान लगाते हुए *He worked hard all his life.* ○ *You'll have to try a bit harder than that.* 2 with great force; heavily ज़ोरदार ढंग से, बहुत ज़ोर से, शक्तिपूर्वक *It was raining/snowing hard.* ○ *He hit her hard across the face.*

**be hard up (for sth)** to have too few or too little of sth, especially money किसी चीज़ की (विशेषतः पैसे की) तंगी होना; अभावग्रस्त

**be hard pressed/pushed/put to do sth** to find sth very difficult to do कोई काम बहुत कठिन लगना *He was hard pressed to explain his wife's sudden disappearance.*

**die hard** ➪ **die** देखिए।

**hard done by** (*BrE*) not fairly treated जिसके साथ न्याय नहीं हुआ *He felt very hard done by when he wasn't chosen for the team.*

**hardback** /ˈhɑːdbæk ˈहाड्बैक्/ *noun* [C] a book that has a hard rigid cover पक्की जिल्द वाली पुस्तक *This book is only available **in hardback**.* ➪ **paperback** देखिए।

**hardboard** /ˈhɑːdbɔːd ˈहाड्बॉड्/ *noun* [U] a type of wooden board made by pressing very small pieces of wood together into thin sheets लकड़ी के चूरे को दबाकर बनाई गई चादरों से बना एक प्रकार का बोर्ड; प्लाई का तख़्ता, हार्डबोर्ड

**hard-boiled** *adj.* (used about an egg) boiled until it is solid inside (अंडा) पूरा उबला (जो अंदर से कठोर हो जाए)

**hard cash** (*AmE* **cold cash**) *noun* [U] money, especially in the form of coins and notes, that you can spend नक़द धनराशि, रोकड़

**hard copy** *noun* [U] (*computing*) information from a computer that has been printed on paper काग़ज़ पर मुद्रित कंप्यूटर-संचित जानकारी, संपठनीय कॉपी; हार्ड कॉपी

**hard core** *noun* [*sing., with sing. or pl. verb*] the members of a group who are the most active समूह के सर्वाधिक सक्रिय सदस्य

**hard currency** *noun* [U] money belonging to a particular country that is easy to exchange and not likely to fall in value देश विशेष की मुद्रा जिसका विनिमय सरल है और जिसके मूल्य के कम होने की संभावना नहीं; सशक्त मुद्रा

**hard disk** *noun* [C] (*computing*) a piece of hard plastic that is fixed inside a computer and is used for storing data and programs permanently कंप्यूटर के अंदर लगा प्लास्टिक खंड जिस पर आँकड़े और प्रोग्राम स्थायी रूप से संचित रहते हैं; हार्ड डिस्क ➪ **floppy disk** देखिए।

**hard drug** *noun* [C, *usually pl.*] a powerful and illegal drug that some people take for pleasure and may become dependent on (**addicted**) शक्तिशाली और ग़ैर-क़ानूनी पदार्थ जिसकी लत लग जाए *Heroin and cocaine are hard drugs.* ➪ **soft drug** देखिए।

**harden** /ˈhɑːdn ˈहाड्न्/ *verb* **1** [I, T] to become or to make sth hard or less likely to change सख़्त बनना या बनाना कि उसमें कोई परिवर्तन न हो सके *The concrete will harden in 24 hours.* ○ *The firm has hardened its attitude on this question.* **2** [T] (*usually passive*) **harden sb (to sth/doing sth)** to make sb less kind or less easily shocked किसी का भावशून्य या कठोर हृदय हो जाना; निष्ठुर *a hardened reporter/criminal* ○ *Police officers get hardened to seeing dead bodies.* **3** [I] (used about a person's face, voice, etc.) to become serious and unfriendly (व्यक्ति का चेहरा, स्वर आदि) गंभीर और कठोर हो जाना

**hard-headed** *adj.* determined and not allowing yourself to be influenced by emotions दृढ़ निश्चयी जिसके भावों में उद्वेलन नहीं होता, अभावुक होना, दृढ़ीभूत होना *a hard-headed businessman*

**hard-hearted** *adj.* not kind to other people and not considering their feelings कठोर चित्त, निर्भय ✪ विलोम **soft-hearted**

**hard-hitting** *adj.* that talks about or criticizes sb/sth in an honest and very direct way सीधे-सीधे और ईमानदारी से की गई आलोचना से युक्त, खरी-खरी बातों वाला; अत्याघाती *a hard-hitting campaign/speech/report*

**hardly** /ˈhɑːdli ˈहाड्लि/ *adv.* **1** almost no; almost not; almost none लगभग कोई नहीं; लगभग कुछ नहीं; लगभग शून्य *There's* ***hardly any*** *coffee left.* ○ *We* ***hardly ever*** *go out nowadays.* ➪ **almost** देखिए। **2** used especially after 'can' and 'could' and before the main verb to emphasize that sth is difficult to do किसी काम में होने वाली कठिनाई पर बल देने के लिए विशेषतः 'can' और 'could' के बाद और मुख्य क्रिया से पहले प्रयुक्त *Speak up I can hardly hear you.* **3** (used to say that sth has just begun, happened, etc.) only just कुछ अभी शुरू हुआ है या घटित हुआ है यह कहने के लिए प्रयुक्त, अभी-अभी *She'd* ***hardly*** *gone to sleep* ***than*** *it was time to get up again.*

> **NOTE** यदि **'hardly'** वाक्य के शुरू में आए तो तुरंत बाद में क्रिया आती है, औपचारिक लेखन में ऐसा प्रयोग पाया जाता है—*Hardly had she gone to sleep than it was time to get up again.*

**4** (used to suggest that sth is unlikely or unreasonable) not really (यह बताने के लिए प्रयुक्त कि कोई बात न तो संभावित है न तर्कयुक्त), बिलकुल नहीं *You can hardly expect me to believe that excuse!* ➪ **barely** और **scarcely** देखिए।

**hard-nosed** *adj.* not affected by feelings or emotions when trying to get what you want अभीष्ट वस्तु की प्राप्ति के प्रयत्न में भावनाओं से उद्वेलित नहीं; सयाना, दुनियादार

**hardship** /ˈhɑːdʃɪp ˈहाड्शिप्/ *noun* [C, U] the fact of not having enough money, food, etc. पर्याप्त धन, भोजन आदि का अभाव, जीवन की मूलभूत सुविधाओं की अपर्याप्तता; तंगहाली *This new tax is going to cause a lot of hardship.*

**hard shoulder** (*AmE* **shoulder**) *noun* [C] (*BrE*) a narrow section of road at the side of a motorway where cars are allowed to stop in an emergency मुख्य सड़क मार्ग पर एक किनारे बनी सँकरी पट्टी जहाँ आवश्यकता होने पर कार रोकी जा सकती है

**hardware** /ˈhɑːdweə(r) ˈहाड्वेअ(र्)/ *noun* [U] **1** the machinery of a computer, not the programmes written for it कंप्यूटर की मशीनरी (न कि कंप्यूटर प्रोगाम) ➪ **software** देखिए। **2** tools and equipment that are used in the house and garden घर और बग़ीचे में इस्तेमाल होने वाले औज़ार *a hardware shop*

**hard-wearing** *adj.* (*BrE*) (used about materials, clothes, etc.) strong and able to last for a long time (वस्त्र आदि सामान) मज़बूत और टिकाऊ

**hardwood** /ˈhɑːdwʊd ˈहाड्वुड्/ *noun* [U, C] hard heavy wood from trees that lose their leaves in winter (**deciduous trees**) ऐसे वृक्षों की कड़ी भारी लकड़ी जिनके पत्ते सर्दियों में झड़ जाते हैं; दृढ़ काष्ठ *tropical hardwoods* ➪ **softwood** देखिए।

**hard-working** *adj.* working with effort and energy परिश्रमी, मेहनती *a hard-working man*

**hardy** /ˈhɑːdi ˈहाडि/ *adj.* (**hardier; hardiest**) strong and able to survive difficult conditions and bad weather शक्तिशाली और कठिन हालात तथा ख़राब मौसम को झेल लेने वाला; सशक्त *a hardy plant* ▶ **hardiness** *noun* [U] सशक्तता

**hare** /heə(r) हेअ(र्)/ *noun* [C] an animal like a rabbit but bigger with longer ears and legs बड़ा ख़रगोश, शशक

**harem** /ˈhærəm ˈहैरम्/ *noun* [C] a number of women living with one man, especially in Muslim societies. The part of the building the women live in is also called a harem हरम; एक पुरुष के साथ रहने वाली अनेक स्त्रियाँ (विशेषतः मुस्लिम समाज में), स्त्रियों का आवास भी हरम कहलाता है

**harm¹** /hɑːm हाम्/ *noun* [U] damage or injury क्षति या चोट *Experienced staff watch over the children to make sure they don't* ***come to any harm.***
IDM **no harm done** (*informal*) used to tell sb that he/she has not caused any damage or injury हानि न होने की बात कहने के लिए प्रयुक्त *'Sorry about what I said to you last night.' 'That's all right, Jai, no harm done!'*
**out of harm's way** in a safe place सुरक्षित स्थान पर *Put the medicine out of harm's way where the children can't reach it.*
**there is no harm in doing sth; it does no harm (for sb) to do sth** there's nothing wrong in doing sth (and sth good may result) जिसे करने में कोई हानि न हो (बल्कि कोई अच्छी बात हो जाए) *I'm sure he'll say no, but there's no harm in asking.*

**harm²** /hɑːm हाम्/ *verb* [T] to cause injury or damage; hurt चोट या क्षति पहुँचाना; नुक़सान करना *Too much sunshine can harm your skin.*

**harmful** /ˈhɑːmfl ˈहाम्फ़्ल्/ *adj.* **harmful (to sb/sth)** causing harm हानिकर *Traffic fumes are harmful to the environment.*

**harmless** /ˈhɑːmləs ˈहाम्लस्/ *adj.* **1** not able or not likely to cause damage or injury; safe अहानिकर; सुरक्षित *You needn't be frightened—these insects are completely harmless.* **2** not likely to upset people लोगों को नाराज़ न करने वाला; अनपकारी *The children can watch that film—it's quite harmless.* ► **harmlessly** *adv.* हानिरहित रूप से; अहानिकर रूप से

**harmonic** /hɑːˈmɒnɪk हाˈमॉनिक्/ *adj.* (*usually before a noun*) (in music) used to describe the way notes are played or sung together to make a pleasing sound (संगीत में) जिसमें स्वर-योजना सामंजस्यपूर्ण और मधुर प्रभावकारी हो; समस्वरित, सुस्वरात्मक

**harmonica** /hɑːˈmɒnɪkə हाˈमॉनिका/ (*BrE* **mouth organ**) *noun* [C] a small musical instrument that you play by moving it across your lips while you are blowing मुँह या होंठों से बजाया जाने वाला वाद्य यंत्र, हारमोनिका; माउथ आर्गन ➪ पृष्ठ 789 पर चित्र देखिए।

**harmonious** /hɑːˈməʊniəs हाˈमोनिअस्/ *adj.* **1** friendly, peaceful and without disagreement **2** (used about musical notes, colours, etc.) producing a pleasant effect when heard or seen together (संगीत स्वर, रंग आदि) मधुर प्रभाव उत्पन्न करने वाला; शांतिदायक ► **harmoniously** *adv.* सामंजस्य के साथ

**harmonize** (*also* **-ise**) /ˈhɑːmənaɪz ˈहामनाइज़्/ *verb* [I] **1 harmonize (with sth)** (used about two or more things) to produce a pleasant effect when seen, heard, etc. together (दो या अधिक वस्तुओं का) परस्पर सामंजस्य बैठाना, संवादी होना **2 harmonize (with sb/sth)** to sing or play music that sounds good combined with the main tune मुख्य स्वर के साथ संयुक्त होकर ऐसे गाना या बजाना कि मधुर प्रभाव उत्पन्न हो; सहस्वर होना ► **harmonization** (*also* **-isation**) /ˌhɑːmənaɪˈzeɪʃn ˌहामनाइˈज़ेश्न्/ *noun* [U] संवादीकरण, सामंजस्य बैठाना

**harmony** /ˈhɑːməni ˈहामनि/ *noun* (*pl.* **harmonies**) **1** [U] a state of agreement or of peaceful existence together सामंजस्य *We need to live more* ***in harmony with*** *our environment.* **2** [C, U] a pleasing combination of musical notes, colours, etc. स्वरों, रंगों आदि का मधुर संयोजन; सहस्वरता *There are some beautiful harmonies in that music.*

**harness¹** /ˈhɑːnɪs ˈहानिस्/ *noun* [C] **1** a set of leather straps that is put around a horse's neck and body so that it can pull sth घोड़े का साज **2** a set of straps for fastening sth to a person's body or for stopping sb from moving around, falling, etc. व्यक्ति के शरीर से बँधे फ़ीते जो उसे गिरने आदि से बचाते हैं *a safety harness*

**harness²** /ˈhɑːnɪs ˈहानिस्/ *verb* [T] **1 harness sth (to sth)** to put a harness on a horse, etc. or to tie a horse, etc. to sth using a harness घोड़े पर साज रखना या घोड़े को किसी वस्तु से फ़ीतों द्वारा बाँधना *Two ponies were harnessed to the cart.* **2** to control the energy of sth in order to produce power or to achieve sth विद्युत उत्पन्न करने या कुछ प्राप्त करने के लिए किसी की ऊर्जा का व्यवस्थित प्रयोग करना *to harness the sun's rays as a source of energy*

**harp** /hɑːp हाप्/ *noun* [C] a large musical instrument which has many strings stretching from the top to the bottom of a frame. You play the harp with your fingers अंगुलियों से बजाए जाने वाला एक बड़ा वाद्य यंत्र जिसकी अनेक तारें एक चौखटे में ऊपर से नीचे तक फैली रहती हैं; हार्प ➪ पृष्ठ 789 पर चित्र देखिए। ► **harpist** *noun* [C] हार्प-वादक

**harpoon** /hɑːˈpuːn हाˈपून्/ *noun* [C] a long thin weapon with a sharp pointed end and a rope tied to it that is used to catch large sea animals (**whales**) व्हेल मछलियों के शिकार का भाला; मछभाला ▶ **harpoon** *verb* [T] मछभाले से शिकार करना

**harrow** /ˈhærəʊ ˈहैरो/ *noun* [C] a piece of farming equipment that is pulled over land that has been turned over (**ploughed**) to break up the earth before planting जोते हुए खेत में बुवाई से पहले मिट्टी के ढेले तोड़ने वाला यंत्र; पटेला

**harrowing** /ˈhærəʊɪŋ ˈहैरोइङ्/ *adj.* making people feel very sad or upset लोगों को दुखी या परेशान कर देने वाला; उत्पीड़क *The programme showed harrowing scenes of the victims of the war.*

**harsh** /hɑːʃ हाश्/ *adj.* **1** very strict and unkind बहुत कठोर और निर्मम *a harsh punishment/criticism* ○ *The judge had some* ***harsh words*** *for the journalist's behaviour.* **2** unpleasant and difficult to live in, look at, listen to, etc. जहाँ रहना, जिसे देखना, सुनना आदि अप्रिय और कठिन हो *She grew up in the harsh environment of New York City.* ○ *a harsh light/voice* **3** too strong or rough and likely to damage sth बहुत तेज़ या खुरदरा और हानिकर *This soap is too harsh for a baby's skin.* ▶ **harshly** *adv.* कठोरता से ▶ **harshness** *noun* [U] कठोरता, रूखापन

**harvest** /ˈhɑːvɪst ˈहाविस्ट्/ *noun* **1** [C, U] the time of year when the grain, fruit, etc. is collected on a farm; the act of collecting the grain, fruit, etc. खेत से फ़सल काटने और इकट्ठा करने का समय; फ़सल काटने और इकट्ठी करने की क्रिया *Farmers always need extra help with the harvest.* **2** [C] the amount of grain, fruit, etc. that is collected जमा की गई फ़सल *This year's wheat harvest was very poor.* ▶ **harvest** *verb* [I, T] फ़सल काटना व इकट्ठी करना ➪ **combine harvester** देखिए।

**has** /həz; *strong form* hæz हज़्; प्रबल रूप हैज़्/ ➪ **have** देखिए।

**has-been** *noun* [C] (*informal*) a person or thing that is no longer as famous, successful or important as before व्यक्ति या वस्तु जो पहले के समान प्रख्यात और प्रभावशाली नहीं रहे, गया-बीता व्यक्ति या वस्तु

**hash** /hæʃ हैश्/ *noun* **1** [U, C] a hot dish of meat mixed together with potato and fried आलू मिले भुने मांस का व्यंजन **2** [U] = **hashish** **3** (**hash sign**)(*BrE*) [C] the symbol (#), especially one on the telephone चिह्न जो प्रायः टेलीफोन के डायल नंबरों के साथ होता है

IDM **make a hash of sth** (*informal*) to do sth badly किसी कार्य को बुरी तरह से करना

**hashish** /ˈhæʃiːʃ ˈहैशीश्/ (*also* **hash**) *noun* [U] a drug made from a plant (**hemp**) that some people smoke for pleasure and which is illegal in many countries गाँजे से बनने वाला नशीला पदार्थ (धूम्रपान के लिए) जो अनेक देशों में ग़ैर-क़ानूनी है; हशीश, चरस

**hasn't** ➪ **has not** का संक्षिप्त रूप

**hassle[1]** /ˈhæsl ˈहैसल्/ *noun* (*informal*) **1** [C, U] a thing or situation that is annoying because it is complicated or involves a lot of effort जटिल और श्रमसाध्य होने के कारण परेशान कर देने वाली वस्तु या स्थिति; परेशानी *It's going to be a hassle having to change trains with all this luggage.* **2** [U] disagreeing or arguing तर्क-वितर्क, बहस-मुबाहिसा *I've decided what to do—please don't give me any hassle about it.*

**hassle[2]** /ˈhæsl ˈहैसल्/ *verb* [T] to annoy sb, especially by asking him/her to do sth many times किसी को झुंझला देना (विशेषतः कोई काम अनेक बार करने के लिए कहकर)

**haste** /heɪst हेस्ट्/ *noun* [U] speed in doing sth, especially because you do not have enough time जल्दी, शीघ्रता *It was obvious that the letter had been written* ***in haste***.

**hasten** /ˈheɪsn ˈहेसन्/ *verb* (*formal*) **1** [I] **hasten to do sth** to be quick to do or say sth कोई काम या बात जल्दी (लगभग तुरंत) करना या कहना *She hastened to apologize.* **2** [T] to make sth happen or be done earlier or more quickly जल्दी या अधिक तेज़ी से कोई काम करवाना; गतिवान बनाना

**hasty** /ˈheɪsti ˈहेस्टि/ *adj.* **1** said or done too quickly जल्दी में कहा या किया हुआ; तीव्र गतिक *He said a hasty 'goodbye' and left.* **2 hasty (in doing sth/to do sth)** (used about a person) acting or deciding sth too quickly or without enough thought (व्यक्ति) जल्दबाज़ *Maybe I was too hasty in rejecting her for the job.* ▶ **hastily** *adv.* जल्दबाज़ी से

**hat** /hæt हैट्/ *noun* [C] a covering that you wear on your head, usually when you are outside (प्रायः घर से बाहर पहना जाने वाला) टोप, हैट, टोपी *to wear a hat*

IDM **at the drop of a hat** ➪ **drop[2]** देखिए।

**hatch[1]** /hætʃ हैच्/ *verb* **1** [I] **hatch (out)** (used about a baby bird, insect, fish, etc.) to come out of an egg (शिशु पक्षी, कीट आदि का) अंडे से बाहर निकलना *Ten chicks hatched (out) this morning.* **2** [T] to make a baby bird, etc. come out of an egg शिशु पक्षी को अंडे से बाहर लाना, अंडे सेना **3** [T] **hatch sth (up)** to think of a plan (usually to do sth bad) षड्यंत्र रचना *He hatched a plan to avoid paying any income tax.*

**hatch²** /hætʃ हैच्/ *noun* [C] **1** an opening in the floor of a ship (**the deck**) through which cargo is lowered जलपोत का डेक जहाँ से माल उतारा-चढ़ाया जाता है **2** an opening in the wall between a kitchen and another room that is used for passing food through कमरे और रसोई के बीच भोजन सामग्री गुज़ारने की छोटी खिड़की **3** the door in a plane or spacecraft विमान या अंतरिक्ष यान का दरवाज़ा

**hatchback** /ˈhætʃbæk ˈहैच्बैक्/ *noun* [C] a car with a large door at the back that opens upwards एक प्रकार की कार जिसमें पीछे लगा दरवाज़ा ऊपर की ओर खुलता है; हैचबैक

**hatchet** /ˈhætʃɪt ˈहैचिट्/ *noun* [C] a tool with a short handle and a heavy metal head with a sharp edge used for cutting wood कुल्हाड़ी ➪ **gardening** पर चित्र देखिए।

**hate¹** /heɪt हेट्/ *verb* [T] **1** to have a very strong feeling of not liking sb/sth at all व्यक्ति या वस्तु के प्रति अत्यधिक अरुचि होना; घृणा करना *I hate it when it's raining like this.* ○ *I hate to see the countryside spoilt.* ➪ **detest** और **loathe** देखिए। इन शब्दों की अर्थव्यंजना अधिक तीव्र है। **2** used as a polite way of saying sorry for sth you would prefer not to have to say ऐसी बात के लिए खेद व्यक्त करने की नम्र अभिव्यक्ति जिसे कहने से आप बचना चाहते हैं *I hate to bother you, but did you pick up my keys by mistake?*

**hate²** /heɪt हेट्/ *noun* **1** [U] a very strong feeling of not liking sb/sth at all; hatred व्यक्ति या वस्तु के लिए तीव्र अरुचि या नापसंदगी; घृणा *Do you feel any hate towards the kidnappers?* **2** [C] a thing that you do not like at all सर्वथा नापसंद वस्तु *Plastic flowers are one of my pet hates* (= the things that I particularly dislike).

**hateful** /ˈheɪtfl ˈहेट्फ़्ल्/ *adj.* **hateful (to sb)** extremely unpleasant अत्यधिक नापसंद, घृणित, घृणास्पद *It was a hateful thing to say.* ✪ पर्याय **horrible**

**hatred** /ˈheɪtrɪd ˈहेट्रिड्/ *noun* [U] **hatred (for/of sb/sth)** a very strong feeling of not liking sb/sth; hate व्यक्ति या वस्तु के लिए अत्यधिक नापसंदगी का भाव; घृणा

**hat-trick** *noun* [C] three points, goals, etc. scored by one player in the same game; three successes achieved by one person एक ही गेम में अकेले खिलाड़ी द्वारा बनाए गए तीन प्वाइंट, गोल आदि; एक ही व्यक्ति को प्राप्त तीन निरंतर (अर्थात बिना विफलता मिले) सफलताएँ *to score a hat-trick*

**haughty** /ˈhɔːti ˈहॉटि/ *adj.* proud, and thinking that you are better than other people घमंडी और स्वयं को दूसरों से बेहतर समझना; दंभी, उद्धत ▶ **haughtily** *adv.* घमंड से

**haul¹** /hɔːl हॉल्/ *verb* [T] to pull sth with a lot of effort or difficulty बहुत मेहनत या कठिनाई से किसी चीज़ को खींचना *A lorry hauled the car out of the mud.*

**haul²** /hɔːl हॉल्/ *noun* **1** [C, *usually sing.*] **a haul (of sth)** a large amount of sth that has been stolen, caught, collected, etc. चुराई, पकड़ी, संगृहीत वस्तुओं की भारी मात्रा *The fishermen came back with a good haul of fish.* **2** [*sing.*] a distance to be travelled यात्रा की दूरी *It seemed **a long haul** back home at night.*

**haunches** /ˈhɔːntʃɪz ˈहॉन्चिज़्/ *noun* [*pl.*] the back end of an animal, including the tops of its back legs; a person's bottom and the tops of his or her legs पशु का पुट्ठा; स्त्री या पुरुष का नितंब *The lion rested on its haunches.*

**haunt¹** /hɔːnt हॉन्ट्/ *verb* [T] **1** (*usually passive*) (used about a ghost of a dead person) to appear in a place regularly (मृतक के भूत का) किसी स्थान पर नियमित रूप से प्रकट होते रहना *The house is said to be haunted.* **2** (used about sth unpleasant or sad) to be always in your mind (दुखद प्रसंग का) दिमाग़ पर छाए रहना *His unhappy face has haunted me for years.*

**haunt²** /hɔːnt हॉन्ट्/ *noun* [C] a place that you visit regularly स्थान जहाँ व्यक्ति नियमित रूप से जाता है; अड्डा *This cafe has always been a favourite haunt of mine.*

**haunting** /ˈhɔːntɪŋ ˈहॉन्टिङ्/ *adj.* having a quality that stays in your mind मन में बस जाने वाला, बार-बार याद आने वाला *a haunting song*

**have¹** /həv; *strong form* hæv हव् ; प्रबल रूप हैव्/ *auxiliary verb* used for forming the perfect tenses पूर्णकाल बनाने के लिए प्रयुक्त सहायक क्रिया ➪ इस शब्दकोश के अंत में **Quick Grammar Reference** देखिए।

**have²** /hæv हैव्/ *verb* [T] **1** (*BrE* **have got**) (*not used in the continuous tenses*) to own or to hold sth; to possess किसी वस्तु का मालिक होना या किसी बात का अधिकारी होना; किसी वस्तु पर अधिकार रखना *I've got a new camera.* ○ *The flat has two bedrooms.* ○ *to have patience/enthusiasm/skill* ○ *Have you got any brothers or sisters?* **2** used with many nouns to talk about doing sth किसी काम के बारे में बताने के लिए अनेक संज्ञाओं के साथ प्रयुक्त *to have a drink/something to eat* ○ *to have an argument/talk/chat* **3** to experience sth किसी बात का अनुभव होना, किसी बात से प्रभावित होना *to have fun* ○ *to have problems/difficulties* ○ *to have* *an idea/an impression/a feeling* **4** (*also* **have got**) (*not used in the continuous tenses*) to be ill with sth किसी को कोई रोग होना *She's got a bad cold.* ○ *to have flu/a headache/cancer/AIDS* **5 have sth done** to arrange for sb to do sth कोई काम करवाना *I have my hair cut every six weeks.* ○ *You should have your eyes tested.* **6** (*also* **have got**) to have a particular duty or plan किसी के पास कोई विशेष काम या योजना होना *Do you have any homework tonight?* ○ *I've got a few things to do this morning, but I'm free later.* **7** (*also* **have got**) (*not used in the continuous tenses*) to hold sb/sth; to keep sth in a particular place व्यक्ति या वस्तु को पकड़ना; किसी वस्तु को विशेष स्थान पर रखना *The dog had me by the leg.* ○ *We've got our TV up on a shelf.* **8** to cause sb/sth to do sth or to be in a particular state किसी से कोई काम करवाना या विशेष मनोदशा में आ जाना *The music soon had everyone dancing.* ○ *I'll have dinner ready when you get home.* **9** to look after or entertain sb किसी की देखभाल या मनोरंजन करना *We're having some people to dinner tomorrow.*

**IDM have had it** used about things that are completely broken, or dead पूरी तरह टूट चुकी या निष्क्रिय वस्तुओं के लिए प्रयुक्त *This television has had it. We'll have to buy a new one.*

**NOTE Have** वाले अन्य मुहावरों के लिए संबंधित संज्ञाओं, विशेषणों आदि की प्रविष्टियों आदि को देखिए। जैसे **not have a clue** की प्रविष्टि **clue** में मिलेगी।

**PHR V have sb on** to trick sb as a joke किसी को मज़ाक में धोखा देना *Don't listen to what Vaibhav says—he's only having you on.*

**have (got) sth on 1** to be wearing sth कुछ पहने होना *She's got a green on.* **2** (*informal*) to have an arrangement to do sth किसी काम में व्यस्त रहना *I've got a lot on this week* (= I'm very busy).

**have sth out** to allow part of your body to be removed शरीर का कोई अंग निकलवाना *to have a tooth/your appendix out*

**haven** /ˈheɪvn ˈहेव्‌न्/ *noun* [C] **a haven (of sth); a haven (for sb/sth)** a place where people or animals can be safe and rest मनुष्यों या पशुओं के लिए सुरक्षित विश्रामस्थल *The lake is a haven for water birds.* ➪ **tax haven** देखिए।

**have to** /ˈhæv tə; ˈhæf tə; ˈहैव़् ट; ˈहैफ़् ट/ *strong form and before vowels* ˈhæv tuː; ˈhæf tuː प्रबल रूप तथा स्वर ध्वनियों से पहले ˈहैव़् टू; ˈहैफ़् टू/ *modal verb* used for saying that sb must do sth or that sth must happen यह कहने के लिए प्रयुक्त कि कोई काम अवश्य किया जाए या कोई बात अवश्य हो *I usually have to work on Saturday mornings.* ○ *We don't have to* (= it's not necessary to) *go to the party if you don't want to.*

**NOTE** वृत्तिवाचक क्रियाओं (modal verbs) के विषय में अधिक जानकारी के लिए इस शब्दकोश के अंत में **Quick Grammar Reference** देखिए।

**havoc** /ˈhævək ˈहैव़क्/ *noun* [U] a situation in which there is a lot of damage or confusion अत्यधिक विनाश या अव्यवस्था की स्थिति; विनाश *The rail strikes will **cause havoc** all over the country.*

**hawk[1]** /hɔːk हॉक्/ *noun* [C] a type of large bird that catches and eats small animals and birds. Hawks can see very well बाज़, (तीव्र दृष्टिक होते हैं) **NOTE** बाज़ एक **bird of prey** (शिकारी पक्षी) है।

**hawk[2]** /hɔːk हॉक्/ *verb* [T] to try to sell things by going from place to place asking people to buy them घर-घर जाकर माल बेचना, फेरी लगाना ► **hawker** *noun* [C] फेरीवाला

**hay** /heɪ हे/ *noun* [U] grass that has been cut and dried for use as animal food पशुओं के खाने की सूखी घास

**hay fever** *noun* [U] an illness that affects the eyes, nose and throat and is caused by breathing in the powder (**pollen**) produced by some plants फूलों का पराग साँस द्वारा अंदर जाने से उत्पन्न रोग (जिसमें आँख, नाक और गले पर असर होता है); परागज ज्वर

**haystack** /ˈheɪstæk ˈहेस्टैक्/ (*also* **hayrick** /ˈheɪrɪk ˈहेरिक्/) *noun* [C] a large firmly packed pile of hay घास का ढेर या चट्टा, गर्री

**haywire** /ˈheɪwaɪə(r) ˈहेवाइअ(र्)/ *adj.*

**IDM be/go haywire** (*informal*) to be or become out of control बेक़ाबू होना या हो जाना

**hazard[1]** /ˈhæzəd ˈहैज़ड्/ *noun* [C] a danger or risk ख़तरा या जोख़िम *Smoking is a serious health hazard.*

**hazard[2]** /ˈhæzəd ˈहैज़ड्/ *verb* [T] to make a guess or to suggest sth even though you know it may be wrong किसी बात का अनुमान लगाना (जो ग़लत भी हो सकती है) *I don't know what he paid for the house but I could **hazard a guess**.*

**hazardous** /ˈhæzədəs ˈहैज़डस्/ *adj.* dangerous ख़तरनाक, जोख़िमभरा ✪ पर्याय **risky**

**haze** /heɪz हेज़्/ *noun* **1** [C, U] air that is difficult to see through because it contains very small drops of water, especially caused by hot weather हलकी धुंध *a heat haze* ➪ **fog** पर नोट देखिए। **2** [*sing.*] air containing sth that makes it difficult to see through it धुंधभरी वायु *a haze of smoke/dust/steam* **3** [*sing.*] a mental state in which you cannot think clearly हलकी भ्रांति, उलझन

**hazel**[1] /ˈheɪzl ˈहेज़्ल्/ *noun* [C] a small tree or bush that produces nuts गिरीदार फल देने वाला पिंघल वृक्ष या झाड़ी, पिंघल का फल

**hazel**[2] /ˈheɪzl ˈहेज़्ल्/ *adj.* (used especially about eyes) light brown in colour (विशेषतः आँखें) हलकी भूरी

**hazelnut** /ˈheɪzlnʌt ˈहेज़्लनट्/ *noun* [C] a small nut that we eat पहाड़ी बादाम, पिंघल फल ➪ **nut** पर चित्र देखिए।

**hazy** /ˈheɪzi ˈहेज़ि/ *adj.* **1** not clear, especially because of heat धुंधभरा, अस्पष्ट (विशेषतः ताप या गरमी के कारण) *The fields were hazy in the early morning sun.* **2** difficult to remember or understand clearly जिसे स्पष्टतया याद करना या समझना कठिन हो *a hazy memory* **3** (used about a person) uncertain, not expressing things clearly (व्यक्ति) अनिश्चयग्रस्त; स्पष्ट अभिव्यक्ति में असमर्थ *She's a bit hazy about the details of the trip.*

**H-bomb** = **hydrogen bomb**

**he**[1] /hi: ही/ *pronoun* (*the subject of a verb*) the male person mentioned earlier (क्रिया का कर्त्ता) पूर्वनिर्दिष्ट पुरुष व्यक्ति *I spoke to Ahmed before he left.* ○ *Look at that little boy—he's going to fall in!*

> **NOTE** किसी पुरुष या महिला के मौखिक रूप से निर्देश के लिए हम **he** या **she, him** या **her** का प्रयोग कर सकते हैं, और लिखित रूप में इन्हें **he/she** या **s/he** इस प्रकार प्रस्तुत किया जा सकता है—*If you are not sure, ask your doctor. He/she can give you further information.* अनौपचारिक शैली में **they, them** या **their** प्रयुक्त किए जा सकते हैं—*Everybody knows what they want.* ○ *When somebody asks me a question I always try to give them a quick answer.* वाक्य को बहुवचनांत भी किया जा सकता है, जैसे—*A baby cries when she/he is tired.* का रूप बदलकर *Babies cry when they are tired.* हो जाता है।

**he**[2] /hi: ही/ *noun* [*sing.*] a male animal नर पशु *Is your cat a he or a she?*

**head**[1] /hed हेड्/ *noun* [C] **1** the part of your body above your neck सिर *She turned her head to look at him.* ➪ **body** पर चित्र देखिए। **2 -headed** (*used to form compound adjectives*) having the type of head mentioned निर्दिष्ट प्रकार के सिर वाला *a bald-headed man* **3** a person's mind, brain or mental ability मस्तिष्क, दिमाग़ *Use your head* (= think)! ○ *A horrible thought entered my head.* **4** the top, front or most important part शीर्ष, आगे का या सर्वाधिक महत्त्वपूर्ण अंश *to sit at the head of the table* ○ *the head of a nail* ○ *the head of the queue* **5** the person in charge of a group of people संस्था या लोगों के समूह का प्रमुख *the head of the family* ○ *Several* ***heads of state*** (= official leaders of countries) *attended the funeral.* ○ *the head waiter* **6** (*also* **head teacher**) the teacher in charge of a school स्कूल का मुख्याध्यापक *Who is going to be the new head?* **7 heads** the side of a coin with the head of a person on it सिक्के का पहलू जिस पर व्यक्ति का सिर बना होता है *Heads or tails? Heads I go first, tails you do.* **8** the white mass of small bubbles on the top of a glass of beer बियर के गिलास में सबसे ऊपर सफ़ेद बुलबुलों का ढेर **9 a head** [*sing.*] the height or length of one head एक सिर के बराबर की लंबाई या ऊँचाई *She's a head taller than her sister.* **10** the part of a machine for playing tapes or videos (**a tape/video recorder**) that touches the tape and changes the electronic signal into sounds and/or pictures टेप-रिकार्डर या वीडियो-रिकार्डर का टेप को स्पर्श करता हिस्सा (जो इलेक्ट्रॉनिक संकेतों को ध्वनि और/या चित्र में बदल देता है)

**IDM a/per head** for each person प्रति व्यक्ति *How much will the meal cost a head?*

**bite sb's head off** ➪ **bite**[1] देखिए।

**come to a head; bring sth to a head** if a situation comes to a head or if you bring it to a head, it suddenly becomes very bad and you have to deal with it immediately किसी स्थिति का प्रतिकूलता की पराकाष्ठा पर पहुँच जाना

**do sb's head in** (*BrE informal*) to make sb upset and confused किसी को परेशानी और उलझन में डाल देना

**get sth into your head; put sth into sb's head** to start or to make sb start believing or thinking sth स्वयं मानने या सोचने लग जाना या दूसरे से भी ऐसा करवाना

**go to sb's head** **1** to make sb too proud किसी में बहुत घमंड भर देना *If you keep telling him how clever he is, it will go to his head!* **2** to make sb drunk किसी को शराब के नशे में बदमस्त कर देना *Wine always goes straight to my head.*

**have a head for sth** to be able to deal with sth easily किसी काम को सरलता से कर लेना *You need a good head for heights if you live on the top floor!* ○ *to have a head for business/figures*

**head first** **1** with your head before the rest of your body सबसे पहले सिर को आगे करके *Don't go down the slide head first.* **2** too quickly or suddenly बहुत जल्दी या एकाएक *Don't rush head first into a decision.*

**head over heels (in love)** loving sb very much; madly किसी से बहुत अधिक प्रेम करना; प्रेम में पागल होना या होकर *Mona's fallen head over heels in love with her new neighbour.*

**hit the nail on the head** ➪ **hit¹** देखिए।

**keep your head** to stay calm शांत रहना

**keep your head above water** to just manage to survive in a difficult situation, especially one in which you do not have enough money कठिन परिस्थिति को झेल लेना/में टिके रहना (विशेषत: जब धन की कमी हो)

**keep your head down** to try not to be noticed दिखाई देने से बचना

**laugh, scream, etc. your head off** to laugh, shout, etc. very loudly and for a long time बहुत ऊँचे और देर तक हंसते, चिल्लाते रहना

**lose your head** ➪ **lose** देखिए।

**make head or tail of sth** to understand sth किसी बात को समझना *I can't make head or tail of this exercise.*

**off the top of your head** ➪ **top¹** देखिए।

**out of/off your head** (*informal*) crazy, often because of the effects of drugs or alcohol प्राय: नशीली दवा या शराब के प्रभाव से असंयत

**put/get your heads together** to make a plan with sb मिल-बैठकर योजना बनाना

**a roof over your head** ➪ **roof** देखिए।

**shake your head** ➪ **shake¹** देखिए।

**take it into your head to do sth** to suddenly decide to do sth that other people consider strange दूसरों को विचित्र लगने वाले काम को करने का अचानक निश्चय कर लेना *I don't know why Arjun took it into his head to enter that marathon!*

**head²** /hed हेड्/ *verb* **1** [I] to move in the direction mentioned निर्दिष्ट दिशा में आगे बढ़ना *The ship headed towards the harbour.* ○ *Where are you heading?* **2** [T] to be in charge of or to lead sth किसी बात का दायित्व लेना या नेतृत्व करना **3** [T] to be at the front of a line, top of a list, etc. किसी पंक्ति में सबसे आगे होना, सूची में सबसे ऊपर होना आदि **4** [T] (*usually passive*) to give a title at the top of a piece of writing किसी लेख को शीर्षक देना *The report was headed 'The State of the Market'.* **5** [T] (in football) to hit the ball with your head (फ़ुटबॉल में) सिर से बॉल को मारना

**PHR V head for** to move towards a place किसी स्थान की ओर बढ़ना *It's getting late—I think it's time to head for home.*

**headache** /ˈhedeɪk ˈहेड्एक्/ *noun* [C] **1** a pain in the head सरदर्द *I've got a splitting* (= very bad) *headache.* ➪ **ache** पर नोट देखिए। **2** a person or thing that causes worry or difficulty निरंतर चिंता या मुश्किल पैदा करने वाला व्यक्ति या वस्तु *Paying the bills is a constant headache.*

**headhunter** /ˈhedhʌntə(r) ˈहेड्हन्ट(र्)/ *noun* [C] a person whose job is to find people to work for a particular company and to persuade them to join it किसी कंपनी के लिए कुशल कर्मचारियों को खोजने तथा लाने वाला व्यक्ति

**heading** /ˈhedɪŋ ˈहेडिङ्/ *noun* [C] the words written as a title at the top of a page or a piece of writing शीर्षक *I've grouped our ideas under three main headings.*

**headland** /ˈhedlənd; -lænd ˈहेड्लन्ड्; -लैन्ड्/ *noun* [C] a narrow piece of land that sticks out into the sea समुद्र में प्रविष्ट सँकरा भूखंड; अंतरीप

**headlight** /ˈhedlaɪt ˈहेड्लाइट्/ (*also* **headlamp** /ˈhedlæmp ˈहेड्लैम्प्/) *noun* [C] one of the two large bright lights at the front of a vehicle वाहन के अग्रभाग में तेज़ चमकती बत्ती; हैडलाइट

**headline** /ˈhedlaɪn ˈहेड्लाइन्/ *noun* **1** [C] the title of a newspaper article printed in large letters above the story समाचारपत्र में लेख, समाचार का शीर्षक **2 the headlines** [*pl.*] the main items of news read on television or radio टेलीविज़न या रेडियो पर प्रस्तुत मुख्य समाचार

**headlong** /ˈhedlɒŋ ˈहेड्लॉङ्/ *adv., adj.* **1** with your head before the rest of your body सिर के बल *I tripped and fell headlong into the road.* **2** too quickly; without enough thought हड़बड़ी में, बहुत जल्दी में; अविचारित *He rushed headlong into buying the business.*

**headmaster** /ˌhedˈmɑːstə(r) ˌहेड्ˈमास्ट(र्)/ *noun* [C] (*old-fashioned*) the man who is in charge of a school स्कूल का प्रधानाध्यापक **NOTE** अब **head** या **headteacher** शब्द का प्रयोग होता है।

**headmistress** /ˌhedˈmɪstrəs ˌहेड्ˈमिस्ट्रस्/ *noun* [C] (*old-fashioned*) the woman who is in charge of a school स्कूल की प्रधानाध्यापिका **NOTE** अब **head** या **headteacher** शब्द का प्रयोग होता है।

**head-on** *adj., adv.* with the front of one car, etc. hitting the front of another दो कारों की आमने-सामने की टक्कर; सम्मुख *a head-on crash*

**headphones** /ˈhedfəʊnz ˈहेड्फ़ोन्ज़्/ *noun* [*pl.*] a piece of equipment worn over the ears that makes it possible to listen to music, the radio, etc. without other people hearing it कानों पर लगाने वाला फ़ोन जिस पर अकेले संगीत सुना जा सकता है; हेडफ़ोन

**headquarters** /ˌhedˈkwɔːtəz ˌहेड्ˈक्वॉटज़्/ *noun* [*pl., with sing. or pl. verb*] (*abbr.* **HQ**) the place from where an organization is controlled; the people who work there किसी संगठन का मुख्यालय; हेडक्वार्टर्स *Where is/are the firm's headquarters?*

**headrest** /ˈhedrest ˈहेड्रेस्ट्/ *noun* [C] the part of a seat or chair that supports a person's head, especially on the front seat of a car सीट या कुरसी का वह हिस्सा जो बैठने वाले के सिर को सहारा देता है (विशेषतः कार की अगली सीटों में), हेडरेस्ट ➪ **car** पर चित्र देखिए।

**headroom** /ˈhedruːm ˈहेड्रूम्/ *noun* [U] **1** the space between the top of a vehicle and an object, for example a bridge, that it drives under वाहन की छत तथा उसके ऊपर की वस्तु (जैसे पुल) के बीच की जगह **2** the space between the top of your head and the inside roof of a vehicle वाहन की अंदरूनी छत और सवारी के सिर के (शीर्ष भाग के) बीच की जगह; शीर्षांतर

**headset** /ˈhedset ˈहेड्सेट्/ *noun* [C] a piece of equipment that you wear on your head that includes a device for listening (**headphones**) and/or a device for speaking into (**a microphone**) सिर पर पहना जाने वाला उपकरण जिसमें हेडफ़ोन और माइक्रोफ़ोन दोनों लगे होते हैं; हेडसेट *The pilot was talking into his headset.*

**headstart** *noun* [*sing.*] an advantage that you have from the beginning of a race or competition किसी खिलाड़ी को दौड़ या स्पर्धा के आरंभ बिंदु से ही प्राप्ति लाभ की स्थिति; हेडस्टार्ट ➪ **start**[4] देखिए

**headstone** /ˈhedstəʊn ˈहेड्स्टोन्/ *noun* [C] a large stone with writing on, used to mark where a dead person is buried मृतक की क़ब्र या समाधि पर उसकी पहचान के लिए लगा पत्थर (जिस पर कुछ लिखा भी होता है); समाधि-शिला ➪ **gravestone** और **tombstone** देखिए।

**headstrong** /ˈhedstrɒŋ ˈहेड्स्ट्रॉङ्/ *adj.* doing what you want, without listening to advice from other people मनमानी करने वाला; हठी, ज़िद्दी

**head teacher** = **head**[1] **6**

**headway** /ˈhedweɪ ˈहेड्वे/ *noun*

**IDM make headway** to go forward or make progress in a difficult situation कठिन परिस्थिति में आगे बढ़ना या प्रगति करना

**headwind** /ˈhedwɪnd ˈहेड्विन्ड्/ *noun* [C] a wind that is blowing towards a person or vehicle, so that it is blowing from the direction in which the person or vehicle is moving सामने से आती हवा; प्रतिकूल पवन ➪ **tailwind** देखिए।

**headword** /ˈhedwɜːd ˈहेड्वड्/ *noun* [C] (*technical*) the first word of an entry in a dictionary, which is followed by an explanation of its meaning शब्दकोश में मुख्य प्रविष्टि (जिसके बाद अर्थ की व्याख्या आती है)

**heal** /hiːl हील्/ *verb* [I, T] **heal (over/up)** to become healthy again; to make sth healthy again पुनः स्वस्थ हो जाना; पुनः स्वस्थ कर देना *The cut will heal up in a few days.* ○ (*figurative*) *Nothing he said could heal the damage done to their relationship.*

**healer** /ˈhiːlə(r) ˈहील(र्)/ *noun* [C] a person who cures people of illnesses and disease using natural powers rather than medicine अपनी प्राकृतिक शक्तियों से (न कि दवाओं से) रोगशमन करने वाला; रोगहर

**health** /helθ हेल्थ्/ *noun* [U] **1** the condition of a person's body or mind व्यक्ति के शरीर या मन की दशा; स्वास्थ्य, सेहत *Fresh fruit and vegetables are good for your health.* ○ *in good/poor health* ○ (*figurative*) *the health of your marriage/finances* **2** the state of being well and free from illness रोगमुक्त और स्वस्थ होने की स्थिति *As long as you have your health, nothing else matters.* **3** the work of providing medical care चिकित्सा सुविधा उपलब्ध कराने का कार्य *health and safety regulations*

**health centre** *noun* [C] a building where a group of doctors see their patients भवन जहाँ डॉक्टर लोग मरीज़ों को देखते हैं; स्वास्थ्य केंद्र, अस्पताल

**health food** *noun* [C, U] natural food that many people think is especially good for your health because it has been made or grown without adding chemicals स्वास्थ्य के लिए हितकर माना जाने वाला प्राकृतिक भोजन

**the health service** *noun* [C] the organization of the medical services of a country देश के चिकित्सा सेवाओं का संगठन, राष्ट्रीय चिकित्सा सेवा

**healthy** /ˈhelθi ˈहेल्थि/ *adj.* (**healthier; healthiest**) **1** not often ill; strong and well निरोग, ठीक-ठाक; सशक्त और स्वस्थ *a healthy child/animal/plant* **2** showing good health (of body or mind) (शारीरिक या मानसिक रूप से) सुस्वस्थ *healthy skin and hair* **3** helping to produce good health स्वास्थ्यप्रद, स्वास्थ्य को लाभ पहुँचाने वाला *a healthy climate/diet/life style* **4** normal and sensible सामान्य और समझदार या विवेकपूर्ण *There was plenty of healthy competition between the brothers.* ✪ विलोम **unhealthy** ▶ **healthily** *adv.* स्वस्थ भाव से

**heap**[1] /hiːp हीप्/ *noun* [C] **1 a heap (of sth)** an untidy pile of sth वस्तुओं का अव्यवस्थित ढेर *a heap of books/papers* ○ *All his clothes are* ***in a heap***

*on the floor!* ➪ **pile** पर नोट देखिए। **2** (*informal*) **a heap (of sth); heaps (of sth)** a large number or amount; plenty बहुत बड़ी संख्या या मात्रा; बहुतायत, प्रचुरता *I've got a heap of work to do.* ○ *There's heaps of time before the train leaves.*

**IDM heaps better, more, older, etc.** (*informal*) much better, etc. कहीं अच्छा

**heap²** /hiːp हीप्/ *verb* [T] **1 heap sth (up)** to put things in a pile चीज़ों का ढेर लगाना; अंबार लगाना *I'm going to heap all the leaves up over there.* ○ *Add six heaped tablespoons of flour* (= in a recipe). **2 heap A on/onto B; heap B with A** to put a large amount of sth on sth/sb किसी स्थान को किसी वस्तु से भर देना, किसी पर कोई चीज़ लाद देना *He heaped food onto his plate.* ○ *The press heaped the team with praise.*

**hear** /hɪə(r) हिअ(र्)/ *verb* (*pt, pp* **heard** /hɜːd हड्/) **1** [I, T] (*not used in the continuous tenses*) to receive sounds with your ears सुनना *Can you speak a little louder—I can't hear very well.* ○ *Did you hear what I said?*

> **NOTE Hear** और **listen** में तुलना कीजिए। प्रायः **hear** का तात्पर्य होता है सुनना बिना आवश्यक (रूप से) प्रयत्न किए; **listen** का तात्पर्य है कुछ सुनने का सचेत या सक्रिय रूप से प्रयास करना—*I always wake up when I hear the milkman come.* ○ *I love listening to music in the evening.* ○ *Listen—I've got something to tell you.* कभी-कभी **hear** और **'listen to'** का अर्थ समान होता है—*We'd better hear what they have to say.*

**2** [T] (*not used in the continuous tenses*) to be told or informed about sth किसी बात को बताया जाना या सूचित किया जाना *I hear that you've been offered a job in Canada.* ○ *'I passed my test!' '**So I've heard**—well done!'*

> **NOTE** यद्यपि यह क्रिया सातत्यबोधक कालों (continuous tenses) में प्रयुक्त नहीं होती तथापि इसका वर्तमान कृदंत रूप (present participle) (= -ing) रूप प्रायः दिखाई पड़ता है—*Not hearing what he'd said over the roar of the machines, she just nodded in reply.*

**3** [T] (used about a judge, a court, etc.) to listen to the evidence in a trial in order to make a decision about it (जज या कचहरी) मुक़दमे की सुनवाई करना (ताकि फ़ैसला किया जा सके); पेशी *Your case will be heard this afternoon.*

**IDM hear! hear!** used for showing that you agree with what sb has just said, especially in a meeting (विशेषतः सभा में) किसी की कही बात से सहमति व्यक्त करने के लिए प्रयुक्त

**won't/wouldn't hear of sth** to refuse to allow sth किसी बात के लिए मना कर देना *I wanted to go to art school but my parents wouldn't hear of it.*

**PHR V hear from sb** to receive a letter, telephone call, etc. from sb किसी का पत्र, फ़ोन आदि आना

**hear of sb/sth** to know that sb/sth exists because you have heard him/her/it mentioned किसी व्यक्ति या वस्तु के अस्तित्व के बारे में जानना (क्योंकि उसके होने की बात आपने सुन रखी है) *Have you heard of the Niagara Falls?*

**hearing** /ˈhɪərɪŋ ˈहिअरिङ्/ *noun* **1** [U] the ability to hear सुनने की क्षमता, श्रवण-शक्ति *Her hearing isn't very good so you need to speak louder.* **2** [*sing.*] a time when evidence is given to a judge in a court of law कचहरी में जज के सामने गवाही; सुनवाई *a court/disciplinary hearing* **3** [*sing.*] a chance to give your opinion or explain your position अपनी राय प्रकट करने या स्थिति स्पष्ट करने का अवसर *to get/give sb a fair hearing*

**hard of hearing** ➪ **hard¹** देखिए।

**in/within sb's hearing** near enough to sb so that he/she can hear what is being said सुनाई पड़ने की सीमा के भीतर

**hearing aid** *noun* [C] a small device for people who cannot hear well that fits inside the ear and makes sounds louder बहरों के सुनने में सहायक छोटी मशीन; हिअरिंग एड

**hearsay** /ˈhɪəseɪ ˈहिअसे/ *noun* [U] things you have heard another person or other people say, which may or may not be true, gossip सुनी-सुनाई बात, दूसरों से सुनी बात जो असत्य भी हो से सकती है

**hearse** /hɜːs हस्/ *noun* [C] a large car used for carrying a dead person to his/her funeral शव ले जाने का वाहन; शवयान

**heart** /hɑːt हाट्/ *noun* **1** [C] the organ inside your chest that sends blood round your body हृदय, दिल *When you exercise your heart beats faster.* ○ *heart disease/failure* ➪ **circulation** देखिए। **2** [C] the centre of a person's feelings and emotions व्यक्ति के मनोभावों का केंद्र *She has a kind heart* (= she is kind and gentle). **3 -hearted** (*used to form compound adjectives*) having the type of feelings or character mentioned निर्दिष्ट प्रकार के भावों वाला *kind-hearted* ○ *cold-hearted* **4** [*sing.*] **the heart (of sth)** the most central or important part of sth; the middle किसी का एकदम केंद्रवर्ती या सर्वाधिक महत्त्वपूर्ण अंश; मध्यवर्ती अंश *Rare plants can be found **in the heart of** the forest.* **5** [C] a symbol that is shaped like a heart, often red or pink and used to show love प्रेम का अभिव्यंजक हृदय की आकृति का

प्रतीक (कोई वस्तु, प्रायः लाल या गुलाबी) *He sent her a card with a big red heart on it.* **6 hearts** [*pl.*] the group (**suit**) of playing cards with red shapes like **hearts 5** on them ताश में लाल रंग के पान के पत्ते (पान की आकृति हृदय के समान होती है) *the queen of hearts* ➪ **card** देखिए। **7** [C] one of the cards from this suit पान का (एक) पत्ता *Play a heart, if you've got one.*

**IDM after your own heart** (used about people) similar to yourself or of the type you like best (व्यक्ति) आपके जैसा या आपकी सर्वाधिक पसंद का

**at heart** really; in fact सचमुच, दिल से; वास्तव में *My father seems strict but he's a very kind man at heart.*

**break sb's heart** to make sb very sad किसी का दिल तोड़ देना, किसी को दुखी करना

**by heart** by remembering exactly; from memory ठीक-ठाक याद करना; स्मृति से, कंठस्थ *Learning lists of words off by heart isn't a good way to increase your vocabulary.*

**a change of heart** ➪ **change**[2] देखिए।

**close/dear/near to sb's heart** having a lot of importance and interest for sb किसी व्यक्ति का आपके लिए बहुत महत्त्वपूर्ण या प्रिय होना

**cross my heart** ➪ **cross**[2] देखिए।

**from the (bottom of your) heart** in a way that is true and sincere हृदय के अंतस्तल से, तहेदिल से, निष्कपट भाव से *I mean what I said from the bottom of my heart.*

**have a heart of gold** to be a very kind person बहुत दयालु व्यक्ति होना

**have/with sb's (best) interests at heart** ➪ **interest**[1] देखिए।

**heart and soul** with a lot of energy and enthusiasm प्रचुर ऊर्जा और उत्साह के साथ

**your heart is not in sth** used to say that you are not very interested in or enthusiastic about sth किसी वस्तु में अधिक रुचि या उत्साह न होने का भाव व्यक्त करने के लिए प्रयुक्त

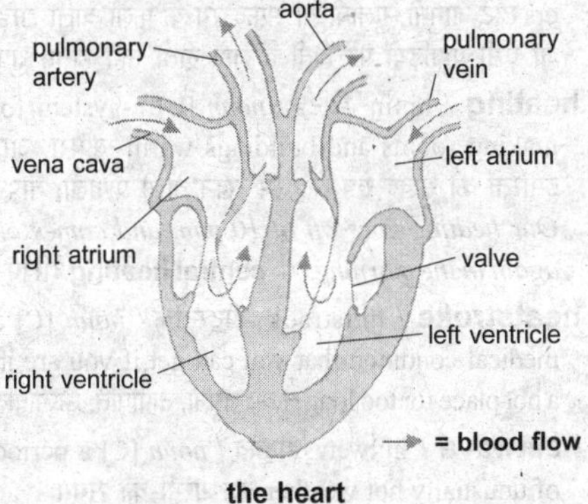

the heart

**your heart sinks** to suddenly feel disappointed or sad एकाएक निराश या दुखी हो जाना *When I saw the queues of people in front of me my heart sank.*

**in your heart (of hearts)** used to say that you know that sth is true although you do not want to admit or believe it यह बताने के लिए प्रयुक्त कि अमुक बात है तो सच परंतु आप ऐसा मानना नहीं चाहते *She knew in her heart of hearts that she was making the wrong decision.*

**lose heart** ➪ **lose** देखिए।

**not have the heart (to do sth)** to be unable to do sth unkind हृदयहीनता न दिखा पाना *I didn't have the heart to say no.*

**pour your heart out (to sb)** ➪ **pour** देखिए।

**set your heart on sth; have your heart set on sth** to decide you want sth very much; to be determined to do or have sth किसी वस्तु के अत्यधिक पसंद होने के निर्णय पर पहुँच जाना; कोई काम करने या कुछ प्राप्त करने का दृढ़ निश्चय कर लेना

**take heart (from sth)** to begin to feel positive and hopeful about sth किसी वस्तु के प्रति अनुकूल और आशावान होने लगना

**take sth to heart** to be deeply affected or upset by sth किसी बात से अत्यधिक प्रभावित या परेशान हो जाना

**to your heart's content** as much as you want जी भर कर

**with all your heart; with your whole heart** completely पूरे दिल से *I hope with all my heart that things work out for you.*

**young at heart** ➪ **young**[1] देखिए।

**heartache** /ˈhɑːteɪk ˈहाट्एक्/ *noun* [U] great sadness or worry घोर व्यथा या चिंता; मनोवेदना

**heart attack** *noun* [C] a sudden serious illness when the heart stops working correctly, sometimes causing death दिल का दौरा, हृदय गति का अनियमित हो जाना; हार्ट अटैक *She's had a heart attack.*

**heartbeat** /ˈhɑːtbiːt ˈहाट्बीट्/ *noun* [C] the regular movement or sound of the heart as it sends blood round the body दिल की धड़कन या धकधक (जिससे शरीर में रक्त प्रवाहित होते रहने की जानकारी मिलती है)

**heartbreak** /ˈhɑːtbreɪk ˈहाट्ब्रेक्/ *noun* [U] very great sadness बहुत गहरी मनोव्यथा, दिल का टूट जाना

**heartbreaking** /ˈhɑːtbreɪkɪŋ ˈहाट्ब्रेकिङ्/ *adj.* making you feel very sad हृदयविदारक; दिल तोड़ देने वाला

**heartbroken** /ˈhɑːtbrəʊkən ˈहाट्ब्रोकन्/ (*also* **broken-hearted**) *adj.* extremely sad because of sth that has happened अत्यंत दुखी, विदीर्ण *Madhu was heartbroken when Vijay left her.*

**heartburn** /ˈhɑːtbɜːn ˈहाट्बन्/ *noun* [U] a pain that feels like sth burning in your chest and that you get when your stomach cannot deal with a particular food अपच के कारण छाती में होने वाली जलन; अम्ल शूल

**hearten** /ˈhɑːtn ˈहाट्न्/ *verb* [T] (*usually passive*) to encourage sb; to make sb feel happier प्रोत्साहित करना, उत्साह बढ़ाना; किसी की प्रसन्नता बढ़ाना ✪ विलोम **dishearten**

**heartening** /ˈhɑːtnɪŋ ˈहाट्निङ्/ *adj.* making you feel more hopeful; encouraging आशावर्धक; उत्साहवर्धक ✪ विलोम **disheartening**

**heartfelt** /ˈhɑːtfelt ˈहाट्फ़ेल्ट्/ *adj.* deeply felt; sincere गहराई से महसूस किया हुआ, हार्दिक; निष्कपट *a heartfelt apology*

**hearth** /hɑːθ हाथ्/ *noun* [C] the place where you have an open fire in the house or the area in front of it घर में चूल्हा जलाने की जगह या चूल्हे के सामने की जगह

**heartily** /ˈhɑːtɪli ˈहाटिलि/ *adv.* **1** with obvious enthusiasm and enjoyment उत्साह और आनंद के साथ, सोत्साह और सानंद *He joined in heartily with the singing.* **2** very much; completely अत्यधिक; पूर्णतया

**heartland** /ˈhɑːtlænd ˈहाट्लैन्ड्/ *noun* [C] the most central or important part of a country, area, etc. किसी देश, क्षेत्र आदि का सर्वाधिक केंद्रीय या महत्त्वपूर्ण भाग *India's industrial heartland*

**heartless** /ˈhɑːtləs ˈहाट्लस्/ *adj.* unkind; cruel निर्मम; क्रूर ▶ **heartlessly** *adv.* निर्ममता से, क्रूरतापूर्वक ▶ **heartlessness** *noun* [U] निर्ममता, क्रूरता

**heart-rending** *adj.* making you feel very sad हृदय-विदारक

**heart-to-heart** *noun* [C] a conversation in which you say exactly what you really feel or think खुले दिल से की गई बातचीत

**hearty** /ˈhɑːti ˈहाटि/ *adj.* **1** showing warm and friendly feelings स्नेहमयी और मैत्रीपूर्ण भावनाओं वाला; हार्दिक *a hearty welcome* **2** loud, happy and full of energy प्रसन्नता तथा ऊर्जा से भरा हुआ; उन्मुक्त *a hearty laugh* **3** large; making you feel full तगड़ा, तीव्र, तेज़; छककर किया जाने वाला (भोजन) *a hearty appetite* **4** showing that you feel strongly about sth हृदय से समर्थित *He nodded his head in hearty agreement.*

**heat**[1] /hiːt हीट्/ *noun* **1** [U] the feeling of sth hot ताप, गरमी *This fire doesn't **give out** much **heat**.* **2** [*sing.*] (*often with 'the'*) hot weather (प्रायः 'the' के साथ) गरमी का मौसम *I like the English climate because I can't stand the heat.* **3** [*sing.*] a thing that produces heat ताप या गरमी उत्पन्न करने वाली वस्तु *Remove the pan from the heat* (= the hot part of the stove). **4** [U] a state or time of anger or excitement क्रोध या उत्तेजना की दशा या क्षण ***In the heat of the moment**, she threatened to resign.* **5** [C] one of the first parts of a race or competition. The winners of the heats compete against other winners until the final result is decided दौड़ या स्पर्धा के प्रथम चरणों में से एक प्रारंभिक दौड़, इसे जीतने वाले ही अंतिम दौड़ में भाग लेते हैं

IDM **be on heat** (used about some female animals) to be ready to have sex because it is the right time of the year (कुछ मादा पशु) संभोग के लिए तैयार (उचित समय होने के कारण)

**heat**[2] /hiːt हीट्/ *verb* [I, T] **heat (sth) (up)** to become or to make sth hot or warm गरम या गुनगुना हो जाना या कर देना *Wait for the oven to heat up before you put the pie in.* ○ *The meal is already cooked but it will need heating up.*

**heated** /ˈhiːtɪd ˈहीटिड्/ *adj.* (used about a person or discussion) angry or excited (व्यक्ति या चर्चा) क्रोधित या उत्तेजनापूर्ण *a heated argument/debate* ▶ **heatedly** *adv.* क्रोध से, उत्तेजित होकर

**heater** /ˈhiːtə(r) ˈहीट(र्)/ *noun* [C] a machine used for making water or the air in a room, car, etc. hotter पानी या कमरे की वायु को गरम करने वाली मशीन; हीटर *an electric/gas heater* ○ *a water heater*

**heath** /hiːθ हीथ्/ *noun* [C] (especially in Britain) an area of open land that is not used for farming and that is often covered with rough grass and other wild plants बंजर भूमि, अजोत भूमि

**heathen** /ˈhiːðn ˈहीद्न्/ *noun* [C] (*old-fashioned*) a person who does not belong to one of the main world religions संसार के मुख्य धर्मों से विमुख व्यक्ति; विधर्मी

**heather** /ˈheðə(r) ˈहेद्र(र्)/ *noun* [U] a low wild plant that grows especially on hills and land that is not farmed and has small purple, pink or white flowers छोटे जामुनी, गुलाबी या सफ़ेद रंग के फूलों वाली झाड़ी जो ऐसी पहाड़ियों पर होती है जहाँ खेती नहीं होती; क्षुप

**heating** /ˈhiːtɪŋ ˈहीटिङ्/ *noun* [U] a system for making rooms and buildings warm कमरों और इमारतों को सुखद रूप से गरम रखने वाली प्रणाली; तापन *Our heating goes off at 10 p.m. and comes on again in the morning.* ➪ **central heating** देखिए।

**heatstroke** /ˈhiːtstrəʊk ˈहीट्स्ट्रोक्/ *noun* [C] a medical condition that you can get if you are in a hot place for too long लू का लगना, तापाघात, ऊष्माघात

**heatwave** /ˈhiːtweɪv ˈहीट्वेव्/ *noun* [C] a period of unusually hot weather तेज़ गरमी का समय

**heave**[1] /hi:v हीव़्/ *verb* **1** [I, T] to lift, pull or throw sb/sth heavy with one big effort सप्रयास किसी भारी व्यक्ति या वस्तु को ऊपर उठाना, खींचना या फेंकना *Take hold of this rope and heave!* ○ *We heaved the cupboard up the stairs.* **2** [I] **heave (with sth)** to move up and down or in and out in a heavy but regular way भारीपन के साथ लगातार ऊपर-नीचे गिरना या अंदर-बाहर जाना *His chest was heaving with the effort of carrying the trunk.* **3** [I] to experience the tight feeling you get in your stomach when you are just about to vomit उलटी आने से पहले पेट में भारीपन महसूस करना *The sight of all that blood made her stomach heave.*

IDM **heave a sigh** to breathe out slowly and loudly धीरे और आवाज़ के साथ साँस लेना *He heaved a sigh of relief when he heard the good news.*

**heave**[2] /hi:v हीव़्/ *noun* [C, U] a strong pull, push, throw, etc. ज़ोर से खींचने, धकियाने, फेंकने आदि की क्रिया

**heaven** /ˈhevn ˈहेव़्न्/ *noun* **1** [*sing.*] the place where, in some religions, it is believed that God lives and where good people go when they die स्वर्ग; कुछ धर्मों की मान्यता के अनुसार ईश्वर का निवासस्थान *to go to/be in heaven* ➪ **hell** देखिए।

> NOTE कुछ अभिव्यक्तियों में **God** के स्थान पर **Heaven** का प्रयोग किया जाता है ➪ **God** पर नोट देखिए।

**2** [U, C] a place or a situation in which you are very happy ऐसा स्थान या स्थिति जिसमें आप प्रसन्न रहते हैं, आनंद या सुख-शांति का स्थान *It was heaven being away from work for a week.* **3 the heavens** [*pl.*] (used in poetry and literature) the sky (कविता और साहित्य में प्रयुक्त) आकाश, आसमान

**heavenly** /ˈhevnli ˈहेव़्नलि/ *adj.* **1** (*only before a noun*) connected with heaven or the sky स्वर्ग, आकाश या अंतरिक्ष से संबंधित *heavenly bodies* (= the sun, moon, stars, etc.) **2** (*informal*) very pleasant; wonderful बहुत आनंदप्रद; आश्चर्यजनक

**heavy** /ˈhevi ˈहेवि़/ *adj.* (**heavier; heaviest**) **1** weighing a lot; difficult to lift or move भारी; जिसे उठाना या हिलाना मुश्किल हो *This box is too heavy for me to carry.* **2** used when asking or stating how much sb/sth weighs व्यक्ति या वस्तु का भार पूछने के लिए प्रयुक्त ***How heavy** is your suitcase?* **3** larger, stronger or more than usual अधिक बड़ा, जोरदार, उग्र या असाधारण *heavy rain* ○ *heavy traffic* ○ *a heavy smoker/drinker* (= a person who smokes/drinks a lot) ○ *The sound of his heavy* (= loud and deep) *breathing told her that he was asleep.* ○ *a heavy sleeper* (= sb who is difficult to wake) **4** serious, difficult or boring गंभीर, कठिन या उबाऊ *His latest novel makes **heavy reading**.* **5** full of hard work; (too) busy परिश्रमपूर्ण, गतिविधिपूर्ण; (अति) व्यस्त *a heavy day/schedule/timetable* **6** (used about a material or substance) solid or thick (सामग्री या पदार्थ) ठोस या मोटा *heavy soil* ○ *a heavy coat* ✪ विलोम **light** (सब अर्थों का) ▶ **heavily** *adv* अत्यधिक, भारीपन से ▶ **heaviness** *noun* [U] भारीपन, गुरुता

IDM **make heavy weather of sth** to make sth seem more difficult than it really is किसी काम को वास्तविकता से अधिक कठिन दिखाना

**heavy-duty** *adj.* not easily damaged and therefore suitable for regular use or for hard physical work टिकाऊ और मज़बूत (अतः नियमित उपयोग या कठोर कामों के लिए उपयुक्त) *a heavy-duty carpet/tyre*

**heavy-handed** *adj.* **1** not showing much understanding of other people's feelings दूसरों की भावनाओं को ठीक से न समझने वाला, संवेदनशीलता-रहित *a heavy-handed approach* **2** using unnecessary force अनावश्यक बल के प्रयोग वाला, धक्काशाही वाला *heavy-handed police methods*

**heavy industry** *noun* [C, U] industry that uses large machinery to produce metal, coal, vehicles, etc. धातु, कोयला उत्पन्न करने के लिए भारी मशीनों का प्रयोग करने वाला उद्योग; भारी उद्योग

**heavy metal** *noun* [U] a style of very loud rock music that is played on electric instruments विद्युत-चालित वाद्यों से बजाया जाने वाला एक प्रकार का ऊँचे स्वर का रॉक संगीत

**heavyweight** /ˈheviweɪt ˈहेविवेट्/ *noun* [C] a person who is in the heaviest weight group in certain fighting sports मुक्केबाजी आदि खेलों में सबसे अधिक वज़नदार खिलाड़ी वर्ग का सदस्य; हैवीवेट *the world heavyweight boxing champion*

**heckle** /ˈhekl ˈहेक्ल्/ *verb* [I, T] to interrupt a speaker at a public meeting with difficult questions or rude comments कठिन प्रश्नों या अशिष्ट टिप्पणियों से वक्ता के सार्वजनिक भाषण में बाधा डालना, टोकाटाकी करना ▶ **heckler** *noun* [C] टोकाटोकी करने वाला

**hectare** /ˈhekteə(r) ˈहेक्टेअ(र्)/ *noun* [C] a measurement of land; 10,000 square metres भूमि की एक माप; दस हज़ार वर्ग मीटर, हेक्टेअर

**hectic** /ˈhektɪk ˈहेक्टिक्/ *adj.* very busy with a lot of things that you have to do quickly अत्यधिक व्यस्त, प्रायः बहुत से कार्य शीघ्र करते हुए ▶ **hectically** /-kli -कलि/ *adv.* अतिव्यस्तता पूर्वक

**he'd** ➪ **he had; he would** का संक्षिप्त रूप

**hedge**[1] /hedʒ हेज्/ *noun* [C] a row of bushes or trees planted close together at the edge of a garden or field to separate one piece of land from another झाड़ीदार बाड़ जो एक खेत या बग़ीचे को दूसरे से अलग करती है

**hedge**[2] /hedʒ हेज्/ *verb* [I] to avoid giving a direct answer to a question प्रश्न का सीधा उत्तर देने से कतराना

**IDM hedge your bets** to protect yourself against losing or making a mistake by supporting more than one person or opinion एक से अधिक व्यक्तियों या विचारों का समर्थन कर संभावित हार या भूल से अपने को बचाना

**hedgehog** /ˈhedʒhɒg ˈहेजहॉग्/ *noun* [C] a small brown animal covered with sharp needles (**prickles**) काँटेदार पीठ वाला एक छोटा भूरा प्राणी; साही, काँटाचूहा

**hedgerow** /ˈhedʒrəʊ ˈहेजरो/ *noun* [C] a row of bushes, etc. especially at the side of a country road or around a field झाड़ियों की क़तार, बाड़ (विशेषतः गाँव की सड़क के साथ-साथ या खेत के चारों ओर) बाड़ पंक्ति

**heed**[1] /hi:d हीड्/ *verb* [T] (*formal*) to pay attention to advice, a warning, etc. सलाह, चेतावनी आदि पर ध्यान देना

**heed**[2] /hi:d हीड्/ *noun* (*formal*)

**IDM take heed (of sb/sth); pay heed (to sb/sth)** to pay careful attention to what sb says किसी के कहे पर विशेष या सावधानी से ध्यान देना *You should take heed of your doctor's advice.*

**heel**[1] /hi:l हील्/ *noun* [C] **1** the back part of your foot एड़ी; पैर का पिछला हिस्सा ➪ **body** पर चित्र देखिए। **2** the part of a sock, etc. that covers your heel ज़ुराब या मोज़े आदि का एड़ी को ढकने वाला हिस्सा, मोज़े की एड़ी **3** the higher part of a shoe under the heel of your foot एड़ी के नीचे आने वाला जूते का ऊपर उठा हिस्सा, जूते की हील या एड़ी *High heels* (= shoes with high heels) *are not practical for long walks.* **4 -heeled** having the type of heel mentioned निर्दिष्ट प्रकार की एड़ी वाला *high-heeled/low-heeled shoes*

**IDM dig your heels in** ➪ **dig**[1] देखिए।

**head over heels** ➪ **head**[1] देखिए।

**heel**[2] /hi:l हील्/ *verb* [T] to repair the heel of a shoe जूते की एड़ी की मरम्मत करना

**hefty** /ˈhefti ˈहेफ़्टि/ *adj.* (*informal*) big and strong or heavy बड़ा और मज़बूत या भारी *a hefty young man*

**hegemony** /hɪˈdʒeməni; -ˈge- हिˈजेमनि; -ˈगे-/ *noun* [U, C] (*pl.* **hegemonies**) (*formal*) control by one country, organization, etc. over other countries, etc. within a particular group समूह विशेष के भीतर एक देश या संगठन का दूसरे पर आधिपत्य; प्राधान्य ▶ **hegemonic** /ˌhedʒɪˈmɒnɪk; ˌhegɪ- ˌहेजिˈमॉनिक्; ˌहेगि-/ *adj.* आधिपत्य-विषयक

**heifer** /ˈhefə(r) ˈहेफ़(र्)/ *noun* [C] a young female cow, especially one that has not yet had a baby (**calf**) जवान बछिया (विशेषतः वह जो अभी ब्याई नहीं)

**height** /haɪt हाइट्/ *noun* **1** [C, U] the measurement from the bottom to the top of a person or thing व्यक्ति या वस्तु की नीचे से ऊपर की माप; ऊँचाई, लंबाई *The nurse is going to check your height and weight.* ○ *We need a fence that's about two metres* ***in height***. ➪ **high** adjective देखिए तथा **tall** पर नोट देखिए। **2** [U] the fact that sb/sth is tall or high लंबाई या ऊँचाई *He looks older than he is because of his height.* **3** [C, U] the distance that sth is above the ground भूमि से ऊपर की तरफ़ की दूरी; ऊँचाई *We are now flying at a height of 10,000 metres.*

**NOTE** विमान ऊँचाई अर्जित **(gain(s))** करता है या खोता **(lose s** है। विमान के संदर्भ में ऊँचाई के लिए शब्द **altitude** औपचारिक प्रयोग है।

**4** [C, *usually pl.*] a high place or area ऊँचा स्थान या इलाक़ा *I can't go up there. I'm afraid of heights.* **5** [U] the strongest or most important part of sth किसी वस्तु का सर्वाधिक सशक्त या महत्त्वपूर्ण अंश; पराकाष्ठा *the height of summer*

**heighten** /ˈhaɪtn ˈहाइट्न्/ *verb* [I, T] to become or to make sth greater or stronger अधिक बड़ा या सशक्त हो जाना या बढ़ाना

**heir** /eə(r) एअ(र्)/ *noun* [C] **heir (to sth)** the person with the legal right to receive (**inherit**) money, property or a title when the owner dies मालिक की मृत्यु के बाद उसकी संपत्ति का क़ानूनी हक़दार व्यक्ति; उत्तराधिकारी, वारिस *He's the heir to a large fortune.*

**NOTE** उत्तराधिकारी स्त्री हो तो कभी-कभी उसे **heiress** कहा जाता है।

**heirloom** /ˈeəlu:m ˈएअलूम्/ *noun* [C] something valuable that has belonged to the same family for many years अनेक वर्षों से एक ही परिवार में रही बहुमूल्य वस्तु, पुश्तैनी चीज़; कुलागत वस्तु

**held** ➪ **hold**[1] का past tense और past participle रूप

**helicopter** /ˈhelɪkɒptə(r) ˈहेलिकॉप्ट(र्)/ (*informal* **chopper**) *noun* [C] a small aircraft that can go straight up into the air. Helicopters have long thin metal parts on top that go round हेलिकॉप्टर

**helium** /ˈhiːliəm ˈहीलिअम्/ *noun* [U] (*symbol* **He**) a very light colourless gas that does not burn, often used to fill objects that float in the air (**balloons**) न जलने वाली बहुत हलकी रंगहीन गैस जो गुब्बारों में भरी जाती है; हीलियम **NOTE** **Helium** एक **noble gas** (अन्य रसायनों से अभिक्रिया न करने वाली गैस) है।

**helix** /ˈhiːlɪks ˈहीलिक्स्/ *noun* [C] (*pl.* **helices** /ˈhiːlɪsiːz ˈहीलिसीज़्/) a shape like a **spiral** (= a long curved line that moves round and round away from a central point) or a line curved round a **cylinder** or **cone** कुंडली मारे सर्प जैसी आकृति या सिलेंडर अथवा शंकु के चारों ओर बनी वक्र रेखा; सर्पिल कुंडली

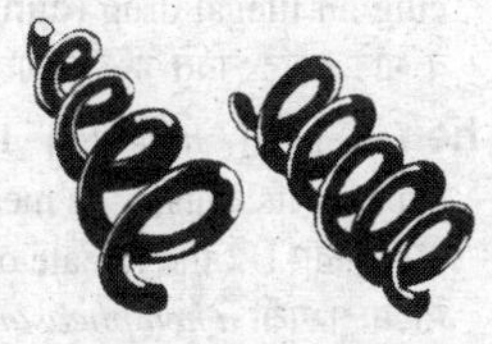

**he'll** /hiːl हील्/ ➪ **he will** का संक्षिप्त रूप

**hell** /hel हेल्/ *noun* **1** [*sing.*] the place where, in some religions, it is believed that the Devil lives and where bad people go to when they die नरक; कुछ धर्मों की मान्यता के अनुसार शैतान का निवासस्थान जहाँ पापी मरने के बाद जाते हैं *to go to/be in hell* ➪ **heaven** देखिए। **2** [C, U] (*informal*) a situation or place that is very unpleasant or painful अत्यंत अप्रिय या कष्टप्रद स्थिति या स्थान; नारकीय *He went through hell when his wife left him.*

> **NOTE** ध्यान रखिए कि कुछ लोगों को **'hell'** का निम्नलिखित अर्थ और इससे बनने वाले मुहावरे अपमानजनक लगते हैं।

**3** [U] (*slang*) used as a swear word to show anger क्रोध व्यक्त करने के लिए अपशब्द के रूप में प्रयुक्त *Oh hell, I've forgotten my money!* **4 the hell** (*slang*) used as a swear word in questions to show anger or surprise प्रश्नवाचक वाक्यों में क्रोध या आश्चर्य व्यक्त करने के लिए अपशब्द के रूप में प्रयुक्त *Why the hell didn't you tell me this before?*

**IDM a/one hell of a...** (*informal*) used to make an expression stronger or to mean 'very' किसी अभिव्यक्ति को अधिक सशक्त बनाने या (अत्यधिक) के अर्थ में प्रयुक्त *He got into a hell of a fight* (= a terrible fight).

**all hell broke loose** (*informal*) there was suddenly a lot of noise and confusion एकाएक बहुत शोर-शराबा हो गया और अफ़रा-तफ़री मच गई, मानो क़हर टूट पड़ा हो

**(just) for the hell of it** (*informal*) for fun मस्ती के लिए

**give sb hell** (*informal*) to speak to sb very angrily or to be very strict with sb किसी से बहुत गुस्से से बोलना या बहुत कड़ाई से पेश आना

**like hell** (*informal*) very much; with a lot of effort अत्यधिक; कड़ी मेहनत के साथ *I'm working like hell at the moment.*

**hellish** /ˈhelɪʃ ˈहेलिश्/ *adj.* terrible; awful भयावह; अत्यधिक अरुचिकर *a hellish experience*

**hello** (*BrE* **hallo**) /həˈləʊ हˈलो/ *exclamation* used when you meet sb, for attracting sb's attention or when you are using the telephone किसी से मिलने पर, किसी का ध्यान खींचने के लिए या फ़ोन करते समय प्रयुक्त

**helm** /helm हेल्म्/ *noun* [C] the part of a boat or ship that is used to guide it. The helm can be a handle or a wheel नाव या जहाज़ का दिशानिर्देश करने वाला अंग; पतवार या पहिया/चाक

**IDM at the helm** in charge of an organization, group of people, etc. किसी संगठन या व्यक्ति समूह का प्रमुख

**helmet** /ˈhelmɪt ˈहेल्मिट्/ *noun* [C] a type of hard hat that you wear to protect your head सिर का बचाव करने वाला एक प्रकार का कड़ा टोप; हेल्मेट

**help[1]** /help हेल्प्/ *verb* **1** [I, T] **help (sb) (with sth); help (sb) (to) do sth; help sb (across, over, out of, into, etc.)** to do sth for sb in order to be useful or to make sth easier for him/her किसी की सहायता करना *Could you help me with the cooking?* ○ *My son's helping in our shop at the moment.* ○ *She helped her grandmother up the stairs* (= supported her as she climbed the stairs). **2** [I, T] to make sth better or easier हालात को बेहतर या अधिक आसान बना देना *If you apologize to him it might help.* ○ *This medicine should help your headache.* **3** [T] **help yourself (to sth)** to take sth (especially food and drink) that is offered to you परोसी गई वस्तु (प्रायः खाद्य और पेय) ले लेना *'If you want another drink, just help yourself.'* **4** [T] **help yourself to sth** to take sth without asking permission; to steal बिना पूछे कोई वस्तु ले लेना; चुरा लेना **5** [I] (*spoken*) used to get sb's attention when you are in danger or difficulty संकट या कठिनाई में किसी से मदद पाना *Help! I'm going to fall!*

**IDM can/can't/couldn't help sth** be able/not be able to stop or avoid doing sth किसी बात को रोकने या उससे कतराने में समर्थ या असमर्थ होना *It was so funny I couldn't help laughing.* ○ *I just couldn't help myself—I had to laugh.*

**a helping hand** some help सहायता, मदद *My neighbour is always ready to give me a helping hand.*

**PHR V** **help (sb) out** to help sb in a difficult situation; to give money to help sb कठिनाई में किसी की मदद करना; सहायतार्थ धन देना

**help²** /help हेल्प्/ *noun* **1** [U] **help (with sth)** the act of helping सहायता, मदद *Do you need any help with that?* ○ *This map isn't much help.* ○ *She stopped smoking **with the help of** her family and friends.* **2** [*sing.*] **a help (to sb)** a person or thing that helps सहायता करने वाला व्यक्ति या वस्तु; मददगार *Your directions were a great help—we found the place easily.*

**helper** /ˈhelpə(r) ˈहेल्पर्(र्)/ *noun* [C] a person who helps (especially with work) सहायक व्यक्ति (विशेषतः काम में), सहायता दाता व्यक्ति, मददगार इनसान

**helpful** /ˈhelpfl ˈहेल्प्फ़ल्/ *adj.* giving help सहायता करने वाला, सहायतापूर्ण, सहायक, सहायता के लिए तत्पर *helpful advice* ▸ **helpfully** /-fəli -फ़लि/ *adv.* सहायतापूर्वक ▸ **helpfulness** *noun* [U] सहायतापूर्वकता

**helping** /ˈhelpɪŋ ˈहेल्पिङ्/ *noun* [C] the amount of food that is put on a plate at one time तश्तरी में एक बार में परोसे भोजन की मात्रा *After two helpings of pasta, I couldn't eat any more.* ➪ **portion** देखिए।

**helpless** /ˈhelpləs ˈहेल्प्लस्/ *adj.* unable to take care of yourself or do things without the help of other people असहाय, लाचार, विवश, बिना दूसरों की सहायता के अपनी देखभाल या अल्प काम करने में असमर्थ *a helpless baby* ▸ **helplessly** *adv.* असहाय भाव से, लाचार या विवश होकर *They watched helplessly as their house went up in flames.* ▸ **helplessness** *noun* [U] सहायताहीनता, लाचारी, विवशता

**hem¹** /hem हेम्/ *noun* [C] the edge at the bottom of a piece of cloth (especially on a skirt, dress or trousers) that has been turned up and sewn स्कर्ट, पैंट आदि पोशाक के सबसे नीचे का किनारा; गोट

**hem²** /hem हेम्/ *verb* [T] (**he<u>mm</u>ing; he<u>mm</u>ed**) to turn up and sew the bottom of a piece of clothing or cloth पोशाक का किनारा बनाना या गोट लगाना **PHR V** **hem sb in** to surround sb and prevent him/her from moving away किसी को ऐसे घेर लेना कि बाहर न जाए *We were hemmed in by the crowd and could not leave.*

**hematite** (*AmE*) = **haematite**

**hemisphere** /ˈhemɪsfɪə(r) ˈहेमिस्फ़िअ(र्)/ *noun* [C] **1** one half of the earth पृथ्वी का आधा भाग; गोलार्ध *the northern/southern/eastern/western hemisphere* **2** the shape of half a ball; half a **sphere** गेंद के आधे भाग की आकृति; अर्धवृत्त, आधा गोला

**hemoglobin** (*AmE*) = **haemoglobin**

**hemophilia, hemophiliac** (*AmE*) = **haemophilia, haemophiliac**

**hemorrhage** (*AmE*) = **haemorrhage**

**hemorrhoids** (*AmE*) = **haemorrhoids**

**hemp** /hemp हेम्प्/ *noun* [U] a plant that is used for making rope and rough cloth and for producing an illegal drug (**cannabis**) सन जिससे रस्सी व मोटे कपड़े बनते हैं और गाँजा तैयार होता है

**hen** /hen हेन्/ *noun* [C] **1** a female bird that is kept for its eggs or its meat मुरग़ी ➪ **chicken** पर नोट देखिए। **2** the female of any type of bird कोई भी मादा पक्षी *a hen pheasant* **NOTE** मुरग़ी के नर को **cock** कहते हैं।

**hence** /hens हेन्स्/ *adv.* (*formal*) for this reason अतएव, इस कारण से, फलतः *I've got some news to tell you—hence the letter.*

**henceforth** /ˌhensˈfɔːθ ˌहेन्स्ˈफ़ॉथ्/ (*also* **henceforward** /ˌhensˈfɔːwəd ˌहेन्स्ˈफ़ॉवड्/) *adv.* (*written*) from now on; in future यहाँ से, अब से; भविष्य में

**henchman** /ˈhentʃmən ˈहेन्च्मन्/ *noun* [C] (*pl.* **-men** /-mən -मन्/) a person who is employed by sb to protect him/her and who may do things that are illegal or violent किसी की रक्षा के लिए नियुक्त व्यक्ति जो ग़ैर-क़ानूनी या हिंसात्मक कार्य भी कर सकता है

**henna** /ˈhenə ˈहेना/ *noun* [U] a reddish-brown colour (**dye**) that is obtained from the henna plant. It is used to colour and decorate the hands, finger nails, etc. मेहँदी

**hen party** (*also* **hen night**) *noun* [*sing.*] a party that a woman who is getting married soon has with her female friends शीघ्र विवाह करने वाली युवती की, सहेलियों के साथ, पार्टी ➪ **stag night** देखिए।

**henpecked** /ˈhenpekt ˈहेन्पेक्ट्/ *adj.* used to describe a husband who always does what his wife tells him to do पत्नी का आज्ञाकारी पति; जोरू का गुलाम

**hepatic** /hɪˈpætɪk हिˈपैटिक्/ *adj.* (*technical*) connected with the **liver** यकृत या जिगर से संबंधित

**hepatic portavein** = **portal vein**

**hepatitis** /ˌhepəˈtaɪtɪs ˌहेपˈटाइटिस्/ *noun* [U] a serious disease of one of the body's main organs (**liver**) यकृत-शोथ, जिगर की सूजन

**hepta-** /ˈheptə ˈहेप्टा/ *prefix* (*used in nouns, adjectives and adverbs*) seven; having seven सात; सात वाला, सप्त *heptathlon* (= an athletics competition, usually one for women, that consists of seven different events)

**heptagon** /ˈheptəgən ˈहेप्टगन्/ *noun* [C] a flat shape with seven straight sides and seven angles सात सीधी रेखाओं और सात कोणों वाली आकृति; सप्तभुज ▶ **heptagonal** /hepˈtægənl हेप्ˈटैगनल्/ *adj.* सप्तभुजीय

**her¹** /hɜ:(r) ह(र्)/ *pronoun* (*the object of a verb or preposition*) the female person that was mentioned earlier पूर्वनिर्दिष्ट स्त्री व्यक्ति, उसे *He told Sheela that he loved her.* ○ *I've got a letter for your mother. Could you give it to her, please?* ➪ **she** और **he** पर नोट देखिए।

**her²** /hɜ:(r) ह(र्)/ *det.* of or belonging to the female person mentioned earlier पूर्वनिर्दिष्ट स्त्री व्यक्ति का या उसके स्वामित्व का या उससे संबद्ध, उसका/के/की *That's her book. She left it there this morning.* ○ *Mala has broken her leg.* ➪ **hers** देखिए।

**herald** /ˈherəld ˈहेरल्ड्/ *verb* [T] (*written*) to be a sign that sth is going to happen soon इस बात का संकेत होना कि कुछ घटित होने वाला है *The minister's speech heralded a change of policy.*

**heraldry** /ˈherəldri ˈहेरल्ड्रि/ *noun* [U] the study of the history of old and important families and their special family symbols (**coats of arms**) प्राचीन और महत्त्वपूर्ण वंशों और उनके विशिष्ट वंशचिह्नों का इतिहास; कुल चिह्न

**herb** /hɜ:b हब्/ *noun* [C] a plant whose leaves, seeds, etc. are used in medicine or in cooking जड़ी-बूटी *Add some herbs, such as rosemary and thyme.* ➪ **spice** देखिए।

**herbaceous** /hɜ:ˈbeɪʃəs हˈबेशस्/ *adj.* (*technical*) connected with plants that have soft **stems** कोमल तने वाले पौधों से संबंधित *a herbaceous plant*

**herbal** /ˈhɜ:bl ˈहब्ल्/ *adj.* made of or using herbs जड़ी-बूटी का, शाक *herbal medicine/remedies*

**herbicide** /ˈhɜ:bɪsaɪd ˈहबिसाइड्/ *noun* [C, U] a chemical substance that farmers use to kill plants that are growing where they are not wanted ग़लत स्थान पर उग आए या अनचाहे पौधों का नाशक रसायन

**herbivore** /ˈhɜ:bɪvɔ:(r) ˈहबिव़ॉ(र्)/ *noun* [C] an animal that only eats grass and plants शाकाहारी प्राणी ➪ **carnivore, insectivore** और **omnivore** देखिए। ▶ **herbivorous** /hɜ:ˈbɪvərəs हबिव़रस्/ *adj.* शाकाहारी *herbivorous dinosaurs*

**herd¹** /hɜ:d हड्/ *noun* [C] a large number of animals that live and feed together साथ रहने और खाने वाले पशुओं का झुंड *a herd of cattle/deer/elephants* ➪ **flock** देखिए।

**herd²** /hɜ:d हड्/ *verb* [T] to move people or animals somewhere together in a group लोगों या पशुओं को झुंड में कहीं ले जाना *The prisoners were herded onto the train.*

**herdsman** /ˈhɜ:dzmən ˈहड्ज़्मन्/ (*pl.* **-men** /-mən -मन्/) *noun* [C] a man who looks after a group of animals पशुओं के झुंड की देखभाल करने वाला व्यक्ति; पशुपालक, चरवाहा

**here¹** /hɪə(r) हिअ(र्)/ *adv.* **1** (*after a verb or a preposition*) in, at or to the place where you are or which you are pointing to जहाँ आप हैं वहाँ या उस ओर, या जिस ओर आप इशारा कर रहे हैं; यहाँ *Come (over) here.* ○ *The school is a kilometre from here.* ○ *Please sign here.* **2** used at the beginning of a sentence to introduce or draw attention to sb/sth किसी व्यक्ति या वस्तु की ओर ध्यान खींचने या उसे प्रस्तुत करने के लिए वाक्य के आरंभ में प्रयुक्त *Here is the nine o'clock news.* ○ *Here comes the bus.* ○ *Here we are* (= we've arrived).

> **NOTE** अंतिम उदाहरण में शब्दों का क्रम पिछले वाक्यों से अलग है। हम कहते हैं—*Here are the children.* परंतु सर्वनाम के साथ वाक्य बनता है—*Here they are.* निम्नलिखित अभिव्यक्ति या वाक्य पर ध्यान दीजिए—**Here you are** इसका प्रयोग तब करते हैं जब कोई व्यक्ति किसी को कुछ देता है—*Here you are—this is that book I was talking about.*

**3** used for emphasizing a noun संज्ञा पर बल देने के लिए प्रयुक्त *I think you'll find this book here very useful.* **4** at this point in a discussion or a piece of writing किसी चर्चा या लेख में इस बिंदु पर *Here the speaker stopped and looked around the room.*

**IDM** **here and there** in various places अनेक स्थानों पर, यहाँ-वहाँ, यत्र-तत्र, सर्वत्र

**here goes** (*informal*) used to say that you are about to do sth exciting, dangerous, etc. कोई ख़तरनाक, उत्तेजक काम शुरू करने से पहले वक्ता द्वारा प्रयुक्त *I've never done a backward dive before, but here goes!*

**here's to sb/sth** used for wishing for the health, success, etc. of sb/sth while holding a drink पानगोष्ठी में गिलास थामे किसी को शुभकामनाएँ देने के लिए प्रयुक्त *Here's to a great holiday!*

**neither here nor there** not important महत्त्वहीन, बेमतलब *My opinion is neither here nor there. If you like the dress then buy it.*

**here²** /hɪə(r) हिअ(र्)/ exclamation used for attracting sb's attention, when offering help or when giving sth to sb सहायता की पेशकश करते हुए या कुछ देते हुए किसी का ध्यान आकृष्ट करने के लिए प्रयुक्त *Here, let me help!*

**hereabouts** /ˌhɪərəˈbaʊts ˌहिअरˈबाउट्स्/ (*AmE* **hereabout**) *adv.* around or near here आसपास या यहाँ से पास

**hereafter** /ˌhɪərˈɑːftə(r) ˌहिअर्ˈआफ़्ट(र्)/ *adv.* (*written*) (used in legal documents, etc.) from now on (क़ानूनी काग़ज़ात आदि में प्रयुक्त) यहाँ से, अब से, भविष्य में

**hereditary** /həˈredɪtri हˈरेडिट्रि/ *adj.* passed on from parent to child माता-पिता से संतान तक पहुँचाया हुआ; पुश्तैनी, आनुवंशिक *a hereditary disease*

**heredity** /həˈredəti हˈरेडटि/ *noun* [U] the process by which physical or mental qualities pass from parent to child वह प्रक्रिया जिसके द्वारा माता-पिता के शारीरिक या मानसिक गुण संतान तक पहुँचते हैं; आनुवंशिकता

**heresy** /ˈherəsi ˈहेरसि/ *noun* [C, U] (*pl.* **heresies**) a (religious) opinion or belief that is different from what is generally accepted to be true अपसिद्धांत, विधर्म, अधर्म

**heretic** /ˈherətɪk ˈहेरटिक्/ *noun* [C] a person whose religious beliefs are believed to be wrong or evil ऐसा व्यक्ति जिसके धार्मिक विश्वास अस्वीकार्य या सदोष माने गए हों; विधर्मी, अधर्मी ▶ **heretical** /həˈretɪkl हˈरेटिक्ल्/ *adj.* विधर्म-संबंधी

**herewith** /ˌhɪəˈwɪð ˌहिअˈविद्/ *adv.* (*formal*) with this letter, etc. इस (पत्र आदि) के साथ *Please fill in the form enclosed herewith.*

**heritage** /ˈherɪtɪdʒ ˈहेरिटिज्/ *noun* [C, *usually sing.*] the traditions, qualities and culture of a country that have existed for a long time and that have great importance for the country एक देश की चिरकालिक तथा महत्त्वपूर्ण मानी गई परंपराएँ, विशेषताएँ और संस्कृति; धरोहर, विरासत

**hermaphrodite** /hɜːˈmæfrədaɪt हˈमैफ्रडाइट्/ *noun* [C] a person, an animal or a flower that has both male and female sexual organs or characteristics व्यक्ति, पशु या पुष्प जिसमें नर और मादा दोनों के यौनांग या लक्षण हों; उभयलिंगी

**hermit** /ˈhɜːmɪt ˈहमिट्/ *noun* [C] a person who prefers to live alone, without contact with other people सामाजिक जीवन से दूर एकांत में रहने वाला व्यक्ति; एकांतवासी, संन्यासी

**hermitage** /ˈhɜːmɪtɪdʒ ˈहमिटिज्/ *noun* [C,U] a place away from society where a **hermit** lives or lived समाज से दूर संन्यासी का निवास स्थान; आश्रम, कुटीर

**hernia** /ˈhɜːniə ˈहनिआ/ (*also* **rupture**) *noun* [C, U] the medical condition in which an organ inside the body, for example the stomach, pushes through the wall of muscle which surrounds it आँत आदि आंतरिक अंग का मांसपेशियों में से बाहर आ जाने का रोग, आँत उतरने का रोग; हर्निया, अंत्रवृद्धि

**hero** /ˈhɪərəʊ ˈहिअरो/ *noun* [C] (*pl.* **heroes**) **1** a person who is admired, especially for having done sth difficult or good प्रशंसित व्यक्ति (विशेषतः कठिन या अच्छा काम करने के लिए), वीर *The team were given a* ***hero's welcome*** *on their return home.* **2** the most important male character in a book, play, film, etc. किसी पुस्तक, नाटक, फ़िल्म आदि में सर्वाधिक महत्त्वपूर्ण पुरुष पात्र; नायक, हीरो *The hero of the film is a little boy.* ➪ **heroine, anti-hero** और **villain** भी देखिए।

**heroic** /həˈrəʊɪk हˈरोइक्/ *adj.* (used about people or their actions) having a lot of courage (व्यक्ति और उनके कार्य) साहसपूर्ण, हिम्मत वाला *a heroic effort* ▶ **heroically** /-kli -क्लि/ *adv.* साहसपूर्वक, हिम्मत से

**heroin** /ˈherəʊɪn ˈहेरोइन्/ *noun* [U] a powerful illegal drug produced from morphine that some people take for pleasure and then cannot stop taking मॉर्फ़ीन से उत्पन्न एक शक्तिशाली ग़ैर-क़ानूनी नशीला पदार्थ; हेरोइन.

**heroine** /ˈherəʊɪn ˈहेरोइन्/ *noun* [C] **1** a woman who is admired, especially for having done sth difficult or good प्रशंसित महिला (विशेषतः कठिन या अच्छा काम करने के लिए); वीरांगना **2** the most important female character in a book, play, film, etc. (पुस्तक, नाटक या फ़िल्म आदि की सर्वाधिक महत्त्वपूर्ण स्त्री पात्र); नायिका ➪ **hero** भी देखिए।

**heroism** /ˈherəʊɪzəm ˈहेरोइज़म्/ *noun* [U] great courage महान साहस, बड़ी बहादुरी, वीरता

**heron** /ˈherən ˈहेरन्/ *noun* [C] a large bird with a long neck and long legs, that lives near water बगुला

**herpes** /ˈhɜːpiːz ˈहपीज़्/ *noun* [U] a contagious disease and that causes painful spots on the skin, especially on the face and sexual organs एक संक्रामक त्वचा-रोग जिसमें त्वचा पर (विशेषतः चेहरे और गुप्तांगों पर) तकलीफ़देह चकत्ते उभर आते हैं; इकलंगी माता, विसर्पिका

**herring** /ˈherɪŋ ˈहेरिङ्/ *noun* [C, U] (*pl.* **herring** or **herrings**) a fish that swims in large groups (**shoals**) in cold seas and is used for food समुद्र के ठंडे पानी वाले भाग में झुंड बना कर रहने वाली मछली जिसे लोग खाते हैं

**IDM** **a red herring** ➪ **red** देखिए।

**herringbone** /ˈherɪŋbəʊn ˈहेरिङ्बोन्/ *noun* [U] a pattern used in cloth consisting of lines of V shape that are parallel to each other कपड़े में डाला

गया एक डिज़ाइन या आकृति जिसमें अंग्रेज़ी अक्षर V के आकार की समानांतर रेखाएँ होती हैं

**hers** /hɜːz हज़्/ *pronoun* of or belonging to her स्त्री का या उससे संबंधित *I didn't have a pen but Hema lent me hers.*

**herself** /hɜːˈself हˈसेल्फ़्/ *pronoun* **1** used when the female who does an action is also affected by it उस स्थिति को व्यक्त करने के लिए प्रयुक्त जब किसी क्रिया को करने वाली स्त्री अपनी क्रिया से स्वयं भी प्रभावित हो, स्वयं को *She hurt herself quite badly when she fell downstairs.* ○ *Isha looked at herself in the mirror.* **2** used to emphasize the female who did the action स्त्री पर बल देने के लिए प्रयुक्त, स्वयं, खुद कोई क्रिया करने वाली *She told me the news herself.* ○ *Has Roshni done this herself* (= or did sb else do it for her)?

IDM **(all) by herself** **1** alone अकेली *She lives by herself.* ➪ **alone** पर नोट देखिए। **2** without help बिना किसी की सहायता के; अकेले *I don't think she needs any help—she can change a tyre by herself.*

**(all) to herself** without having to share अकेले का, जिसमें कोई हिस्सा न बँटाए *Sana has the bedroom to herself now her sister's left home.*

**hertz** /hɜːts हट्स्/ *noun* [C] (*pl.* **hertz**) (*abbr.* **Hz**) (*technical*) a unit for measuring the **frequency** of sound waves ध्वनि-तरंगों की आवृत्ति (फ्रीक्वेंसी) नापने की इकाई; हर्ट्ज़

**he's** ➪ **he is, he has** का संक्षिप्त रूप

**hesitant** /ˈhezɪtənt ˈहेज़िटन्ट्/ *adj.* **hesitant (to do/about doing sth)** slow to speak or act because you are uncertain झिझकने या हिचकने वाला, संकोची, अनिश्चय के कारण बोलने या कुछ करने में मंद *I'm very hesitant about criticizing him too much.* ▶ **hesitancy** /-ənsi -अन्सि/ *noun* [U] हिचक, झिझक, संकोच ▶ **hesitantly** *adv.* हिचकते हुए, संकोचपूर्वक

**hesitate** /ˈhezɪteɪt ˈहेज़िटेट्/ *verb* [I] **1 hesitate (about/over sth)** to pause before you do sth or before you take a decision, usually because you are uncertain or worried किसी बात पर हिचकना, झिझकना, अनिश्चय या चिंता के कारण मंद गति से कुछ करना या निर्णय लेना *He hesitated before going into the room.* ○ *She's still hesitating about whether to accept the job or not.* **2 hesitate (to do sth)** to not want to do sth because you are not sure that it is right कुछ करने में हिचकना या झिझकना *Don't hesitate to phone if you have any problems.* ▶ **hesitation** /ˌheziˈteɪʃn ˌहेज़िˈटेश्न्/ *noun* [C, U] हिचकिचाहट, संकोच *She agreed without a moment's hesitation.*

**hessian** /ˈhesiən ˈहेसिअन्/ (*AmE* **burlap**) *noun* [U] a strong rough brown cloth, used especially for making large bags (**sacks**) बड़े थैले बनाने में प्रयुक्त मज़बूत खुरदुरा भूरा कपड़ा; टाट

**hetero-** /ˈhetərəʊ ˈहेटरो/ *prefix* (*in nouns, adjectives and adverbs*) other; different अन्य; भिन्न, अलग *heterogeneous* ○ *heterosexual* ➪ **homo-** देखिए।

**heterogeneous** /ˌhetərəˈdʒiːniəs ˌहेटरˈजीनिअस्/ *adj.* (*formal*) consisting of different kinds of people or things विभिन्न प्रकार के व्यक्तियों या वस्तुओं वाला, विषमांग, विषमरूप, पचमेल ➪ **homogeneous** देखिए।

**heterosexual** /ˌhetərəˈsekʃuəl ˌहेटरˈसेक्शुअल्/ *adj.* sexually attracted to a person of the opposite sex विपरीतलिंगी व्यक्ति के प्रति कामुक भाव से आकृष्ट ➪ **bisexual** और **homosexual** देखिए। ▶ **heterosexual** *noun* [C] विपरीतलिंगकामी

**heterozygote** /ˌhetərəˈzaɪgəʊt; ˌhetərəʊ- ˌहेटरˈज़ाइगोट; ˌहेटरो-/ *noun* [C] a living thing that has two varying forms of a particular **gene** and whose young may therefore vary in a particular characteristic ऐसा प्राणी जिसमें जीव विशेष के दो भिन्न रूप हों; विषमयुग्मज प्राणी ▶ **heterozygous** /ˌhetərəˈzaɪgəs ˌहेटरˈज़ाइगस्/ *adj.* विषमयुग्मज प्राणी-विषयक

**hewn** /hjuːn ह्यून्/ *adj.* (*old-fashioned*) cut with a large sharp tool तेज़ धार के औज़ार से तराशा हुआ *roughly hewn stone*

**hexa-** /ˈheksə ˈहेक्सा/ (*also* **hex-**) *prefix* (*in nouns, adjectives and adverbs*) six; having six छह; छह वाला, षट् *hexagonal*

**hexagon** /ˈheksəgən ˈहेक्सगन्/ *noun* [C] a shape with six sides छह फलकों वाली आकृति; षड्भुज ▶ **hexagonal** /hekˈsægənl हेक्ˈसैगन्ल्/ *adj.* षड्भुजाकार

**hey** /heɪ हे/ *exclamation* (*informal*) used to attract sb's attention or to show that you are surprised or interested किसी बात में आश्चर्य या रुचि के प्रति दूसरे का ध्यान आकृष्ट करने के लिए प्रयुक्त *Hey, what are you doing?*

IDM **hey presto** people sometimes say 'hey presto' when they have done sth so quickly that it seems like magic जादू की-सी फुरती से काम करने पर प्रयुक्त

**heyday** /ˈheɪdeɪ ˈहेडे/ *noun* [*sing.*] the period when sb/sth was most powerful, successful, rich, etc. व्यक्ति या वस्तु के सर्वाधिक शक्तिशाली, सफल आदि होने का समय, समृद्धि-काल, स्वर्ण-काल, बहार का समय

**HGV** /ˌeɪtʃ dʒiː ˈviː ˌएच् जी ˈव़ी/ *abbr.* (*BrE*) heavy goods vehicle, such as a lorry भारी माल ढोने का वाहन, जैसे ट्रक

**hi** /haɪ हाइ/ *exclamation* (*informal*) an informal word used when you meet sb you know well; hello सुपरिचित के लिए अभिवादन-शब्द; हैलो

**hibernate** /ˈhaɪbəneɪt ˈहाइबनेट्/ *verb* [I] (used about animals) to spend the winter in a state like deep sleep (कुछ पशुओं का) गहरी निद्रा की-सी स्थिति में शीतकाल को बिताना; शीत स्वाप करना ▶ **hibernation** /ˌhaɪbəˈneɪʃn ˌहाइबˈनेश्न्/ *noun* [U] शीतनिद्रा

**hiccup** (*also* **hiccough**) /ˈhɪkʌp ˈहिकप्/ *noun* **1** [C] a sudden, usually repeated sound that is made in the throat and that you cannot control हिचकी **2 (the) hiccups** [*pl.*] a series of hiccups लगातार हिचकी, हिचकी पर हिचकी *Don't eat so fast or you'll* ***get hiccups****!* ○ *If you* ***have the hiccups****, try holding your breath.* **3** [C] a small problem or difficulty छोटी-मोटी समस्या या कठिनाई ▶ **hiccup** (*also* **hiccough**) *verb* [I] हिचकी लेना

**hide¹** /haɪd हाइड्/ *verb* (*pt* **hid** /hɪd हिड्/; *pp* **hidden** /ˈhɪdn ˈहिड्न्/) **1** [T] to put or keep sb/sth in a place where he/she/it cannot be seen; to cover sth so that it cannot be seen व्यक्ति या वस्तु को ऐसी जगह रखना जहाँ कोई देख न सके, छिपाना; किसी वस्तु को ऐसे ढकना कि वह दिखाई न दे, छिपा देना *Where shall I hide the money?* ○ *You couldn't see Ram in the photo—he was hidden behind Shyam.* **2** [I] to be or go in a place where you cannot be seen or found ऐसे स्थान पर होना या जाना जहाँ आप दिखाई न दें या आपका पता न लगे, छिपना *Quick, run and hide!* ○ *The child was hiding under the bed.* **3** [T] **hide sth (from sb)** to keep sth secret, especially your feelings किसी बात को (विशेषतः भावनाओं को) गुप्त रखना *She tried to hide her disappointment from them.*

**hide²** /haɪd हाइड्/ *noun* **1** [C, U] the skin of an animal that will be used for making leather, etc. (चमड़ा आदि बनाने में प्रयुक्त) पशुओं की खाल; पशु चर्म **2** [C] a place from which people can watch wild animals, birds, etc. without being seen वन्य पशुओं, पक्षियों आदि को छिपकर देखने का स्थान

**hide-and-seek** *noun* [U] a children's game in which one person hides and the others try to find him/her लुका-छिपी का खेल (जिसे बच्चे खेलते हैं)

**hideous** /ˈhɪdiəs ˈहिडिअस्/ *adj.* very ugly or unpleasant बहुत भद्दा या अरुचिकर *a hideous sight* ○ *a hideous crime* ▶ **hideously** *adv.* भद्दे तरीक़े से

**hiding** /ˈhaɪdɪŋ ˈहाइडिङ्/ *noun* **1** [U] the state of being hidden छिपे होने की स्थिति; छिपाव, गोपन *The escaped prisoners are believed to be* ***in hiding*** *somewhere in Kanpur.* ○ *to go into hiding* **2** [C, *usually sing.*] (*informal*) a punishment involving being hit hard many times पिटाई, ठुकाई *You deserve a good hiding for what you've done.*

**hierarchy** /ˈhaɪərɑːki ˈहाइअराकि/ *noun* [C] (*pl.* **hierarchies**) a system or organization that has many levels from the lowest to the highest श्रेणीबद्ध संस्था, निम्न-उच्चक्रम, अधिक्रम, पदानुक्रम ▶ **hierarchical** /ˌhaɪəˈrɑːkɪkl ˌहाइअˈराकिक्ल्/ *adj.* अधिक्रमिक, प्रदानुक्रमिक

**hieroglyphics** /ˌhaɪərəˈɡlɪfɪks ˌहाइअरˈग्लिफ़िक्स्/ *noun* [*pl.*] the system of writing that was used in ancient Egypt in which a small picture represents a word or sound प्राचीन मिस्र में प्रचलित चित्रलिपि

**hi-fi** /ˈhaɪ faɪ ˈहाइ-फ़ाइ/ *noun* [C] equipment for playing recorded music that produces high-quality sound रिकार्ड किए संगीत को बजाने का उपकरण (जो उत्कृष्ट स्वर उत्पन्न करता है) ▶ **hi-fi** *adj.* उच्च क्षमता संपन्न *a hi-fi system*

**higgledy-piggledy** /ˌhɪɡldi ˈpɪɡldi ˌहिग्लडि ˈपिग्लडि/ *adv.*, *adj.* (*informal*) not in any order; mixed up together अव्यवस्थित; गड्डमड्ड

**high¹** /haɪ हाइ/ *adj.* **1** (used about things) having a large distance between the bottom and the top (वस्तुएँ) जिनमें निम्नतम से उच्चतम बिंदु तक लंबी दूरी हो, ऊँचा या ऊँची *high cliffs* ○ *What's the highest mountain in the world?* ✪ विलोम **low** ⇨ **height** noun देखिए तथा **tall** पर नोट देखिए। **2** having a particular height ख़ास ऊँचाई का, निर्दिष्ट प्रकार से ऊँचा *The hedge is one metre high.* ○ *knee-high boots* **3** at a level which is a long way from the ground, or from sea level ज़मीन या समुद्र तल से लंबी दूरी के स्तर पर; ऊँचा *a high shelf* ○ *The castle was built on high ground.* ✪ विलोम **low** **4** above the usual or normal level or amount सामान्य स्तर या क़ीमत से ऊपर, ऊँचा, अधिक, तेज़ *high prices* ○ *a high level of unemployment* ○ *Oranges are high in vitamin C.* ✪ विलोम **low** **5** better than what is usual सामान्य से बेहतर *high-quality goods* ○ *Her work is of a very high standard.* ○ *He has a high opinion of you.* ✪ विलोम **low** **6** having an important position उच्च पद पर आसीन *Sameera only joined the company three years ago, but* *she's already quite high up.* **7** morally good उच्च कोटि का, नैतिक रूप से उचित *high ideals* **8** (used about a sound or voice) not deep or low (ध्वनि या स्वर) गहरा या नीचा नहीं, ऊँचा *Dogs can hear very high sounds.* ○ *Women usually have higher voices than men.* ✪ विलोम **low** **9** (*informal*) **high (on sth)** under the influence of drugs, alcohol, etc. (नशीले पदार्थ, शराब आदि के) नशे में **10** (used about a gear in a car) that allows a faster speed (कार का गिअर) जिससे कार की गति बढ़ जाती है, हाई ✪ विलोम **low**

IDM **be left high and dry** to be left without help in a difficult situation कठिनाई में असहाय

**high²** /haɪ हाइ/ *adv.* **1** at or to a high position or level उच्च स्थिति या स्तर पर या उसकी ओर, ऊँचा *The sun was high in the sky.* ○ *I can't jump any higher.* ○ *The plane flew high overhead.* ➪ **height** noun देखिए। **2** (used about a sound) at a high level (ध्वनि) उच्च स्तर की, ऊँचा *How high can you sing?* ✪ विलोम **low**

IDM **high and low** everywhere सब जगह *We've searched high and low for the keys.*

**run high** (used about the feelings of a group of people) to be especially strong (लोगों की भावनाएँ) विशेषतः प्रबल या उफ़ान पर होना *Emotions are running high in the neighbourhood where the murders took place.*

**high³** /haɪ हाइ/ *noun* [C] **1** a high level or point उच्चस्तर या बिंदु, ऊँचाई *Profits reached an all-time high last year.* **2** an area of high air pressure उच्च वायु दाब का क्षेत्र **3** (*informal*) a feeling of great pleasure or happiness that sb gets from doing sth exciting or being successful रोमांचपूर्ण काम करने या सफल होने से प्राप्त अत्यधिक प्रसन्नता की भावना *He was **on a high** after passing all his exams.* ○ *She talked about the **highs and lows** of her career.* **4** (*informal*) a feeling of great pleasure or happiness that may be caused by a drug, alcohol, etc. नशे की मस्ती ✪ विलोम **low** (सब अर्थों का)

IDM **on high** (*formal*) above, in the sky or heaven ऊपर, आकाश या स्वर्ग जैसी ऊँचाई पर *The order came from on high.*

**highbrow** /ˈhaɪbraʊ ˈहाइब्राओ/ *adj.* interested in or concerned with matters that many people would find too serious to be interesting अतिगंभीर या उच्चस्तरीय मामलों से संबंधित; अभिजातवर्गीय, उच्चभ्रू *highbrow newspapers/television programmes*

**high-class** *adj.* of especially good quality विशेष रूप से उच्च कोटि का; उत्कृष्ट *a high-class restaurant*

**High Commissioner** *noun* [C] **1** a senior diplomat who is sent by one Commonwealth country to live in another, to protect the interests of his/her own country राष्ट्रकुल के एक देश का दूसरे देश में नियुक्त प्रतिनिधि; उच्चायुक्त **2** a person who is head of an important international project किसी बड़ी अंतर्राष्ट्रीय परियोजना का प्रमुख या अध्यक्ष *the United Nations High Commissioner for Refugees*

**High Court** *noun* [C] the most important court of law in some countries उच्च न्यायालय, हाई कोर्ट

**higher education** *noun* [U] education and training at a college or university, especially to degree level कॉलेज या विश्वविद्यालय स्तर की शिक्षा, उच्च(तर) शिक्षा ➪ **further education** देखिए।

**high jump** *noun* [*sing.*] the sport in which people try to jump over a bar in order to find out who can jump the highest ऊँची कूद; ऊँचाई पर लगे डंडे को पार करते हुए लगाई गई कूद ➪ **long jump** देखिए।

**highland** /ˈhaɪlənd ˈहाइलन्ड्/ *adj.* **1** in or connected with an elevated land that has mountains पर्वतों वाले भूक्षेत्र में या उससे संबंधित, उच्च भूमि संबंधी *highland streams* ➪ **lowland** देखिए। **2** [*pl.*] in or connected with the part of Scotland where there are mountains (**the Highlands**) स्कॉटलैंड के पर्वतीय प्रदेश खंड में या उससे संबंधित

**high-level** *adj.* **1** involving important people जिसमें महत्त्वपूर्ण व्यक्ति शामिल हैं; उच्चस्तरीय *high-level talks* **2** (*computing*) (of a computer language) similar to an existing language such as English, making it fairly simple to use (कंप्यूटर भाषा) अंग्रेज़ी या हिंदी जैसी भाषा के सदृश, जो प्रयोग करने में काफ़ी सरल हो ✪ विलोम **low-level**

**highlight¹** /ˈhaɪlaɪt ˈहाइलाइट्/ *verb* [T] **1** to emphasize sth so that people give it special attention किसी अंश या चीज़ की ओर लोगों का ध्यान आकृष्ट करने के लिए प्रकाशमय करना *The report highlighted the need for improved safety at football grounds.* **2** to mark part of a text with a different colour, etc. so that people give it more attention लिखित पाठ के अंश को अलग रंग से चिह्नित करना ताकि पाठक उस पर विशेष ध्यान दें **3** to make some parts of a person's hair a lighter colour व्यक्ति के कुछ बालों को हलके रंग में रंग देना *Have you had your hair highlighted?*

**highlight²** /ˈhaɪlaɪt ˈहाइलाइट्/ *noun* **1** [C] the best or most interesting part of sth किसी वस्तु का सर्वोत्तम या सबसे रोचक अंश; मुख्यांश, झलकी *The highlights of the match will be shown on TV tonight.*

**2 highlights** [*pl.*] areas of lighter colour that are put in a person's hair व्यक्ति के हलके रंगे बाल

**highlighter** /ˈhaɪlaɪtə(r) ˈहाइलाइट(र्)/ (*also* **highlighter pen**) *noun* [C] a special pen used for marking words in a text in a bright colour लिखित पाठांश को चमकीले रंग से चिह्नित करने वाला विशेष क़लम, चिह्नक; हाईलाइटर ➪ **stationery** पर चित्र देखिए।

**highly** /ˈhaɪli ˈहाइलि/ *adv.* **1** to a high degree; very काफ़ी अधिक सीमा तक या मात्रा में; अत्यधिक *highly trained/educated/developed* ○ *a highly paid job* ○ *It's highly unlikely that anyone will complain.* **2** with admiration प्रशंसा के साथ *I think very highly of your work.*

**highly strung** *adj.* nervous and easily upset घबराया हुआ और जल्दी परेशान; अति संवेदनशील

**Highness** /ˈhaɪnəs ˈहाइनस्/ *noun* [C] **your/his/her Highness** a title used when speaking about or to a member of a royal family शाही ख़ानदान के सदस्य का निर्देश करने के लिए प्रयुक्त

**high-pitched** *adj.* (used about sounds) very high (ध्वनियाँ) बहुत ऊँची, तीक्ष्ण *a high-pitched voice/whistle* ✪ विलोम **low-pitched**

**high-powered** *adj.* **1** (used about things) having great power (वस्तुएँ) अत्यंत शक्तिशाली *a high-powered engine* **2** (used about people) important and successful (व्यक्ति) महत्त्वपूर्ण और सफल; उच्चाधिकार संपन्न *high-powered executives*

**high-rise** *adj.* (*only before a noun*) (used about a building) very tall and having a lot of floors (भवन) बहुत ऊँचा और बहुमंज़िला, गगनचुंबी

**high school** *noun* [C, U] a school for children who are about 13–18 years old, 13–18 वर्ष के छात्रों के लिए स्कूल; हाई स्कूल

**high season** *noun* [C] (*BrE*) the time of year when a hotel or tourist area receives most visitors होटल या पर्यटन-क्षेत्र का सबसे अनुकूल समय ➪ **low season** देखिए।

**high street** *noun* [C] (*BrE*) (often used in names) the main street of a town (प्रायः नामों में प्रयुक्त) किसी नगर की मुख्य सड़क *The Post Office is in the High Street.*

**high-tech** (*also* **hi-tech**) /ˌhaɪˈtek ˌहाइˈट्रेक्/ *adj.* using the most modern methods and machines, especially electronic ones अत्याधुनिक मशीनों (विशेषतः इलेक्ट्रॉनिक मशीनों) और विधियों का प्रयोग करने वाला *high-tech industries/hospitals*

**high tide** *noun* [U] the time when the sea comes furthest onto the land ज्वार; समुद्री लहरों का तटभूमि पर काफ़ी अंदर तक चले आना ✪ विलोम **low tide**

**highway** /ˈhaɪweɪ ˈहाइवे/ *noun* [C] (*BrE*) a main road (between towns) (नगरों के बीच) मुख्य मार्ग, राजमार्ग, हाइवे ➪ **road** पर नोट देखिए।

**hijack** /ˈhaɪdʒæk ˈहाइजैक्/ *verb* [T] **1** to take control of a plane, etc. by force, usually for political reasons बलप्रयोग द्वारा विमान को क़ाबू कर लेना (प्रायः राजनीतिक कारणों से), विमान का अपहरण कर लेना *The plane was hijacked on its flight to Sydney.* ➪ **kidnap** देखिए। **2** to take control of a meeting, an event, etc. in order to force people to pay attention to sth किसी सभा, कार्यक्रम आदि का नियंत्रण अपने हाथ में ले लेना (ताकि लोग किसी विशेष बात पर ध्यान देने के लिए विवश हो जाएँ), सभा आदि का अपहरण कर लेना *The peace rally was hijacked by right-wing extremists.* ▶ **hijack** *noun* [C] अपहरण *The hijack was ended by armed police.* ▶ **hijacker** *noun* [C] अपहरणकर्ता ▶ **hijacking** *noun* [C, U] अपहरण की क्रिया

**hike** /haɪk हाइक्/ *noun* [C] a long walk in the country देहाती क्षेत्र में लंबी पैदल यात्रा *We went on a twenty-kilometre hike at the weekend.* ▶ **hike** *verb* [I] **NOTE** लंबी पैदल यात्रा में छुट्टियाँ बिताने की बात करने के लिए **go hiking** का प्रयोग होता है—*They went hiking in Kasauli for their holiday.* ▶ **hiker** *noun* [C] पैदल यात्री

**hilarious** /hɪˈleəriəs हिˈलेअरिअस्/ *adj.* extremely funny बहुत मज़ेदार, हास्यक ▶ **hilariously** *adv.* बहुत मज़े से, हास्यकतापूर्वक

**hilarity** /hɪˈlærəti हिˈलैरटि/ *noun* [U] great amusement or loud laughter बहुत मनोविनोद या ठहाका; हास्यकता

**hill** /hɪl हिल्/ *noun* [C] a high area of land that is not as high as a mountain पहाड़ी *There was a wonderful view from the top of the hill.* ➪ **uphill** और **downhill** देखिए।

**hillock** /ˈhɪlək ˈहिलक्/ *noun* [C] a small hill छोटी पहाड़ी, गिरिका

**hillside** /ˈhɪlsaɪd ˈहिल्साइड्/ *noun* [C] the side of a hill पहाड़ी का पार्श्व

**hilltop** /ˈhɪltɒp ˈहिल्टॉप्/ *noun* [C] the top of a hill पहाड़ी की चोटी

**hilly** /ˈhɪli ˈहिलि/ *adj.* having a lot of hills जहाँ बहुत सी पहाड़ियाँ हों; पर्वतीय *The country's very hilly around here.*

**hilt** /hɪlt हिल्ट्/ *noun* [C] the handle of a knife or a similar weapon (**sword**) चाक़ू या तलवार की मूठ **IDM** **to the hilt** to a high degree; completely बड़ी सीमा तक; पूरी तरह *I'll defend you to the hilt.*

**him** /hɪm हिम्/ *pronoun* (*the object of a verb or preposition*) the male person who was mentioned earlier पूर्वनिर्दिष्ट पुरुष व्यक्ति; उसे *I've got a letter for your father—can you give it to him, please?* ➪ **he** पर नोट देखिए।

**himself** /hɪmˈself हिम्ˈसेल्फ़्/ *pronoun* **1** used when the male who does an action is also affected by it जब पुरुष व्यक्ति अपनी क्रिया से स्वयं भी प्रभावित हो, अपने को, खुद को *He cut himself when he was shaving.* ○ *Ravi looked at himself in the mirror.* **2** used to emphasize the male who did the action पुरुष कर्ता पर बल देने के लिए प्रयुक्त; स्वयं, खुद *He told me the news himself.* ○ *Did he write this himself* (= or did sb else do it for him) ?

IDM **(all) by himself 1** alone अकेला *He lives by himself.* ➪ **alone** पर नोट देखिए। **2** without help बिना किसी की सहायता के; अकेले *He should be able to cook a meal by himself.*

**(all) to himself** without having to share अकेले का, जिसमें कोई हिस्सा न बँटाए *Chandan has the bedroom to himself now his brother's left home.*

**hind** /haɪnd हाइन्ड्/ *adj.* (used about an animal's legs, etc.) at the back (पशुओं की टाँगें इत्यादि) पिछला, पिछली (टाँगें)

NOTE इस अर्थ में **back legs** शब्द का प्रयोग भी होता है। अगली टाँगों को **front legs** या **forelegs** कहते हैं।

**hinder** /ˈhɪndə(r) ˈहिन्ड(र्)/ *verb* [T] to make it more difficult for sb/sth to do sth व्यक्ति या वस्तु के लिए कठिनाई पैदा करना, किसी के काम में बाधा डालना *A lot of scientific work is hindered by lack of money.*

**Hindi** *noun* [U] an Indo-European language that is derived from Sanskrit and is written in the Devanagari script. It is the most widely spoken language of north and central India and is one of the official languages of India संस्कृत से व्युत्पन्न एवं देवनागरी लिपि में लिखित एक भारत-यूरोपीय मूल की भाषा; हिंदी, यह मुख्यतः उत्तर तथा मध्य भारत में बोली जाती है एवं भारत की आधिकारिक भाषाओं में से एक है ▶ **Hindi** *adj.* हिंदी का, हिंदी-विषयक

**hindquarters** /ˌhaɪndˈkwɔːtəz ˌहाइन्ड् ˈक्वॉटज़्/ *noun* [*pl.*] the back part of an animal that has four legs, including its two back legs चौपाये जानवर का पिछला हिस्सा (पिछली दो टाँगें सम्मिलित); पुट्ठा

**hindrance** /ˈhɪndrəns ˈहिन्ड्रन्स्/ *noun* [C] a person or thing that makes it difficult for you to do sth, an obstacle or obstruction किसी काम में कठिनाई पैदा करने वाला व्यक्ति या वस्तु, बाधक तत्व; रुकावट, बाधा, विघ्न

**hindsight** /ˈhaɪndsaɪt ˈहाइन्ड्साइट्/ *noun* [U] the understanding that you have of a situation only after it has happened घटना के घटित हो जाने के बाद उपजी समझदारी; पश्चबुद्धि ***With hindsight,*** *I wouldn't have lent him the money.* ➪ **foresight** देखिए।

**Hindu** *noun* [C] a person whose religion is Hinduism हिंदू धर्म का अनुयायी ▶ **Hindu** *adj.* हिंदू-विषयक, हिंदू का *Hindu beliefs*

**Hinduism** *noun* [U] a major religion of India. Hindus believe in many gods and in rebirth हिंदू धर्म; हिंदू लोग बहुदेवतावाद और पुनर्जन्म में विश्वास करते हैं

**Hindustani music** *noun* [U] the main style of classical music of northern India उत्तर भारत की प्रमुख शास्त्रीय संगीत शैली; हिंदुस्तानी संगीत

**hinge[1]** /hɪndʒ हिन्ज्/ *noun* [C] a piece of metal that joins two sides of a box, door, etc. together and allows it to be opened or closed दरवाज़े, संदूक आदि के क़ब्जे जिसके सहारे दरवाज़ा आदि खुलते और बंद होते हैं; संधि

**hinge[2]** /hɪndʒ हिन्ज्/ *verb*

PHR V **hinge on sth** to depend on sth किसी बात पर निर्भर होना *The future of the project hinges on the meeting today.*

**hint[1]** /hɪnt हिन्ट्/ *noun* [C] **1** something that you suggest in an indirect way परोक्ष संकेत, इशारा *If you keep mentioning parties, maybe they'll* ***take the hint*** *and invite you.* **2** sth that suggests what will happen in the future भविष्य में घटित होने वाली बात का संकेत *The first half of the match* ***gave*** *no* ***hint*** *of the excitement to come.* **3** a small amount of sth अंश *There was a hint of sadness in his voice.* **4** a piece of advice or information सलाह या जानकारी *helpful hints*

**hint[2]** /hɪnt हिन्ट्/ *verb* [I, T] **hint (at sth); hint that...** to suggest sth in an indirect way किसी बात का परोक्ष संकेत करना *They only hinted at their great disappointment.* ○ *He hinted that he might be moving to USA.*

**hinterland** /ˈhɪntəlænd ˈहिन्टलैन्ड्/ *noun* [C, *usually sing.*] the areas of a country that are away from the coast, from the banks of a large river or from the main cities समुद्र तट, नदी तट, मुख्य नगरों से दूर का इलाक़ा; पृष्ठ प्रदेश, पश्च या भीतरी प्रदेश *the rural/agricultural hinterland*

**hip**[1] /hɪp हिप्/ *noun* [C] the part of the side of your body above your legs and below your waist कूल्हा, पुट्ठा *He stood there angrily with his hands on his hips.* ○ *the hip bone* ➪ **body** पर चित्र देखिए।

**hip**[2] /hɪp हिप्/ *exclamation*

IDM **hip, hip, hurray/hurrah** shouted three times when a group wants to show that it is pleased with sb or with sth that has happened प्रसन्नता व्यक्त करने की अभिव्यक्ति (जिसे दर्शक वर्ग तीन बार चिल्लाकर बोलता है)

**hippie** (*also* **hippy**) /ˈhɪpi ˈहिपि/ *noun* [C] (*pl.* **hippies**) a person who rejects the usual values and way of life of Western society. Especially in the 1960s, hippies showed that they were different by wearing colourful clothes, having long hair and taking drugs पाश्चात्य समाज की जीवन-शैली और मूल्य व्यवस्था का तिरस्कार करने वाला व्यक्ति; हिप्पी, विशेषतः 1960 के दशक में रंगीन कपड़े, लंबे बाल और नशाखोरी द्वारा हिप्पियों ने अपनी विलक्षणता का प्रदर्शन किया

**hippopotamus** /ˌhɪpəˈpɒtəməs ˌहिपˈपॉटमस्/ *noun* [C] (*pl.* **hippopotamuses** /-sɪz -सिज़्/ or **hippopotami** /-maɪ -माइ/) (*informal* **hippo** /ˈhɪpəʊ ˈहिपो/) a large African animal with a large head and short legs that lives in or near rivers अफ्रीक़ी दरियाई घोड़ा जिसका सिर बड़ा होता है और आँखें छोटी ➪ **pachyderm** पर चित्र देखिए।

**hire**[1] /ˈhaɪə(r) ˈहाइअ(र्)/ *verb* [T] **1** (*AmE* **rent**) **hire sth (from sb)** to have the use of sth for a short time by paying for it किसी वस्तु को किराए पर लेना

NOTE ब्रिटिश अंग्रेज़ी में, किसी वस्तु को थोड़े समय के लिए लेना हो तो **hire** का प्रयोग किया जाता है—*We hired a car for the day.* और बात लंबे समय के लिए हो तो **rent** का प्रयोग होता है—*to rent a house/flat/television* अमेरिकी अंग्रेज़ी में दोनों स्थितियों में **rent** का प्रयोग होता है।

**2** to give sb a job for a short time किसी को थोड़े समय के लिए कोई काम देना *We'll have to hire somebody to mend the roof.*

NOTE अमेरिकी अंग्रेज़ी में **hire** का प्रयोग नौकरियों की चर्चा के संदर्भ में भी होता है—*We just hired a new secretary.*

**3** (*AmE* **rent**) **hire sth (out) (to sb)** to allow sb to use sth for a short fixed period in exchange for money सीमित निश्चित अवधि के लिए किसी को किसी वस्तु का प्रयोग करने देना, किसी वस्तु को किराए पर देना *We hire (out) our vans by the day.*

NOTE यदि अवधि लंबी हो तो ब्रिटिश अंग्रेज़ी में **rent** या **let** का प्रयोग होता है—*Mrs Smith rents out rooms to students.* ○ *We let our house while we were in France for a year.*

**hire**[2] /ˈhaɪə(r) ˈहाइअ(र्)/ *noun* [U] the act of paying to use sth for a short time थोड़े समय के उपयोग के लिए धन देने की क्रिया, किराए पर लेना *Car hire is expensive in this country.* ○ *Do you have bicycles* ***for hire****?*

**his** /hɪz हिज़्/ *det., pronoun* of or belonging to the male person that was mentioned earlier पूर्वनिर्दिष्ट पुरुष व्यक्ति का उससे संबद्ध; उसका/के/की *Govind has hurt his shoulder.* ○ *This is my book so that one must be his.* ➪ **he** पर नोट देखिए।

**hiss** /hɪs हिस्/ *verb* **1** [I, T] to make a sound like a very long 's' to show that you are angry or do not like sth क्रोध या अरुचि व्यक्त करने के लिए सी-सी की लंबी आवाज़ करना *The cat hissed at me.* ○ *The speech was hissed and booed.* **2** [T] to say sth in an angry hissing voice सी-सी करते हुए क्रोध में कुछ कहना; फुफकारना *'Stay away from me!' she hissed.* ► **hiss** *noun* [C] सिसकारी, फुफकार

**histamine** /ˈhɪstəmiːn ˈहिस्टमीन्/ *noun* [U] a chemical substance that is produced by the body if you are injured or have a bad reaction to sth that you touch, eat or breathe घायल होने पर या स्पर्श आदि की प्रतिकूल प्रतिक्रिया स्वरूप शरीर में उत्पन्न रसायन; हिस्टामिन ➪ **antihistamine** देखिए।

**historian** /hɪˈstɔːriən हिˈस्टॉरिअन्/ *noun* [C] a person who studies or who is an expert in history इतिहासकार, इतिहासविद, इतिहासज्ञ

**historic** /hɪˈstɒrɪk हिˈस्टॉरिक्/ *adj.* famous or important in history इतिहास में महत्त्वपूर्ण, ऐतिहासिक (महत्त्व) *The ending of apartheid was a historic event.*

**historical** /hɪˈstɒrɪkl हिˈस्टॉरिकल्/ *adj.* that really lived or happened; connected with real people or events in the past वास्तविक, भौतिक अस्तित्व वाला; इतिहास से संबंधित, ऐतिहासिक *historical events/records* ○ *This house has great historical interest.* ► **historically** /-kli -कलि/ *adv.* ऐतिहासिक रूप से

**history** /ˈhɪstri ˈहिस्ट्रि/ *noun* (*pl.* **histories**) **1** [U] all the events of the past अतीत की घटनाएँ, इतिहास *an important moment in history* ➪ **natural history** देखिए। **2** [C, *usually sing.*] the series of events or facts that is connected with sb/sth किसी व्यक्ति या वस्तु से संबद्ध घटनाएँ या तथ्य; इतिहास *He has a history of violence.* ○ *a patient's medical history* **3** [U] the study of past events अतीतकालीन घटनाओं का अध्ययन; इतिहास *She has* *a degree in history.* ○ *History was my favourite subject at school.* **4** [C] a written description of past events अतीतकालीन घटनाओं का लिखित विवरण; इतिहास *a new history of Asia.*

**NOTE** **History** वह सच है जो वस्तुतः घटित हुआ है। घटनाओं के उस वर्णन को **story** कहते हैं जो संभवतः घटित हुई हों या न हुई हों।

**IDM** **go down in/make history** to be or do sth so important that it will be recorded in history इतिहास में स्थान बन जाना या बना लेना

**the rest is history** used when you are telling a story to say that you are not going to tell the end of the story, because every one knows it already कहानी सुनाते समय यह बताने के लिए प्रयुक्त अभिव्यक्ति कि कहानी का अंत नहीं बताया जा रहा क्योंकि वह सबको पहले से मालूम है

**hit[1]** /hɪt हिट्/ *verb* [T] (*pres. part.* **hitting;** *pt, pp* **hit**) **1** to make sudden, violent contact with sb/sth किसी के साथ अचानक उग्र संपर्क होना, टकराना, प्रहार करना, चोट मारना *The bus left the road and hit a tree.* ○ *to hit somebody in the eye/across the face/on the nose*

**NOTE** **Hit** की अपेक्षा **strike** अधिक औपचारिक शब्द है। **Beat** का अर्थ है अनेक बार प्रहार करना—*He was badly beaten in the attack.*

**2 hit sth (on/against sth)** to knock a part of your body, etc. against sth शरीर के किसी अंग को किसी वस्तु पर रखकर चोट मारना, शरीर के अंग का किसी वस्तु से टकराना *Pawan hit his head on the low beam.* **3** to have a bad or unpleasant effect on sb/sth किसी व्यक्ति या वस्तु पर प्रतिकूल प्रभाव होना *Inner city areas have been badly hit by unemployment.* ○ *Her father's death has hit her very hard.* **4** to experience sth unpleasant or difficult कोई कठिन या अप्रिय अनुभव होना *Things were going really well until we hit this problem.* **5** to reach a place or a level किसी स्थान या स्तर पर पहुँचना *The price of oil hit a new high yesterday.* **6** to suddenly come into sb's mind; to make sb realize or understand sth कोई बात एकाएक मन में आना; किसी को कुछ अहसास कराना या समझाना *I thought I recognized the man's face and then it hit me—he was my old maths teacher!*

**IDM** **hit it off (with sb)** (*informal*) to like sb when you first meet him/her पहली भेंट में किसी को पसंद करना *When I first met Tarun's parents, we didn't really hit it off.*

**hit the nail on the head** to say sth that is exactly right ऐसी बात कहना जो बिलकुल सही हो

**hit the jackpot** to win a lot of money or have a big success (लाटरी आदि में) बहुत-सा पैसा जीत लेना या बड़ी सफलता प्राप्त करना

**PHR V** **hit back (at sb/sth)** to attack (with words) sb who has attacked you किसी पर पलटवार करना, जवाबी हमला करना (प्रायः शब्दों से)

**hit on sth** to suddenly find sth by chance अचानक कुछ पा लेना, सूझ जाना *I finally hit on a solution to the problem.*

**hit out (at sb/sth)** to attack sb/sth किसी व्यक्ति या वस्तु पर हमला बोलना *The man hit out at the policeman.*

**hit[2]** /hɪt हिट्/ *noun* [C] **1** the act of hitting sth किसी पर प्रहार करने का कार्य; प्रहार, आघात *The ship took a* ***direct hit*** *and sank.* ○ *She gave her brother a hard hit on the head.* ➪ **miss** देखिए। **2** a person or thing that is very popular or successful बहुत लोकप्रिय या सफल व्यक्ति या वस्तु *The record was a big hit.* **3** (*computing*) a result of a search on a computer, especially on the Internet कंप्यूटर (विशेषतः इंटरनेट) पर खोज का परिणाम, हिट

**IDM** **make a hit (with sb)** (*informal*) to make a good impression on sb किसी पर अच्छा प्रभाव डालना

**hit-and-miss** (*also* **hit-or-miss**) *adj.* not done in a careful or planned way and therefore not likely to be successful सावधानी से योजनापूर्वक न किया हुआ और फलस्वरूप जिसकी सफलता संदिग्ध है, अटकल-पच्चू, तीर-तुक्का *This method is a bit hit-and-miss, but it usually works.*

**hit-and-run** *adj.* (used about a road accident) caused by a driver who does not stop to help (सड़क दुर्घटना) जिसमें ड्राइवर किसी को मार कर भाग गया है

**hitch[1]** /hɪtʃ हिच्/ *verb* **1** [I, T] (*informal*) to get a lift or a free ride by holding out your hand at the vehicles passing by to your destination वाहन के ड्राइवर से अनुरोध कर उसके साथ अपने गंतव्य तक मुफ़्त यात्रा करना *I managed to hitch to Pune in just six hours.* ○ *We missed the bus so we had to* ***hitch a lift****.* **2** [T] to fasten sth to sth else एक वस्तु को दूसरी के साथ बाँधना *to hitch a trailer to the back of a car*

**hitch[2]** /hɪtʃ हिच्/ *noun* [C] a small problem or difficulty छोटी समस्या या कठिनाई *a technical hitch*

**hitch-hike** (*informal* **hitch**) *verb* [I] to get a lift or free ride by holding out your hand at the vehicles passing to your distination वाहन के ड्राइवर से अनुरोध कर उसके साथ अपने गंतव्य तक मुफ़्त यात्रा करना *He hitch-hiked across Europe.* ▶ **hitch-hiker** *noun* [C] अनुरोध-यात्री, हिच-हाइकर

**hi-tech** = **high-tech**

**hitherto** /ˌhɪðəˈtuː; ˌहिद्रˈटू/ *adv.* (*formal*) until now अभी तक

**HIV** /ˌeɪtʃ aɪˈviː; ˌएच् आइˈव़ी/ *abbr.* human immunodeficiency virus; the **virus** that is believed to cause the illness **AIDS** एड्स का रोग उत्पन्न करने वाला वाइरस, एचआइवी

**hive** /haɪv हाइव़्/ = **beehive**

**hm** *exclamation* (used when you are not sure or when you are thinking about sth) (अनिश्चय या सोचने में व्यस्तता की सूचक ध्वनि) हमम...

**hoard[1]** /hɔːd हॉड्/ *noun* [C] a store (often secret) of money, food, etc. धन, भोजन आदि का (प्रायः गुप्त) भंडार

**hoard[2]** /hɔːd हॉड्/ *verb* [I, T] **hoard (sth) (up)** to collect and store large quantities of sth (often secretly) किसी वस्तु को बड़ी मात्रा में (प्रायः गुप्त रीति से) संचित कर जमा करना

**hoarding** /ˈhɔːdɪŋ ˈहॉडिङ्/ (*BrE*) = **billboard**

**hoarse** /hɔːs हॉस्/ *adj.* (used about a person or his/her voice) sounding rough and quiet, especially because of a sore throat (व्यक्ति या उसका स्वर) फटा-फटा और बैठा हुआ (विशेषतः गले में दर्द के कारण); कर्कश स्वर *a hoarse whisper* ▶ **hoarsely** *adv.* कर्कश स्वर में

**hoax** /həʊks होक्स्/ *noun* [C] a trick to make people believe sth that is not true, especially sth unpleasant कुछ असत्य को सत्य दर्शाने के लिए किया गया छल (प्रायः बुरा), झाँसा-पट्टी *The fire brigade answered the call, but found that it was a hoax.*

**hob** /hɒb हॉब्/ (*AmE* **stovetop**) *noun* [C] the surface on the top of a stove that is used for boiling, frying, etc. स्टोव का ऊपरी सिरा जिस पर खाना बनता है

**hobble** /ˈhɒbl ˈहॉब्ल्/ *verb* [I] to walk with difficulty because your feet or legs are hurt पैरों या टाँगों में दर्द के मारे कठिनाई से चलना, लँगड़ाते हुए चलना *He hobbled home on his twisted ankle.*

**hobby** /ˈhɒbi ˈहॉबि/ *noun* [C] (*pl.* **hobbies**) something that you do regularly for pleasure in your free time ख़ाली समय में अपनी ख़ुशी के लिए नियमित रूप से किया गया काम; शौक़ *Balwinder's hobbies are stamp collecting and surfing the net.* ✪ पर्याय **pastime**

**hockey** /ˈhɒki ˈहॉकि/ *noun* [U] **1** a game that is played on a field (**pitch**) by two teams of eleven players who try to hit a small hard ball into a goal with a curved wooden stick (**hockey stick**) हॉकी (का खेल) **NOTE** अमेरिका में इसे प्रायः **field hockey** कहते हैं ताकि **ice hockey** से इसका अंतर स्पष्ट हो सके। **2** (*AmE*) = **ice hockey**

**hoe** /həʊ हो/ *noun* [C] a garden tool with a long handle that is used for turning the soil and for removing plants that you do not want कुदाली (इससे बग़ीचे की मिट्टी और बेकार के पौधे निकालते हैं) ➪ **gardening** पर चित्र देखिए

**hog[1]** /hɒg हॉग्/ *noun* [C] a male pig that is kept for its meat पालतू सूअर

**IDM** **go the whole hog** (*informal*) to do sth as completely as possible किसी काम को यथासंभव पूरा-पूरा कर डालना

**hog[2]** /hɒg हॉग्/ *verb* [T] (**hogging; hogged**) (*informal*) to take or keep too much or all of sth for yourself अपने हिस्से से अधिक हथिया लेना *The red car was hogging the middle of the road so no one could overtake.*

**Hogmanay** /ˈhɒgməneɪ ˈहॉग्मने/ *noun* [C] the Scottish name for New Year's Eve (31 December) and the celebrations that take place then नव-वर्ष की संध्या (31 दिसंबर) और तब आयोजित समारोह के लिए स्कॉटलैंड में प्रचलित शब्द

**hoist** /hɔɪst हॉइस्ट्/ *verb* [T] to lift or pull sth up, often by using ropes, etc. प्रायः रस्सी आदि के सहारे किसी वस्तु को ऊपर उठाना या खींचना *to hoist a flag/sail*

**hold[1]** /həʊld होल्ड्/ *verb* (*pt, pp* **held** /held हेल्ड्/) **1** [T] to take sb/sth and keep him/her/it in your hand, etc. किसी व्यक्ति या वस्तु को थामे रहना *He held a gun in his hand.* ○ *The woman was holding a baby in her arms.* **2** [T] to keep sth in a certain position किसी वस्तु को विशेष दशा में थामना या बनाए रखना *Hold your head up straight.* ○ *These two screws hold the shelf in place.* **3** [T] to take the weight of sb/sth किसी वस्तु के भार को सँभालना *Are you sure that branch is strong enough to hold you?* **4** [T] to organize an event; to have a meeting, an election, a concert, etc. समारोह मनाना; सभा, चुनाव आदि का आयोजन करना *They're holding a party for his fortieth birthday.* ○ *The Olympic Games are held every four years.* **5** [I] to stay the same उसी स्थिति में बने रहना *I hope this weather holds till the weekend.* ○ *What I said still holds—nothing has changed.* **6** [T] to contain or have space for a particular amount किसी में किसी वस्तु की विशेष मात्रा का समाना *The car holds five people.* ○ *How much does this bottle hold?* **7** [T] to keep a person in a position or place by force किसी व्यक्ति को पकड़े रखना *The terrorists are **holding** three men **hostage**.* ○ *A man is being held at the police station.* **8** [T] to have sth, usually in an official way कोई वस्तु रखना, के पास कोई

वस्तु होना (प्रायः अधिकारिक रूप में) *Does she **hold** an Indian **passport**?* ○ *She holds the world record in the 100 metres.* **9** [T] to have an opinion, etc. कोई राय आदि रखना *They **hold the view** that we shouldn't spend any more money.* **10** [T] to believe that sth is true about a person किसी व्यक्ति के विषय में किसी बात को सच मानना *I **hold** the parents **responsible** for the child's behaviour.* **11** [I, T] (used when you are telephoning) to wait until the person you are calling is ready (फ़ोन करते समय) जवाब की प्रतीक्षा करना *I'm afraid his phone is engaged. Will you **hold the line**?* **12** [T] to have a conversation बातचीत करना *It's impossible to **hold a conversation** with all this noise.*

IDM **Hold it!** (*spoken*) Stop! Don't move! रुको! खड़े रहो!

NOTE **Hold** से बनने वाले मुहावरों के लिए संबंधित संज्ञाओं, विशेषणों आदि की प्रविष्टियाँ देखिए। जैसे **hold your own** की प्रविष्टि **own** में मिलेगी।

PHR V **hold sth against sb** to not forgive sb because of sth he/she has done माफ़ी न देना

**hold sb/sth back** **1** to prevent sb from making progress किसी की प्रगति में बाधक बनना **2** to prevent sb/sth from moving forward किसी को आगे न बढ़ने देना

**hold sth back** **1** to refuse to give some of the information that you have अपने पास की जानकारी देने से इनकार करना **2** to control an emotion and stop yourself from showing what you really feel अपनी हार्दिक भावनाओं को प्रकट न होने देना

PHR V **hold off (sth/doing sth)** to delay sth किसी काम में देरी करना

**hold on** **1** to wait or stop for a moment क्षणभर प्रतीक्षा करना या रुकना *Hold on. I'll be with you in a minute.* **2** to manage in a difficult or dangerous situation कठिन या ख़तरनाक स्थिति में भी जमे रहना *They managed to hold on until a rescue party arrived.*

**hold onto sb/sth** to hold sb/sth tightly किसी व्यक्ति या वस्तु को कसकर पकड़ना *The child held on to his mother; he didn't want her to go.*

**hold onto sth** to keep sth; to not give or sell sth किसी वस्तु को अपने पास ही रखना; किसी वस्तु को न किसी को देना न बेचना *They've offered me a lot of money for this painting, but I'm going to hold onto it.*

**hold out** to last (in a difficult situation) (कठिन स्थिति में) डटे रहना *How long will our supply of water hold out?*

**hold sth out** to offer sth by moving it towards sb in your hand किसी को कोई चीज़ पेश करना *He held out a carrot to the horse.*

**hold out for sth** (*informal*) to cause a delay while you continue to ask for sth माँग पर डटे रहकर काम में देरी करवाना *Union members are holding out for a better pay offer.*

**hold sb/sth up** to make sb/sth late; to cause a delay व्यक्ति या वस्तु को किसी कार्य में देर करने के लिए बाध्य कर देना; देरी करवाना *We were held up by the traffic.*

**hold up sth** to rob a bank, shop, vehicle, etc. using a gun बंदूक़ की नोक पर बैंक, दुकान, वाहन आदि को लूटना

**hold²** /həʊld होल्ड् / *noun* **1** [C] the act or manner of having sb/sth in your hand(s) व्यक्ति या वस्तु को पकड़ने का कार्य या ढंग; पकड़ *to have a firm hold on the rope* ○ *judo/wrestling holds* **2** [*sing.*] **a hold (on/over sb/sth)** influence or control प्रभाव या नियंत्रण *The new government has strengthened its hold on the country.* **3** [C] the part of a ship or an aircraft where cargo is carried जलपोत या विमान में सामान रखने का स्थान ➪ **plane** पर चित्र देखिए।

IDM **catch, get, grab, take, etc. hold (of sb/sth)** **1** to take sb/sth in your hands किसी को पकड़ लेना *I managed to catch hold of the dog before it ran out into the road.* **2** to take control of sb/sth; to start to have an effect on sb/sth व्यक्ति या वस्तु को काबू में कर लेना, किसी व्यक्ति या वस्तु पर किसी बात का असर होने लगना *Mass hysteria seemed to have taken hold of the crowd.*

**get hold of sb** to find sb or make contact with sb किसी का पता लगाना या उससे मिलना *I've been trying to get hold of the complaints department all morning.*

**get hold of sth** to find sth that will be useful उपयोगी चीज़ का पता लगाना *I must try and get hold of a good second-hand bicycle.*

**holdall** /ˈhəʊldɔːl ˈहोल्डॉल् / *noun* [C] a large bag that is used for carrying clothes, etc. when you are travelling बड़ा बैग जिसमें सफ़र करते समय वस्त्रों को रखते हैं; होल्डाल

**holder** /ˈhəʊldə(r) ˈहोल्ड(र्)/ *noun* [C] (*often in compound nouns*) **1** a person who has or holds sth किसी वस्तु को रखने या धारण करने वाला व्यक्ति, धारक (जैसे टिकट-धारक, शेयर-धारक) *a season ticket holder* ○ *the world record holder in the 100 metres* **2** something that contains or holds sth किसी अन्य वस्तु को पकड़ने वाली वस्तु; होल्डर *a toothbrush holder*

**holding company** *noun* [C] a company that is formed to buy shares in other companies which it then controls अन्य कंपनी के शेयरों को ख़रीदकर बनी (नई) कंपनी, होल्डिंग कंपनी

**hold-up** *noun* [C] **1** a delay देरी, देर *'What's the hold-up?' 'There's been an accident ahead of us.'* **2** the act of robbing a bank, etc. using a gun बंदूक़ की नोक पर बैंक आदि को लूटने का काम *The gang have carried out three hold-ups of banks in South Delhi.*

**hole** /həʊl होल्/ *noun* **1** [C] an opening; an empty space in sth solid गड्ढा, छेद; किसी ठोस वस्तु में ख़ाली स्थान, छेद, सुराख़ *The pavement is full of holes.* ○ *There are holes in my socks.* **2** [C] the place where an animal lives in the ground or in a tree ज़मीन में या पेड़ पर पशु-पक्षी के रहने का स्थान; माँद, बिल, विवर, कोटर *a mouse hole* **3** [C] (in golf) the hole in the ground that you must hit the ball into. Each section of the land where you play (**golf course**) is also called a hole (गॉल्फ़ के खेल में) गॉल्फ़ कोर्स में बना छोटा गड्ढा जिसमें गेंद को मारकर पहुँचाया जाता है *an eighteen-hole golf course* **4** [*sing.*] (*informal*) a small dark and unpleasant room, flat, etc. छोटा अँधेरा घटिया कमरा, फ़्लैट आदि *This place is a hole—you can't live here!*

**Holi** *noun* [C, U] an Indian spring festival celebrated in honour of Lord Krishna. During this festival people scatter coloured powders or apply them on each other रंगों का त्योहार होली

**holiday** /ˈhɒlədeɪ ˈहॉलिडे/ *noun* **1** (*AmE* **vacation**) [C, U] a period of rest from work or school (often when you go and stay away from home) स्कूल या काम से आराम का समय; छुट्टियाँ, दीर्घावकाश *We're going to Shimla **for our** summer **holidays** this year.* ○ *Mr Philips isn't here this week. He's away **on holiday**.*

> **NOTE** विशेष कारण से काम पर न जाने को **leave** (छुट्टी) कहते हैं—*sick leave* ○ *maternity leave* (= when you are having a baby) ○ *unpaid leave*

**2** [C] a day of rest when people do not go to work, school, etc. often for religious or national celebrations धार्मिक या राष्ट्रीय उत्सव के कारण विश्राम का दिन, धार्मिक या राष्ट्रीय अवकाश *Next Monday is a holiday.* ○ *New Year's Day is a **bank/public holiday** in Britain.*

> **NOTE** इस अर्थ में **holiday** का प्रयोग ब्रिटिश अंग्रेज़ी के साथ अमेरिकी अंग्रेज़ी में भी होता है; स्वेच्छा से काम पर न जाने को **day off** कहते हैं—*I'm having two days off next week when we move house.*

**holiday camp** *noun* [C] (*BrE*) a place that provides a place to stay and organized entertainment for people on holiday अवकाश-भोगी लोगों के लिए रहने और बाक़ायदा मनोरंजन का स्थान; अवकाश -शिविर

**holidaymaker** /ˈhɒlədeɪmeɪkə(r); -dimeɪ- ˈहॉलडेमेक(र्); -डिमे- / *noun* [C] (*BrE*) a person who is away from home on holiday अवकाश पर रहने वाला व्यक्ति

**hollow**[1] /ˈhɒləʊ ˈहॉलो/ *adj.* **1** with a hole or empty space inside खोखला, पोला *a hollow tree* **2** (used about parts of the face) sinking deep into the face (चेहरे के अंश) अंदर धँसे हुए, चिपके हुए *hollow cheeks* ○ *hollow-eyed* **3** not sincere थोथा, झूठा, बनावटी *a hollow laugh/voice* ○ *hollow promises/threats* **4** (used about a sound) seeming to come from a hollow place (आवाज़) ख़ाली स्थान से आती प्रतीत होती हुई *hollow footsteps*

**hollow**[2] /ˈhɒləʊ ˈहॉलो/ *verb*

**PHR V** **hollow sth out** to take out the inside part of sth किसी वस्तु को खोखला कर देना

**hollow**[3] /ˈhɒləʊ ˈहॉलो/ *noun* [C] an area that is lower than the land around it चारों तरफ़ की ज़मीन से नीची ज़मीन, गड्ढा, घाटी

**holly** /ˈhɒli ˈहॉलि/ *noun* [U] a plant that has shiny dark green leaves with sharp points and red berries in the winter. It is often used as a Christmas decoration चमकीले गहरे हरे नुकीले पत्तों वाला पौधा जिस पर सर्दियों में लाल बेर से फल लगते हैं; (प्रायः क्रिसमस कालीन सजावट में प्रयुक्त); शूलपर्णी

**holocaust** /ˈhɒləkɔːst ˈहॉलकॉस्ट्/ *noun* [C] a situation where a great many things are destroyed and a great many people die विनाश-लीला, विध्वंस *a nuclear holocaust*

**hologram** /ˈhɒləgræm ˈहॉलग्रैम्/ *noun* [C] an image or picture which appears to stand out from the flat surface it is on when light falls on it किसी सतह पर लगी कोई लघु छवि या चित्र जो प्रकाश पड़ने पर अलग से चमकती-उभरती है; होलोग्राम

**holster** /ˈhəʊlstə(r) ˈहोलुस्ट(र्)/ *noun* [C] a leather case for a gun that is fixed to a belt or worn under the arm (बेल्ट या काठी से बंधा) पिस्तौल रखने का चमड़े का खोल, जो कंधे से बग़ल तक लटका रहता है

**holy** /ˈhəʊli ˈहोलि/ *adj.* (**holier; holiest**) **1** connected with God or with religion and therefore very special or important पवित्र, धर्म या ईश्वर से संबंधित होने के कारण अति विशेष या महत्त्वपूर्ण *the Holy Bible/Holy Koran* ○ *holy water* **2** (used about a person) serving God; pure (व्यक्ति) परमेश्वर का सेवक, ईश्वर-भक्त; शुद्धात्मा ▶ **holiness** *noun* [U] पवित्रता

**homage** /ˈhɒmɪdʒ ˈहॉमिज्/ *noun* [U, C, *usually sing.*] (*formal*) **homage (to sb/sth)** something that is said or done to show respect publicly for sb किसी के लिए श्रद्धांजलि, सार्वजनिक रूप से किसी व्यक्ति के लिए कहे गए शब्द या व्यक्त आदर *Thousands came to **pay/do homage** to the dead leader.*

**home¹** /həʊm होम्/ *noun* **1** [C, U] the place where you live or where you feel that you belong निवास-स्थान, घर *She **left home*** (= left her parents' house and began an independent life) *at the age of 21.* ○ *Children from **broken homes*** (= whose parents are divorced) *sometimes have learning difficulties.* ➪ **house** पर नोट देखिए।

**NOTE** ध्यान रहे कि पूर्वसर्ग (preposition) 'to' का **'home'** से पहले प्रयोग नहीं होता—*It's time to go home.* ○ *She's usually tired when she gets/arrives home.* किसी अन्य के घर के विषय में कहने के लिए—*at Reena and Arun's* या *at Reena and Arun's place/house* का प्रयोग होता है।

**2** [C] a place that provides care for a particular type of person or for animals विशेष प्रकार के व्यक्तियों या पशुओं को शरण देने वाला स्थान, शरण-स्थल, आश्रम, शाला (जैसे वृद्धाश्रम, गोशाला) *a children's home* (= for children who have no parents to look after them) ○ *an **old people's home*** **3** [*sing.*] **the home of sth** the place where sth began (किसी का) उद्गम स्थल, मूल स्थान *Greece is said to be the home of democracy.*

**IDM at home 1** in your house, flat, etc. मकान, फ़्लैट आदि में या पर *Is anybody at home?* ○ *Tomorrow we're staying at home all day.* **2** comfortable, as if you were in your own home आराम महसूस करना मानो घर में बैठे हों; सुखपूर्वक *Please make yourself at home.* **3** (used in sport) played in the town to which the team belongs (खेल) निजी स्थान के मैदान पर खेला गया *Manchester City are playing at home on Saturday.*

**IDM romp home/to victory** ➪ **romp** देखिए।

**home²** /həʊm होम्/ *adj.* (*only before a noun*) **1** connected with home घर का, घर से संबंधित; घरेलू *home cooking* ○ *your home address/town* (= with your family) **2** connected with your own country, not with a foreign country अपने देश का, स्वदेशी न कि विदेश का), स्वदेश संबंधी ***The Home Minister** is responsible for **home affairs**.* **3** (used in sport) connected with a team's own sports ground (खेल में) टीम के अपने मैदान से संबंधित स्थानीय (टीम) *The home team has a lot of support.* ○ *a home game* ✪ विलोम **away**

**home³** /həʊm होम्/ *adv.* at, in or to your home or home country घर या स्वदेश पर, में, को *We must be getting home soon.* ○ *She'll be flying home for Diwali.*

**IDM bring sth home to sb** to make sb understand sth fully किसी को कोई बात पूरी तरह समझाना

**drive sth home (to sb)** ➪ **drive¹** देखिए।

**home⁴** /həʊm होम्/ *verb*

**PHR V home in on sb/sth** to move towards sb/sth किसी व्यक्ति या वस्तु की ओर बढ़ना *The police homed in on the house where the thieves were hiding.*

**homecoming** /ˈhəʊmkʌmɪŋ ˈहोम्कमिङ्/ *noun* [C, U] the act of returning home, especially when you have been away for a long time घर वापसी (विशेषतः घर से लंबे समय तक दूर रहने के बाद)

**home-grown** *adj.* (used about fruit and vegetables) grown in your own garden (फल और सब्ज़ियाँ) घर के बग़ीचे में उगाए हुए

**homeland** /ˈhəʊmlænd ˈहोम्लैन्ड्/ *noun* [C] the country where you were born or that your parents came from, or to which you feel you belong स्वदेश, मातृभूमि

**homeless** /ˈhəʊmləs ˈहोम्लस्/ *adj.* **1** having no home जिसका कोई घर नहीं; बेघर **2 the homeless** *noun* [*pl.*] people who have no home बेघर लोग ▶ **homelessness** *noun* [U] गृहहीनता

**homely** /ˈhəʊmli ˈहोम्लि/ *adj.* (*BrE*) (used about a place) simple but also pleasant or welcoming (स्थान) सीधा-सादा तथा ऐसा कि वहाँ आना अच्छा लगे, घर जैसा लगने वाला

**home-made** *adj.* made at home; not bought in a shop घर में बना; बाहर का नहीं *home-made cakes*

**homeopath** (*also* **homoeopath**) /ˈhəʊmiəpæθ ˈहोमिअपैथ्/ *noun* [C] a person who treats sick people using homoeopathy होम्योपैथी का डॉक्टर

**homeopathy** (*also* **homoeopathy**) /ˌhəʊmiˈɒpəθi ˌहोमिˈऑपथि/ *noun* [U] the treatment of a disease by giving very small amounts of a drug that would cause the disease if given in large amounts होम्योपैथी की चिकित्सा पद्धति ▶ **homeopathic** (*also* **homoeopathic**) /ˌhəʊmiəˈpæθɪk ˌहोमिअˈपैथिक्/ *adj.* होम्योपैथी का *homeopathic medicine*

**homeostasis** /ˌhəʊmiəʊˈsteɪsɪs; ˌhɒm- ˌहोमिओˈस्टेसिस्; ˌहॉम्-/ *noun* [U] (*technical*) the process by which the body reacts to changes in order to keep conditions inside the body, for example temperature; the same परिवर्तनों के प्रति शारीरिक प्रतिक्रिया की प्रक्रिया जिसमें शरीर की अंदरूनी दशाएँ स्थिर रहती हैं; समस्थिति

**home page** *noun* [C] (*computing*) the first of a number of pages of information on the Internet that belongs to a person or an organization. A home page contains connections to other pages of information इंटरनेट पर किसी व्यक्ति या संगठन के विभाजन का मुखपृष्ठ, मुखपृष्ठ पर ही अन्य सूचनायुक्त पृष्ठों के संपर्क सूत्र रहते हैं; होम पेज

**home rule** *noun* [U] the right of a country or region to govern itself, especially after another country or region has governed it किसी देश या क्षेत्र का स्वशासन का अधिकार (विशेषतः पराधीनता की स्थिति में), स्वशासन, स्वराज्य, होम रूल

**the Home Secretary** *noun* [C] (*BrE*) a politician in the British Government (**minister**) who is in charge of the Home Office ब्रिटिश सरकार में गृहमंत्री ➪ **the Foreign Secretary** देखिए।

**homesick** /ˈhəʊmsɪk ˈहोम्सिक्/ *adj.* **homesick (for sb/sth)** sad because you are away from home and you miss it घर से दूर रहने के कारण उदास, घर के लिए उदास; गृहासक्त ▶ **homesickness** *noun* [U] गृहासक्ति

**homeward** /ˈhəʊmwəd ˈहोम्वड्/ *adj., adv.* going towards home घर की ओर (का), गृहोन्मुख *the homeward journey* ○ *to travel homeward*

**homework** /ˈhəʊmwɜːk ˈहोम्वक्/ *noun* [U] the written work that teachers give to students to do away from school गृहकार्य; अध्यापक द्वारा छात्रों को घर पर करने के लिए दिया गया लिखित कार्य *Have we got any homework?*

> **NOTE** **Homework** शब्द अगणनीय है, अतः बहुवचन में इसका प्रयोग नहीं होता, यदि एक अकेले गृहकार्य की बात करनी हो तो **a piece of homework** का प्रयोग करना होगा। ➪ **housework** पर नोट देखिए।

**homicidal** /ˌhɒmɪˈsaɪdl ˌहॉमिˈसाइड्ल्/ *adj.* likely to murder sb जो संभवतः किसी की हत्या कर दे, मानव-हत्या के इरादे वाला *a homicidal maniac*

**homicide** /ˈhɒmɪsaɪd ˈहॉमिसाइड्/ *noun* [C, U] (*AmE*) the illegal killing of one person by another; murder एक व्यक्ति द्वारा दूसरे की ग़ैर-क़ानूनी हत्या; हत्या

**homo-** /ˈhɒməʊ; ˈhəʊməʊ ˈहॉमो; ˈहोमो/ *prefix* (*in nouns, adjectives and adverbs*) the same वही, समान, सम- *homogeneous* ○ *homosexual* ➪ **hetero-** देखिए।

**homogeneous** /ˌhɒməˈdʒiːniəs ˌहॉमˈजीनिअस्/ *adj.* (*technical*) made up of parts that are all of the same type एक ही प्रकार के अंशों से निर्मित; समरूप, समांगी ➪ **heterogeneous** देखिए।

**homograph** /ˈhɒməgrɑːf ˈहॉमग्राफ़्/ *noun* [C] (*grammar*) a word that is spelled like another word but has a different meaning and may have a different pronunciation, for example **'bow'**/baʊ बाउ/ and **bow'**/bəʊ बो/ वर्तनी में समान परंतु अर्थ में (और प्रायः उच्चारण में भी) भिन्न शब्द; समलेखी शब्द

**homologous** /həˈmɒləgəs हˈमॉलगस्/ *adj.* **homologous (with sth)** (*technical*) similar in position, structure, etc. to sth else स्थिति, संरचना आदि में दूसरे के समान; समजातीय *The seal's flipper is homologous with the human arm.*

**homonym** /ˈhɒmənɪm ˈहॉमनिम्/ *noun* [C] (*grammar*) a word that is spelt and pronounced like another word but that has a different meaning उच्चारण तथा वर्तनी में समान परंतु अर्थ में भिन्न शब्द; समनाम *'Bank'* (= river bank) *and 'bank'* (= place where money is kept) *are homonyms.*

**homophone** /ˈhɒməfəʊn ˈहॉमफ़ोन्/ *noun* [C] (*grammar*) a word that is pronounced the same as another word but that has a different spelling and meaning उच्चारण में समान परंतु वर्तनी और अर्थ में भिन्न शब्द; समध्वनिक शब्द *'Flower' and 'flour' are homophones.*

**Homo sapiens** /ˌhəʊməʊˈsæpienz ˌहोमोˈसैपिअन्ज़्/ *noun* [U] (*technical*) the kind or **species** of human being that exists now आधुनिक मानव जाति

**homosexual** /ˌhəʊməˈsekʃuəl; ˌhɒm- ˌहोमˈसेक्शुअल्; ˌहॉम्-/ *adj.* sexually attracted to people of the same sex एक ही लिंग के व्यक्ति के प्रति कामुक भाव से आकृष्ट; समलैंगिक ➪ **heterosexual, bisexual, gay** और **lesbian** देखिए। ▶ **homosexual** *noun* [C] समलैंगिक व्यक्ति ▶ **homosexuality** /ˌhəʊməˌsekʃuˈæləti; ˌhɒm- ˌहोमˌसेक्शुˈऐलटि; ˌहॉम्-/ *noun* [U] समलैंगिकता

**homozygote** /ˌhɒməˈzaɪgəʊt; ˌhɒməʊ- ˌहॉमˈज़ाइगोट्; ˌहॉमो-/ *noun* [C] a living thing that has only one form of a particular **gene** and so whose young are more likely to share a particular characteristic ऐसा प्राणी जिसमें एक विशेष जीन का केवल एक ही रूप होता है; समयुग्मज प्राणी ▶ **homozygous** /ˌhɒməˈzaɪgəs ˌहॉमˈज़ाइगस्/ *adj.* समयुग्मजात्मक

**Hon** *abbr.* **1** Honorary; used to show that sb holds a position without being paid for it वेतनरहित पद का धारक; अवैतनिक, मानद *Hon Presi-*

*dent* **2** Honourable: a title for Members of Parliament and some high officials माननीयः सांसदों और अन्य उच्च अधिकारियों के लिए सम्मानसूचक पदवी

**honest** /ˈɒnɪst ˈऑनिस्ट्/ *adj.* **1** (used about a person) telling the truth; not lying to people or stealing (व्यक्ति) सत्याचरण करने वाला, ईमानदार; चोरी आदि असत्याचरण न करने वाला *Just be honest—do you like this skirt or not?* ○ ***To be honest**, I don't think that's a very good idea.* **2** showing honest qualities ईमानदारी के गुणों वाला *an honest face* ○ *I'd like your honest opinion, please.* ✪ विलोम **dishonest** (दोनों अर्थों में) ▶ **honesty** *noun* [U] ईमानदारी, सत्यनिष्ठ ✪ विलोम **dishonesty**

**honestly** /ˈɒnɪstli ˈऑनिस्ट्लि/ *adv.* **1** in an honest way ईमानदारी से, सत्यनिष्ठ भाव से *He tried to answer the lawyer's questions honestly.* **2** used for emphasizing that what you are saying is true कही जा रही बात की सचाई पर बल देने के लिए प्रयुक्त *I honestly don't know where she has gone.* **3** used for expressing disapproval असहमति या नापसंदी व्यक्त करने के लिए प्रयुक्त *Honestly! What a mess!*

**honey** /ˈhʌni ˈहनि/ *noun* [U] **1** the sweet sticky substance that is made by bees and that people eat शहद, मधु **2** a word for 'darling', used especially in American English प्रियजन; 'darling' के लिए अमेरिकी अंग्रेज़ी में प्रयुक्त शब्द

**honeycomb** /ˈhʌnikəʊm ˈहनिकोम्/ *noun* [C, U] a structure of holes (**cells**) with six sides, in which bees keep their eggs and the substance they produce (**honey**) शहद का छत्ता

**honeymoon** /ˈhʌnimuːn ˈहनिमून्/ *noun* [C] a holiday that is taken by a man and a woman who have just got married नवविवाहित दंपत्ति द्वारा आमोद-प्रमोद के लिए ली गई छुट्टी *We went on a world tour for our honeymoon.*

**honk** /hɒŋk हॉङ्क्/ *verb* [I] to sound the horn of a car; to make this sound कार का हॉर्न बजाना; कार के हॉर्न की आवाज़ निकालना

**honorary** /ˈɒnərəri ˈऑनररि/ *adj.* **1** given as an honour (without the person needing the usual certificates, etc.) सम्मान के रूप में प्रदत्त (जिसमें व्यक्ति को नियमित योग्यता के प्रमाण-पत्र की अपेक्षा नहीं होती), सम्मानद्योतक *to be awarded an honorary degree* **2** (*often* **Honorary**) (*abbr.* **Hon**) not paid अवैतनिक *He is the Honorary President.*

**honour**[1] (*AmE* **honor**) /ˈɒnə(r) ˈऑन(र्)/ *noun* **1** [U] the respect from other people that a person, country, etc. gets because of high standards of behaviour and moral character आदर, सम्मान *the guest of honour* (= the most important one) ➪ **dishonour** देखिए। **2** [*sing.*] (*formal*) something that gives pride or pleasure गौरव या प्रसन्नता देने वाली वस्तु, सम्मान की बात *It was a great honour to be asked to speak at the conference.* **3** [U] the quality of doing what is morally right नैतिक रूप से उचित कार्य करने का गुण *I give you my word of honour.* **4 Honours** [*pl.*] the four highest marks you can be given in Bachelor degrees छात्र को बैचलर उपाधि में दिए जा सकने वाले चार उच्चतम अंक; ऑनर्स **5** [C] something that is given to a person officially, to show great respect विशेष सम्मान प्रकट करने के लिए किसी व्यक्ति को आधिकारिक रूप से प्रदत्त वस्तु *He was buried with full military honours* (= with a military ceremony as a sign of respect).

**IDM** **in honour of sb/sth; in sb/sth's honour** out of respect for sb/sth किसी व्यक्ति या वस्तु के सम्मान में *A party was given in honour of the guests from Russia.*

**honour**[2] (*AmE* **honor**) /ˈɒnə(r) ˈऑन(र्)/ *verb* [T] **1 honour sb/sth (with sth)** to show great (public) respect for sb/sth or to give sb pride or pleasure किसी व्यक्ति या वस्तु के प्रति (सार्वजनिक रूप से) विशेष सम्मान प्रदर्शित करना या किसी व्यक्ति को गौरव या प्रसन्नता प्रदान करना *I am very honoured by the confidence you have shown in me.* **2** to do what you have agreed or promised वादे को पूरा करना

**honourable** (*AmE* **honorable**) /ˈɒnərəbl ˈऑनरबल्/ *adj.* **1** acting in a way that makes people respect you; having or showing honour सम्मानजनक; सम्मानपूर्ण ✪ विलोम **dishonourable** **2 the Honourable** (*abbr.* **the Hon**) a title that is given to some high officials and to Members of Parliament when they are speaking to each other कतिपय उच्च अधिकारियों और संसद-सदस्यों द्वारा एक दूसरे के लिए प्रयुक्त संबोधन; माननीय ▶ **honourably** /-əbli -अबलि/ *adv.* सम्मान भाव से, सम्मानजनक रीति से

**Hons** /ɒnz ऑनज़्/ *abbr.* Honours (in Bachelor degrees) (बैचलर उपाधि में) ऑनर्स *Jimmy Bhatia BSc (Hons)*

**hood** /hʊd हुड्/ *noun* [C] **1** the part of a coat, etc. that you pull up to cover your head and neck in bad weather कोट में लगी टोपी जो सिर और गरदन को ढकती है; हुड **2** (*BrE*) a soft cover for a car that has no roof, or a folding cover on a baby's **pram** which can be folded down in good weather बग़ैर छत की कार का कपड़े आदि से बना कवर या बच्चा गाड़ी का फ़ोल्डिंग कवर (जो अच्छे मौसम में लपेटकर रखा जा सकता है) **3** (*AmE*) = **bonnet**[1]

**hoof** /hu:f हूफ़्/ *noun* [C] (*pl.* **hoofs** or **hooves** /hu:vz हूव्ज़्/) the hard part of the foot of horses and some other animals घोड़ा आदि पशुओं का खुर ➪ **paw** देखिए।

**hook**[1] /hʊk हुक्/ *noun* [C] **1** a curved piece of metal, plastic, etc. that is used for hanging sth on or for catching fish किसी वस्तु को टाँगने की खूँटी या मछली पकड़ने का हुक; काँटा *Put your coat on the hook over there.* ○ *a fish-hook* **2** (used in boxing) a way of hitting sb that is done with the arm bent (मुक्केबाज़ी) एक प्रकार का प्रहार जिसमें बाँह मोड़कर घूँसा मारते हैं *a right hook* (= with the right arm)

IDM **off the hook** (used about the top part of a telephone) not in position, so that telephone calls cannot be received (दूरभाष संबंधी) फ़ोन के रिसीवर को इस प्रकार उठाकर रखना जिससे फ़ोन से संपर्क न स्थापित हो

**get/let sb off the hook** (*informal*) to free yourself or sb else from a difficult situation or punishment स्वयं को या किसी को संकट की परिस्थिति या दंड से मुक्त करना *My father paid the money I owed and got me off the hook.*

**hook**[2] /hʊk हुक्/ *verb* **1** [I, T] to fasten or catch sth with a hook or sth in the shape of a hook; to be fastened in this way हुक से बाँधना या (किसी वस्तु को) पकड़ना या हुक के आकार की किसी वस्तु को बाँधना; इस प्रकार से बाँधना *We hooked the trailer to the back of the car.* ○ *The curtain simply hooks onto the rail.* **2** [T] to put sth through a hole in sth else किसी वस्तु को छेद में से निकालते हुए दूसरी से जोड़ना *Hook the rope through your belt.*

PHR V **hook (sth) up (to sth)** to connect sb/sth to a piece of electronic equipment or to a power supply किसी व्यक्ति या वस्तु को किसी विद्युत उपकरण से या बिजली की आपूर्ति से जोड़ना

**hook and eye** *noun* [C] a thing that is used for fastening clothes कपड़ों को बाँधने का आँखनुमा हुक ➪ **button** पर चित्र देखिए।

**hooked** /hʊkt हुक्ट्/ *adj.* **1** shaped like a hook हुक की शकल का *a hooked nose* **2** (*not before a noun*) (*informal*) **hooked (on sth)** enjoying sth very much, so that you want to do it, see it, etc. as much as possible किसी वस्तु का भरपूर आनंद लेना *He is hooked on computer games.*

**hooligan** /ˈhu:lɪgən ˈहूलिगन्/ *noun* [C] a person who behaves in a violent and aggressive way in public places सार्वजनिक स्थानों पर उग्र और आक्रामक आचरण करने वाला व्यक्ति; उपद्रवी, दंगाई, गुंडा *football hooligans* ➪ **lout** और **yob** देखिए। ▶ **hooliganism** /-ɪzəm -इज़म्/ *noun* [U] उपद्रव, दंगा-फ़साद, गुंडागर्दी

**hoop** /hu:p हूप्/ *noun* [C] a large metal or plastic ring धातु या प्लास्टिक का बड़ा छल्ला; छर-पट्टी

**hooray** = **hurray**

**hoot**[1] /hu:t हूट्/ *noun* **1** [C] (*BrE*) a short loud laugh or shout छोटी ज़ोर की हँसी, ठहाका या शोरगुल *hoots of laughter* **2** [*sing.*] (*spoken*) a situation or a person that is very funny अजीबोग़रीब हालत या व्यक्ति *Gagan is a real hoot!* **3** [C] the loud sound that is made by the horn of a vehicle वाहन में लगे भोंपू की आवाज़ **4** [C] the cry of a particular bird (**an owl**) उल्लू की आवाज़

**hoot**[2] /hu:t हूट्/ *verb* [I, T] to sound the horn of a car or to make a loud noise कार का हॉर्न बजाना या ठहाके मारना *The driver hooted (his horn) at the dog but it wouldn't move.* ○ *They hooted with laughter at the suggestion.*

**hoover** /ˈhu:və(r) ˈहूव(र्)/ *verb* [I, T] (*BrE*) to clean a carpet, etc. with a machine that sucks up the dirt धूल सोखने वाली मशीन से क़ालीन आदि को साफ़ करना *This carpet needs hoovering.* ✪ पर्याय **vacuum** ▶ **Hoover™** *noun* [C] हूवर™ ✪ पर्याय **vacuum cleaner**

**hooves** /hu:vz हूव्ज़्/ ➪ **hoof** plural का रूप

**hop**[1] /hɒp हॉप्/ *verb* [I] (**hopping; hopped**) **1** (used about a person) to jump on one leg (व्यक्ति का) एक टाँग के बल उछलना या कूदना **2** (used about an animal or bird) to jump with both or all feet together (पशु या पक्षी का) दोनों या सब पैरों के बल उछलना या कूदना **3 hop (from sth to sth)** to change quickly from one activity or subject to another एक क्रिया या विषय से दूसरे पर जल्दी-जल्दी जाना, जल्दी-जल्दी क्रिया या विषय परिवर्तन करना

IDM **hop it!** (*slang*) Go away! परे हट

PHR V **hop in/into sth; hop out/out of sth** (*informal*) to get in or out of a car, etc. (quickly) (फुरती से) कार आदि में बैठना या उससे उतरना

PHR V **hop on/onto sth; hop off sth** (*informal*) to get onto/off a bus, etc. (quickly) (फुरती से) बस आदि में सवार होना या उससे उतरना

**hop**[2] /hɒp हॉप्/ *noun* **1** [C] a short jump by a person on one leg or by a bird or animal with its feet together व्यक्ति का एक पैर से कूदना या पशु या पक्षी का एक साथ सब पैरों के बल उछलना **2** [C] a tall climbing plant with flowers फूलों वाली लंबी ऊपर चढ़ती बेल **3 hops** [*pl.*] the flowers of this plant that are used in making beer इस बेल के फूल (जिनसे बियर बनती है)

**hope**[1] /həʊp होप्/ *verb* [I, T] **hope that... ; hope to do sth; hope (for sth)** to want sth to happen or be true अनुकूल स्थिति की आशा करना या चाहना कि कुछ घटित हो या कोई बात सच हो, किसी घटना के घटित होने या बात के सच होने की आशा करना *'Is it raining?' '**I hope not**. I haven't got a coat with me.'* ○ *Hoping to hear from you soon* (= at the end of a letter).

**hope**[2] /həʊp होप्/ *noun* **1** [C, U] **(a) hope (of/for sth); (a) hope of doing sth; (a) hope that...** the feeling of wanting sth to happen and thinking that it will किसी घटना के घटित होने की चाह और तदनुकूल सोच, आशा, उम्मीद *Amar has **high hopes** of becoming a jockey* (= is very confident about it). ○ *She never **gave up hope** that a cure for the disease would be found.* **2** [*sing.*] a person, a thing or a situation that will help you get what you want अभीष्ट की प्राप्ति में सहायक व्यक्ति, वस्तु या स्थिति *Please can you help me? You're my last hope.*

IDM **dash sb's hopes (of sth/of doing sth)** ➪ **dash**[2] देखिए।

**in the hope of sth/that...** because you want sth to happen किसी बात की आशा में *I came here in the hope that we could talk privately.*

**pin (all) your hopes on sb/sth** ➪ **pin**[2] देखिए।

**a ray of hope** ➪ **ray** देखिए।

**hopeful** /ˈhəʊpfl ˈहोपफ़्ल्/ *adj.* **1 hopeful (about sth); hopeful that...** believing that sth that you want will happen आशा रखने वाला, आशावान *He's very hopeful about the success of the business.* ○ *The ministers seem hopeful that an agreement will be reached.* **2** making you think that sth good will happen आशाप्रद; अनुकूल घटित होने की सोच पैदा करने वाला *a hopeful sign*

**hopefully** /ˈhəʊpfəli ˈहोपफ़लि/ *adv.* **1** (*informal*) I/We hope; if everything happens as planned मुझे/हमें आशा है; यदि वैसा ही हुआ जैसा सोचा था *Hopefully, we'll be finished by six o'clock.* **2** hoping that what you want will happen आशा करते हुए कि जो हम चाहते हैं वही होगा, अभीष्ट परिणाम की आशा करते हुए *She smiled hopefully at me, waiting for my answer.*

**hopeless** /ˈhəʊpləs ˈहोप्लस्/ *adj.* **1** giving no hope that sth/sb will be successful or get better निराशापूर्ण काम में सफलता या बेहतरी की आशा से रहित *It's hopeless. There is nothing we can do.* **2** (*informal*) **hopeless (at sth)** (*BrE*) (used about a person) often doing things wrong; very bad at doing sth (व्यक्ति) अकसर ग़लत काम करने वाला; एकदम अनाड़ी *I'm absolutely hopeless at tennis.* ▶ **hopelessly** *adv.* निराशापूर्वक *They were hopelessly lost.* ▶ **hopelessness** *noun* [U] निराशावादिता

**horde** /hɔːd हॉड्/ *noun* [C] a very large number of people लोगों का झुंड, भीड़ **2** nomadic tribe ख़ानाबदोश जाति

**horizon** /həˈraɪzn हˈराइज़्न्/ *noun* **1** [*sing.*] the line where the earth and sky appear to meet क्षितिज; वह रेखा जहाँ पृथ्वी और आकाश मिलते प्रतीत होते हैं *The ship appeared on/disappeared over the horizon.* **2 horizons** [*pl.*] the limits of your knowledge or experience ज्ञान या अनुभव की परिधि *Foreign travel is a good way of expanding your horizons.*

IDM **on the horizon** likely to happen soon संभवतः शीघ्र होने वाला; संभावित *There are further job cuts on the horizon.*

**horizontal** /ˌhɒrɪˈzɒntl ˌहॉरिˈज़ॉन्ट्ल्/ *adj.* going from side to side, not up and down; flat or level क्षितिज के समानांतर, एक पार्श्व से दूसरे पार्श्व की ओर (न कि ऊपर और नीचे); समतल *The gymnasts were exercising on the horizontal bars.* ➪ **vertical, perpendicular** तथा **line** भी देखिए। ▶ **horizontally** /-təli -टलि/ *adv.* क्षितिज के अनुरूप

**hormone** /ˈhɔːməʊn ˈहॉमोन्/ *noun* [C] a substance in your body that influences growth and development शरीर की वृद्धि और विकास को प्रभावित करने वाला तत्व; अंतःस्राव, हॉरमोन ▶ **hormonal** /hɔːˈməʊnl हॉˈमोनल्/ *adj.* हॉरमोन संबंधी *the hormonal changes occurring during pregnancy*

**horn** /hɔːn हॉन्/ *noun* [C] **1** one of the hard pointed things that some animals have on their heads (पशुओं के) सींग **2** the thing in a car, etc. that gives a loud warning sound कार आदि का हॉर्न या भोंपू *Don't sound your horn late at night.* ➪ **car** पर चित्र देखिए। **3** one of the family of metal musical instruments that you play by blowing into them फूँक मारकर बजाने का एक वाद्य; तुरही *the French horn*

**hornet** /ˈhɔːnɪt ˈहॉनिट्/ *noun* [C] a black and yellow flying insect that has a very powerful sting तीखा डंक मारने वाला काला-पीला उड़न कीट; हाड़ा, बर्रे, भिड़, ततैया NOTE **Hornet** कीड़ा **wasp** से बड़ा होता है।

**horoscope** /ˈhɒrəskəʊp ˈहॉरस्कोप्/ *noun* [C] (*also* **stars** [*pl.*]) a statement about what is going to happen to a person in the future, based on the position of the stars and planets when he/she was born जन्मपत्री, जन्मकुंडली *What does my horoscope for next week say?* ➪ **astrology** और **zodiac** देखिए।

**horrendous** /hɒˈrendəs हॉˈरेन्डस्/ *adj.* (*informal*) very bad or unpleasant बहुत बुरा या अप्रिय ▶ **horrendously** *adv.* अप्रिय रीति से

**horrible** /ˈhɒrəbl ˈहॉरब्ल्/ *adj.* **1** (*informal*) bad or unpleasant बुरा, दुष्ट या अप्रिय *Don't be so horrible* (= unkind)! ○ *I've got **a horrible feeling** that I've forgotten something.* ✪ पर्याय **horrid** **2** shocking and/or frightening बहुत बुरा और/या भयावह *a horrible murder/death/nightmare* ▶ **horribly** /-əbli -अब्लि/ *adv.* भयावह रूप से

**horrid** /ˈhɒrɪd ˈहॉरिड्/ *adj.* (*informal*) very unpleasant or unkind बहुत अप्रिय या बुरा लगने वाला या हृदयहीन; अमनोहर *horrid weather* ○ *I'm sorry that I was so horrid last night.* ✪ पर्याय **horrible**

**horrific** /həˈrɪfɪk हˈरिफ़िक्/ *adj.* **1** extremely bad and shocking or frightening बहुत बुरा और आघात-कारी या भयावह *a horrific murder/accident/attack* **2** (*informal*) very bad or unpleasant बहुत बुरा या अप्रिय ▶ **horrifically** /-kli -क्लि/ *adv.* अत्यधिक, अप्रिय रूप से *horrifically expensive*

**horrify** /ˈhɒrɪfaɪ ˈहॉरिफ़ाइ/ *verb* [T] (*pres. part.* **horrifying;** *3rd person sing. pres.* **horrifies;** *pt, pp* **horrified**) to make sb feel extremely shocked, disgusted or frightened किसी को अत्यंत आहत, खीजा हुआ या भयभीत करना ▶ **horrifying** *adj.* भयभीत करने वाला

**horror** /ˈhɒrə(r) ˈहॉर(र्)/ *noun* **1** [U, *sing.*] a feeling of great fear or shock बहुत डर या सदमा; दहशत, आतंक *They watched **in horror** as the building collapsed.* **2** [C] something that makes you feel frightened or shocked भयभीत करने वाली या सदमा पहुँचाने वाली कोई वस्तु; त्रासदायक वस्तु *a horror film/story*

**horror film** a film that entertains people by showing frightening or shocking things डरावनी फ़िल्म

**horse** /hɔːs हॉस्/ *noun* **1** [C] a large animal that is used for riding on or for pulling or carrying heavy loads घोड़ा

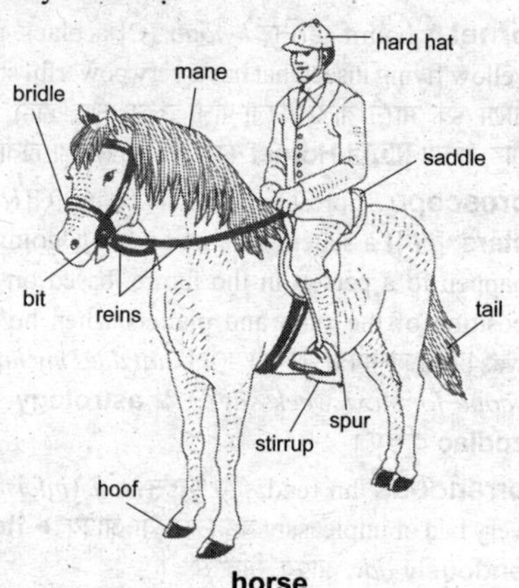

horse

> **NOTE** नर घोड़े को **stallion** कहते हैं, मादा को **mare** (घोड़ी) और (घोड़े के) बच्चे को **foal** कहते हैं।

**2 the horses** [*pl.*] (*informal*) horse racing घुड़दौड़ **IDM on horseback** sitting on a horse घोड़े पर सवार

**horse chestnut** *noun* [C] **1** a large tree that has leaves divided into seven sections and pink or white flowers सात खंडों में विभक्त पत्तों वाला बड़ा वृक्ष जिसमें गुलाबी या सफ़ेद फूल लगते हैं; बनखोर **2** (*informal* **conker**) the nut from this tree इस पेड़ की गिरी

**horseman** /ˈhɔːsmən ˈहॉस्मन्/ *noun* [C] (*pl.* **-men** /-mən -मन्/) a man who rides a horse well घोड़े पर संवारी करने में कुशल व्यक्ति, कुशल घुड़सवार या अश्वारोही *an experienced horseman*

**horsepower** /ˈhɔːspaʊə(r) ˈहॉस्पाउअ(र्)/ *noun* [C] (*pl.* **horsepower**) (*abbr.* **h.p.**) a measurement of the power of an engine इंजन की शक्ति की माप; अश्वशक्ति

**horse racing** (*also* **racing**) *noun* [U] the sport in which a person (**jockey**) rides a horse in a race to win money पेशेवर घुड़सवार वाली घुड़दौड़ जिसमें पैसा दाँव पर लगता है

> **NOTE** घुड़दौड़ का आयोजन **race course** में होता है, लोग प्रायः घुड़दौड़ के परिणामों को लेकर पैसा दाँव पर या **bet** लगाते हैं।

**horseshoe** /ˈhɔːsʃuː ˈहॉस्शू/ (*also* **shoe**) *noun* [C] a U-shaped piece of metal that is fixed to the bottom of a horse's foot (**hoof**). Some people believe that horseshoes bring good luck घोड़े के खुर में लगाने वाली U के आकार की धातु; नाल (कुछ लोग मानते हैं कि नाल से भाग्य अच्छा होता है)

**horsewoman** /ˈhɔːswʊmən ˈहॉस्वुमन्/ *noun* [C] (*pl.* **-women** /-wɪmɪn -विमिन/) a woman who rides a horse well कुशल महिला घुड़सवार या अश्वारोही

**horticulture** /ˈhɔːtɪkʌltʃə(r) ˈहॉटिकल्च(र्)/ *noun* [U] the study or practice of growing flowers, fruit and vegetables उद्यानविद्या या विज्ञान ▶ **horticultural** /ˌhɔːtɪˈkʌltʃərəl ˌहॉटिˈकल्चरल्/ *adj.* उद्यानविद्या-संबंधी

**hose** /həʊz होज़्/ (*also* **hosepipe** /ˈhəʊzpaɪp ˈहोज़्पाइप्/) *noun* [C, U] a long rubber or plastic tube that water can flow through रबर या प्लास्टिक का बना पानी का पाइप ➪ **gardening** पर चित्र देखिए।

**hospice** /ˈhɒspɪs ˈहॉस्पिस्/ *noun* [C] a special hospital where people who are dying are cared for मृत्यु के निकट पहुँचे हुए व्यक्तियों की सेवा-शुश्रूषा करने वाला विशेष अस्पताल

**hospitable** /hɒˈspɪtəbl; ˈhɒspɪtəbl हॉˈस्पिटबल्; ˈहॉस्पिटबल्/ *adj.* (used about a person) friendly and kind to visitors (व्यक्ति) मेहमानों के प्रति मित्रवत और उदार; आतिथ्यकारी, सत्कारशील, मेहमाननवाज़ ✪ विलोम **inhospitable**

**hospital** /ˈhɒspɪtl ˈहॉस्पिट्ल/ *noun* [C] a place where ill or injured people are treated अस्पताल, चिकित्सालय *He was rushed* ***to hospital*** *in an ambulance.* ○ *to be admitted to/discharged from hospital* ○ *a psychiatric/mental hospital*

> **NOTE** जब कोई व्यक्ति अस्पताल जाता है तो अभिव्यक्ति **goes to hospital** या **is in hospital** (बिना शब्द *'the'* के) का प्रयोग होता है जिनका अर्थ है कि वह बीमार है और अस्पताल में उसका इलाज चल रहा है—*His mother's in hospital.* ○ *She cut her hand and had to go to hospital.* **'The hospital'** से किसी एक विशेष अस्पताल का संकेत होता है या इस बात का कि कोई व्यक्ति अस्पताल भवन में थोड़ी देर के लिए आया या गया है—*He went to the hospital to visit Mona.* अस्पताल में जिस व्यक्ति का **doctors** और **nurses** इलाज करते हैं उसे **patient** कहते हैं। दुर्घटना में घायल व्यक्ति को पहले **casualty** विभाग या (*AmE*) **emergency room** में ले जाते हैं।

**hospitality** /ˌhɒspɪˈtæləti ˌहॉस्पिˈटैलटि/ *noun* [U] looking after guests and being friendly and welcoming towards them आतिथ्य-सत्कार, मेहमाननवाज़ी

**host** /həʊst होस्ट्/ *noun* [C] **1** a person who invites guests to his/her house, etc. and provides them with food, drink, etc. अतिथियों का सत्कार करने वाला पुरुष; आतिथेय, मेज़बान ➪ **hostess** देखिए। **2** a person who introduces a television or radio show and talks to the guests टेलीविज़न या रेडियो पर कार्यक्रम प्रस्तुत करने और अतिथियों से बातचीत करने वाला व्यक्ति; होस्ट **3 a host of sth** a large number of people or things लोगों या वस्तुओं की बड़ी संख्या, लोगों के झुंड और वस्तुओं के ढेर **4** an animal or a plant on which another animal or plant lives and feeds पशु या पौधा जिस पर दूसरा पशु या पौधा पलता है; परपोषी (पशु या पौधा) ▶ **host** *verb* [T] मेज़बानी करना, का आयोजन करना *The city is aiming to host the Commonwealth Games in four years' time.*

**hostage** /ˈhɒstɪdʒ ˈहॉस्टिज्/ *noun* [C] a person who is caught and kept prisoner. A hostage may be killed or injured if the person who is holding him/her does not get what he/she is asking for पकड़ा जाकर बंदी बनाया गया व्यक्ति; बंधक (माँग पूरी न होने पर बंधक की हत्या तक की जा सकती है) *The robbers tried to* ***take*** *the staff* ***hostage***. ○ *The hijackers say they will* ***hold*** *the passengers* ***hostage*** *until their demands are met.* ➪ **ransom** देखिए।

**hostel** /ˈhɒstl ˈहॉस्ट्ल/ *noun* [C] **1** a place like a cheap hotel where people can stay when they are living away from home घर से बाहर रहने का अपेक्षाकृत सस्ता स्थान; होस्टल, छात्रावास *a youth hostel* ○ *a student hostel* **2** a building where people who have no home can stay for a short time गृह-विहीन लोगों के लिए थोड़े समय रहने का स्थान

**hostess** /ˈhəʊstəs; -es ˈहोस्टस्; -एस्/ *noun* [C] **1** a woman who invites guests to her house, etc. and provides them with food, drink, etc. अतिथियों का सत्कार करने वाली महिला, महिला-मेज़बान ➪ **host** देखिए। **2** a woman who introduces a television or radio show and talks to the guests टेलीविज़न या रेडियो कार्यक्रम को प्रस्तुत करने और अतिथियों से बातचीत करने वाली महिला; होस्टेस **3** = **air hostess**

**hostile** /ˈhɒstaɪl ˈहॉस्टाइल्/ *adj.* **hostile (to/towards sb/sth)** having very strong feelings against sb/sth व्यक्ति या वस्तु के प्रति अत्यंत उग्र भावनाओं वाला; प्रतिकूल भाव *a hostile crowd* ○ *They are very hostile to any change.*

**hostility** /hɒˈstɪləti हॉˈस्टिलटि/ *noun* **1** [U] **hostility (to/towards sth)** very strong feelings against sb/sth व्यक्ति या वस्तु के प्रति अत्यंत उग्र भावनाएँ; शत्रुता *She didn't say anything but I could sense her hostility.* ✪ पर्याय **animosity** **2 hostilities** [*pl.*] fighting in a war युद्ध में लड़ना, युद्ध की स्थिति

**hot**[1] /hɒt हॉट्/ *adj.* (**hotter; hottest**) **1** having a high temperature गरम, उच्च तापमान वाला, उष्ण *It was* ***boiling hot*** *on the beach.* ○ *Don't touch the plates—they're* ***red hot****!*

> **NOTE** तापमान के निर्देश के लिए शब्दावली **freezing (cold), cold, cool, tepid** (पानी के लिए प्रयुक्त) **warm, hot** या **boiling (hot)** हैं। ➪ **cold**[1] पर नोट देखिए।

**2** (used about food) causing a burning feeling in your mouth (भोजन) मुँह में जलन-सी पैदा कर देने वाला, तीखा *hot curry* ✪ पर्याय **spicy** **3** (*informal*) difficult or dangerous to deal with जिससे निपटना कठिन या ख़तरनाक हो *The defenders found the Italian strikers* ***too hot to handle***. **4** (*informal*) exciting and popular रोमांचक या उत्तेजक और लोकप्रिय *This band is* ***hot stuff****!*

**IDM** **in hot pursuit** following sb who is moving fast किसी का तेज़ी से पीछा करते हुए

**hot**[2] /hɒt हॉट्/ *verb* (**hotting; hotted**)

**PHR V** **hot up** (*BrE informal*) to become more exciting अधिक उत्तेजक हो जाना *The election campaign has really hotted up in the past few days.*

**hot-air balloon** = **balloon**[2]

**hot dog** *noun* [C] a hot sausage in a soft bread roll मुलायम/नरम ब्रेड रोल में गरम गुलमा (सॉसेज); हॉट डॉग

**hotel** /həʊˈtel होˈटेल्/ *noun* [C] a place where you pay to stay when you are on holiday or travelling होटल, अवकाश का यात्रा के समय शुल्क देकर ठहरने का स्थान *to stay in/at a hotel* ○ *I've booked a double room at the Grand Hotel.* ○ *a two-star hotel*

> **NOTE** होटल में **double, single** या **twin-bedded** कमरा बुक कर सकते हैं। होटल पहुँचने पर **check in** या **register** किया जाता है और होटल छोड़कर जाते समय **check out** करते हैं।

**hotelier** /həʊˈteliə(r); -lieɪ होˈटेलिअ(र्); -लिए/ *noun* [C] a person who owns or manages a hotel होटल का मालिक या प्रबंधक

**hothouse** /ˈhɒthaʊs ˈहॉट्हाउस्/ *noun* [C] a heated glass building where plants are grown काँच का तपाया घर जिसमें पौधे उगाए जाते हैं, उष्ण कक्ष; हॉट-हाउस ➪ **greenhouse** देखिए।

**hotline** /ˈhɒtlaɪn ˈहॉट्लाइन्/ *noun* [C] a direct telephone line to a business or organization किसी व्यापार केंद्र या संगठन की सीधी टेलीफ़ोन लाइन; हॉटलाइन

**hotly** /ˈhɒtli ˈहॉट्लि/ *adv.* **1** in an angry or excited way क्रोधित या उत्तेजित होकर *They hotly denied the newspaper reports.* **2** closely and with determination एकदम पीछे-पीछे और दृढ़तापूर्वक *The dog ran off, hotly pursued by its owner.*

**hot-water bottle** *noun* [C] a rubber container that is filled with hot water and put in a bed to warm it गरम पानी से भरी रबर की थैली (बिस्तर गरम करने के लिए); हॉट वाटर बॉटल

**hound**[1] /haʊnd हाउन्ड्/ *noun* [C] a type of dog that is used for hunting or racing शिकार या दौड़ में हिस्सा लेने वाला कुत्ता; शिकारी कुत्ता *a foxhound*

**hound**[2] /haʊnd हाउन्ड्/ *verb* [T] to follow and disturb sb किसी का पीछा करना और उसे परेशान करना *Many famous people complain of being hounded by the press.*

**hour** /ˈaʊə(r) ˈआउअ(र्)/ *noun* **1** [C] a period of 60 minutes एक घंटा, साठ मिनट की अवधि *He studies **for three hours** most evenings.* **2** [C] the distance that you can travel in about 60 minutes लगभग साठ मिनट में तय की जा सकने वाली दूरी *Agra is only three hours away from Delhi.* **3 hours** [*pl.*] the period of time when sb is working or a shop, etc. is open किसी दफ़्तर, दुकान आदि के खुले रहने या काम करने की समयावधि *Employees are demanding shorter **working hours**.* **4** [C] a period of about an hour when sth particular happens लगभग एक घंटे की अवधि जिसमें कोई विशेष बात (जैसे लंच) होती है *I'm going shopping in my **lunch hour**.* ○ *The traffic is very bad in **the rush hour**.* **5 the hour** [*sing.*] the time when a new hour starts (= 1 o'clock, 2 o'clock, etc.) नया घंटा शुरू होने का समय (= 1.00 बजे, 2.00 बजे आदि) *Buses are **on the hour** and at twenty past the hour.* **6 hours** [*pl.*] a long time लंबा समय, काफ़ी देर (तक), कई घंटे, घंटों *He went on speaking **for hours** and hours.*

**IDM** **at/till all hours** at/until any time किसी भी समय तक *She stays out till all hours* (= very late).

**the early hours** ➪ **early** देखिए।

**hourly** /ˈaʊəli ˈआउअलि/ *adj., adv.* **1** done, happening, etc. every hour हर घंटे किया जाने या होने वाला, प्रत्येक घंटे में *an hourly news bulletin* ○ *Trains are hourly.* **2** for one hour एक घंटे के लिए या का *What is your hourly rate of pay?*

**house**[1] /haʊs हाउस्/ *noun* [C] (*pl.* **houses** /ˈhaʊzɪz ˈहाउज़िज़्/) **1** a building that is made for people to live in रहने का मकान *Is yours a four-bedroomed or a three-bedroomed house?* ➪ **bungalow, cottage** और **flat** देखिए।

> **NOTE** **Home** (घर) वह स्थान है जहाँ आप रहते हैं (रहने के अहसास का स्थान), भले ही वह पूरा मकान (house) न हो—*Let's go home to my flat.* वह स्थान भी आपका home है जो आपको अपनेपन का अहसास दे। मकान (house) तो इमारत भर है—*We've only just moved into our new house and it doesn't feel like home yet.*
>
> आप घर को **build, do up, redecorate** या **extend** कर सकते हैं। आप किसी से मकान को **rent** पर ले सकते हैं या किसी को **let** कर सकते हैं। यदि (मकान बदलने) **move house** की बात हो तो आप **estate agent** से संपर्क कर सकते हैं।

**2** [*usually sing.*] all the people who live in one house मकान में रहने वाले सभी लोग *Don't shout. You'll wake the whole house up.* **3** a building that is used for a particular purpose विशेष प्रयोजन की इमारत *a warehouse* **4** a large firm involved in a particular kind of business विशेष प्रकार का व्यापार करने वाली बड़ी फ़र्म, व्यापारिक प्रतिष्ठान *a fashion/publishing house* **5** a restaurant, usually that sells one particular type of food रेस्तराँ (जहाँ प्रायः एक विशेष प्रकार के भोज्य पदार्थ मिलते हैं) *a curry/*

*spaghetti house* ○ *house wine* (= the cheapest wine on a restaurant's menu) **6 House** a group of people who meet to make a country's laws एक जगह मिल-बैठकर देश के लिए क़ानून बनाने वालों का समूह, सदन (के सदस्य) *the House of Commons* ○ *the Houses of Parliament* ➪ **Parliament** पर नोट देखिए। **7** [*usually sing.*] the audience at a theatre or cinema, or the area where they sit रंगमंच या सिनेमा का दर्शक वर्ग या उनके बैठने का स्थान *There was a full house for the play this evening.*

**IDM move house** ➪ **move**[1] देखिए।

**on the house** paid for by the pub, restaurant, etc. that you are visiting; free जिसके लिए अपेक्षित शुल्क पब, रेस्तराँ आदि ने पहले से दे दिया है; निःशुल्क *Your first drink is on the house.*

**get on/along like a house on fire** to immediately become good friends with sb किसी के साथ तुरंत गाढ़ी दोस्ती हो जाना

**house**[2] /haʊz हाउज़्/ *verb* [T] **1** to provide sb with a place to live किसी को रहने के लिए स्थान उपलब्ध कराना, ठहराना *The government must house homeless families.* **2** to contain or keep sth किसी का स्थित होना, किसी वस्तु को स्थान देना *Her office is housed in a separate building.*

**house arrest** *noun* [U] the state of being a prisoner in your own house rather than in a prison कारागार के स्थान पर घर पर ही बंदी बन जाने की स्थिति, घर में नज़रबंदी *to be kept/held/placed* ***under house arrest***

**houseboat** /ˈhaʊsbəʊt ˈहाउस्बोट्/ *noun* [C] a boat on a river, etc. where sb lives and which usually stays in one place रहने की सुविधा से युक्त और नदी में प्रायः एक स्थान पर खड़ी नाव; शिकारा, बजरा, हाउसबोट

**housebound** /ˈhaʊsbaʊnd ˈहाउस्बाउन्ड्/ *adj.* unable to leave your house because you are old or ill वृद्ध या रोगी होने के कारण घर से बाहर जाने में असमर्थ, घर में बंद

**household** /ˈhaʊshəʊld ˈहाउस्होल्ड्/ *noun* [C] all the people who live in one house and the work, money, organization, etc. that is needed to look after them एक ही घर के सब सदस्य और उनका काम, पैसा आदि की आवश्यकताएँ *household expenses*

**householder** /ˈhaʊshəʊldə(r) ˈहाउस्होल्ड(र्)/ *noun* [C] a person who rents or owns a house मकान का मालिक या किराएदार व्यक्ति

**housekeeper** /ˈhaʊskiːpə(r) ˈहाउस्कीप(र्)/ *noun* [C] a person who is paid to look after sb else's house and organize the work in it दूसरे के मकान की व्यवस्था के लिए वेतन पर नियुक्त व्यक्ति; गृह-प्रबंधक

**housekeeping** /ˈhaʊskiːpɪŋ ˈहाउस्कीपिङ्/ *noun* [U] **1** the work involved in looking after a house घर की देखरेख का काम **2** the money that you need to manage a house घर की व्यवस्था के लिए अपेक्षित धन

**house-proud** *adj.* paying great attention to the care, cleaning, etc. of your house घर की व्यवस्था के प्रति बहुत सजग

**house-to-house** *adj.* going to each house घर-घर (जाकर) *The police are making house-to-house enquiries.*

**house-warming** *noun* [C] a party that you have when you have just moved into a new home नव गृह-प्रवेश पर आयोजित पार्टी

**housewife** /ˈhaʊswaɪf ˈहाउस्वाइफ़्/ *noun* [C] (*pl.* **housewives**) a woman who does not have a job outside the home and who spends her time cleaning the house, cooking, looking after her family, etc. नौकरी पर न जाकर घर पर रहते हुए घर की व्यवस्था सँभालने वाली पत्नी; गृहिणी, गृहस्वामिनी

**NOTE** उपर्युक्त काम करने वाला पुरुष **house husband** कहलाता है।

**housework** /ˈhaʊswɜːk ˈहाउस्वक्/ *noun* [U] the work that is needed to keep a house clean and tidy घर को साफ़-सुथरा रखने के लिए अपेक्षित काम-काज; गृहकार्य

> **NOTE** ध्यान रहे कि शिक्षक अपने छात्रों को घर पर करने के लिए जो काम देते हैं उसे **homework** कहते हैं।

**housing** /ˈhaʊzɪŋ ˈहाउज़िङ्/ *noun* [U] houses, flats, etc. for people to live in लोगों के रहने के मकान, फ़्लैट आदि

**housing estate** *noun* [C] an area where there are a large number of similar houses that were built at the same time एक ही समय में एक ही स्थान पर बने एक ही प्रकार के अनेक मकान; हाउसिंग एस्टेट

**housing society** *noun* [C] (especially in India) a term used for a **residential** complex usually consisting of several buildings each having a certain number of flats (विशेषतः भारत में) फ़्लैट युक्त भवनों वाले आवासीय स्थान; रिहायशी स्थल

**hovel** /ˈhɒvl ˈहॉव्‌ल्/ *noun* [C] a house or room that is not fit to live in because it is dirty or in very bad condition बहुत गंदा या टूटा-फूटा होने के कारण रहने के अयोग्य मकान या कमरा

**hover** /ˈhɒvə(r) ˈहॉव(र्)/ *verb* [I] **1** (used about a bird, etc.) to stay in the air in one place (पक्षी, विमान आदि का) आकाश में मँडराना **2** (used about a person) to wait near sb/sth (व्यक्ति का) किसी व्यक्ति या वस्तु के निकट प्रतीक्षा करना *He hovered nervously outside the office.*

**hovercraft** /ˈhɒvəkrɑːft ˈहॉव्रक्राफ़्ट्/ *noun* [C] (*pl.* **hovercraft**) a type of boat that moves over land or water on a cushion of air नरम वायु के सहारे भूमि और जल दोनों पर चलने वाली एक प्रकार की नाव

**how** /haʊ हाउ/ *adv., conj.* **1** (*often used in questions*) in what way किस प्रकार, कैसे *How do you spell your name?* ○ *Can you show me how to use this machine?* **2** used when you are asking about sb's health or feelings किसी व्यक्ति का कुशल-क्षेम पूछने के लिए प्रयुक्त, कैसा/कैसी/कैसे *'How is your mother?' 'She's much better, thank you.'* ○ *How are you feeling today?* ○ *How do you feel about your son joining the army?*

> NOTE **'How'** का प्रयोग केवल स्वास्थ्य की दशा पूछने के लिए होता है, व्यक्ति के चरित्र या चेहरे-मोहरे आदि के विषय में पूछना हो तो **what ... like?** का प्रयोग किया जाता है—*'What is your mother like?' 'Well, she's much taller than me and she's got dark hair.'*

**3** used when you are asking about sb's opinion of a thing or a situation किसी वस्तु या स्थिति के विषय में किसी की राय के लिए प्रयुक्त *How was the weather?* ○ ***How** did the interview **go**?* **4** used in questions when you are asking about the degree, amount, age, etc. of sb/sth प्रश्नवाचक वाक्यों में किसी व्यक्ति या वस्तु की डिग्री, मात्रा, आयु आदि के विषय में पूछने के लिए प्रयुक्त *How old are you?* ○ *How much is that?* **5** used for expressing surprise, pleasure, etc. आश्चर्य, प्रसन्नता आदि व्यक्त करने के लिए प्रयुक्त *She's gone. How strange!* ○ *I can't believe how expensive it is!*

IDM **how/what about...?** ⇨ **about**[2] देखिए।

**how come?** ⇨ **come** देखिए।

**how do you do?** (*formal*) used when meeting sb for the first time पहली बार भेंट होने पर प्रयुक्त

**however** /haʊˈevə(r) हाउˈएव्र(र्)/ *adv., conj.* **1** (*formal*) (used for adding a comment to what you have just said) although sth is true (अभी कही बात के साथ कुछ और कहने के लिए प्रयुक्त) तथापि, तो भी *Sales are poor this month. There may, however, be an increase before Diwali.* **2** (used in questions for expressing surprise) in what way; how (आश्चर्य व्यक्त करने के लिए प्रश्नवाचक वाक्यों में प्रयुक्त) किस तरह; कैसे *However did you manage to find me here?* NOTE इस प्रकार के प्रश्नवाचक वाक्यों में जब आप केवल **how** का प्रयोग करते हैं तो कुछ ख़ास आश्चर्य भाव व्यक्त नहीं होता। **3** in whatever way किसी भी तरह, चाहे जैसे भी *However I sat I couldn't get comfortable.* ○ *You can dress however you like.* **4** (*before an adjective or adverb*) to whatever degree किसी भी तुलनात्मक मात्रा तक *He won't wear a hat however cold it is.* ○ *You can't catch her however fast you run.*

**howl** /haʊl हाउल्/ *verb* [I] to make a long loud sound लंबी ऊँची आवाज़ करना; हूकना *I couldn't sleep because there was a dog howling all night.* ○ *The wind howled around the house.* ▶ **howl** *noun* [C] ऊँची आवाज़

**h.p.** /ˌeɪtʃˈpiː ˌएच ˈपी/ *abbr.* **1** (used about an engine) horsepower हार्सपावर (इंजन के लिए प्रयुक्त) अश्वशक्ति

**HQ** /ˌeɪtʃˈkjuː ˌएच् ˈक्यू/ *abbr.* headquarters मुख्यालय

**hr** (*pl.* **hrs**) *abbr.* hour घंटा *3 hrs 15 min*

**HTML** /ˌeɪtʃ tiː em ˈel ˌएच् टी एम् ˈएल्/ *abbr.* (*computing*) Hypertext Mark-up Language (a system used to mark text for **World Wide Web** pages in order to obtain colours, style, pictures, etc.) हाइपर टेक्स्ट मार्क-अप लैंग्वेज का संक्षिप्त रूप (वर्ल्ड वाइड वेब के पृष्ठों को चिह्नित करने की प्रणाली ताकि अपेक्षित रंग, चित्र आदि प्राप्त किए जा सकें)

**hub** /hʌb हब्/ *noun* [*usually sing.*] **1 the hub (of sth)** the central and most important part of a place or an activity किसी स्थान या गतिविधि का केंद्रीय और सर्वाधिक महत्त्वपूर्ण अंश; केंद्रस्थल, हब *the commercial hub of the city* **2** the central part of a wheel पहिए का केंद्रीय स्थल; चक्रनाभि

**hubbub** /ˈhʌbʌb ˈहबब्/ *noun* [*sing.*, U] **1** the noise made by a lot of people talking at the same time लोगों का शोरगुल **2** a situation in which there is a lot of noise, excitement and activity शोर-शराबा और हलचल; कोलाहल

**hubcap** /ˈhʌbkæp ˈहब्कैप्/ *noun* [C] a round metal cover that fits over the **hub** of a vehicle's wheel वाहन के पहिए पर फ़िट होने वाला गोल धातु-निर्मित ढक्कन

**hubris** /ˈhjuːbrɪs ˈह्यूब्रिस्/ *noun* [U] (in literature) the fact of sb being too proud. A character with this pride usually dies because he/she ignores warnings (साहित्य में) पात्र की हेकड़ी, अक्खड़पन, हेकड़ीबाज़ या अक्खड़ पात्र जो चेतावनियों की उपेक्षा करने के कारण प्रायः मारा जाता है

**huddle**[1] /ˈhʌdl ˈहड्ल्/ *verb* [I] **huddle (up) (together)** **1** to get close to other people because you are cold or frightened ठंड या डर के मारे लोगों का सट-सटकर बैठना *The campers huddled together around the fire.* **2** to make your body as small as possible because you are cold or frightened ठंड या डर के मारे गठरी बन जाना या सिमट जाना *She huddled up in her sleeping bag and* *tried to get some sleep.* ▶ **huddled** *adj.* गठरी बना हुआ, सिमटा हुआ, सटकर बैठा हुआ *We found the children lying huddled together on the ground.*

**huddle²** /ˈhʌdl ˈहड्ल् / *noun* [C] a small group of people or things that are close together थोड़े से व्यक्तियों या वस्तुओं का जमघट; जमावड़ा *They all stood* ***in a huddle****, laughing and chatting.*

**hue** /hju: ह्यू / *noun* [C] **1** (*written*) or (*technical*) a colour; a particular shade of a colour कोई रंग; किसी रंग का विशेष आभा भेद; वर्णिमा, छटा **2** (*formal*) a type of belief or opinion एक प्रकार का विश्वास या राय

IDM **hue and cry** strong public protest about sth किसी मुद्दे का प्रबल सार्वजनिक विरोध

**huff** /hʌf हफ़् / *noun* [C]

IDM **in a huff** (*informal*) in a bad mood because sb has annoyed or upset you नाराज़गी या परेशानी के कारण क्रोधित; क्रोधावेश *Did you see Sagar* ***go off in a huff*** *when he wasn't chosen for the team?*

**hug** /hʌg हग् / *verb* [T] (**hugging; hugged**) **1** to put your arms around sb, especially to show that you love him/her किसी को गले लगाना (विशेषत: उसके प्रति प्रेम व्यक्त करने के लिए) आलिंगन करना **2** to hold sth close to your body किसी वस्तु को शरीर से चिपटा लेना *She hugged the parcel to her chest as she ran.* **3** (used about a ship, car, road, etc.) to stay close to sth (जहाज़, कार आदि का) किसी वस्तु के निकट पहुँचना *to hug the coast* ▶ **hug** *noun* [C] *Niraj's crying—I'll go and give him* ***a hug****.*

**huge** /hju:dʒ ह्यूज् / *adj.* very big बहुत बड़ा, विशाल *a huge amount/quantity/sum/number* ○ *a huge building* ○ *The film was a huge success.* ▶ **hugely** *adv.* अत्यधिक *hugely successful/popular/expensive*

**huh** /hʌ ह / *exclamation* (*informal*) used for expressing anger, surprise, etc. or for asking a question क्रोध, आश्चर्य आदि व्यक्त करने या प्रश्न पूछने के लिए प्रयुक्त *They've gone away, huh? They didn't tell me.*

**hull** /hʌl हल् / *noun* [C] the body of a ship जहाज़ का ढाँचा ➪ **boat** पर चित्र देखिए। **2** the outer covering of some fruits and seeds छिलका (कुछ फलों या बीज़ों का) *The hull of peas were thrown away.*

**hullabaloo** /ˌhʌləbəˈlu: ˌहलबˈलू / *noun* [*sing.*] a lot of loud noise, for example made by people shouting शोरगुल, कोलाहल (लोगों के चीख़ने-चिल्लाने से उत्पन्न)

**hum** /hʌm हम् / *verb* (**humming; hummed**) **1** [I] to make a continuous low noise निरंतर नीची, हलकी आवाज़ करना, भनभन करना *The machine began to hum as I switched it on.* **2** [I, T] to sing with your lips closed गुनगुनाना *You can hum the tune if you don't know the words.* ▶ **hum** *noun* [*sing.*] भनभनाहट, गुनगुनाहट *the hum of machinery/distant traffic*

**human¹** /ˈhju:mən ˈह्यूमन् / *adj.* connected with people, not with animals, machines or gods; typical of people मानव या मनुष्य से संबंधित (पशुओं, मशीनों या देवताओं से नहीं), मानवीय; मानव जाति का प्रतिनिधिक *the human body* ○ *The disaster was caused by* ***human error.*** ▶ **humanly** *adv.* मानवीय रूप से *They did all that was humanly possible to rescue him* (= everything that a human being could possibly do).

**human²** /ˈhju:mən ˈह्यूमन् / (*also* **human being**) *noun* [C] a person एक व्यक्ति, मनुष्य

**humane** /hju:ˈmeɪn ह्यूˈमेन् / *adj.* having or showing kindness or understanding, especially to a person or animal that is suffering सदय या सहानुभूतिपूर्ण (विशेषतः कष्ट पाते व्यक्ति या पशु के प्रति), मानवीय, मानवोचित *Zoo animals must be kept in humane conditions.* ✪ विलोम **inhumane** ▶ **humanely** *adv.* मानवोचित रीति से

**humanitarian** /hju:ˌmænɪˈteəriən ह्यूˌमैनिˈटेअरिअन् / *adj.* concerned with trying to make people's lives better and reduce suffering मनुष्यों के जीवन में सुधार लाने और उनके कष्ट के प्रयत्न से संबंधित; मानवतावादी, लोकोपकारी *Many countries have sent humanitarian aid to the earthquake victims.*

**humanity** /hju:ˈmænəti ह्यूˈमैनटि / *noun* **1** [U] all the people in the world, thought of as a group विश्व के समस्त मानव, मानव जाति, मानवता *crimes against humanity* ✪ पर्याय **the human race** **2** [U] the quality of being kind and understanding दया और सहानुभूति, मानवता *The prisoners were treated with humanity.* ✪ विलोम **inhumanity** **3 (the) humanities** [*pl.*] the subjects of study that are connected with the way people think and behave, for example literature, language, history and **philosophy** मानव-व्यवहार से संबंधित अध्ययन-विषय (साहित्य, भाषा, इतिहास, दर्शन), मानविकी

**human nature** *noun* [U] feelings, behaviour, etc. that all people have in common सब मनुष्यों में समान भावनाएँ, व्यवहार आदि; मानव प्रकृति

**the human race** *noun* [*sing.*] all the people in the world, thought of as a group विश्व के समस्त मानव, मानव जाति, मानवता ✪ पर्याय **humanity**

**human rights** *noun* [*pl.*] the basic freedoms that all people should have, for example the right to say what you think, to travel freely, etc. मूलभूत अधिकार जो सब मनुष्यों को मिलने चाहिए (जैसे अपने विचारों की अभिव्यक्ति, कहीं पर भी जाने की आज़ादी आदि); मानवाधिकार

**humble[1]** /ˈhʌmbl ˈहम्बल्/ *adj.* **1** not thinking that you are better or more important than other people; not proud विनम्र, विनीत; घमंडी नहीं *He became very rich and famous but he always remained a very humble man.* ➪ **humility** noun देखिए। ➪ **modest** देखिए। **2** not special or important विशिष्ट या महत्त्वपूर्ण नहीं, साधारण *She comes from a humble background.* ▶ **humbly** /ˈhʌmbli ˈहम्बलि/ *adv.* विनम्रता से *He apologized very humbly for his behaviour.*

**humble[2]** /ˈhʌmbl ˈहम्बल्/ *verb* [T] to make sb feel that he/she is not as good or important as he/she thought किसी को यह अनुभव कराना कि वह इतना बड़ा नहीं जैसा कि वह सोचता है, विनम्र बनाना, प्रतिष्ठा घटाना, हेकड़ी भुलाना

**humerus** /ˈhjuːmərəs ˈह्यूमरस्/ *noun* [C] the large bone in the top part of the arm between your shoulder and your elbow कंधे और कोहनी के बीच में बाँह के ऊपर की बड़ी हड्डी; प्रगंडिका ➪ **body** पर चित्र देखिए।

**humid** /ˈhjuːmɪd ˈह्यूमिड्/ *adj.* (used about the air or climate) containing a lot of water; damp (वायु या मौसम) सीलनभरा, आर्द्र; नम *Mumbai is hot and humid in summer.* ▶ **humidity** /hjuːˈmɪdəti ह्यूˈमिडटि/ *noun* [U] आर्द्रता, नमी, सीलन

**humiliate** /hjuːˈmɪlieɪt ह्यूˈमिलिएट्/ *verb* [T] to make sb feel very embarrassed किसी को नीचा दिखाना, अवमानित करना *I felt humiliated when the teacher laughed at my work.* ▶ **humiliating** *adj.* अपमानपूर्ण *a humiliating defeat* ▶ **humiliation** /hjuːˌmɪliˈeɪʃn ह्यूˌमिलिˈएशन्/ *noun* [C, U] अपमान, अवमानना

**humility** /hjuːˈmɪləti ह्यूˈमिलिटि/ *noun* [U] the quality of not thinking that you are better than other people विनम्रता, विनयशीलता ➪ **humble** adjective देखिए।

**humorous** /ˈhjuːmərəs ˈह्यूमरस्/ *adj.* amusing or funny विनोदी या हास्यपूर्ण ▶ **humorously** *adv.* विनोदपूर्वक

**humour[1]** (*AmE* **humor**) /ˈhjuːmə(r) ˈह्यूम(र्)/ *noun* [U] **1** the funny or amusing qualities of sb/sth व्यक्ति या वस्तु के विचित्र या हास्यजनक गुण *It is sometimes hard to understand the humour* (= the jokes) *of another country.* **2** being able to see when sth is funny and to laugh at things यह परखने की क्षमता कि कब कौन-सी वस्तु विनोद या हँसी का पात्र होती है *Rani has a good* ***sense of humour****.* **3 -humoured** (*AmE* **-humored**) (*used to form compound adjectives*) having or showing a particular mood विशेष प्रकार के स्वभाव वाला *good-humoured*

**humour[2]** (*AmE* humor) /ˈhjuːmə(r) ˈह्यूम(र्)/ *verb* [T] to keep sb happy by doing what he/she wants किसी की मनचाही बात को मानकर उसे ख़ुश रखना, किसी का मन रखना

**humourless** /ˈhjuːmələs ˈह्यूमलस्/ (*AmE* **humorless**) *adj.* having no sense of fun; serious हँसी-मज़ाक पसंद न करने वाला; गंभीर

**hump** /hʌmp हम्प्/ *noun* [C] a large round lump, for example on the back of an animal who lives in the desert (**camel**) (ऊँट आदि का) कूबड़

**humus** /ˈhjuːməs ˈह्यूमस्/ *noun* [U] a substance made from dead leaves and plants, that you put into the ground to help plants grow सड़े पत्तों और पौधों की खाद; खाद मिट्टी

**hunch[1]** /hʌntʃ हन्च्/ *noun* [C] (*informal*) a thought or an idea that is based on a feeling rather than on facts or information तथ्य या ज्ञान के स्थान पर भावनाओं पर आधारित सोच; अटकल, काल्पनिक अनुमान *I'm not sure, but I've got a hunch that she's got a new job.*

**hunch[2]** /hʌntʃ हन्च्/ *verb* [I, T] to bend your back and shoulders forward into a round shape पीठ और कंधों को गोलाकार आगे की ओर झुकाना, कूबड़ निकालकर चलना या बैठना

**hunchback** /ˈhʌntʃbæk ˈहन्चबैक्/ *noun* [C] a person with a back that has a round lump on it कुबड़ा (व्यक्ति)

**hundred** /ˈhʌndrəd ˈहन्ड्रड्/ *number* **1** (*pl.* **hundred**) 100 सौ (की संख्या) *two hundred* ○ *There were alone hundred people in the room.* ○ *She's a hundred today.*

> **NOTE** किसी संख्या (जैसे 1430) लिखते या बोलते समय **hundred** शब्द के बाद 'and' लगाते हैं—*one thousand four hundred and thirty.*

**2 hundreds** (*informal*) a lot; a large amount ढेर सारा; बड़ी मात्रा या राशि, सैकड़ों *I've got hundreds of things to do today.*

> **NOTE** संख्याओं के विषय में अधिक जानकारी के लिए इस कोश के अंत में Numbers पर special section देखिए।

**hundredth**[1] /ˈhʌndrədθ ˈहन्ड्रड्थ् / *noun* [C] the fraction $\frac{1}{100}$ ; one of a hundred equal parts of sth भिन्न $\frac{1}{100}$ ; किसी वस्तु के सौ समान अंशों में एक अंश, शतांश

**hundredth**[2] /ˈhʌndrədθ ˈहन्ड्रड्थ् / *pronoun, det., adv.* 100th सौवाँ NOTE उदाहरणों के लिए **sixth** की प्रविष्टि देखिए।

**hundredweight** /ˈhʌndrədweɪt ˈहन्ड्रड्वेट् / *noun* [C] (*abbr.* **cwt** ) a measurement of weight तौल या भार का एक माप, टन का बीसवाँ भाग

NOTE तौलवाची शब्दों (weights) के विषय में अधिक जानकारी के विषय में इस कोश के अंत में Numbers पर special section देखिए।

**hung** ➪ **hang** का past tense और past participle रूप

**hunger**[1] /ˈhʌŋgə(r) ˈहङ्ग(र्) / *noun* **1** [U] the state of not having enough food to eat, especially when this causes illness or death भोजन की कमी (विशेषतः जब इससे रोग या मृत्यु हो जाए) *In some parts of the world many people die of hunger each year.* ➪ **thirst** देखिए। **2** [U] the feeling caused by a need to eat खाने की आवश्यकता से उत्पन्न संवेदना या अनुभूति; भूख, क्षुधा *Hunger is one reason why babies cry.*

NOTE ध्यान रहे कि अंग्रेज़ी में *I have hunger* प्रयोग अमान्य है। एकमात्र शुद्ध प्रयोग है—*I am hungry.*

**3** [*sing.*] **a hunger (for sth)** a strong desire for sth किसी वस्तु की प्रबल इच्छा, भूख *a hunger for knowledge/fame/success*

**hunger**[2] /ˈhʌŋgə(r) ˈहङ्ग(र्) / *verb* (*formal*)
PHR V **hunger for/after sth** to have a strong desire for sth किसी वस्तु के लिए अत्यंत इच्छुक होना

**hunger strike** *noun* [C, U] a time when sb (especially a prisoner) refuses to eat because he/she is protesting about sth विरोध स्वरूप भोजन खाने से इनकार करने की क्रिया, भूख-हड़ताल; अनशन *to be/go **on hunger strike***

**hungry** /ˈhʌŋgri ˈहङ्ग्रि / *adj.* (**hungrier; hungriest**) **1** wanting to eat भोजन करने का इच्छुक; भूखा *I'm hungry. Let's eat soon.* ○ *There were hungry children begging for food in the streets.* ➪ **thirsty** देखिए। **2 hungry for sth** wanting sth very much किसी वस्तु के लिए अति-उत्सुक या इच्छुक *I'm hungry for some excitement tonight.*
▶ **hungrily** *adv.* भूख से पीड़ित होकर, उत्सुकता से
IDM **go hungry** to not have any food भूखा रहना

**hunk** /hʌŋk हङ्क् / *noun* [C] **1** a large piece of sth किसी वस्तु का बड़ा टुकड़ा *a hunk of bread/cheese/meat* **2** (*informal*) a man who is big, strong and attractive कद्दावर, मज़बूत और आकर्षक आदमी

**hunt**[1] /hʌnt हन्ट् / *verb* [I, T] **1** to run after wild animals, etc. in order to catch or kill them either for sport or for food शिकार खेलना, शिकार करना *Owls hunt at night.* ○ *Are tigers still hunted in India?*
**2 hunt (for) (sb/sth)** to try to find sb/sth व्यक्ति या वस्तु का पता लगाने की कोशिश करना *The police are still hunting for the murderer.*

**hunt**[2] /hʌnt हन्ट् / *noun* [C] **1** the act of hunting wild animals, etc. वन्य पशुओं का शिकार *a fox-hunt* **2** [*usually sing.*] **a hunt (for sb/sth)** the act of looking for sb/sth that is difficult to find व्यक्ति या वस्तु की ज़ोरदार तलाश *The police have launched a hunt for the missing child.*

**hunter** /ˈhʌntə(r) ˈहन्ट(र्) / *noun* [C] a person that hunts wild animals for food or sport; an animal that hunts its food शिकारी (व्यक्ति जो खेल में या खाने के लिए शिकार करता है); शिकारी (पशु, जो खाने के लिए शिकार करता है)

**hunter-gatherer** /ˌhʌntəˈgæðərə(r) ˌहन्टˈगैद्रर(र्) / *noun* [C] a member of a group of people who do not live in one place but move around and live by hunting and fishing घुमंतू और आखेटजीवी समुदाय का सदस्य

**hunting** /ˈhʌntɪŋ ˈहन्टिङ् / *noun* [U] the act of following and killing wild animals or birds as a sport or for food खेल के रूप में खाने के लिए पशु-पक्षियों का शिकार करने की क्रिया; आखेट-कर्म ➪ **shoot** देखिए।

**hurdle**[1] /ˈhɜːdl ˈहड्ल् / *noun* **1** [C] a type of light fence that a person or a horse jumps over in a race एक प्रकार की हलकी बाड़ जिसे व्यक्ति या घोड़े को दौड़-स्पर्धा में फाँदना होता है; फाँद, बाधा *to clear a hurdle* (= to jump over it successfully) **2 hurdles** [*pl.*] a race in which runners or horses have to jump over hurdles बाधा दौड़ या घुड़दौड़ *the 200-metres hurdles* **3** [C] a problem or difficulty that you must solve or deal with before you can achieve sth समस्या या कठिनाई (जिसका समाधान अपेक्षित है)

**hurdle**[2] /ˈhɜːdl ˈहड्ल् / *verb* [I, T] **hurdle (over sth)** to jump over sth while you are running दौड़ते समय किसी वस्तु को फाँदना

**hurl** /hɜːl हल् / *verb* [T] to throw sth with great force किसी वस्तु को ज़ोर लगाकर फेंकना

**hurray** /həˈreɪ हˈरे / (**hooray** /huˈreɪ हुˈरे /; **hurrah** /həˈrɑː हˈरा /) *exclamation* used for expressing great pleasure, approval, etc. बहुत ख़ुशी, पसंद आदि व्यक्त करने के लिए प्रयुक्त *Hurray! We've won!*
IDM **hip, hip, hurray/hurrah** ➪ **hip**[2] देखिए।

**hurricane** /ˈhʌrɪken ˈहरिकेन्/ *noun* [C] a violent storm with very strong winds बहुत तेज़ हवाओं वाली उग्र आँधी, आँधी-तूफ़ान ➪ **storm** पर नोट देखिए।

**hurried** /ˈhʌrid ˈहरिड्/ *adj.* done (too) quickly शीघ्रता में किया गया, जल्दबाज़ी-भरा *a hurried meal* ▶ **hurriedly** *adv.* जल्दबाज़ी में

**hurry**[1] /ˈhʌri ˈहरि/ *noun* [U] the need or wish to do sth quickly किसी काम को जल्दी करने की आवश्यकता या इच्छा; जल्दबाज़ी, उतावली, हड़बड़ी *Take your time. There's **no hurry**.*

IDM **in a hurry** quickly जल्दी में, हड़बड़ी में, जल्दी-जल्दी में, अधीर, उतावला *She got up late and left in a hurry.*

**in a hurry (to do sth)** wanting to do sth soon; impatient शीघ्र कुछ करने का इच्छुक; अधीर, उतावला *They are in a hurry to get the job done before the winter.*

**in no hurry (to do sth); not in any hurry (to do sth)** **1** not needing or wishing to do sth quickly जिसे जल्दबाज़ी में कुछ करने की न तो विवशता है न इच्छा, जल्दबाज़ी में कुछ करने का अनिच्छुक या ग़ैर-ज़रूरतमंद *We weren't in any hurry so we stopped to admire the view.* **2** not wanting to do sth अनिच्छुक, जल्दी में नहीं *I am in no hurry to repeat that experience.*

**hurry**[2] /ˈhʌri ˈहरि/ *verb* (*pres. part.* **hurrying;** *3rd person sing. pres.* **hurries;** *pt, pp* **hurried**) **1** [I] to move or do sth quickly because there is not much time (समय कम होने के कारण) जल्दी चलना या करना *Don't hurry. There's plenty of time.* ○ *Several people hurried to help.* **2 hurry sb (into sth/doing sth)** [T] to cause sb/sth to do sth, or sth to happen more quickly किसी से अधिक जल्दी में कोई काम करवाना या ऐसा करना कि कोई कार्य जल्दी हो जाए *Don't hurry me. I'm going as fast as I can.* ○ *He was hurried into a decision.* **3** [T] (*usually passive*) to do sth too quickly कोई काम बहुत जल्दी कर देना या किसी काम में बहुत जल्दबाज़ी करना

IDM **hurry up (with sth)** to move or do sth more quickly चलने में या काम करने में जल्दी करना *Hurry up or we'll miss the train.*

**hurt**[1] /hɜːt हट्/ *verb* (*pt, pp* **hurt**) **1** [I, T] to cause sb/yourself physical pain or injury अपने या किसी को तकलीफ़ देना या चोट पहुँचाना *I fell and hurt my arm.* ○ *These shoes hurt; they're too tight.*

> NOTE **Hurt, injure** और **wound** देखिए। सामान्यतः लड़ाई-झगड़े के कारण कोई व्यक्ति चाकू, तलवार, बंदूक़ आदि से **wounded** (ज़ख़्मी) हो सकता है—*a wounded soldier.* लोग दुर्घटना में प्रायः **injured** (चोटग्रस्त) हो जाते हैं—*Five people were killed in the crash and twelve others were injured.* **Hurt** और **injured** का अर्थ समान है परंतु चोट बहुत अधिक न हो तो **hurt** का प्रयोग अधिक प्रचलित है—*I hurt my leg when I fell off my bike.*

**2** [I] to feel painful दर्द महसूस करना *My leg hurts.* ○ ***It hurts** when I lift my leg.* ○ *Where exactly does it hurt?* **3** [T] to make sb unhappy; to upset sb किसी को नाराज़ करना; परेशान करना *His unkind remarks hurt her deeply.* ○ *I didn't want to **hurt** his **feelings**.*

IDM **it won't/wouldn't hurt (sb/sth) (to do sth)** (*informal*) used to say that sb should do sth किसी को कुछ करने के लिए प्रेरित करने हेतु प्रयुक्त *It wouldn't hurt you to help with the housework occasionally.*

**hurt**[2] /hɜːt हट्/ *adj.* **1** injured physically शरीर से चोटग्रस्त, घायल *None of the passengers were **badly/seriously hurt**.* **2** upset and offended by sth that sb has said or done किसी की बात या काम से परेशान और अपमानित *She was **deeply hurt** that she had not been invited to the party.*

**hurt**[3] /hɜːt हट्/ *noun* [U] a feeling of unhappiness because sb has been unkind or unfair to you (किसी की कठोरता या अनुचित व्यवहार से उत्पन्न) पीड़ा, व्यथा

**hurtful** /ˈhɜːtfl ˈहट्फ़्ल्/ *adj.* **hurtful (to sb)** unkind; making sb feel upset and offended निष्ठुर, किसी को परेशान या अपमानित करने वाला

**hurtle** /ˈhɜːtl ˈहट्ल्/ *verb* [I] to move with great speed, perhaps causing danger तेज़ गति से आगे बढ़ना (संभवतः ख़तरा पैदा करते हुए) *The lorry **came hurtling** towards us.*

**husband** /ˈhʌzbənd ˈहज़्बन्ड्/ *noun* [C] a man that a woman is married to पति *Her husband is a doctor.*

**husbandry** /ˈhʌzbəndri ˈहज़्बन्ड्रि/ *noun* [U] farming; looking after animals and food crops कृषि खेती; पशुओं और फ़सलों की देखभाल

**hush**[1] /hʌʃ हश्/ *verb* [I] (*spoken*) used to tell sb to be quiet, to stop talking or crying किसी से रोना या बात कराना बंद करने के लिए कहना, किसी को चुप कराना *Hush now and try to sleep.*

IDM **hush sth up** to hide information to stop people knowing about sth; to keep sth secret लोगों से जानकारी छिपाना; मामले को दबा देना

**hush**[2] /hʌʃ हश्/ *noun* [*sing.*] silence चुप्पी, सन्नाटा

**hush-hush** *adj.* (*informal*) very secret बहुत गोपनीय

**husk** /hʌsk हस्क्/ *noun* [C] the dry outside layer of nuts, fruits and seeds, especially of grain (फलों का) छिलका और (अनाज का) भूसा

**husky**[1] /ˈhʌski ˈहस्कि/ *adj.* (used about a person's voice) sounding rough and quiet as if your throat were dry (व्यक्ति की आवाज़) फटी-फटी और बैठी हुई (मानो गला ख़ुश्क हो)

**husky**[2] /ˈhʌski ˈहस्कि/ *noun* [C] (*pl.* **huskies**) a strong dog with thick fur that is used in teams for pulling heavy loads over snow घने बालों वाला ताक़तवर कुत्ता जो और कुत्तों के साथ मिलकर बर्फ़ पर भारी वज़न वाली गाड़ी खींचता है

**hustle** /ˈhʌsl ˈहस्ल्/ *verb* [T] to push or move sb in a way that is not gentle रूखेपन से किसी को धक्का देना या रास्ते से हटा देना; धकेलना, धकियाना

**hut** /hʌt हट्/ *noun* [C] a small building with one room, usually made of wood or metal झोपड़ी, कुटिया (प्रायः लकड़ी या धातु की बनी, एक कमरे वाली) *a wooden/mud hut*

**hutch** /hʌtʃ हच्/ *noun* [C] a wooden box with a front made of wire, that is used for keeping rabbits or other small animals ख़रगोश आदि छोटे जानवरों को पालने का बक्सा (लकड़ी का बना हुआ और आगे तारों की जाली); दड़बा

**hybrid** /ˈhaɪbrɪd ˈहाइब्रिड्/ *noun* [C] an animal or a plant that has parents of two different types (**species**) दो विभिन्न प्रजातियों के जनकों से उत्पन्न पशु या पौधा, संकर पशु या पौधा; वर्ण संकर *A mule is a hybrid of a male donkey and a female horse.*
▶ **hybrid** *adj.* संकर, मिश्र *a hybrid flower*

**hydrant** /ˈhaɪdrənt ˈहाइड्रन्ट्/ *noun* [C] a pipe in a street from which water can be taken for stopping fires, cleaning the streets, etc. सड़क पर लगा नल जिससे पानी लेकर आग बुझाने, सड़क साफ़ करने आदि का कार्य किया जाता है; बंबा

**hydrate** /ˈhaɪdreɪt; haɪˈdreɪt ˈहाइड्रेट्; हाइˈड्रेट्/ *verb* [T] (*technical*) to make sth take in water किसी को जलयुक्त करना, अंदर पानी जाए ऐसी युक्ति करना
▶ **hydration** /haɪˈdreɪʃn हाइˈड्रेश्न्/ *noun* [U] जलयोजन ➪ **dehydrate** देखिए।

**hydraulic** /haɪˈdrɔːlɪk हाइˈड्रॉलिक्/ *adj.* operated by water or another liquid moving through pipes, etc. under pressure दाब की स्थिति में पाइप आदि में से बहते पानी या अन्य द्रव से चालित; द्रवचालित *hydraulic brakes*

**hydraulics** /haɪˈdrɔːlɪks; -ˈdrɒl- हाइˈड्रॉलिक्स्; -ˈड्रॉल्-/ *noun* **1** [*pl.*] machinery that works by the use of liquid moving under pressure दाब की स्थिति में बदलते द्रव के प्रयोग से काम करने वाली मशीन; द्रवचालित मशीन **2** [U] the science of the use of liquids moving under pressure दाब की स्थिति में गतिशील द्रव के प्रयोग का अध्ययन करने वाला शास्त्र; द्रवचालन विज्ञान

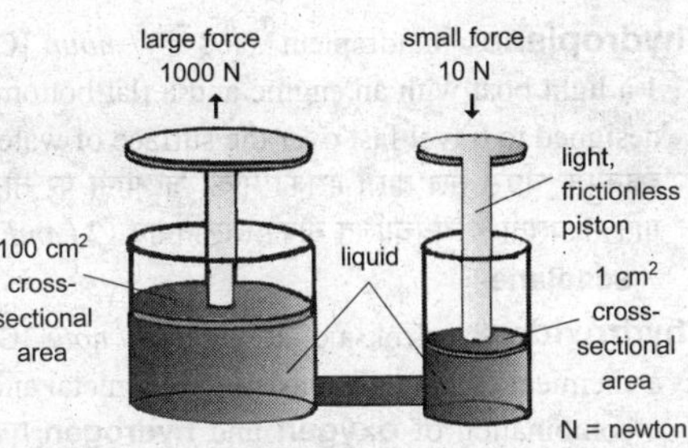

**hydraulic jack**

**hydr(o)-** /ˈhaɪdr(əʊ) ˈहाइड्रो/ *prefix* (*in nouns, adjectives and adverbs*) **1** connected with water जल-संबंधित, जल *hydroelectricity* **2** (*technical*) connected with or mixed with **hydrogen** हाइड्रोजन से संबंधित या मिश्रित या प्रयुक्त

**hydrocarbon** /ˌhaɪdrəˈkɑːbən ˌहाइड्रˈकाबन्/ *noun* [C] (in chemistry) a combination of a very light gas (**hydrogen**) and a substance that is found in all living things (**carbon**). Hydrocarbons are found in petrol, coal and natural gas (रसायनशास्त्र में) हाइड्रोजन और कार्बन का मिश्रण (हाइड्रोकार्बन पेट्रोल, कोयला और प्राकृतिक गैस में पाए जाते हैं)

**hydrochloric acid** /ˌhaɪdrəˌklɒrɪk ˈæsɪd ˌहाइड्रˌक्लॉरिक् ˈऐसिड्/ *noun* [U] (*symbol* **HCl**) (in chemistry) a type of acid containing a very light gas (**hydrogen**) and a greenish-yellow gas with a strong smell (**chlorine**) (रसायन में) हाइड्रोजन और क्लोरीन युक्त एसिड

**hydroelectric** /ˌhaɪdrəʊɪˈlektrɪk ˌहाइड्रोइˈलेक्ट्रिक्/ *adj.* using the power of water to produce electricity; produced by the power of water विद्युत उत्पादन में जल की शक्ति का प्रयोग करने वाला; जल की शक्ति से उत्पन्न किया हुआ *a hydroelectric dam* ○ *hydroelectric power*

**hydrogen** /ˈhaɪdrədʒən ˈहाइड्रजन्/ *noun* [U] (*symbol* **H**) a light colourless gas. Hydrogen and another gas (**oxygen**) form water एक हलकी रंगहीन गैस (हाइड्रोजन और ऑक्सीजन से मिलकर पानी बनता है)

**hydrogen bomb** (*also* **H-bomb**) *noun* [C] a very powerful nuclear bomb बहुत शक्तिशाली नाभकीय बम, हाइड्रोजन बम

**hydrogen peroxide** = **peroxide**

**hydrology** /haɪˈdrɒlədʒi हाइˈड्रॉलजि/ *noun* [U] the scientific study of the earth's water, especially its movement in relation to land भूजल का वैज्ञानिक अध्ययन (विशेषतः जल की भूमि-संबंधित क्रियाशीलता का अध्ययन); भूजलविज्ञान

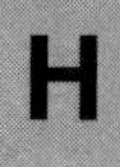


**hydroplane** /ˈhaɪdrəpleɪn ˈहाइड्रप्लेन्/ *noun* [C] **1** a light boat with an engine and a flat bottom, designed to travel fast over the surface of water इंजनयुक्त चौरस तल वाली हलकी नौका जो पानी पर तीव्र गति से चलती है; यंत्रचालित नौका, जलविमान **2** (*AmE*) = **seaplane**

**hydroxide** /haɪˈdrɒksaɪd हाइˈड्रॉक्साइड्/ *noun* [C] a chemical compound consisting of a metal and a combination of **oxygen** and **hydrogen** एक यौगिक रसायन जिसमें किसी धातु और ऑक्सीजन एवं हाइड्रोजन का मिश्रण होता है; हाइड्रो-ऑक्साइड

**hyena** (*also* **hyaena**) /haɪˈiːnə हाइˈईना/ *noun* [C] a wild animal like a dog that lives in Africa and Asia. Hyenas eat the meat of animals that are already dead and can make a sound like a human laugh लकड़बग्घा; अफ़्रीक़ा और एशिया में पाया जाने वाला कुत्ते जैसा जंगली जानवर जो लाशों का मांस खाता है और मनुष्यों की हँसी जैसी आवाज़ निकालता है

**hygiene** /ˈhaɪdʒiːn ˈहाइजीन्/ *noun* [U] (the rules of) keeping yourself and things around you clean, in order to prevent disease मानव शरीर और उसके परिवेश की स्वच्छता (उसके नियम ताकि रोग न हों) *High standards of hygiene are essential when you are preparing food.* ○ *personal hygiene*

**hygienic** /haɪˈdʒiːnɪk हाइˈजीनिक्/ *adj.* clean, without the bacteria that cause disease साफ़ (रोग उत्पन्न करने वाले बैक्टीरिया से मुक्त); स्वास्थ्यकर *hygienic conditions* ▶ **hygienically** /-kli -क्लि/ *adv.* स्वच्छतापूर्वक

**hymn** /hɪm हिम्/ *noun* [C] a religious song that Christians sing together in church, etc. धार्मिक गीत (चर्च आदि में गाया जाने वाला), (वैदिक) मंत्र, स्तोत्र, स्तुति

**hype¹** /haɪp हाइप्/ *noun* [U] advertisements that tell you how good and important a new product, film, etc. is वस्तुओं का गुणगान करने वाले विज्ञापन; हाइप *Don't believe all the hype—the book is rubbish!*

**hype²** /haɪp हाइप्/ *verb* [T] **hype sth (up)** to exaggerate how good or important sth is वस्तुओं की विशेषता को बढ़ा-चढ़ाकर बताना

**hyper-** /ˈhaɪpə(r) ˈहाइप(र्)/ *prefix* (*in adjectives and nouns*) more than normal; too much असाधारण; अत्यधिक *hypercritical* ○ *hypersensitive* ➪ **hypo-** देखिए।

**hyperbole** /haɪˈpɜːbəli हाइˈपबलि/ *noun* [U, C, *usually sing.*] a way of speaking or writing that makes sth sound better, more exciting, dangerous, etc. than it really is किसी वस्तु की विशेषता को बढ़ा-चढ़ाकर बखान करने का ढंग, अतिशयोक्तिपूर्ण कथन; अतिशयोक्ति ✪ पर्याय **exaggeration** *His latest movie is accompanied by the usual hyperbole.*

**hyperlink** /ˈhaɪpəlɪŋk ˈहाइपलिङ्क्/ *noun* [C] (*computing*) a place in an electronic document on a computer that is connected to another electronic document कंप्यूटर स्थित इलेक्ट्रॉनिक डॉक्युमेंट में एक स्थान जो दूसरे इलेक्ट्रॉनिक डॉक्युमेंट से जुड़ा हो; हाइपरलिंक *Click on the hyperlink.*

**hypermarket** /ˈhaɪpəmɑːkɪt ˈहाइपमाकिट्/ *noun* [C] (*BrE*) a very large shop that is usually situated outside a town and sells a wide variety of goods (प्रायः शहर से बाहर स्थित) बहुत बड़ी दुकान जहाँ तरह-तरह का सामान मिलता है

**hyphen** /ˈhaɪfn ˈहाइफ़्न्/ *noun* [C] the mark (–) used for joining two words together (for example *left-handed*, *red-hot*) or to show that a word has been divided and continues on the next line एक चिह्न (–) जो दो शब्दों को जोड़ता है (जैसे माता-पिता) या यह व्यक्त करता है कि किसी विभक्त शब्द का शेष भाग अगली पंक्ति में है; योजक चिह्न, हाइफ़न ➪ **dash** देखिए।

**hyphenate** /ˈhaɪfəneɪt ˈहाइफ़नेट्/ *verb* [T] to join two words together with a hyphen योजक-चिह्न से दो शब्दों को जोड़ना ▶ **hyphenation** /ˌhaɪfəˈneɪʃn ˌहाइफ़ˈनेशन्/ *noun* [U] (हाइफ़न से शब्दों का) संयोजन

**hypnosis** /hɪpˈnəʊsɪs हिप्ˈनोसिस्/ *noun* [U] (the producing of) an unconscious state where sb's mind and actions can be controlled by another person व्यक्ति की निश्चेतनावस्था जिसमें उसके मानसिक और शारीरिक क्रिया-कलाप को अन्य व्यक्ति नियंत्रित करता है; सम्मोहन *She was questioned **under hypnosis**.*

**hypnotize** (*also* **-ise**) /ˈhɪpnətaɪz ˈहिप्नटाइज़्/ *verb* [T] to put sb into an unconscious state where the person's mind and actions can be controlled किसी व्यक्ति को सम्मोहित करना, उसके मानसिक-शारीरिक क्रिया-कलाप को अन्य व्यक्ति द्वारा नियंत्रित किया जाना ▶ **hypnotic** /hɪpˈnɒtɪk हिप्ˈनॉटिक्/ *adj.* सम्मोहक, सम्मोहन-विषयक ▶ **hypnotism** /ˈhɪpnətɪzəm ˈहिप्नटिज़्म्/ *noun* [U] सम्मोहन-विद्या, सम्मोहन-क्रिया ▶ **hypnotist** /ˈhɪpnətɪst ˈहिप्नटिस्ट्/ *noun* [C] सम्मोहन-कर्ता

**hypo-** /ˈhaɪpəʊ ˈहाइपो/ (*also* **hyp-**) *prefix* (*in adjectives and nouns*) under; below normal अधस्तात्, अधः/अधो, अव, नीचे; सामान्य से कम *hypodermic* ○ *hypothermia* ➪ **hyper-** देखिए।

**hypochondria** /ˌhaɪpəˈkɒndriə ˌहाइपˈकॉन्ड्रिआ/ *noun* [U] a mental condition in which sb believes that he/she is ill, even when there is nothing wrong (वास्तविकता के विपरीत) रोगी होने का भ्रम; रोगभ्रम

**hypochondriac** /ˌhaɪpəˈkɒndriæk ˌहाइप ˈकॉन्ड्रिऐक् / *noun* [C] a person who is always worried about his/her health and believes he/she is ill, even when there is nothing wrong (वास्तविकता के विपरीत) किसी व्यक्ति को भ्रम कि वह सदा रोगी रहता है; स्वकाय-दुश्चिंता

**hypocrisy** /hɪˈpɒkrəsi हिˈपॉक्रसि / *noun* [U] behaviour in which sb pretends to have moral standards or opinions that he/she does not really have (वास्तविकता के विपरीत) उच्च नैतिक मानदंड और व्यवहार का ढोंग रचना; पाखंड, ढोंग, मिथ्याचार

**hypocrite** /ˈhɪpəkrɪt ˈहिपक्रिट् / *noun* [C] a person who pretends to have moral standards or opinions which he/she does not really have. Hypocrites say one thing and do another (वास्तविकता के विपरीत) उच्च नैतिक मानदंड और व्यवहार का ढोंग रचने वाला व्यक्ति; पाखंडी, ढोंगी *What a hypocrite! She says she's against the hunting of animals but she's wearing a fur coat.* ▶ **hypocritical** /ˌhɪpəˈkrɪtɪkl ˌहिपˈक्रिटिक्ल् / *adj.* पाखंडपूर्ण ▶ **hypocritically** /-kli -क्लि / *adv.* पाखंडपूर्वक

**hypodermic** /ˌhaɪpəˈdɜːmɪk ˌहाइपˈडमिक् / *noun* a medical instrument with a long needle that is used for putting drugs under the skin (**giving an injection**) त्वचा के नीचे इंजेक्शन लगाने के लिए प्रयुक्त (यंत्र) *a hypodermic needle/syringe*

**hypotenuse** /haɪˈpɒtənjuːz हाइˈपॉटन्यूज़् / *noun* [C] (*mathematics*) the side opposite the **right angle** of a **right-angled** triangle (गणित में) समकोण त्रिभुज का कर्ण

**hypothermia** /ˌhaɪpəˈθɜːmiə ˌहाइपˈथ़मिआ / *noun* [U] a medical condition in which the body temperature is much lower than normal शरीर का तापमान सामान्य से बहुत कम हो जाने की दशा; अपताप

**hypothesis** /haɪˈpɒθəsɪs हाइˈपॉथ़सिस् / *noun* [C] (*pl.* **hypotheses** /-siːz -सीज़् /) an idea that is suggested as the possible explanation for sth but has not yet been found to be true or correct किसी तथ्य को समझाने के लिए मान ली जाने वाली बात, अनुमान पर आधारित (न कि वस्तुतः प्रमाणित) विचार; प्राक्कल्पना

**hypothetical** /ˌhaɪpəˈθetɪkl ˌहाइपˈथ़ेटिक्ल् / *adj.* based on situations that have not yet happened, not on facts प्राक्कल्पना पर आधारित *That's a hypothetical question because we don't know what the situation will be next year.* ▶ **hypothetically** /-kli -क्लि / *adv.* प्राक्कल्पनापूर्वक; प्राक्कल्पना की दृष्टि से, प्राक्कल्पित रूप से

**hysteria** /hɪˈstɪəriə हिˈस्टिअरिआ / *noun* [U] a state in which a person or a group of people cannot control their emotions, for example cannot stop laughing, crying, shouting, etc. व्यक्ति की अपनी भावनाओं पर नियंत्रण खो बैठने की दशा; भावोन्माद, हिस्टीरिया *mass hysteria*

**hysterical** /hɪˈsterɪkl हिˈस्टेरिक्ल् / *adj.* **1** very excited and unable to control your emotions अत्यंत उत्तेजित (जिसका भावनाओं पर नियंत्रण नहीं रहा), उन्मादग्रस्त *hysterical laughter* ○ *She was hysterical with grief.* **2** (*informal*) very funny अत्यंत हास्यजनक ▶ **hysterically** /-kli -क्लि / *adv.* उन्मादपूर्वक

**hysterics** /hɪˈsterɪks हिˈस्टेरिक्स् / *noun* [*pl.*] **1** an expression of extreme fear, excitement or anger that makes sb lose control of his/her emotions उन्माद का दौरा, हिस्टीरिया का दौरा *She* ***went into hysterics*** *when they told her the news.* **2** (*informal*) laughter that you cannot control हँसी का दौरा *The comedian had the audience* ***in hysterics***.

**Hz** *abbr.* hertz; (used in radio) a measure of **frequency** हर्ट्ज़ (रेडियो में प्रयुक्त) फ्रीक्वेंसी की एक माप

# I i

**I, i**[1] /aɪ आइ/ *noun* [C, U] (*pl.* **I's; i's** /aɪz आइज़्/) the ninth letter of the English alphabet अंग्रेज़ी वर्णमाला का नवाँ अक्षर *'Island' begins with an 'I'.*

**I**[2] /aɪ आइ/ *pronoun* (*the subject of a verb*) the person who is speaking or writing वक्ता या लेखक व्यक्ति, मैं *I phoned and said that I was busy.* ○ *I'm not going to fall, am I?*

**iambic** /aɪˈæmbɪk आइˈऐम्बिक्/ *adj.* (*technical*) (used about rhythm in poetry) having one short or weak syllable followed by one long or strong syllable (कविता की लय का संकेत करने के लिए प्रयुक्त) क्रमशः लघु और गुरु चरणों वाला *a poem written in iambic pentameters* (= in lines of ten syllables, five short and five long)

**ice**[1] /aɪs आइस्/ *noun* [U] water that has frozen and become solid जमकर ठोस हो चुका पानी; बर्फ़ *Do you want ice in your orange juice?* ○ *black ice* (= ice on roads, that cannot be seen easily)

**IDM** **break the ice** to say or do sth that makes people feel more relaxed, especially at the beginning of a party or meeting बातचीत शुरू करना, बात छेड़ना (विशेषतः किसी पार्टी या बैठक के आरंभ में)

**cut no ice (with sb)** to have no influence or effect on sb किसी पर कोई प्रभाव न होना

**on ice** **1** (used about wine, etc.) kept cold by being surrounded by ice (मदिरा आदि) बर्फ़ में लगी (इसलिए ठंडी) **2** (used about a plan, etc.) waiting to be dealt with later; delayed (योजना आदि) थोड़े समय के लिए स्थगित; विलंब से, बाद में करने योग्य *We've had to put our plans to go to Australia on ice for the time being.*

**ice**[2] /aɪs आइस्/ (*AmE* **frost**) *verb* [T] to decorate a cake by covering it with a mixture of sugar, butter, chocolate, etc. केक पर शक्कर, बटर, चॉकलेट आदि का सजावटी लेप चढ़ाना ➪ **icing** देखिए।

**PHRV** **ice (sth) over/up** to cover sth or become covered with ice किसी पर बर्फ़ जमना या जमाना *The windscreen of the car had iced over in the night.*

**iceberg** /ˈaɪsbɜːg ˈआइस्बग्/ *noun* [C] a very large block of ice that floats in the sea समुद्र में तैरता विशाल हिमखंड; हिमशैल

**IDM** **the tip of the iceberg** ➪ **tip**[1] देखिए।

**icebox** /ˈaɪsbɒks ˈआइस्बॉक्स्/ (*AmE*) = **fridge**

**ice cap** *noun* [C] (in geography) a layer of ice permanently covering parts of the earth, especially around the North and South Poles (भूगोल में) भूमि के कुछ भागों (विशेषतः उत्तरी और दक्षिणी ध्रुव) पर स्थायी रूप से जमी बर्फ़, हिमशिखर, हिमाच्छद, हिमावरण *the polar ice caps*

**ice-cold** *adj.* very cold बहुत ठंडा *ice-cold beer/lemonade* ○ *Your hands are ice-cold.*

**ice cream** *noun* **1** [U] a frozen sweet food that is made from cream आइस-क्रीम **2** [C] an amount of ice cream that is served to sb, often in a special container (**a cone**) शंकु आदि में भर कर परोसी गई आइस-क्रीम *a strawberry ice cream*

**ice cube** *noun* [C] a small block of ice that you put in a drink to make it cold बर्फ़ का (घन के आकार का) छोटा टुकड़ा (जो पेय पदार्थ को ठंडा करता है)

**iced** /aɪst आइस्ट्/ *adj.* (used about drinks) very cold (पेय) बहुत ठंडा किया हुआ; प्रशीतित *iced tea*

**ice floe** *noun* [C] a large area of ice, floating in the sea समुद्र में तैरती बर्फ़ की चादर, प्लावी हिमखंड

**ice hockey** (*AmE* **hockey**) *noun* [U] a game that is played on ice by two teams who try to hit a small flat rubber object (**a puck**) into a goal with long wooden sticks बर्फ़ (के मैदान) पर खेली जाने वाली हॉकी; आइस-हॉकी

**ice lolly** *noun* [C] (*pl.* **ice lollies**) (*AmE* **popsicle**) a piece of flavoured ice on a stick स्टीक पर जमाई गई ज़ायकेदार बर्फ़ ➪ **lollipop** देखिए।

**ice rink** = **skating rink**

**ice-skate** = **skate**[2]

**ice skating** = **skating 1**

**icicle** /ˈaɪsɪkl ˈआइसिकल्/ *noun* [C] a pointed piece of ice that is formed by water freezing as it falls or runs down from sth लटकती हुई नुकीली बर्फ़

**icing** /ˈaɪsɪŋ ˈआइसिङ्/ (*AmE* **frosting**) *noun* [U] a sweet mixture of sugar and water, milk, butter etc. that is used for decorating cakes केक सजाने के लिए प्रयुक्त शक्कर, दूध आदि का मिश्रण; आइसिंग

**icon** /ˈaɪkɒn ˈआइकॉन्/ *noun* [C] **1** (*computing*) a small picture or symbol on a computer screen that represents a program कंप्यूटर स्क्रीन पर किसी प्रोग्राम का प्रतीक लघुचित्र या प्रतीक; आइकन *Click on the printer icon with the mouse.* **2** a person or thing that is considered to be a symbol of sth किसी वस्तु का प्रतीक बना कोई व्यक्ति या पदार्थ; प्रतिमा, मूर्ति *Madonna and other pop icons of the 1980s* **3** (*also* **ikon**) a picture or figure of an important religious person, used by some types of Christians किसी महत्त्वपूर्ण धार्मिक व्यक्ति का चित्र या आकृति

**icy** /ˈaɪsi ˈआइसि/ *adj.* **1** very cold बहुत ठंडा, बर्फ़ीला *icy winds/water/weather* **2** covered with ice बर्फ़ से ढका, हिमाच्छादित *icy roads*

**ID** /ˌaɪ ˈdiː ˌआइ ˈडी/ *abbr.* (*informal*) identification; identity पहचान; परिचय *an ID card*

**Id** = **Eid**

**I'd** /aɪd आइड्/ ➪ **I had, I would** का संक्षिप्त रूप

**idea** /aɪˈdɪə आइˈडिआ/ *noun* **1** [C] **an idea (for sth); an idea (of sth/of doing sth)** a plan, thought or suggestion, especially about what to do in a particular situation योजना, विचार या सुझाव (विशेषतः इस बारे में कि स्थिति विशेष में क्या किया जाए) *He's* ***got an idea*** *for a new play.* ○ *I had the* ***bright idea*** *of getting Nisha to help me with my homework.* **2** [*sing.*] **an idea (of sth)** a picture or impression in your mind मन में बना चित्र या मन पर पड़ा प्रभाव *You have no idea* (= you can't imagine) *how difficult it was to find a time that suited everybody.* ○ *The programme* ***gave a good idea*** *of what life was like before the war.* **3** [C] **an idea (about sth)** an opinion or belief मत या धारणा *She has her own ideas about how to bring up children.* **4 the idea** [*sing.*] **the idea (of sth/ of doing sth)** the aim or purpose of sth किसी बात का उद्देश्य या प्रयोजन *The idea of the course is to teach the basics of car maintenance.*

IDM **get the idea** to understand the aim or purpose of sth किसी बात के उद्देश्य या प्रयोजन को समझना *Right! I think I've got the idea now.*

**get the idea that...** to get the feeling or impression that... किसी बात का अहसास होना या सूझना या दिमाग़ में आना कि... *Where did you get the idea that I was paying for this meal?*

**have an idea that...** to have a feeling or think that.... मन में भाव या विचार आना कि... *I'm not sure but I have an idea that they've gone on holiday.*

**not have the faintest/foggiest (idea)** ➪ **faint**[1] देखिए।

**ideal**[1] /aɪˈdiːəl आइˈडीअल्/ *adj.* **ideal (for sb/ sth)** the best possible; perfect (व्यक्ति या वस्तु के लिए) यथासंभव सर्वोत्तम; सर्वांगपूर्ण ***In an ideal world*** *there would be no poverty.* ○ *It would be an* ***ideal opportunity*** *for you to practise your English.*

**ideal**[2] /aɪˈdiːəl आइˈडीअल्/ *noun* [C] **1** an idea or principle that seems perfect to you and that you want to achieve सर्वोत्तम लगने वाला विचार या सिद्धांत (जिसे हम प्राप्त करना चाहें), आदर्श *She finds it hard to live up to her parents' high ideals.* ○ *political/ moral/social ideals* **2** [*usually sing.*] **an ideal (of sth)** a perfect example of a person or thing किसी व्यक्ति या वस्तु का सर्वांगपूर्ण उदाहरण *It's my ideal of what a family home should be.*

**idealism** /aɪˈdiːəlɪzəm आइˈडीअलिज़म्/ *noun* [U] the belief that a perfect life, situation, etc. can be achieved, even when this is not very likely यह धारणा कि एक सर्वांगपूर्ण जीवन, स्थिति को प्राप्त किया जा सकता है (भले ही वह पूर्णतया संभव न हो); आदर्शवाद *Young people are usually full of idealism.* ➪ **realism** देखिए। ▶ **idealist** *noun* [C] आदर्शवादी व्यक्ति ▶ **idealistic** /ˌaɪdiəˈlɪstɪk ˌआइडिअˈलिस्टिक्/ *adj.* आदर्शवादी

**idealize** (*also* **-ise**) /aɪˈdiːəlaɪz आइˈडीअलाइज़्/ *verb* [T] to imagine or show sb/sth as being better than he/she/it really is किसी स्थिति को आदर्श के रूप में सोचना या प्रदर्शित करना *Old people often idealize the past.*

**ideally** /aɪˈdiːəli आइˈडीअलि/ *adv.* **1** perfectly पूर्णतया, सब दृष्टियों से *They are ideally suited to each other.* **2** in an ideal situation आदर्श स्थिति में, आदर्शतः *Ideally, no class should be larger than 25.*

**identical** /aɪˈdentɪkl आइˈडेन्टिकल्/ *adj.* **1 identical (to/with sb/sth)** exactly the same as; similar in every detail बिलकुल एक जैसा; सब बातों में समान, सर्वसम *I can't see any difference between these two pens—they look identical to me.* ○ *That watch is identical to the one I lost yesterday.* **2 the identical** (*only before a noun*) the same एकरूप, अभिन्न *This is the identical room we stayed in last year.* ▶ **identically** /-kli -क्लि/ *adv.* अभिन्न रूप से

**identical twin** *noun* [C] one of two children born at the same time from the same mother, and who are of the same sex and look very similar सब बातों में (लिंग, शकल-सूरत आदि) में बहुत समान जुड़वाँ बच्चे

**identification** /aɪˌdentɪfɪˈkeɪʃn आइˌडेन्टिफ़िˈकेशन्/ *noun* [U, C] **1** the process of showing, recognizing or giving proof of who or what sb/sth is व्यक्ति या वस्तु को दिखाने, पहचानने या इस बात का सबूत देने की प्रक्रिया कि वे कौन हैं, व्यक्ति या वस्तु की शिनाख़्त *The identification of the bodies of those killed in the explosion was very difficult.* **2** (*abbr.* **ID**) [U] an official paper, document, etc. that is proof of who you are आधिकारिक पहचान-पत्रक दस्तावेज़ या काग़ज़ात *Do you have any identification?* **3 identification (with sb/sth)** a strong feeling of understanding or sharing the same feelings as sb/sth अपने किसी व्यक्ति या वस्तु के समान समझना या उनके जैसी भावनाएँ रखना, तादात्म्य की अनुभूति होना *children's identification with TV heroes*

**identify** /aɪˈdentɪfaɪ आइˈडेन्टिफ़ाइ/ *verb* [T] (*pres. part.* **identifying;** *3rd person sing. pres.* **identifies;** *pt, pp* **identified**) **identify sb/sth (as sb/sth)** to recognize or be able to say who or what sb/sth is व्यक्ति या वस्तु की पहचान करना या बता सकना कि यह व्यक्ति कौन है या यह वस्तु क्या है *The police need someone to identify the body.* ○ *We must identify the cause of the problem before we look for solutions.*

**PHR V** **identify sth with sth** to think or say that sth is the same as sth else दो वस्तुओं को एक जैसा मानना या बताना *You can't identify nationalism with fascism.*

**identify with sb** to feel that you understand and share what sb else is feeling दूसरे की अनुभूति को समझने और उसमें शामिल होने का अहसास होना *I found it hard to identify with the woman in the film.*

**identify (yourself) with sb/sth** to support or be closely connected with sb/sth किसी व्यक्ति या वस्तु का समर्थन करना या उससे निकटता से जुड़ना *She became identified with the new political party.*

**identity** /aɪˈdentəti आइˈडेन्टटि/ *noun* [C, U] (*pl.* **identities**) who or what a person or a thing is किसी व्यक्ति या वस्तु की पहचान *The region has its own* ***cultural identity****.* ○ *The arrest was a case of mistaken identity* (= the wrong person was arrested).

**identity card** (*also* **ID card**) *noun* [C] a card with your name, photograph, etc. that is proof of who you are नाम, फ़ोटो आदि वाला कार्ड जो किसी व्यक्ति की पहचान का प्रमाण है; पहचान-पत्र

**ideology** /ˌaɪdiˈɒlədʒi ˌआइडिˈऑलजि/ *noun* [C, U] (*pl.* **ideologies**) a set of ideas which form the basis for a political or economic system किसी राजनीतिक या आर्थिक प्रणाली के आधार में स्थित विचार; विचारधारा *Marxist ideology* ▶ **ideological** /ˌaɪdiəˈlɒdʒɪkl ˌआइडिअˈलॉजिकल्/ *adj.* विचारधारा-संबंधी

**idiom** /ˈɪdiəm ˈइडिअम्/ *noun* [C] an expression whose meaning is different from the meanings of the individual words in it मुहावरा, एक ऐसी अभिव्यक्ति जिसका अपना अर्थ उसके शब्दों के अर्थों के कुलयोग से भिन्न हो *The idiom 'bring sth home to sb' means 'make sb understand sth'.*

**idiomatic** /ˌɪdiəˈmætɪk ˌइडिअˈमैटिक्/ *adj.* **1** using language that contains expressions that are natural to sb who learned the language as a child वाक्य व्यवहारिक, स्वाभाविक अभिव्यक्तियों वाला, मातृभाषावत सहज *He speaks good idiomat[ic] English.* **2** containing an idiom मुहावरेदार *a[n] idiomatic expression*

**idiosyncrasy** /ˌɪdiəˈsɪŋkrəsi ˌइडिअˈसिङ्क्रसि/ *noun* [C, U] (*pl.* **idiosyncrasies**) a person's pa[r]ticular way of behaving, thinking, etc., especial[ly] when it is unusual; an unusual characteristic व्यक्ति के व्यवहार, सोच आदि का (विशेषतः असामान्य) तरीका; एक असामान्य विशेषता, प्रकृतिगत विलक्षणता ✪ पर[्याय] **eccentricity** *Eating garlic every morning is o[ne] of his idiosyncrasies.* ○ *The car has its litt[le] idiosyncrasies.* ▶ **idiosyncratic** /ˌɪdiəsɪŋˈkræt[ɪk] ˌइडिअसिङ्ˈक्रैटिक्/ विलक्षण, सनकभरा *His teachi[ng] methods are idiosyncratic but successful.*

**idiot** /ˈɪdiət ˈइडिअट्/ *noun* [C] (*informal*) a ve[ry] stupid person निरा बेवकूफ़ *I was an idiot to forg[et] my passport.* ▶ **idiotic** /ˌɪdiˈɒtɪk ˌइडिˈऑटिक्/ *adj.* बेवकूफ़ी का ▶ **idiotically** /-kli -क्लि/ *ad[v.]* बेवकूफ़ी से

**idle** /ˈaɪdl ˈआइड्ल्/ *adj.* **1** not wanting to wo[rk] hard; lazy मेहनत से जी चुराने वाला, कामचोर; आल[सी] *He has the ability to succeed but he is just* ***bo[ne]*** (= very) ***idle****.* **2** not doing anything; not bei[ng] used निष्क्रिय, अक्रिय; बेकार पड़ा, चालू हालत में न *She can't bear to be idle.* ○ *The factory* ***sto[od]*** ***idle*** *while the machines were being repaire[d].* **3** (*only before a noun*) not to be taken seriou[sly] because it will not have any result व्यर्थ का, निरर्थक, ख़ाली *an idle promise/threat* ○ *idle chatter/curi[os]ity* ▶ **idleness** *noun* [U] ख़ालीपन, सुस्ती ▶ **i[dly]** /ˈaɪdli ˈआइड्लि/ *adv.* सुस्ती से

**idli** *noun* [C] (*pl.* **idlis**) a south Indian steam[ed] cake made from a batter of ground rice a[nd] lentils. It is usually served with **sambar** इडली

**idol** /ˈaɪdl ˈआइड्ल्/ *noun* [C] **1** a person (such [as] a film star or pop musician) who is admired [or] loved समादृत, प्रशंसित या चहेता व्यक्ति (जैसे फ़ि[ल्म] स्टार या पॉप गायक) आराध्य *a pop/football/te[levision] screen idol* **2** a statue that people treat as a g[od] मूर्ति जिसे लोग ईश्वर मानते हैं; देवप्रतिमा, देवमूर्ति

**idolize** (*also* **-ise**) /ˈaɪdəlaɪz ˈआइडलाइज़्/ *verb* to love or admire sb very much or too much कि[सी] से बहुत या बहुत अधिक प्रेम या आदर करना *He is [an] only child and his parents idolize him.*

**idyllic** /ɪˈdɪlɪk इˈडिलिक्/ *adj.* very pleasant a[nd] peaceful; perfect बहुत सुहाना और शांत; सर्वांग[सुंदर] *an idyllic holiday*

**i.e.** /ˌaɪ ˈiː ˌआइ ˈई/ *abbr.* that is; in other wo[rds] अर्थात; दूसरे शब्दों में *deciduous trees, i.e. those wh[ich] lose their leaves in autumn*

**if** /ɪf इफ़्/ *conj.* **1** used in sentences in which one thing only happens or is true when another thing happens or is true यदि, अगर, शर्त, अनुमान या कल्पना का भाव व्यक्त करने के लिए प्रयुक्त *If you see him, give him this letter.* ○ *We won't go to the beach if it rains.* **2** when; every time जब भी; हर बार *If I try to phone her she just hangs up.* ○ *If metal gets hot it expands.* **3** used after verbs such as 'ask', 'know', 'remember' कुछ विशेष क्रियाओं 'ask', 'know', 'remember' के बाद प्रयुक्त *They asked if we would like to go too.* ○ *I can't remember if I posted the letter or not.* ➪ **whether** पर नोट देखिए। **4** used when you are asking sb to do sth or suggesting sth politely विनम्रता से अनुरोध करने या कोई सुझाव देने के लिए प्रयुक्त *If you could just come this way, sir.* ○ *If I might suggest something...*

**IDM as if** ➪ **as** देखिए।

**even if** ➪ **even²** देखिए।

**if I were you** used when you are giving sb advice किसी को परामर्श देने के लिए प्रयुक्त *If I were you, I'd leave now.*

**if it wasn't/weren't for sb/sth** if a particular person or situation did not exist or was not there; without sb/sth यदि वह व्यक्ति न होता या वह बात न होती; व्यक्ति या वस्तु के बिना *If it wasn't for him, I wouldn't stay in this country.*

**if only** used for expressing a strong wish कोई प्रबल इच्छा व्यक्त करने के लिए प्रयुक्त *If only I could drive.* ○ *If only he'd write.*

**igloo** /ˈɪɡluː ˈइग्लू/ *noun* [C] (*pl.* **igloos**) a small house that is built from blocks of hard snow कड़ी बर्फ़ के टुकड़ों से बना छोटा घर; हिमकुटी, इग्लू

**igneous** /ˈɪɡniəs ˈइग्निअस्/ *adj.* (*technical*) (used about rocks) formed when **magma** comes out of a **volcano** and becomes solid ज्वालामुखी से निकले लावा के ठोस हो जाने पर बनी (चट्टानें) ➪ **metamorphic** और **sedimentary** देखिए तथा **rock** पर चित्र देखिए।

**ignite** /ɪɡˈnaɪt इग्ˈनाइट्/ *verb* [I, T] (*formal*) to start burning or to make sth start burning जलना आग लगाना, ज्वलित होना या करना *A spark from the engine ignited the petrol.*

**ignition** /ɪɡˈnɪʃn इग्ˈनिश्न्/ *noun* **1** [C] the electrical system that starts the engine of a car कार के इंजन को स्टार्ट करने वाली विद्युत-प्रणाली *to turn the ignition on/off* ○ *First of all, put the key in the ignition.* ➪ **car** पर चित्र देखिए। **2** [U] the action of starting to burn or making sth start to burn ज्वलन या ज्वालन की क्रिया, जलने या जलाना शुरू करने की क्रिया

**ignominious** /ˌɪɡnəˈmɪniəs ˌइग्नˈमिनिअस्/ *adj.* (*formal*) making you feel embarrassed शरमिंदा करने वाला *The team suffered an ignominious defeat.* ▶ **ignominiously** *adv.* शरमिंदगी के साथ

**ignorance** /ˈɪɡnərəns ˈइग्नरन्स्/ *noun* [U] **ignorance (of/about sth)** a lack of information or knowledge सूचना या ज्ञान का अभाव; अज्ञान *The workers were **in** complete **ignorance** of the management's plans.*

**ignorant** /ˈɪɡnərənt ˈइग्नरन्ट्/ *adj.* **1 ignorant (of/about sth)** not knowing about sth (किसी बात से) अनजान, अनभिज्ञ *Many people are ignorant of their rights.* **2** (*informal*) having or showing bad manners अभद्र, अशिष्ट *an ignorant person/remark*

**ignore** /ɪɡˈnɔː(r) इग्ˈनॉ(र्)/ *verb* [T] to pay no attention to sb/sth व्यक्ति या वस्तु पर कोई ध्यान न देना, की उपेक्षा करना *I said hello to Dolly but she totally ignored me* (= acted as though she hadn't seen me). ○ *Suman ignored her doctor's advice about doing regular exercise.*

**ikon** = **icon 3**

**il-** *prefix* ➪ **in** देखिए।

**ileum** /ˈɪliəm ˈइलिअम्/ *noun* [C] (*pl.* **ilea** /ˈɪliə ˈइलिआ/) one part of the **intestine** छोटी आँत का पिछला भाग; शेषांत्र

**I'll** /aɪl आइल्/ ➪ **I will, I shall** का संक्षिप्त रूप

**ill¹** /ɪl इल्/ *adj.* **1** (*AmE* **sick**) (*not before a noun*) not in good health; not well स्वस्थ नहीं; अस्वस्थ, बीमार *I can't drink milk because it makes me **feel ill**.* ○ *My mother was **taken ill** suddenly last week.* ○ *My grandfather is **seriously ill** in hospital.* ➪ **sick** पर नोट देखिए। **2** (*only before a noun*) bad or harmful ख़राब या हानिकर *He resigned because of **ill health**.* ○ *I'm glad to say I suffered no **ill effects** from all that rich food.* ➪ **illness** noun देखिए।

**ill²** /ɪl इल्/ *adv.* **1** (*often in compounds*) badly or wrongly अनुचित या ग़लत (तरीक़े से) *You would be **ill-advised** to drive until you have fully recovered.* **2** only with difficulty; not easily काफ़ी कठिनाई से; आसानी से नहीं *They could ill afford the extra money for better heating.*

**IDM augur well/ill for sb/sth** ➪ **augur** देखिए।

**bode well/ill (for sb/sth)** ➪ **bode** देखिए।

**illegal** /ɪˈliːɡl इˈलीग्ल्/ *adj.* not allowed by the law ग़ैर-क़ानूनी, अवैध *It is illegal to own a gun without a special licence.* ○ *illegal drugs/immigrants/activities* ✪ विलोम **legal** ✪ पर्याय **unlawful** ▶ **illegally** /-ɡəli -गलि/ *adv.* ग़ैर-क़ानूनी या अवैध तरीक़े से

**illegality** /ˌɪliˈɡæləti ˌइलिˈगैलटि/ *noun* (*pl.* **illegalities**) **1** [U] the state of being illegal ग़ैर-क़ानूनीपन, अवैधता *No illegality is suspected.* **2** [C] an illegal act ग़ैर-क़ानूनी या अवैध कार्य ➪ **legality** देखिए।

**illegible** /ɪˈledʒəbl इˈलेजब्ल्/ *adj.* difficult or impossible to read जिसे पढ़ना कठिन या असंभव हो; अपाठ्य, दुर्वाच्य *Your handwriting is quite illegible.* ✪ विलोम **legible** ▶ **illegibly** /-əbli -अब्लि/ *adv.* दुर्वाच्य रीति से

**illegitimate** /ˌɪləˈdʒɪtəmət ˌइलˈजिटमट्/ *adj.* **1** (*old-fashioned*) (used about a child) born to parents who are not married to each other (शिशु) अविवाहित स्त्री-पुरुष से जन्मा, अवैध; जारज **2** not allowed by law; against the rules ग़ैर-क़ानूनी, अवैध; नियमों के विरुद्ध *the illegitimate use of company money* ✪ विलोम **legitimate** ▶ **illegitimacy** /ˌɪləˈdʒɪtəməsi ˌइलˈजिटमसि/ *noun* [U] अवैधता, नियम-विरुद्धता

**ill-fated** *adj.* not lucky अभागा, भाग्य का मारा *the ill-fated ship, the Titanic*

**illicit** /ɪˈlɪsɪt इˈलिसिट्/ *adj.* (used about an activity or substance) not allowed by law or by the rules of society (कोई गतिविधि या तत्व) क़ानून या समाज के नियमों के विरुद्ध, ग़ैर-क़ानूनी; अवैध *the illicit trade in ivory* ○ *They were having an illicit affair.*

**illiterate** /ɪˈlɪtərət इˈलिटरट्/ *adj.* **1** not able to read or write लिखने या पढ़ने में असमर्थ; निरक्षर, अनपढ़ ✪ विलोम **literate** **2** (used about a piece of writing) very badly written (लेख) रचना की दृष्टि से अत्यंत शिथिल **3** not knowing much about a particular subject विषय-विशेष से अनभिज्ञ या अनजान *computer illiterate* ▶ **illiteracy** /ɪˈlɪtərəsi इˈलिटरसि/ *noun* [U] निरक्षरता *adult illiteracy* ✪ विलोम **literacy**

**illness** /ˈɪlnəs ˈइलनस्/ *noun* **1** [U] the state of being physically or mentally ill शारीरिक या मानसिक बीमारी *He's missed a lot of school through illness.* ○ *There is a history of mental illness in the family.* **2** [C] a type or period of physical or mental ill health शारीरिक या मानसिक बीमारी का एक प्रकार या समय *minor/serious/childhood illnesses* ○ *My dad is just getting over his illness.* ➪ **ill** adjective देखिए तथा **disease** पर नोट देखिए।

**illogical** /ɪˈlɒdʒɪkl इˈलॉजिक्ल्/ *adj.* not sensible or reasonable समझदारी या तर्कसंगति से रहित, नासमझी का या अतर्कसंगत *It seems illogical to me to pay somebody to do work that you could do yourself.* ✪ विलोम **logical** ▶ **illogicality** /ɪˌlɒdʒɪˈkæləti इˌलॉजिˈकैलटि/ *noun* [C, U] (*pl.* **illogicalities**) तर्कसंगतिहीनता ▶ **illogically** /-kli -क्लि/ *adv.* अतर्कसंगत रीति से

**ill-treat** *verb* [T] to treat sb/sth badly or in an unkind way किसी के साथ दुर्व्यवहार करना ▶ **ill-treatment** *noun* [U] दुर्व्यवहार

**illuminate** /ɪˈluːmɪneɪt इˈलूमिनेट्/ *verb* [T] (*formal*) **1** to shine light on sth or to decorate sth with lights किसी वस्तु को प्रकाश से आलोकित करना या बत्तियों से सजाना *The palace was illuminated by spotlights.* **2** to explain sth or make sth clear किसी बात को समझाना या उसे स्पष्ट करना

**illuminating** /ɪˈluːmɪneɪtɪŋ इˈलूमिनेटिङ्/ *adj.* helping to explain sth or make sth clear किसी बात को समझाने या स्पष्ट करने में सहायक *an illuminating discussion*

**illumination** /ɪˌluːmɪˈneɪʃn इˌलूमिˈनेश्न्/ *noun* **1** [U, C] light or the place where a light comes from प्रकाश या प्रकाश का स्रोत **2 illuminations** [*pl.*] (*BrE*) bright colourful lights that are used for decorating a street, town, etc. सड़क, नगर, आदि की सजावट में प्रयुक्त चमकदार रंगबिरंगी बत्तियाँ

**illusion** /ɪˈluːʒn इˈलूश़्न्/ *noun* **1** [C, U] a false idea, belief or impression निराधार विचार, धारणा या प्रभाव; भ्रम *I **have no illusions** about the situation—I know it's serious.* ○ *I think Puneet's **under the illusion** that he will be the new director.* **2** [C] something that your eyes tell you is there or is true but in fact is not (वास्तविकता के विपरीत) किसी वस्तु की सत्ता होने का आभास; दृष्टिभ्रम *That line looks longer, but in fact they're the same length. It's an **optical illusion**.*

**illusory** /ɪˈluːsəri इˈलूसरि/ *adj.* (*formal*) not real, although seeming to be अवास्तविक, मिथ्या, भ्रामक *The profits they had hoped for proved to be illusory.*

**illustrate** /ˈɪləstreɪt ˈइलस्ट्रेट्/ *verb* [T] **1** to explain or make sth clear by using examples, pictures or diagrams उदाहरणों, चित्रों या आरेखों की सहायता से किसी बात को समझना या स्पष्ट करना *These statistics **illustrate the point** that I was making very well.* **2** to add pictures, diagrams, etc. to a book or magazine पुस्तक या पत्रिका में चित्र, आरेख आदि देना *Most cookery books are illustrated.*

**illustration** /ˌɪləˈstreɪʃn ˌइलˈस्ट्रेश्न्/ *noun* **1** [C] a drawing, diagram or picture in a book or magazine पुस्तक या पत्रिका में आरेखन, आरेख या चित्र *colour illustrations* **2** [U] the activity or art of illustrating चित्रों आदि द्वारा समझाने की क्रिया **3** [C] an example that makes a point or an idea clear उदाहरण (जिससे विचारबिंदु या धारणा स्पष्ट हो जाते हैं) *Can you give me an illustration of what you mean?*

**illustrator** /ˈɪləstreɪtə(r) ˈइलस्ट्रेट(र्)/ *noun* [C] a person who draws or paints pictures for books, etc. पुस्तक आदि के लिए आरेखन करने या चित्र बनाने वाला व्यक्ति; चित्रकार, चित्रक

**illustrious** /ɪˈlʌstriəs इˈलसट्रिअस्/ *adj.* (*formal*) famous and successful प्रसिद्ध और सफल

**I'm** /aɪm आइम्/ ➪ **I am** का संक्षिप्त रूप

**im-** *prefix* ➪ **in** देखिए।

**image** /ˈɪmɪdʒ ˈइमिज्/ *noun* [C] **1** the general impression that a person or organization gives to the public जनता के सामने व्यक्ति या संगठन के विषय में सामान्य धारणा *When you meet him, he's very different from his public image.* **2** a mental picture or idea of sb/sth व्यक्ति या वस्तु का मानसिक चित्र या कल्पना *I have an image of my childhood as always sunny and happy.* **3** a picture or description that appears in a book, film or painting पुस्तक, फ़िल्म या चित्रकारी में कोई चित्र या वर्णन *horrific images of war* **4** a copy or picture of sb/sth seen in a mirror, through a camera, on television, computer, etc. व्यक्ति या वस्तु का दर्पण में प्रतिबिंब (कैमरे के माध्यम से या टेलीविज़न, कंप्यूटर आदि पर) *A perfect image of the building was reflected in the lake.* ○ *He's **the (spitting) image of** his father* (= he looks exactly like him).

**imagery** /ˈɪmɪdʒəri ˈइमिजरि/ *noun* [U] language that produces pictures in the minds of the people reading or listening पाठक या श्रोता के मानस में चित्र उभारने वाली भाषा; बिंब-चित्रण *poetic imagery*

**imaginable** /ɪˈmædʒɪnəbl इˈमैजिनबल्/ *adj.* that you can imagine जिसकी कल्पना की जा सके, कल्पनीय, चिंतनीय *Shruti made all the excuses imaginable when she was caught stealing.* ○ *His house was equipped with every imaginable luxury.*

**imaginary** /ɪˈmædʒɪnəri इˈमैजिनरि/ *adj.* existing only in the mind; not real केवल मन में, काल्पनिक; अवास्तविक *Many children have imaginary friends.*

**imagination** /ɪˌmædʒɪˈneɪʃn इˌमैजिˈनेशन्/ *noun* **1** [U, C] the ability to create mental pictures or new ideas मानसिक चित्र या नई धारणाएँ बनाने की क्षमता, रचनात्मक कल्पना *He has a lively imagination.* ○ *She's very clever but she doesn't **have much imagination**.* **2** [C] the part of the mind that uses this ability कल्पनाशक्ति *If you **use** your **imagination**, you should be able to guess the answer.* ▸ **imaginatively** *adv.* कल्पनाशक्ति से

**imaginative** /ɪˈmædʒɪnətɪv इˈमैजिनटिव्/ *adj.* having or showing imagination कल्पना से उत्पन्न, कल्पनाशील *She's always full of imaginative ideas.*

**imagine** /ɪˈmædʒɪn इˈमैजिन्/ *verb* [T] **1 imagine that...; imagine sb/sth (doing/as sth)** to form a picture or idea in your mind of what sth/sb might be like किसी व्यक्ति या वस्तु के विषय में कुछ कल्पना करना, मन में उसका चित्र या उसके विषय में कोई धारणा बनाना *Imagine that you're lying on a beach.* ○ *I can't imagine myself cycling 20 kilometres a day.* **2** to see, hear or think sth that is not true or does not exist असत्य और अस्तित्वहीन वस्तुओं को देखना, सुनना और उनके विषय में सोचना या कल्पना करना *She's always imagining that she's ill but she's fine really.* ○ *I thought I heard someone downstairs, but I must have been **imagining things**.* **3** to think that sth is probably true; to suppose सोचना कि बात शायद सच हो; कल्पना करना *I imagine he'll be coming by car.*

**imam** *noun* [C] **1** the person who leads prayers in a **mosque** इमाम **2 Imam** a title adopted by various Muslim leaders इमाम

**imbalance** /ɪmˈbæləns इम्ˈबैलन्स्/ *noun* [C] **an imbalance (between A and B); an imbalance (in/of sth)** a difference; not being equal भिन्नता; समान न होना, असंतुलन *an imbalance in the numbers of men and women teachers*

**imbecile** /ˈɪmbəsiːl ˈइमबसील्/ *noun* [C] a stupid person मूर्ख व्यक्ति ✪ पर्याय **idiot**

**IMF** /ˌaɪ em ˈef ˌआइ एम् ˈएफ़्/ *abbr.* the International Monetary Fund अंतर्राष्ट्रीय वित्तीय निधि

**imitate** /ˈɪmɪteɪt ˈइमिटेट्/ *verb* [T] **1** to copy the behaviour of sb/sth किसी के आचरण की नक़ल करना; अनुकरण करना *Small children learn by imitating their parents.* **2** to copy the speech or actions of sb/sth, often in order to make people laugh व्यक्ति या वस्तु के बोलने या कुछ करने के ढंग की नक़ल उतारना (प्रायः लोगों को हँसाने के लिए) *She could imitate her mother perfectly.*

**imitation** /ˌɪmɪˈteɪʃn ˌइमिˈटेशन्/ *noun* **1** [C] a copy of sth real किसी वास्तविक वस्तु की प्रतिकृति या नक़ल *Some artificial flowers are good imitations of real ones.* ➪ **genuine** देखिए। **2** [U] the act of copying sb/sth व्यक्ति या वस्तु की नक़ल करना *Good pronunciation of a language is best learnt **by imitation**.* **3** [C] the act of copying the way sb talks and behaves, especially in order to make people laugh लोगों के बोलने और कुछ करने के ढंग की नक़ल लगाना (ताकि लोग हँसे) *Can you **do** any **imitations** of politicians?*

**immaculate** /ɪˈmækjələt इˈमैक्यलट्/ *adj.* **1** perfectly clean and tidy एकदम साफ़-सुथरा *immaculate white shirts* **2** without any mistakes; perfect त्रुटिहीन; परिपूर्ण *His performance of 'Gandhi' was immaculate.* ▶ **immaculately** *adv.* परिपूर्णता से

**immaterial** /ˌɪməˈtɪəriəl ˌइमˈटिअरिअल्/ *adj.* **immaterial (to sb/sth)** not important महत्त्वहीन *It's immaterial to me whether we go today or tomorrow.*

**immature** /ˌɪməˈtjʊə(r) ˌइमˈट्युअ(र्)/ *adj.* **1** not fully grown or developed अविकसित; अपरिपक्व *an immature body* **2** (used about a person) behaving in a way that is not sensible and is typical of people who are much younger (व्यक्ति) नादानी भरा और अपने से छोटे लोगों जैसा आचरण करने वाला; बचकानेपन से पेश आने वाला *I think he's too immature to take his work seriously.* ✪ विलोम **mature**

**immeasurable** /ɪˈmeʒərəbl इˈमेझ़रबल्/ *adj.* (*formal*) too large, great, etc. to be measured अमापनीय, अपरिमित, अपार *to cause immeasurable harm* ○ *Her contribution was of immeasurable importance.* ▶ **immeasurably** /-əbli -अब्लि/ *adv.* अपरिमित रूप से, अत्यधिक *Housing standards have improved immeasurably since the war.*

**immediacy** /ɪˈmiːdiəsi इˈमीडिअसि/ *noun* [U] the quality of being available or seeming to happen close to you and without delay अविलंबता, अव्यवधान, तात्कालिकता या सन्निकटता *Letters do not have the same immediacy as email.*

**immediate** /ɪˈmiːdiət इˈमीडिअट्/ *adj.* **1** happening or done without delay तुरंत होने या किया जाने वाला, तत्काल संपन्न; अविलंब *I'd like an immediate answer to my proposal.* ○ *The government responded with immediate action.* **2** (*only before a noun*) existing now and needing urgent attention अभी का और अत्यावश्यक *Tell me what your immediate needs are.* **3** (*only before a noun*) nearest in time, position or relationship समय, स्थान या संबंध की दृष्टि से निकटतम *They won't make any changes in **the immediate future**.* ○ *He has left most of his money to his immediate family* (= parents, children, brothers and sisters).

**immediately** /ɪˈmiːdiətli इˈमीजिअट्लि/ *adv., conj.* **1** at once; without delay तुरंत; अविलंब *Can you come home immediately after work?* ○ *I couldn't immediately see what he meant.* **2** very closely; directly बहुत निकटता से; सीधे *He wasn't immediately involved in the crime.* **3** nearest in time or position समय या स्थान की दृष्टि से निकटतम, एकदम *Who's the girl immediately in front of Shiva?* ○ *What did you do immediately after the war?* **4** (*BrE*) as soon as ज्यों ही *I opened the letter immediately I got home.*

**immense** /ɪˈmens इˈमेन्स्/ *adj.* very big or great अत्यधिक, असीम, अपार *immense difficulties/importance/power* ○ *She gets immense pleasure from her garden.*

**immensely** /ɪˈmensli इˈमेन्स्लि/ *adv.* extremely; very much अत्यधिक; बहुत ज़्यादा *immensely enjoyable*

**immensity** /ɪˈmensəti इˈमेनसटि/ *noun* [U] an extremely large size आकारगत विशालता *the immensity of the universe*

**immerse** /ɪˈmɜːs इˈमस्/ *verb* [T] **1 immerse sth (in sth)** to put sth into a liquid so that it is covered किसी वस्तु को द्रव में पूरी तरह डुबाना *Make sure the spaghetti is fully immersed in the boiling water.* **2 immerse yourself (in sth)** to involve yourself completely in sth so that you give it all your attention किसी काम में पूरी तरह लीन हो जाना *Rakhi's usually immersed in a book.*

**immersion** /ɪˈmɜːʃn इˈमशन्/ *noun* [U] **1 immersion (in sth)** the act of putting sb/sth into a liquid so that he/she/it is completely covered; the state of being completely covered by a liquid किसी वस्तु को द्रव में पूरी तरह डुबा देने की क्रिया; द्रव में पूरी तरह डूबे होने की स्थिति; निमज्जन, डुबकी *Immersion in cold water resulted in rapid loss of heat.* **2 immersion (in sth)** the state of being completely involved in sth (किसी काम में) पूरी तल्लीनता, पूर्ण ध्यानमग्नता *a two-week immersion course in French* (= in which the student hears and uses only French)

**immigrant** /ˈɪmɪɡrənt ˈइमिग्रन्ट्/ *noun* [C] a person who has come into a foreign country to live there permanently दूसरे देश में आकर वहीं स्थायी रूप से बसने वाला व्यक्ति; आप्रवासी *The government plans to tighten controls to prevent **illegal immigrants**.* ○ *London has a high immigrant population.*

**immigrate** /ˈɪmɪɡreɪt ˈइमिग्रेट्/ *verb* [I] to come to live permanently in a country after leaving your own country आप्रवास करना

**NOTE** 'Immigrate' क्रिया है परंतु इसका प्रयोग बहुत कम होता है। हम सामान्यतया 'be an immigrant' या 'emigrate' कहते हैं जिसका प्रयोग उस स्थान के संबंध में होता है जहाँ से आप्रवासी आया है—*My parents emigrated to this country from Jamaica.* ➪ **emigrate, emigrant** और **emigration** देखिए।

**immigration** /ˌɪmɪˈɡreɪʃn ˌइमिˈग्रेश्न्/ *noun* [U] **1** the process of coming to live permanently in a country that is not your own; the number of people who do this दूसरे देश मे आकर वहाँ स्थायी रूप से बसने की प्रक्रिया, आप्रवासन; आप्रवासियों की संख्या *There are greater controls on immigration than there used to be.* ○ *a fall in immigration* **2** (*also* **immigration control**) the control point at an airport, port, etc. where the official documents of people who want to come into a country are checked हवाई अड्डे, बंदरगाह आदि पर नियंत्रण कक्ष जहाँ आप्रवासियों की आधिकारिक दस्तावेज़ों की जाँच की जाती है *When you leave the plane you have to go through customs and immigration.*

**imminent** /ˈɪmɪnənt ˈइमिनन्ट्/ *adj.* (usually used about sth unpleasant) almost certain to happen very soon (प्रायः अप्रिय बात) बहुत शीघ्र लगभग निश्चित रूप से घटित होने वाली; सन्निकट, आसन्न, अवश्यंभावी *Heavy rainfall means that flooding is imminent.* ▶ **imminently** *adv.* सन्निकट रूप से

**immiscible** /ɪˈmɪsəbl इˈमिसब्ल्/ *adj.* (*technical*) (used about liquids) that cannot be mixed together (द्रव पदार्थ) जिसका परस्पर मिश्रण नहीं हो सकता; अमिश्रणीय ✪ विलोम **miscible**

**immobile** /ɪˈməʊbaɪl इˈमोबाइल्/ *adj.* not moving or not able to move निश्चल; अचल, स्थिर, गतिहीन ✪ विलोम **mobile** ▶ **immobility** /ˌɪməˈbɪləti ˌइमˈबिलटि/ *noun* [U] गतिहीनता, अचलता

**immobilize** (*also* **-ise**) /ɪˈməʊbəlaɪz इˈमोबलाइज़्/ *verb* [T] to prevent sb/sth from moving or working normally व्यक्ति या वस्तु को गति या सामान्यतया कोई काम न करने देना, गतिहीन कर देना; अचल कर देना *This device immobilizes the car to prevent it being stolen.* ✪ विलोम **mobilize**

**immobilizer** (*also* **-iser**) /ɪˈməʊbəlaɪzə(r) इˈमोबलाइज़(र्)/ *noun* [C] a device in a vehicle that prevents thieves from starting the engine when the vehicle is parked वाहन में लगा उपकरण जो इंजन पार्क की हुई गाड़ी को स्टार्ट नहीं होने देता; इंजनरोधी उपकरण

**immoral** /ɪˈmɒrəl इˈमॉरल्/ (used about people or their behaviour) considered wrong or not honest by most people लोग या उनका आचरण जिसे अधिकतर लोग ग़लत या अविश्वसनीय मानते हैं; अनैतिक *It's immoral to steal.* ✪ विलोम **moral** ⇨ **amoral** देखिए। ▶ **immorality** /ˌɪməˈræləti ˌइमˈरैलटि/ *noun* [U] अनैतिकता ✪ विलोम **morality** ▶ **immorally** /-rəli -रलि/ *adv.* अनैतिक रूप से

**immortal** /ɪˈmɔːtl इˈमॉटल्/ *adj.* living or lasting for ever अमर, शाश्वत अनश्वर *Nobody is immortal—we all have to die some time.* ✪ विलोम **mortal** ▶ **immortality** /ˌɪmɔːˈtæləti ˌइमॉˈटैलटि/ *noun* [U] अमरत्व

**immortalize** (*also* **-ise**) /ɪˈmɔːtəlaɪz इˈमॉटलाइज़्/ *verb* [T] to give lasting fame to sb/sth व्यक्ति या वस्तु को स्थायी यश प्रदान करना; अमर कर देना, चिरस्मरणीय बना देना *He immortalized their relationship in a poem.*

**immune** /ɪˈmjuːn इˈम्यून्/ *adj.* **1 immune (to sth)** having natural protection against a certain disease or illness किसी रोग से प्राकृतिक रूप से सुरक्षित; प्रतिरक्षित *You should be immune to measles if you've had it already.* **2 immune (to sth)** not affected by sth किसी भी बात से प्रभावित नहीं; अप्रभावित *You can say what you like—I'm immune to criticism!* **3 immune (from sth)** protected from a danger or punishment संकटग्रस्ट या दंडित होने से सुरक्षित, निरापद या अदंडनीय *Young children are immune from prosecution.*

**immunity** /ɪˈmjuːnəti इˈम्यूनटि/ *noun* [U] the ability to avoid or not be affected by disease, criticism, punishment by law, etc. रोग, आलोचना, क़ानूनन दंडित होना आदि से बचने या प्रभावित न होने की क्षमता; निरापदता, बचाव, प्रतिरक्षण *In many countries people have no immunity to diseases like measles.* ○ *Ambassadors to other countries receive diplomatic immunity* (= protection from prosecution, etc.).

**immunize** (*also* **-ise**) /ˈɪmjʊnaɪz ˈइम्युनाइज़्/ *verb* [T] to make sb immune to a disease, usually by putting a substance (**vaccine**) into his/herbody टीका लगाकर रोग के आक्रमण से बचाना; प्रतिरक्षिकरण करना *Before visiting certain countries you will need to be immunized against cholera.* ✪ पर्याय **inoculate** और **vaccinate** ▶ **immunization** (*also* **-isation**) /ˌɪmjʊnaɪˈzeɪʃn ˌइम्युनाइˈज़ेशन्/ *noun* [C, U] प्रतिरक्षिकरण

**imp** /ɪmp इम्प्/ *noun* [C] (in stories) a small creature like a little devil (कहानियों में) छोटा शैतान

**impact** /ˈɪmpækt ˈइम्पैक्ट्/ *noun* **1** [C, *usually sing.*] **an impact (on/upon sb/sth)** an effect or impression परिणाम या प्रभाव *I hope this anti-smoking campaign will **make/have an impact** on young people.* **2** [U] the action or force of one object hitting another दूसरी से टकराने वाली वस्तु की क्रियाशीलता या शक्ति *The impact of the crash threw the passengers out of their seats.* ○ *The bomb exploded **on impact**.*

**impair** /ɪmˈpeə(r) इम्ˈपेअ(र्)/ *verb* [T] to damage sth or make it weaker किसी वस्तु को क्षतिग्रस्त या अधिक दुर्बल बना देना *Ear infections can result in impaired hearing.*

**impairment** /ɪmˈpeəmənt इम्ˈपेअमन्ट्/ *noun* [U, C] the state of having a physical or mental condition which means that part of your body or brain does not work properly; a particular condition of this sort शारीरिक या मानसिक रूप से क्षतिग्रस्त होने की स्थिति; इस प्रकार की विशिष्ट स्थिति, विशिष्ट क्षति

**impale** /ɪmˈpeɪl इम्ˈपेल्/ *verb* [T] **impale sb/sth (on sth)** to push a sharp pointed object through sb/sth व्यक्ति या वस्तु में कोई नुकीली चीज़ घोंपना *The boy fell out of the tree and impaled his leg on some railings.*

**impalpable** /ɪmˈpælpəbl इम्ˈपैल्पबल्/ *adj.* **1** not easily grasped by the mind; difficult to understand जो आसानी से बोधगम्य न हो, समझने में कठिन; दुर्बोध **2** unable to be felt by touch स्पर्शातीत, अस्फुट ▶ **impalpability** *noun* दुर्बोधता, स्पर्शातीतत्व, अस्फुटता

**impart** /ɪmˈpɑːt इम्ˈपाट्/ *verb* [T] (*formal*) **1 impart sth (to sb)** to pass information, knowledge, etc. to other people अन्य व्यक्तियों को जानकारी पहुँचाना, ज्ञान प्रदान करना **2 impart sth (to sth)** to give a certain quality to sth किसी बात में विशेष प्रभाव जोड़ देना *The low lighting imparted a romantic atmosphere to the room.*

**impartial** /ɪmˈpɑːʃl इम्ˈपाश्ल्/ *adj.* not supporting one person or group more than another; fair जिसमें दो पक्षों में से किसी एक को अधिक प्रमुखता न दी जाए; निष्पक्ष ✪ पर्याय **neutral** ▶ **impartiality** /ɪmˌpɑːʃiˈæləti इम्ˌपाशिˈऐलटि/ *noun* [U] ▶ **impartially** /-ʃəli -शलि/ *adv.* निष्पक्ष रूप से

**impassable** /ɪmˈpɑːsəbl इम्ˈपासबल्/ *adj.* (used about a road, etc.) impossible to travel on because it is blocked (सड़क आदि) अवरोध के कारण जिस पर वाहन का चलना असंभव हो; अलंध्य ✪ विलोम **passable**

**impasse** /ˈæmpɑːs ˈऐम्पास्/ *noun* [C, *usually sing.*] a difficult situation in which no progress can be made because the people involved cannot agree what to do लोगों के सहमत न हो पाने से उत्पन्न कठिन स्थिति जिसमें बात या काम आगे न बढ़ सके; गतिरोध ✪ पर्याय **deadlock** *to break/end the impasse* ○ *Negotiations have reached an impasse.*

**impassioned** /ɪmˈpæʃnd इम्ˈपैश्न्ड्/ *adj.* (*usually before a noun*) (usually used about speech) showing strong feelings about sth भावावेशपूर्ण (भाषण) *an impassioned defence/plea/speech*

**impassive** /ɪmˈpæsɪv इम्ˈपैसिव्/ *adj.* (used about a person) showing no emotion or reaction जो कोई भाव या प्रतिक्रिया व्यक्त न करे, भावशून्य (व्यक्ति); अविचलित ▶ **impassively** *adv.* भावशून्य होकर

**impatient** /ɪmˈpeɪʃnt इम्ˈपेश्न्ट्/ *adj.* **1 impatient (at sth/ with sb)** not able to stay calm and wait for sb/sth; easily annoyed by sb/sth that seems slow जो किसी व्यक्ति या वस्तु के लिए शांतिपूर्वक प्रतीक्षा न कर सके, अधीर, आतुर; व्यग्र *The passengers are getting impatient at the delay.* ○ *It's no good being impatient with small children.* ✪ विलोम **patient** **2 impatient for/to do sth** wanting sth to happen soon किसी बात के लिए उतावला; आतुर *By the time they are sixteen many young people are impatient to leave school.* ▶ **impatience** *noun* [U] अधीरता, आतुरता *He began to explain for the third time with growing impatience.* ▶ **impatiently** *adv.* अधीरता से, आतुरतापूर्वक

**impeach** /ɪmˈpiːtʃ इम्ˈपीच्/ *verb* [T] **impeach sb (for sth)** (used about a court of law, especially in the US and some other countries) to officially accuse a public official of committing a serious crime while he/she is still in office (न्यायालय के लिए प्रयुक्त, विशेषतः अमेरिका में तथा कुछ अन्य देशों में) पद पर रहते हुए गंभीर अपराध करने के लिए सरकारी अधिकारी पर आधिकारिक रूप से दोषारोपण करना; महाभियोग लगाना ▶ **impeachment** *noun* [U, C] महाभियोग **NOTE** भारत में संविधान के उल्लंघन के लिए राष्ट्रपति पर महाभियोग लागू हो सकता है।

**impeccable** /ɪmˈpekəbl इम्ˈपेकबल्/ *adj.* without any mistakes or faults; perfect निर्दोष, त्रुटिहीन; परिपूर्ण ▶ **impeccably** /-bli -ब्लि/ *adv.* बिना किसी त्रुटि के

**impede** /ɪmˈpiːd इम्ˈपीड्/ *verb* [T] (*formal*) to make it difficult for sb/sth to move or go forward व्यक्ति या वस्तु के लिए हिलने-डुलने या आगे बढ़ने में कठिनाई उपस्थित करना, बाधा या अड़चन डालना

**impediment** /ɪmˈpedɪmənt इम्ˈपेडिमन्ट्/ *noun* [C] (*formal*) **1 an impediment (to sth)** something that makes it difficult for a person or thing to move or progress जो व्यक्ति या वस्तु के लिए हिलने-डुलने या आगे बढ़ने में अड़चन या बाधा डाले; अड़चन, बाधा, रुकावट **2** something that makes speaking difficult जो बोलने में कठिनाई उत्पन्न करे, उच्चारण दोष, हकलाहट *a speech impediment*

**impel** /ɪmˈpel इम्ˈपेल्/ *verb* [T] (**impelling; impelled**) **impel sb (to do sth)** if an idea or a feeling impels you to do sth, you feel as if you are forced to do it कुछ करने के लिए बाध्य या प्रेरित

अनुभव करना *He felt impelled to investigate further.* ○ *There are various reasons that impel me to that conclusion.*

**impending** /ɪmˈpendɪŋ इम्ˈपेन्डिङ्/ *adj.* (*only before a noun*) (usually used about sth bad) that will happen soon (अशुभ घटना) जो शीघ्र घटित होगी, आसन्न, सन्निकट *There was a feeling of impending disaster in the air.*

**impenetrable** /ɪmˈpenɪtrəbl इम्ˈपेनिट्रबल्/ *adj.* **1** impossible to enter or go through जिसमें प्रवेश करना या गुज़रना असंभव हो; अभेद्य *The jungle was impenetrable.* **2** impossible to understand जिसे समझना असंभव हो; अगम्य, दुर्बोध *an impenetrable mystery*

**imperative**[1] /ɪmˈperətɪv इम्ˈपेरटिव्/ *adj.* very important or urgent बहुत महत्त्वपूर्ण या आवश्यक; अत्यावश्यक *It's imperative that you see a doctor immediately.*

**the imperative**[2] /ɪmˈperətɪv इम्ˈपेरटिव्/ *noun* [C] (*grammar*) the form of the verb that is used for giving orders क्रिया का आज्ञार्थक रूप, आज्ञार्थक वृत्ति *In 'Shut the door!' the verb is in the imperative.*

**imperceptible** /ˌɪmpəˈseptəbl ˌइम्पˈसेप्टबल्/ *adj.* too small to be seen or noticed इतना छोटा कि दिखने में न आए या जिस पर ध्यान न जाए; अतिसूक्ष्म, अतींद्रिय *The difference between the original painting and the copy was almost imperceptible.* ✪ विलोम **perceptible** ▸ **imperceptibly** /-əbli -अब्लि/ *adv.* बिना दृष्टि या ध्यान में आए *Almost imperceptibly winter was turning into spring.*

**imperfect**[1] /ɪmˈpɜːfɪkt इम्ˈपफ़िक्ट्/ *adj.* with mistakes or faults त्रुटिपूर्ण, सदोष, अधूरा, अपूर्ण *This is a very imperfect system.* ✪ विलोम **perfect** ▸ **imperfection** /ˌɪmpəˈfekʃn ˌइम्पˈफ़ेक्शन्/ *noun* [C, U] अपूर्णता, अधूरापन *They learned to live with each other's imperfections.* ▸ **imperfectly** *adv.* अपूर्ण रूप से

**the imperfect**[2] /ɪmˈpɜːfɪkt इम्ˈपफ़िक्ट्/ *noun* [U] (*grammar*) used for expressing action in the past that is not completed अतीत में अपूर्ण रहे कार्य व्यापार को व्यक्त करने के लिए प्रयुक्त; अपूर्ण क्रिया *In 'I was having a bath', the verb is in the imperfect.* **NOTE** इस काल के लिए अधिक प्रचलित नाम **past continuous** या **past progressive** है।

**imperial** /ɪmˈpɪəriəl इम्ˈपिअरिअल्/ *adj.* **1** connected with an empire or its ruler किसी साम्राज्य या उसके शासक (सम्राट) से संबंधित, साम्राज्य-विषयक या सम्राट-विषयक, शाही, राजसी, साम्राज्यिक *the imperial palace* **2** belonging to a system of weighing and measuring that, in the past, was used for all goods in the UK and is still used for some इंग्लैंड (युनाइटेड किंगडम) में पहले प्रचलित और अंशतः अब भी प्रचलित, नाप तौल पद्धति से संबंधित ➪ **metric, inch, foot, yard, ounce, pound, pint** और **gallon** भी देखिए।

**imperialism** /ɪmˈpɪəriəlɪzəm इम्ˈपिअरिअलि ज़्म्/ *noun* [U] a political system in which a rich and powerful country controls other countries (**colonies**) which are not as rich and powerful as itself साम्राज्यवाद ▸ **imperialist** *noun* [C] साम्राज्यवादी

**impermeable** /ɪmˈpɜːmiəbl इम्ˈपमिअबल्/ *adj.* **impermeable (to sth)** not allowing a liquid or gas to pass through जिसमें से होकर द्रव या गैस नहीं जा सकते; अपारगम्य *impermeable rock* ○ *The container is impermeable to water vapour.* ✪ विलोम **permeable**

**impersonal** /ɪmˈpɜːsənl इम्ˈपसनल्/ *adj.* **1** not showing friendly human feelings; cold in feeling or atmosphere जिसमें मित्रवत मानवीय भावनाएँ नहीं; अनुभूति या वातारण की दृष्टि से भावनाशून्य, तटस्थ या उदासीन *The hotel room was very impersonal.* **2** not referring to any particular person जिसमें विशिष्ट व्यक्ति का निर्देश नहीं; निर्वैयक्तिक *Can we try to keep the discussion as impersonal as possible, please?*

**impersonate** /ɪmˈpɜːsəneɪt इम्ˈपसनेट्/ *verb* [T] to copy the behaviour and way of speaking of a person or to pretend to be a different person रूपारोप करना प्रायः छल करने या धोखा देने के लिए *a comedian who impersonates politicians* ▸ **impersonation** /ɪmˌpɜːsəˈneɪʃn इम्ˌपसˈनेशन्/ *noun* [C, U] पररूपधारण, छद्मव्यक्तिता ▸ **impersonator** *noun* [C] पररूपधारक, छद्मवेशी, बहुरूपिया

**impertinent** /ɪmˈpɜːtɪnənt इम्ˈपटिनन्ट्/ *adj.* (*formal*) not showing respect to sb who is older and more important; rude स्वयं से अधिक महत्त्वपूर्ण एवं ज्येष्ठ व्यक्ति का सम्मान न करते हुए ✪ विलोम **polite, respectful** ▸ **impertinence** *noun* [U] धृष्टता, गुस्ताख़ी ▸ **impertinently** *adv.* धृष्टतापूर्वक, गुस्ताख़ी से

**imperturbable** /ˌɪmpəˈtɜːbəbl ˌइम्पˈटबबल्/ *adj.* (*formal*) not easily worried by a difficult situation जो कठिन स्थिति में जल्दी विचलित नहीं होता; धीर, शांत, अविचलित

**impervious** /ɪmˈpɜːviəs इम्ˈपविअस्/ *adj.* **impervious (to sth)** **1** not affected or influenced by sth जिस पर किसी बात का असर नहीं होता या जो किसी के असर में नहीं आता; अप्रभावनीय *She was impervious to criticism.* **2** not allowing water, etc. to pass through अप्रवेश्य

**impetuous** /ɪmˈpetʃuəs इम्ˈपेचुअस्/ *adj.* acting or done quickly and without thinking जो बिना

विचारे करे या जल्दबाजी में किया जाए *Her impetuous behaviour often got her into trouble.* NOTE इस अर्थ में **impulsive** अधिक प्रचलित है। ▶ **impetuously** *adv.* बिना विचारे, जल्दबाज़ी में

**impetus** /ˈɪmpɪtəs ˈइम्पिटस्/ *noun* [U, *usually sing.*] **(an) impetus (for sth); (an) impetus (to do sth)** something that encourages sth else to happen ऐसी वस्तु जो दूसरी वस्तु की क्रियाशीलता को बढ़ावा दे; प्रेरणा, प्रोत्साहन *This scandal provided the main impetus for changes in the rules.* ○ *I need fresh impetus to start working on this essay again.*

**impinge** /ɪmˈpɪndʒ इम्ˈपिन्ज्/ *verb* [I] (*formal*) **impinge on/ upon sth** to have a noticeable effect on sth, especially a bad one किसी बात का अन्य बात पर सुस्पष्ट असर होना (विशेषतः प्रतिकूल प्रभाव) *I'm not going to let my job impinge on my home life.*

**implant** /ˈɪmplɑːnt ˈइम्प्लान्ट्/ *noun* [C] something that is put into a part of the body in a medical operation, often in order to make it bigger or a different shape शल्य-क्रिया द्वारा शरीर के किसी अंग में रोपी गई वस्तु (ताकि वह अंग अधिक बड़ा या आकृति में भिन्न हो सके)

**implausible** /ɪmˈplɔːzəbl इम्ˈप्लॉज़बल्/ *adj.* not easy to believe जिस पर जल्दी विश्वास न हो सके; अविश्वसनीय *an implausible excuse* ✪ विलोम **plausible**

**implement**[1] /ˈɪmplɪmənt ˈइम्प्लिमन्ट्/ *noun* [C] a tool or instrument (especially for work outdoors) औज़ार या उपकरण (विशेषतः खुले में या घर से बाहर काम के लिए) *farm implements* ➪ **tool** देखिए।

**implement**[2] /ˈɪmplɪment ˈइम्प्लिमन्ट्/ *verb* [T] to start using a plan, system, etc. योजना आदि पर अमल करना, उसे व्यवहार में लाना; कार्यान्वित करना *Some teachers are finding it difficult to implement the government's educational reforms.* ▶ **implementation** /ˌɪmplɪmenˈteɪʃn ˌइम्प्लिमेन्ˈटेशन्/ *noun* [U] क्रियान्वयन, कार्यान्वित

**implicate** /ˈɪmplɪkeɪt ˈइम्प्लिकेट्/ *verb* [T] **implicate sb (in sth)** to show that sb is involved in sth unpleasant, especially a crime यह दिखाना कि व्यक्ति कुकर्म में लिप्त है; लपेटे में लेना, अलिप्त करना *A well-known politician was implicated in the scandal.*

**implication** /ˌɪmplɪˈkeɪʃn ˌइम्प्लिˈकेश्न्/ *noun* **1** [C, *usually pl.*] संलिप्तता **implications (for/of sth)** the effect that sth will have on sth else in the future एक बात का दूसरे पर भविष्य में पड़ने वाला प्रभाव *The new law will **have** serious **implications** for our work.* **2** [C, U] something that is suggested or said indirectly जिसका इशारा किया जाए या जिसे परोक्ष रूप से कहा जाए; व्यंजना, आशय *The implication of what she said was that we had made a bad mistake.* ➪ **imply** verb देखिए। **3** [U] **implication (in sth)** the fact of being involved, or of involving sb, in sth unpleasant, especially a crime किसी कुकर्म में लिप्त होने या अन्य व्यक्ति को लपेटने का काम; फँसाव ➪ **implicate** verb देखिए।

**implicit** /ɪmˈplɪsɪt इम्ˈप्लिसिट्/ *adj.* **1** not expressed in a direct way but understood by the people involved जो स्पष्ट रूप से नहीं कहा गया परंतु संबंधित लोगों ने समझ लिया; अंतर्निहित, विवक्षित *We had an implicit agreement that we would support each other.* ➪ **explicit** देखिए। **2** complete; total पूर्ण; समग्र *I have implicit faith in your ability to do the job.* ▶ **implicitly** *adv.* परोक्ष रूप से, अव्यक्त रूप से

**implore** /ɪmˈplɔː(r) इम्ˈप्लॉ(र्)/ *verb* [T] (*formal*) to ask sb with great emotion to do sth, because you are in a very serious situation (कठिनाई में फँसे व्यक्ति की) अन्य व्यक्ति से याचना करना, अनुनय-विनय करना *She implored him not to leave her alone.* ✪ पर्याय **beg**

**imply** /ɪmˈplaɪ इम्ˈप्लाइ/ *verb* [T] (*pres. part.* **implying**; *3rd person sing. pres.* **implies**; *pt, pp* **implied**) to suggest sth in an indirect way or without actually saying it परोक्ष रूप से अथवा बिना कुछ कहे किसी बात का संकेत करना *He didn't say so—but he implied that I was lying.* ➪ **implication** noun देखिए।

**impolite** /ˌɪmpəˈlaɪt ˌइम्पˈलाइट्/ *adj.* rude अभद्र, अशिष्ट *I think it was impolite of him to ask you to leave.* ✪ विलोम **polite** ▶ **impolitely** *adv.* अभद्रता से

**import**[1] /ˈɪmpɔːt ˈइम्पॉट्/ *noun* **1** [C, *usually pl.*] a product or service that is brought into one country from another किसी देश में दूसरे देश से लाई गई वस्तु या सेवा; आयातित माल या सेवा *What are your country's major imports?* ✪ विलोम **export** **2** [U] (*also* **importation**) the act of bringing goods or services into a country किसी देश में अन्य देश से सामान या सेवाएँ लाने की क्रिया; आयात *new controls on the import of certain goods from abroad*

**import**[2] /ɪmˈpɔːt इम्ˈपॉट्/ *verb* [I, T] **1 import sth (from)** to buy goods, etc. from a foreign country and bring them into your own country अन्य देश से सामान आदि ख़रीदकर अपने देश में लाना; आयात करना *Britain imports wine from Spain.* ○ (*figurative*) *We need to import some extra help from somewhere.* ✪ विलोम **export** **2** (*computing*) to move information onto a program from another program सूचना राशि को एक प्रोग्राम से दूसरे में ले जाना ▶ **importer** आयातक ✪ विलोम **exporter**

**nportance** /ɪmˈpɔːtns इम्ˈपॉटन्स्/ *noun* [U] the quality of being important महत्त्व *The decision was* ***of*** *great* ***importance*** *to the future of the business.*

**nportant** /ɪmˈpɔːtnt इम्ˈपॉटन्ट्/ *adj.* **1 important (to sb); important (for sb/sth) (to do sth); important that...** having great value or influence; very necessary महत्त्वपूर्ण; अत्यावश्यक *an important meeting/decision/factor* ○ *It was important to me that you were there.* **2** (used about a person) having great influence or authority (व्यक्ति) प्रभावशाली या अधिकार संपन्न *He was one of the most important writers of his time.* ▶ **importantly** *adv.* उल्लेखनीय रूप से

**nportation** /ˌɪmpɔːˈteɪʃn ˌइम्पॉˈटेश्न् = **import[1] 2**

**npose** /ɪmˈpəʊz इम्ˈपोज़्/ *verb* **1** [T] **impose sth (on/upon sb/sth)** to make a law, rule, opinion, etc. be accepted by using your power or authority अपनी शक्ति या अधिकार के बल पर क़ानून, नियम आदि को मनवाना, थोपना; आरोपित करना **2** [I] **impose (on/upon sb/sth)** to ask or expect sb to do sth that may cause extra work or trouble किसी पर काम या परेशानी का अतिरिक्त बोझ लादना *I hate to impose on you, but can you lend me some money?* ▶ **imposition** /ˌɪmpəˈzɪʃn इम्पˈज़िशन्/ *noun* [U, C] आरोपण, अधिरोपण *the imposition of military rule*

**nposing** /ɪmˈpəʊzɪŋ इम्ˈपोजिङ्/ *adj.* big and important; impressive बड़ा और महत्त्वपूर्ण; प्रभावशाली *They lived in a large, imposing house near the park.*

**npossible** /ɪmˈpɒsəbl इम्ˈपॉसबल्/ *adj.* **1** not able to be done or to happen असंभव *I find it almost impossible to get up in the morning!* ○ *That's impossible* (= I don't believe it)*!* **2** very difficult to deal with or control जिससे निपटना या नियंत्रित करना बहुत कठिन हो; बेक़ाबू, असाध्य *This is an impossible situation!* ○ *He's always been an impossible child.* ✪ विलोम **possible** ▶ **the impossible** *noun* [*sing.*] असंभव काम *Don't attempt the impossible!* ▶ **impossibility** /ɪmˌpɒsəˈbɪləti इम्ˌपॉसˈबिलटि/ *noun* [C, U] (*pl.* **impossibilities**) असंभवता, अशक्यता *What you are suggesting is a complete impossibility!*

**npossibly** /ɪmˈpɒsəbli इम्ˈपॉसब्लि/ *adv.* extremely अत्यधिक *impossibly complicated*

**npostor** /ɪmˈpɒstə(r) इम्ˈपॉस्टर्/ *noun* [C] a person who pretends to be sb else in order to trick other people छद्मवेशी, पररूपधारक, बहुरूपिया

**impotent** /ˈɪmpətənt ˈइम्पटन्ट्/ *adj.* **1** without enough power to influence a situation or to change things शक्तिहीन, प्रभावहीन, जिसके पास स्थिति को प्रभावित करने या बदलने की पर्याप्त क्षमता न हो **2** (used about men) not capable of having sex (पुरुष) यौनक्रिया में अक्षम, नपुंसक, नामर्द ▶ **impotence** *noun* [U] नपुंसकता, शक्तिहीनता

**impoverish** /ɪmˈpɒvərɪʃ इम्ˈपॉवरिश्/ *verb* [T] (*formal*) to make sb/sth poor or lower in quality व्यक्ति को दरिद्र कर देना या वस्तु की गुणवत्ता गिरा देना ✪ विलोम **enrich**

**impractical** /ɪmˈpræktɪkl इम्ˈप्रैक्टिकल्/ *adj.* **1** not sensible or realistic अव्यावहारिक *It would be impractical to take our bikes on the train.* **2** (used about a person) not good at doing ordinary things that involve using your hands; not good at organizing or planning things (व्यक्ति) जो हाथ से करने के कामों में कुशल नहीं; जिसमें कामों को संगठित करने और योजना बनाने की क्षमता नहीं; अव्यावहारशील ✪ विलोम **practical**

**imprecise** /ˌɪmprɪˈsaɪs ˌइम्प्रिˈसाइस्/ *adj.* not clear or exact जो स्पष्ट या सटीक नहीं *imprecise instructions* ✪ विलोम **precise**

**impress** /ɪmˈpres इम्ˈप्रेस्/ *verb* [T] **1 impress sb (with sth); impress sb that** to make sb feel admiration and respect किसी को प्रशंसा और आदर का अनुभव कराना, प्रभावित करना, मन पर गहरी छाप छोड़ना *She's always trying to impress people with her new clothes.* ○ *It impressed me that he understood immediately what I meant.* **2** (*formal*) **impress sth on/upon sb** to make the importance of sth very clear to sb किसी वस्तु के महत्त्व को किसी के सामने स्पष्टतया बताना, कोई बात किसी के मन में अच्छी तरह बैठाना *I wish you could impress on Jeevan that he must pass these exams.*

**impression** /ɪmˈpreʃn इम्ˈप्रेशन्/ *noun* [C] **1** an idea, a feeling or an opinion that you get about sb/sth किसी व्यक्ति या वस्तु के विषय में धारणा, भावना या राय, प्रभाव, छाप *I'm not sure but* ***I have/get the impression*** *that Tina's rather unhappy.* ○ *I was* ***under the impression*** (= I believed, but I was wrong) *that you were married.* **2** the effect that a person or thing produces on sb else किसी व्यक्ति या वस्तु का दूसरे पर पड़ा प्रभाव *She* ***gives the impression*** *of being older than she really is.* ○ *Do you think I* ***made a good impression on*** *your parents?* **3** an amusing copy of the way a person acts or speaks किसी के हाव-भाव की विनोदपूर्ण नक़ल *My brother can do a good impression of the Prime Minister.* ✪ पर्याय **imitation** **4** a mark that is left when an object has been pressed hard into a surface किसी वस्तु को किसी सतह पर ज़ोर लगाकर दबाने से बना निशान, छाप; निशानी

**impressionable** /ɪmˈpreʃənəbl इम्ˈप्रेशनबल्/ *adj.* easy to influence जो जल्दी किसी के प्रभाव में आ जाए; आशुप्रभावित, अति संवेदनशील *Sixteen is a very impressionable age.*

**impressive** /ɪmˈpresɪv इम्ˈप्रेसिव्/ *adj.* causing a feeling of admiration and respect because of the importance, size, quality, etc. of sth किसी वस्तु के महत्त्व, आकार, गुणवत्ता के कारण उसके प्रति प्रशंसा और सम्मान से युक्त; प्रभावशाली, असरदार *an impressive building/speech* ○ *The way he handled the situation was most impressive.*

**imprint** /ɪmˈprɪnt इम्ˈप्रिन्ट्/ *noun* [C] a mark made by pressing an object on a surface किसी वस्तु को किसी सतह पर दबाने से बना निशान, छाप, मुहर, छापा *the imprint of a foot in the sand*

**imprison** /ɪmˈprɪzn इम्ˈप्रिज़न्/ *verb* [T] (*usually passive*) to put or keep in prison जेल में बंद करना या रखना *He was imprisoned for armed robbery.* ✪ पर्याय **incarcerate** इस अर्थ में अधिक औपचारिक शब्द है। ▶ **imprisonment** *noun* [U] क़ैद, कारावास *She was sentenced to five years' imprisonment.*

**improbable** /ɪmˈprɒbəbl इम्ˈप्रॉबबल्/ *adj.* not likely to be true or to happen जिसके सच निकलने या घटित होने की संभावना नहीं; असंभाव्य *an improbable explanation* ○ *It is **highly improbable** that she will arrive tonight.* ✪ पर्याय **unlikely** ✪ विलोम **probable** ▶ **improbability** /ɪmˌprɒbəˈbɪləti इम्ˌप्रॉबˈबिलटि/ *noun* [U] असंभाव्यता ▶ **improbably** /-əbli -अब्लि/ *adv.* असंभाव्य रूप से

**impromptu** /ɪmˈprɒmptjuː इम्ˈप्रॉम्प्ट्यू/ *adj.* (done) without being prepared or organized बिना तैयारी या व्यवस्था के (किया गया), आशु या तत्काल (आयोजित) *an impromptu party*

**improper** /ɪmˈprɒpə(r) इम्ˈप्रॉप(र्)/ *adj.* **1** illegal or dishonest ग़ैर-क़ानूनी या झूठा *It seems that she had been involved in improper business deals.* **2** not suitable for the situation; rude in a sexual way स्थिति के अनुपयुक्त; स्त्री-पुरुष संबंध की दृष्टि से अनुचित, अशोभनीय, अश्लील *He lost his job for making improper suggestions to several of the women.* ✪ विलोम **proper** ▶ **improperly** *adv.* अनुचित रूप से ✪ विलोम **properly**

**impropriety** /ˌɪmprəˈpraɪəti ˌइम्प्रˈप्राइअटि/ *noun* [U, C] (*pl.* **improprieties**) (*formal*) behaviour or actions that are morally wrong or not appropriate नैतिक दृष्टि से अनुचित या अनुपयुक्त आचरण या कार्य, अनैचित्य, अनुपयुक्तता *She was unaware of the impropriety of her remark.*

**improve** /ɪmˈpruːv इम्ˈप्रूव्/ *verb* [I, T] to become or to make sth better किसी स्थिति का बेहतर होना या उसे बेहतर बनाना, सुधरना या सुधारना *I hope the weather will improve later on.* ○ *Your vocabulary is excellent but you could improve your pronunciation.*

PHR V **improve on/upon sth** to produce sth that is better than sth else किसी वस्तु या स्थिति से बेहतर वस्तु या स्थिति को अंजाम देना *Nobody will be able to improve on that score* (= nobody will be able to make a higher score).

**improvement** /ɪmˈpruːvmənt इम्ˈप्रूवमन्ट्/ *noun* [C, U] **(an) improvement (on/in sth)** (a) change which makes the quality or condition of sb/sth better व्यक्ति या वस्तु की गुणवत्ता या दशा में बेहतरी के लिए परिवर्तन; सुधार *Your written work is in need of some improvement.*

> **NOTE** किसी स्थिति के पहले से बेहतर हो जाने की बात करनी हो तो **improvement in** का प्रयोग करते हैं—*There's been a considerable improvement in your mother's condition.* जब दो स्थितियों में से दूसरी को पहली से बेहतर बताना हो तो **improvement on** का प्रयोग होता है—*These marks are an improvement on your previous ones.*

**improvise** /ˈɪmprəvaɪz ˈइम्प्रवाइज़्/ *verb* [I, T] **1** to make, do, or manage sth without preparation, using what you have जो पास है उसी से तत्काल कुछ व्यवस्था करना *If you're short of teachers today you'll just have to improvise* (= manage somehow with the people that you've got). **2** to play music, speak or act using your imagination instead of written or remembered material (बिना पूर्व तैयारी के) अपनी कल्पना का प्रयोग करते हुए संगीत-रचना, भाषण या अभिनय करना *It was obvious that the actor had forgotten his lines and was trying to improvise.* ▶ **improvisation** /ˌɪmprəvaɪˈzeɪʃn ˌइम्प्रवाइˈज़ेशन्/ *noun* [C, U] कामचलाऊ व्यवस्था; तत्काल रचित कृति

**impudent** /ˈɪmpjədənt ˈइम्प्यडन्ट्/ *adj.* (*formal*) very rude; lacking respect and not polite बहुत अशिष्ट; आदरभाव और नम्रता से रहित, निर्लज्ज ✪ पर्याय **cheeky** इस अर्थ में अधिक अनौपचारिक शब्द है। ▶ **impudently** *adv.* निर्लज्ज भाव से, अशिष्टतापूर्वक ▶ **impudence** *noun* [U] निर्लज्जता, अशिष्टता

**impulse** /ˈɪmpʌls ˈइम्पल्स्/ *noun* [C] **1** [*usually sing.*] **an impulse (to do sth)** a sudden desire to do sth without thinking about the results परिणाम का विचार किए बिना कुछ करने की सहसा उत्पन्न इच्छा, आवेग *She felt a terrible impulse to rush out*

*the house and never come back.* **2** (*technical*) a force or movement of energy that causes a reaction प्रतिक्रिया उत्पन्न करने वाली शक्ति या ऊर्जा की क्रियाशीलता, क्रियाशील ऊर्जा *nerve/electrical impulses*
IDM **on (an) impulse** without thinking or planning and not considering the results सोच-विचार या योजना और परिणाम की चिंता से रहित

**impulsive** /ɪmˈpʌlsɪv इम्ˈपल्सिव़्/ *adj.* likely to act suddenly and without thinking; done without careful thought बिना विचार के सहसा काम करने वाला, आवेगशील; बिना सोच-विचार के किया हुआ, आवेगपूर्ण *an impulsive character* ▶ **impulsively** *adv.* आवेगपूर्वक ▶ **impulsiveness** *noun* [U] आवेगात्मकता

**impure** /ɪmˈpjʊə(r) इम्ˈप्युअ(र्)/ *adj.* **1** not pure or clean; consisting of more than one substance mixed together (and therefore not of good quality) जो शुद्ध या साफ़ न हो, अशुद्ध; मिलावट वाला (इसलिए घटिया), मिलावटी *impure metals* **2** (*old-fashioned*) (used about thoughts and actions connected with sex) not moral; bad (कामभावना विषयक विचार और क्रियाएँ) अनैतिक; दुष्ट ✪ विलोम **pure**

**impurity** /ɪmˈpjʊərəti इम्ˈप्युअरटि/ *noun* (*pl.* **impurities**) **1** [C, *usually pl.*] a substance that is present in small amounts in another substance, making it dirty or of poor quality एक वस्तु में थोड़ी मात्रा में मौजूद अन्य वस्तु (जो उसे गंदा और घटिया बना देती है), अशुद्धता, मिलावट **2** [U] (*old-fashioned*) the state of being morally bad अनैतिकता ➪ **purity** देखिए।

**in**[1] /ɪn इन्/ *adv., prep.*

NOTE संज्ञा वाले विशिष्ट प्रयोगों (जैसे **in time**) के लिए उन संज्ञाओं की प्रविष्टियाँ देखिए। क्रिया वाले विशिष्ट प्रयोगों (जैसे **give in**) के लिए उन क्रियाओं की प्रविष्टियाँ देखिए।

**1** (used to show place) inside or to a position inside a particular area or object (पूर्वसर्ग) (स्थान का निर्देश) अंदर या किसी क्षेत्र या वस्तु के भीतर कोई स्थिति में, के अंदर *He lay **in bed**.* ○ *She put the keys in her pocket.* ○ *His wife's **in hospital**.* ○ *When does the train get in* (= to the station)? **2** at home or at work घर पर या काम पर *She won't **be in** till late today.* **3** (showing time) during a period of time (समय का निर्देश) एक समयावधि के दौरान, में *My birthday is in August.* ○ *You could walk there in about an hour* (= it would take that long to walk there). **4** (showing time) after a period of time (समय का निर्देश) एक समयावधि के बाद, में *I'll be finished in ten minutes.* **5** wearing sth कुछ पहने हुए *a woman in a yellow dress* **6** showing the condition or state of sb/sth व्यक्ति या वस्तु की दशा या स्थिति व्यक्त करने के लिए प्रयुक्त *My father is in poor health.* ○ *This room is **in a mess**!* **7** showing sb's job or the activity sb is involved in नौकरी या काम (जिसमें कोई लगा है) का निर्देश करने के लिए प्रयुक्त *He's got a good job in advertising.* ○ *All her family are in politics* (= they are politicians). ○ *He's in the army.* **8** contained in; forming the whole or part of sth में समाविष्ट; किसी पूर्ण वस्तु का अंग या पूर्ण वस्तु *There are 31 days in January.* ○ *What's in this parcel?* **9** used for saying how things are arranged यह बताने के लिए प्रयुक्त कि चीज़ें कैसे लगाई गई हैं या लगी हैं *We sat in a circle.* ○ *She had her hair in plaits.* **10** used for saying how sth is written or expressed यह बताने के लिए कि लेखन किस उपकरण (जैसे क़लम, पेंसिल) से लिखा गया है या किस भाषा (जैसे हिंदी, अंग्रेज़ी) में लिखा गया है *Please write in pen.* ○ *They were talking **in Italian/French/Polish**.* **11** used with feelings भावनाओं को व्यक्त करने के लिए प्रयुक्त *I watched **in horror** as the plane crashed to the ground.* ○ *He was **in** such **a rage** I didn't dare to speak to him.* **12** used for giving the rate of sth and for talking about numbers किसी वस्तु की दर बताने या संख्या विषयक चर्चा के लिए प्रयुक्त ***One** family **in ten** owns a TV.* **13** used for sth received by sb official पावती की तारीख़ का निर्देश करने के लिए प्रयुक्त *Entries should **be in** by 20 March.* ○ *All applications must be in by Friday.* **14** (used about the sea) at the highest point, when the water is closest to the land (समुद्र) ज्वार का निर्देश करने के लिए प्रयुक्त *The tide's coming in.*

IDM **be in for it/sth** to be going to experience sth unpleasant अप्रिय अनुभव के लिए तैयार *He'll be in for a shock when he gets the bill.* ○ *You'll be in for it when Mum sees what you've done.*

**be/get in on sth** to be included or involved in sth किसी बात में समाविष्ट या उससे लिप्त या उसका अंग बना *I'd like to be in on the new project.*

**have (got) it in for sb** (*informal*) to cause trouble for sb because you dislike him/her नापसंदगी के कारण किसी के लिए मुसीबत खड़ी करना *The boss has had it in for me ever since I asked to be considered for the new post.*

**in**[2] /ɪn इन्/ *noun*

IDM **the ins and outs (of sth)** the details and difficulties (involved in sth) किसी बात के ब्योरे और संभावित कठिनाइयाँ *Will somebody explain the ins and outs of the situation to me?*

**in**[3] /ɪn इन्/ *adj.* (*informal*) fashionable at the moment निर्दिष्ट समय में फ़ैशनेबल *the in place to go* ○ *The colour red is very in this season.*

**in.** *abbr.* inch(es) इंच

**in-** /ɪn इन्/ *prefix* **1** (*also* **il-** /ɪl इल्/; **im-** /ɪm इम्/; **ir-** /ɪr इर्/) (*in adjectives, adverbs and nouns*) not; the opposite of निषेध के अर्थ में प्रयुक्त; विलोम के अर्थ में प्रयुक्त (हिंदी में अ-, अन-, से व्यक्त, जैसे अनैतिक, अनावश्यक) *infinite* ○ *illogical* ○ *immorally* ○ *irrelevance* **2** (*also* **im-** /ɪm इम्/) (*in verbs*) to put into the condition mentioned (शब्द से) निर्दिष्ट दशा में डालना *inflame* ○ *imperil*

**inability** /ˌɪnəˈbɪləti, इनˈबिलटि/ *noun* [*sing.*] **inability (to do sth)** lack of ability, power or skill क्षमता, शक्ति या कौशल की न्यूनता या अभाव *He has a complete inability to listen to other people's opinions.* ➪ **unable** adjective देखिए।

**inaccessible** /ˌɪnækˈsesəbl, इनैक्ˈसेसबल्/ *adj.* very difficult or impossible to reach or contact जहाँ पहुँचना या जिससे संपर्क करना बहुत कठिन या असंभव हो, पहुँच से परे; अगम्य, अनभिगम्य *That beach is inaccessible by car.* ✪ विलोम **accessible** ▶ **inaccessibility** /ˌɪnæksesəˈbɪləti ˌइनैक्सेसˈबिलटि/ *noun* [U] अगम्यता

**inaccurate** /ɪnˈækjərət इन्ˈऐक्यरट्/ *adj.* not correct or accurate; with mistakes जो सही या वास्तविक या यथार्थ न हो; त्रुटियुक्त a*n inaccurate report/description/statement* ✪ विलोम **accurate** ▶ **inaccuracy** /ɪnˈækjərəsi इन्ˈऐक्यरसि/ *noun* [C, U] (*pl.* **inaccuracies**) [C] अशुद्धि, त्रुटि *There are always some inaccuracies in newspaper reports.* ✪ विलोम **accuracy** ▶ **inaccurately** *adv.* ग़लत तरीक़े से

**inaction** /ɪnˈækʃn इन्ˈऐक्शन्/ *noun* [U] doing nothing; lack of action कुछ न करना; निष्क्रियता *The crisis was blamed on the government's earlier inaction.* ✪ विलोम **action**

**inactive** /ɪnˈæktɪv इन्ˈऐक्टिव़्/ *adj.* doing nothing; not active कुछ न करने वाला; निष्क्रिय *The virus remains inactive in the body.* ✪ विलोम **active** ▶ **inactivity** /ˌɪnækˈtɪvəti, इन्ऐक्ˈटिव़टि/ *noun* [U] निष्क्रियता ✪ विलोम **activity**

**inadequate** /ɪnˈædɪkwət इन्ˈऐडिक्वट्/ *adj.* **1 inadequate (for sth/to do sth)** not enough; not good enough अपर्याप्त, नाकाफ़ी; अयोग्य *the problem of inadequate housing* **2** (used about a person) not able to deal with a problem or situation; not confident (व्यक्ति) जो समस्या या स्थिति को निबटा न सके; आत्मविश्वासहीन *There was so much to learn in the new job that for a while I felt totally inadequate.* ✪ विलोम **adequate** ▶ **inadequately** *adv.* अपर्याप्त रीति से, बिना आत्मविश्वास के ▶ **inadequacy** /ɪnˈædɪkwəsi इन्ˈऐडिक्वसि/ *noun* [C, U] (*pl.* **inadequacies**) अपर्याप्तता, आत्मविश्वासहीनता *his inadequacy as a parent*

**inadmissible** /ˌɪnədˈmɪsəbl, इनड्ˈमिसबल्/ *adj.* (*formal*) that cannot be allowed or accepted, especially in a court of law आमान्य, अस्वीकार्य (विशेषतः न्यायालय में) *inadmissible evidence*

**inadvertent** /ˌɪnədˈvɜːtənt, इनड्ˈव़टन्ट्/ *adj.* (used about actions) done without thinking, not on purpose (कार्य) बिना विचारे, बिना प्रयोजन, किया हुआ; अनजाने में किया हुआ; अनवधानी ✪ विलोम **intentional** या **deliberate** ▶ **inadvertently** *adv.* अनजाने में *She had inadvertently left the letter where he could find it.*

**inadvisable** /ˌɪnədˈvaɪzəbl, इनड्ˈव़ाइज़बल्/ *adj.* not sensible; not showing good judgement जिसमें समझदारी न हो, मूर्खतापूर्ण; जिससे अच्छी निर्णय-क्षमता प्रकट न हो; विवेकहीन *It is inadvisable to go swimming when you have a cold.* ✪ विलोम **advisable**

**inalienable** /ɪnˈeɪliənəbl इन्ˈएलिअनबल्/ *adj.* (*formal*) that cannot be taken away from you जो किसी से लिया न जा सके, जिसे किसी से अलग न किया जा सके; अहरणीय, अनन्य

**inane** /ɪˈneɪn इˈनेन्/ *adj.* without any meaning; silly निरर्थक, बेमतलब; बेवकूफ़ीभरा *an inane remark* ▶ **inanely** *adv.* बेवकूफ़ी से

**inanimate** /ɪnˈænɪmət इन्ˈऐनिमट्/ *adj.* not alive in the way that people, animals and plants are जो मनुष्यों, पशुओं और पौधों के समान चेतन न हो; जड़ निर्जीव *A rock is an inanimate object.* ✪ विलोम **animate**

**inappropriate** /ˌɪnəˈprəʊpriət ˌइनˈप्रोप्रिअट्/ *adj.* not suitable अनुपयुक्त *Isn't that dress rather inappropriate for the occasion?* ✪ विलोम **appropriate**

**inarticulate** /ˌɪnɑːˈtɪkjələt ˌइनाˈटिक्यलट्/ *adj.* **1** (used about a person) not able to express ideas and feelings clearly (व्यक्ति) जो अपने विचारों और भावों को स्पष्टता से व्यक्त न कर सके, अवाक्पटु **2** (used about speech) not clear or well expressed (अभिव्यक्ति) अस्पष्ट या जो सुव्यक्त न हो ✪ विलोम **articulate** ▶ **inarticulately** *adv.* अस्पष्टता से

**inasmuch as** /ˌɪnəzˈmʌtʃ əz, इनज़्ˈमच् अज़्/ *conj.* (*formal*) because of the fact that जहाँ तक कि; क्योंकि, चूँकि *We felt sorry for the boys inasmuch as they had not realized that what they were doing was wrong.*

**inattention** /ˌɪnəˈtenʃn, इनˈटेन्शन्/ *noun* [U] lack of attention असावधानी, ध्यान में कमी, अनवधानता *a moment of inattention* ✪ विलोम **attention**

**inattentive** /ˌɪnəˈtentɪv, इनˈटेन्टिव़्/ *adj.* not paying attention असावधान, अन्यमनस्क *One inattentive student can disturb the whole class.* ✪ विलोम **attentive**

**inaudible** /ɪnˈɔːdəbl इन्ˈऑडबल्/ *adj.* not loud enough to be heard जो जल्दी या आसानी से सुनाई न पड़े, कष्टश्राव्य; अश्रव्य ✪ विलोम **audible** ▶ **inaudibly** /-bli -बलि/ *adv.* अश्रव्यतापूर्वक, अश्रव्य रूप से

**inaugurate** /ɪˈnɔːɡjəreɪt इˈनॉग्यरेट्/ *verb* [T] **1** to introduce a new official, leader, etc. at a special formal ceremony विशेष औपचारिक समारोह में किसी नए अफ़सर या नेता आदि का परिचय देना *He will be inaugurated as President next month.* **2** to start, introduce or open sth new (often at a special formal ceremony) कोई नया काम आरंभ करना, सबको उसका परिचय देना (प्रायः विशेष औपचारिक समारोह में) ▶ **inaugural** /ɪˈnɔːɡjərəl इˈनॉग्यरल्/ *adj.* (*only before a noun*) उद्घाटन-संबंधी *the President's inaugural speech* ▶ **inauguration** /ɪˌnɔːɡjəˈreɪʃn इˌनॉग्यˈरेश्न्/ *noun* [C, U] उद्घाटन, शुभारंभ, आग़ाज़

**inauspicious** /ˌɪnɔːˈspɪʃəs ˌइनॉˈस्पिशस्/ *adj.* (*formal*) showing signs that the future will not be good or successful; unlucky जिसमें भविष्य के अनुकूल या सफल न होने के संकेत हों; अशुभ, अमांगलिक *an inauspicious start* ✪ विलोम **auspicious**

**inborn** /ˌɪnˈbɔːn ˌइन्ˈबॉन्/ *adj.* an inborn quality is one that you are born with जन्मजात, नैसर्गिक ✪ पर्याय **innate**

**inbred** /ˌɪnˈbred ˌइन्ˈब्रेड्/ *adj.* produced by breeding among closely related members of a group of animals, people or plants निकट-संबंधित पशुओं, मनुष्यों या पौधों के बीच प्रजनन-क्रिया से उत्पन्न; अंतःप्रजात

**inbreeding** /ˈɪnbriːdɪŋ ˈइन्ब्रीडिङ्/ *noun* [U] breeding between closely related people or animals निकट-संबंधित मनुष्यों या पशुओं के बीच प्रजनन; अंतःप्रजनन

**Inc.** (*also* **inc**) /ɪŋk इङ्क्/ *abbr.* (*AmE*) Incorporated समाविष्ट *Mumbai Drugstores Inc.*

**incalculable** /ɪnˈkælkjələbl इन्ˈकैल्क्यलबल्/ *adj.* very great; too great to calculate अत्यधिक; अनगिनत, बेहिसाब, अगणनीय an incalculable risk

**incapable** /ɪnˈkeɪpəbl इन्ˈकेपबल्/ *adj.* **1 incapable of sth/doing sth** not able to do sth कुछ करने में अक्षम; असमर्थ *She is incapable of hardwork/working hard.* ○ *He's quite incapable of unkindness* (= too nice to be unkind). **2** not able to do, manage or organize anything well किसी काम को अच्छी तरह से करने में अक्षम; अयोग्य *As a doctor, she's totally incapable.* ✪ विलोम **capable**

**incapacitate** /ˌɪnkəˈpæsɪteɪt ˌइन्कˈपैसिटेट्/ *verb* [T] to make sb unable to do sth किसी को कोई काम करने में अक्षम बना देना; पंगु बना देना

**incarcerate** /ɪnˈkɑːsəreɪt इन्ˈकासरेट्/ *verb* [T] (*formal*) (*usually passive*) to put sb in prison or in another place from which he/she cannot escape क़ारागार में रखना, क़ैद करना ✪ पर्याय **imprison** ▶ **incarceration** /ɪnˌkɑːsəˈreɪʃn इन्ˌकासˈरेशन्/ *noun* [U] बंदीकरण, कैद

**incarnation** /ˌɪnkɑːˈneɪʃn ˌइन्काˈनेश्न्/ *noun* [C] **1** a period of life on earth in a particular form पृथ्वी पर एक विशिष्ट रूप में देह-धारण; अवतरण *He believed he was a prince in a previous incarnation.* **2 the incarnation of sth** (a person that is) a perfect example of a particular quality (व्यक्ति) विशिष्ट गुण का सर्वांगपूर्ण उदाहरण, साक्षात मूर्ति *She is the incarnation of goodness.* ➪ **reincarnation** देखिए।

**incendiary** /ɪnˈsendiəri इन्ˈसेन्डिअरि/ *adj.* that causes a fire आग लगाने वाला; दाहक *an incendiary bomb/device*

**incense**[1] /ˈɪnsens ˈइन्सेन्स्/ *noun* [U] a substance that produces a sweet smell when burnt, used especially in religious ceremonies (विशेषतः धार्मिक कार्यक्रमों में प्रयुक्त), लोबान, धूप

**incense**[2] /ɪnˈsens इन्ˈसेन्स्/ *verb* [T] (*usually passive*) to make sb very angry अत्यधिक क्रोधित करना, भड़काना *The decision of the management not to give the bonus this year incensed the employees.*

**incensed** /ɪnˈsenst इन्ˈसेन्स्ट्/ *adj.* **incensed (by/at sth)** very angry अतिक्रुद्ध ✪ पर्याय **furious**

**incentive** /ɪnˈsentɪv इन्ˈसेन्टिव्/ *noun* [C, U] **(an) incentive (for/to sb/sth) (to do sth)** something that encourages you (to do sth) प्रोत्साहन देने वाली वस्तु; प्रेरक *There's no incentive for young people to do well at school because there aren't any jobs when they leave.*

**inception** /ɪnˈsepʃn इन्ˈसेप्शन्/ *noun* [*sing.*] (*formal*) the establishment of an organization, institution, etc. (किसी संगठन या संस्थान आदि का) संस्थापन *The business has grown rapidly since its inception in 2000.*

**incessant** /ɪnˈsesnt इन्ˈसेसन्ट्/ *adj.* never stopping (and usually annoying) अविराम, निरंतर (और प्रायः खीज पैदा करने वाला) *incessant rain/noise/chatter* ➪ **continual** देखिए। ▶ **incessantly** *adv.* अविराम, निरंतर, लगातार

**incest** /ˈɪnsest ˈइनसेस्ट्/ *noun* [U] illegal sex between members of the same family, for example brother and sister एक ही परिवार के सदस्यों (जैसे भाई और बहिन) के बीच ग़ैर-क़ानूनी यौन-संबंध; कौटुंबिक व्यभिचार

**incestuous** /ɪnˈsestjuəs इन्ˈसेस्ट्युअस्/ *adj.* **1** involving illegal sex between members of the same family कौटुंबिक व्यभिचार-संबंधी; व्यभिचारपूर्ण *an incestuous relationship* **2** (used about a group of people and their relationships with each other) too close; not open to anyone outside the group (एक जनसमूह के सदस्यों के पारस्परिक संबंध) अति निकट; बाहर के लोगों का शामिल होना वर्जित *Life in a small community can be very incestuous.*

**inch**[1] /ɪntʃ इन्च्/ *noun* [C] (*abbr.* **in.**) a measure of length; 2.54 centimetres. There are 12 inches in a foot लंबाई की एक माप इंच; 2.54 से. मी. (एक फ़ुट में 12 इंच होते हैं) *He's 5 foot 10 inches tall.* ○ *Three inches of rain fell last night.*

**inch**[2] /ɪntʃ इन्च्/ *verb* [I, T] **inch forward, past, through, etc.** to move slowly and carefully in the direction mentioned निर्दिष्ट दिशा में मंद गति से और सावधानी के साथ आगे बढ़ना; सरकना *He inched (his way) forward along the cliff edge.*

**incidence** /ˈɪnsɪdəns ˈइन्सिडन्स्/ *noun* **1** [*sing.*] (*formal*) **an incidence of sth** the number of times sth (usually sth unpleasant) happens; the rate of sth कोई बात (प्रायः अप्रिय) जितनी बार घटित हो वह संख्या; किसी (प्रायः अप्रिय) घटना घटित होने की दर; किसी बात की दर *a high incidence of crime/disease/unemployment* **2** [U] (*technical*) the way in which a ray of light meets a surface सतह पर रोशनी पड़ने का तरीक़ा; आपतन, संपात *the angle of incidence* ▶ **incident** *adj.* आपतित *the incident ray* (= the one that meets a surface) ○ *the incident angle* (= at which a ray of light meets a surface) ➪ **reflection** पर चित्र देखिए।

**incident** /ˈɪnsɪdənt ˈइन्सिडन्ट्/ *noun* [C] (*formal*) something that happens (especially sth unusual or unpleasant) घटना (विशेषतः असामान्य या अप्रिय) *There were a number of incidents after the football match.* ○ *a diplomatic incident* (= a dangerous or unpleasant situation between countries)

**incidental** /ˌɪnsɪˈdentl ˌइन्सिˈडेन्ट्ल्/ *adj.* **incidental (to sth)** happening as part of sth more important अपेक्षया अधिक महत्त्वपूर्ण वस्तु के अंश के रूप में घटित; आनुषंगिक *The book contains various themes that are incidental to the main plot.*

**incidentally** /ˌɪnsɪˈdentli ˌइन्सिˈडेन्ट्लि/ *adv.* used to introduce extra news, information, etc. that the speaker has just thought of वक्ता को तुरंत सूझी बात (कोई ख़बर, जानकारी आदि) को प्रस्तुत करने के लिए प्रयुक्त शब्द; प्रसंगतः, प्रसंगवश *Incidentally, that new restaurant you told me about is excellent.*

NOTE 'Incidentally' के स्थान पर **by the way** का प्रयोग भी हो सकता है।

**incinerate** /ɪnˈsɪnəreɪt इन्ˈसिनरेट्/ *verb* [T] (*formal*) to destroy sth completely by burning किसी चीज़ को जलाकर राख कर देना; भस्म कर देना

**incinerator** /ɪnˈsɪnəreɪtə(r) इन्ˈसिनरेट(र्)/ *noun* [C] a container or machine for burning rubbish, etc. कूड़ा-करकट को जलाने की मशीन या डिब्बा; भस्मक यंत्र

**incision** /ɪnˈsɪʒn इन्ˈसिश़्न्/ *noun* [C] (*formal*) a cut carefully made into sth (especially into a person's body as part of a medical operation) सावधानी से लगाया गया चीरा (विशेषतः शल्य-क्रिया के दौरान व्यक्ति के शरीर में)

**incisive** /ɪnˈsaɪsɪv इन्ˈसाइसिव़्/ *adj.* **1** showing clear thought and good understanding of what is important, and the ability to express this महत्त्वपूर्ण बातों की अच्छी और स्पष्ट समझ रखने और दर्शाने वाला; तीक्ष्ण *incisive comments/criticism/analysis* ○ *an incisive mind* **2** showing sb's ability to take decisions and act firmly व्यक्ति की निर्णय लेने और दृढ़तापूर्वक अमल में लाने की क्षमता को दर्शाने वाला *an incisive performance*

**incisor** /ɪnˈsaɪzə(r) इन्ˈसाइज़(र्)/ *noun* [C] one of the eight sharp teeth at the front of the mouth that are used for biting सामने के नुकीले काटने वाले आठ दाँतों में से एक; कृंतक, छेदक ➪ **canine** और **molar** देखिए तथा **teeth** पर चित्र देखिए।

**incite** /ɪnˈsaɪt इन्ˈसाइट्/ *verb* [T] **incite sb (to sth)** to encourage sb to do sth by making him/her very angry or excited भड़काना, उकसाना *He was accused of inciting the crowd to violence.* ▶ **incitement** *noun* [C, U] भड़कावा, उकसाव *He was guilty of incitement to violence.*

**incl.** *abbr.* including; inclusive सम्मिलित; संलग्न *total Rs 59.00 incl. tax*

**inclination** /ˌɪnklɪˈneɪʃn ˌइन्क्लिˈनेश़्न्/ *noun* [C, U] **inclination (to do sth); inclination (towards/for sth)** a feeling that makes sb want to behave in a particular way झुकाव, एक विशेष रीति से कुछ करना चाहने की भावना; रुझान *He did not show the* ***slightest inclination*** *to help.* ○ *She had no inclination for a career in teaching.*

**incline**[1] /ɪnˈklaɪn इन्ˈक्लाइन्/ *verb* **1** [I] (*formal*) **incline to/towards sth** to want to behave in a particular way or make a particular choice कोई काम विशेष रीति से करने या किसी विशेष वस्तु को पसंद करने का इच्छुक होना, किसी विशेष बात या काम की ओर झुकाव होना **2** [T] (*formal*) to bend (your head) forward (सिर को) आगे झुकाना *They sat round* *the table, heads inclined, deep in discussion.* **3** [I] **incline towards sth** to be at an angle in a particular direction किसी वस्तु का विशेष दिशा में ढलान होना *The land inclines towards the shore.*

**incline²** /ˈɪnklaɪn ˈइन्क्लाइन्/ *noun* [C] (*formal*) a slight hill ढाल *a steep/slight incline* ✪ पर्याय **slope**

**inclined** /ɪnˈklaɪnd इन्ˈक्लाइन्ड्/ *adj.* **1 inclined (to do sth)** (*not before a noun*) wanting to behave in a particular way प्रवृत्त, इच्छुक, प्रवृत्तियुक्त *I know Amir well so I'm* ***inclined to believe*** *what he says.* **2 inclined to do sth** likely to do sth संभावित रूप से (कुछ) करने वाला, -प्रवण, -शील (जैसे परिवर्तन-प्रवण, परिवर्तनशील) *She's inclined to change her mind very easily.* **3** having a natural ability in the subject mentioned क्षेत्र-विशेष के लिए नैसर्गिक क्षमता संपन्न *to be musically inclined*

**include** /ɪnˈkluːd इन्ˈक्लूड्/ *verb* [T] (*not used in the continuous tenses*) **1** to have as one part; to contain (among other things) को समाविष्ट करना; साथ में रखना *The price of the holiday includes the flight, the hotel and car hire.* ○ *The crew included one woman.* ➪ **contain** पर नोट देखिए। ✪ विलोम **exclude** **2 include sb/sth (as/in/on sth)** to make sb/sth part (of another group, etc.) किसी व्यक्ति या वस्तु को दूसरे समूह का अंग बनाना; शामिल करना *The children immediately included the new girl in their games.* ○ *Everyone was disappointed, myself included.* ▶ **inclusion** /ɪnˈkluːʒn इन्ˈक्लूश़न्/ *noun* [U] समावेश *The inclusion of all that violence in the film was unnecessary.*

**including** /ɪnˈkluːdɪŋ इन्ˈक्लूडिङ्/ *prep.* having as a part को शामिल करते हुए *It costs Rs 990, including postage and packing.* ✪ विलोम **excluding**

**inclusive** /ɪnˈkluːsɪv इन्ˈक्लूसिव्/ *adj.* **1 inclusive (of sth)** (used about a price, etc.) including or containing everything; including the thing mentioned जिसमें (क़ीमत आदि) सम्मिलित हैं; जिसमें निर्दिष्ट वस्तु शामिल है *Is that an inclusive price or are there some extras?* ○ *The rent is inclusive of electricity.* **2** (*only after a noun*) including the dates, numbers, etc. mentioned जिसमें निर्दिष्ट तारीख़े, संख्याएँ आदि शामिल हैं *You are booked at the hotel from Monday to Friday inclusive* (= including Monday and Friday).

> **NOTE** समयावधि का निर्देश करने के लिए अमेरिकी अंग्रेज़ी में प्रायः **through** का प्रयोग होता है **inclusive** का नहीं—*We'll be away from Friday through Sunday.*

**incognito** /ˌɪnkɒgˈniːtəʊ ˌइन्कॉग्ˈनीटो/ *adv.* hiding your real name and identity (especially if you are famous and do not want to be recognized) अपना असली नाम और पहचान को छिपाते हुए (विशेषतः यदि व्यक्ति प्रसिद्ध है और नहीं चाहता कि लोग उसे पहचानें), प्रच्छन्न रूप से, छद्मवेश में; अज्ञात *to travel incognito*

**incoherent** /ˌɪnkəʊˈhɪərənt ˌइन्कोˈहिअरन्ट्/ *adj.* not clear or easy to understand; not saying sth clearly जो स्पष्ट या सुबोध न हो, अस्पष्ट या दुर्बोध, जिसमें अभिव्यक्ति की स्पष्टता न हो; असंगत, असंबद्ध ✪ विलोम **coherent** ▶ **incoherence** *noun* [U] असंगति, असंबद्धता ▶ **incoherently** *adv.* असंगत रूप से

**income** /ˈɪnkʌm; -kəm ˈइन्कम्/ *noun* [C, U] the money you receive regularly as payment for your work or as interest on money you have saved, etc. काम करने के एवज़ में या बचत पर ब्याज के रूप में नियमित रूप से प्राप्त होने वाला धन; आय, आमदनी *It's often difficult for a family to live on one income.*

> **NOTE** हम **monthly** या **annual** आय की बात करते हैं। आय के विषय में बात करते समय शब्द **high** या **low** भी प्रयुक्त होते हैं। आपकी **gross** आय वह है जिस पर आप कर देते हैं। कर देने के बाद की राशि आपकी **net** आय है। ➪ **Pay²** पर नोट देखिए।

**income tax** *noun* [U] the amount of money you pay to the government according to how much you earn आय पर लगने वाला कर; आयकर

**incoming** /ˈɪnkʌmɪŋ ˈइन्कमिङ्/ *adj.* (*only before a noun*) **1** arriving or being received आने वाला या जिसे प्राप्त किया जा रहा है; आवक *incoming flights/passengers* ○ *incoming telephone calls* **2** new; recently elected नया; नवनिर्वाचित *the incoming government*

**incomparable** /ɪnˈkɒmprəbl इन्ˈकॉम्प्रब्ल्/ *adj.* so good or great that it does not have an equal अनुपम, बेजोड़, अतुलनीय, अद्वितीय *incomparable beauty* ➪ **compare** verb देखिए।

**incompatible** /ˌɪnkəmˈpætəbl ˌइन्कम्ˈपैटब्ल्/ *adj.* **incompatible with sb/sth** very different and therefore not able to live or work happily with sb or exist with sth बहुत अलग तरह का और इसलिए दूसरे से असंगत या बेमेल *The working hours of the job are incompatible with family life.* ✪ विलोम **compatible** ▶ **incompatibility** /ˌɪnkəmpætəˈbɪləti ˌइन्कम्पैटˈबिलटि/ *noun* [C, U] (*pl.* **incompatibilities**) असंगति, बेमेलपन

**incompetent** /ɪnˈkɒmpɪtənt इन्ˈकॉम्पिटन्ट्/ *adj.* lacking the necessary skill to do sth well जिसमें उच्च स्तर की कुशलता की कमी है; अक्षम, असमर्थ *He is* *completely incompetent at his job.* ○ *an incompetent teacher/manager* ✪ विलोम **competent** ▶ **incompetent** *noun* [C] अयोग्य *She's a total incompetent at basketball.* ▶ **incompetence** *noun* [U] अयोग्यता ▶ **incompetently** *adv.* बिना योग्यता के, अयोग्यतापूर्वक

**incomplete** /ˌɪnkəmˈpliːt, इनकम्ˈप्लीट्/ *adj.* having a part or parts missing अपूर्ण, अधूरा ✪ विलोम **complete** ▶ **incompletely** *adv.* अधूरे तौर पर, अपूर्ण रूप से

**incomprehensible** /ɪnˌkɒmprɪˈhensəbl इन्ˌकॉम्प्रिˈहेन्सबल्/ *adj.* impossible to understand जिसे समझना असंभव हो; अबोधगम्य *an incomprehensible explanation* ○ *Her attitude is incomprehensible to the rest of the committee.* ✪ विलोम **comprehensible** या **understandable** ▶ **incomprehension** /ɪnˌkɒmprɪˈhenʃn इन्ˌकॉम्प्रिˈहेन्शन्/ *noun* [U] अबोधगम्यता

**inconceivable** /ˌɪnkənˈsiːvəbl ˌइन्कन्ˈसीव़बल्/ *adj.* impossible or very difficult to believe or imagine जिस पर विश्वास करना या जिसके विषय में सोचना असंभव या बहुत कठिन हो; अचिंत्य, अकल्पनीय *It's inconceivable that he would have stolen anything.* ✪ विलोम **conceivable**

**inconclusive** /ˌɪnkənˈkluːsɪv, इन्कन्ˈक्लूसिव़्/ *adj.* not leading to a definite decision or result जो निश्चित निर्णय या परिणाम की ओर न ले जाए; अनिश्चायक, अनिर्णायक *an inconclusive discussion* ○ *inconclusive evidence* (= that doesn't prove anything) ✪ विलोम **conclusive** ▶ **inconclusively** *adv.* अनिश्चायक रूप से

**incongruous** /ɪnˈkɒŋgruəs इन्ˈकॉङ्ग्रुअस्/ *adj.* strange and out of place; not suitable in a particular situation विसंगत, बेमेल; अनुपयुक्त *That huge table looks rather incongruous in such a small room.* ▶ **incongruously** *adv.* असंगतिपूर्वक, बेमेलपन से ▶ **incongruity** /ˌɪnkɒnˈgruːəti ˌइनकॉन्ˈग्रुअटि/ *noun* [U] असंगति, बेमेलपन

**inconsiderate** /ˌɪnkənˈsɪdərət ˌइन्कन्ˈसिडरट्/ *adj.* (used about a person) not thinking or caring about the feelings or needs of other people (व्यक्ति) जो दूसरों की भावनाओं और आवश्यकताओं की परवाह नहीं करता; बेमुरौवत, बेलिहाज़, उदासीन ✪ पर्याय **thoughtless** ✪ विलोम **considerate** ▶ **inconsiderately** *adv.* बेमुरौवती से, बिना लिहाज़ के ▶ **inconsiderateness** *noun* [U] बेमुरौवती, बेलिहाज़ी, उदासीनता

**inconsistent** /ˌɪnkənˈsɪstənt, इनकन्ˈसिसटन्ट्/ *adj.* **1 inconsistent (with sth)** (used about statements, facts, etc.) not the same as sth else; not matching, so that one thing must be wrong or not true (वक्तव्य, तथ्य आदि) दूसरे जैसा नहीं, अनमेल विसंगत (अतएव संभावित रूप से ग़लत या असत्य) त *The witnesses' accounts of the event are inconsistent.* ○ *These new facts are inconsistent wi the earlier information.* **2** (used about a person likely to change (in attitude, behaviour, etc.) s that you cannot depend on him/her (व्यक्ति) जिस रुख, व्यवहार आदि बदल सकते हैं (अतः भरोसेमंद नहीं अस्थिर, परिवर्तनीय ✪ विलोम **consistent** ▶ **inconsistency** /-ənsi -अन्सि/ *noun* [C, U] (*pl.* **inconsistencies**) विसंगति, असंबद्धता, अस्थिरता *There we a few inconsistencies in her argument.* ✪ विलो **consistency** ▶ **inconsistently** *adv.* विसंगत रूप

**inconspicuous** /ˌɪnkənˈspɪkjuəs, इनकन्ˈस्पि क्युअस्/ *adv.* not easily noticed जिस पर आसानी ध्यान न जाए, अविशिष्ट महत्त्वहीन, नगण्य *I tried make myself as* ***inconspicuous*** *as possible that no one would ask me a question.* ✪ विलो **conspicuous** ▶ **inconspicuously** *adv.* अप्रक रूप से

**incontinent** /ɪnˈkɒntɪnənt इन्ˈकॉन्टिनन्ट्/ *a* unable to control the passing of waste (**urine** a **faeces**) from the body जो मलमूत्र-त्याग की क्रिया को नियंत्रित न कर सके; असंयत ▶ **incontinen** *noun* [U] मलमूत्र-त्याग पर नियंत्रणहीनता; असंयति

**inconvenience** /ˌɪnkənˈviːniəns, इनकन्ˈव़ीनिअन् *noun* [U, C] trouble or difficulty, especial when it affects sth that you need to do; a pers or thing that causes this कष्ट या कठिन असुविधा, परेशानी (विशेषतः आवश्यक काम में); असुवि या परेशानी उत्पन्न करने वाला व्यक्ति *We apolog for any inconvenience caused by the dela* ▶ **inconvenience** *verb* [T] असुविधा, परेशानी

**inconvenient** /ˌɪnkənˈviːniənt, इनकन्ˈव़ीनिअ *adj.* causing trouble or difficulty, especially wh it affects sth that you need to do असुविधाज (विशेषतः आवश्यक काम में) *It's a bit inconveni at the moment—could you phone again late* ✪ विलोम **convenient** ▶ **inconveniently** *a* असुविधापूर्ण रीति से, परेशानी से

**incorporate** /ɪnˈkɔːpəreɪt इन्ˈकॉपरेट्/ *verb* **incorporate sth (in/into/within sth)** to m sth a part of sth else; to have sth as a part वस्तु को दूसरी का अंश बनाना, समाविष्ट करना; एक का दूसरी का अंश बनना, समाविष्ट होना *I'd like you incorporate this information into your rep* ✪ पर्याय **include** ▶ **incorporation** /ɪnˌkɔ ˈreɪʃn इन्ˌकॉपˈरेशन्/ *noun* [U] समावेश

**incorporated** /ɪnˈkɔːpəreɪtɪd इन्ˈकॉपरेटिड्/ *adj.* (*abbr.* **Inc.**) (following the name of a company) formed into a legal organization (**corporation**) (किसी कंपनी के नाम के साथ प्रयुक्त) कारपोरेशन (क़ानून-सम्मत संगठन) के रूप में परिणत; निगमित

**incorrect** /ˌɪnkəˈrekt ˌइन्कˈरेक्ट्/ *adj.* not right or true जो शुद्ध, सही या सच न हो; अशुद्ध, ग़लत *Incorrect answers should be marked with a cross.* ✪ विलोम **correct** ▶ **incorrectly** *adv.* अशुद्ध रीति से, ग़लत तरीक़े से

**incorrigible** /ɪnˈkɒrɪdʒəbl इन्ˈकॉरिजबल्/ *adj.* (used about a person or his/her behaviour) very bad; too bad to be corrected or improved (व्यक्ति या उसका आचरण) बहुत ख़राब, असुधार्य, सुधारातीत *an incorrigible liar*

**increase**[1] /ɪnˈkriːs इन्ˈक्रीस्/ *verb* [I, T] **increase (sth) (from A) (to B); increase (sth) (by sth)** to become or to make sth larger in number or amount संख्या या मात्रा में वृद्धि होना या करना, संख्या या मात्रा की दृष्टि से बढ़ना या बढ़ाना *The rate of inflation has increased by 1% to 7%.* ○ *She increased her speed to overtake the lorry.* ✪ विलोम **decrease** या **reduce**

**increase**[2] /ˈɪŋkriːs ˈइङ्क्रीस्/ *noun* [C, U] **(an) increase (in sth)** a rise in the number, amount or level of sth किसी वस्तु की संख्या, मात्रा या स्तर में वृद्धि, बढ़ोतरी *There has been a **sharp increase** of nearly 50% on last year's figures.* ○ *Doctors expect some further increase in the spread of the disease.* ○ *They are demanding a large wage increase.* ✪ विलोम **decrease** या **reduction**

**IDM on the increase** becoming larger or more frequent; increasing बढ़ना या अधिक बार होने लगना; वृद्धि पर *Attacks by monkeys on children are on the increase.*

**increasingly** /ɪnˈkriːsɪŋli इन्ˈक्रीसिङ्लि/ *adv.* more and more अधिकाधिक *It's becoming increasingly difficult/important/dangerous to stay here.*

**incredible** /ɪnˈkredəbl इन्ˈक्रेडबल्/ *adj.* **1** impossible or very difficult to believe जिस पर विश्वास करना असंभव या बहुत कठिन हो; अविश्वसनीय *I found his account of the event incredible.* ✪ विलोम **credible** ➪ **unbelievable** देखिए। **2** (*informal*) extremely good or big बहुत अच्छा या बड़ा *He earns an incredible salary.* ▶ **incredibly** /-əbli -अब्लि/ *adv.* अविश्वसनीय रूप से *We have had some incredibly strong winds recently.*

**incredulous** /ɪnˈkrədjələs इन्ˈक्रेड्यलस्/ *adj.* not willing or not able to believe sth; unbelieving, showing an inability to believe sth अविश्वासी, अविश्वसनीय; संदेहशील *an incredulous look* ✪ विलोम **credulous** ▶ **incredulity** /ˌɪŋkrəˈdjuːləti ˌइन्क्रेˈड्यूलटि/ *noun* [U] अविश्वसनीयता, संदेहशीलता *He gave her a look of surprise and incredulity.*

**increment** /ˈɪŋkrəmənt ˈइङ्क्रमन्ट्/ *noun* [C] **1** a regular increase in the amount of money that sb is paid for his/her job वेतन में नियमित रूप से होने वाली वृद्धि; वेतन-वृद्धि *a salary with annual increments* **2** (*formal*) *an increase in a number or an amount* संख्या या मात्रा में वृद्धि ▶ **incremental** /ˌɪŋkrəˈmentl ˌइङ्क्रˈमन्ट्ल्/ *adj.* वृद्धि से संबंधित *incremental costs* ▶ **incrementally** /-təli -टलि/ *adv.* वृद्धि की दृष्टि से

**incriminate** /ɪnˈkrɪmɪneɪt इन्ˈक्रिमिनेट्/ *verb* [T] to provide evidence that sb is guilty of a crime किसी को अपराध का दोषी सिद्ध करने के लिए सबूत जुटाना; अभिशस्त करना *The police searched the house but found nothing to incriminate the man.*

**incubate** /ˈɪŋkjubeɪt ˈइङ्क्युबेट्/ *verb* **1** [T] to keep an egg at the right temperature so that it can develop and produce a bird (**hatch**) अंडे को सही तापमान पर रखना (ताकि वह विकसित होकर पक्षी को जन्म दे सके); अंडे सेना **2** [I, T] (used about a disease) to develop without showing signs; (used about a person or an animal) to carry a disease without showing signs (रोग का) लक्षण प्रकट किए बिना बढ़ना; (व्यक्ति या पशु) बिना लक्षण प्रकट किए रोग को वहन करना *Some viruses take weeks to incubate.*

**incubation** /ˌɪŋkjuˈbeɪʃn ˌइङ्क्युˈबेश्न्/ *noun* **1** [U] the process of incubating eggs अंडों को सही तापमान पर रखने यज्ञ सेने की प्रक्रिया **2** [C] (*also* **incubation period**) the period between catching a disease and the time when signs of it (**symptoms**) appear रोग से आक्रांत होने और उसके लक्षण प्रकट होने के बीच का समय

**incubator** /ˈɪŋkjubeɪtə(r) ˈइङ्क्युबेट(र्)/ *noun* [C] **1** a machine used in hospitals for keeping small or weak babies alive in controlled conditions अस्पतालों में प्रयुक्त ताप-मशीन, उष्मायित्र (छोटे या दुर्बल शिशुओं को जीवित रखने के लिए) **2** a machine for keeping eggs warm until they break open (**hatch**) अंडे सेने की तापयुक्त मशीन

**incumbent** /ɪnˈkʌmbənt इन्ˈकम्बन्ट्/ *noun* [C] (*formal*) a person who is currently in an official position (व्यक्ति) पदधारी *the present incumbent of the Rashtrapati Bhavan* ▶ **incumbent** *adj.* पदस्थ *the incumbent governor*

**incur** /ɪnˈkɜ:(r) इन्ˈक(र्)/ *verb* [T] (**incurred; incurring**) (*formal*) to suffer the unpleasant results of a situation that you have caused अपनी ग़लती के अप्रिय परिणामों को भुगतना *to incur debts/sb's anger*

**incurable** /ɪnˈkjʊərəbl इन्ˈक्युअरब्ल्/ *adj.* that cannot be cured or made better जिसका इलाज या जिसमें सुधार न हो सके; लाइलाज, असाध्य *an incurable disease* ✪ विलोम **curable** ▶ **incurably** /-əbli -अब्लि/ *adv.* असाध्य रूप से *incurably ill*

**indebted** /ɪnˈdetɪd इन्ˈडेटिड्/ *adj.* **indebted (to sb) (for sth)** very grateful to sb किसी के प्रति अत्यंत कृतज्ञ *I am deeply indebted to my family and friends for all their help.*

**indecent** /ɪnˈdi:snt इन्ˈडीसन्ट्/ *adj.* shocking to many people in society, especially because sth involves sex or the body अशोभनीय, अश्लील, अशोभन *indecent photos/behaviour/language* ○ *You can't wear those tiny swimming trunks—they're indecent!* ✪ विलोम **decent** ▶ **indecency** /-nsi -न्सि/ *noun* [U, *sing.*] अश्लीलता ▶ **indecently** *adv.* अश्लीलतापूर्वक

**indecision** /ˌɪndɪˈsɪʒn ˌइन्डिˈसिश़न्/ (*also* **indecisiveness**) *noun* [U] the state of being unable to decide निश्चय या निर्णय न कर सकने की स्थिति; अनिश्चय, अनिर्णय *His indecision about the future is really worrying me.*

**indecisive** /ˌɪndɪˈsaɪsɪv ˌइन्डिˈसाइसिव्/ *adj.* not able to make decisions easily शीघ्र निर्णय करने में असमर्थ ✪ विलोम **decisive** ▶ **indecisively** *adv.* अनिश्चयपूर्वक

**indeed** /ɪnˈdi:d इन्ˈडीड्/ *adv.* **1** (used for emphasizing a positive statement or answer) really; certainly (स्वीकारात्मक कथन या उत्तर पर बल देने के लिए प्रयुक्त) सचमुच; निश्चित रूप से *'Have you had a good holiday?' 'We have indeed.'* **2** used after 'very' with an adjective or adverb to emphasize the quality mentioned निर्दिष्ट गुण पर बल देने के लिए 'very' युक्त विशेषण या क्रियाविशेषण के बाद प्रयुक्त *Thank you very much indeed.* ○ *She's very happy indeed.* **3** (used for adding information to a statement) in fact (वक्तव्य के साथ कुछ और जानकारी जोड़ने के लिए प्रयुक्त) वस्तुतः *It's important that you come at once. Indeed, it's essential.* **4** used for showing interest, surprise, anger, etc. रुचि, आश्चर्य, क्रोध आदि व्यक्त करने के लिए प्रयुक्त *'They were talking about you last night.' 'Were they indeed!'*

**indefensible** /ˌɪndɪˈfensəbl ˌइन्डिˈफ़ेन्सब्ल्/ *adj.* (used about behaviour, etc.) completely wrong; that cannot be defended or excused (आचरण आदि) पूर्णतया अनुचित; जिसको समर्थित या उपेक्षित न किया जा सके

**indefinable** /ˌɪndɪˈfaɪnəbl ˌइन्डिˈफ़ाइनब्ल्/ *adj.* difficult or impossible to describe जिसका वर्णन करना कठिन या असंभव हो, अवर्णनीय *There was an indefinable atmosphere of hostility.* ▶ **indefinably** /-əbli -अब्लि/ *adv.* अवर्णनीय रूप से

**indefinite** /ɪnˈdefɪnət इन्ˈडेफ़िनट्/ *adj.* not fixed or clear अनिश्चित या अस्पष्ट, अनियत *Our plans are still rather indefinite.* ✪ विलोम **definite**

**the indefinite article** *noun* [C] (*grammar*) the name used for the words a and an, 'a' और 'an' के लिए पारिभाषिक शब्द, अनिश्चायक आर्टिकल ➪ **the definite article** देखिए।

> **NOTE** अनिश्चायक आर्टिकल (indefinite article) पर अधिक जानकारी के लिए इस शब्दकोश के अंत में **Quick Grammar Reference** देखिए।

**indefinitely** /ɪnˈdefɪnətli इन्ˈडेफ़िनट्लि/ *adv.* for a period of time that has no fixed end अनिश्चित काल के लिए *The meeting was postponed indefinitely.*

**indelible** /ɪnˈdeləbl इन्ˈडेलब्ल्/ *adj.* that cannot be removed or washed out जो हटाया या धोया न जा सके; अमिट, अलोप्य, स्थायी *indelible ink* ○ (*figurative*) *The experience made an indelible impression on me.* ▶ **indelibly** /-əbli -अब्लि/ *adv.* अमिट रूप से

**indemnify** /ɪnˈdemnɪfaɪ इन्ˈडेमनिफ़ाइ/ *verb* [T] (*pres. part.* **indemnifying;** *3rd person sing. pres.* **indemnifies;** *pt* **indemnified;** *pt* **indemnified**) (*law*) **1 indemnify sb (against sth)** to promise to pay sb an amount of money if he/she suffers any damage or loss क्षति की पूर्ति के रूप में धन देने की वचनबद्धता **2 indemnify sb (for sth)** to pay sb an amount of money because of the damage or loss that he/she has suffered क्षति की पूर्ति के रूप में किसी को धन देना; हर्जाना देना ▶ **indemnification** /ɪnˌdemnɪfɪˈkeɪʃn इन्ˌडेमनिफ़िˈकेशन्/ *noun* [U] क्षतिपूर्ति, क्षतिपूरण

**indemnity** /ɪnˈdemnəti इन्ˈडेम्नटि/ *noun* (*formal*) **1** [U] protection against damage or loss, especially in the form of a promise to pay for any that happens क्षति से सुरक्षा (विशेषतः धन देने की वचनबद्धता के रूप में) **2** [C] (*pl.* **indemnities**) an amount of money that is given as payment for damage or loss क्षति की पूर्ति के रूप में दी गई धनराशि, हर्जाने की रक़म

**indent** /ɪnˈdent इन्ˈडेन्ट्/ *verb* [I, T] to start a line of writing further from the left-hand side of the page than the other lines हाशिये से हट कर पंक्ति आरंभ करना

**independence** /ˌɪndɪˈpendəns ˌइन्डिˈपेन्डन्स्/ *noun* [U] **independence (from sb/sth)** (used about a person, country, etc.) the state of being free and not controlled by another person, country, etc. (व्यक्ति, देश आदि की) स्वाधीनता, स्वतंत्रता, अन्य व्यक्ति या देश के अधीन न होने की स्थिति, अनधीनता *In 1947 India achieved independence from Britain.* ○ *financial independence*

**NOTE** भारत में **Independence Day** 15 अगस्त को मनाया जाता है। सन् 1947 में इसी दिन भारत ब्रिटेन के आधिपत्य से स्वतंत्र हुआ था।

**independent** /ˌɪndɪˈpendənt ˌइन्डिˈपेन्डन्ट्/ *adj.* 1 **independent (of/from sb/sth)** free from and not controlled by another person, country, etc. अन्य व्यक्ति, देश आदि के नियंत्रण से मुक्त; स्वाधीन, स्वतंत्र *Many former colonies are now independent nations.* ○ *independent schools/television* (= not supported by government money) 2 **independent (of/from sb/sth)** not needing or wanting help जिसे सहायता की न तो आवश्यकता हो न इच्छा; आत्मनिर्भर *I got a part-time job because I wanted to be financially independent from my parents.* ✪ विलोम **dependent** 3 not influenced by or connected with sb/sth जो किसी व्यक्ति या वस्तु के न तो प्रभाव में हो न संपर्क में; निष्पक्ष, अलग *Complaints against the police should be investigated by an independent body.* ○ *Two independent opinion polls have obtained similar results.* ▶ **independently** *adv.* **independently (of sb/sth)** स्वतंत्र रूप से, अलग-अलग *Scientists working independently of each other have had very similar results in their experiments.*

**indescribable** /ˌɪndɪˈskraɪbəbl ˌइन्डिˈस्क्राइबबल्/ *adj.* too good or bad to be described इतना अच्छा या बुरा कि वर्णन न किया जा सके; अवर्णनीय, अकथनीय *indescribable poverty/luxury/noise* ▶ **indescribably** /-əbli -अब्लि/ *adv.* अवर्णनीय रूप से

**indestructible** /ˌɪndɪˈstrʌktəbl ˌइन्डिˈस्ट्रक्टबल्/ *adj.* that cannot be easily damaged or destroyed जिसे आसानी से क्षतिग्रस्त या नष्ट न किया जा सके; अविनाशी, अध्वंस्य

**index** /ˈɪndeks ˈइन्डेक्स्/ *noun* [C] (*pl.* **indexes**) 1 a list in order from A to Z, usually at the end of a book, of the names or subjects that are referred to in the book पुस्तक के अंत में अकारादि क्रम से बनी सूची जिसमें पुस्तक में वर्णित व्यक्तियों या विषयों के नाम होते हैं; अनुक्रमणिका, इंडेक्स *If you want to find all the references to Delhi, look it up in the index.* 2 (*BrE*) = **card index** 3 (*pl.* **indexes** or **indices**) a way of showing how the price, value, rate, etc. of sth has changed क़ीमत, दर आदि में हुए परिवर्तन को दर्शाने का एक प्रकार या पद्धति; सूचकांक *the cost-of-living index* ▶ **index** *verb* [T] सूचीबद्ध करना *The books in the library are indexed by subject and title.*

**index card** *noun* [C] a small card that you can write information on and keep with other cards in a box or file एक छोटा कार्ड जिस पर विवरण अंकित कर अन्य कार्डों के साथ एक बॉक्स या फ़ाइल में रखा जाता है; इंडेक्स कार्ड ➪ **stationery** पर चित्र देखिए।

**index finger** *noun* [C] the finger next to your thumb that you use for pointing अँगूठे के साथ की अंगुली जिसे इशारा करने के लिए प्रयोग में लाते हैं; तर्जनी ✪ पर्याय **forefinger**

**Indian** /ˈɪndiən ˈइन्डिअन्/ *noun* [C], *adj.* 1 (a person) from the Republic of India (व्यक्ति) भारत का, भारतीय *Indian food is famous worldwide.* 2 = **Native American** *The Sioux were a famous Indian tribe.* ➪ **West Indian** देखिए।

**indicate** /ˈɪndɪkeɪt ˈइन्डिकेट्/ *verb* 1 [T] to show that sth is probably true or exists किसी बात के संभवतः सत्य या अस्तित्व में होने का संकेत करना, बताना, दिखाना *Recent research indicates that children are getting too little exercise.* 2 [T] to say sth in an indirect way किसी बात को परोक्ष रीति से कहना; संकेत करना *The spokesman indicated that an agreement was likely soon.* 3 [T] to make sb notice sth, especially by pointing to it किसी व्यक्ति का किसी बात की ओर ध्यान दिलाना (विशेषतः उसकी ओर संकेत करके) *The receptionist indicated where I should sign.* ○ *The boy seemed to be indicating that I should follow him.* 4 [I, T] to signal that your car, etc. is going to turn कार आदि के मुड़ने का इशारा करना *The lorry indicated left but turned right.*

**indication** /ˌɪndɪˈkeɪʃn ˌइन्डिˈकेशन्/ *noun* [C, U] **an indication (of sth/doing sth); an indication that...** something that shows sth; a sign अन्य वस्तु को दिखाने वाली वस्तु; संकेत *There was no indication of a struggle.* ○ *There is every indication that he will make a full recovery.*

**indicative** /ɪnˈdɪkətɪv इन्ˈडिकटिव्/ *adj.* (*formal*) being or giving a sign of sth संकेत या संकेत करने वाला; सूचक, बोधक *Is the unusual weather indicative of climatic changes?*

**indicator** /ˈɪndɪkeɪtə(r) ˈइन्डिकेट(र्)/ *noun* [C] 1 something that gives information or shows sth; a sign कुछ सूचित या प्रदर्शित करने वाली वस्तु; सूचक *The indicator showed that we had plenty of* *petrol.* ○ *The unemployment rate is a reliable indicator of economic health.* **2** (*AmE* **turn signal**) the flashing light on a car, etc. that shows that it is going to turn right or left कार पर लगी रह-रहकर चमकने वाली रोशनी (जो कार के दाएँ या बाएँ जाने का संकेत करती है)

**indices** /ˈɪndɪsiːz ˈइन्डिसीज़् / ➪ **index 3** का plural रूप

**indict** /ɪnˈdaɪt इन्ˈडाइट् / *verb* [T] (*usually passive*) **indict sb (for sb)** (*usually AmE*) (*law*) to officially charge sb with a crime किसी पर अपराध के लिए औपचारिक रूप से अभियोग लगाना; अभ्यारोपण करना *The senator was indicted for murder.*

**indictment** /ɪnˈdaɪtmənt इन्ˈडाइट्मन्ट् / *noun* [C] **1** a written paper that officially accuses sb of a crime औपचारिक अभियोग-पत्र; अभ्यारोपण **2 an indictment (of sth)** something that shows how bad sth is किसी की दुर्दशा-ग्रस्तता का सूचक *The fact that many children leave school with no qualifications is an indictment of our education system.*

**indifference** /ɪnˈdɪfrəns इन्ˈडिफ़्रन्स् / *noun* [U] **indifference (to sb/sth)** a lack of interest or feeling towards sb/sth व्यक्ति या वस्तु के प्रति रुचि या भावना में कमी; उदासीनता *He has always shown indifference to the needs of others.*

**indifferent** /ɪnˈdɪfrənt इन्ˈडिफ़्रन्ट् / *adj.* **1 indifferent (to sb/sth)** not interested in or caring about sb/sth व्यक्ति या वस्तु में रुचि या सोच-विचार से रहित; उदासीन *The manager of the shop seemed indifferent to our complaints.* **2** not very good जो बहुत अच्छा न हो; साधारण *The standard of football in the World Cup was rather indifferent.*
▶ **indifferently** *adv.* उदासीनतापूर्वक

**indigenous** /ɪnˈdɪdʒənəs इन्ˈडिजनस्/ *adj.* (used about people, animals or plants) living or growing in the place where they are from originally (मनुष्य, पशु या पौधे) अपने मूल स्थान में स्थित; स्वदेशी, स्थानीय

**indigestible** /ˌɪndɪˈdʒestəbl ˌइन्डिˈजेस्टबल् / *adj.* (used about food) difficult or impossible for the stomach to deal with (भोजन) जिसका पचना कठिन या असंभव हो; दुष्पच, अपाच्य ✪ विलोम **digestible**

**indigestion** /ˌɪndɪˈdʒestʃən ˌइन्डिˈजेस्चन् / *noun* [U] pain in the stomach that is caused by difficulty in dealing with food भोजन पचने में कठिनाई से उत्पन्न पेट दर्द; बदहज़मी, अपच

**indignant** /ɪnˈdɪgnənt इन्ˈडिग्नन्ट् / *adj.* **indignant (with sb) (about/at sth); indignant that...** shocked or angry because sb has said or done sth that you do not like and do not agree with नापसंद या प्रतिकूल बात या काम से बहुत रुष्ट या क्रुद्ध *They were indignant that they had to pay more for worse services.* ▶ **indignantly** *adv.* रोषपूर्वक, क्रोधपूर्वक

**indignation** /ˌɪndɪgˈneɪʃn ˌइन्डिग्ˈनेश्न् / *noun* [U] **indignation (at/about sth); indignation that** shock and anger मानसिक आघात और क्रोध, रोष *commuters' indignation at the rise in fares*

**indignity** /ɪnˈdɪgnəti इन्ˈडिग्नटि / *noun* [U, C] (*pl.* **indignities**) **indignity (of sth/of doing sth)** a situation that makes you feel embarrassed because you are not treated with respect; an act that causes these feelings सम्मान न मिलने से उत्पन्न परेशानी, तिरस्कार, अनादर, अपमान ✪ पर्याय **humiliation** *The chairman suffered the indignity of being refused admission to the meeting.* ○ *the daily indignities of imprisonment*

**indigo** /ˈɪndɪgəʊ ˈइन्डिगो / *adj.* very dark blue in colour गहरा नीला ▶ **indigo** *noun* [U] नील

**indirect** /ˌɪndəˈrekt; -daɪˈr- ˌइन्डˈरेक्ट्; -डाइˈर- / *adj.* **1** not being the direct cause of sth; not having a direct connection with sth जो किसी का प्रत्यक्ष कारण न हो, परोक्ष; जिसका किसी के साथ प्रत्यक्ष संपर्क न हो; अप्रत्यक्ष *an indirect result* **2** that avoids saying sth in an obvious way घुमाव-फिराव वाला *She gave only an indirect answer to my question.* **3** not going in a straight line or using the shortest route सीधी रेखा में या सबसे छोटे रास्ते से न जाने वाला; चक्करदार *We came the indirect route to avoid driving through Chandigarh.* ✪ विलोम **direct**
▶ **indirectly** *adv.* परोक्ष रीति से ✪ विलोम **directly**
▶ **indirectness** *noun* [U] परोक्षता

**indirect object** *noun* [C] (*grammar*) a person or thing that an action is done to or for व्यक्ति या वस्तु जो कार्य व्यापार का लक्ष्य या विषय हो; परोक्ष कर्म *In the sentence, 'I wrote him a letter', 'him' is the indirect object.* ➪ **direct object** देखिए।

> **NOTE** परोक्ष कार्य (indirect object) के विषय में अधिक जानकारी के लिए इस शब्दकोश के अंत में **Quick Grammar Reference** खंड देखिए।

**indirect speech** (*also* **reported speech**) *noun* [U] (*grammar*) reporting what sb has said, not using the actual words मूल कथन को सूचित करने वाली शैली (जिसमें मूल शब्दों का प्रयोग नहीं होता) अप्रत्यक्ष या परोक्ष कथन ➪ **direct speech** देखिए।

> **NOTE** मोहन के अपने शब्द थे—*'I'll phone again later.'* परोक्ष कथन में वाक्य का रूप होगा—*Mohan said that he would phone again later.*
> परोक्ष कथन (indirect speech) के विषय में अधिक जानकारी के लिए इस शब्दकोश के अंत में **Quick Grammar Reference** खंड देखिए।

**indiscreet** /ˌɪndɪˈskriːt ˌइन्ˈडिस्क्रीट्/ *adj.* not careful or polite in what you say or do वाणी या व्यवहार में असावधान या अभद्र; अविवेकी ✪ विलोम **discreet** ▶ **indiscreetly** *adv.* असावधानी या अभद्रता से; अविवेकपूर्ण तरह से

**indiscretion** /ˌɪndɪˈskreʃn ˌइन्डिˈस्क्रेशन्/ *noun* [C, U] behaviour that is not careful or polite, and that might cause embarrassment or offence असावधानीपूर्ण या अभद्र व्यवहार (जो अपमानजनक लगे); विवेकहीनता

**indiscriminate** /ˌɪndɪˈskrɪmɪnət ˌइन्डिˈस्क्रिमिनट्/ *adj.* done or acting without making sensible judgement or caring about the possible harmful effects लापरवाह; विवेकहीन, नासमझ *He's indiscriminate in his choice of friends.* ▶ **indiscriminately** *adv.* विवेकहीनता के साथ; नासमझी से, अंधाधुंध तरीक़े से

**indispensable** /ˌɪndɪˈspensəbl ˌइन्डिˈस्पेन्सबल्/ *adj.* very important, so that it is not possible to be without it बहुत आवश्यक, जिसके बिना काम न चल सके; अपरिहार्य; अनिवार्य *A car is indispensable nowadays if you live in the country.* ✪ पर्याय **essential** ✪ विलोम **dispensable**

**indisposed** /ˌɪndɪˈspəʊzd ˌइन्डिˈस्पोज़्ड्/ *adj.* (*formal*) **1** (*not before a noun*) unable to do sth because you are ill अस्वस्थ *Sheila is indisposed, so Ravi will perform at the concert tonight.* **2** not willing अनिच्छुक *indisposed to help*

**indisputable** /ˌɪndɪˈspjuːtəbl ˌइन्डिˈस्प्यूटबल्/ *adj.* definitely true; that cannot be shown to be wrong सर्वथा सत्य; पूर्णतः दोषमुक्त, निर्विवाद

**indistinct** /ˌɪndɪˈstɪŋkt ˌइन्डिˈस्टिङ्क्ट्/ *adj.* not clear अस्पष्ट, धुँधला *indistinct figures/sounds/memories* ✪ विलोम **distinct** ▶ **indistinctly** *adv.* अस्पष्ट रूप से

**indistinguishable** /ˌɪndɪˈstɪŋgwɪʃəbl ˌइन्डिˈस्टिङ्ग्विशबल्/ *adj.* **indistinguishable (from sth)** appearing to be the same एक जैसे लगने वाले, जिनमें भेद करना कठिन है; अप्रभेद्य *From a distance the two colours are indistinguishable.* ✪ विलोम **distinguishable**

**individual**[1] /ˌɪndɪˈvɪdʒuəl ˌइन्डिˈविजुअल्/ *adj.* **1** (*only before a noun*) considered separately rather than as part of a group समूह से अलग; अकेला *Each individual animal is weighed and measured before being set free.* **2** for or from one person एक व्यक्ति पर केंद्रित, एक अदद (टुकड़ा आदि) *Children need individual attention when they are learning to read.* **3** typical of one person in a way that is different from other people दूसरों से भिन्न एक व्यक्ति विशिष्ट; व्यक्तिगत *I like her individual style of dressing.*

**individual**[2] /ˌɪndɪˈvɪdʒuəl ˌइन्डिˈविजुअल्/ *noun* [C] **1** one person, considered separately from others or a group एक व्यक्ति (दूसरों से या समूह से अलग रूप में गृहीत) *Are the needs of society more important than the rights of the individual?* **2** (*informal*) a person of the type that is mentioned निर्दिष्ट कोटि का व्यक्ति *She's a strange individual.*

**individualism** /ˌɪndɪˈvɪdʒuəlɪzəm ˌइन्डिˈविजुअलिज़म्/ *noun* [U] **1** the quality of being different from other people and doing things in your own way दूसरों से अलग और अपने ढंग से काम करने की विशिष्टता; वैयक्तिकता *She owes her success to her individualism and flair.* **2** the belief that individual people in society should have the right to make their own decisions, etc., rather than being controlled by the government यह धारणा कि व्यक्तियों को अपने विषय में स्वयं (न कि सरकार को) निर्णय लेने का अधिकार है; व्यक्तिवाद ▶ **individualist** /-əlɪst -अलिस्ट्/ *noun* [C] व्यक्तिवादी *He's a complete individualist in the way he paints.* ▶ **individualistic** /ˌɪndɪˌvɪdʒuəˈlɪstɪk ˌइन्डिˌविजुअˈलिस्टिक्/ (*also* **individualist**) *adj.* व्यक्तिवादपरक *an individualistic culture* ○ *Her music is highly individualistic and may not appeal to everyone.*

**individuality** /ˌɪndɪˌvɪdʒuˈæləti ˌइन्डिˌविजुˈऐलटि/ *noun* [U] the qualities that make sb/sth different from other people or things किसी व्यक्ति या वस्तु को अन्य व्यक्तियों या वस्तुओं से भिन्न बनाने वाले गुणों का समुच्चय; व्यक्तित्व, एकत्व *Young people often try to express their individuality by the way they dress.*

**individually** /ˌɪndɪˈvɪdʒuəli ˌइन्डिˈविजुअलि/ *adv.* separately; one by one अलग-अलग; एक-एक करके *The teacher talked to each member of the class individually.*

**indivisible** /ˌɪndɪˈvɪzəbl ˌइन्डिˈविज़बल्/ *adj.* that cannot be divided or split into smaller pieces जिसे लघुतर खंडों में विभक्त नहीं किया जा सके; अविभाज्य

**indoctrinate** /ɪnˈdɒktrɪneɪt इन्ˈडॉक्ट्रिनेट्/ *verb* [T] to force sb to accept particular beliefs without considering others मतारोपण करना, किसी को विशेष मान्यताओं को मानने के लिए बाध्य करना *For 20 years the people have been indoctrinated by the government.* ▶ **indoctrination** /ɪnˌdɒktrɪˈneɪʃn इन्ˌडॉक्ट्रिˈनेशन्/ *noun* [U] मतारोपण

**indomitable** /ɪnˈdɒmɪtəbl इन्ˈडॉमिटबल् / *adj.* (*formal, approving*) impossible to defeat or frighten, even in a difficult situation; very brave and determined कठिन परिस्थिति में भी अजेय एवं निडर; अदम्य *Despite his illness he has an indomitable spirit.*

**indoor** /ˈɪndɔː(r) ˈइन्डॉ(र्)/ *adj.* (*only before a noun*) done or used inside a building भवन के भीतर किया गया या स्थित; भवनांतर्गत, अंतर्द्वारीय *indoor games* ○ *an indoor swimming pool* ✪ विलोम **outdoor**

**indoors** /ˌɪnˈdɔːz ˌइन्ˈडॉज़्/ *adv.* in or into a building भवन के अंदर या भीतर *Let's go indoors.* ○ *Oh dear! I've left my sunglasses indoors* ✪ विलोम **outdoors** या **out of doors**

**induce** /ɪnˈdjuːs इन्ˈड्यूस्/ *verb* [T] (*formal*) **1** to make or persuade sb to do sth किसी से कुछ काम करवाना या उसके लिए मनाना; राज़ी करना *Nothing could induce him to change his mind.* **2** to cause or produce किसी वस्तु या स्थिति का कारण बनना या उसे उत्पन्न करना; उत्प्रेरण करना *drugs that induce sleep* ○ *a drug-induced coma* **3** (*medical*) to make a woman start giving birth to her baby by giving her special drugs विशेष औषधियाँ देकर माता का प्रसव कराना

**inducement** /ɪnˈdjuːsmənt इन्ˈड्यूस्मन्ट्/ *noun* [C, U] something that is offered to sb to make him/her do sth प्रलोभन, प्रोत्साहन *The player was offered a car as an inducement to join the club.*

**induction** /ɪnˈdʌkʃn इन्ˈडक्शन्/ *noun* **1** [U, C] the process of introducing sb to a new job, skill, organization, etc.; an event at which this takes place किसी को नया काम आदि सिखाना या शुरू करने की प्रक्रिया; अधिष्ठापन, प्रवेश *an induction day for new students* **2** [U] (*technical*) a method of discovering general rules and principles from particular facts and examples विशिष्ट तथ्यों और उदाहरणों से सामान्य नियमों और सिद्धांतों के निर्धारण की विधि; आगमन विधि ➪ **deduction** देखिए। **3** [U] (*technical*) the process by which electricity or **magnetism** passes from one object to another without them touching एक प्रक्रिया जिसके द्वारा विद्युत या चुंबक शक्ति एक वस्तु से दूसरी तक बिना उनका स्पर्श पाए पहुँचती है; प्रेरण, प्रवर्तन

**inductive** /ɪnˈdʌktɪv इन्ˈडक्टिव़्/ *adj.* (*technical*) **1** using particular facts and examples to form general rules and principles जिसमें विशिष्ट तथ्यों और उदाहरणों से सामान्य नियमों और सिद्धांतों का निर्धारण हो; आगमनात्मक *an inductive argument* ○ *inductive reasoning* ➪ **deductive** देखिए। **2** connected with the induction of electricity विद्युत के प्रेरण से संबंधित

**indulge** /ɪnˈdʌldʒ इन्ˈडल्ज्/ *verb* **1** [I, T] **indulge (yourself) (in sth)** to allow yourself to have or do sth for pleasure मौज-मस्ती करना, आनंद के लिए किसी काम में लिप्त होना *I'm going to indulge myself and go shopping for some new clothes.* ○ *Manisha never indulges in gossip.* **2** [T] to give sb/sth what he/she/it wants or needs किसी को उसकी मनचाही या ज़रूरत की चीज़ देना; अनुग्रह करना *You shouldn't indulge that child. It will make him very selfish.* ○ *At the weekends he indulges his passion for fishing.*

**indulgence** /ɪnˈdʌldʒəns इन्ˈडल्जन्स्/ *noun* **1** [U] the state of having or doing whatever you want इच्छापूर्ति में संलिप्तता *to lead a life of indulgence* ○ *Over-indulgence in chocolate makes you fat.* **2** [C] something that you have or do because it gives you pleasure आनंदोपभोग, मज़ा *Ice cream after dinner is my only indulgence.*

**indulgent** /ɪnˈdʌldʒənt इन्ˈडल्जन्ट्/ *adj.* allowing sb to have or do whatever he/she wants सब प्रकार की इच्छापूर्ति करने वाला, लाड़-प्यार करने वाला *indulgent parents* ▶ **indulgently** *adv.* इच्छापूर्ति करते हुए

**industrial** /ɪnˈdʌstriəl इन्ˈडस्ट्रिअल्/ *adj.* **1** (*only before a noun*) connected with industry उद्योग से संबंधित; औद्योगिक *industrial development* ○ *industrial workers* **2** having a lot of factories, etc. जहाँ बहुत-से कल-कारख़ाने हों; उद्योग-प्रधान *an industrial region/country/town*

**industrial action** *noun* [U] action that workers take, especially stopping work, in order to protest about sth to their employers; a strike विरोध प्रकट करने के लिए कर्मचारियों की कार्रवाई (विशेषतः काम रोक देना); हड़ताल *to threaten (to take) industrial action*

**industrialist** /ɪnˈdʌstriəlɪst इन्ˈडस्ट्रिअलिस्ट्/ *noun* [C] a person who owns or manages a large industrial company उद्योगपति

**industrialize** (*also* **-ise**) /ɪnˈdʌstrɪəlaɪz इन्ˈडस्ट्रिअलाइज़्/ *verb* [I, T] to develop industries in a country देश में उद्योगों का विकास करना; उद्योगीकरण करना *Japan industrialized rapidly in the late 19th century.* ▶ **industrialization** (*also* **-isation**) /-eɪʃn -एश्न्/ *noun* [U] देश में उद्योग-विकास, देश का औद्योगिकी-करण

**industrious** /ɪnˈdʌstriəs इन्ˈडस्ट्रिअस्/ *adj.* always working hard कठोर परिश्रमी, अध्यवसायी, उद्यमी

**industry** /ˈɪndəstri ˈइन्डस्ट्रि/ *noun* (*pl.* **industries**) **1** [U] the production of goods in factories कारख़ानों में माल का उत्पादन; उद्योग-धंधे; व्यवसाय *Is British industry being threatened by foreign imports?* ○ *heavy/light industry* **2** [C] the people and activities involved in producing sth, providing a service, etc. वस्तुओं का निर्माण, सेवाएँ उपलब्ध कराना आदि में लगे लोग और गतिविधियाँ *the tourist/catering/entertainment industry*

**inedible** /ɪnˈedəbl इन्ˈएडबल्/ *adj.* (*formal*) not suitable to be eaten जो खाने के लायक न हो; अखाद्य ✪ विलोम **edible**

**ineffective** /ˌɪnɪˈfektɪv ˌइनिˈफ़ेक्टिव्/ *adj.* not producing the effect or result that you want जो अभीष्ट प्रभाव या परिणाम उत्पन्न न करे; निष्प्रभावी ✪ विलोम **effective**

**inefficient** /ˌɪnɪˈfɪʃnt ˌइनिˈफ़िश्न्ट्/ *adj.* not working or producing results in the best way, so that time or money is wasted जो सर्वोत्तम रीति से काम न करे या परिणाम न दे (जिससे समय और पैसे की बरबादी हो), अकुशल, अक्षम *Our heating system is very old and extremely inefficient.* ○ *an inefficient secretary* ✪ विलोम **efficient** ▶ **inefficiency** /-ənsi -अन्सि/ *noun* [U] अक्षमता ▶ **inefficiently** *adv.* अक्षमतापूर्वक

**ineligible** /ɪnˈelɪdʒəbl इन्ˈएलिजबल्/ *adj.* **ineligible (for/to do sth)** without the necessary qualifications, etc. to do or get sth जिसके पास किसी बात के लिए अपेक्षित योग्यता आदि न हो; अपात्र, अयोग्य *She was ineligible for the job because she wasn't a German citizen.* ✪ विलोम **eligible** ▶ **ineligibility** /ɪnˌelɪdʒəˈbɪləti इन्ˌएलिजˈबिलटि/ *noun* [U] अपात्रता, अनुपयुक्तता

**inept** /ɪˈnept इˈनेप्ट्/ *adj.* **inept (at sth)** not able to do sth well कोई काम अच्छे ढंग से करने में असमर्थ; दक्षताहीन, अकुशल *She is totally inept at dealing with people.* ✪ विलोम **adept**

**inequality** /ˌɪnɪˈkwɒləti ˌइनिˈक्वॉलटि/ *noun* [C, U] (*pl.* **inequalities**) (a) difference between groups in society because one has more money, advantages, etc. than the other धन, लाभ आदि की दृष्टि से समाज के विभिन्न वर्गों के बीच असमानता *There will be problems as long as inequality between the races exists.* ✪ विलोम **equality**

**inert** /ɪˈnɜːt इˈनर्ट्/ *adj.* **1** not able to move or act जड़, स्थिर **2** (used about chemical elements) that do not react with other chemicals (रासायनिक तत्वों के लिए प्रयुक्त) अन्य रसायनों के प्रति क्रियाहीन; रासायनिक गुणरहित, निष्क्रिय

> NOTE **Inert gases** को **noble gases** भी कहते हैं। **Helium, argon, krypton** और **neon** ये रासायनिक निष्क्रिय (inert) गैसें हैं।

**inertia** /ɪˈnɜːʃə इˈनर्शा/ *noun* [U] **1** a lack of energy; an inability to move or change ऊर्जा की न्यूनता शक्तिहीनता; निष्क्रियता **2** the physical force that keeps things where they are or keeps them moving in the direction they are travelling वस्तु को स्थिर रखने वाली भौतिक शक्ति-वस्तु एक ही स्थान पर स्थित हो या दिशाविशेष में गति कर रही हो, वस्तु की स्थिति-स्थिरता या गति-स्थिरता, वस्तु की स्थिरता-शक्ति

**inescapable** /ˌɪnɪˈskeɪpəbl ˌइनिˈस्केपबल्/ *adj.* (*formal*) that cannot be avoided जिसे टाला न जा सके; अपरिहार्य *an inescapable conclusion*

**inevitable** /ɪnˈevɪtəbl इन्ˈएविटबल्/ *adj.* that cannot be avoided or prevented from happening जिसे घटित होने से रोका न जा सके, अवश्य होने वाला; अवश्यंभावी *With more cars on the road, traffic jams are inevitable.* ▶ **the inevitable** *noun* [*sing.*] भवितव्यता, नियति *They fought to save the firm from closure, but eventually had to accept the inevitable.* ▶ **inevitability** /ɪnˌevɪtəˈbɪləti इन्ˌएविटˈबिलटि/ *noun* [U] अवश्यंभाविता ▶ **inevitably** /-əbli -अब्लि/ *adv.* अवश्यंभावी रूप से

**inexcusable** /ˌɪnɪkˈskjuːzəbl ˌइनिक्ˈस्क्यूज़बल्/ *adj.* that cannot be allowed or forgiven अक्षम्य, जिसे सहन न किया जा सके *Their behaviour was quite inexcusable.* ✪ पर्याय **unforgivable** ✪ विलोम **excusable**

**inexhaustible** /ˌɪnɪɡˈzɔːstəbl ˌइनिग्ˈज़ॉस्टबल्/ *adj.* that cannot be finished or used up completely जो समाप्त न हो सके या जिसे पूर्णतया समाप्त न किया सके; अक्षय, अपार *Our energy supplies are not inexhaustible.*

**inexpensive** /ˌɪnɪkˈspensɪv ˌइनिक्ˈस्पेन्सिव्/ *adj.* low in price दाम में कम, सस्ता ✪ पर्याय **cheap** ✪ विलोम **expensive** ▶ **inexpensively** *adv.* सस्ते में

**inexperience** /ˌɪnɪkˈspɪəriəns ˌइनिक्ˈस्पीरिअन्स्/ *noun* [U] not knowing how to do sth because you have not done it before किसी काम को करने की जानकारी न होना (क्योंकि उसे पहले नहीं किया); अनुभवहीनता *The mistakes were all due to inexperience.* ✪ विलोम **experience** ▶ **inexperienced** *adj.* अनुभवहीन *He's too young and inexperienced to be given such responsibility.*

**inexplicable** /ˌɪnɪkˈsplɪkəbl ˌइनिक्ˈस्प्लिकबल्/ *adj.* that cannot be explained जिसे समझाया न जा सके, जिसकी व्याख्या न की जा सके; अव्याख्येय *Her sudden disappearance is quite inexplicable.* ✪ विलोम **explicable** ▶ **inexplicably** /-əbli -अब्लि/ *adv.* अव्याख्येय रूप से

**infallible** /ɪnˈfæləbl इन्ˈफ़ैलबल्/ *adj.* **1** (used about a person) never making mistakes or being wrong (व्यक्ति) जो कभी भूलें न करें या ग़लती पर न हो; अमोघ **2** always doing what you are supposed to do ; never failing सदैव अभीष्ट की पूर्ति करने वाला; जिससे

कभी चूक न हो, अचूक *No computer is infallible.* ✪ विलोम **fallible** ▶ **infallibility** /ɪnˌfæləˈbɪləti इन्ˌफ़ैलˈबिलटि / *noun* [U] अचूकपन

**infamous** /ˈɪnfəməs ˈइन्फ़मस् / *adj.* **infamous (for sth)** famous for being bad कुख्यात, बदनाम *The area is infamous for drugs and crime.* ✪ पर्याय **notorious** ⇨ **famous** देखिए।

**infamy** /ˈɪnfəmi ˈइन्फ़मि / *noun* (*formal*) **1** [U] the state of being well known for sth bad or evil बदनामी *a day that will live in infamy* **2** [U, C] (*pl.* **infamies**) an infamous or evil act घृणित कार्य, निंदनीय कार्य, अपकीर्ति *images of horror and infamy*

**infancy** /ˈɪnfənsi ˈइन्फ़न्सि / *noun* [U] the time when you are a baby or young child शिशु होने की अवस्था; शैशव, प्रारंभिक अवस्था (*figurative*) *Research in this field is still in its infancy.*

**infant** /ˈɪnfənt ˈइन्फ़न्ट् / *noun* [C] a baby or very young child शिशु या बच्चा, छोटा बालक अथवा बालिका, छौना या छौनी, नन्हा या नन्ही *There is a high rate of infant mortality* (= many children die when they are still babies). ○ *Mrs Das teaches infants* (= children aged between four and seven).

**NOTE** बोलचाल की या अनौपचारिक भाषा में **baby, toddler** और **child** अधिक प्रचलित हैं।

**infanticide** /ɪnˈfæntɪsaɪd इन्ˈफ़ैन्टिसाइड् / *noun* (*formal*) [U, C] the crime of killing a baby, especially when a parent kills his/her own child शिशु-हत्या (विशेषतः माता-पिता द्वारा अपने शिशु की हत्या)

**infantile** /ˈɪnfəntaɪl ˈइन्फ़न्टाइल् / *adj.* (of behaviour) typical of, or connected with, a baby or very young child and therefore not appropriate for adults or older children (आचरण) शैशव संबंधी और इसलिए बड़ों के अनुपयुक्त, बचकाना *infantile jokes*

**infantry** /ˈɪnfəntri ˈइन्फ़न्ट्रि / *noun* [U, *with sing. or pl. verb*] soldiers who fight on foot पैदल सेना *The infantry was/were supported by heavy gunfire.*

**infant school** *noun* [C] a school for children between the ages of 4 and 7; 4 से 7 वर्ष की आयु के बच्चों का स्कूल, शिशु-पाठशाला; बालवाड़ी

**infatuated** /ɪnˈfætʃueɪtɪd इन्ˈफ़ैचुएटिड् / *adj.* **infatuated (with sb/sth)** having a very strong feeling of love or attraction for sb/sth that usually does not last long and makes you unable to think about anything else प्रेम या आकर्षण की अस्थायी परंतु शक्तिशाली भावना से ग्रस्त; प्रेमोन्मत्त ▶ **infatuation** /ɪnˌfætʃˈeɪʃn इन्ˌफ़ैचुˈएशन् / *noun* [C, U] प्रेमोन्माद, प्रेमांधता

**infect** /ɪnˈfekt इन्ˈफ़ेक्ट् / *verb* [T] **1 infect sb/sth (with sth)** (*usually passive*) to cause sb/sth to have a disease or illness किसी को अस्वस्थता या रोग से आक्रांत करवाना, रोग-संक्रमित होना *We must clean the wound before it becomes infected.* ○ *Many thousands of people have been infected with the virus.* **2** to make people share a particular feeling or emotion लोगों को विशेष अनुभूति या भावना का हिस्सा बनाना *Milind's happiness infected the whole family.*

**infection** /ɪnˈfekʃn इन्ˈफ़ेक्शन्/ *noun* **1** [U] the act of becoming or making sb ill रोगी होने या किसी को रोगी कर देने की क्रिया, संक्रमण, रोग-संचार *A dirty water supply can be a source of infection.* **2** [C] a disease or illness that is caused by harmful bacteria, etc. and affects one part of your body हानिकर बैक्टीरिया या लघु कीटाणु से उत्पन्न अस्वस्थता या बीमारी (जो शरीर के एक अंग को प्रभावित करे); प्रभावन, रोगाणुग्रस्तता *She is suffering from a chest infection.* ○ *an ear infection*

**NOTE** संक्रमण के संभावित कारण हैं **bacteria** या **viruses** जिनके लिए अनौपचारिक शब्द **germs** है।

**infectious** /ɪnˈfekʃəs इनˈफ़ेक्शस् / *adj.* (used about a disease, illness, etc.) that can be easily passed on to another person (अस्वस्थता, बीमारी आदि) एक से दूसरे व्यक्ति तक सरलता से संक्रांत; छुतहा, संसर्गज, संक्रामक *Flu is very infectious.* ○ (*figurative*) *infectious laughter*

**NOTE** **Infectious** रोग वे हैं जो सामान्यतया वायु के द्वारा हमारी सांसों में प्रवेश कर जाते हैं। **Contagious** रोग उन्हें कहते हैं जो एक व्यक्ति दूसरे के संस्पर्श से फैलते हैं।

**infer** /ɪnˈfɜː(r) इन्ˈफ़(र्) / *verb* [T] (**inferring; inferred**) **infer sth (from sth)** to form an opinion or decide that sth is true from the information you have उपलब्ध सूचना के आधार पर कोई राय बनाना या सत्यता का निर्णय करना, से परिणाम निकालना *I inferred from our conversation that he was unhappy with his job.* ▶ **inference** /ˈɪnfərəns ˈइन्फ़रन्स् / *noun* [C] निष्कर्ष

**inferior** /ɪnˈfɪəriə(r) इन्ˈफ़िअरिअ(र्) / *adj.* **inferior (to sb/sth)** low or lower in social position, importance, quality, etc. सामाजिक स्थिति, महत्त्व, गुणवत्ता आदि की दृष्टि से निम्न या निम्नतर स्तर का; घटिया, निकृष्ट *This material is obviously inferior to that one.* ○ *Don't let people make you **feel inferior**.* ✪ विलोम **superior** ▶ **inferior** *noun* [C] निम्न, अवर, छोटा, हीन *She always treats me as her intellectual inferior.* ▶ **inferiority** /ɪnˌfɪəriˈɒrəti इन्ˌफ़िअरिˈऑरटि / *noun* [U] हीनता

**inferiority complex** *noun* [C] the state of feeling less important, clever, successful, etc. than other people अन्य व्यक्तियों की तुलना में महत्त्व आदि की दृष्टि से अपने को हीन समझना; हीन भावना, हीनत्व

**infernal** /ɪnˈfɜːnl इन्ˈफ़नल्/ *adj.* **1** (*only before a noun*) (*old-fashioned*) extremely annoying अत्यंत प्रकोपक, क्षोभक, खिझाने वाला *How I wish that the children would stop making that infernal noise!* **2** (*literary*) belonging to or connected with hell; evil; terrible नारकीय; पैशाचिक; नृशंस *the infernal regions*

**infertile** /ɪnˈfɜːtaɪl इन्ˈफ़टाइल्/ *adj.* **1** (used about a person or animal) not able to have babies or produce young (व्यक्ति या पशु) संतानोत्पादन में असमर्थ, बांझ, वंध्या **2** (used about land) not able to grow strong healthy plants (भूमि) मज़बूत और स्वस्थ पौधे उत्पन्न करने में असमर्थ, अनुपजाऊ, अनुर्वर ✪ विलोम **fertile** ▶ **infertility** /ˌɪnfɜːˈtɪləti ˌइनफ़ˈटिलटि/ *noun* [U] बांझपन, वंध्यात्व *infertility treatment* ✪ विलोम **fertility**

**infested** /ɪnˈfestɪd इन्ˈफ़ेस्टिड्/ *adj.* **infested (with sth)** (used about a place) with large numbers of unpleasant animals or insects in it (स्थान) जहाँ बड़ी संख्या में गंदे प्राणी या कीड़े जमा हो गए हों, कीट आदि से ग्रस्त *The warehouse was infested with rats.* ▶ **infestation** /ˌɪnfeˈsteɪʃn ˌइनफ़ेˈस्टेश्न्/ *noun* [C, U] कीड़ों की भरमार हो जाना, कीटग्रस्तता *an infestation of lice*

**infidel** /ˈɪnfɪdəl ˈइनफ़िडल्/ *noun* [C] (*old-fashioned*) **1** an offensive term used to refer to sb who does not believe in what the speaker considers to be the true religion वक्ता द्वारा प्रचारित सही धर्म में विश्वास न रखने वाले के लिए प्रयुक्त अपमानजनक शब्द **2** sb who rejects a theory or doctrine मत या सिद्धांत को नकारने वाला व्यक्ति; अविश्वासी, संदेहवादी

**infidelity** /ˌɪnfɪˈdeləti ˌइनफ़िˈडेलटि/ *noun* [U, C] (*pl.* **infidelities**) the act of not being faithful to your wife or husband by having a sexual relationship with sb else पति या पत्नी की साथी से बेवफ़ाई (अन्य व्यक्ति से यौन संबंध बनाकर) विश्वासघात **NOTE** इस अर्थ में कम औपचारिक शब्द **unfaithfulness** है।

**infiltrate** /ˈɪnfɪltreɪt ˈइनफ़िल्ट्रेट्/ *verb* [T] to enter an organization, etc. secretly so that you can find out what it is doing गुपचुप तरीक़े से किसी संगठन में घुस जाना (उसके बारे में जानकारी के लिए), घुसपैठ करना *The police managed to infiltrate the gang of terrorists.* ▶ **infiltration** /-eɪʃn -एश्न्/ *noun* [C, U] घुसपैठ ▶ **infiltrator** *noun* [C] घुसपैठिया

**infinite** /ˈɪnfɪnət ˈइनफ़िनट्/ *adj.* **1** very great अत्यधिक, असीम, अपार, अनंत *You need infinite patience for this job.* **2** without limits; that never ends जिसकी सीमाएँ न हों, असीमित, अपरिमित; जिसका कभी अंत न हो, अंतहीन *Supplies of oil are not infinite.* ✪ विलोम **finite**

**infinitely** /ˈɪnfɪnətli ˈइनफ़िनट्लि/ *adv.* very much अत्यधिक, अपरिमित रूप से *Compact discs sound infinitely better than audio cassettes.*

**infinitesimal** /ˌɪnfɪnɪˈtesɪml ˌइनफ़िनिˈटेसिम्ल्/ *adj.* (*formal*) extremely small अत्यंत सूक्ष्म, अत्यल्प, अत्यणु *infinitesimal traces of poison* ○ *an infinitesimal risk* ▶ **infinitesimally** /-məli -मलि/ *adv.* अत्यंत सूक्ष्म रूप से

**infinitive** /ɪnˈfɪnətɪv इन्ˈफ़िनटिव्/ *noun* [C] (*grammar*) the basic form of a verb क्रिया का मूलवर्ती रूप

> **NOTE** अंग्रेज़ी में क्रियार्थक (infinitive) रूप का प्रयोग 'to' के साथ या उसके बिना भी कर सकते हैं। यह उस पर निर्भर करता है कि उससे पहले क्या शब्द आया है—*He can sing.* ○ *He wants to sing.*

**infinity** /ɪnˈfɪnəti इन्ˈफ़िनटि/ *noun* **1** [U] space or time without end अंतहीन स्थान या समय, अनंतता, असीमता *The ocean seemed to stretch over the horizon into infinity.* **2** [U, C] (*symbol*) (in mathematics) the number that is larger than any other that you can think of (गणित) असंख्य संख्या

**infirmary** /ɪnˈfɜːməri इन्ˈफ़मरि/ *noun* [C] (*pl.* **infirmaries**) (used mainly in names) a hospital (मुख्यतया नामों में प्रयुक्त) अस्पताल (किसी के नाम वाला अस्पताल) *The Manchester Royal Infirmary*

**inflamed** /ɪnˈfleɪmd इन्ˈफ़्लेम्ड्/ *adj.* (used about a part of the body) red and swollen or painful because of an infection or injury (शरीर का अंग) लाल और सूजा या दर्द करता हुआ (रोग-संक्रमण या चोट के कारण)

**inflammable** /ɪnˈflæməbl इन्ˈफ़्लैमब्ल्/ *adj.* that burns easily जो आसनी से आग पकड़ ले; ज्वलनशील, तुरंत आग पकड़ने वाला *Petrol is highly inflammable.* ➪ **flammable** देखिए। ✪ विलोम **non-flammable**

**inflammation** /ˌɪnfləˈmeɪʃn ˌइनफ़्लˈमेश्न्/ *noun* [C, U] a condition in which a part of the body becomes red, sore and swollen because of infection or injury शरीर के अंग की एक अवस्था जिसमें वह लाल, तकलीफ़देह और सूजनयुक्त हो जाता है (रोग-संक्रमण या चोट के कारण)

**inflammatory** /ɪnˈflæmətri इन्ˈफ़्लैमट्रि/ *adj.* **1** (*disapproving*) likely to cause very strong feelings of anger उत्तेजक, प्रज्वलनकारी *inflammatory remarks* **2** (*medical*) causing or involving inflammation of a part of the body शरीर में सूजन पैदा करने वाला या उससे संबंधित *inflammatory lung disease*

**inflatable** /ɪnˈfleɪtəbl इन्ˈफ़्लेटबल्/ *adj.* that can or must be filled with air जिसमें हवा भरी जा सके या हवा भरना सर्वथा आवश्यक हो *an inflatable pillow/mattress*

**inflate** /ɪnˈfleɪt इन्ˈफ़्लेट्/ *verb* [I, T] (*formal*) to fill sth with air; to become filled with air हवा भरना, फुलाना; हवा से भरी होना, फूलना **NOTE** इस अर्थ में कम औपचारिक शब्द **blow up** है। ✪ विलोम **deflate**

**inflation** /ɪnˈfleɪʃn इन्ˈफ़्लेशन्/ *noun* [U] a general rise in prices; the rate at which prices rise मूल्यों में सामान्य वृद्धि मुद्रा स्फीति; मूल्यवृद्धि की दर, मुद्रास्फीति की दर *the inflation rate/rate of inflation* ○ *Inflation now stands at 3%.*

**inflect** /ɪnˈflekt इन्ˈफ़्लेक्ट्/ *verb* [I] (*grammar*) if a word inflects, its ending or spelling changes according to its function in the grammar of the sentence; if a language inflects, it has words that do this शब्दों के रूप में परिवर्तन होना, शब्द रूप चलाना, विभक्ति चलाना ▶ **inflected** *adj.* विभक्ति-प्रधान *an inflected language/form/verb*

**inflection** (*also* **inflexion**) /ɪnˈflekʃn इन्ˈफ़्लेक्शन्/ *noun* [C, U] **1** (*grammar*) a change in the form of a word, especially its ending, that changes its function in the grammar of the language, for example -ed, -est शब्द के रूप में (विशेषतः अंत-प्रत्यय में) परिवर्तन (जिससे भाषा के व्याकरण में उसका प्रकार्य बदल जाता है), जैसे -ओं (शिशुओं) **2** the rise and fall of your voice when you are talking बोलते समय सुर में उतार-चढ़ाव ✪ पर्याय **intonation**

**inflexible** /ɪnˈfleksəbl इन्ˈफ़्लेक्सबल्/ *adj.* **1** that cannot be changed or made more suitable for a particular situation; rigid जिसे स्थिति विशेष के अनुसार बदला या अनुकूल न बनाया जा सके, ग़ैर-लचीला; कठोर, अटल *He has a very inflexible attitude to change.* **2** (used about a material) not able to bend or be bent easily (सामान या वस्तुएँ) जो तुरंत न मुड़ सकें या न मोड़ी जा सकें, कड़ा या कड़ी ✪ विलोम **flexible** ▶ **inflexibly** /əbli -अबलि/ *adv.* कठोरता से, ग़ैर-लचीलेपन से ▶ **inflexibility** /ɪnˌfleksəˈbɪləti इन्ˌफ़्लेक्सˈबिलटि/ *noun* [U] कड़ापन, ग़ैर-लचीलापन

**inflict** /ɪnˈflɪkt इन्ˈफ़्लिक्ट्/ *verb* [T] **inflict sth (on sb)** to force sb to have sth unpleasant or sth that he/she does not want किसी को अप्रिय या अनचाही बात मानने के लिए विवश करना, ज़बरदस्ती लादना *Don't inflict your problems on me—I've got enough of my own.*

**in-flight** *adj.* (*only before a noun*) happening or provided during a journey in a plane विमान-यात्रा के दौरान होने वाला या उपलब्ध कराया गया; विमान-यात्राकालीन *in-flight entertainment*

**influence¹** /ˈɪnfluəns ˈइन्फ़्लुअन्स्/ *noun* **1** [U, C] **(an) influence (on/upon sb/sth)** the power to affect, change or control sb/sth व्यक्ति या वस्तु को प्रभावित, परिवर्तन या नियंत्रित करने की शक्ति *Television can have a strong influence on children.* ○ *Nobody should drive while they are **under the influence of** alcohol.* **2** [C] **an influence (on sb/sth)** a person or thing that affects or changes sb/sth व्यक्ति या वस्तु को प्रभावित या परिवर्तित करने वाला व्यक्ति या वस्तु *His new friend has been a good influence on him.* ○ *cultural/environmental influences*

**influence²** /ˈɪnfluəns ˈइन्फ़्लुअन्स्/ *verb* [T] to have an effect on or power over sb/sth so that he/she/it changes व्यक्ति या वस्तु में परिवर्तन लाने के लिए उस पर प्रभाव या शक्ति का उपयोग करना *You must decide for yourself. Don't let anyone else influence you.* ○ *Her style of painting has been influenced by Japanese art.*

**NOTE** **Affect** और **influence** का लगभग एक ही अर्थ है। **Affect** का प्रयोग प्रायः तब होता है जब परिवर्तन की प्रकृति भौतिक हो और यदि विचार या मनोवृत्ति में परिवर्तन की बात हो तो प्रायः **influence** का प्रयोग होता है—*Drinking alcohol can affect your ability to drive.* ○ *TV advertisements have influenced my attitude towards the homeless.*

**influential** /ˌɪnfluˈenʃl ˌइन्फ़्लुˈएन्शल्/ *adj.* **influential (in sth/in doing sth)** having power or influence प्रभावशाली, असरदार *an influential politician* ○ *He was influential in getting the hostages set free.*

**influenza** /ˌɪnfluˈenzə ˌइन्फ़्लुˈएन्ज़ा/ (*formal*) = **flu**

**influx** /ˈɪnflʌks ˈइन्फ़्लक्स्/ *noun* [C, *usually sing.*] **an influx (of sb/sth) (into...)** large numbers of people or things arriving suddenly बड़ी संख्या में लोगों या वस्तुओं का एकाएक कहीं से आना; अंतर्वहन, अंतर्वाही *the summer influx of visitors from abroad*

**info** /ˈɪnfəʊ ˈइन्फ़ो/ *noun* **1** [U] (*informal*) information सूचना, जानकारी *Have you had any more info about the job yet?* **2** **info-** *prefix* (*used in nouns*) connected with information सूचना-विषयक *an infosheet* ○ *Phone now for a free infopack.*

**inform** /ɪnˈfɔːm इन्ˈफ़ॉम्/ *verb* [T] **inform sb (of/about sth)** to give sb information (about sth), especially in an official way किसी को (किसी के विषय में) सूचना देना (विशेषतः आधिकारिक रूप से) *You should inform the police of the accident.* ○ *Do **keep** me **informed** of any changes.*

**PHR V** **inform on sb** to give information to the police, etc. about what sb has done wrong (किसी प्रकार के ग़लत काम के विषय में) पुलिस को सूचना देना *The wife of the killer informed on her husband.*

**informal** /ɪnˈfɔːml इन्ˈफ़ॉम्ल् / *adj.* relaxed and friendly or suitable for a relaxed occasion बेतकल्लुफ़ी का और मित्रवत या इस प्रकार के अवसर के उपयुक्त; अनौपचारिक *Don't get dressed up for the party—it'll be very informal.* ○ *The two leaders had informal discussions before the conference began.* ✪ विलोम **formal** **NOTE** इस शब्दकोश में कतिपय शब्दों या अभिव्यक्तियों को **informal** (अनौपचारिक) कहा गया है। इसका अर्थ है कि मित्रों या सुपरिचित व्यक्तियों से मौखिक बातचीत में उनका प्रयोग किया जा सकता है परंतु लिखित माध्यम के भाषा व्यवहार–ग्रंथ, औपचारिक पत्र आदि में नहीं। ▶ **informality** /ˌɪnfɔːˈmæləti ˌइन्फ़ॉˈमैलटि / *noun* [U] अनौपचारिकता *an atmosphere of informality* ▶ **informally** /-məli -मलि / *adv.* अनौपचारिक रूप से *I was told informally* (= unofficially) *that our plans had been accepted.*

**informant** /ɪnˈfɔːmənt इन्ˈफ़ॉमन्ट् / *noun* [C] a person who gives secret knowledge or information about sb/sth to the police or a newspaper पुलिस या अख़बार को किसी व्यक्ति या वस्तु के विषय में गुप्त रूप से जानकारी देने वाला व्यक्ति; मुख़बिर ➪ **informer** देखिए।

**information** /ˌɪnfəˈmeɪʃn ˌइन्फ़ˈमेश्न् / (*informal* **info**) *noun* [U] **information (on/about sb/sth)** knowledge or facts जानकारी या तथ्य *For further information please send for our fact sheet.* ○ *Can you give me some information about evening classes in Italian, please?*

**NOTE** **Information** शब्द अगणनीय है इसलिए *'I need an information'* प्रयोग अमान्य है। मान्य प्रयोग **a bit** या **piece of information** हैं।

**information superhighway** *noun* [C] (*computing*) a name for a large electronic system such as the Internet that is used for sending information to people एक बृहत इलेक्ट्रॉनिक प्रणाली, जैसे इंटरनेट (सूचना के संप्रेषण के लिए प्रयुक्त); इनफ़र्मेशन सुपर हाइवे

**information technology** *noun* [U] (*abbr.* **IT**) (*computing*) the study or use of electronic equipment, especially computers, for collecting, storing and sending out information सूचना को संचित और संप्रेषित करने के लिए इलेक्ट्रॉनिक उपकरण (विशेषतः कंप्यूटर) का अध्ययन या प्रयोग; सूचना प्रौद्योगिकी, कंप्यूटर के अध्ययन और प्रयोग की जानकारी

**informative** /ɪnˈfɔːmətɪv इन्ˈफ़ॉमटिव् / *adj.* giving useful knowledge or information उपयोगी सूचना या जानकारी देने वाला; सूचनात्मक, ज्ञानप्रद, शिक्षाप्रद

**informed** /ɪnˈfɔːmd इन्ˈफ़ॉम्ड् / *adj.* having knowledge or information about sth किसी वस्तु के विषय में जानकारी से युक्त, किसी बात का जानकार, जानकारीपूर्ण *Consumers cannot make informed choices unless they are told all the facts.*

**informer** /ɪnˈfɔːmə(r) इन्ˈफ़ॉम(र्) / *noun* [C] a criminal who gives the police information about other criminals वह अपराधी जो दूसरे अपराधियों के बारे में पुलिस को जानकारी देता है; सूचक ➪ **informant** देखिए।

**infra-** *prefix* (*in adjectives*) below a particular limit एक विशेष सीमा से नीचे, अव- *infrared* ➪ **ultra-** देखिए।

**infrared** /ˌɪnfrəˈred ˌइन्फ्रˈरेड् / *adj.* (used about light) that is produced by hot objects but cannot be seen (प्रकाश के विषय में प्रयुक्त) तापित या उष्ण वस्तुओं द्वारा उत्पन्न परंतु अदृश्य; अवरक्त ➪ **ultraviolet** देखिए तथा **wavelength** पर चित्र देखिए।

**infrastructure** /ˈɪnfrəstrʌktʃə(r) ˈइन्फ्रस्ट्रक्च(र्) / *noun* [C, U] the basic systems and services that are necessary for a country or an organization, for example buildings, transport, and water and power supplies किसी देश या संगठन के लिए अपेक्षित आधारभूत प्रणालियाँ और सेवाएँ (जैसे भवन, यातायात, पानी और बिजली की आपूर्ति), बुनियादी ढाँचा, अवसरंचना *economic/social/transport infrastructure* ▶ **infrastructural** /ˌɪnfrəˈstrʌktʃərəl ˌइन्फ्रˈस्ट्रक्चरल् / *adj.* बुनियादी ढाँचा विषयक

**infrequent** /ɪnˈfriːkwənt इन्ˈफ्रीक्वन्ट् / *adj.* not happening often कभी-कभी होने वाला; विरल, प्रायिक ✪ विलोम **frequent** ▶ **infrequently** *adv.* विरल रूप से

**infringe** /ɪnˈfrɪndʒ इन्ˈफ्रिन्ज् / *verb* (*formal*) **1** [T] to break a rule, law, agreement, etc. नियम, क़ानून, समझौता आदि तोड़ना, आज्ञा उल्लंघन करना *The material can be copied without infringing copyright.* **2** [I] **infringe on/upon sth** to reduce or limit sb's rights, freedom, etc. किसी के अधिकार, स्वतंत्रता आदि को कम या सीमित कर देना; अतिलंघन करना *She refused to answer questions that infringed on her private affairs.* ▶ **infringement** *noun* [C, U] (अधिकार) हनन, अतिक्रमण

**infuriate** /ɪnˈfjʊərieɪt इन्ˈफ़्युअरिएट् / *verb* [T] to make sb very angry किसी को बहुत क्रुद्ध कर देना ▶ **infuriating** *adj.* क्रोधजनक *an infuriating habit* ▶ **infuriatingly** *adv.* क्रोधजनक रीति से

**infuse** /ɪnˈfjuːz इन्ˈफ़्यूज़् / *verb* **1** [T] **infuse A into B; infuse B with A** (*formal*) to make sb/sth have a particular quality व्यक्ति या वस्तु में विशेष गुण या भावना का संचार करना *Her novels are infused with sadness.* **2** [T] (*formal*) to have an effect on all parts of sth किसी वस्तु के सब अंगों को प्रभावित करना *Politics infuses all aspects of our lives.* **3** [I, T] if you **infuse herbs** or they **infuse**, you put them in hot water until the flavour has passed into the water जड़ी-बूटि आदि को गरम पानी में तब तक रखना जब तक उनकी सुगंध पानी में न पहुँच जाए, जड़ी-बूटी का काढ़ा बनाना, निचोड़ना, अर्क बनाना

**infusion** /ɪnˈfju:ʒn इन्ˈफ़्यूश़न्/ *noun* **1** [C, U] **infusion of sth (into sth)** (*formal*) the act of adding sth to sth else in order to make it stronger or more successful अतिरिक्त वस्तु के संयोग से किसी को अधिक शक्तिशाली या प्रभावकारी बनाने की प्रक्रिया; अनुप्रेरण, अनुप्राणन, निषेचन *an infusion of new talent into teaching* ○ *The company needs an infusion of new blood* (= new employees with new ideas). **2** [C] a drink or medicine made by putting **herbs** in hot water काढ़ा, क्वाथ **3** [C, U] (*medical*) the act of introducing a liquid substance into the body, especially into a **vein** शरीर में, विशेषतया नसों में, द्रव पदार्थ को प्रविष्ट करना

**ingenious** /ɪnˈdʒi:niəs इन्ˈजीनिअस्/ *adj.* **1** (used about a thing or an idea) made or planned in a clever way (वस्तु या विचार) चतुराई से बनाया गया या सोचा गया, कौशलपूर्ण, कुशल *an ingenious plan for making lots of money* ○ *an ingenious device/experiment/invention* **2** (used about a person) full of new ideas and clever at finding solutions to problems or at inventing things (व्यक्ति) नए विचारों से युक्त और समस्याओं के समाधान या नई बातों के आविष्कार में दक्ष; प्रतिभाशाली, मेधावी, विदग्ध ▶ **ingeniously** *adv.* विदग्धता से ▶ **ingenuity** /ˌɪndʒəˈnju:əti ˌइन्जˈन्यूअटि/ *noun* [U] विदग्धता, प्रतिभाशालिता

**ingenuous** /ɪnˈdʒənjuəs इन्ˈजे़न्युअस्/ *adj.* (*formal*) honest, innocent and willing to trust people in a way that sometimes seems foolish निष्कपट और सरल *It is ingenuous to suppose that money did not play a part in his decision.* ✪ विलोम **disingenuous** ▶ **ingenuously** /-li -लि/ *adv.* (*formal*) सरलतापूर्वक

**ingest** /ɪnˈdʒest इन्ˈजे़स्ट्/ *verb* [T] (*technical*) to take food, drugs, etc. into your body, usually by swallowing भोजन, औषधियाँ आदि शरीर के अंदर पहुँचाना (प्रायः निगलकर); अंतर्ग्रहण करना ▶ **ingestion** *noun* [U] अंतर्ग्रहण

**ingot** /ˈɪŋgət ˈइङ्गट्/ *noun* [C] a solid piece of metal, especially gold or silver, usually shaped like a brick (प्रायः ईंट के आकार का) धातुखंड (विशेषतः सोना या चाँदी); निपिंड, शिलिका

**ingrained** /ɪnˈgreɪnd इन्ˈग्रेन्ड्/ *adj.* **ingrained (in sb/sth)** (used about a habit, an attitude, etc.) that has existed for a long time and is therefore difficult to change (आदत, सोच आदि) लंबे समय से चली आ रही, पुरानी और इसलिए जिसे बदलना कठिन हो, गहरा जमा हुआ, पक्का; अंतर्जनित *ingrained prejudices/beliefs*

**ingratiate** /ɪnˈgreɪʃieɪt इन्ˈग्रेशिएट्/ *verb* [T] (*formal*) **ingratiate yourself (with sb)** to make yourself liked by doing or saying things that will please people, especially people who might be useful to you किसी की प्रशंसा कर उसका कृपापात्र बन जाना (विशेषतः अपने लाभ के लिए) किसी का अनुग्रह प्राप्त करना *He was always trying to ingratiate himself with his teachers.* ▶ **ingratiating** *adj.* अनुग्रहकारी *an ingratiating smile* ▶ **ingratiatingly** *adv.* अनुग्रहकारी रीति से

**ingratitude** /ɪnˈgrætɪtju:d इन्ˈग्रैटिट्यूड्/ *noun* [U] (*formal*) the state of not showing or feeling thanks for sth that has been done for you; not being grateful कृतज्ञता का अभाव; कृतघ्नता **NOTE** इस अर्थ में **ungratefulness** कम औपचारिक शब्द है। ✪ विलोम **gratitude**

**ingredient** /ɪnˈgri:diənt इन्ˈग्रीडिअन्ट्/ *noun* [C] **1** one of the items of food you need to make sth to eat किसी खाद्य पदार्थ का घटक *Mix all the ingredients together in a bowl.* **2** one of the qualities necessary to make sth successful सफलता का तत्व *The film has all the ingredients of success.*

**inhabit** /ɪnˈhæbɪt इन्ˈहैबिट्/ *verb* [T] to live in a place किसी स्थान पर रहना, बसना, निवास करना *Are the Aran Islands still inhabited* (= do people live there)?

**inhabitable** /ɪnˈhæbɪtənt इन्ˈहैबिटबल्/ *adj.* that can be lived in रहने लायक, निवास-योग्य *The house was no longer inhabitable after the earthquake.* ✪ विलोम **uninhabitable**

**inhabitant** /ɪnˈhæbɪtənt इन्ˈहैबिटन्ट्/ *noun* [C, *usually pl.*] a person or animal that lives in a place किसी स्थान पर रहने वाला; निवासी, बाशिंदा *The local inhabitants protested at the plans for a new highway.*

**inhale** /ɪnˈheɪl इन्ˈहेल्/ *verb* [I, T] to breathe in साँस लेना *Be careful not to inhale the fumes from the paint.* ✪ विलोम **exhale** ▶ **inhalation**/ˌɪnhəˈleɪʃn ˌइन्हˈलेशन्/ *noun* [U] अंतःश्वसन *They were treated for the effects of smoke inhalation.*

**inhaler** /ɪnˈheɪlə(r) इन्ˈहेल(र्)/ *noun* [C] a small device containing medicine that you breathe in through your mouth, used by people who have problems with breathing औषधियुक्त (छोटी नली के

आकार की) वस्तु जिसे आप मुँह पर रख कर साँस अंदर खींचते हैं (साँस के रोगियों द्वारा प्रयुक्त); प्रश्वसन यंत्र

**inherent** /ɪnˈhɪərənt इन्ˈहिअरन्ट्/ *adj.* **inherent (in sb/sth)** that is a basic or permanent part of sb/sth and that cannot be removed व्यक्ति या वस्तु का मूलवर्ती या स्थायी अंश; अंतर्निहित *The risk of collapse is inherent in any business.* ▶ **inherently** *adv.* अंतर्निहित रूप से *No matter how safe we make them, motorbikes are inherently dangerous.*

**inherit** /ɪnˈherɪt इन्ˈहेरिट्/ *verb* [T] **inherit sth (from sb)** **1** to receive property, money, etc. from sb who has died मृतक की संपत्ति, धन आदि को (उत्तराधिकार या विरासत के रूप में) प्राप्त करना *I inherited quite a lot of money from my mother. She left me Rs 120,000 when she died.* ➪ **heir** देखिए। ➪ **disinherit** देखिए। **2** to receive a quality, characteristic, etc. from your parents or family माता-पिता या परिवार के गुणों को (विरासत के रूप में) प्राप्त करना *She has inherited her father's gift for languages.*

**inheritance** /ɪnˈherɪtəns इन्ˈहेरिटन्स्/ *noun* [C, U] the act of inheriting; the money, property, etc. that you inherit उत्तराधिकार, विरासत; उत्तराधिकार या विरासत के रूप में प्राप्त धन-संपत्ति *inheritance tax*

**inhibit** /ɪnˈhɪbɪt इन्ˈहिबिट्/ *verb* [T] **1** to prevent sth or make sth happen more slowly किसी बात को रोकना या उसकी गति को मंद कर देना; निषेध करना, अवरोध करना *a drug to inhibit the growth of tumours* **2 inhibit sb (from sth/from doing sth)** to make sb nervous and embarrassed so that he/she is unable to do sth किसी को चिंतित और परेशान कर देना (कि वह कुछ कर न सके) *The fact that her boss was there inhibited her from saying what she really felt.* ▶ **inhibited** *adj.* अवरुद्ध *The young man felt shy and inhibited in the roomful of women.* ✪ विलोम **uninhibited**

**inhibition** /ˌɪnhɪˈbɪʃn; ˌɪnɪˈb- ˌइनहिˈबिश्न्; ˌइनिˈब/ *noun* [C, U] a shy or nervous feeling that stops you from saying or doing what you really want अभीष्ट बात को कहने या करने से रोकने वाली संकोच भावना; अंतर्बाधा, अवरोध *After the first day of the course, people started to **lose** their **inhibitions**.*

**inhospitable** /ˌɪnhɒˈspɪtəbl ˌइनहॉˈस्पिटब्ल्/ *adj.* **1** (used about a place) not pleasant to live in, especially because of the weather (स्थान) जहाँ रहना सुखद न हो (विशेषतः मौसम के कारण); अप्रीतिकर *the inhospitable Arctic regions* **2** (used about a person) not friendly or welcoming to guests (व्यक्ति) जो मित्रवत तथा सत्कारशील न हो; असत्कारी, रूखा ✪ विलोम **hospitable**

**inhuman** /ɪnˈhjuːmən इन्ˈह्यूमन्/ *adj.* **1** very cruel and without pity बहुत क्रूर और निर्दय; अमानवीय *inhuman treatment/conditions* **2** not seeming to be human and therefore frightening मानव सदृश नहीं और इसलिए डरावना *an inhuman noise*

**inhumane** /ˌɪnhjuːˈmeɪn ˌइनह्यूˈमेन्/ *adj.* very cruel; not caring if people or animals suffer बहुत निर्मम; मनुष्यों या पशुओं के प्रति असंवेदनशील; अमानवीय *the inhumane conditions in which animals are kept on some large farms* ✪ विलोम **humane**

**inhumanity** /ˌɪnhjuːˈmænəti ˌइनह्यूˈमैनटि/ *noun* [U] very cruel behaviour बहुत निर्मम व्यवहार, अमानवीयता *The 20th century is full of examples of man's inhumanity to man.* ✪ विलोम **humanity**

**inimitable** /ɪˈnɪmɪtəbl इˈनिमिटब्ल्/ *adj.* too good to be satisfactorily copied by anyone अत्युतकृष्ठ, अननुकरणीय *She narrated the incident in her own inimitable style.*

**initial**[1] /ɪˈnɪʃl इˈनिश्ल्/ *adj.* (*only before a noun*) happening at the beginning; first प्रारंभिक; प्रथम *My initial reaction was to refuse, but I later changed my mind.* ○ *the initial stages of our survey*

**initial**[2] /ɪˈnɪʃl इˈनिश्ल्/ *noun* [C, *usually pl.*] the first letter of a name नाम का प्रथम अक्षर, आद्याक्षर *Om Prakash Chandrababu's initials are O.P.C.*

**initial**[3] /ɪˈnɪʃl इˈनिश्ल्/ *verb* [T] (**initia<u>l</u>ling; initia<u>l</u>led** *AmE* **initia<u>l</u>ing; initia<u>l</u>ed**) to mark or sign sth with your initials किसी पर आद्याक्षर अंकित करना *Any changes made when writing a cheque should be initialled by you.*

**initially** /ɪˈnɪʃəli इˈनिशलि/ *adv.* at the beginning; at first शुरू या आरंभ में; पहले *I liked the job initially but it soon got quite boring.*

**initiate** /ɪˈnɪʃieɪt इˈनिशिएट्/ *verb* [T] **1** (*formal*) to start sth आरंभ करना, श्रीगणेश या सूत्रपात करना *to initiate peace talks* **2 initiate sb (into sth)** to explain sth to sb or make him/her experience sth for the first time पहली बार किसी को कोई बात समझाना या कुछ अनुभव कराना *I wasn't initiated into the joys of skiing until I was 30.* **3 initiate sb (into sth)** to bring sb into a group by means of a special ceremony विशेष समारोह के माध्यम से किसी को समुदाय विशेष का सदस्य बनाना *to initiate sb into a secret society* ▶ **initiation** /-eɪʃn -एश्न्/ *noun* [U] दीक्षा, श्रीगणेश, सूत्रपात, अंतःप्रवेश *All the new students had to go through a strange initiation ceremony.*

**initiative** /ɪˈnɪʃətɪv इˈनिशटिव़्/ *noun* **1** [C] official action that is taken to solve a problem or improve a situation समस्या के समाधान या स्थिति में सुधार के लिए की गई आधिकारिक कार्रवाई; पहल *a new government initiative to help people start small businesses* **2** [U] the ability to see and do what is necessary without waiting for sb to tell you आवश्यक उपाय कर लेने की निजी योग्यता या कल्पनाशक्ति *Don't keep asking me how to do it. Use your initiative.* **3 the initiative** [*sing.*] the stronger position because you have done sth first; the advantage पहले शुरुआत करने से बनी सशक्त स्थिति, पहल शक्ति; लाभ की स्थिति *The enemy forces have **lost the initiative**.*

IDM **on your own initiative** without being told by sb else what to do बिना किसी के बताए, अपनी समझ से

**take the initiative** to be first to act to influence a situation स्थिति में परिवर्तन लाने के लिए पहल करना

**inject** /ɪnˈdʒekt इन्ˈजेक्ट्/ *verb* [T] **1** to put a drug under the skin of person's or an animal's body with a needle (**syringe**) सूई से मनुष्य या पशु के शरीर में त्वचा के अंदर दवा पहुँचाना, सूई लगाना, इंजेक्शन लगाना, टीका लगाना **2 inject sth (into sth)** to add sth (किसी वस्तु में) कोई वस्तु डालना *They injected a lot of money into the business.*

**injection** /ɪnˈdʒekʃn इन्ˈजेक्शन्/ *noun* **1** [C, U] **(an) injection (of sth) (into sb/sth)** the act of putting a drug or substance under the skin of a person's or an animal's body with a needle (**a syringe**) सूई (सिरिंज) से मनुष्य या पशु के शरीर में त्वचा के अंदर दवा पहुँचाने की क्रिया; इंजेक्शन *to give sb an injection* ○ *a tetanus injection* ○ *An anaesthetic was administered **by injection**.* ✪ पर्याय **jab** **2** [C] a large amount of sth that is added to sth to help it किसी वस्तु की बड़ी मात्रा जिसके अतिरिक्त प्रयोग से किसी में जान आए *The theatre needs a huge **cash injection** if it is to stay open.* **3** [U, C] the act of forcing liquid into sth किसी में ज़बरदस्ती कोई द्रव डालना *fuel injection*

**injunction** /ɪnˈdʒʌŋkʃn इन्ˈजङ्क्शन्/ *noun* [C] **an injunction (against sb)** an official order from a court of law to do/not do sth विधि-निषेध के विषय में न्यायालय का औपचारिक आदेश; समादेश, निषेधाज्ञा *A court injunction prevented the programme from being shown on TV.*

**injure** /ˈɪndʒə(r) ˈइन्ज(र्)/ *verb* [T] to harm or hurt yourself or sb else physically, especially in an accident शारीरिक चोट पहुँचाना, घायल होना या करना (विशेषतः दुर्घटना में) *The goalkeeper seriously injured himself when he hit the goalpost.* ○ *She fell and injured her back.* ➪ **hurt** पर नोट देखिए।

**injured** /ˈɪndʒəd ˈइन्जड्/ *adj.* **1** physically or mentally hurt शारीरिक या मानसिक रूप से आहत *an injured arm/leg* ○ *injured pride* **2 the injured** *noun* [*pl.*] people who have been hurt घायल लोग *The injured were rushed to hospital.*

**injurious** /ɪnˈdʒʊəriəs इन्ˈजुअरिअस्/ *adj.* (*formal*) harmful or likely to cause damage हानिकारक, अनिष्टकर, क्षतिशील *Smoking is injurious to health.*

**injury** /ˈɪndʒəri ˈइन्जरि/ *noun* [C, U] (*pl.* **injuries**) **injury (to sb/sth)** harm done to a person's or an animal's body, especially in an accident मनुष्य या पशु के शरीर को लगी चोट (विशेषतः दुर्घटना में) *They escaped from the accident with only **minor injuries**.* ○ *Injury to the head can be extremely dangerous.*

**injury time** *noun* [U] (*BrE*) time that is added to the end of a **rugby**, football, etc. match when there has been time lost because of injuries to players फ़ुटबॉल आदि खेल में खिलाड़ियों को चोट लगने से नष्ट समय की पूर्ति के लिए अंत में दिया गया अतिरिक्त समय

**injustice** /ɪnˈdʒʌstɪs इन्ˈजस्टिस्/ *noun* [U, C] the fact of a situation being unfair; an unfair act अन्याय; अन्यायपूर्ण काम *racial/social injustice* ○ *People are protesting about the injustice of the new tax.*

IDM **do sb an injustice** to judge sb unfairly किसी के साथ अन्याय करना *I'm afraid I've done you both an injustice.*

**ink** /ɪŋk इङ्क्/ *noun* [U, C] coloured liquid that is used for writing, drawing, etc. रोशनाई, स्याही, मसि *Please write **in ink**, not pencil.*

**inkling** /ˈɪŋklɪŋ ˈइङ्क्लिङ्/ *noun* [C, *usually sing.*] **an inkling (of sth/that...)** a slight feeling (about sth) (किसी के विषय में) आभास *I had an inkling that something was wrong.*

**inky** /ˈɪŋki ˈइङ्कि/ *adj.* made black with ink; very dark स्याही से गंदा; बहुत काला, काला स्याह *inky fingers* ○ *an inky night sky*

**inlaid** /ˌɪnˈleɪd ˌइन्ˈलेड्/ *adj.* **inlaid (with sth)** (used about furniture, floors, etc.) decorated with designs of wood, metal, etc. that are put into the surface (फ़र्नीचर, फ़र्श आदि) लकड़ी, धातु आदि के डिज़ाइनों को जड़ने से सजावटी *a box inlaid with gold*

**inland** /ˈɪnlænd ˈइन्लैन्ड्/ *adj.* /ˌɪnˈlænd/ *adv.* away from the coast or borders of a country देश के समुद्रतट या सीमाओं से दूर, देश के भीतरी भाग में *The village lies 20 kilometres inland.* ○ *Goods are carried inland along narrow mountain roads.*

**in-laws** *noun* [*pl.*] (*informal*) your husband's or wife's mother and father or other relations पति या पत्नी के माता-पिता या अन्य संबंधी

**inlet** /ˈɪnlet ˈइन्लेट्/ *noun* [C] a narrow area of water that stretches into the land from the sea or a lake समुद्र या झील में से भूमि की ओर गई तंग जलधारा; उपखाड़ी

**inmate** /ˈɪnmeɪt ˈइन्मेट्/ *noun* [C] one of the people living in an institution such as a prison जेल, छात्रावास आदि स्थान पर रहने वाले व्यक्तियों में से एक; संवासी

**inn** /ɪn इन्/ *noun* [C] a small hotel or old pub, usually in the country छोटा होटल या पुरानी मद्यशाला (प्रायः पश्चिम के ग्रामीण क्षेत्रों में); सराय

**innate** /ɪˈneɪt इˈनेट्/ *adj.* (used about an ability or quality) that you have when you are born (योग्यता और गुण) जन्मजात, अंतर्निहित *the innate ability to learn*

**inner** /ˈɪnə(r) ˈइन(र्)/ *adj.* (*only before a noun*) **1** (of the) inside; towards or close to the centre of a place अंदर का, अंदरूनी; किसी स्थान के केंद्र की ओर या उसके निकट, अंदर की तरफ़, भीतरी *The inner ear is very delicate.* ○ *an inner courtyard* ✪ विलोम **outer** **2** (used about a feeling, etc.) that you do not express or show to other people; private (मनोभाव) जिसे आप व्यक्त या प्रदर्शित नहीं करते, अव्यक्त; निजी या व्यक्तिगत *Everyone has inner doubts.*

**inner city** *noun* [C] the poor parts of a large city, near the centre, that often have a lot of social problems बड़े शहर के बीच के भाग में ग़रीबों का इलाक़ा (अनेक सामाजिक समस्याओं से ग्रस्त) ▶ **inner-city** *adj.* अतंस्थ शहर (*only before a noun*) *Inner-city schools often have difficulty in attracting good teachers.*

**inner ear** *noun* [C] the part of your ear that is inside your head and that consists of the organs that control your balance and hearing कान का अंदरूनी भाग (जो श्रवण-शक्ति और संतुलन को नियंत्रित करता है) ➪ **middle ear** देखिए तथा **ear** पर चित्र देखिए।

**innermost** /ˈɪnəməʊst ˈइनमोस्ट्/ *adj.* (*only before a noun*) **1** (used about a feeling or thought) most secret or private (मनोभाव या विचार) सर्वाधिक गुप्त या निजी; व्यक्तिगत *She never told anyone her innermost thoughts.* **2** nearest to the centre or inside of sth केंद्र-स्थल के सबसे निकट या किसी के भीतर *the innermost shrine of the temple*

**inner tube** *noun* [C] a rubber tube filled with air inside a tyre टायर के अंदर की हवा से भरी ट्यूब

**innings** /ˈɪnɪŋz ˈइनिङ्ज़्/ *noun* [C] (*pl.* **innings**) a period of time in a game of cricket when it is the turn of one player or team to hit the ball (**to bat**) क्रिकेट में एक कालावधि जिसमें एक खिलाड़ी या सारी टीम बल्लेबाज़ी करती है; पारी, इनिंग्स

**innocence** /ˈɪnəsns ˈइनसन्स्/ *noun* [U] **1** the fact of not being guilty of a crime, etc. अपराध का दोषी न होने की स्थिति; निर्दोषता *The accused man* ***protested*** *his* ***innocence*** *throughout his trial.* ✪ विलोम **guilt** **2** lack of knowledge and experience of the world, especially of bad things सांसारिक अनुभव (विशेषतः प्रतिकूल) का अभाव; अनुभवहीनता, भोलापन *the innocence of childhood*

**innocent** /ˈɪnəsnt ˈइनसन्ट्/ *adj.* **1 innocent (of sth)** not having done wrong जिसने ग़लत काम नहीं किया; निर्दोष, बेगुनाह, बेक़सूर *An innocent man was arrested by mistake.* ○ *to be innocent of a crime* ✪ पर्याय **blameless** ✪ विलोम **guilty** **2** (*only before a noun*) being hurt or killed in a crime, war, etc. although not involved in it in any way अपराध-कर्म, युद्ध आदि में घायल या मृत (यद्यपि उससे संबधित नहीं या कोई लेना-देना नहीं) ***innocent victims*** *of a bomb blast* ○ *an innocent bystander* **3** not wanting to cause harm or upset sb, although it does अहानिकर, निरीह *He got very aggressive when I asked* ***an innocent question*** *about his past life.* **4** not knowing the bad things in life; believing everything you are told जीवन के कुत्सित पक्ष से अपरिचित, अबोध; सब बातों पर विश्वास कर लेने वाला, सीधा, सरल *She was so innocent as to believe that politicians never lie.* ✪ पर्याय **naive** ▶ **innocently** *adv.* अबोध भाव से *'What are you doing here?' she asked innocently* (= pretending she did not know the answer).

**innocuous** /ɪˈnɒkjuəs इˈनॉक्युअस्/ *adj.* (*formal*) not meant to cause harm or upset sb अहानिकर, सीधा-सादा *I made an* ***innocuous remark*** *about teachers and she got really angry.* ✪ पर्याय **harmless** ▶ **innocuously** *adv.* सीधे-सादे ढंग से

**innovate** /ˈɪnəveɪt ˈइनवेट्/ *verb* [I] to create new things, ideas or ways of doing sth नई वस्तुओं, विचारों या विधियों की रचना करना; नवप्रवर्तन करना, नवपरिवर्तन लाना ▶ **innovation** /ˌɪnəˈveɪʃn ˌइनˈवेशन्/ *noun* [C, U] **(an) innovation (in sth)** [C] नवप्रवर्तन, नवपरिवर्तन *technological innovations in industry* ▶ **innovative** /ˈɪnəvətɪv; ˈɪnəveɪtɪv ˈइनवटिव्; ˈइनवेटिव्/ *adj.* नवप्रवर्तनकारी, नवपरिवर्तनकारी *innovative methods/designs/products* ▶ **innovator** *noun* [C] नवप्रवर्तक, नवपरिवर्तनकार

**innuendo** /ˌɪnjuˈendəʊ ˌइन्युˈएन्डो/ *noun* [C, U] (*pl.* **innuendoes** or **innuendos**) an indirect way of talking about sb/sth, usually suggesting sth bad or rude व्यक्ति या वस्तु के विषय में परोक्ष टिप्पणी (प्रायः अनुचित प्रकार की); कटाक्ष, व्यंग्य *His speech was full of sexual innuendo.*

**innumerable** /ɪˈnjuːmərəbl इˈन्यूमरब्ल्/ *adj.* too many to be counted असंख्य, अनगिनत

**inoculate** /ɪˈnɒkjuleɪt इˈनॉक्युलेट्/ *verb* [T] **inoculate sb (against sth)** to protect a person or animal from a disease by giving him/her/it a mild form of the disease with a needle which is put under the skin (**an injection**) मनुष्य या पशु को इंजेक्शन लगाकर उसका रोग से बचाव करना, बीमारी से बचाव के लिए मनुष्य या पशु को टीका लगाना *The children have been inoculated against measles.* ✪ पर्याय **Immunize** और **vaccinate** ▶ **inoculation** /-eɪʃn -एश्न्/ *noun* [C, U] टीका

**inoffensive** /ˌɪnəˈfensɪv ˌइनˈफ़ेन्सिव़्/ *adj.* not likely to offend or upset sb; harmless जो किसी को नाराज़ या परेशान न करे; अहानिकर, आपत्तिहीन ✪ विलोम **offensive**

**inoperable** /ɪnˈɒpərəbl इन्ˈऑपरब्ल्/ *adj.* (used about a disease) that cannot be cured by a medical operation (रोग) जो शल्यक्रिया से ठीक न हो सके, शल्यक्रियातीत ✪ विलोम **operable**

**inordinate** /ɪnˈɔːdɪnət इन्ˈऑडिनट्/ *adj.* (*formal*) much greater than usual or expected सामान्य या प्रत्याशित से बहुत अधिक, अत्यधिक; अमर्यादित *They spent an **inordinate amount** of time and money on the production.* ▶ **inordinately** *adv.* अत्यधिक

**inorganic** /ˌɪnɔːˈgænɪk ˌइनऑˈगैनिक्/ *adj.* not made of or coming from living things जो सजीवों से निर्मित या प्राप्त नहीं; अजैव *Rocks and metals are inorganic substances.* ✪ विलोम **organic**

**input**[1] /ˈɪnpʊt ˈइनपुट्/ *noun* **1** [C, U] **input (of sth) (into/to sth)** what you put into sth to make it successful; the act of putting sth in किसी वस्तु में डाली गई कोई वस्तु (उसे असरदार या परिणामकारी बनाने के लिए), इनपुट, निवेश; किसी में कुछ डालने की क्रिया *Growing anything in this soil will require heavy inputs of nutrients.* ○ *We need some input from teachers into this book.* **2** [U] the act of putting information into a computer कंप्यूटर में सूचना भरने की क्रिया *The computer breakdown means we have lost the whole day's input.* ➪ **output** देखिए।

**input**[2] /ˈɪnpʊt ˈइनपुट्/ *verb* [T] (*pres. part.* **inputting**; *pt, pp* **input** or **inputted**) to put information into a computer कंप्यूटर में सूचना भरना

**inquest** /ˈɪŋkwest ˈइङ्क्वेस्ट्/ *noun* [C] an official process that tries to find out how sb died किसी मृत्यु के कारणों की खोज की आधिकारिक प्रक्रिया, किसी की मृत्यु के कारणों की न्यायिक जाँच *to hold an inquest*

**inquire, inquirer, inquiring, inquiry** = **enquire, enquirer, enquiring, enquiry**

**inquisition** /ˌɪnkwɪˈzɪʃn ˌइन्क्विˈज़िश्न्/ *noun* **1 the Inquisition** [*sing.*] the organization formed by the Roman Catholic Church to find and punish people who did not agree with its beliefs, especially from the 15th to the 17th century रोमन कैथोलिक चर्च का बनाया संगठन (धर्माधिकरण) जो चर्च की मान्यताओं में विश्वास न करने वालों का पता लगाकर उन्हें दंडित करता था (विशेषतः 15वीं से 17वीं सदी तक); धर्म न्यायाधिकरण **2** [C] (*formal*) a series of questions that sb asks you, especially when he/she asks them in an unpleasant way (कठोरता से पूछे गए) प्रश्न

**inquisitive** /ɪnˈkwɪzətɪv इन्ˈक्विज़टिव़्/ *adj.* **1** too interested in finding out about what other people are doing दूसरों के बारे में जानने का अति-इच्छुक, पूछाताछी करने वाला; प्रश्नशील *Don't be so inquisitive. It's none of your business.* **2** interested in finding out about many different things. विभिन्न वस्तुओं के बारे में जानने का इच्छुक; जिज्ञासु *You need an inquisitive mind to be a scientist.* ▶ **inquisitively** *adv.* जिज्ञासु भाव से ▶ **inquisitiveness** *noun* [U] जिज्ञासा

**insane** /ɪnˈseɪn इन्ˈसेन्/ *adj.* **1** crazy or mentally ill पागल, विक्षिप्त या मानसिक रोगी **2** not showing sensible judgement जो अक़्लमंदी का काम न करे *You must be insane to leave your job before you've found another one.* ➪ **mad** पर नोट देखिए। ▶ **insanely** *adv.* विक्षिप्ततापूर्वक, पागलपन से *insanely jealous* ▶ **insanity** /ɪnˈsænəti इन्ˈसैनटि/ *noun* [U] विक्षिप्तता, पागलपन

**insanitary** /ɪnˈsænətri इन्ˈसैनट्रि/ *adj.* (*formal*) dirty and likely to cause disease अस्वच्छ और रोगकारक *The restaurant was closed because of the insanitary conditions of the kitchen.* ➪ **sanitary** देखिए।

**insatiable** /ɪnˈseɪʃəbl इन्ˈसेशब्ल्/ *adj.* that cannot be satisfied; very great जिसे तृप्त न किया जा सके, अतृप्त; अपरितोष्य, अत्यधिक *an insatiable desire for knowledge* ○ *an insatiable appetite*

**inscribe** /ɪnˈskraɪb इन्ˈस्क्राइब्/ *verb* [T] (*formal*) **inscribe A (on/in B); inscribe B (with A)** to write or cut (**carve**) words on sth किसी वस्तु पर कुछ अंकित या उत्कीर्ण करना, लिखना या खोदना *The names of all the previous champions are inscribed on the cup.* ○ *The book was inscribed with the author's name.*

**inscription** /ɪnˈskrɪpʃn इन्ˈस्क्रिप्श्न्/ *noun* [C] words that are written or cut on sth किसी वस्तु पर अंकित या उत्कीर्ण शब्द *There was an Urdu inscription on the tombstone.*

**insect** /ˈɪnsekt ˈइन्सेक्ट्/ *noun* [C] a small animal with six legs, two pairs of wings and a body which is divided into three parts कीट, कीड़ा, (छह टाँगों और दो डैनों वाला लघुजीव जिसका शरीर तीन भागों में विभक्त होता है) *Ants, flies, beetles, butterflies and mosquitoes are all insects.* ○ *an insect bite/sting* **NOTE** कुछ अन्य लघु जीवों, जैसे मकड़ियों, को भी कीट कहा जाता है यद्यपि तकनीकी तौर पर यह ग़लत है।

**insecticide** /ɪnˈsektɪsaɪd इन्ˈसेक्टिसाइड् / *noun* [C, U] a substance that is used for killing insects कीटनाशक पदार्थ ➪ **pesticide** देखिए।

**insectivore** /ɪnˈsektɪvɔ:(r) इन्ˈसेक्टिवॉ(र्)/ *noun* [C] any animal that eats insects कीटभक्षी प्राणी ➪ **carnivore, herbivore** और **omnivore** भी देखिए।

**insecure** /ˌɪnsɪˈkjʊə(r) ˌइन्सिˈक्योअ(र्)/ *adj.* **1 insecure (about sb/sth)** not confident about yourself or your relationships with other people जिसे अपने ऊपर विश्वास हो ना दूसरों पर; आत्मविश्वासहीन, असुरक्षा-भावना से ग्रस्त *Many teenagers are insecure about their appearance.* **2** not safe or protected असुरक्षित *This ladder feels a bit insecure.* ○ *The future of the company looks very insecure.* ✪ विलोम **secure** ▶ **insecurely** *adv.* असुरक्षित रूप से ➪ **insecurity** /-rəti -रटि/ *noun* [U, C] (*pl* **insecurities**) असुरक्षा *Their aggressive behaviour is really a sign of insecurity.* ✪ विलोम **security**

**insensitive** /ɪnˈsensətɪv इन्ˈसेन्सटिव़् / *adj.* **insensitive (to sth) 1** not knowing or caring how another person feels and therefore likely to hurt or upset him/her दूसरों की भावनाओं की उपेक्षा करने वाला और इस प्रकार उन्हें कष्ट पहुँचाने वाला; संवेदनाहीन *Some insensitive reporters tried to interview the families of the accident victims.* ○ *an insensitive remark* **2 insensitive (to sth)** not able to feel or react to sth प्रतिक्रियाहीन, वेदनाहीन, अनुभव करने में असमर्थ, संवेदनशून्य *insensitive to pain/cold/criticism* ✪ विलोम **sensitive** ▶ **insensitively** *adv.* संवेदनहीन या संवेदनशून्य भाव से ▶ **insensitivity** /ɪnˌsensəˈtɪvəti इन्ˌसेन्सˈटिव़टि/ *noun* [U] संवेदनाहीनता, संवेदनशून्यता

**inseparable** /ɪnˈseprəbl इन्ˈसेप्रब्ल्/ *adj.* that cannot be separated from sb/sth जिसे व्यक्ति या वस्तु से अलग न किया जा सके; अवियोज्य, अपृथक्करणीय *inseparable friends* ✪ विलोम **separable**

**insert** /ɪnˈsɜ:t इन्ˈसट्/ *verb* [T] (*formal*) to put sth into sth or between two things निविष्ट करना, अंतर्निविष्ट करना, अंतःस्थापित करना *I decided to insert an extra paragraph in the text.* ▶ **insertion** /ɪnˈsɜ:ʃn इन्ˈसश्न्/ *noun* [C, U] अंतर्निवेश, सन्निवेश, अंतःस्थापन

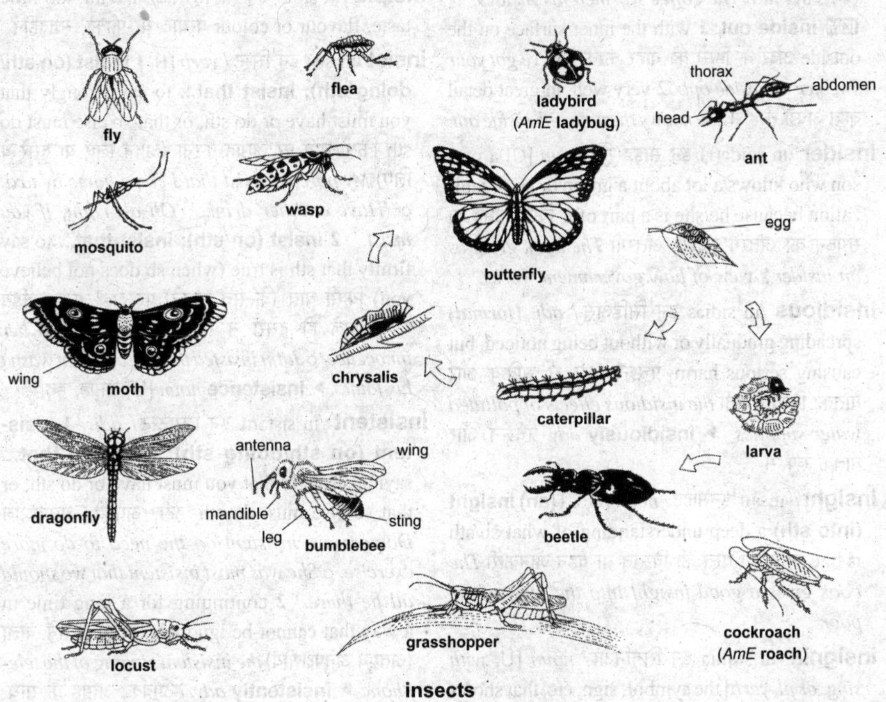

insects

**inshore** /ˈɪnʃɔː(r) ˈइन्शॉ(र्)/ *adj.* /ˌɪnˈʃɔː(r) ˌइन्ˈशॉ(र्)/ *adv.* in or towards the part of the sea that is close to the land समुद्र-तट के पास, समुद्र-तट की ओर; तटसमीपस्थ *inshore fishermen* ○ *Sharks don't often come inshore.*

**inside**[1] /ˌɪnˈsaɪd ˌइन्ˈसाइड्/ *prep., adj., adv.* **1** in, on or to the inner part or surface of sth किसी वस्तु के अंदरूनी भाग या सतह में/पर/की ओर, के भीतर, के अंदर, अंदर या भीतर के *Is there anything inside the box?* ○ *It's safer to be inside the house in a thunderstorm.* **2** (*formal*) (used about time) in less than; within (समय) से कम में; के अंदर *Your photos will be ready inside an hour.* **3** (used about information, etc.) told secretly by sb who belongs to a group, organization, etc. (जानकारी आदि) किसी समूह, संगठन आदि के सदस्यों को गुप्त रूप से दी गई; आंतरिक, भीतरी *The robbers seemed to have had some inside information about the bank's security system.* **4** (*slang*) in prison जेल में

**inside**[2] /ˌɪnˈsaɪd ˌइन्ˈसाइड्/ *noun* **1** [C] the inner part or surface of sth किसी वस्तु का अंदरूनी हिस्सा या सतह, अंदर से, अंदर के हिस्से में *The door was locked from the inside.* ○ *There's a label somewhere **on the inside**.* **2 insides** [*pl.*] (*informal*) the organs inside the body शरीर के आंतरिक अंग, (पेट और आँतें) *The coffee warmed his insides.*

**IDM inside out 1** with the inner surface on the outside अंदर के हिस्से को बाहर करके *You've got your sweater on inside out.* **2** very well, in great detail बहुत अच्छी तरह से *She knows these streets inside out.*

**insider** /ɪnˈsaɪdə(r) इन्ˈसाइड(र्)/ *noun* [C] a person who knows a lot about a group or an organization because he/she is a part of it किसी समूह या संगठन का अंतरंग सदस्य; अंतरंगी *The book gives us an insider's view of how government works.*

**insidious** /ɪnˈsɪdiəs इन्ˈसिडिअस्/ *adj.* (*formal*) spreading gradually or without being noticed, but causing serious harm प्रच्छन्न रूप से सक्रिय और घातक, विश्वासघाती *the insidious effects of polluted water supplies* ▶ **insidiously** *adv.* प्रच्छन्न और घातक रूप से

**insight** /ˈɪnsaɪt ˈइन्साइट्/ *noun* [C, U] **(an) insight (into sth)** a deep understanding of what sb/sth is like व्यक्ति या वस्तु की विस्तृत या गहन जानकारी *The book gives a good insight into the lives of the poor.*

**insignia** /ɪnˈsɪgniə इन्ˈसिग्निआ/ *noun* [U, *with sing. or pl. verb*] the symbol, sign, etc. that shows that sb is a member of, or has a particular position in, a group or an organization प्रतीक, चिह्न (किसी समूह या संगठन में पद या सदस्यता का) अधिचिह्न *His uniform bore the insignia of a captain.*

**insignificant** /ˌɪnsɪgˈnɪfɪkənt ˌइन्सिग्ˈनिफ़िकन्ट्/ *adj.* of little value or importance महत्त्वहीन, उपेक्षणीय, नगण्य, निरर्थक *an insignificant detail* ○ *Working in such a big company made her feel insignificant.* ▶ **insignificance** *noun* [U] महत्त्वहीनता, नगण्यता ▶ **insignificantly** *adv.* नगण्य भाव से

**insincere** /ˌɪnsɪnˈsɪə(r) ˌइन्सिन्ˈसिअ(र्)/ *adj.* saying or doing sth that you do not really believe कपटी, पाखंडी, निष्ठाहीन, अवास्तविक *His apology sounded insincere.* ○ *an insincere smile* ✪ विलोम **sincere** ▶ **insincerely** *adv.* निष्ठाहीन रूप से ▶ **insincerity** /ˌɪnsɪnˈserəti ˌइन्सिन्ˈसेरटि/ *noun* [U] निष्ठाहीनता, असत्यता ✪ विलोम **sincerity**

**insinuate** /ɪnˈsɪnjueɪt इन्ˈसिन्युएट्/ *verb* [T] to suggest sth unpleasant in an indirect way परोक्ष रीति से कोई अप्रिय बात बताना; कटाक्ष करना, आक्षेप करना *She seemed to be insinuating that our work was below standard.* ▶ **insinuation** /ɪnˌsɪnjuˈeɪʃn इन्ˌसिन्युˈएश्न्/ *noun* [C, U] कटाक्ष, आक्षेप ***to make insinuations** about sb's honesty*

**insipid** /ɪnˈsɪpɪd इन्ˈसिपिड्/ *adj.* having too little taste, flavour or colour बेस्वाद या फीका, स्वादहीन

**insist** /ɪnˈsɪst इन्ˈसिस्ट्/ *verb* [I] **1 insist (on sth/doing sth); insist that...** to say strongly that you must have or do sth, or that sb else must do sth किसी बात पर आग्रह करना (अपने लिए या दूसरे के लिए) *My parents insist that I come home by taxi.* ○ *'Have another drink.' 'Oh all right, if you insist.'* **2 insist (on sth); insist that...** to say firmly that sth is true (when sb does not believe you) किसी बात (के सच मानने) पर अड़ जाना, अडिग रहना (भले ही दूसरा न माने) *She insisted on her innocence.* ○ *Jatin insisted that the accident wasn't his fault.* ▶ **insistence** *noun* [U] आग्रह, हठ

**insistent** /ɪnˈsɪstənt इन्ˈसिस्टन्ट्/ *adj.* **1 insistent (on sth/doing sth); insistent that...** saying strongly that you must have or do sth, or that sb else must do sth हठी, आग्रही, आग्रहशील *Doctors are insistent on the need to do more exercise.* ○ *She was most insistent that we should all be there.* **2** continuing for a long time in a way that cannot be ignored देर तक चलने वाला (अतएव अनुपेक्षणीय) *the insistent ringing of the telephone* ▶ **insistently** *adv.* हठपूर्वक, आग्रह के साथ

**insolent** /ˈɪnsələnt ˈइन्सलन्ट्/ *adj.* (*formal*) lacking respect; rude अवमानक; अभद्र, धृष्ट, गुस्ताख़ *insolent behaviour* ▶ **insolence** *noun* [U] ▶ **insolently** *adv.* अवमाननापूर्वक, गुस्ताख़ी से

**insoluble** /ɪnˈsɒljəbl इन्ˈसॉल्यबल्/ *adj.* **1** that cannot be explained or solved जिसे समझाया या हल न किया जा सके; असमाधेय *We faced almost insoluble problems.* **2** that cannot be dissolved in a liquid जो द्रव में घोला न जा सके; अविलेय ✪ विलोम **soluble**

**insolvent** /ɪnˈsɒlvənt इन्ˈसॉल्वन्ट्/ *adj.* (*formal*) not having enough money to pay what you owe धन की कमी के कारण ऋण चुकाने में असमर्थ; दिवालिया ✪ पर्याय **bankrupt** *The company has been declared insolvent.* ▶ **insolvency** /-ənsi -अन्सि/ *noun* [U, C] (*pl.* **insolvencies**) दिवालियापन

**insomnia** /ɪnˈsɒmniə इन्ˈसॉम्निआ/ *noun* [U] inability to sleep सो न सकने का रोग; अनिद्रा *Do you ever suffer from insomnia?* ➪ **sleepless** देखिए।

**insomniac** /ɪnˈsɒmniæk इन्ˈसॉम्निऐक्/ *noun* [C] a person who cannot sleep अनिद्रा का रोगी

**inspect** /ɪnˈspekt इन्ˈस्पेक्ट्/ *verb* [T] **1 inspect sb/sth (for sth)** to look at sth closely or in great detail किसी बात की बारीकी या विस्तार से जाँच करना, निरीक्षण करना *The detective inspected the room for fingerprints.* **2** to make an official visit to make sure that rules are being obeyed, work is being done properly, etc. नियमों के पालन आदि की सरकारी जाँच करना; निरीक्षण करना *All food shops should be inspected regularly.* ▶ **inspection** *noun* [C, U] जाँच, निरीक्षण *The fire prevention service will* ***carry out an inspection*** *of the building next week.* ○ ***On inspection****, the passport turned out to be false.*

**inspector** /ɪnˈspektə(r) इन्ˈस्पेक्ट(र्)/ *noun* [C] **1** an official who visits schools, factories, etc. to make sure that rules are being obeyed, work is being done properly, etc. स्कूलों, कारख़ानों आदि में नियमों के पालन आदि की जाँच करने वाला अधिकारी; निरीक्षक, इंस्पेक्टर *a health and safety inspector* **2** a police officer with quite an important position महत्त्वपूर्ण पुलिस अधिकारी, पुलिस इंस्पेक्टर **3** a person whose job is to check passengers' tickets on buses or trains बसों या रेलगाड़ियों में यात्रियों के टिकटों की जाँच करने वाला व्यक्ति; टिकट-निरीक्षक

**inspiration** /ˌɪnspəˈreɪʃn ˌइन्स्पˈरेश्न्/ *noun* **1** [C, U] **an inspiration (to/for sb); inspiration (to do/for sth)** a feeling, person or thing that makes you want to do sth or gives you exciting new ideas कुछ नया करने या सोचने की इच्छा उत्पन्न करने वाला मनोभाव, व्यक्ति या वस्तु; प्रेरणा *The beauty of the mountains was a great* ***source of inspiration*** *to the writer.* ○ *What gave you the inspiration to become a dancer?* **2** [C] (*informal*) a sudden good idea अचानक मन में आया अच्छा विचार, अंतःप्रेरणा *I've had an inspiration—why don't we go to that new club?*

**inspire** /ɪnˈspaɪə(r) इन्ˈस्पाइअ(र्)/ *verb* [T] **1 inspire sth; inspire sb (to do sth)** to make sb want to do or create sth कुछ करने या रचने की इच्छा उत्पन्न करना; प्रेरित करना *Mahatma Gandhi's autobiography inspired her to go into politics.* **2 inspire sb (with sth); inspire sth (in sb)** to make sb feel, think, etc. sth किसी को कुछ अनुभव कराना या सोचने के लिए प्रेरित करना, अनुप्राणित कर देना, जगाना *to be inspired with enthusiasm* ○ *The guide's nervous manner did not* ***inspire*** *much* ***confidence*** *in us.* ▶ **inspiring** *adj.* प्रेरक, प्रेरणापूर्ण *an inspiring speech.*

**inspired** /ɪnˈspaɪəd इन्ˈस्पाइअड्/ *adj.* influenced or helped by a particular feeling, thing or person विशेष मनोभाव, वस्तु या व्यक्ति द्वारा प्रेरित *The pianist gave an inspired performance.*

**instability** /ˌɪnstəˈbɪləti ˌइन्स्टˈबिलटि/ *noun* [U] the state of being likely to change ऐसी स्थिति जिसमें परिवर्तन संभावित है; अस्थिरता *There are growing signs of political instability.* ➪ **unstable** adjective देखिए। ✪ विलोम **stability**

**install** (*AmE* **instal**) /ɪnˈstɔːl इन्ˈस्टॉल्/ *verb* [T] **1** to put a piece of equipment, etc. in place so that it is ready to be used किसी मशीन को लगाना (ताकि उसका इस्तेमाल आरंभ किया जा सके); व्यवस्थापित करना *We are waiting to have our new computer system installed.* ✪ पर्याय **put in 2 install sb (as sth)** to put sb/sth or yourself in a position or place किसी व्यक्ति, वस्तु या स्वयं को पद (या स्थान) पर स्थापित करना, पदासीन करना *He was installed as President yesterday.* ▶ **installation** /ˌɪnstəˈleɪʃn ˌइन्स्टˈलेश्न्/ *noun* [C, U] स्थापित संयंत्र, प्रतिष्ठापन *a military/nuclear installation* ○ *the installation of a new chairman*

**instalment** (*AmE* **installment**) /ɪnˈstɔːlmənt इन्ˈस्टॉल्मन्ट्/ *noun* [C] **1** one of the regular payments that you make for sth until you have paid the full amount भुगतान की कुल राशि का नियमित रूप से दिया जाने वाला अंश, भुगतान की किस्त *to pay for sth* ***in instalments*** **2** one part of a story that is shown or published as a series शृंखला के रूप में प्रकाशित या प्रदर्शित की जा रही कहानी का एक अंश; कड़ी *Don't miss next week's exciting instalment.*

**instance** /ˈɪnstəns ˈइन्स्टन्स् / *noun* [C] **an instance (of sth)** an example or case (of sth) (किसी वस्तु का) उदाहरण, मिसाल या मामला *There have been several instances of racial attacks in the area.* ○ *In most instances the drug has no side effects.* IDM **for instance** for example उदाहरण के लिए, उदाहरणस्वरूप *There are several interesting places to visit around here—Red Fort, for instance.*

**instant[1]** /ˈɪnstənt ˈइन्स्टन्ट् / *adj.* **1** happening suddenly or immediately अचानक या तत्काल होने वाला; तुरंत, तात्कालिक *The film was an instant success.* **2** (used about food) that can be prepared quickly and easily, usually by adding hot water (खाद्य पदार्थ) जो बहुत शीघ्र और आसानी से तैयार किया जा सके (प्रायः गरम पानी में डालकर), तत्काल (खाद्य पदार्थ) *instant coffee*

**instant[2]** /ˈɪnstənt ˈइन्स्टन्ट् / *noun* [*usually sing.*] **1** a very short period of time क्षण भर, पल भर *Ali thought* ***for an instant*** *and then agreed.* **2** a particular point in time समय का विशिष्ट बिंदु ***At that instant*** *I realized I had been tricked.* ○ *Stop doing that this instant* (= now)*!*

**instantaneous** /ˌɪnstənˈteɪniəs ˌइन्स्टनˈटेनिअस् / *adj.* happening immediately or extremely quickly तत्काल या अतिशीघ्र होने वाला; तात्कालिक, क्षणिक ▶ **instantaneously** *adv.* तत्क्षण, सहसा

**instantly** /ˈɪnstəntli ˈइन्स्टन्ट्लि / *adv.* without delay; immediately अविलंब; तुरंत *I asked him a question and he replied instantly.*

**instead** /ɪnˈsted इन्ˈस्टेड् / *adv., prep.* **instead (of sb/sth/ doing sth)** in the place of sb/sth व्यक्ति या वस्तु के स्थान पर *I couldn't go so my husband went instead.* ○ *You should play football instead of just watching it on TV.*

**instigate** /ˈɪnstɪgeɪt ˈइन्स्टिगेट् / *verb* [T] (*formal*) to make sth start to happen उकसाना, भड़काना ▶ **instigation** /ˌɪnstɪˈgeɪʃn ˌइन्स्टिˈगेश्न् / *noun* [U] उकसावा, भड़कावा

**instil** (*AmE* **instill**) /ɪnˈstɪl इन्ˈस्टिल् / *verb* [T] (**instilling; instilled**) **instil sth (in/into sb)** to make sb think or feel sth किसी के मन में कुछ बैठाना, की शिक्षा देना *Parents should try to instil a sense of responsibility into their children.*

**instinct** /ˈɪnstɪŋkt ˈइन्स्टिङ्क्ट् / *noun* [C, U] the natural force that causes a person or animal to behave in a particular way without thinking or learning about it सहज वृत्ति, स्वाभाविक प्रवृत्ति, नैसर्गिक या मूल प्रवृत्ति *Birds learn to fly* ***by instinct.*** ○ *In a situation like that you don't have time to think—you just* ***act on instinct.*** ▶ **instinctive** /ɪnˈstɪŋktɪv इन्ˈस्टिङ्क्टिव् / *adj.* नैसर्गिक प्रवृत्ति पर आधारित *Your instinctive reaction is to run from danger.* ▶ **instinctively** *adv.* नैसर्गिक रूप से

**institute[1]** /ˈɪnstɪtjuːt ˈइन्स्टिट्यूट् / *noun* [C] an organization that has a particular purpose; the building used by this organization विशेष प्रयोजन वाली कोई संस्था; संस्था का भवन *the Institute of Science and Technology* ○ *institutes of higher education*

**institute[2]** /ˈɪnstɪtjuːt ˈइन्स्टिट्यूट् / *verb* [T] (*formal*) to introduce a system, policy, etc., or start a process कोई प्रक्रिया शुरू करने के लिए किसी प्रणाली, नीति को प्रारंभ करना, संस्थापित करना *The government has instituted a new scheme for youth training.*

**institution** /ˌɪnstɪˈtjuːʃn ˌइन्स्टिˈट्यूश्न् / *noun* **1** [C] a large, important organization that has a particular purpose, such as a bank, a university, etc. विशेष प्रयोजन से स्थापित बड़ा और महत्त्वपूर्ण प्रतिष्ठान (जैसे बैंक, विश्वविद्यालय आदि) संस्थान, प्रतिष्ठान *the financial institutions in the city of Delhi.* **2** [C] a building where certain people with special needs live and are looked after भवन जहाँ विशेष प्रकार की जरूरतों वाले लोग रहते हैं, विशेष प्रकार की जरूरतों वाले लोगों का निवास स्थान *a mental institution* (= a hospital for the mentally ill) ○ *She's been in institutions all her life.* **3** [C] a social custom or habit that has existed for a long time चिरकाल से चली आती सामाजिक प्रथा या व्यवहार *the institution of marriage* **4** [U] the act of introducing a system, policy, etc., or of starting a process कोई प्रक्रिया शुरू करने के लिए किसी प्रणाली, नीति आदि का प्रवर्तन *the institution of new safety procedures*

**institutional** /ˌɪnstɪˈtjuːʃənl ˌइन्स्टिˈट्यूशनल् / *adj.* connected with an institution संस्था-संबंधी, संस्थात्मक, संस्थागत *The old lady is in need of institutional care.*

**instruct** /ɪnˈstrʌkt इन्ˈस्ट्रक्ट् / *verb* [T] **1 instruct sb (to do sth)** to give an order to sb; to tell sb to do sth किसी व्यक्ति को आदेश देना; कुछ करने का निर्देश देना *The soldiers were instructed to shoot above the heads of the crowd.* **2** (*formal*) **instruct sb (in sth)** to teach sb sth किसी को कुछ सिखाना *Children must be instructed in road safety before they are allowed to ride a bicycle on the road.*

**instruction** /ɪnˈstrʌkʃn इन्ˈस्ट्रक्श्न् / *noun* **1 instructions** [*pl.*] detailed information on how you should use sth, do sth, etc. किसी वस्तु के उपयोग, प्रयोग आदि के विषय में विस्तृत निर्देश *Read the instructions on the back of the packet carefully.* ○ *You should always* ***follow the instruc-***

*tions*. 2 [C] **an instruction (to do sth)** an order that tells you what to do or how to do sth 'क्या करें या कैसे करें' के विषय में निर्देश *The guard was under strict instructions not to let anyone in or out.* 3 [U] **instruction (in sth)** the act of teaching sth to sb किसी को कुछ सिखाने की क्रिया; शिक्षण-प्रशिक्षण *The staff need instruction in the use of computers.*

**instructive** /ɪnˈstrʌktɪv इन्ˈस्ट्रक्टिव्/ *adj.* giving useful information उपयोगी सूचना देने वाला, सूचनाप्रद, शिक्षाप्रद ▸ **instructively** *adv.* शिक्षाप्रद रीति से

**instructor** /ɪnˈstrʌktə(r) इन्ˈस्ट्रक्टर्/ *noun* [C] a person whose job is to teach a practical skill or sport प्रायोगिक कौशल या खेल का शिक्षक *a driving/fitness/golf instructor*

**instrument** /ˈɪnstrəmənt ˈइन्स्ट्रमन्ट्/ *noun* [C] 1 a tool that is used for doing a particular job or task कार्य विशेष का उपकरण *surgical/optical/precision instruments* ➪ **tool** पर नोट देखिए। 2 something that is used for playing music संगीत का कोई वाद्य (जैसे सितार) *'What instrument do you play?' 'The violin.'* ➪ पृष्ठ 789 पर चित्र देखिए।

> NOTE **Musical instruments** अनेक प्रकार के होते हैं: (क) **stringed** (तारदार, तंतु वाद्य) — वायलिन, गिटार आदि; (ख) **brass** (पीतल-निर्मित) — सिंही, तुरही आदि (ग) **woodwind** (काष्ठ-निर्मित) — बांसुरी, क्लैरिनेट आदि; (घ) **keyboard** (कुंजी-पटल-युक्त) — पियानो, ऑरगन, सिंथेसाइज़र, आदि। **Percussion instruments** (ताल वाद्य) में ढोल या नगाड़ा, झाँझ या मंजीरा शामिल हैं।

3 something that is used for measuring speed, distance, temperature, etc. in a car, plane or ship कार, विमान या जलपोत में लगा चाल, दूरी, तापमान आदि मापने का उपकरण *the instrument panel of a plane* 4 something that sb uses in order to achieve sth किसी लक्ष्य की प्राप्ति का साधन *The press should be more than an instrument of the government.*

**instrumental** /ˌɪnstrəˈmentl ˌइन्स्ट्रˈमेन्ट्ल्/ *adj.* 1 **instrumental in doing sth** helping to make sth happen किसी बात में सहायक *She was instrumental in getting him the job.* 2 for musical instruments without voices वाद्य (संगीत) *instrumental music*

**insubordinate** /ˌɪnsəˈbɔːdɪnət ˌइनसˈबॉडिनट्/ *adj.* (*formal*) (used about a person or behaviour) not obeying rules or orders (व्यक्ति या आचरण) जो नियमों या आदेशों का पालन न करे; अवज्ञाकारी, दुर्विनीत ▸ **insubordination** /ˌɪnsəˌbɔːdɪˈneɪʃn ˌइनसˌबॉडिˈनेशन्/ *noun* [C, U] अवज्ञापूर्ण आचरण, अविनय *He was dismissed from the army for insubordination.*

**insubstantial** /ˌɪnsəbˈstænʃl ˌइनसब्ˈस्टैन्श्ल्/ *adj.* not large, solid or strong जो बड़ा, कठोर या मज़बूत न हो; कमज़ोर *a hut built of insubstantial materials* ✪ विलोम **substantial**

**insufferable** /ɪnˈsʌfrəbl इन्ˈसफ़रबल्/ *adj.* (*formal*) (used about a person or behaviour) extremely unpleasant or annoying (व्यक्ति या आचरण) अत्यधिक अप्रिय या कष्टप्रद

**insufficient** /ˌɪnsəˈfɪʃnt ˌइनसˈफ़िश्न्ट्/ *adj.* **insufficient (for sth/to do sth)** not enough अपर्याप्त, नाकाफ़ी *The students complained that they were given insufficient time for the test.* ✪ विलोम **sufficient** ▸ **insufficiently** *adv.* अपर्याप्तता

**insular** /ˈɪnsjələ(r) ˈइन्स्यलर्/ *adj.* not interested in or able to accept new people or different ideas जिसे नए व्यक्तियों या भिन्न विचारों में ना रुचि है ना ग्रहणशीलता, संकीर्ण मनोवृत्ति का; तंगदिल, अनुदार ✪ पर्याय **narrow-minded** ▸ **insularity** /ˌɪnsjuˈlærəti ˌइन्स्युˈलैरटि/ *noun* [U] मानसिक संकीर्णता

**insulate** /ˈɪnsjuleɪt ˈइन्स्युलेट्/ *verb* [T] **insulate sth (against/ from sth)** to protect sth with a material that prevents electricity, heat or sound from passing through विद्युत, ताप या ध्वनि रोधन करना *walls are insulated against noise.* ○ (*figurative*) *This industry has been insulated from the effects of competition.* ▸ **insulation** /ˌɪnsjuˈleɪʃn ˌइन्स्युˈलेशन्/ *noun* [U] विद्युत-रोधन, विद्युत-रोधक वस्तु

**insulating tape** *noun* [U] a thin band of sticky material used for covering electrical wires to prevent the possibility of an electric shock बिजली के झटके से बचाव के लिए बिजली की तारों पर चढ़ाया गया चिपचिपी सामग्री का पतला बैंड या पतली पट्टी; इनसुलेटिंग टेप

**insulator** /ˈɪnsjuleɪtə(r) ˈइन्स्युलेटर्/ *noun* [C] a material or device used to prevent heat, electricity or sound from escaping from sth ताप, विद्युत या ध्वनि रोधक यंत्र ➪ **bulb** पर चित्र देखिए।

**insulin** /ˈɪnsjəlɪn ˈइन्स्यलिन्/ *noun* [U] a substance, normally produced by the body itself, which controls the amount of sugar in the blood स्वयं शरीर द्वारा उत्पन्न एक पदार्थ (जो खून में शक्कर की मात्रा को नियंत्रित करता है); इनसुलिन *Some diabetics need to rely on insulin injections.*

**insult[1]** /ɪnˈsʌlt इन्ˈसल्ट्/ *verb* [T] to speak or act rudely to sb (किसी का) अपमान करना *I felt very insulted when I didn't even get an answer to my letter.* ○ *He was thrown out of the hotel for insulting the manager.*

**insult²** /ˈɪnsʌlt ˈइन्सल्ट्/ *noun* [C] a rude comment or action अपमानजनक टिप्पणी या काम *The drivers were standing on the road yelling insults at each other.*

**insulting** /ɪnˈsʌltɪŋ इन्ˈसल्टिङ्/ *adj.* **insulting (to sb/sth)** making sb feel offended अपमानजनक *insulting behaviour/remarks* ○ *That poster is insulting to women.*

**insuperable** /ɪnˈsuːpərəbl इन्ˈसूपरबल्/ *adj.* (*formal*) (used about a problem, etc.) impossible to solve (समस्या) जिसका समाधान असंभव हो; असमाधेय

**insurance** /ɪnˈʃɔːrəns इन्ˈशॉरन्स्/ *noun* **1** [U] **insurance (against sth)** an arrangement with a company in which you pay them regular amounts of money and they agree to pay the costs if, for example, you die or are ill, or if you lose or damage sth बीमा; एक कंपनी के साथ की गई व्यवस्था जिसके अनुसार व्यक्ति उसे नियमित रूप से राशि देता है और कंपनी उसे सुरक्षा देती है, जैसे—मृत्यु, चोरी या हानि पर धन का भुगतान

> **NOTE** बीमा कंपनी को नियमित रूप से दी जाने वाली राशि को **insurance premium** कहते हैं। हम **life, health, car, travel** और **household insurance** ले सकते हैं।

**2** [U] the business of providing insurance बीमा उपलब्ध कराने का व्यापार, बीमा क्षेत्र, बीमा-व्यापार *He works in insurance.* **3** [U, *sing.*] **(an) insurance (against sth)** something you do to protect yourself (against sth unpleasant) (अप्रिय स्थिति से) सुरक्षा के लिए किया गया काम, सुरक्षा-कवच *Many people take vitamin pills as an insurance against illness.*

**insure** /ɪnˈʃɔː(r) इन्ˈशॉ(र्)/ *verb* [T] **1 insure yourself/sth (against/for sth)** to buy or to provide insurance बीमा करवाना या करना *They insured the painting for Rs 10,000 against damage or theft.* **2** (*AmE*) = **ensure**

**insurgent** /ɪnˈsɜːdʒənt इन्ˈसजन्ट्/ *noun* [C] (*usually plural*) (*formal*) a person fighting against the government or armed forces of their own country विद्रोही, बाग़ी *an attack by armed insurgents* ➪ **rebel** देखिए। ▶ **insurgent** *adj.* विद्रोह करने वाला *insurgent groups* ▶ **insurgency** /ɪnˈsɜːdʒənsi इन्ˈसजन्सि/ *noun* [C, U] विद्रोह, विप्लव, बग़ावत *insurgency in Iraq*

**insurmountable** /ˌɪnsəˈmaʊntəbl ˌइन्सˈमाउन्टबल्/ *adj.* (*formal*) (used about a problem, etc.) impossible to solve (समस्या आदि) जिसका समाधान असंभव है; असमाधेय ➪ **surmountable** देखिए।

**insurrection** /ˌɪnsəˈrekʃn ˌइन्सˈरेक्श्न्/ *noun* [C, U] (*formal*) violent action against the rulers of a country or the government देश के शासक या सरकार के विरुद्ध विद्रोह, बग़ावत

**intact** /ɪnˈtækt इन्ˈटैक्ट्/ *adj.* (*not before a noun*) complete; not damaged साबुत; क्षतिग्रस्त नहीं, सही-सलामत *Very few of the buildings* ***remain intact*** *following the earthquake.*

**intake** /ˈɪnteɪk ˈइन्टेक्/ *noun* [C, *usually sing.*] **1** the amount of food, drink, etc. that you take into your body खाद्य, पेय आदि की मात्रा जिसे हम अंतर्ग्रहण करते हैं *The doctor told me to cut down my carbohydrate intake.* **2** the (number of) people who enter an organization or institution during a certain period अवधिविशेष में किसी संस्था में प्रवेश करने वाले व्यक्ति (उनकी संख्या), भरती *This year's intake of students is down 10%.* **3** the act of taking sth into your body, especially breath किसी वस्तु (विशेषतः श्वास) को शरीर के अंदर ले जाने की प्रक्रिया **4** a place where liquid, air, etc. enters a machine द्रव, वायु आदि के प्रवेश के लिए मशीन में बना मुँह

**intangible** /ɪnˈtændʒəbl इन्ˈटैन्जबल्/ *adj.* difficult to describe, understand or measure जिसका वर्णन करना, जिसे समझना या मापना कठिन हो *The benefits of good customer relations are intangible.* ✪ विलोम **tangible**

**integer** /ˈɪntɪdʒə(r) ˈइन्टिज(र्)/ *noun* [C] (*mathematics*) a whole number, such as 3 or 4 but not 3.5 पूर्ण संख्या (जैसे 3 या 4, परंतु 3.5 नहीं) ➪ **fraction** देखिए।

**integral** /ˈɪntɪgrəl ˈइन्टिग्रल्/ *adj.* **1 integral (to sth)** necessary in order to make sth complete किसी वस्तु के पूर्ण बनाने के लिए अपेक्षित, संपूर्णता के लिए आवश्यक *Spending a year in France is* ***an integral part of*** *the university course.* **2** including sth as a part संपूर्णता के भाग के रूप में शामिल (न कि अलग से प्रदत्त) *The car has an integral CD player.*

**integrate** /ˈɪntɪgreɪt ˈइन्टिग्रेट्/ *verb* **1** [T] **integrate sth (into sth); integrate A and B/integrate A with B** to join things so that they become one thing or work together वस्तुओं को ऐसे जोड़ना कि वे एक हो जाएँ या साथ काम करें; एकीकृत करना *The two small schools were integrated into one large one.* ○ *These programs can be integrated with your existing software.* **2** [I, T] **integrate (sb) (into/with sth)** to join in and become part of a group or community, or to make sb do this किसी समूह या समुदाय में शामिल हो

जाना या दूसरे को शामिल कर लेना *It took Amit quite a while to integrate into his new school.* ➪ **segregate** देखिए। ▶ **integration** /ˌɪntɪˈɡreɪʃn ˌइन्टिˈग्रेश्न्/ *noun* [U] एकीकरण *racial integration* ➪ **segregation** देखिए।

**integrity** /ɪnˈteɡrəti इन्ˈटेग्रटि/ *noun* [U] **1** the quality of being honest and having strong moral principles ईमानदारी और दृढ़ नैतिकता, सत्य-निष्ठा *He's a person **of great integrity** who can be relied on to tell the truth.* **2** the state of being united or undivided अखंडता *The integrity of a nation must be maintained.*

**intellect** /ˈɪntəlekt ˈइन्टलेक्ट्/ *noun* **1** [U] the power of the mind to think and to learn मन की सोचने और सीखने की शक्ति, प्रज्ञा-बुद्धि, विचार शक्ति *a woman of considerable intellect* **2** [C] an extremely intelligent person अत्यधिक प्रतिभाशाली व्यक्ति *He was one of the most brilliant intellects of his time.*

**intellectual¹** /ˌɪntəˈlektʃuəl ˌइन्टˈलेक्चुअल्/ *adj.* **1** connected with a person's ability to think in a logical way and to understand things (*only before a noun*) व्यक्ति की तर्कसंगत रूप से सोचने और समझने की क्षमता से संबंधित; बौद्धिक, बुद्धिमतापूर्ण *The boy's intellectual development was very advanced for his age.* **2** (used about a person) enjoying activities in which you have to think deeply about sth (व्यक्ति) चिंतन प्रधान गतिविधियों में मग्न, बौद्धिक विलासी ▶ **intellectually** *adv.* बौद्धिक दृष्टि से

**intellectual²** /ˌɪntəˈlektʃuəl ˌइन्टˈलेक्चुअल्/ *noun* [C] a person who enjoys thinking deeply about things चिंतक, बुद्धिजीवी

**intelligence** /ɪnˈtelɪdʒəns इन्ˈटेलिजन्स्/ *noun* [U] **1** the ability to understand, learn and think समझने, सीखने और सोचने की क्षमता; बुद्धि, समझ, प्रज्ञा *a person of normal intelligence* ○ *an intelligence test* **2** important information about an enemy country शत्रु देश के विषय में महत्त्वपूर्ण सूचना, खुफ़िया जानकारी

**intelligent** /ɪnˈtelɪdʒənt इन्ˈटेलिजन्ट्/ *adj.* having or showing the ability to understand, learn and think; clever समझने, सीखने और सोचने की क्षमता से संपन्न, बुद्धिमान; चतुर *All their children are very intelligent.* ○ *an intelligent question* ▶ **intelligently** *adv.* बुद्धिमत्तापूर्वक

**intelligible** /ɪnˈtelɪdʒəbl इन्ˈटेलिजबल्/ *adj.* (used especially about speech or writing) possible or easy to understand (भाषण या लेखन) जिसे समझना संभव या सरल हो; सुबोध, बोधगम्य ✪ विलोम **unintelligible** ▶ **intelligibility** /ɪnˌtelɪdʒəˈbɪləti इन्ˌटेलिजˈबिलटि/ *noun* [U] बोधगम्यता

**intend** /ɪnˈtend इन्ˈटेन्ड्/ *verb* [T] **1 intend to do sth/doing sth** to plan or mean to do sth कुछ करने की योजना बनाना या इरादा करना *I'm afraid I spent more money than I had intended.* ○ *I certainly don't intend to wait here all day!* ➪ **intention** noun देखिए। **2 intend sth for sb/sth; intend sb to do sth** to plan, mean or make sth for a particular person or purpose विशेष व्यक्ति या प्रयोजन हेतु किसी बात की योजना बनाना, इरादा रखना या निर्माण करना *You shouldn't have read that letter—it wasn't intended for you.* ○ *I didn't intend you to have all the work.*

**intense** /ɪnˈtens इन्ˈटेन्स्/ *adj.* very great, strong or serious बहुत अधिक, उग्र या गंभीर *intense heat/cold/pressure* ○ *intense anger/interest/desire* ▶ **intensely** *adv.* उग्रतापूर्वक, तीव्रतापूर्वक *They obviously dislike each other intensely.* ▶ **intensity** /-səti -सटि/ *noun* [U] उग्रता, तीव्रता, भाव-प्रबलता *I wasn't prepared for the intensity of his reaction to the news.*

**intensifier** /ɪnˈtensɪfaɪə(r) इन्ˈटेन्सिफ़ाइअ(र्)/ *noun* [C] (*grammar*) a word, especially an adjective or an adverb, for example 'so' or 'very', that makes the meaning of another word stronger कोई शब्द, विशेषतः विशेषण या क्रियाविशेषण (जैसे 'so' या 'very') जो अन्य शब्द के अर्थ को तीव्र करे; तीव्रक, रंजक ➪ **modifier** देखिए।

**intensify** /ɪnˈtensɪfaɪ इन्ˈटेन्सिफ़ाइ/ *verb* [I, T] (*pres. part.* **intensifying**; *3rd person sing. pres.* **intensifies**; *pt, pp* **intensified**) to become or to make sth greater or stronger तीव्रतर, प्रबल या उग्रतर हो जाना या कर देना *Fighting in the region has intensified.* ○ *The government has intensified its anti-smoking campaign.* ▶ **intensification** /ɪnˌtensɪfɪˈkeɪʃn इन्ˌटेन्सिफ़िˈकेश्न्/ *noun* [U] तीव्रीकरण, प्रबलता

**intensive** /ɪnˈtensɪv इन्ˈटेन्सिव्/ *adj.* **1** involving a lot of work or care in a short period of time जिसमें सीमित समय में काफ़ी अधिक कार्य या सावधानी की अपेक्षा हो; गहन, प्रबलित *an intensive investigation/course* **2** (used about methods of farming) aimed at producing as much food as possible from the land or money available (खेती की विधि) जिसमें उपलब्ध भूमि और धन की सहायता से यथासंभव अधिकतम उपज लेना लक्ष्य हो; गहन *intensive agriculture* ➪ **extensive** देखिए। ▶ **intensively** *adv.* गहन रूप से

**intensive care** *noun* [U] special care in hospital for patients who are very seriously ill or injured; the department that gives this care बहुत गंभीर रूप से बीमार या घायल रोगियों की विशेष देखभाल; सघन चिकित्सा; यह चिकित्सा सेवा देने वाला विभाग, सघन चिकित्सा कक्ष *She was in intensive care for a week after the car crash.*

**intent**[1] /ɪnˈtent इन्ˈटेन्ट्/ *adj.* **1 intent (on/upon sth)** showing great attention जिसमें पूरा ध्यान लगा हो; लीन, मग्न *She was so intent upon her work that she didn't hear me come in.* **2 intent on/upon sth/doing sth** determined to do sth कुछ करने के लिए दृढ़निश्चय या कृतसंकल्प *He's always been intent on making a lot of money.* ▶ **intently** *adv.* दृढ़ निश्चय के साथ, संकल्पपूर्वक

**intent**[2] /ɪnˈtent इन्ˈटेन्ट्/ *noun* [U] (*formal*) what sb intends to do; intention व्यक्ति जो करने का इरादा करे; इरादा *He was charged with possession of a gun **with intent to** commit a robbery.* ○ *to do sth with evil/ good intent*

IDM **to/for all intents and purposes** in effect, even if not completely true असल में, सभी तरह से (भले ही वह बात पूरी तरह सच न हो) *When they scored their fourth goal the match was, to all intents and purposes, over.*

**intention** /ɪnˈtenʃn इन्ˈटेन्शन्/ *noun* [C, U] **(an) intention (of doing sth/to do sth)** what sb intends or means to do; a plan or purpose जिसे करने का इरादा या इच्छा है, अभिप्राय, इरादा; योजना या प्रयोजन *I **have no intention of** staying indoors on a nice sunny day like this.* ○ *I borrowed the money **with the intention of** paying it back the next day.*

**intentional** /ɪnˈtenʃənl इन्ˈटेन्शनल्/ *adj.* done on purpose, not by chance सोद्देश्य किया गया (अकस्मात्); साभिप्राय *I'm sorry I took your jacket–it wasn't intentional!* ✪ पर्याय **deliberate** ✪ विलोम **unintentional** या **inadvertent** ▶ **intentionally** /-ʃənəli -शनलि/ *adv.* इरादतन, जानबूझकर *I can't believe the boys broke the window intentionally.*

**inter-** /ˈɪntə(r) ˈइन्ट(र्)/ *prefix* (*in verbs, nouns, adjectives and adverbs*) between; from one to another बीच में, अंतर; एक से दूसरे तक; अन्योन्य *interface* ○ *interaction* ○ *international* ➪ **intra-** देखिए।

**interact** /ˌɪntərˈækt ˌइन्टरˈऐक्ट्/ *verb* [I] **1 interact (with sb)** (used about people) to communicate or mix with sb, especially while you work, play or spend time together (व्यक्तियों का) परस्पर बातचीत करना या मिलना-जुलना (विशेषतः काम करते हुए, खेलते हुए या एक साथ समय गुज़ारते हुए) *He is studying the way children interact with each other at different ages.* **2** (of two things) to have an effect on each other (दो वस्तुओं का) एक दूसरे को प्रभावित करना ▶ **interaction** *noun* [U, C] **interaction (between/with sb/sth)** [U] एक-दूसरे पर प्रभाव, अन्योन्य क्रिया *There is a need for greater interaction between the two departments.*

**interactive** /ˌɪntərˈæktɪv ˌइन्टरˈऐक्टिव़्/ *adj.* **1** that involves people working together and having an influence on each other जिसमें लोग साथ-साथ काम करें तथा एक-दूसरे से प्रभावित हों; अन्योन्य क्रियापरक *interactive language-learning techniques* **2** (*computing*) involving direct communication both ways, between the computer and the person using it जिसमें कंप्यूटर तथा प्रयोगकर्ता के बीच दुतरफ़ा संप्रेषण हो *interactive computer games*

**intercept** /ˌɪntəˈsept ˌइन्टˈसेप्ट्/ *verb* [T] to stop or catch sb/sth that is moving from one place to another एक स्थान से दूसरे स्थान पर जाते व्यक्ति या वस्तु को अवरुद्ध करना या पकड़ना; अंतरोधन करना *Detectives intercepted him at the airport.* ▶ **interception** *noun* [U, C] अवरोधन, अंतरावरोधन

**interchangeable** /ˌɪntəˈtʃeɪndʒəbl ˌइन्टˈचेन्जबल्/ *adj.* **interchangeable (with sth)** able to be used in place of each other without making any difference to the way sth works जिसका एक दूसरे के स्थान पर प्रयोग हो सके (बिना किसी बाधा के), विनिमय के योग्य; विनिमेय *Are these two words interchangeable* (= do they have the same meaning)? ▶ **interchangeably** /-əbli -अबलि/ *adv.* विनिमयपूर्वक

**intercom** /ˈɪntəkɒm ˈइन्टकॉम्/ *noun* [C] a system of communication by radio or telephone inside an office, plane, etc.; the device you press or switch on to start using this system किसी कार्यालय, विमान आदि में रेडियो या टेलीफ़ोन द्वारा संचालित संप्रेषण प्रणाली; इस प्रणाली को प्रयोग में लाने वाला उपकरण; इंटरकाम

**interconnect** /ˌɪntəkəˈnekt ˌइन्टकˈनेक्ट्/ *verb* [I, T] **interconnect (A) (with B); interconnect A and B** to connect similar things; to be connected to similar things सदृश वस्तुओं को परस्पर जोड़ना; सदृश वस्तुओं से जुड़ना *electronic networks which interconnect thousands of computers around the world*

**intercontinental** /ˌɪntəˌkɒntɪˈnentl ˌइन्टˌकॉन्टिˈनेन्टल्/ *adj.* between continents दो महाद्वीपों के बीच; अंतरमहाद्वीपीय *intercontinental flights*

**intercostal** /ˌɪntəˈkɒstl ˌइन्टˈकॉस्टल्/ *adj.* (*technical*) between the **ribs** पसलियों के बीच का, अंतरा पर्शुका *intercostal muscles*

**intercourse** /ˈɪntəkɔːs ˈइन्टकॉस्/ = **sex 3**

**interdependent** /ˌɪntədɪˈpendənt ˌइन्टडिˈपेन्डन्ट्/ *adj.* depending on each other परस्पर निर्भर *Exercise and good health are generally interdependent.* ○ *interdependent economies/organizations*
▶ **interdependence** *noun* [U] पारस्परिक निर्भरता

**interest¹** /ˈɪntrəst ˈइन्ट्रस्ट्/ *noun* **1** [U, *usually sing.*] **an interest (in sb/sth)** a desire to learn or hear more about sb/sth or to be involved with sb/sth व्यक्ति या वस्तु के विषय में अधिक जानने सुनने या उससे जुड़ने की इच्छा, रुचि, दिलचस्पी *She's begun to* ***show*** *a great* ***interest*** *in politics.* ○ *I wish he'd* ***take*** *more* ***interest in*** *his children.* ○ *Don't* ***lose interest*** *now!* **2** [U] the quality that makes sth interesting वस्तु को रोचक बनाने वाला गुण, रोचकता, महत्त्व *I thought this article might* ***be of interest to*** *you.* ○ *Computers* ***hold no interest for*** *me.* **3** [C, *usually pl.*] something that you enjoy doing or learning about ऐसा काम जिसे करना या जानना अच्छा लगे; अभिरुचि *What are your interests and hobbies?* **4** [U] **interest (on sth)** the money that you pay for borrowing money from a bank, etc. or the money that you earn when you keep money in a bank, etc. उधार पर दिया जाने वाला या मिलने वाला पैसा; ब्याज, सूद *The* ***interest rate*** *has never been so high/low.* ○ *Some companies offer* ***interest-free*** *loans.*

**IDM** **have/with sb's interests at heart** to want sb to be happy and successful, even though your actions may not show it किसी का भला चाहना (भले ही ऐसा ऊपर से न लगे)

**in sb's interest(s)** to sb's advantage के हित में *Using lead-free petrol is in the public interest.*

**in the interest(s) of sth** in order to achieve or protect sth कुछ प्राप्त करने या बचाव के लिए *In the interest(s) of safety, please fasten your seat belts.*

**interest²** /ˈɪntrəst ˈइन्ट्रस्ट्/ *verb* [T] to make sb want to learn or hear more about sth or to become involved in sth किसी व्यक्ति में कुछ जानने या सुनने का कौतूहल जागृत करना *It might interest you to know that I didn't accept the job.* ○ *The subject of the talk was one that interests me greatly.*

**PHR V** **interest sb in sth** to persuade sb to buy, have, do sth किसी को कोई चीज़ ख़रीदने, लेने आदि के लिए मनाना *Can I interest you in our new brochure?*

**interested** /ˈɪntrəstɪd ˈइन्ट्रसटिड्/ *adj.* **1** (*not before a noun*) **interested (in sth/sb); interested in doing sth; interested to do sth** wanting to know or hear more about sth/sb; enjoying or liking sth/sb किसी व्यक्ति या वस्तु के विषय में अभिरुचि होना *They weren't interested in my news at all!* ○ *I'm really not interested in going to the concert.* ✪ विलोम **uninterested**

> **NOTE** आपको यदि कुछ अच्छा लगे और आप उसके बार में और जानना या सुनना चाहें तो कहा जाएगा कि आप उसमें **interested** हैं। जो व्यक्ति या वस्तु आपको ऐसा महसूस कराए वह **interesting** कहलाएगा।

**2** (*only before a noun*) involved in or affected by sth; in a position to gain from sth किसी में लिप्त या प्रभावित; किसी बात से लाभ प्राप्त करने की स्थिति में होना *As an interested party* (= a person directly involved), *I was not allowed to vote.* ✪ विलोम **disinterested**

**interesting** /ˈɪntrəstɪŋ; -trest- ˈइन्ट्रसटिङ्; ट्रेस्ट्-/ *adj.* **interesting (to do sth); interesting that...** enjoyable and entertaining; holding your attention आनंदप्रद और मनोरंजक; ध्यान को बाँधकर रखने वाला, रोचक *an interesting person/book/idea/job* ○ *It's always interesting to hear about the customs of other societies.* ▶ **interestingly** *adv.* मनोरंजक रीति से

**interface¹** /ˈɪntəfeɪs ˈइन्टफ़ेस्/ *noun* [C] **1** (*computing*) the way a computer program presents information to or receives information from the person who is using it, in particular the **lay out** of the screen and the **menus** सूचना प्रदान करने और प्राप्त करने (विशेषतः स्क्रीन का लेआउट और मेन्यु) के संदर्भ में कंप्यूटर-प्रोग्राम और कंप्यूटर-प्रयोक्ता के बीच संबंध; इंटरफ़ेस *the user interface* **2** (*computing*) an electrical **circuit**, connection or program that joins one device or system to a another वह विद्युत परिचय (सर्किट), संयोजन या प्रोगाम जो एक युक्ति या प्रणाली को दूसरी से जोड़ता है *the interface between computer and printer* **3 an interface (between A and B)** (*written*) the point where two subjects, systems, etc. meet and affect each other दो विषय-क्षेत्रों, प्रणालियों का मिलनबिंदु (जहाँ वे एक दूसरे को प्रभावित भी करते हैं) *the interface between manufacturing and sales*

**interface²** /ˈɪntəfeɪs ˈइन्टफ़ेस्/ *verb* [I, T] **interface (sth) (with sth); interface A and B** (*computing*) to be connected with sth using an interface; to connect sth in this way इंटरफ़ेस का प्रयोग करने वाली वस्तु से संयोजित होना; किसी अन्य वस्तु को इस प्रकार संयोजित करना *The new system interfaces with existing telephone equipment.*

**interfere** /ˌɪntəˈfɪə(r) ˌइन्टˈफ़िअ(र्)/ *verb* [I] **1 interfere (in sth)** to get involved in a situation which does not involve you and where you are not wanted स्वयं अलिप्त रहते हुए दूसरे के मामले में (उसकी इच्छा के विरुद्ध) लिप्त होना, दखल देना; हस्तक्षेप करना *You shouldn't interfere in your children's lives—let them make their own decisions.* **2 interfere (with sb/sth)** to prevent sth from succeeding or to slow down the progress that sb/sth makes किसी काम को पूरा न होने देना या उसकी प्रगति को मंद कर देना *Every time the telephone rings it interferes with my work.* ○ *She never lets her private life interfere with her career.* **3 interfere (with sth)** to touch or change sth without permission बिना अनुमति के किसी वस्तु को स्पर्श या परिवर्तित करना, बाधा डालना *Many people feel that scientists shouldn't interfere with nature.* ▶ **interfering** *adj.* हस्तक्षेप करने वाला, दखलंदाज़ या दस्तंदाज़

**interference** /ˌɪntəˈfɪərəns ˌइन्टˈफ़िअरन्स्/ *noun* [U] **1 interference (in sth)** the act of getting involved in a situation that does not involve you and where you are not wanted स्वयं अलिप्त रहते हुए दूसरे के मामले में (उसकी इच्छा के विरुद्ध) लिप्त होने की क्रिया, हस्तक्षेप, दखलंदाज़ी या दस्तंदाज़ी *I left home because I couldn't stand my parents' interference in my affairs.* **2** extra noise (because of other signals or bad weather) that prevents you from receiving radio, television or telephone signals clearly (अन्य संकेतों या ख़राब मौसम के कारण उत्पन्न) अतिरिक्त आवाज़ या गड़गड़ जो रेडियो, टेलीविज़न या टेलीफ़ोन के संकेतों के स्पष्ट सुनाई देने में बाधक बनती है **3** the combination of two or more wave movements to form a new wave, which may be bigger or smaller than the first दो या अधिक तरंगों के मिलने से बनी नई तरंग (पहली से बड़ी या छोटी)

**interim¹** /ˈɪntərɪm ˈइन्टरिम्/ *adj.* (*only before a noun*) not final or lasting; temporary until sb/sth more permanent is found जो अंतिम या स्थायी नहीं, अंतरिम; तब तक अस्थायी जब तक स्थायी का पता न लग जाए, अंतःकालीन *an interim arrangement* ○ *The deputy head teacher took over* ***in the interim period*** *until a replacement could be found.*

**interim²** /ˈɪntərɪm ˈइन्टरिम्/ *noun*

IDM **in the interim** in the time between two things happening; until a particular event happens दो बातों के घटित होने के बीच का समय; जब तक विशेष घटना हो न जाए

**interior** /ɪnˈtɪəriə(r) इन्ˈटिअरिअ(र्)/ *noun* **1** [C, *usually sing.*] the inside part of sth किसी वस्तु का आंतरिक भाग *I'd love to see the interior of the castle.* ○ *interior walls* ✪ विलोम **exterior** **2 the interior** [*sing.*] the central part of a country or continent that is a long way from the coast समुद्र तट से बहुत दूर किसी देश या महाद्वीप का केंद्रीय भाग या भीतरी प्रदेश **3 the Interior** [*sing.*] a country's own news and affairs that do not involve other countries किसी देश के निजी आंतरिक मामले (जो अन्य देशों से संबंधित नहीं) *the Department of the Interior*

**interior design** *noun* [U] the art or job of choosing colours, furniture, carpets, etc. to decorate the inside of a house भवन के आंतरिक भाग को सजाने (जैसे फ़र्नीचर, रंग आदि का निर्णय करना) की कला या काम, आंतरिक सज्जा ▶ **interior designer** *noun* [C] आंतरिक सज्जाकार, आंतरिक सज्जा विशेषज्ञ

**interjection** /ˌɪntəˈdʒekʃn ˌइन्टˈजेक्शन्/ *noun* [C] (*grammar*) a word or phrase that is used to express surprise, pain, pleasure, etc. (for example Oh!, Hurray! or Wow!) आश्चर्य, पीड़ा, हर्ष आदि (जैसे आह या वाह) व्यक्त करने वाला शब्द; विस्मयादिबोधक ✪ पर्याय **exclamation**

**interlude** /ˈɪntəluːd ˈइन्टलूड्/ *noun* [C] a period of time between two events or activities दो घटनाओं या कार्यक्रमों के बीच का समय, अंतराल, मध्यांतर या मध्यावकाश ➪ **interval** पर नोट देखिए।

**intermarry** /ˌɪntəˈmæri ˌइन्टˈमैरि/ *verb* (*pres. part.* **intermarrying;** *3rd person pres.* **intermarries;** *pt, pp* **intermarried**) [I] to marry sb from a different religion, culture, country, etc. अन्य धर्म, संस्कृति, देश आदि के व्यक्ति से विवाह करना; अंतरजातीय विवाह करना ▶ **intermarriage** /ˌɪntə-ˈmærɪdʒ ˌइन्टˈमैरिज्/ *noun* [U] अंतरजातीय विवाह

**intermediary** /ˌɪntəˈmiːdiəri ˌइन्टˈमीडिअरि/ *noun* [C] (*pl.* **intermediaries**) **an intermediary (between A and B)** a person or an organization that helps two people or groups to reach an agreement, by being a means of communication between them कोई व्यक्ति या संगठन जो दो व्यक्तियों या समूहों के बीच समझौता कराता है (दोनों के बीच संवाद का सेतु बनकर), मध्यस्थ व्यक्ति या मध्यस्थता करने वाला व्यक्ति

**intermediate** /ˌɪntəˈmiːdiət ˌइन्टˈमीडिअट्/ *adj.* **1** situated between two things in position, level, etc. पद, स्तर आदि की दृष्टि से दो वस्तुओं के बीच स्थित; मध्यवर्ती *an intermediate step/stage in a process* **2** having more than a basic knowledge of sth but not yet advanced; suitable for sb who is at this level आरंभिक स्तर से ऊपर का परंतु स्तर से निम्न स्तर का ज्ञान रखने वाला, मध्य स्तर का, माध्यमिक; इस स्तर के व्यक्ति के उपयुक्त *an intermediate student/book/level*

**interminable** /ɪnˈtɜːmɪnəbl इन्ˈटमिनब्ल्/ *adj.* lasting for a very long time and therefore boring or annoying अत्यधिक लंबा होने के कारण उबाऊ, अंतहीन, असीम *an interminable delay/wait/speech* ✪ पर्याय **endless** ▶ **interminably** /-əbli -अब्लि/ *adv.* अंतहीन रूप से

**intermission** /ˌɪntəˈmɪʃn ˌइन्टˈमिश्न्/ *noun* [C] a short period of time separating the parts of a film, play, etc. फ़िल्म, नाटक आदि के अंशों को अलग करने वाली छोटी अवधि, मध्यांतर, अंतराल, अल्पांतर ➪ **interval** पर नोट देखिए।

**intermittent** /ˌɪntəˈmɪtənt ˌइन्टˈमिटन्ट्/ *adj.* stopping for a short time and then starting again several times क्षण-भर रुकते हुए पुनः अनेक बार आरंभ होने वाला, रुक-रुक कर होने वाला, रह-रहकर होने वाला; सविराम, आंतरापिक *There will be intermittent showers.* ▶ **intermittently** *adv.* रुक-रुक कर होते हुए

**intern** /ɪnˈtɜːn इन्ˈटन्/ *verb* [T] (*formal*) **intern sb (in sth)** (*usually passive*) to keep sb in prison for political reasons, especially during a war राजनीतिक कारणों से किसी को जेल में रखना (प्रायः युद्धकाल में), नज़रबंद करना ▶ **internment** *noun* [U] नज़रबंदी

**internal** /ɪnˈtɜːnl इन्ˈटन्ल्/ *adj.* **1** (*only before a noun*) of or on the inside (of a place, person or object) (स्थान, व्यक्ति या वस्तु के) भीतर के या भीतर में, अंदरूनी, भीतरी, आंतरिक *He was rushed to hospital with internal injuries.* **2** happening or existing inside a particular organization संगठन विशेष के अंदर होने वाला या उसमें स्थित *an internal exam* (= one arranged and marked inside a particular school or college) ○ *an internal police inquiry* **3** (used about political or economic affairs) inside a country; not abroad (राजनीतिक या आर्थिक मामले) देश के भीतर, स्वदेशी; देश के बाहर नहीं *a country's internal affairs/trade/markets* ○ *an internal flight* ✪ विलोम **external** ▶ **internally** /-nəli -नलि/ *adv.* आंतरिक रूप से *This medicine is not to be taken internally* (= not swallowed).

**international** /ˌɪntəˈnæʃnəl ˌइन्टˈनैश्नल्/ *adj.* involving two or more countries जिसमें दो या अधिक देश शामिल हों; अंतरराष्ट्रीय *an international agreement/flight/football match* ○ *international trade/law/sport* ➪ **local, national** और **regional** देखिए। ▶ **internationally** /-nəli -नलि/ *adv.* अंतरराष्ट्रीय दृष्टि से या स्तर पर

**the International Date Line** (*also* **the date line**) *noun* [*sing.*] the imagined line that goes from north to south through the Pacific Ocean. The date on the east side is one day earlier than that on the west side प्रशांत महासागर में से होते हुए उत्तर से दक्षिण को जाने वाली कल्पित रेखा (इसके फलस्वरूप पूर्वी भाग में दिवस पश्चिमी भाग की अपेक्षा एक दिन पहले आ जाता है), अंतरराष्ट्रीय तिथि रेखा ➪ **earth** पर चित्र देखिए।

**the Internet** /ˈɪntənet ˈइन्टनेट्/ (*informal* **the Net**) *noun* [*sing.*] (*computing*) the international system of computers that makes it possible for you to see information from all around the world on your computer and to send information to other computers अंतरराष्ट्रीय कंप्यूटर प्रणाली जिसके कारण किसी भी कंप्यूटर पर कोई भी जानकारी प्राप्त करना या दूसरे कंप्यूटर को भेजना संभव होता है; इंटरनेट, अंतर्राष्ट्रीय-कंप्यूटर-तंत्र *I read about it* ***on the Internet.*** ➪ **Intranet** और **World Wide Web** देखिए।

**Interpol** /ˈɪntəpɒl ˈइन्टपॉल्/ *noun* [*sing., with sing or pl. verb*] an international organization that makes it possible for the police forces of different countries to help each other to solve crimes अंतरराष्ट्रीय अपराध पुलिस आयोग; इंटरपोल

**interpret** /ɪnˈtɜːprɪt इन्ˈटप्रिट्/ *verb* **1** [T] **interpret sth (as sth)** to explain or understand the meaning of sth किसी के अर्थ को समझाना या समझना *Your silence could be interpreted as arrogance.* ○ *How would you interpret this part of the poem?* ✪ विलोम **misinterpret** **2** [I] **interpret (for sb)** to translate what sb is saying into another language as you hear it (किसी के लिए) एक भाषा में वक्ता की बात सुनते हुए दूसरी भाषा में मौखिक अनुवाद करते जाना; भाषांतर करना *He can't speak much English so he'll need somebody to interpret for him.*

**interpretation** /ɪnˌtɜːprɪˈteɪʃn इन्ˌटप्रिˈटेश्न्/ *noun* [C, U] **1** an explanation or understanding of sth किसी बात की व्याख्या या बोधन, समझ What's *your interpretation of these statistics?* ○ *What he meant by that remark is* ***open to interpretation*** (= it can be explained in different ways). **2** the way an actor or musician chooses to perform or understand a character or piece of music अभिनेता या संगीतज्ञ द्वारा मूलपात्र या संगीत रचना को प्रस्तुत करने या समझने का प्रकार; व्याख्या *a modern interpretation of 'Shakuntala'*

**interpreter** /ɪnˈtɜːprɪtə(r) इन्ˈटप्रिट(र्)/ *noun* [C] a person whose job is to translate what sb is saying immediately into another language एक भाषा से दूसरी भाषा में मौखिक अनुवाद करने वाला व्यक्ति, मौखिक अनुवादक; भाष्यकार *The president spoke through an interpreter.* ➪ **translator** देखिए।

**interracial** /ˌɪntəˈreɪʃl ˌइन्टˈरेश्ल्/ *adj.* (*only before a noun*) involving people of different races जिसमें अलग-अलग जातियों के लोगों की संलिप्तता हो, अंतरजातीय *interracial marriage*

**interrelate** /ˌɪntərɪˈleɪt ˌइन्टरिˈलेट्/ *verb* [I, T] (*usually passive*) (*formal*) (used about two or more things) to connect or be connected very closely so that each has an effect on the other (दो या अधिक वस्तुएँ) बहुत गहराई से जोड़ना या जुड़ जाना (ऐसे कि प्रत्येक का दूसरे पर प्रभाव पड़े), अंतःसंबंधित होना या करना ▸ **interrelated** *adj.* अंतःसंबंधित

**interrogate** /ɪnˈterəgeɪt इन्ˈटेरगेट्/ *verb* [T] **interrogate sb (about sth)** to ask sb a lot of questions over a long period of time, especially in an aggressive way किसी से लंबी पूछताछ करना (विशेषतः कड़ाई से) *The prisoner was interrogated for six hours.* ▸ **interrogator** *noun* [C] पूछताछ करने वाला, परिप्रश्नक ▸ **interrogation** /ɪnˌterəˈgeɪʃn इन्ˌटेरˈगेशन्/ *noun* [C, U] पूछताछ, परिप्रश्न *The prisoner broke down **under interrogation** and confessed.*

**interrogative**[1] /ˌɪntəˈrɒgətɪv ˌइन्टˈरॉगटिव्/ *adj.* **1** (*formal*) asking a question; having the form of a question प्रश्न पूछते हुए; प्रश्न के रूप में, प्रश्नात्मक *an interrogative tone/gesture/remark* **2** (*grammar*) used in questions प्रश्नों में प्रयुक्त *an interrogative sentence/pronoun/determiner/adverb*

**interrogative**[2] /ˌɪntəˈrɒgətɪv ˌइन्टˈरॉगटिव्/ *noun* [C] (*grammar*) a question word प्रश्नात्मक शब्द *'Who', 'what' and 'where' are interrogatives.*

**interrupt** /ˌɪntəˈrʌpt ˌइन्टˈरप्ट्/ *verb* **1** [I, T] **interrupt (sb/ sth) (with sth)** to say or do sth that makes sb stop what he/she is saying or doing कुछ करते या कहते हुए व्यक्ति को कुछ कह कर कोई हरकतकर रोकना, टोकाटोकी करना *He kept interrupting me with silly questions.* **2** [T] to stop the progress of sth for a short time किसी वस्तु की प्रगति को क्षण भर के लिए रोकना, रुकावट होना या पैदा करना *The programme was interrupted by an important news flash.*

**interruption** /ˌɪntəˈrʌpʃn ˌइन्टˈरप्शन्/ *noun* [U, C] the act of interrupting sb/sth; the person or thing that interrupts sb/sth व्यक्ति या वस्तु को रोकने का कार्य, रुकावट, अवरोध; व्यक्ति या वस्तु के काम में रुकावट उत्पन्न करने वाला व्यक्ति या वस्तु, अवरोधक *I need to work for a few hours without interruption.* ○ *I've had so many interruptions this morning that I've done nothing!*

**intersect** /ˌɪntəˈsekt ˌइन्टˈसेक्ट्/ *verb* [I, T] (used about roads, lines, etc.) to meet or cross each other (सड़कों, रेखाओं, आदि का) एक दूसरे से मिलना या एक दूसरे को काटना *The lines intersect at right angles.*

**intersection** /ˌɪntəˈsekʃn ˌइन्टˈसेक्शन्/ *noun* [C] the place where two or more roads, lines, etc. meet or cross each other स्थान या बिंदु जहाँ दो या अधिक सड़कें, रेखाएँ आदि एक दूसरे से मिलती हैं या एक दूसरे को काटती हैं, कटाव-बिंदु, (गणित) प्रतिच्छेद

**intersperse** /ˌɪntəˈspɜːs ˌइन्टˈस्पस्/ *verb* [T] (*usually passive*) to put things at various points in sth एक वस्तु में अनेक बिंदुओं पर (बीच-बीच में) अन्य वस्तुओं को रख देना, छितराना, अंतः प्रकीर्ण करना *He interspersed his speech with jokes.*

**intertwine** /ˌɪntəˈtwaɪn ˌइन्टˈट्वाइन्/ *verb* [I, T] if two things intertwine or if you intertwine them, they become very closely connected and difficult to separate दो वस्तुओं का परस्पर गुँथना या उन्हें परस्पर गूँथना (ऐसे कि वे गइराई से जुड़ जाएँ और उन्हें अलग करना कठिन हो जाए); अंतर्ग्रथन करना

**interval** /ˈɪntəvl ˈइन्टव्ल्/ *noun* [C] **1** a period of time between two events दो घटनाओं के बीच का समय, अंतराल *There was a long interval between sending the letter and getting a reply.* **2** a short break separating the different parts of a play, film, concert, etc. नाटक, फ़िल्म आदि के अंशों को अलग करने वाला लघु विराम; मध्यांतर **3** [*usually pl.*] a short period during which sth different happens from what is happening for the rest of the time वह लघु अवधि जिसमें किसी घटित हो रही घटना में अन्य घटना व्यवधान उपस्थित करती है *There'll be a few **sunny intervals** between the showers today.*

> NOTE **Interval** के अर्थ के समान अर्थ वाले अन्य शब्द हैं—**intermission, break, recess, interlude** और **pause.** किसी कार्यक्रम के बीच में विराम के लिए ब्रिटिश अंग्रेज़ी में **interval** का प्रयोग होता है और अमेरिकी अंग्रेज़ी में **intermission** का। **Break** का प्रयोग विशेषतः काम और पढ़ाई की अवधि के संदर्भ में होता है; जैसे किसी कार्यालय, फ़ैक्टरी या स्कूल में **a lunch/tea break**—*The children play outside in the breaks at school.* ○ *You've worked so hard you've earned a break.* अमेरिकी अंग्रेज़ी में स्कूल में होने वाले 'ब्रेक' को **(a) recess** कहते हैं। ब्रिटिश अंग्रेज़ी में **recess** लंबी अवधि का विराम है जो विशेषतः संसद और कचहरियों में होता है—*Parliament is in recess.* ○ *the summer recess.* **Interlude** दो घटनाओं के बीच में होने वाला अल्पकालिक विराम को कहते है जिसमें कोई अलग बात घटित होती है—*a peaceful interlude in the fighting* और **a pause** उस अल्पकालिक और अस्थायी विराम को कहते हैं जो कुछ करते या बोलते हुए आता है—*After a moment's pause, she answered.*

**IDM** **at intervals** with time or spaces between समय या स्थान के अंतराल से, बीच-बीच में रुकते या स्थान छोड़ते हुए *I write home **at regular intervals**.* ○ *Plant the trees at two-metre intervals.*

**intervene** /ˌɪntəˈviːn ˌइन्टˈव़ीन्/ *verb* [I] **1 intervene (in sth)** to act in a way that prevents sth happening or influences the result of sth ऐसा काम करना कि कोई बात होने न पाए या उसका परिणाम प्रभावित हो, बीच-बचाव करना *She would have died if the neighbours hadn't intervened.* ○ *to intervene in a dispute* **2** to interrupt sb who is speaking in order to say sth अपनी बात कहने के लिए वक्ता की बात में बाधा पहुँचाना; टोकना **3** (used about events, etc.) to happen in a way that delays sth or stops it from happening (घटनाओं का) इस प्रकार घटित होना जिससे काम में देरी हो या वह रुक जाए, अड़चन डालना *If no further problems intervene we should be able to finish in time.* ▶ **intervention** /ˌɪntəˈvenʃn ˌइन्टˈव़ेन्शन्/ *noun* [U, C] **intervention (in sth)** हस्तक्षेप *military intervention in the crisis*

**intervening** /ˌɪntəˈviːnɪŋ ˌइन्टˈव़ीनिङ्/ *adj.* (*only before a noun*) coming or existing between two events, dates, objects, etc. दो घटनाओं, तारीख़ों, वस्तुओं आदि के बीच में आने या पड़ने वाला; मध्यवर्ती *the intervening years/days/months*

**interview**[1] /ˈɪntəvjuː ˈइन्टव्यू/ *noun* [C] **1 an interview (for sth)** a meeting at which sb is asked questions to find out if he/she is suitable for a job, course of study, etc. साक्षात्कार, इंटरव्यू; प्रश्न पूछकर नौकरी, प्रवेश आदि के लिए प्रत्याशी के उपयुक्त होने का पता लगाने के लिए आयोजित मीटिंग या मुलाक़ात *to attend an interview* **2 an interview (with sb)** a meeting at which a journalist asks sb questions in order to find out his/her opinion, etc. पत्रकार द्वारा प्रश्न पूछकर व्यक्ति विशेष के विचार जानने के लिए आयोजित मीटिंग या मुलाक़ात; इंटरव्यू *There was an interview with the Prime Minister on television last night.* ○ *The actress refused to **give an interview*** (= answer questions).

**interview**[2] /ˈɪntəvjuː ˈइन्टव्यू/ *verb* [T] **1 interview sb (for sth)** to ask sb questions to find out if he/she is suitable for a job, course of study, etc. (किसी काम के लिए) किसी का इंटरव्यू लेना, प्रश्न पूछकर नौकरी, प्रवेश आदि के लिए प्रत्याशी की उपयुक्तता का पता लगाना *How many applicants did you interview for the job?* **2 interview sb (about sth)** to ask sb questions about his/her opinions, private life, etc., especially on the radio or television or for a newspaper, magazine, etc. (किसी विषय में) किसी का इंटरव्यू लेना, किसी व्यक्ति से उसके विचारों, निजी जीवन आदि पर प्रश्न पूछना (विशेषतः रेडियो या टेलीविज़न पर या अख़बार, पत्रिका आदि के लिए) **3 interview sb (about sth)** to ask sb questions at a private meeting निजी मीटिंग में किसी से प्रश्न पूछना या पूछताछ करना *The police are waiting to interview the injured girl.*

**interviewee** /ˌɪntəvjuːˈiː ˌइन्टव्यूˈई/ *noun* [C] a person who is questioned in an interview साक्षात्कार में प्रत्याशी, इंटरव्यू देने वाला व्यक्ति

**interviewer** /ˈɪntəvjuːə(r) ˈइन्टव्यूअ(र्)/ *noun* [C] a person who asks the questions in an interview साक्षात्कार-कर्ता, इंटरव्यू लेने वाला व्यक्ति

**intestine** /ɪnˈtestɪn इन्ˈटेस्टिन्/ *noun* [C, *usually pl.*] the long tube in your body that carries food away from your stomach to the place where it leaves your body आँत; शरीर के अंदर एक लंबी नली जो उदर से भोजन लेकर शरीर के अंत तक पहुँचाती है *the small/large intestine* ✪ पर्याय **gut** कम औपचारिक शब्द है। ⇨ **body** पर चित्र देखिए। ▶ **intestinal** /ɪnˈtestɪnl; ˌɪnteˈstaɪnl इन्ˈटेस्टिनल्; ˌइन्टेˈस्टाइनल्/ *adj.* आँत-संबंधी

**intimacy** /ˈɪntɪməsi ˈइन्टिमसि/ *noun* [U] the state of having a close personal relationship with sb किसी के साथ निजी संबंधों की अति निकटता; घनिष्ठता, अंतरंगता *Their intimacy grew over the years.*

**intimate** /ˈɪntɪmət ˈइन्टिमट्/ *adj.* **1** (used about people) having a very close relationship (व्यक्ति) जिसके साथ बहुत निकट संबंध हों; घनिष्ठ, अंतरंग *They're intimate friends.* **2** very private and personal अत्यधिक निजी और व्यक्तिगत *They told each other their most intimate thoughts and secrets.* **3** (used about a place, an atmosphere, etc.) quiet and friendly (स्थान, वातावरण) शांत और मैत्रीपूर्ण *I know an intimate little restaurant we could go to.* **4** very detailed सुविस्तृत, प्रगाढ़ *He's lived here all his life and has an **intimate knowledge** of the area.* ▶ **intimately** *adv.* घनिष्ठतापूर्वक, विस्तारपूर्वक

**intimation** /ˌɪntɪˈmeɪʃn ˌइन्टिˈमेशन्/ *noun* [C, U] (*formal*) the act of stating sth or of making it known, especially in an indirect way कुछ कहने या ज्ञापित करने की क्रिया (विशेषतः परोक्ष रीति से), सूचना, प्रज्ञापन *There was no intimation from his doctor that his condition was serious.*

**intimidate** /ɪnˈtɪmɪdeɪt इन्ˈटिमिडेट्/ *verb* [T] **intimidate sb (into sth/doing sth)** to frighten or threaten sb, often in order to make him/her do sth किसी को डराना या धमकाना (प्रायः कोई काम करवाने के लिए); अभित्रस्त करना *She refused to be intimidated by their threats.* ▶ **intimidating** *adj.* डराने वाला, धमकी भरा, अभित्रासकीय *The teacher* *had rather an intimidating manner.* ▶ **intimidation** /ɪnˌtɪmɪˈdeɪʃn इन्ˌटिमिˈडेश्न्/ *noun* [U] धमकी, तर्जन, अभित्रास *The rebel troops controlled the area by intimidation.*

**into** /ˈɪntə ˈइन्ट; *before vowels* ˈɪntə; ˈɪntu: स्वर ध्वनियों के पूर्व ˈइन्ट; ˈइनटू/ *prep.* **1** moving to a position inside or in sth (किसी के) अंदर की ओर या अंदर *Come into the house.* ○ *I'm going into town.* ✪ विलोम **out of 1** **2** in the direction of sth किसी की दिशा में, किसी की ओर या किसी के अभिमुख *Please speak into the microphone.* ○ *At this point we were driving into the sun and had to shade our eyes.* **3** to a point at which you hit sth ऐसे स्थानबिंदु पर जहाँ कोई टकरा जाए, में *I backed the car into a wall.* ○ *She walked into a glass door.* **4** showing a change from one thing to another जिसमें एक वस्तु बदलकर दूसरी हो जाए, में *She changed into her jeans.* ○ *Translate the passage into Hindi.* **5** concerning or involving sth किसी से संबंधित या किसी को शामिल करते हुए, के बारे में *an inquiry into safety procedures* **6** used when you are talking about dividing numbers संख्याओं को भाग देने या गुणा करने का निर्देश करने के लिए प्रयुक्त *7 into 28 goes 4 times.*
IDM **be into sth** (*spoken*) to be very interested in sth, for example as a hobby किसी बात में बहुत दिलचस्पी रखना *I'm really into canoeing.*

**intolerable** /ɪnˈtɒlərəbl इन्ˈटॉलरबल्/ *adj.* too bad, unpleasant or difficult to bear or accept इतना ख़राब; बुरा या कठिन कि सहन या स्वीकार न हो सके; असह्य, असहनीय, बर्दाश्त से बाहर *The living conditions were intolerable.* ○ *intolerable pain* ✪ पर्याय **unbearable** ✪ विलोम **tolerable** ➪ **tolerate** verb देखिए। ▶ **intolerably** /-əbli -अब्लि/ *adv.* असह्य रूप से

**intolerant** /ɪnˈtɒlərənt इन्ˈटॉलरन्ट्/ *adj.* **intolerant (of sb/sth)** not able to accept behaviour or opinions that are different from your own जो अपने आचरण या विचारों से भिन्नता को स्वीकार न कर सके, असहिष्णु; असहनशील *She's very intolerant of young children.* ✪ विलोम **tolerant** ▶ **intolerance** *noun* [U] असहिष्णुता, असहनशीलता ✪ विलोम **tolerance** ▶ **intolerantly** *adv.* असहनशीलतापूर्वक

**intonation** /ˌɪntəˈneɪʃn ˌइन्टˈनेश्न्/ *noun* [C, U] the rise and fall of your voice while you are speaking बोलते समय स्वर में उतार-चढ़ाव; अनुतान ✪ पर्याय **inflection**

**intoxicated** /ɪnˈtɒksɪkeɪtɪd इन्ˈटॉक्सिकेटिड्/ *adj.* (*formal*) **1** having had too much alcohol to drink; drunk बहुत अधिक मदिरापान किए हुए; शराब के नशे में धुत **2** very excited and happy बहुत रोमांचित और प्रसन्न *She was intoxicated by her success.* ▶ **intoxication** /ɪnˌtɒksɪˈkeɪʃn इन्ˌटॉक्सिˈकेश्न्/ *noun* [U] नशा

**intra-** *prefix* (*in adjectives and adverbs*) inside; within के अंदर; के भीतर, अंतः *intravenous* ○ *intra-departmental* ➪ **inter-** देखिए।

**Intranet** /ˈɪntrənet ˈइन्ट्रनेट्/ *noun* [C] (*computing*) a system of computers inside an organization that makes it possible for people who work there to look at the same information and to send information to each other एक ही संगठन के भीतर का कंप्यूटर-तंत्र (जिससे उसके कर्मचारी एक ही जानकारी प्राप्त कर सकते हैं तथा जानकारी एक दूसरे को भेज सकते हैं), आंतरिक कंप्यूटर-तंत्र; इंट्रानेट ➪ **Internet** देखिए।

**intransitive** /ɪnˈtrænsətɪv इन्ˈट्रैन्सटिव्/ *adj.* (*grammar*) (*used about a verb*) used without an object जिसका कर्म न हो; अकर्मक ✪ विलोम **transitive**

> NOTE इस शब्दकोश में अकर्मक क्रियाओं (intransitive verbs) का [I] चिह्न से निर्देश किया गया है। अकर्मक क्रियाओं (intransitive verbs) के विषय में अधिक जानकारी के लिए शब्दकोश के अंत में **Quick Grammar Reference** खंड देखिए।

▶ **intransitively** *adv.* अकर्मक (क्रिया) के रूप में

**intrauterine** /ˌɪntrəˈju:tərɑɪn ˌइन्ट्राˈयूटराइन्/ *adj.* (*medical*) inside the **uterus** गर्भाशय के भीतर का ➪ **IUD** देखिए।

**intravenous** /ˌɪntrəˈvi:nəs ˌइन्ट्राˈवीनस्/ *adj.* (*abbr.* IV) (used about drugs or food) going into a **vein** (दवाएँ या भोजन) नसों के अंदर जाने वाला, अंतःशिरा, शिरा आभ्यंतर *an intravenous injection* ▶ **intravenously** *adv.* नसों के अंदर से *The patient had to be fed intravenously.*

**intrepid** /ɪnˈtrepɪd इन्ˈट्रेपिड्/ *adj.* without any fear of danger संकट के भय से रहित; निर्भीक *an intrepid climber*

**intricacy** /ˈɪntrɪkəsi ˈइन्ट्रिकसि/ *noun* **1 intricacies** [*pl.*] **the intricacies of sth** the complicated parts or details of sth किसी वस्तु के जटिल अंश या ब्योरे, *It's difficult to understand all the intricacies of the situation.* **2** [U] the quality of having complicated parts, details or patterns जटिल अंशों, ब्योरों, पैटर्नों से युक्त होने का गुण; जटिलता, पेचीदापन

**intricate** /ˈɪntrɪkət ˈइन्ट्रिकट्/ *adj.* having many small parts or details put together in a complicated way जिसमें अनेक छोटे अंशों या ब्योरों को पेचीदा ढंग से जुटा दिया गया हो, उलझा हुआ, उलझावदार, पेचीदा *an intricate pattern* ○ *The story has an intricate plot.* ▶ **intricately** *adv.* जटिलतापूर्वक

**intrigue**[1] /ɪnˈtriːg इन्ˈट्रीग् / *verb* [T] to make sb very interested and wanting to know more किसी की रुचि या उत्सुकता को जगाना *I was intrigued by the way he seemed to know all about us already.* ▸ **intriguing** *adj.* षड्यंत्रकारी, पहेली-जैसा *an intriguing story*

**intrigue**[2] /ˈɪntriːg ˈइन्ट्रीग् / *noun* [C, U] secret plans to do sth, especially sth bad कुछ (विशेषतः कुकर्म) करने की गुप्त योजना; षड्यंत्र, कुचक्र *The film is about political intrigues against the government.* ○ *His new novel is full of intrigue and suspense.*

**intrinsic** /ɪnˈtrɪnsɪk; -zɪk इन्ˈट्रिन्सिक्; -ज़िक् / *-adj.* (*only before a noun*) belonging to sth as part of its nature; basic (किसी वस्तु की) प्रकृति का अंतरंग; मूलभूत *The object is of no intrinsic value* (= the material it is made of is not worth anything). ▸ **intrinsically** /-kli -क्लि / *adv.* अंतरंग रूप से

**introduce** /ˌɪntrəˈdjuːs ˌइन्ट्रˈड्यूस् / *verb* [T] **1 introduce sth (in/into sth)** to bring in sth new, use sth, or take sth to a place for the first time नई वस्तु लेकर आना, पहली बार प्रयोग में लाना या किसी स्थान पर लाना, प्रस्तुत या पेश करना *The new law was introduced in 1999.* ○ *The company is introducing a new range of cars this summer.* **2 introduce sb (to sb)** to tell two or more people who have not met before what each others' names are दो या अधिक और परस्पर अपरिचित व्यक्तियों का एक दूसरे को अपना नाम आदि बताना या परिचय कराना *'Who's that girl over there?' 'Come with me and I'll introduce you to her.'* **3 introduce yourself (to sb)** to tell sb you have met for the first time what your name is पहली बार मिले व्यक्ति को अपना नाम बताना या परिचय देना *He just walked over and introduced himself to me.* **4 introduce sb to sth** to make sb begin to learn about sth or do sth for the first time किसी व्यक्ति को पहली बार कोई काम सिखाने लगना *This pamphlet will introduce you to the basic aims of our society.* **5** to be the first or main speaker on a radio or television programme telling the audience who is going to speak, perform, etc. रेडियो या टेलीविज़न कार्यक्रम में प्रथम या मुख्य वक्ता होना और लोगों को बताना कि कौन व्यक्ति भाषण, कार्यक्रम आदि देगा, प्रथम या मुख्य वक्ता को सबके सामने पेश या प्रस्तुत करना *May I introduce my first guest on the show tonight—it is Rahul Dravid.*

**NOTE** (प्रायः अवसर के भेद से) ब्रिटेन में एक दूसरे का परिचय कराने के अलग-अलग तरीक़े हैं। औपचारिक परिचय में व्यक्ति की (सामाजिक) उपाधि के बाद उसका कुलनाम आता है। अनौपचारिक परिचय में या बच्चों के परिचय में हम उनका प्रथम नाम बताते हैं। औपचारिक और अनौपचारिक दोनों परिचयों में हम लोगों का परिचय कराते हुए कहते हैं 'this is' न कि 'he/she is' *(informal)—'Ravi, meet Mita.' 'Mrs Sharma, **this is** my daughter, Jaya.'* ○ (*formal*) *'May I introduce you. Dr Walia, **this is** Mr Rao. Mr Rao, Dr Walia.'* परिचय कराने पर अनौपचारिक रूप से कहा जाता है 'Hello' या 'Nice to meet you'. औपचारिक अभिव्यक्ति है 'How do you do?' दूसरा व्यक्ति जवाब में कहता है 'How do you do?' परिचय कराए जाने पर लोग प्रायः हाथ मिलाते हैं।

**introduction** /ˌɪntrəˈdʌkʃn ˌइन्ट्रˈडक्श्न् / *noun* **1** [U] **introduction of sth (into sth)** the action of bringing in sth new; using sth or taking sth to a place for the first time कुछ नया लेकर आने की क्रिया, प्रस्तुति; किसी वस्तु का पहली बार प्रयोग या उसे किसी स्थान पर लाने की क्रिया, प्रथम प्रयोग या प्रस्तुति *the introduction of computers into the classroom* **2** [C, *usually pl.*] the act of telling two or more people each others' names for the first time दो या अधिक लोगों का प्रथम पारस्परिक परिचय *I think I'll get my husband to **make/do the introductions**—he's better at remembering names!* **3** [C] the first part of a book, a piece of written work or a talk which gives a general idea of what is going to follow पुस्तक के आरंभ में या मौखिक चर्चा में आगामी विषय विवेचन की सामान्य रूपरेखा; भूमिका **4** [C] **an introduction (to sth)** a book for people who are beginning to study a subject किसी विषय के प्रारंभिक अध्येताओं के लिए पुस्तक, विषय-प्रवेश कराने वाली पुस्तक *'An Introduction to English Grammar'* **5** [*sing.*] **an introduction to sth** first experience of sth किसी काम का पहला अनुभव *My first job—in a factory—was not a pleasant introduction to work.*

**introductory** /ˌɪntrəˈdʌktəri ˌइन्ट्रˈडक्टरि / *adj.* **1** happening or said at the beginning in order to give a general idea of what will follow आरंभवर्ती या आरंभ में प्रस्तुत (भाषण आदि) (जिसमें आगामी विषय-विवेचन की सामान्य रूपरेखा होती है); परिचयात्मक *an introductory speech/chapter/remark* **2** intended as an introduction to a subject or activity किसी विषय या गतिविधि का परिचय कराने वाला; प्रारंभिक *introductory courses*

**introvert** /ˈɪntrəvɜːt ˈइन्ट्रव़ट् / *noun* [C] a quiet, shy person who prefers to be alone than with other people शांत, लजीला एकांतप्रिय व्यक्ति; अंतर्मुखी व्यक्ति ✪ विलोम **extrovert** ▸ **introverted** *adj.* अंतर्मुख

**intrude** /ɪnˈtruːd इन्ˈट्रूड्/ *verb* [I] **intrude on/upon sb/sth** to enter a place or situation without permission or when you are not wanted किसी स्थान या अवसर पर बिना अनुमति के या लोगों की इच्छा के विपरीत पहुँचना, घुस आना या जाना, घुसपैठ करना, अनधिकार प्रवेश करना *I'm sorry to intrude on your Sunday lunch but the matter was rather urgent.*

**intruder** /ɪnˈtruːdə(r) इन्ˈट्रूड(र्)/ *noun* [C] a person who enters a place without permission and often secretly बिना अनुमति और प्रायः गुप्त रीति से किसी स्थान में प्रवेश करने वाला व्यक्ति; घुसपैठिया, अनधिकार प्रवेश करने वाला व्यक्ति

**intrusion** /ɪnˈtruːʒn इन्ˈट्रूश़न्/ *noun* **1** [C, U] **(an) intrusion (on/upon/into sth)** something that disturbs you or your life when you want to be private निजता या एकांत की चाह के क्षणों में किसी की शांति भंग करने वाली बात, अनुचित हस्तक्षेप *This was another example of press intrusion into the affairs of the royals.* **2** [C] (in geology) a mass of hot liquid rock that has been forced up from below the earth's surface and cooled in between other layers of rock (भूगर्भविज्ञान में) पृथ्वी के नीचे से बलपूर्वक उभरी और चट्टान की अन्य परतों के बीच ठंडी हुई उष्ण द्रवीभूत चट्टान; अंतर्वेधी शैल ▶ **intrusive** /ɪnˈtruːsɪv इन्ˈट्रूसिव्/ *adj.* अनधिकार प्रवेश से संबंधित

**intuition** /ˌɪntjuˈɪʃn ˌइन्ट्यु ˈइश्न्/ *noun* [C, U] the feeling or understanding that makes you believe or know that sth is true without being able to explain why मनोभाव या बुद्धि जो बिना तर्क किए किसी बात को सही माने; अंतःप्रज्ञा, सहजबुद्धि, अंतर्ज्ञान *She knew, by intuition, about his illness, although he never mentioned it.* ▶ **intuitive** /ɪnˈtjuːɪtɪv इन्ˈट्यूइटिव्/ *adj.* अंतर्ज्ञानमूलक ▶ **intuitively** *adv.* अंतर्ज्ञान से *Intuitively, she knew that he was lying.*

**inundate** /ˈɪnʌndeɪt ˈइनन्डेट्/ *verb* [T] (*usually passive*) **1 inundate sb (with sth)** to give or send sb so many things that he/she cannot deal with them all किसी के पास चीज़ों का ढेर लगा देना (कि वह उन सबसे निबट न सके) *We were inundated with applications for the job.* ✪ पर्याय **swamp** **2** (*formal*) to cover an area of land with water ज़मीन का पानी से ढक जाना, बाढ़ आ जाना *After the heavy rains the fields were inundated.* ✪ पर्याय **flood**

**invade** /ɪnˈveɪd इन्ˈव़ेड्/ *verb* **1** [I, T] to enter a country with an army in order to attack and take control of it किसी देश पर आक्रमण कर उस पर अधिकार करने के लिए सेना का उसमें प्रवेश करना, किसी देश पर आक्रमण करना *When did the Huns invade India?* **2** [T] to enter in large numbers, often where sb/sth is not wanted बड़ी संख्या में लोगों का वहाँ पहुँचना जहाँ वे वांछित नहीं, अप्रत्याशित रूप से कहीं पर लोगों की भरमार होना *The whole area has been invaded by tourists.* ➪ **invasion** noun देखिए। ▶ **invader** *noun* [C] आक्रांता, हमलावर

**invalid**[1] /ɪnˈvælɪd इन्ˈव़ैलिड्/ *adj.* **1** not legally or officially acceptable क़ानूनन या आधिकारिक रूप से अमान्य, अप्रामाणिक, अविधिमान्य *I'm afraid your passport is invalid.* **2** not correct according to reason; not based on all the facts जो तर्कयुक्त न हो, तर्कहीन; जो समग्र रूप में तथ्यपुष्ट नहीं, दुर्बल, अशक्त *an invalid argument* **3** (*computing*) (used about an instruction, etc.) of a type that the computer cannot recognize (निर्देश) जिसे कंप्यूटर समझ न सके *an invalid command* ✪ विलोम **valid**

**invalid**[2] /ˈɪnvəlɪd ˈइन्व़लिड्/ *noun* [C] a person who has been very ill for a long time and needs to be looked after लंबे समय से बीमार व्यक्ति (जिसे देखभाल की ज़रूरत है)

**invalidate** /ɪnˈvælɪdeɪt इन्ˈव़ैलिडेट्/ *verb* [T] **1** to show that an idea, a story, an argument, etc. is wrong किसी विचार, कहानी, तर्क आदि को अमान्य ठहराना *This new piece of evidence invalidates his version of events.* **2** if you **invalidate** a document, contract, election, etc., you make it no longer legally or officially valid or acceptable किसी दस्तावेज़, क़रार, चुनाव आदि को अविधिमान्य करना(अर्थात वह क़ानूनी या आधिकारिक दृष्टि से विधिमान्य या स्वीकार्य नहीं रहा) ✪ विलोम **validate** ▶ **invalidation** /ɪnˌvælɪˈdeɪʃn इन्ˌव़ैलि ˈडेश्न्/ *noun* [U] अविधिमान्यकरण, अमान्यकरण

**invaluable** /ɪnˈvæljuəbl इन्ˈव़ैल्युअब्ल्/ *adj.* **invaluable (to/for sb/sth)** extremely useful अत्यधिक उपयोगी, बहुमूल्य *invaluable help/information/support* **NOTE** ध्यान रखिए 'invaluable' को 'valuable' का विलोम न समझिए, 'valuable' का विलोम **valueless** या **worthless** है।

**invariable** /ɪnˈveəriəbl इन्ˈव़ेरिअब्ल्/ *adj.* not changing अपरिवर्तनशील, अपरिवर्ती, अचर

**invariably** /ɪnˈveəriəbli इन्ˈव़ेरिअब्लि/ *adv.* almost always लगभग हमेशा *She invariably arrives late.*

**invasion** /ɪnˈveɪʒn इन्ˈव़ेश़न्/ *noun* **1** [C, U] the action of entering another country with an army in order to take control of it किसी देश पर सेना का आक्रमण *the threat of invasion* **2** [C] the action of entering a place where you are not wanted and disturbing sb अवांछित रूप से किसी स्थान पर प्रवेश *Such questions are an* ***invasion of privacy.*** ➪ **invade** verb देखिए।

**invent** /ɪnˈvent इन्ˈवेन्ट्/ *verb* [T] **1** to think of or make sth for the first time कोई बात प्रथम बार सोचना या वस्तु प्रथम बार बनाना, किसी बात या वस्तु का आविष्कार करना *When was the camera invented?* **2** to say or describe sth that is not true किसी असत्य बात को कहना या बनाना, कोई बात मन से गढ़ लेना, की कल्पना कर लेना *I realized that he had invented the whole story.* ▸ **inventor** *noun* [C] आविष्कारक

**invention** /ɪnˈvenʃn इन्ˈवेन्शन्/ *noun* **1** [C] a thing that has been made or designed by sb for the first time प्रथम बार बनाई या डिज़ाइन की गई वस्तु; आविष्कार *The microwave oven is a very useful invention.* **2** [U] the action or process of making or designing sth for the first time किसी वस्तु को प्रथम बार बनाने या डिज़ाइन करने का कार्य या प्रक्रिया, आविष्कार प्रक्रिया; आविष्करण *Books had to be written by hand before the invention of printing.* **3** [C, U] telling a story or giving an excuse that is not true कहानी गढ़ने या झूठा बहाना बनाने की क्रिया *It was obvious that his story about being robbed was (an) invention.*

**inventive** /ɪnˈventɪv इन्ˈवेन्टिव्/ *adj.* having clever and original ideas मौलिक और चतुराई भरी सूझ वाला; उपज्ञाता ▸ **inventiveness** *noun* [U] मौलिकता, आविष्कारशीलता

**inventory** /ˈɪnvəntri ˈइन्वन्ट्रि/ *noun* [C] (*pl.* **inventories**) a detailed list, for example of all the furniture in a house विस्तृत सूची (जैसे मकान के सारे फ़र्नीचर की सूची) *The landlord is coming to **make an inventory** of the contents of the flat.*

**inverse[1]** /ˌɪnˈvɜːs ˌइन्ˈवस्/ *adj.* (*only before a noun*) opposite in amount or position to sth else मात्रा या पद की दृष्टि से (किसी का) प्रतिलोम या उलटा *A person's wealth is often **in inverse proportion to** their happiness* (= the more money a person has, the less happy he/she is). ▸ **inversely** *adv.* प्रतिलोम रूप से, उलटे क्रम से

**inverse[2]** /ˈɪnvɜːs ˈइन्वस्/ **the inverse** *noun* [*sing.*] (*technical*) the exact opposite of sth किसी वस्तु का सही प्रतिलोम; व्युत्क्रम

**invert** /ɪnˈvɜːt इन्ˈवट्/ *verb* [T] (*formal*) to put sth in the opposite order or position to the way it usually is किसी वस्तु को उसकी सामान्य स्थिति के विपरीत क्रम या स्थिति में रखना, किसी वस्तु को उलटा या औंधा कर देना, पलट देना

**invertebrate** /ɪnˈvɜːtɪbrət इन्ˈवटिब्रट्/ *noun* [C] an animal without a solid line of bones (**backbone**) going along its body बिना रीढ़ का प्राणी, मेरुदंडरहित प्राणी *slugs, worms and other small invertebrates* ✪ विलोम **vertebrate**

**inverted commas** (*BrE*) = **quotation marks** *to put sth **in inverted commas***

**invest** /ɪnˈvest इन्ˈवेस्ट्/ *verb* [I, T] **invest (sth) (in sth) 1** to put money into a bank, business, property, etc. in the hope that you will make a profit लाभ अर्जित करने की आशा में धन को बैंक, व्यापार आदि में डालना, धन का निवेश करना, पूँजी निवेश करना *Many firms have invested heavily in this project.* ○ *I've invested all my money in the company.* **2** to spend money, time or energy on sth that you think is good or useful अच्छी या उपयोगी लगने वाली वस्तु पर पैसा, समय या शक्ति लगाना *I'm thinking of investing in a computer.* ○ *You have to invest a lot of time if you really want to learn a language well.* ▸ **investor** *noun* [C] निवेशक, पैसा लगाने वाला

**investigate** /ɪnˈvestɪgeɪt इन्ˈवेसटिगेट्/ *verb* [I, T] to try to find out all the facts about sth तथ्यों के लिए किसी मामले की छानबीन करना, तहक़ीक़ात करना *A murder was reported and the police were sent to investigate.* ○ *A group of experts are investigating the cause of the crash.* ▸ **investigator** *noun* [C] अन्वेषणकर्ता, जाँचकर्ता

**investigation** /ɪnˌvestɪˈgeɪʃn इन्ˌवेसटिˈगेशन्/ *noun* [C, U] **(an) investigation (into sth)** an official examination of the facts about a situation, crime, etc. किसी स्थिति, अपराध आदि से संबंधित तथ्यों की आधिकारिक जाँच, अन्वेषणकार्य, छान-बीन, तफ़्तीश, तहक़ीक़ात *The airlines are going to **carry out an investigation** into security procedures at airports.* ○ *The matter is still **under investigation**.*

**investigative** /ɪnˈvestɪgətɪv इन्ˈवेसटिगटिव्/ *adj.* activities that involve trying to find out all the facts about sb/sth किसी व्यक्ति या वस्तु में सब तथ्यों का पता लगाने की कोशिश से संबंधित, अन्वेषणात्मक, खोजपरक या खोजी *investigative journalism*

**investment** /ɪnˈvestmənt इन्ˈवेस्ट्मन्ट्/ *noun* **1** [U, C] **(an) investment (in sth)** the act of putting money in a bank, business, property, etc.; the amount of money that you put in बैंक, व्यापार आदि में पैसा लगाने या रखने की क्रिया, निवेशन; निवेशित धन की मात्रा; पूँजी निवेशन *investment in local industry* ○ *The company will have to **make an** enormous **investment** to computerize production.* **2** [C] (*informal*) a thing that you have bought ख़रीदी वस्तु *This coat has been a good investment—I've worn it for three years.*

**invigilate** /ɪnˈvɪdʒɪleɪt इन्ˈविजिलेट्/ *verb* [I, T] (*BrE*) to watch the people taking an exam to make sure that nobody is cheating परीक्षा में परीक्षार्थियों पर निगाह रखना (कि वे ग़लत काम न करें), परीक्षा में निरीक्षण-कार्य करना ▶ **invigilator** *noun* [C] निरीक्षक

**invigorate** /ɪnˈvɪɡəreɪt इन्ˈविगरेट्/ *verb* [I, T] to make sb feel healthy, fresh and full of energy किसी व्यक्ति को स्वस्थ और ऊर्जस्वी बनाना, किसी का बलवर्धन करना, अनुप्राणित करना *I felt invigorated after my run.* ▶ **invigorating** *adj.* बलवर्धनकारी

**invincible** /ɪnˈvɪnsəbl इन्ˈविन्सबल्/ *adj.* too strong or powerful to be defeated इतना सशक्त या बलशाली कि पराजित न किया जा सके; अपराजेय, अजेय

**invisible** /ɪnˈvɪzəbl इन्ˈविज़बल्/ *adj.* **invisible (to sb/sth)** that cannot be seen जो दिखाई न दे; अदृश्य *bacteria that are invisible to the naked eye* ✪ विलोम **visible** ▶ **invisibility** /ɪn,vɪzəˈbɪləti इन्,विज़ˈबिलटि/ *noun* [U] अदृश्यता ▶ **invisibly** /-bli -बलि/ *adv.* अदृश्य रूप से

**invitation** /,ɪnvɪˈteɪʃn ,इन्विˈटेशन्/ *noun* **1** [U] the act of inviting sb or being invited (किसी को) निमंत्रित करने या (किसी के द्वारा) निमंत्रित होने की क्रिया; निमंत्रण *Entry is by invitation only.* ○ *a letter of invitation* **2** [C] **an invitation to sb/sth (to sth/to do sth)** a written or spoken request to go somewhere or do sth किसी स्थान पर जाने या कुछ करने का लिखित या मौखिक अनुरोध, निमंत्रण, न्यौता *Did you get an invitation to the conference?* ○ *a wedding invitation*

> NOTE निमंत्रण को (स्वीकृत) **accept** किया जाता है, या (अस्वीकृत) **turn it down** अथवा **decline** किया जाता है।

**invite** /ɪnˈvaɪt इन्ˈवाइट्/ *verb* [T] **1 invite sb (to/for sth)** to ask sb to come somewhere or to do sth किसी को कहीं आने या कुछ करने के लिए कहना, निमंत्रित करना *We invited all the family to the wedding.* ○ *Successful applicants will be invited for interview next week.* **2** to make sth unpleasant likely to happen किसी अप्रिय बात को घटित करवाना, बुलाना *You're inviting trouble if you carry so much money around.*

PHR V **invite sb back 1** to ask sb to return with you to your home किसी को अपने साथ घर आने के लिए कहना, किसी को जवाबी निमंत्रण देना **2** to ask sb to come to your home a second time, or after you have been a guest at his/her home किसी को दोबारा निमंत्रित करना, या किसी के घर अतिथि बनने के बाद उन्हें निमंत्रण देना

**invite sb in** to ask sb to come into your home किसी को घर के अंदर बुलाना, घर के अंदर आने के लिए कहना

**invite sb out** to ask sb to go out somewhere with you किसी को अपने साथ कहीं चलने के लिए कहना, साथ चलने का निमंत्रण देना *We've been invited out to lunch by the neighbours.*

**invite sb over/round** (*informal*) to ask sb to come to your home किसी को अपने घर आने के लिए कहना, घर आने का निमंत्रण देना

> NOTE 'Invite' के सब अर्थों में **ask** का प्रयोग भी हो सकता है।

**inviting** /ɪnˈvaɪtɪŋ इन्ˈवाइटिङ्/ *adj.* attractive and pleasant आकर्षक और प्रीतिकर *The smell of cooking was very inviting.*

**in vitro** /,ɪnˈviːtrəʊ ,इन्ˈवीट्रो/ *adj., adv.* (*technical*) (used about a process or a reaction) taking place in a glass tube or dish, not inside a living body सजीव शरीर में न होकर किसी वैज्ञानिक उपकरण में होने वाली (जैविक प्रक्रिया); अंतःपात्र *in vitro experiments* ○ *the development of **in vitro fertilization***

**invoice** /ˈɪnvɔɪs ˈइन्वॉइस्/ *noun* [C] an official paper that lists goods or services that you have received and says how much you have to pay for them एक औपचारिक काग़ज़ जिसमें ग्राहक को प्राप्त सामान और सेवाओं की सूची तथा उसके लिए अदा की जाने वाली राशि का विवरण होता है; बीजक, इन्वायस

**involuntary** /ɪnˈvɒləntri इन्ˈवॉलन्ट्रि/ *adj.* done without wanting or meaning to बिना चाहे या मंशा के किया गया; अनैच्छिक, अनभिप्रेत *She gave an involuntary gasp of pain as the doctor inserted the needle.* ✪ विलोम **voluntary** या **deliberate** ▶ **involuntarily** /ɪnˈvɒləntrəli इन्ˈवॉलन्ट्रलि/ *adv.* अनिच्छापूर्वक

**involve** /ɪnˈvɒlv इन्ˈवॉल्व्/ *verb* [T] **1** (*not used in the continuous tenses*) to make sth necessary किसी बात को आवश्यक बनाना, के लिए आवश्यक होना, की अपेक्षा करना *The job involves a lot of travelling.* **2** (*not used in the continuous tenses*) if a situation, an event or an activity involves sb/sth, he/she/it takes part in it किसी प्रसंग, कार्यक्रम या गतिविधि में किसी का शामिल होना *The story involves a woman who went on holiday with her child.* ○ *More than 100 people were involved in the project.*

> NOTE यद्यपि यह क्रिया सातत्यबोधक कालों (continuous tenses) में प्रयुक्त नहीं होती, तथापि इसका -ing युक्त (वर्तमान कृदंत) (present participle) रूप काफ़ी प्रचलित है—*There was a serious accident involving a stolen car.*

**3 involve sb/sth in (doing) sth** to cause sb/sth to take part in or be concerned with sth किसी

व्यक्ति या वस्तु को किसी में उलझाना या उससे जोड़ना *Please don't involve me in your family arguments.* ▸ **involvement** *noun* [C, U] संलिप्तता *The men denied any involvement in the robbery.*

**involved** /ɪnˈvɒlvd इन्ˈवॉल्व्ड्/ *adj.* **1** difficult to understand; complicated जिसे समझना कठिन हो, दुर्बोध; जटिल, पेचीदा *The book has a very involved plot.* **2** (*not before a noun*) **involved (in sth)** closely connected with sth; taking an active part in sth किसी बात से बख़ूबी जुड़ा होना, लिप्त होना; किसी बात में सक्रिय भाग लेना *I'm very involved in local politics.* **3** (*not before a noun*) **involved (with sb)** having a sexual relationship with sb किसी के साथ यौन-संबंध में उलझे होना *He is involved with his new neighbour.*

**inward** /ˈɪnwəd ˈइन्वड्/ *adv., adj.* **1** (*also* **inwards**) towards the inside or centre अंदर की या बीच की ओर *Stand in a circle facing inwards.* **2** inside your mind, not shown to other people मन के भीतर (कि बाहर न दीखे) *my inward feelings* ✪ विलोम **outward**

**inwardly** /ˈɪnwədli ˈइन्वड्लि/ *adv.* in your mind; secretly मन में, मन के अंदर; मन-ही-मन, अंदर-ही-अंदर *He was inwardly relieved that they could not come.*

**iodide** /ˈaɪədaɪd ˈआइअडाइड्/ *noun* [C] a chemical compound consisting of iodine and another chemical element आयोडीन और किसी अन्य रसायन से मिलकर बना यौगिक रसायन; आयोडाइड

**iodine** /ˈaɪədiːn ˈआइअडीन्/ *noun* [U] (*symbol*) **1** a dark-coloured substance that is found in sea water. A purple liquid containing iodine is sometimes used to clean cuts in your skin समुद्र जल में पाया जाने वाला काले रंग का पदार्थ, आयोडीन (आयोडीन युक्त बैंगनी रंग के द्रव से कभी-कभी त्वचा के कटे स्थान को साफ़ किया जाता है)

**ion** /ˈaɪən ˈआइअन्/ *noun* [C] (in chemistry) an atom or a **molecule** that has gained or lost one or more of its parts (**electrons**) and so has a positive or negative electric charge (रसायन शास्त्र में) परमाणु या परमाणु-गुच्छ जिसमें कोई इलेक्ट्रॉन जुड़ या निकल जाता है और इस प्रकार उसमें धनात्मक या ऋणात्मक विद्युत चार्ज आ जाता है; आयन

**ionic** /aɪˈɒnɪk आइˈऑनिक्/ *adj.* **1** of or related to ions आयन का या आयन-विषयक **2** (used about the way chemicals join together) using the electrical pull between positive and negative ions (रसायनों के संयुक्त होने का प्रकार) जिसमें धनात्मक और ऋणात्मक आयनों के बीच विद्युत कर्षण शक्ति का प्रयोग हो *ionic bonds/compounds*

**ionize** (*also* **-ise**) /ˈaɪənaɪz ˈआइअनाइज़्/ *verb* [I, T] (used about atoms and molecules) to gain a positive or negative electric charge by losing or gaining one part (**an electron**) (परमाणुओं और अणुओं का) इलेक्ट्रॉन के निकलने या जुड़ने से धनात्मक या ऋणात्मक विद्युत चार्ज से युक्त हो जाना; आयनीकरण होना

**ionosphere** /aɪˈɒnəsfɪə(r) आइˈऑनस्फ़िअ(र्)/ *noun* [*sing.*] **the ionosphere** the layer of the earth's atmosphere between about 80 and 1000 kilometres above the surface of the earth, that sends radio waves back around the earth पृथ्वी की सतह से 80 से लेकर 1000 किलोमीटर ऊपर तक पृथ्वी के वातावरण की परत जो रेडियो तरंगों को पृथ्वी को लौटाती है; आयन मंडल ➪ **stratosphere** और **troposphere** देखिए।

**IOU** /ˌeaɪ əʊˈjuː ˌआइ ओ ˈयू/ *abbr.* I owe you; a piece of paper that you sign showing that you owe sb some money मैं आपका देनदार हूँ, किसी ऋण की स्वीकृति की रसीद जो किसी के देनदार होने का प्रमाण होता है

**IPA** /ˌaɪ piː ˈeɪ ˌआइ पी ˈए/ *abbr.* the International Phonetic Alphabet अंतर्राष्ट्रीय ध्वनिक वर्णमाला

**IQ** /ˌaɪ ˈkjuː ˌआइ ˈक्यू/ *abbr.* intelligence quotient; a measure of how intelligent sb is बुद्धि लब्धि; किसी की बुद्धिमता की माप *have a high/low IQ* ○ *an IQ of 120*

**irate** /aɪˈreɪt आइˈरेट्/ *adj.* (*formal*) very angry अतिक्रुद्ध, रुष्ट

**iridescent** /ˌɪrɪˈdesnt ˌइरिˈडेसन्ट्/ *adj.* (*formal*) showing many bright colours that seem to change in different lights जिसमें अलग-अलग प्रकाश में चमकदार रंग बदलते दीखें, रंगबिरंगा, सतरंगा, रंगदीप्त ▸ **iridescence** *noun* [U] रंगबिरंगापन, सतरंगापन, रंगदीप्ति

**iridium** /ɪˈrɪdiəm इˈरिडिअम्/ *noun* [U] (*symbol* **Ir**) a very hard yellow-white metal, used especially to mix with other metals to form another metal (**an alloy**) बहुत कड़ा पीत-श्वेत धातु (विशेषतः मिश्रधातु बनाने के लिए अन्य धातुओं के साथ मिश्रण के लिए प्रयुक्त); इरिडियम

**iris** /ˈaɪrɪs ˈआइरिस्/ *noun* [C] the coloured part of your eye आँख की पुतली ➪ **eye** पर चित्र देखिए।

**irk** /ɜːk अक्/ *verb* [T] (*formal* or *literary*) to irritate or annoy sb किसी को खिझाना या क्षुब्ध करना *Jaya's flippant tone irked him*

**irksome** /ˈɜːksəm ˈअक्सम्/ *adj.* annoying and irritating क्षोभनीय, खिझाऊ *She found the restrictions irksome.*

**iron[1]** /ˈaɪən ˈआइअन्/ *noun* **1** [U] (*symbol* **Fe**) a hard strong metal that is used for making steel and is found in small quantities in food and in blood लोहा; एक कड़ी मज़बूत धातु जिससे इस्पात बनता है और जिसके कण अत्यंत अल्प मात्रा में खाद्य पदार्थों और रक्त में पाए जाते हैं *The doctor gave me iron tablets.* ○ *(figurative) The general has an iron* (= very strong) *will.* ➪ **pig iron** देखिए। **2** [C] an electrical instrument with a flat bottom that is heated and used to smooth clothes after you have washed and dried them (कपड़ों की) इस्तरी, आयरन *a steam iron*

**iron[2]** /ˈaɪən ˈआइअन्/ *verb* [I, T] to use an iron to make clothes, etc. smooth कपड़ों पर इस्तरी करना *Could you iron this dress for me?*

> **NOTE** Iron की अपेक्षा **do the ironing** का प्रयोग अधिक होता है—*I usually do the ironing on Sunday.*

**PHR V** **iron sth out** to get rid of any problems or difficulties that are affecting sth समस्याओं या कठिनाइयों से छुटकारा पाना

**the Iron Age** *noun* [*sing.*] the period in human history after the Bronze Age, when people first used iron tools and weapons मानव इतिहास में कांस्य युग के बाद का युग, लौहयुग (इस युग में लोहे के औज़ार और हथियार बनते थे)

**ironic** /aɪˈrɒnɪk आइˈरॉनिक्/ (*also* **ironical** /aɪˈrɒnɪkl आइˈरॉनिकल्/) *adj.* **1** meaning the opposite of what you say जिसमें कही गई बात से उलटा अर्थ निकले; व्यंग्यपूर्ण, व्यंग्यात्मक *Amit sometimes offends people with his ironic sense of humour.* ➪ **sarcastic** देखिए। **2** (used about a situation) strange or amusing because it is unusual or unexpected (स्थिति) विचित्र या हास्यजनक (असामान्य या अप्रत्याशित होने के कारण) *It is ironic that the busiest people are often the most willing to help.* ▶ **ironically** /-kli -कलि/ *adv.* व्यंग्यात्मक रीति से

**ironing** /ˈaɪənɪŋ ˈआइअनिङ्/ *noun* [U] clothes, etc. that need ironing or that have just been ironed कपड़े जिन पर अभी इस्तरी होनी है या अभी-अभी हुई है, इस्तरी के या किए हुए कपड़े *a large pile of ironing* ➪ **iron** पर नोट देखिए।

**ironing board** *noun* [C] a special table that is used for putting clothes on when we are making them smooth with an iron इस्तरी करने की मेज़ (जिस पर इस्तरी के कपड़े डाले जाते हैं)

**irony** /ˈaɪrəni ˈआइरनि/ *noun* (*pl.* **ironies**) **1** [C, U] an unusual or unexpected part of a situation, etc. that seems strange or amusing किसी स्थिति आदि का असामान्य या अप्रत्याशित अंश जो विचित्र या हास्यजनक लगे; विडंबना, व्यंग्य *The irony was that he was killed in a car accident soon after the end of the war.* **2** [U] a way of speaking that shows you are joking or that you mean the opposite of what you say परिहासोक्ति (ऐसी बात) कही जाए कि लगे मज़ाक हो रहा है) या व्यंग्योक्ति (जिसमें, कही गई बात से उलटा अर्थ निकले), व्याजनिंदा या स्तुति *'The English are such good cooks,' he said with heavy irony.*

**irradiate** /ɪˈreɪdieɪt इˈरेडिएट्/ *verb* [T] to treat food with powerful (**radioactive**) rays in order to be able to keep it for a long time सुरक्षित रखने के लिए खाद्य पदार्थों को रेडियो सक्रिय किरणों से उपचारित करना *Irradiated food lasts longer, but some people think it is not safe.*

**irrational** /ɪˈræʃənl इˈरैशन्ल्/ *adj.* not based on reason or clear thought जो तर्क या स्पष्ट चिंतन पर आधारित न हो; तर्कहीन, विवेकहीन, अतार्किक *an irrational fear of spiders* ▶ **irrationality** /ɪˌræʃəˈnæləti इˌरैशˈनैलटि/ *noun* [U] अतार्किकता ▶ **irrationally** /-nəli -नलि/ *adv.* अतार्किक रीति से

**irreconcilable** /ɪˌrekənˈsaɪləbl इˌरेकन्ˈसाइलबल्/ *adj.* (*formal*) (used about people or their ideas and beliefs) so different that they cannot be made to agree (लोग या उनके विचार और विश्वास) इतने अलग कि उनमें सहमति न हो सके; अनमेल, परस्पर विरोधी ▶ **irreconcilably** /-əbli -अबलि/ *adv.* अनमेलपन से, परस्पर विरोधपूर्वक

**irregular** /ɪˈregjələ(r) इˈरेग्यल(र्)/ *adj.* **1** not having a shape or pattern that we recognize or can predict जिसकी आकृति या पैटर्न की पहचान या पूर्वाभास न हो पाए; असम, विषम *an irregular shape* **2** happening at times that you cannot predict जो ऐसे समय घटित हो कि उसका पूर्वाभास न हो सके; अनियमित *His visits became more and more irregular.* **3** not allowed according to the rules or social customs जो नियमों और सामाजिक प्रथाओं के अनुसार न हो, नियम विरुद्ध *It is highly irregular for a doctor to give information about patients without their permission.* **4** (*grammar*) not following the usual rules of grammar जो व्याकरण के सामान्य नियमों का पालन न करे; अव्यवस्थित *irregular verbs* ○ *'Caught' is an irregular past tense form.* ✪ विलोम **regular** अर्थ सं. **1**, **2**, और **4** का ▶ **irregularity** /ɪˌregjəˈlærəti इˌरेग्यˈलैरटि/ *noun* [C, U] अनियमितता (*pl.* **irregularities**) ▶ **irregularly** *adv.* अनियमित रूप से

**irrelevancy** /ɪˈreləvənsi इˈरेलवन्सि / *noun* [C] (*pl.* **irrelevancies**) something that is not important because it is not connected with sth else किसी अन्य से संबंधित न होने के कारण महत्त्वहीन होने की स्थिति; अप्रासंगिकता, असंबद्धता

**irrelevant** /ɪˈreləvənt इˈरेलवन्ट् / *adj.* not connected with sth or important to it किसी वस्तु से असंबद्ध या उसके लिए महत्त्वहीन, अप्रासंगिक, असंबद्ध *That's completely irrelevant to the subject under discussion.* ✪ विलोम **relevant** ▶ **irrelevance** *noun* [U, C] अप्रासंगिकता, असंबद्धता ▶ **irrelevantly** *adv.* अप्रासंगिक या असंबद्ध रूप से

**irreparable** /ɪˈrepərəbl इˈरेपरबल् / *adj.* that cannot be repaired जिस क्षति की पूर्ति न हो सके, जिस स्थिति को सुधारा न जा सके; असुधार्य *Irreparable damage has been done to the forests of Eastern Europe.* ▶ **irreparably** /-əbli -अब्लि / *adv.* असुधारणीय, असंशोध्य रूप से

**irreplaceable** /ˌɪrɪˈpleɪsəbl ˌइरिˈप्लेसबल् / *adj.* (used about sth very valuable or special) that cannot be replaced (कोई बहुमूल्य या विशिष्ट वस्तु) जिसका स्थान कोई न ले सके ✪ विलोम **replaceable**

**irrepressible** /ˌɪrɪˈpresəb ˌइरिˈप्रेसबल् / *adj.* full of life and energy जीवन और ऊर्जा से परिपूर्ण; अदम्य *young people full of irrepressible good humour* ▶ **irrepressibly** /-əbli -अब्लि / *adv.* अदम्यता

**irresistible** /ˌɪrɪˈzɪstəbl ˌइरिˈज़िस्टबल् / *adj.* **1** so strong that it cannot be stopped or prevented इतना शक्तिशाली कि उसका प्रतिरोध या अवरोध न हो; अप्रतिरोध्य *an irresistible urge to laugh* **2 irresistible (to sb)** very attractive अत्यंत आकर्षक *He seems to think he's irresistible to women.* ➪ **resist** verb देखिए। ▶ **irresistibly** /-əbli -अब्लि / *adv.* अप्रतिरोध्य रूप से

**irrespective of** /ɪrɪˈspektɪv əv इरिˈस्पेक्टिव् अव् / *prep.* not affected by बिना किसी बात से प्रभावित हुए *Anybody can take part in the competition, irrespective of age.*

**irresponsible** /ˌɪrɪˈspɒnsəbl,इरिˈस्पॉन्सबल् *adj.* not thinking about the effect your actions will have; not sensible अपने कामों के परिणाम की चिंता न करने वाला, ग़ैर-ज़िम्मेदार; जो अक़्लमंद न हो, मूर्ख *It is irresponsible to let small children go out alone.* ✪ विलोम **responsible** ▶ **irresponsibility** /ˌɪrɪˌspɒnsəˈbɪləti ˌइरिˌस्पॉन्सˈबिलटि / *noun* [U] ग़ैर-ज़िम्मेदारी ▶ **irresponsibly** /-əbli -अब्लि / *adv.* ग़ैर-ज़िम्मेदार तरीक़े से

**irreverent** /ɪˈrevərənt इˈरेवरन्ट् / *adj.* not feeling or showing respect किसी के प्रति आदर का अनुभव न करने वाला या न दिखने वाला; अनादरपूर्ण *This comedy takes an irreverent look at the world of politics.* ▶ **irreverence** *noun* [U] अनादर भाव ▶ **irreverently** *adv.* अनादरपूर्वक

**irreversible** /ˌɪrɪˈvɜːsəbl ˌइरिˈवसबल् / *adj.* that cannot be stopped or changed जिसे रोका या बदला न जा सके; अपरिवर्त्य, अनुत्क्रमणीय *The disease can do irreversible damage to the body.* ▶ **irreversibly** /-əbli -अब्लि / *adv.* अपरिवर्त्य रूप से

**irrigate** /ˈɪrɪɡeɪt ˈइरिगेट् / *verb* [T] to supply water to land and crops using pipes, small canals, etc. पाइपों, छोटी नहरों आदि के द्वारा ज़मीन और फ़सल को पानी पहुँचाना; सींचना ▶ **irrigation** /ˌɪrɪˈɡeɪʃn ˌइरिˈगेश्न् / *noun* [U] सिंचाई

**irritable** /ˈɪrɪtəbl ˈइरिटबल् / *adj.* becoming angry easily जल्दी क्रुद्ध हो जाने वाला; चिड़चिड़ा *to be/feel/get irritable* ▶ **irritability** /ˌɪrɪtəˈbɪləti ˌइरिटˈबिलटि / *noun* [U] चिड़चिड़ापन ▶ **irritably** /-əbli -अब्लि / *adv.* चिड़चिड़ेपन से

**irritant** /ˈɪrɪtənt ˈइरिटन्ट् / *noun* [C] a substance that makes part of your body painful or sore शरीर के किसी अंग में दर्द पैदा कर देने वाला पदार्थ, जलन पैदा करने वाली वस्तु ▶ **irritant** *adj.* उत्तेजक, क्षोभक, दाहोत्पादक, प्रदाहकारी

**irritate** /ˈɪrɪteɪt ˈइरिटेट् / *verb* [T] **1** to make sb angry; to annoy किसी को क्रुद्ध करना; नाराज़ करना, क्षुब्ध करना *It really irritates me the way he keeps repeating himself.* **2** to cause a part of the body to be painful or sore शरीर के किसी अंग में जलन या दर्द पैदा करना *I don't use soap because it irritates my skin.* ▶ **irritation** /ˌɪrɪˈteɪʃn ˌइरिˈटेश्न् / *noun* [C, U] जलन, दर्द

**is** ➪ **be** देखिए।

**Islam** /ɪzˈlɑːm इज़्ˈलाम् / *noun* [U] the religion of Muslim people. Islam teaches that there is only one God and that Muhammad is His Prophet मुसलमानों का धर्म, इस्लाम। इस्लाम सिखाता है कि अल्लाह एक हैं और मुहम्मद उनके पैगंबर हैं ▶ **Islamic** *adj.* इस्लाम-संबंधी, इस्लामी *Islamic law*

**island** /ˈaɪlənd ˈआइलन्ड् / *noun* [C] **1** a piece of land that is surrounded by water पानी से घिरी ज़मीन; द्वीप, टापू *the Andaman and Nicobar islands* **2** = **traffic island**

**islander** /ˈaɪləndə(r) ˈआइलन्ड(र्) / *noun* [C] a person who lives on a small island छोटे द्वीप का वासी

**isle** /aɪl आइल् / *noun* [C] an small island उपद्वीप या टापू *the Isle of Wight* ○ *the British Isle*
**NOTE** नामों के साथ अधिकतर **Isle** का प्रयोग होता है।

**isn't** ➪ **is not** का संक्षिप्त रूप

**isobar** /ˈaɪsəbɑː(r) ˈआइसबा(र्)/ *noun* [C] (*technical*) a line on a weather map that joins places that have the same air pressure at a particular time मौसम के मानचित्र पर खींची रेखा जो उन सब स्थानों को जोड़ती है जिनमें एक विशेष समय में वायु का दाब समान होता है; समदाब रेखा

**isolate** /ˈaɪsəleɪt ˈआइसलेट्/ *verb* [T] **isolate sb/sth (from sb/sth)** to put or keep sb/sth separate from other people or things किसी व्यक्ति या वस्तु को अन्य व्यक्तियों या वस्तुओं से अलग करना या रखना *Some farms were isolated by the heavy snowfalls.* ○ *We need to isolate all the animals with the disease so that the others don't catch it.*

**isolated** /ˈaɪsəleɪtɪd ˈआइसलेटिड्/ *adj.* **1 isolated (from sb/sth)** alone or apart from other people or things अन्य व्यक्ति या वस्तुओं से अलग-थलग *an isolated village deep in the countryside* ○ *I was kept isolated from the other patients.* **2** not connected with others; happening once जो किसी अन्य से नहीं जुड़ा, अकेला, एकाकी; केवल एक बार घटित, इक्का-दुक्का *Is this an isolated case or part of a general pattern?*

**isolation** /ˌaɪsəˈleɪʃn ˌआइसˈलेश्न्/ *noun* [U] **isolation (from sb/sth)** the state of being separate and alone; the act of separating sb/sth अलग और अकेला होने की स्थिति, अलगाव; किसी व्यक्ति या वस्तु को अलग करने का कार्य; पृथक्करण *He lived **in** complete **isolation** from the outside world.* ○ ***In isolation** each problem does not seem bad, but together they are quite daunting.* ➪ **loneliness** और **solitude** देखिए।

**isosceles** /aɪˈsɒsəliːz आइˈसॉसलीज़्/ *adj.* (*mathematics*) (used about a triangle) having two of its three sides the same length (त्रिभुज) जिसकी दो भुजाएँ समान लंबाई की हों; समद्विबाहु ➪ **triangle** पर चित्र देखिए।

**isotherm** /ˈaɪsəθɜːm ˈआइसथर्म्/ *noun* [C] (*technical*) a line on a weather map that joins places that have the same temperature at a particular time मौसम के मानचित्र पर खींची रेखा जो उन सब स्थानों को जोड़ती है जिनमें एक विशेष समय में तापमान समान होता है; समताप रेखा

**isotope** /ˈaɪsətəʊp ˈआइसटोप्/ *noun* [C] (in chemistry) one of two or more forms of a chemical element that have different physical characteristics but the same chemical characteristics (रसायन शास्त्र में) रासायनिक तत्वों में से एक तत्व जिसके भौतिक लक्षण औरों से अलग हों परंतु रासायनिक लक्षण वही हों; आइसोटोप

NOTE समान तत्वों के **isotopes** के केंद्रक में **protons** की संख्या समान (वही) होती है परंतु **neutrons** की संख्या अलग होती है।

**ISP** /ˌaɪ es ˈpiː ˌआइ एस्ˈपी/ *abbr.* Internet Service Provider; a company that provides you with an Internet connection and services such as email, etc. इंटरनेट सेवा प्रदाता; ग्राहकों को इंटरनेट संयोजन तथा इ-मेल जैसी सेवाएँ उपलब्ध कराने वाली कंपनी

**issue¹** /ˈɪʃuː; ˈɪsjuː ˈइशू; ˈइस्यू/ *noun* **1** [C] a problem or subject for discussion चर्चा का मुद्दा या विषय *I want to **raise the issue** of overtime pay at the meeting.* ○ *The government cannot avoid the issue of homelessness any longer.* **2** [C] one in a series of things that are published or produced प्रकाशित या उत्पादित वस्तुओं की शृंखला में एक; अंक *Do you have last week's issue of this magazine?* **3** [U] the act of publishing or giving sth to people प्रकाशित करने का या लोगों को कुछ देने का कार्य *the issue of blankets to the refugees*

IDM **make an issue (out) of sth** to give too much importance to a small problem छोटी समस्या को बहुत बड़ा समझना

**issue²** /ˈɪʃuː; ˈɪsjuː ˈइशू; ˈइस्यू/ *verb* **1** [T] to print and supply sth कोई वस्तु छापना और कहीं/किसी को पहुँचाना *to issue a magazine/newsletter* **2** [T] to give or say sth to sb officially किसी व्यक्ति को आधिकारिक रूप से कुछ देना या कहना, जारी करना *The new employees were issued with uniforms.* ○ *to issue a visa* **3** [I] (*formal*) to come or go out आना या बाहर जाना, निकलना *An angry voice issued from the loudspeaker.*

**isthmus** /ˈɪsməs ˈइस्मस्/ *noun* [C] (in geography) a narrow piece of land, with water on each side, that joins two larger pieces of land (भूगोल में) दोनों ओर पानी से घिरी ज़मीन की तंग पट्टी जो दो बड़े भूखंडों को जोड़ती है; जल डमरूमध्य

**IT** /ˌaɪˈtiː ˌआइˈटी/ *abbr.* (*computing*) Information Technology इन्फ़ॉरमेशन टेक्नॉलजी, सूचना प्रौद्योगिकी

**it** /ɪt इट्/ *pronoun* **1** (*used as the subject or object of a verb, or after a preposition*) the animal or thing mentioned earlier पूर्व-वर्णित पशु या कोई वस्तु *Look at that car. It's going much too fast.* ○ *The children went up to the dog and patted it.*

NOTE **It** का प्रयोग उस शिशु के लिए भी वक्ता कर सकता है जिसे अभी उसके लिंग के बारे में पता नहीं—*Is it a boy or a girl?*

**2** used for identifying a person किसी व्यक्ति की पहचान बताने के लिए प्रयुक्त *It's your Mum on the phone.* ○ *'Who's that?' 'It's the postman.'* **3** used in the position of the subject or object of a verb when the real subject or object is at the end of the sentence वास्तविक कर्ता या कर्म के वाक्य के अंत में आने पर कर्ता के या क्रिया के कर्म के स्थान पर प्रयुक्त *It's hard for them to talk about their problems.* ○ *I think it doesn't really matter what time we arrive.* **4** used in the position of the subject of a verb when you are talking about time, the date, distance, the weather, etc. समय, तारीख़, दूरी, मौसम आदि की चर्चा में क्रिया के कर्ता के स्थान पर प्रयुक्त *It's nearly half past eight.* ○ *It's about 100 kilometres from Jaipur.* **5** used when you are talking about a situation किसी प्रसंग की चर्चा में प्रयुक्त *It gets very crowded here in the summer.* ○ *I'll come at 7 o'clock if it's convenient.* **6** used for emphasizing a part of a sentence वाक्य के किसी अंश पर बल देने के लिए प्रयुक्त *It was Atul who said it, not me.* ○ *It's your health I'm worried about, not the cost.*

IDM **that/this is it** **1** that/this is the answer इसका जवाब वह, यह है या बात बन गई *That's it! You've solved the puzzle!* **2** that/this is the end बस करो *That's it, I've had enough! I'm going home!*

**italics** /ɪˈtælɪks इˈटैलिक्स्/ *noun* [*pl.*] a type of writing or printing in which the letters do not stand straight up लेखन या मुद्रण का एक प्रकार जिसमें अक्षर सीधे नहीं होते, तिरछे अक्षर *All the example sentences in the dictionary are printed **in italics**.* ▸ **italic** *adj.* तिरछा

**itch** /ɪtʃ इच्/ *noun* [C] the feeling on your skin that makes you want to rub or scratch it खाज, खुजली ▸ **itch** *verb* [I] खाज या खुजली होना, खुजलाना *My nose is itching.*

**itchy** /ˈɪtʃi ˈइचि/ *adj.* having or producing an **itch** खुजलीवाला या पैदा करने वाला *This shirt is itchy.* ○ *I feel itchy all over.* ▸ **itchiness** *noun* [U] खुजलाहट

**it'd** /ˈɪtəd ˈइटड्/ ➪ **it had** तथा **it would** का संक्षिप्त रूप

**item** /ˈaɪtəm ˈआइटम्/ *noun* [C] **1** one single thing on a list or in a collection किसी सूची या संग्रह में से एक चीज़; आइटम *Some items arrived too late to be included in the catalogue.* ○ *What is the first item on the agenda?* **2** one single article or object एक अकेली वस्तु; नग, एकक *Can I pay for each item separately?* ○ *an item of clothing* **3** a single piece of news कोई अकेली ख़बर, समाचार *There was an interesting item about Goa in yesterday's news.*

**itemize** (*also* **-ise**) /ˈaɪtəmaɪz ˈआइटमाइज़्/ *verb* [T] to make a list of all the separate items in sth किसी वस्तु से संबंधित अलग-अलग मदों की सूची बनाना, मदवार देना *an itemized telephone bill*

**itinerant** /aɪˈtɪnərənt आइˈटिनरन्ट्/ *adj.* (*only before a noun*) travelling from place to place घूमने या दौरे पर जाने वाला; भ्रमणशील, यात्राशील *an itinerant circus family*

**itinerary** /aɪˈtɪnərəri आइˈटिनररि/ *noun* [C] (*pl.* **itineraries**) a plan of a journey, including the route and the places that you will visit यात्रा-कार्यक्रम (जिसमें यात्रा का मार्ग और स्थल शामिल हैं)

**it'll** /ˈɪtl ˈइट्ल्/ ➪ **it will** का संक्षिप्त रूप

**its** /ɪts इट्स्/ *det.* of or belonging to a thing किसी वस्तु का या उससे संबंधित *The club held its Annual General Meeting last night.* ➪ **it's** पर नोट देखिए।

**it's** /ɪts इट्स्/ ➪ **it is; it has** का संक्षिप्त रूप

> NOTE ध्यान रखिए **it's** 'it is' या 'it has' का संक्षिप्त रूप है। **Its** का अर्थ है 'it' से संबंधित (इसका)—*The bird has broken its wings.*

**itself** /ɪtˈself इट्ˈसेल्फ़्/ *pronoun* **1** used when the animal or thing that does an action is also affected by it किसी पशु या वस्तु का निर्देश करने के लिए प्रयुक्त जब अपनी क्रिया से वह स्वयं प्रभावित हो, अपने (आप) को, स्वयं को *The cat was washing itself.* ○ *The company has got itself into financial difficulties.* **2** used to emphasize sth किसी बात पर बल देने के लिए प्रयुक्त *The building itself is beautiful, but it's in a very ugly part of town.*

IDM **(all) by itself** **1** without being controlled by a person; automatically बिना किसी से नियंत्रित हुए; अपने आप, स्वयंमेव *The central heating comes on by itself before we get up.* **2** alone अकेला *The house stood all by itself on the hillside.* ➪ **alone** पर नोट देखिए।

**IUD** /ˌaɪ juː ˈdiː ˌआइ यू ˈडी/ *noun* [C] intrauterine device; a small metal or plastic object that is placed inside the **uterus** to stop a woman from becoming pregnant (संधि) अंतःगर्भाशय युक्ति; धातु या प्लास्टिक की एक छोटी वस्तु जो स्त्री को गर्भधारण से सुरक्षित करती है, परिवार-नियोजन में सहायक युक्ति या वस्तु

**IV¹** /ˌaɪ ˈviː ˌआइ ˈव़ी/ *abbr.* intravenous शिराओं के अंदर, अंतःशिरा, शिरा अभयंतर; इन्ट्रावीनस

**IV²** /ˌaɪ ˈviː ˌआइ ˈव़ी/ (*AmE*) = **drip² 3**

**I've** /aɪv आइव़्/ ➪ **I have** का संक्षिप्त रूप

**ivory** /ˈaɪvəri ˈआइवरि/ *noun* [U] the hard white substance that the **tusks** of an elephant are made of हाथी-दाँत, गज दंत

**ivy** /ˈaɪvi ˈआइवि/ *noun* [U] a climbing plant that has dark leaves with three or five points तीन या पाँच बिंदु की छाप के पत्तों वाली बेल, सिरपेचे की बेल, सिरपेचा ➪ **plant** पर चित्र देखिए।

# J j

**J, j** /dʒeɪ जे / *noun* [C, U] (*pl.* **J's; j's** /dʒeɪz जेज़्/ the tenth letter of the English alphabet अंग्रेज़ी वर्णमाला का दसवाँ अक्षर *'Jam' begins with a 'j'.*

**jab**[1] /dʒæb जैब् / *verb* [I, T] **jab sb/sth (with sth); jab sth into sb/sth** to push at sb/sth with a sudden, rough movement, usually with sth sharp किसी व्यक्ति या वस्तु में कुछ (प्रायः कोई नुकीली वस्तु) ज़ोर से चुभा देना *She jabbed me in the ribs with her elbow.* ○ *The robber jabbed a gun into my back and ordered me to move.*

**jab**[2] /dʒæb जैब् / *noun* [C] **1** a sudden rough push with sth sharp एकाएक ज़ोरदार धक्का (किसी नुकीली वस्तु से) *He* ***gave*** *me* ***a jab*** *in the ribs with the stick.* **2** (*informal*) the action of putting a drug, etc. under sb's skin with a needle टीका लगाना, इंजेक्शन देना *I'm going to the doctor's to* ***have a*** *typhoid* ***jab*** *today.* ✪ पर्याय **injection**

**Jacaranda** /ˌdʒækəˈrændə ˌजैकˈरैनडा / *noun* [C] a tropical tree which commonly has blue trumpet-shaped flowers and compound leaves नीले तुरहीदार फूलों और संयोजित पत्तों वाला जैकरैंडा का वृक्ष

**jack**[1] /dʒæk जैक् / *noun* [C] **1** a piece of equipment for lifting a car, etc. off the ground, for example in order to change its wheel (पहिया बदलने आदि के लिए) ज़मीन से कार आदि उठाने का उपकरण; जैक ➪ **hydraulic** पर चित्र देखिए। **2** the card between the ten and the queen in a pack of cards ताश में गुलाम का पत्ता ➪ **card** पर नोट देखिए।

**IDM** **a jack of all trades** a person who can do many different types of work, but who perhaps does not do them very well तरह-तरह के काम कर सकने वाला व्यक्ति (परंतु किसी में भी संभवतः पर्याप्त कुशल नहीं); बहुधंधी

**jack**[2] /dʒæk जैक् / *verb*

**PHRV** **jack sth in** (*slang*) to stop doing sth कोई काम करना बंद कर देना *Hitesh got fed up with his job and jacked it in.*

**jack sth up** to lift a car, etc. using a jack जैक के सहारे कार आदि को उठाना *We jacked the car up to change the wheel.*

**jackal** /ˈdʒækl ˈजैकल्/ *noun* [C] a wild animal like a dog that lives in Africa and Asia. Jackals eat the meat of animals that are already dead गीदड़, सियार। यह जानवर एशिया और अफ़्रीक़ा में पाया जाता है और यह मरे हुए जानवरों का मांस खाता है

**jacket** /ˈdʒækɪt ˈजैकिट् / *noun* [C] **1** a short coat with sleeves आस्तीनदार छोटा कोट; जैकेट *Do you have to wear a jacket and tie to work?* ➪ **life jacket** देखिए। **2** a cover for a hot-water **tank** etc. that stops heat from being lost गरम पानी के टैंक पर लगा ढक्कन जो पानी की गरमी को बचाए रखता है; बॉयलर का बाह्यावरण **2** a paper cover for a book that has a hard rigid cover पुस्तक की जिल्द के लिए काग़ज़ का आवरण

**jacket potato** *noun* [C] a potato that is cooked in the oven in its skin अवन में छिलके समेत पकने वाला आलू

**jackfruit** /ˈdʒækfru:t ˈजैक्फ्रूट् / *noun* **1** [C] an Indian evergreen tree cultivated for its large fruit and seeds कटहल का वृक्ष **2** [U, C] a very large edible fruit of this tree कटहल

**jackhammer** /ˈdʒækhæmə(r) ˈजैक्हैम(र्) / (*AmE*) = **pneumatic drill**

**jackknife** /ˈdʒæknaɪf ˈजैक्नाइफ़् / *noun* a large knife with a folding blade खटकेदार चाक़ू जिसको मोड़ा जा सकता है

**the jackpot** /ˈdʒækpɒt ˈजैक्पॉट् / *noun* [C] the largest money prize that you can win in a game किसी खेल की सबसे बड़ी इनाम-राशि

**IDM** **hit the jackpot** ➪ **hit**[1] देखिए।

**Jacuzzi™** /dʒəˈku:zi जˈकूज़ि / *noun* [C] a special bath in which powerful movements of air make bubbles in the water हवा की तेज़ गति से बने बुलबुलों वाले पानी में किया जाने वाला विशेष स्नान; जाकूज़ी

**jade** /dʒeɪd जेड् / *noun* [U] **1** a hard stone that is usually green and is used in making jewellery आभूषण बनाने में प्रयुक्त हरे रंग का रत्न **2** a bright green colour चमकीला हरा रंग ▶ **jade** *adj.* हरे रंग का; हरित

**jaded** /ˈdʒeɪdɪd ˈजेडिड् / *adj.* tired and bored after doing the same thing for a long time without a break लगातार लंबे समय तक एक ही काम करने से थका और ऊबा हुआ; थका-माँदा; थककर चूर

**jagged** /ˈdʒægɪd ˈजैगिड् / *adj.* rough with sharp points नुकीला और खुरदरा *jagged rocks*

**jaggery** /ˈdʒægəri ˈजैगरि / *noun* [U] unrefined coarse brown sugar made from sugar cane juice or palm sap शक्कर, गुड़

**jaguar** /ˈdʒægjuə(r) ˈजैग्युअ(र्) / *noun* [C] a large wild cat with black spots that comes from Central and South America मध्य और दक्षिण अमेरिका में पाया जाने वाला चीते जैसा जानवर; जागुआर ➪ **lion** पर चित्र देखिए।

**jail[1]** /dʒeɪl जेल्/ *noun* [C, U] (a) prison जेल, कारागार *He was **sent to jail** for ten years.* ➪ **prison** पर नोट देखिए।

**jail[2]** /dʒeɪl जेल्/ *verb* [T] to put sb in prison जेल में डालना या बंद करना *She was jailed for ten years.*

**jailer** /ˈdʒeɪlə(r) ˈजेल(र्)/ *noun* [C] (*old-fashioned*) a person whose job is to guard prisoners क़ैदियों का सुरक्षा-अधिकारी; जेलर

**Jain** *noun* [C] a person whose religion is **Jainism** जैन धर्म का उपासक; जैनी *Many Jains go to the Dilwara Temples on pilgrimage.* ▶ **Jain** *adj.* जैन धर्म संबंधी; जैनी *Jain rituals/Jain temples*

**Jainism** *noun* [U] an Indian religion established in about 6 BC by Mahavira. It is based on the principle of non-violence and a belief in **reincarnation** लगभग सन् 6 ईसा पूर्व में भारत में, महावीर द्वारा स्थापित जैन धर्म, यह धर्म अहिंसावाद और पुनर्जन्म के सिद्धांतों को मान्यता देता है

**Jaiphal** *noun* [U] (*IndE*) nutmeg जायफल, जावित्री

**jalebi** *noun* [C] an Indian sweet made of a **coil** of deep-fried **batter** that is soaked briefly in sugar syrup जलेबी

**jam[1]** /dʒæm जैम्/ *noun* **1** [U] (*AmE* **jelly**) a sweet substance that you spread on bread, made by boiling fruit and sugar together ब्रेड पर लगाया जाने वाला मुरब्बा; जैम *a jar of raspberry jam*

> **NOTE** संतरों या नीबुओं से बने जैम को **marmalade** कहते हैं।

**2** [C] a situation in which you cannot move because there are too many people or vehicles बड़ी संख्या में लोगों या वाहनों के आ जाने से उत्पन्न रास्ते की रुकावट; यातायात-अवरोध *a traffic jam* **3** [C] (*informal*) a difficult situation कठिन स्थिति *We're in a bit of a jam without our passports or travel documents.* **4** [C] (*informal*) the act of playing music together with other musicians in a way which has not been planned or prepared first बिना पूर्व तैयारी या नियोजन का अचानक बना संगीत कार्यक्रम (जिसमें अनेक संगीतज्ञ भाग लेते हैं) *a jam session*

**jam[2]** /dʒæm जैम्/ *verb* (**jamming; jammed**) **1** [T] **jam sb/sth in, under, between, etc. sth** to push or force sb/sth into a place where there is not much room तंग जगह में लोगों या वस्तुओं को ठूँस देना *She managed to jam everything into her suitcase.* **2** [I, T] **jam (sth) (up)** to become or to make sth unable to move or work हिलने-डुलने या काम करने में असमर्थ हो जाना या कर देना *Something is jamming (up) the machine.* ○ *I can't open the door. The lock has jammed.* **3** [T] **jam sth (up) (with sb/sth)** (*usually passive*) to fill sth with too many people or things किसी स्थान को बहुत सारे लोगों या वस्तुओं से भर देना *The cupboard was **jammed full** of old newspapers and magazines.* ○*The bus was **jam-packed with*** (= completely full of) *passengers.* **4** [T] to send out signals in order to stop radio programmes, etc. from being received or heard clearly रेडियो कार्यक्रमों के प्रसारित होने या सुने जाने को रोकने वाले संकेत भेजना **5** [I] (*informal*) to play music with other musicians in an informal way without preparing or practising first बिना पूर्व तैयारी के हलके-फुलके ढंग का संगीत कार्यक्रम करना *They continued to jam together and write music and eventually they made their first record.*
**PHR V** **jam on the brakes/jam the brakes on** to stop a car suddenly by pushing hard on the controls (**brakes**) with your feet पैरों के ब्रेक लगाकर झटके से कार रोकना

**Jan.** *abbr.* January जनवरी *1 Jan. 1993*

**jangle** /ˈdʒæŋgl ˈजैङ्ग्ल्/ *verb* [I, T] to make a noise like metal hitting against metal; to move sth so that it makes this noise धातुओं के टकराने जैसी आवाज़ पैदा करना, खड़खड़ाना; झनझनाना, खनखनाना; झनझनाहट, खड़खड़ाहट, खनखनाहट के साथ किसी चीज़ को हिलाना *The baby smiles if you jangle your keys.* ▶ **jangle** *noun* [U] खनखनाहट, झनझनाहट

**janitor** /ˈdʒænɪtə(r) ˈजैनिट(र्)/ (*AmE*) = **caretaker**

**January** /ˈdʒænjuəri ˈजैन्युअरि/ *noun* [U, C] (*abbr.* **Jan**) the first month of the year, coming after December वर्ष का पहला महीना, जनवरी *We're going skiing **in January.*** ○ *last/next January* ○ *We first met **on January** 31st, 1989.* **NOTE** सामान्य प्रयोग है *'on January the seventeenth'* या *'on the seventeenth of January'* या अमेरिकी अंग्रेज़ी मे *'January seventeeth'*. ब्रिटिश और अमेरिकी अंग्रेज़ी, दोनों में महीनों के नाम बड़े अक्षर से आरंभ किए जाते हैं।

**jar[1]** /dʒɑː(r) जा(र्)/ *noun* [C] **1** a container with a lid, usually made of glass and used for keeping food, etc. in ढक्कनदार मर्तबान (प्रायः काँच से बना और खाद्य पदार्थों को रखने के लिए प्रयुक्त); जार *a jam jar* ○ *a large storage jar for flour* **2** the food that a jar contains मर्तबान में रखा खाद्य पदार्थ *a jar of honey/jam/coffee*

**jar[2]** /dʒɑː(r) जा(र्)/ *verb* (**jarring; jarred**) **1** [T] to hurt or damage sth as a result of a sharp knock तेज़ धक्के से चोट खा जाना या कुछ तोड़ बैठना *He fell and jarred his back.* **2** [I] **jar (on sb/sth)** to have an unpleasant or annoying effect अप्रिय या क्षोभकारी प्रभाव होना; विक्षुब्ध होना, खटकना *The dripping tap jarred on my nerves.*

**jargon** /ˈdʒɑːɡən ˈजागन्/ *noun* [U] special or technical words that are used by a particular group of people in a particular profession and that other people do not understand व्यवसाय-विशेष से जुड़े व्यक्तियों द्वारा प्रयुक्त विशिष्ट या तकनीकी शब्द जिन्हें अन्य लोग नहीं समझ पाते *medical/scientific/legal/computer jargon*

**jaundice** /ˈdʒɔːndɪs ˈजॉन्डिस्/ *noun* [U] a medical condition in which the skin and the white parts of the eyes become yellow पीलिया रोग जिसमें त्वचा और आँखों के सफ़ेद अंश पीले हो जाते हैं ▸ **jaundiced** *adj.* पीलिया रोग से ग्रस्त

**javelin** /ˈdʒævlɪn ˈजैव्लिन्/ *noun* **1** [C] a long stick with a pointed end that is thrown in sports competitions खेल स्पर्धाओं में फेंका जाने वाला भाला **2 the javelin** [*sing.*] the event or sport of throwing the javelin as far as possible भाला-फेंक का खेल

**jaw** /dʒɔː जॉ/ *noun* **1** [C] either of the two bones in your face that contain your teeth जबड़ा *the lower/upper jaw* ➪ **body** पर चित्र देखिए। **2 jaws** [*pl.*] the mouth (especially of a wild animal) मुँह (विशेषत: किसी वन्य पशु का) *The lion came towards him with its jaws open.* **3 jaws** [*pl.*] the parts of a tool or machine that are used to hold things tightly किसी औज़ार या मशीन के वस्तुओं को कसकर पकड़ने वाले हिस्से *the jaws of a vice* ➪ **vice** पर चित्र देखिए।

**jawan** *noun* [C] (*in India*) a male police constable or soldier (भारत में) जवान; (पुलीस में) सिपाही, (सेना में) सैनिक *The notice asked all the jawans to assemble at 5 p.m.*

**jawbone** /ˈdʒɔːbəʊn ˈजॉबोन्/ *noun* [C] the bone that forms the lower jaw निचले जबड़े की हड्डी; हन्वस्थि ✪ पर्याय **mandible** ➪ **body** पर चित्र देखिए।

**jazz**[1] /dʒæz जैज़्/ *noun* [U] a style of music with a strong rhythm, originally of African American origin मूलतः अफ्रीकी-अमेरिकी मूल की भारी या प्रबल लय वाली संगीत शैली; जाज़ संगीत *modern/traditional jazz* ➪ **classical, pop** और **rock** भी देखिए।

**jazz**[2] /dʒæz जैज़्/ *verb*

PHR V **jazz sth up** (*informal*) to make sth brighter, more interesting or exciting किसी वस्तु को अधिक चमकदार, रोचक या उत्तेजक बना देना

**jealous** /ˈdʒeləs ˈजेलस्/ *adj.* **1** feeling upset or angry because you think that sb you like or love is showing interest in sb else किसी प्रिय व्यक्ति का किसी अन्य व्यक्ति के प्रति झुकाव के कारण परेशान या क्रुद्ध; ईर्ष्यालु *Tarun seems to get jealous whenever Sarita speaks to another boy!* **2 jealous (of sb/sth)** feeling angry or sad because you want to be like sb else or because you want what sb else has किसी के प्रति ईर्ष्यालु (क्योंकि आप उसके समान होना चाहते हैं या जो उसके पास है वह आप भी चाहते हैं) *He's always been jealous of his older brother.* ○ *I'm very jealous of your new car—how much did it cost?* ✪ पर्याय **envious** ▸ **jealously** *adv.* ईर्ष्यापूर्वक ▸ **jealousy** *noun* [C, U] (*pl.* **jealousies**) ईर्ष्या, डाह

**jeans** /dʒiːnz जीन्ज़्/ *noun* [*pl.*] trousers made of strong, usually blue, cotton cloth (**denim**) नीले डेनिम की या मजबूत सूती पैंट; जीन्स *These jeans are a bit too tight.* ○ *a pair of jeans*

**Jeep™** /dʒiːp जीप्/ *noun* [C] a strong vehicle suitable for travelling over rough ground ऊबड़-खाबड़ ज़मीन के लिए उपयुक्त एक मज़बूत मोटर गाड़ी; जीप

**jeer** /dʒɪə(r) जिअ(र्)/ *verb* [I, T] **jeer (at) sb/sth** to laugh or shout rude comments at sb/sth to show your lack of respect for him/her/it किसी व्यक्ति या वस्तु पर हँसना या फबती कसना (उसके प्रति आदरहीनता दिखाने के लिए) *The spectators booed and jeered at the losing team.* ▸ **jeer** *noun* [C] ताना, फबती *The Prime Minister was greeted with jeers in the Parliament House today.*

**jeera** *noun* [U] (*IndE*) cumin ज़ीरा

**jelly** /ˈdʒeli ˈजेलि/ *noun* (*pl.* **jellies**) (*AmE* **Jell-O™**) **1** [C, U] a soft, solid brightly coloured food that shakes when it is moved. Jelly is made from sugar and fruit juice and is eaten cold at the end of a meal नरम, ठोस चमकदार खाद्य पदार्थ जो आगे-पीछे करने पर हिलता है; जेली, यह शक्कर और फलों के रस से बनती है और इसे भोजन के बाद, ठंडा करके खाते हैं **2** [U] (*AmE*) a type of jam that does not contain any solid pieces of fruit एक प्रकार का जैम जिसमें फल के ठोस टुकड़े नहीं होते

IDM **be/feel like jelly** (used especially about the legs or knees) to feel weak because you are nervous, afraid, etc. (विशेषत: टाँगों या घुटनों में) घबराहट, डर आदि के मारे दुर्बलता अनुभव करना

**turn to jelly** (used about the legs and knees) to suddenly become weak because of fear (टाँगों और घुटनों का) डर के मारे एकाएक कमज़ोर हो जाना

**jellyfish** /ˈdʒelifɪʃ ˈजेलिफ़िश्/ *noun* [C] (*pl.* **jellyfish**) a sea animal with a soft colourless body and long thin parts called **tentacles** that can sting you कोमल रंगहीन शरीर वाला एक जलचर जिसके स्पर्शक डंक मारते हैं; छत्रिक, जेलीफ़िश

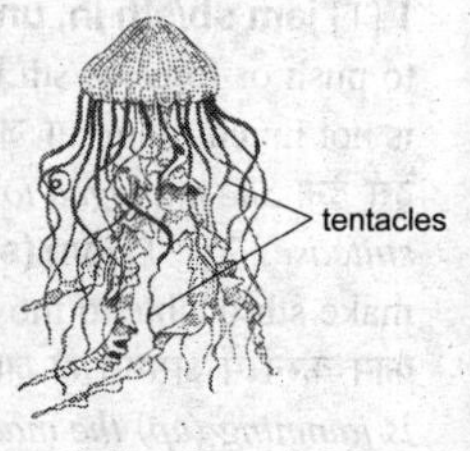

**jeopardize** (*also* **-ise**) /ˈdʒepədaɪz ˈजेपडाइज़्/ *verb* [T] to do sth that may damage sth or put it at risk किसी कार्य द्वारा किसी वस्तु को ख़तरे में डालना या हानि पहुँचाना *He would never do anything to jeopardize his career.*

**jeopardy** /ˈdʒepədi ˈजेपडि/ *noun*

IDM **in jeopardy** in a dangerous position and likely to be lost or harmed ख़तरनाक स्थिति में जिसमें लुप्त या क्षतिग्रस्त होने की संभावना हो *The future of the factory and 15,000 jobs are in jeopardy.*

**jerk**[1] /dʒɜːk जक्/ *verb* [I, T] to move or make sb/sth move with a sudden sharp movement एकाएक तेज़ हरकत से हिलना या हिलाना; झटका खाना या झटका देना *She jerked the door open.* ○ *His head jerked back as the car suddenly set off.* ▶ **jerky** *adj.* झटकेदार ▶ **jerkily** *adv.* झटके से

**jerk**[2] /dʒɜːk जक्/ *noun* [C] **1** a sudden sharp movement झटका **2** (*AmE slang*) a stupid or annoying person बेवक़ूफ़ या खिजाऊ व्यक्ति

**jersey** /ˈdʒɜːzi ˈजज़ि/ *noun* **1** [C] a piece of clothing made of wool that you wear over a shirt कमीज़ के ऊपर पहनने की ऊनी पोशाक, जर्सी

> NOTE इसी पोशाक को **jersey** के अलावा **jumper, pullover** और **sweater** भी कहते हैं।

**2** [U] a soft thin material made of cotton or wool that is used for making clothes सूत या ऊन से बना कोमल पतला कपड़ा जिससे पोशाकें बनती हैं

**jest**[1] /dʒest जेस्ट्/ *noun* [C] a joke or prank; sth said or done to amuse people चुटकुला या मज़ाक़; प्रहसन

IDM **in jest** not said seriously and intended as a joke परिहासपूर्वक कहा गया

**jest**[2] /dʒest जेस्ट्/ *verb* [I] to say or do sth to amuse people मज़ाक़ करना; आमोदित करने के लिए कुछ कहना *How can someone jest about something so important!*

**jester** /ˈdʒestə(r) ˈजेस्‌ट(र्)/ *noun* [C] (usually in the past at the court of kings and queens) a man employed to amuse people by telling jokes, funny stories, etc. (प्रायः पूर्वकाल में राज दरबार में) विदूषक

**Jesus** /ˈdʒiːzəs ˈजीज़स्/ = **Christ**

**jet** /dʒet जेट्/ *noun* [C] **1** a fast modern plane एक आधुनिक तीव्रगामी विमान; जेट विमान *a jet plane/aircraft* **2** a fast, thin current of water, gas, etc. coming out of a small hole एक छोटे छेद से निकलती हुई पानी, गैस आदि की तेज़ पतली धारा

**jet-black** *adj.* very dark black in colour गहरा काला, स्याहा काला

**jet engine** *noun* [C] a powerful engine that makes planes fly by pushing out a current of hot air and gases at the back एक शक्तिशाली इंजन जो पश्च भाग से गरम हवा और गैसों को बाहर धकेलता है जिसके फलस्वरूप विमान उड़ता है; जेट इंजन ➪ **plane** पर चित्र देखिए।

**jet lag** *noun* [U] the tired feeling that people often have after a long journey in a plane to a place where the local time is different लंबी विमान-यात्रा से यात्री को हुई थकावट (गंतव्य स्थान का स्थानीय समय भिन्न होने के कारण); जेट लैग ▶ **jetlagged** *adj.* लंबी विमान यात्रा से थका हुआ

**the jet set** *noun* [*sing.*] the group of rich, successful and fashionable people (especially those who travel around the world a lot) धनी, सफल और फ़ैशनपसंद लोगों का समूह (विशेषतः जो काफ़ी अधिक विदेश यात्रा करते हैं)

**jetty** /ˈdʒeti ˈजेटि/ *noun* [C] (*pl.* **jetties**) (*AmE* **dock**) a stone wall or wooden platform built out into the sea or a river where boats are tied and where people can get on and off them समुद्र तट के जल में बनी पत्थर की दीवार या लकड़ी का प्लेटफ़ॉर्म जिससे नावों को बाँधते हैं और जहाँ लोग चढ़ते-उतरते हैं; जेट्टी, जलपोत; पोतघाट ✪ पर्याय **landing stage**

**Jew** /dʒuː जू/ *noun* [C] a person whose family was originally from the ancient land of Israel or whose religion is Judaism मूल रूप से इज़रायलवासी परिवार का सदस्य या यहूदी धर्म का अनुयायी; यहूदी ▶ **Jewish** *adj.* यहूदी-संबंधित

**jewel** /ˈdʒuːəl ˈजूअल्/ *noun* **1** [C] a valuable stone (for example a diamond) रत्न (जैसे हीरा) **2** [*pl.*] a piece of jewellery or an object that contains precious stones रत्न जटित आभूषण या कोई वस्तु

**jeweller** (*AmE* **jeweler**) /ˈdʒuːələ(r) ˈजूअल(र्)/ *noun* **1** [C] a person whose job is to buy, sell, make or repair jewellery and watches आभूषण और घड़ियाँ ख़रीदने, बेचने, बनाने आदि वाला व्यक्ति; जौहरी **2 the jeweller's** [*sing.*] a shop where jewellery and watches are made, sold and repaired जौहरी की दुकान

**jewellery** (*AmE* **jewelry**) /ˈdʒuːəlri ˈजूअल्रि/ *noun* [U] objects such as rings, etc. that are worn as personal decoration अँगूठियाँ आदि आभूषण *a piece of jewellery*

**jib**[1] /dʒɪb जिब्/ *noun* [C] **1** a small sail in front of the large sail on a boat नाव के बड़े पाल के सामने का छोटा पाल, तिकोना पाल **2** the arm of a **crane**[1] क्रेन की भुजा या डाँड

**jib²** /dʒɪb जिब्/ *verb* [I] (**jibbing; jibbed**) **jib (at sth/at doing sth)** (*old-fashioned*) to refuse to do or accept sth कोई काम करने या बात मानने से इनकार करना *She agreed to attend but jibbed at making a speech.*

**jig¹** /dʒɪg जिग्/ *noun* [C] a type of quick dance with jumping movements; the music for this dance उछल-कूद वाला एक तेज़ नृत्य, जोशीला नाच, जिग; इस नाच का संगीत

**jig²** /dʒɪg जिग्/ *verb* [I] (**jigging; jigged**) **jig about/around** to move about in an excited or impatient way उत्तेजना या आतुरता से घूमना

**jiggle** /ˈdʒɪgl ˈजिगल्/ *verb* [T] (*informal*) to move sth quickly from side to side किसी वस्तु को तेज़ी से एक ओर से दूसरी ओर घुमाना; झुलाना *She jiggled her car keys to try to distract the baby.*

**jigsaw** /ˈdʒɪgsɔː ˈजिग्सॉ/ (*also* **jigsaw puzzle**) *noun* [C] a picture on cardboard or wood that is cut into small pieces and has to be fitted together again गत्ते या लकड़ी के पट्टे पर चित्र जो छोटे टुकड़ों में कटा होता है और इन टुकड़ों को पुनः जोड़कर चित्र पूरा करना होता है; चित्रखंड प्रहेलिका

**jilt** /dʒɪlt जिल्ट्/ *verb* [T] to suddenly end a romantic relationship with sb in an unkind way किसी से प्रेम प्रसंग को एकाएक और कठोरता से समाप्त करना *a jilted lover*

**jingle¹** /ˈdʒɪŋgl ˈजिङ्गल्/ *noun* **1** [*sing.*] a ringing sound like small bells, made by metal objects gently hitting each other धातु से बनी परस्पर टकराती छोटी घंटियों जैसी आवाज़; टनटनाहट, खनखनाहट, झंकार *the jingle of coins* **2** [C] a short simple tune or song that is easy to remember and is used in advertising on television or radio टेलीविज़न या रेडियो के विज्ञापन में प्रयुक्त छोटी सादी धुन या गीत जिसे याद रखना या करना आसान हो

**jingle²** /ˈdʒɪŋgl ˈजिङ्गल्/ *verb* [I, T] to make or cause sth to make a pleasant gentle sound like small bells ringing छोटी खनखनाती घंटियों जैसी सुहानी आवाज़ पैदा करना या करवाना *She jingled the coins in her pocket.*

**jinx** /dʒɪŋks जिङ्क्स्/ *noun* [C, *usually sing.*] (*informal*) bad luck; a person or thing that people believe brings bad luck to sb/sth दुर्भाग्य, अभिशाप; दुर्भाग्य या अभिशाप लाने वाला व्यक्ति या वस्तु, (विश्वास के अनुसार), अशुभ व्यक्ति या वस्तु ▶ **jinx** *verb* [T] दुर्भाग्य लाना ▶ **jinxed** *adj.* अभागा, अभिशप्त *After my third accident in a month, I began to think I was jinxed.*

**the jitters** /ˈdʒɪtəz ˈजिटज़्/ *noun* [*pl.*] (*informal*) feelings of fear or worry, especially before an important event or before having to do sth difficult भय या चिंता (विशेषतः किसी महत्त्वपूर्ण घटना या कठिन काम से पहले) *Just thinking about the exam **gives me the jitters**!*

**jittery** /ˈdʒɪtəri ˈजिटरि/ *adj.* (*informal*) nervous or worried बेचैन या चिंतित

**Jnr** (*also* **Jr.**) *abbr.* (*AmE*) Junior अवराज, छोटा *Jnr*

**job** /dʒɒb जॉब्/ *noun* [C] **1** the work that you do regularly to earn money धन कमाने के लिए नियमित रूप से किया जाने वाला काम; नौकरी *She **took/got a job** as a waitress.* ○ *A lot of people will **lose** their **jobs** if the factory closes.*

> **NOTE** नौकरी ढूँढ़ने के संबंध में किए जाने वाले प्रयोग— **look for, apply for** या **find a job** हैं। नौकरी **well paid/highly paid** या **badly paid** किसी भी तरह की हो सकती है। नौकरी **full-time, part-time, permanent** या **temporary** भी हो सकती है। ➪ **work** पर नोट देखिए।

**2** a task or a piece of work कोई काम या कार्य *I always have a lot of jobs to do in the house at weekends.* ○ *The garage has **done a good/bad job on** our car.* **3** [*usually sing.*] a duty or responsibility कर्तव्य या दायित्व *It's not his job to tell us what we can and can't do.*

**IDM do the job/trick** (*informal*) to get the result that is wanted अभीष्ट परिणाम प्राप्त करना

**have a hard job to do sth/doing sth** ➪ **hard¹** देखिए।

**it's a good job** (*spoken*) it is a good or lucky thing अच्छा या भाग्यशाली कार्य आदि *It's a good job you reminded me—I had completely forgotten!*

**just the job/ticket** (*informal*) exactly what is needed in a particular situation ख़ास परिस्थिति की ख़ास ज़रूरत

**make a bad, good, etc. job of sth** to do sth badly, well, etc. कोई कार्य बुरे, अच्छे आदि तरीक़े से करना

**make the best of a bad job** ➪ **best³** देखिए।

**out of a job** without paid work बेरोज़गार, ख़ाली, बेकार ✪ पर्याय **unemployed**

**jobless** /ˈdʒɒbləs ˈजॉब्लस्/ *adj.* **1** (usually used about large numbers of people) without paid work (बड़ी संख्या में लोग) बेरोज़गार ✪ पर्याय **unemployed** **2 the jobless** *noun* [*pl.*] people without paid work बेरोज़गार लोग ▶ **joblessness** *noun* [U] बेरोज़गारी ✪ पर्याय **unemployment**

**jockey** /ˈdʒɒki ˈजॉकि/ *noun* [C] a person who rides horses in races, especially as a profession

घुड़दौड़ में भाग लेने वाला घुड़सवार (विशेषतः पेशेवर के रूप में); जॉकी ➪ **DJ** देखिए।

**jocular** /ˈdʒɒkjələ(r) ˈजॉक्यल(र्)/ *adj.* (*formal*) **1** humorous or amusing मज़ाक़िया या हास्यक *a jocular comment* **2** (about or of a person) enjoying making people laugh (व्यक्ति) परिहासपूर्ण *jocular in nature* ▶ **jocularity** /ˌdʒɒkjəˈlærəti ˌजॉक्यˈलैरटि/ *noun* [U] मज़ाक़

**jodhpurs** *noun* [*pl.*] special trousers that you wear for riding a horse घुड़सवारी की विशेष पतलून

**joey** /ˈdʒəʊi ˈजोइ/ *noun* [C] a young **kangaroo** or **wallaby** कंगारू या वाल्लाबी का बच्चा ➪ **marsupial** पर चित्र देखिए।

**jog**[1] /dʒɒg जॉग्/ *verb* (**jogging; jogged**) **1** [I] to run slowly, especially as a form of exercise धीरे-धीरे दौड़ना, विशेषतः व्यायाम के रूप में

> **NOTE** व्यायाम या आनंद के लिए **jogging** (दौड़) की बात करनी हो तो अधिक प्रचलित प्रयोग है **go jogging**—*I go jogging most evenings.*

**2** [T] to push or knock sb/sth slightly किसी व्यक्ति या वस्तु को हलके से धक्का या झटका देना *He jogged my arm and I spilled the milk.*

**IDM jog sb's memory** to say or do sth that makes sb remember sth ऐसी बात कहना या काम करना कि कोई बात याद आ जाए

**jog**[2] /dʒɒg जॉग्/ *noun* [*sing.*] **1** a slow run as a form of exercise व्यायाम के रूप में मंद गति की दौड़; जॉग *She **goes for a jog** before breakfast.* **2** a slight push or knock हलका धक्का या झटका

**jogger** /ˈdʒɒgə(r) ˈजॉग(र्)/ *noun* [C] a person who goes jogging for exercise व्यायाम के लिए मंद गति से दौड़ने वाला व्यक्ति; जॉगर

**join**[1] /dʒɔɪn जॉइन्/ *verb* **1** [T] **join A to B; join A and B (together)** to fasten or connect one thing to another एक वस्तु से दूसरी वस्तु को बाँधना या जोड़ना *The Channel Tunnel joins Britain to Europe.* ○ *The two pieces of wood had been carefully joined together.* **2** [I, T] **join (up) (with sb/sth)** to meet or unite (with sb/sth) to form one thing or group (किसी व्यक्ति या वस्तु से) मिलकर या जुड़कर एक वस्तु या समूह बनाना *Do the two rivers join (up) at any point?* **3** [T] to become a member of a club or organization किसी क्लब या संगठन का सदस्य बनना; में शामिल होना *I've joined an aerobics class.* ○ *He joined the company three months ago.* **4** [T] to take your place in sth or to take part in sth किसी में अपनी जगह लेना या भाग लेना *We'd better go and join the queue if we want to see the film.* ○ *Come downstairs and join the party.* **5** [I, T] **join (with) sb in sth/in doing sth/to do sth; join together in doing sth/to do sth** to take part with sb (often in doing sth for sb else) किसी के साथ शामिल होना (प्रायः किसी के लिए कुछ करने की दृष्टि से) *Everybody here joins me in wishing you the best of luck in your new job.*

**IDM join forces (with sb)** ➪ **force**[1] देखिए।

**PHR V join in (sth/doing sth)** to take part in an activity किसी गतिविधि या कार्यक्रम में भाग लेना *Everyone started singing but Firoz refused to join in.*

**join up** to become a member of the army, navy or air force थलसेना, नौसेना या वायुसेना में शामिल होना

**join**[2] /dʒɔɪn जॉइन्/ *noun* [C] a place where two things are fixed or connected वह स्थान जहाँ दो वस्तुओं को बैठाया या जोड़ा गया है; जोड़ *He glued the handle back on so cleverly that you couldn't see the join.*

**joiner** /ˈdʒɔɪnə(r) ˈजॉइन(र्)/ *noun* [C] a person who makes the wooden parts of a building किसी भवन के लकड़ी वाले हिस्सों को बनाने वाला व्यक्ति; बढ़ई ➪ **carpenter** देखिए।

**joinery** /ˈdʒɔɪnəri ˈजॉइनरि/ *noun* [U] the work of a person who makes all the wooden parts of a building (**a joiner**) or the things made by him/her बढ़ई का काम

**joint**[1] /dʒɔɪnt जॉइन्ट्/ *noun* [C] **1** a part of the body where two bones fit together and are able to bend शरीर का वह अंग जहाँ दो हड्डियाँ एक दूसरे के साथ सही बैठती हैं और मुड़ सकती हैं; जोड़, संधि **2** the place where two or more things are fastened or connected together, especially to form a corner वह स्थान जहाँ दो या अधिक वस्तुएँ एक साथ बँधती या जुड़ती हैं; गाँठ **3** a large piece of meat that you cook whole in the oven गोश्त का बड़ा टुकड़ा जो अवन या भट्टी में समूचा पकाया जाता है *a joint of lamb*

**joint**[2] /dʒɔɪnt जॉइन्ट्/ *adj.* (*only before a noun*) shared or owned by two or more people दो या अधिक लोगों की भागीदारी या स्वामित्व वाला; संयुक्त *Have you and your husband got a **joint account** (= a shared bank account)?* ○ *a joint decision* ▶ **jointly** *adv.* संयुक्त रूप से

**joist** /dʒɔɪst जॉइस्ट्/ *noun* [C] a long thick piece of wood or metal that is used to support a floor or ceiling in a building मकान में फ़र्श या छत को थामने वाला लकड़ी या धातु का लंबा मोटा टुकड़ा; कड़ी धरन

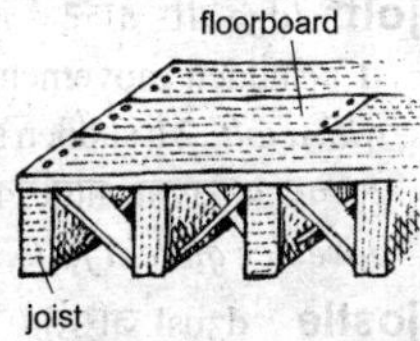

**joke[1]** /dʒəʊk जोक्/ *noun* **1** [C] something said or done to make you laugh, especially a funny story हँसाने वाली कोई बात या काम (विशेषतः कोई विचित्र कथा), चुटकुला, लतीफ़ा *to tell/crack jokes* ○ *I'm sorry, I didn't get the joke* (= understand it). ➪ **joke** देखिए। **2** [*sing.*] a ridiculous person, thing or situation हास्यजनक व्यक्ति, प्रसंग, या परिस्थिति, मज़ाक़ *The salary he was offered was a joke!*

IDM **play a joke/trick on sb** to trick sb in order to amuse yourself or other people अपने को या लोगों को हँसाने के लिए किसी के साथ मज़ाक़ करना

**see the joke** to understand what is funny about a joke or trick मज़ाक़ के मज़ाक़िया अंश को समझ लेना

**take a joke** to be able to laugh at a joke against yourself स्वयं अपने साथ किए मज़ाक़ पर हँस सकना *The trouble with Prateek is he can't take a joke.*

**joke[2]** /dʒəʊk जोक्/ *verb* [I] **1 joke (with sb) (about sth)** to say sth to make people laugh; to tell a funny story लोगों को हँसाने के लिए कुछ कहना, चुटकुले सुनाना; हास्यजनक कहानी सुनाना *She spent the evening laughing and joking with her old friends.* **2** to say sth that is not true because you think it is funny कोई झूठी बात कहना (यह मानते हुए कि लोग हँसेंगे) *I never joke about religion.* ○ *Don't get upset. I was **only joking**!*

IDM **you must be joking; you're joking** (*spoken*) (used to express great surprise) you cannot be serious (अत्यधिक आश्चर्य व्यक्त करने के लिए प्रयुक्त) आप मज़ाक़ कर रहे हैं या यह बात सच नहीं हो सकती

**joker** /ˈdʒəʊkə(r) ˈजोक(र्)/ *noun* [C] **1** a person who likes to tell jokes or play tricks ऐसा व्यक्ति जिसे चुटकुले सुनाना या लोगों के साथ मज़ाक़ करना पसंद हो; मज़ाक़िया, विनोदप्रिय व्यक्ति, जोकर **2** an extra card which can be used instead of any other one in some card games (ताश में) किसी भी पत्ते के बदले प्रयोग होने वाला अतिरिक्त पत्ता; जोकर

**jolly** /ˈdʒɒli ˈजॉलि/ *adj.* happy ख़ुश, प्रसन्नचित्त

**jolt[1]** /dʒəʊlt जोल्ट्/ *verb* [I, T] to move or make sb/sth move in a sudden rough way अचानक झटका खाना या झटका देना *The lorry jolted along the bumpy track.* ○ *The crash jolted all the passengers forward.*

**jolt[2]** /dʒəʊlt जोल्ट्/ *noun* [C, *usually sing.*] **1** a sudden movement झटका *The train stopped with a jolt.* **2** a sudden surprise or shock अप्रत्याशित आश्चर्य या सदमा, मानसिक आघात *His sudden anger gave her quite a jolt.*

**jostle** /ˈdʒɒsl ˈजॉसल्/ *verb* [I, T] to push hard against sb in a crowd भीड़ में धक्का-मुक्की करना

**jot** /dʒɒt जॉट्/ *verb* (**jo*tt*ing; jo*tt*ed**)

PHR V **jot sth down** to make a quick short note of sth जल्दी से संक्षेप में कुछ लिख लेना *Let me jot down your address.*

**joule** /dʒuːl जूल्/ *noun* [C] (in physics) a measurement of energy or **work[2] 7** (भौतिकी में) ऊर्जा या काम को मापने की इकाई; जूल ➪ **kilojoule** देखिए।

**journal** /ˈdʒɜːnl ˈजर्नल्/ *noun* [C] **1** a newspaper or a magazine, especially one in which all the articles are about a particular subject or profession समाचारपत्र या पत्रिका, विशेषतः जिसमें सभी लेख एक विशेष विषय या व्यवसाय पर हों; जर्नल *a medical/scientific journal* **2** a written account of what you have done each day प्रत्येक दिन के काम का लेखा-जोखा; रोज़नामचा, दैनंदिनी, डायरी *Have you read his journal of the years he spent in India?* ➪ **diary** देखिए।

**journalism** /ˈdʒɜːnəlɪzəm ˈजनलिज़म्/ *noun* [U] the profession of collecting and writing about news in newspapers and magazines or talking about it on the television or radio पत्रकारिता (का व्यवसाय); समाचारपत्रों या पत्रिकाओं में समाचारों का संकलन तथा लेखन या टेलीविज़न अथवा रेडियो पर उसकी चर्चा का व्यवसाय

**journalist** /ˈdʒɜːnəlɪst ˈजनलिस्ट्/ *noun* [C] a person whose job is to collect and write about news in newspapers and magazines or to talk about it on the television or radio समाचारपत्रों या पत्रिकाओं में संकलित समाचारों पर लेखन करने वाला या टेलीविज़न अथवा रेडियो पर उनपर चर्चा करने वाला व्यक्ति; पत्रकार ➪ **reporter** देखिए।

**journey** /ˈdʒɜːni ˈजनि/ *noun* [C] the act of travelling from one place to another, usually on land एक स्थान से दूसरे स्थान की यात्रा (प्रायः ज़मीन पर), सफ़र *a two-hour journey* ○ *We'll have to break the journey* (=stop for a rest). ➪ **travel** पर नोट देखिए।

**jovial** /ˈdʒəʊviəl ˈजोविअल्/ *adj.* (used about a person) happy and friendly (व्यक्ति) प्रसन्न और मित्रवत

**joy** /dʒɔɪ जॉइ/ *noun* **1** [U] a feeling of great happiness हर्ष, ख़ुशी, आह्लाद, आनंद *We'd like to wish you joy and success in your life together.* **2** [C] a person or thing that gives you great pleasure बहुत प्रसन्नता देने वाला व्यक्ति या वस्तु; आनंदकर व्यक्ति या वस्तु *the joys of fatherhood* ○ *That class is a joy to teach.* **3** [U] (*BrE informal*) (*used in questions and negative sentences*) success or satisfaction सफलता या संतुष्टि *'I asked again if we could have seats with more leg room but **got no joy** from the check-in clerk.'*

IDM **jump for joy** ➪ **jump[1]** देखिए।

IDM **sb's pride and joy** ➪ **pride[1]** देखिए।

**joyful** /ˈdʒɔɪfl ˈजॉइफ़्ल् / *adj.* very happy बहुत प्रसन्न, ख़ुश या आनंदित *a joyful occasion* ▶ **joyfully** /-fəli -फ़लि / *adv.* आनंदपूर्णता से ▶ **joyfulness** *noun* [U] आनंदपूर्णता

**joyless** /ˈdʒɔɪləs ˈजॉइलस् / *adj.* unhappy अप्रसन्न, निरानंद *a joyless marriage*

**joyriding** /ˈdʒɔɪraɪdɪŋ ˈजॉइराइडिङ् / *noun* [U] the crime of stealing a car and driving it for pleasure, usually in a fast and dangerous way कार चुराकर उसमें घूमने का आनंद लेने का अपराध (प्रायः तेज़ और ख़तरनाक तरीक़े से चलाते हुए), आमोदी सैर करना (विशेषतः चुराई हुई गाड़ी में) ▶ **joyrider** *noun* [C] आमोदी कार-चोर ▶ **joyride** *noun* [C] आमोदी सैर

**joystick** /ˈdʒɔɪstɪk ˈजॉइस्टिक् / *noun* [C] a handle used for controlling movement on a computer, aircraft, etc. कंप्यूटर, विमान आदि के संचालन को नियंत्रित करने का हत्था; हैंडल

**Jr.** *abbr.* = **Jnr**

**jubilant** /ˈdʒuːbɪlənt ˈजूबिलन्ट् / *adj.* (*formal*) extremely happy, especially because of a success अत्यधिक प्रसन्न विशेषतः सफलता प्राप्ति पर; आनंदविभोर *The football fans were jubilant at their team's victory in the cup.*

**jubilation** /ˌdʒuːbɪˈleɪʃn ˌजूबिˈलेश्न् / *noun* [U] (*formal*) great happiness because of a success (सफलता प्राप्ति पर) हर्षोल्लास, आनंदोत्सव

**jubilee** /ˈdʒuːbɪliː ˈजूबिली / *noun* [C] a special anniversary of an event that took place a certain number of years ago, and the celebrations that go with it निश्चित अवधि के उपरांत वर्ष-विशेष में किसी प्रसंग से संबंधित विशिष्ट समारोह; जयंती महोत्सव *It's the company's* ***golden jubilee*** *this year* (= it is fifty years since it was started).

> NOTE **Golden jublee** (स्वर्ण जयंती – 50 वर्ष) के अतिरिक्त **silver jublee** (रजत जयंती – 25 वर्ष) और **diamond jublee** (हीरक जयंती – 60 वर्ष) भी मनाई जाती है।

**Judaism** /ˈdʒuːdeɪɪzəm ˈजूडेइज़म् / *noun* [U] the religion of the Jewish people यहूदियों का धर्म, यहूदी धर्म, यहूदीवाद

**judge**[1] /dʒʌdʒ जज् / *noun* [C] **1** a person in a court of law whose job is to decide how criminals should be punished and to make legal decisions न्यायाधीश, न्यायमूर्ति *The judge sentenced the man to three years in prison.* **2** a person who decides who has won a competition खेल स्पर्धा में निर्णायक *a panel of judges* **3** [usually *sing.*] **a judge of sth** a person who has the ability or knowledge to give an opinion about sth किसी विषय पर मत प्रकट करने की योग्यता या अपेक्षित ज्ञान रखने वाला व्यक्ति; पारखी, गुणग्राहक *You're a good judge of character—what do you think of him?*

**judge**[2] /dʒʌdʒ जज् / *verb* **1** [I, T] to form or give an opinion about sb/sth based on the information you have प्राप्त जानकारी के आधार पर किसी व्यक्ति या वस्तु के विषय में राय बनाना या देना; आँकना ***Judging by/from*** *what he said, his work is going well.* ○ *It's difficult to judge how long the project will take.* **2** [T] to decide the result or winner of a competition खेल-स्पर्धा के परिणाम या विजेता का निर्णय करना; खेल-स्पर्धा में निर्णायक का काम करना *The head teacher will judge the competition.* **3** [T] to form an opinion about sb/sth, especially when you disapprove of him/her/it किसी व्यक्ति या वस्तु के विषय में कोई राय बनाना (विशेषतः उसे नकारते समय) *Don't judge him too harshly—he's had a difficult time.* **4** [T] to decide if sb is guilty or innocent in a court of law न्यायालय में किसी व्यक्ति के अपराधी या निरपराध होने के विषय में निर्णय देना; कचहरी में फ़ैसला सुनाना

**judgement** (*also* **judgment**) /ˈdʒʌdʒmənt ˈजज्मन्ट् / *noun* **1** [U] the ability to form opinions or to make sensible decisions सम्मति स्थिर करने या बुद्धिमतापूर्ण निर्णय करने की योग्यता; निर्णयक्षमता *to have good/poor/sound judgement* **2** [C, U] an opinion formed after carefully considering the information you have प्राप्त जानकारी पर सावधानी से विचार के उपरांत बनी सम्मति *What,* ***in your judgement,*** *would be the best course of action?* **3 judgment** [C] an official decision made by a judge or a court of law न्यायाधीश का निर्णय *The man collapsed when the judgment was read out in court.*

**Judgement Day** (*also* **the Day of Judgement** and **the Last Judgement**) *noun* [*sing.*] the day at the end of the world when, according to some religions, God will judge everyone who has ever lived कुछ धर्मों के अनुसार संसार के अंत या प्रलय का दिन जब परमेश्वर संसार में रह चुके प्राणियों के विषय में अपना निर्णय सुनाएँगे; क़यामत (का दिन)

**judicial** /dʒuːˈdɪʃl जूˈडिश्ल् / *adj.* connected with a court of law, a judge or a legal judgment न्यायालय, न्यायाधीश या क़ानूनी निर्णय से संबंधित, न्यायिक *the judicial system*

**judiciary** /dʒuˈdɪʃəri जूˈडिशरि / *noun* [C, *with sing. or pl. verb*] (*pl.* **judiciaries**) the judges of a country or a state, when they are considered as a group किसी देश या राज्य के न्यायाधीश (समूह के रूप में गृहीत); न्यायपालिका, न्यायतंत्र *an independent judiciary*

**judicious** /dʒuːˈdɪʃəs जूˈडिशस्/ *adj.* (used about a decision or an action) sensible and carefully considered; showing good judgement (निर्णय या कार्रवाई) बुद्धिमत्तापूर्ण और सुविचारित; विवेकपूर्ण विवेक-सम्मान ▶ **judiciously** *adv.* विवेकपूर्ण

**judo** /ˈdʒuːdəʊ ˈजूडो/ *noun* [U] a sport from Asia in which two people fight and try to throw each other to the ground एशिया का एक कुश्ती जैसा खेल; जूडो ➪ **martial arts** देखिए।

**jug** /dʒʌg जग्/ (*also AmE* **pitcher**) *noun* [C] a container with a handle used for holding or pouring liquids द्रव पदार्थ रखने या उड़ेलने के लिए प्रयुक्त मूठदार पात्र; जग *a milk jug* ○ *a jug of water*

**juggle** /ˈdʒʌgl ˈजग्ल्/ *verb* [I, T] **1 juggle (with sth)** to keep three or more objects such as balls in the air at the same time by throwing them one at a time and catching them quickly तीन या अधिक गेंद जैसी वस्तुओं को एक साथ एक-एक करके फुरती से उछालते-पकड़ते रहना; बाज़ीगरी करना **2 juggle sth (with sth)** to try to deal with two or more imporant jobs or activities at the same time एक ही समय में दो या अधिक महत्त्वपूर्ण कामों को करते रहने की कोशिश करना

**juggler** /ˈdʒʌglə(r) ˈजग्ल(र्)/ *noun* [C] a person who juggles to entertain people लोगों का मनोरंजन करने वाला बाज़ीगर

**jugular** /ˈdʒʌgjələ(r) ˈजग्यल(र्)/ (*also* **jugular vein**) *noun* [C] any of the three large tubes (veins) in your neck that carry blood away from your head to your heart गरदन की तीन बड़ी नसों में से एक जो सिर से हृदय तक ख़ून पहुँचाती हैं; कंठ्य धमनी, गल-शिरा

**juice** /dʒuːs जूस्/ *noun* [C,U] **1** the liquid that comes from fruit and vegetables फलों और सब्ज़ियों का रस *carrot/grape fruit/lemon juice* ○ *I'll have an orange juice, please.* **2** the liquid that comes from a piece of meat when it is cooked गोश्त को पकाते समय उससे निकला रस *You can use the juices of the meat to make gravy.* **3** the liquid in your stomach or another part of your body that deals with the food you eat (भोजन पचाने में सहायक) आमाशय या शरीर के किसी अन्य अंग में उत्पन्न द्रव *gastric/digestive juices*

**juicy** /ˈdʒuːsi ˈजूसि/ *adj.* (**juicier**; **juiciest**) **1** containing a lot of juice रस से भरा हुआ; रसदार, रसीला *juicy oranges* **2** (*informal*) (used about information) interesting because it is shocking (सूचना या जानकारी) चौंका देने के कारण रोचक *juicy gossip*

**jukebox** /ˈdʒuːkbɒks ˈजूकबॉक्स्/ *noun* [C] a machine in a cafe or bar, that plays music when money is put in किसी रेस्त्राँ या बार में लगी मशीन जो पैसे डालने पर संगीत सुनाती है; ज्यूकबॉक्स

**Jul.** *abbr.* July जुलाई *4 Jul. 2001*

**July** /dʒuˈlaɪ जुˈलाइ/ *noun* [U, C] (*abbr.* **Jul.**) the seventh month of the year, coming after June वर्ष का सातवाँ महीना; जुलाई

**NOTE** महीनों के वाक्य-प्रयोग की जानकारी के लिए **January** पर नोट और उदाहरण देखिए।

**jumble[1]** /ˈdʒʌmbl ˈजम्ब्ल्/ *verb* [T] (*usually passive*) **jumble sth (up/together)** to mix things together in a confused and untidy way वस्तुओं को बेतरतब ढंग से मिला देना

**jumble[2]** /ˈdʒʌmbl ˈजम्ब्ल्/ *noun* [*sing.*] an untidy group of things वस्तुओं का घाल-मेल *a jumble of papers/ideas*

**jumbo[1]** /ˈdʒʌmbəʊ ˈजम्बो/ *adj.* (*informal*) (*only before a noun*) very large बहुत बड़ा, विशाल, भारी-भरकम, बृहदाकार

**jumbo[2]** /ˈdʒʌmbəʊ ˈजम्बो/ *noun* [C] (*pl.* **jumbos**) (*also* **jumbo jet**) a very large aircraft that can carry several hundred passengers काफ़ी बड़ी संख्या में यात्रियों को ले जाने वाला बृहदाकार विमान; जंबो जेट

**jump[1]** /dʒʌmp जम्प्/ *verb* **1** [I] to move quickly into the air by pushing yourself up with your legs and feet, or by stepping off a high place कूदना; छलाँग लगाना *to jump into the air/off a bridge/onto a chair* ○ *How high can you jump?* **2** [I] to move quickly and suddenly तेज़ी से और एकाएक हरकत करना; कूदना *The telephone rang and she jumped up to answer it.* ○ *A taxi stopped and we jumped in.* **3** [T] to get over sth by jumping कूदकर किसी वस्तु के पार जाना, लाँघना, फाँदना *The dog jumped the fence and ran off down the road.* **4** [I] to make a sudden movement because of surprise or fear आश्चर्य या भय से एकाएक हरकत में आ जाना; चौंकना *'Oh, it's only you—you made me jump,' he said.* **5** [I] **jump (from sth) to sth; jump (by) (sth)** to increase suddenly by a very large amount अचानक बहुत अधिक बढ़ जाना *His salary jumped from Rs 20,000 to Rs 28,000 last year.* ○ *Prices jumped (by) 50% in the summer.* **6** [I] **jump (from sth) to sth** to go suddenly from one point in a series, a story, etc. to another किसी शृंखला या कहानी में एक बिंदु से दूसरे पर एकाएक पहुँच जाना *The book kept jumping from the present to the past.*

**IDM climb/jump on the bandwagon** ➪ **bandwagon** देखिए।

**jump for joy** to be extremely happy about sth किसी विषय में अत्यंत प्रसन्न होना
**jump the gun** to do sth too soon, before the proper time उचित समय से पहले या बारी आने से पहले कोई काम कर डालना
**jump the queue** to go to the front of a line of people (queue) without waiting for your turn अपनी बारी आए बिना पंक्ति में आगे पहुँच जाना, पंक्ति तोड़ कर आगे चले जाना
**jump to conclusions** to decide that sth is true without thinking about it carefully enough बिना अधिक सोचे-विचारे किसी निर्णय पर पहुँच जाना या कोई बात मान लेना, जल्दबाज़ी में किसी परिणाम पर पहुँच जाना
**PHR V** **jump at sth** to accept an opportunity, offer, etc. with enthusiasm उत्साह के साथ किसी अवसर, प्रस्ताव आदि को मानना; किसी अवसर आदि को लपक कर ले लेना *Of course I jumped at the chance to work in New York for a year.*

**jump²** /dʒʌmp जम्प् / *noun* [C] **1** an act of jumping कूदने की क्रिया, कूद, छलाँग *With a huge jump the horse cleared the hedge.* ○ *to do a parachute jump* ➪ **high jump** और **long jump** देखिए। **2 a jump (in sth)** a sudden increase in amount, price or value मात्रा, क़ीमत या मूल्य में अचानक वृद्धि, उछाल **3** a thing to be jumped over वह वस्तु जिसको फाँदना हो *The horse fell at the first jump.*

**jumper** /ˈdʒʌmpə(r) ˈजम्प(र्)/ *noun* [C] **1** (*BrE*) a piece of clothing with sleeves, usually made of wool, that you wear on the top part of your body (प्रायः ऊन से बनी) आस्तीन वाली पोशाक जिसे शरीर के ऊपरी भाग पर पहनते हैं; जंपर ➪ **sweater** पर नोट देखिए। **2** a person or animal that jumps कूदने वाला व्यक्ति या जानवर

**jumpy** /ˈdʒʌmpi ˈजम्पि/ *adj.* (*informal*) nervous or worried बेचैन या चिंतित

**Jun.** *abbr.* June जून *10 Jun. 2001*

**junction** /ˈdʒʌŋkʃn ˈजङ्क्शन्/ *noun* [C] a place where roads, railway lines, etc. meet स्थान जहाँ सड़कें, रेल का पटरियाँ आदि मिलती हैं; जंक्शन

**juncture** /ˈdʒʌŋktʃə(r) ˈजङ्क्च(र्)/ *noun* [U] a particular point in time समय का कोई विशिष्ट क्षण *The cricket match had reached a crucial juncture.*

**June** /dʒu:n जून् / *noun* [U,C] (*abbr.* **Jun**) the sixth month of the year, coming after May वर्ष का छठा महीना; जून

**NOTE** महीनों के वाक्य-प्रयोग की जानकारी के लिए, **January** पर नोट तथा उदाहरण देखिए।

**jungle** /ˈdʒʌŋgl ˈजङ्गल्/ *noun* [C,U] a thick forest in a hot tropical country (उष्णकटिबंधीय देश में) घना जंगल *the jungles of Africa and South America* ➪ **forest** पर नोट देखिए।

**junior¹** /ˈdʒu:niə(r) ˈजूनिअ(र्)/ *adj.* **1 junior (to sb)** having a low or lower position (than sb) in an organization, etc. किसी संगठन आदि में किसी निम्न अवर या किसी से निम्न अवर पद पर आसीन; अवर, जूनिअर, कनिष्ठ *a junior officer/doctor/employee* ○ *A lieutenant is junior to a captain in the army.* **2 Junior** (*abbr.* **Jnr, Jr.**) (*AmE*) used after the name of a son who has the same first name as his father पिता के ही प्रथम नाम वाले पुत्र के नाम के साथ प्रयुक्त *Sammy Davis, Junior* **3** (*BrE*) of or for children below a particular age एक विशेष आयु से कम के बच्चों का या के लिए; जूनियर *the junior athletics championships* ➪ **senior¹** देखिए।

**junior²** /ˈdʒu:niə(r) ˈजूनिअ(र्)/ *noun* **1** [C] a person who has a low position in an organization, etc. किसी संगठन आदि में निम्न पद का व्यक्ति; कनिष्ठ, जूनियर **2** [*sing.*] (with his, her, your etc.) a person who is younger than sb else by the number of years mentioned व्यक्ति जो किसी अन्य से वर्षों की निर्दिष्ट संख्या के अंतर से छोटा है; छोटा *She's two years his junior/his junior by two years.* **3** [C] (*BrE*) a child who goes to junior school जूनियर स्कूल का छात्र *The juniors are having an outing to a museum today.* ➪ **senior²** देखिए।

**junk** /dʒʌŋk जङ्क्/ *noun* [U] (*informal*) things that are old or useless or do not have much value पुरानी, बेकार या कम उपयोग की वस्तुएँ; कबाड़, कूड़ा-करकट *There's an awful lot of junk up in the attic.*

**junk food** *noun* [U] (*informal*) food that is not very good for you but that is ready to eat or quick to prepare तुरंत बनने या खाया जाने वाला खाद्य पदार्थ (जो यद्यपि स्वास्थ्यकर नहीं)

**junta** /ˈdʒʌntə ˈजन्टा/ *noun* [C, *with sing. or pl. verb*] a group, especially of military officers, who rule a country by force बल प्रयोग से देश पर शासन करने वालों (विशेषतः सैन्य अधिकारियों) का समूह; बलात पदासीन शासक-गुट, जुंटा

**Jupiter** /ˈdʒu:pɪtə(r) ˈजूपिट(र्)/ *noun* [*sing.*] the planet that is fifth in order from the sun सूर्य से क्रम में पाँचवा ग्रह; जुपिटर, बृहस्पति ➪ **the solar system** पर चित्र देखिए।

**jurisdiction** /ˌdʒʊərɪsˈdɪkʃn ˌजुअरिस्ˈडिक्शन्/ *noun* [U] legal power or authority; the area in which this power can be used क़ानूनी अधिकार,

न्यायाधिकार; वह क्षेत्र जिस पर न्यायाधिकार लागू होता है, अधिकार-क्षेत्र *That question is outside the jurisdiction of this council.*

**juror** /ˈdʒʊərə(r) ˈजुअर(र्)/ *noun* [C] a member of a jury जूरी का सदस्य

**jury** /ˈdʒʊəri ˈजुअरि/ *noun* [C, *with sing. or pl. verb*] (*pl.* **juries**) **1** a group of members of the public in a court of law who listen to the facts about a crime and decide if sb is guilty or not guilty न्यायालय में जनता के सदस्यों का समूह जो अपराध के मामले को सुनकर अपना निर्णय सुनाता है; जूरी, अभिनिर्णायक *Has/have the jury reached a verdict?* **2** a group of people who decide who the winner is a competition प्रतिस्पर्धा में निर्णायक-मंडल *The jury is/are about to announce the winners.*

**just[1]** /dʒʌst जस्ट्/ *adv* **1** a very short time before अभी-अभी, हाल ही में, एकदम पहले *She's just been to the shops.* ○ *They came here just before Diwali.* **2** at exactly this/that moment, or immediately after ठीक अभी या तुरंत बाद *I was **just going to** phone my mother when she arrived.* ○ ***Just as** I was beginning to enjoy myself, Mohit said it was time to go.* ○ ***Just then** the door opened.* **3** exactly ठीक, बिलकुल *You're **just as** clever as he is.* ○ *The room was too hot before, but now it's **just right.*** ○ *He looks **just like** his father.* ○ *My arm hurts just here.* **4** only केवल *She's just a child.* ○ *Just a minute! I'm nearly ready.* **5** almost not; hardly लगभग नहीं; बड़ी मुश्किल से *I could **only just** hear what she was saying.* ○ *We got to the station **just in** time.* **6** (*often with the imperative*) used for getting attention or to emphasize what you are saying ध्यान आकृष्ट करने के लिए या अपनी बात पर बल देने के लिए प्रयुक्त *Just let me speak for a moment, will you?* ○ *I just don't want to go to the party.* **7** used with 'might', 'may' or 'could' to express a slight possibility हलकी संभावना प्रकट करने के लिए 'might', 'may' या 'could' के साथ प्रयुक्त *This might just/just might be the most important decision of your life.* **8** really; absolutely सचमुच; सर्वथा, बिलकुल *The whole day was just fantastic!*

**IDM all/just the same** ➪ **same** देखिए।

**it is just as well (that...)** it is a good thing यह अच्छा हुआ *It's just as well you remembered to bring your umbrella!* ➪ **well** की प्रविष्टि में **(just) as well (to do sth)** भी देखिए।

**just about** almost or approximately लगभग या के आस-पास *I've just about finished.* ○ *Karan's plane should be taking off just about now.*

**just in case** in order to be completely prepared or safe ज़रूरत पड़ने पर पूरी तरह से तैयार या सुरक्षित रहने के लिए *It might be hot in Jaipur—take your shorts just in case.*

**just now** **1** at this exact moment or during this exact period ठीक इसी क्षण या ठीक इसी अवधि में *I can't come with you just now—can you wait 20 minutes?* **2** a very short time ago एकदम अभी, अभी-अभी *I saw Tony just now.*

**just so** exactly right एकदम वैसा, ठीक उसी तरह

**not just yet** not now, but probably quite soon अभी नहीं, परंतु शायद काफ़ी जल्दी

**just[2]** /dʒʌst जस्ट्/ *adj.* fair and right; reasonable उचित और सही; न्यायसंगत *I don't think that was a very just decision.* ▶ **justly** *adv.* ईमानदारी से

**justice** /ˈdʒʌstɪs ˈजस्टिस्/ *noun* **1** [U] the fair treatment of people न्याय; लोगों के साथ उचित व्यवहार *a struggle for justice* **2** [U] the quality of being fair or reasonable न्यायोचित होने का गुण *Everybody realized the justice of what he was saying.* **3** [U] the law and the way it is used क़ानून और क़ानून का व्यवहार *the criminal justice system* **4** [C] (*AmE*) a judge in a court of law न्यायाधीश, जज

**IDM do justice to sb/sth; do sb/sth justice** to treat sb/sth fairly or to show the real quality of sb/sth किसी व्यक्ति या वस्तु के साथ न्यायोचित बरताव करना या किसी व्यक्ति या वस्तु की वास्तविक गुण प्रकट करना *I don't like him, but to do him justice, he's a very clever man.* ○ *The photograph doesn't do her justice—she's actually very pretty.*

**a miscarriage of justice** ➪ **miscarriage** देखिए।

**justifiable** /ˌdʒʌstɪˈfaɪəbl ˌजस्टिˈफ़ाइअबल्/ *adj.* that you can accept because there is a good reason for it न्यायोचित होने से स्वीकार्य *His action was entirely justifiable.* ▶ **justifiably** /ˈdʒʌstɪfaɪəbli; ˌdʒʌstɪˈfaɪəbli ˈजस्टिफ़ाइअब्लि; ˌजस्टिˈफ़ाइअब्लि/ *adv.* न्यायोचित रूप से

**justification** /ˌdʒʌstɪfɪˈkeɪʃn ˌजस्टिफ़िˈकेश्न्/ *noun* [C, U] **(a) justification (for sth/doing sth)** (a) good reason स्वीकार्य कारण, औचित्य *I can't see any justification for cutting his salary.*

**justify** /ˈdʒʌstɪfaɪ ˈजस्टिफ़ाइ/ *verb* [T] (*pres. part.* **justifying;** *3rd person sing. pres.* **justifies;** *pt, pp* **justified**) to give or be a good reason for sth किसी बात के औचित्य का निरूपण करना, सफ़ाई देना *Can you justify your decision?*

**jut** /dʒʌt जट्/ *verb* [I] (**jutting; jutted**) **jut (out) (from/into/over sth)** to stick out further than the surrounding surface, objects, etc. आसपास की सतहों, वस्तुओं आदि की अपेक्षा बाहर की ओर निकलना; बहिर्विष्ट होना *rocks that jut out into the sea*

**jute** /dʒuːt जूट्/ *noun* [U] thin threads from a plant that are used for making rope and rough cloth (**sackcloth**) जूट, पटसन इससे रस्सियाँ बटी जाती हैं और बोरे बनते हैं

**juvenile** /ˈdʒuːvənaɪl ˈजूव़नाइल्/ *adj.* **1** (*formal*) of, for or involving young people who are not yet adults किशोरों का, के लिए या को शामिल करते हुए; बाल, अल्पवयस्क *juvenile crime* **2** behaving like sb of a younger age; childish कम आयु के व्यक्ति के समान बरताव करने वाला; बचकाना *He's twenty but he is still quite juvenile.* ▶ **juvenile** *noun* [C] किशोर

**juvenile delinquent** *noun* [C] a young person who is guilty of committing a crime किशोर अपराधी

**juxtapose** /ˌdʒʌkstəˈpəʊz ˌजकुस्टˈपोज़्/ *verb* [T] (*formal*) to put two people, things, etc. very close together, especially in order to show how they are different दो व्यक्तियों, वस्तुओं को एक साथ रखना, (विशेषतः उनमें भिन्नता दर्शाने के लिए) *The artist achieves a special effect by juxtaposing light and dark.* ▶ **juxtaposition** /ˌdʒʌkstəpəˈzɪʃn ˌजकुस्टपˈज़िशन्/ *noun* [U] सन्निकटता, सन्निधि

# K k

**K, k**[1] /keɪ के/ *noun* [C, U] (*pl.* **K's; k's** /keɪz केज़्/) the eleventh letter of the English alphabet अंग्रेज़ी वर्णमाला का ग्यारहवाँ अक्षर *'Kajal' begins with a 'K'.*

**K**[2] /keɪ के/ *abbr.* **1** (*informal*) one thousand एक हज़ार *She earns 22K* (= Rs 22,000) *a month.* **2** (*technical*) kelvin केल्विन, तापमान मापने की इकाई

**kabab** *noun* [C] small pieces of meat, vegetables, etc. that are cooked on a stick (**a skewer**) कबाब

**kabaddi** *noun* [U] a game of Indian origin played by two teams of twelve players each, of which seven are on court at a time. A player, from each team while uttering the word 'kabaddi' has to cross the dividing line to the other team; try to touch one or more player(s) of the rival team and then return to their side without being caught कबड्डी (का खेल)

**kaivalya** *noun* [U] (*IndE*) the state of absolute **bliss** or inner freedom; final **emancipation** परमानंद या आंतरिक मुक्ति की दशा; मोक्ष

**kaju** = **cashew**

**kaleidoscope** /kəˈlaɪdəskəʊp कˈलाइडस्कोप्/ *noun* [C] **1** a large number of different things बड़ी संख्या में विभिन्न प्रकार की वस्तुएँ; वैविध्यपूर्ण वस्तुओं का संग्रह **2** a toy that consists of a tube containing mirrors and small pieces of coloured glass. When you look into one end of the tube and turn it, you see changing patterns of colours रंगीन काँच के टुकड़ों से भरी और दर्पणों वाली नली का खिलौना जिसे घुमाने से रंगबिरंगी दृश्यावली दिखाई देती है; सैरबीन नामक खिलौना, बहुमूर्तिदर्शी

**kameez** *noun* [C] a piece of clothing like a long shirt worn by many people from south Asia and the Midddle East (दक्षिण तथा मध्य पूर्वी एशियाई देशों में प्रचलित) लंबा कुरता

**kangaroo** /ˌkæŋgəˈruː ˌकैङ्गˈरू/ *noun* [C] (*pl.* **kangaroos**) an Australian animal that moves by jumping on its strong back legs and that carries its young in a pocket of skin (**a pouch**) on its stomach ऑस्ट्रेलियाई जानवर जो अपनी पिछली मज़बूत टाँगों के बल पर उछलते हुए चलता है और अपने बच्चे को पेट पर लगी थैली में रखता है; कंगारू ➪ **marsupial** पर चित्र देखिए।

**kaolin** /ˈkeɪəlɪn ˈकेअलिन्/ (*also* **china clay**) *noun* [U] a type of fine white clay that is used in some medicines and in making cups, plates, etc. चीनी मिट्टी जिससे प्याले, तश्तरियाँ आदि और कुछ दवाइयाँ बनती हैं

**karaoke** /ˌkæriˈəʊki ˌकैरिˈओकि/ *noun* [U] a type of entertainment in which a machine plays only the music of popular songs so that people can sing the words themselves मशीन द्वारा प्रस्तुत लोकप्रिय गानों की धुन जिस पर लोग अपने स्वर मिलाकर गाते है

**karat** (*AmE*) = **carat**

**karate** /kəˈrɑːti कˈराटि/ *noun* [U] a style of fighting originally from Japan in which the hands and feet are used as weapons जापानी युद्ध-क्रीड़ा जिसमें हाथ व पैर ही शस्त्र होते हैं; कराटे ➪ **martial arts** देखिए।

**karma** *noun* [U] **1** (in Hinduism and Buddhism) the sum of a person's good and bad actions in this and previous states of existence, viewed as affecting their future (हिंदू और बौद्ध धर्म में) मनुष्य के पिछले एवं इस जन्म के कर्म जिससे उसका भविष्य प्रभावित होता है; कर्म **2** (*informal*) the good or bad effect of doing something किसी कार्य का अच्छा या बुरा प्रभाव *good karma*

**kart** /kɑːt काट्/ = **go-kart**

**Kathakali** *noun* [U] a traditional dramatic dance form from Kerala, marked by elaborate facial make-up and **minute** facial gestures केरल राज्य की पारंपरिक नृत्य शैली; कथाकली

**kayak** /ˈkaɪæk ˈकाइऐक्/ *noun* [C] a light narrow boat (**a canoe**) for one person, that you move using with a stick with a flat part at each end (**a paddle**) एक व्यक्ति के प्रयोग की, चप्पू से चलने वाली छोटी नाव

**kebab** = **kabab**

**keel**[1] /kiːl कील्/ *noun* [C] a long piece of wood or metal on the bottom of a boat that stops it falling over sideways in the water नाव की पेंदे में लगा लकड़ी या धातु का लंबा टुकड़ा जो उसे पानी में उलटने नहीं देता; जहाज़ की आधार बिल्ली

**keel**[2] /kiːl कील्/ *verb*

**PHR V** **keel over** to fall over उलटना

**keen** /kiːn कीन्/ *adj.* **1 keen (to do sth/that...)** very interested in sth; wanting to do sth किसी बात में बहुत रुचि रखने वाला; कुछ करने का इच्छुक, लालायित, उत्सुक *They are both keen gardeners.* ○ *I failed the first time but I'm keen to try again.* **2** (used about one of the senses, a feeling, etc.) good or strong (इंद्रियानुभूति, मनोभाव आदि) अच्छा या पुख़्ता, पैना, तीक्ष्ण *Foxes have a keen sense of smell.*

IDM **keen on sb/sth** very interested in or having a strong desire for sb/sth किसी व्यक्ति या वस्तु में बहुत रुचि रखने वाला या उसके लिए बहुत लालायित या उत्सुक *He's very keen on jazz.* ▶ **keenly** *adv.* उत्सुकता से ▶ **keenness** *noun* [U] उत्सुकता

**keep[1]** /ki:p कीप्/ *verb* (*pt, pp* **kept** /kept केप्ट्/) **1** [I] to continue to be in a particular state or position किसी विशेष अवस्था या स्थिति में बने रहना *You must keep warm.* ○ *I still keep in touch with my old school friends.* **2** [T] to make sb/sth stay in a particular state, place or condition किसी व्यक्ति या वस्तु को विशेष स्थिति, स्थान या दशा में बनाए रखना *Please keep this door closed.* ○ *I'm sorry to keep you waiting.* **3** [T] to continue to have sth; to save sth for sb किसी वस्तु को रखे रहना; किसी वस्तु को बचाए या सुरक्षित रखना *You can keep that book—I don't need it any more.* ○ *Can you keep my seat for me till I get back?* **4** [T] to have sth in a particular place किसी वस्तु को किसी विशेष स्थान पर रखना *Where do you keep the matches?* ○ *Keep your passport in a safe place.* **5** [T] **keep doing sth** to continue doing sth or to repeat an action many times किसी काम को करते रहना या बार-बार करना *Keep going until you get to the church and then turn left.* ○ *She keeps asking me silly questions.* **6** [T] to do what you promised or arranged वचनबद्धता या पूर्व-आयोजित कार्यक्रम को निभाना *Can you keep a promise?* ○ *to keep a secret* (= not tell it to anyone) **7** [T] to write down sth that you want to remember याद रखने योग्य बातों को लिख लेना *Keep a record of how much you spend.* ○ *to keep a diary* **8** [I] (used about food) to stay fresh (खाद्य और पेय पदार्थ) ताज़ा बना रहना, ख़राब न होना *Drink up all the milk—it won't keep in this weather.* **9** [T] to support sb with your money धन से किसी का भरण-पोषण करना *You can't keep a family on the money I earn.* **10** [T] to have and look after animals पशुओं को रखना और उनकी देखभाल करना *They keep ducks on their farm.* **11** [T] to delay sb/sth; to prevent sb from leaving किसी व्यक्ति या वस्तु को रोके रखना; किसी व्यक्ति को जाने न देना *Where's the doctor? What's keeping him?*

IDM **keep it up** to continue doing sth as well as you are doing it now किसी काम को इसी प्रकार आगे भी अच्छे ढंग से करते रहना

> NOTE **Keep** वाली अभिव्यक्तियों के लिए संबंधित संज्ञाओं और विशेषणों की प्रविष्टियाँ देखिए, जैसे **keep count** की प्रविष्टि **count** में मिलेगी।

PHR V **keep at it/sth** to continue to work on/at sth किसी काम को करते रहना *Keep at it—we should be finished soon.*

**keep away from sb/sth** to not go near sb/sth किसी व्यक्ति या वस्तु के पास न जाना; से दूर रहना *Keep away from the town centre this weekend.*

**keep sb/sth back** to prevent sb/sth from moving forwards किसी व्यक्ति या वस्तु को आगे न बढ़ने देना *The police tried to keep the crowd back.*

**keep sth back (from sb)** to refuse to tell sb sth किसी को कुछ न बताना; से कुछ छिपाना *I know he's keeping something back; he knows much more than he says.*

**keep sth down** to make sth stay at a low level, to stop sth increasing किसी वस्तु को नीचे के स्तर पर रखना; बढ़ने से रोकना *Keep your voice down.*

**keep sb from sth/from doing sth** to prevent sb from doing sth किसी को कोई काम न करने देना

**keep sth from sb** to refuse to tell sb sth किसी से कोई बात छिपाना

**keep your mouth shut** ➪ **mouth[1]** देखिए।

**keep off sth** to not go near or on sth किसी वस्तु से दूर रहना *Keep off the grass!*

**keep sth off (sb/sth)** to stop sth touching or going on sb/sth किसी व्यक्ति या वस्तु को कुछ छूने या कहीं पहुँचने न देना *I'm trying to keep the flies off the food.*

**keep on (doing sth)** to continue doing sth or to repeat an action many times, especially in an annoying way किसी काम को करते रहना या बार-बार करना (विशेषतः दूसरे को खिझाते हुए) *He keeps on interrupting me.*

**keep on (at sb) (about sb/sth)** to continue talking to sb in an annoying or complaining way खिझाने वाले या शिकायती लहज़े में किसी से कुछ कहते रहना *She kept on at me about my homework until I did it.*

**keep (sb/sth) out (of sth)** to not enter sth; to stop sb/sth entering sth प्रवेश न करना; प्रवेश न करने देना *They put up a fence to keep people out of their garden.*

**keep to sth** to not leave sth; to do sth in the usual, agreed or expected way को न छोड़ना; के साथ बने रहना; किसी काम को अपेक्षित ढंग से करते रहना *Keep to the path!* ○ *He didn't keep to our agreement.*

**keep sth to/at sth** to not allow sth to rise above a particular level किसी वस्तु को स्तर-विशेष से ऊँचा न जाने देना या स्तर-विशेष पर बनाए रखना *We're trying to keep costs to a minimum.*

**keep sth up 1** to prevent sth from falling down किसी वस्तु को गिरने न देना **2** to make sth stay at a high level किसी वस्तु को ऊँचे स्तर पर बनाए रखना *We want to keep up standards of education.* **3** to continue doing sth किसी काम को करते रहना

**keep up (with sb)** to move at the same speed as sb दूसरे की चाल के साथ बने रहना या दूसरे के बराबर चाल बनाए रखना *Can't you walk a bit slower? I can't keep up.*

**keep up (with sth)** to know about what is happening घटती घटनाओं के बारे में जानते रहना *You have to read the latest magazines if you want to keep up.*

**keep**[2] /ki:p कीप्/ *noun* [U] food, clothes and the other things that you need to live; the cost of these things जीवन यापन की सामग्री (भोजन, कपड़े आदि); इन वस्तुओं की लागत

IDM **for keeps** (*informal*) for always हमेशा के लिए *Take it. It's yours for keeps.*

**keeper** /ˈki:pə(r)ˈकीप(र्)/ *noun* [C] **1** a person who guards or looks after sth किसी वस्तु की रक्षा या देखभाल करने वाला व्यक्ति; रखवाला, रक्षक *a zoo-keeper* **2** (*informal*) = **goalkeeper**

**keeping** /ˈki:pɪŋˈकीपिङ्/ *noun*

IDM **in/out of keeping (with sth)** **1** that does/does not look good with sth (किसी के साथ) मेल खाते हुए या बेमेल *That modern table is out of keeping with the style of the room.* **2** in/not in agreement with a rule, belief, etc. नियम, विश्वास आदि के साथ संगत या असंगत *The Council's decision is in keeping with government policy.*

**keg** /keg केग्/ *noun* [C] a round metal or wooden container, used especially for storing beer बियर भर कर रखने का धातु या लकड़ी का गोल पीपा

**kelvin** /ˈkelvɪnˈकेल्विन्/ *noun* [C, U] (*abbr.* **K**) (*technical*) a unit for measuring temperature ताप मापने की इकाई; केल्विन NOTE एक डिग्री **kelvin** एक डिग्री **Celsius** के बराबर होता है। शून्य केल्विन **absolute zero** है।

**kendra** *noun* [C] (*IndE*) a centre for some activity (research, study, business, art, etc.) किसी गतिविधि (अध्ययन, पढ़ाई, व्यापार, कला आदि) का केंद्र *Doordarshan Kendra ○ Sunder Kala Kendra*

**kennel** /ˈkenlˈकेन्ल्/ *noun* [C] a small house for a dog छोटा कुत्ताघ, कुक्कुरशाला

**kept** ➪ **keep**[1] का past tense और past participle रूप।

**kerb** (*AmE* **curb**) /kɜ:b कब्/ *noun* [C] the edge of the path (**the pavement**) along the sides of a road सड़क के दोनों तरफ बने फुटपाथ का किनारा *They stood on the kerb waiting to cross the road.*

**kernel** /ˈkɜ:nl ˈकनल्/ *noun* [C] the inner part of a nut or seed गिरी या बीज का अंदरूनी हिस्सा

**kerosene** /ˈkerəsi:nˈकेरसीन्/ (*AmE*) = **paraffin**

**ketchup** /ˈketʃəpˈकेचप्/ *noun* [U] a cold sauce made from soft red fruit (**tomatoes**) that is eaten with hot or cold food टमाटर की चटनी; केचप

**kettle** /ˈketlˈकेट्ल्/ *noun* [C] a container with a lid, used for boiling water पानी उबालने की केतली *an electric kettle*

**key**[1] /ki: की/ *noun* [C] **1** a metal object that is used for locking a door, starting a car, etc. चाबी *Have you seen my car keys anywhere? ○ We need a spare key to the front door. ○ a bunch of keys* **2** [*usually sing.*] **the key (to sth)** something that helps you achieve or understand sth कुछ प्राप्त करने या समझने में सहायक कोई वस्तु; कुंजी *A good education is the key to success.* **3** one of the parts of a piano, computer, etc. that you press with your fingers to make it work पियानो, कंप्यूटर आदि की कुंजी या की (जिसे दबाकर उन्हें चलाया जाता है) **4** a set of musical notes that is based on one particular note स्वर-विशेष पर आधारित स्वर माला *The concerto is in the key of A minor.* **5** a set of answers to exercises or problems अभ्यासमाला या प्रश्नमाला के उत्तर; कुंजी *an answer key* **6** a list of the symbols and signs used in a map or book, showing what they mean पुस्तक या मानचित्र (नक़्शे) में दिए गए चिह्नों और संकेतों की सूची (उनका अर्थ बताते हुए)

IDM **under lock and key** ➪ **lock**[2] देखिए।

**key**[2] /ki: की/ *verb* [T] **key sth (in)** to put information into a computer or give it an instruction by typing कंप्यूटर में कोई सूचना भरना या टाइप करके उसे निर्देश देना *Have you keyed that report yet? ○ First, key in your password.*

**key**[3] /ki: की/ *adj.* (*only before a noun*) very important अत्यंत महत्त्वपूर्ण *Tourism is a key industry in Rajasthan.*

**keyboard** /ˈki:bɔ:dˈकीबॉड्/ *noun* [C] **1** the set of keys on a piano, computer, etc. पियानो, कंप्यूटर आदि का कुंजीपटल; कीबोर्ड **2** an electrical musical instrument like a small piano छोटे पियानो जैसा विद्युत-चलित वाद्य ➪ 789 पर चित्र देखिए।

**keyhole** /ˈki:həʊlˈकीहोल्/ *noun* [C] the hole in a lock where you put the key ताले का मुहँ या छेद, कुंजी खाँचा

**keynote** /ˈki:nəʊtˈकीनोट्/ *noun* [C] **1** (*usually sing.*) the central idea of a book, a speech, etc. (पुस्तक, भाषण आदि का) मुख्य विचार *This particular issue is the keynote of the election campaign this year. ○ a keynote speech/speaker* (= a very important one, introducing a meeting or its sub-

ject) किसी सभा या उसके विषय का परिचय देने वाला अत्यंत महत्त्वपूर्ण वक्ता या भाषण **2** the note on which a **key** is based कुंजीपटल की कुंजी का स्वर

**key ring** *noun* [C] a ring on which you keep keys चाबियों का छल्ला, की रिंग

**keyword** /ˈkiːwɜːd ˈकीवड्/ *noun* [C] **1** a word that tells you about the main idea or subject of sth मुख्य धारणा या विषयवस्तु का सूचक शब्द *When you're studying a language, the keyword is patience.* **2** a word or phrase that is used to give an instruction to a computer कंप्यूटर को निर्देश देने वाला शब्द, कंप्यूटर निर्देशक शब्द

**kg** *abbr.* kilogram(s) किलोग्राम *weight 10 kg*

**khadi** (*also* **khaddar**) *noun* [U] (in India) a cloth that is hand-woven and is made from a kind of cotton or silk thread made on a spinning wheel (भारत में) खादी का कपड़ा *curtains made of khadi* ▶**khadi** *adj.* खादी से बना *khadi shirt*

**khaki**[1] *adj.* of a pale brownish-yellow colour ख़ाकी रंग का *a khaki uniform*

**khaki**[2] *noun* [U] **1** a pale brownish-yellow colour ख़ाकी (रंग) *His uniform is khaki in colour.* **2** a strong brownish-yellow cloth, especially used for making military uniforms ख़ाकी कपड़ा, विशेषतः सैनिक पोशाक के लिए

**kharif** *noun* [U] (in India) a crop sown in early summer to be harvested in autumn or at the beginning of winter ख़रीफ़ *Crops like rice, maize, bajra, etc. are kharif.* ▶ **kharif** *adj.* ख़रीफ़ी *kharif crops/season*

**kHz** *abbr.* kilohertz; (used in radio) a measure of **frequency** किलोहर्टज़; यह रेडियो तरंगो की फ्रीक्वेंसी मापने की इकाई है

**kick**[1] /kɪk किक्/ *verb* **1** [T] to hit or move sb/sth with your foot पैर से किसी व्यक्ति या वस्तु को ठोकर मारना *He kicked the ball wide of the net.* ○ *The police kicked the door down.* **2** [I, T] to move your foot or feet पैर या पैरों को चलाना या मारना *You must kick harder if you want to swim faster.*

IDM **kick the habit** to stop doing sth harmful that you have done for a long time पुरानी हानिकारक आदत को छोड़ना

**kick yourself** to be annoyed with yourself because you have done sth stupid, missed an opportunity, etc. अपने ऊपर, अपनी मूर्खता, विफलता आदि पर नाराज़ होना

**make, kick up, etc. a fuss** ➪ **fuss**[1] देखिए।

PHR V **kick off** to start a game of football फ़ुटबॉल का खेल शुरू करना

**kick sb out (of sth)** (*informal*) to force sb to leave a place किसी को कहीं से निकाल बाहर करना *to be kicked out of university*

**kick**[2] /kɪk किक्/ *noun* [C] **1** an act of kicking ठोकर या लात मारने की क्रिया; पादप्रहार *She gave the door a kick and it closed.* **2** (*informal*) a feeling of great pleasure, excitement, etc. अत्यधिक प्रसन्नता, रोमांच आदि का भाव *He seems to* ***get a real kick out of*** *driving fast.*

**kick-off** *noun* [C] the start of a game of football फ़ुटबॉल खेल का आरंभ *The kick-off is at 2.30 p.m.*

**kick-start**[1] *verb* [T] **1** to start a motorbike by pushing down on one of the controls with your foot पैर से एक पुरज़े को नीचे दबाकर मोटरसाइकिल चालू करना; किक लगाकर मोटरसाइकिल चालू करना **2** to do sth to help a process or project start more quickly किसी प्रक्रिया या परियोजना को विशेष प्रयत्न के द्वारा अधिक जल्दी शुरू करना

**kick-start**[2] *noun* [C] **1** (*also* **kick-starter**) the part of a motorbike that you push down with your foot in order to start it वह पुरज़ा जिसे किक लगाकर मोटर-साइकिल चालू की जाती है **2** a quick start that you give to sth by taking some action विशेष प्रयत्न द्वारा किसी काम का तेज़ी से आरंभ

**kid**[1] /kɪd किड्/ *noun* **1** [C] (*informal*) a child or young person बच्चा या किशोर *How are your kids?* **2** [C] **kid brother/sister** (*AmE informal*) younger brother/sister छोटा भाई या बहन **3** [C] a young **goat** बकरी का बच्चा; मेमना **4** [U] soft leather made from the skin of a young **goat** मेमने की खाल से बना नरम चमड़ा

**kid**[2] /kɪd किड्/ *verb* [I,T] (**ki<u>dd</u>ing; ki<u>dd</u>ed**) (*informal*) to trick sb/yourself by saying sth that is not true; to make a joke about sth असत्य बात कहकर धोखा या झाँसा देना; किसी को मज़ाक का पात्र बनाना *I didn't mean it. I was only kidding.*

**kiddy** (*also* **kiddie**) /ˈkɪdi ˈकिडि/ *noun* [C] (*pl.* **kiddies**) (*informal*) a child बच्चा

**kidnap** /ˈkɪdnæp ˈकिड्नैप्/ *verb* [T] (**kidna<u>pp</u>ing; kidna<u>pp</u>ed**) to take sb away by force and demand money for his/her safe return किसी का अपहरण करना उसे सुरक्षित छोड़ने के लिए पैसा माँगना, फिरौती माँगना *The child was kidnapped and a ransom of Rs 50,000 was demanded for her release.* ➪ **hijack** देखिए। ▶ **kidnapper** *noun* [C] अपहरणकर्ता, अपहर्ता *The kidnappers demanded Rs 50,000.* ▶ **kidnapping** *noun* [C, U] अपहरण (की क्रिया)

**kidney** /ˈkɪdni ˈकिड्नि / *noun* **1** [C] one of the two organs in the abdomen that separate waste liquid from your blood गुरदा-वृक्क (जो रक्त का शोधन करता है) ➪ **body** पर चित्र देखिए। **2** [U, C] the kidneys of an animal when they are cooked and eaten as food किसी पशु के गुरदे (जिन्हें पका कर खाया जाता है) *steak and kidney pie* ➪ **renal** adjective देखिए।

**kidney bean** *noun* [C] a type of reddish-brown bean, shaped like a **kidney** गुरदे के शकल की लाल-भूरी सेम

**kill**[1] /kɪl किल् / *verb* **1** [I, T] to make sb/sth die किसी को मारना, किसी का मारा जाना *Smoking kills.* ○ *She was killed instantly in the crash.*

> NOTE **Murder** का अर्थ है किसी विशेष कारण से किसी व्यक्ति को मारना—*This was no accident. The old lady was murdered.* **Assassinate** का अर्थ है राजनीतिक कारणों से किसी की हत्या करना—*Gandhiji was assassinated.* **Slaughter** और **massacre** का अर्थ है बड़ी संख्या में लोगों को मारना—*Hundreds of people were massacred when the army opened fire on the crowd.* खाने के लिए पशु को मारने के अर्थ में भी **slaughter** का प्रयोग किया जाता है।

**2** [T] (*informal*) to cause sb pain; to hurt किसी को तकलीफ़ पहुँचाना; दर्द करना, चोट खा जाना *My feet are killing me.* **3** [T] to cause sth to end or fail किसी वस्तु को नष्ट या विफल करवाना *The minister's opposition killed the idea stone dead.* **4** [T] (*spoken*) to be very angry with sb किसी व्यक्ति पर बहुत क्रुद्ध होना *My mum will kill me when she sees this mess.* **5** [T] (*informal*) **kill yourself/sb** to make yourself/sb laugh a lot स्वयं को या किसी और को ख़ूब हँसाना *We were* ***killing ourselves laughing.***

IDM **kill time, an hour, etc.** to spend time doing sth that is not interesting or important while you are waiting for sth else to happen किसी बात की प्रतीक्षा में जैसे-तैसे समय गुज़ारना

**kill two birds with one stone** to do one thing which will achieve two results ऐसा एक काम करना जिसके दो नतीजे निकलें; एक पंथ दो काज करना

PHRV **kill sth off** to cause sth to die or to not exist any more किसी को मार देना, ख़त्म कर देना

**kill**[2] /kɪl किल् / *noun* [*sing.*] **1** the act of killing मारने की क्रिया *Lions often make a kill in the evening.* **2** an animal or animals that have been killed मारा गया प्राणी; मारे गए प्राणी *The eagle took the kill back to its young.*

**killer** /ˈkɪlə(r) ˈकिल(र्) / *noun* [C] a person, animal or thing that kills मारने या हत्या करने वाला व्यक्ति, पशु या कोई वस्तु; हत्यारा, घातक *a killer disease* ○ *He's a dangerous killer who may strike again.*

**killing** /ˈkɪlɪŋ ˈकिलिङ् / *noun* [C] act of killing a person on purpose; a murder कारण-विशेष से किसी व्यक्ति की हत्या *There have been a number of brutal killings in the area recently.*

IDM **make a killing** to make a large profit quickly जल्दी बड़ा लाभ या मुनाफ़ा कमाना

**kiln** /kɪln किल्न्/ *noun* [C] a large oven for baking clay and bricks, drying wood and grain etc. मिट्टी या ईंटें पकाने, लकड़ी और अनाज सुखाने आदि की बड़ी भट्ठी

**kilo** /ˈkiːləʊ ˈकीलो / (*also* **kilogram; kilogramme**) /ˈkɪləɡræm ˈकिलग्रैम् /)*noun* [C] (*pl.* **kilos**) (*abbr.* **kg**) a measure of weight; 1000 grams भार मापने की एक इकाई, किलो, किलोग्राम; एक हज़ार ग्राम

**kilo-** /ˈkɪləʊ ˈकिलो / (*used in nouns, often in units of measurement*) one thousand (प्रायः मापसूचक संज्ञाओं में प्रयुक्त) एक हज़ार, किलो- *kilometre* ○ *kilogram*

**kilohertz** /ˈkɪləhɜːts ˈकिलहर्ट्स् / *noun* [C] (*pl.* **kilohertz**) (*abbr.* **kHz**) (used in radio) a measure of **frequency** (रेडियो में) फ्रीक्वेंसी की एक माप; किलोहर्ट्ज़

**kilojoule** /ˈkɪlədʒuːl ˈकिलजूल् / *noun* [C] (*abbr.* **kJ**) a measurement of the energy that you get from food; 1000 **joules** भोजन से प्राप्त उर्जा की माप की एक इकाई; एक हज़ार जूल

**kilometre** (*AmE* **kilometer**) /ˈkɪləmiːtə(r); kɪˈlɒmɪtə(r) ˈकिलमीट(र्); किˈलॉमिट(र्) / *noun* [C] (*abbr.* **km**) a measure of length; 1000 metres लंबाई की एक माप; एक हज़ार मीटर; किलोमीटर

**kilowatt** /ˈkɪləwɒt ˈकिलवॉट् / *noun* [C] (*abbr.* **kW**) a unit for measuring electrical power; 1000 **watts** विद्युत शक्ति को मापने की इकाई; एक हज़ार वाट

**kilt** /kɪlt किल्ट् / *noun* [C] a skirt with many folds (**pleats**) that is worn by men as part of the national dress of Scotland चुन्नटों वाली स्कर्ट जो स्कॉटलैंड के पुरुषों की राष्ट्रीय पोशाक है

**kimono** /kɪˈməʊnəʊ किˈमोनो / *noun* [C] (*pl.* **kimonos**) a traditional Japanese piece of clothing like a long dress with wide sleeves, worn on formal occasions जापानियों की चौड़े आस्तीनों वाली लंबी पारंपरिक पोशाक जिसे वे विशिष्ट अवसरों पर पहनते हैं

**kin** /kɪn किन् / ➪ **next of kin** देखिए।

**kind**[1] /kaɪnd काइन्ड् / *noun* [C] a group whose members all have the same qualities समान गुणों वाले सदस्यों का वर्ग, प्रकार ***people of all kinds*** ○ *The concert attracted* ***all kinds of*** *people.* ○ ***What kind of*** *car have you got?* ✪ पर्याय **sort** या **type**

**NOTE** याद रखिए, **kind** गणनीय शब्द है इसलिए—*Those kind of dogs are really dangerous.* या *I like all kind of music.* मान्य नहीं है। मान्य प्रयोग है—*That kind of dog is really dangerous./Those kinds of dogs are really dangerous.* और *I like all kinds of music*. **Kinds of** के बाद एकवचनांत संज्ञा (singular noun) या बहुवचनांत संज्ञा (plural noun) आ सकती है—*There are so many kinds of camera/cameras on the market that it's hard to know which is best.*

**IDM a kind of** (*informal*) used for describing sth in a way that is not very clear अस्पष्ट-सी बात का संकेत या करने के लिए प्रयुक्त वर्णन; एक प्रकार का, की, के *I had a kind of feeling that something would go wrong.* ○ *There's a funny kind of smell in here.*

**kind of** (*informal*) slightly; a little bit हलका-सा; थोड़ा-सा *I'm kind of worried about the interview.*

**of a kind 1** the same उसी तरह का या के, एक जैसा या जैसे *The friends were two of a kind—very similar in so many ways.* **2** not as good as it could be इतना अच्छा नहीं जितना हो सकता है; ख़ास नहीं *You're making progress of a kind.*

**kind[2]** /kaɪnd काइन्ड्/ *adj.* **kind (to sb); kind (of sb) (to do sth)** caring about others; friendly and generous परोपकारी; मित्रवत और उदार *Everyone's been so kind to us since we came here!* ○ *It was kind of you to offer, but I don't need any help.* ✪ विलोम **unkind**

**kindergarten** /ˈkɪndəgɑːtn ˈकिन्डगाटन्/ *noun* [C] a school for very young children, aged from about 3 to 5 तीन से पाँच वर्ष की आयु के बच्चों का स्कूल; किंडरगार्टन ➪ **nursery school** देखिए।

**kind-hearted** *adj.* kind and generous दयालु और उदार

**kindle** /ˈkɪndl ˈकिन्ड्ल्/ *verb* [I, T] (*formal*) **1** to start a fire or to make something start to burn सुलगाना या जलाना *to kindle a fire* **2** to make sth, such as an interest, emotion, feeling, start to grow in sb or to get sth started इच्छा, भावनाओं आदि को किसी व्यक्ति में उत्पन्न करना या कुछ शुरू करना *It was her friends who kindled her interest in reading.*

**kindling** /ˈkɪndlɪŋ ˈकिन्ड्लिङ्/ *noun* [U] thin small pieces of wood used for starting a fire आग सुलगाने की लकड़ियाँ

**kindly** /ˈkaɪndli ˈकाइन्ड्लि/ *adv, adj.* **1** in a kind way दयाभाव से, अनुग्रहपूर्वक *The nurse smiled kindly.* **2** (used for asking sb to do sth) please (किसी को कुछ करने हेतु कहने के लिए प्रयुक्त) कृपा करके, कृपापूर्वक *Would you kindly wait a moment?* **3** kind and friendly दयालु और मित्रवत

**kindness** /ˈkaɪndnəs ˈकाइन्ड्नस्/ *noun* [C, U] the quality of being kind; a kind act दयालुता; दयामय कार्य *Thank you very much for all your kindness.*

**kinetic** /kɪˈnetɪk किˈनेटिक्/ *adj.* of or produced by movement गति-विषयक या गतिक; गति-उत्पादित या गतिज गति से संबंधित, गति से उत्पादित *kinetic energy*

**king** /kɪŋ किङ्/ *noun* [C] **1** (the title of) a man who rules a country. A king is usually the son or close relative of the former ruler (किसी देश का) राजा, राजा की उपाधि, पूर्वशासक या उसके निकट संबंधी का पुत्र प्रायः राजा बनता है *The new king was crowned yesterday.* ○ *King Ashoka* ○ (*figurative*) *The lion is the king of the jungle.* ➪ **queen, prince** और **princess** देखिए। **2** one of the four playing cards in a pack with a picture of a king ताश के पत्तों में बादशाह *the king of spades* ➪ **card** पर नोट देखिए। **3** the most important piece in the game of **chess** that can move one square in any direction शतरंज के खेल में बादशाह का मोहरा

**kingdom** /ˈkɪŋdəm ˈकिङ्डम्/ *noun* [C] **1** a country that is ruled by a king or queen राजा या रानी द्वारा शासित देश; राज्य *the United Kingdom* **2** (*technical*) one of the three traditional divisions of the natural world, larger than a **class** or a **phylum** प्रकृति-जगत के तीन पारंपरिक विभाजनों में से एक (जो 'क्लास' या 'फ़ाइलम' से बड़ा होता है) किंगडम, जगत *the animal kingdom*

**kingfisher** /ˈkɪŋfɪʃə(r) ˈकिङ्फ़िश(र्)/ *noun* [C] a small bright blue bird with a long beak, that catches fish in rivers लंबी चोंच वाला छोटा चमकीला नीला पक्षी(जो नदियों से मछली पकड़ता है); कौड़िल्ला, किंगफ़िशर

**king prawn** *noun* [C] a small shellfish that we eat and that becomes pink when cooked खाने की छोटी शंखमीन (जो पकने पर गुलाबी रंग की हो जाती है), बड़ी झींगा मछली, शाहीझींगा **NOTE** शाहीझींगा साधारण झींगा से बड़ी होती है।

**king-size** (*also* **king-sized**) *adj.* bigger than usual सामान्य से बड़ा, शाही *a king-size bed*

**kink** /kɪŋk किङ्क्/ *noun* [C] a turn or bend in sth that should be straight (रस्सी आदि सीधी वस्तुओं में) ऐंठन या बल

**kinship** /ˈkɪnʃɪp ˈकिन्शिप्/ *noun* (*literary*) **1** [U] the relationship between the members of the same family सगोत्रता *the ties of kinship* **2** [U, *sing.*] a feeling of being close to sb because you have similar attitudes or characteristics समान प्रवृति या व्यवहार के कारण बँधुता *They felt a kinship with the local peasants.*

**kiosk** /ˈkiːɒsk ˈकीऑस्क्/ *noun* [C] a very small shop or stall in the street where newspapers, sweets, cigarettes, etc. are sold सड़क पर बनी बहुत छोटी दुकान जहाँ अख़बार, मिठाइयाँ आदि बिकती है; गुमटी, स्टॉल

**kipper** /ˈkɪpə(r) ˈकिप(र्)/ *noun* [C] a type of fish that has been kept for a long time in salt, and then smoked एक प्रकार की मछली जिसे देर तक नमक में लपेट कर रखा जाता है और फिर धुँआरा जाता है

**kiss** /kɪs किस्/ *verb* [I, T] to touch sb with your lips to show love or friendship चूमना, चुंबन करना *He kissed her on the cheek.* ○ *They kissed each other goodbye.* ▶ **kiss** *noun* [C] चुंबन *a kiss on the lips/cheek*

**kit¹** /kɪt किट्/ *noun* **1** [C, U] a set of tools, equipment or clothes that you need for a particular purpose, sport or activity प्रयोजन-विशेष, खेल या किसी गतिविधि के लिए अपेक्षित औज़ारों, उपकरणों या कपड़ों का सेट; किट, उपकरण-समूह *a tool kit* ○ *a drum kit* ○ *football/gym kit* **2** [C] a set of parts that you buy and put together in order to make sth वस्तुएँ बनाने में प्रयुक्त पुरज़ों का बंडल, किट *a kit for a model aeroplane*

**kit²** /kɪt किट्/ *verb* (**kitting; kitted**)

**PHR V** **kit sb/yourself out/up (in/with sth)** to give sb all the necessary clothes, equipment, tools, etc. for sth किसी काम के लिए किसी व्यक्ति को सभी आवश्यक कपड़े, उपकरण आदि देना

**kitchen** /ˈkɪtʃɪn ˈकिचिन्/ *noun* [C] a room where food is prepared and cooked रसोई, रसोई-घर *We usually eat in the kitchen.*

**kite¹** /kaɪt काइट्/ *noun* [C] a toy which consists of a light frame covered with paper or cloth. Kites are flown in the wind on the end of a long piece of string पतंग, गुड्डी *to fly a kite*

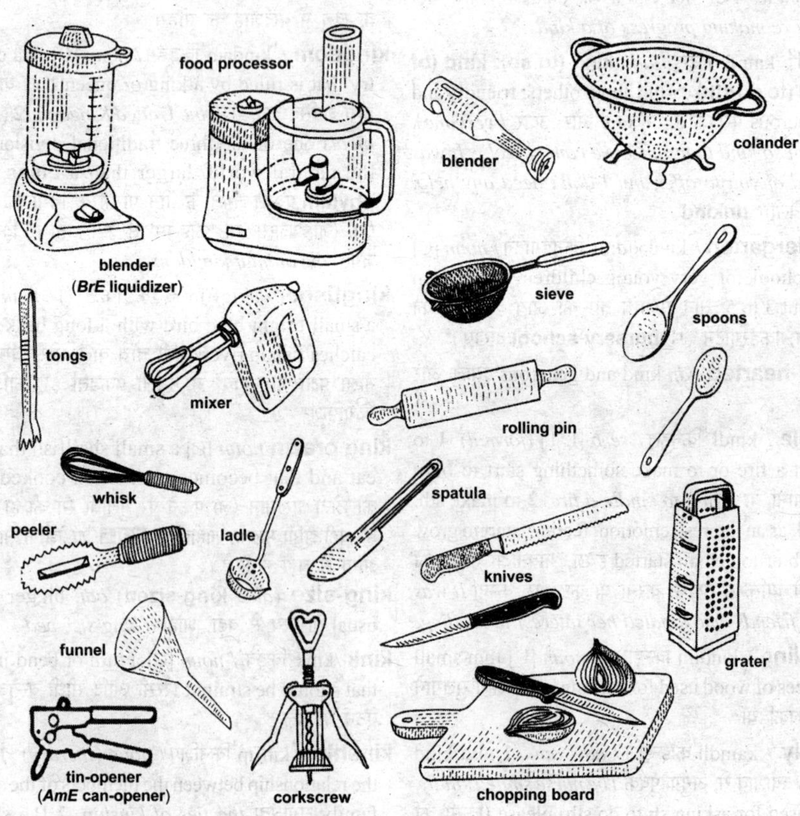


kitchen utensils

**kite**[2] /kaɪt काइट्/ *noun* [C] a large powerful bird (of the hawk family) with strong wings that kills other birds and small animals for food चील

**kith** /kɪθ किथ्/ *noun*

IDM **kith and kin** (*old-fashioned*) people with whom you are connected like friends and relatives मित्र, निकट संबंधी, रिश्तेदार

**kitten** /ˈkɪtn ˈकिट्न्/ *noun* [C] a young cat बिल्ली का बच्चा; बिलौटा

**kitty** /ˈkɪti ˈकिटि/ *noun* [C] (*pl*. **kitties**) **1** a sum of money that is collected from a group of people and used for a particular purpose विशेष प्रयोजन के लिए लोगों से इकट्ठा किया हुआ पैसा; जमा साँझा धन *All the students in the flat put Rs 50 a week into the kitty.* **2** (*spoken*) a way of calling or referring to a cat बिल्ली के लिए सामान्य शब्द या उसे (प्यार से) बुलाने का नाम; किट्टी

**kiwi** /ˈki:wi: ˈकीवी/ *noun* [C] (*pl*. **kiwis**) **1** a New Zealand bird with a long beak and short wings that cannot fly लंबी चोंच और छोटे डैनों वाला न्यू ज़ीलैंड का एक पक्षी जो उड़ नहीं सकता; कीवी **2 kiwi fruit** a fruit with brown skin that is green inside with black seeds अंदर से हरा और भूरे छिलके वाला एक फल जिसके बीज काले होते हैं; कीवी फल

**kJ** *abbr*. kilojoule(s) किलोजूल

**km** *abbr*. kilometre(s) किलोमिटर

**knack** /næk नैक्/ *noun* [*sing*.] (*informal*) **knack (of/for doing sth)** skill or ability to do sth (difficult) that you have naturally or you can learn कोई (कठिन) काम करने की नैसर्गिक या अर्जित कुशलता या योग्यता *Knitting isn't difficult once you've got the knack of it.*

**knapsack** /ˈnæpsæk ˈनैप्सैक्/ *noun* [C] a small **rucksack**-like bag with straps that is usually carried on the back or on the shoulders पट्टे वाला झोला या बोरा जिसे पीठ या कंधों पर बाँधा जा सकता है; नैपसैक

**knead** /ni:d नीड्/ *verb* [T] to press and squeeze a mixture of flour and water (**dough**) with your hands in order to make bread, etc. रोटी आदि बनाने के लिए हाथों से आटा गूँधना

**knee** /ni: नी/ *noun* [C] **1** the place where your leg bends in the middle घुटना *Anjali fell and grazed her knee.* ○ *She was **on her hands and knees** on the floor looking for her earrings.* ➪ **body** पर चित्र देखिए। **2** the part of a pair of trousers, etc. that covers the knee पतलून का वह हिस्सा जो घुटनों पर आता है; पतलून का घुटना *There's a hole in the knee of those jeans.*

IDM **bring sth to its knees** to badly affect an organization, etc. so that it can no longer function किसी संगठन को नाकाम बना देना *The strikes brought the industry to its knees.*

**kneecap** /ˈni:kæp ˈनीकैप्/ *noun* [C] the bone that covers the front of the knee घुटने के सामने के हिस्से की हड्डी, चपनी; जानु-फलक ✪ पर्याय **patella** ➪ **body** पर चित्र देखिए।

**knee-deep** *adj., adv.* up to your knees घुटनों तक गहरा, घुटनों-भर *The water was knee-deep in places.*

**kneel** /ni:l नील्/ *verb* [I] (*pt, pp* **knelt** /nelt नेल्ट्/ or **kneeled**) **kneel (down)** to rest on one or both knees एक या दोनों घुटनों के बल टिकना या बैठना *She knelt down to talk to the child.*

**knew** ➪ **know**[1] का past tense रूप

**knickers** /ˈnɪkəz ˈनिकज़्/ (*AmE* **panties**) *noun* [*pl*.] a piece of underwear for women that covers the area between the waist and the top of the legs महिलाओं की जाँघिया *a pair of knickers*

**knife**[1] /naɪf नाइफ़्/ *noun* [C] (*pl*. **knives** /naɪvz नाइव़्ज़्/) a sharp flat piece of metal (**a blade**) with a handle. A knife is used for cutting things or as a weapon चाक़ू, छुरी, छुरा *The carving knife is very blunt/sharp.* ○ *a knife and fork*

**knife**[2] /naɪf नाइफ़्/ *verb* [T] to deliberately injure sb with a knife किसी को जान-बूझकर चाक़ू मारना या घोंपना ✪ पर्याय **stab**

**knight** /naɪt नाइट्/ *noun* [C] **1** (*especially in Britain*) a person who has been given a title of honour by a king or queen for good work he/she has done and who can use *Sir/Dame* in front of his/her name श्रेष्ठ काम के लिए राजा या रानी द्वारा *Sir/Dame* की उपाधि से सम्मानित पुरुष या महिला (जो इस उपाधि का अपने नाम से पहले प्रयोग कर सकता/सकती है), नाइट *Don Bradman was knighted for his excellence in cricket.* **2** a soldier of a high level who fought on a horse in the Middle Ages 'मध्य युग' में उच्च स्तर का घुड़सवार योद्धा या सैनिक, शूरवीर **3** a piece used in the game of **chess** that is shaped like a horse's head शतरंज का घोड़ा, घोड़े के सिर की शकल का शतरंज का एक मोहरा ▸ **knighthood** ˈnaɪthʊd ˈनाइट्हुड्/ *noun* [C, U] नाइट की उपाधि

**knit** /nɪt निट्/ *verb* [I, T] (**knitting; knitted** or *AmE pt, pp* **knit**) **1** to make sth (for example an article of clothing) with wool using two long needles or a special machine सिलाइयों में या किसी विशेष मशीन से (ऊनी कपड़ा) बुनना *I'm knitting a sweater for my nephew.* ➪ **crochet** देखिए।

**2 knit** (only used in this form) joined closely together गहराई से जुड़ा हुआ, सुसंगठित (केवल इसी रूप में प्रयुक्त) *a **closely/tightly knit** village community*
▶ **knitting** *noun* [U] बुनाई (का काम) *I usually do some knitting while I'm watching TV.*

**knitting needle** = **needle**[2]

**knitwear** /ˈnɪtweə(r) ˈनिट्वेअ(र्)/ *noun* [U] articles of clothing that have been knitted बुने हुए कपड़े या परिधान *the knitwear department*

**knob** /nɒb नॉब्/ *noun* [C] **1** a round switch on a machine (for example a television) that you press or turn किसी मशीन की घुंडी, नॉब (जिसे घुमाने या दबाने से मशीन चलती है) *the volume control knob* **2** a round handle on a door, drawer, etc. दरवाज़े, दराज़ आदि की मूठ

**knock**[1] /nɒk नॉक्/ *verb* **1** [I] **knock (at/on sth)** to make a noise by hitting sth firmly with your hand हाथ से किसी वस्तु पर ज़ोर के प्रहार द्वारा अवाज़ कराना; (दरवाज़े आदि) को खटखटाना *Someone is knocking at the door.* **2** [T] **knock sth (on/against sth)** to hit sb/sth hard, often by accident किसी व्यक्ति या वस्तु को चोट पहुँचाना (प्रायः अचानक या अनजाने में) *He knocked the vase onto the floor.* ○ *to knock sb unconscious* **3** [T] (*informal*) to say bad things about sb/sth; to criticize sb/sth किसी व्यक्ति या विषय के बारे में बुरा भला कहना; किसी की निंदा करना

IDM **knock on wood** ➪ **wood** देखिए।

**knock about/around** (*informal*) to travel and live in various places जगह-जगह की यात्रा करना और वहाँ रहना *Is last week's newspaper still knocking about?*

**knock sb down** to hit sb causing him/her to fall to the ground किसी को (धक्का या घूँसा) मारकर नीचे गिरा देना *The old lady was knocked down by a cyclist.*

**knock sth down** to destroy a building, etc. किसी इमारत आदि को नष्ट कर देना *They knocked down the old factory because it was unsafe.*

**knock off (sth)** (*spoken*) to stop working काम करना बंद कर देना *What time do you knock off?*

**knock sth off** **1** (*informal*) to reduce a price by a certain amount दाम में कटौती करना *He agreed to knock Rs 10 off the price.* **2** (*slang*) to steal sth कोई वस्तु चुरा लेना

**knock sb out** **1** to hit sb so that he/she becomes unconscious or cannot get up again for a while घूँसा मारकर बेहोश कर देना या नीचे गिरा देना **2** (used about a drug, alcohol, etc.) to cause sb to sleep (नशीला पदार्थ, मद्य आदि देकर) किसी को सुला देना

**knock sb out (of sth)** to beat a person or team in a competition so that they do not play any more games in it व्यक्ति या टीम को हराकर स्पर्धा से बाहर कर देना *Sri Lanka was knocked out of the Champions Trophy by Pakistan.*

**knock sb/sth over** to cause sb/sth to fall over किसी व्यक्ति या वस्तु को गिरा देना *Be careful not to knock over the drinks.*

**knock**[2] /nɒk नॉक्/ *noun* [C] a sharp hit from sth hard or the sound it makes किसी कड़ी वस्तु से तेज़ चोट या उससे उत्पन्न आवाज़; प्रहार या खटखटाहट *a nasty knock on the head* ○ *I thought I heard a knock at the door.* ○ (*figurative*) *She has suffered some hard knocks* (= bad experiences) *in her life.*

**knocker** /ˈnɒkə(r) ˈनॉक(र्)/ *noun* [C] a piece of metal fixed to the outside of a door that you hit against the door to attract attention दरवाज़ा खटखटाने की कुंडी

**knock-on** *adj.* (*BrE*) causing other events to happen one after the other परिणामस्वरूप अन्य स्थितियों को जन्म देते हुए *An increase in the price of oil has **a knock-on effect** on other fuels.*

**knockout** /ˈnɒkaʊt ˈनॉक्आउट्/ *noun* [C] **1** a hard hit that causes sb to become unconscious or to be unable to get up again for a while किसी को बेहोश कर देने वाला या पछाड़ देने वाला प्रहार **2** (*BrE*) a competition in which the winner of each game goes on to the next part but the person who loses plays no more games निरस्तीकरण प्रतियोगिता जिसमें पराजित खिलाड़ी प्रतियोगिता से बाहर हो जाता है और विजेता अगले दौर में पहुँच जाता है; नॉकआउट

**knot**[1] /nɒt नॉट्/ *noun* [C] **1** a place where two ends or pieces of rope, string, etc. have been tied together रस्सी, डोरी आदि की गाँठ *to tie/untie a knot* **2** a measure of the speed of a ship; approximately 1.85 kilometres per hour जलपोत की चाल मापने की इकाई; लगभग 1.85 किलोमीटर प्रति घंटा

**knot**[2] /nɒt नॉट्/ *verb* [T] (**knotting; knotted**) to fasten sth together with a knot गाँठ बाँधना

**know**[1] /nəʊ नो/ *verb* (*pt* **knew** /njuː न्यू/; *pp* **known** /nəʊn नोन्/) (*not used in the continuous tenses*) **1** [I, T] **know (about sth); know that** to have knowledge or information in your mind किसी बात या व्यक्ति की जानकारी होना *I don't know much about sport.* ○ *Do you **know the way** to the restaurant?* **2** [T] to be familiar with a person or a place; to have met sb or been somewhere before किसी व्यक्ति या स्थान से परिचित होना; पहले किसी व्यक्ति से मिला होना या किसी स्थान पर गया होना *We've known each other for years.* ○ *I don't know this part of Guwahati.*

**NOTE** पहली बार के परिचय या किसी को देखने और उससे बात करने के प्रसंग में **meet** क्रिया का प्रयोग किया जाता है—*Peter and I met at university in 1997.* मिलने के बाद जब धीरे-धीरे मित्रता हो जाती है तो **get to know sb** प्रयुक्त किया जाता है—*Her sister seems very interesting. I'd like to get to know her better.* **See** और **visit** उन स्थानों के लिए प्रयोग किया जाता है जहाँ पहली बार जाते हैं—*I'd love to go to the States and see/visit San Francisco and New York.*

**3** [T, I] to feel certain; to be sure of sth निश्चित होना; विश्वस्त होना *I just know you'll pass the exam!* ○ ***As far as I know*** (= I think it is true but I am not absolutely sure), *the meeting is next Monday afternoon.* **4** [T] (*only in the past and perfect tenses*) to have seen, heard, or experienced sth (कुछ) देखा, सुना या अनुभव किया हुआ होना *I've known him go a whole day without eating.* ○ *It's been known to snow in June.* **5** [T] (*usually passive*) **know sb/sth as sth** to give sth a particular name; to recognize sb/sth as sth किसी वस्तु को कोई विशिष्ट नाम देना; किसी व्यक्ति या वस्तु को मान्यता देना या स्वीकारना *Chennai was previously known as Madras.* **6** [T] **know how to do sth** to have learned sth and be able to do कुछ सीख लेना और उसे कर पाना *Do you know how to use a computer?*

**NOTE** ध्यान रखिए! क्रिया से पहले **how to** का प्रयोग होता है। *I know use a computer*—कहना अनुचित होगा। उचित प्रयोग है—*I know how to use a computer.*

**7** [T] to have personal experience of sth किसी बात का निजी अनुभव होना *Many people in western countries don't know what it's like to be hungry.*

**NOTE** सातत्यबोधक कालों (continuous tenses) में इस क्रिया का प्रयोग नहीं होता है, परंतु वर्तमान कृदंत (present participle) (= ing form) में यह सामान्यतः प्रयुक्त होता है—*Knowing how he'd react if he found out about it, she kept quiet.*

**IDM God/goodness/Heaven knows 1** I do not know मुझे मालूम नहीं *They've ordered a new car but goodness knows how they're going to pay for it.* **2** used for emphasizing sth किसी बात पर बल देने के लिए प्रयुक्त *I hope I get an answer soon. Goodness knows, I've waited long enough.*

**know better (than that/than to do sth)** to have enough sense to realize that you should not do sth इस विषय में पर्याप्त बोध या समझ होना कि क्या नहीं करना है

**know sth inside out/like the back of your hand** (*informal*) to be very familiar with sth किसी बात से पूरी तरह से परिचित होना

**know what you are talking about** (*informal*) to have knowledge of sth from your own experience व्यक्तिगत अनुभव से कोई बात जानना

**know what's what** (*informal*) to have all the important information about sth; to fully understand sth किसी विषय में सारी आवश्यक जानकारी रखना; किसी बात को पूरी तरह समझना

**let sb know** to tell sb; to inform sb about sth किसी को कुछ बताना; किसी व्यक्ति को किसी वस्तु के विषय में सूचित करना *Could you let me know what time you're arriving?*

**you know** used when the speaker is thinking of what to say next, or to remind sb of sth वक्ता द्वारा तब प्रयुक्त जब उसे आगे की बात तुरंत न सूझे या जब किसी को कुछ याद दिलानी हो *Well, you know, it's rather difficult to explain.* ○ *I've just met Mamta. You know—Varun's sister.*

**you never know** (*spoken*) you cannot be certain आप निश्चयपूर्वक नहीं कह सकते, कहना मुश्किल है या हो सकता है *Keep those empty boxes. You never know, they might come in handy one day.*

**PHR V know of sb/sth** to have information about or experience of sb/sth किसी व्यक्ति या वस्तु के विषय में जानकारी या अनुभव होना *Do you know of any pubs around here that serve food?*

**know**[2] /nəʊ नो/ *noun*

**IDM in the know** (*informal*) having information that other people do not ऐसी बात जानना जो दूसरे न जानते हों; गोपनीय बात का जानकार

**know-all** (*AmE* **know-it-all**) *noun* [C] an annoying person who behaves as if he/she knows everything सर्वज्ञ के समान आचरण करने वाला घमंडी व्यक्ति

**know-how** *noun* [U] (*informal*) practical knowledge of or skill in sth किसी काम का व्यावहारिक ज्ञान या उसमें व्यावहारिक कुशलता

**knowing** /ˈnəʊɪŋ ˈनोइङ्/ *adj.* showing that you know about sth that is thought to be secret गोपनीय बात के जानकार होने का दिखावा करने वाला *a knowing look*

**knowingly** /ˈnəʊɪŋli ˈनोइङ्लि/ *adv* **1** on purpose; deliberately सोद्देश्य रूप से; जान-बूझ कर *I've never knowingly lied to you.* **2** in a way that shows that you know about sth that is thought to be secret गोपनीय बात के जानकार होने का दिखावा करते हुए *He smiled knowingly at her.*

**knowledge** /ˈnɒlɪdʒ ˈनॉलिज् / *noun* **1** [U, *usually sing.*] information, understanding and skills that you have gained through learning or experience शिक्षा या अनुभव से प्राप्त जानकारी, समझ और कौशल *I have* ***a working knowledge*** *of French* (= enough to be able to make myself understood). **2** [U] the state of knowing about a particular fact or situation किसी तथ्य या स्थिति-विशेष के विषय में जानकारी ***To my knowledge*** (= from the information I have, although I may not know everything) *they are still living there.* ○ *She did it* ***without my knowledge*** (= I did not know about it).

IDM **be common/public knowledge** to be sth that everyone knows ऐसी बात होना जो सबको मालूम है; सर्वविदित तथ्य

**knowledgeable** /ˈnɒlɪdʒəbl ˈनॉलिजबल् / *adj.* having a lot of knowledge बहुत कुछ जानने वाला, बहुज्ञ, सुविज्ञ *She's very knowledgeable about history.* ▶ **knowledgeably** /-əbli -अब्लि/ *adv* सुविज्ञ भाव से

**knuckle** /ˈnʌkl ˈनकल् / *noun* [C] the bones where your fingers join the rest of your hand उँगली की गाँठ (जहाँ वह हथेली से जुड़ती है); पोर ➪ **body** पर चित्र देखिए।

**koala** /kəʊˈɑːlə कोˈआला / *noun* [C] an Australian animal with thick grey fur that lives in trees and looks like a small bear घने धूसर रंग के बालों वाला भालू जैसा एक ऑस्ट्रेलियाई पशु जो पेड़ों पर रहता है; कोआला ➪ **marsupial** पर चित्र देखिए।

**koel** *noun* [C] any of the several species of **cuckoos** found in India and Australasia (प्रायः भारत एवं ऑस्ट्रेलेशिया में पाए जाने वाली पक्षी प्रजाति) कोयल

**kolam** *noun* [U, C] decorative designs drawn on the floor, traditionally with rice flour, etc. in southern India चावल के आटे आदि से बनी दक्षिण भारत की पारंपरिक रंगोली; कोलम ➪ **rangoli** देखिए।

**the Koran** (*also* **Quran, Qur'an**) *noun* [*sing.*] the **sacred** book of the Muslims इस्लाम का धर्मग्रंथ; क़ुरान

**kosher** /ˈkəʊʃə(r) ˈकोश(र्) / *adj.* (used about food) prepared according to the rules of Jewish law (भोजन) यहूदी प्रथा के अनुसार तैयार

**kph** /ˌkeɪ piːˈeɪtʃ ˌके पीˈएच् / *abbr.* kilometres per hour किलोमीटर प्रति घंटा

**krill** /krɪl क्रिल् / *noun* [*pl.*] very small shell fish that in the sea around the Antarctic and are eaten by large sea animals (**whales**) दक्षिण ध्रुव प्रदेश में पाई जाने वाली बहुत छोटी शंखमीन जिसे ह्वेल खाती है

**krypton** /ˈkrɪptɒn ˈक्रिप्टॉन् / *noun* [U] (*symbol* **Kr**) a colourless gas that does not react with chemicals, used in **fluorescent** lights फ़्लूरोसेंट ट्यूबों में प्रयुक्त रासायनिक प्रतिक्रियाहीन और रंगहीन गैस

NOTE **Krypton** एक **noble gas** है।

**Kuchipudi** *noun* [U] a classical dance form from Andhra Pradesh (आंध्र प्रदेश का) कुचिपुड़ि नृत्य

**kudos** /ˈkjuːdɒs ˈक्यूडॉस् / *noun* [U] (originally from Greek) a word that is used as an expression of approval and praise for a particular achievement किसी विशेष उपलब्धि पर अनुमोदन और प्रशंसा के लिए प्रयुक्त (ग्रीक मूल की) अभिव्यक्ति; कुडोस

**kulfi** *noun* [C] a cone-shaped Indian ice cream usually made with boiled milk. It comes in various flavours like **pistachio, saffron**, etc. क़ुलफ़ी

**kumkum** *noun* [U] a dark red powder used by married Hindu women to make a mark on the forehead कुमकुम

**kung fu** /ˌkʌŋˈfuː ˌकङ्ˈफ़ू / *noun* [U] a Chinese style of fighting using the feet and hands as weapons हाथों और पैरों से लड़ने की चीनी शैली; कंगफ़ू ➪ **martial arts** देखिए।

**kurta** *noun* [C] a long, loose shirt worn by men and women in south Asia कुरता

**kW** (*also* **kw**) *abbr.* kilowatt(s) किलोवॉट

# L l

**L, l**[1] /el एल् / *noun* [C, U] (*pl.* **L's; l's** /elz एल्ज़् /) the twelfth letter of the English alphabet अंग्रेज़ी वर्णमाला का बारहवाँ अक्षर *'Lake' begins with an 'L'.*

**l**[2] *abbr.* **1** litre(s) लीटर्ज़ **2** (*BrE*) **L** (a sign on a car) learner driver (कार पर संकेत), यह संक्षिप्ति इस संकेत को दर्शाती है कि चालक नौसिखिया है **3 L** large (size) बड़ा (आकार)

**label**[1] /ˈleɪbl ˈलेबल् / *noun* [C] **1** a piece of paper, etc. that is fixed to sth and which gives information about it (सूचना देने वाला) नामचिप्पी, नामपर्ची लेबल *There is a list of all the ingredients on the label.* **2 record label** a company that produces and sells records, CDs, etc. रिकार्ड, सीडी आदि बनाने और बेचने वाली कंपनी

**label**[2] /ˈleɪbl ˈलेबल् / *verb* [T] (**labelling; labelled** *AmE* **labeling; labeled**) **1** (*usually passive*) to fix a label or write information on sth नामचिप्पी लगाना या किसी वस्तु पर सूचना अंकित करना **2 label sb/sth (as) sth** to describe sb/sth in a particular way, especially unfairly किसी को तरीक़े-विशेष में दर्शाना या वर्णन करना, विशेषतः अनुचित रूप से

**labial** /ˈləɪbiəl ˈलेबिअल् / *noun* [C] (*technical*) a speech sound made with the lips, for example m, p, v ओंठों से उत्पन्न ध्वनि, ओष्ठ्य ध्वनि ▶ **labial** *adj.* ओष्ठ्य

**laboratory** /ləˈbɒrətri लˈबॉरट्रि / *noun* [C] (*pl.* **laboratories**) (*informal* **lab**) a room or building that is used for scientific research, testing, experiments, etc. or for teaching about science विज्ञान की प्रयोगशाला (जहाँ विज्ञान से संबंधित परीक्षण और शिक्षण कार्य होते हैं) *The blood samples were sent to the laboratory for analysis.* ○ *a physics laboratory* ⇨ **language laboratory** देखिए।

**laborious** /ləˈbɔːriəs लˈबॉरिअस् / *adj.* needing a lot of time and effort जिसमें बहुत समय और प्रयत्न की अपेक्षा हो; श्रमसाध्य *a laborious task/process/job* ▶ **laboriously** *adv.* श्रमसाध्य रीति से

**labour**[1] (*AmE* **labor**) /ˈleɪbə(r) ˈलेब(र्) / *noun* **1** [U] work, usually of a hard, physical kind कड़ी शारीरिक मेहनत, कठोर श्रम *manual labour* (= work using your hands) **2** [U] workers, when thought of as a group एक समूह के रूप में मज़दूर; श्रमिक वर्ग *There is a shortage of skilled labour.* **3** [U, C, *usually sing.*] the process of giving birth to a baby शिशु को जन्म देने की प्रक्रिया; प्रसव (की स्थिति) *She went into labour in the early hours of this morning.*

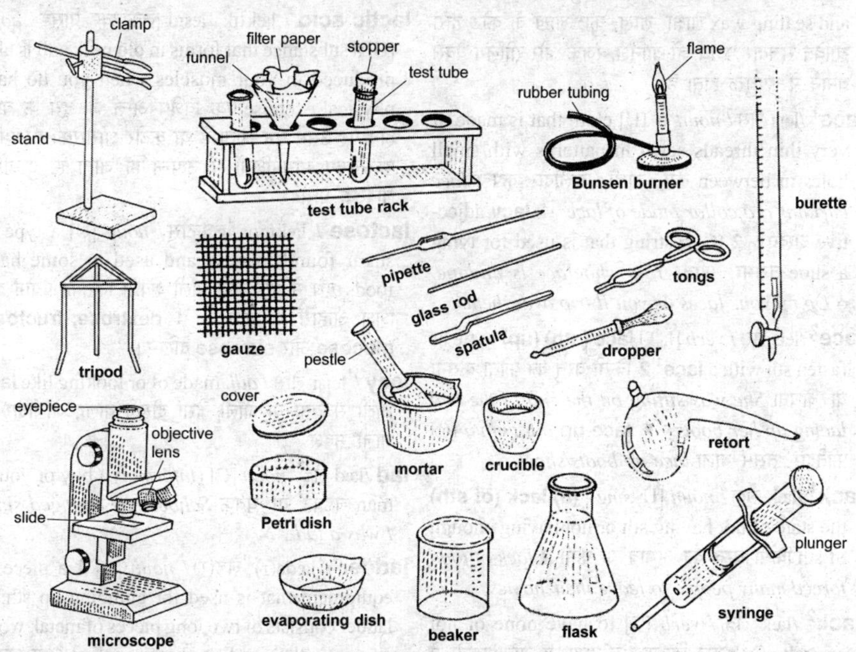


laboratory apparatus

**labour²** (*AmE* **labor**) /ˈleɪbə(r) ˈलेब(र्)/ *verb* [I] **1 labour (away)** to work hard at sth किसी बात के लिए मेहनत करना *She laboured on her book for two years.* **2** to move or do sth with difficulty and effort कठिनाई से और प्रयत्नपूर्वक कोई काम करना

**laboured** (*AmE* **labored**) /ˈleɪbəd ˈलेबड्/ *adj.* done slowly or with difficulty धीरे-धीरे या कठिनाई से किया गया; प्रयासपूर्ण, कठिन *laboured breathing*

**labourer** (*AmE* **laborer**) /ˈleɪbərə(r) ˈलेबर(र्)/ *noun* [C] a person whose job involves hard physical work मज़दूर, श्रमिक *unskilled/farm labourers*

**labour-saving** *adj.* reducing the amount of work needed to do sth जिसमें श्रम की बचत हो; श्रमरक्षी *labour-saving devices such as washing machines and dishwashers*

**labyrinth** /ˈlæbərɪnθ ˈलैबरिन्थ्/ *noun* [C] **1** a complicated set of paths and passages, through which it is difficult to find your way रास्तों और गलियारों की पेचीदी शृंखला जिसमें से रास्ता खोजना कठिन हो; भूलभुलैयाँ **2** an arrangment of membranes and bones in the internal ear which assist in hearing आंतर कर्ण ➪ **ear** पर चित्र देखिए। *a labyrinth of corridors* ✪ पर्याय **maze**

**lac** *noun* [U] a sticky substance produced by certain insects, and used in making varnishes, dyes and sealing wax लाक्षा, लाख; कुछ लाख के कीट द्वारा स्रावित रालदार पदार्थ जो वार्निश, रंजक और सीलिंग वैक्स बनाने में उपयुक्त होता है

**lace¹** /leɪs लेस्/ *noun* **1** [U] cloth that is made of very thin threads sewn in patterns with small holes in between लेस, जाली, जालीदार कपड़ा *lace curtains* ○ *a collar made of lace* ➪ **lacy** adjective देखिए। **2** [C] a string that is used for tying a shoe तसमा, फ़ीता *Your shoelace is undone.* ○ *Do up your laces or you'll trip over them.*

**lace²** /leɪs लेस्/ *verb* [I, T] **lace (sth) (up)** to tie or fasten sth with a **lace¹ 2** किसी वस्तु का फ़ीता कसना या बाँधना *She was sitting on the end of the bed lacing up her boots.* ▶ **lace-up** *adj.*, *noun* [C] फ़ीतेदार, तसमें वाला *lace-up boots/shoes*

**lack¹** /læk लैक्/ *noun* [U, *sing.*] **(a) lack (of sth)** the state of not having sth or not having enough of sth किसी वस्तु का अभाव या कमी *A lack of food forced many people to leave their homes.*

**lack²** /læk लैक्/ *verb* [T] to have none or not enough of sth कुछ बिलकुल न होना या आवश्यकता से कम होना *She seems to lack the will to succeed.*

**lacking** /ˈlækɪŋ ˈलैकिङ्/ *adj.* (*not before a noun*) **1** lacking in sth not having enough of sth जिसमें किसी बात की कमी हो, किसी बात में कम या न्यून *He's certainly not lacking in intelligence.* **2** not present or available अभावयुक्त, जिसका अभाव हो *I feel there is something lacking in my life.*

**lacklustre** /ˈlæklʌstə(r) ˈलैक्लस्ट(र्)/ *adj.* not interesting or exciting; dull जो रोचक या रोमांचक न हो; शिथिल, ढीला-ढाला, बुझा-बुझा *a lacklustre performance*

**laconic** /ləˈkɒnɪk लˈकॉनिक्/ *adj.* (*formal*) using only a few words to say sth अतिसंक्षिप्त, नपा-तुला, सूचनात्मक ▶ **laconically** /-kli -क्लि/ *adv.* नपे-तुले ढंग से, सूचनात्मक रीति से

**lacquer** /ˈlækə(r) ˈलैक(र्)/ *noun* [U] **1** a type of transparent paint that is put on wood, metal, etc. to give it a hard, shiny surface लकड़ी, धातु आदि पर लगाया जाने वाला, पारदर्शी पेंट (चमक लाने के लिए), प्रलाक्षा रस **2** (*old-fashioned*) a liquid that you put on your hair to keep it in place बालों पर लगाया जाने वाला द्रव (जिससे बाल जमें रहें) ✪ पर्याय **hair spray**

**lactate** /lækˈteɪt लैक्ˈटेट्/ *verb* [I] (of a woman or female animal) to produce milk from the body to feed a baby or young animal (स्त्री या मादा पशु द्वारा) अपने बच्चे को अपना दूध पिलाना ▶ **lactation** /lækˈteɪʃn लैक्ˈटेश्न्/ *noun* [U] शिशु को दूध पिलाने की क्रिया; दुग्धस्रवण *the period of lactation*

**lactic acid** /ˌlæktɪk ˈæsɪd ˌलैक्टिक् ˈऐसिड्/ *noun* [U] a substance that forms in old milk and is also produced in your muscles when you do hard physical exercise एक विशेष अम्ल जो दूध के बासी होने पर उसमें बन जाता है या कठोर शारीरिक परिश्रम के फलस्वरूप मांसपेशियों में उत्पन्न हो जाता है; दुग्धाम्ल, लेक्टिक एसिड

**lactose** /ˈlæktəʊs ˈलैक्टोस्/ *noun* [U] a type of sugar found in milk and used in some baby foods दूध में पाई जाने वाली शर्करा जिसका प्रयोग कुछ शिशु आहारों में होता है ➪ **dextrose, fructose, glucose** और **sucrose** देखिए।

**lacy** /ˈleɪsi ˈलेसि/ *adj.* made of or looking like **lace** जाली से बना या जाली जैसा दीखने वाला, जालीदार या जाली सदृश

**lad** /læd लैड्/ *noun* [C] (*informal*) a boy or young man लड़का या युवक *School has changed since I was a lad.*

**ladder** /ˈlædə(r) ˈलैड(र्)/ *noun* [C] **1** a piece of equipment that is used for climbing up sth. A ladder consists of two long pieces of metal, wood or rope with steps fixed between them धातु, लकड़ी या रस्सी की बनी सीढ़ी, निसेनी, ज़ीना (*figurative*) to *climb the ladder of success* ➪ **step ladder** देखिए। **2** (*AmE* **run**) a long hole in the thin pieces of clothing that women wear to cover their legs (**tights** or **stockings**), where the threads have broken स्त्रियों के लंबे मोज़ों में उधड़ा हुआ अंश *Oh no! I've got a ladder in my tights.* ▶ **ladder** *verb* [I, T] सीढ़ी लगाना या बनाना

**laddu** *noun* [C] a popular Indian sweet made from a mixture of various kinds of flour, sugar and **ghee** which is shaped into a ball लड्डू

**laden** /ˈleɪdn ˈलेड्न्/ *adj.* **laden (with sth)** (*not before a noun*) having or carrying a lot of sth बहुत-सी वस्तुएँ लादे हुए या से लदे हुए *The travellers were laden down with luggage.* ○ *The orange trees were laden with fruit.*

**ladle**[1] /ˈleɪdl ˈलेड्ल्/ *noun* [C] a large deep spoon with a long handle, used especially for serving soup करछी, बड़ा चमचा (सूप आदि परोसने के लिए) ➪ **kitchen** पर चित्र देखिए।

**ladle**[2] /ˈleɪdl ˈलेड्ल्/ *verb* [T] to serve food with a ladle करछी से परोसना

**lady** /ˈleɪdi ˈलेडि/ *noun* [C] (*pl.* **ladies**) **1** a polite way of saying 'woman', especially when you are referring to an older woman महिला (विशेषतः वृद्ध) के लिए सम्मानसूचक शब्द *The old lady next door lives alone.* **2** (*formal*) used when speaking to or about a woman or women in a polite way महिला या महिलाओं से/के विषय में शिष्ट रीति से बात करने के लिए प्रयुक्त ***Ladies and gentlemen**!* (= at the beginning of a speech) ○ *Mrs Sharma, there's a lady here to see you.*

**ladybird** /ˈleɪdibɜːd ˈलेडिबड्/ (*AmE* **ladybug** /ˈleɪdibʌg ˈलेडिबग्/) *noun* [C] a small insect that is red or yellow with black spots काले धब्बों वाला लाल या पीले रंग का एक छोटा कीड़ा, सोनापंखी ➪ **insect** पर चित्र देखिए।

**lady's finger** *noun* [C] = **okra**

**lag**[1] /læg लैग्/ *verb* [I] (**lagging; lagged**) **lag (behind) (sb/sth)** to move or develop more slowly than sb/sth किसी व्यक्ति या वस्तु से पीछे रह जाना; पिछड़ जाना

**lag**[2] /læg लैग्/ (*also* **time lag**) *noun* [C] a period of time between two events; a delay दो घटनाओं के बीच का समय; विलंब, देरी ➪ **jet lag** देखिए।

**lager** /ˈlɑːgə(r) ˈलाग(र्)/ *noun* [C, U] (*BrE*) a type of light beer that is golden colour सुनहरे रंग की एक प्रकार की हलकी बियर; लागर *Three pints of lager, please.*

**lagoon** /ləˈguːn लˈगून्/ *noun* [C] a lake of salt water that is separated from the sea by sand or rock खारे पानी की झील (समुद्र के पास बालू या चट्टान से घिरी); समुद्रताल

**laid** ➪ **lay** का past tense और past participle रूप

**laid-back** /ˌleɪd ˈbæk ˌलेड् ˈबैक्/ *adj.* (*informal*) calm and relaxed; seeming not to worry about anything शांत और तनावमुक्त; पूरी तरह से निश्चित दिखने वाला

**lain** ➪ **lie**[2] का past participle रूप

**laissez-faire** /ˌleseɪ ˈfeə(r) ˌलेसे ˈफ़ेअ(र्)/ *noun* [U] the policy of allowing private businesses to develop without government control सरकारी नियंत्रण से मुक्त निजी उद्योग के विकास को छूट देने की नीति; अबंधनीति, अहस्तक्षेप नीति ▶ **laissez-faire** *adj.* अहस्तक्षेप नीति का *a laissez-faire economy* ○ *They have a laissez-faire approach to bringing up their children* (= they give them a lot of freedom).

**lake** /leɪk लेक्/ *noun* [C] a large area of water that is surrounded by land झील, सरोवर *They've gone sailing **on the lake**.* ○ *We all swam **in the lake**.* ○ *Lake Chilka* **NOTE** **Lake** से **pond** छोटा होता है। ➪ **oxbow** पर चित्र देखिए।

**lakh** *noun* [C] (in the Indian system of measurement) one hundred thousand; 1,00,000 (भारतीय मापन प्रणाली में) एक लाख; 1,00,000

**lamb** /læm लैम्/ *noun* **1** [C] a young sheep मेमना ➪ **sheep** पर नोट तथा चित्र देखिए। **2** [U] the meat of a young sheep मेमने का गोश्त *lamb chops*

**lame** /leɪm लेम्/ *adj.* **1** (used mainly about animals) not able to walk properly because of an injury to the leg or foot (प्रायः पशुओं के लिए प्रयुक्त) टाँग या पैर में चोट के कारण लँगड़ा *The horse is lame and cannot work.*

> **NOTE** व्यक्ति के संदर्भ में अब **lame** का प्रयोग नहीं किया जाता। इसके लिए क्रिया और संज्ञा के रूप में **limp** का प्रयोग अधिक होता है—*He's got a limp.* ○ *You're limping. Have you hurt your leg?*

**2** (used about an excuse, argument, etc.) not easily believed; weak (बहाना, युक्ति आदि) जिस पर सरलता से विश्वास न हो; कमज़ोर *a lame excuse*

**lament** /ləˈment लˈमेन्ट्/ *noun* [C] (*formal*) a song, poem or other expression of sadness for sb who has died or for sth that has ended दिवंगत आत्मा या (किसी समाप्त हो चुकी वस्तु) के लिए विलापगीत ▶ **lament** *verb* [T] विलाप करना

**laminated** /ˈlæmɪneɪtɪd ˈलैमिनेटिड्/ *adj.* **1** (used about wood, plastic, etc.) made by sticking several thin layers together (लकड़ी, प्लास्टिक आदि की वस्तु) अनेक पतली तहें चिपका कर बनाई गई; स्तरित, स्तरबंद *laminated glass* **2** covered with thin transparent plastic for protection सुरक्षा के लिए परदर्शी प्लास्टिक से लिपटा हुआ; परतबंद

**lamp** /læmp लैम्प्/ *noun* [C] a device that uses electricity, gas or oil to produce light बिजली, गैस या तेल से जलने वाला लैंप, दीया, चिराग़ *a street lamp* ○ *a table/desk/bicycle lamp* ○ *a sunlamp* ➪ **bicycle** पर चित्र देखिए।

**lamp post** *noun* [C] a tall pole at the side of the road with a light on the top सड़क के पार्श्व में लगा बत्ती का खंभा, दीप स्तंभ; लैंप पोस्ट

**lampshade** /ˈlæmpʃeɪd ˈलैम्प्शेड्/ *noun* [C] a cover for a lamp that makes it look more attractive and makes the light softer लैंपशेड; दीप-छादक (इससे लैंप सुंदर लगता है और रोशनी मद्धिम हो जाती है)

**LAN** /læn लैन्/ *abbr.* (*computing*) local area network (a system for communicating by computer within a large building) स्थानीय संप्रेषण जालतंत्र (एक ही बड़े भवन में कंप्यूटर से संप्रेषण की प्रणाली) ➪ **WAN** देखिए।

**land**[1] /lænd लैन्ड्/ *noun* **1** [U] the solid part of the surface of the earth (= not sea) धरती, ज़मीन, पृथ्वी, स्थल, पृथ्वी की सतह का कड़ा हिस्सा *Penguins can't move very fast on land.* ➪ **ground** पर नोट देखिए। ✪ विलोम **sea** **2** [U] an area of ground भूमि का टुकड़ा, भूक्षेत्र *The land rose to the east.* ○ *She owns 500 acres of land in her native village.* **3** [U] ground, soil or earth of a particular kind विशेष प्रकार की ज़मीन या मिट्टी *The land is rich and fertile.* ○ *arid/barren land* ○ *arable/agricultural/industrial land* **4** [C] (*written*) a country or region कोई देश या क्षेत्र *She died far from her native land.* ○ *to travel to distant lands* ➪ **country** पर नोट देखिए।

**land**[2] /lænd लैन्ड्/ *verb* **1** [I, T] to come down from the air or to bring sth down to the ground आकाश से ज़मीन पर आ जाना या किसी वस्तु को ले आना; उतरना या उतारना *He fell off the ladder and landed on his back.* ○ *The pilot landed the aeroplane safely.* **2** [I, T] to go onto land or put sth onto land from a ship जहाज़ से उतरना या कुछ (सामान) उतारना **3** [T] to succeed in getting sth, especially sth that a lot of people want कुछ पाने में सफल हो जाना (विशेषतः ऐसी वस्तु जिसके लिए स्पर्धा हो) *The company has just landed a million-dollar contract.*

IDM **fall/land on your feet** ➪ **foot**[1] देखिए।

PHR V **land up (in...)** (*BrE informal*) to finish in a certain position or situation किसी विशेष जगह या अवस्था में पहुँच जाना *He landed up in a prison cell for the night.*

**land sb with sb/sth** (*informal*) to give sb sth unpleasant to do, especially because no one else wants to do it किसी से कोई अप्रिय काम करवाना (विशेषतः इसलिए कि और कोई करना नहीं चाहता)

**landfill** /ˈlændfɪl ˈलैन्ड्फ़िल्/ *noun* **1** [C, U] an area of land where large amounts of waste material are buried भूक्षेत्र जहाँ बड़ी मात्रा में अपशिष्ट पदार्थ गाड़ दिए जाते हैं **2** [U] waste material that will be buried; the burying of waste material अपशिष्ट पदार्थ जिसे गड्ढे में गाड़ देना है; अपशिष्ट पदार्थ को गड्ढे में डालने की क्रिया

**landing** /ˈlændɪŋ ˈलैन्डिङ्/ *noun* [C] **1** the action of coming down onto the ground (in an aircraft) (विमान) पृथ्वी पर उतरने की प्रक्रिया *The plane made an* ***emergency landing*** *in a field.* ○ *a crash landing* ○ *a safe landing* ✪ विलोम **take-off** **2** the area at the top of a staircase in a house, or between one staircase and another in a large building मकान में ज़ीने के ऊपर का स्थल या बड़ी इमारत में एक ज़ीने से दूसरे ज़ीने के बीच का स्थल

**landing card** *noun* [C] a form on which you have to write details about yourself when flying to a foreign country एक प्रपत्र जिस पर विदेश की हवाई यात्रा के दौरान व्यक्तिगत ब्योरे देने होते हैं; लैंडिंग कार्ड

**landing gear** *noun* [U] = **undercarriage**

**landing stage** (*AmE* **dock**) *noun* [C] a wooden platform built out into the sea or a river where boats are tied and where people can get on or off them समुद्र के किनारे पानी में बना प्लेटफ़ॉर्म जिससे नावें बँधती हैं और यात्री चढ़ते-उतरते हैं; जेट्टी, अवतरण-पटरा ✪ पर्याय **jetty**

**landing strip** = **airstrip**

**landlady** /ˈlændleɪdi ˈलैन्ड्लेडि/ *noun* [C] (*pl.* **landladies**) **1** a woman who rents a house or room to people for money मकान-मालकिन **2** a woman who owns or manages a pub, small hotel, etc. मदिरालय, छोटे होटल आदि की स्वामिनी या प्रबंधक महिला

**landlocked** /ˈlændlɒkt ˈलैन्ड्लॉक्ट्/ *adj.* completely surrounded by land पूरी तरह से ज़मीन से घिरा हुआ; स्थलरुद्ध

**landlord** /ˈlændlɔːd ˈलैन्ड्लॉड्/ *noun* [C] **1** a person who rents a house or room to people for money मकान-मालिक **2** a person who owns or manages a pub, small hotel, etc. मदिरालय, छोटे होटल आदि का स्वामी या प्रबंधक

**landmark** /ˈlændmɑːk ˈलैन्ड्माक् / *noun* [C] **1** an object (often a building) that can be seen easily from a distance and will help you to recognize where you are दूर से दिखाई देने वाली ऐसी वस्तु (प्रायः कोई इमारत) जिससे आपको पता चलता है कि आप कहाँ हैं; पहचान-चिह्न, सीमा चिह्न *The Gateway of India is one of the historical landmarks of Mumbai.* **2 a landmark (in sth)** an important stage or change in the development of sth किसी परिस्थिति या वस्तु के विकास में महत्त्वपूर्ण दशा या परिवर्तन

**landmine** /ˈlændmaɪn ˈलैन्ड्माइन् / *noun* [C] a bomb placed on or under the ground, which explodes when vehicles or people move over it बारूदी सुरंग

**landowner** /ˈlændəʊnə(r) ˈलैन्ड्ओन(र्) / *noun* [C] a person who owns land, especially a large area of land भूस्वामी (विशेषतः बड़े भूक्षेत्र का स्वामी), ज़मींदार

**landscape**[1] /ˈlændskeɪp ˈलैन्ड्स्केप् / *noun* **1** [C, *usually sing.*] everything you can see when you look across a large area of land विस्तृत मैदान के पार दिखाई देने वाली सभी वस्तुएँ; दृश्यावली, दृश्यभूमि *an urban/industrial landscape* ➪ **scenery** पर नोट देखिए। **2** [C, U] a picture or a painting that shows a view of the countryside; this style of painting ग्रामीण परिवेश को दिखाने वाला चित्र या पेंटिंग; इस प्रकार की पेंटिंग-शैली; भू-दृश्य चित्रण

**landscape**[2] /ˈlændskeɪp ˈलैन्ड्स्केप् / *verb* [T] to improve the appearance of an area of land by changing its design and planting trees, flowers, etc. किसी भूक्षेत्र की रूपरेखा को सुधारना प्रायः उसकी आकृति बदलकर और तरह-तरह की वनस्पतियाँ लगाकर उसकी शकल निखारना; दृश्यभूमि निर्माण करना

**landslide** /ˈlændslaɪd ˈलैन्ड्स्लाइड् / *noun* [C] **1** the sudden fall of a mass of earth, rocks, etc. down the side of a mountain पहाड़ की एक तरफ़ मिट्टी, चट्टानों आदि का अचानक टूटकर नीचे गिरने की क्रिया; भू-स्खलन **2** a great victory for one person or one political party in an election चुनाव में किसी उम्मीदवार या राजनीतिक दल की ज़बरदस्त जीत

**lane** /leɪn लेन् / *noun* [C] **1** a narrow road in the country (देहात में) तंग सड़क *We found a route through country lanes to avoid the traffic jam on the main road.* **2** used in the names of roads सड़कों के नामों में प्रयुक्त *Janpath Lane* **3** a section of a wide road that is marked by painted white lines to keep lines of traffic separate चौड़ी सड़क का एक भाग (यातायात-पट्टी) जिसे सफ़ेद रेखाओं से पेंट कर दिया जाता है (ताकि वाहन अलग-अलग रहें); लेन *a four-lane highway* ○ *the inside/middle/fast/outside lane* **4** a section of a sports track, swimming pool, etc. for one person to go along खेल के मैदान का ट्रैक, स्विमिंगपूल आदि में एक व्यक्ति के लिए खिंची पट्टी (दौड़ने या तैरने का सँकरा मार्ग); लेन **5** a route or path that is regularly used by ships or aircraft जहाज़ या विमान द्वारा नियमित रूप से प्रयुक्त पथ या मार्ग

**language** /ˈlæŋɡwɪdʒ ˈलैङ्ग्विज् / *noun* **1** [C] the system of communication in speech and writing that is used by people of a particular country देश-विशेष के लोगों की मौखिक और लिखित माध्यम की संप्रेषण प्रणाली; भाषा *How many languages can you speak?* ○ *What is your first language* (= your mother tongue)? **2** [U] the system of sounds and writing that human beings use to express their thoughts, ideas and feelings मानव जाति द्वारा अपने विचारों, कल्पनाओं और मनोभावों को व्यक्त करने के लिए प्रयुक्त ध्वनि एवं लेखन की प्रणाली; भाषा *written/spoken language* **3** [U] words of a particular type or words that are used by a particular person or group विशिष्ट व्यक्ति या वर्ग द्वारा प्रयुक्त विशेष शब्द या विशेष प्रकार के शब्द; भाषाशैली, शैली *bad* (= rude) *language* ○ *legal language* ○ *the language of Shakespeare* **4** [U] any system of signs, symbols, movements, etc. that is used to express sth संकेतों, प्रतीक, संचालन मुद्राओं आदि की कोई भी प्रणाली जिससे कुछ अभिव्यक्त हो, भाषा *sign language* (= using your hands, not speaking) ➪ **body language** देखिए। **5** [C, U] (*computing*) a system of symbols and rules that is used to operate a computer कंप्यूटर को संचालित करने के लिए प्रयुक्त संकेतों और नियमों की प्रणाली, कंप्यूटर-भाषा

**language laboratory** *noun* [C] a room in a school or college that contains special equipment to help students to learn foreign languages by listening to tapes, watching videos, recording themselves, etc. भाषा-प्रयोगशाला; विदेशी भाषा सीखने में सहायक इलेक्ट्रॉनिक उपकरणों (टेप, विडियो आदि) से युक्त प्रयोगशाला

**langur** *noun* [C] a long-tailed large monkey usually with a grey or cream-coloured body and a black face, native to S and SE Asia लंबी पूँछ, धूसर या क्रीम रंग का शरीर और काले चेहरे वाला बड़ा बंदर जो दक्षिण और दक्षिण पूर्व एशियाई देशों में पाया जाता है; लंगूर

**lanky** /ˈlæŋki ˈलैङ्कि / *adj.* (used about a person) very tall and thin (व्यक्ति) बहुत लंबा और पतला; छरहरा

**lantern** /ˈlæntən ˈलैन्टन् / *noun* [C] a type of light with a metal frame, glass sides and a light or candle inside that can be carried लालटेन

**lap[1]** /læp लैप्/ *noun* [C] **1** the flat area that is formed by the upper part of your legs when you are sitting down गोद *The child sat quietly on his mother's lap.* **2** one journey around a running track, etc. ट्रैक या दौड़-मार्ग आदि के चारों ओर लगा एक चक्कर *There are three more laps to go in the race.* **3** one part of a long journey लंबी यात्रा का एक भाग

**lap[2]** /læp लैप्/ *verb* (**lapping; lapped**) **1** [I] (used about water) to make gentle sounds as it moves against sth (पानी की लहरों का) तट आदि से टकराते हुए छप-छप करना *The waves lapped against the side of the boat.* **2** [T] **lap sth (up)** (usually used about an animal) to drink sth using the tongue (किसी पशु का) जीभ से (लपलप करते हुए) पानी आदि पीना *The cat lapped up the cream.* **3** [T] to pass another competitor in a race who has been round the track fewer times than you दौड़-प्रतियोगिता में प्रतिस्पर्धी को एक या अधिक चक्कर से पिछाड़ देना

PHR V **lap sth up** (*informal*) to accept sth with great enjoyment without stopping to think if it is good, true, etc. किसी चीज़ को ख़ुशी-ख़ुशी लपक लेना बिना सोचे-समझे कि वह कितनी उपयोगी है

**lapel** /lə'pel ल'पेल्/ *noun* [C] one of the two parts of the front of a coat or jacket that are folded back कोट या जैकिट का गरेबान का मुड़ा हुआ भाग, गरेबान की लौट, मोड़ी, मुड़ी

**lapse[1]** /læps लैप्स्/ *noun* [C] **1** a short time when you cannot remember sth or you are not thinking about what you are doing वह संक्षिप्त अवधि जिसमें आपको कोई बात याद न आए या जो आप कर रहे हों वह दिमाग़ में न रहे; भ्रंश, च्यूति, चूक *a lapse of memory* ○ *The crash was the result of a temporary lapse in concentration.* **2** a period of time between two things that happen दो बातें घटित होने के बीच का समय; व्यवधान, अंतराल *She returned to work after a lapse of ten years.* ➪ **elapse** देखिए। **3** a piece of bad behaviour from sb who usually behaves well ग़लत आचरण (उस व्यक्ति का जो सामान्यतया अच्छा आरचरण करता है); स्खलन

**lapse[2]** /læps लैप्स्/ *verb* [I] **1** (used about a contract, an agreement, etc.) to finish or stop, often by accident (अनुबंध, करार आदि का) समाप्त हो जाना (प्रायः लापरवाही से) *My membership has lapsed because I forgot to renew it.* **2** to become weaker or stop for a short time क्षणभर के लिए क्षीण या लुप्त हो जाना *My concentration lapsed during the last part of the exam.*

PHR V **lapse into sth** to gradually pass into a worse or less active state or condition; to start speaking or behaving in a less acceptable way क्रमशः निम्नतर स्थिति या दशा में आ जाना, अवनत हो जाना; अनुचित ढंग से बोलने या व्यवहार करने लगना *to lapse into silence/a coma*

**laptop** /'læptɒp 'लैप्टॉप्/ *noun* [C] a small computer that is easy to carry and that can use batteries for power बैटरी से चलने वाला छोटा कंप्यूटर जिसे ले चलना आसान होता है; लैपटॉप (कंप्यूटर) ➪ **desktop** और **palmtop** देखिए।

**lard** /lɑ:d लाड्/ *noun* [U] a firm white substance made from melted fat that is used in cooking पिघलाई हुई चरबी से निकला सफ़ेद पदार्थ, भोजन पकाने में प्रयुक्त चरबी

**larder** /'lɑ:də(r) 'लाड(र्)/ *noun* [C] a large cupboard or small room that is used for storing food खाद्य सामग्री को रखने के लिए बड़ी अलमारी या छोटा कमरा; खाद्य-भंडार, भंडार ✪ पर्याय **pantry**

**large** /lɑ:dʒ लाज्/ *adj.* greater in size, amount, etc. than usual; big आकार, मात्रा आदि में सामान्य से अधिक; बड़ा *a large area/house/family/appetite* ○ *We have this shirt in small, medium or large.* ➪ **big** पर नोट देखिए।

IDM **at large 1** as a whole; in general कुल मिलाकर; सामान्य रूप से *He is well known to scientists but not to the public at large.* **2** (used about a criminal, animal, etc.) not caught; free (अपराधी, पशु आदि) जो पकड़ा नहीं गया है; आज़ाद

**by and large** mostly; in general अधिकांशतः; सामान्य रूप से *By and large the school is very efficient.*

**largely** /'lɑ:dʒli 'लाज़्लि/ *adv.* mostly अधिकांशतः *His success was largely due to hard work.*

**large-scale** *adj.* happening over a large area or affecting a lot of people जिसकी क्रियाशीलता का क्षेत्र व्यापक हो या जिससे बड़ी संख्या में लोग प्रभावित हों; बड़े पैमाने पर होने वाला, बड़े परिमाण वाला *large-scale production/unemployment*

**lark** /lɑ:k लाक्/ *noun* [C] a small brown bird that makes a pleasant sound एक छोटी भूरी गाने वाली चिड़िया; लवा चिड़िया, लार्क, भरत पक्षी

**larva** /'lɑ:və 'लावा/ *noun* [C] (*pl.* **larvae** /'lɑ:vi: 'लावी/) an insect at the stage when it has just come out of an egg and has a short fat soft body with no legs अंडे से तुरंत निकला हुआ बिना टाँगों का कीड़ा (जिसका शरीर छोटा, कोमल और भरा हुआ होता है) लार्वा, इल्ली, डिंभक ➪ **pupa** देखिए तथा **insect** पर चित्र देखिए।

**laryngitis** /ˌlærɪn'dʒaɪtɪs ˌलैरिन्'जाइटिस्/ *noun* [U] a mild illness of the throat that makes it difficult to speak गले का हलका रोग जिसके कारण बोलने में कठिनाई होती है; गले की सूजन, कंठशोथ, स्वरयंत्र शोथ

**larynx** /ˈlærɪŋks ˈलैरिङ्क्स् / *noun* [C] the area at the top of your throat that contains the muscles that move to produce the voice (**vocal cords**) गले का ऊपरी भाग जिसमें ध्वनि-उत्पादक मांसपेशियाँ होती हैं, कंठ, स्वरयंत्र ✪ पर्याय **voice box** ➪ **body** तथा **epiglottis** पर चित्र देखिए।

**laser** /ˈleɪzə(r) ˈलेज़(र्)/ *noun* [C] a device that produces a controlled ray of very powerful light that can be used as a tool अत्यधिक शक्तिशाली प्रकाश की सुनियंत्रित किरण उत्पन्न करने वाली युक्ति जिसका उपकरण के रूप में भी प्रयोग हो सकता है; लेज़र

**laser printer** *noun* [C] (*computing*) a machine that produces very good quality printed material from a computer by using a controlled ray of very powerful light (**a laser**) कंप्यूटर से जुड़ा लेज़र चालित मुद्रण-यंत्र; लेज़र-प्रिंटर

**lash**[1] /læʃ लैश्/ *verb* **1** [I, T] (used especially about wind, rain and storms) to hit sth with great force (हवा, वर्षा और आँधी का) किसी वस्तु से ज़ोर से टकराना, थपेड़े मारना *The rain lashed against the windows.* **2** [T] to hit sb with a piece of rope, leather, etc.; to move sth like a piece of rope, leather, etc. violently किसी को कोड़े लगाना; किसी वस्तु (रस्सी या चमड़े का टुकड़ा आदि) को तेज़ी से हिलाना या लहराना **3** [T] **lash A to B; lash A and B together** to tie two things together firmly with rope, etc.दो वस्तुओं को रस्सी आदि से कसकर बाँधना *The two boats were lashed together.*

PHR V **lash out (at/against sb/sth)** to suddenly attack sb/sth (with words or by hitting him/her/it) किसी पर एकाएक हमला करना (तीखे शब्दों के प्रहार से) *The actor lashed out at a photographer outside his house.*

**lash**[2] /læʃ लैश्/ *noun* [C] **1** = **eyelash** **2** a hit with a long piece of rope, leather, etc. (**a whip**) कोड़े से वार

**lass** /læs लैस्/ (*also* **lassie** /ˈlæsi ˈलैसि/) *noun* [C] (*informal*) a girl or young woman लड़की या युवती

NOTE **Lass** का सबसे अधिक प्रचलन स्कॉटलैंड और उत्तरी इंग्लैंड में है।

**lassi** *noun* [U, C] a traditional Indian drink, sweet or salty, made by blending yogurt with water, sugar or salt, and spices like **cardamom**, **cumin**, etc. लस्सी

**lasso** /læˈsuː लैˈसू/ *noun* [C] (*pl.* **lassos** or **lassoes**) a long rope tied in a circle at one end that is used for catching cows and horses पशुओं को पकड़ने के लिए प्रयुक्त गोल फंदे वाली लंबी रस्सी; कमंद, पाश ▶ **lasso** *verb* [T] कमंद या फाँसे से पकड़ना

**last**[1] /lɑːst लास्ट्/ *det., adj., adv.* **1** at the end; after all the others अंत का, अंतिम; सबके बाद, अंत में *December is the last month of the year.* ○ *Our house is the last one on the left.* ○ *She lived alone for the last years of her life.* **2** used about a time, period, event, etc. in the past that is nearest to the present अतीत का समय, अवधि, घटना आदि जो वर्तमान के निकटतम है; पिछला, पिछली, पिछले या पिछली बार *last night/week/Saturday/summer* ○ ***The last time*** *I saw her was in London.* ○ *We'll win this time, because they beat us **last time**.* ○ *When did you last have your eyes checked?* **3** final अंतिम **4** (*only before a noun*) not expected or not suitable जिसकी आशा न हो या जो उपयुक्त न हो अप्रत्याशित या अनुपयुक्त *He's the last person I thought would get the job.* ▶ **lastly** *adv.* अंत में *Lastly, I would like to thank the band who played this evening.* ✪ पर्याय **finally**

IDM **the last/next but one, two, etc.** one, two, etc. away from the last/next पिछले या अगले में से एक, दो आदि स्थान दूर *I live in the next house but one on the right.* ○ *X is the last letter but two of the alphabet* (= the third letter from the end).

**first/last thing** ➪ **thing** देखिए।

**have the last laugh** to be the person, team, etc. who is successful in the end अंततः जीतने वाला व्यक्ति या टीम होना

**have, etc. the last word** to be the person who makes the final decision or the final comment वह व्यक्ति होना जिसका निर्णय या टिप्पणी अंतिम हो

**in the last resort; (as) a last resort** when everything else has failed; the person or thing that helps when everything else has failed जब और कोई रास्ता न बचे; वह व्यक्ति या वस्तु जो तब सहायता करे जब अन्य सभी उपाय विफल हो गए हों

**last but not least** (used before the final item in a list) just as important as all the other items (सूची की अंतिम मद का संकेत करने से पहले प्रयुक्त) उतना ही आवश्यक जितने अन्य

**a last-ditch attempt** a final effort to avoid sth unpleasant or dangerous अप्रिय या ख़तरनाक स्थिति से बचने का अंतिम प्रयास

**the last/final straw** ➪ **straw** देखिए।

**the last minute/moment** the final minute/moment before sth happens किसी बात के घटित होने से पहले का या अंतिम क्षण *We arrived at the last minute to catch the train.* ○ *a last-minute change of plan*

**last**[2] /lɑːst लास्ट्/ *noun, pronoun* **1 the last** (*pl.* **the last**) the person or thing that comes or happens after all other similar people or things

सदृश व्यक्तियों या वस्तुओं की शृंखला में अंतिम व्यक्ति या वस्तु *Arvind was the last to arrive.*

> **NOTE** **The latest** का अर्थ है सबसे ताज़ा या नया। **The last** का अर्थ है वर्तमान से एक पहला (=पिछला)—*His last novel was a huge success, but the latest one is much less popular.*

**2 the last of sth** [*sing.*] the only remaining part or items of sth किसी वस्तु के अवशिष्ट अंश या इकाइयाँ या मदें *We finished the last of the bread at breakfast so we'd better get some more.*

**IDM at (long) last** in the end; finally अंत में; अंततः *After months of separation they were together at last.*

**last³** /lɑːst लास्ट्/ *verb* (*not used in the continuous tenses*) **1** *linking verb* to continue for a period of time कुछ समय तक जारी रहना, चलना, बने रहना *The exam lasts three hours.* ○ *How long does a cricket match last?* ○ **2** [I, T] to continue to be good or to function ठीक हालत में रहना या काम करते रहना, टिकना या टिके रहना *Do you think this weather will last till the weekend?* ○ *It's only a cheap radio but it'll probably last a year or so.* **3** [I, T] to be enough for what sb needs आवश्यकता के लिए पर्याप्त होना *This money won't last me till the end of the month.*

> **NOTE** यद्यपि इस क्रिया का प्रयोग सातत्यबोधक कालों (continuous tenses) में नहीं होता तथापि इसका -ing युक्त वर्तमान कृदंत (present participle) रूप का पर्याप्त प्रचलन है—*An earthquake lasting approximately 20 seconds struck the city last night.*

**lasting** /ˈlɑːstɪŋ ˈलास्टिङ्/ *adj.* continuing for a long time देर तक रहने वाला; (चिर) स्थायी *The museum left a lasting impression on me.*

**last name** = **surname** ➪ **name** पर नोट देखिए।

**latch¹** /lætʃ लैच्/ *noun* [C] **1** a small metal bar that is used for fastening a door or a gate. You have to lift the latch in order to open the door दरवाज़ा या गेट बंद करने के लिए प्रयुक्त धातु निर्मित साँकल, अर्गला, सिटकनी **2** a type of lock for a door that you open with a key from the outside बाहर से खुलने वाला एक विशेष प्रकार का ताला; खटकेदार ताला, (सेफ़्टी) लैच

**latch** /lætʃ लैच्/ *verb*

**PHR V latch on (to sth)** (*informal*) to understand sth किसी बात का समझ में आना या को समझाना *It took them a while to latch on to what she was talking about.*

**late** /leɪt लेट्/ *adj., adv.* **1** near the end of a period of time एक समयावधि के अंत के निकट; परवर्ती *in the late afternoon/summer/twentieth century* ○ *His mother's in her late fifties* (= between 55 and 60). **2** after the usual or expected time सामान्य या प्रत्याशित समय के बाद; विलंब से *She was ten minutes late for school.* ○ *The ambulance arrived too late to save him.* ○ *to stay up late* **3** near the end of the day दिन के अंत के निकट *It's getting late—let's go home.* **4** (*only before a noun*) no longer alive; dead अब जीवित नहीं; दिवंगत *his late wife*

**IDM an early/a late night** ➪ **night** देखिए।

**later on** at a later time बाद में *Later on you'll probably wish that you'd worked harder at school.* ○ *Bye—I'll see you a bit later on.*

**sooner or later** ➪ **soon** देखिए।

**latecomer** /ˈleɪtkʌmə(r) ˈलेट्कम(र्)/ *noun* [C] a person who arrives or starts sth late देर से आने या काम शुरू करने वाला; दीर्घसूत्री

**lately** /ˈleɪtli ˈलेट्लि/ *adv.* in the period of time up until now; recently अब तक के समय में; हाल में, अभी *What have you been doing lately?* ○ *Hasn't the weather been dreadful lately?*

**latent** /ˈleɪtnt ˈलेट्न्ट्/ *adj.* (*usually before a noun*) existing, but not yet very noticeable, active or well developed विद्यमान परंतु प्रकट या सक्रिय नहीं; प्रच्छन्न *latent defects/disease* ○ *latent talent* ▶ **latency** *noun* [U] प्रच्छन्नता

**lateral** /ˈlætərəl ˈलैटरल्/ *adj.* (*usually before a noun*) connected with the side of sth or with movement to the side किसी वस्तु के पार्श्व से या पार्श्व की ओर गति से संबंधित; पार्श्विक *the lateral branches of a tree* ○ *lateral eye movements* ▶ **laterally** *adv.* पार्श्व की ओर से

**latest** /ˈleɪtɪst ˈलेटिस्ट्/ *adj.* very recent or new नवीनतम या आधुनिकतम *the latest fashions/news* ○ *the terrorists' latest attack on the town* ➪ **last** पर नोट देखिए।

**the latest** *noun* [*sing.*] (*informal*) the most recent or the newest thing or piece of news नवीनतम या आधुनिकतम वस्तु या समाचार *This is the very latest in computer technology.* ○ *This is the latest in a series of attacks by this terrorist group.*

**IDM at the latest** no later than the time or the date mentioned निर्दिष्ट तारीख़ या समय के बाद नहीं; देर-से-देर, अधिक-से-अधिक *You need to hand your projects in by Friday at the latest.*

**latex** /ˈleɪteks ˈलेटेक्स्/ *noun* [U] **1** a thick white liquid that is produced by some plants and trees especially rubber trees कुछ पौधों और वृक्षों (विशेषतः रबड़ के वृक्षों) से उत्पन्न गाढ़ा सफ़ेद द्रव; वनस्पति-दूध, रबड़ क्षीर **2** an artificial substance that is used to make paints, **glues** and materials एक कृत्रिम पदार्थ जिससे पेंट, सरेस और अन्य चीज़ें बनती हैं; लेटेक्स

**lathe** /leɪð लेद्/ *noun* [C] a machine that shapes pieces of wood or metal by holding and turning them against a fixed cutting tool ख़राद मशीन (जो लकड़ी या धातु के टुकड़ों को मनचाही शकल देती है)

**lather** /ˈlɑːðə(r)ˈलाद़(र्)/ *noun* [U] a white mass of bubbles that are produced when you mix soap with water साबुन का झाग

**lathi** *noun* [C] (*IndE*) **1** a long stick made of bamboo लाठी; बाँस की लंबी छड़ी **2** (in the Indian subcontinent) a heavy bamboo stick with a metal rim, used as a weapon especially by the police; a baton (भारतीय उपमहाद्वीप में) धातु के किनारे वाली बाँस की भारी छड़, पुलीस द्वारा शस्त्र के रूप में प्रयुक्त; डंडा

**Latin** /ˈlætɪnˈलैटिन/ *noun* [U] the language that was used in ancient Rome प्राचीन रोम में प्रचलित भाषा; लैटिन ▶ **Latin** *adj.* लैटिन भाषा से संबंधित *Latin poetry* ○ *Spanish, Italian and other Latin languages* (= that developed from Latin)

**Latin American** *noun* [C], *adj.* (a person who comes) from Latin America (Mexico or the parts of Central and South America where Spanish or Portuguese is spoken) लैटिन अमेरिका का निवासी (लैटिन अमेरिका में शामिल हैं मेक्सिको, मध्य और दक्षिण अमेरिका के देश, जहाँ स्पैनिश या पुर्तगाली बोली जाती है) *Latin American music*

**latitude** /ˈlætɪtjuːdˈलैटिट्यूड्/ *noun* [U] the distance of a place north or south of the line that we imagine around the middle of the earth (**the equator**) भूमध्य रेखा के उत्तर या दक्षिण की ओर के किसी स्थान की दूरी; अक्षांश **NOTE** अक्षांश को **degrees** में मापा जाता है। ➪ **longitude** देखिए तथा **earth** पर चित्र देखिए।

**latrine** /ləˈtriːn लˈट्रीन्/ *noun* [C] a type of toilet made by digging a hole in the ground ज़मीन में गड्ढा खोदकर बनाया गया शौचघर; पाखाना

**latter** /ˈlætə(r)ˈलैट(र्)/ *adj.* (*formal*) (*only before a noun*) nearer to the end of a period of time; later एक समयावधि के अंत के निकटतर; पिछला, परवर्ती *Interest rates should fall in the latter half of the year.* ▶ **latterly** *adv.* परवर्ती रूप से

**the latter** *noun* [*sing.*], *pronoun* the second (of two people or things that are mentioned) दूसरा, अन्य (पथनिर्दिष्ट दो व्यक्ति या वस्तुओं में) *The options were History and Geography. I chose the latter.*

**NOTE** पथनिर्दिष्ट दो व्यक्तियों या वस्तुओं में जो पहला है उसके लिए **the former** प्रयुक्त होता है।

**lattice** /ˈlætɪsˈलैटिस्/ *noun* [C, U] **1** (*also* **lattice work**) a structure that is made of long thin pieces of wood or metal that cross over each other with spaces shaped like a diamond between them, used as a fence or a support for climbing plants; any structure or pattern like this जाली, झँझरी, जालक (एक दूसरे को काटती हुई तारों या लकड़ी की पट्टियों से बना ढाँचा जिसमें बीच-बीच में हीरे के शकल की खाली जगह होती है यह बाड़ का काम करती है या इस पर बेलें चढ़ाई जाती हैं) *a lattice of branches* **2** an arrangement of points or objects in a regular pattern over an area or in space, for example atoms in **crystal** एक स्थान या अंतरिक्ष में बिंदुओं या वस्तुओं का नियमित पुनरावर्ती विन्यास या बनावट जैसे क्रिस्टल में परमाणु

**laugh[1]** /lɑːf लाफ़्/ *verb* [I] to make the sounds that show you are happy or amused हँसना, हँस कर प्रसन्नता अभिव्यक्त करना *His jokes always make me laugh.* ○ *to laugh out loud*

**IDM** **die laughing** ➪ **die** देखिए।

**PHRV** **laugh at sb/sth** **1** to show, by laughing, that you think sb/sth is funny हँसना, यह व्यक्त करने के लिए कि व्यक्ति या वस्तु विचित्र है *The children laughed at the clown.* **2** to show that you think sb is ridiculous उपहास करना, यह दिखाना कि अमुक आपको अजीब लगता है, किसी की हँसी उड़ाना *Don't laugh at him. He can't help the way he speaks.*

**laugh** /lɑːf लाफ़्/ *noun* [C] **1** the sound or act of laughing हँसने की आवाज़ या क्रिया; हँसी *Her jokes got a lot of laughs.* ○*We all had a good laugh at what he'd written.* **2** (*informal*) a person or thing that is amusing हास्यास्पद लगने वाला व्यक्ति या वस्तु

**IDM** **for a laugh** as a joke मज़ाक़ के तौर पर

**have the last laugh** ➪ **last[1]** देखिए।

**laughable** /ˈlɑːfəblˈलाफ़ब्ल्/ *adj.* deserving to be laughed at; of very poor quality; ridiculous हँसी उड़ाने लायक; निम्नस्तरीय; हास्यास्पद

**laughing stock** *noun* [C] a person or thing that other people laugh at or make fun of (in an unpleasant way) व्यक्ति या वस्तु जिसका लोग मज़ाक़ उड़ाएँ; हँसी का पात्र, हास्यास्पद

**laughter** /ˈlɑːftə(r)ˈलाफ़्ट(र्)/ *noun* [U] the sound or act of laughing हास्य ध्वनि, हँसी; खिलखिलाहट *Everyone roared with laughter.*

**launch[1]** /lɔːntʃ लॉन्च्/ *verb* [T] **1** to send a ship into the water or a spacecraft into the sky (नए) जहाज़ को पानी में उतारना या अंतरिक्ष यान को अंतरिक्ष में

भेजना **2** to start sth new or to show sth for the first time कोई नया काम शुरू करना या किसी वस्तु को पहली बार प्रदर्शित करना *to launch a new product onto the market*

**launch²** /lɔːntʃ लॉन्च् / *noun* [C] **1** [*usually sing.*] the act of launching a ship, spacecraft, new product, etc. जहाज़, अंतरिक्ष यान या कोई उत्पाद आदि को पानी में उतारने आदि की क्रिया; प्रवर्तन, जलावतरण या अंतरिक्ष-प्रक्षेपण आदि **2** a large motor boat बड़ी मोटरनौका, लाँच

**launder** /ˈlɔːndə(r) ˈलॉन्ड(र्) / *verb* [T] **1** (*formal*) to wash and dry clothes, etc. कपड़ों को धोना, सुखाना आदि *freshly laundered sheets* **2** to move money that sb has got illegally into foreign bank accounts or legal businesses so that it is difficult for people to know where the money came from काले धन को विदेशी बैंक में जमा करना या क़ानून-सम्मत व्यापार में लगाना *Most of the money was laundered through Swiss bank accounts.*

**launderette** /lɔːnˈdret लॉन्ˈड्रेट् / (*AmE* **Laundromat**) /ˈlɔːndrəmæt ˈलॉन्ड्रमैट् /) *noun* [C] a type of shop where you pay to wash and dry your clothes in machines एक प्रकार की दुकान जहाँ शुल्क देकर मशीन में कपड़े धोए और सुखाए जा सकते हैं

**laundry** /ˈlɔːndri ˈलॉन्ड्रि /*noun* (*pl.* **laundries**) **1** [U] clothes, etc. that need washing or that are being washed धोए जाने के या धोए जा रहे कपड़े *dirty laundry* **2** [C] a business where you send sheets, clothes, etc. to be washed and dried चादरें, कपड़े आदि धोए और सुखाए जाने के व्यापार की दुकान, धोबीखाना; धुलाई-घर

**lava** /ˈlɑːvə ˈलाव़ा/ *noun* [U] hot liquid rock that comes out of a mountain with an opening in the top (**volcano**) ज्वालामुखी से निकली गरम पिघली चट्टानें, लावा ➩ **volcano** पर चित्र देखिए।

**lavatory** /ˈlævətri ˈलैव़ट्रि / *noun* [C] (*pl.* **lavatories**) (*formal*) **1** a toilet शौचघर, शौचालय **2** a room that contains a toilet, a place to wash your hands, etc. शौच-सुविधा से युक्त कक्ष *Where's the ladies' lavatory, please?* ➩ **toilet** पर नोट देखिए।

**lavender** /ˈlævəndə(r) ˈलैव़न्ड(र्) / *noun* [U] **1** a garden plant with purple flowers that smells very pleasant ख़ुशबूदार बैंगनी फूलों का (बग़ीचे में उगने वाला) पौधा; लैवंडर **2** a light purple colour हलका बैंगनी रंग

**lavish¹** /ˈlævɪʃ ˈलैविश् / *adj.* **1** giving or spending a large amount of money जो बहुत पैसा दे या ख़र्च करे, ख़र्चीला; फिज़ूलख़र्ची *She was always very lavish with her presents.* **2** large in amount or number मात्रा या संख्या में बड़ा *a lavish meal*

**lavish²** /ˈlævɪʃ ˈलैविश् / *verb*

**PHR V** **lavish sth on sb/sth** to give sth generously or in large quantities to sb किसी को उदारतापूर्वक या बड़ी मात्रा में कुछ देना

**law** /lɔː लॉ / *noun* **1** [C] an official rule of a country or state that says what people may or may not do क़ानून, विधि; किसी देश या राज्य का अधिकारिक नियम जो बताता है कि लोग क्या करें या न करें *There's a new law about wearing seat belts in the back of cars.* **2 the law** [U] all the laws in a country or state किसी देश या राज्य के समस्त क़ानून, विधि-संहिता, क़ानून-तंत्र *Stealing is **against the law**.* ○ *to break the law* ○ *to obey the law* ➩ **legal** देखिए। **3** [U] the law as a subject of study or as a profession क़ानून या विधि अध्ययन का विषय या व्यवसाय के *She is studying law.* ○ *My brother works for **a law firm** in Delhi.* ➩ **legal** देखिए। **4** [C] (in science) a statement of what always happens in certain situations or conditions (विज्ञान में) सुनिश्चित परिस्थितियों या दशाओं में सदा घटित होने वाले तथ्यों का कथन; नियम *the laws of mathematics/gravity*

**IDM** **law and order** a situation in which the law is obeyed क़ानून का पालन किए जाने की स्थिति; क़ानून और व्यवस्था

**law-abiding** *adj.* (used about a person) obeying the law (व्यक्ति) क़ानून-पालक *law-abiding citizens*

**lawbreaker** /ˈlɔːbreɪkə(r) ˈलॉब्रेक(र्) / *noun* [C] a person who does not obey the law; a criminal क़ानून को तोड़ने वाला व्यक्ति; अपराधी

**law court** (*also* **court of law**) *noun* [C] a place where legal cases are decided by a judge and often by twelve members of the public (**a jury**) न्यायालय, कचहरी

> **NOTE** न्यायालय में **case** (मुक़दमा) को try (**is tried**) किया जाता है। ➩ **defence, prosecution** और **witness** भी देखिए।

**lawful** /ˈlɔːfl ˈलॉफ़्ल् / *adj.* allowed or recognized by law क़ानून के अनुकूल या क़ानून से मान्य *We shall use all lawful means to obtain our demands.* ➩ **legal** और **legitimate** देखिए।

**lawless** /ˈlɔːləs ˈलॉलस् / *adj.* (used about a person or his/her actions) breaking the law (व्यक्ति या उसका कार्य) क़ानून को तोड़ने वाला, ग़ैर-क़ानूनी, ▶ **lawlessness** *noun* [U] अव्यवस्था, विधि-विहीनता, विधि-विरुद्ध

**lawn** /lɔːn लॉन् / *noun* [C, U] an area of grass in a garden or park that is regularly cut घर, सार्वजनिक उद्यान या बग़ीचे में शाद्वल क्षेत्र; लॉन

**lawnmower** /ˈlɔːnməʊə(r) ˈलॉन्मोअ(र्)/ *noun* [C] a machine that is used for cutting the grass in a garden बग़ीचे की घास काटने की मशीन; घास लावक, घास कर्तक

**lawn tennis** = **tennis**

**lawsuit** /ˈlɔːsuːt ˈलॉसूट्/ *noun* [C] a legal argument in a court of law that is between two people or groups and not between the police and a criminal दो व्यक्तियों या व्यक्ति समूहों के बीच न्यायालय में अभियोग (पुलिस और अपराधी के बीच विवाद के लिए शब्द अलग है)

**lawyer** /ˈlɔːjə(r) ˈलॉय(र्)/ *noun* [C] a person who has a certificate in law and gives legal advice/help वक़ील, अधिवक्त; क़ानूनी सलाह या सहायता देने वाला, क़ानून का प्रमाणित जानकार *to consult a lawyer*

> **NOTE** **Solicitor** वह वकील है जो क़ानूनी परामर्श देता है, क़ानूनी दस्तावेज़ तैयार करता है तथा भूमि के क्रय-विक्रय की व्यवस्था आदि करता है। ब्रिटिश अंग्रेज़ी में **barrister** कचहरी में मुक़दमा लड़ता है और इसके लिए अमेरिकी शब्द **attorney** है।

**lax** /læks लैक्स्/ *adj.* not having high standards; not strict उच्च मानकों से रहित; कठोर नहीं, शिथिल *Their security checks are rather lax.*

**laxative** /ˈlæksətɪv ˈलैक्सटिव्/ *noun* [C] a medicine, food or drink that sb can take to make him/her get rid of solid waste from his/her body more easily पेट साफ़ करने में सहायक कोई औषधि, खाद्य या पेय; रेचक वस्तु, दस्तावर पदार्थ ▶ **laxative** *adj.* रेचक, दस्तावर

**lay¹** /leɪ ले/ *verb* [T] (*pt, pp* **laid** /leɪd लेड्/) **1** to put sb/sth carefully in a particular position or on a surface किसी व्यक्ति या वस्तु को स्थिति विशेष में या किसी सतह पर रखना *He laid the child gently down on her bed.* ○ *'Don't worry,' she said, laying her hand on my shoulder.* **2** to put sth in the correct position for a particular purpose प्रयोजन विशेष से किसी वस्तु को सही स्थिति में रखना या डालना *They're laying new electricity cables in our street.* **3** to prepare sth for use किसी वस्तु को उपयोग के लिए तैयार करना *The police have laid a trap for him and I think they'll catch him this time.* ○ *Can you lay the table please* (= put the knives, forks, plates, etc. on it)? **4** to produce eggs अंडे देना *Hens lay eggs.* **5** (*used with some nouns to give a similar meaning to a verb*) to put डालना, देना *They laid all the blame on him* (= they blamed him). ○ *to lay emphasis on sth* (= emphasize it)

**PHR V** **lay sth down** to give sth as a rule किसी बात को नियम के रूप में व्यवस्थित करना या नियमबद्ध करना *It's all laid down in the rules of the club.*

**lay off (sb)** (*informal*) to stop annoying sb किसी को और तंग न करना *Can't you lay off me for a bit?*

**lay sb off** to stop giving work to sb किसी को काम से हटा देना *They've laid off 500 workers at the car factory.*

**lay sth on** (*informal*) to provide sth कुछ उपलब्ध कराना *They're laying on a trip to Mumbai for everybody.*

**lay sth out 1** to spread out a number of things so that you can see them easily or so that they look nice वस्तुओं को सजाना या प्रदर्शित करना *All the food was laid out on a table in the garden.* **2** to arrange sth in a planned way किसी वस्तु को योजनापूर्वक व्यवस्थित करना

**lay²** /leɪ ले/ *adj.* (*only before a noun*) **1** (used about a religious teacher) who has not been officially trained as a priest (धार्मिक शिक्षक या धर्मशिक्षक) जो पुरोहित के रूप में विधिवत प्रशिक्षित नहीं; अविशेषज्ञ (पुरोहित) *a lay preacher* **2** without special training in or knowledge of a particular subject विषय विशेष का ज्ञान या उसमें विशेष प्रशिक्षण के बिना

**lay³** ⇨ **lie²** का past tense रूप

**layabout** /ˈleɪəbaʊt ˈलेअबाउट्/ *noun* [C] (*BrE informal*) a person who is lazy and does not do much work आलसी व्यक्ति

**lay-by** (*AmE* **rest stop**) *noun* [C] (*pl.* **lay-bys**) an area at the side of a road where vehicles can stop for a short time सड़क के किनारे की जगह जहाँ वाहन कुछ देर के लिए रुक सकते हैं

**layer** /ˈleɪə(r) ˈलेअ(र्)/ *noun* [C] a thickness or quantity of sth that is on sth else or between other things परत, तह *A thin layer of dust covered everything in the room.* ○ *the top/bottom layer* ○ *the inner/outer layer*

**layman** /ˈleɪmən ˈलेमन्/ *noun* [C] (*pl.* **-men** /-mən -मन्/) a person who does not have special training in or knowledge of a particular subject व्यक्ति जिसे विशेष प्रशिक्षण या जानकारी प्राप्त न हो, साधारण जानकार, अविशेषज्ञ, जन साधारण *a medical reference book for the layman*

**laze** /leɪz लेज़्/ *verb* [I] **laze (about/around)** to do very little; to rest or relax बहुत कम काम करना, सुस्त होना; आराम फ़रमाना

**lazy** /ˈleɪzi ˈलेज़ी/ *adj.* (**lazier; laziest**) **1** (used about a person) not wanting to work (व्यक्ति) जो काम न करना चाहे; आलसी, कामचोर *Don't be lazy. Come and give me a hand.* **2** moving slowly or without much energy मंद-मंद या ऊर्जाहीन, सुस्ती-भरा या अलसाया हुआ *a lazy smile* **3** making you feel that you do not want to do very much सुस्ती पैदा करने वाला या सुस्त बना देने वाला *a lazy summer's afternoon* ▸ **lazily** *adv.* सुस्ती से ▸**laziness** *noun* [U] सुस्ती

**lb** *abbr.* pound(s); a measurement of weight equal to about 454 grams पाउन्ड; 454 ग्राम के बराबर भार का एक माप

**LCD** /ˌel siː ˈdiː ˌएल् सी ˈडी / *abbr.* **1** liquid crystal display; a way of showing information in electronic equipment. An elecric current is passed through a special liquid and numbers and letters can be seen on a small screen लिक्विड क्रिस्टल डिस्प्ले, एल सी डी। इलेक्ट्रॉनिक उपकरण पर जानकारी देने की एक पद्धति जिसमें एक विशेष द्रव में विद्युत-धारा को गुज़ारा जाता है और छोटे परदे पर संख्याएँ और अक्षर दिखाई देते हैं *a pocket calculator with LCD* **2** (*mathematics*) = **lowest common denominator**

**leach** /liːtʃ लीच् / *verb* (*technical*) **1** [I] (used about chemicals, etc.) to be removed from soil by liquids passing through it (रसायनों आदि के लिए प्रयुक्त) द्रवों की सहायता से मिट्टी से (रसायनों का) अलग होना **2** [T] (used about liquids) to remove chemicals, etc. from soil by passing through it (द्रव पदार्थ के लिए प्रयुक्त) मिट्टी में (द्रव को) गुज़ार कर उसमें से रसायनों को बाहर निकालना

**lead**[1] /liːd लीड् / *verb* (*pt, pp* **led** /led लेड् /) **1** [T] to go with or in front of a person or animal to show the way or to make him/her/it go in the right direction किसी व्यक्ति या पशु को साथ ले जाना या उसे रास्ता दिखाना या सही दिशा में भेजना *The teacher led the children out of the hall and back to the classroom.* ○ *The receptionist* ***led the way*** *to the boardroom.* ○ *to lead sb by the hand*

> **NOTE** सामान्यतया पर्यटक को या जिसे विशेष सहायता चाहिए उसे **guide** किया जाता है—*to guide visitors around Udaipur* ○ *He guided the blind woman to her seat.* किसी को **direct** करने का अर्थ है उसे समझाना कि वह ठिकाने पर कैसे पहुँचे—*Could you direct me to the nearest Post Office, please?*

**2** [I] (used about a road or path) to go to a place (सड़क या रास्ते का) किसी जगह जाना *I don't think this path leads anywhere.* **3** [I] **lead to sth** to have sth as a result परिणामस्वरूप कोई बात होना *Eating too much sugar can lead to all sorts of health problems.* **4** [T] **lead sb to do sth** to influence what sb does or thinks किसी के काम या सोच को प्रभावित करना *He led me to believe he really meant what he said.* **5** [T] to have a particular type of life एक विशेष प्रकार का जीवन जीना *They lead a very busy life.* ○ *to lead a life of crime* **6** [I, T] to be winning or in first place in front of sb जीत की राह पर होना या किसी से आगे होना *Leander Paes is leading Mahesh Bhupathi by two games to love.* **7** [I, T] to be in control or the leader of sth किसी कार्य का संचालन, निर्देशन या नेतृत्व करना *Who is going to lead the discussion?*

**IDM lead sb astray** to make sb start behaving or thinking in the wrong way किसी के व्यवहार या सोच को ग़लत दिशा में ले जाना; किसी को भटकाना

**PHRV lead up to sth** to be an introduction to or cause of sth किसी स्थिति की ओर ले जाना या उसका कारण बनना

**lead**[2] /liːd लीड् / *noun* **1 the lead** [*sing.*] the first place or position in front of other people or organizations अन्य व्यक्तियों या संगठन में प्रथम स्थान या पद; अगुआई, नेतृत्व *The French athlete has gone* ***into the lead.*** ○ *India has* ***taken the lead*** *in developing computer software for the market.* **2** [*sing.*] the distance or amount by which sb/sth is in front of another person or thing किसी व्यक्ति या वस्तु के अन्य व्यक्ति या वस्तु से आगे रहने का अंतर या मात्रा(वह कितना आगे है) *The company has a lead of several years in the development of the new technology.* **3** [C] the main part in a play, show or other situation किसी नाटक, प्रदर्शन या अन्य स्थिति में मुख्य भूमिका *Who's playing the lead in the new film?* ○ *Neha played* ***a lead role*** *in getting the company back into profit.* **4** [C] a piece of information that may help to give the answer to a problem किसी समस्या के समाधान की ओर ले जाने वाली जानकारी, सुराग़, सूत्र *The police are* ***following*** *all possible* ***leads*** *to track down the killer.* **5** [C] a long chain or piece of leather that is connected to the collar around a dog's neck and used for keeping the dog under control कुत्ते के गरदन के पट्टे से लगी लंबी ज़ंजीर या चमड़े की पट्टी (कुत्ते को क़ाबू में रखने के लिए) *All dogs must be* ***kept on a lead.*** **6** [C] a piece of wire that carries electricity to a piece of equipment किसी उपकरण को विद्युत पहुँचाने वाली तार; लीड

**IDM follow sb's example/lead** ➪ **follow** देखिए।

**lead**[3] /led लेड् / *noun* **1** [U] (*symbol* **Pb**) a soft heavy grey metal. Lead is used in pipes, roofs, etc. सीसा, लेड (जो पाइपों, छतों आदि में इस्तेमाल होता है) **2** [C, U] the black substance inside a pencil that makes a mark when you write पेंसिल के अंदर का काला पदार्थ, ग्रैफ़ाइट, लिखिज, लेड ➪ **stationery** पर चित्र देखिए।

**leader** /ˈliːdə(r) ˈलीड(र्)/ *noun* [C] **1** a person who is a manager or in charge of sth किसी काम का प्रबंधकर्ता या प्रभारी व्यक्ति, नेतृत्व-कर्ता *a weak/strong leader* ○ *She is a natural leader* (= she knows how to tell other people what to do). **2** the person or thing that is best or in first place सर्वोत्तम या प्रथम स्थान पर रहा व्यक्ति या वस्तु *The leader has just finished the third lap.* ○ *The new shampoo soon became a market leader.*

**leadership** /ˈliːdəʃɪp ˈलीडशिप्/ *noun* **1** [U] the state or position of being a manager or the person incharge नेतृत्व *Who will take over the leadership of the party?* **2** [U] the qualities that a leader should have नेतृत्व के गुण *She's got good leadership skills.* **3** [C, *with sing. or pl. verb*] the people who are incharge of a country, organization, etc. किसी देश, संगठन आदि का नेतृत्व करने वाले लोग; नेतागण

**leading** /ˈliːdɪŋ ˈलीडिङ्/ *adj.* **1** best or most important सर्वोत्तम या सबसे महत्त्वपूर्ण *He's one of the leading experts in this field.* ○ *She played a leading role in getting the business started.* **2** that tries to make sb give a particular answer एक विशेष उत्तर देने के लिए प्रेरित करने वाला; संकेतक या सूचक, *The lawyer was warned not to ask the witness* ***leading questions.***

**lead story** *noun* [C] the most important piece of news in a newspaper or on a news programme समाचार-पत्र या समाचार-कार्यक्रम का सबसे महत्त्वपूर्ण समाचार

**leaf[1]** /liːf लीफ़्/ *noun* [C] (*pl.* **leaves** /liːvz लीव्ज़्/) one of the thin, flat, usually green parts of a plant or tree पौधे या वृक्ष का पत्ता *The trees lose their leaves in autumn.* ➪ **tree** पर चित्र देखिए।

**leaf[2]** /liːf लीफ़्/ *verb*

**PHRV** **leaf through sth** to turn the pages of a book, etc. quickly and without looking at them carefully जल्दी-जल्दी और लापरवाही से किसी किताब के पन्ने पलटना

**leaflet** /ˈliːflət ˈलीफ़्लट्/ *noun* [C] a printed piece of paper that gives information about sth. Leaflets are usually given free of charge किसी वस्तु के विषय में सूचना देने वाला मुद्रित काग़ज़ (जो प्रायः मुफ़्त बाँटा जाता है) *I picked up a leaflet advertising a new club.*

**leafy** /ˈliːfi ˈलीफ़ि/ *adj.* **1** having many leaves पत्तियों वाला, पत्तेदार *a leafy bush* **2** (used about a place) with many trees (स्थान) जहाँ अनेक वृक्ष हों, वृक्ष-बहुल

**league** /liːg लीग्/ *noun* [C] **1** a group of sports clubs that compete with each other for a prize स्पोर्ट्स-क्लबों का समूह (जो पुरस्कार के लिए आपस में मुक़ाबला करते हैं); लीग, संघ *the football league* ○ *Which team is top of the league at the moment?* **2** a group of people, countries, etc. that join together for a particular purpose प्रयोजन विशेष से एक साथ जुड़ने वाले लोगों, देशों आदि का समूह; लीग, संघ *the League of Nations* **3** a level of quality, ability, etc. गुणवत्ता, योग्यता आदि का स्तर, वर्ग, श्रेणी या कोटि *He is so much better than the others. They're just not in the same league.*

**IDM** **in league (with sb)** having a secret agreement (with sb) (किसी व्यक्ति के साथ) गुप्त समझौता होना, मिलीभगत होना

**leak[1]** /liːk लीक्/ *verb* **1** [I, T] to allow liquid or gas to get through a hole or crack किसी छेद या दरार में से द्रव या गैस को निकलने देना; रिसना *The boat was leaking badly.* **2** [I] (used about liquid or gas) to get out through a hole or crack (द्रव या गैस का) छेद या दरार में से बाहर निकलना; क्षरण करना *Water is leaking in through the roof.* **3** [T] **leak sth (to sb)** to give secret information to sb किसी को गोपनीय सूचना देना *The committee's findings were leaked to the press before the report was published.*

**PHRV** **leak out** (used about secret information) to become known (गुप्त जानकारी) प्रकट हो जाना; पता चल जाना

**leak[2]** /liːk लीक्/ *noun* [C] **1** a small hole or crack which liquid or gas can get through छेद या दरार जिसमें से द्रव या गैस बाहर निकलती है *There's a leak in the pipe.* ○ *The roof has sprung a leak.* **2** the liquid or gas that gets through a hole छेद में से निकल रहा द्रव या गैस *a gas leak* **3** the act of giving away information that should be kept secret गोपनीय सूचना को प्रकट करने की क्रिया; रहस्योद्घाटन ▶ **leaky** *adj.* सूराख़दार, छिद्रयुक्त, सछिद्र

**leakage** /ˈliːkɪdʒ ˈलीकिज्/ *noun* [C, U] the action of coming out of a hole or crack; the liquid or gas that comes out सूराख़ या दरार में से बाहर निकलने की क्रिया, रिसाव, स्रवण; रिसने वाला द्रव या गैस *a leakage of dangerous chemicals*

**lean[1]** /liːn लीन्/ *verb* (*pt, pp* **leant** /lent लेन्ट्/ or **leaned** /liːnd लीन्ड्/) **1** [I] to move the top part of your body and head forwards, backwards or to the side सिर और शरीर के ऊपर के भाग को आगे, पीछे या पार्श्वों की ओर गति करना; झुकना, झुक जाना *He leaned across the table to pick up the phone.* ○ *She leaned out of the window and waved.* ○ *Just lean back and relax.* **2** [I] to be in a position that is not straight or upright सीधी या खड़ी से भिन्न स्थिति में होना; तिरछे होना *That wardrobe leans to the right.* **3** [I, T] **lean (sth) against/on sth**

to rest against sth so that it gives support; to put sth in this position किसी वस्तु के सहारे शरीर आदि को टिकाना *She had to stop and lean on the gate.* ○ *Please don't lean bicycles against this window.*

**lean²** /liːn लीन्/ *adj.* **1** (used about a person or animal) thin and in good health (व्यक्ति या पशु) छरहरा और स्वस्थ **2** (used about meat) having little or no fat (गोश्त या मांस) चरबी-रहित **3** not producing much अलाभकर, जिसमें अधिक उत्पादन नहीं, क्षीण, अपर्याप्त *a lean harvest*

**leap¹** /liːp लीप्/ *verb* [I] (*pt, pp* **leapt** /lept लेप्ट्/ or **leaped** /liːpt लीप्ट्/) **1** to jump high or a long way ऊँची या लंबी छलाँग लगाना *The horse leapt over the wall.* ○ *A fish suddenly leapt out of the water.* ○ (*figurative*) *Share prices leapt to a record high yesterday.* **2** to move quickly झपाटे से कोई हरकत करना *I looked at the clock and leapt out of bed.* ○ *She leapt back when the pan caught fire.*

**PHR V** **leap at sth** to accept a chance or offer with enthusiasm उत्साह के साथ किसी अवसर या प्रस्ताव को स्वीकार करना *She leapt at the chance to work in television.*

**leap²** /liːp लीप्/ *noun* [C] **1** a big jump एक बड़ी छलाँग *He took a flying leap at the wall but didn't get over it.* ○ (*figurative*) *My heart gave a leap when I heard the news.* **2** a sudden large change or increase in sth किसी बात में अचानक बड़ा परिवर्तन या वृद्धि *The development of penicillin was a great leap forward in the field of medicine.*

**leapfrog** /ˈliːpfrɒɡ ˈलीपफ़्रॉग्/ *noun* [U] a children's game in which one person bends over and another person jumps over his/her back मेंढक-कूद नामक बच्चों का खेल जिसमें एक बच्चा झुकता है और दूसरा उसके ऊपर से मेंढक के समान कूद जाता है

**leap year** *noun* [C] one year in every four, in which February has 29 days instead of 28 हर चौथे वर्ष पड़ने वाला वर्ष (जिसमें फरवरी में 28 के स्थान पर 29 दिन होते हैं); लीप-इयर अधिवर्ष

**learn** /lɜːn लन्/ *verb* (*pt, pp* **learnt** /lɜːnt लन्ट्/ or **learned** /lɜːnd लन्ड्/) **1** [I, T] **learn (sth) (from sb/sth)** to get knowledge, a skill, etc. (from sb/sth) (किसी व्यक्ति या वस्तु से) ज्ञान, कौशल आदि प्राप्त करना, सीखना *Deepa is learning to play the piano.* ○ *to learn a foreign language/a musical instrument* **2** [I] **learn (of/about) sth** to get some information about sth; to find out किसी बात के बारे में जानकारी प्राप्त करना; (किसी बात का) पता चलना *I was sorry to learn about your father's death.* **3** [T] to study sth so that you can repeat it from memory किसी विषय का इस प्रकार अध्ययन करना कि वह याद रहे; किसी बात को सीखकर याद कर लेना **4** [I] to understand or realize समझना या सीख लेना *We should have learned by now that we can't rely on her.* ○ *It's important to learn from your mistakes.*

**IDM** **learn your lesson** to understand what you must do/not do in the future because you have had an unpleasant experience अप्रिय अनुभव से सबक़ सीखना

**learned** /ˈlɜːnɪd ˈलनिड्/ *adj.* having a lot of knowledge from studying; for people who have a lot of knowledge ज्ञानी, विद्वान, पंडित; विद्वानों से संबंधित, विद्वतापूर्ण, पांडित्यपूर्ण

**learner** /ˈlɜːnə(r) ˈलन(र्)/ *noun* [C] a person who is learning जो अभी सीख रहा है या ज्ञान प्राप्त कर रहा है; शिक्षार्थी *a learner driver* ○ *books for young learners*

**learning** /ˈlɜːnɪŋ ˈलनिङ्/ *noun* [U] **1** the process of learning sth किसी बात को सीखने या जानने की प्रक्रिया *new methods of language learning* **2** knowledge that you get from studying अध्ययन से प्राप्त ज्ञान

**lease** /liːs लीस्/ *noun* [C] a legal agreement that allows you to use a building or land for a fixed period of time in return for rent एक क़ानूनी क़रारनामा जिसके अनुसार किसी भवन या भूखंड को निर्धारित अवधि के लिए किराए पर लिखा जाता है; पट्टा, लीज़, इज़ारा *The lease on the flat runs out/expires next year.* ▶ **lease** *verb* [T] पट्टे पर लेना या देना *They lease the land from a local farmer.* ○ *Part of the building is leased out to tenants.*

**leasehold** /ˈliːshəʊld ˈलीसहोल्ड्/ *adj.* (used about property or land) that you can pay to use for a limited period of time (संपत्ति या भूमि) सीमित अवधि के उपयोग के लिए किराए पर, पट्टे पर *a leasehold property* ▶ **leasehold** *noun* [U] पट्टा, पट्टाभूमि ➪ **freehold** देखिए।

**least** /liːst लीस्ट्/ *det., pronoun, adv.* **1** (used as the superlative of **little**) smallest in size, amount, degree, etc. (शब्द 'little' का उत्तमावस्था रूप) मात्रा, डिग्री आदि में सबसे कम; अल्पतम, न्यूनतम *He's got the least experience of all of us.* ○ *You've done the most work, and I'm afraid Anurag has done the least.* **2** less than anyone/anything else; less than at any other time किसी भी अन्य की अपेक्षा कम; किसी भी अन्य समय से कम, कम-से-कम, न्यूनतम *He's the person who needs help least.* ○ *I bought the least expensive tickets.* ✪ विलोम **most**

**IDM at least** 1 not less than, and probably more किसी से कम नहीं और शायद अधिक; कम-से-कम *It'll take us at least two hours to get there.* ○ *You could at least say you're sorry!* 2 even if other things are wrong कम-से-कम, चाहे जो भी हो *It may not be beautiful but at least it's cheap.* 3 used for correcting sth that you have just said अपनी अभी कही बात को सुधारने के लिए प्रयुक्त *I saw him—at least I think I saw him.*

**at the (very) least** not less and probably much more कम नहीं और शायद कहीं अधिक; न्यूनतम *It'll take six months to build at the very least.*

**least of all** especially not विशेषतः नहीं, (तो) बिलकुल नहीं *Nobody should be worried, least of all you.*

**not in the least (bit)** not at all ज़रा भी नहीं, एकदम नहीं *It doesn't matter in the least.* ○ *I'm not in the least bit worried.*

**last but not least** ➪ **last**[1] देखिए।

**to say the least** used to say that sth is in fact much worse, more serious, etc. than you are saying यह बताने के लिए प्रयुक्त कि वास्तविक स्थिति कहीं अधिक गंभीर है *Ajay's going to be annoyed, to say the least, when he sees his car.*

**leather** /ˈleðə(r) ˈलेद्र(र्)/ *noun* [U] the skin of animals which has been specially treated. Leather is used to make shoes, bags, coats, etc. विशेष रूप से उपचारित पशुओं की खाल; चमड़ा *a leather jacket*

**leave**[1] /liːv लीव्/ *verb* (*pt, pp* **left** /left लेफ़्ट्/) 1 [I, T] to go away from sb/sth किसी व्यक्ति या वस्तु से दूर जाना *We should leave now if we're going to get there by eight o'clock.* ○ *I felt sick in class so I left the room.*

> **NOTE** 'Leave sb/sth' स्थायी या अस्थायी रूप से दूर जाना हो सकता है—*He leaves the house at 8.00 every morning.* ○ *He left New York and went to live in Canada.* **Depart** अधिक औपचारिक शब्द है और नावों, रेलगाड़ियों, विमानों आदि के लिए प्रयुक्त होता है—*The 6.15 train for Delhi departs from Platform 3.*

2 [T] to cause or allow sb/sth to stay in a particular place or condition; to not deal with sth किसी व्यक्ति या वस्तु को विशेष स्थान या दशा में रहने देना, छोड़ देना; किसी वस्तु को न छेड़ना, टाल देना *Leave the door open, please.* ○ *Don't leave the iron on when you are not using it.* 3 [T] **leave sth (behind)** to forget to bring sth with you अपने साथ कुछ लाना भूल जाना, छोड़ आना या भूल आना *I'm afraid I've left my homework at home. Can I give it to you tomorrow?* ○ *I can't find my glasses. Maybe I left them behind at work.* 4 [T] to make sth happen or stay as a result परिणामस्वरूप कुछ होने देना, छोड़ देना; शेष रह जाना या शेष छोड़ देना *Don't put that cup on the table. It'll leave a mark.* 5 [T] to not use sth किसी चीज़ का प्रयोग न करना, कुछ छोड़ देना या रहने देना *Leave some milk for me, please.* 6 [T] to put sth somewhere किसी वस्तु को कहीं रख देना, छोड़ देना या आना *Veena left a message on her answer phone.* ○ *I left him a note.* 7 [T] to give sth to sb when you die मृत्यु के समय किसी को कुछ दे जाना, वसीयत में कुछ छोड़ जाना *In his will he left everything to his three sons.* 8 [T] to give the care of or responsibility for sb/sth to another person किसी व्यक्ति या वस्तु की देखभाल या ज़िम्मेदारी किसी और को सौंपना *I'll leave it to you to organize all the food.*

**IDM leave sb/sth alone** to not touch, annoy or speak to sb/sth किसी व्यक्ति या वस्तु को न छूना, न नाराज़ करना, न उससे बात करना; किसी व्यक्ति या वस्तु को अकेले छोड़ देना

**leave go (of sth)** to stop touching or holding sth किसी वस्तु का स्पर्श या पकड़ छोड़ देना *Will you please leave go of my arm.*

**be left high and dry** ➪ **high**[1] देखिए।

**leave sb in the lurch** to leave sb without help in a difficult situation कठिनाई में किसी को बेसहारा छोड़ देना

**leave sth on one side** ➪ **side**[1] देखिए।

**PHR V leave sb/sth out (of sth)** to not include sb/sth किसी व्यक्ति या वस्तु को शामिल न करना *This doesn't make sense. I think the typist has left out a line.*

**leave**[2] /liːv लीव्/ *noun* [U] a period of time when you do not go to work नौकरी से अवकाश की अवधि; छुट्टी *Diplomats working abroad usually get a month's home leave each year.* ○ *annual leave* ○ *sick leave* ➪ **holiday** पर नोट देखिए।

**leaves** ➪ **leaf**[1] का plural रूप

**lecture** /ˈlektʃə(r) ˈलेक्च(र्)/ *noun* [C] **1 a lecture (on/about sth)** a talk that is given to a group of people to teach them about a particular subject, especially as part of a university course अध्यापन कार्य के अंतर्गत श्रोता वर्ग को विषय विशेष का ज्ञान देने के लिए दिया गया भाषण; व्याख्यान, लेक्चर *The college has asked a journalist to come and give a lecture on the media.* 2 a serious talk to sb that explains what he/she has done wrong or how he/she should behave ग़लत काम करने पर या सही व्यवहार सिखाने के लिए डाँट या आलोचना *We got a lecture from a policeman about playing near the railway track.* ► **lecture** *verb* [I, T] पढ़ाना, डाँटना या नसीहत देना *Ashish lectures in Gandhian Studies at the university.* ○ *The policeman lectured the boys about playing on the road.*

**lecturer** /ˈlektʃərə(r) ˈलेक्चर(र्)/ *noun* [C] a person who gives talks to teach people about a subject, especially as a job in a university विषय विशेष को छात्रों को पढ़ाने के लिए व्याख्यान देने वाला व्यक्ति; (विशेषतः विश्वविद्यालय में) व्याख्याता, प्राध्यापक, लेक्चरर

**LED** /ˌel iː ˈdiː ˌएलु ई ˈडी/ *abbr* light emitting diode (a device that produces a light on electrical and electronic equipment) लाइट इमिटिंग डायोड (किसी विद्युत संचालित या इलेक्ट्रॉनिक उपकरण पर प्रकाश करने वाली युक्ति)

**led** ➪ **lead**[1] देखिए।

**ledge** /ledʒ लेज्/ *noun* [C] a narrow shelf underneath a window, or a narrow piece of rock that sticks out on the side of a cliff or mountain खिड़की के नीचे का ख़ाना या पटिया, ऊँची खड़ी चट्टान अथवा पर्वत की ओर आगे को निकली तंग शिला, शिला–फलक, तलशिखा

**lee** /liː ली/ *noun* [*sing.*] the side or part of a hill, building, etc. that provides protection from the wind पहाड़ी, इमारत आदि का हवा से बचाव करने वाला पार्श्व या हिस्सा *We built the house* ***in the lee of*** *the hill.* ➪ **leeward** और **windward** देखिए।

**leech** /liːtʃ लीच्/ *noun* [C] a small creature with a soft body and no legs that usually lives in water. Leeches fasten themselves to other creatures and drink their blood जोंक, जलोका; कोमल शरीर और बिना पैरों वाले ये क्षुद्र जंतु पानी में रहते हैं। ये अन्य प्राणी से कस कर चिपट कर उसका रक्त चूसते हैं

**leek** /liːk लीक्/ *noun* [C] a long thin vegetable that is white at one end with thin green leaves हरी पत्तियों वाली एक पतली सब्ज़ी जिसका एक सिरा सफ़ेद होता है; मंदना

**leeward** /ˈliːwəd ˈलीवड्/ *adj.* on the side of a hill, building, etc. that is protected from the wind पहाड़ी, इमारत आदि के हवा से बचाव करने वाले पार्श्व की ओर ➪ **lee** और **windward** देखिए।

**left**[1] ➪ **leave**[1] का past tense और past participle रूप

**left**[2] /left लेफ़्ट्/ *adj.* **1** on the side where your heart is in the body बायाँ (जिधर हृदय होता है) *I've broken my left arm.* ✪ विलोम **right 2** still available after everything else has been taken or used अन्य सब कुछ समाप्त हो जाने के बाद भी उपलब्ध कुछ, बाक़ी *Is there any bread left?* ○ *How much time do we have left?*

**left**[3] /left लेफ़्ट्/ *adv.* to or towards the left बाईं ओर *Turn left just past the Post Office.* ✪ विलोम **right**

**left**[4] /left लेफ़्ट्/ *noun* **1** [U] the left side बाईं तरफ़ *Our house is just* ***to/on the left of*** *that tall building.* ✪ विलोम **right 2 the Left** [*with sing. or pl. verb*] political groups who support the ideas and beliefs of **socialism** समाजवादी विचारों और मान्यताओं के समर्थक राजनीतिक दल; वामदल, वामपंथी

**left-hand** *adj.* (*only before a noun*) of or on the left बाईं ओर का या बाईं ओर *the left-hand side of the road* ○ *a left-hand drive car*

**left-handed** *adj., adv.* **1** using the left hand rather than the right hand (दाएँ हाथ के स्थान पर) बाएँ हाथ से काम करने वाला; खब्बू, वामहस्तिक *Are you left-handed?* ○ *I write left-handed.* **2** made for left-handed people to use खब्बुओं द्वारा प्रयोग के लिए बना *left-handed scissors*

**leftovers** /ˈleftəʊvəz ˈलेफ़्टओवज़्/ *noun* [*pl.*] food that has not been eaten when a meal has finished भोजन खा लिए जाने के बाद बचा हुआ; उच्छिष्ट

**left wing** *noun* [*sing.*] **1** [*with sing. or pl. verb*] the members of a political party, group, etc. that want more social change than the others in their party किसी राजनीतिक दल, समूह आदि के वे सदस्य जो अन्य सदस्यों की अपेक्षा अधिक सामाजिक परिवर्तन के बड़े पक्षधर वर्ग हैं; सामाजिक क्रांति का पक्षधर वर्ग *the left wing of the Labour Party* **2** the left side of the field in some team sports कुछ दल-आधारित खेलों में बायाँ पक्ष *He plays on the left wing for Mohun Bagan.* ▶ **left-wing** *adj.* वामपक्षीय ✪ विलोम **right-wing**

**leg** /leg लेग्/ *noun* [C] **1** one of the parts of the body on which a person or animal stands or walks (मनुष्य या पशु की) टाँग *A spider has eight legs.* ○ *She sat down and crossed her legs.* ➪ **body** पर चित्र देखिए। **2** one of the parts of a chair, table, etc. on which it stands (कुरसी, मेज़ आदि की) टाँग, पाया *the leg of a chair/table* ○ *a chair/table leg* **3** the part of a pair of trousers, shorts, etc. that covers the leg (पतलून, निकर आदि की) टाँग वाला हिस्सा, पाँयचा *There's a hole in the leg of my trousers/my trouser leg.* **4** one part or section of a journey, competition, etc. किसी यात्रा, प्रतियोगिता आदि का एक अंश या खंड, यात्रा का चरण *The band are in Germany on the first leg of their world tour.*

IDM **pull sb's leg** ➪ **pull**[1] देखिए।

**stretch your legs** ➪ **stretch**[1] देखिए।

**legacy** /ˈlegəsi ˈलेगसि/ *noun* [C] (*pl.* **legacies**) money or property that is given to you after sb dies, because he/she wanted you to have it दिवंगत व्यक्ति द्वारा छोड़ी गई धनराशि या संपत्ति, रिक्थ, वसीयत, संपदा

**legal** /ˈliːɡl ˈलीगल् / *adj.* **1** (*only before a noun*) using or connected with the law क़ानूनी, क़ानून-विषयक *legal advice* ○ *to take legal action against sb* ○ *the legal profession* **2** allowed by law क़ानून-सम्मत, विधि-सम्मत *It is not legal to own a gun without a licence.* ✪ विलोम **illegal** ➪ **lawful** और **legitimate** देखिए। ▶ **legally** /ˈliːɡəli ˈलीगलि / *adv.* क़ानूनी तौर पर, क़ानूनन *Schools are legally responsible for the safety of their pupils.*

**legality** /liːˈɡæləti लीˈगैलटि / *noun* [U] the state of being legal क़ानून-सम्मत होने की स्थिति; वैधता ➪ **illegality** देखिए।

**legalize** (*also* **-ise**) /ˈliːɡəlaɪz ˈलीगलाइज़् / *verb* [T] to make sth legal किसी बात को क़ानून-सम्मत बनाना, वैद्य बनाना, क़ानूनी रूप देना ▶ **legalization** (*also* **-isation**) /ˌliːɡəlaɪˈzeɪʃn ˌलीगलाइˈज़ेश्न् / *noun* [U] वैधीकरण

**legend** /ˈledʒənd ˈलेजन्ड् / *noun* **1** [C] an old story that may or may not be true प्राचीन कथा (जिसका सत्य या असत्य होना प्रासंगिक नहीं); आख्यान, किंवदंती, दंतकथा, लोककथा *the legend of Hanuman* **2** [U] such stories when they are grouped together लोककथा-समूह *According to legend, Hanuman is the son of Pavan, the God of Wind.* **3** [C] a famous person or event प्रसिद्ध व्यक्ति या घटना *a movie/jazz/cricket legend* ▶ **legendary** /ˈledʒəndri ˈलेजन्ड्रि / *adj.* पौराणिक, सुप्रसिद्ध *the legendary heroes of Greek myths* ○ *Madonna, the legendary pop star*

**leggings** /ˈleɡɪŋz ˈलेगिङ्ज़् / *noun* [*pl.*] a piece of women's clothing that fits tightly over both legs from the waist to the feet, like a very thin pair of trousers महिलाओं की तंग चुस्त या पतलून की तरह की पतली पोशाक; लेगिंग

**legible** /ˈledʒəbl ˈलेजबल् / *adj.* that is clear enough to be read easily इतना साफ़ कि पढ़ने में आसानी हो; सुवाच्य, सुपाठ्य *His writing is so small that it's barely legible.* ✪ विलोम **illegible** ➪ **readable** देखिए। ▶ **legibility** /ˌledʒəˈbɪləti ˌलेजˈबिलटि / *noun* सुपाठ्यता, सुवाच्यता ▶ **legibly** /-zəbli -जब्लि / *adv.* सुपाठ्य या सुवाच्य रीति से

**legislate** /ˈledʒɪsleɪt ˈलेजिस्लेट् / *verb* [I] **legislate (for/against sth)** to make a law or laws विधि या क़ानून बनाना

**legislation** /ˌledʒɪsˈleɪʃn ˌलेजिस्ˈलेश्न् / *noun* [U] **1** a group of laws क़ानून-समूह, विधि-समूह *The government is introducing new legislation to help small businesses.* **2** the process of making laws क़ानून बनाने की प्रक्रिया; विधि-निर्माण, विधायन

**legislative** /ˈledʒɪslətɪv ˈलेजिस्लटिव् / *adj.* (*formal*) (*only before a noun*) connected with the act of making laws विधि-निर्माण से संबंधित *a legislative assembly/body/council*

**legislature** /ˈledʒɪsleɪtʃə(r) ˈलेजिस्लेच(र्) / *noun* [C] (*formal*) a group of people who have the power to make and change laws क़ानून बनाने और बदलने का अधिकार रखने वाले व्यक्तियों का समूह; विधान-मंडल

**legitimate** /lɪˈdʒɪtɪmət लिˈजिटिमट् / *adj.* **1** reasonable or acceptable तर्कसंगत या स्वीकार्य *a legitimate excuse/question/concern* **2** allowed by law विधिसंगत, क़ानून से मान्य; वैद्य *Could he earn so much from legitimate business activities?* ➪ **lawful** और **legal** देखिए। **3** (*old-fashioned*) (used about a child) having parents who are married to each other (संतान) विवाहित माता-पिता से उत्पन्न ✪ विलोम **illegitimate** ▶ **legitimacy** /lɪˈdʒɪtɪməsi लिˈजिटिमसि / *noun* [U] वैधता, तर्कसंगति *I intend to challenge the legitimacy of his claim.* ▶ **legitimately** *adv.* वैध रूप से

**legume** /ˈleɡjuːm; lɪˈɡjuːm ˈलेग्यूम्; लिˈग्यूम् / *noun* [C] (*technical*) any plant that has seeds in long **pods.** Peas and beans are legumes बीज वाली फलियों का पौधा, शिंबजातीय पौधा (जैसे मटर और सेम)

**leisure** /ˈleʒə(r) ˈलेश़(र्) / *noun* [U] the time when you do not have to work; free time समय जिसमें काम नहीं करना होता; ख़ाली समय, फ़ुरसत *Shorter working hours mean that people have more leisure.* ○ *leisure activities*

**IDM** **at your leisure** (*formal*) when you have free time फ़ुरसत में *Look through the catalogue at your leisure and then order by telephone.*

**leisure centre** *noun* [C] a public building where you can do sports and other activities in your free time सार्वजनिक भवन जहाँ लोग फ़ुरसत में आकर खेल आदि के द्वारा अपना मनोरंजन करते हैं; मनोरंजन केंद्र

**leisurely** /ˈleʒəli ˈलेश़लि / *adj.* without hurry फ़ुरसत वाला, विश्रामपूर्ण, चैनभरा *a leisurely Sunday breakfast* ○ *I always cycle at a leisurely pace.*

**lemon** /ˈlemən ˈलेमन् / *noun* [C, U] a yellow fruit with sour juice that is used for giving flavour to food and drink नींबू *a slice of lemon* ○ *Add the juice of two lemons.* ➪ **fruit** पर चित्र देखिए।

**lemonade** /ˌleməˈneɪd ˌलेमˈनेड् / *noun* [C, U] **1** (*BrE*) a colourless sweet drink with a lot of bubbles in it रंगहीन झागदार मधुर पेय **2** a drink that is made from fresh lemon juice, sugar and water ताज़े नींबू के रस, चीनी और पानी से बना पेय; शिकंजवी, नींबू का शर्बत

**lemur** /ˈliːmə(r) ˈलीमर्‌/ *noun* [C] an animal like a monkey, with thick fur and a long tail, that lives in trees in Madagascar. There are many different types of lemur मडगास्कर देश के वृक्षों पर रहने वाला बंदर जैसा पशु जिसके बाल घने और पूँछ लंबी होती है; लीमर

**lend** /lend लेन्ड्/ *verb* [T] (*pt, pp* **lent** /lent लेन्ट्/) **1 lend sb sth; lend sth to sb** to allow sb to use sth for a short time or to give sb money that must be paid back after a certain period of time थोड़े समय के लिए उधार देना *Could you lend me Rs 100 until Friday?* ○ *He lent me his bicycle.* ✪ विलोम **borrow** NOTE यदि बैंक आदि आपको ऋण देता है तो उसे निश्चित समय में सूद (**interest**) समेत चुकाना पड़ता है। **2** (*formal*) **lend sth (to sth)** to give or add sth कुछ देना या बढ़ाना *to lend advice/support* ○ *This evidence lends weight to our theory.*

IDM **lend (sb) a hand/lend a hand (to sb)** to help sb किसी व्यक्ति की सहायता करना

PHR V **lend itself to sth** to be suitable for sth किसी के लिए उपयुक्त होना

**lender** /ˈlendə(r) ˈलेन्ड(र्)/ *noun* [C] a person or organization that lends sth, especially money ऋण (विशेषतः धन) देने वाला व्यक्ति या संगठन; ऋणदाता

**length** /leŋθ लेङ्थ्/ *noun* **1** [U, C] the size of sth from one end to the other; how long sth is किसी वस्तु की लंबाई *to measure the length of a room* ○ *The tiny insect is only one millimetre **in length**.* ➪ **width** और **breadth** देखिए। **2** [U] the amount of time that sth lasts समय की अवधि (जिसमें कोई चीज़ बनी रहती है), समय की व्याप्ति, समय का विस्तार *Many people complained about the **length of time** they had to wait.* ○ *the length of a class/speech/film* **3** [U] the number of pages in a book, a letter, etc. किसी पुस्तक, पत्र आदि के पृष्ठों की संख्या **4** [C] the distance from one end of a swimming pool to the other तरण ताल के एक सिरे से दूसरे तक की दूरी *I can swim a length in thirty seconds.* **5** [C] a piece of sth long and thin किसी लंबी और पतली वस्तु (जैसे डोरी) का टुकड़ा *a length of material/rope/string*

IDM **at length** for a long time or in great detail काफ़ी देर तक या काफ़ी विस्तार से *We discussed the matter at great length.*

**go to great lengths** to make more effort than usual in order to achieve sth कुछ पाने के लिए सामान्य से अधिक प्रयास करना

**the length and breadth of sth** to or in all parts of sth किसी वस्तु के सब हिस्सों तक या हिस्सों में *They travelled the length and breadth of India.*

**lengthen** /ˈleŋθən ˈलेङ्थ्न्/ *verb* [I, T] to become longer or to make sth longer लंबा हो जाना या किसी वस्तु को लंबा कर देना

**lengthways** /ˈleŋθweɪz ˈलेङ्थ्वेज़्/ (*also* **lengthwise** /ˈleŋθwaɪz ˈलेङ्थ्वाइज़्/) *adv.* in a direction from one end to the other of sth किसी वस्तु के एक सिरे से दूसरे सिरे तक की दिशा में; लंबाई में *Fold the paper lengthwise.*

**lengthy** /ˈleŋθi ˈलेङ्थि/ *adj.* very long बहुत लंबा, दीर्घ

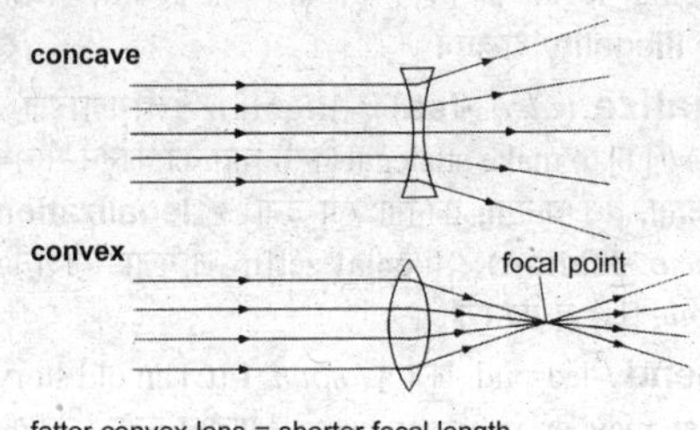


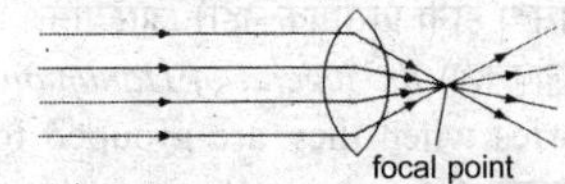


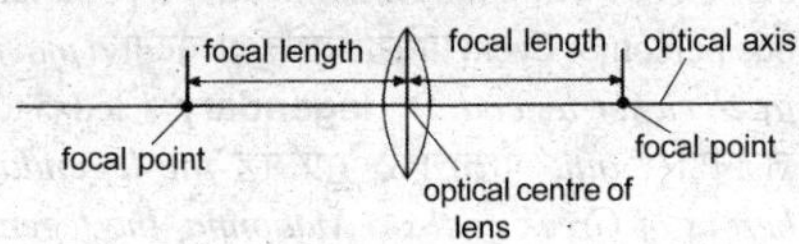


**lenses**

**lenient** /ˈliːniənt ˈलीनिअन्ट्/ *adj.* (used about a punishment or person who punishes) not as strict as expected (दंड या दंड देने वाला व्यक्ति) जो आशा के अनुरूप कठोर न हो; नरम, सौम्य ▶ **lenience** (*also* **leniency** /-ənsi -अन्सि/) *noun* [U] नरमी सौम्यता ▶ **leniently** *adv.* नरमी से

**lens** /lenz लेन्ज़्/ *noun* [C] (*pl.* **lenses**) **1** a curved piece of glass that makes things look bigger, clearer, etc. when you look through it लेन्स, ताल

NOTE कुछ लोग **contact lenses** लगाते हैं ताकि चीज़ें अधिक साफ़ दिखाई दें। कैमरे पर **zoom** या **telephoto lens** लगाया जाता है।

**2** = **contact lens** **3** the transparent part of the eye, behind the round hole in the middle of the eye (**pupil**), that changes shape in order to direct light so that you can see clearly आँख में पुतली के पीछे पारदर्शी अंग जो प्रकाश को नियंत्रित करने के लिए अपनी आकृति बदलता है (ताकि साफ़ दिखाई दे) ➪ **eye** पर चित्र देखिए।

**Lent** /lent लेन्ट्/ *noun* [U] a period of 40 days starting in February or March, when some Christians stop doi ng or eating certain things for religious reasons फ़रवरी-मार्च में चालीस दिन की अवधि जिसमें कुछ ईसाई लोग धार्मिक कारणों से खान-पान या कुछ आदतों पर रोक लगाते हैं; ईसाइयों का चालीसा, ईस्टर से पहले के चालीस दिन *I'm giving up smoking for Lent.*

**lent** ➪ **lend** का past tense और past participle रूप

**lentil** /ˈlentl ˈलेन्ट्ल्/ *noun* [C] a small brown, orange or green seed that can be dried and used in cooking दाल *lentil soup/stew*

**Leo** /ˈliːəʊ ˈलीओ/ *noun* [U] the fifth sign of the **zodiac**, the Lion सिंह राशि

**leopard** /ˈlepəd ˈलेपड्/ *noun* [C] a large wild animal of the cat family that has yellow fur with dark spots. Leopards live in Africa and Southern Asia तेंदुआ, चीता(अफ्रीक़ा और दक्षिण एशिया मूल का)

> **NOTE** मादा तेंदुआ को **leopardess** और बच्चे को **cub** कहते हैं। ➪ **lion** पर चित्र देखिए।

**leotard** /ˈliːətɑːd ˈलीअटाड्/ *noun* [C] a piece of clothing that fits the body tightly from the neck down to the top of the legs. Leotards are worn by dancers or women doing certain sports गरदन से पैर तक की तंग पोशाक जिसे नर्तक या नर्तकियाँ या कुछ खेलों में महिलाएँ पहनती हैं

**leper** /ˈlepə(r) ˈलेप(र्)/ *noun* [C] a person who has leprosy कुष्ठ रोग से पीड़ित व्यक्ति; कोढ़ी

**leprosy** /ˈleprəsi ˈलेप्रसि/ *noun* [U] a serious infectious disease that affects the skin, nerves, etc. and can cause parts of the body to fall off छूत की एक गंभीर बीमारी जिसका त्वचा आदि पर असर होता है और शरीर के कुछ अंग गल कर गिर जाते हैं; कुष्ठ रोग, कोढ़

**lesbian** /ˈlezbiən ˈलेज़्बिअन्/ *noun* [C] a woman who is sexually attracted to other women कामुकता पूर्वक अन्य स्त्रियों के प्रति आकर्षित होने वाली स्त्री; समलिंगी कामुक स्त्री ▶ **lesbian** *adj.* स्त्री समलिंग-कामुकता से संबंधित या समलिंग-कामुक *a lesbian relationship* ▶ **lesbianism** *noun* [U] स्त्री-समलिंग-कामुकता ➪ **gay** और **homosexual** देखिए।

**less¹** /les लेस्/ *det., pronoun, adv.* **1** (*used with uncountable nouns*) a smaller amount (of) किसी वस्तु की कुछ कम मात्रा, कम *It took less time than I thought.* ○ *I'm too fat—I must try to eat less.*

> **NOTE** बहुवचनांत क्रियाओं (plural verbs) के साथ **less** का प्रयोग कभी-कभी दिखाई पड़ता है—*less cars* परंतु **fewer** को ही शुद्ध प्रयोग माना जाता है—*fewer cars.*

**2** not so much (as) अन्य के समान नहीं, जितना दूसरा उतना नहीं, कम *He's less intelligent than his brother.* ○ *People work less well when they're tired.* ✪ विलोम **more**

**IDM** **less and less** becoming smaller and smaller in amount or degree मात्रा में कमतर होते जाना

**more or less** ➪ **more²** देखिए।

**less²** /les लेस्/ *prep.* taking a certain number or amount away; minus निश्चित संख्या या मात्रा को घटाकर *You'll earn Rs 100 an hour, less tax.*

**lessee** /leˈsiː लेˈसी/ *noun* [C] (in law) a person who has a legal agreement (**a lease**) allowing him/her use of a building, an area of land, etc. (क़ानून में) किसी भवन, भूखंड आदि को प्रयोग के लिए पट्टे पर लेने वाला व्यक्ति; पट्टेदार

**lessen** /ˈlesn ˈलेसन्/ *verb* [I, T] to become less; to make sth less कम हो जाना; कम कर देना *The medicine will lessen your pain.*

**lesser** /ˈlesə(r) ˈलेस(र्)/ *adj., adv.* (*only before a noun*) not as great/much as जितना अन्य है उतना नहीं, अपेक्षाकृत कम *He is guilty and so, to a lesser extent, is his wife.* ○ *a lesser-known artist*

**IDM** **the lesser of two evils** the better of two bad things दो बुराइयों में से कमतर (बुराई)

**lesson** /ˈlesn ˈलेसन्/ *noun* [C] **1** a period of time when you learn or teach sth समयावधि जिसमें हम कुछ सीखते हैं या सिखाते हैं *I want to take extra lessons in English conversation.* ○ *a driving lesson* **2** something that is intended to be or should be learnt सबक़, सीख *I hope we can learn some lessons from this disaster.*

**IDM** **learn your lesson** ➪ **learn** देखिए।

**teach sb a lesson** ➪ **teach** देखिए।

**lessor** /leˈsɔː(r) लेˈसॉ(र्)/ *noun* [C] (in law) a person who gives sb the use of a building, an area of land, etc., having made a legal agreement (**a lease**) (क़ानून में) किसी भवन, भूखंड आदि को प्रयोग के लिए पट्टे पर देने वाला व्यक्ति; पट्टाकार

**let** /let लेट्/ *verb* [T] (*pres. part.* **letting**; *pt, pp* **let**) **1 let sb/sth do sth** to allow sb/sth to do sth; to make sb/sth able to do sth किसी व्यक्ति या वस्तु को कुछ करने देना; किसी व्यक्ति वस्तु को कुछ करने के योग्य बनाना *My parents let me stay out till 11 o'clock.* ○ *I wanted to borrow Bharat's bike but he wouldn't let me.* ○ *This ticket lets you travel anywhere in the city for a day.*

> **NOTE** **Let** का प्रयोग कर्मवाच्य (passive) में नहीं हो सकता। इसके लिए **to** के साथ **allow** या **permit** का प्रयोग ही मान्य है—*They let him take the exam again.* ○ *He was allowed to take the exam again.* ➪ **allow** पर नोट देखिए।

**2** to allow sth to happen किसी बात को होने देना *He's let the dinner burn again!* ○ *Don't let the fire go out.* **3** used for offering help to sb किसी को सहायता की पेशकश करने के लिए प्रयुक्त *Let me help you carry your bags.* **4** to allow sb/sth to go somewhere किसी व्यक्ति या वस्तु को कहीं जाने या आने देना *Open the windows and let some fresh air in.* ○ *She was let out of prison yesterday.* **5** used for making suggestions about what you and other people can do किसी को कुछ करने का सुझाव देने के लिए प्रयुक्त *'Let's go to the cinema tonight.' 'Yes, let's.'*

NOTE इस अर्थ में **let** का निषेधात्मक (negative) रूप **let's not** है—*Let's not go to that awful restaurant again.*

**6 let sth (out) (to sb)** to allow sb to use a building, room, etc. in return for rent किसी को किराए पर मकान, कमरा आदि देना *They let out two rooms to students.* ○ *There's a flat to let in our block.* ➪ **hire** पर नोट देखिए।

IDM **let alone** and certainly not की बात तो बिलकुल नहीं *We haven't decided where we're going yet, let alone booked the tickets.*

**let sb/sth go; let go of sb/sth** to stop holding sb/sth किसी व्यक्ति या वस्तु को पकड़े न रहना, छोड़ देना *Let me go. You're hurting me!* ○ *Hold the rope and don't let go of it.*

**let sb know** ➪ **know**[1] देखिए।

**let me see; let's see** used when you are thinking or trying to remember sth यह व्यक्त करने के लिए प्रयुक्त कि आप कुछ सोचने या याद करने की कोशिश कर रहे हैं *Where did I put the car keys? Let's see. I think I left them by the telephone.*

**let sth slip** to accidentally say sth that you should keep secret अचानक कोई बात कह बैठना (जो अन्यथा गुप्त रहनी चाहिए)

**let's say** for example उदाहरण के लिए या सुझाव के रूप में *You could work two mornings a week, let's say Tuesday and Friday.*

**let yourself go 1** to relax without worrying what other people think (अपने मामले में) दूसरों की सोच की चिंता न करना **2** to allow yourself to become untidy, dirty, etc. अपने मामले में लापरवाह हो जाना

PHR V **let sb down** to not do sth that you promised to do for sb; to disappoint sb किसी के साथ किए वादे को तोड़ देना; किसी को निराश कर देना

**let on (about sth) (to sb)** to tell sb a secret किसी को रहस्य की बात बताना *He didn't let on how much he'd paid for the vase.*

**let sb off** to not punish sb, or to give sb a less serious punishment than expected दंड न देना या अपेक्षा से कम दंड देना *He expected to go to prison but they let him off with a fine.*

**let sth out** to make a sound with your voice मुँह से चीख़ आदि निकालना *to let out a scream/sigh/groan/yell*

**lethal** /ˈliːθl ˈलीथ्ल्/ *adj.* that can cause death or great damage मृत्युकारक, घातक, अत्यंत हानिकारक *a lethal weapon/drug* ▶ **lethally** /ˈliːθəli ˈलीथ्लि/ *adv.* घातक रूप से

**lethargy** /ˈleθədʒi ˈलेथ्जि/ *noun* [U] the feeling of being very tired and not having any energy बहुत थकान या कमज़ोरी ▶ **lethargic** /ləˈθɑːdʒɪk लˈथाजिक्/ *adj.* बहुत थका, कमज़ोर

**letter** /ˈletə(r) ˈलेट(र्)/ *noun* [C] **1** a written or printed message that you send to sb (लिखा हुआ या मुद्रित) पत्र *I got a letter from Mohit this morning.* ○ *I'm writing* ***a thank-you letter*** *to my uncle for the gift he sent.* **2** a written or printed sign that represents a sound in a language भाषा में ध्वनि का लिखित या मुद्रित प्रतीक; अक्षर *'Z' is the last letter of the English alphabet.*

NOTE बहुत सी लिपियों, जैसे अंग्रेज़ी (रोमन) के अक्षरों को **capitals** या **small** में लिखा जा सकता है—*Is 'east' written with a capital or a small 'e'?*

**letter box** *noun* [C] **1** a hole in a door or wall for putting letters, etc. through दरवाज़े या दीवार में बना सुराख़ जिसमें से पत्र आदि भीतर डाले जाते हैं **2** (*AmE* **mailbox**) a small box near the main door of a building or by the road in which letters are left for the owner to collect किसी भवन या सड़क पर लगा एक छोटा डिब्बा जिसमें भवन-स्वामी के पत्र डाल दिए जाते हैं; मेल बॉक्स **3** = **post box**

**lettuce** /ˈletɪs ˈलेटिस्/ *noun* [C, U] a plant with large green leaves which are eaten cold in salads सलाद पत्ते का पौधा *a lettuce leaf*

**leucocyte** /ˈluːkəsaɪt ˈलूकसाइट्/ *noun* [C] (*technical*) a white blood cell रक्त का श्वेत कण, श्वेताणु; श्वेत कोशिका

**leukaemia** (*AmE* **leukemia**) /luːˈkiːmɪə लूˈकीमिआ/ *noun* [U] a serious disease of the blood which often results in death रक्त का गंभीर रोग जिससे प्रायः मृत्यु हो जाती है; श्वेतरक्तता, ल्यूकीमिया

**levee** /ˈlevi ˈलेवि/ *noun* [C] (in geography) a low wall built at the side of a river to prevent it from flooding (भूगोल में) नदी के किनारे बनी नीची दीवार ताकि नदी में बाढ़ न आए ➪ **flood plain** पर चित्र देखिए।

**level**[1] /ˈlevl ˈलेव्ल्/ *noun* [C] **1** the amount, size or number of sth (compared to sth else) (अन्य की तुलना में) किसी वस्तु की मात्रा, आकार या संख्या *a low level of unemployment ○ high stress/pollution levels* **2** the height, position, standard, etc. of sth किसी वस्तु की ऊँचाई, अवस्था, मानदंड आदि (की दृष्टि से उसका स्तर) *He used to play tennis at a high level. ○ an intermediate-level student ○ top-level discussions* **3** a way of considering sth किसी बात पर विचार करने का तरीक़ा *on a spiritual/personal/professional level* **4** a flat surface or layer चपटी सतह या परत *a multi-level shopping centre*

**level**[2] /ˈlevl ˈलेव्ल्/ *adj.* **1** with no part higher than any other; flat जिसमें किसी अंश की ऊँचाई दूसरे से अधिक नहीं, बराबर की (ऊँचाई); समतल *Make sure the shelves are level before you fix them in position. ○ level ground ○ a level teaspoon of sugar* **2 level (with sb/sth)** at the same height, standard or position समान ऊँचाई, मानदंड या अवस्था पर *The boy's head was level with his father's shoulder. ○ The teams are level on 34 points.*

IDM **a level playing field** a situation in which everyone has an equal chance of success सब के लिए सफलता हेतु समान अवसर की स्थिति

**level**[3] /ˈlevl ˈलेव्ल्/ *verb* [T] (**levelling; levelled** *AmE* **leveling; leveled**) to make sth flat, equal or level किसी वस्तु को समतल, समान या हमवार करना *Mohun Bagan levelled the score with a late goal. ○ Many buildings were levelled* (= destroyed) *in the earthquake.*

PHR V **level sth at sb/sth** to aim sth at sb/sth किसी व्यक्ति या वस्तु को निशाना बनाना *They levelled serious criticisms at the standard of teaching.*

**level off/out** to become flat, equal or level समतल, समान या चौरस हो जाना

**level crossing** (*AmE* **railroad crossing**) *noun* [C] a place where a railway crosses the surface of a road समान तल पर सड़क का वह स्थान जहाँ से रेलगाड़ी या रेलपटरी गुज़रती या पारगमन होती है; समपार

**level-headed** *adj.* calm and sensible; able to make good decisions in a difficult situation शांत और समझदार; कठिन परिस्थिति में सही निर्णय लेने में समर्थ; संतुलित

**lever** /ˈliːvə(r) ˈलीव़(र्)/ *noun* [C] **1** a handle that you pull or push in order to make a machine, etc. work मशीन आदि को चलाने के लिए मूठ या हत्था (जिसे खींचा या खिसकाया जाता है); लीवर, हैंडिल *Pull the lever towards you. ○ the gear lever in a car* **2** a bar or tool that is used to lift or open sth when you put pressure or force on one end एक सिरे पर दबाव डालकर या ताक़त लगाकर किसी वस्तु को ऊपर उठाने के लिए प्रयुक्त छड़ या औज़ार; लीवर, उत्तोलक *You need to get the tyre off with a lever.*

▶ **lever** *verb* [T] लीवर से कुछ उठाना या चलाना *The police had to lever the door open.*

**leverage** /ˈliːvərɪdʒ ˈलीव़रिज्/ *noun* [U] the act of using a lever to lift or open sth; the force needed to do this किसी वस्तु को उठाने या खोलने के लिए लीवर का प्रयोग; इस काम के लिए अपेक्षित शक्ति

**levy** /ˈlevi ˈलेवि/ verb [T] (*pres. part.* **levying;** *3rd pesson. sing. pres.* **levies;** *pt,pp* **levid**) (*written*) **levy sth (on sb)** to officially demand and collect money, etc. क़ानूनी तौर पर धन की माँग करना और जमा करना, क़ानूनन उगाही करना

**lexicon** /ˈleksɪkən ˈलेक्सिकन्/ *noun* **1** (*also* **the lexicon**) [*sing.*] all the words and phrases used in a particular language or subject; all the words and phrases used and known by a particular person or group of people किसी विषय-क्षेत्र या भाषा की समूची शब्द संपदा; विशेष व्यक्ति या व्यक्ति-समुदाय को ज्ञात और उसके द्वारा प्रयुक्त समस्त शब्दकोश; शब्दावली **2** [C] a list of words from A to Z on a particular subject or in a language किसी भाषा में विशिष्ट विषय-क्षेत्र से संबंधित आदि से अंत तक समस्त शब्दों का संग्रह; संपूर्ण शब्दसंग्रह *a lexicon of technical scientific terms*

**liability** /ˌlaɪəˈbɪləti ˌलाइअˈबिलटि/ *noun* (*pl.* **liabilities**) **1** [U] **liability (for sth)** the state of being responsible for sth किसी बात का उत्तरदायित्व *The company cannot accept liability for damage to cars in this car park.* **2** [C] (*informal*) a person or thing that can cause a lot of problems, cost a lot of money, etc. व्यक्ति या वस्तु जो बहुत-सी समस्याएँ उत्पन्न करे, बहुत-सा ख़र्चा करवाए आदि; एक मुसीबत **3** [C, *usually pl.*] = **debt**

**liable** /ˈlaɪəbl ˈलाइअबल्/ *adj.* (*not before a noun*) **1 liable to do sth** likely to do sth कुछ करने की संभावना से युक्त *We're all liable to fall asleep while driving when we are very tired.* **2 liable to sth** likely to have or suffer from sth किसी समस्या से ग्रस्त होने की संभावना से युक्त *The area is liable to floods.* **3 liable (for sth)** (in law) responsible for sth (क़ानून में) किसी बात के लिए उत्तरदायी

**liaise** /liˈeɪz लिˈएज़्/ *verb* [I] **liaise (with sb/sth)** to work closely with a person, group, etc. and give him/her/it regular information about what you are doing किसी व्यक्ति, दल आदि के साथ घनिष्ठतापूर्वक काम करना तथा अपने कार्य की प्रगति के विषय में उसे सूचित करते रहना

**liaison** /liˈeɪzn लिˈएज़्न् / *noun* **1** [U, *sing.*] **liaison (between A and B)** communication between two or more people or groups that work together साथ काम करने वाले व्यक्तियों या समूहों के बीच संपर्क या संप्रेषण **2** [C] a secret sexual relationship गुप्त यौन संबंध

**liar** /ˈlaɪə(r)ˈलाइअ(र्) / *noun* [C] a person who does not tell the truth असत्यभाषी व्यक्ति, झूठा व्यक्ति *She called me a liar.* ➪ **lie** verb और **lie** noun देखिए।

**libel** /ˈlaɪblˈलाइब्ल् / *noun* [C, U] the act of printing a statement about sb that is not true and would give people a bad opinion of him/her किसी व्यक्ति की प्रतिष्ठा को चोट पहुँचाते हुए उसके विषय में असत्य वक्तव्य को प्रकाशित करने का कार्य; अपमान-लेख *The singer is suing the newspaper for libel.* ▶ **libel** *verb* [T] (**libelling; libelled** *AmE* **libeling; libeled**) अपमान-लेख प्रकाशित करना *The actor claims he was libelled in the magazine article.*

**liberal** /ˈlɪbərəlˈलिबरल् / *adj.* **1** accepting different opinions or kinds of behaviour; tolerant भिन्न मतों और व्यवहारों के प्रति उदार; सहिष्णु *He has very liberal parents.* **2** (in politics) believing in or based on principles of commercial freedom, freedom of choice, and avoiding extreme social and political change (राजनीति में) अतिवादी सामाजिक और राजनीतिक परिवर्तन से असहमत तथा व्यापार और प्राथमिकताओं के मामले में खुलेपन के सिद्धांत पर आधारित या उसमें विश्वास करने वाला; उदारतावादी *liberal policies/politicians* **3** not strictly limited in amount or variety मात्रा या विविधता की दृष्टि से दृढ़तया सीमित या बद्ध न होना ▶ **liberal** *noun* [C] उदार *He's always considered himself a liberal.* ▶ **liberalism** /-ɪzəm इज़्म् / *noun* [U] उदारवाद

**liberally** /ˈlɪbərəliˈलिबरलि / *adv.* freely or in large amounts खुलकर या भरपूर; उदारतापूर्वक

**liberate** /ˈlɪbəreɪtˈलिबरेट् / *verb* [T] **liberate sb/sth (from sth)** to allow sb/sth to be free किसी व्यक्ति या वस्तु को आज़ाद या मुक्त करना *India was liberated in 1947.* ▶**liberation** /ˌlɪbəˈreɪʃn ˌलिबˈरेश्न् / *noun* [U] ˌआज़ादी या मुक्ति, स्वतंत्रता

**liberated** /ˈlɪbəreɪtɪdˈलिबरेटिड् / *adj.* free from traditional opinions or ways of behaving that might limit you in what you think or do परंपरागत धारणाओं और व्यवहार-सरणियों के बंधन से मुक्त

**liberty** /ˈlɪbətiˈलिबटि / *noun* [C, U] (*pl.* **liberties**) the freedom to go where you want, do what you want, etc. मनचाही जगह पर जाने, मनचाहा काम करने आदि की आज़ादी *We must defend our civil liberties at all costs.* ➪ **freedom** देखिए।

IDM **at liberty (to do sth)** free or allowed to do sth कोई काम करने के लिए स्वतंत्र या अनुमति-प्राप्त *You are at liberty to leave when you wish.*

**Libra** /ˈliːbrəˈलीब्रा / *noun* [U] the seventh sign of the **zodiac,** the Scales तुला राशी

**librarian** /laɪˈbreəriən लाइˈब्रेअरिअन् / *noun* [C] a person who works in or is incharge of a library पुस्तकालय में काम करने वाला या उसका अध्यक्ष (व्यक्ति)

**library** /ˈlaɪbrəri; ˈlaɪbri ˈलाइब्ररि; ˈलाइब्रि/ *noun* [C] (*pl.* **libraries**) **1** a room or building that contains a collection of books, etc. that can be looked at or borrowed पुस्तकालय (भवन) *My library books are due back tomorrow.* ➪ **bookshop** देखिए। **2** a private collection of books, etc. पुस्तकों आदि का निजी संग्रह

**lice** ➪ **louse** का plural रूप

**licence** (*AmE* **license**) /ˈlaɪsnsˈलाइसन्स् / *noun* **1** [C] **a licence (for sth/to do sth)** an official paper that shows you are allowed to do or have sth कोई विशेष काम करने या कोई वस्तु रखने की अनुमति देने वाला आधिकारिक पत्र; सरकारी या क़ानूनी अनुमति-पत्र, लाइसेंस, अनुज्ञप्ति *Do you have a licence for this gun?* ○ *The shop has applied for a licence to sell alcoholic drinks.* ➪ **driving licence** देखिए। **2** [U] (*formal*) **licence (to do sth)** permission or freedom to do sth कुछ करने की अनुमति, आज़ादी या छूट *The soldiers were given licence to shoot if they were attacked.*

**licence plate** (*AmE* **license plate**) = **number plate**

**license**[1] /ˈlaɪsnsˈलाइसन्स् / *verb* [T] to give official permission for sth कोई काम करने की आधिकारिक अनुमति देना *Is that gun licensed?*

**license**[2] (*AmE*) = **licence**

**lichen** /ˈlaɪkən; ˈlɪtʃənˈलाइकन्; ˈलिचन्/ *noun* [U, C] a very small grey or yellow plant that spreads over the surface of rocks, walls and trees and does not have any flowers बहुत छोटा भूरा या पीला पुष्पहीन पौधा जो चट्टानों, दीवारों और वृक्षों पर छा जाता है; शैवाक

**lick** /lɪk लिक् / *verb* [T] to move your tongue across sth किसी वस्तु पर जीभ फेरना, किसी वस्तु को चाटना *The child licked the spoon clean.* ○ *I licked the envelope and stuck it down.* ▶ **lick** *noun* [C] चाटने की क्रिया

**licorice** = **liquorice**

**lid** /lɪd लिड् / *noun* [C] **1** the top part of a box, pot, etc. that can be lifted up or taken off किसी बक्से, बरतन आदि का ढक्कन **2** = **eyelid**

**lie**[1] /laɪ लाइ / *verb* [I] (*pres. part.* **lying;** *pt, pp* **lied**) **lie (to sb) (about sth)** to say or write sth that you know is not true कोई असत्य बात कहना या लिखना *He lied about his age in order to join the army.* ○ *How could you lie to me!* ▶ **lie** *noun* [C] असत्य या झूठी बात, असत्य/झूठ *to tell a lie* ○ *That story about his mother being ill was just* ***a pack of lies****.*

> **NOTE** किसी की भावनाओं को चोट नहीं पहुँचाने के लिए कहा गया झूठ को **white lie** कहते हैं। ➪ **liar** और **fib** देखिए।

**lie**[2] /laɪ लाइ / *verb* [I] (*pres. part* **lying;** *pt* **lay** /leɪ ले /; *pp pt* **lain** /leɪn लेन् /) **1** to be in or move into a flat or horizontal position (so that you are not standing or sitting) सपाट या क्षैतिज स्थिति में होना (खड़े या बैठे रहने से भिन्न), लेटना, पड़े होना *He lay on the sofa and went to sleep.* ○ *to lie on your back/side/front* ○ *The book lay open in front of her.*

> **NOTE** याद रखिए शब्द **lie** का प्रयोग किसी वस्तु के संदर्भ में नहीं होता है। यदि किसी वस्तु को सपाट स्थिति में रखा जाता है तो उसके लिए अभिव्यक्ति **lay** (it down) प्रयुक्त होती है—*to lay a book on a desk.*

**2** to be or stay in a certain state or position एक विशेष स्थिति या अवस्था में होना या पड़े होना *Snow lay thick on the ground.* ○ *They are young and their whole lives* ***lie ahead*** *of them.* **3 lie (in sth)** to exist or to be found somewhere (किसी का) कहीं पर होना या मिलना *The problem lies in deciding when to stop.*

**IDM lie in wait (for sb)** to hide somewhere waiting to attack, surprise or catch sb किसी पर आक्रमण करने, उसे चकित करने या पकड़ने के लिए कहीं पर छिपकर बैठना, ताक लगाना, प्रतीक्षा करना

**lie low** to try not to attract attention to yourself चुपचाप रहना (कि आप पर ध्यान न जाए)

**PHR V lie about/around** to relax and do nothing (बिना कुछ किए) आराम फ़रमाना

**lie back** to relax and do nothing while sb else works, etc. दूसरे काम करें और स्वयं आराम करना

**lie behind sth** to be the real hidden reason for sth किसी परिस्थिति के लिए कोई वास्तविक गुप्त कारण होना *We may never know what lay behind his decision to resign.*

**lie down** (used about a person) to be in or move into a flat or horizontal position so that you can rest आराम करने के लिए सपाट या पड़ी अवस्था में होना या चले जाना, लेट कर आराम करना **NOTE** इसी से संबंधित अभिव्यक्ति **have a lie-down** है।

**lie in** (*informal*) to stay in bed later than usual because you do not have to get up उठने का समय हो जाने के बाद भी (कोई काम न होने के कारण) बिस्तर में पड़े रहना **NOTE** इसी से संबंधित अभिव्यक्ति **have a lie-in** है। ➪ **oversleep** देखिए।

**lie with sb (to do sth)** (*informal*) to be sb's responsibility to do sth कोई काम किसी की ज़िम्मेदारी होना

**lie detector** *noun* [C] a piece of equipment that can show if a person is telling the truth or not उपकरण जो यह संकेत दे पाता है कि कोई व्यक्ति सच बोल रहा है या नहीं

**Lieut.** (*also* **Lt** ) *abbr.* Lieutenant लेफ़्टिनेंट

**lieutenant** /lefˈtenənt लेफ़्ˈटेनन्ट्/ *noun* [C] an officer at a middle level in the army, navy or air force स्थल सेना, नौ सेना या वायु सेना में एक मध्यस्तरी अधिकारी; लेफ़्टिनेंट

**life** /laɪf लाइफ़् / *noun* (*pl.* **lives** /laɪvz लाइव़्ज़् /) **1** [U] the quality that people, animals or plants have when they are not dead व्यक्तियों, पशुओं या पौधों की जीवित अवस्था; जीवन, ज़िंदगी *Do you believe in life after death?* ○ *to bring sb/come back to life* **2** [U] living things सजीव वस्तुएँ *Life on earth began in a very simple form.* ○ *plant life* **3** [C, U] the state of being alive as a human being मनुष्य का जीवन, मानव के रूप में अस्तित्व *Would you* ***risk*** *your* ***life*** *to protect your property?* ○ *Doctors fought all night to* ***save*** *her* ***life****.* **4** [C, U] the period during which sb/sth is alive or exists किसी व्यक्ति या वस्तु के जीवित रहने या बने रहने की अवधि, आस्तित्व की कालावधि; जीवन, आयु *I've lived in this town* ***all*** *my* ***life****.* ○ *I spent my early life in Mussorie.* ○ *to have a short/long/exciting life* **5** [U] the things that you may experience while you are alive मानव जीवन की घटनाएँ, अनुभव आदि *Life can be hard for a single parent.* ○ *I'm not happy with the situation, but I suppose* ***that's life****.* **6** [C, U] a way of living जीने का ढंग *They went to America to* ***start a new life****.* **7** [U] energy; activity स्फूर्ति, ऊर्जा; सक्रियता, ज़िंदादिली *Young children are* ***full of life****.* ○ *These streets* ***come to life*** *in the evenings.* **8** [U] something that really exists and is not just a story, a picture, etc. वास्तविक जीवन (किसी कहानी, चित्र आदि से भिन्न) *I wonder what that actor's like* ***in real life****.* ○ *Do you draw people* ***from life*** *or from photographs?*

**IDM a fact of life** ➪ **fact** देखिए।

**the facts of life** ➪ **fact** देखिए।

**full of beans/life** ➪ **full**[1] देखिए।

**get a life** (*spoken*) used to tell sb to stop being boring and do sth more interesting किसी को कुछ रुचिकर करने या होने के लिए प्रयुक्त

**lose your life** ➪ **lose** देखिए।

**a matter of life and/or death** ➪ **matter**[1] देखिए।

**take your (own) life** to kill yourself आत्महत्या करना

**a walk of life** ➪ **walk**[2] देखिए।

**a/sb's way of life** ➪ **way**[1] देखिए।

**have the time of your life** ➪ **time**[1] देखिए।

**life-and-death** (*also* **life-or-death**) *adj.* (*only before a noun*) very serious or dangerous बहुत गंभीर या ख़तरनाक *a life-and-death struggle/matter/decision*

● **lifebelt** /ˈlaɪfbelt ˈलाइफ़्बेल्ट् / (*also* **lifebuoy** /ˈlaɪfbɔɪ ˈलाइफ़्बॉइ /) *noun* [C] (*BrE*) a ring that is made from light material which will float. A lifebelt is thrown to a person who has fallen into water to stop him/her from sinking (जीवन) रक्षा-पेटी (हलकी सामग्री से बना पानी पर तैरने वाला एक बड़ा छल्ला जिसे डूबते व्यक्ति की ओर फेंका जाता है ताकि वह उसके सहारे डूबने से बच सके)

**lifeboat** /ˈlaɪfbəʊt ˈलाइफ़्बोट् / *noun* [C] **1** a small boat that is carried on a large ship and that is used to escape from the ship if it is in danger of sinking (जीवन) रक्षा-नौका (जहाज़ के डूबने का ख़तरा होने पर लोगों के प्राण बचाने के लिए इस नौका का प्रयोग किया जाता है) **2** a special boat that is used for rescuing people who are in danger at sea समुद्र में संकटग्रस्त लोगों को बचाने के लिए प्रयुक्त विशेष नौका; जीवनरक्षा-नौका; जीवन-तरी

**life cycle** *noun* [C] the series of forms into which a living thing changes as it develops प्राणियों और वनस्पतियों का जीवन-चक्र *the life cycle of a frog*

**life expectancy** *noun* [C, U] (*pl.* **life expectancies**) the number of years that a person is likely to live व्यक्ति की संभावित जीवन-अवधि या आयु

**lifeguard** /ˈlaɪfgɑːd ˈलाइफ़्गाड् / *noun* [C] a person at a beach or swimming pool whose job is to rescue people who are in difficulty in the water जीवन-रक्षक व्यक्ति (लोगों को कठिनाई से उबारने के लिए समुद्र-तट या स्विमिंग पूल पर नियुक्त); गोताख़ोर रक्षक

**life jacket** *noun* [C] a plastic or rubber jacket without sleeves that can be filled with air. A life jacket is used to make sb float if he/she falls into water जीवन रक्षा-जैकेट (बिना आस्तीन की प्लास्टिक या रबर से बनी जैकेट जिसमें हवा भर देते हैं जिसे पहना व्यक्ति पानी में गिरने पर डूबने से बच जाता है)

**lifeless** /ˈlaɪfləs ˈलाइफ़्लस् / *adj.* **1** dead or appearing to be dead निष्प्राण या निष्प्राणवत **2** without energy or interest; dull स्फूर्ति या रुचि से रहित; सुस्त, ढीलाढाला

**lifelike** /ˈlaɪflaɪk ˈलाइफ़्लाइक् / *adj.* looking like a real person or thing वास्तविक व्यक्ति जैसा दिखने वाला, जीता-जागता-सा, सजीव के समान *The flowers are made of silk but they are very lifelike.*

**lifeline** /ˈlaɪflaɪn ˈलाइफ़्लाइन् / *noun* [C] something that is very important for sb and that he/she depends on किसी व्यक्ति के लिए कोई बहुत आवश्यक वस्तु जिसके ऊपर वह निर्भर है; जीवन-रेखा *For many old people their telephone is a lifeline.*

**lifelong** /ˈlaɪflɒŋ ˈलाइफ़्लॉङ् / *adj.* (*only before a noun*) for all of your life जीवन भर के लिए; आजीवन *a lifelong friend*

**life-size(d)** *adj.* of the same size as the real person or thing व्यक्ति या वस्तु के वास्तविक आकार का, पूरे कद का; आदमकद *a life-sized statue*

**lifespan** /ˈlaɪfspæn ˈलाइफ़्स्पैन् / *noun* [C] the length of time that sth is likely to live, work, last, etc. जीवन-अवधि *A mosquito has a lifespan of only a few days.*

**life story** *noun* [C] (*pl.* **life stories**) the story of sb's life किसी व्यक्ति की जीवन-कथा

**lifestyle** /ˈlaɪfstaɪl ˈलाइफ़्स्टाइल् / *noun* [C] the way that you live जीवन-शैली

**life support** *noun* [U] the fact of being kept alive by a special machine विशेष मशीन की सहायता से किसी को जीवित रखने की स्थिति *After the accident he was* ***on life support*** *for a week.*

**life-support machine** *noun* [C] a piece of equipment in a hospital that keeps sb alive when he/she cannot breathe without help रोगी के स्वयं साँस लेने में असमर्थ होने पर उसे जीवित रखने में सहायक मशीन

**lifetime** /ˈlaɪftaɪm ˈलाइफ़्टाइम् / *noun* [C] the period of time that sb is alive जीवन-काल, सारी उम्र, आजीवन

**lift**[1] /lɪft लिफ़्ट् / verb **1** [T] **lift sb/sth (up)** to move sb/sth to a higher level or position किसी व्यक्ति या वस्तु को उच्चतर स्तर या स्थिति में ले जाना, ऊपर उठाना *He lifted the child up onto his shoulders.* ○ *Lift your arm very gently and see if it hurts.* **2** [T] to move sb/sth from one place or position to another किसी व्यक्ति या वस्तु को एक स्थान (या स्थिति) से हटाकर दूसरे स्थान पर (या स्थिति में) रखना *She lifted the suitcase down from the rack.* **3** [T] to end or remove a rule, law, etc. किसी नियम, क़ानून आदि को समाप्त करना या हटाना *The ban on public meetings has been lifted.* **4** [I, T] to become or make sb happier ख़ुशी बढ़ना या बढ़ाना *The news lifted our spirits.* **5** [I] (used about clouds, fog, etc.) to rise up and disappear (बादल, धुंध आदि का) छँट जाना, ऊपर उड़ जाना या ग़ायब हो जाना *The mist lifted towards the end of the morning.* **6** [T] (*informal*) **lift sth (from sb/sth)** to steal or copy sth किसी वस्तु की चोरी करना या नक़ल लगाना *Most of his essay was lifted straight from the textbook.* ➪ **shoplifting** देखिए।

**PHR V** **lift off** (used about a spacecraft) to rise straight up from the ground (अंतरिक्ष यान का) ज़मीन से सीधे ऊपर उठना

**lift²** /lɪft लिफ़्ट्/ *noun* **1** (*AmE* **elevator**) [C] a machine in a large building that is used for carrying people or goods from one floor to another लिफ़्ट (बड़ी इमारतों में लगी मशीन जो लोगों को या सामान को एक मंजिल से दूसरी पर ले जाती है) *It's on the third floor so we'd better* ***take the lift.*** **2** [C] a free ride in a car, etc. कार आदि में मुफ़्त की सवारी *Can you* ***give*** *me* ***a lift*** *to the station, please?* ○ *I got a lift from a passing car.* **3** [*sing.*] (*informal*) a feeling of being happier or more confident than before प्रसन्नता या आत्म-विश्वास में वृद्धि *Her words of encouragement* ***gave*** *the whole team* ***a lift.*** **4** [*sing.*] the action of moving or being moved to a higher position उत्थान की प्रक्रिया, उच्चतर स्थिति में पहुँचने या पहुँचाने की प्रक्रिया

**IDM** **thumb a lift** ➪ **thumb²** देखिए।

**lift-off** *noun* [C] the start of the flight of a spacecraft when it leaves the ground अंतरिक्ष यान की उड़ान का आरंभ

**ligament** /ˈlɪɡəmənt ˈलिगमन्ट्/ *noun* [C] a strong band of tissue in a person's or animal's body that holds the bones, etc. together मनुष्य या पशु के शरीर के अंदर एक ऊतक जो हड्डियों को जोड़ती है; स्नायु अस्थिबंध

**light¹** /laɪt लाइट्/ *noun* **1** [U, C] the energy from the sun, a lamp, etc. that allows you to see things प्रकाश, रोशनी *a beam/ray of light* ○ *The light was too dim for us to read by.* **2** [C] something that produces light, for example an electric lamp प्रकाश देने वाली वस्तु (जैसे बिजली का बल्ब) *Suddenly all the lights went out/came on.* ○ *the lights of the city in the distance* **3** [C] something, for example a match, that can be used to light a cigarette, start a fire, etc. सिगरेट, आग आदि जलाने के लिए प्रयुक्त कोई वस्तु, जैसे माचिस *Have you got a light?*

**IDM** **bring sth/come to light** to make sth known or to become known किसी बात की जानकारी करवाना या जानकारी होना, किसी बात को प्रकाश में लाना या बात का प्रकाश में आना

**cast light on sth** ➪ **cast¹** देखिए।

**give sb/get the green light** ➪ **green¹** देखिए।

**in a good, bad, etc. light** (used about the way that sth is seen or described by other people) well, badly, etc.(किसी विषय में लोगों की धारणा व्यक्त करने के लिए प्रयुक्त) अनुकूल या प्रतिकूल रूप में *The newspapers often portray his behaviour in a bad light.*

**in the light of** because of; considering के प्रकाश में, के कारण; पर विचार करते हुए

**set light to sth** to cause sth to start burning किसी वस्तु को आग लगाना या जलाना

**shed light on sth** ➪ **shed²** देखिए।

**light²** /laɪt लाइट्/ *adj.* **1** not of great weight हलका (अधिक भारी नहीं) *Carry this bag—it's the lightest.* ○ *I've lost weight—I'm five kilos lighter than I used to be.* ○ *light clothes* (= for summer) ✪ विलोम **heavy** **2** having a lot of light सुप्रकाशित, रोशनीदार, प्रकाशमय *In summer it's still light at 7 o'clock.* ○ *a light room* ✪ विलोम **dark** **3** (used about a colour) pale (रंग) फीका, हलका *a light-blue sweater* ✪ विलोम **dark** **4** not great in amount, degree, etc. मात्रा, डिग्री आदि में अधिक नहीं; हलका *Traffic in Chandigarh is light on Sundays.* ○ *a light prison sentence* ○ *a light wind* ○ *a light breakfast* **5** not using much force; gentle जिसमें अधिक ताक़त न लगे, हलका; कोमल *a light touch on the shoulder* **6** not hard or tiring जो कठिन या थकाने वाला न हो; हलका, हलका-फुलका *light exercise* ○ *light entertainment/reading* **7** (used about sleep) not deep (नींद) जो गहरी न हो; हलकी *I'm a light sleeper, so the slightest noise wakes me.* ▶ **lightness** *noun* [U] हलकापन

**light³** /laɪt लाइट्/ *verb* (*pt, pp* **lit** or **lighted**) **1** [I, T] to begin or to make sth begin to burn किसी वस्तु का जलने लगना या किसी वस्तु को जलाने लगना *The gas oven won't light.* ○ *to light a fire*

> **NOTE** सामान्यतः **lighted** का प्रयोग संज्ञा के पहले विशेषण के रूप में होता है और **lit** का प्रयोग क्रिया के भूत कृदंत (past participle) रूप में होता है—*Candles were lit in memory of the dead.* ○ *The church was full of lighted candles.*

**2** [T] to give light to sth रोशनी करना *The street is well/badly lit at night.* ○ *We only had a small torch to light our way.*

**PHR V** **light (sth) up 1** to make sth bright with light किसी वस्तु को रोशनी से जगमगा देना *The fire works lit up the whole sky.* **2** (used about sb's face, eyes, etc.) to become bright with happiness or excitement (व्यक्ति का चेहरा, आँखें आदि) प्रसन्नता या रोमांच से चमक उठना **3** to start smoking a cigarette सिगरेट जलाना

**light⁴** /laɪt लाइट्/ *adv.* without much luggage कम सामान के साथ *I always travel light.*

**light bulb** = **bulb 1**

**lighten** /ˈlaɪtn ˈलाइट्न्/ *verb* [I, T] **1** to become lighter in weight or to make sth lighter भार में हलका हो जाना या कर देना **2** to become or to make sth brighter अधिक प्रकाशमय हो जाना या कर देना

**lighter** /ˈlaɪtə(r) ˈलाइट(र्)/ = **cigarette lighter**

**light-headed** *adj.* feeling slightly ill and not in control of your thoughts and movements जो हलका अस्वस्थ हो और अपने विचारों और क्रिया-कलापों को नियंत्रित करने मे असमर्थ; प्रलापीपन

**light-hearted** *adj.* **1** intended to be funny and enjoyable जो अजीब और मज़ेदार हो **2** happy and without problems प्रफुल्ल और चिंतामुक्त

**lighthouse** /ˈlaɪthaʊs ˈलाइट्हाउस्/ *noun* [C] a tall building with a light at the top to warn and guide ships near the coast समुद्रतट पर बनी एक बहुत ऊँची इमारत जिसकी चोटी से प्रकाश फेंका जाता है जो कि तटवर्ती जहाजों को संभावित ख़तरे की चेतावनी देता है और मार्गदर्शन देता है; प्रकाशगृह

**lighting** /ˈlaɪtɪŋ ˈलाइटिङ्/ *noun* [U] the quality or type of lights used in a room, building, etc. किसी कमरे, इमारत आदि की प्रकाश-व्यवस्था

**lightly** /ˈlaɪtli ˈलाइट्लि/ *adv.* **1** gently; with very little force कोमलता से; हलके से *He touched her lightly on the arm.* **2** only a little; not much बहुत थोड़ा; अधिक नहीं *lightly cooked/spiced/whisked* **3** not seriously; without serious thought बिना गंभीरता के, हलके ढंग से; बिना गंभीर विचार के *We do not take our customers' complaints lightly.*

IDM **get off/be let off lightly** to avoid serious punishment or trouble भारी दंड या परेशानी से बच जाना

**lightning[1]** /ˈlaɪtnɪŋ ˈलाइट्निङ्/ *noun* [U] a bright flash of light that appears in the sky during a storm, and is usually followed by **thunder** आकाश की बिजली, तड़ित *The tree was **struck by lightning** and burst into flames.* ○ *a flash of lightning*

**lightning[2]** /ˈlaɪtnɪŋ ˈलाइट्निङ्/ *adj.* (*only before a noun*) very quick or sudden बहुत फुरतीला या अचानक, आकस्मिक *a lightning attack*

**lightweight** /ˈlaɪtweɪt ˈलाइट्वेट्/ *noun* [C], *adj.* **1** a person who is in one of the lightest weight groups in certain fighting sports मुक्केबाज़ी आदि खेलों में न्यूनतम भार-वर्गों में आने वाला खिलाड़ी; लाइटवेट (मुक्केबाज़ आदि) *a lightweight boxing champion* **2** (a thing) weighing less than usual सामान्य से कम भार की या हलकी *a lightweight suit for the summer*

**light year** *noun* [C] (*technical*) the distance that light travels in one year, about $9.46 \times 10^{12}$ kilometres प्रकाश वर्ष; एक वर्ष में प्रकाश द्वारा तय की जाने वाली दूरी जो लगभग $9.46 \times 10^{12}$ किलोमीटर होती है

**lignite** /ˈlɪgnaɪt ˈलिग्नाइट्/ *noun* [U] a soft brown type of coal भूरा कोयला

**likable** = **likeable**

**like[1]** /laɪk लाइक्/ *verb* [T] **1 like sb/sth; like doing sth; like to do sth; like sth about sb/sth** to find sb/sth pleasant; to enjoy sth किसी व्यक्ति या वस्तु का अच्छा लगना; किसी वस्तु का आनंद लेना *I like playing tennis.* ○ *She didn't like it when I shouted at her.* ○ *The job seems strange at first, but you'll **get to like** it.* ✪ विलोम **dislike**

> NOTE जब **like** का अर्थ हो कि '...की आदत है' या 'लगता है कि यह बात ठीक है कि...' तो इसके बाद संज्ञार्थक क्रिया रूप (infinitive) का प्रयोग किया जाता है—*I like to get up early so that I can go for a run before breakfast.*

**2** to want चाहना *We can go whenever you like.* ○ *I didn't like to disturb you while you were eating.*

> NOTE **Would like** में **want** की अपेक्षा अधिक विनम्रता का भाव है—*Would you like something to eat?* ○ *I'd like to speak to the manager.* **Would like** के बाद सदा संज्ञार्थक क्रिया रूप (infinitive) आता है, -ing युक्त क्रिया रूप का प्रयोग कभी नहीं किया जाता है।

IDM **if you like** used for agreeing with sb or suggesting sth in a polite way सहमति व्यक्त करने और विनम्रतापूर्वक सुझाव देने के लिए प्रयुक्त *'Shall we stop for a rest?' 'Yes, if you like.'*

**like the look/sound of sb/sth** to have a good impression of sb/sth after seeing or hearing about him/ her/it किसी व्यक्ति या वस्तु को देखकर या उसके विषय में जानकर उससे प्रभावित होना

**like[2]** /laɪk लाइक्/ *prep., conj.* **1** similar to sb/sth किसी व्यक्ति या वस्तु के सदृश *You **look** very/just/exactly **like** your father.* ○ *Your house is **nothing like** how I imagined it.*

> NOTE किसी व्यक्ति से किसी अन्य व्यक्ति या वस्तु का वर्णन जानने के लिए **'What's he/she/it like?'** अभिव्यक्ति का प्रयोग किया जाता है—*Tell me about your town. What's it like?* ○ *What was it like being interviewed on TV?*

**2** (*in compounds*) in the manner of; similar to

के जैसा; के सदृश *childlike innocence/simplicity* ○ *a very lifelike statue* **3** in the same way as sb/sth किसी व्यक्ति या वस्तु के समान *Stop behaving like children.* ○ *She can't draw like her sister can.* **4** for example; such as उदाहरण के लिए; जैसे *They enjoy most team games, like football and rugby.* **5** typical of a particular person किसी विशेष व्यक्ति का प्रतिनिधिक, केवल किसी विशेष व्यक्ति जैसा *It was just like Meera to be late.* **6** (*informal*) as if मानो *She behaves like she owns the place.* **7** (*slang*) (used before saying what sb said, how sb felt, etc.) (किसने क्या कहा, किसको कैसा लगा आदि बताने से पहले प्रयुक्त) *When I saw the colour of my hair I was like 'Wow, I can't believe it!'*

IDM **like anything** (*spoken*) very much, fast, hard, etc.बहुत अधिक, तेज़, कठोर आदि *We had to pedal like anything to get up the hill.*

**nothing like** ➪ **nothing** देखिए।

**something like** about; approximately लगभग, के आस-पास *The temple took something like 20 years to build.*

**that's more like it** (used to say that sth is better than before) (यह बताने के लिए प्रयुक्त कि कोई स्थिति पहले से बेहतर है) *The sun's coming out now—that's more like it!*

**like**[3] /laɪk लाइक्/ *noun* **1** [*sing.*] a person or thing that is similar to sb/sth else किसी अन्य व्यक्ति या वस्तु के सदृश व्यक्ति या वस्तु *I enjoy going round castles, old churches **and the like.*** ○ *She was a great singer, and we may never see her like/the like of her again.* **2 likes** [*pl.*] things that you like पसंदीदा बातें या चीज़ें *Tell me about some of your **likes and dislikes*** ▸ **like** *adj.* (*formal*) समान, सदृश, तुल्य

**likeable** (*also* **likable**) /ˈlaɪkəbl ˈलाइकब्ल्/ *adj.* (used about a person) easy to like; pleasant (व्यक्ति) जो तुरंत पसंद आ जाए; आकर्षक, मनोहर

**likelihood** /ˈlaɪklihʊd ˈलाइक्लिहुड्/ *noun* [U] the chance of sth happening; how likely sth is to happen किसी बात के घटित होने का अवसर, संभावना का अवसर; संभाव्यता, संभावना की मात्रा *There seems very little likelihood of success.*

**likely** /ˈlaɪkli ˈलाइक्लि/ *adj., adv.* (**likelier; likeliest**) **1 likely (to do sth)** probable or expected संभावित या प्रत्याशित; अपेक्षित *Do you think it's likely to rain?* ○ *It's not likely that the boss will agree.* **2** probably suitable संभवतः उपयुक्त, संभावित *a likely candidate for the job* ✪ विलोम **unlikely**

IDM **not likely!** (*informal*) certainly not बिलकुल नहीं

**liken** /ˈlaɪkən ˈलाइकन्/ *verb* [T] (*formal*) **liken sb/sth to sb/sth** to compare one person or thing with another किसी व्यक्ति या वस्तु की दूसरे से तुलना करना *This young artist has been likened to M.F. Hussain.*

**likeness** /ˈlaɪknəs ˈलाइक्नस्/ *noun* [C, U] the fact of being similar in appearance; an example of this आकृति में एक जैसा होने की स्थिति, साम्यता, सदृश्यता; इस स्थिति का उदाहरण *The witness's drawing turned out to be **a good likeness** of the attacker.*

**likewise** /ˈlaɪkwaɪz ˈलाइक्वाइज़्/ *adv.* (*formal*) the same; in a similar way वैसा ही, वही; उसी प्रकार *I intend to send a letter of apology and suggest that you do likewise.*

**liking** /ˈlaɪkɪŋ ˈलाइकिङ्/ *noun* [*sing.*] **a liking (for sb/sth)** the feeling that you like sb/sth किसी व्यक्ति या वस्तु को पसंद करने का मनोभाव; पसंद, रुचि *I have a liking for spicy food.*

IDM **too... for your liking** that you do not like because he/she/it has too much of a particular quality किसी को इसलिए नापसंद करना कि उसकी कोई विशेषता बहुत अधिक मात्रा में हो *The music was a bit too loud for my liking.*

**lilac** /ˈlaɪlək ˈलाइलक्/ *noun* [C, U], *adj.* **1** a tree or large bush that has large purple or white flowers in spring वसंत में खिलने वाले बड़े बैंगनी या सफ़ेद फूलों वाला वृक्ष या बड़ी झाड़ी; नीलक वृक्ष **2** (of) a pale purple colour फीके बैंगनी रंग का

**lily** /ˈlɪli ˈलिलि/ *noun* [C] (*pl.* **lilies**) a type of plant that has large white or coloured flowers in the shape of a bell घंटी के आकार के बड़े सफ़ेद या रंगीन फूलों का एक पौधा; कुमुदिनी, लिली ➪ **water lily** देखिए।

**limb** /lɪm लिम्/ *noun* [C] **1** a leg or an arm of a person व्यक्ति की टाँग या बाँह **2** one of the main branches of a tree वृक्ष की कोई प्रमुख शाखा

IDM **out on a limb** without the support of other people बिना किसी की सहायता के, अपने बूते

**lime** /laɪm लाइम्/ *noun* **1** [C] a fruit that looks like a small green lemon कागज़ी नींबू ➪ **fruit** पर चित्र देखिए। **2** [U] (*also* **lime green**) a yellowish-green colour पीलापन लिए हरा रंग **3** [U] a white substance that is used for making cement and also for adding to soil to improve its quality चूना (सीमेंट बनाने तथा मृदा की गुणवत्ता में सुधार के लिए प्रयुक्त)

**the limelight** /ˈlaɪmlaɪt ˈलाइम्लाइट्/ *noun* [U] the centre of public attention जनसामान्य के ध्यान का केंद्र होने की स्थिति; लोकप्रसिद्धि, सार्वजनिक ख्याति *to be in/out of the limelight*

**limestone** /ˈlaɪmstəʊn ˈलाइम्स्टोन्/ *noun* [U] a type of hard white **sedimentary** rock that is used for building or for making cement चूना-पत्थर (मकान या सीमेंट बनाने में प्रयुक्त)

**limit**[1] /ˈlɪmɪt ˈलिमिट्/ *noun* [C] **1** the greatest or smallest amount of sth that is allowed or possible किसी वस्तु की अधिकतम या न्यूनतम मात्रा जो संभव या मान्य हो; सीमा; हद *a speed/age/time limit* ○ *He was fined for exceeding the speed limit.* **2** the boundary edge of a place or area किसी स्थान या क्षेत्र की सीमा, हद *the city limits* ○ *Trucks are not allowed within a two-kilometre limit of the town centre.*

**IDM** **off limits** (*AmE*) = **out of bounds**

**within limits** only up to a reasonable point or amount केवल तर्कसंगत बिंदु या मात्रा तक

**limit**[2] /ˈlɪmɪt ˈलिमिट्/ *verb* [T] **limit sb/sth (to sth)** to keep sb/sth within or below a certain amount, size, degree or area किसी व्यक्ति या वस्तु को एक निश्चित मात्रा, आकार, डिग्री या क्षेत्र के भीतर या उससे कम रखना *In China families are limited to just one child.*

**limitation** /ˌlɪmɪˈteɪʃn ˌलिमिˈटेश्न्/ *noun* **1** [C, U] **(a) limitation (on sth)** the act of limiting or controlling sth; a condition that puts a limit on sth किसी वस्तु को सीमित या नियंत्रित करने की क्रिया, सीमा-निर्धारण; किसी वस्तु को कहीं तक सीमित करने वाली शर्त, प्रतिबंध *There are no limitations on what we can do.* **2** [*pl.*] **limitations** things that you cannot do वे काम जो आप नहीं कर सकते, सीमाएँ *It is important to know your own limitations.*

**limited** /ˈlɪmɪtɪd ˈलिमिटिड्/ *adj.* small or controlled in number, amount, etc. संख्या, मात्रा आदि की दृष्टि से कम या नियंत्रित, सीमित *Book early because there are only a limited number of seats available.* ✪ विलोम **unlimited**

**limited company** *noun* [C] (*abbr.* **Ltd**) a company whose owners only have to pay a limited amount of its debts if it fails इस प्रकार की कंपनी जिसके बंद हो जाने पर उसके मालिकों को सीमित (न की पूरी) मात्रा में ही ऋण लौटाना पड़े

**limousine** /ˌlɪməziːn; ˌlɪməˈziːn ˌलिमज़ीन्; ˌलिमˈज़ीन्/ (*informal* **limo** /ˈlɪməʊ ˈलिमो/) *noun* [C] a large expensive car that usually has a sheet of glass between the driver and the passengers in the back एक लंबी महँगी शाही कार जिसमें ड्राइवर और पिछली सीट के यात्रियों के बीच शीशे की पट्टी का परदा होता है; लिमज़ीन

**limp**[1] /lɪmp लिम्प्/ *verb* [I] to walk with difficulty because you have hurt your leg or foot चोट के कारण लँगड़ाकर चलना, लँगड़ाना ▶ **limp** *noun* [*sing.*] लँगड़ापन, लँगड़ी चाल *to walk with a limp*

**limp**[2] /lɪmp लिम्प्/ *adj.* not firm or strong अशक्त, निस्तेज *You should put those flowers in water before they go limp.*

**line**[1] /laɪn लाइन्/ *noun* [C] **1** a long thin mark on the surface of sth or on the ground रेखा (किसी वस्तु की सतह या ज़मीन पर लंबा बारीक निशान), लकीर *to draw a line* ○ *a straight/wiggly/dotted line* ○ *The old lady had lines on her forehead.* **2** a row of people, things, words on a page, etc. लोगों,

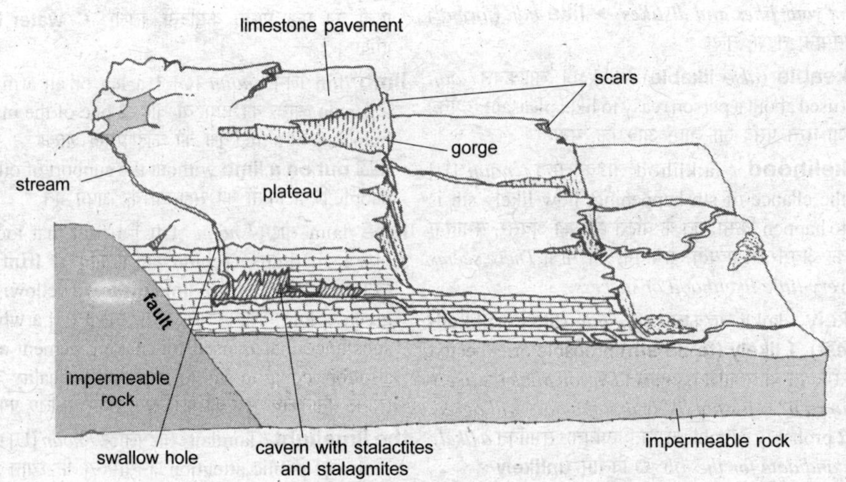


**limestone landscape**

वस्तुओं, को पृष्ठ पर शब्दों आदि की क़तार; पंक्ति *There was a long line of people waiting at the Post Office.* ○ *a five-line poem* **3** a border or limit between one place or thing and another एक स्थान या वस्तु और दूसरे स्थान या वस्तु के बीच सीमा-रेखा; हद *to cross state lines* ○ *There's a thin line between showing interest and being nosy.* **4** a direction or course of movement, thought or action गति, विचार या क्रिया की दिशा या मार्ग *The two countries' economies are developing **along** similar **lines**.* **5** a piece of rope or string रस्सी या डोरी *a fishing line* **6** a telephone or electricity wire or connection टेलीफ़ोन या बिजली की तार या संयोजन; लाइन *I'm sorry—the line is engaged. Can you try again later?* ○ *I'll just check for you. Can you **hold the line** (= wait)?* **7** a section of railway track रेल मार्ग का कोई खंड, रेलवे लाइन **8 lines** [*pl.*] the words that are spoken by an actor in a play, etc. किसी नाटक, फ़िल्म आदि में अभिनेता द्वारा बोले गए शब्द **9** a company that provides transport by air, ship, etc. वायुमार्ग, जलमार्ग आदि द्वारा यातायात की सुविधा उपलब्ध कराने वाली कंपनी *an airline* **10** [*sing.*] one type of goods in a shop, etc. किसी दुकान आदि में अकेले एक प्रकार का समान **11** the place where an army is fighting वह स्थान जहाँ सेना लड़ रही है; मोरचा; पंक्ति *There's renewed fighting on **the frontline**.* **12** a series of people in a family, things or events that follow one another in time कालक्रम से एक दूसरे के बाद आने वाली वस्तुओं, घटनाओं, परिवार के लोगों की शृंखला, परंपरा *He comes from **a long line of** musicians.* **13** something that you do as a job, do well, or enjoy doing मनपसंद व्यापार, धंधा, पेशा, व्यवसाय *What **line of business/work** are you in?*

IDM **draw the line at sth/doing sth** ➪ **draw**[1] देखिए।

**drop sb a line** ➪ **drop**[1] देखिए।

**in line for sth** likely to get sth कुछ पाने की संभावना से युक्त *You could be in line for promotion if you keep working like this.*

**in line with sth** similar to sth; in agreement with sth किसी वस्तु के सदृश; किसी वस्तु के अनुकूल *These changes will bring the industry in line with the new laws.*

**somewhere along/down the line** at some time; sooner or later कभी-न-कभी; पहले या बाद में

**take a hard line (on sth)** ➪ **hard**[1] देखिए।

**toe the (party) line** ➪ **toe**[2] देखिए।

**line**[2] /laɪn लाइन्/ *verb* [T] **1** (*often passive*) to cover the inside surface of sth with a different material किसी वस्तु में अस्तर लगाना **2** to form lines or rows along sth क़तारें लगाना *Crowds lined the streets to watch the race.*

PHR V **line up (for sth)** (*AmE*) to form a line of people; to queue लोगों का क़तार में लगना; पंक्तिबद्ध होना

**line sth up** (*informal*) to arrange or organize sth किसी को व्यवस्थित करना *She lined the bottles up on the shelf.*

**lined** /laɪnd लाइन्ड्/ *adj.* **1** covered in lines झुर्रीदार, झुर्रियोंभरा, रेखायुक्त, रूलदार *a face lined with age* ○ *lined paper* **2 -lined** (*used in compounds*) having the object mentioned all along the side(s); having the inside surface covered with the material mentioned जिस वस्तु के सारे किनारे के साथ-साथ निर्दिष्ट वस्तुएँ हों; जिसके अंदर की सतह पर निर्दिष्ट सामान लगा हो, -वाला, -दार *a tree-lined avenue* ○ *fur-lined boots*

**linen** /ˈlɪnɪn ˈलिनिन्/ *noun* [U] **1** a type of strong cloth that is made from a natural substance (**flax**) फ्लैक्स-नामक एक प्राकृतिक पदार्थ से बना मज़बूत कपड़ा; लिनन **2** sheets and other cloth coverings used in the house on a bed, table, etc. पलंग, मेज़ आदि की चादरें और अन्य खोल, ग़िलाफ़ आदि *bedlinen*

**liner** /ˈlaɪnə(r) ˈलाइन(र्)/ *noun* [C] **1** a large ship that carries people, etc. long distances यात्रियों को लेकर दूर-दूर तक जाने वाला बड़ा जलपोत; लाइनर ➪ **boat** पर चित्र देखिए। **2** something that is put inside sth else to keep it clean or protect it. A liner is thrown away after it has been used किसी वस्तु को साफ़ रखने के लिए उसके अंदर लगाई गई अस्तरनुमा चीज़ (जिसे प्रायः इस्तेमाल के बाद फेंक दिया जाता है) *a dustbin liner*

**linger** /ˈlɪŋgə(r) ˈलिङ्ग(र्)/ *verb* [I] **linger (on)** to stay somewhere or do sth for longer than usual किसी जगह देर तक रुके रहना या कोई काम देर तक करते रहना *His eyes lingered on the money in her bag.*

**lingerie** /ˈlænʒəri ˈलैन्ज़रि/ *noun* [U] (used in shops, etc.) women's underwear (दुकान आदि पर प्रयुक्त) महिलाओं का अधोवस्त्र

**lingua franca** /ˌlɪŋgwə ˈfræŋkə ˌलिङ्ग्वा ˈफ्रैङ्का/ *noun* [*usually sing.*] (*technical*) a shared language of communication used by people who are speakers of different languages भिन्न भाषाएँ बोलने वालों की सहभागी भाषा; संपर्क भाषा *English has become a lingua franca in many parts of the world.*

**linguist** /ˈlɪŋgwɪst ˈलिङ्ग्विस्ट्/ *noun* [C] **1** a person who knows several foreign languages well विदेशी भाषाओं का अच्छा जानकार; भाषाविद **2** a person who studies languages or **linguistics** भाषाज्ञानी, भाषाशास्त्री

mane
lioness
cub
lion

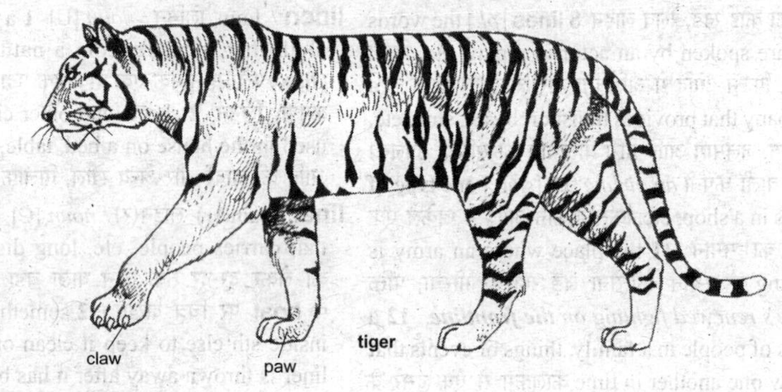
tiger
claw
paw

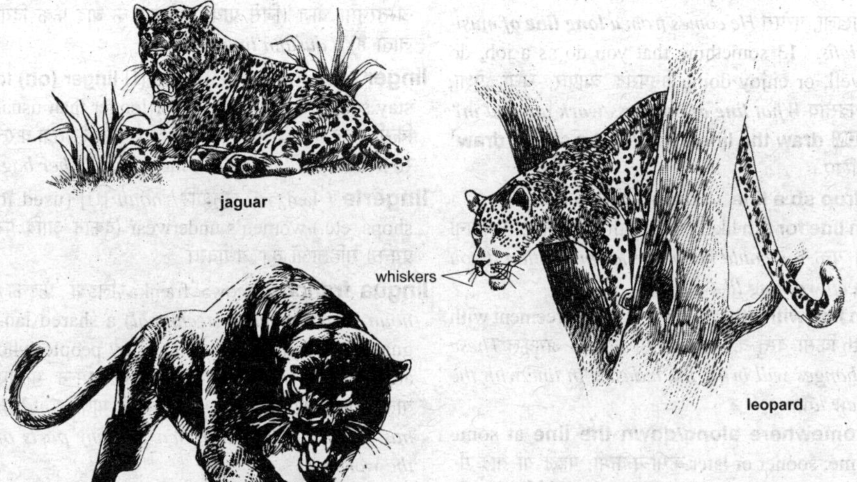
jaguar
whiskers
leopard
panther

**linguistic** /lɪŋˈgwɪstɪk लिङ्ˈग्विसटिक्/ *adj.* connected with language or the study of language भाषा या भाषा विज्ञान से संबंधित; भाषावैज्ञानिक

**linguistics** /lɪŋˈgwɪstɪks ˈलिङ्ˈग्विसटिक्स्/ *noun* [U] the scientific study of language भाषा का वैज्ञानिक अध्ययन; भाषाविज्ञान, भाषाशास्त्र

**lining** /ˈlaɪnɪŋ ˈलाइनिङ्/ *noun* [C, U] material that covers the inside surface of sth अस्तर, लाइनिंग *I've torn the lining of my coat.*

**IDM every cloud has a silver lining** ➪ **cloud**[1] देखिए।

**link**[1] /lɪŋk लिङ्क्/ *noun* [C] **1 a link (between A and B); a link (with sb/sth)** a connection or relationship between two or more people or things दो या अधिक व्यक्तियों या वस्तुओं के बीच संपर्कसूत्र या संबंध *There is a strong link between smoking and heart disease.* **2** one ring of a chain किसी शृंखला की एक कड़ी **3** a means of travelling or communicating between two places दो स्थानों के बीच यात्रा करने या संवाद स्थापित करने का साधन *To visit similar websites to this one, click on the links at the bottom of the page.*

**link**[2] /lɪŋk लिङ्क्/ *verb* [T] **link A to/with B; link A and B (together)** to make a connection between two or more people or things व्यक्तियों या वस्तुओं के बीच संपर्कसूत्र या संबंध स्थापित करना, व्यक्तियों या वस्तुओं को जोड़ना *The new bridge will link the island to the mainland.* ○ *The computers are linked together in a network.*

**PHR V link up (with sb/sth)** to join together (with sb/sth) (व्यक्ति या वस्तु के साथ) जोड़ना *All our branches are linked up by computer.*

**linking verb** *noun* [C] (*grammar*) a verb such as (be) or (become) that connects a subject with the adjective or noun that describes it; 'be' या 'become' ऐसी क्रिया जो कर्ता को उस विशेषता या संज्ञा से जोड़ती है, जिसका वह वर्णन करती है; संयोजक क्रिया *In 'She became angry', the verb 'became' is a linking verb.*

**link-up** *noun* [C] the joining together or connection of two or more things वस्तुओं के परस्पर जुड़ने या संपर्क होने की क्रिया, जुड़ाव या मेल-जोल

**linoleum** /lɪˈnəʊliəm लिˈनोलिअम्/ (*informal* **lino** /ˈlaɪnəʊ ˈलाइनो/) *noun* [U] strong, shiny material used for covering floors फ़र्श पर बिछाने वाला मज़बूत चमकदार कपड़ा; लिनोलियम

**lint** /lɪnt लिन्ट्/ *noun* [U] **1** soft cotton cloth used for covering and protecting injuries घावों को ढकने और सुरक्षित रखने के लिए प्रयुक्त नरम सूती कपड़ा; फाहा **2** small soft pieces of wool, cotton, etc. that stick on the surface of clothes, etc. कपड़ों आदि की सतह पर चिपक जाने वाले ऊन, सूत आदि के छोटे-छोटे नरम टुकड़े

**lintel** /ˈlɪntl ˈलिन्ट्ल्/ *noun* [C] a piece of wood or stone over a door or window दरवाज़े या खिड़की के ऊपर लगी लकड़ी या पत्थर; सोहावटी, लिंटल

**lion** /ˈlaɪən ˈलाइअन्/ *noun* [C] a large animal of the cat family that lives in Africa and parts of southern Asia. Male lions have a large amount of hair around their head and neck (**a mane**) शेर, सिंह ➪ पृष्ठ 706 पर चित्र देखिए।

**IDM the lion's share (of sth)** (*BrE*) the largest or best part of sth when it is divided किसी वस्तु के विभाजन के बाद उसका सबसे बड़ा या अच्छा हिस्सा

**lioness** /ˈlaɪənes ˈलाइअनेस्/ *noun* [C] a female lion शेरनी ➪ पृष्ठ 706 पर चित्र देखिए।

**lip** /lɪp लिप्/ *noun* [C] **1** either of the two soft edges at the opening of your mouth ओंठ, होंठ *top/upper lip* ○ *bottom/lower lip* ➪ **body** पर चित्र देखिए। **2 -lipped** (*used to form compound adjectives*) having the type of lips mentioned निर्दिष्ट प्रकार के ओंठों वाला *thin-lipped* **3** the edge of a cup or sth that is shaped like a cup प्याले या प्यालेनुमा वस्तु का किनारा

**IDM purse your lips** ➪ **purse**[2] देखिए।

**lipase** /ˈlaɪpeɪz ˈलाइपेज़्/ *noun* [U] an enzyme that makes fats change into acids and alcohol वसाओं को अम्लों और ऐल्कोहॉल में बदल देने वाला एक एन्ज़ाइम

**lip-read** *verb* [I, T] (*pt, pp* **lip-read** /-red -रेड्/) to understand what sb is saying by looking at the movements of his/her lips व्यक्ति के ओंठों की हरक़त से उसकी बात को समझ जाना

**lipstick** /ˈlɪpstɪk ˈलिपस्टिक्/ *noun* [C, U] a substance that is used for giving colour to your lips लिपस्टिक *to put on some lipstick* ○ *a new lipstick*

**liquefy** /ˈlɪkwɪfaɪ ˈलिक्विफ़ाइ/ *verb* [I, T] (*pres. part.* **liquefying;** *3rd person sing. pres.* **liquefies;** *pt, pp* **liquefied**) (*formal*) to become liquid; to make sth liquid द्रव हो जाना; किसी वस्तु को द्रव बना देना; द्रवीकरण करना

**liqueur** /lɪˈkjʊə(r) लिˈक्युअ(र्)/ *noun* [U, C] a strong sweet alcoholic drink that is sometimes drunk in small quantities after a meal तेज़ और मीठी शराब जो कभी-कभी भोजन के बाद थोड़ी मात्रा में ली जाती है

**liquid** /ˈlɪkwɪd ˈलिक्विड्/ *noun* [C, U] a substance, for example water, that is not solid or a gas and that can flow or be poured द्रव पदार्थ, तरल पदार्थ (न ठोस न गैस) ▶ **liquid** *adj.* द्रव, तरल

**liquidate** /ˈlɪkwɪdeɪt ˈलिक्विडेट् / *verb* [T] **1** to close a business because it has no money left धनाभाव के कारण व्यापार को बंद कर देना, व्यापार का दिवाला निकाल देना **2** to destroy or remove sb/sth that causes problems समस्याकारी व्यक्ति या वस्तु को हटा या समाप्त कर देना; परिसमाप्त करना ▶ **liquidation** /ˌlɪkwɪˈdeɪʃn ˌलिक्विˈडेश्न् / *noun* [U] दिवाला *If the company doesn't receive a big order soon, it will have to* ***go into liquidation****.*

**liquid crystal display** *noun* [C] = **LCD**

**liquidity** /lɪˈkwɪdəti लिˈक्विडटि / *noun* [U] (*technical*) the state of owning things of value that can be exchanged for cash नक़द धन और मूल्यवान वस्तुओं के बीच विनिमेयता, नक़दी, तरलता

**liquidize** (*also* **-ise**) /ˈlɪkwɪdaɪz ˈलिक्विडाइज़् / *verb* [T] to cause sth to become liquid किसी वस्तु को तरल बनाना ▶ **liquidizer** (*also* **-iser**) = **blender**

**liquor** /ˈlɪkə(r) ˈलिक(र्) / *noun* [U] (*AmE*) strong alcoholic drinks; spirits तेज़ शराब

**liquorice** (*AmE* **licorice**) /ˈlɪkərɪʃ ˈलिकरिश् / *noun* [U] a black substance, made from a plant, that is used in some sweets मुलेठी, जेठी मधु (रत्ती के पौधे से बना पदार्थ जो कुछ मिठाइयों में डाला जाता है)

**lisp** /lɪsp लिस्प् / *noun* [C] a speech fault in which 's' is pronounced as 'th' 'स्' को 'थ्' बोलने का उच्चारण दोष; तुतलाहट, थथलाहट *He speaks with a slight lisp.* ▶ **lisp** *verb* [I, T] तुतलाना, थथलाना

**list** /lɪst लिस्ट् / *noun* [C] a series of names, figures, items, etc. that are written, printed or said one after another सूची, तालिका (जिसमें नामों, चित्रों आदि को क्रम से लिखा, छापा या बोला जाता है) *a checklist of everything that needs to be done* ○ *a waiting list* ○ *Your name is third* ***on the list****.* ▶ **list** *verb* [T] सूची बनाना *to list items in alphabetical order*

**listen** /ˈlɪsn ˈलिसन् / *verb* [I] **1 listen (to sb/sth)** to pay attention to sb/sth in order to hear him/her/it किसी बात को सुनने के लिए उस पर ध्यान देना *Now please listen carefully to what I have to say.* ○ *to listen to music/the radio* ➪ **hear** पर नोट देखिए। **2 listen to sb/sth** to take notice of or believe what sb says किसी की बात पर ध्यान देना और उसे मानना *You should listen to your parents' advice.* ▶ **listen** *noun* [*sing.*] (*informal*) श्रवण, सुनाई *Have a listen and see if you can hear anything.*

**PHR V** **listen (out) for sth** to wait to hear sth कुछ सुनने की प्रतीक्षा करना *to listen (out) for a knock on the door*

**listen in (on/to sth)** to listen to sb else's private conversation किसी अन्य की निजी बातचीत को सुनना *Have you been listening in on my phone calls?*

**listener** /ˈlɪsənə(r) ˈलिसन(र्) / *noun* [C] a person who listens (ध्यान से) सुननेवाला, श्रोता *When I'm unhappy I always phone Chandan—he's such a good listener.* ○ *The new radio show has attracted a record number of listeners.*

**listless** /ˈlɪstləs ˈलिस्ट्लस् / *adj.* tired and without energy थका और सुस्त, निरुत्साही ▶ **listlessly** *adv.* थककर, सुस्ती से

**lit** ➪ **light**[3] का past tense और past participle रूप

**liter** (*AmE*) = **litre**

**literacy** /ˈlɪtərəsi ˈलिटरसि / *noun* [U] the ability to read and write लिखने व पढ़ने की योग्यता; साक्षरता ✪ विलोम **illiteracy**

**literal** /ˈlɪtərəl ˈलिटरल् / *adj.* **1** (used about the meaning of a word or phrase) original or basic (शब्द का अर्थ) प्रथम, आदिम या मूल *The adjective 'big-headed' is hardly ever used in its literal sense.* ➪ **figurative** और **metaphor** देखिए। **2** (used when translating, etc.) dealing with each word separately without looking at the general meaning (अनुवाद के संदर्भ में प्रयुक्त) जिसमें अलग-अलग शब्दों का अर्थ दिया जाता है (बिना समग्र अर्थ पर ध्यान दिए); शाब्दिक

**literally** /ˈlɪtərəli ˈलिटरलि / *adv.* **1** according to the basic or original meaning of the word, etc. शब्द के मूल, आदिम या आद्य अर्थ के अनुसार; शब्दशः *You can't translate these idioms literally.* **2** (*informal*) used for emphasizing sth किसी बात पर बल देने के लिए प्रयुक्त *We were literally frozen to death* (= we were very cold).

**literary** /ˈlɪtərəri ˈलिटररि / *adj.* of or concerned with literature साहित्य का या साहित्य-विषयक, साहित्यिक *literary criticism* ○ *a literary journal*

**literate** /ˈlɪtərət ˈलिटरट् / *adj.* **1** able to read and write पढ़ने व लिखने में सक्षम ✪ विलोम **illiterate** ➪ **literacy** noun तथा **numerate** देखिए। **2** well educated सुशिक्षित

**literature** /ˈlɪtrətʃə(r) ˈलिट्रच(र्) / *noun* [U] **1** writing that is considered to be a work of art. Literature includes novels, plays and poetry कलात्मक माना जाने वाला लेखन जैसे उपन्यास, नाटक, कविता; साहित्य *Sanskrit literature* **2 literature (on sth)** printed material about a particular subject किसी विषय पर मुद्रित सामग्री

**lithium** /ˈlɪθiəm ˈलिथिअम् / *noun* [U] (*symbol* **Li**) a soft, very light, silver-white metal that is used in batteries बैटरियों में प्रयुक्त नरम, बहुत हलकी, चाँदी जैसी सफ़ेद धातु; लिथियम

**litigant** /ˈlɪtɪgənt ˈलिटिगन्ट्/ *noun* [C] (*technical*) a person who is taking legal action in a court of law न्यायालय में मुक़दमा लड़ने वाला व्यक्ति, वादी और प्रतिवादी

**litigate** /ˈlɪtɪgeɪt ˈलिटिगेट्/ *verb* [I, T] (*technical*) to take legal action in a court of law न्यायालय में मुक़दमा लड़ना, वाद अभियोजित करना ▶ **litigator** *noun* [C] वादी

**litigation** /ˌlɪtɪˈgeɪʃn ˌलिटिˈगेश्न्/ *noun* [U] (*technical*) the process of taking legal action in a court of law न्यायालय में मुक़दमा लड़ने की प्रक्रिया; मुक़दमा, वाद

**litmus** /ˈlɪtməs ˈलिट्मस्/ *noun* [U] a substance that turns red when it touches an acid and blue when it touches an **alkali** एक विशेष पदार्थ जो अम्ल के स्पर्श से लाल और क्षार के स्पर्श से नीला हो जाता है; लिटमस ➪ **pH** पर चित्र देखिए।

**litre** (*AmE* **liter**) /ˈliːtə(r) ˈलीट(र्)/ *noun* [C] (*abbr.* **l**) a measure of liquid द्रव की एक माप *ten litres of petrol* ○ *a litre bottle of wine*

**litter** /ˈlɪtə(r) ˈलिट(र्)/ *noun* **1** [U] pieces of paper, rubbish, etc. that are left in a public place सार्वजनिक स्थल पर जमा कूड़ा-कचरा **2** [C] all the young animals that are born to one mother at the same time एक ही समय में एक ही माँ से जन्मे सभी पशु बच्चे *a litter of six puppies* ▶ **litter** *verb* [T] कचरा फैलाना *The streets were littered with rubbish.*

**litter bin** *noun* [C] a container to put rubbish in, in the street or a public building सड़क या सार्वजनिक भवन पर रखा कूड़ादान

**little[1]** /ˈlɪtl ˈलिट्ल्/ *adj.* **1** not big; small बड़ा नहीं; छोटा *Do you want the big one or the little one?* ○ *a little mistake/problem*

> **NOTE** **Little** का प्रयोग प्रायः किसी अन्य विशेषण के साथ (प्रविशेषण के रूप में) होता है—*a little old lady* ○ *a cute little kitten* ○ *What a funny little shop!* ➪ **small** पर नोट देखिए।

**2** (used about distance or time) short (दूरी या समय) थोड़ा या थोड़ी *Do you mind waiting **a little while**?* ○ *We only live **a little way** from here.* **3** young (उम्र में) छोटा *a little girl/boy*

**little[2]** /ˈlɪtl लिट्ल्/ *adv., pronoun, det.* (**less; least**) **1** (also as a noun after **the**) not much or not enough ('the' के साथ संज्ञा के रूप में भी प्रयुक्त) अधिक नहीं या पर्याप्त नहीं, कम *a little-known author* ○ *There is little hope that she will recover.* **2 a little** a small amount of sth किसी वस्तु की थोड़ी मात्रा, थोड़ी-सी *I like a little sugar in my tea.* ○ *Could I have a little help, please?* **3** rather; to a small degree कुछ-कुछ; ज़रा *This skirt is a little too tight.*

> **NOTE** 'A little' की अपेक्षा **'a little bit'** या **a bit** का प्रयोग अधिक होता है—*I was feeling a little bit tired so I decided not to go out.*

**IDM** **little by little** slowly धीरे-धीरे *After the accident her strength returned little by little.*

**littoral** /ˈlɪtərəl ˈलिटरल्/ *noun* [C] (*technical*) the part of a country that is near the coast किसी देश का समुद्रतट के निकट का भाग, समुद्रतटवर्ती *the littoral state of Goa* ▶ **littoral** *adj.* तटवर्तीय

**live[1]** /lɪv लिव्/ *verb* **1** [I] to have your home reside in a particular place रहना, किसी विशेष स्थान पर घर होना; निवास करना *Where do you live?* ○ *He still lives with his parents.* **2** [I] to be or stay alive जीवित होना या रहना *She hasn't got long to live.* ○ *to live to a great age* **3** [I, T] to pass or spend your life in a certain way एक विशेष रीति से जीवन जीना *to live a quiet life* ○ *to live in comfort/poverty* **4** [I] to enjoy all the opportunities of life fully जीवन के सब अवसरों का भरपूर आनंद लेना *I want to live a bit before settling down and getting married.*

**IDM** **live/sleep rough** ➪ **rough[3]** देखिए।

**PHR V** **live by sth** to follow a particular belief or set of principles विशेष मान्यताओं या सिद्धांतों को मानना

**live by doing sth** to get the money, food, etc. you need by doing a particular activity कोई विशेष काम कर रोज़ी-रोटी कमाना *They live by fishing.*

**live for sb/sth** to consider sb/sth to be the most important thing in your life किसी व्यक्ति या वस्तु को अपने जीवन की सबसे महत्त्वपूर्ण बात मानना *He felt he had nothing to live for after his wife died.*

**not live sth down** to be unable to make people forget sth bad or embarrassing that you have done लोगों का किसी व्यक्ति की ग़लती को भुला न पाना

**live it up** to enjoy yourself in an exciting way, spending a lot of money जीवन का भरपूर आनंद लेना; (प्रायः खुला ख़र्च करके) शान से रहना

**live off sb/sth** to depend on sb/sth in order to live जीवित रहने या जीवन-यापन करने के लिए किसी वस्तु या व्यक्ति पर निर्भर रहना *Ganesh lives off tinned food.* ○ *She could easily get a job but she still lives off her parents.*

**live on** to continue to live or exist जीवन या अस्तित्व का बने रहना *R.D. Burman is dead but his music lives on.*

**live on sth** **1** to have sth as your only food एक-मात्र भोजन के रूप में कोई वस्तु लेना *to live on bread and water* **2** to manage to buy what you need to live जीवित रहने के लिए आवश्यक वस्तुओं को ख़रीद सकना *I don't know how they live on so little money!*

**live out sth 1** to actually do sth that you only imagined doing before जो पहले सोचा भर था उसे वस्तुतः कर देना *to live out your dreams/fantasies* **2** to spend the rest of your life in a particular way एक विशेष प्रकार से शेष जीवन गुज़ारना

**live through sth** to survive an unpleasant experience अप्रिय अनुभव को झेल लेना *She lived through two wars.*

**live together** to live in the same house, etc. as sb and have a sexual relationship with him/her सहवास करना; एक ही घर में पति-पत्नी के रूप में रहना

**live up to sth** to be as good as expected अपेक्षा के अनुसार अच्छा होना *Children sometimes find it hard to live up to their parents' expectations.*

**live with sb** = **live together**

**live with sth** to accept sth unpleasant that you cannot change नियति को बरबस स्वीकार करना *It can be hard to live with the fact that you are getting older.*

**live²** /laɪv लाइव़् / *adj., adv.* **1** having life; not dead सजीव, सप्राण; मृत नहीं, जीवित *Have you ever touched a **real live** snake?* **2** (used about a radio or television programme) seen or heard as it is happening (रेडियो या टेलीविज़न कार्यक्रम) घटित होने के साथ-साथ ही प्रसारित भी; सीधा, लाइव, प्रत्यक्ष *live coverage of the Olympic Games* ○ *to go out live on TV* **3** performed or performing for an audience दर्शकों या श्रोताओं के सामने सजीव रूप में प्रस्तुत *That pub has live music on Saturdays.* **4** (used about a bomb, bullet, etc.) that has not yet exploded (बम, गोली आदि) जो अभी विस्फोटित नहीं हुआ हो **5** (used about a wire, etc.) carrying electricity (तार, आदि) जिसमें बिजली चल रही हो

**livelihood** /ˈlaɪvlihʊd ˈलाइव़्लिहुड् / *noun* [C, *usually sing.*] the way that you earn money धन अर्जित करने का ढंग; आजीविका, रोज़ी *to lose your livelihood*

**lively** /ˈlaɪvli ˈलाइव़्लि / *adj.* (**livelier; liveliest**) full of energy, interest, excitement, etc. चुस्ती, रुचि, रोमांच आदि से भरपूर; जानदार, ज़िंदादिल *lively children* ○ *The town is quite lively at night.*

**liven** /ˈlaɪvn ˈलाइव़्न् / *verb*

PHR V **liven (sb/sth) up** to become or make sb/sth become more interesting and exciting किसी व्यक्ति या वस्तु का अधिक रुचिकर और उत्तेजक हो जाना; किसी को जानदार कर देना *Once the band began to play the party livened up.*

**liver** /ˈlɪvə(r) ˈलिव़(र्) / *noun* **1** [C] the part of your body that cleans your blood यकृत, जिगर (रक्त की शुद्धि करने वाला शरीरांग) ➪ **body** पर चित्र देखिए। **2** [U] the liver of an animal when it is cooked and eaten as food भोजन के रूप में खाया जाने वाला का पशु का जिगर; कलेजी *fried liver and onions*

**lives** ➪ **life** का plural रूप

**livestock** /ˈlaɪvstɒk ˈलाइव़्स्टॉक् / *noun* [U] animals that are kept on a farm, such as cows, pigs, sheep, etc. मवेशी; गाय, सूअर, भेड़ आदि जैसे पशु, पशुधन

**living¹** /ˈlɪvɪŋ ˈलिव़िङ् / *adj.* **1** alive now वर्तमान में जीवित *He has no living relatives.* ➪ **alive** पर नोट देखिए। **2** still used or practised now वर्तमान में भी प्रयुक्त या व्यवहृत; समकालिक *living languages/traditions* ✪ विलोम **dead**

**living²** /ˈlɪvɪŋ ˈलिव़िङ् / *noun* **1** [C, *usually sing.*] money to buy things that you need in life जीवन की आवश्यक वस्तुएँ ख़रीदने के लिए धन; जीविका *What do you do for a living?* **2** [U] your way or quality of life जीवन-शैली, रहन-सहन *The cost of living has risen in recent years.* ○ *The standard of living is very high in that country.*

**living room** (*BrE* **sitting room**) *noun* [C] the room in a house where people sit, relax, watch television, etc. together सबके बैठने-उठने का कमरा; बैठक

**lizard** /ˈlɪzəd ˈलिज़ड् / *noun* [C] a small reptile with four legs, dry skin and a long tail छिपकली, गोधिका

**load¹** /ləʊd लोड् / *noun* [C] **1** something (heavy) that is being or is waiting to be carried ढोया जा रहा या ढोया जाने वाला सामान; बोझ, वज़न *a truck carrying a load of sand* **2** (*often in compounds*) the quantity of sth that can be carried ढोयी जाने वाली वस्तु की मात्रा, खेप, लदान *bus loads of tourists* **3 loads (of sth)** [*pl.*] (*informal*) a lot (of sth) (किसी वस्तु के) ढेर *There are loads of things to do in Mumbai in the evenings.*

IDM **a load of rubbish, etc.** (*informal*) nonsense बक़वास

**load²** /ləʊd लोड् / *verb* **1** [I, T] **load (sth/sb) (up) (with sth); load (sth/sb) (into/onto sth)** to put a large quantity of sth into or onto sb/sth कोई वस्तु बड़ी मात्रा में किसी में भर देना या किसी पर लाद देना *They loaded the plane (up) with supplies.* **2** [I] to receive a load (पर) लदान होना *The ship is still loading.* **3** [I, T] to put a program or disk into a computer कंप्यूटर में कोई प्रोग्राम या डिस्क डालना या लोड करना *First, switch on the machine and load the disk.* ○ *The program is now loading.* **4** [T] to put sth into a machine, a weapon, etc. so that it can be used किसी यंत्र, हथियार आदि में कुछ डालना (ताकि वह काम कर सके) *to load film into a camera* ○ *to load a gun* ✪ विलोम **unload**

**loaded** /ˈləʊdɪd ˈलोडिड्/ *adj.* **1 loaded (with sth)** carrying a load; full and heavy (किसी वस्तु से) लदा हुआ; भरा हुआ और भारी या वज़नदार **2** (used especially about a gun or a camera) containing a bullet, a film, etc. (बंदूक़ या कैमरा) जिसमें गोली, फ़िल्म आदि डली हो **3** giving an advantage लाभ देने वाला *The system is loaded in their favour.* **4** (*informal*) (*not before a noun*) having a lot of money; rich बहुत पैसे वाला; धनी

**loaf** /ləʊf लोफ़्/ *noun* [C] (*pl.* **loaves** /ləʊvz लोव्ज़्/) bread that is baked in one piece and can be cut into pieces एक बड़े आकार में पकाई गई डबलरोटी जिसे बाद में टुकड़ों में काटा जाता है *a loaf of bread*

**loam** /ləʊm लोम्/ *noun* [U] (*technical*) good quality soil containing sand, clay and dead plants अच्छी क़िस्म की मिट्टी, दोमट मिट्टी, उपजाऊ मिट्टी (जिसमें रेत, चिकनी मिट्टी और मरे पौधे या सड़े पत्ते होते हैं)

**loan** /ləʊn लोन्/ *noun* **1** [C] money, etc. that sb/sth lends you उधार, ऋण *to take out a bank loan* ○ *to pay off a loan* **2** [U] the act of lending sth or the state of being lent उधार देने का कार्य या दिया गया उधार या ऋण *The books are* ***on loan*** *from the library.* ▶ **loan** *verb* [T] (*formal*) **loan sth (to sb)** (किसी व्यक्ति को) कोई वस्तु उधार देना या ऋण के रूप में देना

**loath** /ləʊθ लोथ्/ *adj.* **loath to do sth** (*formal*) not willing to do sth (कोई काम करने का) अनिच्छुक

**loathe** /ləʊð लोद्/ *verb* [T] (*not used in the continuous tenses*) to hate sb/sth किसी व्यक्ति या वस्तु से नफ़रत करना

**NOTE** यद्यपि इस क्रिया का प्रयोग सातत्यबोधक कालों (continuous tenses) में नहीं होता तथापि इसका **-ing** युक्त वर्तमान कृदंत (present participle) रूप का प्रयोग पर्याप्त प्रचलित है—*Loathing the thought of having to apologize, she knocked on his door.*

▶ **loathsome** /ˈləʊðsəm ˈलोद्सम्/ *adj.* घृणा उत्पन्न करने वाला ▶ **loathing** *noun* [U] घृणा

**loaves** = **loaf** का plural रूप

**lob** /lɒb लॉब्/ *verb* [I, T] (**lobbing; lobbed**) (*sport*) to hit, kick or throw a ball high into the air, so that it lands behind your opponent गेंद को ऐसे ऊपर मारना या फेंकना कि वह प्रतिपक्षी खिलाड़ी के पीछे गिरे ▶ **lob** *noun* [C] इस प्रकार से फेंकी गई गेंद

**lobby**[1] /ˈlɒbi ˈलॉबि/ *noun* [C] (*pl.* **lobbies**) **1** the area that is just inside a large building, where people can meet and wait बड़े भवन में प्रतीक्षा-कक्ष, लॉबी *a hotel lobby* **2** [*with sing. or pl. verb*] a group of people who try to influence politicians to do or not do sth व्यक्तियों का समूह जो राजनेताओं के किसी मुद्दे के पक्ष या विपक्ष में सहमत कराने का प्रयत्न करता है *the anti-smoking lobby*

**lobby**[2] /ˈlɒbi ˈलॉबि/ *verb* [I, T] (*pres. part.* **lobbying;** *3rd person sing. pres.* **lobbies;** *pt, pp* **lobbied**) to try to influence a politician or the government to do or not do sth किसी राजनेता या सरकार को किसी मुद्दे के पक्ष या विपक्ष में सहमत कराने का प्रयत्न करना; लॉबी करना

**lobe** /ləʊb लोब्/ *noun* [C] **1** = **ear lobe** **2** one part of an organ of the body, especially the brain or lungs किसी शरीरांग का एक भाग विशेषतः मस्तिष्क या फेफड़े का; पालि

**lobster** /ˈlɒbstə(r) ˈलॉबूस्ट(र्)/ *noun* **1** [C] a large shellfish that has eight legs. A lobster is bluish-black but it turns red when it is cooked समुद्री झींगा, महाचिंगट; आँठ टाँगों वाला यह झींगा नीला-काला होता है मगर पकने पर लाल हो जाता है ➪ **shellfish** पर चित्र देखिए। **2** [U] a cooked lobster eaten as food खाने के लिए पकाया हुआ समुद्री झींगा

**local**[1] /ˈləʊkl ˈलोकूल्/ *adj.* of a particular place (near you) स्थानीय *local newspapers/radio* ○ *the local doctor/policeman/butcher* ➪ **international, national** और **regional** देखिए। ▶ **locally** *adv.* स्थानीय स्तर पर *I do most of my shopping locally.*

**local**[2] /ˈləʊkl ˈलोकूल्/ *noun* [C] **1** [*usually pl.*] a person who lives in a particular place स्थान विशेष में रहने वाला व्यक्ति *The locals seem very friendly.* **2** (*BrE informal*) a pub that is near your home where you often go to drink घर के निकट की मधुशाला

**local government** *noun* [U, *BrE*] the system of government of a town or an area by elected representatives of the people who live there किसी शहर या क्षेत्र के निर्वाचित प्रतिनिधियों द्वारा संचालित प्रशासन; स्थानीय स्वशासन, स्थानीय सरकार

**localize** (*also* **-ise**) /ˈləʊkəlaɪz ˈलोकलाइज़्/ *verb* [T] to limit sth to a particular place or area किसी बात को स्थान या क्षेत्र विशेष तक सीमित कर देना; स्थानीयकरण करना

**local time** *noun* [U] the time at a particular place in the world स्थान-विशेष का या स्थानीय समय *We arrive in Singapore at 2 o'clock in the afternoon, local time.*

**locate** /ləʊˈkeɪt लोˈकेट्/ *verb* [T] **1** to find the exact position of sb/sth किसी व्यक्ति या वस्तु के सही ठिकाने का पता लगाना *The damaged ship has been located two kilometres off the coast.* **2** to put or build sth in a particular place स्थान-विशेष पर किसी वस्तु को रखना या बनाना; स्थापित करना ▶ **located** *adj.* स्थित *Where exactly is your office located?*

**location** /ləʊˈkeɪʃn लोˈकेश्न् / *noun* **1** [C] a place or position कोई स्थान या ठिकाना *Several locations have been suggested for the new office block.* **2** [U] the action of finding where sb/sth is किसी व्यक्ति या वस्तु के ठिकाने का पता लगाने का कार्य; स्थान निर्धारण करना **IDM on location** (used about a film, television programme, etc.) made in a suitable place outside a **studio** (फ़िल्म, टेलीविज़न कार्यक्रम आदि) स्टूडियो से बाहर किसी उपयुक्त स्थान पर निर्मित *The series was filmed on location in Thailand.*

**loch** /lɒk लॉक् / *noun* [C] the Scottish word for a lake (स्कॉट्टिश भाषा में) झील *the Loch Ness Monster*

**lock**[1] /lɒk लॉक् / *verb* **1** [I, T] to close or fasten (sth) so that it can only be opened with a key (किसी वस्तु पर) ताला लगाना *Have you locked the car?* ○ *The door won't lock.* ✪ विलोम **unlock** **2** [T] to put sb/sth in a safe place and lock it (किसी व्यक्ति या वस्तु) को सुरक्षित स्थान पर ताला लगाकर रखना *Lock your passport in a safe place.* **3** [T] **be locked in sth** to be involved in an angry argument, etc. with sth, or to be holding sb very tightly किसी के साथ विवाद में उलझना या किसी को कसके थामे रहना *The two sides were locked in a bitter dispute.* ○ *They were locked in a passionate embrace.*

**PHR V lock sth away** to keep sth in a safe or secret place that is locked किसी ताला-जड़े सुरक्षित या गुप्त स्थान पर किसी वस्तु को रखना

**lock sb in/out** to lock a door so that a person cannot get in/out दरवाज़े पर ताला लगा देना ताकि व्यक्ति बाहर न जा सके या अंदर न आ सके *I locked myself out of the house and had to climb in through the window.*

**lock (sth) up** to lock all the doors, windows, etc. of a building किसी इमारत के सभी दरवाज़ों, खिड़कियों आदि पर ताला लगा देना *Make sure that you lock up before you leave.*

**lock sb up** to put sb in prison किसी को जेल में डाल देना

**lock**[2] /lɒk लॉक् / *noun* [C] **1** something that is used for fastening a door, lid, etc. so that you need a key to open it again ताला *to turn the key in the lock* ➪ **padlock** देखिए। **2** a part of a river or a canal where the level of water changes. Locks have gates at each end and are used to allow boats to move to a higher or lower part of the canal or river नदी या तरह का वह भाग जहाँ जल का स्तर भिन्न हो जाता है; जलपाश बाँध के प्रत्येक सिरे पर द्वार बने होते हैं और नावों के आवागमन के लिए इन्हें खोला-बंद किया जाता है

**IDM pick a lock** ➪ **pick**[1] देखिए।

**under lock and key** in a locked place ताला-जड़े स्थान पर, ताला लगा कर

**locker** /ˈlɒkə(r) ˈलॉक(र्) / *noun* [C] a small cupboard that can be locked in a bank, school or sports centre, where you can leave your clothes, books, etc. स्कूल, बैंक या खेल केंद्र आदि में बनी छोटी अलमारी जिसमें अपना सामान रखकर ताला लगा सकते हैं; लॉकर, ताले वाली अलमारी

**locket** /ˈlɒkɪt ˈलॉकिट् / *noun* [C] a piece of jewellery that you wear on a chain around your neck and which opens so that you can put a picture, etc. inside (एक आभूषण जिसे ज़ंजीर में डालकर गरदन में पहना जाता है और खोलने पर जिसमें कोई चित्र दिखाई देता है); लॉकेट

**locksmith** /ˈlɒksmɪθ ˈलॉक्स्मिथ् / *noun* [C] a person who makes and repairs locks तालासाज़

**locomotion** /ˌləʊkəˈməʊʃn ˌलोकˈमोश्न् / *noun* [U] (*formal*) movement or the ability to move गमन, गति, संचलन की क्षमता

**locomotive**/ˌləʊkəˈməʊtɪv ˌलोकˈमोटिव़् / = **engine 2**

**locust** /ˈləʊkəst ˈलोकस्ट् / *noun* [C] a flying insect from Africa and Asia that moves in very large groups, eating and destroying large quantities of plants टिड्डी (अफ़्रीका और एशिया में पाया जाने वाल एक उड़न-कीट जो बड़े झुंड बनाकर ढेर-सारे पौधों को खाता और नष्ट करता चलता है) ➪ **insect** पर चित्र देखिए।

**lodge**[1] /lɒdʒ लॉज् / *verb* **1** [I] to pay to live in sb's house with him/her किसी व्यक्ति के मकान में किराए पर रहना *He lodged with a family for his first term at university.* **2** [I, T] to become firmly fixed or to make sth do this किसी बात का मन में पक्के तौर पर बैठ जाना या उसे बैठा लेना **3** [T] (*formal*) to make an official statement complaining about sth किसी बात की आधिकारिक रूप से शिक़ायत दर्ज कराना

**lodge**[2] /lɒdʒ लॉज् / *noun* [C] **1** a room at the entrance to a large building such as a college or factory बड़े भवन का प्रवेश कक्ष **2** a small house in the country ग्रामीण अंचल में छोटा मकान **3** = **lodging 2**

**lodger** /ˈlɒdʒə(r) ˈलॉज(र्) / *noun* [C] a person who pays rent to live in a house as a member of the family किसी मकान में परिवार का अंग बनकर रहने वाला किराएदार ➪ **boarder** देखिए।

**lodging** /ˈlɒdʒɪŋ ˈलॉजिङ् / *noun* **1** [C, U] a place where you can stay ठहरने का स्थान, अस्थायी आवास *The family offered full board and lodging* (= a room and all meals) *in exchange for English lessons.* **2** (*old-fashioned*) **lodgings** [*pl.*] a room or rooms in sb's house where you can pay to stay किराए का कमरा या कमरे

**loft** /lɒft लॉफ़्ट् / *noun* [C] the room or space under the roof of a house or other building अटारी, परछत्ती, उत्क्षा ➪ **attic** देखिए।

**lofty** /ˈlɒfti ˈलॉफ़्टि / *adj.* (**loftier; loftiest**) (*formal*) **1** (of buildings, mountains, etc.) very tall and impressive (भवन, पर्वत आदि) बहुत ऊँचा और प्रभावशाली *lofty mountains/towers* **2** (*usually before a noun*) (*approving*) (of a thought, aim, etc.) of high moral quality, or noble character (विचार, लक्ष्य आदि) उच्च नैतिक गुणवत्ता या उत्कृष्ट आचरण *lofty principles/ambitions/ideals* **3** (*disapproving*) proud and arrogant अहंकारी एवं हेकड़ीबाज़ *lofty tone* ▶ **loftily** /ˈlɑftɪli ˈलॉफ़्टिलि / *adv.* उच्चता से, ऊँचाइपूर्ण, अहंकारपूर्वक

**log**[1] /lɒg लॉग् / *noun* [C] **1** a thick piece of wood that has fallen or been cut from a tree लकड़ी का लट्ठा (जो पेड़ से गिर कर अलग हुआ है या काटा गया है) **2** (*also* **logbook**) the official written record of a ship's or an aircraft's journey जहाज़ या विमान की यात्रा का आधिकारिक लिखित रिकार्ड *to keep a log*

**log**[2] /lɒg लॉग् / *verb* [T] (**logging; logged**) to keep an official written record of sth किसी काम का आधिकारिक रिकार्ड रखना

**PHR V** **log in/on** to perform the actions that allow you to start using a computer system कंप्यूटर सिस्टम को सक्रिय करने के लिए आवश्यक क्रियाएँ करना *You need to key in your password to log on.*

**log off/out** to perform the actions that allow you to finish using a computer system कंप्यूटर प्रणाली को निष्क्रिय करने के लिए आवश्यक क्रियाएँ करना; निष्क्रिय करना

**logarithm** /ˈlɒgərɪðəm ˈलॉगरिद्रम् / (*informal* **log**) *noun* [C] one of a series of numbers arranged in lists (**tables**) that allow you to solve problems in mathematics by adding or subtracting numbers instead of multiplying or dividing लघुगणक; लघुगणक तालिका में क्रम से संख्याएँ दी हुई होती हैं। यहाँ संख्याओं में गुणा या भाग करने के लिए संख्याओं के सामने दिए अंकों को जोड़ा या घटाया जाता है। तत्पश्चात एक अन्य तालिका से गुणनफल या भागफल ज्ञात हो जाता है

**loggerheads** /ˈlɒgəhedz ˈलॉगहेड्ज़् / *noun*

**IDM** **at loggerheads (with sb)** strongly disagreeing (with sb) (किसी व्यक्ति से) घोर असहमत

**logic** /ˈlɒdʒɪk ˈलॉजिक् / *noun* [U] **1** a sensible reason or way of thinking युक्तिसंग तर्क या विचार *There is no logic in your argument.* **2** the science of using reason तर्कशास्त्र

**logical** /ˈlɒdʒɪkl ˈलॉजिकल् / *adj.* **1** seeming natural, reasonable or sensible जो स्वाभाविक, युक्तिसंगत या तर्कयुक्त प्रतीत हो *As I see it, there is only one logical conclusion.* ✪ विलोम **illogical** **2** thinking in a sensible way युक्तिसंग रीति से विचार करने वाला *a logical mind* ▶ **logically** /ˈlɒdʒɪkli ˈलॉजिक्लि / *adv.* युक्तिसंगत रीति से

**logjam** /ˈlɒgdʒæm ˈलॉग्जैम् / *noun* [C] **1** a mass of **logs** that are floating on a river and blocking it नदी में तैरते और रुकावट पैदा करते ढेरों लट्ठे **2** a difficult situation in which you cannot make progress easily because there are too many things to do रुकावटों-भरी कठिन स्थिति

**logo** /ˈləʊgəʊ ˈलोगो / *noun* [C] (*pl.* **logos**) a printed symbol or design that a company or an organization uses as its special sign मुद्रित प्रतीक या डिज़ाइन जिसे कोई कंपनी या संगठन अपने एक विशेष चिह्न के रूप में प्रयुक्त करती है; लोगो

**loiter** /ˈlɔɪtə(r) ˈलॉइट(र्) / *verb* [I] to stand or walk around somewhere for no obvious reason अकारण कहीं खड़े हो जाना या इधर-उधर घूमना; मटरगश्ती या आवारागर्दी करना

**Lok Sabha** *noun* [U] the lower house of the Indian Parliament लोक सभा

**lollipop** /ˈlɒlipɒp ˈलॉलिपॉप् / (*also* **lolly**) *noun* [C] a sweet on a stick एक सींकदार मिठाई, लॉलीपॉप, चूसनीय मिठाई ➪ **ice lolly** देखिए।

**lone** /ləʊn लोन् / *adj.* (*only before a noun*) **1** without any other people; alone बिना संगी-साथी के; अकेला *a lone swimmer* ✪ पर्याय **solitary** **2** (used about a parent) single; without a partner (माता या पिता) अकेला बिना अपने साथी का *a support group for lone parents*

**lonely** /ˈləʊnli ˈलोन्लि / *adj.* (**lonelier; loneliest**) **1** unhappy because you are not with other people किसी का साथ न होने से उदास *to feel sad and lonely* **2** (used about a situation or a period of time) sad and spent alone (स्थिति या कालावधि) उदासीभरी और अकेलेपन की **3** (*only before a noun*) far from other people and places where people live एकांत और सुनसान में रहने वाला ➪ **alone** पर नोट देखिए। ▶ **loneliness** *noun* [U] एकाकीपन ➪ **solitude** और **isolation** देखिए।

**loner** /ˈləʊnə(r) ˈलोन(र्) / *noun* [C] (*informal*) a person who prefers being alone to being with other people औरों के साथ की अपेक्षा अकेलेपन को पसंद करने वाला व्यक्ति; एकांतप्रिय व्यक्ति

**lonesome** /ˈləʊnsəm ˈलोन्सम् / *adj.* (*AmE*) lonely or making you feel lonely अकेला या अकेलेपन का अहसास कराने वाला ➪ **alone** पर नोट देखिए।

**long¹** /lɒŋ लॉङ्/ *adj.* (**longer** /ˈlɒŋɡə(r) ˈलॉङ्ग(र्)/ **longest** /ˈlɒŋɡɪst ˈलॉङ्गिस्ट्/) **1** measuring or covering a large amount in distance or time दूरी या समय की बड़ी मात्रा में व्याप्त, दूर या लंबा *She has lovely long hair.* ○ *We had to wait a long time.* ○ *a very long journey/book/corridor* **2** used for asking or talking about how much something measures in length, distance or time किसी वस्तु की लंबाई, दूरी या समय की माप पूछने या बात करने के लिए प्रयुक्त ***How long** is the film?* ○ *The insect was only two millimetres long* ➪ **length** noun देखिए।
✪ विलोम **short**

IDM **a long shot** a person or thing that probably will not succeed, win, etc. सफलता की संभावना से वंचित व्यक्ति या वस्तु

**at (long) last** ➪ **last²** देखिए।

**at the longest** not longer than the stated time निर्दिष्ट समय से अधिक देर नहीं, अधिक-से-अधिक, देर-से-देर *It will take a week at the longest.*

**go a long way** (used about money, food, etc.) to be used for buying a lot of things, feeding a lot of people, etc. (धन, भोजन आदि का) लंबे समय तक चलना, बहुतों के लिए सहायक होना

**have a long way to go** to need to make a lot more progress before sth can be achieved लक्ष्य प्राप्ति के लिए काफ़ी अधिक प्रयत्न की आवश्यकता होना

**in the long run** after a long time; in the end लंबे समय के बाद; अंत में

**in the long/short term** ➪ **term¹** देखिए।

**long²** /lɒŋ लॉङ्/ *adv.* (**longer** /-ŋɡə(r) -ङ्ग(र्)/, **longest** /-ŋɡɪst -ङ्गिस्ट्/) **1** for a long time लंबे समय तक *You shouldn't have to wait long.* ○ *I hope we don't have to wait much longer.* ○ *They won't be gone for long.*

> NOTE **Long** और **a long time** दोनों का प्रयोग समय की अभिव्यक्ति के लिए होता है। स्वीकारात्मक वाक्यों में सामान्यतया **a long time** का प्रयोग होता है—*They stood there for a long time.* **Long** का प्रयोग केवल स्वीकारात्मक वाक्यों में अन्य क्रियाविशेषण (जैसे 'too' 'enough', 'ago') के साथ होता है—*We lived here long ago.* ○ *I've put up with this noise long enough. I'm going to make a complaint.* **Long** और **a long time** दोनों का प्रश्नवाचक वाक्यों में प्रयोग हो सकता है—*Were you away long/a long time?* परंतु निषेधवाचक वाक्यों में **long** और **a long time** में कभी-कभी अर्थ का अंतर आ जाता है—*I haven't been here long* (= I arrived only a short time ago). ○ *I haven't been here for a long time* (= it is a long time since I was last here).

**2** a long time before or after a particular time or event एक विशेष समय या घटना के बहुत पहले या बाद *We got married **long before** we moved here.* ○ *Don't worry–they'll be here **before long**.* **3** for the whole of the time that is mentioned बताए गए सारे समय तक *The baby cried **all night long**.*

IDM **as/so long as** on condition that; provided (that) किसी शर्त पर, बशर्ते (कि) *As long as no problems arise we should get the job finished by Friday.*

**no/not any longer** not any more अब (और) नहीं *They no longer live here.* ○ *They don't live here any longer.*

**long³** /lɒŋ लॉङ्/ *verb* [I] **long for sth; long (for sb) to do sth** to want sth very much, especially sth that is not likely किसी वस्तु की बहुत चाह होना (विशेषतः जब संभावना अनुकूल न हो) *She longed to return to India.* ▶ **longing** *noun* [C, U] लालसा, चाहत *a longing for peace* ▶ **longingly** *adv.* लालसा के साथ

**long-distance** *adj., adv.* (used about travel or communication) between places that are far from each other (यात्रा या संचार) लंबी दूरी का *to phone long-distance*

**longevity** /lɒnˈdʒevəti लॉन्ˈजेव़टि/ *noun* [U] (*formal*) long life; the fact of lasting a long time लंबा जीवन; दीर्घ आयु *Elephants are known for their longevity.* ○ *He prides himself on the longevity of the company.*

**longhand** /ˈlɒŋhænd ˈलॉङ्हैन्ड्/ *noun* [U] ordinary writing that is not typed and does not use any special signs or short forms हाथ की साधारण लिखाई जिसमें विशेष चिह्नों या संक्षिप्त रूपों का प्रयोग नहीं होता ➪ **shorthand** देखिए।

**long-haul** *adj.* (*only before a noun*) connected with the transport of people or goods over long distances लोगों या सामान की लंबी दूरी की यात्रा या ढुलाई से संबंधित *a long-haul flight*

**longitude** /ˈlɒndʒɪtjuːd; ˈlɒŋɡɪ- ˈलॉन्जिट्यूड्; ˈलॉङ्गि-/ *noun* [U] the distance of a place east or west of a line from the North Pole to the South Pole that passes through Greenwich in London. Longitude is measured in degrees मानचित्र के अनुसार लंदन में ग्रीनिच से गुज़रते हुए उत्तरी से दक्षिणी ध्रुव तक जाने वाली रेखा के पूर्व या पश्चिम में किसी स्थान की (उस रेखा से) दूरी; देशांतर रेखा, इसे डिग्रियों में मापा जाता है ➪ **latitude** देखिए तथा **earth** पर चित्र देखिए।

**longitudinal wave** *noun* [C] (*technical*) a wave that **vibrates** in the direction that it is moving देशांतरीय लहर (वह लहर जो अपनी गति की दिशा में कंपन करती है) ➪ **transverse wave** देखिए।

**long jump** *noun* [*sing.*] the sport in which people try to jump as far as possible लंबी कूद ➪ **high jump** देखिए।

**long-life** *adj.* made to last for a long time देर तक चलने वाली *a long-life battery* ○ *long-life milk*

**long-lived** *adj.* that has lived or lasted for a long time जो देर तक जीवित रहा हो या चला हो; दीर्घायु या दीर्घकालीन *a long-lived dispute*

**long-range** *adj.* **1** of or for a long period of time starting from the present लंबी समयावधि का या के लिए, दीर्घावधि वाला *the long-range weather forecast* **2** that can go or be sent over long distances जो लंबी दूरी तक जा सके या प्रक्षेपित हो सके; दूरमार, दूरप्रहारी *long-range nuclear missiles*

**longshore drift** /ˌlɒŋʃɔːˈdrɪftˌलॉङ्शॉˈड्रिफ़्ट्/ *noun* [U] (in geography) the movement of sand, etc. along a beach caused by waves hitting the beach at an angle and going back in a straight line (भूगोल में) समुद्र तट पर रेत आदि की हरकत जो लहरों के तट से, टकराकर सीधे लौटने की क्रिया से उत्पन्न होती है; वेलांचली प्रवाह, तटीय प्रवाह

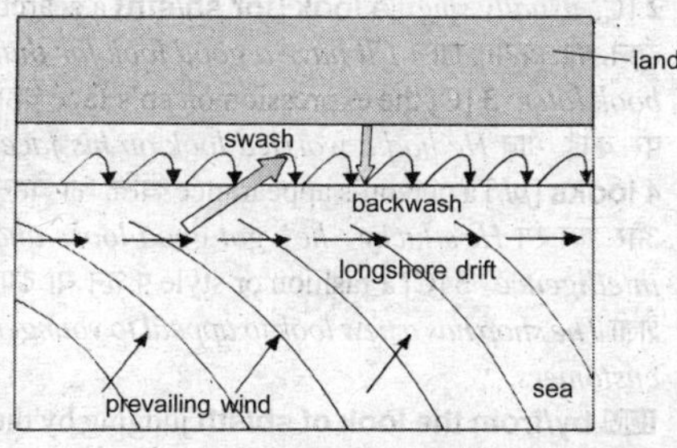

**longshore drift**

**long-sighted** (*AmE* **far-sighted**) *adj.* able to see things clearly only when they are quite far away केवल लंबी दूरी की वस्तुओं को ही साफ़ देखने में सक्षम; दीर्घदृष्टि ✪ विलोम **short-sighted** (*AmE* **near-sighted**) ➪ **short-sighted** पर चित्र देखिए।

**long-standing** *adj.* that has lasted for a long time जो देर तक चलता रहा है; (बहुत) पुराना, चिरकालिक *a long-standing arrangement*

**long-suffering** *adj.* (used about a person) having a lot of troubles but not complaining (व्यक्ति) अनेक कष्टों से ग्रस्त (परंतु मूक)

**long-term** *adj.* of or for a long period of time लंबी अवधि का या के लिए; दीर्घावधिक *long-term planning*

**long wave** *noun* [U] (*abbr.* **LW**) the system of sending radio signals using sound waves of 1000 metres or more एक हज़ार मीटर या अधिक दूर जाने वाली ध्वनि तरंगों पर आधारित रेडियो संकेतों की प्रेषण पद्धति, एक हज़ार मीटर से अधिक दूर जाने वाली रेडियो तरंग; लॉंग वेव ➪ **short wave** और **medium wave** देखिए।

**long-winded** *adj.* (used about sth that is written or spoken) boring because it is too long (लेख या कथन) अनावश्यक रूप से लंबा होने के कारण उबाऊ; शब्दाडंबर

**loo** /luː लू/ *noun* [C] (*pl.* **loos**) (*BrE informal*) toilet शौचालय ➪ **toilet** पर नोट देखिए।

**look¹** /lʊk लुक्/ *verb* **1** [I, T] **look (at sth)** to turn your eyes in a particular direction (in order to pay attention to sb/sth) (किसी व्यक्ति या वस्तु को ध्यान से) देखना *Sorry, I wasn't looking. Can you show me again?* ○ *Look carefully at this picture.*

> NOTE **See** शब्द में केवल देखने की बात है, ध्यान से देखने की नहीं—*I saw a girl riding past on a horse.* परंतु **look** में ध्यानपूर्वक देखने की विशेषता है—*Look carefully. Can you see anything strange?*

**2** [I] **look (for sb/sth)** to try to find (sb/sth) (किसी व्यक्ति या वस्तु का पता लगाने की कोशिश करना *We've been looking for you everywhere. Where have you been?* ○ *to look for work.* **3** *linking verb* **look (like sb/sth) (to sb); look (to sb) as if... /as though...** to seem or appear प्रतीत होना या लगना *to look tired/ill/sad/well/happy* ○ *The boy looks like his father.* **4** [I] used for asking sb to listen to what you are saying किसी व्यक्ति को यह कहने के लिए प्रयुक्त कि वह आपकी बात सुने *Look, Wasim, I know you are busy but could you give me a hand?* **5** [I] to face a particular direction दिशा-विशेष के सामने होना *This room looks south so it gets the sun.* **6** [I] **look to do sth** to aim to do sth किसी काम को लक्ष्य बनाना *We are looking to double our profits over the next five years.*

IDM **look bad; not look good** to be considered bad manners कोई बात अशिष्ट लगना *It'll look bad if we get there an hour late.*

**look good** to seem to be encouraging कोई बात अच्छी या आशाजनक लगना *This year's sales figures are looking good.*

**look sb in the eye** to look straight at sb without feeling embarrassed or afraid बिना संकोच या भय के किसी व्यक्ति को सीधे देखना; किसी व्यक्ति को आँख से आँख मिलाकर देखना

**(not) look yourself** to (not) look as well or healthy as usual हमेशा की तरह ठीक या स्वस्थ (न) दीखना

**look on the bright side (of sth)** to think only about the good side of a bad situation and be happy and hopeful किसी प्रतिकूल स्थिति के अनुकूल पक्ष पर ध्यान देना और ख़ुश तथा आशान्वित रहना

**never/not look back** to become and continue being successful सफल होना तथा निरंतर सफल होते रहना

**PHR V look after sb/sth/yourself** to be responsible for or take care of sb/sth/yourself किसी व्यक्ति, वस्तु या स्वयं की देखभाल करना *The old lady's son looked after all her financial affairs.*

**look ahead** to think about or plan for the future भविष्य के बारे में सोचना या योजना बनाना

**look at sth** 1 to examine or study sth किसी वस्तु की जाँच करना या उसका अध्ययन करना *The government is looking at ways of reducing unemployment.* 2 to read sth कुछ पढ़ना *Could I look at the newspaper when you've finished with it?* 3 to consider sth किसी बात पर विचार करना, कोई बात समझना *Different races and nationalities look at life differently.*

**look back (on sth)** to think about sth in your past पिछली बातें याद करना

**look down on sb/sth** to think that you are better than sb/sth किसी को तुच्छ या हेय दृष्टि से देखना, स्वयं को किसी अन्य से बेहतर समझना

**look forward to sth/doing sth** to wait with pleasure for sth to happen आने वाली स्थिति की सहर्ष प्रतीक्षा करना *I'm really looking forward to the weekend.*

**look into sth** to study or try to find out sth किसी बात की जाँच-पड़ताल करना *A committee was set up to look into the causes of the accident.*

**look on** to watch sth happening without taking any action किसी घटना के घटित होते समय दर्शक मात्र बने रहना; घटना को घटते देखते भर रहना (कोई कार्रवाई न करना) *All they could do was look on as the house burned.*

**look on sb/sth as sth; look on sb with sth** to think of sb/sth in a particular way किसी वस्तु या व्यक्ति के विषय में ख़ास तरह से सोचना *They seem to look on me as someone who can advise them.*

**look out** to be careful or to pay attention to sth dangerous चारों ओर ध्यान बनाए रखना और सावधान रहना ताकि कोई दुर्घटना न हो जाए, इस अभिव्यक्ति का प्रयोग चेतावनी के अर्थ में किया जाता है *She must look out for her health.*

**look out (for sb/sth)** to pay attention in order to see, find or avoid sb/sth किसी को देखने, ढूँढ़ने या उससे बचने के लिए सतर्क रहना *Look out for thieves!*

**look round** 1 to turn your head in order to see sb/sth किसी व्यक्ति या वस्तु को देखने के लिए सिर घुमाना 2 to look at many things (before buying sth) (ख़रीदने से पहले) अनेक वस्तुएँ देखना *She looked round but couldn't find anything she liked.*

**look round sth** to walk around a place looking at things चीज़ों को देखते-देखते किसी स्थान के सब ओर घूमना *to look round a town/shop/museum*

**look through sth** to read sth quickly किसी वस्तु को तुरंत पढ़ लेना, उस पर नज़र डालना

**look to sb for sth; look to sb to do sth** to expect sb to do or to provide sth किसी से कुछ आशा करना (काम की या कुछ पाने की) *He always looked to his father for advice.*

**look up** 1 to move your eyes upwards to look at sb/sth किसी व्यक्ति या वस्तु को ध्यान से देखने के लिए नज़रें ऊपर उठाना *She looked up and smiled.* 2 (*informal*) to improve (में) सुधार होना *Business is looking up.*

**look sth up** to search for information in a book पुस्तक में कोई जानकारी खोजना *to look up a word in a dictionary*

**look up to sb** to respect and admire sb किसी का सम्मान और प्रशंसा करना

**look²** /lʊk लुक्/ *noun* 1 [C] the act of looking देखने की क्रिया *Have a look at this article.* ○ *Take a close look at the contract before you sign it.* 2 [C, *usually sing.*] **a look (for sb/sth)** a search ढूँढ़ने की क्रिया; खोज *I'll have a good look for that book later.* 3 [C] the expression on sb's face चेहरे पर कोई भाव *He had a worried look on his face.* 4 **looks** [*pl.*] a person's appearance व्यक्ति का चेहरा और रूप-रंग *He's lucky—he's got good looks and intelligence.* 5 [C] a fashion or style फ़ैशन या ढंग; शैली *The shop has a new look to appeal to younger customers.*

**IDM by/from the look of sb/sth** judging by the appearance of sb/sth किसी व्यक्ति या वस्तु के रूप या आकृति से अनुमान लगाते हुए *It's going to be a fine day by the look of it.*

**like the look/sound of sb/sth** ➪ **like¹** देखिए।

**look-in** *noun*

**IDM (not) give sb a look-in; (not) get/have a look-in** (*informal*) to (not) give sb, or to (not) have a chance to do sth किसी को कुछ (न) देना, या कुछ करने का मौका (न) देना

**-looking** /ˈlʊkɪŋ ˈलुकिङ्/ *suffix* (*used to form compound adjectives*) having the appearance mentioned बताई हुई शकल-सूरत वाला *an odd-looking building* ○ *He's very good-looking.*

**lookout** /ˈlʊkaʊt ˈलुक्आउट्/ *noun* [C] (a person who has) the responsibility of watching to see if danger is coming; the place this person watches from आगामी ख़तरे पर निगाह रखने के लिए उत्तरदायी व्यक्ति; वह स्थान जहाँ से निगाह रखी जाती है *One of the gangs acted as lookout.*

IDM **be on the lookout for sb/sth; keep a lookout for sb/sth** to pay attention in order to see, find or avoid sb/sth किसी व्यक्ति या वस्तु को देखने, ढूँढ़ने या उससे कन्नी काटने के लिए ध्यान देना

**loom**[1] /luːm लूम्/ *noun* [C] a machine that is used for making cloth (**weaving**) by passing pieces of thread across and under other pieces (कपड़ा बुनने का) करघा

**loom**[2] /luːm लूम्/ verb [I] **loom (up)** to appear as a shape that is not clear and in a way that seems frightening धुँधली और डरावनी शकल में दिखाई पड़ना *The mountain loomed (up) in the distance.*

**loony** /ˈluːni ˈलूनि/ *noun* [C] (*pl.* **loonies**) (*slang*) a person who is crazy सनकी या झक्की व्यक्ति; विक्षिप्त **loony** *adj.* सनकी, विक्षिप्त

**loop** /luːp लूप्/ *noun* [C] a curved or round shape made by a line curving round and joining or crossing itself फंदा, छल्ला *a loop in a rope* ○ *The road goes around the lake in a loop.* ▶ **loop** *verb* [I, T] (से) फंदा बनाना या डालना *He was trying to loop a rope over the horse's head.*

**loophole** /ˈluːphəʊl ˈलूपहोल्/ *noun* [C] a way of avoiding sth because the words of a rule or law are badly chosen बच निकलने का रास्ता (क्योंकि नियम या क़ानून की भाषा त्रुटिपूर्ण है)

**loose**[1] /luːs लूस्/ *adj.* **1** not tied up or shut in sth; free बंधनमुक्त; खुला *The horse managed to* ***get loose*** *and escape.* ○ *I take the dog to the woods and* ***let him loose****.* **2** not firmly fixed ढीला, जो मज़बूती से जमा हुआ न हो *a loose tooth* **3** not contained in sth or joined together छुट्टी या अलग-अलग *loose change* (= coins) ○ *some loose sheets of paper* **4** not fitting closely; not tight जो ठीक से फ़िट न हो; जो कसा न हो, ढीला *These trousers don't fit. They're much too loose round the waist.* ✪ विलोम **tight** **5** not completely accurate or the same as sth जो पूर्णतया शुद्ध या मूल के समान न हो; शिथिल *a loose translation* ▶ **loosely** *adv.* शिथिल रूप से *The film is loosely based on the life of Dhirubhai Ambani.*

IDM **all hell broke loose** ➪ **hell** देखिए।

**at a loose end** having nothing to do and feeling bored बिना कुछ काम के और ऊबता हुआ

**loose**[2] /luːs लूस्/ *noun*

IDM **on the loose** escaped and dangerous भागा हुआ और ख़तरनाक *a lion on the loose from a zoo*

**loose-leaf** *adj.* (used about a book, file, etc.) with pages that can be removed or added separately (पुस्तक, फ़ाइल आदि) जिसके पन्नों को अलग से हटाया या जोड़ा जा सके, अलग-अलग पन्नों वाला

**loosen** /ˈluːsn ˈलूसन्/ *verb* [I, T] to become or make sth less tight ढीला हो जाना या कर देना *to loosen your tie/belt* ○ *Don't loosen your grip on the rope or you'll fall.*

PHR V **loosen (sb/sth) up** to relax or move more easily तनाव रहित होना या अधिक आराम महसूस करना *These exercises will help you to loosen up.*

**loot**[1] /luːt लूट्/ *verb* [I, T] to steal things from shops or buildings during a war, a **riot**, a fire, etc. युद्ध, दंगा आदि में इमारतों या दुकानों से सामान लूटना ▶ **looting** *noun* [U] लूट-मार

**loot**[2] /luːt लूट्/ *noun* [U] **1** money and valuable objects taken by soldiers from the enemy after winning a battle युद्ध में विजयी सेना द्वारा लूटा माल, युद्ध धन, युद्ध लूट **2** (*informal*) money and valuable objects that have been stolen by thieves चोरों द्वारा चुराया गया क़ीमती माल, चोरी माल

**lop** /lɒp लॉप्/ *verb* [T] (**lopping; lopped**) to cut branches off a tree किसी वृक्ष की शाखाएँ काटना

PHR V **lop sth off/away** to cut sth off/away किसी वस्तु को काटकर अलग कर देना

**lopsided** /ˌlɒpˈsaɪdɪd ˌलॉप्ˈसाइडिड्/ *adj.* with one side lower or smaller than the other जिसका एक सिरा दूसरे से नीचा या छोटा हो; तिरछा, एकतरफ़ा *a lopsided smile*

**lorry** /ˈlɒri ˈलॉरि/ (*BrE*) *noun* [C] (*pl.* **lorries**) (*AmE* **truck**) a large strong motor vehicle that is used for carrying goods by road सड़क मार्ग से माल ढोने के लिए प्रयुक्त बड़ा मोटर वाहन; ट्रक, लारी

**lose** /luːz लूज़्/ *verb* (*pt, pp* **lost** /lɒst लॉस्ट्/) **1** [T] to become unable to find sth (किसी वस्तु को) खो देना, न पा सकना *I've lost my purse. I can't find it anywhere.* **2** [T] to no longer have sb/sth किसी व्यक्ति या वस्तु को गँवा देना, खो देना *She lost a leg in the accident.* ○ *He lost his wife last year* (= she died). ○ *to lose your job* **3** [T] to have less of sth किसी वस्तु का कम हो जाना या हानि उठाना *to lose weight/interest/patience* ○ *The company is losing money all the time.* ✪ विलोम **gain** **4** [I, T] to not win; to be defeated जीतना न पाना; हार जाना *We played well but we lost 2–1.* ○ *to lose a court case/an argument* **5** [T] to waste time, a chance, etc. समय, मौक़ा आदि गँवाना या बरबाद करना *Hurry up! There's* ***no time to lose****.* **6** [I, T] to become poorer (as a result of sth) (किसी बात के फलस्वरूप) हानि उठाना *The company lost on the deal.* **7** [T] (*informal*) to cause sb not to understand sth किसी व्यक्ति को कोई बात समझने न देना *You've totally lost me! Please explain again.*

**IDM** **give/lose ground (to sb/sth)** ➪ **ground**[1] देखिए।
**keep/lose your cool** ➪ **cool**[3] देखिए।
**keep/lose count (of sth)** ➪ **count**[2] देखिए।
**keep/lose your temper** ➪ **temper** देखिए।
**keep/lose track of sb/sth** ➪ **track**[1] देखिए।
**lose your bearings** to become confused about where you are अपने बारे में भ्रम में पड़ जाना
**lose face** to lose the respect of other people दूसरों की नज़र में गिर जाना, दूसरों से मिलने वाले सम्मान से वंचित हो जाना
**lose your head** to become confused or very excited भ्रमित या बहुत उत्तेजित हो जाना
**lose heart** to stop believing that you will be successful in sth you are trying to do हिम्मत हार बैठना; किसी काम में सफलता के प्रति आत्मविश्वासी न रहना
**lose it** (*spoken*) to go crazy or suddenly become unable to control your emotions सनक सवार हो जाना या एकाएक भावनाओं पर नियंत्रण खो बैठना
**lose your life** to be killed मारा जाना, जान गँवाना
**lose sight of sb/sth** to no longer be able to see sb/sth किसी व्यक्ति या वस्तु का दीखना बंद हो जाना *We eventually lost sight of the animal in some trees.* ○ *(figurative) We mustn't lose sight of our original aim.*
**lose your touch** to lose a special skill or ability विशेष कुशलता या योग्यता से वंचित हो जाना
**lose touch (with sb/sth)** to no longer have contact (with sb/sth) (किसी व्यक्ति या वस्तु से) संपर्क टूट जाना *I've lost touch with a lot of my old school friends.*
**a losing battle** a competition, fight, etc. in which it seems that you will not be successful ऐसी स्पर्धा, संघर्ष आदि जिसमें विफलता अधिक संभावित है
**win/lose the toss** ➪ **toss** देखिए।
**PHR V** **lose out (on sth/to sb)** (*informal*) to be at a disadvantage हानि उठाने की स्थिति में होना *If a teacher pays too much attention to the bright students, the others lose out.*

**loser** /ˈluːzə(r) ˈलूज़(र्)/ *noun* [C] **1** a person who is defeated हार जाने वाला व्यक्ति, असफल व्यक्ति *He is a bad loser. He always gets angry if I beat him.* **2** a person who is never successful सदा असफल व्यक्ति **3** a person who suffers because of a particular situation, decision, etc. विशेष स्थिति, निर्णय आदि के कारण हानि उठाने वाला व्यक्ति; परिस्थिति का शिकार व्यक्ति

**loss** /lɒs लॉस्/ *noun* **1** [C, U] **(a) loss (of sth)** the state of no longer having sth or not having as much as before; the act of losing sth किसी वस्तु की हानि या क्षति; कुछ खो देने की क्रिया *loss of blood/sleep* ○ *The plane crashed causing great* ***loss of life.*** **2** [C] **a loss (of sth)** the amount of money which is lost by a business व्यापार में गँवाए धन की मात्रा *The firm made a loss of five million rupees.* ➪ **profit** देखिए। **3** [C] **a loss (to sb)** the disadvantage that is caused when sb/sth leaves or is taken away; the person or thing that causes this disadvantage किसी व्यक्ति या वस्तु के जाने से उत्पन्न अभाव की स्थिति; अभाव की स्थिति उत्पन्न करने वाला व्यक्ति या वस्तु *If she leaves, it/she will be a big loss to the school.*
**IDM** **at a loss** not knowing what to do or say पता न चले कि क्या किया या कहा जाए; किंकर्तव्यविमूढ़
**cut your losses** to stop wasting time or money on sth that is not successful असफल हो चुके प्रयास पर और अधिक पैसा या समय न गँवाना

**lost**[1] ➪ **lose** का past tense और past participle रूप

**lost**[2] /lɒst लॉस्ट्/ *adj.* **1** unable to find your way; not knowing where you are रास्ता खोज पाने में असमर्थ; दिशा-ज्ञान से रहित *This isn't the right road—we're completely lost!* ○ *If you* ***get lost****, stop and ask someone the way.* **2** that cannot be found or that no longer exists ग़ायब या नष्ट *The letter must have* ***got lost*** *in the post.* **3** unable to deal with a situation or to understand sth स्थिति से निपटने या उसे समझने में असमर्थ; चकराया हुआ *Sorry, I'm lost. Could you explain the last part again?* **4 lost on sb** not noticed or understood by sb न जिस पर ध्यान गया न जो समझ में आया, जो बेकार साबित हुआ *The humour of the situation was completely lost on Nisha.*
**IDM** **get lost** (*slang*) used to rudely tell sb to go away अशिष्ट रूप से किसी को चले जाने के लिए कहने के लिए प्रयुक्त
**a lost cause** a goal or an aim that cannot be achieved अप्राप्य या दुष्प्राप्य लक्ष्य या उद्देश्य
**lost for words** not knowing what to say कहने के लिए शब्द न होना

**lost property** *noun* [U] things that people have lost or left in a public place and that are kept in a special office for the owners to collect गुमशुदा सामान

**lot**[1] /lɒt लॉट्/ *noun* **1** [C] **a lot (of sth); lots (of sth)** a large amount or number of things or people ढेरों वस्तुएँ या लोग *There seem to be* ***quite a lot of*** *new shops opening.* ○ ***An awful lot of*** (= very many) *people will be disappointed if the match is cancelled.*

**NOTE** निषेधवाचक और प्रश्नवाचक वाक्यों में **much** और **many** अधिक प्रचलित हैं—*A lot of girls go to dancing classes, but not many boys.* ○ *'How much would a car like that cost?' 'A lot!'*

**2** [*sing., with sing. or pl. verb*] all of sth; the whole of a group of things or people सारा-का-सारा; किसी समूह की सारी वस्तुएँ या सारे लोग *When we opened the bag of potatoes **the whole lot** was/were bad.* ○ *You count those kids and I'll count **this lot**.* **3** [C] an object or group of objects that are being sold at a public sale (**an auction**) नीलामी का सामान (एक वस्तु या वस्तुओं का समूह) *Lot 27 is six chairs.* **4** [*sing.*] the quality or state of your life; your fate जीवन की गुणवत्ता या दशा; भाग्य, नियति *I'm quite happy with my lot in life.* **5** [C] (*AmE*) an area of land used for a particular purpose प्रयोजन-विशेष से संबंधित कोई भूखंड *a parking lot*

**IDM** **draw lots** ➪ **draw[1]** देखिए।

**lot[2]** /lɒt लॉट्/ *adv.* (*informal*) **1 a lot; lots** (*before adjectives and adverbs*) very much अत्यधिक *a lot bigger/better/faster* ○ *They see lots more of each other than before.* **2 a lot** very much or often अत्यधिक या बहुत बार ***Thanks a lot**—that's very kind.* ○ *It generally rains a lot at this time of year.*

**a lot of** /əˈlɒt əv अˈलॉट् अव़्/ (*informal* **lots of** /ˈlɒts əvˈलॉट्स् अव़्/) *det.* a large amount or number of (sb/sth) (किसी व्यक्ति या वस्तु की) बड़ी संख्या या मात्रा, ढेर-सा *There's been a lot of rain this year.* ○ *Lots of love, Bhanu* (= an informal ending for a letter).

**lotion** /ˈləʊʃn ˈलोश्न्/ *noun* [C, U] liquid that you use on your hair or skin बालों या त्वचा पर लगाया जाने वाला द्रव; लोशन *suntan lotion*

**lottery** /ˈlɒtəri ˈलॉटरि/ *noun* [C] (*pl.* **lotteries**) a way of making money for the government, for charity, etc. by selling tickets with numbers on them and giving prizes to the people who have bought certain numbers which are chosen by chance लॉटरी

**loud** /laʊd लाउड्/ *adj., adv.* **1** making a lot of noise; not quiet बहुत आवाज़ करता हुआ; कोलाहलपूर्ण *Can you turn the television down, it's too loud.* ○ *Could you speak a bit louder—the people at the back can't hear.* ✪ विलोम **quiet** या **soft**

**NOTE** **Loud** का प्रयोग शोर या शोर उत्पन्न करने वाली वस्तु के लिए होता है—*a loud noise/bang* ○ *loud music.* **Noisy** का प्रयोग शार मचाने वाले व्यक्ति या पशु के लिए और शोर-भरे स्थान, कार्यक्रम आदि के लिए होता है—*a noisy road/party/engine/child*

**2** (used about clothes or colours) too bright (कपड़े या रंग) बहुत चमकीला, शोख़ *a loud shirt* ▶ **loudly** *adv.* शोर मचाते हुए, ऊँचे स्वर में ▶ **loudness** *noun* [U] (स्वर की) प्रबलता, उच्चता

**IDM** **out loud** so that people can hear it इतने ऊँचे कि सुनने में आसानी हो *Shall I read this bit out loud to you?*

**loudspeaker** /ˌlaʊdˈspiːkə(r) ˌलाउड्ˈस्पीक(र्)/ *noun* [C] **1** (*also* **speaker**) the part of a radio, CD player, etc. which the sound comes out of रेडियो, सीडी प्लेयर आदि में लगा स्पीकर **2** a piece of electrical equipment for speaking, playing music, etc. to a lot of people ध्वनि-विस्तारक (यंत्र); लाउडस्पीकर

**lounge[1]** /laʊndʒ लाउन्ज्/ *noun* [C] **1** a comfortable room in a house or hotel where you can sit and relax घर या होटल में आराम करने का आरामदेह कमरा; लाउंज **2** the part of an airport where passengers wait हवाई अड्डे पर यात्रियों के लिए प्रतीक्षा-कक्ष; लाउंज *the departure lounge*

**lounge[2]** /laʊndʒ लाउन्ज्/ *verb* [I] **lounge (about/around)** to sit, stand or lie in a lazy way अलसाते हुए बैठना, खड़े होना या लेटना *People were lounging on the beach*

**louse** /laʊs लाउस्/ *noun* [C] (*pl.* **lice** /laɪs लाइस्/) a small insect that lives on the bodies of animals and people जूँ, चीलर

**lousy** /ˈlaʊzi ˈलाउज़ि/ *adj.* (*informal*) very bad बहुत बुरा *We had lousy weather on holiday.*

**lout** /laʊt लाउट्/ *noun* [C] a young man who behaves in a rude, rough or stupid way अशिष्ट या बेवकूफ़ युवक ➪ **hooligan** और **yob** देखिए।

**lovable** (*also* **loveable**) /ˈlʌvəbl ˈलव़ब्ल्/ *adj.* having a personality or appearance that is easy to love प्यारा लगने वाला, आकर्षक *a lovable little boy*

**love[1]** /lʌv लव़्/ *noun* **1** [U] a strong feeling that you have when you like sb/sth very much प्रेम, प्यार *a mother's love for her children* ○ *to **fall in love** with sb* ○ *a love song/story* **2** [U, *sing.*] a strong feeling of interest in or enjoyment of sth किसी काम में गहरी रुचि या किसी वस्तु से प्राप्त होने वाला आनंद *a love of adventure/nature/sport* **3** [C] a person, a thing or an activity that you like very much व्यक्ति, वस्तु या क्रिया जो बहुत पसंद हो *His great love was always music.* **4** [U] (used in tennis) a score of zero (टेनिस में) शून्य का स्कोर *The score is forty-love.*

**IDM** **give/send sb your love** to give/send sb a friendly message किसी व्यक्ति को मैत्रीपूर्ण या प्रेमपूर्ण संदेश देना *Give Mona my love when you next see her.*

**(lots of) love (from)** used at the end of a letter to a friend or a member of your family मित्र या परिवार के सदस्य को संबोधित पत्र के अंत में लिखे जाने वाले शब्द; को ढेरों प्यार *See you soon. Love, Rajan*

**love²** /lʌv लव् / *verb* [T] **1** to like sb/sth in the strongest possible way किसी से प्रेम या प्यार करना *She loves her children.* **2** to like or enjoy sth very much किसी वस्तु या काम का बहुत अच्छा लगना *I love the summer!* ○ *I really love swimming in the sea.* ○ **3 would love sth/to do sth** used to say that you would very much like sth/to do sth यह कहने के लिए प्रयुक्त कि कोई बात आपको बहुत अच्छी लगती है *'Would you like to come?' 'I'd love to'.* ○ *'What about a drink?' 'I'd love one.'* ○ *We'd love you to come and stay with us.*

**love affair** *noun* [C] **1** a sexual relationship between two people who love each other but are not married अविवाहित स्त्री-पुरुष में प्रेम-संबंध (कामुकतापूर्ण) *She had a love affair with her tennis coach.* **2** a great enthusiasm for sth किसी वस्तु के प्रति-अति उत्साह *His love affair with bikes started when he was still a teenager.*

**lovely** /ˈlʌvli ˈलव्लि / *adj.* **(lovelier; loveliest) 1** beautiful or attractive सुंदर या आकर्षक *a lovely room/voice/expression* ○ *You look lovely with your hair short.* **2** enjoyable or pleasant; very nice आनंदप्रद या रुचिकर; बहुत बढ़िया *We had a lovely holiday.* ► **loveliness** *noun* [U] मनोहरता, रमणीयता

IDM **lovely and warm, peaceful, fresh, etc.** used for emphasizing how good sth is because of the quality mentioned ऊँची गुणवत्ता के कारण किसी वस्तु के पसंद आने की बात पर बल देने के लिए प्रयुक्त *These blankets are lovely and soft.*

**lover** /ˈlʌvə(r) ˈलव़(र्) / *noun* [C] **1** a partner in a sexual relationship with sb who he/she is not married to प्रेमी *The park was full of young lovers holding hands.* **2** a person who likes or enjoys the thing mentioned निर्दिष्ट वस्तु को पसंद करने या उससे आनंदित होने वाला व्यक्ति; प्रेमी *a music lover* ○ *an animal lover*

**loving** /ˈlʌvɪŋ ˈलव़िङ् / *adj.* **1** feeling or showing love or care स्नेहशील, प्यार-भरा *She's very loving towards her brother.* **2 -loving** (*used to form compound adjectives*) loving the thing or activity mentioned निर्दिष्ट वस्तु या क्रिया को बहुत पसंद करने वाला *a fun-loving girl* ► **lovingly** *adv.* प्रेमपूर्वक

**low¹** /ləʊ लो / *adj., adv.* **1** close to the ground or to the bottom of sth ज़मीन या किसी वस्तु के निम्नतम स्तर के निकट; नीचे *Hang that picture a bit higher, it's much too low!* ○ *That plane is flying very low.* **2** below the usual or normal level or amount सामान्य स्तर या मात्रा से कम *Temperatures were very low last winter.* ○ *low wages* ○ *low-fat yoghurt* **3** below what is normal or acceptable in quality, importance or development गुणवत्ता, महत्त्व या विन्यास के सामान्य या स्वीकार्य स्तर से नीचे; निम्न *a low standard of living* ○ *low status* **4** (used about a sound or voice) deep or quiet (आवाज़ या स्वर) गहरा या शांत, नीचा *His voice is already lower than his father's.* ○ *A group of people in the library were speaking in low voices.* **5** not happy and lacking energy उदास और सुस्त *He's been **feeling** a bit **low** since his illness.* **6** (used about a light, an oven, etc.) made to produce only a little light or heat बत्ती, अँगीठी आदि) धीमा, हलका, मंद *Cook the rice on a low heat for 20 minutes.* ○ *The low lighting adds to the restaurant's atmosphere.* **7** (used about a gear in a car) that allows a slower speed (कार का गियर) जिससे गति धीमी हो जाती है, निचला ✪ विलोम **high** (सब अर्थों का)

IDM **high and low** ⇨ **high²** देखिए।

**lie low** ⇨ **lie²** देखिए।

**run low (on sth)** to start to have less of sth than you need; to be less than is needed कोई वस्तु ज़रूरत से कम मिलने लगना; कोई वस्तु ज़रूरत से कम होने लगना *We're running low on coffee—shall I go and buy some?*

**low²** /ləʊ लो/ *noun* [C] a low point, level, figure, etc. निम्न बिंदु, स्तर, संख्या आदि *Unemployment has fallen to a new low.* ✪ विलोम **high**

**low-down** *noun* [*sing.*] (*informal*)

IDM **give sb/get the low-down (on sb/sth)** to tell sb/be told the true facts or secret information (about sb/sth) किसी को किसी के विषय में तथ्य बताना या गुप्त जानकारी देना

**lower¹** /ˈləʊə(r) ˈलोअ(र्) / *adj.* (*only before a noun*) below sth or at the bottom of sth निचला *She bit her lower lip.* ○ *the lower deck of a ship* ✪ विलोम **upper**

**lower²** /ˈləʊə(r) ˈलोअ(र्) / *verb* [T] **1** to make or let sb/sth go down नीचे उतारना या करना *They lowered the boat into the water.* ○ *to lower your head/eyes* **2** to make sth less in amount, quality, etc. किसी वस्तु की मात्रा, गुणवत्ता आदि को कम करना *The virus lowers resistance to other diseases.* ○ *Could you **lower** your **voice** slightly? I'm trying to sleep.* ✪ विलोम **raise**

**lower case** *noun* [U] letters that are written or printed in their small form; not in capital letters (मुद्रण या लेखन में) अक्षरों का छोटा रूप, छोटे अक्षर; बड़े अक्षरों में नहीं *The text is all in lower case.* ○ *lower-case letters* ✪ विलोम **upper case**

**lowest common denominator** *noun* [C] (*abbr.* **LCD**) (*mathematics*) the smallest number that the bottom numbers of a group of **fractions** can be divided into exactly लघुतम समापवर्त्य

**low-key** *adj.* quiet and not wanting to attract a lot of attention शांत और धूम-धड़ाका-रहित *The wedding will be very low-key. We're only inviting ten people.*

**lowland** /ˈləʊlənd ˈलोलन्ड्/ *noun* [C, *usually pl.*] a flat area of land at about sea level नीची ज़मीन, लगभग समुद्र के स्तर की ज़मीन *the lowlands near the coast* ○ *lowland areas*

**low-level** *adj.* (*computing*) (used about a computer language) not like an existing language, but using a system of numbers that a computer can understand and act on; similar to **machine code** (कंप्यूटर भाषा) सामान्य भाषा से भिन्न अंकों की पद्धति जिसे कंप्यूटर समझता है, कंप्यूटर-ग्राह्य अंक पद्धति की भाषा; मशीन कोड के सदृश ✪ विलोम **high-level**

**low-lying** *adj.* (used about land) near to sea level; not high (भूमि) समुद्रतल के निकट; निचली

**low-pitched** *adj.* (used about sounds) deep; low (ध्वनि) गहरी; निम्न, नीची *a low-pitched voice* ✪ विलोम **high-pitched**

**low season** *noun* [C] (*BrE*) the time of year when a hotel or tourist area receives fewest visitors वह अवधि जिसमें होटलों या पर्यटन केंद्रों में पर्यटकों की संख्या बहुत कम हो जाती है; अल्पपर्यटक काल ➪ **high season** देखिए।

**low tide** *noun* [U] the time when the sea is at its lowest level (समुद्र में) भाटा *At low tide you can walk out to the island.* ✪ विलोम **high tide**

**loyal** /ˈlɔɪəl ˈलॉइअल्/ *adj.* (used about a person) not changing in your friendship or beliefs (व्यक्ति) निष्ठावान *a loyal friend/supporter* ✪ पर्याय **faithful** ✪ विलोम **disloyal** ▶ **loyally** *adv.* निष्ठापूर्वक ▶ **loyalty** /ˈlɔɪəlti ˈलॉइअल्टि/ *noun* [C, U] (*pl.* **loyalties**) निष्ठा

**lozenge** /ˈlɒzɪndʒ ˈलॉज़िन्ज्/ *noun* [C] **1** (*mathematics*) a figure with four sides in the shape of a diamond that has two opposite angles more than $90^0$ and the other two less than $90^0$ ऐसा चतुर्भुज जिसके दो आमने-सामने के कोण $90^0$ से अधिक हों और अन्य दो कोण $90^0$ से कम हों; पतंगाकार ➪ **shape** पर चित्र देखिए। **2** a sweet that you suck if you have a cough or a sore throat खाँसी या गले में सूजन के लिए ली जाने वाली चूसने की मीठी टिकिया

**LPG** /ˌel piː ˈdʒiː ˌएॅल पी ˈजी/ *abbr.* Liquefied Petroleum Gas, commonly known as cooking gas लिक्विफाइड पेट्रोलियम गैस, सामान्यतः कुकिंग गैस के नाम से प्रसिद्ध, खाना बनाने का गैस

**L-plate** *noun* [C] a sign with a large red letter L (for 'learner') on it, that you fix to a car to show that the driver is learning to drive लाल रंग का अक्षर 'L' (लर्नर) का संकेत जो ड्राइविंग सीखने वाले कार पर लगाते हैं

**Lt** *abbr.* (*written*) Lieutenant लेफ्टिनेंट

**Ltd** *abbr.* (*BrE*) (used about private companies) Limited (ग़ैर-सरकारी कंपनियों के लिए प्रयुक्त) लिमिटेड *Pierce and Co. Ltd*

**lubricant** /ˈluːbrɪkənt ˈलूब्रिकन्ट्/ *noun* [C, U] a substance, for example oil, that makes the parts of a machine work easily and smoothly तेल जैसा चिकना पदार्थ जिसको लगाने से मशीन के पुरज़े आसानी से बिना रुकावट काम करते हैं; ल्युब्रिकैंट, चिकनाई

**lubricate** /ˈluːbrɪkeɪt ˈलूब्रिकेट्/ *verb* [T] to put oil, etc. onto or into sth so that it works smoothly किसी मशीन आदि में चिकनाई या ल्युब्रिकैंट डालना ▶ **lubrication** /ˌluːbrɪˈkeɪʃn ˌलूब्रिˈकेश्न्/ *noun* [U] तेल या चिकनाई डालने की क्रिया

**lucid** /ˈluːsɪd ˈलूसिड्/ *adj.* (*formal*) **1** (used about sth that is said or written) clear and easy to understand (भाषण या लेखन) समझने में स्पष्ट और सरल, सुबोध *a lucid style/description* **2** (used about a person's mind) not confused; clear and normal (व्यक्ति की सोच) सुलझी हुई; स्पष्ट और सुबोध ▶ **lucidly** *adv.* स्पष्टता और सुबोधता से ▶ **lucidity** /luːˈsɪdəti लूˈसिडटि/ *noun* [U] स्पष्टता और सुबोधता

**luck** /lʌk लक्/ *noun* [U] **1** success or good things that happen by chance सौभाग्य; संयोग से प्राप्त सफलता या सुखद वस्तुएँ *We'd like to **wish** you lots of **luck** in your new career.* ○ ***With** a bit of **luck**, we'll finish this job today.* **2** chance; the force that people believe makes things happen (विश्वास के अनुसार) घटनाओं को प्रेरित करने वाली शक्ति; संयोग, भाग्य *There's no skill in this game—it's all luck.* ○ *to have good/bad luck*

IDM **bad luck!; hard luck!** used to show pity for sb किसी व्यक्ति पर तरस खाने के लिए प्रयुक्त *'Bad luck. Maybe you'll win next time.'*

**be in/out of luck** to be lucky/to not be lucky भाग्यशाली होना या न होना *I was in luck—they had only one ticket left!*

**good luck (to sb)** used to wish that sb is successful किसी को सफल होने की शुभकामनाएँ देने के लिए प्रयुक्त *Good luck! I'm sure you'll get the job.* **worse luck** ⇨ **worse** देखिए।

**lucky** /ˈlʌki ˈलकि / *adj.* **(luckier; luckiest) 1** (used about a person) having good luck (व्यक्ति) भाग्यशाली *He's lucky to be alive after an accident like that.* ○ *With so much unemployment, I* ***count myself lucky*** *that I've got a job.* **2** (used about a situation, event, etc.) having a good result (स्थिति, घटना आदि) जिसमें परिणाम अनुकूल हो *It's lucky I got here before the rain started.* ○ *a lucky escape* **3** (used about a thing) bringing success or good luck (वस्तु) सौभाग्यप्रद *a lucky number* ○ *It was not my lucky day.* ✪ विलोम **unlucky** ▶ **luckily** *adv.* सौभाग्य से *Luckily, I remembered to bring some money.*

IDM **you'll be lucky** used to tell sb that sth that he/she is expecting will probably not happen किसी को यह बताने के लिए प्रयुक्त कि उसकी मनचाही शायद न हो *You're looking for a good English restaurant? You'll be lucky!*

**lucrative** /ˈluːkrətɪv ˈलूक्रटिव् / *adj.* (*formal*) allowing sb to earn a lot of money जिसमें अच्छा पैसा हो; लाभप्रद *a lucrative contract/business*

**ludicrous** /ˈluːdɪkrəs ˈलूडिक्रस् / *adj.* very silly; ridiculous बहुत बेतुका; हास्यास्पद *What a ludicrous idea!* ▶ **ludicrously** *adv.* हास्यास्पद रूप से

**lug** /lʌg लग् / *verb* [T] **(lugging; lugged)** (*informal*) to carry or pull sth very heavy with great difficulty किसी भारी वस्तु को दम लगाकर ढोना या खींचना

**luggage** /ˈlʌgɪdʒ ˈलगिज् / *noun* [U] bags, suitcases, etc. used for carrying a person's clothes and things on a journey कपड़े एवं यात्रा का समान ले जाने के लिए (थैले, सूटकेस आदि) *'How much luggage are you taking with you?' 'Only one suitcase.'* ○ *You're only allowed one piece of* ***hand luggage*** (= a bag that you carry with you on the plane). ✪ पर्याय **baggage**

**luggage rack** *noun* [C] a shelf above the seats in a train or bus for putting your bags, etc. on रेलगाड़ी में सीटों के ऊपर सामान रखने की जगह

**lukewarm** /ˌluːkˈwɔːm ˌलूक् ˈवॉम् / *adj.* **1** (used about liquids) only slightly warm (द्रव) हलका गरम गुनगुना **2 lukewarm (about sb/sth)** not showing much interest; not keen मंद उत्साह वाला; उदासीन

**lull¹** /lʌl लल् / *noun* [C, *usually sing.*] **a lull (in sth)** a short period of quiet between times of activity गतिविधि के विभिन्न चरणों में संक्षिप्त विराम की स्थिति; शांति, मंदी

**lull²** /lʌl लल् / *verb* [T] **1** to make sb relaxed and calm किसी को शांत करना *She sang a song to* ***lull*** *the children* ***to sleep.*** **2 lull sb into sth** to make sb feel safe, and not expecting anything bad to happen किसी को सुरक्षित महसूस कराना (कि कुछ बुरा नहीं होगा) *Our first success* ***lulled us into a false sense of security.***

**lullaby** /ˈlʌləbaɪ ˈललबाइ / *noun* [C] (*pl.* **lullabies**) a gentle song that you sing to help a child to go to sleep (बच्चों के लिए) लोरी

**lumber¹** /ˈlʌmbə(r) ˈलम्ब(र्) / (*AmE*) = **timber 1**

**lumber²** /ˈlʌmbə(r) ˈलम्ब(र्) / *verb* **1** [I] to move in a slow, heavy way मंदगति से, भारी क़दमों से चलना *A family of elephants lumbered past.* **2** [T] (*informal*) **lumber sb (with sb/sth)** (*usually passive*) to give sb a responsibility or job that he/she does not want किसी को उसका अनचाहा दायित्व या काम सौंपना

**luminous** /ˈluːmɪnəs ˈलूमिनस् / *adj.* that shines in the dark अँधेरे में चमकने वाला *a luminous watch*

**lump¹** /lʌmp लम्प् / *noun* [C] **1** a piece of sth solid of any size or shape ढेला, डला, पिंड *a lump of coal/cheese/wood* ○ *The sauce was full of lumps.* **2** a swelling under the skin सूजन, गुमड़ा या गूमड़ *You'll have a bit of a lump on your head where you banged it.*

IDM **have/feel a lump in your throat** to feel pressure in your throat because you are about to cry रो उठने की प्रक्रिया में गले में दबाव महसूस करना

**lump²** /lʌmp लम्प् / *verb* [T] **lump A and B together; lump A (in) with B** to put or consider different people or things together in the same group अलग-अलग व्यक्तियों या वस्तुओं को एक ही वर्ग में रख देना या मान लेना

IDM **lump it** (*informal*) to accept sth unpleasant because you have no choice विकल्प के अभाव में अप्रिय को स्वीकार करना; 'मन मार कर ले लेना' *That's the deal—like it or lump it.*

**lump sum** *noun* [C] an amount of money paid all at once rather than in several smaller amounts एकमुश्त राशि

**lumpy** /ˈlʌmpi ˈलमपि / *adj.* full of or covered with lumps थुलथुल, मोटा, ढेलों से युक्त *This bed is very lumpy.* ✪ विलोम **smooth**

**lunacy** /ˈluːnəsi ˈलूनसि / *noun* [U] very stupid behaviour पागलपन *It was lunacy to drive so fast in that terrible weather.* ✪ पर्याय **madness**

**lunar** /ˈluːnə(r) ˈलून(र्) / *adj.* (*usually before a noun*) connected with the moon चंद्रमा-संबंधी *a lunar spacecraft/eclipse/landscape*

**lunatic**[1] /ˈluːnətɪk ˈलूनटिक्/ *noun* [C] (*informal*) a person who behaves in a stupid way doing crazy and often dangerous things पागलपन का आचरण करने वाला व्यक्ति ✪ पर्याय **madman**

**lunatic**[2] /ˈluːnətɪk ˈलूनटिक्/ *adj.* stupid; crazy बेवकूफ़; झक्की *a lunatic idea*

**lunch** /lʌntʃ लन्च्/ *noun* [C, U] a meal that you have in the middle of the day मध्याह्न कालीन भोजन; लंच *Hot and cold lunches are served between 12 and 2.* ○ *What would you like for lunch?* ▶ **lunch** *verb* [I] (*formal*) मध्याह्न कालीन भोजन करना या खाना

**luncheon** /ˈlʌntʃən ˈलन्चन्/ *noun* [C, U] (*formal*) lunch लंच

**lunch hour** *noun* [C, *usually sing.*] the time around the middle of the day when you stop work or school to have lunch लंच का अवकाश (दोपहर को) *I went to the shops in my lunch hour.*

**lunchtime** /ˈlʌntʃtaɪm ˈलन्चटाइम्/ *noun* [C,U] the time around the middle of the day when lunch is eaten लंच या भोजन (करने) का समय (दोपहर में) *I'll meet you at lunchtime.*

**lung** /lʌŋ लङ्/ *noun* [C] one of the two organs of your body that are inside your chest and are used for breathing फेफड़ा ➪ **body** पर चित्र देखिए।

**lunge** /lʌndʒ लन्ज्/ *noun* [C, *usually sing.*] **a lunge (at sb); a lunge (for sb/sth)** a sudden powerful forward movement of the body, especially when trying to attack sb/sth झपट्टा *She made a lunge for the ball.* ▶ **lunge** *verb* [I] झपटना *He lunged towards me with a knife.*

**lungi** *noun* [C] (*IndE*) a kind of cloth white or coloured, usually wrapped around the waist the two ends of which are knotted together. It is worn in various ways in different parts of India, Bangladesh and Myanmar एक प्रकार की सफ़ेद या रंगीन धोती, भारत, बांग्लादेश तथा म्यांमार के विभिन्न क्षेत्रों का पहनावा; लुंगी ➪ **dhoti** देखिए।

**lurch** /lɜːtʃ लच्/ *noun* [C, *usually sing.*] a sudden movement forward or to one side एकाएक आगे की ओर या एक तरफ़ लुढ़कने की क्रिया ▶ **lurch** *verb* [I] लुढ़कना

IDM **leave sb in the lurch** ➪ **leave**[1] देखिए।

**lure**[1] /lʊə(r) लुअ(र्)/ *verb* [T] to persuade or trick sb to go somewhere or do sth, usually by offering him/her sth nice प्रलोभन देकर किसी को धोखे से कहीं ले जाना या कुछ करवाना *Young people are lured to the city by the prospect of a job and money.*

**lure**[2] /lʊə(r) लुअ(र्)/ *noun* [C] the attractive qualities of sth प्रलोभन, आकर्षण *the lure of money/fame/adventure*

**lurid** /ˈlʊərɪd; ˈljʊə- ˈलुअरिड्; ˈल्युअ-/ *adj.* **1** having colours that are too bright, in a way that is not attractive भड़कीला (परंतु आकर्षक या मनोहर नहीं) *a lurid purple and orange dress* **2** (used about a story or a piece of writing) deliberately shocking, especially because of violent or unpleasant detail (कोई कहानी या रचना) सनसनीख़ेज़ (विशेषतः हिंसात्मक और अप्रिय विवरण के कारण) ▶ **luridly** *adv.* भड़कीले रूप में

**lurk** /lɜːk लक्/ *verb* [I] to wait somewhere secretly especially in order to do sth bad or illegal कहीं छिपकर बैठना, विशेषतः किसी पर हमला करने के लिए *I thought I saw somebody lurking among the trees.*

**luscious** /ˈlʌʃəs ˈलशस्/ *adj.* (used about food) tasting very good (खाद्य पदार्थ) अत्यंत स्वादु *luscious fruit*

**lush** /lʌʃ लश्/ *adj.* (used about plants or gardens) growing very thickly and well (पौधे या बग़ीचे) घने और हरे-भरे

**lust**[1] /lʌst लस्ट्/ *noun* **1** [U] **lust (for sb)** strong sexual desire प्रबल कामवासना **2** [C, U] **(a) lust (for sth)** (a) very strong desire to have or get sth किसी वस्तु को पास रखने या पाने की प्रबल इच्छा *a lust for power* ○ *(a) lust for life* (= enjoyment of life)

**lust**[2] /lʌst लस्ट्/ *verb* [I] **lust (after sb); lust (after/for sth)** to feel a very strong desire for sb/sth किसी व्यक्ति या वस्तु के लिए अत्यधिक इच्छुक होना; लालायित होना *to lust for power/success/fame*

**lustful** /ˈlʌstfl ˈलस्ट्फ़्ल्/ *adj.* full of sexual desire कामुकतापूर्ण, कामुक *lustful thoughts* ▶ **lustfully** /-fəli -फ़लि/ *adv.* कामुकतापूर्वक

**luxurious** /lʌgˈʒʊəriəs लग्ˈशुअरिअस्/ *adj.* very comfortable; full of expensive and beautiful things बहुत आरामदेह; मँहगी और सुंदर विलास की वस्तुओं से भरा हुआ, विलासितापूर्ण *a luxurious hotel* ▶ **luxuriously** *adv.* विलासितापूर्वक

**luxury** /ˈlʌkʃəri ˈलक्शरि/ *noun* (*pl.* **luxuries**) **1** [U] the enjoyment of expensive and beautiful things; a very comfortable and enjoyable situation विलास की वस्तुओं का आनंद; बहुत आरामदेह और आंनदप्रद स्थिति; विलासिता *to lead **a life of luxury*** ○ *a luxury hotel/car/yacht* **2** [C] something that is enjoyable and expensive that you do not really need विलास की वस्तु (जो आवश्यक नहीं) *luxury goods, such as wine and chocolates* **3** [U, *sing.*] a pleasure which you do not often have दुर्लभ आनंद *It was (an) absolute luxury to do nothing all weekend.*

**LW** *abbr.* = **long wave** ➪ **wavelength** पर चित्र देखिए।

**lychee** *noun* [C] a small fruit with thick rough red skin, that is white inside and has a large stone लीची का फल

**lymph** /lɪmf लिम्फ़्/ *noun* [U] a colourless liquid containing white blood cells that cleans the inside of your body and helps to prevent infections from spreading मानव शरीर में श्वेत रक्त कोशिकाओं वाला रंगहीन द्रव जो संक्रमण को फैलने नहीं देता; लसीका ▶ **lymphatic** /lɪmˈfætɪk लिम्ˈफ़ैटिक्/ *adj.* (*only before a noun*) लसीका-संबंधी *the lymphatic system*

**lymph node** (*also* **lymph gland**) *noun* [C] a small hard mass in your body through which **lymph** passes शरीर में गाँठ जिसमें से होकर लसीका जाता है

**lymphocyte** /ˈlɪmfəsaɪt ˈलिम्फ़साइट्/ *noun* [C] (*technical*) a type of **leucocyte** एक प्रकार की छोटी श्वेत रक्तकोशिका; लसीका कोशिका, लसीकाणु

**lynch** /lɪntʃ लिन्च्/ *verb* [T] (used about a crowd of people) to kill sb who is thought to be guilty of a crime, usually by hanging him/her, without a legal trial in a court of law (लोगों की भीड़ द्वारा) किसी तथाकथित अपराधी को (प्रायः फाँसी पर लटकाकर) ग़ैर-क़ानूनी तरीक़े से मार दिया जाना

**lyric** /ˈlɪrɪk ˈलिरिक्/ *adj.* (used about poetry) expressing personal feelings and thoughts (कविता) निजी मनोभावों और विचारों की व्यंजक; आत्माभिव्यंजक

**lyrical** /ˈlɪrɪkl ˈलिरिक्ल्/ *adj.* like a song or a poem, expressing strong personal feelings आत्माभिव्यंजक गीत या कविता के समान; प्रगीत

**lyrics** /ˈlɪrɪks ˈलिरिक्स्/ *noun* [*pl.*] the words of a song गीत के शब्द

# M m

**M, m**[1] /em एम्/ *noun* [C, U] (*pl.* **M's; m's** /emz एम्ज़्/) the thirteenth letter of the English alphabet अंग्रेज़ी वर्णमाला का तेरहवाँ अक्षर *'Mitali' begins with an 'M'.*

**M**[2] *abbr.* **1** (*also* **med**) medium (size) मध्यम (आकार) **2 M** (*BrE*) used with a number to show the name of a **motorway** मोटरमार्ग का नाम दर्शाने के लिए संख्या के साथ प्रयुक्त *heavy traffic on the M25* **3 m** metre(s) मीटर्स, मीटर(ों) *a 500 m race* **4 m** million(s) मिलियन्स, लाख(ों) *population 10 m*

**MA** /ˌem ˈeɪ ˌएम् ˈए/ *abbr.* Master of Arts; a second degree that you receive when you complete a more advanced course or piece of research in an arts subject at university or college एम. ए., मास्टर आफ़ आर्ट्स; विश्वविद्यालय या कॉलेज की स्नातकोत्तर उपाधि ➪ **BA** और **MSc** देखिए।

**ma 'am** /mæm; mɑːm मैम्; माम्/ *noun* [*sing.*] (*AmE*) used as a polite way of addressing a woman महिलाओं के लिए सम्मानजनक संबोधन; मैम ➪ **sir** देखिए।

**mac** /mæk मैक्/ (*also* **mackintosh**) /ˈmækɪntɒʃ ˈमैकिन्टॉश्/) *noun* [C] (*BrE*) a coat that is made to keep out the rain वर्षा से बचने का कोट, (रबड़ की) बरसाती

**macabre** /məˈkɑːbrə मˈकाब्र/ *adj.* unpleasant and frightening because it is connected with death (मृत्यु से संबंधित होने के कारण) अप्रिय और डरावना *a macabre tale/joke/ritual*

**macaroni** /ˌmækəˈrəʊni ˌमैकˈरोनि/ *noun* [U] a type of dried Italian food made from flour and water (**pasta**) in the shape of short tubes छोटी नलियों के आकार में (पास्ता से बना) एक प्रकार का इटैलियन खाद्य पदार्थ; मैकरोनी

**mace** /meɪs मेस्/ *noun* **1** [C] a special stick, carried as a sign of authority by an official such as a **mayor** सत्ता का प्रतीक विशेष दंड; राजदंड **2** [C] a large heavy stick that has a head with metal points on it, used in the past as a weapon गदा नामक प्राचीन अस्त्र (एक बड़ा और भारी दंड जिसके सिर पर धातुनिर्मित उभरे बिंदु होते हैं) **3** [U] the dried outer covering of **nutmegs** used in cooking as a spice जावित्री (मसाला)

**Mach** /mɑːk; mæk माक्; मैक्/ *noun* [U] (often followed by a number) a measurement of speed, used especially for aircraft. Mach 1 is the speed of sound (प्रायः किसी संख्या से अनुगामित) गति की एक माप (विशेषतः विमान के लिए) माक, (माक 1 ध्वनि की गति है)

**machete** /məˈʃeti मˈशेटि/ *noun* [C] a broad heavy knife used as a cutting tool and as a weapon चौड़ा भारी चाक़ू (जो काटने का औज़ार है और हथियार भी), छुरा; खंजर

**machine** /məˈʃiːn मˈशीन्/ *noun* [C] (*often in compounds*) a piece of equipment with moving parts that is designed to do a particular job. A machine usually needs electricity, gas, steam, etc. in order to work मशीन, यंत्र *a washing/sewing/knitting machine* ○ *a machine for making pasta* ➪ **tool** पर नोट देखिए।

**machine code** *noun* [U] (*computing*) a language used for computer programs in which instructions are written in the form of numbers so that a computer can understand and act on them कंप्यूटर प्रोग्राम के लिए प्रयुक्त (विशेष) भाषा जिसमें निर्देशों को संख्याओं के रूप में लिखा जाता है ताकि कंप्यूटर उसे समझकर तदनुसार कार्य कर सके, अंक-भाषा; मशीन कोड

**machine-gun** *noun* [C] a gun that fires bullets very quickly and continuously मशीन-गन (ऐसी बंदूक़ जो तेज़ गति से लगातार गोलियाँ दाग़ती है)

**machine-readable** *adj.* (*computing*) (of data) in a form that a computer can understand (डाटा) ऐसे रूप में जिसे कंप्यूटर समझ सके; कंप्यूटर-ग्राह्य

**machinery** /məˈʃiːnəri मˈशीनरि/ *noun* [U] machines in general, especially large ones; the moving parts of a machine सभी प्रकार की मशीनें (विशेषतः बड़ी मशीनें), मशीनरी; किसी मशीन के गतिमान पुरज़े, यंत्र समूह *farm/agricultural/industrial machinery*

**machine tool** *noun* [C] a tool for cutting or shaping metal, wood, etc., driven by a machine धातु, लकड़ी आदि को काटने या गढ़ने का मशीन-चालित औज़ार; मशीन टूल

**machinist** /məˈʃiːnɪst मˈशीनिस्ट्/ *noun* [C] **1** a person whose job is operating a machine, especially machines used in industry for cutting and shaping things, or a sewing machine मशीन को परिचालित करने वाला व्यक्ति (विशेषतः वस्तुओं को काटने और गढ़ने वाली औद्योगिक मशीनें या सिलाई-मशीन); मशीन-परिचालक **2** a person whose job is to make or repair machines मशीनें बनाने और सुधारने वाले व्यक्ति; यंत्रकार

**macho** /ˈmætʃəʊ ˈमैचो/ *adj.* (*informal*) (used about a man or his behaviour) having typically male qualities like strength and courage, but using them in an aggressive way (व्यक्ति या उसका आचरण) शक्ति और साहस जैसे पुरुषोचित गुणों वाला (परंतु उनके प्रयोग में आक्रामक) *He's too macho to ever admit he was wrong and apologize.*

**mackerel** /ˈmækrəl ˈमैक्रल्/ *noun* [C, U] (*pl.* **mackerel**) a sea fish with greenish-blue bands on its body that you can eat कुछ-कुछ हरी-नीली पट्टियों वाली खाने की समुद्री मछली; बाँगड़ा मछली

**mackintosh** = **mac**

**macro** /ˈmækrəʊ ˈमैक्रो/ *noun* [C] (*pl.* **macros**) (*computing*) a single instruction that a computer automatically reads as a set of instructions necessary to do a particular task कंप्यूटर के लिए अकेला (बृहत) निर्देश जिसे वह स्वचालित रूप से निर्देश समुच्चय के रूप में ग्रहण करता है ताकि विशिष्ट कार्य को निष्पादित किया जा सके; मैक्रो

**macro-** /ˈmækrəʊ ˈमैक्रो/ (*used in nouns, adjectives and adverbs*) large; on a large scale बृहत; बृहत-स्तरीय *macroeconomics* ✪ विलोम **micro-**

**macrobiotic** /ˌmækrəʊbaɪˈɒtɪk ˌमैक्रोबाइˈऑटिक्/ *adj.* (used about food) that is grown without using chemicals and is thought to make us live longer (खाद्य पदार्थ) रसायन-प्रयोग रहित और इसलिए आयुवर्धक माना जाने वाला; दीर्घजीवी

**macrocosm** /ˈmækrəʊkɒzəm ˈमैक्रोकॉज़म्/ *noun* [C] (*technical*) any large complete structure that contains smaller structures, for example the universe कोई भी बड़ा पूरा ढाँचा जिसमें छोटे ढाँचे अंतर्निहित हों (जैसे ब्रह्मांड) ➪ **microcosm** देखिए।

**mad** /mæd मैड्/ *adj.* **1** having a mind that does not work normally; mentally ill पागल, विक्षिप्त; मानसिक रोगी

> **NOTE** मानसिक रूप से विक्षिप्त व्यक्ति के लिए आजकल **mad** या **insane** का प्रयोग नहीं होता है। आधुनिक प्रयोग **mentally ill** है।

**2** (*BrE*) not at all sensible; crazy बिलकुल बेसमझ निपट मूर्ख; सनकी *You must be mad to drive in this weather.* **3** (*not before a noun*) **mad (at/with sb) (about sth)** very angry अत्यंत क्रुद्ध *His laziness **drives me mad!*** ○ (*AmE*) *Don't **get/go mad** at him. He didn't mean to do it.* **4** (*informal*) **mad about/on sb/sth** liking sb/sth very much जिसे कोई व्यक्ति या वस्तु अत्यधिक पसंद हो, के पीछे पागल *He's mad on computer games at the moment.* **5** not controlled; wild or very excited बेक़ाबू; उच्छृंखल या बहुत उत्तेजित *When Abhishek Bachchan appeared on the hotel balcony his fans **went mad.***

**madam** /ˈmædəm ˈमैडम्/ *noun* [*sing.*] **1** (*formal*) used as a polite way of speaking to a woman, especially to a customer in a shop or restaurant महिलाओं के लिए आदरपूर्ण संबोधन (विशेषतः दुकान या रेस्तराँ में महिला ग्राहक के लिए) *Can I help you, madam?* ➪ **sir** देखिए। **2 Madam** used for beginning a formal letter to a woman when you do not know her name नाम से अपरिचित महिला को लिखे औपचारिक पत्र में संबोधन *Dear Madam, I am writing in reply to the advertisement.*

**madame** /məˈdɑːm मˈड़ाम्/ *noun* (*pl.* **Mesdames** /meɪˈdæːm मेˈड़ैम्/) a title used especially to address or refer to a French or a French-speaking woman, usually a married one फ्राँसीसी मूल या फ्राँसीसी भाषी महिला (प्रायः विवाहित) के लिए प्रयुक्त संबोधन

**mad cow disease** = **BSE**

**maddening** /ˈmædnɪŋ ˈमैड्निङ्/ *adj.* that makes you very angry or annoyed जो किसी को अत्यधिक क्रुद्ध या नाराज़ कर दे, किसी को पागल बना देने वाला *She has some really maddening habits.* ▶ **maddeningly** *adv.* पागल बना देने वाले ढंग से

**made** ➪ **make**[1] का past tense और past participle रूप

**IDM made to measure** ➪ **measure**[2] देखिए।

**madly** /ˈmædli ˈमैड्लि/ *adv.* **1** in a wild or crazy way अंधाधुंध, बेतहाशा, उद्धत या सनकी *They were rushing about madly.* **2** (*informal*) very; extremely बहुत; अत्यधिक *They're madly in love.*

**madman** /ˈmædmən ˈमैड्मन्/ *noun* [C] (*pl.* **madmen** /-mən -मन्/) a person who behaves in a wild or crazy way पागल व्यक्ति, विक्षिप्त व्यक्ति ✪ पर्याय **lunatic**

**madness** /ˈmædnəs ˈमैड्नस्/ *noun* [U] crazy or stupid behaviour that could be dangerous पागलपन, सनकभरा या मूर्खतापूर्ण आचरण जो ख़तरनाक हो सकता है *It would be madness to take a boat out in such rough weather.*

**maestro** /ˈmaɪstrəʊ ˈमाइस्ट्रो/ *noun* [C] (*pl.* **maestros** /ˈmaɪstrəʊs ˈमाइस्ट्रोस्/ or **maestri** /ˈmaɪstri ˈमाइस्ट्रि/) a title used to refer to someone who is very skilled or gifted in a specified art especially a musician, **conductor**, performer, etc. 'Maestro' is an Italian word that literally means 'master' आचार्य, संगीताचार्य; माइस्ट्रो इतालियन मूल का शब्द है जिसका अर्थ है आचार्य *Maestro Zubin Mehta*

**mafia** /ˈmæfiə ˈमैफ़िआ/ *noun* **1 the Mafia** [*sing.*] a secret international organization of criminals active especially in Italy and the US ईटली और अमेरिका में सक्रिय विधि-विरोधी गुप्त अपराधी गुट; माफ़िया **2** [C] a closely knit group of trusted **associates** who use ruthless and criminal methods to get advantages for themselves विश्वस्त सहयोगियों का विधि-विरोधी संगठन; माफ़िआ

**magazine** /ˌmægəˈziːn ˌमैगˈज़ीन्/ (*informal* **mag** /mæg मैग्/) *noun* [C] a type of large thin book with a paper cover that you can buy every week or month containing articles, photographs, etc. often on a particular topic पत्रिका, मैगज़ीन *a woman's/computer/gardening magazine*

**magenta** /məˈdʒentə मˈजे़न्टा/ *adj.* reddish-purple in colour लाली लिए हुए बैंगनी रंग का; मैजंटा ▶ **magenta** *noun* [U] मैजंटा रंग

**maggot** /ˈmægət ˈमैगट्/ *noun* [C] a young insect before it grows wings and legs and becomes a fly नवजात कीड़ा (जिसके अभी पंख और टाँगे नहीं है और जो उड़ नहीं सकता); लार्वा, इल्ली

**magic[1]** /ˈmædʒɪk ˈमैजिक्/ *noun* [U] **1** the secret power that some people believe can make strange or impossible things happen if you say special words or do special things (विशेष शब्दों या क्रियाओं के प्रयोग द्वारा) असाधारण या असंभव बातें कर दिखाने वाली एक गुप्त शक्ति; जादू, इंद्रजाल ➪ **black magic** देखिए। **2** the art of doing tricks that seem impossible in order to entertain people लोगों के मनोरंजन के लिए असंभव लगने वाले करतब दिखाने की कला, हाथ की सफ़ाई का खेल **3** a special quality that makes sth seem wonderful विशेष गुण जिसके कारण कोई बात अद्भुत लगे; सम्मोहक प्रभाव *I'll never forget the magic of that moment.*

**magic[2]** /ˈmædʒɪk ˈमैजिक्/ *adj.* **1** used in or using magic जादू में प्रयुक्त या जादूभरा *a magic spell/potion/charm/trick* ○ *There is no magic formula for passing exams—just hard work.* **2** having a special quality that makes sth seem wonderful किसी बात को अद्भुत-सा बना देने वाले गुण से युक्त, सम्मोहन का प्रभाव युक्त *Respect is the magic ingredient in our relationship.* ▶ **magically** /-kli -कलि/ *adv.* जादू का-सा असर छोड़ते हुए

**magical** /ˈmædʒɪkl ˈमैजिक्ल्/ *adj.* **1** that seems to use magic जादू का सा असर छोड़ने वाला; जादुई *a herb with magical powers to heal* **2** wonderful and exciting आश्चर्यजनक और उत्तेजक या रोमांचक *Our holiday was absolutely magical.*

**magician** /məˈdʒɪʃn मˈजिश्न्/ *noun* [C] **1** a person who performs magic tricks to entertain people जादूगर, बाज़ीगर ➪ **conjuror** देखिए। **2** (in stories) a man who has magic powers (कहानियों में वर्णित) जादुई शक्तियों वाला पात्र, चमत्कारी पुरुष,मायावी ➪ **wizard** देखिए।

**magisterial** /ˌmædʒɪˈstɪəriəl ˌमैजिˈस्टिअरिअल्/ *adj.* **1** (especially of a person or their behaviour) having or seeming to have power or authority (विशेषतः व्यक्ति या उसका व्यवहार) शक्ति या प्राधिकार युक्त होना या विदित होना *her magisterial presence* **2** (of a book or piece of writing) having great knowledge or understanding (पुस्तक या लेख की) पूर्ण जानकारी या समझदारी से *his magisterial account of the history of India* **3** (*only before a noun*) connected with or related to a magistrate दंडाधीशसंबंधी ▶ **magisterially** /ˌmædʒɪˈstɪəriəli ˌमैजिस्ˈस्टिअरिअलि/ *adv.* अधिकारिक तरीक़े से

**magistrate** /ˈmædʒɪstreɪt ˈमैजिस्ट्रेट्/ *noun* [C] an official who acts as a judge in cases involving less serious crimes दंडनायक, मजिस्ट्रेट; मामूली अपराधों के मुक़दमों का प्राधिकारी

**magma** /ˈmægmə ˈमैग्मा/ *noun* [U] (*technical*) very hot liquid rock found below the earth's surface पृथ्वी के नीचे बहुत गरम द्रवीभूत चट्टान; मैगमा ➪ **volcano** पर चित्र देखिए।

**magnanimous** /mægˈnænɪməs मैग्ˈनैनिमस्/ *adj.* kind, generous and forgiving (especially towards an enemy or a competitor that you have beaten) दयालु, उदार और क्षमाशील (विशेषतः पराजित शत्रु या प्रतियोगी के प्रति)

**magnate** /ˈmægneɪt ˈमैग्नेट्/ *noun* [C] a person who is rich, powerful and successful, especially in business धनी, शक्तिशाली और सफल व्यक्ति (विशेषतः व्यापार में) *a media/property/shipping magnate*

**magnesium** /mægˈniːziəm मैग्ˈनीज़िअम्/ *noun* [U] (*symbol* **Mg**) a light, silver-white metal that burns with a bright white flame एक हलकी, चाँदी जैसी सफ़ेद धातु जिसमें से चमकीली सफ़ेद लौ निकलती है; मैगनीशियम

**magnet** /ˈmægnət ˈमैग्नट्/ *noun* [C] a piece of iron, steel, etc. that can attract and pick up other metal objects चुंबक

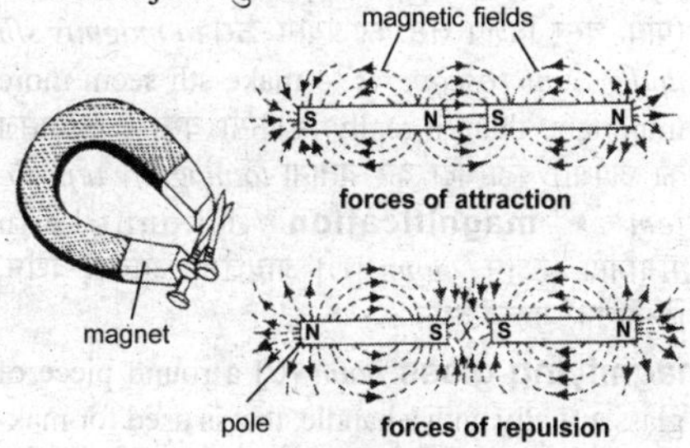

magnet

**magnetic** /mægˈnetɪk मैग्ˈनेटिक्/ *adj.* **1** having the ability to attract metal objects चुंबकीय *a magnetic tape/disk* (= containing electronic information which can be read by a computer or other machine) **2** having a quality that strongly attracts people चुंबकीय आकर्षणयुक्त व्यक्तित्व *a magnetic personality*

**magnetic field** *noun* [C] an area around a magnet or materials that behave like a magnet, where there is a force that will attract some metals towards it चुंबक या चुंबकवत वस्तुओं के चारों ओर का क्षेत्र (जिसमें चुंबकीय शक्ति काम करती है); चुंबकीय क्षेत्र

**magnetic north** *noun* [U] (*technical*) the direction that is approximately north as it is shown on a **compass** चुंबक द्वारा दर्शाई गई (लगभग वही) उत्तर दिशा ➪ **true north** देखिए।

**magnetism** /ˈmæɡnətɪzəm ˈमैग्नटिज़म्/ *noun* [U] **1** a characteristic of magnets that causes attraction or repulsion चुंबकत्व, चुंबकशक्ति (विद्युत धारा द्वारा लोहे जैसी वस्तुओं में उत्पन्न विशेष गुण जिसके कारण वस्तुएँ एक-दूसरे की ओर आकृष्ट होती हैं या एक-दूसरे से दूर हट जाती हैं) **2** qualities that strongly attract people लोगों को प्रबल रूप से आकृष्ट करने वाली विशेषताएँ; व्यक्तित्व आकर्षण *Nobody could resist his magnetism.*

**magnetize** (*also* **-ise**) /ˈmæɡnətaɪz ˈमैग्नटाइज़्/ *verb* [T] **1** to make sth behave like a **magnet** किसी वस्तु को चुंबकीय गुणों वाला बना देना, चुंबकित कर देना **2** (*written*) to strongly attract sb किसी व्यक्ति को प्रबल रूप से आकृष्ट करना

**magnificent** /mæɡˈnɪfɪsnt मैग्ˈनिफ़िसन्ट्/ *adj.* extremely impressive and attractive अत्यधिक प्रभावशाली और आकर्षक, भव्य, शानदार ▶ **magnificence** /-sns -सन्स्/ *noun* [U] भव्यता, वैभव ▶ **magnificently** *adv.* भव्यता से

**magnify** /ˈmæɡnɪfaɪ ˈमैग्निफ़ाइ/ *verb* [T] (*pres. part.* **magnifying**; *3rd person sing. pres.* **magnifies**; *pt, pp* **magnified**) **1** to make sth look bigger than it is, usually using a special piece of equipment किसी वस्तु को (अपने आकार से) बड़ा दिखाना (प्रायः वस्तु विशेष लेंस का प्रयोग कर) *to magnify sth under a microscope* **2** to make sth seem more important than it really is किसी वस्तु को (असल की अपेक्षा) बड़ा-चढ़ा कर बताना *to magnify a problem* ▶ **magnification** /ˌmæɡnɪfɪˈkeɪʃn ˌमैग्निफ़िˈकेश्न्/ *noun* [U] आवर्धन, आकार-वर्धन, विस्तीर्णन, महत्त्व-वर्धन

**magnifying glass** *noun* [C] a round piece of glass, usually with a handle, that is used for making things look bigger than they are मूठदार गोल लेंस जो वस्तुओं को बड़ा करके दिखाता है; आवर्धक लेंस

**magnitude** /ˈmæɡnɪtjuːd ˈमैग्निट्यूड्/ *noun* [U] the great size or importance of sth किसी वस्तु का बड़ा आकार या महत्त्व

**magnum opus** /ˌmæɡnəm ˈəʊpəs ˌमैग्नम् ˈओपस्/ *noun* [*sing.*] an artist's or writer's most important or best work. It is a Latin phrase that literally means 'great work' किसी कलाकार या लेखक की प्रधान कृति या सर्वोत्तम रचना *'Mona Lisa' is Leonardo Da Vinci's magnum opus.*

**maha** *adj.* (*IndE*) very large or great बहुत बड़ा या प्रमुख *Mahasabha ○ Maharaja/Maharani*

**mahal** *noun* (*IndE*) a palace; a large mansion महल; विशाल भवन

**Maharaja** (*also* **maharaja**) *noun* [C] (*IndE*) (in the past) a great Indian king; an Indian ruler of a big state usually ranking above a raja (विगत में) प्रमुख भारतीय शासक; महाराजा *Maharaja of Jaipur*

**Maharani** (*also* **maharani**) *noun* [C] (*IndE*) the title of a queen; the wife or widow of a **maharaja** महारानी

**Mahatma** (*also* **mahatma**) *noun* [C] (*IndE*) a term of respect for a person who is regarded with **reverence**; a great spiritual being, a great soul महात्मा; आध्यात्मिक व्यक्ति, एक महान आत्मा *Mahatma Gandhi*

**mahogany** /məˈhɒɡəni मˈहॉगनि/ *noun* [U] hard dark reddish-brown wood (from a tropical tree) that is used for making furniture फ़र्नीचर बनाने में प्रयुक्त सख़्त गहरे, लाल-भूरे रंग की लकड़ी (और उसका वृक्ष जो उष्णकटिबंधीय क्षेत्र में होता है), महॉगनी (वृक्ष और उसकी लकड़ी)

**mahout** (*also* **mahavat**) *noun* [C] (*IndE*) a person who drives, trains and looks after elephants महावत

**maid** /meɪd मेड्/ *noun* [C] a woman whose job is to clean in a hotel or large house होटल या बड़े भवन में सफ़ाई आदि घरेलू काम करने वाली महिला, कामवाली; घरेलू सहायिका ➪ **chambermaid** देखिए।

**maidan** *noun* (*IndE*) a large open ground or playfield in a town or village मैदान *Pragati Maidan in Delhi*

**maiden name** /ˈmeɪdn neɪm ˈमेड्न् नेम्/ *noun* [C] a woman's family name before marriage महिला का विवाह से पहले का कुलनाम ➪ **née** देखिए।

**maiden voyage** /ˌmeɪdn ˈvɔɪɪdʒ ˌमेड्न् ˈवॉइइज्/ *noun* [C] the first journey of a new ship नए जलपोत की प्रथम यात्रा

**mail** /meɪl मेल्/ (*also BrE* **post**) *noun* [U] **1** the system for collecting and sending letters and packages डाक-व्यवस्था *to send a parcel by air mail/surface mail* **2** the letters, etc. that you receive डाक से भेजे या प्राप्त पत्र आदि *junk mail* (= letters, usually advertising sth, that are sent to people although they have not asked for them) ➪ **post** पर नोट देखिए। **3** = **email** ▶ **mail** *verb* [T] (*AmE*) डाक से पत्र आदि को भेजना

**mailbox** /ˈmeɪlbɒks ˈमेलबॉक्स् / *noun* [C] **1** (*AmE*) = **letter box 2** **2** (*AmE*) = **postbox** **3** a computer program that receives and stores electronic messages (**email**) इलेक्ट्रॉनिक संदेश को प्राप्त और संगृहित करने वाला कंप्यूटर प्रोग्राम, ई-मेल का मेलबॉक्स (संदेश-संग्रहस्थल)

**mailing list** *noun* [C] a list of the names and addresses of people to whom advertising material or information is regularly sent by a business or an organization लोगों के नामों और पत्तों का सूची जिन्हें कोई संगठन विज्ञापन-सामग्री या सूचनाएँ नियमित रूप से भेजता है

**mail order** *noun* [U] a method of shopping. You choose what you want from a special book (**a catalogue**) and the goods are then sent to you by post डाक से ख़रीदारी का तरीक़ा

**maim** /meɪm मेम् / *verb* [T] to hurt sb so badly that part of his/her body can no longer be used ऐसी गहरी चोट करना कि व्यक्ति का अंग बेकार हो जाए, किसी को अपंग बना देना

**main[1]** /meɪn मेन् / *adj.* (*only before a noun*) most important सबसे महत्त्वपूर्ण *My main reason for wanting to learn English is to get a better job.* ○ *a busy main road* ✪ पर्याय **chief**

**IDM** **in the main** (*formal*) generally; mostly सामान्य रूप से; अधिकांशतः *We found Bengali people very friendly in the main.*

**main[2]** /meɪn मेन् / *noun* **1** [C] a large pipe or wire that carries water, gas or electricity between buildings भवनों के बीच पानी या गैस का बड़ा पाइप या बिजली की बड़ी तार *The water main has burst.* **2 the mains** [*pl.*] (*BrE*) the place where the supply of gas, water or electricity to a building starts; the system of providing these services to a building वह स्थान जहाँ से किसी भवन को गैस, पानी या बिजली की आपूर्ति शुरू होती है; किसी भवन को ये सेवाएँ उपलब्ध कराने की व्यवस्था या पद्धति *Turn the water off at the mains.* ○ *mains gas/water/electricity*

**mainframe** /ˈmeɪnfreɪm ˈमेन्फ्रेम् / (*also* **mainframe computer**) *noun* [C] (*computing*) a large powerful computer, usually the centre of a system (**network**) that is shared by many people (**users**) एक बड़ा और शक्तिशाली कंप्यूटर जिससे अनेक कंप्यूटर-प्रयोक्ता जुड़े रहते हैं; मेनफ्रेम

**mainland** /ˈmeɪnlænd ˈमेन्लैन्ड् / *noun* [*sing.*] the main part of a country or continent, not including the islands around it किसी देश या द्वीप का मुख्य भाग (जिसमें उसके चारों ओर के द्वीप नहीं आते); महाद्वीप *mainland China*

**mainline** /ˈmeɪnlaɪn ˈमेन्लाइन् / *adj.* (*AmE*) belonging to the system, or connected with the ideas that most people accept or believe in ऐसी व्यवस्था से संबंधित या ऐसे विचारों से संबंधित जिन्हें अधिकतम लोग मानते हो; मुख्यधारा ✪ पर्याय **mainstream**

**mainly** /ˈmeɪnli ˈमेन्लि / *adv.* mostly मुख्य रूप से, अधिकांशतः, अधिकतर *The students here are mainly from Japan.*

**mainsail** /ˈmeɪnseɪl; ˈmeɪnsl ˈमेन्सेल्; ˈमेन्सल् / *noun* [C] the largest and most important sail on a boat or ship किसी नाव या जहाज़ का सबसे बड़ा और सबसे ज़रूरी पाल ➪ **boat** पर चित्र देखिए।

**mainstay** /ˈmeɪnsteɪ ˈमेन्स्टे / *noun* [C] a person or thing that is the most important part of sth, which makes it possible for it to exist or to be successful किसी वस्तु, गतिविधि आदि के अस्तित्व या सफलता का मुख्य आधार (व्यक्ति या वस्तु) *Agriculture is the mainstay of the country's economy.*

**mainstream** /ˈmeɪnstriːm ˈमेन्स्ट्रीम् / *noun* [*sing.*] **the mainstream** the ideas and opinions that are considered normal because they are shared by most people; the people who hold these opinions and beliefs अधिकतम लोगों में प्रचलित सामान्य विचार और मत; मुख्यधारा, सामान्य विचार और मत रखने वाले लोग *The Green Party is not in the mainstream of British politics.* ▶ **mainstream** *adj.* मुख्यधारा विषयक

**maintain** /meɪnˈteɪn मेन्ˈटेन् / *verb* [T] **1** to make sth continue at the same level, standard, etc. किसी वस्तु को उसी स्तर, मानक आदि पर बनाए रखना, जारी रखना *We need to maintain the quality of our goods but not increase the price.* ○ *to maintain law and order* **2** to keep sth in good condition by checking and repairing it regularly किसी वस्तु की नियमित जाँच और मरम्मत करते हुए उसे सही हालत में रखना, किसी वस्तु का रख-रखाव करना *to maintain a road/building/machine* **3** to keep saying that sth is true even when others disagree or do not believe it किसी बात को सच माने रहना (भले ही दूसरे असहमत हों या उसे सच न मानें) *She has always maintained her innocence.* **4** to support sb with your own money अपने धन से किसी का पालन-पोषण करना *He has to maintain two children from his previous marriage.*

**maintenance** /ˈmeɪntənəns ˈमेन्टनन्स् / *noun* [U] **1** keeping sth in good condition रख-रखाव *This house needs a lot of maintenance.* ○ *car maintenance* **2** (*BrE*) money that sb must pay regularly to a former wife, husband or partner especially when they have had children together पूर्व पत्नी या

पति को क़ानूनन मिलने वाला गुज़ारा भत्ता (विशेषतः दोनों को विवाहित जीवन में संतानें होने पर) *He has to pay maintenance to his ex-wife.*

**maisonette** /ˌmeɪzəˈnet ˌमेज़ˈनेट्/ *noun* [C] (*BrE*) a flat on two floors that is part of a larger building बड़ी इमारत में दो मंज़िलों पर बना फ़्लैट

**maize** /meɪz मेज़्/ (*AmE* **corn**) *noun* [U] a tall plant that produces yellow grains in a large mass (**a cob**) मक्का, मक्की

> NOTE मक्का के पीले दाने, जिन्हें सब्ज़ी की तरह खाया जाता है, **sweetcorn** कहलाते हैं। ➪ **cereal** पर चित्र देखिए।

**Maj.** *abbr.* (*written*) Major; an officer of a middle level in the army or the US air force मेजर; स्थल सेना या अमेरिकी वायु सेना में मध्य स्तर का एक अधिकारी

**majestic** /məˈdʒestɪk मˈजेस्टिक्/ *adj.* impressive because of its size or beauty प्रभावशाली, शानदार (विशाल या सुंदर होने के कारण) *a majestic mountain/landscape* ▸ **majestically** /-kli -क्लि/ *adv.* शानदार ढंग से

**majesty** /ˈmædʒəsti ˈमैजस्टि/ *noun* (*pl.* **majesties**) **1** [U] the impressive and attractive quality that sth has किसी वस्तु की प्रभावशालिता और आकर्षकता; विभूति *the splendour and majesty of the palace and its gardens* **2 His/Her/Your Majesty** [C] (*formal*) used when speaking to or about a royal person शाही ख़ानदान के सदस्य का निर्देश करने या उसे संबोधित करने के लिए प्रयुक्त *Her Majesty the Queen*

**major**[1] /ˈmeɪdʒə(r) ˈमेज(र्)/ *adj.* **1** (*only before a noun*) very large, important or serious बहुत बड़ा, महत्त्वपूर्ण या गंभीर *The patient needs major heart surgery.* ○ *There haven't been any major problems.* ✪ विलोम **minor** **2** of one of the two types of **key**[1] **4** in which music is usually written संगीत-स्वरयोजना की (दो प्रकारों में से एक) कुंजी *the key of D major* ➪ **minor** देखिए।

**major**[2] /ˈmeɪdʒə(r) ˈमेज(र्)/ *noun* **1** (*abbr.* **Maj.**) [C] an officer of a middle level in the army or the US air force स्थल सेना या अमेरिकी वायु सेना में मध्यस्तर का एक अधिकारी; मेजर **2** [C] (*AmE*) the main subject or course of a student at college or university; the student who studies it कॉलेज या विश्वविद्यालय में छात्र का मुख्य विषय या पाठ्यक्रम; इसका अध्ययन करने वाला छात्र *Her major is French.*

**major**[3] /ˈmeɪdʒə(r) ˈमेज(र्)/ *verb*

PHR V **major in sth** (*AmE*) to study sth as your main subject at college or university कॉलेज या विश्वविद्यालय में किसी विषय का मुख्य विषय के रूप में अध्ययन करना

**major general** *noun* [C] an officer of a high level in the army स्थल सेना में उच्च स्तर का एक अधिकारी; मेजर जनरल

**majority** /məˈdʒɒrəti मˈजॉरटि/ *noun* (*pl.* **majorities**) **1** [*sing., with sing. or pl. verb*] **majority (of sb/sth)** the largest number or part of a group of people or things लोगों या वस्तुओं के समूह ही सबसे बड़ी संख्या या अंश; बहुमत, बहुलांश *The majority of students in the class come/comes from Japan.* ○ *This treatment is not available in* ***the vast majority*** *of hospitals.* ✪ विलोम **minority** **2** [C, *usually sing.*] **majority (over sb)** (in an election) the difference in the number of votes for the person/party who came first and the person/party who came second चुनाव में प्रथम और द्वितीय स्थान पर आए उम्मीदवार या दल के बीच मतों की संख्या में अंतर *He was elected by/with a majority of almost 5000 votes.* NOTE **Overall majority** का मतलब है अन्य उम्मीदवारों या दलों के कुल मिलाकर मतों से अधिक मत। ➪ **absolute majority** देखिए।

IDM **be in the/a majority** to form the largest number or part of sth किसी वस्तु की सबसे बड़ी संख्या होना या उसका सबसे बड़ा अंश होना, किसी का बहुमत होना *Women are in the majority in the teaching profession.*

**make**[1] /meɪk मेक्/ *verb* (*pt, pp* **made** /meɪd मेड्/) **1** [T] to produce or create sth कुछ उत्पन्न या सृजित करना *to make bread* ○ *Cheese is* ***made from*** *milk.* ○ *Those cars are* ***made in*** *Pune.* **2** [T] (*used with nouns*) to perform a certain action किसी विशिष्ट क्रिया को निष्पन्न करना *to make a mistake* ○ *to make a guess/comment/statement/suggestion* ○ *I've made an appointment to see the doctor.*

> NOTE ऐसे प्रयोगों के समकक्ष एक अलग क्रिया भी मिलती है, उदाहरण के लिए **decide** = **make a decision**. यदि 'make' + संज्ञा का प्रयोग हो रहा है तो उसके साथ एक विशेषण भी आ सकता है—*He made the right decision.* ○ *They made a generous offer.*

**3** [T] to cause a particular effect, feeling, situation, etc. विशेष प्रभाव, मनोभाव आदि उत्पन्न करना या का कारण बनना *The film made me cry.* ○ *You don't need to know much of a language to* ***make yourself understood.*** ○ *to make trouble/a mess/a noise* **4** [T] to force sb/sth to do sth किसी व्यक्ति या वस्तु को कुछ करने के लिए बाध्य करना *You can't make her come with us if she doesn't want to.* ○ *They made him wait at the police station all day.*

> NOTE कर्मवाच्य (passive) में शब्द **to** का प्रयोग अनिवार्य है—*He was made to wait at the police station.*

5 [T] used with money, numbers and time धन, संख्याएँ और समय के वाचक शब्दों के साथ प्रयुक्त *How much do you think he makes* (= earns) *a month?* ○ *5 and 7 make 12.* **6** *linking verb* to make sb/sth become sth; to have the right qualities to become sth किसी व्यक्ति या वस्तु को कुछ बना देना; कुछ बनने के लिए उपयुक्त गुणों वाला होना *She was made* (= given the job of) *President.* ○ *You can borrow some money this time, but don't* ***make a habit of*** *it.* **7** *linking verb* to become sth; to achieve sth कुछ बन जाना; कोई लक्ष्य प्राप्त कर लेना *I'm hoping to make head of department by the time I'm thirty.* **8** to manage to reach a place or go somewhere किसी स्थान पर पहुँच जाना या कहीं चले जाना *We should make Jaipur by about 10 p.m.* ○ *I can't make the meeting next week.*

IDM **make do with sth** to use sth that is not good enough because nothing better is available जो मिले उसी से काम चलाना *If we can't get limes, we'll have to make do with lemons.*

**make it** to manage to do sth; to succeed कोई काम कर सकना; (किसी काम में) सफल हो जाना *She'll never make it as an actress.* ○ *He's badly injured—it looks like he might not make it* (= survive).

**make the most of sth** to get as much pleasure, profit, etc. as possible from sth किसी वस्तु का पूरा या यथासंभव अधिकतम उपयोग कर लेना *You won't get another chance—make the most of it!*

NOTE **Make** से बनने वाली अन्य अभिव्यक्तियों के लिए, संबंधित संज्ञाओं और विशेषणों की प्रविष्टियाँ देखिए, जैसे **make amends** के लिए **amends** देखिए।

IDM **make for sb/sth** to move towards sb/sth किसी व्यक्ति या वस्तु की ओर बढ़ना

**make for sth** to help or allow sth to happen किसी बात में सहायक होना या कोई बात होने देना *Arguing all the time doesn't make for a happy marriage.*

**be made for sb/each other** to be well suited to sb/each other दो व्यक्तियों का एक-दूसरे के लिए उपयुक्त होना *Javed and Alisha seem made for each other.*

**make sb/sth into sb/sth** to change sb/sth into sb/sth किसी व्यक्ति या वस्तु को किसी अन्य रूप में परिवर्तित कर देना *She made her spare room into an office.*

**make sth of sb/sth** to understand the meaning or nature of sb/sth किसी व्यक्ति या वस्तु के अभिप्राय या स्वभाव को समझना *What do you make of Kabir's letter?*

**make off (with sth)** (*informal*) to leave or escape in a hurry, for example after stealing sth जल्दबाज़ी में चले जाना या निकल भागना (उदाहरण के लिए कुछ चुराकर) *Someone's made off with my wallet!*

**make sb/sth out** **1** to understand sb/sth किसी व्यक्ति या वस्तु को समझना (कि वह वस्तुतः क्या है या क्या चाहता है) *I just can't make him out.* **2** to be able to see or hear sb/sth; to manage to read sth किसी व्यक्ति या वस्तु को देख या सुन सकना; किसी वस्तु को पढ़ लेना या पढ़ने में सफल हो जाना *I could just make out her signature.*

**make out that... ; make yourself out to be sth** to say that sth is true and try to make people believe it किसी बात को सच मानना तथा अन्य लोगों से भी ऐसा ही मनवाना *He made out that he was a millionaire.* ○ *She's not as clever as she makes herself out to be.*

**make (yourself/sb) up** to put powder, colour, etc. on your/sb's face to make it look attractive चेहरे को आकर्षक बनाने के लिए उस पर पाउडर, रंग आदि लगाना

**make sth up** **1** to form sth किसी का निर्माण करना *the different groups that make up our society* **2** to invent sth, often sth that is not true कुछ गढ़ लेना (बहाना, कहानी आदि) *to make up an excuse* **3** to make a number or an amount complete; to replace sth that has been lost (कमी वाली) किसी विशेष संख्या या मात्रा को पूरा करना; किसी क्षति की पूर्ति करना *We need one more person to make up our team.*

**make up for sth** to do sth that corrects a bad situation किसी कमी को पूरा करने के लिए कुछ करना *Her enthusiasm makes up for her lack of experience.*

**make it up to sb** (*informal*) to do sth that shows that you are sorry for what you have done to sb or that you are grateful for what he/she has done for you (दूसरे के प्रति) अपनी ग़लती या (अपने प्रति) दूसरे के उपकार को मानना *You've done me a big favour. How can I make it up to you?*

**make (it) up (with sb)** to become friends again after an argument झगड़े के बाद सुलह हो जाना या कर लेना *Has she made it up with him yet?*

**make²** /meɪk मेक्/ *noun* [C] the name of the company that produces sth किसी वस्तु का उत्पादन करने वाली कंपनी का नाम *'What make is your television?' 'It's a Sony.'*

IDM **on the make** always trying to make money for yourself, especially in a dishonest way हमेशा पैसा बनाने के चक्कर में रहना (विशेषतः बेईमानी से) *The country is being ruined by politicians on the make.*

**make-believe** *noun* [U] things that sb imagines or invents that are not real बहाना, छल, ढोंग

**maker** /ˈmeɪkə(r) ˈमेक(र्)/ *noun* [C] a person, company or machine that makes sth किसी वस्तु का निर्माता व्यक्ति, कंपनी या मशीन *a film-maker* ○ *If it doesn't work, send it back to the maker.* ○ *an ice cream maker*

**makeshift** /ˈmeɪkʃɪft ˈमेक्शिफ़्ट्/ *adj.* made to be used for only a short time until there is sth better अस्थायी, कामचलाऊ *makeshift shelters of old cardboard boxes*

**make-up** *noun* 1 [U] powder, cream, etc. that you put on your face to make yourself more attractive. Actors use make-up to change their appearance when they are acting (चेहरे को अधिक आकर्षक बनाने के लिए प्रयुक्त) पाउडर, क्रीम आदि शृंगार-सामग्री, अभिनेता अभिनय के समय आकृति बदलने के लिए इसका प्रयोग करते हैं *to put on/take off make-up* ➪ **cosmetic**[1] तथा **make (yourself/sb) up** देखिए। 2 [*sing.*] a person's character व्यक्ति का चरित्र *He can't help his temper. It's part of his make-up.*

**making** /ˈmeɪkɪŋ ˈमेकिङ्/ *noun* [*sing.*] the act of doing or producing sth; the process of being made कुछ करने या बनाने की क्रिया; कुछ बनने की प्रक्रिया *breadmaking* ○ *This movie has been three years in the making.*

IDM **be the making of sb** to be the reason that sb is successful किसी व्यक्ति की सफलता में कारण होना *University was the making of Priyanka.*

**have the makings of sth** to have the necessary qualities for sth किसी वस्तु में (किसी अन्य वस्तु के निर्माण के लिए) अपेक्षित गुण होना *The book has the makings of a good film.*

**mal-** /mæl मैल्/ *prefix* (*used in nouns, verbs and adjectives*) bad or badly; not correct or correctly ख़राब या ख़राब तरीक़े से; ग़लत या ग़लत तरीक़े से *malnutrition* ○ *maltreat*

**Malabar** *noun* [U] the region lying between the Western Ghats and the Arabian Sea in southern India. Also known as the Malabar Coast, it is famous for its tropical forests (दक्षिण भारत में) पश्चिमी घाट और अरब सागर के बीच का क्षेत्र; मालाबार तट, यह उष्णप्रदेशीय वन के लिए प्रसिद्ध है

**maladjusted** /ˈmæləd͡ʒʌstɪd ˈमैलजस्टिड्/ *adj.* (used about a person) not able to behave well with other people (व्यक्ति) जिसकी औरों से बन न सके; कुसमंजित, कुसमायोजित

**malady** /ˈmælədi ˈमैलडि/ *noun* [C] (*pl.* **maladies**) 1 (*formal*) a serious problem अप्रिय और गंभीर अवस्था 2 (*old-fashioned*) a disease or an **ailment** बीमारी, व्याधि, रोग

**malaria** /məˈleəriə मˈलेअरिआ/ *noun* [U] a serious disease in hot countries that you get from the bite of a small flying insect (**a mosquito**) उष्ण देशों में मिलने वाली गंभीर बीमारी जो मच्छर के काटने से होती है; मलेरिया ▶ **malarial** *adj.* मलेरिया संबंधी *a malarial mosquito*

**male** /meɪl मेल्/ *adj.* belonging to the sex that does not give birth to babies or produce eggs नर, पुरुष (गर्भ धारण करने में असमर्थ लिंग से संबंधित) *a male goat* ○ *a male model/nurse* ➪ **masculine** और **female** पर नोट देखिए। ▶ **male** *noun* [C] नर *The male of the species has a white tail.*

**malformation** /ˌmælfɔːˈmeɪʃn ˌमैल्फ़ॉˈमेश्न्/ *noun* 1 [C] a part of the body that is not formed correctly शरीर का वह अंग जिसकी रचना में विकृति है; विकृति, अपरचना *foetal malformations* 2 [U] the state of not being correctly formed विकृत होने की दशा, में विकृति

**malice** /ˈmælɪs ˈमैलिस्/ *noun* [U] a wish to hurt other people दूसरों को मानसिक पीड़ा पहुँचाने की अभिलाषा, दुर्भावना ▶ **malicious** /məˈlɪʃəs मˈलिशस्/ *adj.* विद्वेषी, दुर्भावनाशील ▶ **maliciously** *adv.* दुर्भावनापूर्वक

IDM **with malice aforethought** (*technical*) with the deliberate intention of committing a crime or harming sb किसी के प्रति सोची-समझी दुर्भावना के साथ

**malign**[1] /məˈlaɪn मˈलाइन्/ *verb* [T] (*formal*) to say or write bad things about sb/sth publicly especially in a unfair manner दुर्भावनापूर्वक लेख से या मौखिक निंदा करके किसी को सार्वजनिक रूप से बदनाम करना

**malign**[2] /məˈlaɪn मˈलाइन्/ *adj.* (*formal*) (*usually before a noun*) causing harm or harmful अनिष्टकर, हानिकर, क्षतिकर *a malign effect*

**malignant** /məˈlɪgnənt मˈलिग्नन्ट्/ *adj.* (used about a disease (**cancer**) that spreads in the body, or a growing mass (**a tumour**) caused by disease) likely to cause death if not controlled (कैंसर या किसी रोग के कारण बनी गाँठ) जिससे मृत्यु भी हो सकती है यदि वह नियंत्रित न हो सके; घातक *He has a malignant brain tumour.* ✪ विलोम **benign**

**mall** /mæl; mɔːl मैल्; मॉल्/ = **shopping centre**

**malleable** /ˈmæliəbl ˈमैलिअब्ल्/ *adj.* 1 (*technical*) (used about metals, etc.) that can be hit or pressed into shape easily without breaking or cracking (धातुएँ आदि पदार्थ) जिन्हें पीट या दबाकर आसानी से गढ़ा जा सकता है बिना उनके टूटे या उनमें दरार पड़े; आघात-वर्धनीय, पिटवाँ 2 (used about people, ideas, etc.) easily influenced or changed (व्यक्ति, विचार आदि) जो आसानी से प्रभावित या परिवर्तित हो जाते हैं ▶ **malleability** /ˌmæliəˈbɪləti ˌमैलिअˈबिलटि/ *noun* [U] आघातवर्धनीयता, पिटवाँपन

**mallet** /ˈmælɪt ˈमैलिट्/ *noun* [C] a heavy wooden hammer लकड़ी का भारी हथौड़ा; मुँगरी ➪ **tool** पर चित्र देखिए।

**malnutrition** /ˌmælnjuːˈtrɪʃn ˌमैलन्यूˈट्रिशन्/ *noun* [U] bad health that is the result of not having enough food or enough of the right kind of food कुपोषण; पर्याप्त भोजन या सही प्रकार के पर्याप्त भोजन के अभाव से उत्पन्न अस्वस्थता ▶ **malnourished** /ˌmælˈnʌrɪʃt ˌमैलˈनरिश्ट्/ *adj.* कुपोषित *The children were badly malnourished.*

**malpractice** /ˌmælˈpræktɪs ˌमैलˈप्रैक्टिस्/ *noun* [U, C] (*law*) careless, wrong or illegal behaviour while in a professional job व्यावसायिक कार्य में असावधानीपूर्ण, अनुचित या ग़ैर-क़ानूनी आचरण; कदाचार, अनाचार *medical malpractice* ○ *He is standing trial for alleged malpractices.*

**malt** /mɔːlt मॉल्ट्/ *noun* [U] grain that is used for making beer and **whisky** जौ, यव (जिससे बियर और व्हिस्की बनती हैं), मॉल्ट

**maltose** /ˈmɔːltəʊz ˈमॉल्टोज़्/ *noun* [U] a sugar that chemicals in the body make from **starch** शरीर के रसायनों द्वारा स्टार्च से बनाई गई शर्करा, मॉल्टोज़

**maltreat** /ˌmælˈtriːt ˌमैलˈट्रीट्/ *verb* [T] (*formal*) to treat a person or animal in a cruel or unkind way किसी मनुष्य या प्राणी से निर्ममता का व्यवहार करना, दुर्व्यवहार करना ▶ **maltreatment** *noun* [U] दुर्व्यवहार

**mammal** /ˈmæml ˈमैमल्/ *noun* [C] an animal of the type that gives birth to live babies, not eggs, and feeds its young on milk from its own body स्तनपायी प्राणी (जो, अंडे नहीं, जीवित बच्चे पैदा करते हैं और उन्हें अपना दूध पिलाते हैं) *Whales, dogs and humans are mammals.*

**mammary** /ˈmæməri ˈमैमरि/ *adj.* (*only before a noun*) (*medical*) connected with the breasts स्तन-संबंधी *mammary glands* (= parts of the breast that produce milk)

**mammoth** /ˈmæməθ ˈमैमथ्/ *adj.* very big विशाल

**man[1]** /mæn मैन्/ *noun* (*pl.* **men** /men मेन्/) **1** [C] an adult male person पुरुष, आदमी, वयस्क पुरुष **2** [C] a person of either sex, male or female इनसान, व्यक्ति (पुरुष या स्त्री) *All men are equal.* ○ *No man could survive long in such conditions.* **3** [U] the human race; human beings मानव जाति; मानव जन *Early man lived by hunting.* ○ *the damage man has caused to the environment* **4** [C] (*often in compounds*) a man who comes from a particular place; a man who has a particular job or interest किसी विशेष स्थान का निवासी व्यक्ति; विशेष व्यवसाय या रुचि वाला व्यक्ति *a Frenchman* ○ *a businessman* ○ *sportsmen and women*

IDM **the man in the street** (*BrE*) an ordinary man or woman जन साधारण, आम आदमी

**the odd man/one out** ➪ **odd** देखिए।

**man[2]** /mæn मैन्/ *verb* [T] (**manning; manned**) to operate sth or to provide people to operate sth किसी वस्तु का परिचालन करना या उसके लिए व्यक्ति उपलब्ध कराना *The telephones are manned 24 hours a day.*

**manage** /ˈmænɪdʒ ˈमैनिज्/ *verb* **1** [I, T] (*often with* **can** *or* **could**) to succeed in doing or dealing with sth difficult; to be able to do sth कोई कठिन काम करने या निपटाने में सफल होना; कुछ कर सकना *However did you manage to find us here?* ○ *I can't manage this suitcase. It's too heavy.* **2** [T] to be incharge or control of sth किसी काम का प्रभारी या नियंत्रक होना *She manages a small advertising business.* ○ *You need to manage your time more efficiently.* **3 [I] manage (without/with sb/sth); manage (on sth)** to deal with a difficult situation; to continue in spite of difficulties कठिन स्थिति से निबटना; कठिनाइयों के बावजूद काम करते रहना *My grandmother couldn't manage without her neighbours.*

**manageable** /ˈmænɪdʒəbl ˈमैनिजबल्/ *adj.* not too big or too difficult to deal with इतना बड़ा या कठिन नहीं कि सँभाला न जा सके, नियंत्रण या संचालन योग्य

**management** /ˈmænɪdʒmənt ˈमैनिज्मन्ट्/ *noun* **1** [U] the control or organization of sth संचालन, प्रबंधन, मैनेजमेंट *Good classroom management is vital with large groups of children.* **2** [C, U] the people who control a business or company प्रबंधक वर्ग, मैनेजमेंट *The hotel is now **under new management**.*

> NOTE एकवचन शब्द के रूप में **management** के साथ एकवचन (singular) या बहुवचन (plural) क्रिया प्रयुक्त होती है—*The management is/are considering making some workers redundant.*

**manager** /ˈmænɪdʒə(r) ˈमैनिज(र्)/ *noun* [C] **1** a man or woman who controls an organization or part of an organization प्रबंधक, संचालक (पुरुष या महिला); मैनेजर *a bank manager* **2** a person who looks after the business affairs of a singer, actor, etc. गायक, अभिनेता आदि के व्यापारिक हितों की देखभाल करने वाला व्यक्ति; मैनेजर **3** a person who is incharge of a sports team खेल टीम का प्रभारी व्यक्ति; मैनेजर *the England manager*

**manageress** /ˌmænɪdʒəˈres ˌमैनिजˈरेस्/ *noun* [C] the woman who is incharge of a shop or restaurant किसी दुकान या रेस्तराँ की प्रभारी महिला

**managerial** /ˌmænəˈdʒɪəriəl ˌमैनˈजिअरिअल्/ *adj.* connected with the work of a manager मैनेजर के काम से संबंधित, प्रबंध-संबंधी, प्रबंधक-संबंधी *Do you have any managerial experience?*

**managing director** *noun* [C] a person who controls a business or company किसी व्यापार या कंपनी का सर्वोच्च प्रमुख; प्रबंध निदेशक

**mandarin** /ˈmændərɪn ˈमैन्डरिन्/ *noun* [C] a type of small orange एक प्रकार का छोटा संतरा; मेंडारिन संतरा **2** (*also* **Mandarin**) the official language of China चीन देश की अधिकारिक भाषा मैंडरिन

**mandate** /ˈmændeɪt ˈमैन्डेट्/ *noun* [C, *usually sing.*] the power that is officially given to a group of people to do sth, especially after they have won an election अधिदेश, शासनदेश, जनादेश (विशेषत: चुनाव जीतने के बाद) *The union leaders had a clear mandate from their members to call a strike.*

**mandatory** /ˈmændətəri; mænˈdeɪtəri ˈमैन्डटरि; मैन्ˈडेटरि/ *adj.* (*formal*) that you must do, have, obey, etc. क़ानूनन आवश्यक, अनिवार्य *The crime carries a mandatory life sentence.* ✪ पर्याय **obligatory** ✪ विलोम **optional**

**mandible** /ˈmændɪbl ˈमैन्डिब्ल्/ *noun* [C] (*technical*) **1** the lower of the two bones in your face that contain your teeth (मनुष्य का) जबड़ा, अधोहनु, चिबुकास्थि ✪ पर्याय **jawbone** ⇨ **body** पर चित्र देखिए। **2** either of the two parts that are at the front and on either side of an insect's mouth, used especially for biting and crushing food चिबुकास्थि; कीड़े के निचले जबड़े का हिस्सा ⇨ **insect** पर चित्र देखिए।

**mane** /meɪn मेन्/ *noun* [C] the long hair on the neck of a horse or male lion घोड़े या नर शेर के लंबे बाल; अयाल ⇨ **lion** पर चित्र देखिए।

**man-eater** /ˈmæniːtə(r) ˈमैनीईट(र्)/ *noun* [C] a wild animal like a tiger that can kill and eat a human being नरभक्षी, आदमख़ोर *Sometimes tigers become man-eaters.* ▶ **man-eating** *adj.* (*only before a noun*) नरभक्षी *a man-eating tiger*

**maneuver** = **manoeuvre**

**mangalsutra** *noun* [C] (in India) a gold ornament strung from a string of black beads, a gold chain or a yellow thread that is put around the bride's neck during the wedding ceremony मंगलसूत्र

**manganese** /ˈmæŋɡəniːz ˈमैङ्गनीज़्/ *noun* [U] (*symbol* **Mn**) a type of hard grey metal एक प्रकार की सख़्त भूरी या धूसर धातु; मैंगनीज़

**mangle** /ˈmæŋgl ˈमैङ्गल्/ *verb* [T] (*usually passive*) to damage sth so badly that it is difficult to see what it looked like originally किसी वस्तु को क्षत-विक्षत कर देना, विकृत कर देना *The highway was covered with the mangled wreckage of cars.*

**mango** /ˈmæŋɡəʊ ˈमैङ्गो/ *noun* [C] (*pl.* **mangoes**) a tropical fruit that has a yellow and red skin and is yellow inside आम (का फल) ⇨ **fruit** पर चित्र देखिए।

**mangrove** /ˈmæŋɡrəʊv ˈमैङ्ग्रोव्/ *noun* [C] a tropical tree that grows in wet ground at the edge of rivers and has some roots that are above ground दलदल में या नदियों के छोर पर उगने वाला एक उष्ण कटिबंधीय वृक्ष जिसकी कुछ जड़ें ज़मीन पर होती है; वनस्पति गरान

**manhole** /ˈmænhəʊl ˈमैन्होल्/ *noun* [C] a hole in the street with a lid over it through which sb can go to look at the pipes, wires, etc. that are underground सड़क पर बना एक ढक्कनदार बड़ा गड्ढा; मैनहोल (इसके अंदर जाकर ज़मीन के नीचे लगे पाइपों, तारों आदि को जाँचा जा सकता है)

**manhood** /ˈmænhʊd ˈमैन्हुड्/ *noun* [U] the state of being a man rather than a boy (लड़का न होकर) पुरुष होना; पुरुषत्व

**mania** /ˈmeɪniə ˈमेनिआ/ *noun* **1** [C] (*informal*) a great enthusiasm for sth उत्साह का अतिरेक, (किसी बात के लिए) अति-उत्साह; उन्माद *World Cup mania is sweeping the country.* **2** [U] a serious mental illness that may cause sb to be very excited or violent गंभीर मनोरोग जिसमें रोगी अत्यंत उत्तेजित या हिंसक हो उठता है; उन्माद-रोग

**maniac** /ˈmeɪniæk ˈमेनिऐक्/ *noun* [C] **1** a person who behaves in a wild and stupid way विक्षिप्त, उन्मत्त व्यक्ति *to drive like a maniac* **2** a person who has a stronger love of sth than is normal किसी वस्तु के प्रति असाधारण रूप से आकृष्ट व्यक्ति, अति-आसक्त व्यक्ति, उन्माद-रोगी *a football maniac*

**manic** /ˈmænɪk ˈमैनिक्/ *adj.* **1** full of nervous energy or excited activity उन्मादग्रस्त *His behaviour became more manic as he began to feel stressed.* **2** (*medical*) connected with **(mania)** उन्माद-रोग से संबंधित

**manicure** /ˈmænɪkjʊə(r) ˈमैनिक्युअ(र्)/ *noun* [C, U] treatment to make your hands and fingernails look attractive हाथों और नाख़ूनों को सुंदर बनाने की क्रिया; नख-प्रसाधन

**manifest** /ˈmænɪfest ˈमैनिफ़ेस्ट्/ *verb* [I, T] (*formal*) **manifest (sth/itself) (in/as sth)** to show sth or to be shown clearly किसी वस्तु को स्पष्टतया प्रकट करना या प्रकट होना *Mental illness can manifest itself in many forms.* ▶ **manifest** *adj.* सुस्पष्ट, प्रत्यक्ष रूप से व्यक्त *manifest failure/anger* ▶ **manifestly** *adv.* सुस्पष्ट रूप से

**manifestation** /ˌmænɪfeˈsteɪʃn ˌमैनिफ़ेˈस्टेश्न्/ *noun* [C, U] (*formal*) a sign that sth is happening प्रकटीकरण; कुछ घटित होने का संकेत

**manifesto** /ˌmænɪˈfestəʊ ˌमैनिˈफ़ेस्टो / *noun* [C] (*pl.* **manifestos**) a written statement by a political party that explains what it hopes to do if it becomes the government in the future घोषणापत्र; किसी राजनीतिक दल का औपचारिक वक्तव्य कि सत्ता में आने पर उसका क्या कार्यक्रम रहेगा

**manifold**[1] /ˈmænɪfəʊld ˈमैनिफ़ोल्ड् / *adj.* (*formal*) many; of many different types अनेक; अनेक प्रकार का, विविध

**manifold**[2] /ˈmænɪfəʊld ˈमैनिफ़ोल्ड् / *noun* [C] (*technical*) a pipe or an enclosed space with several openings for taking gases in and out of a car engine कार के इंजन में पाइप या परिबद्ध जगह जिसमें गैस भरने और निकालने के अनेक छेद बने होते है, मैनिफ़ोल्ड, बहुछिद्री नली

**manipulate** /məˈnɪpjuleɪt मˈनिप्युलेट् / *verb* [T] **1** to influence sb so that he/she does or thinks what you want किसी को अपने पक्ष में प्रभावित कर लेना (कि वह वही करे या सोचे जो आप चाहते है) *Clever politicians know how to manipulate public opinion.* **2** to use, move or control sth with skill कुशलतापूर्वक किसी वस्तु का उपयोग करना उसे हिलाना-डुलाना या नियंत्रित करना *The doctor manipulated the bone back into place.* ▶ **manipulation** /məˌnɪpjuˈleɪʃn मˌनिप्युˈलेश्न् / *noun* [C, U] कुशलतापूर्वक कार्य-संचालन, हस्तकौशल, व्यवहार-कौशल

**manipulative** /məˈnɪpjələtɪv मˈनिप्यलटिव् / *adj.* **1** skilful at influencing sb or forcing sb to do what you want, often in an unfair way दूसरों को (प्रायः चालाकी से) अपनी बात मनवाने में दक्ष, व्यवहार-कुशल **2** (*formal*) connected with the ability to move things with your hands skilfully हस्तकौशल से संबंधित *manipulative skills such as typing and knitting*

**mankind** /mænˈkaɪnd मैन्ˈकाइन्ड् / *noun* [U] all the people in the world संसार के समस्त लोग; मानवता *A nuclear war would be a threat to all mankind.* ➪ **man** पर नोट देखिए।

**manly** /ˈmænli ˈमैन्लि / *adj.* typical of or suitable for a man पुरुष का प्रतिनिधिक या उसके उपयुक्त; पुरुषोचित, मर्दाना *a deep manly voice* ▶ **manliness** *noun* [U] पुरुषोचित-भाव, मर्दानापन

**man-made** *adj.* made by people, not formed in a natural way; artificial मानव-निर्मित (प्राकृतिक रूप से निर्मित नहीं); कृत्रिम *man-made fabrics such as nylon and polyester*

**manner** /ˈmænə(r) ˈमैन(र्) / *noun* **1** [*sing.*] the way that you do sth or that sth happens (किसी काम को करने का या कुछ घटित होने का) तरीक़ा, रीति ***He acted** in a civilized **manner**.* **2** [*sing.*] the way that sb behaves towards other people दूसरों से व्यवहार करने का तरीक़ा, व्यवहार, आचरण *to have an aggressive/a relaxed/a professional manner* **3 manners** [*pl.*] a way of behaving that is considered acceptable in your country or culture किसी देश या समाज में सही माना जाने वाला व्यवहार या आचरण *In some countries it is bad manners to show the soles of your feet.*

IDM **all manner of...** every kind of... सब तरह से... *You meet all manner of people in my job.*

**mannerism** /ˈmænərɪzəm ˈमैनरिज़म् / *noun* [C] sb's particular way of speaking or a particular movement he/she often does किसी व्यक्ति के व्यवहार की विचित्रता (बोलने या अन्य कामों में), व्यक्तिगत व्यवहार-वैचित्र्य

**manoeuvre**[1] (*AmE* **maneuver**) /məˈnuːvə(r) मˈनूव़(र्) / *noun* **1** [C] a movement that needs care or skill सावधानी या कुशलता की अपेक्षा वाली क्रिया *Parking the car in such a small space would be a tricky manoeuvre.* **2** [C, U] something clever that you do in order to win sth, trick sb, etc. कुछ हासिल करने, किसी को ठगने आदि के लिए चालाकी भरी हरकत, चालबाज़ी *political manoeuvre(s)* **3 manoeuvres** [*pl.*] a way of training soldiers when large numbers of them practise fighting in battles युद्ध-कला में सैनिकों का प्रशिक्षण; युद्धाभ्यास

**manoeuvre**[2] (*AmE* **maneuver**) /məˈnuːvə(r) मˈनूव़(र्) / *verb* [I, T] to move (sth) to a different position using skill निपुणता से किसी वस्तु को हिलाना या संचालित करना *The driver was manoeuvring his lorry into a narrow gateway.*

**manor** /ˈmænə(r) ˈमैन(र्) / (*also* **manor house**) *noun* [C] a large house in the country that has land around it ग्रामीण अंचल में बड़ा भवन जिसके साथ ज़मीन लगी हो, ज़मींदार का घर, सामंत-भवन

**manpower** /ˈmænpaʊə(r) ˈमैन्पाउअ(र्) / *noun* [U] the people that you need to do a particular job किसी काम को करने के लिए अपेक्षित व्यक्ति या लोग; श्रमशक्ति *There is a shortage of skilled manpower in the computer industry.*

**mansion** /ˈmænʃn ˈमैन्श्न् / *noun* [C] a very large house बड़ा भवन, कोठी, हवेली

**manslaughter** /ˈmænslɔːtə(r) ˈमैन्स्लॉट(र्) / *noun* [U] the crime of killing sb without intending to do so अनजाने में की ग़ैर-इरादतन मानव-हत्या ➪ **murder** देखिए।

**mantelpiece** /ˈmæntlpiːs ˈमैन्ट्ल्पीस् / *noun* [C] a narrow shelf above the space in a room where a fire goes कमरे में चिमनी वाली अँगीठी पर बनी ताक

**mantle** /ˈmæntl ˈमैन्ट्ल्/ *noun* [*sing.*] (in geology) the part of the earth between the surface (**crust**) and the centre (**core**) (भूविज्ञान में) भूमि के मध्य बिंदु और सतह के बीच का भू-अंश ➪ **seismic** पर चित्र देखिए।

**mantra** *noun* [C] **1** a word or a prayer that is chanted or sung शब्द या प्रार्थना जिसका जाप किया जाता है या गाया जाता है; मंत्र *Gayatri mantra* **2** a commonly repeated word or phrase साधारणतया दोहराया गया शब्द या वाक्यांश; मंत्र *Today's self-help books usually carry the magic mantra 'easy-to-follow'.*

**manual¹** /ˈmænjuəl ˈमैन्युअल्/ *adj.* using your hands; operated by hand जिसमें हाथों का प्रयोग हो; हस्त-चालित *Office work can sometimes be more tiring than **manual work**. ○ a skilled manual worker ○ Does your car have a manual or an automatic gear box?* ▶ **manually** *adv.* हाथ या हाथों से

**manual²** /ˈmænjuəl ˈमैन्युअल्/ *noun* [C] a book that explains how to do or operate sth किसी वस्तु को परिचालित करने का तरीक़ा बताने वाली पुस्तक; परिचालन-निर्देशपुस्तिका *a training manual ○ a car manual*

**manufacture** /ˌmænjuˈfæktʃə(r) ˌमैन्युˈफ़ैक्च(र्)/ *verb* [T] to make sth in large quantities using machines मशीनों द्वारा बड़ी मात्रा में कुछ बनाना; निर्माण, उत्पादन करना *a local factory that manufactures furniture ○ manufacturing industries* ✪ पर्याय **produce** ▶ **manufacture** *noun* [U] निर्माण, उत्पादन *The manufacture of chemical weapons should be illegal.*

**manufacturer** /ˌmænjuˈfæktʃərə(r) ˌमैन्युˈफ़ैक्चर(र्)/ *noun* [C] a person or company that makes sth उत्पादन या निर्माण करने वाला व्यक्ति या कंपनी, उत्पादक, निर्माता *a car manufacturer*

**manure** /məˈnjʊə(r) मˈन्युअ(र्)/ *noun* [U] the waste matter from animals that is put on the ground in order to make plants grow better गोबर की खाद ➪ **fertilizer** देखिए।

**manuscript** /ˈmænjuskrɪpt ˈमैन्युस्क्रिप्ट्/ *noun* [C] **1** a copy of a book, piece of music, etc. before it has been printed पुस्तक, संगीत-रचना आदि की पांडुलिपि या मुद्रण-पूर्व प्रति **2** a very old book or document that was written by hand हस्तलिखित अति प्राचीन ग्रंथ या दस्तावेज़

**many** /ˈmeni ˈमेनि/ *det., pronoun* (*used with plural nouns or verbs*) **1** a large number of people or things लोगों या वस्तुओं की बड़ी संख्या, बहुत सारे, अनेक *Have you made many friends at school yet? ○ There are **too many** mistakes in this essay.*

NOTE सकारात्मक वाक्यों में **many** का प्रयोग काफ़ी औपचारिक लगता है—*Many schools teach computing nowadays.* अनौपचारिक भाषण या लेखन में प्रायः **a lot of** का प्रयोग होता है—*A lot of schools teach computing nowadays.* तथापि नकारात्मक वाक्यों और प्रश्नों में **many** का हमेशा प्रयोग हो सकता है और वह औपचारिक भी नहीं लगता—*I don't know many cheap places to eat. ○ Are there many hotels in this town?*

**2** used to ask about the number of people or things, or to refer to a known number लोगों या वस्तुओं की संख्या के बारे में पूछने के लिए या किसी ज्ञात संख्या का निर्देश करने के लिए प्रयुक्त *I don't work **as many** hours as you. ○ There are **half/twice as many** boys as girls in the class.* **3** (*used to form compound adjectives*) having a lot of the thing mentioned जिसमें निर्दिष्ट वस्तु बड़ी मात्रा में हो, अनेक (कोणों) वाला, बहु (कोणीय) *a many-sided shape* **4 many a** (*formal*) (*used with a singular noun and verb*) a large number of की बड़ी संख्या, अनेक *I've heard him say that many a time.*

IDM **a good/great many** very many बहुत ही ज़्यादा

**Maori** /ˈmaʊri ˈमाउरि/ *noun* [C] (*pl.* **Maori** or **Maoris**) a member of the race of people who were the original inhabitants of New Zealand माओरी, न्यूज़ीलैंड के मूल निवासियों की जाति, माओरी जाति का सदस्य ▶ **Maori** *adj.* माओरी-संबंधित

**map** /mæp ˈमैप्/ *noun* [C] a drawing or plan of (part of) the surface of the earth that shows countries, rivers, mountains, roads, etc. पृथ्वी का मानचित्र या नक़्शा जिस पर विभिन्न देश नदियाँ, पहाड़, सड़कें आदि दिखाई जाती हैं *a road/street map ○ I can't find Chattisgarh **on the map**.* NOTE मानचित्रों या नक़्शों की पुस्तक को **atlas** कहते हैं। ▶ **map** *verb* [T] (**mapping; mapped**) मानचित्र में दिखाना *The region is so remote it has not yet been mapped.*

**maple** /ˈmeɪpl ˈमेप्ल्/ *noun* [C] a tree that has leaves with five points and that produces a very sweet liquid that is **edible** पंचकोण पत्तों वाला एक वृक्ष जिसमें से खाने योग्य बहुत मीठा द्रव निकलता है, मैपिल *maple syrup*

**Mar.** *abbr.* March मार्च *17 Mar. 1956*

**marathon** /ˈmærəθən ˈमैरथन्/ *noun* [C] **1** a long-distance running race, in which people run about 42 kilometres or 26 miles लगभग 42 किलोमीटर या 26 मील की एक लंबी दूरी की दौड़ स्पर्धा; मैराथन **2** an activity that lasts much longer than expected आशा से अधिक देर तक चलने वाली क्रिया *The interview was a real marathon.*

**marble** /ˈmɑːbl ˈमाब्ल्/ *noun* **1** [U] a hard attractive stone that is used to make statues and parts of buildings संगमरमर *a marble statue* **2** [C] a small ball of coloured glass that children play with बच्चों के खेलने का रंगबिरंगा कंचा **3 marbles** [U] the children's game that you play by rolling marbles along the ground trying to hit other marbles बच्चों का कंचों का खेल

**March** /mɑːtʃ माच्/ *noun* [U, C] (*abbr.* **Mar.**) the third month of the year, coming after February वर्ष का तीसरा महीना; मार्च

> **NOTE** महीनों के नामों के वाक्य-प्रयोग विधि के लिए **January** पर नोट और उदाहरण देखिए।

**march¹** /mɑːtʃ माच्/ *verb* **1** [I] to walk with regular steps (like a soldier) (सैनिक के समान) क़दम से क़दम मिलाते हुए चलना, मार्च करना *The President saluted as the troops marched past.* **2** [I] to walk in a determined way दृढ़ निश्चय के साथ चलना *She marched up to the manager and demanded an apology.* **3** [T] to make sb walk or march somewhere किसी को चलाते या मार्च कराते हुए कहीं ले जाना *The prisoner was marched away.* **4** [I] to walk in a large group to protest about sth किसी बात के विरोध में जुलूस बना कर चलना, जुलूस में मार्च करना *The demonstrators marched through the centre of town.*

**march²** /mɑːtʃ माच्/ *noun* [C] **1** an organized walk by a large group of people who are protesting about sth किसी बात के विरोध में जुलूस का संगठित प्रयाण या मार्च *a peace march* ➪ **demonstration** देखिए। **2** a journey made by marching मार्च करते हुए यात्रा *The soldiers were tired after their long march.*

**mare** /meə(r) मेअ(र्)/ *noun* [C] a female horse घोड़ी ➪ **horse** पर नोट देखिए।

**marg** *noun* (*IndE*) a path, way or road रास्ता, पथ या सड़क *Mahatama Gandhi Marg*

**margarine** /ˌmɑːdʒəˈriːn ˌमाजˈरीन्/ *noun* [U] a food that is similar to butter, made of animal or vegetable fats पशु या वनस्पति की वसा से बना मक्खन जैसा खाद्य पदार्थ, कृत्रिम मक्खन; मार्जरीन

**margin** /ˈmɑːdʒɪn ˈमाजिन्/ *noun* [C] **1** the empty space at the side of a page in a book, etc. पुस्तक आदि के पृष्ठ पर किनारे की ख़ाली जगह; हाशिया **2** [*sing.*] the amount of space, time, votes, etc. by which you win sth (सामान्यतः) अंतर, समय, वोट आदि की मात्रा जितने से विजय मिली हो *He won by a wide/narrow/comfortable margin.* **3** the amount of profit that a company makes on sth कंपनी द्वारा अर्जित लाभ की मात्रा **4** the area around the edge of sth किसी चीज़ के किनारे का चारों तरफ़ का स्थान; सीमांत, उदांत *the margins of the Pacific Ocean* **5** (*usually sing.*) an amount of space, time, etc. that is more than you need स्थान, समय आदि की मात्रा जो आवश्यकता से अधिक हो, अतिरेक स्थान समय आदि; गुंजाइश *It is a complex operation with little* ***margin for error***.

**marginal** /ˈmɑːdʒɪnl ˈमाजिन्ल्/ *adj.* small in size or importance जिसका आकार या महत्त्व कम हो; गौण, मामूली, हाशिए पर *The differences are marginal.* ▶ **marginally** *adv.* मामूली रूप से *In most cases costs will increase only marginally.*

**marigold** /ˈmærigəʊld ˈमैरिगोल्ड्/ *noun* [C] a plant of the daisy family, also known as calendula, with bright yellow or orange flowers गेंदा

**marijuana** /ˌmærəˈwɑːnə ˌमैरˈवाना/ *noun* [U] a drug that is smoked and is illegal in many countries गाँजे जैसा नशीला पदार्थ जो अनेक देशों में ग़ैर-क़ानूनी है

**marina** /məˈriːnə मˈरीना/ *noun* [C] a small area of water (**a harbour**) designed for pleasure boats बंदरगाह के पास (मनोरजंन) नौका विहार के लिए छोटा जल-क्षेत्र; मैरीना

**marinade** /ˌmærɪˈneɪd ˌमैरिˈनेड्/ *noun* [C, U] a mixture of oil, spices, etc. which you leave meat or fish in for a long time before it is cooked in order to make it softer or give it a particular flavour मांस-मछली पकाने में प्रयुक्त तेल, मसालों आदि का मिश्रण; मैरिनेड (पकाने से पहले इस मिश्रण में मांस-मछली को देर तक रखते हैं ताकि वह नरम हो जाए और पकने पर ख़ास स्वाद दे)

**marinate** /ˈmærɪneɪt ˈमैरिनेट्/ (*also* **marinade**) *verb* [I, T] if you marinate food or it marinates, you leave it in a mixture of oil, spices, etc. (**a marinade**) for a long time before it is cooked in order to make it softer or give it a particular flavour मैरिनेट; मांस-मछली को पकाने से पूर्व मैरिनेड में डालकर देर तक रखना (ताकि वह नरम हो जाए और पकाने पर ख़ास स्वाद दे)

**marine¹** /məˈriːn मˈरीन्/ *adj.* **1** connected with the sea समुद्र से संबंधित; समुद्री *the study of marine life* **2** connected with ships or sailing जहाज़ों या समुद्र-यात्रा से संबंधित, जहाज़ों या समुद्र-यात्रा विषयक *marine insurance*

**marine²** /məˈriːn मˈरीन्/ *noun* [C] a soldier who has been trained to fight on land or at sea ज़मीन या समुद्र में लड़ने के लिए प्रशिक्षित सैनिक, थलसैनिक या नौसैनिक

**marital** /ˈmærɪtl ˈमैरिट्ल्/ *adj.* (*only before a noun*) connected with marriage विवाह-संबंधी, वैवाहिक *marital problems*

**marital status** *noun* [U] (*written*) (used on official documents) if you are married, single, divorced, etc. व्यक्ति की वैवाहिक स्थिति (विवाहित, अविवाहित, तलाक़शुदा, आदि होने का तथ्य जिसका उल्लेख आधिकारिक दस्तावेज़ों में किया जाता है

**maritime** /ˈmærɪtaɪm ˈमैरिटाइम्/ *adj.* connected with the sea or ships समुद्र या जहाज़ों से संबंधित; समुद्री या जहाज़ी

**mark[1]** /mɑːk माक्/ *noun* [C] **1** a spot or line that spoils the appearance of sth निशान या लकीर (जिससे किसी की शकल बिगड़ जाए) *There's a dirty mark on the front of your shirt.* ○ *If you put a hot cup down on the table it will **leave a mark**.* ➪ **birth mark** देखिए। **2** something that shows who or what sb/sth is, especially by making him/her/it different from others किसी की पहचान का निशान (जिससे वह औरों से अलग लगे) *My horse is the one with the white mark on its face.* **3** a written or printed symbol that is a sign of sth किसी बात का संकेत करने वाला लिखित या मुद्रित चिह्न *a question/punctuation/exclamation mark* **4** a sign of a quality or feeling गुणवत्ता या मनोभाव का प्रतीक *They stood in silence for two minutes as **a mark of respect**.* **5** a number or letter you get for school work that tells you how good your work was स्कूल-कार्य आदि में प्राप्त अंक *She got very good marks in the exam.* ○ *The **pass mark** is 60 out of 100.* **6** the level or point that sth/sb has reached वह स्तर या बिंदु जहाँ कोई व्यक्ति या वस्तु पहुँचे *The race is almost at the half-way mark.* **7** an effect that people notice and will remember लोगों के ध्यान को आकृष्ट करने वाला स्मरणीय प्रभाव *The time he spent in prison **left** its **mark on** him.* ○ *He was only eighteen when he first **made** his **mark** in politics.* **8** a particular model or type of sth किसी वस्तु का विशेष माडल या टाइप *the new SL 53 Mark III*

> **NOTE** ध्यान रखिए **mark** का प्रयोग, स्वयं वस्तु या उसकी निर्माता कंपनी के लिए नहीं हो सकता। इसके लिए उपयुक्त शब्द है **brand** या **make**—*What make is your car?* ○ *What brand of coffee do you buy?*

**9** (*formal*) a person or an object towards which sth is directed; a target व्यक्ति या वस्तु जिसकी ओर कुछ प्रेषित किया जाए; लक्ष्य *the arrow hit/missed its mark* ○ *His judgement of the situation is **wide of the mark*** (= wrong). **10** the unit of money in Germany जर्मनी की मुद्रा, मार्क

**IDM on your marks, get set, go!** used at the start of a sports race दौड़-स्पर्धा को आरंभ कराने के लिए प्रयुक्त वाक्य

**quick, slow, etc. off the mark** quick, slow, etc. in reacting to a situation किसी परिस्थिति के प्रभाव का फुरती या सुस्ती से सामना करना

**mark[2]** /mɑːk माक्/ *verb* [T] **1** to put a sign on sth किसी वस्तु पर कोई निशान लगाना *We marked the price on all items in the sale.* ○ *I'll mark all the boxes I want you to move.* **2** to spoil the appearance of sth by making a mark on it किसी वस्तु पर निशान लगाकर उसे गंदा कर देना या विरूप कर देना *The white walls were dirty and marked.* **3** to show where sth is or where sth happened किसी वस्तु या घटना का स्थान दर्शाना *The route is marked in red.* **4** to celebrate or officially remember an important event किसी महत्त्वपूर्ण अवसर को समारोह-पूर्वक मनाना *The ceremony marked the fiftieth anniversary of the opening of the school.* **5** to be a sign that sth new is going to happen कुछ नया होने का संकेत होना *This decision marks a change in government policy.* **6** to look at sb's school, etc. work, show where there are mistakes and give it a number or letter to show how good it is छात्रों या परीक्षार्थियों के उत्तर पत्रों का मूल्यांकन करना (नंबर देते हुए) *Why did you mark that answer wrong?* ○ *He has fifty exam papers to mark.* **7** (in sport) to stay close to a player of the opposite team so that he/she cannot play easily (खेल में) विरोधी खिलाड़ी के साथ चिपके रहना (ताकि वह खुलकर न खेल सके)

**IDM mark sb/sth down as/for sth** to decide that sb/sth is of a particular type or suitable for a particular use किसी व्यक्ति या वस्तु को किसी विशेष रूप में या काम के लिए चिह्नित करना *From the first day of school, the teachers marked Varun down as a troublemaker.*

**mark sth out** to draw lines to show the position of sth किसी वस्तु के स्थान-निर्धारण के लिए निशान लगाना *Spaces for each car were marked out in the car park.*

**mark sth up/down** to increase/decrease the price of sth that you are selling बिक्री के माल के दाम घटाना या बढ़ाना *All goods have been marked down by 15 per cent.*

**marked** /mɑːkt माक्ट्/ *adj.* clear; noticeable स्पष्ट; उल्लेखनीय *There has been a marked increase in vandalism in recent years.* ▶ **markedly** /ˈmɑːkɪdli ˈमाकिड्लि/ *adv.* स्पष्टतया, उल्लेखनीय रूप से *This years sales have risen markedly.*

**marker** /ˈmɑːkə(r) ˈमाक(र्)/ *noun* [C] something that shows the position of sth किसी वस्तु की स्थिति को चिह्नित करने वाला; मार्कर *I've highlighted the important sentences with a marker pen.* ➪ **stationery** पर चित्र देखिए।

**market**[1] /ˈmɑːkɪt ˈमाकिट्/ *noun* **1** [C] a place where people go to buy and sell things बाज़ार, मार्केट (जहाँ वस्तुएँ बिकती और ख़रीदी जाती हैं) *a market stall/trader/town ○ a cattle/fish/meat market* ➪ **flea market, hypermarket** और **supermarket** देखिए। **2** [C] business or commercial activity; the amount of buying or selling of a particular type of goods व्यापारिक या वाणिज्यिक गतिविधि; विशेष प्रकार के माल की ख़रीद-फ़रोख़्त (की मात्रा) *The company currently has a 10 per cent share of the market. ○ the property/job market* **3** [C, U] a country, an area or a group of people that buys sth; the number of people who buy sth देश, भूक्षेत्र या व्यक्ति-समूह जिनमें माल की खपत हो सके; ख़रीदारों की पर्याप्त संख्या, मार्केट *The company is hoping to expand into the European Market. ○ There's no market for very large cars when petrol is so expensive.* ➪ **black market** और **stock market** देखिए।

IDM **on the market** available to buy ख़रीदने के लिए उपलब्ध, बाज़ार में (उपलब्ध) *This is one of the best cameras on the market.*

**market**[2] /ˈmɑːkɪt ˈमाकिट्/ *verb* [T] to sell sth with the help of advertising विज्ञापन द्वारा माल बेचना *The car company is trying to market a petrol car.*

**marketable** /ˈmɑːkɪtəbl ˈमाकिटबल्/ *adj.* that can be sold easily because people want it जिसे बेचना आसान हो (माँग के कारण)

**market day** *noun* [C, U] the day of the week when a town usually has a market सप्ताह का वह दिन जब बस्ती में बाज़ार लगता है, बाज़ार का दिन *All the farmers come to town on market day.*

**market garden** *noun* [C] a type of farm where vegetables and fruit are grown for sale बिक्री के लिए सब्ज़ियाँ और फल उगाने वाला फ़ार्म

**marketing** /ˈmɑːkɪtɪŋ ˈमाकिटिङ्/ *noun* [U] the activity of showing and advertising a company's products in the best possible way किसी कंपनी के माल को सर्वोत्तम रीति से प्रदर्शित और विज्ञापित करना *Effective marketing will lead to increased sales. ○ the marketing department*

**marketing mix** *noun* [C] (*technical*) the combination of things that a company decides to try in order to persuade people to buy a product बिक्री बढ़ाने का फ़ार्मुला-मिश्रण

**market place** *noun* **1 the market place** [*sing.*] the activity of competing with other companies to buy and sell goods, services, etc. माल, सेवाएँ आदि की ख़रीद-फ़रोख़्त में कंपनियों के बीच प्रतिस्पर्धा का स्थल **2** [C] the place in a town where a market is held बस्ती में बाज़ार लगने का स्थान

**market price** *noun* [C] the price that people in general will pay for sth at a particular time (किसी वस्तु का) बाज़ार-भाव (समय विशेष में कोई वस्तु किस दर पर बिक रही है)

**market research** *noun* [U] the study of what people want to buy and why ख़रीदारी की प्रवृत्तियों का अध्ययन *to carry out/do market research*

**market town** *noun* [C] a town that has a regular market, or that had one in the past वह बस्ती जिसमें बाक़ायदा बाज़ार हो या पहले कभी था

**marking** /ˈmɑːkɪŋ ˈमाकिङ्/ *noun* [C, *usually pl.*] shapes, lines and patterns of colour on an animal or a bird, or painted on a road, vehicle, etc. किसी पशु या पक्षी पर या सड़क, वाहन आदि पर बनी रंगीन आकार, रेखाएँ और आकृतियाँ

**marksman** /ˈmɑːksmən ˈमाक्स्मन्/ *noun* [C] (*pl.* **-men** /-mən -मन्/) a person who can shoot very well with a gun (बढ़िया) निशानेबाज़, लक्ष्यवेधी

**mark-up** *noun* [C, *usually sing.*] the difference between the cost of producing sth and the price it is sold at किसी वस्तु के लागत-मूल्य और बिक्री-मूल्य में अंतर

**marmalade** /ˈmɑːməleɪd ˈमामलेड्/ *noun* [U] a type of jam that is made from oranges or lemons संतरों या नीबुओं का मुरब्बा

**maroon** /məˈruːn मˈरून्/ *adj., noun* [U] (of) a dark brownish-red colour गहरे भूरे-लाल रंग का, गहरा भूरा-लाल; करौंदिया

**marooned** /məˈruːnd मˈरून्ड्/ *adj.* in a place that you cannot leave किसी स्थान पर अवरुद्ध *The sailors were marooned on a desert island.*

**marquee** /mɑːˈkiː माˈकी/ *noun* [C] a very large tent that is used for parties, shows, etc. पार्टियों, कार्यक्रमों आदि के लिए प्रयुक्त बहुत बड़ा टेंट या तंबू; शामियाना

**marriage** /ˈmærɪdʒ ˈमैरिज्/ *noun* **1** [C, U] the state of being husband and wife पति-पत्नी होने की स्थिति; विवाह, शादी *a happy marriage* **2** [C] a wedding ceremony विवाह-संस्कार *The marriage took place at a registry office in Delhi.* ➪ **wedding** पर नोट देखिए।

**married** /ˈmærid ˈमैरिड्/ *adj.* **1 married (to sb)** having a husband or wife विवाहित *a married man/woman/couple ○ They're planning to* ***get***

*married* in the summer. ✪ विलोम **unmarried** या **single** 2 (*only before a noun*) connected with marriage विवाह-संबंधी; वैवाहिक *How do you like married life?*

**marrow** /ˈmærəʊ मैरो/ *noun* 1 [C, U] a large vegetable with green skin that is white inside कुम्हड़ा, लौकी जैसी तरकारी 2 = **bone marrow**

**marry** /ˈmæri ˈमैरि/ *verb* (*pres. part.* **marrying;** *3rd person sing. pres.* **marries;** *pt, pp* **married**) 1 [I, T] to take sb as your husband or wife विवाह करना, किसी को पति या पत्नी के रूप में ग्रहण करना *They married when they were very young.*

NOTE **Marry** की अपेक्षा **get married (to sb)** अधिक प्रचलित है—*When are Shikha and Shekhar getting married?* ○*They got married in 2000.*

2 [T] to join two people together as husband and wife दो व्यक्तियों को पति-पत्नी के रूप में मिला देना, (दो व्यक्तियों का) विवाह कराना *We asked the local priest to marry us.* ➪ **marriage** noun देखिए।

**Mars** /mɑːz माज़्/ *noun* [*sing.*] the red planet, that is fourth in order from the sun मंगल ग्रह (जो क्रम में सूर्य से चौथे स्थान पर है) ➪ **Martian** देखिए तथा **the solar system** पर चित्र देखिए।

**marsh** /mɑːʃ माश्/ *noun* [C, U] an area of soft wet land दलदल, कछार प्रदेश ▶ **marshy** *adj.* दलदल वाला, कछारी

**marshal** /ˈmɑːʃl ˈमाश्ल्/ *noun* [C] 1 a person who helps to organize or control a large public event किसी बड़े सार्वजनिक कार्यक्रम को संगठित या नियंत्रित करने में सहायक व्यक्ति; मार्शल *Marshals are directing traffic in the car park.* 2 (*AmE*) an officer of a high level in the police or fire department or in a court of law पुलिस, अग्निशमन विभाग या न्यायालय में एक उच्चपद का अधिकारी; मार्शल

**marsupial** /mɑːˈsuːpiəl माˈसूपिअल्/ *noun* [C] any Australian animal that carries its baby in a pocket of skin (**pouch**) on the mother's stomach कोई भी ऑस्ट्रेलियाई पशु जिसमें मादा अपने बच्चे को पेट पर लगी थैली में ले जाती हैं, शिशुधानी वाले पशु *Kangaroos are marsupials.* ▶ **marsupial** *adj.* शिशुधानी वाले पशुओं से संबंधित

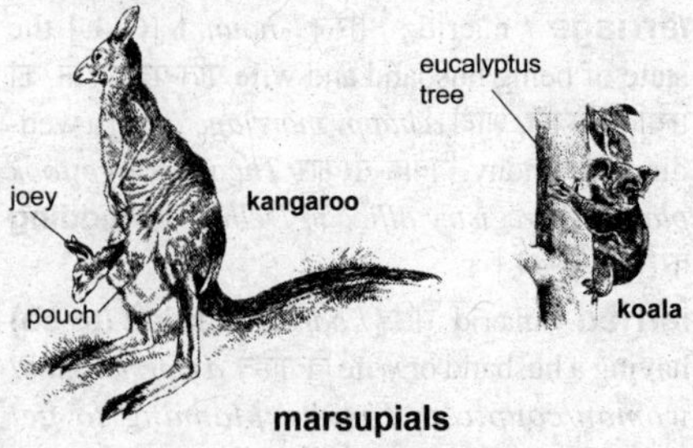

**marsupials**

**martial** /ˈmɑːʃl ˈमाश्ल्/ *adj.* (*formal*) connected with war युद्ध-संबंधी, सामरिक

**martial arts** *noun* [*pl.*] fighting sports such as **karate** or **judo** in which you use your hands and feet as weapons कराटे या जूडो जैसे युद्धात्मक खेल जिसमें खिलाड़ी के हाथ-पैर ही उसके अस्त्र होते हैं

**martial law** *noun* [U] a situation in which the army of a country instead of the police controls an area during a time of trouble किसी देश के संकट-काल में पुलिस के स्थान पर सेना द्वारा स्थिति पर नियंत्रण; सैनिक शासन, फ़ौजी क़ानून, मार्शल लॉ *The city remains under martial law.*

**Martian** /ˈmɑːʃn ˈमाशन्/ *noun* [C] (in stories) a creature that comes from the planet Mars (कथाओं में) मंगल ग्रह का प्राणी

**martyr** /ˈmɑːtə(r) ˈमाट(र्)/ *noun* [C] 1 a person who is killed because of what he/she believes अपने विश्वासों के कारण आत्मबलिदान करने वाला व्यक्ति; शहीद, बलिदानी 2 a person who tries to make people feel sorry for him/her लोगों की सहानुभूति अर्जित करने के लिए प्रयत्नशील व्यक्ति *Don't be such a martyr! You don't have to do all the housework.* ▶ **martyrdom** /ˈmɑːtədəm ˈमाटडम्/ *noun* [U] बलिदान, शहादत

**marvel** /ˈmɑːvl ˈमाव़्ल्/ *noun* [C] a person or thing that is wonderful or that surprises you स्वयं अद्भुत या दूसरों को चकित कर देने वाला व्यक्ति या वस्तु; चमत्कार, चमत्कारी व्यक्ति या वस्तु *the marvels of modern technology* ▶ **marvel** *verb* [I] (**marvelling; marvelled** *AmE* **marveling; marveled**) (*formal*) **marvel (at sth)** (किसी बात पर) अत्यंत आश्चर्यचकित होना *We marvelled at how much they had managed to do.*

**marvellous** (*AmE* **marvelous**) /ˈmɑːvələs ˈमाव़लस्/ *adj.* very good; wonderful बहुत बढ़िया; आश्चर्यजनक *a marvellous opportunity* ▶ **marvellously** (*AmE* **marvelously**) *adv.* आश्चर्यजनक रूप से

**Marxism** /ˈmɑːksɪzəm ˈमाक्सिज़म्/ *noun* [U] the political and economic thought of Karl Marx कार्ल मार्क्स के राजनीतिक और आर्थिक विचार; मार्क्सवाद ➪ **communism, socialism** और **capitalism** देखिए। ▶ **Marxist** *noun* [C], *adj.* मार्क्सवादी *Marxist ideology*

**marzipan** /ˈmɑːzɪpæn ˈमाज़िपैन्/ *noun* [U] a food that is made of sugar, egg and **almonds**. Marzipan is used to make sweets or to put on cakes शक्कर, अंडा और बादाम से बना खाद्य पदार्थ (जिसे अन्य मिठाइयों में डाला जाता है, या केक पर लगाया जाता है)

**masc** *abbr.* masculine पुल्लिंग

**mascara** /mæˈskɑːrə मैˈस्कारा/ *noun* [U] a beauty product that is used to make the hairs around your eyes (**eyelashes**) dark and attractive बरौनियों का अंजन, बरौनियाँ रँगने की प्रसाधन

**mascot** /ˈmæskət; -skɒt ˈमैस्कट्; -स्कॉट्/ *noun* [C] a person, animal or thing that is thought to bring good luck सौभाग्यप्रद माने जाने वाला व्यक्ति, पशु या वस्तु; शुभंकर

**masculine** /ˈmæskjəlɪn ˈमैस्क्यलिन्/ *adj.* 1 typical of or looking like a man; connected with men पुरुषोचित या पुरुष-सा दीखने वाला, मर्दाना; पुरुष-विषयक *a deep, masculine voice* ○ *Her short hair makes her look quite masculine.* ➪ **feminine** और **female** पर नोट देखिए। 2 (*abbr.* **masc**) (*grammar*) belonging to a class of words that refer to male people or animals and often have a special form नर प्राणियों के वाचक शब्दों से संबंधित जिसकी रूप रचना प्रायः विशेष होती है; पुंजातीय, पुरुष वाचक, पुल्लिंग *'He' is a masculine pronoun.* 3 (*abbr.* **masc**) (*grammar*) (in the grammar of some languages) belonging to a certain class of nouns, pronouns or adjectives (कुछ भाषाओं के व्याकरण में) संज्ञा शब्दों, सर्वनामों या विशेषणों के वर्ग विशेष से संबंधित *The French word for 'sun' is masculine.* ➪ **feminine** और **neuter** देखिए। ▶ **masculinity** /ˌmæskjuˈlɪnəti ˌमैस्क्युˈलिनटि/ *noun* [U] पुंसत्व, पुरुषत्व, मर्दानगी

**mash** /mæʃ मैश्/ *verb* [T] to mix or crush sth until it is soft वस्तुओं को मिलते-मिलाते या कुचल कर नरम बना देना *mashed potatoes*

**masjid** *noun* [C] = **mosque**

**mask¹** /mɑːsk मास्क्/ *noun* [C] something that you wear that covers your face or part of your face. People wear masks in order to hide or protect their faces or to make themselves look different. नक़ाब; चेहरे या चेहरे के अंश को ढकने वाला आवरण, मुखौटा (इसका प्रयोग चेहरे को छिपाने या बचाने या बदला हुआ दीखने के लिए होता है) ➪ **gas mask** और **goggles** देखिए।

**mask²** /mɑːsk मास्क्/ *verb* [T] 1 to cover or hide your face with a mask नक़ाब से चेहरा ढकना या छिपाना, नक़ाब पहनना *a masked gunman* 2 to hide a feeling, smell, fact, etc. मनोभाव, गंध, सचाई आदि को छिपाना *He masked his anger with a smile.*

**masochism** /ˈmæsəkɪzəm ˈमैसकिज़म्/ *noun* [U] the enjoyment of pain, or of what most people would find unpleasant पीड़ा या अप्रिय अनुभव में सुखानुभूति, कष्ट भोग-जन्य आनंद; स्वपीड़नरति *He swims in the sea even in winter—that's sheer masochism!* ➪ **sadism** देखिए। ▶ **masochist** /-kɪst -किस्ट्/ *noun* [C] कष्टभोग में सुख अनुभव करने वाला; स्वपीड़क ▶ **masochistic** /ˌmæsəˈkɪstɪk ˌमैसˈकिस्टिक्/ *adj.* कष्टभोगजन्य सुख से संबंधित, स्वपीड़न से संबंधित

**mason** /ˈmeɪsn ˈमेस्न्/ *noun* [C] 1 a person who makes things from stone राजमिस्तरी जो पत्थर का काम करता है 2 = **Freemason**

**masonry** /ˈmeɪsənri ˈमेसन्रि/ *noun* [U] the parts of a building that are made of stone किसी भवन के पत्थर से बने अंश; राजगीरी

**masquerade** /ˌmæskəˈreɪd; ˌmɑːsk- मैस्कˈरेड्; ˌमास्क्-/ *noun* [C] a way of behaving that hides the truth or sb's true feelings सत्य या सच्चे मनोभावों को छिपाने वाला आचरण ▶ **masquerade** *verb* [I] **masquerade as sth** छद्म आचरण करना, छंद्मवेश धारण करना *Two people, masquerading as doctors, knocked at the door and asked to see the child.*

**mass¹** /mæs मैस्/ *noun* 1 [C] **a mass (of sth)** a large amount or number of sth किसी वस्तु की बड़ी मात्रा या संख्या, पिंड, पुंज, ढेर *a dense mass of smoke* ○ (*informal*) *There were masses of people at the market today.* 2 **the masses** [*pl.*] ordinary people when considered as a political group जनसाधारण (राजनीतिक दृष्टि से) 3 [U] (in physics) the quantity of material that sth contains (भौतिकी में) किसी वस्तु में निहित सामग्री की मात्रा; भार, द्रव्यमान 4 **Mass** [C, U] the ceremony in some Christian churches when people eat bread and drink wine in order to remember the last meal that Christ had before he died ईसाई चर्च में आयोजित समारोह जिसमें लोग, मृत्यु से पहले ईसा के अंतिम भोजन की स्मृति में, डबल रोटी और मदिरा का सेवन करते हैं; मास *to go to Mass*

**mass²** /mæs मैस्/ *adj.* (*only before a noun*) involving a large number of people or things जिसमें बड़ी संख्या में लोग या वस्तुएँ सम्मिलित हों *a mass murderer*

**mass³** /mæs मैस्/ *verb* [I, T] to come together or bring people or things together in large numbers लोगों या वस्तुओं का बड़ी संख्या में इकट्ठा होना या उन्हें इकट्ठा करना *The students massed in the square.*

**massacre** /ˈmæsəkə(r) ˈमैसक(र्)/ *noun* [C] the killing of a large number of people or animals बड़ी संख्या में लोगों या पशुओं का मारा जाना; हत्याकांड, कत्लेआम ▶ **massacre** *verb* [T] बड़ी संख्या में हत्याएँ करना, हत्याकांड रचना या करना ➪ **kill** पर नोट देखिए।

**massage** /ˈmæsɑːʒ ˈमैसाश़्/ *noun* [C, U] the act of rubbing and pressing sb's body in order to reduce pain or to help him/her relax मालिश, अभ्यंजन *to give sb a massage* ▶ **massage** *verb* [T] की मालिश करना, अभ्यंजन करना

**massive** /ˈmæsɪv ˈमैसिव्/ *adj.* very big अत्यधिक, भारी-भरकम *a massive increase in prices* ✪ पर्याय **huge** ▶ **massively** *adv.* अत्यधिक

**mass media** *noun* [*pl.*] newspapers, television and radio that reach a large number of people अख़बार, टेलीविज़न और रेडियो जो विशाल जन-समुदाय तक पहुँचते हैं, जनसंचार-माध्यम, जनसंपर्क-माध्यम

**mass number** *noun* [C] (*technical*) the total number of **protons** and **neutrons** in an atom एक परमाणु में प्रोटोन्स और न्यूट्रोन्स की कुल संख्या

**mass-produce** *verb* [T] to make large numbers of similar things by machine in a factory कारख़ाने में मशीन द्वारा बड़े पैमाने पर एक ही प्रकार की वस्तुएँ बनाना *mass-produced goods* ▶ **mass production** *noun* [U] बड़े पैमाने पर उत्पादन

**mast** /mɑːst मास्ट्/ *noun* [C] **1** a tall wooden or metal pole for a flag, a ship's sails, etc. झंडे, जहाज़ के पाल आदि के लिए लंबा लकड़ी या धातु का डंडा; मस्तूल (जहाज़ का) ➪ **boat** पर चित्र देखिए। **2** a tall pole that is used for sending out radio or television signals रेडियो या टीवी के संकेत भेजने के लिए प्रयुक्त लंबा डंडा

**master[1]** /ˈmɑːstə(r) ˈमास्‌ट(र्)/ *noun* [C] **1** a person who has great skill at doing sth किसी काम में विशेष रूप से दक्ष व्यक्ति *a master builder* ○ *an exhibition of work by French masters* (= painters) **2** (*old-fashioned*) a male teacher (usually in a private school) पुरुष शिक्षक (प्रायः किसी प्राइवेट स्कूल में) *the chemistry master* **3** a film or tape from which copies can be made (मूल) फ़िल्म या टेप जिससे प्रतिलिपियाँ बन सकती हैं

**master[2]** /ˈmɑːstə(r) ˈमास्‌ट(र्)/ *verb* [T] **1** to learn how to do sth well किसी काम को अच्छे ढंग से करना सीखना *It takes a long time to master a foreign language.* **2** to control sth किसी पर नियंत्रण स्थापित करना *to master a situation*

**mastermind** /ˈmɑːstəmaɪnd ˈमास्‌टमाइन्ड्/ *noun* [C] a very clever person who has planned or organized sth किसी काम की योजना बनाने या सुव्यवस्थित करने में अति कुशल व्यक्ति; शातिर दिमाग़ *The mastermind behind the robbery was never caught.* ▶ **mastermind** *verb* [T] चतुराई से योजना बनाना *The police failed to catch the man who masterminded the robbery.*

**masterpiece** /ˈmɑːstəpiːs ˈमास्‌टपीस्/ *noun* [C] a work of art, music, literature, etc. that is of the highest quality कला, संगीत, साहित्य आदि की अतिश्रेष्ठ रचना

**Master's degree** (*also* **Master's**) *noun* [C] a second or higher university degree. You usually get a Master's degree by studying for one or two years after your first degree विश्वविद्यालय की दूसरी या उच्चतर उपाधि (जो पहली उपाधि के एक या दो वर्ष के अध्ययनोपरांत मिलती है), मास्टर उपाधि *Master of Arts* (*MA*) ○ *Master of Science* (*MSc*) ➪ **Bachelor's degree** देखिए।

**mastery** /ˈmɑːstəri ˈमास्‌टरि/ *noun* [U] **1 mastery (of sth)** great skill at doing sth किसी काम में उच्च दक्षता, किसी पर अधिकार *His mastery of the violin was quite exceptional for a child.* **2 mastery (of/over sb/sth)** control over sb/sth किसी व्यक्ति या वस्तु पर स्वामित्व या अधिकार *The battle was fought for mastery of the seas.*

**mat** /mæt मैट्/ *noun* [C] **1** a piece of carpet or other thick material that you put on the floor फ़र्श पर बिछाने का, ग़लीचे या किसी अन्य मोटी वस्तु का टुकड़ा; चटाई *a doormat* ➪ **rug** देखिए। **2** a small piece of material that you put under sth on a table मेज़ पर रखी वस्तु के नीचे रखा जाने वाला (चटाईनुमा) टुकड़ा; मैट *a table mat* ○ *a mouse mat*

**match[1]** /mætʃ मैच्/ *noun* **1** [C] a small stick of wood, cardboard, etc. that you use for starting a fire, lighting a cigarette, etc. दियासलाई, माचिस की तीली *to light/strike a match* ○ *a box of matches* **2** [C] an organized game or sports event कोई व्यवस्थित खेल या खेल-कूद कार्यक्रम; मैच *a tennis/football match* **3** [*sing.*] **a match for sb; sb's match** a person or thing that is as good as or better than sb/sth else किसी व्यक्ति या वस्तु के बराबर का अन्य व्यक्ति या वस्तु, बराबरी का जोड़ *Charu is no match for her mother when it comes to cooking* (= she doesn't cook as well as her mother). **4** [*sing.*] a person or thing that combines well with sb/sth else किसी व्यक्ति या वस्तु का जोड़ीदार अन्य व्यक्ति या वस्तु; जोड़ीदार *Raghav and Reena are a **perfect match** for each other.*

**match[2]** /mætʃ मैच्/ *verb* **1** [I, T] to have the same colour or pattern as sth else; to look good with sth else रंग या पैटर्न की दृष्टि से मेल खाना; दूसरी वस्तु के साथ अच्छा लगना या जमना *That shirt doesn't match your jacket.* **2** [T] to find sb/sth that is like or suitable for sb/sth else किसी व्यक्ति या वस्तु का जोड़ीदार ढूँढ़ना *The agency tries to match single people with suitable partners.* **3** [T] to be as good as or better than sb/sth else बराबर का या कुछ बेहतर होना *The two teams are very evenly matched.*

PHR V **match up** to be the same (दूसरे के) सदृश होना, एक जैसा होना *The statements of the two witnesses don't match up.*

**match sth up (with sth)** to fit or put sth together (with sth else) (किसी अन्य वस्तु के साथ) मेल बैठाना *What you have to do is match up each star with his or her pet.*

**match up to sb/sth** to be as good as sb/sth किसी व्यक्ति या वस्तु के अनुरूप होना *The film didn't match up to my expectations*

**matchbox** /ˈmætʃbɒks ˈमैचूबॉक्स्/ *noun* [C] a small box for matches माचिस की डिबिया

**matchstick** /ˈmætʃstɪk ˈमैचुस्टिक्/ *noun* [C] the thin wooden part of a match माचिस की तीली

**mate**[1] /meɪt मेट्/ *noun* [C] **1** (*informal*) a friend or sb you live, work or do an activity with मित्र या साथी, सहकार्यकर्ता *He's an old mate of mine.* ○ *a flatmate/classmate/team-mate/playmate* **2** (*BrE slang*) used when speaking to a man किसी पुरुष से बात करने में प्रयुक्त शब्द (प्रायः संबोधन) *Can you give me a hand, mate?* **3** one of a male and female pair of animals, birds, etc. पशुओं, पक्षियों आदि का नर या मादा साथी *The female sits on the eggs while her mate hunts for food.* **4** an officer on a ship जहाज़ पर नियुक्त एक अधिकारी; मेट

**mate**[2] /meɪt मेट्/ *verb* **1** [I] (used about animals and birds) to have sex and produce young (पशुओं और पक्षियों का) यौन-संसर्ग द्वारा संतानोत्पत्ति करना *Pandas rarely mate in zoos.* **2** [T] to bring two animals together so that they can mate यौन-संसर्ग के लिए दो युवा पशुओं को मिलाना ✪ पर्याय **breed**

**material**[1] /məˈtɪəriəl मˈटिअरिअल्/ *noun* **1** [C, U] a substance that can be used for making or doing sth कुछ बनाने या कुछ करने के लिए प्रयुक्त पदार्थ, सामग्री, माल, सामान *raw materials* ○ *writing/teaching/building materials* **2** [C, U] cloth (for making clothes, etc.) कपड़ा (पोशाक आदि बनाने के लिए) *Is there enough material for a dress?* **3** [U] facts or information that you collect before you write a book, article, etc. पुस्तक, लेख आदि लिखने के लिए संचित सामग्री (तथ्य या जानकारियाँ)

**material**[2] /məˈtɪəriəl मˈटिअरिअल्/ *adj.* **1** connected with real or physical things rather than the spirit or emotions भौतिक (न कि आध्यात्मिक या भावनात्मक) *We should not value material comforts too highly.* ➪ **spiritual** देखिए। **2** important and needing to be considered महत्त्वपूर्ण और विचारणीय *material evidence* **NOTE** इस अर्थ में यह शब्द (विशेष) प्रचलित नहीं है, परंतु **immaterial** देखिए। ▸ **materially** *adv.* भौतिकत्य से

**materialism** /məˈtɪəriəlɪzəm मˈटिअरिअलिज़म्/ *noun* [U] the belief that money and possessions are the most important things in life धन आदि भौतिक वस्तुओं को जीवन में सर्वाधिक महत्त्वपूर्ण मानने की प्रवृत्ति; भौतिकवाद ▸ **materialist** /-lɪst -लिस्ट्/ *noun* [C] भौतिकवादी ▸ **materialistic** /məˌtɪəriəˈlɪstɪk मˌटिअरिअˈलिस्टिक्/ *adj.* भौतिकवादी

**materialize** (*also* **-ise**) /məˈtɪəriəlaɪz मˈटिअरिअलाइज़्/ *verb* [I] to become real; to happen वास्तविकता बनना; घटित होना *The pay rise that they had promised never materialized.*

**maternal** /məˈtɜːnl मˈटर्नल्/ *adj.* **1** behaving as a mother would behave; connected with being a mother मातृ-सुलभ, माँ-जैसा; मातृत्व-विषयक *maternal love/instincts* **2** (*only before a noun*) related through your mother's side of the family परिवार में मातृ-पक्ष से संबंधित; ममेरा या ममेरी *your maternal grandfather* ➪ **paternal** देखिए।

**maternity** /məˈtɜːnəti मˈटनटि/ *adj.* connected with women who are going to have or have just had a baby आसन्न-प्रसवा या सद्यःप्रसूता माता से संबंधित; प्रसवा *maternity clothes* ○ *the hospital's maternity ward* ➪ **paternity** देखिए।

**mathematician** /ˌmæθəməˈtɪʃn ˌमैथम ˈटिश्न्/ *noun* [C] a person who studies or is an expert in mathematics गणितज्ञ

**mathematics** /ˌmæθəˈmætɪks ˌमैथ्ˈमैटिक्स्/ *noun* [U] the science or study of numbers, quantities or shapes गणितशास्त्र **NOTE** ब्रिटिश अंग्रेज़ी में संक्षिप्त है **maths** और अमेरिकी अंग्रेज़ी में **math**—*Maths/math is my favourite subject.* ➪ **Arithmetic, algebra** और **geometry** भी देखिए। ▸ **mathematical** /ˌmæθəˈmætɪkl ˌमैथ्ˈमैटिकल्/ *adj.* गणितीय *mathematical calculations* ▸ **mathematically** /ˌmæθəˈmætɪki ˌमैथ्ˈमैटिक्लि/ *adv.* गणित(शास्त्र) की दृष्टि से

**matinée** /ˈmætɪneɪ ˈमैटिने/ *noun* [C] an afternoon performance of a play, film, etc. किसी नाटक, फ़िल्म आदि का अपराह्नकालीन प्रदर्शन

**matriarch** /ˈmeɪtriɑːk ˈमेट्रिआक्/ *noun* [C] a woman who is the head of a family or social group किसी परिवार या सामाजिक समुदाय की प्रमुख महिला; कुलमाता ➪ **patriarch** देखिए।

**matriarchal** /ˌmeɪtriˈɑːkl ˌमेट्रिˈआकल्/ *adj.* (used about a society or system) controlled by women rather than men; passing power, property, etc. from mother to daughter rather than from father to son (समाज या उसकी व्यवस्था के लिए प्रयुक्त) महिलाओं द्वारा नियंत्रित (पुरुषों द्वारा नहीं), मातृसत्तात्मक; जिसमें परिवार की सत्ता, संपत्ति आदि माता से पुत्री के पास जाती है (न कि पिता से पुत्र के पास), मातृ-प्रधान ➪ **patriarchal** देखिए।

**matriarchy** /ˈmeɪtriɑːki ˈमेट्रिआकि/ *noun* [C, U] (*pl.* **matriarchies**) a social system that gives power and control to women rather than men सामाजिक व्यवस्था जिसमें परिवार की सत्ता और नियंत्रण महिलाओं के पास रहते हैं (न कि पुरुषों के पास), मातृ-सत्ता, मातृ-तंत्र ➪ **patriarchy** देखिए।

**matricide** /ˈmætrɪsaɪd ˈमैट्रिसाइड् / *noun* [U] (*formal*) the crime of killing your mother अपनी माँ की हत्या का अपराध, मातृ-हत्या, मातृघात ➪ **patricide** देखिए।

**matrimony** /ˈmætrɪməni ˈमैट्रिमनि / *noun* [U] (*formal*) the state of being married विवाहित होने की स्थिति, वैवाहिक जीवन; विवाह दांपत्यावस्था ▶ **matrimonial** /ˌmætrɪˈməʊniəl ˌमैट्रिˈमोनिअल् / *adj.* वैवाहिक

**matrix** /ˈmeɪtrɪks ˈमेट्रिक्स् / *noun* [C] (*pl.* **matrices** /ˈmeɪtrɪsiːz ˈमेट्रिसीज़्/) **1** (in mathematics) an arrangement of numbers, symbols, etc. in rows and columns, treated as a single quantity (गणित में) एकल राशि के रूप में गृहीत, संख्याओं, प्रतीकों आदि की पंक्तियों और स्तंभों में व्यवस्था; मैट्रिक्स **2** (*formal*) the social, political, etc. situation from which a society or person grows and develops सामाजिक, राजनीतिक आदि स्थिति जिससे समाज या व्यक्ति का संवर्धन और विकास होता है *the European cultural matrix* **3** (*formal*) a system of lines, roads, etc. that cross each other, forming a series of squares or shapes in between एक दूसरे को काटती और बीच-बीच में वर्गाकार या अन्य आकृतियाँ बनाती, रेखाओं, सड़कों आदि की व्यवस्था, जाल, तंत्र ✪ पर्याय **network** *a matrix of paths* **4** (*technical*) a **mould** in which sth is shaped किसी वस्तु को आकार विशेष देने के लिए प्रयुक्त साँचा **5** (*technical*) a mass of rock in which minerals, precious stones, etc. are found in the ground एक बड़ी चट्टान जिसके नीचे की ज़मीन में खनिज, रत्न आदि पाए जाते हैं, आधार-पत्थर

**matron** /ˈmeɪtrən मेट्रन् / *noun* [C] **1** (*old-fashioned*) a nurse who is in charge of the other nurses in a hospital नर्सों की अध्यक्ष नर्स, प्रधान नर्स; मेट्रन **2** a woman who works as a nurse in a school स्कूल में नर्स के रूप में काम करने वाली महिला, स्कूल में आवास-अधीक्षिका, स्कूल मेट्रन

**matt** (*AmE* **matte**) /mæt मैट् / *adj.* not shiny फीका, निष्प्रभ *This paint gives a matt finish.* ➪ **gloss** देखिए।

**matted** /ˈmætɪd ˈमैटिड् / *adj.* (used especially about hair) forming a thick mass, especially because it is wet and/or dirty (विशेषतः बालों के विषय में प्रयुक्त) उलझे हुए ढेर-सा (विशेषतः भीगा और/या गंदा होने के कारण)

**matter**[1] /ˈmætə(r) ˈमैट(र्) / *noun* **1** [C] a subject or situation that you must think about and give your attention to विचारणीय और ध्यान देने योग्य विषय या प्रसंग *Finding a job will be* ***no easy matter****.* ○ *to simplify/complicate matters* **2** [*sing.*] **the matter (with sb/sth)** the reason sb/sth has a problem or is not good मामला, बात समस्या या परेशानी *She looks sad.* ***What's the matter*** *with her?* ○ *There seems to be* ***something the matter*** *with the car.* **3** [U] all physical substances; a substance of a particular kind (सब प्रकार के) भौतिक पदार्थ; एक विशेष प्रकार की सामग्री *Matter is of three kinds—solids, liquid and gas.* **4** [U] the contents of a book, film, etc. पुस्तक, फ़िल्म आदि की विषय-वस्तु *I don't think the* ***subject matter*** *of this programme is suitable for children.*

IDM **a matter of hours, miles, etc.** used to say that sth is not very long, far, expensive, etc. यह कहने के लिए प्रयुक्त कि कोई वस्तु बहुत लंबी, दूर, महँगी आदि नहीं है *The fight lasted a matter of seconds.*

**a matter of life and/or death** extremely urgent and important अत्यधिक आवश्यक और महत्त्वपूर्ण, जीवन मृत्यु का प्रश्न

**another/a different matter** something much more serious, difficult, etc. कुछ और ही बात होना, अधिक गंभीर, कठिन आदि मामला होना *I can speak a little Japanese, but reading it is quite another matter.*

**as a matter of fact** to tell the truth; in reality सच तो यह है कि... ; वस्तुतः *I like him very much, as a matter of fact.*

**for that matter** as far as sth is concerned किसी स्थिति से संबंधित *Manav is really fed up with his course. I am too, for that matter.*

**to make matters/things worse** ➪ **worse** देखिए।

**a matter of course** something that you always do; the usual thing to do हमेशा किया जाने वाला काम; नियमित कार्रवाई *Goods leaving the factory are checked as a matter of course.*

**a matter of opinion** a subject on which people do not agree ऐसा मामला जिस पर प्रायः सभी लोग सहमत नहीं होते, अपनी-अपनी राय *'I think the government is doing a good job.' 'That's a matter of opinion.'*

**(be) a matter of sth/doing sth** a situation in which sth is needed ऐसी स्थिति जिसमें किसी बात की अपेक्षा हो *Learning a language is largely a matter of practice.*

**no matter who, what, where, etc.** whoever, whatever, wherever, etc. चाहे कुछ भी हो, किया या कहा जाए, आदि *They never listen no matter what you say.*

**matter**[2] /ˈmætə(r) ˈमैट(र्) / *verb* [I] **matter (to sb)** (*not used in the continuous tenses*) to be important महत्त्व की बात होना ***It doesn't*** *really* ***matter*** *how much it costs.*

**matter-of-fact** *adj.* said or done without showing any emotion, especially when it would seem more normal to express your feelings तथ्यात्मक; बिना भावुक हुए कहा या किया गया (विशेषतः जब भावुकता का प्रदर्शन अधिक स्वाभाविक होता) *He was very matter-of-fact about his illness.*

**mattress** /ˈmætrəs ˈमैट्रस्/ *noun* [C] a large soft thing that you lie on to sleep, usually put on a bed गद्दा

**mature** /məˈtʃʊə(r) मˈचुअ(र्)/ *adj.* **1** fully grown or fully developed पूर्णतया विकसित *a mature tree/bird/animal* **2** behaving in a sensible adult way बड़ों जैसा समझदारी का आचरण करने वाला; प्रौढ़, परिपक्व *Is she mature enough for such responsibility?* ✪ विलोम **immature** ▶ **mature** *verb* [I] परिपक्व होना *He matured a lot during his two years at college.* ▶ **maturity** /məˈtʃʊərəti मˈचुअरटि/ *noun* [U] परिपक्वता

**maul** /mɔːl मॉल्/ *verb* [T] (usually used about a wild animal) to attack and injure sb (किसी वन्य जीव का) किसी पर आक्रमण कर उसे घायल कर देना

**mauve** /məʊv मोव्/ *adj., noun* [U] (of) a pale purple colour फीके बैंगनी रंग का, कासनी रंग

**maverick** /ˈmævərɪk ˈमैव़रिक्/ *noun* [C] a person who does not behave or think like everyone else, but who has independent, unusual opinions औरों के समान न होकर, स्वतंत्र और अपने ढंग से सोचने वाला व्यक्ति, स्वतंत्रचेता व्यक्ति ▶ **maverick** *adj.* स्वतंत्रचेता

**max** /mæks मैक्स्/ *abbr.* maximum अधिकतम *max temp 21°C*

**maxim** /ˈmæksɪm ˈमैक्सिम्/ *noun* [C] a few words that express a rule for good or sensible behaviour सूक्ति, नीतिवचन सिद्धांतवाक्य, सूत्र *Our maxim is: 'If a job's worth doing, it's worth doing well.'*

**maximize** (*also* **-ise**) /ˈmæksɪmaɪz ˈमैक्सिमाइज़्/ *verb* [T] to increase sth as much as possible किसी वस्तु को अधिक से अधिक बढ़ाना *to maximize profits* ✪ विलोम **minimize**

**maximum** /ˈmæksɪməm ˈमैक्सिमम्/ *noun* [*sing.*] (*abbr.* **max**) the greatest amount or level of sth that is possible, allowed, etc. किसी वस्तु का यथासंभव अधिकतम परिमाण या स्तर *The bus can carry a maximum of 40 people.* ○ *That is the maximum we can afford.* ✪ विलोम **minimum** ▶ **maximum** *adj.* (*only before a noun*) अधिकतम *a maximum speed of 120 kilometres per hour*

**May** /meɪ मे/ *noun* [U, C] the fifth month of the year, coming after April वर्ष का पाँचवाँ महीना; मई

> NOTE महीनों के नामों के वाक्य-प्रयोग विधि के लिए **January** पर नोट और उदाहरण देखिए।

**may** /meɪ मे/ *modal verb* (*negative* **may not**) **1** used for saying that sth is possible यह बताने के लिए प्रयुक्त कि कोई बात संभव है। किसी बात के संभव होने का अर्थ व्यक्त करने के लिए प्रयुक्त *You may be right.* ○ *They may have forgotten the meeting.* **2** used as a polite way of asking for and giving permission अनुमति माँगने और देने के लिए प्रयुक्त शिष्ट शब्द *May I use your phone?* ○ *You may not take photographs in the museum.* **3** used for contrasting two facts दो सचाइयों में वैषम्य या विरोध दिखाने के लिए प्रयुक्त *He may be very clever but he can't do anything practical.* **4** (*formal*) used for expressing wishes and hopes इच्छाएँ और आशाओं को व्यक्त करने के लिए प्रयुक्त *May you both be very happy.*

> NOTE वृत्तिवाचक क्रियाओं (modal verbs) के विषय में अधिक जानकारी के लिए इस शब्दकोश के अंत में **Quick Grammar Reference** देखिए।

IDM **may/might as well (do sth)** ➪ **well**[1] देखिए।

**maybe** /ˈmeɪbi ˈमेबि/ *adv.* perhaps; possibly शायद, कदाचित; संभवतः *There were three, maybe four armed men.* ○ *Maybe I'll accept the invitation and maybe I won't.* ➪ **perhaps** पर नोट देखिए।

**May Day** *noun* [C] 1st May पहली मई (की तारीख़), मई दिवस

> NOTE पारंपरिक रूप से यूरोप में **May Day** को वसंतोत्सव के रूप में मनाया जाता है और कुछ देशों में श्रमिकों के सम्मान में श्रमिक दिवस के रूप में मनाया जाता है।

**mayonnaise** /ˌmeɪəˈneɪz ˌमेअˈनेज़्/ *noun* [U] a cold thick pale yellow sauce made with eggs and oil अंडों और तेल से बनी ठंडी गाढ़ी हलकी-पीली चटनी; मेयनेज़

**mayor** /meə(r) मेअ(र्)/ *noun* [C] a person who is elected to be the leader of the group of people (**a council**) who manage the affairs of a town or city मेयर, महापौर, नगर-प्रतिनिधियों की परिषद का चुना हुआ नेता

**mayoress** /meəˈres मेअˈरेस्/ *noun* [C] a woman mayor, or a woman who is married to or helps a mayor महिला मेयर या मेयर की पत्नी या उसकी सहायिका

**maze** /meɪz मेज़्/ *noun* [C] a system of paths which is designed to confuse you so that it is difficult to find your way out भूल-भुलैयाँ, रास्तों का ऐसा जाल जो भटका दे और बाहर निकलना कठिन हो जाए (*figurative*) *a maze of winding streets* ✪ पर्याय **labyrinth**

**MBA** /ˌem biː ˈeɪ ˌएम बी ˈए/ *abbr.* Master of Business Administration; an advanced university degree in business एम.बी.ए.; व्यापार-प्रबंधन की उच्च शैक्षिक उपाधि

**MBE** /ˌem biːˈiː ˌएम् बीˈई/ *noun* [C] the abbreviation for 'Member of the Order of the British Empire'; an honour given to some people in Britain because they have achieved something special (संक्षिप्त) एम. बी. ई., ब्रिटिश साम्राज्य व्यवस्था का सदस्य; (किसी क्षेत्र में) विशेष उपलब्धि के लिए ब्रिटेनवासी को दिया जाने वाला सम्मान *She was made an MBE in 2001.*

**MD** /ˌemˈdiː ˌएम्ˈडी/ *abbr.* Doctor of Medicine एम. डी., डॉक्टर ऑफ मेडिसिन

**me** /miː मी/ *pronoun* used by the speaker to refer to himself/herself कर्ता द्वारा स्वयं के लिए प्रयुक्त *He telephoned me yesterday.* ○ *She wrote to me last week.*

**meadow** /ˈmedəʊ ˈमेडो/ *noun* [C] a field of grass घास का मैदान, घास स्थली

**meagre** (*AmE* **meager**) /ˈmiːgə(r) ˈमीग(र्)/ *adj.* too small in amount बहुत कम, स्वल्प *a meagre salary*

**meal** /miːl मील्/ *noun* [C] the time when you eat or the food that is eaten at that time भोजन का समय या भोजन *Shall we **go out for a meal** on Friday?* ○ *a heavy/light meal*

> **NOTE** दिन के समय के मुख्य भोजन **breakfast, lunch** और **dinner** हैं। गौण भोजन हैं **tea** और **supper** (परंतु **dinner** पर नोट देख लीजिए)। इनके बीच के समय में जो खाया जाए वह **snack** है।

**IDM a square meal** ➪ **square²** देखिए।

**mealtime** /ˈmiːltaɪm ˈमील्टाइम्/ *noun* [C] the time at which a meal is usually eaten भोजन का समय

**mean¹** /miːn मीन्/ *verb* [T] (*pt, pp* **meant** /ment मेन्ट्/) **1** (*not used in the continuous tenses*) to express, show or have as a meaning अर्थ को व्यक्त करना, दिखाना या उससे युक्त होना ***What does** this word **mean?*** ○ *The bell means that the lesson has ended.*

> **NOTE** यद्यपि यह क्रिया सातत्यबोधक कालों (continuous tenses) में प्रयुक्त नहीं होती तथापि इसका -ing युक्त रूप वर्तमान कृदंत (present participle) रूप काफ़ी प्रचलित है—*The weather during filming was terrible, meaning that several scenes had to be reshot later.*

**2** to want or intend to say sth; to refer to sb/sth कुछ कहने की इच्छा या इरादा होना; किसी व्यक्ति या वस्तु का निर्देश करना *I only meant that I couldn't come tomorrow—any other day would be fine.* ○ ***I see what you mean**, but I'm afraid it's not possible.*

> **NOTE** **Mean** का प्रयोग कोई राय होने ('to have the opinion that') का अर्थ व्यक्त करने के लिए नहीं हो सकता। इसके लिए हम कहते हैं—*'I think that'* या *'In my opinion...' I think that she'd be silly to buy that car.*
> **I mean** का प्रयोग प्रायः बातचीत में तब होता है जब हम अपनी बात को समझाना चाहते हैं या उसमें कुछ और जोड़ना चाहते हैं—*What a terrible summer—I mean it's rained almost all the time.* **I mean** का प्रयोग अपनी बात की ग़लती को ठीक करने के लिए भी होता है—*We went there on Tuesday, I mean Thursday.*

**3** (*usually passive*) **mean (sb) to do sth; mean sth (as/for sth/sb); mean sb/sth to be sth** to intend sth; to be supposed to be/do sth कुछ इरादा होना; कोई बात होने या करने को मान लिया जाना *I'm sure she didn't mean to upset you.* ○ *She meant the present to be for both of us.* ○ *It was only meant as a joke.* ○ **4** to make sth likely; to cause किसी बात को संभावित बनाना; (किसी स्थिति का) कारण बनना *The shortage of teachers means that classes are larger.* **5 mean sth (to sb)** to be important to sb किसी के लिए महत्त्व की बात होना *This job means a lot to me.* ○ *Money means nothing to her.* **6** to be serious or sincere about sth किसी बात के प्रति गंभीर या सच्चा होना *He said he loved me but I don't think he meant it!*

**IDM be meant to be sth** to be considered or said to be sth किसी वस्तु को कुछ माना या कहा जाना *That restaurant is meant to be excellent.*

**mean well** to want to be kind and helpful but usually without success किसी का शुभ चाहना (परंतु प्रायः उसमें सफल न हो पाना) *My mother means well but I wish she'd stop treating me like a child.*

**mean²** /miːn मीन्/ *adj.* **1 mean (with sth)** wanting to keep money, etc. for yourself rather than let other people have it कंजूस, स्वार्थी *It's no good asking him for any money—he's much too mean.* ○ *They're mean with the food in the canteen.* **2 mean (to sb)** (used about people or their behaviour) unkind (व्यक्ति या व्यक्तियों का आचरण के लिए प्रयुक्त) संकुचित मनोवृत्ति वाला *It was mean of him not to invite you too.* **3** (*only before a noun*) average औसत *What is the mean annual temperature in Delhi?* ► **meanness** *noun* [U] कंजूसी, संकुचित मनोवृत्ति

**meander** /miˈændə(r) मिˈऐन्ड(र्)/ *verb* [I] **1** (used about a river, road, etc.) to have a lot of curves and bends (नदी, सड़क आदि का) काफ़ी टेढ़ा-मेढ़ा और घुमावदार होना **2** (used about a person or animal) to walk or travel slowly or without any definite direction (मनुष्य या पशु का) मंद गति से चलना या निरुद्देश्य घूमना-फिरना ► **meander** *noun* [C] मोड़, घुमाव *the meanders of a river* ➪ **oxbow** पर चित्र देखिए।

**meaning** /ˈmiːnɪŋ ˈमीनिङ्/ *noun* **1** [C, U] the thing or idea that sth represents; what sb is trying to communicate किसी(शब्द) के द्वारा निर्दिष्ट वस्तु या विचार; अर्थ, जिसे संप्रेषित करने का प्रयत्न किया जा रहा है; तात्पर्य, प्रयोजन *This word has two different meanings in English.* ○ *What's the meaning of the last line of the poem?* **2** [U] the purpose or importance of an experience किसी अनुभव का प्रयोजन या महत्त्व *With his child dead there seemed to be no meaning in life.*

**meaningful** /ˈmiːnɪŋfl ˈमीनिङ्फ़्ल्/ *adj.* **1** useful, important or interesting उपयोगी, महत्त्वपूर्ण या रोचक, सार्थक, सोद्देश्य *Most people need a meaningful relationship with another person.* **2** (used about a look, expression, etc.) trying to express a certain feeling or idea (देखने का तरीक़ा, चेहरे का भाव आदि) जो किसी मनोभाव या विचार विशेष को प्रकट करने का प्रयत्न करे; अर्थ-भरा, प्रयोजनपूर्ण *They kept giving each other meaningful glances across the table.* ► **meaningfully** /-fəli -फ़लि/ *adv.* सार्थक या सोद्देश्य रूप से

**meaningless** /ˈmiːnɪŋləs ˈमीनिङ्लस्/ *adj.* without meaning, reason or sense निरर्थक, तर्कहीन *The figures are meaningless if we have nothing to compare them with.*

**means** /miːnz मीन्ज़्/ *noun* (*pl.* **means**) **1** [C] **a means (of doing sth)** a method of doing sth साधन, कुछ करने का उपाय *Do you have any means of transport* (= a car, bicycle, etc.)? ○ *Is there any means of contacting your husband?* **2** [*pl.*] (*formal*) all the money that sb has किसी व्यक्ति की पूरी संपत्ति, आर्थिक सामर्थ *This car is* ***beyond the means of*** *most people.*

IDM **by all means** used to say that you are happy for sb to have or do sth किसी की कोई बात ख़ुशी-ख़ुशी मानने का भाव व्यक्त करने के लिए प्रयुक्त, ज़रूर, निश्चय ही *'Can I borrow your newspaper?' 'By all means.'*

**by means of** by using का प्रयोग करके, के द्वारा *We got out of the hotel by means of the fire escape.*

**by no means; not by any means** (used to emphasize sth) not at all किसी बात पर बल देने के लिए प्रयुक्त) हरगिज़ नहीं, कदापि नहीं *I'm by no means sure that this is the right thing to do.*

**a means to an end** an action or thing that is not important in itself but is a way of achieving sth else साधन की अपेक्षा साध्य की महत्ता बताने के लिए प्रयुक्त, किसी साध्य का साधन *I don't enjoy my job, but it's a means to an end.*

**meant** ⇨ **mean[1]** का past tense और past participle रूप

**meantime** /ˈmiːntaɪm ˈमीन्टाइम्/ *noun*

IDM **in the meantime** in the time between two things happening दो बातें घटित होने के बीच के समय में, बीच के समय में, इस बीच *Our house isn't finished so in the meantime we're living with my mother.*

**meanwhile** /ˈmiːnwaɪl ˈमीन्वाइल्/ *adv.* during the same time or during the time between two things happening उसी समय के दौरान या दो घटनाएँ घटित होने के बीच के समय में *Prayag was at home studying. Omar, meanwhile, was out with his friends.*

**measles** /ˈmiːzlz ˈमीज़्ल्ज़्/ *noun* [U] a common infectious disease, especially among children, in which your body feels hot and your skin is covered in small red spots खसरा

NOTE **Measles** शब्द देखने में बहुवचनांत संज्ञा है परंतु इसके साथ एकवचनांत क्रिया प्रयुक्त होती है—*a measles vaccine.*

**measly** /ˈmiːzli ˈमीज़्लि/ *adj.* (*informal*) much too small in size, amount or value आकार, मात्रा या क़ीमत में बहुत कम, नगण्य *All that work for this measly amount of money!*

**measurable** /ˈmeʒərəbl ˈमेश़रब्ल्/ *adj.* **1** that can be measured जिसे मापा जा सके **2** (*usually before a noun*) large enough to be noticed or to have a clear and noticeable effect इतना बड़ा कि दिखाई पड़े या जिसका स्पष्ट और दिखाई पड़ने वाला प्रभाव हो, स्पष्ट या सुदृश्य, दर्शनीय *measurable improvements* ► **measurably** /-əbli -अब्लि/ *adv.* स्पष्ट रूप से *Working conditions have changed measurably in the last ten years.*

**measure[1]** /ˈmeʒə(r) ˈमेश़(र्)/ *verb* **1** [I, T] to find the size, weight, quantity, etc. of sb/sth in standard units by using an instrument उपकरण का प्रयोग करते हुए किसी व्यक्ति मानक इकाइयों में या वस्तु के आकार, भार, मात्रा आदि का पता लगाना, किसी को मापना *to measure the height/width/length/depth of sth* ○ *Could you measure the table to see if it will fit into our room?* **2** *linking verb* to be a certain height, width, length, etc. किसी ख़ास ऊँचाई, चौड़ाई, लंबाई आदि का होना, किसी ख़ास नाप का होना *The room measures five metres across.* **3** [T] **measure sth (against sth)** to judge the value or effect of sth किसी वस्तु के मूल्य या प्रभाव को आँकना *Our sales do not look good when measured against those of our competitors.*

PHR V **measure up (to sth)** to be as good as you need to be or as sb expects you to be आवश्यकता या आशा के अनुरूप होना *Did the holiday measure up to your expectations?*

**measure²** /ˈmeʒə(r) ˈमेश़(र्)/ *noun* **1** [C, *usually pl.*] an action that is done for a special reason विशेष कारण से की गई कोई कार्रवाई, उपाय *The government is to **take** new **measures** to reduce inflation.* ○ *As a temporary measure, the road will have to be closed.* **2** [*sing.*] (*formal*) **a/some measure of sth** a certain amount of sth; some किसी वस्तु की ख़ास मात्रा; कुछ, सीमित *The play achieved a measure of success.* **3** [*sing.*] a way of understanding or judging sth किसी बात को समझने या आँकने का तरीक़ा, कसौटी, मानदंड *The school's popularity is a measure of the teachers' success.* **4** [C] a way of describing the size, amount, etc. of sth किसी वस्तु का आकार, मात्रा आदि बताने का तरीक़ा, नापने का उपाय; युक्ति *A metre is a measure of length.* ⇨ **tape measure** देखिए।

IDM **for good measure** in addition to sth, especially to make sure that there is enough अतिरिक्त रूप में (विशेषतः यह सुनिश्चित करने के लिए कि चीज़ कम न पड़े या काफ़ी मात्रा में उपलब्ध रहे) *He made a few extra sandwiches for good measure.*

**made to measure** specially made or perfectly suitable for a particular person, use, etc. विशेष व्यक्ति, आदि के लिए विशेषतया निर्मित या पूर्णतया उपयुक्त *I'm getting a suit made to measure for the wedding.*

**measurement** /ˈmeʒəmənt ˈमेश़मन्ट्/ *noun* **1** [C] a size, amount, etc. that is found by measuring मापने से मालूम किया गया आकार, परिमाण आदि; माप, नाप *What are the exact measurements of the room* (= how wide, long, etc. is it)? **2** [U] the act or process of measuring sth किसी वस्तु को मापने का कार्य या प्रक्रिया

**meat** /miːt मीट्/ *noun* [U] the parts of animals or birds that people eat पशुओं या पक्षियों का मांस जो खाया जाता है; गोश्त *She doesn't eat meat—she's a vegetarian.* ○ *meat-eating animals*

**meatball** /ˈmiːtbɔːl ˈमीट्बॉल्/ *noun* [C] a small round ball of meat, usually eaten hot with a sauce गोश्त या क़ीमे का गोला (जिसे प्रायः चटनी के साथ खाते हैं)

**meaty** /ˈmiːti ˈमीटि/ *adj.* **1** like meat, or containing a lot of meat गोश्त जैसा, गोश्त वाला या मांसल *meaty sausages* **2** large and fat बड़ा और मोटा या भारी *meaty tomatoes* **3** containing a lot of important or good ideas जिसमें अनेक महत्त्वपूर्ण या उत्तम विचार हों, विचारपूर्ण, सारगर्भित *a meaty topic for discussion*

**Mecca** /ˈmekə ˈमेका/ *noun* **1** [*sing.*] the city in Saudi Arabia where Muhammad was born, which is the centre of Islam सऊदी अरब का शहर मक्का जो मुहम्मद साहब का जन्मस्थान और इस्लाम धर्म का केंद्र स्थल है **2 mecca** [C, *usually sing.*] a place that many people wish to visit because of a particular interest विशेष कारण से महत्त्वपूर्ण कोई भी स्थान (नगर या देश), जहाँ संबंधित रुचि वाले लोग आना चाहते हैं *Italy is a mecca for art lovers.*

**mechanic** /məˈkænɪk मˈकैनिक्/ *noun* **1** [C] a person whose job is to repair and work with machines यंत्रों या मशीनों का काम (मरम्मत आदि) करने वाला व्यक्ति, मिस्तरी; मैकेनिक *a car mechanic* **2 mechanics** [U] the science of how machines work यंत्रों या मशीनों की कार्यपद्धति का वैज्ञानिक अध्ययन; यांत्रिकी, यंत्रगति-विज्ञान **3 the mechanics** [*pl.*] the way in which sth works or is done कुछ करने या संचालित होने की रीति; प्रक्रिया, क्रियाविधि *Don't ask me—I don't understand the mechanics of the legal system.*

**mechanical** /məˈkænɪkl मˈकैनिकल्/ *adj.* **1** connected with or produced by machines मशीनों से संबंधित या उत्पन्न *a mechanical pump* ○ *mechanical engineering* ○ *mechanical problems* **2** (used about a person's behaviour) done like a machine, as if you are not thinking about what you are doing (व्यक्ति का आचरण) मशीन के समान, यंत्रवत, बँधा-सधा (जिसमें सोच-विचार का स्थान नहीं) *He played the piano in a dull and mechanical way.*
▶ **mechanically** /məˈkænɪkli मˈकैनिक्लि/ *adv.* मशीनी ढंग से, यांत्रिकतापूर्वक

**mechanism** /ˈmekənɪzəm ˈमेकनिज़म्/ *noun* [C] **1** a set of moving parts in a machine that does a certain task विशेष काम करने वाले मशीन के सचल कल-पुरज़े *Our car has an automatic locking mechanism.* **2** the way in which sth works or is done कुछ करने या संचालित होने की विधि; क्रियाविधि *I'm afraid there is no mechanism for dealing with your complaint.*

**mechanize** (*also* **-ise**) /ˈmekənaɪz ˈमेकनाइज़्/ *verb* [T] to use machines instead of people to do work (मनुष्यों के स्थान पर) मशीनों से काम करना *We have mechanized the entire production process.*
▶ **mechanization** (*also* **-isation**) /ˌmekənaɪˈzeɪʃn ˌमेकनाइˈज़ेश्न्/ *noun* [U] मशीनीकरण

**medal** /ˈmedl ˈमेड्ल्/ *noun* [C] a small flat piece of metal, usually with a design and words on it, which is given to sb who has shown courage or as a prize in a sporting event मेडल, तमग़ा, पदक (जो साहस-प्रदर्शन के लिए या खेल-स्पर्धा में विजेता को दिया जाता है) *to win a gold/silver/bronze medal in the Olympics*

**medallion** /məˈdæliən मˈडैलिअन्/ *noun* [C] a small round piece of metal on a chain which is worn as jewellery around the neck गरदन में पहनने का ज़ंजीर वाला आभूषण जिसमें गोलाकार फलक लगा होता है

**medallist** (*AmE* **medalist**) /ˈmedəlɪst ˈमेडलिस्ट्/ *noun* [C] a person who has won a medal, especially in sport पदक-विजेता (विशेषतः खेल में) *an Olympic gold medallist*

**meddle** /ˈmedl ˈमेड्ल्/ *verb* [I] **meddle (in/with sth)** to take too much interest in sb's private affairs or to touch sth that does not belong to you दूसरों के निजी मामलों में ज़रूरत से ज्यादा रुचि लेना या पराई चीज़ से छेड़-छाड़ करना; हस्तक्षेप करना *She criticized her mother for meddling in her private life.*

**media** /ˈmiːdiə ˈमीडिआ/ *noun* [*pl.*] television, radio and newspapers used as a means of communication संप्रेषण के माध्यम के रूप में प्रयुक्त टीवी, रेडियो और अख़बार; मीडिया *The reports **in the media** have been greatly exaggerated.* ➪ **mass media** और **the press** देखिए।

> **NOTE** **Media** बहुवचनांत संज्ञा (plural noun) है परंतु कभी-कभी इसका प्रयोग एकवचनांत क्रिया (singular verb) के साथ भी होता है—*The media always take/takes a great interest in the lives of cricketers.*

**mediaeval** = **medieval**

**median¹** /ˈmiːdiən ˈमीडिअन्/ *adj.* (*only before a noun*) (*technical*) **1** having a value in the middle of a series of values मूल्य-शृंखला के मध्य जिसका मूल्य स्थिर हो; माध्यिका *the median age/price* **2** situated in or passing through the middle मध्य में स्थिर या मध्य में से जाता हुआ *a median point/line* **3 median strip** (*AmE*) = **central reservation**

**median²** /ˈmiːdiən ˈमीडिअन्/ *noun* [C] **1** the middle value of a series of numbers arranged in order of size आकार (बड़ा-छोटा) के क्रम में व्यवस्थित संख्याओं की मध्यवर्ती मूल्य; माध्यिका **2** a straight line passing from a point of a triangle to the centre of the opposite side त्रिभुज के किसी बिंदु से गुज़रती सीधी रेखा जो सामने की भुजा के मध्य-बिंदु पर पहुँचती है, मध्यांतर या मध्यम रेखा

**media studies** *noun* [U, *pl.*] the study of newspapers, television, radio, etc., especially as an academic subject समाचारपत्र टेलीविज़न, रेडियो आदि का अध्ययन (विशेषतः एक शैक्षिक विषय के रूप में), मीडिया-विमर्श

**mediate** /ˈmiːdieɪt ˈमीडिएट्/ *verb* [I, T] **mediate (in sth) (between A and B)** to try to end a disagreement between two or more people or groups व्यक्तियों या व्यक्ति समूहों के बीच मतभेद समाप्त करने का यत्न करना; मध्यस्थता करना *As a supervisor she had to mediate between her colleagues and the management.* ▶ **mediation** /ˌmiːdiˈeɪʃn ˌमीडिˈएश्न्/ *noun* [U] मध्यस्थता ▶ **mediator** *noun* [C] मध्यस्थ

**medical¹** /ˈmedɪkl ˈमेडिक्ल्/ *adj.* connected with medicine and the treatment of illness औषधि और रोग के उपचार से संबंधित; डॉक्टरी *medical treatment/care* ○ *the medical profession* ▶ **medically** /-kli -क्लि/ *adv.* डॉक्टरी तौर पर

**medical²** /ˈmedɪkl ˈमेडिक्ल्/ *noun* [C] an examination of your body by a doctor to check your state of health डॉक्टर द्वारा शरीर की जाँच (ताकि स्वास्थ्य की दशा पता लगे) *to have a medical checkup*

**medication** /ˌmedɪˈkeɪʃn ˌमेडिˈकेश्न्/ *noun* [C, U] (*AmE*) medicine that a doctor has given to you डॉक्टर द्वारा दी गई दवाएँ *Are you on any medication?*

**medicinal** /məˈdɪsɪnl मˈडिसिन्ल्/ *adj.* useful for curing illness or infection रोग या संक्रमण के उपचार में उपयोगी *medicinal plants*

**medicine** /ˈmedsn ˈमेड्सन्/ *noun* **1** [U] the science of preventing and treating illness रोग की रोकथाम और उपचार का शास्त्र, चिकित्सा-शास्त्र *to study medicine* **2** [C, U] a substance, especially a liquid, that you take in order to cure an illness रोग का उपचार करने वाली दवा (विशेषतः द्रव) ***Take this medicine** three times a day.* ○ *cough medicine*

**medieval** (*also* **mediaeval**) /ˌmediˈiːvl ˌमेडिˈईव्ल्/ *adj.* connected with the period in history between about 1100 and 1500 AD (**the Middle Ages**) इतिहास के मध्यकाल (सन् 1100 से 1500 ई॰) से संबंधित *medieval architecture*

**mediocre** /ˌmiːdiˈəʊkə(r) ˌमीडिˈओक(र्)/ *adj.* of not very high quality औसत दर्जे का (उच्च कोटि का नहीं), दरम्याना, साधारण *a mediocre performance* ▶ **mediocrity** /ˌmiːdiˈɒkrəti ˌमीडिˈऑक्रटि/ *noun* [U] दरम्यानापन, साधारणता

**meditate** /ˈmedɪteɪt ˈमेडिटेट्/ *verb* [I] **meditate (on/upon sth)** to think carefully and deeply, especially for religious reasons or to make your mind calm ध्यानपूर्वक और गहराई से चिंतन करना (विशेषतः धार्मिक कारणों से या मन को शांत करने के लिए) मनन करना, ध्यान लगाना *I've been meditating on what you said last week.* ▶ **meditation** /ˌmedɪˈteɪʃn ˌमेडिˈटेश्न्/ *noun* [U] मनन, ध्यान, साधना

**the Mediterranean** /ˌmedɪtəˈreɪniən ˌमेडिटˈरेनिअन्/ (*informal* **the Med**) *noun* [*sing.*], *adj.* (of) the Mediterranean Sea or the countries around it भूमध्यसागर का या उसके निकटवर्ती देशों का *Mediterranean cookery/climate*

**medium[1]** /ˈmi:diəm ˈमीडिअम्/ *adj.* **1** in the middle between two sizes, lengths, temperatures, etc.; average दो आकारों, लंबाईयों, तापमानों आदि के मध्य का, मध्यम, बीच का; औसत *She was of medium height.* ○ *a medium-sized car/town/ dog* **2** (used about meat) cooked until it is brown all the way through (मांस) सारा भूरा होने तक पका हुआ ➪ **rare** और **well done** देखिए।

**medium[2]** /ˈmi:diəm ˈमीडिअम्/ *noun* **1** [C] (*pl.* **media** or **mediums**) a means you can use to express or communicate sth कुछ व्यक्त या संप्रेषित करने का माध्यम *English is the medium of instruction in the school.* ➪ **media** और **mass media** देखिए। **2** [C, U] medium size मध्यम आकार *Have you got this shirt in (a) medium?* **3** [C] (*pl.* **mediums**) a person who says that he/she can speak to the spirits of dead people मृत व्यक्तियों की आत्माओं से बात करने का दावा करने वाला व्यक्ति, माध्यम, माध्य व्यक्ति **4** (in biology) a substance that sth exists or grows in or that it travels through (जीव विज्ञान में) ऐसा पदार्थ जिसमें कोई वस्तु बनी रहती हे या बढ़ती है या जिसमें से होकर गुज़रती है; माध्यम *Good clean garden soil is the best sowing medium.*

**medium wave** *noun* [U] (*abbr.* **MW**) the system of sending out radio signals using sound waves between 100 and 1000 metres रेडियो संकेतों को प्रसारित करने की प्रणाली जिसमें 100 और 1000 मीटर के बीच की ध्वनि तरंगों का प्रयोग होता है ➪ **long wave** और **short wave** देखिए।

**medley** /ˈmedli ˈमेड्लि/ *noun* [C] **1** a piece of music consisting of several tunes or songs played one after the other without a break ऐसी संगीत रचना जिसमें एक बाद एक निरंतर बजने वाली विभिन्न धुनों या गीतों का मिश्रण होता है; स्वर-मिश्रण, गीत-मिश्रण **2** a mixture of different things विभिन्न वस्तुओं का मिश्रण; सम्मिश्रण *a medley of styles/flavours*

**meek** /mi:k मीक्/ *adj.* (used about people) quiet, and doing what other people say without asking questions (व्यक्ति) शांत और आज्ञाकारी, दब्बू ▶ **meekly** *adv.* चुपचाप ▶ **meekness** *noun* [U] दब्बूपन

**meet** /mi:t मीट्/ *verb* (*pt, pp* **met** /met मेट्/) **1** [I, T] to come together by chance or because you have arranged it एक स्थान पर आना (संयोग से या योजनानुसार), मिलना *I just met Kareem on the train.* ○ *What time shall we meet for lunch?* **2** [I, T] to see and know sb for the first time किसी को पहली बार देखना और जानना, से मिलना *Where did you first meet your husband?* ○ *Have you two met before?* **3** [T] to go to a place and wait for sb/sth to arrive कहीं जाना और किसी व्यक्ति या वस्तु के पहुँचने की प्रतीक्षा करना *I'll come and meet you at the station.* **4** [I, T] to play, fight, etc. together as opponents in a sports competition खेल-स्पर्धा में मुक़ाबला करना *These two teams met in last year's final.* ○ *Yamaha will meet Suzuki in the second round.* **5** [T] to experience sth, often sth unpleasant कुछ अनुभव करना (प्रायः अप्रिय बात) *We will never know how he met his death.* **6** [I, T] to touch, join or make contact with स्पर्श करना, जुड़ना या संपर्क स्थापित करना *The two roads meet not far from here.* ○ *His eyes met hers.* **7** [T] to be enough for sth; to be able to deal with sth किसी बात के लिए पर्याप्त होना; किसी स्थिति से निपट सकना *The money that I earn is enough to meet our basic needs.* ○ *to meet a challenge*

IDM **make ends meet** ➪ **end[1]** देखिए।

**there is more to sb/sth than meets the eye** sb/sth is more interesting or complicated than he/she/it seems कोई व्यक्ति या वस्तु वस्तुतः उससे अधिक रोचक या ज़टिल है जितना बाहर से लगता है या कोई बात जैसी बाहर से लगे उससे अधिक वस्तुतः गंभीर हो *Do you think there's more to their relationship than meets the eye?*

PHR V **meet up (with sb)** to meet sb, especially after a period of being apart किसी से मिलना (विशेषतः कुछ समय अलग रहने के बाद) *I have a few things I need to do now, but let's meet up later.*

**meet with sb** (*AmE*) to meet sb, especially for discussion किसी व्यक्ति से मिलना (विशेषतः विचार-विमर्श के लिए) *The President met with his advisers early this morning.*

**meet with sth** to get a particular answer, reaction or result विशेष उत्तर, प्रक्रिया या परिणाम प्राप्त करना *to meet with success/failure/opposition*

**meeting** /ˈmi:tɪŋ ˈमीटिङ्/ *noun* **1** [C] an organized occasion when a number of people come together in order to discuss or decide sth सभा, गोष्ठी, बैठक (विचार-विमर्श या कुछ निश्चित करने के लिए) *The group **holds** regular **meetings** all year.* ○ *We need to **have a meeting** to discuss these matters.*

> NOTE 'मीटिंग' को **call, arrange** या **organize** किया जाता है। इसे **cancel** या **postpone** भी किया जाता है।

**2** [*sing.*] the people at a meeting सभा में उपस्थित लोग *The meeting was in favour of the new proposals.* **3** [C] the coming together of two or more people लोगों का एक साथ आना, लोगों का जमाव *Durga Puja is a time of family meetings and reunions.*

**mega-** /ˈmegə ˈमेगा/ *prefix* (*used in nouns*) **1** (*informal*) very large or great बहुत बड़ा या विशाल *a megastore* **2** (used in units of measurement) one million (माप की इकाई के रूप में प्रयुक्त) दस लाख *a megawatt* **3** (*computing*) 1048576 (= $2^{20}$)

**megaphone** /ˈmegəfəʊn ˈमेगाफ़ोन्/ *noun* [C] a piece of equipment that you speak through to make your voice sound louder when speaking to a crowd भीड़ को संबोधित करने के लिए ध्वनि-विस्तारक यंत्र; मेगाफ़ोन, भोंपू

**meiosis** /maɪˈəʊsɪs माइˈओसिस्/ *noun* [U] (*technical*) the division of a cell in two stages that results in four cells, each with half the **chromosomes** of the original cell शरीर की कोशिका का विभक्त होकर दो कोशिकाएँ बनना (जिसमें से प्रत्येक में मूल कोशिका के आधे गुणसूत्र हो); अर्धसूत्री विभाजन ➪ **mitosis** देखिए।

**melancholy** /ˈmelənkəli; -kɒli ˈमेलन्कलि; कॉलि/ *noun* [U] (*formal*) a feeling of sadness which lasts for a long time चिरकाल तक रहने वाली विषाद-भावना या उदासी ▶ **melancholy** *adj.* विषादपूर्ण, उदास

**melanin** /ˈmelənɪn ˈमेलनिन्/ *noun* [U] a dark substance in the skin and hair that causes the skin to change colour in the sun's light त्वचा और सिर में एक काला पदार्थ जिसके कारण सूर्य के प्रकाश से त्वचा का रंग बदल जाता है

**melee** /ˈmeleɪ ˈमेले/ *noun* [C, *sing.*] a situation in which a crowd of people are in a hurry or pushing each other in a confused way ऐसा जमावड़ा जिसमें लोग जल्दबाज़ी में होते हैं या उलटे-सीधे एक दूसरे को धकेलते हैं, भीड़-भक्कड़

**mellow** /ˈmeləʊ ˈमेलो/ *adj.* **1** (used about colours or sounds) soft and pleasant (वर्ण या ध्वनि) मृदु और मनोरम **2** (used about people) calm and relaxed (लोग) शांत और तनावमुक्त *My dad's grown mellower as he's got older.* ▶ **mellow** *verb* [I, T] मृदु बनना या बनाना *Experience had mellowed her views about many things.*

**melodic** /məˈlɒdɪk मˈलॉडिक्/ *adj.* **1** (*only before a noun*) connected with the main tune in a piece of music संगीत-रचना की मुख्य धुन से संबंधित *The melodic line is carried by the flute.* **2** = **melodious**

**melodious** /məˈləʊdiəs मˈलोडिअस्/ (*also* **melodic**) *adj.* pleasant to listen to, like music श्रुतिमधुर, सुरीला *a rich melodious voice*

**melodrama** /ˈmelədrɑːmə ˈमेलड्रामा/ *noun* [C, U] a story, play or film in which a lot of exciting things happen and in which people's emotions are stronger than in real life भावुकतापूर्ण उत्तेजना-प्रधान कथा, नाटक या फ़िल्म; अतिनाटक या अतिकथा

**melodramatic** /ˌmelədrəˈmætɪk ˌमेलड्रˈमैटिक्/ *adj.* (used about a person's behaviour) making things seem more exciting or serious than they really are (व्यक्ति का आचरण) अवास्तविक रूप से उत्तेजक, सनसनीख़ेज़ *Don't be so melodramatic, Shubham—of course you're not going to die!*

**melody** /ˈmelədi ˈमेलडि/ *noun* [C] (*pl.* **melodies**) a song or tune; the main tune of a piece of music गति या धुन; किसी संगीत रचना की मुख्य धुन

**melon** /ˈmelən ˈमेलन्/ *noun* [C, U] a large roundish fruit with a thick yellow or green skin and a lot of seeds ख़रबूज़ा (फल)

**melt** /melt ˈमेल्ट्/ *verb* **1** [I, T] to change or make sth change from a solid to a liquid by means of heat ताप से पिघलना या पिघलाना *When we got up in the morning the snow had melted.* ○ *First melt the butter in a saucepan.* ➪ **thaw** देखिए। **2** [I] (used about sb's feelings, etc.) to become softer or less strong (व्यक्ति के मनोभावों का) अधिक कोमल हो जाना, पसीजना *My heart melted when I saw the baby.*

**PHR V** **melt away** to disappear चले जाना, ग़ायब हो जाना, विघटित हो जाना *The crowd slowly melted away when the speaker had finished.*

**melt sth down** to heat a metal or glass object until it becomes liquid ताप से धातु या काँच को पूरी तरह गला देना

**melting point** *noun* [U, C] the temperature at which a substance will melt तापमान जिस पर कोई पदार्थ पिघल जाता है; गलनांक, द्रवणांक

**melting pot** *noun* [C] a place where a lot of different cultures, ideas, etc. come together विभिन्न संस्कृतियों, विचारधाराओं का मिलन-स्थल

**member** /ˈmembə(r) ˈमेम्ब(र्)/ *noun* [C] a person, an animal or a thing that belongs to a group, club, organization, etc. किसी वर्ग, क्लब, संगठन आदि से संबंधित व्यक्ति, पशु या वस्तु, किसी संगठन आदि का सदस्य *All the members of the family were there.* ○ *to become a member of a club* ○ *a member of staff*

**Member of Parliament** *noun* [C] (*abbr.* **MP**) a person who has been elected to represent people from a particular area in Parliament क्षेत्र विशेष से संसद के लिए चुना गया व्यक्ति; संसद-सदस्य, सांसद *the MP for Kanpur*

**membership** /ˈmembəʃɪp ˈमेम्बशिप्/ *noun* **1** [U] the state of being a member of a group, organization, etc. किसी वर्ग, संगठन आदि की सदस्यता *To **apply for membership**, please fill in the enclosed form.* ○ *a membership card/fee* **2** [C, U] the people who belong to a group, organization, etc.

किसी वर्ग, संगठन आदि के सदस्य व्यक्ति *Membership has fallen in the past year* (= the number of members).

**membrane** /ˈmembreɪn ˈमेम्ब्रेन् / *noun* [C] a thin skin which covers certain parts of a person's or an animal's body झिल्ली, मनुष्य या पशु के कुछ अंगों को ढकने वाली महीन त्वचा

**memento** /məˈmentəʊ मˈमेन्टो / *noun* [C] (*pl.* **mementoes; mementos**) something that you keep to remind you of sb/sth स्मृति-चिह्न

**memo** /ˈmeməʊ ˈमेमो / *noun* [C] (*pl.* **memos**) (*formal* **memorandum**) a note sent from one person or office to another within an organization एक ही संगठन के भीतर एक व्यक्ति या कार्यालय द्वारा दूसरे को भेजा नोट; ज्ञापन, मीमो

**memoirs** /ˈmemwɑːz ˈमेम्वाज़् / *noun* [*pl.*] a person's written account of his/her own life and experiences जीवनवृत्त, जीवनचरित्र ✪ पर्याय **autobiography**

**memorabilia** /ˌmemərəˈbɪliə ˌमेमरˈबिलिआ / *noun* [U] things that people buy because they are connected with a famous person, event, etc. प्रसिद्ध व्यक्तियों, घटनाओं आदि की याद दिलाने वाली वस्तुएँ (जिन्हें लोग ख़रीदते है); स्मृति-चिह्न *Beatles/Titanic/war memorabilia*

**memorable** /ˈmemərəbl ˈमेमरबल् / *adj.* worth remembering or easy to remember स्मरणीय, स्मरण करने योग्य या जिसे स्मरण करना सरल हो ▸ **memorably** *adv.* स्मरणीय रूप से

**memorandum** /ˌmeməˈrændəm ˌमेमˈरैन्डम् / (*pl.* **memoranda** /-də -डा /) (*formal*) = **memo**

**memorial** /məˈmɔːriəl मˈमॉरिअल् / *noun* [C] **a memorial (to sb/sth)** something that is built or done to remind people of an event or a person स्मारक; किसी घटना या व्यक्ति का स्मरण कराने के लिए निर्मित कोई वस्तु या कार्य *a memorial to the victims of the bombing* ○ *a war memorial* ○ *a memorial service*

**memorize** (*also* **-rise**) /ˈmeməraɪz ˈमेमराइज़् / *verb* [T] to learn sth so that you can remember it exactly किसी बात को भली-भाँति याद कर लेना; कंठस्थ करना *Actors have to memorize their lines.*

**memory** /ˈmeməri ˈमेमरि / *noun* (*pl.* **memories**) **1** [C] a person's ability to remember things स्मरणशक्ति; याददाश्त *to have a good/bad memory* ○ *The drug can affect your short-term memory.* **2** [C, U] the part of your mind in which you store things that you remember स्मृतिकोश *That day remained firmly **in** my **memory** for the rest of my life.* ○ *Are you going to do your speech **from memory**, or are you going to use notes?* **3** [C] something that you remember स्मृति-याद *That is one of my happiest memories.* ○ *childhood memories* **4** [C, U] the part of a computer where information is stored कंप्यूटर का वह भाग जहाँ सूचना संचित रहती है, कंप्यूटर की मेमोरी *This computer has a 640k memory/640k of memory.*

**IDM in memory of sb** in order to remind people of sb who has died दिवंगत आत्मा की स्मृति में *A service was held in memory of the dead.*

**jog sb's memory** ⇨ **jog**[1] देखिए।

**refresh your memory** ⇨ **refresh** देखिए।

**men** ⇨ **man**[1] का plural रूप

**menace** /ˈmenəs ˈमेनस् / *noun* **1** [C] **a menace (to sb/sth)** a danger or threat ख़तरा या ख़तरे की आशंका *The new road is a menace to everyone's safety.* **2** [U] a quality, feeling, etc. that is threatening or frightening धमकी, घुड़की *He spoke with menace in his voice.* **3** [C] a person or thing that causes trouble कष्टप्रद (व्यक्ति या वस्तु) ▸ **menace** *verb* [T] धमकी देना, जोखिम में डालना ▸ **menacing** *adj.* धमकी-भरा

**mend**[1] /mend मेन्ड् / *verb* [T] to repair sth that is damaged or broken क्षतिग्रस्त वस्तु की मरम्मत करना *Can you mend the hole in this sweater for me?* ✪ पर्याय **repair**

**mend**[2] /mend मेन्ड् / *noun*

**IDM be on the mend** (*informal*) to be getting better after an illness or injury बीमारी या चोट के बाद सुधरना

**menial** /ˈmiːniəl ˈमीनिअल् / *adj.* (used about work) not skilled or important (काम) जिसमें दक्षता की अपेक्षा नहीं या महत्त्वहीन, छोटे स्तर का *a menial job*

**meningitis** /ˌmenɪnˈdʒaɪtɪs ˌमेनिन्ˈजाइटिस् / *noun* [U] a dangerous illness which affects the brain and the inside of the bones in your back (**the spinal cord**) मस्तिष्क की झिल्ली में सूजन का गंभीर रोग; मेनिनजाइटिस्

**the menopause** /ˈmenəpɔːz ˈमेनपॉज़् / *noun* [*sing.*] the time when a woman stops losing blood once a month (**menstruating**) and can no longer have children. This usually happens around the age of 50 रजोनिवृत्ति; लगभग 50 वर्ष की आयु में महिलाओं के मासिक धर्म का बंद हो जाना और फलस्वरूप गर्भधारण-क्षमता का समाप्त हो जाना

**menstrual** /ˈmenstruəl ˈमेन्स्ट्रुअल् / *adj.* connected with the time when a woman loses blood once a month (**menstruates**) मासिक धर्म संबंधी *The average length of a woman's **menstrual cycle** is 28 days.*

**menstruate** /ˈmenstrueɪt ˈमेन्स्ट्रुएट् / *verb* [I] (*formal*) (used about women) to lose blood once a month from the part of the body where a baby would develop (**the womb**) (महिलाओं के) मासिक धर्म होना, प्रति मास गर्भाशय से रक्तस्राव होना NOTE **To have a period** इसके लिए कम औपचारिक अभिव्यक्ति है। ▶ **menstruation** /ˌmenstruˈeɪʃn ˌमेन्स्ट्रुˈएशन् / *noun* [U] मासिक धर्म, रजोधर्म

**mental** /ˈmentl ˈमेन्ट्ल् / *adj.* (*only before a noun*) **1** connected with or happening in the mind; involving the process of thinking मन से संबंधित या मन में होने वाला, मानसिक; जिसमें सोचने की प्रक्रिया चले, दिमाग़ी *It's fascinating to watch a child's mental development.* **2** connected with illness of the mind मानसिक रोग से संबंधित *a mental disorder/illness* ▶ **mentally** /ˈmentəli ˈमेन्टलि / *adv.* मानसिक रूप से, दिमाग़ी तौर पर *She's mentally ill.*

**mental arithmetic** *noun* [U] adding, multiplying, etc. numbers in your mind without writing anything down or using a **calculator** लिखे बिना या कैलक्युलेटर के प्रयोग बिना मन में संख्याओं का जोड़, गुणा आदि करना

**mentality** /menˈtæləti मेन्ˈटैलटि / *noun* [C] (*pl.* **mentalities**) a type of mind or way of thinking एक प्रकार का मन या सोच, मानसिक, मनोवृत्ति *I just can't understand his mentality!* ○ *the criminal mentality*

**mention** /ˈmenʃn ˈमेन्शन् / *verb* [T] to say or write sth about sb/sth without giving much information (बोलने/लिखने में) किसी व्यक्ति या वस्तु का उल्लेख या ज़िक्र करना (न कि विस्तार से बताना) *He mentioned (to me) that he might be late.* ○ *Did she mention what time the film starts?*

IDM **don't mention it** used as a polite reply when sb thanks you for sth धन्यवाद के उत्तर में प्रयुक्त शिष्ट शब्दावली *'Thank you for all your help.' 'Don't mention it.'*

**not to mention** (used to emphasize sth) and also; as well as (किसी बात पर बल देने के लिए प्रयुक्त) साथ ही; के अतिरिक्त *This is a great habitat for birds, not to mention other wildlife.* ▶ **mention** *noun* [C, U] उल्लेख *It was odd that there wasn't even a mention of the riots in the newspaper.*

**mentor** /ˈmentɔ:(r) ˈमेन्टॉ(र्) / *noun* [C] an experienced person who advises and helps sb with less experience over a period of time अनुभवी परामर्शदाता (कम अनुभवी व्यक्ति के लिए) ▶ **mentoring** *noun* [U] परामर्श देने की क्रिया *a mentoring programme*

**menu** /ˈmenju: ˈमेन्यू / *noun* [C] **1** a list of the food that you can choose at a restaurant रेस्तराँ में उपलब्ध पदार्थों की सूची (अभीष्ट चुनने के लिए) *I hope there's soup on the menu.* ○ *They do a special lunchtime menu here.* **2** a list of choices in a computer program which is shown on the screen किसी कंप्यूटर प्रोग्राम में विकल्पों की सूची (जो स्क्रीन पर दिखाई जाती है) *a pull-down menu*

**mercenary[1]** /ˈmɜ:sənəri ˈमसनरि / *adj.* interested only in making money जिस काम में केवल पैसा बनाने की बात हो; धन लोलुप *His motives are entirely mercenary.*

**mercenary[2]** /ˈmɜ:sənəri ˈमसनरि / *noun* [C] (*pl.* **mercenaries**) a soldier who fights for any group or country that will pay him/her भाड़े के या भृतक सैनिक

**merchandise** /ˈmɜ:tʃəndaɪs; -daɪz ˈमचन्डाइस्; -डाइज़् / *noun* [U] (*formal*) goods that are for sale बिक्री की वस्तुएँ

**merchandising** /ˈmɜ:tʃəndaɪzɪŋ ˈमचन्डाइज़िङ् / *noun* [U] **1** (*AmE*) (*technical*) the activity of selling goods, or of trying to sell them, by advertising or showing them विज्ञापन या प्रदर्शन के द्वारा माल को बेचने या बेचने का प्रयत्न करने की क्रिया **2** products connected with a popular film, person or event; the process of selling these goods लोकप्रिय फ़िल्म, व्यक्ति या कार्यक्रम से जुड़ी हुई (बिक्री की) वस्तुएँ; इन वस्तुओं को बेचने की प्रक्रिया *millions of rupees worth of Krish merchandising*

**merchant** /ˈmɜ:tʃənt ˈमचन्ट् / *noun* [C] a person whose job is to buy and sell goods, usually of one particular type, in large amounts बड़ा व्यापारी (जो प्रायः एक साथ ख़ास प्रकार का माल बेचता है)

**the merchant navy** *noun* [C, *with sing. or pl. verb*] a country's commercial ships and the people who work on them देश की व्यापारिक जहाज़रानी (जहाज़ और उसके कर्मचारी)

**merciful** /ˈmɜ:sɪfl ˈमसिफ़्ल् / *adj.* feeling or showing mercy दयावान, सहृदय *His death was a merciful release from pain.* ▶ **mercifully** /-fəli -फ़लि / *adv.* सदय भाव से

**merciless** /ˈmɜ:sɪləs ˈमसिलस् / *adj.* showing no mercy दयाहीन या निर्मम ▶ **mercilessly** *adv.* दयाहीनता या निर्ममता से

**Mercury** /ˈmɜ:kjəri ˈमक्यरि / *noun* [*sing.*] the planet that is nearest to the sun बुध ग्रह (जो सूर्य के सबसे अधिक पास है) ➪ **the solar system** पर चित्र देखिए।

**mercury** /ˈmɜːkjəri ˈमक्यरि / *noun* [U] (*symbol* **Hg**) a heavy silver-coloured metal that is usually in liquid form. Mercury is used in instruments that measure temperature (**thermometers**) पारा (चाँदी जैसी भारी धातु जो प्रायः द्रव रूप में इस्तेमाल होती है। पारे का प्रयोग थर्मामीटर में होता है)

**mercy** /ˈmɜːsi ˈमसि / *noun* [U] kindness shown by sb/sth who has the power to make sb suffer दया, रहम (उस व्यक्ति द्वारा जो दूसरे को पीड़ित करने में समर्थ हो) *The rebels were shown no mercy. They were taken out and shot.*

**IDM at the mercy of sb/sth** having no power against sb/sth that is strong शक्तिशाली के सामने कमज़ोर साबित होना, किसी के रहमोक़रम पर होना, किसी की दया पर निर्भर होना *The climbers spent the night on the mountain at the mercy of the wind and rain.*

**mere** /mɪə(r) मिअ(र्) /*adj.* (*only before a noun*) **1** (used for emphasizing how small or unimportant sth is) nothing more than (किसी वस्तु की स्वल्पता पर बल देने के लिए प्रयुक्त) *Ninety per cent of the country's land is owned by a mere two per cent of the population.* **2** used to say that just the fact that sb/sth is present in a situation is enough to have an influence इस बात पर बल देने के लिए प्रयुक्त के किसी व्यक्ति या वस्तु की उपस्थिति ही प्रभाव के लिए पर्याप्त है *The mere thought of giving a speech in public makes me feel sick.*

**IDM the merest** even a very small amount of sth किसी वस्तु की अत्यल्प मात्रा *The merest smell of the fish market made her feel ill.*

**merely** /ˈmɪəli ˈमिअलि / *adv.* (*formal*) only; just केवल; मात्र *I don't want to place an order. I am merely making an enquiry.*

**merge** /mɜːdʒ मज् / *verb* **1** [I] **merge (with/into sth); merge (together)** to become part of sth larger में विलय या विलीन हो जाना, अपने से बड़े का हिस्सा बन जाना *Three small companies merged into one large one.* ○ *This stream merges with the river a few miles downstream.* **2** [T] to join things together so that they become one वस्तुओं का मिलाकर एक कर देना *We have merged the two classes into one.*

**merger** /ˈmɜːdʒə(r) ˈमज(र्) / *noun* [C, U] **a merger (with sb/sth); a merger (between/of A and B)** the act of joining two or more companies together दो या अधिक कंपनियों को संयुक्त करने का कार्य, कंपनियों का विलय

**meridian** /məˈrɪdiən मˈरिडिअन् / *noun* [C] a line that we imagine on the surface of the earth that joins the North Pole to the South Pole and passes through a particular place स्थान विशेष के ऊपर से जाती उत्तरी और दक्षिणी ध्रुवों को मिलाने वाली एक कल्पित रेखा; याम्योत्तर रेखा *the Greenwich Meridian* ➪ **longitude** देखिए तथा **earth** पर चित्र देखिए।

**meringue** /məˈræŋ मˈरैङ् / *noun* [C, U] a mixture of sugar and egg whites that is cooked in the oven; a cake made from this अवन में पकाया गया शक्कर और अंडे की सफ़ेदी का मिश्रण; इस मिश्रण से बना केक

**merit**[1] /ˈmerɪt ˈमेरिट् / *noun* **1** [U] the quality of being good गुण, ख़ूबी, अच्छाई *There is a lot of merit in her ideas.* ○ *He got the job **on merit**, not because he's the manager's son.* **2** [C, *usually pl.*] an advantage or a good quality of sb/sth (किसी व्यक्ति या वस्तु का) लाभ या गुण *Each case must be judged separately on its own merits* (= not according to general principles).

**merit**[2] /ˈmerɪt ˈमेरिट् / *verb* [T] (*formal*) to be good enough for sth; to deserve किसी बात के लिए पर्याप्त और उपयुक्त होना; के योग्य होना *This suggestion merits further discussion.*

**meritocracy** /ˌmerɪˈtɒkrəsi ˌमेरिˈटॉक्रसि / *noun* [C] (*pl.* **meritocracies**) **1** [C, U] a country or social system where people get power or money on the basis of their ability योग्यता के आधार पर लोगों को सत्ता या धन की प्राप्ति का अवसर देने वाला समाज या देश, गुणवानों को महत्त्व देने वाला समाज; गुणतंत्र, योग्यता-आधारित सामाजिक व्यवस्था **2 the meritocracy** [*sing.*] the group of people with power in this kind of social system गुणतंत्र में सत्ताधारी वर्ग

**meritorious** /ˌmerɪˈtɔːriəs ˌमेरिˈटॉरिअस् / *adj.* (*formal*) deserving great praise or reward; having merit सराहनीय; गुणवान

**mermaid** /ˈmɜːmeɪd ˈममेड् / *noun* [C] (in stories) a woman who has the tail of a fish instead of legs and who lives in the sea जलपरी, मत्स्य कन्या, (कथाओं में) कल्पित समुद्रवासी सुंदरी जिसकी टाँगों के स्थान पर मछली की पूँछ होती है

**merriment** /ˈmerimənt ˈमेरिमन्ट् / *noun* [U] laughter and enjoyment आमोद-प्रमोद

**merry** /ˈmeri ˈमेरि / *adj.* (**merrier; merriest**) **1** happy आनंदित, प्रभुदित *merry laughter* ○ ***Merry Christmas*** (= used to say you hope sb has a happy holiday) **2** (*informal*) slightly drunk हलका मदोन्मत ▶ **merrily** *adv.* सानंद

**merry-go-round** (*BrE* **roundabout** *AmE* **carousel**) *noun* [C] a big round platform that turns round and round and has model animals, etc. on it for children to ride on बच्चों के मनोरंजन का घुमौआ झूला; चक्रदोला, हिंडोला

**mesh** /meʃ ˈमेश् / *noun* [C, U] material that is like a **net** जाल, जाली *a fence made of wire mesh*

**mesmerize** (*also* **-ise**) /ˈmezməraɪz ˈमेज़्मराइज़् / *verb* [T] to hold sb's attention completely किसी के ध्यान को पूर्ण रूप से आकर्षित कर लेना, मंत्रमुग्ध या सम्मोहित कर लेना *The audience seemed to be mesmerized by the speaker's voice.*

**mesophyll** /ˈmesəʊfɪl ˈमेसोफ़िल् / *noun* [U] (*technical*) the material that the inside of a leaf is made of वह वस्तु जिससे पत्री का आंतरिक भाग बना होता है; पर्णमध्य, मध्यपर्ण

**mesosphere** /ˈmesəsfɪə(r); ˈmez- ˈमेसस्फ़िअ(र्); ˈमेज़्- / *noun* [*sing.*] **the mesosphere** the region of the earth's atmosphere between about 50 and 80 kilometres above the surface of the earth, above the **stratosphere** and below the **thermosphere** पृथ्वी की सतह के ऊपर 50 और 80 किलोमीटर के बीच का पर्यावरण-क्षेत्र जो समताप और बाह्य वायुमंडल के मध्य में होता है; मध्यमंडल

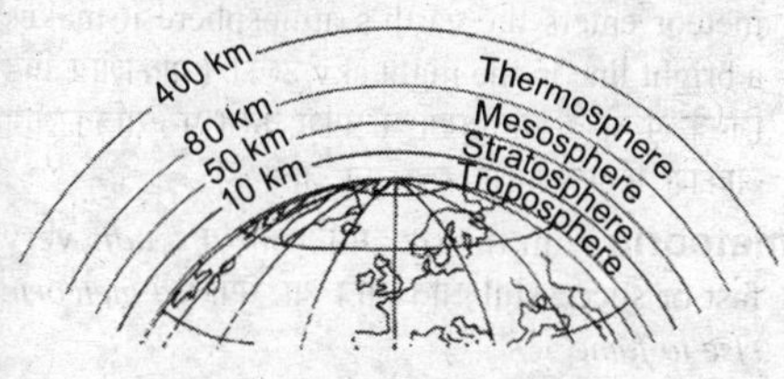


**mesosphere**

**mess¹** /mes मेस् / *noun* **1** [C, *usually sing.*] the state of being dirty or untidy; a person or thing that is dirty or untidy गंदगी या अव्यवस्था; गंदा या अव्यवस्थित व्यक्ति या वस्तु *The kitchen's* ***in a*** *terrible* ***mess****!* ○ *You can paint the door, but don't* ***make a mess****!* **2** [*sing.*] the state of having problems or troubles समस्याग्रस्त या झंझट-भरा होने की स्थिति *The company is* ***in a*** *financial* ***mess****.* ○ *to* ***make a mess*** *of your life*

**mess²** /mes मेस् / *verb* [T] (*AmE informal*) to make sth dirty or untidy गंदा या मैला कर देना *Don't mess your hands.*

**PHRV** **mess about/around** **1** to behave in a silly and annoying way मूर्खतापूर्ण और खिजाने वाले ढंग से व्यवहार करना **2** to spend your time in a relaxed way without any real purpose बिना मतलब बेफ़िक्री से समय गुज़ारना, मौज-मस्ती करना, आवारागर्दी करना *We spent Sunday just messing around at home.*

**mess sb about/around** to treat sb in a way that is not fair or reasonable, for example by changing your plans without telling him/her किसी व्यक्ति के साथ सही व्यवहार न करना (जैसे उसे बिना बताए अपना कार्यक्रम बदल लेना)

**mess about/around with sth** to touch or use sth in a careless way असावधानी से किसी वस्तु का स्पर्श या उपयोग करना *It is dangerous to mess about with fireworks.*

**mess sth up** **1** to make sth dirty or untidy गंदा या मैला कर देना **2** to do sth badly or spoil sth किसी काम को ख़राब तरीक़े से करना या बिगाड़ देना *I really messed up the last question in the exam.*

**mess with sb/sth** to deal or behave with sb/sth in a way that you should not किसी व्यक्ति के साथ अनुचित आचरण करना, वस्तु को ठीक से न बरतना *You shouldn't mess with people's feelings.*

**mess³** /mes मेस् / *noun* [C] a place where people from the armed forces, have their meals together and socialize सेना का भोजन कक्ष जहाँ सैनिक भोजन एवं सामाजिक मनोरंजन के लिए मिलते हैं; मेस

**message** /ˈmesɪdʒ ˈमेसिज् / *noun* **1** [C] a written or spoken piece of information that you send to or leave for a person when you cannot speak to him/her लिखित या मौखिक रूप से प्रेषित संदेश (जब संबोधित व्यक्ति से साक्षात बात न हो सके) *Mr Khanna is not here at the moment. Can I* ***take a message****?* ○ *If he's not in I'll* ***leave a message*** *on his answering machine.* **2** [*sing.*] an important idea that a book, speech, etc. is trying to communicate पुस्तक, भाषण आदि में व्यक्त महत्त्वपूर्ण विचार या संदेश *The advertising campaign is trying to get the message across that smoking kills.*

**IDM** **get the message** (*informal*) to understand what sb means even if it is not clearly stated किसी के मंतव्य या आशय को समझ लेना (भले ही स्पष्ट रूप से प्रकट न किया गया हो) *He finally got the message and went home.*

**messenger** /ˈmesɪndʒə(r) ˈमेसिन्ज(र्) / *noun* [C] a person who carries a message संदेशवाहक

**Messiah** (*also* **messiah**) /məˈsaɪə मˈसाइआ / *noun* [C] a person, for example Jesus Christ, who is expected to come and save the world मसीहा, व्यक्ति (जैसे ईसा) जिससे विश्व की रक्षा हेतु पृथ्वी पर आने की आशा की जाती है, परमेश्वर का अवतार माना जाने वाला व्यक्ति

**Messrs** *abbr.* (used as the plural of Mr before a list of men's names and before names of business firms) (Mr का बहुवचन) सूचीबद्ध पुरुषों और व्यापारिक प्रतिष्ठानों के नामों से पहले प्रयुक्त *Messrs Sinha, Singh and Shah* ○ *Messrs T Bhatt and Co.*

**messy** /ˈmesi ˈमेसि / *adj.* (**messier; messiest**) **1** dirty or untidy गंदा या मैला-कुचैला *a messy room*

2 that makes sb/sth dirty गंदगी फैलाने वाला *Painting the ceiling is a messy job.* **3** having or causing problems or trouble समस्याग्रस्त या झंझट भरा *a messy divorce*

**met** ➪ **meet** का past tense रूप

**meta-** /ˈmetə ˈमेटा/ *prefix* (*used in nouns, adjectives and verbs*) **1** connected with a change of position or state स्थिति या दशा में परिवर्तन से संबंधित *metamorphosis* ○ *metabolism* **2** higher; beyond उच्चतर, अधि- (जैसे अधिनायक); के परे *metaphysics*

**metabolism** /məˈtæbəlɪzəm मˈटैबलिज़्म्/ *noun* [U, *sing.*] the chemical processes in plants or animals that change food into energy and help them grow पेड़-पौधों और जंतुओं में होने वाली रासायनिक प्रक्रियाएँ जो भोजन को ऊर्जा में परिवर्तित कर देती हैं जिससे उनकी वृद्धि होती है; चयापचयन, उपपाचन *An athlete has a faster metabolism than most ordinary people.* ▶ **metabolic** /ˌmetəˈbɒlɪk ˌमेटˈबॉलिक्/ *adj.* चपापचयी, उपापचयी *a high/low metabolic rate*

**metal** /ˈmetl ˈमेट्ल्/ *noun* [C, U] a type of solid substance that is usually hard and shiny and that heat and electricity can travel through धातु *metals such as tin, iron, gold and steel* ○ *to recycle scrap metal* ○ *a metal bar/pipe*

**metallic** /məˈtælɪk मˈटैलिक्/ *adj.* **1** connected with metal or metals धातु से संबंधित *metallic alloys* **2** looking like metal or making a noise like one piece of metal hitting another धातु जैसी दीखने वाली या धातुओं के टकराने की-सी आवाज़; धात्विक *a metallic blue car* ○ *harsh metallic sounds*

**metallurgist** /məˈtælədʒɪst मˈटैलजिस्ट्/ *noun* [C] a scientist who studies metals and their uses धातुविज्ञानी

**metallurgy** /məˈtælədʒi मˈटैलजि/ *noun* [U] the scientific study of metals and their uses धातुविज्ञान

**metamorphic** /ˌmetəˈmɔːfɪk ˌमेटˈमॉफ़िक्/ *adj.* (*technical*) (used about rocks) that have been changed by heat or pressure (चट्टानों के लिए प्रयुक्त) ताप या दाब से परिवर्तित ➪ **igneous** और **sedimentary** देखिए तथा **rock** पर चित्र देखिए।

**metamorphosis** /ˌmetəˈmɔːfəsɪs ˌमेटˈमॉफ़सिस्/ *noun* [C] (*pl.* **metamorphoses** /-əsiːz -असीज़्/) (*formal*) a complete change of form (as part of natural development) (प्राकृतिक विकास-प्रक्रिया के अंतर्गत) पूर्ण रूप से आकृति में परिवर्तन; रूपांतरण *the metamorphosis of a tadpole into a frog*

**metaphor** /ˈmetəfə(r) ˈमेटफ़(र्)/ *noun* [C, U] a word or phrase that is used in an imaginative way to show that sb/sth has the same qualities as another thing. 'Her words were a knife in his heart' is a metaphor एक वस्तु की दूसरी से पूरी समानता दिखाने के लिए किसी शब्द का कल्पनाशील प्रयोग; रूपक (उदाहरण 'Her words were a knife in his heart' में 'knife' रूपक है); लक्षणा ➪ **figurative**, **literal** और **simile** देखिए। ▶ **metaphorical** /ˌmetəˈfɒrɪkl ˌमेटˈफ़ॉरिकल्/ *adj.* रूपकात्मक, लाक्षणिक ▶ **metaphorically** /-kli -क्लि/ *adv.* रूपकात्मक दृष्टि से, लाक्षणिक दृष्टि से

**metaphysics** /ˌmetəˈfɪzɪks ˌमेटˈफ़िज़िक्स्/ *noun* [U] the area of **philosophy** that deals with the nature of existence, truth and knowledge दर्शनशास्त्र की शाखा जिसमें अस्तित्व, सत्य और ज्ञान का अध्ययन होता है; तत्वमीमांसा

**mete** /miːt मीट्/ *verb*

**PHR V** **mete sth out (to sb)** (*formal*) to give sb a punishment or harsh treatment किसी को दंड देना या उससे कठोरपूर्वक पेश आना

**meteor** /ˈmiːtiə(r); -ɔː(r) ˈमीटिअ(र्); -ऑ(र्)/ *noun* [C] a small piece of rock, etc. in space. When a meteor enters the earth's atmosphere it makes a bright line in the night sky उल्का (आकाशीय पिंड जिनके पृथ्वी के वातावरण में प्रवेश करने पर रात्रिकालीन आकाश में प्रकाशमयी रेखा बन जाती है)

**meteoric** /ˌmiːtiˈɒrɪk ˌमीटिˈऑरिक्/ *adj.* very fast or successful अति तीव्र या सफल *a meteoric rise to fame*

**meteorologist** /ˌmiːtiəˈrɒlədʒɪst ˌमीटिअˈरॉलजिस्ट्/ *noun* [C] a person who studies the weather मौसम-विज्ञानी

**meteorology** /ˌmiːtiəˈrɒlədʒi ˌमीटिअˈरॉलजि/ *noun* [U] the study of the weather and climate मौसम-विज्ञान ▶ **meteorological** /ˌmiːtiərəˈlɒdʒɪkl ˌमीटिअरˈलॉजिकल्/ *adj.* मौसम-विज्ञान संबंधी

**meter** /ˈmiːtə(r) ˈमीट(र्)/ *noun* [C] **1** a piece of equipment that measures the amount of gas, water, electricity, voltage, etc. you have used गैस, पानी, बिजली आदि के उपयोग की मात्रा को मापने वाला उपकरण; मीटर *a voltmeter* **2** (*AmE*) = **metre** ▶ **meter** *verb* [T] मीटर के प्रयोग से मापना *Is your water metered?*

**methane** /ˈmiːθeɪn ˈमीथेन्/ *noun* [U] (*symbol* $CH_4$) a gas without colour or smell, that burns easily and that we can use to produce heat रंग या गंध से रहित ज्वलनशील गैस जो ताप उत्पन्न करती है; मीथेन

**methanol** /ˈmeθənɒl ˈमेथ़नॉल्/ *noun* [U] (*symbol* $CH_3OH$) a poisonous form of alcohol that is colourless, has no smell and changes easily into a gas ऐलकोहल का विषैला रूप जो रंग और गंध से रहित होता है और सरलता से गैस में बदल जाता है; मेथनॉल

**method** /ˈmeθəd ˈमेथ़ड्/ *noun* [C] a way of doing sth रीति, विधि *What method of payment do you prefer? Cash, cheque or credit card?* ○ *modern teaching methods*

**methodical** /məˈθɒdɪkl मˈथ़ॉडिकल्/ *adj.* having or using a well-organized and careful way of doing sth सावधानी से और सुव्यवस्थित रीति से किया (काम) या करने वाला (व्यक्ति) *Payal is a very methodical worker.* ▸ **methodically** /-kli -कलि/ *adv.* सुव्यवस्थित रीति से

**methodist** /ˈmeθədɪst ˈमेथ़डिस्ट्/ *noun* [C] (a member) of a Protestant Church that was started by John Wesley in the 18th century, 18वीं सदी में जॉन वेस्ले द्वारा स्थापित एक प्रोटेस्टेंट चर्च का सदस्य; मेथोडिस्ट

**methodology** /ˌmeθəˈdɒlədʒi ˌमेथ़ˈडॉलजि/ (*pl.* **methodologies**) *noun* [C, U] a way of doing sth based on particular principles and methods विशिष्ट सिद्धांतों और विधियों पर आधारित कार्यप्रणाली *language teaching methodologies* ▸ **methodological** /ˌmeθədəˈlɒdʒɪkl ˌमेथ़डˈलॉजिकल्/ *adj.* कार्यप्रणालीविषयक

**methylated spirits** /ˌmeθəleɪtɪd ˈspɪrɪts ˌमेथ़लेटिड् ˈस्पिरिट्स्/ (*informal* **meths** /ˌmeθs ˌमेथ़्स्/) *noun* [U] a type of alcohol that you cannot drink, used as a fuel for lighting and heating and for cleaning off dirty marks एक प्रकार का न पीने योग्य ऐलकोहल (जलाने, गरम करने और गंदे धब्बे दूर करने के लिए प्रयुक्त); मेथिलेटिड स्पिरिट, मद्यसार

**meticulous** /məˈtɪkjələs मˈटिक्यलस्/ *adj.* giving or showing great attention to detail; very careful ब्योरों पर बहुत ध्यान देने वाला या ब्योरों को बहुत ध्यान से दिखाने वाला; बहुत सतर्क, अति सावधान ▸ **meticulously** *adv.* अत्यंत सतर्कता के साथ, अति सावधानी से

**metonymy** /məˈtɒnəmi मˈटॉनमि/ *noun* [U] (*technical*) the act of referring to sth by the name of sth else that is closely connected with it, for example using the White House for the US President एक वस्तु का उससे अति निकटता से संबंधित दूसरी वस्तु से निर्देश करना (जैसे अमेरिकी राष्ट्रपति को 'the White House' कहना, क्योंकि वह राष्ट्रपति का निवास स्थान है); लाक्षणिकता

**metre** (*AmE* **meter**) /ˈmiːtə(r) ˈमीट(र्)/ *noun* **1** [C] (*abbr.* **m**) a measure of length; 100 centimetres लंबाई की एक माप; 100 सेंटीमीटर्स *a two-metre high wall* ○ *Who won the 100 metres?* **2** metres used in the name of races दौड़ों के नामों के साथ प्रयुक्त *She came second in the 100 metres.* **3** [U, C] the arrangement of strong and weak **stresses** in lines of poetry that produces the rhythm; a particular example of this कविता में छंद (लघु-गुरु वर्ण या प्रबल-दुर्बल बलाघातों की विशिष्ट व्यवस्था जिससे कविता में लय उत्पन्न होती है); कोई विशेष छंद

**metric** /ˈmetrɪk ˈमेट्रिक्/ *adj.* using the system of measurement that is based on metres, grams, litres, etc. (**the metric system**) जिसमें मिट्रिक पद्धति पर आधारित मापन-प्रणाली का प्रयोग हुआ हो; परिमाणात्मक ➪ **imperial** देखिए।

**metrication** /ˌmetrɪˈkeɪʃn ˌमेट्रिˈकेश्न्/ *noun* [U] the process of changing from measuring in imperial system to using the **metric system** मीट्रिक पद्धति को अपनाने का प्रक्रिया; मीट्रीकरण, मीटरीकरण

**the metric system** *noun* [*sing.*] the system of measurement that uses the metre, the kilogram and the litre as basic units मीटर, किलोग्राम और लिटर को मूल इकाईयों के रूप में प्रयुक्त करने वाली मापन-प्रणाली; मीट्रिक पद्धति

**metric ton** (*also* **tonne**) *noun* [C] a unit for measuring weight, equal to 1000 kilograms भार मापने की एक इकाई (1000 किलोग्राम के बराबर)

**metro** /ˈmetrəʊ ˈमेट्रो/ *noun* [*sing.*] **1** an underground train system in a large city भूमिगत रेल सेवा (नगर या बड़े शहर की) *She travels to work by metro.* **2** (*IndE*) a large and important city बड़ा और प्रमुख शहर *Fashion is ever changing in the metros like Delhi, Mumbai and Kolkata.*

**metropolis** /məˈtrɒpəlɪs मˈट्रॉपलिस्/ *noun* [C] a very large city बहुत बड़ा शहर; महानगर ▸ **metropolitan** /ˌmetrəˈpɒlɪtən ˌमेट्रˈपॉलिटन्/ *adj.* महानगरीय, महानगर-विषयक

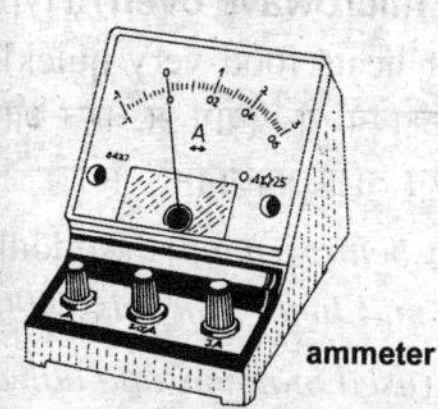
ammeter

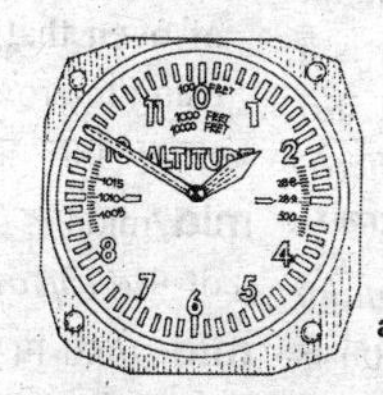

altimeter

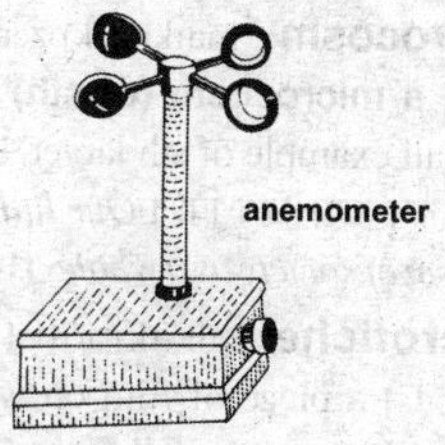
anemometer

meters

**mezzanine** /ˈmezəniːn ˈमेज़नीन्/ *noun* [C] a floor that is built between two floors of a building and is smaller than the other floors दुछत्ती, म्यानी, (दो तल्लों के) बीच का तल्ला (जो दोनों से छोटा होता है); मध्यतल

**mg** *abbr.* milligram(s) मिलीग्राम, मि.ग्रा.

**MHz** *abbr.* megahertz; (used in radio) a measure of **frequency** मेगाहर्ट्ज़ (रेडियो में प्रयुक्त) फ्रीक्वेंसी की एक माप

**miaow** /miˈaʊ मिˈआउ/ *noun* [C] the sound that a cat makes बिल्ली की आवाज़, म्याऊँ-म्याऊँ ▶ **miaow** *verb* [I] म्याऊँ-म्याऊ करना ➪ **purr** देखिए।

**mice** = **mouse** का plural रूप

**micro-** /ˈmaɪkrəʊ ˈमाइक्रो/ *prefix* (*used in nouns, adjectives and adverbs*) small; on a small scale छोटा, लघु; छोटे पैमाने पर, लघुस्तरीय *microchip* ○ *micro-organism* ✪ विलोम **macro-**

**microbe** /ˈmaɪkrəʊb ˈमाइक्रोब्/ *noun* [C] an extremely small living thing that you can only see with a special piece of equipment (**a microscope**) and that can cause disease अति सूक्ष्म जीवाणु (जिसे केवल सूक्ष्मदर्शी द्वारा देखा जा सकता है और जो रोग का कारण बन सकता है); रोगाणु

**microbiologist** /ˌmaɪkrəʊbaɪˈɒlədʒɪst ˌमाइक्रोबाइˈऑलजिस्ट्/ *noun* [C] a scientist who studies very small living things सूक्ष्म जीवों का वैज्ञानिक अध्ययन करने वाला; सूक्ष्मजीवविज्ञानी

**microbiology** /ˌmaɪkrəʊbaɪˈɒlədʒi ˌमाइक्रोबाइˈऑलजि/ *noun* [U] the scientific study of very small living things सूक्ष्म जीवों का वैज्ञानिक अध्ययन; सूक्ष्मजीवविज्ञान

**microchip** /ˈmaɪkrəʊtʃɪp ˈमाइक्रोचिप्/ (*also* **chip**) *noun* [C] a very small piece of a special material (**silicon**) that is used inside a computer, etc. to make it work कंप्यूटर के अंदर प्रयुक्त सिलिकॉन का सूक्ष्म खंड (जो कंप्यूटर को सक्रिय करता है); माइक्रोचिप या चिप

**microcomputer** /ˈmaɪkrəʊkəmpjuːtə(r) ˈमाइक्रोकम्प्यूट(र्)/ *noun* [C] (*computing*) a small computer that contains a **microprocessor** माइक्रोप्रोसेसर युक्त बहुत छोटा कंप्यूटर

**microcosm** /ˈmaɪkrəʊkɒzəm ˈमाइक्रोकॉज़्म्/ *noun* [C] **a microcosm (of sth)** something that is a small example of sth larger किसी भी बृहदाकार वस्तु का लघु रूप; अणु विश्व *Our little village is a microcosm of society as a whole.* ➪ **macrocosm** देखिए।

**microfiche** /ˈmaɪkrəʊfiːʃ ˈमाइक्रोफ़ीश्/ *noun* [C, U] a piece of film on which information is stored in very small print लघु फ़िल्म जिसमें बहुत महीन प्रिंट में सूचना संचित रहती है

**microgram** /ˈmaɪkrəʊɡræm ˈमाइक्रोग्रैम्/ *noun* [C] (*symbol* **µg**) (*technical*) a unit for measuring weight. There are one million micrograms in one gram भार तोलने की इकाई, माइक्रोग्राम (एक ग्राम में दस लाख माइक्रोग्राम होते हैं)

**micrometre** /ˈmaɪkrəʊmiːtə(r) ˈमाइक्रोमीट(र्) *noun* [C] (*symbol* **µm**) (*technical*) a unit for measuring length. There are one million micrometres in one metre लंबाई नापने की इकाई, माइक्रोमीटर (एक मीटर में दस लाख माइक्रोमीटर होते हैं)

**micron** /ˈmaɪkrɒn ˈमाइक्रॉन्/ *noun* [C] = **micrometre**

**micro-organism** *noun* [C] a very small living thing that you can only see with a special piece of equipment (**a microscope**) सूक्ष्म जीव (जिसे केवल सूक्ष्मदर्शी द्वारा देखा जा सकता है)

**microphone** /ˈmaɪkrəfəʊn ˈमाइक्रोफ़ोन्/ (*also* **mike**) *noun* [C] a piece of electrical equipment that is used for making sounds louder or for recording them ध्वनि वर्धक या उसे रिकार्ड करने वाला विद्युत उपकरण; माइक्रोफ़ोन

**microprocessor** /ˌmaɪkrəʊˈprəʊsesə(r) ˌमाइक्रोˈप्रोसेस(र्)/ *noun* [C] (*computing*) a small unit of a computer that contains all the functions of the **central processing unit** कंप्यूटर का वह भाग जो सेंट्रल प्रोसेसिंग यूनिट का काम करता है; माइक्रो-प्रोसेसर

**microscope** /ˈmaɪkrəskəʊp ˈमाइक्रोस्कोप्/ *noun* [C] a piece of equipment that makes very small objects look big enough for you to be able to see them सूक्ष्मदर्शी (एक यंत्र जिसमें बहुत वस्तुएँ इतनी बड़ी दिखाई देती है कि हम इन्हें सरलता से देख सकें) *to examine sth* ***under a microscope*** ➪ **laboratory** पर चित्र देखिए।

**microscopic** /ˌmaɪkrəˈskɒpɪk ˌमाइक्रˈस्कॉपिक्/ *adj.* too small to be seen without a microscope इतना छोटा कि केवल सूक्ष्मदर्शी द्वारा दिखाई दे

**microwave** /ˈmaɪkrəweɪv ˈमाइक्रवेव्/ *noun* [C] **1** a short electric wave that is used for sending radio messages and for cooking food रेडियो-संकेतों को भेजने और भोजन पकाने के लिए प्रयुक्त सूक्ष्म विद्युत तरंग; माइक्रो-वेव **2** (*also* **microwave oven**) a type of oven that cooks or heats food very quickly using microwaves माइक्रोवेवों के प्रयोग से बहुत शीघ्र भोजन बनाने या गरम करने वाली बक्सानुमा अँगीठी

**mid** /mɪd मिड्/ *adj.* (*only before a noun*) the middle of मध्य *I'm away from mid June.* ○ *the mid 1990s*

**mid-** /mɪd मिड्/ *prefix* (*used in nouns and adjectives*) in the middle of के मध्य में *mid-afternoon* ○ *a mid-air collision*

**midday** /ˌmɪdˈdeɪ ˌमिड्ˈडे/ *noun* [U] at or around twelve o'clock in the middle of the day दिन के मध्य में ठीक या लगभग बारह बजे, मध्याह्न, दोपहर को *We arranged to meet **at midday**.* ○ *the heat of the midday sun* ✪ पर्याय **noon** ➪ **midnight** देखिए।

**middle¹** /ˈmɪdl ˈमिड्ल्/ *noun* **1** [*sing.*] **the middle (of sth)** the part, point or position that is at about the same distance from the two ends or sides of sth किसी वस्तु का मध्य भाग (किसी वस्तु के दो छोरों से समान दूरी पर स्थित उसका अंश; बिंदु या स्थिति) *the white line **in the middle of** the road* ○ *Here's a photo of me with my two brothers. I'm the one **in the middle**.*

> **NOTE** **Centre** और **middle** के अर्थों में बहुत समानता है, तथापि किसी वस्तु के पूरी तरह से मध्य बिंदु के लिए 'centre' का प्रयोग होता है—*How do you find the centre of a circle?* ○ *The bee stung me **right in the middle** of my back.* जब समय की अवधि के मध्य भाग की बात करनी हो तो केवल **middle** का प्रयोग होगा—*in the middle of the night* ○ *the middle of July*

**2** [C] (*informal*) your waist (व्यक्ति की कमर) *I want to lose weight around my middle.*

**IDM** **be in the middle of sth/doing sth** to be busy doing sth किसी काम में व्यस्त *Can you call back in five minutes—I'm in the middle of a meeting.*

**in the middle of nowhere** a long way from any town किसी भी बस्ती से काफ़ी दूर

**middle²** /ˈmɪdl ˈमिड्ल्/ *adj.* (*only before a noun*) in the middle बीच में या का; मध्यवर्ती *I wear my ring on my middle finger.*

**middle age** *noun* [U] the time when you are about 40 to 60 years old मध्य वय, अधेड़ अवस्था (40 से 60 के बीच की उम्र) *a woman in early middle age* ▶ **middle-aged** *adj.* मध्य वय का, अधेड़ *a middle-aged man*

**the Middle Ages** noun [*pl.*] the period of European history from about 1100 to 1500 AD यूरोपीय इतिहास में मध्य युग (सन् 1100–1500 ई॰ तक)

**the middle class** *noun* [*sing.*] (*also* **the middle classes**) [*pl.*] the group of people in a society who are neither very rich nor very poor and that includes professional and business people समाज का वह वर्ग जो न बहुत धनी है न निर्धन और जिसमें नौकरी-पेशा और व्यापारी आते हैं; मध्यवर्ग ▶ **middle class** *adj.* मध्यवर्गीय *They're middle class.* ○ *a middle-class background* ➪ **the upper class** और **the working class** देखिए।

**middle ear** *noun* [*sing.*] the central part of your ear behind your **eardrum** कान के परदे के पीछे का मध्यवर्ती भाग; मध्यकर्ण ➪ **inner ear** देखिए तथा **ear** पर चित्र देखिए।

**the Middle East** *noun* [*sing.*] an area that covers SW Asia and NE Africa दक्षिण-पूर्वी एशियाई तथा उत्तर-पूर्वी अफ़्रीक़ी क्षेत्र ➪ **Far East** देखिए।

**middleman** /ˈmɪdlmæn ˈमिड्ल्मैन्/ *noun* [C] (*pl.* **-men** /-men -मेन्/) **1** a person or company who buys goods from the company that makes them and then sells them to sb else उत्पादन करने वाली कंपनी से माल लेकर दूसरों के बेचने वाली कंपनी या व्यक्ति; दलाल (व्यक्ति), बिचौलिया **2** a person who helps to arrange things between two people who do not want to meet each other एक दूसरे से भिन्न व्यक्तियों को मिलाने वाला व्यक्ति; मध्यस्थल

**middle-of-the-road** *adj.* (used about people, policies, etc.) not extreme; acceptable to most people (व्यक्ति, नीतियाँ आदि) अतिवादी नहीं; अधिकतर व्यक्तियों को स्वीकार्य, मध्यममार्गी

**middle school** *noun* [C] (*BrE*) a school for children aged between 9 and 13 मिडिल स्कूल; 9 से 13 की उम्र के बच्चों का स्कूल

**midge** /mɪdʒ मिज्/ *noun* [C] a very small flying insect that can bite people बहुत छोटा काटने वाला मच्छर; मशकाम ✪ पर्याय **gnat**

**midget** /ˈmɪdʒɪt ˈमिजिट्/ *noun* [C] a very small person बौना आदमी **NOTE** ध्यान रखिए कुछ लोग इस शब्द को अपमानजनक मानते हैं।

**midnight** /ˈmɪdnaɪt ˈमिड्नाइट्/ *noun* [U] twelve o'clock at night रात के बारह बजे, मध्यरात्रि, ठीक आधी-रात *They left the party **at midnight**.* ○ *The clock struck midnight.* ➪ **midday** देखिए।

**midriff** /ˈmɪdrɪf ˈमिड्रिफ़्/ *noun* [C] the part of your body between your chest and your waist छाती और कमर के बीच का भाग; मध्यपट

**midst** /mɪdst मिड्स्ट्/ *noun* [U] the middle of sth; among a group of people or things किसी वस्तु का मध्य; लोगों या वस्तुओं के बीच *The country is **in the midst of** a recession.* ○ *They realized with a shock that there was an enemy **in their midst**.*

**midsummer** /ˌmɪdˈsʌmə(r) ˌमिड्ˈसम(र्)/ *noun* [U] the time around the middle of summer ग्रीष्म ऋतु का मध्य *a beautiful midsummer's evening*

**midway** /ˌmɪdˈweɪ ˌमिड्ˈवे/ *adj., adv.* in the middle of a period of time or between two places समयावधि के मध्य या दो स्थानों के बीच *The village lies midway between two large towns.* ✪ पर्याय **halfway**

**midweek** /ˌmɪdˈwiːk ˌमिड्ˈवीक्/ *noun* [U] the middle of the week (= Tuesday, Wednesday and

Thursday) सप्ताह का मध्य (मंगलवार, बुधवार और गुरूवार ▶ **midweek** *adv.* सप्ताह के मध्य में *If you travel midweek it will be less crowded.*

**midwife** /ˈmɪdwaɪf ˈमिड्वाइफ़् / *noun* [C] (*pl.* **midwives** /-waɪvz -वाइव्ज़् /) a person who has been trained to help women give birth to babies शिशु जन्म की प्रक्रिया में माता की सहायता करने के लिए प्रशिक्षित व्यक्ति; दाई, धात्री

**midwifery** /ˌmɪdˈwɪfəri ˌमिड्ˈवाइफ़रि / *noun* [U] the work of a midwife दाई का काम, प्रसूति-विद्या

**midwinter** /ˌmɪdˈwɪntə(r)ˌमिड्ˈविन्ट(र्) / *noun* [U] the time around the middle of winter मध्यशीत

**might**[1] /maɪt माइट् / *modal verb* (*negative* **might not**; *short form* **mightn't** /ˈmaɪtnt ˈमाइट्न्ट् /) **1** used for saying that sth is possible किसी बात की 'संभावना' का अर्थ व्यक्त करने के लिए प्रयुक्त *'Where's Vinay?' 'He might be upstairs.' I think I might have forgotten the tickets.* **2** (*BrE formal*) used to ask for sth or suggest sth very politely अति नम्र भाव से कुछ माँगने या कोई देने के लिए प्रयुक्त *I wonder if I might go home half an hour early today?* **3** used as the form of 'may' when you report what sb has said वक्ता के मूल कथन को रिपोर्ट करने में प्रयुक्त 'may' का परोक्ष रूप (प्रत्यक्ष कथन में 'may' का परोक्ष कथन में 'might' हो जाना) *He said he might be late* (= his words were, 'I may be late').

**NOTE** वृत्तिवाचक क्रियाओं (modal verbs) के विषय में अधिक जानकारी के लिए इस कोश के अंत में **Quick Grammar Reference** देखिए।

**IDM may/might as well (do sth)** ➪ **well**[1] देखिए। **you, etc. might do sth** used when you are angry to say what sb could or should have done क्रोधपूर्वक दूसरे को नसीहत देने वाली भाषा में प्रयुक्त *They might at least have phoned if they're not coming.* **I might have known** used for saying that you are not surprised that sth has happened किसी घटना पर आश्चर्य न होने को व्यक्त करने के लिए प्रयुक्त *I might have known he wouldn't help.*

**might**[2] /maɪt माइट् / *noun* [U] (*formal*) great strength or power प्रचुर बल या शक्ति, पराक्रम *I pushed **with all** my **might**, but the rock did not move.*

**mighty**[1] /ˈmaɪti ˈमाइटि / *adj.* (**mightier; mightiest**) very strong or powerful महाबली, पराक्रमी, अतिशक्तिशाली

**mighty**[2] /ˈmaɪti ˈमाइटि / *adv.* (*AmE informal*) very बहुत *That's mighty kind of you.*

**migraine** /ˈmaɪgreɪn ˈमाइग्रेन् / *noun* [C, U] very bad pain in your head that makes you feel sick; a severe headache अस्वस्थता की अनुभूति कराने वाला सिर का दर्द; तेज़ सिर दर्द

**migrant** /ˈmaɪgrənt ˈमाइग्रन्ट् / *noun* [C] **1** a person who moves from place to place looking for work काम के लिए जगह-जगह जाने वाला व्यक्ति, प्रवासी (व्यक्ति) *migrant workers* **2** a bird or an animal that moves from one place to another according to the season मौसम के अनुसार स्थान-परिवर्तन करते रहने वाला पक्षी या पशु, प्रवासी (पक्षी या पशु)

**migrate** /maɪˈgreɪt माइˈग्रेट् / *verb* [I] **1** (used about animals and birds) to travel from one part of the world to another at the same time every year (पशुओं और पक्षियों का) प्रतिवर्ष एक ही समय विश्व के एक भाग से दूसरे में प्रवास करना **2** (used about a large number of people) to go and live and work in another place (बड़ी संख्या में लोगों का) अन्य स्थान पर जाना, वहाँ रहना और काम करना *Many country people were forced to migrate to the cities to look for work.* ➪ **emigrate** देखिए। ▶ **migration** /maɪˈgreɪʃn माइˈग्रेशन् / *noun* [C, U] प्रवास

**migratory** /ˈmaɪgrətri; maɪˈgreɪtəri ˈमाइग्रट्रि; माइˈग्रेट्रि / *adj.* (used about animals and birds) travelling from one part of the world to another at the same time every year (पशु और पक्षी) प्रतिवर्ष एक ही समय में विश्व के एक भाग से दूसरे में प्रवास करने वाले; प्रवासशील

**mike** /maɪk माइक् / (*informal*) = **microphone**

**milage** = **mileage**

**mild** /maɪld माइल्ड् / *adj.* **1** not strong; not very bad नरम; हलका *a mild soap* ○ *a mild winter* ○ *a mild punishment* **2** (used about food) not having a strong taste (खाद्य पदार्थ) जो स्वाद में तीखा न हो, मृदु *mild cheese* **3** kind and gentle दयालु और भद्र, शांत, मृदु स्वभाव का *He's a very mild man—you never see him get angry.* ▶ **mildness** *noun* [U] मृदुलता, मृदुता, सौम्यता

**mildew** /ˈmɪldju: ˈमिल्ड्यू / *noun* [U] a living white substance (**fungus**) that grows on walls, plants, food, etc. in warm wet conditions फफूँदी, भुकड़ी (जो हलकी गरम और सीलनभरी दशाओं में दीवारों, पेड़-पौधों और खाद्य पदार्थों पर आ जाती है)

**mildly** /ˈmaɪldli ˈमाइल्ड्लि / *adv.* **1** not very; slightly अधिक नहीं; हलका-सा *mildly surprised* **2** in a gentle way मृदु भाव से, भद्रतापूर्वक

**mile** /maɪl माइल् / *noun* **1** [C] a measure of length; 1.6 kilometres. There are 1760 yards in a mile दूरी की एक नाप; मील; 1.6 किलोमीटर (एक मील में 1760 गज होते है) *The nearest beach is seven miles away.* ○ *It's a seven-mile drive to the beach.* **2** [C] a lot बड़ी मात्रा में, काफ़ी अधिक *He missed the target by a mile.* ○ *I'm feeling miles better this* *morning.* **3 miles** [*pl.*] a long way काफ़ी दूर *How much further is it? We've walked miles already.* ○ *From the top of the hill you can see **for miles**.* IDM **see, hear, tell, spot, etc. sb/sth a mile off** (*informal*) used to say that sb/sth is very obvious यह कहने के लिए प्रयुक्त कि बात एकदम साफ़ है *He's lying—you can tell that a mile off.*

**mileage** (*also* **milage**) /ˈmaɪlɪdʒ ˈमाइलिज्/ *noun* **1** [C, U] the distance that has been travelled, measured in miles तय की गई दूरी जो मीलों में नापी गई है, मील-दूरी; माइलेज *The car is five years old but it has a low mileage.* **2** [U] (*informal*) the amount of use that you get from sth किसी वस्तु के उपयोग से प्राप्त लाभ *The newspapers got a lot of mileage out of the scandal.*

**mileometer** *noun* [C] = **milometer**

**milestone** /ˈmaɪlstəʊn ˈमाइलुस्टोन्/ *noun* [C] a very important event अत्यंत महत्त्वपूर्ण घटना, विशेष उपलब्धि *The concert was a milestone in the band's history*

**militant** /ˈmɪlɪtənt ˈमिलिटन्ट्/ *adj.* willing to use force to get what you want अभीष्ट की प्राप्ति के लिए बल प्रयोग या तगड़ा दबाव डालने के लिए तत्पर, जुझारू, संघर्ष का इच्छुक; युयुत्सु, लड़ाका *The workers were in a very militant mood.* ▶ **militant** *noun* [C] लड़ाका, युद्धोत्सुक, उग्रवादी ▶ **militancy** /-ənsi -अन्सि/ *noun* [U] उग्रवाद

**military** /ˈmɪlətri ˈमिलट्रि/ *adj.* (*only before a noun*) connected with soldiers or the army, navy, etc. सैनिक का या सैन्य-विषयक; सैन्य *All men in that country have to do two years' **military service**.* ○ *to take military action*

**militia** /məˈlɪʃə मˈलिशा/ *noun* [C, *with sing. or pl. verb*] a group of people who are not professional soldiers but who have had military training सैनिक प्रशिक्षण प्राप्त लोग परंतु पेशेवर सैनिक नहीं, नागरिक सेना, सहायक सेना

**milk**[1] /mɪlk मिल्क्/ *noun* [U] **1** a white liquid that is produced by women and female animals to feed their babies. People drink the milk of some animals and use it to make butter and cheese दूध *skimmed/low-fat milk* ○ *a bottle/carton of milk* **2** the juice of some plants or trees that looks like milk कुछ पेड़ों या पौधों का दूधिया रस *coconut milk*

**milk**[2] /mɪlk मिल्क्/ *verb* [T] **1** to draw milk from a cow, **goat**, etc. (गाय, बकरी आदि का) दुध दुहना **2** to get as much money, advantage, etc. for yourself from sb/sth as you can, without caring about others किसी व्यक्ति या वस्तु से अधिकाधिक स्वार्थ-सिद्धि कर लेना (बिना औरों के हितों की परवाह किए)

**milkman** /ˈmɪlkmən ˈमिल्क्मन्/ *noun* [C] (*pl.* **-men** /-mən; -men -मन्; -मेन्/) a person who takes milk to people's houses every day प्रतिदिन घर-घर जाकर दूध पहुँचाने वाला व्यक्ति; दूधवाला; दूधिया, ग्वाला

**milkshake** /ˈmɪlkʃeɪk ˈमिल्क्शेक्/ *noun* [C, U] a drink made of milk with an added flavour of fruit or chocolate दूध के साथ फल या चॉकलेट के मिश्रण से बना पेय; मिल्कशेक

**milk tooth** *noun* [C] any of the first set of teeth in young children that fall out and are replaced by others (बच्चों के) दूध के दाँत

**milky** /ˈmɪlki ˈमिल्कि/ *adj.* like milk, or made with milk दूध जैसा या दूध से बना *milky white skin* ○ *milky coffee*

**the Milky Way** *noun* [*sing.*] = **the Galaxy**

**mill**[1] /mɪl मिल्/ *noun* [C] **1** a factory that is used for making certain kinds of material फ़ैक्टरी, मिल (जहाँ ख़ास तरह का माल बनता है) *a cotton/paper/steel mill* **2** a building that contains a large machine that was used in the past for grinding grain into flour (पुराने ज़माने की) आटा चक्की वाली इमारत *a windmill* **3** a kitchen tool that is used for making sth into powder कुछ पीसने की छोटी मशीन (प्रायः रसोई में प्रयुक्त) *a pepper mill*

**mill**[2] /mɪl मिल्/ *verb* [T] to produce sth in a mill फ़ैक्टरी में कोई वस्तु बनाना

PHR V **mill about/around** (*informal*) (used about a large number of people or animals) to move around in a place with no real purpose (लोगों या जानवरों का) आवारागर्दी करना, बेमतलब इधर-उधर घूमना-फिरना

**millennium** /mɪˈleniəm मिˈलेनिअम्/ *noun* [C] (*pl.* **millennia** /-niə -निआ/ or **millenniums**) a period of 1000 years एक हजार वर्ष की अवधि; सहस्त्राब्दी *We are at the start of the new millennium.*

**millet** /ˈmɪlɪt ˈमिलिट्/ *noun* [U] a plant with a lot of small seeds that are used as food for people and birds बाजरा ➪ **cereal** पर चित्र देखिए।

**milli-** /ˈmɪli ˈमिलि/ *prefix* (*used in nouns, often in units of measurement*) one **thousandth** (प्रायः माप की इकाइयों में पूर्वपद) एक हज़ारवाँ *millisecond* ○ *millimetre*

**millibar** /ˈmɪlibɑː(r) ˈमिलिबा(र्)/ (*also* **bar**) *noun* [C] a unit for measuring the pressure of the atmosphere वातावरण के दाब को मापने की इकाई

**milligram** (*also* **milligramme**) /ˈmɪlɪɡræm ˈमिलिग्रैम्/ *noun* [C] (*abbr.* **mg**) a measure of weight. There are 1000 milligrams in a gram भार तोलने की इकाई (एक ग्राम में 1000 मिलिग्राम होते हैं)

**millilitre** (*AmE* **milliliter**) /ˈmɪliliːtə(r) ˈमिलिलीट(र्)/ *noun* [C] (*abbr.* **ml**) a measure of liquid. There are 1000 millilitres in a litre द्रव नापने की इकाई (एक लीटर में 1000 मिलिलीटर होते हैं)

**millimetre** (*AmE* **millimeter**) /ˈmɪlimiːtə(r) ˈमिलिमीट(र्)/ *noun* [C] (*abbr.* **mm**) a measure of length. There are 1000 millimetres in a metre लंबाई नापने की इकाई (एक मीटर में 1000 मिलिमीटर होते हैं)

**millinery** /ˈmɪlɪnəri ˈमिलिनरि/ *noun* [U] the business of making or selling women's hats and other articles महिलाओं के हैट और अन्य वस्तुएँ बनाने या बेचने का काम

**million** /ˈmɪljən ˈमिल्यन्/ *number* **1** 1,000,000 दस लाख, मिलियन *Nearly 60 million people live in Britain.* ○ *Millions of people are at risk from the disease.*

> **NOTE** एक मिलियन से बड़ी संख्या का निर्देश करने के लिए **'million'** के साथ बहुवचन प्रत्यय **'s'** नहीं लगता— *six million people.* संख्याओं के वाक्य-प्रयोग के उदाहरणों के लिए **six** देखिए।

**2 a million; millions (of)** (*informal*) a very large amount अत्यधिक विशाल मात्रा *I still have a million things to do.* ○ *There are millions of reasons why you shouldn't go.*

> **NOTE** संख्याओं के विषय में अधिक जानकारी के लिए इस शब्दकोश के अंत में **numbers** पर विशेष खंड देखिए।

**millionaire** /ˌmɪljəˈneə(r) ˌमिल्यˈनेअ(र्)/ *noun* [C] a person who has a million pounds, dollars, etc.; a very rich person लखपति, करोड़पति; बहुत धनी व्यक्ति

**millionth**[1] /ˈmɪljənθ ˈमिल्यन्थ्/ *pronoun, det.* 1,000,000th दस लाखवाँ

**millionth**[2] /ˈmɪljənθ ˈमिल्यन्थ्/ *noun* [C] one of a million equal parts of sth दस लाखवाँ अंश *a millionth of a second*

**millipede** /ˈmɪlɪpiːd ˈमिलिपीड्/ *noun* [C] a small animal like an insect with a long thin body divided into many sections, each with two pairs of legs सहस्त्रपाद; (एक बड़ा कीड़ा जिसका लंबा पतला शरीर अनेक खंडों में विभक्त होता है और प्रत्येक खंड में दो जोड़ी टाँगें होती हैं)

**milometer** (*also* **mileometer**) /maɪˈlɒmɪtə(r) माइˈलॉमिट(र्)/ (*AmE* **odometer**) *noun* [C] a piece of equipment in a vehicle that measures the number of miles you have travelled वाहन में लगा यंत्र जो तय की गई दूरी को मीलों में नापता है; माइलोमीटर ⇨ **car** पर चित्र देखिए।

**mime** /maɪm माइम्/ (*AmE* **pantomime**) *noun* [U, C] the use of movements of your hands and body and the expression on your face to tell a story or to act sth without speaking; a performance using this method of acting मूकाभिनय, कहानी सुनाने के लिए शब्दों के स्थान पर हस्त-संचालन और मुख-मुद्राओं का प्रयोग करने की प्रणाली; इस प्रणाली में प्रस्तुत कार्यक्रम; स्वाँग, मूकाभिनय *The performance consisted of dance, music and mime.* ▶ **mime** *verb* [I, T] स्वाँग भरना; बिना बोले केवल इशारों से कहानी सुनाना

**mimic**[1] /ˈmɪmɪk ˈमिमिक्/ *verb* [T] (*pres. part.* **mimicking;** *pt, pp* **mimicked**) to copy sb's behaviour, movements, voice, etc. in an amusing way मज़ाकिया ढंग से दूसरों की नक़ल उतारना

**mimic**[2] /ˈmɪmɪk ˈमिमिक्/ *noun* [C] a person who can copy sb's behaviour, movements, voice, etc. in an amusing way मज़ाकिया ढंग से दूसरों के व्यवहार, हरकतों आवाज़ आदि की नक़ल उतारने वाला; नक़लची, स्वाँगी ▶ **mimicry** /ˈmɪmɪkri ˈमिमिक्रि/ *noun* [U] नक़ल, स्वाँग

**min.** *abbr.* **1** minimum न्यूनतम *min. temp tomorrow 2°C* **2** minute(s) मिनट *fastest time: 6 min*

**minaret** *noun* [C] a tall thin tower, usually forming part of a building where Muslims meet and pray (**a mosque**) मस्जिद की मीनार

**mince** /mɪns मिन्स्/ (*BrE*) *noun* [U] meat that has been cut into very small pieces with a special machine क़ीमा; विशेष मशीन से बहुत छोटे टुकड़ों में काटा गया गोश्त, क़ीमा ▶ **mince** *verb* [T] क़ीमा करना, काटकर टुकड़े करना

**mincemeat** /ˈmɪnsmiːt ˈमिन्स्मीट्/ *noun* [U] a mixture of dried fruit, nuts, sugar, etc. (but no meat) that is used as a filling for sweet dishes, especially mince pies सूखे मेवे, चीनी आदि (परंतु गोश्त नहीं) का मिश्रण जिसे मीठी कचौरिओं में भरा जाता है

**mincepie** *noun* [C] a small round cake with a mixture of dried fruit, sugar, etc. (**mincemeat**) inside, traditionally eaten at Christmas time सूखे मेवे, चीनी आदि के मिश्रण से भरा छोटा गोल केक (जो पारंपरिक रूप से क्रिसमस के समय खाया जाता है)

**mind**[1] /maɪnd माइन्ड्/ *noun* [C, U] the part of your brain that thinks and remembers; your thoughts, feelings and intelligence चित्त, मन (मस्तिष्क का वह अंश जो सोचता और याद रखता है); व्यक्ति के विचार, मनोभाव और बुद्धि *He has a brilliant mind.* ○ *Not everybody has the right sort of mind for this work.*

**at/in the back of your mind** ⇨ **back**[1] देखिए।

**IDM be in two minds (about sth/doing sth)** to not feel sure of sth किसी बात के बारे में निश्चित न हो

पाना, दुचित्ता होना, दुविधाग्रस्त होना *I'm in two minds about leaving Ria alone in the house while we're away.*

**be/go out of your mind** (*informal*) to be or become crazy or very worried सनकी या बहुत चिंतित होना या हो जाना *I was going out of my mind when Tina didn't come home on time.*

**bear in mind (that); bear/keep sb/sth in mind** to remember or consider (that); to remember sb/sth याद रखना या विचार करना (कि); किसी व्यक्ति या वस्तु को याद रखना *We'll bear/keep your suggestion in mind for the future.*

**bring/call sb/sth to mind** to be reminded of sb/sth; to remember sb/sth किसी व्यक्ति या वस्तु की याद दिलाना; किसी व्यक्ति या वस्तु को याद करना

**cast your mind back** ➪ **cast**[1] देखिए।

**change your mind** ➪ **change**[1] देखिए।

**come/spring to mind** if sth comes/springs to mind, you suddenly remember or think of it एकाएक कोई बात मन में आ जाना (याद आ जाना या उस पर सोचने लगना)

**cross your mind** ➪ **cross**[2] देखिए।

**ease sb's mind** ➪ **ease**[2] देखिए।

**frame of mind** ➪ **frame**[1] देखिए।

**give sb a piece of your mind** ➪ **piece**[1] देखिए।

**go clean out of your mind** ➪ **clean**[3] देखिए।

**have/keep an open mind** ➪ **open**[1] देखिए।

**have sb/sth in mind (for sth)** to be considering sb/sth as suitable for sth; to have a plan किसी व्यक्ति या वस्तु को किसी काम के उपयुक्त समझने पर विचार करना; कोई योजना बनाना *Who do you have in mind for the job?*

**keep your mind on sth** to continue to pay attention to sth किसी बात पर ध्यान केंद्रित रखना *Keep your mind on the road while you're driving!*

**make up your mind** to decide (किसी बात का) निश्चय करना *I can't make up my mind which sweater to buy.*

**on your mind** worrying you (किसी बात पर) चिंताग्रस्त होना *Don't bother her with that. She's got enough on her mind already.*

**prey on sb's mind** ➪ **prey**[2] देखिए।

**put/set sb's mind at rest** to make sb stop worrying किसी को चिंतामुक्त कर देना *The results of the blood test set his mind at rest.*

**slip your mind** ➪ **slip**[1] देखिए।

**speak your mind** ➪ **speak** देखिए।

**state of mind** ➪ **state**[1] देखिए।

**take sb's mind off sth** to help sb not to think or worry about sth किसी व्यक्ति को किसी बात पर ज़्यादा सोचने या चिंता न करने देना

**to my mind** in my opinion मेरे विचार से *To my mind, this is a complete waste of time!*

**mind**[2] /maɪnd माइन्ड्/ *verb* **1** [I, T] (*especially in questions, answers and negative sentences*) to feel annoyed, upset or uncomfortable about sth/sb किसी वस्तु या व्यक्ति से नाराज़ होना, परेशान हो जाना या उसकी बात का बुरा मानना *Do you mind having to travel so far to work every day?* ○ *'Would you like tea or coffee?' 'I don't mind.'* (= I'm happy to have either) ○ *I wouldn't mind a break right now* (= I would like one). **2** [T] (used in a question as a polite way of asking sb to do sth or for permission to do sth) could you...?; may I...? (कुछ करने का नम्र अनुरोध करने या उसकी अनुमति माँगने का अर्थ देने वाले प्रश्नवाचक वाक्य में प्रयुक्त) क्या आप... क्या मैं...? *Would you mind closing the window for me?* ○ *Do you mind driving? I'm feeling rather tired.* **3** [T] used to tell sb to be careful of sth or to pay attention to sb/sth किसी बात के विषय में सावधानी बरतने या उस पर ध्यान देने की सलाह देने के लिए प्रयुक्त *It's a very low doorway so mind your head.* ○ *Don't mind me! I won't disturb you.* **4** [T] (*BrE*) to look after or watch sb/sth for a short time थोड़े समय के लिए किसी व्यक्ति या वस्तु की देख-भाल करना या उस पर निगाह रखना *Could you mind my bag while I go and get us some drinks?*

IDM **mind you** used for attracting attention to a point you are making or for giving more information अपनी बात की ओर दूसरे का ध्यान आकृष्ट करने या अधिक जानकारी देने के लिए प्रयुक्त अभिव्यक्ति *Pratik seems very tired. Mind you, he has been working very hard recently.*

**mind your own business** used to tell sb to pay attention to his/her affairs, not other people's अपने काम से सरोकार रखना, दूसरों के काम से नहीं, ऐसा कहने के लिए प्रयुक्त अभिव्यक्ति *Stop asking me personal questions and mind your own business!*

**never mind** used to tell sb not to worry as it doesn't matter किसी अमहत्त्वपूर्ण बात के लिए चिंता नहीं करने के लिए प्रयुक्त *'I forgot to post your letter.' 'Never mind, I'll do it later.'*

**mind out** (*informal*) used to tell sb to get out of the way रास्ते से हट जाओ *Mind out! There's a car coming.*

**mind-boggling** *adj.* (*informal*) difficult to imagine, understand or believe कल्पनातीत, समझ से बाहर; अविश्वसनीय *Mind-boggling amounts of money were being discussed.*

**-minded** /ˈmaɪndɪd ˈमाइन्डिड्/ *adj.* (*compound adjectives*) **1** having the type of mind mentioned

निर्दिष्ट प्रकार के मन वाला (जैसे हिंदी में 'उदारमना', महामना), -मना *a strong-minded/open-minded/narrow-minded person* **2** interested in the thing mentioned निर्दिष्ट वस्तु में दिलचस्पी रखने वाला (जैसे हिंदी में 'धन-प्रेमी', 'धर्म-प्रेमी'), -प्रेमी *money-minded*

**minder** /ˈmaɪndə(r) ˈमाइन्डर्(र्)/ *noun* [C] a person whose job is to look after and protect sb/sth किसी की देख-भाल और सुरक्षा का काम करने वाला व्यक्ति *My son goes to a childminder so that I can work part-time.*

**mindful** /ˈmaɪndfl ˈमाइन्ड्फ़ुल्/ *adj.* **mindful of sb/sth; mindful that...** (*formal*) remembering sb/sth and considering him/her/it when you do sth सावधान, सचेत, सतर्क, जागरुक *mindful of our responsibilities* ○ *Mindful of the danger of tropical storms, I decided not to go out.* ✪ पर्याय **conscious**

**mindless** /ˈmaɪndləs ˈमाइन्ड्लस्/ *adj.* **1** done or acting without thought and for no particular reason नासमझी-भरा, बुद्धिहीन *mindless violence* **2** not needing thought or intelligence जिसमें सोचने या समझने की आवश्यकता नहीं; यंत्रवत *a mindless and repetitive task*

**mine**[1] /maɪn माइन्/ *pronoun* of or belonging to me मुझसे संबंधित या मेरा *Don't take your car—you can come in mine.* ○ *May I introduce a friend of mine* (= one of my friends)? ➪ **my** देखिए।

**mine**[2] /maɪn माइन्/ *noun* [C] **1** a deep hole, or a system of passages under the ground where minerals such as coal, tin, gold, etc. are dug खान, खदान (कोयले, टीन, सोना आदि की) *a coal/salt/gold mine* ➪ **quarry** देखिए। **2** a bomb that is hidden under the ground or under water and explodes when sb/sth touches it बारूदी सुरंग (ज़मीन या पानी के नीचे रखा बम जो किसी के छू लेने से फट जाता है) *The car went over a mine and blew up.*

**mine**[3] /maɪn माइन्/ *verb* **1** [I, T] to dig in the ground for minerals such as coal, tin, gold, etc. कोयला, टीन, सोना आदि खनिजों के लिए ज़मीन में गहरे खोदना *Diamonds are mined in South Africa.* ➪ **mining** देखिए। **2** [T] to put **mines**[2] **2** in an area of land or sea ज़मीन या समुद्र के नीचे किसी स्थान पर बारूदी सुरंगें बिछाना

**minefield** /ˈmaɪnfiːld ˈमाइन्फ़ील्ड्/ *noun* [C] **1** an area of land or sea where **mines**[2] **2** have been hidden बारूदी सुरंग क्षेत्र **2** a situation that is full of hidden dangers or difficulties गुप्त ख़तरों या कठिनाइयों से भरी स्थिति *a political minefield*

**miner** /ˈmaɪnə(r) ˈमाइन(र्)/ *noun* [C] a person whose job is to work in a **mine**[2] **1** to get coal, salt, tin, etc. खान-कर्मी (खान में काम करने वाला); खनिक

**mineral** /ˈmɪnərəl ˈमिनरल्/ *noun* [C] a natural substance such as coal, salt, oil, etc. especially one that is found in the ground. Some minerals are also present in food and drink and are very important for good health खनिज पदार्थ (ज़मीन के नीचे पाए जाने वाले कोयला, नमक, तेल आदि प्राकृतिक पदार्थ, कुछ खनिज खाद्य और पेय पदार्थों में पाए जाने वाले पदार्थ स्वास्थ्यवर्धक होते हैं) *a country rich in minerals* ○ *the recommended daily intake of vitamins and minerals*

**mineral water** *noun* [U] water that comes straight from a place in the ground (**a spring**), which contains minerals or gases and is thought to be good for your health सीधे ज़मीन के स्रोतों या चश्मों से प्राप्त पानी जिसमें स्वास्थ्यवर्धक खनिज या गैसें होती हैं; खनिज जल, मिनरल वाटर

**mingle** /ˈmɪŋgl ˈमिङ्गल्/ *verb* [I, T] **mingle A and B (together); mingle (A) (with B)** to mix with other things or people अन्य वस्तुओं या व्यक्तियों से मिलना, में घुल-मिल जाना *His excitement was mingled with fear.* ○ *to mingle with the rich and famous*

**mini-** /ˈmɪni ˈमिनि/ (*used to form compound nouns*) very small बहुत छोटा (आकार, लंबाई आदि में), लघु *a miniskirt* ○ *minigolf*

**miniature** /ˈmɪnətʃə(r) ˈमिनच(र्)/ *noun* [C] a small copy of sth which is much larger बड़े आकार की वस्तु का लघु रूप *a miniature camera*

**IDM in miniature** exactly the same as sb/sth else but in a very small form किसी की लघु प्रतिकृति (आकृति मूलवत, आकार लघु)

**minibus** /ˈmɪnibʌs ˈमिनिबस्/ *noun* [C] (*BrE*) a small bus, usually for no more than 12 people छोटी बस (प्रायः बारह सवारियों तक के लिए), मिनि-बस ➪ **bus** देखिए।

**minidisc** /ˈmɪnidɪsk ˈमिनिडिस्क्/ *noun* [C] a disc like a small **CD** that can record and play sound or data छोटी सीडी जैसी डिस्क (जो आवाज़ या सूचना-सामाग्री को रिकार्ड या पुनः प्रस्तुत कर सकती है); मिनि-डिस्क

**minimal** /ˈmɪnɪməl ˈमिनिमल्/ *adj.* very small in amount, size or level; as little as possible मात्रा, आकार या स्तर में बहुत कम; यथासंभव न्यूनतम *The project must be carried out at minimal cost.*

**minimize** (*also* **-ise**) /ˈmɪnɪmaɪz ˈमिनिमाइज़्/ *verb* [T] **1** to make sth as small as possible (in amount or level) (मात्रा या स्तर की दृष्टि से) यथासंभव न्यूनतम कर देना *We shall try to minimize the risks to the public.* **2** to try to make sth seem less important than it really is **3** (*computing*) to make sth small on a computer screen कंप्यूटर स्क्रीन पर किसी वस्तु का आकार घटा देना ✪ विलोम **maximize**

**minimum¹** /ˈmɪnɪməm ˈमिनिमम्/ *noun* [*sing.*] the smallest amount or level that is possible or allowed न्यूनतम (मात्रा या स्तर जो संभव या स्वीकार्य हो) *I need a minimum of seven hours' sleep.* ○ *We will try and* ***keep*** *the cost of the tickets to a minimum.* ✪ विलोम **maximum**

**minimum²** /ˈmɪnɪməm ˈमिनिमम्/ *adj.* (*only before a noun*) the smallest possible or allowed; extremely small न्यूनतम संभव या स्वीकार्य; बहुत छोटा *to introduce a national* ***minimum wage*** (= the lowest wage that an employer is legally allowed to pay) ✪ विलोम **maximum** ▶ **minimum** *adv.* न्यूनतम रूप से *We'll need Rs 200 minimum for expenses.*

**mining** /ˈmaɪnɪŋ ˈमाइनिङ्/ *noun* [U] (*often used to form compound nouns*) the process or industry of getting minerals, metals, etc. out of the ground by digging खुदाई कर जमीन से खनिजों, धातुओं, आदि को निकालने की प्रक्रिया या इस कार्य का उद्योग; खनन-उद्योग *coal/tin/gold mining*

**minister** /ˈmɪnɪstə(r) ˈमिनिस्ट(र्)/ *noun* [C] **1 Minister** (*AmE* **Secretary**) a member of the government, often the head of a government department मंत्रिमंडल का सदस्य (प्रायः किसी मंत्रालय का प्रमुख), मंत्री *the Minister for Trade and Industry* ➪ **Prime Minister** और **Cabinet Minister** भी देखिए। **2** a priest in some Protestant churches (कुछ प्रोटेस्टैंट चर्चों में) पुरोहित, पादरी ➪ **vicar** देखिए।

**ministerial** /ˌmɪnɪˈstɪəriəl ˌमिनिˈस्टिअरिअल्/ *adj.* connected with a government minister or department मंत्री या मंत्रालय से संबंधित

**ministry** /ˈmɪnɪstri ˈमिनिस्ट्रि/ *noun* [C] (*pl.* **ministries**) (*also* **department**) a government department that has a particular area of responsibility एक सरकारी विभाग जिसका अपना कार्यक्षेत्र होता है; मंत्रालय *the Ministry of Defence*

**minivan** /ˈmɪnivæn ˈमिनिवैन्/ (*AmE*) = **people carrier**

**mink** /mɪŋk मिङ्क्/ *noun* [C] a small wild animal that is kept for its thick brown fur which is used to make expensive coats एक छोटा वन्य पशु जिसके फ़र से महँगे कोट बनते हैं; मिंक

**minor¹** /ˈmaɪnə(r) ˈमाइनर्/ *adj.* **1** not very big, serious or important (when compared with others) जो अधिक बड़ा, गंभीर या आवश्यक न हो (औरों की तुलना में), गौण, छोटा, कम महत्त्वपूर्ण *It's only a minor problem. Don't worry.* ○ *She's gone into hospital for a minor operation.* ✪ विलोम **major** **2** of one of the two types of **key¹ 4** in which music is usually written संगीत-रचना के लिए अपेक्षित दो प्रकार की कुंजियों में से एक से संबंधित, माइनर *a symphony in F minor* ➪ **major** देखिए।

**minor²** /ˈmaɪnə(r) ˈमाइनर्/ *noun* [C] (used in law) a person who is not legally an adult (क़ानून में) अवयस्क, नाबालिग़ (18 वर्ष से कम आयु का)

**minority** /maɪˈnɒrəti माइˈनॉरटि/ *noun* [C] (*pl.* **minorities**) **1** [*usually sing., with sing. or pl. verb*] the smaller number or part of a group; less than half छोटी संख्या या समूह का अपेक्षाकृत छोटा अंश, अल्पांश; आधे से कम (की संख्या), अल्पसंख्या *Only a minority of teenagers become/becomes involved in crime.* ✪ विलोम **majority** **2** a small group of people who are of a different race or religion to most of the people in the community or country where they live जाति या धर्म की दृष्टि से अल्पसंख्यक वर्ग *Schools in Britain need to do more to help children of* ***ethnic/racial minorities.***

IDM **be in a/the minority** to be the smaller of two groups अपेक्षाकृत छोटे समूह का सदस्य होना, दूसरे वर्ग से संख्या में कम होना *Men are in the minority in the teaching profession.* ➪ **in a/the majority** देखिए।

**mint** /mɪnt मिन्ट्/ *noun* **1** [U] a type of plant (**a herb**) whose leaves are used to give flavour to food, drinks, toothpaste, etc. पुदीना (पौधा) (जिसके पत्तों से खाद्य और पेय पदार्थों आदि में विशेष स्वाद आ जाता है) *kababs with mint sauce* **2** [C] a type of sweet with a strong fresh flavour एक प्रकार की मीठी गोली जिसका स्वाद तीखा तथा ताज़ा होता है **3** [*sing.*] the place where money in the form of coins and notes is made by the government टकसाल (जहाँ सरकारी व्यस्था के अंतर्गत सिक्के ढलते हैं और नोट छपते हैं) ▶ **mint** *verb* [T] सिक्के ढालना और नोट छापना *freshly minted coins*

**minus¹** /ˈmaɪnəs ˈमाइनस्/ *prep.* **1** (used in sums) less; subtract; take away (संख्याओं में प्रयुक्त) कम; घटा, ऋण कम करना, घटना *Six minus two is four* $(6 - 2 = 4)$. ✪ विलोम **plus** **2** (used about a number) below zero (संख्या) शून्य से कम या नीचे *The temperature will fall to minus 10°C.* **3** (*informal*) without sth that was there before पहले वाली वस्तु के बिना; विहीन, रहित *We're going to be minus a car for a while.*

**minus²** /ˈmaɪnəs ˈमाइनस्/ *noun* [C] **1** (*also* **minus sign**) (*symbol* –) the symbol which is used in mathematics to show that a number is below zero or that you should subtract the second number from the first गणित में प्रयुक्त ऋण चिह्न जो यह दर्शाता है कि कोई संख्या शून्य से कम या नीचे है, किसी दूसरी संख्या को पहली संख्या से घटाने के लिए

प्रयुक्त चिह्न (–) **2** (*also* **minus point**) (*informal*) a negative quality; a disadvantage नकारात्मक गुण; हानि, नुक़सान *Let's consider the pluses and minuses of moving out of the city.* ✪ विलोम **plus**

**minus³** /ˈmaɪnəs ˈमाइनस् / *adj.* **1** (used in mathematics) lower than zero (गणित में प्रयुक्त) शून्य से कम; ऋणात्मक *a minus figure* **2** (*not before a noun*) (used in a system of grades given for school work) slightly lower than स्कूल-कार्य के लिए अंक देने की प्रणाली में प्रयुक्त) बिंदु विशेष से कुछ कम *I got A minus (A–) for my essay.* ✪ विलोम **plus**

**minuscule** /ˈmɪnəskjuːl ˈमिनस्क्यूल् / *adj.* extremely small अति सूक्ष्म

**minute¹** /ˈmɪnɪt ˈमिनिट् / *noun* **1** [C] (*abbr.* **min.**) one of the 60 parts that make up one hour; 60 seconds मिनट (एक घंटे का 60वाँ अंश); साठ सेकंडों की इकाई *It's twelve minutes to nine.* ○ *The programme lasts for about fifty minutes.* **2** [*sing.*] (*spoken*) a very short time; a moment अत्यल्प समय; क्षणभर ***Just/Wait a minute*** (= wait)! *You've forgotten your notes.* ○ *Have you got a minute?—I'd like to talk to you.* **3 the minutes** [*pl.*] a written record of what is said and decided at a meeting सभा या बैठक के लिए गए निर्णयों का लिखित विवरण; कार्यवृत्त **4** each of the 60 equal parts of a degree, used in measuring angles (कोणों को नापने में प्रयुक्त) एक डिग्री का 60वाँ अंश *37 degrees 30 minutes (37° 30')*

IDM **(at) any minute/moment (now)** (*informal*) very soon बहुत शीघ्र, किसी भी क्षण *The plane should be landing any minute now.*

**in a minute** very soon बहुत शीघ्र (केवल) एक मिनट में *I'll be with you in a minute.*

**the last minute/moment** ➪ **last¹ 1** देखिए।

**the minute/moment (that)** as soon as ज्यों ही *I'll tell him you rang the minute (that) he gets here.*

**this minute** immediately; now इसी क्षण; अभी-अभी *I don't know what I'm going to do yet—I've just found out this minute.*

**up to the minute** (*informal*) having the most recent information नवीनतम, इस क्षण तक का *For up-to-the-minute information on flight times, phone this number*

**minute²** /maɪˈnjuːt माइˈन्यूट् / *adj.* (*superlative* **minutest**) (*no comparative*) **1** very small बहुत महीन, अति सूक्ष्म *I couldn't read his writing. It was minute!* **2** very exact or accurate एकदम सही या ठीक-ठाक या यथार्थ *She was able to describe the man **in minute detail/the minutest detail**.*

**miracle** /ˈmɪrəkl ˈमिरक्ल् / *noun* **1** [C] a wonderful event that seems impossible and that is believed to be caused by God or a god दैवीय घटना, चमत्कार (जिसका कर्ता स्वयं ईश्वर या किसी देवता को माना जाता है) **2** [*sing.*] a lucky thing that happens that you did not expect or think was possible (आशा या सोच के विपरीत घटी) शुभ घटना *It's a miracle (that) nobody was killed in the crash.*

IDM **work/perform miracles** to achieve very good results चमत्कार कर देना, बहुत अच्छे परिणाम देना *The new diet and exercise programme have worked miracles for her.*

**miraculous** /mɪˈrækjələs मिˈरैक्यलस् / *adj.* completely unexpected and very lucky सर्वथा अप्रत्याशित और बहुत शुभ; चमत्कारपूर्ण *She's made a miraculous recovery.* ▶ **miraculously** *adv.* चमत्कारी ढंग से

**mirage** /ˈmɪrɑːʒ; mɪˈrɑːʒ ˈमिराश़्; मिˈराश़् / *noun* [C] an image you think you see in very hot weather, for example water in a desert, but which does not really exist घोर ग्रीष्म ऋतु में दिखाई देने वाली भ्रामक वस्तु (जिसका वस्तुतः अस्तित्व नहीं होता, जैसे मरूस्थल में जल); मरु मरीचिका **2** a hope or wish that cannot be achieved मरीचिका, मृग तृष्णा *His victory in the election is just a mirage.*

**mirror** /ˈmɪrə(r) ˈमिर(र्) / *noun* [C] a piece of special flat glass that you can look into in order to see yourself or what is behind you दर्पण, शीशा *to look **in the mirror*** ○ *a **rear-view mirror*** (= in a car, so that the driver can see what is behind) ○ *a **mirror image***

NOTE दर्पण छवियों को **reflect** करता है और दर्पण में जो हम देखते हैं वह **reflection** होता है।

▶ **mirror** *verb* [T] प्रतिबिंबित करना *The trees were mirrored in the lake.*

**mirth** /mɜːθ मश़् / *noun* [U] (*written*) amusement or laughter मनोरंजन या हँसी, हास्य

**mis-** /mɪs मिस् / *prefix* (*used in verbs and nouns*) bad or wrong; badly or wrongly अप्रिय या अनुचित; अप्रिय या अनुचित रूप से *misbehaviour* ○ *misunderstand*

**misapprehension** /ˌmɪsæprɪˈhenʃn ˌमिसऐप्रिˈहेन्शन् / *noun* [U, C] (*formal*) to have the wrong idea about sth or to believe sth is true when it is not ग़लतफ़हमी, मिथ्याबोध *I was **under the misapprehension** that this course was for beginners.*

**misbehave** /ˌmɪsbɪˈheɪv ˌमिस्बिˈहेव् / *verb* [I] to behave badly दुर्व्यवहार करना ✪ विलोम **behave**

▶ **misbehaviour** (*AmE* **misbehavior**) /ˌmɪsbɪˈheɪvjə(r) ˌमिस्बिˈहेव्य(र्)/ *noun* [U] दुर्व्यवहार, दुराचार

**misc.** *abbr.* miscellaneous विविध, फुटकर

**miscalculate** /ˌmɪsˈkælkjuleɪt ˌमिस्ˈकैल्क्युलेट्/ *verb* [I, T] to make a mistake in calculating or judging a situation, an amount, etc. गणना करने या किसी स्थिति को समझने या आँकने में भूल करना ▶ **miscalculation** /ˌmɪskælkjuˈleɪʃn ˌमिस्कैल्क्युˈलेश्न्/ *noun* [C, U] अशुद्ध गणना, ग़लत अनुमान

**miscarriage** /ˈmɪskærɪdʒ ˈमिस्कैरिज्/ *noun* [C, U] (*medical*) giving birth to a baby before it is fully developed, causing its death (चिकित्सा) गर्भपात, गर्भस्राव (समय से पूर्व शिशु का जन्म और फलस्वरूप उसकी मृत्यु) ➪ **abortion** देखिए।

IDM **a miscarriage of justice** an occasion when sb is punished for a crime that he/she did not do न्याय-हत्या, ग़लत निर्णय (जिसने अपराध नहीं किया उसे अपराधी मानने का निर्णय)

**miscarry** /ˌmɪsˈkæri ˌमिस्ˈकैरि/ *verb* [I] (*pres. part.* **miscarrying;** *3rd person sing. pres.* **miscarries;** *pt, pp* **miscarried**) to give birth to a baby before it is ready to be born, with the result that it cannot live समय से पूर्व शिशु का जन्म होना और फलस्वरूप उसकी मृत्यु हो जाना; गर्भपात या गर्भस्राव होना

**miscellaneous** /ˌmɪsəˈleɪniəs ˌमिसˈलेनिअस्/ *adj.* (*abbr.* **misc.**) consisting of many different types or things विविध, फुटकर *a box of miscellaneous items for sale*

**mischief** /ˈmɪstʃɪf ˈमिस्चिफ़्/ *noun* [U] bad behaviour (usually of children) that is not very serious (बच्चों की) शरारत, नटखटपन *The children in Class 9 are always* ***getting into mischief.***

**mischievous** /ˈmɪstʃɪvəs ˈमिस्चिव़स्/ *adj.* (usually used about children) liking to behave badly and embarrassing or annoying people (प्रायः बच्चों के लिए प्रयुक्त) शरारती, नटखट ▶ **mischievously** *adv.* शरारतभरे ढंग से

**miscible** /ˈmɪsəbl ˈमिसब्ल्/ *adj.* (*technical*) (used about liquids) that can be mixed together (द्रव) जिन्हें परस्पर मिलाया जा सकता है, परस्पर मिश्रणीय; विलयी ✪ विलोम **immiscible**

**misconception** /ˌmɪskənˈsepʃn ˌमिस्कन्ˈसेप्श्न्/ *noun* [C] a wrong idea or understanding of sth (किसी बात के विषय में) भ्रांत धारणा, ग़लतफ़हमी *It is a popular misconception* (= many people wrongly believe) *that people need meat to be healthy.*

**misconduct** /ˌmɪsˈkɒndʌkt ˌमिस्ˈकॉन्डक्ट्/ *noun* [U] (*formal*) unacceptable behaviour, especially by a professional person अनुचित आचरण (विशेषतः पेशेवर व्यक्ति द्वारा); कदाचार *The doctor was dismissed for* ***gross*** (= very serious) ***misconduct.***

**misconstrue** /ˌmɪskənˈstruː ˌमिस्कन्ˈस्ट्रू/ *verb* [T] (*formal*) **misconstrue sth (as sth)** to understand sb's words or actions wrongly किसी व्यक्ति के कहे और किए शब्दों और कार्यों को ग़लत समझ लेना ➪ **construe** देखिए।

**misdemeanour** (*AmE* **misdemeanor**) /ˌmɪsdɪˈmiːnə(r) ˌमिस्डिˈमीन(र्)/ *noun* [C] something slightly bad or wrong that a person does; a crime that is not very serious किसी के द्वारा किया गया कुछ बुरा या ग़लत आचरण; अपराध जो अधिक संगीन या गंभीर नहीं ➪ **felony** देखिए।

**misdirect** /ˌmɪsdəˈrekt ˌमिस्डˈरेक्ट्/ *verb* [T] **1** to send sb/sth in the wrong direction or to a wrong place किसी व्यक्ति या वस्तु को ग़लत निर्देश देना या विमार्गन करना **2** (*formal*) to use sth like funds, etc. for unsuitable purposes or in a way that is inappropriate to a particular situation धन आदि को अनुप्युक्त उद्देश्य के लिए प्रयोग करना जो विशिष्ट परिस्थिति के प्रतिकूल हो **2** (*legal*) to provide incorrect legal information ग़लत क़ानूनी सूचना देना

**miser** /ˈmaɪzə(r) ˈमाइज़(र्)/ *noun* [C] a person who loves to have a lot of money but hates to spend it कंजूस, कृपण ▶ **miserly** *adj.* कृपण समान, कंजूसी-भरा

**miserable** /ˈmɪzrəbl ˈमिज़्रब्ल्/ *adj.* **1** very unhappy बहुत उदास, दयनीय *Oh dear, you look miserable. What's wrong?* **2** unpleasant; making you feel unhappy अप्रिय; खिन्न कर देने वाला *What miserable weather* (= grey, cold and wet)*!* ✪ पर्याय **dismal** **3** too small or of bad quality बहुत कम या (गुणवत्ता में) घटिया, निकृष्ठ *I was offered a miserable salary so I didn't take the job.* ▶ **miserably** /ˈmɪzrəbli ˈमिज़्रब्लि/ *adv.* दयनीय भाव से, बुरी तरह से *I stared miserably out of the window.* ○ *He* ***failed miserably*** *as an actor.*

**misery** /ˈmɪzəri ˈमिज़रि/ *noun* [U, C] (*pl.* **miseries**) great unhappiness or suffering घोर निराशा या व्यथा, तकलीफ़, परेशानी, दुर्दशा *I couldn't bear to see him in such misery.* ○ *the miseries of war*

IDM **put sb out of his/her misery** (*informal*) to stop sb worrying about sth by telling the person what he/she wants to know किसी की परेशानियों का अंत कर देना या किसी को परेशानियों से बाहर निकाल लेना *Put me out of my misery—did I pass or not?*

**put sth out of its misery** to kill an animal because it has an illness or injury that cannot be treated असाध्य रोग से ग्रस्त या बुरी तरह से घायल पशु की दया-हत्या कर देना (उसे मार देना ताकि उसकी पीड़ाओं का अंत हो जाए)

**misfire** /ˌmɪsˈfaɪə(r) ˌमिस्ˈफ़ाइअ(र्)/ *verb* [I] to fail to have the intended result or effect अभीष्ट परिणाम या प्रभाव उत्पन्न न कर पाना *The plan misfired.*

**misfit** /ˈmɪsfɪt ˈमिस्फ़िट्/ *noun* [C] a person who is not accepted by other people, especially because his/her behaviour or ideas are very different अनुपयुक्त व्यक्ति (अन्य लोगों के साथ संबंध की दृष्टि से, आचरण या विचारों की अत्यधिक भिन्नता के कारण)

**misfortune** /ˌmɪsˈfɔːtʃuːn ˌमिस्ˈफ़ॉचून्/ *noun* [C, U] (*formal*) (an event, accident, etc. that brings) bad luck or disaster दुर्भाग्य, विपत्ति या अनर्थ *I hope I don't ever **have the misfortune to** meet him again.*

**misgiving** /ˌmɪsˈɡɪvɪŋ ˌमिस्ˈगिविङ्/ *noun* [C, U] a feeling of doubt, worry or suspicion संदेह, चिंता या शंका का भाव; अविश्वास *I **had serious misgivings** about leaving him on his own.*

**misguided** /ˌmɪsˈɡaɪdɪd ˌमिस्ˈगाइडिड्/ *adj.* wrong because you have understood or judged a situation badly गुमराह, पथभ्रष्ट (वस्तुस्थिति को समझने या आँकने में भूल के कारण)

**mishap** /ˈmɪshæp ˈमिस्हैप्/ *noun* [C, U] a small accident or piece of bad luck that does not have serious results मामूली दुर्घटना या अशुभ प्रसंग *to have a slight mishap*

**misinform** /ˌmɪsɪnˈfɔːm ˌमिसिन्ˈफ़ॉम्/ *verb* [T] (*formal*) to give sb the wrong information (किसी को) ग़लत सूचना देना *I think you've been misinformed—no one is going to lose their job.*

**misinterpret** /ˌmɪsɪnˈtɜːprɪt ˌमिसिन्ˈटप्रिट्/ *verb* [T] **misinterpret sth (as sth)** to understand sth wrongly किसी बात का ग़लत अर्थ लगाना *His comments were misinterpreted as a criticism of the project.* ✪ विलोम **interpret** ▶ **misinterpretation** /ˌmɪsɪntɜːprɪˈteɪʃn ˌमिसिनूटप्रिˈटेश्न्/ *noun* [C, U] ग़लत या भ्रांत व्याख्या *Parts of the speech were open to misinterpretation* (= easy to understand wrongly).

**misjudge** /ˌmɪsˈdʒʌdʒ ˌमिस्ˈजज्/ *verb* [T] **1** to form a wrong opinion of sb/sth, usually in a way which is unfair to him/her/it किसी व्यक्ति या वस्तु के विषय में ग़लत धारणा बना लेना (प्रायः अनुचित रूप से) **2** to guess time, distance, etc. wrongly समय, दूरी आदि के बारे में ग़लत अनुमान लगाना *He completely misjudged the speed of the other car and almost crashed.* ▶ **misjudgement** (*also* **misjudgment**) *noun* [C, U] ग़लत अनुमान, भ्रांत धारणा

**mislay** /ˌmɪsˈleɪ ˌमिस्ˈले/ *verb* [T] (*pres. part.* **mislaying;** *3rd person sing. pres.* **mislays;** *pt, pp* **mislaid** /-leɪd -लेड्/) to lose sth, usually for a short time, because you cannot remember where you put it किसी वस्तु को कहीं रखकर भूल जाना कि वह कहाँ रखी है (प्रायः थोड़े समय के लिए), किसी वस्तु को ग़लत स्थान पर रख देना (प्रायः थोड़े समय के लिए)

**mislead** /ˌmɪsˈliːd ˌमिस्ˈलीड्/ *verb* [T] (*pt, pp* **misled** /-led -लेड्/) to make sb have the wrong idea or opinion about sb/sth किसी व्यक्ति या वस्तु के विषय में ग़लत धारणा देना; गुमराह या पथभ्रष्ट करना ▶ **misleading** *adj.* गुमराह या पथभ्रष्ट करने वाला; भ्रामक *a misleading advertisement*

**mismanage** /ˌmɪsˈmænɪdʒ ˌमिस्ˈमैनिज्/ *verb* [T] to manage or organize sth badly कुप्रबंध या दुर्व्यवस्था करना ▶ **mismanagement** *noun* [U] कुप्रबंध, दुर्व्यवस्था

**misogynist** /mɪˈsɒdʒɪnɪst मिˈसॉजिनिस्ट्/ *noun* [C] (*formal*) a man who hates women नारी-द्वेषी, पुरुष संबंधी ▶ **misogynistic** /mɪˌsɒdʒɪˈnɪstɪk मिˌसॉजिˈनिस्टिक्/ (*also* **misogynist**) *adj.* नारी-द्वेष संबंधी ▶ **misogyny** /mɪˈsɒdʒɪni मिˈसॉजिनि/ *noun* [U] नारी-द्वेष

**misplaced** /ˌmɪsˈpleɪst ˌमिस्ˈप्लेस्ट्/ *adj.* given to sb/sth that is not suitable or good enough to have it अनुपयुक्त व्यक्ति या वस्तु को अर्पित; अपात्र-गत *misplaced loyalty*

**misprint** /ˈmɪsprɪnt ˈमिस्प्रिंट्/ *noun* [C] a mistake in printing or typing मुद्रण या टंकण में ग़लती, मुद्रण-दोष

**mispronounce** /ˌmɪsprəˈnaʊns ˌमिस्प्रˈनाउन्स्/ *verb* [T] to say a word or letter wrongly किसी शब्द का अशुद्ध उच्चारण करना *People always mispronounce my surname.* ▶ **mispronunciation** /ˌmɪsprənʌnsiˈeɪʃn ˌमिस्प्रननसिˈएश्न्/ *noun* [C, U] अशुद्ध उच्चारण

**misread** /ˌmɪsˈriːd ˌमिसˈरीड्/ *verb* [T] (*pt, pp* **misread** /-ˈred -रेड्/) **misread sth (as sth)** to read or understand sth wrongly किसी बात को ग़लत समझ लेना, कुछ का कुछ समझ बैठना *He misread my silence as a refusal.*

**misrepresent** /ˌmɪsrepriˈzent ˌमिस्रेप्रिˈज़ेन्ट्/ *verb* [T] (*usually passive*) to give a wrong description of sb/sth किसी व्यक्ति या वस्तु के विषय में ग़लत विवरण देना *In the newspaper article they were misrepresented as uncaring parents.* ▶ **misrepresentation** /ˌmɪsreprɪzenˈteɪʃn ˌमिस्रेप्रिज़ेन्ˈटेश्न्/ *noun* [C, U] मिथ्या या अयथार्थ निरूपण

**Miss**[1] /mɪs मिस्/ used as a title before the family name of a young woman or a woman who is not married अविवाहित युवती या महिला के कुल नाम से पहले प्रयुक्त उपाधि; कुमारी, मिस, सुश्री

**NOTE** **Miss, Mrs, Ms** और **Mr** ये सब उपाधियाँ हैं जो व्यक्ति के कुलनाम के पहले लगती हैं, न कि उसके प्रथम नाम के पहले यदि वह कुलनाम का अंग बनकर प्रयुक्त नहीं होता। सही प्रयोग है—*Is there a Miss (Tanya) Singh here?* न कि *Miss Tanya* ○ *'Dear Miss Garg,' the letter began.*

**miss**[2] /mɪs मिस्/ *verb* **1** [I, T] to fail to hit, catch, etc. sth (किसी वस्तु को मारने, पकड़ने आदि में) चूकना, चूक जाना *She tried to catch the ball but she missed.* ○ *The bullet narrowly missed his heart.* **2** [T] to not see, hear, understand, etc. sb/sth किसी व्यक्ति या वस्तु को देखने, सुनने, समझने आदि में असफल होना *The house is on the corner so **you can't miss it**.* ○ *They completely **missed the point** of what I was saying.* **3** [T] to arrive too late for sth or to fail to go to or do sth कहीं पर बहुत देर से पहुँचना या कहीं पर पहुँच न पाना या कुछ कर न पाना *Hurry up or you'll miss the plane!* ○ *Of course I'm coming to your wedding. I **wouldn't miss it for the world*** (= used to emphasize that you really want to do sth). **4** [T] to feel sad because sb is not with you any more, or because you have not got or cannot do sth that you once had or did किसी व्यक्ति का साथ छूट जाने पर या (पहले की अपेक्षा अब किसी काम के लिए) अशक्त हो जाने पर दुखी होना *What did you miss most when you lived abroad?* **5** [T] to notice that sb/sth is not where he/she/it should be किसी व्यक्ति या वस्तु के अपने स्थान से ग़ायब हो जाने पर ध्यान जाना *When did you first miss your handbag?* **6** [T] to avoid sth unpleasant अप्रिय स्थिति से बचना *If we leave now, we'll miss the rush-hour traffic.*

**PHR V** **miss sb/sth out** to not include sb/sth किसी व्यक्ति या वस्तु का छूट जाना *You've missed out several important points in your report.*

**miss out (on sth)** to not have a chance to have or do sth किसी बात का अवसर चूक जाना *You'll miss out on all the fun if you stay at home.*

**miss**[3] /mɪs मिस्/ *noun* [C] a failure to hit, catch or reach sth किसी वस्तु को मारने, पकड़ने या कहीं पहुँचने में विफलता *After several misses he finally managed to hit the target.*

**IDM** **give sth a miss** (*BrE informal*) to decide not to do or have sth कुछ न करने या न रखने का निर्णय *I think I'll give aerobics a miss tonight.*

**a near miss** ⇨ **near**[1] देखिए।

**missile** /ˈmɪsaɪl ˈमिसाइल्/ *noun* [C] **1** a powerful exploding weapon that can be sent long distances through the air प्रक्षेपास्त्र (शक्तिशाली विस्फोटक अस्त्र जिसे वायु में बहुत दूर तक प्रक्षेपित किया जा सकता है) *nuclear missiles* **2** an object or weapon that is fired from a gun or thrown in order to hurt sb or damage sth बंदूक़ से दाग़ी या फेंकी हुई वस्तु या हथियार (जो चोट या नुक़सान पहुँचाए) *The rioters threw missiles such as bottles and stones.*

**missing** /ˈmɪsɪŋ ˈमिसिङ्/ *adj.* **1** lost, or not in the right or usual place गुम; अपने स्थान से ग़ायब या अनुपस्थित *a missing person* ○ *Two files have **gone missing** from my office.* **2** (used about a person) not present after a battle, an accident, etc. but not known to have been killed (व्यक्ति) युद्ध, दुर्घटना आदि के बाद जो दिखाई न पड़े और न जिसके मारे जाने की ख़बर हो; लापता, अज्ञात *Many soldiers were listed as **missing in action**.* **3** not included, often when it should have been लुप्त (जो अपने स्थान पर दिखाई न पड़े) *Fill in the missing words in the text.*

**mission** /ˈmɪʃn ˈमिशन्/ *noun* [C] **1** an important official job that sb is sent somewhere to do, especially to another country कोई महत्त्वपूर्ण शासकीय कार्य (जिसे कोई, विशेषतः अन्य देश में जाकर पूरा या संपन्न करता है) *Your mission is to send back information about the enemy's movements.* **2** a group of people who are sent to a foreign country to perform a special task विशेष उद्देश्य से विदेश में भेजा गया प्रतिनिधिमंडल *an Indian trade mission to China* **3** a special journey made by a spacecraft or military aircraft अंतरिक्ष यान या सैनिक यान द्वारा की गई विशेष यात्रा *a mission to the moon* **4** a place where people are taught about the Christian religion, given medical help, etc. by people who are sent from another country to do this (**missionaries**) ईसाई मिशनरियों का प्रशिक्षण केंद्र जहाँ चिकित्सीय सहायता भी प्रदान की जाती है **5** a particular task which you feel it is your duty to do विशिष्ट कार्य जिसे करना कर्तव्य माना जाता है *Her work with the poor was more than just a job—it was her **mission in life**.*

**missionary** /ˈmɪʃənri ˈमिशन्रि/ *noun* [C] (*pl.* **missionaries**) a person who is sent to a foreign country to teach about the Christian religion (विदेश में कार्यरत) ईसाई-धर्म प्रचारक, विदेश में रह कर ईसाई धर्म का प्रचार करने वाले मिशनरि

**mission statement** *noun* [C] an official statement of the aims of a company or an organization किसी कंपनी या संगठन के उद्देश्यों का अधिकारिक विवरण

**misspell** /ˌmɪsˈspel ˌमिस्ˈस्पेल्/ *verb* [T] (*pt, pp* **misspelled** or **misspelt** /ˌmɪsˈspelt ˌमिस्ˈस्पेल्ट्/) to spell sth wrongly किसी शब्द की अशुद्ध वर्तनी करना

**misspent** /ˌmɪsˈspent ˌमिस्ˈस्पेन्ट्/ *adj.* (of time or money) used in a foolish way; wasted (समय या धन) जिसका प्रयोग बुद्धिमानी से नहीं किया गया; बरबाद, नष्ट

**mist¹** /mɪst मिस्ट्/ *noun* [C, U] a cloud made of very small drops of water in the air just above the ground, that makes it difficult to see कुहासा (जल की नन्हीं बूँदों से आकाश में बने बादल जिसके कारण देखने में कठिनाई होती है) *The fields were covered in mist.* ➪ **fog** देखिए तथा **weather** पर नोट देखिए। ▶ **misty** *adj.* कुहासा-भरा *a misty morning* ➪ **foggy** देखिए।

**mist²** /mɪst मिस्ट्/ *verb*

PHR V **mist (sth) up/over** to cover or be covered with very small drops of water that make it difficult to see कुहासा छा जाना *My glasses keep misting up.*

**mistake¹** /mɪˈsteɪk मिˈस्टेक्/ *noun* [C] something that you think or do that is wrong भूल, त्रुटि, ग़लती *Try not to **make** any **mistakes** in your essays.* ○ *a spelling mistake*

IDM **by mistake** as a result of being careless ग़लती से *The terrorists shot the wrong man by mistake.*

> NOTE **Mistake** की अपेक्षा **error** अधिक औपचारिक है—*a computing error.* **Fault** के प्रयोग से ग़लती के लिए ज़िम्मेदार व्यक्ति या वस्तु का संकेत मिलता है—*The accident wasn't my fault. The other driver pulled out in front of me.* **Fault** का प्रयोग किसी व्यक्ति या वस्तु की समस्या या दुर्बलता बताने के लिए भी होता है—*a technical fault*

**mistake²** /mɪˈsteɪk मिˈस्टेक्/ *verb* [T] (*pt* **mistook** /mɪˈstʊk मिˈस्टुक्/; *pp* **mistaken** /mɪˈsteɪkən मिˈस्टेकन्/) **1 mistake A for B** to think wrongly that sb/sth is sb/sth else किसी व्यक्ति या वस्तु को ग़लती से कोई अन्य व्यक्ति या वस्तु समझ लेना, पहचानने-समझने में ग़लती कर देना *I'm sorry, I mistook you for a friend of mine.* **2** to be wrong about sth किसी बात को ग़लत समझ लेना *I think you've mistaken my meaning.*

**mistaken** /mɪˈsteɪkən मिˈस्टेकन्/ *adj.* wrong; not correct ग़लत, भ्रांतिपूर्ण; अयथार्थ *a case of mistaken identity* ○ *a mistaken belief/idea* ▶ **mistakenly** *adv.* भूल से

**mister** ➪ **Mr** देखिए।

**mistletoe** /ˈmɪsltəʊ ˈमिसल्टो/ *noun* [U] a plant with white berries and green leaves. Mistletoe grows on trees सफ़ेद बेरियों और हरी पत्तियों वाली बेल (जो वृक्षों पर उगती है); मिसिलटो

> NOTE ब्रिटेन में क्रिसमस के समय मिसिलटो को घरों में आंतरिक सज्जा के लिए लगाया जाता है।

**mistook** ➪ **mistake²** का past tense रूप

**mistreat** /ˌmɪsˈtriːt ˌमिसˈट्रीट्/ *verb* [T] to be cruel to a person or animal किसी व्यक्ति या पशु के प्रति निर्दय होना या से दुर्व्यवहार करना *The owner of the zoo was accused of mistreating the animals.* ▶ **mistreatment** *noun* [U] दुर्व्यवहार

**mistress** /ˈmɪstrəs ˈमिस्ट्रेस्/ *noun* [C] a man's (usually a married man's) mistress is a woman that he is having a regular sexual relationship with and who is not his wife किसी पुरुष की रखैल (जिससे पुरुष के नियमित यौन संबंध है परंतु जो उसकी पत्नी नहीं); उपपत्नी

**mistrust** /ˌmɪsˈtrʌst ˌमिस्ˈट्रस्ट्/ *verb* [T] to have no confidence in sb/sth because you think he/she/it may be harmful किसी व्यक्ति या वस्तु पर अविश्वास करना (क्योंकि वह हानि पहुँचा सकता है) *I always mistrust politicians who smile too much.* ▶ **mistrust** *noun* [U, *sing.*] अविश्वास *She has a deep mistrust of strangers.* ➪ **distrust** देखिए।

**misty** /ˈmɪsti ˈमिस्टि/ ➪ **mist¹** देखिए।

**misunderstand** /ˌmɪsʌndəˈstænd ˌमिसअन्डˈस्टैन्ड्/ *verb* [I, T] (*pt, pp* **misunderstood** /-ˈstʊd -ˈस्टुड्/) to understand sb/sth wrongly किसी व्यक्ति या वस्तु को समझने में ग़लती करना *I misunderstood the instructions and answered too many questions.*

**misunderstanding** /ˌmɪsʌndəˈstændɪŋ ˌमिसअनड स्टैन्डिङ्/ *noun* **1** [C, U] a situation in which sb/sth is not understood correctly ग़लतफ़हमी, भ्रांति *The contract is written in both languages to avoid any misunderstanding.* **2** [C] a disagreement or an argument मतभेद या विवाद

**misuse** /ˌmɪsˈjuːz ˌमिस्ˈयूज़्/ *verb* [T] to use sth in the wrong way or for the wrong purpose अनुचित रीति या प्रयोजन से किसी वस्तु का प्रयोग करना, किसी वस्तु का दुरुपयोग करना *These chemicals can be dangerous if misused.* ▶ **misuse** /ˌmɪsˈjuːs ˌमिस्ˈयूस्/ *noun* [C, U] अनुचित प्रयोग, दुरुपयोग

**mite** /maɪt माइट्/ *noun* [C] a very small creature like a spider that lives on plants and animals and in carpets, etc. मकड़ी जैसा बहुत छोटा जंतु जो पेड़-पौधों, पशुओं, क़ालीनों आदि में छुपा रहता है; कुटकी

**mitigate** /ˈmɪtɪɡeɪt ˈमिटिगेट्/ *verb* [T] (*formal*) to make sth less serious, painful, unpleasant, etc. (किसी बात की गंभीरता, पीड़ा, अरोचकता आदि को) कम कर देना

**mitigating** /ˈmɪtɪɡeɪtɪŋ ˈमिटिगेटिङ्/ *adj.* (*formal*) (*only before a noun*) providing a reason that explains sb's actions or why he/she committed a crime, which makes it easier to understand so that the punishment may be less harsh किसी अपराध के कारण को समझने तथा संभावित क्षमादान में सहायक; प्रशमन, अल्पीकरण *mitigating circumstances/factors*

**mitosis** /maɪˈtəʊsɪs माइˈटोसिस्/ *noun* [U] (*technical*) the division of a cell of the body that results in two cells, each with the same number of **chromosomes** as the original cell शरीर की एक कोशिका का दो कोशिकाओं में विभाजन जिनमें गुणसूत्रों की संख्या समान रहती है; सूत्री विभाजन, समसूत्रण ➪ **meiosis** देखिए।

**mitten** /ˈmɪtn ˈमिट्न्/ *noun* [C] a type of glove that has one part for the thumb and another part for all four fingers एक प्रकार का दस्ताना जिसमें एक हिस्सा अँगूठे के लिए और दूसरा चारों अँगुलियों के लिए होता है; निरंगुल दस्ताना ➪ **glove** देखिए।

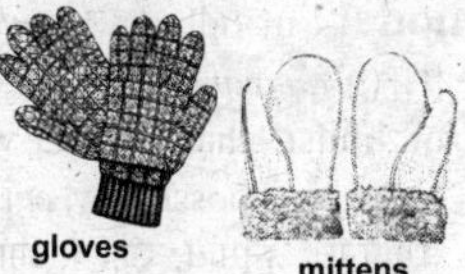


**mix¹** /mɪks मिक्स्/ *verb* **1** [I, T] **mix (A) (with B); mix (A and B) (together)** if two or more substances mix or if you mix them, they combine to form a new substance दो वस्तुओं का मिलकर एक नई वस्तु बनना या दो वस्तुओं को मिलाकर एक नई वस्तु बनाना *Oil and water don't mix.* ○ *to mix cement* (= to make cement by mixing other substances) **2** [I] **mix (with sb)** to be with and talk to other people सबसे मिलना-जुलना, सबसे मिलकर बात करना *He mixes with all types of people at work.*

IDM **be/get mixed up in sth** (*informal*) to be/ become involved in sth bad or unpleasant कुछ बुरा या अरुचिकर होना या में संलिप्त होना

PHRV **mix sth up** to put something in the wrong order किसी वस्तु को बेतरतीब उलटा-पुलटा या गड्ड-मड्ड कर देना *He was so nervous that he dropped his speech and got the pages all mixed up.*

**mix sb/sth up (with sb/sth)** to confuse sb/sth with sb/sth else एक व्यक्ति या वस्तु को ग़लती से दूसरा व्यक्ति या वस्तु समझ लेना *I always get him mixed up with his brother.*

**mix²** /mɪks मिक्स्/ *noun* **1** [C, *usually sing.*] a group of different types of people or things विभिन्न प्रकारों के लोगों या वस्तुओं का एकीकृत समूह *We need a good racial mix in the police force.* **2** [C, U] a special powder that contains all the substances needed to make sth. You add water or another liquid to this powder एक विशेष पाउडर जिसमें कुछ बनाने के लिए अपेक्षित सभी वस्तुएँ होती है; मिक्स (इसमें पानी या कोई अन्य द्रव केवल मिलाना होता है) *cake mix* ○ *idli mix*

**mixed** /mɪkst मिक्स्ट्/ *adj.* **1** being both good and bad अच्छा और बुरा दोनों; मिश्रित ***I have mixed feelings** about leaving my job.* **2** made or consisting of different types of person or thing अलग-अलग प्रकार के व्यक्तियों या वस्तुओं से बना या उन्हें समाविष्ट किए हुए, मिला-जुला *mixed school* ○ *a mixed salad*

**mixed doubles** *noun* [U] a game of tennis, etc. in which there is a man and woman on each side टेनिस के खेल आदि में दोनों ओर पुरुष-महिला युगल का, मिश्रित युगल

**mixed-up** *adj.* (*informal*) confused because of emotional problems भावनात्मक समस्याओं से परेशान *He has been very mixed-up since his parents' divorce.*

**mixer** /ˈmɪksə(r) ˈमिक्स(र्)/ *noun* [C] a machine that is used for mixing sth मिश्रण करने वाली मशीन; मिक्सर *a food/cement mixer* ➪ **kitchen** पर चित्र देखिए।

**mixture** /ˈmɪkstʃə(r) ˈमिक्स्च(र्)/ *noun* **1** [*sing.*] a combination of different things विभिन्न वस्तुओं का मिश्रण *Monkeys eat a mixture of leaves and fruit.* **2** [C, U] a substance that is made by mixing other substances together अनेक वस्तुओं को परस्पर मिलाकर बनाई गई एक वस्तु; मिश्रण *cake mixture* ○ *a mixture of eggs, flour and milk*

**mix-up** *noun* [C] (*informal*) a mistake in the planning or organization of sth किसी वस्तु के योजना-निर्माण या संगठन में हुई त्रुटि *There was a mixup and we were given the wrong ticket.*

**ml** *abbr.* millilitre(s) मिलिलिटर *contents 75 ml*

**mm** *abbr.* millimetre(s) मिलिमीटर *a 35 mm camera*

**moan** /məʊn मोन्/ *verb* [I] **1** to make a low sound because you are in pain, very sad, etc. दर्द या दुख आदि से कराहना, क्रंदन करना *to moan with pain* **2** (*informal*) to keep complaining about sth स्वर में रोनी आवाज में आलोचना करते रहना; शिकायत करना *The English are always moaning about the weather.* ▶ **moan** *noun* [C] कराहट, क्रंदन

**moat** /məʊt मोट्/ *noun* [C] a long wide channel that is dug around a castle and filled with water to make it difficult for enemies to attack किले के चारों और बनी पानी से भरी खाई, खंदक (जो शत्रु के लिए बाधा बनती है)

**mob¹** /mɒb मॉब्/ *noun* [C, *with sing. or pl. verb*] a large crowd of people that may become violent or cause trouble भीड़ (जो उग्र या कष्ट का कारण बन सकती है)

**mob²** /mɒb मॉब्/ *verb* [T] (**mobbing; mobbed**) to form a large crowd around sb, for example in order to see or touch him/her किसी व्यक्ति के चारों और भीड़ लगा लेना (उसे देखने या छूने के लिए) *The band was mobbed by fans as they left the hotel.*

**mobile**[1] /ˈməʊbaɪl ˈमोबाइल् / *adj.* able to move or be moved easily जो गति कर सके या जिसे गतिशील बनाया जा सके; गतिशील *My daughter is much more mobile now she has her own car.* ✪ विलोम **immobile** ▶ **mobility** /məʊˈbɪləti मोˈबिलटि / *noun* [U] गतिशीलता

**mobile**[2] /ˈməʊbaɪl ˈमोबाइल् / *noun* [C] **1** a decoration that you hang from the ceiling and that moves when the air around it moves छत से लटकी सजावटी वस्तु जो वायु चलने से हिलने-डुलने या आंदोलित होने लगती है **2** = **mobile phone**

**mobile home** *noun* [C] (*AmE*) a building that can be moved on wheels, and is used for living in चलता-फिरता घर, चल गृह

**mobile phone** (*also* **mobile; cellphone**) *noun* [C] a telephone that you can carry around with you एक प्रकार का टेलीफ़ोन जिसे चलते फिरते आप अपने साथ रख सकते हैं; चल भाष, मोबाइल फ़ोन

**mobilize** (*also* **-ise**) /ˈməʊbɪlaɪz ˈमोबिलाइज़् / *verb* **1** [T] to organize people or things to do sth (कुछ करने के लिए) लोगों या वस्तुओं को संगठित करना *They mobilized the local residents to oppose the new development.* **2** [I, T] (used about the army, navy, etc.) to get ready for war (थलसेना, नौसेना आदि का) युद्ध के लिए तैयार होना या उसे करना, सेना का लामबंद होना या सेना को लामबंद करना ✪ पर्याय **immobilize**

**mock**[1] /mɒk मॉक् / *verb* [I, T] (*formal*) to laugh at sb/sth in an unkind way or to make other people laugh at him/her/it किसी की हँसी उड़वाना, परिहास का पात्र बनाना या बनवाना

> **NOTE** **Laugh at** और **make fun of** ये अभिव्यक्तियाँ कम औपचारिक और अधिक प्रचलित है।

**mock**[2] /mɒk मॉक् / *adj.* (*only before a noun*) not real or genuine नक़ली, दिखावटी, बनावटी, अवास्तविक *He held up his hands in mock surprise.* ○ *a mock* (= practice) *exam*

**mock**[3] /mɒk मॉक् / *noun* [C, *usually pl.*] a practice exam that you do before the official one (ब्रिटेन में) औपचारिक परीक्षा से पहले आयोजित अनौपचारिक (अभ्यास) परीक्षा

**mockery** /ˈmɒkəri ˈमॉकरि / *noun* **1** [U] comments or actions that are intended to make sb/sth seem ridiculous उपहास, हँसी (ऐसी टिप्पणियाँ और क्रियाएँ जिनसे किसी का उपहास हो) *She couldn't face any more of their mockery.* **2** [*sing.*] an action, a decision, etc. that is a failure and that is not as it is should be विफलता का सूचक कार्य, निर्णय आदि *It was a mockery of a trial.*

**IDM** **make a mockery of sth** to make sth seem ridiculous or useless ऐसा काम करना कि कोई बात हास्यास्पद, निरुपयोगी या निष्फल लगे, किसी (गंभीर) बात का मज़ाक़-सा बना देना

**mock-up** *noun* [C] a model of sth that shows what it will look like or how it will work नमूने की वस्तु (मशीन आदि); मूल वस्तु की प्रतिदर्श या नमूना

**modal** /ˈməʊdl ˈमोड्ल् / (*also* **modal verb**) *noun* [C] (*grammar*) a verb, for example 'might', 'can' or 'must' that is used with another verb for expressing possibility, permission, intention, etc. संभावना, अनुमति, उद्देश्य आदि का अर्थ व्यक्त करने के लिए मुख्य क्रिया के साथ प्रयुक्त (सहायक) क्रिया, जैसे **might, can** या **must**; वृत्तिवाचक क्रिया

> **NOTE** वृत्तिवाचक क्रियाओं (modal verbs) के विषय में अधिक जानकारी के लिए इस शब्दकोश के अंत में **Quick Grammar Reference** देखिए।

**mode** /məʊd मोड् / *noun* [C] **1** a type of sth or way of doing sth किसी वस्तु या कोई काम करने का प्रकार *a mode of transport/life* **2** one of the ways in which a machine can work मशीन के काम करने की एक रीति *Switch the camera to automatic mode.* **3** (*technical*) a particular arrangement of notes in music for example the musical **scale** system संगीत में स्वरों की विशिष्ट व्यवस्था (जैसे स्वरग्राम), राग, थाट *major/minor mode* **4** the most frequent number or value in a group of numbers संख्याओं के एक वर्ग में अधिकतम वाली संख्या या मूल्य बहुलक; मोड समूह

**model**[1] /ˈmɒdl ˈमॉड्ल् / *noun* [C] **1** a copy of sth that is usually smaller than the real thing किसी वस्तु का नमूना, प्रतिरूप (प्रायः मूल वस्तु से छोटा); मॉडल *a model aeroplane* **2** one of the machines, vehicles, etc. that is made by a particular company किसी विशेष कंपनी द्वारा निर्मित मशीन, वाहन आदि (जो अपनी श्रृंखला का प्रतिनिधित्व करते हैं); मॉडल *The latest models are on display at the show.* **3** a person or thing that is a good example to copy अनुकरणीय व्यक्ति या वस्तु, आदर्श प्रतिमान *a model student* ○ *Children often use older brothers or sisters as* ***role models*** (= copy the way they behave). **4** a person who is employed to wear clothes at a fashion show or for magazine photographs फ़ैशन शो में या पत्रिका में फ़ोटो हेतु नए परिधानों के प्रदर्शन के लिए नियुक्त युवक या युवती; मॉडल **5** a person who is painted, drawn or photographed by an artist व्यक्ति जिसका कलाकार चित्र बनाता है, रेखांकन करता है या फ़ोटो खींचता है; मॉडल

**model**[2] /ˈmɒdl ˈमॉड्ल् / *verb* (**modelling; modelled** *AmE* **modeling; modeled**) **1** [T] **model sth/yourself on sb/sth** to make sth/yourself similar to sth/sb else किसी वस्तु या स्वयं को अन्य वस्तु या व्यक्ति के सदृश बनाना, आदर्श या प्रतिमान के रूप में लेना *The house is modelled on a Roman villa.* **2** [I, T] to wear and show clothes at a fashion show or for photographs फ़ैशन शो या फ़ोटो के लिए नए वस्त्रों को पहनकर उनका प्रदर्शन करना, फ़ैशन शो आदि में मॉडल के रूप में कार्य करना *to model swimsuits* **3** [I, T] to make a model of sth किसी वस्तु से मॉडल तैयार करना, को गढ़ना *This clay is difficult to model.*

**modelling** (*AmE* **modeling**) /ˈmɒdəlɪŋ ˈमॉडलिङ् / *noun* [U] the work of a fashion model फ़ैशन मॉडल द्वारा किया जाने वाला काम; मॉडलिंग

**modem** /ˈməʊdem ˈमोडेम् / *noun* [C] a piece of equipment that connects two or more computers together by means of a telephone line so that information can go from one to the other टेलीफ़ोन लाइन द्वारा कंप्यूटरों को परस्पर जोड़ने वाला यंत्र (ताकि सूचना-सामग्री एक कंप्यूटर से दूसरी में जा सके); मोडेम

**moderate**[1] /ˈmɒdərət ˈमॉडरट् / *adj.* **1** being, having, using, etc. neither too much nor too little of sth मध्यम स्तर का (न बहुत अधिक न बहुत कम) *a moderate speed* ○ *We've had a moderate amount of success.* **2** having or showing opinions, especially about politics, that are not extreme अतिवाद से मुक्त विचारों वाला (विशेषतः राजनीति), संतुलनशील, मध्यमार्गी *moderate policies/views* ➪ **extreme** और **radical** देखिए। ▶ **moderately** *adv.* औसत दर्जे का *His career has been moderately successful.*

**moderate**[2] /ˈmɒdəreɪt ˈमॉडरेट् / *verb* [I, T] to become or to make sth less strong or extreme उग्रता में कमी होना या करना, संतुलित होना या करना *The union moderated its original demands.*

**moderate**[3] /ˈmɒdərət ˈमॉडरट् / *noun* [C] a person whose opinions, especially about politics, are not extreme संतुलित विचारों वाला व्यक्ति (विशेषतः राजनीति में), मध्यमार्गी ➪ **extremist** देखिए।

**moderation** /ˌmɒdəˈreɪʃn ˌमॉडˈरेश्न् / *noun* [U] **1** the quality of being reasonable and not being extreme संतुलन, संयम *Alcohol can harm unborn babies even if it's taken **in moderation**.* **2** (in education) the process of making sure that the same standards are used by different people in marking exams, etc. (शिक्षा में) उत्तरपत्रों के मूल्यांकन के लिए प्रश्नपत्रों के समान मानकों को तैयार करने की प्रक्रिया, प्रश्नपत्रों का परिसीमन

**modern** /ˈmɒdn ˈमॉड्न् / *adj.* **1** of the present or recent times वर्तमान या हाल का; आधुनिक *Pollution is one of the major problems in the modern world.* ○ *modern history* **2** (used about styles of art, music, etc.) new and different from traditional styles (कला, संगीत आदि की शैली) पारंपरिक शैलियों से भिन्न और नवीन; आधुनिक *modern jazz/architecture* **3** with all the newest methods, equipment, designs, etc.; up to date जिसमें नवीनतम विधियाँ, उपकरण, आकृतियाँ आदि हों; नवीन *It is one of the most modern hospitals in the country.* ➪ **old-fashioned** देखिए।

**modernity** /məˈdɜːnəti मˈडनटि / *noun* [U] (*written*) the condition of being new and modern आधुनिकता

**modernize** (*also* **-ise**) /ˈmɒdənaɪz ˈमॉडनाइज़् / *verb* [T] to make sth suitable for use today using new methods, styles, etc. नई विधियों, शैलियों आदि के प्रयोग से किसी वस्तु को आधुनिक परिस्थितियों के अनुकूल बनाना ▶ **modernization** (*also* **-isation**) /ˌmɒdənaɪˈzeɪʃn ˌमॉडनाइˈज़ेशन् / *noun* [U] आधुनिकीकरण, आधुनिक बनाना *The house is large but is in need of modernization.*

**modern languages** *noun* [*pl.*] languages that are spoken now आधुनिक भाषाएँ

**modest** /ˈmɒdɪst ˈमॉडिस्ट् / *adj.* **1** not talking too much about your own abilities, good qualities, etc. विनम्र, विनीत (अपनी क्षमताओं आदि का बखान न करने वाला) *She got the best results in the exam but she was too modest to tell anyone.* ➪ **humble** और **proud** देखिए। **2** not very large बहुत अधिक नहीं, साधारण *a modest pay increase* **3** (used about a woman's clothes) not showing much of the body (महिला का परिधान) जो शरीर को अधिक अनावृत न करे; मर्यादित, शालीन ▶ **modesty** *noun* [U] शालीनता, विनम्रता ▶ **modestly** *adv.* शालीनता से, विनम्रतापूर्वक

**modifier** /ˈmɒdɪfaɪə(r) ˈमॉडिफ़ाइअ(र्) / *noun* [C] (*grammar*) a word, such as an adjective or adverb, that describes another word, or changes its meaning in some way विशेषण या क्रियाविशेषण (जो दूसरे शब्द की विशेषता बताता है या उसके अर्थ में आंशिक परिवर्तन कर देता है); विशेषक ➪ **intensifier** देखिए।

**modify** /ˈmɒdɪfaɪ ˈमॉडिफ़ाइ / *verb* [T] (*pres. part* **modifying;** *3rd person sing. pres.* **modifies;** *pt, pp* **modified**) to change sth slightly किसी वस्तु में अंशतः परिवर्तन करना ▶ **modification** /ˌmɒdɪfɪˈkeɪʃn ˌमॉडिफ़िˈकेशन् / *noun* [C, U] आंशिक परिवर्तन

**modular** /ˈmɒdjələ(r) ˈमाड्यलर्/ *adj.* (*technical*) (used about machines, buildings, etc.) consisting of separate parts or units that can be joined together (यंत्र, भवन आदि) जिसमें अनेक स्वतंत्र भाग या इकाइयाँ हों जिन्हें आवश्यकतानुसार जोड़ा जा सके

**module** /ˈmɒdju:l ˈमॉड्यूल्/ *noun* [C] a unit that forms part of sth bigger ऐसी इकाई जो अपने से बड़ी इकाई का अंग है, बड़ी संरचना की छोटी परंतु स्वतंत्र इकाई *You must complete three modules* (= courses that you study) *in your first year.*

**mohair** /ˈməʊheə(r) ˈमोहेअ(र्)/ *noun* [U] very soft wool that comes from a **goat** बकरी की बहुत कोमल ऊन; मोहेर

**Mohammed** = **Muhammad**

**Mohiniattam** *noun* [U] a traditional dance form from Kerala. It is a graceful dance and is usually performed as a solo **recital** by women महिलाओं द्वारा प्रदर्शित केरल प्रदेश का एकल नृत्य; मोहिनिअट्टम

**moist** /mɔɪst मॉइस्ट्/ *adj.* slightly wet; damp हलका गीला; नम, आर्द्र *Her eyes were moist with tears.* ○ *Keep the soil moist or the plant will die.* ➪ **wet** पर नोट देखिए। ▶ **moisten** /ˈmɔɪsn ˈमॉइसन्/ *verb* [I, T] नम करना, भिगोना, गीला करना

**moisture** /ˈmɔɪstʃə(r) ˈमॉइस्चर्/ *noun* [U] water in small drops on a surface, in the air, etc. नमी, आर्द्रता

**moisturize** (*also* **-ise**) /ˈmɔɪstʃəraɪz ˈमॉइस्चराइज़्/ *verb* [I, T] to put special cream on your skin to make it less dry विशेष क्रीम के प्रयोग से त्वचा की शुष्कता कम होना या करना

**moisturizer** (*also* **-iser**) /ˈmɔɪstʃəraɪzə(r) ˈमॉइस्चराइज़र्/ *noun* [C, U] a special cream that you put on your skin to make it less dry त्वचा की शुष्कता कम करने वाली विशेष क्रीम; मोइश्चराइज़र

**molar** /ˈməʊlə(r) ˈमोलर्/ *noun* [C] one of the large teeth at the back of your mouth दाढ़, चर्वण-दंत ➪ **canine** और **incisor** देखिए तथा **teeth** पर चित्र देखिए।

**molasses** /məˈlæsɪz मˈलैसिज़्/ (*AmE*) = **treacle**

**mold** (*AmE*) = **mould**

**moldy** (*AmE*) = **mouldy**

**mole** /məʊl मोल्/ *noun* [C] **1** a small dark spot on a person's skin that never goes away त्वचा पर तिल (जो सदा रहता है) ➪ **freckle** देखिए। **2** a small animal with dark fur that lives underground and is almost blind छछूँदर **3** (*informal*) a person who works in one organization and gives secret information to another organization घर का भेदिया ✪ पर्याय **spy** **4** (in chemistry) a unit for measuring the amount of a substance (रसायनशास्त्र में) किसी पदार्थ की मात्रा को मापने की इकाई; अणु

**molecule** /ˈmɒlɪkju:l ˈमॉलिक्यूल्/ *noun* [C] the smallest unit into which a substance can be divided without changing its chemical nature अणु (किसी पदार्थ की लघुतम इकाई जिसकी रासायनिक प्रकृति अक्षुण्ण रहती है) ➪ **atom** देखिए। ▶ **molecular** /məˈlekjələ(r) मˈलेक्यलर्/ *adj.*

**molest** /məˈlest मˈलेस्ट्/ *verb* [T] to attack sb, especially a child, in a sexual way किसी के (विशेषतः बच्चे के) साथ कामुकतापूर्ण छेड़छाड़ करना

**mollify** /ˈmɒlɪfaɪ ˈमॉलिफ़ाइ/ *verb* [T] (*pres. part.* **mollifying;** *3rd person sing. pres.* **mollifies;** *pt, pp* **mollified**) (*formal*) to make sb feel less angry or upset किसी के क्रोध या परेशानी को कम करना, किसी अशांत व्यक्ति को शांत करना *His explanation failed to mollify her.*

**mollusc** (*AmE* **mollusk**) /ˈmɒləsk ˈमॉलस्क्/ *noun* [C] any creature with a soft body that is not divided into different sections, and usually a hard outer shell. Molluscs can live either on land or in water मृदु कवच धारी जंतु कोमल और अखंड शरीर के जंतु जो सामान्यतया कठोर आवरण युक्त कोष में रहते हैं (जल में या भूमि पर) *Snails and mussels are molluscs.*

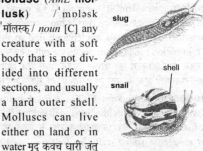

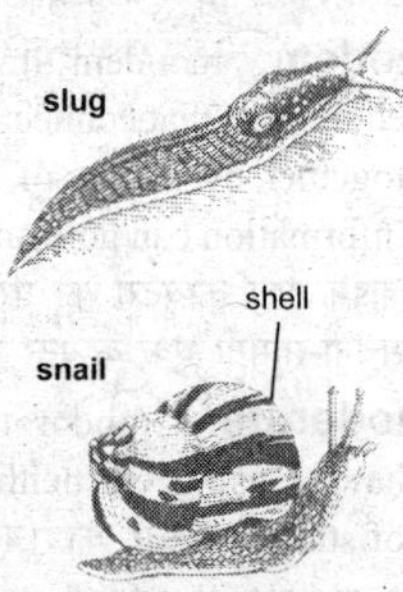


**molt** (*AmE*) = **moult**

**molten** /ˈməʊltən ˈमोल्टन्/ *adj.* (used about metal or rock) made liquid by very great heat (धातु या चट्टान) अत्यधिक ताप से द्रवीभूत

**mom** (*AmE*) = **mum**

**moment** /ˈməʊmənt ˈमोमन्ट्/ *noun* **1** [C] a very short period of time अत्यल्पसमय *One moment, please* (= please wait). ○ *Arun left just a few moments ago.* **2** [*sing.*] a particular point in time समय का विशिष्ट बिंदु, क्षण *Just at that moment my mother arrived.* ○ *the moment of birth/death*

IDM **(at) any minute/moment (now)** ➪ **minute**[1] देखिए।

**at the moment** now इस क्षण, अभी *I'm afraid she's busy at the moment. Can I take a message?*

**for the moment/present** for a short time; for now कुछ समय के लिए; इस समय, फ़िलहाल *I'm not very happy at work but I'll stay there for the moment.*

**in a moment** very soon क्षण-भर में, बहुत जल्दी *Just wait here. I'll be back in a moment.*

**the last minute/moment** ➪ **last**[1] देखिए।
**the minute/moment (that)** ➪ **minute**[1] देखिए।
**on the spur of the moment** ➪ **spur**[1] देखिए।

**momentary** /ˈməʊməntri ˈमोमन्ट्रि / *adj.* lasting for a very short time क्षणिक ▶ **momentarily** /ˈməʊməntrəli ˈमोमन्ट्रलि / *adv.* क्षण-भर के लिए

**momentous** /məˈmentəs मˈमेन्टस् / *adj.* very important अत्यंत महत्त्वपूर्ण *a momentous decision/event/change*

**momentum** /məˈmentəm मˈमेन्टम् / *noun* [U] the ability to keep increasing or developing; the force that makes sth move faster and faster वृद्धि या विकास की गतिशीलता या निरंतरता; किसी की गति को अधिकाधिक बढ़ाने वाली शक्ति; संवेगबल *The environmental movement is **gathering momentum**.*

**mommy** (*AmE*) = **mummy 1**

**Mon.** *abbr.* Monday सोमवार *Mon. 6 June*

**monarch** /ˈmɒnək ˈमॉनक् / *noun* [C] a king or queen राजा या रानी, शासक, अधिपति

**monarchy** /ˈmɒnəki ˈमॉनकि / *noun* (*pl.* **monarchies**) **1** [*sing.*, U] the system of government or rule by a king or queen राजा या रानी के आधिपत्यवाली शासन-प्रणाली; राजतंत्र **2** [C] a country that is governed by a king or queen राजा या रानी द्वारा शासित देश ➪ **republic** देखिए।

**monastery** /ˈmɒnəstri ˈमॉनस्ट्रि / *noun* [C] (*pl.* **monasteries**) a place where **monks** live together मठ, विहार ➪ **convent** देखिए।

**Monday** /ˈmʌndeɪ; -di ˈमन्डे; -डि / *noun* [C, U] (*abbr.* **Mon.**) the day of the week after Sunday सोमवार *I finish work a bit later **on Mondays/on a Monday**.*

**NOTE** लिखते समय दिनों के नाम सदा बड़े अक्षर से प्रारंभ किए जाते हैं।

**monetary** /ˈmʌnɪtri ˈमनिट्रि / *adj.* connected with money वित्त-संबंधी, वित्तीय *the government's monetary policy*

**money** /ˈmʌni ˈमनि / *noun* [U] the means of paying for sth or buying sth (= coins or notes) धन, पैसा (सिक्के या नोट) *Will you **earn** more **money** in your new job?* ○ *The new road will **cost** a lot **of money**.* ➪ **pocket money** देखिए।
**IDM** **be rolling in money/in it** ➪ **roll**[2] देखिए।
**get your money's worth** to get full value for the money you have spent पैसा, दाम वसूल कर लेना, व्यय किए गए धन का पूरा लाभ प्राप्त करना

**mongoose** /ˈmɒŋɡuːs ˈमॉङ्गूस् / *noun* [C] (*pl.* **mongooses**) a small animal with fur that lives in hot countries and kills snakes, rats, etc. नेवला

**mongrel** /ˈmʌŋɡrəl ˈमङ्ग्रल् / *noun* [C] a dog that has parents of different types (**breeds**) द्विजातीय नस्ल का कुत्ता, वर्णसंकर कुत्ता ➪ **pedigree** देखिए।

**monitor**[1] /ˈmɒnɪtə(r) ˈमॉनिट(र्) / *noun* [C] **1** a machine that shows information or pictures on a screen like a television; a screen that shows information from a computer टेलीविज़न के समान परदे पर चित्र आदि दिखाने वाली मशीन; कंप्यूटर सूचना-सामग्री प्रदर्शित करने वाला परदा, कंप्यूटर का मानिटर **2** a machine that records or checks sth रिकार्ड या जाँच-पड़ताल करने वाली मशीन *A monitor checks the baby's heartbeat.*

**monitor**[2] /ˈmɒnɪtə(r) ˈमॉनिट(र्) / *verb* [T] to check, record or test sth regularly for a period of time निश्चित समयावधि तक नियमित रूप से किसी बात की जाँच-पड़ताल या उसे रिकार्ड करना *Pollution levels in the lake are closely monitored.*

**monk** /mʌŋk मॉङ्क् / *noun* [C] a member of a religious group of men who live in a special building (**monastery**) and do not get married or have possessions किसी धार्मिक समूह का सदस्य जो मठों में वैरागी जीवन व्यतीत करते हैं; संन्यासी, मुनि, वैरागी ➪ **nun** देखिए।

**monkey** /ˈmʌŋki ˈमङ्कि / *noun* [C] an animal with a long tail that lives in hot countries and can climb trees बंदर, वानर ➪ **ape** देखिए।
**NOTE** **Chimpanzees** और **gorillas** वस्तुतः 'apes' में आते हैं। परंतु कभी-कभी उन्हें 'monkeys' में भी शामिल कर लिया जाता है। ➪ **primate** देखिए।
**IDM** **monkey business** (*informal*) silly or dishonest behaviour मूर्खतापूर्ण या बेईमानी का आचरण

**monkey wrench** = **adjustable spanner**

**mono** /ˈmɒnəʊ ˈमॉनो / *adj.* (used about recorded music or a system for playing it) having the sound coming from one direction only (रिकार्ड किया हुआ संगीत या संगीत वाद्य-प्रणाली) जिसमें केवल एक ओर से आवाज़ आती है, एक पक्षीय ध्वनि-व्यवस्था वाला (रिकार्ड किया संगीत) ➪ **stereo** देखिए।

**mono-** /ˈmɒnəʊ ˈमॉनो / *prefix* (*used in nouns and adjectives*) one; single एक; एकल *monorail* ○ *monolingual*

**monochrome** /ˈmɒnəkrəʊm ˈमॉनक्रोम् / *adj.* (used about a photograph or picture) using only black, white and shades of grey (फ़ोटो या चित्र) जिसमें केवल श्याम, श्वेत और धूसर रंगों का प्रयोग हो; इकरंगा

**monoculture** /ˈmɒnəʊkʌltʃə(r) ˈमॉनोकल्च(र्) / *noun* [U] (*technical*) the growing of a single crop in a particular area किसी विशेष क्षेत्र में केवल एक फ़सल उत्पन्न होने की स्थिति

**monogamy** /məˈnɒgəmi मˈनॉगमि/ *noun* [U] the fact or custom of being married to only one person at a particular time एक समय में केवल एक व्यक्ति से विवाह और उसकी प्रथा, एकविवाह प्रथा ➪ **bigamy** और **polygamy** देखिए। ▶ **monogamous** /məˈnɒgəməs मˈनॉगमस्/ *adj.* एकविवाही *a monogamous society*

**monolingual** /ˌmɒnəˈlɪŋgwəl ˌमॉनˈलिङ्ग्वल्/ *adj.* using only one language जिसमें केवल एक भाषा का प्रयोग हो; एकभाषिक *That is a monolingual dictionary.* ➪ **bilingual** देखिए।

**monolith** /ˈmɒnəlɪθ ˈमॉनलिथ्/ *noun* [C] a large single standing block of stone, especially one that was put there by people living in ancient times एक ही पत्थर से बना बहुत बड़ा खंभा (विशेषत: प्राचीन युग के निवासियों द्वारा स्थापित); एकाश्मक स्तंभ ▶ **monolithic** /ˌmɒnəˈlɪθɪk ˌमॉनˈलिथिक्/ *adj.* एकाश्म

**monologue** (*also AmE* **monolog**) /ˈmɒnəlɒg ˈमॉनलॉग्/ *noun* [C] a long speech by one person, for example in a play अकेले व्यक्ति का लंबा भाषण (जैसे नाटक में), एकालाप; स्वगत भाषण ➪ **soliloquy** देखिए।

**monopolize** (*also* **-ise**) /məˈnɒpəlaɪz मˈनॉपलाइज़्/ *verb* [T] to control sth so that other people cannot share it किसी वस्तु पर केवल एक व्यक्ति या संगठन द्वारा नियंत्रण कर लेना, एकाधिपत्य स्थापित करना, एकाधिकार करना *She completely monopolized the conversation. I couldn't get a word in.*

**monopoly** /məˈnɒpəli मˈनॉपलि/ *noun* [C] (*pl.* **monopolies**) **a monopoly (on/in sth)** **1** the control of an industry or service by only one company; a type of goods or a service that is controlled in this way किसी उद्योग या सेवा-क्षेत्र पर केवल एक कंपनी का नियंत्रण, एकाधिकार; इस रीति से नियंत्रित सामग्री या सेवा *The company has a monopoly on broadcasting international football.* **2** the complete control, possession or use of sth; something that belongs to only one person or group and is not shared किसी वस्तु पर पूर्ण नियंत्रण स्वामित्व या उसका पूर्ण उपयोग; केवल एक व्यक्ति या समूह के स्वामित्व वाली वस्तु (जिसमें अन्य किसी की भागीदारी नहीं)

**monorail** /ˈmɒnəʊreɪl ˈमॉनोरेल्/ *noun* [C] a railway in which the train runs on a single track, usually high above the ground केवल एक पटरी पर (प्राय: भूसतह से काफ़ी ऊँचे) चलने वाली रेलगाड़ी; मोनोरेल

**monosodium glutamate** /ˌmɒnəsəʊdiəm ˈgluːtəmeɪt ˌमॉनसोडिअम् ˈग्लूटमेट्/ *noun* [U] (*abbr.* **MSG**) a chemical mixture (**compound**) that is sometimes added to food to improve its flavour खाद्य पदार्थों में स्वाद-वृद्धि के लिए डाला जाने वाला रासायनिक मिश्रण

**monosyllabic** /ˌmɒnəsɪˈlæbɪk ˌमॉनसिˈलैबिक्/ *adj.* **1** having only one syllable जिसमें केवल एक अक्षर हो, एकाक्षरी **2** (used about a person or his/her way of speaking) saying very little, in a way that appears rude to other people (किसी व्यक्ति के बोलने का ढंग) जिसमें बहुत कम शब्दों का प्रयोग हो (जिससे लोगों लगे को लगे कि वक्ता अशिष्ट है) *He gave monosyllabic replies to everything I asked him.*

**monosyllable** /ˈmɒnəsɪləbl ˈमॉनसिलबल्/ *noun* [C] a short word, such as 'leg', that has only one syllable एकाक्षरी शब्द (जैसे leg)

**monotonous** /məˈnɒtənəs मˈनॉटनस्/ *adj.* never changing and therefore boring परिवर्तन-रहित और अतएव उबाऊ, अरोचक, नीरस *monotonous work* ○ *a monotonous voice* ▶ **monotonously** *adv.* विरसता से

**monotony** /məˈnɒtəni मˈनॉटनि/ *noun* [U] the state of being always the same and therefore boring परिवर्तन-हीनता और अतएव अरोचकता की स्थिति; विरसता *the monotony of working on a production line*

**monozygotic** /ˌmɒnəʊzaɪˈgɒtɪk ˌमॉनोज़ाइˈगॉटिक्/ *adj.* (*technical*) (used about **twins**) from the same egg and therefore **identical** (जुड़वाँ बच्चे) एक ही अंडे से उत्पन्न अत: आकृति में समान; एकयुग्मज

**monsoon** /ˌmɒnˈsuːn ˌमॉन्ˈसून्/ *noun* [C] the season when it rains a lot in Southern Asia; the rain that falls during this period दक्षिणी एशिया की वर्षा ऋतु, मानसून; मानसून की वर्षा

**monster** /ˈmɒnstə(r) ˈमॉन्स्ट(र्)/ *noun* [C] (in stories) a creature that is large, ugly and frightening (कथाओं में) दैत्य, राक्षस (बड़ा कुरूप और भयावह प्राणी) (*figurative*) *The murderer was described as a dangerous monster.*

**monstrosity** /mɒnˈstrɒsəti मॉन्ˈस्ट्रॉसटि/ *noun* [C] (*pl.* **monstrosities**) something that is very large and ugly, especially a building बहुत बड़ी और कुरूप वस्तु (विशेषत: कोई भवन)

**monstrous** /ˈmɒnstrəs ˈमॉन्स्ट्रस्/ *adj.* **1** that people think is shocking and unacceptable because it is morally wrong or unfair लोगों को स्तब्ध कर देने वाला और अस्वीकार्य (अनैतिक या अनुचित होने के कारण), नितांत असंगत *It's monstrous that she earns less than he does for the same job!* **2** very large (and often ugly or frightening) बहुत बड़ा (और प्राय: कुरूप या भयावह), दैत्याकार *a monstrous spider/wave*

**month** /mʌnθ मन्थ् / *noun* [C] **1** one of the twelve periods of time into which the year is divided महीना, मास, माह *They are starting work next month.* ○ *Have you seen this month's Sportstar?* **2** the period of about four weeks from a certain date in one month to the same date in the next, for example 13 May to 13 June; a calendar month किसी महीने की किसी एक तारीख़ से अगले महीने की उसी तारीख़ की लगभग चार सप्ताह की अवधि (जैसे 13 मई से 13 जून); एक कैलेंडर *'How long will you be away?' 'For about a month.'* ○ *a six-month course*

**monthly[1]** /ˈmʌnθli ˈमन्थ्लि / *adj., adv.* (happening or produced) once every month मासिक ; जो प्रति मास एक बार होने वाला आए, प्रति माह या हर महीने *a monthly meeting/magazine/visit* ○ *Are you paid weekly or monthly?*

**monthly[2]** /ˈmʌnθli ˈमन्थ्लि / *noun* [C] (*pl.* **monthlies**) a magazine that is published once a month मासिक पत्रिका

**monument** /ˈmɒnjumənt ˈमॉन्युमन्ट् / *noun* [C] **a monument (to sb/sth) 1** a building or statue that is built to remind people of a famous person or event स्मारक, कीर्तिस्तंभ (किसी प्रसिद्ध व्यक्ति या घटना की स्मृति में निर्मित कोई भवन या अन्य स्थान **2** an old building or other place that is of historical importance ऐतिहासिक महत्त्व का कोई प्राचीन भवन या अन्य स्थान

**monumental** /ˌmɒnjuˈmentl ˌमॉन्यु ˈमेन्ट्ल् / *adj.* (*only before a noun*) very great, large or important अति विशाल या महत्त्वपूर्ण, चिरस्मरणीय *a monumental success/task/achievement*

**moo** /muː मू / *noun* [C] the sound that a cow makes ▶ **moo** *verb* [I] गाय का रँभाना

**mood** /muːd मूड् / *noun* **1** [C, U] the way that you are feeling at a particular time (समय विशेष में व्यक्ति की) मनोदशा, मनःस्थिति *to be in a bad/good mood* (= to feel angry/happy) ○ *Turn that music down a bit—I'm not* ***in the mood for*** *it.* **2** [C] a time when you are angry or bad-tempered क्रोध या चिड़चिड़ाहट का समय *Dolly's in one of her moods again.* ✪ पर्याय **temper 3** [*sing.*] the way that a group of people feel about sth किसी बात के विषय में व्यक्तियों के समूह का सोच *The mood of the crowd suddenly changed and violence broke out.*

**moody** /ˈmuːdi ˈमूडि / *adj.* **1** often changing moods in a way that people cannot predict अस्थिर मनोदशा वाला (जिसका पूर्वानुमान असंभव हो) *You never know where you are with Anurag because he's so moody.* **2** bad-tempered or unhappy, often for no particular reason (प्रायः बिना कारण) चिड़चिड़ा बदमिज़ाज, कलहप्रिय, तुनकमिज़ाज या खिन्न ▶ **moodily** *adv.* तुनकमिज़ाजी से ▶ **moodiness** *noun* [U] तुनकमिज़ाजी, मनोदशा की अस्थिरता

**moon** /muːn मून् / *noun* **1 the moon** [*sing.*] the object that shines in the sky at night and that moves around the earth once every 28 days चंद्रमा, चाँद

> NOTE चंद्रमा की विभिन्न दशाओं के लिए अलग-अलग शब्द हैं—**new moon**, **full moon**, **half-moon** या **crescent moon** ➪ **lunar** adjective देखिए।

**2** [C] an object like the moon that moves around another planet उपग्रह—*How many moons does Neptune have?*

IDM **once in a blue moon** ➪ **once** देखिए।

**over the moon** (*BrE informal*) extremely happy and excited about sth किसी बात पर बहुत प्रसन्न और रोमांचित

**moonlight** /ˈmuːnlaɪt ˈमूनलाइट् / *noun* [U] light that comes from the moon चंद्रमा का प्रकाश, चंद्रकिरण, चाँदनी, ज्योत्स्ना *The lake looked beautiful in the moonlight.*

**moonlit** /ˈmuːnlɪt ˈमूनलिट् / *adj.* lit by the moon चाँदनी-भरा, ज्योत्स्ना-स्नान

**moor[1]** /mɔː(r) मॉ(र्) / (*also* **moorland** /ˈmɔːlənd ˈमॉलन्ड् /) *noun* [C, U] a wild open area of high land that is covered with grass and **heather** घास से ढका उच्च भूमि का खुला वन्य क्षेत्र, बंजर या अनुर्वर भूमि *We walked across* ***the moors****.* ➪ **heath** देखिए।

**moor[2]** /mɔː(r) मॉ(र्) / *verb* [I, T] **moor (sth to sth)** to fasten a boat to the land or to an object in the water with a rope or chain रस्सा या मोटे तार से नाव को पानी में या भूमि पर लगे खंभे आदि से बाँधना

**mooring** /ˈmɔːrɪŋ ˈमॉरिङ् / *noun* [C, *usually pl.*] a place where a boat is tied; the ropes, chains, etc. used to fasten a boat वह स्थान जहाँ नाव बाँधी जाए, नौ-बंध, बाँध-घाट; नाव बाँधने की रस्सियाँ, ज़ंजीर आदि

**moose** /muːs मूस् / (*AmE*) = **elk**

**mop[1]** /mɒp मॉप् / *noun* [C] a tool for washing floors that consists of a long stick with thick strings, pieces of cloth or a **sponge** on the end फ़र्श साफ़ करने लंबे डंडे वाला ब्रश (जिसमें किनारे पर कपड़ा, स्पंज या मोटे तार लगे होते है), पोंछा

**mop[2]** /mɒp मॉप् / *verb* [T] (**mopping; mopped**) **1** to clean a floor with water and a mop पोंछा और पानी से फ़र्श साफ़ करना, फ़र्श पर पोंछा लगाना **2** to remove liquid from sth using a dry cloth सूखे कपड़े से पसीना, द्रव आदि साफ़ करना *to mop your forehead with a handkerchief*

**PHR V** **mop sth up** to get rid of liquid from a surface with a mop or dry cloth पोंछे या सूखे कपड़े से कोई द्रव पदार्थ पूरी तरह से साफ़ करना

**mope** /məʊp मोप् / *verb* [I] **mope (about/around)** to spend your time doing nothing and feeling sorry for yourself because you are unhappy उदासी में बेकार बैठे या घूमते-फिरते रहना

**moped** /ˈməʊped ˈमोपेड् / *noun* [C] a type of small, not very powerful motorbike छोटी, कम शक्तिशाली मोटरसाइकिल; मोपेड

**moraine** /məˈreɪn मˈरेन् / *noun* [U] (in geography) earth, stones, etc., that have been carried along by a mass of ice (**a glacier**) and left when it melted (भूगोल में) पिघलने पर ग्लेशियर द्वारा लाया और जमा किया गया मिट्टी, पत्थर आदि; हिमोढ ➪ **glacial** पर चित्र देखिए।

**moral**[1] /ˈmɒrəl ˈमॉरल् / *adj.* **1** (*only before a noun*) concerned with what is right and wrong उचित-अनुचित से संबंधित; नैतिक *Some people refuse to eat meat* ***on moral grounds*** (= because they believe it to be wrong). ○ *a moral dilemma/issue/question* **2** having a high standard of behaviour that is considered good and right by most people नैतिकतापूर्ण आचरण *She has always led a very moral life.* ✪ विलोम **immoral** ➪ **amoral** देखिए।

**IDM** **moral support** help or encouragement that you give to sb who is nervous or worried परेशान या चिंतित व्यक्ति को सहायता या समर्थन; नैतिक समर्थन *I went to the dentist's with him just to give him some moral support.*

**moral**[2] /ˈmɒrəl ˈमॉरल् / *noun* **1 morals** [*pl.*] standards of good behaviour अच्छे आचरण के मानदंड, सदाचार, नैतिकता *These people appear to have no morals.* **2** [C] a lesson in the right way to behave that can be learnt from a story or an experience किसी कथा या अनुभव से प्राप्त सीख, शिक्षा, निष्कर्ष *The moral of the play is that friendship is more important than money.*

**morale** /məˈrɑːl मˈराल् / *noun* [U] how happy, sad, confident, etc. a group of people feel at a particular time (समय विशेष में किसी व्यक्ति समूह का) मनोबल *The team's morale was low/high before the match* (= they felt worried/confident). ○ *to boost/raise/improve morale*

**moralistic** /ˌmɒrəˈlɪstɪk ˌमॉरˈलिस्टिक् / *adj.* (*formal*) having or showing very fixed ideas about what is right and wrong, especially when this causes you to judge other people's behaviour नैतिकता के विषय में रूढ़िवादी; नीतिवादात्मक

**morality** /məˈræləti मˈरैलटि / *noun* [U] principles concerning what is good and bad or right and wrong behaviour उचित-अनुचित विचार के सिद्धांत; नैतिकता *a debate about the morality of abortion* ✪ विलोम **immorality**

**moralize** (*also* **-ise**) /ˈmɒrəlaɪz ˈमॉरलाइज़् / *verb* [I] **moralize (about/on sth)** to tell other people what the right or wrong way to behave is दूसरों को नैतिकता का उपदेश देना

**morally** /ˈmɒrəli ˈमॉरलि / *adv.* connected with standards of what is right or wrong नैतिक रूप से

**morass** /məˈræs मˈरैस् / *noun* **1** [*sing.*] a complicated and dangerous situation that is especially difficult to escape from जटिल और संकटपूर्ण परिस्थिति जिससे बचना कठिन हो *a morass of lies and deceit* **2** [C] an area of low soft wet marshy land दलदली क्षेत्र

**moratorium** /ˌmɒrəˈtɔːriəm ˌमॉरˈटॉरिअम् / *noun* [C] **a moratorium (on sth)** a temporary stopping of an activity, especially by official agreement किसी गतिविधि पर अस्थायी प्रतिबंध (विशेषतः शासन की सहमति से) *The convention called for a two-year moratorium on commercial whaling.*

**morbid** /ˈmɔːbɪd ˈमॉबिड् / *adj.* showing interest in unpleasant things, for example disease and death अप्रिय वस्तुओं (जैसे रोग, मृत्यु) में रुचि रखने वाला

**more**[1] /mɔː(r) मॉ(र्) / *det., pronoun* a larger number or amount of people or things; sth extra as well as what you have व्यक्तियों या वस्तुओं की अधिक बड़ी संख्या या मात्रा; जो है वह भी (और) साथ ही और भी, से अधिक *There were* ***more*** *people* ***than*** *I expected.* ○ *We had more time than we thought.* ✪ विलोम **less** या **fewer**

**IDM** **more and more** an increasing amount or number अधिकाधिक *There are more and more cars on the road.*

**what's more** (used for adding another fact) also; in addition (कुछ और जोड़ने के लिए प्रयुक्त) साथ ही; के अतिरिक्त *The hotel was awful and what's more it was miles from the beach.*

**more**[2] /mɔː(r) मॉ(र्) / *adv.* **1** used to form the comparative of many adjectives and adverbs अनेक विशेषणों और क्रियाविशेषणों के तुलनात्मक रूप बनाने के लिए प्रयुक्त *She was* ***far/much more*** *intelligent* ***than*** *her sister.* ○ *a course for more advanced students* ○ *Please write more carefully.* ✪ विलोम **less** **2** to a greater degree than usual or than sth else सामान्य या अन्य से अपेक्षाकृत अधिक *I like him* ***far/much more*** *than his wife.* ✪ विलोम **less**

IDM **not any more** not any longer अब नहीं *She doesn't live here any more.*

**more or less** approximately; almost लगभग कुछ अंश तक; क़रीब-क़रीब, कमोबेश, न्यूनाधिक *We are more or less the same age.*

**moreover** /mɔːrˈəʊvə(r) मॉरˈओव़(र्)/ *adv.* (*written*) (used for adding another fact) also; in addition (कुछ और जोड़ने के लिए प्रयुक्त) साथ ही; के अतिरिक्त *This firm did the work very well. Moreover, the cost was not too high.*

**morgue** /mɔːg मॉग्/ *noun* [C] a building where dead bodies are kept until they are buried or burned शव-गृह ➪ **mortuary** देखिए।

**morning** /ˈmɔːnɪŋ ˈमॉनिङ्/ *noun* [C, U] **1** the early part of the day between the time when the sun rises and midday प्रातःकाल, सुबह, सवेरा *Bye, see you* ***in the morning*** (= tomorrow morning). ○ *I've been studying hard* ***all morning***. **2** the part of the night that is after midnight मध्यरात्रि के बाद का समय, भोर में, तड़के *I was woken by a strange noise in* ***the early hours of the morning***. ○ *He didn't come home until three* ***in the morning***.

NOTE 'Morning', 'afternoon' या 'evening' से पहले विशेषण 'early' या 'late' लगने पर पूर्वसर्ग (preposition) **in** का प्रयोग सर्वथा आवश्यक है—*The accident happened in the early morning.* ○ *We arrived in the late afternoon.* अन्य विशेषणों के साथ **on** का प्रयोग होता है—*School starts on Monday morning.* ○ *They set out on a cold, windy afternoon.* 'This', 'tomorrow', 'yesterday' से पहले किसी पूर्वसर्ग (preposition) का प्रयोग नहीं होता—*Let's go swimming this morning.* ○ *I'll phone Leena tomorrow evening.*
**Good morning** औपचारिक अभिव्यक्ति है जिसका प्रयोग प्रातःकाल में अभिवादन के रूप में होता है। यदि स्थिति कम औपचारिक हो तो केवल Morning कहना काफ़ी है—*Morning Kiran, how are you today?*

**moron** /ˈmɔːrɒn ˈमॉरॉन्/ *noun* [C] (*informal*) a rude way of referring to sb who you think is very stupid मूर्ख लगने वाले व्यक्ति के लिए प्रयुक्त शब्द; बुद्धू, बेवक़ूफ़ *Stop treating me like a moron!* ▶ **moronic** /məˈrɒnɪk मˈरॉनिक्/ *adj.* मूर्खतापूर्ण

**morose** /məˈrəʊs मˈरोस्/ *adj.* bad-tempered, and not saying much to other people बदमिज़ाज, असौम्य (और अपने तक सीमित) ▶ **morosely** *adv.* असौम्य भाव से

**morphine** /ˈmɔːfiːn ˈमॉफ़ीन्/ *noun* [U] a powerful drug that is used for reducing pain दर्द-निवारक प्रभावकारी औषधि; मॉरफ़ीन

**morphology** /mɔːˈfɒlədʒi मॉˈफ़ॉलजि/ *noun* [U] (*technical*) **1** the form and structure of animals and plants, studied as a science जीव-जंतुओं और पेड़-पौधों के रूप और संरचना या बनावट का वैज्ञानिक अध्ययन; आकृति-विज्ञान **2** the form of words, studied as a branch of **linguistics** शब्दों के रूप का भाषावैज्ञानिक अध्ययन, शब्दरूप विज्ञान ➪ **grammar** देखिए। ▶ **morphological** /ˌmɔːfəˈlɒdʒɪkl ˌमॉफ़ˈलॉजिकल्/ *adj.* शब्दरूप विज्ञान-संबंधी

**Morse code** /ˌmɔːsˈkəʊd ˌमॉस्ˈकोड्/ *noun* [U] **1** a system of communication developed by Samuel Morse in which the letters of the alphabet are coded as a combination of dots and dashes so that messages can either be sent using light, sound or wireless सैम्युअल मॉर्स द्वारा विकसित अंग्रेज़ी वर्णमाला के अक्षरों को बिंदु एवं डैश के रूप में संहित कर उन्हें विद्युत, ध्वनि या वायरलैस सिगनल के रूप में संकेत भेजने की प्रणाली; मॉर्स कोड **2** a method of sending messages using these signals मॉर्स कोड द्वारा संदेश भेजने की पद्धति

**morsel** /ˈmɔːsl ˈमॉसल्/ *noun* [C] a very small piece of sth, usually food किसी वस्तु (प्रायः भोजन) का बहुत छोटा टुकड़ा, (भोजन का) कौर, ग्रास

**mortal**[1] /ˈmɔːtl ˈमॉट्ल्/ *adj.* **1** that cannot live forever and must die मरणधर्मा, नश्वर, मर्त्य *We are all mortal.* ✪ विलोम **immortal** **2** (*written*) that will result in death प्राणघातक (जिसका परिणाम मृत्यु हो) *a mortal wound/blow* ○ *to be in mortal danger* ➪ **fatal** देखिए। **3** very great or extreme अत्यधिक या चरम *They were in mortal fear of the enemy.* ▶ **mortally** /-təli -टलि/ *adv.* अत्यधिक रूप से, प्राणघातक रूप से

**mortal**[2] /ˈmɔːtl ˈमॉट्ल्/ *noun* [C] (*formal*) a human being मनुष्य

**mortality** /mɔːˈtæləti मॉˈटैलटि/ *noun* [U] **1** the number of deaths in one period of time or in one place समय विशेष या स्थान विशेष में मरने वालों की संख्या, मृत्यु-संख्या *Infant mortality is high in the region.* **2** the fact that nobody can live for ever नश्वरता *He didn't like to think about his own mortality.*

**mortar** /ˈmɔːtə(r) ˈमॉट(र्)/ *noun* **1** [U] a mixture of cement, sand and water used in building for holding bricks and stones together मकान बनाने का मसाला (सीमेंट, रेत और पानी का मिश्रण जिससे ईंटों और पत्थरों को जोड़ा और जमाया जाता है) **2** [C] a type of heavy gun that fires a type of bomb high into the air एक प्रकार की भारी तोप; मॉर्टर तोप **3** [C] a small heavy bowl used when crushing food, etc. into powder with a special object (**a pestle**) खरल, ऊखल, ओखली ➪ **laboratory** पर चित्र देखिए।

**mortgage** /ˈmɔːɡɪdʒ ˈमॉगिज़्/ *noun* [C] money that you borrow in order to buy a house or flat मकान या फ़्लैट ख़रीदने के लिए उधार लिया पैसा; आवास-ऋण, रेहन *We took out a Rs 40,000 mortgage.*

NOTE सामान्यतया उधार देने वाली संस्थाएँ हैं **bank** या **building society** जो ब्याज दर या **rate of interest** तय करती हैं जिसे **loan** पर उन संस्थाओं को देना आवश्यक होता है।

**mortician** /mɔːˈtɪʃn मॉˈटिश्न्/ (*AmE*) = **undertaker**

**mortify** /ˈmɔːtɪfaɪ ˈमॉटिफ़ाइ/ *verb* [T] (*usually passive*) (*pres. part.* **mortifying;** *3rd person sing. pres.* **mortifies;** *pt, pp* **mortified**) (*formal*) to make sb feel very embarrassed किसी को बहुत लज्जित या अपमानित कर देना *She **was mortified to** realize he had heard every word she said.* ▶ **mortification** /ˌmɔːtɪfɪˈkeɪʃn ˌमॉटिफ़िˈकेशन्/ *noun* [U] अपमान, अवमानता ▶ **mortifying** *adj.* लज्जाजनक *How mortifying to have to apologize to him!*

**mortise** (*also* **mortice**) /ˈmɔːtɪs ˈमॉटिस्/ *noun* [C] (*technical*) a hole cut in a piece of wood, etc. to receive the end of another piece of wood, so that the two are held together खाँचा, खम (लकड़ी आदि में बना सूराख जिसमें दूसरे छोर से डाला लकड़ी आदि का टुकड़ा जुड़ जाता है)

**mortuary** /ˈmɔːtʃəri ˈमॉचरि/ *noun* [C] (*pl.* **mortuaries**) a room, usually in a hospital, where dead bodies are kept before they are buried or burned शव-गृह (प्रायः अस्पताल में), शवागार ➪ **morgue** देखिए।

**mosaic** /məʊˈzeɪk मोˈज़ेइक्/ *noun* [C, U] a picture or pattern that is made by placing together small coloured stones, pieces of glass, etc. छोटे रंगीन पत्थरों, काँच के टुकड़ों को जमाकर बनाया गया चित्र या पैटर्न, चित्रिल चित्र वर्ण योजना; पच्चीकारी, मोज़ेक

**Moslem** = **Muslim**

**mosque** /mɒsk मॉस्क्/ *noun* [C] a building where Muslims meet and pray मस्जिद; वह इमारत जहाँ मुसलमान इकट्ठा होकर नमाज़ पढ़ते हैं

**mosquito** /məˈskiːtəʊ; mɒs- मˈस्कीटो; मॉस्- / *noun* [C] (*pl.* **mosquitoes**) a small flying insect that lives in hot countries and bites people or animals to drink their blood. Some types of mosquito spread a very serious disease (**malaria**) मच्छर, मशक ➪ **insect** पर चित्र देखिए।

**moss** /mɒs मॉस्/ *noun* [C, U] a small soft green plant, with no flowers, that grows in wet places, especially on rocks or trees काई, शैवाल, मॉस (नमीदार स्थानों, विशेषतः चट्टानों या वृक्षों, पर उगने वाली पुष्पहीन महीन कोमल हरी वनस्पति) ▶ **mossy** *adj.* काईदार

**most¹** /məʊst मोस्ट्/ *det. pronoun* **1** (used as the superlative of 'many' and 'much') greatest in number or amount (संख्या या मात्रा में) अधिकतम *Who got the most points?* ○ *We all worked hard but I did the most.* ✪ विलोम **least** या **fewest** **2** nearly all of a group of people or things (व्यक्तियों या वस्तुओं के समूह में) लगभग सभी *Most people in this country have a television.* ○ *I like most Italian food.*

NOTE यदि **most** के बाद **the, this, my** आदि से युक्त संज्ञा का प्रयोग हो तो **most of** का प्रयोग अनिवार्य है—*Most of my friends were able to come to the wedding.* ○ *It rained most of the time we were at Mumbai.*

IDM **at (the) most** not more than a certain number, and probably less अधिक-से अधिक, एक विशेष संख्या से अधिक नहीं (संभवतः कम ही) *There were 20 people there, at the most.*

**make the most of sth** ➪ **make¹** देखिए।

**most²** /məʊst मोस्ट्/ *adv.* **1** used to form the superlative of many adjectives and adverbs अनेक विशेषणों और क्रियाविशेषणों का उत्तमावस्था का रूप बनाने के लिए प्रयुक्त *It's the most beautiful house I've ever seen.* ○ *I work most efficiently in the morning.* ✪ विलोम **least** **2** more than anyone/anything else सबसे अधिक *What do you miss most when you're abroad?* ✪ विलोम **least** **3** (*formal*) very अत्यंत, बहुत *We heard a most interesting talk about Japan.*

**mostly** /ˈməʊstli ˈमोस्ट्लि/ *adv.* in almost every case; almost all the time अधिकांशतः, मुख्यतया, अधिकतर *Our students come mostly from Japan.*

**motel** /məʊˈtel मोˈटेल्/ *noun* [C] a hotel near a main road for people who are travelling by car कार-यात्रियों के लिए मुख्य सड़क के निकट बना होटल; मोटल

**moth** /mɒθ मॉथ्/ *noun* [C] an insect with a hairy body and large wings that usually flies at night. Some moths eat cloth and leave small holes in your clothes कपड़ों में लगने वाला कीड़ा; कपड़कीड़ा, शलभ, पतंगा ➪ **insect** पर चित्र देखिए।

**mothball** /ˈmɒθbɔːl ˈमॉथ्बॉल्/ *noun* [C] a small ball made of a chemical substance that protects clothes in cupboards from moths कपड़कीड़े मारने की फ़िनाइल की गोली

**mother¹** /ˈmʌðə(r) ˈमद़(र्)/ *noun* [C] the female parent of a person or an animal माँ, माता, जननी (मनुष्य या पशु को जन्म देने वाली मादा) ➪ **mum, mummy** और **stepmother** देखिए।

**mother**[2] /ˈmʌðə(r) ˈमद़र्/ *verb* [T] to look after sb as a mother does किसी व्यक्ति की माँ के समान देख-भाल करना *Stop mothering me—I can look after myself!*

**motherhood** /ˈmʌðəhʊd ˈमद़हुड्/ *noun* [U] the state of being a mother मातृत्व

**mother-in-law** *noun* [C] (*pl.* **mothers-in-law**) the mother of your husband or wife पति या पत्नी की माँ; सास

**motherland** /ˈmʌðəlænd ˈमद़लैन्ड्/ *noun* [C] (*formal*) the country where you or your family were born and which you feel a strong emotional connection with मातृभूमि, जन्मभूमि

**motherly** /ˈmʌðəli ˈमद़लि/ *adj.* having the qualities of a good mother माता-सदृश, मातृ-सुलभ *motherly love*

**mother tongue** *noun* [C] the first language that you learned to speak as a child मातृभाषा; शैशव में सीखी प्रथम भाषा

**motif** /məʊˈtiːf मोˈटीफ़्/ *noun* [C] a picture or pattern on sth किसी वस्तु का चित्र या डिज़ाइन

**motion**[1] /ˈməʊʃn ˈमोश्न्/ *noun* **1** [U] movement or a way of moving गति या गति करने का प्रकार *The motion of the ship made us all feel sick.* ○ *Pull the lever to* ***set*** *the machine* ***in motion*** (= make it start moving). ➪ **slow motion** देखिए। **2** [C] a formal suggestion at a meeting that you discuss and vote on किसी बैठक में चर्चा और मतदान हेतु प्रस्तुत प्रस्ताव *The motion was carried/rejected by a majority of eight votes.*

**motion**[2] /ˈməʊʃn ˈमोश्न्/ *verb* [I, T] **motion to sb (to do sth); motion (for) sb (to do sth)** to make a movement, usually with your hand, that tells sb what to do हाथ हिलाकर किसी को इशारा करना (बुलाने आदि के लिए) *I motioned to the waiter.* ○ *The manager motioned for me to sit down.*

**motionless** /ˈməʊʃnləs ˈमोश्नलस्/ *adj.* not moving गतिहीन, जड़

**motivate** /ˈməʊtɪveɪt ˈमोटिव़ेट्/ *verb* [T] **1** (*usually passive*) to cause sb to act in a particular way विशेष प्रकार से कुछ करने का कारण बनना, प्रेरित करना *Her reaction was motivated by fear.* **2** to make sb want to do sth, especially sth that involves hardwork and effort किसी को किसी (परिश्रमपूर्ण) काम के लिए प्रोत्साहित या अभिप्रेरित करना *Our new teacher certainly knows how to motivate his classes.* ▶ **motivated** *adj.* अभिप्रेरित *highly motivated students* ▶ **motivation** /ˌməʊtɪˈveɪʃn ˌमोटिˈव़ेश्न्/ *noun* [C, U] अभिप्रेरण *He's clever enough, but he lacks motivation.*

**motive** /ˈməʊtɪv ˈमोटिव़्/ *noun* [C, U] **(a) motive (for sth/doing sth)** a reason for doing sth, often sth bad प्रयोजन, इरादा (प्रायः कुत्सित) *The police couldn't discover a motive for the murder.*

**motor**[1] /ˈməʊtə(r) ˈमोट(र्)/ *noun* [C] a device that uses petrol, gas, electricity, etc. to produce movement and makes a machine, etc. work पेट्रोल, गैस, विद्युत आदि से चलने वाला यंत्र जिससे मशीनें आदि चलती हैं, मोटर *The washing machine doesn't work. I think something is wrong with the motor.*

> **NOTE** कारों और मोटर-साइकिलों के संदर्भ में **engine** शब्द का प्रयोग होता है (**motor** का नहीं) तथापि कारों को कभी-कभी औपचारिक रूप से **motor cars** कह देते हैं।

**motor**[2] /ˈməʊtə(r) ˈमोट(र्)/ *adj.* (*only before a noun*) **1** having or using the power of an engine or a motor इंजन या मोटर से युक्त *a motor vehicle* **2** connected with vehicles that have engines, especially cars इंजन-युक्त वाहनों (विशेषतः कारों) से संबंधित *the motor industry* ○ *motor racing*

**motorbike** /ˈməʊtəbaɪk ˈमोटबाइक्/ (*formal* **motorcycle**) *noun* [C] a vehicle that has two wheels and an engine मोटर-साइकिल

**motor boat** *noun* [C] a small fast boat that has a motor मोटर-बोट

**motor car** (*BrE formal*) = **car 1**

**motorcycle** /ˈməʊtəsaɪkl ˈमोटसाइक्ल्/ (*formal*) = **motorbike**

**motorcyclist** /ˈməʊtəsaɪklɪst ˈमोटसाइक्लिस्ट्/ *noun* [C] a person who rides a motorbike मोटर-साइकिल-सवार

**motoring** /ˈməʊtərɪŋ ˈमोटरिङ्/ *noun* [U] driving in a car मोटर-वाहन, कार-यात्रा *a motoring holiday*

**motorist** /ˈməʊtərɪst ˈमोटरिस्ट्/ *noun* [C] a person who drives a car कार-चालक, कार-यात्री ➪ **pedestrian** देखिए।

**motorized** (*also* **-ised**) /ˈməʊtəraɪzd ˈमोटराइज़्ड्/ *adj.* (*only before a noun*) that has an engine इंजन-चलित, मोटर-चालित *a motorized wheelchair*

**motorway** /ˈməʊtəweɪ ˈमोटवे/ (*AmE* **expressway; freeway**) *noun* [C] a wide road connecting cities that is specially built for fast traffic नगरों को जोड़ने वाली, विशेषतः तीव्रगामी यातायात के लिए बनी चौड़ी सड़क

**mottled** /ˈmɒtld ˈमॉट्ल्ड्/ *adj.* marked with shapes of different colours without a regular pattern बेतरतीब डिज़ाइन की रंगबिरंगी आकृतियों वाला; चित्तीदार, चितकबरा *the mottled skin of a snake*

**motto** /ˈmɒtəʊ ˈमॉटो/ *noun* [C] (*pl.* **mottoes** or **mottos**) a short sentence or phrase that expresses the aims and beliefs of a person, a group, an organization, etc. किसी व्यक्ति, समूह, संगठन आदि के उद्देश्यों और मान्यताओं को व्यक्त करने वाला वाक्य या वाक्यांश, ध्येय वाक्य या वाक्यांश *'Live and let live' —that's my motto.*

**mould**[1] (*AmE* **mold**) /məʊld मोल्ड्/ *noun* **1** [C] a container that you pour a liquid or substance into. The liquid then becomes solid (**sets**) in the same shape as the container, for example after it has cooled or cooked साँचा (एक ऐसा डिब्बा जिसमें डाला गया द्रव या अन्य पदार्थ जम या पक जाने पर उसी की शकल ले लेता है) **2** [C, *usually sing.*] a particular type एक विशिष्ट प्रकार; मोल्ड *She doesn't fit into the usual mould of sales directors.* **3** [U] a soft green or black substance like fur (**fungus**) that grows in wet places or on old food ▸ **mouldy** (*AmE* **moldy**) *adj.* फफूँदा-भरा *The cheese had gone mouldy.*

**mould**[2] (*AmE* **mold**) /məʊld मोल्ड्/ *verb* [T] **mould A (into B); mould B (from/out of A)** to make sth into a particular shape or form by pressing it or by putting it into a **mould**[1] **1** साँचे में डालकर किसी वस्तु को विशेष आकृति देना *First mould the dough into a ball.* ○ *a bowl moulded from clay*

**moult** (*AmE* **molt**) /məʊlt मोल्ट्/ *verb* [I] (used about an animal or a bird) to lose hairs or feathers before growing new ones (पशुओं के) बाल और (पक्षियों के) पर झड़ना (बाद में नए निकलने के लिए); निर्मोचन करना

**mound** /maʊnd माउन्ड्/ *noun* [C] **1** a large pile of earth or stones; a small hill मिट्टी या पत्थरों का टीला; एक छोटी पहाड़ी **2** (*spoken*) **a mound (of sth)** a pile or a large amount of sth किसी वस्तु का ढेर या बड़ी मात्रा *I've got a mound of work to do.*

**mount**[1] /maʊnt माउन्ट्/ *verb* **1** [T] to organize sth कुछ आयोजित करना *to mount a protest/a campaign/an exhibition/an attack* **2** [I] to increase gradually in level or amount किसी वस्तु के स्तर या मात्रा में वृद्धि होना, स्तर या मात्रा बढ़ना *The tension mounted as the end of the match approached.* **3** [T] (*written*) to go up sth or up on to sth किसी वस्तु पर या के ऊपर चढ़ जाना *He mounted the platform and began to speak.* **4** [I, T] to get on a horse or bicycle घोड़े या साइकिल पर सवार होना या चढ़ना ✪ विलोम **dismount** **5** [T] **mount sth (on/onto/in sth)** to fix sth firmly on sth else किसी वस्तु को किसी अन्य वस्तु पर जमाना, जड़ना या मढ़ना *The gas boiler was mounted on the wall.*

**PHR V** **mount up** to increase (often more than you want) बढ़ जाना (आशा से अधिक) *When you're buying food for six people the cost soon mounts up.*

**mount**[2] /maʊnt माउन्ट्/ *noun* [C] (*abbr.* **Mt**) (used in names) a mountain (नामों में प्रयुक्त) कोई पर्वत *Mt Everest*

**mountain** /ˈmaʊntən ˈमाउन्टन्/ *noun* [C] **1** a very high hill पर्वत, पहाड़ *Which is the highest mountain in the world?* ○ *mountain roads/scenery/villages* **2 a mountain (of sth)** a large amount of sth किसी वस्तु की बड़ी मात्रा, ढेर सारी (कोई) वस्तु *I've got a mountain of work to do.* ○ *the problem of Europe's butter mountain* (= the large amount of butter that has to be stored because it is not needed)

**mountain bike** *noun* [C] a bicycle with a strong frame, wide tyres and many different **gears**, designed for riding on rough ground ऊबड़-खाबड़ या ऊँची-नीची ज़मीन पर चलाने की अनेक गिअर वाली साइकिल (जिसके टायर चौड़े और ढाँचा मज़बूत होता है), माउंटेन बाइक

**mountaineering** /ˌmaʊntəˈnɪərɪŋ ˌमाउन्टˈनिअरिङ्/ *noun* [U] the sport of climbing mountains पहाड़ों पर चढ़ने का खेल, पर्वतारोहण का अभियान ▸ **mountaineer** /-ˈnɪə(r) -ˈनिअ(र्)/ *noun* [C] पर्वतारोही

**mountain lion** (*AmE*) = **puma**

**mountainous** /ˈmaʊntənəs ˈमाउन्टनस्/ *adj.* **1** having many mountains अनेक पहाड़ों वाला, पर्वत-बहुल *a mountainous region* **2** very large in size or amount आकार या मात्रा में बहुत बड़ा; भीमकाय, पर्वताकार *The mountainous waves made sailing impossible.*

**mountainside** /ˈmaʊntənsaɪd ˈमाउन्टन्साइड्/ *noun* [C] the land on the side of a mountain पर्वत की ओर की भूमि

**mounted** /ˈmaʊntɪd ˈमाउन्टिड्/ *adj.* riding a horse घोड़े पर सवार, घुड़सवार *mounted police*

**mounting** /ˈmaʊntɪŋ ˈमाउन्टिङ्/ *adj.* (*only before a noun*) increasing बढ़ता हुआ *mounting unemployment/tension*

**mourn** /mɔːn मॉन्/ *verb* [I, T] **mourn (for/over) sb/sth** to feel and show great sadness, especially because sb has died दुख या शोक मनाना (विशेषतः किसी की मृत्यु पर) *She is still mourning (for) her child.* ▸ **mourning** *noun* [U] शोकमग्न, दुखी *He wore a black armband to show he was **in mourning**.*

**mourner** /ˈmɔːnə(r) ˈमॉन(र्)/ *noun* [C] a person who goes to a funeral as a friend or relative of the person who has died शवयात्रा में भाग लेने वाला मृतक का मित्र या संबंधी; शोकार्त

**mournful** /ˈmɔːnfl ˈमॉन्फ़्ल्/ *adj.* (*written*) very sad शोकग्रस्त, बहुत दुखी, मातमी *a mournful song* ▶ **mournfully** /-fəli -फ़लि/ *adv.* शोकपूर्ण भाव से

**mouse** /maʊs माउस्/ *noun* [C] (*pl.* **mice** /maɪs माइस्/) **1** a very small animal with fur and a long thin tail चूहा, मूषक

> **NOTE** **Rats, hamsters** आदि के समान **mice** भी **rodent** परिवार में आते हैं।

**2** a piece of equipment, connected to a computer, for moving around the screen and entering commands without touching the keys कंप्यूटर का माउस (जिसे कुंजियों को बिना छुए हम कंप्यूटर-स्क्रीन के चारों और घुमाते हैं और अपेक्षित आदेशों या कमांडस को प्रविष्ट करते हैं) *Use the mouse to drag the icon to a new position.*

**mousse** /muːs मूस्/ *noun* [C, U] **1** a type of light food that is made by mixing together cream and egg whites and adding another food for flavour क्रीम और अंडे की सफ़ेदी के मिश्रण मे किसी अन्य खाद्य पदार्थ को मिलाने से बना एक प्रकार का हलका भोज्य पदार्थ; मूस *(a) chocolate/salmon mousse* **2** a light substance containing a lot of bubbles that you use to make your hair stay in a particular style बालों में लगाने का एक बुलबुलेदार हलका पदार्थ (ताकि केशसज्जा जमी रहे)

**moustache** /məˈstɑːʃ मˈस्टाश्;/ (*AmE* **mustache**) *noun* [C] hair that grows on a man's top lip, between the mouth and nose मूँछ

**mouth[1]** /maʊθ माउथ्/ *noun* [C] (*pl.* **mouths**/ maʊðz माउद्ज़्/) **1** the part of your face that you use for eating and speaking मुख, मुह *to open/close your mouth* ➪ **body** पर चित्र देखिए। **2 -mouthed** /maʊðd माउद्ड्/ (*used to form compound adjectives*) having a particular type of mouth or a particular way of speaking विशेष प्रकार के मुख या बोलने के ढंग वाला *We stared open-mouthed in surprise.* ○ *He's a loud-mouthed bully.* **3** the place where a river enters the sea नदी का मुहाना (जहाँ वह समुद्र में मिलती है)

**IDM** **keep your mouth shut** (*informal*) to not say sth to sb because it is a secret or because it will upset or annoy him/her (अपना) मुँह बंद रखना, कुछ न कहना (बात को गुप्त रखने या दूसरे को नाराज़गी या परेशानी से बचाने के लिए)

**mouth[2]** /maʊð माउद्/ *verb* [I, T] to move your mouth as if you were speaking but without making any sound वक्ता का ओंठों को ऐसे चलाना या हिलाना कि लगे वह कुछ कह रहा है (परंतु बिना आवाज़ किए) *Vinay was outside the window, mouthing something to us.*

**mouthful** /ˈmaʊθfʊl ˈमाउथ्फ़ुल्/ *noun* **1** [C] the amount of food or drink that you can put in your mouth at one time खाद्य या पेय पदार्थ की एक बार में मुँह में आने वाली मात्रा; कौर, ग्रास, निवाला **2** [*sing.*] a word or phrase that is long or difficult to say लंबा या उच्चारण में कठिन शब्द या वाक्यांश *Her name is a bit of a mouthful.*

**mouth organ** = **harmonica**

**mouthpiece** /ˈmaʊθpiːs ˈमाउथ्पीस्/ *noun* [C] **1** the part of a telephone, musical instrument, etc. that you put in or near your mouth टेलीफ़ोन, संगीत वाद्य उपकरण आदि का वह भाग जो मुँह में या मुँह के निकट रखा जाता है (बोलने, बजाने आदि के लिए); मुखिका, माउथपीस **2** a person, newspaper, etc. that a particular group uses to express its opinions समूह विशेष के विचारों को व्यक्त करने वाला व्यक्ति, समाचार-पत्र आदि; प्रतिनिधि, प्रवक्ता, मुखपत्र

**mouth-watering** *adj.* (used about food) that looks or smells very good (भोजन) सुगंधित, सुशोमन या स्वादिष्ट, मुँह में पानी लाने वाला

**movable** /ˈmuːvəbl ˈमूवबल्/ *adj.* that can be moved जिसे हिलाया या चलाया जा सके; चल, चलनशील ✪ विलोम **fixed** ➪ **portable** और **mobile** देखिए।

**move[1]** /muːv मूव्/ *verb* **1** [I, T] to change position or to put sth in a different position स्थान बदलना या किसी वस्तु को अन्य स्थान पर ले जाना, हिलना या हिलाना; खिसकना या खिसकाना *The station is so crowded you **can hardly move**.* ○ *The meeting has been moved to Thursday.* **2** [I, T] **move along, down, over, up, etc.** to move (sth) further in a particular direction in order to make space for sb/sth else (किसी वस्तु का) विशेष दिशा मे हटना या उसे हटाना (ताकि अन्य के लिए जगह निकल आए) *If we move up a bit, Raj can sit here too.* ○ *Move your head down—I can't see the screen.* **3** [I, T] to change the place where you live, work, study, etc. (निवास, नौकरी, अध्ययन आदि करने का) स्थान बदलना *Our neighbours are moving to Mumbai next week.* ○ *to **move house*** **4** [I] **move (on/ahead)** to make progress प्रगति करना, आगे बढ़ना *When the new team of builders arrived things started moving very quickly.* **5** [I] to take action कार्रवाई करना *Unless we move quickly lives will be lost.* **6** [T] to cause sb to have strong feelings, especially of sadness भावनाओं (विशेषतः उदासी की) के उमड़ने का कारण बनाना *Many people were **moved to tears** by reports of the massacre.*

**IDM** **get moving** to go, leave or do sth quickly फुरती से कहीं जाना या कुछ करना

**get sth moving** to cause sth to make progress किसी काम को आगे बढ़ाना

PHR V **move in (with sb)** to start living in a house (with sb) (किसी व्यक्ति के साथ) मकान में रहने लगना

**move on (to sth)** to start doing or discussing sth new कोई नया काम या नए प्रसंग पर चर्चा आरंभ करना

**move off** (used about a vehicle) to start a journey; to leave (वाहन का) चलने लगना या चलना आरंभ करना; चल पड़ना, छूटना

**move out** to leave your old home पुराना घर छोड़ना

**move²** /mu:v मूव् / *noun* [C] **1** a change of place or position स्थान या स्थिति में परिवर्तन *She was watching every move I made.* **2** a change in the place where you live or work निवास-स्थान या कार्य-स्थान में परिवर्तन *a move to a bigger house* **3** action that you take because you want to achieve a particular result उद्देश्य पूर्ति के लिए उठाया गया क़दम *Both sides want to negotiate but neither is prepared to **make the first move**. ○ Asking him to help me was **a good move**.* **4** (in chess and other games) a change in the position of a piece (शतरंज और अन्य खेलों में) मोहरे की चाल *It's your move.*

IDM **be on the move** to be going somewhere कहीं जाने को तैयार होना

**get a move on** (*informal*) to hurry जल्दी करना *I'm late. I'll have to get a move on.*

**make a move** to start to go somewhere कहीं के लिए चलना शुरू करना *It's time to go home. Let's make a move.*

**movement** /ˈmu:vmənt ˈमूव्मन्ट् / *noun* **1** [C, U] an act of moving गति, संचलन, हिलने-डुलने की क्रिया *The dancer's movements were smooth and controlled. ○ The seat belt doesn't allow much freedom of movement.* **2** [C, U] an act of moving or being moved from one place to another स्थान-परिवर्तन (करने या होने की क्रिया) *the slow movement of the clouds across the sky* **3** [C, *usually sing.*] **a movement (away from/towards sth)** a general change in the way people think or behave समाज की सोच या आचरण में सामान्य परिवर्तन *There's been a movement away from the materialism of the 1980s.* **4 movements** [*pl.*] a person's actions or plans during a period of time एक समयावधि में व्यक्ति की चेष्टाएँ या योजनाएँ *Detectives have been watching the man's movements for several weeks.* **5** [C] a group of people who have the same aims or ideas समान उद्देश्यों या विचारों से प्रेरित कोई व्यक्ति-समूह *I support the Animal Rights movement.*

**movie** /ˈmu:vi ˈमूवि / *noun* (*AmE*) **1** = **film¹ 1** *Shall we go and **see a movie**? ○ a movie theater* (= cinema) **2 the movies** [*pl.*] = **cinema** *Let's **go to the movies**.*

**moving** /ˈmu:vɪŋ ˈमूविङ् / *adj.* **1** causing strong feelings, especially of sadness भावावेश (विशेषतः विषाद) को जन्म देने वाली; हृदयस्पर्शी, प्रभावशाली *a deeply moving speech/story* **2** that moves चल, गतिमान *It's a computerized machine with few moving parts.*

**mow** /məʊ मो / *verb* [I, T] (*pt* **mowed;** *pp* **mown** /məʊn मोन् / or **mowed**) to cut grass using a machine (**a mower**) विशेष मशीन से घास काटना *to mow the lawn*

IDM **mow sb down** to kill sb with a gun or a car बंदूक़ (चलाकर) या कार से (कुचल कर) किसी को मार देना

**mower** /ˈməʊə(r) ˈमोअ(र्) / *noun* [C] a machine for cutting grass घास काटने की मशीन, घास लावक यंत्र, घास कर्तक *a lawnmower ○ an electric mower*

**MP** /ˌemˈpi: ˌएम्ˈपी / *abbr.* Member of Parliament संसद-सदस्य, सांसद

**mph** /ˌem pi: ˈeɪtʃ ˌएम् पी ˈएच् / *abbr.* miles per hour मील प्रति घंटा *a 70 mph speed limit*

**MPV** /ˌempi:ˈvi: ˌएम् पी ˈवी / *noun* [C] the abbreviation for 'multi-purpose vehicle', a large car like a van बहु प्रयोजनात्मक वाहन का संक्षिप्त रूप (बड़े आकार की बंद मोटरगाड़ी वैन) ✪ पर्याय **people carrier**

**Mr** /ˈmɪstə(r) ˈमिस्ट(र्) / used as a title before the name of a man पुरुष के नाम से पहले प्रयुक्त शब्द, श्री *Mr (Anil) Kumar* ➪ **Miss** पर नोट देखिए।

**mridangam** *noun* [C] a barrel-shaped drum from South India, especially used in **Carnatic music** कर्नाटक संगीत में प्रयुक्त, दक्षिण भारतीय ढोलक; मृदंग ➪ पृष्ठ 789 पर चित्र देखिए।

**Mrs** /ˈmɪsɪz ˈमिसिज़् / used as a title before the name of a married woman विवाहित महिला के नाम से पहले प्रयुक्त शब्द, श्रीमती *Mrs (Sunita) Ray* ➪ **Miss** देखिए।

**MS** /ˌem ˈes ˌएम् ˈएस् / *abbr.* multiple sclerosis मल्टिपल स्कलेरॉसिस

**Ms** /mɪz; məz मिज़्; मज़् / used as a title before the family name of a woman who may or may not be married (विवाहित या अविवाहित) महिला के कुलनाम से पहले प्रयुक्त शब्द सुश्री *Ms (Dolly) Rawat*

NOTE कुछ महिलाएँ अपने नाम से पहले **Mrs** या **Miss** लगाने की अपेक्षा **Ms** लगाना अधिक पसंद करती हैं। यदि हमें मालूम न हो कि महिला विवाहित हैं या अविवाहित तो हम भी उनके नाम से पहले इस शब्द का प्रयोग कर सकते हैं। **Miss** पर भी नोट देख लीजिए।

**MSc** /ˌem es ˈsiː ˌएम् एस् ˈसी / *abbr.* Master of Science: a second degree that you receive when you complete a more advanced course or piece of research in a science subject at university or college मास्टर ऑफ साइंस; विज्ञान विषय में मास्टर उपाधि विश्वविद्यालय द्वारा प्रदत्त ➪ **BSc** और **MA** देखिए।

**MSG** /ˌem es ˈdʒiː ˌएम् एस् ˈजी / *abbr.* monosodium glutamate मोनोसोडियम ग्लुटमेट

**Mt** *abbr.* Mount माउंट *Mt Everest*

**mth** (*AmE* **mo**) (*pl.* **mths;** *AmE* **mos**) *abbr.* month मास, महीना *6 mths old*

**much** /mʌtʃ मच् / *det., pronoun, adv.* **1** (used with uncountable nouns, mainly in negative sentences and questions, or after ***as, how, so, too***) a large amount of sth (अगणनीय संज्ञाओं में, मुख्यतया निषेधवाचक और प्रश्नवाचक वाक्य अथवा as, how, so, too के बाद प्रयुक्त) किसी वस्तु की अधिक मात्रा *You've given me **too much** food.* ○ ***How much** time have you got?*

> **NOTE** सामान्य कथनों में हम **a lot of** का प्रयोग करते हैं (**much** का नहीं)—*I've got a lot of experience.*

**2** to a great degree बड़ी सीमा तक *I don't like her very much.* ○ *much taller/prettier/harder* ○ *much more interesting/unusual* **3** (*with past participles used as adjectives*) very अत्यधिक *She was much loved by all her friends.*

**IDM** **much the same** very similar अत्यधिक समान *Softball is much the same as baseball.*

**nothing much** ➪ **nothing** देखिए।

**not much good (at sth)** not skilled (at sth) (किसी कार्य में) विशेष कुशल नहीं; अकुशल *I'm not much good at singing.*

**not much of a**... not a good... (विशेष) अच्छा नहीं *She's not much of a cook.*

**not up to much** ➪ **up** देखिए।

**muck¹** /mʌk मक् / *noun* [U] **1** the waste from farm animals, used to make plants grow better पालतू पशुओं का गोबर जो खाद का काम करता है ✪ पर्याय **manure** **2** (*informal*) dirt or mud गंदगी या कीचड़

**muck²** /mʌk मक् / *verb* (*informal*)

**PHR V** **muck about/around** to behave in a silly way or to waste time मूर्खता का आचरण करना या समय नष्ट करना *Stop mucking around and come and help me!*

**muck sth up** to do sth badly; to spoil sth किसी काम को लापरवाही या असावधानी से करना; काम बिगाड़ देना *I was so nervous that I completely mucked up my interview.*

**mucous membrane** *noun* [C] a thin layer of skin that covers the inside of the nose and mouth and the outside of other organs in the body, producing a sticky substance (**mucus**) to stop these parts from becoming dry श्लेष्मल झिल्ली (नाक और मुँह के अंदर और अन्य अंगों के बाहर त्वचा की महीन परत जिससे श्लेष्मा उत्पन्न होता है जो इन अंगों को शुष्क नहीं होने देता)

**mucus** /ˈmjuːkəs ˈम्यूकस् / *noun* [U] (*formal*) a sticky substance that is produced in some parts of the body, especially the nose श्लेष्मा, बलग़म, कफ़ ▶ **mucous** /ˈmjuːkəs ˈम्यूकस् / *adj.* श्लेष्मल, श्लेष्मा-उत्पादक *mucous glands*

**mud** /mʌd मड् / *noun* [U] soft, wet earth कीचड़, पंक *He came home from the football match **covered in mud**.*

**muddle** /ˈmʌdl ˈमड्ल् / *verb* [T] **1 muddle sth (up)** to put things in the wrong place or order or to make them untidy वस्तुओं को उलटा-सीधा रख देना या उन्हें [illegible] कर देना *Try not to **get** those papers **muddled up**.* **2 muddle sb (up)** to confuse sb किसी व्यक्ति को चकरा देना, उलझन में डाल देना *I do my homework and schoolwork in separate books so that I don't **get muddled up**.* ▶ **muddle** *noun* [C, U] अस्त व्यस्तता, गड़बड़ी, भ्रम *If you **get in a muddle,** I'll help you.* ▶ **muddled** *adj.* चकराया हुआ, विभ्रांत

**muddy** /ˈmʌdi ˈमडि / *adj.* full of or covered in mud कीचड़-भरा, पंकिल, गँदला *muddy boots* ○ *It's very muddy down by the river.*

**mudflat** /ˈmʌdflæt ˈमड्फ़्लैट् / *noun* [C] (*pl.* **mudflats**) an area of flat wet land that is covered by the sea when it is at its highest level (**high tide**) ज्वार के समय समुद्रतट का भाग जो कीचड़ से भर जाता है

**mudguard** /ˈmʌdgɑːd ˈमड्गाड् / *noun* [C] a curved cover over the wheel of a bicycle or motorbike मडगार्ड (साइकिल या मोटरसाइकिल के पहियों पर लगा घुमावदार ढक्कन जो उन्हें कीचड़ से बचाता है)

**muesli** /ˈmjuːzli ˈम्यूज़्लि / *noun* [U] food made of grains, nuts, dried fruit, etc that you eat with milk for breakfast अन्न; मेवों आदि का मिश्रण जो नाश्ते में दूध के साथ लिया जाता है

**muezzin** /muːˈezɪn म्यूˈएज़िन् / *noun* [C] a man who calls Muslims to come to a special building (**a mosque**) to pray (मस्जिद का) मुअज़्ज़िन (जो प्रार्थना के लिए मुसलमानों को मस्जिद बुलाता है, अज़ान देता है)

**muffin** /ˈmʌfɪn ˈमफ़िन् / *noun* [C] **1** (*AmE* **English muffin**) a type of bread roll often eaten hot with butter मक्खन के साथ गरम-गरम खाया जाने वाला एक प्रकार का ब्रैडरौल; मफ़िन **2** a type of small cake एक प्रकार का छोटा केक

**muffle** /ˈmʌfl ˈमफ़्ल्/ *verb* [T] to make a sound quieter and more difficult to hear आवाज़ को कम कर देना या दबा देना (ताकि आसानी से सुनाई न दे) *He put his hand over his mouth to muffle his laughter.* ▶ **muffled** *adj.* (आवाज़) दबी हुई, मंद *I heard muffled voices outside.*

**muffler[1]** /ˈmʌflə(r) ˈमफ़्ल(र्)/ *noun* [C] (*old-fashioned*) a thick scarf worn around the neck for warmth मफ़लर, गुलुबंद

**muffler[2]** /ˈmʌflə(r) ˈमफ़्ल(र्)/ = (*AmE*) **silencer**

**mug[1]** /mʌg मग्/ *noun* [C] **1** a large cup with straight sides and a handle मूठदार बड़ा कप; मग *a coffee mug* ○ *a mug of tea* **2** (*informal*) a person who seems stupid मूर्ख-सा व्यक्ति

**mug[2]** /mʌg मग्/ *verb* [T] (**mugging; mugged**) to attack and rob sb in the street रास्ते में किसी पर हमला कर उसे लूट लेना *Keep your wallet out of sight or you'll* ***get mugged***. ▶ **mugger** *noun* [C] लुटेरा ➪ **thief** पर नोट देखिए। ▶ **mugging** *noun* [C, U] लूट-मार *The mugging took place around midnight.*

**muggy** /ˈmʌgi ˈमगि/ *adj.* (used about the weather) warm and slightly wet in an unpleasant way (**humid**) (मौसम) उमस-भरा

**Muhammad** (*also* **Mohammed**) *noun* [*sing.*] the **prophet** who started the religion of Islam इस्लाम के संस्थापक पैगंबर हज़रत मुहम्मद

**mulch** /mʌltʃ मल्च्/ *noun* [C, U] (*technical*) material, for example dead leaves, that you put around a plant to protect its base and its roots, to improve the quality of the soil or to stop **weeds** from growing पेड़-पौधों की जड़ों को हानिप्रद जंगली पौधों के प्रभाव से बचाने के लिए उन्हें ढकने के लिए प्रयुक्त सड़े पत्ते आदि का कचरा (जो खाद का काम भी करता है), घास-पात, पलवार ▶ **mulch** *verb* [T] पत्तों से ढकना

**mule** /mju:l म्यूल्/ *noun* [C] an animal that is used for carrying heavy loads and whose parents are a horse and a **donkey** खच्चर (घोड़े और गधे के मेल से उत्पन्न वज़नदार सामान ले जाने के लिए प्रयुक्त पशु)

**mull** /mʌl मल्/ *verb*

**PHR V** **mull sth over** to think about sth carefully and for a long time किसी विषय पर सावधानी के साथ देर तक सोचना, चिंतन करना *Don't ask me for a decision right now. I'll have to mull it over.*

**mulligatawny** *noun* [C] a kind of spicy soup, originally from India भारतीय मूल का चटपटा सूप, शोरबा ➪ **rasam** देखिए।

**multi-** /ˈmʌlti ˈमल्टि/ (*used in nouns and adjectives*) more than one; many एक से अधिक; अनेक, बहु *multicoloured* ○ *a multimillionaire*

**multicultural** /ˌmʌltiˈkʌltʃərəl ˌमल्टिˈकल्चरल्/ *adj.* for or including people of many different races, languages, religions and traditions बहु-सांस्कृतिक (विभिन्न जातियों, भाषाओं, धर्मों और परंपराओं के लोगों वाला या उनके उपयोग का) *a multicultural society*

**multilateral** /ˌmʌltiˈlætərəl ˌमल्टिˈलैटरल्/ *adj.* involving more than two groups of people, countries, etc. बहु-पक्षीय (जिसमें अनेक व्यक्ति-समूहों, देशों आदि की भागीदारी हो) ➪ **unilateral** देखिए।

**multimedia** /ˌmʌltiˈmi:diə ˌमल्टिˈमीडिआ/ *adj.* (*only before a noun*) (*computing*) using sound, pictures and film in addition to text on a screen बहु-माध्यमी, (जो स्क्रीन पर लिखित सामग्री के अतिरिक्त ध्वनि, चित्र और फ़िल्म के प्रदर्शन का भी माध्यम है) *multimedia systems/products*

**multinational** /ˌmʌltiˈnæʃnəl ˌमल्टिˈनैश्नल्/ *adj.* existing in or involving many countries बहु-राष्ट्रीय (जो अनेक देशों में फैला हो या जिसमें अनेक देश शामिल हों) *multinational companies* ▶ **multinational** *noun* [C] बहुराष्ट्रीय संगठन *The company is owned by Ford, the US multinational.*

**multiple[1]** /ˈmʌltɪpl ˈमल्टिपल्/ *adj.* involving many people or things or having many parts बहुल, बहुविध या बहुखंड, (जिसमें अनेक लोग या वस्तुएँ शामिल हों या जिसके अनेक अंग खंड हों) *multiple choice question* ○ *multiple fractures*

**multiple[2]** /ˈmʌltɪpl ˈमल्टिपल्/ *noun* [C] a number that can be divided by another number without any remainder वह संख्या जो किसी अन्य संख्या से, शेष न छोड़ते हुए, पूरी-पूरी विभाजित हो जाए; गुणज, अपवर्त्य *12, 18 and 24 are multiples of 6.*

**multiple-choice** *adj.* (used about exam questions) showing several different answers from which you have to choose the right one (परीक्षा का प्रश्न) बहु-विकल्पी (जिसके एक से अधिक उत्तर संभावित हों जिनमें से शुद्ध का चयन किया जाए)

**multiple sclerosis** /ˌmʌltɪpl skləˈrəʊsɪs ˌमल्टिपल् स्क्लˈरोसिस्/ *noun* [U] (*abbr.* **MS**) a serious disease which causes you to slowly lose control of your body and become less able to move एक गंभीर रोग जिसमें रोगी अपने शरीर का नियंत्रण क्रमशः खोते हुए दुर्बल होता जाता है

**multiply** /ˈmʌltɪplaɪ ˈमल्टिप्लाइ/ *verb* (*pres. part.* **multiplying;** *3rd person sing. pres.* **multiplies;** *pt, pp* **multiplied**) **1** [I, T] **multiply A by B** to increase a number by the number of times mentioned किसी अंक को निर्दिष्ट संख्या से गुणा करना *2 multiplied by 4 makes 8* (2×4 = 8) ✪ विलोम **divide** 2 [I, T] to increase or make sth increase by a very large amount किसी वस्तु का बहुत बढ़ना या उसे बहुत बढ़ाना *We've multiplied our profits over the last two years.* ▶ **multiplication** /ˌmʌltɪplɪˈkeɪʃn ˌमल्टिप्लि'केश्न्/ *noun* [U] गुणा करने की क्रिया; गुणन ➪ **division, addition** और **subtraction** देखिए।

**multi-purpose** *adj*. that can be used for several different purposes बहु-प्रयोजनात्मक (जिससे अनेक प्रयोजन सिद्ध हों *a multi-purpose tool/machine*

**multitasking** /ˌmʌltiˈtɑːskɪŋ ˌमल्टि'टास्किङ्/ *noun* [U] **1** (*computing*) the ability of a computer to operate several programs at the same time कंप्यूटर की एक ही समय में अनेक प्रोग्रामों को परिचालित करने की क्षमता; बहु-कार्य निष्पादन **2** the ability of a person to do more than one thing at time एक ही समय में अनेक कार्यों को करने की क्षमता

**multitude** /ˈmʌltɪtjuːd 'मल्टिट्यूड्/ *noun* [C] (*formal*) a very large number of people or things लोगों का जमघट या वस्तुओं का ढेर, लोगों या वस्तुओं की बड़ी संख्या

**mum** /mʌm मम्/ (*AmE* **mom** /mɒm मॉम्/) *noun* [C] (*informal*) mother मम, माँ *Is that your mum?* ○ *Can I have a lemonade, Mum?* ➪ **mummy** देखिए।

**mumble** /ˈmʌmbl 'मम्बल्/ *verb* [I, T] to speak quietly without opening your mouth properly, so that people cannot hear the words मुँह ही मुँह में बोलना (कि शब्द सुनाई न दें), बुदबुदाना, फुसफुसाना *I can't hear if you mumble.* ➪ **mutter** देखिए।

**mummy** /ˈmʌmi 'ममि/ *noun* [C] (*pl.* **mummies**) **1** (*AmE* **mommy** /ˈmɒmi 'मॉमि/) (*informal*) (used by or to children) mother (बच्चों द्वारा माँ के लिए प्रयुक्त) ममी, माँ *Here comes your mummy now.* **2** the dead body of a person or animal which has been kept by rubbing it with special oils and covering it in cloth मनुष्य या पशु का शव (कपड़े में लिपटा व विशेष लेप लगाकर); ममी *an Egyptian mummy*

**mumps** /mʌmps मम्प्स्/ *noun* [U] an infectious disease, especially of children, that causes the neck to swell गलसुआ विशेषतः बच्चों को होने वाला एक संक्रमणशील रोग जिसमें गरदन सूज जाती है *to have/catch (the) mumps*

**munch** /mʌntʃ मन्च्/ *verb* [I, T] **munch (on sth)** to bite and eat sth noisily किसी वस्तु को काटना और आवाज़ करते हुए खाना, चबड़-चबड़ कर खाना *He sat there munching (on) an apple.*

**mundane** /mʌnˈdeɪn मन्'डेन्/ *adj*. ordinary; not interesting or exciting साधारण, मामूली; रोचक या उत्तेजक नहीं *a mundane job*

**municipal** /mjuːˈnɪsɪpl म्यू'निसिप्ल्/ *adj*. connected with a town or city that has its own local government ऐसे नगर या टाउन से संबंधित जहाँ स्थानीय स्वशासन हो, नगरीय, नगरपालिका-संबंधी *municipal buildings* (= the town hall, public library, etc.)

**munitions** /mjuːˈnɪʃnz म्यू'निश्न्ज़्/ *noun* [*pl.*] military supplies, especially bombs and guns सैन्य सामान (विशेषतः बम, तोपें और बंदूकें)

**mural** /ˈmjʊərəl 'म्युअरल्/ *noun* [C] a large picture painted on a wall भित्तिचित्र (दीवार पर बनाया बड़ा चित्र)

**murder** /ˈmɜːdə(r) 'मड(र्)/ *noun* **1** [C, U] the crime of killing a person illegally and on purpose ग़ैर-क़ानूनी रूप से और जान-बूझकर किसी व्यक्ति को मार देने का अपराध, मानव हत्या का अपराध *to **commit murder*** ○ *the murder victim/weapon* ➪ **manslaughter** देखिए। **2** [U] (*informal*) a very difficult or unpleasant experience कठिन या अप्रिय अनुभव *It's murder trying to work when it's as hot as this.*

**IDM** **get away with murder** to do whatever you want without being stopped or punished मनचाहा काम करना (बिना किसी के रोके या दंडित हुए) *He lets his students get away with murder.* ▶ **murder** *verb* [I, T] मानव-हत्या होना या करना ➪ **kill** देखिए। ▶ **murderer** *noun* [C] मानव-हत्यारा, हत्यारा

**murderous** /ˈmɜːdərəs 'मडरस्/ *adj*. intending or likely to murder हत्या के इरादे या संभावना वाला; हिंसक

**murky** /ˈmɜːki 'मकि/ *adj*. dark and unpleasant or dirty अंधकारमय और अप्रिय या मलिन *The water in the river looked very murky.* ○ (*figurative*) *According to rumours, the new boss had a murky past.*

**murmur** /ˈmɜːmə(r) 'मम(र्)/ *verb* [I, T] to say sth in a low quiet voice निम्न मंद स्वर में कुछ कहना; बड़बड़ाना, भुनभुनाना *He murmured a name in his sleep.* ▶ **murmur** *noun* [C] बड़बड़ाहट, भुनभुनाहट

**muscle** /ˈmʌsl 'मसल्/ *noun* [C, U] one of the parts inside your body that you can make tight or relax in order to produce movement मांसपेशी *Riding a bicycle is good for developing the leg muscles.* ○ *Lifting weights builds muscle.*

**muscular** /ˈmʌskjələ(r) 'मस्क्यल(र्)/ *adj*. **1** connected with the muscles मांसपेशियों से संबंधित *muscular pain/tissue* **2** having large strong muscles मज़बूत बड़ी मांसपेशियों वाला, हट्टा-कट्टा *a muscular body*

**muse**[1] /mju:z म्यूज़् / *verb* [I] **1 muse (about/on/over/upon sth)** to think carefully about sth for a time, without noticing what is happening around you एकाग्रचित होकर चिंतन करना (आस-पास हो रही बातों पर ध्यान दिए बिना) *She looked out to sea, musing on what he had said.* **2** to say sth, usually to yourself, in a way that shows you are thinking carefully about it मनन या चिंतन करते हुए स्वयं से कुछ कहना *'I wonder if I should tell him?' she mused.*

**muse**[2] /mju:z म्यूज़् / *noun* [C] a person or spirit that gives a writer, painter, musician, etc. ideas and the desire to create things किसी लेखक, चित्रकार, संगीतज्ञ आदि की प्रेरक शक्ति (व्यक्ति या कोई दैवीय सत्ता) *He felt that his muse had deserted him* (= that he could no longer write, paint, etc).

**museum** /mjuˈzi:əm म्युˈज़ीअम् / *noun* [C] a building where collections of valuable and interesting objects are kept and shown to the public बहुमूल्य और रोचक वस्तुओं का संग्रहालय और प्रदर्शन-स्थल; संग्रहालय, म्यूज़ियम *Have you been to the National Museum in Delhi?*

**mushroom** /ˈmʌʃrʊm; -ru:m ˈमशरुम्; -रूम् / *noun* [C] a type of plant which grows very quickly, has a flat or rounded top and can be eaten as a vegetable कुकुरमुत्ता, छत्रक, खुंबी, मशरूम

> **NOTE** कुकुरमुत्ता एक प्रकार का **fungus** है। केवल, कुछ **fungi** खाने योग्य होते हैं। विषैली फफूँदियों (**fungi**) के कुछ प्रकारों को **toadstool** कहते हैं।

**music** /ˈmju:zɪk ˈम्यूज़िक् / *noun* [U] **1** an arrangement of sounds in patterns to be sung or played on instruments संगीत *classical/pop/rock music* ○ *to write/compose music* ○ *a music lesson/teacher*

**musical**[1] /ˈmju:zɪkl ˈम्यूज़िकल् / *adj.* **1** connected with music संगीत-विषयक *Can you play a musical instrument* (= the piano, the violin, the trumpet, etc.)? **2** interested in or good at music संगीत-प्रेमी या संगीत-निपुण *He's very musical.* **3** having a pleasant sound like music संगीत के समान मधुर (स्वर वाला), संगीतमय, संगीतात्मक *a musical voice* ▶ **musically** /-kli -कलि/ *adv.* संगीतात्मक रीति से

**musical**[2] /ˈmju:zɪkl ˈम्यूज़िकल् / *noun* [C] a play or film which has singing and dancing in it संगीत-नृत्यमय नाटक या फ़िल्म

**musician** /mjuˈzɪʃn म्यूˈज़िश्न् / *noun* [C] a person who plays a musical instrument or writes music, especially as a job संगीतकार, वादक या स्वर-लिपि लेखक (विशेषतः नौकरी के रूप में)

**musket** /ˈmʌskɪt ˈमस्किट् / *noun* [C] an early type of long gun that was used by soldiers in the past पुराने ज़माने में सैनिकों द्वारा प्रयुक्त पुरानी तरह की लंबी बंदूक़

**Muslim** /ˈmʊzlɪm ˈमुज़्लिम् / (*also* **Moslem** /ˈmɒzləm ˈमॉज़्लम् /) *noun* [C] a person whose religion is Islam मुस्लिम, मुसलमान, इस्लाम धर्म का अनुयायी व्यक्ति ▶ **Muslim** (*also* **Moslem**) *adj.* मुस्लिम-विषयक, मुस्लिम या मुसलमानी *Muslim traditions/beliefs*

**muslin** /ˈmʌzlɪn ˈमज़्लिन् / *noun* [U] thin cotton cloth that is almost transparent, used, especially in the past, for making clothes and curtains मलमल, लगभग पारदर्शी महीन सूती कपड़ा जिससे (विशेषतः विगत युग में) कपड़े और परदे बनते थे

**mussel** /ˈmʌsl ˈमसल् / *noun* [C] a type of small sea animal (**a shellfish**) that can be eaten, with a black shell in two parts सीपी में रहने वाली खाने की छोटी समुद्री मछली (जिसका काला खोल दो भागों में विभक्त रहता है) ➪ **shellfish** पर चित्र देखिए।

**must**[1] /məst; *strong form* mʌst मस्ट्; प्रबल रूप मस्ट् / *modal verb* (*negative* **must not;** *short form* **mustn't** /ˈmʌsnt ˈमसन्ट् /) **1** used for saying that it is necessary that sth happens किसी बात के घटित होने की आवश्यकता बताने के लिए प्रयुक्त, आवश्यकता-बोधक, आवश्यकता का भाव व्यक्त करने के लिए प्रयुक्त *I must remember to go to the bank today.* ○ *You mustn't take photographs in here. It's forbidden.* **2** used for saying that you feel sure that sth is true किसी बात की सचाई के विषय निश्चित होने का भाव व्यक्त करने के लिए प्रयुक्त, निश्चितता का भाव व्यक्त करने के लिए प्रयुक्त *Have something to eat. You must be hungry.* ○ *I can't find my cheque book. I must have left it at home.* **3** used for giving sb advice परामर्श देने के लिए प्रयुक्त *You really must see that film. It's wonderful.*

> **NOTE** वृतिवाचक क्रियाओं (modal verbs) के विषय में अधिक जानकारी के लिए इस शब्दकोश के अंत में **Quick Grammar Reference** देखिए।

**must**[2] /mʌst मस्ट् / *noun* [C] a thing that you strongly recommend नितांत आवश्यक वस्तु; अनिवार्य *This book is a must for all science fiction fans.*

**mustache** /ˈmʌstæʃ ˈमस्टैश् / (*AmE*) = **moustache**

**mustard** /ˈmʌstəd ˈमस्टड् / *noun* [U] a cold yellow or brown sauce that tastes hot and is eaten in small amounts with meat राई, सरसों

**muster** /ˈmʌstə(r) ˈमस्ट(र्) / *verb* **1** [T] to find as much support, courage, etc. as you can (किसी के लिए यथासंभव अधिकतम समर्थन, साहस आदि) जुटाना, बटोरना, एकत्र करना *We mustered all the support we could for the project.* ✪ पर्याय **summon**

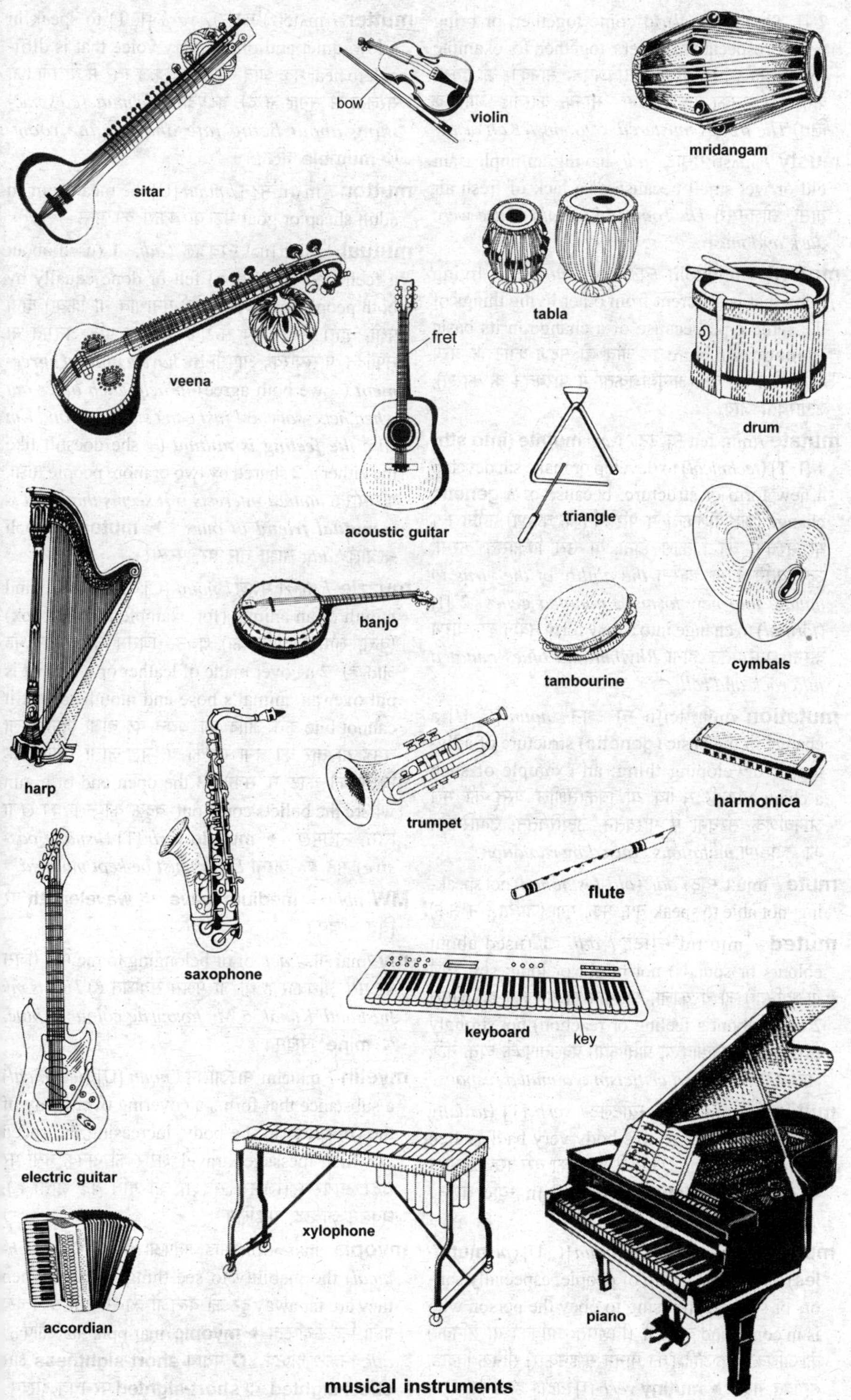


musical instruments

**2** [I, T] (*technical*) to come together, or bring people, especially soldiers, together, for example for military action लोगों (विशेषतः सैनिकों) को इकट्ठा करना या उनका इकट्ठा होना (सैनिक कार्रवाई आदि के लिए) *The troops mustered.* ○ *to muster an army*

**musty** /ˈmʌsti ˈमस्टि/ *adj.* having an unpleasant old or wet smell because of a lack of fresh air बासी, सीलनभरी *The rooms in the old house were dark and musty.*

**mutant** /ˈmjuːtənt ˈम्यूटन्ट्/ *noun* [C] a living thing that is different from other living things of the same type because of a change in its basic (**genetic**) structure वह जीव जो सदृश कोटि के अन्य जीवों से भिन्न हो (आनुवंशिकता में परिवर्तन के कारण); उत्परिवर्ती जीव

**mutate** /mjuːˈteɪt म्यूˈटेट्/ *verb* **mutate (into sth)** **1** [I, T] (*technical*) to develop or make sth develop a new form or structure, because of a **genetic** change (आनुवंशिकता में परिवर्तन के कारण) नवीन रूप या संरचना का विकास होना या उसे विकसित करना, उत्परिवर्तन होना, करना *the ability of the virus to mutate into new forms* ○ *mutated genes* **2** [I] (*formal*) to change into a new form नवीन रूप धारण करना, परिवर्तित होना *Rhythm and blues mutated into rock and roll.*

**mutation** /mjuːˈteɪʃn म्यूˈटेश्न्/ *noun* [C, U] a change in the basic (**genetic**) structure of a living or developing thing; an example of such a change किसी सजीव या विकासशील वस्तु की मूल आनुवंशिक संरचना में परिवर्तन, उत्परिवर्तन; उत्परिवर्तन का उदाहरण *mutations caused by radiation*

**mute** /ˈmjuːt ˈम्यूट्/ *adj.* (*old-fashioned*) not speaking; not able to speak चुप; मूक, गूँगा (जो बोल न सके)

**muted** /ˈmjuːtɪd ˈम्यूटिड्/ *adj.* **1** (used about colours or sounds) not bright or loud; soft (वर्ण या ध्वनियाँ) जो चटकीला, द्युतिमान या प्रबल न हो; कोमल **2** (used about a feeling or reaction) not strongly expressed (मनोभाव या प्रतिक्रिया) प्रबलतापूर्वक व्यक्त नहीं, अप्रबल, मंदित *muted criticism* ○ *a muted response*

**mutilate** /ˈmjuːtɪleɪt ˈम्यूटिलेट्/ *verb* [T] (*usually passive*) to damage sb's body very badly, often by cutting off parts किसी के शरीर का बुरी तरह अंग-भंग कर देना ▶ **mutilation** /ˌmjuːtɪˈleɪʃn ˌम्यूटिˈलेश्न्/ *noun* [C, U] अंग-भंग

**mutiny** /ˈmjuːtəni ˈम्यूटनि/ *noun* [C, U] (*pl.* **mutinies**) an act of a group of people, especially sailors or soldiers, refusing to obey the person who is in command व्यक्तियों (विशेषतः नाविकों या सैनिकों) का अधिकारी के आदेश को मानने से इनकार; सैनिक विद्रोह, बग़ावत, ग़दर ▶ **mutiny** *verb* [I] विद्रोह होना या करना

**mutter** /ˈmʌtə(r) ˈमट(र्)/ *verb* [I, T] to speak in a low, quiet and often angry voice that is difficult to hear मंद, शांत और प्रायः क्रुद्ध स्वर में बोलना (जो सरलता से सुनाई न दे); बुदबुदाना *He muttered something about being late and left the room.* ➪ **mumble** देखिए।

**mutton** /ˈmʌtn ˈमट्न्/ *noun* [U] the meat from an adult sheep or goat भेड़ या बकरी का मांस

**mutual** /ˈmjuːtʃuəl ˈम्यूचुअल्/ *adj.* **1** (used about a feeling or an action) felt or done equally by both people involved (कोई मनोभाव या क्रिया) दोनों पक्षों द्वारा समान रूप से एक दूसरे के प्रति अनूभूत या संपादित, पारस्परिक, आपसी *We have* ***a mutual agreement*** (= we both agree) *to help each other out when necessary.* ○ *I just can't stand her and I'm sure* ***the feeling is mutual*** (= she doesn't like me either). **2** shared by two or more people साझा, पारस्परिक *mutual interests* ○ *It seems that Tina is* ***a mutual friend*** *of ours.* ▶ **mutually** /-uəli -उअलि/ *adv.* साझा तौर पर, परस्पर

**muzzle** /ˈmʌzl ˈमज़्ल्/ *noun* [C] **1** the nose and mouth of an animal (for example a dog or fox) (कुत्ते, लोमड़ी आदि का) थूथन (जिसमें नाक और मुँह आते हैं) **2** a cover made of leather or wire that is put over an animal's nose and mouth so that it cannot bite कुत्ते आदि की थूथन पर बाँधा जाने वाला चमड़े या तार का बना मुसका या मुख-जाली (ताकि वह किसी को काट न सके) **3** the open end of a gun where the bullets come out बंदूक़ की नली का खुला सिरा, नालमुख ▶ **muzzle** *verb* [T] (*usually passive*) मुँह बंद करना *Dogs must be kept muzzled.*

**MW** *abbr.* = **medium wave** ➪ **wavelength** पर चित्र देखिए।

**my** /maɪ माइ/ *det.* of or belonging to me मेरा (जिस पर मेरा अधिकार है या जो मुझसे संबंधित है) *This is my husband, Kunal.* ○ *My favourite colour is blue.* ➪ **mine**[1] देखिए।

**myelin** /ˈmaɪəlɪn ˈमाइअलिन्/ *noun* [U] (*technical*) a substance that forms a covering over many of the (**nerves**) in the body, increasing the speed at which messages travel शरीर की अनेक नसों पर चढ़ा आवरण (जिससे संदेशों की गति बढ़ जाती है); धवलमज्जाच्छद, माइलिन

**myopia** /maɪˈəʊpiə माइˈओपिआ/ *noun* [U] (*technical*) the inability to see things clearly when they are far away दूर की वस्तुओं को स्पष्टता से न देख पाना, निकट-दृष्टिता ▶ **myopic** /maɪˈɒpɪk माइˈऑपिक्/ *adj.* निकट दृष्टिक ✪ पर्याय **short-sightness** और **short-sighted** ➪ **short-sighted** पर चित्र देखिए

**myself** /maɪˈself माइˈसेल्फ़् / *pronoun* **1** used when the person who does an action is also affected by it मै स्वयं (जब कर्ता भी प्रभावित हो) *I saw myself in the mirror.* ○ *I felt rather pleased with myself.* **2** used to emphasize the person who does the action मै स्वयं (जब कर्ता पर बल दिया जाए) *I'll speak to her myself.* ○ *I'll do it myself* (= if you don't want to do it for me).

IDM **(all) by myself 1** alone अकेला *I live by myself.* ➪ **alone** पर नोट देखिए। **2** without help बिना किसी की सहायता के, स्वयं *I painted the house all by myself.*

**mysterious** /mɪˈstɪəriəs मिˈस्टिअरिअस् / *adj.* **1** that you do not understand or cannot explain; strange समझने या समझाने से परे; अद्भुत, रहस्यमय *Several people reported seeing mysterious lights in the sky.* **2** (used about a person) keeping sth secret or refusing to explain sth (व्यक्ति) किसी भेद को छिपाए हुए या बताने से इनकार करने वाला *They're being very mysterious about where they're going this evening.* ▶ **mysteriously** *adv.* रहस्यमय ढंग से

**mystery** /ˈmɪstri ˈमिस्टरि / *noun* (*pl.* **mysteries**) **1** [C] a thing that you cannot understand or explain जो न समझ में आए न समझाया जा सके, समझने या समझाने से परे, रहस्य, भेद की बात *The cause of the accident is a complete mystery.* **2** [U] the quality of being strange and secret and full of things that are difficult to explain रहस्यमयता, रहस्य *There's a lot of mystery surrounding this case.* **3** [C] a story, film or play in which crimes or strange events are only explained at the end रहस्यपूर्ण कथा, फ़िल्म या नाटक (जिसमें अपराधों या अद्भुत घटनाओं का ख़ुलासा या समाधान अंतिम भाग में होता है)

**mystic** /ˈmɪstɪk ˈमिस्टिक् / *noun* [C] a person who spends his/her life developing his/her spirit and communicating with God or a god ईश्वर या किसी देवता के साथ संवाद-स्थापना की साधना में आजीवन रत व्यक्ति, रहस्य-साधक संत

**mystical** /ˈmɪstɪkl ˈमिस्टिक्ल् / (*also* **mystic** /ˈmɪstɪk ˈमिस्टिक् /) *adj.* connected with the spirit; strange and wonderful अध्यात्म से संबंधित, आध्यात्मिक; अद्भुत और आश्चर्यजनक, रहस्यात्मक *Watching the sun set over the island was an almost mystical experience.*

**mysticism** /ˈmɪstɪsɪzəm ˈमिस्टिसिज़म् / *noun* [U] the belief that you can reach complete truth and knowledge of God or gods by prayer, thought and development of the spirit अध्यात्मवाद, रहस्यवाद

**mystify** /ˈmɪstɪfaɪ ˈमिस्टिफ़ाइ / *verb* [T] (*pres. part.* **mystifying;** *3rd person sing. pres.* **mystifies;** *pt, pp* **mystified**) to make sb confused because he/she cannot understand sth किसी को उलझन में डाल देना (क्योंकि वह बात समझ नहीं सका) *I was mystified by the strange note he'd left behind.*

**mystique** /mɪˈstiːk मिˈस्टीक् / *noun* [U, *sing.*] the quality of having hidden or secret characteristics that makes sb/sth seem interesting or attractive रहस्यमय कौशलों से संपन्न होने की विशेषता (जिससे कोई व्यक्ति या वस्तु रोचक या आकर्षक बन जाती है), रहस्यमयता

**myth** /mɪθ मिथ् / *noun* [C] **1** a story from past times, especially one about gods and men of courage. Myths often explain natural or historical events मिथक, पौराणिक कथा (जो विशेषतया देवताओं और वीर पुरुषों के विषय में होती हैं और जिनमें प्राय: प्राकृतिक या ऐतिहासिक घटनाओं का वर्णन होता है) **2** an idea or story which many people believe but that does not exist or is false मनगढ़ंत, काल्पनिक विचार या कथा *The idea that money makes you happy is a myth.*

**mythical** /ˈmɪθɪkl ˈमिथिक्ल् / *adj.* **1** existing only in **myths 1** जो केवल मिथकों में हो, मिथकीय *mythical beasts/heroes* **2** not real or true; existing only in the imagination यथार्थ या सत्य नहीं; केवल काल्पनिक

**mythology** /mɪˈθɒlədʒi मिˈथ़ॉलजि / *noun* [U] very old stories and the beliefs contained in them पौराणिक कथाएँ और उनमें निहित विश्वास *Greek and Roman mythology* ▶ **mythological** /ˌmɪθəˈlɒdʒɪkl ˌमिथ़ˈलॉजिक्ल् / *adj.* पौराणिक कथाओं से संबंधित; पौराणिक *mythological beasts/figures/ stories*

# N n



**N, n**[1] /en एन् / *noun* [C, U] (*pl.* **N' s; n' s** /enz एन्ज़् /) the fourteenth letter of the English alphabet अंग्रेज़ी वर्णमाला का चौदहवाँ अक्षर *'Naresh' begins with an 'N'.*

**N**[2] *abbr.* **1** (*AmE* **No**) north(ern) उत्तरी *N Delhi* **2** the abbreviation for 'newton'; a unit of force, 'newton' की संक्षिप्ति; बल की एक इकाई

**nab** /næb नैब् / *verb* [T] (**nabbing, nabbed**) (*informal*) **1** to catch or arrest sb who is doing sth wrong दोषी व्यक्ति को पकड़ना या हिरासत में लेना *The police nabbed the criminal yesterday.* **2** to take or get sth before anyone else can get to it छीन लेना या झपट लेना *Someone nabbed my sandwich while I was away.*

**nadeswaram** *noun* [C] a long conical Indian **reed 2** instrument, similar to the 'shehnai'. Considered **auspicious** it is played at temples, weddings and as an accompaniment to **Carnatic music** मंदिरों, विवाह समारोह तथा कर्नाटक संगीत में बजाए जाने वाला शहनाई जैसा वाद्य यंत्र; नादस्वरम

**nadir** /ˈneɪdɪə(r) ˈनेडिअ(र्) / *noun* [*sing.*] (*written*) the worst moment of a particular situation स्थिति विशेष का सबसे बुरा समय; अधोबिंदु *She is at the nadir of her career.* ✪ विलोम **zenith**

**nag** /næg नैग् / *verb* (**nagging; nagged**) **1** [I, T] **nag (at) sb** to continuously complain to sb about his/her behaviour or to ask him/her to do sth many times किसी के आचरण की लगातार शिकायत करते रहना या कोई काम करने के लिए बार-बार कहना, किसी बात के लिए किसी के पीछे पड़ जाना *My parents are always nagging (at) me to work harder.* **2** [T] to worry or irritate sb continuously किसी को लगातार चिंता में डालना या गुस्सा दिलाना *a nagging doubt/headache*

**nail** /neɪl नेल् / *noun* [C] **1** the thin hard layer that covers the ends of your fingers and toes नाख़ून, नख *finger nails/toenails* **2** a small thin piece of metal that is used for holding pieces of wood together, hanging pictures on, etc. कील *to hammer in a nail* ➪ **bolt** पर चित्र देखिए। ► **nail** *verb* [T]

IDM **hit the nail on the head** ➪ **hit**[1] देखिए।

PHR V **nail sb down (to sth)** to make a person say clearly what he/she wants or intends to do किसी व्यक्ति को अपनी इच्छा या इरादा स्पष्टतया बताने के लिए विवश करना *She says she'll visit us in the summer but I can't nail her down to a definite date.*

**nail brush** *noun* [C] a small brush for cleaning your fingernails नाख़ूनों को साफ करने का ब्रश

**nail file** *noun* [C] a small metal tool with a rough surface that you use for shaping your nails नाख़ूनों को गढ़ने के लिए उन पर चलाने की रेती

**nail polish** (*BrE* **nail varnish**) *noun* [U] a liquid that people paint on their nails to give them colour नाख़ूनों को रँगने की पालिश

**naive** (*also* **naïve**) /naɪˈiːv नाइˈईव् / *adj.* without enough experience of life and too ready to believe or trust other people जिसे जीवन का पर्याप्त अनुभव नहीं और जो दूसरों पर तुरंत विश्वास या भरोसा कर लेता है; भोला-भाला *I was too naive to realize what was happening.* ○ *a naive remark/question/view* ✪ पर्याय **innocent** ► **naively** (*also* **naïvely**) *adv.* भोलेपन से *She naively accepted the first price he offered.* ► **naivety** (*also* **naïvety** /naɪˈiːvəti नाइˈईव़टि /) *noun* [U] भोलापन

**naked** /ˈneɪkɪd ˈनेकिड् / *adj.* **1** not wearing any clothes वस्त्ररहित, नग्न, नंगा *He came to the door naked except for a towel.* ○ *naked shoulders/arms* ➪ **bare** और **nude** देखिए। **2** (*only before a noun*) (used about sth that is usually covered) not covered (प्रायः ढकी रहने वाली वस्तु के लिए प्रयुक्त) जो ढका न हो, खुला आवरण या खोल-रहित *a naked flame/bulb/light* **3** (*only before a noun*) clearly shown or expressed in a way that is often shocking एकदम प्रकट या बीभत्स रीति से प्रदर्शित; नंगा *naked aggression/ambition/fear*

IDM **the naked eye** the normal power of your eyes without the help of glasses, a machine, etc. केवल आँख, सामान्य दृष्टि शक्ति, चश्मे, यंत्र आदि की सहायता के बिना *Bacteria are too small to be seen with the naked eye.*

**name**[1] /neɪm नेम् / *noun* **1** [C] a word or words by which sb/sth is known व्यक्ति या वस्तु का नाम *What's your name, please?* ○ *Do you know the name of this flower?* **2** [*sing.*] an opinion that people have of a person or thing किसी व्यक्ति या वस्तु के विषय में लोगों की राय, ख्याति या कुख्याति *That area of Delhi has rather a bad name.* ✪ पर्याय **reputation** **3** [C] a famous person कोई प्रसिद्ध व्यक्ति *All the big names in show business were invited to the party.*

IDM **by name** using the name of sb/sth किसी व्यक्ति या वस्तु के नाम से *It's a big school but the head teacher knows all the children by name.*

**call sb names** ➪ **call**[1] देखिए।

**in the name of sb; in sb's name** for sb/sth; officially belonging to sb किसी व्यक्ति या वस्तु के लिए; अधिकारिक रूप से किसी के नाम *The contract is in my name.*

**in the name of sth** used to give a reason or excuse for an action, even when what you are doing might be wrong किसी नाम पर, किसी काम के लिए कोई कारण या बहाना बनाना (भले ही काम ग़लत हो) *They acted in the name of democracy.*

**IDM make a name for yourself; make your name** to become well known and respected नाम कमाना, यश अर्जित करना *She made a name for herself as a journalist.*

**NOTE** व्यक्ति का **first name** (*AmE* प्रायः **given name**) नवजात शिशु का वह नाम है जो माता-पिता रखते या निश्चित करते हैं। ईसाई देशों में कभी-कभी इसे **Christian name** भी कहा जाता है। माता-पिता शिशु के प्रथम नाम के बाद उसका एक और नाम रख सकते हैं जिसे **middle name** कहते हैं। इस नाम का व्यवहार सीमित स्तर पर केवल औपचारिक, आधिकारिक दस्तावेजों में होता है जहाँ दोनों नामों को **forenames** कहा जाता है। **Surname** शब्द का व्यवहार प्रायः **family name** (परंपरा प्राप्त) के लिए होता है। विवाह के पश्चात महिला अपने पति के कुलनाम को अपना सकती है। ऐसा होने पर महिला का पूर्व कुलनाम उसका **maiden name** कहलाता है।

**name²** /neɪm नेम्/ *verb* [T] **1 name sb/sth (after sb)** to give sb/sth a name किसी व्यक्ति या वस्तु का कोई विशेष नाम रखना, का नामकरण करना *Columbia was named after Christopher Columbus.*

**NOTE** किसी को किसी विशेष नाम से निर्दिष्ट किए जाने की बात हो तो उसके लिए **be called** का प्रयोग होता है—*Their youngest son is called Mohit.*

**2** to say what the name of sb/sth is किसी के नाम को प्रकट करना या किसी का नाम बताना *The journalist refused to name the person who had given her the information.* ○ *Can you name all the planets?* **3** to state sth exactly कोई बात सही-सही बताना *Name your price we'll pay it!*

**nameless** /ˈneɪmləs ˈनेम्लस्/ *adj* **1** without a name or with a name that you do not know अनाम, नाम-रहित या अज्ञात नामा **2** whose name is kept a secret जिसका नाम गुप्त रहे *a well-known public figure who shall* ***remain nameless***

**namely** /ˈneɪmli ˈनेम्लि/ *adv.* (used for giving more detail about what you are saying) that is to say (कही गई बात का विस्तार करने के लिए प्रयुक्त) अर्थात, यानी *There is only one person who can overrule the death sentence, namely the President.*

**namesake** /ˈneɪmseɪk ˈनेम्सेक्/ *noun* [C] a person who has the same name as another हमनाम, नामराशि (ऐसा व्यक्ति जिसका वही नाम हो जो दूसरे का है)

**nan** (*also* **naan**) /nɑːn नान्/ *noun* [C, U] a type of flat Indian bread नान

**nanny** /ˈnæni ˈनैनि/ *noun* [C] (*pl.* **nannies**) a woman whose job is to look after a family's children and who usually lives in the family home परिवार के बच्चों की नर्स या आया (जो सामान्यतः परिवार के साथ ही रहती है)

**nanny goat** *noun* [C] a female **goat** बकरी ➪ **billy goat** देखिए।

**nano-** /ˈnænəʊ ˈनैनो/ *prefix* (*technical*) (*used in nouns and adjectives, especially in units of measurement*) one **billionth** किसी वस्तु का दस अरबवाँ अंश, $10^{-9}$ अंश *nanosecond*

**nap** /næp नैप्/ *noun* [C] a short sleep that you have during the day झपकी (दिन के समय की अल्प निद्रा) ➪ **snooze** देखिए। ▶ **nap** *verb* [I] (**napping; napped**) झपकी लेना

**nape** /neɪp नेप्/ *noun* [*sing.*] the back part of your neck गरदन का पिछला भाग, गद्दी, घाटिका

**napthalene** /ˈnæfθəliːn ˈनैफ़्थलीन्/ *noun* [U] a white **crystalline** aromatic substance produced by the **distillation** of **coal tar** or petroleum that is used in the manufacture of dyes, mothballs, etc. तारकोल या पेट्रोलियम के आवसन से बनी फ़िनाइल की गोलियाँ जो रंग और कीटनाशक दवाओं के निर्माण में प्रयुक्त होती हैं

**napkin** /ˈnæpkɪn ˈनैप्किन्/ *noun* [C] a piece of cloth or paper that you use when you are eating to protect your clothes or for cleaning your hands and mouth भोजन करते समय कपड़ों को ख़राब होने से बचाने या हाथ-मुँह पोंछने के लिए प्रयुक्त कपड़ा या काग़ज़; नैपकिन *a paper napkin* ✪ पर्याय **serviette**

**nappy** /ˈnæpi ˈनैपि/ *noun* [C] (*pl.* **nappies**) (*AmE* **diaper**) a piece of soft thick cloth or paper that a baby or very young child wears around its bottom and between its legs पोतड़ा या डाइपर; नैपी *Does his nappy need changing?* ○ *disposable nappies* (= that you throw away when they have been used)

**narcotic** /nɑːˈkɒtɪk नाˈकॉटिक्/ *noun* [C] **1** a powerful illegal drug that affects your mind in a harmful way शक्तिशाली नशीला पदार्थ (जो मन पर बुरा प्रभाव डालता है); स्वापक **2** a substance or drug that relaxes you, stops pain, or makes you sleep ऐसी दवा या पदार्थ जो तनाव दूर करे, दर्द मिटाए या नींद लाए, शमनकारी औषधि ▶ **narcotic** *adj.* शमनकारी या नशीली दवा से संबंधित

**narrate** /nəˈreɪt नˈरेट्/ *verb* [T] (*formal*) to tell a story कथा का वर्णन करना, कहानी सुनाना ▶ **narration** /nəˈreɪʃn नˈरेश्न्/ *noun* [C, U] कथावर्णन, विवरण

**narrative** /ˈnærətɪv ˈनैरटिव़्/ *noun* (*formal*) **1** [C] the description of events in a story कथा में घटनाओं का वर्णन **2** [U] the process or skill of telling a story कहानी सुनाने की प्रक्रिया या कला; वृतांत, आख्यान

**narrator** /nəˈreɪtə(r) नˈरेट(र्)/ *noun* [C] the person who tells a story or explains what is happening in a play, film, etc. कथा का वर्णन करने वाला या नाटक, फ़िल्म आदि में घटित होने वाली बातों को समझाने वाला व्यक्ति; कथा-वाचक, वर्णन-कर्त्ता

**narrow** /ˈnærəʊ ˈनैरो/ *adj.* **1** having only a short distance from side to side तंग, संकीर्ण *The bridge is too narrow for two cars to pass.* ✪ विलोम **wide** या **broad** **2** not large छोटा, सीमित *a narrow circle of friends* **3** by a small amount बहुत थोड़े अंतर से, बाल-बाल (बचाव आदि) *That was a very narrow escape. You were lucky.* ○ *a narrow defeat/victory* ▶ **narrow** *verb* [I, T] तंग, संकीर्ण होना या करना *The road narrows to 50 metres.* ▶ **narrowness** *noun* [U] तंगी, संकीर्णता

**PHRV** **narrow sth down** to make a list of things smaller वस्तुओं की सूची को छोटा करना *The police have narrowed down their list of suspects to three.*

**narrowly** /ˈnærəʊli ˈनैरोलि/ *adv.* only by a small amount बहुत ही थोड़े अंतर से

**narrow-minded** *adj.* not wanting to accept new ideas or the opinions of other people if they are not the same as your संकीर्ण मानसिकता वाला (जो नए या अपने विचारों से भिन्न विचारों को स्वीकार नहीं करता) ✪ पर्याय **insular** ✪ विलोम **broad-minded**

**NASA** /ˈnæsə ˈनैसा/ *abbr.* National Aeronautics and Space Administration; a US government organization that does research into space and organizes space travel नेशनल एअरोनॉटिक्स एंड स्पेस एडमिनिस्ट्रेशन; अमेरिकी सरकार का एक संगठन जो अंतरिक्ष-अनुसंधान तथा अंतरिक्ष-यात्रा का आयोजन करता है

**nasal** /ˈneɪzl ˈनेज़्ल्/ *adj.* **1** of or for the nose नाक का या नाक के लिए, नासिका-संबंधी **2** produced partly through the nose अंशत नाक में से उत्पन्न, नासिक्य *a nasal voice*

**nasty** /ˈnɑːsti ˈनास्टि/ *adj.* (**nastier; nastiest**) very bad or unpleasant बहुत बुरा या अप्रिय *When she was asked to leave she **got/turned nasty**.* ○ *a nasty bend in the road* ▶ **nastily** *adv.* बहुत बुरी तरह ▶ **nastiness** *noun* [U] घोर बुराई

**nation** /ˈneɪʃn ˈनेश्न्/ *noun* [C] a country or all the people in a country राष्ट्र या समस्त राष्ट्रवादी *a summit of the leaders of seven nations*

**national[1]** /ˈnæʃnəl ˈनैश्नल्/ *adj.* connected with all of a country; typical of a particular country राष्ट्रीय; राष्ट्र विशेष का प्रतिनिधिक *Here is today's national and international news.* ○ *a national newspaper* ➪ **international, regional** और **local** भी देखिए। ▶ **nationally** *adv.* राष्ट्रीय स्तर पर

**national[2]** /ˈnæʃnəl ˈनैश्नल्/ *noun* [C, *usually pl.*] (*formal*) a citizen of a particular country किसी देश का नागरिक

**national anthem** *noun* [C] the official song of a country that is played at public events राष्ट्रगान (किसी देश का आधिकारिक गान जो सार्वजनिक कार्यक्रमों में प्रस्तुत किया, गाया या बजाया जाता है)

**nationalism** /ˈnæʃnəlɪzəm ˈनैश्नलिज़म्/ *noun* [U] **1** the desire of a group of people who share the same race, culture, language, etc. to form an independent country जाति, संस्कृति, भाषा आदि कीं समानता के आधार पर एक स्वतंत्र राष्ट्र-बनाने की जन-भावना **2** a feeling of love or pride for your own country; a feeling that your country is better than any other राष्ट्र-प्रेम की भावना, राष्ट्रीयता; अपने राष्ट्र को अन्य से श्रेष्ठ बनाने की भावना, राष्ट्रवाद

**nationalist** /ˈnæʃnəlɪst ˈनैश्नलिस्ट्/ *noun* [C] a person who wants his/her country or region to become independent अपने देश या क्षेत्र को स्वतंत्र देखने का इच्छुक व्यक्ति; राष्ट्रीयता-वादी, राष्ट्रवादी

**nationalistic** /ˌnæʃnəˈlɪstɪk ˌनैश्नˈलिस्टिक्/ *adj.* having strong feelings of love for or pride in your own country so that you think it is better than any other उत्कट राष्ट्र-प्रेम, उग्र राष्ट्रवाद से संबंधित; राष्ट्रीयतामूलक **NOTE** अहंकार-पूर्ण अभियान के अर्थ देने के कारण **nationalistic** की व्यंजना प्रायः निंदात्मक होती है।

**nationality** /ˌnæʃəˈnæləti ˌनैशˈनैलटि/ *noun* [C, U] (*pl.* **nationalities**) the state of being legally a citizen of a particular nation or country किसी राष्ट्र की नागरिकता *to have French nationality* ○ *students of many nationalities* ○ *to have **dual nationality*** (= of two countries)

**nationalize** (*also* **-ise**) /ˈnæʃnəlaɪz ˈनैश्नलाइज़्/ *verb* [T] to put a company or organization under the control of the government किसी कंपनी या संगठन का राष्ट्रीयकरण करना (उसे सरकारी नियंत्रण में लेना) ✪ विलोम **privatize** ▶ **nationalization** (*also* **-isation**) /ˌnæʃnəlaɪˈzeɪʃn ˌनैश्नलाइˈज़ेश्न्/ *noun* [U] राष्ट्रीयकरण

**national park** *noun* [C] a large area of beautiful land that is protected by the government so that the public can enjoy it राष्ट्रीय पार्क

**nationwide** /ˌneɪʃnˈwaɪd ˌनेश्न्ˈवाइड्/ *adj., adv.* over the whole of a country राष्ट्रव्यापी *The police launched a nationwide hunt for the killer.*

**native**[1] /ˈneɪtɪv ˈनेटिव्/ *adj.* **1** (*only before a noun*) connected with the place where you were born or where you have always lived जन्म स्थान या निवास-स्थान से संबंधित *your native language/country/city* ○ *native Londoners* **2** (*only before a noun*) connected with the people who originally lived in a country before other people, especially white people, came to live there किसी स्थान के मूल निवासियों से संबंधित *native art/dance* **NOTE** ध्यान रखिए **native** का यह अर्थ कभी-कभी अपमानजनक लगता है। **3 native (to...)** (used about an animal or plant) living or growing naturally in a particular place (जंतु या पौधा) स्थान विशेष का मूल निवासी या वहाँ पर मूलतः उत्पन्न *This plant is native to South America.* ○ *a native species/habitat*

**native**[2] /ˈneɪtɪv ˈनेटिव्/ *noun* [C] **1** a person who was born in a particular place स्थान विशेष में जन्मा व्यक्ति, (जन्म से) निवासी *a native of New York* **2** [*usually pl.*] (*old-fashioned*) the people who were living in Africa, America, etc. originally, before the Europeans arrived there (यूरोपीय लोगों के आगमन से पूर्व के) अफ़्रीका, अमेरिका आदि के मूल निवासी **NOTE Native** शब्द का यह अर्थ अब अपमानजनक माना जाता है।

**Native American** (*also* **American Indian**) *adj., noun* [C] (of) a member of the race of people who were the original inhabitants of America अमेरिका का मूल निवासी (मूलतः अमेरिका में बसी जाति का कोई सदस्य)

**native speaker** *noun* [C] a person who speaks a language as his/her first language and has not learned it as a foreign language किसी भाषा को अपनी प्रथम भाषा (न कि विदेशी भाषा के रूप में अर्जित भाषा) के रूप में प्रयुक्त करने वाला व्यक्ति, देशीय भाषा-भाषी, स्वभाषा-भाषी *All their Spanish teachers are native speakers.*

**NATO** (*also* **Nato**) /ˈneɪtəʊ ˈनेटो/ *abbr.* North Atlantic Treaty Organization; a group of European countries, Canada and the US, who agree to give each other military help if necessary नाटो; नॉर्थ अटलांटिक ट्रीटि ऑर्गनाइज़ेशन (यूरोपीय देशों, कनाडा और अमेरिका का संयुक्त सैन्य संगठन)

**natural**[1] /ˈnætʃrəl ˈनैचरल्/ *adj.* **1** (*only before a noun*) existing in nature; not made or caused by human beings प्रकृति में विद्यमान, प्राकृतिक, मानव-प्रेरित या निर्मित नहीं; नैसर्गिक *I prefer to see animals in their* ***natural habitat*** *rather than in zoos.* ○ *She died of* ***natural causes*** (= of old age or illness). **2** usual or normal स्वाभाविक, या प्राकृत *It's natural to feel nervous before an interview.* ✪ विलोम **unnatural** **3** that you had from birth or that was easy for you to learn जन्मजात या सहज *a natural gift for languages* **4** (*only before a noun*) (used about parents or their children) related by blood (माता-पिता और उनके बच्चे) रक्त से संबंधित; सगा *She's his stepmother, not his natural mother.*

**natural gas** *noun* [U] gas that is found under the ground or the sea, and that we burn for light and heat प्राकृतिक गैस (पृथ्वी या समुद्र के नीचे पाई जाने वाली, रोशनी या ताप उत्पन्न करने के लिए प्रयुक्त)

**natural history** *noun* [U] the study of plants and animals पेड़-पौधों और जीव-जंतुओं का वैज्ञानिक अध्ययन; प्रकृति-विज्ञान

**naturalist** /ˈnætʃrəlɪst ˈनैच्‌रलिस्ट्/ *noun* [C] a person who studies plants and animals पेड़-पौधों और जीव-जंतुओं का वैज्ञानिक अध्ययन करने वाला; प्रकृति-विज्ञानी

**naturalize** (*also* **-ise**) /ˈnætʃrəlaɪz ˈनैच्‌रलाइज़्/ *verb* [T] (*usually passive*) to make sb a citizen of a country where he/she was not born किसी विदेशी को नागरिकता देना ▶ **naturalization** (*also* **-isation**) /ˌnætʃrəlaɪˈzeɪʃn ˌनैच्‌रलाइˈज़ेश्न्/ *noun* [U] नागरिकीकरण

**naturally** /ˈnætʃrəli ˈनैच्‌रलि/ *adv.* **1** of course; as you would expect निश्चित रूप से; प्रत्याशित स्वाभाविक रूप से *The team was naturally upset about its defeat.* **2** in a natural way; not forced or made artificially नैसर्गिक रूप से; कृत्रिम रूप से आरोपित या निर्मित नहीं *naturally wavy hair* ○ *naturally cheerful person* **3** in a way that is relaxed and normal शांत और सामान्य भाव से, सहज भाव से *Don't try and impress people. Just* ***act naturally***.

**natural selection** *noun* [U] the process by which those animals and plants which are best suited to the conditions in which they live have more young and live longer वह प्रक्रिया जिसके द्वारा अनुकूलतम परिस्थितियों में रहने वाले जीव-जंतुओं और पेड़-पौधों के परिवार बड़े बनते हैं और वे दीर्घजीवी होते हैं; प्राकृतिक या सहज वरण

**nature** /ˈneɪtʃə(r) ˈनेच(र्)/ *noun* **1** [U] all the plants, animals, etc. in the universe and all the things that happen in it that are not made or caused by people प्रकृति, ब्रह्मांड में स्थित समस्त पेड़-पौधे, जीव-जंतु आदि और उसमें होने वाली सब क्रिया जो मानव-निर्मित या प्रेरित नहीं *the forces of nature* (e.g. volcanoes, hurricanes, etc.) ○ *the wonders/beauties of nature* **2** [C, U] the qualities or character of a person or thing किसी व्यक्ति या वस्तु की विशेषताएँ या उसका स्वभाव *He's basically honest* ***by nature***. ○ *It's* ***human nature*** *never to be completely satisfied.* **3** [*sing.*] a type or sort of sth किसी व्यक्ति का प्रकार या भेद *I'm not very interested in things of that nature.* ○ *books of a scientific nature* **4 -natured** (*used to form compound adjectives*) having a particular quality or type of character विशेष प्रकार की विशेषता या स्वभाव वाला *a kind-natured man*

**IDM second nature** ➪ **second**[1] देखिए।

**naughty** /ˈnɔːti ˈनॉटि / *adj.* (*BrE*) (used when you are talking to or about a child) badly behaved; not obeying (बच्चों के विषय में प्रयुक्त) शरारती, नटखट; कहना न मानने वाला, उद्दंड *It was very naughty of you to wander off on your own.* ▶ **naughtily** *adv.* नटखटपन से ▶ **naughtiness** *noun* [U] नटखटपन

**nausea** /ˈnɔːziə ˈनॉज़िआ / *noun* [U] the feeling that you are going to **vomit** मिचली, मतली, उबकाई (उल्टी होने की अनुभूति) ➪ **sick 2** देखिए।

**nauseate** /ˈnɔːzieɪt ˈनॉज़िएट् / *verb* [T] to cause sb to feel sick or disgusted किसी को बीमार-सा कर देना या खिझा देना, उसका जी फेर देना, उसमें घृणा पैदा कर देना ▶ **nauseating** *adj.* बीमार-सा कर देने वाला, खिझाऊ या जी फेर देने वाला; घृणाकारक

**nautical** /ˈnɔːtɪkl ˈनॉटिकल् / *adj.* connected with ships, sailors or sailing जहाजों, नाविकों या नौका यात्रा से संबंधित

**nautical mile** (*also* **sea mile**) *noun* [C] a unit for measuring distance at sea; 1852 metres समुद्र में दूरी मापने की इकाई (जो 1852 मीटर होती है), समुद्री मील

**naval** /ˈneɪvl ˈनेवल् / *adj.* connected with the navy नौसेना-विषयक, नौसैनिक *a naval base/officer/battle*

**navel** /ˈneɪvl ˈनेवल् / (*informal* **belly button**) *noun* [C] the small hole or lump in the middle of your stomach नाभि

**navigable** /ˈnævɪɡəbl ˈनैविगबल् / *adj.* (used about a river or narrow area of sea) that boats can sail along (नदी या तंग समुद्री पट्टी) जहाँ नौकाएँ चल सकें; नौ-चालन के योग्य

**navigate** /ˈnævɪɡeɪt ˈनैविगेट् / *verb* **1** [I] to use a map, etc. to find your way to somewhere गंतव्य का मार्ग ढूँढ़ने के लिए मानचित्र आदि का प्रयोग करना *If you drive, I'll navigate.* **2** [T] (*written*) to sail a boat along a river or across a sea नदी या समुद्र में नौ-चालन करना ▶ **navigator** *noun* [C] जलयान या विमान का पथ-निर्देशक ▶ **navigation** /ˌnævɪˈɡeɪʃn ˌनैविˈगेशन् / *noun* [U] जलयान या नौका और विमान का पथ-निर्देशन

**navy** /ˈneɪvi ˈनेवि / *noun* [C] (*pl.* **navies**) the part of a country's armed forces that fights at sea in times of war नौ-सेना *to join the navy* ○ *Their son is* ***in the Navy***. **NOTE** जब शब्द **navy** एकवचनांत (singular) में प्रयुक्त होता है तो उसके साथ एकवचनांत (singular) या बहुवचनांत (plural) क्रिया भी प्रयुक्त होती है —*The Navy is/are introducing a new warship this year.* ➪ **Army, air force** और **merchant navy** देखिए तथा **naval** adjective देखिए।

**navy blue** (*also* **navy**) *adj.*, *noun* [U] (of) a very dark blue colour गहरा नीला रंग

**Nazi** /ˈnɑːtsi ˈनाट्सि / *noun* [C] **1** a member of the National Socialist party which controlled Germany from 1933 to 1945 नाज़ी (1933 से 1945 तक जर्मनी में सत्तालीन नैशनल सोशलिस्ट पार्टी का सदस्य) **2** a person who uses their power in a cruel way; a person with extreme and unreasonable views about race अपने अधिकारों का निर्दय रीति से प्रयोग करने वाला व्यक्ति; जाति के विषय में अतिवादी और अविवेकी विचारों वाला व्यक्ति, घोर जातिवादी व्यक्ति ▶ **Nazi** *adj.* निर्दय, अतिवादी और अविवेकी ▶ **Nazism** /ˈnɑːtsɪzəm ˈनाट्सिज़म् / *noun* [U] नाज़ीवाद

**NB** (*also* **nb**) /ˌen ˈbiː ˌएन् ˈबी / *abbr.* (used before a written note) take special notice of (लिखित टिप्पणी से पहले प्रयुक्त) विशेष ध्यान दीजिए *NB There is an extra charge for reservations.*

**NE** *abbr.* north-east उत्तर-पूर्व *NE India*

**near**[1] /nɪə(r) निअ(र्) / *adj.*, *adv.*, *prep.* **1** not far away in time or distance; close (समय या स्थान की दृष्टि से) बहुत दूर नहीं; पास, समीप, निकट *We're hoping to move to Wales* ***in the near future*** (= very soon). ○ *Where's the nearest Post Office?*

**NOTE Close** और **near** के अर्थ प्रायः समान हैं परंतु कुछ वाक्यांशों में उनमें से किसी एक का ही प्रयोग हो सकता है—*a close friend/relative* ○ *the near future* ○ *a close contest.* ➪ **Next** पर नोट देखिए।

**2 near-** (*used to form compound adjectives*) almost लगभग, प्रायः *a near-perfect performance*

**IDM close/dear/near to sb's heart** ➪ **heart** देखिए।

**a near miss** a situation where sth nearly hits you or where sth bad nearly happens करीब से निशाना चूक जाने की स्थिति, करीबी चूक या कुछ बुरा लगभग घट जाने की स्थिति, करीबी बचाव

**nowhere near** far from से दूर, से बहुत कम, बिलकुल भी नहीं *We've sold nowhere near enough tickets to make a profit.*

**near**[2] /nɪə(r) निअ(र्) / *verb* [T, I] to get closer to sth in time or distance (समय या स्थान की दृष्टि से)

किसी के निकट आना *At last we were nearing the end of the project.*

**nearby** /ˌnɪəˈbaɪ, निअˈबाइ / *adj., adv.* not far away in distance (स्थान की दृष्टि से) अधिक दूर नहीं, निकट-स्थित *A new restaurant has opened nearby.* ○ *We went out to a nearby restaurant.*

**NOTE** विशेषण के रूप में **nearby** केवल संज्ञा से पहले आता है।

**nearly** /ˈnɪəli ˈनिअलि / *adv.* almost; not completely or exactly लगभग; पूरी तरह या बिलकुल सही तौर पर नहीं, करीब-करीब *It's nearly five years since I've seen him.* ○ *It's not far now. We're nearly there.*

**IDM** **not nearly** much less than; not at all से काफ़ी कम; बिलकुल भी नहीं *It's not nearly as warm as it was yesterday.*

**near-sighted** = **short-sighted 1**

**neat** /ni:t नीट् / *adj.* **1** arranged or done carefully; tidy and in order सुव्यवस्थित; साफ़-सुथरा *Please keep your room* ***neat and tidy****.* ○ *neat rows of figures* **2** (used about a person) liking to keep things tidy and in order (व्यक्ति) व्यवस्था-प्रिय *The new secretary was very neat and efficient.* **3** simple but clever सरल और चातुर्यपूर्ण *a neat solution/explanation/idea/trick* **4** (*AmE spoken*) good; nice अच्छा; बढ़िया *That's a really neat car!* **5** (*AmE* **straight**) (used about an alcoholic drink) on its own, without ice, water or any other liquid (मदिरा) शुद्ध, ख़ालिस (जिसमें बर्फ़, पानी आदि कुछ नहीं) *a neat whisky* ▶ **neatly** *adv.* सफ़ाई से *neatly folded clothes* ▶ **neatness** *noun* [U] सफ़ाई, सुव्यवस्था

**nebula** /ˈnebjələ ˈनेब्यला / *noun* [C] (*pl.* **nebulae** /-li: -ली /) a bright area in the night sky that is caused by a mass of dust or gas or by a large cloud of stars that are far away नीहारिका (धुएँ, गैस या दूरस्थ तारावली के कारण आकाश में बना प्रकाशपुंज), तारा धुंध

**necessarily** /ˈnesəsərəli; ˌnesəˈserəli ˈनेससरलि; ˌनेसˈसेरलि / *adv.* used to say that sth cannot be avoided or has to happen अनिवार्य रूप से *The number of tickets available is necessarily limited.*

**IDM** **not necessarily** used to say that sth might be true but is not definitely or always true किसी बात के सत्य होने की संभावना व्यक्त करने के लिए प्रयुक्त

**necessary** /ˈnesəsəri ˈनेससरि / *adj.* **necessary (for sb/sth) (to do sth)** that is needed for a purpose or a reason (प्रयोजन विशेष या कारण विशेष से) आवश्यक, ज़रूरी *A good diet is necessary for a healthy life.* ○ *If necessary I can take you to work that day.* ✪ विलोम **unnecessary**

**necessitate** /nəˈsesɪteɪt नˈसेसिटेट् / *verb* [T] (*formal*) to make sth necessary किसी बात को आवश्यक या अपेक्षित बना देना

**necessity** /nəˈsesəti नˈसेसटि / *noun* (*pl.* **necessities**) **1** [U] **necessity (for sth/to do sth)** the need for sth; the fact that sth must be done or must happen (किसी वस्तु की) आवश्यकता, अपेक्षा; (किसी बात की) अनिवार्यता *Is there any necessity for change?* ○ *They sold the car* ***out of necessity*** (= because they had to). **2** [C] something that you must have आवश्यक वस्तु *Clean water is an absolute necessity.*

**neck** /nek नेक् / *noun* **1** [C] the part of your body that joins your head to your shoulders गरदन, ग्रीवा *She wrapped a scarf around her neck.* ○ *Giraffes have long necks.* ➪ **body** पर चित्र देखिए। **2** [C] the part of a piece of clothing that goes round your neck वस्त्र का गरदन वाला भाग *a polo-neck/V-neck sweater* ○ *The neck on this shirt is too tight.* **3** [C] the long narrow part of sth किसी वस्तु का गरदन-नुमा भाग *the neck of a bottle* **4 -necked** (*used to form compound adjectives*) having the type of neck mentioned निर्दिष्ट प्रकार की गरदन वाला *a round-necked sweater*

**IDM** **by the scruff (of the/your neck)** ➪ **scruff** देखिए।

**neck and neck (with sb/sth)** equal or level with sb in a race or competition दौड़ या स्पर्धा में बराबरी के स्तर पर

**up to your neck in sth** having a lot of sth to deal with किसी काम में पूरी तरह लिप्त होना, किसी वस्तु के बहुल होने की स्थिति से निपटना *We're up to our necks in work at the moment.*

**necklace** /ˈnekləs ˈनेक्लस् / *noun* [C] a piece of jewellery that you wear around your neck कंठहार, कंठी, नेकलेस

**neckline** /ˈneklaɪn ˈनेक्लाइन् / *noun* [C] the edge of a piece of clothing, especially a woman's, which fits around or below the neck वस्त्र (विशेषतया महिलाओं के वस्त्र) का वह किनारा जो गरदन के चारों ओर या कुछ नीचे आता है *a dress with a low/round neckline*

**necktie** /ˈnektaɪ ˈनेक्टाइ / (*AmE*) = **tie[1] 1**

**nectar** /ˈnektə(r) ˈनेक्ट(र्) / *noun* [U] **1** the sweet liquid that bees collect from flowers to make **honey** शहद बनाने के लिए मधुमक्खियों द्वारा फूलों से एकत्रित मधुर द्रव; मकरंद **2** the thick juice of some fruit, used as a drink किसी फल का गाढ़ा रस (पेय के रूप में प्रयुक्त) *apricot nectar*

**nectarine** /ˈnektəriːn ˈनेक्टरीन्/ *noun* [C] a soft round red and yellow fruit that looks like a **peach** with smooth skin शफ़तालू

**née** /neɪ ने/ *adj.* used in front of the family name that a woman had before she got married महिला के विवाह-पूर्व कुलनाम का निर्देश करने के लिए प्रयुक्त *Mili Mitra née Sen* ➪ **maiden name** देखिए।

**need**[1] /niːd नीड्/ *verb* [T] (*not usually used in the continuous tenses*) **1 need sb/sth (for sth/to do sth)** if you need sth, you want it or must have it किसी को किसी वस्तु की आवश्यकता होना *All living things need water.* ○ *I need a new film for my camera.* ○ *Does Roshni need any help?* **2** to have to; to be obliged to कुछ करना आवश्यक होना; किसी बात की बाध्यता होना *Do we need to buy the tickets in advance?* ○ *You didn't need to bring any food but it was very kind of you.*

NOTE मुख्य क्रिया **need** का प्रश्नवाचक रूप है **do I need?** आदि और भूतकाल का रूप है **needed** (प्रश्नवाचक रूप में **did you need?** आदि तथा नकारात्मक रूप में **didn't need**)

**3 need (sth) doing** if sth needs doing, it is necessary or must be done किसी वस्तु या व्यक्ति के लिए कुछ आवश्यक या अनिवार्य होना *This jumper needs washing.*

NOTE इस क्रिया का सामान्यतया सातत्यबोधक कालों (continuous tenses) में प्रयोग नहीं होता तथापि इसका -ing युक्त वर्तमान कृदंत (present participle) रूप बड़ी संख्या में दिखाई पड़ता है—*Patients needing emergency treatment will go to the top of the waiting list.*

**need**[2] /niːd नीड्/ *modal verb* (*not used in the continuous tenses; used mainly in questions or negative sentences after* if *and* whether *or with words like* hardly, only, never) to have to; to be obliged to कुछ करना आवश्यक होना; किसी बात की बाध्यता होना *Need we pay the whole amount now?* ○ *You needn't come to the meeting if you're too busy.* ○ *I* ***hardly need*** *remind you* (= you already know) *that this is very serious.*

NOTE तीनों पुरुषों में वर्तमान काल रूप है **need**; निषेधात्मक रूप **need not (needn't)**; प्रश्नवाचक रूप **need I?**, आदि।
अतीत की घटना की चर्चा के लिए प्रयुक्त भूत कृदंत रूप (past participle) के साथ **needn't have** यह प्रदर्शित करता है कि आपने अवश्य कुछ 'किया था' परंतु बाद में लगा कि वह करना आवश्यक 'नहीं था' —*I needn't have gone to the hospital* (= I went but it wasn't necessary). अनियतात्मक वाक्यांश **didn't need to** सामान्यतया यह व्यक्त करता है कि आपने कोई काम इसलिए 'नहीं' किया क्योंकि आपको 'पहले से ही' मालूम था कि वह काम आवश्यक नहीं—*I didn't need to go to the hospital* (= I didn't go because it wasn't necessary). वृत्तिवाचक क्रियाओं (modal verbs) के विषय में अधिक जानकारी के लिए इस शब्दकोश के अंत में **Quick Grammar Reference** देखिए।

**need**[3] /niːd नीड्/ *noun* **1** [U, *sing.*] **need (for sth); need (for sb/sth) to do sth** a situation in which you must have or do sth (किसी व्यक्ति या वस्तु की) आवश्यकता, अनिवार्यता *There's* ***no need for*** *you to come if you don't want to.* ○ *Do phone me if you* ***feel the need*** *to talk to someone.* **2** [C, *usually pl.*] the things that you must have आवश्यकताएँ, आवश्यक वस्तुएँ *He doesn't earn enough to pay for his basic needs.* ○ *Parents must consider their children's emotional as well as their physical needs.* **3** [U] the state of not having enough food, money or support (भोजन, धन या सहायता की दृष्टि से) अभाव की स्थिति *a campaign to help families* ***in need***

**needle** /ˈniːdl ˈनीड्ल्/ *noun* [C] **1** a small thin piece of metal with a point at one end and a hole (**an eye**) at the other that is used for sewing सूई (कपड़ा सीने की) *to thread a needle with cotton* ➪ **pins** और **needles** भी देखिए। **2** (*also* **knitting needle**) one of two long thin pieces of metal or plastic with a point at one end that are used for knitting सलाई (ऊन आदि बुनने की) **3** the sharp metal part of a **syringe** इंजेक्शन की सूई **4** a thin metal part on a scientific instrument that moves to point to the correct measurement or direction घड़ी आदि यांत्रिक उपकरणों की सूई (जो सही माप-तोल या दिशा बताती है) **5** the thin, hard pointed leaf of certain trees that stay green all year कुछ बारहमासी वृक्षों के महीन तीखी नोंक वाले पत्ते *pine needles*

**needless** /ˈniːdləs ˈनीड्लस्/ *adj.* that is not necessary and that you can easily avoid अनावश्यक, ग़ैर-ज़रूरी ➪ **unnecessary** देखिए। ▶ **needlessly** *adv.* अनावश्यक रूप से

**needlework** /ˈniːdlwɜːk ˈनीड्ल्वक्/ *noun* [U] sth that you sew by hand, especially for decoration (हाथ की) बुनाई-कढ़ाई का काम (विशेषतः सजावट के लिए)

**needy** /ˈniːdi ˈनीडि/ *adj.* **1** not having enough money, food, clothes, etc. अभावग्रस्त (पर्याप्त धन, भोजन आदि की दृष्टि से); ज़रूरतमंद **2 the needy** *noun* [*pl.*] people who do not have enough money, food, clothes, etc. अभावग्रस्त या ज़रूरतमंद लोग

**neg.** *abbr.* negative निषेधात्मक, नकारात्मक

**neem** *noun* [C] a large, usually evergreen tree commonly found in India that has small pointed leaves. Different parts of the tree are used in the preparation of medicines as well as in insecticides नीम का पेड़

**negative**[1] /ˈnegətɪv ˈनेगटिव़्/ *adj.* **1** bad or harmful बुरा या हानिप्रद *The effects of the new rule have been rather negative.* **2** only thinking about the bad qualities of sb/sth व्यक्ति या वस्तु का नकारात्मक पक्ष *I'm feeling very negative about my job—in fact I'm thinking about leaving.* ○ *If you go into the match with a negative attitude, you'll never win.* **3** (used about a word, phrase or sentence) meaning 'no' or 'not' (शब्द, वाक्यांश या वाक्य) 'न' या 'नहीं' का अर्थ देने वाला *a negative sentence* ○ *His reply was negative/He gave a negative reply* (= he said 'no'). ✪ विलोम **affirmative** **4** (used about a medical or scientific test) showing that sth has not happened or has not been found (डॉक्टरी या वैज्ञानिक परीक्षण) लक्ष्यगत वस्तु की दृष्टि से नकारात्मक परिणाम वाला *The results of the tuberculosis test were negative.* **5** (used about a number) less than zero (संख्या) शून्य से कम, ऋण संख्या ✪ विलोम **positive** (सभी अर्थों का) ▶ **negatively** *adv.* नकारात्मक रूप से

**negative**[2] /ˈnegətɪv ˈनेगटिव़्/ *noun* [C] **1** a word, phrase or sentence that says or means 'no' or 'not' निषेध ('न', 'नहीं,) के अर्थ वाला शब्द, वाक्यांश या वाक्य *Aisha answered **in the negative*** (= she said no). ○ *'Never', 'neither' and 'nobody' are all negatives.* ✪ विलोम **affirmative** **2** a piece of film from which we can make a photograph. The light areas of a negative are dark on the final photograph and the dark areas are light फ़ोटो की निगेटिव फ़िल्म (निगेटिव और फ़ोटो में धुँधले-उजले पक्षों की अदला-बदली हो जाती है या में परस्पर परिवर्तन हो जाता है)

**neglect** /nɪˈglekt निˈग्लेक्ट्/ *verb* [T] **1** to give too little or no attention or care to sb/sth किसी व्यक्ति या वस्तु की उपेक्षा करना (बहुत कम ध्यान देना, बिलकुल ध्यान न देना या ख़याल न रखना) *Don't neglect your health.* ○ *The old house had stood neglected for years.* **2 neglect to do sth** to fail or forget to do sth कोई बात छोड़ देना या भूल जाना *He neglected to mention that he had spent time in prison.* ▶ **neglect** *noun* [U] उपेक्षा *The garden was like a jungle after years of neglect.* ▶ **neglected** *adj.* उपेक्षित *neglected children*

**negligence** /ˈneglɪdʒəns ˈनेग्लिजन्स्/ *noun* [U] not being careful enough; lack of care *The accident was a result of negligence.* ▶ **negligent** /ˈneglɪdʒənt ˈनेग्लिजन्ट्/ *adj.* असावधान; उपेक्षाशील ▶ **negligently** *adv.* असावधानी से, उपेक्षापूर्वक

**negligible** /ˈneglɪdʒəbl ˈनेग्लिजब्ल्/ *adj.* very small and therefore not important नगण्य, उपेक्षणीय

**negotiable** /nɪˈgəʊʃiəbl निˈगोशिअब्ल्/ *adj.* that can be decided or changed by discussion जिसे बातचीत से तय किया जा सके या बदला जा सके *The price is not negotiable/non-negotiable.*

**negotiate** /nɪˈgəʊʃieɪt निˈगोशिएट्/ *verb* **1** [I] **negotiate (with sb) (for/about sth)** to talk to sb in order to decide or agree about sth किसी मुद्दे पर निर्णय या समझौते के लिए किसी से बातचीत करना; परक्रामण करना *The unions are still negotiating with management about this year's pay claim.* **2** [T] to decide or agree sth by talking about it बातचीत द्वारा किसी निर्णय पर पहुँचना या समझौता करना *to negotiate an agreement/a deal/a settlement* **3** [T] to get over, past or through sth difficult किसी कठिनाई पर पार पाना या किसी बाधा को पार करना *To escape, prisoners would have to negotiate a five-metre wall.* ▶ **negotiator** *noun* [C] वार्ताकार, समझौता-वार्ताकार

**negotiation** /nɪˌgəʊʃiˈeɪʃn निˌगोशिˈएश्न्/ *noun* [pl., U] discussions at which people try to decide or agree sth वार्ता (किसी निर्णय या समझौते पर पहुँचने के लिए लोगों में बातचीत) *to enter into/break off negotiations* ○ *The pay rise is still **under negotiation**.*

**Negro** /ˈniːgrəʊ ˈनीग्रो/ *noun* [C] (*pl.* **Negroes**) (*old-fashioned*) a black person (जाति की दृष्टि से) काला व्यक्ति, नीग्रो, हबशी **NOTE** ध्यान रखिए यह शब्द अब अपमानजनक माना जाता है।

**neigh** /neɪ ने/ *noun* [C] the long high sound that a horse makes घोड़े की हिनहिनाहट ▶ **neigh** *verb* [I] घोड़े का हिनहिनाना

**neighbour** (*AmE* **neighbor**) /ˈneɪbə(r) ˈनेब(र्)/ *noun* [C] **1** a person who lives near you पड़ोसी (व्यक्ति), प्रतिवेशी *our **next-door neighbours*** **2** a person or thing that is near or next to another साथ वाला या बग़ल वाला, पड़ोसी व्यक्ति या देश आदि *Britain's nearest neighbour is France.* ○ *Try not to look at what your neighbour is writing.*

**neighbourhood** (*AmE* **neighborhood**) /ˈneɪbəhʊd ˈनेबहुड्/ *noun* [C] a particular part of a town and the people who live there शहर का कोई मुहल्ला; पड़ोस, प्रतिवेश

**neighbouring** (*AmE* **neighboring**) /ˈneɪbərɪŋ ˈनेबरिङ्/ *adj.* (*only before a noun*) near or next to समीपस्थ, निकटवर्ती, पड़ोस का *Farmers from neighbouring villages come into town each week for the market.*

**neighbourly** (*AmE* **neighborly**) /ˈneɪbəli ˈनेबलि/ *adj.* friendly and helpful मित्रवत और सहायक; पड़ोसाना

**neither** /ˈnaɪðə(r); ˈniːðə(r) ˈनाइद्र(र्); ˈनीद्र(र्)/ *det., pronoun, adv.* **1** (used about two people or things) not one and not the other (व्यक्ति या वस्तुएँ) न यह न वह *Neither of the teams played very well.* ○ *'Would you like tea or juice?' 'Neither, thank you. I'm not thirsty.'*

> **NOTE** ध्यान दीजिए कि **neither** के बाद एकवचन संज्ञा और क्रिया आती है—*Neither day was suitable. Neither of* के बाद आने वाला संज्ञा या सर्वनाम एकवचन या बहुवचन हो सकता है—*Neither of the days is/are suitable.*

**2** also not; not either यह भी नहीं; दोनों में से कोई भी नहीं *I don't eat meat and neither does Vijay.* ○ *'I don't like fish.' 'Neither do I.'* ○ (*informal*) *'I don't like fish.' 'Me neither.'*

> **NOTE** इस अर्थ में **nor** का प्रयोग भी इसी प्रकार हो सकता है *'I don't like fish.' 'Nor do I.'* ध्यान दीजिए कि **not...either** के प्रयोग में शब्दों का क्रम बदल जाता है—*I haven't seen that film.' 'I haven't either.'*

**3 neither ... nor** not ... and not न तो ... और न ... *Neither Vijay nor I eat meat.*

> **NOTE** **Neither ... nor** के साथ आने वाली क्रिया एकवचन या बहुवचन हो सकती है—*Neither Sheena nor Meena was/were at the meeting.*

**nemesis** /ˈneməsɪs ˈनेमसिस्/ *noun* [U, *sing.*] (*formal*) a punishment or defeat that sb deserves and cannot avoid दंड या पराजय जिससे उसका पात्र बच नहीं सकता; नियति

**neo-** /ˈniːəʊ ˈनीओ/ *prefix* (*used in adjectives and nouns*) new; in a later form नया, नव-, नव्य; उत्तरवर्ती, परवर्ती या बाद के रूप में *neo-Georgian* ○ *neo-fascist*

**Neolithic** /ˌniːəˈlɪθɪk ˌनीअˈलिथिक्/ *adj.* referring to the later part of the **Stone Age** नव पाषाणकालीन, नव प्रस्तर कालिक

**neon** /ˈniːɒn ˈनीऑन्/ *noun* [U] (*symbol* **Ne**) a type of gas that does not react with anything and is used for making bright lights and signs एक प्रकार की प्रतिक्रिया-हीन गैस जो बत्तियों और विज्ञापन-पट्टों को चमकदार बनाती है, निओन गैस **NOTE** **Neon** एक **noble gas** है।

**nephew** /ˈnefjuː; ˈnevjuː ˈनेफ़्यू; ˈनेव्यू/ *noun* [C] the son of your brother or sister, or the son of your husband's or wife's brother or sister भाई का पुत्र (भतीजा) या बहन का पुत्र (भानजा) या पति के भाई या बहन अथवा पत्नी के भाई या बहन का पुत्र; भतीजा, भानजा ➪ **niece** देखिए।

**nepotism** /ˈnepətɪzəm ˈनेपटिज़म्/ *noun* [U] using your power or influence to give unfair advantage to your family, especially by giving them jobs अपने अधिकार या प्रभाव से परिवार के सदस्यों का अनुचित लाभ (विशेषतः नौकरी देना) पहुँचाना; भाई-भतीजावाद, कुनबापरस्ती

**Neptune** /ˈneptjuːn ˈनेप्ट्यून्/ *noun* [*sing.*] the planet that is eighth in order from the sun सूर्य से आठवाँ ग्रह; वरुण ➪ **the solar system** पर चित्र देखिए।

**nerd** /nɜːd नड्/ *noun* [C] a person who is not fashionable and has a boring hobby पुरानी चाल का ओर उबाऊ शौक़ पालने वाला आदमी, खूसट आदमी ▸ **nerdy** *adj.* पुराने ढंग का और उबाऊ

**nerve** /nɜːv नव्/ *noun* **1** [C] one of the long thin threads in your body that carry feelings or other messages to and from your brain स्नायु, नस, तंत्रिका **2 nerves** [*pl.*] worried, nervous feelings घबराहट, परेशानी *Breathing deeply should help to* ***calm/steady your nerves***. ○ *I was* ***a bag of nerves*** *before my interview.* **3** [U] the courage that you need to do sth difficult or dangerous कठिनाई या ख़तरे का सामना करने का साहस *Rajiv didn't have the nerve to ask his father for more money.* ○ *Some pilots* ***lose their nerve*** *and can't fly any more.* **4** [*sing.*] a way of behaving that people think is not acceptable धृष्ट आचरण *You've got a nerve, calling me lazy!*

**IDM** **get on sb's nerves** (*informal*) to annoy sb or make sb angry किसी को नाराज़ या क्रुद्ध कर देना

**nerve cell** *noun* [C] a cell that carries information between the brain and the other parts of the body स्नायु कोशिका (जो मस्तिष्क और शरीर के अन्य अंगों के बीच सूचना का वहन करती है) ✪ पर्याय **neuron**

**nerve-racking** *adj.* making you very nervous or worried तंत्रिकोत्पीड़क; बहुत आशंकित या चिंतित कर देने वाला

**nervous** /ˈnɜːvəs ˈनवस्/ *adj.* **1 nervous (about/of sth/doing sth)** worried or afraid चिंतित या भयभीत *I always* ***get nervous*** *just before a match.* ○ *a nervous laugh/smile/voice* **2** connected with the nerves of the body स्नायु-विषयक, स्नायविक *a nervous disorder* ▸ **nervously** *adv.* चिंतित या भयभीत होकर ▸ **nervousness** *noun* [U] चिंता या भय

**nervous breakdown** (*also* **breakdown**) *noun* [C] a time when sb suddenly becomes so unhappy that he/she cannot continue living and working normally अत्यधिक विषाद से उत्पन्न असामान्यता *to have a nervous breakdown*

**the nervous system** *noun* [C] your brain and all the nerves in your body मस्तिष्क तथा समस्त स्नायु-मंडल

**nest** /nest नेस्ट्/ *noun* [C] **1** a structure that a bird builds to keep its eggs and babies in (पक्षियों का) घोंसला, नीड़ **2** the home of certain animals or insects कुछ जंतुओं या कीटों का घर; बाँबी *a wasps' nest* ▶ **nest** *verb* [I] घोंसला बनाना

**nestle** /ˈnesl ˈनेस्ल्/ *verb* [I, T] to be or go into a position where you are comfortable, protected or hidden आरामदेह, सुरक्षित या गुप्त स्थिति में होना या चले जाना *The baby nestled her head on her mother's shoulder.*

**net¹** /net नेट्/ *noun* **1** [U] material that has large, often square, spaces between the threads जाल, नेट **2** [C] a piece of net that is used for a particular purpose विशेष प्रयोजन का जाल *a tennis/fishing/mosquito net* ➪ **safety net** देखिए। **3** the net [*sing.*] = **the Internet**

IDM **surf the net** ➪ **surf²** देखिए।

**net²** /net नेट्/ *verb* [T] (**netting; netted**) **1** to catch sth with a net; to kick a ball into a net किसी को जाल में फँसाना; गेंद को मारकर (गोल के) जाल में पहुँचाना **2** to gain sth as a profit लाभ के रूप में कुछ प्राप्त करना

**net³** (*also* **nett**) /net नेट्/ *adj.* **net (of sth)** (used about a number or amount) from which nothing more needs to be taken away (संख्या या मात्रा) शेष, शुद्ध, निवल (जिसमें से अब कुछ निकालना नहीं) *I earn about Rs 15,000 net* (= after tax, etc. has been paid). ○ *The net weight of the jam is 350 g* (= not including the jar). ○ *a net profit* ✪ विलोम **gross**

**netball** /ˈnetbɔːl ˈनेट्बॉल्/ *noun* [U] a game that is played by two teams of seven players, usually women. Players score by throwing the ball through a high net hanging from a ring नेट बॉल (सात-सात खिलाड़ियों, प्रायः महिला खिलाड़ियों की दो टीमों का खेल जिसमें छल्ले से ऊँचाई पर लटके नेट में बॉल को फ़ेंका जाता है)

**netting** /ˈnetɪŋ ˈनेटिङ्/ *noun* [U] material that is made of long pieces of string, thread, wire, etc. that are tied together with spaces between them जाली

**nettle** /ˈnetl ˈनेट्ल्/ *noun* [C] a wild plant with hairy leaves. Some nettles make your skin red and painful if you touch them बिच्छू पौधा (जंगली और रेशेदार पत्तों वाला पौधा जिसे छूने पर बिच्छू के काटने का-सा दर्द होता है)

**network** /ˈnetwɜːk ˈनेट्वक्/ *noun* [C] **1** a system of roads, railway lines, nerves, etc. that are connected to each other परस्पर संयुक्त सड़कों, रेलवे लाइनों, नसों आदि का जाल या तंत्र *an underground railway network* **2** a group of people or companies that work closely together परस्पर घनिष्ठता से जुड़े लोगों या कंपनियों का समूह *We have a network of agents who sell our goods all over the country.* **3** a number of computers that are connected together so that information can be shared परस्पर जुड़े अनेक कंप्यूटर (ताकि सूचना में सहभागिता हो सके) **4** a group of television or radio companies that are connected and that send out the same programmes at the same time in different parts of a country एक ही कार्यक्रम को एक ही समय में देश के विभिन्न भागों में प्रसारित करने के लिए एक साथ जुड़ी टेलीविज़न या रेडियो कंपनियों का समूह

**neuro-** /ˈnjʊərəʊ ˈन्युअरो/ *prefix* (*used in nouns, adjectives and adverbs*) connected with the nerves स्नायुओं से संबंधित, स्नायविक, स्नायु *neuroscience* ○ *a neurosurgeon*

**neurologist** /njʊəˈrɒlədʒɪst न्युअˈरॉलजिस्ट्/ *noun* [C] a scientist who studies nerves and treats their diseases स्नायुरोग-विशेषज्ञ, स्नायुविज्ञानी

**neurology** /njʊəˈrɒlədʒi न्युअˈरॉलजि/ *noun* [U] the scientific study of nerves and their diseases स्नायु-विज्ञान ▶ **neurological** /ˌnjʊərəˈlɒdʒɪkl ˌन्युअरˈलॉजिक्ल्/ *adj.* स्नायुविज्ञान-विषयक, स्नायुवैज्ञानिक *neurological damage/diseases*

**neuron** /ˈnjʊərɒn ˈन्युअरॉन्/ (*also* **neurone** /ˈnjʊərəʊn ˈन्युअरोन्/) *noun* [C] (*technical*) a cell that carries information between the brain and the other parts of the body स्नायु-कोशिका (जो मस्तिष्क और शरीर के अन्य अंगों के बीच सूचना वहन करती है) ✪ पर्याय **nerve cell**

**neurosis** /njʊəˈrəʊsɪs न्युअˈरोसिस्/ *noun* [C] (*pl.* **neuroses** /-əʊsiːz -ओसीज़्/) (*medical*) a mental illness that causes strong feelings of fear and worry (चिकित्सा) गंभीर भय और चिंता को जन्म देने वाला एक मनोरोग, मनस्ताप का स्नायु-रोग

**neurotic** /njʊəˈrɒtɪk न्युअˈरॉटिक्/ *adj.* **1** worried about things in a way that is not normal अकारण चिंतित, विक्षिप्त-सा **2** (*medical*) suffering from a neurosis मनस्ताप का रोगी

**neuter¹** /ˈnjuːtə(r) ˈन्यूट(र्)/ *adj.* (used about a word in some languages) not **masculine** or **feminine** according to the rules of grammar (कुछ भाषाओं में कुछ शब्द) जो व्याकरण के अनुसार नपुंसकलिंगी होते हैं

**neuter²** /ˈnjuːtə(r) ˈन्यूट(र्)/ *verb* [T] to remove the sexual parts of an animal किसी पशु को नपुंसक बनाना (उसके प्रजननांगों को निकाल लेना) ➪ **castrate** देखिए।

**neutral**[1] /ˈnjuːtrəl ˈन्यूट्रल्/ *adj.* **1** not supporting or belonging to either side in an argument, war, etc. किसी विवाद, युद्ध आदि में तटस्थ *I don't take sides when my brothers argue—I* ***remain neutral.*** ○ *The two sides agreed to meet on neutral ground.* **2** having or showing no strong qualities, emotions or colour हलका, मंद (तीखेपन से रहित) *neutral colours* ○ *a neutral tone of voice* **3** (in chemistry) neither acid nor **alkaline** (रसायन शास्त्र में) न अम्ल न क्षार ➪ **pH** पर चित्र देखिए। **4** (in physics) having neither a positive nor a negative charge (भौतिक विज्ञान) न धन-विद्युत न ऋण-विद्युत

**neutral**[2] /ˈnjuːtrəl ˈन्यूट्रल्/ *noun* [U] the position of the **gears** in a vehicle when no power is sent from the engine to the wheels वाहन में न्यूट्रल गिअर (जब इंजिन से पहियों में शक्ति-प्रवाह बंद रहता है)

**neutrality** /njuːˈtræləti न्यूˈट्रैलटि/ *noun* [U] the state of not supporting either side in an argument, war, etc. किसी विवाद, युद्ध आदि में तटस्थता

**neutralize** (*also* **-ise**) /ˈnjuːtrəlaɪz ˈन्यूट्रलाइज़्/ *verb* [T] **1** to take away the effect of sth किसी वस्तु को निष्प्रभावी कर देना *to neutralize a threat* **2** to have an effect on a substance so that it becomes neither an acid nor an **alkali** किसी पदार्थ को न तो अम्लीय रहने देना न क्षारीय **3** to make a country or area **neutral** किसी देश या क्षेत्र को युद्ध में तटस्थ घोषित कर देना

**neutron** /ˈnjuːtrɒn ˈन्यूट्रॉन्/ *noun* [C] one of the three types of **particles** that form all atoms. Neutrons have no electric charge परमाणु के तीन घटकों में से एक (न्यूट्रॉन में विद्युत चार्ज नहीं होता) ➪ **electron** और **proton** देखिए।

**never** /ˈnevə(r) ˈनेव़(र्)/ *adv.* **1** at no time; not ever कभी नहीं; कदापि नहीं *I've never been to Paris.* ○ (*formal*) *Never before has such a high standard been achieved.* **2** used for emphasizing a negative statement निषेधात्मक प्रकथन पर बल देने के लिए प्रयुक्त *Rohit never so much as looked at us* (= he didn't even look at us). ○ *'I got the job!' 'Never!'* (= expressing surprise)

**IDM** **never mind** ➪ **mind**[2] देखिए।

**you never know** ➪ **know**[1] देखिए।

**nevertheless** /ˌnevəðəˈles ˌनेव़द़ˈलेस्/ *adv., conj.* (*formal*) in spite of that तथापि, ऐसा होने पर भी *It was a cold, rainy day. Nevertheless, more people came than we had expected.* ✪ पर्याय **nonetheless**

**new** /njuː न्यू/ *adj.* **1** that has recently been built, made, discovered, etc. नया (बना, खोजा आदि) *a new design/film/hospital* ○ *new evidence* ✪ विलोम **old** **2** different or changed from what was before जो पहले था उससे भिन्न या परिवर्तित *I've just started reading a new book.* ○ *to make new friends* ✪ विलोम **old** **3 new (to sb)** that you have not seen, learnt, etc. before जो पहले न देखा हो, न जाना हो आदि *This type of machine is new to me.* ○ *to learn a new language* **4 new (to sth)** having just started being or doing sth (अस्तित्व में आने या करने की दृष्टि से) अभी-अभी आरंभ *a new parent* ○ *She's new to the job and needs a lot of help.*

▶ **newness** *noun* [U] नयापन

**IDM** **break fresh/new ground** ➪ **ground**[1] देखिए।

**news reporter** = **reporter**

**New Age** *adj.* connected with a way of life that rejects modern Western values and is based on spiritual ideas and beliefs आधुनिक पाश्चात्य जीवन-मूल्यों को नकारने वाली और आध्यात्मिक विचारों और मान्यताओं पर आधारित अभिनव जीवन-शैली *a New Age festival*

**newborn** /ˈnjuːbɔːn ˈन्यूबॉन्/ *adj.* (*only before a noun*) (used about a baby) that has been born very recently (शिशु) अभी जन्मा, नवजात

**newcomer** /ˈnjuːkʌmə(r) ˈन्यूकम(र्)/ *noun* [C] a person who has just arrived in a place किसी स्थान पर अभी पहुँचा व्यक्ति, नवागत व्यक्ति

**newfangled** /ˌnjuːˈfæŋgld ˌन्यूˈफ़ैङ्गल्ड्/ *adj.* new or modern in a way that the speaker does not like ऐसा नया या आधुनिक जो अरुचिकर लगे, अति-आधुनिक (अटपटा-सा लगने वाला)

**newly** /ˈnjuːli ˈन्यूलि/ *adv.* (*usually before a past participle*) recently हाल का *the newly appointed Minister of Health*

**newly-wed** *noun* [C, *usually pl.*] a person who has recently got married नव-विवाहित व्यक्ति

**new moon** *noun* [*sing.*] the moon when it appears as a thin curved line नव चंद्र, दूज का चाँद ➪ **full moon** देखिए।

**news** /njuːz न्यूज़्/ *noun* **1** [U] information about sth that has happened recently समाचार, ख़बर *Have you had any news from Naina recently?* ○ *That's news to me* (= I didn't know that).

> **NOTE** **News** अगणनीय (uncountable) संज्ञा है। यदि किसी एक समाचार की बात करनी हो तो 'a piece of news' वाक्यांश का प्रयोग होता है—*We had two pieces of good news yesterday.*

**2 the news** [*sing.*] a regular programme giving the latest news on the radio or television रेडियो या टेलीविज़न का नियमित समाचार-कार्यक्रम *We always watch the nine o'clock news on television.* ○ *I heard about the accident* ***on the news.***

**IDM** **break the news (to sb)** to be the first to tell sb about sth important that has happened किसी महत्त्वपूर्ण घटना का सबसे पहले समाचार देना

**newsagent** /ˈnjuːzeɪdʒənt ˈन्यूज़्एजन्ट् / (*AmE* **newsdealer**) *noun* **1** [C] a person who owns or works in a shop that sells newspapers and magazines, etc. समाचार पत्र-पत्रिका विक्रेता **2 the newsagent's** [*sing.*] a shop that sells newspapers, magazines, etc. पत्र-पत्रिकाएँ बेचने की दुकान

**newsflash** /ˈnjuːzflæʃ ˈन्यूज़्फ़्लैश् / *noun* [C] a short report on television or radio, which often interrupts the normal programme to give information about an important event that has just happened टेलीविज़न या रेडियो के चल रहे किसी कार्यक्रम को रोककर सुनाया जाने वाला संक्षिप्त समाचार (अभी घटी महत्त्वपूर्ण घटना से संबंधित)

**newsletter** /ˈnjuːzletə(r) ˈन्यूज़्लेट(र्) / *noun* [C] a printed report about a club or an organization that is sent regularly to members and other people who may be interested किसी क्लब या संघ की लघु पत्रिका (सदस्यों को नियमित रूप से प्रेषित), संवाद पत्रिका, समाचारिका

**newspaper** /ˈnjuːzpeɪpə(r) ˈन्यूज़्पेप(र्) / *noun* **1** (*also* **paper**) [C] large folded pieces of paper printed with news, advertisements and articles on various subects. Newspapers are printed and sold either every day or every week समाचार-पत्र, अख़बार *a daily/weekly/Sunday newspaper* ○ *a newspaper article* ○ *I read about it **in the newspaper**.* **2** (*also* **paper**) [C] an organization that produces a newspaper समाचार-पत्र निकालने वाली संस्था *Which newspaper does he work for?* **3** [U] the paper on which newspapers are printed अख़बार का काग़ज़ *We wrapped the plates in newspaper so they would not get damaged.*

> **NOTE** **Journalists** और **reporters** अख़बारों के लिए समाचार एकत्रित करते हैं। **Editor** तय करता है कि क्या छपेगा।

**newsreader** /ˈnjuːzriːdə(r) ˈन्यूज़्रीड(र्) / (*also* **newscaster** / ˈnjuːzkɑːstə(r) ˈन्यूज़्कास्ट(र्) /) *noun* [C] a person who reads the news on the radio or television रेडियो या टेलीविज़न पर समाचार पढ़ने वाला व्यक्ति, समाचार-वाचक, समाचार प्रसारक

**news reporter** *noun* [C] = **reporter**

**news-stand** (*AmE*) = **bookstall**

**the New Testament** *noun* [*sing.*] the second part of the Bible, that describes the life and teachings of Jesus Christ बाइबिल का दूसरा खंड जिसमें ईसा के जीवन और शिक्षाओं का विवरण है; न्यू टेस्टामेंट ➪ **the Old Testament** देखिए।

**newton** / ˈnjuːtən ˈन्यूटन् / *noun* [C] (*abbr.* **N**) a unit of force. One newton is equal to the force that would give a mass of one kilogram an **acceleration** of one metre per second शक्ति की इकाई, न्यूटन (एक न्यूटन उस शक्ति के बराबर है जो एक किलोग्राम के पिंड को एक मीटर प्रति सेकंड का त्वरण देता है

**new year** (*also* **New Year**) *noun* [*sing.*] the first few days of January जनवरी के आरंभिक दिन *New Year's Eve* (= 31 December) ○ *New Year's Day* (= 1 January)

**next** /nekst नेक्स्ट् / *adj., adv.* **1** (*usually with 'the'*) coming immediately after sth in order, space or time; closest (प्रायः 'the' के साथ) (स्थान या समय की दृष्टि से) अगला; सबसे पास, निकटतम *The next bus leaves in 20 minutes.* ○ *The next name on the list is Parvati.*

> **NOTE** **Nearest** और **next** देखिए। **Next** का अर्थ है (घटनाओं या स्थानों की शृंखला में) आगामी या अगला—*When is your next appointment?* ○ *Turn left at the next traffic lights.* **Nearest** का अर्थ है (स्थान या समय की दृष्टि से) सबसे पास का या निकटतम—*Where's the nearest supermarket?*

**2** (used without the before days of the week, months, seasons, years, etc.) the one immediately following the present one) (सप्ताह के दिनों, महीनों, ऋतुओं, वर्षों आदि के नामों से पहले 'the' के बिना प्रयुक्त) वर्तमान के बाद एकदम अगला *See you again next Monday.* ○ *Let's go camping next weekend.* **3** after this or after that; then इसके या उसके बाद; तब *I wonder what will happen next.* ○ *I know Jai arrived first, but who came next?* ○ *It was 10 years until I next saw her.* **4 the next** *noun* [*sing.*] the person or thing that is next अगला(पढ़ने वाला) व्यक्ति या वस्तु *If we miss this train we'll have to wait two hours for the next.*

**IDM** **last/next but one, two etc.** ➪ **last[1]** देखिए।

**next door** *adj., adv.* in or into the next house or building अगले मकान या भवन में या उसके भीतर ठीक बग़ल वाला, एकदम बाजूवाला *our **next-door neighbours*** ○ *The school is **next door to** an old people's home.*

**next of kin** *noun* [C] (*pl.* **next of kin**) your closest living relative or relatives निकटतम जीवित संबंधी *My husband is my next of kin.*

**next to** *prep.* **1** at the side of sb/sth; beside किसी व्यक्ति वस्तु के बग़ल में; से अगला *He sat down next to Gita.* ○ *There's a public telephone next to the bus stop.* **2** in a position after sth (क्रम में) किसी के बाद *Next to English my favourite subject is Maths.*

IDM **next to nothing** almost nothing लगभग शून्य *We took plenty of money but we've got next to nothing left.*

**nexus** /ˈneksəs ˈनेक्सस्/ *noun* [C, *usually sing.*] (*formal*) a complicated series of connections between different people or things विभिन्न व्यक्तियों या वस्तुओं के बीच जटिल संबंध

**nib** /nɪb निब्/ *noun* [C] the metal point of a pen पेन का निब ➪ **stationery** पर चित्र देखिए।

**nibble** /ˈnɪbl ˈनिबल्/ *verb* [I, T] to eat sth by taking small bites किसी वस्तु को टुकड़े-टुकड़े कर के खाना, कुतरना *The bread had been nibbled by mice.* ▸ **nibble** *noun* [C] कुतरने की क्रिया

**nice** /naɪs नाइस्/ *adj.* **1** pleasant, enjoyable or attractive सुहाना या मनोरम, आनंदप्रद या आकर्षक *It would be nice to spend more time at home.* ○ *'Hi, I'm Tony.' 'I'm Ray—**nice to meet you**.'* **2 nice (to sb); nice (of sb) (to do sth); nice (about sth)** kind; friendly दयालु; मित्रवत *Everyone was very nice to me when I fell ill.* ○ *It was really nice of Deepa to help us.* **3** (*informal*) used before adjectives and adverbs to emphasize how pleasant or suitable sth is विशेषणों और क्रियाविशेषणों से पहले (किसी वस्तु की) मनोरमता या अनुकूलता पर बल देने के लिए प्रयुक्त *It's nice and warm by the fire.* ○ *a nice long chat* ▸ **nicely** *adv.* कृपापूर्वक, मनोरम रूप से ▸ **niceness** *noun* [U] मनोरमता, कृपालुता

**niche** /nɪtʃ; niːʃ निच्; नीश्/ *noun* [C] **1** a job, position, etc. that is suitable for you अनुकूल या उपयुक्त नौकरी, पद आदि *to find your niche in life* **2** (in business) an opportunity to sell a particular product to a particular group of people (व्यापार में) विशिष्ट व्यक्ति-वर्ग को विशिष्ट वस्तु बेचने का अवसर या गुंजाइश **3** a place in a wall that is further back, where a statue, etc. can be put दीवार में आला (मूर्ति आदि रखने के लिए), ताक

**nick[1]** /nɪk निक्/ *noun* [C] a small cut in sth (किसी वस्तु में) खाँच या काट

IDM **in good/bad nick** (*BrE slang*) in a good/bad state or condition अच्छी या बुरी दशा में

**in the nick of time** only just in time ऐन मौके पर, एकदम ठीक समय पर

**nick[2]** /nɪk निक्/ *verb* [T] **1** to make a very small cut in sb/sth (किसी व्यक्ति या वस्तु में) छोटी-सी काट लगाना **2** (*BrE slang*) to arrest sb किसी व्यक्ति को गिरफ़्तार करना या बंदी बनाना **3** (*BrE slang*) to steal sth कोई वस्तु चुराना

**nickel** /ˈnɪkl ˈनिकल्/ *noun* **1** [U] (*symbol* **Ni**) a hard silver-white metal that is often mixed with other metals निकल (धातु)

**nickname** /ˈnɪkneɪm ˈनिक्नेम्/ *noun* [C] an informal name that is used instead of your real name, usually by your family or friends वास्तविक नाम के बदले प्रायः परिवार के सदस्यों या मित्रों द्वारा प्रयुक्त अनौपचारिक नाम, मुँहबोला नाम, घर का नाम, छोटा नाम, उपनाम ▸ **nickname** *verb* [T] अनौपचारिक नाम रखना

**nicotine** /ˈnɪkətiːn ˈनिकटीन्/ *noun* [U] the poisonous chemical substance in tobacco तंबाकू में पाया जाने वाला विषैला रसायन, निकोटीन

**niece** /niːs नीस्/ *noun* [C] the daughter of your brother or sister; the daughter of your husband's or wife's brother or sister भाई की पुत्री (भतीजी) या बहन की पुत्री (भाँजी); पति या पत्नी की भतीजी, भाँजी ➪ **nephew** देखिए।

**niggle** /ˈnɪgl ˈनिग्ल्/ *verb* **1** [I, T] **niggle (at) sb** to annoy or worry sb (किसी व्यक्ति को) नाराज़ या चिंतित या परेशान कर देना *His untidy habits really niggled her.* **2** [I] **niggle (about/over sth)** to complain or argue about things that are not important मामूली बातों को लेकर शिकायत करना या उन पर बहस करना

**niggling** /ˈnɪglɪŋ ˈनिग्लिङ्/ *adj.* not very serious (but that does not go away) मामूली (परंतु बरक़रार) यथावत *niggling doubts* ○ *a niggling injury*

**night** /naɪt नाइट्/ *noun* [C, U] **1** the part of the day when it is dark and when most people sleep रात, रात्रि *The baby cried **all night**.* ○ *It's a long way home. Why don't you **stay the night**?* **2** the time between late afternoon and when you go to bed देर शाम (का समय) *He doesn't get home until 8 o'clock **at night**.* ○ *I went out with Katrina **the other night*** (= a few nights ago).

> NOTE **Night** के साथ अनेक पूर्वसर्गों (prepositions) का प्रयोग होता है। **At** का प्रयोग सबसे अधिक होता है—*I'm not allowed out after 11 o'clock at night.* प्रायः रात को जो काम किया जाता है उसके लिए **by** का प्रयोग होता है—*These animals sleep by day and hunt by night.* अभी गुज़री रात का निर्देश करने के लिए **in/during** का प्रयोग होता है—*I woke up twice in the night.* **On** का प्रयोग तब किया जाता है जब किसी विशेष रात के विषय में चर्चा करनी हो—*On the night of Saturday 30 June.* **Tonight** का अर्थ है आज की रात या शाम—*Where are you staying tonight?*

IDM **an early/a late night** an evening when you go to bed earlier/later than usual ऐसी शाम जब प्रतिदिन की अपेक्षा जल्दी या देर से सोने जाएँ

**a night out** an evening that you spend out of the house enjoying yourself घर से बाहर जाकर मनोरंजन करने की शाम

**in the/at dead of night** ➪ **dead²** देखिए।

**good night** said late in the evening, before you go home or before you go to sleep देर शाम घर लौटने से या रात को सोने से पहले प्रयुक्त अभिवादन, शुभ रात्रि, शब्बा ख़ैर

**nightclub** /ˈnaɪtklʌb ˈनाइट्क्लब् / *noun* [C] = **club¹ 2**

**nightdress** /ˈnaɪtdres ˈनाइट्ड्रेस् / (*informal* **nightie**) /ˈnaɪti ˈनाइटि / *noun* [C] a loose dress that a girl or woman wears in bed महिलाओं की रात्रिकालीन ढीली-ढाली पोशाक

**nightingale** /ˈnaɪtɪŋgeɪl ˈनाइटिङ्गेल् / *noun* [C] a small brown bird that has a beautiful song बुलबुल (मधुर कंठ वाला छोटा भूरा पक्षी)

**nightlife** /ˈnaɪtlaɪf ˈनाइट्लाइफ़् / *noun* [U] the entertainment that is available in the evenings in a particular place (स्थान विशेष पर उपलब्ध) रात्रिकालीन आमोद-प्रमोद की व्यवस्था *It's a small town with very little nightlife.*

**nightly** /ˈnaɪtli ˈनाइट्लि / *adj., adv.* happening every night प्रत्येक रात का *a nightly news bulletin*

**nightmare** /ˈnaɪtmeə(r) ˈनाइट्मेअ(र्) / *noun* [C] **1** a frightening or unpleasant dream डरावना या अप्रिय सपना, दुःस्वप्न *I had a terrible nightmare about being stuck in a lift last night.* **2** (*informal*) an experience that is very unpleasant or frightening बहुत अप्रिय या डरावना अनुभव, अत्यंत कटु अनुभव *Travelling in the rush hour can be a real nightmare.*

**night-time** *noun* [U] the time when it is dark रात का समय

**nightwatchman** /naɪt ˈwɒtʃmən नाइट् ˈवॉच्मन् / *noun* [C] **1** (*pl.* **nightwatchmen** /-mən -मन् /) a person who guards a building at night रात का चौकीदार **2** (in cricket) a player, usually a bowler, who is sent to bat at the end of the day in a test match with the intention of saving a regular batsman's wicket (क्रिकेट में) नाइटवॉचमेन; टेस्ट मैच में बल्लेबाज़ का विकेट सुरक्षित रखने के लिए दिन के अंत में भेजा गया खिलाड़ी (प्रायः बॉलर)

**nil** /nɪl निल् / *noun* [U] the number 0 (especially as the score in some games) शून्य की संख्या (0) प्रायः खेलों में गणना के लिए स्कोर *We won two-nil/ by two goals to nil.* ➪ **zero** पर नोट देखिए।

**nimble** /ˈnɪmbl ˈनिम्बल् / *adj.* able to move quickly and lightly फुरतीला ▶ **nimbly** /ˈnɪmbli ˈनिम्बलि / *adv.* फुरतीलेपन से

**nimbostratus** /ˌnɪmbəʊˈstrɑːtəs; -ˈstreɪtəs ˌनिम्बो ˈस्ट्राटस्; -ˈस्ट्रेटस् / *noun* [U] (*technical*) a type of cloud that forms a thick grey layer at a low level, from which rain or snow often falls (प्रायः बरसने वाला) कम ऊँचाई पर बना घना बादल, वर्षाउत्तरी मेघ

**nimbus** /ˈnɪmbəs ˈनिम्बस् / *noun* [C, usually *sing.*] (*technical*) a large grey rain cloud दूर तक फैला घना बादल, विशाल वर्षा-मेघ

**nine** /naɪn नाइन् / *number* 9 नौ (की संख्या)

> **NOTE** संख्यावाची शब्दों के वाक्य-प्रयोग के उदाहरणों के लिए **six** की प्रविष्टि देखिए।

**IDM** **nine to five** the hours that you work in most offices नौ से पाँच (का कार्यालय-समय) *a nine-to-five job*

**nineteen** /ˌnaɪnˈtiːn ˌनाइन्ˈटीन् / *number* 19 उन्नीस (की संख्या)

> **NOTE** संख्यावाची शब्दों के वाक्य-प्रयोग के उदाहरणों के लिए **six** की प्रविष्टि देखिए।

**nineteenth** /ˌnaɪnˈtiːnθ ˌनाइन्ˈटीन्थ् / *noun, det., adv.* 19th उन्नीसवाँ ➪ **sixth** की प्रविष्टि के उदाहरण देखिए।

**ninetieth** /ˈnaɪntiəθ ˈनाइन्टिअथ् / **1** *noun, det., adv.* 90th नब्बेवाँ ➪ **sixth** की प्रविष्टि के उदाहरण देखिए। **2** *noun* [C] one of 90 equal parts of sth नब्बेवाँ भाग

**ninety** /ˈnaɪnti ˈनाइन्टि / *number* 90 नब्बे (की संख्या)

> **NOTE** संख्यावाची शब्दों के वाक्य-प्रयोग के उदाहरणों के लिए **sixty** की प्रविष्टि देखिए।

**ninth¹** /naɪnθ नाइन्थ् / *noun* [C] the fraction ¹⁄₉; one of nine equal parts of sth भिन्न संख्या ¹⁄₉; नौवाँ भाग ➪ **sixth** की प्रविष्टि के उदाहरण देखिए।

**ninth²** /naɪnθ नाइन्थ् / *det., adv.* 9th नौवाँ ➪ **sixth** की प्रविष्टि के उदाहरण देखिए।

**nip** /nɪp निप् / *verb* (**nipping; nipped**) **1** [I, T] to give sb/sth a quick bite or to quickly squeeze a piece of sb's skin between your thumb and finger (किसी को) फुरती से काट लेना या चिकोटी काटना *She nipped him on the arm.* **2** [I] (*BrE spoken*) to go somewhere quickly and/or for a short time फुरती से कहीं जाना (थोड़े समय के लिए) ▶ **nip** *noun* [C] चिकोटी, काट

**IDM** **nip sth in the bud** to stop sth bad before it develops or gets worse किसी अप्रिय स्थिति को बढ़ने या बिगड़ने से पहले रोक देना

**nipple** /ˈnɪpl ˈनिप्ल् / *noun* [C] either of the two small dark circles on either side of your chest. A baby can suck milk from his/her mother's breast through the nipples महिला के स्तन का अग्रभाग (जिससे शिशु दूध पीता है)

**nit** /nɪt निट्/ *noun* [C] the egg of a small insect that lives in the hair of people or animals (मनुष्यों या पशुओं के बालों में रहने वाली) लीख, लिक्षा (एक लघु कीट का अंडा)

**nit-picking** *adj., noun* [U] the habit of finding small mistakes in sb's work or paying too much attention to small, unimportant details छिद्रान्वेषण या नुक्ता चीनी करना या मामूली बातों पर बहुत अधिक समय नष्ट करना

**nitrate** /ˈnaɪtreɪt ˈनाइट्रेट् / *noun* [U, C] a compound containing **nitrogen**. Nitrates are often used to improve the quality of soil नाइट्रोजन से बना यौगिक, नाइट्रेट (इनके प्रयोग से मिट्टी मृदा की उपजाऊ शक्ति बढ़ती है)

**nitric acid** /ˌnaɪtrɪkˈæsɪd ˌनाइट्रिक्ˈऐसिड्/ *noun* [U] (*symbol* **$HNO_3$**) a powerful acid that can destroy most substances and is used to make explosive substances and other chemical products नाइट्रिक एसिड (एक शक्तिशाली विनाशकारी पदार्थ जो विस्फोटक एवं अन्य रासायनिक पदार्थों को बनाने में प्रयुक्त होता है)

**nitrify** /ˈnaɪtrɪfaɪ ˈनाइट्रिफ़ाइ / *verb* [T] (*pres. part.* **nitrifying;** *3rd person sing. pres.* **nitrifies;** *pt, pp* **nitrified**) to change a substance into a compound that contains **nitrogen** किसी पदार्थ को नाइट्रोजन-युक्त यौगिक में परिवर्तित करना (किसी पदार्थ का) नाइट्रीकरण करना ➪ **nitrates** देखिए।

**nitrogen** /ˈnaɪtrədʒən ˈनाइट्रजन् / *noun* [U] (*symbol* **N**) a gas that has no colour, taste or smell. Nitrogen forms about 80 % of the air around the earth नाइट्रोजन गैस (रंग-स्वाद-गंधहीन और पृथ्वी के 80% वायुमंडल में व्याप्त)

**nitrogen dioxide** *noun* [U] a reddish-brown poisonous gas. Nitrogen dioxide is formed when some metals dissolve in **nitric acid** नाइट्रोजन डाइ-ऑक्साइड गैस (लाल-भूरे रंग की विषैली गैस जो नाइट्रिक एसिड में कुछ धातुओं के घुलने से बनती है)

**the nitty-gritty** /ˌnɪtiˈɡrɪti ˌनिटिˈग्रिटि / *noun* [*sing.*] (*spoken*) the most important facts, not the small or unimportant details किसी प्रसंग के सर्वाधिक महत्त्वपूर्ण तथ्य (न कि छोटे-मोटे ब्योरे)

**No.** (*also* **no.**) (*pl.* **Nos; nos**) *abbr.* number संख्या, सं॰ *No. 10 Mahabat Khan Road* ○ *telephone no. 51236409*

**no¹** /nəʊ नो / *det., adv.* **1** not any; not a कोई नहीं; नहीं, एक भी नहीं *I have no time to talk now.* ○ *Alice is feeling no better this morning.* **2** used for saying that sth is not allowed किसी बात के निषिद्ध होने की सूचना देने के लिए प्रयुक्त *No smoking.* ○ *No parking.*

**no²** /nəʊ नो / *exclamation* **1** used for giving a negative reply (किसी बात के जवाब में) 'नहीं' कहने के लिए प्रयुक्त या नकारात्मक उत्तर देने के लिए प्रयुक्त *'Would you like something to eat?'*, *'**No thank you**.'* ✪ विलोम **Yes, please** ○ *'Can I borrow the car?' 'No, you can't.'*

> **NOTE** निषेध-व्यंजक कथन से सहमत होने के लिए शब्द **no** का प्रयोग भी किया जा सकता है—*'This programme's not very good.' 'No, you're right. It isn't.'* ✪ विलोम **yes**

**2** used for expressing surprise or shock आश्चर्य या आकस्मिक क्षोभ प्रकट करने के लिए प्रयुक्त *'Mohit's had an accident.' 'Oh, no!'*

**nobility** /nəʊˈbɪləti नोˈबिलटि/ *noun* **1 the nobility** [*sing., with sing. or pl. verb*] the group of people who belong to the highest social class and have special titles such as **Duke** or **Duchess** समाज का संभ्रांत वर्ग (जैसे ब्रिटिश समाज में ड्यूक या डचेस) ✪ पर्याय **aristocracy** **2** [U] (*formal*) the quality of having courage and honour साहसी और स्वाभिमानी होने का गुण

**noble¹** /ˈnəʊbl ˈनोबल् / *adj.* **1** honest; full of courage and care for others ईमानदार; साहसी और परोपकारी *a noble leader* ○ *noble ideas/actions* **2** belonging to the highest social class कुलीन, संभ्रांत या अभिजात वर्ग का *a man of noble birth* ▶ **nobly** /ˈnəʊbli ˈनोब्लि / *adv.* भलमनसाहसता से

**noble²** /ˈnəʊbl ˈनोबल् / *noun* [C] (in past times) a person who belonged to the highest social class and had a special title (विगत युग में) समाज के उच्चतम स्तर से संबंधित व्यक्ति (जिसकी एक विशेष उपाधि होती थी) **NOTE** **Peer** इसके लिए आजकल अधिक प्रचलित शब्द है।

**nobleman** /ˈnəʊblmən ˈनोबल्मन् / or **noblewoman** /ˈnəʊblwʊmən ˈनोबल्वुमन् / *noun* (*pl.* **noblemen** or **noblewomen**) a person who belongs by rank, title or birth to the highest social class; a member of the nobility (वर्ग, पदवी या जन्म से) समाज के कुलीन वर्ग के व्यक्ति; कुलीन वर्ग का सदस्य ➪ **aristocrat** देखिए।

**noble gas** *noun* [C] (in chemistry) any of a group of gases that do not react with other chemicals (रसायनशास्त्र में) कोई भी ऐसी गैस जिसमें अन्य रसायनों के संयोग से प्रतिक्रिया न हो; अहानिकर गैस

> **NOTE** **Noble gases** को **inert gases** भी कहते हैं। इनमें **argon, helium, krypton** और **neon** शामिल हैं।

**nobody¹** /ˈnəʊbədi ˈनोबडि / (*also* **no one** /ˈnəʊ wʌn ˈनो वन् /) *pronoun* no person; not anyone कोई व्यक्ति नहीं; कोई भी नहीं *He screamed but nobody came to help him.* ○ *No one else was around.*

**NOTE** *The, his, her, those* आदि शब्दों या किसी सर्वनाम से पहले **none of** का प्रयोग अनिवार्य है— *None of my friends remembered my birthday.* ○ *I've asked all my classmates but none of them are free.*

**nobody**[2] /nəʊbədi ˈनोबडि / *noun* [C] (*pl.* **nobodies**) a person who is not important or famous नगण्य व्यक्ति (ऐसा व्यक्ति जो न महत्त्वपूर्ण है न प्रसिद्ध), नाचीज़ इनसान *She rose from being a nobody to a superstar.*

**nocturnal** /nɒkˈtɜːnl नॉक्ˈटनॅल् / *adj.* **1** (used about animals and birds) awake and active at night and asleep during the day (पशु और पक्षी) रात में जागने वाले और दिन में सोने वाले निशाचर और दिवाशायी *Owls are nocturnal birds.* ✪ विलोम **diurnal** **2** (*written*) happening in the night रात्रिकालीन *a nocturnal adventure*

**nod** /nɒd नॉड् / *verb* [I, T] (**no<u>dd</u>ing; no<u>dd</u>ed**) to move your head up and down as a way of saying 'yes' or as a sign to sb to do sth सिर हिलाना-अपनी स्वीकृति जतलाने या किसी को काम करने का इशारा करने के लिए; नवाना *Everybody at the meeting nodded in agreement.* ○ *Nod your head if you understand what I'm saying and shake it if you don't.* ▶ **nod** *noun* [C] नवाई, नगन

**PHR V** **nod off** (*informal*) to fall asleep for a short time झपकी लेना

**node** /nəʊd नोड् / *noun* [C] (*technical*) **1** (in botany) a place on the long thin part **(stem)** of a plant from which a branch or leaf grows (जीव-विज्ञान में) वृक्ष के तने में गाँठ जहाँ से शाखाएँ या पत्तियाँ फूटती हैं **2** (in maths) a point at which two lines or systems meet or cross (गणितशास्त्र में) वह बिंदु जहाँ दो रेखाएँ या तंत्र मिलते हैं या एक-दूसरे को काटते हैं **3** (in zoology) a small hard mass, especially near a place where two bones meet **(joint)** in the human body (जीवविज्ञान में) मानव शरीर में हड्डियों के जोड़ के निकट एक कड़ा मांसपिंड; गूमड़ ➪ **lymph node** देखिए।

**nodule** /ˈnɒdjuːl ˈनॉड्यूल् / *noun* [C] a small round lump, especially on a plant एक छोटा गोलाकार पिंड (विशेषतः पौधे पर)

**noise** /nɔɪz नॉइज़् / *noun* [C, U] a sound, especially one that is loud or unpleasant आवाज़ (विशेषतः ऊँची और अप्रिय), शोर, कोलाहल *Try not to* ***make a noise*** *if you come home late.* ○ *What an awful noise!*

**noiseless** /ˈnɔɪzləs ˈनॉइज़लस् / *adj.* making no sound नीरव, मौन, शांत ▶ **noiselessly** *adv.* नीरव भाव से

**noisy** /ˈnɔɪzi ˈनॉइज़ि / *adj.* (**noisier; noisiest**) making a lot of or too much noise; full of noise शोर मचाने वाला; शोर-भरा, कोलाहलपूर्ण *The clock was so noisy that it kept me awake.* ○ *noisy children/traffic/crowds* ➪ **loud** पर नोट देखिए। ▶ **noisily** *adv.* शोर मचाते हुए

**nomad** /ˈnəʊmæd ˈनोमैड् / *noun* [C] a member of a **tribe** that moves with its animals from place to place ख़ानाबदोश या घुमंतू जनजाति का व्यक्ति (ये अपने पशुओं के साथ जगह-जगह घूमते रहते हैं) ▶ **nomadic** /nəʊˈmædɪk/ *adj.* ख़ानाबदोश

**no-man's-land** *noun* [U, *sing.*] an area of land between the borders of two countries or between two armies during a war and which is not controlled by either दो देशों की सीमाओं पर स्थित या दो युद्धरत सेनाओं के मध्य की भूमि जिस पर दोनों में से किसी का अधिकार नहीं होता; असैन्य-क्षेत्र, अवांतर या मध्यवर्ती भूमि

**nomenclature** /nəˈmenklətʃə(r) नˈमेनक्लच(र्) / *noun* [U, C] (*formal*) a system of naming things, especially in science वस्तुओं का नाम रखने की प्रणाली (विशेषतः विज्ञान में) नामकरण-प्रणाली, नाम-प्रद्धति *zoological nomenclature*

**nominal** /ˈnɒmɪnl ˈनॉमिनल् / *adj.* **1** being sth in name only but not in reality नाममात्र का (न कि वास्तव में) *the nominal leader of the country* (= sb else is really in control) **2** (used about a price, sum of money, etc.) very small; much less than normal (मूल्य, धनराशि आदि) नगण्य, अत्यल्प; सामान्य से बहुत कम *Because we are friends he only charges me* ***a nominal rent.*** ▶ **nominally** /-nəli -नलि / *adv.* नाममात्र के लिए

**nominate** /ˈnɒmɪneɪt ˈनॉमिनेट् / *verb* [T] nominate sb/sth (for/as sth) to formally suggest that sb/sth should be given a job, role, prize, etc. किसी व्यक्ति या वस्तु को नौकरी, दायित्व, पुरस्कार आदि देने का औपचारिक सुझाव देना, किसी को किसी प्रयोजन से नामित करना *I would like to nominate Ram Prakash as chairman.* ○ *The novel has been nominated for the Booker Prize.* ▶ **nomination** /ˌnɒmɪˈneɪʃn ˌनॉमिˈनेशन् / *noun* [C, U] नामन, नामांकन, नाम-निर्देशन

**nominative** /ˈnɒmɪnətɪv ˈनॉमिनटिव् / *noun* [C] (*grammar*) (in some languages) the form of noun, a pronoun or an adjective when it is the subject of a verb (कुछ भाषाओं में) संज्ञा, सर्वनाम या विशेषण जो वाक्य में क्रिया का कर्त्ता बनता है ▶ **nominative** *adj.* कर्त्ता के रूप में प्रयुक्त, कर्तरि प्रयुक्त *nominative pronouns* ➪ **accusative, dative, genitive** और **vocative** देखिए।

**nominee** /ˌnɒmɪˈniː ˌनॉमिˈनी / *noun* [C] a person who is suggested for an important job, prize, etc.

किसी महत्त्वपूर्ण कार्य या पुरस्कार के लिए मनोनित व्यक्ति; नामित व्यक्ति, नॉमिनी

**non-** /nɒn नॉन्/ (*used to form compounds*) not नहीं, अ-/अन-, ग़ैर- *non-biodegradable* ○ *non-flammable*

**nona-** / nɒnə; nəʊnə ˈनॉना; ˈनोना / (*used in nouns and adjectives*) nine; having nine नौ; नौ वाला *nonagenarian* (= a person who is between 90, and 99 years old)

**non-academic** *adj.* connected with technical or practical subjects rather than subjects of interest to the mind ग़ैर-शैक्षिक, शैक्षिकेतर (तकनीकी या व्यावहारिक क्षेत्रों से संबंधित, न कि मानव-व्यवहार के अध्ययन-क्षेत्रों से)

**non-alcoholic** *adj.* (used about drinks) not containing any alcohol (पेय) ऐलकोहल-रहित *non-alcoholic drinks*

**non-aligned** *adj.* (used about a country) not providing support for or receiving support from any of the powerful countries in the world (देश) संसार के सशक्त देशों को न समर्थन देने वाला न उनसे प्राप्त करने वाला; निर्गुट, गुट-निरपेक्ष ✪ विलोम **aligned**

**nonchalant** /ˈnɒnʃələnt ˈनॉन्शलन्ट् / *adj.* not feeling or showing interest or excitement about sth उदासीन (किसी वस्तु के प्रति कोई मनोभाव, रुचि या आकर्षण अनुभव न करने वाला) ▶ **nonchalance** /-ləns -लन्स् / *noun* [U] उदासीनता ▶ **nonchalantly** *adv.* उदासीन भाव से

**non-committal** *adj.* not saying or showing exactly what your opinion is or which side of an argument you agree with अवचनबद्ध, अप्रतिबद्ध (जो न अपने विचार स्पष्टतया प्रकट करे न विवाद में किसी का पक्ष ले)

**nonconformist** /ˌnɒnkənˈfɔːmɪst ˌनॉन्कन्ˈफ़ॉमिस्ट् / *noun* [C] a person who behaves or thinks differently from most other people in society जिसके विचार या आचरण समाज के बहुसंख्यक अंश से भिन्न हैं, परंपरा-विरोधी व्यक्ति ✪ विलोम **conformist** ▶ **nonconformist** *adj.* परंपरा-विरोधी

**nondescript** /ˈnɒndɪskrɪpt ˈनॉन्डिस्क्रिप्ट् / *adj.* not having any interesting or unusual qualities जिसमें कोई आकर्षक या असाधारण गुण न हो, साधारण, मामूली

**none**[1] /nʌn नन् / *pronoun* **none (of sb/sth)** not any, not one (of a group of three or more) कोई भी नहीं, एक भी नहीं (तीन या अधिक समूह में से) *They gave me a lot of information but none of it was very helpful.* ○ *'Have you brought any books to read?' 'No, none.'*

**NOTE** **None of** का प्रयोग बहुवचनांत संज्ञा (plural noun) के साथ हो तो अर्थ के अनुसार एकवचन (singular) या बहुवचन क्रिया (plural verb) प्रयुक्त हो सकती है। यदि हमारा तात्पर्य किसी (समूह) में से कोई एक नहीं है, तो इस बात पर बल देने के लिए आएगी बहुवचन क्रिया (plural verb)—*None of these trains goes to Lucknow.* यदि तात्पर्य है 'किसी (समूह) में से कोई भी नहीं' तो बहुवचन क्रिया (plural noun) प्रयुक्त होती है—*None of the children like spinach.* यदि हम दो व्यक्तियों या वस्तुओं के विषय में बात कर रहे हों तो हम **neither** का प्रयोग करेंगे (**none** का नहीं)—*Neither of my brothers lives nearby.*

**None** और **no** के प्रयोग में अंतर पर ध्यान दीजिए। **No** का प्रयोग हमेशा संज्ञा से पहले ही होगा, परंतु **none** का प्रयोग होने पर संज्ञा लुप्त हो जाएगी—*I told him that I had **no money** left.* ○ *When he asked me how much money I had left, I told him that I had **none**.*

**none**[2] /nʌn नन् / *adv.*

**IDM** **none the wiser/worse** knowing no more than before; no worse than before जानकारी में वृद्धि नहीं, ज्यों का त्यों; जानकारी में कमी नहीं *We talked for a long time but I'm still **none the wiser**.*

**none too happy, clean, pleased, etc.** (*informal*) not very happy, clean, pleased, etc. बहुत अधिक प्रसन्न, साफ, प्रमुदित आदि नहीं

**nonentity** /nɒnˈentəti: नॉनˈऐन्टटि / *noun* [C] (*pl.* **nonentities**) a person without any significant quality or character or someone who has not achieved anything important अवस्तु, अस्तित्वहीन व्यक्ति

**nonetheless** /ˌnʌnðəˈles ˌननद्रˈलेस् / *adv.* in spite of this fact तथापि, फिर भी, इसके बावजूद भी *It won't be easy but they're going to try nonetheless.* ✪ पर्याय **nevertheless**

**non-existent** *adj.* not existing or not available अस्तित्वहीन या अनुपलब्ध

**non-fiction** *noun* [U] writing that is about real people, events and facts वास्तविक या वस्तुतः विद्यमान व्यक्तियों, घटनाओं और तथ्यों के विषय में लेखन, वास्तविकता-मूलक लेखन, अकाल्पनिक लेखन *You'll find biographies in the non-fiction section of the library.* ✪ विलोम **fiction**

**nonplussed** /ˌnɒnˈplʌst ˌनॉन्ˈप्लस्ट् / *adj.* confused; not able to understand उलझन-ग्रस्त; समझने में असमर्थ

**non-renewable** *adj.* (used about natural sources of energy such as gas or oil) that cannot be replaced after use (गैस या तेल जैसे ऊर्जा के प्राकृतिक स्रोत) जिन्हें (एक बार के बाद) दुबारा प्रयोग में नहीं लाया जा सकता; अपूर्य, अनवीकरणीय

**nonsense** /ˈnɒnsns ˈनॉन्सन्स् / *noun* [U] **1** ideas, statements or beliefs that you think are ridiculous or not true हास्यास्पद या असत्य विचार, वक्तव्य या मान्यताएँ *Don't **talk nonsense**!* **2** silly or unacceptable behaviour निरर्थक, असंगत या अनर्गल आचरण *The head teacher won't stand for any nonsense.*

**nonsensical** /nɒnˈsensɪkl नॉन् ˈसेन्सिकल् / *adj.* ridiculous; without meaning हास्यास्पद; बेतुका या असंगत

**non-smoker** *noun* [C] a person who does not smoke cigarettes or **cigars** धूम्रपान न करने वाला व्यक्ति, अधूम्रपायी व्यक्ति ✪ पर्याय **smoker** ▸ **non-smoking** *adj.* धूम्रपान-वर्जित *Would you like a table in the smoking or the non-smoking section?*

**non-starter** *noun* [C] a person, plan or idea that has no chance of success व्यक्ति, योजना या विचार जिसकी सफलता की संभावना नहीं

**non-stick** *adj.* (used about a pan, etc.) covered with a substance that prevents food from sticking to it (कढ़ाई आदि) जिस पर कुछ चिपकता नहीं

**non-stop** *adj., adv.* without a stop or a rest जिसका कोई विराम या विश्राम बिंदु या स्थल न हो, अविराम या अविश्राम, बिना रुके, सीधे *a non-stop flight to Delhi from London* ○ *He talked non-stop for two hours about his holiday.*

**non-violence** *noun* [U] fighting for political or social change without using force, for example by not obeying laws शक्ति का प्रयोग किए बिना राजनीतिक या सामाजिक परिवर्तन के लिए संघर्ष, (जैसे क़ानून को न मानकर) (सविनय अवज्ञा आंदोलन के माध्यम से); अहिंसा ▸ **non-violent** *adj.* अहिंसक

**noodle** /ˈnuːdl ˈनूड्ल् / *noun* [C, *usually pl.*] long thin strips of food made of flour, egg and water that are cooked in boiling water or used in soups सेंवई जैसा चीनी खाद्य पदार्थ; नूडल

**nook** /nʊk नुक् / *noun* [C] a small quiet place or corner (in a house, garden, etc.) छोटा शांत स्थल, एक्रांत या कोना (मकान, बग़ीचा आदि में)

**IDM** **every nook and cranny** (*informal*) every part of a place किसी स्थान के हर हिस्से में

**noon** /nuːn नून् / *noun* [U] 12 o'clock in the middle of the day; midday दोपहर, दिन के मध्य 12.00 बजे; मध्याह्न ***At noon** the sun is at its highest point in the sky.* ⇨ **midnight** देखिए।

**no one** = **nobody**[1]

**noose** /nuːs नूस् / *noun* [C] a circle that is tied in the end of a rope and that gets smaller as one end of the rope is pulled (रस्सी के एक किनारे बना) फंदा, जो रस्सी खींचने से छोटा होता जाता है; पाश

**nor** /nɔː(r) नॉ(र्) / *conj., adv.* **1 neither ... nor ...** and not और न (ही) *I have neither the time nor the inclination to listen to his complaints again.* **2** (*used before a positive verb to agree with sth negative that has just been said*) also not; neither भी नहीं; दोनों में से कोई भी नहीं *'I don't like football.' 'Nor do I.'* ○ *'We haven't been to America.' 'Nor have we.'* ✪ पर्याय इस अर्थ में **neither** का प्रयोग भी उसी प्रकार (nor की तरह) किया जा सकता है—*'I won't be here tomorrow.' 'Nor/Neither will I.'* **3** (*used after a negative statement to add some more information*) also not (कही गई बात में कुछ और जोड़ने के लिए नकारात्मक कथन के बाद प्रयुक्त) भी नहीं *Michael never forgot her birthday. Nor their wedding anniversary for that matter.*

**Nordic** /ˈnɔːdɪk ˈनॉडिक् / *adj.* **1** connected with Scandinavia, Finland and Iceland स्कैंडिनेविया, फ़िनलैंड और आइसलैंड से संबंधित; नॉर्डिक **2** typical of a member of a European race of people who are tall and have blue eyes and fair hair नॉर्डिक लोगों जैसा (यह एक यूरोपीय जाति है जिसके लोग लंबे, उनकी आँखें नीली और बाल शुभ्र होते हैं) *Nordic features*

**norm** /nɔːm नॉम् / *noun* [C] (*often with 'the'*) a situation or way of behaving that is usual or expected (प्रायः 'the' के साथ) सामान्य या प्रत्याशित आचरण वाली स्थिति या कार्यशैली; मानक, मानदंड

**normal**[1] /ˈnɔːml ˈनॉमल् / *adj.* typical, usual or ordinary; what you expect प्रतिनिधिक, सामान्य या साधारण औसत; जिसकी आशा हो, प्रत्याशित *I'll meet you at the normal time.* ○ *It's quite normal to feel angry in a situation like this.* ✪ विलोम **abnormal**

**normal**[2] /ˈnɔːml ˈनॉमल् / *noun* [U] the usual or average state, level or standard सामान्य या औसत स्थिति, स्तर या माप-दंड *temperatures above/below normal* ○ *Things are **back to normal** at work now.*

**normality** /nɔːˈmæləti नॉ ˈमैलटि / (*AmE* **normalcy** /ˈnɔːmlsi ˈनॉम्लसि /) *noun* [U] the state of being normal सामान्य होने की स्थिति

**normalize** (*also* **-ise**) /ˈnɔːməlaɪz ˈनॉमलाइज़् / *verb* [I, T] (*written*) to become or make sth become normal again or return to how it was before पुनः सामान्य हो जाना या कर देना *The two countries agreed to normalize relations* (= return to a normal, friendly relationship, for example after a disagreement or a war).

**normally** /ˈnɔːməli ˈनॉमलि/ *adv.* **1** usually सामान्यतया *I normally leave the house at 8 o'clock.* ○ *Normally he takes the bus.* **2** in the usual or ordinary way सामान्य या औसत ढंग से *His heart is beating normally.*

**north[1]** /nɔːθ नॉथ्/ *noun* [*sing.*] (*abbr.* **N**) (*also* **the north**) **1** the direction that is on your left when you watch the sun rise; one of the four main directions that we give names to **(the points of the compass)** सूर्योदय देखने की स्थिति में बाईं ओर की दिशा, उत्तर दिशा; क़ुतुबनुमा या दिक्सूचक में अंकित चार बिंदुओं में से एक *I live **to the north of*** (= further north than) *the Qutub Minar.* ➪ **compass** पर चित्र देखिए। **2** (*also* **the North**) the northern part of any country, city, region or the world किसी देश, नगर, क्षेत्र या विश्व का उत्तरी भाग *I live in the north of Delhi.* ➪ **south, east, west, magnetic north** और **true north** देखिए।

**north[2]** /nɔːθ नॉथ्/ *adj., adv.* **1** (*also* **North**) (*only before a noun*) in the north उत्तर में स्थित, उत्तरी *The new offices will be in North Bangalore.* ○ *The north wing of the hospital was destroyed in a fire.* **2** to or towards the north उत्तर दिशा में या उत्तर की ओर *The house faces north.* ○ *Is Kashmir north of Rajasthan?* **3** (used about a wind) coming from the north (वायु) उत्तर से आने वाली; उत्तरी

**North Atlantic Drift** *noun* [*sing.*] a current of warm water in the Atlantic Ocean, that has the effect of making the climate of NW Europe warmer अटलांटिक सागर की उष्ण जलधारा जिससे उत्तर-पूर्वी यूरोप की जलवायु गरम हो जाती है

**northbound** /ˈnɔːθbaʊnd ˈनॉथ्बाउन्ड्/ *adj.* travelling or leading towards the north उत्तर की ओर जाने वाला या बढ़ता हुआ; उत्तरोन्मुख *northbound traffic*

**north-east[1]** *noun* [*sing.*] (*abbr.* **NE**) (*also* **the North-East**) the direction or a region halfway between north and east उत्तर और पूर्व के मध्य की दिशा या क्षेत्र, पूर्वोत्तर या उत्तर-पर्व

**north-east[2]** *adj., adv.* in, from or to the north-east of a place or country किसी स्थान या देश के उत्तर-पूर्व या पूर्वोत्तर में, से या की ओर *the north-east coast of Australia* ○ *If you look north-east you can see the sea.* ➪ **compass** पर चित्र देखिए।

**north-easterly** *adj.* **1** towards the north-east उत्तर-पूर्व की ओर *in a north-easterly direction* **2** (used about a wind) coming from the north-east (वायु) उत्तर-पूर्व या पूर्वोत्तर से आने वाली, उत्तर-पूर्वी या पूर्वोत्तरी

**north-eastern** *adj.* (*only before a noun*) connected with the north-east of a place or country किसी स्थान या देश के उत्तर-पूर्व या पूर्वोत्तर से संबंधित, उत्तर-पूर्वी या पूर्वोत्तरी

**north-eastward(s)** *adv.* towards the north-east उत्तर-पूर्व या पूर्वोत्तर की ओर, उत्तर-पूर्वोन्मुख या पूर्वोत्तरोन्मुख *Follow the highway north-eastward.*

**northerly** /ˈnɔːðəli ˈनॉद़्लि/ *adj.* **1** to, towards or in the north उत्तर को/की ओर या उत्तर में, उत्तरीय *Keep going in a northerly direction.* **2** (used about a wind) coming from the north (वायु) उत्तर की ओर से आने वाली; उत्तरी

**northern** (*also* **Northern**) /ˈnɔːðən ˈनॉद़न्/ *adj.* of, in or from the north of a place किसी स्थान से उत्तर की ओर का, उत्तर में से *She has a northern accent.* ○ *in northern Australia*

**northerner** (*also* **Northerner**) /ˈnɔːðənə(r) ˈनॉद़न(र्)/ *noun* [C] a person who was born in or who lives in the northern part of a country किसी देश के उत्तरी भाग में जन्मा या रहने वाला व्यक्ति; उत्तरवासी ✪ विलोम **southerner**

**northernmost** /ˈnɔːðənməʊst ˈनॉद़न्मोस्ट्/ *adj.* furthest north उत्तर दिशा में सबसे दूर का या दूरतम; सुदूर उत्तरी *the northernmost island of Japan*

**the North Pole** *noun* [*sing.*] the point on the Earth's surface which is furthest north पृथ्वी की सतह पर उत्तर में दूरतम स्थान; उत्तरी ध्रुव ➪ **earth** पर चित्र देखिए।

**northward** /nɔːθwəd ˈनॉथ्वड्/ (*also* **northwards**) *adv., adj.* towards the north उत्तर की ओर, उत्तरोन्मुख *Continue northwards out of the city for about five kilometres.* ○ *in a northward direction*

**north-west[1]** *adj., adv.* in, from or to the north-west of a place or country किसी स्थान या देश के उत्तर-पश्चिम, पश्चिमोत्तर में/से या को *the north-west coast of Gujarat.* ○ *Our house faces north-west.* ➪ **compass** पर चित्र देखिए।

**north-west[2]** *noun* [*sing.*] (*abbr.* **NW**) (*also* **the North-West**) the direction or region halfway between north and west उत्तर और पश्चिम के मध्य की दिशा या क्षेत्र

**north-westerly** *adj.* **1** towards the north-west उत्तर-पश्चिम या पश्चिमोत्तर की ओर *in a north-westerly direction* **2** (used about a wind) coming from the north-west (वायु) उत्तर-पश्चिम या पश्चिमोत्तर से आने वाली, उत्तर-पश्चिमी या पश्चिमोत्तरी

**north-western** *adj.* (*only before a noun*) connected with the north-west of a place or country किसी स्थान या देश के उत्तर-पश्चिम या पश्चिमोत्तर से संबंधित, उत्तर-पश्चिमोत्तरी

**north-westward(s)** *adv.* towards the north-west उत्तर-पश्चिम या पश्चिमोत्तर की ओर *Follow the highway north-westward for ten kilometres.*

**nose**[1] /nəʊz नोज़्/ *noun* [C] **1** the part of your face, above your mouth, that is used for breathing and smelling नाक, नासिका ➪ **body** पर चित्र देखिए। **2 -nosed** (*used to form compound adjectives*) having the type of nose mentioned निर्दिष्ट प्रकार की नाक वाला *red-nosed* ○ *big-nosed* **3** the front part of a plane, spacecraft, etc. वायुयान, अंतरिक्ष यान आदि का अग्रभाग ➪ **plane** पर चित्र देखिए।

IDM **blow your nose** ➪ **blow**[1] देखिए।

**follow your nose** ➪ **follow** देखिए।

**look down your nose at sb/sth** (*BrE informal*) to think that you are better than sb else; to think that sth is not good enough for you अपने को दूसरों से बेहतर समझना; किसी वस्तु को अपने योग्य न समझना

**poke/stick your nose into sth** (*spoken*) to be interested in or try to become involved in sth which does not concern you दूसरों के मामलों में टाँग अड़ाना

**turn your nose up at sth** (*informal*) to refuse sth because you do not think it is good enough for you किसी बात पर नाक-भौं सिकोड़ना (उसे अपने लायक न मानना)

**nose**[2] /nəʊz नोज़्/ *verb* [I] (used about a vehicle) to move forward slowly and carefully (वाहन) मंद गति और सावधानी से आगे बढ़ना

PHR V **nose about/around** (*informal*) to look for sth, especially private information about sb सूँघ-सूँघ कर पता लगाना (विशेषतः किसी की निजी बातों का)

**nosebleed** /ˈnəʊzbliːd ˈनोज़्ब्लीड् / *noun* [C] a sudden flow of blood that comes from your nose नकसीर (नाक से ख़ून का एकाएक प्रवाह)

**nosedive** /ˈnəʊzdaɪv ˈनोज़्डाइव् / *noun* [C] a sudden sharp fall or drop एकाएक गिरावट या कमी *Oil prices **took a nosedive** in the crisis.* ▶ **nosedive** *verb* [I] एकाएक गिरावट या कमी आना

**nostalgia** /nɒˈstældʒə नॉˈस्टैल्जा / *noun* [U] a feeling of pleasure, mixed with sadness, when you think of happy times in the past अतीत के सुखद प्रसंगों की याद से उभरी आनंद और विषाद की मिश्रित भावना; गृहातुरता *She was suddenly filled with **nostalgia for** her childhood days.* ▶ **nostalgic** /-dʒɪk -जिक् / *adj.* अतीत की सुखद स्मृति में खोया हुआ; गृहातुर ▶ **nostalgically** /-dʒɪkli -जिक्लि / *adv.* अतीत की सुखद स्मृति में डूबते हुए

**nostril** /nɒstrəl ˈनॉस्ट्रल्/ *noun* [C] one of the two openings at the end of your nose that you breathe through नथुना, नासाछिद्र ➪ **body** पर चित्र देखिए।

**nosy** (*also* **nosey**) /ˈnəʊzi ˈनोज़ि / *adj.* too interested in other people's personal affairs दूसरों के निजी मामलों में बहुत रुचि रखने वाला, ताक-झाँकिया *a nosy neighbour*

**not** /nɒt नॉट् / *adv.* **1** used to form the negative with the verbs **be**, **do** and **have** (**auxilliary verb**) and with verbs such as **can**, **must**, **will**, etc. (**modal verbs**). *Not* is often pronounced or written *n't* in informal situations सहायक क्रियाओं 'be', 'do' और 'have' तथा 'can', 'must', 'will' आदि वृत्तिवाचक क्रियाओं के साथ निषेधवाचक वाक्य बनाने में प्रयुक्त अनौपचारिक प्रसंगों में not का उच्चारणगत या लिखित रूप *'n't'* होता है *I cannot/can't see from here.* ○ *You're German, aren't you?* **2** used to give the following word or phrase a negative meaning एकदम अगले शब्द या वाक्यांश को निषेध का अर्थ देने के लिए प्रयुक्त *He told me not to telephone.* ○ *She accused me of not telling the truth.* **3** used to give a short negative reply संक्षेप में 'न' कहने के लिए प्रयुक्त *'Do you think they'll get caught in the storm?' 'I hope not.'* (= I hope that they will not.) ○ *'Can I borrow Rs 20?'* ***'Certainly not!'*** **4** used with or to give a negative possibility निषेध की संभावना व्यक्त करने के लिए 'or' के साथ प्रयुक्त *Shall we tell her **or not**?*

IDM **not at all 1** used as a way of replying when sb has thanked you धन्यवाद का उत्तर देने में प्रयुक्त *'Thanks for the present.' 'Not at all, don't mention it.'* **2** used as a way of saying 'no' or 'definitely not' 'नहीं' या 'बिलकुल नहीं' कहने के लिए प्रयुक्त *'Do you mind if I come too?' 'Not at all.'*

**not only... (but) also** used for emphasizing the fact that there is something more to add कहने के लिए कुछ और भी है, इस बात पर बल देने के लिए प्रयुक्त *They not only have two houses in Mumbai, they also have one in Kolkata.*

**notable** /ˈnəʊtəbl ˈनोटब्ल् / *adj.* **notable (for sth)** interesting or important enough to receive attention (पर्याप्त रोचक या महत्त्वपूर्ण होने के कारण) ध्यान देने योग्य *The area is notable for its wildlife.*

**notably** /ˈnəʊtəbli ˈनोटब्लि / *adv.* used for giving an especially important example of what you are talking about चर्चित प्रसंग का विशेषतया उल्लेखनीय उदाहरण देने के लिए प्रयुक्त, विशेष रूप से *Several politicians, most notably the Prime Minister and the Home Secretary, have given the proposal their full support.*

**notation** /nəʊˈteɪʃn नो'टेश्न् / *noun* [U, C] a system of symbols that represent information, especially in mathematics, science and music (विशेषतः) गणित, विज्ञान और संगीत की विषय-वस्तु की अंकन-पद्धति

**notch¹** /nɒtʃ नॉच् / *noun* [C] **1** a level on a scale of quality गुणवत्ता के मापक्रम का एक स्तर, बिंदु या दर्जा *This meal is certainly **a notch above** the last one we had here.* **2** a cut in an edge or surface in the shape of a V or a circle, sometimes used to help you count sth (किसी वस्तु में बना) V या शून्य के आकार का खाँचा (कभी-कभी कुछ गिनने के लिए प्रयुक्त)

**notch²** /nɒtʃ नॉच् / *verb*

**PHR V notch sth up** to score or achieve sth कोई वस्तु बना लेना या पा लेना *Lewis notched up his best ever time in the 100 metres.*

**note¹** /nəʊt नोट् / *noun* **1** [C] some words that you write down quickly to help you remember sth किसी बात को याद रखने में सहायक फुरती से लिखी गई संक्षिप्त भाषा, फुरती से टाँके गए शब्द और वाक्यांश; विवरण *I'd better **make a note of** your name and address.* ○ ***Keep a note of** who has paid and who hasn't.* **2** [C] a short letter छोटा पत्र, पुरज़ा, नोट, रुक्का *If Raj's not at home we'll leave a note for him.* **3** [C] a short explanation or extra piece of information that is given at the back of a book, etc. or at the bottom or side of a page टिप्पणी, पाद-टिप्पणी (पुस्तक के अंत में पृष्ठ के नीचे या किनारे दिया गया संक्षिप्त स्पष्टीकरण या अतिरिक्त जानकारी) ➪ **footnote** देखिए। **4** [C] (*also* **banknote**) (*AmE* **bill**) a piece of paper money करेंसी नोट, काग़ज़ी सिक्का *I'd like the money in ten-rupee notes, please.* **5** [C] a single musical sound made by a voice or an instrument; a written sign that represents a musical sound संगीत का स्वर (मौखिक या वाद्य से उत्पन्न); संगीत के स्वर का चिह्न *I can only remember the first few notes of the song.* **6** [*sing.*] something that shows a certain quality or feeling जिससे कोई विशेषता या भाव प्रकट हो *The meeting ended on a rather unpleasant note.*

**IDM compare notes (with sb)** ➪ **compare** देखिए।

**take note (of sth)** to pay attention to sth and be sure to remember it किसी बात पर ध्यान देना और उसे निश्चयपूर्वक याद रखना या किसी बात पर पक्के तौर पर ध्यान देना

**note²** /nəʊt नोट् / *verb* [T] **1** to notice or pay careful attention to sth किसी बात पर ग़ौर करना या अच्छी तरह ध्यान देना *He noted a slight change in her attitude towards him.* ○ *Please note that this office is closed on Tuesdays.* **2** to mention sth किसी बात का उल्लेख करना *I'd like to note that the project has so far been extremely successful.*

**PHR V note sth down** to write sth down so that you remember it किसी बात को लिख देना (ताकि वह याद रहे)

**notebook** /ˈnəʊtbʊk ˈनोट्बुक् / *noun* [C] a small book in which you write things that you want to remember कापी, नोटबुक

**noted** /ˈnəʊtɪd ˈनोटिड् / *adj.* (*formal*) **noted (for/as sth)** well known; famous जाना-माना, विख्यात; प्रसिद्ध *The hotel is noted for its food.*

**notepad** /ˈnəʊtpæd ˈनोट्पैड् / *noun* [C] some sheets of paper in a block that are used for writing things on नोटपैड

**notepaper** /ˈnəʊtpeɪpə(r) ˈनोट्पेप(र्) / *noun* [U] paper that you write letters on पत्र लिखने में प्रयुक्त काग़ज़, पत्र-काग़ज़

**noteworthy** /ˈnəʊtwɜːði ˈनोट्वदि / *adj.* interesting or important; that is worth noticing रोचक या महत्त्वपूर्ण, उल्लेखनीय; ध्यान देने योग्य, विचारणीय

**nothing** /ˈnʌθɪŋ ˈनथिङ् / *pronoun* not anything; nothing कुछ नहीं; नगण्य, शून्यप्राय *I'm bored—there's **nothing to do** here.* ○ *There was **nothing else** to say.* ➪ **zero** पर नोट देखिए।

**IDM be/have nothing to do with sb/sth** to have no connection with sb/sth किसी व्यक्ति या वस्तु से कुछ लेना-देना नहीं *That question has nothing to do with what we're discussing.* ○ *Put my diary down—it's nothing to do with you.*

**come to nothing** ➪ **come** देखिए।

**for nothing** **1** for no good reason or with no good result बिना पुष्ट कारण के, अकारण, व्यर्थ ही में; बिना अनुकूल या वांछित परिणाम के, निष्फल रूप में, बेकार *His hardwork was all for nothing.* **2** for no payment; free बिना भुगतान किए; मुफ़्त में, निःशुल्क *Children under four are allowed in for nothing.*

**nothing but** only केवल, सिर्फ़ *He does nothing but sit around watching TV all day.*

**nothing like** **1** not at all like के जैसा बिल्कुल नहीं *She looks nothing like either of her parents.* **2** not at all; not nearly बिल्कुल नहीं; लगभग नहीं *There's nothing like enough food for all of us.*

**nothing much** not a lot of sth; nothing of importance अधिक नहीं; कोई विशेष बात नहीं *It's a nice town but there's nothing much to do in the evenings.*

**(there's) nothing to it** (it's) very easy (इसमें) कुछ भी नहीं, (यह) बहुत आसान हैं *You'll soon learn—there's nothing to it really.*

**there is/was nothing (else) for it (but to do sth)** there is/was no other action possible (इसके सिवाय) कोई चारा नहीं था *There was nothing for it but to resign.*

**notice**[1] /ˈnəʊtɪs ˈनोटिस्/ *noun* **1** [U] the act of paying attention to sth or knowing about sth किसी बात पर ध्यान देने या किसी के विषय में जानने की क्रिया *The protests are finally making the government* ***take notice****.* ○ ***Take no notice of*** *what he said—he was just being silly.* ○ *Some people don't take any notice of* (= choose to ignore) *speed limits.* **2** [C] a piece of paper or a sign giving information, a warning, etc. that is put where everyone can read it नोटिस, सूचना, चेतावनी (लिखित या मुद्रित) (सबकी जानकारी के लिए) *There's a notice on the board saying that the meeting has been cancelled.* ○ *The notice said 'No dogs allowed'.* **3** [U] a warning that sth is going to happen चेतावनी (आगे होने वाली बात की) *I can't produce a meal* ***at*** *such* ***short notice****!* ○ *The swimming pool is closed* ***until further notice*** (= until we are told that it will open again).

**notice**[2] /ˈnəʊtɪs ˈनोटिस्/ *verb* [I, T] (*not usually used in the continuous tenses*) to see and become conscious of sth किसी बात को देखना और सतर्क हो जाना *'What kind of car was the man driving?' 'I'm afraid I didn't notice.'* ○ *I noticed (that) he was carrying a black briefcase.*

**noticeable** /ˈnəʊtɪsəbl ˈनोटिसबल्/ *adj.* easy to see or notice जो सहज ही दिखाई पड़े या जिस पर सहज ही ध्यान जाए, स्पष्ट या ध्यानाकर्षक *The scar from the accident was hardly noticeable.* ▶ **noticeably** /-əbli -अब्लि/ *adv.* स्पष्टतया, ध्यानाकर्षक या उल्लेखनीय रूप से

**noticeboard** /ˈnəʊtɪsbɔːd ˈनोटिस्बॉड्/ (*AmE* **bulletin board**) *noun* [C] a board on a wall for putting written information where everyone can read it नोटिस-बोर्ड, सूचना-पट्ट

**notify** /ˈnəʊtɪfaɪ ˈनोटिफ़ाइ/ *verb* [T] (*pres. part.* **notifying;** *3rd person sing. pres.* **notifies;** *pt, pp* **notified**) **notify sb (of sth)** to inform sb about sth officially किसी विषय पर आधिकारिक रूप से किसी को सूचित करना, अधिसूचित करना ▶ **notification** /ˌnəʊtɪfɪˈkeɪʃn ˌनोटिफ़िˈकेश्न्/ *noun* [C, U] अधिसूचना, अधिसूचन (अधिसूचित करने की क्रिया)

**notion** /ˈnəʊʃn ˈनोश्न्/ *noun* [C] **a notion (that.../of sth)** something that you have in your mind; an idea मन में कोई बात, ख़याल; विचार, धारणा *I had a vague notion that I had seen her before.*

**notional** /ˈnəʊʃənl ˈनोशनल्/ *adj.* existing only in the mind; not based on facts or reality ख़याली, काल्पनिक; तथ्यों या वास्तविकता पर आधारित नहीं

**notoriety** /ˌnəʊtəˈraɪəti ˌनोटराइअटि/ *noun* [U] the state of being well known for sth bad बदनाम, कुख्याति

**notorious** /nəʊˈtɔːriəs नोˈटॉरिअस्/ *adj.* **notorious (for/as sth)** well known for sth bad बदनामी, कुख्याति *a notorious drug dealer* ○ *This road is notorious for the number of accidents on it.* ✪ पर्याय **infamous** ▶ **notoriously** *adv.* कुख्यात रूप से, बदनाम होकर या बदनामी के साथ

**notwithstanding** /ˌnɒtwɪθˈstændɪŋ ˌनॉट्विथ्ˈस्टैन्डिङ्/ *prep., adv.* (*written*) in spite of sth के बावजूद (भी)

**nougat** /ˈnuːɡɑː ˈनूगा/ *noun* [U] a hard sweet containing nuts that is pink or white in colour गुलाबी या सफ़ेद रंग की मेवों वाली एक कड़ी मिठाई

**nought** /nɔːt नॉट्/ (*AmE* **zero**) *noun* [C] the figure 0 शून्य का अंक *A million is written with six noughts.* ○ *We say 0.1 'nought point one'.*

IDM **noughts and crosses** a game for two players in which each person tries to win by writing three 0s or three Xs in a line दो खिलाड़ियों वाला एक खेल जिसमें खिलाड़ी को जीतने के लिए एक ही पंक्ति में तीन शून्य (0) या तीन एक्स (X) लिखने होते हैं

**noun** /naʊn नाउन्/ *noun* [C] (*grammar*) a word that is the name of a thing, an idea, a place or a person संज्ञा; वस्तु, विचार, स्थान या व्यक्ति के नाम का सूचक शब्द *'Water', 'happiness', 'James' and 'India' are all nouns.* ➪ **countable** और **uncountable** देखिए।

**nourish** /ˈnʌrɪʃ ˈनरिश्/ *verb* [T] **1** to give sb/sth the right kind of food so that he/she/it can grow and be healthy (किसी को) पोषक भोजन देकर पुष्ट और स्वस्थ बनाना **2** (*formal*) to allow a feeling, an idea, etc. to grow stronger किसी मनोभाव, विचार आदि को बढ़ावा देना ▶ **nourishment** *noun* [U] पोषण, संवर्धन

**Nov.** *abbr.* November नवंबर *17 Nov. 2001*

**nova** /ˈnəʊvə ˈनोवा/ *noun* [C] (*pl.* **novae** /-viː -व़ी/ or **novas**) (*technical*) a star that suddenly becomes much brighter for a short period ऐसा तारा जिसका प्रकाश क्षणभर के लिए बहुत तीव्र हो जाए; नवतारा ➪ **supernova** देखिए।

**novel**[1] /nɒvl ˈनॉव्ल्/ *noun* [C] a book that tells a story about people and events that are not real उपन्यास, कल्पना-प्रसूत कथा *a romantic/historical/detective novel*

**novel**[2] /ˈnɒvl ˈनॉव्ल्/ *adj.* new and different नया और भिन्न *That's a novel idea! Let's try it.*

**novelist** /ˈnɒvəlɪst ˈनॉवलिस्ट्/ *noun* [C] a person who writes novels उपन्यासकार

**novelty** /ˈnɒvlti ˈनॉव्ल्टि/ *noun* (*pl.* **novelties**) **1** [U] the quality of being new and different

नवीनता और भिन्नता *The novelty of her new job soon wore off.* **2** [C] something new and unusual नई और असाधारण-सी वस्तु *It was quite a novelty not to have to get up early.* **3** [C] a small, cheap object that is sold as a toy or decoration छोटा और सस्ता खिलौना या सजावट का सामान

**November** /nəʊˈvembə(r) नोˈवे़म्ब(र्)/ *noun* [U, C] (*abbr.* **Nov.**) the eleventh month of the year, coming after October नवंबर (का महीना)

NOTE महीनों के नामों के वाक्य-प्रयोग विधि के लिए **January** पर नोट तथा उसके उदाहरण देखिए।

**novice** /ˈnɒvɪs ˈनॉविस्/ *noun* [C] a person who is new and without experience in a certain job, situation, etc. किसी विशेष काम, परिस्थिति आदि के लिए नया और अनुभवहीन व्यक्ति; नौसिखिया ✪ पर्याय **beginner**

**now** /naʊ नाउ/ *adv., conj.* **1** (at) the present time अब, इस समय ***From now on** I'm going to work harder.* ○ ***Up till now** we haven't been able to afford a house of our own.* ○ *He will be on his way home **by now**.* ○ *I can manage **for now** but I might need some help later.* **2** immediately तुरंत, अभी *You must go to the doctor **right now**.* **3** used to introduce or to emphasize what you are saying, or while pausing to think अपनी बात को प्रस्तुत करने या उस पर बल देने, या सोचने के लिए क्षण-भर रुकने का अर्थ व्यक्त करने के लिए प्रयुक्त *Now listen to what he's saying.* ○ *What does he want now?* ○ *Now, let me think.* NOTE इस अर्थ में **now then** का प्रयोग भी होता है—*Now then, what was I saying?* **4 now (that)...** because of the fact that अब (क्योंकि), क्योंकि बात यह है कि *Now (that) the children have left home we can move to a smaller house.*

IDM **any moment/second/minute/day (now)** ➪ **any** देखिए।

**(every) now and again/then** from time to time; occasionally समय-समय पर; कभी-कभी *We see each other now and then, but not very often.*

**just now** ➪ **just**[1] देखिए।

**right now** ➪ **right**[2] देखिए।

**nowadays** /ˈnaʊədeɪz ˈनाउअडेज़्/ *adv.* at the present time (when compared with the past) आजकल (पहले की तुलना में) *I don't go to London much nowadays* (= but I did in the past). ✪ पर्याय **today**

**nowhere** /ˈnəʊweə(r) ˈनोवेअ(र्)/ *adv.* not in or to any place; not anywhere किसी स्थान में या पर; कहीं नहीं *I'm afraid there's nowhere to stay in this village.* ○ *I don't like it here, but there's **nowhere else** for us to sit.*

IDM **get nowhere (with sth)** to not make any progress with sth किसी मामले में प्रगति न होना

**in the middle of nowhere** ➪ **middle**[1] देखिए।

**nowhere near** ➪ **near**[1] देखिए।

**noxious** /ˈnɒkʃəs ˈनॉक्शस्/ *adj.* (*formal*) harmful or poisonous हानिकर या विषैला *noxious gases*

**nozzle** /ˈnɒzl ˈनॉज़्ल्/ *noun* [C] a narrow tube that is put on the end of a pipe to control the liquid or gas coming out पाइप की ट्यूबदार टोंटी ➪ **gardening** पर चित्र देखिए।

**nr** *abbr.* (used in addresses) near (चिट्ठी के पतों पर प्रयुक्त) के पास *YMCA, nr Parliament Street*

**nuance** /ˈnjuːɑːns ˈन्यूआन्स्/ *noun* [C] a very small difference in meaning, feeling, sound, etc. अर्थ, मनोभाव, ध्वनि आदि में सूक्ष्म अंतर

**nuclear** /ˈnjuːkliə(r) ˈन्यूक्लिअ(र्)/ *adj.* **1** using, producing or resulting from the energy that is produced when the central part (**nucleus**) of an atom is split आणविक या नाभिकीय ऊर्जा *nuclear energy* ○ *a nuclear power station* ➪ **atomic** देखिए। **2** connected with the nucleus of an atom परमाणु के नाभिक से संबंधित *nuclear physics*

**nuclear disarmament** *noun* [U] stopping the use and development of nuclear weapons परमाणु-अस्त्रों के प्रयोग और विकास पर विराम, परमाणिक निःस्त्रीकरण

**nuclear fission** = **fission**

**nuclear-free** *adj.* not having or allowing nuclear weapons or nuclear energy जहाँ परमाणु-अस्त्र या परमाणु-ऊर्जा की न उपस्थिति हो न अनुमति; परमाणु-मुक्त *This town has been declared a nuclear-free zone.*

**nuclear fusion** = **fusion**

**nuclear physics** *noun* [U] the scientific study of the centres (**nuclei**) of atoms, especially of how energy can be produced from them परमाणु-नाभिकों का वैज्ञानिक अध्ययन (विशेषतः ऊर्जा-उत्पादन की विधि की दृष्टि से); परमाण्विक भौतिकी

**nuclear reactor** (*also* **reactor**) *noun* [C] a very large machine that produces nuclear energy परमाणु-ऊर्जा उत्पन्न करने का संयंत्र; परमाणु-रिएक्टर

**nucleic acid** /njuːˌkliːɪk ˈæsɪd न्यूˌक्लीक् ˈऐसिड्/ *noun* [U] either of two acids (**DNA** and **RNA**), that are present in all living cells सभी सजीव कोशिकाओं में उपस्थित दो एसिडों – DNA और RNA – में से कोई एक

**nucleus** /njuːkliəs ˈन्यूक्लिअस्/ *noun* [C] (*pl.* **nuclei** /-kliaɪ -क्लिआइ/) **1** the central part of an atom or of certain cells परमाणु या कतिपय कोशिकाओं का केंद्रीय भाग **2** the central or most important part of sth किसी वस्तु का केंद्रीय या सबसे महत्त्वपूर्ण अंश

**nude**[1] /nju:d न्यूड्/ *adj.* not wearing any clothes वस्त्ररहित, नग्न ➪ **bare** और **naked** भी देखिए।
▶ **nudity** /ˈnju:dəti ˈन्यूड्टि/ *noun* [U] नग्नता

**nude**[2] /nju:d न्यूड्/ *noun* [C] a picture or photograph of a person who is not wearing any clothes वस्त्ररहित व्यक्ति का चित्र या फ़ोटो

IDM **in the nude** not wearing any clothes नग्नावस्था में

**nudge** /nʌdʒ नज्/ *verb* [T] to touch or push sb/sth with your elbow किसी व्यक्ति या वस्तु को कोहनी से स्पर्श करना या धक्का देना ▶ **nudge** *noun* [C] धक्का *to give sb a nudge*

**nuisance** /ˈnju:sns ˈन्यूसन्स्/ *noun* [C] a person, thing or situation that annoys you or causes you trouble परेशानी पैदा करने वाला व्यक्ति, वस्तु या स्थिति *It's a nuisance having to queue for everything.*

**null** /nʌl नल्/ *adj.*

IDM **null and void** (*written*) not valid in law क़ानूनन अमान्य

**numb** /nʌm नम्/ *adj.* not able to feel anything; not able to move सुन्न (अंग); जड़ *I'll give you an injection and the tooth will* ***go numb***. ○ *My fingers were numb with cold.* ▶ **numb** *verb* [T] सुन्न या जड़ कर देना *We were numbed by the dreadful news.* ▶ **numbness** *noun* [U] सुन्नता, संज्ञा- शून्यता या जड़ीभूतता

**number**[1] /ˈnʌmbə(r) ˈनम्ब(र्)/ *noun* **1** [C] a word or symbol that indicates a quantity संख्या (मात्रा-सूचक शब्द या संकेत) *The numbers 2, 4, 6, etc. are* ***even numbers*** *and 1, 3, 5, etc. are* ***odd numbers***. ○ *a three-figure number* (= from 100 to 999) **2** [C] a group of numbers that is used to identify sb/sth किसी व्यक्ति या वस्तु की पहचान कराने वाली संख्या-क्रम *a telephone number* ○ *a code number* **3** [C, U] **a number (of sth)** a quantity of people or things व्यक्तियों या वस्तुओं की संख्या *Pupils in the school have doubled* ***in number*** *in recent years.* ○ *There are* ***a number of*** (= several) *things I don't understand.* **4** [C] (*abbr.* **No.**) (*symbol #*) used before a number to show the position of sth in a series एक श्रृंखला में किसी वस्तु का क्रम स्थान दिखाने के लिए प्रयुक्त; क्रमांक *Room No. 347* **5** [C] a copy of a magazine, newspaper, etc. समाचार पत्र, पत्रिका आदि की प्रति *Back numbers of 'New Scientist' are available from the publishers.* **6** [C] (*informal*) a song or dance गान या नृत्य

IDM **any number of** very many अनेकानेक *There could be any number of reasons why she hasn't arrived yet.*

**in round figures/numbers** ➪ **round**[1] देखिए।

**opposite number** ➪ **opposite** देखिए।

**number**[2] /ˈnʌmbə(r) ˈनम्ब(र्)/ *verb* [T] **1** to give a number to sth किसी वस्तु को कोई संख्या देना या लगाना *The houses are numbered from 1 to 52.* **2** used for saying how many people or things there are व्यक्तियों या वस्तुओं की संख्या बताने के लिए प्रयुक्त *Our forces number 40,000.*

**number plate** (*AmE* **license plate**) *noun* [C] the sign on the front and back of a vehicle that shows a particular combination of numbers and letters (**the registration number**) वाहन के आगे और पीछे लगी वाहन की पंजीकरण संख्या बताने या दिखाने वाली प्लेट (इस संख्या में अंक भी होते हैं अक्षर भी)

**numeracy** /ˈnju:mərəsi ˈन्यूमरसि/ *noun* [U] a good basic knowledge of mathematics; the ability to work with and understand numbers अंकगणित के मूलतत्वों का अच्छा ज्ञान, बुनियादी या आधारिक अंक-ज्ञान; अंक-ज्ञान और अंक-व्यवहार की क्षमता *standards of literacy and numeracy*

**numeral** /ˈnju:mərəl ˈन्यूमरल्/ *noun* [C] a sign or symbol that represents a quantity मात्रा या संख्या का सूचक चिह्न या प्रतीक, अंक, संख्यात्मक *Roman numerals* (= I, II, III, IV, etc.)

**numerate** /ˈnju:mərət ˈन्यूमरट्/ *adj.* having a good basic knowledge of mathematics अंकगणित के मूल तत्वों का अच्छा जानकार; गणन कुशल ➪ **literate** देखिए।

**numerator** /ˈnju:məreɪtə(r) ˈन्यूमरेट(र्)/ *noun* [C] (*mathematics*) the number above the line in a **fraction**, for example the 3 in ¾ भिन्न में रेखा के ऊपर की संख्या, अंश (जैसा ¾ में 3) ➪ **denominator** देखिए।

**numerical** /nju:ˈmerɪkl न्यूˈमेरिकल्/ *adj.* of or shown by numbers संख्याओं से सूचित, संख्यात्मक या संख्यावार *to put sth* ***in numerical order***

**numerous** /ˈnju:mərəs ˈन्यूमरस्/ *adj.* (*formal*) existing in large numbers; many बहुत सारे, बड़ी संख्या में; अनेक

**nun** /nʌn नन्/ *noun* [C] a member of a religious group of women who live together in a special building (**a convent**) away from other people साध्वी (किसी धार्मिक समुदाय की तपस्विनी जो अन्य सदस्यों के साथ पृथक आश्रम में रहती है) ➪ **monk** देखिए।

**nurse**[1] /nɜ:s नस्/ *noun* [C] a person who is trained to look after sick or injured people रोगियों और घायलों की देखभाल के लिए प्रशिक्षित व्यक्ति (पुरुष या महिला), नर्स *a male nurse* ○ *a psychiatric nurse*

**nurse**[2] /nɜːs नस्/ *verb* **1** [T] to take care of sb who is sick or injured; to take care of an injury रोगी या घायल की परिचर्या करना; चोट का इलाज करवाना *She nursed her mother back to health.* ○ *Ahmed is still nursing a back injury.* **2** [T] to hold sb/sth in a loving way किसी व्यक्ति या वस्तु को प्यार से हाथों या गोद में लेना *He nursed the child in his arms.* **3** [T] (*formal*) to have a strong feeling or idea in your mind for a long time लंबी अवधि तक किसी प्रबल भाव या विचार को मन में रखना *Rahul had long nursed the hope that Raima would marry him.* **4** [I, T] to feed a baby or young animal with milk from the breast; to drink milk from the mother's breast स्तनों से मनुष्य या पशु के शिशु को दूध पिलाना; माँ के स्तनों से दूध पीना

**nursery** /ˈnɜːsəri ˈनसरि/ *noun* [C] (*pl.* **nurseries**) **1** a place where small children and babies are looked after so that their parents can go to work शिशुपालन-गृह, शिशु-सदन, नर्सरी (जहाँ शिशुओं के माता-पिता काम पर जाने से पहले उन्हें छोड़ जाते हैं) ➪ **créche** देखिए। **2** a place where young plants are grown and sold पौध-शाला, नर्सरी (जहाँ छोटे पौधे उगाए और बेचे जाते है)

**nursery rhyme** *noun* [C] a traditional poem or song for young children परंपरागत शिशुगीत, बालगीत

**nursery school** (*also* **playgroup; playschool**) *noun* [C] a school for children aged from three to five शिशु-पाठशाला (तीन से पाँच वर्ष तक के शिशुओं के लिए), नर्सरी स्कूल ➪ **kindergarten** देखिए।

**nursing** /ˈnɜːsɪŋ ˈनसिङ्/ *noun* [U] the job of being a nurse नर्स के रूप में कार्य करना, नर्स का कार्य, नर्सिंग (का व्यवसाय)

**nursing home** *noun* [C] a small private hospital, often for old people छोटा निजी अस्पताल, नर्सिंग होम (प्रायः वृद्धों के लिए)

**nurture**[1] /ˈnɜːtʃə(r) ˈनच(र्)/ *verb* [T] **1** to look after and protect sb/sth while he/she/it are growing and developing बढ़ते बच्चों या पौधों आदि की देखभाल और रक्षा करना, पालना-पोसना **2** to encourage sth to develop and to help it succeed विकास और सफलता-प्राप्ति के लिए प्रोत्साहित करना *This is a talent which should be nurtured.*

**nurture**[2] /ˈnɜːtʃə(r) ˈनच(र्)/ *noun* [U] care, encouragement and support for sb/sth while he/she/it is growing and developing बढ़ते बच्चों या पौधों आदि की देखभाल, प्रोत्साहन और सहायता

**nut** /nʌt नट्/ *noun* [C] **1** a dry fruit that consists of a hard shell with a seed inside. Many types of nuts can be eaten कड़े छिलके वाला मेवा (अख़रोट, बादाम, काजू आदि) (कई प्रकार के मेवे खाए जा सकते हैं) **2** a small piece of metal with a round hole in the middle through which you screw a long round piece of metal (**a bolt**) to fasten things together (बोल्ट में लगाने का) नट, टिबरी या क़ाबला ➪ **bolt** पर चित्र देखिए।

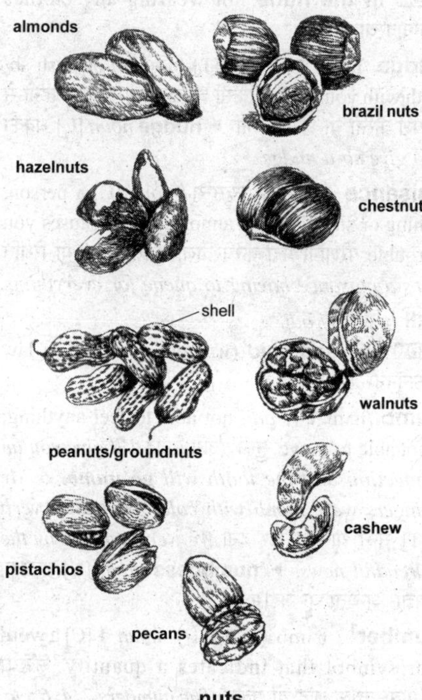


nuts

**nutcrackers** /ˈnʌtkrækəz ˈनट्क्रैकज़्/ *noun* [*pl.*] a tool that you use for breaking open the shell of a nut अख़रोट आदि मेवों के छिलकों को तोड़ने या काटने वाला सरौता

**nutmeg** /ˈnʌtmeg ˈनट्मेग्/ *noun* [C, U] a type of hard seed that is often made into powder and used as a spice in cooking जायफल; (एक प्रकार का कठोर दाना जिसे पीसकर खाने के मसालों के रूप में प्रयोग करते हैं)

**nutrient** /ˈnjuːtriənt ˈन्यूट्रिअन्ट्/ *noun* [C] (*technical*) a substance that is needed to keep a living thing alive and to help it grow पोषक तत्व (जीवन-रक्षा और शारीरिक विकास के लिए आवश्यक) भोजक, पुष्टिकर *Plants get minerals and other nutrients from the soil.*

**nutrition** /njuˈtrɪʃn न्युˈट्रिश्न्/ *noun* [U] the food that you eat and the way that it affects your health स्वास्थ्य को पुष्ट करने वाला भोजन, पोषाहार ▶ **nutritional** /-ʃənl -शनल्/ *adj.* पोषण संबंधी, आहार विषयक

**nutritious** /nju'trɪʃəs न्यु'ट्रिशस्/ *adj.* (used about food) very good for you (भोजन) पोषक तत्वों से युक्त

**nuts** /nʌts नट्स्/ *adj.* (*informal*) (*not before a noun*) crazy पागल *She's driving me nuts with her stupid questions.*

**nutshell** /'nʌtʃel 'नट्शेल्/ *noun*

IDM **in a nutshell** using few words संक्षेप में

**nutty** /'nʌti 'नटि/ *adj.* containing or tasting of nuts मेवों वाला या मेवों के स्वाद वाला

**nuzzle** /'nʌzl 'नज़्ल्/ *verb* [I, T] to press or rub sb/sth gently with the nose किसी को हलके-से नाक से दबाना या रगड़ना

**NW** *abbr.* north-west(ern) उत्तर-पश्चिमी *NW Australia*

**nylon** /'naɪlɒn 'नाइलॉन्/ *noun* [U] a very strong man-made material that is used for making clothes, rope, brushes, etc. नाइलोन (जिससे कपड़े, रस्सियाँ, ब्रश आदि बनाते हैं)

**nymph** /nɪmf निम्फ़्/ *noun* [C] (in Greek and Roman stories) a spirit in the form of a young woman that lives in rivers, woods, etc. (ग्रीक, रोमन तथा अन्य देशों की कथाओं में कल्पित) परी, अप्सरा (जो वनों, नदियों आदि में रहती है)

# O o

**O, o** /əʊ ओ/ *noun* [C, U] (*pl.* **O's; o's** /əʊz ओज़्/) **1** the fifteenth letter of the English alphabet अंग्रेज़ी वर्णमाला का पंद्रहवाँ अक्षर (o) *'Orange' begins with an 'O'.* **2** (used when you are speaking) zero (बोलचाल में प्रयुक्त) शून्य *My number is five o nine double four* (= 50944). ➪ **zero** पर नोट देखिए।

**oak** /əʊk ओक्/ *noun* **1** (*also* **oak tree**) [C] a type of large tree with hard wood that is common in many northern parts of the world शाहबलूत वृक्ष (इसकी लकड़ी सख़्त होती है और यह विश्व के उत्तरी भागों में काफ़ी पाया जाता है) NOTE शाहबलूत के फल को **acorn** कहते हैं। **2** [U] the wood from the oak tree शाहबलूत की लकड़ी *a solid oak table*

**oar** /ɔ:(r) ऑ(र्)/ *noun* [C] a long pole that is flat and wide at one end and that you use for moving a small boat through water **(rowing)** ➪ **paddle** देखिए तथा **boat** पर चित्र देखिए।

**oasis** /əʊˈeɪsɪs ओˈएसिस्/ *noun* [C] (*pl.* **oases** /-si:z -सीज़्/) a place in the desert where there is water and where plants grow नख़लिस्तान, मरूद्वीप, मरूद्यान (मरूभूमि में जल और पेड़-पौधों वाला क्षेत्र)

**oath** /əʊθ ओथ्/ *noun* [C] **1** a formal promise शपथ (औपचारिक रूप से ली गई सौगंध) *They have to* ***swear/take an oath*** *of loyalty.* **2** (*old-fashioned*) = **swear word**

IDM **be on/under oath** to have made a formal promise to tell the truth in a court of law न्यायालय में सच कहने के लिए शपथ-बद्ध

**oatmeal** /ˈəʊtmi:l ˈओट्मील्/ *noun* [U] **1** flour made from a particular type of grain **(oats)** that is used to make biscuits, cakes, etc. जई का आटा (जिससे बिस्कुट, केक आदि बनते हैं) **2** a pale brown colour हलका भूरा रंग

**oats** /əʊts ओट्स्/ *noun* [*pl.*] a type of grain that is used as food for people and animals जई, जुई, जुंदरी (जिससे मनुष्यों और पशुओं के खाद्य पदार्थ बनते हैं) ➪ **cereal** पर चित्र देखिए।

**obedient** /əˈbi:diənt अˈबीडिअन्ट्/ *adj.* **obedient (to sb/sth)** doing what you are told to do आज्ञाकारी *As a child he was always obedient to his parents.* ✪ विलोम **disobedient** ▶ **obedience** *noun* [U] आज्ञाकारिता ▶ **obediently** *adv.* आज्ञापालन करते हुए

**obese** /əʊˈbi:s ओˈबीस्/ *adj.* (used about people) very fat, in a way that is not healthy (व्यक्ति) बहुत मोटा, स्थूलकाय (जो स्वस्थ होने का लक्षण नहीं) ▶ **obesity** /əʊˈbi:səti ओˈबीसटि/ *noun* [U] मोटापा, स्थूलता

**obey** /əˈbeɪ अˈबे/ *verb* [I, T] to do what you are told to do आज्ञा का पालन करना *Soldiers are trained to obey orders* ✪ विलोम **disobey**

**obituary** /əˈbɪtʃuəri अˈबिचुअरि/ *noun* [C] (*pl.* **obituaries**) a piece of writing about a person's life that is printed in a newspaper soon after he/she has died शोक-समाचार, निधन-सूचना (व्यक्ति के निधनोपरांत समाचार पत्रों में उसका जीवन-वृत्त)

**object**[1] /ˈɒbdʒɪkt ˈऑब्जिक्ट्/ *noun* [C] **1** a thing that can be seen and touched, but is not alive वस्तु जिसे देखा और स्पर्श किया जा सकता है, परंतु उसमें चेतना नहीं होती वस्तु, पदार्थ *The shelves were filled with objects of all shapes and sizes.* ○ *everyday/household objects* **2** an aim or purpose लक्ष्य या उद्देश्य *Making money is his sole object in life.* **3 the object of sth** (*written*) a person or thing that causes a feeling, interest, thought, etc. किसी मनोभाव, रुचि, विचार आदि को प्रेरित या जाग्रत करने वाला व्यक्ति या वस्तु *the object of his desire/affections/interest* **4** (*grammar*) the noun or phrase describing the person or thing that is affected by the action of a verb कर्म (क्रिया की कार्यशीलता से प्रभावित व्यक्ति या वस्तु का सूचक संज्ञा शब्द या वाक्यांश)

NOTE निम्नलिखित वाक्यों—*I sent a letter to Meera.* ○ *I sent Meera a letter.* में **'a letter'** क्रिया का **direct object** है और 'Meera' उसका **indirect object** है। ➪ **subject** देखिए।

IDM **money, etc. is no object** money, etc. is not important or is no problem पैसे की कोई बात नहीं (लक्ष्य की दृष्टि से पैसा न महत्त्वपूर्ण है न समस्या) *They always want the best. Expense is no object.*

**object**[2] /əbˈdʒekt अब्ˈजेक्ट्/ *verb* **1** [I] **object (to sb/sth); object (to doing sth/to sb doing sth)** to not like or to be against sb/sth किसी व्यक्ति या वस्तु को नापसंद करना, उसके विरुद्ध होना *Many people object to the new tax.* ○ *I object to companies trying to sell me things over the phone.* **2** [T] to say a reason why you think sth is wrong किसी बात के ग़लत होने का कारण बताना, ऐतराज़ करना, आपत्ति उठाना *'I think that's unfair,' he objected.* ▶ **objector** *noun* [C] आपत्तिकर्ता

**objection** /əbˈdʒekʃn अब्ˈजेक्शन्/ *noun* [C] an **objection (to sb/sth); an objection (to doing sth/to sb doing sth)** a reason why you do not like or are against sb/sth आपत्ति, ऐतराज़; किसी व्यक्ति या वस्तु के प्रति नापसंदगी या विरोध का कारण *We listed* *our objections to the proposed new road.* ○ ***I have no objection*** *to you using my desk while I'm away.*

**objectionable** /əbˈdʒekʃənəbl अब्ˈजेक्शनब्ल्/ *adj.* very unpleasant आपत्ति-योग्य, अत्यंत अप्रिय

**objective**[1] /əbˈdʒektɪv अब्ˈजेक्टिव़्/ *noun* [C] **1** something that you are trying to achieve; an aim वह वस्तु जिसकी प्राप्ति के लिए हम प्रयत्नशील हों; लक्ष्य, ध्येय *Our objective is to finish by the end of the year.* ○ *to achieve your objective* **2** (*also* **objective lens**) (*technical*) the **lens** that is nearest to the object being looked at in a **microscope** (जो लेन्स सूक्ष्मवीक्षण यंत्र से देखी जा रही वस्तु के सबसे निकट हो; अभिदृश्यक लेन्स ➪ **laboratory** पर चित्र देखिए।

**objective**[2] /əbˈdʒektɪv अब्ˈजेक्टिव़्/ *adj.* not influenced by your own personal feelings; considering only facts व्यक्तिगत भावनाओं से प्रभावित नहीं; केवल तथ्यों पर आधारित; वस्तुनिष्ठ *Please try and give an objective report of what happened.* ○ *It's hard to be objective about your own family.* ✪ विलोम **subjective** ▶ **objectively** *adv.* वस्तुनिष्ठ रूप से ▶ **objectivity** /ˌɒbdʒekˈtɪvəti ˌऑब्जेक्ˈटिव़टि/ *noun* [U] वस्तुनिष्ठता

**obligation** /ˌɒblɪˈgeɪʃn ˌऑबलिˈगेश्न्/ *noun* [C, U] **(an) obligation (to sb) (to do sth)** the state of having to do sth because it is a law or duty, or because you have promised क़ानूनी बाध्यता या कर्तव्य-भावना, या वचनबद्धता *The shop is* ***under*** *no* ***obligation*** *to give you your money back.* ○ *We* ***have an obligation*** *to help people who are in need.*

**obligatory** /əˈblɪgətri अˈब्लिगट्रि/ *adj.* (*formal*) that you must do अनिवार्य, बाध्यकर *It is obligatory to get insurance before you drive a car.* ✪ विलोम **optional**

**oblige** /əˈblaɪdʒ अˈब्लाइज्/ *verb* **1** [T] (*usually passive*) to force sb to do sth किसी व्यक्ति को बाध्य करना (किसी काम के लिए) *Rima was obliged to find a job after her father died.* **2** [I, T] (*formal*) to do what sb asks; to be helpful किसी के अनुरोध पर उसका काम करना; (किसी के लिए) सहायक होना *If you ever need any help, I'd be happy to oblige.* ▶ **obliged** *adj.* उपकृत, अनुगृहीत, आभारी *Thanks for your help. I'm* ***much obliged*** *to you.* ▶ **obliging** *adj.* उपकारी, अनुग्रह करने वाला *I asked my neighbour for advice and he was very obliging.*

**oblique**[1] /əˈbliːk अˈब्लीक्/ *adj.* **1** not expressed or done in a direct way अप्रत्यक्ष रूप से व्यक्त या संपादित; परोक्ष ✪ पर्याय **indirect** **2** (used about a line) at an angle; sloping (रेखा) कोण बनाती, तिरछी; ढलवाँ **3** used to describe an angle that is not an angle of 90° तिर्यक कोण 90 डिग्री से छोटा कोण, *The extension was built at an oblique angle to the house.* ▶ **obliquely** *adv.* परोक्ष रूप से

**oblique**[2] /əˈbliːk अˈब्लीक्/ *noun* [C] (*BrE*) = **slash**[2] **3**

**obliterate** /əˈblɪtəreɪt अˈब्लिटरेट्/ *verb* [T] (*formal*) (*usually passive*) to remove all signs of sth by destroying or covering it completely किसी वस्तु के सब चिह्नों को मिटा देना (उन्हें पूर्णतया नष्ट करना या छिपा देना); मिटाना

**oblivion** /əˈblɪviən अˈब्लिविअन्/ *noun* [U] **1** a state in which you do not realize what is happening around you, usually because you are unconscious or asleep चेतना-शून्यता की स्थिति (क्योंकि व्यक्ति बेहोश, संज्ञाहीन या सोया हुआ है) *I was in a state of complete oblivion.* **2** the state in which sb/sth has been forgotten and is no longer famous or important किसी व्यक्ति या वस्तु को लोगों द्वारा भुला दिया जाने की स्थिति; विस्मृति, गुमनामी, अप्रसिद्धि *His work* ***faded into oblivion*** *after his death.*

**oblivious** /əˈblɪviəs अˈब्लिविअस्/ *adj.* **oblivious (to/of sb/sth)** not noticing or realizing what is happening around you आस-पास होने वाली घटनाओं से बेख़बर *She was completely oblivious of all the trouble she had caused.*

**oblong** /ˈɒblɒŋ ˈऑब्लॉङ्/ *adj., noun* [C] (of) a shape with two long sides and two short sides and four angles of 90° (**right angles**) आयताकार (ऐसे चतुर्भुज जिसमें दो भुजाएँ लंबी हों, दो छोटी और चारों कोने समकोण हों) ➪ **rectangle** देखिए।

**obnoxious** /əbˈnɒkʃəs अब्ˈनॉक्शस्/ *adj.* extremely unpleasant, especially in a way that offends people बहुत बुरा लगने वाला; घृणित, घिनौना

**oboe** /ˈəʊbəʊ ओबो/ *noun* [C] a musical instrument made of wood that you play by blowing through it शहनाई या नफ़ीरी जैसा वाद्य (जिसे फूँक मार कर बजाया जाता है)

**obscene** /əbˈsiːn अब्ˈसीन्/ *adj.* **1** connected with sex in a way that most people find disgusting and which causes offence अश्लील *obscene books/gestures/language* **2** very large in size or amount in a way that some people find unacceptable आकार या मात्रा की दृष्टि से इतना अधिक कि अशोभनीय लगे *He earns an obscene amount of money.*

**obscenity** /əbˈsenəti अब्ˈसेनटि/ *noun* (*pl.* **obscenities**) **1** [C] sexual words or acts that shock people and cause offence अश्लील शब्द या चेष्टाएँ (लोगों को स्तब्ध कर देने वाली और अपमानजनक)

*He shouted a string of obscenities out of the car window.* **2** [U] sexual language or behaviour, especially in books, plays, etc. which shocks people and causes offence अश्लील भाषा का आचरण (विशेषतः पुस्तकों में, जो लोगों के लिए स्तब्धकारी और अपमानजनक हो)

**obscure[1]** /əbˈskjʊə(r) अब्ˈस्क्युअ(र्)/ *adj.* **1** not well known अप्रसिद्ध *an obscure Spanish poet* **2** not easy to see or understand जो आसानी से दिखाई न पड़े या समझ में न आए, धुँधला या दुर्बोध ***For some obscure reason**, he decided to give up his well-paid job, to become a writer.* ▶ **obscurity** /əbˈskjʊərəti अब्ˈस्क्युअरटि/ *noun* [U] अप्रसिद्धि, दुर्बोधता

**obscure[2]** /əbˈskjʊə(r) अब्ˈस्क्युअ(र्)/ *verb* [T] to make sth difficult to see or understand किसी वस्तु या प्रसंग को धुँधला या दुर्बोध बना देना

**observance** /əbˈzɜːvəns अब्ˈज़व़न्स्/ *noun* [U, *sing.*] **observance (of sth)** the practice of obeying or following a law, custom, etc. क़ानून, प्रथा आदि का पालन या प्रथा आदि का अनुसरण

**observant** /əbˈzɜːvənt अब्ˈज़व़न्ट्/ *adj.* good at noticing things around you आस-पास की अच्छी खोज-ख़बर रखने वाला; चौकस, सतर्क *An observant passerby gave the police a full description of the men.*

**observation** /ˌɒbzəˈveɪʃn ˌऑब्ज़ˈव़ेश्न्/ *noun* **1** [U] the act of watching sb/sth carefully, especially to learn sth किसी व्यक्ति या वस्तु का सावधानी से निरीक्षण (विशेषतः कुछ जानने के लिए) *My research involves the observation of animals in their natural surroundings.* ○ *The patient is being kept* ***under observation***. **2** [U] the ability to notice things निरीक्षण या प्रेक्षण-क्षमता *Scientists need good* ***powers of observation.*** **3** [C] **an observation (about/on sth)** something that you say or write about sth टिप्पणी, कथन *He began by making a few general observations about the sales figures.* ➪ **remark** और **comment** भी देखिए।

**observatory** /əbˈzɜːvətri अब्ˈज़व़ट्रि/ *noun* [C] (*pl.* **observatories**) a building from which scientists can watch the stars, the weather, etc. वेधशाला (वह भवन जहाँ से वैज्ञानिक तारों, मौसम आदि का प्रेक्षण-निरीक्षण करते हैं)

**observe** /əbˈzɜːv अब्ˈज़व्/ *verb* [T] **1** to watch sb/sth carefully, especially to learn more about him/her/it किसी व्यक्ति या वस्तु का ध्यानपूर्वक निरीक्षण (विशेषतः उसके विषय में जानकारी बढ़ाने के लिए) *We observed the birds throughout the breeding season.* **2** (*formal*) to see or notice sb/sth किसी व्यक्ति या वस्तु को देखना या उस पर ध्यान देना *A man and a woman were observed leaving by the back door.* **3** (*formal*) to make a comment कोई टिप्पणी करना *'We're late,' she observed.* **4** (*formal*) to obey a law, rule, etc. क़ानून, नियम आदि का पालन करना *to observe the speed limit*

**observer** /əbˈzɜːvə(r) अब्ˈज़व़(र्)/ *noun* [C] **1** a person who watches sb/sth दर्शक *According to observers, the plane exploded shortly after take-off.* **2** a person who attends a meeting, lesson, etc. to watch and listen but who does not take part प्रेक्षण (किसी बैठक, कक्षा-पाठ आदि में उपस्थित व्यक्ति जो कार्रवाई को देखता-सुनता है परंतु उसमें भाग नहीं लेता)

**obsess** /əbˈses अब्ˈसेस्/ *verb* [T] (*usually passive*) **be obsessed (about/with sb/sth)** to completely fill your mind so that you cannot think of anything else किसी बात को दिमाग़ में ऐसे भर लेना कि कुछ और न सूझे, किसी बात से मन का पूर्णतया आविष्ट या ग्रस्त हो जाना *He became obsessed with getting his revenge.*

**obsession** /əbˈseʃn अब्ˈसेश्न्/ *noun* **obsession (with sb/sth)** **1** [U] the state in which you can only think about one person or thing so that you cannot think of anything else मनोग्रस्तता (ऐसी मानसिक स्थिति जिसमें केवल एक व्यक्ति या वस्तु के विषय में ही सोचा जा सके) *the tabloid press's obsession with the sordid details of the affair* **2** [C] a person or thing that you think about too much व्यक्ति या वस्तु जिसके विषय में कोई बहुत अधिक सोचे

**obsessive** /əbˈsesɪv अब्ˈसेसिव़्/ *adj.* thinking too much about one particular person or thing; behaving in a way that shows this किसी व्यक्ति या वस्तु विशेष के विषय में बहुत अधिक सोचने वाला, ख़ब्ती; ख़ब्तभरा आचरण करने वाला *He's obsessive about not being late.* ○ *obsessive cleanliness*

**obsolete** /ˈɒbsəliːt ˈऑब्सलीट्/ *adj.* no longer useful because sth better has been invented प्रयोग की दृष्टि से पुरानी पड़ चुकी (क्योंकि उसका स्थान नई वस्तु ने ले लिया है); प्रयोगबाह्य, अब अप्रचलित, अव्यवहृत

**obstacle** /ˈɒbstəkl ˈऑब्स्टक्ल्/ *noun* [C] **an obstacle (to sth/doing sth)** something that makes it difficult for you to do sth or go somewhere बाधा, अड़चन, अवरोध *Not speaking a foreign language was a major obstacle to her career.*

**obstacle course** *noun* [C] **1** a series of objects that competitors in a race have to climb over, under, through, etc. बाधा-दौड़ के लिए संयोजित बाधाकारी वस्तुओं की शृंखला या बाधाकारी वस्तुओं वाला मार्ग **2** a series of difficulties that people have to deal with in order to achieve a particular aim विशिष्ट लक्ष्य की प्राप्ति के मार्ग में आने वाली बाधाओं की शृंखला **3** (*AmE*) = **assault course**

**obstetrician** /ˌɒbstəˈtrɪʃn ˌऑबस्ट्ˈट्रिश्न्/ *noun* [C] a hospital doctor who looks after women who are pregnant प्रसूति-विज्ञान चिकित्सक, यह गर्भिणी महिलाओं की चिकित्सा करता या करती है

**obstetrics** /əbˈstetrɪks अब्ˈस्टेट्रिक्स्/ *noun* [U] the area of medicine connected with the birth of children प्रसूति-विज्ञान

**obstinate** /ˈɒbstɪnət ˈऑब्स्टिनट्/ *adj.* refusing to change your opinions, way of behaving, etc. when other people try to persuade you to हठी, दुराग्रही दूसरों के लाख कहने पर भी, अपनी बात से न हटने वाला व्यक्ति *an obstinate refusal to apologize* ✪ पर्याय **stubborn** ▶ **obstinacy** /ˈɒbstɪnəsi ˈऑब्स्टिनसि/ *noun* [U] दुराग्रह, हठ ▶ **obstinately** *adv.* दुराग्रहपूर्वक

**obstruct** /əbˈstrʌkt अब्ˈस्ट्रक्ट्/ *verb* [T] to stop sth from happening or sb/sth from moving either by accident or deliberately किसी के काम में अड़चन डालना या रुकावट पैदा करना (अनजाने में या जानबूझ कर) *Could you move on, please? You're obstructing the traffic if you park there.*

**obstruction** /əbˈstrʌkʃn अब्ˈस्ट्रक्श्न्/ *noun* **1** [U] the act of stopping sth from happening or moving बाधा, रुकावट, अड़चन, अवरोध **2** [C] a thing that stops sb/sth from moving or doing sth बाधक वस्तु *This car is **causing an obstruction**.*

**obstructive** /əbˈstrʌktɪv अब्ˈस्ट्रक्टिव्/ *adj.* trying to stop sb/sth from moving or doing sth बाधाकारी या बाधक; अवरोधक

**obtain** /əbˈteɪn अब्ˈटेन्/ *verb* [T] (*formal*) to get sth कुछ प्राप्त करना *to obtain advice/information/permission*

**obtainable** /əbˈteɪnəbl अब्ˈटेनब्ल्/ *adj.* that you can get प्राप्य, सुलभ *That make of vacuum cleaner is no longer obtainable.*

**obtuse** /əbˈtjuːs अब्ˈट्यूस्/ *adj.* (*formal*) slow to or not wanting to understand sth मंदबुद्धि ▶ **obtuseness** *noun* [U] मंदबुद्धिता या बुद्धि की मंदता

**obtuse angle** *noun* [C] (*mathematics*) an angle between 90° and 180° अधिक कोण, 90 और 180 डिग्री के बीच का कोण ➪ **acute angle, reflex angle** और **right angle** देखिए तथा **angle** पर चित्र देखिए।

**obvious** /ˈɒbviəs ˈऑब्विअस्/ *adj.* **obvious (to sb)** easily seen or understood; clear जो आसानी से दिखाई दे या समझ में आए; स्पष्ट ***For obvious reasons**, I'd prefer not to give my name.* ○ *His disappointment was obvious to everyone.* ▶ **obviously** *adv.* स्पष्ट रूप से *There has obviously been a mistake.*

**occasion** /əˈkeɪʒn अˈकेश्न्/ *noun* **1** [C] a particular time when sth happens अवसर, मौका, समय विशेष जब कुछ घटित हो *I have met Jai on two occasions.* **2** [C] a special event, ceremony, etc. कोई विशेष कार्यक्रम, कर्म-कांड आदि *Their wedding was a memorable occasion.* **3** [*sing.*] the suitable or right time (for sth) किसी बात का उपयुक्त या सही समय *I shall tell her what I think if the occasion arises* (= if I get the chance).

> NOTE जब यह निर्देश करना हो कि किसी कार्य के लिए समय सही या उपयुक्त है तो शब्द **occasion** प्रयुक्त होता है—*I saw them at the funeral, but it was not a suitable occasion for discussing holiday plans.* **Opportunity** या **chance** का अर्थ है, अमुक काम को करना संभव है—*I was only in Delhi for one day and I didn't get the opportunity/chance to visit the Qutub Minar.*

IDM **on occasion(s)** sometimes but not often कभी-कभी (न कि प्रायः)

**occasional** /əˈkeɪʒənl अˈकेशनल्/ *adj.* done or happening from time to time but not very often कभी-कभार या यदा-कदा (न कि अधिक बार) किया जाने या होने वाला; अनियत, कदाचित, अवसरोचित *We have the occasional argument but most of the time we get on.* ▶ **occasionally** /-nəli -नलि/ *adv.* कभी-कभी, प्रसंगवश *We see each other occasionally.*

**occlusion** /əˈkluːʒn अˈक्लूश़्न्/ *noun* (*technical*) **1** [U] the closing or blocking of a **blood vessel** or an organ of the body शरीर के किसी अंग की रुधिर वाहिका का बंद हो जाना या उसमें अवरोध आना **2** [C] a process by which, when a band of cold air meets and passes a band of warm air in the atmosphere, the warm air is pushed upwards off the earth's surface पृथ्वी की सतह से उष्ण वायु के ऊपर की ओर जाने की प्रक्रिया (जब वायुमंडल में शीतल वायु की पट्टी उष्ण वायु पट्टी से मिलते हुए आगे बढ़ जाती है)

**occult** /ˈɒkʌlt ˈऑकल्ट्/ *adj.* **1** (*only before a noun*) connected with magic powers and things that cannot be explained by reason or science जादुई, रहस्यात्मक (तर्क या विज्ञान से परे) **2 the occult** /əˈkʌlt अˈकल्ट्/ *noun* [*sing.*] magic powers, ceremonies, etc. जादू-टोना, तंत्र-मंत्र

**occupant** /ˈɒkjəpənt ˈऑक्यपन्ट्/ *noun* [C] a person who is in a building, car, etc. at a particular time समय विशेष में किसी भवन में रहने वाला, कार में बैठा हुआ (आदि) व्यक्ति, दख़लकार, अधिभोक्ता

**occupation** /ˌɒkjuˈpeɪʃn ˌऑक्युˈपेश्न्/ *noun* **1** [C] (*written*) a job or profession; the way in which you spend your time नौकरी या व्यवसाय; समय-यापन का ढंग *Please state your occupation* *on the form.* ➪ **work²** पर नोट देखिए। **2** [U] the act of the army of one country taking control of another country; the period of time that this situation lasts एक देश की सेना का दूसरे देश पर अधिकार कर लेना, सैनिक आधिपत्य; सैनिक आधिपत्य की अवधि *the Roman occupation of Britain* **3** [U] the act of living in or using a room, building, etc. कमरे, भवन आदि में रहना या उसका उपयोग करना; अधिभोग

**occupational** /ˌɒkjuˈpeɪʃənl ˌऑक्यु ˈपेशनल्/ *adj.* (*only before a noun*) connected with your work व्यवसाय-विषयक *Accidents are an* ***occupational hazard*** (= a risk connected with a particular job) *on building sites.*

**occupied** /ˈɒkjupaɪd ˈऑक्युपाइड्/ *adj.* **1** (*not before a noun*) being used by sb किसी के द्वारा उपयोग में लाया जा रहा भरा हुआ, घिरा हुआ (ख़ाली नहीं) *Is this seat occupied?* **2** busy doing sth किसी काम में व्यस्त *Looking after the children keeps me fully occupied.* ➪ **preoccupied** देखिए। **3** (used about a country or a piece of land) under the control of another country (कोई देश या भूक्षेत्र) किसी अन्य देश के आधिपत्य में

**occupier** /ˈɒkjupaɪə(r) ˈऑक्युपाइअ(र्)/ *noun* [C] (*written*) a person who owns, lives in or uses a house, piece of land, etc. वह व्यक्ति जो किसी भवन, भूक्षेत्र आदि का स्वामी, निवासी या उपयोगकर्ता हो; अधिभोक्ता व्यक्ति

**occupy** /ˈɒkjupaɪ ˈऑक्युपाइ/ *verb* [T] (*pres. part.* **occupying;** *3rd person sing. pres.* **occupies;** *pt, pp* **occupied**) **1** to fill a space or period of time स्थान या समय घेरना *The large table occupied most of the room.* ✪ पर्याय **take up** **2** (*formal*) to live in or use a house, piece of land, etc. किसी भवन, भूक्षेत्र आदि में रहना या उसका उपयोग करना **3** to take control of a building, country, etc. by force किसी भवन, देश आदि पर बलपूर्वक अधिकार कर लेना **4 occupy sb/yourself** to keep sb/yourself busy किसी व्यक्ति या स्वयं को व्यस्त रखना

**occur** /əˈkɜː(r) अˈक(र्)/ *verb* [I] (**occurring; occurred**) **1** (*formal*) to happen, especially in a way that has not been planned कुछ घटित हो जाना (प्रायः अचानक) *The accident occurred late last night.* ➪ **happen** पर नोट देखिए। **2** to exist or be found somewhere होना या कहीं पाया जाना *The virus occurs more frequently in children.* **3 occur to sb** (used about an idea or a thought) to come into your mind (भाव या विचार) मन में आना, सूझना *It never occurred to Sunil that his wife might be unhappy.*

**occurrence** /əˈkʌrəns अˈकरन्स्/ *noun* [C] something that happens or exists घटना (जो घटित या विद्यमान हो)

**ocean** /ˈəʊʃn ˈओशन्/ *noun* **1** [U] (*AmE*) the mass of salt water that covers most of the surface of the earth विशाल जलराशि, विस्तृत जलसमूह *Two thirds of the earth's surface is covered by ocean.* **2** [C] (*also* **Ocean**) one of the five main areas into which the water is divided महासागर (विशाल जलराशि के पाँच खंडों में से एक) *the Atlantic/Indian/Pacific Ocean* ➪ **sea** देखिए।

IDM **a drop in the ocean** ➪ **drop²** देखिए।

**oceanic** /ˌəʊʃiˈænɪk ˌओशिˈऐनिक्/ *adj.* connected with the oceans महासागर से संबंधित

**oceanography** /ˌəʊʃəˈnɒgrəfi ˌओशˈनॉग्रफ़ि/ *noun* [U] the scientific study of the ocean महासागर का वैज्ञानिक अध्ययन; समुद्र-विज्ञान

**ochre** (*AmE* **ocher**) /ˈəʊkə(r) ˈओक(र्)/ *noun* [U] a pale brownish-yellow colour हलका पीला-भूरा रंग, गेरु ▶ **ochre** *adj.* गेरुआ

**o'clock** /əˈklɒk अˈक्लॉक्/ *adv.* used after the numbers one to twelve for saying what the time is समय बताने के लिए एक से बारह तक की संख्याओं के बाद प्रयुक्त, बजे (जैसे दो बजे) *Lunch is at twelve o'clock.*

> NOTE ध्यान रखिए **O'clock** का प्रयोग केवल पूरे घंटों के बाद ही हो सकता है—*We arranged to meet a 5 o'clock.* ○ *It's 5 o' clock already and he's still not here.*

**Oct.** *abbr.* October अक्तूबर *13 Oct. 2001*

**octa-** /ˈɒktə ˈऑक्टा/ *prefix* (*used in nouns, adjectives and adverbs*) eight; having eight आठ; आठ वाला, अष्ट- (जैसे अष्टकोणीय) *octagon* ○ *octagonal*

**octagon** /ˈɒktəgən ˈऑक्टगन्/ *noun* [C] a shape that has eight straight sides अष्टभुज, आठ सीधी भुजाओं वाली आकृति ▶ **octagonal** /ɒkˈtægənl ऑक्ˈटैगनल्/ *adj.* अष्टभुजाकार, अष्टभुजीय

**octane** /ˈɒkteɪn ˈऑक्टेन्/ *noun* [U] a chemical substance in petrol that is used for measuring its quality पेट्रोल में उपस्थित एक रसायन जिसके आधार पर पेट्रोल की गुणवत्ता आँकी जाती है; ऑक्टेन *high-octane fuel*

**octo-** /ˈɒktəʊ ˈऑक्टो/ *prefix* (*used in nouns, adjectives and adverbs*) eight; having eight आठ; आठ वाला, अष्ट- *octogenarian*

**October** /ɒkˈtəʊbə(r) ऑक्ˈटोब(र्)/ *noun* [U, C] (*abbr.* **Oct.**) the tenth month of the year, coming after September वर्ष का दसवाँ महीना, अक्तूबर

> NOTE महीनों के नामों की वाक्य-प्रयोग विधि के लिए **January** पर नोट तथा उदाहरण देखिए।

**octopus** /ˈɒktəpəsˈऑक्टपस्/ *noun* [C] (*pl.* **octopuses**) a sea animal with a soft body and eight long arms **(tentacles)** कोमल शरीर और आठ लंबी भुजाओं वाला समुद्री जीव अष्ट स्पर्शक समुद्री जीव (समुद्री हाथी); अष्टभुज

**odd** /ɒd ऑड्/ *adj.* **1** strange; unusual विचित्र; असाधारण *There's something odd about him.* ○ *It's a bit odd that she didn't phone to say she couldn't come.* ✪ पर्याय **peculiar** **2 odd-** (*used to form compound adjectives*) strange or unusual in the way mentioned निर्दिष्ट प्रकार से विचित्र या असाधारण *an odd-sounding name* **3** (*only before a noun*) not regular or fixed; happening sometimes जो व्यवस्थित या निश्चित न हो; कभी-कभी होने वाला *He makes the odd mistake, but nothing very serious.* **4** (*only before a noun*) that is left after other similar things have been used अन्य सदृश वस्तुओं के प्रयोग से बचा हुआ; अवशिष्ट *He made the bookshelves out of a few odd bits of wood.* **5** not with the pair or set it belongs to; not matching जो अपने युग्म या सेट से जुड़ा न हो, वियुग्म, इकल्ला; मेल न खाने वाला, अनमेल *You're wearing odd socks.* **6** (used about a number) that cannot be divided by two (संख्या) विषम (जो दो से विभक्त न हो सके) *One, three, five and seven are all odd numbers.* ✪ विलोम **even** **7** (usually used after a number) a little more than (प्रायः किसी संख्या के बाद प्रयुक्त) किसी से कुछ अधिक *'How old do you think he is?' 'Well, he must be thirty-odd, I suppose.'* ▶ **oddly** *adv.* विचित्र रूप से (विचित्र बात है कि) ***Oddly enough**, the most expensive tickets sold fastest.* ▶ **oddness** *noun* [U] विचित्रता

IDM **the odd man/one out** one that is different from all the others in a group वर्ग के अन्य सदस्यों से भिन्न, अलग-थलग पड़ा (व्यक्ति) *Her brothers and sisters were much older than she was. She was always the odd one out.*

**oddity** /ˈɒdəti ˈऑडटि/ *noun* (*pl.* **oddities**) [C] a person or thing that is unusual असामान्य, विचित्र व्यक्ति या वस्तु अनोखापन

**odd jobs** *noun* [*pl.*] small jobs or tasks of various types फुटकर काम, अनेक प्रकार के छोटे काम

**oddment** /ˈɒdmənt ˈऑड्मन्ट्/ *noun* [C, *usually pl.*] (*BrE*) a small piece of material, wood, etc. that is left after the rest has been used इस्तेमाल हो जाने के बाद बची वस्तुएँ (लकड़ी आदि), फुटकर सामान

**odds** /ɒdz ऑड्ज़्/ *noun* [*pl.*] **the odds (on/against sth/sb)** the degree to which sth is likely to happen; the probability of sth happening वह सीमा या मात्रा जहाँ तक कोई घटना घट सकती है या संभावित है; किसी घटना के घटित होने की संभाव्यता *The odds on him surviving are very slim* (= he will probably die). ○ *The odds are against you* (= you are not likely to succeed). ○ *The odds are in your favour* (= you are likely to succeed).

IDM **against (all) the odds** happening although it seemed impossible समस्त प्रतिकूलताओं के होते हुए भी

**be at odds (with sb) (over sth)** to disagree with sb about sth किसी व्यक्ति से किसी बात पर मतभेद होना, अनबन होना

**be at odds (with sth)** to be different from sth, when the two things should be the same किसी वस्तु से भिन्न हो जाना (आशा और संभावना के विपरीत)

**odds and ends** (*BrE informal*) small things of little value or importance बेकार का-सा छुटपुट सामान

**ode** /əʊd ओड्/ *noun* [C] a poem that is written for a special occasion or that speaks to a particular person or thing विशेष अवसर के लिए या विशेष व्यक्ति या वस्तु को लक्ष्य कर लिखी गई कविता, संबोधन कविता *Keats's 'Ode to a Nightingale'*

**odious** /ˈəʊdiəs ˈओडिअस्/ *adj.* (*formal*) extremely unpleasant अत्यधिक अरुचिकर

**Odissi** *noun* [U] (*IndE*) a traditional dance form from the state of Orissa which originated in the temples ओडिसी; उड़ीसा का पारंपरिक नृत्य (मंदिरों में उत्पन्न)

**odometer** /əʊˈdɒmɪtə(r) ओˈडॉमिट(र्)/ (*AmE*) = **milometer**

**odour** (*AmE* **odor**) /ˈəʊdə(r) ˈओड(र्)/ *noun* [C] (*formal*) a smell (often an unpleasant one) गंध (प्रायः बुरी)

**odourless** (*AmE* **odorless**) /ˈəʊdələs ˈओडलस्/ *adj.* without a smell गंधरहित

**odyssey** /ˈɒdɪsi ˈऑडिसि/ *noun* (*pl.* **odysseys**) **1** (*literary*) a long eventful and adventurous journey or experience घटनापूर्ण एवं साहसिक भ्रमण **2 Odyssey** an epic poem written by the Greek poet, Homer, describing an adventurous journey यूनानी कवि होमर द्वारा कृत भ्रमण महाकाव्य 'ऑडसी'

**oesophagus** (*AmE* **esophagus**) /iˈsɒfəgəs इˈसॉफ़गस्/ *noun* [C, *usually sing.*] (*formal*) the tube through which food passes from your mouth to your stomach भोजन की नली (जो भोजन को मुख से आमाशय या उदर तक पहुँचाती है) ✪ पर्याय **gullet** ➪ **body** तथा **epiglottis** पर चित्र देखिए।

**oestrogen** (*AmE* **estrogen**) /ˈi:strədʒən ˈईस्ट्रजन्/ *noun* [U] a substance (**hormone**) produced in a woman's body that makes her develop female physical and sexual characteristics and that causes the body to prepare to become pregnant अंडाशय-रस (स्त्री के शरीर में उत्पन्न होने वाला विशेष हार्मोन जिसके प्रभाव से वह कामुक रूप से आकर्षक तथा गर्भधारण के लिए तत्पर हो जाती है) ➪ **progesterone** और **testosterone** देखिए।

**of** /əv; *strong form* ɒv अव्; प्रबल रूप ऑव्/ *prep.* **1** belonging to, connected with, or part of sth/sb किसी व्यक्ति या वस्तु के स्वामित्ववाला, से संबंधित या उसका भाग; का *the back of the book* ○ *the leader of the party* ○ *a friend of mine* (= one of my friends) **2** made, done or produced by sb किसी व्यक्ति द्वारा बनाया हुआ, किया हुआ या उत्पादित; का *the poems of Rabindranath Tagore* **3** used for saying what sb/sth is or what a thing contains or is made of यह बताने के लिए प्रयुक्त कि किसी व्यक्ति या वस्तु की क्या विशेषता है या उसमें क्या (रखा) है, या वह किससे बनी है; का *a woman of intelligence* ○ *It's made of silver.* **4** showing sb/sth किसी व्यक्ति या वस्तु को दिखाते हुए; का *a map of Jaipur* ○ *a photograph of my parents* **5** showing that sb/sth is part of a larger group यह दिखाते हुए कि कोई व्यक्ति या वस्तु किसी बड़े समूह का अंग है; अंगागि-संबंध का द्योतक *some of the people* ○ *three of the houses* **6** with measurements, directions and expressions of time and age माप-तोल की इकाइयों, दिशाओं तथा समय और युग के वाचक शब्दों के साथ प्रयुक्त *a girl of 12* ○ *an increase of 2.5%* **7** indicating the reason for or cause of sth किसी बात की तर्कपूर्णता या उसके होने के कारण का संकेत करने वाला; से *He died of pneumonia.* **8** with some adjectives कुछ विशेषणों के साथ प्रयुक्त *I'm proud of you.* ○ *She's jealous of her.* **9** with some verbs कुछ क्रियाओं के साथ प्रयुक्त *This perfume smells of roses.* ○ *It reminds me of you.* **10** used after a noun describing an action to show either who did the action or who it happened to ऐसे कार्य के सूचक संज्ञा शब्द के बाद प्रयुक्त जो यह दिखाए कि कार्य किसने किया या उससे कौन प्रभावित हुआ; का *the arrival of the president* (= he arrives) ○ *the murder of the president* (= he is murdered)

**off**[1] /ɒf ऑफ़्/ *adv., prep.*

> **NOTE** अनेक क्रियाओं के साथ विशेष प्रयोग जैसे **go off**, की जानकारी, के लिए उनकी क्रिया की प्रविष्टियाँ देखिए।

**1** down or away from a place or a position on sth किसी स्थान या वस्तु की स्थिति से नीचे, दूर या परे *to fall off a ladder/motorbike/wall* ○ *I* ***must be off*** (= I must leave here). *It's getting late.* ○ (*figurative*) *We've got off the subject.* **2** used with verbs that mean 'remove' or 'separate' 'को हटाना' या 'से अलग होने' का अर्थ देने वाली क्रियाओं के साथ प्रयुक्त *She took her coat off.* ○ *He shook the rain off his umbrella.* **3** joined to and leading away from किसी स्थान से जुड़े बिंदु से निकलते हुए *My road is off the Ring Road.* **4** at some distance from sth किसी से कुछ दूर (स्थान या समय की दृष्टि से) *Sri Lanka is just off the south coast of India.* ○ *Holi is still a long way off* (= it is a long time till then). **5** (used about a machine, a light, etc.) not connected, working or being used (कोई मशीन, बत्ती आदि) काम न करते हुए, बंद *Please make sure the TV/light/heating is off.* ✪ विलोम **on** **6** not present at work, school, etc. काम, स्कूल आदि से अनुपस्थिति या छुट्टी पर *She's* ***off work/off sick*** *with a cold.* ○ *I'm having a day off* (= a day's holiday) *next week.* **7** (used about a plan or arrangement) not going to happen; cancelled (कोई योजना या व्यवस्था) क्रियान्वित न होने वाली; रद्द *The meeting/wedding/trip is off.* ✪ विलोम **on** **8** cheaper; less by a certain amount अधिक सस्ता; निर्दिष्ट राशि को घटाते हुए *cars with Rs 4000 off* ○ *Rs 4000 off the price of a car* **9** not eating or using sth किसी वस्तु को न खाते हुए या प्रयोग में न लाते हुए *The baby's off his food.*

**IDM** **off and on; on and off** sometimes; starting and stopping कभी-कभी; यदा-कदा; शुरू होते और रुकते हुए, रुक-रुक कर *It rained on and off all day.*

**off limits** (*AmE*) forbidden; not to be entered by sb वर्जित, निषिद्ध; जहाँ जाना मना हो

**off the top of your head** ➪ **top** देखिए।

**well/badly off** having/not having a lot of money अच्छी स्थिति में, संपन्न या विपन्न

**off**[2] /ɒf ऑफ़्/ *adj.* (*not before a noun*) **1** (used about food or drink) no longer fresh enough to eat or drink (खाद्य या पेय पदार्थ) बासी पड़ चुका *The milk's off.* **2** (*spoken*) unfriendly मित्रवत नहीं, उखड़ा हुआ-सा *My boss was rather off with me today.*

**off-** /ɒf ऑफ़्/ *prefix* (*used in nouns, adjectives, verbs and adverbs*) not on; away from पर उपस्थित नहीं; से दूर *offstage* ○ *off load*

**offal** /ˈɒfl ˈऑफ़ल्/ *noun* [U] the heart and other organs of an animal, used as food पशुओं का कलेजा आदि अंग जो खाने के काम आते हैं

**off chance** *noun* [*sing.*] a slight possibility हल की संभावना *She popped round* ***on the off chance*** *of finding him at home.*

**off day** *noun* [C] (*informal*) a day when things go badly or you do not work well ढीला-ढाला हो जाने का दिन; कार्यकुशलता में कमी वाला दिन *Even the best players have off days occasionally.*

**offence** (*AmE* **offense**) /əˈfens अˈफ़ेन्स्/ *noun* **1** [C] (*formal*) **an offence (against sth)** a crime; an illegal action अपराध; ग़ैर-क़ानूनी काम *to commit an offence* ○ *a criminal/minor/serious/sexual offence* **2** [U] **offence (to sb/sth)** the act of upsetting or insulting sb किसी व्यक्ति को परेशान या अपमानित करने का काम *I didn't mean to **cause** you any **offence**.*

**IDM take offence (at sth)** to feel upset or hurt by sb/sth किसी व्यक्ति या वस्तु के कारण परेशानी या मानसिक क्लेश अनुभव करना

**offend** /əˈfend अˈफ़ेन्ड्/ *verb* **1** [T] (*usually passive*) to hurt sb's feelings; to upset sb किसी की भावनाओं को चोट पहुँचाना; किसी को परेशान करना *I hope they won't be offended if I don't come.* ○ *He felt offended that she hadn't written for so long.* **2** [I] (*formal*) to do sth illegal; to commit a crime ग़ैर-क़ानूनी काम करना; अपराध करना

**offender** /əˈfendə(r) अˈफ़ेन्ड(र्)/ *noun* [C] **1** (*formal*) a person who breaks the law or commits a crime क़ानून तोड़ने वाला या अपराधी व्यक्ति ***Young offenders** should not be sent to adult prisons.* ○ *a first offender* (= sb who has committed a crime for the first time) **2** a person or thing that does sth wrong कोई ग़लत काम करने वाला व्यक्ति या वस्तु

**offensive[1]** /əˈfensɪv अˈफ़ेन्सिव्/ *adj.* **1 offensive (to sb)** unpleasant; insulting अप्रिय; अपमानजनक *offensive behaviour/language/remarks* ✪ विलोम **inoffensive** **2** (*formal*) (*only before a noun*) used for or connected with attacking आक्रमण करने के लिए प्रयुक्त या आक्रमण-विषयक *offensive weapons* ✪ विलोम **defensive** ▶ **offensively** *adv.* आक्रमण या अपमानजनक रीति से

**offensive[2]** /əˈfensɪv अˈफ़ेनसिव्/ *noun* [C] a military attack सैन्य आक्रमण

**IDM be on the offensive** to be the first to attack, rather than waiting for others to attack you आक्रमण में पहल करना (न कि विपक्ष की पहल की प्रतीक्षा करना)

**offer[1]** /ˈɒfə(r) ˈऑफ़(र्)/ *verb* **1** [T] **offer sth (to sb) (for sth); offer (sb) sth** to ask if sb would like sth or to give sb the chance to have sth किसी को कोई वस्तु पेश करना या उसे कोई वस्तु लेने का अवसर देना *He offered his seat on the bus to an old lady.* ○ *I've been offered a job in London.* **2** [I] **offer (to do sth)** to say or show that you will do sth for sb if he/she wants किसी को उसकी इच्छित वस्तु का प्रस्ताव करना *I don't want to do it but I suppose I'll have to offer.* ○ *My brother's offered to help me paint the fence.* **3** [T] to make sth available or to provide the opportunity for sth किसी को कोई वस्तु उपलब्ध करना या उसे करने का अवसर प्रदान करना *The job offers plenty of opportunity for travel.*

**offer[2]** /ˈɒfə(r) ˈऑफ़(र्)/ *noun* [C] **1 an offer (of sth); an offer (to do sth)** a statement offering to do sth or give sth to sb किसी के लिए कुछ करने या उसे कुछ देने का प्रस्ताव *She accepted my offer of help.* ○ *Thank you for your kind offer to help.*

**NOTE** हम offer (प्रस्ताव) को **make, accept, refuse, turn down** या **withdraw** कर सकते हैं।

**2 an offer (of sth) (for sth)** an amount of money that you say you will give for sth किसी वस्तु के लिए प्रस्तावित धनराशि *They've made an offer for the house.* ○ *We've turned down* (= refused) *an offer of Rs 90,000.* **3** a low price for sth in a shop, usually for a short time किसी वस्तु के लिए दुकान पर घोषित कम क़ीमत (प्रायः सीमित समय के लिए) *See below for details of our special holiday offer.*

**IDM on offer 1** for sale or available बिक्री के लिए उपलब्ध *The college has a wide range of courses on offer.* **2** (*BrE*) for sale at a lower price than usual for a certain time नियमित से घटे दाम पर बिक्री के लिए (प्रायः निश्चित अवधि के लिए) *Leather jackets are on offer until next week.*

**or nearest offer; ono** ➪ **near[1]** देखिए।

**offering** /ˈɒfərɪŋ ˈऑफ़रिङ्/ *noun* [C] something that is given or produced for other people to watch, enjoy, etc. अन्य लोगों के आनंदोपयोग आदि के लिए प्रस्तुत कोई वस्तु; भेंट

**offhand[1]** /ˌɒfˈhænd ˌऑफ़्ˈहैन्ड्/ *adj.* (used about behaviour) not showing any interest in sb/sth in a way that seems rude (आचरण) लापरवाही-भरा (ऐसा कि रूखा लगे) *an offhand manner/voice*

**offhand[2]** /ˌɒfˈhænd ˌऑफ़्ˈहैन्ड्/ *adv.* without having time to think; immediately बिना तैयारी के; तुरंत *I can't tell you what it's worth offhand.*

**office** /ˈɒfɪs ˈऑफ़िस्/ *noun* **1** [C] a room, set of rooms or a building where people work, usually sitting at desks कार्यालय, दफ़्तर *I usually get to the office at about 9 o'clock.* ○ *The firm's **head office** (= the main branch of the company) is in Bangalore.* ○ *Please phone again during **office hours**.* **2** [C] (*often used to form compound nouns*) a room or building that is used for a particular purpose, especially for providing a service विशेष प्रयोजन (विशेषतः कोई सेवा उपलब्ध कराने) के लिए प्रयुक्त कोई कमरा या भवन; दफ़्तर *the tax/ticket/tourist office* ➪ **booking office, box office** और **post office** देखिए। **3 Office** *[sing.]* a government department, including the people who work there and the work they do सरकारी कार्यालय या विभाग (जिसमें वहाँ काम करने वाले और उनका काम भी शामिल है) *the Foreign/Home Office* **4** [U] an official position, often as part of a government or other organization कोई आधिकारिक पद (प्रायः सरकार या अन्य किसी संगठन के अंग के रूप में) *The Congress Party has been **in office** since May 2004.*

**office block** *noun* [C] a large building that contains offices, usually belonging to more than one company बड़ा भवन जिसमें अनेक कार्यालय हों (प्रायः अलग-अलग कंपनियों के); कार्यालय खंड

**officer** /ˈɒfɪsə(r) ˈऑफ़िस(र्)/ *noun* [C] **1** a person who is in a position of authority in the armed forces सेना का अफ़सर, अधिकारी *an army/air-force officer* **2** a person who is in a position of authority in the government or a large organization सरकार या किसी बड़े संगठन में अधिकारी *a prison/customs/welfare officer* **3** = **police officer** ➪ **official²** पर नोट देखिए।

**official¹** /əˈfɪʃl अˈफ़िश्ल्/ *adj.* **1** (*only before a noun*) connected with the position of sb in authority अधिकारी के पद से संबंधित, पदीय, शासकीय *official duties/responsibilities* **2** accepted and approved by the government or some other authority सरकार अथवा किसी अन्य अधिकार-संपन्न संगठन द्वारा स्वीकृत और अनुमोदित; आधिकारिक, अधिकृत *The scheme has not yet received official approval.* ○ *The country's official language is English.* **3** that is told to the public, but which may or may not be true औपचारिक (जो सबके सामने आए परंतु जो सच न हो या सच भी हो) *The official reason for his resignation was that he wanted to spend more time with his family.* ✪ विलोम **unofficial**

**official²** /əˈfɪʃl अˈफ़िश्ल्/ *noun* [C] a person who has a position of authority अधिकार-संपन्न व्यक्ति, अधिकारी, अफसर *The reception was attended by MPs and high-ranking officials.*

> **NOTE** **Official** वह है जिसके पास किसी संगठन में प्रायः सरकार में दायित्वपूर्ण पद हो—*senior government officials.* **Officer** वह है जिसके पास सशस्त्र सेनाओं या पुलिस बल में दूसरों को आदेश देने का अधिकार हो तथापि कभी-कभी इस शब्द का प्रयोग **official** के समानार्थक शब्द के रूप में भी होता है—*She's a tax officer in the Civil Service.*

**officialdom** /əˈfɪʃldəm अˈफ़िश्ल्डम्/ *noun* [U] groups of people in positions of authority in large organizations who seem more interested in following the rules than in being helpful अफ़सरशाही, बाबू-तंत्र (वस्तुतः सहायता करने के स्थान पर केवल नियमों के अनुसार चलने में दिलचस्पी रखने वाले अफ़सरों की मंडली)

**officially** /əˈfɪʃəli अˈफ़िशलि/ *adv.* **1** that is done publicly and by sb in a position of authority आधिकारिक रूप से *The new school was officially opened last week.* **2** according to a particular set of laws, rules, etc. विशिष्ट क़ानूनों, नियमों आदि के समुच्चय के अनुसार, नियमानुसार *Officially we don't accept children under six, but we'll make an exception in this case.*

**officious** /əˈfɪʃəs अˈफ़िशस्/ *adj.* too ready to tell other people what to do and use the power you have to give orders दूसरों को बिन माँगे अवांछित सलाह देने और बात-बात पर हुकुम चलाने वाला, अफ़सराना, दस्तंदाज

**offing** /ˈɒfɪŋ ˈऑफ़िङ्/ *noun*
**IDM** **in the offing** (*informal*) likely to appear or happen soon शीघ्र प्रकट या घटित होने वाला

**off-licence** (*AmE* **liquor store**) *noun* [C] a shop which sells alcoholic drinks in bottles and cans शराब की दुकान

**off-line** *adj., adv.* (*computing*) not directly controlled by or connected to a computer or to the Internet जो कंप्यूटर या इंटरनेट से सीधे नियंत्रित या जुड़ा न हो; ऑफ़-लाइन

**offload** /ˌɒfˈləʊd ˌऑफ़्लोड्/ *verb* [T] (*informal*) **offload sth (on/onto sb)** to give away sth that you do not want to sb else अवांछित वस्तु से छुटकारा पाना (किसी दूसरे को सौंपकर) *It's nice to have someone you can offload your problems onto.*

**off-peak** *adj., adv.* (*only before a noun*) available, used or done at a less popular or busy time जो अपेक्षया कम माँग वाले या कम व्यस्त समय में उपलब्ध हो, इस्तेमाल हो या किया जाए *an off-peak train ticket/bus pass/phone call* ○ *It's cheaper to travel off-peak.* ➪ **peak** देखिए।

**off-putting** *adj.* (*BrE*) unpleasant in a way that stops you from liking sb/sth अप्रीतिकर

**offset** /ˈɒfset ˈऑफ़्सेट्/ *verb* [T] (**offsetting;** *pt, pp* **offset**) to make the effect of sth less strong or noticeable किसी बात के असर को कम कर देना, क्षति की पूर्ति कर देना, कमी पूरी करना *The disadvantages of the scheme are more than offset by the advantages.*

**offshoot** /ˈɒfʃuːt ˈऑफ़्शूट्/ *noun* [C] a thing that develops from sth else, especially a small organization that develops from a larger one किसी अन्य की शाखा या प्रशाखा (विशेषतः किसी बड़े संगठन से जन्मा छोटा संगठन)

**offshore** /ˌɒfˈʃɔː(r) ˌऑफ़्ˈशॉ(र्)/ *adj.* in the sea but not very far from the land समुद्र में (परंतु तट के समीप), अपतट *an offshore oil rig*

**offside** *adj.* **1** /ˌɒfˈsaɪd ˌऑफ़्ˈसाइड्/ (used about a player in football) in a position that is not allowed by the rules of the game (फ़ुटबॉल में खिलाड़ी) विपक्ष के हिस्से में नियम-विरुद्ध रीति से पहले सिरे पर पहुँचा हुआ; ऑफ़साइड **2** /ˈɒfsaid ˈऑफ़्साइड्/ (*BrE*) (used about a part of a vehicle) on the side that is furthest away from the edge of the road (वाहन का भाग) सड़क के सिरे से सबसे दूर वाला

**offspring** /ˈɒfsprɪŋ ˈऑफ़्स्प्रिङ्/ *noun* [C] (*pl.* **offspring**) (*formal*) a child or children; the young of an animal संतान या संतानें; पशु का शावक या बच्चा *to produce/raise offspring*

**off-white** *adj.* not pure white एकदम सफ़ेद नहीं (कुछ पीलापन लिए सूद), श्वेताभ

**often** /ˈɒfn; ˈɒftən ˈऑफ़्न्; ˈऑफ़्टन्/ *adv.* **1** many times; frequently अनेक बार; बार-बार *We often go swimming at the weekend.* ○ ***How often** should you go to the dentist?* **2** in many cases; commonly अनेक मामलों में; प्रायः *Old houses are often damp.*

IDM **every so often** sometimes; from time to time कभी-कभी, यदा-कदा; समय-समय पर

**more often than not** usually सामान्यतया

**ogre** /ˈəʊɡə(r) ˈओग(र्)/ *noun* [C] **1** (in children's stories) a very large, cruel and frightening creature that eats people (बालकथाओं में) नरभक्षी दानव, दैत्य **2** a person who is unpleasant and frightening अप्रिय और डरावना व्यक्ति

**Oh** (*also* **O**) /əʊ ओ/ *exclamation* used for reacting to sth that sb has said, for emphasizing what you are saying, or when you are thinking of what to say next अपनी प्रतिक्रिया व्यक्त करने के लिए, अपनी बात पर बल देने के लिए या 'आगे क्या कहना है' यह सोचते समय प्रयुक्त *'I'm a teacher.' 'Oh? Where?'* ○ *'Oh no!' she cried as she began to read the letter.*

**ohm** /əʊm ओम्/ *noun* [C] (*technical*) (*symbol* Ω) a unit for measuring electrical **resistance** विद्युत की प्रतिरोध शक्ति (ताप या विद्युत को गुज़रने न देना) को मापने की इकाई, वैद्युत प्रतिरोध मात्रक; ओम ➪ **resistor** पर चित्र देखिए।

**oil** /ɔɪl ऑइल्/ *noun* [U] **1** a thick dark liquid that comes from under the ground and is used as a fuel or to make machines work smoothly तैल, तेल, खनिज तेल **2** a thick liquid that comes from animals or plants and is used in cooking भोजन पकाने में प्रयुक्त (गाढ़ा) तेल (पशुओं या पौधों से प्राप्त) *cooking/vegetable/sunflower/olive oil* ▶ **oil** *verb* [T] चिकनाई के लिए तेल डालना; चिकनाना

**oilfield** /ˈɔɪlfiːld ˈआइल्फ़ील्ड्/ *noun* [C] an area where there is oil under the ground or under the sea तैल-क्षेत्र (पृथ्वी या समुद्र के नीचे तेल वाले क्षेत्र)

**oil painting** *noun* [C] a picture that has been painted using paint made with oil तैल-चित्र

**oil rig** (*also* **rig**) *noun* [C] a large platform in the sea with equipment for getting oil out from under the sea समुद्र में बड़ा प्लैटफ़ार्म जिस पर समुद्र के नीचे से तेल निकालने की मशीनें लगी होती हैं; आइल-रिग

**oilseed rape** /ˌɔɪlsiːd ˈreɪp ˌऑइलसीड् ˈरेप्/ = **rape³**

**oil slick** (*also* **slick**) *noun* [C] an area of oil that floats on the sea, usually after a ship carrying oil has crashed समुद्र के पानी पर तैरती तेल की परत (प्रायः तेलवाहक जहाज़ के ध्वंसन से फैली)

**oil well** (*also* **well**) *noun* [C] a hole that is made deep in the ground or under the sea in order to obtain oil तेल-कूप (पृथ्वी या समुद्र के नीचे खनिज तेल निकालने के लिए बनाया गया गहरा कुआँ)

**oily** /ˈɔɪli ˈऑइलि/ *adj.* covered with oil or like oil तेल से चुपड़ा, तैलीय या तेल जैसा *oily food* ○ *Mechanics always have oily hands.*

**ointment** /ˈɔɪntmənt ˈऑइन्ट्मन्ट्/ *noun* [C, U] a smooth substance that you put on sore skin or on an injury to help it get better मलहम, यह चिकना मुलायम होता है तथा फटे अथवा चोट खाए अंग पर हम लगाते हैं

**OK¹** (*also* **okay**) /əʊˈkeɪ ओˈके/ *adj., adv., exclamation* (*informal*) **1** all right; good or well enough ठीक-ठाक; ठीक या अच्छा *'Did you have a nice day?' 'Well, it was OK, I suppose.'* ○ *Is it okay if I come at about 7 p.m.?* **2** yes; all right हाँ; बिलकुल ठीक *'Do you want to come with us?' 'OK.'*

**OK²** (*also* **okay**) /ˌəʊˈkeɪ ˌओˈके/ *noun* [*sing.*] agreement or permission सहमति या अनुमति *As soon as my parents **give** me **the OK**, I'll come and stay with you.*

**OK³** (*also* **okay**) /ˌəʊˈkeɪ ˌओˈके/ (*3rd person sing. pres.* **OK's**; *pres. part.* **OK'ing**; *pt, pp* **OK'd**) *verb* [T] (*informal*) **OK sth (with sb)** to officially agree to something or allow it to happen औपचारिक सहमति या अनुमति देना *If you need time off, you have to OK it with your boss.*

**okra** /ˈəʊkrə; ˈɒkrə ˈओक्रा; ˈऑक्रा/ *noun* [U] the green seed cases of the **okra** plant, eaten as a vegetable भिंडी

**old** /əʊld ओल्ड्/ *adj.* **1** that has existed for a long time; connected with past times पुराना, बहुत पहले से चला आता; प्राचीन *This house is quite old.* ○ *old ideas/traditions* ✪ विलोम **new** या **modern** **2** (used about people and animals) having lived a long time (मनुष्य या पशु) बड़ी आयु का *He's only 50 but he looks older.* ○ *to **get/grow** old* ✪ विलोम **young** **3** (used with a period of time or with *how*) of a particular age (विशिष्ट समयावधि के लिए या 'how' के साथ प्रयुक्त) विशेष आयु का या अवस्था वाला *The book is aimed at eight- to ten-year-olds.* ○ *How old are you?* ➪ **age** पर नोट देखिए।

> **NOTE** **Older** और **oldest** शब्द **old** के नियमित तुलनापरक और उत्तमावस्था के रूप हैं—*My father's older than my mother.* ○ *I'm the oldest in the class.* **Elder** और **eldest** का प्रयोग लोगों की (विशेषतः एक ही परिवार के) आयु की तुलना के लिए किया जाता है तथापि इनका प्रयोग 'than' के साथ नहीं हो सकता है।

**4 the old** *noun* [*pl.*] old people वृद्ध लोग ➪ **the elderly** और **the aged** देखिए। **5** having been used a lot घिसा-पिटा, जीर्ण-शीर्ण *I got rid of all my old clothes.* ✪ विलोम **new** ➪ **second-hand** देखिए। **6** (*only before a noun*) former; previous पहले का; पूर्ववर्ती *I earn more now than I did in my old job.* **7** (*only before a noun*) known for a long time चिरकाल से परिचित *She's a very old friend of mine. We knew each other at school.* **8** (*only before a noun*) (*informal*) used for emphasizing that sth has little importance or value किसी वस्तु की निरुपयोगिता पर बल देने के लिए प्रयुक्त *I write any old rubbish in my diary.*

**IDM** **be an old hand (at sth)** to be good at sth because you have done it often before किसी काम में मँजा हुआ या अनुभवी होना

**old age** *noun* [U] the part of your life when you are old वृद्धावस्था, बुढ़ापा *He's enjoying life **in** his **old age**.* ➪ **youth** देखिए।

**old-age pension** *noun* [U] money paid by the state to people above a certain age वृद्धावस्था की पेंशन

**old-fashioned** *adj.* **1** usual in the past but not now पुरानी चाल का (अब अप्रचलित) *old-fashioned clothes/ideas* **2** (used about people) believing in old ideas, customs, etc. (लोग) पुरानी बातों, रीति-रिवाज़ों आदि में विश्वास करने वाले; रूढ़िवादी, दक़ियानूस *My parents are quite old-fashioned about some-things.* ➪ **modern** और **unfashionable** देखिए।

**the Old Testament** *noun* [*sing.*] the first part of the Bible that tells the history of the Jewish people बाइबिल का प्रथम खंड (यहूदी जाति के इतिहास से संबंधित) दि ओल्ड टेस्टामेंट ➪ **the New Testament** देखिए।

**olive** /ˈɒlɪv ˈऑलिव्/ *noun* **1** [C] a small green or black fruit with a bitter taste, used for food and oil जैतून का फल (खाने और तेल निकालने के लिए प्रयुक्त) *Fry the onions in a little olive oil.* ➪ **virgin olive oil** देखिए। **2** (*also* **olive green**) [U], *adj.* (of) a colour between yellow and green जैतून की तरह हरा, जैतूनी हरा (पीला-हरा)

**the Olympic Games** (*also* **the Olympics** /əˈlɪmpɪks अˈलिम्पिक्स्/) *noun* [*pl.*] an international sports competition which is organized every four years in a different country अंतरर्ष्ट्रीय खेल प्रतियोगिता (जो प्रति चार वर्ष बाद अलग देश में आयोजित की जाती है) ओलंपिक खेल *to win a medal at/in the Olympics* ▶ **Olympic** *adj.* (*only before a noun*) ओलंपिक *Who holds the Olympic record for the 1500 metres?*

**ombudsman** /ˈɒmbʊdzmən; -mæn ˈऑम्बुड्ज़्मन्; -मैन्/ *noun* [C] (*pl.* **-men** /-mən -मन्/) a government official who deals with complaints made by ordinary people against public organizations सार्वजनिक संस्थाओं के विरुद्ध जन-साधारण की शिकायतों पर सुनवाई करने वाला उच्च शासकीय अधिकारी; लोकपाल, लोकायुक्त

**omega** /ˈəʊmɪgə ˈओमिगा/ *noun* [C] the last letter of the Greek alphabet (Ω, ω) ग्रीक वर्णमाला का अंतिम अक्षर

**omelette** (*also* **omelet**) /ˈɒmlət ˈऑम्लट्/ *noun* [C] a dish made of eggs that have been mixed together very fast (**beaten**) and fried अंडे से बनी खाद्य वस्तु, आमलेट

**omen** /ˈəʊmən ˈओमन्/ *noun* [C] a sign of sth that will happen in the future भविष्य में होने वाली बात का संकेत; शकुन, सगुन *a good/bad omen for the future*

**ominous** /ˈɒmɪnəs ˈऑमिनस्/ *adj.* suggesting that sth bad is going to happen अशुभसूचक *Those black clouds look ominous.*

**omission** /əˈmɪʃn अˈमिश्न्/ *noun* [C, U] something that has not been included; the act of not including sb/sth शामिल (समाविष्ट) होने से रह गई वस्तु, चूक; शामिल (समाविष्ट) न करने की क्रिया, छूट *There were several omissions on the list of names.*

**omit** /əˈmɪt अˈमिट्/ *verb* [T] (**omitting; omitted**) **1** to not include sth; to leave sth out किसी वस्तु को शामिल न करना; किसी वस्तु को छोड़ देना *Several verses of the song can be omitted.*

**omni-** /ˈɒmni ˈऑम्नि/ (*used in nouns, adjective and adverbs*) of all things; in all ways or places सब वस्तुओं का; सब प्रकार से या स्थानों पर, सर्व, बहु *omnivore*

**omniscient** /ɒmˈnɪsiənt ऑम्ˈनिसिअन्ट्/ *adj.* (*formal*) knowing everything सर्वज्ञ *The novel has an omniscient narrator.* ▶ **omniscience** /-siəns -सिअन्स्/ *noun* [U] सर्वज्ञता

**omnivore** /ˈɒmnɪvɔː(r) ˈऑम्निवॉ(र्)/ *noun* [C] an animal that eats both plants and meat वनस्पति और मांस दोनों खाने वाला पशु; सर्वभक्षी पशु ➪ **carnivore, herbivore** और **insectivore** देखिए। ▶ **omnivorous** /ɒmˈnɪvərəs ऑम्ˈनिवरस्/ *adj.* सर्वभक्षी, सर्वसमावेशी, सर्वसंग्रही *an omnivorous diet*

**on** /ɒn ऑन्/ *adv., prep.*

**NOTE** अनेक क्रियाओं और संज्ञाओं के साथ **on** के विशेष प्रयोगों, जैसे **get on, on holiday,** के लिए संबंधित क्रिया और संज्ञा की प्रविष्टियाँ देखिए।

**1** (*formal* **upon**) supported by, fixed to or touching sth, especially a surface जब कोई वस्तु किसी अन्य वस्तु, विशेषतः उसकी सतह पर स्थित, संलग्न अथवा संबद्ध होती है, या सतह का संस्पर्श करती है, तब हम upon का प्रयोग करते हैं; पर, के ऊपर *on the table/ceiling/wall* ○ *We sat on the beach/grass/floor.* ○ *Write it down on a piece of paper.* **2** in a place or position किसी स्थान या स्थिति में, पर *on a farm/housing estate/campsite* ○ *a house on the river/seafront/border* ○ *I live on the other side of town.* **3** showing direction दिशा दिखाते हुए, की ओर *on the right/left* ○ *on the way to school* **4** used with ways of travelling and types of travel यात्रा करने के और यात्राओं के प्रकार सूचक शब्दों के साथ प्रयुक्त, से/के द्वारा, पर *on the bus/train/plane* ○ *We came* ***on foot*** (= we walked). ○ *Raju went past on his bike.* **NOTE** ध्यान दीजिए कि **in the car** ऐसा प्रयोग होता है। **5** with expressions of time समय सूचक शब्दों के साथ *on Monday* ○ *on Christmas Day* ○ *on your birthday* **6** working; being used काम करते हुए; प्रयुक्त होते हुए *All the lights were on.* ○ ***Switch*** *the television* ***on***. ✪ विलोम **off** **7** wearing sth; carrying sth in your pocket or bag कुछ पहने हुए; जेब या थैले में कुछ ले जाते हुए *What did she* ***have on***? ○ *to* ***put*** *your shoes/coat/hat/make-up* ***on*** **8** about sth किसी वस्तु के विषय में, किसी वस्तु पर *We've got a test on irregular verbs tomorrow.* ○ *a talk/a book/an article on Japan* **9** happening or arranged to happen चलते या घटित होते हुए या घटित होने के लिए योजित *What's on at the cinema?* ○ *Is the meeting still on, or has it been cancelled?* **10** using sth; by means of sth किसी वस्तु का प्रयोग करते हुए; किसी वस्तु की सहायता से *I was (talking)* ***on the phone*** *to Lata.* ○ *Dinesh spends most evenings* ***on the Internet***. **11** showing the thing or person that is affected by an action or is the object of an action उस व्यक्ति या वस्तु को दर्शाते हुए जो किसी क्रिया या क्रिया के लक्ष्य-बिन्दु से प्रभावित हो; पर, के ऊपर *Divorce can have a bad effect on children.* ○ *He spends a lot on clothes.* **12** using drugs or medicine; using a particular kind of food or fuel नशीली दवाओं या औषधियों का प्रयोग करते हुए; विशेष प्रकार के भोजन या ईंधन का प्रयोग करते हुए; से *to be on medication/antibiotics/heroin* ○ *Gorillas live on leaves and fruit.* ○ *Does this car run on petrol or diesel?* **13** receiving a certain amount of money निश्चित धनराशि प्राप्त करते हुए *What will you be on* (= how much will you earn) *in your new job?* ○ *He's been (living) on unemployment benefit since he lost his job.* **14** showing that sth continues किसी काम की निरंतरता को दर्शाते हुए *The man shouted at us but we walked on.* ○ *The speeches went* ***on and on*** *until everyone was bored.* **15** showing the reason for or basis for sth किसी बात का कारण या आधार को दर्शाते हुए *She doesn't eat meat* ***on principle***. ○ *The film is* ***based on*** *a true story.* **16** compared to की तुलना में *Sales are up 10% on last year.* **17** immediately; soon after तुरंत; के बाद तत्काल *He telephoned her on his return from New Delhi.* **18** paid for by sb जिसके लिए किसी व्यक्ति ने पैसा दिया *The drinks are on me!*

**IDM** **from now/then on** starting from this/that time and continuing अब से या तब से *From then on she never smoked another cigarette.*

**not on** (*informal*) not acceptable मंजूर नहीं, अस्वीकार्य *No, you can't stay out that late. It's just not on.*

**off and on; on and off** ➪ **off**[1] देखिए।

**be/go on at sb** ➪ **go**[1] देखिए।

**once** /wʌns वन्स्/ *adv., conj.* **1** one time only; on one occasion केवल एक बार; एक बार *I've only been to France once.* ○ *once a week/month/year* **2** at some time in the past; formerly अतीत में कभी; पहले (समय में) *This house was once the village school.* **3** as soon as; when जैसे ही; जब *Once you've practised a bit you'll find that it's quite easy.*

**IDM** **all at once** all at the same time or suddenly सब के सब उसी समय या अचानक *People began talking all at once.* ○ *All at once she got up and left the room.*

**at once 1** immediately; now तुरंत; अभी *Come here at once!* **2** at the same time एक ही समय, एक साथ *I can't hear if you all speak at once.*

**just this once; (just) for once** on this occasion only केवल इसी अवसर पर *Just this once, I'll help you with your homework.*

**once again; once more** one more time; another time एक बार फिर; फिर कभी *Once again the train was late.* ○ *Let's listen to that track once more.*

**once and for all** now and for the last time अभी और सदा के लिए *You've got to make a decision once and for all.*

**once in a blue moon** (*informal*) very rarely; almost never बहुत कम; लगभग कभी नहीं

**once in a while** sometimes but not often कभी-कभी (बार-बार नहीं)

**once upon a time** (used at the beginning of a children's story) a long time ago; in the past (किसी बाल-कथा के आरंभ में प्रयुक्त) बहुत पहले; अतीत में *Once upon a time there was a beautiful princess in China.*

**oncoming** /ˈɒnkʌmɪŋ ˈऑन्कमिङ्/ *adj.* (*only before a noun*) coming towards you पास आता हुआ *oncoming traffic*

**one**[1] /wʌn वन्/ *pronoun, det., noun* [C] **1** (the number) 1 एक, (संख्या) 1 *The journey takes one hour.* ○ *If you take* (= subtract) *one from ten it leaves nine.* ➪ **first** देखिए।

> **NOTE** संख्याओं के वाक्य-प्रयोग के उदाहरणों के लिए **six** देखिए।

**2** (used when you are talking about a time in the past or future without actually saying when) a certain (अतीत या भविष्य के किसी समय की सामान्य चर्चा के लिए प्रयुक्त) किसी *He came to see me one evening last week.* ○ *We must go and visit them one day.* **3** used with the other, another or other(s) to make a contrast वैषम्य दिखाने के लिए 'the other', 'another' या 'others' के साथ प्रयुक्त *The twins are so alike that it's hard to tell one from the other.* **4 the one** used for emphasizing that there is only one of sth 'केवल एक' या 'अकेला' अर्थ पर बल देने के लिए प्रयुक्त *She's the one person I trust.* ○ *We can't all get in the one car.*

**IDM (all) in one** all together or combined एक में सब कुछ, एक साथ *It's a phone and fax machine all in one.*

**one after another/the other** first one, then the next, etc. बारी-बारी से *One after another the winners went up to get their prizes.*

**one at a time** separately; individually पृथक रूप से; व्यक्तिशः, एक समय में एक *I'll deal with the problems one at a time.*

**one by one** separately; individually अलग-अलग; एक-एक करके *One by one, people began to arrive at the meeting.*

**one or two** a few एक-दो, कुछ *I've borrowed one or two new books from the library.*

**one**[2] /wʌn वन्/ *pronoun, noun* [C] **1** used instead of repeating a noun दोहराई जाने वाली संज्ञा के लिए प्रयुक्त *I think I'll have an apple. Would you like one?* **2 one of** a member (of a certain group) (किसी समूह का) सदस्य, में से कोई एक *He's staying with one of his friends.* ○ *One of the children is crying.*

> **NOTE One of** के बाद हमेशा बहुवचनांत संज्ञा आती है परंतु क्रिया एकवचन में रहती है क्योंकि कर्ता के स्थान पर **one** का प्रयोग होता है—*One of our assistants is ill.* ○ *One of the buses was late.*

**3** used after this, that, which or after an adjective instead of a noun 'this', 'that', 'which' या किसी विशेषण, न कि संज्ञा के बाद प्रयुक्त *'Which dress do you like?' 'This one.'* ○ *That idea is a very good one.* **4 the one/the ones** used before a group of words that show which person or thing you are talking about उन शब्दों से पहले प्रयुक्त जो यह दर्शाते हैं कि किस व्यक्ति या वस्तु विशेष की चर्चा की जा रही है *My house is the one after the post office.* ○ *If you find some questions difficult, leave out the ones you don't understand.* **5** (*formal*) used for referring to people in general, including the speaker or writer लोगों का (वक्ता या लेखक समेत) सामान्य रूप से निर्देश करने के लिए प्रयुक्त *One must be sure of one's facts before criticizing other people.*

**NOTE One** का ऐसा प्रयोग बहुत औपचारिक है। दैनिक व्यवहार की अंग्रेजी में सामान्यतया **you** का प्रयोग होता है।

**one another** *pronoun* each other एक-दूसरे से या को, परस्पर *We exchanged news with one another.*

**one-off** *noun* [C], *adj.* (*informal*) something that is made or that happens only once केवल एक बार होने या किया जाने वाला, केवल एक बार का, एक बारगी *a one-off payment/opportunity*

**onerous** /ˈəʊnərəs ˈओनरस्/ *adj.* (*formal*) difficult and needing a lot of effort कठिन और प्रयत्नसाध्य

**oneself** /wʌnˈself वन्ˈसेल्फ़्/ *pronoun* (*formal*) **1** used when the person who does an action is also affected by it कर्ता का स्वयं कार्य से प्रभावित होने पर प्रयुक्त, ख़ुद, स्वयं *One can teach oneself to play the piano but it is easier to have lessons.* **2** used to emphasize sth किसी बात पर बल देने के लिए प्रयुक्त *One could easily arrange it all oneself.*

**IDM (all) by oneself 1** alone अकेले ही ➪ **alone** पर नोट देखिए। **2** without help बिना सहायता के

**one-sided** *adj.* **1** (used about an opinion, an argument, etc.) showing only one point of view; not balanced (कोई सम्मति, तर्क आदि) एकपक्षीय, इकतरफ़ा; असंतुलित *Some newspapers give a very one-sided view of politics.* **2** (used about a relationship or a competition) not equal (संबंध या स्पर्धा) असमान, ग़ैर-बराबरी का *The match was very one-sided—we lost 12–1.*

**one-to-one** (*also* **one-on-one**) *adj., adv.* between only two people केवल दो व्यक्तियों के बीच, प्रत्येक के लिए अलग-अलग; एकैक *one-to-one English lessons* (= one teacher to one student)

**one-way** *adj.* (*usually before a noun*) **1** (used about roads) that you can only drive along in one direction (सड़क) जिस पर केवल एक ही दिशा में जा सकें, इकतरफ़ा *a one-way street* **2** (*AmE*) (used about a ticket) that you can use to travel somewhere but not back again (टिकट) जिस पर केवल एक ओर की यात्रा हो सके, एक ओर का *a one-way ticket* ✪ पर्याय **single** ✪ विलोम **return**

**ongoing** /ˈɒngəʊɪŋ ˈऑन्गोइङ्/ *adj.* (*only before a noun*) continuing to exist now अब तक चला आता, जारी, चालू, सतत *It's an ongoing problem.*

**onion** /ˈʌnjən ˈअन्यन्/ *noun* [C, U] a white or red vegetable with many layers. Onions are often used in cooking and have a strong smell that makes some people cry प्याज़ *a kilo of onions* ○ *onion soup* ➪ **vegetable** पर चित्र देखिए।

**online** /ˌɒnˈlaɪn ˌऑन्ˈलाइन्/ *adj., adv.* (*computing*) controlled by or connected to a computer or to the Internet कंप्यूटर या इंटरनेट से संबंधित या जुड़ा हुआ; ऑनलाइन *an online ticket booking system* ○ *I'm studying French online.*

**onlooker** /ˈɒnlʊkə(r) ˈऑन्लुक(र्)/ *noun* [C] a person who watches sth happening without taking part in it द्रष्टामात्र, प्रक्षेक, तमाशबीन (किसी बात को निर्लिप्त भाव से देखने वाला व्यक्ति)

**only** /ˈəʊnli ˈओन्लि/ *adj., adv., conj.* (*only before a noun*) **1** with no others existing or present अकेला (जहाँ कोई दूसरा न हो), एकमात्र *I was the only woman in the room.* ○ *This is the only dress we have in your size.* **2** and no one or nothing else; no more than केवल, सिर्फ़ (और कोई नहीं या और कुछ नहीं; किसी से अधिक नहीं) *She only likes pop music.* ○ *I've only asked a few friends to the party.* **3** the most suitable or the best सबसे उपयुक्त या सर्वोत्तम *It's so cold that the only thing to do is to sit by the fire.*

> **NOTE** अंग्रेजी लिखते समय **only** को प्रायः उस शब्द से 'पहले' रखते हैं जिससे वह (अर्थ की दृष्टि से) संबंधित हो। अंग्रेजी बोलते समय हमें **only** का क्रम नहीं बदलना होता, केवल संबंधित शब्द पर बलाघात देना पर्याप्त है—*I only spoke to ˈRaj* (= I spoke to Raj and no one else). ○ *I only ˈspoke to Raj* (= I spoke to Raj but I didn't do anything else).

**4** (*informal*) except that; but को छोड़कर: किंतु *The film was very good, only it was a bit too long.*

**IDM** **if only** ➪ **if** देखिए।

**not only...but also** both...and दोनों, 'अमुक भी' और 'अमुक भी' *He not only did the shopping but he also cooked the meal.*

**only just 1** not long ago हाल ही में, कुछ ही समय पहले, अधिक समय नहीं हुआ *I've only just started this job.* **2** almost not; hardly लगभग नहीं; मुश्किल से *We only just had enough money to pay for the meal.*

**only child** *noun* [C] a child who has no brothers or sisters एकमात्र संतान

**onomatopoeia** /ˌɒnəˌmætəˈpiːə ˌऑन ˌमैटˈपीआ/ *noun* [U] (*technical*) the fact of words containing sounds similar to the noises they describe, for example 'hiss' or 'thud'; the use of words like this in a piece of writing शब्दों का ध्वनि-विन्यास संबंधित (वास्तविक) ध्वनियों के अनुसार होना, ध्वनि-अनुकरण (जैसे 'hiss', 'thud'); ध्वनि-अनुकरणात्मक शब्द ▶**onomatopoeic** /-ˈpiːɪk -ˈपीइक्/ *adj.* ध्वनि-अनुकरणमूलक

**onset** /ˈɒnset ˈऑन्सेट्/ *noun* [*sing.*] **the onset (of sth)** the beginning (often of sth unpleasant) आरंभ (प्रायः किसी अप्रिय स्थिति का) *the onset of winter/a headache*

**onslaught** /ˈɒnslɔːt ˈऑन्स्लॉट्/ *noun* [C] **an onslaught (on/against sb/sth)** a violent or strong attack उग्र आक्रमण या तीखा विरोध या प्रचण्ड अभियान *an onslaught on government policy*

**onto** (*also* **on to**) /ˈɒntə; *before vowels* ˈɒntu ˈऑन्ट; स्वर ध्वनियों के पूर्व ˈऑन्टु/ *prep.* to a position on sth किसी वस्तु के ऊपर *The cat jumped onto the sofa.* ○ *The crowd ran onto the pitch.*

**IDM** **be onto sb** (*informal*) to have found out about sth illegal that sb is doing किसी की ग़ैर-क़ानूनी गतिविधि को खोज निकालना *The police were onto the car thieves.*

**be onto sth** to have some information, etc. that could lead to an important discovery कुछ जानकारी आदि होना (जिससे कोई महत्त्वपूर्ण खोज हो सके)

**onwards** /ˈɒnwədzˈऑन्वड्ज़्/ (*also* **onward**) /ˈɒnwədˈऑन्वड्/) *adv.* **1 from... onwards** continuing from a particular time समय विशेष के बाद *From September onwards it usually begins to get colder.* **2** (*formal*) forward आगे की ओर *The road stretched onwards into the distance.*

**ooze** /uːz ऊज़्/ *verb* [I, T] **ooze from/out of sth; ooze (with) sth** to flow slowly out or to allow sth to flow slowly out किसी वस्तु का मंद गति से बाहर निकलना या उसे निकलने देना; स्राव, रिसाव *Blood oozed from the cut on his head.* ○ *The fruit was oozing with juice.*

**op** /ɒp ऑप्/ (*spoken*) = **operation**[1]

**opaque** /əʊˈpeɪk ओˈपेक्/ *adj.* **1** that you cannot see through अपारदर्शी *opaque glass in the door* **2** (*formal*) difficult to understand; not clear दुर्बोध; अस्पष्ट ✪ विलोम **transparent**

**OPEC** /ˈəʊpekˈओपेक्/ *abbr.* Organization of Petroleum Exporting Countries ओपेक-पेट्रोलियम निर्यातक देशों का संगठन

**open**[1] /ˈəʊpən ˈओपन्/ *adj.* **1** not closed or covered खुला, अनढका या अनावृत *She stared at me with her eyes wide open.* ○ *The curtains were open so that we could see into the room.* **2 open (to sb/sth); open (for sth)** available for people to enter, visit, use, etc.; not closed to the public जनता के लिए खुला (प्रवेश, भ्रमण, उपयोग आदि के लिए); जनता के लिए बंद नहीं *The hotel damaged by the bomb is now* ***open for business*** *again.* ○ *The gardens are* ***open to the public*** *in the summer.* ✪ विलोम **closed** या **shut** **3** not keeping feelings and thoughts hidden भावों और विचारों को न छिपाने वाला, निष्कपट *He looked at him with open dislike.* **4** (*only before a noun*) (used about an area of land) away from towns and buildings; (used about an area of sea) at a distance from the land (भूक्षेत्र) शहरों और भवनों से दूर खुला (मैदान); (समुद्र का भाग) तट से दूर, खुला (समुद्र) *open country* **5** (*not before a noun*) not finally decided; still being considered अनिर्णीत (जिस पर अंतिम निर्णय नहीं हुआ); विचाराधीन *Let's leave the details open.*

IDM **have/keep an open mind (about/on sth)** to be ready to listen to or consider new ideas and suggestions नए विचारों और सुझावों को सुनने या समझने के लिए तैयार; उदारमनस्क

**in the open air** outside खुले में, बाहर *Somehow, food eaten in the open air tastes much better.*

**keep an eye open/out (for sb/sth)** ➪ **eye**[1] देखिए।

**open to sth** willing to receive sth सुनने आदि को तैयार *I'm always open to suggestions.*

**with your eyes open** ➪ **eye**[1] देखिए।

**with open arms** in a friendly way that shows that you are pleased to see sb or have sth प्रसन्नतापूर्वक, उत्साह के साथ *The unions welcomed the government's decision with open arms.*

**open**[2] /ˈəʊpənˈओपन्/ *verb* **1** [I, T] to move sth or part of sth so that it is no longer closed; to move so as to be no longer closed किसी बंद वस्तु (दरवाज़े आदि) को खोलना; खोलने के लिए खिसकाना *This window won't open—it's stuck.* ○ *The book opened at the very page I needed.* ✪ विलोम **close** या **shut** **2** [I, T] to make it possible for people to enter a place जनता के प्रवेश के लिए किसी स्थान को खोलना *The museum opens at 10 a.m.* ○ *Police finally opened the road six hours after the accident.* ✪ विलोम **close** या **shut** **3** [I, T] to start आरंभ करना (खाता आदि खोलना) *The chairman opened the meeting by welcoming everybody.* ○ *I'd like to open a bank account.* ✪ विलोम **close** **4** [T] (*computing*) to start a program or file so that you can use it on the screen नए प्रोग्राम या फ़ाइल को खोलना (ताकि उसे स्क्रीन पर लाया जा सके) ✪ विलोम **close**

IDM **open fire (at/on sb/sth)** to start shooting गोलियाँ चलाने लगना, गोलाबारी करना *He ordered his men to open fire.*

PHR V **open into/onto sth** to lead to another room, area or place किसी कमरे, इलाक़े या जगह की ओर निकलना *This door opens onto the garden.*

**open out** to become wider फैल जाना *The lane opens out into the highway.*

**open up 1** to talk about what you feel and think खुलकर बात करना **2** to open a door दरवाज़ा खोलना

**open (sth) up 1** to become available or to make sth available कुछ उपलब्ध होना या उपलब्ध कराना *When I left school all sorts of opportunities opened up for me.* **2** to start business काम शुरू करना *The restaurant opened up last year.*

**the open**[3] /ˈəʊpən ˈओपन्/ *noun* [*sing.*] outside or in the countryside बाहर या देहात में *After working in an office I like to be* ***out in the open*** *at weekends.*

IDM **bring sth out into the open; come out into the open** to make sth known publicly; to be known publicly किसी बात को सार्वजनिक करना; किसी बात का सार्वजनिक होना *I'm glad our secret has come out into the open at last.*

**open-air** *adj.* not inside a building भवन के बाहर, खुले मैदान में *an open-air swimming pool*

**open cast** /ˈəʊpənkɑːst ˈओपन्कास्ट्/ *adj.* in open cast mines, coal is taken out of the ground near the surface खुली कटान वाली (खान जिसमें कोयला लगभग ज़मीन पर से ही इकट्ठा कर लिया जाता है)

**open day** *noun* [C] a day when the public can visit a place that they cannot usually go into जिस दिन जनता के लिए प्रवेश खुला हो *Ria's school is having an open day next month.*

**opener** /ˈəʊpnə(r) ˈओपून(र्)/ *noun* [C] (*in compound nouns*) a thing that takes the lid, etc. off sth ढक्कन आदि खोलने का औज़ार; ओपनर *a tin-opener* ○ *a bottle-opener*

**opening** /ˈəʊpnɪŋ ˈओपूनिङ्/ *noun* [C] **1** a space or hole that sb/sth can go through छेद या सुराख (जिसमें से कोई या कुछ जा सके) *We were able to get through an opening in the hedge.* **2** the beginning or first part of sth किसी वस्तु का आरंभ या पहला खंड *The film is famous for its dramatic opening.* **3** a ceremony to celebrate the first time a public building, road, etc. is used किसी सार्वजनिक भवन, सड़क आदि का उदघाटन या शुभारंभ *the opening of the new hospital* **4** a job which is available नौकरी के लिए रिक्त स्थान *We have an opening for a sales manager at the moment.* **5** a good opportunity अच्छा अवसर *I'm sure she'll be a great journalist—all she needs is an opening.* ▶ **opening** *adj.* (*only before a noun*) *the opening chapter of a book* ○ *the opening ceremony of the Olympic Games*

**openly** /ˈəʊpənli ˈओपन्लि/ *adv.* honestly; not keeping anything secret निष्ठापूर्वक; निश्छल भाव से (बिना कुछ छिपाए) *I think you should discuss your feelings openly with each other.*

**open-minded** *adj.* ready to consider new ideas and opinions नए विचारों और मतों का स्वागत करने वाला; उदारमनस्क

**openness** /ˈəʊpənnəs ˈओपन्नस्/ *noun* [U] the quality of being honest and ready to talk about your feelings मस्तिष्क और हृदय का खुलापन

**open-plan** *adj.* (used about a large area indoors) not divided into separate rooms (घर के अंदर बड़ा स्थान) खुला हुआ, बड़ा हाल (अलग-अलग कमरों में विभक्त नहीं) *an open-plan office*

**the Open University** *noun* [*sing.*] a university that offers distance education to students who study mainly at home. Their work is sent to them by post and there are special television and radio programmes for them खुला या मुक्त विश्वविद्यालय, ओपन यूनिवर्सिटी (विद्यार्थी घर पर रहकर पढ़ते हैं, उन्हें अध्ययन सामग्री भेजी जाती है तथा उनके लिए रेडियो और टीवी पर विशेष कार्यक्रम प्रस्तुत किए जाते हैं) *Indira Gandhi Open University*

**opera** /ˈɒprə ˈऑप्रा/ *noun* [C, U] a play in which the actors (**opera singers**) sing the words to music; works of this kind performed as entertainment ऑपेरा, संगीत-प्रधान नाटक; मनोरंजन के लिए आयोजित ऑपेरा-कार्यक्रम *Do you like opera?* ○ *a comic opera* ➪ **soap opera** देखिए।

**operable** /ˈɒpərəbl ˈऑपरबल्/ *adj.* (used about a disease) that can be cured by a medical operation (रोग) शल्यक्रिया से उपचारयोग्य ✪ विलोम **inoperable**

**opera house** *noun* [C] a theatre where operas are performed संगीत-नाटक आयोजित करने की रंगशाला; ऑपेरा-हाउस

**operate** /ˈɒpəreɪt ˈऑपरेट्/ *verb* **1** [I, T] to work, or to make sth work काम करना, परिचालित होना या किसी वस्तु को परिचालित करना *I don't understand how this machine operates.* ○ *These switches here operate the central heating.* **2** [I, T] to do business; to manage sth व्यापार करना; प्रबंधन करना *The firm operates from its central office in New Delhi.* **3** [I] to act or to have an effect सक्रिय होना या प्रभाव डालना *Several factors were operating to our advantage.* **4** [I] **operate (on sb/sth) (for sth)** to cut open a person's body in hospital in order to deal with a part that is damaged, infected, etc. रोग-निवारण के लिए रोगी की शल्यक्रिया करना *The surgeon is going to operate on her in the morning.* ○ *He was operated on for appendicitis.*

**operatic** /ˌɒpəˈrætɪk ˌऑपˈरैटिक्/ *adj.* connected with opera ऑपेरा-विषयक *operatic music*

**operating system** *noun* [C] a computer program that organizes a number of other programs at the same time कंप्यूटर प्रोग्राम जो साथ ही साथ अन्य प्रोग्रामों को व्यवस्थित करता है; प्रचालन-तंत्र

**operating theatre** (*also* **theatre**) *noun* [C] a room in a hospital where operations are performed अस्पताल में आपरेशन-कक्ष

**operation** /ˌɒpəˈreɪʃn ˌऑपˈरेश्न्/ *noun* **1** [C] (*spoken* **op**) the process of cutting open a patient's body in order to deal with a part inside शल्य-क्रिया, आपरेशन *He **had an operation** to remove his appendix.* **2** [C] an organized activity that involves many people doing different things अनेक व्यक्तियों का भिन्न कार्य करने का संगठित प्रयास *A rescue operation was mounted to find* *the missing children.* **3** [C] a business or company involving many parts ऐसा व्यापार या व्यापारिक प्रतिष्ठान जिसमें अनेक खंड हों **4** [C] an act performed by a machine, especially a computer किसी मशीन (विशेषतः कंप्यूटर) द्वारा परिचालित कार्य **5** [U] the way in which you make sth work परिचालन *The operation of these machines is extremely simple.*

IDM **be in operation; come into operation** to be/start working or having an effect व्यवहार में आना, लागू हो जाना, काम करने लगना *The new tax system will come into operation in the spring.*

**operational** /ˌɒpəˈreɪʃənl ˌऑपˈरेशन्‌ल् / *adj.* **1** (*usually before a noun*) connected with the way a business, machine, system, etc. works किसी व्यापार, मशीन, प्रणाली आदि के परिचालन से संबंधित **2** (*not before a noun*) ready for use काम करने को तैयार, परिचालनीय, प्रयोगार्ह *The new factory is now fully operational.* **3** (*only before a noun*) connected with military operations सैन्य कार्रवाई विषयक

**operative** /ˈɒpərətɪv ˈऑपरटिव़् / *adj.* (*formal*) **1** working, able to be used; in use सक्रिय प्रयोग-योग्य; प्रयोगाधीन *The new law will be operative from 1 May.* **2** connected with a medical operation शल्य-क्रिया-संबंधी

**operator** /ˈɒpəreɪtə(r) ˈऑपरेट(र्) / *noun* [C] **1** a person whose job is to connect telephone calls, for the public or in a particular building टेलीफ़ोन का ऑपरेटर (टेलीफ़ोन की कॉलों को मिलाने वाला व्यक्ति) *Dial 9 for the operator.* ○ *a switchboard operator* **2** a person whose job is to work a particular machine or piece of equipment मशीन का ऑपरेटर, विशेष मशीन को चलाने वाला व्यक्ति *a computer operator* **3** a person or company that does certain types of business विशेष प्रकार का व्यापार करने वाला व्यक्ति या कंपनी, विशेष व्यापार आयोजक व्यक्ति या कंपनी *a tour operator*

**opinion** /əˈpɪnjən अˈपिन्यन् / *noun* **1** [C] **an opinion (of sb/sth); an opinion (on/about sth)** what you think about sb/sth सम्मति, राय *She asked me for my opinion of her new hairstyle and I told her.* ○ ***In my opinion****, you're making a terrible mistake.* **2** [U] what people in general think about sth किसी मुद्दे पर जनमत *Public opinion is in favour of a change in the law.*

IDM **be of the opinion that....** (*formal*) to think or believe that... सोचना या मानना कि, किसी की कोई राय होना

**have a good/high opinion of sb/sth; have a bad/low/poor opinion of sb/sth** to think that sb/sth is good/bad किसी के विषय में अच्छी या ख़राब राय होना

**a matter of opinion** ➪ **matter**[1] देखिए।

**opinion poll** = **poll**[1] **1**

**opium** /ˈəʊpiəm ˈओपिअम् / *noun* [U] a powerful drug that is made from the seeds of a **poppy** (= a type of flower) अफ़ीम

**opp.** *abbr.* opposite के सामने, प्रतिमुख, विरोधी।

**opponent** /əˈpəʊnənt अˈपोनन्ट् / *noun* [C] **1** (in sport or competitions) a person who plays against sb (खेल या स्पर्धाओं में) प्रतिद्वंद्वी *They are the toughest opponents we've played against.* **2 an opponent (of sth)** a person who disagrees with sb's actions, plans or beliefs and tries to stop or change them विरोधी *the President's political opponents*

**opportune** /ˈɒpətjuːn ˈऑपट्यून् / *adj.* (*formal*) **1** (used about a time) suitable for doing sth or for sth to happen कुछ करने या होने के लिए उपयुक्त *I waited for an opportune moment to ask him.* **2** done or happening at the right time to be successful समयानुकूल, अवसरोचित *the opportune visit of the managing director* ✪ विलोम **inopportune**

**opportunism** /ˌɒpəˈtjuːnɪzəm ˌऑपˈट्यूनिज़म् / *noun* [U] the practice of using situations unfairly to get an advantage for yourself without thinking about how your actions will affect other people (दूसरों के हितों की चिंता किए बिना) केवल अपने लिए अनुचित रूप से लाभ उठाने की प्रवृत्ति; अवसरवादिता, मौक़ापरस्ती *political opportunism*

**opportunist** /ˌɒpəˈtjuːnɪst ˌऑपˈट्यूनिस्ट् / (*also* **opportunistic**) *adj.* (*usually before a noun*) making use of an opportunity, especially to get an advantage for yourself; not done in a planned way जैसा अवसर मिले वैसा, यथावसर (विशेषतः अपने लाभ के लिए); योजनाबद्ध तरीक़े से न किया हुआ, अनियोजित *an opportunist crime* ▶ **opportunist** *noun* [C] अवसरवादी, मौक़ापरस्त *Eighty per cent of burglaries are committed by casual opportunists.*

**opportunistic** /ˌɒpətjuːˈnɪstɪk ˌऑपट्यूˈनिस्टिक् / *adj.* **1** = **opportunist** **2** (*only before a noun*) (*medical*) harmful to people whose **immune system** has been made weak by disease or drugs (रोग या नशीले पदार्थों के कारण) क्षीण प्रतिरक्षा शक्तिवाले व्यक्तियों के लिए हानिकर *an opportunistic infection*

**opportunity** /ˌɒpəˈtjuːnəti ˌऑपˈट्यूनटि / *noun* [C, U] (*pl.* **opportunities**) **an opportunity (for sth/to do sth)** a chance to do sth that you would like to do; a situation or a time in which it is possible to do sth that you would like to do

अवसर, सुअवसर, मौक़ा; उपयुक्त, अवसरानुकूल स्थिति या समय *I have a **golden opportunity** to go to America now that my sister lives there.* ○ *When we're finally alone, I'll **take the opportunity** to ask him a few personal questions.* ➪ **occasion** पर नोट देखिए।

**oppose** /əˈpəʊz अˈपोज़्/ *verb* [T] to disagree with sb's beliefs, actions or plans and to try to change or stop them किसी का विरोध करना (उसके विचारों, कार्यों या योजनाओं से सहमत न होना और उन्हें बदलने या अवरुद्ध करने का प्रयास करना) *They opposed the plan to build a new road.*

**opposed** /əˈpəʊzd अˈपोज़्ड्/ *adj.* **opposed to sth** disagreeing with a plan, action, etc.; believing that sth is wrong विरुद्ध, असहमत; किसी बात को ग़लत मानने वाला *She has always been strongly opposed to experiments on animals.*

IDM **as opposed to** (used to emphasize the difference between two things) rather than; and not (दो वस्तुओं में अंतर पर बल देने के लिए प्रयुक्त) के विपरीत; न कि *Your work will be judged by quality, as opposed to quantity.*

**opposite** /ˈɒpəzɪt ˈऑपज़िट्/ *adj., adv., prep.* **1** in a position on the other side of sb/sth; facing किसी व्यक्ति या वस्तु के दूसरी तरफ़; सामने *The old town and the new town are on opposite sides of the river.* ○ *You sit there and I'll sit opposite.*

NOTE कभी-कभी **opposite** का प्रयोग संज्ञा के बाद होता है—*Write your answer in the space opposite.*

**2** completely different विपरीत *I can't walk with you because I'm going in the opposite direction.* ○ *the opposite sex* (= the other sex) ▶ **opposite** *noun* [C] विलोम *'Hot' is **the opposite of** 'cold'.*

IDM **your opposite number** a person who does the same job or has the same position as you in a different company, organization, team, etc. समकक्ष पदाधिकारी (भिन्न संगठन, टीम आदि में समान पद पर आसीन या समान कार्य करने वाला व्यक्ति) *The Prime Minister met his Italian opposite number.*

**opposition** /ˌɒpəˈzɪʃn ˌऑपˈज़िश्न्/ *noun* [U] **1** opposition (to sb/sth) the feeling of disagreeing with sth and the action of trying to change it असहमति, विरोध *He expressed strong opposition to the plan.* **2 the opposition** [*sing.*] the person or team who you compete against in sport, business, etc. खेल, व्यापार आदि में प्रतिद्वंद्वी व्यक्ति या दल *We need to find out what the opposition is doing.* **3 the Opposition** [*sing.*] the politicians or the political parties that are in Parliament but not in the government प्रतिपक्ष (संसद या विधायिका में राजनेता या राजनीतिक दल जो सत्ता में नहीं है) *the leader of the Opposition* ○ *Opposition MPs* NOTE अर्थ संख्या **2** और **3** में **opposition** के साथ एकवचनांत (singular) या बहुवचनांत (plural) क्रिया प्रयुक्त हो सकती है।

**oppress** /əˈpres अˈप्रेस्/ *verb* [T] (*usually passive*) to treat a group of people in a cruel and unfair way by not allowing them the same freedom and rights as others लोगों पर अत्याचार करना (उन्हें अधिकारों से वंचित करना), उनका दमन या उत्पीड़न करना ▶ **oppressed** *adj.* उत्पीड़ित *an oppressed minority* ▶ **oppression** *noun* [U] अत्याचार, दमन, उत्पीड़न *a struggle against oppression*

**oppressive** /əˈpresɪv अˈप्रेसिव्/ *adj.* **1** allowing no freedom; controlling by force स्वतंत्रता का अपहरण करते हुए, दमनकारी; बल-प्रयोग से नियंत्रित करते हुए, अत्याचारी **2** (used especially about heat or the atmosphere) causing you to feel very uncomfortable (ताप या वायुमंडल) परेशान करने वाला, कष्टप्रद

**opt** /ɒpt ऑप्ट्/ *verb* [I] **opt to do sth/for sth** to choose or decide to do or have sth after thinking about it सोच-विचार के बाद चयन या निर्णय करना

PHR V **opt out (of sth)** to choose not to take part in sth; to decide to stop being involved in sth किसी बात में भाग न लेने का विकल्प चुनना; किसी बात में लिप्त न होने का निर्णय करना

**optic** /ˈɒptɪk ˈऑप्टिक्/ *adj.* connected with the eye or the sense of sight नेत्र या दृष्टि से संबंधित चाक्षुष या दृष्टि-विषयक *the **optic nerve*** (= from the eye to the brain) ➪ **eye** पर चित्र देखिए।

**optical** /ˈɒptɪkl ˈऑप्टिकल्/ *adj.* connected with the sense of sight दृष्टि-विषयक, दृष्टि-शक्ति बढ़ाने से संबंधित *optical instruments*

**optical illusion** *noun* [C] an image that tricks the eye and makes you think you can see sth that you cannot दृष्टि-भ्रम (जो वस्तुतः नहीं है उसे देखने का भ्रम)

**optician** /ɒpˈtɪʃn ऑप्ˈटिश्न्/ *noun* [C] a person whose job is to test eyes, sell glasses, etc. आँखों की जाँच करना, चश्मा बेचना आदि काम करने वाला व्यक्ति *I have to go to the optician's* (= the shop) *for an eye test.*

**optics** /ˈɒptɪks ˈऑप्टिक्स्/ *noun* [U] the scientific study of sight and light दृष्टि और प्रकाश का वैज्ञानिक अध्ययन, दृष्टि-व-प्रकाश विज्ञान

**optimal** /ˈɒptɪməl ˈऑप्टिमल्/ = **optimum**[1]

**optimism** /ˈɒptɪmɪzəm ˈऑप्टिमिज़म्/ *noun* [U] the feeling that the future will be good or successful भविष्य के अच्छा या अनुकूल होने का भाव; आशावादिता, भविष्य की सफलता में विश्वास *There is* *considerable optimism that the economy will improve.* ✪ विलोम **pessimism** ▶ **optimist** *noun* [C] आशावादी व्यक्ति ✪ विलोम **pessimist**

**optimistic** /ˌɒptɪˈmɪstɪk ˌऑप्टिˈमिस्टिक्/ *adj.* **optmistic (about sth/that...)** expecting good things to happen or sth to be successful; showing this feeling स्थितियों की अनुकूलता या प्रयत्नों में सफलता की आशा करने वाला; आशापूर्ण, आशान्वित *I've applied for the job but I'm not very optimistic that I'll get it.* ✪ विलोम **pessimistic** ▶ **optimistically** /-kli -कलि/ *adv.* आशापूर्वक ✪ विलोम **pessimistically**

**optimum** /ˈɒptɪməm ˈऑप्टिमम्/ *adj.* (*only before a noun*) **1** (*also* **optimal**) the best possible, giving the best possible results यथासंभव सर्वोत्तम अनुकूलता, अनुकूलतम परिणाम देने वाला **2 the optimum** *noun* [*sing.*] the best possible result or the best set of conditions to get good results अनुकूलतम परिणाम, सर्वोत्तम परिस्थितियाँ (जिनमें अच्छे परिणाम प्राप्त हों)

**option** /ˈɒpʃn ˈऑप्शन्/ *noun* [U, C] something that you can choose to do; the freedom to choose विकल्प; चयन की स्वतंत्रता *Students **have the option** of studying part-time or full-time.* ○ *If you're late again, you will give us **no option but to** dismiss you.* ✪ पर्याय **choice**

**optional** /ˈɒpʃənl ˈऑप्शन्ल्/ *adj.* that you can choose or not choose वैकल्पिक (जिसे आप चुन या छोड़ सकते हैं) *an optional subject at school* ✪ विलोम **compulsory** या **obligatory**

**or** /ɔ:(r) ऑ(र्)/ *conj.* **1** used in a list of possibilities or choices या अथवा (संभावनाओं या विकल्पों की सूची में प्रयुक्त) *Would you like to sit here or next to the window?* ○ *Are you interested or not?* ○ *For the main course, you can have peas, eggs or fish.* ➪ **either... or** देखिए। **2** if not; otherwise नहीं तो; अन्यथा *Don't drive so fast or you'll have an accident!* ✪ पर्याय **or else** और **otherwise** का भी इस अर्थ में प्रयोग हो सकता है **3** (*after a negative*) and neither; and not दोनों में से कोई नहीं; और न ही *She hasn't phoned or written to me for weeks.* ○ *I've never been either to Mumbai or Pune.* ➪ **neither... nor** देखिए। **4** used between two numbers to show approximately how many दो संख्याओं के बीच प्रयुक्त (लगभग कितने यह दिखाने के लिए) *I've been there five or six times.* **5** used before a word or phrase that explains or comments on what has been said before पूर्वोक्त को समझाने या उस पर कुछ कहने का अर्थ देने वाले शब्द या वाक्यांश से पहले प्रयुक्त *twenty per cent of the population, or one in five*

IDM **or else** ➪ **else** देखिए।

**or so** about लगभग *You should feel better in three days or so.*

**or something/somewhere** (*spoken*) used for showing that you are not sure, cannot remember or do not know which thing or place किसी वस्तु या स्थान की जानकारी के विषय में अनिश्चय का भाव दर्शाने के लिए प्रयुक्त *She's a computer programmer or something.*

**oracle** /ˈɒrəkl ˈऑरकल्/ *noun* [C] **1** (in ancient Greece) a place where people could go to ask the gods for advice and information about the future; the priest through whom the gods were thought to give their message प्राचीन ग्रीस में एक स्थान जहाँ लोग भविष्य के विषय में देववाणी सुनने जाते थे; लोगों की मान्यता के अनुसार देववाणी सुनाने वाले पुरोहित *They consulted the oracle at Delphi.* **2** (in ancient Greece) the advice or information that the gods gave, which often had a hidden meaning प्राचीन ग्रीस में होने वाली अप्रत्यक्ष अर्थ या आशय वाली देववाणी **3** [*usually sing.*] a person or book that gives valuable advice or information उपयोगी परामर्श या जानकारी देने वाला व्यक्ति या ग्रंथ, विवेकी व्यक्ति या ज्ञानवर्धक ग्रंथ *My sister's the oracle on financial matters.*

**oral[1]** /ˈɔ:rəl ˈऑरल्/ *adj.* **1** spoken, not written बोला हुआ, मौखिक (न कि लिखित) *an oral test* **2** concerning or using the mouth मुख से या उसके प्रयोग से संबंधित *oral hygiene* ➪ **aural** देखिए। ▶ **orally** *adv.* मौखिक रूप से *You can ask the questions orally or in writing.* ○ *This medicine is taken orally* (= is swallowed).

**oral[2]** /ˈɔ:rəl ˈऑरल्/ *noun* [C] a spoken exam मौखिक परीक्षा *I've got my geography oral next week.*

**orange[1]** /ˈɒrɪndʒ ˈऑरिन्ज्/ *noun* **1** [C, U] a round fruit with a thick skin that is divided into sections (**segments**) inside and is a colour between red and yellow संतरा, नारंगी *orange juice/peel* ○ *an orange tree* ➪ **fruit** पर चित्र देखिए। **2** [U, C] a drink made from oranges or with the taste of oranges; a glass of this drink नारंगी का रस या नारंगी के स्वाद वाला पेय; गिलास भर यह पेय या इस पेय से भरा गिलास **3** [U, C] the colour of this fruit, between red and yellow नारंगी रंग (लाल और पीले के बीच का)

**orange[2]** /ˈɒrɪndʒ ˈऑरिन्ज्/ *adj.* of the colour orange नारंगी के रंग का, नारंगी *orange paint*

**orange squash** *noun* [C, U] a drink made by adding water to an orange-flavoured liquid नारंगी का शरबत , ऑरेंज-स्क्वॉश

**orang-utan** /ɔːˌræŋuːˈtæn ऑˌरैङ्यूˈटैन् / *noun* [C] a large **ape** with long arms and reddish hair, that lives in Borneo and Sumatra लंबी बाँहों और कुछ-कुछ लाल बालों वाला एक प्रकार का बड़ा बंदर (जो बोर्नियो और सुमात्रा में रहता है), ओरंग उटान, वनमानुष

**orator** /ˈɒrətə(r) ˈऑरट(र्) / *noun* [C] (*formal*) a person who is good at making public speeches कुशल सार्वजनिक वक्ता

**orbit** /ˈɔːbɪt ˈऑबिट् / *noun* [C, U] a curved path taken by a planet or another object as it moves around another planet, star, moon, etc. ग्रह-उपग्रह का परिक्रमा-पथ (वह गोलाकार या अंडाकार पथ जिस पर कोई ग्रह या अन्य आकाशीय पिंड अन्य ग्रह आदि की परिक्रमा करे), कक्षा ➪ **season** पर चित्र देखिए।

▶ **orbit** *verb* [I, T] परिक्रमा करना

**orbital** /ˈɔːbɪtl ˈऑबिट्ल् / *adj.* **1** (used about a road) built around the outside of a city or town to reduce the amount of traffic travelling through the centre (सड़क) नगर के चारों ओर बनी (नगर के मध्य का यातायात घटाने के लिए); वृत्ताकार **2** connected with the orbit of a planet or another object in space (ग्रह या अन्य आकाशीय पिंड के परिक्रमा-पथ या कक्षा से संबंधित; कक्षीय, ग्रहपक्षीय) ▶ **orbital** *noun* [C, *usually sing.*] मुद्रिका-पथ, परिक्रमा-पथ

**orchard** /ˈɔːtʃəd ˈऑचड् / *noun* [C] a piece of land on which fruit trees are grown फलों का बाग़, फलोद्यान *an apple orchard*

**orchestra** /ˈɔːkɪstrə ˈऑकिस्ट्रा / *noun* [C] a large group of musicians who play different musical instruments together, led by one person (**a conductor**) वाद्यवृंद (एक संचालक के निर्देशन में भिन्न-भिन्न वाद्यों को बजाने वाले वादकों का दल), ऑर्केस्ट्रा *a symphony orchestra*

> **NOTE** ऑर्केस्ट्रा में सामान्यतया शास्त्रीय संगीत प्रस्तुत किया जाता है। पॉप संगीत, जाज़ आदि **group** या **band** द्वारा पेश किए जाते हैं।

▶ **orchestral** /ɔːˈkestrəl ऑˈकेस्ट्रल् / *adj.* वाद्यवृंद-विषयक

**orchestration** /ˌɔːkɪˈstreɪʃn ˌऑकिˈस्ट्रेशन् / *noun* [U] **1** the way that a piece of music is written so that an orchestra can play it वाद्यवृंद के लिए संगीत-रचना, वृंदवादन **2** (*written*) the careful organization of a complicated plan or event, done secretly किसी जटिल योजना या कार्यक्रम को सतर्कतापूर्वक गुप्त रीति से संगठित करने की क्रिया

**orchid** /ˈɔːkɪd ˈऑकिड् / *noun* [C] a beautiful and sometimes rare type of plant that has flowers of unusual shapes and bright colours विचित्र-सी आकृति के और चटकीले रंग के फूलों वाला एक सुंदर (और दुर्लभ) पौधा; आर्किड

**ordain** /ɔːˈdeɪn ऑˈडेन् / *verb* [T] (*usually passive*) **ordain sb (as) (sth)** to make sb a priest of the Church किसी व्यक्ति को चर्च का पुरोहित बनाना, दीक्षा देना, पुरोहित का अभिषेक करना *He was ordained (as) a priest last year.* ➪ **ordination** noun देखिए।

**ordeal** /ɔːˈdiːl; ˈɔːdiːl ऑˈडील्; ˈऑडील् / *noun* [C, *usually sing.*] a very unpleasant or difficult experience अत्यंत अप्रिय या कठिन अनुभव, अग्नि-परीक्षा

**order[1]** /ˈɔːdə(r) ˈऑड(र्) / *noun* **1** [U, C] the way in which people or things are arranged in relation to each other व्यवस्थित क्रम, सिलसिला *a list of names in* ***alphabetical order*** ○ *Try to put the things you have to do* ***in order of importance.*** **2** [U] an organized state, where everything is in its right place व्यवस्था *I really must* ***put*** *my notes* ***in order****, because I can never find what I'm looking for.* ✪ विलोम **disorder** **3** [C] **an order (for sb) (to do sth)** sth that you are told to do by sb in a position of authority आदेश, आज्ञा, हुक्म *In the army, you have to* ***obey orders*** *at all times.* ○ *She* ***gave the order*** *for the work to be started.* **4** [U] the situation in which laws, rules, authority, etc. are obeyed शांति व्यवस्था *Following last week's riots, order has now been restored.* ➪ **disorder** देखिए। **5** [C, U] **an order (for sth)** a request asking for sth to be made, supplied or sent किसी वस्तु के निर्माण, आपूर्ति आदि का अनुरोध, आर्डर, क्रयादेश *The company has just received a major export order.* ○ *The book I need is* ***on order*** (= they are waiting for it to arrive). **6** [C] a request for food or drinks in a hotel, restaurant, etc.; the food or drinks you asked for होटल आदि में खाद्य या पेय पदार्थों के लिए अनुरोध; माँगे गए खाद्य या पेय पदार्थ *Can I* ***take your order*** *now, sir?*

**IDM** **in order to do sth** with the purpose or intention of doing sth; so that sth can be done कुछ करने के लिए; ताकि कुछ किया जा सके *We left early in order to avoid the traffic.*

**in/into reverse order** ➪ **reverse[3]** देखिए।

**in working order** (used about machines, etc.) working properly, not broken (मशीनें) चालू हालत में, क्रियाशील स्थिति में

**law and order** ➪ **law** देखिए।

**out of order** 1 (used about a machine, etc.) not working properly or not working at all (मशीनें) ख़राब या बेकार *I had to walk up to the tenth floor because the lift was out of order.* 2 (*informal*) (used about a person's behaviour) unacceptable, because it is rude, etc. (व्यक्ति का आचरण) अनुचित, धृष्टतापूर्ण *That comment was completely out of order!*

**order²** /ˈɔ:də(r) ˈऑड(र्)/ *verb* 1 [T] **order sb (to do sth)** to use your position of authority to tell sb to do sth or to say that sth must happen आदेश, आज्ञा या हुक्म देना *I'm not asking you to do your homework, I'm ordering you!* ○ *The company was ordered to pay compensation to its former employees.* 2 [T] to ask for sth to be made, supplied or sent somewhere किसी वस्तु के निर्माण, आपूर्ति या कहीं भेजने की माँग करना *The shop didn't have the book I wanted so I ordered it.* 3 [I, T] **order (sb) (sth); order (sth) (for sb)** to ask for food or drinks in a restaurant, hotel, etc. किसी रेस्तराँ आदि में खाद्य या पेय पदार्थों के लिए अनुरोध करना या की माँग करना *Are you ready to order yet, madam?* ○ *Can you order me a sandwich while I make a phone call?*

**PHR V** **order sb about/around** to keep telling sb what to do and how to do it किसी काम के विषय में किसी को कहते रहना *Stop ordering me about! You're not my father.*

**order form** *noun* [C] a form that is filled in by sb ordering goods from a factory shop, etc. क्रयादेश-पत्र, ऑर्डर-फ़ॉर्म

**orderly¹** /ˈɔ:dəli ˈऑडलि/ *adj.* 1 arranged or organized in a tidy way सुव्यवस्थित *an orderly office/desk* 2 well behaved; peaceful सुशील; शांत प्रकृति का ✪ विलोम **disorderly**

**orderly²** /ˈɔ:dəli ˈऑडलि/ *noun* [C] (*pl.* **orderlies**) an untrained worker ( in a hospital or army etc.) who attends to a superior officer अर्दली (अफ़सरों के साथ रहने वाला तथा उनके छोटे-मोटे काम करने वाला व्यक्ति)

**ordinal** /ˈɔ:dɪnl ˈऑडिनल्/ (*also* **ordinal number**) *noun* [C] a number that shows the order or position of sth in a series क्रमसूचक संख्या *'First', 'second', and 'third' are ordinals.* ➪ **cardinal** देखिए।

**ordinance** /ˈɔ:dɪnəns ˈऑडिनन्स्/ *noun* [C] (*formal*) an order or rule made by a government or sb in a position of authority प्राधिकारी अध्याधेश; सरकार या विशिष्ट अधिकारी द्वारा जारी आदेश या नियम

**ordinarily** /ˈɔ:dnrəli ˈऑडिन्रलि/ *adv.* usually; generally प्रायः; सामान्यतः *Ordinarily, I don't work as late as this.*

**ordinary** /ˈɔ:dnri ˈऑडिन्रि/ *adj.* normal; not unusual or different from others साधारण; अन्यों से असामान्य या अलग नहीं, अन्यों के समान *It's interesting to see how ordinary people live in other countries.*

**IDM** **out of the ordinary** unusual; different from normal असाधारण; सामान्य से भिन्न

**ordination** /ˌɔ:dɪˈneɪʃn ˌऑडिˈनेशन्/ *adj* the act or ceremony of making sb a priest of the Church किसी व्यक्ति को चर्च का पुरोहित बनाने की प्रक्रिया या अनुष्ठान, दीक्षा-दान, पुरोहिताभिषेक ➪ **ordain** verb देखिए।

**ordnance** /ˈɔ:dnəns ˈऑड्नन्स्/ *noun* [C] military supplies consisting of ammunition, equipment, etc. युद्ध सामग्री, गोला-बारूद, अस्त्र-शस्त्र आदि

**ore** /ɔ:(r) ऑ(र्)/ *noun* [C, U] rock or earth from which metal can be taken कच्ची धातु (पत्थर या मिट्टी के रूप में, जिससे धातु निकाली जाती है); अयस्क *iron ore*

**organ** /ˈɔ:gən ˈऑगन्/ *noun* [C] 1 one of the parts inside your body that have a particular function शरीर का कोई अवयव या अंग (जो कोई विशेष काम करे) ***vital organs*** (= those such as the heart and liver which help to keep you alive) ○ *sexual/reproductive organs* 2 a large musical instrument like a piano with pipes through which air is forced. Organs are often found in churches नलियों वाला (पियानो सदृश) बड़ा वाद्य यंत्र जिसे फूँककर बजाया जाता है (प्रायः चर्चों में प्रयुक्त), ऑर्गन *organ music*
▸ **organist** *noun* [C] ऑर्गन-वादक

**organic** /ɔ:ˈgænɪk ऑˈगैनिक्/ *adj.* 1 (used about food or farming methods) produced by or using natural materials, without artificial chemicals प्राकृतिक सामग्री के प्रयोग से उत्पादित (खाद्य पदार्थ) या उसका प्रयोग करने वाली (कृषि की विधियाँ) *organic vegetables* ○ *organic farming* 2 produced by or existing in living things सजीवों से उत्पन्न या उनमें उपस्थित; जैविक *organic compounds/molecules* ✪ विलोम **inorganic** ▸ **organically** /-kli -क्लि/ *adv.* जैविक रीति से *organically grown/produced*

**organism** /ˈɔ:gənɪzəm ˈऑगनिज़म्/ *noun* [C] a living thing, especially one that is so small that you can only see it with a special instrument (**a microscope**) अति सूक्ष्म जीव (केवल सूक्ष्मवीक्षण यंत्र से देखने योग्य); अवयव

**organization** (*also* **-isation**) /ˌɔ:gənaɪˈzeɪʃn ˌऑगनाइˈज़ेशन्/ *noun* 1 [C] a group of people who form a business, club, etc. together in order to achieve a particular aim संगठन (विशेष प्रयोजन से किसी व्यापार, क्लब आदि को व्यवस्थित करने वाले व्यक्तियों का समूह) *She works for a voluntary organization helping homeless people.* **2** [U] the activity of making preparations or arrangements for sth किसी कार्यक्रम की तैयारी या व्यवस्था करने की क्रिया *An enormous amount of organization went into the festival.* 3 [U] the way in which sth is organized, arranged or prepared किसी गतिविधि को संगठित, व्यवस्थित करने का तरीक़ा ✪ विलोम **disorganization** ▶ **organizational** (*also* **-isational**) /-ʃənl -शनल्/ *adj.* संगठन-विषयक, सांगठनिक *The job requires a high level of organizational ability.*

**organize** (*also* **-ise**) /ˈɔːɡənaɪz ˈऑगनाइज़्/ *verb* **1** [T] to plan or arrange an event, activity, etc. संगठित करना (उसकी किसी कार्यक्रम, गतिविधि आदि की योजना बनाना या उसकी व्यवस्था करना) *The school organizes trips to various places of interest.* **2** [I, T] to put or arrange things into a system or logical order वस्तुओं को किसी व्यवस्था या तर्कयुक्त क्रम में रखना; संगठित करना *Can you decide what needs doing? I'm hopeless at organizing.* ○ *You need to organize your work more carefully.* ▶ **organizer** (*also* **-iser**) *noun* [C] संगठनकर्ता, व्यवस्थापक, आयोजक *The organizers of the concert said that it had been a great success.*

**organized** (*also* **-ised**) /ˈɔːɡənaɪzd ˈऑगनाइज़्ड्/ *adj.* **1** arranged or planned in the way mentioned निर्दिष्ट रीति से व्यवस्थित या योजनाबद्ध *a carefully/badly/well-organized trip* **2** (used about a person) able to plan your work, life, etc. well (व्यक्ति) सुव्यवस्थित *I wish I were as organized as you!* ✪ विलोम **disorganized** (अर्थ सं॰ 1 और 2 के लिए) **3** (*only before a noun*) involving a large number of people working together to do sth in a way that has been carefully planned सुव्यवस्थित, सुसंगठित (जिसमें अनेक लोग सुनियोजित रीति से एक साथ काम करें) *an organized campaign against cruelty to animals* ○ *organized crime* (= done by a large group of professional criminals)

**orgasm** /ˈɔːɡæzəm ˈऑगैज़म्/ *noun* [U, C] the point of greatest sexual pleasure कामोत्तेजना का चरम बिंदु, रति-निष्पत्ति *to have an orgasm*

**orgy** /ˈɔːdʒi ˈऑजि/ *noun* [C] (*pl.* **orgies**) **1** a party, involving a lot of eating, drinking and sexual activity रंगरलियाँ, विलासोत्सव **2 an orgy (of sth)** a period of doing sth in a wild way, without control अमर्यादित व्यवहार *an orgy of destruction*

**the Orient** /ˈɔːriənt ˈऑरिअन्ट्/ *noun* [*sing.*] (*formal*) the eastern part of the world especially East Asian countries विश्व के पूर्वी भाग के देश (विशेषतः पूर्वी एशियाई देश)

**orient** /ˈɔːrient ˈऑरिएन्ट्/ (*also* **orientate** /ˈɔːriənteɪt ˈऑरिअन्टेट्/) *verb* [T] **orient yourself** to find out where you are; become familiar with a place स्वयं को पहचानना; किसी स्थान से परिचित होना ➪ **disorientate** देखिए।

**oriental** (*also* **Oriental**) /ˌɔːriˈentl ˌऑरिˈएन्ट्ल्/ *adj.* (*old-fashioned*) coming from or belonging to the East of Far East पूर्व या सुदूर पूर्व के देशों का; प्राच्य **NOTE** ध्यान रखिए अनेक लोग इस शब्द को अब अपमानजनक मानते हैं। बेहतर शब्द **Asian** है।

**oriented** /ˈɔːrientɪd ˈऑरिएन्टिड्/ (*also* **orientated** /ˈɔːriənteɪtɪd ˈऑरिअन्टेटिड्/) *adj.* for or interested in a particular type of person or thing विशेष प्रकार के व्यक्ति के लिए या विशेष प्रकार की वस्तु में रुचि रखने वाला *The shop sells male-oriented products.* ○ *She's very career orientated.*

**orienteering** /ˌɔːriənˈtɪərɪŋ ˌऑरिअन्ˈटिअरिङ्/ *noun* [U] a sport in which you find your way across an area on foot, using a map and an instrument that shows direction (**a compass**) किसी क्षेत्र या भूखंड में पदयात्रा करते हुए (मानचित्र और दिक्सूचक यंत्र की सहायता से) अपने गंतव्य पर पहुँचने का खेल

**orifice** /ˈɒrɪfɪs ˈऑरिफ़िस्/ *noun* [C] (*formal*) a hole or opening, especially in the body छिद्र या विवर (विशेषतः शरीर में)

**origin** /ˈɒrɪdʒɪn ˈऑरिजिन्/ *noun* [C, U] **1** (*often used in the plural*) the point from which sth starts; the cause of sth उद्गत-बिंदु; स्रोत *This particular tradition* ***has its origins in*** *Punjab.* ○ *Many English words are* ***of*** *French* ***origin***. **2** (*often used in the plural*) the country, race, culture, etc. that a person comes from व्यक्ति का देश, जाति, संस्कृति आदि जिससे उसका मूलतः संबंध है; मूल *people of African origin*

**original[1]** /əˈrɪdʒənl अˈरिजनल्/ *adj.* **1** (*only before a noun*) first; earliest (before any changes or developments) (किसी परिवर्तन या विकास से पूर्व) प्रथम; आदिम; मूल *The original meaning of this word is different from the meaning it has nowadays.* **2** new and interesting; different from others of its type नया और रोचक; सदृश वस्तुओं से भिन्न, मौलिक *There are no original ideas in his work.* **3** made or created first, before copies मूल (प्रति) *'Is that the original painting?' 'No, it's a copy.'*

**original²** /əˈrɪdʒənl अˈरिजनल् / *noun* [C] the first document, painting, etc. that was made; not a copy किसी चित्र आदि का मूल रूप, मूल प्रति; नक़ल या प्रतिलिपि नहीं *Could you make a photocopy of my birth certificate and give the original back to me?*

**originality** /əˌrɪdʒəˈnæləti अˌरिजˈनैलटि / *noun* [U] the quality of being new and interesting नयापन और रोचकता; मौलिकता

**originally** /əˈrɪdʒənəli अˈरिजनलि / *adv.* **1** in the beginning, before any changes or developments मूल रूप से *I'm from Maharashtra originally, but I left there when I was very young.* **2** in a way or style that is new and different from any others नए और कुछ अपने ढंग से, मौलिकता के साथ *She has a talent for expressing simple ideas originally.*

**originate** /əˈrɪdʒɪneɪt अˈरिजिनेट् / *verb* [I] (*formal*) to happen or appear for the first time in a particular place or situation स्थान या अवसर विशेष पर पहली बार घटित या प्रकट होना

**ornament** /ˈɔːnəmənt ˈऑनमन्ट् / *noun* [C] an object that you have because it is attractive, not because it is useful. Ornaments are used to decorate rooms, etc. अलंकार, सजावटी वस्तु (गहना आदि)

**ornamental** /ˌɔːnəˈmentl ˌऑनˈमेन्ट्ल् / *adj.* made or put somewhere in order to look attractive, not for any practical use आलंकारिक, सजावटी

**ornate** /ɔːˈneɪt ऑˈनेट् / *adj.* covered with a lot of small complicated designs as decoration अत्यधिक अलंकृत

**ornithology** /ˌɔːnɪˈθɒlədʒi ˌऑनिˈथॉलजि / *noun* [U] the study of birds पक्षियों का वैज्ञानिक अध्ययन, पक्षी-विज्ञान ▶ **ornithologist** /-ɪst -इस्ट् / *noun* [C] पक्षी-विज्ञानी

**orographic** /ɒrəˈgræfɪk ऑरˈग्रैफ़िक् / *adj.* (*technical*) connected with mountains, especially with their position and shape पर्वतीय, पर्वतों से संबंधित (विशेषतया उनकी स्थिति और आकृति की दृष्टि से)

**orphan** /ˈɔːfn ˈऑफ़्न् / *noun* [C] a child whose parents are dead अनाथ ▶ **orphan** *verb* [T] (*usually passive*) अनाथ कर देना या हो जाना *She was orphaned when she was three and went to live with her grandparents.*

**orphanage** /ˈɔːfənɪdʒ ˈऑफ़निज् / *noun* [C] a home for children whose parents are dead अनाथालय NOTE इस अर्थ में **children's home** अधिक प्रचलित है।

**ortho-** /ˈɔːθəʊ ˈऑथो / *prefix* (*used in nouns, adjectives and adverbs*) correct; standard शुद्ध; मानक *orthography*

**orthodox** /ˈɔːθədɒks ˈऑथडॉक्स् / *adj.* **1** that most people believe, do or accept; usual रूढ़िवादी (जिसे अधिकतर लोग मानें, जिस पर आचरण करें); सामान्य, बहुमान्य *orthodox opinions/methods* ✪ विलोम **unorthodox** **2** (in certain religions) closely following the old, traditional beliefs, ceremonies, etc. (कुछ धर्मों में) पुरातनपंथी (प्राचीन, परंपरागत विश्वास, अनुष्ठान आदि का अनुसरण करने वाले) *an orthodox Jew* ○ *the Greek Orthodox Church*

**orthography** /ɔːˈθɒgrəfi ऑˈथॉग्रफ़ि / *noun* [U] (*formal*) the system of spelling in a language भाषा की वर्तनी-व्यवस्था ▶ **orthographic** /ˌɔːθəˈgræfɪk ˌऑथˈग्रैफ़िक् / *adj.* वर्तनी-संबंधी

**orthopaedics** (*AmE* **orthopedics**) /ˌɔːθəˈpiːdɪks ˌऑथˈपीडिक्स् / *noun* [U] the area of medicine connected with injuries and diseases of the bones or muscles विकलांग-चिकित्सा (अस्थियों या मांसपेशियों की क्षति और रोगों की चिकित्सा) ▶ **orthopaedic** (*AmE* **orthopedic**) *adj.* विकलांग-चिकित्सा संबंधी

**oscillate** /ˈɒsɪleɪt ˈऑसिलेट् / *verb* [I] (*formal*) **(between A and B)** **1** to keep changing from one extreme of feeling or behaviour to another, and back again किसी मनोभाव या आचरण के चरम-बिंदुओं के बीच डोलना, झूलना या दोलायमान होना *Her moods oscillated between joy and depression.* **2** (*technical*) to keep moving from one position to another and back again किसी वस्तु का दो स्थितियों के बीच डोलते रहना *Watch how the needle oscillates as the current changes.* **3** (*technical*) (used about electric current, radio waves, etc.) to change in strength or direction at regular times (विद्युत, रेडियो तरंगों आदि का) लगातार शक्ति या दिशा बदलना ▶ **oscillation** *noun* [C, U] दोलन

**oscilloscope** /əˈsɪləskəʊp अˈसिलस्कोप् / *noun* [C] (*technical*) a piece of equipment that shows changes in electrical current as waves in a line on a screen दोलन दर्शी (विद्युत धारा के तरंगों में परिवर्तित होने की क्रिया को परदे पर एक रेखा के रूप में दर्शाने वाला यंत्र)

**osmosis** /ɒzˈməʊsɪs ऑज़ˈमोसिस् / *noun* [U] (*technical*) the gradual passing of a liquid through a thin layer of material (**a membrane**) द्रव-संक्रमण (द्रव का झिल्ली में से मंदगति से गुज़रना) *Water passes into the roots of a plant* ***by osmosis***.

**ostensible** /ɒˈstensəbl ऑˈस्टेन्सबल् /*adj.* (*only before a noun*) seeming or stated to be real or true, but not necessarily real or true वास्तविक जैसा पर वास्तविक नही; निर्दिष्ट, दिखावटी *The ostensible reason she gave for her absence was illness.*

**ostentatious** /ˌɒstenˈteɪʃəs ˌऑस्टेन्ˈटेशस् / *adj.* **1** expensive or noticeable in a way that is intended to impress other people तड़क-भड़क वाला, आडंबरपूर्ण (महँगा या दिखावटी कि लोग प्रभावित हों) *ostentatious gold jewellery* **2** behaving in a way that is intended to impress people with how rich or important you are आडंबर-पूर्ण, प्रदर्शन-प्रिय (जिसमें समृद्धि या महत्त्व का ऐसा प्रदर्शन हो कि लोग प्रभावित हों) ▶ **ostentatiously** *adv.* आडंबरपूर्वक

**osteo-** /ˈɒstiəʊ ˈऑस्टिओ / (*used in nouns and adjectives*) connected with bones अस्थि-विषयक *osteopath*

**osteopath** /ˈɒstiəpæθ ˈऑस्टिअपैथ् / *noun* [C] a person whose job involves treating some diseases and physical problems by pressing and moving the bones and muscles अस्थि-चिकित्सक (अस्थियों और मांसपेशियों को दबा या हिलाकर उनके रोगों और विकृतियों की चिकित्सा करने वाला व्यक्ति) ➪ **chiropractor** देखिए।

**osteoporosis** /ˌɒstiəʊpəˈrəʊsɪs ˌऑस्टिओपˈरोसिस् / *noun* [U] a medical condition in which the bones become weak and are easily broken अस्थिसुषिरता; (अस्थियों की दुर्बलता और भंगुरता का रोग)

**ostracize** (*also* **-ise**) / ˈɒstrəsaɪz ˈऑस्ट्रसाइज़् / *verb* [T] (*formal*) to refuse to allow sb to be a member of a social group; to refuse to meet or talk to sb किसी व्यक्ति का सामाजिक बहिष्कार करना; किसी व्यक्ति से मिलने या बात करने से इनकार करना

**ostrich** /ˈɒstrɪtʃ ˈऑस्ट्रिच् / *noun* [C] a very large African bird with a long neck and long legs, which can run very fast but which cannot fly शुतुरमुर्ग़ (लंबी गरदन और टाँगों वाला बड़े आकार का अफ़्रीक़ी पक्षी जो बहुत तेज़ दौड़ता है परंतु उड़ नहीं सकता)

**other** /ˈʌðə(r) ˈअद़(र्) / *det., pronoun* **1** in addition to or different from the one or ones that have already been mentioned (पूर्व-निर्दिष्ट व्यक्तियों या वस्तुओं) के अतिरिक्त या उनसे भिन्न *I hadn't got any other plans that evening so I accepted their invitation.* ○ *She doesn't care what other people think.*

> **NOTE** **An** के बाद शब्द **other** आए तो उसे **another** लिखा जाता है।

**2** (*after 'the', 'my', 'your', 'his', 'her', etc. with a singular noun*) the second of two people or things, when the first has already been mentioned दो व्यक्तियों या वस्तुओं में दूसरा (जब पहले व्यक्ति या वस्तु का निर्देश हो चुका हो) *I can only find one sock. Have you seen the other one?* **3** (*after 'the', 'my', 'your', 'his', 'her', etc. with a plural noun*) the rest of a group or number of people or things व्यक्तियों या वस्तुओं के समूह में से शेष रहा (व्यक्ति या वस्तु) *Their youngest son still lives with them but their other children have left home.* ○ *I'll have to wear this shirt because all my others are dirty.*

**IDM** **every other** ➪ **every** देखिए।

**in other words** used for saying sth in a different way दूसरे शब्दों में *My boss said she would have to let me go. In other words, she sacked me.*

**one after another/the other** ➪ **one**[1] देखिए।

**other than** (*usually after a negative*) apart from; except (for) के अतिरिक्त; को छोड़कर *The plane was a little late, but other than that the journey was fine.*

**the other day/morning/week** recently, not long ago हाल ही में, कुछ दिन पहले *An old friend rang me the other day.*

**the other way round** ➪ **round**[2] देखिए।

**sb/sth/somewhere or other** ➪ **or** देखिए।

**otherwise** /ˈʌðəwaɪz ˈअद़वाइज़् / *adv., conj.* **1** (used for stating what would happen if you do not do sth or if sth does not happen) if not नहीं तो, अन्यथा (नकारात्मक संभावना को व्यक्त करने के लिए प्रयुक्त) *You have to press the red button, otherwise it won't work.* **2** apart from that उस बात के अतिरिक्त *I'm a bit tired but otherwise I feel fine.* **3** in a different way to the way mentioned; differently (निर्दिष्ट से) भिन्न प्रकार से; दूसरे ढंग से

**otter** /ˈɒtə(r) ˈऑट(र्) / *noun* [C] a river animal with brown fur that eats fish ऊदबिलाव (भूरे रोओं वाला जंतु जो नदी में रहता है और मछली खाता है)

**ouch** /aʊtʃ आउच् / *exclamation* used when reacting to a sudden feeling of pain एकाएक उठे दर्द को व्यक्त करने के लिए प्रयुक्त

**ought to** /ˈɔːt tə; ˈऑट् ट *before vowels and in final position* ˈɔːt tuː ˈऑट् टू /) *modal verb* (*negative* **ought not to;** *short form* **oughtn't to** /ˈɔːtnt tə ˈऑटन्ट् ट / *before vowels and in final position* / ˈɔːtnt tuː ˈऑटन्ट् टू /) **1** used to say what sb should do चाहिए सूचक (जो यह बताए कि क्या करना चाहिए) *You ought to visit your parents more often.* ○ *He oughtn't to have been driving so fast.* **2** used to say what should happen or what you expect संभावना सूचक (जो यह बताए कि क्या हो सकता है, संभावित है या प्रत्याशित है) *She ought to pass her test.* ○ *There ought to be more buses in the rush hour.* **3** used for asking for and giving advice about what to do कुछ करने का परामर्श माँगने और देने के लिए प्रयुक्त *You ought to read this book. It's really interesting.*

**NOTE** वृत्तिवाचक क्रियाओं (modal verbs) के विषय में अधिक जानकारी के लिए इस शब्दकोश के अंत में **Quick Grammar Reference** देखिए।

**ounce** /aʊns आउन्स् / *noun* 1 [C] (*abbr.* **oz**) a measure of weight; 28.35 grams. There are 16 ounces in a pound आउंस, तौल की एक माप; 28.35 ग्राम (एक पाउंड में 16 आउंस होते हैं) *For this recipe you need 4 ounces of flour.* 2 [*sing.*] **an ounce of sth** (*usually in negative statements*) a very small amount of sth ज़रा-सा भी *He hasn't got an ounce of imagination.*

**our** /ɑː(r); ˈaʊə(r) आ(र्); ˈआउअ(र्) / *det.* of or belonging to us हमारा (जिसके हम स्वामी हैं या जो हमसे संबंधित हैं) *Our house is at the bottom of the road.* ○ *This is our first visit to Shimla.*

**ours** /ɑːz; ˈaʊəz अ ज़्; ˈआउअज़् / *pronoun* the one or ones belonging to us वह जो हमारा है, हमारे वाला *Their garden is quite nice but I prefer ours.*

**ourselves** /ɑːˈselvz; ˌaʊəˈs- आ ˈसेल्व्ज़्; ˌआउअˈस्- / *pronoun* 1 used when the people who do an action are also affected by it हम स्वयं, अपने आपको (तब प्रयुक्त जब करने वाला अपने काम से प्रभावित भी हो) *Let's forget all about work and just enjoy ourselves.* ○ *They asked us to wait so we sat down and made ourselves comfortable.* 2 used to emphasize sth हम ही या हमीं (किसी बात पर बल देने के लिए प्रयुक्त) *Do you think we should paint the flat ourselves* (= or should we ask sb else to do it for us)?

**IDM** **(all) by ourselves** 1 alone अकेले *Now that we're by ourselves, could I ask you a personal question?* ➪ **alone** देखिए। 2 without help बिना किसी सहायता के *We managed to move all our furniture into the new flat by ourselves.*

**oust** /aʊst आउस्ट् / *verb* [T] (*written*) **oust sb (from/as sth)** to force sb out of a job or position of power, especially in order to take his/her place किसी को नौकरी या अधिकार के पद से निकाल बाहर करना (विशेषतया उसका स्थान हथियाने के लिए) *He was ousted as chairman.*

**out** /aʊt आउट् / *adv., prep.*

**NOTE** विभिन्न क्रियाओं के साथ out के विशेष प्रयोग (जैसे **look out**) के लिए उन क्रियाओं की प्रविष्टि देखिए।

1 away from the inside of a place बाहर (किसी स्थान के भीतरी भाग से दूर) *He opened the drawer and took a fork out.* ○ *Can you show me the way out?* ➪ **out of** देखिए। 2 not at home or in your place of work घर, दफ़्तर या कार्यस्थल से बाहर (वहाँ पर नहीं) *My manager was out when she called.* ○ *I'd love a night out—I'm bored with staying at home.* 3 a long distance away from a place, for example from land or your country किसी स्थान से (जैसे तट या स्वदेश से) काफ़ी दूर *The current is quite strong so don't swim too far out.* 4 (used about the sea) when the water is furthest away from the coast or beach (समुद्र) जब पानी तट से बहुत दूर हो, जब भाटे की स्थिति हो *Don't swim when the tide is on the way out.* 5 used for showing that sth is no longer hidden प्रकट अवस्था में, सबके सामने (जब किसी वस्तु के छिपे न रहने की बात दर्शानी हो) *I love the spring when all the flowers are out.* ○ *The secret's out now. There's no point pretending any more.* 6 made available to the public; published जनता के लिए उपलब्ध; प्रकाशित *There'll be a lot of controversy when her book comes out next year.* 7 in a loud voice; clearly ऊँचे स्वर में; स्पष्टतया *She cried out in pain.* 8 not in fashion अप्रचलित, फ़ैशन से बाहर *Short skirts are out this season.* 9 (*spoken*) not possible or acceptable जो संभव या स्वीकार्य न हो *I'm afraid Friday is out. I've got a meeting that day.* 10 (used about a player in a game or sport) not allowed to continue playing (खिलाड़ी का खेल से) बाहर हो जाना, आगे खेलने पर रोक लग जाना *If you get three answers wrong, you're out.* 11 (used about a ball, etc. in a game or sport) not inside the playing area and therefore not allowed (गेंद का खेल के मैदान से) बाहर चले जाने पर अमान्य होना 12 (used when you are calculating sth) making or containing a mistake; wrong (गिनती करते हुए) ग़लती कर जाना या ग़लत हो जाना; ग़लत, अशुद्ध *My guess was only out by a few centimetres.* 13 (used about a light or a fire) not on; not burning (बत्ती या आग) बुझी हुई; न जलती हुई *The lights are out. They must be in bed.* ○ *Once the fire was completely out, experts were sent in to inspect the damage.*

**IDM** **be out for sth; be out to do sth** to try hard to get or do sth किसी बात पर आमादा हो जाना *I'm not out for revenge.*

**out-and-out** complete संपूर्ण, मुकम्मल *It was out-and-out war between us.*

**out loud** = **aloud**

**out-** /aʊt आउट् / *prefix* 1 (*used in verbs*) greater, better, further, longer, etc. अपेक्षया अधिक बड़ा, अच्छा, दूर, लंबा आदि *outdo* ○ *outrun* 2 (*used in nouns and adjectives*) outside; away from बाहर का, बाह्य; से दूर, दूरवर्ती *outbuildings* ○ *outpatient*

**the outback** /ˈaʊtbæk ˈआउट्बैक् / *noun* [*sing.*] the part of a country (especially Australia) which is a long way from the coast and towns, where few people live किसी देश (विशेषतः ऑस्ट्रेलिया) का वह भाग जो समुद्र तट और छोटे शहरों से काफ़ी दूर हो (और जहाँ आबादी भी कम हो)

**outboard motor** /ˌaʊtbɔːd ˈməʊtə(r) ˌआउट्बॉड् ˈमोट(र्)/ *noun* [C] an engine that can be fixed to a boat नाव में लग सकने वाला इंजन ➪ **boat** पर चित्र देखिए।

**outbreak** /ˈaʊtbreɪk ˈआउट्ब्रेक्/ *noun* [C] the sudden start of sth unpleasant (especially a disease or violence) किसी अप्रिय स्थिति (विशेषतः रोग या हिंसा) का एकाएक विस्फोट होना, भड़क उठना, प्रकोप *an outbreak of cholera/fighting*

**outburst** /ˈaʊtbɜːst ˈआउट्बस्ट्/ *noun* [C] a sudden expression of a strong feeling, especially anger शक्तिशाली मनोभाव (विशेषतः क्रोध) की अभिव्यक्ति; भड़ास *Afterwards, she apologized for her outburst.*

**outcast** /ˈaʊtkɑːst ˈआउट्कास्ट्/ *noun* [C] a person who is no longer accepted by society or by a group of people समाज या समूह विशेष से बहिष्कृत *a social outcast*

**outclass** /ˌaʊtˈklɑːs ˌआउट्ˈक्लास्/ *verb* [T] (*usually passive*) to be much better than sb/sth, especially in a game or competition किसी व्यक्ति या वस्तु से बहुत बढ़कर होना (विशेषतया खेल या स्पर्धा में)

**outcome** /ˈaʊtkʌm ˈआउट्कम्/ *noun* [C] the result or effect of an action or an event किसी क्रिया या घटना का परिणाम या प्रभाव

**outcrop** /ˈaʊtkrɒp ˈआउट्क्रॉप्/ *noun* [C] (in geography) a large mass of rock that stands above the surface of the ground (भूगोल में) चट्टान का अविर्भाव जो पृथ्वी की सतह से ऊँचा होता है; चट्टान शैल

**outcry** /ˈaʊtkraɪ ˈआउट्क्राइ/ *noun* [C, *usually sing.*] (*pl.* **outcries**) a strong protest by a large number of people because they disagree with sth जनता का शक्तिशाली विरोध (किसी बात के अस्वीकार्य होने के कारण) *The public outcry forced the government to change its mind about the new tax.*

**outdated** /ˌaʊtˈdeɪtɪd ˌआउट्ˈडेटिड्/ *adj.* not useful or common any more; old-fashioned बेकार हो चुका, प्रचलन से बाहर; पुरानी चाल का *A lot of the computer equipment is getting outdated.*

**outdo** /ˌaʊtˈduː ˌआउट्ˈडू/ *verb* [T] (*pres. part.* **outdoing**; *3rd person sing. pres.* **outdoes** /-ˈdʌz -ˈडज़्/; *pt*, **outdid** /-ˈdɪd -ˈडिड्/; *pp* **outdone** /-ˈdʌn -ˈडन्/) to do sth better than another person; to be more successful than sb else किसी काम को अन्य व्यक्ति से बेहतर करना; अन्य व्यक्ति से बढ़कर होना ***Not to be outdone*** (= not wanting anyone else to do better), *she tried again.*

**outdoor** /ˈaʊtdɔː(r) ˈआउट्डॉ(र्)/ *adj.* (*only before a noun*) happening, done, or used outside, not in a building घर के बाहर (का) *an outdoor swimming pool ○ outdoor clothing/activities* ✪ विलोम **indoor**

**outdoors** /ˌaʊtˈdɔːz ˌआउट्ˈडॉज़्/ *adv.* outside a building घर से बाहर, खुले में *It's a very warm evening so why don't we eat outdoors?* ✪ पर्याय **out of doors** ✪ विलोम **indoors** ➪ **outside** देखिए।

**outer** /ˈaʊtə(r) ˈआउट(र्)/ *adj.* (*only before a noun*) **1** on the outside of sth बाहरी, बाह्य *the outer layer of skin on an onion* **2** far from the inside or the centre of sth केंद्र, बीच या भीतर से काफ़ी दूर का *the outer suburbs of a city* ✪ विलोम **inner**

**outermost** /ˈaʊtəməʊst ˈआउटमोस्ट्/ *adj.* (*only before a noun*) furthest from the inside or centre; most distant केंद्र या भीतर से सर्वाधिक दूर; बहुत दूर ✪ विलोम **innermost**

**outer space** = **space**[1] **2**

**outfit** /ˈaʊtfɪt ˈआउट्फ़िट्/ *noun* [C] a set of clothes that are worn together for a particular occasion or purpose विशेष अवसर पर या विशेष प्रयोजन से एक साथ पहनने के कपड़ों का सेट *I'm going to buy a whole new outfit for the party.*

**outgoing** /ˈaʊtgəʊɪŋ ˈआउट्गोइङ्/ *adj.* **1** friendly and interested in other people and new experiences सबसे मित्रवत तथा उनमें और नए अनुभवों में रुचि रखने वाला, सामाजिकता प्रिय, मिलनसार **2** (*only before a noun*) leaving a job or a place पद को छोड़कर या बाहर जाने वाला, पदमुक्त या बहिर्गामी *the outgoing president/government ○ Put all the outgoing mail in a pile on that table.* ✪ विलोम **incoming**

**outgoings** /ˈaʊtgəʊɪŋz ˈआउट्गोइङ्ज़्/ *noun* [*pl.*] (*BrE*) an amount of money that you spend regularly for example every week or month प्रति माह या सप्ताह व्यय होने वाली धनराशि, मासिक या साप्ताहिक व्यय ✪ विलोम **income**

**outgrow** /ˌaʊtˈgrəʊ ˌआउट्ˈग्रो/ *verb* [T] (*pt.* **outgrew** /-ˈgruː -ˈग्रू/ *pp* **outgrown** /-ˈgrəʊn -ˈग्रोन्/) to become too old or too big for sth किसी वस्तु के प्रयोग की दृष्टि से अधिक आयु का या बड़ा हो जाना (आयु या लंबाई बढ़ जाने के कारण किसी वस्तु का प्रयोग न कर पाना); अपवृद्धि होना

**outing** /ˈaʊtɪŋ ˈआउटिङ्/ *noun* [C] a short trip for pleasure सैर-सपाटा, उल्लास-यात्रा, आमोद-विहार, भ्रमण *to go on an outing to the zoo*

**outlandish** /aʊtˈlændɪʃ आउट्ˈलैन्डिश् / *adj.* very strange or unusual अति विचित्र या असाधारण, अजीबोग़रीब या ग़ैर-मामूली *outlandish clothes*

**outlast** /ˌaʊtˈlɑːst ˌआउट्ˈलास्ट् / *verb* [T] to continue to exist or to do sth for a longer time than sb/sth अन्य की अपेक्षा देर तक बने रहना या जीवित रहना या कोई काम करते रहना

**outlaw[1]** /ˈaʊtlɔː ˈआउट्लॉ / *verb* [T] to make sth illegal किसी बात को ग़ैर-क़ानूनी घोषित करना; अवैध

**outlaw[2]** /ˈaʊtlɔː ˈआउट्लॉ / *noun* [C] (*old-fashioned*) (used in past times) a person who has done sth illegal and is hiding to avoid being caught ग़ैर-क़ानूनी घोषित व्यक्ति (जो बंदी होने से बचने के लिए छिपा रहता है); विधि-बहिष्कृत

**outlay** /ˈaʊtleɪ ˈआउट्ले / *noun* [C, *usually sing.*] **outlay (on sth)** money that is spent, especially in order to start a business or project लागत, व्यय (विशेषतया कोई व्यापार या परियोजना आरंभ करने में लगी धनराशि)

**outlet** /ˈaʊtlet ˈआउट्लेट् / *noun* [C] **an outlet (for sth)** **1** a way of expressing and making good use of strong feelings, ideas or energy सशक्त भावों, विचारों या ऊर्जा की अभिव्यक्ति और सदुपयोग का मार्ग *Gautam found an outlet for his aggression in boxing.* **2** a shop, business, etc. that sells goods made by a particular company or of a particular type विशेष कंपनी का या विशेष प्रकार का सामान बेचने वाली दुकान, कंपनी आदि *fast food/retail outlets* **3** a pipe through which a gas or liquid can escape गैस या द्रव की निकासी का पाइप

**outline[1]** /ˈaʊtlaɪn ˈआउट्लाइन् / *noun* [C] **1** a description of the most important facts or ideas about sth रूपरेखा *a brief outline of Indian history* **2** a line that shows the shape or outside edge of sb/sth व्यक्ति या वस्तु की आकृति या बाह्य सीमा दर्शाने वाली रेखा; बहिर्रेखा *She could see the outline of a person through the mist.*

**outline[2]** /ˈaʊtlaɪn ˈआउट्लाइन् / *verb* [T] **outline sth (to sb)** to tell sb or give the most important facts or ideas about sth (किसी वस्तु की) रूपरेखा बनाना

**outlive** /ˌaʊtˈlɪv ˌआउट्ˈलिव् / *verb* [T] to live or exist longer than sb/sth व्यक्ति या वस्तु की अपेक्षा अधिक समय तक जीना या जीवित रहना

**outlook** /ˈaʊtlʊk ˈआउट्लुक् / *noun* [C] **1 an outlook (on sth)** your attitude to or feeling about life and the world दृष्टिकोण (जीवन और जगत के प्रति मनोवृत्ति या भावना) *an optimistic outlook on life* **2 outlook (for sth)** what will probably happen संभावना *The outlook for the economy is not good.*

**outlying** /ˈaʊtlaɪɪŋ ˈआउट्लाइङ् / *adj.* (*only before a noun*) far from the centre of a town or city दूरवर्ती, बहिर्वर्ती (नगर के केंद्र से दूर, बाहर की ओर) *The bus service to the outlying villages is very poor.*

**outmoded** /ˌaʊtˈməʊdɪd ˌआउट्ˈमोडिड् / *adj.* (*only before a noun*) no longer common or fashionable जो अब फ़ैशन या प्रचलन में नहीं रहा, पुरानी शैली का

**outnumber** /ˌaʊtˈnʌmbə(r) ˌआउट्ˈनम्ब(र्) / *verb* [T] (*usually passive*) to be greater in number than an enemy, another team, etc. शत्रु, दूसरी टीम आदि से संख्या में अधिक होना *The demonstrators were heavily out numbered by the police.* ○ *The enemy troops outnumbered us by three to one.*

**out of** *prep.* **1** (*used with verbs expressing movement*) away from the inside of sth में से *She took her purse out of her bag.* ○ *to get out of bed* ✪ विलोम **into** **2** away from or no longer in a place or situation किसी स्थान या परिस्थिति से दूर या वहाँ अनुपस्थित *He's out of the country on business.* ○ *The doctors say she's* ***out of danger***. **3** at a distance from a place किसी स्थान से दूर *We live a long way out of London.* **4** used for saying which feeling causes you to do sth के कारण, के मारे (कुछ करने के पीछे की भावना को व्यक्त करने के लिए प्रयुक्त) *I was only asking out of curiosity.* **5** used for saying what you use to make sth else से (किसी वस्तु को बनाने में प्रयुक्त सामग्री का निर्देश करने के लिए प्रयुक्त) *What is this knife* ***made out of****?* ○ *to be made out of wood/metal/plastic/gold* **6** from among a number or set किसी संख्या या समूह में से *Nine out of ten people prefer this model.* **7** from; having sth as its source से; किसी वस्तु का स्रोत *I copied the recipe out of a book.* ○ *I paid for it out of the money I won on the lottery.* **8** used for saying that you no longer have sth किसी वस्तु के (अब) न रहने का संकेत करने के लिए प्रयुक्त *to be out of milk/sugar/tea* ○ *He's been* ***out of work*** *for months.* **9** used for saying that sth is not as it should be किसी वस्तु के निष्क्रिय हो जाने का संकेत करने के लिए प्रयुक्त *My notes are all* ***out of order*** *and I can't find the right page.*

IDM **be/feel out of it** to be/feel lonely and unhappy because you are not included in sth अकेला-सा पड़ जाना *I don't speak French so I felt rather out of it at the meeting.*

IDM **out of bounds** ➪ **bounds** देखिए।

**out of order** ➪ **order[1]** देखिए।

**out-of-work** *adj.* unable to find a job; unemployed जो नौकरी न पा सके; बेकार *an out-of-work actor*

**outpatient** /ˈaʊtpeɪʃnt ˈआउट्पेशन्ट्/ *noun* [C] a person who goes to a hospital for treatment but who does not stay there during the night बहिरंग रोगी (अस्पताल में चिकित्सा कराने आने वाला रोगी जिसे वहीं रहने के लिए प्रविष्ट नहीं किया जाता)

**outpost** /ˈaʊtpəʊst ˈआउट्पोस्ट्/ *noun* [C] **1** a small military camp away from the main army, used for watching an enemy's movements, etc. सेना की सीमा-चौकी (सेना के मुख्य शिविर से दूर छोटा शिविर जो शत्रु की गतिविधियों पर नज़र रखता है) **2** a small town or group of buildings in a lonely part of a country एक छोटा शहर या किसी एकाकी गाँव में भवनों का समूह

**output** /ˈaʊtpʊt ˈआउटपुट्/ *noun* [U, C] **1** the amount that a person or machine produces व्यक्ति या मशीन द्वारा उत्पादित मात्रा, उत्पादन मात्रा **2** the information that a computer produces कंप्यूटर द्वारा प्रस्तुत सूचना-राशि (कंप्यूटर का) आउटपुट ➪ **input** देखिए। **3** the power, energy, etc. produced by a piece of equipment किसी उपकरण द्वारा उत्पादित शक्ति, ऊर्जा आदि *an output of 100 watts* **4** the place where power, energy, etc. leaves a system किसी सिस्टम में शक्ति, ऊर्जा आदि का निष्क्रमण-बिंदु

**outrage** /ˈaʊtreɪdʒ ˈआउट्रेज्/ *noun* **1** [C] something that is very bad or wrong and that causes you to feel great anger अत्यधिक रोष उत्पन्न करने वाली दुर्व्यवस्था *It's an outrage that such poverty should exist in the 21st century.* **2** [U] great anger अत्यधिक क्रोध *a feeling of outrage* ▶ **outrage** *verb* [T] अत्यधिक क्रोध दिलाना

**outrageous** /aʊtˈreɪdʒəs आउट्ˈरेजस्/ *adj.* that makes you very angry or shocked अति क्रोधजनक, अपमानजनक *outrageous behaviour/prices* ▶ **outrageously** *adv.* अत्यधिक क्रोध दिलाते हुए, अपमानपूर्वक

**outright** /ˈaʊtraɪt ˈआउट्राइट्/ *adj., adv.* **1** open and direct; in an open and direct way साफ़-साफ़ और सीधा; खुले और सीधे तौर पर *She told them outright what she thought about it.* **2** complete and clear; completely and clearly पूर्ण और स्पष्ट; पूर्णतया और स्पष्टतया *an outright victory* ○ *to win outright* **3** not gradually; immediately एक ही बार में (न क़िस्तों या टुकड़ों में); तत्काल *They were able to buy the house outright.*

**outrun** /ˌaʊtˈrʌn ˌआउट्ˈरन्/ *verb* [T] (*pres. part.* **outrunning**; *pt* **outran** /-ˈræn -ˈरैन्/; *pp* **outrun**) to run faster or further than sb/sth किसी व्यक्ति या वस्तु से अधिक तेज़ या दूर भागना *He couldn't outrun his pursuers.*

**outset** /ˈaʊtset ˈआउट्सेट्/ *noun*

IDM **at/from the outset (of sth)** at/from the beginning (of sth) आरंभ से या में ही

**outside¹** /ˌaʊtˈsaɪd ˌआउट्ˈसाइड्/ *adv., prep.* **1** in, at or to a place that is not in a room or not in a building (कक्ष, भवन आदि से) बाहर *Please wait outside for a few minutes.* ○ *Leave your muddy boots outside the door.* ➪ **outdoors** और **out of doors** (**door** की प्रविष्टि में) देखिए। **2** (*AmE* **outside of**) not in के अंदर नहीं, के बाहर या बाद *You may do as you wish outside office hours.* ○ *a small village just outside Jaipur*

**outside²** /ˈaʊtsaɪd ˈआउट्साइड्/ *adj.* (*only before a noun*) **1** of or on the outer side or surface of sth किसी वस्तु की बाहरी ओर या सतह से संबंधित या उस पर *the outside walls of a building* **2** not part of the main building (मुख्य भवन से) बाहर का *an outside toilet* **3** not connected with or belonging to a particular group or organization विशिष्ट समूह या संगठन से संबंधित या उस तक सीमित नहीं; बाह्य *We can't do all the work by ourselves. We'll need outside help.* **4** (used about a chance or possibility) very small (अवसर या संभावना) बहुतकम, अत्यल्प

IDM **the outside world** people, places, activities, etc. that are away from the area where you live and your own experience of life आपके निवास-क्षेत्र और जीवन-अनुभव की परिधि से दूर का जगत (व्यक्ति, स्थान, गतिविधियाँ आदि)

**outside³** /ˌaʊtˈsaɪd ˌआउट्ˈसाइड्/ *noun* **1** [C, *usually sing.*] the outer side or surface of sth किसी वस्तु की बाहरी सतह *There is a list of all the ingredients on the outside of the packet.* **2** the area that is near or round a building, etc. बाहर की ओर से (किसी भवन के निकट या आस-पास का क्षेत्र) *We've only seen the church from the outside.* **3** [*sing.*] the part of a road, a track, etc. that is away from the side that you usually drive on, run on, etc. किसी सड़क, ट्रैक आदि का बाहर की ओर पड़ने वाला भाग *The other runners all overtook him on the outside.* ✪ विलोम **inside** (सब अर्थों का)

IDM **at the outside** at the most अधिक-से-अधिक *It will take us three days at the outside.*

**outsider** /ˌaʊtˈsaɪdə(r) ˌआउट्ˈसाइड(र्)/ *noun* [C] **1** a person who is not accepted as a member of a particular group जो व्यक्ति समूह विशेष का अंतरंग सदस्य न हो; बाह्य, बाहरी **2** a person or animal in a race or competition that is not expected to win दौड़ या स्पर्धा में भाग लेने वाला ऐसा व्यक्ति या पशु जिसके जीतने की आशा नहीं ✪ विलोम **favourite**

**outsize** /ˈaʊtsaɪz ˈआउट्साइज़्/ *adj.* (often used about clothes) larger than usual (कपड़े) सामान्य से अधिक बड़े, अधिनाप

**outskirts** /ˈaʊtskɜːts ˈआउट्स्कट्स्/ *noun* [*pl.*] the parts of a town or city that are furthest from the centre नगर या बस्ती का बाहरी भाग (नगर या बस्ती के केंद्र से सर्वाधिक दूर का हिस्सा) सीमांत, बाह्यांचल *They live **on the outskirts** of Patna.*

**outspoken** /aʊtˈspəʊkən आउट्ˈस्पोकन्/ *adj.* saying exactly what you think or feel although you may shock or upset other people मुँह-फट, स्पष्टवक्ता, खरा बोलने वाला *Lalita is very outspoken in her criticism.*

**outstanding** /aʊtˈstændɪŋ आउट्ˈस्टैन्डिङ्/ *adj.* **1** extremely good; excellent अत्यंत अच्छा; उत्कृष्ट *The results in the exams were outstanding.* **2** not yet paid, done or dealt with शेष, अवशिष्ट, बक़ाया *Some of the work is still outstanding.* ○ *outstanding debts/issues*

**outstandingly** /aʊtˈstændɪŋli आउट्ˈस्टैन्डिङ्लि/ *adv.* extremely; very well अत्यधिक; बहुत अच्छा *outstandingly good*

**outstretched** /ˌaʊtˈstretʃt ˌआउट्ˈस्ट्रेच्ट्/ *adj.* reaching as far as possible दूर तक पहुँचने वाला, फैलाया हुआ *He came towards her with his arms outstretched.*

**outstrip** /ˌaʊtˈstrɪp ˌआउट्ˈस्ट्रिप्/ *verb.* (**outstripping; outstripped**) **1** to become larger or greater in quantity than something else मात्रा में अधिक या विशाल होना *Demand is outstripping supply.* **2** to be better than sb or be more successful किसी व्यक्ति से बेहतर या अधिक सफल होना *We are hoping to outstrip our competitors.* **3** to be faster than sb or sth किसी व्यक्ति या वस्तु से तेज़ होना *She ran so fast that soon she had outstripped other runners.*

**outward** /ˈaʊtwəd ˈआउट्वड्/ *adj.* (*only before a noun*) **1** on the outside बाहरी, बाह्य *Despite her cheerful outward appearance, she was in fact very unhappy.* **2** (used about a journey) going away from the place that you will return to later (यात्रा) जाने की दिशा की ओर; बहिर्गामी ✪ विलोम **return** **3** away from the centre or from a particular point बाहरी, बाह्य (केंद्र या विशेष स्थान-बिंदु से दूर *outward movement/pressure* ✪ विलोम **inward** ▶ **outwardly** *adv.* बाहर से *He remained outwardly calm so as not to frighten the children.*

**outwards** /ˈaʊtwədz ˈआउट्वड्ज़्/ (*AmE* **outward**) *adv.* towards the outside or away from the place where you are बाहर की ओर या जहाँ आप हैं वहाँ से दूर *This door opens outwards.*

**outweigh** /ˌaʊtˈweɪ ˌआउट्ˈवे/ *verb* [T] to be more in amount or importance than sth किसी वस्तु से मात्रा या महत्त्व में अधिक होना *The advantages outweigh the disadvantages.*

**outwit** /ˌaʊtˈwɪt ˌआउट्ˈविट्/ *verb* [T] (**outwitting; outwitted**) to gain an advantage over sb by doing sth clever दूसरे को चतुराई में मात देना या उससे बढ़कर होना

**oval** /ˈəʊvl ˈओव्ल्/ *adj., noun* [C] shaped like an egg; a shape like that of an egg अंडे के आकार का; अंडे का-सा आकार ➪ **shape** पर चित्र देखिए।

**ovary** /ˈəʊvəri ˈओव़रि/ *noun* [C] (*pl.* **ovaries**) **1** one of the two parts of the female body that produce eggs नारी शरीर में अंडा उत्पन्न करने वाला अंग; अंडाशय **2** (*technical*) the part of a plant that produces seeds पौधे में बीज उत्पन्न करने वाला अंश ➪ **flower** पर चित्र देखिए।

**ovation** /əʊˈveɪʃn ओˈव़ेशन्/ *noun* [C] an enthusiastic reaction given by an audience when it likes sb/sth very much. The people in the audience make a noise with their hands (**clap**) and shout (**cheer**) and often stand up उत्साहपूर्ण स्वागत (प्रायः खड़े होकर ताली बजाते और हो हल्ला करते हुए); अभिनंदन *The dancers got **a standing ovation** at the end of the performance.*

**oven** /ˈʌvn ˈअव़न्/ *noun* [C] a box-like **equipment** with a door. You put things inside an oven to cook them बक्सनुमा अँगीठी, ओवन *Cook in a hot oven for 50 minutes.* ○ *a microwave oven*

**over**[1] /ˈəʊvə(r) ˈओव़(र्)/ *adv., prep.*

> **NOTE** अनेक क्रियाओं के साथ इस शब्द के विशेष प्रयोग (जैसे **get over sth**) के लिए उनकी क्रिया की प्रविष्टियाँ देखिए।

**1** straight above sth, but not touching it किसी वस्तु से सीधे ऊपर (उसे न छूते हुए) *There's a painting over the bookcase.* ○ *We watched the plane fly over.* ➪ **above** देखिए। **2** covering sth किसी वस्तु को ढकते हुए *He was holding a towel over the cut.* ○ *She hung her coat over the back of the chair.* **3** across to the other side of sth किसी वस्तु के दूसरी तरफ़, आर-पार *The horse jumped over the fence.* ○ *a bridge over the river* **4** on or to the other side दूसरी ओर *The student turned the paper over and read the third question.* **5** down or sideways from an upright position ऊपर से नीचे की ओर या तिरछे *He leaned over to speak to the woman next to him.* ○ *I fell over in the street this morning.* **6** above or more than a number, price, etc. निर्धारित संख्या, क़ीमत आदि से अधिक *She lived in*

*Canada for over 10 years.* ○ *suitable for children aged 10 and over* **7** used for expressing distance दूरी का अर्थ व्यक्त करने के लिए प्रयुक्त *He's over in America at the moment.* ○ *Sit down* ***over there.*** **8** not used; still remaining अप्रयुक्त; शेष, बचा हुआ *There are a lot of cakes* ***left over*** *from the party.* **9** (used with all) everywhere ('all' के साथ प्रयुक्त) चारों ओर, सर्वत्र *There was blood* ***all over the place.*** ○ *I can't find my glasses. I've looked all over for them.* **10** used for saying that sth is repeated किसी काम की पुनरावृत्ति का सूचक *You'll have to start* ***all over again*** (= from the beginning). ○ *She kept saying the same thing* ***over and over again.*** **11** about; on the subject of के विषय में; किसी बात पर *We quarrelled over money.* **12** during के दौरान *We met several times over the Christmas holiday.*

**over²** /ˈəʊvə(r) ˈओव़(र्)/ *adj.* finished समाप्त *The exams are all over now.*

**over-** /ˈəʊvə(r) ˈओव़(र्)/ *prefix* (*used in nouns, verbs, adjectives and adverbs*) **1** more than usual; too much सामान्य से अधिक; अत्यधिक, अति- *oversleep/overeat* ○ *overcrowded/overexcited* **2** completely पूर्णतया *overjoyed* **3** upper; outer; extra ऊपरी; बाहरी; अतिरिक्त *overcoat* ○ *overtime* **4** over; above ऊपर; ऊँचे *overcast* ○ *overhang*

**overall¹** /ˌəʊvərˈɔːl ˌओव़र्ˈऑल्/ *adv., adj.* **1** including everything; total कुल मिलाकर; सकल, समग्र *What will the overall cost of the work be?* **2** generally; when you consider everything सामान्यतया; सब कुछ दृष्टि में रखते हुए *Overall, I can say that we are pleased with the year's work.*

**overall²** /ˈəʊvərɔːl ˈओव़र्ऑल्/ *noun* [C] a piece of clothing like a coat that you wear over your clothes to keep them clean when you are working काम करते समय सामान्य कपड़ों के ऊपर पहना जाने वाला कपड़ा

**overawe** /ˌəʊvərˈɔː ˌओवर्ˈऑ/ *verb* [T] (*usually passive*) to impress sb so much that he/she feels nervous or frightened किसी को अत्यधिक प्रभावित करना (कि वह डर-सा जाए)

**overbalance** /ˌəʊvəˈbæləns ˌओव़ˈबैलन्स्/ *verb* [I] to lose your balance and fall संतुलन खो देना (और गिर जाना)

**overbearing** /ˌəʊvəˈbeərɪŋ ˌओव़ˈबेअरिङ्/ *adj.* having an unpleasant way of telling other people what to do दूसरों पर रौब जमाने वाला; दबंग

**overboard** /ˈəʊvəbɔːd ˈओव़बॉड्/ *adv.* over the side of a boat or ship into the water नाव या जलपोत पर से पानी में

IDM **go overboard (on/about/for sb/sth)** to be too excited or enthusiastic about sb/sth व्यक्ति या वस्तु के विषय में अत्यधिक उत्तेजित या उत्साहित होना

**overcast** /ˌəʊvəˈkɑːst ˌओव़ˈकास्ट्/ *adj.* (used about the sky) covered with cloud (आकाश) मेघाच्छन्न

**overcharge** /ˌəʊvəˈtʃɑːdʒ ˌओव़ˈचाज्/ *verb* [I, T] to ask sb to pay too much money for sth किसी बात के लिए बहुत अधिक दाम वसूलना *The taxi driver overcharged me.* ➪ **charge** देखिए।

**overcoat** /ˈəʊvəkəʊt ˈओव़कोट्/ *noun* [C] a long thick coat that you wear in cold weather ओवरकोट (सर्दियों में कपड़ों के ऊपर पहना जाने वाला बड़ा कोट)

**overcome** /ˌəʊvəˈkʌm ˌओव़ˈकम्/ *verb* [T] (*pt* **overcame** /-ˈkeɪm -ˈकेम्/; *pp* **overcome**) **1** to manage to control or defeat sb/sth व्यक्ति या वस्तु को पराजित या नियंत्रित कर लेना *She tried hard to overcome her fear of flying.* **2** (*usually passive*) to be extremely strongly affected by sth किसी बात से अभिभूत हो जाना

**overcook** /ˌəʊvəˈkʊk ˌओव़ˈकुक्/ *verb* [T] to cook food for too long भोजन को अधिक देर तक पकाना ✪ विलोम **undercook**

**overcrowded** /ˌəʊvəˈkraʊdɪd ˌओव़ˈक्राउडिड्/ *adj.* (used about a place) with too many people inside (स्थान) लोगों से ठसाठस भरा हुआ

**overdo** /ˌəʊvəˈduː ˌओव़ˈडू/ *verb* [T] (*pt* **overdid** /-ˈdɪd -ˈडिड्/; *pp* **overdone** /-ˈdʌn- ˈडन्/) **1** to use or do too much of sth किसी वस्तु के प्रयोग में या किसी काम में अति कर देना **2** to cook sth too long किसी वस्तु को अधिक देर तक पकाना *The meat was overdone.*

IDM **overdo it/things** to work, etc. too hard किसी काम आदि में अत्यधिक परिश्रम करना *Exercise is fine but don't overdo it.*

**overdose** /ˈəʊvədəʊs ˈओव़डोस्/ *noun* [C] an amount of a drug or medicine that is too large and so is not safe नशीले पदार्थ या औषधि की सामान्य से काफ़ी अधिक मात्रा (जो परिणाम की दृष्टि से असुरक्षित हो) *to take an overdose of sleeping pills* ➪ **dose** देखिए।

**overdraft** /ˈəʊvədrɑːft ˈओव़ड्राफ़्ट्/ *noun* [C] an amount of money that you have spent that is greater than the amount you have in your bank account; an arrangement with your bank that allows you to spend more money than you have बैंक के खाते में जमा राशि से अधिक निकाली गई धनराशि, ओवरड्राफ़्ट; बैंक के साथ ओवरड्राफ़्ट की व्यवस्था

**overdrawn** /ˌəʊvəˈdrɔːn ˌओव़ˈड्रॉन्/ *adj.* having spent more money than you have in your bank account बैंक में अपने खाते में जमा राशि से अधिक राशि का निकाल लिया जाना *I checked my balance and discovered I was overdrawn.*

**overdue** /ˌəʊvəˈdjuː ˌओव़ˈड्यू/ *adj.* late in arriving, happening, being paid, returned, etc. (कहीं पहुँचना, कुछ घटित होना, कुछ भुगतान होना आदि में) जिसे देरी हो जाए, विलंबित, ओवरड्यू *an overdue library book* ○ *Her assignment is a week overdue.*

**overeat** /ˌəʊvərˈiːt ˌओव़र्ˈईट्/ *verb* [I] to eat more than is necessary or healthy अपेक्षित या मर्यादित मात्रा से अधिक खाना; अध्यशन

**overestimate** /ˌəʊvərˈestɪmeɪt ˌओव़र्ˈएस्टिमेट्/ *verb* [T] to guess that sb/sth is bigger, better, more important, etc. than he/she/it really is किसी व्यक्ति या वस्तु का वास्तविकता से अधिक बड़ा, बेहतर आदि होने का अनुमान लगाना; अधिमूल्यांकन *I overestimated how much we could paint in a day.* ✪ विलोम **underestimate**

**overfishing** /ˌəʊvəˈfɪʃɪŋ ˌओव़ˈफ़िशिङ्/ *noun* [U] the process of taking so many fish from the sea, a river, etc. that the number of fish in it becomes very low समुद्र आदि से इतनी अधिक मछलियाँ निकाल लेना कि वहाँ उनकी संख्या काफ़ी कम हो जाए

**overflow** /ˌəʊvəˈfləʊ ˌओव़ˈफ़्लो/ *verb* **1** [I, T] **overflow (with sth)** to be so full that there is no more space पूरा भर जाने के कारण जगह न रहना, बह निकलना या उमड़ना *The tap was left on and the bucket overflowed.* ○ *The roads are overflowing with cars.* **2** [I] **overflow (into sth)** to be forced out of a place or a container that is too full बहुत अधिक भरे किसी स्थान या डिब्बे में से बरबस बाहर आ जाना *The crowd overflowed into the street.*

**overgrazing** /ˌəʊvəˈgreɪzɪŋ ˌओव़ˈग्रेज़िङ्/ *noun* [U] allowing animals such as cows to eat the grass on an area of land for too long so that the grass disappears completely and the land can no longer be used पशुओं का किसी भूखंड की सारी घास चर जाना

**overgrown** /ˌəʊvəˈgrəʊn ˌओव़ˈग्रोन्/ *adj.* covered with plants that have grown too big and untidy बेढंगे तौर पर बहुत बढ़ चुके पौधों से ढका हुआ, अतिवृद्धि को प्राप्त

**overhang** /ˌəʊvəˈhæŋ ˌओव़ˈहैङ्/ *verb* [I, T] (*pt, pp* **overhung**) to stick out above sth else किसी वस्तु के ऊपर से लटका हुआ; प्रलंबित होना *The overhanging trees kept the sun off us.*

**overhaul** /ˌəʊvəˈhɔːl ˌओव़ˈहॉल्/ *verb* [T] to look at sth carefully and change or repair it if necessary किसी वस्तु की पूर्णतः मरम्मत करना *to overhaul an engine* ▶ **overhaul** /ˈəʊvəhɔːl ˈओव़हॉल्/ *noun* [C] पूरी जाँच और मरम्मत

**overhead** /ˈəʊvəhed ˈओव़हेड्/ *adj., adv.* above your head सिर के ऊपर से जाने वाला; ऊर्ध्वस्थ *overhead electricity cables* ○ *A helicopter flew overhead.*

**overheads** /ˈəʊvəhedz ˈओव़हेड्ज़्/ *noun* [*pl.*] money that a company must spend on things like heat, light, rent, etc. किसी कंपनी के बँधे ख़र्चे (प्रकाश-व्यवस्था, किराया आदि) पर होने वाले नियमित व्यय

**overhear** /ˌəʊvəˈhɪə(r) ˌओव़ˈहिअ(र्)/ *verb* [T] (*pt, pp* **overheard** /-ˈhɜːd -ˈहड्/) to hear what sb is saying by accident, when he/she is speaking to sb else and not to you संयोग से किसी की (किसी अन्य को कही) बात सुन लेना

**overjoyed** /ˌəʊvəˈdʒɔɪd ˌओव़ˈजॉइड्/ *adj.* (*not before a noun*) **overjoyed (at sth/to do sth)** very happy अत्यंत प्रसन्न, आनंद-विभोर

**overland** /ˈəʊvəlænd ˈओव़लैन्ड्/ *adj., adv.* not by sea or by air स्थल मार्ग से (न कि जल मार्ग या वायु मार्ग से) *an overland journey* ○ *We travelled overland to India.*

**overlap** /ˌəʊvəˈlæp ˌओव़ˈलैप्/ *verb* [I, T] (**overlapping; overlapped**) **1** when two things overlap, part of one covers part of the other एक वस्तु का दूसरी के कुछ अंश को ढक लेना; अधिव्याप्त करना या होना *Make sure that the two pieces of material overlap.* **2** to be partly the same as sth अंशतः समान होना *Our jobs overlap to some extent.* ▶ **overlap** /ˈəʊvəlæp ˈओव़लैप्/ *noun* [C, U] अतिव्याप्ति, अतिव्यापन

**overleaf** /ˌəʊvəˈliːf ˌओव़ˈलीफ़्/ *adv.* on the other side of the page पृष्ठ के दूसरी तरफ़ *Full details are given overleaf.*

**overload** /ˌəʊvəˈləʊd ˌओव़ˈलोड्/ *verb* [T] **1** (*usually passive*) to put too many people or things into or onto sth बहुत सारे व्यक्ति या वस्तुएँ किसी में या पर लाद देना; अतिभारित करना *an overloaded vehicle* **2 overload sb (with sth)** to give sb too much of sth किसी को कोई वस्तु (काम, सूचना आदि) अत्यधिक मात्रा में दे देना *to be overloaded with work/information* **3** to put too much electricity through sth किसी वस्तु के माध्यम से विद्युत प्रणाली पर अतिभार डालना *If you use too many electrical appliances at one time you may overload the system.*

**overlook** /ˌəʊvəˈlʊk ˌओव़ˈलुक्/ *verb* [T] **1** to fail to see or notice sth किसी वस्तु को देखने या उस पर ध्यान देने से चूक जाना, अनदेखी कर जाना *to overlook a spelling mistake* ○ *She felt that her opinion had been completely overlooked.* **2** to see sth wrong but decide to forget it (ग़लत होता हुआ) देखकर भी (उस पर) ध्यान न देना, देखी-अनदेखी करना *I will overlook your behaviour this time but don't let it happen again.* **3** to have a view over sth किसी स्थान का ऊपर से दिखाई देना या किसी स्थान का ऊपर से पूरा दृश्य देखना *My room overlooks the sea.*

**overnight** /ˌəʊvəˈnaɪt ˌओव़ˈनाइट्/ *adj., adv.* **1** for one night एक रात के लिए *an overnight bag* ○ *We stayed overnight in Jaipur.* **2** (happening) very suddenly एकाएक, रातोंरात, बहुत शीघ्र *She became a star overnight.*

**overpass** /ˈəʊvəpɑːs ˈओव़पास्/ (*AmE*) = **flyover**

**overpay** /ˌəʊvəˈpeɪ ˌओव़ˈपे/ *verb* [T] (*pt, pp* **overpaid**) (*usually passive*) to pay sb too much; to pay sb more than his/her job is worth किसी को बहुत अधिक (वेतन) देना; काम को देखते हुए उचित से अधिक पैसा देना *He is grossly overpaid for what he does.* ✪ विलोम **underpay**

**overpopulated** /ˌəʊvəˈpɒpjuleɪtɪd ˌओव़ˈपॉप्युलेटिड्/ *adj.* (used about a country or city) with too many people living in it (देश या नगर) अत्यधिक जनसंख्या वाला ▶ **overpopulation** /ˌəʊvəˌpɒpjuˈleɪʃn ˌओव़ˌपॉप्युˈलेश्न्/ *noun* [U] अपेक्षित से अधिक जनसंख्या

**overpower** /ˌəʊvəˈpaʊə(r) ˌओव़ˈपाउअ(र्)/ *verb* [T] to be too strong for sb किसी व्यक्ति को अत्यधिक शक्ति से दबा देना *The fireman was overpowered by the heat and smoke.* ▶ **overpowering** *adj.* अत्यंत शक्तिशाली *an overpowering smell*

**overrate** /ˌəʊvəˈreɪt ˌओव़ˈरेट्/ *verb* [T] (*usually passive*) to think that sth/sb is better than he/she/it really is व्यक्ति या वस्तु का वास्तविकता से अधिक मूल्यांकन करना, अधिमूल्यांकन करना ✪ विलोम **underrate**

**overreach** /ˌəʊvəˈriːtʃ ˌओव़ˈरीच्/ *verb* [I] **overreach yourself** to fail by trying to do or achieve more than is possible संभाव्य से अधिक प्राप्त करने का प्रयत्न करने के कारण असफल होना; अतिश्रम के कारण विफल होना *In making these promises, the organization had clearly overreached itself.*

**overreact** /ˌəʊvəriˈækt ˌओव़रिˈऐक्ट्/ *verb* [I] **over react (to sth)** to react too strongly, especially to sth unpleasant अपेक्षा से अधिक सशस्त्र प्रतिक्रिया करना (विशेषतः किसी अप्रिय वस्तु के विषय में) ▶ **overreaction** /-ˈækʃn -ˈऐक्श्न्/ *noun* [*sing.*, U] अधि-प्रतिक्रिया या अति-प्रतिक्रिया

**override** /ˌəʊvəˈraɪd ˌओव़ˈराइड्/ *verb* [T] (*pt* **overrode** /-ˈrəʊd -ˈरोड्/; *pp* **overridden** /-ˈrɪdn -ˈरिड्न्/) **1** to use your authority to reject sb's decision, order, etc. अपने अधिकार से किसी निर्णय, आदेश आदि को अस्वीकार कर देना *They overrode my protest and continued with the meeting.* **2** to be more important than sth किसी अन्य की अपेक्षा अधिक महत्त्वपूर्ण होना **3** to stop sth being done automatically in order to control it yourself किसी काम के स्वतः होने को निरस्त करते हुए उसे अपने नियंत्रण में लेना *You need a special password to override the safety lock.*

**overriding** /ˌəʊvəˈraɪdɪŋ ˌओव़ˈराइडिङ्/ *adj.* (*only before a noun*) more important than anything else किसी अन्य की अपेक्षा अधिक महत्त्वपूर्ण *Our overriding concern is safety.*

**overrule** /ˌəʊvəˈruːl ˌओव़ˈरूल्/ *verb* [T] to use your authority to change what sb else has already decided or done अपने अधिकार से किए जा चुके निर्णय या काम को बदल देना *The Supreme Court overruled the High Court judge's decision.*

**overrun** /ˌəʊvəˈrʌn ˌओव़ˈरन्/ *verb* (*pt* **overran** /-ræn -ˈरैन्/; *pp* **overrun**) **1** [T] (*usually passive*) to spread all over an area in great numbers बड़ी संख्या में किसी इलाक़े में सर्वत्र फैल जाना *The city was overrun by rats.* **2** [I, T] to use more time or money than expected आशा से अधिक समय या धन लग जाना या लगा देना *The meeting overran by 30 minutes.*

**overseas** /ˌəʊvəˈsiːz ˌओव़ˈसीज़्/ *adj.* (*only before a noun*) *adv.* in, to or from another country that you have to cross the sea to get to समुद्र पार अन्य देश में या से *overseas students studying in Britain* ○ *Priya has gone to live overseas.*

**oversee** /ˌəʊvəˈsiː ˌओव़ˈसी/ *verb* [T] (*pt* **oversaw** /-ˈsɔː -ˈसॉ/; *pp* **overseen** /-ˈsiːn -ˈसीन्/) to watch sth to make sure that it is done properly किसी काम पर निगाह रखना (कि वह ठीक से हो), निरीक्षण करना

**overshadow** /ˌəʊvəˈʃædəʊ ˌओव़ˈशैडो/ *verb* [T] **1** to cause sb/sth to seem less important or successful अन्य के महत्त्व या उपलब्धि को कम कर देना *Swati always seemed to be overshadowed by her sister.* **2** to cause sth to be less enjoyable किसी अवसर की प्रसन्नता को कम कर देना

**oversight** /ˈəʊvəsaɪt ˈओव़साइट्/ *noun* [C, U] something that you do not notice or do (that you should have noticed or done) कुछ करने या ध्यान देने में भूल या चूक (जिसकी आशा न हो), असावधानी, अनवधान

**oversimplify** /ˌəʊvəˈsɪmplɪfaɪ ˌओव़ˈसिम्प्लिफ़ाइ/ *verb* [I, T] (*pres. part.* **oversimplifying;** *3rd person sing. pres.* **oversimplifies;** *pt, pp* **oversimplified**) to explain sth in such a simple way that its real meaning is lost किसी बात की इतनी सरल व्याख्या करना कि उसका वास्तविक अर्थ सुरक्षित न रह पाए, अतिसरल कर देना

**oversleep** /ˌəʊvəˈsliːp ˌओव़ˈस्लीप्/ *verb* [I] (*pt, pp* **overslept** /-ˈslept -ˈस्लेप्ट्/) to sleep longer than you should have done अधिक देर तक सोते रहना *I overslept and was late for school.* ➪ **lie in** और **sleep in** भी देखिए।

**overstate** /ˌəʊvəˈsteɪt ˌओव़ˈस्टेट्/ *verb* [T] to say sth in a way that makes it seem more important than it really is किसी बात को बढ़ा-चढ़ा कर कहना ताकि वह और महत्त्वपूर्ण लगे ✪ विलोम **understate**

**overstep** /ˌəʊvəˈstep ˌओव़ˈस्टेप्/ *verb* [T] (*pres. part.* **overstepping;** *pt, pp* **overstepped**) to go further than an acceptable limit सीमा का अतिक्रमण करना

**overt** /ˈəʊvɜːt ˈओव़ट्/ *adj.* (*only before a noun*) (*formal*) done in an open way and not secretly खुले तौर पर किया गया, प्रकट, प्रत्यक्ष, खुला ✪ विलोम **covert** ▶ **overtly** *adv.* प्रकट या प्रत्यक्ष रूप से

**overtake** /ˌəʊvəˈteɪk ˌओव़ˈटेक्/ *verb* [I, T] (*pt* **overtook** /-ˈtʊk -ˈटुक्/; *pp* **overtaken** /-ˈteɪkən -ˈटेकन्/) to go past another person, car, etc. because you are moving faster (वाहन, व्यक्ति आदि के) पीछे से आकर आगे निकल जाना *The lorry overtook me on the bend.*

**overthrow** /ˌəʊvəˈθrəʊ ˌओव़ˈथ्रो/ *verb* [T] (*pt* **overthrew** /-ˈθruː -ˈथ्रू/; *pp* **overthrown** /-ˈθrəʊn -ˈथ्रोन्/) to remove a leader or government from power, by using force बलप्रयोग से किसी नेता या सरकार को सत्ता से हटा देना, नेता या सरकार का तख़्ता उलट देना ▶ **overthrow** /ˈəʊvəθrəʊ ˈओव़थ्रो/ *noun* [*sing.*] बलात सत्ताच्युति

**overtime** /ˈəʊvətaɪm ˈओव़टाइम्/ *noun* [U] time that you spend at work after your usual working hours; the money that you are paid for this (सामान्य कार्य घंटों के बाद) काम में लगा अतिरिक्त समय, अधिसमय, ओवरटाइम; अधिसमय, समयोपरि या ओवरटाइम भत्ता *Beena did 10 hours' overtime last week.* ▶ **overtime** *adv.* निर्धारित समय के बाद, समयोपरि *I have been working overtime for weeks.*

**overtone** /ˈəʊvətəʊn ˈओव़टोन्/ *noun* [C, *usually pl.*] something that is suggested but not expressed in an obvious way परोक्ष रूप से (न कि प्रत्यक्षतया) कही गई बात; व्यंजना *Some people claimed there were racist overtones in the advertisement.*

**overture** /ˈəʊvətʃʊə(r); -tjʊə(r) ˈओव़चुअ(र्); -ट्युअ(र्)/ *noun* [C, *usually pl.*] (*formal*) an act of being friendly towards sb, especially because you want to be friends, to start a business relationship, etc. मैत्री, व्यापारिक संबंध आदि बढ़ाने के लिए पहल या संकेत कदम

**overturn** /ˌəʊvəˈtɜːn ˌओव़ˈटन्/ *verb* **1** [I, T] to turn over so that the top is at the bottom उलट जाना या उलटा देना *The car overturned but the driver escaped unhurt.* **2** [T] to officially decide that a decision is wrong and change it क़ानून की दृष्टि से ग़लत पाए गए निर्णय को उलट देना या बदल देना

**overview** /ˈəʊvəvjuː ˈओव़व्यू/ *noun* [C] a general description of sth without any details किसी प्रसंग का (विस्तार-रहित) सामान्य विवरण, विहंगावलोकन

**overweight** /ˌəʊvəˈweɪt ˌओव़ˈवेट्/ *adj.* too heavy or fat बहुत भारी या मोटा *I'm a bit overweight—I think I might go on a diet.* ➪ **fat** पर नोट देखिए। ✪ विलोम **underweight**

**overwhelm** /ˌəʊvəˈwelm ˌओव़ˈवेल्म्/ *verb* [T] (*usually passive*) **1** to cause sb to feel such a strong emotion that he/she does not know how to react अभिभूत हो जाना *The new world champion was overwhelmed by all the publicity.* **2** to be so powerful, big, etc., that sb cannot deal with it पराजित कर देना, हावी हो जाना *He overwhelmed his opponent with his superb technique.* ○ *The television company were overwhelmed by complaints.*

**overwhelming** /ˌəʊvəˈwelmɪŋ ˌओव़ˈवेल्मिङ्/ *adj.* extremely great or strong अत्यधिक महान या शक्तिशाली, तीव्र *Anu had an overwhelming desire to return home.* ▶ **overwhelmingly** *adv.* अत्यधिक सशक्त रूप से

**overwork** /ˌəʊvəˈwɜːk ˌओव़ˈवक्/ *verb* [T] to make sb work too hard किसी से बहुत अधिक काम करवाना *The staff are overworked and underpaid.* ▶ **overwork** *noun* [U] अतिश्रम

**oviparous** /əʊˈvɪpərəs ओˈविपरस्/ *adj.* (*technical*) (used about animals) producing eggs rather than live babies (जंतुओं के संबंध में प्रयुक्त) अंडा देने वाले, न कि जीवित शिशु पैदा करने वाले प्राणी ➪ **viviparous** देखिए।

**ovulate** /ˈɒvjuleɪt ˈऑव्‌युलेट्/ *verb* [I] (used about a woman or female animal) to produce an egg (**ovum**) (मादा प्राणी के लिए प्रयुक्त) अंडा देना, अंडाणु उत्पन्न करना ▸ **ovulation** /ˌɒvjuˈleɪʃn ˌऑव्‌युˈलेशन्/ *noun* [U] अंडोत्सर्ग

**ovule** /ˈɒvjuːl ˈऑव्‌यूल्/ *noun* [C] (*technical*) (in plants that produce seeds) the part of the **ovary** that contains the female cell that becomes the seed बीज वाले पौधों में बीजाशम का वह भाग जिसमें मादा कोशिका रहती है जो कि आगे चलकर बीज बनता है; डिम्ब ➪ **flower** पर चित्र देखिए।

**ovum** /ˈəʊvəm ˈओव़म्/ *noun* [C] (*pl.* **ova** /ˈəʊvə ˈओव़ा/) an egg produced by a woman or female animal मादाजंतु द्वारा उत्पन्न अंडा; अंडाणु

**ow** /aʊ ओ/ *exclamation* used when reacting to a sudden feeling of pain पीड़ा के कारण अचानक निकली ध्वनि के लिए प्रयुक्त; आह!

**owe** /əʊ ओ/ *verb* [T] **1 owe sth (to sb); owe sb for sth** to have to pay money to sb for sth that he/she has done or given किसी की उसके किसी कार्य या किसी वस्तु के देने के बदले में देनदार होना *I owe Katrina a lot of money.* ○ *I still owe you for that bread you bought yesterday.* **2** to feel that you should do sth for sb or give sth to sb, especially because he/she has done sth for you यह अहसास कि आप उसके लिए कुछ करें या उसे कुछ दें विशेषतः इसलिए कि उसने आप के लिए कुछ किया है *Kamini owes me an explanation.* ○ *I owe you an apology.* **3 owe sth (to sb/sth)** to have sth (for the reason given) किसी परिणाम का आधार, कारण समझना *She said she owes her success to hardwork and determination.*

**owing** /ˈəʊɪŋ ˈओइङ्/ *adj.* (*only before a noun*) **owing (to sb)** not yet paid देनदार

**owing to** *prep.* because of के कारण *The match was cancelled owing to bad weather.*

**owl** /aʊl आउल्/ *noun* [C] a bird with large eyes that hunts small animals at night उल्लू, इसकी बड़ी-बड़ी आँखें होती हैं और यह रात में छोटे प्राणियों का शिकार करता है

**own[1]** /əʊn ओन्/ *det., pronoun* **1** used to emphasize that sth belongs to a particular person इस पर बल डालने के लिए प्रयुक्त कि कोई वस्तु या व्यक्ति विशेष की है *I saw him do it with **my own** eyes.* ○ *Rani would like her own room/a room **of her own**.* **2** used to show that sth is done or made without help from another person यह दिखाने के लिए प्रयुक्त कि बिना किसी अन्य की सहायता के कुछ किया या बनाया जा सकता है *The children are old enough to get their own breakfast.*

**IDM come into your own** to have the opportunity to show your special qualities अपनी विशेष योग्यताओं को दिखाने का अवसर पाना

**hold your own (against sb/sth)** to be as strong, good, etc. as sb/sth else किसी अन्य व्यक्ति या वस्तु के समान बलशाली, शुभ आदि होना

**(all) on your, etc. own 1** alone अपने दम पर, अपने बूते पर *Poonam lives all on her own.* ➪ **alone** पर नोट देखिए। **2** without help बिना किसी की सहायता के *I managed to repair the car all on my own.*

**get/have your own back (on sb)** (*informal*) to hurt sb who has hurt you किसी व्यक्ति को, जिसने आपको चोट पहुँचाई है, चोट पहुँचाना

**own[2]** /əʊn ओन्/ *verb* [T] to have sth belonging to you; to possess किसी वस्तु का स्वामी बनना *We don't own the house. We just rent it.* ○ *a privately owned company*

**PHR V own up (to sth)** (*informal*) to tell sb that you have done sth wrong किसी को यह बताना कि आपने कुछ ग़लत किया है *None of the children owned up to breaking the window.* ➪ **confess** देखिए।

**owner** /ˈəʊnə(r) ˈओन(र्)/ *noun* [C] a person who owns sth किसी वस्तु का मालिक *a house/dog owner*

**ownership** /ˈəʊnəʃɪp ˈओनशिप्/ *noun* [U] the state of owning sth मालिक होने की दशा; स्वामित्व *in private/public **ownership***

**ox** /ɒks ऑक्स्/ *noun* [C] (*pl.* **oxen** /ˈɒksn ˈऑक्सन्/) a male cow that has been **castrated**. Oxen are used in some places for pulling or carrying heavy loads बैल ➪ **bull** देखिए।

**oxbow** /ˈɒksbəʊ ˈऑक्स्बो/ *noun* [C] (in geography) a bend in a river that almost forms a full circle; a lake that forms when this bend is separated from the river due to erosion (भूगोल में) चाप झील

**oxbow lake**

**oxide** /ˈɒksaɪd ˈऑक्साइड्/ *noun* [C, U] a combination of **oxygen** and another chemical element ऑक्साइड; ऑक्सीजन और अन्य रासायनिक तत्व का संयोजन *iron oxide*

**oxidize** (*also* **-ise**) /ˈɒksɪdaɪzˈऑक्सिडाइज़्/ *verb* [I,T] to combine or to make sth combine with **oxygen** किसी वस्तु में ऑक्सीजन मिलाना या कोई वस्तु ऑक्सीजन से मिलाना ► **oxidization** (*also* **-isation**) /ˌɒksɪdaɪˈzeɪʃn ˌऑक्सिडाइˈज़ेश्न्/ (*also* **oxidation** /ˌɒksɪˈdeɪʃn ˌऑक्सिˈडेश्न्/) *noun* [U] ऑक्सिकरण, उपचयन

**oxygen** /ˈɒksɪdʒənˈऑक्सिजन्/ *noun* [U] (*symbol* **O**) a gas that you cannot see, taste or smell. Plants and animals cannot live without oxygen ऑक्सीज़न; एक गैस जिसे न आप देख सकते हैं, न सूंघ सकते हैं और न आप उसका स्वाद ले सकते हैं। पौधे और प्राणी बिना ऑक्सीजन के जीवित नहीं रह सकते

**oxygenate** /ˈɒksɪdʒəneɪtˈऑक्सिजनेट्/ *verb* [T] to add **oxygen** to sth किसी में ऑक्सीजन मिलाना

**oxymoron** /ˌɒksɪˈmɔːrɒn ˌऑक्सिˈमॉरॉन्/ *noun* [C] a phrase that combines two words that seem to be the opposite of each other, such as a *deafening silence* ऐसा वाक्यांश जिसके दोनों शब्द विपरीत या विरोधी अर्थ वाले हैं जैसे कि *cruel kindness*

**oyster** /ˈɔɪstə(r)ˈऑइस्ट(र्)/ *noun* [C] a shellfish that we eat. Some oysters produce precious jewels (**pearls**) शंखमीन जिसे लोग खाते हैं कुछ शंखमीनों से मोती मिलते हैं ➪ **shellfish** पर चित्र देखिए।

**oz** *abbr.* ounce(s) आउंस *Add 4 oz flour.*

**ozone** /ˈəʊzəʊnˈओज़ोन्/ *noun* [U] a poisonous gas which is a form of **oxygen** एक जहरीली गैस जो कि ऑक्सीजन की एक प्रकार की गैस है

**ozone-friendly** *adj.* (used about cleaning products, etc.) not containing chemicals that could harm **the ozone layer** ऐसे शोधक उत्पादन जिनमें ओज़ोन गैस की सतह को नुक़सान पहुँचाने वाले कोई हानिकारक रसायन न हो

**the ozone layer** *noun* [*sing.*] the layer of the gas (**ozone**) high up in the atmosphere that helps to protect the earth from the dangerous rays of the sun वायुमंडल में ऊँचाई पर ओज़ोन गैस की सतह जो कि सूर्य की हानिकारक किरणों से पृथ्वी को बचाने में सहायक होती है *a hole in the ozone layer* ➪ **CFC** देखिए।

# P p

**P, p[1]** /piː पी / *noun* [C, U] (*pl.* **P's; p's** /piːz पीज़् /) the sixteenth letter of the English alphabet अंग्रेज़ी वर्णमाला का सोलहवाँ अक्षर *'Pencil' begins with a 'P'.*

**p[2]** *abbr.* **1** (*pl.* **pp**) page पृष्ठ *See p 94.* ○ *pp 63–96* **2 P** (on a road sign) parking (मार्ग चिह्न) वाहनस्थल; किसी वाहन के खड़े रहने के स्थल का सूचक चिह्न

**PA** /ˌpiː ˈeɪ ˌपी ˈए / *abbr., noun* [C] (*BrE*) personal assistant; a **secretary** for just one manager वैयक्तिक सहायक जो अपने अधिकारी के पत्रों का टंकण तथा टेलीफ़ोनों के उत्तर आदि देता है

**p.a.** *abbr.* per annum; in or for a year प्रति वर्ष; एक वर्ष में या के लिए *salary Rs 200,000 p.a.*

**paan** (*also* **pan**) *noun* [C, U] (*IndE*) **1 betel** leaf पान का पत्ता **2** betel leaf that is stuffed with a mixture of **areca nut**, lime, etc. for eating सुपारी, चूना आदि युक्त खाने का पान

**pace[1]** /peɪs पेस् / *noun* **1** [U, *sing.*] **pace (of sth)** the speed at which you walk, run, etc. or at which sth happens चलने, दौड़ने आदि या कुछ घटित होने की गति; चाल *to run at a steady/gentle pace* ○ *Students are encouraged to work at their own pace* (= as fast or as slowly as they like). **2** [C] the distance that you move when you take one step एक क़दम में तय की जाने वाली दूरी; क़दम *Take two paces forward and then stop.*

IDM **keep pace (with sb/sth)** to move or do sth at the same speed as sb/sth else; to change as quickly as sth else is changing उसी चाल से गति या कुछ कार्य करना जितना कि अन्य व्यक्ति कर रहे हैं; अन्य व्यक्ति की भाँति चाल या गति बदलना *Wages are not keeping pace with inflation.*

**set the pace** to move or do sth at the speed that others must follow उस गति से चलना या कार्य करना जिसका अन्य लोगों को अनुसरण करना पड़े *Pinto set the pace for the first three kilometres*

**pace[2]** /peɪs पेस् / *verb* [I, T] to walk up and down in the same area many times, especially because you are nervous or angry एक ही जगह में इधर से उधर बार-बार चलते रहना, विशेषतः घबराहट या क्रोध में

**pacemaker** /ˈpeɪsmeɪkə(r) ˈपेस्मेक(र्) / *noun* [C] **1** a machine that helps to make a person's heart beat regularly or more strongly एक मशीन जो व्यक्ति के हृदय की धड़कन को नियमित रूप से या अधिक बलशाली रीति से धड़कने देती है; गतिचालकयंत्र **2** a person in a race who sets the speed that the others must follow दौड़ में वह व्यक्ति जो उस चाल (गति) को निर्धारित करता है जिस पर अन्य व्यक्तियों को दौड़ना है

**pachyderm** /ˈpækɪdɜːm ˈपैकिडम् / *noun* [C] (*technical*) a type of animal with a very thick skin, for example an elephant एक अत्यधिक मोटी चमड़ी वाला प्राणी, जैसे कि हाथी, गैंडा, दरियाई घोड़ा आदि

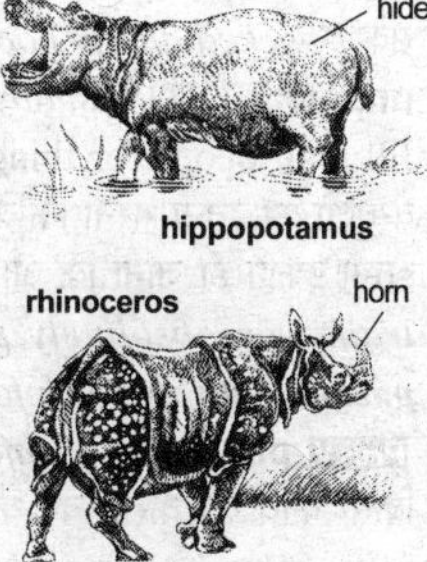

pachyderms

**pacifier** /ˈpæsɪfaɪə(r) ˈपैसिफ़ाइअ(र्) / = **dummy 3**

**pacifism** /ˈpæsɪfɪzəm ˈपैसिफ़िज़म् / *noun* [U] the belief that all wars are wrong and that you should not fight in them यह आस्था कि युद्ध सदैव अनुचित होते हैं और उस में कभी शामिल नहीं होना चाहिए; शांतिवाद ▶ **pacifist** /-fɪst फ़िस्ट्/ *noun* [C] शांतिवादी

**pacify** /ˈpæsɪfaɪ ˈपैसिफ़ाइ / *verb* [T] (*pres. part.* **pacifying;** *3rd person sing. pres.* **pacifies;** *pt, pp* **pacified**) to make sb who is angry or upset be calm or quiet किसी नाराज़ या परेशान व्यक्ति को शांत एवं स्थिर करना

**pack[1]** /pæk पैक् / *noun* [C] **1** a set of things that are supplied together for a particular purpose वस्तुओं का समुच्चय जो विशेष प्रयोजन के लिए एक साथ दिया जाता है *These batteries are sold in packs of four.* ○ (*figurative*) *Everything she told me was **a pack of lies**.* ➪ **package, packet** और **parcel** देखिए। **2** (*AmE*) = **packet[1]** **3** a bag that you carry on your back झोला जिसे पीठ पर वहन किया जा सकता है ✪ पर्याय **rucksack** या **backpack** **4** [*with sing. or pl. verb*] a group of wild animals that hunt together वन्य पशुओं का समूह जो एक साथ झुंड के रूप में शिकार करते हैं *a pack of dogs/wolves* **5** a large group of similar people or things, especially one that you do not like or approve of समान व्यक्तियों या वस्तुओं का बड़ा समूह, विशेषतः वह जो पसंद या स्वीकार्य न हो *We avoided a pack of journalists waiting outside.* **6** (*AmE* **deck**) a compelete set of playing cards ताश की गड्डी ➪ **card** पर नोट देखिए।

**pack[2]** /pæk पैक् / *verb* **1** [I, T] to put your things into a suitcase, etc. before you go away or go on holiday छुट्टियों पर बाहर जाने के पूर्व सूटकेस आदि में अपना सामान रखना *I'll have to pack my suitcase in the morning.* ○ *Have you packed your* *toothbrush?* ✪ विलोम **unpack** 2 [I, T] to put things into containers so they can be stored, transported or sold किसी सामान रखने वाली वस्तु में चीज़ों को रखना ताकि उनका भंडारण, वहन या विक्रय हो सके *I packed all my books into boxes.* ✪ विलोम **unpack** 3 [T] (*usually passive*) (*informal*) to fill with people or things until crowded or full वस्तुओं को इतना भरना कि वे पूरी तरह भर जाएँ; लोगों का इतना इकट्ठा हो जाना कि और लोग वहाँ न समा पाएँ *The train was absolutely packed.* ○ *The book is **packed with** useful information.*

**PHRV pack sth in** (*informal*) to stop doing sth किसी कार्य को करना बंद कर देना *I've packed in my job.* ○ *I've had enough of you boys arguing—just pack it in, will you!*

**pack sth in/into sth** to do a lot in a short time कम समय में बहुत कुछ कर डालना *They packed a lot into their three days in Rome.*

**pack sth out** (*usually passive*) to fill sth with people किसी स्थल को लोगों से पूरा भर देना *The bars **are packed out** every night.*

**pack up** (*informal*) 1 to finish working or doing sth कोई काम पूरा कर डालना *There was nothing else to do so we packed up and went home.* 2 (used about a machine, engine, etc.) to stop working (मशीन, इंजन आदि का) काम करना बंद हो जाना; ख़राब हो जाना *My old car packed up last week so now I cycle to work.*

**package** /ˈpækɪdʒ ˈपैकिज्/ *noun* [C] 1 (*BrE*) something, or a number of things, covered in paper or in a box काग़ज़ में लिपटी या डिब्बे में रखी कुछ या बहुत-सी वस्तुएँ *There's a large package on the table for you.* ➪ **pack, packet** और **parcel** देखिए। 2 a number of things that must be bought or accepted together वस्तुओं का समुच्चय जिसे एक साथ ख़रीदना या स्वीकार करना पड़ता है; पैकेज *a word-processing package* ○ *a financial aid package* 3 (*AmE*) = **packet**[1] और **parcel** ► **package** *verb* [T] डिब्बे या काग़ज़ में वस्तुएँ को लपेटना *Goods that are attractively packaged sell more quickly.*

**package holiday** (*AmE* **package tour**) *noun* [C] a holiday that is organized by a company for a fixed price that includes the cost of travel, hotels, etc. निश्चित धनराशि पर पर्यटन की पूरी व्यवस्था जिस में यात्रा-भाड़ा, होटल का किराया आदि सब शामिल हैं

**packaging** /ˈpækɪdʒɪŋ ˈपैकिजिङ्/ *noun* [U] all the materials (boxes, bags, paper, etc.) that are used to cover or protect goods before they are sold डिब्बा, क़ाग़ज़ आदि सभी पदार्थ जो बेचने के पूर्व सामान को ढके या सुरक्षित रखते हैं

**packed lunch** *noun* [C] food that you prepare at home and take with you to eat at work or school भोजन जो घर पर बनता है और कार्य-स्थल या स्कूलों में खाने के लिए ले जाया जाता है

**packer** /ˈpækə(r) ˈपैक(र्)/ *noun* [C] a person, company or machine that puts goods, especially food, into boxes, plastic, paper, etc. to be sold व्यक्ति, कंपनी या मशीन जो सामान को, विशेषतः भोज्य पदार्थ को बेचने से पहले प्लास्टिक, काग़ज़ आदि में बंद करता है

**packet** /ˈpækɪt ˈपैकिट्/ *noun* 1 (*AmE* **pack; package**) [C] a small box, bag, etc. in which things are packed to be sold in a shop छोटा डिब्बा, थैली आदि जिसमें किसी वस्तु को बेचने के लिए बंद किया जाता है; पैकेट ***a packet of** sweets/biscuits/crisps* ○ *a cigarette packet* ➪ **pack, package** और **parcel** देखिए। 2 [*sing.*] (*spoken*) a large amount of money बड़ी मात्रा में धनराशि *That new kitchen must have cost them a packet.* 3 [C] (*computing*) an amount of data that is sent through a computer **network** डाटा की मात्रा जो कंप्यूटर जाल-तंत्र द्वारा भेजी जाती है

**packing** /ˈpækɪŋ ˈपैकिङ्/ *noun* [U] 1 the act of putting your clothes, possessions, etc. into boxes or cases in order to take or send them somewhere बक्सों या डिब्बों में सामान बाँधने की क्रिया कहीं ले जाने या भेजने हेतु *We're going on holiday tomorrow so I'll **do my packing** tonight.* 2 (*BrE*) soft material that you use to stop things from being damaged or broken when you are sending them somewhere सामान बाँधने में प्रयुक्त मुलायम पदार्थ जो वहन के दौरान सामान को टूट-फूट से बचाता है *The price of the book includes **postage and packing**.*

**packing case** *noun* [C] a wooden box that you put things in before they are sent somewhere or stored लकड़ी का बक्सा जिसमें वस्तुओं को अन्यत्र भेजने या भंडारित करने के पूर्व रखते हैं

**pact** /pækt पैक्ट्/ *noun* [C] a formal agreement between two or more people, groups or countries दो या दो से अधिक व्यक्तिओं, समूहों या देशों के बीच औपचारिक समझौता

**pad**[1] /pæd पैड्/ *noun* [C] 1 a thick piece of soft material, used for cleaning or protecting sth or to make sth a different shape मुलायम पदार्थ का मोटा टुकड़ा जो किसी वस्तु को साफ करने या सुरक्षित रखने के लिए अथवा किसी वस्तु को भिन्न-भिन्न आकृति देने के लिए प्रयुक्त किया जाता है *Remove eye make-up with cleanser and a cotton-wool pad.* ○ *a jacket with shoulder pads* 2 a number of pieces of paper that are fastened together at one end काग़ज़ के बहुत-से टुकड़े जो एक सिरे से साथ-साथ बंधे हुए हों

*a notepad* **3** the place where a spacecraft takes off वह स्थल जहाँ से अंतरिक्ष यान उड़ान भरता है *a launch pad* **4** the soft part on the bottom of the feet of some animals, for example dogs and cats कुछ प्राणियों, जैसे कुत्ते, बिल्ली के पैर के नीचे का मुलायम भाग

**pad[2]** /pæd पैड्/ *verb* (**padding; padded**) **1** [T] **pad sth (with sth)** (*usually passive*) to fill or cover sth with soft material in order to protect it, make it larger or more comfortable, etc. किसी वस्तु को मुलायम पदार्थ से भर या ढक देना ताकि वह सुरक्षित रहे, कुछ बड़े आकार की दिखे या अधिक आरामदेह हो सके *I sent the photograph frame in a padded envelope.* **2** [I] **pad about, along, around, etc.** to walk quietly, especially because you are not wearing shoes बिना आवाज़ किए चलना क्योंकि जूते नहीं पहने हैं *He got up and padded into the bathroom.* **PHR V** **pad sth out** to make a book, speech, etc. longer by adding things that are not necessary किसी किताब, भाषण आदि को कुछ अनावश्यक सामग्री जोड़कर कुछ बड़ा रूप देना

**padding** /ˈpædɪŋ ˈपैडिङ्/ *noun* [U] soft material that is put inside sth to protect it or to make it larger, more comfortable, etc. मुलायम पदार्थ जो किसी वस्तु के भीतर भर दिया जाता है ताकि वह सुरक्षित रहे, कुछ बड़े आकार की दिखे या अधिक आरामदेह हो

**paddle[1]** /ˈpædl ˈपैड्ल्/ *noun* [C] a short pole that is flat and wide at one or both ends and that you use for moving a small boat through water नाव चलाने का चप्पू, डाँड ➪ **boat** पर चित्र देखिए।

**paddle[2]** /ˈpædl ˈपैड्ल्/ *verb* **1** [I, T] to move a small boat through water using a short pole that is flat and wide at one or both ends चप्पू के सहारे छोटी नाव को पानी में चलाना *We paddled down the river.* ➪ **row** देखिए। **2** [I] to walk in water that is not very deep छिछले पानी में चलना *The children paddled in the stream.*

**paddock** /ˈpædək ˈपैडक्/ *noun* [C] a small field where horses are kept एक छोटा भूक्षेत्र जहाँ घोड़े रखे जाते हैं

**paddy** /ˈpædi ˈपैडि/ (*also* **paddy field**) *noun* [C] (*pl.* **paddies**) a field with rice being grown in water पानी से भरा भूक्षेत्र जिसमें धान उगाते हैं **2** rice that has not been processed in any way and is still in its husk or rice as a growing crop चावल जिसे संसाधित नहीं किया गया है और जो छिलके में हो; विकासमय चावल की फ़सल

**padlock** /ˈpædlɒk ˈपैड्लॉक्/ *noun* [C] a type of lock that you can use for fastening gates, bicycles, etc. मुख्य द्वार, साइकिल आदि के लिए प्रयुक्त ताला ▸ **padlock** *verb* [T] **padlock sth (to sth)** किसी वस्तु से किसी वस्तु को ताले द्वारा बाँध देना *I padlocked my bicycle to a post.*

**Padma Bhushan** *noun* [C, U] an Indian civilian decoration that is awarded by the Government of India for distinguished service to the nation, in any field पद्म भूषण; किसी भी क्षेत्र में राष्ट्र की विशिष्ट सेवा के लिए पुरस्कार स्वरूप, भारत सरकार द्वारा प्रदान किए जाने वाली प्रतिष्ठित भारतीय अलंकृत उपाधि

> **NOTE** भारतीय सरकार द्वारा प्रदत्त नागरिक सम्मान (असैनिक) के लिए अलंकृत उपाधियाँ (विशेष पदानुक्रम में) **Bharat Ratna, Padma Vibhushan, Padma Bhushan** तथा **Padma Shri** हैं।

**Padma Shri** *noun* [C, U] a civilian decoration conferred on a distinguished Indian by the Government of India पद्म श्री; भारत सरकार द्वारा किसी विशिष्ट भारतीय नागरिक को दी गई अलंकृत उपाधि ➪ **Padma Bhushan** पर नोट देखिए।

**Padma Vibhushan** *noun* [C, U] India's second highest civilian decoration conferred on a distinguished Indian by the Government of India भारत रत्न के बाद उच्चतम उपाधि जो भारत सरकार अति विशिष्ट सेवा के लिए प्रदान करती है; पद्म विभूषण ➪ **Padma Bhushan** पर नोट देखिए।

**padyatra** *noun* [C, U] (*IndE*) a long walk undertaken as a (social, political or religious) demonstration in order to highlight an issue of public importance पदयात्रा; पैदल मार्च द्वारा जनहित के विषय को प्रकाशमय करने हेतु किया गया (सामाजिक, राजनीतिक या धार्मिक) प्रदर्शन

**paed-** (*AmE* **ped-**) /pi:d पीड्/ *prefix* (*used in nouns and adjectives*) connected with children बाल-विषयक *paediatrics*

**paediatrician** (*AmE* **pediatrician**) /ˌpi:diəˈtrɪʃn ˌपीडिअˈट्रिशन्/ *noun* [C] a doctor who deals with the diseases of children बाल चिकित्सक; बाल-रोगों का इलाज करने वाला चिकित्सक

**paediatrics** (*AmE* **pediatrics**) /ˌpi:diˈætrɪks ˌपीडिˈऐट्रिक्स्/ *noun* [U] the area of medicine connected with the diseases of children चिकित्सा-शास्त्र का वह क्षेत्र जिसका संबंध बाल-रोगों से है ▸ **paediatric** (*AmE* **pediatric**) *adj.* बाल-चिकित्सा संबंधी

**paedophile** (*AmE* **pedo-**) /ˈpi:dəʊfaɪl ˈपीडोफ़ाइल्/ *noun* [C] a person who is sexually attracted to children व्यक्ति जो बच्चों के प्रति कामुकता भाव से आकर्षित रहता है

**paedophilia** (*AmE* **pedo-**) /ˌpi:dəˈfɪliə ˌपीडˈफ़िलिआ/ *noun* [U] the condition of being sexually attracted to children; sexual activity with children बच्चों के साथ कामुकता भाव से आकर्षित होने की स्थिति; बच्चों के साथ कामुकतापूर्ण व्यवहार

**paella** /paɪˈelə पाइˈएला/ *noun* [U, C] a Spanish dish made with rice, meat, fish and vegetables चावल, मांस, मछली और सब्जियों से बना एक स्पेनिश व्यंजन

**pagan** /ˈpeɪgən ˈपेगन्/ *adj.* having religious beliefs that do not belong to any of the main world religions उन धार्मिक विश्वासों का जो मुख्य विश्व धर्मों में नही पाए जाते; विधर्म ▶ **pagan** *noun* [C] विधर्मी

**page**[1] /peɪdʒ पेज्/ *noun* [C] **1** (*abbr.* **p**) one or both sides of a piece of paper in a book, magazine, etc. किसी पुस्तक, पत्रिका आदि का पन्ना; पृष्ठ *The letter was three pages long.* ○ *the **front page** of a newspaper* **2** (*computing*) a section of data or information that can be shown on a computer screen at any one time डाटा या सूचना का एक खंड जो किसी एक समय में कंप्यूटर के परदे पर प्रदर्शित किया जा सकता है ➪ **home page** देखिए।

**page**[2] /peɪdʒ पेज्/ *verb* [T] to call sb by sending a message to a small machine (**a pager**) that sb carries, or by calling sb's name publicly through a device fixed to the wall (**a loudspeaker**) एक छोटी मशीन (पेजर) के माध्यम से किसी व्यक्ति को संदेश भेजकर बुलाना या उसके नाम से दीवार पर लगे लाउडस्पीकर द्वारा पुकारना

**pageant** /ˈpædʒənt ˈपैजन्ट्/ *noun* [C] **1** a type of public entertainment at which people dress in clothes from past times and give outdoor performances of scenes from history लोक आमोद-प्रमोद का एक प्रकार जिसमें लोग पुराने युग की वेशभूषा में इतिहास के प्राचीन दृश्यों का खुले में अभिनय करते हैं; झांकी, शोभायात्रा **2** (*AmE*) = **beauty contest**

**pageantry** /ˈpædʒəntri ˈपैजन्ट्रि/ *noun* [U] the feeling and appearance of a big, colourful ceremony विशाल रंगारंग रमणीय आयोजन, भव्य प्रदर्शन *Millions of people enjoyed the pageantry of the Olympic opening ceremony on television.*

**pager** /ˈpeɪdʒə(r) ˈपेज(र्)/ *noun* [C] a small machine that you carry, that makes a sound when sb sends you a message एक छोटा उपकरण जिसे आप अपने साथ ले जा सकते हैं और जो किसी अन्य व्यक्ति द्वारा संदेश भेजे जाने पर आवाज़ करता है ✪ पर्याय **bleeper**

**pagoda** /pəˈgəʊdə पˈगोडा/ *noun* [C] a Buddhist temple in India or South-East Asia which usually is in the in the form of a tall tower with several levels, each of which has its own roof (भारत या दक्षिण-पूर्व-एशियाई देशों में) एक बुर्ज तथा अनेक तलों वाला बौद्ध मंदिर जिसकी प्रत्येक तल की अपनी छत होती है; पगोडा, स्तूप

**paid** ➪ **pay**[2] का past tense और past participle रूप

**paid-up** *adj.* (*only before a noun*) having paid all the money that you owe, for example to become a member of a club जितनी कुल धनराशि देनी है उसे दे देना, जैसे किसी क्लब के सदस्य बनने हेतु *He's a fully paid-up member of Friends of the Earth.*

**pail** /peɪl पेल्/ (*old-fashioned*) = **bucket** *a pail of water*

**pain**[1] /peɪn पेन्/ *noun* **1** [C, U] the unpleasant feeling that you have when a part of your body has been hurt or when you are ill शरीर के किसी अंग पर चोट या किसी रोग से पीड़ित होने के कारण उत्पन्न दर्द; पीड़ा, वेदना *to **be in pain*** ○ *He screamed with pain.*

> **NOTE** एक दीर्घकालिक निरंतर दर्द के लिए शब्द **ache** का तथा अचानक हुए लघुकालिक तीव्र दर्दों के लिए शब्द **pain** का प्रयोग करते हैं। इसलिए हम सामान्यतया कहते हैं—*I've got earache/backache/toothache/ a headache* किंतु—*He was admitted to hospital with pains in his chest.*

**2** [U] sadness that you feel because sth bad has happened उदासी, दुख क्योंकि कोई बुरी घटना हो गई है *the pain of losing a parent*

**IDM be a pain (in the neck)** (*spoken*) a person, thing or situation that makes you angry or annoyed क्रोधित या परेशान करने वाला व्यक्ति, वस्तु, या परिस्थिति

**pain**[2] /peɪn पेन्/ *verb* [T] (*formal*) to make sb feel sad or upset किसी को दुखी या परेशान कर देना ***It pains me** to think how much money we've wasted.*

**pained** /peɪnd पेन्ड्/ *adj.* showing that you are sad or upset दुखी या परेशान *a pained expression*

**painful** /ˈpeɪnfl ˈपेन्फ़्ल्/ *adj.* **painful (for sb) (to do sth) 1** that causes pain or hurts दर्द या पीड़ा उत्पन्न करने वाला; पीड़ादायी *A wasp sting can be very painful.* **2** making you feel upset or embarrassed परेशान या व्याकुल करने वाला *The break-up of their marriage was very painful for the children.* ▶ **painfully** /-fəli -फ़लि/ *adv.* दुखदायी रूप से

**painkiller** /ˈpeɪnkɪlə(r) ˈपेन्किल(र्)/ *noun* [C] a drug that is used for reducing pain पीड़ा कम करने के लिए प्रयुक्त औषधि

**painless** /ˈpeɪnləs ˈपेन्लस्/ *adj.* that does not cause pain जो पीड़ा नहीं उत्पन्न करता है; पीड़ाहीन, अकष्टकर *The animals' death is quick and painless.* ▶ **painlessly** *adv.* पीड़ाहीन रीतिं से

**pains** /peɪnz पेन्ज़् / *noun*
**IDM be at/take (great) pains to do sth; take (great) pains (with/over sth)** to make a special effort to do sth well अच्छी तरह से करने का विशेष प्रयास करना *He was at pains to hide his true feelings.*

**painstaking** /ˈpeɪnzteɪkɪŋ ˈपेन्ज़्टेकिङ् / *adj.* very careful and taking a long time and effort अत्यधिक सावधानी से लंबी अवधि में व परिश्रम द्वारा किया गया; अध्यवसायी *The painstaking search of the wreckage gave us clues as to the cause of the crash.*
▶ **painstakingly** *adv.* अत्यधिक सावधानीपूर्वक, श्रमसाध्य रीति से

**paint¹** /peɪnt पेन्ट् / *noun* **1** [U] coloured liquid that you put onto a surface to decorate or protect it रंगीन द्रव जो किसी सतह पर साज-सज्जा या सुरक्षा हेतु लगाया जाता है *green/orange/yellow paint* ○ *The door will need another* ***coat of paint***. **2** [U] coloured liquid that you can use to make a picture चित्र बनाने में प्रयुक्त रंगीन द्रव *oil paint* ○ *watercolour paint* **3 paints** [*pl.*] a collection of tubes or blocks of paint that an artist uses for painting pictures रंगों से भरे ट्यूब या पिंडो का समूह जिसका प्रयोग चित्रकार चित्रांकन में करता है

**paint²** /peɪnt पेन्ट् / *verb* [I, T] **1** to put paint onto a surface or an object किसी सतह या वस्तु पर रंग लगाना या पोतना *We painted the fence.* ○ *The walls were painted pink.* **2** to make a picture of sb/sth using paints रंगों द्वारा किसी व्यक्ति या वस्तु का चित्र बनाना *We painted some animals on the wall.*

**paintbox** /ˈpeɪntbɒks ˈपेन्ट्बॉक्स् / *noun* [C] a box that contains blocks or tubes of paint of many colours एक डिब्बा जिसमें अनेक रंगों से भरे ट्यूब या पिंड रखे हुए होते हैं

**paintbrush** /ˈpeɪntbrʌʃ ˈपेन्ट्ब्रश् / *noun* [C] a brush that you use for painting with रंग करने या भरने का ब्रश

**painter** /ˈpeɪntə(r) ˈपेन्ट(र्) / *noun* [C] **1** a person whose job is to paint buildings, walls, etc. व्यक्ति जिसका काम भवनों, दीवारों आदि को रंगना है; रंगसाज **2** a person who paints pictures व्यक्ति जो रंगीन चित्र बनाता है; चित्रकार

**painting** /ˈpeɪntɪŋ ˈपेन्टिङ् / *noun* **1** [C] a picture that sb has painted चित्र जिसको किसी व्यक्ति ने रंगों से भरा हो *a famous painting by MF Hussain* **2** [U] the act of painting pictures or buildings किसी चित्र या इमारत को रंगने की क्रिया; रंगाई *She studies Indian painting.*

**paintwork** /ˈpeɪntwɜːk ˈपेन्ट्वक् / *noun* [U] a painted surface, especially on a vehicle रंगा हुआ पृष्ठ, विशेषतया वाहन पर

**pair¹** /peə(r) पेअ(र्) / *noun* [C] **1** two things of the same type that are used or worn together एक ही प्रकार की दो वस्तुएँ जिनको साथ-साथ प्रयुक्त किया या पहना जाता है; जोड़ा, युग्म *a pair of shoes/gloves/earrings* **2** a thing that consists of two parts that are joined together वस्तु जिसके दो अंश हैं और जो साथ-साथ जुड़े हुए हैं *a pair of scissors/glasses/trousers* **3** [*with pl. verb*] two people or animals that are doing sth together दो व्यक्ति या प्राणी जो साथ मिलकर कोई कार्य कर रहे हैं *These boxers have fought several times, and tonight the pair meet again.*

**NOTE Couple** का प्रयोग उन दो व्यक्तियों के संबंध में किया जाता है जो कि विवाहित-युग्म हैं या वैसा संबंध रखते हैं।

**IDM in pairs** two at a time एक समय में दो; जोड़े में *These earrings are only sold in pairs.* ○ *The students were working in pairs.*

**pair²** /peə(r) पेअ(र्) / *verb*
**PHR V pair (sb/sth) off (with sb)** to come together, especially to form a romantic relationship; to bring two people together for this purpose साथ-साथ होना, विशेषतः प्रेमसंबंध बनाने के लिए; प्रेमसंबंध हो जाए इस हेतु दो व्यक्तिओं को साथ-साथ रखना *She's always trying to pair me off with her brother.*
**pair up (with sb)** to join together with another person or group to work, play a game, etc. कार्य, खेल आदि में किसी अन्य व्यक्ति या समूह के साथ-साथ जुड़ जाना *I paired up with another student and we did the project together.*

**paisa** *noun* [C] (*pl.* **paise**) a unit of money that is used in India, Pakistan and Nepal. There are 100 paise in one rupee पैसा; भारत, पाकिस्तान और नेपाल में प्रचलित मुद्रा की एक इकाई। एक रुपये में सौ पैसे होते हैं

**pajamas** (*AmE*) = **pyjamas**

**pakhawaj** *noun* [C] a barrel-shaped Indian **percussion** instrument similar to the **mridangam**. It is usually used as an **accompaniment** for **Odissi** dancers and occasionally for **Kathak** पखावज; मृदंगम जैसा ढोल के आकार का ताल वाद्य। इसका प्रयोग सामान्यतः ओड़िसी और कभी-कभी कथक नृत्य में होता है

**palace** /ˈpæləs ˈपैलस् / *noun* [C] a large house that is or was the home of a king or queen विशाल भवन जहाँ राजा या रानी रहते थे या रहते हैं, महल, राजभवन; प्रासाद

**palaeontologist** (*AmE* **paleo-**) /ˌpæliɒnˈtɒlədʒɪst; ˌpeɪli- ˌपैलिऑन्ˈटॉलजिस्ट्; ˌपेलि-/ *noun* [C] a person who studies very old dead animals or plants in **fossils** व्यक्ति जो जीवाश्मों में अतिप्राचीन मृत जीवों या पौधों का अध्ययन करता है; जीवाश्मविज्ञानी

**palaeontology** (*AmE* **paleo-**) /ˌpæliɒnˈtɒlədʒi; ˌpeɪli- ˌपैलिऑन्ˈटॉलजि; ˌपेलि-/ *noun* [U] the scientific study of **fossils** जीवाश्मों का वैज्ञानिक अध्ययन; जीवाश्मिकी

**palanquin** /ˌpælənˈkiːn ˌपैलन्ˈकीन्/ *noun* [C] a big covered box-like vehicle usually with a seat for one person. It is attached to poles and is carried on shoulders by four or six men पालकी

**palate** /ˈpælət ˈपैलट्/ *noun* [C] the top part of the inside of your mouth मुख के अंदर का ऊपरी भाग; तालू

**palatial** /pəˈleɪʃəl पˈलेशल्/ *adj.* (used about a room or building) like a palace; extremely large and spacious(कमरा या भवन) महलनुमा; अत्यधिक विशाल एवं विस्तीर्ण, भव्य *a palatial house*

**pale** /peɪl पेल्/ *adj.* **1** (used about a person or his/her face) having skin that is light in colour, often because of fear or illness (किसी व्यक्ति या उसके चेहरे के लिए प्रयुक्त) जिसकी त्वचा पीली पड़ गई है, प्रायः भय या किसी बीमारी के कारण *She has a pale complexion.* ○ *I felt myself **go/turn pale** with fear.* ➪ **pallor** noun तथा **pallid** adjective देखिए। **2** not bright or strong in colour (रंग) फ़ीका, धुँधला *a pale yellow dress* ✪ विलोम **dark** ▶ **pale** *verb* [I] पीला पड़ जाना

**palette** /ˈpælət ˈपैलट्/ *noun* [C] **1** a small thin board with a curved edge on which an artist mixes colours when painting, with a hole for the thumb to hold it by रंग पट्टिका **2** (*usually sing.*) (*technical*) the colours used by a particular artist or the colours in a particular painting किसी विशिष्ट कलाकार द्वारा उपयोग किए गए रंग या किसी विशिष्ट चित्रकला के रंग *Browns, greens and blues are typical of Leonardo da Vinci's palette.* **3** the range of colours that are available in a computer program कंप्यूटर प्रोग्राम में उपलब्ध रंगों के विभिन्न वर्ण

**pall** /pɔːl पॉल्/ *verb* [I] to become less interesting or important कम रोचक या कम महत्त्व का हो जाना *After a few months, the excitement of his new job began to pall.*

**pallid** /ˈpælɪd ˈपैलिड्/ *adj.* (used about a person or his/her face) light in colour, especially because of illness (किसी व्यक्ति या उसके चेहरे के लिए प्रयुक्त) पीला, विशेषतः किसी बीमारी के कारण *His pallid complexion made him look unhealthy.* ➪ **pale** देखिए।

**pallor** /ˈpælə(r) ˈपैल(र्)/ *noun* [U] pale colouring of the face, especially because of illness or fear डर या बीमारी के कारण चेहरे का पीलापन

**palm**[1] /pɑːm पाम्/ *noun* [C] **1** the flat, inner surface of your hand हाथ की हथेली, करतल *She held the coins tightly in the palm of her hand.* ➪ **body** पर चित्र देखिए। **2** (*also* **palm tree**) a tall straight type of tree that grows in hot countries. Palms have a lot of large leaves at the top but no branches खजूर, ताड़; यह उष्णप्रधान देशों में सीधा, ऊँचा पेड़ होता है इस की शाखाएँ नहीं होती किंतु चोटी पर बहुत-सी बड़ी-बड़ी पत्तियाँ होती हैं ➪ **plant** पर चित्र देखिए।

**palm**[2] /pɑːm पाम्/ *verb*

**PHR V** **palm sb off (with sth)** (*informal*) to persuade sb to believe sth that is not true in order to stop him/her asking questions or complaining किसी व्यक्ति को ऐसा समझाना-बुझाना कि वह किसी असत्यता पर विश्वास कर ले और सवाल-जवाब करना छोड़ दे या शिकायत न करे

**palm sth off (on sb)** to persuade sb to accept sth that he/she does not want किसी व्यक्ति को ऐसी वस्तु लेने के लिए राज़ी कर लेना जिसे वह नहीं चाहता *She's always palming off the worst jobs on her assistant.*

**palmistry** /ˈpɑːmɪstri ˈपामिस्ट्रि/ *noun* [U] the art or practice of supposedly predicting the future and describing the character of a person by looking at the lines and other features of the hand, especially the palms and fingers हाथ की रेखाओं को देखकर किसी व्यक्ति का भविष्यकाल या स्वभाव बताने की कला; हस्तरेखाशास्त्र ▶ **palmist** /ˈpɑːmɪst ˈपामिस्ट्/ *noun* [C] हस्तरेखापंडित

**palm oil** *noun* [U] oil that we get from the fruit of a **palm tree** that is used in cooking and in making soap, candles, etc. खजूर के फल से निकला तेल जो खाना बनाने, साबुन या मोमबत्ती आदि तैयार करने में प्रयुक्त होता है

**palmtop** /ˈpɑːmtɒp ˈपाम्टॉप्/ *noun* [C] (*computing*) a very small computer that can be held on the **palm** of one hand एक बहुत छोटा कंप्यूटर जिसे हथेली में ले सकते हैं ➪ **desktop** और **laptop** देखिए।

**palpitate** /ˈpælpɪteɪt ˈपैल्पिटेट्/ *verb* [I] (of the heart) to beat rapidly or irregularly, especially because of fear or excitement (दिल का) ज़ोर से या अनियमित रूप से धड़कना, विशेषतः डर या उत्तेजना के कारण ▶ **palpitation** /ˌpælpɪˈteɪʃn ˌपैल्पिˈटेशन्/ *noun* [C, *usually pl.*] दिल की तेज़ धड़कन, डर या उत्तेजना के कारण

**palsy** /ˈpɔːlzi ˈपॉल्ज़ि/ = **cerebral palsy**

**paltry** /ˈpɔːltri ˈपॉल्ट्रि/ *adj.* too small to be considered important or useful इतना छोटा कि उसका न तो कुछ महत्त्व है और न उपयोगिता; तुच्छ, नगण्य *a paltry sum of money*

**the pampas** /ˈpæmpəs ˈपैम्पस्/ *noun* [*sing.*] the large area of land in South America that has no trees and is covered in grass दक्षिण अमेरिका का विशाल भूक्षेत्र जहाँ कोई पेड़ नहीं है और जो पूरा-पूरा घास से भरा है; पम्पास

**pamper** /ˈpæmpə(r) ˈपैम्प(र्)/ *verb* [T] to take care of sb very well and make him/her feel as comfortable as possible किसी व्यक्ति की बहुत अच्छी देखभाल करना और उसे यथासंभव आराम पहुँचाना

**pamphlet** /ˈpæmflət ˈपैम्फ़्लट्/ *noun* [C] a very thin book with a paper cover containing information about a particular subject काग़ज़ के आवरण वाला बहुत कम पन्नों की पुस्तिका जिसमें एक विशिष्ट विषय के संबंध में ही सूचना दी जाती है; पैम्फ़लेट

**pan** /pæn पैन्/ *noun* [C] a metal container with a handle or handles that is used for cooking food in; the contents of a pan हत्थेदार छिछला पात्र, जो भोजन बनाने में काम आता है; पैन; पैन में स्थित सामग्री *Cook the spaghetti in a large pan of boiling water.*

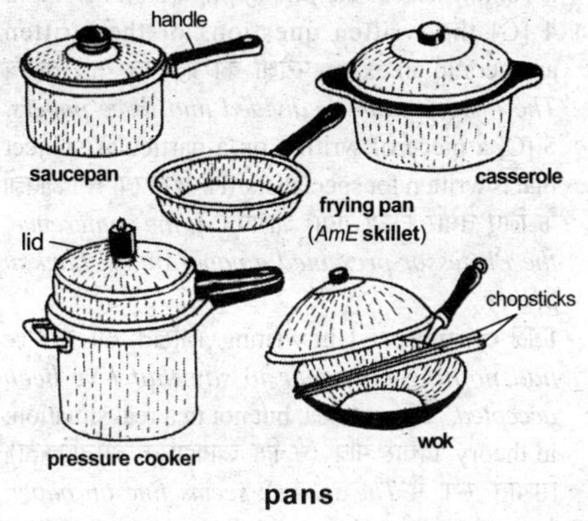


**pans**

**pan²** = **paan**

**pan-** /pæn पैन्/ *prefix* (*used in adjectives and nouns*) including all of sth; connected with the whole of sth पूरा-पूरा शामिल; किसी वस्तु की परिपूर्णता से संबंधित *pan-African*

**panacea** /ˌpænəˈsiːə ˌपैनˈसीआ/ *noun* [C] something that will cure all diseases or solve all problems and difficulties; a universal remedy रोग तथा किसी संकटमय परिस्थिति की सभी कठिनाइयों का निवारक; सर्वरोगहर *Education is panacea for all social evils.*

**pancake** /ˈpænkeɪk ˈपैन्केक्/ *noun* [C] a type of very thin round cake that is made by frying a mixture of flour, milk and eggs (**batter**) आटा, दूध और अंडे के घोल को तलने से बना बहुत पतला गोल केक

**panchayat** *noun* [C] (*in India*) the local governing body of a village; a village council (भारत में) गाँव की स्थानीय प्रशासनिक इकाई, पंचायत; ग्राम पंचायत

**pancreas** /ˈpæŋkriəs ˈपैङ्क्रिअस्/ *noun* [C] an organ near the stomach that produces the substance that controls the amount of sugar in the blood (**insulin**) and which helps your body to deal with (**digest**) the food you eat अग्न्याशय, यह उदर के पास स्थित एक शरीर-अंग है जो ऐसा तत्त्व (इंसुलिन) उत्पन्न करता है जो रक्त में शर्करा को नियंत्रित करता है और खाए हुए आहार के पाचन में सहायक होता है ▶ **pancreatic** /ˌpæŋkriˈætɪk ˌपैङ्क्रिˈऐटिक्/ *adj.* अग्न्याशयी

**panda** /ˈpændə ˈपैन्डा/ *noun* [C] a large black and white bear that comes from China सफ़ेद और काले रंग तथा बड़े आकार का चीनी भालू, पंडा

**pandemic** /pænˈdemɪk पैन्ˈडेमिक्/ *noun* [C] a disease that spreads over a whole country or the whole world देशव्यापी या विश्वव्यापी कोई महामारी ▶ **pandemic** *adj.* महामारी-विषयक ➪ **endemic** और **epidemic** देखिए।

**pandemonium** /ˌpændəˈməʊniəm ˌपैन्डˈमोनिअम्/ *noun* [U] a state of great noise and confusion हुल्लड़बाज़ी, बहुत शोर और अव्यवस्था, भारी गड़बड़ी

**pander** /ˈpændə(r) ˈपैन्ड(र्)/ *verb*

PHR V **pander to sb/sth** to do or say exactly what sb wants especially when this is not reasonable दूसरे का पूरा समर्थन या अनुसरण करना, विशेषतः ग़लत बात में भी *He refuses to pander to his boss's demands.*

**pane** /peɪn पेन्/ *noun* [C] a piece of glass in a window, etc. खिड़की आदि में जड़ा (एक) शीशा *a windowpane*

**panel** /ˈpænl ˈपैन्ल्/ *noun* [C] **1** a square or rectangular piece of wood, metal or glass that forms part of a door or wall दरवाज़े या दीवार में जड़ा वर्गाकार या आयातकार लकड़ी, धातु या काँच का फलक; पैनल **2** [*with sing. or pl. verb*] a group of people who give their advice or opinions about sth; a group of people who discuss topics of interest on television or radio किसी विषय पर परामर्श या सम्मति देने वाले व्यक्तियों का समूह; सलाहकार-मंडल, पैनल; टीवी या रेडयो पर सामयिक मुद्दों पर चर्चा करने वाले व्यक्तियों का समूह; वार्ताकार-मंडल, पैनल *a panel of judges*

(= in a competition) ○ *a panel game* (= a TV game show with two teams) **3** a flat surface that contains the equipment for controlling a vehicle, machine, etc. वाहन, मशीन आदि में लगा फलक जिस पर नियंत्रणकारी यंत्र होता है; पैनल *a control/display panel*

**panelling** (*AmE* **paneling**) /ˈpænəlɪŋ ˈपैनलिङ्/ *noun* [U] square or rectangular pieces of wood used to cover and decorate walls, ceilings, etc. दीवार, भीतरी छत आदि पर अलंकरण हेतु आयताकार लकड़ी की पट्टिका श्रेणी

**panellist** (*AmE* **panelist**) /ˈpænəlɪst ˈपैनलिस्ट्/ *noun* [C] a member of a **panel** सलाहकार या वार्ताकार-मंडल, का सदस्य

**pang** /pæŋ पैङ्/ *noun* [C, *usually pl.*] a sudden strong feeling of emotional or physical pain अचानक उत्पन्न शारीरिक या मानसिक गहरी पीड़ा; टीस, कसक, हूक *hunger pangs* ○ *a pang of jealousy*

**panic** /ˈpænɪk ˈपैनिक्/ *noun* [C, U] a sudden feeling of fear that cannot be controlled and stops you from thinking clearly एकाएक उपजा डर जो नियंत्रित न हो सके और स्पष्टता से सोचने न दे; संत्रास, भीषिका, आतंक *People fled in panic as the fire spread.* ○ *There was a mad panic when the fire alarm went off.* ▶ **panic** *verb* [I] (**panicking; panicked**) डर जाना, आतंकित हो जाना *Stay calm and don't panic.*

**panic-stricken** /ˈpænɪk strɪkn ˈपैनिक् स्ट्रिकन्/ *adj.* very frightened in a way that stops you from thinking clearly आतंकित, संत्रस्त

**panorama** /ˌpænəˈrɑːmə ˌपैनˈरामा/ *noun* [C] a view over a wide area of land किसी बड़े क्षेत्र का दृश्य, परिदृश्य, दृश्यावली, दृश्यपटल ▶ **panoramic** /ˌpænəˈræmɪk ˌपैनˈरैमिक्/ *adj.* परिदृश्यात्मक

**pant** /pænt पैन्ट्/ *verb* [I] to breathe quickly, for example after running or because it is very hot हाँफना (जैसे दौड़ने के बाद या गरमी के मारे) ▶ **pant** *noun* [C] तेज़ी से ली गई साँस, हँफनी

**panther** /ˈpænθə(r) ˈपैन्थ(र्)/*noun* [C] a large wild animal of the cat family with black fur काला तेंदुआ ➪ **lion** पर चित्र देखिए।

**panties** /ˈpæntiz ˈपैन्टिज़्/ (*AmE*) = **knickers**

**pantry** /ˈpæntri ˈपैन्ट्रि/ *noun* [C] (*pl.* **pantries**) a small room where food is kept रसोई-भंडार, भंडार घर ✪ पर्याय **larder**

**pants** /pænts पैन्ट्स्/ *noun* [*pl.*] **1** (*BrE*) = **underpants** **2** (*AmE*) = **trousers**

**pantyhose** /ˈpæntihəʊz ˈपैन्टिहोज़्/ (*AmE*) = **tights**

**papad** *noun* [C, U] a thin, crisp south Asian food item that is made from ground lentils. It is roasted or deep fried in oil before eating पापड़; भारत और श्रीलंका में लोकप्रिय पिसी दाल से बना खाद्य पदार्थ जिसे भून कर या तल कर खाया जाता है

**paparazzi** /ˌpæpəˈrætsi ˌपैपˈरैट्सि/ *noun* [*pl.*] photographers who follow famous people around in order to get pictures of them to sell to a newspaper or magazine फ़ोटो के लिए प्रसिद्ध व्यक्तियों का पीछा करने वाले फ़ोटोग्राफर

**papaya** /pəˈpaɪə पˈपाइआ/ (*also* **pawpaw** /ˈpɔːpɔː ˈपॉपॉ/) *noun* [C] a large tropical fruit which is sweet and orange inside and has small black seeds पपीता

**paper** /ˈpeɪpə(r) ˈपेप(र्)/ *noun* **1** [U] a material made in thin sheets that you use for writing or drawing on, covering things, etc. काग़ज़ *a piece/sheet of paper* ○ *a paper handkerchief*

**NOTE** काग़ज़ों के कुछ प्रकार हैं **filter paper, tissue paper, toilet paper** और **writing paper**.

**2** [C] = **newspaper**[1] *Where's today's paper?* **3 papers** [*pl.*] important letters or pieces of paper that have information written on them महत्त्वपूर्ण काग़ज़ात, दस्तावेज़ *The document you want is somewhere in the pile of papers on her desk.* **4** [C] the written questions or the written answers in an exam परीक्षा का प्रश्नपत्र या उत्तरपत्र *The history exam is divided into three papers.* **5** [C] a piece of writing on a particular subject that is written for specialists (किसी विषय पर विशेषज्ञों के लिए तैयार किया गया) शोधपत्र *At the conference, the Professor presented a paper on Sri Lankan poetry.*

**IDM** **on paper** **1** in writing लिखित रूप में *I've had nothing on paper to say that I've been accepted.* **2** as an idea, but not in a real situation; in theory विचार मात्र (न कि व्यावहारिक वास्तविकता); सिद्धांत रूप में *The scheme seems fine on paper, but would it work in practice?*

**paperback** /ˈpeɪpəbæk ˈपेपबैक्/ *noun* [C, U] a book that has a paper cover काग़ज़ के ज़िल्द की पुस्तक; पेपरबैक *The novel is available **in paperback**.* ➪ **hardback** देखिए।

**paper boy** *noun* [C] a boy who takes newspapers to people's houses घर-घर अख़बार पहुँचाने वाला लड़का

**paper clip** *noun* [C] a small piece of bent wire that is used for holding pieces of paper together काग़ज़ों को एक साथ रखने के लिए प्रयुक्त क्लिप; पेपर क्लिप ➪ **stationery** पर चित्र देखिए।

**paperweight** /ˈpeɪpəweɪt ˈपेपवेट्/ *noun* [C] a small heavy object that you put on top of loose papers to keep them in place अलग-अलग काग़ज़ों को उनके स्थान पर दबाकर रखने वाली छोटी भारी वस्तु; पेपरवेट

**paper tiger** *noun* [C] a person or thing that seems dangerous or powerful, but in fact is not काग़ज़ी शेर, मिट्टी का शेर (ख़तरनाक या शक्तिशाली प्रतीत होने वाला व्यक्ति जो वस्तुतः वैसा नहीं)

**paperwork** /ˈpeɪpəwɜːk ˈपेपवक्/ *noun* [U] **1** the written work that is part of a job, such as writing letters and reports and filling in forms, etc. नौकरी में किया जाने वाला लेखन-कार्य जैसे पत्र, रिपोर्ट लिखना, फ़ार्म भरना आदि; काग़ज़ी कार्य *I hate doing paperwork.* **2** documents that need to be prepared, collected, etc. in order for a piece of business to be completed किसी कार्य से संबंधित आवश्यक काग़ज़ात *Some of the paperwork is missing from this file.*

**paprika** /ˈpæprɪkə ˈपैप्रिका/ *noun* [U] a red powder made from a sweet red pepper that you can use in cooking भोजन में प्रयुक्त एक तरह की पिसी लाल मिर्च जो तीखी नही होती

**papyrus** /pəˈpaɪrəs पˈपाइरस्/ *noun* (*pl.* **papyri** /pəˈpaɪriː पˈपाइरी/) **1** [U] a tall plant with a thick **stem** that grows in water एक प्रकार का सरकंडा; पपीरस, पटेरा **2** [U] paper made from the **stems** of the papyrus plant, used in ancient Egypt for writing and drawing on पपीरस के पौधे से बना काग़ज़ (प्राचीन मिस्र में प्रयुक्त) **3** [C] a document or piece of paper made of papyrus पपीरस के काग़ज़ पर तैयार किया गया दस्तावेज़ या काग़ज़

**par** /pɑː(r) पा(र्)/ *noun* [U] (in golf) the standard number of times a player should hit the ball in order to complete a particular hole or series of holes (गोल्फ़ के खेल में) गेंद को मारकर छेदों में डालने के लिए निर्धारित बारियों की संख्या

IDM **below par** (*informal*) not as good or as well as usual सामान्य से कम अच्छा

**on a par with sb/sth** of an equal level, standard, etc. to sb/sth else समान स्तर या गुणवत्ता का

**par.** (*also* **para.**) *abbr.* paragraph अनुच्छेद

**para-** /ˈpærə ˈपैरा/ *prefix* (*used in nouns and adjectives*) **1** beyond के परे; अतिरिक्त *paranormal* **2** similar to but not official or not fully qualified के सदृश (परंतु अधिकृत या पूर्ण योग्यता संपन्न नहीं) *a paramedic* ○ *paramilitary*

**parable** /ˈpærəbl ˈपैरब्ल्/ *noun* [C] a short story that teaches a lesson, especially one told by Jesus in the Bible नीतिकथा; शिक्षाप्रद कथा (विशेषतः बाइबिल में)

**parabola** /pəˈræbələ पˈरैबला/ *noun* [C] a curve like the path of an object that is thrown through the air and falls back to earth आकाश में फेंकी वस्तु के पृथ्वी पर लौटने के मार्ग जैसी वक्र रेखा; परवलय ▶ **parabolic** /ˌpærəˈbɒlɪk ˌपैरˈबॉलिक्/ *adj.* परवलयाकार *parabolic curves*

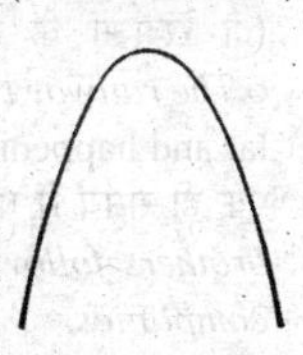

**parachute** /ˈpærəʃuːt ˈपैरशूट्/ *noun* [C] a piece of equipment that opens and lets the person fall to the ground slowly when he/she jumps from a plane विमान से छलाँग लगाने वाले व्यक्ति द्वारा धीमी गति से ज़मीन पर उतरने के लिए प्रयुक्त हवाई छतरी; पैराशूट ▶ **parachute** *verb* [I] पैराशूट से उतरना

**parade** /pəˈreɪd पˈरेड्/ *noun* [C] an occasion when a group of people stand or walk in a line so that people can look at them परेड, क़वायद, जुलूस *a military parade* ○ *a fashion parade*

**paradise** /ˈpærədaɪs ˈपैरडाइस्/ *noun* **1** (*usually* **Paradise**) [U] the perfect place where some people think that good people go after they die स्वर्ग ✪ पर्याय **heaven** **2** [C] a perfect place आनंद धाम, पूर्णतया सुखद स्थल *This beach is a paradise for windsurfers.*

**paradox** /ˈpærədɒks ˈपैरडॉक्स्/ *noun* [C] a situation or statement with two or more parts that seem strange or impossible together विरोधी विशेषताओं वाला कथन या स्थिति; विरोधाभास, अंतर्विरोध *It's a paradox that some countries produce too much food while in other countries people are starving.* ▶ **paradoxical** /ˌpærəˈdɒksɪkl ˌपैरˈडॉक्सिक्ल्/ *adj.* विरोधाभासी ▶ **paradoxically** /ˌpærəˈdɒksɪkli ˌपैरˈडॉक्सिक्लि/ *adv.* विरोधाभासी रीति से

**paraffin** /ˈpærəfɪn ˈपैरफ़िन्/ (*also* **kerosene**) *noun* [U] a type of oil that is burned to produce heat or light एक प्रकार का तेल जिससे ताप और प्रकाश उत्पन्न होते हैं; पैराफ़िन

**paragraph** /ˈpærəgrɑːf ˈपैरग्राफ़्/ *noun* [C] a part of a piece of writing that consists of one or more sentences. A paragraph always starts on a new line पैराग्राफ़, अनुच्छेद (इसे सदा नई पंक्ति से आरंभ करते हैं)

**parakeet** /ˈpærəkiːt ˈपैरकीट्/ *noun* [C] a small bird usually with green feathers and a long tail that lives in hot countries लंबी पूँछ वाला छोटा तोता, ढेलहरी तोता, टुइयाँ, यह गरम देशों में पाया जाता है

**parallel**[1] /ˈpærəlel ˈपैरलेल्/ *adj., adv.* **1 parallel (to sth)** (used about two lines, etc.) with the same distance between them for all their length (दो रेखाओं के संबंध में) समानांतर *parallel lines* ○ *The railway runs parallel to the road.* **2** similar and happening at the same time एक जैसे और एक ही समय में घटित; सदृश और समकालिक *The two brothers followed parallel careers in different companies.*

**parallel**[2] /ˈpærəlel ˈपैरलेल्/ *noun* [C, U] a person, thing or situation that is similar to another one in a different situation, place or time व्यक्ति, वस्तु या परिस्थिति जो किसी अन्य परिस्थिति, स्थान या समय में विद्यमान व्यक्ति, वस्तु या परिस्थिति के समान हो; सादृश्य, समानता *Tagore's literary genius is* ***without parallel.***

square rectangle rhombus rhomboid

**parallelograms**

**parallelogram** /ˌpærəˈleləgræm ˌपैरˈलेलग्रैम्/ *noun* [C] (*technical*) a flat shape with four straight sides. The opposite sides are parallel and equal to each other चार भुजाओं की एक समतलीय आकृति जिसकी विपरीत भुजाएँ परस्पर समानांतर और समान होती हैं; समांतर चतुर्भुज

**paralyse** (*AmE* **paralyze**) /ˈpærəlaɪz ˈपैरलाइज़्/ *verb* [T] **1** to make a person unable to move his/her body or a part of it व्यक्ति का ऐसा हो जाना कि वह अपने शरीर या उस के अंग को हिला-डुला न सके; लक़वे से प्रभावित होना *Mihir is paralysed from the waist down.* **2** to make sb/sth unable to work in a normal way ऐसी स्थिति उत्पन्न करना कि कोई व्यक्ति या वस्तु सामान्य रीति से कार्य न कर सके ▶ **paralysis** /pəˈræləsɪs पˈरैलसिस्/ *noun* [U] लक़वा; कार्य करने आदि में नितांत असमर्थता *The disease can cause paralysis or even death.* ○ *There has been complete paralysis of the railway system.*

**paramedic** /ˌpærəˈmedɪk ˌपैरˈमेडिक्/ *noun* [C] a person who has had special training in treating people who are hurt or ill, but who is not a doctor or nurse (पूर्ण प्रशिक्षित चिकित्सक की तुलना में) सीमित प्रशिक्षण प्राप्त चिकित्सक, सहायक चिकित्सक

**parameter** /pəˈræmɪtə(r) पˈरैमिट(र्)/ *noun* [C, *usually pl.*] (*formal*) something that decides or limits the way in which sth can be done किसी काम को करने का तरीक़ा, निर्धारित या नियंत्रित करने वाला तत्व; पैरामीटर, प्राचल *to set/define the parameters* ○ *We had to work within the parameters that had already been established.*

**paramilitary** /ˌpærəˈmɪlətri ˌपैरˈमिलट्रि/ *adj.* organized in the same way as, but not belonging to, an official army अर्धसैनिक; सेना के समान ही संगठित किंतु सेना के अंग नहीं *a paramilitary group*

**paramount** /ˈpærəmaʊnt ˈपैरमाउन्ट्/ *adj.* (*formal*) most important सर्वाधिक महत्त्वपूर्ण *Safety is paramount in car design.*

**Paramvir Chakra** *noun* [C, U] India's highest military honour, it is awarded by the Government of India for great courage and bravery in war (भारतीय सरकार द्वारा प्रदत्त) भारत का उच्चतम सैनिक सम्मान परमवीर चक्र, यह युद्ध में अत्यधिक साहस और पराक्रम के लिए दिया जाता है

**paranoia** /ˌpærəˈnɔɪə ˌपैरˈनॉइआ/ *noun* [U] **1** a type of mental illness in which you wrongly believe that other people want to harm you इस ग़लत विश्वास पर आधारित एक मानसिक रोग कि अन्य व्यक्ति आपको हानि पहुँचाना चाहते हैं; मिथ्या संदेह या वहम का रोग, भ्रांति रोग **2** (*informal*) a feeling of fear and suspicion of other people दूसरों से भय की और उन पर संदेह करने की प्रवृत्ति; वहम

**paranoid** /ˈpærənɔɪd ˈपैरनॉइड्/ *adj.* wrongly believing that other people are trying to harm you or are saying bad things about you इस मिथ्या संदेह से ग्रस्त कि अन्य लोग हानि पहुँचाना चाहते है या दुर्व्यवहार कर रहे हैं

**paraphernalia** /ˌpærəfəˈneɪliə ˌपैरफ़ˈनेलिआ/ *noun* [U] a large number of different objects that you need for a particular purpose प्रयोजन-विशेष के लिए अपेक्षित ढेर सारी विविध वस्तुएँ; साज-सामान

**paraphrase** /ˈpærəfreɪz ˈपैरफ्रेज़्/ *verb* [T] to express sth again using different words so that it is easier to understand एक ही बात को भिन्न शब्दों में दुबारा कहना ताकि उसे समझने में आसानी हो; अन्वयांतर, शब्दांतरण, भावानुवाद करना ▶ **paraphrase** *noun* [C] अन्वयांतर, शब्दांतरण, भावानुवाद

**parasite** /ˈpærəsaɪt ˈपैरसाइट्/ *noun* [C] a plant or an animal that lives in or on another plant or animal and gets its food from it. Parasites sometimes cause disease परजीवी वनस्पति या जंतु, ये रोगों का कारण भी बन सकते हैं ▶ **parasitic** /ˌpærəˈsɪtɪk ˌपैरˈसिटिक्/ *adj.* परजीवी, परजीवी द्वारा उत्पन्न

**parasol** /ˈpærəsɒl ˈपैरसॉल्/ *noun* [C] an umbrella that you use to protect yourself from the sun धूप से बचाने वाला छाता, छोटा छाता

**paratha** (*also* **parantha**) *noun* [C, U] a flat thick piece of Indian bread, usually made with wheat flour but without yeast. It is often stuffed with vegetables like boiled potatoes, radish or cauliflower, etc. and is fried on a **griddle** (आलू, मूली, गोभी आदि का) पराँठा जिसे तवे पर तल कर बनाते हैं

**paratrooper** /ˈpærətru:pə(r) ˈपैरट्रूप(र्)/ *noun* [C] a soldier in the **paratroops** छाताधारी सेना का एक सैनिक

**paratroops** /ˈpærətru:ps ˈपैरट्रूप्स्/ *noun* [*pl.*] soldiers who are trained to jump from planes using a **parachute** पैराशूट की सहायता से विमान से कूदने के लिए प्रशिक्षित सैनिक

**parboil** /ˈpɑ:bɔɪl ˈपाबॉइल्/ *verb* [T] to partly cook food, especially vegetables, by boiling खाद्य पदार्थ, विशेषतः सब्ज़ियों को थोड़ा पकने तक उबालना

**parcel** /ˈpɑ:sl ˈपासल्/ (*AmE* **package**) *noun* [C] something that is covered in or put in a special envelope paper and sent to sb, especially by mail काग़ज़ में लपेटी गई या विशेष लिफ़ाफ़े में बंद की गई वस्तु जिसे विशेषतः डाक द्वारा किसी को भेजा जाता है; पार्सल ➪ **pack, package** और **packet** देखिए।

**parched** /pɑ:tʃt पाच्ट्/ *adj.* very hot and dry, or very thirsty बहुत गरम और सूखा, या बहुत प्यासा *Can I have a drink? I'm parched!* ○ *parched landscape*

**parchment** /ˈpɑ:tʃmənt ˈपाच्मन्ट्/ *noun* **1** [U] a material made from the skin of animals such as sheep, goat, etc. This was used in the past for writing on चर्म पत्र; भेड़, बकरी आदि के चर्म से बना लेखन पत्र **2** [C] a piece of writing on such material चर्म पत्र पर लिखित लेख *ancient parchment scrolls* **3** [U] a thick and stiff yellowish white paper resembling the parchment made from animal skin सघन और सख़्त पीला-सफ़ेद काग़ज़ जो चर्म पत्र जैसा प्रतीत होता है

**pardon[1]** /ˈpɑ:dn ˈपाड्न्/ (*also* **pardon me**) *exclamation* **1** used for asking sb to repeat what he/she has just said because you did not hear or understand it बात को दुबारा कहने का अनुरोध करने के लिए प्रयुक्त (क्योंकि हम बात को पहले सुन या समझ नहीं सके) **2** used by some people to mean 'sorry' or 'excuse me' कुछ लोगों द्वारा 'sorry' या 'excuse me' के अर्थ में प्रयुक्त

**pardon[2]** /ˈpɑ:dn ˈपाड्न्/ *noun* [C, U] an official decision not to punish sb for a crime अपराधी को औपचारिक क्षमादान

> **NOTE** 'Sorry' कहने के लिए औपचारिक अभिव्यक्ति है—**do beg your pardon**—*Oh, I do beg your pardon. I had no idea this was your seat.* इसका प्रयोग तब भी किया जा सकता है जब वक्ता से अपनी बात दोहराने के लिए कहना हो।

▶ **pardon** *verb* [T] **pardon sb (for sth/ doing sth)** किसी को क्षमा करना

**pare** /peə(r) पेअ(र्)/ *verb* [T] **1 pare sth (off/ away)** to remove the thin outer layer of sth किसी वस्तु का छिलका उतारना, छीलना *First, pare the rind from the lemon.* ○ *She pared the apple.* **2 pare sth (back/down)** to gradually reduce the size or amount of sth किसी वस्तु के आकार या मात्रा को धीरे-धीरे कम करना *The training budget has been pared back to a minimum.* ○ *The workforce has been **pared to the bone*** (= reduced to the lowest possible level). **3** (*BrE*) to cut away the edges of sth, especially your nails, in order to make them smooth किसी वस्तु (विशेषतः नाख़ून) को काटना (उसे चिकना बनाने के लिए)

**parent** /ˈpeərənt ˈपेअरन्ट्/ *noun* [C] **1** a person's mother or father माता या पिता

> **NOTE** **Single parent** उस माता या पिता को कहते हैं जो अकेले ही (बिना दूसरे की सहायता के) अपनी संतान का पालन-पोषण करता है। **Foster-parent** वह व्यक्ति है जो ऐसे बच्चे का पालन-पोषण करे जो क़ानूनन उसकी अपनी संतान नहीं हो।

**2** a company that owns smaller companies of the same type मूल कंपनी (जिसकी उसी प्रकार की छोटी कंपनियाँ हों) *a parent company*

**parentage** /ˈpeərəntɪdʒ ˈपेअरन्टिज्/ *noun* [U] (*formal*) the origin of a person's parents and who they are मातृ-पितृत्व, जनकत्व (किसी व्यक्ति के माता-पिता का निर्धारण) *a young American of Indian parentage* ○ *Nothing is known of her parentage and background.*

**parental** /pəˈrentl पˈरेन्ट्ल्/ *adj.* (*only before a noun*) of a parent or parents माता या पिता अथवा माता-पिता से संबंधित *parental support/advice*

**parentheses** /pəˈrenθəsi:z पˈरेन्थ़सीज़्/ (*AmE*) = **bracket[1] 1**

**parenthesis** /pəˈrenθəsɪs पˈरेन्थ़सिस्/ *noun*
**IDM** **in parenthesis** as an extra comment or piece of information अतिरिक्त टिप्पणी या सूचना के रूप में अंकित

**parenthood** /ˈpeərənthʊd ˈपेअरन्ट्हुड्/ *noun* [U] the state of being a parent माता या पिता होने की स्थिति; जनकत्व

**parish** /ˈpærɪʃ ˈपैरिश्/ *noun* [C] an area or a district which has its own church; the people who live in this area क्षेत्र या जिला जिसका अपना चर्च हो; पल्ली; इस क्षेत्र के निवासी *the parish church*
▶ **parishioner** /pəˈrɪʃənə(r) पˈरिशन(र्)/ *noun* [C] पल्ली-वासी

**parity** /ˈpærəti ˈपैरटि/ *noun* [U] **1** (*formal*) **parity (with sb/sth); parity (between A and B)**

the state of being equal, especially the state of having equal pay or position समानता, विशेषतः वेतन या पद की दृष्टि से *Prison officers are demanding pay parity with the police force.* **2** (*technical*) (in finance) the fact of the units of money of two different countries being equal (वित्तीय दृष्टि से) दो देशों की मुद्रा की समानता *to achieve parity with the dollar*

**park**[1] /pɑ:k पाक्/ *noun* [C] **1** an open area in a town, often with grass or trees, where people can go to walk, play, etc. सार्वजनिक उद्यान, पार्क *Let's go for a walk in the park.* **2** (*in compounds*) a large area of land that is used for a special purpose विशेष प्रयोजन से प्रयुक्त बड़ा भूखंड, पार्क *a national park* ○ *a theme park*

**park**[2] /pɑ:k पाक्/ *verb* [I, T] to leave the vehicle that you are driving somewhere for a period of time वाहन पार्क करना *You can't park in the centre of town.* ○ *Somebody's parked their car in front of the exit.*

**parka** /ˈpɑ:kə ˈपाका/ *noun* [C] a warm jacket or coat with a part for covering your head (**a hood**) टोपी-लगी गरम जैकेट

**parking** /ˈpɑ:kɪŋ ˈपाकिङ्/ *noun* [U] the action of leaving a car, lorry, etc. somewhere for a time वाहन की पार्किंग *The sign said 'No Parking'.*

> **NOTE** जहाँ अनेक कारें पार्क की जा सकें उसे **car park** और जहाँ केवल एक कार की जगह हो उसे **parking space** कहते हैं।

**parking lot** (*AmE*) = **car park**

**parking ticket** *noun* [C] a piece of paper that orders you to pay money (**a fine**) for parking your car where it is not allowed निषिद्ध स्थान पर वाहन पार्किंग के लिए जुरमाना भरने की परची; पार्किंग टिकट

**Parkinson's disease** /ˈpɑ:kɪnsnz dɪzi:z ˈपाकिन्सन्ज़् डिज़ीज़्/ *noun* [U] a disease that gets worse over a period of time and causes the muscles to become weak and the arms and legs to shake मांसपेशियों के दुर्बल हो जाने के कारण अंगों के काँपने का रोग; काँपा, कँपनी, झूलन रोग, पार्किसन्स डिज़ीज़

**parliament** /ˈpɑ:ləmənt ˈपालमन्ट्/ *noun* [C] **1** the group of people who are elected to make and change the laws of a country देश के लिए क़ानून बनाने या बने हुए क़ानून को बदलने के लिए निर्वाचित व्यक्तियों का समूह; संसद

> **NOTE** **Parliament** शब्द स्वयं एकवचन है परंतु इसके साथ क्रिया एकवचनांत भी हो सकता है, बहुवचनांत भी।

**2 Parliament** [*sing.*] the parliament of India भारत की संसद; पार्लियामेंट *a Member of Parliament (MP)*

> **NOTE** भारत की संसद में दो सदन हैं the **Rajya Sabha** जिसके सदस्य नियुक्त या मानित होते हैं निर्वाचित नहीं तथा the **Lok Sabha** जिसके सदस्य लोगों द्वारा उनके क्षेत्रों (**constituencies**) का प्रतिनिधित्व करने के लिए चुने जाते हैं।

**parliamentary** /ˌpɑ:ləˈmentri ˌपालˈमेन्ट्रि/ *adj.* (*only before a noun*) connected with parliament संसद-विषयक, संसदीय

**parlour** (*AmE* **parlor**) /ˈpɑ:lə(r) ˈपाल(र्)/ *noun* [C] **1** (*old-fashioned*) a sitting-room in a private house for entertaining visitors, etc. अतिथियों के लिए बैठक *She led him to the parlour and asked him to be seated.* **2** (*in compounds*) a shop or store that provides specified goods or services विशिष्ट वस्तुओं या सेवाओं की दुकान *an ice cream parlour* ○ *a beauty parlour*

**parody** /ˈpærədi ˈपैरडि/ *noun* [C, U] (*pl.* **parodies**) a piece of writing, speech or music that copies the style of sb/sth in a funny way किसी शैली की हास्यजनक नक़ल (लेखन, भाषण या संगीत द्वारा); विद्रूपिका, पैरोडी *a parody of a spy novel* ▶ **parody** *verb* [T] (*pres. part.* **parodying;** *3rd person sing. pres.* **parodies;** *pt, pp* **parodied**) हास्यजनक नक़ल उतारना

**parole** /pəˈrəʊl पˈरोल्/ *noun* [U] permission that is given to a prisoner to leave prison early on the condition that he/she behaves well सदाचरण की शर्त पर क़ैदी की जेल से समयपूर्व रिहाई; पैरोल *He's going to be released **on parole**.*

**parrot** /ˈpærət ˈपैरट्/ *noun* [C] a type of tropical bird with a curved beak and usually with very bright feathers. Parrots that are kept as pets can be trained to copy what people say तोता (पालतू तोते सिखाने पर मनुष्यों की वाणी को दोहरा सकते हैं)

**parrot-fashion** *adv.* without understanding the meaning of sth अर्थ को बिना समझे, लगातार रटते हुए *to learn sth parrot-fashion*

**Parsee** (*also* **parsi**) *noun* [C] a follower of **Zoroastrianism** whose ancestors originally came to India from Persia in the 7th and the 8th centuries AD ज़रदुश्त धर्म का अनुयायी जिसके पूर्वज सातवीं तथा आठवीं सदियों में फ़ारस से भारत आए थे

**parsley** /ˈpɑ:sli ˈपासलि/ *noun* [U] a plant (**herb**) with very small leaves that are used for adding taste to or decorating food एक प्रकार का पुदीने जैसा पौधा जिसके पत्तों के प्रयोग से भोजन अधिक स्वादिष्ट हो जाता है

**parsnip** /ˈpɑːsnɪp ˈपास्निप्/ *noun* [C] a long thin white vegetable, that grows under the ground मिट्टी के नीचे उगने वाली लंबी, पतली व सफ़ेद रंग की सब्ज़ी

**part**[1] /pɑːt पाट्/ *noun* 1 [C, U] **(a) part (of sth)** one of the pieces, areas, periods, things, etc. that together with others forms the whole of sth; some, but not all of sth अंश, भाग, खंड, हिस्सा *Which part of Gujarat do you come from?* ○ *The film is good* ***in parts.*** ○ ***spare parts*** *for a car* 2 [C] a role or character in a play, film, etc. नाटक, फ़िल्म आदि में कोई भूमिका या पात्र *He played the part of Akbar.* ○ *I had a small part in the school play.* 3 **parts** [*pl.*] a region or area कोई प्रदेश या क्षेत्र *Are you from these parts?* 4 [C] a section of a book, television series, etc. किसी पुस्तक, टीवी धारावाहिक आदि का खंड या भाग *You can see part two of this programme at the same time next week.* 5 [C] an amount or quantity (of a liquid or substance) (किसी द्रव या पदार्थ की) निश्चित मात्रा या राशि *Use one part cleaning fluid to ten parts water.*

IDM **the best/better part of sth** most of sth; more than half of sth, especially a period of time किसी वस्तु का अधिकांश; किसी वस्तु (विशेषतः किसी कालावधि का) आधे से अधिक अंश *They've lived here for the best part of 40 years.*

**for the most part** usually or mostly सामान्यतः या अधिकांशतः

**for my, his, their, etc. part** speaking for myself, etc.; personally अपनी, उसकी (आदि की) ओर से; व्यक्तिगत रूप से

**have/play a part (in sth)** to be involved in sth किसी बात में संलिप्त होना, किसी काम से जुड़ जाना

**in part** not completely अंशतः *The accident was, in part, the fault of the driver.*

**on the part of sb/on sb's part** made, done or felt by sb किसी के द्वारा बनाया या किया गया; की ओर से *There is concern on the part of the teachers that class sizes will increase.* ○ *I'm sorry. It was a mistake on my part.*

**take part (in sth)** to join with other people in an activity किसी गतिविधि में भाग लेना *Everybody took part in the discussion.*

**part**[2] /pɑːt पाट्/ *verb* 1 [I, T] (*formal*) **part (sb) (from sb)** to leave or go away from sb; to separate people or things किसी से अलग होना (साथ छोड़कर जाना); लोगों या वस्तुओं को अलग करना *We exchanged telephone numbers when we parted.* ○ *He hates being parted from his children for long.* 2 [I, T] to move apart; to make things or people move apart अलग होना; वस्तुओं या व्यक्तियों को अलग करना *Her lips were slightly parted.* 3 [T] to separate the hair on the head with a comb so as to make a clear line कंघी से सिर में माँग निकालना *She parts her hair in the middle.* ➪ **parting** देखिए।

IDM **part company (with sb/sth)** to go different ways or to separate after being together साथ रहने के बाद संबंध तोड़ लेना या अलग हो जाना

PHRV **part with sth** to give or sell sth to sb किसी व्यक्ति को कोई वस्तु देना या बेचना *When we went to live in Mumbai, we had to part with our dogs.*

**part**[3] /pɑːt पाट्/ *adv.* not completely one thing and not completely another अंशतः एक और अंशतः अन्य *She's part Sindhi and part Marathi.*

**partake** /pɑːˈteɪk पाˈटेक्/ *verb* [I] (*pt* **partook** /-ˈtʊk -ˈटुक्/; *pp* **partaken** /-ˈteɪkən -ˈटेकन्/) (*old-fashioned*) 1 (**partake of sth**) to eat or drink something कुछ खाना या पीना *Would you care to partake of some tea and a piece of cake?* 2 (**partake in sth**) to join in some activity किसी गतिविधि में भाग लेना, शामिल होना, भागीदार होना *They preferred not to partake in the merrymaking.* 3 **partake of sth** (*literary*) to have a particular quality, etc. to a certain degree मात्रा-विशेष में कोई विशिष्ट गुण आदि होना *She has a self-confident manner that partakes of arrogance.*

**part exchange** *noun* [U] a way of buying sth, such as a car, in which you give your old one as some of the payment for a more expensive one आंशिक विनिमय जिसमें कोई पुरानी वस्तु और कुछ धनराशि देकर नई वस्तु ख़रीदी जाती है

**partial** /ˈpɑːʃl ˈपाश्ल्/ *adj.* 1 not complete आंशिक *The project was only a partial success.* 2 (*old-fashioned*) **partial to sb/sth** liking sth very much किसी वस्तु को अत्यधिक पसंद करने वाला *He's very partial to ice cream.* ▶ **partially** *adv.* अंशतः

**partiality** /ˌpɑːʃiˈæləti ˌपाशिˈऐलटि/ *noun* [U] (*formal*) the unfair support of one person, team, etc. above another किसी व्यक्ति, टीम आदि के प्रति पक्षपात *The referee was accused of partiality towards the home team.* ✪ विलोम **impartiality** ➪ **impartial** देखिए।

**participant** /pɑːˈtɪsɪpənt पाˈटिसिपन्ट्/ *noun* [C] a person who takes part in sth किसी काम में भाग लेने वाला व्यक्ति; सहभागी

**participate** /pɑːˈtɪsɪpeɪt पाˈटिसिपेट्/ *verb* [I] **participate (in sth)** to take part or become involved in sth किसी काम में भाग लेना या उससे जुड़

जाना *Students are encouraged to participate in sporting activities.* ▶ **participation** /pɑːˌtɪsɪˈpeɪʃn पाˌटिसिˈपेश्न्/ *noun* [U] सहभागिता, भागीदारी

**participle** /ˈpɑːtɪsɪpl; ˌpɑːˈtɪsipl ˈपाटिसिपल्; ˌपाˈटिसिपल्/ *noun* [C] (*grammar*) a word that is formed from a verb and that ends in **-ing** (present participle) or **-ed, -en,** etc. (past participle). Participles are used to form tenses of the verb, or as adjectives कृदंत रूप; क्रियाओं की कालरचना के लिए या विशेषण के रूप में प्रयुक्त शब्द (जैसे क्रिया के अंत में 'ing' लगाने से वर्तमान कृदंत रूप तथा '-ed,' '-en' आदि लगाकर भूत कृदंत रूप बनता है) *'Hurrying' and 'hurried' are the present and past participles of 'hurry'.*

**particle** /ˈpɑːtɪkl ˈपाटिकल्/ *noun* [C] **1** a very small piece; a bit बहुत छोटा-सा अंश; कण *dust particles* ➪ **alpha particle** देखिए। **2** (*grammar*) a small word that is not as important as a noun, verb or adjective नियत (सार्थक लघु शब्द परंतु संज्ञा, क्रिया या विशेषण की तुलना में गौण) *In the phrasal verb 'break down', 'down' is an adverbial particle.*

**particular** /pəˈtɪkjələ(r) पˈटिक्यल(र्)/ *adj.* **1** (*only before a noun*) used to emphasize that you are talking about one person, thing, time, etc. and not about others (व्यक्ति, वस्तु, समय आदि) विशेष, ख़ास *Is there any particular dish you enjoy making?* **2** (*only before a noun*) greater than usual; special सामान्य से अधिक; विशेष या विशिष्ट *This article is of particular interest to me.* **3** connected with one person or thing and not with others एक व्यक्ति या वस्तु से संबंधित (न कि सब से) *Everybody has their own particular problems.* **4 particular (about/over sth)** (*not before a noun*) careful about choosing what you want; difficult to please आसानी से संतुष्ट न होने वाला; चुनने में सतर्क *Some people are extremely particular about what they eat.* ➪ **fussy** देखिए।

**IDM in particular** especially विशेष रूप से *Is there **anything in particular** you'd like to do this weekend?*

**particularly** /pəˈtɪkjələli पˈटिक्यललि/ *adv.* especially; more than usual or more than others विशेष रूप से; सामान्य से अधिक या अन्य से अधिक *I'm particularly interested in Indian history.* ○ *The match was excellent, particularly the second half.*

**particulars** /pəˈtɪkjələz पˈटिक्यलज़्/ *noun* [*pl.*] (*formal*) facts or details about sb/sth व्यक्ति या वस्तु के विषय में तथ्य या ब्योरे *The police took down all the particulars about the missing child.*

**parting** /ˈpɑːtɪŋ ˈपाटिङ्/ *noun* **1** [C, U] saying goodbye to, or being separated from, another person (usually for quite a long time) दूसरे को अलविदा कहने या उससे (प्रायः लंबे समय के लिए) अलग होने की क्रिया **2** [C] the line in a person's hair where it is divided in two with a comb सिर में बालों की माँग *a side/centre parting* ➪ **part** देखिए।

**partisan**[1] /ˌpɑːtɪˈzæn; ˈpɑːtɪzæn ˌपाटिˈज़ैन्; ˈपाटिज़ैन्/ *adj.* showing too much support for one person, group or idea, especially without considering it carefully कट्टर (किसी व्यक्ति, समूह या विचार को अत्यधिक समर्थन देते हुए, विशेषतः बिना ध्यानपूर्वक अनुचिंतन के); अंधभक्त *Most newspapers are politically partisan.* ▶ **partisanship** *noun* [U] अंधभक्ति

**partisan**[2] /ˌpɑːtɪˈzæn; ˈpɑːtɪzæn ˌपाटिˈज़ैन्; ˈपाटिज़ैन्/ *noun* [C] **1** a person who strongly supports a particular leader, group or idea विशेष नेता, समूह या विचार का कट्टर समर्थक व्यक्ति **2** a member of an armed group that is fighting secretly against enemy soldiers who have taken control of its country देश पर क़ब्ज़ा जमाने वाली शत्रु सेना से गुप्त रूप से लड़ने वाली सशस्त्र दल का सदस्य; गुरिल्ला देशभक्त सैनिक

**partition** /pɑːˈtɪʃn पाˈटिश्न्/ *noun* **1** [C] something that divides a room, office, etc. into two or more parts, especially a thin or temporary wall कमरा, कार्यालय आदि को दो या अधिक हिस्सों में विभक्त करने वाली वस्तु (प्रायः पतली या अस्थायी दीवार); विभाजक दीवार **2** [U] the division of a country into two or more countries एक देश का दो या अधिक देशों में विभाजन ▶ **partition** *verb* [T] विभाजित करना *to partition a country/room*

**partly** /ˈpɑːtli ˈपाट्लि/ *adv.* not completely अंशतः, आंशिक रूप से *She was only partly responsible for the mistake.*

**partner** /ˈpɑːtnə(r) ˈपाट्न(र्)/ *noun* [C] **1** the person that you are married to or live with as if you are married विवाहित या विवाहित जैसे जीवन का संगी या साथी **2** one of the people who owns a business व्यापार में भागीदार या साझेदार *business partners* **3** a person that you are doing an activity with as a team, for example dancing or playing a game नृत्य, खेल आदि में साथी; जोड़ीदार **4** a country or an organization that has an agreement with another परस्पर समझौते में बँधा देश या संगठन ▶ **partner** *verb* [T] भागीदार या जोड़ीदार बनना *Jaspal partnered his brother in the doubles, and they won the gold medal.*

**partnership** /ˈpɑːtnəʃɪp ˈपाट्नशिप्/ *noun* **1** [U] the state of being a partner in business व्यापार में भागीदारी या साझेदारी *Radha went into partnership with her sister and opened a shop in Sarojini Nagar.* **2** [C] a relationship between two people, organizations, etc. दो व्यक्तियों, संगठनों आदि में संबंध, भागीदारी *Marriage is a partnership for life.* **3** [C] a business owned by two or more people साझा व्यापार

**part of speech** *noun* [C] (*grammar*) one of the groups that words are divided into, for example noun, verb, adjective, etc. संज्ञा, क्रिया, विशेषण आदि में विभक्त शब्द; शब्दभेद

**partridge** /ˈpɑːtrɪdʒ ˈपाट्रिज्/ *noun* [C] a brown bird with a round body and a short tail, that people hunt for sport or food तीतर; इस भूरे रंग की चिड़िया का शरीर गोल-गोल होता है, छोटी-सी पूँछ होती है और लोग इसे खेल या भोजन के लिए पकड़ते हैं

**part-time** *adj., adv.* for only a part of the working day or week अंशकालिक *She's got a part-time job.* ⇨ **full-time** देखिए।

**party** /ˈpɑːti ˈपाटि/ *noun* [C] (*pl.* **parties**) **1** a social occasion to which people are invited in order to eat, drink and enjoy themselves पार्टी, प्रीतिभोज, दावत *When we've moved into our new house we're going to* ***have a party***. ○ *a birthday/dinner party* **2** (*also* **Party**) a group of people who have the same political aims and ideas and who are trying to win elections to parliament, etc. राजनीतिक दल **3** (*often in compounds*) a group of people who are working, travelling, etc. together (एक साथ काम, यात्रा आदि करने वालों का) दल, टोली *a party of tourists* **4** (*formal*) one of the people or groups of people involved in a legal case मुक़दमे में एक पक्ष (एक व्यक्ति या व्यक्ति-समूह) *the guilty/innocent party* ⇨ **third party** देखिए।

**pass[1]** /pɑːs पास्/ *verb* **1** [I, T] to move past or to the other side of sb/sth किसी व्यक्ति या वस्तु से आगे या उसके दूसरी तरफ़ निकल जाना *The street was crowded and the two buses couldn't pass.* ○ *I passed him in the street but he didn't say hello.*

> **NOTE** **Pass** का भूतकालीन रूप **passed** है, **past** नहीं। वस्तुतः शब्द **past** विशेषण या पूर्वसर्ग है—*The summer months passed slowly.* ○ *The past week was very hot.*

**2** [I, T] **pass (sth) along, down, through, etc. (sth)** to go or move, or make sth move, in the direction mentioned निर्दिष्ट दिशा में किसी वस्तु का गुज़रना या उसे गुज़ारना *A plane passed overhead.* ○ *We'll have to pass the wire through the window.* **3** [T] **pass sth (to sb)** to give sth to sb किसी को कुछ देना *Could you pass (me) the salt, please?* **4** [I, T] **pass (sth) (to sb)** (in some sports) to kick, hit or throw the ball to sb on your own team (कुछ खेलों में) गेंद को अपनी टीम के किसी खिलाड़ी की तरफ़ बढ़ाना (ठोकर मार कर, या फेंक कर) **5** [I] (used about time) to go by (समय) गुज़रना, बीतना *At least a year has passed since I last saw them.* ○ *It was a long journey but the time passed very quickly.* **6** [T] to spend time, especially when you are bored or waiting for sth समय बिताना, गुज़ारना, विशेषतः ऊब जाने पर या किसी की प्रतीक्षा में *I'll have to think of something to do to* ***pass the time*** *in hospital.* **7** [I, T] to achieve the necessary standard in an exam, test, etc. परीक्षा में पास या सफल होना *Good luck in the exam! I'm sure you'll pass.* ✪ विलोम **fail** **8** [T] to test sb/sth and say that sb it is good enough किसी व्यक्ति या वस्तु को परीक्षा में पास करना *The examiner passed most of the students.* **9** [T] to officially approve a law, etc. by voting किसी क़ानून आदि को मतदान द्वारा आधिकारिक रूप से अनुमोदित या पास करना *One of the functions of Parliament is to* ***pass*** *new* ***laws***. **10** [T] **pass sth (on sb/sth)** to give an opinion, a judgement, etc. सम्मति, निर्णय आदि देना *The judge passed sentence on the young man* (= said what his punishment would be). **11** [I] to be allowed or accepted किसी बात को होने देना या सहना *I didn't like what they were saying but I* ***let it pass***.

**IDM** **pass the buck (to sb)** to make sb else responsible for a difficult situation किसी कठिनाई की ज़िम्मेदारी किसी दूसरे पर डालना

**pass water** (*formal*) to get rid of waste liquid from your body मूत्र का विसर्जन करना, पेशाब करना

**PHR V** **pass away** used as a polite way of saying 'die' निधन होने के अर्थ में प्रयुक्त शिष्ट शब्द

**pass by (sb/sth)** गुज़रना *I pass by your house on the way to work.*

**pass sth down** to give or teach sth to people who will live after you have died एक पीढ़ी से दूसरी पीढ़ी को कोई वस्तु देना या सिखाना

**pass for sb/sth** to be accepted as sb/sth that he/she/it is not किसी व्यक्ति या वस्तु को ऐसे रूप में स्वीकार करना जो वस्तुतः वह नहीं है *His mother looks so young she'd pass for his sister.*

**pass sb/sth off (as sb/sth)** to say that a person or a thing is sth that sb it is not किसी व्यक्ति या वस्तु को ग़लत रूप में कुछ और बताना *He tried to pass the work off as his own.*

**pass sth on (to sb)** to give sth to sb else, especially after you have been given it or used it yourself स्वयं को मिली वस्तु या स्वयं द्वारा प्रयुक्त की जा चुकी वस्तु को किसी अन्य व्यक्ति को देना *Could you pass the message on to Mr Roberts?*

**pass out** to become unconscious बेहोश हो जाना ✪ पर्याय **faint** ✪ विलोम **come round/to**

**pass²** /pɑːs पास्/ *noun* [C] **1** a successful result in an exam परीक्षा में सफलता *The pass mark is 50%.* ○ *Grades A, B and C are passes.* ✪ विलोम **fail** **2** an official piece of paper that gives you permission to enter or leave a building, travel on a bus or train, etc. (किसी स्थान पर आने-जाने का) अनुमति-पत्र; पास *Show your student pass when you buy a ticket.* **3** the act of kicking, hitting or throwing the ball to sb on your own team in some sports गेंद को अपनी ही टीम के दूसरे खिलाड़ी की तरफ़ बढ़ाने की क्रिया **4** a road or way over or through mountains पर्वतों में होकर निकली सड़क या रास्ता; दर्रा a *mountain pass*

**passable** /ˈpɑːsəbl ˈपासबल्/ *adj.* **1** good enough but not very good पर्याप्त अच्छा (परंतु बहुत अच्छा नहीं); संतोषजनक *My Urdu is not brilliant but it's passable.* **2** (*not before a noun*) (used about roads, rivers, etc.) possible to use or cross; not blocked (सड़कें, नदियाँ आदि) जिन्हें प्रयोग या पार करना संभव हो; अवरुद्ध नहीं ✪ विलोम **impassable**

**passage** /ˈpæsɪdʒ ˈपैसिज्/ *noun* **1** [C] (*also* **passageway**) a long, narrow way with walls on either side that connects one place with another दो स्थानों को जोड़ने वाला लंबा, तंग रास्ता जिसके दोनों ओर दीवारें हों; गलियारा *a secret underground passage* **2** [C] a tube in your body which air, liquid, etc. can pass through शरीर में स्थित वायु, द्रव आदि के गुज़रने की नली *the nasal passages* **3** [C] a short part of a book, a speech or a piece of music किसी पुस्तक, भाषा या संगीत-रचना का छोटा अंश *The students were given a passage from the novel to study.* **4** [*sing.*] the process of passing गुज़रने की प्रकिया *His painful memories faded with **the passage of time**.*

**passbook** /ˈpɑːsbʊk ˈपासबुक्/ *noun* [C] a small book containing a record of the money you put into and take out of your savings account at a bank or post office धारक के बैंक या डाक-घर में जमा राशि, बचत खाता एवं निकासी का हिसाब रखने वाली छोटी किताब; पासबुक

**passenger** /ˈpæsɪndʒə(r) ˈपैसिन्ज(र्)/ *noun* [C] a person who is travelling in a car, bus, train, plane, etc. but who is not driving it or working on it (स्वयं वाहन चालक न होकर) बस, ट्रेन आदि में यात्रा करने वाला व्यक्ति; यात्री, मुसाफ़िर

**passer-by** *noun* [C] (*pl.* **passers-by**) a person who is walking past sb/sth राहगीर, राह चलता व्यक्ति

**passing¹** /ˈpɑːsɪŋ ˈपासिङ्/ *adj.* (*only before a noun*) **1** lasting for only a short time; brief केवल थोड़े समय का; अल्पकालिक *a passing phase/thought/interest* **2** going past गुज़रता हुआ *I stopped a passing car and asked for help.*

**passing²** /ˈpɑːsɪŋ ˈपासिङ्/ *noun* [U] the process of going by गुज़रने की प्रक्रिया *the passing of time*

**IDM** **in passing** done or said quickly, while you are thinking or talking about sth else जल्दी में किया या कहा गया (किसी के बारे में सोचते या चर्चा करते हुए); यों ही, ऐसे ही *He mentioned the house in passing but he didn't give any details.*

**passion** /ˈpæʃn ˈपैश्न्/ *noun* **1** [C, U] (a) very strong feeling, especially of love, hate or anger बहुत प्रबल मनोभाव, भावावेश (विशेषतः प्रेम, घृणा या क्रोध का) *He was a violent man, controlled by his passions.* **2** [*sing.*] **a passion (for sb)** very strong sexual love or attraction तीव्र कामवासना या आकर्षण *He longed to tell Sakshi of his passion for her.* **3** [*sing.*] **a passion for sth** a very strong liking for or interest in sth किसी वस्तु के लिए बहुत आकर्षण, पसंदगी या रुचि *He has a passion for history.*

**passionate** /ˈpæʃənət ˈपैशनट्/ *adj.* **1** showing or caused by very strong feelings भावावेशपूर्ण *The President gave a passionate speech about patriotism.* **2** showing or feeling very strong love or sexual attraction बहुत प्रेमवश या कामुकतापूर्ण *a passionate kiss* ▶ **passionately** *adv.* उत्कटतापूर्वक *He believes passionately in democracy.*

**passive** /ˈpæsɪv ˈपैसिव़्/ *adj.* **1** showing no reaction, feeling or interest; not active जो कोई प्रतिक्रिया, भावना या रुचि न दिखाए; निष्क्रिय *Some people prefer to play a passive role in meetings.* **2** used about the form of a verb or a sentence when the subject of the sentence is affected by the action of the verb कर्मवाच्य; वह क्रियारूप या वाक्य जिसमें वाक्य का कर्ता क्रिया से प्रभावित होता है *In the sentence 'He was bitten by a dog', the verb is passive.*

**NOTE** उक्त के लिए 'The verb is in the passive'. भी कहा जा सकता है। ➪ **active** देखिए। ▶ **passively** *adv.* निष्क्रिय रूप से

**Passover** /ˈpɑːsəʊvə(r) ˈपासओव़(र्)/ *noun* [*sing*] the most important Jewish festival, which is celebrated in spring and lasts seven or eight days यहूदियों का सबसे बड़ा त्योहार जो वसंत ऋतु में सात-आठ दिन चलता है; पासोवर, पास्का

**passport** /ˈpɑːspɔːt ˈपास्पॉट्/ *noun* [C] **1** an official document that identifies you as a citizen of a particular country and that you have to show when you enter or leave a country (विदेश यात्रा के लिए आवश्यक आधिकारिक दस्तावेज़ जिसमें व्यक्ति की राष्ट्रीयता या नागरिकता का विवरण होता है; पासपोर्ट **2 a passport to sth** a thing that makes it possible to achieve sth कुछ प्राप्त करने में सहायक वस्तु *a passport to success*

**password** /ˈpɑːswɜːd ˈपास्वड्/ *noun* [C] **1** a secret word or phrase that you need to know in order to be allowed into a place गुप्त शब्द या वाक्यांश (किसी स्थान में प्रवेश पाने के लिए अपेक्षित); पास्वर्ड **2** a series of letters or numbers that you must type into a computer or computer system in order to be able to use it अक्षरों या संख्याओं की शृंखला जिसे कंप्यूटर चलाने के लिए कंप्यूटर में टाइप करना सर्वथा आवश्यक है (कंप्यूटर का) पासवर्ड *Please enter your password.*

**past**[1] /pɑːst पास्ट्/ *adj.* **1** already gone; belonging to a time before the present जो बीत चुका है, पिछला; वर्तमान से पहले का, अतीत या भूत काल का *in past centuries/times* ○ *I'd rather forget some of my past mistakes.* **2** (*only before a noun*) just finished, last हाल का; पिछला *He's had to work very hard during the past year.*

**past**[2] /pɑːst पास्ट्/ *prep., adv.* **1** (used when telling the time) after; later than (समय बताने के लिए प्रयुक्त) बजकर; के बाद *It's ten (minutes) past three.* ○ *It was past midnight when we got home.* **2** from one side to the other of sb/sth; further than or on the other side of sb/sth किसी व्यक्ति या वस्तु को पार करके; किसी व्यक्ति या वस्तु से और आगे या उसके दूसरी ओर *He walked straight past me.* ○ *She looked right past me without realizing who I was.* **3** above or further than a certain point, limit or age किसी विषेश बिंदु, सीमा या आयु से ऊपर या उसके परे *Unemployment is now past the two million mark.* ○ *I'm so tired that I'm **past caring*** (= I don't care any more) *what we eat.*

**IDM** **not put it past sb (to do sth)** (used with would) to think sb is capable of doing sth bad ('would' के साथ प्रयुक्त) यह सोचना कि कोई बुरा काम करने में सक्षम है *I wouldn't put it past him to do a thing like that.*

**past it** (*informal*) too old काफ़ी वृद्ध या पुराना

**past**[3] /pɑːst पास्ट्/ *noun* **1 the past** [*sing.*] the time that has gone by; the things that happened before now अतीत काल; पिछली बातें *in the recent/distant past* ○ *The art of writing letters seems to be **a thing of the past**.* **2** [C] a person's life and career before now किसी व्यक्ति का पिछला जीवन और पेशा *We know nothing about his past.* **3 the past** [*sing.*] = **the past tense**

**pasta** /ˈpæstə ˈपैस्टा/ *noun* [U] an Italian food made from flour, eggs and water, formed into different shapes, cooked, and usually served with a sauce आटा, अंडे और पानी से विभिन्न आकृतियों में बना इटैलियन खाद्य पदार्थ जो विशेष तरह के चटनी के साथ खाया जाता है; पास्ता

**paste**[1] /peɪst पेस्ट्/ *noun* **1** [C, U] a soft, wet mixture, usually made of a powder and a liquid and sometimes used for sticking things लेई, पेस्ट *wallpaper paste* ○ *Mix the flour and milk into a paste.* **2** [U] (*usually used in compound nouns*) a soft mixture of food that you can spread onto bread, etc. लेईनुमा भोज्य पदार्थ जिसे डबलरोटी आदि पर लगाकर खाया जाता है *fish/chicken paste*

**paste**[2] /peɪst पेस्ट्/ *verb* [T] **1** to stick sth to sth else using paste or a similar substance **(glue)** लेई या गोंद से एक वस्तु को दूसरी से चिपकाना *He pasted the picture into his book.* **2** (*computing*) to copy or move text into a document from somewhere else कंप्यूटर पाठ की प्रतिलिपि करना या उसे अन्य स्थान से लाकर दस्तावेज़ में जोड़ना *This function allows you to **cut and paste** text.*

**pastel** /ˈpæstl ˈपैस्ट्ल्/ *adj.* (used about colours) pale; not strong (रंग) फीका; गहरा नहीं

**pasteurized** (*also* **-ised**) /ˈpɑːstʃəraɪzd ˈपास्चराइज़्ड्/ *adj.* (used about milk or cream) free from bacteria because it has been heated and then cooled using a special process (दूध या क्रीम) जीवाणु रहित किया हुआ (गरम करने के बाद ठंडा करके); पाश्चरीकृत

**pastiche** /pæˈstiːʃ पैˈस्टीश/ *noun* (*written*) **1** [C] a work of art, piece of writing, etc. that is created by deliberately copying the style of sb/sth else किसी व्यक्ति या वस्तु की सावधानी से नक़ल करके बनाई गई कलाकृति, लिखित रचना आदि *a pastiche of the classic detective story* **2** [C] a work of art, etc. that consists of a variety of different styles विभिन्न शैलियों के मिश्रण वाली कलाकृति आदि; मिश्रित रचना **3** [U] the art of creating a pastiche मिश्रित रचना बनाने की कला

**pastime** /ˈpɑːstaɪm ˈपास्टाइम्/ *noun* [C] something that you enjoy doing when you are not working मनबहलाव के लिए ख़ाली समय में किया गया कार्य ✪ पर्याय **hobby**

**pastoral** /ˈpɑːstərəl ˈपासटरल् / *adj.* **1** (connected with the work of a priest or a teacher) giving help and advice on personal matters rather than on matters of religion or education (पुरोहित या शिक्षक द्वारा) किसी को निजी मामलों में, न कि धर्म या शिक्षा पर, सलाह देने से संबंधित; पुरोहितीय, शिक्षकीय **2** connected with pleasant country life रमणीय ग्रामीण जीवन से संबंधित

**past participle** = **participle**

**the past perfect** (*also* **the pluperfect**) *noun* [*sing.*] (*grammar*) the tense of a verb that describes an action that was finished before another event happened पूर्ण भूतकाल

> **NOTE** भूत कृदंत (past perfect) के विषय में अतिरिक्त जानकारी के लिए इस शब्दकोश के अंत में **Quick Grammar Reference** देखिए।

**pastry** /ˈpeɪstri ˈपेस्ट्रि / *noun* (*pl.* **pastries**) **1** [U] a mixture of flour, fat and water that is rolled out flat and cooked as a base or covering for pies, etc. पेस्ट्री **2** [C] a small cake made with pastry पेस्ट्री से बना छोटा केक

**the past tense** (*also* **the past**) *noun* [*sing.*] (*grammar*) the form of a verb used to describe actions in the past क्रिया का भूतकाल रूप *The past (tense) of the verb 'come' is 'came'.*

> **NOTE** भूत काल (past tense) के विषय में अतिरिक्त जानकारी के लिए इस शब्दकोश के अंत में **Quick Grammar Reference** देखिए।

**pasture** /ˈpɑːstʃə(r) ˈपास्च(र्) / *noun* [C, U] a field or land covered with grass, where cows, etc. can feed घास वाला मैदान जहाँ गौएँ आदि पशु घास चरते हैं; चरागाह, गोचर भूमि

**pasty** /ˈpæsti ˈपैस्टि / *noun* [C] (*pl.* **pasties**) (*BrE*) a small pie containing meat and/or vegetables गोश्त या सब्ज़ियों से भरा छोटा केक

**pat**[1] /pæt पैट् / *verb* [T] (**patting; patted**) to touch sb/sth gently with a flat hand, especially as a sign of friendship, care, etc. थपथपाना, विशेषतः मैत्री, कुशल-क्षेम की चिंता आदि के संकेत के रूप में

**pat**[2] /pæt पैट् / *noun* [C] a gentle friendly touch with a flat hand हलकी व मैत्रीपूर्ण थपकी *He gave her knee an affectionate pat.*

**IDM a pat on the back (for sth/doing sth)** approval for sth good that a person has done अच्छे काम के लिए व्यक्ति को प्रोत्साहन *She deserves a pat on the back for all her hard work.*

**pat**[3] /pæt पैट् / *adj.*, *adv.* (*only before a noun*) (used about an answer, comment, etc.) said in a quick or simple way that does not sound natural or realistic (उत्तर, टिप्पणी आदि) तुरंत या सीधे दिया गया, जो स्वाभाविक या वास्तविकतापूर्ण न लगे

**patch**[1] /pætʃ पैच् / *noun* [C] **1 a patch (of sth)** a part of a surface that is different in some way from the area around it किसी सतह पर आस-पास के क्षेत्र से भिन्न प्रकार का हिस्सा *Drive carefully. There are patches of ice on the roads.* ○ *a bald patch* **2** a piece of material that you use to cover a hole in clothes, etc. कपड़ों आदि के छेद को ढकने के लिए लगाया गया कपड़े का टुकड़ा; पैबंद *I sewed patches on the knees of my jeans.* **3** a small piece of material that you wear over one eye, usually because the eye is damaged घायल आँख की सुरक्षा के लिए पहनी पट्टी **4** a small piece of land, especially for growing vegetables or fruit सब्ज़ी या फल उगाने के लिए प्रयुक्त ज़मीन का टुकड़ा *a vegetable patch*

**IDM go through a bad patch** (*BrE informal*) to experience a difficult or unhappy period of time कठिन समय में से गुज़रना

**not a patch on sb/sth** (*BrE informal*) not nearly as good as sb/sth किसी व्यक्ति या वस्तु जैसा अच्छा नहीं *Her new book isn't a patch on her others.*

**patch**[2] /pætʃ पैच् / *verb* [T] to cover a hole in clothes, etc. with a piece of material in order to repair it कपड़ो में बने छेद को कपड़े आदि के टुकड़े से ढकना; पैबंद लगाना *patched jeans*

**PHR V patch sth up** **1** to repair sth, especially in a temporary way by adding a new piece of material किसी वस्तु की मरम्मत करना (विशेषतः कामचलाऊ तौर पर कुछ जोड़कर) **2** to stop arguing with sb and to be friends again झगड़े का निपटारा करना और पुनः मित्र बन जाना *Have you tried to **patch things up** with her?*

**patchwork** /ˈpætʃwɜːk ˈपैचवक् / *noun* [U] a type of sewing in which small pieces of cloth of different colours and patterns are sewn together रंग-बिरंगे और विविध डिज़ाइन वाले कपड़ों के टुकड़ों से बना सिलाई का काम; पैबंदकारी, पैचवर्क

**patchy** /ˈpætʃi ˈपैचि / *adj.* **1** existing or happening in some places but not others यहाँ-वहाँ विद्यमान, असमान रूप से बिखरा हुआ *patchy fog/clouds/rain* **2** not complete; good in some parts but not in others अधूरा; कुछ बातों में अच्छा और अन्य में दुर्बल *My knowledge of Tamil is rather patchy.*

**pâté** /ˈpæteɪ ˈपैटे / *noun* [U] food that is made by making meat, fish or vegetables into a smooth, thick mixture that is served cold and spread on bread, etc. एक खाद्य पदार्थ जो मांस, मछली या सब्जियों का गाढ़ा मिश्रण होता है और ब्रेड पर लगाकर खाया जाता है *liver pâté*

**patella** /pəˈtelə पˈटेला / (*technical*) = **kneecap**

**patent**[1] /ˈpeɪtnt ˈपेट्न्ट्/ *adj.* (*formal*) clear; obvious स्पष्ट, साफ़; प्रकट, प्रत्यक्ष *a patent lie* ▶ **patently** *adv.* स्पष्ट या प्रकट रूप से

**patent**[2] /ˈpætnt ˈpeɪtnt ˈपैट्न्ट्; ˈपेट्न्ट्/ *noun* [C, U] the official right to be the only person to make, use or sell a product or an invention; the document that shows this is your right किसी उत्पाद, वस्तु या आविष्कार को बनाने, प्रयोग करने या बेचने पर केवल एक व्यक्ति का अधिकार; पेटेंट, एकस्व अधिकार, पेटेंट का दस्तावेज़ ▶ **patent** *verb* [T] पेटेंट कराना या प्राप्त करना

**patent leather** *noun* [U] a type of leather with a hard, shiny surface, used especially for making shoes and bags एक प्रकार का कड़ा चमकदार चमड़ा (विशेषत: जूते और थैले बनाने में प्रयुक्त)

**paternal** /pəˈtɜːnl पˈटन्ल्/ *adj.* (*only before a noun*) **1** behaving as a father would behave; connected with being a father पिता-सदृश; पिता से संबंधित **2** related through the father's side of the family परिवार में पिता के पक्ष से संबंधित (व्यक्ति) *my paternal grandparents* ➪ **maternal** देखिए।

**paternalism** /pəˈtɜːnəlɪzəm पˈटनलिज़म्/ *noun* [U] (*technical*) the system in which a government or an employer protects the people who are governed or employed by providing them with what they need, but does not give them any responsibility or freedom of choice ऐसी व्यवस्था जिसमें शासक अपनी जनता की या नियोक्ता अपने कर्मचारियों की आवश्यकताएँ पूरी करता है परंतु उन्हें न तो कोई दायित्व और न चयन की स्वतंत्रता देता है; पितृसत्तावाद, पैतृकशासन ▶ **paternalistic** /pəˌtɜːnəˈlɪstɪk पˌटनˈलिस्टिक्/ (*also* **paternalist**) *adj.* पितातुल्य व्यवहार वाला, पितृ-वृत्ति वाला *a paternalistic employer/state*

**paternity** /pəˈtɜːnəti पˈटनटि/ *noun* [U] the fact of being the father of a child पितृत्व *paternity leave* (= time that the father of a new baby is allowed to have away from work) ➪ **maternity** देखिए।

**path** /pɑːθ पाथ्/ *noun* [C] **1** a way across a piece of land that is made by or used by people walking पगडंडी, रास्ता *the garden path*

> **NOTE** **Pathway** का भी यही अर्थ है—*There was a narrow pathway leading down the cliff.* ➪ **footpath** देखिए।

**2** the line along which sb/sth moves; the space in front of sb/sth as he/she/it moves वह रेखा जिस पर कोई व्यक्ति या वस्तु चले; पथ; किसी व्यक्ति या वस्तु के सामने की ख़ाली जगह जिस पर वह चले *He threw himself* ***into the path of*** *an oncoming vehicle.* ➪ **flight path** देखिए तथा **diffract** पर चित्र देखिए।

**pathetic** /pəˈθetɪk पˈथ़ेटिक्/ *adj.* **1** causing you to feel pity or sadness दयनीय, करुणाजनक *the pathetic cries of the hungry children* **2** (*informal*) very bad, weak or useless बहुत ख़राब, दुर्बल, बेकार या महत्त्वहीन *What a pathetic performance! The team deserved to lose.* ▶ **pathetically** /-kli -क्लि/ *adv.* अत्यंत ख़राब रूप से, दयनीय भाव से

**pathetic fallacy** *noun* [U, *sing.*] (*technical*) (used in art and literature) the act of describing animals and things as having human feelings (साहित्य में) पशुओं और वस्तुओं को मानवीय भावनाओं से युक्त दिखाना; भावाभास, संवेदन-आरोप

**patho-** /ˈpæθəʊ ˈपैथ़ो/ *prefix* (*used in nouns, adjectives and adverbs*) connected with disease रोग-विषयक *pathology*

**pathological** /ˌpæθəˈlɒdʒɪkl ˌपैथ़ˈलॉजिक्ल्/ *adj.* **1** caused by feelings that you cannot control; not reasonable or sensible नियंत्रणहीन भावनाओं से उत्पन्न; अविवेकपूर्ण *He's a pathological liar* (= he cannot stop lying). ○ *pathological fear/hatred/violence* **2** caused by or connected with disease or illness रोग से उत्पन्न या संबंधित *pathological depression* **3** (*medical*) connected with pathology रोगविज्ञान या पैथालॉजी से संबंधित ▶ **pathologically** /-kli -क्लि/ *adv.* रोगविज्ञान की दृष्टि से

**pathologist** /pəˈθɒlədʒɪst पˈथ़ॉलजिस्ट्/ *noun* [C] a doctor who is an expert in pathology, and examines dead bodies to find out why a person has died रोगविज्ञानी जो मृतक की मृत्यु का कारण जानने के लिए उसके शव की परीक्षा भी करता है

**pathology** /pəˈθɒlədʒi पˈथ़ॉलजि/ *noun* [U] (*medical*) the scientific study of diseases of the body रोगविज्ञान

**pathos** /ˈpeɪθɒs ˈपेथ़ॉस्/ *noun* [U] (in literature) the power of a performance, description, etc. to produce feelings of sadness or pity (साहित्य में) विषाद या करुणा के भावों उत्पन्न करने वाला प्रदर्शन या वर्णन

**patience** /ˈpeɪʃns ˈपेश्न्स्/ *noun* [U] **1 patience (with sb/sth)** the quality of being able to stay calm and not get angry, especially when there is a difficulty or you have to wait a long time धैर्य, धीरज, सहनशक्ति; शांत रहना और क्रोध में न आना, (विशेषत: कठिनाई या लंबी प्रतीक्षा के समय) *I've got no patience with people who don't even try.* ○ *to* ***lose patience*** *with sb* ✪ विलोम **impatience** **2** (*AmE* **solitaire**) a card game for only one player ताश का एक खेल जो अकेले खेला जाता है

**patient[1]** /ˈpeɪʃnt ˈपेश्न्ट्/ *adj.* **patient (with sb/sth)** able to stay calm and not get angry, especially when there is a difficulty or you have to wait a long time धैर्यशाली, धीरजवाला, सहनशील *She's very patient with young children.* ✪ विलोम **impatient** ▶ **patiently** *adv.* धैर्यपूर्वक *to wait patiently*

**patient[2]** /ˈpeɪʃnt ˈपेश्न्ट्/ *noun* [C] a person who is receiving medical treatment रोगी जिसका इलाज चल रहा हो *a hospital patient* ○ *He's one of Dr Batra's patients.*

**patio** /ˈpætiəʊ ˈपैटिओ/ *noun* [C] (*pl.* **patios** /-əʊz ओज़्/) a flat, hard area, usually behind a house, where people can sit, eat, etc. outside मकान के पीछे बना पक्का स्थान (जहाँ लोग खुले में उठ-बैठ, खा-पी सकते हैं) ➪ **balcony, verandah** और **terrace** देखिए।

**patriarch** /ˈpeɪtriɑːk ˈपेट्रिआक्/ *noun* [C] a man who is the head of a family or social group परिवार या किसी सामाजिक समुदाय का पुरुष मुखिया ➪ **matriarch** देखिए।

**patriarchal** /ˌpeɪtriˈɑːkl ˌपेट्रिˈआक्ल्/ *adj.* (used about a society or system) controlled by men rather than women; passing power, property, etc. from father to son rather than from mother to daughter (समाज या सामाजिक व्यवस्था) पुरुष-प्रधान या पुरुषों द्वारा शासित; सत्ता, संपत्ति आदि का पिता से पुत्र को (न कि माता से पुत्री को) हस्तांतरित ➪ **matriarchal** देखिए।

**patriarchy** /ˈpeɪtriɑːki ˈपेट्रिआकि/ *noun* [C, U] (*pl.* **patriarchies**) a social system that gives power and control to men rather than women पितृतंत्र; पुरुष-प्रधान सामाजिक व्यवस्था ➪ **matriarchy** देखिए।

**patricide** /ˈpætrɪsaɪd ˈपैट्रिसाइड्/ *noun* [U] (*formal*) the crime of killing your father पिता की हत्या ➪ **matricide** देखिए।

**patriot** /ˈpeɪtriət ˈपेट्रिअट्/ *noun* [C] a person who loves his/her country and is ready to defend it against an enemy देशभक्त, राष्ट्रप्रेमी ▶ **patriotism** /ˈpeɪtriətɪzəm; ˈpæt- ˈपेट्रिअटिज़म्; ˈपैट-/ *noun* [U] देशभक्ति, राष्ट्रप्रेम

**patriotic** /ˌpeɪtriˈɒtɪk; ˌpæt-ˌपेट्रिˈऑटिक्; ˌपैट्-/ *adj.* having or showing great love for your country देशभक्ति पूर्ण; राष्ट्रप्रेम से युक्त ▶ **patriotically** /-kli -क्लि/ *adv.* देशभक्ति के भाव से

**patrol[1]** /pəˈtrəʊl पˈट्रोल्/ *verb* [I, T] (**patrolling; patrolled**) to go round an area, a building, etc. at regular times to make sure that it is safe and that nothing is wrong सुरक्षा की दृष्टि से किसी इलाक़े, भवन आदि का नियमित रूप से चक्कर लगाना; गश्त लगाना

**patrol[2]** /pəˈtrəʊl पˈट्रोल्/ *noun* **1** [C, U] the act of going round an area, building, etc. at regular times to make sure that it is safe and that nothing is wrong सुरक्षा की दृष्टि से किसी इलाक़े, भवन आदि का नियमित रूप से चक्कर लगाने की क्रिया; गश्त *a police car* ***on patrol*** *in the area* **2** [C] a group of soldiers, vehicles, etc. that patrol sth गश्ती लगाने वाले सैनिकों, वाहनों आदि का दल; गश्ती दल *a naval/police patrol* ○ *a patrol car/boat*

**patron** /ˈpeɪtrən ˈपेट्रन्/ *noun* [C] **1** a person who gives money and support to artists, writers and musicians कलाकारों, लेखकों और संगीतज्ञों की धन से सहायता करने वाला व्यक्ति; सरंक्षक, आश्रयदाता *a patron of the arts* **2** a famous person who supports an organization such as a charity and whose name is used in advertising it प्रसिद्ध व्यक्ति जो किसी धर्माथ संस्था की सहायता करता है और जिसका नाम विज्ञापन में छापा जाता है; समर्थक, संरक्षक ➪ **sponsor** देखिए। **3** (*formal*) a person who uses a particular shop, theatre, restaurant, etc. किसी विशेष दुकान, थिएटर, रेस्तराँ आदि का नियमित प्रयोग करने वाला व्यक्ति; नियमित ग्राहक *This car park is for patrons only.*

**patronage** /ˈpætrənɪdʒ; ˈpeɪt- ˈपैट्रनिज्; ˈपेट्-/ *noun* [U] (*formal*) **1** the support, especially financial, that is given to a person or an organization by a patron संरक्षक द्वारा व्यक्ति या संगठन को दी गई सहायता (विशेषतः आर्थिक) *Patronage of the arts comes mainly from businesses and private individuals.* **2** the system by which an important person gives help or a job to sb in return for his/her support किसी प्रसिद्ध व्यक्ति द्वारा किसी व्यक्ति से प्राप्त समर्थन के बदले कोई सहायता या नौकरी देने की क्रिया; संरक्षणात्मक व्यवहार **3** (*AmE*) the support that a person gives a shop, restaurant, etc. by spending money there किसी व्यक्ति द्वारा किसी दुकान, रेस्तराँ आदि में पैसा ख़र्च कर उनका संरक्षण व समर्थन करने की क्रिया

**patronize** (*also* **-ise**) /ˈpætrənaɪz ˈपैट्रनाइज़्/ *verb* [T] **1** to treat sb in a way that shows that you think you are better, more intelligent, experienced, etc. than he/she is किसी अन्य व्यक्ति को अपने से छोटा, कम बुद्धिमान और अनुभवी समझ कर उस पर कृपाभाव का व्यवहार करना **2** (*formal*) to be a regular customer of a shop, restaurant, etc. किसी दुकान, रेस्तराँ आदि का नियमित ग्राहक बनना ▶ **patronizing** (*also* **-ising**) *adj.* कृपाभाववाला *I really hate that patronizing smile of hers.* ▶ **patronizingly** (*also* **-isingly**) *adv.* कृपाभाव से

**patter** /ˈpætə(r) ˈपैटə(र्)/ *noun* **1** [*sing.*] the sound of many quick light steps or knocks on a surface पट-पट ध्वनि, पड़पड़ाहट तेज़ क़दमों की या किसी सतह पर

पट-पट की आवाज़ *the patter of the children's feet on the stairs* **2** [U, *sing.*] fast continuous talk by sb who is trying to sell you sth or entertain you लोगों को कुछ ख़रीदने के लिए प्रेरित करने या उनका मनोरंजन करने के लिए व्यक्ति की लगातार की बात *sales patter* ▶ **patter** *verb* [I] लगातार बोलना, पट-पट ध्वनि करना

**pattern** /ˈpætn ˈपैट्न्/ *noun* [C] **1** the way in which sth happens, develops, or is done कुछ घटित होने, विकसित होने या किए जाने का ढंग; रीति, तरीक़ा, पैटर्न *Her days all seemed to follow the same pattern.* ○ *changing patterns of behaviour/work/weather* **2** an arrangement of lines, shapes, colours, etc. as a design डिज़ाइन के रूप में पंक्तियों, आकृतियों, रंगों आदि की व्यवस्था; पैटर्न, प्रतिकृति *a shirt with a floral pattern on it* ✪ पर्याय **design** **3** a design, a set of instructions or a shape to cut around that you use in order to make sth कुछ बनाने के लिए प्रयुक्त, दिशानिर्देश या आकृति विशेष, डिज़ाइन नमूना

**patterned** /ˈpætənd ˈपैटन्ड्/ *adj.* decorated with a **pattern 2** किसी पैटर्न से अलंकृत

**pauper** /ˈpɔːpə(r) ˈपॉप(र्)/ *noun* [C] (*old-fashioned*) a very poor person दरिद्र, कंगाल *He died a pauper.*

**pause[1]** /pɔːz पॉज़्/ *noun* **1** [C] **a pause (in sth)** a short period of time during which sb stops talking or stops what he/she is doing किसी क्रिया या बातचीत में लघु विराम *He continued playing for 20 minutes without a pause.* ➪ **interval** पर नोट देखिए। **2** (*also* **pause button**) [U] a control on a video, CD, DVD player, etc. that allows you to stop playing or recording for a short time वीडियो प्लेयर सीडी, डीविडी आदि पर गति व समर्थन करने की क्रिया को अल्पकालिक विराम देने के लिए लगा बटन

**pause[2]** /pɔːz पॉज़्/ *verb* [I] **pause (for sth)** to stop talking or doing sth for a short time before continuing बातचीत या कोई काम करते हुए अल्पकाल के लिए रुकना

**pave** /peɪv पेव़्/ *verb* [T] **pave sth (with sth)** (*usually passive*) to cover an area of ground with flat stones (**paving stones**) or bricks सपाट पत्थरों या ईंटों से भूखंड को ढकना

**pavement** /ˈpeɪvmənt ˈपेव़्मन्ट्/ (*AmE* **sidewalk**) *noun* [C] a hard flat area at the side of a road for people to walk on सड़क के किनारे की पटरी (पैदल चलने वालों के लिए)

**pavilion** /pəˈvɪliən पˈव़िलिअन्/ *noun* [C] a building at a sports ground where players can change their clothes and take rest खेल के मैदान के साथ खिलाड़ियों के उपयोग के लिए बना भवन; पैविलियन

**paving stone** *noun* [C] a flat piece of stone that is used for covering the ground मैदान पर बिछाने वाला पत्थर

**paw[1]** /pɔː पॉ/ *noun* [C] the foot of animals such as dogs, cats, bears, etc. पशुओं का पंजा ➪ **lion** पर चित्र देखिए।

**paw[2]** /pɔː पॉ/ *verb* [I, T] **paw (at) sth** (used about an animal) to touch or scratch sb/sth several times with a paw (पशु का) व्यक्ति या वस्तु को पंजे से बार-बार छूना या खुरचना *The dog pawed at my sleeve.*

**pawn[1]** /pɔːn पॉन्/ *noun* [C] **1** (in the game of chess) one of the eight pieces that are of least value and importance (शतरंज में) सबसे छोटा मोहरा; प्यादा **2** a person who is used or controlled by other more powerful people अन्य सशक्त व्यक्तियों द्वारा अपनी स्वार्थ-सिद्धि के लिए प्रयुक्त व्यक्ति

**pawn[2]** /pɔːn पॉन्/ *verb* [T] to leave a valuable object with a **pawnbroker** in return for money. If you cannot pay back the money after a certain period, the object can be sold or kept उधार उठाने के लिए साहूकार के पास कोई क़ीमती वस्तु बंधक या रेहन रखना। उधार न चुकाने पर बंधक वस्तु ज़ब्त हो जाती है

**pawnbroker** /ˈpɔːnbrəʊkə(r) ˈपॉन्ब्रोक(र्)/ *noun* [C] a person who lends money to people when they leave sth of value with him/her क़ीमती वस्तु अपने पास बंधक रख कर किसी को पैसा उधार देने वाला व्यक्ति; साहूकार, महाजन

**pay[1]** /peɪ पे/ *verb* (*pt, pp* **paid**) **1** [I, T] **pay (sb) (for sth); pay (sb) sth (for sth)** to give sb money for work, goods, services, etc. किसी काम, सामान, सेवा आदि के लिए भुगतान करना *She is very **well paid**.* ○ *We paid the dealer Rs 30,000 for the car.* **2** [T] **pay sth (to sb)** to give the money that you owe for sth (देनदारी का) पैसा चुकाना *Have you paid her the rent yet?* **3** [I, T] to make a profit; to be worth doing लाभ कमाना; लाभप्रद होना *It would pay you to get professional advice before making a decision.* **4** [I] **pay (for sth)** to suffer or be punished because of your beliefs or actions अपने विश्वासों और कार्यों की क़ीमत चुकाना (कष्ट उठाना या सज़ा भुगतना) *You'll pay for that remark!*

IDM **be paid in arrears** ➪ **arrears** देखिए।

**pay attention (to sb/sth)** to listen carefully to or to take notice of sb/sth किसी व्यक्ति की बात ध्यान से सुनना या किसी वस्तु पर ध्यान देना

**pay sb a compliment; pay a compliment to sb** to say that you like sth about sb किसी बात के लिए किसी व्यक्ति की प्रशंसा करना

**pay your respects (to sb)** (*formal*) to visit sb as a sign of respect आदरपूर्वक किसी के पास आना *Hundreds came to pay their last respects to her* (= to go to her funeral).

**pay tribute to sb/sth** to say good things about sb/sth and show your respect for sb/sth किसी की प्रशंसा करना (उसके प्रति आदर दिखाने के लिए)

**put paid to sth** to destroy or finish sth किसी वस्तु को नष्ट या समाप्त करना *The bad weather put paid to our picnic.*

PHR V **pay sth back (to sb)** to give money back to sb that you borrowed from him/her किसी का उधार चुकाना *Can you lend me Rs 500? I'll pay you back/I'll pay it back to you on Friday.*

**pay sb back (for sth)** to punish sb for making you or sb else suffer किसी पर पलटवार करना, किसी से बदला लेना *What a mean trick! I'll pay you back one day.*

**pay off** (*informal*) to be successful किसी काम में सफल होना *All her hard work has paid off! She passed her exam.*

**pay sth off** to pay all the money that you owe for sth पूरा उधार चुका देना *to pay off a debt/mortgage*

**pay up** (*informal*) to pay the money that you owe उधार का पैसा लौटाना *If you don't pay up, we'll take you to court.*

**pay²** /peɪ पे/ *noun* [U] money that you get regularly for work that you have done नियमित रूप से किसी कार्य को करने पर प्राप्त धनराशि; वेतन, तनख़्वाह

NOTE किसी कार्य को नियमित रूप से करने पर प्राप्त धन को **pay** (वेतन) कहते हैं। **Wages** (मजदूरी) नक़द में रोज़ाना या हफ़्तावार दी जाती है। **Salary** प्रति मास मिलती है तथा यह राशि आपके बैंक एकाउंट में सीधे भी पहुँचती है। व्यावसायिक सेवाओं जैसे डॉक्टर, वकील आदि को उनके कार्य के लिए **fee** दी जाती है। किसी कार्य को एक बार या अनियमित रूप से करने पर किए गए भुगतान को **payment** कहते हैं। नियमित रूप से कार्य करने पर दी गई तथा बचत की गई धनराशि पर प्राप्त ब्याज को **income** कहते हैं।

**payable** /ˈpeɪəbl ˈपेअबल्/ *adj.* that should or must be paid देय, जो देना है *A 10% deposit is payable in advance.* ○ ***Make the cheque payable to*** *the State Bank of India.*

**payee** /ˌpeɪˈiː ˌपेˈई/ *noun* [C] (*written*) a person that money, especially a cheque, is paid to भुगतान, विशेषतः चेक, पाने वाला

**payment** /ˈpeɪmənt ˈपेमन्ट्/ *noun* **payment (for sth)** **1** [U] the act of paying sb or of being paid किसी व्यक्ति को भुगतान देने या किसी व्यक्ति द्वारा भुगतान पाने की प्रक्रिया *I did the work last month but I haven't had any payment for it yet.* ➪ **pay²** पर नोट देखिए। **2** [C] an amount of money that you must pay धनराशि जिसका भुगतान अवश्य करना है *They asked for a payment of Rs 1000 as a deposit.*

**payroll** /ˈpeɪrəʊl ˈपेरोल्/ *noun* **1** [C] a list of people employed by a company showing the amount of money to be paid to each of them नियुक्त व्यक्तियों की सूची जिसमें प्रत्येक के आगे प्राप्य धनराशि का उल्लेख; वेतन चिट्ठा *There are 70 people* ***on the payroll.*** **2** (*usually sing.*) the total amount paid by a company to its employees कंपनी द्वारा अपने कर्मचारियों को भुगतान की कुल धनराशि

**PC** /ˌpiːˈsiː ˌपीˈसी/ *abbr* **1** (*computing*) personal computer; a computer that is designed for one person to use at work or at home व्यक्तिगत कंप्यूटर; कंप्यूटर जिसका डिज़ाइन कार्यस्थल या घर पर एक व्यक्ति के कार्य करने के लिए किया गया है **2** (in UK) police constable; an officer of the lowest position (यूके में) निम्नतम स्थिति का अफ़सर, पुलिस कांस्टेबल

**PE** /ˌpiːˈiː ˌपीˈई/ *abbr.* physical education शारीरिक शिक्षा *a PE lesson*

**pea** /piː पी/ *noun* [C] a small round green seed that is eaten as a vegetable. A number of peas grow together in a long thin case (**a pod**) मटर, मटर के दाने एक लंबी फली में होते हैं ➪ **vegetable** पर चित्र देखिए।

**peace** /piːs पीस्/ *noun* [U] **1** a situation or a period of time in which there is no war or violence in a country or area ऐसी स्थिति या समयावधि जब किसी देश या प्रदेश में युद्ध या हिंसा न हो; शांति *The two communities now manage to live* ***in peace*** *together.* ○ *A United Nations force has been sent in to* ***keep the peace.*** **2** the state of being calm or quiet शांति की स्थिति जहाँ कोई हलचल आदि न हो *He longed to escape from the city to the* ***peace and quiet*** *of the countryside.*

**peaceful** /ˈpiːsfl ˈपीस्फ़ल्/ *adj.* **1** not wanting or involving war, violence or argument शांतिपूर्ण; युद्ध, हिंसा या तर्क-वितर्क हीन *a peaceful protest/demonstration/solution* **2** calm and quiet शांत और नीरव *a peaceful village* ▶ **peacefully** /-fəli -फ़लि/ *adv.* शांतिपूर्वक *The siege ended peacefully.* ▶ **peacefulness** *noun* [U] शांतिप्रियता

**peacekeeping** /ˈpiːskiːpɪŋ ˈपीस्कीपिङ्/ *adj.* (*only before a noun*) intended to help keep the peace and prevent war or violence in a place where this is likely युद्ध या हिंसा की स्थिति की संभावना में शांति बनाए हुए *a United Nations peacekeeping force*

**peacetime** /ˈpi:staɪm ˈपीस्टाइम् / *noun* [U] a period when a country is not at war देश की वह समय-अवधि जब वह युद्धग्रस्त नहीं है

**peach** /pi:tʃ पीच् / *noun* **1** [C] a soft round fruit with orange-red skin. A peach is soft inside and has a large stone in its centre आड़ू का फल। इसके बीच में गुठली होती है और उस पर मुलायम गूदा होता है **2** [U] a pinkish-orange colour गुलाबीपन लिए नारंगी रंग

**peacock** /ˈpi:kɒk ˈपीकॉक् / *noun* [C] a large bird with beautiful long blue and green tail feathers that it can lift up and spread out मोर

**peak[1]** /pi:k पीक् / *noun* [C] **1** the point at which sth is the highest, best, strongest, etc. वह बिंदु जहाँ कोई वस्तु उच्चतम, सर्वोत्तम, प्रबलतम आदि स्थिति में हो *a man **at the peak of** his career* **2** the pointed top of a mountain पहाड़ का नुक़ीला शीर्ष भाग *snow-covered peaks* ➪ **glacial** पर चित्र देखिए। **3** the rigid front part of a cap that sticks out above your eyes टोपी का वह न मुड़ने वाला अग्रभाग जो आँखों के ठीक ऊपर होता है

**peak[2]** /pi:k पीक् / *adj.* (*only before a noun*) used to describe the highest level of sth, or a time when the greatest number of people are doing or using sth किसी वस्तु का सर्वोच्च स्तर या वह समय जब सर्वाधिक लोग कुछ कर रहे हों या प्रयोग में ला रहे हों *Summer is the peak period for most hotels.* ○ *The athletes are all in peak condition.* ➪ **off-peak** देखिए।

**peak[3]** /pi:k पीक् / *verb* [I] to reach the highest point or value उच्चतम बिंदु या मूल्य पर पहुँचना *Sales peak just before Diwali.*

**peal** /pi:l पील् / *noun* [C] the loud ringing of a bell or bells घंटे-घंटियों की ज़ोरदार बजने की ध्वनि (*figurative*) *peals of laughter* ► **peal** *verb* [I] (घंटियों का) जोर से बजना

**peanut** /ˈpi:nʌt ˈपीनट् / *noun* **1** (*also* **groundnut**) [C] a nut that grows under the ground that we eat मूंगफली ➪ **nut** पर चित्र देखिए। **2 peanuts** [*pl.*] (*informal*) a very small amount of money बहुत ही थोड़ी रक़म *We get paid peanuts for doing this job.*

**pear** /peə(r) पेअ(र्) / *noun* [C] a fruit that has a yellow or green skin and is white inside. Pears are thinner at the top than at the bottom नाशपाती का फल

**pearl** /pɜ:l पर्ल् / *noun* [C] a small, hard, round, white object that grows inside the shell of a type of shellfish (**an oyster**). Pearls are used to make jewellery एक प्रकार के शंखमीन के खोल के भीतर उगने वाली छोटी कड़ी गोल और श्वेत वस्तु; मोती रत्नजड़ित आभूषणों में प्रयुक्त होते हैं *pearl earrings*

**peasant** /ˈpeznt ˈपेज़न्ट् / *noun* [C] (used especially in past times) a person who owns or rents a small piece of land on which he/she grows food and keeps animals in order to feed his/her family (प्राचीन प्रयोग) वह व्यक्ति जो स्वयं की या किराए पर लिए छोटे भूखंड पर अपने परिवार के भरणपोषण हेतु खाद्यान्न उत्पन्न करता है तथा पशुओं का पालन करता है; किसान, खेतिहर

**peat** /pi:t पीट् / *noun* [U] a soft black or brown natural substance that is formed from dead plants just under the surface of the ground in cool, wet places. It can be burned as a fuel or put on the garden to make plants grow better धरती की सतह के अंदर ठंडे एवं गीले स्थानों में सड़ी-गली घास पात से बना काला या भूरा प्राकृतिक पदार्थ; यह जलाने के काम या बग़ीचे में खाद के काम आती है; पंस, पाँस

**pebble** /ˈpebl ˈपेबल् / *noun* [C] a smooth round stone that is found in or near water पत्थर का गोल चिकना टुकड़ा जो नदी, समुद्र आदि में या उनके पास मिलता है; रोड़ी, बजरी

**pecan** /ˈpi:kən ˈपीकन् / *noun* [C] a type of nut that we eat एक प्रकार का कठोर-आवरण वाला फल जिसे खाया जाता है ➪ **nut** पर चित्र देखिए।

**peck** /pek पेक् / *verb* [I, T] **1 peck (at) sth** (used about a bird) to eat or bite sth with its beak (चिड़ियों के संबंध में) चोंच से खाना या कुतरना **2** (*informal*) to kiss sb quickly and lightly किसी व्यक्ति का द्रुत और कोमल चुंबन करना *She pecked him on the cheek and then left.* ► **peck** *noun* [C] चंचु-प्रहार, द्रुत चुंबन

**peckish** /ˈpekɪʃ ˈपेकिश् / *adj.* (*informal*) hungry भूखा

**pectoral** /ˈpektərəl ˈपेक्टरल् / *adj.* on or connected with the chest or breast of a fish or animal मछली या किसी पशु के वक्षस्थल पर या से संबंधित *pectoral fins* ➪ **dorsal** और **ventral** देखिए।

**pectorals** /ˈpektərəlz ˈपेक्ट़रल्ज़ / (*informal* **pecs** /peks पेक्स् /) *noun* [*pl.*] the muscles of the chest वक्षस्थल की मांसपेशियाँ

**peculiar** /pɪˈkju:liə(r) पिˈक्यूलिअ(र्) / *adj.* **1** unusual or strange असामान्य, अज़ीब, विचित्र *There's a very peculiar smell in here.* ✪ पर्याय **odd** **2 peculiar to sb/sth** only belonging to one person or found in one place केवल किसी एक व्यक्ति का या केवल एक ही स्थान पर मिलने वाला *a species of bird peculiar to South East Asia*

**peculiarity** /pɪˌkjuːliˈærəti पि ˌक्यूलिˈऐरटि / *noun* (*pl.* **peculiarities**) **1** [C] a strange or unusual characteristic, quality or habit कोई विचित्र या असामान्य लक्षण, गुण या आदत *There are some peculiarities in her behaviour.* **2** [C] a characteristic or a quality that only belongs to one particular person, thing or place लक्षण या गुण जो केवल एक व्यक्ति, वस्तु या स्थान पर पाया जाता है; विशिष्टता *the cultural peculiarities of the English* **3** [U] the quality of being strange or unusual विचित्रता, असामान्यता

**peculiarly** /pɪˈkjuːliəli पिˈक्यूलिअलि / *adv.* **1** in a strange and unusual way विचित्र या असामान्य रीति से *Leela is behaving very peculiarly.* **2** especially; very विशेष तौर से, अत्यधिक रूप में *Laila's laugh can be peculiarly annoying.* **3** in a way that is especially typical of one person, thing or place ऐसी व्यवहार-रीति से जो किसी एक व्यक्ति, वस्तु या स्थान पर विशिष्टतः मिलती है *a peculiarly French custom*

**ped-** (*AmE*) = **paed-**

**pedagogical** /ˌpedəˈgɒdʒɪkl ˌपेडˈगॉजिकल् / *adj.* connected with ways of teaching अध्यापन या शिक्षण पद्धति से संबंधित, शिक्षा-शास्त्रीय

**pedal** /ˈpedl ˈपेड्ल् / *noun* [C] the part of a bicycle or other machine that you push with your foot in order to make it move or work पेडल, बाइसिकल या अन्य मशीन का वह भाग जिसे, उसे चलाने या कार्यशील करने के लिए अपने पैरों से दबाते हैं ➪ **bicycle** पर चित्र देखिए। ▶ **pedal** *verb* [I, T] (**pedalling; pedalled** *AmE* **pedaling; pedaled**) पेडल द्वारा चलाना *She had to pedal hard to get up the hill.*

**pedantic** /pɪˈdæntɪk पिˈडैन्टिक् / *adj.* too worried about rules or details नियमों और विवरणों पर अत्यधिक ध्यान रखने वाला; पंडिताऊ ▶ **pedantically** /-kli -क्लि / *adv.* अध्यापकीय या पंडिताऊ रूप से

**peddle** /ˈpedl ˈपेड्ल् / *verb* [I] **1** to go from place to place selling something कुछ बेचने के लिए फेरी लगाना *The farmer came to the city to peddle his surplus mangoes.* **2** to illegally sell stolen goods or drugs चुराया माल या मादक द्रव अवैध रूप से बेचना **3** (*disapproving*) to spread an idea in order to get people to accept it (अमान्य) किसी विचार को प्रचारित करना ताकि जनता उसे स्वीकार करे

**pedestal** /ˈpedɪstl ˈपेडिस्ट्ल् / *noun* [C] the base on which a column, statue, etc. stands आधार जिस पर कोई स्तंभ या मूर्ति आदि खड़ी की जाती है; स्तंभ्याधार IDM **put on a pedestal** to admire or idolize someone किसी को सराहना या पूजना *Children put their parents on a pedestal.*

**pedestrian** /pəˈdestriən पˈडेस्ट्रिअन् / *noun* [C] a person who is walking in the street (not travelling in a vehicle) व्यक्ति जो सड़क पर पैदल चल रहा है (न कि वाहन में) ➪ **motorist** देखिए।

**pedestrian crossing** (*AmE* **crosswalk**) *noun* [C] a place for pedestrians to cross the road वह स्थान जहाँ पैदल चलने वाले सड़क को पार करते हैं ➪ **zebra crossing** देखिए।

**pediatrician** (*AmE*) = **paediatrician**

**pediatrics** (*AmE*) = **paediatrics**

**pedigree**[1] /ˈpedɪgriː ˈपेडिग्री / *noun* [C] **1** an official record of the parents, grandfather, grandmother, etc. from which an animal has been bred किसी पशु के माता-पिता, पितामह, मातामह आदि का अधिकारिक अभिलेख ➪ **mongrel** देखिए। **2** a person's family history, especially when this is impressive व्यक्ति का पारिवारिक इतिवृत्त, विशेषतः जब यह प्रभावशाली हो; वंशावली, वंशानुक्रम

**pedigree**[2] /ˈpedɪgriː ˈपेडिग्री / *adj.* (*only before a noun*) (used about an animal) of high quality because the parents, grandfather, grandmother, etc. are all of the same breed and specially chosen (किसी पशु के लिए प्रयुक्त) उच्च गुणवत्ता वाला क्योंकि उसके माता-पिता व पूर्वज एक ही प्रजाति के तथा विशेष तौर से चुने हुए थे

**pedlar** /ˈpedlə(r) ˈपेड्लर्(र्) / *noun* [C] **1** a person who travels from place to place trying to sell something, usually small objects छोटी-मोटी वस्तुओं को जगह-जगह बेचने वाला; खोमचे वाला, फेरी वाला **2** a person who sells stolen goods or illegal drugs अवैध मादक द्रव या चोरी की वस्तुएँ बेचने वाला व्यक्ति *a drug pedlar* **3** someone who spreads an idea or a view widely ऐसा व्यक्ति जो विचार या मत को प्रचारित करता है

**pedophile** (*AmE*) = **paedophile**

**pee** /piː पी / *verb* [I] (*informal*) to get rid of waste water from your body; to urinate पेशाब करना ▶ **pee** *noun* [U, *sing.*] पेशाब करने की क्रिया

**peek** /piːk पीक् / *verb* [I] (*informal*) **peek (at sth)** to look at sth quickly and secretly because you should not be looking at it किसी व्यक्ति या घटना को एक क्षण के लिए तथा छिप कर देखना (विशेषतः जब इस प्रकार देखना अनुचित है) *No peeking at your presents before your birthday!* ▶ **peek** *noun* [*sing.*] झाँकी *to have a quick peek*

**peel**[1] /piːl पील् / *verb* **1** [T] to take the skin off a fruit or vegetable फल या सब्ज़ी का छिलका छीलना या उतारना; विशल्कन *Could you peel the potatoes, please?* **2** [I, T] **peel (sth) (off/away/back)**

to come off or to take sth off a surface in one piece or in small pieces किसी सतह से पूरा-पूरा या टुकड़े-टुकड़े में किसी चिपकी वस्तु को अलग कर देना *I peeled off the price label before handing her the present.*

IDM **keep your eyes peeled/skinned (for sb/sth)** = **eye**[1]

**peel**[2] /pi:l पील्/ *noun* [U] the skin of a fruit or vegetable फल या सब्ज़ी का छिलका *apple/potato peel* ➪ **rind** और **skin** देखिए।

**peeler** /ˈpi:lə(r) ˈपील(र्)/ *noun* [C] a special knife for taking the skin off fruit and vegetables फल या सब्ज़ी के छिलके को छीलने वाला विशेष चाकू; पीलर *a potato peeler* ➪ **kitchen** पर चित्र देखिए।

**peep**[1] /pi:p पीप्/ *verb* [I] **1 peep (at sth)** to look at sth quickly and secretly, especially through a small opening ताक-झाँक करना, लुक-छिप कर देखना; विशेषतः छोटे छेद से क्षणभर के लिए छिप कर देखना **2** to be in a position where a small part of sb/sth can be seen उस स्थिति में होना जहाँ किसी व्यक्ति या वस्तु का छोटा भाग दिखाई पड़े *The moon is peeping out from behind the clouds.*

**peep**[2] /pi:p पीप्/ *noun* [*sing.*] (*informal*) **1** a quick look एक क्षणिक अवलोकन, क्षणभर के लिए देखने की क्रिया ***Have a peep*** *in the bedroom and see if the baby is asleep.* **2** a sound आवाज़ *There hasn't been a peep out of the children for hours.*

**peepul** = **pipal**

**peer**[1] /pɪə(r) पिअ(र्)/ *noun* [C] a person who is of the same age or position in society as you व्यक्ति जो समाज में समान स्थान पर या आयु का हो; समकक्ष व्यक्ति *Children hate to look stupid in front of their peers.*

**peer**[2] /pɪə(r) पिअ(र्)/ *verb* [I] **peer (at sb/sth)** to look closely or carefully at sb/sth, for example because you cannot see very well किसी व्यक्ति या वस्तु को समीप से और ध्यानपूर्वक देखना, क्योंकि वह अन्यथा स्पष्ट नहीं दिखाई दे रही है *He peered at the photo, but it was blurred.*

**peer group** *noun* [C] a group of people who are all of the same age and social position उन लोगों का समूह जिनकी आयु और सामाजिक प्रतिष्ठा एक समान हो

**peeved** /pi:vd पीव्ड्/ *adj.* (*informal*) quite angry or annoyed क्रुद्ध और नाराज़

**peevish** /ˈpi:vɪʃ ˈपीविश्/ *adj.* easily annoyed by things that are not important चिड़चिड़ा; कम महत्त्व की वस्तुओं या घटनाओं से सहज रूप से नाराज़ ▸ **peevishly** *adv.* चिड़चिड़ेपन से

**peg**[1] /peg पेग्/ *noun* [C] **1** a piece of wood, metal, etc. on a wall or door that you hang your coat on दीवार या द्वार पर लकड़ी या धातु का ऐसा टुकड़ा पर कुछ लटकाया जा सके; खूँटी, खूँटा **2** (*also* **tent peg**) a piece of metal that you push into the ground to keep one of the ropes of a tent in place धातु का नुकीला टुकड़ा जिसे भूमि में गाड़ा जाता है और टेंट की रस्सियों को उस से बाँधते हैं; खूँटी **3** (*also* **clothes peg**, *AmE* **clothes pin**) a type of small wooden or plastic object used for fastening wet clothes to a clothes line लकड़ी या प्लास्टिक की वस्तु जिससे डोर पर गीले कपड़े को जकड़ देते हैं ताकि डोर या डोरी से गिर न सके; चिमटी

**peg**[2] /peg पेग्/ *verb* [T] (**pegging; pegged**) **1 peg sth (out)** to fix sth with a peg किसी वस्तु को खूँटे से बाँधना **2 peg sth (at/to sth)** to fix or keep sth at a certain level वस्तु को एक विशेष स्तर पर स्थिर बनाए रखना *Wage increases were pegged at 5%.*

**pelican** /ˈpelɪkən ˈपेलिकन्/ *noun* [C] a large bird that lives near water in warm countries. A pelican has a large beak that it uses for catching and holding fish एक बड़ा पक्षी जो कि उष्ण देशों में जल के समीप रहता है। पेलिकन; पेलिकन की बड़ी चोंच होती है जिस से वह मछली पकड़ता है

**pellet** /ˈpelɪt ˈपेलिट्/ *noun* [C] **1** a small hard ball of any substance, often of soft material that has become hard किसी कोमल पदार्थ की ऐसी छोटी कड़ी गोली जो सूख कर सख़्त हो गई है; ढेला, गोली **2** a very small metal ball that is fired from a gun बंदूक़ से निकली बहुत छोटी गोली; छर्रा *shotgun pellets*

**pelt** /pelt पेल्ट्/ *verb* **1** [T] to attack sb/sth by throwing things किसी वस्तु को किसी पर फेंक कर वार करना, ढेले चलाना या मारना **2** [I] **pelt (down)** (used about rain) to fall very heavily मूसलाधार वर्षा होना *It's absolutely pelting down.* **3** [I] (*informal*) to run very fast बहुत तेज़ दौड़ना *Some kids pelted past us.*

**pelvis** /ˈpelvɪs ˈपेल्विस्/ *noun* [C] (*pl.* **pelvises**) the set of wide bones at the bottom of your back, to which your leg bones are joined व्यक्ति की पीठ में नीचे स्थित चौड़ी हड्डियों का समुच्चय जिससे टांगें जुड़ी होती हैं; श्रोणी ➪ **body** पर चित्र देखिए। ▸ **pelvic** /ˈpelvɪk ˈपेल्विक्/ *adj.* श्रोणीय

**pen** /pen पेन्/ *noun* [C] **1** an object that you use for writing in ink रोशनाई से लिखने में प्रयुक्त क़लम, पेन *a ballpoint/felt-tip/marker/fountain pen* **2** a small piece of ground with a fence around it that is used for keeping animals in एक छोटा भू-क्षेत्र जिसके चारों ओर घेर या बाड़ लगी है और जिसमें पशुओं को रखा जाता है; बाड़ा

**penal** /ˈpi:nl ˈपीनल्/ *adj.* (*only before a noun*) connected with punishment by law क़ानूनी दंड से संबंधित *the penal system*

**penalize** (*also* **-ise**) /ˈpiːnəlaɪz ˈपीनलाइज़्/ *verb* [T] **1** to punish sb for breaking a law or rule क़ानून या नियम भंग करने पर किसी को दंड देना **2** to cause sb to have a disadvantage किसी को हानि की स्थिति में डालना *Children should not be penalized because their parents cannot afford to pay.*

**penalty** /ˈpenəlti ˈपेनल्टि/ *noun* [C] (*pl.* **penalties**) **1** a punishment for breaking a law, rule or contract क़ानून, नियम या संविदा तोड़ने पर मिलने वाला दंड *the death penalty* ○ *What's the maximum penalty for rash driving?* **2** a disadvantage or sth unpleasant that happens as the result of sth किसी बात के परिणामस्वरूप कोई अप्रिय घटना या हानि *I didn't work hard enough and I* ***paid the penalty****. I failed all my exams.* **3** (in sport) a punishment for one team and an advantage for the other team because a rule has been broken (खेलों में) नियम भंग करने पर एक टीम को दंड और दूसरी टीम को उस दंड से लाभ *The referee awarded a penalty to the home team.*

**the penalty area** *noun* [C] the marked area in front of the goal in football फ़ुटबॉल में गोल के आगे का चिह्नित भूक्षेत्र

**penance** /ˈpenəns ˈपेनन्स्/ *noun* [C, U] a punishment that you give yourself to show you are sorry for doing sth wrong किसी ग़लत काम करने पर दुखी होते हुए अपने को कोई दंड देना; प्रायश्चित

**pence** ➪ **penny** का plural रूप

**pencil¹** /ˈpensl ˈपेन्सल्/ *noun* [C, U] an object that you use for writing or drawing. Pencils are usually made of wood and contain a thin stick of a black or coloured substance लिखने या अंकन के लिए प्रयुक्त वस्तु; पेंसिल, यह लकड़ी की होती है इसमें काले या रंगीन पदार्थ की दंडिका पड़ी होती है *Write* ***in pencil****, not ink.* ➪ **stationery** पर चित्र देखिए।

**pencil²** /ˈpensl ˈपेन्सल्/ *verb* [T] (**pencilling; pencilled** *AmE* **penciling; penciled**) to write or draw sth with a pencil पेंसिल से अंकित करना या लिखना

**PHR V** **pencil sth/sb in** to write down the details of an arrangement that might have to be changed later किसी क्रमविन्यास का विवरण लिखना जो कि बाद में बदला जा सके *Shall we pencil the next meeting in for the 14th of September?*

**pencil case** *noun* [C] a small bag or box that you keep pens, pencils, etc. in क़लम, पेंसिल आदि रखने का एक छोटा डिब्बा; पेंसिल बॉक्स

**pencil sharpener** *noun* [C] an instrument that you use for making pencils sharp पेंसिल नुकीली बनाने में प्रयुक्त एक उपकरण; पेंसिल शार्पनर ➪ **stationery** पर चित्र देखिए।

**pendant** /ˈpendənt ˈपेन्डन्ट्/ *noun* [C] a small attractive object that you wear on a chain around your neck एक छोटा आकर्षक आभूषण जो गले की चेन में डालकर पहना जाता हैं; पेंडेंट

**pending** /ˈpendɪŋ ˈपेन्डिङ्/ *adj., prep.* (*formal*) **1** waiting to be done or decided विचाराधीन, अनिर्णीत *The judge's decision is still pending.* **2** until sth happens जब तक कि कोई घटना घटित न हो जाए; लंबित *He took over the leadership pending the elections.*

**pendulum** /ˈpendjələm ˈपेन्ड्यलम्/ *noun* [C] **1** a chain or stick with a heavy weight at the bottom that moves regularly from side to side to work a clock जंजीर या दंडिका जिस के नीचे भारी वजन है और जो कि अग़ल-बग़ल नियमित घूमते हुए घड़ी को चलाता है; पेंडुलम, लोलक **2** a way of describing a situation that changes from one thing to its opposite ऐसी स्थिति का वर्णन जो कि किसी एक स्थिति से विपरीत स्थिति में परिवर्तित होती है *Since last year's election, the pendulum of public opinion has swung against the government.*

**penetrate** /ˈpenɪtreɪt ˈपेनिट्रेट्/ *verb* [I, T] **1** to go through or into sth, especially when this is difficult किसी वस्तु में, विशेषतः कठिनाई से, भीतर जाना; भेदना; घुसना *The knife penetrated ten centimetres into his chest.* **2** to manage to understand sth difficult किसी कठिन वस्तु को समझने का प्रयास करना *Scientists have still not penetrated the workings of the brain.* **3** to be understood or realized समझ या जानने में आने वाला *I was back at home when the meaning of her words finally penetrated.* ▶ **penetration** /ˌpenɪˈtreɪʃn ˌपेनिˈट्रेश्न्/ *noun* [U] वेधन, प्रवेश, भेदन

**penetrating** /ˈpenɪtreɪtɪŋ ˈपेनिट्रेटिङ्/ *adj.* **1** (used about sb's eyes or of a way of looking) making you feel uncomfortable because it seems sb knows what you are thinking (किसी व्यक्ति की आँखो या हावभाव के लिए प्रयुक्त) मन को पढ़ पाने वाला और इस कारण बेचैनी उत्पन्न करने वाला *a penetrating look/stare/gaze* ○ *penetrating blue eyes* **2** showing that you have understood sth completely and quickly यह दिखाते हुए कि कुछ पूरी तरह से और क्षणभर में समझ आ गया है *a penetrating question/comment* **3** that can be heard, felt, smelled, etc. a long way away जो बहुत दूर से सुनी, सूंघी या अनुभव आदि की जा सके

**penfriend** /ˈpenfrend ˈपेन्फ्रेन्ड्/ (*AmE* **pen pal**) *noun* [C] a person that you become friendly with by exchanging letters, often a person that you have never met व्यक्ति जो पत्राचार के माध्यम से मित्र बना है, प्रायः बिना साक्षात मिले; पत्रमित्र

**penguin** /ˈpeŋgwɪn ˈपेङ्ग्विन्/ *noun* [C] a black and white sea bird that cannot fly and that lives in the Antarctic अंटार्कटिक (दक्षिण ध्रुव) में बसी श्वेत-श्याम समुद्री पक्षी जो उड़ नहीं पाता; पेंग्विन

**penicillin** /ˌpenɪˈsɪlɪn ˌपेनिˈसिलिन्/ *noun* [U] a substance that is used as a medicine (**an antibiotic**) for preventing and treating diseases and infections caused by bacteria बैक्टीरिया जनित रोगों और संक्रमण के निवारण एवं उपचार के लिए ऐंटीबायटिक औषधि के रूप में प्रयुक्त पदार्थ; पेनिसिलीन

**peninsula** /pəˈnɪnsjələ पˈनिन्स्यला/ *noun* [C] an area of land that is almost surrounded by water भूक्षेत्र जो लगभग जल से घिरा हुआ है; प्रायद्वीप

**penis** /ˈpiːnɪs ˈपीनिस्/ *noun* [C] the male sex organ that is used for getting rid of waste liquid and having sex पुरुष-इंद्रिय जो पेशाब निकालने और संभोग के लिए प्रयुक्त होता है; शिश्न

**penitent** /ˈpenɪtənt ˈपेनिटन्ट्/ *adj.* (*formal*) sorry for having done sth wrong कुछ अनुचित कर बैठने के लिए खेदपूर्ण

**penitentiary** /ˌpenɪˈtenʃəri ˌपेनिˈटेन्शरि/ *noun* [C] (*pl.* **penitentiaries**) (*AmE*) a prison कारागार, जेल

**penknife** /ˈpennaɪf ˈपेन्नाइफ़्/ *noun* [C] (*pl.* **penknives**) a small knife with parts used for cutting (**blades**), opening bottles, etc. that fold safely away when not being used एक छोटा चाकू जिस के कुछ भाग काटने, बोतल खोलने आदि के काम आते हैं तथा जो प्रयोग न आने की स्थिति में सुरक्षित रखने के लिए बंद कर दी जाती है; पेन-नाइफ़, जेबी चाकू

**penniless** /ˈpeniləs ˈपेनिलस्/ *adj.* having no money; poor निर्धन, जिस के पास कुछ भी धनराशि न हो

**penny** /ˈpeni ˈपेनि/ *noun* [C] (*pl.* **pence** /pens पेन्स् or **pennies**) **1** (*abbr.* **p**) a small brown British coin. There are a hundred pence in a pound पेनी, एक छोटा भूरा ब्रिटिश सिक्का; एक पाउंड में 100 पेंस होते हैं *a fifty-pence piece/coin* **2** (*AmE*) a cent एक सेन्ट

**pension** /ˈpenʃn ˈपेन्श्न्/ *noun* [C] money that is paid regularly by a government or company to sb who has stopped working (**retired**) because of old age or who cannot work because he/she is ill सेवानिवृत्त या पदनिवृत्त व्यक्ति को सरकार या कंपनी द्वारा नियमित रूप से मिलने वाली धनराशि; पेंशन ▶ **pensioner** *noun* [C] सेवानिवृत या पदनिवृत व्यक्ति

**penta-** /ˈpentə ˈपेन्टा/ *prefix* (*used in nouns, adjectives and adverbs*) five; having five पाँच, पाँचवाला, पंच- *pentathlon*

**pentagon** /ˈpentəgən ˈपेन्टगन्/ *noun* **1** [C] a shape that has five straight sides आकृति जिसकी पांच ऋजु भुजाएँ होती हैं; पंचभुज **2 the Pentagon** [*sing.*] a large government building near Washington DC in the US that contains the main offices of the US military forces; the military officials who work there अमेरिका में वाशिंगटन डीसी के समीप एक विशाल सरकारी इमारत जहाँ अमेरिकन सैन्यबलों के मुख्यालय हैं; पेंटागॉन, सैनिक अधिकारी जो वहाँ कार्य करते हैं

**pentathlon** /penˈtæθlən पेन्ˈटैथ्लन्/ *noun* [C] a sports competition in which you have to take part in five different events प्रतियोगिता जिसमें आप को पाँच भिन्न-भिन्न खेलों में भाग लेना होता है; पेंटाथलॉन

**penthouse** /ˈpenthaʊs ˈपेन्ट्हाउस्/ *noun* [C] an expensive flat at the top of a tall building ऊँचे भवन की सबसे ऊँची मंज़िल पर बना क़ीमती फ़्लैट

**pent-up** /ˌpentˈʌp ˌपेन्ट्ˈअप्/ *adj.* (*only before a noun*) (used about feelings) that you hold inside and do not express (भावनाओं के लिए प्रयुक्त) जो भीतर मन में हों पर अभिव्यक्त नहीं किए गए हों; दबी (भावनाएँ) *pent-up anger*

**penultimate** /penˈʌltɪmət पेन्ˈअल्टिमट्/ *adj.* (in a series) the one before the last one (श्रेणी में), अंतिम के ठीक पूर्व *'Y' is the penultimate letter of the alphabet.*

**penumbra** /pəˈnʌmbrə पˈनम्ब्रा/ *noun* [C] (*technical*) **1** the outer part of a **shadow**, that is less dark than the central part छाया का बहिर्भाग जो कि केंद्रीय भाग की तुलना में कम काला होता है; उपच्छाया **2** a dark area on the earth caused by the moon, or a dark area on the moon caused by the earth, during a **partial eclipse** चंद्रग्रहण जिसमें चंद्रमा का कुछ अंश प्रकाशमान रहता है; आंशिक चंद्रग्रहण ➪ **umbra** देखिए तथा **shadow** पर चित्र देखिए।

**people** /ˈpiːpl ˈपीप्ल्/ *noun* **1** [*pl.*] more than one person एक से अधिक व्यक्ति, लोग *How many people are coming to the party?*

> **NOTE** ध्यान रखिए **person** के बहुवचन रूप **persons** के स्थान पर लगभग सदैव **people** का प्रयोग किया जाता है। **Persons** अति औपचारिक प्रयोग है और सामान्यतः क़ानूनी भाषा में प्रयुक्त होता है—*Persons under the age of 18 are not permitted to buy cigarettes.*

**2** [C] (*pl.* **peoples**) (*formal*) all the men, women and children who belong to a particular place or race किसी स्थान या प्रजाति के सभी पुरुष, महिलाएँ और बच्चे *The President addressed the American people.* ○ *the French-speaking peoples of the world* **3** [*pl.*] men and women who work in a particular activity पुरुष एवं स्त्रियाँ जो किसी विशेष गतिविधि में संलग्न हैं *business/sports people* **4 the people** [*pl.*] the ordinary citizens of a country देश के आम नागरिक *The President is popular because he listens to the people.*

**peon** /ˈpiːən ˈपीअन्/ *noun* [C] (in India and some other South East Asian countries) an office messenger; an attendant (भारत और कुछ दक्षिण एशियाई देशों में) पत्रवाह; चपरासी

**people carrier** (*AmE* **minivan**) *noun* [C] a large car, like a van, designed to carry up to eight people एक बड़ी कार, जैसे कि वैन, जो आठ व्यक्तियों तक को ले जा सकती है ✪ पर्याय **MPV**

**pepper[1]** /ˈpepə(r) ˈपेप(र्)/ *noun* **1** [U] a black or white powder with a hot taste that is used for flavouring food काली मिर्च, इसे भोजन में समूचा या पीस कर तेज़ स्वाद के लिए डालते हैं *salt and pepper shaker* **2** [C] a green, red or yellow vegetable that is almost empty inside लाल, हरी या पीली मिर्च जिसकी सब्ज़ी बनाते हैं। मिर्च भीतर से लगभग खाली होती है

**pepper[2]** /ˈpepə(r) ˈपेप(र्)/ *verb* [T] **pepper sb/sth with sth** (*usually passive*) to hit sb/sth with a series of small objects, especially bullets किसी व्यक्ति या वस्तु को गोली, छर्रे आदि मारना *The wall had been peppered with bullets.*

**peppercorn** /ˈpepəkɔːn ˈपेपकॉन्/ *noun* [C] a dried berry from a tropical plant, that is pressed into small pieces or powder to make pepper काली मिर्च का दाना। इसे छोटा-छोटा कूट कर या महीन पीस कर भोजन में प्रयुक्त करते हैं

**peppermint** /ˈpepəmɪnt ˈपेपमिन्ट्/ *noun* **1** [U] a natural substance with a strong fresh flavour that is used in sweets and medicines प्रबल अच्छा ज़ायक़ा देने वाला एक प्राकृतिक पदार्थ। यह मिठाई या टॉफ़ी और दवाइयों के काम में आता है; पेपरमिन्ट **2** (*also* **mint**) [C] a sweet with a peppermint flavour मिंट, पेपरमिंट के स्वाद वाली एक मिठाई या टॉफ़ी

**pepsin** /ˈpepsɪn ˈपेप्सिन्/ *noun* [U] (*technical*) the main **enzyme** in the stomach that breaks down **protein** उदर में स्थित मुख्य एन्ज़ाइम जो प्रोटीन को भंग करता है

**pep talk** /ˈpep tɔːk ˈपेप् टॉक्/ *noun* [C] (*informal*) a speech that is given to encourage people or to make them work harder लोगों का उत्साह बढ़ाने वाला या उन्हें और अधिक श्रम से कार्य करने का जोश दिलाने वाला भाषण

**per** /pə(r) *strong form* pɜː(r) प(र्); प्रबल रूप प(र्)/ *prep.* for each (प्रत्येक) प्रति, के अनुसार *The speed limit is 110 kilometres per hour.* ○ *Rooms cost Rs 60 per person per night.*

**per capita** /pə ˈkæpɪtə प ˈकैपिटा/ *adj.* for each person प्रति व्यक्ति *Per capita income rose sharply last year.* ▶ **per capita** *adv.* प्रति व्यक्ति की दृष्टि से *average earnings per capita*

**perceive** /pəˈsiːv पˈसीव्/ *verb* [T] (*formal*) **1** to notice or realize sth इंद्रियों द्वारा ग्रहण करना, देखना, जानना, बोध होना *Scientists failed to perceive how dangerous the level of pollution had become.* **2** to understand or think of sth in a particular way किसी बात को किसी विशेष दृष्टिकोण से समझना या सोचना *I perceived his comments as a criticism.* ➪ **perception** देखिए।

**per cent** (*AmE* **percent**) *adj., adv., noun* [C, *with sing. or pl. verb*] (*pl.* **per cent**) (*symbol* %) in or of each hundred; one part in every hundred प्रतिशत, सौ का सौवाँ अंश *You get 10% off if you pay cash.* ○ *The price of bread has gone up* ***by 20 per cent*** *in two years.*

**percentage** /pəˈsentɪdʒ पˈसेन्टिज्/ *noun* [C, *with sing. or pl. verb*] the number, amount, rate, etc. of sth, expressed as if it is part of a total which is a hundred; a part or share of a whole प्रतिशतता, प्रतिशत दर; कुल योग को सौ मान कर उसका शतांश निकालना; किसी पूर्ण का अंश या भाग *What percentage of people voted in the last election?*

**perceptible** /pəˈseptəbl पˈसेप्टब्ल्/ *adj.* (*formal*) that can be seen or felt बोधगम्य, प्रतीत या दिखाई पड़ने वाला *a barely perceptible change in colour* ✪ विलोम **imperceptible** ▶ **perceptibly** /-əbli -अब्लि/ *adv.* अवगम्यता से

**perception** /pəˈsepʃn पˈसेप्शन्/ *noun* **1** [U] the ability to notice or understand sth इंद्रियों द्वारा ग्रहण या बोध; प्रत्यक्षण **2** [C] a particular way of looking at or understanding sth; an opinion एक दृष्टिकोण विशेष; राय, मत *What is your perception of the situation?* ➪ **perceive** verb देखिए।

**perceptive** /pəˈseptɪv पˈसेप्टिव् / *adj.* (*formal*) quick to notice or understand things किसी वस्तु को तुरंत समझने वाला, सु-ग्रहणशील ▶ **perceptively** *adv.* अवबोधकता से

**perch[1]** /pɜːtʃ पच्/ *verb* **1** [I] (used about a bird) to sit on a branch, etc. किसी शाखा पर बैठना **2** [I, T] to sit or be put on the edge of sth किसी वस्तु के एक सिरे पर बैठना या रखना *The house was perched on the edge of a cliff.*

**perch[2]** /pɜːtʃ पच्/ *noun* [C] a branch (or a bar in a cage) where a bird sits पेड़ की शाखा या पिंजरे की मध्यदंडिका जिस पर पक्षी बैठता है

**percolate** /ˈpɜːkəleɪt ˈपकलेट्/ *verb* **1** [I] (*technical*) (used about a liquid, gas, etc.) to move gradually through a surface that has very small holes or spaces in it (द्रव, गैस आदि के लिए प्रयुक्त) महीन छलनी या कपड़े से छानना; छोटे छिद्रों से रिसना या बहना *Water had percolated down through the rocks.* **2** [I, T] to make coffee in a special pot (**a percolator**); to be made in this way कॉफ़ी यंत्र (परकोलेटर) से काफ़ी बनाना; इस प्रकार स्रवण होना या बनना ▶ **percolation** /pɜːkəˈleɪʃn पकˈलेशन्/ *noun* [U] रिसन, अंतःस्रवण

**percolator** /ˈpɜːkəleɪtə(r) ˈपकलेट(र्)/ *noun* [C] a pot for making coffee, in which boiling water is forced up a central tube and then comes down again through the coffee कॉफ़ी यंत्र, इसमें उबलता पानी एक मध्यवर्ती ट्यूब में बलपूर्वक ऊपर फ़ेंका जाता है और फिर उबलता पानी कॉफ़ी के बीच में से नीचे आता है; स्राविन्न ➪ **cafetière** देखिए।

**percussion** /pəˈkʌʃn पˈकशन्/ *noun* [U] drums and other instruments that you play by hitting them ड्रम, ढोलक आदि वाद्य यंत्र जो समाघात से बजाए जाते हैं

**perennial** /pəˈreniəl पˈरेनिअल्/ *adj.* **1** that happens often or that lasts for a long time चिरस्थायी या निरंतर; शाश्वत *a perennial problem* **2** (used about plants) living for two years or more (पौधों के लिए प्रयुक्त) दो या अधिक वर्षों तक जीवित रहने वाले; बहुवर्षी

**perfect[1]** /ˈpɜːfɪkt ˈपफ़िक्ट्/ *adj.* **1** completely good; without faults or weaknesses पूर्णतः अच्छा, परिपूर्ण; दोषरहित *The car is two years old but it is still in perfect condition.* ✪ विलोम **imperfect** **2 perfect (for sb/sth)** exactly suitable or right सर्वथा उपयुक्त या सही *Kiran would be perfect for the job.* **3** (*only before a noun*) complete; total पूर्ण; सर्वथा, समग्रतः *What he was saying made perfect sense to me.* ○ *a perfect stranger* **4** used to describe the tense of a verb that is formed with has/have/had and the past participle अंग्रेज़ी व्याकरण में 'has/have/had' के साथ भूत कृदंत जोड़ने से बना क्रिया का काल; पूर्ण (काल) ▶ **perfectly** *adv.* सही रूप से; दोषरहित ढंग से *He played the piece of music perfectly.*

**perfect[2]** /pəˈfekt पˈफ़ेक्ट्/ *verb* [T] to make sth perfect परिष्कृत करना, त्रुटिरहित बनाना *Vinay is spending a year in England to perfect his English.*

**perfection** /pəˈfekʃn पˈफ़ेक्शन्/ *noun* [U] the state of being perfect or without fault परिपूर्णता या दोषहीनता *The vegetable dish was cooked **to perfection**.*

**perfectionist** /pəˈfekʃənɪst पˈफ़ेक्शनिस्ट्/ *noun* [C] a person who always does things as well as he/she possibly can and who expects others to do the same ऐसा व्यक्ति जो अपना काम उत्तम रीति से करे तथा दूसरों से भी वैसी ही आशा करे; पूर्णतावादी

**the perfect tense** (*also* **the perfect**) *noun* [*sing.*] (*grammar*) the tense of a verb that is formed with has/have/had and the past participle अंग्रेज़ी व्याकरण में 'has/have/had' के साथ भूत कृदंत जोड़ने से बना 'क्रिया का काल; पूर्ण काल *'I've finished' is in the present perfect tense.*

NOTE पूर्ण काल (perfect tense) के विषय में अधिक जानकारी के लिए इस शब्दकोश के अंत में **Quick Grammar Reference** देखिए।

**perforate** /ˈpɜːfəreɪt ˈपफ़रेट्/ *verb* [T] to make a hole or holes in sth किसी वस्तु में छोटे-छोटे छेद करना; छेदित करना

**perforation** /ˌpɜːfəˈreɪʃn ˌपफ़ˈरेशन्/ *noun* **1** [C] a series of small holes in paper, etc. that make it easy for you to tear काग़ज़ आदि में बने छोटे-छोटे छेद (ताकि काग़ज़ को आसानी से फाड़ा जा सके) **2** [U] the action of making a hole or holes in sth किसी वस्तु में छेद करने की क्रिया; छिद्रण

**perform** /pəˈfɔːm पˈफ़ॉम्/ *verb* **1** [T] (*formal*) to do a piece of work or sth that you have been ordered to do कोई काम आदि करना जिसके लिए आदेश है *to perform an operation/an experiment/a task* **2** [I, T] to take part in a play or to sing, dance, etc. in front of an audience दर्शकों के सामने अभिनय या गायन, नृत्य आदि का कार्यक्रम प्रस्तुत करना *She is currently performing at the National Theatre.* **3** [I] **perform (well/badly/poorly)** to work or function well or badly अच्छे या ख़राब ढंग से काम करना *The company has not been performing well recently.* IDM **work/perform miracles** ➪ **miracle** देखिए।

**performance** /pəˈfɔːməns पˈफ़ॉमन्स्/ *noun* **1** [C] the act of performing sth in front of an audience; something that you perform दर्शकों के सामने कार्यक्रम प्रस्तुत करने की क्रिया; कार्यक्रम *What time does the performance start?* **2** [C] the way a person performs in a play, concert, etc. व्यक्ति का अभिनय या प्रदर्शन का ढंग *His moving performance in the film won him an Oscar.* **3** [C] the way in which you do sth, especially how successful you are किसी कार्य को करने का ढंग (विशेषतः सफलता की दृष्टि से) *The company's performance was disappointing last year.* **4** [U] (used about a machine, etc.) the ability to work well (मशीन आदि की) ठीक प्रकार से कार्य करने की योग्यता *This car has a high-performance engine.* **5** [U, *sing.*]

(*formal*) the act or process of doing a task, an action, etc. किसी कार्य का निष्पादन *the performance of your duties*

**performer** /pəˈfɔːmə(r) पˈफ़ॉम(र्)/ *noun* [C] **1** a person who performs for an audience दर्शकों के सामने प्रदर्शन करने वाला व्यक्ति; प्रदर्शक *a stage performer* **2** a person or thing that behaves or works in the way mentioned निर्दिष्ट रीति से कुछ करने वाला व्यक्ति या वस्तु; निष्पादक *Divya is an excellent performer in exams.*

**perfume** /ˈpɜːfjuːm ˈपफ़्यूम्/ *noun* [C, U] **1** (*BrE* **scent**) a liquid with a sweet smell that you put on your body to make yourself smell nice सुगंधित द्रव पदार्थ जिसे सुगंध के लिए शरीर पर छिड़का जाता है; इत्र *Are you wearing perfume?* **2** a pleasant, often sweet, smell सुहानी (प्रायः मधुर) सुगंध

**perhaps** /pəˈhæps; præps पˈहैप्स्; प्रैप्स्/ *adv.* (used when you are not sure about sth) possibly; maybe (किसी विषय में अनिश्चय का भाव प्रकट करने के लिए प्रयुक्त) संभवतः, शायद, कदाचित *Perhaps he's forgotten.* ○ *She was, perhaps, one of the most famous writers of the time.*

> NOTE **Perhaps** और **maybe** के अर्थ समान हैं। प्रायः अपने कथन में शिष्टता के प्रदर्शन के लिए इनका प्रयोग किया जाता है—*Perhaps I could borrow your book, if you're not using it?* ○ *Maybe I'd better explain the meaning to you*

**peril** /ˈperəl ˈपेरल्/ *noun* (*written*) **1** [U] great danger गंभीर ख़तरा, संकट *A lack of trained nurses is putting patients' lives* ***in peril***. **2** [C] sth that is very dangerous बहुत ख़तरनाक स्थिति या वस्तु *the perils of drug abuse* ▸ **perilous** /ˈperələs ˈपेरलस्/*adj.* ख़तरनाक, जोखिम-भरा NOTE इस अर्थ में **danger** और **dangerous** अधिक प्रचलित शब्द हैं।

**perimeter** /pəˈrɪmɪtə(r) पˈरिमिट(र्)/ *noun* [C] **1** the outside edge or limit of an area of land किसी भूक्षेत्र का बाहरी किनारा या सीमा; परिधि **2** (in geometry) the circumference of any plane area (रेखा-गणित में) परिमाप *the perimeter fence of the army camp*

**period** /ˈpɪəriəd ˈपिअरिअड्/ *noun* [C] **1** a length of time समय की लंबाई, अवधि, मियाद *The scheme will be introduced for a six-month trial period.* ○ *Her son is going through a difficult period at the moment.* **2** a lesson in school पाठशाला में पाठ का समय; पीरियड, घंटा *We have five periods of English a week.* **3** the time every month when a woman loses blood from her body स्त्रियों के मासिक रक्तस्राव का समय **4** (*AmE*) = **full stop**

**periodic** /ˌpɪəriˈɒdɪk ˌपिअरिˈऑडिक्/ (*also* **periodical** /-kl -क्ल्/) *adj.* happening fairly regularly नियमित रूप से होने वाला *We have periodic meetings to check on progress.* ▸ **periodically** /-kli -क्लि/ *adv.* नियत समय पर, समय-समय पर *All machines need to be checked periodically.*

**periodical** /ˌpɪəriˈɒdɪkl ˌपिअरिˈऑडिक्ल्/ *noun* [C] (*formal*) a magazine that is produced regularly नियत समय पर प्रकाशित होने वाली पत्रिका; नियतकालिक

**the periodic table** *noun* [*sing.*] a table of all the chemical elements, arranged according to the number of parts with a positive electric charge (**protons**) that they each have in their centre (**nucleus**) सभी रासायनिक तत्वों की सारणी या तालिका, इसमें तत्वों का पूर्वापर या उत्तराधर क्रम उन के केंद्र में स्थित प्रोटोनों (धनात्मक वैद्युत आवेश की अंश संख्या) के अनुक्रम में होता है; आवर्त सारणी

**peripheral**[1] /pəˈrɪfərəl पˈरिफ़रल्/ *adj.* **1** (*formal*) **peripheral (to sth)** not as important as the main aim, part, etc. of sth (मुख्य उद्देश्य आदि की तुलना में) कम महत्त्वपूर्ण, गौण **2** (*technical*) connected with the outer edge of a particular area क्षेत्र विशेष के बाहरी सिरे से संबंधित; परिधीय, परिरेखीय *the peripheral nervous system* ○ *peripheral vision* **3** (*computing*) (used about equipment) connected to a computer (यंत्र) कंप्यूटर के साथ जुड़ा हुआ *a peripheral device* ▸ **peripherally** /pəˈrɪfərəli पˈरिफ़रलि/ *adv.* गौण रूप से, बाह्य रूप से

**peripheral**[2] /pəˈrɪfərəl पˈरिफ़रल्/ *noun* [C] (*computing*) a piece of equipment that is connected to a computer, for example a **printer** कंप्यूटर से जुड़ा हुआ कोई उपकरण (जैसे प्रिंटर)

**periphery** /pəˈrɪfəri पˈरिफ़रि/ *noun* [C, *usually sing.*] (*pl.* **peripheries**) (*formal*) **1** the outer edge of a particular area क्षेत्र-विशेष का बाहरी सिरा; परिधि *industrial development* ***on the periphery of*** *the town* **2** the less important part of sth, for example of a particular activity or of a social or political group किसी वस्तु (जैसे कोई विशेष गतिविधि या सामाजिक वर्ग या राजनीतिक दल) का कम महत्त्वपूर्ण भाग; किसी वस्तु का गौण अंश *minor parties* ***on the periphery of*** *Indian politics*

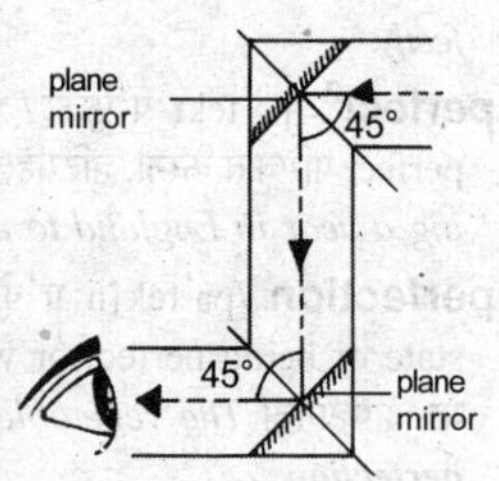


**periscope** /ˈperɪskəʊp ˈपेरिस्कोप्/ *noun* [C] a device like a long tube, containing mirrors which allow you to see over the top of sth, used especially in a **submarine** to see above the surface of the sea (विशेषतः) पनडुब्बी में लगा यंत्र जिससे जल के नीचे रहकर भी समुद्र तल के ऊपर देखा जा सकता है; पेरिस्कोप

**perish** /ˈperɪʃ ˈपेरिश्/ *verb* [I] (*written*) to die or be destroyed मर जाना या नष्ट हो जाना *Thousands perished in the war.*

**perishable** /ˈperɪʃəbl ˈपेरिशब्ल्/ *adj.* (used about food) that will go bad quickly (भोजन) जल्दी ख़राब हो जाने वाला नष्ट हो जाने वाला ✪ विलोम **non-perishable**

**peristalsis** /ˌperɪˈstælsɪs ˌपेरिˈस्टैल्सिस्/ *noun* [U] (*technical*) the movements that the large tubes inside the body make automatically to push sth out or along शरीर के अंदर शिराओं के सिकुड़ने की क्रिया (ताकि कोई वस्तु उसमें से या उसके सहारे बाहर निकाली जा सके); क्रमाकुंचन

**perjury** /ˈpɜːdʒəri ˈपजरि/ *noun* [U] (*formal*) the act of telling a lie in a court of law न्यायालय में असत्य कथन, झूठी गवाही, शपथ-भंग ▶ **perjure** /ˈpɜːdʒə(r) ˈपज(र्)/ *verb* [T] **perjure yourself** झूठी गवाही देना *She admitted that she had perjured herself while giving evidence.*

**perk[1]** /pɜːk पक्/ *verb*

**PHR V** **perk (sb/sth) up** to become or make sb become happier and have more energy अधिक प्रफुल्लित और स्फूर्तिमान होना या बनाना

**perk[2]** /pɜːk पक्/ *noun* [C] (*informal*) something extra that you get from your employer in addition to money वेतन के अतिरिक्त प्राप्त सुविधा या लाभ *Travelling abroad is one of the perks of the job.*

**perm** /pɜːm पम्/ *noun* [C] the treatment of hair with special chemicals in order to make it curly बालों को लहरदार या घुँघराला बनाने के लिए विशेष रसायनों का प्रयोग ➪ **wave** देखिए। ▶ **perm** *verb* [T] (बालों को) घुँघराला बनाना *She has had her hair permed.*

**permafrost** /ˈpɜːməfrɒst ˈपमफ़्रॉस्ट्/ *noun* [U] (*technical*) a layer of soil that is permanently frozen, in very cold regions of the world स्थायी तुषार भूमि; विश्व के बहुत ठंडे क्षेत्रों में स्थायी रूप से जमी भूमि

**permanent** /ˈpɜːmənənt ˈपमनन्ट्/ *adj.* lasting for a long time or forever; that will not change देर तक या सदा के लिए रहने वाला, स्थायी; अपरिवर्तित, जो न बदले *The accident left him with a permanent scar.* ○ *Are you looking for a permanent or a temporary job?* ▶ **permanence** *noun* [U] स्थायित्व ▶ **permanently** *adv.* स्थायी रूप से *Has she left Delhi permanently?*

**permeable** /ˈpɜːmiəbl ˈपमिअब्ल्/ *adj.* allowing a liquid or gas to pass through (जिसमें से द्रव पदार्थ या गैस आर-पार चले जाएँ); पारगम्य *A frog's skin is permeable to water.* ✪ विलोम **impermeable** ▶ **permeability** /ˌpɜːmiəˈbɪləti ˌपमिअˈबिलटि/ *noun* [U] पारगम्यता

**permeate** /ˈpɜːmieɪt ˈपमिएट्/ *verb* [I, T] (*formal*) **1** (of a liquid or gas) to pass through a **porous** material (द्रव्य या गैस का) छिद्रिल वस्तु से पारगमन करना *Rain water permeates through the ground.* **2** (of a smell or gas) to spread through a room or fill every part of something (गंध या गैस का) कमरे में फैल जाना या किसी वस्तु के प्रत्येक भाग में समा जाना *The smell of flowers permeated the house.* **3** (of an idea, etc.) to affect every part of something (विचार आदि) पूर्णतः प्रभावित करना, व्याप्त होना *a belief that permeates all levels of society*

**permissible** /pəˈmɪsəbl पˈमिसब्ल्/ *adj.* (*formal*) **permissible (for sb) (to so sth)** that is allowed by law or by a set of rules क़ानून या नियमों द्वारा अनुमति योग्य; अनुज्ञेय *They have been exposed to radiation above the permissible level.*

**permission** /pəˈmɪʃn पˈमिश्न्/ *noun* [U] **permission (for sth); permission (for sb) (to do sth)** the act of allowing sb to do sth, especially when this is done by sb in a position of authority कुछ करने की अनुमति, विशेषतः किसी अधिकारी द्वारा दी गई *I'm afraid you can't leave **without permission**.* ○ *to **ask/give permission** for sth*

> **NOTE** ध्यान रखिए **permission** अगणनीय है। अनुमति देने वाले पत्र को **permit** कहते हैं।

**permissive** /pəˈmɪsɪv पˈमिसिव्/ *adj.* having, allowing or showing a lot of freedom that many people do not approve of, especially in sexual matters किसी मामले (विशेषतः यौन व्यवहार) में अनुचित रूप से अत्यधिक छूट लेना, देना या उसका दिखावा करना

**permit[1]** /pəˈmɪt पˈमिट्/ *verb* (**permitting; permitted**) **1** [T] (*formal*) to allow sb to do sth or to allow sth to happen किसी बात की अनुमति देना या कोई बात होने देना *You are not permitted to smoke in the hospital.* ○ *His visa does not permit him to work in the UK.* ➪ **allow** पर नोट देखिए। **2** [I, T] to make sth possible किसी बात को संभव बनाना *There will be a bonfire on Saturday, **weather permitting**.*

**permit[2]** /ˈpɜːmɪt ˈपमिट्/ *noun* [C] an official document that says you are allowed to do sth, especially for a limited period of time आधिकारिक रूप से अनुमति देने वाला पत्र (विशेषतः सीमित समय के लिए); अनुमति-पत्र, परमिट *Next month I'll have to apply for a new **work permit**.*

**peroxide** /pəˈrɒksaɪd पˈरॉक्साइड्/ (*also* **hydrogen peroxide**) *noun* [U] a colourless liquid that is used to kill bacteria and to make hair a lighter colour एक रंगहीन द्रव (बैक्टीरिया मारने और बालों का रंग हलका करने के लिए प्रयुक्त); परॉक्साइड

**perpendicular** /ˌpɜːpənˈdɪkjələ(r) ˌपपन्ˈडिक्यल(र्)/ *adj.* **1** at an angle of 90° to sth किसी वस्तु के 90° कोण पर; अभिलंब, लंबवत *Are the lines perpendicular to each other?* ⇨ **horizontal** और **vertical** देखिए। **2** pointing straight up; upright सीधे ऊपर की ओर; सीधा खड़ा *The path was almost perpendicular* (= it was very steep).

**perpetrate** /ˈpɜːpətreɪt ˈपपट्रेट्/ *verb* [T] (*formal*) **perpetrate sth (against/upon/on sb)** to commit a crime or do sth wrong or evil कोई अपराध, ग़लत काम या बुरा काम करना *to perpetrate a crime/fraud/massacre* ○ *violence perpetrated against women and children* ▶ **perpetration** /ˌpɜːpəˈtreɪʃn ˌपपˈट्रेश्न्/ *noun* [U] अपराध-कर्म

**perpetual** /pəˈpetʃuəl पˈपेचुअल्/ *adj.* **1** continuing for a long period of time without stopping लगातार लंबे समय तक बना रहने वाला; अविरल, शाश्वत *They lived in perpetual fear of losing their jobs.* **2** frequently repeated in a way which is annoying बार-बार घटित होने वाला (ऐसे कि परेशान करे) *How can I work with these perpetual interruptions?* ▶ **perpetually** /-tʃuəli -चुअलि/ *adv.* निरंतर, लगातार

**perpetuate** /pəˈpetʃueɪt पˈपेचुएट्/ *verb* [T] (*formal*) to cause sth to continue for a long time लंबे समय तक क़ायम या बनाए रखना *to perpetuate an argument*

**perplexed** /pəˈplekst पˈप्लेक्स्ट्/ *adj.* not understanding sth; confused जिसे कोई बात समझ में न आए; किंकर्तव्य-विमूढ़, हतबुद्धि, भ्रमित

**perquisite** /ˈpɜːkwɪzɪt ˈपक्विज़िट्/ *noun* (*formal*) **1** [*usually pl.*] = **perk**[2] **2 perquisite (of sb)** something special like a privilege to which a person has a special right because of his social position सामाजिक प्रतिष्ठा के कारण विशेष अधिकार या सुविधा; अनुलाभ *Higher education used to be the perquisite of the rich in pre-independent India.*

**per se** /ˌpɜː ˈseɪ ˌप ˈसे/ *adv.* a word used to say that something is considered alone, by or in itself and not in connection with something or someone बिना किसी व्यक्ति या वस्तु से संबंधित, स्वतः अपने आप *The actors were good per se but the movie was very badly made.*

**persecute** /ˈpɜːsɪkjuːt ˈपसिक्यूट्/ *verb* [T] **1 persecute sb (for sth)** (*often passive*) to treat sb in a cruel and unfair way, especially because of race, religion or political beliefs किसी व्यक्ति को सताना या अत्याचार करना, विशेषतः जाति, धर्म या राजनीतिक विश्वासों के कारण **2** to deliberately annoy sb and make his/her life unpleasant जान-बूझ कर किसी को परेशान करना और उसके जीवन को दूभर बना देना ▶ **persecution** /ˌpɜːsɪˈkjuːʃn ˌपसिˈक्यूश्न्/ *noun* [C, U] अत्याचार, उत्पीड़न *the persecution of minorities* ▶ **persecutor** /ˈpɜːsɪkjuːtə(r) ˈपसिक्यूट(र्)/ *noun* [C] अत्याचारी, उत्पीड़क

**persevere** /ˌpɜːsɪˈvɪə(r) ˌपसिˈविअ(र्)/ *verb* [I] **persevere (at/in/with sth)** to continue trying to do or achieve sth that is difficult किसी कठिन काम को करने या उसमें सफल होने की कोशिश करते रहना; अध्यवसाय करना *The treatment is painful but I'm going to persevere with it.* ▶ **perseverance** *noun* [U] अध्यवसाय, दृढ़ता

**persist** /pəˈsɪst पˈसिस्ट्/ *verb* [I] **1 persist (in sth/doing sth)** to continue doing sth even though other people say that you are wrong or that you cannot do it (लोगों द्वारा निरुत्साहित किए जाने के बावजूद) किसी कार्य को निरंतर करते रहना *If you persist in making so much noise, I shall call the police.* **2** to continue to exist अस्तित्व बनाए रहना *If your symptoms persist you should consult your doctor.* ▶ **persistence** *noun* [U] दृढ़ता, आग्रह *Finally her persistence was rewarded and she got what she wanted.*

**persistent** /pəˈsɪstənt पˈसिस्टन्ट्/ *adj.* **1** determined to continue doing sth even though people say that you are wrong or that you cannot do it (लोगों द्वारा मना या निरुत्साहित किए जाने के बावजूद) किसी काम को करते रहने के लिए कृत संकल्प *Some salesmen can be very persistent.* **2** lasting for a long time or happening often लंबे समय तक रहने वाला या बार-बार होने वाला; चिरस्थायी या सतत *a persistent cough* ▶ **persistently** *adv.* लगातार, आग्रहपूर्वक

**person** /ˈpɜːsn ˈपसन्/ *noun* [C] (*pl.* **people**) **1** a man or woman; a human being पुरुष या महिला; व्यक्ति, मनुष्य, इनसान *I would like to speak to the person in charge.*

> **NOTE** कुछ अति औपचारिक मामलों में **person** का बहुवचन रूप **persons** मान्य है। ⇨ **people** पर नोट देखिए।

**2 -person** (*used to form compound nouns*) a person doing the job mentioned निर्दिष्ट काम करने वाला व्यक्ति *a salesperson/spokesperson*

3 (*grammar*) one of the three types of pronouns in grammar. 'I/we' are the first person, 'you' is the second person and 'he/she/it/they' are the third person अंग्रेज़ी व्याकरण में सर्वनाम का एक प्रकार; 'I/we' उत्तम पुरुष है, 'you' मध्यम पुरुष 'he/she/it/they' अन्य पुरुष

IDM **in person** seeing or speaking to sb face to face (not speaking on the telephone or writing a letter) आमने-सामने; किसी को प्रत्यक्ष देखते या उससे बात करते हुए (फ़ोन पर या पत्र द्वारा नहीं)

**personal** /ˈpɜːsənl ˈपसन्ल्/ *adj.* **1** (*only before a noun*) of or belonging to one particular person व्यक्ति-विशेष का या उससे संबंधित; व्यक्तिगत, वैयक्तिक *personal belongings* ○ *Judges should not let their* ***personal feelings*** *influence their decisions.* **2** concerning your feelings, health or relationships with other people व्यक्ति की निजी भावनाओं, स्वास्थ्य या अन्य व्यक्तियों से संबंधों के विषय में *I should like to speak to you in private. I have something personal to discuss.* ○ *Do you mind if I ask you a* ***personal question****?* **3** not connected with a person's job or official position किसी व्यक्ति की नौकरी या आधिकारिक स्थिति से असंबंधित; निजी *Please keep personal phone calls to a minimum.* ○ *I try not to let work interfere with my* ***personal life****.* **4** (*only before a noun*) done by a particular person rather than by sb who is acting for him/her व्यक्ति-विशेष द्वारा स्वयं; व्यक्तिगत रूप से (न कि उसके प्रतिनिधि द्वारा) *The Prime Minister made a personal visit to the flood victims in hospital.* **5** (*only before a noun*) made or done for one particular person rather than for a large group of people or people in general एक विशेष व्यक्ति के लिए (न कि किसी व्यक्ति-समूह या सब लोगों के लिए) *We offer a personal service to all our customers.* **6** speaking about sb's appearance or character in an unpleasant or unfriendly way किसी व्यक्ति के रूप-रंग या चरित्र के विषय में अरुचिकर या द्वेषभाव से टिप्पणी करते हुए, व्यक्तिगत आलोचना करते हुए *It started as a genral discussion but then people started to* ***get personal*** *and an argument began.* **7** (*only before a noun*) connected with the body शारीरिक *personal hygiene* ○ *She's always worrying about her personal appearance.*

**personal assistant** = **PA**

**personal computer** = **PC 1**

**personality** /ˌpɜːsəˈnæləti ˌपसˈनैलटि/ *noun* (*pl.* **personalities**) **1** [C, U] the different qualities of a person's character that make him/her different from other people व्यक्ति के विशेष गुण जो उसे दूसरों से भिन्न, और इसलिए विशेष, बनाते हैं; व्यक्तित्व *Mohini has a kind personality.* **2** [U] the quality of having a strong, interesting and attractive character सशक्त, रोचक और आकर्षक होने का गुण *A good entertainer needs a lot of personality.* **3** [C] a famous person (especially in sport, on television, etc.) प्रसिद्ध व्यक्ति (विशेषतः खेल, टीवी आदि क्षेत्रों में) *a television personality*

**personalize** (*also* **-ise**) /ˈpɜːsənəlaɪz ˈपसनलाइज़्/ *verb* [T] (*usually passive*) to mark sth with your name, etc. to show that it belongs to you व्यक्तिगत संबद्धता दिखाने के लिए किसी वस्तु पर अपना नाम आदि अंकित करना *a car with a personalized number plate*

**personally** /ˈpɜːsənəli ˈपसनलि/ *adv.* **1** used to show that you are expressing your own opinion निजी तौर पर अपनी ओर से (यह दिखाने के लिए प्रयुक्त कि व्यक्तिगत राय प्रकट की जा रही है *Personally, I think that nurses deserve more money.* **2** done by you yourself, not by sb else acting for you स्वयं के द्वारा, न कि अन्य के द्वारा *I will deal with this matter personally.* **3** in a way that is connected with one particular person rather than a group of people किसी एक व्यक्ति के लिए (न कि सबके लिए) *I wasn't talking about you personally—I meant all teachers.* **4** in a way that is intended to offend नाराज़ करने के उद्देश्य से व्यक्त *Please don't* ***take it personally****, but I would just rather be alone this evening.* **5** in a way that is connected with sb's private life, rather than his/her job किसी के निजी जीवन के विषय में (न कि उस के काम के संबंध में)

**personal pronoun** *noun* [C] (*grammar*) any of the pronouns 'I, me, she, her, he, him, we, us, you, they, them' अंग्रेज़ी व्याकरण में पुरुषवाचक सर्वनाम 'I, me, she, her, he, him, we, us, you, they, them'

**personal stereo** *noun* [C] a small machine that plays CDs or cassettes that you can carry round with you and listen to through a wire which goes in each ear (**headphones**) केवल एक व्यक्ति के उपयोग का स्टीरियो (स्टीरियो सीडी या कैसेट बजाने वाली एक छोटी मशीन जिसे व्यक्ति अपने साथ रखकर हैडफोन से संगीत आदि सुनता है)

**personify** /pəˈsɒnɪfaɪ पˈसॉनिफ़ाइ/ *verb* [T] (*pres. part.* **personifying;** *3rd person sing.* **personifies;** *pt, pp* **personified**) **1** to be an example in human form of a particular quality किसी गुण विशेष का मानव रूप में उदाहरण होना *She is kindness personified.* **2** to describe an object or a feeling as if it were a person, for example in a poem (कविता में) किसी वस्तु या मनोभाव को मानव रूप में चित्रित करना ▶ **personification** /pəˌsɒnɪfɪˈkeɪʃn पˌसॉनिफ़िˈकेश्न्/ *noun* [C, U] मानवीकरण

**personnel** /ˌpɜːsəˈnel ˌपर्सˈनेल् / *noun* **1** [*pl.*] the people who work for a large organization or one of the armed forces किसी संगठन या सेना के किसी अंग के कार्यकर्ता, स्टाफ़, कार्यकर्ता-वर्ग *sales/medical/technical personnel* **2** (*also* **personnel department**) [U, *with sing. or pl. verb*] the department of a large company or organization that deals with employing and training people किसी कंपनी या संगठन के स्टाफ़ को नियुक्त और प्रशिक्षित करने वाला विभाग; कार्मिक विभाग *Personnel is/are currently reviewing pay scales.*

**perspective** /pəˈspektɪv पˈस्पेक्टिव् / *noun* **1** [U] the ability to think about problems and decisions in a reasonable way without exaggerating them समस्या को जानने और निर्णय लेने का सही दृष्टिकोण; परिप्रेक्ष्य *Hearing about others' experiences often helps to* ***put*** *your own problems* ***into perspective*** (= makes them seem less important than you thought). ○ *Try to* ***keep*** *these issues* ***in perspective*** (= do not exaggerate them). **2** [C] your opinion or attitude towards sth किसी बात के विषय में व्यक्ति-विशेष का दृष्टिकोण या मत *Try and look at this from my perspective.* **3** [U] the art of drawing on a flat surface so that some objects appear to be farther away than others सपाट सतह पर ऐसा चित्रण कि कुछ वस्तुएँ औरों से काफ़ी दूर दिखाई पड़ें

**Perspex™** /ˈpɜːspeks ˈपर्स्पेक्स् / *noun* [U] a strong transparent plastic material that is often used instead of glass मज़बूत पारदर्शी प्लास्टिक जो प्रायः काँच के स्थान पर प्रयुक्त होता है

**perspire** /pəˈspaɪə(r) पˈस्पाइअ(र्) / *verb* [I] (*formal*) to lose liquid through your skin when you are hot; to sweat पसीना बहाना; पसीना आना ▶ **perspiration** /ˌpɜːspəˈreɪʃn ˌपर्स्पˈरेशन् / *noun* [U] पसीना; पसीना आने की प्रक्रिया **NOTE** इस अर्थ में **sweat** अधिक प्रचलित है।

**persuade** /pəˈsweɪd पˈस्वेड् / *verb* [T] **1 persuade sb (to do sth); persuade sb (into sth/doing sth)** to make sb do sth by giving him/her good reasons समझा-बुझाकर किसी को काम के लिए राज़ी करना, मनाना *It was difficult to persuade Leela to change her mind.* ○ *We eventually persuaded Sanjay into coming with us.* ✪ विलोम **dissuade** **2** (*formal*) **persuade sb that...; persuade sb (of sth)** to make sb believe sth किसी को किसी बात पर विश्वास करवा लेना *She had persuaded herself that she was going to fail.* ○ *The jury was not persuaded of her innocence.* ➪ **convince** देखिए।

**persuasion** /pəˈsweɪʒn पˈस्वेश़न् / *noun* **1** [U] the act of persuading sb to do sth or to believe sth किसी को कुछ करने या मानने के लिए राज़ी करने की क्रिया; प्रत्यायन *It took a lot of persuasion to get Anjali to agree.* **2** [C] (*formal*) a religious or political belief धार्मिक या राजनीतिक मत या विश्वास *politicians of all persuasions*

**persuasive** /pəˈsweɪsɪv पˈस्वेसिव् / *adj.* able to persuade sb to do or believe sth कुछ करने या मानने के लिए राज़ी करने में समर्थ; प्रत्यायी *the persuasive power of advertising* ▶ **persuasively** *adv.* राज़ी करके, मनाकर ▶ **persuasiveness** *noun* [U] विश्वास करा लेने का गुण; प्रत्ययकारिता

**pertinent** /ˈpɜːtɪnənt ˈपटिनन्ट् / *adj.* (*formal*) closely connected with the subject being discussed चर्चाधीन विषय से गहरे संबंधित; संगत, प्रासंगिक *to ask a pertinent question*

**perturb** /pəˈtɜːb पˈटब् / *verb* [T] (*formal*) to make sb worried or upset किसी को चिंतित या परेशान कर देना ▶ **perturbed** *adj.* चिंतित या परेशान

**peruse** /pəˈruːz पˈरूज़् / *verb* [T] (*formal* or *humorous*) to read sth, especially in a careful way ध्यानपूर्वक पढ़ना, अवलोकन करना *A copy of the minutes of the meeting is available for you to peruse at your leisure.* ▶ **perusal** /pəˈruːzəl पˈरूज़ल् / *noun* [U] ध्यानपूर्वक पढ़ने की क्रिया; अवलोकन *The report was published after careful perusal.*

**pervade** /pəˈveɪd पˈव़ेड् / *verb* [T] (*formal*) to spread through and be noticeable in every part of sth सर्वत्र फैल जाना, व्याप्त होना *A sadness pervades most of her novels.*

**pervasive** /pəˈveɪsɪv पˈव़ेसिव् / *adj.* that is present in all parts of sth सर्वत्र, व्याप्त, व्यापक *a pervasive mood of pessimism*

**perverse** /pəˈvɜːs पˈव़स् / *adj.* (*formal*) liking to behave in a way that is not acceptable or reasonable or that most people think is wrong तर्कविरूद्ध या अमान्य व्यवहार करने वाला व्यक्ति, दुष्कर्म में रहने वाला, विकृत रुचि वाला *Dinesh gets perverse pleasure from shocking his parents.* ▶ **perversely** *adv.* विकृत भाव से, उद्दंडता पूर्वक ▶ **perversity** *noun* [U] विकृतता, उद्दंता

**perversion** /pəˈvɜːʃn पˈव़श़न् / *noun* [U, C] **1** sexual behaviour that is not considered normal or acceptable by most people विकृत यौन-व्यवहार, आम रूप से अस्वाभाविक और अस्वीकार्य यौन-आचरण **2** the action of changing sth from right to wrong or from good to bad सकारात्मक स्थिति (जैसे सच) को नकारात्मक (जैसे झूठ) में बदल देने की क्रिया; विलोमत्व, प्रतीयता *That statement is a perversion of the truth.*

**pervert**[1] /pə'vɜːt प'वर्ट्/ *verb* [T] **1** to change a system, process, etc. in a bad way किसी प्रणाली, प्रक्रिया आदि को बदल कर विकृत या भ्रष्ट कर देना *to pervert the course of justice* (= to deliberately prevent the police from finding out the truth about a crime) **2** to cause sb to think or behave in a way that is not moral or acceptable व्यक्ति को सुविचार से विमुख करना

**pervert**[2] /'pɜːvɜːt 'पर्वर्ट्/ *noun* [C] a person whose sexual behaviour is not thought to be natural or normal by most people आम मत में अस्वाभाविक या अस्वीकार्य यौन-आचरण करने वाला व्यक्ति

**pessimism** /'pesɪmɪzəm 'पेसिमिज़म्/ *noun* [U] **pessimism (about/over sth)** the state of expecting or believing that bad things will happen and that sth will not be successful अनिष्ट और असफलता की आशंका से पीड़ित रहने की मनःस्थिति; निराशावादिता ✪ विलोम **optimism** ▸ **pessimistic** /ˌpesɪ'mɪstɪk ˌपेसि'मिस्टिक्/ *adj.* निराशावादी ✪ विलोम **optimistic** ▸ **pessimistically** /-kli -क्लि/ *adv.* निराशावादी ढंग से ✪ विलोम **optimistically**

**pessimist** /'pesɪmɪst 'पेसिमिस्ट्/ *noun* [C] a person who always thinks that bad things will happen or that sth will be not be successful निराशावादी व्यक्ति ✪ विलोम **optimist**

**pest** /pest पेस्ट्/ *noun* [C] **1** an insect or animal that destroys plants, food, etc. पौधों, खाद्य पदार्थों को हानि पहुँचाने वाला कीट, पशु या पक्षी **2** (*informal*) a person or thing that annoys you चिढ़ पैदा करने वाला व्यक्ति या वस्तु *That child is such a pest!*

**pester** /'pestə(r) 'पेस्टर्(र्)/ *verb* [T] **pester sb (for sth); pester sb (to do sth)** to annoy sb, for example by asking him/her sth many times व्यक्ति को परेशान कर देना (एक बात को अनेक बार पूछ कर या अन्य प्रकार से) *to pester sb for money* ○ *The kids kept pestering me to take them to the park.*

**pesticide** /'pestɪsaɪd 'पेस्टिसाइड्/ *noun* [C, U] a chemical substance that is used for killing animals, especially insects, that eat food crops कीटनाशक रसायन जो अन्न की फसलें खा जाने वाले कीटों आदि को नष्ट करता है ➪ **insecticide** देखिए।

**pestilence** /'pestɪləns 'पेस्टिलन्स्/ *noun* [U, *sing.*] (*old-fashioned* or *literary*) any fatal disease that spreads quickly and kills a large number of people महामारी, जनपदमारी

**pestle** /'pesl 'पेसल्/ *noun* [C] a small heavy tool with a round end used for crushing food, etc. into powder in a special bowl (**a mortar**) मूसल ➪ **laboratory** पर चित्र देखिए।

**pet** /pet पेट्/ *noun* [C] **1** an animal or bird that you keep in your home for pleasure rather than for food or work पालतू पशु या पक्षी जिसे मनबहलाव के लिए पाला जाता है *Dogs make very good pets. a pet dog/cat/bird* ○ *a pet shop* (= where pets are sold) **2** a person who is treated as a favourite दुलारा व्यक्ति *the teacher's pet*

**petal** /'petl 'पेट्ल्/ *noun* [C] one of the thin soft coloured parts of a flower फूल की पंखुड़ी ➪ **flower** पर चित्र देखिए।

**peter** /'piːtə(r) 'पीट(र्)/ *verb*

PHR V **peter out** to slowly become smaller, quieter, etc. and then stop शनैः शनैः समाप्त हो जाना

**pet hate** *noun* [C] sth that you particularly do not like विशेष रूप से नापसंद वस्तु, कार्य आदि *Filling in forms is one of my pet hates.*

**petition** /pə'tɪʃn प'टिश्न्/ *noun* [C] a written document, signed by many people, that asks a government, etc. to do or change sth याचिका, अर्ज़ी; औपचारिक अनुरोध-पत्र जिस पर अनेक व्यक्ति हस्ताक्षर कर सरकार आदि से कुछ अनुरोध करते हैं *More than 50,000 people signed the petition protesting about the new law.* ▸ **petition** *verb* [I, T] अर्ज़ी देना, याचिका प्रस्तुत करना

**Petri dish** /'petri dɪʃ; 'piːtri 'पेट्रि डिश्; 'पीट्रि/ *noun* [C] (*technical*) a covered dish that is not very deep, used for growing bacteria, etc. in हलका गहरा व ढक्कन वाला पात्र (बैक्टीरिया आदि को उत्पन्न करने के लिए प्रयुक्त) ➪ **laboratory** पर चित्र देखिए।

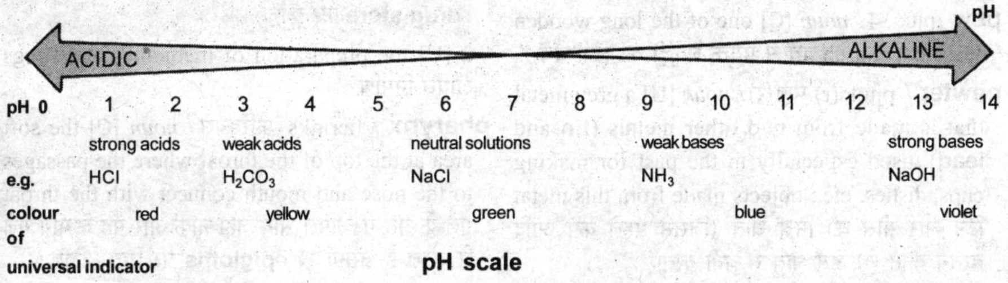

**pH scale**

**petrified** /ˈpetrɪfaɪd ˈपेट्रिफ़ाइड् / *adj.* very frightened अत्यधिक भयभीत

**petro-** /ˈpetrəʊˈपेट्रो / *prefix* (*used in nouns, adjectives and adverbs*) **1** connected with rocks चट्टानों से संबंधित *petrology* **2** connected with petrol पेट्रोल से संबंधित *petrochemical*

**petrochemical** /ˌpetrəʊˈkemɪkl ˌपेट्रोˈकेमिक्ल् / *noun* [C] any chemical substance obtained from petrol or natural gas पेट्रोल या प्राकृतिक गैस से प्राप्त रासायनिक पदार्थ

**petrol** /ˈpetrəlˈपेट्रल् / (*AmE* **gas; gasoline**) *noun* [U] the liquid that is used as fuel for vehicles such as cars and motorbikes पेट्रोल ➪ **diesel** देखिए।

**petroleum** /pəˈtrəʊliəm पˈट्रोलिअम् / *noun* [U] mineral oil that is found under the ground or sea and is used to make petrol, plastic and other types of chemical substances खनिज तेल जिससे पेट्रोल, प्लास्टिक और अन्य प्रकार के रासायनिक तत्व तैयार होते हैं; पेट्रोलियम

**petrol station** (*AmE* **gas station**) *noun* [C] a place where you can buy petrol and other things for your car पेट्रोल स्टेशन ➪ **garage** देखिए।

**pet subject** *noun* [C] a subject that you are very interested in or that you feel very strongly about प्रिय विषय

**petticoat** /ˈpetɪkəʊtˈपेटिकोट् / *noun* [C] (*BrE old-fashioned*) a skirt-like article of clothing for women to be worn under a skirt, dress or sari. It often has pleats or a lace edge साया, पेटिकोट

**petty** /ˈpetiˈपेटि / *adj.* **1** small and unimportant छोटा और नगण्य *He didn't want to get involved with the petty details.* ○ *petty crime/theft* (= that is not very serious) **2** unkind or unpleasant to other people (for a reason that does not seem very important) दूसरों के प्रति निर्दयी या अप्रिय (बिना किसी विशेष कारण के) *petty jealousy/revenge*

**petty cash** *noun* [U] a small amount of money kept in an office for small payments छोटे भुगतानों के लिए कार्यालय में रखी धनराशि

**pew** /pjuː प्यू / *noun* [C] one of the long wooden seats in a church चर्च में प्रयुक्त लकड़ी की लंबी बेंच

**pewter** /ˈpjuːtə(r)ˈप्यूट(र्) / *noun* [U] a grey metal that is made from two other metals (**tin** and **lead**), used especially in the past for making cups, dishes, etc.; objects made from this metal टिन और सीसे की मिश्र धातु (जिससे पहले कप आदि बरतन बनते थे); इस धातु से बनी वस्तुएँ

**PG** /ˌpiːˈdʒiː ˌपीˈजी / *abbr.* (in Britain, USA, etc.) (used about films in which there are scenes that are not suitable for children) parental guidance (ब्रिटेन, अमेरिका आदि में) बच्चों के लिए अनुपयुक्त दृश्यों वाली फ़िल्म के लिए प्रयुक्त निर्देश

**pH** /ˌpiːˈeɪtʃ ˌपीˈएच् / *noun* [*sing.*] a measurement of the level of acid or **alkali** in a substance किसी पदार्थ में अम्ल या क्षार के स्तर को मापने की इकाई पृष्ठ 887 पर चित्र देखिए। **NOTE** 7 से कम pH मूल्य अम्ल का और 7 से ऊपर pH मूल्य क्षार का संकेत करता है।

**phagocyte** /ˈfæɡəsaɪt ˈफ़ैगसाइट् / *noun* [C] (*technical*) a type of cell in the body that can surround smaller cells or small pieces of material and take them into itself (शरीर में एक प्रकार की कोशिका जो छोटी कोशिकाओं और वस्तुखंडों को अपने में लीन कर लेती है); भक्षक कोशिका

**phantom** /ˈfæntəm ˈफ़ैन्टम् / *noun* [C] **1** (*written*) the spirit of a dead person that is seen or heard by sb who is still living भूत-प्रेत **NOTE** इस अर्थ में शब्द **ghost** अधिक प्रचलित है। **2** something that you think exists, but that is not real काल्पनिक सत्ता वाली वस्तु *phantom fears/illnesses*

**pharmaceutical** /ˌfɑːməˈsjuːtɪkl; -ˈsuː- ˌफ़ामˈस्यूटिक्ल्; -ˈसू- / *adj.* connected with the production of medicines and drugs औषधियों और दवाओं के निर्माण से संबंधित *pharmaceutical companies*

**pharmacist** /ˈfɑːməsɪst ˈफ़ामसिस्ट् / = **chemist**[1]

**pharmacology** /ˌfɑːməˈkɒlədʒi ˌफ़ामˈकॉलजि / *noun* [U] (*technical*) the scientific study of drugs and their use in medicine मूल दवा (भेषज) और औषध-निर्माण में उसके उपयोग का वैज्ञानिक अध्ययन; औषधशास्त्र, भेषजगुणविज्ञान ▶ **pharmacological** /ˌfɑːməkəˈlɒdʒɪkl ˌफ़ामकˈलॉजिक्ल् / *adj.* औषधशास्त्रीय *pharmacological research*

**pharmacy** /ˈfɑːməsi ˈफ़ामसि / *noun* (*pl.* **pharmacies**) **1** [C] a shop or part of a shop where medicines and drugs are prepared and sold दवा और औषध बनाने और बेचने की दुकान; औषध-विक्रय केंद्र, औषधशाला

> **NOTE** दवाएँ बेचने की दुकान को ब्रिटिश अंग्रेज़ी में **a chemist's (shop)** और अमेरिकन अंग्रेज़ी में **drug store** कहते हैं।

**2** [U] the preparation of medicines and drugs औषध-निर्माण

**pharynx** /ˈfærɪŋks ˈफ़ैरिङ्क्स् / *noun* [C] the soft area at the top of the throat where the passages to the nose and mouth connect with the throat गले के अंत में कोमल भाग जहाँ नाक और मुँह के मार्ग गले से जुड़ते हैं; ग्रसनी ➪ **epiglottis** पर चित्र देखिए।

**phase**[1] /feɪz फ़ेज़्/ *noun* [C] a stage in the development of sth किसी वस्तु के विकास की अवस्था या चरण *Jaya went through a difficult phase when she started school.*

**phase**[2] /feɪz फ़ेज़्/ *verb*

**PHRV phase sth in** to introduce or start using sth gradually in stages over a period of time किसी वस्तु को एक समयावधि में क्रमशः चरणों में या क्रमावस्था में प्रस्तुत करना या उसका प्रयोग आरंभ करना *The metric system was phased in over several years.*

**phase sth out** to stop using sth gradually in stages over a period of time एक समयावधि में किसी वस्तु का क्रमशः चरणों में प्रयोग बंद कर देना *The older machines are gradually being phased out and replaced by new ones.*

**PhD** /ˌpi: eɪtʃ ˈdi: ˌपी एच ˈडी/ *abbr.* Doctor of philosophy; an advanced university degree that you receive when you complete a piece of research on a special subject किसी विषय में अनुसंधान कार्य पूरा करने पर विश्वविद्यालय द्वारा प्रदान की गई उपाधि; विद्या वाचस्पति *She has a PhD in History.* ✪ पर्याय **DPhil**

**pheasant** /ˈfeznt ˈफ़ेज़न्ट्/ *noun* [C] (*pl.* **pheasants** or **pheasant**) a type of bird with a long tail. The males have brightly coloured feathers चेड़; लंबी पूंछ वाला एक पक्षी, नर के चमकीले पंख होते हैं

**phenomenal** /fəˈnɒmɪnl फ़ˈनॉमिनल्/ *adj.* very great or impressive असाधारण या उल्लेखनीय *phenomenal success* ▶ **phenomenally** /-nəli -नलि/ *adv.* असाधारण रूप से

**phenomenon** /fəˈnɒmɪnən फ़ˈनॉमिनन्/ *noun* [C] (*pl.* **phenomena** /-mɪnə -मिना/) a fact or an event in nature or society, especially one that is not fully understood प्रकृति या समाज में कोई सचाई या घटना, विशेषतः ऐसी जो पूरी तरह समझ में न आए *Acid rain is not a natural phenomenon. It is caused by pollution.*

**phew** /fju: फ़्यू/ *exclamation* a sound which you make to show that you are hot, tired or happy that sth bad did not happen or has finished अशुभ के न घटने पर राहत, थकान या प्रसन्नता व्यक्त करने के लिए व्यक्त ध्वनि, *Phew, it's hot!* ○ *Phew, I'm glad that the interview's over!*

**philanthropist** /fɪˈlænθrəpɪst फ़िˈलैन्थ्रपिस्ट्/ *noun* [C] a rich person who helps the poor and those in need, especially by giving money दान आदि के द्वारा ज़रुरतमंदों की सहायता करने वाला व्यक्ति; परोपकारी व्यक्ति, लोकोपकारक

**philanthropy** /fɪˈlænθrəpi फ़िˈलैन्थ्रपि/ *noun* [U] (*formal*) the practice of helping the poor and those in need, especially by giving money दान आदि के द्वारा ज़रूरतमंदों की सहायता; परोपकार, लोकोपकार ▶ **philanthropic** /ˌfɪlənˈθrɒpɪk ˌफ़िलन्ˈथ्रॉपिक/ *adj.* परोपकारी, लोकोपकारी *philanthropic work* ▶ **philanthropically** /ˌfɪlənˈθrɒpɪkli ˌफ़िलन्ˈथ्रॉपिक्लि/ *adv.* परोपकार या लोकोपकार की भावना से

**philately** /fɪˈlætəli फ़िˈलैटलि/ *noun* [U] (*technical*) the collection and study of postage stamps डाक टिकट संग्रह एवं संकलन व उनका अध्ययन ▶ **philatelic** /ˌfɪləˈtælɪk ˌफ़िलˈटलिक्/ *adj.* टिकट संग्रह एवं संकलन संबंधी

**philo-** (*also* **phil-**) /ˈfɪləʊ ˈफ़िलो/ *prefix* (*used in nouns, adjectives, verbs and adverbs*) liking प्रिय लगना, -प्रेमी, -प्रिय *philoprogenitive/philanthropist*

**philosopher** /fəˈlɒsəfə(r) फ़ˈलॉसफ़(र्)/ *noun* [C] a person who has developed a set of ideas and beliefs about the meaning of life दार्शनिक व्यक्ति, दर्शन शास्त्र में रुचि लेने वाला व्यक्ति

**philosophical** /ˌfɪləˈsɒfɪkl ˌफ़िलˈसॉफ़िकल्/ (*also* **philosophic**) *adj.* **1** of or concerning philosophy दर्शन-विषयक *a philosophical debate* **2 philosophical (about sth)** staying calm and not getting upset or worried about sth bad that happens अशुभ घटने पर भी शांतचित्त और स्थिरमति *He is quite philosophical about failing the exam and says he will try again next year.* ▶ **philosophically** /-kli -क्लि/ *adv.* शांतभाव से

**philosophy** /fəˈlɒsəfi फ़ˈलॉसफ़ि/ *noun* (*pl.* **philosophies**) **1** [U] the study of ideas and beliefs about the meaning of life दर्शन-शास्त्र **2** [C] a set of beliefs that tries to explain the meaning of life or give rules about how to behave जीवन का अर्थ समझने वाली या नैतिक व्यवहार के नियमों का निर्धारण करने वाली जीवन-दृष्टि; जीवन-दर्शन *Her philosophy is 'If a job's worth doing, it's worth doing well.'*

**phlegm** /flem फ़्लेम्/ *noun* [U] the thick substance that is produced in your nose and throat when you have a cold कफ़, बलग़म

**phlegmatic** /flegˈmætɪk फ़्लेग्ˈमैटिक्/ *adj.* (*formal*) not easily made angry or upset; calm जल्दी क्रोध में न आने वाला; शांतचित्त

**phloem** /ˈfləʊem ˈफ़्लोएम/ *noun* [U] (*technical*) the material in a plant containing very small tubes that carry sugars and other substances down from the leaves पौधे में बहुत छोटी नलियों वाला पदार्थ

जो पत्तों से शर्करा तथा अन्य पदार्थ नीचे ले जाता है; वल्कल ➪ **flower** पर चित्र देखिए।

**phobia** /ˈfəʊbiə ˈफ़ोबिआ/ *noun* [C] (*often used in compounds*) a very strong fear or hatred that you cannot explain (किसी वस्तु के प्रति) अत्यधिक भय या घृणा जिसका कारण समझाया नहीं जा सकता *arachnophobia* (= fear of spiders)

**phone** /fəʊn फ़ोन्/ *noun* (*informal*) **1** [U] = **telephone 1** फ़ोन, दूरभाष *a phone conversation* ○ *You can book the tickets* ***over the/by phone***. **2** [C] = **telephone 2** *The phone is ringing—could you answer it?* ▶ **phone** *verb* [I, T] फ़ोन आना, फ़ोन करना *Did anybody phone while I was out?* ○ *Could you phone the restaurant and book a table?* ✪ पर्याय **ring** या **call**

**IDM** **on the phone/telephone** **1** using the telephone फ़ोन पर या से **2** having a telephone in your home किसी के पास फ़ोन होना *I'll have to write to her because she's not on the phone.*

**phone book** = **telephone directory**

**phone box** = **telephone box**

**phonecard** /ˈfəʊnkɑːd ˈफ़ोन्काड्/ *noun* [C] a small plastic card that you can use to pay for calls in a public telephone box सार्वजनिक टेलिफ़ोन पर फ़ोन करने के ख़र्च के भुगतान के लिए प्रयुक्त प्लास्टिक कार्ड; फ़ोन कार्ड

**phone-in** *noun* [C] a radio or television programme during which you can ask a question or give your opinion by telephone रेडियो या टीवी का कार्यक्रम जिसमें श्रोता फ़ोन से प्रश्न पूछ सकते हैं या अपनी राय दे सकते हैं

**phonetic** /fəˈnetɪk फ़ˈनेटिक्/ *adj.* **1** connected with the sounds of human speech; using special symbols to represent these sounds मानव-भाषा की ध्वनियों से संबंधित; इन ध्वनियों को प्रकट करने वाले विशेष चिह्नों का प्रयोग करते हुए *the phonetic alphabet* ➪ **transcribe** देखिए। **2** (used about spelling) having a close relationship with the sounds represented (वर्तनी) उच्चारण के अनुसार *Spanish spelling is phonetic, unlike English spelling.* ▶ **phonetically** /-kli -क्लि/ *adv.* ध्वन्यात्मक दृष्टि से

**phonetics** /fəˈnetɪks फ़ˈनेटिक्स्/ *noun* [U] the study of the sounds of human speech मानव-भाषा की ध्वनियों का वैज्ञानिक अध्ययन; ध्वनि-विज्ञान

**phoney** (*AmE* **phony**) /ˈfəʊni ˈफ़ोनि/ *adj.* not real; false अवास्तविक, नक़ली; बनावटी *She spoke with a phoney Russian accent.* ▶ **phoney** (*AmE* **phony**) *noun* [C] अवास्तविक वस्तु आदि

**phono-** /ˈfəʊnəʊ ˈफ़ोनो/ *prefix* (*used in nouns, adjectives and adverbs*) connected with sound or sounds ध्वनि-विषयक *phonetic* ○ *phonics*

**phosphate** /ˈfɒsfeɪt ˈफ़ॉस्फ़ेट्/ *noun* [C, U] (in chemistry) any salt or compound containing phosphorus, used in industry or for helping plants to grow (रसायन शास्त्र में) फ़ॉसफ़ेट; फ़ॉसफ़ोरस-युक्त कोई भी लवण या यौगिक (औद्योगिक उत्पादनों में या पौधों को संवर्धित या विकसित करने के लिए प्रयुक्त)

**phosphorescent** /ˌfɒsfəˈresənt ˌफ़ॉस्फ़ˈरेसन्ट्/ *adj.* (*technical*) **1** producing a faint light in the dark स्फुरदीप्ति **2** producing light without heat or with so little heat that it cannot be felt ऐसी रोशनी उत्पन्न करने वाला जिस में गरमी न हो या इतनी कम हो कि महसूस न हो सके ▶ **phosphorescence** /-səns -सन्स्/ *noun* [U] स्फुरदीप्ति

**phosphorus** /ˈfɒsfərəs ˈफ़ॉस्फ़रस्/ *noun* [U] (*symbol* **P**) a chemical element found in several different forms, including as a poisonous, pale yellow substance that shines in the dark and starts to burn as soon as it is placed in air एक रासायनिक तत्व जो विविध रूपों में मिलता है, इसका एक रूप है विषैला हलका पीला पदार्थ जो अँधेरे में चमकता है और वायु का स्पर्श पाते ही जल उठता है; फ़ॉसफ़ोरस

**photo** /ˈfəʊtəʊ ˈफ़ोटो/ *noun* [C] (*pl.* **photos** /-təʊz -टोज़्/) (*informal*) = **photograph**

**photo-** /ˈfəʊtəʊ ˈफ़ोटो/ *prefix* (*used in nouns, adjectives and adverbs*) **1** connected with light प्रकाश-विषयक या प्रकाश से संबंधित *photosynthesis* **2** connected with photography फ़ोटोग्राफ़ी से संबंधित *photocopier*

**photocopier** /ˈfəʊtəʊkɒpiə(r) ˈफ़ोटोकॉपिअ(र्)/ *noun* [C] a machine that makes copies of documents by photographing them दस्तावेज़ों की (उनके फ़ोटो लेकर) प्रतिलिपियाँ बनाने वाली मशीन; फ़ोटोकॉपियर

**photocopy** /ˈfəʊtəʊkɒpi ˈफ़ोटोकॉपि/ *noun* [C] (*pl.* **photocopies**) a copy of a document, a page in a book, etc. that is made by a photocopier फ़ोटोकॉपियर से बनी किसी दस्तावेज़ आदि की प्रतिलिपि; फ़ोटोकॉपी ✪ पर्याय **Xerox™** ▶ **photocopy** *verb* [I, T] (*pres. part.* **photocopying**; *3rd person sing. pres.* **photocopies**; *pt, pp* **photocopied**) फ़ोटोकॉपियर से दस्तावेज़ आदि की प्रतिलिपि बनाना

**photograph** /ˈfəʊtəɡrɑːf ˈफ़ोटग्राफ़्/ (*also* **photo**) *noun* [C] a picture that is taken with a camera कैमरे से लिया गया चित्र; फ़ोटो, छायाचित्र *to take a photograph* ○ *She looks younger in real life than she does* ***in the photograph***. ➪ **negative** और **slide** देखिए। ▶ **photograph** *verb* [T] फ़ोटो लेना

**photographer** /fəˈtɒɡrəfə(r) फ़ˈटॉग्राफ़(र्)/ *noun* [C] a person who takes photographs फ़ोटोग्राफ़र, छायाचित्रकार ➪ **cameraman** देखिए।

**photographic** /ˌfəʊtəˈɡræfɪk ˌफ़ोटˈग्रैफ़िक्/ *adj.* connected with photographs or photography फ़ोटो या फ़ोटोग्राफ़ी से संबंधित

**photography** /fəˈtɒɡrəfi फ़ˈटॉग्रफ़ि/ *noun* [U] the skill or process of taking photographs फ़ोटो लेने की कला या प्रक्रिया; फ़ोटोग्राफ़ी, छायाचित्रकारी

**photon** /ˈfəʊtɒn ˈफ़ोटॉन्/ *noun* [C] a unit of a certain type of energy (**electromagnetic energy**), for example light एक विशेष प्रकार की ऊर्जा (जैसे प्रकाश) की इकाई; फ़ोटोन

**photosynthesis** /ˌfəʊtəʊˈsɪnθəsɪs ˌफ़ोटोˈसिनृथसिस्/ *noun* [U] the process by which green plants turn **carbon dioxide** and water into food using energy from sunlight सूर्य के प्रकाश से हरे पौधों द्वारा कार्बन डाइ-ऑक्साइड और जल को भोजन का रूप देने की प्रक्रिया; फ़ोटोसिंथीसिस, प्रकाश-संश्लेषण

**phototropism** /ˌfəʊtəʊˈtrəʊpɪzəm ˌफ़ोटोˈट्रोपिज़म/ *noun* [U] (*technical*) the action of a plant turning towards or away from light किसी वनस्पति का प्रकाश के प्रति आकर्षण या उससे विकर्षण; प्रकाशानुवर्तन ▸ **phototropic** *adj.* प्रकाशानुवर्तन से संबंधित

**phrasal verb** /ˌfreɪzl ˈvɜːb ˌफ़्रेज़ल् ˈव़ब्/ *noun* [C] (*grammar*) a verb that is combined with an adverb or a preposition, or sometimes both, to give a new meaning, such as 'look after' or 'put sb off' क्रियाविशेषण या पूर्वसर्ग या दोनों के संयोग से बनी क्रिया जिसका अपना ही अर्थ होता है; पदबंधीय क्रिया जैसे 'look after' या 'put sb off'

**phrase**[1] /freɪz फ़्रेज़्/ *noun* [C] a group of words that are used together. A phrase does not contain a full verb एक साथ प्रयुक्त शब्दसमुच्चय, पदबंध, वाक्यांश या पदबंध में क्रिया का पूर्ण रूप प्रयुक्त नहीं होता *'First of all' and 'a bar of chocolate' are phrases.* ➪ **sentence** देखिए।

**phrase**[2] /freɪz फ़्रेज़्/ *verb* [T] to express sth in a particular way विशेष रीति से शब्दविन्यास करना *The statement was phrased so that it would offend no one.*

**phylum** /ˈfaɪləm ˈफ़ाइलम्/ *noun* [C] (*pl.* **phyla** /-lə -ला/) a group into which animals, plants, etc. are divided, smaller than a **kingdom**[2] and larger than a **class**[1] **4** जाति या संघ जिसमें पशु, पौधों आदि का वर्गीकरण किया जाता है; फ़ाइलम। यह 'किंगडम' से छोटा और 'क्लास' से बड़ा होता है

**physical** /ˈfɪzɪkl ˈफ़िज़िकल्/ *adj.* **1** connected with your body rather than your mind शारीरिक *physical fitness/strength/disabilities* **2** (*only before a noun*) connected with real things that you can touch, or with the laws of nature जीवन की वास्तविक भौतिक वस्तुओं या प्रकृति के नियमों से संबंधित *physical geography* (= the natural features on the face of the earth) **3** (*only before a noun*) connected with the study of natural forces (**physics**) and things that are not alive भौतिक विज्ञान और जड़ वस्तुओं से संबंधित ▸ **physically** /-kli -क्लि/ *adv.* शारीरिक या भौतिक रूप से, प्रकृति के नियमानुसार *to be physically fit* ○ *It will be physically impossible to get to Noida before 10 p.m.*

**physical education** *noun* [U] (*abbr.* **PE**) sport and exercise that is taught in schools शारीरिक शिक्षा; स्कूलों में सिखाए जाने वाले खेल और व्यायाम

**physician** /fɪˈzɪʃn फ़िˈज़िश्न्/ (*AmE formal*) = **doctor**[1] **1**

**physicist** /ˈfɪzɪsɪst ˈफ़िज़िसिस्ट्/ *noun* [C] a person who studies or is an expert in physics भौतिक विज्ञानी

**physics** /ˈfɪzɪks ˈफ़िज़िक्स्/ *noun* [U] the scientific study of natural forces such as light, sound, heat, electricity, pressure, etc. प्रकाश, ध्वनि, ताप, विद्युत, दाब आदि प्राकृतिक शक्तियों का वैज्ञानिक अध्ययन; भौतिक विज्ञान

**physio-** /ˈfɪziəʊ ˈफ़िज़िओ/ *prefix* (*used in nouns, adjectives and adverbs*) **1** connected with nature प्रकृति से संबंधित; प्राकृतिक **2** connected with **physiology** शरीर क्रिया-विज्ञान से संबंधित

**physiologist** /ˌfɪziˈɒlədʒɪst ˌफ़िज़िˈऑलजिस्ट्/ *noun* [C] a scientist who studies how living things function शरीर क्रिया-विज्ञानी

**physiology** /ˌfɪziˈɒlədʒi ˌफ़िज़िˈऑलजि/ *noun* [U] the scientific study of how living things function शरीर क्रिया-विज्ञान

**physiotherapist** /ˌfɪziəʊˈθerəpɪst ˌफ़िज़िओˈथ्रेरपिस्ट्/ *noun* [C] a person who is trained to use physiotherapy फ़िज़ियोथेरापी द्वारा इलाज करने वाला व्यक्ति; फ़िज़ियोथेरापिस्ट

**physiotherapy** /ˌfɪziəʊˈθerəpi ˌफ़िज़िओˈथ्रेरपि/ (*AmE* **physical therapy**) *noun* [U] the treatment of disease or injury by exercise, light, heat, rubbing the muscles (**massage**), etc. व्यायाम, प्रकाश, ताप, मांसपेशियों की मालिश आदि के द्वारा की जाने वाली चिकित्सा; फ़िजियोथेरापी

**physique** /fɪˈziːk फ़िˈज़ीक्/ *noun* [C] the size and shape of a person's body व्यक्ति के शरीर का रूपाकार, शारीरिक गठन, डील-डौल *a strong muscular physique*

**pi** /paɪ पाइ/ *noun* [*sing.*] the symbol π used to show the relation between the **circumference** of a circle and its **diameter** that is about 3.14159 वृत्त की परिधि और उसके व्यास के संबंध को दिखाने के लिए प्रयुक्त चिह्न विशेष जिसका मूल्य लगभग 3.14159 है

**pianist** /ˈpɪənɪst ˈपिअनिस्ट्/ *noun* [C] a person who plays the piano पियानोवादक

**piano** /piˈænəʊ पिˈऐनो/ *noun* [C] (*pl.* **pianos** /-nəʊz -नोज़्/) a large musical instrument that you play by pressing down black and white keys एक बड़ा वाद्य जिसकी काली और सफ़ेद कुंजियों को दबाकर बजाया जाता है; पियानो *an upright piano* ○ *a grand piano* ➪ पृष्ठ 789 पर चित्र देखिए।

> **NOTE** सामान्य रूप से प्रचलित प्रयोग हैं 'play **the** piano, **the** violin, **the** guitar' इत्यादि (अर्थात शब्द **the** का प्रयोग विशेषतया होता है)—*I've been learning the piano for four years.* आधुनिक संगीत जैसे जाज़, रॉक आदि की चर्चा में अधिक प्रचलित प्रयोग play drums, guitar, etc. हैं (जिनमें शब्द **the** प्रयुक्त नहीं होता है)—*He plays bass in a band.* ○ *This recording features Miles Davis on trumpet.*

**piccolo** /ˈpɪkələʊ ˈपिकलो/ *noun* [C] (*pl.* **piccolos**) a musical instrument like a small **flute** छोटी बाँसुरी जैसा वाद्य

**pick[1]** /pɪk पिक्/ *verb* [T] **1** to choose sb/sth from a group of people or things (व्यक्तियों या वस्तुओं के समूह में से) चुनना, चयन करना, छाँटना *I was upset not to be picked for the team.* ○ *Have I picked a bad time to visit?* **2** to take a flower, fruit or vegetable from the place where it is growing (फूल या फल) चुनना, बीनना (जहाँ से उगाए जा रहे हों) *to pick flowers/grapes/cotton* **3** to remove a small piece or pieces of sth with your fingers अँगुलियों से कुरेदना या खुरचना *Don't pick your nose!* ○ *She picked a hair off her jacket.* **4 pick your way across, over, through, etc. sth** to walk carefully, choosing the best places to put your feet सावधानी से चलना; सावधानी से क़दम रखना

**IDM have a bone to pick with sb** ➪ **bone[1]** देखिए।

**pick a fight (with sb)** to start a fight with sb deliberately किसी से जानबूझकर लड़ने या झगड़ने लगना

**pick a lock** to open a lock without using a key बिना चाबी लगाए ताला खोल लेना (किसी अन्य युक्ति के द्वारा)

**pick and choose** to choose only the things that you like or want very much मनपसंद या मनचाही वस्तुएँ चुनना

**pick sb's pocket** to steal money, etc. from sb's pocket or bag किसी की जेब या थैले से पैसे चुरा लेना

**PHR V pick at sth** **1** to eat only small amounts of food because you are not hungry (भूख न लगने के कारण) रोटी आदि के टुकड़ों को टूँगना या कुतरना (छोटे-छोटे टुकड़े खाना) **2** to touch sth many times with your fingers किसी वस्तु को अँगुलियों से अनेक बार छूना

**pick on sb** to behave unfairly or in a cruel way towards sb किसी व्यक्ति से अनुचित या निर्मम तरीक़े से पेश आना

**pick sb/sth out** to choose or recognize sb/sth from a number of people or things; identify अनेक व्यक्तियों या वस्तुओं में से एक को चुनना या उसकी पहचान करना; पहचानना या पहचान करना *I immediately picked Yamini out in the photo.*

**pick up** to become better; to improve (दशा) बेहतर हो जाना; (दशा में) सुधार होना

**pick sb up** to collect sb, in a car, etc. किसी को कार आदि में बैठा लेना *We've ordered a taxi to pick us up at 4 a.m.*

**pick sb/sth up** **1** to take hold of and lift sb/sth (व्यक्ति या वस्तु को) पकड़कर उठाना *Lalita picked up the child and gave him a cuddle.* **2** to receive an electronic signal, sound or picture इलेक्ट्रॉनिक संकेत, ध्वनि या चित्र को प्राप्त करना *In the north of France you can pick up English television programmes.*

**pick sth up** **1** to learn sth without formal lessons (सुन-देखकर ही) बिना औपचारिक प्रशिक्षण के कुछ सीख लेना या जान लेना *Jaya picked up a few words of Tamil on holiday.* **2** to get or find sth कोई वस्तु प्राप्त करना या ढूँढ़ लेना *I picked up this book at the market.* **3** to go and get sth; to collect sth जाकर (कोई वस्तु) ले लेना; बटोर लेना *I have to pick up my jacket from the cleaner's.*

**pick[2]** /pɪk पिक्/ *noun* **1** [*sing.*] the one that you choose; your choice चुनी हुई, छाँटी हुई वस्तु; मनपसंद वस्तु *You can have whichever cake you like* ○ ***Take your pick.*** **2** [*sing.*] the best of a group सर्वोत्तम *You can see **the pick of** the new films at this year's festival.* **3** (*also* **pickaxe** *AmE* **pickax** /ˈpɪkæks ˈपिक्ऐक्स्/) [C] a tool that consists of a curved iron bar with sharp points at both ends, fixed onto a wooden handle. Picks are used for breaking stones or hard ground गैंती, खोदनी ➪ **gardening** पर चित्र देखिए।

**picket** /ˈpɪkɪt ˈपिकिट्/ *noun* [C] a worker or group of workers who stand outside the entrance to a building to protest about sth, especially in order to stop people entering a factory, etc. during a strike हड़ताल के दौरान कार्यस्थल में कार्यकर्ताओं के प्रवेश को रोकते कर्मचारी, हड़ताली कर्मचारी ▶ **picket** *verb* [I, T] धरना देना, पिकेटिंग करना

**pickle** /ˈpɪkl ˈपिक्ल्/ *noun* **1** [C, *usually pl.*] (*BrE*) food such as fruit or vegetables that is put in salt water or **vinegar** so that it can be kept for a long time before being eaten सिरके या नमकीन जल के प्रयोग से बना अचार **2** [U] a thick sauce-like food with a strong flavour made from fruit and vegetables that have been preserved in oil फलों और सब्ज़ियों से बनी स्वाद में तीखा अचार **3** [C] (*AmE*) = **gherkin** ▶ **pickle** *verb* [T] अचार डालना *pickled onions*

**pickpocket** /ˈpɪkpɒkɪt ˈपिक्पॉकिट्/ *noun* [C] a person who steals things from other people's pockets or bags in public places जेबकतरा, गिरहकट, पॉकिटमार

**pickup** /ˈpɪkʌp ˈपिक्अप्/ (*also* **pickup truck**) *noun* [C] a type of vehicle that has an open part with low sides at the back माल ढोने की खुली गाड़ी; पिकअप

**picky** /ˈpɪki ˈपिकि/ *adj.* (*informal*) (used about a person) liking only certain things and difficult to please (व्यक्ति) केवल ख़ास-ख़ास वस्तुएँ पसंद करने वाला और आसानी से संतुष्ट न होने वाला; मीनमेखी, नख़रेबाज़ ➪ **fussy** देखिए।

**picnic** /ˈpɪknɪk ˈपिक्निक्/ *noun* [C] a meal that you take with you to eat outdoors सैर-सपाटे के लिए (साथ ले जाकर) बाहर जाकर खाया जाने वाला भोजन; वनभोज *We had a picnic on the beach.* ▶ **picnic** *verb* [I] (*pres. part.* **picnicking;** *pt, pp* **picnicked**) सैर-सपाटे के दौरान बाहर ले जाकर भोजन खाना

**pictogram** /ˈpɪktəgræm ˈपिक्टग्रैम्/ *noun* [C] (*technical*) **1** a picture representing a word or phrase किसी शब्द या वाक्यांश का प्रतीक चित्र; चित्राक्षर **2** a diagram that uses pictures to represent amounts or numbers of a particular thing चित्रों द्वारा वस्तु विशेष की कुल मात्रा या संख्या को दर्शाने वाला रेखाचित्र नक़्शा या ख़ाका

**pictorial** /pɪkˈtɔːriəl पिकˈटॉरिअल्/ *adj.* expressed in pictures चित्रों द्वारा अभिव्यक्त करते हुए; सचित्र, चित्रमय, *pictorial representations of objects*

**picture¹** /ˈpktʃə(r) ˈपिक्च(र्)/ *noun* [C] **1** a painting, drawing or photograph चित्र, पेंटिंग, आरेख, फ़ोटो *Who painted the picture in the hall?* ○ *The teacher asked us to* ***draw a picture*** *of our houses.* **2** an image on a television screen टीवी के परदे पर प्रकट आकृति या छवि *They showed pictures of the crash on the news.* **3** a description of sth that gives you a good idea of what it is like किसी वस्तु के रूपाकार का अच्छा-ख़ासा अनुमान कराने वाला वर्णन *The police are trying to build up a picture of exactly what happened.*

**picture²** /ˈpɪktʃə(r) ˈपिक्च(र्)/ *verb* [T] **1 picture sb/sth (as sth)** to imagine sth in your mind मन में छवि बनाना *I can't picture Inder as a father.* **2** to make a picture of sb/sth किसी व्यक्ति या वस्तु का चित्र बनाना *She is pictured here with her parents.*

**picturesque** /ˌpɪktʃəˈresk ˌपिक्चˈरेस्क्/ *adj.* (usually used about an old building or place) attractive (प्रायः कोई पुराना भवन या स्थान) आकर्षक, मनोरम *a picturesque fishing village*

**pie** /paɪ पाइ/ *noun* [C, U] a type of food consisting of fruit, meat or vegetables inside a pastry case फल, मांस या सब्ज़ियों से भरी पेस्ट्री; पाइ *apple pie* ○ *meat pie*

**piece¹** /piːs पीस्/ *noun* [C] **1** an amount or example of sth एक अदद चीज़, एक की संख्या में कोई वस्तु, एक पृथक उदाहरण *a piece of paper* ○ *a piece of advice/information/news* **2** one of the parts that sth is made of अंश, भाग, हिस्सा *We'll have to* ***take*** *the engine* ***to pieces*** *to find the problem.* **3** one of the parts into which sth breaks टुकड़ा, खंड *The plate fell to the floor and smashed* ***to pieces***. ○ *The vase lay* ***in pieces*** *on the floor.* **4 a piece (on/about sb/sth)** an article in a newspaper or magazine समाचार-पत्र या पत्रिका में कोई लेख *There's a good piece on Sri Lanka in today's paper.* **5** a single work of art, music, etc.. कला, संगीत आदि की एक रचना *He played a piece by Ravi Shankar.* **6** one of the small objects that you use when you are playing games such as **chess** शतरंज के खेल में कोई मोहरा **7** a coin of the value mentioned निर्दिष्ट मूल्य का कोई सिक्का *a fifty-paise piece*

IDM **bits and pieces** ➪ **bit¹** देखिए।

**give sb a piece of your mind** to speak to sb angrily because of sth he/she has done किसी से गुस्से में कुछ कहना (उसके ग़लती करने पर)

**go to pieces** to be no longer able to work or behave normally because of a difficult situation कठिनाई से घबराकर स्वयं पर संयम खो बैठना

**in one piece** not broken or injured समूचा, साबुत, या बिना चोट खाए, सही-सलामत *I've only been on a motorbike once, and I was just glad to get home in one piece.*

**a piece of cake** (*informal*) something that is very easy बहुत आसान बात या कार्य

**piece²** /piːs पीस्/ *verb*

PHR V **piece sth together 1** to discover the truth about sth from different pieces of information विभिन्न सूत्रों से किसी वस्तु के विषय में सचाई का पता लगाना *Detectives are trying to piece together the* *last few days of the man's life.* **2** to put sth together from several pieces टुकड़ों को जोड़कर एक करना

**piecemeal** /ˈpi:smi:l ˈपीस्मील्/ *adj., adv.* done or happening a little at a time खंड-खंड करके किया गया या संपन्न हुआ (कार्य); थोड़ा-थोड़ा करके

**piece rate** *noun* [C] an amount of money paid for each thing or amount of sth that a worker produces प्रति वस्तु दर या मज़दूर के बनाए माल की मात्रा

**pie chart** *noun* [C] a diagram consisting of a circle divided into parts to show the size of particular parts in relation to the whole खंडों में विभक्त वृत्त का आरेख जिसमें पूर्ण वृत्त के संदर्भ में उसके खंडों का आकार दिखाया गया हो; पाइ चार्ट ➪ **chart**[1] पर चित्र देखिए।

**pier** /pɪə(r) पिअ(र्)/ *noun* [C] a large wooden or metal structure that is built out into the sea from the land. Boats can stop at piers so that people or goods can be taken on or off ज़मीन से समुद्र में बना लोहे या लकड़ी का ढाँचा जहाँ नावें रुकती हैं और यात्री चढ़ते-उतरते हैं या माल को लादा-उतारा जाता है; पोतघाट

**pierce** /pɪəs पिअस्/ *verb* **1** [T] to make a hole in sth with a sharp point नुकीले औज़ार से किसी वस्तु में छेद करना *I'm going to* ***have my ears pierced****.* **2** [I, T] **pierce (through/into) sth** to manage to go through or into sth किसी वस्तु में से गुज़र जाना या उसके अंदर घुस जाना *A scream pierced the air.*

**piercing** /ˈpɪəsɪŋ ˈपिअसिङ्/ *adj.* **1** (used about the wind, pain, a loud noise, etc.) strong and unpleasant (हवा, दर्द, ऊँची आवाज़ आदि के लिए प्रयुक्त) ज़ोरदार तेज़ और बुरी, कष्टकर **2** (used about sb's eyes or a look) seeming to know what you are thinking (आँखें या दृष्टि) जो मन की बात मानो पढ़ ले

**piety** /ˈpaɪəti ˈपाइअटि/ *noun* [U] a way of behaving that shows a deep respect for God and religion ईश्वर और धर्म के प्रति सम्मान का द्योतक आचरण; धर्मपरायणता ➪ **pious** adjective देखिए।

**pig**[1] /pɪg पिग्/ *noun* [C] **1** a fat pinkish animal with short legs and a short tail सूअर

> **NOTE** नर सूअर को **boar**, मादा को **sow** और बच्चे को **piglet** कहते हैं। बड़े सूअर के आवाज़ करने को **grunt** कहते हैं और बच्चे के आवाज़ को **squeal**।

**2** (*informal*) an unpleasant person or a person who eats too much अप्रिय या पेटू व्यक्ति

**pig**[2] /pɪg पिग्/ *verb* [T] (**pigging; pigged**) (*slang*) **pig yourself** to eat too much बहुत अधिक खा जाना

**PHR V** **pig out (on sth)** (*slang*) to eat too much of sth कोई वस्तु बड़ी मात्रा में खा जाना

**pigeon** /ˈpɪdʒɪn ˈपिजिन्/ *noun* [C] a fat grey bird that often lives in towns कबूतर, कपोत

**pigeon-hole** *noun* [C] one of a set of small open boxes that are used for putting papers or letters in पत्र आदि डालने या काग़ज़ात रखने के लिए छोटे-छोटे ख़ानों में से कोई एक

**piggyback** /ˈpɪgibæk ˈपिगिबैक्/ *noun* [C] the way of carrying sb, especially a child, on your back किसी को (विशेषतः बच्चे को) पीठ पर लादकर ले जाना *to give sb a piggyback*

**piggy bank** *noun* [C] a small box, often shaped like a pig, that children save money in बच्चों की (प्रायः सूअर के आकार की) ग़ोलक (जिसमें वे पैसे बचाकर रखते हैं)

**pig-headed** *adj.* (*informal*) not prepared to change your mind or say that you are wrong ज़िद्दी, विचार बदलने या ग़लती मानने के लिए अनिच्छुक; अड़ियल ➪ **stubborn** और **obstinate** देखिए।

**pig iron** *noun* [U] a form of iron that is not pure कच्चा लोहा, ढलवाँ लोहा

**piglet** /ˈpɪglət ˈपिग्लट्/ *noun* [C] a young pig सूअर का शावक

**pigment** /ˈpɪgmənt ˈपिग्मन्ट्/ *noun* [C, U] a substance that gives colour to things रंजक पदार्थ जिसके प्रयोग से चीज़ों पर रंग आ जाता है *The colour of your skin depends on the amount of pigment in it.*

**pigsty** /ˈpɪgstaɪ ˈपिग्स्टाइ/ (*also* **sty** *AmE* **pigpen**) *noun* [C] (*pl.* **pigsties**) a small building where pigs are kept सूअरों को रखने की जगह, सूअर-बाड़ा

**pigtail** /ˈpɪgteɪl ˈपिग्टेल्/ (*AmE* **braid**) *noun* [C] hair that is tied together in one or two thick pieces made by crossing three pieces of hair over each other (**plaiting**) केश-विन्यास की एक शैली जिसमें बालों की तीन छोटी लटों को गूँथ कर एक या दो बड़ी लटों में सजाया जाता है; लंबी चोटी, वेणी

**pilchard** /ˈpɪltʃəd ˈपिल्चड्/ *noun* [C] a small sea fish that you can eat खाने की छोटी समुद्री मछली; पिल्चर्ड

**pile**[1] /paɪl पाइल्/ *noun* [C] **1** a number of things lying on top of one another, or an amount of sth lying in a mass एक के ऊपर एक करके रखी वस्तुओं का ढेर; वस्तुओं का अंबार *a pile of books/sand* ○ *He put the coins* ***in neat piles****.* ○ *She threw the clothes* ***in a pile*** *on the floor.*

> **NOTE** **Pile** साफ़-सुथरा और ठीक-ठाक हो सकता है, बेढंगा भी। **Heap** बेढंगा और बेतरतीब होता है।

**2** (*usually pl.*) (*informal*) **piles of sth** a lot of sth बड़ी मात्रा या राशि *I've got piles of work to do this evening.* **3 piles** [*pl.*] = **haemorrhoids**

**pile**[2] /paɪl पाइल्/ *verb* [T] **1 pile sth (up)** to put things one on top of the other to form a pile

वस्तुओं का ढेर बना देना (एक के ऊपर दूसरी को रखकर) *We piled the boxes in the corner.* **2 pile A on(to) B; pile B with A** to put a lot of sth on top of sth किसी एक वस्तु पर अन्य वस्तुओं का ढेर लगा देना *She piled the papers on the desk.* ○ *The desk was piled with papers.*

**PHR V pile into, out of, off, etc. sth** (*informal*) to go into, out of, off, etc. sth quickly and all at the same time तेज़ी से एक साथ अंदर-बाहर आना-जाना *The children piled onto the bus.*

**pile up** (used about sth bad) to increase in quantity (प्रतिकूल स्थिति का) मात्रा में बढ़ना, जमा होते जाना *Our problems are really piling up.*

**pile-up** *noun* [C] a crash that involves several cars, etc. कई मोटर गाड़ियों की भिड़ंत *a multiple pile-up on the highway*

**pilfer** /ˈpɪlfə(r) ˈपिल्फ़(र्)/ *verb* to steal something in small quantity or of little value, especially from the place where you work छिटपुट चोरी, विशेषतः कार्यस्थल से *She was caught pilfering stationery from the office.*

**pilgrim** /ˈpɪlgrɪm ˈपिल्ग्रिम्/ *noun* [C] a person who travels a long way to visit a religious place तीर्थयात्री

**pilgrimage** /ˈpɪlgrɪmɪdʒ ˈपिल्ग्रिमिज्/ *noun* [C, U] a long journey that a person makes to visit a religious place तीर्थयात्रा

**pill** /pɪl पिल्/ *noun* **1** [C] a small round piece of medicine that you swallow दवा की गोली *Take one pill, three times a day after meals.* ○ *a sleeping pill* ➪ **tablet** देखिए। **2 the pill** [*sing.*] a pill that some women take regularly so that they do not become pregnant महिलाओं द्वारा प्रयुक्त गर्भ-निरोधक गोली *She is* ***on the pill.***

**pillar** /ˈpɪlə(r) ˈपिल(र्)/ *noun* [C] **1** a column of stone, wood or metal that is used for supporting part of a building पत्थर, लकड़ी या लोहे आदि का खंभा (भवन के किसी भाग को थामे रखने के लिए प्रयुक्त); स्तंभ **2** a person who has a strong character and is important to sb/sth दृढ़ चरित्र वाला व किसी के लिए महत्त्वपूर्ण व्यक्ति *Neeraj was a* ***pillar of strength*** *to his sister when she was ill.*

**pillion** /ˈpɪliən ˈपिलिअन्/ *noun* [C] a seat for a passenger behind the driver on a motorbike मोटर-साइकिल पर (सहयात्री के लिए) पीछे की सीट ▶ **pillion** *adv.* मोटर-साइकिल पर पीछे *to ride pillion on a motorbike*

**pillow** /ˈpɪləʊ ˈपिलो/ *noun* [C] a large cushion that you put under your head when you are in bed तकिया, सिरहाना

**pillowcase** /ˈpɪləʊkeɪs ˈपिलोकेस्/ *noun* [C] a thin soft cloth cover for a pillow तकिये का गिलाफ़

**pilot¹** /ˈpaɪlət ˈपाइलट्/ *noun* [C] a person who flies an aircraft विमान-चालक, पायलट *an airline pilot*

**pilot²** /ˈpaɪlət ˈपाइलट्/ *verb* [T] **1** to operate the controls of a vehicle, especially an aircraft or a boat किसी वाहन को संचालित करना, विशेषतः विमान या नाव को *to pilot a ship* **2** to lead sb/sth through a difficult situation कठिनाई में किसी का मार्गदर्शन करना *The booklet pilots you through the process of starting your own business.* **3** to be the first to test sth that will be used by everyone किसी ऐसी वस्तु का सबसे पहले परीक्षण करना जो बाद में आम प्रयोग में लाई जाएगी *The new exam is being piloted in schools in Delhi.*

**pilot³** /ˈpaɪlət ˈपाइलट्/ *adj.* (*only before a noun*) done as an experiment or to test sth that will be used by everyone प्रयोगात्मक या परीक्षणात्मक *The pilot scheme will run for six months.*

**pimple** /ˈpɪmpl ˈपिम्पल्/ *noun* [C] a small raised spot on your skin त्वचा पर छोटी फुंसी; मुहाँसा

**PIN** /pɪn पिन्/ (*also* **PIN number**) *noun* [C, *usually sing.*] personal identification number; a number given to you by your bank so that you can use a plastic card to take out money from a cash machine व्यक्ति की पहचान कराने वाली संख्या जो कैश मशीन से कार्ड द्वारा पैसा में प्रयोग के लिए ग्राहक को बैंक जारी करता है; व्यक्तिगत जानकारी संख्या, पिन नंबर

**pin¹** /pɪn पिन्/ *noun* [C] **1** a short thin piece of metal with a round head at one end and a sharp point at the other. Pins are used for fastening together pieces of cloth, paper, etc. कपड़े के टुकड़ों, कागज़ आदि को नत्थी करने की पिन **2** a thin piece of wood or metal that is used for a particular purpose विशेष प्रयोजन के लिए लकड़ी या धातु का पिन *a hairpin* ○ *a two-pin plug* ➪ **stationery** पर चित्र देखिए।

**pin²** /pɪn पिन्/ *verb* [T] (**pinning; pinned**) **1 pin sth to/on sth; pin sth together** to fasten sth with a pin or pins पिन या पिनों से किसी को जकड़ना, नत्थी करना *Could you pin this notice on the board, please?* **2 pin sb/sth against, to, under, etc. sth** to make sb/sth unable to move by holding or pressing down on sb/it किसी को पकड़ कर या दबोच कर जकड़े रखना *He caught his brother and pinned him to the floor.* ○ *He was pinned under the fallen tree.*

**IDM** **pin (all) your hopes on sb/sth** to believe completely that sb/sth will help you or will succeed (किसी काम में सहायता या सफलता के लिए) किसी व्यक्ति या वस्तु पर अपनी सभी आशाएँ केंद्रित करना

**PHRV** **pin sb down** 1 to hold sb so he/she cannot move किसी को पकड़ कर जकड़े रखना 2 to force sb to decide sth or to say exactly what he/she is going to do किसी को निर्णय कर लेने के लिए या इरादा साफ़-साफ़ बताने के लिए विवश करना

**pin sth down** to describe or explain exactly what sth is किसी बात का सही-सही निरूपण करना

**pinafore** /ˈpɪnəfɔː(r) ˈपिनफ़ॉ(र्)/ *noun* [C] (*old-fashioned*) a piece of clothing or a dress that a woman can wear over her normal clothes to keep them clean when she is cooking or doing dirty jobs महिलाओं द्वारा कपड़ों पर पहना जाने वाला वस्त्र ताकि घर का काम करते समय कपड़े ख़राब न हों; पिनाफ़ोर, बालापोश ➪ **apron** देखिए।

**pincer** /ˈpɪnsə(r) ˈपिन्स(र्)/ *noun* 1 **pincers** [*pl.*] a tool made of two crossed pieces of metal that is used for holding things, pulling nails out of wood, etc. (कील आदि निकालने की) चिमटी, सड़ँसी 2 [C] one of the two sharp, curved front legs of some shellfish that are used for holding things केकड़े आदि की दो नुकीली आगे की टाँगें (कुछ पकड़ने के लिए) ➪ **shellfish** पर चित्र देखिए।

**pinch**[1] /pɪntʃ पिन्च्/ *verb* 1 [T] to hold a piece of sb's skin tightly between your thumb and first finger, especially in order to hurt sb किसी को चिकोटी काटना (ताकि उसे दर्द हो) *Puneet pinched his brother and made him cry.* 2 [I, T] to hold sth too tight, often causing pain किसी को बहुत कसकर पकड़ना, प्रायः दर्द करते हुए *I've got a pinched nerve in my neck.* 3 [T] (*informal*) to steal चुराना *Who's pinched my pen?*

**pinch**[2] /pɪntʃ पिन्च्/ *noun* [C] 1 the holding of sb's skin tightly between your finger and thumb चिकोटी *She gave him a little pinch on the arm.* 2 the amount of sth that you can pick up with your thumb and first finger चुटकी भर मात्रा *a pinch of salt*

**IDM** **at a pinch** used to say that sth can be done if it is really necessary यदि बहुत ज़रूरी हो तो, कहने के लिए प्रयुक्त *We really need three cars but we could manage with two at a pinch.*

**take sth with a pinch of salt** to think that sth is probably not true or accurate किसी बात के सच या सही होने में शक करना

**pinched** /pɪntʃt पिन्च्ट्/ *adj.* (used about sb's face) thin and pale because of illness or cold (चेहरा) (बीमारी या ठंड के कारण) उतरा हुआ और पीला

**pine**[1] /paɪn पाइन्/ *noun* 1 [C] (*also* **pine tree**) a tall **evergreen** tree that has thin sharp leaves (**needles**) देवदार या चीड़ का पेड़ (फ़र्नीचर निर्माण में प्रयुक्त) 2 [U] the wood from pine trees (which is often used for making furniture) देवदार या चीड़ की लकड़ी *a pine table*

**pine**[2] /paɪn पाइन्/ *verb* [I] **pine (for sb/sth)** to be very unhappy because sb has died or gone away (किसी के न रहने या दूर चले जाने के कारण) दुखी होना *The dog sat outside, pining for its owner.*

**pineapple** /ˈpaɪnæpl ˈपाइनऐप्ल्/ *noun* [C, U] a large sweet fruit that is yellow inside and has a thick brown skin with sharp points. Pineapples grow in hot countries अनन्नास (का फल) ➪ **fruit** पर चित्र देखिए।

**pine nut** (*BrE* **pine kernel**) *noun* [C] the white seed of some **pine** trees, used in cooking देवदार या चीड़ का सफ़ेद दाना (भोजन बनाने में प्रयुक्त)

**ping** /pɪŋ पिङ्/ *noun* [C] a short high noise that is made by a small bell or by a metal object hitting against sth घंटी की तेज़ टनटन या धातु के टकराने से उत्पन्न टनटनाहट *The lift went ping and the doors opened.* ▶ **ping** *verb* [I] टनटन होना

**ping-pong** (*informal*) = **table tennis**

**pink** /pɪŋk पिङ्क्/ *adj.*, *noun* [U] (of) a pale red colour गुलाबी रंग

**pinnacle** /ˈpɪnəkl ˈपिनक्ल्/ *noun* [C] 1 the most important or successful part of sth किसी का सर्वोत्कृष्ट भाग; शिखर, पराकाष्ठा *She is at the pinnacle of her career.* 2 a high pointed rock on a mountain पहाड़ पर ऊँची नुकीली चट्टान; शिखरिका

**pinpoint** /ˈpɪnpɔɪnt ˈपिन्पॉइन्ट्/ *verb* [T] 1 to find the exact position of sth किसी वस्तु की एकदम सही स्थिति का पता लगाना *to pinpoint a place on the map* 2 to describe or explain exactly what sth is किसी बात का सही-सही निरूपण करना *First we have to pinpoint the cause of the failure.*

**pins and needles** *noun* [*pl.*] a strange, sometimes painful feeling that you get in a part of your body after it has been in one position for too long and when the blood is returning to it एक ही स्थिति में देर तक रहने के कारण किसी अंग में चुभती झनझनाहट

**pint** /paɪnt पाइन्ट्/ *noun* [C] 1 (*abbr.* **pt**) a measure of liquid; 0.57 of a litre. There are 8 pints in a gallon द्रव की एक माप, पाइंट (0.57 लिटर, 1 एक गैलान में 8 पाइंट होते हैं) *a pint of milk* **NOTE** एक अमेरिकी पाइंट 0.47 लिटर का होता है। 2 (*BrE informal*) a pint of beer एक पाइंट बियर

**pin-up** *noun* [C] (*informal*) a picture of an attractive person, made to be put on a wall; a person who appears in these pictures दीवार पर लगाने के लिए सुंदर व्यक्ति का चित्र; इन चित्रों में बना व्यक्ति

**pioneer** /ˌpaɪəˈnɪə(r) ˌपाइअˈनिअ(र्)/ *noun* [C] **1 a pioneer (in/of sth)** a person who is one of the first to develop an area of human knowledge, culture, etc. मानवीय ज्ञान, संस्कृति आदि के क्षेत्र में अग्रणी व्यक्ति *Yuri Gagarin was one of the pioneers of space exploration.* **2** a person who is one of the first to go and live in a particular area किसी नई जगह पर सबसे पहले बसने वालों में से एक, किसी नए स्थान का अन्वेषक *the pioneers of the American West* ▶ **pioneer** *verb* [T] सबसे पहले खोजना *a technique pioneered in India*

**pious** /ˈpaɪəs ˈपाइअस्/ *adj.* having or showing a deep belief in religion धर्म में गहरा विश्वास करने या प्रदर्शित करने वाला; भक्त, धर्मपरायण ▶ **piously** *adv.* भक्तीभाव से ➪ **piety** noun देखिए।

**pip** /pɪp पिप्/ *noun* [C] (*BrE*) the small seed of an apple, a lemon, an orange, etc. सेब, नींबू, संतरे आदि का बीज

**pipal** *noun* [C] a fig tree native to India and SE Asia with broad pointed leaves. It is regarded as sacred by Buddhists (Buddha having attained **enlightenment** under the tree) and also by **Hindus** and **Jains** पीपल का वृक्ष, भारतीय मूल का चौड़े और नुकीले पत्तों वाला अंजीर का वृक्ष, बौद्ध धर्म में पावन वृक्ष (गौतम बुद्ध को इसी वृक्ष के नीचे ज्ञान प्राप्त हुआ था) तथा हिंदू एवं जैन धर्मों में भी मान्य पावन वृक्ष

**pipe¹** /paɪp पाइप्/ *noun* [C] **1** a tube that carries gas or liquid पाइप (गैस या द्रव के निकलने के लिए), नली या नल *Waste water is carried away down the drainpipe.* **2** a tube with a small bowl at one end that is used for smoking tobacco तंबाकू पीने वाला पाइप *to smoke a pipe* **3** a simple musical instrument that consists of a tube with holes in it. You blow into it to play it छेदयुक्त नली वाला वाद्य यंत्र; पाइप

**pipe²** /paɪp पाइप्/ *verb* [T] to carry liquid or gas in pipes पाइप में से द्रव या गैस कहीं पहुँचाना *Water is piped to all the houses in the village.*

**PHR V** **pipe up** (*informal*) to suddenly say sth एकाएक बोल पड़ना *Suddenly Shirin piped up with a question.*

**pipeline** /ˈpaɪplaɪn ˈपाइप्लाइन्/ *noun* [C] a line of pipes that are used for carrying liquid or gas over a long distance पाइपों से बनी जिसमें द्रव या गैस को दूर तक पहुँचाया जाता है; पाइपलाइन, बड़ी नली

**IDM** **in the pipeline** being planned or prepared जिसकी योजना, तैयारी की जा रही है, योजनाधीन या निर्माणाधीन

**piper** /ˈpaɪpə(r) ˈपाइप(र्)/ *noun* [C] a person who plays music on a pipe, or who plays a musical instrument that is typical in Scotland (**the bagpipes**) वाद्य यंत्र पाइप या बैगपाइप (स्काटलैंड में प्रचलित) बजाने वाला व्यक्ति; पाइपर

**pipette** /pɪˈpet पिˈपेट्/ *noun* [C] (*technical*) a narrow tube used in a **laboratory** for measuring or moving small amounts of liquids प्रयोगशाला में प्रयुक्त तंग नली (अल्प मात्रा में द्रव को मापने या ले जाने के लिए प्रयुक्त) ➪ **laboratory** पर चित्र देखिए।

**piping¹** /ˈpaɪpɪŋ ˈपाइपिङ्/ *noun* [U] **1** pipes of the type or length mentioned विशिष्ट प्रकार या निर्दिष्ट लंबाई की नली या नलियाँ *The extent of lead piping is 20 metres.* **2** a narrow strip of folded cloth that is used to decorate the edge of a piece of clothing, cushion, etc. कपड़ों, गद्दियाँ आदि में सजावट के लिए किनारों पर लगी कपड़े की मुड़ी हुई पतली पट्टी; पाइपिंग *a red dress with gold piping* **3** the sound of a pipe or pipes being played वेणुवादन की ध्वनि

**piping²** /ˈpaɪpɪŋ ˈपाइपिङ्/ *adj.* (of a person's voice) high (व्यक्ति की आवाज़) तीव्र, चिंघाड़

**piping hot** *adj.* (of liquids or food) very hot (पेय या खाद्य सामग्री) गरमागरम

**piracy** /ˈpaɪrəsi ˈपाइरसि/ *noun* [U] **1** the crime of attacking ships in order to steal from them जहाज़ों से चोरी करने के लिए उन पर हमला; समुद्री डकैती, जलदस्युता **2** the illegal copying of books, video, tapes, etc. पुस्तकों, विडियो टेप आदि की अवैध नक़ल; साहित्यिक-कलात्मक चोरी

**pirate¹** /ˈpaɪrət ˈपाइरट्/ *noun* [C] **1** (usually in the past or in stories) a criminal who attacks ships in order to steal from them जलदस्यु, समुद्री डाकू (कहानियों में वर्णित या पिछले ज़माने में होने वाला) **2** a person who copies books, video tapes, computer programs, etc. in order to sell them illegally पुस्तक आदि की अवैध नक़ल को चोरी से बेचने वाला; कृतिचोर

**pirate²** /ˈpaɪrət ˈपाइरट्/ *verb* [T] to make an illegal copy of a book, video tape, etc. in order to sell it पुस्तक आदि की अवैध नक़ल करना (बेचने के लिए); साहित्यिक-कलात्मक चोरी करना

**Pisces** /ˈpaɪsiːz ˈपाइसीज़्/ *noun* [U] the twelfth sign of the **zodiac**, the Fishes मीन राशि

**pistachio** /pɪˈstæʃiəʊ; -ˈstɑːʃiəʊ पिˈस्टैशिओ; -ˈस्टाशिओ/ (*also* **pistachio nut**) *noun* [C] (*pl.* **pistachios**) the small green nut of an Asian tree पिस्ता ➪ **nut** पर चित्र देखिए।

**pistil** /ˈpɪstɪl ˈपिस्टिल्/ *noun* (*technical*) the female organs of a flower, which receive the **pollen**

and produce seeds फूल का बीजोत्पादक मादा हिस्सा; स्त्रीकेसर, गर्भकेसर

**pistol** /ˈpɪstl ˈपिस्ट्ल् / *noun* [C] a small gun that you hold in one hand पिस्तौल, तमंचा

**piston** /ˈpɪstən ˈपिस्टन् / *noun* [C] a piece of metal in an engine, etc. that fits tightly inside a tube (**cylinder**). The piston is moved up and down inside the tube and causes other parts of the engine to move इंजन की एक नली के अंदर कसकर बैठाया हुआ धातुखंड जो इंजन के अन्य भागों को गतिमान् करता है; पिस्टन ⇨ **hydraulic** पर चित्र देखिए।

**pit**[1] /pɪt पिट् / *noun* **1** [C] a large hole that is made in the ground गड्ढा, गर्त *They dug a large pit to bury the treasure.* **2** [C] = **coal mine 3 the pits** [*pl.*] the place on a motor racing track where cars stop for fuel, new tyres, etc. during a race कारों के दौड़-मार्ग पर वह स्थान जहाँ कारें पेट्रोल, नए टायर आदि लेती हैं; कार-दौड़-विश्राम स्थल

**IDM be the pits** (*slang*) to be very bad बहुत ख़राब होना *The food in that restaurant is the pits!*

**pit**[2] /pɪt पिट् / *verb* [T] (**pitting; pitted**) to make small holes in the surface of sth किसी सतह पर छोटे-छोटे गड्ढे या सुराख़ बनाना *The front of the building was pitted with bullet marks.*

**PHR V pit A against B** to test one person or thing against another in a fight or competition मुक़ाबले में एक व्यक्ति या वस्तु के विरुद्ध दूसरे को खड़ा करना *The two strongest teams were pitted against each other in the final.*

**pitch**[1] /pɪtʃ पिच् / *noun* **1** [C] a special area of ground where you play certain sports कुछ खेल जैसे क्रिकेट, खेलने के लिए मैदान का विशेष क्षेत्र; पिच, खेल-पट्टी *a football/hockey/cricket pitch* ⇨ **court** और **field** देखिए। **2** [*sing.*] the strength or level of feelings, activity, etc. भावनाओं, गतिविधियों आदि की तीव्रता या स्तर *The children's excitement almost reached fever pitch.* **3** [U] how high or low a sound is, especially a musical note स्वर की ऊँचाई का स्तर (विशेषतः संगीत में) **4** [C] talk or arguments used by sb who is trying to sell sth or persuade sb to do sth किसी काम के लिए प्रेरित करने वाले तर्क या बातें *a sales pitch* ○ *to make a pitch for sth*

**pitch**[2] /pɪtʃ पिच् / *verb* **1** [T] to set sth at a particular level किसी वस्तु को स्तर-विशेष पर स्थापित करना *The talk was pitched at people with far more experience than me.* **2** [I, T] to throw sth/sb; to be thrown (गेंद आदि को) फेंकना; कुछ फेंका जाना *Dilshad pitched his can into the bushes.* **3** [T] to put up a tent or tents तंबू लगाना *They pitched their tents in the valley.* **4** [T] **pitch sth (at sb)** to try to sell a product to a particular group of people or in a particular way कुछ ख़ास लोगों को या ख़ास तरीक़े से कोई ख़ास चीज़ बेचने की कोशिश करना *This new breakfast cereal is being pitched at kids.*

**PHR V pitch in** (*informal*) to join in and work together with other people दूसरों के साथ एकजुट होकर काम करना *Everybody pitched in to clear up the flood damage.*

**pitch-black** *adj.* completely dark; with no light at all घुप्प अँधेरा; रोशनी एकदम नहीं

**pitcher** /ˈpɪtʃə(r) ˈपिच(र्) / *noun* [C] **1** a large container for holding and pouring liquids द्रव पदार्थों के लिए बड़ा बर्तन (सुराही, घड़ा, जग आदि); पिचर **2** (in baseball) the player who throws (**pitches**) the ball to a player from the other team, who tries to hit it (बेसबॉल में) विरोधी दल को बॉल फेंकने वाला खिलाड़ी

**pitchfork** /ˈpɪtʃfɔːk ˈपिच्फ़ॉक् / *noun* [C] a farm tool like a fork with a long handle and two or three sharp metal points. It is used for lifting and moving dried cut grass (**hay**) खेतों में घास इकट्ठी करने आदि के लिए प्रयुक्त औज़ार; पाँचा ⇨ **gardening** पर चित्र देखिए।

**piteous** /ˈpɪtiəs ˈपिटिअस् / *adj.* (*formal*) that makes you feel pity or sadness दयनीय, करुणाजनक ▶ **piteously** *adv.* दयनीय ढंग से

**pitfall** /ˈpɪtfɔːl ˈपिट्फ़ॉल् / *noun* [C] a danger or difficulty, especially one that is hidden or not obvious ख़तरा या झमेला (विशेषतः जिसका पता न चले)

**pith** /pɪθ पिथ् / *noun* [U] the white substance inside the skin of an orange, lemon, etc. संतरे, नींबू आदि फल का गूदा, मज्जा

**pithy** /ˈpɪθi ˈपिथि / *adj.* expressed in a clear, direct way स्पष्टता से व्यक्त, सारगर्भित *a pithy comment*

**pitiful** /ˈpɪtɪfl ˈपिटिफ़्ल् / *adj.* causing you to feel pity or sadness दयनीय, कारुणिक *the pitiful groans of the wounded soldiers* ▶ **pitifully** /ˈpɪtɪfəli ˈपिटिफ़लि / *adv.* दयनीय ढंग से

**pitiless** /ˈpɪtiləs ˈपिटिलस् / *adj.* having or showing no pity for other people's suffering निर्दय, निष्करुण ▶ **pitilessly** *adv.* निर्दयतापूर्वक

**pittance** /ˈpɪtns ˈपिटन्स् / *noun* [*usually sing.*] a very small amount of money that is less than what sb needs or deserves, received for example as a wage or allowance (आवश्यकता या योग्यतानुसार नहीं) अल्पवेतन या राशि; ख़ैरात *He works for a pittance.*

**pituitary** /pɪˈtjuːɪtəri पिˈट्यूइटरि / (*also* **pituitary gland**) *noun* [C] (*pl.* **pituitaries**) a small organ at the base of the brain that produces substances that affect growth and sexual development (**hormones**) मस्तिष्क के मूल में स्थित हार्मोन-उत्पादक लघु अवयव; पिट्यूटरी ग्लैंड, पीयूष-ग्रंथि

**pity**[1] /ˈpɪti ˈपिटि/ *noun* **1** [U] a feeling of sadness that you have for sb/sth that is suffering or in trouble दया, करुणा, तरस, रहम *The situation is his fault so I don't feel any pity for him.* **2** [*sing.*] something that makes you feel a little sad or disappointed थोड़ा दुखी या निराश करने वाली बात *'You're too late. Tina left five minutes ago.' 'Oh, **what a pity**!'* ○ *It's a pity that Bina couldn't come to the party.*

IDM **take pity on sb** to help sb who is suffering or in trouble because you feel sorry for him/her किसी पर तरस खाकर उसकी मदद करना

**pity**[2] /ˈpɪti ˈपिटि/ *verb* [T] (*pres. part.* **pitying;** *3rd person sing. pres.* **pities;** *pt, pp* **pitied**) to feel pity or sadness for sb who is suffering or in trouble दुखी या संकटग्रस्त व्यक्ति पर दया करना

**pivot**[1] /ˈpɪvət ˈपिवट्/ *noun* [C] **1** the central point on which sth turns or balances पहिए आदि की धुरी या कीली **2** the central or most important person or thing केंद्रबिंदु या सबसे महत्त्वपूर्ण व्यक्ति या वस्तु *West Africa was the pivot of the cocoa trade.*

**pivot**[2] /ˈpɪvət ˈपिवट्/ *verb* [I] to turn or balance on a central point धुरी पर घुमाना या संतुलित करना ▸ **pivotal** *adj.* धुरीय, मूलभूत

**pixel** /ˈpɪksl ˈपिक्सल्/ *noun* [C] (*computing*) any of the very small individual areas on a computer screen, which together form the whole image कंप्यूटर स्क्रीन पर अति सूक्ष्म अपने में संपूर्ण क्षेत्रों में से एक जो मिलकर पूरा चित्र बनाते हैं

**pixie** /ˈpɪksi ˈपिक्सि/ *noun* [C] (in children's stories) a creature like a small person with pointed ears that has magic powers (परी कथाओं में) नुकीले कान तथा जादुई शक्तियों वाला नाटा व्यक्ति

**pizza** /ˈpiːtsə ˈपीट्सा/ *noun* [C, U] an Italian dish consisting of a flat round bread base with vegetables, cheese, meat, etc. on top, which is cooked in an oven इटैलियन खाद्य जिसमें सपाट गोल ब्रेड पर सब्ज़ी, पनीर, मांस आदि रख कर ओवन में पकाया जाता है; पिज़्ज़ा

**pkt** *abbr.* ⇨ **packet** का संक्षिप्त रूप

**pl.** *abbr.* (*grammar*) ⇨ **plural** का संक्षिप्त रूप

**placard** /ˈplækɑːd ˈप्लैकाड्/ *noun* [C] a large written or printed notice that is put in a public place or carried on a stick in a protest march सूचना पत्रक; बड़े आकार की लिखी या छपी सूचना जिसे छड़ी पर चिपकाकर सार्वजनिक स्थान पर रखा जाता है या (विरोध प्रदर्शन में ले जाया जाता है)

**placate** /pləˈkeɪt प्लˈकेट्/ *verb* [T] to make sb feel less angry about sth किसी को शांत करना

**place**[1] /pleɪs प्लेस्/ *noun* [C] **1** a particular position or area विशेष स्थिति या क्षेत्र *Show me the exact place where it happened.* ○ *This would be a good place to sit down and have a rest.* **2** a particular village, town, country, etc. विशेष ग्राम, नगर, देश आदि *Which places did you go to in Sri Lanka?* ○ *Manali is a very beautiful place.* **3** a building or an area that is used for a particular purpose (विशेष काम के लिए) कोई भवन या क्षेत्र *The nearby cafe is a popular **meeting place** for young people.* ○ *The town is full of inexpensive eating places.* **4** a seat or position that can be used by sb/sth (किसी के प्रयोग के लिए) कोई स्थान पद या स्थिति *They went into the classroom and sat down in their places.* ○ *Go on ahead and **save** me **a place** in the queue.*

> NOTE शब्द **place** से तात्पर्य है किसी व्यक्ति या वस्तु के लिए कोई स्थान या स्थिति। जहाँ कार आदि पार्क की जाती हैं उसके लिए शब्द **space** का प्रयोग भी होता है। **Space** और **room** ख़ाली स्थानों का संकेत करते हैं—*This piano **takes up** too much **space**.* ○ *There is enough **room for** three people in the back of the car.*

**5** [*sing.*] your position in society; your role (व्यक्ति की) समाज में स्थिति; भूमिका, कर्तव्य *I feel **it is not my place** to criticize my boss.* **6** an opportunity to study at a college, play for a team, etc. (किसी संस्था में पढ़ने, टीम में खेलने आदि का) अवसर *Sheila has got a place to study law at Delhi.* ○ *Laila is now sure of a place on the team.* **7** the usual or correct position or occasion for sth किसी वस्तु के लिए सामान्य या उचित स्थिति या अवसर *The room was tidy. Everything had been put away **in its place**.* ○ *A funeral is not the place to discuss business.* **8** the position of a number after the **decimal point** दशमलव बिंदु के बाद की संख्या *Your answer should be correct to three decimal places.* **9** [*sing.*] (*spoken*) a person's home (व्यक्ति का) घर, रहने की जगह *Her parents have got a place in Darjeeling.* **10** [*usually sing.*] the position that you have at the end of a race, competition, etc. खेल-कूद, स्पर्धा के अंत में प्राप्त स्थान *Manish finished **in second place**.*

IDM **all over the place** everywhere सर्वत्र, सब जगह

**change/swap places (with sb)** to take sb's seat, position, etc. and let him/her have yours किसी से स्थान, स्थिति आदि की अदला-बदली करना

**fall/slot into place** (used about sth that is complicated or difficult to understand) to become organized or clear in your mind (किसी जटिल या कठिन स्थिति का) व्यवस्थित या स्पष्ट हो जाना *After two weeks in my new job, everything suddenly started to fall into place.*

**in my, your, etc. place/shoes** in my, your, etc. situation or position (मेरी, आपकी आदि) स्थिति या दशा में *If I were in your place I would wait a year before getting married.*

**in place 1** in the correct or usual position उचित या हमेशा के स्थान पर *Use tape to hold the picture in place.* **2** (used about plans or preparations) finished and ready to be used (योजनाएँ या तैयारियाँ) पूरी और इस्तेमाल के लिए उपलब्ध

**in place of sb/sth; in sb/sth's place** instead of sb/sth व्यक्ति या वस्तु के स्थान पर

**in the first, second, etc. place** (*informal*) used when you are giving a list of reasons for sth or explaining sth; firstly, secondly, etc. पहली बात, दूसरी बात आदि (कारण गिनाने या कुछ समझाने के लिए प्रयुक्त); पहला, दूसरा आदि

**out of place 1** not suitable for a particular situation किसी स्थिति विशेष के लिए अनुपयुक्त *I felt very out of place among all those teenagers.* **2** not in the correct or usual place सही या हमेशा के स्थान पर नहीं

**put sb in his/her place** to show that sb is not as clever, important, etc. as he/she believes किसी को उसकी हैसियत या औक़ात बता देना *It really put her in her place when she failed to qualify for the race.*

**put yourself in sb's place** to imagine that you are in the same situation as sb else मन-ही मन अपने को दूसरे की स्थिति में देखना

**take place** (used about a meeting, an event, etc.) to happen (बैठक, घटना आदि का) घटित होना *The ceremony took place in an ancient church.*

**place²** /pleɪs प्लेस्/ *verb* [T] **1** (*formal*) to put sth carefully or deliberately in a particular position विशेष स्थान पर कोई वस्तु रखना (सावधानी से या जानबूझकर) *The chairs had all been placed in neat rows.* ○ *The poster was placed where everyone could see it.* **2** to put sb in a particular position or situation किसी को विशेष दशा या स्थिति में डाल देना *His behaviour placed me in a difficult situation.* ○ *to place sb in charge* **3** used to express the attitude that sb has to sb/sth किसी के विषय में कोई धारणा रखना *We placed our trust in you and you failed us.* ○ *The blame for the disaster was placed firmly on the company.* **4** (*usually in negative statements*) to recognize sb/sth and be able to identify sb/it किसी को पहचान लेना या सकना *Her face is familiar but I just can't place her.* **5** to give instructions about sth or to ask for sth to happen किसी को निर्देश या आदेश देना *to place a bet on sth* ○ *to place an order for sth*

**place name** *noun* [C] the name of a city, town, etc. किसी स्थान (नगर, क़स्बा आदि) का नाम

**placenta** /plə'sentə प्ल'सेन्टा/ *noun* [C] the material inside the part of a woman's body where a baby grows (**womb**) which protects the baby and supplies the food through a tube (**umbilical cord**) अपरा, गर्भनाल, खेड़ी (माता के गर्भाशय का अंग जो शिशु को सुरक्षा देता है और भोजन पहुँचाता है)

**placid** /'plæsɪd 'प्लैसिड्/ *adj.* (used about a person or an animal) calm and not easily excited (व्यक्ति या पशु) शांत और जल्दी उत्तेजित न होने वाला ▶ **placidly** *adv.* शांत भाव से

**plagiarism** /'pleɪdʒərɪzəm 'प्लेजरिज़म्/ *noun* [U, C] the act of copying another person's ideas, words or work and pretending they are your own; sth that has been copied in this way किसी के विचारों, शब्दों या कृति को अपना बता कर प्रयोग करने की क्रिया; इस प्रकार चोरी किए गए विचार आदि ▶ **plagiarize** (*also* **-ise**) /'pleɪdʒəraɪz 'प्लेजराइज़्/ *verb* [T, I] दूसरों के विचार आदि की चोरी करना, साहित्यिक चोरी करना

**plague¹** /pleɪg प्लेग्/ *noun* **1** [C, U] any infectious disease that spreads quickly and kills many people तेज़ी से फैलने वाला कोई भी संक्रामक रोग जिससे बड़ी संख्या में रोगियों की मृत्यु हो जाती है **2 the plague** [U] an infectious disease spread by rats that causes swellings on the body, a very high temperature and often results in death चूहों से फैलने वाला संक्रमणात्मक रोग; प्लेग, इसमें रोगी का शरीर सूज जाता है, तापमान बढ़ जाता है और प्रायः मृत्यु हो जाती है **3** [C] **a plague of sth** a large number of unpleasant animals or insects that come into an area at one time किसी इलाक़े में बड़ी संख्या में गंदे पशुओं या कीड़े-मकोड़ों का एक ही वक़्त में आ जाना *a plague of ants/locusts*

**plague²** /pleɪg प्लेग्/ *verb* [T] to cause sb/sth a lot of trouble किसी के लिए मुसीबतें खड़ी करना *The project was plagued by a series of disasters.*

**plaice** /pleɪs प्लेस्/ *noun* [C, U] (*pl.* **plaice**) a type of flat sea fish that we eat (खाने की) एक प्रकार की चपटी, समुद्री मछली

**plain¹** /pleɪn प्लेन्/ *adj.* **1** easy to see, hear or understand; clear देखने, सुनने, समझने में आसान; स्पष्ट *She **made it plain that** she didn't want to see me* *again.* **2** (used about people, thoughts, actions, etc.) saying what you think; direct and honest (व्यक्ति, विचार, कार्य आदि) मन की बात कह देने वाले, जैसा अंदर वैसा बाहर कहने वाले; सीधे व स्पष्ट *I'll be plain with you. I don't like the idea.* **3** simple in style; not decorated or complicated सादा; सजावट या उलझाव वाले नहीं *My father likes plain Indian cooking.* **4** (*only before a noun*) all one colour; without a pattern on it एक ही रंग का; बिना पैटर्न का *a plain blue jumper* **5** (used especially about a woman or girl) not beautiful or attractive (स्त्री या लड़की) सुंदर या आकर्षक नहीं, सादी, मामूली शकल-सूरत की *She's a rather plain child.*

**plain²** /pleɪn प्लेन् / *noun* [C] a large area of flat land with few trees कम वृक्षों वाला बड़ा समतल इलाक़ा; बड़ा सपाट मैदान

**plain³** /pleɪn प्लेन् / *adv.* (*spoken*) completely पूर्णतः *That's plain silly.*

**plain clothes** *adj.* (used about a police officer) in ordinary clothes; not uniform (पुलिस अफ़सर) सादे कपड़ों में; वरदी में नहीं *a plain-clothes detective* ▶ **plain clothes** *noun* [*pl.*] सादे कपड़ों में पुलिस अफ़सर *officers **in plain clothes***

**plain flour** *noun* [U] flour that does not contain a powder (**baking powder**) which makes cakes, etc. rise बेकिंग पाउडर रहित आटा, सादा आटा ➪ **self-raising flour** देखिए।

**plainly** /ˈpleɪnli ˈप्लेन्लि / *adv.* **1** clearly स्पष्टतया *He was plainly very upset.* **2** using simple words to say sth in a direct and honest way स्पष्टवादिता से *She told him plainly that he was not doing his job properly.* **3** in a simple way, without decoration बिना सजावट के व सादे ढंग से *She was plainly dressed and wore no make-up.*

**plaintiff** /ˈpleɪntɪf ˈप्लेन्टिफ़् / *noun* [C] a person who starts a legal action against sb in a court of law अदालत में किसी पर मुक़दमा दायर करने वाला; वादी, मुद्दई ➪ **defendant** देखिए।

**plaintive** /ˈpleɪntɪv ˈप्लेन्टिव् / *adj.* sounding sad, especially in a weak complaining way दुखी, कातर (विशेषतः शिकायती लहजे में) ▶ **plaintively** *adv.* कातर भाव से

**plait** /plæt प्लैट् / (*AmE* **braid**) *verb* [T] to cross three or more long pieces of hair, rope, etc. over and under each other to make one thick piece बालों आदि की तीन लटों से चोटी बनाना ▶ **plait** *noun* [C] बालों की चोटी

**plan¹** /plæn प्लैन् / *noun* **1** [C] **a plan (for sth/to do sth)** an idea or arrangement for doing or achieving sth in the future योजना, विचार (किसी काम या कुछ करने के लिए) *There has been **a change of plan**—we're meeting at the restaurant.* ○ *If everything **goes according to plan*** (= happens as we planned) *we should be home by midnight.* **2** [C] a detailed map of a building, town, etc. मकान, शहर आदि का पूरा विवरण देने वाला नक़्शा ***a street plan** of Delhi.* **3 plans** [*pl.*] detailed drawings of a building, machine, road, etc. that show its size, shape and measurements किसी भवन, मशीन, सड़क आदि के (आकार, शकल और माप के) ब्योरे वाले नक़्शे *We're getting an architect to **draw up** some **plans** for a new kitchen.* **4** [C] a diagram that shows how sth is to be organized or arranged विषय वस्तु आदि की व्यवस्था को प्रदर्शित करने वाली; रूपरेखा *Before you start writing an essay, it's a good idea to make a brief plan.*

**plan²** /plæn प्लैन् / *verb* (**pla<u>nn</u>ing; pla<u>nn</u>ed**) **1** [I, T] **plan (sth) (for sth)** to decide, organize

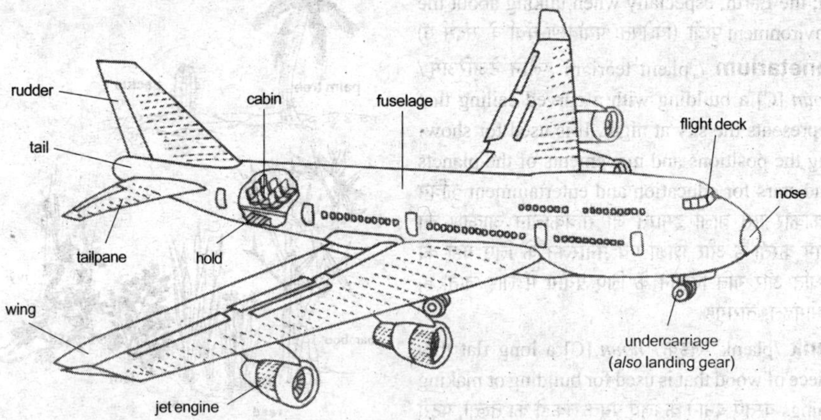


**plane**

or prepare for sth you want to do in the future भविष्य के कामों के विषय में निर्णय करना, उन्हें व्यवस्थित या उनकी तैयारी करना; योजना बनाना *to plan for the future* ○ *You need to plan your work more carefully.* 2 [I, T] **plan (on sth/doing sth); plan (to do sth)** to intend or expect to do sth कुछ करने का इरादा या उसकी आशा करना *I'm planning on having a holiday in July.* ○ *We plan to arrive at about 4 o'clock.* 3 [T] to make a diagram or a design of sth किसी वस्तु का आरेख या नक़्शा बनाना *The new shopping centre is very badly planned.* ▶ **planning** *noun* [U] योजना-निर्माण (की क्रिया); नियोजन *The project requires careful planning.*

**plane[1]** /pleɪn प्लेन्/ *noun* [C] 1 a vehicle that can fly through the air, with wings and one or more engines विमान, वायुयान, हवाई जहाज़ *Has her plane landed yet?* ➪ पृष्ठ 901 पर चित्र देखिए। 2 a tool used for making the surface of wood smooth by taking very thin pieces off it बढ़ई का रंदा; एक औज़ार जिसे चलाकर लकड़ी की सतह चिकनी की जाती है ➪ **tool** पर चित्र देखिए। 3 (*technical*) a flat surface समतल सतह

**plane[2]** /pleɪn प्लेन्/ *verb* [T] to make the surface of a piece of wood flat and smooth using a **plane[1] 2** रंदे से लकड़ी की सतह को चिकना करना

**plane[3]** /pleɪn प्लेन्/ *adj.* (*only before a noun*) (*technical*) completely flat; level पूर्णत: सपाट; समतल *a plane mirror*

**planet** /ˈplænɪt ˈप्लैनिट्/ *noun* 1 [C] a very large round object in space that moves around the sun or another star ग्रह (अंतरिक्ष में एक पिंड जो सूर्य या दूसरे तारे की परिक्रमा करता है) *the planets of our solar system* 2 **the planet** [*sing.*] the world we live in; the Earth, especially when talking about the environment पृथ्वी (विशेषत: पर्यावरण-चर्चा के संदर्भ में)

**planetarium** /ˌplænɪˈteəriəm ˌप्लैनिˈटेअरिअम्/ *noun* [C] a building with a curved ceiling that represents the sky at night. It is used for showing the positions and movements of the planets and stars for education and entertainment कृत्रिम वक्राकार छत वाली इमारत जो रात्रिकालीन आकाश का काम करती है और शिक्षा एवं मनोरंजन के लिए ग्रहों की स्थिति और गति दिखाने के लिए प्रयोग में लाई जाती है; नभोमंडल, तारागृह

**plank** /plæŋk प्लैङ्क्/ *noun* [C] a long flat thin piece of wood that is used for building or making things वस्तुएँ बनाने के लिए प्रयुक्त लकड़ी का तख़्ता, पटरा ➪ **vice** पर चित्र देखिए।

**plankton** /ˈplæŋktən ˈप्लैङ्क्टन्/ *noun* [U, *pl.*] the very small forms of plant and animal life that live in seas, rivers, lakes, etc. समुद्र, नदी या झील में रहने वाले सूक्ष्म जीव (वनस्पति या जंतु)

**planned economy** (*also* **command economy**) *noun* [C] an economy in which levels of pay, prices, production, etc. are decided by the government शासन-नियंत्रण अर्थव्यवस्था जिसमें कर्मचारियों के वेतन, वस्तुओं के मूल्य, उत्पादन आदि का निर्णय सरकार करती है

**planner** /ˈplænə(r) ˈप्लैन(र्)/ *noun* [C] 1 (*also* **town planner**) a person whose job is to plan the growth and development of a town नगर के विकास और संवर्धन की योजना का निर्माता 2 a person who makes plans for a particular area of activity कार्यक्षेत्र-विशेष के लिए योजना का निर्माता *curriculum planners* 3 a book, computer program, etc. that contains dates and is used for recording information, arranging meetings, etc. तिथियों वाली पुस्तक, कंप्यूटर प्रोग्राम आदि जिसमें आवश्यक जानकारी, बैठकों की व्यवस्था आदि दर्ज होते हैं

**plant[1]** /plɑːnt प्लान्ट्/ *noun* [C] 1 a living thing that grows in the ground and usually has leaves, a long thin green central part (**a stem**) and roots पौधा *a tomato plant* ○ *a plant pot* (= a container for plants) ➪ **flower** पर चित्र देखिए। 2 a very

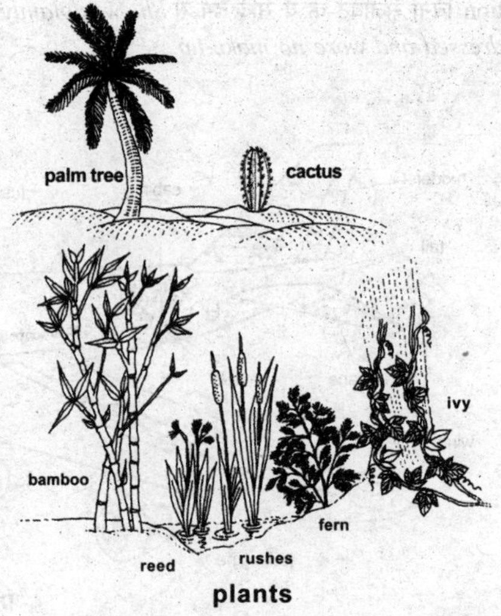

plants

large factory बहुत बड़ा कारख़ाना; फ़ैक्टरी, प्लांट, संयंत्र *a car plant* ○ *a nuclear reprocessing plant*

**plant**[2] /plɑːnt प्लान्ट्/ *verb* [T] **1** to put plants, seeds, etc. in the ground to grow ज़मीन में उगने के लिए पौधे लगाना, बीज बोना **2 plant sth (with sth)** to cover or supply a garden, area of land, etc. with plants बग़ीचे, खेत आदि में सब जगह पौधे लगा देना या बीज बो देना *The field's been planted with wheat this year.* **3** to put yourself/sth firmly in a particular place or position स्थान-विशेष या पद-विशेष पर अपनी स्थिति को सुदृढ़ कर लेना *He planted himself in the best seat.* **4 plant sth (on sb)** to hide sth, especially sth illegal, in sb's clothing, property, etc., often in order to make him/her seem guilty of a crime किसी के यहाँ (उसके घर, कपड़ों आदि में) कोई गै. र-क़ानूनी वस्तु छिपाकर रख देना प्रायः उसे अपराधी साबित करने के लिए *The police think that terrorists may have* ***planted the bomb***. ○ *The women claimed that the drugs had been planted on them.*

**plantain** /ˈplæntɪn; -teɪn ˈप्लैनूटिन्; -टेन्/ *noun* [C, U] a fruit similar to a **banana** but larger and less sweet, that is cooked and eaten as a vegetable केले जैसा, परंतु उससे बड़ा और कम मीठा, फल जिसे सब्ज़ी की तरह प्रयुक्त किया जाता है

**plantation** /plɑːnˈteɪʃn प्लान्ˈटेश्न्/ *noun* [C] **1** a large area of land, especially in a hot country, where tea, cotton, tobacco, etc. are grown चाय, कपास, तंबाकू आदि उगाने के लिए बड़े खेत (विशेषतः गरम देशों में) *a coffee plantation* **2** an area of land where trees are grown to produce wood अरण्य भूमि, वनस्थली

**plaque** /plɑːk प्लाक्/ *noun* **1** [C] a flat piece of stone or metal, usually with names and dates on it, that is fixed on a wall in memory of a famous person or event दीवार में लगाई गई पत्थर या धातु की पट्टिका जिस पर व्यक्ति या घटना की स्मृति में उसका नाम और तिथि अंकित होते हैं, स्मृति-पट्टिका; फलक **2** [U] a harmful substance that forms on your teeth दाँतों पर जम जाने वाली हानिकर परत

**plasma** /ˈplæzmə ˈप्लैज़्मा/ (*also* **plasm** /ˈplæzəm ˈप्लाज़म्/) *noun* [U] the colourless liquid part of blood, in which the blood cells, etc. float रक्त का रंगहीन तरल भाग जिसमें रक्त-कोशिकाएँ तैरती हैं; प्लाविका, प्लाज़्मा

**plaster**[1] /ˈplɑːstə(r) ˈप्लास्ट(र्)/ *noun* **1** [U] a mixture of a special powder and water that becomes hard when it is dry. Plaster is put on walls and ceilings to form a smooth surface दीवार, छत आदि पर लगाने का प्लास्टर जो पानी में विशेष चूरा मिलाने से बनता है; पलस्तर **2** (*also* **sticking plaster**) [C] a small piece of sticky material that is used to cover a cut, etc. on the body घाव आदि पर चिपकाने के लिए प्रयुक्त एक चिपचिपी वस्तु; प्लास्टर **3** (*also* **plaster of Paris**) [U] a white powder that is mixed with water and becomes hard when dry. It is used for putting round broken bones, etc. until they get better टूटी हड्डी पर उपचार के लिए लगाया गया प्लास्टर *When Dev broke his leg it was* ***in plaster*** *for six weeks.*

**plaster**[2] /ˈplɑːstə(r) ˈप्लास्ट(र्)/ *verb* [T] **1** to cover a wall, etc. with **plaster**[1] **1** to make the surface smooth दीवार आदि पर प्लास्टर करना (सतह को चिकना करने के लिए) **2 plaster sb/sth (in/with sth)** to cover sb/sth with a large amount of sth किसी व्यक्ति, स्थान या वस्तु को किसी अन्य वस्तु से पाट देना *He plastered his walls with posters.*

**plaster cast** *noun* [C] **1** a case made of **plaster of Paris** that covers a broken bone and protects it टूटी हड्डी की सुरक्षा के लिए उसे ढक कर रखने वाला प्लास्टर आफ़ पैरिस से बना साँचा **2** a copy of sth, made using **plaster of Paris** प्लास्टर ऑफ़ पैरिस से बनी किसी वस्तु की नक़ल या प्रतिकृति *They took a plaster cast of the teeth for identification purposes.*

**plastic**[1] /ˈplæstɪk ˈप्लैस्टिक्/ *noun* [C, U] a light, strong material that is made with chemicals and is used for making many different sorts of objects रसायनों से बनी हलकी मज़बूत वस्तु जिससे अनेक तरह की वस्तुएँ बनती हैं; प्लास्टिक

**plastic**[2] /ˈplæstɪk ˈप्लैस्टिक्/ *adj.* made of plastic प्लास्टिक से बना *plastic cups* ○ *a plastic bag*

**plastic surgery** *noun* [U] a medical operation to repair or replace damaged skin or to improve the appearance of a person's face or body क्षतिग्रस्त त्वचा के उपचार या व्यक्ति के चेहरे या शरीर के बाहरी रूप में सुधार के लिए शल्य-क्रिया; प्लास्टिक सर्जरी ➪ **facelift** और **surgery** भी देखिए।

**plate**[1] /pleɪt प्लेट्/ *noun* [C] **1** a flat, usually round, dish for eating or serving food from प्लेट, तश्तरी (जिस पर भोजन रखकर परोसा या खाया जाता है) *a plastic/paper/china plate* ○ *a plate of food*

> NOTE मुख्य भोजन (प्रायः औपचारिक अवसरों में) **dinner plate** में रखकर खाया जाता है। ब्रेड आदि को **side plate** में रखा जाता है। अन्न से बने पदार्थ या फिरनी आदि पुडिंग **bowl** में खाए जाते है।

**2** a thin flat piece of metal or glass धातु या काँच की पतली चद्दर *a steel/metal plate* **3** a flat piece of metal with sth written on it नाम आदि से अंकित धातु-पट्टिका *The brass plate beside the door said*

*'Dr Walia'*. **4** metal that has a thin covering of gold or silver सोने या चाँदी की पत्तर चढ़ी धातु *gold/silver plate* **5** (in geology) one of the sheets of rock that cover the earth's surface (भूविज्ञान में) भूसतह बनाने वाली बड़ी चट्टान की परत ➪ **plate tectonics** देखिए।

**plate²** /pleɪt प्लेट्/ *verb* [T] (*usually passive*) (*technical*) **1** to cover a metal with a thin layer of another metal, especially gold or silver किसी अन्य धातु (विशेषतः सोना या चाँदी) की पतली चद्दर चढ़ी कोई धातु *a silver ring plate with gold* **2** to cover sth with sheets of metal or another hard substance धातु की चद्दरों या अन्य किसी कठोर पदार्थ से किसी वस्तु (जैसे दीवार) को मढ़ देना *The walls of the vault were plated with steel.*

**plateau** /ˈplætəʊ ˈप्लैटो/ *noun* [C] (*pl.* **plateaus** /-təʊ -टो/ **1** a large high area of flat land ऊँचाई पर स्थित फैली हुई समतल भूमि; पठार ➪ **limestone** पर चित्र देखिए। **2** a state where there is little development or change स्थिर स्थिति (जिसमें विकास या परिवर्तन की संभावना नगण्य हो) *House prices seem to have* ***reached a plateau***.

**plateful** /ˈpleɪtfʊl ˈप्लेट्फ़ुल्/ *noun* [C] the amount of food that a **plate 1** can hold थाली-भर भोजन

**platelet** /ˈpleɪtlət ˈप्लेट्लट्/ *noun* [C] a very small blood cell, shaped like a disc. Platelets make your blood become thicker so that it **clots** when you cut yourself तश्तरी के आकार की बहुत छोटी रक्त-कोशिका; प्लेटलट इससे रक्त गाढ़ा होता है और कभी किसी अंग के कट जाने पर ख़ून का बहना रुक जाता है

**plate tectonics** *noun* [U] (in geology) the movements of the large sheets of rock (**plates**) that form the earth's surface; the scientific study of these movements (भूविज्ञान में) भूसतह बनाने वाली चट्टान की बड़ी परतों में होने वाली हलचल; इस हलचल की क्रिया का वैज्ञानिक अध्ययन ➪ **continental drift** देखिए।

**platform** /ˈplætfɔːm ˈप्लैट्फ़ॉम्/ *noun* [C] **1** the place where you get on or off trains at a railway station रेलवे स्टेशन का प्लेटफ़ार्म *Which platform does the train to Jaipur leave from?* **2** a flat surface, higher than the level of the floor or ground, on which public speakers or performers stand so that the audience can see them सभा-मंडप का ऊँचा चबूतरा (जहाँ से वक्ता भाषण देते हैं या कलाकार अपना प्रदर्शन करते हैं) **3** [*usually sing.*] the ideas and aims of a political party who want to be elected चुनाव लड़ने वाले राजनीतिक दल के विचार और उद्देश्य *They fought the election on a platform of low taxes.*

**platinum** /ˈplætɪnəm ˈप्लैटिनम्/ *noun* [U] (*symbol* **Pt**) a silver-grey metal that is often used for making expensive jewellery एक हलके रुपहले रंग की धातु जिससे महँगे आभूषण बनते हैं; प्लेटिनम *a platinum wedding ring*

**platonic** /pləˈtɒnɪk प्लˈटॉनिक्/ *adj.* (used about a relationship between two people) friendly but not sexual (दो व्यक्तियों के बीच संबंध) वासनारहित मैत्री वाला, निष्काम (प्रेम)

**platoon** /pləˈtuːn प्लˈटून्/ *noun* [C] a small group of soldiers छोटी सैनिक टुकड़ी, पलटन

**plausible** /ˈplɔːzəbl ˈप्लॉज़बल्/ *adj.* that you can believe; reasonable विश्वसनीय; तर्कसंगत *a plausible excuse* ✪ विलोम **implausible**

**play¹** /pleɪ प्ले/ *verb* **1** [I] **play (with sb/sth)** to do sth to enjoy yourself; to have fun खेलना; मज़े करना *The children have been playing on the beach all day.* ○ *Ria's found a new friend to play with.* **2** [I, T] to take part in a game or sport किसी खेल में भाग लेना *She played him at table tennis and won.* ○ *Who's Brazil playing next in the World Cup?* **3** [I, T] **play (sth) (on sth)** to make music with a musical instrument कोई वाद्य यंत्र बजाना *to play the piano/guitar/trumpet* ○ *She played a few notes on the violin.* **4** [T] to turn on a CD, video, tape, etc. so that it produces sound कोई सीडी वीडियो, टेप आदि बजाना *Shall I play the CD for you again?* **5** [I, T] to act in a play, film, television programme, etc.; to act the role of sb किसी नाटक, फ़िल्म, टीवी कार्यक्रम आदि में भाग लेना; किसी चरित्र की भूमिका करना *Riya is going to play Shakuntala.*

> **NOTE** **Play a part, role** आदि का प्रयोग प्रायः आलंकारिक रूप में होता है—*India has played an active part in the recent discussions.* ○ *Jatin played a key role in organizing the protest.*

**6** [I] (*formal*) to move quickly and lightly लहराना, नाचना, अठखेलियाँ करना *Sunlight played on the surface of the sea.*

> **NOTE** **Play** से बनने वाले मुहावरों के लिए संबंधित संज्ञाओं, विशेषणों आदि की प्रविष्टियाँ देखिए। उदाहरण के लिए **play it by ear** की प्रविष्टि **ear** में मिलेगी।

**PHR V** **play at sth/being sth** to do sth with little interest or effort बिना विशेष रुचि या प्रयास के कोई कार्य करना *He's only playing at studying. He'd prefer to get a job now.* ○ *What is that driver playing at* (= doing)?

**play sth back (to sb)** to turn on and watch or listen to a film, tape, etc. that you have recorded

रिकॉर्ड किए हुए टेप, फ़िल्म आदि को चलाना (देखना या सुनना) *Play that last scene back to me again.*

**play sth down** to make sth seem less important than it really is किसी बात के वास्तविक महत्त्व को कम करके दिखाना *to play down a crisis*

**play A off against B** to make people compete or argue with each other, especially for your own advantage लोगों को एक दूसरे से भिड़ा देना, विशेषतः अपने लाभ के लिए *I think she enjoys playing one friend off against another.*

**play on sth** to use and take advantage of sb's fears or weaknesses किसी के भय या दुर्बलता का (अनुचित) लाभ उठाना और स्वार्थपूर्ति में उसका उपयोग करना *This advertising campaign plays on people's fears of illness.*

**play (sb) up** (*informal*) to cause sb trouble or pain किसी को परेशान करना या तकलीफ़ पहुँचाना *The car always plays up in wet weather.*

**play**[2] /pleɪ प्ले / *noun* **1** [C] a piece of writing performed by actors in the theatre, or on television or radio रंगमंच, टीवी या रेडियो पर प्रस्तुत नाटक *Would you like to see a play while you're in Mumbai?* ○ *a radio/television play*

> NOTE अभिनेता और अभिनेत्रियाँ नाटक को **rehearse** करते हैं। थियेटर कंपनी, ड्रामा ग्रुप आदि नाटक को **produce** करते हैं। नाटक का मंचन प्रायः **stage** पर होता है।

**2** [U] the playing of a game or sport खेल, खेल-प्रदर्शन *Bad weather stopped play yesterday.*

> NOTE हम टेनिस, फ़ुटबॉल आदि के लिए **play** का प्रयोग करते हैं परंतु **a play** of tennis ऐसा प्रयोग नहीं किया जा सकता। सही प्रयोग है **a game** of tennis.

**3** [U] activity done for enjoyment only, especially by children केवल मनबहलाव की कोई क्रिया (विशेषतः बच्चों की) *Young children learn through play.* ○ *the happy sound of children **at play*** **4** [U] a control on a video or cassette player, etc. that you press to start the tape running वीडियो या कैसेट प्लेयर आदि पर कोई नियंत्रणकारी बटन (जिसे दबाकर टेप को चलाया जाता है) *Put the video into the machine then **press play**.*

IDM **fair play** ⇨ **fair**[1] देखिए।

**playback singer** *noun* [C] (*IndE*) a singer who records songs for use in films and the actors mouth (= move their lips as if they were singing) the words of the songs for the camera पार्शर्व गायक *Lata Mangeshkar is a well-known playback singer of India.*

**playboy** /ˈpleɪbɔɪ ˈप्लेबॉइ / *noun* [C] a rich man who spends his time enjoying himself भोग-विलास में मग्न धनी व्यक्ति; खिलंदड़ा, रसिक

**player** /ˈpleɪə(r) ˈप्लेअ(र्) / *noun* [C] **1** a person who plays a game or sport खिलाड़ी *a game for four players* ○ *She's an excellent tennis player.* **2** (*used to form compound nouns*) a machine on which you can listen to sound that has been recorded on CD, tape, etc. सीडी, कैसेट आदि को बजाने की मशीन *a CD/cassette player* **3** a person who plays a musical instrument वाद्य यंत्र को बजाने वाला व्यक्ति; वादक *a piano player*

**playful** /ˈpleɪfl ˈप्लेफ़्ल् / *adj.* **1** done or said in fun; not serious विनोदपूर्ण रीति से कहा या किया गया; हलका-फुलका, अगंभीर *a playful remark* **2** full of fun; wanting to play विनोदप्रिय, विनोदी स्वभाव का; खेलने का इच्छुक, खेलवाड़ी *a playful puppy*

**playground** /ˈpleɪgraʊnd ˈप्लेग्राउन्ड् / *noun* [C] an area of land where children can play खेल का मैदान, क्रीड़ा-स्थल *the school playground*

**playgroup** /ˈpleɪgru:p ˈप्लेग्रूप् / (*also* **playschool** /ˈpleɪsku:l ˈप्लेस्कूल् /) (*BrE*) = **nursery school**

**playhouse** /ˈpleɪhaʊs ˈप्लेहाउस् / *noun* **1** [*sing.*] used in the name of some theatres कुछ थियेटरों के नाम में प्रयुक्त *the Liverpool Playhouse* **2** [C] a model of a house for children to play in मकान का लघु नमूना जिसमें बच्चे खेलते हैं

**playing card** = **card 4**

**playing field** *noun* [C] a large field used for sports such as cricket and football क्रिकेट, फ़ुटबॉल आदि खेलने का बड़ा मैदान

IDM **a level playing field** ⇨ **level**[2] देखिए।

**play-off** *noun* [C] a match between two teams or players who have equal scores to decide the winner बराबरी पर छूटे खिलाड़ियों या टीमों के बीच निर्णायक मैच

**plaything** /ˈpleɪθɪŋ ˈप्लेथिङ् / *noun* [C] (*formal*) a toy कोई खिलौना

**playtime** /ˈpleɪtaɪm ˈप्लेटाइम् / *noun* [C, U] a period of time between lessons when children at school can go outside to play पाठशाला में पढ़ाई के बीच खेलने का समय

**playwright** /ˈpleɪraɪt ˈप्लेराइट् / *noun* [C] a person who writes plays for the theatre, television or radio नाटककार

**plea** /pli: प्ली / *noun* [C] **1** (*formal*) **a plea (for sth)** an important and emotional request सशक्त और भावुक निवेदन; याचना, अपील *a plea for help* **2 a plea of sth** a statement made by or for sb in a court of law न्यायालय में सफ़ाई या दलील *a plea of guilty/not guilty*

**plead** /pli:d प्लीड् / *verb* **1** [I] **plead (with sb) (to do/for sth)** to ask sb for sth in a very strong and serious way गंभीरतापूर्वक याचना करना, चिरौरी करना *She pleaded with him not to leave her.* ○ *He pleaded for mercy.* **2** [I, T] to state in a court of law that you did or did not do a crime न्यायालय में सफ़ाई देना *The defendant **pleaded not guilty** to the charge of theft.* **3** [I, T] **plead (sth) (for sb/sth)** (used especially about a lawyer in a court of law) to support sb's case (वकील द्वारा न्यायालय में) किसी की वकालत करना *He needs the very best lawyer to plead (his case) for him.* **4** [T] to give sth as an excuse or explanation for sth किसी मामले में कुछ बहाना बनाना या सफ़ाई देना *He pleaded family problems as the reason for his lack of concentration.*

**pleasant** /ˈpleznt ˈप्लेज़्न्ट्/ *adj.* nice, enjoyable or friendly सुहाना, आनंददायक या अनुकूल *a pleasant evening/climate/place/view* ○ *a pleasant smile/voice/manner* ✪ विलोम **unpleasant** ▶**pleasantly** *adv.* सुखद ढंग से, सुखपूर्वक

**please**[1] /pli:z प्लीज़्/ *exclamation* **1** used as a polite way of asking for sth or telling sb to do sth (किसी से विनम्र अनुरोध करने के लिए प्रयुक्त) कृपया *Come in, please.* ○ *Please don't spend too much money.* **2** used when you are accepting an offer of sth politely किसी की पेशकश को मान लेने के लिए शिष्टोक्ति; जी हाँ, हाँ जी *'Sugar?' 'Yes, please.'* ✪ विलोम **no, thank you**

**please**[2] /pli:z प्लीज़्/ *verb* **1** [I, T] to make sb happy; to satisfy किसी को खुश या प्रसन्न करना; संतुष्ट करना *There's just no pleasing some people* (= some people are impossible to please). **2** [I] (not used as the main verb in a sentence; used after words like 'as', 'what', 'whatever', 'anything', etc.) to want; to choose (वाक्य में यह शब्द मुख्य क्रिया बन कर नहीं आता अपितु 'as', 'what', 'whatever', 'anything' आदि के बाद इसका प्रयोग होता है) चाहना; पसंद करना *You can't always **do as you please**.* ○ *She has so much money she can buy anything she pleases.*

IDM **please yourself** to be able to do whatever you want अपनी इच्छा के अनुसार कुछ कर पाना; अपनी मन मरज़ी कर पाना *Without anyone else to cook for, I can please myself what I eat.*

**pleased** /pli:zd प्लीज़्ड्/ *adj.* (*not before a noun*) **pleased (with sb/sth); pleased to do sth; pleased that...** happy or satisfied about sth किसी बात के लिए प्रसन्न या संतुष्ट *Jai seems very pleased with his new car.* ○ *We're **only too pleased** (= very happy) to help.* ➪ **glad** पर नोट देखिए। ✪ विलोम **displeased**

**pleasing** /ˈpli:zɪŋ ˈप्लीज़िङ्/ *adj.* giving you pleasure and satisfaction सुखकर और संतोषप्रद *The exam results are very pleasing this year.* ✪ विलोम **displeasing**

**pleasurable** /ˈpleʒərəbl ˈप्लेशरबल्/ *adj.* (*formal*) enjoyable ख़ुशी प्रदान करने वाला, सुखद *a pleasurable experience*

**pleasure** /ˈpleʒə(r) ˈप्लेश़(र्)/ *noun* **1** [U] the feeling of being happy or satisfied प्रसन्नता या संतुष्टि *Parents **get** a lot **of pleasure out of** watching their children grow up.* ○ ***It gives me great pleasure** to introduce our next speaker.* **2** [U] enjoyment (rather than work) आनंद (न कि कोई काम) *What brings you to Paris—business or pleasure?* **3** [C] an event or activity, that you enjoy or that makes you happy सुखद या आनंददायक घटना या गतिविधि *It's been a pleasure to work with you.* ○ *'Thanks for your help.' **'It's a pleasure.'***

IDM **take (no) pleasure in sth/doing sth** to (not) enjoy (doing) sth कुछ करने का आनंद लेना या न लेना

**with pleasure** used as a polite way of saying that you are happy to do sth कुछ करने में खुशी होगी, यह करने के लिए प्रयुक्त *'Could you give me a lift into town?' 'Yes, with pleasure.'*

**pleat** /pli:t प्लीट्/ *noun* [C] a permanent **fold** that is sewn or pressed into a piece of cloth कपड़े की चुनट (स्थायी रूप से सिली गई) *a skirt with pleats at the front*

**plebiscite** /ˈplebɪsɪt; -saɪt ˈप्लेबिसिट्; -साइट्/ *noun* [C] (*technical*) **a plebiscite (on sth)** a vote by the people of a country or a region on a question that is very important किसी महत्त्वपूर्ण प्रश्न पर किसी देश या क्षेत्र की जनता का मतदान द्वारा निर्णय; जनमत-संग्रह *to hold a plebiscite on the country's future system of government*

**plectrum** /ˈplektrəm ˈप्लेक्ट्रम्/ *noun* [C] a small piece of plastic, metal, etc., that you use to play the strings of a guitar or similar musical instrument instead of using your fingers गिटार, सितार आदि के तार बजाने के लिए प्रयुक्त प्लास्टिक या धातु का छोटा टुकड़ा; मिज़राब

**pledge** /pledʒ प्लेज्/ *noun* [C] **a pledge (to do sth)** a formal promise or agreement औपचारिक वचन या सहमति ▶ **pledge** *verb* [T] **pledge (sth) (to sb/sth)** कुछ करने के लिए औपचारिक वचन देना *The Government has pledged Rs 250,000 to help the victims of the crash.*

**plenary** /ˈpliːnəri ˈप्लीनरि / *adj.* (used about meetings, etc.) that should be attended by everyone who has the right to attend (बैठक, अधिवेशन आदि) जिसमें सभी अधिकार प्राप्त सदस्यों की उपस्थिति आवश्यक हो; पूर्ण, परिपूर्ण *The new committee holds its first* ***plenary session*** *this week.* ▶ **plenary** *noun* [C] (*pl.* **plenaries**) पूर्ण अधिवेशन *the opening/final plenary of the conference*

**plentiful** /ˈplentɪfl ˈप्लेन्टिफ़्ल् / *adj.* available in large amounts or numbers बड़ी मात्रा में राशि में उपलब्ध *Fruit is plentiful at this time of year.* ✪ विलोम **scarce**

**plenty** /ˈplenti ˈप्लेन्टि / *pronoun, adv.* **1 plenty (of sb/sth)** as much or as many of sth as you need प्रचुर, बहुतायत, भरपूर, जितना चाहिए उतना भर *'Shall I get some more coffee?' 'No, we've still got plenty.'* ○ *There's still plenty of time to get there.* ○ **2** (before 'more') a lot ('more' से पहले प्रयुक्त) प्रचुर, ख़ूब सारा *There's plenty more ice cream.* **3** (*informal*) (with 'big', 'long', 'tall', etc. followed by enough) easily ('big', 'long', 'tall' आदि के बाद 'enough' के साथ प्रयुक्त) आसानी से *'This shirt's too small.' 'Well, it looks plenty big enough to me.'*

**pliable** /ˈplaɪəbl ˈप्लाइअब्ल् / (*also* **pliant** /ˈplaɪənt ˈप्लाइअन्ट् /) *adj.* **1** easy to bend or shape जो आसानी से मुड़ सके या आकृति में ढाला जा सके; लचीला, नम्य **2** (used about a person) easy to influence (व्यक्ति) आसानी से प्रभावित होने वाला

**pliers** /ˈplaɪəz ˈप्लाइअज़् / *noun* [*pl.*] a tool made of two crossed pieces of metal with handles, that is used for holding things firmly and for cutting wire वस्तुओं को कसकर पकड़ने और तार काटने के लिए प्रयुक्त चिमटा, चिमटी; प्लास *a pair of pliers* ➪ **tool** पर चित्र देखिए।

**plight** /plaɪt प्लाइट् / *noun* [*sing.*] (*formal*) a bad or difficult state or situation दुर्दशा; प्रतिकूल या कठिन दशा या स्थिति

**plinth** /plɪnθ प्लिन्थ् / *noun* [C] a block of stone on which a column or statue stands पत्थर जिसपर खंभा या मूर्ति खड़ी हो; कुरसी, प्लिंथ

**plod** /plɒd प्लॉड् / *verb* [I] (**plodding; plodded**) **plod (along/on) 1** to walk slowly and in a heavy or tired way भारी क़दमों से या थकी चाल से (धीरे-धीरे) चलना *We plodded on through the rain for nearly an hour.* **2** to make slow progress, especially with difficult or boring work मंदगति से काम में प्रगति करना, विशेषतः जब काम कठिन या उबाऊ हो

**plonk¹** /plɒŋk प्लॉङ्क् / *verb* [T] (*spoken*) **1 plonk sth (down)** to put sth down on sth, especially noisily or carelessly किसी वस्तु को नीचे रखना (विशेषतः झनझनाते हुए या लापरवाही के साथ) *Just plonk your bag down anywhere.* **2 plonk (yourself) (down)** to sit down heavily and carelessly लापरवाही के साथ धम्म से नीचे बैठना *He just plonked himself down in front of the TV.*

**plop¹** /plɒp प्लॉप् / *noun* [C, *usually sing.*] a sound like that of a small object dropping into water छपछप ध्वनि; पानी में किसी छोटी वस्तु के गिरने की आवाज़

**plop²** /plɒp प्लॉप् / *verb* [I] (**plopping; plopped**) to fall making a plopping noise छपछप करते हुए गिरना *The frog plopped back into the water.*

**plot¹** /plɒt प्लॉट् / *noun* [C] **1** the series of events which form the story of a novel, film, etc. नाटक या उपन्यास का कथानक, कथावस्तु *The play had a very weak plot.* ○ *I can't follow the plot of this novel.* **2 a plot (to do sth)** a secret plan made by several people to do sth wrong or illegal कुचक्र (ग़लत या ग़ैर-क़ानूनी काम करने की गुप्त योजना); षड्यंत्र *a plot to kill the president* **3** a small piece of land, used for a special purpose किसी विशेष उपयोग के लिए अंकित छोटा भूखंड *a plot of land*

**plot²** /plɒt प्लॉट् / *verb* (**plotting; plotted**) **1** [I, T] **plot (with sb) (against sb)** to make a secret plan to do sth wrong or illegal षड्यंत्र या कुचक्र रचना *They were accused of plotting against the government.* ○ *The terrorists had been plotting this campaign for years.* **2** [T] to mark sth on a map, diagram, etc. मानचित्र, आरेख आदि पर कुछ अंकित करना *to plot the figures on a graph*

**plough** (*AmE* **plow**) /plaʊ प्लाउ / *noun* [C] a large farm tool which is pulled by a **tractor** or by an animal. A plough turns the soil over ready for seeds to be planted हल, लांगल; खेती का बड़ा औज़ार जिसे ट्रैक्टर या जानवर खींचता है। इससे मिट्टी को बोआई के लिए तैयार किया जाता है ➪ **snowplough** देखिए। ▶ **plough** *verb* [I, T] हल चलाना या जोतना (*figurative*) *The book was long and boring but I managed to plough through it* (= read it with difficulty).

**ploy** /plɔɪ प्लॉइ / *noun* [C] **a ploy (to do sth)** something that you say or do in order to get what you want or to persuade sb to do sth (मनचाही वस्तु पाने या किसी को मनाने के लिए कही गई बात या किया गया काम); चाल, तिकड़म, युक्ति

**pluck¹** /plʌk प्लक् / *verb* [T] **1 pluck sth/sb (from sth/out)** to remove or take sth/sb from a place कहीं से कोई वस्तु हटाना या छीन लेना *He plucked the letter from my hands.* **2** to pull the feathers out of a dead bird in order to prepare it for cooking मृत पक्षी के पंख नोचना (प्रायः पकाने के पूर्व) **3** to make the strings of a musical instrument play notes by moving your fingers across them तार वाले वाद्य पर अँगुलियाँ चलाकर उसे बजाना

IDM **pluck up courage** to try to get enough courage to do sth कुछ करने का साहस जुटाना

PHR V **pluck at sth** to pull sth gently several times किसी वस्तु को अनेक बार हलके-से खींचना (जैसे बच्चे का माँ के कपड़े खींचना)

**pluck²** /plʌk प्लक्/ *noun* [U] (*informal*) courage and determination साहस और दृढ़ निश्चय ▶ **plucky** *adj.* साहसी, हिम्मती

**plug¹** /plʌg प्लग्/ *noun* [C] **1** a plastic or rubber object with two or three metal pins, which connects a piece of electrical equipment to the electricity supply बिजली का प्लग; प्लास्टिक या रबर से बना जिसमें दो या तीन पिन होते हैं **2** a round piece of rubber or plastic that you use to block the hole in a bath, etc. स्नानगृह आदि में छेद बंद करने वाली रबड़ या प्लास्टिक की डाट; प्लग **3** a mention that sb makes of a new book, film, etc. in order to encourage people to buy or see it नई पुस्तक, फ़िल्म आदि की प्रशंसा ताकि लोग पुस्तक ख़रीदें या फ़िल्म देखें

**plug²** /plʌg प्लग्/ *verb* [T] (**plugging; plugged**) **1** to fill or block a hole with sth that fits tightly into it किसी वस्तु से छेद को अच्छी तरह भरना या बंद करना *He managed to plug the leak in the pipe.* **2** (*informal*) to say good things about a new book, film, etc. in order to make people buy or see it नई पुस्तक, फ़िल्म आदि की प्रशंसा करना ताकि लोग उसे ख़रीदें या देखें *They're really plugging that song on the radio at the moment.*

PHR V **plug sth in** to connect a piece of electrical equipment to the electricity supply or to another piece of equipment किसी विद्युत उपकरण को बिजली की आपूर्ति या अन्य उपकरण से जोड़ना *Is the microphone plugged in?* ✪ विलोम **unplug**

**plughole** /ˈplʌghəʊlˈप्लग्होल्/ *noun* [C] (*BrE*) a hole in a bath, etc. where the water flows away स्नानगृह आदि में डाट का सूराख़ जहाँ से पानी बाहर बह जाता है

**plum** /plʌm प्लम्/ *noun* [C] a soft, round fruit with red or yellow skin and a stone in the middle आलूचा, आलूबुख़ारा

**plumage** /ˈplu:mɪdʒˈप्लूमिज्/ *noun* [U] the feathers covering a bird's body पक्षियों के पर

**plumb¹** /plʌm प्लम्/ *verb* [T] **1** to measure the depth of water or check whether things like a wall, etc. are vertical by using a lead weight suspended from a line साहुल सूत्र से पानी की गहराई नापना या दीवार की लंबता जाँचना **2** to successfully and completely understand something mysterious by carefully examining it सावधानीपूर्वक जाँच-पड़ताल कर किसी रहस्य को पूर्णतया समझना; ताड़ लेना *plumbing the mysteries of the human psyche* ✪ पर्याय **fathom**

IDM **plumb the depths of sth** to experience the worst of sth unpleasant अत्यधिक बुरा या अप्रिय अनुभव करना *His latest novel plumbs the depths of horror and violence.*

PHR V **plumb sth... in** (*BrE*) to connect something like toilets, washing machines, etc. to the water supply in a building शौचालय, वॉशिंग मशीन आदि को किसी भवन की जलापूर्ति से जोड़ना

**plumb²** /plʌm प्लम्/ *adv.* **1** (*used before prepositions*) exactly यथार्थता से, बिल्कुल सही तरह से *He was running plumb in the middle of the road.* **2** (*old-fashioned*) (*AmE informal*) completely पूर्णतया *He's plumb crazy.*

**plum line** *noun* [C] a lead weight suspended from a line, that is used for measuring the depth of water or for checking whether things like a wall, etc. are vertical साहुल

**plumber** /ˈplʌmə(r)ˈप्लम(र्)/ *noun* [C] a person whose job is to put in or repair water pipes, baths, toilets, etc. नल का मिस्तरी, नलकार

**plumbing** /ˈplʌmɪŋˈप्लमिङ्/ *noun* [U] **1** all the pipes, taps, etc. in a building किसी भवन में लगे सारे नल, टोंटियाँ आदि **2** the work of a person who puts in and repairs water pipes, taps, etc. नल के मिस्तरी का काम (पानी के नल, टोंटी आदि लगाना, उनकी मरम्मत करना)

**plume** /plu:m प्लूम्/ *noun* [C] **1** a quantity of smoke that rises in the air हवा में उठता धुएँ का अंबार **2** a large feather or group of feathers, often worn as a decoration सजावट के लिए (टोपी आदि पर) लगाया बड़ा पंख या पंखों का गुच्छा

**plummet** /ˈplʌmɪtˈप्लमिट्/ *verb* [I] (*formal*) to fall suddenly and quickly from a high level or position ऊँचे स्तर या पद से अचानक और तेज़ी से गिरना *Share prices plummeted to an all-time low.* ○ *The jet plummeted into a row of houses.* ✪ पर्याय **plunge**

**plump¹** /plʌmp प्लम्प्/ *adj.* (used about a person or an animal) pleasantly fat (व्यक्ति या पशु) मोटा-ताज़ा, गोल-मटोल (जो देखने में अच्छा लगे) *the baby's plump cheeks*

**plump**[2] /plʌmp प्लम्प्/ *verb*

**PHR V plump (yourself/sb/sth) down** to sit down or to put sb/sth down heavily धड़ाम से नीचे बैठना या किसी वस्तु को रखना *She plumped herself down by the fire.*

**plump for sb/sth** (*BrE informal*) to choose or decide to have sb/sth किसी वस्तु या व्यक्ति को पसंद करना या उसके पक्ष में निर्णय करना *I think I'll plump for the roast chicken, after all.*

**plunder** /ˈplʌndə(r) ˈप्लन्ड(र्)/ *noun* [U] the action of stealing from people or places, especially during war or fighting; the goods that are stolen लोगों से या जगह-जगह से सामान की लूटपाट (विशेषतः युद्ध या दंगों में); लूट का सामान ▶ **plunder** *verb* [I, T] लूटना, विशेषतः युद्ध या दंगों में

**plunge**[1] /plʌndʒ प्लन्ज्/ *verb* **1** [I] **plunge (into sth/in)** to jump, drop or fall suddenly and with force अचानक ज़ोरों से छलाँग लगाना, गिरना या गिर जाना, डुबकी लगाना *He ran to the river and plunged in.* ○ (*figurative*) *Share prices plunged overnight.* **2** [T] **plunge sth in/into sth** to push sth suddenly and with force into sth ताक़त के साथ कहीं कुछ घुसाना *He plunged the knife into the table in anger.* **3** [T] to cause sb/sth to suddenly be in the state mentioned व्यक्ति या वस्तु को किसी विशेष स्थिति या दशा में डाल देना *The country has been plunged into chaos by the floods.* **4** [I] **plunge into (doing) sth** to start doing sth with energy and enthusiasm शक्ति और उत्साह के साथ कोई काम आरंभ करना *Think carefully before you plunge into buying a house.*

**plunge**[2] /plʌndʒ प्लन्ज्/ *noun* [C] a sudden jump, drop or fall आकस्मिक छलाँग या गिरावट *I slipped and took a plunge in the river.* ○ *the plunge in house prices*

**IDM take the plunge** to decide to do sth difficult after thinking about it for quite a long time काफ़ी सोच-विचार के बाद कोई कठिन काम करने का निर्णय लेना *After going out together for five years, they took the plunge and got married.*

**plunge pool** *noun* [C] (in geography) an area of deep water that is formed by water falling from above (**a waterfall**) (भूगोल में) ऊपर से गिरते झरने के जल से बना कुंड

**plunger** /ˈplʌndʒə(r) ˈप्लन्ज(र्)/ *noun* [C] a part of a piece of equipment that can be pushed down, for example in a **syringe** किसी उपकरण (जैसे इंजेक्शन) का नीचे धकेला जाना वाला भाग; मूसल, मज्जक ➪ **laboratory** पर चित्र देखिए।

**pluperfect** /ˌpluːˈpɜːfɪkt ˌप्लूˈपफ़िक्ट्/ = **the past perfect**

**plural** /ˈplʊərəl ˈप्लुअरल्/ *noun* [C] (*grammar*) the form of a noun, verb, etc. which refers to more than one person or thing बहुवचन रूप *The plural of 'boat' is 'boats'.* ○ *The verb should be **in the plural**.* ▶ **plural** *adj.* बहुवचन का सूचक ➪ **singular** देखिए।

**plus**[1] /plʌs प्लस्/ *prep.* **1** and; added to और; मिला कर *Two plus two is four (2 + 2 = 4).* ✪ विलोम **minus** **2** in addition to; and also के अतिरिक्त; साथ ही *You have to work five days a week plus every other weekend.*

**plus**[2] /plʌs प्लस्/ *noun* [C] **1** the sign (**+**) योग का चिह्न ✪ विलोम **minus** **2** an advantage of a situation स्थिति में लाभ की बात *Her experience in advertising was a plus in her job.*

**plus**[3] /plʌs प्लस्/ *adj.* (*only before a noun*) **1** or more या अधिक, इंगित संख्या या मात्रा से अधिक *I'd say there were 30,000 plus at the match.* **2** (used for marking work done by students) slightly above (छात्रों के शैक्षिक कार्य के मूल्यांकन में प्रयुक्त) कुछ अधिक *I got a B plus (= B+) for my homework.* ✪ विलोम **minus**

**plush** /plʌʃ प्लश्/ *adj.* comfortable and expensive आरामदेह और महँगा *a plush hotel*

**Pluto** /ˈpluːtəʊ ˈप्लूटो/ *noun* [*sing.*] a dwarf planet that moves round the sun and comes after the eighth planet Neptune यम वामन ग्रह, प्लूटो, जो आठवें ग्रह नेपच्यून के बाद आता है ➪ **the solar system** पर चित्र देखिए।

**plutonium** /pluːˈtəʊniəm प्लूˈटोनिअम्/ *noun* [U] a dangerous (**radioactive**) substance used especially as a fuel in nuclear power stations प्लूटोनियम एक ख़तरनाक रेडियोधर्मी तत्व जो विशेष रूप से परमाणु ऊर्जा उत्पादन केंद्रों में ईंधन के रूप में प्रयुक्त किया जाता है; प्लूटोनियम

**ply** /plaɪ प्लाइ/ *verb* (*pres. part.* **plying;** *3rd person sing. pres.* **plies;** *pt, pp* **plied**) [I, T] to try to sell services or goods to people, especially on the street लोगों को सेवा उपलब्ध कराना या माल बेचना विशेषतः सड़क पर *Boat owners were **plying their trade** to passing tourists.* ○ *to ply for business*

**PHR V ply sb with sth** to keep giving sb food and drink, or asking sb questions किसी को खाने-पीने का सामान लगातार देते रहना या सवाल पूछते रहना *They plied us with food from the moment we arrived.*

**plywood** /ˈplaɪwʊd ˈप्लाइवुड्/ *noun* [U] board made by sticking several thin layers of wood together लकड़ी की अनेक पतली परतें चिपकाकर बनाया गया बोर्ड

**p.m.** (*AmE* **P.M.**) /ˌpiː ˈem ˌपी ˈएम् / *abbr.* post meridiem; after midday दोपहर के बाद; अपराह्न में *2 p.m.* (= 2 o'clock in the afternoon) ○ *11.30 p.m.* (= 11.30 in the evening)

**pneumatic** /njuː ˈmætɪk न्यू ˈमैटिक् / *adj.* **1** filled with air हवा से भरा हुआ *a pneumatic tyre* **2** worked by air under pressure दबाव के साथ भरी हवा से काम करने वाला *pneumatic tools*

**pneumatic drill** (*AmE* **jackhammer**) *noun* [C] a large powerful tool, worked by air pressure, used especially for breaking up road surfaces हवा के दबाव से काम करने वाला शक्तिशाली बड़ा बरमा (मशीन) जिसे विशेषत सड़क की सतह को तोड़ने के लिए प्रयुक्त किया जाता है; वातिल बरमा, न्यूमेटिक ड्रिल ➪ **tools** पर चित्र देखिए।

**pneumonia** /njuː ˈməʊniə न्यू ˈमोनिआ / *noun* [U] a serious illness of the lungs which makes breathing difficult फेफड़ों की गंभीर बीमारी जिसके कारण साँस लेने में कठिनाई होती है; निमोनिया

**PO** /ˌpiː ˈəʊ ˌपी ˈओ / *abbr.* (*used in compound nouns*) Post Office, डाक-ख़ाना *a PO box*

**poach** /pəʊtʃ पोच् / *verb* [T] **1** to cook food (especially fish or eggs) gently in a small amount of liquid मछली या अंडों आदि को थोड़े द्रव में हलके ताप से पकाना **2** to hunt animals illegally ग़ैर-क़ानूनी ढंग से पशुओं का शिकार करना **3** to take an idea from sb else and use it as though it is your own किसी अन्य व्यक्ति के विचार को अपने नाम से प्रयोग में लाना **4** to take members of staff from another company in an unfair way अन्य कंपनी के कर्मचारियों को अनुचित तरीक़े से अपने साथ कर लेना

**poacher** /ˈpəʊtʃə(r) ˈपोच(र्) / *noun* [C] a person who hunts animals illegally ग़ैर-क़ानूनी ढंग से शिकार करने वाला व्यक्ति, शिकार-चोर

**PO box** *noun* [C] a place in a post office where letters, packages, etc. are kept until they are collected by the person they were sent to डाकघर में रखा बक्सा जिसमें प्रेषिनी (डाक पाने वाला) की डाक (पत्र, पैकेट आदि) सुरक्षित रखी जाती है (तब तक जब तक वह उसे ले न जाए) *The address is PO Box 4287, Chandigarh, India.*

**pocket[1]** /ˈpɒkɪt ˈपॉकिट् / *noun* [C] **1** a piece of material like a small bag that is sewn inside or on a piece of clothing and is used for carrying things in जेब, पॉकेट *He always walks with his hands in his trouser pockets.* ○ *a pocket dictionary/calculator* (= one small enough to fit in your pocket) **2** a small bag or container that is fixed to the inside of a car door, suitcase, etc. and used for putting things in कार का दरवाज़ा, सूटकेस आदि में वस्तुएँ रखने की थैली *There are safety instructions in the pocket of the seat in front of you.* **3** used to talk about the amount of money that you have to spend ख़र्च करने के लिए उपलब्ध धनराशि *They sell cars to suit every pocket.* ○ *The school couldn't afford a CD player, so the teacher bought one* ***out of*** *his* ***own pocket***. **4** a small area or group that is different from its surroundings अपने आस-पास से अलग तरह का छोटा क्षेत्र या व्यक्तिसमूह *pockets of warm water* ➪ **air pocket** देखिए।

IDM **pick sb's pocket** ➪ **pick[1]** देखिए।

**pocket[2]** /ˈpɒkɪt ˈपॉकिट् / *verb* [T] **1** to put sth in your pocket किसी वस्तु को जेब में रखना *He took the letter and pocketed it quickly.* **2** to steal or win money पैसा चोरी कर लेना या जीत लेना

**pocketbook** /ˈpɒkɪtbʊk ˈपॉकिट्बुक् / *noun* [C] **1** a small book or notebook छोटी पुस्तक या नोटबुक, पॉकेट-बुक **2** (*AmE*) = **wallet**

**pocket money** *noun* [U] (*AmE* **allowance**) an amount of money that parents give a child to spend, usually every week जेब-ख़र्च; माता-पिता द्वारा प्रायः प्रति सप्ताह बच्चे को ख़र्च के लिए दिया गया पैसा

**pod** /pɒd पॉड् / *noun* [C] the long, green part of some plants, such as peas and beans, that contains the seeds मटर, सेम आदि की फली

**podiatrist** /pəˈdaɪətrɪst पˈडाइअट्रिस्ट् / (*AmE*) = **chiropodist**

**podiatry** /pəˈdaɪətri पˈडाइअट्रि / (*AmE*) = **chiropody**

**podium** /ˈpəʊdiəm ˈपोडिअम् / *noun* [C] a small platform for a speaker, a performer, etc. to stand on छोटा मंच जिस पर वक्ता, कलाकार आदि खड़े होते हैं

**poem** /ˈpəʊɪm ˈपोइम् / *noun* [C] a piece of writing arranged in short lines. Poems try to express thoughts and feelings with the help of sound and rhythm कविता

**poet** /ˈpəʊɪt ˈपोइट् / *noun* [C] a person who writes poems कवि

**poetic** /pəʊˈetɪk पोˈएटिक् / (*also* **poetical** /-tɪkl -टिक्ल् ) *adj.* connected with poets or like a poem कवि-विषयक या कविता के सदृश या काव्योचित ▸ **poetically** /-kli -क्लि / *adv.* काव्यात्मक रीति से

**poetry** /ˈpəʊətri ˈपोअट्रि / *noun* [U] a collection of poems; poems in general कविताओं का संग्रह; सब प्रकार की कविताएँ *Kalidasa's poetry and plays* ○ *Do you like poetry?* ➪ **prose** देखिए।

**poignant** /ˈpɔɪnjənt ˈपॉइन्यन्ट्/ *adj.* causing sadness or pity करुणाजनक या मार्मिक *a poignant memory* ▶ **poignancy** /-jənsi -यन्सि/ *noun* [U] मार्मिकता ▶ **poignantly** *adv.* मार्मिक रूप से

**point**[1] /pɔɪnt पॉइन्ट्/ *noun* **1** [C] a particular fact, idea or opinion that sb expresses किसी के द्वारा प्रस्तुत विशिष्ट तथ्य, विचार या सम्मति; प्वाइंट *You **make** some interesting **points** in your essay.* ○ *I see your point but I don't agree with you.* **2 the point** [*sing.*] the most important part of what is being said; the main piece of information चर्चा का सबसे महत्त्वपूर्ण अंश; मुख्य बात *It makes no difference how much it costs—**the point is** we don't have any money!* ○ *She always talks and talks and takes ages to **get to the point**.* **3** [C] an important idea or thought that needs to be considered महत्त्वपूर्ण धारणा या विचार जो विचार करने योग्य हो *'Have you checked what time the last bus back is?' 'That's a point—no I haven't.'* **4** [C] a detail, characteristic or quality of sb/sth व्यक्ति या वस्तु का विशेष पहलू, लक्षण या गुण *Make a list of your **strong points** and your **weak points*** (= good and bad qualities). **5** [*sing.*] **the point (of/in sth/doing sth)** the meaning, reason or purpose of sth किसी बात का अर्थ, उद्देश्य या उसके लिए तर्क *She's said no, so **what's the point** of telephoning her again?* ○ ***There's no point** in talking to my parents—they never listen.* **6** [C] (*often in compounds*) a particular place, position or moment विशिष्ट स्थान, स्थिति या क्षण *The library is a good **starting point** for that sort of information.* ○ *He has reached the **high point** of his career.* ○ *He waved to the crowd and it was **at that point** that the shot was fired.* **7** [C] the thin sharp end of sth किसी वस्तु की नोक *the point of a pin/needle/pencil* **8** [C] a small round mark used when writing parts of numbers संख्याओं के अंशों के लिखने में प्रयुक्त छोटा बिंदु; दशमलव का चिह्न *She ran the race in 11.2 (eleven point two) seconds.* **9** [C] a single mark in some games, sports, etc. that you add to others to get the score खेलों में अर्जित किया जाने वाला अंक *to score a point* ○ *Paes needs two more points to win the match.* **10** [C] a unit of measurement for certain things कुछ वस्तुओं में माप की इकाई *The value of the dollar has fallen by a few points.*

**IDM be on the point of doing sth** just going to do sth कुछ करने ही लगना *I was on the point of going out when the phone rang.*

**beside the point** ➪ **beside** देखिए।

**have your, etc. (good) points** to have some good qualities कुछ अच्छे गुण होना *Jai has his good points, but he's very unreliable.*

**make a point of doing sth** to make sure you do sth because it is important or necessary (महत्त्वपूर्ण या आवश्यक होने से) किसी कार्य का निष्पादन सुनिश्चित करना *I made a point of locking all the doors and windows before leaving the house.*

**point of view** a way of looking at a situation; an opinion दृष्टिकोण; सम्मति *From my point of view it would be better to wait a little longer.*
✪ पर्याय **viewpoint** या **standpoint**

**prove your/the case/point** ➪ **prove** देखिए।

**a sore point** ➪ **sore**[1] देखिए।

**sb's strong point** ➪ **strong** देखिए।

**take sb's point** to understand and accept what sb is saying किसी की बात को समझना और मान लेना

**to the point** connected with what is being discussed; relevant चर्चा के विषय से संबंधित; संगत, प्रासंगिक *His speech was short and to the point.*

**up to a point** partly आंशिक रूप से *I agree with you up to a point.*

**point**[2] /pɔɪnt पॉइन्ट्/ *verb* **1** [I] **point (at/to sb/sth)** to show where sth is or to draw attention to sth using your finger, a stick, etc. अँगुली, छड़ी आदि से किसी वस्तु की स्थिति दिखाना या किसी की ओर लोगों का ध्यान आकृष्ट करना *'I'll have that one,' she said, pointing to a chocolate cake.* **2** [I, T] **point (sth) (at/towards sb/sth)** to aim (sth) in the direction of sb/sth किसी व्यक्ति या वस्तु की ओर निशाना साधना *She pointed the gun at the target and fired.* **3** [I] to face in a particular direction or to show that sth is in a particular direction किसी दिशा-विशेष के सामने होना या किसी दिशा-विशेष में किसी वस्तु के स्थित होने का संकेत करना *The sign pointed towards the highway.* ○ *Turn round until you're pointing north.* **4** [I] **point to sth** to show that sth is likely to exist, happen or be true किसी बात के अस्तित्व में होने, घटित होने या सत्य होने की संभावना का संकेत करना *Research points to a connection between diet and cancer.*

**PHR V point sth out (to sb)** to make sb look at sth; to make sth clear to sb किसी वस्तु को संकेत द्वारा किसी व्यक्ति को दिखाना; किसी व्यक्ति को कोई बात स्पष्ट करना *The guide pointed out all the places of interest to us on the way.* ○ *I'd like to point out that we haven't got much time left.*

**point-blank** *adj., adv.* **1** (used about a shot) from a very close position (गोली का निशाना) बहुत समीप से बनाया गया *He was shot in the head **at***

*point-blank range*. **2** (used about sth that is said) very direct and not polite; not allowing any discussion (कही गई बात) एकदम सीधी और रूखी; जिसमें विचार-विमर्श की गुंजाइश नहीं *She told him point-blank to get out of the house and never comeback.*

**pointed** /ˈpɔɪntɪd ˈपॉइन्टिड्/ *adj.* **1** having a sharp end नुकीला *a pointed stick/nose* **2** (used about sth that is said) critical of sb in an indirect way (किसी के लिए कही गई बात) परोक्ष रूप से आलोचनापूर्ण या निंदात्मक *She made a pointed comment about people who are always late.* ▶ **pointedly** *adv.* लक्ष्य करके, संकेत करते हुए

**pointer** /ˈpɔɪntə(r) ˈपॉइन्ट(र्)/ *noun* [C] **1** a piece of helpful advice or information सहायक या उपयोगी सलाह या जानकारी *Could you **give** me some **pointers** on how best to tackle the problem?* **2** a small arrow on a computer screen that you move by moving the mouse कंप्यूटर स्क्रीन पर तीर जैसा चिह्न जिसे माउस की सहायता से घुमाया जाता है) **3** a stick that is used to point to things on a map, etc. मानचित्र आदि पर किसी का संकेत करने के लिए प्रयुक्त पतली छड़ी

**pointless** /ˈpɔɪntləs ˈपॉइन्ट्लस्/ *adj.* without any use or purpose व्यर्थ, निरर्थक *It's pointless to try and make him agree.* ▶ **pointlessly** *adv.* निरर्थक रूप से ▶ **pointlessness** *noun* [U] निरर्थकता

**poise** /pɔɪz पॉइज़्/ *noun* [U] a calm, confident way of behaving शांत या स्थिर और आत्मविश्वासपूर्ण आचरण

**poised** /pɔɪzd पॉइज़्ड्/ *adj.* **1** not moving but ready to move किसी हरकत के लिए तैयार (परंतु वस्तुतः करना शेष) *'Shall I call the doctor or not?' he asked, his hand poised above the telephone.* **2 poised (to do sth)** ready to act; about to do sth कुछ करने को तैयार; जो तुरंत कुछ करने वाला हो *The government is poised to take action if the crisis continues.* **3** calm and confident संतुलित और आत्मविश्वासपूर्ण

**poison**[1] /ˈpɔɪzn ˈपॉइज़न्/ *noun* [C, U] a substance that kills or harms you if you eat or drink it विष, ज़हर *rat poison* ○ *poison gas*

**poison**[2] /ˈpɔɪzn ˈपॉइज़न्/ *verb* [T] **1** to kill, harm or damage sb/sth with poison किसी व्यक्ति या वस्तु को विष देकर मारना या हानि पहुँचाना **2** to put poison in sth किसी वस्तु में विष मिला देना, विषाक्त करना *The cup of coffee had been poisoned.* **3** to spoil or ruin sth किसी वस्तु को बिगाड़ देना या नष्ट कर देना *The quarrel had poisoned their relationship.* ▶ **poisoned** *adj.* विषैला, ज़हरीला *a poisoned drink*

**poisoning** /ˈpɔɪzənɪŋ ˈपॉइज़निङ्/ *noun* [U] the giving or taking of poison or a dangerous substance विष या कोई हानिकारक वस्तु देने या लेने की क्रिया *He got **food poisoning** from eating fish that wasn't fresh.*

**poisonous** /ˈpɔɪzənəs ˈपॉइज़नस्/ *adj.* **1** causing death or illness if you eat or drink it घातक (जिसे खाने या पीने से मृत्यु या कोई रोग हो जाए), विषाक्त **2** (used about animals, etc.) producing and using poison to attack its enemies (पशु आदि) विषैला, ज़हरीला *He was bitten by a poisonous snake.* **3** very unpleasant and intended to upset sb बहुत कुरुचिपूर्ण और मन को अशांत कर देने वाला *She wrote him a poisonous letter criticizing his behaviour.*

**poke** /pəʊk पोक्/ *verb* **1** [T] to push sb/sth with a finger, stick or other long, thin object अँगुली, छड़ी या किसी लंबी पतली वस्तु से व्यक्ति या वस्तु को कोंचना, कुरेदना *Be careful you don't poke yourself in the eye with that stick!* **2** [I, T] **poke (sth) into, through, out of, down, etc. sth** to move or to push sth quickly into sth or in a certain direction किसी वस्तु या दिशा-विशेष में फुरती से किसी वस्तु को घुमाना या धकेलना *He poked the stick down the hole to see how deep it was.* ○ *A child's head poked up from behind the wall.* ▶ **poke** *noun* [C] कुरेदन

IDM **poke fun at sb/sth** to make jokes about sb/sth, often in an unkind way किसी व्यक्ति या वस्तु का मज़ाक़ उड़ाना (प्रायः अभद्रता या निर्दयता से)

**poke/stick your nose into sth** ⇨ **nose**[1] देखिए।

**poker** /ˈpəʊkə(r) ˈपोक(र्)/ *noun* **1** [U] a type of card game usually played to win money ताश का एक खेल (प्रायः जुए के लिए) **2** [C] a metal stick for moving the coal or wood in a fire जलते कोयले या लकड़ी को हिलाने की धातु की छड़ी; कुरेदनी

**polar** /ˈpəʊlə(r) ˈपोल(र्)/ *adj.* (*only before a noun*) of or near the North or South Pole उत्तरी या दक्षिणी ध्रुव का/के निकट; ध्रुव प्रदेशीय *the polar regions*

**polar bear** *noun* [C] a large white bear that lives in the area near the North Pole उत्तरी ध्रुव के निकट रहने वाला बड़ा सफ़ेद भालू

**polarize** (*also* **-ise**) /ˈpəʊləraɪz ˈपोलराइज़्/ *verb* **1** [I, T] (*formal*) to separate or make people separate into two groups with completely opposite opinions व्यक्तियों को पूर्णतः विपरीत विचार वाले दो समूहों में बाँट देना; ध्रुवीकरण करना *Public opinion has polarized on this issue.* **2** [T] (*technical*) to make waves of light, etc. **vibrate** in a single direction प्रकाश तरंग आदि को किसी एक दिशा में तरंगित करना **3** [T] (*technical*) to make sth have two

**poles 3** with opposite qualities किसी वस्तु को विपरीत गुणों वाले दो ध्रुवों में व्यवस्थित कर देना *to polarize a magnet* ▶ **polarization** (*also* **-isation**) /ˌpəʊləraɪˈzeɪʃn ˌपोलराइˈज़ेशन् / *noun* [U] ध्रुवीकरण

**pole** /pəʊl पोल् / *noun* [C] **1** a long, thin piece of wood or metal, used especially to hold sth up लकड़ी या धातु का डंडा या लट्ठा (विशेषतः किसी वस्तु को सँभालने के लिए) *a flagpole* ○ *a tent pole* **2** either of the two points at the exact top and bottom of the earth पृथ्वी का उत्तरी या दक्षिणी ध्रुव (मानचित्र में एकदम शीर्ष या तल पर प्रदर्शित) *the North/South Pole* ➪ **earth** पर चित्र देखिए। **3** either of the two ends of a **magnet**, or the positive or negative points of an electric battery चुंबक के दो सिरों में से कोई एक या बिजली की बैटरी का धनात्मक या ऋणात्मक बिंदु ➪ **magnet** पर चित्र देखिए।

**the pole vault** *noun* [C] the sport of jumping over a high bar with the help of a long pole लग्गा-कूद का खेल जिसमें खिलाड़ी लंबे डंडे की सहायता से ऊँची लगी छड़ के ऊपर से कूदता है; पोल-वॉल्ट

**police[1]** /pəˈliːs पˈलीस् / *noun* [*pl.*] the official organization whose job is to make sure that people obey the law, and to prevent and solve crime क़ानून और व्यवस्था बनाए रखने के लिए शासकीय संगठन; पुलिस बल *Dial 100 if you need to* ***call the police***. ○ *Kamal wants to join* ***the police force*** *when he finishes school.* ○ *the local* ***police station***

> **NOTE** **Police** बहुवचनांत संज्ञा (plural noun) है जिसके साथ सदा बहुवचनांत क्रिया (plural verb) आती है। पुलिस के एक सिपाही वाले (पुरुष या स्त्री) के अर्थ में **'a police'** का प्रयोग ग़लत है। पुलिस संगठन के अर्थ में **police** शब्द के साथ **the** का प्रयोग आवश्यक है—*There were over 100 police on duty.* ○ *The police are investigating the murder.*

**police[2]** /pəˈliːs पˈलीस् / *verb* [T] to keep control in a place by using the police or a similar official group पुलिस या इसी प्रकार के अन्य संगठन की सहायता से क़ानून और व्यवस्था बनाए रखना *The cost of policing football games is extremely high.*

**police constable** (*also* **constable**) *noun* [C] (*BrE*) (*abbr.* **PC**) a police officer of the lowest position (**rank**) सबसे छोटे पद का पुलिस वाला, पुलिसजन, पुलिस का सिपाही, पुलिस कांस्टेबल

**police officer** (*also* **officer**) (*also* **policeman, policewoman**) *noun* [C] a member of the police पुलिस बल का सदस्य

**police state** *noun* [C] a country where people's freedom, especially to travel and to express political opinions, is controlled by the government, with the help of the police किसी देश की ऐसी व्यवस्था जिसमें सरकार जनता की आज़ादी, विशेषतः घूमने-फिरने और राजनीतिक मत प्रकट करने, पर पुलिस की सहायता से अंकुश लगा दे; पुलिस राज

**policy** /ˈpɒləsi ˈपॉलसि / *noun* (*pl.* **policies**) **1** [C, U] **policy (on sth)** a plan of action agreed or chosen by a government, a company, etc. सरकार, कंपनी आदि की नीति, कार्य-योजना *It is company policy not to allow smoking in meetings.* **2** [C, U] a way of behaving that you think is best in a particular situation स्थिति विशेष के लिए किसी व्यक्ति की सर्वोत्तम कार्ययोजना *It's my policy only to do business with people I like.* **3** [C] a document that shows an agreement that you have made with an insurance company: an insurance policy बीमा कंपनी के साथ हुए क़रार का दस्तावेज़, बीमा पॉलिसी

**polio** /ˈpəʊliəʊ ˈपोलिओ / *noun* [U] a serious disease which can cause you to lose the power in certain muscles कुछ मांसपेशियों के कमज़ोर पड़ जाने का गंभीर रोग; पोलियो

**polish[1]** /ˈpɒlɪʃ ˈपॉलिश् / *verb* [T] to make sth shine by rubbing it and often by putting a special cream or liquid on it जूते, मेज़ आदि को पॉलिश से चमकाना *to polish your shoes/a table*

**PHR V** **polish sth off** (*informal*) to finish sth, especially food, quickly किसी काम, विशेषतः भोजन, को जल्दी समाप्त करना *The two of them polished off a whole chicken for dinner!*

**polish[2]** /ˈpɒlɪʃ ˈपॉलिश् / *noun* **1** [U] a cream, liquid, etc. that you put on sth to clean it and make it shine जूते आदि को चमकाने की क्रीम, द्रव वस्तु, पॉलिश *a tin of shoe polish* **2** [*sing.*] the action of polishing sth पॉलिश से चमकाने की क्रिया *I'll* ***give*** *the glasses* ***a polish*** *before the guests arrive.*

**polished** /ˈpɒlɪʃt ˈपॉलिश्ट् / *adj.* **1** shiny because of polishing चमकदार (पॉलिश लगाने से) *polished wood floors* **2** (used about a performance, etc.) of a high standard उच्च स्तर का (काम, प्रदर्शन आदि) *Most of the actors gave* ***a polished performance***.

**politburo** /ˈpɒlɪtˌbjʊərəʊ ˈपॉलिट्ˌब्युअरो / *noun* [C] (*pl.* **politburos**) the most important committee of a communist party with the power to decide on policy, especially in the former USSR किसी देश, विशेषतः पूर्व सोवियत संघ की कम्युनिस्ट पार्टी की सबसे महत्त्वपूर्ण समिति, पॉलिटब्यूरो

**polite** /pəˈlaɪt पˈलाइट् / *adj.* having good manners and showing respect for others सुशील और दूसरों का सम्मान करने वाला; नम्र, शिष्ट *The assistants in that shop are always very helpful and polite.*

○ *He gave me a polite smile.* ✪ विलोम **impolite** या **impertinent** ▶ **politely** *adv*. नम्रतापूर्वक, शिष्टता से ▶ **politeness** *noun* [U] नम्रता, शिष्टता

**political** /pəˈlɪtɪkl पˈलिटिक्ल्/ *adj.* **1** connected with politics and government राजनीतिक, राजनीति और सरकार से संबंधित *a political leader/debate/party* ○ *She has very strong political opinions.* **2** (used about people) interested in politics (व्यक्ति) राजनीति में रुचि रखने वाला **3** concerned with the competition for power inside an organization संगठन के अंदर सत्ता के लिए स्पर्धा से संबंधित *I suspect he was dismissed for political reasons.* ▶ **politically** *adv.* राजनीतिक दृष्टि से *Politically he's fairly right wing.*

**political asylum** *noun* [U] protection given by a state to a person who has left his/her own country for political reasons राजनीतिक कारणों से स्वदेश छोड़ने वाले व्यक्ति को अन्य देश द्वारा दी गई सुरक्षा; राजनीतिक शरण

**politically correct** *adj.* (*abbr.* **PC**) used to describe language or behaviour that carefully avoids offending particular groups of people ऐसे आचरण और भाषा व्यवहार से संबंधित जिसमें विशिष्ट व्यक्ति समूह की भावनाओं का ध्यान रखा जाए ▶ **political correctness** *noun* [U] ऐसी भाषा व आचरण

**politician** /ˌpɒləˈtɪʃn ˌपॉलˈटिश्न्/ *noun* [C] a person whose job is in politics, especially one who is a member of parliament or of the government राजनीतिक गतिविधियों में संलग्न व्यक्ति, विशेषतः संसद या सरकार का सदस्य; राजनेता *Politicians of all parties supported the war.*

**politics** /ˈpɒlətɪks ˈपॉलटिक्स्/ *noun* **1** [U, *with sing. or pl. verb*] the work and ideas that are connected with governing a country, a town, etc. ऐसे कार्य और अभिमत जिनका संबंध किसी देश का शासन चलाने से हो; राजनीति *to go into politics* ○ *Politics has/have never been of great interest to me.* **2** [*pl.*] a person's political opinions and beliefs किसी व्यक्ति के राजनीतिक विचार और विश्वास *His politics are extreme.* **3** [U, *with sing. or pl. verb*] matters concerned with competition for power between people in an organization किसी संगठन के सदस्यों में सत्ता के लिए स्पर्धा से संबंधित मामले *I never get involved in office politics.* **4** (*AmE* **Political Science**) [U] the scientific study of government राजनीतिशास्त्र *a degree in Politics*

**poll¹** /pəʊl पोल्/ *noun* [C] **1** (*also* **opinion poll**) a way of finding out public opinion by asking a number of people their views on sth किसी मुद्दे पर अनेक व्यक्तियों से उनकी राय जानकर जनमत का निर्धारण; जनमत-सर्वेक्षण *This was voted best drama series in a viewers' poll.* **2** the process of voting in a political election; the number of votes given चुनाव में मतदान; मतों की संख्या, मत-गणना *The country will **go to the polls** (= vote) in June.*

**poll²** /pəʊl पोल्/ *verb* [T] **1** to receive a certain number of votes in an election चुनाव में मत प्राप्त करना *The Congress Party candidate polled over 3000 votes.* **2** to ask members of the public their opinion on a subject किसी मुद्दे पर लोगों की राय जानना *Of those polled, only 20 per cent were in favour of changing the law.*

**pollen** /ˈpɒlən ˈपॉलन्/ *noun* [U] a fine, usually yellow, powder which is formed in flowers. It makes other flowers of the same type produce seeds when it is carried to them by the wind, insects, etc. फूल के पराग कण; पराग कणों को हवा, कीड़े आदि उसी प्रकार के अन्य फूलों तक पहुँचाते हैं और फलस्वरूप फूलों में बीज बन जाते हैं ➪ **flower** पर चित्र देखिए।

**pollen count** *noun* [C, *usually sing.*] a number that shows how much pollen is in the air वायु में विकीर्ण पराग कणों की संख्या; पराग-मापक

**pollen tube** *noun* [C] a tube which grows when pollen lands on the top of the female part in the middle of a flower (**stigma**) to carry the male cell to the part that contains the female cell (**ovule**) (पुष्प के मध्य भाग में मादा अंश पर पराग कणों के एकत्र होने से बनी नली जो नर कोशिका को मादा कोशिका तक पहुँचाती है; पराग-नली ➪ **flower** पर चित्र देखिए।

**pollinate** /ˈpɒləneɪt ˈपॉलनेट्/ *verb* [T] to put a fine powder (**pollen**) into a flower or plant so that it produces seeds पराग खींचना; फूल या पौधे में पराग कणों का पहुँचना जिससे उसमें बीज बने ▶ **pollination** /ˌpɒləˈneɪʃn ˌपॉलˈनेश्न्/ *noun* [U] पराग खींचने की क्रिया; परागण

**polling** /ˈpəʊlɪŋ ˈपोलिङ्/ *noun* [U] **1** the activity of voting in an election मतदान की प्रक्रिया *Polling has been heavy since 8 a.m.* **2** the act of asking questions in order to find out public opinion जनमत जानने के लिए लोगों से प्रश्न पूछने की क्रिया

**polling booth** (*AmE* **voting booth**) *noun* [C] a small, partly enclosed place where you stand to mark your card in order to vote in an election मतदान-कक्ष

**polling day** *noun* [U, C] (*BrE*) a day on which people vote in an election मतदान दिवस

**polling station** *noun* [C] (*usually BrE*) a building where you go to vote in an election मतदान केंद्र

**poll tax** *noun* [*sing.*] a fixed amount of money to be paid for local services. by all adults in a particular area मथौट; व्यक्ति-कर (स्थानीय सेवाओं के लिए प्रति व्यक्ति के हिसाब से लगने वाला कर)

**pollutant** /pəˈluːtənt पˈलूटन्ट्/ *noun* [C] a substance that pollutes air, rivers, etc. प्रदूषक पदार्थ (वायु, नदियों आदि को प्रदूषित करने वाला पदार्थ)

**pollute** /pəˈluːt पˈलूट्/ *verb* [T] to make air, rivers, etc. dirty and dangerous (वायु, नदियों आदि को) प्रदूषित करना *Traffic fumes are polluting our cities.* ○ *The beach has been polluted with oil.*

**pollution** /pəˈluːʃn पˈलूश्न्/ *noun* [U] **1** the action of making the air, water, etc. dirty and dangerous वायु, नदियों आदि को प्रदूषित करने की प्रक्रिया; प्रदूषण *Major steps are being taken to control the pollution of beaches.* **2** substances that pollute प्रदूषणकारी पदार्थ *The rivers are full of pollution.*

**polo** /ˈpəʊləʊ ˈपोलो/ *noun* [U] a game for two teams of horses and riders. The players try to score goals by hitting a ball with long wooden hammers पोलो; चौगान का खेल। यह घुड़सवारों के दलों के बीच खेला जाता है। खिलाड़ी लंबी छड़ियों से गेंद को मार कर गोल करते हैं

**polo neck** *noun* [C] a high collar on a piece of clothing that is rolled over and that covers most of your neck; a piece of clothing with this type of collar स्वेटर आदि का लपेटा जाने वाला कॉलर जो अधिकांश गरदन को ढक लेता है; गोल कॉलर; गोल कॉलर वाला कपड़ा (स्वेटर आदि)

**poly** /ˈpɒli ˈपॉलि/ (*pl.* **polys**) (*informal*) = **polytechnic**

**poly-** /ˈpɒli ˈपॉलि/ *prefix* (*used in nouns, adjectives and adverbs*) many अनेक, बहु- *polygamy*

**polyester** /ˌpɒliˈestə(r) ˌपॉलिˈएस्ट(र्)/ *noun* [U] an artificial material that is used for making clothes, etc. कपड़े आदि बनाने में प्रयुक्त एक प्रकार की कृत्रिम सामग्री; पॉलिस्टर

**polyethylene** (*AmE*) = **polythene**

**polygamy** /pəˈlɪɡəmi पˈलिगमि/ *noun* [U] the custom of having more than one wife at the same time बहुपत्नी प्रथा ➪ **bigamy** और **monogamy** देखिए। ▶ **polygamous** /pəˈlɪɡəməs पˈलिगमस्/ *adj.* बहुपत्नी प्रथा से संबंधित *a polygamous society*

**polygon** /ˈpɒlɪɡən ˈपॉलिगन्/ *noun* [C] a flat shape with at least three, and usually five or more, angles and straight sides न्यूनतम तीन और प्रायः पाँच या अधिक सीधी भुजाओं वाली समतल आकृति; बहुभुज ▶ **polygonal** /pəˈlɪɡənl पˈलिगन्ल्/ *adj.* बहुभुजी

**polymer** /ˈpɒlɪmə(r) ˈपॉलिम(र्)/ *noun* [C] (*technical*) a natural or artificial chemical compound consisting of large **molecules** बड़े आकार के अणुओं वाला एक प्रकार का प्राकृतिक या कृत्रिम रासायनिक यौगिक; बहुलक, पॉलिमर

**polyp** /ˈpɒlɪp ˈपॉलिप्/ *noun* [C] **1** (*medical*) a small lump that grows inside the body, especially in the nose. It is caused by disease but is usually harmless शरीर, विशेषतः नाक, में उभरा छोटा मांसपिंड जो प्रायः हानिकर नहीं होता; पॉलिप **2** a small and very simple sea creature with a body shaped like a tube एक छोटा और बहुत साधारण समुद्री जीव जिसका शरीर एक नली की शकल का होता है

**polystyrene** /ˌpɒliˈstaɪriːn ˌपॉलिˈस्टाइरीन्/ *noun* [U] a light firm plastic substance that is used for packing things so that they do not get broken वस्तुओं की पैकिंग में प्रयुक्त एक हलका मज़बूत प्लास्टिक से बना पदार्थ; पॉलिस्ट्रीन

**polytechnic** /ˌpɒliˈteknɪk ˌपॉलिˈट्रेक्निक्/ (*informal* **poly**) *noun* [C] a college for students who are 18 or over, offering more practical courses than those at traditional universities. In Britain since 1992 polytechnics have been recognized as universities (ब्रिटेन में) 18 या अधिक आयु के छात्रों को तकनीकी व्यावहारिक शिक्षा देने वाला कॉलेज (1992 से इन कॉलेजों को विश्वविद्यालय का दर्जा मिल गया है); पॉलिटेक्नीक

**polythene** /ˈpɒlɪθiːn ˈपॉलिथ्रीन्/ (*AmE* **polyethylene** /ˌpɒliˈeθəliːn ˌपॉलिˈएथ्रलीन्/) *noun* [U] a type of very thin plastic material, often used to make bags for food, etc. or to keep things dry एक प्रकार का बहुत महीन प्लास्टिक इसे खाद्य पदार्थों के लिए थैलियाँ बनाने में प्रयुक्त किया जाता है ताकि उन्हें शुष्क अवस्था में रखा जा सके; पॉलिथीन

**polyunsaturated** /ˌpɒliʌnˈsætʃəreɪtɪd ˌपॉलिअन्ˈसैचरेटिड्/ *adj.* (used about fats and oils) having the type of chemical structure that is thought to be good for your health (चरबियाँ और तेल) स्वास्थ्य के लिए लाभकारी रसायनों वाले *polyunsaturated margarine* ➪ **saturated** और **unsaturated** देखिए।

**pomegranate** /ˈpɒmɪɡrænɪt ˈपॉमिग्रैनिट्/ *noun* [C] a round fruit with thick smooth skin that is red inside and full of seeds अनार (का फल) ➪ **fruit** पर चित्र देखिए।

**pomp** /pɒmp पॉम्प्/ *noun* [U] the impressive nature of a large official occasion or ceremony (किसी बड़े औपचारिक समारोह का) तड़क-भड़क, ठाट-बाट

**pompous** /ˈpɒmpəs ˈपॉम्पस्/ *adj.* showing that you think you are more important than other people, for example by using long words that sound impressive स्वयं को दूसरों से अधिक महत्त्वपूर्ण समझते हुए और भाषा व्यवहार में इसका प्रदर्शन करते हुए; तड़क-भड़क वाला, आडंबरपूर्ण NOTE इस शब्द के प्रयोग से निंदा या आलोचना ध्वनित होती है।

**pond** /pɒnd पॉन्ड्/ *noun* [C] an area of water that is smaller than a lake तालाब (झील से छोटा जलक्षेत्र)

> NOTE **Lake** प्रायः बड़ी होती है जिसमें नावें चल सकती हैं—*Lake Chilka.* **Pond** इतना बड़ा भी हो सकता है कि पशु वहाँ पानी पिएँ या इतना छोटा भी कि बग़ीचे में बन जाए—*We have a fish pond in our garden.* **Pool** बहुत छोटे जलक्षेत्र को कहते हैं—*When the tide went out, pools of water were left among the rocks.* परंतु कृत्रिम pool बड़ा हो सकता है—*a swimming pool.* **Puddle** वह छोटा जलक्षेत्र है जो वर्षा से बन जाता है।

**ponder** /ˈpɒndə(r) ˈपॉन्ड(र्)/ *verb* [I, T] **ponder (on/over sth)** to think about sth carefully or for a long time किसी विषय पर गंभीरतापूर्वक या देर तक सोचना

**Pongal** *noun* **1** [C, U] the harvest festival that is celebrated in January in Tamil Nadu when newly harvested rice is cooked पोंगल; तमिलनाडु का फ़सल कटाई का त्यौहार जो जनवरी मास में मनाया जाता है तथा नई कटी चावल की फ़सल को इस दिन पकाया जाता है **2** [U] a dish made of rice, lentils, pepper and cumin or rice, seasoned milk, sugar, jaggery, etc. This is popular in South India (दक्षिण भारत में लोकप्रिय) चावल और मूंग दाल तथा काली मिर्च और जीरा या सिझाया दूध, चीनी, गुड़ आदि से बना व्यंजन

**Pontiff** /pɒnˈtɪf पॉन् ˈटिफ़्/ *noun* [C] (*formal*) **pope** पोप (= रोमन कैथोलिक चर्च का मुख्य पादरी)

**pony** /ˈpəʊni ˈपोनि/ *noun* [C] (*pl.* **ponies**) a small horse टट्टू (एक प्रकार का छोटी जाति का घोड़ा)

**ponytail** /ˈpəʊniteɪl ˈपोनिटेल्/ *noun* [C] long hair that is tied at the back of the head and that hangs down in one piece लंबे बालों की लटकती हुई इकहरी चोटी, पोनीटेल

**pony-trekking** (*AmE* **trail riding**) *noun* [U] the activity of riding horses for pleasure in the country शौक़िया घुड़सवारी; देहाती इलाक़े में मनोरंजन हेतु टट्टू की सवारी

**poodle** /ˈpu:dl ˈपूड्ल्/ *noun* [C] a type of dog with thick curly fur that is sometimes cut into a special pattern धुँघराले बालों वाला कुत्ता जिसके बालों को किसी विशिष्ट आकृति में भी काटा जाता है

**pool[1]** /pu:l पूल्/ *noun* **1** [C] **a pool (of sth)** a small amount of liquid lying on a surface किसी सतह पर थोड़ी मात्रा में जमा कोई द्रव पदार्थ *There's a huge pool of water on the kitchen floor.* ➪ **pond** पर नोट देखिए। **2** [C] a small area of light छोटा प्रकाश-क्षेत्र *a pool of light* **3** [C] = **swimming pool** *He swam ten lengths of the pool.* **4** [C] a quantity of money, goods, etc. that is shared between a group of people समूह के सदस्यों की साझा संपत्ति (धनराशि, उपयोगी सामान, आदि) सामूहिक निधि या सामान *There is a pool of cars that anyone in the company can use.* **5** [U] a game that is played on a table with 16 coloured and numbered balls. Two players try to hit these balls into holes in the table (**pockets**) with long thin sticks (**cues**) स्नूकर, बिलियर्ड जैसा एक खेल यह खेल दो खिलाड़ियों के बीच एक मेज़ पर 16 रंग-बिरंगी और संख्याओं से अंकित गेंदों से खेला जाता है जिसमें खिलाड़ी एक लंबी छड़ी से गेंदों को मारकर मेज़ की थैलियों में डालते हैं ➪ **billiards** और **snooker** देखिए।

**pool[2]** /pu:l पूल्/ *verb* [T] to collect money, ideas, etc. together from a number of people लोगों से धन, विचार आदि एकत्रित करना (सामान्य लाभ के लिए) *If we pool our ideas we should come up with a good plan.*

**poor** /pɔ:(r) पॉ(र्)/ *adj.* **1** not having enough money to have a comfortable life ग़रीब, निर्धन *The family was too poor to buy new clothes.* ○ *Richer countries could do more to help poorer countries.* ✪ विलोम **rich** **2 the poor** *noun* [*pl.*] people who do not have enough money to have a comfortable life ग़रीब लोग, निर्धन वर्ग **3** of low quality or in a bad condition गुणवत्ता में कम या दुर्दशाग्रस्त *Mona is in very poor health.* ○ *The industry has a poor safety record.* **4** used when you are showing that you feel sorry for sb किसी के लिए सहानुभूति दिखाने के लिए प्रयुक्त *Poor Dev! He's very upset!*

**poorly[1]** /ˈpɔ:li ˈपॉलि/ *adv.* not well; badly अच्छा नहीं, काफ़ी कम; बुरी तरह से *a poorly paid job*

**poorly[2]** /ˈpɔ:li ˈपॉलि/ *adj.* (*BrE informal*) not well; ill अच्छा नहीं, अस्वस्थ; बीमार *I'm feeling a bit poorly.*

**pop[1]** /pɒp पॉप्/ *verb* (**popping; popped**) **1** [I, T] to make a short sudden sound like a small explosion; to cause sth to do this तड़ाक या फट्-सी आवाज़ करना; ऐसी आवाज़ पैदा करना *He popped the balloon.* **2** [I] **pop across, down, out, etc.** to come or go somewhere quickly or suddenly जल्दी-से या अचानक कहीं आना या जाना *I'm just popping out to the shops.* **3** [T] **pop sth in, into, etc. sth** to put or take sth somewhere quickly or suddenly जल्दी-से या अचानक कहीं कुछ रख देना या लेना *She popped the note into her bag.*

**PHR V** **pop in** to make a quick visit थोड़ी देर के लिए मिलने आना *Why don't you pop in for a cup of tea?*

**pop out** to come out (of sth) suddenly or quickly (कहीं से) अचानक या जल्दी बाहर निकल आना *Her eyes nearly popped out of her head in surprise.*

**pop up** (*informal*) to appear or happen when you are not expecting it अप्रत्याशित रूप से प्रकट या घटित होना

**pop²** /pɒp पॉप्/ *noun* **1** [U] (*also* **pop music**) modern music that is most popular among young people युवावर्ग में बहुत लोकप्रिय आधुनिक संगीत; पॉप संगीत *a pop group* ➪ **jazz, rock** और **classical** भी देखिए। **2** [C] a short sudden sound like a small explosion तड़ाक या फट् जैसी आवाज़ *There was a loud pop as the champagne cork came out of the bottle.*

**pop.** *abbr.* population आबादी, जनसंख्या *pop. 12 m*

**popcorn** /ˈpɒpkɔːn ˈपॉप्कॉर्न्/ *noun* [U] a type of corn that is heated until it bursts and forms light whitish balls that are eaten with salt or sugar sprinkled on them मक्की का लावा, पॉपकॉर्न

**pope** /pəʊp पोप्/ *noun* [C] the head of the Roman Catholic Church रोमन कैथोलिक चर्च का सर्वोच्च धर्मगुरु; पोप

**poplar** /ˈpɒplə(r) ˈपॉप्ल(र्)/ *noun* [C] a tall straight tree with soft wood पहाड़ी पीपल (ऊँचा सीधा नरम लकड़ी वाला पेड़)

**poppadum** = **papad**

**popper** /ˈpɒpə(r) ˈपॉप(र्)/ (*also* **press stud** *AmE* **snap**) *noun* [C] two round pieces of metal or plastic that you press together in order to fasten a piece of clothing कमीज़ के कफ़ आदि को जकड़ने वाले दो गोल बटन (धातु या प्लास्टिक के) ➪ **button** पर चित्र देखिए।

**poppy** /ˈpɒpi ˈपॉपि/ *noun* [C] (*pl.* **poppies**) a bright red wild flower that has small black seeds गहरे लाल रंग का एक जंगली फूल जिसमें छोटे काले बीज, खसखस, होते हैं; पोस्त, पोस्ता

**Popsicle™** /ˈpɒpsɪkl ˈपॉप्सिक्ल्/ *noun* [C] (*AmE*) = **ice lolly**

**popular** /ˈpɒpjələ(r) ˈपॉप्यल(र्)/ *adj.* **1 popular (with sb)** liked by many people or by most people in a group लोकप्रिय, अधिकतर लोगों को पसंद *a popular holiday resort* ○ *He's always been very popular with his pupils.* ✪ विलोम **unpopular** **2** made for the tastes and knowledge of ordinary people जनसाधारण की रुचि और ज्ञानसार के अनुकूल *The popular newspapers seem more interested in scandal than news.* **3** (*only before a noun*) of or for a lot of people जनता का या जनता के लिए *The programme is being repeated* ***by popular demand***.

**popularity** /ˌpɒpjuˈlærəti ˌपॉप्यु ˈलैरटि/ *noun* [U] the quality or state of being liked by many people लोकप्रियता *The band's popularity is growing.*

**popularize** (*also* **-ise**) /ˈpɒpjʊləraɪz ˈपॉप्युलराइज़्/ *verb* [T] to make a lot of or make most people like sth किसी वस्तु को लोकप्रिय बनाना *The film did a lot to popularize her novels.*

**popularly** /ˈpɒpjələli ˈपॉप्यललि/ *adv.* by many people; generally अधिकतर लोगों द्वारा; सामान्य रूप से *Sachin Tendulkar is popularly known as the Master Blaster.*

**populate** /ˈpɒpjuleɪt ˈपॉप्युलेट्/ *verb* [T] (*usually passive*) to fill a particular area with people किसी स्थान में आबादी होना *Parts of the country are very thinly populated.*

**population** /ˌpɒpjuˈleɪʃn ˌपॉप्यु ˈलेश्न्/ *noun* **1** [C, U] the number of people who live in a particular area, city or country किसी विशेष क्षेत्र, नगर, देश में रहने वालों की संख्या; जनसंख्या, आबादि *What is the population of your country?* ○ *an increase/a fall in population* **2** [C] all the people who live in a particular place or all the people or animals of a particular type that live somewhere विशेष स्थान पर रहने वाले समस्त व्यक्ति या कहीं पर रहने वाले विशेष प्रकार के समस्त व्यक्ति या जीव-जंतु *the local population* ○ *the male/female population*

**porcelain** /ˈpɔːsəlɪn ˈपॉसलिन्/ *noun* [U] a hard white substance that is used for making expensive cups, plates, etc. महँगे कप, प्लेट आदि बनाने में प्रयुक्त; चीनी मिट्टी

**porch** /pɔːtʃ पॉच्/ *noun* [C] **1** (*BrE*) a small covered area at the entrance to a house or church घर या चर्च का ढका हुआ प्रवेश द्वार; पोर्च, द्वारमंडप **2** (*AmE*) = **veranda**

**porcupine** /ˈpɔːkjupaɪn ˈपॉक्युपाइन्/ *noun* [C] an animal covered with long thin sharp parts (**quills**) which it can lift up to protect itself when it is attacked एक जंतु जिसके शरीर पर पतले नुकीले कांटे से लगे होते हैं जो किसी प्राणी के आक्रमण के समय ऊपर खड़े हो जाते हैं; साही

**pore¹** /pɔː(r) पॉ(र्)/ *noun* [C] one of the small holes in your skin through which sweat can pass रोमकूप, रोएँ का छेद

**pore²** /pɔː(r) पॉ(र्)/ *verb*

**PHR V** **pore over sth** to study or read sth very carefully (किसी वस्तु को) बहुत सावधानी से पढ़ना या उसका अध्ययन करना

**pork** /pɔːk पॉक्/ *noun* [U] meat from a pig सूअर का मांस ➪ **bacon** देखिए।

**pornography** /pɔːˈnɒgrəfi पॉˈनॉग्रफ़ि/ (*informal* **porn** /pɔːn पॉन्/) *noun* [U] books, magazines, films, etc. that describe or show sexual acts in order to cause sexual excitement कामवासना उत्तेजित करने के लिए यौनक्रियाओं का वर्णन करने वाली पुस्तकें, पत्रिकाएँ, फ़िल्में आदि ▶ **pornographic** /ˌpɔːnəˈgræfɪk ˌपॉनˈग्रैफ़िक्/ *adj.* अश्लील

**porous** /ˈpɔːrəs ˈपॉरस्/ *adj.* allowing liquid or air to pass through slowly छिद्रिल (ऐसा कि द्रव या हवा रिस सके), सरंध्र *porous rock* ✪ विलोम **non-porous**

**porpoise** /ˈpɔːpəs ˈपॉपस्/ *noun* [C] a sea animal with a pointed nose that lives in groups. Porpoises are similar to **dolphins** but smaller नुकीली नाक वाला डॉलफ़िन से मिलता-जुलता समुद्री जीव जो समूह बनाकर रहता है

**porridge** /ˈpɒrɪdʒ ˈपॉरिज्/ *noun* [U] a soft, thick white food that is made from a type of grain (**oats**) boiled with milk or water and eaten hot दलिया (दूध या पानी में पका)

**port** /pɔːt पॉट्/ *noun* **1** [C, U] an area where ships stop to let goods and passengers on and off वह स्थल जहाँ ज़हाज़ सवारियों को या माल को उतारने-चढ़ाने के लिए खड़े रहते हैं; बंदरगाह *a fishing port* ○ *The damaged ship reached port safely.* **2** [C] a town or city that has a large area of water where ships load cargo, etc. बंदरगाह से लगा शहर, पत्तन *Mumbai is a major port.* **3** [U] a strong sweet red wine एक तेज़ मीठी लाल शराब **4** [U] the side of a ship that is on your left when you are facing towards the front of the ship जहाज़ का पार्श्व (जो सामने मुँह करने पर बाईं ओर होता है) ✪ विलोम **starboard**

**portable** /ˈpɔːtəbl ˈपॉटबल्/ *adj.* that can be moved or carried easily जिसे आसानी से हिलाया या कहीं ले जाया जा सके; सुवाह्य *a portable television* ➪ **movable** और **mobile** देखिए।

**portal** /ˈpɔːtl ˈपॉट्ल्/ *noun* [C] a **website** that is used as a point of entry to the Internet, where information has been collected that will be useful to a person interested in particular kinds of things इंटरनेट का प्रवेश द्वार का काम करने वाली वेब-साइट (इंटरनेट पर विविध प्रकार की सूचनाएँ संगृहीत रहती हैं); पोर्टल *a business/health/children's portal*

**portal vein** (*also* **hepatic portal vein**) *noun* [C] (*medical*) a vein that takes blood from the stomach and other organs near the stomach to the **liver** आमाशय और निकटवर्ती अंगों से रक्त को गुर्दे तक पहुँचाने वाली शिरा; निर्वाहिका शिरा

**porter** /ˈpɔːtə(r) ˈपॉट(र्)/ *noun* [C] **1** a person whose job is to carry suitcases, etc. at a railway station, airport, etc. रेलवे स्टेशन आदि पर सामान ले जाने वाला व्यक्ति; कुली, हमाल **2** a person whose job is to be in charge of the entrance of a hotel or other large building होटल या किसी बड़े भवन का द्वारपाल, दरबान

**portfolio** /ˌpɔːtˈfəʊliəʊ ˌपॉट्ˈफ़ोलिओ/ *noun* (*pl.* **portfolios**) **1** a thin flat case used for carrying papers, drawings, etc. पेटिका; काग़ज़ात, आरेख आदि का बस्ता **2** a collection of photographs, drawings, documents, etc. that you carry as an example of your work, especially when applying for a job छायाचित्र, आरेख, काग़ज़ात आदि का संग्रह जो रोज़गार के प्रयोग के लिए कार्य को दर्शाता है **3** (*finance*) a list of shares owned by a particular person or organization किसी विशिष्ट व्यक्ति या संस्था के शेयर की सूची **4** (*BrE formal*) the specific area of responsibility of a Minister सरकार के किसी मंत्री का कार्य विभाग *the Information and Broadcasting portfolio*

**porthole** /ˈpɔːthəʊl ˈपॉट्होल्/ *noun* [C] a small round window in a ship जहाज़ में छोटी गोल खिड़की, पोत-झरोखा, मोखा

**portion** /ˈpɔːʃn ˈपॉश्न्/ *noun* [C] **a portion (of sth)** **1** a part or share of sth किसी वस्तु का भाग या अंश *What portion of your salary goes on tax?* ○ *We must both accept a portion of the blame.* **2** an amount of food for one person (especially in a restaurant) एक व्यक्ति के लिए भोजन (विशेषतः रेस्तराँ में) *Could we have two extra portions of chips, please?* ➪ **helping** देखिए।

**portrait** /ˈpɔːtreɪt ˈपॉट्रेट्/ *noun* [C] **1** a picture, painting or photograph of a person किसी व्यक्ति का चित्र, पेंटिंग या फ़ोटो *to paint sb's portrait* **2** a description of sb/sth in words व्यक्ति या वस्तु का शब्दों में वर्णन; शब्दचित्र

**portray** /pɔːˈtreɪ पॉˈट्रे/ *verb* [T] **1** to show sb/sth in a picture; to describe sb/sth in a piece of writing किसी को चित्र में दर्शाना; किसी का लेख में वर्णन या चित्रण करना *Tanya portrayed life in 19th century India in her book.* **2 portray sb/sth as sth** to describe sb/sth in a particular way किसी का विशेष प्रकार से वर्णन या चित्रण करना *In many of his novels life is portrayed as being hard.* **3** to act the part of sb in a play or film नाटक या फ़िल्म में किसी पात्र की भूमिका निभाना *In this film she portrays a very old woman.* ▶ **portrayal** /pɔːˈtreɪəl पॉˈट्रेअल्/ *noun* [C] चित्रण, वर्णन

**pose[1]** /pəʊz पोज़्/ *verb* **1** [T] to create or give sb sth that he/she has to deal with किसी के लिए कोई प्रश्न उत्पन्न या प्रस्तुत करना (जिसे निपटाया जाना हो) *to pose a problem/threat/challenge/risk* किसी को निपटाने के लिए कुछ दे देना या कुछ परेशानी उत्पन्न कर देना *to pose* (= ask) *a question* **2** [I] to sit or stand in a particular position for a painting, photograph, etc. चित्र, फ़ोटो आदि के लिए विशिष्ट मुद्रा में बैठना या खड़ा होना *After the wedding we all posed for photographs.* **3** [I] **pose as sb/sth** to pretend to be sb/sth कोई दूसरा होने का ढोंग रचना *The robbers got into the house by posing as telephone engineers.* **4** [I] to behave in a way that is intended to impress people who see you प्रभावित करने के लिए दिखावा करना *They hardly swam at all. They just sat posing at the side of the pool.*

**pose[2]** /pəʊz पोज़्/ *noun* [C] **1** a position in which sb stands, sits, etc. especially in order to be painted or photographed चित्र बनवाने या फ़ोटो खिंचवाने के लिए खड़ा होने, बैठने आदि की मुद्रा **2** a way of behaving that is intended to impress people who see you लोगों को प्रभावित करने के लिए दिखावा; आडंबर

**posh** /pɒʃ पॉश्/ *adj.* (*informal*) **1** fashionable and expensive लोकप्रिय शैली का और महँगा *We went for a meal in a really posh hotel.* **2** (*BrE*) (used about people) belonging to or typical of a high social class (व्यक्ति) समाज के उच्च वर्ग से संबंधित या उसका प्रतिनिधिक

**position[1]** /pəˈzɪʃn पˈज़िश्न्/ *noun* **1** [C, U] the place where sb/sth is or should be किसी का स्थान (वर्तमान या उपयुक्त) *Are you happy with the position of the chairs?* ○ *All the dancers were* ***in position*** *waiting for the music to begin.* **2** [C, U] the way in which sb/sth sits or stands, or the direction that sth is pointing in किसी के बैठने या खड़ा होने का ढंग या इंगित की जा रही दिशा *My leg hurts when I* ***change position****.* ○ *Turn the switch to the off position.* **3** [C, *usually sing.*] the state or situation that sb/sth is in किसी की तत्कालीन दशा या स्थिति *I'm in a very* ***difficult position****.* ○ *I'm not* ***in a position*** *to help you financially.* **4** [C] **a position (on sth)** what you think about sth; your opinion किसी विषय में सोच, धारणा; मत *What is your position on smoking?* **5** [C, U] the place or level of a person, company, team, etc. compared to others तुलनात्मक दृष्टि से व्यक्ति, कंपनी आदि का स्थान या स्तर *the position of women in society* ○ *Wealth and position are very important to some people.* **6** [C] a job नौकरी, पद *There have been over a hundred applications for the position of Sales Manager.* ✪ पर्याय **post** **7** [C] the part you play in a team game टीम वाले खेल में स्थान, पोज़ीशन (जिस पर खिलाड़ी खेलता है) *Dev can play any position except goalkeeper.*

**position[2]** /pəˈzɪʃn पˈज़िश्न्/ *verb* [T] to put sb/sth in a particular place or position किसी को विशेष स्थान या स्थिति में रखना *Mandira positioned herself near the door so she could get out quickly.*

**positive** /ˈpɒzətɪv ˈपॉज़टिव़् / *adj.* **1** thinking or talking mainly about the good things in a situation, in a way that makes you or sb else feel hopeful and confident किसी स्थिति के अच्छे पक्ष के विषय में ऐसे सोचना या बातें करना कि अपना और दूसरे का विश्वास बढ़े; रचनात्मक, सकारात्मक ***Positive thinking*** *will help you to succeed.* ✪ विलोम **negative** **2 positive (about sth/that...)** certain; sure सुनिश्चित; पक्का *Are you positive that this is the woman you saw?* **3** clear; definite स्पष्ट; संदेहरहित *There is no positive evidence that he is guilty.* ○ *to take positive action* **4** (used about a medical or scientific test) showing that sth has happened or is present (डॉक्टरी या वैज्ञानिक परीक्षण) जो यह दिखाए कि कोई रोग हुआ है या कुछ (रोग का कारण) मौजूद है *Two athletes tested positive for steroids.* ✪ विलोम **negative** **5** (used about a number) more than zero (संख्या) शून्य से अधिक ✪ विलोम **negative**

**positively** /ˈpɒzətɪvli ˈपॉज़टिव़्लि / *adv.* **1** with no doubt; firmly निस्संदेह; पक्के तौर पर *I was positively convinced that I was doing the right thing.* **2** in a way that shows you are thinking about the good things in a situation, not the bad किसी स्थिति में सकारात्मक ढंग से (केवल अच्छी बातें) सोचते हुए *Thinking positively helps many people deal with stress.* **3** (used about a person's way of speaking or acting) in a confident and hopeful way (व्यक्ति का बोलने या काम करने का ढंग) आत्मविश्वासपूर्वक और अनुकूल की आशा के साथ *The team played cautiously for the first 10 minutes, then continued more positively.* **4** (*informal*) (used for emphasizing sth) really; extremely किसी बात पर बल देने के लिए प्रयुक्त सचमुच; अत्यधिक *He wasn't just annoyed—he was positively furious!*

**possess** /pəˈzes पˈज़ेस्/ *verb* [T] (*not used in the continuous tenses*) **1** (*formal*) to have or own sth किसी वस्तु को अधिकार में रखना या उस पर स्वामित्व होना *They lost everything they possessed in the fire.* ○ *Parul possesses a natural ability to make people laugh.* **2** to influence sb or to make sb do sth किसी के मन-मस्तिष्क को प्रभावित कर लेना या उसे कुछ करने के लए मजबूर करना *What possessed you to say a thing like that!*

**NOTE** यद्यपि यह क्रिया सातत्यबोधक कालों (continuous tenses) में प्रयुक्त नहीं होती तथापि इसका (-ing युक्त) वर्तमान कृदंत (present participle) रूप काफ़ी प्रचलित है—*Any student possessing the necessary qualifications will be considered for the course.*

**possession** /pəˈzeʃn पˈज़ेश्न्/ *noun* **1** [U] the state of having or owning sth किसी पर अधिकार या स्वामित्व *The gang were caught* ***in possession of*** *stolen goods.* ○ *Enemy forces managed to* ***take possession of*** *the town.* **2** [C, *usually pl.*] something that you have or own वस्तु जिस पर अधिकार या स्वामित्व है *Vikas packed all his possessions and left.*

**possessive** /pəˈzesɪv पˈज़ेसिव़् / *adj.* **1 possessive (of/about sb/sth)** not wanting to share sb/sth (वस्तुओं को) किसी के साथ बाँटने का अनिच्छुक, (वस्तुओं पर) काबिज़ होने की मनोवृत्ति वाला *Sonu is so possessive with his toys—he won't let his friends play with them.* **2** (*grammar*) used to describe words that show who or what a person or thing belongs to संबंधवाचक (व्यक्ति और वस्तु का संबंध दिखाने वाला) *'My', 'your' and 'his' are possessive adjectives.* ○ *'Mine', 'yours' and 'his' are possessive pronouns.*

**possessor** /pəˈzesə(r) पˈज़ेस(र्)/ *noun* [C] a person who has or owns sth किसी वस्तु पर अधिकार या स्वामित्व रखने वाला व्यक्ति; स्वामी, मालिक, कब्ज़ेदार

**possibility** /ˌpɒsəˈbɪləti ˌपॉसˈबिलटि/ *noun* (*pl.* **possibilities**) **1** [U, C] **(a) possibility (of sth/doing sth); (a) possibility that...** the fact that sth might exist or happen, but is not likely to किसी तथ्य के होने की या किसी घटना के घटित होने की संभावना *There's not much possibility of rain tonight.* ○ *There is* ***a strong possibility*** *that the fire was started deliberately.* **2** [C] one of the different things that you can do in a particular situation or in order to achieve sth विशेष परिस्थिति में या कुछ प्राप्त करने के लिए उपलब्ध विकल्प *There is a wide range of possibilities open to us.*

**possible** /ˈpɒsəbl ˈपॉसबल्/ *adj.* **1** that can happen or be done संभव (जो घटित हो सके या किया जा सके), शक्य *I'll phone you as soon* ***as possible.*** ○ *The doctors did* ***everything possible*** *to save his life.* ✪ विलोम **impossible** **2** that may be suitable or acceptable उपयुक्त या स्वीकार्य *There are four possible candidates for the job.* ➪ **probable** देखिए। **3** used after adjectives to emphasize that sth is the best, worst, etc. of its type किसी वस्तु के उत्कृष्ट, निकृष्ट होने पर बल देने के लिए विशेषण के बाद प्रयुक्त *Alone and with no job or money, I was in the worst possible situation.*

**possibly** /ˈpɒsəbli ˈपॉसब्लि/ *adv.* **1** perhaps; maybe शायद; संभवत: *'Will you be free on Sunday?' 'Possibly.'* **2** (used for emphasizing sth) according to what is possible (किसी पर बल देने के लिए प्रयुक्त) यथासंभव, जो संभव है उसके अनुसार *I will leave as soon as I possibly can.*

**post¹** /pəʊst पोस्ट्/ *noun* **1** (*AmE* **mail**) [U] the system or organization for collecting and dealing with letters, packages, etc. चिट्ठियों, बंडलों आदि को एकत्र करने और निपटाने की व्यवस्था या ऐसा करने वाला संगठन; डाक व्यवस्था *The document is too valuable to send* ***by post.*** ○ *If you hurry you might* ***catch the post*** (= post it before everything is collected). **2** (*AmE* **mail**) [U] letters, packages, etc. that are collected or brought to your house चिट्ठियाँ, बंडल आदि (जिन्हें एकत्र और वितरित किया जाता है) *Has the post come yet this morning?* ○ *There wasn't any post for you.* **3** [C] a job नौकरी, पद *The post was advertised in the local newspaper.* ✪ पर्याय **position** **4** [C] a place where sb is on duty or is guarding sth स्थान जहाँ कोई व्यक्ति तैनात हो; व्यक्ति का कार्यस्थल या पहरा देने का स्थान *The soldiers had to remain at their posts all night.* **5** [C] an upright piece of metal or wood that is put in the ground to mark a position or to support sth धातु या लकड़ी का खंभा जिसे किसी वस्तु की स्थिति अंकित करने या उसे सहारा देने के लिए ज़मीन में गाड़ा जाता है *a goal post* ○ *Can you see a signpost anywhere?*

**IDM by return (of post)** ➪ **return²** देखिए।

**post²** /pəʊst पोस्ट्/ *verb* [T] **1** (*AmE* **mail**) to send a letter, package, etc. by post पत्र, बंडल आदि डाक से भेजना *This letter was posted in New Delhi yesterday.*

**NOTE** **Post** शब्द (संज्ञा और क्रिया) ब्रिटिश अंग्रेज़ी में अधिक प्रचलित है और **mail** अमेरिकन अंग्रेज़ी में। परंतु ब्रिटिश अंग्रेज़ी में संज्ञा के रूप में **mail** का भी प्रायः प्रयोग होता है। इसके अतिरिक्त **airmail** और **surface mail** शब्दों पर भी ध्यान दिया जाए।

**2** to send sb to go and work somewhere किसी को कहीं तैनात करना *After two years in Delhi, Rosa was posted to the Bangalore office.* **3** to put sb on guard or on duty in a particular place किसी को कहीं पहरे पर या ड्यूटी पर लगाना *Policemen were posted outside the building.* **4** (*formal*) (*often passive*) to put a notice where everyone can see it (कहीं) नोटिस आदि लगाना (जहाँ सब उसे देख सकें) *The exam results will be posted on the main noticeboard.*

**post-** /pəʊst पोस्ट्/ *prefix* (*used in nouns, verbs and adjectives*) after पश्च-, उत्तर, के बाद *postgraduate* ○ *post-war* ➪ **ante-** और **pre-** देखिए।

**postage** /ˈpəʊstɪdʒ ˈपोस्‌टिज्/ *noun* [U] the amount that you must pay to send a letter, package etc. डाक-व्यय, डाक-शुल्क

**postage stamp** = **stamp[1] 1**

**postal** /ˈpəʊstl ˈपोस्‌ट्‌ल्/ *adj.* connected with the sending and collecting of letters, packages, etc. डाक-विषयक पत्रादि भेजने और एकत्र करने से संबंधित

**postal order** (*also* **money order**) *noun* [C] a piece of paper that you can buy at a post office that represents a certain amount of money. A postal order is a safe way of sending money by post पोस्टल आर्डर (डाकघर से मिलने वाला निश्चित मूल्य-राशि का काग़ज़ जो राशि को सुरक्षित रूप से भेजने का एक माध्यम है)

**postbox** /ˈpəʊstbɒks ˈपोस्ट्‌बॉक्स्/ (*also* **letter box,** *AmE* **mailbox**) *noun* [C] a box in a public place where you put letters, etc. that you want to send पत्र पेटी (जिसमें भेजने-योग्य पत्र आदि डाले जाते हैं); लेटर बॉक्स ➪ **pillar box** देखिए।

**postcard** /ˈpəʊstkɑːd ˈपोस्ट्‌काड्/ *noun* [C] a card that you write a message on and send to sb. Postcards may have a picture on one side and are usually sent without an envelope पोस्टकार्ड

**postcode** /ˈpəʊstkəʊd ˈपोस्ट्‌कोड्/ (*IndE* **pin code;** *AmE* **ZIP code**) *noun* [C] a group of letters and/or numbers that you put at the end of an address पते के अंत में लिखे जाने वाले अक्षर और/या अंक (भारत में पिन कोड)

**poster** /ˈpəʊstə(r) ˈपोस्‌ट(र्)/ *noun* [C] **1** a large printed picture or a notice in a public place, often used to advertise sth सार्वजनिक स्थान पर (प्रायः विज्ञापन के लिए) बड़ा चित्र या नोटिस; पोस्टर **2** a large picture printed on paper that is put on a wall for decoration सजावट के लिए दीवार पर लगाने का बड़ा मुद्रित चित्र; पोस्टर

**posterity** /pɒˈsterəti पॉˈस्टेरटि/ *noun* [U] the future and the people who will be alive then वंशज; भावी पीढ़ियाँ *We should look after our environment for the sake of posterity.*

**postgraduate** /ˌpəʊstˈgrædʒuət ˌपोस्ट्ˈग्रैजुअट्/ *noun* [C] a person who is doing further studies at a university after taking his/her first degree स्नातकोत्तर कक्षा का छात्र ➪ **graduate** और **undergraduate** देखिए।

**posthumous** /ˈpɒstjʊməs ˈपॉस्‌ट्युमस्/ *adj.* given or happening after sb has died मरणोपरांत, निधनोत्तर *a posthumous medal for bravery*
▶ **posthumously** *adv.* मरणोपरांत, मृत्यु के पश्चात

**posting** /ˈpəʊstɪŋ ˈपोस्‌टिङ्/ *noun* [C] a job in another country that you are sent to do by your employer किसी व्यक्ति की (मूल स्थान से) अन्यत्र तैनाती या पदस्थता

**Post-it™** (*also* **Post-it note**) *noun* [C] a small piece of coloured, sticky paper that you use for writing a note on, and that can be easily removed नोट लिखने के लिए छोटा रंगीन चिपकने वाला काग़ज़ (जिसे आसानी से निकाला जा सकता है) ➪ **stationery** पर चित्र देखिए।

**postman** /ˈpəʊstmən ˈपोस्ट्‌मन्/ (*AmE* **mailman**) *noun* [C] (*pl.* **-men** /-mən -मन्/) a person whose job is to collect letters, packages, etc. and take them to people's houses डाकिया, चिट्ठीरसाँ, पत्रवाहक

**postmark** /ˈpəʊstmɑːk ˈपोस्ट्‌माक्/ *noun* [C] an official mark over a stamp on a letter, package, etc. that says when and where it was posted चिट्ठी आदि पर सरकारी मोहर जिससे भेजे जाने के समय और स्थान का पता चलता है

**post-mortem** /ˌpəʊstˈmɔːtəm ˌपोस्ट्ˈमॉटम्/ *noun* [C] a medical examination of a dead body to find out how the person died (मृत्यु का कारण जानने के लिए) डॉक्टरी शव-परीक्षा, पोस्ट-मार्टम

**post-natal** /ˌpəʊstˈneɪtl ˌपोस्ट्ˈनेट्‌ल्/ *adj.* (*only before a noun*) connected with the period after the birth of a baby शिशु के जन्म के बाद की अवधि से संबंधित; जन्मोत्तर, प्रसवोत्तर ➪ **antenatal** देखिए।

**post office** *noun* [C] **1** a place where you can buy stamps, post packages, etc. डाक-ख़ाना, डाकघर, पोस्ट ऑफ़िस **2 the Post Office** the national organization that is responsible for collecting and dealing with letters, packages, etc. डाक-व्यवस्था के लिए राष्ट्रीय संगठन, सरकार का डाक-विभाग

**postpone** /pəˈspəʊn पˈस्पोन्/ *verb* [T] to arrange that sth will happen at a later time than the time you had planned; to delay नियोजित घटना, कार्यक्रम आदि को स्थगित करना; विलंब से करना *The match was postponed because of rain.* ➪ **cancel** देखिए।
▶ **postponement** *noun* [C, U] स्थगन-क्रिया

**postscript** /ˈpəʊstskrɪpt ˈपोस्ट्‌स्क्रिप्ट्/ *noun* [C] an extra message or extra information that is added at the end of a letter, note, etc. पत्र आदि के अंत में जोड़ा गया अतिरिक्त अंश (सूचना या संदेश) ➪ **PS** देखिए।

**posture** /ˈpɒstʃə(r) ˈपॉस्‌च(र्)/ *noun* [C, U] the way that a person sits, stands, walks, etc. किसी व्यक्ति की बैठने, खड़ा होने, चलने आदि की मुद्रा *Poor posture can lead to backache.*

**post-war** *adj.* existing or happening in the period after the end of a war, especially the Second World War युद्ध (विशेषतः द्वितीय मध्ययुद्ध) के बाद का; युद्धोत्तर

**pot**[1] /pɒt पॉट्/ *noun* [C] **1** a round container that is used for cooking food in भिगौना, बरतन, हँडिया (जिसमें भोजन बनाया जाता है) **2** a container that you use for a particular purpose विशेष प्रयोजन से प्रयुक्त कोई पात्र (गमला आदि) *a flowerpot* ○ *a pot of paint* **3** the amount that a pot contains पात्र में आने वाली (किसी वस्तु की) मात्रा *We drank two pots of tea.*

**pot**[2] /pɒt पॉट्/ *verb* [T] (**potting; potted**) **1** to put a plant into a pot filled with soil (मिट्टी भरे) गमले में पौधा लगाना **2** to hit a ball into one of the pockets in the table in the game of **pool, billiards** or **snooker** पूल, बिलियर्ड्स या स्नूकर में मेज़ के किसी छेद में गेंद डालना *He potted the black ball into the corner pocket.*

**potable** /ˈpəʊtəbl ˈपोटब्ल्/ *adj.* (*formal*) (used about water) safe to drink (पानी) पीने के लिए सुरक्षित

**potassium** /pəˈtæsiəm पˈटैसिअम्/ *noun* [U] (*symbol* **K**) a soft silver-white metal that exists mainly in mixtures (**compounds**) which are used in industry and farming रजत के समान शुभ्र कोमल धातु जो उद्योग और कृषि में प्रयुक्त यौगिकों में मुख्यतः पाई जाती है; पोटैशियम

**potato** /pəˈteɪtəʊ पˈटेटो/ *noun* [C, U] (*pl.* **potatoes**) a round vegetable that grows under the ground with a brown, yellow or red skin. Potatoes are white or yellow inside आलू *mashed potato* ○ *to peel potatoes* ➪ **vegetable** पर चित्र देखिए।

**potato crisp** (*AmE* **potato chip**) = **crisp**[2]

**potent** /ˈpəʊtnt ˈपोट्न्ट्/ *adj.* strong or powerful शक्तिशाली या प्रभावकारी *a potent drug/drink* ▶ **potency** /ˈpəʊtnsi ˈपोट्न्सि/ *noun* [U] शक्ति, प्रभाव

**potential**[1] /pəˈtenʃl पˈटेन्श्ल्/ *adj.* (*only before a noun*) that may possibly become sth, happen, be used, etc. जिसके कुछ होने, प्रयोग में आने आदि की संभावना हो; संभाव्य *Wind power is a potential source of energy.* ○ *potential customers* ▶ **potentially** /pəˈtenʃəli पˈटेन्शलि/ *adv.* संभवतः

**potential**[2] /pəˈtenʃl पˈटेन्श्ल्/ *noun* [U] the qualities or abilities that sb/sth has but that may not be fully developed yet व्यक्ति या वस्तु में विद्यमान गुण या क्षमताएँ जो अभी तक पूर्णतया विकसित नहीं *That boy **has great potential** as an athlete.*

**potential energy** *noun* [U] (*technical*) the form of energy that an object gains as it is lifted उठाए जाने पर पिंड को प्राप्त ऊर्जा; स्थितिज उर्जा

**pothole** /ˈpɒthəʊl ˈपॉट्होल्/ *noun* [C] **1** a hole in the surface of a road that is formed by traffic and bad weather (यातायात और ख़राब मौसम से) सड़क पर बना गड्ढा **2** a deep hole in rock that is formed by water over thousands of years and often leads to underground rooms (**caves**) हज़ारों वर्षों से पानी के प्रभाव से चट्टान में बना छेद (जो प्रायः नीचे गुफाओं तक पहुँचता है), जल गर्तिका

**potholing** /ˈpɒthəʊlɪŋ ˈपॉट्होलिङ्/ *noun* [U] the sport of climbing down inside **potholes 2**, walking through underground tunnels, etc. जल गर्तिकाओं से नीचे उतरने, भूमिगत सुरंगों में से गुज़रने आदि का खेल *to go potholing*

**pot plant** *noun* [C] (*BrE*) a plant that you keep indoors घर के भीतर रखने का पौधा

**potter**[1] /ˈpɒtə(r) ˈपॉट(र्)/ (*AmE* **putter**) *verb* [I] **potter (about/around)** to spend your time doing small jobs or things that you enjoy without hurrying मस्ती से समय बिताना (मनपसंद छोटे-छोटे काम करते हुए व बिना जल्दबाज़ी के)

**potter**[2] /ˈpɒtə(r) ˈपॉट(र्)/ *noun* [C] a person who makes pots, dishes, etc. (**pottery**) from baked clay कुम्हार

**pottery** /ˈpɒtəri ˈपॉटरि/ *noun* (*pl.* **potteries**) **1** [U] pots, dishes, etc. that are made from baked clay मिट्टी के बर्तन (प्याले, प्लेटें आदि) **2** [U] the activity or skill of making dishes, etc. from clay मिट्टी के बर्तन बनाने की क्रिया या कला *a pottery class* **3** [C] a place where clay pots and dishes are made कुम्हार का कारख़ाना

**potty** /ˈpɒti ˈपॉटि/ *noun* [C] (*pl.* **potties**) a plastic bowl that young children use when they are too small to use a toilet छोटे बच्चों का मल त्याग पात्र; शौच पात्र

**pouch** /paʊtʃ पाउच्/ *noun* [C] **1** a small leather bag चमड़े की छोटी थैली; पाउच **2** a pocket of skin on the stomach of some female animals, for example **kangaroos**, in which they carry their babies कुछ मादा पशुओं (जैसे कंगारू) की बच्चा रखने की थैली ➪ **marsupial** पर चित्र देखिए।

**poultice** /ˈpəʊltɪs ˈपोल्टिस्/ *noun* [C] a soft substance that you spread on a cloth and put on the skin to reduce pain or swelling गर्म औषधियुक्त पट्टी (दर्द या सूजन कम करने वाली); पुलटिस

**poultry** /ˈpəʊltri ˈपोल्ट्रि/ *noun* **1** [*pl.*] birds, for example chickens, ducks, etc. that are kept for their eggs or their meat अंडो व माँस के लिए पाली गई बतख़ आदि **2** [U] the meat from these birds मुरग़ियों आदि का माँस

**pounce** /paʊns पाउन्स्/ *verb* [I] **pounce (on sb/sth)** to attack sb/sth by jumping suddenly on him/her/it किसी पर एकाएक झपटते हुए हमला करना (*figurative*) *He was quick to pounce on any mistakes I made.*

**pound[1]** /paʊnd पाउन्ड्/ *noun* **1** [C] (*also* **pound sterling**) (*symbol* **£**) the unit of money in Britain; one hundred pence (100 p) पाउंड (ब्रिटेन की मुद्रा); सौ पेंस *Madhuri earns £16,000 a year.* ○ *Can you change a ten-pound note?* **2** [*sing.*] **the pound** the value of the British pound on international money markets अंतरराष्ट्रीय मुद्रा बाज़ार में ब्रिटिश पाउंड की क़ीमत *The pound has fallen against the dollar.* ○ *How many yen are there **to the pound**?* **3** [C] (*abbr.* **lb**) a measurement of weight, equal to 0.454 of a kilogram तौल की इकाई, पाउंड; (0.454 किलोग्राम के बराबर) *The carrots cost 30p a pound.* ○ *Half a pound of mushrooms, please.*

**pound[2]** /paʊnd पाउन्ड्/ *verb* **1** [I] **pound (at/against/on sth)** to hit sth hard many times making a lot of noise किसी वस्तु को अनेक बार पीटना या कूटना; (ऊँची आवाज़ पैदा करते हुए) तड़ातड़ मारना *She pounded on the door with her fists.* **2** [I] **pound along, down, up, etc.** to walk with heavy, noisy steps in a particular direction (किसी दिशा में) पैर-पटकते हुए जाना, धमा-चौकड़ी मचाना *Ravi went pounding up the stairs three at a time.* **3** [I] (used about your heart, blood, etc.) to beat quickly and loudly (हृदय, रक्त आदि का) तेज़ी से और ऊँची आवाज़ के साथ धड़कना *Her heart was pounding with fear.* **4** [T] to hit sth many times to break it into smaller pieces किसी वस्तु को चूर-चूर कर देना (मार-मार कर चूरा बना देना)

**pour** /pɔː(r) पॉ(र्)/ *verb* **1** [T] to make a liquid or other substance flow steadily out of or into a container द्रव या अन्य पदार्थ को उड़ेलना *Pour the sugar into a bowl.* **2** [I] (used about a liquid, smoke, light, etc.) to flow out of or into sth quickly and steadily, and in large quantities (द्रव, धुआँ, प्रकाश आदि का) तेज़ी से लगातार और बड़ी मात्रा में बाहर निकलना या अंदर आना *Tears were pouring down her cheeks.* ○ *She opened the curtains and sunlight poured into the room.* **3** [T] **pour sth (out)** to serve a drink to sb by letting it flow from a container into a cup or glass कप या गिलास में पेय पदार्थ परसना *Have you poured out the tea?* **4** [I] **pour (down) (with rain)** to rain heavily मूसलाधार (पानी) बरसना *The rain poured down all day long.* ○ *I'm not going out. It's pouring with rain.* **5** [I] to come or go somewhere continuously in large numbers बड़ी संख्या में लोगों का लगातार कहीं आना या जाना *People were pouring out of the station.*

**IDM** **pour your heart out (to sb)** to tell sb all your personal problems, feelings, etc. किसी के सामने दिल खोल देना (निजी समस्याएँ बताना, मनोभाव प्रकट करना आदि)

**PHR V** **pour sth out** to speak freely about what you think or feel about sth that has happened to you किसी बात पर अपने अनुभव के बारे में खुलकर बोलना *to pour out all your troubles*

**pout** /paʊt पाउट्/ *verb* [I] to push your lips, or your bottom lip, forward to show that you are annoyed about sth or to look sexually attractive दोनों होंठ, या निचला होंठ, आगे की ओर निकालना (खीझ प्रकट करने या आकर्षक दीखने के लिए) ▶ **pout** *noun* [C] ऐसी मुखमुद्रा

**poverty** /ˈpɒvəti ˈपॉव़टि/ *noun* [U] the state of being poor ग़रीबी, निर्धनता *There are millions of people in this country who are living **in poverty**.*

**poverty-stricken** *adj.* very poor बहुत ग़रीब, ग़रीबी का मारा, अभावग्रस्त

**POW** /ˌpiː əʊ ˈdʌbljuː ˌपी ओ ˈडब्ल्यू/ *abbr.* prisoner of war युद्ध बंदी

**powder** /ˈpaʊdə(r) ˈपाउड(र्)/ *noun* [U, C] a dry substance that is in the form of very small grains चूर्ण या चूरा पाउडर, (किसी भी वस्तु का) *washing powder* ○ *Grind the spices into a fine powder.* ▶ **powder** *verb* [T] पाउडर लगाना (मुँह आदि पर)

**powdered** /ˈpaʊdəd ˈपाउडड्/ *adj.* (used about a substance that is usually liquid) dried and made into powder (प्रायः द्रव रूप में उपलब्ध पदार्थ) सुखाकर पाउडर बनाया हुआ; चूर्णित *powdered milk/soup*

**power[1]** /ˈpaʊə(r) ˈपाउअ(र्)/ *noun* **1** [U] **power (over sb/sth); power (to do sth)** the ability to control people or things or to do sth लोगों या वस्तुओं को नियंत्रित या कोई काम करने की योग्यता; सामर्थ्य, क्षमता *The aim is to give people more power over their own lives.* ○ *to have sb **in your power*** ○ ***It's not in my power*** (= I am unable) *to help you.* **2** [U] political control of a country or area किसी देश या क्षेत्र पर राजनीतिक नियंत्रण; सत्ता *When did this government **come to power**?* ○ *to take/seize power* **3** [C] **the power (to do sth)** the right or authority to do sth कुछ करने का अधिकार *Do the* *police have the power to stop cars without good reason?* **4** [C] a country with a lot of influence in world affairs or that has great military strength विश्व के मामलों को अत्यधिक प्रभावित करने वाला या प्रचुर सैन्य शक्ति संपन्न देश; महाशक्ति *a military/economic power* ➪ **superpower** और **world power** देखिए। **5 powers** [*pl.*] a particular ability of the body or mind शरीर या मन की विशिष्ट शक्ति *He has great powers of observation.* ○ *She had to use all her powers of persuasion on him.* **6** [U] the energy or strength that sb/sth has व्यक्ति या वस्तु की ऊर्जा, ताक़त या शक्ति *The ship was helpless against the power of the storm.* ○ *I've lost all power in my right arm.* **7** [U] energy that can be collected and used for operating machines, making electricity, etc. मशीन के संचालन, विद्युत निर्माण आदि के लिए संचित और प्रयुक्त ऊर्जा *nuclear/wind/solar power* ○ *This car has power steering.*

**power²** /ˈpaʊə(r) ˈपाउअ(र्)/ *verb* [T] to supply energy to sth to make it work किसी वस्तु (यंत्र आदि) को चलाने के लिए उसे ऊर्जा प्रदान करना *What powers the motor in this machine?* ▶ **-powered** *adj.* शक्तियुक्त *a solar-powered calculator* ○ *a high-powered engine*

**power cut** *noun* [C] a time when the supply of electricity stops, for example during a storm विद्युत की आपूर्ति में अस्थायी रूप से रुकावट की अवधि (जैसे आँधी चलने पर)

**powerful** /ˈpaʊəfl ˈपाउअफ़्ल्/ *adj.* **1** having a lot of control or influence over other people शक्तिशाली, प्रभावशाली, असरदार *a powerful nation* ○ *He's one of the most powerful directors in Hollywood.* **2** having great strength or force शक्तिशाली, सशक्त, ताक़तवर *a powerful car/engine/telescope* ○ *a powerful swimmer* **3** having a strong effect on your mind or body मन या शरीर को अत्यधिक प्रभावित करने वाला; प्रभावशाली, असरदार *The Prime Minister made a powerful speech.* ○ *a powerful drug* ▶ **powerfully** /-fəli -फ़लि/ *adv.* शक्तिशाली ढंग से, सशक्त रूप से

**powerless** /ˈpaʊələs ˈपाउअलस्/ *adj.* **1** without strength, influence or control शक्ति, प्रभाव या नियंत्रण-क्षमता से रहित; शक्तिहीन **2 powerless to do sth** completely unable to do sth कुछ करने में पूर्णतया असमर्थ *I stood and watched him struggle, powerless to help.*

**power point** (*BrE*) = **socket 1**

**power station** (*AmE* **power plant**) *noun* [C] a place where electricity is made (**generated**) बिजली-घर

**pp** *abbr.* **1 pp.** pages पृष्ठ *See pp. 100–178.* **2** (*also* **p.p.**) 'on behalf of' हस्ताक्षर से पहले '(किसी) की ओर से' के अर्थ के लिए प्रयुक्त संक्षिप्ति *p.p. Mohit Arora* (= from Mohit Arora but signed by sb else because he is away)

**PR** /ˌpiː ˈɑː(r) ˌपी ˈआ(र्)/ *abbr.* **1** public relations जन-संपर्क **2** proportional representation आनुपातिक प्रतिनिधित्व

**practicable** /ˈpræktɪkəbl ˈप्रैक्टिकब्ल्/ *adj.* (used about an idea, a plan or a suggestion) able to be done successfully (कोई विचार, योजना या सुझाव) जिसे सफलतापूर्वक किया जा सके, व्यवहार्य, व्यावहारिक, साध्य *The scheme is just not practicable.* ✪ विलोम **impracticable**

**practical¹** /ˈpræktɪkl ˈप्रैक्टिक्ल्/ *adj.* **1** concerned with actually doing sth rather than with ideas or thought व्यावहारिक (न कि काल्पनिक या सैद्धांतिक) *Have you got any* ***practical experience*** *of working on a farm?* ➪ **theoretical** देखिए। **2** that is likely to succeed; right or sensible संभवतः फलदायी; सही या विवेकपूर्ण *We need to find a practical solution to the problem.* **3** very suitable for a particular purpose; useful प्रयोजन-विशेष के लिए बहुत उपयुक्त; उपयोगी *a practical little car, ideal for the city* **4** (used about people) making sensible decisions and good at dealing with problems (व्यक्ति) विवेकी और व्यवहार-कुशल *We must be practical. It's no good buying a house we cannot afford.* ✪ विलोम **impractical** (अर्थ सं. **2**, **3** और **4** के लिए) **5** (used about a person) good at making and repairing things (व्यक्ति) वस्तुओं के निर्माण व मरम्मत में कुशल; सक्रिय, कार्यकुशल

**practical²** /ˈpræktɪkl ˈप्रैक्टिक्ल्/ *noun* [C] (*informal*) a lesson or an exam where you do or make sth rather than just writing प्रायोगिक पाठ या परीक्षा *He passed the theory paper but failed the practical.*

**practicality** /ˌpræktɪˈkæləti ˌप्रैक्टिˈकैलटि/ (*pl.* **practicalities**) *noun* **1** [U] the quality of being suitable and realistic, or likely to succeed उपयुक्त और वास्तविक या संभावित रूप से फलदायी होने का गुण; व्यावहारिकता *I am not convinced of the practicality of the scheme.* **2 practicalities** [*pl.*] the real facts rather than ideas or thoughts वास्तविक तथ्य (न कि कल्पनाएँ या विचार) *Let's look at the practicalities of the situation.*

**practical joke** *noun* [C] a trick that you play on sb that makes him/her look silly and makes other people laugh किसी से ऐसा मज़ाक़ कि वह मूर्ख लगे और दूसरे उस पर हँसें; व्यावहारिक परिहास

**practically** /ˈpræktɪkli ˈप्रैक्टिक्लि/ *adv.* **1** (*spoken*) almost; very nearly लगभग; क़रीब-क़रीब *My essay is practically finished now.* **2** in a realistic or sensible way व्यावहारिक रीति से, यथार्थपरक या समझदारी के तरीक़े से

**practice** /ˈpræktɪs ˈप्रैक्टिस्/ *noun* **1** [U] action rather than ideas or thought व्यवहार, प्रयोग (न कि कल्पनाएँ या विचार) *the **theory and practice** of language teaching* ○ *I can't wait to **put** what I've learnt **into practice**.* **2** [C, U] (*formal*) the usual or expected way of doing sth in a particular organization or situation; a habit or custom संस्था या स्थिति-विशेष में कोई काम करने का रिवाज़ी या अपेक्षानुकूल तरीक़ा; आदत, रिवाज़ या प्रथा *It is standard practice not to pay bills until the end of the month.* **3** [C, U] (a period of) doing an activity many times or training regularly so that you become good at it अभ्यास, रियाज़ (कुशलता-प्राप्ति के लिए कोई काम अनेक बार करने या उसे नियमित रूप से सीखने की क्रिया) *piano/football practice* ○ *His accent should improve **with practice**.* **4** [U] the work of a doctor or lawyer डॉक्टरी या वक़ालत *Dr Khanna doesn't work in a hospital. He's in **general practice*** (= he's a family doctor). **5** [C] the business of a doctor, dentist or lawyer चिकित्सक, दंत-चिकित्सक, वक़ील आदि का व्यवसाय *a successful medical/dental practice*

IDM **be/get out of practice** to find it difficult to do sth because you have not done it for a long time अभ्यास छूट जाने के कारण कोई काम करने में कठिनाई होना *I'm not playing very well at the moment. I'm really out of practice.*

**in practice** in reality व्यवहार में, वास्तविक रूप से *Prisoners have legal rights, but in practice these rights are not always respected.*

**practise** (*AmE* **practice**) /ˈpræktɪs ˈप्रैक्टिस्/ *verb* [I, T] **1** to do an activity or train regularly so that you become very good at sth अभ्यास करना, रियाज़ करना (कुशलता प्राप्ति के लिए कोई काम नियमित रूप से करना या उसे सीखना) *If you want to play a musical instrument well, you must practise every day.* ○ *He always wants to **practise** his English **on** me.* **2** to be involved in religious activities regularly or publicly नियमित रूप से या सार्वजनिक तौर पर गतिविधियों में भाग लेना *a practising Catholic/Jew/Muslim* **3 practise (sth/as sth)** to work as a doctor or lawyer डॉक्टरी या वक़ालत करना *She's practising as a lawyer in Lucknow.* ○ *He was banned from practising medicine.*

**practised** (*AmE* **practiced**) /ˈpræktɪst ˈप्रैक्टिस्ट्/ *adj.* **practised (in sth)** very good at sth, because you have done it a lot or often किसी काम में निपुण (उसे अनेक बार करने या प्रायः करते रहने के फलस्वरूप) *He was practised in the art of inventing excuses.*

**practitioner** /prækˈtɪʃənə(r) प्रैक्ˈटिशन(र्)/ *noun* [C] (*formal*) a person who works as a doctor, dentist or lawyer व्यवसाय से डॉक्टर, दंत-चिकित्सक या वक़ील ➪ **GP** देखिए।

**pragmatic** /prægˈmætɪk प्रैग्ˈमैटिक्/ *adj.* dealing with problems in a practical way rather than by following ideas or principles व्यावहारिक, यथार्थवादी (न कि सिद्धांतवादी या कल्पनाशील)

**pragmatism** /ˈprægmətɪzəm ˈप्रैग्मटिज़म्/ *noun* [U] (*formal*) thinking about solving problems in a practical and sensible way rather than by having fixed ideas व्यावहारिकता, यथार्थवादिता (न कि सिद्धांतप्रियता) ▶ **pragmatist** /-tɪst -टिस्ट्/ *noun* [C] व्यावहारिकतावादी, यथार्थवादी *Most successful teachers are pragmatists and realists.*

**prairie** /ˈpreəri ˈप्रेअरि/ *noun* [C] a very large area of flat land covered in grass with few trees (especially in North America) लगभग वृक्षहीन घास का बड़ा मैदान (विशेषतः उत्तरी अमेरिका में); शाद्वल प्रदेश

**praise[1]** /preɪz प्रेज़्/ *verb* [T] **praise sb/sth (for sth)** to say that sb/sth is good and should be admired व्यक्ति या वस्तु की प्रशंसा करना, उसे सराहना *The fireman was praised for his courage.*

**praise[2]** /preɪz प्रेज़्/ *noun* [U] what you say when you are expressing admiration for sb/sth प्रशंसा, सराहना (के शब्द) *The survivors were full of praise for the paramedics.*

**praiseworthy** /ˈpreɪzwɜːði ˈप्रेज़्वद्रि/ *adj.* that should be admired and recognized as good प्रशंसनीय, सराहनीय

**pram** /præm प्रैम्/ (*AmE* **baby carriage**) *noun* [C] a small vehicle on four wheels for a young baby, pushed by a person on foot चार पहियों की बच्चा गाड़ी; प्रैम

**prance** /prɑːns प्रान्स्/ *verb* [I] to move about with quick, high steps, often because you feel proud or pleased with yourself (घमंड या खुशी के मारे) अकड़कर चलना, इठलाना

**prawn** /prɔːn प्रॉन्/ (*AmE* **shrimp**) *noun* [C] a small shellfish that we eat and that becomes pink when cooked झींगा (मछली) ➪ **shrimp** देखिए तथा **shellfish** पर चित्र देखिए।

**pray** /preɪ प्रे / *verb* [I, T] **pray (to sb) (for sb/sth)** to speak to God or a god in order to give thanks or to ask for help (ईश्वर या देवी या देवता से) प्रार्थना करना *They knelt down and prayed for peace.*

**prayer** /preə(r) प्रेअ(र्) / *noun* **1** [C] **a prayer (for sb/sth)** the words that you use when you speak to God or a god (ईश्वर या देवी या देवता से) प्रार्थना (के शब्द) *Let's **say a prayer** for all the people who are ill.* **2** [U] the act of speaking to God or a god प्रार्थना (की क्रिया) *to kneel **in prayer***

**pre-** /pri: प्री / *prefix* (*used in verbs, nouns and adjectives*) before पूर्व-, प्राक्-, पूर्ववर्ती *prepay* ○ *preview* ○ *pre-war* ➪ **ante-** और **post-** देखिए।

**preach** /pri:tʃ प्रीच् / *verb* **1** [I, T] to give a talk (**a sermon**) on a religious subject किसी धार्मिक विषय पर प्रवचन करना; उपदेश करना **2** [T] to say that sth is good and persuade other people to accept it किसी बात को अच्छा कहना और लोगों को उसे मानने के लिए प्रेरित करना; किसी बात की शिक्षा या सीख देना *I always preach caution in situations like this.* **3** [I] to give sb advice on how to behave, on what is considered morally acceptable, etc., in a way that people find boring or annoying नैतिकता या व्यवहार पर भाषण पिलाना *I'm sorry, I didn't mean to preach.*

**preacher** /ˈpri:tʃə(r) ˈप्रीच(र्) / *noun* [C] a person who gives religious speech (**sermons**) धर्मोपदेशक

**preamble** /pri:ˈæmbl प्री ˈऐम्बल् / *noun* [C, U] (*formal*) an introduction or a preface, for example to a book, a written document, speech, etc. that explains its purpose अपने प्रयोजन का व्याख्यान करने हेतु किसी पुस्तक, लेख या भाषण का प्राक्कथन या आमुख; प्रस्तावना, उद्देशिका *The Preamble highlights the salient features of the Constitution of India.*

**precarious** /prɪˈkeəriəs प्रि ˈकेअरिअस् / *adj.* not safe or certain; dangerous असुरक्षित या अनिश्चित; ख़तरनाक ▶ **precariously** *adv.* ख़तरनाक ढंग से

**precaution** /prɪˈkɔ:ʃn प्रि ˈकॉश्न् / *noun* [C] **a precaution (against sth)** something that you do now in order to avoid danger or problems in the future भविष्य के ख़तरे या समस्या से बचने के लिए किया गया उपाय; एहतियात, सावधानी *You should always **take the precaution of** locking your valuables in the hotel safe.* ○ *precautions against fire/theft* ▶ **precautionary** /prɪˈkɔ:ʃənəri प्रि ˈकॉशनरि / *adj.* एहतियाती

**precede** /prɪˈsi:d प्रि ˈसीड् / *verb* [I, T] (*written*) to happen, come or go before sb/sth किसी अन्य व्यक्ति या वस्तु से पहले होना, जाना या आना, पूर्ववर्ती होना (स्थान, समय या क्रम में) *the table on the preceding page*

**precedence** /ˈpresɪdəns ˈप्रेसिडन्स् / *noun* [U] **precedence (over sb/sth)** the right that sb/sth has to come before sb/sth else because he/she/it is more important (महत्त्व की दृष्टि से व्यक्ति या वस्तु की) वरीयता, प्राथमिकता, पूर्ववर्तिता; किसी अन्य से पहले आने का अधिकार *In business, making a profit seems to **take precedence** over everything else.*

**precedent** /ˈpresɪdənt ˈप्रेसिडन्ट् / *noun* [C, U] an official action or decision that has happened in the past and that is considered as an example or rule to follow in the same situation later पहले लिया गया कोई निर्णय जो उसी प्रकार की परवर्ती स्थिति के लिए उदाहरण या पूर्वनियम का काम करे; नज़ीर, पूर्विका ***set a precedent*** ○ *Such protests are **without precedent** in recent history.* ➪ **unprecedented** देखिए।

**precinct** /ˈpri:sɪŋkt ˈप्रीसिङ्क्ट् / *noun* **1** [C] (*BrE*) a special area of shops in a town where cars are not allowed किसी नगर में दुकानों के लिए निर्धारित क्षेत्र (जहाँ कारों का प्रवेश निषिद्ध हो) *a shopping precinct* **2** [C] (*AmE*) a part of a town that has its own police station नगर का वह क्षेत्र जिसका अपना पुलिस थाना हो **3 precincts** [*pl.*] (*formal*) the area near or around a building किसी भवन के आसपास का क्षेत्र *the hospital and its precincts*

**precious** /ˈpreʃəs ˈप्रेशस् / *adj.* **1** of great value (usually because it is rare or difficult to find) क़ीमती, बहुमूल्य (सामान्यतः दुर्लभ होने के कारण) *In overcrowded Mumbai, every small piece of land is precious.* **2** loved very much अत्यंत प्रिय *The painting was very precious to her.*

**precious metal** *noun* [C] a metal which is very rare and valuable and often used in jewellery (सोना, चाँदी आदि) बहुमूल्य धातु (बहुधा आभूषण बनाने में प्रयुक्त) *Gold and platinum are precious metals.*

**precious stone** (*also* **stone**) *noun* [C] a stone which is very rare and valuable and often used in jewellery (हीरा आदि) बहुमूल्य रत्न (बहुधा आभूषण बनाने में प्रयुक्त) *diamonds and other precious stones*

**precipice** /ˈpresəpɪs ˈप्रेसपिस् / *noun* [C] a very steep side of a high mountain or cliff खड़ी चट्टान

**precipitate**[1] /prɪˈsɪpɪteɪt प्रि ˈसिपिटेट् / *verb* [T] (*formal*) **1** to make sth, especially sth bad, happen suddenly or sooner than it should किसी घटना को (विशेषतः प्रतिकूल घटना को) अचानक या समय से पूर्व घटित करना या होने देना **2 precipitate sb/sth into sth** to suddenly force sb/sth into a particular state or condition किसी व्यक्ति या वस्तु को अचानक किसी विशेष दशा या स्थिति में धकेल देना *The president's assassination precipitated the country into war.*

**precipitate²** /prɪˈsɪpɪtət प्रि'सिपिटट् / *adj.* (*formal*) (used about an action or a decision) happening very quickly or suddenly and usually without enough care and thought (कोई कार्य या निर्णय) बिना सोचे-समझे अचानक या जल्दबाज़ी में किया गया ▶ **precipitately** *adv.* उतावलेपन के साथ

**precipitate³** /prɪˈsɪpɪteɪt प्रि'सिपिटेट् / *noun* [C] (*technical*) a solid substance that has been separated from a liquid in a chemical process रासायनिक प्रक्रिया द्वारा द्रव से अलग किया गया ठोस पदार्थ; अवक्षेप

**precipitation** /prɪˌsɪpɪˈteɪʃn प्रि,सिपि'टेश्न् / *noun* **1** [U] (*technical*) rain, snow, etc. that falls; the amount of this that falls (पड़ने वाली) बरसात, बर्फ़, आदि; बरसात, बर्फ़ आदि की पड़ी मात्रा **2** [U, C] a chemical process in which solid material is separated from a liquid वह रासायनिक प्रक्रिया जिसमें ठोस पदार्थ को द्रव से अलग किया जाता है; अवक्षेपण

**precipitous** /prɪˈsɪpɪtəs प्रि'सिपिटस् / *adj.* (*formal*) **1** very steep and often dangerous प्रपाती, बहुत उन्नत और ख़तरनाक *the precipitous slopes of the mountains* **2** fast and great तीव्र एवं अधिक *a precipitous decline in scooter sales* **3** done very quickly without enough thought or care; rash लापरवाही से जल्दबाज़ी में किया गया; प्रपाती *a precipitous action* ▶ **precipitously** *adv.* लापरवही से, उतावलेपन से

**precis** /ˈpreɪsiː 'प्रेसी / *noun* [C, U] (*pl.* **precis** /-siːz -सीज़् /) a short version of a speech or written text that contains only the most important points किसी भाषण या लेख का सारांश जिसमें केवल मुख्यतम बातें हों ✪ पर्याय **summary**

**precise** /prɪˈsaɪs प्रि'साइस् / *adj.* **1** clear and accurate स्पष्ट और सही *precise details/instructions/measurements* ○ *He's in his forties—well, forty-four, **to be precise**.* ○ ✪ विलोम **imprecise** **2** (*only before a noun*) exact; particular पूर्णतया ठीक, त्रुटिहीन; विशिष्ट *I'm sorry. I can't come just **at this precise moment**.* **3** (used about a person) taking care to get small details right (व्यक्ति) छोटे ब्योरों के (भी) सही होने के विषय में सावधान *He's very precise about his work.*

**precisely** /prɪˈsaɪsli प्रि'साइस्लि / *adv.* **1** exactly सही-सही *The time is 10.03 a.m. precisely.* ✪ पर्याय **exactly** **2** used to emphasize that sth is very true or obvious किसी बात के एकदम सच या सुस्पष्ट होने पर बल देने के लिए प्रयुक्त *It's precisely because I care about you that I got so angry when you stayed out late.* **3** (*spoken*) (used for agreeing with a statement) yes, that is right(कथन से सहमति व्यक्त करने के लिए प्रयुक्त) हाँ, बिलकुल ठीक *'So, if we don't book now, we probably won't get a flight?' 'Precisely.'*

**precision** /prɪˈsɪʒn प्रि'सिश़्न् / *noun* [U] the quality of being clear or exact स्पष्ट या यथार्थ होने का गुण; स्पष्टता या यथार्थता *The plans were drawn with great precision.*

**preclude** /prɪˈkluːd प्रि'क्लूड् / *verb* [T] (*formal*) **preclude sth; preclude sb from doing sth** to prevent sth from happening or sb from doing sth; to make sth impossible कोई बात होने न देना या किसी को कोई काम करने न देना; किसी बात को असंभव बना देना *Lack of time precludes any further discussion.* ○ *His religious beliefs precluded him/his serving in the army.*

**precocious** /prɪˈkəʊʃəs प्रि'कोशस् / *adj.* (used about children) having developed certain abilities and ways of behaving at a much younger age than usual (बच्चा) सामान्य से कम आयु में (अपने से बड़ों की) योग्यताएँ विकसित कर लेने वाला; छोटी आयु में बड़ों जैसा आचरण करने वाला; अकालपक्व, पूर्वविकसित *a precocious child who started her acting career at the age of 5* **NOTE** इस शब्द से हलकी आलोचना व्यक्त या ध्वनित होती है।

**preconceived** /ˌpriːkənˈsiːvd ,प्रीकन्'सीव्ड् / *adj.* (*only before a noun*) (used about an idea or opinion) formed before you have enough information or experience (विचार या सम्मति) पर्याप्त जानकारी या अनुभव होने से पहले बना ली गई; पूर्व-अवधारित

**preconception** /ˌpriːkənˈsepʃn ,प्रीकन्'सेप्श्न् / *noun* [C] an idea or opinion that you have formed about sb/sth before you have enough information or experience पर्याप्त जानकारी या अनुभव होने से पहले निर्मित विचार या सम्मति; पूर्व-धारणा

**precondition** /ˌpriːkənˈdɪʃn ,प्रीकन्'डिश्न् / *noun* [C] (*written*) **a precondition (for/of sth)** something that must happen or exist before sth else can exist or be done (किसी बात या काम की) पूर्व शर्त ✪ पर्याय **prerequisite**

**predator** /ˈpredətə(r) 'प्रेडट(र्) / *noun* [C] an animal that kills and eats other animals अन्य जीवों को मारने और खाने वाला जानवर; परजीवभक्षी, हिंसक पशु

**predatory** /ˈpredətri 'प्रेडट्रि / *adj.* **1** (*technical*) (used about an animal) living by killing and eating other animals (जानवर) अन्य जीवों को मार और खाकर जीवित रहने वाला; परजीवभक्षी **2** (*written*) (used about a person) using weaker people for his/her own financial or sexual advantage (व्यक्ति) स्वयं के आर्थिक लाभ या यौन शोषण के लिए दुर्बलों का शोषण करने वाला

**predecessor** /ˈpriːdɪsesə(r) 'प्रीडिसेस(र्) / *noun* [C] **1** the person who was in the job or position before the person who is in it now पूर्ववर्ती अधिकारी (जो इसके पूर्व इसी नौकरी में या पद पर रह चुका है) **2** a thing such as a machine, that has been followed or replaced by sth else वस्तु से पूर्व प्रचलित मशीन आदि वस्तु ➪ **successor** देखिए।

**predicament** /prɪˈdɪkəmənt प्रि ˈडिकमन्ट्/ *noun* [C] an unpleasant and difficult situation that is hard to get out of अप्रिय और कठिन स्थिति जिससे बाहर निकलना कठिन हो

**predicate** /ˈpredɪkeit ˈप्रेडिकेट्/ *noun* [C] (*grammar*) the part of a sentence which has the verb, and which tells us what the subject is or does. In the sentence—*'He went cycling after returning from school'* the predicate is *'went cycling after returning from school'* (वाक्य में) कर्ता या उसके उद्देश्य के विषय में जो कहा जाए; विधेय ➪ **object**[1] देखिए।

**predicative** /prɪˈdɪkətɪv प्रि ˈडिकटिव्/ *adj.* (*grammar*) (used about an adjective) not used before a noun (विशेषण) जो संज्ञा से पहले प्रयुक्त नहीं होता, विधेय के रूप में प्रयुक्त; विधेयात्मक *You cannot say 'an asleep child' because 'asleep' is a predicative adjective.*

> **NOTE** जो विशेषण संज्ञा से पहले प्रयुक्त हो सके उसे गुणवाचक विशेषण (**attributive**) कहते हैं। अनेक विशेषण, जैसे 'big', विधेयात्मक (**predicative**) भी हो सकते हैं और गुणवाचक (**attributive**) भी— *The house is big.* ○ *It's a big house.*

▶ **predicatively** *adv.* विधेयात्मक रूप से *'Asleep' can only be used predicatively.*

**predict** /prɪˈdɪkt प्रि ˈडिक्ट्/ *verb* [T] to say that sth will happen in the future (किसी बात की) भविष्यवाणी करना *Scientists still cannot predict exactly when earthquakes will happen.*

**predictable** /prɪˈdɪktəbl प्रि ˈडिक्टबल्/ *adj.* **1** that was or could be expected to happen जिसका घटित होना प्रत्याशित है; पूर्वानुमेय *The match had a predictable result.* **2** (used about a person) always behaving in a way that you would expect and therefore rather boring (व्यक्ति) जिसके व्यवहार के विषय में पहले से बताया जा सके (अतएव अरुचिकर) *I knew you were going to say that—you're so predicatable* ▶ **predictably** *adv.* पूर्वानुमेय रूप से

**prediction** /prɪˈdɪkʃn प्रि ˈडिक्शन्/ *noun* [C, U] saying what will happen; what sb thinks will happen भविष्यकथन; पूर्वानुमान *The exam results confirmed my predictions.*

**predominance** /prɪˈdɒmɪnəns प्रि ˈडॉमिनन्स्/ *noun* [*sing.*] the state of being more important or greater in number than other people or things संख्या की दृष्टि से किसी की प्रधानता (अन्य व्यक्तियों या वस्तुओं की अपेक्षा) *There is a predominance of Japanese tourists in Hawaii.*

**predominant** /prɪˈdɒmɪnənt प्रि ˈडॉमिनन्ट्/ *adj.* most noticeable, powerful or important सबसे अधिक दिखाई पड़ने वाला, स्पष्टतया दर्शनीय, सशक्त या महत्त्वपूर्ण *The predominant colour was blue.*

**predominantly** /prɪˈdɒmɪnəntli प्रि ˈडॉमिनन्ट्लि/ *adj.* mostly; mainly अधिकांशतः, मुख्यतः *The population of the island is predominantly Spanish.*

**predominate** /prɪˈdɒmɪneɪt प्रि ˈडॉमिनेट्/ *verb* [I] (*formal*) **predominate (over sb/sth)** to be most important or greatest in number महत्त्व या संख्या में सबसे अधिक होना *Private interest was not allowed to predominate over public good.*

**pre-empt** /priˈempt प्रि ˈएम्प्ट्/ *verb* [T] (*formal*) **1** to prevent sth from happening by taking action to stop it किसी बात को (उस पर रोक लगाकर) होने न देना *Her departure pre-empted any further questions.* ○ *A good training course will pre-empt many problems.* **2** to do or say sth before sb else does किसी अन्य से पहले कोई काम कर देना या कुछ कह देना *She was just about to apologize when he pre-empted her.*

**preen** /priːn प्रीन्/ *verb* **1** [I, T] (of a bird) to clean and tidy its feathers with its beak **2** [T] **preen yourself** (*usually disapproving*) to spend too much time making yourself look attractive and then admiring your appearance स्वयं को सँवारने में बहुत समय व्यतीत करना और अपने रूप को निहारना *Will you stop preening yourself in front of the mirror?*

**preface** /ˈprefəs ˈप्रेफ़स्/ *noun* [C] a written introduction to a book that explains what it is about or why it was written पुस्तक के प्रतिपाद्य का लेखक द्वारा आरंभ में संक्षिप्त परिचय; निवेदन, प्रस्तावना,

**prefect** /ˈpriːfekt ˈप्रीफ़ेक्ट्/ *noun* [C] an older girl or boy in a school who has special duties and responsibilities. Prefects often help to make sure that the younger school children behave properly स्कूल में छोटे छात्रों में अनुशासन के लिए उत्तरदायी बड़ा छात्र (लड़का या लड़की); प्रिफ़ेक्ट

**prefer** /prɪˈfɜː(r) प्रि ˈफ़(र्)/ *verb* [T] (**preferring; preferred**) **prefer sth (to sth); prefer to do sth; prefer doing sth** (*not used in the continuous tenses*) to choose sth rather than sth else; to like sth better एक के स्थान पर दूसरे को चुनना; (तुलना में) किसी वस्तु को अधिक पसंद करना *Would you prefer tea or coffee?* ○ *My parents would prefer me to study law at university.*

**NOTE** **Prefer** के विभिन्न प्रयोगों पर ध्यान दीजिए—*Helen prefers going by train to flying* (= generally or usually). ○ *Helen **would prefer to go** by train rather than (to) fly* (= on this occasion). **Prefer** काफ़ी औपचारिक शब्द है। *Would you prefer tea or coffee?* कहने की अपेक्षा हम कह सकते हैं—*Would you rather have tea or coffee?* इसी प्रकार—*I prefer skating to skiing.* इसकी अपेक्षा हम कह सकते हैं—*I like skating better than skiing.* यद्यपि इस क्रिया का सातत्यबोधक कालों (continuous tenses) में प्रयोग नहीं होता तथापि इसका (= ing युक्त रूप) वर्तमान कृदंत (present participle) रूप पर्याप्त प्रचलित है—*Their elder son had gone to work in London, preferring not to join the family firm.*

**preferable** /ˈprefrəbl ˈप्रेफ़्रबल्/ *adj.* **preferable (to sth/doing sth)** better or more suitable बेहतर या अधिक उपयुक्त *Going anywhere is preferable to staying at home for the weekend.*

**preferably** /ˈprefrəbli ˈप्रेफ़्रब्लि/ *adv.* used to show which person or thing would be better or preferred, if you are given a choice यह दिखाने के लिए प्रयुक्त कि तुलना में किसी व्यक्ति या वस्तु को अधिक पसंद किया जाएगा *Give me a ring tonight—preferably after 7 o'clock.*

**preference** /ˈprefrəns ˈप्रेफ़्रन्स्/ *noun* **1** [C, U] **(a) preference (for sth)** an interest in or desire for one thing more than another एक की अपेक्षा दूसरी में अधिक रुचि; (किसी को किसी पर) अधिमान्यता, तरज़ीह *What you wear is entirely a matter of **personal preference**.* ○ *Please list your choices **in order of preference*** (= put the things you want most first on the list). **2** [U] special treatment that you give to one person or group rather than to others (अन्य की अपेक्षा) किसी व्यक्ति या समूह पर दिखाई गई कृपादृष्टि *When allocating accommodation, we will **give preference to** families with young children.*

**preferential** /ˌprefəˈrenʃl ˌप्रेफ़ˈरेन्शल्/ *adj.* (*only before a noun*) giving or showing special treatment to one person or group rather than to others (अन्य की अपेक्षा) किसी व्यक्ति या समूह पर कृपादृष्टि दिखाते हुए; वरणात्मक, तरज़ीही *He gets a **preferential treatment** at office.*

**prefix** /ˈpriːfɪks ˈप्रीफ़िक्स्/ *noun* [C] (*grammar*) a letter or group of letters that you put at the beginning of a word to change its meaning पूर्वसर्ग; शब्द के आरंभ में लगा वह अक्षर या अक्षर समूह जिससे शब्द का अर्थ बदल जाता है ➪ **affix[2]** और **suffix** देखिए।

**pregnancy** /ˈpregnənsi ˈप्रेग्नन्सि/ *noun* (*pl.* **pregnancies**) [U, C] the state of being pregnant गर्भावस्था

**pregnant** /ˈpregnənt ˈप्रेग्नन्ट्/ *adj.* (used about a woman or female animal) having a baby developing in her body (महिला या मादा पशु) गर्भवती (जिसके शरीर के अंदर शिशु पल रहा है) *Latika is five-months pregnant.* ○ *to get pregnant* **NOTE** हम इन अभिव्यक्तियों का प्रयोग भी कर सकते हैं—*Latika is expecting a baby.* या *Latika is going to have a baby.*

**prehensile** /prɪˈhensaɪl प्रिˈहेन्साइल्/ *adj.* (*technical*) (used about part of an animal's body) able to hold things (पशु के शरीर का कोई अंग) जो वस्तुओं को पकड़, थाम या सँभाल सके; परिग्राही *the monkey's prehensile tail* ➪ **primate** पर चित्र देखिए।

**prehistoric** /ˌpriːhɪˈstɒrɪk ˌप्रीहिˈस्टॉरिक्/ *adj.* from the time in history before events were written down इतिहास में घटनाओं के लिखित विवरण से पूर्व का; प्रागैतिहासिक, इतिहास-पूर्व

**prejudice[1]** /ˈpredʒudɪs ˈप्रेजुडिस्/ *noun* [C, U] **prejudice (against sb/sth)** a strong unreasonable feeling of not liking or trusting sb/sth, especially when it is based on his/her/its race, religion or sex किस व्यक्ति या वस्तु के प्रति प्रबल नापसंदगी या अविश्वास, विशेषतः उसकी जाति, धर्म या लिंग के कारण; पूर्वाग्रह *a victim of **racial prejudice***

**prejudice[2]** /ˈpredʒudɪs ˈप्रेजुडिस्/ *verb* [T] **1 prejudice sb (against sb/sth)** to influence sb so that he/she has an unreasonable or unfair opinion about sb/sth किसी को (किसी व्यक्ति या वस्तु के प्रति) इस तरह प्रभावित करना कि उसके मन में व्यक्ति या वस्तु के प्रति असंगत या अनुचित धारणा बन जाए; पूर्वाग्रहग्रस्त करना *The newspaper stories had prejudiced the jury against him.* **2** to have a harmful effect on sb/sth किसी व्यक्ति या वस्तु पर हानिकर प्रभाव होना *Continuing to live with her violent father may prejudice the child's welfare.*

**prejudiced** /ˈpredʒədɪst ˈप्रेजडिस्ट्/ *adj.* not liking or trusting sb/sth for no other reason than his/her/its race, religion or sex पूर्वाग्रस्त (किसी व्यक्ति या वस्तु को नापसंद या उस पर अविश्वास करने वाला, उसकी जाति, धर्म या लिंग के कारण)

**preliminary[1]** /prɪˈlɪmɪnəri प्रिˈलिमिनरि/ *adj.* coming or happening before sth else that is more important (तुलना में) अधिक महत्त्वपूर्ण स्थिति से पहले आने या होने वाला, प्रारंभिक, प्राथमिक

**preliminary[2]** /prɪˈlɪmɪnəri प्रिˈलिमिनरि/ *noun* [C, *usually pl.*] (*pl.* **preliminaries**) an action or event that is done before and in preparation for another event किसी महत्त्वपूर्ण घटना से पहले होने वाली गतिविधियों या की जाने वाली तैयारी; प्रारंभिक उपाय या चरण

**prelude** /ˈpreljuːd ˈप्रेल्यूड्/ *noun* [C] **1** a short piece of music, especially an introduction to a longer piece मुख्य संगीत से पहले (उसकी प्रस्तावना में) प्रस्तुत लघु संगीत; पूर्वरंग **2** (*written*) **prelude (to sth)** an action or event that happens before sth else or that forms an introduction to sth घटना जो किसी अधिक महत्त्वपूर्ण भावी घटना की प्रस्तावना के रूप में घटित हो

**premature** /ˈpremətʃə(r); ˌpreməˈtʃʊə(r) ˈप्रेमच(र्); ˌप्रेमˈचुअ(र्)/ *adj.* **1** happening before the normal or expected time सामान्य या प्रत्याशित समय से पहले घटित, समय-पूर्व *Her baby was premature* (= born before the expected time). **2** acting or happening too soon बहुत जल्दी घटित या किया गया; अपरिपक्व *I think our decision was premature. We should have thought about it for longer.* ▶ **prematurely** *adv.* असमय, अपक्वता या समय-पूर्वता से

**premeditated** /ˌpriːˈmedɪteɪtɪd ˌप्रीˈमेडिटेटिड्/ *adj.* (used about a crime) planned in advance (अपराध) पहले से योजनाबद्ध या नियोजित

**premier¹** /ˈpremiə(r) ˈप्रेमिअ(र्)/ *adj.* (*only before a noun*) most important; best महत्त्व में सर्वप्रथम; सर्वोत्तम *a premier chef* ○ *the Premier Division* (= in football)

**premier²** /ˈpremiə(r) ˈप्रेमिअ(र्)/ *noun* [C] (used especially in newspapers) the leader of the government of a country (**prime minister**) (विशेषतः अख़बारों या मीडिया में प्रयुक्त) प्रधानमंत्री

**premiere** /ˈpremieə(r) ˈप्रेमिअ(र्)/ *noun* [C] the first public performance of a play, film, etc. नाटक, फ़िल्म आदि का पहला सार्वजनिक प्रदर्शन

**premise** /ˈpremɪs ˈप्रेमिस्/ *noun* [C] (*formal*) an idea or theory that forms the basis for a reasonable line of argument विचार या सिद्धांत जिस पर कोई तर्क आधारित हो *He research is based on the premise stated earlier.* ▶ **premise** *verb* to base sth like an argument, etc. on an idea or theory आधार वाक्य के रूप में कहना या पूर्वकथन करना *He premised his reasoning on the theory that all people are equally capable of good and evil.*

**premises** /ˈpremɪsɪz ˈप्रेमिसिज़्/ *noun* [*pl.*] the building and the land around it that a business owns or uses कोई भूखंड और उस पर बनी इमारतें (जो किसी संस्था की हों या उसके प्रयोग में हों) परिसर *Smoking is not allowed **on the premises**.*

**premium** /ˈpriːmiəm ˈप्रीमिअम्/ *noun* [C] **1** an amount of money that you pay regularly to a company for insurance against accidents, damage, etc. बीमे की क़िस्त *a monthly premium of Rs 250* **2** an extra payment भुगतान की कुछ अतिरिक्त राशि, अधिशुल्क *You must pay a premium for express delivery.*

**premonition** /ˌpriːməˈnɪʃn; ˌpremə- ˌप्रीमˈनिश्न्; ˌप्रेम-/ *noun* [C] **a premonition (of sth)** a feeling that sth unpleasant is going to happen in the future आगामी संकट की मन-ही मन अनुभूति; पूर्वानुमान, पूर्वबोध *a premonition of disaster*

**prenatal** /ˌpriːˈneɪtl ˌप्रीˈनेट्ल्/ *adj.* (especially *AmE*) = **antenatal** ➪ **post-natal** देखिए।

**preoccupation** /priˌɒkjuˈpeɪʃn प्रिˌऑक्युˈपेश्न्/ *noun* [U, C] **preoccupation (with sth)** the state of thinking and/or worrying continuously about sth किसी बात के विषय में लगातार सोचने या चिंता करने की मनःस्थिति; ध्यानमग्नता *She was irritated by his preoccupation with money.*

**preoccupied** /priˈɒkjupaɪd प्रिˈऑक्युपाइड्/ *adj.* **preoccupied (with sth)** not paying attention to sb/sth because you are thinking or worrying about sb/sth else किसी व्यक्ति या वस्तु के विषय में सोचते या चिंता करते रहने के कारण किसी अन्य पर ध्यान न देते हुए; चिंतामग्न ➪ **occupied** देखिए।

**preoccupy** /priˈɒkjupaɪ प्रिˈऑक्युपाइ/ *verb* [T] (*pres. part.* **preoccupying;** *3rd person sing. pres.* **preoccupies;** *pt, pp* **preoccupied**) to fill sb's mind so that he/she does not think about anything else; to worry किसी को किसी बात में तल्लीन कर देना; चिंता करना

**preparation** /ˌprepəˈreɪʃn ˌप्रेपˈरेश्न्/ *noun* **1** [U] getting sb/sth ready (व्यक्ति या वस्तु की) तैयारी *The team has been training hard **in preparation for** the big game.* ○ *exam preparation* **2** [C, *usually pl.*] **preparation (for sth/to do sth)** something that you do to get ready for sth किसी बात के लिए की गई तैयारियाँ *We started to **make preparations** for the wedding six months ago.*

**preparatory** /prɪˈpærətri प्रिˈपैरट्रि/ *adj.* done in order to get ready for sth (किसी बात की) तैयारी के लिए किया गया; आरंभिक

**preparatory school** (*also* **prep school**) *noun* [C] **1** (*BrE*) a private school for children aged between 7 and 13, 7 से 13 की आयु के बच्चों के लिए प्राइवेट स्कूल **2** (*AmE*) a private school that prepares students for college or university कॉलेज या विश्वविद्यालय के लिए छात्रों को आवश्यक तैयारी कराने वाला प्राइवेट स्कूल

**prepare** /prɪˈpeə(r) प्रि'पेअ(र्)/ *verb* [I, T] **prepare (sb/sth) (for sb/sth)** to get ready or to make sb/sth ready व्यक्ति या वस्तु का तैयार होना या उसे तैयार करना *Bina helped me prepare for the exam.* ○ *to prepare a meal*

**IDM** **be prepared for sth** to be ready for sth difficult or unpleasant किसी कठिन या अप्रिय स्थिति के लिए तैयार होना या तैयार रहना

**be prepared to do sth** to be ready and happy to do sth कोई काम करने के लिए सहर्ष तैयार होना *I am not prepared to stay here and be insulted.*

**preponderance** /prɪˈpɒndərəns प्रि'पॉन्डरन्स्/ *noun* [*sing.*] if there is a **preponderance** of one type of people or things in a group, there are more of them than others समूह में (अन्यों की तुलना में) किसी एक प्रकार के व्यक्तियों या वस्तुओं की (प्रभाव, संख्या आदि में) प्रधानता ✪ पर्याय **predominance**

**preponderant** /prɪˈpɒndərənt प्रि'पॉन्डरन्ट्/ *adj.* (*formal*) (*usually used before a noun*) larger in number or more important than other people or things in a group समूह में अन्य व्यक्तियों या वस्तुओं में संख्या या महत्त्व की दृष्टि से अधिक

**prepone** /priˈpəʊn प्रि'पोन्/ *verb* [T] (*IndE*) to change the time or date of an event so that it takes place earlier; to advance something (सामान्यतः दक्षिण एशिया में प्रयुक्त) किसी घटना के समय या तारीख़ को परिवर्तित करना ताकि वह समय से पहले घटित हो; (कुछ) आगे बढ़ाना *The reception was preponed from 18th December to 15th December.*

**preposition** /ˌprepəˈzɪʃn ˌप्रेप'ज़िशन्/ *noun* [C] (*grammar*) a word or phrase that is used before a noun or pronoun to show place, time, direction, etc. स्थान, समय, दिशा आदि के संकेत के लिए संज्ञा या सर्वनाम से पहले प्रयुक्त शब्द या वाक्यांश; पूर्वसर्ग *'In', 'for', 'to' and 'out of' are all prepositions.*

**preposterous** /prɪˈpɒstərəs प्रि'पॉस्टरस्/ *adj.* silly; ridiculous; not to be taken seriously मूर्खतापूर्ण; हास्यास्पद; गंभीरता से लेने योग्य नहीं

**prerequisite** /ˌpriːˈrekwəzɪt ˌप्री'रेकुवज़िट्/ *noun* [C] **a prerequisite (for/of sth)** something that is necessary for sth else to happen or exist किसी अन्य बात के घटित होने या अस्तित्व में रहने के लिए आवश्यकता; पूर्वापेक्षा

**prerogative** /prɪˈrɒgətɪv प्रि'रॉगटिव्/ *noun* [C] a special right that sb/sth has किसी व्यक्ति या वस्तु का विशेष अधिकार; प्राधिकार *It is the Prime Minister's prerogative to fix the date of the election.*

**Pres.** *abbr.* President राष्ट्रपति

**prescribe** /prɪˈskraɪb प्रि'स्क्राइब्/ *verb* [T] **1** to say what medicine or treatment sb should have किसी के लिए दवा या इलाज तय करना; नुसख़ा लिखना *Can you prescribe something for my cough please, doctor?* **2** (*formal*) (used about a person or an organization with authority) to say that sth must be done (विशिष्ट अधिकार संपन्न व्यक्ति या संस्था द्वारा) कुछ निर्धारित करना *The law prescribes that the document must be signed in the presence of two witnesses.*

**prescription** /prɪˈskrɪpʃn प्रि'स्क्रिप्शन्/ *noun* [C, U] a paper on which a doctor has written the name of the medicine that you need. You take your prescription to the **chemist's** and get the medicine there डॉक्टर का लिखा दवा का परचा; नुसख़ा *Some medicines are only available **on prescription*** (= with a prescription from a doctor).

**presence** /ˈprezns 'प्रेज़्न्स्/ *noun* **1** [U] the fact of being in a particular place (स्थान विशेष में या पर) उपस्थिति, मौजूदगी *He apologized to her **in the presence of** the whole family.* ○ *an experiment to test for the presence of oxygen* ✪ विलोम **absence** **2** [*sing.*] a number of soldiers or police officers who are in a place for a special reason विशेष कारण से किसी स्थान पर उपस्थित सैनिक या पुलिसकर्मी *There was a huge police presence at the demonstration.*

**present¹** /ˈpreznt 'प्रेज़्न्ट्/ *adj.* **1** (*only before a noun*) existing or happening now वर्तमान, मौजूदा, इस समय का *We hope to overcome our present difficulties very soon.* **2** (*not before a noun*) being in a particular place स्थान-विशेष में/पर विद्यमान, उपस्थित, मौजूद *There were 200 people present at the meeting.* ✪ विलोम **absent**

**IDM** **the present day** modern times वर्तमान समय, आधुनिक युग *In some countries traditional methods of farming have survived to the present day.*

**present²** /ˈpreznt 'प्रेज़्न्ट्/ *noun* **1** [C] something that you give to sb or receive from sb भेंट, उपहार, तोहफ़ा *a birthday/wedding/Christmas present*

**NOTE** **Gift** अधिक औपचारिक शब्द है और अकसर दुकानों पर या सूची पत्रों में प्रयुक्त होता है।

**2** (*usually* **the present**) [*sing.*] the time now वर्तमान समय *We live **in the present** but we must learn from the past.* ○ *I'm rather busy **at present**.* **3 the present** [*sing.*] = **the present tense**

**IDM** **for the moment/present** ➪ **moment** देखिए।

**present³** /prɪˈzent प्रि'ज़ेन्ट्/ *verb* [T] **1 present sb with sth; present sth (to sb)** to give sth to sb, especially at a formal ceremony किसी को

कुछ देना (विशेषतः औपचारिक अवसर पर); भेंट या उपहार देना *All the dancers were presented with flowers.* ○ *Flowers were presented to all the dancers.* **2 present sth (to sb)** to show sth that you have prepared to people (किसी के सामने) प्रस्तुत करना *Good teachers try to present their material in an interesting way.* **3 present sb with sth; present sth (to sb)** to give sb sth that has to be dealt with निपटाने के लिए कुछ प्रस्तुत करना; किसी के लिए कुछ उत्पन्न करना *Learning English presented no problem to him.* ○ *The manager presented us with a bill for the broken chair.* **4** to introduce a television or radio programme टीवी या रेडियो कार्यक्रम प्रस्तुत करना **5** to show a play, etc. to the public (नाटक आदि का) सार्वजनिक प्रदर्शन करना, मंचन करना *The Theatre Royal is presenting a new production of 'Julius Caesar'.* **6 present sb (to sb)** to introduce sb to a person in a formal ceremony औपचारिक कार्यक्रम में किसी व्यक्ति से परिचय कराना *The teams were presented to the President before the game.*

**presentable** /prɪˈzentəbl प्रिˈज़ेन्टब्ल्/ *adj.* good enough to be seen by people you do not know well अपरिचितों के सामने लाने योग्य, प्रस्तुति योग्य; प्रदेय

**presentation** /ˌprezn̩ˈteɪʃn ˌप्रेज़्न्ˈटेश्न्/ *noun* **1** [C, U] the act of giving or showing sth to sb किसी व्यक्ति के सामने प्रस्तुति (विशेषतः नई वस्तु या विचार या कलाकृति की) *The head will now* ***make a presentation*** *to the winners of the competition.* **2** [U] the way in which sth is shown, explained, offered, etc. to people किसी वस्तु का प्रस्तुतीकरण; प्रदर्शित, व्याख्या, अर्पित आदि करने का ढंग *Untidy presentation of your work may lose you marks.* **3** [C] a meeting at which sth, especially a new product or idea, or piece of work, is shown or explained to a group of people सार्वजनिक कार्यक्रम में प्रस्तुतीकरण (विशेषतः नई वस्तु या विचार या कलाकृति का प्रदर्शन या परिचय-व्याख्या) *Each student has to* ***give a*** *short* ***presentation*** *on a subject of his/her choice.* **4** [C] a formal ceremony at which a prize, etc. is given to sb पुरस्कार वितरण समारोह

**presenter** /prɪˈzentə(r) प्रिˈज़ेन्ट(र्)/ *noun* [C] a person who introduces a television or radio programme टीवी या रेडियो कार्यक्रम का प्रस्तुतकर्ता

**presently** /ˈprezntli ˈप्रेज़्न्ट्लि/ *adv.* **1** soon; shortly शीघ्र; कुछ ही देर में *I'll be finished presently.* **2** (*written*) after a short time थोड़ी देर बाद *Presently I heard the car door shut.* **3** (*AmE*) now; currently इस समय; संप्रति *The management are presently discussing the matter.*

**present participle** *noun* [C] (*grammar*) the form of the verb that ends in *-ing* अंग्रेज़ी व्याकरण में '-ing' से समाप्त होने वाला क्रिया रूप; वर्तमान कृदंत

**the present perfect** *noun* [*sing.*] (*grammar*) the form of a verb that expresses an action done in a time period from the past to the present, formed with the present tense of **have** and the past participle of the verb अंग्रेज़ी व्याकरण में पूर्ण वर्तमान; आसन्न भूत; विगत से वर्तमान की अवधि में हुए कार्य-व्यापार का अर्थ देने वाला क्रिया रूप जो वर्तमान काल रूप *have* और क्रिया के भूत कृदंत रूप से मिल कर बनता है *'I've finished', 'She hasn't arrived' and 'I've been studying' are all* ***in the present perfect***.

> NOTE कालों (tenses) पर अधिक जानकारी के लिए इस शब्दकोश के अंत में **Quick Grammar Reference** देखिए।

**the present tense** *noun* [C] (*also* **the present**) [*sing.*] (*grammar*) the tense of the verb that you use when you are talking about what is happening or what exists now वर्तमान काल; घटित होती हुई घटना या जो स्थिति अब है, उसके बारे में चर्चा के लिए प्रयुक्त क्रिया का काल

**preservative** /prɪˈzɜːvətɪv प्रिˈज़व़टिव़्/ *noun* [C, U] a substance that is used for keeping food, etc. in good condition भोजन आदि को ख़राब होने से सुरक्षित रखने के लिए प्रयुक्त पदार्थ; परिरक्षक, प्रिज़र्वेटिव

**preserve** /prɪˈzɜːv प्रिˈज़व़्/ *verb* [T] to keep sth safe or in good condition किसी वस्तु को सुरक्षित या अच्छी हालत में रखना *They've managed to preserve most of the wall paintings in the caves.* ▶ **preservation** /ˌprezəˈveɪʃn ˌप्रेज़ˈव़ेश्न्/ *noun* [U] सुरक्षा, हिफ़ाज़त, परिरक्षण

**preside** /prɪˈzaɪd प्रिˈज़ाइड्/ *verb* [I] to be in charge of a discussion, meeting, etc. (परिचर्चा, बैठक आदि की) अध्यक्षता करना

PHR V **preside over sth** to be in control of or responsible for sth किसी परिस्थिति पर नियंत्रण रखना या उसके लिए उत्तरदायी होना

**presidency** /ˈprezɪdənsi ˈप्रेज़िडन्सि/ *noun* (*pl.* **presidencies**) **1 the presidency** [*sing.*] the position of being president राष्ट्रपति या अध्यक्ष होने की स्थिति; राष्ट्रपतित्व, अध्यक्षता **2** [C] the period of time that sb is president राष्ट्रपति का कार्यकाल, अध्यक्षता की अवधि

**president** /ˈprezɪdənt ˈप्रेज़िडन्ट्/ *noun* [C] **1** (*also* **President**) the leader of a republic राष्ट्र का अध्यक्ष, राष्ट्रपति *the President of India* ○ *the US President* **2** the person with the highest position in some organizations किसी संस्था का सर्वोच्च अधिकारी या

अध्यक्ष ▶ **presidential** /ˌprezɪˈdenʃl ˌप्रेज़िˈडेन्शल् / *adj.* राष्ट्रपति-विषयक, अध्यक्षीय *presidential elections*

**press¹** /pres प्रेस् / *noun* **1** (*usually* **the press**) [*sing., with sing. or pl. verb*] newspapers and the journalists who work for them पत्र, समाचार और उनमें काम करने वाले पत्रकार *The story has been reported on TV and* ***in the press***. ○ *the local/national press* **2** [*sing.*, U] what or the amount that is written about sb/sth in newspapers समाचारपत्रों में किसी व्यक्ति या वस्तु के विषय में प्रकाशित सामग्री *This company has had* ***a bad press*** *recently.* ○ *The strike got very little press.* **3** [C, U] a machine for printing books, newspapers, etc.; the process of printing them पुस्तक आदि छापने की मशीन, मुद्रणयंत्र, छापाख़ाना; पुस्तक आदि छापने की प्रक्रिया *All details were correct at the time of* ***going to press***. **4** [C] a business that prints books, etc. मुद्रण या प्रकाशन व्यवसाय *Oxford University Press* **5** [C] an act of pushing sth firmly दबाव डालने की क्रिया ***Give*** *that button* ***a press*** *and see what happens.*

**press²** /pres प्रेस् / *verb* **1** [I, T] to push sth firmly ज़ोर से दबाना *Just press that button and the door will open.* ○ *He pressed the lid firmly shut.* **2** [T] to put weight onto sth, for example in order to get juice out of it किसी वस्तु को दबाना रस आदि निकालने के लिए; पेरना, निचोड़ना *to press grapes* **3** [T] to make a piece of clothing smooth by using an iron कपड़े पर इस्तरी करना *This shirt needs pressing.* **4** [T] to hold sb/sth firmly in a loving way व्यक्ति या वस्तु को मज़बूती के साथ प्यार से सँभालना *She pressed the photo to her chest.* **5** [I] **press across, against, around, etc. (sth)** (used about people) to move in a particular direction by pushing (लोगों को) दिशा-विशेष में धकेलना *The crowd pressed against the wall of policemen.* **6** [I, T] **press (sb) (for sth/to do sth)** to try to persuade or force sb to do sth किसी व्यक्ति को कुछ करने के लिए मनाना या उस पर दबाव डालना *I pressed them to stay for dinner.* ○ *to press sb for an answer* **7** [T] to express or repeat sth in an urgent way किसी बात को अत्यावश्यक रीति से व्यक्त करना या दोहराना *I don't want to press the point, but you still owe me money.*

**IDM be hard pressed/pushed/put to do sth** ➪ **hard²** देखिए।

**be pressed for sth** to not have enough of sth किसी बात की तंगी महसूस करना *I must hurry. I'm really pressed for time.*

**bring/press charges (against sb)** ➪ **charge¹** देखिए।

**PHR V press ahead/forward/on (with sth)** to continue doing sth even though it is difficult or hard work कठिन या श्रम-साध्य होने के बावजूद किसी काम को करते जाना *They pressed on with the building work in spite of the bad weather.*

**press conference** *noun* [C] a meeting when a famous or important person answers questions from newspaper and television journalists पत्रकार सम्मेलन या बैठक जिसमें कोई प्रसिद्ध या महत्त्वपूर्ण व्यक्ति अख़बार और टीवी के पत्रकारों के प्रश्नों के उत्तर देता है; सम्मेलन, संवाददाता सम्मेलन, प्रेस कांफ्रेंस *to hold a press conference*

**pressing** /ˈpresɪŋ ˈप्रेसिङ् / *adj.* that must be dealt with immediately; urgent तुरंत करने या निपटाने योग्य; अत्यवाश्यक

**press stud** *noun* [C] = **popper**

**press-up** (*AmE* **push-up**) *noun* [C] a type of exercise in which you lie on your front on the floor and push your body up with your arms एक प्रकार का व्यायाम जिसमें फ़र्श पर औंधे मुँह लेटकर बाँहों से शरीर को ऊपर उठाना होता है *I do 50 press-ups every morning.*

**pressure** /ˈpreʃə(r) ˈप्रेश(र्) / *noun* **1** [U] the force that is produced when you press on or against sth (किसी वस्तु को दबाने या धकेलने से उत्पन्न शक्ति; दबाव *Apply pressure to the cut and it will stop bleeding.* ○ *The pressure of the water caused the dam to crack.* **2** [C, U] the force that a gas or liquid has when it is contained inside sth गैस या द्रव के किसी वस्तु के अंदर बंद होने पर बनी ऊर्जा; दाब *high/low blood pressure* ○ *You should check your tyre pressures regularly.* **3** [C, U] worries or difficulties that you have because you have too much to deal with; stress किसी स्थिति के भारी-भरकम होने से उत्पन्न चिंताएँ या कठिनाइयाँ; तनाव, दबाव, परेशानी *financial pressures* ○ *I find it difficult to cope with pressure at work.*

**IDM put pressure on sb (to do sth)** to force sb to do sth किसी पर कुछ करने के लिए दबाव डालना *The press is putting pressure on him to resign.*

**under pressure 1** being forced to do sth दबाव में *Ananya was under pressure from her parents to leave school and get a job.* **2** worried or in difficulty because you have too much to deal with (काम के बोझ से) चिंतित या परेशान *I perform poorly under pressure, so I hate exams.* **3** (used about liquid or gas) contained inside sth or sent somewhere using force (द्रव या गैस) किसी वस्तु में बंद या बलपूर्वक दाब से अन्यत्र धकेला गया *Water is forced out through the hose under pressure.*

▶ **pressure** *verb* [T] = **pressurize**

**pressure cook** *verb* [T] (*IndE*) to cook in a **pressure cooker** प्रेशर कुकर में पकाना

**pressure cooker** *noun* [C] a strong metal pot with a tight lid, that cooks food quickly using steam under high pressure उच्च दाब से बनी गैस के द्वारा शीघ्र भोजन बनाने का धातु-निर्मित और कसे ढक्कन वाला बरतन; प्रेशर-कुकर ➪ **pan** पर चित्र देखिए।

**pressure group** *noun* [C, *with sing. or pl. verb*] a group of people who are trying to influence what a government or other organization does व्यक्तियों का समूह जो सरकार या किसी संस्था के कामों को प्रभावित करने की कोशिश करता है; दबाव-गुट

**pressurize** (*also* **-ise**) /ˈpreʃəraɪz ˈप्रेशराइज़्/ (*also* **pressure**) *verb* [T] **pressurize sb (into sth/doing sth)** to use force or influence to make sb do sth किसी से कुछ करवाने के लिए उस पर दबाव डालना *Some workers were pressurized into taking early retirement.*

**pressurized** (*also* **-ised**) /ˈpreʃəraɪzd ˈप्रेशराइज़्ड्/ *adj.* (used about air in an aircraft) kept at the pressure at which people can breathe (विमान में वायु) ऐसे दाब पर रखी गई जिससे लोग (आसानी से) साँस ले सकें

**prestige** /preˈstiːʒ प्रेˈस्टीश़्/ *noun* [U] the respect and admiration that people feel for a person because he/she has a high social position or has been very successful उच्च सामाजिक पद पर स्थित या अत्यंत सफल रहे व्यक्ति के प्रति आदर और प्रशंसा का भाव; प्रतिष्ठा, ख्याति ▶ **prestigious** /preˈstɪdʒəs प्रेˈस्टिजस्/ *adj.* प्रतिष्ठित, ख्यातिप्राप्त *a prestigious prize/ school/job*

**presumably** /prɪˈzjuːməbli प्रिˈज़्यूमब्लि/ *adv.* used to say sth is possibly true संभवतः *Presumably this rain means the match will be cancelled?*

**presume** /prɪˈzjuːm प्रिˈज़्यूम्/ *verb* [T] to think that sth is true even if you do not know for sure; to suppose किसी बात की पक्की जानकारी न होने पर भी उसे सच मान लेना; किसी बात की कल्पना कर लेना या धारणा बना लेना *The house looks empty so I presume they are away on holiday.* ▶ **presumption** /prɪˈzʌmpʃn प्रिˈज़म्प्श्न्/ *noun* [C] परिकल्पना, धारणा, संभावना

**presumptuous** /prɪˈzʌmptʃuəs प्रिˈज़म्प्चुअस्/ *adj.* confident that sth will happen or that sb will do sth without making sure first, in a way that annoys people बिना सुनिश्चित हुए ज़रूरत से अधिक आत्मविश्वासपूर्ण (ऐसा कि दूसरों को बुरा लगे); अक्खड़, ढीठ

**presuppose** /ˌpriːsəˈpəʊz ˌप्रीसˈपोज़्/ *verb* [T] (*formal*) **1** to accept sth as true or existing and act on that basis, before it has been shown to be true किसी बात को बिना सिद्ध हुए सत्य या अस्तित्वयुक्त मान लेना और तदनुसार कार्रवाई करना *Teachers sometimes presuppose a fairly high level of knowledge by the students.* ✪ पर्याय **presume** **2** to depend on sth in order to exist or be true (किसी के) सत्य या अस्तित्व में होने के लिए किसी बात पर निर्भर होना; (किसी बात का) शर्त के रूप में आवश्यक होना *His argument presupposes that it does not matter who is in power.*

**pretence** (*AmE* **pretense**) /prɪˈtens प्रिˈटेन्स्/ *noun* [U, *sing.*] an action that makes people believe sth that is not true प्रदर्शन, ढोंग, दिखावा *She was unable to keep up the pretence that she loved him.*
**IDM** **on/under false pretences** ➪ **false** देखिए।

**pretend** /prɪˈtend प्रिˈटेन्ड्/ *verb* [I, T] **1** to behave in a particular way in order to make other people believe sth that is not true प्रदर्शन, ढोंग या दिखावा करना *You can't just pretend that the problem doesn't exist.* ○ *Parul is not really asleep. She's just pretending.* **2** (used especially about children) to imagine that sth is true as part of a game (विशेषतः बच्चों के लिए प्रयुक्त) खेल-खेल में किसी बात के सच होने की कल्पना करना *The kids were under the bed pretending to be snakes.*

**pretentious** /prɪˈtenʃəs प्रिˈटेन्शस्/ *adj.* trying to appear more serious or important than you really are वास्तविकता से अधिक गंभीर या बड़ा होने का दिखावा करने वाला; मिथ्याभिमानी, आडंबरी, बनावटी

**pretext** /ˈpriːtekst ˈप्रीटेक्स्ट्/ *noun* [C] a reason that you give for doing sth that is not the real reason बहाना, हीला *Tariq left* ***on the pretext of*** *having an appointment at the dentist's.*

**pretty**[1] /ˈprɪti ˈप्रिटि/ *adj.* (**prettier; prettiest**) attractive and pleasant to look at or hear दिखने या सुनने में अच्छा और आकर्षक *a pretty girl/smile/ dress/garden/name*

> **NOTE** **Pretty** का प्रयोग सामान्यतः पुरुषों या लड़कों के लिए नहीं किया जाता। **Good-looking** का प्रयोग सबके लिए हो सकता है। पुरुषों के लिए प्रायः **handsome** का प्रयोग होता है। ➪ **Beautiful** पर भी नोट देखिए।

▶ **prettily** *adv.* आकर्षक या सुंदर ढंग से, अच्छी तरह *The room is prettily decorated.* ▶ **prettiness** *noun* आकर्षण, सुन्दरता, मनोहरता

**pretty**[2] /ˈprɪti ˈप्रिटि/ *adv.* (*informal*) quite; fairly काफ़ी; बहुत कुछ *The film was pretty good but not fantastic.* ○ *I'm pretty certain that Amit will agree.* ➪ **rather** पर नोट देखिए।

IDM **pretty much/nearly/well** almost; very nearly लगभग; क़रीब-क़रीब *I won't be long. I've pretty well finished.*

**prevail** /prɪˈveɪl प्रि ˈव़ेल् / *verb* [I] **1** to exist or be common in a particular place or at a particular time स्थान-विशेष या समय-विशेष में (किसी बात का) विद्यमान या प्रचलन में होना **2** (*formal*) **prevail (against/over sb/sth)** to win or be accepted, especially after a fight or discussion किसी की विजय होना या किसी को मान लिया जाना (विशेषतः संघर्ष या विचार-विमर्श में) *In the end justice prevailed and the men were set free.*

**prevailing** /prɪˈveɪlɪŋ प्रि ˈव़ेलिङ् / *adj.* (*only before a noun*) **1** existing or most common at a particular time समय-विशेष में विद्यमान या सर्वाधिक प्रचलित *the prevailing mood of optimism* **2** (used about the wind) most common in a particular area (वायु) क्षेत्र-विशेष में व्याप्त; प्रबल, प्रधान, हावी *The prevailing wind is from the south-west.*

**prevalent** /ˈprevələnt ˈप्रेव़लन्ट् / *adj.* (*formal*) most common in a particular place at a particular time स्थान-विशेष में समय-विशेष पर सर्वाधिक प्रचलित *The prevalent atmosphere was one of fear.* ▶ **prevalence** /-ləns लन्स् / *noun* [U] प्रचलन, प्रधानता

**prevent** /prɪˈvent प्रि ˈव़ेन्ट् / *verb* [T] **prevent sb/sth (from) (doing sth)** to stop sth happening or to stop sb doing sth किसी बात को होने न देना या किसी को कोई काम करने से रोक देना *This accident could have been prevented.* ○ *Her parents tried to prevent her from going abroad.* NOTE **Stop** की अपेक्षा **prevent** अधिक औपचारिक है। ▶ **prevention** *noun* [U] रोकथाम, निवारण *accident/crime prevention*

**preventable** /prɪˈventəbl प्रि ˈव़ेन्टबल् / *adj.* that can be prevented जिसकी रोकथाम हो सके; निवार्य, निरोध्य *Many accidents are preventable.*

**preventive** /prɪˈventɪv प्रि ˈव़ेन्टिव़् / (*also* **preventative** /prɪˈventətɪv प्रि ˈव़ेन्टटिव़् /) *adj.* intended to stop or prevent sth from happening किसी बात को रोकने या न होने देने की मंशा वाला; निवारक *preventative medicine*

**preview** /ˈpriːvjuː ˈप्रीव़्यू / *noun* [C] a chance to see a play, film, etc. before it is shown to the general public पूर्वदर्शन (नाटक, फ़िल्म आदि के सार्वजनिक प्रदर्शन से पहले का प्रदर्शन), पूर्वसमीक्षा

**previous** /ˈpriːviəs ˈप्रीव़िअस् / *adj.* coming or happening before or earlier किसी से पहले या जल्दी आने या होने वाला; पूर्व, पूर्ववर्ती, पिछला, पहले का *Do you have previous experience of this type of work?* ▶ **previously** *adv.* पहले, पूर्व में *Before I moved to Mumbai I had previously worked in Delhi.*

**prey[1]** /preɪ प्रे / *noun* [U] an animal or bird that is killed and eaten by another animal or bird एक पशु या पक्षी द्वारा मार कर खाया गया अन्य पशु या पक्षी; शिकार *The eagle is a bird of prey* (= it kills and eats other birds or small animals).

**prey[2]** /preɪ प्रे / *verb*

IDM **prey on sb's mind** to cause sb to worry or think about sth किसी व्यक्ति को किसी बात के लिए चिंतित कर देना या सोचने के लिए विवश करना *The thought that he was responsible for the accident preyed on the train driver's mind.*

PHR V **prey on sth** (used about an animal or bird) to kill and eat other animals or birds (पशु या पक्षी द्वारा) दूसरे पशुओं या पक्षियों का शिकार करना (मार कर खा जाना) *Owls prey on mice and other small animals.*

**price[1]** /praɪs प्राइस् / *noun* **1** [C] the amount of money that you must pay in order to buy sth (किसी वस्तु को ख़रीदने के लिए देय धनराशि); मूल्य, क़ीमत, दाम *We can't afford to buy the car at that price.* ○ *There's no price on* (= written on) *this jar of coffee.*

NOTE **Charge** वह राशि है जिसे किसी वस्तु के इस्तेमाल के लिए देना होता है—*Is there a charge for parking here?* ○ *admission charges.* **Cost** सेवाओं या वस्तुओं की सामान्य क़ीमत है न कि वास्तविक धनराशि—*The cost of electricity is going up.* ○ *the cost of living.* **Price** (क़ीमत) वह राशि है जिसे कुछ ख़रीदने के लिए देना होता है। क़ीमतों को बढ़ाया **raise/increase**, घटाया **reduce/bring down**, या स्थिर **freeze** किया जा सकता है। क़ीमतों के बढ़ने के लिए **rise/go up** जैसे शब्द प्रयुक्त किए जाते हैं तथा कीमतों के घटने के लिए शब्द **fall/go down** प्रयुक्त किए जाते हैं।

**2** [*sing.*] unpleasant things that you have to experience in order to achieve sth or as a result of sth कुछ पाने के लिए या किसी बात के फलस्वरूप होने वाला कटु अनुभव; क़ीमत, मूल्य *She won the elections but at a heavy price.*

IDM **at a price** costing a lot of money or involving sth unpleasant बहुत महँगा या कटु अनुभव वाला *Fame and success never come without a price.*

**at any price** even if the cost is very high or if it will have unpleasant results किसी भी क़ीमत पर; चाहे कितना भी पैसा लगे या कितने ही कटु अनुभव हों *Ravi was determined to succeed at any price.*

**not at any price never**; under no circumstances कभी नही; किसी भी क़ीमत पर नहीं

**price²** /praɪs प्राइस्/ *verb* [T] to fix the price of sth or to write the price on sth किसी वस्तु का मूल्य तय करना या उस पर लिखना *The books were all priced at between Rs 100 and Rs 250.*

**priceless** /ˈpraɪsləs ˈप्राइसलस्/ *adj.* of very great value बहुमूल्य, बहुत क़ीमती *priceless jewels and antiques* ➪ **worthless, valuable** और **invaluable** देखिए।

**price list** *noun* [C] a list of the prices of the goods that are on sale बिक्री की वस्तुओं के दामों की सूची; मूल्य-सूची

**pricey** /ˈpraɪsi ˈप्राइसि/ *adj.* (*informal*) expensive महँगा *a pricey restaurant*

**prick¹** /prɪk प्रिक्/ *verb* [T] to make a small hole in sth or to cause sb pain with a sharp point किसी वस्तु में छेद करना या किसी को कोई नुकीली चीज़ चुभोना *He pricked the balloon with a pin.*

IDM **prick up your ears** (used about an animal) to hold up the ears in order to listen carefully to sth (पशु का) अपने कान खड़े करना (किसी आवाज़ को सावधानी से सुनने के लिए) (*figurative*) *Madhav pricked up his ears when he heard his name mentioned.*

**prick²** /prɪk प्रिक्/ *noun* [C] the sudden pain that you feel when sth sharp goes into your skin चुभने से उत्पन्न दर्द; चुभन

**prickle¹** /ˈprɪkl ˈप्रिक्ल्/ *noun* [C] one of the sharp points on some plants and animals कुछ पौधों और पशुओं पर काँटेनुमा बाल *Hedgehogs are covered in prickles.* ➪ **spine** देखिए।

**prickle²** /ˈprɪkl ˈप्रिक्ल्/ *verb* [I] to have or make sb/sth have an uncomfortable feeling on the skin (डर आदि के कारण) त्वचा में चुभन पैदा होना या करना *His skin prickled with fear.*

**prickly** /ˈprɪkli ˈप्रिक्लि/ *adj.* **1** covered with sharp points काँटेदार *a prickly bush* **2** causing an uncomfortable feeling on the skin (त्वचा में) चुभन पैदा करने वाला **3** (*informal*) (used about a person) easily made angry (व्यक्ति) जल्दी क्रोधित हो जाने वाला; गुस्सैल

**pride¹** /praɪd प्राइड्/ *noun* **1** [U, *sing.*] **pride (in sth/doing sth)** the feeling of pleasure that you have when you or people who are close to you do sth good or own sth good अपनी या मित्रों की उपलब्धि पर होने वाला आंनद या हर्ष; गर्व, अभिमान *I take a great **pride** in my work.* ○ *You should **feel pride** in your achievement.* **2** [U] the respect that you have for yourself स्वाभिमान, आत्म-गौरव *You'll hurt his pride if you refuse to accept the present.* **3** [U] the feeling that you are better than other people दूसरों से अपने को बेहतर समझने का भाव; घमंड **4** [*sing.*] **the pride of sth/sb** a person or thing that is very important or of great value to sth/sb व्यक्ति या वस्तु जो किसी के लिए बहुत महत्त्वपूर्ण या मूल्यवान हो; गौरव *The new stadium was the pride of the whole town.* ➪ **proud** adjective देखिए।

IDM **sb's pride and joy** a thing or person that gives sb great pleasure or satisfaction (किसी को) बहुत हर्ष या संतुष्टि देने वाली वस्तु या व्यक्ति

**pride²** /praɪd प्राइड्/ *verb*

PHR V **pride yourself on sth/doing sth** to feel pleased about sth good or clever that you can do अपने काम पर गर्व अनुभव करना *Armaan prides himself on his ability to cook.*

**priest** /priːst प्रीस्ट्/ *noun* [C] a person who performs religious ceremonies in some religions पुरोहित, पुजारी (धार्मिक अनुष्ठान करने वाला व्यक्ति) NOTE कुछ धर्मों में महिला पुरोहित को **priestess** कहा जाता है।

**prim** /prɪm प्रिम्/ *adj.* (used about a person) always behaving in a careful or formal way and easily shocked by anything that is rude (व्यक्ति) ऐसा शिष्टता प्रिय (व्यक्ति) जो दूसरों की अशिष्टता से तुरंत परेशान हो जाए; तकल्लुफ़-मिज़ाज, औपचारिक ▶ **primly** *adv.* औपचारिकता से

**primarily** /ˈpraɪmərəli; praɪˈmerəli ˈप्राइमरलि; प्राइˈमेरलि/ *adv.* more than anything else; mainly मुख्य रूप से *The course is aimed primarily at beginners.*

**primary¹** /ˈpraɪməri ˈप्राइमरि/ *adj.* **1** most important; main सबसे बड़ा; मुख्य, प्रधान *Smoking is one of the primary causes of lung cancer.* **2** connected with the education of children between about 5 and 11 years old पाँच से ग्यारह वर्ष की आयु के बच्चों की शिक्षा से संबंधित; प्राथमिक शिक्षा, विद्यालय आदि *Their children are at primary school.*

**primary²** /ˈpraɪməri ˈप्राइमरि/ (*also* **primary election**) *noun* [C] (*pl.* **primaries**) (*AmE*) an election in which people from a particular area vote to choose a **candidate** for a future important election प्रथम चरण का चुनाव

**primary colour** *noun* [C] any of the colours red, yellow or blue. You can make any other colour by mixing primary colours in different ways मूल रंग लाल, पीला या नीला। इन्हें तरह-तरह से मिलाकर अन्य अनेक रंग बनाए जा सकते हैं

**primate** /ˈpraɪmeɪt ˈप्राइमेट्/ *noun* [C] any animal that belongs to the group that includes humans, monkeys and animals like monkeys without a tail (**apes**) मानवों, वानरों और वानर-सदृश पशुओं के समूह का कोई प्राणी; नर-वानर, विकसित प्राणी वर्ग का जीव, प्राइमेट

**primates**

**prime**[1] /praɪm प्राइम्/ *adj.* (*only before a noun*) **1** main; the first example of sth that sb would think of or choose मुख्य, प्रधान; सर्वाधिक उपयुक्त *Seema is a prime candidate as the next team captain.* **2** of very good quality; best उत्कृष्ट; सर्वोत्तम *prime pieces of meat* **3** having all the typical qualities सर्वगुणसंपन्न, सर्वश्रेष्ठ *That's **a prime example** of what I was talking about.*

**prime**[2] /praɪm प्राइम्/ *noun* [*sing.*] the time when sb is strongest, most beautiful, most successful, etc. शक्ति, सौंदर्य आदि की दृष्टि से श्रेष्ठतम अवस्था; शिखर-काल *Several of the team are **past their prime**.* ○ *to be **in the prime of life***

**prime**[3] /praɪm प्राइम्/ *verb* [T] **prime sb (for/with sth)** to give sb information in order to prepare him/her for sth आवश्यक जानकारी आदि देकर किसी को किसी काम के लिए तैयार करना *The politician had been well primed with all the facts before the interview.*

**prime minister** *noun* [C] (*abbr.* **PM**) the leader of the government in some countries, for example India, Britain, etc. प्रधानमंत्री (भारत, ब्रिटेन आदि देशों में) ➪ **minister** देखिए।

**prime number** *noun* [C] (*mathematics*) a number that can be divided exactly only by itself and 1, for example 7, 17 and 41 रूढ़ या अभाज्य संख्या (जैसे 7, 17 और 41)

**primeval** (*also* **primaeval**) /praɪˈmiːvl प्राइˈमीव्ल्/ *adj.* from the earliest period of the history of the world, very ancient विश्व के इतिहास के प्राचीनतम युग का; अति प्राचीन, पुरातन, आद्यकालिक

**primitive** /ˈprɪmətɪv ˈप्रिमटिव्/ *adj.* **1** very simple and not developed अत्यंत साधारण और अविकसित *The washing facilities in the camp were very primitive.* **2** (*only before a noun*) connected with a very early stage in the development of humans or animals मानव या पशु जगत के विकास की अत्यंत आरंभिक अवस्था से संबंधित; आदिम, आदिकालीन *Primitive man lived in caves and hunted wild animals.*

**primrose** /ˈprɪmrəʊz ˈप्रिम्रोज़्/ *noun* [C] a yellow spring flower पीले रंग का वसंती जंगली फूल; पीतसेवती

**prince** /prɪns प्रिन्स्/ *noun* [C] **1** a son or other close male relative of a king or queen राजा या रानी का पुत्र या कोई अन्य निकट संबंधी पुरुष; राजकुमार **2** the male ruler of a small country किसी छोटे देश का शासक; युवराज

**princess** /ˌprɪnˈses ˌप्रिन्ˈसेस्/ *noun* [C] **1** a daughter or other close female relative of a king or queen राजा या रानी की पुत्री या कोई अन्य निकट संबंधी स्त्री; राजकुमारी **2** the wife of a prince राजकुमार की पत्नी

**principal**[1] /ˈprɪnsəpl ˈप्रिन्सप्ल्/ *adj.* (*only before a noun*) most important; main सबसे महत्त्वपूर्ण; मुख्य *the principal characters in a play* ► **principally** /-pli -प्लि/ *adv.* मुख्य रूप से *Our products are designed principally for the European market.*

**principal**[2] /ˈprɪnsəpl ˈप्रिन्सप्ल्/ *noun* [C] the head of some schools, colleges, etc. स्कूल, कॉलेज आदि का प्राचार्य; प्रिंसिपल

**principle** /ˈprɪnsəpl ˈप्रिन्सप्ल्/ *noun* **1** [C, U] a rule for good behaviour, based on what a person believes is right अच्छे आचरण का नियम (व्यक्ति की सदाचार विषयक मान्यता पर आधारित) *He doesn't eat meat **on principle**.* ○ *She refuses to wear fur. It's **a matter of principle** with her.* **2** [C] a basic general law, rule or idea सामान्य सिद्धांत, नियम या विचार *The system works **on the principle that** hot air rises.* ○ *The course teaches the basic principles of car maintenance.*

**IDM** **in principle** in general, but possibly not in detail सिद्धांत रूप में, सामान्यतः (परंतु विस्तृत रूप से नहीं) *His proposal sounds fine in principle, but there are a few points I'm not happy about.*

**print**[1] /prɪnt प्रिन्ट्/ *verb* **1** [I, T] to put words, pictures, etc. onto paper by using a special machine छापना, मुद्रित करना *How much did it cost to print the posters?* **2** [T] to produce books, newspapers, etc. in this way पुस्तक, समाचार-पत्र आदि छापना *Fifty thousand copies of the textbook were printed.* **3** [T] to include sth in a book, newspaper, etc. किसी बात को पुस्तक आदि में शामिल

करना या छापना *The newspaper should not have printed the photographs of the crash.* **4** [T] to make a photograph from a piece of negative film निगेटिव से फ़ोटो बनाना **5** [I, T] to write with letters that are not joined together अक्षरों को जोड़े बिना लिख देना *Please print your name clearly at the top of the paper.* **6** [T] to put a pattern onto cloth, paper, etc. कपड़े, काग़ज़ आदि पर छपाई करना
▶ **printing** *noun* [U] मुद्रण-क्रिया
PHR V **print (sth) out** to print information from a computer onto paper कंप्यूटर से प्रिंट निकालना या लेना *I'll just print out this file.*

**print²** /prɪnt प्रिन्ट् / *noun* **1** [U] the letters, words, etc. in a book, newspaper, etc. पुस्तक आदि में छपे अक्षर, शब्द आदि; टाइप, मुद्रण *The print is too small for me to read without my glasses.* **2** [U] used to refer to the business of producing newspapers, books, etc. समाचार पत्र, पुस्तक आदि के प्रकाशन का व्यवसाय *the print unions/workers* **3** [C] a mark that is made by sth pressing onto sth else चिह्न, निशान या छाप (किसी वस्तु को अन्य पर दबाने से बना) *The police are searching the room for fingerprints.* ○ *footprints in the snow* **4** [C] a picture that was made by printing मुद्रित चित्र या मुद्रण-क्रिया से बना चित्र **5** [C] a photograph (when it has been printed from a negative) (निगेटिव से बना) फ़ोटो *I ordered an extra set of prints for my friends.*
IDM **in print 1** (used about a book) still available from the company that published it (पुस्तक) प्रकाशक के पास अब भी उपलब्ध; (प्रकाशक से) प्राप्य **2** (used about a person's work) published in a book, newspaper, etc. (व्यक्ति की रचना) पुस्तक, समाचार पत्र आदि में प्रकाशित
**out of print** (used about a book) no longer available from the company that published it; not being printed anymore (पुस्तक) प्रकाशक के पास अब उपलब्ध नहीं; (प्रकाशक से) अप्राप्य; जिसका मुद्रण अब बंद हो चुका हो

**printer** /ˈprɪntə(r) ˈप्रिन्ट(र्) / *noun* [C] **1** a person or company that prints books, newspapers, etc. मुद्रक (व्यक्ति या कंपनी जो पुस्तक, समाचार पत्र आदि मुद्रित करे) **2** a machine that prints out information from a computer onto paper कंप्यूटर की सूचना-राशि को मुद्रित करने वाला; मुद्रक यंत्र *a laser printer*

**printing press** (*also* **press**) *noun* [C] a machine that is used for printing books, newspapers, etc. छापाख़ाना, प्रेस; पुस्तक आदि छापने वाली मशीन

**printout** /ˈprɪntaʊt ˈप्रिन्ट्आउट् / *noun* [C, U] information from a computer that is printed onto paper कंप्यूटर में संचित सूचना की (प्रिंटर से) मुद्रित प्रति

**prior** /ˈpraɪə(r) ˈप्राइअ(र्) / *adj.* (*only before a noun*) coming before or earlier पूर्ववर्ती, (किसी से) पहले या शुरू में आने वाला

**prioritize** (*also* **-ise**) /praɪˈɒrətaɪz प्राइˈऑरटाइज़् / *verb* **1** [I, T] to put tasks, problems, etc. in order of importance, so that you can deal with the most important first (महत्त्व की दृष्टि से) करने योग्य कार्यों, समस्याओं आदि का क्रम तय करना (ताकि सबसे आवश्यक को पहले निपटाया जा सके; विभिन्न मुद्दों को प्राथमिकता-क्रम में रखना *You should make a list of all the jobs you have to do and prioritize them.* **2** [T] (*formal*) to treat sth as being more important than other things किसी बात को अन्य बातों से अधिक महत्त्वपूर्ण मानना *The organization was formed to prioritize the needs of older people.*

**priority** /praɪˈɒrəti प्राइˈऑरटि / *noun* (*pl.* **priorities**) **1** [U] **priority (over sb/sth)** the state of being more important than sb/sth or of coming before sb/sth else महत्त्व पर आधारित क्रम की दृष्टि से; अग्रता, वरीयता *We **give priority** to families with small children.* ○ *Emergency cases **take priority** over other patients in hospital.* **2** [C] something that is most important or that you must do before anything else सबसे महत्त्वपूर्ण या सबसे पहले करने योग्य काम; प्राथमिकता *Our **top priority** is to get food and water to the refugee camps.* ○ *I'll **make it** my **priority** to sort out your problem.*

**prior to** *prep.* (*formal*) before किसी से पहले *Passengers are asked to report to the check-in desk prior to departure.*

**prise** /praɪz प्राइज़् / (*AmE* **prize, pry**) *verb* [T] **prise sth off, apart, open, etc.** to use force to open sth, remove a lid, etc. दरवाज़ा, ढक्कन आदि खोलने के लिए ज़ोर लगाना *He prised the door open with an iron bar.*

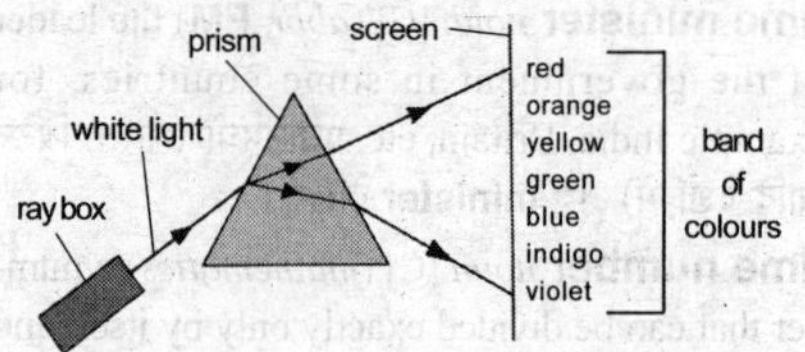

white light can be split into its components using a prism

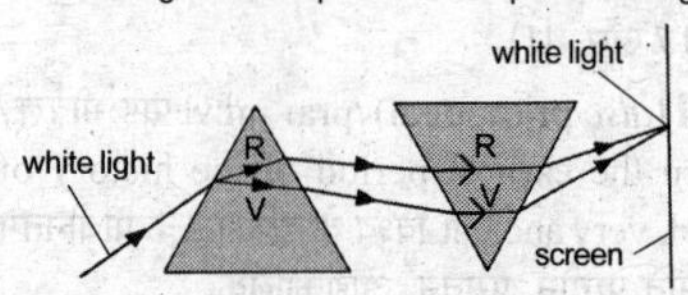

splitting and recombining the colours in white light
R = red V = violet

**prisms**

**prism** /ˈprɪzəm ˈप्रिज़म्/ *noun* [C] **1** a solid object with ends that are parallel and of the same size and shape, and with sides whose opposite edges are equal and parallel एक समपार्श्व ठोस वस्तु जिसके एक पार्श्व के किनारे दूसरे पार्श्व के किनारों के समानांतर तथा आकार एवं आकृति की दृष्टि से समान होते हैं; प्रिज़्म ➪ **solid** पर चित्र देखिए। **2** a transparent glass or plastic object which separates light that passes through it into the seven different colours काँच या प्लास्टिक की वस्तु जो अपने ऊपर पड़ती हुई प्रकाश-रेखा सात अलग-अलग रंगों में बाँट देती है

**prison** /ˈprɪzn ˈप्रिज़न्/ (*also* **jail**) *noun* [C, U] a building where criminals are kept as a punishment जेल, कारागार, क़ैदखाना *The terrorists were* ***sent to prison*** *for 25 years.* ○ *He will be* ***released from prison*** *next month.* ➪ **imprison** और **jail** देखिए।

**NOTE** जब अभिव्यक्तियाँ goes **to prison** या **is in prison** का प्रयोग **'the'** के बिना होता है तो वह यह दर्शाती हैं कि कोई व्यक्ति जेल गया है या जेल में है तथा उसे वहाँ बंदी के रूप में रहना होता है—*He was sent to prison for two years.* 'The prison' से किसी विशिष्ट जेल का बोध होता है या यह भास होता है कि कोई व्यक्ति केवल लघु काल के लिए जेल में भेंट आदि के लिए गया है—*The politician visited the prison and said that conditions were poor.*

**prisoner** /ˈprɪznə(r) ˈप्रिज़्नर्(र्)/ *noun* [C] a person who is being kept in prison बंदी, क़ैदी *a political prisoner*

**prisoner of war** *noun* [C] (*pl.* **prisoners of war**) (*abbr.* **POW**) a soldier, etc. who is caught by the enemy during a war and who is kept in prison until the end of the war युद्ध में शत्रु द्वारा बंदी बनाया गया सैनिक जो युद्ध होने तक क़ैद में रहता है; युद्धबंदी

**privacy** /ˈprɪvəsi ˈप्रिव़सि/ *noun* [U] **1** the state of being alone and not watched or disturbed by other people (व्यक्ति की) एकांतता की स्थिति (जिसमें उसे न कोई देखे न उसकी शांति भंग करे) *There is not much privacy in large hospital wards.* **2** the state of being free from the attention of the public लोगों की नज़र से बचे रहने की स्थिति *The actress claimed that the photographs were an* ***invasion of privacy***.

**private**[1] /ˈpraɪvət ˈप्राइव़ट्/ *adj.* **1** belonging to or intended for one particular person or group and not to be shared by others केवल एक व्यक्ति या समूह से संबंधित (अन्य सदस्यों से सहभाजित नहीं) निजी; व्यक्तिगत *This is private property. You may not park here.* ○ *a private letter/conversation* **2** not connected with work or business निजी (नौकरी या व्यवसाय से संबंधित नहीं) *He never discusses his* ***private life*** *with his colleagues at work.* **3** owned, done or organized by a person or company, and not by the government किसी एक व्यक्ति या कंपनी का (न कि सरकारी) *a private hospital/school* (= you pay to go there) ○ *a private detective* (= one who is not in the police) ➪ **public** देखिए। **4** with no one else present एकांतिक (जहाँ दूसरे लोग न हों) *I would like a private interview with the personnel manager.* **5** not wanting to share thoughts and feelings with other people अपने विचार या भाव दूसरों को न बताने वाला *He's a very private person.* **6** (used about classes, lessons, etc.) given by a teacher to one student or a small group for payment (कक्षा-पाठ, अध्ययन आदि) शुल्क लेकर अध्यापक द्वारा एक छात्र या छोटे समूह के लिए आयोजित *Anu gives private English lessons at her house.* ▶ **privately** *adv.* निजी या व्यक्तिगत रूप से

**private**[2] /ˈpraɪvət ˈप्राइव़ट्/ *noun* [C] a soldier of the lowest level सबसे छोटे स्तर का सैनिक, मामूली सिपाही

**IDM in private** with no one else present अकेले में (जब कोई और न हो) *May I speak to you in private?*

**privatize** (*also* **-ise**) /ˈpraɪvɪtaɪz ˈप्राइव़िटाइज़्/ *verb* [T] to sell a business or an industry that was owned by the government to a private company सरकारी संरक्षण के व्यापार या उद्योग को निजी कंपनी को बेचना; व्यापार या उद्योग निजीकरण करना *The distribution of electricity in the city has been privatized.* ✪ विलोम **nationalize** ▶ **privatization** (*also* **-isation**) /ˌpraɪvɪtaɪˈzeɪʃn ˌप्राइव़िटाइˈज़ेश्न्/ *noun* [U] व्यापार या उद्योग का निजीकरण

**privilege** /ˈprɪvəlɪdʒ ˈप्रिव़लिज्/ *noun* **1** [C, U] a special right or advantage that only one person or group has (केवल एक व्यक्ति या समूह का) विशेष अधिकार या लाभ; विशेषाधिकार *Prisoners who behave well* ***enjoy*** *special* ***privileges***. **2** [*sing.*] a special advantage or opportunity that gives you great pleasure हर्षानुभूति कराने वाला विशेष लाभ; सौभाग्य, अवसर *It was a great privilege to hear her sing.*

**privileged** /ˈprɪvəlɪdʒd ˈप्रिव़लिज्ड्/ *adj.* having an advantage or opportunity that most people do not have विशेष सुविधा या अवसर से संपन्न विशेषाधिकार-संपन्न *Only* ***a privileged few*** *are allowed to enter this room.* ○ *I feel very privileged to be playing for the national team.* ✪ विलोम **underprivileged**

**prize**[1] /praɪz प्राइज़्/ *noun* [C] something of value that is given to sb who is successful in a race, competition, game, etc. पुरस्कार, इनाम में *She won* ***first prize*** *in the competition.* ○ *a prizewinning novel*

**prize²** /praɪz प्राइज़् / *adj.* (*only before a noun*) winning, or good enough to win, a prize पुरस्कार प्राप्त; पुरस्कार जीतने या जीत सकने वाला *a prize flower display*

**prize³** /praɪz प्राइज़् / *verb* [T] to consider sth to be very valuable किसी वस्तु को मूल्यवान (उत्कृष्ट) समझना *This picture is one of my most prized possessions.*

**prize⁴** /praɪz प्राइज़् / (*AmE*) = **prise**

**pro** /prəʊ प्रो / *noun* [C] (*pl.* **pros**) (*informal*) **1** a person who plays or teaches a sport for money पैसे के लिए खेलने या खेल सिखाने वाला व्यक्ति; पेशेवर खिलाड़ी *a golf pro* **2** a person who has a lot of skill and experience बहुत दक्ष और अनुभवी व्यक्ति ✪ पर्याय **professional**

IDM **the pros and cons** the reasons for and against doing sth किसी कार्य आदि के लाभ और हानि *We should consider all the pros and cons before reaching a decision.*

**pro-** /prəʊ प्रो / *prefix* (*used in adjectives*) in favour of; supporting के पक्ष में; समर्थन में *pro-democracy* ○ *pro-European*

**proactive** /ˌprəʊˈæktɪv ˌप्रोˈऐक्टिव़् / *adj.* controlling a situation by making things happen rather than waiting for things to happen and then reacting to them घटनाओं की सक्रियता को स्वयं आरंभ करने वाला, न कि प्रतिक्रिया हेतु उनके स्वयं घटित होने तक प्रतीक्षारत; अग्रसक्रिय, निश्चयपूर्वक सक्रिय ➪ **reactive** देखिए। ▶ **proactively** *adv.* अग्रसक्रियता के साथ

**probability** /ˌprɒbəˈbɪləti ˌप्रॉबˈबिलटि / *noun* (*pl.* **probabilities**) **1** [U, *sing.*] how likely sth is to happen (किसी बात की) संभावना *At that time there seemed little probability of success.* **2** [C] something that is likely to happen संभावित स्थिति *Closure of the factory now seems a probability.*

**probable** /ˈprɒbəbl ˈप्रॉबब्ल् / *adj.* that you expect to happen or to be true; likely संभावित; अपेक्षित, संभावनीय ✪ विलोम **improbable** ➪ **possible** देखिए।

NOTE ध्यान दीजिए **probable** और **likely** का अर्थ समान है परंतु इनके प्रयोग-संदर्भों में भिन्नता है— *It's* ***probable that*** *he will be late.* ○ *He is* ***likely to be*** *late.*

**probably** /ˈprɒbəbli ˈप्रॉबब्लि / *adv.* almost certainly लगभग निश्चित रूप से; संभवतः *I will phone next week, probably on Wednesday.*

**probation** /prəˈbeɪʃn प्रˈबेश्न् / *noun* [U] **1** a system that allows sb who has committed a crime not to go to prison if he/she goes to see to an official (**a probation officer**) regularly for a fixed period of time अपराधियों की परिवीक्षा-पद्धति जिसमें अपराधी जेल नहीं जाता परंतु एक विशेष अधिकारी के सम्मुख नियत अवधि तक नियमित रूप से उपस्थित होता है *Jatin is* ***on probation*** *for two years.* **2** a period of time at the start of a new job when you are tested to see if you are suitable परिवीक्षा-काल जिसमें नव-नियुक्त व्यक्ति की योग्यता की परख की जाती है *a three-month probation period*

**probe¹** /prəʊb प्रोब् / *verb* [I, T] **1 probe (into sth)** to ask questions in order to find out secret or hidden information रहस्य या गुप्त बातें मालूम करने के लिए सवाल पूछना *The newspapers are now probing into the President's past.* **2** to examine or look for sth, especially with a long thin instrument किसी की जाँच करना या कुछ खोजना (विशेषतः किसी लंबे पतले उपकरण से) *The doctor probed the cut for pieces of broken glass.* ▶ **probing** *adj.* खोजी, खोजपरक *to ask probing questions*

**probe²** /prəʊb प्रोब् / *noun* [C] **1** the process of asking questions, collecting facts, etc. in order to find out hidden information about sth (छिपाई बातें मालूम करने के लिए) सवाल पूछने, तथ्य एकत्रित करने आदि की प्रक्रिया; जाँच *a police probe into illegal financial dealing* **2** a long thin tool that you use for examining sth that is difficult to reach, especially a part of the body एक सलाईनुमा उपकरण विशेषतः शरीर के एकदम अंदरूनी अंगों की जाँच के लिए

**problem** /ˈprɒbləm ˈप्रॉब्लम् / *noun* [C] **1** a thing that is difficult to deal with or to understand समस्या, मसला जिससे निपटना या जिसे समझना कठिन हो ***solve the problem*** ○ *The company will* ***face problems*** *from unions if it sacks workers.* ○ *I can't play because I've got* ***a problem with*** *my knee.* **2** a question that you have to solve by thinking about it प्रश्न जिसका हल काफ़ी सोचने से निकले *a maths/logic problem*

**problematic** /ˌprɒbləˈmætɪk ˌप्रॉब्लˈमैटिक् / (**problematical** /-kl -कल् /) *adj.* difficult to deal with or to understand; full of problems; not certain to be successful जिसे निपटाना या समझना कठिन हो, समस्यात्मक; समस्याओं से भरा हुआ, समस्याग्रस्त या समस्यापूर्ण; जिसकी सफलता में संदेह हो, अनिश्चित *Finding replacement parts for such an old car could be problematic.* ✪ विलोम **unproblematic**

**procedure** /prəˈsiːdʒə(r) प्रˈसीज(र्) / *noun* [C, U] the usual or correct way for doing sth कुछ करने का सामान्य या सही ढंग; प्रक्रिया *What's the procedure for making a complaint?*

**proceed** /prəˈsiːd प्रˈसीड्/ *verb* [I] **1** (*formal*) to continue doing sth; to continue being done कुछ करना जारी रखना; कोई बात होते रहना *The building work was proceeding according to schedule.* **2** (*formal*) **proceed (with sth/to do sth)** to start doing the next thing after finishing the last one पिछले को पूरा कर अगले चरण की ओर बढ़ना *Once he had calmed down he proceeded to tell us what had happened.*

**proceedings** /prəˈsiːdɪŋz प्रˈसीडिङ्ज़्/ *noun* [*pl.*] **1 proceedings (against sb/for sth)** legal action क़ानूनी कार्रवाई *to start divorce proceedings* **2** events that happen, especially at a formal meeting, ceremony, etc. किसी औपचारिक बैठक, समारोह आदि की कार्रवाई *The proceedings were interrupted by demonstrations.*

**proceeds** /ˈprəʊsiːdz ˈप्रोसीड्ज़्/ *noun* [*pl.*] **proceeds (of/ from sth)** money that you get when you sell sth कुछ बेचने से प्राप्त धन *The proceeds from the sale will go to charity.*

**process**[1] /ˈprəʊses ˈप्रोसेस्/ *noun* [C] **1** a series of actions that you do for a particular purpose किसी विशेष प्रयोजन से की गई क्रियाओं की शृंखला *We've just begun the complicated process of selling the house.* **2** a series of changes that happen naturally स्वाभाविक रूप से होने वाले परिवर्तनों की शृंखला *Mistakes are part of the learning process.*

**IDM in the process** while you are doing sth else कुछ अन्य काम करते हुए *We bathed the dog yesterday—and we all got very wet in the process.*

**in the process of sth/doing sth** in the middle of doing sth किसी कार्य के दौरान; की प्रक्रिया में *They are in the process of moving house.*

**process**[2] /ˈprəʊses ˈप्रोसेस्/ *verb* [T] **1** to treat sth, for example with chemicals, in order to keep it, change it, etc. सुरक्षित रखने, परिवर्तित करने आदि के लिए किसी वस्तु पर रसायनों आदि का प्रयोग करना *Cheese is processed so that it lasts longer.* ○ *I sent two rolls of film away to be processed.* **2** to deal with information, for example on a computer कंप्यूटर आदि पर सूचना को साधना या संसाधित करना *It will take about 10 days to process your application.* ○ *data processing*

**procession** /prəˈseʃn प्रˈसेशन्/ *noun* [C, U] a number of people, vehicles, etc. that move slowly in a line, especially as part of a ceremony लोगों, वाहनों आदि का पंक्ति बनाकर मंद गति से चलने की गतिविधि, विशेषतः किसी समारोह के प्रसंग में; जुलूस, शोभायात्रा *to walk **in procession*** ○ *a funeral procession*

**processor** /ˈprəʊsesə(r) ˈप्रोसेस(र्)/ *noun* [C] **1** a machine or a person that processes things वस्तुओं को साधने या संसाधित करने वाली मशीन; प्रोसेसर, संसाधक ➪ **food processor** और **word processor** भी देखिए। **2** (*computing*) a part of a computer that controls all the other parts of the system कंप्यूटर का वह भाग जो समस्त अंगों को नियंत्रित करता है; प्रोसेसर

**proclaim** /prəˈkleɪm प्रˈक्लेम्/ *verb* [T] (*written*) to make sth known officially or publicly किसी बात की औपचारिक या सार्वजनिक रूप से घोषणा करना *The day was proclaimed a national holiday.* ▶ **proclamation** /ˌprɒkləˈmeɪʃn ˌप्रॉक्लˈमेशन्/ *noun* [C, U] औपचारिक या सार्वजनिक घोषणा *to make a proclamation of war*

**procrastinate** /preʊˈkræstɪneɪt प्रोˈक्रैस्टिनेट्/ *verb* [I] (*formal*) to put off till another day or time, doing sth that you should do because you do not want to do it अनिच्छा के कारण किसी कार्य को स्थगित करना; टालना *Stop procrastinating—just go and finish your assignment.* ▶ **procrastination** /preʊˌkræstɪˈneɪʃn प्रोˌक्रैस्टिˈनेशन्/ *noun* [U] the act of putting off doing sth that you should do till another day or time, because you do not want to do it (अनिच्छा के कारण कार्य में) टालमटोल, विलंब, स्थगन *Procrastination may cause one to lose a good opportunity.*

**procure** /prəˈkjʊə(r) प्रˈक्युअ(र्)/ *verb* [T] (*written*) **procure sth (for sb)** to obtain sth, especially with difficulty कुछ प्राप्त करना विशेषतः कठिनाई से *I managed to procure two tickets for the match.*

**prod** /prɒd प्रॉड्/ *verb* [I, T] (**prodding; prodded**) to push or press sb/sth with your finger or a pointed object उँगली या नुकीली वस्तु से किसी को धकेलना या दबाना, कोंचना या छेड़ना (*figurative*) *Rita works quite hard but she does need prodding occasionally.* ▶ **prod** *noun* [C] धक्का, कोंचने की क्रिया *to give the fire a prod with a stick* ▶ **prodding** *noun* [C] कोंचने, छेड़ने, धकियाने या दबाने की क्रिया

**prodigal** /ˈprɒdɪgəl ˈप्रॉडिगल्/ *adj.* (*formal*) **1** spending money freely and rather wastefully फ़िज़ूलख़र्च, अपव्ययी, खर्चीला ✪ पर्याय **extravagant** **2** (*old-fashioned*) very generous अत्यंत उदार ▶ **prodigality** *noun* अपव्यय, फ़िज़ूलख़र्ची

**NOTE prodigal son/daughter** a person who leaves home without the approval of the family to lead a **prodigal** life but who is sorry later and returns home वह व्यक्ति जो घर वालों की मरज़ी के ख़िलाफ़ अपव्ययी जीवन व्यतीत करने के लिए घर छोड़ देता है तथा बाद में पश्चाताप करता है और घर लौट आता है

**prodigious** /prəˈdɪdʒəs प्रˈडिजस्/ *adj.* very large or powerful and surprising बहुत बड़ा या शक्तिशाली और आश्चर्यजनक *He seemed to have a prodigious amount of energy.*

**prodigy** /ˈprɒdədʒi ˈप्रॉडजि/ *noun* [C] (*pl.* **prodigies**) a child who is unusually good at sth विलक्षण प्रतिभा संपन्न बालक या बालिका *Shankar Mahadevan was a **child prodigy**.* ➪ **genius** देखिए।

**produce[1]** /prəˈdjuːs प्रˈड्यूस्/ *verb* [T] **1** to make sth to be sold, especially in large quantities (किसी वस्तु का) उत्पादन करना (विशेषतः बड़े परिमाण में) *The factory produces 20,000 cars a year.* ✪ पर्याय **manufacture** **2** to grow or make sth by a natural process प्राकृतिक प्रक्रिया से कुछ उगाना या उत्पन्न करना *This region produces most of the country's wheat.* ○ (*figurative*) *He's the greatest athlete this country has produced.* **3** to create sth using skill कौशल द्वारा कुछ रचना या सृजित करना *The children have produced some beautiful pictures for the exhibition.* **4** to cause a particular effect or result विशेष प्रभाव या परिणाम उत्पन्न करना *Her remarks produced roars of laughter.* **5** to show sth so that sb else can look at or examine it अवलोकनार्थ या परीक्षणार्थ कुछ प्रस्तुत करना *to produce evidence in court* **6** to be in charge of preparing a film, play, etc. so that it can be shown to the public फ़िल्म, नाटक आदि को सार्वजनिक प्रदर्शन के लिए तैयार करने का दायित्व वहन करना; फ़िल्म आदि का निर्माण करना *She is producing 'Shakuntala' at the local theatre.*

**produce[2]** /ˈprɒdjuːs ˈप्रॉड्यूस्/ *noun* [U] food, etc. that is grown on a farm and sold खेत की उपज (फल आदि) *fresh farm produce*

**producer** /prəˈdjuːsə(r) प्रˈड्यूस(र्)/ *noun* [C] **1** a person, company or country that makes or grows sth किसी वस्तु का निर्माता या उत्पादक (व्यक्ति, कंपनी या देश) *India is a major producer of tea.* **2** a person who deals with the business side of organizing a play, film, etc. नाटक, फ़िल्म आदि के प्रदर्शन से संबंधित व्यापारिक गतिविधि का प्रभारी व्यक्ति; निर्माता **3** a person who arranges for sb to make a programme for television or radio, or a record (किसी व्यक्ति के द्वारा) टीवी या रेडियो के कार्यक्रम या रिकार्ड के निर्माण की व्यवस्था करने वाला व्यक्ति

**product** /ˈprɒdʌkt ˈप्रॉडक्ट्/ *noun* [C] **1** something that is made in a factory or that is formed naturally कारख़ाने में निर्मित या प्राकृतिक प्रक्रिया से बनी वस्तु *dairy/meat/pharmaceutical/software products* ○ *Carbon dioxide is one of the waste products of this process.* **2 product of sth** the result of sth किसी बात का परिणाम *The industry's problems are the product of government policy.* **3** the amount that you get if you multiply one number by another दो संख्याओं को गुणा करने से प्राप्त संख्या; गुणनफल *The product of three and five is fifteen.*

**production** /prəˈdʌkʃn प्रˈडक्शन्/ *noun* **1** [U] the making or growing of sth, especially in large quantities किसी वस्तु का उत्पादन (विशेषतः बड़े परिमाण में) *The latest model will be **in production** from April.* ○ *mass production* **2** [U] the amount of sth that is made or grown उत्पादित या उत्पन्न वस्तु की मात्रा *a rise/fall in production* ○ *a high level of production* **3** [C] a play, film or programme that has been made for the public (सार्वजनिक प्रदर्शन के लिए) नाटक, फ़िल्म या कार्यक्रम

IDM **on production of sth** when you show sth को दिखाने पर *You can get a ten per cent discount on production of your membership card.*

**productive** /prəˈdʌktɪv प्रˈडक्टिव़्/ *adj.* **1** that makes or grows sth, especially in large quantities उत्पादित या उत्पन्न करने वाला (विशेषतः बड़े परिमाण में); उत्पादनकारी *The company wants to sell off its less productive factories.* **2** useful (because results come from it) उपयोगी, फलप्रद *a productive discussion* ▶ **productivity** /ˌprɒdʌkˈtɪvəti ˌप्रॉडक्ˈटिव़टि/ *noun* [U] उत्पादकता

**Prof.** *abbr.* (*written*) Professor शिक्षक, प्रोफेसर

**profane** /prəˈfeɪn प्रˈफ़ेन्/ *adj.* **1** showing a lack of respect for sacred or holy things धर्मनिंदक, अधार्मिक *profane language/behaviour* **2** (*technical*) not connected with religion or holy things; secular धार्मिक या पावन वस्तुओं से संबंधित नहीं; धर्मनिरपेक्ष *A discussion was organized on topics both sacred and profane.* ▶ **profanity** /prəˈfænəti प्रˈफ़ैनटि *noun* [C, U] अधर्मिता, अपवित्रता

**profess** /prəˈfes प्रˈफ़ेस्/ *verb* [T] (*formal*) **1** to say that sth is true or correct, even when it is not किसी बात के सच या सही होने का दावा करना (प्रायः झूठा) *Meera professed to know nothing at all about it, but I did not believe her.* **2** to state honestly that you have a particular belief, feeling, etc. अपने विश्वास, मनोभाव आदि को ईमानदारी से व्यक्त करना *He professed his hatred of war.*

**profession** /prəˈfeʃn प्रˈफ़ेशन्/ *noun* [C] **1** a job that needs a high level of training and/or education जीविका, पेशा, व्यवसाय (जिसके लिए उच्च प्रशिक्षण और/या शिक्षा अपेक्षित है) *the medical/legal/teaching profession* ○ *She's thinking of entering the nursing profession.* ➪ **work[1]** देखिए। **2 the...**

**profession** [*with sing. or pl. verb*] all the people who work in a particular profession किसी विशिष्ट पेशे के सब व्यक्ति *The legal profession is/are trying to resist the reforms.*

IDM **by profession** as your job पेशे या व्यवसाय से *Gautam is an accountant by profession.*

**professional**[1] /prəˈfeʃənl प्रˈफ़ेशनल् / *adj.* **1** (*only before a noun*) connected with a job that needs a high level of training and/or education उच्च स्तरीय प्रशिक्षण और/या शिक्षा की अपेक्षा वाले व्यवसाय या पेशे से संबंधित; व्यावसायिक, पेशेवराना *Get professional advice from your lawyer before you take any action.* **2** doing sth in a way that shows skill, training or care निपुणता, प्रशिक्षण या सावधानी के साथ (कुछ) करते हुए *The police are trained to deal with every situation in a calm and professional manner.* ○ *Her application was neatly typed and looked very professional.* ✪ विलोम **unprofessional** **3** doing a sport, etc. as a job or for money; (used about a sport, etc.) done by people who are paid पैसे के लिए खेलने वाला, पेशेवर (खिलाड़ी); वेतनभोगी खिलाड़ियों द्वारा खेला जाने वाला (खेल) *He's planning to **turn professional** after the Olympics.* ○ *professional football* ✪ विलोम **amateur**

**professional**[2] /prəˈfeʃənl प्रˈफ़ेशनल् / *noun* [C] **1** a person who works in a job that needs a high level of training and/or education उच्च प्रशिक्षण और/या शिक्षा की अपेक्षा वाली नौकरी करने वाला व्यक्ति, पेशेवर व्यक्ति; व्यावसायिक, प्रोफ़ेशनल **2** (*informal* **pro**) a person who plays or teaches a sport, etc. for money पेशेवर खिलाड़ी या खेल-प्रशिक्षक; पैसा लेकर खेलने या खेल आदि का प्रशिक्षण देने वाला व्यक्ति **3** (*informal* **pro**) a person who has a lot of skill and experience अति निपुण या अनुभवी व्यक्ति

**professionalism** /prəˈfeʃənəlɪzəm प्रˈफ़ेशनलिज़म् / *noun* [U] a way of doing a job that shows great skill and experience अत्यधिक निपुणता और अनुभव की अपेक्षा वाला काम करने का ढंग; व्यावसायिक गुण, व्यावसायिकता *We were impressed by the professionalism of the staff.*

**professionally** /prəˈfeʃənəli प्रˈफ़ेशनलि / *adv.* **1** in a way that shows great skill and experience व्यावसायिक रूप से; अत्यधिक निपुणता और अनुभव प्रदर्शित करते हुए **2** for money; by a professional person पैसे के लिए; पेशेवर व्यक्ति द्वारा *Rahul plays the guitar professionally.*

**professor** /prəˈfesə(r) प्रˈफ़ेस(र्) / *noun* [C] (*abbr.* **Prof.**) **1** a university teacher of the highest level सर्वोच्च स्तर का विश्वविद्यालयी शिक्षक; प्रोफ़ेसर *She's professor of English at Allahabad University.* **2** (*AmE*) a teacher at a college or university कॉलेज या विश्वविद्यालय का शिक्षक

**proficient** /prəˈfɪʃnt प्रˈफ़िशन्ट् / *adj.* **proficient (in/at sth/doing sth)** able to do a particular thing well; skilled किसी विशेष काम को करने में दक्ष; निपुण, कुशल *We are looking for someone who is proficient in Hindi.* ▶ **proficiency** *noun* [U] **proficiency (in sth/doing sth)** निपुणता, दक्षता *a certificate of proficiency in English*

**profile** /ˈprəʊfaɪl ˈप्रोफ़ाइल् / *noun* [C] **1** a person's face or head seen from the side, not the front मानव चेहरे का एक बग़ल का चित्र (न कि सामने का); पार्श्वचित्र, पार्श्विका *I did a sketch of him **in profile**.* **2** a short description of sb/sth that gives useful information किसी व्यक्ति का संक्षिप्त परिचय (उसके विषय में उपयोगी जानकारी देने वाला); रूपरेखा, ख़ाका *We're building up a profile of our average customer.*

IDM **a high/low profile** a way of behaving that does/does not attract other people's attention लोगों का ध्यान आकृष्ट करने या न करने वाला व्यवहार *I don't know much about the subject—I'm going to keep a low profile at the meeting tomorrow.*

**profit**[1] /ˈprɒfɪt ˈप्रॉफ़िट् / *noun* [C, U] the money that you make when you sell sth for more than it cost you लागत से अधिक दाम पर बेचने से प्राप्त धन; नफ़ा, लाभ, फ़ायदा *Did you **make a profit on** your house when you sold it?* ○ *I'm hoping to sell my shares **at a profit**.* ➪ **loss** देखिए।

**profit**[2] /ˈprɒfɪt ˈप्रॉफ़िट् / *verb* [I, T] (*formal*) **profit (from/by sth)** to get an advantage from sth; to give sb an advantage किसी से लाभ प्राप्त करना, फ़ायदा मिलना; किसी को लाभ या फ़ायदा पहुँचाना *Common people will profit most from the tax reforms.*

**profitable** /ˈprɒfɪtəbl ˈप्रॉफ़िटबल् / *adj.* **1** that makes money लाभकारी, फ़ायदेमंद; जिसमें धन की प्राप्ति हो *a profitable business* **2** helpful or useful (किसी बात में) सहायक या उपयोगी *We had a very profitable discussion yesterday.* ▶ **profitably** *adv.* लाभ उठाते हुए, लाभप्रद ढंग से *to spend your time profitably* ▶ **profitability** /ˌprɒfɪtəˈbɪləti ˌप्रॉफ़िटˈबिलटि / *noun* [U] लाभप्रदता

**profit and loss account** *noun* [C] (*technical*) a written record of the amounts of money that a business or organization earns and spends in a particular period अवधि-विशेष में किसी व्यापार या संगठन का आय-व्यय का लिपिबद्ध विवरण; लाभ-हानि लेखा

**pro forma** /ˌprəʊˈfɔːmə ˌप्रोˈफ़ॉमा/ *adj.* (*usually before a noun*) (*technical*) **1** (used especially about a document) prepared in order to show the usual way of doing sth or to provide a standard method कुछ करने का सामान्य ढंग या मानक पद्धति बताने वाला (दस्तावेज़); प्रोफ़ॉर्मा, प्रपत्र, निदर्शन-पत्र से संबंधित *a pro-forma letter* ○ *pro-forma instructions* **2** (used about a document) sent in advance अग्रिम (दस्तावेज़) *a pro-forma invoice* (= a document that gives details of the goods being sent to a customer) ▶ **pro forma** *noun* [C] प्रपत्र, निदर्शन-पत्र *I enclose a pro forma for you to complete, sign and return.*

**profound** /prəˈfaʊnd प्रˈफ़ाउन्ड्/ *adj.* **1** very great; that you feel very strongly अत्यधिक, प्रबल; मन को अत्यधिक प्रभावित करने वाला, हार्दिक *The experience had a profound influence on her.* **2** needing or showing a lot of knowledge or thought अत्यधिक ज्ञान या विचार से पूर्ण या उसकी अपेक्षा वाला *He's always making profound statements about the meaning of life.* ▶ **profoundly** *adv.* अत्यधिक *I was profoundly relieved to hear the news.*

**profuse** /prəˈfjuːs प्रˈफ़्यूस्/ *adj.* (*formal*) given or produced in great quantity अत्यधिक मात्रा में, प्रचुर *profuse apologies* ▶ **profusely** *adv.* प्रचुरता से *She apologized profusely for being late.*

**profusion** /prəˈfjuːʒn प्रˈफ़्यूश़न्/ *noun* (*with sing. or pl. verb*) a very large quantity of sth किसी वस्तु की बहुत बड़ी मात्रा; प्रचुरता *a profusion of colours/flowers* ○ *Roses grew* ***in profusion*** *against the old wall.*

**progeny** /ˈprɒdʒəni ˈप्रॉजनि/ *noun* [*pl.*] (*formal* or *humorous*) someone's children; the young or offspring of animals or plants संतान; पशु और पौधों के नवागत (शावक या पादप)

**progesterone** /prəˈdʒestərəʊn प्रˈजेसटरोन्/ *noun* [U] a substance (**hormone**) produced in the bodies of women and female animals which prepares the body to become pregnant महिलाओं और मादा पशुओं के शरीर में उत्पन्न विशेष हॉरमोन जो उनके गर्भ धारण करने में सहायक होता है। ➪ **oestrogen** और **testosterone** देखिए।

**prognosis** /prɒgˈnəʊsɪs प्रॉग्ˈनोसिस्/ *noun* [C] (*pl.* **prognoses** /-siːz -सीज़्/) **1** (*medical*) an opinion, based on medical experience, of the likely development of a disease or an illness डॉक्टरी अनुभव के आधार पर रोग का पूर्वानुमान; पूर्वलक्षण **2** (*formal*) a judgement about how sth is likely to develop in the future किसी के भावी विकास के विषय में अंकन *The prognosis is for more people to work part-time in the future.*

**program¹** /ˈprəʊgræm ˈप्रोग्रैम्/ *noun* [C] **1** a set of instructions that you give to a computer so that it will do a particular task कंप्यूटर का प्रोग्राम विशिष्ट कार्य संपादन के लिए कंप्यूटर को दिए गए निर्देश *to write a program*

> **NOTE** कंप्यूटर-विषयक चर्चा के संदर्भ में अमेरिकी और ब्रिटिश अंग्रेज़ी में मान्य वर्तनी **program** है। अन्य संदर्भों में ब्रिटिश वर्तनी **programme** है और अमेरिकी वर्तनी **program** है।

**2** (*AmE*) = **programme¹**

**program²** /ˈprəʊgræm ˈप्रोग्रैम्/ *verb* [I, T] (**programming; programmed**) to give a set of instructions to a computer, etc. to make it perform a particular task कंप्यूटर को निर्देश देना (विशिष्ट कार्य संपादन के लिए)

**programme¹** (*AmE* **program**) /ˈprəʊgræm ˈप्रोग्रैम्/ *noun* [C] **1** a show or other item that is sent out on the radio or television रेडियो या टीवी का कार्यक्रम *a TV/radio programme* ○ *We've just missed an interesting programme on elephants.* **2** a plan of things to do; a scheme कार्यक्रम, प्रोग्राम; योजना *What's (on) your programme today* (= what are you going to do today)? ○ *The leaflet outlines the government's programme of educational reforms.* **3** a little book or piece of paper which you get at a concert, a sports event, etc. that gives you information about what you are going to see किसी समारोह, खेल आदि के कार्यक्रम का विवरण

**programme²** /ˈprəʊgræm ˈप्रोग्रैम्/ (*AmE* **program**) *verb* [T] (**programming; programmed;** *AmE* **programing; programed**) **1** to plan for sth to happen at a particular time किसी काम के लिए योजना बनाना (कि वह कब होगा) *The road is programmed for completion next May.* **2** to make sb/sth work or act automatically in a particular way किसी वस्तु को विशिष्ट रीति से स्वतः कार्य करने हेतु योजनाबद्ध करना या प्रोग्रामित करना *The lights are programmed to come on as soon as it gets dark.*

**programmer** /ˈprəʊgræmə(r) ˈप्रोग्रैम(र्)/ *noun* [C] a person whose job is to write programs for a computer कंप्यूटर के लिए प्रोग्रामों की रचना करने वाला व्यक्ति; प्रोग्रैमर

**progress¹** /ˈprəʊgres ˈप्रोग्रेस्/ *noun* [U] **1** movement forwards or towards achieving sth आगे की ओर या लक्ष्य की ओर गति; प्रगति *Amit's* ***making progress*** *at school.* ○ *to make slow/steady/rapid/good progress* **2** change or improvement in society समाज में परिवर्तन या सुधार *scientific progress* IDM **in progress** happening now प्रगति पर; इस समय चलता हुआ *Silence! Examination in progress.*

**progress²** /prəˈgres प्रˈग्रेस्/ *verb* [I] **1** to become better; to develop (well) प्रगति करना; विकास करना *Medical knowledge has progressed rapidly in the last 20 years.* **2** to move forward; to continue आगे बढ़ना; जारी रहना *I got more and more tired as the evening progressed.*

**progression** /prəˈgreʃn प्रˈग्रेशन्/ *noun* [C, U] **(a) progression (from sth) (to sth)** movement forward or a development from one stage to another आगे बढ़ने या एक दशा से दूसरी दशा में विकसित होने की प्रक्रिया; प्रगति *You've made the progression from beginner to intermediate level.*

**progressive** /prəˈgresɪv प्रˈग्रेसिव़् / *adj.* **1** using modern methods and ideas आधुनिक कार्य-पद्धतियों और विचारों वाला; प्रगतिशील *a progressive school* **2** happening or developing steadily क्रमिक; लगातार घटित या विकसित होने वाला *a progressive reduction in the number of staff*

**progressively** /prəˈgresɪvli प्रˈग्रेसिव़्लि / *adv.* steadily; a little at a time लगातार, अनवरत रूप से; थोड़ा-थोड़ा करके *The situation became progressively worse.*

**the progressive tense** *noun* [*sing.*] (*grammar*) = **the continuous tense**

**prohibit** /prəˈhɪbɪt प्रˈहिबिट् / *verb* [T] (*formal*) **prohibit sb/sth (from doing sth)** to say that sth is not allowed by law; to forbid क़ानून द्वारा किसी बात को मना करना; निषेध करना, प्रतिबंध लगाना *The law prohibits children under 18 from buying cigarettes.*

**prohibition** /ˌprəʊɪˈbɪʃn ˌप्रोइˈबिशन् / *noun* **1** [C] (*formal*) **a prohibition (on/against sth)** a law or rule that forbids sth किसी बात का निषेध करने वाला क़ानून या नियम; निषेधाज्ञा *There is a prohibition on the carrying of knives.* **2** [U] the action of stopping sth being done or used, especially by law किसी काम या किसी वस्तु के प्रयोग पर प्रतिबंध (विशेषतः क़ानून के द्वारा) *the prohibition of alcohol in the 1920s*

**prohibitive** /prəˈhɪbətɪv प्रˈहिबटिव़् / *adj.* (used about a price or cost) so high that it prevents people from buying sth or doing sth (क़ीमत या लागत) इतनी अधिक कि लोग कोई वस्तु ख़रीद न सकें या कोई काम कर न सकें; ख़रीद के लिए हतोत्साहक *The price of houses in South Delhi is prohibitive.* ▸ **prohibitively** *adv.* हतोत्साहक रूप से

**project¹** /ˈprɒdʒekt ˈप्रॉजेक्ट् / *noun* [C] **1** a piece of work, often involving many people, that is planned and organized carefully परियोजना, प्रकल्प; योजनाबद्ध और सावधानी से व्यवस्थित कार्य जिसमें प्रायः अनेक लोगों की भागीदारी होती है *a major project to reduce pollution in our rivers* **2** a piece of school work in which the student has to collect information about a certain subject and then write about it विषय-विशेष पर छात्र द्वारा सामग्री एकत्रित कर उसके विषय में लेखन *Our group chose to do a project on rainforests.*

**project²** /prəˈdʒekt प्रˈजेक्ट् / *verb* **1** [T] (*usually passive*) to plan sth that will happen in the future भविष्योन्मुखी कार्य-योजना बनाना *the band's projected world tour* **2** [T] (*usually passive*) to guess or calculate the size, cost or amount of sth किसी वस्तु के आकार, लागत या मात्रा का अनुमान या हिसाब लगाना *a projected increase of 10%* **3** [T] **project sth (on/onto sth)** to make light, a picture from a film, etc. appear on a flat surface or screen किसी चौरस सतह या परदे पर प्रकाश, फ़िल्म की तस्वीर आदि को प्रक्षेपित करना **4** [T] to show or represent sb/sth/ yourself in a certain way विशेष तरीक़े से किसी को पेश करना *The government is trying to project a more caring image.* **5** [I] (*formal*) to stick out बाहर की ओर निकलना *The balcony projects one metre out from the wall.* **6** [T] to send or throw sth upwards or away from you अपने से दूर या ऊपर की ओर भेजना या फेंकना *The projected missiles did not hit their target.*

**projectile** /prəˈdʒektaɪl प्रˈजेक्टाइल् / *noun* [C] (*formal* or *technical*) **1** an object, such as a bullet, that is fired from a gun or other weapon बंदूक़ या किसी हथियार से दाग़ी गई गोली आदि कोई वस्तु **2** any object that is thrown as a weapon प्रक्षिप्त किया जाने वाला अस्त्र; प्रक्षेपास्त्र

**projection** /prəˈdʒekʃn प्रˈजेक्शन् / *noun* **1** [C] a guess about a future amount, situation, etc. based on the present situation वर्तमान स्थिति के आधार पर भविष्य की बातों (धनराशि, स्थिति आदि) का अनुमान *sales projections for the next five years* **2** [U] the act of making light, a picture from a film, etc. appear on a surface किसी सतह पर फ़िल्म आदि (के चित्र) का प्रक्षेपण; परदे पर फ़िल्म आदि का प्रदर्शन, छायाचित्रण

**projector** /prəˈdʒektə(r) प्रˈजेक्टर(र्) / *noun* [C] a piece of equipment that projects pictures or films onto a screen or wall चित्रों या फ़िल्मों को परदे या दीवार पर प्रक्षेपित या प्रदर्शित करने वाली मशीन; प्रोजेक्टर, प्रक्षेपण-यंत्र *a film/slide/overhead projector*

**proletariat** /ˌprəʊlɪˈteəriət ˌप्रोलि'टेअरिअट्/ *noun* [*sing.*] **1** (often used with reference to Marxism) working class people especially those who do not own any property (मार्क्सवाद से संबंधित) श्रमजीवी, संपत्तिहीन श्रमिक वर्ग ➪ **bourgeoisie** देखिए। **2** the lowest class of people in ancient Rome प्राचीन रोम के समाज का सबसे पिछड़ा वर्ग

**proliferate** /prəˈlɪfəreɪt प्र'लिफ़रेट्/ *verb* [I] (*formal*) to increase quickly in number संख्या की दृष्टि से (किसी वस्तु की) तीव्रता से वृद्धि होना; प्रफलन होना ▶ **proliferation** /prəˌlɪfəˈleɪʃn प्रˌलिफ़'रेशन्/ *noun* [U] त्वरित संख्या-वृद्धि, संख्या में तेज़ी से बढ़ोतरी; बहुजनन, प्रफलन

**prolific** /prəˈlɪfɪk प्र'लिफ़िक्/ *adj.* (used especially about a writer, artist, etc.) producing a lot (विशेषतः लेखक, कलाकार आदि) प्रचुर मात्रा में कृतियों की रचना करने वाला; बहुसर्जक, बहुकृतिक *a prolific goal scorer*

**prologue** /ˈprəʊlɒg 'प्रोलॉग्/ *noun* [C] a piece of writing or a speech that introduces a play, poem, etc. नाटक, कविता आदि को प्रस्तुत करने वाला लेख या भाषण; प्रस्तावना ➪ **epilogue** देखिए।

**prolong** /prəˈlɒŋ प्र'लॉङ्/ *verb* [T] to make sth last longer किसी वस्तु आदि की अवधि बढ़ाना

**prolonged** /prəˈlɒŋd प्र'लॉङ्ड्/ *adj.* continuing for a long time लंबी अवधि तक रहने वाला *There was a prolonged silence before anybody spoke.*

**prom** /prɒm प्रॉम्/ *noun* [C] **1** = **promenade** **2** (*AmE*) a formal dance that is held by a high school class at the end of a school year सत्र के अंत में हाई स्कूल छात्रों द्वारा प्रस्तुत औपचारिक नृत्य; छात्र-नृत्य

**promenade** /ˌprɒməˈnɑːd ˌप्रॉम'नाड्/ (*also* **prom**) *noun* [C] a wide path where people walk beside the sea in a town on the coast तटीय शहर में समुद्र के साथ-साथ (लोगों के लिए बना) चौड़ा विचरण-पथ; तटपथ

**prominent** /ˈprɒmɪnənt 'प्रॉमिनन्ट्/ *adj.* **1** important or famous महत्त्वपूर्ण या प्रसिद्ध *a prominent political figure* **2** noticeable; easy to see साफ़ दीखने वाला; जो आसानी से दीख सके *The church is the most prominent feature of the village.* ▶ **prominence** *noun* [U] प्रमुखता *The newspaper gave the affair great prominence.* ▶ **prominently** *adv.* प्रमुखता से

**promiscuous** /prəˈmɪskjuəs प्र'मिस्क्युअस्/ *adj.* having sexual relations with many people अनेक व्यक्तियों के साथ यौन-संबंध रखने वाला; व्यभिचारी (व्यक्ति) ▶ **promiscuity** /ˌprɒmɪsˈkjuːəti ˌप्रॉमिस्'क्यूअटि/ *noun* [U] व्यभिचार

**promise**[1] /ˈprɒmɪs 'प्रॉमिस्/ *verb* **1** [I, T] **promise (to do sth); promise (sb) that...** to say definitely that you will do or not do sth or that sth will happen किसी काम को करने या न करने या कुछ होने का वचन देना, वादा करना *She promised to write every week* ○ *She promised not to forget to write.* **2** [T] **promise sth (to sb); promise sb sth** to say definitely that you will give sth to sb किसी को कुछ देने का वचन देना *Can you promise your support?* ○ *My dad has promised me a bicycle.* **3** [T] to show signs of sth, so that you expect it to happen किसी (प्रत्याशित) बात के घटित होने के संकेत देना *It promises to be an exciting occasion.*

**promise**[2] /ˈprɒmɪs 'प्रॉमिस्/ *noun* **1** [C] **a promise (to do sth/that...)** a written or spoken statement or agreement that you will or will not do sth वादा या वचन, प्रतिज्ञा ***make a promise*** ○ ***Keep** your **promise** to always do your homework.* ○ *You should never **break a promise**.* **2** [U] signs that you will be able to do sth well or be successful कुछ करने में सक्षम या सफल होने के संकेत *He showed great promise as a musician.*

**promising** /ˈprɒmɪsɪŋ 'प्रॉमिसिङ्/ *adj.* showing signs of being very good or successful उत्कृष्ट या सफल होने के संकेत देने वाला *a promising young writer*

**promontory** /ˈprɒməntri 'प्रॉमनट्रि/ *noun* [C] (*pl.* **-ies**) a long narrow area of highland that goes out into the sea समुद्र में अंदर तक जाने वाली भूमि की तंग पट्टी; अंतरीप *a rocky promontory overlooking the bay*

**promote** /prəˈməʊt प्र'मोट्/ *verb* [T] **1** to encourage sth; to help sth to happen or develop किसी बात को प्रोत्साहित करना; किसी बात के होने या बढ़ने में सहायता करना *to promote good relations between countries* **2 promote sth (as sth)** to advertise sth in order to increase its sales or make it popular किसी वस्तु की बिक्री या लोकप्रियता बढ़ाने के लिए प्रचार करना *The new face cream is being promoted as a miracle cure for wrinkles.* **3 promote sb (from sth) (to sth)** (*often passive*) to give sb a higher position or more important job किसी व्यक्ति को पदोन्नति या पहले से बड़ी नौकरी देना *He's been promoted from assistant manager to manager.* ✪ विलोम **demote**

**promoter** /prəˈməʊtə(r) प्र'मोट(र्)/ *noun* [C] a person who organizes or provides the money for an event किसी कार्यक्रम का आयोजन करने या उसके लिए धन देने वाला व्यक्ति

**promotion** /prəˈməʊʃn प्र'मोशन्/ *noun* **1** [C, U] **promotion (to sth)** a move to a higher position or more important job पदोन्नति या अधिक बड़ी नौकरी की प्राप्ति *The new job is a promotion* *for her.* ✪ विलोम **demotion** **2** [U, C] things that you do in order to advertise a product and increase its sales किसी वस्तु के प्रचार और विक्रय में वृद्धि के लिए किए गए काम; प्रचार-प्रसार *It's all part of a special promotion of the new book.* **3** [U] (*formal*) **promotion (of sth)** the activity of trying to make sth develop or become accepted by people किसी काम के विकास या लोगों तक उसे पहुँचाने की गतिविधि; संवर्धन, बढ़ावा तथा जन-स्वीकृति *We need to work on the promotion of health, not the treatment of disease.*

**prompt**[1] /prɒmpt प्रॉम्प्ट्/ *adj.* **1** immediate; done without delay अत्यावश्यक; बिना बिलंब किया (कार्य) *We need a prompt decision on this matter.* **2 prompt (in doing sth/to do sth)** (*not before a noun*) (used about a person) quick; acting without delay (व्यक्ति) तत्पर, मुस्तैद; बिना विलंब काम करने वाला *We are always prompt in paying our bills.* ○ *She was prompt to point out my mistake.*

**prompt**[2] /prɒmpt प्रॉम्प्ट्/ *verb* **1** [T] to cause sth to happen; to make sb decide to do sth कुछ होने का कारण बनना; किसी को कोई निर्णय लेने के लिए प्रेरित करना *What prompted you to give up your job?* **2** [I, T] to encourage sb to speak by asking questions or to remind an actor of his/her words in a play प्रश्न पूछकर वक्ता को बोलने के लिए प्रोत्साहित करना; नाटक; के अभिनेता या अभिनेत्री को (नेपथ्य से) उसके संवाद की याद दिलाते जाना या उसका अनुबोधन करना *The speaker had to be prompted several times.* ▶ **prompting** *noun* [U] याद दिलाने की क्रिया, अनुबोधन *He apologized without any prompting.*

**prompt**[3] /prɒmpt प्रॉम्प्ट्/ *noun* [C] **1** a word or words said to an actor to remind him/her of what to say next अभिनेता को (नेपथ्य से) याद दिलाया गया अगला संवाद *When she forgot her lines I had to give her a prompt.* **2** (*computing*) a sign on a computer screen that shows that the computer has finished what it was doing and is ready for more instructions कंप्यूटर स्क्रीन पर उभरा संकेत जो बताता है कि वर्तमान कार्य समाप्त हुआ और अब अगले निर्देशों की प्रतीक्षा है; प्राम्प्ट *Wait for the prompt to come up then type in your password.*

**promptly** /ˈprɒmptli ˈप्रॉम्प्ट्लि/ *adv.* **1** immediately; without delay तुरंत; बिना विलंब किए *I invited her to dinner and she promptly accepted.* **2** (*also* **prompt**) at exactly the time that you have arranged; punctually एकदम निर्धारित समय पर; समय से, वक्त की पाबंदी से *We arrived promptly at 12 o'clock.* ○ *I'll pick you up at 7 o'clock prompt.*

**promulgate** /ˈprɒməlgeɪt ˈप्रॉमल्गेट्/ *verb* [T] **1** (*usually passive*) to promote an idea, a belief, a cause, etc. among many people विचार, विश्वास आदि को लोगों में प्रख्यात या प्रचारित करना **2** to officially announce a new law or system नए क़ानून या प्रणाली की औपचारिक रूप से घोषणा करना ▶ **promulgation** /ˌprɒməlˈgeɪʃn ˌप्रॉमल्ˈगेशन्/ *noun* [U] प्रख्यापन, प्रचालन, क़ानून के लागू होने की घोषणा

**prone** /prəʊn प्रोन्/ *adj.* **prone to sth/to do sth** likely to suffer from sth or to do sth bad किसी रोग से पीड़ित होने या ग़लती करने की संभावना से ग्रस्त *prone to infection/injury/heart attacks/errors* ○ *to be **accident-prone*** (= to have a lot of accidents)

**prong** /prɒŋ प्रॉङ्/ *noun* [C] **1** each of the two or more long pointed parts of a fork खाने के काँटे का कोई एक नुकीला भाग **2** each of the separate parts of an attack, argument, etc. that sb uses to achieve sth लक्ष्य प्राप्ति के उद्देश्य से प्रेरित आक्रमण, तर्क आदि के विभिन्न अंगें में कोई एक **3 -pronged** (*used to form compound adjectives*) having the number or type of prongs mentioned तरफ़ा *a three-pronged attack*

**pronoun** /ˈprəʊnaʊn ˈप्रोनाउन्/ *noun* [C] (*grammar*) a word that is used in place of a noun or a phrase that contains a noun सर्वनाम *'He', 'it', 'hers', 'me', 'them', etc. are all pronouns.* ➪ **personal pronoun** भी देखिए।

**pronounce** /prəˈnaʊns प्रˈनाउन्स्/ *verb* **1** [T] to make the sound of a word or letter in a particular way किसी शब्द या ध्वनि का विशेष रीति से उच्चारण करना *You don't pronounce the 'b' at the end of 'comb'.* ○ *How do you pronounce your surname?* ➪ **pronunciation** noun देखिए। **2** [T] (*formal*) to say or give sth formally, officially or publicly कोई बात औपचारिक, आधिकारिक या सार्वजनिक रूप से कहना; घोषित करना *The judge will pronounce the sentence today.* **3** [I, T] (*formal*) **pronounce (on sth)** to give your opinion on sth, especially formally किसी बात पर अपनी राय, सम्मति देना विशेषतः औपचारिक रूप से *The play was pronounced 'brilliant' by all the critics.*

**pronounced** /prəˈnaʊnst प्रˈनाउन्स्ट्/ *adj.* very noticeable; obvious एकदम साफ़ दिखने वाला; प्रकट सुस्पष्ट *His English is excellent although he speaks with a pronounced French accent.*

**pronunciation** /prəˌnʌnsiˈeɪʃn प्रˌनन्सिˈएशन्/ *noun* **1** [U, C] the way in which a particular letter word or sound is said किसी शब्द या ध्वनि का उच्चारण *American pronunciation* ➪ **pronounce**

verb देखिए। **2** [U] a person's way of speaking a word or a letter किसी व्यक्ति-विशेष का उच्चारण (बोलने का विशेष ढंग) *His grammar is good but his pronunciation is awful!*

**proof** /pru:f प्रूफ़्/ *noun* **1** [U] **proof (of sth); proof that...** information, documents, etc. which show that sth is true किसी बात को सत्य सिद्ध करने वाली जानकारी, दस्तावेज़ आदि; प्रमाण, सबूत *'We need some **proof of identity**,' the shop assistant said.* ○ *You've got no proof that Jai took the money.* ➪ **prove** verb देखिए। **2** [C, *usually pl.*] (*technical*) a first copy of printed material that is produced so that mistakes can be corrected मुद्रित सामग्री की पहली प्रति जिसमें ग़लतियाँ सुधारी जा सकती हैं; प्रूफ़, शोध्यपत्र

**-proof** /pru:f प्रूफ़्/ *suffix* (*used to form compound adjectives*) able to protect against the thing mentioned निर्दिष्ट वस्तु से सुरक्षा देने वाला, -अभेद्य, -सह *a soundproof room* ○ *bulletproof glass* ○ *a waterproof/windproof jacket*

**prop¹** /prɒp प्रॉप्/ *verb* [T] (**propping; propped**) to support sb/sth or keep sb/sth in position by putting him/her/it against or on sth व्यक्ति या वस्तु को (टेक लगाकर या उसे किसी पर रखकर) सहारा देना *I'll use this book to prop the window open.* ○ *He propped his bicycle against the wall.*

**PHR V** **prop sth up** to support sth that would otherwise fall किसी वस्तु को सहारा देना (जिसके बिना वह गिर सकती है)

**prop²** /prɒp प्रॉप्/ *noun* [C] **1** a stick or other object that you use to support sth or to keep sth in position सहारा देने या सही स्थिति में रखने के लिए प्रयुक्त छड़ी या कोई अन्य वस्तु; टेक *Rescuers used props to stop the roof of the tunnel collapsing.* **2** [*usually pl.*] an object that is used in a play, film, etc. नाटक, फ़िल्म आदि में प्रयुक्त कोई वस्तु (परदे, फ़र्नीचर आदि) *He's responsible for all the stage props, machinery and lighting.*

**propaganda** /ˌprɒpəˈgændə ˌप्रॉपˈगैन्डा/ *noun* [U] information and ideas that may be false or exaggerated, which are used to gain support for a political leader, party, etc. (राजनीतिक नेता, दल आदि के लिए समर्थन जुटाने में प्रयुक्त) असत्य या अतिशयोक्तिपूर्ण जानकारी और विचार; मतप्रचार, दुष्प्रचार

**propagate** /ˈprɒpəgeɪt ˈप्रॉपगेट्/ *verb* [I, T] to produce new plants from a parent plant मूल पौधे से नए पौधे उत्पन्न करना ▶ **propagation** /ˌprɒpəˈgeɪʃn ˌप्रॉपˈगेशन्/ *noun* [U] वनस्पति-प्रजनन

**propane** /ˈprəʊpeɪn ˈप्रोपेन्/ *noun* [U] a colourless gas that is found in natural gas and petrol and that we use as a fuel for cooking and heating प्राकृतिक गैस और पेट्रोल में उपलब्ध रंगहीन गैस जिसे भोजन आदि पकाने के लिए ईंधन के रूप में तथा ताप उत्पन्न करने में प्रयुक्त किया जाता है; प्रोपेन गैस

**propel** /prəˈpel प्रˈपेल्/ *verb* [T] (**propelling; propelled**) to move, drive or push sb/sth forward or in a particular direction आगे की ओर या दिशा-विशेष में व्यक्ति या वस्तु को धकेलना या चलाना

**propeller** /prəˈpelə(r) प्रˈपेल(र्)/ *noun* [C] a device with several flat metal parts (**blades**) which turn round very fast in order to make a ship or a plane move तेज़ी से घूमने वाला पंखनुमा यंत्र (जो जलपोत या विमान को धकेलता है); नोदक, प्रोपेलर

**propensity** /prəˈpensəti प्रˈपेन्सटि/ *noun* [C] (*pl.* **propensities**) (*formal*) **a propensity (for sth); a propensity (for doing sth); a propensity (to do sth)** a habit of behaving in a particular way विशेष प्रकार की प्रवृति (प्रायः अनुचित) *He showed a propensity for violence.* ○ *She has a propensity to exaggerate.*

**proper** /ˈprɒpə(r) ˈप्रॉप(र्)/ *adj.* **1** (*especially BrE*) (*only before a noun*) right, suitable or correct उचित, उपयुक्त या सही *If you're going skiing you must have the proper clothes.* ○ *I've got to get these pieces of paper in the proper order.* **2** that you consider to be real or good enough वास्तविक या पर्याप्त अच्छे ढंग से *I didn't see much of the flat yesterday. I'm going to go today and have a proper look.* **3** (*formal*) socially and morally acceptable सामाजिक और नैतिक दृष्टि से स्वीकार्य; समुचित, समीचीन मर्यादानुसार, मर्यादित *I think it would be only proper for you to apologize.* ✪ विलोम **improper** **4** (*only before a noun*) real or main यथार्थ या मुख्य *We travelled through miles of suburbs before we got to the city proper.*

**properly** /ˈprɒpəli ˈप्रॉपलि/ *adv.* **1** (*BrE*) correctly; in an acceptable way सही तरीक़े से; उचित रीति से *The teacher said I hadn't done my homework properly.* ○ *These shoes don't fit properly.* **2** in a way that is socially and morally acceptable; politely सामाजिक और नैतिक मर्यादा के अनुसार; शिष्टता से *If you two children can't behave properly then we'll have to go home.* ✪ विलोम **improperly**

**proper name** (*also* **proper noun**) *noun* [C] (*grammar*) a word which is the name of a particular person or place and begins with a **capital letter** व्यक्तिवाचक संज्ञा (व्यक्ति या स्थान का नाम जो अंग्रेज़ी में लिखते समय बड़े अक्षर से आरंभ होता है) *'Arun' and 'Agra' are proper names.*

**property** /ˈprɒpəti ˈप्रॉपटि/ *noun* (*pl.* **properties**) **1** [U] a thing or things that belong to sb (किसी के) स्वामित्व वाली वस्तु या वस्तुएँ *The sack contained* ***stolen property***. ○ *This file is government property.* ➪ **lost property** देखिए। **2** [U] land and buildings भूमि और भवन; संपत्ति, जायदाद *Property prices vary enormously from area to area.* **3** [C] one building and the land around it एक भवन और उससे लगी भूमि, घर और ज़मीन *There are a lot of empty properties in the area.* **4** [C, *usually pl.*] (*formal*) a special quality or characteristic that a substance, etc. has किसी वस्तु का विशेष गुण या वैशिष्ट्य *Some plants have healing properties.*

**prophecy** /ˈprɒfəsi ˈप्रॉफ़सि/ *noun* [C] (*pl.* **prophecies**) a statement about what is going to happen in the future भविष्यवाणी *to fulfil a prophecy* (= to make it come true)

**prophesy** /ˈprɒfəsaɪ ˈप्रॉफ़साइ/ *verb* [T] (*pres. part.* **prophesying;** *3rd person sing. pres.* **prophesies;** *pt, pp* **prophesied**) to say what you think will happen in the future भविष्यवाणी करना *to prophesy disaster/war*

**prophet** /ˈprɒfɪt ˈप्रॉफ़िट्/ *noun* [C] **1** (*also* **Prophet**) (in the Christian, Jewish and Muslim religions) a person who is sent by God to teach the people and give them messages from God (ईसाई, यहूदी और इस्लाम धर्मों में) पैग़ंबर जिन्हें ईश्वर ने जनता को ईश्वरीय संदेश देने के लिए धरती पर भेजा है **2** a person who says what will happen in the future भविष्यवक्ता ▸ **prophetic** /prəˈfetɪk प्रˈफ़ेटिक्/ *adj.* पैग़ंबरी, भविष्यसूचक

**prophylactic[1]** /ˌprɒfɪˈlæktɪk ˌप्रॉफ़िˈलैकटिक्/ *adj.* (*medical*) done or used in order to prevent a disease रोगनिरोधी; रोग को रोकने के लिए किया गया या प्रयुक्त *prophylactic treatment*

**prophylactic[2]** /ˌprɒfɪˈlæktɪk ˌप्रॉफ़िˈलैकटिक्/ *noun* [C] (*formal* or *technical*) a medicine, device or course of action that prevents disease रोगनिरोधी औषध, युक्ति या कार्यकलाप

**propitiate** /prəˈpɪʃieɪt प्रˈपिशिएट्/ *verb* [T] (*formal*) to make peace with somebody who is angry by trying to please them किसी नाराज़ या रूष्ट व्यक्ति को शांत कर लेना और संतुष्ट करना; मना लेना ▸ **propitiation** *noun* [U] अनुनय

**propitious** /prəˈpɪʃəs प्रˈपिशस्/ *adj.* favourable; likely to produce a successful result अनुकूल; संभवतः सफल परिणाम उत्पन्न करने वाला *It was a propitious time to start a new business.*

**proportion** /prəˈpɔːʃn प्रˈपॉश्न्/ *noun* **1** [C] a part or share of a whole पूर्ण का एक भाग या अंश *A large proportion of the earth's surface is covered by sea.* **2** [U] **proportion (of sth to sth)** the relationship between the size or amount of two things आकार या मात्रा की दृष्टि से एक वस्तु का दूसरी वस्तु से संबंध; अनुपात *The proportion of men to women in the college has changed dramatically over the years.* **3 proportions** [*pl.*] the size or shape of sth किसी वस्तु का आकार या आकृति *a room of odd proportions* ○ *Political unrest is reaching alarming proportions.*

IDM **in proportion** the right size in relation to other things अन्य वस्तुओं से सही संबंध में; उपयुक्त अनुपात में *to draw sth in proportion* ○ *She's so upset that it's hard for her to keep the problem in proportion* (= to her it seems more important or serious than it really is).

**in proportion to sth 1** by the same amount or number as sth else; relative to मात्रा या संख्या में दूसरे के समान; के अनुपात में *Salaries have not risen in proportion to inflation.* **2** compared with की तुलना में *In proportion to the number of students as a whole, there are very few women.*

**out of proportion (to sth) 1** too big, small, etc. in relation to other things दूसरों की तुलना में अधिक बड़ा, छोटा आदि **2** too great, serious, important, etc. in relation to sth दूसरे से संबंध की दृष्टि से कहीं अधिक बड़ा, गंभीर, महत्त्वपूर्ण आदि; अनुपात से बहुत अधिक *His reaction was completely out of proportion to the situation.*

**proportional** /prəˈpɔːʃənl प्रˈपॉशनल्/ *adj.* **proportional (to sth)** of the right size, amount or degree compared with sth else किसी अन्य की तुलना में सही आकार, मात्रा या डिग्री का; उचित अनुपात में, समानुपातिक *Salary is proportional to years of experience.* ▸ **proportionally** *adv.* आनुपातिक दृष्टि से, सही अनुपात में

**proportional representation** *noun* [U] (*abbr.* **PR**) a system that gives each political party in an election a number of representatives in parliament in direct relation to the number of votes its **candidates** receive चुनाव में उम्मीदवारों का मिलने वाले वोटों के समानुपात में संसद आदि में प्रतिनिधित्व देने की व्यवस्था; समानुपातिक प्रतिनिधित्व ➪ **representation** देखिए।

**proportionate** /prəˈpɔːʃənət प्रˈपॉशनट्/ *adj.* in due proportion समानुपाती, बराबर ▸ **proportionately** /-tli -ट्लि/ *adv.* समानुपातिकता से, बराबरी से *He divided the cake proportionately into six pieces.*

**proposal** /prəˈpəʊzl प्रˈपोज़ल्/ *noun* [C] **1 a proposal (for/to do sth); a proposal that...** a plan that is formally suggested औपचारिक प्रस्ताव, सुझाव *a new proposal for raising money* ○ *May I* ***make a proposal*** *that we all give an equal amount?* **2** an act of formally asking sb to marry you विवाह-प्रस्ताव

**propose** /prəˈpəʊz प्रˈपोज़्/ *verb* **1** [T] to formally suggest sth as a possible plan or action किसी योजना या कार्यक्रम को विचारार्थ प्रस्तुत करना *At the meeting a new advertising campaign was proposed.* **2** [T] to intend to do sth; to have sth as a plan कुछ करने का इरादा रखना; किसी काम की योजना बनाना *What do you propose to do now?* **3** [I, T] **propose (to sb)** to ask sb to marry you (किसी से) विवाह के लिए प्रस्ताव रखना *to propose marriage* **4** [T] **propose sb for/as sth** to suggest sb for an official position किसी औपचारिक पद के लिए किसी का नाम प्रस्तुत करना *I'd like to propose Anirudh Sharma as Chairperson.*

**proposition** /ˌprɒpəˈzɪʃn ˌप्रॉपˈज़िशन्/ *noun* [C] **1** an idea, a plan or an offer, especially in business; a suggestion कोई विचार, योजना या प्रस्ताव (विशेषतः व्यवसाय के क्षेत्रों में); सुझाव *A month's holiday in Sri Lanka is an* ***attractive proposition.*** **2** an idea or opinion that sb expresses about sth किसी बात के विषय में व्यक्त विचार या सम्मति *That's a very interesting proposition. Are you sure you can prove it?*

**proprietor** /prəˈpraɪətə(r) प्रˈप्राइअट(र्)/ *noun* [C] (*feminine* **proprietress** /prəˈpraɪətres प्रˈप्राइअट्रेस्/) the owner of a business, a hotel, etc. किसी व्यवसाय, होटल आदि का मालिक, स्वामी

**prose** /prəʊz प्रोज़्/ *noun* [U] written or spoken language that is not poetry कविता से भिन्न लिखित या मौखिक भाषा प्रयोग का खंड; गद्य *to write* ***in prose*** ➪ **poetry** देखिए।

**prosecute** /ˈprɒsɪkjuːt ˈप्रॉसिक्यूट्/ *verb* [I, T] **prosecute sb (for sth)** to officially charge sb with a crime and try to show that he/she is guilty, in a court of law अदालत में किसी पर औपचारिक रूप से अपराध का अभियोग लगाना या दोषारोपण करना *the prosecuting counsel/lawyer/attorney* ○ *He was prosecuted for theft.* ➪ **defend** देखिए।

**prosecution** /ˌprɒsɪˈkjuːʃn ˌप्रॉसिˈक्यूशन्/ *noun* **1** [U, C] the process of officially charging sb with a crime and of trying to show that he/she is guilty, in a court of law अदालत में किसी के विरुद्ध अपराध के लिए अभियोग प्रक्रिया *to bring a prosecution against sb* ○ *Failure to pay your parking fine will result in prosecution.* **2 the prosecution** [*with sing. or pl. verb*] a person or group of people who try to show that sb is guilty of a crime in a court of law अभियोजन पक्ष (व्यक्ति या व्यक्ति समूह जो अदालत में किसी पर अभियोग चलाए) *The prosecution claim/claims that Rohit was driving at 100 kilometres per hour.* ➪ **defence** देखिए।

**prosecutor** /ˈprɒsɪkjuːtə(r) ˈप्रॉसिक्यूट(र्)/ *noun* [C] **1** a public official who charges sb with a crime and tries to show that he/she is guilty in a court of law अदालत में किसी पर अपराध के लिए अभियोग लगाने वाला सरकारी अधिकारी; अभियोजक *the public/state prosecutor* **2** a lawyer who leads the case against the accused person (**the defendant**) in a court of law अदालत में अभियुक्त के विरुद्ध अभियोग-प्रक्रिया का नेतृत्व करने वाला सरकारी वकील

**prosody** /ˈprɒsədi ˈप्रॉसडि/ *noun* [U] (*technical*) the patterns of sounds and rhythms in poetry and speech; the study of this कविता और वाणी में ध्वनियों और लयों के पैटर्न; छंदों का व्यवस्थित अध्ययन; छंदशास्त्र

**prospect** /ˈprɒspekt ˈप्रॉस्पेक्ट्/ *noun* **1** [U, *sing.*] **prospect (of sth/of doing sth)** the possibility that sth will happen कुछ घटित होने की संभावना, आसार *There's little prospect of better weather before next week.* **2** [*sing.*] **prospect (of sth/of doing sth)** a thought about what may or will happen in the future भविष्य में जो हो सकता है या होने वाला है उसका विचार; संभावना, आशा *The prospect of becoming a father filled Jatin with happiness.* **3 prospects** [*pl.*] chances of being successful in the future भविष्य में सफलता के अवसर, आसार, संभावना *good job/career/promotion prospects*

**prospective** /prəˈspektɪv प्रˈस्पेक्टिव्/ *adj.* likely to be or to happen; possible संभावित; संभव *prospective changes in the law*

**prospectus** /prəˈspektəs प्रˈस्पेक्टस्/ *noun* [C] a small book which gives information about a school or college in order to advertise it स्कूल या कॉलेज के विषय में जानकारी देने वाली (प्रचारार्थ) पुस्तिका नियमावली

**prosper** /ˈprɒspə(r) ˈप्रॉस्प(र्)/ *verb* [I] to develop in a successful way; to be successful, especially with money सफलतापूर्वक विकसित होना, फलना-फूलना; धन की दृष्टि से समृद्ध होना

**prosperity** /prɒˈsperəti प्रॉˈस्पेरटि/ *noun* [U] the state of being successful, especially with money समृद्धि (धन की दृष्टि से) *Tourism has brought prosperity to many parts of Kerala.*

**prosperous** /ˈprɒspərəs ˈप्रॉस्परस्/ *adj.* rich and successful समृद्ध (धनी और सफल)

**prostate** /ˈprɒsteɪt ˈप्रॉस्ट्रेट्/ (*also* **prostate gland**) *noun* [C] a small organ in a man's body near the **bladder** that produces a liquid in which **sperm** is carried पुरुष के मूत्राशय के पास स्थित ग्रंथि; पुरःस्थ या प्रोस्टेट ग्रंथि

**prostitute** /ˈprɒstɪtjuːt ˈप्रॉस्टिट्यूट्/ *noun* [C] a person, especially a woman, who earns money by having sex with people वेश्या

**prostitution** /ˌprɒstɪˈtjuːʃn ˌप्रॉस्टिˈट्यूशन्/ *noun* [U] working as a prostitute वेश्यावृत्ति

**prostrate** /prɒˈstreɪt प्रॉˈस्ट्रेट्/ *adj.* lying flat on the ground, facing downwards नीचे मुँह कर ज़मीन पर सीधा लेटा हुआ; साष्टांग, दंडवत प्रणाम करता हुआ

**protagonist** /prəˈtægənɪst प्रˈटैगनिस्ट्/ *noun* [C] (*formal*) (in literature) the main character in a play, film or book (साहित्य में) किसी नाटक, फ़िल्म या पुस्तक का प्रधान पात्र; नायक

**protease** /ˈprəʊtieɪz ˈप्रोटिएज़्/ *noun* [U] (*technical*) an **enzyme** that breaks down **protein** प्रोटीन को विखंडित करने वाला एंज़ाइम; प्रोटिएस

**protect** /prəˈtekt प्रˈटेक्ट्/ *verb* [T] **protect sb/sth (against/from sth)** to keep sb/sth safe; to defend sb/sth व्यक्ति या वस्तु को सुरक्षित रखना; व्यक्ति या वस्तु की रक्षा करना *Parents try to protect their children from danger as far as possible.* ○ *Bats are a **protected species*** (= they must not be killed).

**protection** /prəˈtekʃn प्रˈटेक्शन्/ *noun* [U] **protection (against/from sth)** the act of keeping sb/sth safe so that he/she/it is not harmed or damaged सुरक्षा, हिफ़ाज़त *Vaccination gives protection against diseases.* ○ *After the attack he was put **under** police **protection**.*

**protectionism** /prəˈtekʃənɪzəm प्रˈटेक्शनिज़्म्/ *noun* [U] (*technical*) the principle or practice of protecting a country's own industry by taxing foreign goods विदेशी माल पर कर लगाकर अपने देश के उद्योगों को संरक्षण प्रदान करने का सिद्धांत या व्यवहार; संरक्षणवाद की नीति ▸ **protectionist** /-ʃənɪst -शनिस्ट्/ *adj.* संरक्षणात्मक *protectionist measures/policies*

**protective** /prəˈtektɪv प्रˈटेक्टिव्/ *adj.* **1** (*only before a noun*) that prevents sb/sth from being damaged or harmed व्यक्ति या वस्तु को नुक़सान से बचाने वाला; रक्षात्मक *In certain jobs workers need to wear protective clothing.* **2 protective (of/towards sb/sth)** wanting to keep sb/sth safe व्यक्ति या वस्तु को सुरक्षित रखने की प्रवृत्तिवाला; रक्षाकारी *Female animals are very protective of their young.*

**protector** /prəˈtektə(r) प्रˈटेक्टर्(र्)/ *noun* [C] a person who protects sb/sth व्यक्ति या वस्तु की रक्षा करने वाला व्यक्ति; रक्षक

**protein** /ˈprəʊtiːn ˈप्रोटीन्/ *noun* [C, U] a substance found in food such as meat, fish, eggs and beans. It is important for helping people and animals to grow and be healthy गोश्त, मछली, अंडों, दूध आदि में बहुलता से उपलब्ध और मनुष्यों तथा पशुओं के शारीरिक विकास और स्वस्थ रहने में सहायक पदार्थ; प्रोटीन

**protest[1]** /ˈprəʊtest ˈप्रोटेस्ट्/ *noun* [U, C] **protest (against sth)** a statement or action that shows that you do not like or approve of sth किसी बात की नापसंदगी या अस्वीकृति दिखाने वाला वक्तव्य या कार्य; विरोध *He resigned **in protest** against the decision.* ○ *The union organized a protest against the redundancies.*

IDM **under protest** not happily and after expressing disagreement असहमति व्यक्त करते हुए और अनिच्छा के साथ *Farida agreed to pay in the end but only under protest.*

**protest[2]** /prəˈtest प्रˈटेस्ट्/ *verb* **1** [I, T] **protest (about/ against/at sth)** to say or show that you do not approve of or agree with sth, especially publicly (विशेषतः सार्वजनिक) विरोध प्रदर्शन करना *Students have been protesting against the government's decision.* NOTE अमेरिकन अंग्रेज़ी में **protest** का प्रयोग preposition के बिना होता है—*They protested the government's handling of the situation.* **2** [T] to say sth firmly, especially when others do not believe you किसी बात को दृढ़तापूर्वक कहना विशेषतः जब अन्य लोग संदेह करें *She has always **protested** her **innocence**.*

NOTE शब्द **protest** में अधिक दृढ़ता का भाव है और **complain** की अपेक्षा अधिक गंभीर मामलों में इसका प्रयोग होता है। ग़लत और अनुचित व्यवहार पर **protest** किया जाता है। कोई वस्तु घटिया हो या बात अधिक गंभीर न हो तो शब्द **complain** प्रयुक्त किया जाता है—*to protest about a new tax* ○ *to complain about the poor weather.*

▸ **protester** *noun* [C] विरोध-प्रदर्शनकारी *Protesters blocked the road outside the factory.*

**Protestant** /ˈprɒtɪstənt ˈप्रॉटिस्टन्ट्/ *noun* [C] a member of the Christian church that separated from the Catholic church in the 16th century ईसाई धर्म के प्रोटेस्टेंट चर्च का अनुयायी। यह चर्च कैथोलिक चर्च से 16 वीं शताब्दी में अलग हुआ था ▸ **Protestant** *adj.* प्रोटेस्टेंट *a Protestant church* ⇨ **Roman Catholic** देखिए।

**proto-** /ˈprəʊtəʊ ˈप्रोटो/ *prefix* (*used in nouns and adjectives*) original; from which others develop मूल; जिससे अन्य विकसित हुए; आद्य, आदिम *prototype*

**protocol** /ˈprəʊtəkɒl ˈप्रोटकॉल्/ *noun* **1** [U] (*formal*) a system of fixed rules and formal behaviour used at official meetings, usually between governments औपचारिक अवसरों पर सुनिश्चित नियमों और प्रक्रियाओं की व्यवस्था (प्रायः दो सरकारों के मध्य); औपचारिक शिष्टाचार *a breach of protocol* ○ *the protocol of diplomatic visits* **2** [C] (*technical*) the first or original version of a written agreement, especially one between countries; an extra part added to a written agreement (विशेषतः दो सरकारों के बीच हुई) लिखित संधि का प्रथम या मूल रूप; लिखित संधि में जोड़ा गया अतिरिक्त अंश, विज्ञप्ति *the first Geneva Protocol* ○ *It is set out in a legally binding protocol which forms part of the treaty.* **3** [C] (*computing*) a set of rules that control the way information is sent between computers कंप्यूटरों के बीच सूचना के आदान-प्रदान के नियम **4** [C] (*technical*) a plan for carrying out a scientific experiment or medical treatment वैज्ञानिक प्रयोग या डॉक्टरी उपचार को क्रियान्वित करने की योजना

**proton** /ˈprəʊtɒn ˈप्रोटॉन्/ *noun* [C] one of the three types of **particles** that form all atoms. Protons have a positive electric charge अणु के तीन घटक अंश में से एक; प्रोटोन। प्रोटोन में धनात्मक विद्युत चार्ज होता है ➪ **electron** और **neutron** देखिए।

**prototype** /ˈprəʊtətaɪp ˈप्रोटटाइप्/ *noun* [C] the first model or design of sth from which other forms will be developed किसी वस्तु का आदिप्ररूप (मॉडल या डिज़ाइन, जिससे दूसरे रूप विकसित हों)

**protozoan** /ˌprəʊtəˈzəʊən ˌप्रोटˈज़ोअन्/ *noun* [C] (*pl.* **protozoans** or **protozoa** /-ˈzəʊə -ˈज़ोआ/) a very small living thing, usually with only one cell, that can only be seen using a special piece of equipment that makes it look bigger (**a microscope**) प्रायः एक कोशिका वाला अत्यंत लघु जीव जो केवल सूक्ष्मदर्शी या माइक्रोस्कोप से ही दिखाई देता है; आदिजंतु, प्रोटोज़ोआ

**protrude** /prəˈtruːd प्रˈट्रूड्/ *verb* [I] **protrude (from sth)** to stick out from a place or surface (सतह आदि का) बाहर की ओर निकलना *protruding eyes/teeth*

**protrusion** /prəˈtruːʒn प्रˈट्रूश़्न्/ *noun* [C, U] (*formal*) a thing that sticks out from a place or surface; the fact of doing this बाहर की ओर निकली हुई वस्तु, बाहर की ओर निकला होना; बहिःसरण *a protrusion on the rock face*

**protuberance** /prəˈtjuːbərəns प्रˈट्यूबरन्स्/ *noun* [C] (*formal*) a round part that sticks out from a surface किसी सतह से उभरा हुआ गोल अंश; उभार, गुमटा, गोल सूजन या उभार, प्रावर्ध *The diseased trees have protuberances on their trunks.*

**proud** /praʊd प्राउड्/ *adj.* **1 proud (of sb/sth); proud to do sth/that...** feeling pleased and satisfied about sth that you own or have done किसी उपलब्धि पर हर्षित और संतुष्ट; गर्वित या गर्वयुक्त, गौरवान्वित *They are very proud of their new house.* ○ *I feel very proud to be part of such a successful organization.* **2** feeling that you are better and more important than other people अहंकारी, अभिमानी *Now she's at university she'll be much too proud to talk to us!* **3** having respect for yourself and not wanting to lose the respect of others स्वाभिमानी, खुद्दार *He was too proud to ask for help.* ➪ **pride** noun देखिए। ▶ **proudly** *adv.* गर्वपूर्वक *'I did all the work myself,' he said proudly.*

**prove** /pruːv प्रूव्/ *verb* (*pp* **proved;** *AmE* **proven**) **1** [T] **prove sth (to sb)** to use facts and evidence to show that sth is true किसी बात को (तथ्यों और प्रमाणों के द्वारा) सत्य सिद्ध करना *She tried to prove her innocence to the court.* ○ *He felt he needed* ***to prove a point*** (= show other people that he was right). ➪ **proof** noun देखिए। **2** *linking verb* to show a particular quality over a period of time (समय के दौरान) कोई विशेष बात साबित होना, निकलकर आना या पता चलना *The job proved more difficult than we'd expected.* **3** [T] **prove yourself (to sb)** to show other people how good you are at doing sth and/or that you are capable of doing sth (किसी काम में) लोगों के सामने अपनी क्षमता सिद्ध करना *He constantly feels that he has to prove himself to others.*

**proven** /ˈprəʊvn; ˈpruːvn ˈप्रोव्न्; ˈप्रूव्न्/ *adj.* that has been shown to be true सत्य सिद्ध किया गया; प्रमाणित या सिद्ध *a proven fact*

**proverb** /ˈprɒvɜːb ˈप्रॉव़ब्/ *noun* [C] a short well-known sentence or phrase that gives advice or says that sth is generally true in life कहावत, लोकोक्ति *'Too many cooks spoil the broth,' is a proverb.* ➪ **saying** देखिए।

**proverbial** /prəˈvɜːbiəl प्रˈव़बिअल्/ *adj.* **1** (*only before a noun*) used to show you are referring to a well-known phrase (**a proverb**) यह दिखाने के लिए प्रयुक्त कि आप किसी प्रसिद्ध उक्ति की चर्चा या का संकेत कर रहे हैं *Let's not count our proverbial chickens.* **2** well known and talked about by a lot of people लोकप्रसिद्ध, जाना-माना

**provide** /prəˈvaɪd प्र 'वाइड् / *verb* [T] **provide sb (with sth); provide sth (for sb)** to give sth to sb or make sth available for sb to use; to supply sth किसी को कुछ देना या प्रयोग के लिए उपलब्ध कराना; किसी वस्तु की आपूर्ति *This book will provide you with all the information you need.* ○ *We provide accommodation for students.* ➪ **provision** noun देखिए।

**PHR V** **provide for sb** to give sb all that he/she needs to live, for example food and clothing किसी के जीवन-यापन के साधन (जैसे भोजन, कपड़े) देना **provide for sth** to make preparations to deal with sth that might happen in the future भविष्य के लिए तैयारी करना; पूर्वोपाय करना *We did not provide for such a large increase in prices.*

**provided** /prəˈvaɪdɪd प्र 'वाइडिड् / (*also* **providing**) *conj.* **provided/providing (that)** only if; on condition that यदि; इस शर्त पर कि, बशर्ते कि *She agreed to go and work abroad provided (that) her family could go with her.*

**province** /ˈprɒvɪns 'प्रॉव़िन्स् / *noun* **1** [C] one of the areas that some countries are divided into with its own local government देश का कोई प्रांत या प्रदेश जो स्वायत्तशासी होता है या अपना शासन स्वयं चलाता है *Canada has ten provinces.* ➪ **county** और **state** देखिए। **2 the provinces** [*pl.*] (*BrE*) the part of a country that is outside the most important city (**the capital**) राजधानी के अतिरिक्त देश के विभिन्न भाग

**provincial** /prəˈvɪnʃl प्र 'व़िन्शल् / *adj.* **1** (*only before a noun*) connected with one of the large areas that some countries are divided into प्रांतीय, प्रादेशिक *provincial governments/elections* **2** connected with the parts of a country that do not include its most important city राजधानी से भिन्न प्रदेशों से संबंधित *a provincial town/newspaper* **3** (used about a person or his/her ideas) not wanting to consider new or different ideas or fashions (व्यक्ति या उसके विचार) नए या भिन्न विचारों या लोकप्रिय शैलियों को अपनाने का अनिच्छुक, संकीर्ण दृष्टि वाला *provincial attitudes*

**provision** /prəˈvɪʒn प्र 'व़िश़न् / *noun* **1** [U] the giving or supplying of sth to sb or making sth available for sb to use किसी को कुछ देने या पहुँचाने अथवा उपयोग हेतु कुछ उपलब्ध कराने की क्रिया; अभिपूर्ति *The council is responsible for the provision of education and social services.* **2** [U] **provision for sb/sth** preparations that you make to deal with sth that might happen in the future भविष्य की स्थितियों से निपटने की तैयारी *She made **provision for** (= planned for the financial future of) the children in the event of her death.* **3 provisions** [*pl.*] (*formal*) supplies of food and drink, especially for a long journey खाद्य और पेय सामग्री (विशेषतः लंबी यात्रा के लिए) ➪ **provide** verb देखिए।

**provisional** /prəˈvɪʒənl प्र 'व़िशनल् / *adj.* only for the present time, that is likely to be changed in the future केवल वर्तमान तक सीमित, जिसमें भविष्य में परिवर्तन संभावित हो; अनंतिम, अंतरकालीन, कच्चा *The provisional date for the next meeting is 18 November.* ○ *a **provisional driving licence*** (= that you use when you are learning to drive) ▶ **provisionally** /-nəli -नलि / *adv.* अनंतिम रूप से *I've only repaired the bike provisionally—we'll have to do it properly later.*

**proviso** /prəˈvaɪzəʊ प्र 'वाइज़ो / *noun* [C] (*pl.* **provisos**) a condition that must be accepted before an agreement can be made समझौते या संधि के होने से पहले की शर्त जिसे मानना अनिवार्य हो, अनिवार्य पूर्व शर्त; प्रतिबंध *He agreed to the visit **with the proviso that** they should stay no longer than a week.*

**provocation** /ˌprɒvəˈkeɪʃn ˌप्रॉव़ 'केशन् / *noun* [U, C] doing or saying sth deliberately to try to make sb angry or upset; sth that is said or done to cause this किसी को क्रोधित या परेशान करने के लिए जान-बूझकर की गई बात, हरकत आदि *You should never hit children, even **under** extreme **provocation**.* ➪ **provoke** verb देखिए।

**provocative** /prəˈvɒkətɪv प्र 'वॉकटिव़् / *adj.* **1** intended to make sb angry or upset or to cause an argument किसी को क्रोधित या नाराज़ या विवाद में घसीटने की मंशा से किया गया; भड़काऊ *He made a provocative remark about a woman's place being in the home.* **2** intended to cause sexual excitement कामोत्तेजक ▶ **provocatively** *adv.* भड़काऊ या कामोत्तेजक ढंग से

**provoke** /prəˈvəʊk प्र 'वोक् / *verb* [T] **1** to cause a particular feeling or reaction विशेष भाव या प्रतिक्रिया उत्पन्न करना; उकसाना, उभाड़ना *an article intended to provoke discussion* **2 provoke sb (into sth/into doing sth)** to say or do sth that you know will make a person angry or upset किसी को जान-बूझकर क्रोधित या नाराज़ करना (ऐसी बात कहना या ऐसा काम करना); भड़काना *The lawyer claimed his client was provoked into acts of violence.* ➪ **provocation** noun देखिए।

**prow** /praʊ प्राउ / *noun* [C] the front part of a ship or boat जहाज़ या नाव का (नुकीला) अग्रभाग; पोताग्र **NOTE** जहाज़ के पिछले हिस्से को **stern** कहते हैं।

**prowess** /ˈpraʊəs ˈप्राउअस् / *noun* [U] (*formal*) great skill at doing sth उत्कृष्ट निपुणता, कौशल, विशिष्ट प्रवीणता *academic/sporting prowess*

**prowl** /praʊl प्राउल् / *verb* [I, T] **prowl (about/ around)** (used about an animal that is hunting or a person who is waiting for a chance to steal sth or do sth bad) to move around an area quietly so that you are not seen or heard (शिकार ढूँढ़ता कोई पशु या चोरी की मंशा से प्रतीक्षा करता कोई व्यक्ति), चुपचाप व गोपनीय रीति से दबे पाँव इधर-उधर विचरना *I could hear someone prowling around outside so I called the police.* **NOTE** 'Prowl' कर रहे व्यक्ति के लिए **on the prowl** का प्रयोग होता है। ▶ **prowler** *noun* [C] विचरण करता पशु या व्यक्ति *The police arrested a prowler outside the hospital.*

**proximity** /prɒkˈsɪməti प्रॉक्ˈसिमटि / *noun* [U] (*formal*) **proximity (of sb/sth) (to sb/sth)** the state of being near to sb/sth in distance or time (स्थान और समय की दृष्टि से) निकटता *An advantage is the proximity of the new offices to the airport.*

**proxy** /ˈprɒksi ˈप्रॉक्सि / *noun* [U] the authority that you give to sb to act for you if you cannot do sth yourself किसी अन्य का प्रतिनिधित्व करने का अधिकार, प्रतिनिधित्व, मुख़्तारी *to vote* ***by proxy***

**prude** /pruːd प्रूड् / *noun* [C] a person who is easily shocked by anything connected with sex यौन विषयों में अति संकोची व्यक्ति, अतिलज्जालु व्यक्ति ▶ **prudish** *adj.* अतिलज्जालु

**prudent** /ˈpruːdnt ˈप्रूड्न्ट् / *adj.* (*formal*) sensible and careful when making judgements and decisions; avoiding unnecessary risks मूल्यांकन और निर्णय करने में सावधान और विवेकपूर्ण; अनावश्यक ख़तरों से बचते हुए *It would be prudent to get some more advice before you invest your money.* ✪ विलोम **imprudent** ▶ **prudence** *noun* [U] विवेकशीलता ▶ **prudently** *adv.* विवेपूर्वक

**prune[1]** /pruːn प्रून् / *noun* [C] a dried fruit (**plum**) सुखाया हुआ आलूबुख़ारा

**prune[2]** /pruːn प्रून् / *verb* [T] to cut branches or parts of branches off a tree or bush in order to make it a better shape किसी पेड़ या झाड़ी को काँटना-छाँटना ताकि वह सुंदर दिखाई दे

**pry** /praɪ प्राइ / *verb* (*pres. part.* **prying;** *3rd person sing. pres.* **pries;** *pt, pp* **pried**) **1** [I] **pry (into sth)** to try to find out about other people's private affairs दूसरों के निजी मामलों को जानने की कोशिश करना, ताक-झाँक करना *I'm sick of you prying into my personal life.* **2** [T] (*AmE*) = **prise**

**PS** (*also* **ps**) /ˌpiː ˈes ˌपी ˈएस् / *abbr.* (used for adding sth to the end of a letter) postscript (पत्र के अंत में कुछ जोड़ने के लिए प्रयुक्त) पश्चलेख; पुनश्चः *Love Raman. PS I'll bring the car.*

**psalm** /sɑːm साम् / *noun* [C] a sacred song, poem or prayer that praises God, especially one in the Bible ईश्वर की स्तुति में गाया गया स्तोत्र गान या प्रार्थना (विशेषतः बाइबल से) *Book of Psalms*

**pseudo-** /ˈsuːdəʊ; ˈsjuː- सूडो; ˈस्यू- / *prefix* (*used in nouns, adjectives and adverbs*) not genuine; false or pretended जो प्रामाणिक न हो; छद्म, नक़ली *pseudonym* ○ *pseudo-science*

**pseudocode** /ˈsuːdəʊkəʊd; ˈsjuː- ˈसूडोकोड्; स्यू- / *noun* [C] (*computing*) a very simple form of computer language used in program design प्रोग्राम डिज़ाइन के लिए प्रयुक्त एक सरल कंप्यूटर-भाषा

**pseudonym** /ˈsuːdənɪm; ˈsjuː- ˈसूडनिम्; स्यू- / *noun* [C] a name used by sb, especially a writer, instead of his/her real name छद्मनाम, उपनाम (असली नाम के बदले प्रयुक्त, विशेषतः किसी लेखक द्वारा)

**psych** /saɪk साइक् / *verb*

**PHR V** **psych yourself up** (*informal*) to prepare yourself in your mind for sth difficult मन-ही-मन कठिनाई का सामना करने के लिए तैयार होना *I've got to psych myself up for this interview.*

**psyche** /ˈsaɪki ˈसाइकि/ *noun* [C] (*formal*) the mind; your deepest feelings and attitudes मन, चित्त; गहनतम भावनाएँ और मनोवृत्तियाँ *the human/ female/ national psyche*

**psychedelic** /ˌsaɪkəˈdelɪk ˌसाइकˈडेलिक् / *adj.* (used about art, music, clothes, etc.) having bright colours or patterns or strange sounds (कला, संगीत, कपड़े आदि) चटकीले रंगों या आकृतियों वाला (कपड़ा) या विचित्र ध्वनियों वाला (संगीत)

**psychiatrist** /saɪˈkaɪətrɪst साइˈकाइअट्रिस्ट् / *noun* [C] a doctor who is trained to treat people with mental illness मानसिक रोगों का चिकित्सक; मनोरोग-चिकित्सक

**psychiatry** /saɪˈkaɪətri साइˈकाइअट्रि / *noun* [U] the study and treatment of mental illness मनोरोग अध्ययन और चिकित्सा ➪ **psychology** देखिए। ▶ **psychiatric** /ˌsaɪkiˈætrɪk ˌसाइकिˈऐट्रिक्/ *adj.* मनोरोग-विषयक, मनश्चिकित्सा-संबंधी *a psychiatric hospital/unit/nurse*

**psychic** /ˈsaɪkɪk ˈसाइकिक् / *adj.* (used about a person or his/her mind) having unusual powers that cannot be explained, for example knowing what sb else is thinking or being able to see into the future मनस्तत्व; (व्यक्ति या उसका चित्त) असाधारण

शक्तियों वाला और इंद्रियातीत-ज्ञानेंद्रियों की पहुँच से बाहर (जैसे दूसरों के मन को पढ़ लेना या भविष्य को जान लेना)

**psycho** /ˈsaɪkəʊ ˈसाइको/ = **psychopath**

**psycho-** /ˈsaɪkəʊ ˈसाइको/ (*also* **psych-**) *prefix* (*used in nouns, adjectives and adverbs*) connected with the mind मन से संबंधित, मनो- *psychology* ○ *psychiatrist*

**psychoanalysis** /ˌsaɪkəʊəˈnæləsɪs ˌसाइकोअˈनेलसिस्/ (*also* **analysis**) *noun* [U] a method of treating sb with a mental illness by asking about his/her past experiences, feelings, dreams, etc. in order to find out what is making him/her ill मनोरोग से ग्रस्त व्यक्ति के उपचार की एक विधि, जिसमें रोग का कारण जानने के लिए रोगी के विगत अनुभवों, मनोभावों, स्वप्नों आदि की जानकारी का उपयोग किया जाता है; मनो-विश्लेषण; मनोरोग-विश्लेषण ▶ **psychoanalyse** (*AmE* **-yze**) /ˌsaɪkəʊˈænəlaɪz ˌसाइकोˈऐनलाइज़्/ *verb* [T] मनो-विश्लेषण करना

**psychoanalyst** /ˌsaɪkəʊˈænəlɪst ˌसाइकोˈऐनलिस्ट्/ *noun* [C] a person who treats sb with a mental illness by using psychoanalysis मनोविश्लेषक, मनोरोग-विश्लेषक

**psychological** /ˌsaɪkəˈlɒdʒɪkl ˌसाइकˈलॉजिकल्/ *adj.* **1** connected with the mind or the way that it works मन से या मानसिक प्रक्रियाओं से संबंधित; मनोगत *Her ordeal caused her long-term psychological damage.* **2** connected with the study of the mind and the way people behave (**psychology**) मनोवैज्ञानिक ▶ **psychologically** /-kli -क्लि/ *adv.* मानसिक या मनोवैज्ञानिक रूप से *Psychologically, it was a bad time to be starting a new job.*

**psychologist** /saɪˈkɒlədʒɪst साइˈकॉलजिस्ट्/ *noun* [C] a scientist who studies the mind and the way that people behave व्यक्तियों के मन और व्यवहार की रीति का अध्ययन करने वाला वैज्ञानिक; मनोविज्ञानी

**psychology** /saɪˈkɒlədʒi साइˈकॉलजि/ *noun* **1** [U] the scientific study of the mind and the way that people behave व्यक्तियों के मन और व्यवहार की रीति का वैज्ञानिक अध्ययन; मनोविज्ञान *child psychology* ➪ **psychiatry** देखिए। **2** [*sing.*] the type of mind that a person or group of people has व्यक्ति या वर्ग के मानसिक लक्षण *If we understood the psychology of the killer we would have a better chance of catching him.*

**psychopath** /ˈsaɪkəpæθ ˈसाइकपैथ्/ (*spoken* **psycho**) *noun* [C] a person who has a serious mental illness that may cause him/her to hurt or kill other people गंभीर मनोरोग से ग्रस्त व्यक्ति जो अपने या दूसरों के साथ हिंसात्मक व्यवहार कर सकता है; मनोरोगी, मनोविकृत

**psychosis** /saɪˈkəʊsɪs साइˈकोसिस्/ *noun* [C, U] (*pl.* **psychoses** /-siːz -सीज़्/) a very serious mental illness that affects your whole personality व्यक्ति के समूचे व्यक्तित्व को विकृत कर देने वाला एक गंभीर मनोरोग; मनोविकृति, मनोविक्षिप्ति ▶ **psychotic** /saɪˈkɒtɪk साइˈकॉटिक्/ *adj.*, *noun* [C] मनोविक्षिप्ति-ग्रस्त, मनोविक्षिप्त *a psychotic patient/individual*

**psychosomatic** /ˌsaɪkəʊsəˈmætɪ ˌसाइकोसˈमैटिक्/ *adj.* (of an illness) caused by mental problems rather than physical problems (रोग) मानसिक (न कि शारीरिक) समस्याओं से उत्पन्न

**psychotherapy** /ˌsaɪkəʊˈθerəpi ˌसाइकोˈथ़ेरपि/ *noun* [U] the treatment of mental illness by discussing sb's problems rather than by giving him/her drugs मनोरोग-चिकित्सा जिसमें रोगी को दवाएँ देने के स्थान पर उसकी समस्याओं के विषय में बात की जाती है

**PT** /ˌpiːˈtiː ˌपीˈटी/ *abbr.* physical training शारीरिक प्रशिक्षण

**pt** (*pl.* **pts**) *abbr.* **1** pint पाइंट (माप) *2 pints milk* **2** (in a game or competition) point खेल या प्रतियोगिता में मिले अंक; पॉइंट *Anand 5 pts, Anuj 3 pts*

**PTO** (*also* **pto**) /ˌpiː tiːˈəʊ ˌपी टीˈओ/ *abbr.* (at the bottom of a page) please turn over पृष्ठ के अंत में अंकित संक्षिप्ति जिसका अर्थ है कृपया पृष्ठ पलटिए

**pub** /pʌb पब्/ (*formal* **public house**) *noun* [C] a place where people go to buy and drink alcohol and that also often serves food सार्वजनिक मदिरालय, मधुशाला, पब

**puberty** /ˈpjuːbəti ˈप्यूबटि/ *noun* [U] the time when a child's body is changing and becoming physically like that of an adult वह समय जब बालक या बालिका में यौवन के लक्षण प्रकट होने लगें; यौवनारंभ, वयःसंधि

**pubic** /ˈpjuːbɪk ˈप्यूबिक्/ *adj.* of the area around the sexual organs जनेंद्रियों के आस-पास का *pubic hair*

**public¹** /ˈpʌblɪk ˈपब्लिक्/ *adj.* **1** (*only before a noun*) connected with ordinary people in general, not those who have an important position in society जन-साधारण से संबंधित (न कि समाज के उच्च वर्ग से) लोक-/जन- ***Public opinion*** *was not in favour of the war.* ○ *How much public support is there for the government's policy?* **2** provided for the use of people in general; not private आम, सार्वजनिक जन-साधारण के उपयोग का; जो निजी न हो *a public library/telephone* **3** known by many people जो सबको मालूम हो; सर्वविदित *We're going to* ***make*** *the news* ***public*** *soon.* ➪ **private** देखिए। ▶ **publicly** /-kli -क्लि/ *adv.*

सार्वजनिक रूप से, खुले आम *The company refused to admit publicly that it had acted wrongly.*

**IDM be common/public knowledge** ➪ **knowledge** देखिए।

**go public** **1** to tell people about sth that is a secret गोपनीय बात को सार्वजनिक करना (सबको बता देना) *The sacked employee went public with his stories of corruption inside the company.* **2** (used about a company) to start selling shares to the public (कंपनी द्वारा) अपने शेयर जनता को बेचना आरंभ करना

**in the public eye** often appearing on television, in magazines, etc. लोगों की नज़र में बार-बार आने वाला (टीवी पर तथा पत्रिकाओं आदि में प्रायः दिखाई पड़ने वाला)

**public²** /ˈpʌblɪk ˈपब्लिक्/ *noun* [*with sing. or pl. verb*] **1 the public** people in general जनता *The museum is **open to the public**. ○ The police have asked for help from **members of the public**.* **2** a group of people who are all interested in sth or who have sth in common एक जैसी रुचि या विशेषताओं वाले लोगों का समूह *the travelling public*

**IDM in public** when other people are present सबके सामने *This is the first time that Ms Sharma has spoken about her experience in public.*

**publican** /ˈpʌblɪkən ˈपब्लिकन्/ *noun* [C] a person who owns or manages a pub मदिरालय का मालिक या प्रबंधक

**publication** /ˌpʌblɪˈkeɪʃn ˌपब्लिˈकेश्न्/ *noun* **1** [U] the act of printing a book, magazine, etc. and making it available to the public (पुस्तक, पत्रिका आदि को) प्रकाशित करने की क्रिया; प्रकाशन *His latest book has just been accepted for publication.* **2** [C] a book, magazine, etc. that has been published प्रकाशित पुस्तक, पत्रिका आदि; प्रकाशन **3** [U] the action of making sth known to the public किसी बात को सार्वजनिक करने की क्रिया *the publication of exam results*

**public company** (*also* **public limited company**) *noun* [C] (*BrE*) a large company that sells shares in itself to the public सार्वजनिक कंपनी; ऐसी बड़ी कंपनी जो अपने शेयर जनता को बेचती है

**public convenience** *noun* [C] a toilet in a public place that anyone can use सार्वजनिक शौचालय

**public house** (*formal*) = **pub**

**publicity** /pʌbˈlɪsəti पब्ˈलिसटि/ *noun* [U] **1** notice or attention given by the newspapers, television, etc. to sth/sb समाचारपत्रों, टीवी आदि द्वारा व्यक्ति या वस्तु को दिया नोटिस या दिया ध्यान; प्रचार *to seek/avoid publicity* **2** the business of attracting people's attention to sth/sb; advertising व्यक्ति या वस्तु की ओर ध्यान आकृष्ट करने का काम; विज्ञापन *There has been a lot of publicity for this film.*

**publicize** (*also* **-ise**) /ˈpʌblɪsaɪz ˈपब्लिसाइज़्/ *verb* [T] to attract people's attention to sth किसी वस्तु को प्रचारित करना (उसकी ओर लोगों का ध्यान आकृष्ट करना) *The event has been well publicized and should attract a lot of people.*

**public relations** *noun* (*abbr.* **PR**) **1** [*pl.*] the state of the relationship between an organization and the public किसी संस्था और जनता के बीच संपर्क की स्थिति; जनसंपर्क *Giving money to local charities is good for public relations.* **2** [U] the job of making a company, organization, etc. popular with the public किसी कंपनी, संस्था आदि को अच्छे ढंग से जनता के सामने प्रस्तुत करने का काम *a Public Relations Officer*

**public school** *noun* [C] **1** (in Britain, especially in England) a private school for children aged between 13 and 18. Parents have to pay to send their children to one of these schools. Many of the children at public schools live (**board**) there while they are studying (ब्रिटेन, विशेषतः इंग्लैंड, में और अब भारत में भी) 13 से 18 से वर्ष के बच्चों के लिए प्राइवेट स्कूल (माता-पिता इन बच्चों का ख़र्चा उठाते हैं और अनेक बच्चे छात्रावासों में रहते हैं) **2** (in the US, Australia, Scotland and other countries) a local school that provides free education (अमेरिका, ऑस्ट्रेलिया, स्कॉटलैंड और अन्य देशों में) सबको निःशुल्क शिक्षा देने वाला स्थानीय स्कूल; पब्लिक स्कूल

**public-spirited** *adj.* always ready to help other people and the public in general जनहित की भावना से प्रेरित; लोकहितैषी

**public transport** *noun* [U] (the system of) buses, trains, etc. that run according to a series of planned times and that anyone can use सार्वजनिक यातायात व्यवस्था *to travel by/on public transport*

**publish** /ˈpʌblɪʃ ˈपब्लिश्/ *verb* **1** [I, T] to prepare and print a book, magazine, etc. and make it available to the public (पुस्तक, पत्रिका आदि को) प्रकाशित करना *This dictionary has been published by Oxford University Press.* **2** [T] (used about a writer, etc.) to have your work put in a book, magazine, etc. (लेखक आदि का) पुस्तक, लेख आदि प्रकाशित करना *Dr Verma has published several articles on the subject.* **3** [T] to make sth known to the public जनता के सामने प्रस्तुत करना *Large companies must publish their accounts every year.*

**publisher** /ˈpʌblɪʃə(r) ˈपब्लिश(र्)/ *noun* [C] a person or company that publishes books, magazines, etc. पुस्तकों, पत्रिका आदि को प्रकाशित करने वाला व्यक्ति या कंपनी; प्रकाशक

**publishing** /ˈpʌblɪʃɪŋ ˈपब्लिशिङ्/ *noun* [U] the business of preparing books, magazines, etc. to be printed and sold प्रकाशन-व्यवसाय *She's aiming for a career in publishing.*

**pudding** /ˈpʊdɪŋ ˈपुडिङ्/ *noun* [C, U] (*BrE*) **1** any sweet food that is eaten at the end of a meal भोजन के अंत में खाया जाने वाला मीठा पकवान (फ़िरनी आदि), पुडिंग *What's for pudding today?* **NOTE** इस अर्थ में **dessert** अधिक औपचारिक शब्द है। ➪ **sweet** देखिए। **2** a type of sweet food that is made from bread, flour or rice with eggs, milk, etc. ब्रेड, मैदा या चावल, अंडे, दूध आदि से बना मीठा पकवान *rice pudding*

**puddle** /ˈpʌdl ˈपड्ल्/ *noun* [C] a small pool of water or other liquid, especially rain, that has formed on the ground किसी द्रव, विशेषत: बरसाती पानी, से बना छोटा ताल; बरसाती पोखरा, डबरा, डबरी ➪ **pond** पर नोट देखिए।

**puff[1]** /pʌf पफ़्/ *verb* **1** [I, T] (used about air, smoke, wind, etc.) to blow or come out in clouds (हवा, धुएँ आदि का) उड़ना या बादलों के आकार में, सघन रूप में बाहर आना *Smoke was puffing out of the chimney.* **2** [I, T] to smoke a cigarette, pipe etc. सिगरेट, पाइप आदि पीना *to puff on a cigarette* **3** [I] to breathe loudly or quickly, for example when you are running हाँफना *He was puffing hard as he ran up the hill.* **4** [I] **puff along, in, out, up,** etc. to move in a particular direction with loud breaths or small clouds of smoke शोर करते हुए या धुएँ के बादल छोड़ते हुए किसी विशेष दिशा में बढ़ना *The train puffed into the station.*

**PHR V** **puff sth out/up** to cause sth to become larger by filling it with air हवा भर कर फुला देना *The trumpet player was puffing out his cheeks.*

**puff up** (used about part of the body) to become swollen (शरीर का) फूल जाना; सूज जाना *Her arm puffed up when she was stung by a wasp.*

**puff[2]** /pʌf पफ़्/ *noun* [C] **1** a small amount of air, smoke, wind, etc. that is blown or sent out हवा का झोंका; धुएँ आदि की फूँक *a puff of smoke* **2** one breath that you take when you are smoking a cigarette or pipe सिगरेट या पाइप का कश *to take/have a puff on a cigarette*

**puffed** /pʌft पफ़्ट्/ (*also* **puffed out**) *adj.* finding it difficult to breathe, for example because you have been running हाँफता हुआ (जैसे भागते समय)

**puffin** /ˈpʌfɪn ˈपफ़िन्/ *noun* [C] a North Atlantic sea bird with a large brightly coloured beak उत्तरी एटलांटिक का बड़ी और चटकीली चोंच वाला एक पक्षी ➪ **seabird** पर चित्र देखिए।

**puffy** /ˈpʌfi ˈपफ़ि/ *adj.* (used about a part of a person's body) looking soft and swollen (व्यक्ति के शरीर का अंग) जो नरम और सूजा हुआ लगे *Your eyes look a bit puffy. Have you been crying?*

**pug mark** /ˌpʌgˈmaːk ˌपग्ˈमाक्/ *noun* [C] the trail or footprint of an animal पशु के पदचिह्न

**puke** /pjuːk प्यूक्/ *verb* [I, T] to vomit उल्टी करना, वमन करना ▶ **puke** *noun* [U] उल्टी, वमन

**pulao** *noun* [U] a rice dish cooked with meat or vegetables. The rice can be **seasoned** with various spices पुलाव

**pull[1]** /pʊl पुल्/ *verb* **1** [I, T] to use force to move sb/sth towards yourself व्यक्ति या वस्तु को अपनी ओर खींचना *I pulled on the rope to make sure that it was secure.* ○ *They managed to pull the child out of the water.* **2** [T] **pull sth on, out, up, down, etc.** to move sth in the direction that is described निर्दिष्ट दिशा में किसी वस्तु को खींचना *She pulled her sweater on.* ○ *She pulled on her sweater.* ○ *I switched off the TV and pulled out the plug.* **3** [T] to hold or be fastened to sth and move it along behind you in the direction that you are going किसी को थाम या बाँधकर पीछे-पीछे घसीटना (गति की अनुकूल दिशा में) *That cart is too heavy for one horse to pull.* **4** [I, T] to move your body or a part of your body away with force (शरीर या उसके अंग को) तेज़ी से झटक देना, झटके से खींच लेना *I pulled back my fingers just as the door slammed.* **5** [T] to damage a muscle, etc. by using too much force (अधिक ज़ोर लगाने के कारण) मांसपेशियों का खिंच जाना *I've **pulled a muscle** in my thigh.*

**IDM** **make/pull faces/a face (at sb)** ➪ **face[1]** देखिए।

**pull sb's leg** (*informal*) to play a joke on sb by trying to make him/her believe sth that is not true किसी की टाँग खींचना, झाँसा देकर किसी का मज़ाक़ बनाना

**pull out all the stops** (*informal*) to make the greatest possible effort to achieve sth कुछ पाने के लिए यथासंभव कोशिश करना

**pull your punches** (*informal*) (*usually used in negative sentences*) to be careful what you say or do in order not to shock or upset anyone कुछ कहने या करने में सावधानी बरतना (कि दूसरे को न धक्का लगे न परेशानी हो) *The film pulls no punches in its portrayal of urban violence.*

**pull strings** to use your influence to gain an advantage अपने फ़ायदे के लिए प्रभाव का इस्तेमाल करना

**pull your weight** to do your fair share of the work किसी काम में अपनी हिस्सेदारी निभाना

PHRV **pull away (from sb/sth)** to start moving forward, leaving sb/sth behind व्यक्ति या वस्तु को वहीं छोड़ते हुए चल देना *We waved as the bus pulled away.*

**pull sth down** to destroy a building किसी इमारत को गिरा देना या ढहाना

**pull in (to sth); pull into sth** **1** (used about a train) to enter a station (रेलगाड़ी का) स्टेशन पर पहुँचना **2** (used about a car, etc.) to move to the side of the road and stop (कार आदि का) सड़क के किनारे लगातार रुक जाना

**pull sth off** (*informal*) to succeed in sth किसी काम में सफल होना *to pull off a business deal*

**pull out** (used about a car, etc.) to move away from the side of the road (कार आदि का) सड़क के किनारे से आगे बढ़ जाना *I braked as a car suddenly pulled out in front of me.*

**pull out (of sth)** (used about a train) to leave a station (रेलगाड़ी का) स्टेशन से रवाना होना

**pull (sb/sth) out (of sth)** (to cause sb/sth) to leave sth (व्यक्ति या वस्तु) से कुछ छुड़वाना, को छोड़ना, से बाहर निकल आना *The Americans have pulled their forces out of the area.* ○ *We've pulled out of the deal.*

**pull sth out** to take sth out of a place suddenly or with force कहीं से कुछ अचानक या झटके से बाहर निकाल लेना *She walked into the bank and pulled out a gun.*

**pull over** (used about a vehicle or its driver) to slow down and move to the side of the road (कार या उसके चालक का) गति मंद करते हुए सड़क के किनारे हो जाना *I pulled over to let the ambulance pass.*

**pull through (sth)** to survive a dangerous illness or a difficult time ख़तरनाक बीमारी या कठिनाई से पार पा लेना या निकल आना

**pull together** to do sth or work together with other people in an organized way and without fighting दूसरों के साथ मिलकर एकता और सहयोग की भावना से कोई काम करना

**pull yourself together** to control your feelings and behave in a calm way अपनी भावनाओं पर नियंत्रण रखकर शांत भाव से आचरण करना *Pull yourself together and stop crying.*

**pull up** (to cause a car, etc.) to stop कार आदि को रोक देना

**pull²** /pʊl पुल्/ *noun* **1** [C] **a pull (at/on sth)** the action of moving sb/sth towards you using force व्यक्ति या वस्तु को अपनी ओर खींचने की क्रिया; खिंचाई, कर्षण *I gave a pull on the rope to check it was secure.* **2** [*sing.*] a physical force or an attraction that makes sb/sth move in a particular direction खींच, भौतिक शक्ति या आकर्षण (जो व्यक्ति या वस्तु को किसी ओर धकेले) *the earth's gravitational pull* ○ *He couldn't resist the pull of the city.* **3** [*sing.*] the act of taking a breath of smoke from a cigarette सिगरेट का कश खींचने की क्रिया

**pulley** /ˈpʊli ˈपुलि/ *noun* [C] a piece of equipment, consisting of a wheel and a rope, that is used for lifting heavy things गरारी, घिरनी, पुली (भारी सामान उठाने की मशीन जिसमें एक रस्सी और चरखी होती है)

**pullover** /ˈpʊləʊvə(r) ˈपुल्ओव़(र्)/ *noun* [C] a knitted woollen piece of clothing for the upper part of the body, with long sleeves and no buttons बिना बटन और पूरी बाँह का ऊनी स्वेटर; पुलोवर ➪ **sweater** पर नोट देखिए।

**pulmonary** /ˈpʌlmənəri ˈपल्मनरि/ *adj.* (*technical*) connected with the lungs फेफड़ों का या से संबंधित *the pulmonary artery* ➪ **heart** पर चित्र देखिए।

**pulp** /pʌlp पल्प्/ *noun* **1** [*sing.*, U] a soft substance that is made especially by pressing sth किसी वस्तु को मसलने या कूटने-पीटने से बनी गूदे जैसी नरम चीज़ *Mash the beans to a pulp.* ➪ **wood pulp** देखिए। **2** [U] the soft inner part of some fruits or vegetables फलों या साग-सब्ज़ियों का गूदा

**pulpit** /ˈpʊlpɪt ˈपुल्पिट्/ *noun* [C] a raised platform in a church where the priest stands when he/she is speaking चर्च में बना मंच जहाँ से पादरी प्रवचन करते हैं; प्रवचन-मंच

**pulsar** /ˈpʌlsɑ:(r) ˈपल्सा(र्)/ *noun* [C] (*technical*) a star that cannot be seen but that sends out fast regular radio signals अदृश्य तारा जो तीव्र गति से नियमित रेडियो संकेत भेजता है; पलसार ➪ **quasar** देखिए।

**pulsate** /pʌlˈseɪt पल्ˈसेट्/ *verb* [I] to move or shake with strong regular movements नियमित गति से तेज़ी के साथ हरकत करना या काँपना, स्पंदित होना *a pulsating rhythm*

**pulse**[1] /pʌls पल्स्/ *noun* **1** [C, *usually sing.*] the regular beating in your body as blood is pushed around it by your heart. You can feel your pulse at your wrist, neck, etc. (नाड़ी, कलाई, गरदन में महसूस होने वाली) धड़कन, स्पंदन जो हृदय द्वारा शरीर में एक प्रवाह को गति देने से उत्पन्न होती है *Your pulse rate increases after exercise.* ○ *to feel/take sb's pulse* (= to count how many times it beats in one minute) **2 pulses** [*pl.*] the seeds of some plants such as beans and peas that are cooked and eaten as food दालें

**pulse**[2] /pʌls पल्स्/ *verb* [I] to move with strong regular movements तीव्र नियमित गति से हरकत करना; स्पंदित होना, फड़कना, धड़कना

**pulverize** (*also* **-ise**) /ˈpʌlvəraɪz ˈपलवराइज़्/ *verb* [T] (*formal*) to crush sth into a fine powder किसी वस्तु को कूट कर उसका महीन चूरा बना देना, किसी वस्तु को चूर-चूर कर देना; संपेषित करना *pulverized bones*

**puma** /ˈpjuːmə ˈप्यूमा/ (*AmE* **cougar** or **mountain lion**) *noun* [C] a large American wild animal of the cat family, with yellowish-brown or greyish fur लाल-भूरे या धूसर राख जैसे रंग के बालों वाला अमेरिकी बिलाव

**pumice** /ˈpʌmɪs ˈपमिस्/ (*also* **pumice stone**) *noun* [U] a type of grey stone that is very light in weight. It is used as a powder for cleaning and polishing, and in larger pieces for rubbing on the skin to make it softer बहुत हलका धूसर या मटमैले रंग का पत्थर जो चूरे के रूप में सफ़ाई और पालिश करने तथा बड़े टुकड़ों के रूप में त्वचा को कोमल बनाने के लिए उस पर रगड़ने के काम आता है; झाँवा, झामक

**pump**[1] /pʌmp पम्प्/ *verb* **1** [T] to force a gas or liquid to go in a particular direction दिशा-विशेष में गैस या द्रव को धकेलना; पंप करना *Your heart pumps blood around your body.* **2** [I] (used about a liquid) to flow in a particular direction as if forced by a pump (द्रव का) पंप के दबाव से दिशा-विशेष की ओर बहना *Blood was pumping out of the wound.* **3** [I, T] to be moved or to move sth very quickly up and down or in and out किसी वस्तु का तेज़ी से ऊपर-नीचे या अंदर-बाहर हिलना या हिलाना *He pumped his arms up and down to keep warm.*

PHR V **pump sth into sth/sb** to put a lot of sth into sth/sb व्यक्ति या वस्तु को किसी चीज़ से भर देना या में कुछ भर देना *He pumped all his savings into the business.*

**pump sth up** to fill sth with air, for example by using a pump पंप आदि से किसी में हवा भरना *to pump up a car tyre*

**pump**[2] /pʌmp पम्प्/ *noun* [C] **1** a machine that is used for forcing a gas or liquid in a particular direction गैस या द्रव पदार्थ को दिशा विशेष में धकेलने, बलपूर्वक निकालने या भरने की मशीन; पंप *Have you got a bicycle pump?* ○ *a petrol pump* ⇨ **bicycle** पर चित्र देखिए। **2** [*usually pl.*] a flat woman's shoe with no fastening स्त्रियों के बिना फ़ीते के जूते *ballet pumps*

**pump-action** *adj.* (used about a machine or device) that you operate using a pumping action of your hand or arm हाथ या बाँह से पंप-क्रिया द्वारा संचालित (यंत्र या उपकरण) *a pump-action spray/shotgun*

**pumpkin** /ˈpʌmpkɪn ˈपम्पकिन्/ *noun* [C, U] a very large round fruit with thick orange-coloured skin that is cooked and eaten as a vegetable कद्दू, सीताफल ⇨ **vegetable** पर चित्र देखिए।

**pun** /pʌn पन्/ *noun* [C] an amusing use of a word that can have two meanings or of different words that sound the same दो अर्थों वाले या एक-समान उच्चारण परंतु भिन्न अर्थों वाले शब्दों का विनोदी प्रयोग; श्लेष (अलंकार)

**punch**[1] /pʌntʃ पन्च्/ *verb* [T] **1 punch sb (in/on sth)** to hit sb/sth hard with your closed hand (**fist**) किसी को मुक्का या घूँसा मारना *to punch sb on the nose* ○ *He punched the air when he heard the good news.* **2** to make a hole in sth with a special tool (**a punch**) पंच मशीन से किसी में छेद करना *He punched a hole in the ticket.*

**punch**[2] /pʌntʃ पन्च्/ *noun* **1** [C] a hard hit with your closed hand (**fist**) घूँसा, ज़ोरदार मुक्का **2** [C] a machine or tool that you use for making holes in sth छेद करने की मशीन; पंच, छेदक, छेदन यंत्र *a ticket punch* ○ *a hole punch* **3** [U] a drink made from wine, fruit juice and sugar मदिरा, फलों के रस और चीनी के मिश्रण से बना एक पेय पदार्थ

IDM **pull your punches** ⇨ **pull**[1] देखिए।

**punchline** /ˈpʌntʃlaɪn ˈपन्चलाइन्/ *noun* [C] the last and most important words of a joke or story किसी विनोद (वार्ता) या कहानी की अंतिम और सबसे महत्त्वपूर्ण पंक्ति, अंतिम पंक्ति, पंच लाइन

**punch-up** *noun* [C] (*BrE informal*) a fight in which people hit each other मुक्का-युद्ध (मुक्कों से लड़ना), मुक्केबाज़ी

**punctual** /ˈpʌŋktʃuəl ˈपङ्क्चुअल्/ *adj.* doing sth or happening at the right time; not late सही समय पर कुछ करने या होने वाला, वक्त का पाबंद, समय पालक; विलंब न करने वाला, समयनिष्ठ *It is important to be punctual for your classes.* NOTE इस संदर्भ में रेलगाड़ी, बस आदि के लिए **on time** का प्रयोग होता है, punctual का नहीं। ▶ **punctuality** /ˌpʌŋktʃuˈæləti

ˌपङ्क्चुˈऐलटि / *noun* [U] वक्त की पाबंदी, समय-पालन *Japanese trains are famous for their punctuality.* ▸ **punctually** *adv.* ठीक समय पर

**punctuate** /ˈpʌŋktʃueɪt ˈपङ्क्चुएट्/ *verb* **1** [T] **punctuate sth (with sth)** to interrupt sth many times बीच-बीच में बाधित करना *Her speech was punctuated with bursts of applause.* **2** [I, T] to divide writing into sentences and phrases by adding full stops, question marks, etc. विराम-चिह्न लगाना

**punctuation** /ˌpʌŋktʃuˈeɪʃn ˌपङ्क्चुˈएश्न्/ *noun* [U] the marks used for dividing writing into sentences and phrases लिखने में प्रयुक्त विराम आदि चिह्न (जिनसे वाक्य और वाक्यांश अलग दिखाई पड़ते हैं) ***Punctuation marks*** *include full stops, commas and question marks.*

**puncture** /ˈpʌŋktʃə(r) ˈपङ्क्च(र्)/ *noun* [C] a small hole made by a sharp point, especially in a bicycle or car tyre किसी नुकीली चीज़ से किया गया छोटा छेद (विशेषतः साइकिल या कार के टायर में); पंचर ▸ **puncture** *verb* [I, T] छेद होना या करना

**pungent** /ˈpʌndʒənt ˈपन्जन्ट्/ *adj.* (used about a smell) very strong (गंध) बहुत तीखी

**punish** /ˈpʌnɪʃ ˈपनिश्/ *verb* [T] **punish sb (for sth/for doing sth)** to make sb suffer because he/she has done sth bad or wrong (ग़लती या बुरे काम के लिए) किसी को दंड देना *The children were severely punished for telling lies.*

**punishable** /ˈpʌnɪʃəbl ˈपनिशबल्/ *adj.* **punishable (by sth)** (used about a crime, etc.) that you can be punished for doing (अपराध) आदि दंडित करने योग्य, दंडनीय *a punishable offence* ○ *In some countries drug smuggling is punishable by death.*

**punishing** /ˈpʌnɪʃɪŋ ˈपनिशिङ्/ *adj.* that makes you very tired or weak थकाने या पस्त कर देने वाला *The Prime Minister had a punishing schedule, visiting five countries in five days.*

**punishment** /ˈpʌnɪʃmənt ˈपनिश्मन्ट्/ *noun* [C, U] the action or way of punishing sb किसी को दंड देने का कार्य या ढंग; दंड, सज़ा *He was excluded from school for a week as a punishment.* ○ ***capital punishment***

**punitive** /ˈpjuːnətɪv ˈप्यूनटिव्/ *adj.* (*formal*) **1** intended as a punishment दंडात्मक; दंड के रूप में प्रयुक्त *to take punitive measures against sb* **2** very harsh and that people find difficult to pay बहुत कठोर, जिसे झेलना कठिन हो *punitive taxation*

**punk** /pʌŋk पङ्क्/ *noun* **1** [U] a type of loud music that was popular in Britain in the late 1970s and early 1980s. Punk deliberately tried to offend people with traditional views and behaviour एक प्रकार का हो हल्ले वाला संगीत जो ब्रिटेन में 1970 के अंतिम वर्षों ओर 1980 के अरंभिक वर्षों के दौरान लोकप्रिय हुआ था। इसमें जानबूझकर परंपरागत मूल्यों की अवमानना की जाती थी; पंक संगीत **2** [C] a person who likes punk music and often has brightly coloured hair and unusual clothes पंक संगीत का प्रेमी (गहरे रंगे हुए बाल और अजीबोगरीब पोशाक में)

**punt** /pʌnt पन्ट्/ *noun* [C] a long narrow boat with a flat bottom and square ends which is moved by pushing a long pole against the bottom of a river चौरस पेंदे और चौकोर किनारों वाली लंबी तंग नाव; डोंगी। इसे लंबे डंडे को नदी के तल से टिकाते हुए चलाया जाता है ▸ **punt** *verb* [I, T] डोंगी चलाना या खेना *to go punting*

**puny** /ˈpjuːni ˈप्यूनि/ *adj.* very small and weak बहुत छोटा और दुर्बल

**pup** /pʌp पप्/ *noun* [C] **1** = **puppy 2** the young of some animals, for example **seals** सील मछली आदि का बच्चा

**pupa** /ˈpjuːpə ˈप्यूपा/ *noun* [C] (*pl.* **pupae** /-piː -पी/) an insect in the stage of development before it becomes an adult insect विकसित होता हुआ कीट, पूर्ण विकास से पहले की अवस्था में; प्यूपा, कोषित ➪ **larva** देखिए।

> **NOTE** तितली या पतंगे के प्यूपा को **chrysalis** कहते हैं।

**pupil** /ˈpjuːpl ˈप्यूपल्/ *noun* [C] **1** a child in school स्कूल में पढ़ने वाला छात्र *There are 28 pupils in my class.* **2** a person who is taught artistic, musical, etc. skills by an expert विशेषज्ञ द्वारा कला-कौशल का प्रशिक्षण ले रहा छात्र *He was a pupil of Ravi Shankar.* ➪ **student** देखिए। **3** the round black hole in the middle of your eye आँखों की पुतली (गोल काला बिंदु) ➪ **eye** पर चित्र देखिए।

**puppet** /ˈpʌpɪt ˈपपिट्/ *noun* [C] **1** a model of a person or an animal that you can move by pulling the strings which are tied to it or by putting your hand inside it and moving your fingers कठपुतली (मानव या पशु के आकार में) **2** a person or an organization that is controlled by sb else दूसरों की इच्छानुसार काम करने वाला व्यक्ति या संस्था *The occupying forces set up a puppet government.*

**puppy** /ˈpʌpi ˈपपि/ *noun* [C] (*pl.* **puppies**) (*also* **pup**) a young dog पिल्ला (कुत्ते का छोटा बच्चा)

**purchase** /ˈpɜːtʃəs ˈपचस्/ *noun* (*formal*) **1** [U] the action of buying sth कुछ ख़रीदने की क्रिया; ख़रीदारी, क्रय *to take out a loan for the purchase of a car* **2** [C] something that you buy ख़रीदी गई वस्तु *These shoes were a poor purchase—they're falling apart already.* ○ *to make a purchase* ▶ **purchase** *verb* [T] ख़रीदना, क्रय करना *Many employees have the opportunity to purchase shares in the company they work for.*

**purchaser** /ˈpɜːtʃəsə(r) ˈपचस(र्)/ *noun* [C] (*formal*) a person who buys sth ख़रीदार, क्रेता *The purchaser of the house agrees to pay a deposit of 10 per cent.* ➪ **vendor** देखिए।

**pure** /pjʊə(r) प्युअ(र्)/ *adj.* **1** not mixed with anything else शुद्ध (बिना मिलावट का) *pure orange juice/silk/alcohol* **2** clean and not containing any harmful substances स्वच्छ और हानिकर पदार्थों से रहित *pure air/water* ✪ विलोम **impure** **3** (*only before a noun*) complete and total पूर्ण और समग्र *We met by pure chance.* **4** (used about a sound, colour or light) very clear; perfect (ध्वनि, रंग या प्रकाश) बहुत साफ़; परिपूर्ण *She was dressed in pure white.* **5** (*only before a noun*) (used about an area of learning) concerned only with increasing your knowledge rather than having practical uses (शिक्षा का कोई क्षेत्र) सिद्धांत प्रधान (न कि व्यावहारिक उपयोग से संबंधित) *pure mathematics* ✪ विलोम **applied** **6** not doing or knowing anything evil or anything that is connected with sex पवित्र, निष्पाप, शुद्ध *a young girl still pure in mind and body* ✪ विलोम **impure**

**purée** /ˈpjʊəreɪ ˈप्युअरे/ *noun* [C, U] a food that you make by cooking a fruit or vegetable and then pressing and mixing it until it is smooth and liquid गाढ़े द्रव के रूप में तैयार फल या सब्ज़ियों का खाद्य पदार्थ *apple/tomato purée*

**purely** /ˈpjʊəli ˈप्युअलि/ *adv.* only or completely केवल, पूर्ण रूप से *It's not purely a question of money.*

**purge** /pɜːdʒ पज्/ *verb* [T] **purge sth (of sb); purge sb (from sth)** to remove people that you do not want from a political party or other organization राजनीतिक दल, संस्था आदि से अनचाहे वर्ग के सदस्यों को हटाना; शुद्धिकरण करना ▶ **purge** *noun* [C] शुद्धीकरण, सफ़ाई *The General carried out a purge of his political enemies.*

**puri** (*also* **poori**) *noun* [C] (in India) a small round unleavened wheat bread that is deep fried until it puffs up and turns brown. It is usually served with vegetables or chickpeas पूरी

**purify** /ˈpjʊərɪfaɪ ˈप्युअरिफ़ाइ/ *verb* [T] (*pres. part.* **purifying;** *3rd person sing. pres.* **purifies;** *pt, pp* **purified**) to remove dirty or harmful substances from sth किसी वस्तु को शुद्ध या साफ़ करना; अशुद्ध या हानिकर तत्वों को दूर करना, शोधन करना *purified water*

**puritan** /ˈpjʊərɪtən ˈप्युअरिटन्/ *noun* [C] a person who has high moral standards and who thinks that it is wrong to enjoy yourself नैतिकता पर बहुत अधिक बल देने वाला व्यक्ति जो भोग-विलास को ग़लत मानता है; शुद्धाचारवादी ▶ **puritan** (*also* **puritanical** /ˌpjʊərɪˈtænɪkl ˌप्युअरिˈटैनिक्ल्/) *adj.* निस्स्वार्थ नैतिकतापरक, शुद्धिवादी *a puritan attitude to life*

**purity** /ˈpjʊərəti ˈप्युअरटि/ *noun* [U] the state of being pure शुद्धता, पवित्रता *to test the purity of the air* ➪ **impurity** देखिए।

**purl** /pɜːl पल्/ *noun* [U] a simple stitch used in knitting बुनाई में सादा फंदा

**purple** /ˈpɜːpl ˈपप्ल्/ *adj.*, *noun* [U] (of) a reddish-blue colour बैंगनी (रंग का), नील-लोहित, जामुनी *His face was purple with rage.*

**purport** /pəˈpɔːt पˈपॉट्/ *verb* [I] (*formal*) to give the impression of being sth or of having done sth, when this may not be true कोई विशेष अभिप्राय होने या उत्पन्न करने का आभास देना (भले ही वह सच न हो) *The book does not purport to be a true history of the period.*

**purpose** /ˈpɜːpəs ˈपपस्/ *noun* **1** [C] the aim or intention of sth (किसी का) प्रयोजन, उद्देश्य, आशय या इरादा *The main purpose of this meeting is to decide what we should do next.* ○ *You may only use the telephone for business purposes.* **2 purposes** [*pl.*] what is needed in a particular situation स्थिति-विशेष की अपेक्षाएँ, आवश्यकताएँ ***For the purposes of*** *this demonstration, I will use model cars.* **3** [U] a meaning or reason that is important to you व्यक्ति-विशेष के अनुसार सार्थक बात (अर्थ या तर्क) *A good leader inspires people with a* ***sense of purpose.*** **4** [U] the ability to plan sth and work hard to achieve it योजना बनाने और तदनुसार कार्य करने का सामर्थ्य *I was impressed by his* ***strength of purpose.***

IDM **to/for all intents and purposes** ➪ **intent²** देखिए।

**on purpose** not by accident; with a particular intention संयोग से नहीं; विशेष इरादे से, जान-बूझकर, इरादतन *'You've torn a page out of my book!' 'I'm sorry, I didn't do it on purpose.'* ✪ पर्याय **deliberately**

**purposeful** /ˈpɜːpəsfl ˈपपस्फ़ल्/ *adj.* having a definite aim or plan विशेष प्रयोजन या योजना वाला, सोद्देश्य, कृतसंकल्प *Gautam strode off down the street looking purposeful.* ▶ **purposefully** /ˈpɜːpəsfli ˈपपस्फ़लि/ *adv.* सप्रयोजन, संकल्प के साथ

**purposely** /ˈpɜːpəsli ˈपपस्लि/ *adv.* with a particular intention विशेष इरादे से *I purposely waited till everyone had gone so that I could speak to you in private.* ✪ पर्याय **deliberately**

**purr** /pɜː(r) प(र्)/ *verb* [I] (used about a cat) to make a continuous low sound that shows pleasure (बिल्ली का) घुरघुराना (आनंद प्रकट करने के लिए) ➪ **miaow** देखिए।

**purse¹** /pɜːs पस्/ *noun* [C] **1** a small bag made of leather, etc., for carrying coins and often also paper money, used especially by women पर्स, चमड़े आदि की छोटी थैली, बटुआ (विशेषतः महिलाओं द्वारा प्रयुक्त) ➪ **wallet** देखिए। **2** (*AmE*) = **handbag**

**purse²** /pɜːs पस्/ *verb*

IDM **purse your lips** to press your lips together to show that you do not like sth (नापसंदी प्रकट करने के लिए) होंठ बिचकाना

**purser** /ˈpɜːsə(r) ˈपस(र्)/ *noun* [C] the person on a ship who looks after the accounts and deals with passengers' problems जहाज़ पर हिसाब-किताब रखने और यात्रियों की देखभाल करने वाला अधिकारी; पर्सर, पोतनीस

**pursue** /pəˈsjuː पˈस्यू/ *verb* [T] (*formal*) **1** to follow sb/sth in order to catch him/her/it किसी का पीछा करना (उसे पकड़ने के लिए) *The robber ran off pursued by two policemen.* NOTE **Chase** की अपेक्षा **pursue** अधिक औपचारिक शब्द है। **2** to try to achieve sth or to continue to do sth over a period of time कुछ पाने की कोशिश करना या किसी काम में लगे रहना (अरसे तक) *to pursue a career in banking* ○ *She didn't seem to want to pursue the discussion so I changed the subject.*

**pursuer** /pəˈsjuːə(r) पˈस्यूअ(र्)/ *noun* [C] a person who is following and trying to catch sb/sth किसी का पीछा करने वाला व्यक्ति

**pursuit** /pəˈsjuːt पˈस्यूट्/ *noun* **1** [U] the action of trying to achieve or get sth कुछ पाने की कोशिश *the pursuit of pleasure* **2** [C] an activity that you do either for work or for pleasure व्यवसाय, धंधा या मनोविनोद संबंधी कार्यकलाप *outdoor/leisure pursuits*

IDM **in hot pursuit** ➪ **hot¹** देखिए।

**in pursuit (of sb/sth)** trying to catch or get sb/sth (किसी का) पीछा करने या (कुछ) पाने की कोशिश में *He neglected his family in pursuit of his own personal ambitions.*

**pus** /pʌs पस्/ *noun* [U] a thick yellowish liquid that may form in a part of your body that has been hurt पस, मवाद, पीप

**push¹** /pʊʃ पुश्/ *verb* **1** [I, T] to use force to move sb/sth forward or away from you किसी को आगे की ओर या अपने से दूर धकेलना, ठेलना *She pushed him into the water.* ○ *to push a pram* **2** [I, T] to move forward by pushing sb/sth दूसरे को धकेल कर आगे की ओर बढ़ना *Jatin pushed his way through the crowd.* ○ *People were **pushing and shoving** to try to get to the front* **3** [I, T] to press a switch, button, etc., for example in order to start a machine (किसी मशीन को चालू करने आदि के लिए) कोई स्विच, बटन आदि दबाना *Push the red button if you want the bus to stop.* **4** [T] **push sb (to do sth /into doing sth); push sb (for sth)** to try to make sb do sth that he/she does not want to do किसी को उसका अनचाहा काम करने के लिए मजबूर करना *My friend pushed me into entering the competition.* ○ *She will not work hard unless you push her.* **5** [T] (*informal*) to try to make sth seem attractive, for example so that people will buy it किसी वस्तु को आकर्षक बनाने का प्रयत्न करना (ताकि लोग उसे ख़रीदें) *They are launching a major publicity campaign to push their new product.*

IDM **be hard pressed/pushed/put to do sth** ➪ **hard²** देखिए।

**be pushed for sth** (*informal*) to not have enough of sth किसी वस्तु की कमी अनुभव करना *Hurry up. We're really **pushed for time**.*

PHR V **push sb about/around** to give orders to sb in a rude and unpleasant way रूखे और अप्रिय ढंग से किसी को आदेश देना *Don't let your boss push you around.*

**push ahead/forward (with sth)** to continue with sth किसी काम को जारी रखना

**push for sth** to try hard to get sth कुछ पाने की जी तोड़ कोशिश करना *Jai is pushing for a pay rise.*

**push in** to join a line of people waiting for sth by standing in front of others who were there before you प्रतीक्षारत लोगों की कतार के बीच में घुस जाना (कई लोगों को धकेलते हुए)

**push on** to continue a journey यात्रा जारी रखना *Although it was getting dark, we decided to push on.*

**push sb/sth over** to make sb/sth fall down by pushing him/her/it किसी को धकेलकर गिरा देना

**push²** /pʊʃ पुश्/ *noun* [C] an act of pushing धक्का, ठेल *Can you help me **give** the car **a push** to get it started?* ○ *The car windows opened at the push of a button.*

**IDM** **at a push** (*informal*) if it is really necessary (but only with difficulty) यदि अत्यावश्यक हो तो (तो भी मुश्किल से) *We can get ten people round the table at a push.*

**give sb the push** to tell sb you no longer want him/her in a relationship, or in a job किसी से संबंध समाप्त कर देना या नौकरी से निकाल देना

**push button** *adj.* (*only before a noun*) (used about a machine, etc.) that you work by pressing a button (मशीन आदि) बटन दबाने से चलने वाली, दाब-बटन, पुश-बटन *a radio with push-button controls*

**pushchair** /ˈpʊʃtʃeə(r) ˈपुशचेअ(र्)/ (*BrE* **buggy**) *noun* [C] a chair on wheels that you use for pushing a young child in पहिएदार बच्चागाड़ी

**pusher** /ˈpʊʃə(r) ˈपुश(र्)/ *noun* [C] a person who sells illegal drugs ग़ैर-क़ानूनी नशीले पदार्थ बेचने वाला

**pushover** /ˈpʊʃəʊvə(r) ˈपुशओव़(र्)/ *noun* [C] (*informal*) **1** something that is easy to do or win सरल काम या सरलता से प्राप्य वस्तु **2** a person who is easy to persuade to do sth व्यक्ति जिसे मनाना आसान हो

**push-up** (*AmE*) = **press-up**

**pushy** /ˈpʊʃi ˈपुशि/ *adj.* (*informal*) (used about a person) trying hard to get what you want, in a way that seems rude (व्यक्ति) अभीष्ट वस्तु पाने के लिए ढीठ होकर प्रयत्न करने वाला

**puss** /pʊs पुस्/ *noun* [C] used when you are speaking to or calling a cat बिल्ली से बात करने या उसे पुकारने के लिए प्रयुक्त (शब्द)

**pussy** /ˈpʊsi ˈपुसि/ *noun* [C] (*informal*) a cat बिल्ली

**put** /pʊt पुट्/ *verb* [T] (*pres. part.* **putting;** *pt, pp* **put**) **1** to move sb/sth into a particular place or position किसी को किसी स्थान या स्थिति में रखना या डालना *She put the book on the table.* ○ *When do you put the children to bed?* **2** to fix sth to or in sth else किसी में या पर कुछ लगाना *Can you put* (= sew) *a button on this shirt?* ○ *We're going to put a picture on this wall.* **3** to write sth कुछ लिखना *Lunch 12.30 p.m. on Friday? I'll put it in my diary.* ○ *What did you put for question number 2?* **4 put sb/sth in/into sth** to bring sb/sth into the state or condition mentioned किसी को निर्दिष्ट स्थिति या दशा में लाना *This sort of weather always puts me in a bad mood.* ○ *I was **put in charge** of the project.* ○ *It was time to **put** our ideas **into practice**.* **5** to make sb/sth feel sth or be affected by sth किसी को कुछ अनुभव कराना या किसी से प्रभावित होना ***put pressure on*** ○ ***put the blame on*** ○ *to **put a stop to** cheating in tests.* **6** to give or fix a particular value or importance to sb/sth किसी को विषेश महत्त्व देना या उसका विशेष मूल्य निर्धारित करना *We'll have to **put a limit on** how much we spend.* **7** to say or express sth कुछ कहना या व्यक्त करना *To **put it another way**, you're sacked.* ○ ***Put simply**, he just wasn't good enough.*

**IDM** **put it to sb that** (*formal*) to suggest to sb that sth is true (किसी के सामने) किसी बात को सच बताना *I put it to you that this man is innocent.*

**put together** (*used after a noun or nouns*) (referring to a group of people or things) combined; in total (व्यक्ति या वस्तु का निर्देश करने वाले संज्ञापद या संज्ञापदों के बाद प्रयुक्त) को मिलाकर; कुल मिलाकर, कुल योग में *You got more presents than the rest of the family put together.*

> **NOTE** **Put** से बनने वाले अन्य मुहावरों के लिए संबधित संज्ञाओं, विशेषणों आदि की प्रविष्टियाँ देखिए। उदाहरण के लिए **put an end to sth** की प्रविष्टि **end** में मिलेगी।

**PHR V** **put sth/yourself across/over** to say what you want to say clearly, so that people can understand it अपनी बात स्पष्ट रूप से कहना (ताकि लोग उसे समझ सकें) *He didn't put his ideas across very well at the meeting.*

**put sth aside** **1** to save sth, especially money, to use later भविष्य के लिए कुछ (विशेषतः धन) बचाकर रखना **2** to ignore or forget sth किसी बात की उपेक्षा करना या उसे भूल जाना *We agreed to put aside our differences and work together.*

**put sb away** (*informal*) to send sb to prison किसी को जेल में डालना

**put sth away** **1** to put sth where you usually keep it because you have finished using it (काम हो जाने के बाद) वस्तुओं को सँभाल लेना *Put the tools away if you've finished with them.* **2** to save money to spend later भविष्य के लिए पैसे की बचत करना

**put sth back** **1** to return sth to its place किसी वस्तु को वापस उसकी जगह पर रखना *to put books back on the shelf* **2** to move sth to a later time किसी आयोजन आदि को स्थगित करना *The meeting's been put back until next week.* ✪ विलोम **bring sth forward** **3** to change the time shown on a clock to an earlier time घड़ी का समय पीछे करना *We have to put the clocks back tonight.* ✪ विलोम **put sth forward**

**put sb/sth before/above sb/sth** to treat sb/sth as more important than sb/sth else किसी व्यक्ति या वस्तु को दूसरे पर तरजीह देना *He puts his children before anything else.*

**put sth by** to save money to use later पैसा बचाना (बाद में ख़र्च करने के लिए) *Her grandparents had put some money by for her wedding.*
**put sb down** 1 (*informal*) to say things to make sb seem stupid or foolish किसी को नीचा दिखाना 2 to put a baby to bed बच्चे को सुलाना
**put sth down** 1 to stop holding sth and put it on the floor, a table, etc. किसी वस्तु को नीचे, मेज़ आदि पर रख देना *The policeman persuaded him to put the gun down.* 2 to write sth कुछ लिखना *I'll put that down in my diary.* 3 to pay part of the cost of sth कुल मूल्य का कुछ अंश देना *We put down a 10% deposit on a car.* 4 (used about a government, an army or the police) to stop sth by force (सरकार, सेना या पुलिस द्वारा) किसी स्थिति को बलपूर्वक दबा देना *to put down a rebellion* 5 to kill an animal because it is old, sick or dangerous पशु को मार देना (बूढ़ा, बीमार या ख़तरनाक होने के कारण) *The dog was put down after it attacked a child.*
**put sth down to sth** to believe that sth is caused by sth किसी को किसी बात का कारण बताना *I put his bad exam results down to laziness rather than a lack of ability.*
**put yourself/sb forward** to suggest that you or another person should be considered for a job, etc. नौकरी आदि के लिए अपना या किसी का नाम पेश करना *His name was put forward for the position of chairman.*
**put sth forward** 1 to change the time shown on a clock to a later time घड़ी का समय आगे करना *They put the clocks forward in spring.* ✪ विलोम **put sth back** 2 to suggest sth कोई सुझाव पेश करना *She put forward a plan to help the homeless.*
**put sth in** 1 to fix equipment or furniture in position so that it can be used किसी यंत्र या फर्नीचर को फिट करना (प्रयोग में लाने के लिए) *We're having a shower put in.* ✪ पर्याय **install** 2 to include a piece of information, etc. in sth that you write अपने लेख आदि में कोई जानकारी आदि शामिल करना 3 to ask for sth officially (औपचारिक रूप से) किसी वस्तु की माँग करना *to put in an invoice/request*
**put sth in; put sth into sth/into doing sth** to spend time, etc. on sth किसी काम में समय लगाना *She puts all her time and energy into her business.*
**put sb off (sb/sth/doing sth)** 1 to make sb not like sb/sth or not want to do sth किसी के मन में किसी बात या काम के लिए अरुचि पैदा कर देना *The accident put me off driving for a long time.* 2 to say to a person that you can no longer do what you had agreed किसी को टाल देना; पूर्वनिश्चित कार्यक्रम को स्थगित कर देना *They were coming to stay last weekend but I had to put them off at the last moment.* 3 to make sb unable to give his/her attention to sth किसी को किसी पर ध्यान केंद्रित न करने देना *Don't stare at me—you're putting me off!*
**put sth off** to turn or switch a light off बत्ती बुझाना *She put off the light and went to sleep.*
**put sth off; put off doing sth** to move sth to a later time; to delay doing sth किसी बात या काम को स्थगित करना; किसी काम में विलंब करना *She put off writing her essay until the last minute.*
**put sth on** 1 to dress yourself in sth कुछ ऊपर से पहन लेना या धारण करना *Put on your coat!* ○ *I'll have to put my glasses on.* 2 to cover an area of your skin with sth त्वचा पर कुछ लगाना या मलना *You'd better put some sunscreen on.* 3 to switch on a piece of electrical equipment किसी विद्युत उपकरण को चालू करना *It's too early to put the lights on yet.* 4 to make a tape, a CD, etc. begin to play टेप, सीडी आदि लगाना *Let's put some music on.* 5 to become heavier, especially by the amount mentioned भार बढ़ा लेना (विशेषतः निर्दिष्ट मात्रा में) ***I put on weight** very easily.* ✪ विलोम **lose** 6 to organize or prepare sth for people to see or use लोगों के लिए कुछ आयोजित या तैयार करना (कि वे उसे देखें या प्रयोग करें) *The school is putting on 'Hamlet'.* ○ *They put on extra trains in the summer.* 7 to pretend to be feeling sth; to pretend to have sth कुछ महसूस होने का बहाना बनाना; अपने पास कुछ होने या रखने का दिखावा करना *He's not angry with you really—he's just putting it on.*
**put sth on sth** 1 to add an amount of money, etc. to the cost or value of sth किसी वस्तु की लागत या क़ीमत को बढ़ाना *The government want to put more tax on the price of a packet of cigarettes.* 2 to bet money on sth किसी पर (पैसे का) दाँव लगाना *He put all his money on a horse.* ✪ पर्याय **bet**
**put sb out** 1 to give sb trouble or extra work किसी को तकलीफ़ पहुँचाना या उसका काम बढ़ा देना *He put his hosts out by arriving very late.* 2 to make sb upset or angry किसी को परेशान या क्रोधित कर देना *I was quite put out by their selfish behaviour.*
**put sth out** 1 to make sth stop burning किसी जलती हुई वस्तु को बुझा देना *to put out a fire* ✪ पर्याय **extinguish** 2 to switch off a piece of electrical equipment किसी विद्युत उपकरण (पंखा आदि) को बंद कर देना *They put out the lights and locked the door.* 3 to take sth out of your house and leave it किसी को घर से बाहर कर उससे पीछा छुड़ाना *to put the rubbish out* 4 to give or tell the public sth, often on the television or radio or in newspapers जनता

को कोई सूचना देना (प्रायः टीवी, रेडियो, समाचार-पत्र के ज़रिए) *The police put out a warning about the escaped prisoner.*

**put yourself out** (*informal*) to do sth for sb, even though it brings you trouble or extra work किसी की कुछ सहायता करना (कुछ अतिरिक्त कष्ट उठाकर या परिश्रम करके) *'I'll give you a lift home.' 'I don't want you to put yourself out. I'll take a taxi.'*

**put sth/yourself over** ➪ **put sth/yourself across/ over**

**put sb through sth** to make sb experience sth unpleasant किसी को मुसीबत में डालना

**put sb/sth through** to make a telephone connection that allows sb to speak to sb किसी को फ़ोन लगाना, फ़ोन का नंबर मिलाना *Could you put me through to Rekha, please?*

**put sth to sb** to suggest sth to sb; to ask sb sth किसी को कोई सुझाव देना; किसी से कुछ पूछना *I put the question to her.*

**put sth together** to build or repair sth by joining its parts together पुरज़े जोड़कर कुछ बनाना या मरम्मत करना *The furniture comes with instructions on how to put it together.*

**put sb up** to give sb food and a place to stay किसी के ठहरने, खान-पान आदि की व्यवस्था करना *She had missed the last train home, so I offered to put her up for the night.*

**put sth up** **1** to lift or hold sth up किसी वस्तु को ऊपर उठाना या सँभालना *Put your hand up if you know the answer.* **2** to build sth किसी वस्तु का निर्माण करना *to put up a fence/tent* **3** to fix sth to a wall, etc. so that everyone can see it प्रदर्शन के लिए किसी वस्तु को दीवार आदि पर लगाना *to put up a notice* **4** to increase sth किसी वस्तु में बढ़ोतरी करना *Some shops put up their prices just before Diwali.*

**put up sth** to try to stop sb attacking you आक्रमण का सामना करना *The old lady put up a struggle against her attacker.*

**put up with sb/sth** to suffer sb/sth unpleasant and not complain about it परेशानी उठाना पर शिकायत न करना *I don't know how they put up with this noise.*

**putrid** /ˈpjuːtrɪd ˈप्यूट्रिड्/ *adj.* **1** (used about dead animals and plants) smelling bad after being dead for some time (मृत पशु और पौधे) बदबूदार, दुर्गंधपूर्ण **2** (*informal*) very unpleasant बहुत अप्रिय *The food there was putrid.*

**putt** /pʌt पट्/ *verb* [I, T] (used in golf) to hit the ball gently when it is near the hole (गोल्फ़ में) गेंद को हलके से मारना (गड्ढा पास होने पर)

**putter** /ˈpʌtə(r) ˈपट(र्)/ (*AmE*) = **potter**[1]

**putty** /ˈpʌti ˈपटि/ *noun* [U] a soft substance that is used for fixing glass into windows that becomes hard when dry खिड़कियों में शीशा लगाने के लिए प्रयुक्त एक नरम चीज़ जो सूखकर कड़ी हो जाती है; पुटीन

**puzzle[1]** /ˈpʌzl ˈपज़्ल्/ *noun* [C] **1** [*usually sing.*] something that is difficult to understand or explain; a mystery जिसे समझना या समझाना कठिन हो; गूढ़ बात, रहस्य *The reasons for his actions have remained a puzzle to historians.* **2** a game or toy that makes you think a lot खेल या खिलौना जिसके लिए बहुत सोचना पड़े; पहेली *a crossword/jigsaw puzzle* ○ *I like to* ***do puzzles****.*

**puzzle[2]** /ˈpʌzl ˈपज़्ल्/ *verb* **1** [T] to make sb feel confused because he/she does not understand sth किसी को उलझन में डाल देना (बात को समझ न पाने के कारण) *Her strange illness puzzled all the experts.* **2** [I] **puzzle over sth** to think hard about sth in order to understand or explain it (किसी के विषय में) गंभीर चिंतन करना (समझने या समझाने के लिए) *to puzzle over a mathematical problem*

**PHR V** **puzzle sth out** to find the answer to sth by thinking hard गंभीर चिंतन द्वारा समस्या का समाधान ढूँढ़ लेना

**puzzled** /ˈpʌzld ˈपज़्ल्ड्/ *adj.* not able to understand or explain sth (किसी बात को) समझने या समझाने में असमर्थ, उलझन-ग्रस्त *a puzzled expression*

**PVC** /ˌpiː viː ˈsiː ˌपी व़ी ˈसी/ *noun* [U] a strong plastic material used to make clothing, pipes, floor coverings, etc. प्लास्टिक से बनी मज़बूत पदार्थ जो कपड़े, पाइप आदि बनाने में प्रयुक्त होता है; पी वी सी

**pygmy[1]** (*also* **pigmy**) /ˈpɪgmi ˈपिग्मि/ *noun* [C] (*pl.* **pygmies; pigmies**) **1 Pygmy** a member of a race of very small people living in parts of Africa and SE Asia अफ़्रीक़ा और दक्षिण-पूर्व एशिया की बौनी मानव जाति का सदस्य; पिग्मी **2** a very small person or thing or one that is weak in some way बौना या किसी रूप में दुर्बल व्यक्ति या वस्तु

**pygmy[2]** (*also* **pigmy**) /ˈpɪgmi ˈपिग्मि/ *adj.* (*only before a noun*) used to describe a plant or **species** of animal that is much smaller than other similar kinds बौनी प्रजाति का (पौधा या पशु) *a pygmy shrew*

**pyjamas** (*AmE* **pajamas**) /pəˈdʒɑːməz पˈजामज़्/ *noun* [*pl.*] loose trousers and a loose jacket or **T-shirt** that you wear in bed पायजामा, पाजामा (रात को सोते समय पहनने की ढीली पोशाक) **NOTE** अन्य संज्ञा से पहले आने पर **pyjama** (**'s'** के बिना), प्रयुक्त किया जाएगा *pyjama trousers*

**pylon** /ˈpaɪlən ˈपाइलन्/ *noun* [C] a tall metal tower that supports heavy electrical wires ऊँचा धातु-निर्मित तोरणनुमा खंभा जिस पर विद्युत-तार डाले जाते हैं

**pyramid** /ˈpɪrəmɪd ˈपिरमिड्/ *noun* [C] a shape with a flat base and three or four sides in the shape of triangles चौरस आधार और त्रिभुजनुमा तीन या चार पार्श्वों वाली आकृति; पिरामिड ➪ **solid** पर चित्र देखिए। ▶ **pyramidal** /ˈpɪrəmɪdl ˈपिरमिड्ल्/ *adj.* पिरामिड-विषयक

**pyre** /ˈpaɪə(r) ˈपाइअ(र्)/ *noun* [C] a large pile of wood on which a dead body is placed and burned as a part of a funeral ceremony चिता; लकड़ियों का ढेर जिसपर शव जलाते हैं

**python** /ˈpaɪθən ˈपाइथन्/ *noun* [C] a large snake that kills animals by squeezing them very hard अजगर (साँप) जो पशुओं को बुरी तरह भींचकर मार डालता है

# Q q

**Q, q**[1] /kju: क्यू/ *noun* [C, U] (*pl.* **Q's; q's** /kju:z क्यूज़्/) the seventeenth letter of the English alphabet अंग्रेजी वर्णमाला का सत्रहवाँ अक्षर *'Queen' begins with a 'Q'.*

**Q**[2] *abbr.* question प्रश्न *Qs 1–5 are compulsory.*

**qt** *abbr.* quart(s) क्वार्ट्ज़

**quack**[1] /kwæk क्वैक्/ *noun* [C] the sound that a duck makes बत्तख़ की काँ-काँ ▶ **quack** *verb* [I] बतख़ का या बतख़ की तरह काँ-काँ करना

**quack**[2] /kwæk क्वैक्/ *noun* [C] (*informal, disapproving*) a person who pretends to have medical knowledge or skill and practices medicine without any formal training in the subject कठवैद; नीम हकीम या डॉक्टर होने का पाखंड करने वाला व्यक्ति

**quad** /kwɒd क्वॉड्/ **1** = **quadrangle** **2** (*informal*) = **quadruplet**

**quad-** /kwɒd क्वॉड्/ *prefix* (*used in nouns, adjectives, verbs and adverbs*) four; having four चार; चार वाला; चतु:- (चतुष्कोण) *quadruple*

**quadrangle** /ˈkwɒdræŋgl ˈक्वॉड्रैङ्ग्ल्/ (*also* **quad**) *noun* [C] a square open area with buildings round it in a school, college, etc. चतुष्कोणीय खुला स्थान जिसके चारों ओर अनेक भवन हों (प्रायः स्कूल, कॉलेज आदि में)

**quadrant** /ˈkwɒdrənt ˈक्वॉड्रन्ट्/ *noun* [C] **1** a quarter of a circle or of its **circumference** वृत्त का चौथाई भाग; चतुर्थांश ➪ **circle** पर चित्र देखिए। **2** an instrument for measuring angles, especially to check your position at sea or to look at stars कोण-मापी यंत्र (स्थिति जानने के लिए विशेषतः नौ-चालन या तारों की दशा देखने में प्रयुक्त)

**quadri-** /ˈkwɒdri ˈक्वॉड्रि/ *prefix* (*used in nouns, adjectives, verbs and adverbs*) four; having four चार; चार वाला, चतु:- (जैसे चतुर्भुज) *quadrilateral*

**quadrilateral** /ˌkwɒdrɪˈlætərəl ˌक्वॉड्रि ˈलैटरल्/ *noun* [C] a flat shape with four straight sides चतुर्भुज (चार सीधी भुजाओं वाली चौरस आकृति) ▶ **quadrilateral** *adj.* चतुर्भुजीय

**quadruped** /ˈkwɒdrʊped ˈक्वॉड्रुपेड्/ *noun* [C] any creature with four feet चौपाया जानवर; चतुष्पाद ➪ **biped** देखिए।

**quadruple** /kwɒˈdru:pl क्वॉˈड्रूप्ल्/ *verb* [I, T] to multiply or be multiplied by four चौगुना करना या चार से गुणा करना या गणित होना; चतुर्गण

**quadruplet** /ˈkwɒdrʊplət ˈक्वॉड्रुप्लट्/ (*also informal* **quad**) *noun* [C] one of four children or animals that are born to one mother at the same time एक ही माँ के एक ही समय में जन्मे चार बच्चों या पशु-शावकों में से एक

**quail** /kweɪl क्वेल्/ *noun* **1** [C] a small brown bird whose meat and eggs we eat बटेर (एक छोटी भूरी चिड़िया जिसका मांस और अंडा खाया जाता है) **2** [U] the meat of this bird बटेर का मांस

**quaint** /kweɪnt क्वेन्ट्/ *adj.* attractive or unusual because it seems to belong to the past आकर्षक या अनूठा (अतीत की वस्तु होने के कारण), अनोखा

**quake**[1] /kweɪk क्वेक्/ *verb* [I] (used about a person) to shake (व्यक्ति का) काँपना *to quake with fear*

**quake**[2] /kweɪk क्वेक्/ (*informal*) = **earthquake**

**qualification** /ˌkwɒlɪfɪˈkeɪʃn ˌक्वॉलिफ़िˈकेश्न्/ *noun* **1** [C] an exam that you have passed or a course of study that you have completed (पास की गई) परीक्षा या (पूरा किया गया) पाठ्यक्रम, योग्यता, अर्हता *to **have a** teaching/nursing **qualification*** ○ *She left school at 16 with no formal qualifications.* **2** [C] a skill or quality that you need to do a particular job विशेष कार्य के लिए अपेक्षित निपुणता या गुण; परिगुण *Is there a height qualification for the police force?* **3** [C, U] something that limits the meaning of a general statement or makes it weaker सामान्य अर्थ को सीमित या दुर्बल करने वाला सीमाकारक *I can recommend him for the job **without qualification.*** ○ *She accepted the proposal with only a few qualifications.* **4** the fact of doing what is necessary in order to be able to do a job, play in a competition, etc. नौकरी करने, खेल-प्रतियोगिता में भाग लेने आदि के लिए अपेक्षित अर्हता

**qualified** /ˈkwɒlɪfaɪd ˈक्वॉलिफ़ाइड्/ *adj.* **1 qualified (for sth/to do sth)** having passed an exam or having the knowledge, experience, etc. in order to be able to do sth किसी कार्य को करने के लिए प्रशिक्षण-प्राप्त या उस कार्य का जानकार, अनुभवी आदि; अर्हता-प्राप्त योग्य *a fully qualified doctor* **2** not complete; limited अधूरा जो पूर्ण न हो; सीमित *My boss gave only qualified approval to the plan.* ✪ विलोम **unqualified**

**qualify** /ˈkwɒlɪfaɪ ˈक्वॉलिफ़ाइ/ *verb* (*pres. part.* **qualifying;** *3rd person sing. pres.* **qualifies;** *pt, pp* **qualified**) **1** [I] **qualify (as sth)** to pass the examination that is necessary to do a particular job; to have the qualities that are necessary for sth किसी विशेष कार्य के लिए अपेक्षित परीक्षा प्राप्त करना; किसी बात के लिए उपयुक्त या पर्याप्त होना *It takes five years to qualify as a doctor.* ○ *A cup of coffee and a sandwich doesn't really qualify as a meal.* **2** [I, T] **qualify (sb) (for sth/to do sth)** to have or give sb the right to have or do sth किसी बात के लिए अधिकार पाना या किसी को किसी काम के लिए अधिकार देना *How many years must you work to qualify for a pension?* ○ *This exam will qualify me to teach music.* **3** [I] **qualify (for sth)** to win the right to enter a competition or continue to the next part किसी प्रतियोगिता में प्रवेश का पात्र होना या उसके अगले चरण में भाग लेने का अधिकारी होना *Our team has qualified for the final.* **4** [T] to limit the meaning of a general statement or make it weaker किसी सामान्य वक्तव्य के अर्थ को सीमित या हलका कर देना *To qualify what I said earlier, I did not mean that she can't do the work but that she will need help.*

**qualitative** /ˈkwɒlɪtətɪv ˈक्वॉलिटटिव़् / *adj.* (*formal*) connected with how good sth is, rather than with how much of it there is गुणात्मक या गुण-परक (न कि मात्रा परक) किसी वस्तु के गुणों या विशेषताओं से संबंधित (न कि उसके परिमाण से) *qualitative analysis/research*

**quality** /ˈkwɒləti ˈक्वॉलटि / *noun* (*pl.* **qualities**) **1** [U, *sing.*] how good or bad sth is (किसी वस्तु की) उत्कृष्टता का स्तर (कम या अधिक); गुणवत्ता *to be of good/poor/top quality* ○ ***quality of life*** **2** [U] a high standard or level उच्च स्तर, दर्जा या कोटि *Aim for quality rather than quantity in your writing.* **3** [C] something that is typical of a person or thing (व्यक्ति या वस्तु की/को) विशेषता, गुण *Vicky has all the qualities of a good manager.*

**qualm** /kwɑːm क्वाम् / *noun* [C, *usually pl.*] a feeling of doubt or worry that what you are doing may not be morally right (किसी बात के नैतिक औचित्य के विषय में) आशंका या चिंता *I don't* ***have*** *any* ***qualms about*** *asking them to lend us some money.*

**quandary** /ˈkwɒndəri ˈक्वॉन्डरि / *noun* (*pl.* **quandaries**) [C, *usually sing.*] a state of not being able to decide what to do; a difficult situation (किसी बात को लेकर) असमंजस, दुविधा; कठिन स्थिति *I'm* ***in a quandary****—should I ask her or not?*

**quantify** /ˈkwɒntɪfaɪ ˈक्वॉन्टिफ़ाइ / *verb* [T] (*pres. part.* **quantifying;** *3rd person sing. pres.* **quantifies;** *pt, pp* **quantified**) to describe or express sth as an amount or a number किसी स्थिति को परिमाण या संख्या की शब्दावली में व्यक्त करना; परिमाणित करना ▶ **quantifiable** /ˈkwɒntɪfaɪəbl ˈक्वॉन्टिफ़ाइअब्ल् / *adj.* परिमाणनात्मक ▶ **quantification** /ˌkwɒntɪfɪˈkeɪʃn ˌक्वॉन्टिफ़िˈकेश्न् / *noun* [U] परिमाणन

**quantitative** /ˈkwɒntɪtətɪv ˈक्वॉन्टिटटिव़् / *adj.* (*formal*) connected with the amount or number of sth rather than with how good it is परिमाणपरक न कि गुणवत्तापरक *quantitative analysis/research*

**quantity** /ˈkwɒntəti ˈक्वॉन्टटि / *noun* (*pl.* **quantities**) [C, U] **1** a number or an amount of sth किसी वस्तु का परिमाण (संख्या या मात्र); तादाद *Add a small quantity of salt.* ○ *It's cheaper to buy goods* ***in large quantities.*** **2** a large number or amount of sth (किसी वस्तु की) बड़ी संख्या या मात्रा; बडी तादाद *It's cheaper to buy goods* ***in quantity.***
IDM **an unknown quantity** ➪ **unknown**[1] देखिए।

**quantity surveyor** *noun* [C] (*BrE*) a person whose job is to calculate the quantity of materials needed for building sth, how much it will cost and how long it will take निर्माण-सामग्री के परिमाण आदि का सर्वेक्षण-कर्त्ता; परिमाण-सर्वेक्षक किसी वस्तु के निर्माण के लिए आवश्यक सामग्री का हिसाब लगाने वाला व्यक्ति (सामग्री कितनी लगेगी, क्या लागत आएगी, चीज़ कब तैयार होगी आदि)

**quantum** /ˈkwɒntəm ˈक्वॉन्टम् / *noun* [C] (*pl.* **quanta** /-tə -टा /) (*technical*) a very small quantity of **electromagnetic** energy विद्युत-चुंबकीय ऊर्जा की अत्यल्प मात्रा या प्रमात्र; क्वांटम

**quarantine** /ˈkwɒrəntiːn ˈक्वॉरन्टीन् / *noun* [U] a period of time when a person or animal that has or may have an infectious disease must be kept away from other people or animals छूत की बीमारी वाले व्यक्ति या पशु को (दूसरे व्यक्तियों या पशुओं से) अलग रखने की अवधि; संगरोध (-अवधि)

**quarrel**[1] /ˈkwɒrəl ˈक्वॉरल् / *noun* [C] **1 a quarrel (about/ over sth)** an angry argument or disagreement झगड़ा या विवाद (बातचीत में) *We sometimes* ***have a quarrel*** *about who should do the washing-up.* ➪ **argument** और **fight**[2] **3** देखिए। **2 a quarrel with sb/sth** a reason for complaining about or disagreeing with sb/sth व्यक्ति या वस्तु के विषय में शिकायत का कारण या असहमति *I have no quarrel with what has just been said.*

**quarrel**[2] /ˈkwɒrəl ˈक्वॉरल् / *verb* [I] (**quarrelling; quarrelled** *AmE* **quarreling; quarreled**) **1 quarrel (with sb) (about/over sth)** to have an angry argument or disagreement बातों से झगड़ना, विवाद करना *The children are always quarrelling!* ➪ **argue** और **fight**[1] **4** देखिए। **2 quarrel with sth** to disagree with sth किसी बात पर झगड़ना

**quarrelsome** /ˈkwɒrəlsəm ˈक्वॉरल्सम् / *adj.* (used about a person) liking to argue with other people (व्यक्ति) झगड़ालू, कलहप्रिय

**quarry[1]** /ˈkwɒri ˈक्वॉरि / *noun* (*pl.* **quarries**) **1** [C] a place where sand, stone, etc. is dug out of the ground बालू, पत्थर आदि की खदान या खान ➪ **mine** देखिए। **2** [*sing.*] a person or animal that is being hunted शिकार किया जाने वाला मनुष्य या पशु

**quarry[2]** /ˈkwɒri ˈक्वॉरि / *verb* [I, T] (*pres. part.* **quarrying;** *3rd person sing. pres.* **quarries;** *pt, pp* **quarried**) to dig stone, sand, etc. out of the ground ज़मीन से बालू, पत्थर आदि निकालना; उत्खनन करना *to quarry for marble*

**quart** /kwɔːt क्वॉट् / *noun* [C] (*abbr:* **qt**) a measure of liquid; 1.14 litres. There are 2 pints in a quart द्रव की एक माप; 1.14 लिटर (एक इकाई में दो पिंट होते है) NOTE अमेरिकी क्वार्ट 0.94 लिटर का होता है।

**quarter** /ˈkwɔːtə(r) ˈक्वॉट(र्) / *noun* **1** [C] one of four equal parts of sth चौथा भाग, चतुर्थांश, चौथाई *The programme lasts for three quarters of an hour.* ○ *a kilometre and a quarter* **2** [*sing.*] 15 minutes before or after every hour हर घंटे के 15 मिनट पहले या बाद में (क्रमशः पौने या सवा से व्यक्त जैसे पौने दो या सवा दो) ***(a) quarter past*** *six.* ○ ***(a) quarter to*** *three.* NOTE अमेरिकी अंग्रेज़ी के प्रयोग हैं, '(a) quarter **after**' और '(a) quarter **of**' *I'll meet you at (a) quarter after six.* ○ *It's a quarter of three.* **3** [C] a period of three months तीन महीने की अवधि; तिमाही, त्रिमास *You get a gas bill every quarter.* **4** [C] a part of a town, especially a part where a particular group of people live नगर का कोई इलाक़ा (विशेषतः वह जहाँ वर्ग-विशेष के लोग रहते हैं) *the Chinese quarter of the city* **5** [C] a person or group of people who may give help or information or who have certain opinions विशेष मदद या जानकारी देने या सोच रखने वाला व्यक्ति या वर्ग; व्यक्तिसमूह **6** [C] (in the US or Canada) a coin that is worth 25 cents (¼ dollar) (अमेरिका या कनाडा में) 25 सेंट का सिक्का (¼ डालर) **7 quarters** [*pl.*] a place that is provided for people, especially soldiers, to live in आवास-भवन (विशेषतः सैनिकों के लिए) **8** [C] four ounces of sth; ¼ of a pound चार आउंस की माप; चौथाई पाउंड *a quarter of mushrooms*

IDM **at close quarters** ➪ **close[3]** देखिए।

**quarter-final** *noun* [C] one of the four matches between the eight players or teams left in a competition क्वार्टर-फ़ाइनल (किसी प्रतियोगिता की अंतिम आठ टीमों या खिलाड़ियों के बीच खेले जाने वाले चार मैचों में से एक) ➪ **semi-final** देखिए।

**quarterly** /ˈkwɔːtəli ˈक्वॉटलि / *adj., adv.* (produced or happening) once every three months तिमाही, त्रैमासिक (तीन माह में एक बार होने या बनने वाला) *a quarterly magazine*

**quartet** /kwɔːˈtet क्वॉˈट्रेट् / *noun* [C] **1** four people who sing or play a piece of music together चार सहगायकों या सहवादकों का समूह; क्वार्टेट **2** a piece of music for four people to sing or play together चार सहगायकों या सहवादकों का सहगान या सहवादन; चतुष्पदी, चौराग, क्वार्टेट **3** any group of four persons or things चतुष्टयः, चतुष्टक, क्वार्टेट

**quartz** /kwɔːts क्वॉट्स् / *noun* [U] a type of hard rock that is used in making very accurate clocks or watches क्वार्ट्ज़ (एक प्रकार का कड़ा पत्थर जो एकदम सही समय देने के लिए घड़ियों में प्रयुक्त होता है); स्फटिक, काचमणि

**quasar** /ˈkweɪzɑː(r) ˈक्वेज़ा(र्) / *noun* [C] (*technical*) a large object like a star, that is far away and that shines very brightly and sometimes sends out strong radio signals बहुत दूर और बहुत चमकदार एक प्रकार का तारा जो कभी-कभी शक्तिशाली रेडियों संकेत भेजता है; क्वासर ➪ **pulsar** देखिए।

**quash** /kwɒʃ क्वॉश् / *verb* [T] (*formal*) **1** to say that an official decision is no longer true or legal आधिकारिक निर्णय को रद्द कर देना **2** to stop or defeat sth by force बल प्रयोग से किसी को दबा या कुचल देना *to quash a rebellion*

**quasi-** /ˈkweɪzaɪ; -saɪ ˈक्वेज़ाइ; -साइ / *prefix* (*used in adjectives and nouns*) **1** that appears to be sth but is not really so जो जैसा लगे वैसा वस्तुतः हो न, -वत्/-सा/-प्राय (जैसे सत्यवत, सत्य-सा, सत्यप्राय) *a quasi-scientific explanation* **2** partly; almost अर्ध-, आंशिक; लगभग *a quasi-official body*

**quay** /kiː की / *noun* [C] a platform where goods and passengers are loaded on and off boats बंदरगाहों पर जहाज़ों से माल उतारने-लादने का प्लेटफ़ार्म, ऊँचा चबूतर; (जहाज़ी) घाट

**quayside** /ˈkiːsaɪd ˈकीसाइड् / *noun* [*sing.*] the area of land that is near a quay (जहाज़ी) घाट से लगी ज़मीन

**queasy** /ˈkwiːzi ˈक्वीज़ि / feeling sick; wanting to vomit खुद को अस्वस्थ अनुभव करने वाला; वमन करने का इच्छुक

**queen** /kwiːn क्वीन् / *noun* [C] **1** (*also* **Queen**) the female ruler of a country (किसी देश की) शासिका, महारानी *Queen Elizabeth* ➪ **king, prince** और **princess** देखिए। **2** (*also* **Queen**) the wife of a king राजा की पत्नी; रानी **3** the largest and most important female in a group of insects कीट-समूह में सबसे बड़ी और प्रभावशाली मादा; रानी मक्खी *the queen* *bee* **4** one of the four playing cards in a pack with a picture of a queen (ताश की) बेग़म (रानी के चित्र वाले ताश के चार पत्तों में से कोई एक) *the queen of hearts* ➪ **card** पर नोट देखिए। **5** (in chess) the most powerful piece, that can move any distance and in all directions (शतरंज में) रानी; वज़ीर

**queer** /kwɪə(r) क्विअ(र्)/ *adj.* (*old-fashioned*) strange or unusual विचित्र, अजीब या असामान्य *His face was a queer pink colour.*

**quell** /kwel क्वेल्/ *verb* [T] (*formal*) to end sth किसी को दबाना या कुचलना; दमन करना

**quench** /kwentʃ क्वेन्च्/ *verb* [T] to satisfy your feeling of thirst by drinking a liquid (पानी आदि पीकर) प्यास बुझाना *He drank some juice to quench his thirst.*

**query** /ˈkwɪəri ˈक्विअरि/ *noun* [C] (*pl.* **queries**) a question, especially one asking for information or expressing a doubt about sth प्रश्न (विशेषतः कोई जानकारी पाने या किसी बात के विषय में संदेह व्यक्त करने के लिए); पृच्छा *Does anyone have any queries?* ▶ **query** *verb* [T] (*pres. part.* **querying;** *3rd person sing. pres.* **queries;** *pt, pp* **queried**) पूछताछ करना *We queried the bill but were told it was correct.*

**quest** /kwest क्वेस्ट्/ *noun* [C] (*formal*) a long search for sth that is difficult to find लंबी खोज या तलाश (कुछ दुष्कर वस्तु के लिए) *the quest for happiness/knowledge/truth*

**question**[1] /ˈkwestʃən ˈक्वेसचन्/ *noun* **1** [C] **a question (about/on sth)** a sentence or phrase that asks for an answer (किसी विषय में) प्रश्न, सवाल (किसी बात का उत्तर पाने के लिए प्रयुक्त वाक्य या वाक्यांश) ***to ask a question*** ○ *In the examination, you must* ***answer*** *five* ***questions*** *in one hour.* **2** [C] a problem or difficulty that needs to be discussed or dealt with विचारणीय या समाधान की अपेक्षा वाली समस्या या कठिनाई ***to raise the question*** ○ ***The question is,*** *how are we going to raise the money?* **3** [U] doubt or uncertainty संदेह या अनिश्चय की स्थिति *His honesty is* ***beyond question.*** ○ *The results of the report were accepted* ***without question.***

IDM **(be) a question of sth/of doing sth** a situation in which sth is needed किसी बात की अपेक्षा वाली स्थिति; मामला *It's not difficult—it's just a question of finding the time to do it.*

**in question** that is being considered or talked about विचाराधीन, मुद्दा *The lawyer asked where she was on the night in question.*

**no question** of no possibility of (की) कोई संभावना नहीं, (का) कोई सवाल नहीं *There is no question of him leaving the hospital yet.*

**out of the question** impossible असंभव, नामुमकिन *A new car is out of the question. It's just too expensive.*

**question**[2] /ˈkwestʃən ˈक्वेसचन्/ *verb* [T] **1 question sb (about/on sth)** to ask sb a question or questions (किसी से) कोई प्रश्न या सवाल पूछना *The police questioned him for several hours.* **2** to express or feel doubt about sth किसी विषय में संदेह व्यक्त या अनुभव करना *to question sb's sincerity/honesty*

**questionable** /ˈkwestʃənəbl ˈक्वेसचनब्ल्/ *adj.* **1** that you have doubts about; not certain संदिग्ध; अनिश्चित *It's questionable whether we'll be able to finish in time.* **2** likely to be dishonest or morally wrong जिसके अनुचित या अनैतिक होने की संभावना हो, शंका करने योग्य *questionable motives* ✪ विलोम **unquestionable**

**question mark** *noun* [C] the sign (?) that you use when you write a question प्रश्न चिह्न (?)

**questionnaire** /ˌkwestʃəˈneə(r) ˌक्वेसचˈनेअ(र्)/ *noun* [C] a list of questions that are answered by many people. A questionnaire is used to collect information about a particular subject प्रश्नों की ऐसी सूची जिसका उत्तर अनेक व्यक्ति दें; प्रश्नावली (विषय-विशेष के संबंध में जानकारी इकट्ठा करने के लिए प्रयुक्त) *to complete/fill in a questionnaire*

**question tag** (*also* **tag**) *noun* [C] a short phrase such as 'isn't it?' or 'did you?' at the end of a sentence that changes it into a question and is often used to ask sb to agree with you वाक्य के अंत में प्रयुक्त 'isn't it?' या 'did you?' जैसा लघु वाक्यांश जो वाक्य को प्रश्नवाचक बना देता है (दूसरे को अपने साथ सहमत कराने के लिए प्रयुक्त), प्रश्नकर/प्रश्न टैग, नत्थी प्रश्न *You told the truth, didn't you?*

**queue** /kju: क्यू/ (*AmE* **line**) *noun* [C] a line of people, cars, etc. that are waiting for sth or to do sth (किसी प्रतीक्षा में लोगों, कारों आदि की पंक्ति, कतार या लाइन; क्यू ***wait in a queue*** ○ ***join a queue*** ○ ***form a queue*** ▶ **queue** *verb* [I] **queue (up) (for sth)** (किसी काम के लिए प्रतीक्षा में) क्यू या लाइन लगाना; पंक्तिबद्ध होना *to queue for a bus*

IDM **jump the queue** ➪ **jump**[1] देखिए।

**quiche** /ki:ʃ कीश्/ *noun* [C, U] a type of food made of pastry filled with a mixture of eggs and milk with cheese, onion, etc. and cooked in the oven. You can eat quiche hot or cold विशेष प्रकार की पेस्ट्री जिसमें अंडों, दूध, पनीर, प्याज़ आदि का मिश्रण भरा होता है (अवन में पकी इस पेस्ट्री को ठंडा खा सकते हैं या गरम भी)

**quick**[1] /kwɪk क्विक् / *adj.* **1** done with speed; taking or lasting a short time फुरती से किया गया; थोड़ा समय लेने या रहने वाला *May I make a quick telephone call?* ○ *We need to make a quick decision.* **2 quick (to do sth)** doing sth at speed or in a short time तेज ी से या तुरंत कुछ करते हुए *It's quicker to travel by train.* ○ *She was quick to point out all my mistakes I had made.*

> **NOTE** **Fast** का प्रयोग अधिकतर शीघ्रगामी व्यक्ति या वस्तु के लिए किया जाता है—*a fast horse/car/runner.* **Quick** का प्रयोग अधिकतर फुरती से किए गए काम के लिए होता है—*a quick decision/visit.*

**3** used to form compound adjectives यौगिक विशेषणों में पूर्वपद *quick-thinking* ○ *quick-drying paint*

**IDM** **(as) quick as a flash** very quickly बहुत शीघ्र, बिजली की-सी फुरती से

**IDM** **quick/slow on the uptake** ➪ **uptake**[1] देखिए।

**quick**[2] /kwɪk क्विक् / *adv.* (*informal*) quickly जल्दी; तेज़ी से *Come over here quick!*

**quicken** /ˈkwɪkən ˈक्विकन् / *verb* [I, T] (*written*) **1** to become quicker or make sth quicker तीव्र हो जाना या कर देना *She felt her heartbeat quicken as he approached.* ○ *He quickened his pace to catch up with them.* **2** (*written*) to become more active; to make sth more active और अधिक सक्रिय हो जाना या कर देना *His interest quickened as he heard more about the plan.*

**quickly** /ˈkwɪkli ˈक्विक्लि / *adv.* fast; in a short time जल्दी, शीघ्र; थोड़े समय में *I'd like you to get here as quickly as possible.*

**quicksand** /ˈkwɪksænd ˈक्विकसैन्ड् / *noun* [U] (*also* **quicksands**) [*pl.*] deep wet sand that you sink into if you walk on it बालू वाली दलदल, बलुआ दलदल; बालू-पंक

**quid** /kwɪd क्विड् / *noun* [C] (*pl.* **quid**) (*BrE informal*) a pound (in money); £ 1 पाउंड की मुद्रा *Can you lend me a couple of quid until tomorrow?*

**quiet**[1] /ˈkwaɪət ˈक्वाइअट् / *adj.* **1** with very little or no noise शांत, ख़ामोश *Be quiet!* ○ *His voice was quiet but firm.* ✪ विलोम **loud** **2** without much activity or many people जहाँ न अधिक क्रियाशीलता हो न लोग हों, शांत; ख़ामोश *The streets are very quiet on Sundays.* ○ *Business is quiet at this time of year.* **3** (used about a person) not talking very much (व्यक्ति) अधिक न बोलते हुए; शांत, ख़ामोश *He's very quiet and shy.* ▸ **quietly** *adv.* शांतिपूर्वक, ख़ामोशी से *Try and shut the door quietly!* ▸ **quietness** *noun* [U] शांति, ख़ामोशी

**IDM** **keep quiet about sth; keep sth quiet** to say nothing about sth किसी मामले में चुप या ख़ामोश रहना

**quiet**[2] /ˈkwaɪət ˈक्वाइअट् / *noun* [U] the state of being calm and without much noise or activity शांति और बहुत कम शोरगुल या हरकत *the* ***peace and quiet*** *of the countryside*

**IDM** **on the quiet** secretly चोरी-छिपे *He's given up smoking but he still has an occasional cigarette on the quiet.*

**quieten** /ˈkwaɪətn ˈक्वाइअट्न् / *verb* [T] to make sb/sth quiet व्यक्ति या वस्तु को शांत या चुप करा देना

**PHRV** **quieten (sb/sth) down** to become quiet or to make sb/sth quiet शांत हो जाना या किसी को शांत कर देना *When you've quietened down, I'll tell you what happened.*

**quill** /kwɪl क्विल् / *noun* [C] **1** (*also* **quill feather**) a large feather from the wing or tail of a bird पक्षी का बड़ा पंख (डैने या पूँछ से) **2** (*also* **quill pen**) a pen made from a quill feather पक्षी के पंख से बनी क़लम **3** one of the long, thin, sharp points on the body of a **porcupine** साही या सेही का काँटा

**quilt** /kwɪlt क्विल्ट् / *noun* [C] a cover for a bed that has a thick warm material, for example feathers, inside it रज़ाई, लिहाफ़ ➪ **duvet** देखिए।

**quinine** /kwɪˈniːn क्विˈनीन् / *noun* [U] a drug made from the **bark** of a South American tree, used in the past to treat a tropical disease (**malaria**) मलेरिया की दवा; कुनैन (एक दक्षिण अमेरिकी वृक्ष की छाल से बनी)

**quintessential** /ˌkwɪntɪˈsenʃl ˌक्विन्टिˈसेन्शल् / *adj.* being the perfect example of sth सर्वोत्कृष्ट *He was the quintessential tough guy.* ▸ **quintessence** /kwɪnˈtesns क्विन्ˈटेसन्स् / *noun* [*sing.*] सारतत्व, निचोड़, सर्वोत्कृष्टता का उदाहरण *It was the quintessence of an Indian palace.* ▸ **quintessentially** /-ʃəli -शलि / *adv.* सर्वोत्कृष्ट रूप से *a sense of humour that is quintessentially British*

**quintet** /kwɪnˈtet क्विन्ˈटेट् / *noun* [C] **1** a group of five people who sing or play music together सहगान या सहवादन करने वाले पाँच व्यक्तियों का दल **2** a piece of music for five people to sing or play together पंचक; पाँच व्यक्तियों द्वारा सहगान **3** any group of five persons or things क्विनटेट; (व्यक्ति या वस्तु) पाँच का समूह

**quintuplet** /ˈkwɪntʊplət ˈक्विन्टुप्लट् / *noun* [C] one of five children or animals that are born to one mother at the same time एक ही माँ के एक साथ जन्मे पाँच बच्चों में से कोई एक

**quirk** /kwɜːk क्वक्/ *noun* [C] **1** an aspect of sb's character or behaviour that is strange अजीब आदत या व्यवहार *You'll soon get used to the boss's little quirks.* **2** a strange thing that happens by chance विचित्र आकस्मिक घटना *By* ***a strange quirk of fate*** *they met again several years later.* ▶ **quirky** *adj.* विचित्र *Some people don't like his quirky sense of humour.*

**quit** /kwɪt क्विट्/ *verb* (*pres. part.* **quitting;** *pt, pp* **quit**) **1** [I, T] **quit (as sth)** to leave a job, etc. or to go away from a place कोई नौकरी या स्थान छोड़ना *She quit as manager of the volleyball team.* **2** [T] (*AmE informal*) to stop doing sth कुछ करना बंद कर देना या छोड़ देना *to quit smoking* **3** [I, T] (*computing*) to close a computer program कंप्यूटर पर चलते प्रोग्राम को बंद कर देना

**quite** /kwaɪt क्वाइट्/ *adv.* **1** not very; to a certain degree; rather अधिक नहीं; किसी हदतक; अपेक्षाकृत *The film's quite good.* ○ *They had to wait quite a long time.* ➪ **rather** पर नोट देखिए। **2** (used for emphasizing sth) completely; very (किसी बात पर बल देने के लिए प्रयुक्त) पूर्णतया; बहुत अधिक *Are you quite sure you don't mind?* **3** used for showing that you agree with or understand sth सहमत होने या समझ लेने का भाव दिखाने के लिए प्रयुक्त *'He'll find it difficult.' 'Well, quite* (= I agree).'

IDM **not quite** used for showing that there is almost enough of sth, or that it is almost suitable ज़्यादा नहीं मगर काफ़ी, लगभग पर्याप्त *There's not quite enough bread for breakfast.* ○ *These shoes don't quite fit.*

**quite a** used for showing that sth is unusual किसी स्थिति की असामान्यता प्रकट करने के लिए प्रयुक्त; अच्छा-ख़ासा *It's quite a climb to the top of the hill.*

**quite a few; quite a lot (of)** a fairly large amount or number अच्छी ख़ासी संख्या या मात्रा *We've received quite a few enquiries.*

**quite enough** used for emphasizing that no more of sth is wanted or needed यह बताने के लिए प्रयुक्त कि कोई वस्तु और नहीं चाहिए; बहुत, काफ़ी *I've had quite enough of listening to you two arguing!* ○ *That's quite enough juice, thanks.*

**quits** /kwɪts क्विट्स्/ *adj.*

IDM **be quits (with sb)** (*informal*) if two people are quits, it means that neither of them owes the other anything बराबर; हिसाब चुकता होना *You buy me a drink and then we're quits.*

**quiver**[1] /ˈkwɪvə(r) ˈक्विव़(र्)/ *verb* [I] to shake slightly हलके-से काँपना; थरथराना *to quiver with rage/excitement/fear* ✪ पर्याय **tremble** ▶ **quiver** *noun* [C] कंपन, स्पंदन, थरथराहट

**quiver**[2] /ˈkwɪvə(r) ˈक्विव़(र्)/ *noun* [C] a long narrow case for carrying arrows तरकस, तूणीर

**quiz**[1] /kwɪz क्विज़्/ *noun* [C] (*pl.* **quizzes**) a game or competition in which you have to answer questions खेल या प्रतियोगिता जिसमें प्रश्नों के उत्तर देने होते हैं; प्रश्नोत्तरी *a quiz programme on TV* ○ *a general knowledge quiz*

**quiz**[2] /kwɪz क्विज़्/ (*3rd person sing. pres.* **quizzes;** *pres. part.* **quizzing;** *pt* **quizzed**) *verb* [T] to ask sb a lot of questions in order to get information जानकारी पाने के लिए (किसी से) ढेरों प्रश्न करना; पूछ-ताछ करना

**quizzical** /ˈkwɪzɪkl ˈक्विज़िकल्/ *adj.* (used about a look, smile, etc.) seeming to ask a question (दृष्टि, मुसकान आदि) मानो प्रश्न करती हुई; प्रश्नभरी ▶ **quizzically** /-kli -क्लि/ *adv.* प्रश्नात्मक ढंग से, प्रश्न करने के ढंग से

**quorum** /ˈkwɔːrəm ˈक्वॉरम्/ *noun* [*sing.*] the smallest number of people that must be at a meeting before it can make official decisions गणपूर्ति, कोरम (सदस्यों की वह न्यूनतम संख्या जिसके होने पर ही बैठक में निर्णय लिए जा सकें)

**quota** /ˈkwəʊtə ˈक्वोटा/ *noun* [C] the number or amount of sth that is allowed or that you must do नियतांश, कोटा (किसी उद्देश्य से व्यक्तियों या वस्तुओं की निर्धारित संख्या या मात्रा) *We have a fixed quota of work to get through each day.*

**quotation** /kwəʊˈteɪʃn क्वोˈटेश्न्/ (*informal* **quote**) *noun* [C] **1** a phrase from a book, speech, play, etc, that sb repeats because it is interesting or useful किसी पुस्तक, भाषण, नाटक आदि का उद्धृत किया जाने वाला रोचक या उपयोगी वाक्यांश; उद्धरण, अवतरण *a quotation from Rabindranath* **2** a statement that says how much a piece of work will probably cost किसी काम की संभावित लागत का विवरण; भाव, दर, कोटेशन *You should get quotations from three different builders.* ➪ **estimate** देखिए।

**quotation marks** (*also* **speech marks**) (*informal*) (*also* **quotes,** *BrE* **inverted commas**) *noun* [*pl.*] the signs '...' or "..." that you put around a word, a sentence, etc to show that it is what sb said or wrote, that it is a title, or that you are using it in a special way उद्धरण चिह्न (उद्धृत शब्द, वाक्य आदि के दोनों ओर लगने वाले चिह्न '...' "...")

**quote** /kwəʊt क्वोट्/ *verb* **1** [I, T] **quote (sth) (from sb/sth)** to repeat exactly sth that sb else has said or written before पहले कही या लिखी गई बात को सही-सही दोहराना, दूसरे के शब्दों को उद्धृत करना *The minister asked the newspaper not to quote him.* **2** [T] to give sth as an example to support what you are saying अपने कथन की पुष्टि में किसी बात को मिसाल के तौर पर पेश करना **3** [I, T] to say what the cost of a piece of work, etc. will probably be किसी काम आदि कि संभावित लागत का विवरण देना

**quotient** /ˈkwəʊʃnt ˈक्वोशन्ट्/ *noun* [C] (*technical*) a number which is the result when one number is divided by another भागफल, लब्धि (एक संख्या को दूसरी से विभाजित करने पर प्राप्त संख्या) ➪ **IQ** देखिए।

# R r

**R, r**[1] /ɑ:(r) आ(र्)/*noun* [C, U] (*pl.* **R's; r's** /ɑ:z आज़्/) the eighteenth letter of the English alphabet अंग्रेज़ी वर्णमाला का अठारहवाँ अक्षर *'Rabbit' begins with an 'R'.*

**R**[2] *abbr.* river नदी *R Ganga ○ R Kaveri*

**rabbi** /ˈræbaɪ ˈरैबाइ/ *noun* [C] (*pl.* **rabbis**) a Jewish religious leader and teacher of Jewish law रब्बी; यहूदियों का धार्मिक गुरु (और यहूदी क़ानून का विशेषज्ञ)

**rabbit** /ˈræbɪt ˈरैबिट्/ *noun* [C] a small animal with long ears ख़रगोश, शशक *a wild rabbit ○ a rabbit hutch* (= a cage for rabbits) **NOTE** ख़रगोश के लिए बच्चों की भाषा में शब्द **bunny** है।

**rabbit warren** *noun* [C] a system of holes and underground tunnels where wild rabbits live जंगली ख़रगोशों का बाड़ा (धरती में बने सूराख और सुरंगें)

**rabble** /ˈræbl ˈरैब्ल्/ *noun* [C] a noisy crowd of people who are or may become violent शोरगुल करती या हिंसा पर उतारू भीड़; असंगठित भीड़

**rabi** *noun* [U] (in Indian subcontinent) a crop sown in autumn or early winter and harvested in spring or at the beginning of summer (भारतीय उपमहाद्वीप में) रबि; शरद ऋतु या शीत ऋतु में बीजी गई फ़सल जिसकी वसंत या ग्रीष्म ऋतु में कटाई होती है *Wheat is the major rabi crop of India.* ➪ **kharif** देखिए।

**rabies** /ˈreɪbi:z ˈरेबीज़्/ *noun* [U] a very dangerous disease that a person can get if he/she is bitten by an animal that has the disease एक ख़तरनाक छूत का रोग (जो इस रोग से ग्रस्त पशु के काटने से किसी व्यक्ति को हो सकता है); रेबीज़

**race**[1] /reɪs रेस्/ *noun* **1** [C] **a race (against/with sb/sth); a race for sth/to do sth** a competition between people, animals, cars, etc. to see which is the fastest or to see which can achieve sth first दौड़-प्रतियोगिता (व्यक्तियों, पशुओं, कारों आदि की) *to run/win/lose a race ○ to come first/second/last **in a race** ○ the race to find a cure for AIDS ○ Rescuing victims of the earthquake is now **a race against time**.* **2 the races** [*pl.*] (*BrE*) an occasion when a number of horse races are held in one place एक ही स्थान पर घुड़दौड़ों का कार्यक्रम **3** [C, U] one of the groups into which people can be divided according to the colour of their skin, their hair type, the shape of their face, etc. (मानव) जाति (त्वचा का रंग, बालों का प्रकार, चेहरे की शकल आदि से निर्धारित मनुष्यों का वर्ग) ➪ **human race** देखिए। **4** [C] a group of people who have the same language, customs, history, etc. समान भाषा, संस्कृति, इतिहास आदि वाले लोगों का वर्ग

**IDM the rat race** ➪ **rat** देखिए।

**race**[2] /reɪs रेस्/ *verb* **1** [I, T] **race (against/with sb/sth); race sb/sth** to have a competition with sb/sth to find out who is the fastest or to see who can do sth first दौड़-प्रतियोगिता में भाग लेना, किसी से दौड़ में स्पर्धा करना *I'll race you home.* **2** [I, T] to go very fast or to move sb/sth very fast तेज़ चलना या किसी को तेज़ चलाकर ले जाना *We raced up the stairs. ○ The child had to be raced to hospital.* **3** [T] to make an animal or a vehicle take part in a race दौड़-प्रतियोगिता में (घोड़ा आदि) किसी पशु या (कार आदि) वाहन को दौड़ाना

**racecourse** /ˈreɪskɔ:s ˈरेस्कॉस्/ (*AmE* **racetrack**) *noun* [C] a place where horse races take place घुड़दौड़ का मैदान; रेसकोर्स

**racehorse** /ˈreɪshɔ:s ˈरेस्हॉस्/ *noun* [C] a horse that is trained to run in races घुड़दौड़ का घोड़ा

**race relations** *noun* [*pl.*] the relations between people of different races who live in the same town, area, etc. एक ही स्थान, शहर आदि में रहने वाली मानव जातियों के बीच संबंध

**race track** /ˈreɪstræk ˈरेस्ट्रैक्/ *noun* [C] **1** a track for races between runners, cars, bicycles, etc. धावकों, कारों, साइकिलों आदि के लिए दौड़ का मैदान **2** (*AmE*) = **racecourse**

**racial** /ˈreɪʃl ˈरेश्ल्/ *adj.* connected with people's race; happening between people of different races मानव जातियों से संबंधित; विभिन्न मानव जातियों में होने वाला *racial tension/discrimination* ▶ **racially** /-ʃəli -शलि/ *adv.* जाति-संबंधी, जातीय दृष्टि से *a racially mixed school*

**racing** /ˈreɪsɪŋ ˈरेसिङ्/ *noun* [U] **1** = **horse racing** **2** the sport of taking part in races दौड़ों (में भाग लेने) का खेल *motor racing ○ a racing driver/car*

**racism** /ˈreɪsɪzəm ˈरेसिज़म्/ *noun* [U] the belief that some races of people are better than others; unfair ways of treating people of different races जातिवाद (कुछ जातियों को दूसरी जातियों से उत्कृष्ट मानना); भिन्न जाति के लोगों से अनुचित व्यवहार *to take measures to combat racism* ▶ **racist** /ˈreɪsɪst ˈरेसिस्ट्/ *noun* [C], *adj.* जातिवादी *He's a racist. ○ racist beliefs/views/remarks*

**rack**[1] /ræk रैक्/ *noun* [C] (*often in compounds*) a piece of equipment, usually made of bars, that you can put things in or on (प्रायः) सरियों से बना ढाँचा (जिसके अंदर या ऊपर सामान रखा जाता है); रैक luggage rack ➪ **laboratory** पर चित्र देखिए।

IDM **go to rack and ruin** to be in or get into a bad state because of a lack of care लापरवाही के कारण तबाह हो जाना

**rack**[2] /ræk रैक्/ *verb*

IDM **rack your brains** to try hard to think of sth or remember sth किसी बात को सोचने या याद करने की भरपूर कोशिश करना

**racket** /ˈrækɪt ˈरैकिट्/ *noun* **1** [*sing.*] (*informal*) a loud noise शोरगुल, हल्ला *Stop making that terrible racket!* **2** [C] an illegal way of making money ग़ैर-क़ानूनी ढंग से पैसा बनाने का काम; धोखाधड़ी *a drugs racket* **3** (*also* **racquet**) [C] a piece of sports equipment that you use to hit the ball with in sports such as tennis and **badminton** रैकेट (जैसे बैडमिंटन तथा टेनिस के खेलों में प्रयुक्त)

**racy** /ˈreɪsi ˈरेसि/ *adj.* (used especially about speech and writing) having a style that is exciting and amusing, often in a way that is connected with sex (भाषण या लेखन) उत्तेजक और मनोरंजक (प्रायः अश्लीलता का स्पर्श लिए) *a racy novel*

**radar** /ˈreɪdɑː(r) ˈरेडा(र्)/ *noun* [U] a system that uses radio waves for finding the position of moving objects, for example ships and planes रडार (चलते जहाज़, उड़ते विमान आदि की स्थिति का पता लगाने के लिए रेडियो तरंगों का उपयोग करने वाली उपकरण-प्रणाली) *This plane is hard to detect by radar.* ➪ **sonar** देखिए।

**radiant** /ˈreɪdiənt ˈरेडिअन्ट्/ *adj.* **1** showing great happiness उल्लासपूर्ण *a radiant smile* **2** sending out light or heat प्रकाश या ताप को बिखेरने वाला; विकिरणकारी *the radiant heat/energy of the sun*

**radiate** /ˈreɪdieɪt ˈरेडिएट्/ *verb* **1** [T] (used about people) to clearly show a particular quality or emotion in your appearance or behaviour (व्यक्ति का) मुखाकृति या व्यवहार द्वारा किसी विशिष्ट गुण या भावना का स्पष्ट प्रदर्शन करना *She radiated self-confidence in the interview.* **2** [T] to send out light or heat प्रकाश या ताप को बिखेरना, विकिरण करना **3** [I] to go out in all directions from a central point केंद्र से सब दिशाओं में फैलना *Narrow streets radiate from the village square.*

**radiation** /ˌreɪdiˈeɪʃn ˌरेडिˈएश्न्/ *noun* [U] **1** powerful and very dangerous rays that are sent out from certain substances. You cannot see or feel radiation but it can cause serious illness or death कुछ पदार्थों से निकलकर फैलने वाली शक्तिशाली और ख़तरनाक किरणें (इन्हें हम देख या महसूस नहीं कर सकते परंतु इनसे गंभीर रोग या मृत्यु हो सकती है) ➪ **radioactive** देखिए। **2** heat, light or energy that is sent out from sth किसी वस्तु से फैलने वाला ताप, प्रकाश या ऊर्जा *ultraviolet radiation*

**radiator** /ˈreɪdieɪtə(r) ˈरेडिएटə(र्)/ *noun* [C] **1** a piece of equipment that is usually fixed to the wall and is used for heating a room. Radiators are made of metal and filled with hot water रेडिएटर (कमरा गरम करने का धातु-निर्मित और गरम पानी से भरा यंत्र जिसे दीवार पर लगाया जाता है) **2** a piece of equipment that is used for keeping a car engine cool कार का रेडिएटर (जो इंजन को ठंडा रखता है)

**radical**[1] /ˈrædɪkl ˈरैडिकल्/ *adj.* **1** (used about changes in sth) very great; complete (परिवर्तन) अत्यधिक; पूर्ण *The tax system needs radical reform.* ○ *radical change* **2** wanting great social or political change क्रांतिकारी सामाजिक या राजनीतिक परिवर्तन का इच्छुक *to have radical views* ➪ **moderate**[1] और **extreme**[2] देखिए। ▶ **radically** /ˈrædɪkli ˈरैडिक्लि/ *adv.* आमूल, मूल रूप से, मूलतः *The First World War radically altered the political map of Europe.*

**radical**[2] /ˈrædɪkl ˈरैडिकल्/ *noun* [C] a person who wants great social or political change क्रांतिकारी सामाजिक या राजनीतिक परिवर्तन का इच्छुक व्यक्ति; उग्र सुधारवादी ➪ **moderate**[3] और **extremist** देखिए।

**radii** ➪ **radius** का plural रूप

**radio** /ˈreɪdiəʊ ˈरेडिओ/ *noun* (*pl.* **radios**) **1** (*often* **the radio**) [U, *sing.*] the activity of sending out programmes for people to listen to; the programmes that are sent out रेडियो; लोगों के लिए कार्यक्रमों का प्रसारण; प्रसारित कार्यक्रम *to* ***listen to the radio*** ○ *I heard an interesting report* ***on the radio*** *this morning.* **2** [C] a piece of equipment that is used for receiving and/or sending radio messages or programmes (on a ship, plane, etc. or in your house) रेडियो सेट (उपकरण); जहाज़, विमान, घर आदि पर रेडियो संदेश या कार्यक्रम भेजने या प्राप्त करने वाला उपकरण

> NOTE रेडियो को चलाने के अर्थ में आप **put, switch, turn on** या **off** शब्द प्रयोग कर सकते हैं। इसकी आवाज़ बढ़ाने या घटाने के लिए सामान्यतः अभिव्यक्तियाँ **turn up** या **(turn) down** का प्रयोग किया जा सकता है।

**3** [U] the sending or receiving of messages through the air by electrical signals विद्युत संकेतों या रेडियो तरंगों द्वारा वायु के माध्यम से संदेशों को भेजने या प्राप्त करने की क्रिया *to keep in radio contact* ○ *radio signals/waves* ▶ **radio** *verb* [I, T] (*pt, pp* **radioed**) रेडियो तरंगों द्वारा भेजना या से प्राप्त करना

**radio-** /ˈreɪdiəʊ ˈरेडिओ/ *prefix* (*used in nouns, adjectives and adverbs*) **1** connected with radio waves or the activity of sending out radio or television programmes (**broadcasting**) रेडियो तरंगों या रेडियो, टीवी कार्यक्रमों के प्रसारण से संबंधित *a radio-controlled car* **2** connected with **radioactivity** रेडियो सक्रियता या विकिरणशीलता से संबंधित *radiographer*

**radioactive** /ˌreɪdiəʊˈæktɪv ˌरेडिओˈऐक्‌टिव्/ *adj.* sending out powerful and very dangerous rays that are produced when atoms are broken up. These rays cannot be seen or felt but can cause serious illness or death रेडियो सक्रिय या विकिरणशील (अणु-विखंडन से उत्पन्न शक्तिशाली और ख़तरनाक किरणें बिखेरने वाला) (इन किरणों को देखा या महसूस नहीं किया जा सकता परंतु इनसे गंभीर रोग या मृत्यु हो सकती है) *the problem of the disposal of radioactive waste from power stations* ➪ **radiation** देखिए। ► **radioactivity** /ˌreɪdiəʊækˈtɪvəti ˌरेडिओऐक्ˈटिव़टि/ *noun* [U] रेडियो-सक्रियता, विकिरणशीलता

**radiographer** /ˌreɪdiˈɒɡrəfə(r) ˌरेडिˈऑग्रफ़(र्)/ *noun* [C] a person who is trained to take pictures of your bones, etc. (**X-rays**) in a hospital or to use them for the treatment of certain illnesses रेडियोग्राफर; अस्पताल में शरीर के अंगों (हड्डियों आदि) की फ़ोटो, एक्स-रे लेने वाला व्यक्ति ताकि कुछ ख़ास रोगों के उपचार में सहायता मिल सके

**radish** /ˈrædɪʃ ˈरैडिश्/ *noun* [C] a small red vegetable that is white inside or a long white vegetable with a strong taste. You eat radishes in salads मूली ➪ **vegetable** पर चित्र देखिए।

**radium** /ˈreɪdiəm ˈरेडिअम्/ *noun* [U] (*symbol* **Ra**) a chemical element. Radium is a white **radioactive** metal used in the treatment of some serious diseases रेडियम (एक रासायनिक तत्व), रेडियम सफ़ेद रंग का रेडियो-सक्रिय या विकिरणशील धातु है जो कुछ गंभीर रोगों के इलाज के काम आता है

**radius** /ˈreɪdiəs ˈरेडिअस्/ *noun* [C] (*pl.* **radii**) /-diaɪ -डिआइ/ **1** the distance from the centre of a circle to the outside edge वृत्त का व्यासार्ध; त्रिज्या (वृत्त के केंद्र से परिधि तक की दूरी) ➪ **diameter** और **circumference** देखिए तथा **circle** पर चित्र देखिए। **2** a circular area that is measured from a point in its centre अपने केंद्रबिंदु से मापा गया गोलाकार क्षेत्र; घेरा *The wreckage of the plane was scattered over a radius of several kilometres.* **3** (*medical*) the shorter bone of the two bones in the lower part of your arm between your wrist and your elbow (चिकित्सा) बाँह की कलाई से कुहनी तक की छोटी हड्डी, बहिः प्रकोष्ठिका ➪ **ulna** देखिए तथा **arm** पर चित्र देखिए।

**radon** /ˈreɪdɒn ˈरेडॉन्/ *noun* [U] (*symbol* **Rn**) a chemical element. Radon is a colourless **radioactive** gas used in the treatment of some serious diseases रेडन (एक रासायनिक तत्व); रेडन एक रंगहीन रेडियो-सक्रिय या विकिरणशील गैस है जो कुछ गंभीर रोगों के इलाज के काम आती है

**raffle** /ˈræfl ˈरैफ़्ल्/ *noun* [C] a way of making money for a charity or a project by selling tickets with numbers on them. Later some numbers are chosen and the tickets with these numbers on them win prizes लॉटरी; (अच्छे कार्यों के लिए नंबर वाले ऐसे टिकट बेचकर धनसंग्रह का काम जिनमें से चुने हुए टिकटों पर इनाम दिए जाते हैं)

**raft** /rɑːft राफ़्ट्/ *noun* [C] a flat structure made of pieces of wood tied together and used as a boat or a floating platform बेड़ा; लकड़ी के लट्ठों को जोड़कर बनाया गया बेड़ा जो नाव या बहते चबूतरे या प्लेटफ़ार्म का काम करता है

**rafter** /ˈrɑːftə(r) ˈराफ़्ट(र्)/ *noun* [C] one of the long pieces of wood that support a roof छत को सहारा देने वाली (लकड़ी की कड़ी; शहतीर, धरन)

**rag** /ræɡ रैग्/ *noun* **1** [C, U] a small piece of old cloth that you use for cleaning साफ़ करने के लिए पुराना कपड़ा; चिथड़ा, लत्ता **2 rags** [*pl.*] clothes that are very old and torn फटे-पुराने कपड़े

**raga** *noun* [C] (in Indian classical music) a series of musical notes on which a melody is based and which expresses different moods for different times of the day (भारतीय शास्त्रीय संगीत में) दिवस के विभिन्न समय के लिए विभिन्न मनःस्थिति के राग

**rage[1]** /reɪdʒ रेज्/ *noun* [C, U] a feeling of violent anger that is difficult to control क्रोधोन्माद (उग्र क्रोध जिसे नियंत्रित करना कठिन हो) *He was trembling with rage.* ○ *to fly into a rage*

**rage[2]** /reɪdʒ रेज्/ *verb* [I] **1 rage (at/against/about sb/ sth)** to show great anger about sth, especially by shouting किसी बात पर बहुत क्रोध करना (विशेषतः चिल्लाते हुए) *He raged against the injustice of it all.* **2** (used about a battle, disease, storm, etc.) to continue with great force (युद्ध, रोग, आँधी आदि का) ज़ोर-शोर से जारी रहना *The battle raged for several days.* ► **raging** *adj.* (*only before a noun*) ज़ोरदार, प्रचंड *a raging headache*

**ragged** /ˈræɡɪd ˈरैगिड्/ *adj.* **1** (used about clothes) old and torn (कपड़ों के लिए प्रयुक्त) फटे-पुराने; जीर्ण-शीर्ण **2** not straight; untidy ऊबड़-खाबड़; खुरदुरा, कटा-फटा *a ragged edge/coastline*

**ragi** *noun* [U] a kind of millet that is widely grown as a cereal in the **arid** areas of Africa and Asia;

finger millet रागी; अफ़्रीक़ा और एशिया में अनाज की तरह उपजाई जाने वाली एक प्रकार की ज्वार

**raid** /reɪd रेड्/ *noun* [C] **a raid (on sth)** **1** a short surprise attack on an enemy by soldiers, ships or aircraft थल-सैनिकों, पानी के जहाज़ों या विमानों से शत्रु पर अचानक आक्रमण *an air raid* **2** a surprise visit by the police looking for criminals or illegal goods अपराधियों को, या चोरी का माल ढूँढ़ती पुलिस का छापा **3** a surprise attack on a building in order to steal sth कुछ चुराने की मंशा से किसी इमारत पर अचानक बोला धावा *a bank raid* ▶ **raid** *verb* [T] छापा मारना, धावा बोलना *Police raided the club at dawn this morning.*

**rail** /reɪl रेल्/ *noun* **1** [C] a wooden or metal bar fixed to a wall, which you can hang things on (दीवार में लगी) चीज़ें टाँगने की रेलिंग या छड़ *a towel/curtain/picture rail* **2** [C] a bar which you can hold to stop you from falling (on stairs, from a building, etc.) (इमारतों आदि में ज़ीने पर लगी) रेलिंग (जो सीढ़ियाँ चढ़ते समय सहारा देने का काम करती है) **3** [C, *usually pl.*] each of the two metal bars that form the track that trains run on रेल की पटरियाँ **4** [U] the railway system; trains as a means of transport रेल यातायात व्यवस्था; यातायात के साधन के रूप में रेलगाड़ियाँ *rail travel/services/fares*

**railing** /ˈreɪlɪŋ ˈरेलिङ्/ *noun* [C, *usually pl.*] a fence (around a park, garden, etc.) that is made of metal bars (पार्क, बाग़ आदि के चारों ओर) लोहे की छड़ों से बनी बाड़; रेलिंग, जंगला

**railway** /ˈreɪlweɪ ˈरेल्वे/ (*AmE* **railroad**) *noun* [C] **1** (*BrE* **railway line**) the metal lines on which trains travel between one place and another रेलगाड़ियों के आने-जाने के लिए लोहे की पटरियाँ; रेलवे लाइन **2** the whole system of tracks, the trains and the organization and people needed to operate them रेलवे, समग्र रेल-तंत्र (जिसमें रेल की पटरियाँ, रेलगाड़ियाँ, प्रबंध व्यवस्था तथा रेल कर्मचारी आते हैं) *He works in the railways.* ○ *a railway engine/company*

**railway station** = **station[1] 1**

**rain[1]** /reɪn रेन्/ *noun* **1** [U] the drops of water that falls from the sky वर्षा, बारिश *Take your umbrella, **it looks like rain*** (= as if it is going to rain). ○ *It's **pouring with rain*** (= the rain is very heavy). ➪ **shower 3, acid rain** देखिए तथा **weather** पर नोट देखिए। **2 rains** [*pl.*] (in tropical countries) the time of the year when there is a lot of rain (उष्णप्रदेशीय देशों में) बरसात का मौसम
**IDM** **(as) right as rain** ➪ **right[1]** देखिए।

**rain[2]** /reɪn रेन्/ *verb* **1** [I] (used with it) to fall as rain ('it' के साथ प्रयुक्त) वर्षा होना, पानी बरसना *Is it **raining hard**?* **2** [I, T] **rain (sth) (down) (on sb/sth)** to fall or make sth fall on sb/sth in large quantities किसी पर किसी वस्तु की बौछार होना या करना *Bombs rained down on the city.*
**PHRV** **be rained off** to be cancelled or to have to stop because it is raining वर्षा के कारण (कार्यक्रम का) रद्द होना या उसे रद्द करना

**rainbow** /ˈreɪnbəʊ ˈरेन्बो/ *noun* [C] an arch of many colours that sometimes appears in the sky when the sun shines through rain इंद्रधनुष

**rain check** *noun* (*AmE*)
**IDM** **take a rain check on sth** (*spoken*) to refuse an invitation or offer but say that you might accept it later किसी निमंत्रण या प्रस्ताव को अस्वीकार करना (यह कहते हुए कि बाद में स्वीकार करेंगे)

**raincoat** /ˈreɪnkəʊt ˈरेन्कोट्/ *noun* [C] a long light waterproof coat which keeps you dry in the rain बरसाती, रेनकोट

**raindrop** /ˈreɪndrɒp ˈरेन्ड्रॉप्/ *noun* [C] a single drop of rain वर्षा की एक बूँद, वर्षा-बिंदु

**rainfall** /ˈreɪnfɔːl ˈरेन्फ़ॉल्/ *noun* [U, *sing.*] the total amount of rain that falls in a particular place during a month, year, etc. किसी स्थान पर विशेष अवधि में हुई वर्षा की कुल मात्रा; वर्षा

**rainforest** /ˈreɪnfɒrɪst ˈरेन्फ़ॉरिस्ट्/ *noun* [C] a thick forest in tropical parts of the world that have a lot of rain वर्षा-प्रचुर वन (अत्यंत गरम क्षेत्रों के), भारी वर्षा वाले घने जंगल *the Amazon rainforest*

**rainwater** /ˈreɪnwɔːtə(r) ˈरेन्वॉट(र्)/ *noun* [U] water that has fallen as rain वर्षा-जल, बरसाती पानी

**rainy** /ˈreɪni ˈरेनि/ *adj.* having or bringing a lot of rain अत्यधिक वर्षा वाला, बरसाती, वर्षा बहुल *a rainy day* ○ *the rainy season*
**IDM** **keep/save sth for a rainy day** to save sth, especially money, for a time when you really need it ज़रूरत के समय के लिए धन आदि बचा कर रखना

**raise** /reɪz रेज़्/ *verb* [T] **1** to lift sth up (कुछ) ऊपर उठाना *If you want to leave the room raise your hand.* ○ *He raised himself up on one elbow.* **2 raise sth (to sth)** to increase the level of sth or to make sth better or stronger किसी वस्तु के स्तर में वृद्धि करना या उसे बेहतर या अधिक सशक्त करना *to raise taxes/salaries/prices* ○ ***raise the standards*** ○ *to **raise your voice*** (= speak loudly or angrily) ✪ विलोम **lower** (अर्थ सं. 1 और 2 के लिए) **3** to get money from people for a particular purpose विशेष उद्देश्य के लिए लोगों से धनसंग्रह करना *We are doing* *a sponsored walk to* ***raise money*** *for charity.* ○ *a* ***fund-raising*** *event* **4** to introduce a subject that needs to be talked about or dealt with चर्चा योग्य विषय पर चर्चा आरंभ करना, कोई विषय विचार के लिए सम्मुख रखना *I would like to* ***raise the subject*** *of money.* ○ *This* ***raises the question*** *of why nothing was done before.* **5** to cause a particular reaction or emotion कोई विशेष प्रतिक्रिया या मनोभाव उत्पन्न करना *The neighbours* ***raised the alarm*** (= told everybody there was a fire/an emergency) *when they saw smoke coming out of the window.* ○ *to* ***raise hopes/fears/suspicions*** *in people's minds* **6** to look after a child or an animal until he/she is an adult किसी बच्चे या पशु के बड़ा होने तक उसका पालन-पोषण करना *You can't* ***raise a family*** *on what I earn.* ➪ **bring sb up** देखिए। **7** to breed animals or grow a particular plant for a special purpose प्रजनन द्वारा पशुओं की संख्या बढ़ाना या विशेष प्रयोजन से किसी विशेष पौधे को उगाना

**IDM** **raise your eyebrows** to show that you are surprised or that you do not approve of sth किसी बात पर आश्चर्य या असहमति प्रकट करना

**raisin** /ˈreɪzn ˈरेज़्न् / *noun* [C] a dried grape, used in cakes, etc. किशमिश ➪ **sultana** देखिए।

**rake** /reɪk रेक् / *noun* [C] a garden tool with a long handle and a row of metal teeth, used for collecting leaves or making the earth smooth (खेत या बग़ीचे में काम आने वाला) पाँचा (लंबे हत्थे और धातु निर्मित दाँतों वाला औज़ार जो पत्ते इकट्ठे करने या धरती को समतल बनाने के काम आता है) ➪ **gardening** पर चित्र देखिए। ▶ **rake** *verb* [T] पाँचे से कुछ इकट्ठा करना या समतल बनाना *to rake up the leaves*

**PHR V** **rake sth in** (*informal*) to earn a lot of money, especially when it is done easily ख़ूब पैसा कमाना (विशेषतः बिना विशेष श्रम के) *She's been* ***raking it in*** *since she got promoted.*

**rake sth up** to start talking about sth that it would be better to forget भूलने योग्य मामले को फिर से उठा देना *Don't rake up all those old stories again.*

**rally**[1] /ˈræli ˈरैलि / *noun* [C] (*pl.* **rallies**) **1** a large public meeting, especially one held to support a political idea रैली; बड़ी जनसभा (विशेषतः राजनीतिक समर्थन के लिए आयोजित) **2** (*BrE*) a race for cars or motorbikes on public roads आम सड़कों पर कारों या मोटर-साइकिलों की दौड़ **3** (used in tennis and similar sports) a series of hits of the ball before a point is won (टेनिस या उसके सदृश कोई खेल में) बॉल को लगातार मारने की क्रिया (जब तक अंक प्राप्त न हो जाए)

**rally**[2] /ˈræli ˈरैलि / *verb* (*pres. part.* **rallying;** *3rd person sing. pres.* **rallies;** *pt, pp* **rallied**) **1** [I, T] **rally (sb/sth) (around/behind/to sb)** to come together or to bring people together in order to help or support sb/sth लोगों का इकट्ठा होना या लोगों को इकट्ठा करना (किसी की सहायता या समर्थन के लिए) *The cabinet rallied behind the Prime Minister.* **2** [I] to get stronger, healthier, etc. after an illness or a period of weakness बीमारी या दुर्बलता के बाद पुनः स्वास्थ्य-लाभ करना

**PHR V** **rally round** to come together to help sb किसी की सहायता के लिए इकट्ठे हो जाना *When I was in trouble my family all rallied round.*

**RAM** /ræm रैम् / *abbr.* (*computing*) random-access memory (computer memory in which data can be changed or removed and can be looked at in any order) रैंडम-एक्सेस मेमरी (कंप्यूटर-स्मृति-कोश जिसमें सूचना-सामग्री को परिवर्तित या विलोपित किया जा सकता है तथा क्रम बदल-बदल कर उसे देखा जा सकता है) *32 megabytes of RAM*

**ram**[1] /ræm रैम् / *noun* [C] a male sheep मेढ़ा, भेड़ा ➪ **sheep** पर नोट तथा चित्र देखिए।

**ram**[2] /ræm रैम् / *verb* [T] (**ra<u>mm</u>ing; ra<u>mm</u>ed**) to crash into sth or push sth with great force किसी वस्तु को ज़ोर से टक्कर या धक्का मारना

**Ramzan** (*also* **ramadan**) /ˈrəmzɑːn ˈरम्ज़ान् / *noun* [C, U] a period of a month when, for religious reasons, Muslims do not eat anything from early morning until the sun goes down in the evening रमज़ान का महीना (इस अवधि में मुसलमान धार्मिक कारणों से सुबह से सूर्यास्त तक निराहार रहते हैं) ➪ **Eid** देखिए।

**ramble**[1] /ˈræmbl ˈरैम्बल् / *verb* [I] **1** to walk in the countryside for pleasure ग्रामीण अंचल में सैर-सपाटा करना *to go rambling* **2 ramble (on) (about sth)** to talk for a long time in a confused way (बोलते-बोलते) विषय से बहक जाना

**ramble**[2] /ˈræmbl ˈरैम्बल् / *noun* [C] a long, organized walk in the country for pleasure ग्रामीण अंचल में व्यवस्थित सैर सपाटा

**rambler** /ˈræmblə(r) ˈरैम्ब्ल(र्) / *noun* [C] **1** (*BrE*) a person who walks in the countryside for pleasure, especially as part of an organized group व्यवस्थित दल के सदस्य के रूप में ग्रामीण अंचल में सैर-सपाटा करने वाला व्यक्ति **2** a plant that grows up walls, fences, etc. दीवारों, बाड़ों आदि पर चढ़ने वाली बेल

**rambling** /ˈræmblɪŋ ˈरैम्ब्लिङ् / *adj.* **1** (used about speech or writing) very long and confused (भाषण या लेखन) बहुत लंबा और बहका-बहका **2** (used about a building) spreading in many directions (इमारत) इधर-उधर फैली हुई *a rambling old house*

**ramp** /ræmp रैम्प् / *noun* [C] **1** a path going up or down which you can use instead of steps or stairs to get from one place to a higher or lower place ऊपर-नीचे के तलों को जोड़ने वाली ढाल, रैम्प (जिसे चढ़ने-उतरने के लिए सीढ़ियों के बदले इस्तेमाल किया जा सकता है) *There are ramps at both entrances for wheelchair access.* **2** an artificial slope made of wood etc. for models to walk while displaying clothes jewellery etc. during a fashion show कृत्रिम ढलाऊ भूमि जिसपर मॉडल चलकर परिधान, गहने आदि का (फ़ैशन शो में) प्रदर्शन करते हैं

**rampage[1]** /ræmˈpeɪdʒ रैमˈपेज् / *verb* [I] to move through a place in a violent group, usually breaking things and attacking people झुंड बनाकर क्रोधोन्माद में कहीं से दौड़ते-भागते गुज़रना (प्रायः तोड़फोड़ और लोगों पर हमला करते हुए), हिंसात्मक व्यवहार करना *The football fans rampaged through the town.*

**rampage[2]** /ˈræmpeɪdʒ ˈरैम्पेज् / *noun*

IDM **be/go on the rampage** to move through a place in a violent group, usually breaking things and attacking people झुंड बनाकर क्रोधोन्माद में कहीं से दौड़ते-भागते गुज़रना (प्रायः तोड़फोड़ और लोगों पर हमला करते हुए)

**rampant** /ˈræmpənt ˈरैम्पन्ट् / *adj.* (used about sth bad) existing or spreading everywhere in a way that is very difficult to control (बुरी चीज़ों का) अनियंत्रित रूप से सर्वत्र विद्यमान होना या फैलना *Car theft is rampant in this town.*

**ramshackle** /ˈræmʃækl ˈरैम्शैक्ल् / *adj.* (usually used about a building) old and needing repair (प्रायः इमारत) पुरानी और टूटी-फूटी; जर्जर

**ran** ➪ **run[1]** का past tense रूप

**ranch** /rɑːntʃ रैन्च् / *noun* [C] a large farm, especially in the US or Australia, where cows, horses, sheep, etc. are kept बड़ा पशु-फ़ार्म (विशेषतः अमेरिका या ऑस्ट्रेलिया में)

**rancid** /ˈrænsɪd ˈरैन्सिड् / *adj.* if food containing fat is **rancid**, it tastes or smells unpleasant because it is no longer fresh बासी और विकृत गंध वाली खाद्य सामग्री *rancid butter*

**random** /ˈrændəm ˈरैन्डम् / *adj.* chosen by chance सांयोगिक, बेतरतीब, अनियमित, यादृच्छिक *For the opinion poll they interviewed* ***a random selection*** *of people in the street.* ▶ **randomly** *adv.* यादृच्छिक रूप से

IDM **at random** without thinking or deciding in advance what is going to happen बिना पूर्व विचार या निर्णय के; यदृच्छया, यों ही *The competitors were chosen at random from the audience.*

**random-access memory** *noun* [U] (*computing*) = **RAM**

**rang** ➪ **ring[2]** का past tense रूप

**range[1]** /reɪndʒ रेन्ज् / *noun* **1** [C, *usually sing.*] **a range (of sth)** a variety of things that belong to the same group एक ही प्रकार की विभिन्न वस्तुएँ *The course will cover a* ***whole range*** *of topics.* ○ *a* ***wide range*** *of clothes* **2** [C] the limits between which sth can vary ऐसी सीमाएँ जिनके भीतर कोई वस्तु घट-बढ़ सकती है *That car is outside my* ***price range.*** ○ *I don't think this game is suitable for all* ***age ranges.*** **3** [C, U] the distance that it is possible for sb/sth to travel, see, hear, etc. यात्रा करने, कुछ देखने-सुनने आदि की अधिकतम दूरी *Keep* ***out of range of*** *the guns.* ○ *The gunman shot the policeman* ***at close range.*** ○ *They can pick up signals* ***at a range of*** *400 metres.* **4** [C] a line of mountains or hills पर्वतों या पहाड़ियों की शृंखला या पंक्ति

**range[2]** /reɪndʒ रेन्ज् / *verb* [I] **1 range between A and B; range from A to B** to vary between two amounts, sizes, etc., including all those between them दो मात्राओं, आकारों आदि के बीच बदलते रहना *The ages of the students range from 15 to 50.* **2 range (from A to B)** to include a variety of things in addition to those mentioned (दो सीमाओं के भीतर) पूर्व निर्दिष्ट वस्तुओं के साथ विविध वस्तुओं का शामिल होना, एक सीमाबिंदु से दूसरे के बीच में अनेक वस्तुओं का होना

**rangoli** *noun* [U, C] a popular Indian art form in which a pattern is made on the floor, commonly outside homes, usually with finely ground rice powder and colours. Sometimes flower petals are also used to make these decorative patterns रंगोली (रंगों या फूलों की)

**rank[1]** /ræŋk रैङ्क् / *noun* **1** [C, U] the position, especially a high position, that sb has in an organization such as the army, or in society सेना, समाज आदि में किसी व्यक्ति की (प्रायः उच्च) स्थिति या पद *General is one of the highest ranks in the army.* ○ *She's much higher in rank than I am.* **2** [C] a group or line of things or people वस्तुओं या व्यक्तियों का वर्ग या पंक्ति *a taxi rank* **3 the ranks** [*pl.*] the ordinary soldiers in the army; the members of any large group सेना के जवान, साधारण सैनिक, किसी बड़े समूह के सदस्य *At the age of 43, he was forced to* ***join the ranks of*** *the unemployed.*

IDM **the rank and file** the ordinary soldiers in the army; the ordinary members of an organization सेना के जवान, साधारण सैनिक; किसी संस्था के साधारण सदस्य

**rank²** /ræŋk रैङ्क्/ *verb* [I, T] **rank (sb/sth) (as sth)** (*not used in the continuous tenses*) to give sb/sth a particular position on a scale according to importance, quality, success, etc.; to have a position of this kind व्यक्ति या वस्तु की उसके महत्त्व, गुणवत्ता, सफलता आदि के अनुसार स्थिति निर्धारित करना; इस प्रकार किसी का किसी स्थिति में या पद पर होना *She's ranked as one of the world's top players.* ○ *a high-ranking police officer*

**rankle** /ˈræŋkl ˈरैङ्क्ल्/ *verb* [I, T] **rankle (with sb)** if an event or a remark rankles, you still remember it angrily because it upset or annoyed you a lot क्रोधवश कुछ याद रखना क्योंकि किसी (व्यक्ति) से आप नाराज़ या खिन्न हैं; चुभना, कसकना *Her immature comments still rankled with him.*

**ransack** /ˈrænsæk ˈरैन्सैक्/ *verb* [T] **ransack sth (for sth)** to search a place, making it untidy and causing damage, usually because you are looking for sth सामान को उलट-पुलट करते हुए और हानि पहुँचाते हुए किसी स्थान पर वस्तु विशेष की खोजबीन करना *The house had been ransacked by burglars.*

**ransom** /ˈrænsəm ˈरैन्सम्/ *noun* [C, U] the money that you must pay to free sb who has been captured illegally and who is being kept as a prisoner फिरौती (अपहरण कर बंदी बना लिए गए व्यक्ति को छुड़ाने के लिए माँगी या दी गई धनराशि) *The kidnappers demanded a ransom of Rs 500,000 for the boy's release.*

IDM **hold sb to ransom** to keep sb as a prisoner and say that you will not free him/her until you have received a certain amount of money किसी को बंधक बनाकर रखना (फिरौती मिलने तक) ➪ **hostage** देखिए।

**rant** /rænt रैन्ट्/ *verb* [I] **rant (on) (about sth)/ rant (at sb)** (*disapproving*) to speak or complain about sth in a loud, angry and rather confused way उच्च, क्रुद्ध स्वर और संभ्रमित प्रकार से बोलना या शिकायत करना ▸ **rant** *noun* [C] थोथी निंदा

IDM **rant and rave** to show that you are angry by shouting or complaining loudly for a long time लंबे समय तक चीख़कर या शिकायत करके अपनी नाराज़गी दिखाना

**rap¹** /ræp रैप्/ *noun* **1** [C] a quick, sharp hit or knock on a door, window, etc. खिड़की, दरवाज़े आदि पर खटखटाहट *There was a sharp rap on the door.* **2** [C, U] a style or a piece of music with a fast strong rhythm, in which the words are spoken fast, not sung एक प्रकार का तीव्र लय युक्त संगीत (जिसमें गायक, गाने के स्थान पर तीव्र गति से बोलता है); रैप संगीत

**rap²** /ræp रैप्/ *verb* (**rapping; rapped**) **1** [I, T] to hit a hard object or surface several times quickly and lightly, making a noise किसी सतह (दरवाज़ा आदि) को खटखटाना *She rapped angrily on/at the door.* **2** [T] (*informal*) (used mainly in newspaper headlines) to criticize sb strongly (सामाचारपत्रों के शीर्षकों में प्रयुक्त) किसी की तीखी आलोचना करना *Minister raps police over rise in crime.* **3** [I] to speak the words of a song (**a rap**) that has music with a very fast strong rhythm रैप संगीत गाना

**rape¹** /reɪp रेप्/ *verb* [T] to force a person to have sex when he/she does not want to, using threats or violence किसी से बलात्कार या दुष्कर्म करना (प्रायः धमकाकर या हिंसापूर्वक)

**rape²** /reɪp रेप्/ *noun* **1** [U, C] the crime of forcing sb to have sex when he/she does not want to बलात्कार, दुष्कर्म *to commit rape* **2** [*sing.*] (*written*) **the rape (of sth)** the destruction of sth beautiful किसी सुंदर वस्तु का विनाश **3** (*also* **oilseed rape**) [U] a plant with bright yellow flowers, that farmers grow as food for farm animals and for its seeds, which are used to make oil तिलहन *a field of rape* ○ *rape oil/seed*

**rapid** /ˈræpɪd ˈरैपिड्/ *adj.* happening very quickly or moving with great speed द्रुत (गति से होने वाला) या द्रुतगामी *She made rapid progress and was soon the best in the class.* ▸ **rapidity** /rəˈpɪdəti रˈपिडटि/ *noun* [U] (*formal*) द्रुत गति, द्रुतता, तेज़ी, शीघ्रता *The rapidity of change has astonished most people.* ▸ **rapidly** *adv.* द्रुत गति से

**rapids** /ˈræpɪdz ˈरैपिड्स्/ *noun* [*pl.*] a part of a river where the water flows very fast over rocks नदी का वह भाग जहाँ पानी चट्टानों पर से होते हुए तेज़ी से बहता है; क्षिप्रिका

**rapist** /ˈreɪpɪst ˈरेपिस्ट्/ *noun* [C] a person who forces sb to have sex when he/she does not want to बलात्कारी, दुष्कर्मी

**rappel** /ræˈpel रैˈपेल्/ (*AmE*) = **abseil**

**rapport** /ræˈpɔː(r) रैˈपॉ(र्)/ *noun* [*sing.*, U] **(a) rapport (with sb); (a) rapport (between A and B)** a friendly relationship in which people understand each other very well मैत्री संबंध जिसमें लोग एक-दूसरे को अच्छी तरह समझते हैं, आपसी समझदारी पर आधारित घनिष्ठता; सौहार्द *She understood the importance of establishing a close rapport with clients.* ○ *Honesty is essential if there is to be good rapport between patient and therapist.*

**rapt** /ræpt रैप्ट्/ *adj.* (*written*) so interested in one particular thing that you do not notice anything else तन्मय, तल्लीन, एकनिष्ठ (कि किसी अन्य बात का पता ही न चले) *a rapt audience* ○ *She listened to the speaker with rapt attention.*

**rapture** /ˈræptʃə(r) ˈरैप्च(र्)/ *noun* [U] a feeling of extreme happiness हर्षातिरेक, अत्यधिक आनंद; हर्षोन्माद **IDM go into raptures (about/over sb/sth)** to feel and show that you think that sb/sth is very good किसी बात से आनंदविभोर हो जाना *I didn't like the film much but my sister went into raptures about it.*

**rapturous** /ˈræptʃərəs ˈरैप्चरस्/ *adj.* (*usually before a noun*) expressing extreme pleasure or enthusiasm for sb/sth व्यक्ति या वस्तु को लेकर हर्षोन्मादपूर्ण, हर्षोन्मत *rapturous applause*

**rare** /reə(r) रेअ(र्)/ *adj.* **1 rare (for sb/sth to do sth); rare (to do sth)** not done, seen, happening, etc. very often दुर्लभ, विरल (बहुत कम किया जाने, दीखने या होने वाला) *a rare bird/flower/plant* **2** (used about meat) not cooked for very long so that the inside is still red (मांस) अधपका (इसलिए अंदर से अब भी लाल) *a rare steak* ➪ **medium** और **well done** देखिए। ▶ **rarely** *adv.* विरले ही *People rarely live to be 100 years old.*

**raring** /ˈreərɪŋ ˈरेअरिङ्/ *adj.* **raring to do sth** wanting to start doing sth very much कुछ करने को अति आतुर या उत्सुक *They were raring to try out the new computer.*

**rarity** /ˈreərəti ˈरेअरटि/ *noun* (*pl.* **rarities**) **1** [C] a thing or a person that is unusual and is therefore often valuable or interesting दुर्लभ वस्तु या विरले प्रकार का व्यक्ति (अतएव बहुमूल्य या रोचक) *Women lorry drivers are still quite a rarity.* **2** [U] the quality of being rare दुर्लभता, विरलता *The rarity of this stamp increases its value a lot.*

**rasam** *noun* [U] a kind of thin soup prepared especially in South India by adding lentils and certain spices like pepper and **cumin** to a diluted mix of tomatoes and tamarind water रसम ➪ **mulligatawny** देखिए।

**rascal** /ˈrɑːskl ˈरास्कल्/ *noun* [C] a person, especially a child, who shows a lack of respect for other people and enjoys playing tricks on them उद्धत या शरारती व्यक्ति (विशेषतः बच्चा) **NOTE** किसी को **rascal** कहने का मतलब है कि आप उससे बहुत अधिक नाराज़ नहीं हैं।

**rash¹** /ræʃ रैश्/ *noun* **1** [C, *usually sing.*] an area of small red spots that appear on your skin when you are ill or have a reaction to sth (बीमारी में या प्रतिक्रियावश) शरीर पर उभरे छोटे-छोटे लाल दाने; चकत्ते *He **came out in a rash** where the plant had touched him.* **2** [*sing.*] **a rash (of sth)** a series of unpleasant events of the same kind happening close together एक के बाद एक घटित होने वाली दुखद घटनाएँ

**rash²** /ræʃ रैश्/ *adj.* (used about people) doing things that might be dangerous or bad without thinking about the possible results first; (used about actions) done in this way (व्यक्ति) जल्दबाज़ या उतावला और अविवेकी; (काम) जल्दबाज़ी में किया गया; अविवेकपूर्ण *a rash decision/promise* ▶ **rashly** *adv.* जल्दबाज़ी में

**raspberry** /ˈrɑːzbəri ˈराज़्बरि/ *noun* [C] (*pl.* **raspberries**) a small, soft, red fruit which grows on bushes मकोप, रसभरी (का फल) *raspberry jam* ➪ **fruit** पर चित्र देखिए।

**rat** /ræt रैट्/ *noun* [C] an animal like a large mouse बड़ा चूहा, मूषक **NOTE** चूहे **rodents** में आते हैं। **IDM rat race** the way of life in which everyone is only interested in being better or more successful than everyone else एक दूसरे से आगे बढ़ने के लिए अंधाधुंध दौड़, कड़ी प्रतियोगिता, तेज़ होड़ा-होड़ी

**rate¹** /reɪt रेट्/ *noun* [C] **1** a measurement of the speed at which sth happens or the number of times sth happens or exists during a particular period दर (किसी घटना के घटित होने की चाल या उसकी आवृत्ति या अवधि विशेष में उसकी विद्यमानता की आवृत्ति) *The **birth rate** is falling.* ○ *The population is increasing **at the rate of** less than 0.5% a year.* **2** a fixed amount of money that sth costs or that sb is paid किसी वस्तु के लिए निर्धारित क़ीमत या किसी को किया गया भुगतान *We offer special reduced rates for students.* ➪ **first-rate** और **second-rate** देखिए।
**IDM at any rate** (*spoken*) **1** used when you are giving more exact information about sth बहरहाल, हर स्थिति में (किसी विषय में अधिक सही जानकारी देते समय प्रयुक्त) *He said that they would be here by ten. At any rate, I think that's what he said.* **2** whatever else might happen चाहे जो (भी) हो *Well, that's one good piece of news at any rate.*
**the going rate (for sth)** ➪ **going²** देखिए।

**rate²** /reɪt रेट्/ *verb* (*not used in continuous tenses*) **1** [I, T] to say how good you think sb/sth is व्यक्ति या वस्तु का मूल्यांकन होना या करना *She's rated among the best tennis players of all time.* ○ *The match rated as one of their worst defeats.* **2** [T] to be good, important, etc. enough to be treated in a particular way (महत्त्व आदि की दृष्टि से) विशेष उल्लेख योग्य माना जाना *The accident wasn't very serious—it didn't rate a mention in the local newspaper.*

**rather** /ˈrɑːðə(r) ˈराद़(र्)/ *adv.* quite; to some extent काफ़ी; किसी हद तक *It was a rather nice day.* ○ *I was rather hoping that you'd be free on Friday.*

NOTE 'बहुत अधिक नहीं' के अर्थ में **fairly, quite, rather** और **pretty** इन सबका प्रयोग हो सकता है। इनमें **fairly** सबसे दुर्बल है और **rather** एवं **pretty** सबसे सबल हैं। **Fairly** और **quite** अधिकतर सकारात्मक अर्थ देने वाले शब्दों के साथ प्रयुक्त होते हैं—*The room was fairly tidy.* कटु आलोचना या नकारात्मक व्यंजना के लिए **rather** का प्रयोग होता है—*This room's rather untidy.* परंतु सकारात्मक अर्थ वाले शब्द के साथ **rather** के प्रयोग का तात्पर्य है आश्चर्य और हर्ष की अभिव्यक्ति—*The new teacher is actually rather nice, though he doesn't look very friendly.*

IDM **or rather** used as a way of correcting sth you have said, or making it more exact अपने पूर्वकथन को सही करने या उसे अधिक सटीक बनाने के लिए प्रयुक्त *She lives in Delhi, or rather she lives in a suburb of Delhi.*

**rather than** instead of; in place of के बजाय; के स्थान पर *I think I'll just have a sandwich rather than a full meal.*

**would rather... (than)** would prefer to (को) अधिक पसंद होना *I'd rather go to the cinema than watch television.*

**ratify** /ˈrætɪfaɪ ˈरैटिफ़ाइ/ *verb* [T] (*pres. part.* **ratifying;** *3rd person sing. pres.* **ratifies;** *pt, pp* **ratified**) to make an agreement officially acceptable by voting for or signing it किसी समझौते की औपचारिक संपुष्टि करना (मतदान या हस्ताक्षर द्वारा) ▶ **ratification** /ˌrætɪfɪˈkeɪʃn ˌरैटिफ़िˈकेश्न्/ *noun* [U] संपुष्टि, अनुसमर्थन *The agreement is subject to ratification by the Parliament.*

**rating** /ˈreɪtɪŋ ˈरेटिङ्/ *noun* [C] **1** a measurement of how popular, important, good, etc. sth is किसी की लोकप्रियता, महत्त्व, श्रेष्ठता आदि की माप **2** (*usually* **the ratings**) a set of figures showing the number of people who watch a particular television programme, etc., used to show how popular the programme is टीवी के किसी विशेष कार्यक्रम के दर्शकों की संख्या बताने वाला अंक-समुच्चय (कार्यक्रम की लोकप्रियता की माप)

**ratio** /ˈreɪʃiəʊ ˈरेशिओ/ *noun* [C] **ratio (of A to B)** the relation between two numbers which shows how much bigger one quantity is than another अनुपात (दो संख्याओं के बीच संबंध जो बताता है कि एक संख्या दूसरी से कितनी बड़ी है) *The ratio of boys to girls in this class is three to one* (= there are three times as many boys as girls).

**ration** /ˈræʃn ˈरैश्न्/ *noun* [C] a limited amount of food, petrol, etc. that you are allowed to have when there is not enough for everyone to have as much as he/she wants राशन, खाद्य पदार्थ, पेट्रोल आदि की नियम द्वारा मर्यादित मात्रा (कमी के दिनों में) ▶ **ration** *verb* [T] मर्यादित करना *In the desert water is strictly rationed.* ▶ **rationing** *noun* [U] राशनिंग, सीमांकन

**rational** /ˈræʃnəl ˈरैशनल्/ *adj.* **1** (used about a person) able to use logical thought rather than emotions to make decisions (व्यक्ति) विवेकशील; समझदार (निर्णय करने में भावनाओं के स्थान पर तर्कबुद्धि का प्रयोग करने वाला) ✪ विलोम **irrational** **2** based on reason; sensible or logical तर्क पर आधारित; विवेकपूर्ण या तर्कसंगत *There must be a rational explanation for why he's behaving like this.* ▶ **rationally** *adv.* विवेकपूर्वक

**rationale** /ˌræʃəˈnɑːl ˌरैशˈनाल्/ *noun* [C] (*formal*) **the rationale (behind/for/of sth)** the principles or reasons which explain a particular decision, course of action, belief, etc. विशिष्ट निर्णय, कार्रवाई, धारणा आदि के आधारवर्ती सिद्धांत या तर्क *What is the rationale behind these new exams?*

**rationalize** (*also* **-ise**) /ˈræʃnəlaɪz ˈरैश्नलाइज़्/ *verb* **1** [I, T] to find reasons that explain why you have done sth (perhaps because you do not like the real reason) किसी कार्य का औचित्य-स्थापन करना (वास्तविक कारण को संभवतः छिपाने के लिए) **2** [T] make a business or a system better organized किसी व्यवसाय या व्यवस्था को बेहतर ढंग से सुसंगठित करना ▶ **rationalization** (*also* **-isation**) /ˌræʃnəlaɪˈzeɪʃn ˌरैश्नलाइˈज़ेश्न्/ *noun* [C, U] सुव्यवस्थीकरण, औचित्य-स्थापन

**rattle**[1] /ˈrætl ˈरैट्ल्/ *verb* 1 [I, T] to make a noise like hard things hitting each other or to shake sth so that it makes this noise खड़खड़ाना, किसी वस्तु को ऐसे हिलाना कि खड़खड़ की आवाज़ हो *The windows were rattling all night in the wind.* ○ *He rattled the money in the tin.* **2** [T] (*informal*) to make sb suddenly become worried किसी को अचानक चिंतित कर देना *The news of his arrival really rattled her.*

PHR V **rattle sth off** to say a list of things you have learned very quickly जल्दी-जल्दी लोगों या वस्तुओं के नाम बताना *She rattled off the names of every player in the team.*

**rattle**[2] /ˈrætl ˈरैट्ल्/ *noun* [C] **1** a toy that a baby can shake to make a noise बच्चों का झुनझुना **2** a noise made by hard things hitting each other खड़खड़ की आवाज़; खड़खड़ाहट

**rattlesnake** /ˈrætlsneɪk ˈरैट्ल्स्नेक् / *noun* [C] a poisonous American snake that makes a noise by moving the end of its tail quickly when it is angry or afraid रैटल-सर्प (एक विषैला अमेरिकी साँप जो क्रुद्ध या भयभीत होने पर अपनी पूँछ से खड़खड़ की ध्वनि उत्पन्न करता है)

**raucous** /ˈrɔːkəs ˈरॉकस् / *adj.* (used about people's voices) loud and unpleasant (लोगों की आवाज़) ऊँची और कर्णकटु; कर्कश

**rava** *noun* [U] coarsely ground wheat; semolina (used in Indian cooking) (भारतीय पाक-कला में प्रयुक्त) सूजी

**ravage** /ˈrævɪdʒ ˈरैविज् / *verb* [T] to damage sth very badly; to destroy sth किसी चीज़ को बुरी तरह नुक़सान पहुँचाना; किसी वस्तु को नष्ट करना

**rave¹** /reɪv रेव् / *verb* [I] **1** (*informal*) **rave (about sb/sth)** to say very good things about sb/sth व्यक्ति या वस्तु की अत्यधिक प्रशंसा करना *Everyone's raving about her latest record!* **2** to speak angrily or wildly गुस्से से बोलना या पागल की तरह प्रलाप करना

**rave²** /reɪv रेव् / *noun* [C] (*BrE*) a large party held outside or in an empty building, at which people dance to electronic music इलेक्ट्रॉनिक संगीत पर थिरकते लोगों की बड़ी पार्टी (खुली जगह पर या किसी ख़ाली इमारत में)

**raven** /ˈreɪvn ˈरेव़न् / *noun* [C] a large black bird that has an unpleasant voice कर्कश ध्वनि वाला एक बड़ा काला पक्षी (चमकीला कौआ, डोम कौआ)

**ravenous** /ˈrævənəs ˈरैवनस् / *adj.* very hungry बहुत भूखा; मरभुक्खा ▶ **ravenously** *adv.* मरभुक्खेपन से

**rave review** *noun* [C] an article in a newspaper, etc. that says very good things about a new book, film, play, etc. किसी पुस्तक, फ़िल्म, नाटक आदि की अतिप्रशंसापूर्ण समीक्षा (अख़बार आदि में)

**ravine** /rəˈviːn रˈव़ीन् / *noun* [C] a narrow deep valley with steep sides खड़े पार्श्वों वाली गहरी संकरी घाटी; दर्रा

**raving** /ˈreɪvɪŋ ˈरेविङ् / *adj.*, *adv.* (*informal*) used to emphasize a particular state or quality विशेष स्थिति या विशेषता पर बल देने के लिए प्रयुक्त *He went raving mad.*

**raw** /rɔː रॉ / *adj.* **1** not cooked कच्चा; न पकाया हुआ *Raw vegetables are good for your health.* **2** in the natural state; not yet made into anything प्राकृतिक अवस्था में; कच्ची स्थिति में, अनगढ़ *raw materials* (= that are used to make things in factories, etc.) **3** used about an injury where the skin has come off from being rubbed (घाव) हरा, छिला हुआ (रगड़ खाने से जिसकी त्वचा अपने स्थान से हट गई है)

**ray** /reɪ रे / *noun* [C] a line of light, heat or energy प्रकाश, ताप या ऊर्जा की रेखा *the sun's rays* ○ *ultraviolet rays* ➪ **X-ray** देखिए।

IDM **a ray of hope** a small chance that things will get better आशा की किरण, बेहतरी का हलका संकेत

**raze** /reɪz रेज़् / *verb* [T] (*usually passive*) to completely destroy a building, town, etc. so that nothing is left (भवन, शहर आदि) पूर्णतः नष्ट कर देना; ध्वस्त करना *The building was razed to the ground.*

**razor** /ˈreɪzə(r) ˈरेज़(र्) / *noun* [C] a sharp instrument which people use to cut off the hair from their skin (**shave**) (दाढ़ी बनाने या बाल साफ़ करने का) रेज़र; उस्तरा *an electric razor* ○ *a disposable razor*

**razor blade** *noun* [C] the thin sharp piece of metal that you put in a razor रेज़र (में लगाने) का ब्लेड

**Rd** *abbr.* road रोड, सड़क *Jai Singh Rd*

**re** /riː री / *prep.* (*written*) used at the beginning of a business letter, etc. to introduce the subject that it is about पत्र के विषय का संकेत करने के लिए प्रयुक्त शब्द; संदर्भ *Re: travel expenses*

**re-** /riː री/ *prefix* (*used in verbs and related nouns, adjectives and adverbs*) again दोबारा, फिर से, पुनः *rebuild* ○ *reappearance*

**reach¹** /riːtʃ रीच् / *verb* **1** [T] to arrive at a place or condition that you have been going towards उद्दिष्ट स्थान पर या स्थिति में पहुँचना *to* ***reach an agreement*** ○ *The team reached the semi-final last year.* ○ *to reach a decision/conclusion/compromise* **2** [I, T] **reach (out) (for sb/sth); reach (sth) (down)** to stretch out your arm to try and touch or get sth हाथ या बाँह बढ़ाना (कुछ छूने या लेने की कोशिश में) *The child reached out for her mother.* ○ *She reached into her bag for her purse.* **3** [I, T] to be able to touch sth किसी वस्तु को छू पाना *I can't reach the top shelf.* ○ *I need a longer ladder. This one won't reach.* **4** [T] to communicate with sb, especially by telephone; contact किसी से बात करना ( विशेषतः फ़ोन पर); संपर्क स्थापित करना *You can reach me at this number.*

**reach²** /riːtʃ रीच् / *noun* [U] the distance that you can stretch your arm दूरी जहाँ तक हाथ बढ़ सके; पहुँच

IDM **beyond/out of (sb's) reach 1** outside the distance that you can stretch your arm (किसी की) पहुँच के बाहर *Keep this medicine out of the reach of children.* **2** not able to be got or done by sb जो प्राप्त न हो सके या किया न जा सके, सामर्थ्य के बाहर *A job like that is beyond his reach.*

**within (sb's) reach** 1 inside the distance that you can stretch your arm (किसी की) पहुँच के भीतर 2 able to be achieved by sb जिसे प्राप्त किया जा सकता है, प्राप्ति के सामर्थ्य के भीतर We *could sense that victory was within our reach.*

**within (easy) reach of sth** not far from sth (किसी से) अधिक दूर नहीं (किसी की) (आसान) पहुँच के भीतर

**react** /riˈækt रिˈऐक्ट्/ *verb* [I] **1 react (to sth) (by doing sth)** to do or say sth because of sth that has happened or been said प्रतिक्रिया व्यक्त करना (कोई क्रिया करना या कुछ कहना) *He reacted to the news by shouting.* ○ *The players reacted angrily to the decision.* **2 react (to sth)** to become ill after eating, breathing, etc. a particular substance कुछ खाने, सूँघने आदि से बीमार हो जाना **3 react (with sth/together)** (used about a chemical substance) to change after coming into contact with another substance (किसी रासायनिक तत्व में) दूसरे तत्व के संपर्क से परिवर्तन आ जाना

**PHR V** **react against sb/sth** to behave or talk in a way that shows that you do not like the influence of sb/sth (for example authority, your family, etc.) किसी व्यक्ति या वस्तु के अप्रीतिकर आचरण पर नकारात्मक प्रतिक्रिया करना (व्यवहार या वाणी द्वारा)

**reaction** /riˈækʃn रिˈऐक्शन्/ *noun* 1 [C, U] **(a) reaction (to sb/sth)** something that you do or say because of sth that has happened (किसी की) प्रतिक्रिया (व्यवहार या वाणी द्वारा व्यक्त) *Could we have your reaction to the latest news, Prime Minister?* ○ *I shook him to try and wake him up but there was no reaction.* 2 [C, U] **(a) reaction (against sb/sth)** behaviour that shows that you do not like the influence of sb/sth (for example authority, your family, etc.) किसी व्यक्ति या वस्तु के अप्रीतिकर आचरण पर नकारात्मक प्रतिक्रिया 3 [C] **a reaction (to sth)** a bad effect that your body experiences because of sth that you have eaten, touched or breathed (किसी वस्तु को खाने, छूने या सूँघने से) शरीर पर पड़ा कुप्रभाव *She had an* ***allergic reaction*** *to something in the food.* 4 [C, *usually pl.*] the physical ability to act quickly when sth happens किसी घटना पर त्वरित प्रतिक्रिया का शारीरिक सामर्थ्य *If the other driver's reactions hadn't been so good, there would have been an accident.* 5 [C, U] (*technical*) a chemical change produced by two or more substances coming into contact with each other रासायनिक क्रिया, अभिक्रिया (दो या अधिक तत्वों के संपृक्त होने से उत्पन्न रासायनिक परिवर्तन)

**reactionary** /riˈækʃənri रिˈऐक्शन्रि/ *noun* [C] (*pl.* **reactionaries**) a person who tries to prevent political or social change प्रतिक्रियावादी व्यक्ति (राजनीतिक या सामाजिक परिवर्तन में बाधक व्यक्ति) ▶ **reactionary** *adj.* प्रतिक्रियात्मक, प्रतिगामी *reactionary views/politics/groups*

**reactive** /riˈæktɪv रिˈऐक्टिव्/ *adj.* 1 (*formal*) showing a reaction or response प्रतिक्रिया या अनुक्रिया प्रकट करने वाला; प्रतिक्रियाकारी, अनुक्रियाकारी ➪ **proactive** देखिए। 2 (used about chemicals) whose chemical characteristics will change when mixed with another substance (रसायन) जिनके रासायनिक गुण अन्य पदार्थ के साथ मिलने से परिवर्तित हो जाएँ

**reactivity** /ˌriːækˈtɪvəti ˌरीऐक्ˈटिव़िटि/ *noun* [U] (*technical*) the degree to which a substance shows chemical change when mixed with another substance किसी पदार्थ में दूसरे पदार्थ के साथ मिश्रण से उत्पन्न रासायनिक परिवर्तन की मात्रा

**reactor** /riˈæktə(r) रिˈऐक्टर्/ = **nuclear reactor**

**read**[1] /riːd रीड्/ *verb* (*pt, pp* **read**/red रेड्/) 1 [I, T] to look at words or symbols and understand them पढ़ना (शब्दों या प्रतीकों को देखना और समझना) *He never learnt to read and write.* ○ *Have you read any good books lately?* 2 [I, T] **read (sb) (sth); read sth (to sb)** to say written words to sb (किसी को) पढ़कर सुनाना *My father used to read me stories when I was a child.* ○ *I hate reading out loud.* 3 [T] to be able to understand sth from what you can see (किसी वस्तु को) देखकर बात समझ लेना, भाँप लेना *Profoundly deaf people train to* ***read lips***. ○ *I've no idea what he'll say—I can't* ***read*** *his* ***mind****!* 4 [T] to show words or a sign of sth (किसी के) शब्द या संकेत प्रदर्शित करना *The sign read 'Keep Left'.* 5 [T] (*formal*) to study a subject at university (विश्वविद्यालय आदि में किसी विषय का) अध्ययन करना *She read Modern Languages at Cambridge.*

**PHR V** **read sth into sth** to think that there is a meaning in sth that may not really be there किसी में कुछ अर्थ मान लेना (जो संभवतः उसमें न हो)

**read on** to continue reading; to read the next part of sth पढ़ते जाना; किसी का अगला भाग पढ़ना

**read sth out** to read sth to other people अन्य लोगों को पढ़कर सुनाना

**read sth through** to read sth to check details or to look for mistakes ब्योरों को जाँचने या ग़लती ढूँढ़ने के लिए पढ़ना *I read my essay through a few times before handing it in.*

**read up on sth** to find out everything you can about a subject किसी विषय का विस्तार से अध्ययन करना

**read**[2] /riːd रीड्/ *noun* [*sing.*] (*informal*) a period or the action of reading पढ़ने की अवधि या क्रिया *Her detective novels are usually **a good read**.*

**readable** /ˈriːdəbl ˈरीडब्ल्/ *adj.* **1** able to be read पढ़ने-लायक; पठनीय *machine-readable data* ➪ **legible** देखिए। **2** easy or interesting to read पढ़ने में आसान या रोचक

**reader** /ˈriːdə(r) ˈरीड(र्)/ *noun* [C] **1** a person who reads sth (a particular newspaper, magazine, type of book, etc.) पाठक (विशेष समाचार पत्र, पत्रिका, पुस्तक आदि को पढ़ने वाला व्यक्ति) *She's an avid reader of science fiction.* **2** (*with an adjective*) a person who reads in a particular way विशेष ढंग से पढ़ने वाला *a fast/slow reader* **3** a book for practising reading पढ़ने के अभ्यास में सहायक पुस्तक; पाठ्य-पुस्तक, रीडर

**readership** /ˈriːdəʃɪp ˈरीडशिप्/ *noun* [*sing.*] the number of people who regularly read a particular newspaper, magazine, etc. पाठक-संख्या (विशेष समाचार पत्र, पत्रिका आदि को पढ़ने वालों की संख्या) *The newspaper has a readership of 200,000.*

**readily** /ˈredɪli ˈरेडिलि/ *adv.* **1** easily, without difficulty आसानी से, बिना कठिनाई के *Most vegetables are **readily available** at this time of year.* **2** without pausing; without being forced बेहिचक; स्वेच्छा से *He readily admitted that he was wrong.*

**readiness** /ˈredinəs ˈरेडिनस्/ *noun* [U] **1 readiness (for sth)** the state of being ready or prepared (किसी बात के लिए) तत्परता या मुस्तैदी **2 readiness (to do sth)** the state of being prepared to do sth without arguing or complaining बिना बहस या शिकायत कुछ करने की तत्परता; स्वेच्छा, उत्कंठा *The bank have indicated their readiness to lend him the money.*

**reading** /ˈriːdɪŋ ˈरीडिङ्/ *noun* **1** [U] what you do when you read पढ़ाई, पठन-क्रिया *Her hobbies include painting and reading.* **2** [U] books, articles, etc. that are intended to be read पढ़ने के काम की पुस्तकें, लेख आदि; पाठ्य-सामग्री *The information office gave me a pile of reading matter to take away.* **3** [C] the particular way in which sb understands sth किसी बात को समझने का विशेष ढंग; विचार, व्याख्या *What's your reading of the situation?* **4** [C] the number or measurement that is shown on an instrument किसी उपकरण पर प्रदर्शित संख्या या माप; रीडिंग (मीटर आदि पर) *a reading of 20°C*

**readjust** /ˌriːəˈdʒʌst ˌरीअˈड्जस्ट्/ *verb* **1** [I] **readjust (to sth)** to get used to a different or new situation भिन्नतया नई स्थिति का अभ्यस्त होना, से तालमेल बैठाना *After her divorce, it took her a long time to readjust to being single again.* **2** [T] to change or move sth slightly (किसी वस्तु को) हलके से बदलना या हिलाना-डुलाना, सही करना, ठीक-ठाक करना ▶ **readjustment** *noun* [C, U] तालमेल बैठाने की क्रिया

**read-only memory** *noun* [U] (*computing*) = **ROM**

**ready** /ˈredi ˈरेडि/ *adj.* **1 ready (for sb/sth); ready (to do sth)** prepared and able to do sth or to be used कुछ करने या इस्तेमाल होने के लिए तैयार और सक्षम *He isn't ready to take his driving test.* ○ *I'll go and **get** the dinner **ready**.* ○ ***Have** your money **ready** before you get on the bus.* **2 ready to do sth; ready (with/for sth)** prepared and happy to do sth कुछ करने के लिए तैयार और ख़ुश *I know it's early, but I'm **ready for bed**.* **3** *adv.* (*used to form compound adjectives*) that has already been made or done; not done especially for you बना-बनाया या किया-कराया; किसी के लिए विशेषतया निर्मित नहीं *ready-cooked food* ○ *There are no **ready-made** answers to this problem—we'll have to find our own solution.*

**reagent** /riˈeɪdʒənt रिˈएजन्ट्/ *noun* [C] (*technical*) a substance used to cause a chemical reaction, especially in order to find out if another substance is present रीएजेंट; रासायनिक क्रिया उत्पन्न करने वाला पदार्थ (विशेषतः दूसरे पदार्थ की उपस्थिति का पता लगाने के लिए); अभिकर्मक, प्रतिकर्मक

**real**[1] /ˈriːəl; rɪəl ˈरीअल्; रिअल्/ *adj.* **1** actually existing, not imagined असली, वास्तविक, काल्पनिक नहीं *The film is based on real life.* ○ *We have a real chance of winning.* **2** actually true; not only what people think is true वस्तुतः सत्य; लोगों की धारणा मात्र से सत्य नहीं *The name he gave to the police wasn't his real name.* **3** (*only before a noun*) having all, not just some, of the qualities necessary to really be sth सर्वगुण संपन्न; पूर्ण रूप से *She was my first real girlfriend.* **4** natural, not false or artificial प्राकृतिक, कृत्रिम या नक़ली नहीं *This shirt is real silk.* **5** (*only before a noun*) (used to emphasize a state, feeling or quality) strong or big (स्थिति, मनोभाव या विशेषता पर बल देने के लिए प्रयुक्त) सशक्त, बड़ा *Money is a real problem for us at the moment.* ○ *He made a real effort to be polite.*
IDM **for real** genuine or serious ईमानदारी वाला या गंभीर *Her tears weren't for real.* ○ *Was he for real when he offered you the job?*

**the real thing** something genuine, not a copy असली ची ज़, नक़्ली नहीं *This painting is just a copy. The real thing is in a gallery.*

**real²** /ˈri:əl; rɪəl ˈरीअल्; रिअल् / *adv.* (*AmE informal*) very; really बहुत; वास्तव में

**real estate** *noun* [U] property in the form of land and buildings भू और भवन संपत्ति; ज़मीन, जायदाद

**real estate agent** (*AmE*) = **estate agent**

**realism** /ˈri:əlɪzəm ˈरीअलिज़्म् (*also BrE*) ˈrɪə- ˈरिअ- / *noun* [U] **1** behaviour that shows that you accept the facts of a situation and are not influenced by your feelings स्थिति की वास्तविकता को समझने और भावनाओं से प्रभावित न होने वाला आचरण; यथार्थवादिता ➪ **idealism** देखिए। **2** (in art, literature, etc.) showing things as they really are (कला, साहित्य आदि में) यथार्थवाद, वास्तववाद

**realist** /ˈri:əlɪst ˈरीअलिस्ट् (*also BrE*) ˈrɪə- ˈरिअ- / *noun* [C] **1** a person who accepts the facts of a situation, and does not try to pretend that it is different स्थिति की वास्तविकता को ईमानदारी से स्वीकार करने वाला व्यक्ति; यथार्थवादी व्यक्ति *I'm a realist—I don't expect the impossible.* **2** an artist or writer who shows things as they really are यथार्थवादी कलाकार या लेखक

**realistic** /ˌri:əˈlɪstɪk ˌरीअˈलिस्टिक् (*also BrE*) ˌrɪə- ˌरिअ- / *adj.* **1** sensible and understanding what it is possible to achieve in a particular situation स्थिति-विशेष में जो हो सकता है उसे बुद्धिमानी से समझते हुए, स्थिति की असलियत को समझते हुए *We have to be realistic about our chances of winning.* **2** showing things as they really are वस्तुओं को उनकी वास्तविकता में दिखाते हुए; वास्तववादी *a realistic drawing/description* **3** not real but appearing to be real वास्तविक या असली जैसा (न कि वास्तविक या असली) *The monsters in the film were very realistic.* ▶ **realistically** /ˌrɪəˈlɪstɪkli ˌरिअˈलिस्टिक्लि / *adv.* वास्तविक रूप से

**reality** /riˈæləti रिˈऐलटि / *noun* (*pl.* **realities**) **1** [U] the way life really is, not the way it may appear to be or how you would like it to be वास्तविकता, यथार्थ (जीवन जैसा है वैसा, न कि जैसा वह लग सकता है या जैसा हमें पसंद है) *I enjoyed my holiday, but now it's back to reality.* ○ *We have to **face reality** and accept that we've failed.* **2** [C] a thing that is actually experienced, not just imagined वास्तविक अनुभव (न कि काल्पनिक) *Films portray war as heroic and exciting, but the reality is very different.*

IDM **in reality** in fact, really (not the way sth appears or has been described) वास्तव में, यथार्थतः (न कि जैसा वह लगता है या वर्णित है) *People say this is an exciting city but in reality it's rather boring.*

**realize** (*also* **-ise**) /ˈrɪəlaɪz ˈरिअलाइज़् / *verb* [T] **1** to know and understand that sth is true or that sth has happened जानना और समझना (सचाई या भौतिक वास्तविकता को) *I'm sorry I mentioned it, I didn't realize how much it upset you.* ○ *Didn't you realize (that) you needed to bring money?* **2** to become conscious of sth or that sth has happened, usually sometime later किसी बात या कुछ घटित होने का एहसास होना (प्रायः देर से) *When I got home, I realized that I had left my keys at the office.* **3** to make sth that you imagined become reality किसी कल्पना का यथार्थ रूप ग्रहण कर लेना, सोची हुई बात का असलियत में बदल जाना *His worst fears were realized when he saw the damage caused by the fire.* ▶ **realization** (*also* **-isation**) /ˌrɪəlaɪˈzeɪʃn ˌरिअलाइˈज़ेश्न् / *noun* [U] अनुमति, (कार्य) सिद्धि

**really** /ˈrɪəli ˈरिअलि / *adv.* **1** actually; in fact वास्तव में; सचमुच *I couldn't believe it was really happening.* ○ *She wasn't really angry, she was only pretending.* **2** very; very much बहुत; बहुत अधिक *I'm really tired.* ○ *I really hope you enjoy yourself.* **3** used as a question for expressing surprise, interest, doubt, etc. आश्चर्य, रुचि, संदेह आदि व्यक्त करने के लिए प्रश्न रूप में प्रयुक्त (शब्द) *'She's left the job.' 'Really? When did that happen?'* **4** (*used in negative sentences*) used to make what you are saying less strong निषेधवाचक वाक्यों के प्रभाव को कम करने के लिए प्रयुक्त (शब्द) *I don't really agree with that.* **5** used in questions when you are expecting sb to answer 'No' नकारात्मक उत्तर की आशा में प्रश्नात्मक वाक्य में प्रयुक्त (शब्द) *You don't really expect me to believe that, do you?*

**real time** *noun* [U] (*computing*) the fact that there is only a very short time between a computer system receiving information and dealing with it कंप्यूटर द्वारा सूचना-प्राप्ति और प्रक्रमण के बीच समय के अत्यल्प होने की वास्तविकता; वास्तविक (अत्यल्प) समय *To make the training realistic the simulation operates **in real time**.* ○ *real-time missile guidance systems*

**reap** /ri:p रीप् / *verb* [T] to cut and collect a crop (corn, wheat, etc.) फ़सल काट कर सँभालना (*figurative*) *Work hard now and you'll **reap the benefits** later on.*

**reappear** /ˌriːəˈpɪə(r) ˌरीअˈपिअ(र्)/ *verb* [I] to appear again or be seen again पुनः प्रकट या पेश होना या दिखाई देना ▶ **reappearance** /-rəns -रन्स्/ *noun* [C, U] पुनःप्रकटन, दोबारा पेशी

**reappraisal** /ˌriːəˈpreɪzl ˌरीअˈप्रेज़्ल्/ *noun* [C, U] the new examination of a situation, way of doing sth, etc. in order to decide if any changes are necessary किसी स्थिति, कार्यविधि आदि का पुनर्मूल्यांकन (परिवर्तन की आवश्यकता की दृष्टि से)

**rear**[1] /rɪə(r) रिअ(र्)/ *noun* [*sing.*] **1 the rear** the back part पिछला हिस्सा, पिछवाड़ा या पृष्ठ भाग *Smoking is only permitted at the rear of the bus.* **2** the part of your body that you sit on; bottom शरीर का हिस्सा जिसके बल बैठते हैं; नितंब ▶ **rear** *adj.* पृष्ठ, पिछला *the rear window/lights of a car*

IDM **bring up the rear** to be the last one in a race, a line of people, etc. (किसी दौड़, लोगों की कतार आदि में) सबसे पीछे होना

**rear**[2] /rɪə(r) रिअ(र्)/ *verb* **1** [T] to look after and educate children बच्चों के पालन-पोषण और शिक्षा की व्यवस्था करना *This generation of children will be reared without fear of war.* **2** [T] to breed and look after animals on a farm, etc. (फ़ार्म आदि पर) पशुओं के प्रजनन और पालन की व्यवस्था करना *to rear cattle/poultry* **3** [I] **rear (up)** (used about horses) to stand only on the back legs (घोड़ों का) पिछली टाँगों के बल खड़ा होना

**rearrange** /ˌriːəˈreɪndʒ ˌरीअˈरेन्ज्/ *verb* [T] **1** to change the position or order of things वस्तुओं को पुनर्व्यवस्थित करना (उनका स्थान या क्रम बदलना) **2** to change a plan, meeting, etc. that has been fixed पूर्वनिर्धारित बैठक, योजना आदि में परिवर्तन करना *The match has been rearranged for next Wednesday.*

**rear-view mirror** *noun* [C] a mirror in which a driver can see the traffic behind दर्पण या शीशा जिसमें ड्राइवर पीछे का दृश्य देख सकता है; रियर-व्यू मिरर ➪ **car** पर चित्र देखिए।

**reason**[1] /ˈriːzn ˈरीज़्न्/ *noun* **1** [C] **a reason (for sth/for doing sth); a reason why.../that...** a cause or an explanation for sth that has happened or for sth that sb has done कारण, व्याख्या या औचित्य-वर्णन (किसी घटना या कार्य का) *He said he couldn't come but he didn't* ***give a reason.*** ○ ***For some reason*** *they can't give us an answer until next week.* **2** [C, U] **(a) reason (to do sth); (a) reason (for sth/for doing sth)** something that shows that it is right or fair to do sth युक्ति, दलील (किसी काम के सही या उचित होने की) ***I have reason*** *to believe that you've been lying.* ○ *You* ***have every reason*** (= you are completely right) *to be angry.* **3** [U] the ability to think and to make sensible decisions विवेक, तर्क-शक्ति (सोचने और बुद्धिमानी के निर्णय करने की क्षमता) *Only human beings are capable of reason.* **4** [U] what is right or acceptable सही या स्वीकार्य बात *I tried to persuade him not to drive but he just wouldn't* ***listen to reason.*** ○ *I'll pay anything* ***within reason*** *for a ticket.*

IDM **it stands to reason** (*informal*) it is obvious if you think about it यह समझ में आने वाली बात है

**reason**[2] /ˈriːzn ˈरीज़्न्/ *verb* [I, T] to form a judgement or an opinion, after thinking about sth in a logical way कोई निर्णय करना या राय बनाना (तर्कयुक्त सोच-विचार के बाद)

PHR V **reason with sb** to talk to sb in order to persuade him/her to behave or think in a more reasonable way किसी को समझाना-बुझाना (कि वह अधिक समझदारी से व्यवहार करे या सोचे)

**reasonable** /ˈriːznəbl ˈरीज़्नबल्/ *adj.* **1** fair, practical and sensible उचित व्यवहार और विवेकपूर्ण *I think it's reasonable to expect people to keep their promises.* ○ *I tried to be reasonable even though I was very angry.* **2** acceptable and appropriate in a particular situation (स्थिति-विशेष में) स्वीकार्य और उपयुक्त *He made us a reasonable offer for the car.* ✪ विलोम **unreasonable** **3** (used about prices) not too expensive (क़ीमतें) उचित, बहुत अधिक नहीं *We sell good quality food at reasonable prices.* **4** quite good, high, big, etc. but not very कुछ या काफ़ी हद तक (अच्छा, ऊँचा, बड़ा आदि) *His work is of a reasonable standard.*

**reasonably** /ˈriːznəbli ˈरीज़्नब्लि/ *adv.* **1** fairly or quite (but not very) पर्याप्त या काफ़ी (परंतु बहुत नहीं) *The weather was reasonably good but not brilliant.* **2** in a sensible and fair way तर्कयुक्त रूप से, समझदारी वाले और सही तरीक़े से

**reasoning** /ˈriːzənɪŋ ˈरीज़निङ्/ *noun* [U] the process of thinking about sth and making a judgement or decision तर्क; तर्कपूर्ण आधार (किसी बात के विषय में सोच-विचार के साथ राय बनाने या फ़ैसला करने की क्रिया) *What's the reasoning behind his sudden decision to leave?*

**reassurance** /ˌriːəˈʃɔːrəns ˌरीअˈशॉरन्स्/ *noun* [U, C] advice or help that you give to sb to stop him/her worrying or being afraid आश्वासन (चिंता और भय से मुक्ति के लिए परामर्श या सहायता) *I need some reassurance that I'm doing things the right way.*

**reassure** /ˌriːəˈʃɔː(r) ˌरीअˈशॉ(र्)/ *verb* [T] to say or do sth in order to stop sb worrying or being afraid किसी को आश्वस्त करना (चिंता या भय से मुक्त होने के लिए) *The mechanic reassured her that the engine was fine.* ▶ **reassuring** *adj.* आश्वासनकारी ▶ **reassuringly** *adv.* आश्वासनपूर्वक

**rebate** /ˈriːbeɪt ˈरीबेट्/ *noun* [C] a sum of money that is given back to you because you have paid too much (अधिक भुगतान हो जाने के कारण) लौटाई गई राशि *to get a tax rebate*

**rebel¹** /ˈrebl ˈरेब्ल्/ *noun* [C] **1** a person who fights against his/her country's government because he/she wants things to change राजद्रोही; सत्ता-विरोधी व्यक्ति (परिवर्तन की इच्छा से राज्य-शासन से संघर्ष करने वाला व्यक्ति) **2** a person who refuses to obey people in authority or to accept rules विद्रोही; बाग़ी (अधिकारियों के आदेश या नियमों को न मानने वाला व्यक्ति) *At school he had a reputation as a rebel.*

**rebel²** /rɪˈbel रिˈबेल्/ *verb* [I] (**rebelling; rebelled**) **rebel (against sb/sth)** to fight against authority, society, a law, etc. सत्ता, समाज, किसी क़ानून आदि के विरुद्ध संघर्ष करना *She rebelled against her parents by marrying a man she knew they didn't approve of.*

**rebellion** /rɪˈbeljən रिˈबेल्यन्/ *noun* [C, U] **1** an occasion when some of the people in a country try to change the government, using violence राजद्रोह (हिंसा द्वारा देश में सत्ता-परिवर्तन का प्रयास) **2** the action of fighting against authority or refusing to accept rules अधिकारियों के विरुद्ध संघर्ष या नियमों की अवमानना *Voting against the leader of the party was an act of open rebellion.*

**rebellious** /rɪˈbeljəs रिˈबेल्यस्/ *adj.* not doing what authority, society, etc. wants you to do उद्धत, अक्खड़ (शासन, समाज आदि की अवज्ञा करने वाला) *rebellious teenagers*

**reboot** /ˌriːˈbuːt ˌरीˈबूट्/ *verb* [T, I] (*computing*) if you reboot a computer or if it reboots, you turn it off and then turn it on again immediately कंप्यूटर का तैयार होना या को तैयार करना बंद होने या करने के तुरंत बाद दोबारा चालू होने या करने के लिए

**rebound** /rɪˈbaʊnd रिˈबाउन्ड्/ *verb* [I] **rebound (from/off sth)** to hit sth/sb and then go in a different direction (किसी का) टकरा कर दूसरी तरफ चले जाना (या लौटना) *The ball rebounded off a defender and went into the goal.* ▶ **rebound** /ˈriːbaʊnd ˈरीबाउन्ड्/ *noun* [C] प्रतिक्षेप

**rebuff** /rɪˈbʌf रिˈबफ़्/ *noun* [C] an unkind refusal of an offer or suggestion अक्खड़ ढंग से प्रस्ताव या सुझाव की अस्वीकृति ▶ **rebuff** *verb* [T] अक्खड़ ढंग से बात मानने से इनकार करना

**rebuild** /ˌriːˈbɪld ˌरीˈबिल्ड्/ *verb* [T] (*pt, pp* **rebuilt** /ˌriːˈbɪlt ˌरीˈबिल्ट्/) to build sth again (किसी वस्तु को) फिर से बनाना, का पुनर्निमाण करना *Following the storm, a great many houses will have to be rebuilt.*

**rebuke** /rɪˈbjuːk रिˈब्यूक्/ *verb* [T] (*formal*) to speak angrily to sb because he/she has done sth wrong किसी को झाड़ पिलाना, डाँटना-फटकारना (ग़लती पर) ▶ **rebuke** *noun* [C] झाड़, डाँट-फटकार

**recall** /rɪˈkɔːl रिˈकॉल्/ *verb* [T] **1** to remember sth (a fact, event, action, etc.) from the past अतीत की कोई बात (तथ्य, घटना, क्रिया आदि) याद करना *She couldn't recall meeting him before.* **2** to order sb to return; to ask for sth to be returned किसी व्यक्ति को वापस बुलाना; किसी वस्तु को वापस मँगाना *The company has recalled all the fridges that have this fault.*

**recap** /ˈriːkæp ˈरीकैप्/ (**recapping; recapped**) (*spoken*) (*written* **recapitulate** /ˌriːkəˈpɪtʃuleɪt ˌरीकˈपिचुलेट्/) *verb* [I, T] to repeat or look again at the main points of sth to make sure that they have been understood किसी बात के मुख्य बिंदुओं को दोहराना या उनका पुनरावलोकन करना (बात को समझ लिए जाने की पुष्टि के लिए) *Let's quickly recap what we've done in today's lesson.*

**recapture** /ˌriːˈkæptʃə(r) ˌरीˈकैप्च(र्)/ *verb* [T] **1** to win back sth that was taken from you by an enemy or a competitor शत्रु या प्रतिस्पर्धा द्वारा कब्ज़ा की गई वस्तुओं को पुनः प्राप्त कर लेना *Government troops have recaptured the city.* **2** to catch a person or animal that has escaped (क़ैद से) निकल भागे व्यक्ति या पशु को पकड़ लेना **3** to create or experience again sth from the past अतीत के प्रसंग को पुनः सृजन या अनुभव करना *The film brilliantly recaptures life in the 1930s.*

**recede** /rɪˈsiːd रिˈसीड्/ *verb* [I] **1** to move away and begin to disappear दूर जाना और ओझल होने लगना *The coast began to recede into the distance.* **2** (used about a hope, fear, chance, etc.) to become smaller or less strong (आशा, भय, संयोग आदि) कम हो जाना या मंद पड़ जाना **3** (used about a man's hair) to fall out and stop growing at the front of the head (पुरुष के सिर का) आगे से गंजा हो जाना *He's got a **receding hairline**.*

**receipt** /rɪˈsiːt रिˈसीट्/ *noun* **1** [C] **a receipt (for sth)** a piece of paper that is given to show that you have paid for sth रसीद (प्राप्त वस्तु की) *Keep the receipt in case you want to exchange the shirt.* **2** [U] (*formal*) **receipt (of sth)** the act of receiving sth प्राप्ति (कुछ प्राप्त करने की क्रिया)

**receive** /rɪˈsiːv रिˈसीव़् / *verb* [T] **1 receive sth (from sb/sth)** to get or accept sth that sb sends or gives to you प्राप्त या स्वीकार करना (दूसरे के द्वारा भेजी या दी गई वस्तु को) *to receive a phone call/a prize/a letter* **2** to experience a particular kind of treatment or injury विशेष प्रकार का बरताव या सुलूक मिलना या चोट खाना *We received a warm welcome from our hosts.* ○ *He received several cuts and bruises in the accident.* **3** (*often passive*) to react to sth new in a particular way विशेष प्रकार की प्रतिक्रिया करना *The film has been well received by the critics.*

**received pronunciation** = **RP**

**receiver** /rɪˈsiːvə(r) रिˈसीव़(र्) / *noun* [C] **1** (*also* **handset**) the part of a telephone that is used for listening and speaking टेलीफ़ोन का रिसीवर (सुनने-बोलने के लिए प्रयुक्त टेलीफ़ोन उपकरण); चोंगा **2** a piece of television or radio equipment that changes electronic signals into sounds or pictures टीवी या रेडियो का रिसीवर (इलेक्ट्रॉनिक संकेतों को ध्वनि या चित्र में बदलने वाला उपकरण)

**recent** /ˈriːsnt ˈरीसन्ट् / *adj.* that happened or began only a short time ago हालिया; कुछ ही देर पहले का, हाल का ***In recent years*** *there have been many changes.* ○ *This is a recent photograph of my daughter.*

**recently** /ˈriːsntli ˈरीसन्ट्लि / *adv.* not long ago अधिक पहले नहीं, हाल ही में *She worked here until quite recently.* ○ *Have you seen Parul recently?*

**NOTE Recently** से समय-बिंदु और समयावधि दोनों का निर्देश मिलता है। समय-बिंदु के निर्देश में सामान्य भूतकाल का प्रयोग होता है—*He got married recently.* समयावधि के निर्देश में पूर्ण वर्तमान या सातत्यबोधक पूर्ण वर्तमान काल प्रयुक्त होते हैं—*I haven't done anything interesting recently.* ○ *She's been working hard recently.* **Lately** से केवल समयावधि का निर्देश मिलता है और इसके साथ केवल पूर्ण वर्तमान या सातत्यबोधक पूर्ण वर्तमान आते हैं—*I've seen a lot of films lately.* ○ *I've been spending too much money lately.*

**receptacle** /rɪˈseptəkl रिˈसेप्टकल् / *noun* [C] **1 a receptacle (for sth)** (*formal*) a container for putting sth in कुछ रखने का पात्र; आधान, (जैसे संदूक, थैला) **2** the rounded area at the top of a **stem** that supports the head of a flower तने के शीर्ष पर गोलाकार स्थान जो फूल के अग्रभाग को थामता है; पुष्पधर ➪ **flower** पर चित्र देखिए।

**reception** /rɪˈsepʃn रिˈसेप्शन् / *noun* **1** [U] the place inside the entrance of a hotel or office building where guests or visitors go when they first arrive किसी होटल या दफ़्तर का स्वागत-कक्ष; रिसेप्शन *Leave your key* ***at/in reception***. ○ *the reception desk* **2** [C] a formal party to celebrate sth or to welcome an important person महत्त्वपूर्ण व्यक्तियों के सम्मान में आयोजित औपचारिक स्वागत-समारोह ***a wedding reception*** ○ *There will be an official reception at the embassy for the visiting ambassador.* **3** [*sing.*] the way people react to sth लोगों की प्रतिक्रिया *The play got a mixed reception* (= some people liked it, some people didn't). **4** [U] the quality of radio or television signals रेडियो या टीवी संकेतों की गुणवत्ता (स्पष्टता का स्तर) *TV reception is very poor where we live.*

**receptionist** /rɪˈsepʃənɪst रिˈसेप्शनिस्ट् / *noun* [C] a person who works in a hotel, office, etc. answering the telephone and dealing with visitors and guests when they arrive होटल, दफ़्तर आदि के स्वागत-कक्ष में नियुक्त व्यक्ति (जो फ़ोन सुनना अतिथियों का स्वागत करना आदि करता है); स्वागतकर्त्ता, रिसेप्शनिस्ट *a hotel receptionist*

**receptive** /rɪˈseptɪv रिˈसेप्टिव़् / *adj.* **receptive (to sth)** ready to listen to new ideas, suggestions, etc. नए विचारों, सुझावों आदि को सुनने के लिए तैयार; ग्रहणशील

**recess** /rɪˈses रिˈसेस् / *noun* **1** [C, U] a period of time when Parliament, committees, etc. do not meet मध्यावकाश (संसद, समितियों आदि की बैठक आदि के बीच अवकाश का समय) **2** [U] a short break during a trial in a court of law अदालत की कार्रवाई में अल्पकालिक विराम **3** (*AmE*) = **break² 3** ➪ **interval** पर नोट देखिए। **4** [C] part of a wall that is further back than the rest, forming a space दीवार का पीछे को हटा हुआ भाग (ख़ाली जगह बनाते हुए) **5** [C] a part of a room that receives very little light कमरे का बहुत कम रोशनी वाला भाग

**recession** /rɪˈseʃn रिˈसेशन् / *noun* [C, U] a period when the business and industry of a country is not successful (किसी देश के व्यापार और उद्योग में) मंदी का दौर *The country is now* ***in recession***.

**recessive** /rɪˈsesɪv रिˈसेसिव़् / *adj.* (*technical*) a **recessive** physical characteristic only appears in a child if he/she has two **genes** for this characteristic, one from each parent दो जीन (माता से एक, पिता से एक) के लक्षण प्रदर्शित करने वाला (बच्चा या बच्ची); अप्रभावी ➪ **dominant** देखिए।

**recharge** /ˌriːˈtʃɑːdʒ ˌरीˈचाज् / *verb* [T, I] to fill a battery with electrical power; to fill up with electrical power बैटरी में पुनः विद्युत शक्ति भरना, बैटरी को

रिचार्ज करना; (किसी को) विद्युत शक्ति से भर देना *He plugged the drill in to recharge it.* ➪ **charge** देखिए। ▶ **rechargeable** *adj.* रिचार्ज करने योग्य *rechargeable batteries*

**recipe** /ˈresəpi ˈरेसपि/ *noun* [C] **1 a recipe (for sth)** the instructions for cooking or preparing sth to eat. A recipe tells you what to use **(the ingredients)** and what to do भोजन बनाने या कोई खाने की चीज़ तैयार करने के निर्देश; पाकविधि *a recipe for chocolate cake* **2 a recipe for sth** the way to get or produce sth कुछ पाने या बनाने का उपाय *Putting Dinesh in charge of the project is **a recipe for disaster**.*

**recipient** /rɪˈsɪpiənt रिˈसिपिअन्ट्/ *noun* [C] (*formal*) a person who receives sth कुछ प्राप्त करने वाला व्यक्ति; प्राप्तकर्ता

**reciprocal** /rɪˈsɪprəkl रिˈसिप्रक्ल्/ *adj.* involving two or more people or groups who agree to help each other or to behave in the same way towards one another पारस्परिक एक दूसरे के हित में दो व्यक्तियों या वर्गों के बीच होने वाला *The arrangement is reciprocal. They help us and we help them.*

**reciprocate** /rɪˈsɪprəkeɪt रिˈसिप्रकेट्/ *verb* **1** [T, I] (*formal*) **reciprocate (sth) (with sth)** to behave or feel towards sb in the same way as he/she behaves or feels towards you परस्पर आदान-प्रदान करना (भावनाओं या आचरण का), दो व्यक्तियों का एक दूसरे के प्रति समान भाव रखना या आचरण करना *They wanted to reciprocate the kindness that had been shown to them.* ○ *He smiled but his smile was not reciprocated.* **2** [I] (*technical*) to move backwards and forwards in a straight line सीध में आगे-पीछे गति करना *a reciprocating action/movement* ▶ **reciprocation** /rɪˌsɪprəˈkeɪʃn रिˌसिप्रˈकेश्न्/ *noun* [U] आदान-प्रदान

**recital** /rɪˈsaɪtl रिˈसाइट्ल्/ *noun* [C] a formal public performance of music or poetry संगीत-प्रस्तुति या कविता पाठ का सार्वजनिक कार्यक्रम *a piano recital* ➪ **concert** देखिए।

**recitation** /ˌresɪˈteɪʃn ˌरेसिˈटेश्न्/ *noun* [U, C] an act of saying aloud a piece of poetry or prose that you have learned, for people to listen to (कविता या गद्य) प्रपठन

**recite** /rɪˈsaɪt रिˈसाइट्/ *verb* [I, T] to say aloud a piece of writing, especially a poem or a list, from memory (याद की हुई) कविता आदि रचना सुनाना

**reckless** /ˈrekləs ˈरेक्लस्/ *adj.* not thinking about possible bad or dangerous results that could come from your actions दुःसाहसी (अपनी हरकतों के संभावित दुष्परिणामों या ख़तरों के प्रति लापरवाह) *reckless driving* ▶ **recklessly** *adv.* दुःसाहस के साथ, लापरवाही से

**reckon** /ˈrekən ˈरेकन्/ *verb* [T] (*informal*) **1** to think; to have an opinion about sth मानना, समझना; किसी विषय में कोई विचार होना *She's very late now. I reckon (that) she isn't coming.* ○ *I think she's forgotten. What do you reckon?* **2** to calculate sth approximately मोटे तौर पर कोई हिसाब लगाना *I reckon the journey will take about half an hour.* **3** to expect to do sth कुछ करने की आशा करना *I wasn't reckoning to pay so much.*

**PHR V** **reckon on sth** to expect sth to happen and therefore to base a plan or action on it कुछ करने के लिए किसी बात की आशा करना, कोई योजना बनाने या किसी काम के लिए किसी बात पर निर्भर होना *I didn't book in advance because I wasn't reckoning on tickets being so scarce.*

**reckon (sth) up** to calculate the total amount or number of sth किसी वस्तु की कुल मात्रा या संख्या का हिसाब लगाना

**reckon with sb/sth** to think about sb/sth as a possible problem किसी व्यक्ति या वस्तु को संभावित समस्या मानना

**reckoning** /ˈrekənɪŋ ˈरेकनिङ्/ *noun* **1** [U, C] the act of calculating sth, especially in a way that is not very exact मोटा हिसाब, अनुमान **2** [C, *usually sing.*, U] (*formal*) a time when sb's actions will be judged to be right or wrong and they may be punished शुभ या अशुभ कर्मों के अनुसार दंडित होने का समय, क़यामत का दिन *In the **final reckoning** truth is rewarded.* ○ *Officials concerned with environmental policy predict that **a day of reckoning** will come.*

**IDM** **in/into/out of the reckoning** (*BrE*) (especially in sport) among/not among those who are likely to win or be successful (विशेषतः खेल में) जीतने या सफल होने वालों में शामिल या शामिल नहीं *Ganguly is fit again and should come into the reckoning.*

**reclaim** /rɪˈkleɪm रिˈक्लेम्/ *verb* [T] **1 reclaim sth (from sb/sth)** to get back sth that has been lost or taken away खोया हुआ या अन्यत्र ले जाया गया सामान (किसी से) वापस पाना *Reclaim your luggage after you have been through passport control.* **2** to get back useful materials from waste products बेकार हो चुकी चीज़ों से (आवश्यक प्रक्रिया द्वारा) उपयोगी वस्तुएँ प्राप्त कर लेना **3** to make wet land suitable for use दलदल को काम लायक बनाना ▶ **reclamation** /ˌrekləˈmeɪʃn ˌरेक्लˈमेश्न्/ *noun* [U] सुधार, उद्धार, भूमि-उद्धार

**recline** /rɪˈklaɪn रिˈक्लाइन्/ *verb* [I] to sit or lie back in a relaxed and comfortable way आराम

के साथ (सहारा लेते हुए) बैठना या लेटना ▶ **reclining** *adj.* सहारे वाली, ढलानदार *The car has **reclining seats**.*

**recluse** /rɪˈklu:s रिˈक्लूस्/ *noun* [C] **1** a person who lives alone and who maintains very little contact with other people or society एकांतवासी *to lead the life of a recluse* **2** a religious person who lives a life away from other people and society विरागी, संन्यासी ▶ **reclusive** *adv.* एकांतप्रिय *a reclusive lifestyle*

**recognition** /ˌrekəgˈnɪʃn ˌरेकग्ˈनिशन्/ *noun* **1** [U] the fact that you can identify sb/sth that you see किसी को पहचानने की क्रिया *When I arrived no sign of recognition showed on her face at all.* **2** [U, *sing.*] the act of accepting that sth exists, is true or is official किसी का (सत्य या आधिकारिक होने के रूप में) मान्यता देने की क्रिया **3** [U] a public show of respect for sb's work or actions किसी के अच्छे कार्यों की सार्वजनिक प्रशंसा *She has **received** public **recognition** for her services to charity.* ○ *Please accept this gift **in recognition of** the work you have done.*

**recognizable** (*also* **-isable**) /ˈrekəgnaɪzəbl; ˌrekəgˈnaɪzəbl ˈरेकग्नाइज़बल्; ˌरेकग्ˈनाइज़बल्/ *adj.* **recognizable (as sb/sth)** that can be identified as sb/sth व्यक्ति या वस्तु विशेष के रूप में पहचानने लायक; अभिज्ञेय *He was barely recognizable with his new short haircut.* ▶ **recognizably (***also* **-isably)** /-əbli -अबलि/ *adv.* अभिज्ञेय रूप से, ऐसे कि पहचाना जा सके

**recognize** (*also* **-ise**) /ˈrekəgnaɪz ˈरेकग्नाइज़्/ *verb* [T] **1** to know again sb/sth that you have seen or heard before किसी को पहचानना (पहले देखे या सुने को दुबारा जानना) *I recognized him but I couldn't remember his name.* **2** to accept that sth is true किसी बात को सत्य के रूप में स्वीकार करना **3** to accept sth officially किसी को आधिकारिक रूप से स्वीकृति प्रदान करना; मान्यता देना *My qualifications are not recognized in other countries.* **4** to show officially that you think sth that sb has done is good किसी के अच्छे काम या उपलब्धि को आधिकारिक रूप से मानना; क़दर करना

**recoil** /rɪˈkɔɪl रिˈकॉइल्/ *verb* [I] to quickly move away from sb/sth unpleasant अप्रिय व्यक्ति या वस्तु से (घबराकर या घृणा से) पीछे हटना *She recoiled in horror at the sight of the snake.*

**recollect** /ˌrekəˈlekt ˌरेकˈलेक्ट्/ *verb* [I, T] to remember sth, especially by making an effort किसी बात को याद करना (विशेषतः कुछ प्रयास के पश्चात) *I don't recollect exactly when it happened.*

**recollection** /ˌrekəˈlekʃn ˌरेकˈलेक्शन्/ *noun* **1** [U] **recollection (of sth/doing sth)** the ability to remember अनुस्मरण, संस्मृति *I **have no recollection** of promising to lend you money.* **2** [C, *usually pl.*] something that you remember याद, स्मृति *I have only vague recollections of the movie*

**recommend** /ˌrekəˈmend ˌरेकˈमेन्ड्/ *verb* [T] **1 recommend sb/sth (to sb) (for/as sth)** to say that sb/sth is good and that sb should try or use him/her/it किसी की (किसी से) (किसी काम के लिए) सिफ़ारिश करना, अनुशंसा करना *Which film would you recommend?* ○ *Doctors don't always recommend drugs as the best treatment for every illness.* **2** to tell sb what you strongly believe he/she should do किसी को (कोई विशेष काम करने की) सलाह देना *I recommend that you get some legal advice.* ○ *I wouldn't recommend (your) travelling on your own. It could be dangerous.* ➪ **suggest** देखिए।

**recommendation** /ˌrekəmenˈdeɪʃn ˌरेकमेन्ˈडेशन्/ *noun* **1** [C, U] saying that sth is good and should be tried or used (किसी बात की) सिफ़ारिश, अनुशंसा *I visited Goa **on** a friend's **recommendation** and I really enjoyed it.* **2** [C] a statement about what should be done in a particular situation संस्तुति, सिफ़ारिश (स्थिति-विशेष में करने योग्य बातों के विषय में टिप्पणी) *In their report on the crash, the committee **make** several **recommendations** on how safety could be improved.*

**recompense** /ˈrekəmpens ˈरेकम्पेन्स्/ *verb* [T] (*formal*) **recompense sb (for sth)** to give money, etc. to sb for special efforts or work or because you are responsible for a loss he/she has suffered किसी को विशेष प्रयास या काम करने के लिए या किसी को हुई क्षति की पूर्ति में धन आदि देना *The airline has agreed to recompense us for the damage to our luggage.* ▶ **recompense** *noun* [*sing.*, U] क्षतिपूर्ति *Please accept this cheque **in recompense** for our poor service.*

**reconcile** /ˈrekənsaɪl ˈरेकन्साइल्/ *verb* [T] **1 reconcile sth (with sth)** to find a way of dealing with two ideas, situations, statements, etc. that seem to be opposite to each other परस्पर विपरीत प्रतीत होने वाली स्थितियों में ताल-मेल बैठाना *She finds it difficult to reconcile her career ambitions with her responsibilities to her children.* **2** (*often passive*) **reconcile sb (with sb)** to make people become friends again after an argument झगड़े के बाद दो व्यक्तियों में पुनः मेल-मिलाप करा देना *After years of not speaking to each other, she and her parents were eventually reconciled.* **3 reconcile yourself to sth** to accept an unpleasant situation because there is nothing you can do to change it (विवश होकर) अप्रिय स्थिति को स्वीकार कर लेना या से समझौता कर लेना ▶ **reconciliation** /ˌrekənsɪliˈeɪʃn ˌरेकन्सिलिˈएश्न्/ *noun* [*sing*., U] पुनः मेल-मिलाप, सामंजस्य, समन्वय *The negotiators are hoping to bring about a reconciliation between the two sides.*

**reconnaissance** /rɪˈkɒnɪsns रिˈकॉनिसन्स्/ *noun* [C, U] the study of a place or area for military reasons सैन्य कारणों से किसी स्थान या क्षेत्र का सर्वेक्षण *The plane was shot down while on a reconnaissance mission over enemy territory.*

**reconnoitre** /ˌrekəˈnɔɪtə(r) ˌरेकˈनॉइट(र्)/ *verb* [I, T] to obtain information about an area, especially for military purposes (किसी क्षेत्र का) सैन्य जानकारी के लिए टोह लेना या जाँच पड़ताल करना *A naval patrol was sent to reconnoitre the approaches to the bay.*

**reconsider** /ˌriːkənˈsɪdə(r) ˌरीकन्ˈसिड(र्)/ *verb* [I, T] to think again about sth, especially because you may want to change your mind (किसी बात पर) पुनःविचार करना (विशेषतः जब निर्णय बदलने की ज़रूरत हो)

**reconstruct** /ˌriːkənˈstrʌkt ˌरीकन्ˈस्ट्रक्ट्/ *verb* [T] **1** to build again sth that has been destroyed or damaged नष्ट या क्षतिग्रस्त वस्तु का पुनर्निर्माण करना **2** to get a full description or picture of sth using the facts that are known एकत्रित जानकारी के आधार पर स्थिति का पूरा खाका तैयार करना *The police are trying to reconstruct the victim's movements on the day of the murder.* ▶ **reconstruction** /-ˈstrʌkʃn -ˈस्ट्रक्श्न्/ *noun* [C, U] पुनर्निर्माण, पुनःकल्पन, पुनर्रचना *a reconstruction of the crime using actors*

**record**[1] /ˈrekɔːd ˈरेकॉड्/ *noun* **1** [C] **a record (of sth)** a written account of what has happened, been done, etc. घटित घटनाओं और किए गए कामों का लिपिबद्ध विवरण; अभिलेख, रिकॉर्ड *The teachers* ***keep records*** *of the children's progress.* ○ *medical records* **2** [*sing.*] the facts, events, etc. that are known (and sometimes written down) about sb/sth व्यक्ति या वस्तु के विषय में ज्ञात तथ्य, घटनाएँ आदि (कभी-कभी लिपिबद्ध), व्यक्ति या वस्तु का पिछला इतिहास *The police said that the man had* ***a criminal record*** (= he had been found guilty of crimes in the past). ○ *This airline has a bad safety record.* **3** [C] (*also* **album**) a thin, round piece of plastic which can store music so that you can play it when you want ग्रामोफ़ोन का रिकॉर्ड **4** [C] the best performance or the highest or lowest level, etc. ever reached in sth, especially in sport किसी क्षेत्र में (विशेषतः खेल में) सर्वोत्तम प्रदर्शन या उपलब्धि का उच्चतम या निम्नतम स्तर *She's hoping to* ***break the record*** *for the 100 metres.* ○ *He did it* ***in record time*** (= very fast).

IDM **be/go on (the) record (as saying)** to say sth publicly or officially so that it may be written down and repeated सार्वजनिक या आधिकारिक वक्तव्य (लिपिबद्ध होने या दोहराए जाने योग्य) *He didn't want to go on the record as either praising or criticizing the proposal.*

**off the record** if you tell sb sth off the record, it is not yet official and you do not want it to be repeated publicly (वक्तव्य या बयान) जो न आधिकारिक हो न लोगों के लिए, व्यक्तिगत रूप से, निजी स्तर पर *She told me off the record that she was going to resign.*

**put/set the record straight** to correct a mistake by telling sb the true facts सही तथ्यों की सहायता से पहले की ग़लती को सुधारना

**record**[2] /rɪˈkɔːd रिˈकॉड्/ *verb* **1** [T] to write down or film facts or events so that they can be referred to later and will not be forgotten तथ्यों या घटनाओं को भविष्य में उपयोग के लिए लिपिबद्ध या फ़िल्मांकित करना *He recorded everything in his diary.* ○ *At the inquest the coroner* ***recorded a verdict*** *of accidental death.* **2** [I, T] to put music, a film, a programme, etc. onto a CD or cassette so that it can be listened to or watched again later संगीत, फ़िल्म, कार्यक्रम आदि को सीडी या कैसेट पर रिकॉर्ड करना (ताकि बाद में उसे सुना या देखा जा सके) *The band has recently recorded a new album.*

**record-breaking** *adj.* (*only before a noun*) the best, fastest, highest, etc. ever अब तक का सर्वश्रेष्ठ, उच्चतम आदि, वर्तमान कीर्तिमान को भंग या नए कीर्तिमान को स्थापित करने वाला; कीर्तिमान-भंजक या स्थापक *We did the journey in record-breaking time.*

**recorder** /rɪˈkɔːdə(r) रिˈकॉड(र्)/ *noun* [C] **1** a machine for recording sound and/or pictures ध्वनियों, चित्रों को रिकॉर्ड करने वाली मशीन *a tape/cassette/video recorder* **2** a type of musical instrument that is often played by children. You play it by blowing through it and covering the holes in it with your fingers (बाँसुरी के समान बजाया जाने वाला) बच्चों का एक संगीत यंत्र

**recording** /rɪˈkɔːdɪŋ रिˈकॉडिङ्/ *noun* **1** [C] sound or pictures that have been put onto a cassette, CD, film, etc. (कैसेट, सीडी आदि पर) रिकॉर्ड किया गया चित्र या ध्वनि *the recording of Sonu Nigam's songs* **2** [U] the process of making a cassette, record, film, etc. कैसेट, रिकॉर्ड, फ़िल्म आदि बनाने की प्रक्रिया *a recording session/studio*

**record player** *noun* [C] a machine that you use for playing records रिकॉर्ड बजाने की मशीन; रिकॉर्ड प्लेयर

**recount** /rɪˈkaʊnt रिˈकाउन्ट्/ *verb* [T] (*formal*) to tell a story or describe an event कोई कहानी सुनाना या घटना का वर्णन करना

**recourse** /rɪˈkɔːs रिˈकॉस्/ *noun* [C] (*formal*) having to use sth or ask sb for help in a difficult situation कठिन समय में उपयोग की वस्तु या सहायता का स्रोत; शरण, सहारा, आश्रय *She made a complete recovery without recourse to surgery.*

**recover** /rɪˈkʌvə(r) रिˈकव़(र्)/ *verb* **1** [I] **recover (from sth)** to become well again after you have been ill बीमारी के बाद स्वास्थ्य लाभ करना *It took him two months to recover from the operation.* **2** [I] **recover (from sth)** to get back to normal again after a bad experience, etc. कष्टप्रद अनुभव आदि के बाद पुनः सामान्य स्थिति में आना *The old lady never really recovered from the shock of being robbed.* **3** [T] **recover sth (from sb/sth)** to find or get back sth that was lost or stolen खोयी हुई वस्तु को ढूँढ़ लेना या चोरी गई वस्तु को पुनः पा लेना *Police recovered the stolen goods from a warehouse in Khandala.* **4** [T] to get back the use of your senses, control of your emotions, etc. (भावनात्मक दृष्टि से) फिर से भला-चंगा या चुस्त-दुरुस्त हो जाना

**recovery** /rɪˈkʌvəri रिˈकव़रि/ *noun* **1** [*usually sing.*, U] **recovery (from sth)** a return to good health after an illness or to a normal state after a difficult period of time बीमारी के बाद स्वास्थ्य-लाभ या कठिन समय के बाद सामान्य अवस्था *to make a good/quick/speedy/slow recovery* ○ *She's **on the road to recovery*** (= getting better all the time) *now.* ○ *the prospects of **economic recovery*** **2** [U] **recovery (of sth/sb)** getting back sth that was lost, stolen or missing खोये जाने या चोरी होने के बाद वस्तु की पुनःप्राप्ति

**recreation** /ˌrekriˈeɪʃn ˌरेक्रिˈएश्न्/ *noun* [U, *sing.*] enjoying yourself and relaxing when you are not working; a way of doing this मनोरंजन, मन-बहलाव; कोई मनोरंजन-क्रिया *the need to improve facilities for leisure and recreation* ▶ **recreational** /ˌrekriˈeɪʃənl ˌरेक्रिˈएशन्ल्/ *adj.* मनोरंजन-संबंधी *recreational activities*

**recrimination** /rɪˌkrɪmɪˈneɪʃn रिˌक्रिमिˈनेश्न्/ *noun* [C, *usually pl.*, U] an angry statement accusing sb of sth, especially in answer to a similar statement from him/her किसी विषय में किसी व्यक्ति द्वारा दूसरे पर पलट कर लगाया गया आरोप-प्रत्यारोप विशेषतः दूसरे के द्वारा लगाए गए आरोप के जवाब में *bitter recriminations*

**recruit**[1] /rɪˈkruːt रिˈक्रूट्/ *noun* [C] a person who has just joined the army or another organization सेना या ऐसे ही किसी संगठन में अभी भरती हुआ व्यक्ति; रंगरूट

**recruit**[2] /rɪˈkruːt रिˈक्रूट्/ *verb* [I, T] to find new people to join a company, an organization, the armed forces, etc. किसी कंपनी, संगठन, सशस्त्र सेना आदि में नई भरती करना ▶ **recruitment** *noun* [U] भरती

**rectal** /ˈrektəl ˈरेक्टल्/ ➪ **rectum** देखिए।

**rectangle** /ˈrektæŋgl ˈरेक्टैङ्ग्ल्/ *noun* [C] a shape with four straight sides and four angles of 90 degrees (**right angles**). Two of the sides are longer than the other two आयात ✪ पर्याय **oblong** ➪ **shape** पर चित्र देखिए। ▶ **rectangular** /rekˈtæŋgjələ(r) रेक्ˈटैङ्ग्यल(र्)/ *adj.* आयताकार

**rectify** /ˈrektɪfaɪ ˈरेक्टिफ़ाइ/ *verb* [T] (*pres. part.* **rectifying;** *3rd person sing. pres.* **rectifies;** *pt, pp* **rectified**) (*formal*) to correct sth that is wrong अशुद्ध को शुद्ध करना

**rector** /ˈrektə(r) ˈरेक्ट(र्)/ *noun* [C] (in the Church of England) a priest in charge of a certain area (**a parish**) (इंग्लैंड के चर्च में) पुरोहित (जो क्षेत्र विशेष का प्रभारी होता है)

**rectum** /ˈrektəm ˈरेक्टम्/ *noun* [C] the end section of the tube through which solid waste leaves the body मलद्वार, गुदा ▶ **rectal** *adj.* गुदा-संबंधी

**recuperate** /rɪˈkuːpəreɪt रिˈकूपरेट्/ *verb* [I] (*formal*) **recuperate (from sth)** to get well again after an illness or injury बीमारी या चोट के बाद पनुः स्वस्थ होना ▶ **recuperation** /rɪˌkuːpəˈreɪʃn रिˌकूपˈरेश्न्/ *noun* [U] स्वास्थ्य-लाभ

**recur** /rɪˈkɜː(r) रिˈक(र्)/ *verb* [I] (**recurring; recurred**) to happen again or many times दोबारा या अनेक बार घटित होना; पुनरावृत्त होना *a recurring problem/illness/nightmare* ▶ **recurrence** /rɪˈkʌrəns रिˈकरन्स्/ *noun* [C, U] पुनरावृत्ति ▶ **recurrent** /rɪˈkʌrənt रिˈकरन्ट्/ *adj.* पुनरावर्तक

**recycle** /ˌriːˈsaɪkl ˌरीˈसाइक्ल्/ *verb* [T] **1** to put used objects and materials through a process so that they can be used again इस्तेमाल की जा चुकी वस्तुओं को पुनः इस्तेमाल के लिए तैयार करना, पुनः चक्रित करना; पुनश्चक्रण *recycled paper* ○ *Aluminium cans can be recycled.* **2** to keep used objects and materials and use them again इस्तेमाल की जा चुकी वस्तुओं को सँभाल कर रखना और उन्हें फिर से इस्तेमाल करना *Don't throw away your plastic carrier bags—recycle them!* ▶ **recyclable** *adj.* पुनः इस्तेमाल करने योग्य; पुनः प्रयोग्य *Most plastics are recyclable.*

**red** /red रेड्/ *noun* [C, U], *adj.* (**redder; reddest**) **1** (of) the colour of blood लाल (रंग का), ख़ून के रंग का *red wine* ○ *She was dressed in red.*

NOTE 'लाल रंग के विभिन्न आभा-भेदों का निर्देश करने वाले शब्द **crimson, maroon** और **scarlet** हैं।

**2** a colour that some people's faces become when they are embarrassed, angry, shy, etc. झेंपने, गुस्सा होने, शर्माने आदि से चेहरे पर आया रंग; लाल *He went bright red when she spoke to him.* ○ *to turn/be/go red in the face* **3** (used about a person's hair or an animal's fur) (of) a colour between red, orange and brown (मनुष्य का बाल या पशु का फ़र) ललौहा-भूरा *She's got red hair and freckles.*

IDM **be in the red** to have spent more money than you have in the bank, etc. बैंक में जमा राशि से अधिक ख़र्च कर देना *I'm Rs 500 in the red at the moment.* ✪ विलोम **be in the black**

**catch sb red-handed** ➪ **catch**[1] देखिए।

**a red herring** an idea or a subject which takes people's attention away from what is really important जो वस्तुतः महत्त्वपूर्ण है उससे ध्यान हटा लेने वाला विचार या विषय, ध्यान बँटाने वाली बात

**see red** (*informal*) to become very angry बहुत क्रोधित होना, क्रोध से लाल-पीला होना, आपे से बाहर होना

**red card** *noun* [C] (in football) a card that is shown to a player who is being sent off the field for doing sth wrong (फ़ुटबॉल में) लाल कार्ड (गंभीर नियमोल्लंघन पर मैदान से बाहर किए जाने वाले खिलाड़ी को दिखाया जाने वाला कार्ड) ➪ **yellow card** देखिए।

**the red carpet** *noun* [*sing.*] a piece of red carpet that is put outside to receive an important visitor; a special welcome for an important visitor सम्मानित अतिथि के स्वागत में बिछाया गया लाल कालीन; सम्मानित अतिथि का हार्दिक स्वागत *I didn't expect to be given the red carpet treatment!*

**the Red Cross** *noun* [*sing.*] an international organization that takes care of people who are suffering because of war or natural disasters. Its full name is 'the International Movement of the Red Cross and the Red Crescent' रेडक्रॉस (युद्ध या प्राकृतिक विपदाओं से पीड़ित लोगों की देखभाल करने वाली अंतरराष्ट्रीय संस्था)

**redcurrant** /ˌredˈkʌrənt ˌरेड्ˈकरन्ट्/ *noun* [C] a small red berry that you can eat खाने की छोटी लाल बेरी जैसा फल *redcurrant jelly*

**redden** /ˈredn ˈरेड्न्/ *verb* [I, T] to become red or to make sth red चेहरे का लाल हो जाना या कर देना

NOTE इस अर्थ में **go red** या **blush** अधिक प्रचलित प्रयोग है।

**reddish** /ˈredɪʃ ˈरेडिश्/ *adj.* fairly red in colour कुछ-कुछ लाल, ललछौहाँ, रक्ताभ

**redeem** /rɪˈdiːm रिˈडीम्/ *verb* [T] **1** to prevent sth from being completely bad किसी को पूर्णतया घटिया होने से बचा लेना *The **redeeming feature** of the job is the good salary.* **2 redeem yourself** to do sth to improve people's opinion of you, especially after you have done sth bad लोगों की नज़रों में अच्छा बनने के लिए कुछ करना (विशेषतः कोई ग़लत काम करने के बाद)

**redemption** /rɪˈdempʃn रिˈडेम्पूश्न्/ *noun* [U] (according to the Christian religion) the action of being saved from evil (ईसाई धर्म में) दुष्कर्म से बचाव या पाप से सुरक्षा या मुक्ति

IDM **beyond redemption** too bad to be saved or improved इतना ख़राब कि बचाव या सुधार संभव न हो, सुधार से परे

**redevelop** /ˌriːdɪˈveləp ˌरीडिˈवेलप्/ *verb* [T] to build or arrange an area, a town, a building, etc. in a different and more modern way किसी क्षेत्र, शहर, इमारत आदि को पुनर्विकसित करना *They're redeveloping the town centre.* ▶ **redevelopment** *noun* [U] पुनर्विकास

**redhead** /ˈredhed ˈरेड्हेड्/ *noun* [C] a person, usually a woman, who has red hair लाल बालों वाला व्यक्ति (प्रायः महिला)

**red-hot** *adj.* (used about a metal) so hot that it turns red (धातु) ख़ूब गरम (इसलिए लाल), रक्ततप्त, जलता हुआ

**redial** /ˌriːˈdaɪəl ˌरीˈडाइअल्/ *verb* [I, T] (on a telephone) to call the same number that you have just called (टेलीफ़ोन पर) अभी डायल किए नंबर को दुबारा डायल करना

**redistribute** /ˌriːdɪˈstrɪbjuːt; ˌriːˈdɪs- ˌरीडिˈस्ट्रिब्यूट्; ˌरीˈडिस्-/ *verb* [T] to share sth out among people in a different way from before भिन्न तरीक़े से लोगों में कुछ बाँटना; पुनर्वितरण करना ▶ **redistribution** /ˌriːdɪstrɪˈbjuːʃn ˌरीडिस्ट्रिˈब्यूश्न्/ *noun* [U] पुनर्वितरण

**redo** /ˌriːˈduː ˌरीˈडू/ *verb* [T] (*3rd person sing. pres.* **redoes** /-ˈdʌz ˈडज़्/; *pt* **redid** /-ˈdɪd -ˈडिड्/; *pp* **redone** /-ˈdʌn -ˈडन्/) to do sth again or differently कोई काम दोबारा या भिन्न प्रकार से करना *A whole day's work had to be redone.* ○ *We've just redone the bathroom* (= decorated it differently).

**red pepper** *noun* [C] = **pepper**[1] **2**

**red tape** *noun* [U] official rules that must be followed and papers that must be filled in, which seem unnecessary and often cause delay and difficulty in achieving sth दफ़्तरी मामलों में (प्रायः अनावश्यक और देरी एवं कठिनाई पैदा करने वाली) काग़ज़ी कार्रवाई, लालफ़ीताशाही

**reduce** /rɪˈdju:s रि'ड्यूस्/ *verb* [T] **1 reduce sth (from sth) (to sth); reduce sth (by sth)** to make sth less or smaller in quantity, price, size, etc. मात्रा, क़ीमत, आकार आदि की दृष्टि से घटाना; छोटा करना *The sign said 'Reduce speed now'.* ✪ विलोम **increase 2 reduce sb/sth (from sth) to sth** (*often passive*) to force sb/sth into a particular state or condition, usually a bad one व्यक्ति या वस्तु को विशिष्ट स्थिति (प्रायः बदतर) में ला देना या धकेल देना *One of the older boys **reduced** the small child **to tears**.*

**reduction** /rɪˈdʌkʃn रि'डक्शन्/ *noun* **1** [C, U] **reduction (in sth)** the action of becoming or making sth less or smaller पहले से कम या छोटा होने या करने की क्रिया; कमी, घटाव, कटौती *a sharp reduction in the number of students* **2** [C] the amount by which sth is made smaller, especially in price कटौती की मात्रा (विशेषतः दाम में) *There were massive reductions in the June sales.*

**redundant** /rɪˈdʌndənt रि'डन्डन्ट्/ *adj.* **1** (used about employees) no longer needed for a job and therefore out of work (कर्मचारी) ग़ैर-ज़रूरी और इसलिए बेकार, फ़ालतू, अतिरिक्त *When the factory closed 800 people were **made redundant**.* **2** not necessary or wanted अनिवार्य या इच्छित नहीं ▶ **redundancy** /-dənsi -डन्सि/ *noun* [C, U] (*pl.* **redundancies**) बेकारी, फ़ालतू, अतिरिक्त *redun-dancy pay*

**reed** /ri:d रीड्/ *noun* [C] **1** a tall plant, like grass, that grows in or near water सरकंडा, नरकट, नरकुल (जो पानी में या उसके पास उगता है) ➪ **plant** पर चित्र देखिए। **2** a thin piece of wood at the end of some musical instruments which produces a sound when you blow through it (बाँसुरी जैसे) कुछ वाद्य यंत्रों में लगी लकड़ी की छोटी पत्ती (जो फूँक मारने पर आवाज़ उत्पन्न करती है); कंपिका, रीड

**reef** /ri:f रीफ़्/ *noun* [C] a long line of rocks, plants, etc. just below or above the surface of the sea (समुद्र के जल में थोड़ा नीचे या सतह पर बनी) चट्टानों, वनस्पतियों आदि की शृंखला; शैलभित्ति, जलशैल *a coral reef*

**reek** /ri:k रीक्/ *verb* [I] **reek (of sth)** to smell strongly of sth unpleasant दुर्गंध देना, बदबू मारना *His breath reeked of tobacco.* ▶ **reek** *noun* [*sing.*] दुर्गंध, बदबू

**reel[1]** /ri:l रील्/ *noun* [C] a round object that thread, wire, film for cameras, etc. is put around रील, चरख़ी (जिस पर धागा, तार, कैमरे की फ़िल्म आदि लपेटे जाते हैं) *a cotton reel* ○ *a reel of film* ➪ **spool** देखिए तथा **gardening** पर चित्र देखिए।

**reel[2]** /ri:l रील्/ *verb* **1** [I] to walk without being able to control your legs, for example because you are drunk or you have been hit (नशे में होने या चोट खा जाने के कारण) लड़खड़ाते या डगमगाते हुए चलना **2** [I] to feel very shocked or upset about sth (किसी बात से) आहत होना या परेशानी महसूस करना *His mind was still reeling from the shock of seeing her again.* **3** [T] **reel sth in/out** to put sth on or take sth off a reel रील पर लपेटना या रील पर से उतारना *to reel in a fish*

**PHRV reel sth off** to say or repeat sth from memory quickly and without having to think about it धड़ाधड़ बोलना या दोहराना *She reeled off a long list of names.*

**re-entry** *noun* [U] **re-entry (into sth) 1** the act of returning to a place or an area of activity that you used to be in अपने पुराने स्थान या कार्यक्षेत्र में लौटकर आने की क्रिया; पुनःप्रवेश *She feared she would not be granted re-entry into Britain.* **2** (*technical*) the return of a spacecraft into the earth's atmosphere अंतरिक्ष यान की पृथ्वी के वायुमंडल में वापसी *The capsule gets very hot on re-entry.*

**ref.** *abbr.* reference संदर्भ *ref. no. 3456*

**refectory** /rɪˈfektri रि'फ़ेक्ट्रि/ *noun* [C] (*pl.* **refectories**) (*BrE old-fashioned*) a large room in a college, school, etc. where meals are served कॉलेज, स्कूल आदि में भोजन-कक्ष

**refer** /rɪˈfɜ:(r) रि'फ़(र्)/ *verb* (**refer<u>r</u>ing; refer<u>r</u>ed**) **1** [I] **refer to sb/sth (as sth)** to mention or talk about sb/sth व्यक्ति या वस्तु के विषय में उल्लेख या चर्चा करना *When he said 'some students', do you think he was referring to us?* ○ *She always referred to Mohan as 'that nice man'.* **2** [I] **refer to sb/sth** to describe or be connected with sb/sth व्यक्ति या वस्तु का वर्णन करना या उससे संबंध बताना *The term 'adolescent' refers to young people between the ages of 12 and 17.* **3** [I] **refer to sb/sth** to find out information by asking sb or by looking in a book, etc. अपेक्षित जानकारी के लिए किसी से पूछना या पुस्तक आदि देखना *If you don't understand a word you may refer to your dictionaries.* **4** [T] **refer sb/sth to sb/sth** to send sb/sth to sb/sth else for help or to be dealt with व्यक्ति या वस्तु को दूसरे व्यक्ति या वस्तु के पास सहायता या अपेक्षित कार्रवाई के लिए भेजना *The doctor has referred me to a specialist.*

**referee** /ˌrefəˈri: ˌरेफ़'री/ *noun* [C] **1** (*informal* **ref**) the official person in sports such as football who controls the match and prevents players from breaking the rules (फ़ुटबॉल आदि खेलकूद में)

रेफ़री, निर्णायक NOTE टेनिस आदि खेलों में निर्णायक को **umpire** कहते हैं। 2 (*BrE*) a person who gives information about your character and ability, usually in a letter, for example when you are hoping to be chosen for a job किसी की (जैसे नौकरी के उम्मीदवार की) योग्यता आदि को (प्रायः पत्र द्वारा) प्रमाणित करने वाला व्यक्ति; रेफ़री *Her teacher agreed to **act as her referee**.* ▶ **referee** *verb* [I, T] रेफ़री का काम करना, रेफ़री होना

**reference** /ˈrefrəns ˈरेफ़्रन्स्/ *noun* 1 [C, U] **(a) reference (to sb/sth)** a written or spoken comment that mentions sb/sth व्यक्ति या वस्तु के विषय में लिपिबद्ध या मौखिक वक्तव्य; उल्लेख, ज़िक्र *The article **made a** direct **reference** to a certain member of the royal family.* 2 [U] looking at sth for information जानकारी पाने के लिए कुछ देखने की क्रिया *The guidebook might be useful **for future reference**.* 3 [C] a note, especially in a book, that tells you where certain information came from or can be found विशिष्ट जानकारी का उद्‌गम या स्रोत बताने वाली टिप्पणी (विशेषतः पुस्तक में), पुस्तक आदि में संदर्भ-सूची (ग्रंथों की) 4 [C] (*abbr.* **ref.**) (used on business letters, etc.) a special number that identifies a letter, etc. (व्यापारिक पत्र आदि में) पत्र आदि की पहचान बताने वाली विशिष्ट संस्था; पत्रांक, पत्र संख्या, संदर्भ, हवाला *Please quote our reference when replying.* 5 [C] a statement or letter describing a person's character and ability that is given to a possible future employer (नौकरी के इच्छुक) व्यक्ति के चरित्र और योग्यता का प्रमाणपत्र (भावी नियोक्ता या मालिक के उपयोग के लिए) *My boss gave me a good reference.*

IDM **with reference to sb/sth** (*formal*) about or concerning sb/sth व्यक्ति या वस्तु के विषय में या उससे संबंधित *I am writing with reference to the advertisment dated 10 April.*

**reference book** *noun* [C] a book that you use to find a piece of information जानकारी देने वाला ग्रंथ; संदर्भ-ग्रंथ *dictionaries, encyclopedias and other reference books*

**referendum** /ˌrefəˈrendəm ˌरेफ़ˈरेन्डम्/ *noun* [C, U] (*pl.* **referendums** or **referenda** /-də -डा/) an occasion when all the people of a country can vote on a particular political question विशिष्ट राजनीतिक मुद्दे पर जनमत संग्रह *to hold a referendum*

**refill** /ˌriːˈfɪl ˌरीˈफ़िल्/ *verb* [T] to fill sth again (किसी को) फिर से भरना *Can I refill your glass?* ▶ **refill** /ˈriːfɪl ˈरीफ़िल्/ *noun* [C] फिर से भरा जाने वाला पदार्थ; रीफ़िल (पेन आदि का) *a refill for a pen*

**refine** /rɪˈfaɪn रिˈफ़ाइन्/ *verb* [T] 1 to make a substance pure and free from other substances (मिलावट दूर कर) किसी पदार्थ को शुद्ध करना *to refine sugar/oil* 2 to improve sth by changing little details छोटे-मोटे परिवर्तन लाकर किसी में सुधार करना *to refine a theory*

**refined** /rɪˈfaɪnd रिˈफाइन्ड्/ *adj.* 1 (used about a substance) that has been made pure by having other substances taken out of it (पदार्थ) मिलावट दूर कर शुद्ध हुआ; शोधित, परिष्कृत *refined sugar/oil/flour* 2 (used about a person) polite; having very good manners (व्यक्ति) शिष्ट विनीत; सुसंस्कृत ✪ विलोम **unrefined** (अर्थ सं. 1 और 2 के लिए) 3 improved and therefore producing a better result परिमार्जित (और अतएव फलदायक)

**refinement** /rɪˈfaɪnmənt रिˈफ़ाइन्मन्ट्/ *noun* 1 [C] a small change that improves sth सुधार के लिए थोड़ा-सा परिवर्तन *The new model has electric windows and other refinements.* 2 [U] good manners and polite behaviour सुरुचिपूर्ण आचार और शिष्ट व्यवहार

**refinery** /rɪˈfaɪnəri रिˈफ़ाइनरि/ *noun* [C] (*pl.* **refineries**) a factory where a substance is made pure by having other substances taken out of it मिलावट दूर कर किसी वस्तु को शुद्ध करने का कारख़ाना, (तेल आदि) शोधक कारख़ाना *an oil/sugar refinery*

**reflect** /rɪˈflekt रिˈफ़्लेक्ट्/ *verb* 1 [T] to send back light, heat or sound from a surface (किसी सतह से) प्रकाश, ताप या ध्वनि को वापस भेजना या परावर्तित करना *The windows reflected the bright morning sunlight.* 2 [T] **reflect sb/sth (in sth)** (*usually passive*) to show an image of sb/sth on the surface of sth such as a mirror, water or glass दर्पण, जल आदि में व्यक्ति या वस्तु का प्रतिबिंब दिखना *She caught sight of herself reflected in the shop window.* 3 [T] to show or express sth कुछ दिखाना या व्यक्त करना *His music reflects his interest in African culture.* 4 [I] **reflect (on/upon sth)** to think, especially deeply and carefully, about sth किसी बात पर चिंतन करना (विशेषतः गहराई और सावधानी से)

PHR V **reflect (well, badly, etc.) on sb/sth** to give a particular impression of sb/sth व्यक्ति या वस्तु के विषय में विशेष प्रकार का (अच्छा या बुरा) प्रभाव छोड़ना *It reflects badly on the whole school if some of its pupils misbehave in public.*

**reflection** (*BrE* **reflexion**) /rɪˈflekʃn रिˈफ़्लेक्श्न्/ *noun* 1 [C] an image that you see in a mirror, in water or on a shiny surface (दर्पण, जल या किसी चमकदार सतह पर दिखने वाला) प्रतिबिंब *He admired his reflection in the mirror.* 2 [U] the sending back of light, heat or sound from a surface किसी

सतह से प्रकाश, ताप या ध्वनि की वापसी; परावर्तन **3** [C] a thing that shows what sb/sth is like किसी चीज़ का आभास (कि वह कैसी है) *Your clothes are a reflection of your personality.* **4** [*sing.*] **a reflection on/upon sb/sth** something that causes people to form a good or bad opinion about sb/sth व्यक्ति या वस्तु के विषय में टिप्पणी (अच्छी या बुरी) *Parents often feel that their children's behaviour is a reflection on themselves.* **5** [U, C] careful thought about sth सावधानीपूर्वक किया गया विचार *a book of his **reflections on** fatherhood*

**IDM on reflection** after thinking again पुनर्विचार के बाद *I think, on reflection, that we were wrong.*

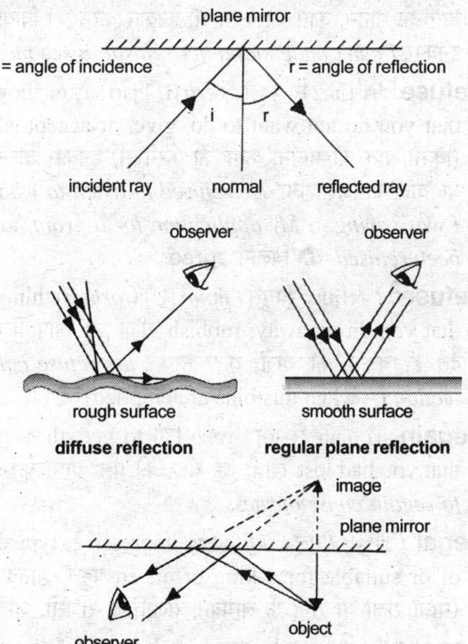


**reflection**

**reflective** /rɪˈflektɪv रिˈफ़्लेक्टिव़् / *adj.* **1** (*written*) (used about a person, mood, etc.) thinking deeply about things (व्यक्ति, मनोदशा आदि) विचारशील *a reflective expression* **2** (used about a surface) sending back light or heat (कोई सतह) प्रकाश या ताप को लौटाने वाला; परावर्तनशील *Wear reflective strips when you're cycling at night.* **3 reflective (of sth)** showing what sth is like (कुछ) दिखाने वाला

**reflector** /rɪˈflektə(r) रिˈफ़्लेक्टर्(र्)/ *noun* [C] **1** a surface that sends back (**reflects**) light, heat or sound that hits it प्रकाश, ताप या ध्वनि को परावर्तित करने वाली सतह **2** a small piece of glass or plastic on a bicycle or on clothing that can be seen at night when light shines on it साइकिल या किसी कपड़े पर लगा और रात के समय प्रकाश पड़ने पर चमकने वाला छोटा काँच या प्लास्टिक का टुकड़ा; रिफ़्लेक्टर

**reflex** /ˈri:fleks ˈरीफ़्लेक्स् / *noun* **1** [C] (*also* **reflex action**) a sudden movement or action that you make without thinking (बिना पूर्व विचार के) एकाएक हुई हरकत या क्रिया; प्रतिवर्ती क्रिया *She put her hands out as a reflex to stop her fall.* **2 reflexes** [*pl.*] the ability to act quickly when necessary आवश्यकता के समय तुरंत सक्रिय हो जाने की योग्यता *A good tennis player needs to have excellent reflexes.*

**reflex angle** *noun* [C] (*mathematics*) an angle of more than 180 degree, 180 अंश से बड़ा कोण ➪ **acute angle, obtuse angle** और **right angle** देखिए तथा **angle** पर चित्र देखिए।

**reflexion** (*BrE*) = **reflection**

**reflexive** /rɪˈfleksɪv रिˈफ़्लेक्सिव़् / *adj., noun* [C] (*grammar*) (a word or verb form) showing that the person who performs an action is also affected by it निजवाचक (शब्द या क्रिया रूप जो यह दिखाए कि कार्य को करने वाला भी उससे प्रभावित होता है); आत्मवाचक *In 'He cut himself', 'himself' is a **reflexive pronoun**.*

**reform** /rɪˈfɔ:m रिˈफ़ॉम् / *verb* **1** [T] to change a system, the law, etc. in order to make it better व्यवस्था, क़ानून आदि में सुधार लाना **2** [I, T] to improve your behaviour; to make sb do this व्यक्ति का अपने आचरण को सुधारना; दूसरे के आचरण को सुधारना *Our prisons aim to reform criminals, not simply to punish them.* ▶ **reform** *noun* [C, U] सुधार

**reformation** /ˌrefəˈmeɪʃn ˌरेफ़ˈमेश्न् / *noun* **1** [U] (*formal*) the act of improving or changing sb/sth व्यक्ति या वस्तु में सुधार या परिवर्तन **2 the Reformation** [*sing.*] new ideas in religion in 16th century Europe that led to changes in the Roman Catholic Church and the forming of the Protestant Churches; the period in history when these changes were taking place, 16 वीं सदी में यूरोप में हुआ धर्म सुधार आंदोलन (जिसके फलस्वरूप रोमन कैथोलिक चर्च में परिवर्तन हुए और प्रोटेस्टेंट चर्च स्थापित हुआ); (इतिहास में) यह धर्म सुधार आंदोलन काल

**reformer** /rɪˈfɔ:mə(r) रिˈफ़ॉम(र्)/ *noun* [C] a person who tries to change society and make it better समाज में सुधार के लिए प्रयत्नशील व्यक्ति; समाज-सुधारक

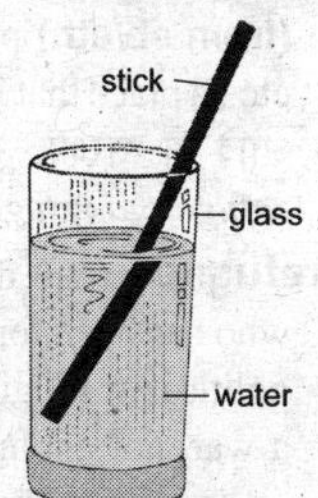


**refract** /rɪˈfrækt रिˈफ़्रैक्ट् / *verb* [T] (in physics) (used about water, glass, etc.) to make a ray of light change direction when it goes through at an angle (भौतिक विज्ञान में) (पानी, काँच आदि का) प्रकाश रेखा का

दिशा-परिवर्तन करना (जब प्रकाश एक कोण में से गुज़रे), अपवर्तन करना ▶ **refraction** *noun* [U] अपवर्तन

**refrain[1]** /rɪˈfreɪn रिˈफ्रेन्/ *verb* [I] (*formal*) **refrain (from sth/from doing sth)** to stop yourself doing sth; to not do sth कुछ करने से अपने को रोकना; कोई (ख़ास) काम न करना *Please refrain from smoking in the hospital.*

**refrain[2]** /rɪˈfreɪn रिˈफ्रेन्/ *noun* [C] (*formal*) a part of a song which is repeated, usually at the end of each verse गीत में टेक (जो प्रायः प्रत्येक छंद के अंत में दोहाराई जाती है) ✪ पर्याय **chorus**

**refresh** /rɪˈfreʃ रिˈफ्रेश्/ *verb* [T] to make sb/sth feel less tired or less hot and full of energy again व्यक्ति या वस्तु की थकावट दूर करना, नई स्फूर्ति देना *He looked refreshed after a good night's sleep.*

IDM **refresh your memory (about sb/sth)** to remind yourself about sb/sth व्यक्ति या वस्तु के विषय में याद ताज़ा करना *Could you refresh my memory about what we said on this point last week?*

**refreshing** /rɪˈfreʃɪŋ रिˈफ्रेशिङ्/ *adj.* **1** pleasantly new or different प्रियकर रूप से नया या भिन्न *It makes **a refreshing change** to meet somebody who is so enthusiastic.* **2** making you feel less tired or hot थकावट दूर करने वाला; स्फूर्तिदायक *a refreshing swim/shower/drink*

**refreshment** /rɪˈfreʃmənt रिˈफ्रेश्मन्ट्/ *noun* **1 refreshments** [*pl.*] light food and drinks that are available at a cinema, theatre or other public places (सिनेमा, थिएटर तथा अन्य सार्वजनिक स्थलों आदि में उपलब्ध) अल्पाहार, नाश्ता **2** [U] (*formal*) the fact of making sb feel stronger and less tired or hot; food or drink that helps to do this तरोताज़ा होने की स्थिति, ताज़गी; ताज़गी देने वाले खाद्य और पेय पदार्थ

**refrigerate** /rɪˈfrɪdʒəreɪt रिˈफ्रिजरेट्/ *verb* [T] to make food, etc. cold in order to keep it fresh सुरक्षित रखने के लिए भोजन आदि को ठंडा करना; भोजन का प्रशीतन करना ▶ **refrigeration** /rɪˌfrɪdʒəˈreɪʃn रिˌफ्रिजˈरेशन्/ *noun* [U] प्रशीतन ▶ **refrigerator** (*formal*) = **fridge**

**refuge** /ˈrefju:dʒ ˈरिफ़्यूज्/ *noun* [C, U] **refuge (from sb/sth)** protection from danger, trouble, etc.; a place that is safe किसी ख़तरा, अशांति, परेशानी आदि से सुरक्षा; सुरक्षित स्थान, शरणस्थल *to **take refuge*** ○ *a refuge for the homeless*

**refugee** /ˌrefjuˈdʒi: ˌरेफ़्युˈजी/ *noun* [C] a person who has been forced to leave his/her country for political or religious reasons, or because there is a war, not enough food, etc. शरणार्थी *a refugee camp* ➪ **fugitive** और **exile** देखिए।

**refund** /ˈri:fʌnd ˈरीफ़न्ड्/ *noun* [C] a sum of money that is paid back to you, especially because you have paid too much or you are not happy with sth you have bought वापस किया गया धन (विशेषतः अधिक भुगतान हो जाने या ख़रीदी वस्तु के पसंद न आने के कारण) *to claim/demand/get a refund* ▶ **refund** /rɪˈfʌnd; ˈri:fʌnd रिˈफ़न्ड्; ˈरीफ़न्ड्/ *verb* [T] धन वापस करना ▶ **refundable** *adj.* वापस करने योग्य; प्रतिदेय *The security deposit is not refundable.*

**refusal** /rɪˈfju:zl रिˈफ़्यूज़्ल्/ *noun* [U, C] **(a) refusal (of sth); (a) refusal (to do sth)** saying or showing that you will not do, give or accept sth (किसी बात को मानने, काम को करने से) इनकार करने की क्रिया; इनकार *I can't understand her refusal to see me.*

**refuse[1]** /rɪˈfju:z रिˈफ़्यूज़्/ *verb* [I, T] to say or show that you do not want to do, give, or accept sth (किसी बात को मानने, काम को करने से) इनकार करना या बात नामंज़ूर होना *He refused to listen to what I was saying.* ○ *My application for a grant has been refused.* ✪ विलोम **agree**

**refuse[2]** /ˈrefju:s ˈरेफ़्यूस्/ *noun* [U] (*formal*) things that you throw away; rubbish चीज़ें जो आप फेंक देते हैं, बेकार की चीज़ें; कूड़ा-करकट *the refuse collection* (= when dustbins are emptied)

**regain** /rɪˈgeɪn रिˈगेन्/ *verb* [T] to get sth back that you had lost खोयी हुई चीज़ को पुनः प्राप्त करना *to regain consciousness*

**regal** /ˈri:gl ˈरीगल्/ *adj.* very impressive; typical of or suitable for a king or queen बहुत शानदार (मानो राजा या रानी के लायक); राजोचित, राजसी, शाही

**regard[1]** /rɪˈgɑ:d रिˈगाड्/ *verb* [T] **1 regard sb/sth as sth; regard sb/sth (with sth)** to think of sb/sth (in the way mentioned) व्यक्ति या वस्तु को वैसा समझना जैसा बताया गया हो या व्यक्ति या वस्तु को यथानिर्दिष्ट रूप से समझना *Her work is highly regarded* (= people have a high opinion of it). ○ *In some villages newcomers are regarded with suspicion.* **2** (*formal*) to look at sb/sth for a while व्यक्ति या वस्तु को क्षणभर के लिए देखना

IDM **as regards sb/sth** (*formal*) in connection with sb/sth किसी व्यक्ति या वस्तु के संबंध में *What are your views as regards this proposal?*

**regard[2]** /rɪˈgɑ:d रिˈगाड्/ *noun* **1** [U] **regard to/for sb/sth** attention to or care for sb/sth किसी व्यक्ति या वस्तु के प्रति ध्यान या उसके लिए चिंता *He shows little regard for other people's feelings.* **2** [U, *sing.*] **(a) regard (for sb/sth)** a feeling of admiration for sb/sth; respect किसी व्यक्ति या वस्तु

के लिए कोमल भावनाएँ; आदर, सम्मान *She obviously **has** great **regard** for your ability.* **3 regards** [*pl.*] (used especially to end a letter politely) kind thoughts; best wishes (विशेषतः पत्र के अंत में, शिष्टता की दृष्टि से) शेष कृपा सद्भाव के साथ; शुभकामनाएँ *Please **give my regards to** your parents.*

IDM **in/with regard to sb/sth; in this/that/one regard** (*formal*) about sb/sth; connected with sb/sth किसी व्यक्ति या वस्तु के विषय में; किसी व्यक्ति या वस्तु के संबंध में *With regard to the details—these will be finalized later.*

**regarding** /rɪˈɡɑːdɪŋ रिˈगाडिङ्/ *prep.* (*formal*) about or in connection with के विषय में या के संबंध में *Please write if you require further information regarding this matter.*

**regardless** /rɪˈɡɑːdləs रिˈगाड्लस्/ *adv.*, *prep.* **regardless (of sb/sth)** paying no attention to sb/sth; treating problems and difficulties as unimportant किसी की परवाह न करते हुए; कठिनाइयों और समस्याओं को महत्त्वहीन या बेअसर मानते हुए *I suggested she should stop but she **carried on regardless**.* ○ *Everybody will receive the same amount, regardless of how long they've worked here.*

**regatta** /rɪˈɡætə रिˈगैटा/ *noun* [C] an event at which there are boat races नौका-दौड़ का उत्सव या मेला

**reggae** /ˈreɡeɪ ˈरेगे/ *noun* [U] a type of West Indian music with a strong rhythm वेस्ट इंडीज़ का भारी लययुक्त संगीत

**regime** /reɪˈʒiːm रेˈश़ीम्/ *noun* [C] a method or system of government, especially one that has not been elected in a fair way शासनप्रणाली या व्यवस्था (विशेषतः ऐसी जो निष्पक्ष रूप से निर्वाचित नहीं) *a military/fascist regime*

**regiment** /ˈredʒɪmənt ˈरेजिमन्ट्/ [C, *with sing. or pl. verb*] a group of soldiers in the army who are commanded by a particular officer (**a colonel**) रेजिमेंट (कर्नल के नेतृत्व में सैन्य टुकड़ी) ▸ **regimental** /ˌredʒɪˈmentl ˌरेजिˈमेन्ट्ल्/ *adj.* रेजिमेंट से संबंधित

**regimented** /ˈredʒɪmentɪd ˈरेजिमेन्टिड्/ *adj.* (*formal*) (too) strictly controlled (बहुत) कठोरता से अनुशासित

**region** /ˈriːdʒən ˈरीजन्/ *noun* [C] **1** a part of the country or the world; a large area of land देश या विश्व का कोई भाग, क्षेत्र; (ज़मीन का) कोई बड़ा इलाक़ा *desert/tropical/polar regions* ○ *This region of India is very mountainous.* ➪ **district** पर नोट देखिए। **2** an area of your body शरीर का कोई (बड़ा) हिस्सा

IDM **in the region of sth** about or approximately लगभग या के आस-पास *There were somewhere in the region of 30,000 people at the rally.*

**regional** /ˈriːdʒənl ˈरीजन्ल्/ *adj.* connected with a particular region क्षेत्र-विशेष से संबंधित; क्षेत्रीय *regional accents* ➪ **local, international** और **national** देखिए।

**register¹** /ˈredʒɪstə(r) ˈरेजिस्टर्/ *verb* **1** [I, T] to put a name on an official list किसी नाम को बाक़ायदा सूचीबद्ध करना, नाम का पंजीकरण करना *You should register with a doctor nearby.* ○ *All births, deaths and marriages must be registered.* **2** [I, T] to show sth or to be shown on a measuring instrument (थर्मामीटर आदि) किसी मापन-उपकरण पर कुछ दर्ज करना या दर्ज होना *The thermometer registered 32°C.* ○ *The earthquake registered 6.4 on the Richter scale.* **3** [T] to show feelings, opinions, etc. मनोभावों, विचारों आदि को व्यक्त रूप देना *Her face registered intense dislike.* **4** [I, T] (*often used in negative sentences*) to notice sth and remember it; to be noticed and remembered किसी पर ध्यान देना और उसे याद रखना; किसी पर ध्यान जाना और उसका याद रहना *He told me his name but it didn't register.* **5** [T] to send a letter or package by special (**registered**) post पत्र या बंडल को पंजीकृत या रजिस्टर्ड डाक से भेजना

**register²** /ˈredʒɪstə(r) ˈरेजिस्टर्/ *noun* **1** [C] an official list of names, etc. or a book that contains this kind of list नाम आदि की अधिकृत सूची या ऐसी सूची वाली कॉपी; पंजिका, रजिस्टर *the electoral register* (= of people who are able to vote in an election) **2** [C, U] the type of language (formal or informal) that is used in a piece of writing लेखन में प्रयुक्त भाषा का प्रयोगमूलक भेद (औपचारिक या अनौपचारिक प्रयुक्ति, रजिस्टर)

**registered post** *noun* [U] (*BrE*) a way of sending things by post that you pay extra for. If your letter or package is lost the post office will make a payment to you पंजीकृत या रजिस्टर्ड डाक (इसके लिए अतिरिक्त शुल्क देना होता है और खो जाने की स्थिति में डाक विभाग भेजने वाले को मुआवज़ा देता है)

**registered trademark** *noun* [C] (*symbol* ®) the sign or name of a product, etc. that is officially recorded and protected so that nobody else can use it किसी उत्पादित वस्तु का चिह्न या नाम जो क़ानूनी तौर पर दर्ज और सुरक्षित रहता है (ताकि कोई दूसरा उसका इस्तेमाल न कर सके); रजिस्टर्ड ट्रेडमार्क या व्यापारिक चिह्न

**register office** = **registry office**

**registrar** /ˌredʒɪˈstrɑː(r); ˈredʒɪstrɑː(r)ˌरेजिˈस्ट्रा(र्); ˈरेजिस्ट्रा(र्)/ *noun* [C] **1** a person whose job is to keep official lists, especially of births, marriages and deaths पंजीकरण-अधिकारी; रजिस्ट्रार (जन्म, विवाह तथा मृत्यु आदि से संबंधित अधिकृत सूचियों का प्रभारी अधिकारी) **2** a person who is responsible for keeping information about the students at a college or university कॉलेज या विश्वविद्यालय का रजिस्ट्रार; कुल सचिव (छात्रों से संबंधित मामलों का प्रभारी अधिकारी)

**registration** /ˌredʒɪˈstreɪʃn ˌरेजिˈस्ट्रेश्न्/ *noun* [U] putting sb/sth's name on an official list (व्यक्ति या वस्तु के नाम का) पंजीकरण, अधिकृत सूची में व्यक्ति या वस्तु का नाम डालना *Registration for evening classes will take place on 8 September.*

**registration number** *noun* [C] the numbers and letters on the front and back of a vehicle that are used to identify it पंजीकरण संख्या (वाहन की पहचान के लिए उसके आगे और पीछे अंकित अंक और अक्षर)

**registry** /ˈredʒɪstri ˈरेजिस्ट्रि/ *noun* [C] (*pl.* **registries**) a place where official lists are kept पंजीगृह रजिस्टर रखने का स्थान; पंजी कार्यालय

**registry office** (*also* **register office**) *noun* [C] an office where a marriage can take place and where births, marriages and deaths are officially written down पंजीकरण कार्यालय (जहाँ विवाह संपन्न होते हैं और जन्म, विवाह और मृत्यु का लेखा-जोखा रहता है) ➪ **wedding** पर नोट देखिए।

**regressive** /rɪˈgresɪv रिˈग्रेसिव्/ *adj.* becoming or making sth less advanced पीछे की ओर जाने या ले जाने वाली; पश्चगामी, प्रतिगामी *The policy has been condemned as a regressive step.*

**regret**[1] /rɪˈgret रिˈग्रेट्/ *verb* [T] (**regretting; regretted**) **1** to feel sorry that you did sth or that you did not do sth दुखी या खिन्न होना (कुछ कर देने या न कर पाने के लिए) *I hope you won't regret your decision later.* ○ *Do you regret not taking the job?* **2** (*formal*) used as a way of saying that you are sorry for sth किसी बात पर खेद व्यक्त करने के रूप में प्रयुक्त; (को) खेद है *I regret to inform you that your application has been unsuccessful.*

**regret**[2] /rɪˈgret रिˈग्रेट्/ *noun* [C, U] a feeling of sadness about sth that cannot now be changed खेद, दुख (उस बात के लिए जिसे अब बदला नहीं जा सकता) *He has regrets about his illiteracy.* ▶ **regretful** /-fl -फ़्ल्/ *adj.* उदास, खिन्न *a regretful look/smile* ▶ **regretfully** /-fəli -फ़लि/ *adv.* खेदपूर्वक

**regrettable** /rɪˈgretəbl रिˈग्रेटब्ल्/ *adj.* that you should feel sorry or sad about खेदजनक, शोचनीय *It is regrettable that the police were not informed sooner.* ▶ **regrettably** /-əbli -अब्लि/ *adv.* शोचनीय रूप से

**regular**[1] /ˈregjələ(r) ˈरेग्यल(र्)/ *adj.* **1** having the same amount of space or time between each thing or part नियमित; जहाँ प्रत्येक वस्तु या उसके अंग के बीच स्थान की मात्रा या समय की अवधि समान हो *Nurses checked her blood pressure* ***at regular intervals.*** ○ *The fire alarms are tested* ***on a regular basis.*** ✪ विलोम **irregular** **2** done or happening often प्रायः किया जाने या घटित होते रहने वाला *The doctor advised me to take regular exercise.* ○ *Accidents are* ***a regular occurrence*** *on thisroad.* **3** going somewhere or doing sth often प्रायः कहीं जाते या कुछ करते रहने वाला *a regular customer* ○ *We're regular visitors to Goa.* **4** normal or usual साधारण, सामान्य *Who is your regular dentist?* **5** not having any individual part that is different from the rest सम, सममित; जिसका कोई अकेला अंश बाक़ी अंशों से भिन्न न हो *regular teeth/features* ○ *a regular pattern* ✪ विलोम **irregular** **6** fixed or permanent नियत या स्थायी *a regular income/job* ○ *a regular soldier/army* **7** (*AmE*) standard, average or normal औसत या सामान्य *Regular or large fries?* **8** (*grammar*) (*used about a noun, verb, etc.*) having the usual or expected plural, verb form, etc. (संज्ञा, क्रिया आदि) नियमित या अपेक्षित बहुवचन संज्ञारूप, क्रियारूप आदि *'Walk' is a regular verb.* ✪ विलोम **irregular** ▶ **regularly** *adv.* नियमित रूप से, नियत अंतराल पर *to have a car serviced regularly* ▶ **regularity** /ˌregjuˈlærəti ˌरेग्युˈलैरटि/ *noun* [U, C] नियमितता *Aircraft passed overhead with monotonous regularity.*

**regular**[2] /ˈregjələ(r) ˈरेग्यल(र्)/ *noun* [C] **1** (*informal*) a person who goes to a particular shop, bar, restaurant, etc. very often नियमित ग्राहक (विशेष दुकान, रेस्तराँ आदि का) **2** a person who usually does a particular activity or sport नियमित खिलाड़ी (विशिष्ट खेल का) **3** a permanent member of the army, navy, etc. नियमित सैनिक (स्थल, नौ या वायु सेना का)

**regulate** /ˈregjuleɪt ˈरेग्युलेट्/ *verb* [T] **1** to control sth by using laws or rules किसी को नियंत्रित करना (क़ानून या नियम की सहायता से) **2** to control a machine, piece of equipment, etc. किसी मशीन, उपकरण (आदि को नियंत्रित या व्यवस्थित करना) *You can regulate the temperature in the car with this dial.*

**regulation** /ˌregjuˈleɪʃn ˌरेग्यु ˈलेश्न्/ *noun* **1** [C, *usually pl.*] an official rule that controls how sth is done नियम या क़ानून (कुछ नियंत्रित करने का) *to observe/obey the safety regulations* ○ *The plans must comply with EU regulations.* **2** [U] the control of sth by using rules नियमों की सहायता से किसी पर नियंत्रण *state regulation of imports and exports*

**regur** (*also* **black-cotton soil**) *noun* [U] (in India) a rich black soil in which cotton is grown (भारत में) रेगर दुमट जिसमें कपास की खेती होती है

**regurgitate** /rɪˈgɜːdʒɪteɪt रिˈगजिटेट्/ *verb* [T] **1** (*formal*) to bring food that has been swallowed back up into the mouth again भोजन को उगलना *The bird regurgitates half-digested fish to feed its young.* **2** to repeat sth you have heard or read without really thinking about it or understanding it सुनी या पढ़ी बात को दोहराना (बिना उसके विषय में सोचे या उसे समझे) *He's just regurgitating what his father says.*

**rehabilitate** /ˌriːəˈbɪlɪteɪt ˌरीअˈबिलिटेट्/ *verb* [T] to help sb to live a normal life again after an illness, being in prison, etc. अस्वस्थ होने, क़ैद में रहने आदि के बाद सामान्य जीवन बिताने में किसी की सहायता करना ▶ **rehabilitation** /ˌriːəˌbɪlɪˈteɪʃn ˌरीअˌबिलिˈटेश्न्/ *noun* [U] पुनर्वासन *a rehabilitation centre for drug addicts*

**rehearsal** /rɪˈhɜːsl रिˈहसल्/ *noun* [C, U] the time when you practise a play, dance, piece of music, etc. before you perform it for other people नाटक, नृत्य, संगीत आदि का पूर्वाभ्यास (उसके सार्वजनिक प्रदर्शन से पहले) *a dress rehearsal* (= when all the actors wear their stage clothes) ▶ **rehearse** /rɪˈhɜːs रिˈहस्/ *verb* [I, T] पूर्वाभ्यास करना

**reign** /reɪn रेन्/ *verb* [I] **1 reign (over sb/sth)** (used about a king or queen) to rule a country (राजा या रानी का) किसी देश पर शासन करना (*figurative*) *the reigning world champion* **2 reign (over sb/sth)** to be in charge of a business or an organization किसी व्यापारिक प्रतिष्ठान या संस्था का प्रमुख होना **3** to be present as the most important quality of a particular situation स्थिति-विशेष में किसी बात का सर्वाधिक प्रभावशाली होना *Chaos reigned after the first snow of the winter.* ▶ **reign** *noun* [C] शासन

**reimburse** /ˌriːɪmˈbɜːs ˌरीइम्ˈबस्/ *verb* [T] (*formal*) to pay money back to sb किसी व्यक्ति को पैसा लौटाना, व्यय की प्रतिपूर्ति करना *The company will reimburse you in full for your travelling expenses.*

**rein** /reɪn रेन्/ *noun* [C, *usually pl.*] a long thin piece of leather that is held by the rider and used to control a horse's movements घोड़े की लगाम, रास ➪ **horse** पर चित्र देखिए।

**reincarnation** /ˌriːɪnkɑːˈneɪʃn ˌरीइन्काˈनेश्न्/ *noun* **1** [U] the belief that people who have died can live again in a different body पुनर्जन्म (मृत व्यक्ति का भिन्न शरीर धारण कर पुनः जीवन प्राप्त करना) *Do you believe in reincarnation?* **2** [C] a person or animal whose body is believed to contain the soul of a dead person पुर्नजन्म-प्राप्त या पुर्नजन्म व्यक्ति या पशु (जिसमें किसी मृत व्यक्ति की आत्मा है, विश्वास के अनुसार) *He believes he is the reincarnation of an Egyptian princess.* ➪ **incarnation** देखिए।

**reindeer** /ˈreɪndɪə(r) ˈरेन्डिअ(र्)/ *noun* [C] (*pl.* **reindeer**) a type of large brownish wild animal that eats grass and lives in Arctic regions रेनडियर; उत्तरी ठंडे प्रदेशों में पाया जाने वाला (हिरण जैसा) बड़ा भूरा-सा वन्य पशु

**reinforce** /ˌriːɪnˈfɔːs ˌरीइन्ˈफ़ॉस्/ *verb* [T] to make sth stronger अधिक मज़बूत करना, सुदृढ़ करना *Concrete can be reinforced with steel bars.*

**reinforcement** /ˌriːɪnˈfɔːsmənt ˌरीइन्ˈफ़ॉस्मन्ट्/ *noun* **1** [U] making sth stronger सुदृढ़ करने की क्रिया; सृदृढ़ीकरण *The sea wall is weak in places and needs reinforcement.* **2 reinforcements** [*pl.*] extra people who are sent to make an army, navy, etc. stronger कुमक, अतिरिक्त सेना (जल, थल सेना को सुदृढ़ बनाने के लिए भेजे अतिरिक्त सैनिक)

**reinstate** /ˌriːɪnˈsteɪt ˌरीइन्ˈस्टेट्/ *verb* [T] **1 reinstate sb (in/as sth)** to give back a job or position that was taken from sb किसी को उसके पूर्व पद या नौकरी पर वापस लेना *He was cleared of the charge of theft and reinstated as Head of Security.* **2** to return sth to its former position or role किसी को उसका पूर्व पद या दायित्व लौटाना ▶ **reinstatement** *noun* [U] बहाली, पुनः स्थापना

**reject¹** /rɪˈdʒekt रिˈजेक्ट्/ *verb* [T] to refuse to accept sb/sth व्यक्ति या वस्तु को अस्वीकार करना (मानने से इनकार करना) *The plan was rejected as being impractical.* ▶ **rejection** *noun* [C, U] अस्वीकृति, नामंज़ूरी *Gargi got a rejection from Delhi University.* ○ *There has been total rejection of the new policy.*

**reject²** /ˈriːdʒekt ˈरीजेक्ट्/ *noun* [C] a person or thing that is not accepted because he/she/it is not good enough (घटिया होने के कारण) अस्वीकृत वस्तु (या व्यक्ति) *Rejects are sold at half price.*

**rejoice** /rɪˈdʒɔɪs रिˈजॉइस्/ *verb* [I] (*formal*) **rejoice (at/over sth)** to feel or show great happiness बहुत हर्षित होना या हर्ष मनाना ▶ **rejoicing** *noun* [U] हर्षोल्लास *There were scenes of rejoicing when the war ended.*

**rejoin** /ˌriːˈdʒɔɪn ˌरीˈजॉइन्/ *verb* [T, I] to join sb/sth again after leaving him/her/it किसी के साथ फिर से मिल जाना

**rejuvenate** /rɪˈdʒuːvəneɪt रिˈजूव़नेट्/ *verb* [T] (*usually passive*) to make sb/sth feel or look younger किसी को युवा बना देना ▶ **rejuvenation** /rɪˌdʒuːvəˈneɪʃn रिˌजूव़ˈनेश्न्/ *noun* [U] पुनर्यौवन

**relapse** /rɪˈlæps रिˈलैप्स्/ *verb* [I] to become worse again after an improvement सुधरने के बाद फिर से बिगड़ जाना; पुनरावर्तन *He relapsed into his old bad habits after he lost his job.* ▶ **relapse** /ˈriːlæps ˈरीलैप्स्/ *noun* [C] पुनर्विकृति (स्वास्थ्य या आदत में) *The patient had a relapse and then died.*

**relate** /rɪˈleɪt रिˈलेट्/ *verb* [T] **1 relate A to/with B** to show or make a connection between two or more things वस्तुओं, स्थितियों आदि में संबंध दिखाना या स्थापित करना *The report relates heart disease to high levels of stress.* **2** (*formal*) **relate sth (to sb)** to tell a story to sb किसी को कोई कहानी सुनाना *He related his side of the story to a journalist.*

PHR V **relate to sb/sth 1** to be concerned or involved with sth किसी से संबंधित होना या किसी का ज़िक्र करना **2** to be able to understand how sb feels किसी के मनोभावों को समझ पाना *Some teenagers find it hard to relate to their parents.*

**related** /rɪˈleɪtɪd रिˈलेटिड्/ *adj.* **related (to sb/sth) 1** connected with sb/sth व्यक्ति या वस्तु से संबंधित *The rise in the cost of living is directly related to the price of oil.* **2** of the same family एक ही परिवार का होना, पारिवारिक संबंध से जुड़े होना *We are related by marriage.*

**relation** /rɪˈleɪʃn रिˈलेश्न्/ *noun* **1 relations** [*pl.*] **relations (with sb); relations (between A and B)** the way that people, groups, countries, etc. feel about or behave towards each other (लोगों, वर्गों, देशों आदि के बीच) संबंध (एक दूसरे के प्रति सोच/के साथ व्यवहार का ढंग) *The police officer stressed that good relations with the community were essential.* **2** [U] **relation (between sth and sth); relation (to sth)** the connection between two or more things किन्हीं दो या अधिक वस्तुओं के बीच संबंध *There seems to be little relation between the cost of the houses and their size.* ○ *Their salaries **bear no relation** to the number of hours they work.* **3** [C] a member of your family (आपके) परिवार का सदस्य, नातेदार, रिश्तेदार, संबंधी व्यक्ति) *a close/distant relation* ✪ पर्याय **relative**

> NOTE निम्नलिखित दोनों अभिव्यक्तियाँ मान्य हैं— *'What relation are you to each other?'* और *'Are you any relation to each other?'*

IDM **in/with relation to sb/sth 1** concerning sb/sth व्यक्ति या वस्तु के संबंध में *Many questions were asked, particularly in relation to the cost of the new buildings.* **2** compared with से तुलना करने पर, की अपेक्षा *Prices are low in relation to those in other parts of Asia.*

**relationship** /rɪˈleɪʃnʃɪp रिˈलेश्न्शिप्/ *noun* [C] **1 a relationship (with sb/sth); a relationship (between A and B)** the way that people, groups, countries, etc. feel about or behave towards each other (किसी के साथ या किन्हीं दो व्यक्ति, संगठनों या देशों के बीच) संबंध *The relationship between the parents and the school has improved greatly.* **2 a relationship (with sb); a relationship (between A and B)** a friendly or loving connection between people (किसी के साथ या किन्हीं दो व्यक्तियों के बीच) मैत्रीपूर्ण या प्रेममय संबंध *to **have a relationship** with sb* ○ *He has a close relationship with his brother?* **3 a relationship (to sth); a relationship (between A and B)** the way in which two or more things are connected (किसी के साथ या किन्हीं दो के बीच) संबंधित होने का ढंग या संबंध का प्रकार) *Is there a relationship between violence on TV and the increase in crime?* **4 a relationship (to sb); a relationship (between A and B)** a family connection पारिवारिक संबंध, रिश्ता, नाता *'What is your relationship to Ramit?' 'He's married to my cousin.'*

**relative**[1] /ˈrelətɪv ˈरेलटिव़्/ *adv.* **1 relative (to sth)** when compared to sb/sth else किसी अन्य व्यक्ति या वस्तु से तुलना करने पर अन्य व्यक्ति, वस्तु; सापेक्ष *the position of the earth relative to the sun* ○ *They live in relative luxury.* **2** (*grammar*) referring to an earlier noun, sentence or part of a sentence *In the phrase 'the lady who lives next door' 'who' is a **relative pronoun** and 'who lives next door' is a **relative clause***

> NOTE संबंधवाचक उपवाक्यों (relative clauses) पर अधिक जानकारी के लिए शब्दकोश के अंत में **Quick Grammar Reference** देखिए।

**relative**[2] /ˈrelətɪv ˈरेलटिव़्/ *noun* [C] a member of your family (आपके) परिवार का सदस्य, नातेदार, रिश्तेदार, संबंधी (व्यक्ति) *a close/distant relative* ✪ पर्याय **relation**

**relatively** /ˈrelətɪvli ˈरेलटिव़्लि/ *adv.* to quite a large degree, especially when compared to others काफ़ी बड़ी मात्रा में या सीमा तक (विशेषतः अन्य की तुलना मे); अपेक्षाकृत, अपेक्षया *Spanish is a relatively easy language to learn.*

**relativity** /ˌreləˈtɪvəti ˌरेलˈटिव़टि/ *noun* [U] (in physics) Einstein's belief that all movement is affected by space, light, time and **gravity** (भौतिक विज्ञान में) सापेक्षता का सिद्धांत, सापेक्षवाद (आइंस्टाइन की मान्यता कि सब प्रकार की गति स्थान, प्रकाश, समय और गुरुत्वाकर्षण से प्रभावित होती है अर्थात तत्सापेक्ष होती है)

**relax** /rɪˈlæks रिˈलैक्स्/ *verb* **1** [I] to rest while you are doing sth enjoyable, especially after work or effort आराम फ़रमाना, विश्राम करना (विशेषतः काम या श्रम के बाद) *This holiday will give you a chance to relax.* ○ *They spent the evening relaxing in front of the television.* **2** [I] to become calmer and less worried तनावमुक्त होना, अधिक शांत और चिंतामुक्त हो जाना *Relax—everything's going to be OK!* **3** [I, T] to become or make sb/sth become less hard or tight व्यक्ति या वस्तु का तनावमुक्त या शिथिल होना, उसे तनावमुक्त या शिथिल करना *Don't relax your grip on the rope!* ○ *A hot bath will relax you after a hard day's work.* **4** [T] to make rules or laws less strict नियमों को शिथिल करना

**relaxation** /ˌri:lækˈseɪʃn ˌरीलैक्ˈसेश्न्/ *noun* **1** [C, U] something that you do in order to rest, especially after work or effort विश्राम, आराम (विशेषतः काम या श्रम के बाद) *Everyone needs time for rest and relaxation.* **2** [U] making sth less strict, tight or strong (किसी को) शिथिल करने की क्रिया; शिथिलता, ढील

**relaxed** /rɪˈlækst रिˈलैक्स्ट्/ *adj.* not worried or tense तनावमुक्त, निश्चिंत, बेफ़िक्र *The relaxed atmosphere made everyone feel at ease.*

**relaxing** /rɪˈlæksɪŋ रिˈलैक्सिंग/ *adj.* pleasant, helping you to rest and become less worried सुहाना, आराम देने और चिंता घटाने वाला, सुखद *a quiet relaxing holiday*

**relay[1]** /rɪˈleɪ; ˈri:leɪ रिˈले; ˈरीले/ *verb* [T] (*pt, pp* **relayed**) **1** to receive and then pass on a signal or message संकेत या संदेश को (प्राप्त कर) आगे भेजना *Instructions were relayed to us by phone.* **2** (*BrE*) to put a programme on the radio or television रेडियो या टीवी पर कार्यक्रम प्रसारित करना

**relay[2]** /ˈri:leɪ ˈरीले/ (*also* **relay race**) *noun* [C] a race in which each member of a team runs, swims, etc. one part of the race टीम के सदस्यों की सहयोगात्मक दौड़ (जिसमें प्रत्येक सदस्य अपना हिस्सा पूरा करता है); चौकी दौड़, रिले रेस

**release[1]** /rɪˈli:s रिˈलीस्/ *verb* [T] **1 release sb/sth (from sth)** to allow sb/sth to be free व्यक्ति या वस्तु को (किसी से या कहीं से) मुक्त करना, जाने देना *He's been released from prison.* ○ *(figurative) His firm released him for two days a week to go on a training course.* **2** to stop holding sth so that it can move, fly, fall, etc. freely किसी वस्तु को खुला छोड़ देना, बंधन ढीला करना *Thousands of balloons were released at the ceremony.* ○ *(figurative) Crying is a good way to release pent-up emotions.* **3** to move sth from a fixed position (किसी वस्तु को) आबद्ध स्थिति से मुक्त या शिथिल करना; छुड़ाना *He released the handbrake and drove off.* **4** to allow sth to be known by the public कुछ वस्तु या परिस्थिति को सार्वजनिक होने देना *The identity of the victim has not been released.* **5** to make a film, record, etc. available so the public can see or hear it फ़िल्म, रिकॉर्ड आदि को सार्वजनिक उपयोग के लिए उपलब्ध कराना; विमोचन करना *Their new single is due to be released next week.*

**release[2]** /rɪˈli:s रिˈलीस्/ *noun* [C, U] **1 (a) release (of sth) (from sth)** the freeing of sth or the state of being freed किसी की मुक्ति या मुक्ति की स्थिति *The release of the hostages took place this morning.* ○ *I had a great feeling of release when my exams were finished.* **2** a book, film, record, piece of news, etc. that has been made available to the public; the act of making sth available to the public सार्वजनिक उपयोग के लिए जारी पुस्तक, फ़िल्म, रिकॉर्ड आदि; सार्वजनिक उपयोग के लिए जारी करने की क्रिया; विमोचन *a press release* ○ *The film won't **be/go on release** until March.*

**relegate** /ˈrelɪgeɪt ˈरेलिगेट्/ *verb* [T] to put sb/sth into a lower level or position व्यक्ति या वस्तु का स्तर या पद घटाना; पदावनत करना *The team finished bottom and were relegated to the second division.* ▶ **relegation** /ˌrelɪˈgeɪʃn ˌरेलिˈगेश्न्/ *noun* [U] पदावनति

**relent** /rɪˈlent रिˈलेन्ट्/ *verb* [I] **1** to finally agree to sth that you had refused नरम पड़ जाना (अंत में वह मान लेना जो पहले अमान्य था) *Her parents finally relented and allowed her to go to the concert.* **2** to become less determined, strong, etc. शिथिल पड़ जांना, ज़ोर कम हो जाना *The heavy rain finally relented and we went out.*

**relentless** /rɪˈlentləs रिˈलेन्ट्लस्/ *adj.* not stopping or changing लगातार, अनवरत, निरंतर *the relentless fight against crime* ▶ **relentlessly** *adv.* लगातार, अनवरत भाव से *The sun beat down relentlessly.*

**relevant** /ˈreləvənt ˈरेलवन्ट् / *adj.* **relevant (to sb/sth)** **1** connected with what is happening or being talked about प्रांसगिक, संबद्ध (विचार किए जा रहे विषय या जो हो रहा है उससे संबद्ध) *Much of what was said was not directly relevant to my case.* **2** important and useful महत्त्वपूर्ण और उपयोगी *Many people feel that poetry is no longer relevant in today's world.* ✪ विलोम **irrelevant** ▶ **relevance** *noun* [U] प्रासंगिकता *I honestly can't see the relevance of what he said.*

**reliable** /rɪˈlaɪəbl रिˈलाइअब्ल् / *adj.* that you can trust विश्वसनीय, भरोसेमंद *Japanese cars are usually very reliable.* ○ *Is he a reliable witness?* ✪ विलोम **unreliable** ➪ **rely** verb देखिए। ▶ **reliability** /rɪˌlaɪəˈbɪləti रि,लाइअˈबिलटि / *noun* [U] विश्वसनीयता ▶ **reliably** /-əbli -अब्लि / *adv.* विश्वसनीय रूप से *I have been reliably informed that there will be no trains tomorrow.*

**reliance** /rɪˈlaɪəns रिˈलाइअन्स् / *noun* [U] **reliance on sb/sth** **1** being able to trust sb/sth व्यक्ति या वस्तु पर विश्वास या भरोसा *Don't* ***place*** *too much reliance on her promises.* **2** not being able to live or work without sb/sth; being dependent on sb/sth किसी व्यक्ति या वस्तु के बिना रहना या काम करना असंभव होने की स्थिति, अपरिहार्यता; व्यक्ति या वस्तु पर निर्भरता, अनिवार्यता ➪ **rely** verb देखिए।

**reliant** /rɪˈlaɪənt रिˈलाइअन्ट् / *adj.* **reliant on sb/sth** not being able to live or work without sb/sth निर्भर, अवलंबित *They are totally reliant on the state for financial support.* ➪ **rely** verb देखिए तथा **self-reliant** देखिए।

**relic** /ˈrelɪk ˈरेलिक् / *noun* [C] an object, tradition, etc. from the past that still survives today अवशेष (वर्तमान तक सुरक्षित अतीत की वस्तु, परंपरा आदि)

**relief** /rɪˈliːf रिˈलीफ़् / *noun* **1** [U, *sing.*] **relief (from sth)** the feeling that you have when sth unpleasant stops or becomes less strong कष्ट, चिंता आदि से राहत या चैन *It was a great relief to know they were safe.* ○ *to breathe* ***a sigh of relief*** ○ ***To my relief,*** *he didn't argue with me.* **2** [U] the removal or reduction of pain, worry, etc. दर्द, चिंता आदि की समाप्ति या कमी; आराम *These tablets provide pain relief for up to four hours.* **3** [U] money or food that is given to help people who are in trouble or difficulty राहत-सहायता (पीड़ितों के सहायतार्थ धन या भोजन) *disaster relief for the flood victims* **4** [U] a reduction in the amount of tax you have to pay कर में राहत (कर के रूप में देय राशि में कटौती)

**relief map** *noun* [C] (in geography) a map that uses different colours to show the different heights of hills, valleys, etc. (भूगोल में) उभारदार नक़्शा (ऐसा नक़्शा जिसमें घाटियों, अलग-अलग ऊंचाई की पहाड़ियों आदि को भिन्न-भिन्न रंगों द्वारा दिखाया जाता है)

**relieve** /rɪˈliːv रिˈलीव् / *verb* [T] to make an unpleasant feeling or situation stop or get better कष्ट या चिंता में राहत पहुँचाना *This injection should* ***relieve the pain.*** ○ *We played cards to relieve the boredom.*

**PHR V** **relieve sb of sth** (*formal*) to take sth away from sb किसी से कुछ ले लेना *to relieve sb of responsibility*

**relieved** /rɪˈliːvd रिˈलीव्ड् / *adj.* pleased because your fear or worry has been taken away चिंतामुक्त, भारमुक्त *I was very relieved to hear that you weren't seriously hurt.*

**religion** /rɪˈlɪdʒən रिˈलिजन् / *noun* **1** [U] the belief in a god or gods and the activities connected with this ईश्वर, देवताओं में विश्वास और संबंधित दार्शनिक विचारधारा तथा कर्म-कांड **2** [C] one of the systems of beliefs that is based on a belief in a god or gods एकेश्वरवाद या बहुदेवतावाद पर आधारित धार्मिक विश्वास; धर्म *Representatives of all the major world religions were present at the talks.*

**religious** /rɪˈlɪdʒəs रिˈलिजस् / *adj.* **1** connected with religion धार्मिक, धर्म-विषयक *religious faith* **2** having a strong belief in a religion धर्मनिष्ठ, धर्मपरायण *a deeply religious person*

**religiously** /rɪˈlɪdʒəsli रिˈलिजस्लि / *adv.* **1** very carefully or regularly बहुत सावधानी से या नियमपूर्वक *She stuck to the diet religiously.* **2** in a religious way धार्मिक रीति से

**relinquish** /rɪˈlɪŋkwɪʃ रिˈलिङ्क्विश् / *verb* [T] (*formal*) to stop having or doing sth त्याग देना, छोड़ देना (कोई वस्तु या काम) **NOTE** इस अर्थ में **give up** अधिक प्रचलित है।

**relish**[1] /ˈrelɪʃ ˈरेलिश् / *verb* [T] to enjoy sth or to look forward to sth very much किसी वस्तु का आनंद लेना या किसी बात की उत्सुकता से प्रतीक्षा करना *I don't* ***relish the prospect*** *of getting up early tomorrow.*

**relish**[2] /ˈrelɪʃ ˈरेलिश् / *noun* **1** [U] (*written*) great enjoyment अत्यंत आनंद *She accepted the award with obvious relish.* **2** [U, C] a thick, cold sauce made from fruit and vegetables फल और सब्ज़ियों से बनी गाढ़ी ठंडी चटनी

**relive** /ˌriːˈlɪv ˌरीˈलिव् / *verb* [T] to remember sth and imagine that it is happening again किसी अनुभव को कल्पना में फिर से दोहराना या जीना

**reload** /ˌriːˈləʊd ˌरीˈलोड्/ *verb* [I, T] to put sth into a machine again किसी वस्तु (गोली आदि) को मशीन में दोबारा भरना *to reload a gun* ○ *to reload a disk into a computer*

**reluctant** /rɪˈlʌktənt रिˈलक्टन्ट्/ *adj.* **reluctant (to do sth)** not wanting to do sth because you are not sure it is the right thing to do (कोई विशेष कार्य करने का) अनिच्छुक (उसके औचित्य में कुछ संदेह के कारण) ▶ **reluctance** *noun* [U] कार्य-विशेष के प्रति अनिच्छा या हिचक *Tony left* ***with obvious reluctance***. ▶ **reluctantly** *adv.* अनिच्छापूर्वक, हिचकते हुए

**rely** /rɪˈlaɪ रिˈलाइ/ *verb* [I] (*pres. part.* **relying**; *3rd person sing. pres.* **relies**; *pt, pp* **relied**) **rely on/upon sb/sth (to do sth)** **1** to need sb/sth and not be able to live or work properly without him/her/it किसी पर निर्भर होना (ठीक ढंग से रह पाने या कुछ कर पाने के लिए) *The old lady had to rely on other people to do her shopping for her.* **2** to trust sb/sth to work or behave well किसी पर भरोसा या विश्वास करना (किसी काम के लिए) *Can I rely on you to keep a secret?* ➪ **reliance** noun देखिए तथा **reliable** और **reliant** भी देखिए।

**remain** /rɪˈmeɪn रिˈमेन्/ *verb* **1** *linking verb* to stay or continue in the same place or condition एक ही स्थान या दशा में रहना या बने रहना *to remain silent/standing/seated* ○ *Jeevan went to live in America but his family remained behind in India.* **2** [I] to be left after other people or things have gone बाक़ी रह जाना (दूसरों के चले जाने के बाद) *They spent the two remaining days of their holidays buying presents to take home.* **3** [I] to still need to be done, said or dealt with कुछ करने, कहने या निपटाने को बाक़ी रह जाना *It* ***remains to be seen*** (= we do not know yet) *whether we've made the right decision.* ○ *Although he seems very pleasant,* ***the fact remains*** *that I don't trust him.*

**remainder** /rɪˈmeɪndə(r) रिˈमेन्ड(र्)/ *noun* [*sing., with sing. or pl. verb*] (*usually* **the remainder**) the people, things, etc. that are left after the others have gone away or been dealt with; the rest बचे हुए व्यक्ति या वस्तुएँ आदि (दूसरों के चले जाने या निपट जाने के बाद); शेष, बाक़ी

**remains** /rɪˈmeɪnz रिˈमेन्ज़्/ *noun* [*pl.*] **1** what is left behind after other parts have been used or taken away बाक़ी बचा हुआ भाग (अन्य भागों के इस्तेमाल हो जाने के बाद) *The builders found the remains of a Roman mosaic floor.* **2** (*formal*) a dead body (some times one that has been found somewhere a long time after death) मृत शरीर (कभी-कभी ऐसा जो मृत्यु होने के काफ़ी देर बाद कहीं पड़ा मिला हो), पार्थिव अवशेष *Human remains were discovered in the wood.*

**remand** /rɪˈmɑːnd रिˈमान्ड्/ *noun* [U] (*BrE*) the time before a prisoner's trial takes place क़ैदी पर मुक़दमा शुरू होने से पहले का समय; रिमांड *a remand prisoner* ▶ **remand** *verb* [T] (क़ैदी को) हवालात वापस भेजना *The man was* ***remanded in custody*** (= sent to prison until the trial).

IDM **on remand** (used about a prisoner) waiting for the trial to take place (क़ैदी) रिमांड पर (मुक़दमा शुरू होने की प्रतीक्षा में/हवालात में बंद)

**remark** /rɪˈmɑːk रिˈमाक्/ *verb* [I, T] **remark (on/upon sb/sth)** to say or write sth; to comment कुछ कहना या लिखना; टिप्पणी करना *A lot of people have remarked on the similarity between them.* ➪ **observation** और **comment** देखिए। ▶ **remark** *noun* [C] टिप्पणी, कथन

**remarkable** /rɪˈmɑːkəbl रिˈमाकब्ल्/ *adj.* unusual and surprising in a way that people notice असाधारण और आश्चर्यजनक (ध्यान देने योग्य) *That is a remarkable achievement for someone so young.* ▶ **remarkably** /-əbli -अब्लि/ *adv.* उल्लेखनीय या आश्चर्यजनक रूप से

**remedial** /rɪˈmiːdiəl रिˈमीडिअल्/ *adj.* **1** aimed at improving or correcting a situation सुधारात्मक या उपचारात्मक **2** helping people who are slow at learning sth मंदबुद्धियों के लिए सहायक *remedial English classes*

**remedy**[1] /ˈremədi ˈरेमडि/ *noun* [C] (*pl.* **remedies**) **a remedy (for sth)** **1** something that makes you better when you are ill or in pain दर्द या बीमारी को ठीक करने वाली कोई वस्तु; इलाज, उपाय *Hot lemon with honey is a good remedy for colds.* **2** a way of solving a problem समस्या का समाधान *There is no easy remedy for unemployment.*

**remedy**[2] /ˈremədi ˈरेमडि/ *verb* [T] (*pres. part.* **remedying**; *3rd person sing. pres.* **remedies**; *pt, pp* **remedied**) to change or improve sth that is wrong or bad सुधारना (ग़लत या अनुचित को)

**remember** /rɪˈmembə(r) रिˈमेम्ब(र्)/ *verb* [I, T] **1 remember (sb/sth); remember (doing sth); remember that** to have sb/sth in your mind or to bring sb/sth back into your mind व्यक्ति या वस्तु का ध्यान रहना या उसे याद करना ***As far as I can remember***, *I haven't seen him before.* ○ *I'm sorry. I don't remember your name.* **2 remember (sth/to do sth)** to not forget to do what you have to do करने योग्य काम को करना न भूलना या कुछ करना न भूलना *I remembered to buy the coffee.* ○ *Remember to turn the lights off before you leave.*

**NOTE** ध्यान दीजिए, remember **to do** something का प्रयोग तब होता है जब आपको कुछ करना याद हो तथा आप उसे करना नहीं भूलते—*Remember to take your keys when you go out.* Remember **doing** something से यह ज्ञात होता है कि कुछ करने की याद या उसकी तस्वीर आपके मन में है—*I remember leaving my keys on the table last night.*

**3** [T] to give money, etc. to sb/sth व्यक्ति को पैसा आदि देना *to remember sb in your will* **4** (*formal*) to think about and show respect for sb who is dead दिवंगत आत्मा को याद करना (आदरपूर्वक उसका उल्लेख करना)

**IDM** **remember me to sb** used when you want to send good wishes to a person you have not seen for a long time ऐसे व्यक्ति को नमस्कार कहने या शुभकामनाएँ भेजने के लिए प्रयुक्त जिसे बहुत दिनों से नहीं देखा *Please remember me to your wife.* ➪ **remind** पर नोट देखिए।

**remembrance** /rɪˈmembrəns रिˈमेम्ब्रन्स्/ *noun* [U] (*formal*) thinking about and showing respect for sb who is dead दिवंगत आत्मा की स्मृति *a service **in remembrance of** those killed in the war*

**remind** /rɪˈmaɪnd रिˈमाइन्ड्/ *verb* [T] **1 remind sb (about/of sth); remind sb (to do sth/that)** to help sb to remember sth, especially sth important that he/she has to do किसी को कुछ याद दिलाना (विशेषतः किसी ख़ास बात के लिए) *Can you remind me of your address?* ○ *He reminded the children to wash their hands.* **2 remind sb of sb/sth** to cause sb to remember sb/sth किसी को किसी व्यक्ति या वस्तु की याद दिलाना *That smell reminds me of school.* ○ *You remind me of your father.*

**reminder** /rɪˈmaɪndə(r) रिˈमाइन्ड(र्)/ *noun* [C] something that makes you remember sth याद दिलाने वाली वस्तु (पत्र आदि); स्मरण-पत्र *We received a reminder that we hadn't paid the electricity bill.*

**reminisce** /ˌremɪˈnɪs ˌरेमिˈनिस्/ *verb* [I] **reminisce (about sb/sth)** to talk about pleasant things that happened in the past अतीत की सुखद बातों की चर्चा करना

**reminiscence** /ˌremɪˈnɪsns ˌरेमिˈनिसन्स्/ *noun* [C, U] (*often pl.*) the act of remembering, talking or writing about events or experiences remembered from the past संस्मरण, संस्मृति; (बीते हुए दिनों की) घटनाओं या अनुभवों को याद करना, के बारे में मौखिक या लिखित वर्णन देने की क्रिया *his reminiscences of his early days in Parliament.* ○ *reminiscences of the war*

**reminiscent** /ˌremɪˈnɪsnt ˌरेमिˈनिसन्ट्/ *adj.* (*not before a noun*) that makes you remember sb/sth; similar to व्यक्ति या वस्तु का स्मरण कराने वाला; के सदृश *His suit was reminiscent of an old army uniform.*

**remit** /rɪˈmɪt रिˈमिट्/ *verb* [T] (**remitting; remitted**) (*formal*) **1 remit sth (to sb)** to send money, etc. as a payment to a person or place (पैसा आदि) किसी व्यक्ति या स्थान को भुगतान करना *Payment will be remitted to you in full.* **2** to cancel sb's debt or free sb from duty or punishment कर्ज़ माफ़ करना, कर्त्तव्य या सज़ा से छूट देना *to remit somebody's fees* **3** (of God) to forgive sins (ईश्वर का) पाप को माफ़ करना

**PHRV** **remit sth to sb** (*usually passive*) (in law) to send a matter for decision to another authority, for example to refer a case to a lower court (क़ानून में) कोई विशेष मामला निर्णय के लिए अन्य न्यायालय के सुपुर्द करना

**remittance** /rɪˈmɪtns रिˈमिट्न्स्/ *noun* **1** [C] (*formal*) money that is sent to sb in order to pay for sth प्रेषित धन (प्रायः किसी भुगतान के लिए) *Kindly return the completed form with your remittance **at the reception**.* **2** [U] the act of sending money to sb in order to pay for sth धन-प्रेषण (भुगतान हेतु) *Remittance can be made by cash or card.*

**remnant** /ˈremnənt ˈरेम्नन्ट्/ *noun* [C] a piece of sth that is left after the rest has gone किसी का बचा हुआ टुकड़ा *These few trees are the remnants of a huge forest.*

**remorse** /rɪˈmɔːs रिˈमॉस्/ *noun* [U] **remorse (for sth/ doing sth)** a feeling of sadness because you have done sth wrong पश्चात्ताप (ग़लती करने का दुख), ग्लानि, अनुताप *She was filled with remorse for what she had done.* ▶ **remorseful** /-fl -फ़्ल्/ *adj.* पश्चात्तापी, ग्लानिपूर्ण, अनुपात

**remorseless** /rˈmɔːsləs रिˈमॉसलस्/ *adj.* **1** showing no pity निर्दय **2** not stopping or becoming less strong न रुकने वाला या कमज़ोर पड़ता हुआ *a remorseless attack on sb* ▶ **remorselessly** *adv.* निर्दयतापूर्वक

**remote** /rɪˈməʊt रिˈमोट्/ *adj.* **1 remote (from sth)** far away from where other people live (किसी स्थान से) बहुत दूर, दूरवर्ती *a remote island in the Bay of Bengal* **2** far away in time (समय की दृष्टि से) बहुत दूर *the remote past/future* **3** not very great थोड़ा, कम *I haven't **the remotest** idea who could have done such a thing.* ○ *a remote possibility* **4** not very friendly or interested in other people अलग रहने वाला, अमित्रवत या दूसरों में दिलचस्पी न लेने वाला; बेमिलनसार *He seemed rather remote.* ▶ **remoteness** *noun* [U] दूरी

**remote control** *noun* **1** [U] a system for controlling sth from a distance दूर से किसी को नियंत्रित करने की व्यवस्था, दूर नियंत्रण प्रणाली *The doors can be opened by remote control.* **2** (*also* **remote**) [C] a piece of equipment for controlling sth from a distance दूर से नियंत्रित करने वाली मशीन; दूरस्थ नियंत्रण (यंत्र)

**remotely** /rɪˈməʊtli रिˈमोट्लि/ *adv.* (*used in negative sentences*) to a very small degree; at all (निषेधवाचक वाक्यों में प्रयुक्त) बहुत ही कम; बिलकुल भी *I'm not remotely interested in your problems.*

**removable** /rɪˈmu:vəbl रिˈमूवबल्/ *adj.* (*usually before a noun*) that can be taken off or out of sth जिसे (कहीं से) हटाया या बाहर निकाला जा सके ✪ पर्याय **detachable**

**removal** /rɪˈmu:vl रिˈमूवल्/ *noun* **1** [U] the action of taking sb/sth away व्यक्ति या वस्तु को हटा लेने की क्रिया; निराकरण *the removal of restrictions/regulations/rights* **2** [C, U] the activity of moving from one house to live in another मकान बदलने का काम *a removal van*

**remove** /rɪˈmu:v रिˈमूव्/ *verb* [T] (*formal*) **1 remove sb/sth (from sth)** to take sb/sth off or away व्यक्ति या वस्तु को हटा या मिटा देना *Remove the saucepan from the heat.* ○ *to remove doubts/fears/problems* **NOTE** इस अर्थ में **take off, out** आदि कम औपचारिक प्रयोग हैं। **2 remove sb (from sth)** to make sb leave his/her job or position किसी को नौकरी या पद से हटा देना

**removed** /rɪˈmu:vd रिˈमूव्ड्/ *adj.* (*not before a noun*) far or different from sth किसी से दूर या अलग *Hospitals today are **far removed from** what they were fifty years ago.*

**remover** /rɪˈmu:və(r) रिˈमूव(र्)/ *noun* [C, U] a substance that cleans off paint, dirty marks, etc. रंग मिटाने या दाग़, मैल आदि साफ़ करने वाला पदार्थ *make-up/nail polish remover*

**the Renaissance** /rɪˈneɪsns रिˈनेसन्स्/ *noun* [*sing.*] the period in Europe during the 14th, 15th and 16th centuries when people became interested in the ideas and culture of ancient Greece and Rome and used them in their own art, literature, etc. पुनर्जागरण काल; 14वीं, 15वीं, 16वीं शताब्दी की अवधि (जिसमें प्राचीन यूनान और रोम के विचारों और संस्कृति में लोगों की रुचि जाग्रत हुई और उन्होंने अपनी कला, साहित्य आदि में उसका उपयोग किया) *Renaissance art/drama/music*

**renal** /ˈri:nl ˈरीनल्/ *adj.* involving or connected to your **kidneys** गुरदों पर असर डालने वाला या उनसे संबंधित; वृक्कीय *renal failure*

**render** /ˈrendə(r) ˈरेन्ड(र्)/ *verb* [T] (*written*) **1** to cause sb/sth to be in a certain condition व्यक्ति या वस्तु को किसी स्थिति में डाल देना *She was rendered speechless by the attack.* **2** to give help, etc. to sb किसी को सहायता आदि देना *to render sb a service/render a service to sb*

**rendezvous** /ˈrɒndɪvu:; -deɪ- ˈरॉन्डिवू; -डे-/ *noun* [C] (*pl.* **rendezvous** /-vu:z -वूज़्/) **1 a rendezvous (with sb)** a meeting that you have arranged with sb किसी के साथ तय हुई भेंट, पूर्व निश्चित भेंट *Sameer had a secret rendezvous with Deeya.* **2** a place where people often meet ऐसा स्थान जहाँ (वर्ग-विशेष के) लोग प्रायः मिलते हैं; मिलन स्थल *The cafe is a popular rendezvous for students.*

**renegade** /ˈrenɪgeɪd ˈरेनिगेड्/ *noun* [C] (*formal*) **1** (*often used as an adjective*) a person who leaves one political, religious, etc. group to join another that has very different views स्वपक्षत्यागी (व्यक्ति); जो अपने पक्ष को छोड़कर दूसरे विरोधी पक्ष में शामिल हो जाए **2** a person who decides to live outside a group or society because he/she has different opinions भिन्न विचारों के कारण किसी ख़ास समूह या समाज से अलग हो जाने वाला व्यक्ति; विद्रोही, बाग़ी, अवज्ञाकारी *teenage renegades*

**renew** /rɪˈnju: रिˈन्यू/ *verb* [T] **1** to start sth again (किसी काम को) फिर से शुरू करना *renewed outbreaks of violence* ○ *to renew a friendship* **2** to give sb new strength or energy (किसी में) नई शक्ति या ऊर्जा का संचार करना *After a break he set to work with renewed enthusiasm.* **3** to make sth valid for a further period of time अधिक समय के लिए किसी को वैध बनाना, किसी (अनुबंध आदि का) नवीनीकरण करना *to renew a contract/passport/library book* ▶ **renewal** /-ˈnju:əl -ˈन्यूअल्/ *noun* [C, U] नवीकरण *When is your passport due for renewal?*

**renewable** /rɪˈnju:əbl रिˈन्यूअबल्/ *adj.* **1** (used about sources of energy) that will always exist (ऊर्जा के स्रोत) स्थायी *renewable resources such as wind and solar power* ✪ विलोम **non-renewable** **2** that can be continued or replaced with a new one for another period of time जिसका एक और बार के लिए नवीकरण हो सके; नवीकरणीय

**renounce** /rɪˈnaʊns रिˈनाउन्स्/ *verb* [T] (*formal*) to say formally that you no longer want to have sth or to be connected with sth किसी पर दावा या स्वामित्व बाक़ायदा छोड़ देना; त्याग देना ➪ **renunciation** noun देखिए।

**renovate** /ˈrenəveɪt ˈरेनवेट्/ *verb* [T] to repair an old building and put it back into good condition

पुरानी इमारत की मरम्मत कर उसे बढ़िया बना देना, नूतन करना ▶ **renovation** /ˌrenəˈveɪʃn ˌरेनˈव़ेश्न्/ *noun* [C, U] नवीकरण, मरम्मत *The house is in need of complete renovation.*

**renown** /rɪˈnaʊn रिˈनाउन्/ *noun* [U] (*formal*) fame and respect that you get for doing sth especially well प्रसिद्धि और आदर ▶ **renowned** *adj.* प्रसिद्ध **renowned (for/as sth)** *The region is renowned for its food.*

**rent**[1] /rent रेन्ट्/ *noun* [U, C] money that you pay regularly for the use of land, a house or a building (ज़मीन, मकान या इमारत) का किराया *a high/low rent* ○ *She was allowed to live there* ***rent-free*** *until she found a job.*

**rent**[2] /rent रेन्ट्/ *verb* [T] **1 rent sth (from sb)** to pay money for the use of land, a building, a machine, etc. (ज़मीन, मकान, मशीन आदि का) किराया देना *Do you own or rent your television?* ○ *to rent a flat* ➪ **hire**[1] **1** पर नोट देखिए। **2 rent sth (out) (to sb)** to allow sb to use land, a building, a machine, etc. for money किसी को ज़मीन, मकान, मशीन आदि किराए पर देना *We could rent out the small bedroom to a student.* ➪ **hire**[1] **3** देखिए। **3** (*AmE*) = **hire**[1] **1** **4** (*AmE*) = **hire**[1] **3**

**rental** /ˈrentl ˈरेन्ट्ल्/ *noun* [C, U] money that you pay when you rent a telephone, television, etc. (किराए पर लिए टेलीफ़ोन आदि के) किराए की राशि

**renunciation** /rɪˌnʌnsiˈeɪʃn रिˌनन्सिˈएश्न्/ *noun* [U] (*formal*) saying that you no longer want sth or believe in sth किसी वस्तु या विश्वास को औपचारिक रूप से त्याग देना; परित्याग ➪ **renounce** verb देखिए।

**reorganize** (*also* **-ise**) /riˈɔːgənaɪz रिˈऑगनाइज़्/ *verb* [I, T] to organize sth again or in a new way पुनः या नए तरीक़े से किसी को संगठित करना ▶ **reorganization** (*also* **-isation**) /riˌɔːgənaɪˈzeɪʃn रिˌऑगनाइˈज़ेश्न्/ *noun* [C, U] पुनर्गठन

**rep** /rep रेप्/ (*informal*) (*also* **representative**) *noun* [C] a person whose job is to travel round a particular area and visit companies, etc., to sell the products of the firm for which he/she works किसी कंपनी का एजेंट या प्रतिनिधि (जो अपनी कंपनी का माल बेचने के लिए एक विशेष इलाक़े में घूम-घूम कर ख़रीदारों से संपर्क करता है) *a sales rep*

**repair**[1] /rɪˈpeə(r) रिˈपेअ(र्)/ *verb* [T] to put sth old or damaged back into good condition किसी पुरानी या क्षतिग्रस्त वस्तु की मरम्मत करना *These cars can be expensive to repair.* ○ *How much will it cost to have the TV repaired?* ✪ पर्याय **fix** or **mend** ➪ **irreparable** देखिए।

**repair**[2] /rɪˈpeə(r) रिˈपेअ(र्)/ *noun* [C, U] something that you do to fix sth that is damaged क्षतिग्रस्त वस्तु की मरम्मत *The road is in need of repair.* ○ *The bridge is under repair.* ○ *The bike was damaged* ***beyond repair.***

IDM **in good, bad, etc. repair** in a good, bad, etc. condition अच्छी, बुरी आदि हालत में

**repatriate** /ˌriːˈpætrieɪt ˌरीˈपैट्रिएट्/ *verb* [T] to send sb back to his/her own country स्वदेश वापस भेज देना ▶ **repatriation** /ˌriːˌpætriˈeɪʃn ˌरीˌपैट्रिˈएश्न्/ *noun* [C, U] स्वदेश-वापसी, देश-प्रत्यावर्तन, प्रत्यावासन

**repay** /rɪˈpeɪ रिˈपे/ *verb* [T] (*pt, pp* **repaid** /rɪˈpeɪd रिˈपेड्/) **1 repay sth (to sb); repay (sb)** sth to pay back money that you owe to sb किसी से लिया पैसा उसे वापस देना; उधार चुकाना *to repay a debt/loan* **2 repay sb (for sth)** to give sth to sb in return for help, kindness, etc. सहायता, दया आदि के बदले किसी को कुछ देना *How can I ever repay you for all you have done for me?*

**repayable** /rɪˈpeɪəbl रिˈपेअब्ल्/ *adj.* that you can or must pay back जिसे वापस करना संभव या अनिवार्य हो; प्रतिदेय, शोध्य *The loan is repayable over three years.*

**repayment** /rɪˈpeɪmənt रिˈपेमन्ट्/ *noun* **1** [U] paying sth back किसी वस्तु को वापस देना; चुकौती *the repayment of a loan* **2** [C] money that you must pay back to sb/sth regularly नियमित वापसी या चुकौती की राशि *I make monthly repayments on my loan.*

**repeal** /rɪˈpiːl रिˈपील्/ *verb* [T] (*formal*) to officially make a law no longer valid किसी क़ानून को औपचारिक रूप से रद्द करना

**repeat**[1] /rɪˈpiːt रिˈपीट्/ *verb* **1** [I, T] **repeat (sth/yourself)** to say, write or do sth again or more than once किसी बात को दोबारा या अनेक बार कहना, लिखना या करना *Could you repeat what you just said?* ○ *Raise and lower your left leg ten times, then repeat with the right.* **2** [T] **repeat sth (to sb)** to say or write sth that sb else has said or written or that you have learnt किसी दूसरे के लिखे, कहे या पहले से याद किए को सुनाना (कहना या लिखना) *Please don't repeat what you've heard here to anyone.* ○ *Repeat each sentence after me.* ➪ **repetition** noun देखिए।

**repeat**[2] /rɪˈpiːt रिˈपीट्/ *noun* [C] something that is done, shown, given, etc. again दोहराई गई बात *I think I've seen this programme before—it must be a repeat.*

**repeated** /rɪˈpiːtɪd रिˈपीटिड्/ *adj.* (*only before a noun*) done or happening many times अनेक बार किया जाने या होने वाला; पुनरावृत्त *There have been repeated accidents on this stretch of road.* ▶ **repeatedly** *adv.* बार-बार *I've asked him repeatedly not to leave his bicycle there.*

**repel** /rɪˈpel रिˈपेल्/ *verb* [T] (**repelling; repelled**) **1** to send or push sb/sth back or away किसी व्यक्ति या वस्तु को पीछे या दूर भेज या धकेल देना **2** to make sb feel disgusted वितृष्ण या घृणा पैदा कर देना *The dirt and smell repelled her.* ➪ **repulsion** noun देखिए।

**repellent**[1] /rɪˈpelənt रिˈपेलन्ट्/ *noun* [C, U] a chemical substance that is used to keep insects, etc. away कीड़ों आदि को भगाने वाला रासायनिक पदार्थ

**repellent**[2] /rɪˈpelənt रिˈपेलन्ट्/ *adj.* causing a strong feeling of disgust विकर्षक, घृणाजनक, घिनौना *a repellent smell*

**repent** /rɪˈpent रिˈपेन्ट्/ *verb* [I, T] (*formal*) **repent (sth); repent of sth** to feel and show that you are sorry about sth bad that you have done पछताना, पश्चात्ताप करना (किसी बुरे काम के लिए) *to repent of your sins* ○ *He repented his hasty decision.* ▶ **repentance** *noun* [U] /-əns -अन्स्/ पश्चात्ताप, पछताना ▶ **repentant** /-ənt -अन्ट्/ *adj.* पश्चात्तापी, पछताने वाला

**repercussion** /ˌriːpəˈkʌʃn ˌरीपˈकश्न्/ *noun* [C, *usually pl.*] an unpleasant effect or result of sth you do (आपके किए का) दुष्प्रभाव या दुष्परिणाम *His resignation will **have** serious **repercussions**.*

**repertoire** /ˈrepətwɑː(r) ˈरेपट्वा(र्)/ *noun* [C] **1** all the plays or music that an actor or a musician knows and can perform नाटकों, गानों आदि का पूरा संग्रह जिसे अभिनेता या गायक जानते हैं और प्रस्तुत कर सकते हैं; रंगपटल *He must have sung every song in his repertoire last night.* **2** all the things that a person is able to do वे सब काम जो कोई व्यक्ति कर सकता है

**repetition** /ˌrepəˈtɪʃn ˌरेपˈटिश्न्/ *noun* [U, C] doing sth again; sth that you do or that happens again पुनरावृति; दोहराई हुई वस्तु *to learn by repetition* ○ *Let's try to avoid a repetition of what happened last Friday.* ➪ **repeat** verb देखिए।

**repetitive** /rɪˈpetətɪv रिˈपेटटिव्/ (*also* **repetitious** /ˌrepəˈtɪʃəs ˌरेपˈटिशस्/) *adj.* not interesting because the same thing is repeated many times अरुचिकर, उबाऊ (बार-बार दोहराए जाने के कारण)

**replace** /rɪˈpleɪs रिˈप्लेस्/ *verb* [T] **1 replace sb/sth (as/with sb/sth)** to take the place of sb/sth; to use sb/sth in place of another person or thing किसी व्यक्ति या वस्तु का स्थान लेना; किसी व्यक्ति या वस्तु के स्थान पर दूसरे को ले आना *Teachers will never be replaced by computers in the classroom.* **2 replace sb/sth (with sb/sth)** to exchange sb/sth for sb/sth that is better or newer किसी व्यक्ति या वस्तु को बेहतर या नए व्यक्ति या वस्तु से बदल देना *We will replace any goods that are damaged.* **3** to put sth back in the place where it was before किसी वस्तु को वापस उसके स्थान पर रख देना *Please replace the books on the shelves when you have finished with them.* NOTE इस अर्थ में **put back** अधिक प्रचलित और कम औपचारिक प्रयोग है।

**replaceable** /rɪˈpleɪsəbl रिˈप्लेसब्ल्/ *adj.* that can be replaced जिसके स्थान पर दूसरा आ सके; प्रतिस्थापनीय ✪ विलोम **irreplaceable**

**replacement** /rɪˈpleɪsmənt रिˈप्लेस्मन्ट्/ *noun* **1** [U] exchanging sb/sth for sb/sth that is better or newer किसी व्यक्ति या वस्तु का बेहतर या नए व्यक्ति या वस्तु से विनिमय *The carpets are in need of replacement.* **2** [C] a person or thing that will take the place of sb/sth स्थानापन्न (किसी व्यक्ति या वस्तु के स्थान लेने वाला दूसरा व्यक्ति या वस्तु)

**replay**[1] /ˈriːpleɪ ˈरीप्ले/ *noun* [C] **1** (*BrE*) a sports match that is played again because neither team won the first time दोबारा खेला गया मैच (पहली बार निर्णय न होने के कारण; रिप्ले **2** something on the television, on a film or a cassette tape that you watch or listen to again टीवी, फ़िल्म या कैसेट पर दोबारा देखने या सुनने योग्य चीज़; रिप्ले *Now let's see **an action replay** of that tremendous goal!*

**replay**[2] /ˌriːˈpleɪ ˌरीˈप्ले/ *verb* [T] **1** to play a sports match, etc. again because neither team won the first time मैच दोबारा खेलना (पहली बार निर्णय न होने के कारण) **2** to play again sth that you have recorded रिकॉर्ड किए हुए को दोबारा चलाना या बजाना *They kept replaying the goal over and over again.*

**replenish** /rɪˈplenɪʃ रिˈप्लेनिश्/ *verb* [T] (*formal*) **replenish sth (with sth)** (*formal*) to replace what has been used up and make sth full again (कुछ) भरना या पूरा करना; पुनर्भरण करना *Food supplies have to be replenished.* ▶ **replenishment** *noun* [U] पुनर्भरण, आपूरण, भराई

**replete** /rɪˈpliːt रिˈप्लीट्/ *adj.* (*not before a noun*) (*formal*) **replete with sth** filled with sth; full supply of sth भरा हुआ; परिपूर्ण, अघाया हुआ *That dictionary is replete with detailed illustrations.*

**replica** /ˈreplɪkə ˈरेप्लिका/ *noun* [C] **a replica (of sth)** an exact copy of sth (किसी वस्तु की) ठीक-ठीक नक़ल; प्रतिकृति

**replicate** /ˈreplɪkeɪt ˈरेप्लिकेट्/ *verb* [T] (*formal*) to copy sth exactly किसी वस्तु की प्रतिकृति या हूबहू नक़ल करना या बनाना ▶ **replication** /ˌreplɪˈkeɪʃn ˌरेप्लिˈकेश्न्/ *noun* [U, C] प्रतिकृति, नक़ल

**reply** /rɪˈplaɪ रिˈप्लाइ/ *verb* [I, T] (*pres. part.* **replying;** *3rd person sing. pres.* **replies;** *pt, pp* **replied**) **reply (to sb/sth) (with sth)** to say, write or do sth as an answer to sb/sth जवाब या उत्तर के रूप में किसी को कुछ कहना, लिखना या कुछ करना *I wrote to Shalini but she hasn't replied.* ○ *'Yes, I will,' Seema replied.* ○ *to reply to a question* ➪ **answer**[1] पर नोट देखिए। ▶ **reply** *noun* [C, U] (*pl.* **replies**) उत्तर, जवाब *Ali nodded* ***in reply to*** *my question.*

**report**[1] /rɪˈpɔːt रिˈपॉट्/ *verb* **1** [I, T] **report (on sb/sth) (to sb/sth); report sth (to sb)** to give people information about what you have seen, heard, done, etc. लोगों को देखे, सुने या किए आदि की जानकारी, रिपोर्ट या विवरण देना *Several people reported seeing/having seen the boy.* ○ *The company reported huge profits last year.* **2** [I, T] **report (on) sth** (in a newspaper or on the television or radio) to write or speak about sth that has happened (अख़बार, टीवी या रेडियो पर) घटित घटना के विषय में लिखना या बोलना *The paper sent a journalist to report on the events.* **3** [T] **report sb (to sb) (for sth)** to tell a person in authority about an accident, a crime, etc. or about sth wrong that sb has done किसी व्यक्ति या अधिकारी को दुर्घटना, अपराध किसी के कुछ ग़लत आचरण के बारे में बताना या रिर्पोट देना *All accidents must be reported to the police.* ○ *The boy was reported missing early this morning.* **4** [I] **report (to sb/sth) for sth** to tell sb that you have arrived किसी को अपने पहुँचने की सूचना देना *On your arrival, please report to the reception desk.* **5** [T] (*formal*) **be reported to be/as sth** used to say that you have heard sth said, but you are not sure if it is true बताया जाता है रिर्पोट के अनुसार (ऐसी बात की सूचना देने के लिए प्रयुक्त जिसकी प्रामाणिकता असंदिग्ध नहीं) *The 70-year-old actor is reported to be/as being comfortable in hospital.*

PHR V **report back (on sth) (to sb)** to give information to sb about sth that he/she has asked you to find out about किसी को किसी बात पर माँगी गई जानकारी देना *One person in each group will then report back to the class on what you've decided.*

**report to sb** (*not used in the continuous tenses*) to have sb as your manager in the company or organization that you work for उच्चतर अधिकारी के प्रति जवाबदेह होना

NOTE यद्यपि यह क्रिया सातत्यबोधक कालों (continuous tenses) में प्रयुक्त नहीं होती तथापि इसका (-ing युक्त) वर्तमान कृदंत रूप (present participle) काफ़ी प्रचलित है—*A new team was put together for the project, reporting to Rahul Sharma.*

**report**[2] /rɪˈpɔːt रिˈपॉट्/ *noun* [C] **1 a report (on/of sth)** a written or spoken description of what you have seen, heard, done, studied, etc. रिपोर्ट, विवरण (देखे, सुने, किए, पढ़े आदि का लिपिबद्ध या मौखिक वर्णन) *newspaper reports* ○ *a first-hand report* (= from the person who saw what happened) **2** a written statement about the work of a student at school, college, etc. स्कूल, कॉलेज आदि के छात्र की रिपोर्ट (उसकी प्रगति, उपलब्धि या व्यवहार का लिखित विवरण) *to get a good/bad report*

**reportedly** /rɪˈpɔːtɪdli रिˈपॉटिड्लि/ *adv.* (*written*) according to what some people say कथित रूप से, लोगों के कथनानुसार *The band have reportedly decided to split up.*

**reported speech** = **indirect speech**

NOTE अधिक जानकारी के लिए इस शब्दकोश के अंत में **Quick Grammar Reference** देखिए।

**reporter** /rɪˈpɔːtə(r) रिˈपॉट(र्)/ *noun* [C] a person who writes about the news in a newspaper or speaks about it on the television or radio रिपोर्टर, संवाददाता (ख़बरों के विषय में अख़बारों में लिखने वाला या टीवी, रेडियो पर बोलने वाला व्यक्ति) ➪ **journalist** देखिए।

**represent** /ˌreprɪˈzent ˌरेप्रिˈज़ेन्ट्/ *verb* **1** [T] to act or speak in the place of sb else; to be the representative of a group or country किसी का प्रतिनिधित्व करना (उसके स्थान पर काम करना या बोलना); किसी वर्ग या देश का प्रतिनिधि होना *You will need a lawyer to represent you in court.* ○ *It's an honour for an athlete to represent his or her country.* **2** (*linking verb*) to be the result of sth; to be sth किसी बात का परिचायक होना; कुछ होना *These results represent a major breakthrough in our understanding of cancer.* **3** [T] to be a picture, sign, example, etc. of sb/sth किसी व्यक्ति या वस्तु का चित्र, संकेत, उदाहरण आदि होना *The yellow lines on the map represent minor roads.* **4** [T] to describe sb/sth in a particular way व्यक्ति या वस्तु का विशिष्ट प्रकार से वर्णन करना

**representation** /ˌreprɪzenˈteɪʃn ˌरेप्रिज़ेन्ˈटेश्न्/ *noun* **1** [U, C] the way that sb/sth is shown or described; something that shows or describes sth व्यक्ति या वस्तु का प्रतिनिधित्व (चित्रण या वर्णन का प्रकार); प्रतिनिधित्व (चित्रण या वर्णन) करने वाली वस्तु *The article complains about the representation of women in* *advertising.* **2** [U] (*formal*) having sb to speak for you किसी को अपना प्रतिनिधि बनाने की क्रिया; प्रतिनिधायन ➪ **proportional representation** देखिए।

**representative**[1] /ˌreprɪˈzentətɪv ˌरेप्रिˈज़ेन्टटिव़् / *adj.* **representative (of sb/sth)** typical of a larger group to which sb/sth belongs किसी बड़े वर्ग का प्रतिनिधित्व (जिससे व्यक्ति या वस्तु का संबंध है) *Tonight's audience is not representative of national opinion.*

**representative**[2] /ˌreprɪˈzentətɪv ˌरेप्रिˈज़ेन्टटिव़् / *noun* [C] **1** a person who has been chosen to act or speak for sb else or for a group व्यक्ति या वर्ग का प्रतिनिधि **2** (*formal*) = **rep**

**repress** /rɪˈpres रिˈप्रेस् / *verb* [T] **1** to control an emotion or to try to prevent it from being shown or felt मनोभाव को नियंत्रित करना या प्रकट या महसूस न होने देना *She tried to repress her anger.* **2** to limit the freedom of a group of people लोगों की स्वतंत्रता का दमन करना ▶ **repression** /rɪˈpreʃn रिˈप्रेश्न् / *noun* [U] दमन, निग्रह, निरोध *protests against government repression*

**repressed** /rɪˈprest रिˈप्रेस्ट् / *adj.* **1** (used about a person) having emotions and desires that he/she does not show or express (व्यक्ति) भावनाओं और आकांक्षाओं को दमित किए हुए **2** (used about an emotion) that you do not show (मनोभाव) दमित, निरुद्ध (रोका या दबाया हुआ) *repressed anger/desire*

**repressive** /rɪˈpresɪv रिˈप्रेसिव़् / *adj.* that limits people's freedom दमनकारी (लोगों की स्वतंत्रता का दमन करने वाला); निरोधी *a repressive government*

**reprieve** /rɪˈpriːv रिˈप्रीव़् / *verb* [T] to stop or delay the punishment of a prisoner who was going to be punished by death मृत्युदंड प्राप्त व्यक्ति की सज़ा को रोकना या उसे कुछ देर का विराम देना; प्रविलंबन करना ▶ **reprieve** *noun* [C] प्राणदंड-स्थगन या विराम, विलंबन *The judge granted him a last-minute reprieve.*

**reprimand** /ˈreprɪmɑːnd ˈरेप्रिमान्ड् / *verb* [T] **reprimand sb (for sth)** to tell sb officially that he/she has done sth wrong (ग़लत काम करने पर) किसी की भर्त्सना करना, फटकार लगाना (औपचारिक रूप से) ▶ **reprimand** *noun* [C] भर्त्सना, फटकार *a severe reprimand*

**reprisal** /rɪˈpraɪzl रिˈप्राइज़्ल् / *noun* [C, U] punishment, especially by military force, for harm that one group of people does to another बदले की कार्रवाई (विशेषतः सेना द्वारा); प्रतिशोध

**reproach** /rɪˈprəʊtʃ रिˈप्रोच् / *verb* [T] **reproach sb (for/with sth)** to tell sb that he/she has done sth wrong; to blame sb ग़लती पर किसी को डाँटना या फटकारना; किसी को धिक्कारना *You've nothing to reproach yourself for. It wasn't your fault.* ▶ **reproach** *noun* [C, U] निंदा, आलोचना *His behaviour is **beyond reproach** (= cannot be criticized).* ▶ **reproachful** /-fl -फ़ुल् / *adj.* निंदात्मक *a reproachful look* ▶ **reproachfully** /-fəli -फ़लि / *adv.* निंदात्मक ढंग से

**reproduce** /ˌriːprəˈdjuːs ˌरीप्रˈड्यूस् / *verb* **1** [T] to produce a copy of sth किसी की नक़ल बनाना, किसी को पुनः बनाना *It is very hard to reproduce a natural environment in the laboratory.* **2** [I] (used about people, animals and plants) to produce young (व्यक्ति या पशु-पौधे का) प्रजनन करना, संतान को जन्म देना

**reproduction** /ˌriːprəˈdʌkʃn ˌरीप्रˈडक्श्न् / *noun* **1** [U] the process of producing babies or young संतान उत्पन्न करने की प्रक्रिया; प्रजनन, संतानोत्पादन *sexual reproduction* **2** [U] the production of copies of sth किसी वस्तु की प्रतियाँ तैयार करना *Digital recording gives excellent sound reproduction.* **3** [C] a copy of a painting, etc. चित्र आदि की प्रतिलिपि या नक़ल

**reproductive** /ˌriːprəˈdʌktɪv ˌरीप्रˈडक्टिव़् / *adj.* connected with the production of young animals, plants, etc. प्रजनन या संतानोत्पादन से संबंधित; प्रजननकारी *the male reproductive organs*

**reproof** /rɪˈpruːf रिˈप्रूफ़् / *noun* [C, U] (*formal*) something that you say to sb when you do not approve of what he/she has done फटकार, भर्त्सना (अनुचित काम पर)

**reptile** /ˈreptaɪl ˈरेप्टाइल् / *noun* [C] an animal that has cold blood and a skin covered in scales, and whose young come out of eggs, for example **crocodiles** and snakes सरीसृप; रेंगने वाला जीव, जैसे मगरमच्छ, साँप (इनका ख़ून ठंडा होता है एवं त्वचा छिलके वाली, और इनके बच्चों का जन्म अंडों से होता है) ➪ **amphibian** देखिए।

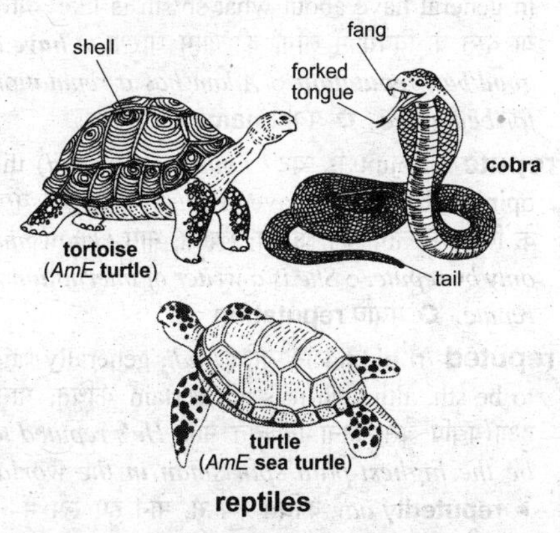

**reptiles**

**republic** /rɪˈpʌblɪk रि ˈपब्लिक् / *noun* [C] a country that has an elected government and an elected leader (**president**) गणतंत्र; गणतांत्रिक राज्य (जिसकी सरकार और नेता दोनों निर्वाचित होते हैं) *the Republic of Ireland* ➪ **monarchy** देखिए।

**republican** /rɪˈpʌblɪkən रि ˈपब्लिकन् / *noun* [C] **1** a person who supports the system of an elected government and leader गणतंत्र समर्थक व्यक्ति (जो सरकार और उसके नेता के निर्वाचित होने का समर्थन करे) ▸ **republican** *adj*. गणतंत्रात्मक

**repudiate** /rɪˈpju:dieɪt रि ˈप्यूडिएट् / *verb* [T] to say that you refuse to accept or believe sth खंडन करना, किसी बात को स्वीकार करने या मानने से इनकार करना *to repudiate a suggestion/an accusation* ▸ **repudiation** /rɪˌpju:diˈeɪʃn रि,प्यूडि ˈएशन् / *noun* [U] खंडन, अस्वीकरण

**repugnant** /rɪˈpʌgnənt रि ˈपग्नन्ट् / *adj*. (*usually not before a noun*) (*formal*) **repugnant (to sb)** making you feel disgust अत्यधिक अरुचिकर, बेहद नापसंद *We found his suggestion absolutely repugnant.*

**repulsion** /rɪˈpʌlʃn रि ˈपल्शन् / *noun* [U] **1** a strong feeling of not liking sth that you find extremely unpleasant अत्यधिक अरुचि, नफ़रत, जुगुप्सा **2** the force by which objects push each other away प्रतिकर्षण (वस्तुओं को एक दूसरे से दूर धकेलने वाली शक्ति) *the forces of attraction and repulsion* ➪ **repel** verb देखिए तथा **magnet** पर चित्र देखिए।

**repulsive** /rɪˈpʌlsɪv रि ˈपल्सिव् / *adj*. that causes a strong feeling of disgust घोर नफ़रत पैदा करने वाला; घृणास्पद ➪ **repel** verb देखिए। ▸ **repulsion** *noun* [U] घृणा, नफ़रत, जुगुप्सा

**reputable** /ˈrepjətəbl ˈरेप्यटब्ल् / *adj*. that is known to be good प्रतिष्ठित, ख्यातिप्राप्त ✪ विलोम **disreputable**

**reputation** /ˌrepjuˈteɪʃn ˌरेप्यु ˈटेशन् / *noun* [C] **a reputation (for/as sth)** the opinion that people in general have about what sb/sth is like व्यक्ति या वस्तु के विषय में लोगों की आम धारणा *to have a **good/bad reputation*** ○ *Adam has a reputation for being late.* ✪ पर्याय **name**

**repute** /rɪˈpju:t रि ˈप्यूट् / *noun* [U] (*formal*) the opinion that people have of sb/sth व्यक्ति या वस्तु के विषय में लोगों की धारणा; ख्याति, नाम *I know him only by repute.* ○ *She is a writer of international repute.* ✪ पर्याय **reputation**

**reputed** /rɪˈpju:tɪd रि ˈप्यूटिड् / *adj*. generally said to be sth, although it is not certain कथित, माना हुआ(यद्यपि वैसा होना निश्चित नहीं) *He's reputed to be the highest-paid sportsman in the world.* ▸ **reputedly** *adv*. कथित रूप से, माने हुए रूप में

**request[1]** /rɪˈkwest रि ˈक्वेस्ट् / *noun* [C, U] **request (for sth/that...)** an act of asking for sth (किसी बात के लिए) अनुरोध या निवेदन; प्रार्थना *a request for help* ○ ***make a request*** ○ *to grant/turn down a request*

**request[2]** /rɪˈkwest रि ˈक्वेस्ट् / *verb* [T] (*formal*) **request sth (from/of sb)** to ask for sth किसी बात के लिए (किसी से) अनुरोध या निवेदन करना *Passengers are requested not to smoke on this bus.* ○ *to request a loan from the bank* **NOTE** शब्द **request** अधिक औपचारिक है **ask** की अपेक्षा।

**require** /rɪˈkwaɪə(r) रि ˈक्वाइअ(र्) / *verb* [T] **1** to need sth (किसी बात की) आवश्यकता होना *a situation that requires tact and diplomacy* **NOTE** शब्द **need** की अपेक्षा **require** अधिक औपचारिक है। **2** (*often passive*) to officially demand or order sth किसी बात की अधिकृत रूप से माँग करना या कोई आदेश देना, से अपेक्षा होना, के लिए आवश्यक होना *Passengers are required by law to wear seat belts.*

**requirement** /rɪˈkwaɪəmənt रि ˈक्वाइअमन्ट् / *noun* [C] something that you need or that you must do or have अपेक्षा, ज़रूरत, माँग *university entrance requirements*

**requisite** /ˈrekwɪzɪt ˈरेक्विज़िट् / *adj*. (*only before a noun*) (*formal*) necessary for a particular purpose विशेष प्रयोजन के लिए आवश्यक या अपेक्षित *She lacks the requisite experience for the job.* ▸ **requisite** *noun* [C] **a requisite (for/of sth)** (किसी बात के लिए या की) ज़रूरत; आवश्यकता, अपेक्षा *toilet requisites* ○ *A university degree has become a requisite for entry into most professions.* ➪ **prerequisite** देखिए।

**rescind** /rɪˈsɪnd रि ˈसिन्ड् / *verb* [T] (*formal*) to officially state that a law, contract, decision, etc. is no longer valid किसी क़ानून, अनुबंध, निर्णय आदि को अधिकृत रूप से निरस्त, रद्द या मंसूख़ करना

**rescue** /ˈreskju: ˈरेस्क्यू / *verb* [T] **rescue sb/sth (from sb/sth)** to save sb/sth from a situation that is dangerous or unpleasant (ख़तरनाक या अप्रिय स्थिति से) व्यक्ति या वस्तु को बचाना या का उद्धार करना *He rescued a child from drowning.* ▸ **rescue** *noun* [C, U] बचाव, उद्धार *Ten fishermen were saved in a daring sea rescue.* ○ *rescue workers/boats/helicopters* ▸ **rescuer** *noun* [C] उद्धारक, बचाने वाला

**research** /rɪˈsɜ:tʃ रि ˈसच् / *noun* [U] **research (into/on sth)** a detailed and careful study of sth to find out more information about it किसी विषय में या पर अनुसंधान या शोधकार्य (किसी विषय के ज्ञान में वृद्धि के लिए उसका विस्तृत और सुविचारित अध्ययन)

*scientific/medical/historical research* ○ ***market research*** ▸ **research** *verb* [I, T] **research (into/in/on sth)** अनुसंधान या शोधकार्य करना *They're researching into ways of reducing traffic in the city centre.*

**researcher** /rɪˈsɜːtʃə(r) रि'सच(र्)/ *noun* [C] a person who does research अनुसंधानकर्त्ता, शोधार्थी

**resemble** /rɪˈzembl रि'ज़ेम्बल्/ *verb* [T] to be or look like sb/sth else दूसरे व्यक्ति या वस्तु जैसा होना या दिखना *Lata resembles her brother.* ▸ **resemblance** /rɪˈzembləns रि'ज़ेम्ब्लन्स्/ *noun* [C, U] **(a) resemblance (between A and B); (a) resemblance (to sb/sth)** सादृश्य, समानता *a family resemblance* ○ *The boys bear no resemblance to their father.*

**resent** /rɪˈzent रि'ज़ेन्ट्/ *verb* [T] to feel angry about sth because you think it is unfair (अनुचित प्रतीत होने के कारण) किसी बात का बुरा मानना या पर नारा ज़ होना *I resent his criticism.* ○ *Lalita bitterly resented being treated differently from the men.* ▸ **resentful** /-fl -फ़ल्/ *adj.* नाराज़, रुष्ट ▸ **resentment** *noun* [*sing.*, U] नाराज़गी, रोष *to feel resentment towards sb/sth*

**reservation** /ˌrezəˈveɪʃn ˌरेज़ 'वेश्न्/ *noun* **1** [C] a seat, table, room, etc. that you have booked आरक्षित स्थान (सीट, टेबल, कमरा आदि) *I'll phone the restaurant to **make a reservation**.* **2** [C, U] a feeling of doubt about sth (such as a plan or an idea) (किसी योजना, विचार आदि के विषय में) शंका *I have some **reservations** about letting Kirti go out alone.*

**reserve¹** /rɪˈzɜːv रि'ज़व्/ *verb* [T] **reserve sth (for sb/sth)** **1** to keep sth for a special reason or to use at a later time विशेष प्रयोजन से या भविष्य में इस्तेमाल के लिए किसी चीज़ को सुरक्षित रखना *The car park is reserved for hotel guests only.* **2** to ask for a seat, table, room, etc. to be available at a future time; to book सीट, टेबल, कमरा आदि आरक्षित कराना, बुक कराना *to reserve theatre tickets*

**reserve²** /rɪˈzɜːv रि'ज़व्/ *noun* **1** [C, *usually pl.*] something that you keep for a special reason or to use at a later date विशेष प्रयोजन से या भविष्य में उपयोग के लिए सुरक्षित कोई वस्तु *The US has huge oil reserves.* **2** [C] an area of land where the plants, animals, etc. are protected by law क़ानून द्वारा सुरक्षित भूभाग (वहाँ के पौधे, पशु आदि) *a nature reserve* ○ *He works as a warden on a **game reserve** in Kenya.* **3** [U] the quality of being shy or keeping your feelings hidden संकोच या मनोभाव का गोपन या छिपाव *It took a long time to breakdown her reserve and get her to relax.* **4** [C] (in sport) a person who will play in a game if one of the usual members of the team cannot play (खेल में) रिज़र्व खिलाड़ी (नियमित खिलाड़ी के असमर्थ होने पर खेलने के लिए उपलब्ध)

IDM **in reserve** that you keep and do not use unless you need to आवश्यकता के समय उपयोग के लिए बचाकर रखा गया *Keep some money in reserve for emergencies.*

**reserved** /rɪˈzɜːvd रि'ज़र्व्ड्/ *adj.* shy and keeping your feelings hidden संकोची तथा मनोभावों को छिपाकर रखने वाला ✪ विलोम **unreserved**

**reservoir** /ˈrezəvwɑː(r) 'रेज़व्वा(र्)/ *noun* [C] a large lake where water is stored to be used by a particular area, city, etc. बड़ा जलाशय (जिसमें विशेष क्षेत्र, नगर आदि के लिए जल संचित हो)

**reshuffle** /ˌriːˈʃʌfl ˌरी'शफ़ल्/ *verb* [I, T] to change around the jobs that a group of people do, for example in the Government समूह के सदस्यों के कामों में फेरबदल करना (जैसे सरकारी तंत्र में) ▸ **reshuffle** /ˈriːʃʌfl 'रीशफ़ल्/ *noun* [C] फेरबदल *a Cabinet reshuffle*

**reside** /rɪˈzaɪd रि'ज़ाइड्/ *verb* [I] (*formal*) **reside (in/at...)** to have your home in or at a particular place किसी स्थान पर रहना, निवास करना

**residence** /ˈrezɪdəns 'रेज़िडन्स्/ *noun* **1** [U] the state of having your home in a particular place (किसी स्थान पर) निवास, रिहायश *The family applied for permanent residence in the United States.* ○ *a **hall of residence** for college students* **2** [C] = **residency⁴**

**residency** /ˈrezɪdənsi 'रेज़िडन्सि/ *noun* (*pl.* **residencies**) (*formal*) **1** [U, C] = **residence¹** *She has been granted permanent residency in Britain.* **2** [U, C] the period of time that an artist, a writer or a musician spends working for a particular institution संस्था-विशेष में किसी कलाकार, लेखक या संगीतज्ञ के कार्यरत रहने की अवधि **3** [U, C] (*AmE*) the period of time when a doctor working in a hospital receives special advanced training किसी डॉक्टर के किसी अस्पताल में उच्चस्तरीय विशेष प्रशिक्षण के लिए कार्यरत रहने की अवधि **4** (*also* **residence**) [C] (*formal*) the official house of sb important in the government, etc. किसी बड़े सरकारी अधिकारी आदि का अधिकृत निवास

**resident** /ˈrezɪdənt 'रेज़िडन्ट्/ *noun* [C] **1** a person who lives in a place (किसी स्थान का) निवासी (व्यक्ति) *local residents* **2** a person who is staying in a hotel किसी होटल में ठहरा व्यक्ति *The hotel bar is open only to residents.* ▸ **resident** *adj.* रहने वाला; निवासी

**residential** /ˌreziˈdenʃl ˌरेज़िˈडेन्शल् / *adj.* **1** (used about a place or an area) that has houses rather than offices, large shops or factories (स्थान या क्षेत्र) आवासी, रिहायशी (जहाँ रहने के मकान हों, न कि दफ़्तर, स्कूल या फ़ैक्टरियाँ) *They live in a quiet residential area.* **2** that provides a place for sb to live रहने से संबंधित *This home provides residential care for the elderly.*

**residual** /rɪˈzɪdjuəl रिˈज़िड्युअल् / *adj.* (*only before a noun*) (*formal*) left at the end of a process अवशिष्ट (किसी प्रक्रिया के अंत में) बचा हुआ *There are still a few residual problems with the computer program.*

**residue** /ˈrezɪdju: ˈरेज़िड्यू / *noun* [C, *usually sing.*] (*formal*) what is left after the main part of sth is taken or used अवशेष, (किसी वस्तु के मुख्य भाग के प्रयोग में आने के बाद) बचा हुआ अंश *The washing powder left a white residue on the clothes.*

**resign** /rɪˈzaɪn रिˈज़ाइन् / *verb* **1** [I, T] **resign (from/as) (sth)** to leave your job or position नौकरी या पद छोड़ना या से त्यागपत्र देना *He's resigned as chairman of the committee.* **2** [T] **resign yourself to sth/doing sth** to accept sth that is unpleasant but that you cannot change किसी अप्रिय स्थिति को स्वीकार कर लेना (उसे बदलने में असमर्थता के कारण) *Hemant resigned himself to the fact that he would not be selected in the team.*

**resignation** /ˌrezɪgˈneɪʃn ˌरेज़िग्ˈनेशन् / *noun* **1** [C, U] **resignation (from sth)** a letter or statement that says you want to leave your job or position औपचारिक त्यागपत्र (नौकरी या पद छोड़ने के लिए पत्र या वक्तव्य) *to hand in your resignation* ○ *a letter of resignation* **2** [U] the state of accepting sth unpleasant that you cannot change अप्रिय स्थिति को स्वीकार कर लेने की स्थिति (उसे बदलने में असमर्थता के कारण)

**resigned** /rɪˈzaɪnd रिˈज़ाइन्ड् / *adj.* **resigned (to sth/doing sth)** accepting sth that is unpleasant but that you cannot change अप्रिय स्थिति को स्वीकार करने या सहने को तैयार (उसे बदलने में असमर्थता के कारण) *Ben was resigned to the fact that he would never be an athlete.*

**resilient** /rɪˈzɪliənt रिˈज़िलिअन्ट् / *adj.* strong enough to deal with illness, a shock, change, etc. रोग, आघात, परिवर्तन आदि से सँभलने में समर्थ; प्रतिस्कंदी ▶ **resilience** *noun* [U] रोग आदि से सँभलने का सामर्थ्य; प्रतिस्कंदन

**resin** /ˈrezɪn ˈरेज़िन् / *noun* [U] **1** a sticky substance that is produced by some trees and is used in making **varnish** medicine, etc. राल; कुछ वृक्षों से प्राप्त एक चिपचिपा पदार्थ जो वार्निश, दवाइयाँ आदि बनाने में इस्तेमाल होता है **2** an artificial substance that is used in making plastics प्लास्टिक बनाने में प्रयुक्त राल जैसा एक कृत्रिम पदार्थ

**resist** /rɪˈzɪst रिˈज़िस्ट् / *verb* **1** [I, T] to try to stop sth happening or to stop sb from doing sth; to fight back against sth/sb कुछ घटित होने से या किसी को कुछ करने से रोकने की कोशिश करना; व्यक्ति या वस्तु का प्रतिरोध या विरोध करना *The government are resisting pressure to change the law.* ○ *to resist arrest* **2** [T] to stop yourself from having or doing sth that you want to have or do अपने को रोकना (अभीष्ट वस्तु को प्राप्त करने से या अभीष्ट काम करने से) *I couldn't resist telling Leela what we'd bought for her.*

**resistance** /rɪˈzɪstəns रिˈज़िस्टन्स् / *noun* **1** [U] **resistance (to sb/sth)** trying to stop sth from happening or to stop sb from doing sth; fighting back against sb/sth कुछ घटित होने या किसी को कुछ करने से रोकने की क्रिया; व्यक्ति या वस्तु का प्रतिरोध या विरोध *The government troops overcame the resistance of the rebel army.* **2** [U] **resistance (to sth)** the power in a person's body not to be affected by disease व्यक्ति की रोग-प्रतिरोधन शक्ति **3** [C, U] (*technical*) (*symbol* **R**) the fact of a substance not **conducting** heat or electricity; a measurement of this गरमी या बिजली का प्रतिरोध करने की शक्ति; ऐसी शक्ति की माप

**resistant** /rɪˈzɪstənt रिˈज़िस्टन्ट् / *adj.* **resistant (to sth)** **1** not wanting sth and trying to prevent sth happening किसी बात का अनिच्छुक या उसे घटित होने से रोकने के लिए प्रयत्नशील; प्रतिरोध करने वाला *resistant to change* **2** not harmed or affected by sth प्रतिरोधी (किसी बात से न तो क्षतिग्रस्त न ही प्रभावित) *This watch is water-resistant.*

**resistor** /rɪˈzɪstə(r) रिˈज़िस्टर्(र्) / *noun* [C] (*technical*) a device that does not allow electric current to flow through it freely in a **circuit** विद्युत शक्ति को परिपथ पर खुलकर प्रवाहित होने से रोकने वाला उपकरण

Resistance is measured in ohms (Ω). A resistor of 100 Ω is a much greater obstacle to the flow of current than a resistor of 10 Ω.

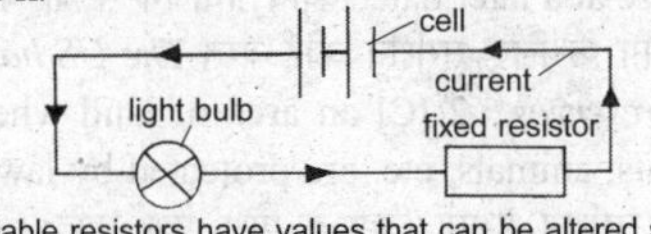


Variable resistors have values that can be altered so it is possible to adjust the current flowing in the circuit.

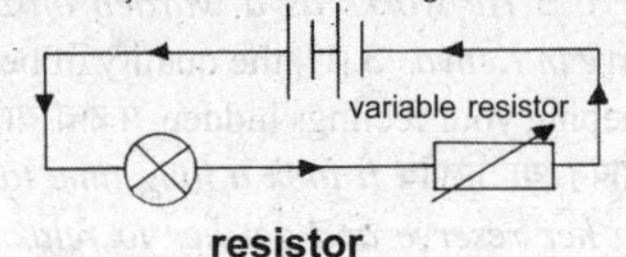


**resistor**

**resolute** /ˈrezəluːt ˈरेज़लूट्/ *adj.* having or showing great determination दृढ़निश्चयी, कृतसंकल्प *a resolute refusal to change* ✪ पर्याय **determined** ▶ **resolutely** *adv.* दृढ़तापूर्वक

**resolution** /ˌrezəˈluːʃn ˌरेज़ˈलूश्न्/ *noun* **1** [U] the quality of being firm and determined दृढ़ता, संकल्पबद्धता **2** [U] solving or settling a problem, dispute, etc. समस्या, विवाद आदि का समाधान या निपटारा **3** [C] a formal decision that is taken after a vote by a group of people किसी सभा द्वारा स्वीकृत प्रस्ताव *The UN resolution condemned the invasion.* **4** [C] a firm decision to do or not to do sth कुछ करने या न करने का पक्का निर्णय

**resolve** /rɪˈzɒlv रिˈज़ॉल्व्/ *verb* (*formal*) **1** [T] to find an answer to a problem किसी समस्या का हल निकालना *Most of the difficulties have been resolved.* **2** [I, T] to decide sth and be determined not to change your mind कोई निर्णय करना और उस पर डटे रहना; कृतसंकल्प *He resolved never to repeat the experience.*

**resonance** /ˈrezənəns ˈरेज़नन्स्/ *noun* **1** [U] (*formal*) (used about sound) the quality of being **resonant** (ध्वनि के लिए प्रयुक्त) अनुनाद, गूँज *the strange and thrilling resonance of her voice* **2** [C, U] (*technical*) the sound produced in an object by sound of a similar **frequency** from another object प्रतिध्वनि (किसी वस्तु में समान आवृत्ति वाले अन्य पदार्थ की ध्वनि से उत्पन्न ध्वनि); अनुनाद **3** [U, C] (*formal*) (in a piece of writing, music, etc.) the power to bring images, feelings, etc. into the mind of the person reading or listening; the images, etc. produced in this way (किसी लेख या संगीत आदि में) पाठक या श्रोता के मन में चित्र, भाव आदि उपस्थित करने की शक्ति; इस प्रकार उपस्थित चित्र, भाव आदि

**resonant** /ˈrezənənt ˈरेज़नन्ट्/ *adj.* **1** (used about a sound) deep, clear and continuing for a long time (ध्वनि) गहरी, स्पष्ट और गुंजायमान *a deep resonant voice* **2** (*technical*) causing sounds to continue for a long time गुंजायमान ध्वनियों को उत्पन्न करने वाला *resonant frequencies* **3** having the power to bring images, feelings, memories, etc. into your mind किसी के मस्तिष्क में चित्रों, भावों, स्मृतियों आदि को उपस्थित करने की क्षमता *a poem filled with resonant imagery*

**resonate** /ˈrezəneɪt ˈरेज़नेट्/ *verb* [I] (*formal*) **1** (used about a voice, an instrument, etc.) to make a deep, clear sound that continues for a long time (स्वर, उपकरण आदि का) गहरी, स्पष्ट और गुंजायमान ध्वनि उत्पन्न करना *Her voice resonated through the theatre.* **2 resonate (with sth)** (used about a place) to be filled with sound; to make a sound continue longer (किसी स्थान का) आवाज़ से भर जाना; ध्वनि को गुंजायमान कर देना *The room resonated with the chatter of 100 people.* **3 resonate (with sb/sth)** to remind sb of sth; to be similar to what sb thinks or believes किसी को कुछ याद दिलाना; किसी के सोच या मान्यताओं से अनुकूलता अनुभव करना *These issues resonated with the voters.*

PHR V **resonate with sth** (*formal*) to be full of a particular quality or feeling विशेष गुण या मनोभाव से परिपूर्ण होना *She makes a simple story resonate with complex themes and emotions.*

**resort[1]** /rɪˈzɔːt रिˈज़ॉट्/ *noun* [C] a place where a lot of people go to on holiday लोगों की अवकाश-कालीन आनंद-स्थली, सैरगाह *a seaside/ski resort*

IDM **in the last resort; (as) a last resort** ➪ **last[1]** देखिए।

**resort[2]** /rɪˈzɔːt रिˈज़ॉट्/ *verb* [I] **resort to sth/doing sth** to do or use sth bad or unpleasant because you feel you have no choice (विवशता में किसी भी (अरुचिकर) उपाय का सहारा लेना *After not sleeping for three nights I finally resorted to sleeping pills.*

**resounding** /rɪˈzaʊndɪŋ रिˈज़ाउन्डिङ्/ *adj.* (*only before a noun*) **1** very loud बहुत ऊँची आवाज़ वाला *resounding cheers* **2** very great उल्लेखनीय, असाधारण *a resounding victory/win/defeat/success*

**resource** /rɪˈsɔːs; -ˈzɔːs रिˈसॉस्; -ˈज़ॉस्/ *noun* [C, *usually pl.*] a supply of sth, a piece of equipment, etc. that is available for sb to use उपयोग के लिए उपलब्ध सामग्री; संसाधन *Russia is rich in* ***natural resources*** *such as oil and minerals.*

**resourceful** /rɪˈzɔːsfl; -ˈsɔːs- रिˈज़ॉस्फ़्ल्; -ˈसॉस्/ *adj.* good at finding ways of doing things उपाय-कुशल, चतुर, साधनसंपन्न

**respect[1]** /rɪˈspekt रिˈस्पेक्ट्/ *noun* **1** [U] **respect (for sb/sth)** the feeling that you have when you admire or have a high opinion of sb/sth व्यक्ति या वस्तु के प्रति आदर-भावना *I* ***have*** *little* ***respect*** *for people who are arrogant.* ○ *to win/lose sb's respect* ➪ **self-respect** देखिए। **2** [U] **respect (for sb/sth)** polite behaviour or care towards sb/sth that you think is important बड़ों का ध्यान या लिहाज़ *We should all treat older people with more respect.* ✪ विलोम **disrespect** **3** [C] a detail or point कोई बात या कोई दृष्टि ***In what respects*** *do you think things have changed in the last ten years?* ○ *Her performance was brilliant* ***in every respect.***

IDM **with respect to sth** (*formal*) about or concerning sth किसी के विषय या संबंध में

**pay your respects** ➪ **pay[1]** देखिए।

**respect²** /rɪˈspekt रिˈस्पेक्ट्/ *verb* [T] **1 respect sb/sth (for sth)** to admire or have a high opinion of sb/sth व्यक्ति या वस्तु का आदर करना *I respect him for his honesty.* **2** to show care for or pay attention to sb/sth व्यक्ति या वस्तु का लिहाज़ करना या उस का ध्यान रखना *We should respect other people's cultures and values.* ▶ **respectful** /-fl -फ़्ल्/ *adj.* **respectful (to/towards sb)** आदरपूर्ण, श्रद्धायुक्त *The crowd listened in respectful silence.* ✪ विलोम **disrespectful** ▶ **respectfully** /-fəli -फ़लि/ *adv.* आदरपूर्वक, श्रद्धापूर्वक

**respectable** /rɪˈspektəbl रिˈस्पेक्टब्ल्/ *adj.* **1** considered by society to be good, proper or correct सम्मान-योग्य, आदरणीय (समाज में अच्छा, उचित या सही माना जाने वाला) *a respectable family* ○ *He combed his hair and tried to look respectable for the interview.* **2** quite good or large काफ़ी अच्छा या काफ़ी बड़ा *a respectable salary* ▶ **respectability** /rɪˌspektəˈbɪləti रिˌस्पेक्टˈबिलटि/ *noun* [U] सम्माननीयता

**respective** /rɪˈspektɪv रिˈस्पेक्टिव्/ *adj.* (*only before a noun*) belonging separately to each of the people who have been mentioned अपना-अपना (निर्दिष्ट व्यक्तियों में प्रत्येक से अलग-अलग संबंधित) *They all left for their respective destinations.*

**respectively** /rɪˈspektɪvli रिˈस्पेक्टिव्लि/ *adv.* in the same order as sb/sth that was mentioned क्रमशः, क्रमानुसार (उसी क्रम में जिसमें व्यक्ति या वस्तु का पहले निर्देश हुआ है) *Reena and Raju, aged 17 and 19, respectively.*

**respiration** /ˌrespəˈreɪʃn ˌरेस्पˈरेश्न्/ *noun* [U] **1** (*formal*) breathing श्वसन; साँस लेने या छोड़ने की क्रिया **2** (*technical*) a process by which living things produce energy from food. Respiration usually needs **oxygen** सजीवों द्वारा भोजन से ऊर्जा प्राप्त करने की प्रक्रिया (जिसमें प्रायः ऑक्सीजन की आवश्यकता होती है)

**respirator** /ˈrespəreɪtə(r) ˈरेस्परेट(र्)/ *noun* [C] **1** a piece of equipment that makes it possible for sb to breathe over a long period when he/she is unable to do so naturally श्वसन-सहायक यंत्र, (प्राकृतिक रूप से श्वसन में असमर्थ होने पर) श्वसन क्रिया में रोगी की लंबे समय तक सहायता करने वाला उपकरण *She was put on a respirator.* **2** a device worn over the nose and mouth to allow sb to breathe in a place where there is a lot of smoke, gas, etc. श्वास-यंत्र (धुएँ, गैस आदि वाले स्थान पर साँस लेने के लिए नाक और मुँह पर पहना जाने वाला यंत्र)

**respiratory** /rəˈspɪrətri; ˈrespərətri रˈस्पिरट्रि; ˈरेस्परट्रि/ *adj.* connected with breathing श्वसन-विषयक *the respiratory system* ○ *respiratory diseases*

**respire** /rɪˈspaɪə(r) रिˈस्पाइअ(र्)/ *verb* [I] (*technical*) to breathe साँस लेना-छोड़ना

**respite** /ˈrespaɪt ˈरेस्पाइट्/ *noun* [*sing.*, U] **respite (from sth)** a short period of rest from sth that is difficult or unpleasant (कठिन या अप्रिय स्थिति से) थोड़े समय का विश्राम; थोड़ी फ़ुरसत *There was a brief respite from the fighting.*

**respond** /rɪˈspɒnd रिˈस्पॉन्ड्/ *verb* [I] **1** (*formal*) **respond (to sb/sth) (with/by sth)** to say or do sth as an answer or reaction to sth उत्तर या प्रतिक्रिया में कुछ कहना या करना *He responded to my question with a nod.* ○ *Ben responded to the manager's criticism by scoring two goals.* ✪ पर्याय **reply 2 respond (to sb/sth)** to have or show a good or quick reaction to sb/sth व्यक्ति या वस्तु के प्रति अनुकूल या त्वरित प्रतिक्रिया होना या प्रदर्शित करना *The patient did not respond well to the new treatment.*

**response** /rɪˈspɒns रिˈस्पॉन्स्/ *noun* [C, U] **(a) response (to sb/sth)** an answer or reaction to sb/sth (व्यक्ति या वस्तु को) उत्तर या प्रतिक्रिया *I've sent out twenty letters of enquiry but I've had no responses yet.* ○ *The government acted **in response to** economic pressure.*

**responsibility** /rɪˌspɒnsəˈbɪləti रिˌस्पॉन्सˈबिलटि/ *noun* (*pl.* **responsibilities**) **1** [U, C] **responsibility (for sb/sth); responsibility (to do sth)** a duty to deal with sth so that it is your fault if sth goes wrong उत्तरदायित्व; ज़िम्मेदारी, जवाबदेही (किसी के प्रति, किसी काम के लिए) *I refuse to **take responsibility** if anything goes wrong.* ○ *I feel that I have*

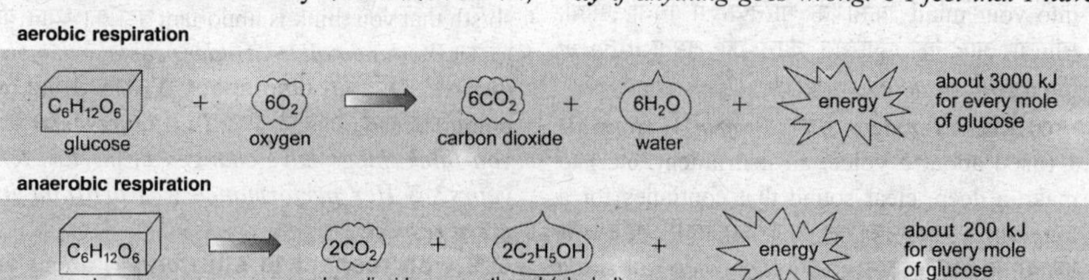


respiration

***a responsibility*** *to help them—after all, they did help me.* **2** [U] the fact of sth being your fault; blame किसी बात का दोष; ग़लती का दोष *No group has yet admitted responsibility for planting the bomb.*

IDM **shift the blame/responsibility (for sth) (onto sb)** ➪ **shift**[1] देखिए।

**responsible** /rɪˈspɒnsəbl रि'स्पॉन्सब्ल्/ *adj.* **1** (*not before a noun*) **responsible (for sb/sth); responsible (for doing sth)** having the job or duty of dealing with sb/sth, so that it is your fault if sth goes wrong उत्तरदायी, ज़िम्मेदार, जवाबदेह (किसी के प्रति, किसी काम के लिए) *The school is responsible for the safety of the children in school hours.* ○ *The manager is responsible for making sure the shop is run properly.* **2** (*not before a noun*) **responsible (for sth)** being the person whose fault sth is ग़लती के लिए ज़िम्मेदार *Who was responsible for the accident?* **3** (*not before a noun*) **responsible (to sb/sth)** having to report to sb/sth with authority, or to sb who you are working for, about what you are doing अपने किए के लिए जवाबदेह (अधिकारी को या जिसके हम प्रतिनिधि हैं उसे) *Members of Parliament are responsible to the electors.* **4** (used about a person) that you can trust to behave well and in a sensible way (व्यक्ति) उचित और समझदारी के आचरण के लिए भरोसे लायक; विश्वसनीय *Manisha is responsible enough to take her little sister to school.* ✪ विलोम **irresponsible** **5** (used about a job) that is important and that should be done by a person who can be trusted (कार्य) महत्त्वपूर्ण और विश्वसनीय व्यक्ति द्वारा करने योग्य

**responsibly** /rɪˈspɒnsəbli रि'स्पॉन्सब्लि/ *adv.* in a sensible way that shows that you can be trusted जिम्मेदारी से, भरोसेमंद तरीक़े से *They can be relied on to act responsibly.*

**responsive** /rɪˈspɒnsɪv रि'स्पॉन्सिव्/ *adj.* paying attention to sb/sth and reacting in a suitable or positive way व्यक्ति या वस्तु का ध्यान रखने वाला और उपयुक्त या अनुकूल प्रतिक्रिया करने वाला; प्रतिसंवेदी *By being responsive to changes in the market, the company has had great success.*

**rest**[1] /rest रेस्ट्/ *verb* **1** [I] to relax, sleep or stop after a period of activity or because of illness (सक्रिय रहने या बीमारी के बाद) सुस्ताना; सोना या आराम करना *We've been walking for hours. Let's rest here for a while.* **2** [T] to not use a part of your body for a period of time because it is tired or painful शरीर के किसी अंग को कुछ समय के लिए विश्राम देना (उसके थके या दर्द में होने के कारण) *Your knee will get better as long as you rest it as much as you can.* **3** [I, T] **rest (sth) on/against sth** to place sth in a position where it is supported by sth else; to be in such a position (किसी वस्तु को किसी दूसरी वस्तु पर) टिकाना, टेकना; सहारा लेना या देना, टेक लगाना या लगना *She rested her head on his shoulder and went to sleep.*

IDM **let sth rest** to not talk about sth any longer किसी विषय पर बात न करना

PHR V **rest on sb/sth** to depend on sb/sth or be based on sth व्यक्ति या वस्तु पर निर्भर होना या किसी पर आधारित होना *The whole theory rests on a very simple idea.*

**rest**[2] /rest रेस्ट्/ *noun* **1** [C, U] a period of relaxing, sleeping or doing nothing विश्राम, आराम (सुस्ताना, सोना या कुछ न करना) *I'm going upstairs to* ***have a rest****.* ○ *I sat down to* ***give*** *my bad leg* ***a rest****.* **2 the rest (of sb/sth)** [*sing., with sing. or pl. verb*] the part that is left; the ones that are left बाकी बचा हुआ, शेष; अन्य, बाकी रह गए *We had lunch and spent the rest of the day on the beach.* ○ *She takes no interest in what happens in the rest of the world.* **3** [C, U] (in music) a period of silence between notes; a sign for this (संगीत में) स्वरों के बीच विराम, यति; विराम या यति का चिह्न

IDM **at rest** not moving स्थिर, निश्चल *At rest the insect looks like a dead leaf.*

**come to rest** to stop moving (चलती हुई वस्तु का) रुक जाना *The car crashed through a wall and came to rest in a field.*

**put/set your/sb's mind at rest** ➪ **mind**[1] देखिए।

**restaurant** /ˈrestrɒnt 'रेस्ट्रॉन्ट्/ *noun* [C] a place where you can buy and eat a meal रेस्तराँ, भोजनालय *a fast food/hamburger restaurant* ○ *a Chinese/an Italian/a Thai restaurant* ➪ **cafe** और **takeaway** देखिए।

**restful** /ˈrestfl 'रेस्ट्फ़्ल्/ *adj.* giving a relaxed, peaceful feeling सुखद, शांतिप्रद *I find this piece of music very restful.*

**restitution** /ˌrestɪˈtjuːʃn ˌरेस्टि'ट्यूशन्/ *noun* [U] **restitution (of sth) (to sb/sth)** **1** (*formal*) the act of giving back sth that was lost or stolen to its owner खोई या चुराई हुई वस्तु की उसके मालिक को वापसी **2** (in law) payment, usually money, for some harm or wrong that sb has suffered (क़ानून में) चोट आदि के लिए व्यक्ति को मुआवज़ा

**restless** /ˈrestləs 'रेस्ट्लस्/ *adj.* **1** unable to relax or be still because you are bored, nervous or impatient बेचैन, अशांत या निश्चेष्ट (ऊब जाने, घबरा जाने या अधीर हो जाने के कारण) *The children always get restless on long journeys.* **2** (used about a period of time) without sleep or rest (समयावधि) निद्रा या विश्राम रहित ▸ **restlessly** *adv.* बैचेनी से

**restoration** /ˌrestəˈreɪʃn ˌरेस्टˈरेश्न्/ *noun* **1** [C, U] the return of sth to its original condition; the things that are done to achieve this किसी वस्तु की मूल दशा में वापसी, मरम्मत, जीर्णोद्धार, मूल रूप निरूपण; इसके लिए उठाए गए क़दम *The house is in need of restoration.* **2** [U] the return of sth to its original owner किसी वस्तु की उसके असली मालिक को वापसी *the restoration of stolen property to its owner*

**restore** /rɪˈstɔː(r) रिˈस्टॉ(र्)/ *verb* [T] **restore sb/sth (to sb/sth)** **1** to put sb/sth back into his/her/its former condition or position व्यक्ति या वस्तु को उसकी पूर्व दशा या स्थिति में लाना *She restores old furniture as a hobby.* ○ *In the recent elections, the former president was restored to power.* **2 restore sth to sb** (*formal*) to give sth that was lost or stolen back to sb खोई या चुराई वस्तु को लौटाना, वापस करना

**restrain** /rɪˈstreɪn रिˈस्ट्रेन्/ *verb* [T] **restrain sb/sth (from sth/doing sth)** to keep sb or sth under control; to prevent sb or sth from doing sth व्यक्ति या वस्तु को नियंत्रण में रखना; व्यक्ति या वस्तु को कुछ करने से रोकना *I had to restrain myself from saying something rude.*

**restrained** /rɪˈstreɪnd रिˈस्ट्रेन्ड्/ *adj.* not showing strong feelings शांत, भावहीन

**restraint** /rɪˈstreɪnt रिˈस्ट्रेन्ट्/ *noun* **1** [U] the quality of behaving in a calm or controlled way शांत या नियंत्रित व्यवहार; संयम *It took a lot of restraint on my part not to scold him.* ○ *Soldiers have to exercise **self-restraint** even when provoked.* **2** [C] **a restraint (on sb/sth)** a limit or control on sth (किसी पर) प्रतिबंध या नियंत्रण *Are there any restraints on what the newspapers are allowed to publish?*

**restrict** /rɪˈstrɪkt रिˈस्ट्रिक्ट्/ *verb* [T] **restrict sb/sth (to sth/ doing sth)** to put a limit on sb/sth व्यक्ति या वस्तु पर (किसी बात के लिए) पाबंदी लगाना *There is a plan to restrict the use of cars in the area.*

**restricted** /rɪˈstrɪktɪd रिˈस्ट्रिक्टिड्/ *adj.* controlled or limited नियंत्रित या सीमित *There is only restricted parking available.*

**restriction** /rɪˈstrɪkʃn रिˈस्ट्रिक्श्न्/ *noun* **restriction (on sth)** **1** [C] something (sometimes a rule or law) that limits the number, amount, size, freedom, etc. of sb/sth प्रतिबंधात्मक व्यवस्था (नियम या क़ानून), रोक, पाबंदी (संख्या, मात्रा, आकार आदि की दृष्टि से) *parking restrictions in the town centre* ○ *The government is to **impose** tighter **restrictions** on the number of immigrants permitted to settle in this country.* **2** [U] the action of limiting the freedom of sb/sth प्रतिबंध, रोक (किसी की आज़ादी सीमित करने वाला काम) *This ticket permits you to travel anywhere, without restriction.*

**restrictive** /rɪˈstrɪktɪv रिˈस्ट्रिक्टिव्/ *adj.* limiting; preventing people from doing what they want सीमित करने वाला; लोगों को मनचाहे काम करने से रोकने वाला; प्रतिबंधक

**rest room** *noun* [C] (*AmE*) a public toilet in a hotel, shop, restaurant, etc. होटल, दुकान, रेस्तराँ आदि में सार्वजनिक शौचालय ➪ **toilet** पर नोट देखिए।

**result[1]** /rɪˈzʌlt रिˈज़ल्ट्/ *noun* **1** [C] something that happens because of sth else; the final situation at the end of a series of actions परिणाम, नतीजा, फल (किसी अन्य बात के कारण घटित स्थिति); अंतिम स्थिति (घटनाओं की शृंखला की) *The traffic was very heavy and **as a result** I arrived late.* ○ *This wasn't really the result that I was expecting.* **2** [C, U] a good effect of an action किसी कार्य का अच्छा प्रभाव *He has tried very hard to find a job, until now without result.* ○ *The treatment is beginning to show results.* **3** [C] the score at the end of a game, competition or election किसी खेल, प्रतियोगिता या चुनाव के अंत में स्थिति, परिणाम या नतीजा *Have you heard today's football results?* ○ *The results of this week's competition will be published next week.* **4** [C, *usually pl.*] the mark given for an exam or test परीक्षा या परीक्षण में प्राप्त अंक *When do you **get** your exam **results**?* **5** [C] something that is discovered by a medical test डॉक्टरी परीक्षण या जाँच का नतीजा या रिपोर्ट *I'm still waiting for the result of my X-ray.* ○ *The result of the test was negative.*

**result[2]** /rɪˈzʌlt रिˈज़ल्ट्/ *verb* [I] **result (from sth)** to happen or exist because of sth (किसी अन्य बात के कारण) कुछ घटित होना या मौजूद होना, परिणाम होना या निकलना *Ninety per cent of the deaths in road accidents resulted from injuries to the head.*

**PHR V** **result in sth** to cause sth to happen; to produce sth as an effect किसी बात के घटित होने का कारण बनना; परिणामस्वरूप कुछ प्राप्त करना, उत्पन्न करना या बनाना *There has been an accident on the highway, resulting in long delays.*

**resume** /rɪˈzuːm; -ˈzjuː- रिˈज़ूम; -ˈज़्यू-/ *verb* [I, T] to begin again or continue after a pause or interruption पुनः आरंभ होना या करना, जारी रहना या रखना (विराम या बाधा के बाद) *Normal service will resume as soon as possible.*

**resumé** /ˈrezjumeɪ ˈरेज़्यूमे/ (*AmE*) = **CV**

**resumption** /rɪˈzʌmpʃn रिˈज़म्प्शन्/ *noun* [*sing.*, U] (*written*) beginning again or continuing after a pause or interruption पुनः आरंभ होने या करने या जारी रहने की क्रिया (विराम या बाधा के बाद); पुनरारंभ

**resurgence** /rɪˈsɜːdʒəns रिˈसजन्स्/ *noun* [C, *usually sing.*] (*formal*) the return and growth of an activity that had stopped (किसी मृतप्राय गतिविधि का) पुनरुज्जीवन *a resurgence of interest in the artist's work*

**resurrect** /ˌrezəˈrekt ˌरेज़ˈरेक्ट्/ *verb* [T] to bring back sth that has not been used or has not existed for a long time (लंबे समय तक अनुपयुक्त या अनुपस्थित वस्तु का) पुनर्जीवित करना

**resurrection** /ˌrezəˈrekʃn ˌरेज़ˈरेक्शन्/ *noun* **1** [U] bringing back sth that has not existed or not been used for a long time (लंबे समय तक अनुपयुक्त या अनुपस्थित वस्तु का) पुनरुज्जीवन **2 the Resurrection** [*sing.*] (in the Christian religion) the return to life of Jesus Christ (ईसाई धर्म में) मृत्यु के बाद ईसा का पुनः जीवित हो उठना; मृतोत्थान

**resuscitate** /rɪˈsʌsɪteɪt रिˈससिटेट्/ *verb* [T] to bring sb who has stopped breathing back to life (लगभग निष्प्राण हो चुके व्यक्ति को) पुनः होश में लाना या जीवित करना *Unfortunately, all efforts to resuscitate the patient failed.* ▶ **resuscitation** /rɪˌsʌsɪˈteɪʃn रिˌससिˈटेश्न्/ *noun* [U] पुनः होश में लाने की क्रिया; पुनरुज्जीवन *mouth-to-mouth resuscitation*

**retail** /ˈriːteɪl ˈरीटेल्/ *noun* [U] the selling of goods to the public in shops, etc. दुकानों आदि पर सामान की खुदरा या फुटकर बिक्री (आम ग्राहकों को) ➪ **wholesale** देखिए।

**retailer** /ˈriːteɪlə(r) ˈरीटेल(र्)/ *noun* [C] a person or company who sells goods to the public in a shop खुदरा या फुटकर विक्रेता व्यक्ति या कंपनी

**retain** /rɪˈteɪn रिˈटेन्/ *verb* [T] (*formal*) to keep or continue to have sth; not to lose किसी वस्तु को रखना या बनाए रखना या रखे रहना; न गँवाना *Despite all her problems, she has managed to retain a sense of humour.* ➪ **retention** noun देखिए।

**retaliate** /rɪˈtælieɪt रिˈटैलिएट्/ *verb* [I] **retaliate (against sb/sth)** to react to sth unpleasant that sb does to you by doing sth unpleasant in return किसी के दुर्व्यवहार का जवाब कटु व्यवहार से देना, बदले की कार्रवाई करना ▶ **retaliation** /rɪˌtæliˈeɪʃn रिˌटैलिˈएश्न्/ *noun* [U] **retaliation (against sb/sth) (for sth)** बदले की कार्रवाई, प्रतिकार *The terrorist group said that the shooting was **in retaliation** for the murder of one of its members.*

**retarded** /rɪˈtɑːdɪd रिˈटाडिड्/ *adj.* slower to develop than normal अपूर्ण विकसित, मंदगति से विकसित

**retch** /retʃ रेच्/ *verb* [I] to make sounds and movements as if you are going to vomit, but without bringing any food up from your stomach मिचली होना, उबकाई आना (वमन क्रिया वाली हरकतें करना परंतु वस्तुतः वमन न होना)

**retention** /rɪˈtenʃn रिˈटेन्श्न्/ *noun* [U] the action of keeping sth or of being kept किसी वस्तु को रखने या वस्तु के रखने जाने की क्रिया; धारण, अवधारण, प्रतिधारण ➪ **retain** verb देखिए।

**rethink** /ˈriːθɪŋk; ˌriːˈθɪŋk ˈरीथिङ्क्; ˌरीˈथिङ्क्/ *verb* [I, T] (*pt, pp* **rethought** /-ˈθɔːt -ˈथॉट्/) to think about sth again because you probably need to change it किसी इरादे आदि पर पुनर्विचार करना (इसलिए कि शायद उसे बदलना पड़े) *The government has been forced to rethink its economic policy.*

**reticent** /ˈretɪsnt ˈरेटिस्न्ट्/ *adj.* **reticent (about sth)** not wanting to tell people about things (किसी विषय में) लोगों से बातें करने को अनिच्छुक; अल्पभाषी *He is extremely reticent about his personal life.* ▶ **reticence** noun [U] अल्पभाषिता

**retina** /ˈretɪnə ˈरेटिना/ *noun* [C] the area at the back of your eye that is sensitive to light and sends an image of what is seen to your brain दृष्टिपटल, रेटिना; (आँख में पीछे का हिस्सा जो प्रकाश के प्रति संवेदनशील है और जो हम देखते हैं उसे मस्तिष्क को संप्रेषित करता है) ➪ **eye** पर चित्र देखिए।

**retinue** /ˈretɪnjuː ˈरेटिन्यू/ *noun* [C, *with sing. or pl. verb*] a group of people who travel with an important person to provide help and support किसी महत्त्वपूर्ण व्यक्ति के साथ सेवकों का दल; अनुचर वर्ग

**retire** /rɪˈtaɪə(r) रिˈटाइअ(र्)/ *verb* [I] **1 retire (from sth)** to leave your job and stop working, usually because you have reached a certain age सेवा से निवृत्त होना या अवकाश प्राप्त करना, रिटायर होना (प्रायः सेवानिवृत्ति की आयु पर) *Most people in the company retire at 60.* ○ *Injury forced her to retire from professional athletics.* **2** to leave and go to a quiet or private place (घर छोड़ कर) किसी शांत या निजी स्थान पर चले जाना, एकांतवास को चले जाना

**retired** /rɪˈtaɪəd रिˈटाइअड्/ *adj.* having stopped work permanently सेवानिवृत्त, अवकाश-प्राप्त, रिटायर्ड *a retired teacher*

**retirement** /rɪˈtaɪəmənt रिˈटाइअमन्ट्/ *noun* **1** [C, U] the act of stopping working permanently सेवानिवृत्ति, अवकाश-ग्रहण *She has decided to **take early retirement**.* ○ *The former world champion* *has announced his retirement from the sport.* 2 [*sing*., U] the situation or period after retiring from work सेवानिवृत्ति के बाद की स्थिति या समय *We all wish you a long and happy retirement.*

**NOTE** सेवानिवृत्ति हो जाने वाले व्यक्ति को नियमित रूप से मिलने वाली राशि **pension** कहलाती है। इसे सरकार देती है या वह संस्था जहाँ व्यक्ति सेवारत था।

**retiring** /rɪˈtaɪərɪŋ रिˈटाइअरिङ्/ *adj.* (used about a person) shy and quiet (व्यक्ति) एकांतप्रिय, संकोची

**retort[1]** /rɪˈtɔːt रिˈटॉट्/ *verb* [T] to reply quickly to what sb says, in an angry or amusing way किसी की बात का तुरंत जवाब देना (चिढ़कर या विनोदी ढंग से) *'Who asked you for your opinion?' she retorted.*

**retort[2]** /rɪˈtɔːt रिˈटॉट्/ *noun* [C] 1 a quick, angry or amusing reply त्वरित; खीझ भरा या विनोदपूर्ण उत्तर *an angry retort* 2 a round glass vessel with a long neck bent downwards that is used in a **laboratory** for distilling water लंबी तंग मुड़ी हुई टोंटी वाली बोतल जो प्रयोगशाला में जल आसवन के काम आती है ➪ **laboratory** पर चित्र देखिए।

**retrace** /rɪˈtreɪs रिˈट्रेस्/ *verb* [T] to repeat a past journey, series of events, etc. (ठीक उसी रास्ते) लौटना, पिछली बातों को दोहराना, आदि *If you **retrace** your **steps**, you might see where you dropped the ticket.*

**retract** /rɪˈtrækt रिˈट्रैक्ट्/ *verb* [I, T] (*formal*) to say that sth you have said is not true अपनी बात से पीछे हट जाना, पूर्व कथन को वापस ले लेना; मुकर जाना *When he appeared in court, he retracted the confession he had made to the police.*

**retreat[1]** /rɪˈtriːt रिˈट्रीट्/ *verb* [I] 1 (used about an army, etc.) to move backwards in order to leave a battle or in order not to become involved in a battle (सेना का) मोर्चे से पीछे हट जाना (हारकर या फिर से तैयार होने के लिए) *The order was given to retreat.* ✪ विलोम **advance** 2 to move backwards; to go to a safe or private place पीछे हटना; एकांतवास में चले जाना *(figurative) She seems to retreat into a world of her own sometimes.*

**retreat[2]** /rɪˈtriːt रिˈट्रीट्/ *noun* 1 [C, U] the action of moving backwards, away from a difficult or dangerous situation दूर और पीछे हटने की क्रिया (कठिन या ख़तरनाक स्थिति से) *The invading forces are now in retreat.* ✪ विलोम **advance** 2 [C] a private place where you can go when you want to be quiet or to rest एकांत स्थान (शांति या विश्राम के लिए) *a country retreat*

**retrial** /ˌriːˈtraɪəl ˌरीˈट्राइअल्/ *noun* [C, *usually sing*.] a new trial for a person whose criminal offence has already been judged once in a court of law किसी पर दोबारा मुक़दमा चलाने की क्रिया; पुनःविचारण *The judge ordered a retrial because new evidence had appeared.*

**retribution** /ˌretrɪˈbjuːʃn ˌरेट्रिˈब्यूश्न्/ *noun* [U] (*written*) **retribution (for sth)** punishment for a crime अपराध की सज़ा

**retrieve** /rɪˈtriːv रिˈट्रीव़्/ *verb* [T] 1 **retrieve sth (from sb/sth)** to get sth back from the place where it was left or lost (किसी वस्तु को) पुनः प्राप्त करना (वहाँ से जहाँ वह छूटी या खोई थी) *Police divers retrieved the body from the canal.* 2 (*computing*) to find information that has been stored (मेमोरी में) संचित सूचना को प्राप्त करना *The computer can retrieve all the data about a particular customer.* 3 to make a bad situation or a mistake better; to put sth right किसी दुर्व्यवस्था या त्रुटि को सुधारना; किसी बात को सही कर देना *The team was losing two-nil at half-time but they managed to **retrieve the situation** in the second half.* ▶ **retrieval** /-vl -व़्ल्/ *noun* [U] पुनः प्राप्ति; सुधार

**retro-** /ˈretrəʊ ˈरेट्रो/ *prefix* (*used in nouns, adjectives and adverbs*) back or backwards पीछे या पीछे की ओर, पश्च-, अधः या अधो- *retrospective*

**retrograde** /ˈretrəgreɪd ˈरेट्रग्रेड्/ *adj.* (*formal*) (used about an action) making a situation worse or returning to how sth was in the past (कार्य) स्थिति को बदतर बनाने वाला पतनोन्मुख या पूर्व स्थिति पर लौट आने वाला या प्रतिगामी *The closure of the factory is a **retrograde step**.*

**retrospect** /ˈretrəspekt ˈरेट्रस्पेक्ट्/ *noun*

**IDM** **in retrospect** thinking about sth that happened in the past, often seeing it differently from the way you saw it at that time पुरानी बातों पर विचार करते हुए (प्रायः वर्तमान में कुछ नए ढंग से सोचने की भूमिका पर); पश्चदर्शन *In retrospect, I can see what a stupid mistake it was.*

**retrospective** /ˌretrəˈspektɪv ˌरेट्रˈस्पेक्टिव़्/ *adj.* 1 looking again at the past पुनः अतीत को देखते हुए; अतीतलक्षी, पश्चदर्शी *a retrospective analysis of historical events* 2 (used about laws, decisions, payments, etc.) intended to take effect from a date in the past (क़ानून, निर्णय, भुगतान आदि) पिछली तारीख़ से लागू, पूर्व-प्रभावी *Is this new tax law retrospective?* ▶ **retrospectively** *adv*. पूर्व प्रभाव से, भूतलक्षी प्रभाव से

**return[1]** /rɪˈtɜːn रिˈटन्/ *verb* 1 [I] **return (to/from)** to come or go back to a place कहीं पहुँचना या लौटना *I leave on 10 July and return on 6 August.* ○ *I shall be returning to this country in six months.* 2 [I] **return (to sth/doing sth)** to go back to the former or usual activity, situation, condition, etc. वापस जाना, लौटना (पिछले या रोज़मर्रा के कार्यकलाप की ओर, स्थिति में, दशा में आदि) *The strike is over and they will* ***return to work*** *on Monday.* ○ *It is hoped that train services will* ***return to normal*** *soon.* **3** [I] to come back; to happen again लौट आना; दोबारा होना *If the pain returns, make another appointment to see me.* **4** [T] **return sth (to sb/ sth)** to give, send, put or take sth back कुछ वापस देना, भेजना, रखना या लेना *I've stopped lending him things because he never returns them.* ○ *Application forms must be returned by 14 March.* **5** [T] to react to sth that sb does, says or feels by doing, saying or feeling sth similar किसी के कुछ करने, कहने या अनुभव करने की उसी प्रकार से (कर, कह या अनुभव कर) प्रतिक्रिया व्यक्त करना *I've phoned them several times and left messages but they haven't returned any of my calls.* ○ *We'll be happy to return your hospitality if you ever come to our country.* **6** [T] (*in tennis*) to hit or throw the ball back (टेनिस में) गेंद को मार या फेंक कर लौटाना

**return²** /rɪˈtɜːn रिˈटन्/ *noun* **1** [*sing.*] **a return (to/from)** coming or going back to a place or to a former activity, situation or condition लौट कर आने या जाने की क्रिया(किसी स्थान पर, पिछले कार्यकलाप की ओर या स्थिति या दशा में) *I'll contact you* ***on*** *my* ***return*** *from holiday.* ○ *He has recently made a return to form* (= started playing well again). **2** [U] giving, sending, putting or taking sth back किसी वस्तु को वापस देने, भेजने या रखने की क्रिया *I demand the immediate return of my passport.* **3** [C] (in tennis) the act of hitting or throwing the ball back (टेनिस में) गेंद को मार या फेंककर लौटाने की क्रिया *She hit a brilliant return.* **4** [C, U] **(a) return (on sth)** the profit from a business, etc. व्यापार आदि से लाभ *This account offers high returns on all investments.* **5** [C] (*BrE* **return ticket,** *AmE* **round trip; round trip ticket**) a ticket to travel to a place and back again दोनों तरफ का यात्रा-टिकट, लौटा फेरी का टिकट *A* ***day return*** *to Delhi, please.* ○ *Is the* ***return fare*** *cheaper than two singles?* ✪ विलोम **single** या **one-way** **6** (*also* **the return key**) [*sing.*] the button on a computer that you press when you reach the end of a line or of an instruction (कंप्यूटर) रिटर्न-की, कंप्यूटर पर वह बटन जिसे पंक्ति या निर्देश के अंत तक पहुँचने पर दबाया जाता है

**IDM** **by return (of post)** (*BrE*) immediately; by the next post तुरंत; लौटती डाक, वापसी डाक

**in return (for sth)** as payment or in exchange (for sth); as a reaction to sth किसी के भुगतान स्वरूप या बदले में; किसी की प्रतिक्रिया में *Please accept this present in return for all your help.*

**returnable** /rɪˈtɜːnəbl रिˈटनबल्/ *adj.* that can or must be given or taken back जिसे वापस देना या लेना संभव या अनिवार्य हों; लौटाऊ *a non-returnable deposit*

**reunion** /riːˈjuːniən रीˈयूनिअन्/ *noun* **1** [C] a party or occasion when friends or people who worked together meet again after they have not seen each other for a long time पुनर्मिलन (की) पार्टी या अवसर (पुराने मित्रों या साथियों से लंबे वियोग के बाद) *The college holds an annual reunion for former students.* **2** [C, U] **a reunion (with sb/between A and B)** coming together again after being apart (लंबे वियोग के बाद) पुनर्मिलन *The released hostages had an emotional reunion with their families at the airport.*

**reunite** /ˌriːjuːˈnaɪt ˌरीयूˈनाइट/ *verb* [I, T] **reunite (A with/and B)** to come together again; to join two or more people, groups, etc. together again पुनर्मिलन होना; व्यक्तियों, समूहों आदि का पुनर्मिलन करा देना *The missing child was found by the police and reunited with his parents.*

**Rev.** *abbr.* Reverend रेवरेंड, पादरी

**rev¹** /rev रेव़्/ *verb* [I, T] (**re<u>vv</u>ing; re<u>vv</u>ed**) **rev (sth) (up)** when an engine revs or when you rev it, it turns quickly and noisily इंजन का परिक्रमण करना (तेज़ी से और आवाज़ करते हुए घूमना)

**rev²** /rev रेव़् / *noun* [C] (*informal*) (used when talking about an engine's speed) one complete turn (इंजन का) एक परिक्रमण (एक पूरा चक्कर) *4000 revs per minute* ➪ **revolution** देखिए।

**reveal** /rɪˈviːl रिˈव़ील्/ *verb* [T] **1 reveal sth (to sb)** to make sth known that was secret or unknown before ( गुप्त या पूर्वतः अज्ञात वस्तु को) प्रकट करना, रहस्य खो लेना *He refused to reveal any names to the police.* **2** to show sth that was hidden before (जो पहले छुपा था उसे) दिखाना, प्रदर्शित करना *The X-ray revealed a hairline fracture in her right hand.*

**revealing** /rɪˈviːlɪŋ रिˈवीलिङ्/ *adj.* **1** allowing sth to be known that was secret or unknown before (गुप्त या पूर्वतः अज्ञात वस्तु को) प्रकट करने वाला, अर्थपूर्ण, सारगर्भित *This book provides a revealing insight into the world of politics.* **2** allowing sth to be seen that is usually hidden, especially sb's body सामान्यतः ढकी रहने वाली वस्तु (विशेषतः शरीर) को उघड़ा देने वाला; पारदर्शक *a very revealing swimsuit*

**revel** /ˈrevl ˈरेव़ल्/ *verb* (**reve<u>ll</u>ing; reve<u>ll</u>ed** *AmE* **reve<u>l</u>ing; reve<u>l</u>ed**)

**PHR V** **revel in sth/doing sth** to enjoy sth very much (किसी बात का) भरपूर आनंद लेना *He likes being famous and revels in the attention he gets.*

**revelation** /ˌrevəˈleɪʃn ˌरेव़ˈलेश्न्/ *noun* **1** [C] something that is made known, that was secret or unknown before, especially sth surprising रहस्योद्घाटन; (गुप्त या पूर्वतः अज्ञात विशेषतः किसी आश्चर्यकारी बात का) प्रकटीकरण *This magazine is full of revelations about the private lives of the stars.* **2** [*sing.*] a thing or a person that surprises you and makes you change your opinion about sb/sth आश्चर्यकारी वस्तु या व्यक्ति (जो किसी के बारे में आपका विचार बदल दे)

**revenge** /rɪˈvendʒ रिˈव़ेन्ज्/ *noun* [U] **revenge (on sb) (for sth)** something that you do to punish sb who has hurt you, made you suffer, etc. (किसी से किसी बात का) बदला, प्रतिशोध (चोट के बदले चोट) *He made a fool of me and now I want to* ***get*** *my* ***revenge***. ○ *to* ***take revenge*** ○ *The shooting was* ***in revenge*** *for an attack by the nationalists.* ➪ **vengeance** देखिए। ▶ **revenge** *verb* [T] **revenge yourself on sb** किसी से बदला लेना *She revenged herself on her enemy.* ➪ **avenge** देखिए।

**revenue** /ˈrevənjuː ˈरेव़न्यू/ *noun* [U, *pl.*] money regularly received by a government, company, etc. सरकार, कंपनी आदि की नियमित आय; राजस्व *Revenue from income tax rose last year.*

**reverberate** /rɪˈvɜːbəreɪt रिˈव़बरेट्/ *verb* [I] **1** (used about a sound) to be repeated several times as it comes off different surfaces (ध्वनि का) गूँजना, प्रतिध्वनित होना *Her voice reverberated around the hall.* ✪ पर्याय **echo** **2 reverberate (with/to sth)** (used about a place) to seem to shake because of a loud noise (कमरा आदि स्थान) मारे शोर के हिलने-सा लगना या तीव्र ध्वनि से कंपायमान हो जाना *The hall reverberated with the sound of music and dancing.*

**revere** /rɪˈvɪə(r) रिˈव़िअ(र्)/ *verb* [T] (*usually passive*) (*formal*) **revere sb/sth (as sth)** to feel great respect or admiration for sb/sth किसी व्यक्ति या वस्तु के लिए बहुत आदर या प्रशंसा का भाव रखना, व्यक्ति या वस्तु में श्रद्धा रखना *He is revered as one of the greatest musicians of his generation.*

**reverence** /ˈrevərəns ˈरेव़रन्स्/ *noun* [U] (*formal*) **reverence (for sb/sth)** a feeling of great respect श्रद्धा

**Reverend** (*also* **reverend**) /ˈrevərənd ˈरेव़रन्ड्/ *adj.* (*abbr.* **Rev.**) the title of a Christian priest इसाई पादरी की उपाधि; रेवरेंड

**reverent** /ˈrevərənt ˈरेव़रन्ट्/ *adj.* (*formal*) showing respect श्रद्धालु

**reversal** /rɪˈvɜːsl रिˈव़सल्/ *noun* [U, C] the action of changing sth to the opposite of what it was before; an occasion when this happens विपरीत के लिए बदलाव; विपरीत के लिए बदलाव होने की क्रिया *The government insists that there will be no reversal of policy.* ○ *The decision taken yesterday was a complete reversal of last week's decision.*

**reverse[1]** /rɪˈvɜːs रिˈव़स्/ *verb* **1** [T] to put sth in the opposite position to normal or to how it was before पहले किए का उलटा या विपरीत करना *Today's results have reversed the order of the top two teams.* **2** [T] to exchange the positions or functions of two things or people दो व्यक्तियों या वस्तुओं के पदों या क्रियाओं की अदला-बदली करना *Leela and her husband have reversed roles—he stays at home now and she goes to work.* **3** [I, T] to go backwards in a car, etc.; to make a car go backwards (वाहन में) पीछे की ओर जाना; वाहन को पीछे को चलाना *It might be easier to reverse into that parking space.* ○ *He reversed his brand new car into a wall.*

**IDM** **reverse (the) charges** (*BrE*) to make a telephone call that will be paid for by the person who receives it ऐसा फ़ोन करना जिसमें पाने वाला भुगतान करे *Phone us when you get there, and reverse the charges.* ○ *a reverse charge call*

**reverse[2]** /rɪˈvɜːs रिˈव़स्/ *noun* **1** [*sing.*] **the reverse (of sth)** the complete opposite of what was said just before, or of what is expected पूर्णतः विपरीत (जो अभी कहा गया है या जो अपेक्षित है उसका) *Of course I don't dislike you—quite the reverse* (= I like you very much). ○ *This course is the exact reverse of what I was expecting.* **2** (*also* **reverse gear**) [U] the control in a car, etc. that allows it to move backwards कार को पीछे ले जाने के लिए प्रयुक्त गियर; रिवर्स गियर *Leave the car* ***in reverse*** *while it's parked on this hill.*

**IDM** **in reverse** in the opposite order, starting at the end and going backwards to the beginning विपरीत क्रम में, अंत से प्रारंभ की ओर

**reverse[3]** /rɪˈvɜːs रिˈव़स्/ *adj.* opposite to what is expected or has just been described विपरीत (उसके कि जो अपेक्षित है या अभी कहा गया है)

**IDM** **in/into reverse order** starting with the last one and going backwards to the first one विपरीत क्रम में, अंतिम से प्रथम की ओर *The results will be announced in reverse order.*

**reversible** /rɪˈvɜːsəbl रि'व़सबल्/ *adj.* 1 (used about clothes) that can be worn with either side on the outside (पोशाक) उलटवाँ, पलटवाँ (जिसे उलट या पलट कर पहना जा सके) *a reversible coat jacket* 2 (used about a process, an action or a disease) that can be changed so that sth returns to its original state or situation (कोई प्रक्रिया, क्रिया या रोग) जिसे ऐसे बदला जा सके कि वह अपनी मूल दशा या स्थिति में पहुँच जाए; प्रतिवर्त्य ✪ विलोम **irreversible**

**revert** /rɪˈvɜːt रि'व़ट्/ *verb* [I] **revert (to sth)** to return to a former state or activity पूर्व दशा या क्रिया में लौट जाना *The land will soon revert to jungle if it is not farmed.* ○ *If the experiment is unsuccessful we will revert to the old system.*

**review**[1] /rɪˈvjuː रि'व्यू/ *noun* 1 [C, U] the examining or considering again of sth in order to decide if changes are necessary (किसी बात का) पुनः परीक्षण या उस पर पुनर्विचार (उसमें परिवर्तन की आवश्यकता पर निर्णय हेतु) *There will be a review of your contract after the first six months.* ○ *The system is in need of review.* 2 [C] a look back at sth in order to check, remember, or be clear about sth (किसी का) पुनरीक्षण या पुनर्विलोकन (उसे जाँचने, याद करने या स्पष्टता से समझने के लिए) *a review of the major events of the year* 3 [C] a newspaper or magazine article, or an item on television or radio, in which sb gives an opinion on a new book, film, play, etc. पुस्तक, फ़िल्म आदि की (लिपिबद्ध या मौखिक) समीक्षा (अख़बार, पत्रिका, टीवी या रेडियो पर) *The film got bad reviews.*

**review**[2] /rɪˈvjuː रि'व्यू/ *verb* [T] 1 to examine or consider sth again in order to decide if changes are necessary (किसी बात का) पुनः परीक्षण या उस पर पुनर्विचार करना (उसमें परिवर्तन की आवश्यकता पर निर्णय हेतु) *Your salary will be reviewed after one year.* 2 to look at or think about sth again to make sure that you understand it किसी का पुनर्विलोकन या उस पर पुनर्विचार करना उसे ठीक से समझने की पुष्टि के लिए *Let's review what we've done in class this week.* 3 to write an article or to talk on television or radio, giving an opinion on a new book, film, play, etc. (रेडियो या टीवी पर वार्ता या पत्रिका में लेख के रूप में पुस्तक आदि की समीक्षा करना) *In this week's edition our film critic reviews the latest films.*

**reviewer** /rɪˈvjuːə(r) रि'व्यूअ(र्)/ *noun* [C] a person who writes about new books, films, etc. (नई पुस्तक फ़िल्म आदि का) समीक्षक

**revise** /rɪˈvaɪz रि'वाइज़्/ *verb* 1 [T] to make changes to sth in order to correct or improve it किसी वस्तु में परिवर्तन करना (उसे शुद्ध करने या सुधारने के लिए), संशोधन या परिशोधन करना *The book has been revised for this new edition.* ○ *I revised my opinion of him when I found out that he had lied.* 2 [I, T] (*BrE*) **revise (for sth)** to read or study again sth that you have learnt, especially when preparing for an exam पढ़े हुए को दोहराना (विशेषतः परीक्षा की तैयारी के लिए); पुनरावृत्ति करना *I can't come out tonight. I'm revising for my exam.* ○ *None of the things I had revised came up in the exam.*

**revision** /rɪˈvɪʒn रि'विश़न्/ *noun* 1 [C, U] the changing of sth in order to correct or improve it किसी में परिवर्तन करने की क्रिया (उसे शुद्ध करने या सुधारने के लिए), संशोधन या परिशोधन *It has been suggested that the whole system is in need of revision.* 2 [U] (*BrE*) the work of reading or studying again sth you have learnt, especially when preparing for an exam पढ़े हुए को दोहराने की क्रिया (विशेषतः परीक्षा की तैयारी के लिए); दुहराई, पुनरावृत्ति *I'm going to have to **do** a lot of **revision** for History.*

**revival** /rɪˈvaɪvl रि'वाइवल्/ *noun* 1 [C, U] the act of becoming or making sth strong or popular again पुनः सशक्त या जनप्रिय होना या करना; पुनरुज्जीवन *economic revival* ○ *a revival of interest in traditional farming methods* 2 [C] a new performance of a play that has not been performed for sometime नाटक का पुनः मंचन (कुछ अंतराल के बाद) *a revival of the musical 'The Sound of Music'*

**revive** /rɪˈvaɪv रि'वाइव्/ *verb* [I, T] 1 to become or to make sb/sth strong or healthy again; to come or to bring sb back to life or consciousness किसी का पुनरुज्जीवित होना या करना; किसी का पुनः जीवित होना या करना *Hopes have revived for an early end to the fighting.* ○ *Attempts were made to revive him but he was already dead.* 2 to become or to make sth popular again; to begin to do or use sth again पुनः जनप्रिय होना या करना; पुनः प्रचलन होना या करना *Public interest in athletics has revived now that the national team is doing well.* ○ *to revive an old custom*

**revoke** /rɪˈvəʊk रि'वोक्/ *verb* [T] (*formal*) to officially cancel sth so that it is no longer valid किसी वस्तु (जैसे क़ानून) को रद्द करना

**revolt** /rɪˈvəʊlt रि'वोल्ट्/ *verb* 1 [I] **revolt (against sb/sth)** to protest in a group, often violently, against the person or people in power किसी व्यक्ति या सत्ताधारी के विरुद्ध सामूहिक विद्रोह करना (प्रायः हिंसात्मक रीति से) *A group of generals revolted against the government.* 2 [T] to make sb feel disgusted or ill किसी के मन में घृणा भर देना *The sight and smell of the meat revolted him.*

➪ **revulsion** noun देखिए। ▶ **revolt** *noun* [C, U] विद्रोह *The people rose* ***in revolt*** *against the corrupt government.*

**revolting** /rɪˈvəʊltɪŋ रिˈवोल्टिङ्/ *adj.* extremely unpleasant; disgusting अत्यंत अरुचिकर; घृणाजनक

**revolution** /ˌrevəˈluːʃn ˌरेव़ˈलूशन्/ *noun* **1** [C, U] action taken by a large group of people to try to change the government of a country, especially by violent action क्रांति (जनसमूह द्वारा शासन व्यवस्था को बदलने का प्रयास विशेषतः हिंसक रीति से) *the French Revolution of 1789* ○ *a country on the brink of revolution* **2** [C] **a revolution (in sth)** a complete change in methods, opinions, etc., often as a result of progress किसी की कार्यपद्धति आदि में आमूल परिवर्तन (प्रायः प्रगति के फलस्वरूप) *the Industrial Revolution* **3** [C, U] a movement around sth; one complete turn around a central point (for example in a car engine) परिक्रमण (किसी वस्तु के चारों ओर का चक्कर); किसी केंद्रबिंदु के चारों और एक पूरा चक्कर (जैसे कार के इंजन में) *400 revolutions per minute* ➪ **rev**[2] देखिए।

**revolutionary**[1] /ˌrevəˈluːʃənəri ˌरेव़ˈलूशनरि/ *adj.* **1** connected with or supporting political revolution क्रांतिकारी (राजनीतिक क्रांति से संबंधित या उसका समर्थक) *the revolutionary leaders* **2** producing great changes; very new and different अत्यधिक परिवर्तनकारी; कायापलट करने वाला *a revolutionary new scheme to ban cars from the city centre*

**revolutionary**[2] /ˌrevəˈluːʃənəri ˌरेव़ˈलूशनरि/ *noun* [C] (*pl.* **revolutionaries**) a person who starts or supports action to try to change the government of a country, especially by using violent methods क्रांतिकारी व्यक्ति (शासन-व्यवस्था को बदलने के लिए हिंसात्मक प्रयासों का प्रवर्तक या समर्थक व्यक्ति)

**revolutionize** (*also* **-ise**) /ˌrevəˈluːʃənaɪz ˌरेव़ˈलूशनाइज़्/ *verb* [T] to change sth completely, usually improving it किसी को पूरी तरह बदल देना, क्रांति ले आना (प्रायः उसमें सुधार के साथ) *a discovery that could revolutionize the treatment of mental illness*

**revolve** /rɪˈvɒlv रिˈव़ॉल्व़्/ *verb* [I] to move in a circle around a central point किसी केंद्रीय बिंदु के चारों ओर चक्कर लगाना, वृत्ताकार घूमना *The earth revolves around the sun.*

**PHR V** **revolve around sb/sth** to have sb/sth as the most important part किसी व्यक्ति या वस्तु का सबसे महत्त्वपूर्ण होना या किसी बात के केंद्र में होना *Her life revolves around the family.*

**revolver** /rɪˈvɒlvə(r) रिˈव़ॉल्व़(र्)/ *noun* [C] a type of small gun with a container for bullets that turns round रिवॉल्वर; एक प्रकार की छोटी बंदूक़

**revolving** /rɪˈvɒlvɪŋ रिˈवॉल्विङ्/ *adj.* that goes round in a circle चक्राकार घूमने वाला *revolving doors*

**revulsion** /rɪˈvʌlʃn रिˈव़ल्शन्/ *noun* [U] a feeling of disgust (because sth is extremely unpleasant) घृणा या जुगुप्सा का भाव (घिनौनी चीज़ के कारण) ➪ **revolt** verb देखिए।

**reward**[1] /rɪˈwɔːd रिˈवॉड्/ *noun* **reward (for sth/doing sth)** **1** [C, U] something that you are given because you have done sth good, worked hard, etc. पुरस्कार, इनाम (अच्छा काम करने, मेहनत करने आदि के लिए प्रशंसा के रूप में दी गई कोई वस्तु) *Winning the match was* ***just reward*** *for all the effort.* **2** [C] an amount of money that is given in exchange for helping the police, returning sth that was lost, etc. (पुलिस की सहायता करने, खोई वस्तु लौटाने आदि के लिए) प्रशंसा स्वरूप दी गई धनराशि *Police are offering a reward for information leading to a conviction.*

**reward**[2] /rɪˈwɔːd रिˈवॉड्/ *verb* [T] **reward sb (for sth/for doing sth)** (*usually passive*) to give sth to sb because he/she has done sth good, worked hard, etc. किसी को पुरस्कार देना (अच्छा काम करने, परिश्रम करने आदि के लिए) *Eventually her efforts were rewarded and she got a job.*

**rewarding** /rɪˈwɔːdɪŋ रिˈवॉडिङ्/ *adj.* (used about an activity, job, etc.) giving satisfaction; making you happy because you think it is important, useful, etc. (कोई गतिविधि, नौकरी आदि) संतोषप्रद; आनंदप्रद (महत्त्वपूर्ण, उपयोगी आदि लगने के कारण)

**rewind** /ˌriːˈwaɪnd ˌरिˈवाइन्ड्/ *verb* [T] (*pt, pp* **rewound**) to make a video or cassette tape go backwards विडियो कैसेट या टेप को पीछे करना या उलटा घुमाना *Please rewind the tape at the end of the film.* ▶ **rewind** *noun* [U] पीछे करने या उलटा घुमाने की क्रिया ➪ **fast forward** देखिए।

**rewrite** /ˌriːˈraɪt ˌरीˈराइट्/ *verb* [T] (*pt* **rewrote** /-ˈrəʊt -ˈरोट्/; *pp* **rewritten** /-ˈrɪtn -ˈरिट्न्/) to write sth again in a different or better way किसी बात को दोबारा लिखना (भिन्न रूप से या बेहतर तरीक़े से)

**rhetoric** /ˈretərɪk ˈरेटरिक्/ *noun* [U] (*formal*) a way of speaking or writing that is intended to impress or influence people but is not always sincere वाग्मिता, वाक्पटुता (प्रभावपूर्ण रीति से या लोगों को प्रभावित करने के लिए कुछ कहने या लिखने की कला, कभी-कभी केवल दिखावे के लिए) ▶ **rhetorical** /rɪˈtɒrɪkl रिˈटॉरिक्ल्/ *adj.* वाक्पटुता-विषयक, आलंकारिक ▶ **rhetorically** /rɪˈtɒrɪkli रिˈटॉरिक्लि/ *adv.* वाक्पटुतापूर्वक, आलंकारिक रीति से

**rhetorical question** *noun* [C] a question that does not expect an answer प्रश्नालंकार, भाषणगत प्रश्न (ऐसा प्रश्न जिसका उत्तर अपेक्षित नहीं, अभिव्यक्ति की शोभा)

**rheumatism** /ˈruːmətɪzəm ˈरूमटिज़म्/ *noun* [U] an illness that causes pain in muscles and where your bones join together (**the joints**) संधिवात, गठिया (का रोग)

**rhino** /ˈraɪnəʊ ˈराइनो/ (*pl.* **rhinos**) (*informal*) = **rhinoceros**

**rhinoceros** /raɪˈnɒsərəs राइˈनॉसरस्/ *noun* [C] (*pl.* **rhinoceros** or **rhinoceroses**) a large animal from Africa or Asia, with a thick skin and with one or two horns on its nose गैंडा (अफ़्रीक़ा या एशिया में पाया जाता है) ➪ **pachyderm** पर चित्र देखिए।

**rhomboid** /ˈrɒmbɔɪd ˈरॉम्बॉइड्/ *noun* [C] (*technical*) a flat shape with four straight sides, with only the opposite sides and angles equal to each other समानांतर असमचतुर्भुज (सीधी भुजाओं वाली चौरस आकृति जिसके केवल आमने-सामने की भुजाएँ और कोण एक दूसरे के समान होते हैं) ➪ **parallelogram** पर चित्र देखिए।

**rhombus** /ˈrɒmbəsˈरॉम्बस्/ *noun* [C] (*mathematics*) a flat shape with four equal sides and four angles which are not 90° समचतुर्भुज (भुजाएँ समान परंतु कोण 90° के नहीं) ➪ **parallelogram** पर चित्र देखिए।

**rhubarb** /ˈruːbɑːb ˈरूबाब्/ *noun* [U] a plant with long red parts (**stalks**) that can be cooked and eaten as fruit रेवत चीनी, रेबंद चीनी (का पौधा, लंबे लाल डंठल वाला जो खाने के काम आता है)

**rhyme[1]** /raɪm राइम्/ *noun* **1** [C] a word that has the same sound as another तुक, अंत्यानुप्रास (शब्दगत ध्वनियों की समानता), क़ाफ़िया **2** [C] a short piece of writing, or sth spoken, in which the word at the end of each line sounds the same as the word at the end of the line before it तुकांत अभिव्यक्ति (लिखित या मौखिक) ➪ **nursery rhyme** देखिए। **3** [U] the use of words in a poem or song that have the same sound, especially at the ends of lines तुकांत कविता या गीत; तुकबंदी *All of his poetry was written* ***in rhyme.***

**rhyme[2]** /raɪm राइम्/ *verb* **1** [I] **rhyme (with sth)** to have the same sound as another word; to contain lines that end with words that sound the same शब्दों की तुक मिलना; किसी रचना का तुकांत होना (रचना की पंक्तियों के अंत, समान ध्वनि वाले शब्दों का प्रयोग होना) *'Tough' rhymes with 'stuff'.* **2** [T] **rhyme sth (with sth)** to put together words that have the same sound (शब्दों, पंक्तियों की) तुक मिलना

**rhythm** /ˈrɪðəm ˈरिद्रम्/ *noun* [C, U] a regular repeated pattern of sound or movement लय, ताल (ध्वनि या गति की नियमित आवृत्ति का पैटर्न) *He's a terrible dancer because he has no* ***sense of rhythm.*** ○ *He tapped his foot* ***in rhythm*** *with the music.* ▶ **rhythmic** /ˈrɪðmɪk ˈरिद्मिक्/ (*also* **rhythmical** /ˈrɪðmɪkl ˈरिद्मिकल्/) *adj.* लयबद्ध, तालबद्धपूर्वक *the rhythmic qualities of African music* ▶ **rhythmically** /-kli -क्लि/ *adv.* लय या तालपूर्वक

**ria** /ˈriːə ˈरीआ/ *noun* [C] (in geography) a long narrow area of water formed when a river valley floods (भूगोल में) नदी में बाढ़ से बना लंबा तंग नाला गहरी घाटी; रीआ

**rib** /rɪb रिब्/ *noun* [C] one of the curved bones that go round your chest पसली की हड्डी, पर्शुका *He's so thin that you can see his ribs.* ➪ **body** पर चित्र देखिए।

**ribbon** /ˈrɪbən ˈरिबन्/ *noun* [C, U] a long, thin piece of material that is used for tying or decorating sth फ़ीता, रिबन (किसी वस्तु को बाँधने या सजाने के लिए)

**ribbon lake** *noun* [C] (in geography) a long narrow lake (भूगोल में) लंबी तंग झील ➪ **glacial** पर चित्र देखिए।

**ribcage** /ˈrɪbkeɪdʒ ˈरिब्केज्/ *noun* [C] the structure of curved bones (**ribs**) that surrounds and protects the chest पसली-पिंजर, पर्शुका-पिंजर (पसली की हड्डी के चारों ओर का ढांचा जो छाती को सुरक्षा देता है)

**rice** /raɪs राइस्/ *noun* [U] short, thin, white or brown grain from a plant that grows on wet land in hot countries. We cook and eat rice धान, चावल *boiled/fried/steamed rice* ➪ **cereal** पर चित्र देखिए।

**rich** /rɪtʃ रिच्/ *adj.* **1** having a lot of money or property; not poor धनी, अमीरी (धन और संपत्ति वाला); ग़रीब नहीं *a rich family/country* ○ *one of the richest women in the world* ➪ **wealthy** देखिए। ✪ विलोम **poor** **2 the rich** *noun* [*pl.*] people with a lot of money or property धनी लोग, पैसे वाले **3 rich in sth** containing a lot of sth भरपूर बहुलतापूर्वक, बहुतायत वाला *Oranges are rich in vitamin C.* **4** (used about food) containing a lot of fat, oil, sugar or cream and making you feel full quickly (खाद्य पदार्थ) प्रचुर वसा, तेल, चीनी या क्रीम वाला (जो जल्दी पेट भर दे) *a rich chocolate cake* **5** (used about soil) containing the substances that make it good for growing plants in (मिट्टी) उपज बढ़ाने वाली वस्तुओं से युक्त **6** (used about colours, sounds or smells) strong and deep (रंग, ध्वनि, गंध) तेज़ और गाढ़ा, गंभीर या उत्कट ▶ **richness** *noun* [U] अमीरी, समृद्धि, प्रचुरता

**riches** /ˈrɪtʃɪz ˈरिचिज़्/ *noun* [*pl.*] (*formal*) a lot of money or property प्रचुर धन-संपत्ति ✪ पर्याय **wealth**

**richly** /ˈrɪtʃli ˈरिच्लि/ *adv.* **1** in a generous way उदारता से, भरपूर *She was richly rewarded for her hard work.* **2** in a way that people think is right उचित रूप से, सही तौर पर (लोगों की दृष्टि में) *His promotion was **richly deserved**.*

**the Richter scale** /ˈrɪktə skeɪl ˈरिक्टर स्केल्/ *noun* [*sing.*] a system for measuring how strong a movement of the earth's surface (**an earthquake**) is भूकंप की शक्ति के मापन की प्रणाली *an earthquake measuring 7 **on the Richter scale***

**rickets** /ˈrɪkɪts ˈरिकिट्स्/ *noun* [U] a disease of children caused by a lack of good food that makes the bones become soft and badly formed, especially in the legs सूखा रोग (पोषक आहार के अभाव में बच्चों को होने वाला अस्थिरोग जिसमें विशेषतः टाँगों की हड्डियाँ नरम पड़कर मुड़ जाती हैं)

**rickety** /ˈrɪkəti ˈरिकटि/ *adj.* likely to break; not strongly made जर्जर, टुटियल; दुर्बल *a rickety old fence* ○ *rickety furniture*

**rickshaw** *noun* [C] a small light vehicle with two wheels used in some Asian countries to carry people over short distances. The rickshaw is pulled by a person walking or riding a bicycle रिक्शा (कुछ एशियाई देशों में प्रयुक्त)

**ricochet** /ˈrɪkəʃeɪ ˈरिकशे/ *verb* [I] (*pt, pp* **ricocheted** /-ʃeɪd -शेड्/) **ricochet (off sth)** (used about a moving object) to fly away from a surface after hitting it (गोली आदि गतिमान वस्तु का) सतह से टकरा कर छिटक जाना, उछटना, छटकना *The bullet ricocheted off the wall and grazed his shoulder.*

**rid** /rɪd रिड्/ *verb* [T] (*pres. part.* **ridding**; *pt, pp* **rid**) (*formal*) **rid yourself/sb/sth of sb/sth** to make yourself/sb/sth free from sb/sth that is unpleasant or not wanted अप्रिय या अनचाहे व्यक्ति या वस्तु से पीछा छुड़ाना (अपना या दूसरे का) *He was unable to rid himself of his fears and suspicions.* ○ *He was a nuisance and we're **well rid** of him* (= it will be much better without him).

**IDM** **get rid of sb/sth** to make yourself free of sb/sth that is annoying you or that you do not want; to throw sth away बुरी लगने वाली या अनचाही वस्तु/व्यक्ति से पिंड छुड़ाना; (किसी चीज़ को) फेंक देना *Let's get rid of that old chair and buy a new one.*

**riddance** /ˈrɪdns ˈरिड्न्स्/ *noun*

**IDM** **good riddance (to sb/sth)** (*spoken*) used for expressing pleasure or satisfaction that sb/sth that you do not like has gone अनचाहे व्यक्ति या वस्तु से छुटकारा मिलने पर ख़ुशी या संतोष व्यक्त करने के लिए प्रयुक्त

**ridden**[1] ➪ **ride**[1] का past participle रूप

**ridden**[2] /ˈrɪdn ˈरिड्न्/ *adj.* (*formal*) (*used in compound adjectives*) full of से भरा हुआ, (से) ग्रस्त *She was guilt-ridden.* ○ *She was ridden with guilt.*

**riddle** /ˈrɪdl ˈरिड्ल्/ *noun* [C] **1** a difficult question that you ask people for fun that has a clever or amusing answer पहेली, बुझौवल **2** a person, thing or event that you cannot understand or explain पेचीदा व्यक्ति, वस्तु या घटना (ऐसा जिसे समझा या समझाया न जा सके)

**riddled** /ˈrɪdld ˈरिड्ल्ड्/ *adj.* **riddled with sth** full of sth, especially sth unpleasant किसी (विशेषतः अवांछित) वस्तु से भरा हुआ *This essay is riddled with mistakes.*

**ride**[1] /raɪd राइड्/ *verb* (*pt* **rode** /rəʊd रोड्/; *pp* **ridden** /ˈrɪdn ˈरिड्न्/) **1** [I, T] to sit on a horse, etc. and control it as it moves घोड़े आदि पर सवार होना (और उसे क़ाबू में रखना) *We rode through the forest.* ○ *Which horse is Vinay riding in the next race?* **2** [I, T] to sit on a bicycle, motorbike, etc. and control it as it moves साइकिल आदि पर सवार होना (और उसे क़ाबू में रखना) *He jumped onto his motorbike and rode off* (= went away). ○ *Can Ravi ride a bike yet?* **3** [I] (*AmE*) to travel as a passenger in a bus, car, etc. बस, कार आदि में यात्री के रूप में सफ़र करना ▶ **rider** *noun* [C] सवार, घुड़सवार

**ride**[2] /raɪd राइड्/ *noun* [C] **1** a short journey on a horse or bicycle, or in a car, bus, etc. घोड़ा, साइकिल, कार, बस आदि की सवारी (थोड़ी दूर की) *It's only a short bus/train ride into Karol Bagh.* ○ *We went for a bike ride on Saturday.* **2** used to describe what a journey or trip is like यह बताने के लिए प्रयुक्त कि यात्रा कैसी रही *a smooth/bumpy/comfortable ride* **3** a large machine at an amusement park which you pay to go on for amusement or excitement; an occasion when you go on one of these मनोरंजन पार्क में झूला (मन बहलाव या उत्तेजनापूर्ण आनंद के लिए); झूले की सवारी *My favourite **fairground ride** is the roller coaster.*

**IDM** **take sb for a ride** (*informal*) to cheat or trick sb किसी को धोखा देना

**ridge** /rɪdʒ रिज्/ *noun* [C] **1** a long, narrow piece of highland along the top of hills or mountains पहाड़ियों या पहाड़ों के शिखर पर का लंबा तंग उठा हुआ हिस्सा **2** a line where two surfaces meet at an angle रेखा या लकीर जहाँ दो सतहें एक कोण पर मिलती हैं

**ridicule** /ˈrɪdɪkjuːl ˈरिडिक्यूल्/ *noun* [U] unkind laughter or behaviour that is intended to make sb/sth appear silly किसी की खिल्ली उड़ाने वाली निर्लज्ज हँसी या आचरण *He had become an object* *of ridicule.* ▶ **ridicule** *verb* [T] खिल्ली उड़ाना, मज़ाक बनाना *The idea was ridiculed by everybody present.*

**ridiculous** /rɪˈdɪkjələs रिˈडिक्यलस् / *adj.* very silly or unreasonable मूर्खतापूर्ण या बेतुका *They're asking a ridiculous* (= very high) *price for that house.* ▶ **ridiculously** *adv.* बेतुकेपन से

**riding** /ˈraɪdɪŋ ˈराइडिङ् / (*AmE* **horseback riding**) *noun* [U] the sport or hobby of riding a horse घुड़सवारी का खेल या शौक़ *riding boots* ○ *a riding school*

**rife** /raɪf राइफ़् / *adj.* (*not before a noun*) (*formal*) (used especially about bad things) very common (विशेषतः बुरी बातें) फैली हुई; बहुविदित, सर्वविदित *Rumours are rife that his wife has left him.*

**rifle¹** /ˈraɪfl ˈराइफ़्ल्/ *noun* [C] a long gun that you hold against your shoulder to shoot with राइफ़ल (लंबी नली की बंदूक़)

**NOTE** हम राइफ़ल को **load, aim** और **fire** करते हैं।

**rifle²** /ˈraɪfl ˈराइफ़्ल् / *verb* [I, T] **rifle (through) sth** to search sth usually in order to steal from it किसी वस्तु को ढूंढना (प्रायः उसे चुराने की दृष्टि से) *I caught him rifling through the papers on my desk.*

**rift** /rɪft रिफ़्ट् / *noun* [C] **1** a serious disagreement between friends, groups, etc. that stops their relationship from continuing मित्रों, संगठनों आदि में गंभीर मतभेद, मनमुटाव (जो संबंधों को बीच में ही ख़त्म कर दे) *a growing rift between the brothers* **2** a very large crack or opening in the ground, a rock, etc. ज़मीन, चट्टान आदि में बड़ी दरार या छेद

**rift valley** *noun* [C] (in geography) a valley with steep sides formed when two parallel cracks develop in the earth's surface and the land between them sinks (भूगोल में) विभ्रंश घाटी (घाटी जिसके पार्श्व, ज़मीन पर दो समानांतर दरारें बन जाने और बीच की ज़मीन के धँस जाने के फलस्वरूप सीधी खड़ी शकल में आ जाते हैं)

**rig¹** /rɪg रिग् / *verb* [T] (**rigging; rigged**) to arrange or control an event, etc. in an unfair way, in order to get the result you want घाँधली करना (अपने अनुकूल परिणाम के लिए किसी गतिविधि को अनुचित रूप से प्रभावित करना) *They claimed that the competition had been rigged.*

**PHR V** **rig sth up** to make sth quickly, using any materials you can find जल्दी से कुछ बना देना (जो भी सामान मिले उसी से) *We tried to rig up a shelter using our coats.*

**rig²** /rɪg रिग् / = **oil rig**

**rigging** /ˈrɪgɪŋ ˈरिगिङ् / *noun* [U] the ropes, etc. that support a ship's sails मस्तूल-पाल बाँधने वाली रस्सियाँ आदि

**right¹** /raɪt राइट् / *adj.* **1** correct; true शुद्ध, सही; सच *You were right about the weather—it did rain.* ○ *'You're Chinese, aren't you?' 'Yes, **that's right**.'* **2 right (for sb/sth)** best; most suitable सर्वोत्तम; सबसे उपयुक्त *I hope I've made **the right decision**.* ○ *I am sure we've chosen the right person for the job.* ○ *I would help you to wash the car, but I'm not wearing the right clothes.* **3** (used about behaviour, actions, etc.) fair; morally and socially correct (आचरण, कार्य आदि) उचित; नैतिक और सामाजिक दृष्टि से ठीक *It's not right to treat people so badly.* ○ *What do you think is **the right thing** to do?* ✪ विलोम **wrong** अर्थ सं॰ **1**, **2** और **3** के लिए **4** healthy or normal; as it should be स्वस्थ या सामान्य; जैसा होना चाहिए वैसा ठीक-ठाक *The car exhaust doesn't sound right—it's making a funny noise.* ○ *I don't feel quite right today* (= I feel ill). **5** on or of the side of the body that faces east when a person is facing north दायाँ, दाहिना *Most people write with their right hand.* ○ *He's blind in his right eye.* ✪ विलोम **left** **6** (*BrE spoken*) (used for emphasizing sth bad) real or complete (किसी सदोष बात पर बल देने के लिए प्रयुक्त) एकदम या पूरी तरह *I'll look a right idiot in that hat!* ▶ **rightness** *noun* [U] न्यायशीलता

**IDM** **get/start off on the right/wrong foot (with sb)** ➪ **foot¹** देखिए।

**get on the right/wrong side of sb** ➪ **side¹** देखिए।

**on the right/wrong track** ➪ **track¹** देखिए।

**put/set sth right** to correct sth or deal with a problem किसी (ख़राब) चीज़ को ठीक कर देना या समस्या को हल कर देना *There's something wrong with the lawnmower. Do you think you'll be able to put it right?*

**right (you are)** (*spoken*) yes, I will or yes, I agree; OK हामी भरना, कुछ स्वीकार करने के लिए मंजूरी देने के लिए प्रयुक्त *'See you later.' 'Right you are!'*

**(as) right as rain** completely healthy and normal पूरी तरह से स्वस्थ और सामान्य

**right²** /raɪt राइट् / *adv.* **1** exactly; directly एकदम ठीक; एकदम सीधे *The train was right on time.* ○ *He was sitting right beside me.* **2** correctly; in the way that it should happen or should be done सही तरीक़े से; जैसे होना या करना चाहिए वैसे *Have I spelt your name right?* ○ *Nothing seems to be going right for me at the moment.* ✪ विलोम **wrong** **3** all the way; completely सारा का सारा; पूरी तरह *Did you watch the film right to the end?* ○ *There's* *a high wall that goes right round the house.* **4** to the right side दाहिने ओर *Turn right at the traffic lights.* ✪ विलोम **left** **5** immediately तुरंत, फ़ौरन *Wait here a minute—I'll **be right back**.* **6** (*spoken*) (used for preparing sb for sth that is about to happen) get ready; listen (जो बात होने को है उसके लिए आगाह करने हेतु प्रयुक्त) *Have you got your seat belts on? Right, off we go.*

IDM **right/straight away** ➪ **away** देखिए।

**right now** at this moment; exactly now इसी क्षण; एकदम अभी *We can't discuss this right now.*

**serve sb right** ➪ **serve** देखिए।

**right³** /raɪt राइट्/ *noun* **1** [U] what is morally good and fair नैतिक रूप से मान्य और उचित *Does a child of ten really understand the difference between right and wrong?* ○ *You **did right** to tell me what happened.* ✪ विलोम **wrong** **2** [*sing.*] the right side or direction दाहिना पार्श्व या दिशा *We live in the first house **on the right**.* ○ *Take the first right and then the second left.* ✪ विलोम **left** **3** [U, C] **the right (to sth/to do sth)** a thing that you are allowed to do according to the law; a moral authority to do sth क़ानून-सम्मत बात; नैतिक अधिकार ***human rights*** ○ ***civil rights*** ○ *animal rights campaigners* **4 the Right** [*sing.,with sing. or pl. verb*] the people or political parties who are against social change दक्षिण पंथी व्यक्ति या राजनीतिक दल (सामाजिक परिवर्तन का विरोधी)

IDM **be in the right** to be doing what is correct and fair सही और न्यायोचित बात के पक्ष में *You don't need to apologize. You were in the right and he was in the wrong.*

**by rights** according to what is fair or correct जो उचित या सही हो उसके अनुसार; न्यायसंगत रूप से *By rights, half the profit should be mine.*

**in your own right** because of what you are yourself and not because of other people अपनी योग्यता के आधार पर (न कि अन्य लोगों के कारण)

**within your rights (to do sth)** acting in a reasonable or legal way युक्ति संगत और क़ानून सम्मत दृष्टि से *You are quite within your rights to demand to see your lawyer.*

**right⁴** /raɪt राइट्/ *verb* [T] to put sb/sth/yourself back into a normal position किसी को सही स्थिति में वापस ले आना *The boat tipped over and then righted itself again.*

IDM **right a wrong** to do sth to correct an unfair situation or sth bad that you have done किसी अनुचित बात या ग़लत काम को सुधार कर सही करना

**right angle** *noun* [C] (*mathematics*) an angle of 90° समकोण (90° का कोण) *A square has four right angles.* ➪ **acute angle, obtuse angle** और **reflex angle** देखिए तथा **angle** पर चित्र देखिए।

**right-angled** *adj.* having or consisting of a right angle (= an angle of 90°) समकोणीय *a right-angled triangle* ➪ **triangle** पर चित्र देखिए।

**righteous** /ˈraɪtʃəs ˈराइचस्/ *adj.* (*formal*) that you think is morally good or fair नैतिक रूप से मान्य या उचित *righteous anger/indignation* ➪ **self-righteous** देखिए।

**rightful** /ˈraɪtfl ˈराइट्फ़्ल्/ *adj.* (*only before a noun*) (*formal*) legally or morally correct; fair क़ानूनन या नैतिक दृष्टि से सही; न्यायोचित ▶ **rightfully** /-fəli -फ़लि/ *adv.* न्यायोचित रूप से

**right-hand** *adj.* (*only before a noun*) of or on the right of sb/sth (किसी का) दाहिना या दाहिने ओर का *The postbox is on the right-hand side of the road.* ○ *in the top right-hand corner of the screen*

**right-handed** *adj.* using the right hand for writing, etc. and not the left दाहिने हाथ से लिखना आदि करने वाला, दक्षिण हस्त चालक

**right-hand man** *noun* [*sing.*] the person you depend on most to help and support you in your work सबसे विश्वस्त और सहायक व्यक्ति *the President's right-hand man*

**rightly** /ˈraɪtli ˈराइट्लि/ *adv.* correctly or fairly सही तौर पर या उचित रूप से *He's been sacked and **quite rightly**, I believe.*

**right of way** *noun* (*pl.* **rights of way**) **1** [C, U] (*BrE*) a path across private land that the public may use; legal permission to go into or through another person's land निजी ज़मीन में से आम रास्ता; किसी दूसरे की ज़मीन में या में से जाने का क़ानूनी अधिकार *Walkers have right of way through the farmer's field.* **2** [U] (used in road traffic) the fact that a vehicle in a particular position is allowed to drive into or across a road before another vehicle in a different position (सड़क यातायात में) किसी वाहन का मार्गाधिकार (सामने से आते वाहन से पहले सड़क पार या के पार जाने का अधिकार) *He should have stopped—I had the right of way.*

**right wing** *noun* [*sing., with sing. or pl. verb*] the people in a political party who are against social change राजनीतिक दल में दक्षिण पंथी धड़ा (जो सामाजिक परिवर्तन का विरोध करता है) ▶ **right-wing** *adj.* दक्षिणपंथी *a right-wing government* ✪ विलोम **left-wing**

**rigid** /ˈrɪdʒɪd ˈरिजिड्/ *adj.* **1** not able to or not wanting to change or be changed किसी को बदलने में असमर्थ या परिवर्तित होने का अनिच्छुक **2** difficult to bend; stiff कठिनाई से मुड़ने वाला; कड़ा, कठोर *a rucksack with a rigid frame* ○ *She was rigid with fear.* ▶ **rigidity** /rɪˈdʒɪdəti रिˈजिडटि/ *noun* [U] कड़ापन, कठोरता ▶ **rigidly** *adv.* कठोरता से *The speed limit must be rigidly enforced.*

**rigor mortis** /ˌrɪɡə ˈmɔːtɪs ˌरिगˈमॉटिस्/ *noun* [U] the process by which the body becomes difficult to bend or move after death मृत्यु के बाद शव में आने वाली अकड़न, शव-काठिन्य

**rigorous** /ˈrɪɡərəs ˈरिगरस्/ *adj.* done very carefully and with great attention to detail बहुत सावधानी और बारीक़ी से किया गया; परिशुद्ध *Rigorous tests are carried out on the drinking water.* ▶ **rigorously** *adv.* परिशुद्धता के साथ

**rigour** (*AmE* **rigor**) /ˈrɪɡə(r) ˈरिग(र्)/ *noun* (*formal*) **1** [U] doing sth carefully with great attention to detail बहुत सावधानी और बारीक़ी से कुछ करने की क्रिया *The tests were carried out with rigour.* **2** [U] the quality of being strict कड़ाई, सख़्ती, कठोरता *the full rigour of the law* **3** [C, *usually pl.*] difficult conditions कठोर परिस्थितियाँ

**rim** /rɪm रिम्/ *noun* [C] an edge at the top or outside of sth that is round किसी गोलाकार वस्तु का किनारा (उसके शीर्ष पर या बाहर की ओर) *the rim of a cup*

**rind** /raɪnd राइन्ड्/ *noun* [C, U] the thick hard skin on the outside of some fruits, some types of cheese, meat, etc. कुछ फलों आदि का ऊपरी कड़ा छिलका

> **NOTE** नींबू या नारंगी के छिलकों को **rind** या **peel** कहते हैं। केले आदि के नरम छिलके को **skin** कहा जाता है।

**ring**[1] /rɪŋ रिङ्/ *noun* **1** [C] a piece of jewellery that you wear on your finger अँगूठी, मुद्रिका *a gold/diamond/wedding ring* ○ *an engagement ring* **2** [C] (*usually in compound nouns*) a round object of any material with a hole in the middle छल्ला (किसी भी चीज़ से बना) *curtain rings* ○ *a key ring* (= for holding keys) **3** [C] a round mark or shape घेरा (गोल निशान या आकार) *The coffee cup left a ring on the table top.* ○ *Stand in a ring and hold hands.* **4** [C] the space with seats all around it where a performance, boxing match, etc. takes place सर्कस आदि का प्रांगण (जहाँ प्रदर्शन आदि प्रस्तुत किए जाते हैं) *a circus/boxing ring* **5** (*AmE* **burner**) [C] one of the round parts on the top of an electric or gas cooker on which you can put pans बिजली या गैस के चूल्हे का बर्नर (गोलाकार खंड जिस पर बर्तन रखते हैं) **6** [C] a number of people who are involved in sth that is secret or not legal चोरी-चोरी या ग़ैर-क़ानूनी काम करने वालों की टोली, गुट *a spy/drugs ring* **7** [C] the sound made by a bell; the action of ringing a bell घंटी की आवाज़; घंटी बजाने की क्रिया *There was a ring at the door.* **8** [*sing.*] **a ring of sth** a particular quality that words or sounds have शब्दों या ध्वनियों का विशेष गुण *What the man said **had a ring of truth** about it* (= sounded true).

**IDM give sb a ring** (*BrE informal*) to telephone sb किसी को फ़ोन करना *I'll give you a ring in the morning.*

**ring**[2] /rɪŋ रिङ्/ *verb* (*pt* **rang** /ræŋ रैङ्/; *pp* **rung** /rʌŋ रङ्/) **1** [I, T] (*AmE* **call**) **ring (sb/sth) (up)** to telephone sb/sth किसी को या किसी बात के लिए फ़ोन करना *What time will you ring tomorrow?* ○ *I rang up yesterday and booked the hotel.* ✪ पर्याय **phone** **2** [I, T] to make a sound like a bell or to cause sth to make this sound घंटी जैसी आवाज़ करना या घंटी बजाना *Is that the phone ringing?* ○ *We rang the door bell but nobody answered.* **3** [I] **ring (for sb/sth)** to ring a bell in order to call sb, ask for sth, etc. किसी को बुलाने, कुछ पूछने आदि के लिए घंटी बजाना *'Did you ring, sir?' asked the stewardess.* ○ *Could you ring for a taxi, please?* **4** [I] (used about words or sounds) to have a certain effect when you hear them (शब्दों या ध्वनियों का) कुछ प्रभाव होना *Her words didn't **ring true*** (= you felt that you could not believe what she said). **5** [I] **ring (with sth)** to be filled with loud sounds गूँजना, प्रतिध्वनित होना *The music was so loud it made my ears ring.* **6** [T] (*pt, pp* **ringed**) (*often passive*) to surround sb/sth को घेर लेना या से घिर जाना **7** [T] (*AmE* **circle**) (*pt, pp* **ringed**) to draw a circle around sth किसी के चारों ओर घेरा बनाना या खींचना

**IDM ring a bell** to sound familiar or to remind you, not very clearly, of sb/sth परिचित-सा लगना या किसी की (धुँधली-सी) याद दिलाना *'Do you know Leela Rai?' 'Well, the name rings a bell.'*

**PHR V ring (sb) back** (*BrE*) to telephone sb again or to telephone sb who has telephoned you दोबारा फ़ोन करना या किसी को जवाबी फ़ोन करना *I can't talk now—can I ring you back?*

**ring in** (*BrE*) to telephone a television or radio show, or the place where you work टीवी या रेडियो कार्यस्थल कार्यक्रम को या अपने (दफ़्तर, स्कूल आदि) को फ़ोन करना *Mandira rang in sick this morning.*

**ring out** to sound loudly and clearly ऊँची और साफ़ आवाज़ में बजना

**ring binder** *noun* [C] (*BrE*) a file for holding papers, in which metal rings go through the edges of the pages, holding them in place धातु के छल्लों वाली फ़ाइल (काग़ज़ों को सँभाले रखने के लिए) ➪ **stationery** पर चित्र देखिए।

**ringleader** /ˈrɪŋliːdə(r) ˈरिङ्लीड(र्)/ *noun* [C] a person who leads others in crime or in causing trouble अपराधियों या शरारतियों के गुट का नेता *The ring leaders were jailed for 15 years.*

**ringroad** *noun* [C] (*BrE*) a road that is built all around a town so that traffic does not have to go into the town centre मुद्रिका पथ; वलायाकार मार्ग (नगर के चारों ओर बनी सड़क ताकि यातायात नगर के अंदरूनी भागों में प्रवेश न करे) ➪ **bypass**[1] देखिए।

**ringworm** /ˈrɪŋwɜːm ˈरिङ्वम्/ *noun* [U] a skin disease that produces round red areas, especially on the head or the feet दाद (एक त्वचा-रोग, विशेषत: सिर और पैरों पर)

**rink** /rɪŋk रिङ्क्/ = **skating rink**

**rinse** /rɪns रिन्स्/ *verb* [T] to wash sth in water in order to remove soap or dirt पानी से धोना (साबुन या मैल निकालने के लिए), खँगालना, प्रछारना *Rinse your hair thoroughly after each shampoo.* ▶ **rinse** *noun* [C] धोने, खँगालने की क्रिया

**riot** /ˈraɪət ˈराइअट्/ *noun* [C] a situation in which a group of people behave in a violent way in a public place, often as a protest दंगा, बलवा, हंगामा (लोगों द्वारा किसी सार्वजनिक स्थान पर, प्राय: विरोधस्वरूप) ▶ **riot** *verb* [I] उपद्रव मचाना, दंगा करना *There is a danger that the prisoners will riot if conditions do not improve.* ▶ **rioter** *noun* [C] उपद्रवी, दंगाई

IDM **run riot** 1 to behave in a wild way without any control हंगामा करना, क़ाबू के बाहर होना *At the end of the football match, the crowd ran riot.* 2 (used about your imagination, feelings, etc.) to allow sth to develop and continue without trying to control it (कल्पना, भावनाओं आदि का) अनियंत्रित हो जाना

**riotous** /ˈraɪətəs ˈराइअटस्/ *adj.* 1 wild or violent; lacking in control ऊधमी या हिंसापूर्ण; बेक़ाबू 2 wild and full of fun धमा-चौकड़ी वाला

**RIP** /ˌɑːr aɪ ˈpiː ˌआर् आइ ˈपि/ *abbr.* (used on graves) rest in peace (क़ब्रों पर अंकित) ईश्वर शांति दे

**rip**[1] /rɪp रिप्/ *verb* (**ripping; ripped**) 1 [I, T] to tear or be torn quickly and suddenly (किसी वस्तु) को चीर देना या का चिर जाना (तेज़ी से और अचानक) *He **ripped** the letter **in half/two** and threw it in the bin.* ○ *The blast of the bomb ripped the house apart.* 2 [T] to remove sth quickly and violently often by pulling it तेज़ी से और ज़ोर लगाकर किसी वस्तु को हटाना (प्राय: खींचकर) *He ripped the poster from the wall.*

PHR V **rip through sth** to move very quickly and violently through sth तेज़ी और ज़ोर से घुसकर किसी वस्तु के आर-पार चले जाना *The house was badly damaged when fire ripped through the first floor.*

**rip sb off** (*informal*) to cheat sb by charging too much money for sth किसी को बुरी तरह ठगना

**rip sth up** to tear sth into small pieces फाड़कर टुकड़े-टुकड़े कर देना

**rip**[2] /rɪp रिप्/ *noun* [C] a long tear (in material, etc.) लंबा चीरा (कपड़ा आदि चीज़ में)

**ripe** /raɪp राइप्/ *adj.* 1 (used about fruit, grain, etc.) ready to be picked and eaten (फल, अनाज आदि) पका हुआ 2 **ripe (for sth)** ready for sth or in a suitable state for sth (किसी स्थिति के लिए तैयार या उपयुक्त) ▶ **ripen** /raɪpən राइपन्/ *verb* [I, T] पकना, पकाना

**rip-off** *noun* [C, *usually pl.*] (*informal*) something that costs a lot more than it should उचित मूल्य से अधिक मूल्य वाली महँगी वस्तु

**ripple** /ˈrɪpl ˈरिपल्/ *noun* [C] 1 a very small wave or movement on the surface of water छोटी सी लहर या पानी की हलकी सी हरकत 2 [*usually sing.*] **a ripple (of sth)** a sound that gradually becomes louder and then quieter again; a feeling that gradually spreads through a person or a group of people आवाज़ का क्रमिक उतार-चढ़ाव; व्यक्ति या व्यक्तिसमूह के मन में धीरे-धीरे व्याप्त होने वाला कोई भाव *a ripple of laughter* ▶ **ripple** *verb* [I, T] लहराना, लहरें बनाना

**rise**[1] /raɪz राइज़्/ *noun* 1 [C] **a rise (in sth)** an increase in an amount, a number or a level वृद्धि (मात्रा, संख्या या स्तर में) *There has been a **sharp rise** in the number of people out of work.* ✪ विलोम **drop** या **fall** 2 [C] (*AmE* **raise**) an increase in the money you are paid for the work you do वेतन में वृद्धि *I'm hoping to **get a rise** next April.* ○ *a 10% **pay rise*** 3 [*sing.*] **the rise (of sth)** the process of becoming more powerful or important किसी का उत्थान और अभ्युदय (अधिक शक्तिशाली या महत्त्वपूर्ण हो जाने की प्रक्रिया) *The rise of fascism in Europe.* ○ *her meteoric **rise to fame/power***

IDM **give rise to sth** (*formal*) to cause sth to happen or exist किसी बात के होने का कारण बनना, किसी बात को जन्म देना

**rise**[2] /raɪz राइज़्/ *verb* [I] (*pt* **rose** /rəʊz रोज़्/; *pp* **risen** /ˈrɪzn ˈरिज़्न्/) 1 to move upwards, to become higher, stronger or to increase ऊपर उठना, चढ़ना या ऊपर की ओर जाना, बढ़ना *Smoke was rising from the chimney.* ○ *The temperature has risen to nearly 40°C.* ✪ विलोम **fall** 2 (*written*) to get up from a chair, bed, etc. कुरसी, बिस्तर आदि से

उठना *The audience rose and applauded the singers.* **3** (used about the sun, moon, etc.) to appear above the horizon (सूर्य, चंद्रमा आदि का) उदय होना, क्षितिज पर प्रकट होना *The sun rises in the east and sets in the west.* ✪ विलोम **set** **4** to become more successful, powerful, important, etc. उन्नति करना (अधिक सफल, शक्तिशाली, बड़ा आदि होना) *He **rose through the ranks** to become managing director.* ○ *She **rose to power** in the 90s.* **5** to be seen above or higher than sth else दूसरी वस्तुओं से ऊपर या ऊँचा दिखाई देना (पर्वत आदि का) **6** to come from (कहीं से कुछ) आना *Shouts of protest rose from the crowd.* **7 rise (up) (against sb/sth)** to start fighting against your ruler, government, etc. शासक, शासन आदि के विरुद्ध संघर्ष करना ▸ **rising** *adj.* उठान, वृद्धि *the rising cost of living* ○ *a rising young rock star*

IDM **rise to the occasion, challenge, task, etc.** to show that you are able to deal with a problem, etc. successfully किसी समस्या आदि का सफलतापूर्वक सामना करने की योग्यता दिखाना

**risk**[1] /rɪsk रिस्क्/ *noun* **1** [C, U] **(a) risk (of sth/that...); (a) risk (to sb/sth)** a possibility of sth dangerous or unpleasant happening; a situation that could be dangerous or have a bad result ख़तरा, किसी ख़तरनाक या अप्रिय बात के घटित हो जाने की संभावना; स्थिति जो ख़तरनाक या नुक़सानदेह हो सकती है, जोख़िम या हानि का ख़तरा *Don't **take** any **risks** when you're driving.* ○ *Scientists say pesticides **pose a risk** to wildlife.* ○ *If we don't leave early enough we **run the risk** of missing the plane.* ○ *Small children are most **at risk** from the disease.* **2** [*sing.*] a person or thing that might cause danger ख़तरे या जोख़िम का कारण व्यक्ति या वस्तु *If he knows your real name he's a security risk.*

IDM **at your own risk** having the responsibility for whatever may happen अपनी ज़िम्मेदारी पर *This building is in a dangerous condition—enter at your own risk.*

**at the risk of sth/doing sth** even though there could be a bad effect or loss किसी बात या काम का जोख़िम उठाते हुए *He rescued the girl at the risk of his own life.*

**risk**[2] /rɪsk रिस्क्/ *verb* [T] **1** to take the chance of sth unpleasant happening ख़तरा मोल लेना *If you don't work hard now you risk failing your exams.* **2** to put sth or yourself in a dangerous position किसी को या अपने को जोख़िम में डालना *The man had to **risk** his **life** to save the little boy.*

**risky** /ˈrɪski ˈरिस्कि/ *adj.* **(riskier; riskiest)** involving the possibility of sth bad happening; dangerous जोख़िम की संभावना वाला, जोख़िम भरा; ख़तरनाक

**rite** /raɪt राइट्/ *noun* [C] a ceremony performed by a particular group of people, often for religious purposes वर्ग विशेष द्वारा (प्रायः धार्मिक प्रयोजन से) किया गया अनुष्ठान

**ritual** /ˈrɪtʃuəl ˈरिचुअल्/ *noun* [C, U] an action, ceremony or process which is always done the same way अनुष्ठान, कर्मकांड (हमेशा ही समान ढंग से किया जाने वाला कार्य, संस्कार या प्रक्रिया) *(a) religious ritual* ▸ **ritual** *adj.* कर्मकांड-परक ▸ **ritually** *adv.* कर्मकांड-पूर्वक

**rival**[1] /ˈraɪvl ˈराइव्ल्/ *noun* [C] a person or thing that is competing with you प्रतिद्वंद्वी व्यक्ति या वस्तु *It seems that we're rivals for the sales manager's job.*

**rival**[2] /ˈraɪvl ˈराइव्ल्/ *verb* [T] **(rivalling; rivalled** *AmE* **rivaling; rivaled) rival sb/sth (for/in sth)** to be as good as sb/sth किसी व्यक्ति या वस्तु की बराबरी करना *Nothing rivals skiing for sheer excitement.*

**rivalry** /ˈraɪvlri ˈराइव्ल्रि/ *noun* [C, U] (*pl.* **rivalries) rivalry (with sb); rivalry (between A and B)** competition between people, groups, etc. प्रतिद्वंद्विता, प्रतिस्पर्धा (व्यक्तियों, समूहों आदि में) *There was a lot of rivalry between the sisters.*

**river** /ˈrɪvə(r) ˈरिव़(र्)/ *noun* [C] a large, natural flow of water that goes across land and into the sea नदी, दरिया *the River Ganga* ○ *He sat down on the bank of the river to fish.*

> NOTE नदी के समुद्र में मिलने के लिए अभिव्यक्ति **flows** into the sea प्रयुक्त होती है। इस मिलन स्थल को **mouth** कहते हैं। नाव नदी पर चलती है (sails **on** the river)। नदी में चलने या बहने के लिए अभिव्यक्तियाँ walk, sail, etc. **up** or **down river** प्रयुक्त होती हैं।

**riverside** /ˈrɪvəsaɪd ˈरिव़साइड्/ *noun* [*sing.*] the land next to a river नदी तट *a riverside hotel*

**rivet**[1] /ˈrɪvɪt ˈरिव़िट्/ *noun* [C] a metal pin for fastening two pieces of metal or other thick materials together दो धातुखंडों को जोड़ने की (विशेष) कील, कीलक, रिवेट

**rivet**[2] /ˈrɪvɪt ˈरिव़िट्/ *verb* [T] (*usually passive*) to keep sb very interested आकर्षण या रुचि को बनाए रखना *I was riveted by her story.* ▸ **riveting** *adj.* रुचिपूर्ण, रुचिकर

**rm** *abbr.* room रूम, कमरा

**RNA** /ˌɑːr en ˈeɪ ˌआर् एन् ˈए/ *noun* [U] a chemical that is found in the cells of all animals and plants सब पशुओं और पौधों की कोशिकाओं में पाया जाने वाला एक रसायन; आर एन ए

**roach** /rəʊtʃ रोच्/ (*AmE*) = **cockroach**

**road** /rəʊd रोड्/ *noun* **1** [C] a way between places, with a hard surface which cars, buses, etc. can drive along सड़क, रोड *Turn left off the* ***main*** (= important) ***road***. ○ *road signs*

> NOTE **Roads** (*AmE* **highways**) शहरों और गाँवों को जोड़ती है—*a* ***road map*** *of Punjab*. शहर या गाँव के अंदर जिस सड़क के किनारे इमारतें हों उसे प्रायः **street** कहते हैं। शहर से बाहर की सड़कों के लिए **street** शब्द का प्रयोग नहीं होता—*a street map of Chandigarh*. जिस चौड़ी सड़क के साथ-साथ पेड़ लगे हों या इमारतें खड़ी हो उसे **avenue** कहते हैं। **Highways** (*AmE* **freeways/expressways**) वे सड़क हैं जिन पर दो या तीन **lanes** वाले **carriageways** बने होते हैं ताकि यातायात शहरों के बाहर से निकलते हुए तीव्र गति से लंबी दूरियाँ तय कर सकें।

**2 Road** (*abbr.* **Rd**) [*sing.*] used in names of roads, especially in towns रोड (सड़कों के नाम के साथ प्रयुक्त शब्द विशेषतः शहरों में) *1 Jai Singh Road, New Delhi*
IDM **by road** in a car, bus, etc. सड़क मार्ग से (बस, कार आदि में) *It's going to be a terrible journey by road—let's take the train.*
**on the road** travelling सफ़र में *We were on the road for 14 hours.*

**roadblock** /ˈrəʊdblɒk ˈरोड्ब्लॉक्/ *noun* [C] a barrier put across a road by the police or army to stop traffic (पुलिस या सेना द्वारा यातायात रोकने के लिए) सड़क के आर-पार खड़ी की गई रुकावट; सड़कबंदी

**roadside** /ˈrəʊdsaɪd ˈरोड्साइड्/ *noun* [C, *usually sing.*] the edge of a road सड़क का किनारा *a roadside cafe*

**road tax** *noun* [C, U] a tax which the owner of a vehicle has to pay to be allowed to drive it on public roads सड़क-कर, रोड टैक्स (सार्वजनिक सड़कों के उपयोग के लिए वाहन के मालिक द्वारा देय कर)

**the roadway** /ˈrəʊdweɪ ˈरोड्वे/ *noun* [*sing.*] the part of the road used by cars, etc.; not the side of the road सड़क मार्ग (सड़क का वह हिस्सा जिस पर कारें आदि चलें; सड़क के किनारे का हिस्सा नहीं)

**roadworks** /ˈrəʊdwɜːks ˈरोड्वर्क्स्/ *noun* [*pl.*] work that involves repairing or building roads सड़क के निर्माण या मरम्मत का कार्य

**roadworthy** /ˈrəʊdwɜːði ˈरोड्वर्दि/ *adj.* (used about a vehicle) in good enough condition to be driven on the road (वाहन) सड़क पर चलने लायक (हालत में), मार्गयोग्य ► **roadworthiness** *noun* [U] मार्गयोग्यता

**roam** /rəʊm रोम्/ *verb* [I, T] to walk or travel with no particular plan or aim बिना किसी योजना या लक्ष्य के घूमना-फिरना या सफ़र करना *Gangs of youths were roaming the streets looking for trouble.*

**roar** /rɔː(r) रॉ(र्)/ *verb* 1 [I] to make a loud, deep sound ठहाके लगाना *She* ***roared with laughter*** *at the joke.* ○ *The lion opened its huge mouth and roared.* **2** [I, T] to shout sth very loudly ज़ोर से चिल्लाते हुए कुछ कहना **3** [I] **roar along, down, past, etc.** to move in the direction mentioned, making a loud, deep sound गरजते, दहाड़ते या ज़ोर से शोर करते हुए जाना (निर्दिष्ट दिशा में) *A motorbike roared past us.* ► **roar** *noun* [C] ठहाका, शोर-गुल, गर्जन, दहाड़ *the roar of heavy traffic on the main road* ○ *roars of laughter*

**roaring** /ˈrɔːrɪŋ ˈरॉरिङ्/ *adj.* **1** making a very loud noise ज़ोर से शोर करते हुए, गरजते या दहाड़ते हुए **2** (used about a fire) burning very well (आग) तेज़ी से जलते हुए **3** very great ज़ोरदार, अत्यधिक *a roaring success*

**roast**[1] /rəʊst रोस्ट्/ *verb* **1** [I, T] to cook or be cooked in an oven or over a fire आग में या अवन में भूनना या पकाना *a smell of roasting meat* ○ *to roast a chicken* ➪ **cook** पर नोट देखिए। **2** [T] to heat and dry sth भूनना *roasted peanuts* ► **roast** *adj.* (*only before a noun*) पका, भुना *roast chicken/potatoes/chestnuts*

**roast**[2] /rəʊst रोस्ट्/ *noun* **1** [C, U] a piece of meat that has been cooked in an oven अँगीठी में पकाया गोश्त **2** [C] an outdoor meal at which food is cooked over a fire घर से बाहर भोजन बनाने और खाने का कार्यक्रम ➪ **barbecue** देखिए।

**rob** /rɒb रॉब्/ *verb* [T] (**robbing; robbed**) **rob sb/sth (of sth)** **1** to take money, property, etc. from a person or place illegally (किसी व्यक्ति या स्थान से पैसा आदि) लूटना *to rob a bank* ➪ **steal** पर नोट देखिए। **2 rob sb/sth (of sth)** to take sth away from sb/sth that he/she/it should have (किसी को उसके प्राप्य से) वंचित करना *His illness robbed him of the chance to play for his country.*

**robber** /ˈrɒbə(r) ˈरॉब(र्)/ *noun* [C] a person who steals from a place or a person, especially using violence or threats लुटेरा डाकू ➪ **thief** पर नोट देखिए।

**robbery** /ˈrɒbəri ˈरॉबरि/ *noun* [C, U] (*pl.* **robberies**) the crime of stealing from a place or a person, especially using violence or threats लूटमार, डाका *They were found guilty of* ***armed robbery*** (= using a weapon).

**robe** /rəʊb रोब्/ *noun* [C] **1** a long, loose piece of clothing, especially one worn at ceremonies लाबादा, ढीली लंबी पोशाक (विशेषतः विशेष कार्यक्रमों पर पहनी जाने वाली) **2** (*AmE*) = **dressing gown**

**robin** /ˈrɒbɪn ˈरॉबिन्/ *noun* [C] a small brown bird with a bright red chest चमकीले लाल रंग की छाती वाली भूरे रंग की चिड़िया; रॉबिन

**robot** /ˈrəʊbɒt ˈरोबॉट्/ *noun* [C] a machine that works automatically and can do some tasks that a human can do मनुष्य की तरह काम करने वाली स्वचालित मशीन; रोबोट, यंत्र-मानव *These cars are built by robots.*

**robust** /rəʊˈbʌst रोˈबस्ट्/ *adj.* strong and healthy तगड़ा और स्वस्थ

**rock[1]** /rɒk रॉक्/ *noun* **1** [U] the hard, solid material that forms part of the surface of the earth पत्थर की चट्टान *layers of rock formed over millions of years* **2** [C, *usually pl.*] a large mass of rock that sticks out of the sea or the ground समुद्र तल या ज़मीन से निकली बड़ी चट्टान *The ship hit the rocks and started to sink.* **3** [C] a single large piece of rock एकल चट्टान खंड *The beach was covered with rocks that had broken away from the cliffs.* **4** [C] (*AmE*) a small piece of rock that can be picked up; a stone पत्थर का छोटा टुकड़ा *The boy threw a rock at the dog.* **5** (*also* **rock music**) [U] a type of pop music with a very strong beat, played on electric guitars, etc. रॉक संगीत (एक प्रकार का तेज़ विद्युत गिटार आदि पर बजाया जाने वाला, पॉप संगीत) *I prefer jazz to rock.* ○ *a rock singer/band* ➪ **classical, jazz** और **pop** देखिए। **6** [U] (*BrE*) a type of hard sweet made in long, round sticks एक प्रकार की मिठाई (कड़ी और लंबी छड़ियों के रूप में बनी)

IDM **on the rocks** **1** (used about a marriage, business, etc.) having problems and likely to fail (विवाह, व्यापार आदि) समस्याग्रस्त और असफल होने के कगार पर **2** (used about drinks) served with ice but no water (पेय पदार्थ) केवल बर्फ़ के साथ (किंतु पानी नहीं) *whisky on the rocks*

**rock[2]** /rɒk रॉक्/ *verb* **1** [I, T] to move backwards and forwards or from side to side; to make sb/sth do this आगे-पीछे या दाएँ-बाएँ हिलना; इस प्रकार किसी को हिलाना *boats rocking gently on the waves* ○ *He rocked the baby in his arms to get her to sleep.* **2** [T] to shake sth violently किसी वस्तु को ज़ोर से हिलाना, झकझोर देना *The city was rocked by a bomb blast/earthquake.* **3** [T] to shock sb किसी को आघात पहुँचाना

IDM **rock the boat** to do sth that causes problems or upsets people लोगों के लिए समस्याएँ पैदा करना या उन्हें परेशान कर देना

**rock and roll** (*also* **rock 'n' roll**) *noun* [U] a type of music with a strong beat that was most popular in the 1950s रॉक एंड रॉल (विशेष प्रकार का तेज़ गति वाला संगीत, 1950 के दशक में विशेष लोकप्रिय)

**rock bottom** *noun* [U] the lowest point निम्नतम बिंदु *He **hit rock bottom** when he lost his job.* ○ *rock-bottom prices*

**rock climbing** *noun* [U] the sport of climbing rocks and mountains with ropes, etc. चढ़ाई-क्रीड़ा (चट्टानों और पहाड़ों पर रस्सी आदि से चढ़ने का खेल)

**rocket[1]** /ˈrɒkɪt ˈरॉकिट्/ *noun* [C] **1** a vehicle that is used for travel into space रॉकेट, अंतरिक्ष यात्रा के लिए प्रयुक्त यान, अंतिरिक्ष यान *a space rocket* ○ *to launch a rocket* **2** a weapon that travels through the air and that carries a bomb प्रक्षेपास्त्र (हवा में बम को अपने साथ ले जाने वाला अस्त्र) ✪ पर्याय **missile** **3** a **firework** that shoots high into the air and explodes in a beautiful way when you light it with a flame अग्निबाण (आकाश में छोड़ी आतिशबाज़ी जो ख़ूबसूरत ढंग से रंग-बिरंगा प्रकाश फैलाते हुए बिखर जाती है)

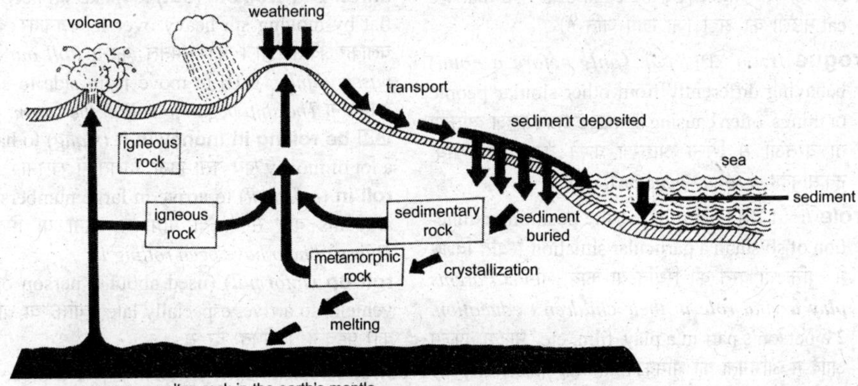

**the rock cycle**

**rocket²** /ˈrɒkɪt ˈरॉकिट्/ *verb* [I] to increase or rise very quickly तेज़ी से बढ़ना या ऊपर उठना *Property prices have rocketed recently.*

**rocky** /ˈrɒki ˈरॉकि/ *adj.* covered with or made of rocks चट्टानों से भरा या बना हुआ; चट्टानी *a rocky road/coastline*

**rod** /rɒd रॉड्/ *noun* [C] (*often in compounds*) a thin straight piece of wood, metal, etc. छड़, सरिया, सलाई (लकड़ी, धातु आदि की) *a fishing rod* सरिया ⇨ **laboratory** पर चित्र देखिए।

**rode** ⇨ **ride¹** का past tense रूप

**rodent** /ˈrəʊdnt ˈरोड्न्ट्/ *noun* [C] a type of small animal, such as a rat, a rabbit, a mouse, etc., which has strong sharp front teeth कुतरने वाला जीव (जैसे चूहा, ख़रगोश आदि, जिसके आगे के दाँत मज़बूत और तेज़ होते हैं)

**rodents**

**rodeo** /ˈrəʊdiəʊ; rəʊˈdeɪəʊ ˈरोडिओ; रोˈडेओ/ *noun* [C] (*pl.* **rodeos**) a competition or performance in which people show their skill in riding wild horses, catching cows, etc. बदमस्त घोड़ों पर सवारी आदि की प्रतियोगिता या प्रदर्शन

**roe** /rəʊ रो/ *noun* [U] the eggs of a fish that we eat मछली का अंडा (जो खाए जाते हैं)

**rogue** /rəʊg रोग्/ *adj.* (*only before a noun*) behaving differently from other similar people or things, often causing damage अपने सदृश व्यक्तियों या वस्तुओं से भिन्न आचरण करने वाला और प्रायः नुक़सानदेह *a rogue gene/program*

**role** /rəʊl रोल्/ *noun* [C] **1** the position or function of sb/sth in a particular situation स्थिति विशेष में व्यक्ति या वस्तु की स्थिति या कार्य; भूमिका *Parents **play a** vital **role** in their children's education.* **2** a person's part in a play, film, etc. नाटक, फ़िल्म आदि में अभिनेता की भूमिका *She was chosen to **play the role** of Mumtaz Mahal.* ○ *a **leading role** in the film*

**role play** *noun* [C, U] an activity, used especially in teaching, in which a person acts a part अभिनयात्मक गतिविधि, विशेषतः शिक्षण में (अभिनय की सहायता से आंशिक शिक्षण)

**roll¹** /rəʊl रोल्/ *noun* [C] **1** something made into the shape of a tube by turning it round and round itself बेलन के आकार में लपेटी हुई वस्तु *a roll of film/wallpaper* **2** bread baked in a round shape for one person to eat गोला आकार में सिकी हुई ब्रेड **3** moving or making sth move by turning over and over गोल-गोल घूमने या (किसी वस्तु को) घुमाने की क्रिया *Everything depended on one roll of the dice.* **4** an official list of names नामों की अधिकृत सूची, नामावली *the electoral roll* (= the list of people who can vote in an election) **5** a long, low sound लगातार आती नीची आवाज़, मंद ध्वनि *a roll of drums* **6** a movement from side to side लुढ़काव

**roll²** /rəʊl रोल्/ *verb* **1** [I, T] to move by turning over and over; to make sth move in this way गोल-गोल घूमते हुए जाना; किसी वस्तु को गोल-गोल घुमाते हुए चलाना *The apples fell out of the bag and rolled everywhere.* ○ *Delivery men were rolling barrels across the yard.* **2** [I] to move smoothly, often on wheels सहज रूप से चलना (प्रायः पहियों पर), बहना *The car began to roll back down the hill.* ○ *Tears were rolling down her cheeks.* **3** [I, T] **roll (sth) (over)** to turn over and over; to make sth do this लगातार लोटना, लुढ़कना या लिपटना; किसी वस्तु को लुढ़काना या लपेटना *The horse was rolling in the dirt.* ○ *The car rolled over in the crash.* ○ *We rolled the log over to see what was underneath.* **4** [I, T] **roll (sth) (up)** to make sth into the shape of a ball or tube गोल या बेलन के आकार में लपेटना *He was rolling himself a cigarette.* ○ *The insect rolled up when I touched it.* ✪ विलोम **unroll** **5** [T] **roll sth (out)** to make sth become flat by moving sth heavy over it वज़नदार वस्तु चलाकर किसी चीज़ को समतल करना *Roll out the pastry thinly.* **6** [I] to move from side to side डगमगाना *The ship began to roll in the storm.*

**IDM be rolling in money/in it** (*slang*) to have a lot of money ख़ूब पैसा होना, दौलत में खेलना

**roll in** (*informal*) to arrive in large numbers or amounts बड़ी संख्या या मात्रा में आना या मिलना *Offers of help have been rolling in.*

**roll up** (*informal*) (used about a person or a vehicle) to arrive, especially late (व्यक्ति या वाहन का) पहुँचना, विशेषतः देर से

**roller** /ˈrəʊlə(r) ˈरोल(र्)/ *noun* [C] **1** a piece of equipment or part of a machine that is shaped like a tube and used, for example, to make sth flat or to help sth move कोई बेलनाकार उपकरण या मशीन का अंग (जो किसी को समतल करे या चलाए) बेलन, रोलर *a roller blind on a window* **2** [*usually pl.*] a small plastic tube that you roll hair around in order to make the hair curly प्लास्टिक की छोटी बेलनाकार कंघी (बालों को घुंघराला बनाने के लिए)

**Rollerblade**™ /ˈrəʊləbleɪd ˈरोलब्लेड्/ *noun* [C] a boot with one row of narrow wheels on the bottom जूता जिसके तले पर छोटे-छोटे पहिए लगे होते हैं (स्केटिंग का जूता) *a pair of Rollerblades* ▶ **rollerblade** *verb* [I] रोलरब्लेडिंग करना

**roller coaster** *noun* [C] a narrow metal track at a **fairground** that goes up and down and round tight bends, and that people ride on in a special vehicle for fun मेले में तीखे मोड़ों पर ऊपर-नीचे जाने और चारों ओर घूमने वाला तंग रोल-पथ (लोग इस पथ के वाहन पर मन बहलाव के लिए सवारी करते हैं); रॉलर-कोस्टर

**roller skate** (*also* **skate**) *noun* [C] a type of shoe with small wheels on the bottom एक प्रकार का जूता जिसके नीचे छोटे पहिए लगे होते है; रॉलर-स्केट *a pair of roller skates* ▶ **roller skate** *verb* [I] रॉलर-स्केटिंग करना ▶ **roller skating** *noun* [U] रॉलर-स्केटिंग

**rolling pin** *noun* [C] a piece of wood, etc. in the shape of a tube, that you use for making pastry flat and thin before cooking लकड़ी आदि का बेलन (रोटी आदि बनाने के लिए) ➪ **kitchen** पर चित्र देखिए।

**ROM** /rɒm रॉम्/ *noun* [U] (*computing*) the abbreviation for 'read-only memory' (computer memory that contains instructions or data that cannot be changed or removed) 'रीड-ओनली' मेमोरी का संक्षिप्त रूप (कंप्यूटर स्मृति या मेमोरी जिसमें आवश्यक निर्देश या सूचना-सामग्री स्थायी रूप से रहते हैं, उन्हें परिवर्तित या मिटाया नहीं जा सकता) ➪ **CD-ROM** देखिए।

**Roman** /ˈrəʊmən ˈरोमन्/ *adj.* **1** connected with ancient Rome or the Roman Empire प्राचीन रोम या रोमन साम्राज्य से संबंधित; रोमन *Roman coins* ○ *the Roman invasion of Britain* **2** connected with the modern city of Rome आधुनिक रोम (नगर) से संबंधित ▶ **Roman** *noun* [C] रोमवासी

**the Roman alphabet** *noun* [*sing.*] the letters A to Z, used especially in Western European languages, A से Z तक रोमन वर्णमाला (विशेषतः पश्चिमी यूरोप की भाषाओं में प्रयुक्त)

**Roman Catholic** (*also* **Catholic**) *noun* [C], *adj.* (a member) of the Christian Church which has the Pope as its head पोप की अध्यक्षता वाले ईसाई चर्च का (सदस्य), रोमन कैथोलिक; कैथोलिक *She's a Roman Catholic.* ➪ **Protestant** देखिए।

**Roman Catholicism** (*also* **Catholicism**) *noun* [U] the beliefs of the Roman Catholic Church रोमन कैथोलिक चर्च की मान्यताएँ

**romance** /rəʊˈmæns रोˈमैन्स्/ *noun* **1** [C] a love affair प्रेम-प्रसंग *The film was about a teenage romance.* **2** [U] a feeling or atmosphere of love or of sth new, special and exciting प्रेम या किसी नई, विशेष और उत्तेजक वस्तु का अनुभव या वातावरण **3** [C] a novel about a love affair प्रेम कथा *historical romances*

**Roman numeral** *noun* [C] one of the letters used by the ancient Romans to represent numbers and still used today, in some situations. In this system I = 1, V = 5, X = 10, L = 50, C = 100, D = 500, M = 1000 and these letters are used in combinations to form other numbers रोमन अंक प्रणाली (प्राचीन रोमवासियों द्वारा प्रयुक्त वर्णमाला के अक्षर, जो संख्याओं का प्रतिनिधित्व करते हैं और कुछ प्रसंगों में अब भी इस्तेमाल होते हैं। इस प्रणाली के अनुसार समीकरण है I = 1, V = 5, X = 10, L = 50, C = 100, D = 500, M = 1000 इन अक्षरों को संयुक्त कर अन्य संख्याएँ बनाई जाती हैं) *Henry VIII*

**romantic**[1] /rəʊˈmæntɪk रोˈमैन्टिक्/ *adj.* **1** having a quality that strongly affects your emotions or makes you think about love; showing feelings of love भावुकतापूर्ण और प्रेमोद्दीपक; प्रेम दिखाने वाला, रूमानी *a romantic candlelit dinner* ○ *He isn't very romantic—he never says he loves me.* **2** involving a love affair प्रेम-प्रसंग वाला, रूमानी *Reports of a romantic relationship between the two film stars have been strongly denied.* **3** having or showing ideas about life that are emotional rather than real or practical भावुक और कल्पनाशील (न कि वास्तविक या व्यावहारिक) *He has a romantic idea that he'd like to live on a farm in Scotland.* ▶ **romantically** /rəʊˈmæntɪkli रोˈमैन्टिक्लि/ *adv.* रूमानीपन से

**romantic**[2] /rəʊˈmæntɪk रोˈमैन्टिक्/ *noun* [C] a person who has ideas that are not based on real life or that are not very practical रोमांटिक, कल्पनाशील व्यक्ति (वास्तविक या व्यावहारिक जीवन से दूर रहने वाला व्यक्ति)

**romanticize** (*also* **-ise**) /rəʊˈmæntɪsaɪz रोˈमैन्टिसाइज़्/ *verb* [I, T] to make sth seem more interesting, exciting, etc. than it really is किसी चीज़ को रूमानी बनाना (असलियत से अधिक से अधिक रोचक, उत्तेजक आदि बनाना)

**romp** /rɒmp रॉम्प्/ *verb* [I] (used about children and animals) to play in a happy and noisy way

(बच्चों और पशुओं का) उछल-कूद मचाना (ख़ुशी के मारे और शोर मचाते हुए) ▶ **romp** *noun* [C] उधम, उछल-कूद

**IDM** **romp home/to victory** to win easily सरलता से जीत जाना *India romped to a 4–0 victory over New Zealand.*

**roof** /ru:f रूफ़्/ *noun* [C] (*pl.* **roofs**) **1** the part of a building, vehicle, etc. which covers the top of it (भवन, वाहन आदि की) छत *a flat/sloping/tiled roof* ○ *the roof of a car* ○ *The library and the sports hall are* ***under one roof*** (= in the same building). **2** the highest part of the inside of sth किसी वस्तु के अंदर का उच्चतम अंग या बिंदु *The roof of the cave had collapsed.* ○ *The soup burned the roof of my mouth.*

**IDM** **a roof over your head** somewhere to live रहने के लिए कोई जगह, सिर पर छत, आश्रय-स्थल, ठौर *I might not have any money, but at least I've got a roof over my head.*

**roof rack** *noun* [C] a structure that you fix to the roof of a car and use for carrying luggage or other large objects कार की छत पर सामान रखने का सींकचा; लगेज़ कैरियर

**rooftop** /ˈru:ftɒp ˈरूफ़टॉप्/ *noun* [C, *usually pl.*] the outside of the roofs of buildings भवनों की छतों के ऊपरी भाग *From the tower we looked down over the rooftops of the city.*

**room** /ru:m; rʊm रूम्; रुम्/ *noun* **1** [C] a part of a house or building that has its own walls, floor and ceiling कमरा (किसी घर या भवन का एक हिस्सा जिसकी अपनी दीवारें, फ़र्श और भीतरी छत होते हैं) *a sitting/dining/living room* ○ *I sat down in the waiting room until the doctor called me.* **2** [U] **room (for sb/sth); room (to do sth)** space; enough space ख़ाली जगह या स्थान; पर्याप्त रिक्त स्थान *These chairs* ***take up*** *too much* ***room***. ○ *How can we* ***make room*** *for all the furniture?* ➪ **space** देखिए तथा **place**[1] पर नोट देखिए। **3** [U] **room for sth** the opportunity or need for sth (किसी चीज़ की) गुंजाइश या ज़रूरत *There's* ***room for improvement*** *in your work* (= it could be much better). ○ *The lack of time gives us very little* ***room for manoeuvre***.

**room cooler** = **air cooler**

**roomful** /ˈru:mfʊl; ˈrʊm- ˈरूमफ़ुल्; ˈरुम्-/ *noun* [C] a large number of people or things in a room कमरे में भरे अनेक लोग या वस्तुएँ

**room-mate** *noun* [C] a person that you share a room with in a flat, etc. कमरा साथी (कमरे में आपके साथ रहने वाला व्यक्ति)

**room service** *noun* [U] a service provided in a hotel, by which guests can order food and drink to be brought to their rooms कक्षीय सेवा, रूम सर्विस (होटल में उपलब्ध सेवा जिसमें आदेश देने पर, भोजन आदि व्यक्ति के कक्ष में पहुँचाए जाते हैं) *He ordered coffee from room service.*

**roomy** /ˈru:mi ˈरूमि/ *adj.* (**roomier; roomiest**) having plenty of space पर्याप्त जगह वाला लंबा-चौड़ा खुला, विस्तृत *a roomy house/car*

**roost** /ru:st रूस्ट्/ *noun* [C] a place where birds rest or sleep पक्षियों का बसेरा (विश्राम या शयन का स्थान) ▶ **roost** *verb* [I] पक्षियों का बसेरा करना, विश्राम करना

**rooster** /ˈru:stə(r) ˈरूस्ट(र्)/ (*AmE*) = **cock**[1] **1**

**root**[1] /ru:t रूट्/ *noun* **1** [C] the part of a plant that grows under the ground and takes in water and food from the soil (पेड़-पौधों की) जड़ (जो ज़मीन के अंदर रहकर मिट्टी से आहार लेती है) *The deep roots of these trees can cause damage to buildings.* ○ ***root vegetables*** *such as carrots and radishes* ➪ **flower** पर चित्र देखिए। **2** [C] the part of a hair or tooth that is under the skin and that holds it in place on the body बाल या दाँत की जड़ **3 roots** [*pl.*] the feelings or connections that you have with a place because you have lived there or your family came from there जड़ें (अपने पूर्व निवास या परिवार के मूलस्थल से लगाव या संबंध) *She's proud of her Indian roots.* **4** [C] the basic cause or origin of sth किसी बात का मूल कारण या उद्‌गम *Let's try and get to the* ***root of the problem***. ➪ **square root** देखिए।

**root**[2] /ru:t रूट्/ *verb*

**PHR V** **root about/around (for sth)** to search for sth by moving things सामान इधर-उधर फैलाते हुए कुछ ढूँढ़ना *What are you rooting around in my desk for?*

**root for sb** to give support to sb who is in a competition, etc. प्रतियोगिता आदि में भाग ले रहे व्यक्ति का हौंसला बढ़ाना

**root sth out** to find and destroy sth bad completely किसी बुरी चीज़ को ढूँढ़कर जड़ से उखाड़ देना, पूरी तरह से नष्ट कर देना

**rope**[1] /rəʊp रोप्/ *noun* [C, U] very thick, strong string that is used for tying or lifting heavy things, climbing up, etc. रस्सी *We need some rope to tie up the boat with.*

**show sb/know/learn the ropes** to show sb/ know/learn how a job should be done किसी को काम करने का तरीक़ा दिखाना, बताना या सिखाना

**rope**[2] /rəʊp रोप्/ *verb* [T] **rope A to B; rope A and B together** to tie sb/sth with a rope व्यक्ति या वस्तु को रस्सी से बाँधना

IDM **rope sb in (to do sth)** (*informal*) to persuade sb to help in an activity, especially when he/she does not want to किसी काम में साथ देने के लिए मनाना (विशेषतः जब वह इच्छुक न हो)

**rope sth off** to put ropes round or across an area in order to keep people out of it किसी स्थान को रस्सियों से घेर लेना (ताकि लोग अंदर न आएँ)

**rosary** /ˈrəʊzəri ˈरोज़रि/ *noun* [C] (*pl.* **rosaries**) a string of small round pieces of wood, etc. used by some Roman Catholics for counting prayers सुमिरनी, जयमाला (लकड़ी आदि के दानों की माला जिससे भक्त लोग प्रार्थनाओं की गिनती करते हैं)

**rose**[1] ⇨ **rise**[2] का past tense रूप

**rose**[2] /rəʊz रोज़्/ *noun* [C] a flower with a sweet smell, that grows on a bush that usually has sharp points (**thorns**) growing on it गुलाब का फूल

**rosé** /ˈrəʊzeɪ ˈरोज़े/ *noun* [U] pink wine गुलाबी रंग की शराब या वाइन; रोज़े

**rosette** /rəʊˈzet रोˈज़ेट्/ *noun* [C] a decoration made from long pieces of coloured material (**ribbons**) that you wear on your clothes. Rosettes are given as prizes or worn to show that sb supports a particular political party लंबे फ़ीतों से बना (गुलाब की शकल का) बिल्ला (जो प्रतियोगियों को पुरस्कार स्वरूप प्रदान किया जाता है या जिसे किसी राजनीतिक दल को समर्थन व्यक्त करने के लिए कपड़ों पर लगाया जाता है)

**roster** /ˈrɒstə(r) ˈरॉस्टर(र्)/ = **rota**

**rostrum** /ˈrɒstrəm ˈरॉस्ट्रम्/ *noun* [C] a platform that sb stands on to make a public speech, etc. भाषण आदि देने के लिए मंच, चबूतरा

**rosy** /ˈrəʊz ˈरोज़ि/ *adj.* (**rosier; rosiest**) **1** pink and pleasant in appearance गुलाबी और देखने में सुंदर *rosy cheeks* **2** full of good possibilities अनुकूल संभावनाओं से परिपूर्ण; उज्जवल *The future was looking rosy.*

**rot** /rɒt रॉट्/ *verb* [I, T] (**rotting; rotted**) to go bad or make sth go bad as part of a natural process (किस चीज़) का सड़ना या ख़राब होना या को सड़ाना या ख़राब करना (प्राकृतिक प्रक्रिया के अंतर्गत) *Too many sweets will rot your teeth!* ✪ पर्याय **decay** ▶ **rot** *noun* [U] सड़न, विगलन

**rota** /ˈrəʊtə ˈरोटा/ (*also AmE* **roster**) *noun* [C] a list of people who share a certain job or task and the times that they are each going to do it एक साथ किसी काम को करने वाले लोगों की नाम-सूची और कार्यक्रमावली; रोस्टर *We organize the cleaning* ***on a rota***.

**rotary** /ˈrəʊtəri ˈरोटरि/ *adj.* moving in circles round a central point धुरी पर घूमने वाला; चक्रिल, घूर्णक

**rotate** /rəʊˈteɪt रोˈटेट्/ *verb* [I, T] **1** to turn in circles round a central point; to make sth do this धुरी पर घूमना या घुमाना, चक्कर लगाना या लगवाना; घूर्णन करना *The earth rotates on its axis.* **2** to happen in turn or in a particular order; to make sth do this किसी बात का बारी-बारी से या विशेष क्रम में होना या करना *We rotate the duties so that nobody is stuck with a job they don't like.*

**rotation** /rəʊˈteɪʃn रोˈटेशन्/ *noun* [C, U] **1** movement in circles around a central point धुरी पर वृत्ताकार आवर्तन; घूर्णन *one rotation every 24 hours* **2** happening or making things happen in a particular order किसी बात का विशेष क्रम में होना या उसे विशेष क्रम में करना *The company is chaired by all the members* ***in rotation***.

**rotor** /ˈrəʊtə(r) ˈरोटर(र्)/ *noun* [C] a part of a machine that turns around a central point मशीन का धूरी पर घूमने वाला भाग; रोटर *rotor blades on a helicopter*

**rotten** /ˈrɒtn ˈरॉटन्/ *adj.* **1** (used about food and other substances) old and not fresh enough or good enough to use (खाद्य और अन्य वस्तुएँ) बासी, सड़ा-गला *rotten vegetables* **2** (*informal*) very unpleasant बहुत बेकार (की बात) *That was a rotten thing to say!* **3** (*spoken*) used to emphasize that you are angry प्रबल क्रोध को व्यक्त करने के लिए प्रयुक्त *You can keep your rotten job!*

**rouge** /ruːʒ रूज़्/ *noun* [U] (*old-fashioned*) a red powder or cream used for giving more colour to the cheeks रूज़; गालों की लाली बढ़ाने वाला पाउडर या क्रीम ⇨ **blusher** देखिए।

**rough**[1] /rʌf रफ़्/ *adj.* **1** not smooth, soft or level खुरदरा (चिकना, कोमल या समतल नहीं) *rough ground* **2** violent; not calm or gentle उग्र; शांत या कोमल नहीं, रूखा *You can hold the baby, but don't be rough with him.* ○ *The sea was rough and half the people on the boat were seasick.* **3** made or done quickly or without much care; approximate जल्दी में या कुछ लापरवाही से किया हुआ; मोटा-मोटा, अनुमानित *a rough estimate* ○ *Can you give me a rough idea of what time you'll be arriving?* **4** (*informal*) looking or feeling ill बीमार-सा *You look a bit rough—are you feeling all right?* ▶ **roughness** *noun* [U] रूखापन

**IDM be rough (on sb)** be unpleasant or unfortunate for sb किसी के लिए अप्रिय या अशुभ होना

**rough²** /rʌf रफ़्/ *noun*

**IDM in rough** done quickly without worrying about mistakes, as a preparation for the finished piece of work or drawing जल्दी में और भूलों की चिंता के बिना किया गया (किसी काम को पूरा करने की तैयारी के रूप में), कच्चा काम

**take the rough with the smooth** to accept difficult or unpleasant things in addition to pleasant things प्रिय-अप्रिय को समान रूप से स्वीकार करना

**rough³** /rʌf रफ़्/ *adv.* in a rough way अनगढ़ या उग्र ढंग से *One of the boys was told off for playing rough.*

**IDM live/sleep rough** to live or sleep outdoors, usually because you have no home or money खुले में रहना या सोना (प्रायः घर या धन के अभाव में)

**rough⁴** /rʌf रफ़्/ *verb*

**IDM rough it** to live without all the comfortable things that you usually have जैसे-तैसे काम चलाना, अभ्यस्त सुविधाओं के बिना रहना *You have to rough it a bit when you go camping.*

**roughage** /ˈrʌfɪdʒ ˈरफ़िज्/ *noun* [U] the types or parts of food (**fibre**) which help your stomach to deal with other foods खाद्य पदार्थों का रेशेदार हिस्सा, चोकर, मोटाझोंटा अंश (भोजन को पचाने में सहायक) रुक्षांश

**roughen** /ˈrʌfn ˈरफ़्न्/ *verb* [T] to make sth less smooth or soft (किसी वस्तु को) खुरदरा या रूखा बनाना

**roughly** /ˈrʌfli ˈरफ़्लि/ *adv.* **1** in a violent way; not gently उग्रता के साथ (न कि शांत भाव से) *He grabbed her roughly by her arm.* **2** not exactly; approximately मोटे तौर पर; अंदाज़न *It took roughly three hours I suppose.*

**roulette** /ruːˈlet रूˈलेट्/ *noun* [U] a game in which a ball is dropped onto a moving wheel that has holes with numbers on them. The players bet on which hole the ball will be in when the wheel stops रुलेट का खेल (जिसमें गेंद को घूमते हुए संख्यांकित पहिए पर डाला जाता है और पहिया जिस संख्या पर रुकता है उस संख्या पर बाजी लगाई जाती है)

**round¹** /raʊnd राउन्ड्/ *adj.* having the shape of a circle or a ball गोल (वृत्त या गेंद के आकार का) *a round table*

**IDM in round figures/numbers** given to the nearest 10, 100, 1000, etc.; not given in exact numbers निकटतम शून्यांत संख्याओं में; एकदम सही संख्या में नहीं

**round²** /raʊnd राउन्ड्/ *adv., prep.*

> **NOTE** अनेक क्रियाओं के साथ मिल कर बनने वाले विशेष प्रयोगों (पदबंधीय क्रिया-संरचना) के लिए संबंधित verb की प्रविष्टि देखिए।

**1** in a circle or curve; on all sides of sth वृत्ताकार या वक्राकार; (किसी वस्तु के) सभी ओर *He had a bandage right round his head.* ○ *We were just talking about Ravi and he came* ***round the corner.*** ○ *(figurative) It wasn't easy to see a way round the problem* (= a way of solving it). **2** in a full circle पूर्ण वृत्त के आकार में *The wheels spun* ***round and round*** *but the car wouldn't move.* **3** turning to look or go in the opposite direction घूमकर या विपरीत दिशा में जाकर *Don't* ***look round*** *but the teacher's just come in.* ○ *She* ***turned*** *the car* ***round*** *and drove off.* **4** from one place, person, etc. to another एक (स्थान, व्यक्ति आदि) के बाद दूसरे को, बारी-बारी से प्रत्येक को *Pass the photographs* ***round*** *for everyone to see.* **5** in or to a particular area or place किसी विशेष इलाक़े या स्थान में, की तरफ़ *Do you live round here?* ○ *I'll come round to see you at about 8 o'clock.* **6** in or to many parts of sth किसी वस्तु के अधिकतर हिस्सों में, की तरफ़ *Let me* ***show*** *you* ***round*** *the house.*

**IDM round about (sth)** in the area near a place; approximately किसी स्थान के आस-पास; अंदाज़न *We hope to arrive round about 6 p.m.*

**the other way round** in the opposite way or order विपरीत दिशा या क्रम में *My appointment's at 3 o'clock and Leena's is at 3.15—or was it the other way round?*

> **NOTE** **Around** का वही अर्थ हैं जो **round** का और यह शब्द अमेरिकी अंग्रेज़ी में अधिक प्रचलित है।

**round³** /raʊnd राउन्ड्/ *noun* [C] **1** a number or series of events, etc. दौर (घटनाओं का दौर या शृंखला) *a further round of talks with other European countries* **2** a regular series of visits, etc., often as part of a job फेरा, गश्त (नौकरी या काम के सिलसिले में) *The postman's round takes him about three hours.* ○ *Dr Sharma is on his daily round of the wards.* **3** a number of drinks (one for all the people in a group) (मंडली या पानगोष्टि के सदस्य के रूप में) एक व्यक्ति की पेय ख़रीदने की बारी *It's my round* (= it's my turn to buy the drinks). **4** one part of a game or competition किसी खेल या प्रतियोगिता का एक हिस्सा, दौर या चक्र *India will play Sri Lanka in the next round.* **5** (*in golf*) one game, usually of 18 holes (गोल्फ़ में) एक गेम (प्रायः 18 गड्ढों वाला) *to play a round of golf* **6** a bullet or a number of bullets, fired from a gun बंदूक़ से दाग़ी गोली या गोलियाँ *He fired several rounds at us.* **7** a short, sudden period of loud noise ऊँची आवाज़ में संक्षिप्त आकस्मिक प्रशंसा-प्रक्रिया; लहर, चक्र *The last speaker got the biggest* ***round of applause.***

**round[4]** /raʊnd राउन्ड्/ *verb* [T] to go round sth घेरे या चक्कर में घूमना *The police car rounded the corner at high speed.*

PHR V **round sth off** to do sth that completes a job or an activity किसी काम या गतिविधि को पूरा करने के अंतर्गत कुछ करना *We rounded off the meal with coffee and chocolates.*

**round sb/sth up** to bring sb/sth together in one place व्यक्तियों या वस्तुओं को इकट्ठा करना *The teacher rounded up the children.*

**round sth up/down** to increase/decrease a number, price, etc. to the nearest whole number किसी संख्या, क़ीमत आदि को निकटतम पूर्ण संख्या तक बढ़ाना या घटाना

**roundabout[1]** /ˈraʊndəbaʊt राउन्डबाउट्/ *noun* [C] **1** a circle where several roads meet, that all the traffic has to go round in the same direction चौराहे का गोल चक्कर (जिसको चक्कर लगाते हुए ट्रैफ़िक को जाना होता है) **2** a round platform made for children to play on. They sit or stand on it and sb pushes it round चरखी झूला, चक्करदार झूला (बच्चों के खेलने के लिए) **3** = **merry-go-round**

**roundabout[2]** /ˈraʊndəbaʊt ˈराउन्डबाउट्/ *adj.* longer than is necessary or usual; not direct अधिक लंबा (आवश्यकता से या सामान्य से); घुमाव-फिराव वाला (सीधा नहीं) *We got lost and came by a rather roundabout route.*

**rounders** /ˈraʊndəz ˈराउन्डज़्/ *noun* [U] a British game that is similar to baseball बेसबॉल जैसा एक ब्रिटिश खेल

**round trip** *noun* [C] **1** a journey to a place and back again किसी स्थान की चक्राकार या वापसी यात्रा, जाने-आने की यात्रा *It's a four-kilometre round trip to the centre of town.* **2** (*AmE*) = **return[2] 5**

**roundworm** /ˈraʊndwɜːm ˈराउन्ड्वर्म्/ *noun* [C] a **worm** that lives inside the bodies of pigs, humans and some other animals गोल कृमि (सुअरों, मनुष्यों और कुछ अन्य पशुओं के शरीरों में पलने वाला कृमि)

**rouse** /raʊz राउज़्/ *verb* [T] **1** (*formal*) to make sb wake up (किसी को) जगाना *She was sleeping so soundly that I couldn't rouse her.* **2** to make sb/sth very angry, excited, interested, etc. किसी को अत्यंत क्रोधित, उत्तेजित, रुचियुक्त कर देना

**rousing** /ˈraʊzɪŋ ˈराउज़िङ्/ *adj.* exciting and powerful उत्तेजक और प्रभावशाली *a rousing speech*

**rout** /raʊt राउट्/ *verb* [T] to defeat sb completely (किसी को) बुरी तरह हरा देना ▶ **rout** *noun* [C] बुरी या पूर्ण हार

**route** /ruːt रूट्/ *noun* [C] **1 a route (from A) (to B)** a way from one place to another एक स्थान से दूसरे स्थान तक जाने का रास्ता *What is the most direct route from Noida to Delhi?* ○ *I got a leaflet about the bus routes from the information office.* **2 a route to sth** a way of achieving sth कुछ प्राप्त करने का मार्ग या उपाय *Hard work is the only route to success.*

**routine[1]** /ruːˈtiːn रूˈटीन्/ *noun* **1** [C, U] the usual order and way in which you regularly do things नेम, नित्यक्रम, रुटीन (नियमित रूप से कुछ करने का सामान्य तरीक़ा और क्रम) *Make exercise part of your daily routine.* **2** [U] tasks that have to be done again and again and so are boring उबाऊ काम (बार-बार किए जाने के फलस्वरूप) **3** [C] a series of movements, jokes, etc. that are part of a performance शृंखलाबद्ध क्रियाएँ आदि (जो किसी प्रदर्शन का अंग होती है, जैसे नृत्य में पदसंचालन) *a dance/comedy routine* **4** [C] (*computing*) a list of instructions that make a computer able to perform a particular task कंप्यूटर के लिए निर्देशों की सूची (ताकि वह कृत्य-विशेष संपन्न कर सके)

**routine[2]** /ruːˈtiːn रूˈटीन्/ *adj.* **1** normal and regular; not unusual or special सामान्य और नियमित; असामान्य या विशेष नहीं *The police would like to ask you some routine questions.* **2** boring; not exciting उबाऊ; उत्तेजक या रोचक नहीं *It's a very routine job, really.*

**routinely** /ruːˈtiːnli रूˈटीनली/ *adv.* regularly; as part of a routine नियमित रूप से; रुटीन के अंतर्गत *The machines are routinely checked every two months.*

**row[1]** /rəʊ रो/ *noun* [C] **1** a line of people or things व्यक्तियों या वस्तुओं की पंक्ति, कतार *a row of books* ○ *The children were all standing **in a row** at the front of the class.* **2** a line of seats in a theatre, cinema, etc. थियेटर, सिनेमा आदि में सीटों की पंक्ति या कतार, लाइन *Our seats were in the back row.* ○ *a front-row seat*

IDM **in a row** one after another; without a break एक के बाद दूसरा, लगातार; बिना अंतराल के, अविराम *It rained for four days in a row.*

**row[2]** /rəʊ रो/ *verb* **1** [I, T] to move a boat through the water using long thin pieces of wood with flat parts at the end (**oars**) चप्पुओं से नाव खेना *We often go rowing on the lake.* **2** [T] to carry sb/sth in a boat that you row खेते हुए नाव में सैर कराना *Could you row us over to the island?* ➪ **paddle** देखिए। ▶ **row** *noun* [*sing.*] नौका-विहार

**row³** /raʊ राओ/ *noun* 1 [C] **a row (about/over sth)** a noisy argument or serious disagreement between two or more people, groups, etc. (लोगों में) किसी बात पर झगड़ा *When I* ***have a row*** *with my sister, I always try to make up as soon as possible.* ○ *A row has broken out between the main parties over education.* 2 [*sing.*] a loud noise शोर, हो-हल्ला *What a row! Could you be a bit quieter?* ▶ **row** *verb* [I] झगड़ना **row (with sb) (about/over sth)** *Paroma and I are always rowing about money!*

**rowdy** /ˈraʊdi ˈराउडि/ *adj.* noisy and likely to cause trouble शोर मचाने वाला और उपद्रवी *a rowdy group of football fans* ○ *rowdy behaviour* ▶ **rowdily** *adv.* शोर मचाते या झगड़ते हुए ▶ **rowdiness** *noun* [U] उपद्रव, हुल्लड़बाज़ी

**rowing boat** (*AmE* **row boat**) /ˈrəʊbəʊt ˈरोबोट्/) *noun* [C] a small boat that you move through the water using long thin pieces of wood with flat parts at the end (**oars**) चप्पू-चालित नौका ➪ **boat** पर चित्र देखिए।

**royal** /ˈrɔɪəl ˈरॉइअल्/ *adj.* 1 connected with a king or queen or a member of their family राजकीय, शाही (राजा या रानी या राजपरिवार से संबंधित) *the royal family* 2 (used in the names of organizations) supported by a member of the royal family (संस्थाओं या संगठनों के नाम के साथ प्रयुक्त शब्द), राजपरिवार के किसी सदस्य द्वारा पोषित ▶ **royal** *noun* [C] (*informal*) राजपरिवार का सदस्य *the Queen, the Princes and other royals*

**royal blue** *adj., noun* (of) deep bright blue गहरे चमकदार नीले रंग का

**Royal Highness** *noun* [C] **His/Her/Your Royal Highness** used when you are speaking to or about a member of the royal family राजपरिवार के सदस्य के लिए प्रयुक्त (संबोधन में या उनसे संबंधित चर्चा में)

**royalty** /ˈrɔɪəlti ˈरॉइअल्टि/ *noun* (*pl.* **royalties**) 1 [U] members of the royal family राजपरिवार के सदस्य 2 [C] an amount of money that is paid to the person who wrote a book, piece of music, etc. every time his/her work is sold or performed रॉयल्टि; लेखक को उसकी प्रत्येक रचना या कलाकार को प्रत्येक प्रदर्शन पर मिलने वाली धनराशि *The author earns a 2 per cent royalty on each copy sold.*

**RP** /ˌɑːˈpiː ˌआˈपी/ *noun* [U] received pronunciation; the standard form of British pronunciation सामान्य स्वीकृत उच्चारण; मानक ब्रिटिश उच्चारण

**rpm** /ˌɑː piːˈem ˌआ पीˈएम्/ *abbr.* revolutions per minute प्रति-मिनट परिक्रमण *an engine speed of 2500 rpm*

**RSI** /ˌɑːr esˈaɪ ˌआर् एस्ˈआइ/ *noun* [U] repetitive strain injury; pain and swelling, especially in the wrists and hands, caused by doing the same movement many times in a job or an activity पुनरावर्ती खिंचाव से उत्पन्न शारीरिक कष्ट; किसी काम में एक ही क्रिया की पुनरावृत्ति से उत्पन्न दर्द और सूजन (विशेषतः कलाइयों और हाथों में)

**RSVP** /ˌɑːr es viːˈpiː ˌआर् एस् वीˈपी/ *abbr.* (used on invitations) please reply (निमंत्रण पत्रों में प्रयुक्त) उत्तरापेक्षी

**rub** /rʌb रब्/ *verb* (**rubbing; rubbed**) 1 [I, T] to move your hand, a cloth, etc. backwards and forwards on the surface of sth while pressing firmly (किसी सतह को) रगड़ना *Raju rubbed his hands together to keep them warm.* ○ *The cat rubbed against my leg.* 2 [T] **rub sth in (to sth)** to put a cream, liquid, etc. onto a surface by rubbing किसी सतह पर क्रीम आदि मलना *Apply a little of the lotion and rub it into the skin.* 3 [I, T] **rub (on/against sth)** to press on/against sth, often causing pain or damage (किसी पर या के साथ) मसलना (प्रायः दर्द करते या क्षति पहुँचाते हुए) *These new shoes are rubbing my heels.* ▶ **rub** *noun* [C]

IDM **rub salt into the wound/sb's wounds** to make a situation that makes sb feel bad even worse जले पर नमक छिड़कना, दुर्दशा को बदतर बना देना

**rub shoulders with sb** to meet and spend time with famous people बड़े लोगों से मिलना-जुलना और उनके साथ रहना *As a journalist you rub shoulders with the rich and famous.*

**rub it/sth in** to keep reminding sb of sth embarrassing that he/she wants to forget किसी को अप्रिय बात याद दिलाते रहना *I know it was a stupid mistake, but there's no need to rub it in!*

**rub off (on/onto sb)** (used about a good quality) to be passed from one person to another (कोई अच्छा गुण) एक व्यक्ति से दूसरे तक पहुँचाना *Let's hope some of her enthusiasm rubs off onto her brother.*

**rub sth off (sth)** to remove sth from a surface by rubbing मल कर निकाल देना (निशान, धूल आदि को) *He rubbed the dirt off his boots.*

PHR V **rub sth out** to remove the marks made by a pencil, chalk, etc. using a rubber, cloth, etc. पेंसिल आदि के निशान रबड़ आदि से मिटाना *That answer is wrong. Rub it out.*

**rubber** /ˈrʌbə(r) ˈरब(र्)/ *noun* 1 [U] a strong substance that can be stretched and does not allow water to pass through it, used for making tyres, boots, etc. Rubber is made from the juice of a tropical tree or is produced using chemicals

रबड़ *a rubber ball* ○ *rubber gloves* ○ *foam rubber* **2** [C] (*AmE* **eraser**) a small piece of rubber that you use for removing pencil marks from paper; soft material used for removing chalk marks or pen marks from a board पेंसिल से लिखे को मिटाने वाला रबड़; बोर्ड या तख़्ते पर के खड़िया या क़लम के निशान मिटाने वाली नरम चीज़ ➪ **stationery** पर चित्र देखिए।

**rubber band** (*also* **elastic band**) *noun* [C] a thin circular piece of rubber that is used for holding things together चीज़ों को पकड़े रखने वाला रबड़ का पतला गोल छल्ला *Her hair was tied back with a rubber band.* ➪ **stationery** पर चित्र देखिए।

**rubber stamp** *noun* [C] **1** a small tool that you hold in your hand and use for printing the date, the name of an organization, etc. on a document रबड़ की मोहर जिससे किसी दस्तावेज़ पर तारीख़, संख्या का नाम आदि अंकित किए जाते हैं; रबर स्टाम्प ➪ **stationery** पर चित्र देखिए। **2** a person or group who gives official approval to sth without thinking about it first बिना पूर्व विचार के किसी मुद्दे का आधिकारिक अनुमोदन कर देने वाला व्यक्ति या गुट, आँख मूँद कर किसी मामले की पुष्टि करने वाला व्यक्ति या गुट ▶ **rubber-stamp** *verb* [T] आँख मूँद कर (किसी मामले की) पुष्टि करना *The committee have no real power—they just rubber-stamp the chairman's ideas.*

**rubbery** /ˈrʌbəri ˈरबरि/ *adj.* like rubber रबड़-जैसा *This meat is rubbery.*

**rubbish** /ˈrʌbɪʃ ˈरबिश्/ (*AmE* **garbage**; **trash**) *noun* [U] **1** things that you do not want any more; waste material बेकार की चीज़ें; कूड़ा-करकट, रद्दी माल *The dustmen collect the rubbish every Monday.* ○ *a rubbish bin* ➪ **waste** देखिए। **2** something that you think is bad, silly or wrong कोई बात जो बुरी, बेवक़ूफ़ीभरी या गलत लगे, अनर्गल प्रलाप, बेकार की बात *I thought that film was absolute rubbish.* ○ *Don't talk such rubbish.*

**rubbish tip** = **tip**[1] **4**

**rubble** /ˈrʌbl ˈरबूल्/ *noun* [U] pieces of broken brick, stone, etc., especially from a damaged building ईंट, पत्थर आदि के टुकड़े, मलवा (विशेषतः टूटे मकान का)

**rubella** /ru:ˈbelə रूˈबेला/ = **German measles**

**ruby** /ˈru:bi ˈरूबि/ *noun* [C] (*pl.* **rubies**) a type of precious stone that is red माणिक, लाल (रत्न), रूबी

**ruby wedding** *noun* [C] the 40th anniversary of a wedding विवाह की चालीसवीं वर्षगाँठ ➪ **diamond wedding, golden wedding** और **silver wedding** देखिए।

**rucksack** /ˈrʌksæk ˈरक्सैक्/ *noun* [C] (*BrE*) a bag that you use for carrying things on your back पीठथैला (चीज़ें पीठ पर लाद कर ले जाने का थैला) ✪ पर्याय **backpack** या **pack**

**rudder** /ˈrʌdə(r) ˈरड(र्)/ *noun* [C] a piece of wood or metal that is used for controlling the direction of a boat or plane पतवार, कर्ण (नाव या विमान की दिशा नियंत्रित करने वाला काष्ठ या धातु खंड) ➪ **boat** पर चित्र देखिए।

**rude** /ru:d रूड्/ *adj.* **1 rude (to sb) (about sb/sth)** not polite अशिष्ट (किसी के प्रति)(किसी बात पर) *It's rude to interrupt when people are speaking.* ○ *I think it was rude of them not to phone and say that they weren't coming.* ✪ पर्याय **impolite** **2** connected with sex, using the toilet, etc. in a way that might offend people अश्लील, भद्दा *a rude joke/word/gesture* **3** (*written*) sudden and unpleasant (लिखित) आकस्मिक और अरुचिकर *If you're expecting any help from him, you're in for a rude shock.* ▶ **rudely** *adv.* अशिष्टतापूर्वक ▶ **rudeness** *noun* [U] अशिष्टता

**rudimentary** /ˌru:dɪˈmentri ˌरूडिˈमेनट्रि/ *adj.* (*formal*) very basic or simple प्रारंभिक या साधारण

**rudiments** /ˈru:dɪmənts ˈरूडिमन्ट्स्/ *noun* [*pl.*] **the rudiments (of sth)** (*formal*) the most basic or important facts of a particular subject, skill, etc. विशिष्ट विषय, कौशल आदि के सर्वथा प्रारंभिक या महत्त्वपूर्ण तथ्य

**ruffle** /ˈrʌfl ˈरफ़्ल्/ *verb* [T] **1 ruffle sth (up)** to make sth untidy or no longer smooth किसी चीज़ को उलटा-पुलटा या बेतरतीब कर देना *to ruffle sb's hair* **2** (*passive*) to make sb annoyed or confused (किसी को) परेशान कर देना या उलझन में डाल देना

**rug** /rʌg रग्/ *noun* [C] **1** a piece of thick material that covers a small part of a floor क़ालीन, ग़लीचा ➪ **carpet** और **mat** देखिए। **2** a large piece of thick cloth that you put over your legs or around your shoulders to keep warm, especially when travelling मोटी चादर, कंबल आदि (गरमी के लिए टाँगों या कंधों पर डाले जाने वाले, विशेषतः यात्रा के दौरान)

**rugby** /ˈrʌgbi ˈरग्बि/ *noun* [U] a form of football that is played by two teams of 13 or 15 players with an ball that can be carried, kicked or thrown रगबी, एक प्रकार का फुटबॉल का खेल (जिसमें 13 या 15 खिलाड़ी होते हैं, गेंद अंडाकार होती है जिसे खिलाड़ी पैरों से मारने के अलावा हाथों से उठाकर ले जाते हैं या फेंकते हैं; रगबी

**NOTE** खेल का शीर्षक **Rugby League** हो तो दल में 13 खिलाड़ी होंगे और **Rugby Union** हो तो 15।

**rugged** /ˈrʌgɪd ˈरगिड्/ *adj.* **1** (used about land) rough, with a lot of rocks and not many plants (ज़मीन) ऊबड़-खाबड़ (जिसमें पेड़-पौधे कम और पत्थर के टुकड़े अधिक हों) **2** (used about a man) strong and attractive (व्यक्ति) तगड़ा और सुंदर **3** strong and made for difficult conditions मज़बूत और कठिन परिस्थितियों के लिए निर्मित (वाहन आदि)

**ruin**[1] /ˈruːɪn ˈरूइन्/ *verb* [T] **1** to damage sth so badly that it loses all its value, pleasure, etc. किसी चीज़ को तबाह कर देना, बरबाद कर देना (कि वह बिलकुल बेकार हो जाए) *a ruined building* ○ *That one mistake ruined my chances of getting the job.* **2** to cause sb to lose all his/her money, hope of being successful, etc. किसी को उसके धन, सफलता की आशा, आदि से वंचित कर देना *The cost of the court case nearly ruined them.*

**ruin**[2] /ˈruːɪn ˈरूइन्/ *noun* **1** [U] the state of being destroyed or very badly damaged तबाही, बरबादी, विनाश *The city was in a state of ruin.* **2** [U] the cause or state of having lost all your money, hope of being successful, etc. धन की बरबादी, सफलता की आशा की समाप्ति आदि या उसका कारण *Many small companies are facing* ***financial ruin****.* **3** [C] the parts of a building that are left standing after it has been destroyed or badly damaged खंडहर, भग्नावशेष *the ruins of the ancient city of Hampi*

**IDM go to rack and ruin** ➪ **rack**[1] देखिए।

**in ruin(s)** badly damaged or destroyed बुरी तरह क्षतिग्रस्त *After the accident her life seemed to be in ruins.*

**ruinous** /ˈruːɪnəs ˈरूइनस्/ *adj.* causing serious problems, especially with money गंभीर समस्याएँ उत्पन्न करने वाला (विशेषतः रुपये-पैसे के मामले में)

**rule**[1] /ruːl रूल्/ *noun* **1** [C] an official statement that tells you what you must or must not do in a particular situation or when playing a game खेल आदि का नियम, क़ायदा *to* ***obey/break a rule*** ○ *It's* ***against the rules*** *to smoke in this area.* ○ *The company have strict* ***rules and regulations*** *governing employees' dress.* **2** [C] a piece of advice about what you should do in a particular situation स्थिति विशेष के लिए परामर्श, सलाह *When you run a marathon, the* ***golden rule*** *is—don't start too fast.* **3** [*sing.*] what is usual सामान्य स्थिति ***As a general rule****, women live longer than men.* ○ *I don't read much* ***as a rule****.* **4** [C] (in a language) a description of what is usual or correct भाषा में प्रयोग या शुद्धता संबंधी नियम *What is the rule for forming the past tense?* **5** [U] government; control सरकारी नियंत्रण, शासन *The country is* ***under*** *military* ***rule****.*

**IDM bend the rules** ➪ **bend**[1] देखिए।

**a rule of thumb** a simple piece of practical advice, not involving exact details or figures व्यवहारिक या कामचलाऊ तरीक़ा (सही ब्योरों या आँकड़ों से पुष्ट नहीं)

**work to rule** to follow the rules of your job in a very strict way in order to cause delay, as a form of protest against your employer or your working conditions (देरी करने की मंशा से) नियम के अनुसार (कम से कम) काम करना (मालिक या नियोजक से या नौकरी की परिस्थियों को लेकर विरोधस्वरूप) ➪ **work-to-rule** देखिए।

**rule**[2] /ruːl रूल्/ *verb* [I, T] **1 rule (over sb/sth)** to have the power over a country, group of people, etc. देश, जनता आदि पर शासन करना *Ashoka ruled over a vast empire.* ○ (*figurative*) *His whole life was ruled by his ambition to become President.* **2 rule (on sth); rule (in favour of/against sb/sth); rule (that)** to make an official decision औपचारिक रूप से निर्णय देना *The judge will rule on whether or not the case can go ahead.*

**PHRV rule sb/sth out** to say that sb/sth is not possible, cannot do sth, etc.; to prevent sth किसी मामले को अवैध ठहराना, खारिज कर देनाः किसी बात को न होने देना *The government has ruled out further increases in train fares next year.*

**ruler** /ˈruːlə(r) ˈरूल(र्)/ *noun* [C] **1** a person who rules a country, etc. देश आदि का शासक व्यक्ति **2** a straight piece of wood, plastic, etc. marked in **centimetres** or **inches**, that you use for measuring sth or for drawing straight lines (लकड़ी या प्लास्टिक का) पैमाना, पटरी, फ़ुटा, चपती, रेखनी

**ruling**[1] /ˈruːlɪŋ ˈरूलिङ्/ *adj.* (*only before a noun*) with the most power in an organization, country, etc. किसी संस्था, देश आदि में सबसे अधिक प्रभावशाली *the ruling political party*

**ruling**[2] /ˈruːlɪŋ ˈरूलिङ्/ *noun* [C] an official decision अधिकारिक निर्णय

**rum** /rʌm रम्/ *noun* [C, U] a strong alcoholic drink that is made from the juice of a plant from which sugar is made (**sugar cane**) गुड़ की शराब, रम

**rumble** /ˈrʌmbl ˈरम्बल्/ *verb* [I] to make a deep heavy sound गड़गड़ाना, घड़घड़ाना *I was so hungry that my stomach was rumbling.* ▸ **rumble** *noun* [*sing.*] गड़गड़ाहट, घड़घड़ाहट *a rumble of thunder*

**ruminant** /ˈruːmɪnənt ˈरूमिनन्ट्/ *noun* [C] any animal that brings back food from its stomach and **chews** it again पशु का जुगाली करना *Cows and sheep are both ruminants.* ▸ **ruminant** *adj.* जुगाली करने वाला

**rummage** /ˈrʌmɪdʒ ˈरमिज्/ *verb* [I] to move things and make them untidy while you are looking for sth कुछ ढूँढ़ते हुए चीज़ें इधर-उधर फैलाना *Nina rummaged through the drawer looking for the tin-opener.*

**rumour[1]** (*AmE* **rumor**) /ˈruːmə(r) ˈरूम(र्)/ *noun* [C, U] **(a) rumour (about/of sb/sth)** (a piece of) news or information that many people are talking about but that is possibly not true अफ़वाह, उड़ती खबर, जनप्रवाद (लोगों के बीच चर्चित ऐसी ख़बर या जानकारी जिसकी सचाई संदिग्ध हो) ***Rumour has it*** (= people are saying) *that Leena has resigned.* ○ *to confirm/deny a rumour* (= to say that it is true/not true)

**rumour[2]** (*AmE* **rumor**) /ˈruːmə(r) ˈरूम(र्)/ *verb* [T] (*usually passive*) **be rumoured** to be reported as a rumour and possible but may not be true अफ़वाह के रूप में प्रसारित ***It's widely rumoured that*** *they are getting married.* ○ *They are rumoured to be getting married.*

**rump** /rʌmp रम्प्/ *noun* [C] the back end of an animal जानवर का पुट्ठा, पृष्ठभाग *rump steak* (= meat from the rump)

**run[1]** /rʌn रन्/ *verb* [I, T] (*pres. part.* **running**; *pt* **ran** /ræn रैन्/; *pp* **run**) **1** [I, T] to move using your legs, going faster than a walk दौड़ना (टाँगों के सहारे, चलने से अधिक तेज़, गति करना) *I had to run to catch the bus.* ○ *I often* ***go running*** *in the evenings* (= as a hobby). ○ *I ran nearly ten kilometres this morning.* **2** [I, T] to move, or move sth, quickly in a particular direction विशेष दिशा में तेज़ गति से चलना (भागना) या किसी को चलाना (भगाना, दौड़ाना) *I've been running around after the kids all day.* ○ *The car ran off the road and hit a tree.* ○ *She ran her finger down the list of passengers.* **3** [I] to lead from one place to another; to be in a particular position एक स्थान से दूसरे स्थान तक लाना; स्थिति-विशेष में होना *The road runs along the side of a lake.* **4** [T] to organize or be in charge of sth; to provide a service किसी की व्यवस्था करना या दायित्व वहन करना; कोई सेवा उपलब्ध कराना *She runs a restaurant.* ○ *They run English courses all the year round.* **5** [I, T] to operate or function; to make sth do this (मशीन आदि का) चालू होना चलना या काम करना; चालू करना, चलाना *The engine is running very smoothly now.* ○ *We're running a new computer program today.* **6** [I] to operate at a particular time विशेष समय पर संचालित होना या चलना *All the trains are* ***running late*** *this morning.* ○ *We'd better hurry up—we're running behind schedule.* **7** [T] to use and pay for a vehicle वाहन का प्रयोग करना और उसके लिए ख़र्च करना *It costs a lot to run a car.* **8** [I] to continue for a time कुछ समय के लिए जारी रहना, चलना *My contract has two months left to run.* ○ *The play ran for nearly two years in a Kolkata theatre.* **9** [I, T] (used about water or other liquid) to flow; to make water flow (जल या अन्य द्रव) का बहना; को बहाना *When it's really cold, my nose runs.* ○ *I can hear a tap running somewhere.* ○ *to run a bath/a tap* **10** [I] **run with sth** to be covered with flowing water बहते पानी या द्रव से सन जाना *My face was running with sweat.* **11** [I] (used about the colour in material, etc.) to spread, for example when the material is washed (किसी चीज़ में लगे रंग का) फैल जाना (धोए जाने पर आदि) *Don't put that red shirt in the washing machine. It might run.* **12** [I] **run (for sth)** to be one of the people hoping to be chosen (**a candidate**) in an election किसी पद के लिए चुनाव में खड़ा होना *He's running for president.* **13** [T] to publish sth in a newspaper or magazine अख़बार या पत्रिका में कुछ प्रकाशित करना *'The Independent' is running a series of articles on pollution.* **14** [T] **run a test/check (on sth)** to do a test or check on sth किसी पर परीक्षण करना या किसी की जाँच करना *They're running checks on the power supply to see what the problem is.*

**IDM be running at** to be at a certain level किसी विशेष स्तर पर होना

**run for it** to run in order to escape बच निकलने के लिए भागना

> **NOTE** **Run** से बनने वाले अन्य मुहावरों के लिए संबंधित संज्ञाओं, विशेषणों आदि की प्रविष्टियाँ देखिए। जैसे **run in the family** की प्रविष्टि **family** में मिलेगी।

**PHR V run across sb/sth** to meet or find sb/sth by chance संयोग से किसी से भेंट हो जाना या किसी का पता लग जाना

**run after sb/sth** to try to catch sb/sth किसी को पकड़ने की कोशिश करना

**run away** to escape from somewhere कहीं से निकल भागना *He's run away from home.*

**run sb/sth down** **1** to hit a person or an animal with your vehicle वाहन से किसी व्यक्ति या पशु को चोट पहुँचाना या कुचल देना *She was run down by a bus.* **2** to criticize sb/sth किसी की आलोचना या निंदा करना *He's always running her down in front of other people.*

**run (sth) down** to stop functioning gradually; to make sth do this धीरे-धीरे काम करना बंद कर देना या करवा देना *Turn the lights off or you'll run the battery down.*

**run into sb** to meet sb by chance किसी से अचानक भेंट हो जाना

**run into sth** to have difficulties or a problem कठिनाइयों या समस्या का सामना करना *If you run into any problems, just let me know.*

**run (sth) into sb/sth** to hit sb/sth with a car, etc. कार आदि से किसी को टक्कर मारना *He ran his car into a brick wall.*

**run sth off** to copy sth, using a machine मशीन द्वारा नक़ल तैयार करना

**run off with sth** to take or steal sth कुछ ले जाना या चुरा लेना

**run out (of sth)** to finish your supply of sth; to come to an end किसी वस्तु की आपूर्ति समाप्त हो जाना; (अवधि आदि) समाप्त हो जाना *We've run out of coffee.* ○ *Time is running out.*

**run sb/sth over** to hit a person or an animal with your vehicle वाहन से व्यक्ति या वस्तु को चोट पहुँचाना या कुचल देना *The child was run over as he was crossing the road.*

**run through sth** to discuss or read sth quickly जल्दी-जल्दी किसी बात की चर्चा करना या कुछ पढ़ देना *She ran through the names on the list.*

**run²** /rʌn रन्/ *noun* **1** [C] an act of running on foot दौड़ *I* ***go for a*** *three-mile* ***run*** *every morning.* ○ *The prisoner tried to* ***make a run for it*** (= to escape on foot). **2** [C] a journey by car, train, etc. (कार, रेलगाड़ी आदि से) यात्रा *The bus driver was picking up kids on the school run.* **3** [*sing.*] a series of similar events or sth that continues for a very long time एक जैसी अनेक घटनाएँ या देर तक चलने वाली स्थिति, दौर, अवधि *We've had a run of bad luck recently.* **4** [*sing.*] **a run on sth** a sudden great demand for sth किसी वस्तु की अचानक भारी माँग **5** [C] a point in the games of base ball and cricket बेसबॉल और क्रिकेट में (स्कोर किया गया) रन

IDM **in the long run** ⇨ **long¹** देखिए।

**on the run** hiding or trying to escape from sb/sth कहीं पर छिपा होना या कहीं से भाग निकलने की कोशिश करना *The escaped prisoner is still on the run.*

**runaway¹** /ˈrʌnəweɪ रनअवे/ *adj.* **1** out of control बेक़ाबू, नियंत्रण-हीन *a runaway horse/car/train* **2** happening very easily सरलता से होने वाला *a runaway victory*

**runaway²** /ˈrʌnəweɪ रनअवे/ *noun* [C] a person, especially a child, who has left or escaped from somewhere भगोड़ा व्यक्ति (विशेषतः बच्चा), जो कहीं से चला जाए या भाग निकले ऐसा व्यक्ति

**run-down** *adj.* **1** (used about a building or place) in bad condition (भवन या स्थान) बुरी हालत में, जर्जर अवस्था में *a run-down block of flats* **2** very tired and not healthy बहुत थका हुआ और बीमार-सा

**rung¹** /rʌŋ रङ्/ *noun* [C] one of the bars that form the steps of a ladder सीढ़ी का डंडा जिस पर पैर रखते हैं

**rung²** ⇨ **ring²** का past participle रूप

**runner** /ˈrʌnə(r) ˈरन(र्)/ *noun* [C] **1** a person or an animal that runs, especially in a race दौड़ने वाला या धावक व्यक्ति या पशु (विशेषतः किसी दौड़ में) *a long-distance runner* **2** a person who takes guns, drugs, etc. illegally from one country to another बंदूक़ों, नशीली वस्तुओं आदि को अवैध रूप से एक देश से दूसरे देश में ले जाने वाला व्यक्ति

**runner-up** *noun* [C] (*pl.* **runners-up**) the person or team that finished second in a race or competition किसी दौड़ या प्रतियोगिता में द्वितीय स्थान पर आया व्यक्ति; उपविजेता

**running¹** /ˈrʌnɪŋ रनिङ्/ *noun* [U] **1** the action or sport of running दौड़ की क्रिया या खेल *How often do you* ***go running****?* ○ *running shoes* **2** the process of managing a business or other organization किसी व्यवसाय या संस्था का संचालन *She's not involved in the day-to-day running of the office.* ○ *the* ***running costs*** *of a car* (= petrol, insurance, repairs, etc.)

IDM **in/out of the running (for sth)** (*informal*) having/not having a good chance of getting or winning sth सफलता या कार्यसिद्धि की संभावना होना या न होना

**running²** /ˈrʌnɪŋ रनिङ्/ *adj.* **1** used after a number and a noun to say that sth has happened a number of times in the same way without a change लगातार, क्रम से (संख्यावाचक शब्द और संज्ञा के बाद यह बताने के लिए प्रयुक्त कि कोई बात एक ही तरह से अनेक बार घटित हुई है) *Our school has won the competition for four years running.* **2** (*only before a noun*) flowing or available from a tap (used about water) (पानी) टोंटी से बहता हुआ या वहाँ से प्राप्त *There is no running water in the cottage.* **3** (*only before a noun*) not stopping; continuous न रुकने वाला; निरंतर, अविराम *a running battle between two rival gangs*

**running commentary** *noun* [C] a spoken description of sth while it is happening (किसी चल रहे कार्यक्रम का) आँखों देखा हाल

**runny** /ˈrʌni ˈरनि/ *adj.* (*informal*) **1** containing more liquid than is usual or than you expected सामान्य स्तर पर आशा से अधिक तरल *runny jam* **2** (used about your eyes or nose) producing too much liquid (आँखें या नाक) बहुत अधिक पानी बहाती हुई, तरल *Their children always seem to have runny noses.*

**run-of-the-mill** *adj.* ordinary, with no special or interesting characteristics साधारण, मामूली (विशेष या रोचक गुणों से रहित) *a run-of-the-mill job*

**run-up** *noun* [*sing.*] **1** the period of time before a certain event किसी विशेष घटना से पहले की समयावधि *the run-up to the election* **2** (in sport) a run that people do in order to be going fast enough to do an action (खेल में) तेज़ी से गेंद फेंकने आदि की क्रिया से पहले की दौड़

**runway** /ˈrʌnweɪ ˈरन्वे/ *noun* [C] a long piece of ground with a hard surface where aircraft take off and land at an airport हवाई अड्डे पर विमान के उड़ान भरने और उतरने के लिए पट्टी या पथ; धावन-पथ, रनवे

**rupee** *noun* [C] (*pl.* **rupees**) the common name for currencies used in India, Pakistan, Sri Lanka, Nepal, etc. रुपया (भारत, पाकिस्तान, श्रीलंका, नेपाल आदि देशों की मुद्रा)

**rupture** /ˈrʌptʃə(r) ˈरप्च(र्)/ *noun* [C, U] **1** a sudden bursting or breaking अचानक हुआ विस्फोट, फटन या दरार **2** (*formal*) the sudden ending of good relations between two people or groups दो व्यक्तियों या वर्गों में एकाएक संबंध-विच्छेद, अच्छे संबंधों की समाप्ति ▶ **rupture** *verb* [I, T] फटन होना; (संबंध) विच्छेद करना *Her appendix ruptured and she had to have emergency surgery.* फटन होना; (संबंध) विच्छेद करना

**rural** /ˈrʊərəl ˈरुअरल्/ *adj.* connected with the country, not the town देहाती, ग्रामीण (न कि शहरी) ➪ **urban** और **rustic** देखिए।

**ruse** /ruːz रूज़्/ *noun* [C] a trick or clever plan चाल या छल; धोखा

**rush**[1] /rʌʃ रश्/ *verb* **1** [I, T] to move or do sth with great speed, often too fast प्रायः बहुत तेज़ी से चलना, गति करना या कोई काम करना *I rushed back home when I got the news.* ○ *Don't rush off—I want to talk to you.* ○ *We had to rush our meal.* **2** [T] to take sb/sth to a place very quickly तेज़ी से किसी को कहीं पहुँचाना *He suffered a heart attack and **was rushed to hospital**.* **3** [I, T] **rush (sb) (into sth/into doing sth)** to do sth or make sb do sth without thinking about it first किसी को बिना सोचे-समझे कुछ करने के लिए विवश करना या स्वयं ऐसा करना *Don't let yourself be rushed into marriage.* ○ *Don't rush me—I'm thinking!*

IDM **be rushed/run off your feet** ➪ **foot**[1] देखिए।

**rush**[2] /rʌʃ रश्/ *noun* **1** [*sing.*] a sudden quick movement रेल-पेल, हबड़-धबड़; एकाएक तेज़ हलचल *At the end of the match there was a rush for the exits.* ○ *I was so nervous, all my words came out **in a rush**.* **2** [*sing.*, U] a situation in which you are in a hurry and need to do things quickly जल्दबाज़ी की हालत *I can't stop now. I'm **in a terrible rush**.* ○ *Don't hurry your meal. There's no rush.* **3** [*sing.*] **a rush (on sth)** a time when many people try to get sth (किसी वस्तु की) भारी माँग का समय *There's been a rush to buy petrol before the price goes up.* **4** [*sing.*] a time when there is a lot of activity and people are very busy बहुत हलचल और व्यस्तता का समय *We'll leave early to avoid the rush.* **5** [C] a type of tall grass that grows near water तालाब आदि के पास उगने वाला एक प्रकार का पौधा; भादा, जलबेंत, नड़ या सरपत ➪ **plant** पर चित्र देखिए।

**rush hour** *noun* [C] the times each day when there is a lot of traffic because people are travelling to or from work प्रतिदिन भारी ट्रैफ़िक का समय *rush-hour traffic*

**rust** /rʌst रस्ट्/ *noun* [U] **1** a reddish-brown substance that forms on the surface of iron, etc., caused by the action of air and water (लोहे आदि पर लगा) जंग, मोरचा (वायु और जल की मिलन-क्रिया के कारण) ▶ **rust** *verb* [I, T] जंग खाना, मोरचा लगना; जंग खाने या मोरचा लगने का कारण बनना *Some parts of the car had rusted.* **2** a reddish-brown colour similar to the colour of rust जंग के रंग का, भूरा-लाल *a rust-colour sari*

**rustic** /ˈrʌstɪk ˈरस्टिक्/ *adj.* typical of the country or of country people; simple देहाती, ग्रामीण (क्षेत्र या व्यक्तियों से संबंधित); सीधा-सादा *The whole area is full of rustic charm.* ➪ **rural** और **urban** देखिए।

**rustle** /ˈrʌsl ˈरस्ल्/ *verb* [I, T] to make a sound like dry leaves or paper moving सरसराना, फड़फड़ाना (सूखे पत्तों या काग़ज़ों में हरकत होने की-सी आवाज़ पैदा करना) *There was a rustling noise in the bushes.* ▶ **rustle** *noun* [*sing.*] सरसराहट, खरखराहट

PHR V **rustle sth up (for sb)** (*informal*) to make or find sth quickly for sb and without planning किसी के लिए बिना तैयारी के और तुरंत कोई वस्तु बना देना या प्राप्त कर लेना *I can rustle you up a quick snack.*

**rusty** /ˈrʌsti ˈरस्टि/ *adj.* **1** (used about metal objects) covered with a brownish substance (**rust**) as a result of being in contact with water and air (धातु-निर्मित वस्तुएँ) ज़ंग खाई हुई; मोरचेदार *rusty tins* **2** (used about a skill) not as good as it was because you have not used it for a long time (कोई कौशल) अप्रयोग या अभ्यास के कारण विस्मृतप्राय *My French is rather rusty.*

**rut** /rʌt रट्/ *noun* [C] a deep track that a wheel makes in soft ground (मुलायम भूमि पर) पहियों की लीक **IDM** **be in a rut** to have a boring way of life that is difficult to change उकताहट भरा या नीरस जीवन बिताना, जीवन में नीरसता या उकताहट आ जाना

**ruthless** /ˈru:θləs ˈरूथ्लस्/ *adj.* (used about people and their behaviour) hard and cruel; determined to get what you want and showing no pity to others (व्यक्ति और उनका आचरण) कठोर और निर्मम; इच्छापूर्ति पर अटल और दूसरों के प्रति असंवेदनशील *a ruthless dictator* ▶ **ruthlessly** *adv.* निर्ममतापूर्वक ▶ **ruthlessness** *noun* [U] निर्ममता

**rye** /raɪ राइ/ *noun* [U] a plant that is grown in colder countries for its grain, which is used to make flour and also an alcoholic drink (**whisky**) राई (ठंडे देशों में उगने वाला पौधा जिसके दाने से आहार का आटा और व्हिस्की, शराब बनते हैं) ➪ **cereal** पर चित्र देखिए।

# S s

**S, s**[1] /es एस्/ *noun* [C, U] (*pl.* **S's; s's** /ˈesɪz ˈएसिज़्/) the nineteenth letter of the English alphabet अंग्रेज़ी वर्णमाला का उन्नीसवाँ अक्षर *'Sam' begins with an 'S'.*

**S**[2] *abbr.* **1** small (size) छोटा (आकार में) **2** (*AmE* **So**) south(ern) दक्षिण का, दक्षिणी *S Delhi*

**sabbath** /ˈsæbəθ ˈसैबथ्/ **the Sabbath** *noun* [*sing.*] the day of the week for rest and prayer in certain religions (Sunday for Christians, Saturday for Jews) कुछ धर्मों में साप्ताहिक विश्राम और ईश्वर-प्रार्थना का दिन (ईसाईयों के लिए रविवार, यहूदियों के लिए शनिवार)

**sabotage** /ˈsæbətɑːʒ ˈसैबटाश़्/ *noun* [U] damage that is done on purpose and secretly in order to prevent an enemy or a competitor being successful, for example by destroying machinery, roads, bridges, etc. अंतर्ध्वंस; जान-बूझ कर और गुप्त रूप से वाहन, मशीनरी आदि को पहुँचाई गई क्षति (ताकि शत्रु या प्रतिस्पर्धी को उसका लाभ न मिल सके), उद्देश्यपूर्ण ध्वंस-लीला, तोड़-फोड़ *industrial/economic/military sabotage* ▶ **sabotage** *verb* [T] जान-बूझ कर तोड़-फोड़ करना

**saccharin** /ˈsækərɪn ˈसैकरिन्/ *noun* [U] a very sweet chemical substance that can be used instead of sugar सैकरीन; चीनी के स्थान पर प्रयुक्त एक मीठा रासायनिक पदार्थ

**sachet** /ˈsæʃeɪ ˈसैशे/ *noun* [C] a small plastic or paper packet that contains a small amount of liquid or powder प्लास्टिक या काग़ज़ का छोटा पैकेट (जिसमें थोड़ी मात्रा में कोई द्रव या पाउडर भरा हो) *a sachet of shampoo/sugar/coffee*

**sack**[1] /sæk सैक्/ *noun* [C] a large bag made from a rough heavy material, paper or plastic, used for carrying or storing things बोरा, बोरी (किसी खुरदरी मोटी चीज़, काग़ज़ या प्लास्टिक से निर्मित तथा समान को ले जाने या उसे इकट्ठा करने के लिए प्रयुक्त) *sacks of flour/potatoes*

IDM **get the sack** (*BrE*) to be told by your employer that you can no longer continue working for him/her (usually because you have done sth wrong) किसी कर्मचारी का नौकरी से बर्ख़ास्त होना (ग़लत काम करने के कारण) *Tarun got the sack for poor work.*

**give sb the sack** (*BrE*) to tell an employee that he/she can no longer continue working for you (because of bad work, behaviour, etc.) किसी कर्मचारी को नौकरी से बर्ख़ास्त करना (अक्षमता, अनुचित व्यवहार आदि के कारण) *Tarun's work wasn't good enough and he was given the sack.*

**sack**[2] /sæk सैक्/ (*AmE* **fire**) *verb* [T] to tell an employee that he/she can no longer work for you (because of bad work, bad behaviour, etc.) किसी कर्मचारी को नौकरी से बर्ख़ास्त करना (अक्षमता, अनुचित आचरण आदि के कारण) *Her boss has threatened to sack her if she's late again.*

**sackcloth** /ˈsækklɒθ ˈसैक्क्लॉथ्/ (*also* **sacking** /ˈsækɪŋ ˈसैकिङ्/) *noun* [U] a rough cloth that is used for making large bags (**sacks**) टाट (जिससे बोरियाँ बनती हैं)

**sacred** /ˈseɪkrɪd ˈसेक्रिड्/ *adj.* **1** connected with God, a god or religion ईश्वर; किसी देवता या धर्म से संबंधित *The Koran is the sacred book of Muslims.* **2** too important and special to be changed or harmed पवित्र, पावन (इतना महत्त्वपूर्ण या विशिष्ट कि उसमें कोई परिवर्तन या क्षति न की जा सके) *a sacred tradition*

**sacrifice**[1] /ˈsækrɪfaɪs ˈसैक्रिफ़ाइस्/ *noun* [U, C] **1** giving up sth that is important or valuable to you in order to get or do sth that seems more important; sth that you give up in this way (अधिक बड़ी उपलब्धि के लिए) किसी विशेष या मूल्यवान वस्तु का त्याग; इस प्रकार किया गया कुछ त्याग *If we're going to have a holiday this year, we'll have to **make** some sacrifices.* **2 sacrifice (to sb)** the act of offering sth to a god, especially an animal that has been killed in a special way; an animal, etc. that is offered in this way किसी देवता को बलि चढ़ाई गई कोई वस्तु (विशेषतः विशेष रीति से वध किया गया पशु), चढ़ावा; बलि चढ़ाया गया पशु

**sacrifice**[2] /ˈsækrɪfaɪs ˈसैक्रिफ़ाइस्/ *verb* **1** [T] **sacrifice sth (for sb/sth)** to give up sth that is important or valuable to you in order to get or do sth that seems more important (अधिक बड़ी उपलब्धि के लिए) किसी विशेष या मूल्यवान वस्तु का त्याग करना *She is not willing to sacrifice her career in order to have children.* **2** [I, T] to kill an animal and offer it to a god, in order to please the god किसी देवता को पशु की बलि चढ़ाना (उसे प्रसन्न करने के लिए)

**sacrilege** /ˈsækrəlɪdʒ ˈसैक्रलिज्/ *noun* [U, *sing.*] treating a religious object or place without the respect that it deserves पवित्र वस्तु या स्थान का अपमान; अपवित्रीकरण

**sad** /sæd सैड्/ *adj.* (**sadder; saddest**) **1 sad (to do sth); sad (that...)** unhappy or causing sb to feel unhappy उदास या उदास करने वाला *That's one of the saddest stories I've ever heard!* ○ *a sad poem/song/film* **2** bad or unacceptable बुरा, ख़राब, दुखद *It's a sad state of affairs when your best friend doesn't trust you.* ▶ **sadden** /ˈsædn ˈसैड्न्/ *verb* [T] (*formal*) दुखी या उदास करना *The news of your father's death saddened me greatly.* ▶ **sadness** *noun* [C, U] उदासी, दुख

**saddle** /ˈsædl ˈसैड्ल्/ *noun* [C] **1** a seat, usually made of leather, that you put on a horse so that you can ride it (प्रायः चमड़े से बनी) घोड़े की ज़ीन, काठी (सवार के बैठने के लिए) ⇨ **horse** पर चित्र देखिए। **2** a seat on a bicycle or motorbike साइकिल या मोटरसाइकिल की सीट ⇨ **bicycle** पर चित्र देखिए। ▶ **saddle** *verb* [T] ज़ीन या काठी कसना

**PHR V** **saddle sb with sth** to give sb a responsibility or task that he/she does not want किसी को कोई दायित्व या काम सौंपना, उसकी इच्छा के विपरीत

**sadism** /ˈseɪdɪzəm ˈसेडिज़म्/ *noun* [U] getting pleasure, especially sexual pleasure, from hurting other people दूसरे को यातना देकर प्राप्त सुख, विशेषतः यौन-सुख ⇨ **masochism** देखिए।

**sadist** /ˈseɪdɪst ˈसेडिस्ट्/ *noun* [C] a person who gets pleasure, especially sexual pleasure, from hurting other people दूसरे को यातना देकर सुख, विशेषतः यौन-सुख प्राप्त करने वाला व्यक्ति; परपीड़क ▶ **sadistic** /səˈdɪstɪk सˈडिस्टिक्/ *adj.* परपीड़नात्मक ▶ **sadistically** /səˈdɪstɪkli सˈडिस्टिक्लि/ *adv.* परपीड़तपूर्वक

**sadly** /ˈsædli ˈसैड्लि/ *adv.* **1** unfortunately दुर्भाग्य से; दुख की बात है कि *Sadly, after eight years of marriage they had grown apart.* **2** in a way that shows unhappiness दुखद ढंग से **3** in a way that is wrong ग़लत ढंग से, अफ़सोस के साथ *If you think that I've forgotten what you did, you're **sadly mistaken**.*

**sae** /ˌes eɪ ˈiː ˌएस् एˈई/ *abbr.* stamped addressed envelope टिकट-लगा और पता-लिखा लिफ़ाफ़ा

**safari** /səˈfɑːri सˈफ़ारि/ *noun* [C, U] (*pl.* **safaris**) a trip to see or hunt wild animals, especially in East Africa वन्य पशु दर्शन या आखेट के लिए सैर (विशेषतः पूर्वी अफ़्रीक़ा में) *to be/go **on safari***

**safe**[1] /seɪf सेफ़्/ *adj.* **1** (*not before a noun*) **safe (from sb/sth)** free from danger; not able to be hurt जिसे कोई ख़तरा न हो, जिसे क्षति न पहुँचाई जा सके; सुरक्षित *She didn't **feel safe** in the house on her own.* ○ *Keep the papers where they will be safe from fire.* **2 safe (to do sth); safe (for sb)** not likely to cause danger, harm or risk जो किसी के लिए ख़तरा, हानिप्रद न हो; निरापद *Don't sit on that chair, it isn't safe.* ○ *She's a very safe driver.* ○ *I think **it's safe to say** that the situation is unlikely to change for sometime.* **3** (*not before a noun* ) not hurt, damaged or lost जो चोटग्रस्त, क्षतिग्रस्त या गुमशुदा न हो; सही-सलामत, सकुशल *After the accident he checked that all the passengers were safe.* ○ *After five days the child was found, **safe and sound**.* **4** based on good evidence सशक्त साक्ष्य पर आधारित; विश्वस्त, विश्वसनीय *a safe verdict* ▶ **safely** *adv.* कुशलपूर्वक *I rang my parents to tell them I had arrived safely.*

**IDM** **in safe hands** with sb who will take good care of you सुरक्षित हाथों में

**on the safe side** not taking risks; being very careful ख़तरा मोल न लेते हुए; बहुत सावधानी के साथ

**safe**[2] /seɪf सेफ़्/ *noun* [C] a strong metal box or cupboard with a special lock that is used for keeping money, jewellery, documents, etc. in (पैसा, गहना, दस्तावेज़ आदि रखने की) तिजोरी, सेफ़ (मज़बूत धातु निर्मित और विशेष ताले वाला बक्सा या अलमारी)

**safeguard** /ˈseɪfɡɑːd ˈसेफ़्गाड्/ *noun* [C] **a safeguard (against sb/sth)** something that protects against possible dangers ▶ **safeguard** *verb* [T] संभावित ख़तरों से सुरक्षा देने वाली वस्तु *to safeguard sb's interests/rights/privacy*

**safety** /ˈseɪfti ˈसेफ़्टि/ *noun* [U] the state of being safe; not being dangerous or in danger सुरक्षित रहने की स्थिति, सुरक्षा; (दूसरों के लिए) ख़तरनाक या (स्वयं) ख़तरे में या संकटग्रस्त न होना ***road safety*** (= the prevention of road accidents) ○ *New **safety measures** have been introduced on trains.*

**safety belt** = **seat belt**

**safety net** *noun* [C] **1** a net that is placed to catch sb who is performing high above the ground if he/she falls बचाव-जाल, बचाव करने वाला जाल (ऊँचाई पर प्रदर्शन करते कलाकार के नीचे गिर पड़ने की स्थिति में; सेफ़्टी नेट **2** an arrangement that helps to prevent disaster (usually with money) if sth goes wrong घोर आकस्मिक संकट (विशेषतः धन-संबंधित) से बचाव की व्यवस्था

**safety pin** *noun* [C] a metal pin with a point that is bent back towards the head, which is covered so that it cannot be dangerous सेफ़्टीपिन

**safety valve** *noun* [C] a device in a machine that allows steam, gas, etc. to escape if the pressure becomes too great सेफ़्टी वाल्व; मशीन को सुरक्षा देने वाला उपकरण (जो भाप, गैस आदि का दबाव बढ़ने पर उसे बाहर जाने देता है)

**saffron** /ˈsæfrən ˈसैफ़्रन्/ *noun* [U] **1** a bright yellow powder from a flower (**crocus**), that is used in cooking to give colour to food केसर, जाफ़रान (केसर के पौधे) से प्राप्त चमकीला पीला पाउडर जिसके प्रयोग से खाद्य पदार्थों में रंग आ जाता है) **2** a bright orange-yellow colour नारंगी-पीला रंग, केसरिया रंग ▶ **saffron** *adj.* नारंगी-पीला, केसरिया, जाफ़रानी

**sag** /sæg सैग्/ *verb* [I] (**sagging; sagged**) to hang or to bend down, especially in the middle लटक या झुक जाना (विशेषतः बीच में से)

**saga** /ˈsɑːgə ˈसागा/ *noun* [C] a very long story; a long series of events बहुत लंबी कहानी; घटनाओं की लंबी शृंखला

**Sagittarius** /ˌsædʒɪˈteəriəs ˌसैजिˈटेअरिअस्/ *noun* [U] the ninth sign of the **zodiac**, the Archer धनु राशि; राशिचक्र की नौवीं राशि

**sago** /ˈseɪgəʊ ˈसेगो/ *noun* [U] hard white grains made from the soft inside of a type of tree (**palm**), often cooked with milk to make a sweet dish साबूदाना, सागू *sago pudding*

**said** ➪ **say**[1] का past tense और past participle रूप

**sail**[1] /seɪl सेल्/ *verb* **1** [I] (used about a boat or ship and the people on it) to travel on water in a ship or boat of any type (नाव या जहाज़ और उसकी सवारियों का) नदी या समुद्र में जल में यात्रा करना *I stood at the window and watched the ships sailing by.* ○ *to sail round the world* **2** [I, T] to travel in and control a boat with sails, especially as a sport पाल वाली नाव में यात्रा करना (विशेषतः एक खेल के रूप में) *My father is teaching me to sail.* ○ *I've never sailed this kind of yacht before.*

NOTE मौज-मस्ती के लिए नौका-विहार करने को **go sailing** कहते हैं।

**3** [I] to begin a journey on water नदी या समुद्र यात्रा आरंभ करना *When does the ship sail?* ○ *We sail for Singapore at six o'clock tomorrow morning.* **4** [I] to move somewhere quickly in a smooth or proud way किसी स्थान पर वेग पूर्वक सहज भाव से या अकड़ते हुए जाना या पहुँचाना *The ball sailed over the fence and into the neighbour's garden.* ○ *Madhuri sailed into the room, completely ignoring all of us.*

IDM **sail through (sth)** to pass a test or exam easily आसानी से कोई परीक्षा पास कर लेना या जाँच में खरा उतरना

**sail**[2] /seɪl सेल्/ *noun* **1** [C] a large piece of strong material that is fixed onto a ship or boat. The wind blows against the sail and moves the ship along जहाज़ या नाव का पाल (जिससे हवा टकराती है और जहाज़ या नाव को चलाती है) **2** [*sing.*] a trip on water in a ship or boat with a sail पाल वाली नाव या जहाज़ पर सैर **3** [C] any of the long parts that the wind moves round that are fixed to a building (**windmill**) पवनचक्की का फट्टा (जिसे हवा घुमाती है)

IDM **set sail** ➪ **set**[1] देखिए।

**sailboard** /ˈseɪlbɔːd ˈसेलबॉड्/ = **windsurfer 1**

**sailing** /ˈseɪlɪŋ ˈसेलिङ्/ *noun* [U] the sport of being in, and controlling, small boats with sails पाल वाली नौका को चलाने का खेल (उसमें स्वयं बैठकर); पाल नौकायन खेल

**sailing boat** (*AmE* **sailboat** /ˈseɪlbəʊt ˈसेलबोट्/) *noun* [C] a boat with a sail or sails पाल या पालों वाली नाव

**sailor** /ˈseɪlə(r) ˈसेल(र्)/ *noun* [C] a person who works on a ship or a person who sails a boat नाविक (जहाज़ का कर्मचारी या नाव को चलाने वाला)

**saint** /seɪnt; sənt सेन्ट्; सन्ट्/ *noun* [C] **1** a very good or religious person who is given special respect after death by the Christian church पवित्रात्मा, संत, सेंट; (कोई उत्कृष्ट या धार्मिक व्यक्ति जिसे ईसाई चर्चा उसकी मृत्यु के बाद विशेष सम्मान देता है)

NOTE जब **saint** शब्द को उपाधि के रूप में प्रयुक्त किया जाता है तो इसे बड़े अक्षर से लिखा जाता है—*Saint Patrick.* स्थानों, चर्चों आदि के नामों में सामान्यतः संक्षित रूप **St** का प्रयोग होता है—*St Andrew's Church.* नामों से पहले **saint** का उच्चारण /sənt सन्ट्/ होता है।

**2** a very good, kind person श्रेष्ठ, दयालु व्यक्ति; महात्मा

**sake** /seɪk सेक्/ *noun* [C]

IDM **for Christ's/God's/goodness'/Heaven's/pity's, etc. sake** (*spoken*) used to emphasize that it is important to do sth or to show that you are annoyed किसी काम को अवश्य करने पर बल देने या नाराज़गी व्यक्त करने के लिए प्रयुक्त *For goodness' sake, hurry up!* ○ *Why have you taken so long, for God's sake?* NOTE **For God's sake** की अभिव्यक्ति और विशेषतः **for Christ's sake** काफ़ी वज़नदार है जिनके प्रयोग से कुछ लोग नाराज़ भी हो सकते हैं।

**for the sake of sb/sth; for sb's/sth's sake in order to help sb/sth** *is order to help sb/sth* किसी की सहायता करने के लिए *Don't go to any trouble for my sake.* ○ *They only stayed together for the sake of their children/for their children's sake.*

**for the sake of sth/of doing sth** in order to get or keep sth; for the purpose of sth किसी वस्तु को प्राप्त करने या सुरक्षित रखने के लिए; किसी उद्देश्य से *She gave up her job for the sake of her health.*

**salad** /ˈsæləd ˈसैलड्/ *noun* [C, U] a mixture of vegetables, usually not cooked, that you often eat together with other foods सलाद (मिली-जुली सब्ज़ियाँ प्रायः कच्ची, जो भोजन के साथ खाई जाती हैं) *All main courses are served with chips or salad.*

**salamander** /ˈsæləmændə(r) ˈसैलमैन्ड(र्)/ *noun* [C] a small thin animal with four legs and a long tail, of the type that lives both on land and in water (**amphibian**). Salamanders often have bright colours on their skin सरट, गिरगिट (जल और स्थल दोनों पर रहने वाला छोटा प्राणी जिसकी खाल प्रायः चमकीली होती है) ➪ **lizard** देखिए तथा **amphibian** पर चित्र भी देखिए।

**salary** /ˈsæləri ˈसैलरि/ *noun* [C, U] (*pl.* **salaries**) the money that a person receives (usually every month) for the work he/she has done तनख़्वाह, वेतन (काम के लिए प्रायः प्रति माह मिलने वाली राशि) *My salary is paid directly into my bank account.* ○ *a high/low salary* ➪ **pay**[2] पर नोट देखिए।

**sale** /seɪl सेल्/ *noun* **1** [C, U] the action of selling or being sold; the occasion when sth is sold बिक्री, विक्रय (वस्तुओं को बेचना या वस्तुओं का बिकना); बिक्री का अवसर या आयोजन *The sale of alcohol to any one under the age of 25 is forbidden.* ○ *a sale of used toys* **2 sales** [*pl.*] the number of items sold बिक्री की मात्रा (बेची गई वस्तुओं की तादाद) *Sales of personal computers have increased rapidly.* ○ *The company reported excellent sales figures.* **3 sales** [U] (*also* **sales department**) the part of a company that deals with selling its products किसी कंपनी का बिक्री विभाग *Prachi works in sales/ in the sales department.* ○ *a sales representative/ sales rep* **4** [C] a time when shops sell things at prices that are lower than usual वस्तुओं की सस्ते दामों पर बिक्री *The sale starts on December 28th.* ○ *I got several bargains **in the sales**.*

IDM **for sale** offered for sb to buy बिकाऊ *This painting is not for sale.* ○ *Our neighbours have **put** their house **up for sale**.*

**on sale 1** available for sb to buy, especially in shops ख़रीदने के लिए उपलब्ध (विशेषतः दुकानों पर) *This week's edition is on sale now at your local news agents.* **2** (*AmE*) offered at a lower price than usual सामान्य दामों से सस्ते दामों पर उपलब्ध

**sales clerk** (*also* **clerk**) (*AmE*) = **shop assistant**

**salesman** /ˈseɪlzmən ˈसेल्ज़्मन्/ *noun* [C] (*pl.* **-men** /-men -मेन्/) a man whose job is selling things to people सामान बेचने के लिए नियुक्त पुरुष; सेल्समैन

**salesperson** /ˈseɪlzpɜːsn ˈसेल्ज़्पसन्/ *noun* [C] (*pl.* **salespeople** /ˈseɪlzpiːpl ˈसेल्ज़्पीपल्/) a person whose job is selling things to people, especially in a shop सामान बेचने के लिए नियुक्त व्यक्ति (विशेषतः दुकान पर)

**saleswoman** /ˈseɪlzwʊmən ˈसेल्ज़्वुमन्/ *noun* [C] (*pl.* **-women** /-wɪmɪn -विमिन्/) a woman whose job is selling things to people सामान बेचने के लिए नियुक्त महिला; सेल्सवुमन

**salient** /ˈseɪliənt ˈसेलिअन्ट्/ *adj.* (*only before a noun*) most important or noticeable सर्वाधिक महत्त्वपूर्ण या सबसे अधिक दिखाई पड़ने वाला

**saline** /ˈseɪlaɪn ˈसेलाइन्/ *adj.* (*technical*) containing salt रासायनिक नमक से भरा हुआ; लवणीय *a saline solution*

**saliva** /səˈlaɪvə सˈलाइव़ा/ *noun* [U] the liquid that is produced in the mouth लार, लाला ➪ **spit** देखिए।

**sallow** /ˈsæləʊ ˈसैलो/ *adj.* (used about a person's skin or face) having a slightly yellow colour that does not look healthy (व्यक्ति की त्वचा या चेहरा) अस्वस्थता का सूचक पीलापन लिए हुए; पीला, फीका

**salmon** /ˈsæmən ˈसैमन्/ *noun* [C, U] (*pl.* **salmon**) a large fish with silver skin and pink meat that we eat सामन मछली (बड़ी मछली जिसकी त्वचा रुपहली तथा मांस गुलाबी होता है और खाया जाता है) *smoked salmon*

**salmonella** /ˌsælməˈnelə ˌसैलमˈनेला/ *noun* [U] a type of bacteria that causes food poisoning भोजन को विषाक्त कर देने वाला बैक्टीरिया

**salon** /ˈsælɒn ˈसैलॉन्/ *noun* [C] a shop where you can have beauty or hair treatment or where you can buy expensive clothes सौंदर्य प्रसाधन या केशचर्या या महँगे कपड़े बेचने की दुकान; सैलून

**saloon** /səˈluːn सˈलून्/ (*AmE* **sedan**) *noun* [C] a car with a fixed roof and a separate area (**boot**) for luggage कार जिसकी छत स्थिर सामान रखने की जगह अलग से बनी होती है; सैलून कार, सेडान

**salt**[1] /sɔːlt (*BrE*) sɒlt सॉल्ट्/ *noun* **1** [U] a common white substance that is found in sea water and the earth. Salt is used in cooking for flavouring food नमक (भोजन में और स्वाद वर्धन के लिए प्रयुक्त) *Season with **salt and pepper**.* ○ *Add a pinch* (= a small amount) *of salt.* **2** [C] (in chemistry) a chemical mixture (**compound**) of a metal and an acid (रसायनशास्त्र में) धातु और अम्ल का यौगिक; लवण, साल्ट ▸ **salt** *adj.* नमकीन, खारा *salt water*

IDM **rub salt into the wound/sb's wounds** ➪ **rub** देखिए।

**take sth with a pinch of salt** ➪ **pinch**[2] देखिए।

**salt²** /sɔːlt सॉल्ट्/ *verb* [T] (*usually passive*) to put salt on or in sth किसी वस्तु में या पर नमक डालना *salted peanuts*

**saltwater** /ˈsɔːltwɔːtə(r) ˈसॉल्ट्वॉट(र्)/ *adj.* living in the sea समुद्र में रहने वाला, समुद्री *a saltwater fish* ➪ **freshwater** देखिए।

**salty** /ˈsɒlti ˈसॉल्टि/ *adj.* having the taste of or containing salt नमक के स्वाद वाला या नमक से भरा हुआ; नमकीन, खारा *I didn't like the meat, it was too salty.*

**salute** /səˈluːt सˈलूट्/ *noun* [C] **1** an action that a soldier, etc. does to show respect, by holding his/her hand to the forehead सैनिक आदि द्वारा अभिवादन; सैल्यूट (हाथ को माथे पर ले जाकर किया गया सम्मान-प्रदर्शन), सलामी *to give a salute* **2** something that shows respect for sb सम्मानद्योतक वस्तु या कार्य *The next programme is **a salute to** all the freedom fighters of India.* ▸ **salute** *verb* [I, T] सैल्यूट मारना, अभिवादन करना *The soldiers saluted as they marched past the general.*

**salvage¹** /ˈsælvɪdʒ ˈसैल्व्रिज्/ *noun* [U] saving things that have been or are likely to be lost or damaged, especially in an accident or a disaster; the things that are saved सामान को नष्ट या क्षतिग्रस्त होने से बचाने की क्रिया (विशेषतः दुर्घटना या घोर संकट के समय); भ्रंशोद्धार, बचाया हुआ सामान *a salvage operation/company/team*

**salvage²** /ˈsælvɪdʒ ˈसैल्व्रिज्/ *verb* [T] **salvage sth (from sth)** to manage to rescue sth from being lost or damaged; to rescue sth or a situation from disaster किसी को नष्ट या क्षतिग्रस्त होने से बचाने की व्यवस्था करना; किसी वस्तु या स्थिति को संकटग्रस्त होने से बचाना *They salvaged as much as they could from the house after the fire.*

**salvation** /sælˈveɪʃn सैल्ˈव्रेशन्/ *noun* **1** [U] (in the Christian religion) being saved from the power of evil (ईसाई धर्म में) शैतान के प्रभाव से बचाव **2** [U, *sing.*] a thing or person that rescues sb/sth from danger, disaster, etc. संकटमोचक वस्तु या व्यक्ति

**sambar** (*also* **sambhar**) *noun* [U] a kind of soup from the southern regions of India that is prepared by using **lentils**, vegetables and spices साँबर

**same** /seɪm सेम्/ *adj., adv., pronoun* **1 the same... (as sb/sth); the same... that...** not different, not another or other; exactly the one or ones that you have mentioned before अलग नहीं, कोई और या अन्य नहीं; वही एकदम पहले वाला *My brother and I had the same teacher at school.* ○ *This one looks **exactly the same** as that one.* **2 the same... (as sb/sth); the same... that...** exactly like the one already mentioned पूर्व निदिष्ट के पूर्णतया समान *I wouldn't buy the same car again* (= the same model of car). ○ *We treat all the children in the class the same.*

> **NOTE** **A same...** प्रयोग मान्य नहीं है। इस अभिप्राय को व्यक्त करने के लिए **the same sort of** का प्रयोग होता है—*I'd like the same sort of job as my father.*

**IDM** **all/just the same** in spite of this/that; anyway इस या उस के बावजूद; चाहे जो भी हो हर हालत में *I understand what you're saying. All the same, I don't agree with you.* ○ *I don't need to borrow any money but thanks all the same for offering.*

**at the same time 1** together; at one time एक साथ; एक ही समय पर *I can't think about more than one thing at the same time.* **2** on the other hand; however इसके विपरीत; तथापि *It's a very good idea but at the same time it's rather risky.*

**much the same** ➪ **much** देखिए।

**on the same wavelength** able to understand sb because you have similar ideas and opinions (विचारों में समानता के कारण) दूसरे को समझने में समर्थ

**(the) same again** (*spoken*) a request to be served or given the same drink as before पहले वाला ही चाहिए (मदिरापान के संदर्भ में अनुरोध)

**same here** (*spoken*) the same thing is also true for me वही बात मेरे साथ भी; 'मैं भी' *'I'm bored.' 'Same here.'*

**(the) same to you** (*spoken*) used as an answer when sb says sth rude to you or wishes you sth अशिष्ट शब्द या अभिवादन के उत्तर में प्रयुक्त *'Best of luck!' 'Same to you!'* ○ *'Have a good weekend.' 'The same to you.'*

**samosa** *noun* [C] a popular triangular-shaped fried **snack** stuffed with spiced vegetables or meat समोसा

**sample** /ˈsɑːmpl ˈसाम्पल्/ *noun* [C] a small number or amount of sb/sth that is looked at, tested, examined, etc. to find out what the rest is like नमूना (व्यक्तियों की थोड़ी संख्या या वस्तुओं की थोड़ी मात्रा जिसकी जाँच के आधार पर शेष व्यक्ति या वस्तु के विषय में पता चले कि वे कैसे या कैसी हैं) *a **random sample** of students/clients* ○ *to take a blood sample* ○ *a free sample of shampoo* ✪ पर्याय **specimen** ▸ **sample** *verb* [T] नमूना लेना या परीक्षण करना *I got a chance to sample the local food when I was in Goa.*

**sanatorium** /ˌsænəˈtɔːriəm ˌसैनˈटॉरिअम्/ (*AmE* **sanitarium**) *noun* [C] a type of hospital where patients who need a long period of treatment for an illness can stay आरोग्य-निवास; स्वास्थ्य-सुधार केंद्र, सैनिटोरियम (लंबी बीमारी से पीड़ित रोगियों के उपचार और स्वास्थ्य-लाभ के लिए अस्पताल जैसा स्थान)

**sanction[1]** /ˈsæŋkʃn ˈसैङ्क्शन्/ *noun* **1** [C, *usually pl.*] **sanctions (against sb)** an official order that limits business, contact, etc. with a particular country, in order to make it do sth, such as obeying international law किसी देश से व्यापार, संपर्क आदि पर आधिकारिक दंडात्मक प्रतिबंध (उसे अंतरराष्ट्रीय क़ानून के पालन आदि के लिए बाध्य करने हेतु) *Economic sanctions were imposed on any country that refused to sign the agreement.* **2** [U] (*formal*) official permission to do or change sth आधिकारिक अनुमति, मंज़ूरी, संस्वीकृति (किसी काम की) **3** [C] a punishment for breaking a rule or law (नियम या क़ानून के भंग के लिए) दंड

**sanction[2]** /ˈsæŋkʃn ˈसैङ्क्शन्/ *verb* [T] to give official permission for sth (किसी बात के लिए) आधिकारिक अनुमति, मंज़ूरी या संस्वीकृति देना

**sanctity** /ˈsæŋktəti ˈसैङ्क्टटि/ *noun* [U] **1 sanctity (of sth)** the quality of being important enough to make it worth protecting and preserving अत्यंत महत्त्वपूर्ण होने के कारण सुरक्षा एवं संरक्षण के योग्य होने की अवस्था या परिस्थिति *the sanctity of marriage* **2** the state of being holy पवित्रता की अवस्था *a life of sanctity, like that of Kabir*

**sanctuary** /ˈsæŋktʃuəri ˈसैङ्क्चुअरि/ *noun* (*pl.* **sanctuaries**) **1** [C] a place where birds or animals are protected from being hunted पशु-पक्षियों के सुरक्षित विचरण का स्थान; अभयारण्य **2** [C, U] a place where sb can be safe from enemies, the police, etc. सुरक्षित शरणस्थल (शत्रु, पुलिस आदि की पहुँच से परे)

**sand** /sænd सैन्ड्/ *noun* **1** [U] a powder consisting of very small grains of rock, found in deserts and on beaches बालू, रेत **2 the sands** [*pl.*] a large area of sand बड़ा रेतीला इलाक़ा

**sandal** /ˈsændl ˈसैन्ड्ल्/ *noun* [C] a type of light, open shoe that people wear when the weather is warm सैंडल (पैरों में पहनने की विशेष प्रकार की चप्पल या जूता)

**sandalwood** /ˈsændlwʊd ˈसैन्ड्ल्वुड्/ *noun* [U] a type of light coloured hard wood of an evergreen tree that gives sweet smelling oil which is used to make pleasant smelling liquid (**perfume**) संदल; चंदन की लकड़ी (जिससे चंदन तेल निकलता है और इत्र बनता है)

**sandbank** /ˈsændbæŋk ˈसैन्ड्बैङ्क्/ *noun* [C] an area of sand that is higher than the sand around it in a river or the sea नदी या समुद्र का रेतीला तट; सैकत

**sandbar** /ˈsændbɑː(r) ˈसैन्ड्बा(र्)/ *noun* [C] (in geography) a long mass of sand at the point where a river meets the sea that is formed by the movement of the water बालू-भित्ति (नदी के समुद्र से मिलने के स्थान पर पानी में हलचल के कारण बनी बालू की लंबी दीवार)

**sandcastle** /ˈsændkɑːsl ˈसैन्ड्कासल्/ *noun* [C] a pile of sand that looks like a castle, made by children playing on a beach (समुद्र पर खेल-खेल में) बच्चों द्वारा बनाया रेत का क़िला

**sand dune** = **dune**

**sandpaper** /ˈsændpeɪpə(r) ˈसैन्ड्पेप(र्)/ *noun* [U] strong paper with sand on one side that is used for rubbing surfaces in order to make them smooth बालू-काग़ज़, रेगमाल (सतह को चिकना बनाने के लिए प्रयुक्त रेत-चिपका मज़बूत काग़ज़)

**sandstone** /ˈsændstəʊn ˈसैन्ड्स्टोन्/ *noun* [U] a type of stone that is formed of grains of sand tightly pressed together and that is used in building बलुआ पत्थर (बालू के कणों को कसकर दबाने से बना, भवन-निर्माण में प्रयुक्त)

**sandstorm** /ˈsændstɔːm ˈसैन्ड्स्टॉम्/ *noun* [C] a storm in a desert in which sand is blown into the air by strong winds रेतीली आँधी, रेतीला तूफ़ान

**sandwich[1]** /ˈsænwɪdʒ ˈसैन्विज्/ *noun* [C] two slices of bread with food between them सैंडविच (ब्रेड के दो टुकड़े जिनके बीच में खाद्य वस्तु हो) *a chicken/cheese sandwich*

**sandwich[2]** /ˈsænwɪdʒ ˈसैन्विज्/ *verb* [T] **sandwich sb/sth (between sb/sth)** to place sb/sth in a very narrow space between two other things or people दो व्यक्तियों या वस्तुओं के बीच किसी को रखना या दबाना, बीच में ठूँसना

**sandwich course** *noun* [C] (*BrE*) a course of study which includes periods of working in business or industry सांतराल पाठ्यक्रम, सैंडविच कोर्स (ऐसी पढ़ाई जिसमें बीच-बीच में व्यापार या उद्योग क्षेत्र में काम करते रहना शामिल है)

**sandy** /ˈsændi ˈसैन्डि/ *adj.* covered with or full of sand रेतीला; बलुआ (रेत या बालू से ढका या भरा हुआ)

**sane** /seɪn सेन्/ *adj.* **1** (used about a person) mentally normal; not crazy (व्यक्ति) मानसिक रूप से सामान्य दशावाला, स्वस्थचित्त; सनकी नहीं, समझदार *No sane person would do anything like that.* **2** (used about a person or an idea, a decision, etc.) sensible; showing good judgement (व्यक्ति, विचार या निर्णय) विवेकपूर्ण; अच्छी निर्णयशक्ति वाला ✪ विलोम **insane** ➪ **sanity** noun देखिए।

**sang** ➪ **sing** का past tense रूप

**sangh** *noun* [U] (*IndE*) a society for something; an association or an organization (किसी प्रयोजन हेतु) समाज; संघ, संगठन *Chatra Sangh*

**sanitarium** /ˌsænəˈteəriəm ˌसैनˈटेअरिअम्/ (*AmE*) = **sanatorium**

**sanitary** /ˈsænətri ˈसैनट्रि/ *adj.* connected with the protection of health, for example how human waste is removed स्वास्थ्य-रक्षा-विषयक (जैसे सफ़ाई कैसे रखी जाए) *Sanitary conditions in the refugee camps were terrible.* ➪ **insanitary** देखिए।

**sanitary towel** (*AmE* **sanitary napkin**) *noun* [C] a thick piece of soft material that women use to take in and hold blood lost during their period माहवारी के दिनों में महिलाओं द्वारा प्रयुक्त पैड या गद्दी ➪ **tampon** देखिए।

**sanitation** /ˌsænɪˈteɪʃn ˌसैनिˈटेश्न्/ *noun* [U] the equipment and systems that keep places clean, especially by removing human waste सफ़ाई के उपकरण (विशेषतः मल साफ़ करने के)

**sanity** /ˈsænəti ˈसैनटि/ *noun* [U] **1** the state of having a normal healthy mind मन के स्वस्थ होने की स्थिति; स्वस्थचित्तता **2** the state of being sensible and reasonable समझदार और विवेकी होने की स्थिति; विवेकपूर्णता ✪ विलोम **insanity** ➪ **sane** adjective देखिए।

**sank** ➪ **sink**[1] का past tense रूप

**Sanskrit** *noun* [U] an ancient language of India and one of the oldest languages of the Indo-European family संस्कृत

**Santa Claus** /ˈsæntə klɔːz ˈसैन्टा क्लॉज़्/ = **Father Christmas**

**sap**[1] /sæp सैप्/ *noun* [U] the liquid in a plant or tree सत्व; पेड़ों या पौधों से स्वयं निकलता हुआ रस

**sap**[2] /sæp सैप्/ *verb* [T] (**sapping; sapped**) **sap (sb of) sth** to make sb/sth weaker; to destroy sth gradually (किसी को) कमज़ोर करना; धीरे-धीरे नष्ट करना *Years of failure have sapped (him of) his confidence.*

**sapling** /ˈsæplɪŋ ˈसैप्लिङ्/ *noun* [C] a young tree छोटा पौधा या पादप

**sapphire** /ˈsæfaɪə(r) ˈसैफ़ाइअ(र्)/ *noun* [C, U] a bright blue precious stone नीलम, नील मणि

**sarcasm** /ˈsɑːkæzəm ˈसाकैज़म्/ *noun* [U] the use of words or expressions to mean the opposite of what they actually say. People use sarcasm in order to criticize other people or to make them look silly कटाक्ष; व्यंग्यपूर्ण टिप्पणी; (जिसका अभिप्रेत अर्थ सामान्य शब्दार्थ के विपरीत हो और जिसे दूसरों की निंदा या अपमान करने के लिए प्रयुक्त किया जाए ➪ **ironic** देखिए। ▶ **sarcastic** /sɑːˈkæstɪk साˈकैस्टिक्/ *adj.* व्यंग्यात्मक *a sarcastic comment* ▶ **sarcastically** /sɑːˈkæstɪkli साˈकैस्टिक्लि/ *adv.* व्यंग्यपूर्वक

**sardine** /ˌsɑːˈdiːn ˌसाˈडीन्/ *noun* [C] a type of very small silver-coloured fish that we cook and eat सार्डीन मछली (बहुत छोटी रुपहली मछली जिसे खाया जाता है) *a tin of sardines*

**sari** /ˈsɑːriː ˈसारी/ *noun* [C] a garment that consists of a long piece of cloth that women, particularly in the Indian subcontinent, wear draped around their bodies साड़ी (भारतीय महिलाओं का परिधान)

**sarong** /səˈrɒŋ सˈरॉङ्/ *noun* [C] a long piece of material folded around the body from the waist or the chest, worn by Malaysian and Indonesian men and women सरौंग; मलेशिया और इंडोनेशिया के स्त्रियों-पुरुषों द्वारा बाँधा जाने वाला पेटीकोट नुमा परिधान या लुंगी

**sash** /sæʃ सैश्/ *noun* [C] a long piece of material that is worn round the waist or over the shoulder, often as part of a uniform कंधे से कमर तक पहुँचने वाला या कमर के चारों तरफ़ बाँधा जाने वाला कपड़े का लंबा टुकड़ा; कमरबंद

**Sat.** *abbr*. Saturday शनिवार *Sat. 2 May*

**sat** ➪ **sit** का past tense और past participle रूप

**Satan** /ˈseɪtn ˈसेट्न्/ *noun* [*sing.*] a name for the Devil शैतान ➪ **devil** देखिए।

**satchel** /ˈsætʃəl ˈसैचल्/ *noun* [C] a bag, often carried over the shoulder, used by school children for taking books to and from school स्कूल में किताबें ले जाने का बच्चों का बैग; बस्ता

**satellite** /ˈsætəlaɪt ˈसैटलाइट्/ *noun* [C] **1** an electronic device that is sent into space and moves around the earth or another planet for a particular purpose कृत्रिम उपग्रह (विशेष प्रयोजन से अंतरिक्ष में भेजा गया इलेक्ट्रॉनिक उपकरण जो पृथ्वी या अन्य ग्रह की परिक्रमा करता है) *a weather/communications satellite* **2** a natural object that moves round a bigger object in space प्राकृतिक उपग्रह (अंतरिक्ष में भेजा गया इलेक्ट्रॉनिक उपकरण जो पृथ्वी या अन्य ग्रह की परिक्रमा करता है)

**satellite dish** (*also* **dish**) *noun* [C] a large, circular piece of equipment that people have on the outside of their houses, that receives signals from a **satellite 1** so that they can receive satellite television सैटलाइट डिश (घरों के बाहर लगा तश्तरीनुमा उपकरण जो कृत्रिम उपग्रह से संकेत प्राप्त करता है ताकि घरों तक सैटलाइट टेलीविज़न पहुँच सके)

**satellite television** (*also* **satellite TV**) *noun* [U] television programmes that are sent out using a **satellite 1** कृत्रिम उपग्रह की सहायता से प्रचारित टीवी कार्यक्रम

**satin** /ˈsætɪn ˈसैटिन्/ *noun* [U] a type of cloth that is smooth and shiny साटन (एक प्रकार का चिकना और चमकदार कपड़ा) *a satin dress/ribbon*

**satire** /ˈsætaɪə(r) ˈसैटाइअ(र्)/ *noun* **1** [U] the use of humour to attack a person, an idea or behaviour that you think is bad or silly (ख़राब या मूर्ख व्यक्ति, विचार या आचरण पर) किया गया व्यंग्य (उनकी आलोचना में) **2** [C] **a satire (on sb/sth)** a piece of writing or a play, film, etc. that uses satire व्यंग्य रचना या नाटक, फ़िल्म आदि *a satire on political life* ▶ **satirical** /səˈtɪrɪkl सˈटिरिकल्/ *adj.* व्यंग्यात्मक *a satirical magazine* ▶ **satirically** /səˈtɪrɪkli सˈटिरिक्लि/ *adv.* व्यंग्यपूर्वक

**satirize** (*also* **-ise**) /ˈsætəraɪz ˈसैटराइज़्/ *verb* [T] to use satire to show the faults in a person, an organization, a system, etc. किसी व्यक्ति, संस्था, प्रणाली आदि के दोषों पर व्यंग्य करना

**satisfaction** /ˌsætɪsˈfækʃn ˌसैटिस्ˈफ़ैक्श्न्/ *noun* [U, C] the feeling of pleasure that you have when you have done, got or achieved what you wanted; sth that gives you this feeling संतुष्टि (अभीष्ट उद्देश्य या वस्तु की उपलब्धि या कार्य को संपन्न करने पर प्रसन्नता); संतुष्टि देने वाली वस्तु *We finally found a solution that was **to** every one's **satisfaction**.* ○ *She was about to **have the satisfaction of** seeing her book in print.* ✪ विलोम **dissatisfaction**

**satisfactory** /ˌsætɪsˈfæktəri ˌसैटिस्ˈफ़ैक्टरि/ *adj.* good enough for a particular purpose; acceptable संतोषजनक (उद्देश्य विशेष के लिए पर्याप्त); स्वीकार्य *This piece of work is not satisfactory. Please do it again.* ✪ विलोम **unsatisfactory** ▶ **satisfactorily** /-tərəli -टरलि/ *adv.* संतोषजनक रूप से *Work is progressing satisfactorily.*

**satisfied** /ˈsætɪsfaɪd ˈसैटिसफ़ाइड्/ *adj.* **satisfied (with sb/sth)** pleased because you have had or done what you wanted अभीष्ट काम को संपन्न करने या वस्तु को प्राप्त करने पर प्रसन्न; संतुष्ट *a satisfied smile* ✪ विलोम **dissatisfied**

**satisfy** /ˈsætɪsfaɪ ˈसैटिसफ़ाइ/ *verb* [T] (*pres. part.* **satisfying**; *3rd person sing. pres.* **satisfies**; *pt, pp* **satisfied**) **1** to make sb pleased by doing or giving him/her what he/she wants किसी को उसका अभीष्ट काम कर या वस्तु देकर प्रसन्न या संतुष्ट करना *Nothing satisfies him—he's always complaining.* **2** to have or do what is necessary for sth किसी बात के लिए अपेक्षित वस्तु का होना या काम करना, पूरा करना, संतुष्ट करना *Make sure you **satisfy** the entry **requirements** before you apply to the university.* ○ *I had a quick look inside the parcel just to **satisfy** my **curiosity**.* **3 satisfy sb (that)** to show or give proof to sb that sth is true or has been done किसी बात की सचाई का या काम हो जाने का सबूत देना या उसे प्रदर्शित करना; आश्वस्त होना *Once the police were satisfied that they were telling the truth, they were allowed to go.*

**satisfying** /ˈsætɪsfaɪɪŋ ˈसैटिसफ़ाइइङ्/ *adj.* pleasing, giving satisfaction हर्षप्रद, संतोषप्रद *I find it satisfying to see people enjoying something I've cooked.*

**satsuma** /sætˈsuːmə सैट्ˈसूमा/ *noun* [C] a type of small orange एक प्रकार की छोटी नारंगी

**saturate** /ˈsætʃəreɪt ˈसैचरेट्/ *verb* [T] **1** to make sth extremely wet (किसी चीज़ को) ख़ूब भिगो देना, तर-बतर कर देना; सराबोर करना **2** to fill sth so completely that it is impossible to add any more किसी चीज़ को पूरी तरह भर देना या पाट देना (कि उसमें और न समा सके); संतृप्त करना *The market is saturated with cheap imports.* ▶ **saturation** /ˌsætʃəˈreɪʃn ˌसैचˈरेश्न्/ *noun* [U] अत्यधिकतम, संतृप्ति

**saturated** /ˈsætʃəreɪtɪd ˈसैचरेटिड्/ *adj.* **1** completely wet तर-बतर, सराबोर **2** (*technical*) (used about fats in food) that are not easily dealt with by the body because of their chemical structure (खाद्य पदार्थों में वसा) दुष्पाच्य; जिसे पचाना कठिन हो (वसा की रासायनिक संरचना के कारण) ➪ **polyunsaturated** और **unsaturated** देखिए।

**saturation point** *noun* [U, *sing.*] **1** the stage at which no more of sth can be accepted or added because there is already too much of it or too many of them अत्यधिकता या संतृप्ति की स्थिति *The market for mobile phones is reaching saturation point.* **2** (in chemistry) the stage at which no more of a substance can be taken in by a liquid or **vapour** (रसायनशास्त्र में) द्रव या वाष्प की संतृप्ति की स्थिति

**Saturday** /ˈsætədeɪ; -di ˈसैटडे; -डी/ *noun* [C, U] (*abbr.* **Sat.**) the day of the week after Friday शनिवार

**NOTE** दिनों के नाम हमेशा बड़े अक्षरों से लिखे जाते हैं। इन नामों के वाक्य-प्रयोग के उदाहरणों के लिए **Monday** की प्रविष्टि देखिए।

**Saturn** /ˈsætɜːn; -tən ˈसैटन्/ *noun* [*sing.*] the planet that is sixth in order from the sun and that has rings around it शनि ग्रह (क्रम में सूर्य से छठा ग्रह जिसके चारों ओर वृत्त होते हैं) ➪ **the solar system** पर चित्र देखिए।

**sauce** /sɔːs सॉस्/ *noun* [C, U] a thick hot or cold liquid that you eat on or with food सॉस, चटनी *The chicken was served in a delicious sauce.* ○ *ice cream with hot chocolate sauce* ➪ **gravy** देखिए।

**saucepan** /ˈsɔːspən ˈसॉसपन्/ *noun* [C] a round metal pot with a handle that is used for cooking things on top of a stove भोजन पकाने का गोलधातु-निर्मित मुठ्ठीदार बरतन; डेगची

**saucer** /ˈsɔːsə(r) ˈसॉस(र्)/ *noun* [C] a small round plate that you put under a cup तश्तरी, प्लेट

**sauna** /ˈsɔːnə ˈसॉना/ *noun* [C] **1** a type of bath where you sit in a room that is very hot वाष्प स्नान (गरम कमरे में किया जाने वाला) *to have a sauna* **2** the room that you sit in to have a sauna वाष्प स्नान का स्नानघर

**saunter** /ˈsɔːntə(r) ˈसॉन्ट(र्)/ *verb* [I] to walk without hurrying टहलना; चहल-क़दमी करना (बिना जल्दबाज़ी घूमना-फिरना)

**sausage** /ˈsɒsɪdʒ ˈसॉसिज्/ *noun* [C, U] a mixture of meat cut into very small pieces, spices, etc. that is made into a long thin shape. Some sausage is eaten cold in slices; other types are cooked and then served whole गुलमा; लंगोचा (लंबी पतली शकल में बना मसालेदार गोश्त जिसका छोटा टुकड़ा ठंडा खाया जाता है और पूरा टुकड़ा पका कर गरम) *garlic/liver sausage* ○ *We had sausages and chips for lunch.*

**savage** /ˈsævɪdʒ ˈसैविज्/ *adj.* very cruel or violent अति निर्दय, हिंसक या बर्बर *He was the victim of a savage attack.* ○ *The book received savage criticism.* ▶ **savage** *verb* [T] हिंसा का शिकार होना या बनाना *The boy died after being savaged by a wolf.* ▶ **savagely** *adv.* घोर निर्ममतापूर्वक, बर्बरतापूर्वक ▶ **savagery** /ˈsævɪdʒri ˈसैविज्रि/ *noun* [U] घोर निर्ममता, बर्बरता

**savannah** (*also* **savanna**) /səˈvænə सˈवैना/ *noun* [U] a wide flat open area of land, especially in Africa, that is covered with grass but has few trees घास का बड़ा मैदानी क्षेत्र (विशेषतः अफ़्रीक़ा में)

**save**[1] /seɪv सेव्/ *verb* **1** [T] **save sb/sth (from sth/from doing sth)** to keep sb/sth safe from death, harm, loss, etc. किसी को बचाना, रक्षा करना (मृत्यु, क्षति, हानि आदि से) *to **save** sb's **life*** ○ *to save sb from drowning* **2** [I, T] **save (sth) (up) (for sth)** to keep or not spend money so that you can use it later पैसा ख़र्च न करना या बचाकर रखना (भविष्य के लिए) *I'm saving up for a new bike.* ○ *Do you manage to save any of your wages?* **3** [T] to keep sth for future use भविष्य के लिए कुछ बचा कर या सुरक्षित रखना *I'll be home late so please save me some dinner.* ○ *Save that box. It might come in useful.* **4** [I, T] **save (sb) (sth) (on) sth** to avoid wasting time, money, etc. समय, धन आदि को बरबाद न करना *It will save you twenty minutes on the journey if you take the express train.* ○ *This car will save you a lot on petrol.* **5** [T] **save (sb) sth/doing sth** to avoid, or make sb able to avoid, doing sth unpleasant or difficult अप्रिय या कठिन स्थिति से (स्वंय) बचना या (दूसरे को) बचाना *If you make an appointment it will save you waiting.* **6** [T] to store information in a computer by giving it a special instruction विशेष निर्देश देकर कंप्यूटर में सूचना या प्रोग्राम को सुरक्षित करना *Don't forget to save the file before you close it.* **7** [T] to stop a goal being scored in sports such as football, **hockey**, etc. गोल बचाना (फ़ुटबॉल, हॉकी आदि खेलों में)

IDM **keep/save sth for a rainy day** ➪ **rainy** देखिए।

**save face** to prevent yourself losing the respect of other people (अपनी) लाज बचाना

**save**[2] /seɪv सेव्/ *noun* [C] (in football, etc.) the action of preventing a goal from being scored (फ़ुटबॉल आदि में) गोल बचाने की कार्य; गोल का बचाव *The goalkeeper made a great save.*

**saver** /ˈseɪvə(r) ˈसेव(र्)/ *noun* [C] **1** a person who saves money for future use (भविष्य में प्रयोग के लिए) पैसा बचाने वाला व्यक्ति *The rise in interest rates is good news for savers.* **2** (*often used in compounds*) a thing that helps you save time, money, or the thing mentioned समय, धन आदि को बचाने में सहायक वस्तु

**saving** /ˈseɪvɪŋ ˈसेविङ्/ *noun* **1** [C] **a saving (of sth) (on sth)** an amount of time, money, etc. that you do not have to use or spend (समय, धन आदि की) बचत *The sale price represents a saving of 25% on the usual price.* **2 savings** [*pl.*] money that you have saved for future use भविष्य के लिए बचाया गया धन; बचत *All our savings are in the bank.*

**saviour** (*AmE* **savior**) /ˈseɪvjə(r) ˈसेव्य(र्)/ *noun* [C] a person who rescues or saves sb/sth from danger, loss, death, etc. (संकट, हानि, मृत्यु आदि से) किसी को छुड़ाने या बचाने वाला व्यक्ति; परित्राता, उद्धारक

**savoury** (*AmE* **savory**) /ˈseɪvəri ˈसेवरि/ *adj.* (used about food) having a taste that is not sweet but salty (खाद्य पदार्थ) मीठे से भिन्न स्वाद का; नमकीन आदि ➪ **sweet** देखिए।

**saw**[1] ➪ **see** का past tense रूप

**saw**[2] /sɔː सॉ/ *noun* [C] a tool that is used for cutting wood, etc. A saw has a long flat metal part (**a blade**) with sharp teeth on it, and a handle at one or both ends आरा (लकड़ी चीरने का) ➪ **tool** पर चित्र देखिए। ▶ **saw** *verb* [I, T] (*pt* **sawed**; *pp* **sawn** /sɔːn सॉन्/) चीरना, (आरी से) काटना *to saw through the trunk of a tree* ○ *He sawed the log up into small pieces.* NOTE अमेरिकी अंग्रेज़ी में भूत कृदंत (past participle) रूप **sawed** है।

**sawdust** /ˈsɔːdʌst ˈसॉडस्ट्/ *noun* [U] very small pieces of wood that fall like powder when you are cutting a large piece of wood लकड़ी का बुरादा

**saxophone** /ˈsæksəfəʊn ˈसैक्सफ़ोन्/ (*informal* **sax**) *noun* [C] a metal musical instrument that you play by blowing into it. Saxophones are especially used for playing modern music, for example **jazz** सैक्सोफ़ोन; फूँक मार कर बजाने का धातु-निर्मित वाद्य यंत्र (विशेषतः जाज़ जैसे आधुनिक संगीत में प्रयुक्त) *This track features Dexter Gordon on the saxophone.* ➪ पृष्ठ 789 पर चित्र देखिए।

**say**[1] /seɪ से/ *verb* [T] (*3rd person sing. pres.* **says** /sez सेज़्/; *pt, pp* **said** /sed सेड्/) **1 say sth (to sb); say that; say sth (about sb)** to speak or tell sb sth, using words (शब्दों की सहायता से) (किसी को कुछ) कहना; बोलना *They just sat there without saying anything.* ○ ***It is said that** cats have nine lives.*

NOTE **Say या tell?** वक्ता के अपने शब्दों के लिए या परोक्ष कथन में **that** के साथ प्रायः **say** का प्रयोग होता है—*'I'll catch the 9 o'clock train,' he said.* ○ *He said that he would catch the 9 o'clock train.* ध्यान रखिए जब आप किसी को कुछ कहते हैं तो **say to** प्रयुक्त होता है—*He said to me that he would catch the 9 o'clock train.* **Tell** के बाद हमेशा कोई संज्ञा या सर्वनाम आता है, यह बताने के लिए कि किससे बात की जा रही है—*He told me that he would catch the 9 o'clock train.* आदेश या परामर्श देने के बारे में बात करने के लिए भी **tell** का प्रयोग हो सकता है—*I told them to hurry up.* ○ *She's always telling me what I ought to do.*

**2** to express an opinion on sth राय व्यक्त करना (किसी विषय में) *It's **hard to say** what I like about the book.* ○ *'When will it be finished?' '**I couldn't say*** (= I don't know).' **3** (used about a book, notice, etc.) to give information (पुस्तक, सूचना आदि से) कोई जानकारी मिलना *The map says the hotel is just past the railway bridge.* ○ *The sign clearly says 'No pets allowed'.* **4 say sth (to sb)** to show a feeling, a situation, etc. without using words कोई भाव, स्थिति आदि व्यक्त करना (बिना शब्दों का प्रयोग किए) *His angry look said everything about the way he felt.* **5** to imagine or guess sth about a situation; to suppose किसी स्थिति के बारे में कुछ सोचना या अनुमान करना; कल्पना करना *We will need, say, Rs 500,000 for a new car.* ○ *Say you don't get a place at university, what will you do then?*

IDM **go without saying** to be clear, so that you do not need to say it बात का खुद स्पष्ट होना (कि कुछ कहना ही न पड़े) *It goes without saying that the children will be well looked after at all times.*

**have a lot, nothing, etc. to say for yourself** to have a lot, nothing, etc. to say in a particular situation किसी विशेष स्थिति में कहने के लिए बहुत कुछ होना, कुछ न होना, आदि *Late again! What have you got to say for yourself?*

**I must say** (*spoken*) used to emphasize your opinion अपनी बात पर बल देने के लिए प्रयुक्त *I must say, I didn't believe him at first.*

**I wouldn't say no** (*spoken*) used to say that you would like sth अपनी पसंद पर बल देने के लिए प्रयुक्त *'Coffee?' 'I wouldn't say no.'*

**Say when** (*spoken*) used to tell sb to say when you have poured enough drink in his/her glass or put enough food on his/her plate शराब का प्याला दोबारा भरने से या प्लेट में और खाना परोसने से रुकने हेतु पूछने के लिए प्रयुक्त

**that is to say** which means अर्थात; दूसरे शब्दों में *We're leaving on Friday, that's to say in a week's time.*

**say**[2] /seɪ से/ *noun* [*sing*., U] **(a) say (in sth)** the authority or right to decide sth (कोई मामला तय करने की) शक्ति या अधिकार *I'd like to have some say in the arrangements for the party.*

IDM **have your say** to express your opinion अपनी राय व्यक्त करना *Thank you for your comments. Now let somebody else have their say.*

**saying** /ˈseɪɪŋ ˈसेइङ्/ *noun* [C] a well-known phrase that gives advice about sth or says sth that many people believe is true कहावत; लोकोक्ति (कुछ परामर्श देने वाली या किसी, बात को सच मानने वाली जग प्रसिद्ध उक्ति) *'Love is blind' is an old saying.* ➪ **proverb** देखिए।

**scab** /skæb स्कैब्/ *noun* [C, U] a mass of dried blood that forms over a part of the body where the skin has been cut or broken (कटने या फटने से बने) घाव पर जमने वाली पपड़ी; खुरंड ➪ **scar** देखिए।

**scabies** /ˈskeɪbiːz ˈस्केबीज़् / *noun* [U] a skin disease that causes small red spots and makes your skin feel uncomfortable so that you want to rub or scratch it खुजली, खारिश

**scaffold** /ˈskæfəʊld ˈस्कैफ़ोल्ड् / *noun* [C] a platform on which criminals were killed in past times by hanging फाँसी का तख़्ता

**scaffolding** /ˈskæfəldɪŋ ˈस्कैफ़ल्डिङ् / *noun* [U] long metal poles and wooden boards that form a structure which is put next to a building so that people who are building, painting, etc. can stand and work on it भवन-निर्माण के लिए प्रयुक्त ढाँचा; पाड़, (धातु के लंबे डंडों और लकड़ी के तख़्तों से बना मचान जिस पर खड़े होकर कारीगर काम करते हैं)

**scalar** /ˈskeɪlə(r) ˈस्केल(र्) / *adj.* (*mathematics*) (used about a measurement or a quantity) having size but no direction (माप या मात्रा) आकारमय परंतु दिशारहित; अदिश ▶ **scalar** *noun* [C] सोपान, अधिक्रम ➪ **vector** पर नोट और चित्र देखिए।

**scald** /skɔːld स्कॉल्ड् / *verb* [T] to burn sb/sth with very hot liquid गरम द्रव से किसी व्यक्ति या वस्तु को जला देना *I scalded my arm badly when I was cooking.* ▶ **scald** *noun* [C] गरम द्रव के पड़ने से उत्पन्न जलन ▶ **scalding** *adj.* उबलता हुआ *scalding hot water*

**scale[1]** /skeɪl स्केल् / *noun* **1** [C, U] the size of sth, especially when compared to other things किसी वस्तु का आकार, पैमाना (विशेषतः तुलनात्मक दृष्टि से) *We shall be making the product* ***on a large scale*** *next year.* ○ *At this stage it is impossible to estimate* ***the full scale of*** *the disaster.* **2** [C] a series of marks on a tool or piece of equipment that you use for measuring sth नापने का पैमाना; पटरी, फ़ुटा *The ruler has one scale in centimetres and one scale in inches.* **3** [C] a series of numbers, amounts, etc. that are used for measuring or fixing the level of sth (किसी वस्तु को मापने या स्तर-निर्धारण के लिए प्रयुक्त) अंकों, मात्राओं आदि की शृंखला; पैमाना, स्केल, मापक्रम *The earthquake measured 6.5 on the Richter scale.* ○ *the new pay scale for nurses* ➪ **Beaufort scale** और **the Richter scale** देखिए। **4** [C] the relationship between the actual size of sth and its size on a map or plan वास्तविक आकार और मानचित्र में प्रदर्शित, आकार में संबंध; अनुपात *The map has a scale of one centimetre to a kilometre.* ○ *a scale of 1: 50,000* (= one to fifty thousand) **5 scales** [*pl.*] a piece of equipment that is used for weighing sb/sth भार तोलने की मशीन; तुला, तराज़ू *I weighed it on the kitchen scales.* **6** [C] a series of musical notes which go up or down in a fixed order. People play or sing scales to improve their technical ability संगीत में स्वरक्रम; सरगम *the scale of C major* **7** [C] one of the small flat pieces of hard material that cover the body of some fish and animals मछली आदि का कवच; शल्क *the scales of a snake* ➪ **fish** पर चित्र देखिए।

**scale[2]** /skeɪl स्केल् / *verb* [T] to climb up a high wall, steep cliff, etc. ऊँची दीवार या खड़ी चट्टान आदि पर चढ़ना **PHR V scale sth up/down** to increase/decrease the size, number, importance, etc. of sth आकार, संख्या, महत्त्व आदि का बढ़ना या घटना *Police have scaled up their search for the missing boy.*

**scallop** /ˈskɒləp ˈस्कॉलप् / *noun* [C] a shell fish that we eat, with two flat round shells that fit together घोंघा, शंबूक

**scalp** /skælp स्कैल्प् / *noun* [C] the skin on the top of your head that is under your hair सिर की खाल; शिरोवल्क

**scalpel** /ˈskælpəl ˈस्कैल्पल् / *noun* [C] a small knife that is used by doctors (**surgeons**) when they are doing operations सर्जन का चाक़ू (शल्य-क्रिया में प्रयुक्त)

**scam** /skæm स्कैम् / *noun* [C] a clever but dishonest plan for making money पैसे कमाने का चतुर परंतु कपटपूर्ण योजना; स्कैम *stamp paper scam* ○ *share market scam*

**scamper** /ˈskæmpə(r) ˈस्कैम्प(र्) / *verb* [I] (used especially about a child or small animal) to run quickly (विशेषतः बच्चे या छोटे पशु का) तेज़ी से हड़बड़ाकर दौड़ना

**scan[1]** /skæn स्कैन् / *verb* [T] (**scanning; scanned**) **1** to look at or read every part of sth quickly until you find what you are looking for किसी चीज़ के प्रत्येक अंश को जल्दी-जल्दी देखना (अभीष्ट को खोज लेने तक) *Kareena scanned the list untils she found her own name.* **2** (used about a machine) to examine what is inside a person's body or inside an object such as a suitcase (मशीन का) शरीर के या सूटकेस आदि के अंदरुनी भाग का सूक्ष्म निरीक्षण करना *Machines scan all the luggage for bombs and guns.* **3 scan sth (into sth); scan sth (in)** (*computing*) to use a special machine (**a scanner**) to change printed words or pictures into electronic text in order to put them in the memory of a computer स्कैनर (एक प्रतिलिपि करने वाले उपकरण) का चित्रों को ग्रहण करना या मुद्रित शब्दों को इलेक्ट्रॉनिक टैक्स्ट में परिवर्तित करना (कंप्यूटर के स्मृतिकोश में उन्हें सुरक्षित रखने के लिए) *Text and pictures can be scanned into the computer.*

**scan**[2] /skæn स्कैन्/ *noun* **1** [C] a medical test in which a machine produces a picture of the inside of a person's body on a computer screen after taking **X-rays** एक डॉक्टरी परीक्षण जिसमें मशीन एक्स-रे की सहायता से, व्यक्ति के शरीर के अंदर का चित्र कंप्यूटर-स्क्रीन पर उपस्थित करती है *to do/have a brain scan* **2** [C] a medical test for pregnant women in which a machine uses **ultrasound** to produce a picture of a baby inside its mother's body गर्भवती महिलाओं के लिए डॉक्टरी परीक्षण जिसमें मशीन गर्भस्थित शिशु का चित्र प्रस्तुत करती है *The scan showed the baby was in the normal position.* **3** [*sing.*] the act of looking quickly through sth written or printed, usually in order to find sth लिखित या मुद्रित सामग्री को तेज़ी से जाँचना (सामान्यतया कुछ पता लगाने के लिए) *a scan of the newspapers*

**scandal** /ˈskændl ˈस्कैन्ड्ल्/ *noun* **1** [C, U] an action, a situation or behaviour that shocks people; the public feeling that is caused by such behaviour बदनामी वाला काम, आचरण या स्थिति (जिससे लोगों को आघात पहुँचे); ऐसे आचरण से आहत जनभावना (क्रोध आदि) *The chairman resigned after being involved in a financial scandal.* ○ *There was no suggestion of scandal in his private life.* **2** [U] talk about sth bad or wrong that sb has or may have done बदनामी का क़िस्सा, कलंकवार्ता *to spread scandal about sb*

**scandalize** (*also* **-ise**) /ˈskændəlaɪz ˈस्कैन्डलाइज़्/ *verb* [T] to cause sb to feel shocked by doing sth that he/she thinks is bad or wrong ख़राब या ग़लत समझे जाने वाले काम से दूसरों को विक्षुब्ध करना

**scandalous** /ˈskændələs ˈस्कैन्डलस्/ *adj.* very shocking or wrong अत्यंत विक्षोभकारी या अनुचित *It is scandalous that so much money is wasted.*

**Scandinavia** /ˌskændɪˈneɪviə ˌस्कैन्डिˈनेविआ/ *noun* [*sing.*] the group of countries in northern Europe that consists of Denmark, Norway and Sweden. Sometimes Finland and Iceland are also said to be part of Scandinavia उत्तरी यूरोप के कुछ देशों डेनमार्क, नार्वे, स्वीडन (आइसलैंड और फ़िनलैंड भी) का समूह; स्कैंडनेविया ▶ **Scandinavian** *adj., noun* [C] स्कैंडनेविया-विषयक

**scanner** /ˈskænə(r) ˈस्कैन(र्)/ *noun* [C] an electronic machine that can look at, record or send images or electronic information स्कैनर (एक इलेक्ट्रॉनिक यंत्र जो चित्रों या इलेक्ट्रॉनिक जानकारी को देखता, रिकॉर्ड करता या प्रेषण-योग्य करता है) *The scanner can detect cancer at an early stage.* ○ *I used the scanner to send the pictures by email.*

**scant** /skænt स्कैन्ट्/ *adj.* (*only before a noun*) not very much; not as much as necessary अत्यल्प (बहुत अधिक नहीं); अपर्याप्त (जितना अपेक्षित हो उतना नहीं)

**scanty** /ˈskænti ˈस्कैन्टि/ *adj.* too small in size or amount संख्या या मात्रा में बहुत कम; अत्यल्प *We didn't learn much from the scanty information they gave us.* ▶ **scantily** *adv.* अल्पमात्रा में; बहुत कम *I realized I was too scantily dressed for the cold weather.*

**scapegoat** /ˈskeɪpɡəʊt ˈस्केप्गोट्/ *noun* [C] a person who is punished for things that are not his/her fault बलि का बकरा (दूसरों की ग़लती के लिए दंडित व्यक्ति) *When Akansha was sacked she felt she had been* ***made a scapegoat*** *for all the company's problems.*

**scapula** /ˈskæpjʊlə ˈस्कैप्युला/ (*formal*) = **shoulder blade** ➪ **body** पर चित्र देखिए।

**scar** /skɑː(r) स्का(र्)/ *noun* [C] **1** a mark on the skin that is caused by a cut that skin has grown over त्वचा पर चोट का निशान; दाग़ *The operation didn't leave a very big scar.* ➪ **scab** देखिए। **2** an area of a hill or cliff where there is rock with nothing covering it and no grass पहाड़ी या ऊँची खड़ी चट्टान पर घास-रहित क्षेत्र या नंगी जगह *a kilometre long limestone scar* ➪ **limestone** पर चित्र देखिए। ▶ **scar** *verb* [I, T] (**scarring; scarred**) विक्षत होना *Wasim's face was* ***scarred for life*** *in the accident.*

**scarce** /skeəs स्केअस्/ *adj.* not existing in large quantities; hard to find विरल (अधिक मात्रा में उपलब्ध नहीं); दुर्लभ *Food for birds and animals is scarce in the winter.* ✪ विलोम **plentiful** ▶ **scarcity** /ˈskeəsəti ˈस्केअसटि/ *noun* [C, U] (*pl.* **scarcities**) विरलता, दुर्लभता, अभाव *(a) scarcity of food/jobs/ resources*

**scarcely** /ˈskeəsli ˈस्केअस्लि/ *adv.* **1** only just; almost not बहुत ही कम, मुश्किल से; नहीं के बराबर *There was scarcely a car in sight.* ○ *She's not a friend of mine. I scarcely know her.* ➪ **hardly** देखिए। **2** used to suggest that sth is not reasonable or likely किसी बात की तर्कहीनता या असंभाव्यता को व्यक्त करने के लिए प्रयुक्त *You can scarcely expect me to believe that after all you said before.*

**scare**[1] /skeə(r) स्केअ(र्)/ *verb* **1** [T] to make a person or an animal frightened (व्यक्ति या वस्तु को) डरा देना, भयभीत कर देना *The sudden noise scared us all.* ○ *It scares me to think what might happen.* **2** [I] to become frightened डर जाना *I don't scare easily, but when I saw the gun I was terrified.*

**PHR V** **scare sb/sth away/off** to make a person or animal leave or stay away by frightening them (व्यक्ति या पशु को) डराकर भगा देना

**scare²** /skeə(r) स्केअ(र्)/ *noun* [C] **1** a feeling of being frightened डर, भय *It wasn't a serious heart attack but it gave him a scare.* **2** a situation where many people are afraid or worried about sth आतंक, संत्रास, दुश्चिंता *Last night there was a **bomb scare** in the city centre.*

**scarecrow** /ˈskeəkrəʊ ˈस्केअक्रो/ *noun* [C] a very simple model of a person that is put in a field to frighten away the birds बिजूरवा; डराना (व्यक्तियों को डराकर भगाने के लिए खेत में लगाया आदमी का पुतला)

**scared** /skeəd स्केअड्/ *adj.* **scared (of sb/sth); scared (of doing sth/to do sth)** frightened भयभीत *Are you scared of the dark?* ○ *Everyone was too scared to move.*

**scarf** /skɑːf स्काफ़्/ *noun* [C] (*pl.* **scarves** /skɑːvz स्काव्ज़्/ or **scarfs** /skɑːfs स्काफ़्स्/) **1** a long thin piece of cloth, usually made of wool, that you wear around your neck to keep warm स्कार्फ़; रुमाल (प्रायः ऊन का जो गरम रखने के लिए गरदन के चारों ओर लपेटा जाता है) **2** a square piece of cloth that women wear around their neck or shoulders or over their heads महिलाओं का दुपट्टा (जो गरदन, कंधों या सिर पर लिया जाता है)

**scarlet** /ˈskɑːlət ˈस्कालट्/ *adj., noun* [U] (of) a bright red colour सिंदूरी रंग

**scarlet fever** *noun* [U] a serious disease that is passed from one person to another and that makes sb very hot and get red marks on the skin लोहित ज्वर; स्कारलेट फ़ीवर (एक संक्रामक ज्वर जिसमें शरीर बहुत तपता है और त्वचा पर चकत्ते निकल आते हैं)

**scarp** /skɑːp स्काप्/ *noun* [C] (in geography) a very steep piece of land (भूगोल में) बहुत ढालू ज़मीन; कगार

**scary** /ˈskeəri ˈस्केअरि/ *adj.* (**scarier; scariest**) (*informal*) frightening डरावना, भयानक *a scary ghost story* ○ *It was a bit scary driving in the mountains at night.*

**scathing** /ˈskeɪðɪŋ ˈस्केदिङ्/ *adj.* expressing a very strong negative opinion about sb/sth; very critical किसी के विषय में अत्यंत निषेधात्मक विचार वाला, अत्यंत कठोर, अत्यंत कटु *a scathing attack on the new leader* ○ *scathing criticism*

**scatter** /ˈskætə(r) ˈस्कैट(र्)/ *verb* **1** [I] (used about a group of people or animals) to move away quickly in different directions (लोगों या पशुओं के समूह का) तितर-बितर हो जाना, विभिन्न दिशाओं में तेज़ी से बिखर जाना **2** [T] to drop or throw things in different directions over a wide area वस्तुओं को इधर-उधर बिखरा देना; छितरा देना *The wind scattered the papers all over the room.*

**scattered** /ˈskætəd ˈस्कैटड्/ *adj.* spread over a large area or happening several times during a period of time इधर-उधर बिखरा हुआ या एक समयावधि में अनेक बार घटित *There will be sunny intervals with scattered showers today.*

**scavenge** /ˈskævɪndʒ ˈस्कैविन्ज्/ *verb* [I, T] to look for food, etc. among waste and rubbish कूड़े-कचरे और गंदगी में से खाने का सामान ढूँढ़ना ▶ **scavenger** *noun* [C] कूड़े-कचरे में से खाना ढूँढ़ने वाला पशु आदि *Scavengers steal the food that the lion has killed.*

**scenario** /səˈnɑːriəʊ सˈनारिओ/ *noun* [C] (*pl.* **scenarios**) **1** one way that things may happen in the future भावी घटनाओं का परिदृश्य *A likely scenario is that the company will get rid of some staff.* **2** a description of what happens in a play or film नाटक या फ़िल्म की दृश्यावली

**scene** /siːn सीन्/ *noun* **1** [C] the place where sth happened घटनास्थल *the scene of a crime/an accident* ○ *An ambulance was **on the scene** in minutes.* **2** [C] an occasion when sb expresses great anger or another strong emotion in public तीव्र क्रोध या अन्य भावनाओं का सार्वजनिक प्रदर्शन *There was quite a scene when she refused to pay the bill.* **3** [C] one part of a book, play, film, etc. in which the events happen in one place पुस्तक, नाटक या फ़िल्म का घटनाक्रम (एक स्थान पर संपन्न) *The first scene of 'Hamlet' takes place on the castle walls.* **4** [C, U] what you see around you in a particular place स्थान-विशेष का दृश्य; नज़ारा *Her new job was no better, but at least it would be a **change of scene**.* **5 the scene** [*sing.*] the way of life or the present situation in a particular area of activity विशिष्ट जीवन शैली या गतिविधि-विशेष की वर्तमान स्थिति *The political scene in Eastern Europe is very confused.* ○ *the fashion scene*

IDM **set the scene (for sth)** **1** to create a situation in which sth can easily happen or develop किसी बात के (घटित होने या विकास के) अनुकूल स्थिति का निर्माण करना *His arrival set the scene for another argument.* **2** to give sb the information and details that he/she needs in order to understand what comes next आगामी दृश्य की पूर्वपीठिका निर्मित करना (उसे समझने में सहायक अपेक्षित जानकारी देना) *The first part of the programme was just setting the scene.*

**scenery** /ˈsiːnəri ˈसीनरि/ *noun* [U] **1** the natural beauty that you see around you in the country प्राकृतिक दृश्य *The scenery is exquisite in the mountains.* **2** the furniture, painted cloth, boards, etc.

that are used on the stage in a theatre रंगमंच की सज्जा (फ़र्नीचर, परदे आदि) *The scenery is changed during the interval.*

> **NOTE** ग्रामीण अंचल में कोई इलाक़ा आकर्षक लगे तो हम कहते हैं कि इसकी **scenery** सुंदर है। किसी क्षेत्र की घास, पौधे आदि जिस ढंग से व्यवस्थित हों वह वहाँ का **landscape** है—*Trees and hedges are a typical feature of the British landscape.* ○ *an urban landscape* (= in a city or town). ऊँचे स्थान पर बैठकर खिड़की से बाहर या नीचे देखने पर हमें वहाँ का **view** मिलता है—*There was a marvellous view of the sea from our hotel room.* ➪ **country 3** पर नोट देखिए।

**scenic** /ˈsiːnɪk ˈसीनिक्/ *adj.* having beautiful scenery सुंदर दृश्यों वाला

**scent** /sent सेन्ट्/ *noun* **1** [C, U] a pleasant smell सुगंध, ख़ुशबू *This flower has no scent.* **2** [C, U] the smell that an animal leaves behind and that some other animals can follow किसी पशु की गंध जिसकी सहायता से दूसरे पशु उसके पीछे-पीछे जाते हैं **3** [U] a liquid with a pleasant smell that you wear on your skin to make it smell nice इत्र, अतर (सुगंधित द्रव जिसे शरीर पर लगाते हैं) ✪ पर्याय **perfume** **4** [*sing.*] the feeling that sth is going to happen भावी घटना का एहसास *The scent of victory was in the air.* ▶ **scent** *verb* [T] कुछ सूँघना *The dog scented a rabbit and shot off.* ▶ **scented** *adj.* सुगंधित

**sceptre** (*AmE* **scepter**) /ˈseptə(r) ˈसेप्ट(र्)/ *noun* [C] a decorated rod carried by a king or queen on ceremonial occasions as a symbol of their power राजदंड; अधिकार दंड जिसे राजा या रानी औपचारिक अवसरों पर धारण करते हैं

**sceptic** (*AmE* **skeptic**) /ˈskeptɪk ˈस्केप्टिक्/ *noun* [C] a person who doubts that sth is true, right, etc. किस बात की सच्चाई, औचित्य आदि में संशय करने वाला; संशयवादी, संशयात्मा ▶ **sceptical** (*AmE* **skeptical**)/ˈskeptɪkl ˈस्केप्टिक्ल्/ *adj.* **sceptical (of/about sth)** संशयी, संशयवादी *Many doctors are sceptical about the value of alternative medicine.*

**scepticism** (*AmE* **skepticism**) /ˈskeptɪsɪzəm ˈस्केप्टिसिज़म्/ *noun* [U] a general feeling of doubt about sth; a feeling that you are not likely to believe sth किसी विषय में संशय; अविश्वास की भावना

**schedule¹** /ˈʃedjuːl ˈशेड्यूल्/ *noun* **1** [C, U] a plan of things that will happen or of work that must be done होने वाली बातों या किए जाने वाले काम की योजना; समयसारणी, कार्य-योजना *Madhuri has a busy schedule for the next few days.* ○ *to be ahead of/behind schedule* (= to have done more/less than was planned) **2** (*AmE*) = **timetable**

**schedule²** /ˈʃedjuːl ˈशेड्यूल्/ *verb* [T] **schedule sth (for sth)** to arrange for sth to happen or be done at a particular time किसी बात की समयसारणी या कार्य-योजना को क्रियान्वित करना *We've scheduled the meeting for Monday morning.* ○ *The train was scheduled to arrive at 10.07 a.m.*

**scheduled flight** *noun* [C] a plane service that leaves at a regular time each day or week एक निश्चित समय पर प्रतिदिन या प्रति सप्ताह जाने वाली विमान की उड़ान ➪ **charter flight** देखिए।

**scheme¹** /skiːm स्कीम्/ *noun* [C] **1 a scheme (to do sth/for doing sth)** an official plan or system for doing or organizing sth आधिकारिक योजना या प्रणाली (कोई काम करने या कुछ आयोजित करने की सुनियोजित व्यवस्था) *a new scheme to provide houses in the area* ○ *a local scheme for recycling newspapers* **2** a clever plan to do sth षड्यंत्र *He's thought of a new scheme for making money fast.* ➪ **colour scheme** देखिए।

**scheme²** /skiːm स्कीम्/ *verb* [I, T] to make a secret or dishonest plan षड्यंत्र रचना *She felt that everyone was scheming to get rid of her.*

**schist** /ʃɪst शिस्ट्/ *noun* [U] (*technical*) a type of rock formed of layers of different minerals, that breaks naturally into thin flat pieces परतदार चट्टान; (विभिन्न खनिजों की परतों से बनी एक प्रकार की चट्टान जिसके प्राकृतिक प्रक्रिया में चौरस टुकड़े बन जाते हैं)

**schizophrenia** /ˌskɪtsəˈfriːniə ˌस्किट्सˈफ्रीनिआ/ *noun* [U] a serious mental illness in which a person confuses the real world and the world of the imagination and often behaves in strange and unexpected ways एक गंभीर मनोरोग जिसमें रोगी वास्तविक और काल्पनिक संसार में भेद नहीं कर पाता तथा विचित्र एवं अनपेक्षित रीति से आचरण करता है; मनोविदलता, खंडित मनस्कता ▶ **schizophrenic** /ˌskɪtsəˈfrenɪk ˌस्किट्सˈफ्रेनिक्/ *adj.*, *noun* [C] मनोविदलित; खंडित मनस्कता वाला

**scholar** /ˈskɒlə(r) ˈस्कॉल(र्)/ *noun* [C] **1** a person who studies and has a lot of knowledge about a particular subject विद्वान, पंडित (विषय-विशेष का) **2** a person who has passed an exam or won a competition and has been given some money (**a scholarship**) to help pay for his/her studies (परीक्षा या प्रतियोगिता में सफल होकर) शिक्षावृत्ति पाने वाला विद्यार्थी या छात्र *a UGC research scholar*

**scholarly** /ˈskɒləli ˈस्कॉललि/ *adj.* **1** (used about a person) spending a lot of time studying and having a lot of knowledge about an academic subject अध्ययनशील और विषयमर्मज्ञ (व्यक्ति) **2** connected with academic study विद्याध्ययन से संबंधित

**scholarship** /ˈskɒləʃɪp ˈस्कॉलशिप्/ *noun* **1** [C] an amount of money that is given to a person who has passed an exam or won a competition, in order to help pay for his/her studies शिक्षावृत्ति (परीक्षा या प्रतियोगिता में सफल होने वाले व्यक्ति को अध्ययन-हेतु मिलने वाली धनराशि; छात्रवृत्ति *to win a scholarship to Oxford* **2** [U] serious study of an academic subject विषय-विशेष का गंभीर अध्ययन; विद्वता, पांडित्य

**school** /skuːl स्कूल्/ *noun* **1** [C] the place where children go to be educated स्कूल, विद्यालय, पाठशाला *Where did you **go to school**?* **2** [U] the time you spend at a school; the process of being educated in a school स्कूल में व्यतीत किया गया समय; स्कूल में पढ़ने की प्रक्रिया *Their children are still **at school**.*

**NOTE** छात्र या शिक्षक के रूप में स्कूल जाने की बात हो तो केवल **school** (**'the'** रहित) का प्रयोग होता है—*Where do your children go to school?* ○ *I enjoyed being at school.* यदि किसी अन्य प्रयोजन से या माता-पिता के रूप में स्कूल जाने की बात हो तो **the school** का प्रयोग किया जाता है—*I have to go to the school on Thursday to talk to John's teacher.* स्कूल के बारे में अधिक जानकारी देनी हो तो **'a'** या **'the'** का प्रयोग अवश्य किया जाता है—*Rani goes to the school in the next village.* ○ *She teaches at a school for children with learning difficulties.*

**3** [*sing., with sing. or pl. verb*] all the students and teachers in a school विद्यालय के सब छात्र और शिक्षक *The whole school cheered the winner.* **4** (*used to form compounds*) connected with school विद्यालय से संबंधित *children **of school age*** ○ *The bus was full of **schoolchildren**.* ○ ***schoolteachers*** ○ ***schooldays***. **5** [C] a place where you go to learn a particular subject विषय-विशेष का अध्ययन केंद्र; अध्ययन-शाला *a language/driving/drama/business school* **6** [C] (*AmE*) a college or university कॉलेज या विश्वविद्यालय *management school* **7** [C] a department of a university that teaches a particular subject विश्वविद्यालय में विषय-विशेष के अध्ययन का विभाग *the school of languages at Delhi University* **8** [C] a group of writers, painters, etc. who have the same ideas or style समान विचारधारा या शैली वाले लेखकों या चित्रकारों का वर्ग *the Kangra school of painting* **9** [C] a large group of fish swimming together (एक साथ तैरती) मछलियों का गोल

**IDM** **a school of thought** the ideas or opinions that one group of people share एक वर्ग की विचारधारा; संप्रदाय *There are various schools of thought on this matter.*

**schoolboy** /ˈskuːlbɔɪ ˈस्कूलबॉइ/ *noun* [C] a boy who goes to school विद्यालय में पढ़ने वाला लड़का; स्कूली-छात्र

**schoolgirl** /ˈskuːlgɜːl ˈस्कूलगल्/ *noun* [C] a girl who goes to school विद्यालय में पढ़ने वाली लड़की; स्कूल-छात्रा

**schooling** /ˈskuːlɪŋ ˈस्कूलिङ्/ *noun* [U] the time that you spend at school; your education स्कूल-शिक्षा की अवधि; स्कूल में शिक्षा

**schoolteacher** /ˈskuːltiːtʃə(r) ˈस्कूलटीच(र्)/ *noun* [C] a person whose job is teaching in a school विद्यालय का शिक्षक; स्कूल-शिक्षक

**schooner** /ˈskuːnə(r) ˈस्कून(र्)/ *noun* [C] **1** a sailing ship with two or more **masts** दो या अधिक पालों वाली नाव **2** a tall glass for beer or **sherry** बियर या शेरी (एक तरह का शराब) पीने का बड़ा गिलास

**schwa** /ʃwɑː श्वा/ *noun* [C] (*technical*) a vowel sound in parts of words that are not emphasized (**stressed**), for example the 'a' in 'about' or the 'e' in 'moment'; the symbol that represents this sound, /ə अ/ श्वा; उदासीन स्वर (स्वरों में वह स्वर जिसके उच्चारण पर बल नहीं दिया जाता जैसे about में 'a', moment में 'e'; उदासीन स्वर को /ə अ/ चिह्न द्वारा प्रकट किया जाता है)

**science** /ˈsaɪəns ˈसाइन्स्/ *noun* **1** [U] the study of and knowledge about the physical world and natural laws भौतिक जगत और प्रकृति के नियमों का अध्ययन और ज्ञान; विज्ञान *Modern science has discovered a lot about the origin of life.* ○ *Fewer young people are studying science at university.* ⇨ **arts** देखिए। **2** [C] one of the subjects into which science can be divided विज्ञान की कोई शाखा (जीवविज्ञान, रसायनविज्ञान आदि) *Biology, chemistry and physics are all sciences.*

**NOTE** मानव जाति तथा मानव समाज का अध्ययन **social science** कहलाता है।

**science fiction** (*also* **sci-fi**) *noun* [U] books, films, etc. about events that take place in the future, often involving travel in space भविष्य की घटनाओं (प्रायः अंतरिक्ष यात्रा वाली) पर कथाएँ, फ़िल्में आदि; विज्ञान-कथा

**scientific** /ˌsaɪənˈtɪfɪk ˌसाइन्ˈटिफ़िक्/ *adj.* **1** connected with or involving science विज्ञान से संबंधित या विज्ञान को साथ लेते हुए; वैज्ञानिक *We need more funding for scientific research.* ○ *scientific instruments* **2** (used about a way of thinking or of doing sth) careful and logical (सोच-विचार और काम) सावधानीपूर्ण और तर्कसंगत *a scientific study of the way people use language* ► **scientific-**

**ally** /ˌsaɪənˈtɪfɪkli ˌसाइन्ˈटिफ़िक्लि / *adv.* वैज्ञानिक ढंग से *Sorting out the files won't take long if we do it scientifically.*

**scientist** /ˈsaɪəntɪst ˈसाइन्टिस्ट् / *noun* [C] a person who studies or teaches science, especially biology, chemistry or physics विज्ञान (की शाखाओं, विशेषतः जीवविज्ञान, रसायन विज्ञान या भौतिक विज्ञान) का अध्ययन या अध्यापन करने वाला व्यक्ति; वैज्ञानिक, विज्ञानविद्

**sci-fi** /ˈsaɪ faɪ ˈसाइ फ़ाइ / (*informal*) = **science fiction**

**scissors** /ˈsɪzəz ˈसिज़ज़् / *noun* [*pl.*] a tool for cutting things that consists of two long, flat, sharp pieces of metal that are joined together कैंची **NOTE** **Scissors** बहुवचनांत संज्ञा है—*These scissors are blunt.* **'A scissors'** प्रयोग अशुद्ध है, शुद्ध प्रयोग है—**a pair of scissors.**

**scoff** /skɒf स्कॉफ़् / *verb* **1** [I] **scoff (at sb/sth)** to speak about sb/sth in a way that shows you think that he/she/it is stupid or ridiculous किसी व्यक्ति या वस्तु की हँसी उड़ाना, को ताना मारना **2** [T] (*BrE informal*) to eat a lot of sth quickly कोई वस्तु जल्दी-जल्दी प्रचुर मात्रा में खाना; भकोसना

**scold** /skəʊld स्कोल्ड् / *verb* [I, T] **scold sb (for sth/for doing sth)** to speak angrily to sb because he/she has done sth bad or wrong (ख़राब या ग़लत काम के लिए) किसी को डाँटना; डपटना, फटकारना

**scone** /skɒn; skəʊn स्कॉन्; स्कोन् / *noun* [C] a small, simple cake, usually eaten with butter छोटा, सादा केक (जो प्रायः मक्खन लगाकर खाया जाता है)

**scoop**[1] /sku:p स्कूप् / *noun* [C] **1** a tool like a spoon used for picking up ice cream, flour, grain, etc. कलछी (आइसक्रीम, आटा अनाज के दाने आदि उठाने या निकालने के लिए) **2** the amount that one scoop contains कलछी भर (कोई वस्तु) **3** an exciting piece of news that is reported by one newspaper, television or radio station before it is reported anywhere else किसी एक अख़बार, टीवी या रेडियो चैनल द्वारा सबसे पहले दी गई कोई सनसनीखेज़ ख़बर; स्कूप

**scoop**[2] /sku:p स्कूप / *verb* [T] **1 scoop sth (out/up)** to make a hole in sth or to take sth out by using a scoop or sth similar कलछी (या कलछी जैसी चीज़ से) कुछ उठाना या निकालना *Scoop out the middle of the pineapple.* **2 scoop sb/sth (up)** to move or lift sb/sth using a continuous action किसी व्यक्ति या वस्तु को हिलाना या उठाना (लगातार) हरकत करते हुए *He scooped up the child and ran.* **3** to win a big or important prize कोई बड़ा या महत्त्वपूर्ण पुरस्कार जीतना *The film has scooped all the awards this year.* **4** to get a story before all other newspapers, television stations, etc. सबसे पहले कोई ख़बर देना

**scooter** /ˈsku:tə(r) ˈस्कूट(र्) / *noun* [C] **1** a light motorbike with a small engine स्कूटर **2** a child's toy with two wheels that you stand on and move by pushing one foot against the ground बच्चों की दोपहिया खिलौनानुमा गाड़ी (जिसे एक पैर ज़मीन रखते हुए धकेला जाता है)

**scope** /skəʊp स्कोप् / *noun* **1** [U] **scope (for sth/to do sth)** the chance or opportunity to do sth किसी बात की गुंजाइश; कुछ करने की संभावना या अवसर *The job offers plenty of scope for creativity.* **2** [*sing.*] the variety of subjects that are being discussed or considered कार्य-क्षेत्र; व्याप्ति या विस्तार (चर्चाधीन या विचाराधीन विषय-वैविध्य) *The government was unwilling to extend the scope of the inquiry.*

**scorch** /skɔ:tʃ स्कॉच् / *verb* [T] to burn sth so that its colour changes but it is not destroyed किसी वस्तु को झुलसाना (इस प्रकार जलाना कि वह बदरंग हो जाए पर नष्ट न हो) *I scorched my blouse when I was ironing it.*

**scorching** /ˈskɔ:tʃɪŋ ˈस्कॉचिङ् / *adj.* very hot बहुत गरम; झुलसाने वाला *It was absolutely scorching on Tuesday.*

**score**[1] /skɔ:(r) स्कॉ(र्) / *noun* **1** [C] the number of points, goals, etc. that sb/sth gets in a game, competition, exam, etc. खेल, प्रतियोगिता आदि में बनाए गोल, प्राप्त अंक आदि का लेखा; स्कोर ○ *The score is 3–2 to Mohun Bagan.* ○ *The top score in the test was 80%.* **2 scores** [*pl.*] very many बहुत सारे *Scores of people have written to offer their support.* **3** [C] the written form of a piece of music लिपिबद्ध रूप में संगीत-रचना

**IDM** **on that score** as far as that is concerned जहाँ तक इस या उस बात का संबंध है; इस या उस पर *Ritu will be well looked after. Don't worry on that score.*

**score**[2] /skɔ:(r) स्कॉ(र्) / *verb* [I, T] to get points, goals, etc. in a game, competition, exam, etc. खेल, प्रतियोगिता, परीक्षा आदि में गोल बनाना, अंक प्राप्त करना आदि; स्कोर करना *The team still hadn't scored by half-time.* ○ *Varun scored the highest marks in the exam.*

**scoreboard** /ˈskɔ:bɔ:d ˈस्कॉबॉड् / *noun* [C] a large board that shows the score during a game, competition, etc. खेल, प्रतियोगिता आदि का स्कोर (बनाए गए गोल, प्राप्त अंक आदि) दिखाने वाला बोर्ड; स्कोर बोर्ड

**scorn**[1] /skɔːn स्कॉन् / *noun* [U] **scorn (for sb/sth)** the strong feeling that you have when you do not respect sb/sth घृणा, अवज्ञा, अनादर-भाव, तिरस्कार

**scorn**[2] /skɔːn स्कॉन् / *verb* [T] **1** to feel or show a complete lack of respect for sb/sth किसी व्यक्ति या वस्तु के प्रति अनादरभाव रखना; उसका तिरस्कार करना *The President scorned his critics.* **2** to refuse to accept help or advice, especially because you are too proud (घमंड में आकर) दूसरे की सहयता या सलाह को न मानना; उसका तिरस्कार करना *The old lady scorned all offers of help.* ▶ **scornful** /-fl -फ़ल् / *adj.* तिरस्कारपूर्ण, अवज्ञापूर्ण *a scornful look/smile/remark* ▶ **scornfully** /-fəli -फ़लि / *adv.* तिरस्कारपूर्वक, अवज्ञापूर्ण

**Scorpio** /ˈskɔːpiəʊ ˈस्कॉपिओ / *noun* [U] the eighth sign of the **zodiac**, the Scorpion राशिचक्र में आठवीं राशि; वृश्चिक

**scorpion** /ˈskɔːpiən ˈस्कॉपिअन् / *noun* [C] a creature which looks like a large insect and lives in hot countries. A scorpion has a long curved tail with a poisonous sting in it बिच्छू, वृश्चिक

**Scot** /skɒt स्कॉट् / *noun* [C] a person who comes from Scotland स्कॉटलैंड का निवासी

**Scotch** /skɒtʃ स्कॉच् / *noun* [U, C] a strong alcoholic drink (**whisky**) that is made in Scotland; a glass of this स्कॉटलैंड की ह्विस्की, स्कॉच; गिलासभर स्कॉच ➪ **Scottish** पर नोट देखिए।

**Scotch tape**™ (*AmE*) = **Sellotape**

**Scots** /skɒts स्कॉट्स् / *adj.* of or connected with people from Scotland स्कॉटलैंड का या वहाँ के निवासियों से संबंधित ➪ **Scottish** पर नोट देखिए।

**Scottish** /ˈskɒtɪʃ ˈस्कॉटिश् / *adj.* of or connected with Scotland, its people, culture, etc. स्कॉटलैंड, वहाँ के निवासियों, संस्कृति आदि का या उनसे संबंधित; स्कॉटिश

> NOTE **Scots** शब्द से केवल स्कॉटलैंड के निवासियों का बोध होता है—*a Scots piper.* **Scottish** शब्द, स्कॉटलैंड तथा वहाँ के निवासियों और वस्तुओं सभी के लिए प्रयुक्त होता है—*Scottish law/dancing/music* ○ *She speaks with a strong Scottish accent.* **Scotch** से ह्विस्की और अन्य कुछ खाद्य पदार्थों का संकेत होता है लोगों का नहीं।

**scoundrel** /ˈskaʊndrəl ˈस्काउन्ड्रल् / *noun* [C] (*old-fashioned*) a man who behaves very badly towards other people, especially by being dishonest दुष्ट, बदनाम, बेईमान

**scour** /ˈskaʊə(r) ˈस्काउअ(र्) / *verb* [T] **1** to clean sth by rubbing it hard with sth rough खुरदरी वस्तु से रगड़कर साफ़ करना; माँजना *to scour a dirty pan* **2** to search a place very carefully because you are looking for sb/sth व्यक्ति या वस्तु की खोज में किसी स्थान की बारीक़ी से या गहराई से तलाशी लेना

**scourge** /skɜːdʒ स्कज् / *noun* [C] a person or thing that causes a lot of trouble or suffering महाकष्ट या विपत्ति का कारण व्यक्ति या वस्तु *Rahul Dravid was the scourge of the Pakistani bowlers.*

**scout** /skaʊt स्काउट् / *noun* [C] **1 Scout** (*also* **Boy Scout**) a member of an organization (**the Scouts**), originally for boys, that teaches young people how to look after themselves and encourages them to help others. Scouts do sport, learn useful skills, go camping, etc. स्काउट; बालचर (लड़कों का स्वयंसेवी संगठन जो युवाओं में आत्मनिर्भरता तथा परोपकार भावना को प्रोत्साहित करता है। बालचरों की गतिविधियाँ हैं खेल, उपयोगी कौशलों का अभ्यास, कैम्पिंग आदि ➪ **Guide** देखिए। **2** a soldier who is sent on in front of the rest of the group to find out where the enemy is or which is the best route to take सैनिकों के आगे-आगे चलने वाला गुप्तचर सिपाही (जो शत्रु की स्थिति तथा वहाँ पहुँचने के सर्वोत्तम रास्ते का पता लगाता हैं)

**scowl** /skaʊl स्काउल् / *noun* [C] a look on your face that shows you are angry or in a bad mood चढ़ी हुई त्योरी; तेवर, भ्रू-भंग (नाक-भौं चढ़े हुए) ▶ **scowl** *verb* [I] त्योरी चढ़ाना, तेवर दिखाना, नाक-भौं सिकोड़ना

**scrabble** /ˈskræbl ˈस्क्रैबल् / *verb* [I] to move your fingers or feet around quickly, trying to find sth or get hold of sth कुछ ढूँढ़ने या पाने के लिए उँगलियाँ या पैर घुमाना; कुछ टटोलना *She scrabbled about in her purse for some coins.*

**scraggy** /ˈskrægi ˈस्क्रैगि / *adj.* (*BrE*) (of people or animals) very thin and unhealthy looking (व्यक्ति या पशु) अत्यंत पतला और अस्थिप्राय दिखाई पड़ने वाला *a scraggy old cat*

**scramble** /ˈskræmbl ˈस्क्रैम्बल् / *verb* [I] **1** to climb quickly up or over sth using your hands to help you; to move somewhere quickly हाथों के सहारे जल्दी-जल्दी ऊपर की ओर या किसी वस्तु के ऊपर चढ़ना; जल्दी-जल्दी कहीं जाना *He **scrambled to his feet*** (= off the ground). ○ *The children scrambled into the car.* **2 scramble (for sth/to do sth)** to fight or move quickly to get sth which a lot of people want छीना-झपटी करना (ऐसी वस्तु के लिए जिसे दूसरे भी चाहते हैं) *People stood up and began scrambling for the exits.* ○ *Everyone was scrambling to get the best bargains.* ▶ **scramble** *noun* [*sing.*] चढ़ाई, छीना-झपटी

**scrambled egg** *noun* [U] (*also* **scrambled eggs**) [*pl.*] eggs mixed together with milk and then cooked in a pan कड़ाही या पैन में पकाया अंडों और दूध का मिश्रण; अंडा भुर्जी

**scrap**[1] /skræp स्क्रैप् / *noun* **1** [C] a small piece of sth किसी चीज़ का टुकड़ा *a scrap of paper/cloth* ○ *scraps of food* **2** [U] something that you do not want any more but that is made of material that can be used again रद्दी सामान, कूड़ा-करकट (जिसमें प्रयुक्त माल से दोबारा कुछ बनाया जा सके) *The old car was sold* ***for scrap***. ○ *scrap paper* **3** [C] (*informal*) a short fight or argument झगड़ा, तू तू-मैं मैं

**scrap**[2] /skræp स्क्रैप् / *verb* [T] (**scrapping; scrapped**) to get rid of sth that you do not want any more (अनचाही हो चुकी चीज़ से) छुटकारा पाना *I think we should scrap that idea.*

**scrapbook** /ˈskræpbʊk ˈस्क्रैप्बुक् / *noun* [C] a large book with empty pages that you can stick pictures, newspaper articles, etc. in कतरन-रजिस्टर (खाली पृष्ठों वाला रजिस्टर जिस पर चित्र, अख़बार में छपे लेख आदि की कतरनें चिपकाई जाएँ); स्क्रैपबुक

**scrape**[1] /skreɪp स्क्रेप् / *verb* **1** [T] **scrape sth (down/ out/ off)** to remove sth from a surface by moving a sharp edge across it firmly चाक़ू आदि से किसी सतह पर लगी चीज़ हटाना; खुरचना *Scrape all the mud off your boots before you come in.* **2** [T] **scrape sth (against/ along/on sth)** to damage or hurt sth by rubbing it against sth rough or hard किसी खुरदरी या कठोर चीज़ से रगड़ खाकर चोट लगा लेना *Mir fell and scraped his knee.* ○ *Sunita scraped the car against the wall.* **3** [I, T] **scrape (sth) against/along/on sth to rub (sth)** against sth and make a sharp unpleasant noise खड़खड़ करते हुए दो चीज़ों को आपस में रगड़ना *The branches scraped against the window.* **4** [T] to manage to get or win sth with difficulty कठिन प्रयास से कुछ लेना या हासिल करना *I just scraped a pass in the maths exam.*

PHR V **scrape by** to manage to live on the money you have, but with difficulty कठिनाई से गुज़ारा करना *We can just scrape by on my salary.*

**scrape through (sth)** to succeed in doing sth with difficulty बड़ी मुश्किल से कुछ कर पाना *to scrape through an exam* (= just manage to pass it)

**scrape sth together/up** to get or collect sth together with difficulty बड़ी मुश्किल से चीजें हासिल करना या बटोरना

**scrape**[2] /skreɪp स्क्रेप् / *noun* [C] **1** the action or unpleasant sound of one thing rubbing against another खड़खड़ाहट (दो वस्तुओं को परस्पर रगड़ने से उत्पन्न) **2** damage or an injury caused by rubbing against sth rough खरोंच, चोट (पुरानी चीज़ से रगड़ खाकर) *I got a nasty scrape on my knee.* **3** (*informal*) a difficult situation that was caused by your own stupid behaviour (अपनी मूर्खता से बनी) कठिनाई की स्थिति; खुद बुलाई मुसीबत

**scrap heap** *noun* [C] a large pile of objects, especially metal, that are no longer wanted रद्दी हो चुकी वस्तुओं, विशेषतः धातु-खंडों का ढेर

IDM **on the scrap heap** not wanted any more रद्दी की टोकरी में, कूड़े के ढेर पर *Many of the unemployed feel that they are on the scrap heap.*

**scrappy** /ˈskræpi ˈस्क्रैपि / *adj.* not organized or tidy and so not pleasant to see बेतरतीब या अव्यवसस्थित और भद्दा *a scrappy essay/football match*

**scratch**[1] /skrætʃ स्क्रैच् / *verb* **1** [I, T] **scratch (at sth)** to rub your skin with your nails, especially because it is irritating you (**itching**) नाख़ूनों से त्वचा को खरोंचना (खुजली के कारण) *Don't scratch at your insect bites or they'll get worse.* ○ *She sat and scratched her head as she thought about the problem.* **2** [I, T] to make a mark on a surface or a slight cut on a person's skin with sth sharp चाक़ू आदि से किसी सतह या व्यक्ति की त्वचा को खुरचना; कुरेदना *The cat will scratch if you annoy it.* ○ *The table was badly scratched.* **3** [I] to make a sound by rubbing a surface with sth sharp (तेज़ धार वाली वस्तु से) खरोंच कर कर्कश शब्द उत्पन्न करना *The dog was scratching at the door to go outside.* **4** [T] to use sth sharp to make or remove a mark चाक़ू आदि से निशान बनाना या मिटाना *He scratched his name on the top of his desk.* ○ *I tried to scratch the paint off the table.*

**scratch**[2] /skrætʃ स्क्रैच् / *noun* **1** [C] a cut, mark or sound that was made by sb/sth sharp rubbing a surface (किसी सतह की रगड़न के फलस्वरूप) खरोंच निशान या खड़खड़ाहट *There's a scratch on the car door.* **2** [*sing.*] an act of scratching part of the body because it is irritating you (**itching**) खुजली, खुजलाहट, ख़राश *The dog had a good scratch.*

IDM **from scratch** from the very beginning एकदम आरंभ से; शून्य से *I'm learning Marathi from scratch.*

**(be/come) up to scratch** (*informal*) (to be/become) good enough

**scrawl** /skrɔːl स्क्रॉल् / *verb* [I, T] to write sth quickly in an untidy and careless way लापरवाही से जल्दी-जल्दी कुछ लिख देना; घसीट मार कर लिखना; घसीटना *He scrawled his name across the top of the paper.* ▶ **scrawl** *noun* [*sing.*] घसीट; घसीट मार कर लिखा हुआ *Her signature was just a scrawl.* ➪ **scribble** देखिए।

**scream**[1] /skri:m स्क्रीम् / *verb* [I, T] **scream (sth) (out) (at sb)** to cry out loudly in a high voice because you are afraid, excited, angry, in pain, etc. ज़ोर से चीख़ना (डर, उत्तेजना, गुस्सा, दर्द आदि के कारण) *She saw a rat and screamed out.* ○ *He screamed with pain.* ○ *He clung to the edge of the cliff, screaming for help.* ➪ **shout** देखिए।

**scream**[2] /skri:m स्क्रीम् / *noun* **1** [C] a loud cry in a high voice ज़ोर की चीख़ *a scream of pain* **2** [*sing.*] (*informal*) a person or thing that is very funny अजीबोग़रीब व्यक्ति या वस्तु *Sarita's a real scream.*

**scree** /skri: स्क्री / *noun* [U, C] (in geography) a steep area of small loose stones, especially on a mountain (भूगोल में) कंकड़ों वाली ढाल (विशेषतः पहाड़ पर); शैल-मलबा

**screech** /skri:tʃ स्क्रीच् / *verb* [I, T] to make an unpleasant loud, high sound चीख़ कर बोलना, कर्कश ध्वनि निकालना *'Get out of here,' she screeched at him.* ➪ **shriek** देखिए। ▶ **screech** *noun* [*sing.*] चीख, चीत्कार, कर्कश ध्वनि *the screech of brakes*

**screen**[1] /skri:n स्क्रीन् / *noun* **1** [C] a flat vertical surface that is used for dividing a room or keeping sb/sth out of sight परदा, कर्टन *The nurse pulled the screen round the bed.* **2** [C] the glass surface of a television or computer where the picture or information appears टीवी या कंप्यूटर का स्क्रीन **3** [C] the large flat surface on which films are shown सिनेमा का बड़ा परदा **4** [*sing.*, U] films or television in general (सामान्य रूप से) फ़िल्में या टीवी (फ़िल्मों या टीवी का परदा या स्क्रीन) *Some actors look better in real life than on screen.*

**screen**[2] /skri:n स्क्रीन् / *verb* [T] **1 screen sb/sth (off) (from sb/sth)** to hide or protect sb/sth from sb/sth else (परदे आदि की सहायता से) कुछ छिपाना, आड़ में करना या किसी चीज़ को हानिग्रस्त होने से बचाना *The bed was screened off while the doctor examined him.* ○ *to screen your eyes from the sun* **2 screen sb (for sth)** to examine or test sb to find out if he/she has a particular disease or if he/she is suitable for a particular job रोग-विशेष की जानकारी के लिए रोगी की या नौकरी-विशेष के लिए उम्मीदवार की उपयुक्तता की जाँच करना *All women over 50 should be screened for breast cancer.* ○ *The Ministry of Defence screens all job applicants.* **3** to show sth on television or in a cinema टीवी या सिनेमा में कुछ (फ़िल्म या कोई दृश्य) दिखाना

**screen saver** *noun* [C] a computer program that replaces what is on the screen with a moving image if the computer is not used for certain amount of time एक कंप्यूटर प्रोग्राम जिसमें स्क्रीन की सामग्री के स्थान पर एक सचल चित्र आ जाता है (यदि कुछ समय तक कंप्यूटर को काम में न लाया जाए); स्क्रीन सेवर

**screw**[1] /skru: स्क्रू / *noun* [C] a thin pointed piece of metal used for fixing two things, for example pieces of wood, together. You turn a screw with a special tool (**a screwdriver**) पेंच, स्क्रू ➪ **bolt** पर चित्र देखिए।

**screw**[2] /skru: स्क्रू / *verb* **1** [T] **screw sth (on, down, etc.)** to fasten sth with a screw or screws (किसी वस्तु को) पेंच कस कर जमाना *The bookcase is screwed to the wall.* ○ *The lid is screwed down so you can't remove it.* **2** [I, T] to fasten sth, or to be fastened, by turning किसी वस्तु को पेंच से कसना या किसी वस्तु पर पेंच कसना *The legs screw into holes in the underside of the seat.* ○ *Make sure that you screw the top of the jar on tightly.* **3 screw sth (up) (into sth)** to squeeze sth, especially a piece of paper, into a tight ball किसी वस्तु (विशेषतः काग़ज़ का टुकड़ा) को ज़ोर से दबाकर गेंदनुमा बना देना *He screwed the letter up into a ball and threw it away.*

**PHR V** **screw (sth) up** (*slang*) to make a mistake and cause sth to fail ग़लती कर कोई काम बिगाड़ देना *You'd better not screw up this deal.*

**screw your eyes, face, etc. up** to change the expression on your face by nearly closing your eyes, in pain or because the light is strong (दर्द या तेज़ रोशनी के कारण) आँखें मीचते हुए मुँह बनाना

**screwdriver** /ˈskru:draɪvə(r) ˈस्क्रूड्राइव़(र्) / *noun* [C] a tool that you use for turning screws पेंचकस, स्क्रूड्राइवर ➪ **tool** पर चित्र देखिए।

**scribble** /ˈskrɪbl ˈस्क्रिब्ल् / *verb* [I, T] **1** to write sth quickly and carelessly लापरवाही से जल्दी-जल्दी कुछ लिखना, घसीट मारना, घसीटना *to scribble a note down on a pad* ➪ **scrawl** देखिए। **2** to make marks with a pen or pencil that are not letters or pictures पेन या पेंसिल से निरर्थक चिह्न बनाना *The children had scribbled all over the walls.* ▶ **scribble** *noun* [C, U] घसीट लिखाई

**script** /skrɪpt स्क्रिप्ट् / *noun* **1** [C] the written form of a play, film, speech, etc. नाटक, फ़िल्म, भाषण आदि लिपिबद्ध रूप में; आलेख, पटकथा, स्क्रिप्ट *Who wrote the script for the movie?* **2** [C, U] a system of writing लेखन-प्रणाली, लिपि *Hindi/Urdu/Bangla script*

**scripture** /ˈskrɪptʃə(r) ˈस्क्रिप्च(र्) / *noun* [U] (*also* **the scriptures**) [*pl.*] books of religious importance for particular religions, such as the Bible for Christians धर्म-विशेष का धार्मिक ग्रंथ; धर्मग्रंथ (जैसे, ईसाईयों की बाइबिल)

**scroll[1]** /skrəʊl स्क्रोल् / *noun* [C] a long roll of paper with writing on it काग़ज़ का खर्रा (जिस पर कुछ लिखा हो)

**scroll[2]** /skrəʊl स्क्रोल् / *verb* [I] **scroll (up/down)** to move text up and down or left and right on a computer screen कंप्यूटर स्क्रीन पर लिखे हुए को ऊपर-नीचे या दाएँ-बाँए चलाना या घुमाना

**scroll bar** *noun* [C] a tool on a computer screen that you use to move the text up and down or left and right कंप्यूटर स्क्रीन पर लिखे हुए को ऊपर-नीचे या दाएँ-बाएँ चलाने वाला टूल; स्क्रॉलबार

**scrotum** /ˈskrəʊtəm ˈस्क्रोटम् / *noun* [C] the bag of skin that contains the two roundish male sex organs (**testicles**) अंडकोश, फ़ोता

**scrounge** /skraʊndʒ स्क्राउन्ज् / *verb* [I, T] (*informal*) **scrounge (sth) (from/off sb)** to get sth by asking another person to give it to you instead of making an effort to get it for yourself (स्वयं प्रयत्नपूर्वक प्राप्त करने के बजाय दूसरों की चीज़ उनसे झटक लेना) उस चीज़ को दूसरों से झटक लेना *Mona is always scrounging money off her friends.*

**scrub[1]** /skrʌb स्क्रब् / *verb* [I, T] (**scrubbing; scrubbed**) **1 scrub (sth) (down/out)** to clean sth with soap and water by rubbing it hard, often with a brush (प्रायः ब्रश से) अच्छी तरह रगड़कर (किसी को ) साबुन और पानी से साफ़ करना; माँजना *to scrub (down) the floor/walls* **2 scrub (sth) (off/out); scrub (sth) (off sth/out of sth)** to remove sth or be removed by scrubbing रगड़ कर (किसी वस्तु को) हटाना या रगड़ने से हिट या मिट जाना *to scrub the dirt off the walls* ○ *I hope these coffee stains will scrub out.*

**scrub[2]** /skrʌb स्क्रब् / *noun* **1** [*sing.*] an act of cleaning sth by rubbing it hard, often with a brush (प्रायः ब्रश से) अच्छी तरह रगड़ कर हटाने का कार्य; सफ़ाई *This floor needs a good scrub.* **2** [U] small trees and bushes that grow in an area that has very little rain झाड़-झंखाड़ (बहुत कम वर्षा वाले इलाक़े में) **3** (*also* **scrubland**) /ˈskrʌblənd ˈस्क्रबुलन्ड् / [U] an area of dry land covered with small bushes and trees झाड़-झंखाड़ वाला इलाक़ा

**scruff** /skrʌf स्क्रफ़् / *noun*

**IDM by the scruff (of the/your neck)** by the back of the/your neck गरदन पकड़कर

**scruffy** /ˈskrʌfi ˈस्क्रफ़ि / *adj.* dirty and untidy गंदा और मैला *He always looks so scruffy.* ○ *scruffy jeans*

**scrum** /skrʌm स्क्रम् / *noun* [C] the part of a game of **rugby** when several players put their heads down in a circle and push against each other to try to get the ball (रगबी में) घेरा बनाकर सिर नीचे किए हुए खिलाड़ियों का गेंद के लिए धक्कम-धक्का

**scruples** /ˈskru:plz ˈस्क्रूपल्ज़् / *noun* [*pl.*] a feeling that stops you from doing sth that you think is morally wrong ग़लत काम करने में हिचक; नैतिक संकोच *I've got no scruples about asking them for money* (= I don't think it's wrong).

**scrupulous** /ˈskru:pjələs ˈस्क्रूप्यलस् / *adj.* **1** very careful or paying great attention to detail अति सावधान या ब्योरों पर अधिक ध्यान देने वाला *a scrupulous investigation into the causes of the disaster* **2** careful to do what is right or honest सही या सच के प्रति सर्तक; धर्मसाध्य ✪ विलोम **unscrupulous** ▶ **scrupulously** *adv.* अति सावधानी से, नियमनिष्ठापूर्वक *scrupulously clean/honest/tidy*

**scrutinize** (*also* **-ise**) /ˈskru:tɪnaɪz ˈस्क्रूटिनाइज़् / *verb* [T] (*written*) to look at or examine sth carefully (किसी वस्तु को) सावधानी से देखना या जाँचना *The customs official scrutinized every page of my passport.* ▶ **scrutiny** /ˈskru:təni ˈस्क्रूटनि / *noun* [U] अति सावधानी से की गई जाँच; सूक्ष्म परीक्षण *The police kept all the suspects under close scrutiny.*

**scuba-diving** /ˈsku:bə daɪvɪŋ ˈस्कूबा डाइविङ् / *noun* [U] swimming underwater using special equipment for breathing श्वासयंत्र के साथ गोताख़ोरी *to go scuba-diving*

**scuff** /skʌf स्कफ़् / *verb* [T] to make a mark on your shoes or with your shoes, for example by kicking sth or by rubbing your feet along the ground पैर घसीटते हुए या ठोकर मारते हुए ऐसे चलना कि जूतों पर या जूतों से ज़मीन पर निशान बन जाएँ

**scuffle** /ˈskʌfl ˈस्कफ़ल् / *noun* [C] a short, not very violent fight हाथापाई, हाथाबाँही

**sculptor** /ˈskʌlptə(r) ˈस्कल्प्ट(र्) / *noun* [C] a person who makes figures or objects (**sculptures**) from stone, wood, etc. मूर्तिकार; बुत-तराश, शिल्पी (पत्थर, लकड़ी आदि से प्रतिमाएँ या वस्तु बनाने वाला)

**sculpture** /ˈskʌlptʃə(r) ˈस्कल्प्च(र्) / *noun* **1** [U] the art of making figures or objects from stone, wood, clay, etc. मूर्तिकला (पत्थर, लकड़ी, मिट्टी आदि से प्रतिमाओं या वस्तुओं का निर्माण **2** [C, U] a work or works of art that are made in this way इस प्रकार निर्मित मूर्ति या मूर्तियाँ

**scum** /skʌm स्कम् / *noun* [U] **1** a dirty or unpleasant substance on the surface of a liquid मलफेन (किसी द्रव की सतह पर झाग की शकल में जमा गंदगी); गंदी झिल्ली **2** (*slang*) an insulting word for people that you have no respect for सम्मान के अयोग्य व्यक्ति के लिए अपमानजनक शब्द; नीच *Drug dealers are scum.*

**scurry** /ˈskʌri ˈस्करि/ *verb* [I] (*pres. part.* **scurrying;** *3rd person sing. pres.* **scurries;** *pt, pp* **scurried**) to run quickly with short steps; to hurry छोटे-छोटे तेज़ क़दमों से आगे बढ़ना; जल्दी करना या मचाना

**scurvy** /ˈskɜːvi ˈस्कवि/ *noun* [U] a disease caused by a lack of **vitamin C** विटामिन 'सी' की कमी से उत्पन्न रोग (जिसमें मसूड़ों से ख़ून आता है); स्कर्वी

**scuttle** /ˈskʌtl ˈस्कट्ल्/ *verb* [I] to run quickly with short steps or with the body close to the ground छोटे क़दमों से या काफ़ी झुकते हुए तेज़ भागना *The spider scuttled away when I tried to catch it.*

**scythe** /saɪð साइद्/ *noun* [C] a tool with a long handle and a long, curved piece of metal with a very sharp edge (**a blade**). You use a scythe to cut long grass, corn, etc. हँसिया, दराँती

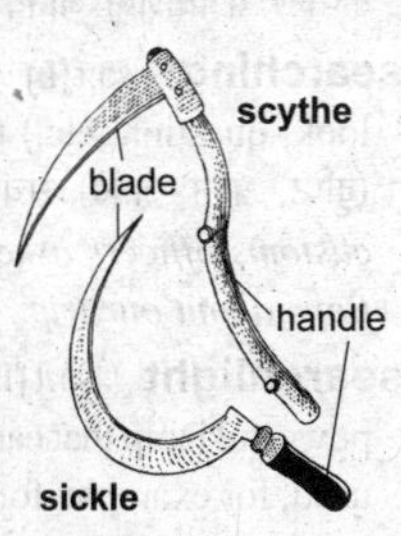


**SE** *abbr.* south-east(ern) दक्षिण-पूर्वी *SE Asia*

**sea** /siː सी/ *noun* **1** (*often* **the sea**) [U] the salt water that covers large parts of the surface of the earth (सामान्यतः) समुद्र, सागर *Do you live* ***by the sea?*** ○ *to travel* ***by sea*** ○ *There were several people swimming* ***in the sea.*** **2** (*often* **Sea**) [C] a particular large area of salt water. A sea may be part of the ocean or may be surrounded by land विशिष्ट समुद्री क्षेत्र (जो चाहे महासागर का अंश हो या ज़मीन से घिरा हो) *the Mediterranean Sea* ○ *the Arabian Sea* ➪ **ocean** देखिए। **3** [*sing.*] (*also* **seas**) [*pl.*] the state or movement of the waves of the sea समुद्र की लहरों की स्थिति या गति *The boat sank in heavy* (= rough) *seas off the Indian coast.* **4** [*sing.*] a large amount of sb/sth close together व्यक्तियों या वस्तुओं की घनीभूत बड़ी संख्या या मात्रा

**IDM at sea 1** sailing in a ship समुद्र यात्रा में *They spent about three weeks at sea.* **2** not understanding or not knowing what to do उलझन में, परेशान; किंकर्तव्यविमूढ़

**sea anemone** *noun* [C] a small, brightly coloured sea creature that lives on rocks and looks like a flower एक छोटा चमकीला समुद्री जीव (जो फूल जैसा दीखता है और चट्टानों पर रहता है) ➪ **anemone** देखिए।

**the seabed** /ˈsiːbed ˈसीबेड्/ *noun* [*sing.*] the floor of the sea समुद्र का अधस्तल ➪ **wave** पर चित्र देखिए।

seabirds

**seabird** /ˈsiːbɜːd ˈसीबड्/ *noun* [C] any bird that lives close to the sea and gets its food from it समुद्री पक्षी (समुद्र के पास रहने वाला और समुद्र से भोजन पाने वाला पक्षी) ➪ **waterbird** देखिए।

**seafood** /ˈsiːfuːd ˈसीफ़ूड्/ *noun* [U] fish and shell fish from the sea that can be eaten समुद्री खाद्य (समुद्र से प्राप्त खाने की मछलियाँ और घोंघे आदि शंखमीन)

**the sea front** *noun* [*sing.*] the part of a town facing the sea तटीय नगर का भाग; समुद्र की ओर खुलता हुआ नगर का भाग *The hotel is right* ***on the sea front.*** ○ *to walk* ***along the sea front***

**seagull** /ˈsiːgʌl ˈसीगल्/ = **gull**

**seal¹** /siːl सील्/ *noun* [C] **1** a grey animal with short fur that lives in and near the sea and that eats fish. Seals have no legs and swim with the help of short flat arms (**flippers**) एक समुद्री पशु; सील (समुद्र में या उसके निकट रहने वाला, मदमैले रंग का और छोटे फ़र वाला मछली खाने वाला जीव जिसकी टाँगें नहीं होती और जो हाथ जैसे पंखों की सहायता से तैरता है) **2** an official design or mark that is put on a document, an envelope, etc. to show that it is genuine or that it has not been opened सील, मोहर (किसी दस्तावेज़, लिफ़ाफ़े आदि पर लगाया जाने का अधिकारिक डिज़ाइन या चिह्न जो यह प्रदर्शित करता है वह प्रामाणिक है या उसे किसी ने बीच में खोला नहीं है) **3** a small piece of paper, metal, plastic, etc. on a packet, bottle, etc. that you must break before you can open it किसी पैकेट, बोतल आदि पर लगा काग़ज़, धातु या प्लास्टिक आदि का टुकड़ा (जिसे तोड़कर ही बोतल आदि को खोला जा सकता है); सील **4** something that stops air or liquid from getting in or out of something किसी वस्तु में से वायु या द्रव को बाहर जाने से रोकने के लिए प्रयुक्त पदार्थ *The seal has got worn out and oil is escaping.*

**seal²** /siːl सील्/ *verb* [T] **1 seal sth (up/down)** to close or fasten a package, envelope, etc. किसी पैकेट, लिफ़ाफ़े आदि को बंद करना या बाँधना *The parcel was sealed with tape.* ○ *to seal (down) an envelope*

**2 seal sth (up)** to fill a hole or cover sth so that air or liquid does not get in or out वायु या द्रव को अंदर जाने या बाहर निकलने से रोकने के लिए छेद को भरना या ढकना या बंद करना *The food is packed in sealed bags to keep it fresh.* **3** (*formal*) to make sth sure, so that it cannot be changed or argued about किसी बात को पक्का या सुनिश्चित करना (ताकि उसमें बदलाव या बहस की गुंजाइश न रहे) *to seal an agreement*

**PHR V seal sth off** to stop any person or thing from entering or leaving an area or building किसी स्थान पर लोगों या वस्तुओं के आने-जाने पर रोक लगाना *The building was sealed off by the police.*

**sea level** *noun* [U] the average level of the sea, used for measuring the height of places on land समुद्र तल (समुद्र-जल का औसत स्तर जिसकी सहायता से पृथ्वी के विभिन्न स्थानों की ऊँचाई मापी जाती है) *The town is 500 metres above sea level.*

**sea lion** *noun* [C] a type of large animal that lives in the sea and on land and uses two flat arms (**flippers**) to move through the water जलसिंह (समुद्र और पृथ्वी दोनों पर रहने वाला एक बड़ा जीव जो हाथनुमा पंखों से पानी में तैरता है)

**seam** /siːm सीम्/ *noun* [C] **1** the line where two pieces of cloth are sewn together कपड़े की सिलाई की सीवन (दो वस्त्र खंडों को एक साथ सीने से बनी रेखा) **2** a layer of coal under the ground ज़मीन के नीचे कोयले की परत

**seaman** /ˈsiːmən ˈसीमन्/ *noun* [C] (*pl.* **-men** /-mən -मन्/) a sailor नाविक

**seance** (*also* **séance**) /ˈseɪɒ̃s ˈसेऑन्स्/ *noun* [C] a meeting at which people try to talk to the spirits of dead people प्रेतात्मा-संवाद गोष्ठी (वह बैठक जिसमें दिवंगत आत्माओं से संवाद का प्रयास किया जाए), मृत की आत्मा बुलाना

**seaplane** /ˈsiːpleɪn ˈसीप्लेन्/ (*also AmE* **hydroplane**) *noun* [C] a plane that can take off from and land on water समुद्र जल से उड़ने और वहीं उतर सकने वाला विमान; समुद्री विमान

**search¹** /sɜːtʃ सर्च्/ *verb* [I, T] **search (sb/sth) (for sb/sth); search (through sth) (for sth)** to examine sb/sth carefully because you are looking for sth; to look for sth that is missing अभीष्ट वस्तु की खोज में किसी की बारीकी से जाँच करना; खोई हुई वस्तु को तलाशना *The men were arrested and searched for drugs.* ○ *They are still searching for the missing child.* ○ *I started searching the Web for interesting sites.*

**search²** /sɜːtʃ सर्च्/ *noun* **1** [C, U] an act of trying to find sb/sth, especially by looking carefully for him/her/it किसी की तलाश (विशेषतः बारीकी से जाँच कर) *the search for the missing boy* ○ *She walked round for hours* ***in search of*** (= looking for) *her missing dog.* **2** [C] (*computing*) an act of looking for information in a computer **database** or **network** कंप्यूटर से डाटाबेस या नेटवर्क में (अभीष्ट) सूचना-सामग्री या जानकारी की खोज *to do a search on the Internet* ○ *a* ***search engine*** (= a program that does searches)

**searcher** /ˈsɜːtʃə(r) ˈसर्च(र्)/ *noun* [C] **1** a person who is looking for sb/sth किसी को खोजने वाला; खोजकर्ता, अन्वेषक **2** a program that allows you to look for particular information on a computer कंप्यूटर में विशिष्ट जानकारी की खोज में सहायक प्रोग्राम

**searching** /ˈsɜːtʃɪŋ ˈसर्चिङ्/ *adj.* (used about a look, question, etc.) trying to find out the truth (दृष्टि, प्रश्न आदि) सचाई की खोज में सहायक *The customs officers asked a lot of searching questions about our trip.*

**searchlight** /ˈsɜːtʃlaɪt ˈसर्चलाइट्/ *noun* [C] a powerful lamp that can be turned in any direction, used, for example, for finding people or vehicles at night सर्चलाइट; घूमने वाली बहुत तेज़ बत्ती (रात के समय व्यक्तियों या वाहनों को खोजने में प्रयुक्त), खोज-बत्ती

**search party** *noun* [C] a group of people who look for sb who is lost or missing खोजी दल (खो गए या लापता व्यक्तियों को खोजने वालों का दल)

**search warrant** *noun* [C] an official piece of paper that gives the police the right to search a building, etc. तलाशी का वारंट (आधिकारिक पत्र जो पुलिस को किसी इमारत आदि की तलाशी लेने का अधिकार देता है)

**seashell** /ˈsiːʃel ˈसीशेल्/ *noun* [C] the empty shell of a small animal that lives in the sea छोटे समुद्री जीव का ख़ाली खोल या कोष

**seashore** /ˈsiːʃɔː(r) ˈसीशॉ(र्)/ (*usually* **the seashore**) *noun* [U] the part of the land that is next to the sea समुद्र तट *We were looking for shells* ***on the seashore****.*

**seasick** /ˈsiːsɪk ˈसीसिक्/ *adj.* feeling sick or vomiting because of the movement of a boat or ship नाव या जहाज़ की यात्रा में बीमार हो जाने वाला या जहाज़ी मतली का रोगी *to feel/get/be seasick* ▶ **seasickness** *noun* [U] जहाज़ी मतली ⇨ **airsick, carsick** और **travel-sick** देखिए।

**seaside** /ˈsiːsaɪd ˈसीसाइड्/ *noun* (*usually* **the seaside**) [*sing.*] an area on the coast, especially one where people go on holiday समुद्र तट का क्षेत्र (विशेषतः जहाँ लोग छुट्टियाँ मनाने जाते हैं) *to go to the seaside* ○ *a seaside town*

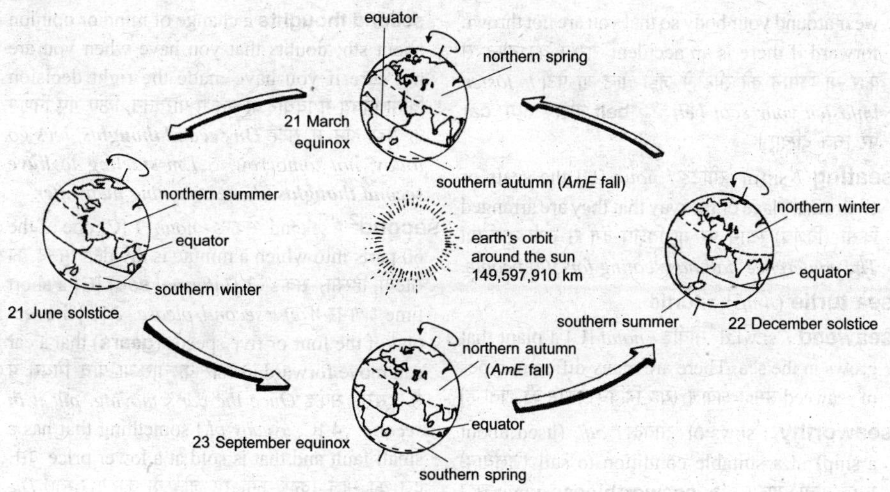


**the seasons**

**season¹** /ˈsi:zn ˈसीज़न्/ *noun* [C] **1** one of the periods of different weather into which the year is divided मौसम; ऋतु (प्राकृतिक वातावरण की दृष्टि से वर्ष का एक विभाग) *In cool countries the four seasons are spring, summer, autumn and winter.* **2** the period of the year when sth is common or popular or when sth usually happens or is done वर्ष का वह समय जब कोई विशेष गतिविधि प्रायः सर्वत्र हो या लोकप्रिय हो *the holiday/football season*

IDM **in season 1** (used about fresh foods) available in large quantities (ताज़े खाद्य पदार्थ) बड़ी मात्रा में उपलब्ध **2** (used about a female animal) ready to have sex (मादा पशु) यौन-संसर्ग के लिए तैयार

**out of season 1** (used about fresh foods) not available in large quantities (ताज़े फल, सब्ज़ियाँ आदि) सीमित मात्रा में उपलब्ध **2** (used about a place where people go on holiday) at the time of year when it is least popular with tourists (छुट्टियाँ मनाने के स्थान की) वह अवधि जब पर्यटकों की संख्या बहुत कम होती है

**season²** /ˈsi:zn ˈसीज़न्/ *verb* [T] to add salt, pepper, spices, etc. to food in order to make it taste better मिर्च-मसाले डालकर भोजन को छौंकना; बघारना ▶ **seasoning** *noun* [C, U] छौंक, बघार *Add seasoning to the soup and serve with bread.*

**seasonal** /ˈsi:zənl ˈसीज़नल्/ *adj.* happening or existing at a particular time of the year मौसमी (ख़ास मौसम में होने या मिलने वाला) *There are a lot of seasonal jobs in the summer.*

**seasoned** /ˈsi:znd ˈसीज़न्ड्/ *adj.* having a lot of experience of sth (किसी कार्यक्षेत्र में) अति-अनुभवी *a seasoned traveller*

**season ticket** *noun* [C] a ticket that allows you to make a particular journey by bus, train, etc. or to go to a theatre or watch a sports team as often as you like for a fixed period of time मियादी टिकट; सीज़न टिकट (जिसकी सहायता से नियत अवधि तक नाटकों या खेलों के कार्यक्रम में जितनी बार चाहें उतनी बार जा सकते हैं)

**seat¹** /si:t सीट्/ *noun* [C] **1** something that you sit on बैठने का आसन, स्थान या सीट *Please **take a seat** (= sit down).* ○ *the back/driving/passenger seat of a car* **2** the part of a chair, etc. that you sit on कुरसी आदि की सीट **3** a place in a theatre, on a plane, etc. where you pay to sit सिनेमा घर; विमान आदि की सीट (जिसके लिए भुगतान करना होता है) *There are no seats left on that flight.* **4** a place on a council or in a parliament that you win in an election विधान मंडल या संसद का पद (जो चुनाव में जीती जाती है) *to win/lose a seat*

IDM **be in the driving seat** to be the person, group, etc. that has the most powerful position in a particular situation स्थिति-विशेष में सबसे प्रभावशाली व्यक्ति, दल आदि होना, अगुआ या अग्रणी होना, सबसे आगे का व्यक्ति या दल होना

**take a back seat** ➪ **back²** देखिए।

**seat²** /si:t सीट्/ *verb* [T] **1** (*usually passive*) (*formal*) to sit down बैठना *Please be seated.* **2** to have seats or chairs for a particular number of people नियत संख्या में लोगों को बैठाना (उनके लिए कुरसियों आदि की व्यवस्था करना

**seat belt** (*also* **safety belt**) *noun* [C] a strap that is fixed to the seat in a car or plane and that you wear around your body so that you are not thrown forward if there is an accident सुरक्षा की दृष्टि से कार या विमान की सीट में जड़ी बेल्ट या पेटी *to fasten unfasten your seat belt* ➪ **belt** देखिए तथा **car** पर चित्र देखिए।

**seating** /ˈsiːtɪŋ ˈसीटिङ्/ *noun* [U] the seats or chairs in a place or the way that they are arranged किसी (विशेष) स्थान पर या विशेष ढंग से लगी कुरसियाँ *The conference hall has seating for 500 people.*

**sea turtle** (*AmE*) = **turtle**

**seaweed** /ˈsiːwiːd ˈसीवीड्/ *noun* [U] a plant that grows in the sea. There are many different types of seaweed समुद्री शैवाल (यह विविध प्रकार की होती है)

**seaworthy** /ˈsiːwɜːði ˈसीवर्दी/ *adj.* (used about a ship) in a suitable condition to sail (जलयान) समुद्र-यात्रा योग्य ▸ **seaworthiness** *noun* [U] समुद्र-यात्रा योग्यता

**sebaceous** /sɪˈbeɪʃəs सिˈबेशस्/ *adj.* (*usually before a noun*) (*technical*) producing a substance like oil in the body स्निग्ध पदार्थ उत्पन्न करने वाली वसामय (ग्रंथि); तैलजनक *the sebaceous glands in the skin*

**sec** /sek सेक्/ *noun* [C] (*informal*) = **second² 2**

**secateurs** /ˌsekəˈtɜːz ˌसेकˈटज़्/ *noun* [*pl.*] (*BrE*) a garden tool like a pair of strong scissors, used for cutting plants and small branches क़लम कैंची; कैंचा (पौधों को तराशने का औज़ार) *a pair of secateurs* ➪ **gardening** पर चित्र देखिए।

**secede** /sɪˈsiːd सिˈसीड्/ *verb* [I] **secede (from sth)** (*formal*) (used about a state, country, etc.) to officially leave an organization of states, countries, etc. and become independent (राज्य, देश आदि का) राज्यों, देशों के संघ को आधिकारिक रूप से छोड़ देना और स्वतंत्र हो जाना *The Republic of Panama seceded from Colombia in 1903.*

**secluded** /sɪˈkluːdɪd सिˈक्लूडिड्/ *adj.* far away from other people, roads, etc.; very quiet निर्जन (लोगों की बस्ती से बहुत दूर); एकांत, बहुत शांत *a secluded beach/garden* ▸ **seclusion** /sɪˈkluːʒn सिˈक्लूश़न्/ *noun* [U]

**second¹** /ˈsekənd ˈसेकन्ड्/ *pronoun, det., adv., noun* 2nd दूसरा, द्वितीय *I came* ***second*** *in the competition.* ○ ***the second*** *of January*

**IDM** **second nature (to sb)** something that has become a habit or that you can do easily because you have done it so many times आदत बन चुका आचरण (बार-बार करने के कारण) *With practice, typing becomes second nature.*

**second thoughts** a change of mind or opinion about sth; doubts that you have when you are not sure if you have made the right decision किसी विषय में विचार या मत में परिवर्तन; किए गए निर्णय के सही होने में संदेह ***On second thoughts****, let's go today, not tomorrow.* ○ *I'm starting to* ***have second thoughts*** *about accepting their offer.*

**second²** /ˈsekənd ˈसेकन्ड्/ *noun* **1** [C] one of the 60 parts into which a minute is divided मिनट का साठवाँ हिस्सा; सेकंड **2** (*informal* **sec**) [C] a short time क्षणभर *Wait a second, please.* **3** [U] the second of the four or five speeds (**gears**) that a car can move forward in कार के चार या पाँच गियरों में से दूसरा; सेकंड *Once the car's moving, put it* ***in second.*** **4** [C, *usually pl.*] something that has a small fault and that is sold at a lower price दूसरे दर्जे का माल (कुछ कमी रह जाने के कारण सस्ता) *The clothes are all seconds.* **5** [C] (*formal*) **a second (in sth)** the second-best result in a university degree दूसरा सर्वोत्तम परिणाम या स्थान विश्वविद्यालय की परीक्षा में) *to get an upper/a lower second in physics*

**second³** /ˈsekənd ˈसेकन्ड्/ *verb* [T] to support sb's suggestion or idea at a meeting so that it can then be discussed and voted on बैठक में किसी सुझाव या विचार का अनुमोदन करना (चर्चा एवं मतदान हेतु)

**second⁴** /sɪˈkɒnd सिˈकॉन्ड्/ *verb* [T] **second sb (from sth) (to sth)** to move sb from his/her job for a fixed period of time to do another job नियत अवधि के लिए किसी को दूसरे काम में लगाना (अपने काम से हटाकर) *Our teacher has been seconded to another school for a year.* ▸ **secondment** *noun* [U, C] प्रतिनियुक्ति, अस्थायी स्थानांतरण *to be on secondment*

**secondary** /ˈsekəndri ˈसेकन्ड्रि/ *adj.* **1** less important than sth else (दूसरे की अपेक्षा) गौण *Other people's opinions are secondary—it's my opinion that counts.* **2** caused by or developing from sth else किसी अन्य से उत्पन्न या विकसित

**secondary school** *noun* [C] a school for children aged from 11 to 18, 11 से 18 की आयु के छात्रों का विद्यालय; माध्यमिक विद्यालय, सेकंडरी स्कूल

**second-best¹** *adj.* not quite the best but the next one after the best सर्वोत्तम के बाद का *the second-best time in the 100-metres race* ➪ **best** देखिए।

**second-best²** *noun* [U] something that is not as good as the best, or not as good as you would like सर्वोत्तम या अभीष्ट स्तर के बाद की वस्तु *I'm not prepared to accept second-best.*

**second class** *noun* [U] (*also* **standard class**) ordinary accommodation in a train, boat, etc. रेलगाड़ी, नाव आदि में दूसरा दर्जा; द्वितीय श्रेणी

**second-class** *adj.* 1 (*also* **standard class**) used about ordinary accommodation in a train, etc. (रेलगाड़ी आदि में) द्वितीय श्रेणी; दूसरे दर्जे का *a second-class ticket ○ a second-class compartment* 2 (used about a university degree) of the level that is next after first-class (विश्वविद्यालय की उपाधि) द्वितीय श्रेणी का *a second-class honours degree in geography* 3 of little importance महत्त्वहीन, दूसरे दर्जे का, उपेक्षणीय *Old people should not be treated as second-class citizens.* ▶ **second-class** *adv.* द्वितीय श्रेणी में *to travel second-class*

**second cousin** *noun* [C] the child of your mother's or father's **cousin** आपके माता या पिता के (चचेरे, ममेरे, मौसेरे, फुफेरे) भाई या बहन के बच्चे

**second-degree** *adj.* (*only before a noun*) 1 (*AmE*) (used about murder) not of the most serious kind (हत्या का अपराध) गंभीर श्रेणी का नहीं 2 (used about burns) of the second most serious of three kinds, causing the skin to form bubbles (**blisters**) but not leaving any permanent marks (जले के लिए प्रयुक्त) जले के तीन प्रकारों में से दूसरा गंभीरतम प्रकार (जिसमें त्वचा पर छाले तो पड़ जाते हैं परंतु अंत में पक्का दाग़ नहीं रहता) ➪ **first-degree** और **third-degree** देखिए।

**second floor** *noun* [C] the floor in a building that is two floors above the lowest floor भवन की दूसरी मंजिल (भूतल की मंजिल से दो मंजिल ऊपर *I live on the second floor. ○ a second-floor flat*

**the second hand** *noun* [C] the hand on some clocks and watches that shows seconds (कुछ) घड़ियों में सेकंड की सूई

**second-hand** *adj., adv.* 1 already used or owned by sb else पूर्व प्रयुक्त या पहले किसी और का; पुराना *a second-hand car ○ I bought this camera second-hand.* ➪ **old** देखिए। 2 (used about news or information) that you heard from sb else, and did not see or experience yourself (समाचार या जानकारी) किसी अन्य से प्राप्त न कि स्वयं देखी या जानी; सुनी-सुनाई न कि आँखों देखी ➪ **hand** देखिए।

**second language** *noun* [C] a language that is not the language that you learned first, as a child, but which you learn because it is used, often for official purposes, in your country प्रथम से भिन्न द्वितीय भाषा (प्रायः प्रशासनिक या औपचारिक कार्यों के लिए प्रयुक्त) *French is the second language of several countries in Africa.*

**secondly** /ˈsekəndli ˈसेकन्ड्लि/ *adv.* (used when you are giving your second reason or opinion) also दूसरी बात; दूसरे (दूसरा तर्क या मत देते हुए प्रयुक्त) *Firstly, I think it's too expensive and secondly, we don't really need it.*

**the second person** *noun* [*sing.*] (*grammar*) the set of pronouns and verb forms that you use when you talk to sb मध्यम पुरुष (के सर्वनाम और क्रियापद) *In the phrase 'you are', the verb 'are' is in the second person and the word 'you' is a second-person pronoun.* ➪ **the first person** और **the third person** देखिए।

**second-rate** *adj.* of poor quality घटिया, मामूली *a second-rate poet*

**secrecy** /ˈsiːkrəsi ˈसीक्रसि/ *noun* [U] being secret or keeping sth secret गोपनीयता (किसी चीज़ का गोपनीय होना या उसे गोपनीय रखना) *I must stress the importance of secrecy in this matter.*

**secret**[1] /ˈsiːkrət ˈसीक्रट्/ *noun* 1 [C] something that is not or must not be known by other people गोपनीय बात (जो दूसरों को न पता हो न पता चले), दूसरों से छिपाने योग्य बात *to **keep a secret** ○ to let sb in on/tell sb a secret ○ **It's no secret that** they don't like each other* (= everybody knows). 2 [*sing.*] **the secret (of/to sth/doing sth)** the only way or the best way of doing or achieving sth एकमात्र या सर्वोत्तम उपाय (कुछ करने या पाने का रहस्य) *What is the secret of your success* (= how did you become so successful)?

IDM **in secret** without other people knowing बिना दूसरों के जाने, छिप-छिप कर *to meet in secret*

**secret**[2] /ˈsiːkrət ˈसीक्रट्/ *adj.* 1 **secret (from sb)** that is not or must not be known by other people गोपनीय (दूसरों से छिपाने योग्य) *We have to **keep** the party **secret** from Shilpa. ○ a secret address* 2 used to describe actions that you do not tell anyone about दूसरों से छिपा कर किए जाने वाले काम *a secret admirer ○ secret meeting* ▶ **secretly** *adv.* गुप्त रूप से *The government secretly agreed to pay the kidnappers.*

**secret agent** (*also* **agent**) *noun* [C] a person who tries to find out secret information especially about the government of another country गुप्तचर (विशेषतः विदेशों में कार्यरत) ➪ **spy** देखिए।

**secretarial** /ˌsekrəˈteəriəl ˌसेक्रˈटेअरिअल्/ *adj.* involving or connected with the work that a secretary does सचिव के कार्य से संबंधित; सचिवीय *secretarial skills/work*

**secretariat** /ˌsekrəˈteəriət ˌसेक्रˈटेअरिअट्/ *noun* [C] the department of a large international or political organization, especially the office of a

**Secretary General**, that manages the way the organization is run सचिवालय; (किसी बड़े अंतरराष्ट्रीय या राजनीतिक विशेषतः महासचिव का कार्यालय, जिस पर संगठनों को संचालित करने का दायित्व होता है)

**secretary** /ˈsekrətri ˈसेक्रट्रि/ *noun* [C] (*pl.* **secretaries**) **1** a person who works in an office. A secretary types letters, answers the telephone, keeps records, etc. दफ़्तर में काम करने वाला व्यक्ति (जो टाइप करना, फ़ोन का काम देखना, रिकार्ड सँभालना आदि करता है); सेक्रेटरी, सचिव *the director's personal secretary* **2** an official of a club or society who is responsible for keeping records, writing letters, etc. किसी क्लब या सोसाइटी का अधिकारी (जिस पर रिकार्ड सँभालने, पत्राचार करने आदि का दायित्व होता है) **3** (*AmE*) the head of a government department, chosen by the President राष्ट्रपति द्वारा नियुक्त किसी विभाग का अध्यक्ष; सचिव, सेक्रेटरी **4** (*BrE*) = **Secretary of State 1**

**Secretary General** *noun* [C] the person who is in charge of the department which runs a large international or political organization महासचिव; किसी बड़े अंतरराष्ट्रीय या राजनीतिक संगठन को संचालित करने वाले कार्यालय का प्रभारी अधिकारी)

**Secretary of State** *noun* [C] **1** (*also* **Secretary**) (in Britain) the head of one of the main government departments (ब्रिटेन में) सरकार के किसी प्रमुख विभाग या मंत्रालय का अध्यक्ष मंत्री (भारतीय व्यवस्था में) *the Secretary of State for Defence* **2** (in the US) the head of the government department that deals with foreign affairs (अमेरिका में) विदेश सचिव (विदेशी मामलों के विभाग का अध्यक्ष; सेक्रेटरी आफ़ स्टेट

**secrete** /sɪˈkriːt सिˈक्रीट्/ *verb* [T] **1** (used about a part of a plant, animal or person) to produce a liquid पौधे, पशु या व्यक्ति के किसी अंग का विशेष प्रकार का द्रव निकालना **2** (*formal*) to hide sth in a secret place किसी गुप्त स्थान पर कुछ छिपाना

**secretion** /sɪˈkriːʃn सिˈक्रीशन्/ *noun* (*formal*) [C, U] a liquid that is produced by a plant or an animal; the process by which the liquid is produced पौधे या पशु द्वारा उत्पादित द्रव; स्राव, स्राव की प्रक्रिया *The frog covers itself in a poisonous secretion for protection.*

**secretive** /ˈsiːkrətɪv ˈसीक्रटिव्/ *adj.* liking to keep things secret from other people बातों को दूसरों से छिपाने के स्वभाव वाला; गोपनशील, गोपनप्रिय *Nita is very secretive about her private life.* ▶ **secretively** *adv.* गोपनप्रिय रति से ▶ **secretiveness** *noun* [U] गोपनप्रियता

**secret police** *noun* [C, *with sing. or pl. verb*] a police force that works secretly to make sure that people behave as their government wants खुफिया या गुप्तचर पुलिस (जो गुप्त रूप से यह देखती है कि जनता शासन के अनुकूल आचरण कर रही है या नहीं)

**the secret service** *noun* [*sing.*] the government department that tries to find out secret information about other countries and governments गुप्तचर सेवा (विशेषतः विदेशों के लिए)

**sect** /sekt सेक्ट्/ *noun* [C] a group of people who have a particular set of religious or political beliefs. A sect has often broken away from a larger group संप्रदाय, पंथ (विशेष धार्मिक या राजनीतिक विश्वासों वाला वर्ग जो अपने से बड़े वर्ग से अलग होने के फलस्वरूप बनता है)

**sectarian** /sekˈteəriən सेक्ˈटेअरिअन्/ *adj.* connected with the differences that exists between religious groups सांप्रदायिक, पंथिक (विभिन्न धार्मिक वर्गों की भिन्नताओं से संबंधित) *sectarian violence*

**section** /ˈsekʃn ˈसेक्शन्/ *noun* [C] **1** one of the parts into which sth is divided खंड, भाग *the financial section of a newspaper* ○ *The library has an excellent reference section.* **2** a view or drawing of sth as if it was cut from the top to the bottom so that you can see the inside किसी वस्तु का दृश्य या आरेख या चित्र (लगे कि उसे ऊपर से नीचे तक काटा गया है ताकि अंदर का हिस्सा दिखाई पड़े); कर्तन *The illustration shows a section through a leaf.*

**sector** /ˈsektə(r) ˈसेक्ट(र्)/ *noun* [C] **1** a part of the business activity of a country देश की व्यापारिक गतिविधि का भाग या क्षेत्र *The manufacturing sector has declined in recent years.* ○ *the public/private sector* **2** a part of an area or of a large group of people किसी क्षेत्र या बड़े जनवर्ग का अंश, टोला, मुहल्ला, अंचल, सेक्टर *the residential sector of the city* **3** (*mathematics*) a part of a circle that is between two straight lines drawn from the centre to the edge त्रिज्य-खंड, वृत्त-खंड त्रिज्याओं के बीच का क्षेत्र ➪ **circle** पर चित्र देखिए।

**secular** /ˈsekjələ(r) ˈसेक्यल(र्)/ *adj.* not concerned with religion धर्म से संबंधित नहीं; लौकिक

**secure[1]** /sɪˈkjʊə(r) सिˈक्युअ(र्)/ *adj.* **1** free from worry or doubt; confident संदेह या चिंता से मुक्त; आश्वस्त, सुरक्षित *Children need to **feel secure**.* ○ *to be financially secure* ✪ विलोम **insecure** **2** not likely to be lost; safe जिसमें हानि संभावित नहीं; सुरक्षित, निरापद *Business is good so his job is secure.* ○ *a secure investment* **3** not likely to fall or be broken; firmly fixed जिसका गिरना या टूटना संभावित नहीं; मज़बूती से जमा हुआ *That ladder doesn't* *look very secure.* **4 secure (against/from sth)** well locked or protected भलीभाँति तालाबंद या सुरक्षित *Make sure the house is secure before you go to bed.* ▶ **securely** *adv.* मज़बूती से *All doors and windows must be securely fastened at night.*

**secure**[2] /sɪˈkjʊə(r) सिˈक्युअ(र्)/ *verb* [T] **1 secure sth (to sth)** to fix or lock sth firmly किसी वस्तु को अच्छी तरह जमा देना या जकड़ देना *The load was secured with ropes.* ○ *Secure the rope to a tree or a rock.* **2 secure sth (against/from sth)** to make sth safe किसी वस्तु को सुरक्षित करना *The sea wall needs strengthening to secure the town against flooding.* **3** to obtain or achieve sth, especially by having to make a big effort किसी वस्तु को प्राप्त करना या उपलब्ध करना (विशेषतः बहुत प्रयत्न के बाद *The company has secured a contract to build ten planes.*

**security** /sɪˈkjʊərəti सिˈक्युअरटि/ *noun* (*pl.* **securities**) **1** [U] the state of feeling safe and being free from worry; protection against the difficulties of life सुरक्षित और चिंतामुक्त होने की स्थिति, सुरक्षा और चिंतामुक्ति; जीवन की कठिनाइयों से सुरक्षा *Children need the security of a stable home environment.* ○ *financial/job security* ✪ विलोम **insecurity** **2** [U] things that you do to protect sb/sth from attack, danger, thieves, etc. (हमला, ख़तरा, चोरों आदि से बचाव के लिए) सुरक्षा व्यवस्था *Security was tightened at the airport before the president arrived.* ○ *The robbers were caught on the bank's* ***security cameras.*** **3** [U] the section of a large company or organization that deals with the protection of buildings, equipment and staff (भवन, उपकरण एवं कर्मचारियों की सुरक्षा हेतु) किसी कंपनी या संस्था का सुरक्षा विभाग *If you see a suspicious bag, contact airport security immediately.* **4** [C, U] something of value that you use when you borrow money. If you cannot pay the money back then you lose the thing you gave as security प्रतिभूति; ज़मानत (ऋण न लौटाने की दशा में जो ज़ब्त हो जाती है)

**sedan** /sɪˈdæn सिˈडैन्/ *noun* [C] (*AmE*) = **saloon**

**sedate**[1] /sɪˈdeɪt सिˈडेट्/ *adj.* quiet, calm and well behaved शांत, गंभीर एवं सौम्य

**sedate**[2] /sɪˈdeɪt सिˈडेट्/ *verb* [T] to give sb a drug or medicine to make him/her feel calm or want to sleep किसी को शांत करने या सुलाने के लिए नशीली गोली या दवाई देना *The lion was sedated and treated by a vet.* ▶ **sedation** /sɪˈdeɪʃn सिˈडेश्न्/ *noun* [U] प्रशमन, प्रशांति *The doctor put her* ***under sedation.***

**sedative** /ˈsedətɪv ˈसेडटिव्/ *noun* [C] a drug or medicine that makes you feel calm or want to sleep कोई नशीला पदार्थ या औषधि जिसे लेकर व्यक्ति शांत हो जाए या सोने लगे; शामक ➪ **tranquillizer** देखिए।

**sedentary** /ˈsedntri ˈसेड्न्ट्रि/ *adj.* involving a lot of sitting down; not active जिसमें व्यक्ति देर तक बैठा रहे; सक्रिय नहीं *a sedentary lifestyle/job*

**sediment** /ˈsedɪmənt ˈसेडिमन्ट्/ *noun* [C, U] a thick substance that forms at the bottom of a liquid तलछट; द्रव के तले पर जमा गाढ़ा पदार्थ

**sedimentary** /ˌsedɪˈmentri ˌसेडिˈमेन्ट्रि/ *adj.* (*technical*) used about rocks formed from the sand, stones, mud, etc. that are at the bottom of lakes, rivers, etc. झीलों, नदियों आदि के तल पर जमा रेत, पत्थर, कीचड़ आदि से बनी; तलछटी शैल ➪ **igneous** और **metamorphic** देखिए तथा **rock** पर चित्र देखिए।

**sedimentation** /ˌsedɪmenˈteɪʃn ˌसेडिमेन्ˈटेश्न्/ *noun* [U] (*technical*) the process of leaving **sediment** तलछट का जमा होना (झील, नदी आदि में); तलछटन

**sedition** /sɪˈdɪʃn सिˈडिश्न्/ *noun* [U] (*formal*) the use of words or actions that are intended to encourage people to be or act against a government राजद्रोह; जनता को शासन के विरोध में खड़े होने के लिए प्रेरित करने वाला आचरण (वाणी का व्यवहार या कार्य) ▶ **seditious** *adj.* राजद्रोहात्मक, राजद्रोही

**seduce** /sɪˈdjuːs सिˈड्यूस्/ *verb* [T] **1 seduce sb (into sth/doing sth)** to persuade sb to do sth he/she would not usually agree to do किसी को किसी बात का प्रलोभन देना (उस बात के लिए तैयार करना जो वह सामान्यतया नहीं करता) *Special offers seduce customers into spending their money.* **2** to persuade sb to have sex with you यौन-संबंध के लिए राज़ी करना; फुसलाना ▶ **seduction** /sɪˈdʌkʃn सिˈडक्श्न्/ *noun* [C, U] विलोभ, फुसलाहट

**seductive** /sɪˈdʌktɪv सिˈडक्टिव्/ *adj.* **1** sexually attractive सम्मोहक, मोहक; कामुक रूप से आकर्षक *a seductive smile* **2** attractive in a way that makes you want to have or do sth आकर्षक (इस रूप में कि आप उससे सहमत हो जाएँ) *a seductive argument/opinion* (= one which you are tempted to agree with)

**see** /siː सी/ *verb* (*pt* **saw** /sɔː सॉ/; *pp* **seen** /siːn सीन्/) **1** [I, T] to become conscious of sth, using your eyes; to use the power of sight देखना, नेत्रों द्वारा प्रत्यक्ष करना; दृष्टि-शक्ति का प्रयोग करना *On a clear day you can see for miles.* ○ *He looked for her but couldn't see her in the crowd.* ➪ **look**[1] पर नोट देखिए। **2** [T] to look at or watch a film, play, television programme, etc. फ़िल्म, नाटक आदि

देखना *Did you see that programme on sharks last night?* ○ *Have you seen Ram Gopal Verma's latest film?* **3** [T] to find out sth by looking, asking or waiting देखकर, पूछकर या प्रतीक्षा कर बात का पता लगाना ***Go and see** who is at the door.* ○ *I saw in the paper that they're building a new theatre.* **4** [T] to spend time with sb; to visit sb किसी के साथ कुछ समय रहना; किसी के पास जाना, किसी से मिलना *I saw Arun at the weekend and we had dinner together.* ○ *You should see a doctor about that cough.* **5** [I, T] to understand sth; to realize sth किसी बात को समझना; कुछ महसूस करना *Do you **see what I mean**?* ○ *She doesn't **see the point in** spending so much money on a car.* **6** [T] to have an opinion about sth किसी विषय में कोई विचार होना या रखना *How do you see the situation developing?* **7** [T] to imagine sth as a future possibility भावी स्थिति के रूप में किसी बात की कल्पना करना *I can't see her changing her mind.* **8** [T] to do what is necessary in a situation; to make sure that sb does sth (किसी स्थिति में) जो आवश्यक हो वह करना, ध्यान देना; पक्का करना कि काम हो जाए *I'll see that he gets the letter.* **9** [T] to go with sb, for example to help or protect him/her साथ चल कर किसी को कहीं पहुँचाना (सहायता या सुरक्षा की दृष्टि से) *He was willing to see me home.* ○ *I'll see you to the door.* **10** [T] to be the time when an event happens किसी घटना के घटित होने का साक्षी होना *Last year saw huge changes in the education system.*

**IDM as far as I can see** ➪ **far²** देखिए।

**as far as the eye can see** ➪ **far²** देखिए।

**let me see; let's see** ➪ **let** देखिए।

**see eye to eye (with sb)** to agree with sb; to have the same opinion as sb किसी के साथ सहमत होना; दोनों या सब का एकमत होना *We don't always see eye to eye on political matters.*

**see if** to try to do sth कुछ करने का प्रयास करना *I'll see if I can find time to do it.* ○ *See if you can undo this knot.*

**see you around** (*informal*) used for saying goodbye to sb you have made no arrangement to see again जिससे जल्दी मिलना निश्चित न हो उसे अलविदा कहने के लिए प्रयुक्त

**see you (later)** used for saying goodbye to sb you expect to see soon or later that day जिससे जल्दी मिलना निश्चित हो उसे अलविदा कहने के लिए प्रयुक्त

**you see** used for giving a reason किसी बात का कोई कारण बताने के लिए प्रयुक्त *She's very unhappy. She had worked very hard for the test, you see.*

**PHR V see about sth/doing sth** to deal with sth कोई काम निपटाना *I've got to go to the bank to see about my credit card.*

**see sb off** to go with sb to the railway station, the airport, etc. in order to say goodbye to him/her रेलवे स्टेशन, एअरपोर्ट आदि तक साथ जाकर (किसी को) विदा देना

**see through sb/sth** to be able to see that sb/sth is not what he/she/it appears को भाँप जाना (कि बात वस्तुतः सच नहीं), के धोखे में न आना *The police immeditely saw through his story.*

**see to sb/sth** to do what is necessary in a situation; to deal with sb/sth किसी बात पर ध्यान देना, यथापेक्षित करना; किसी से निपटना या किसी को निपटाना *I'll see to the travel arrangements and you book the hotel.*

**seed** /siːd सीड्/ *noun* **1** [C, U] the small hard part of a plant from which a new plant of the same kind can grow बीज *a packet of sunflower seeds* **2** [C] the start of a feeling or event that continues to grow किसी मनोभाव या घटना का आरंभ (जो बाद में बढ़ता या बढ़ती जाए) **3** [C] a good player in a sports competition, especially tennis, who is given a rank and is expected to finish in a high rank किसी खेल (विशेषतः टेनिस) का वरीयता प्राप्त श्रेष्ठ खिलाड़ी जिसकी वरीयता क्रम में उच्च श्रेणी में बने रहने की संभावना हो

**seeded** /ˈsiːdɪd ˈसीडिड्/ *adj.* (used about a player or a team in a sports competition) of a high rank and expected to finish in a high position (खिलाड़ी या दल) उच्च वरीयता प्राप्त और संभावित रूप से श्रेष्ठ; मानांकित

**seedless** /ˈsiːdləs सीड्लस्/ *adj.* (used about fruit) having no seeds (फल) बेदाना, निर्बीज *seedless grapes*

**seedling** /ˈsiːdlɪŋ ˈसीड्लिङ्/ *noun* [C] a very young plant or tree that has grown from a seed छोटा नया पौधा या बीज से निकला पौधा; नवोद्भिद्

**seedy** /ˈsiːdi ˈसीडि/ *adj.* dirty and unpleasant; possibly connected with illegal or immoral activities गंदा और ख़राब; अवैध या अनैतिक कार्यों के शक के घेरे में *a seedy hotel/neighbourhood*

**seeing** /ˈsiːɪŋ ˈसीइङ्/ (*also* **seeing that; seeing as**) *conj.* (*informal*) because; as यह देखते हुए कि, क्योंकि; जैसा कि *Seeing as we're going the same way, I'll give you a lift.*

**seek** /siːk सीक्/ *verb* [T] (*pt, pp* **sought** /sɔːt सॉट्/) (*formal*) **1** to try to find or get sth कुछ ढूँढ़ने या पाने की कोशिश करना; तलाश करना *Politi-*

*cians are still seeking a peaceful solution.* **2 seek sth (from sb)** to ask sb for sth (किसी से) कुछ माँगना, लेना या अनुरोध करना *You should seek advice from a lawyer.* **3 seek (to do sth)** to try to do sth कुछ करने का यत्न करना *They are still seeking to find a peaceful solution to the conflict.* **4 -seeking** (*used to form compound adjectives*) looking for or trying to get the thing mentioned निर्दिष्ट वस्तु को चाहने या पाने की कोशिश करनेवाला, -अपेक्षी *attention-seeking behaviour* ○ *a heat-seeking missile*

**seeker** /ˈsiːkə(r) ˈसीक(र्)/ *noun* [C] (*often used in compounds*) a person who is trying to find or get the thing mentioned निर्दिष्ट वस्तु को ढूँढ़ने या पाने की कोशिश करने वाला व्यक्ति; अर्थी व्यक्ति *an attention seeker* ○ *asylum seekers*

**seem** /siːm सीम्/ *linking verb* **seem (to sb) (to be) sth; seem (like) sth** (*not used in the continuous tenses*) to give the impression of being or doing sth; to appear कुछ होने या करने की प्रतीति कराना; प्रतीत होना, लगाना *It seems to me that we have no choice.* ○ *This machine doesn't seem to work.*

**seeming** /ˈsiːmɪŋ ˈसीमिङ्/ *adj.* (*only before a noun*) appearing to be sth कुछ लगता हुआ, कुछ प्रतीत होता हुआ *Despite her seeming enthusiasm, Sulekha didn't really help much.* ▶ **seemingly** *adv.* प्रकट रूप से *a seemingly endless list of complaints*

**seen** ➪ **see** का past participle रूप

**seep** /siːp सीप्/ *verb* [I] (used about a liquid) to flow very slowly through sth (द्रव का) रिसना (किसी वस्तु के अंदर धीरे-धीरे जाना) *Water started seeping in through small cracks.*

**see-saw** *noun* [C] an outdoor toy for children that consists of a long piece of wood that is balanced in the middle. One child sits on each end of the see-saw and one goes up while the other goes down झूला पट्टी; झुलने वाला तख़्ता, झुलावा

**seethe** /siːð सीद्/ *verb* [I] **1** to be very angry क्रोध से उबलना *I was absolutely seething.* **2 seethe (with sth)** to be very crowded बहुत भीड़ भरा होना *The streets were seething with people.*

**segment** /ˈsegmənt ˈसेग्मन्ट्/ *noun* [C] **1** a section or part of sth किसी का खंड या भाग *I've divided the sheet of paper into three segments.* ○ *a segment of the population* ➪ **circle** पर चित्र देखिए। **2** one of the parts into which an orange can be divided नारंगी की फाँक

**segmentation** /ˌsegmenˈteɪʃn ˌसेग्मेन्ˈटेश्न्/ *noun* [U, C, *usually pl.*] (*technical*) the act of dividing sth into different parts; one of these parts किसी वस्तु को विभिन्न खंडों में विभक्त करने की क्रिया; खंडीकरण, एक खंड (खंडीकरण के फलस्वरूप) *the segmentation of social classes*

**segregate** /ˈsegrɪgeɪt ˈसेग्रिगेट्/ *verb* [T] **segregate sb/sth (from sb/sth)** to separate one group of people or things from the rest व्यक्तियों या वस्तुओं के एक समूह को दूसरे से अलग करना *The two groups of football fans were segregated to avoid trouble.* ➪ **integrate** देखिए। ▶ **segregation** /ˌsegrɪˈgeɪʃn ˌसेग्रिˈगेश्न्/ *noun* [U] पृथक्करण *racial segregation* (= separating people of different races)

**seismic** /ˈsaɪzmɪk ˈसाइज़्मिक्/ *adj.* connected with or caused by movements in the earth's surface (**earthquakes**) भूकंप से संबंधित या उससे उत्पन्न; भूकंपीय

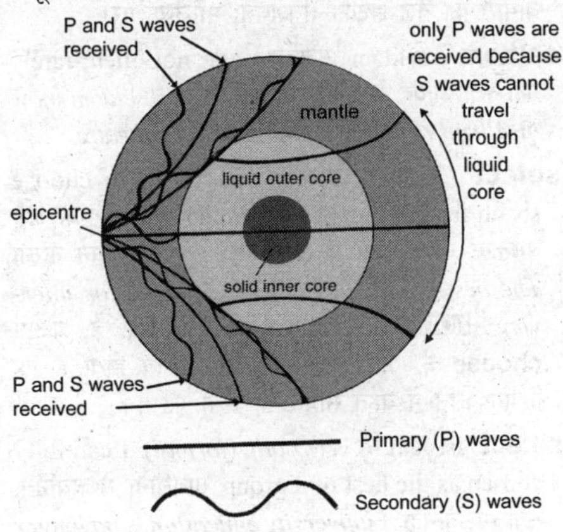


**paths of seismic waves through the earth**

**seismograph** /ˈsaɪzməgrɑːf ˈसाइज़्मग्राफ़्/ *noun* [C] an instrument that measures and records information about **earthquakes** भूकंपमापी यंत्र, भूकंपलेखी

**seismology** /saɪzˈmɒlədʒi साइज़्ˈमॉलजि/ *noun* [U] the scientific study of movements in the earth's surface (**earthquakes**) भूकंप-विज्ञान

**seize** /siːz सीज़्/ *verb* [T] **1** to take hold of sth suddenly and firmly; to grab sth किसी वस्तु को एकाएक और कसकर पकड़ लेना; छीन लेना, झपट लेना *The thief seized her handbag and ran off with it.* ○ (*figurative*) *to seize a chance/an opportunity* **2** to take control or possession of sb/sth किसी को

कब्ज़े में कर लेना या हथिया लेना *The police seized 50 kilograms of illegal drugs.* **3** (*usually passive*) (used about an emotion) to affect sb suddenly and very strongly (किसी भाव से) एकाएक तथा अत्यधिक आक्रांत हो जाना *I felt myself seized by panic.*

**PHRV** **seize (on/upon) sth** to make use of a good and unexpected chance अच्छे और आकस्मिक अवसर का लाभ उठाना *He seized on a mistake by the goalkeeper and scored.*

**seize up** (used about a machine) to stop working because it is too hot, does not have enough oil, etc. (मशीन का) चलते-चलते रुक जाना (बहुत गरम हो जाने, तेल चुक जाने आदि के कारण)

**seizure** /ˈsiːʒə(r) ˈसीश़(र्)/ *noun* **1** [U] using force or legal authority to take control or possession of sth बलप्रयोग से या क़ानूनन किसी वस्तु पर नियंत्रण या आधिपत्य *the seizure of 30 kilos of heroin by the police* **2** [C] a sudden strong attack of an illness, especially one affecting the brain किसी बीमारी का तेज़ झटका (विशेषतः मस्तिष्क पर)

**seldom** /ˈseldəm ˈसेल्डम्/ *adv.* not often; rarely यदा-कदा; शायद ही कभी, कदाचित *There is seldom snow in Athens.* ○ *I very seldom go to the theatre.*

**select**[1] /sɪˈlekt सिˈलेक्ट्/ *verb* [T] to choose sb/sth from a number of similar things एक जैसे व्यक्तियों या वस्तुओं में से एक को चुनना; चयन करना *The best candidates will be selected for interview.* **NOTE** **Select** अधिक औपचारिक है, बजाए **choose** के, और इससे यह भी ध्वनित होता है कि निर्णय करने में बहुत सावधानी बरती गई है।

**select**[2] /sɪˈlekt सिˈलेक्ट्/ *adj.* (*formal*) **1** carefully chosen as the best of a group सावधानी से चयनित, सर्वोत्तम; चुनिंदा *A university education is no longer the privilege of* ***a select few****.* **2** used or owned by rich people धनी व्यक्तियों द्वारा प्रयुक्त या उनका अपना या उनके स्वामित्व वाला

**selection** /sɪˈlekʃn सिˈलेक्श्न्/ *noun* **1** [U] choosing or being chosen चयन करना या चुना जाना; चयन *The manager is responsible for team selection.* **2** [C] a number of people or things that have been chosen चुने गए लोग या वस्तुएँ; चयन, संकलन, चयनिका *a selection of hits from the fifties and sixties* **3** [C] a number of things from which you can chose वस्तुएँ जिनमें से चुनाव करना है; संग्रह *This shop has a very good selection of toys.*

**selective** /sɪˈlektɪv सिˈलेक्टिव्/ *adj.* **1** careful when choosing चयन करने में सावधान; चयनशील *She's very selective about who she invites to her parties.* **2** being careful about what or who you choose चयन करने में सावधानी बरतते हुए; चयन प्रधान *selective schools/education* ▶ **selectively** *adv.* चयनात्मकता के साथ

**self** /self सेल्फ़्/ *noun* [C] (*pl.* **selves** /selvz सेल्व्ज़्/) a person's own nature or qualities व्यक्ति का अपना स्वभाव या अपने गुण *It's good to see you back to* ***your old self*** *again* (= feeling well or happy again). ○ *Her spiteful remark revealed her* ***true self*** (= what she was really like).

**self-** *prefix* (*used in nouns and adjectives*) of, to or by yourself or itself आत्म-, स्वयं-, स्वतः-, स्व- (अपना, अपने को या अपने से या स्वयं) *self-control* ○ *self-addressed* ○ *self-taught*

**self-addressed envelope** = **stamped addressed envelope**

**self-assured** *adj.* = **assured**

**self-assurance** *noun* [U] = **assurance**[2]

**self-catering** *adj.* (*BrE*) (used about a holiday or a place to stay) where meals are not provided for you so you cook them yourself (अवकाश का दिन या ठहरने का स्थान) जहाँ भोजन स्वयं बनाना पड़े

**self-centred** (*AmE* **self-centered**) *adj.* thinking only about yourself and not about other people आत्म-केंद्रित (केवल अपनी चिंता करने वाला); स्वार्थी, ख़ुदगर्ज़ ➪ **selfish** देखिए।

**self-confessed** *adj.* admitting that you are sth or do sth that most people consider to be bad आत्म-घोषित (जो अपनी ग़लती मान ले)

**self-confident** *adj.* feeling sure about your own value and abilities आत्मविश्वासी ➪ **confident** देखिए। ▶ **self-confidence** *noun* [U] आत्मविश्वास *Many women lack the self-confidence to apply for senior jobs.*

**self-conscious** *adj.* too worried about what other people think about you आत्मचेतन (अपने विषय में दूसरों के विचारों को लेकर अति चिंतित; आत्म प्रबुद्ध ▶ **selfconsciously** *adv.* आत्मचेतन भाव से ▶ **selfconsciousness** *noun* [U] आत्मचेतना

**self-contained** *adj.* (*BrE*) (used about a flat, etc.) having its own private entrance, kitchen and bathroom (फ़्लैट आदि) स्वतः पूर्ण, जिसमें सभी सुविधाएँ (प्रवेशद्वार, रसोई, स्नानघर) किसी दूसरे के साथ बटीं हुई न हों

**self-control** *noun* [U] the ability to control your emotions and appear calm even when you are angry, afraid, excited, etc. आत्मनियंत्रण (अपनी भावनाओं पर नियंत्रण रखने की क्षमता) *to lose/keep your self-control*

**self-defence** (*AmE* **self defense**) *noun* [U] the use of force to protect yourself or your property आत्मरक्षा (अपनी या अपनी संपत्ति की रक्षा के लिए बलप्रयोग) *Laila is learning karate for self-defence.* ○ *to shoot sb* ***in self-defence*** (= because they are going to attack you)

**self-destruct** *verb* [I] to destroy him-/her-/itself अपना नाश करना ▶ **self-destructive** आत्मनाशी *adj.* ▶ **self-destruction** *noun* [U] आत्मनाश

**self-discipline** *noun* [U] the ability to make yourself do sth difficult or unpleasant आत्मानुशासन (अति-कठिन या अपने को नापसंद कार्यों में स्वयं को लगाने की योग्यता) *It takes a lot of self-discipline to give up smoking.*

**self-employed** *adj.* working for yourself and earning money from your own business स्वनियोजित (अपने लिए काम करने वाला और निजी व्यवसाय से धनार्जन करने वाला)

**self-esteem** *noun* [U] a good opinion of your own character and abilities आत्मसम्मान (अपने चरित्र और क्षमताओं के लिए सम्मान का भाव) *a man with high/low self-esteem*

**self-evident** *adj.* that does not need any proof or explanation; clear जिसे प्रमाण-पुष्ट करने या समझाने की आवश्यकता नहीं, स्वतः प्रमाण; सुस्पष्ट

**self-explanatory** *adj.* clear and easy to understand; not needing to be explained स्वतः स्पष्ट, सुबोध; जिसे समझाने की आवश्यकता नहीं, स्वस्पष्टीकारक *The book's title is self-explanatory.*

**self-important** *adj.* thinking that you are more important than other people अपने को दूसरों से बड़ा मानने वाला; अहंकारी ▶ **self-importance** *noun* [U] अहंकार ▶ **self-importantly** *adv.* अहंकार-पूर्वक

**self-indulgent** *adj.* allowing yourself to have or do things you enjoy (sometimes when it would be better to stop yourself) असंयमी, विषयासक्त (सांसारिक भोगों में अबाध रूप से लीन) ▶ **self-indulgence** *noun* [C, U] असंयम, विषयासक्ति

**self-interest** *noun* [U] thinking about what is best for yourself rather than for other people स्वार्थ, आत्महित

**selfish** /ˈselfɪʃ ˈसेल्‌फ़िश्/ *adj.* thinking only about your own needs or wishes and not about other people's स्वार्थी *a selfish attitude/selfish behaviour!* ✪ विलोम **unselfish** या **selfless** ➪ **self-centred** देखिए। ▶ **selfishly** *adv.* स्वार्थ भाव से, ख़ुदग़रज़ी के साथ ▶ **selfishness** *noun* [U] स्वार्थ भाव, स्वार्थता

**selfless** /ˈselfləs ˈसेल्‌फ़्लस्/ *adj.* thinking more about other people's needs or wishes than your own निःस्वार्थ

**self-made** *adj.* having become rich or successful by your own efforts अपने निजी प्रयासों से धनी या सफल होने वाला; स्वनिर्मित, कर्मठ *a self-made millionaire*

**self-pity** *noun* [U] the state of thinking too much about your own problems or troubles and feeling sorry for yourself आत्मदया; अपनी ही समस्याओं या परेशानियों में डूबा तथा खुद के लिए दुखी

**self-portrait** *noun* [C] a picture that you draw or paint of yourself आत्मचित्र; स्वयं निर्मित अपना चित्र या आरेख

**self-raising flour** (*AmE* **self-rising flour**) *noun* [U] flour that contains a substance that makes cakes, etc. rise during cooking ख़मीर वाला आटा (जिससे केक आदि बनते समय फूल उठते हैं), स्वयं फूलने वाला आटा ➪ **plain flour** देखिए।

**self-reliant** *adj.* not depending on help from anyone else आत्मनिर्भर ➪ **reliant** देखिए।

**self-respect** *noun* [U] a feeling of confidence and pride in yourself आत्मसम्मान, स्वाभिमान *Old people need to keep their dignity and self-respect.* ➪ **respect** देखिए। ▶ **self-respecting** *adj.* स्वाभिमानी (*usually in negative sentences*) *No self-respecting language student* (= nobody who is serious about learning a language) *should be without this book.*

**self-restraint** *noun* [U] the ability to stop yourself doing or saying sth that you want to because you know it is better not to आत्मसंयम, आत्मनिग्रह *She* ***exercised*** *all her* ***self-restraint*** *and kept quiet.*

**self-righteous** *adj.* believing that you are always right and other people are wrong, so that you are better than other people स्वयं को हमेशा सही (और दूसरों को ग़लत) और इसलिए ख़ुद को दूसरों से बेहतर मानने वाला; दंभी ➪ **righteous** देखिए। ▶ **self-righteously** *adv.* दंभपूर्वक ▶ **self-righteousness** *noun* [U] आत्मधर्माभिमानिता, दंभ

**self-rising flour** (*AmE*) = **self-raising flour**

**self-sacrifice** *noun* [U] giving up what you need or want, in order to help others आत्मबलिदान, आत्मत्याग

**self-satisfied** *adj.* too pleased with yourself or with what you have done आत्मसंतुष्ट (अपने से या अपने काम से अति प्रसन्न) ✪ पर्याय **smug**

**self-service** *adj.* (used about a shop, restaurant, etc.) where you serve yourself and then pay at a special desk (**a cash desk**) स्वयं-सेवा (ऐसी दुकान, रेस्तराँ आदि के लिए प्रयुक्त जहाँ ग्राहक अपना सामान खुद लेता है तथा कांउटर पर ख़ुद भुगतान करता है)

**self-study** *noun* [U] the activity of learning about sth without a teacher to help you स्वयं अध्ययन (शिक्षक की सहायता के बिना संपन्न अध्ययन); स्वयं शिक्षा, स्वशिक्षा ▶ **self-study** *adj*. स्वयं शिक्षात्मक, स्वशिक्षात्मक

**self-styled** *adj*. (*only before a noun*) using a name or title that you have given yourself, especially when you do not have the right to do it स्वघोषित, स्वकथित; (अपने लिए किसी नाम या उपाधि की घोषणा करते हुए, विशेषतः अनधिकृत रूप से) *the self-styled king of fashion*

**self-sufficient** *adj*. able to produce or provide everything that you need without help from or having to buy from others आत्मनिर्भर

**sell** /sel सेल् / *verb* (*pt, pp* **sold** /səʊld सोल्ड् /) **1** [I, T] **sell (sb) (sth) (at/for sth); sell (sth) (to sb) (at/for sth)** to give sth to sb who pays for it and is then the owner of it किसी को कुछ बेचना (दाम लेकर वस्तु देना, और ग्राहक का वस्तु का स्वामी हो जाना) *We are going to sell our car.* ○ *He sold his guitar for Rs 500.* **2** [T] to offer sth for people to buy ख़रीदने के लिए ग्राहक को कुछ पेश करना *to sell insurance/advertising space/stamps* **3** [I, T] to be bought by people in the way or in the numbers mentioned; to be offered at the price mentioned निर्दिष्ट प्रकार से या संख्या में बिकना; निर्दिष्ट दाम पर बिक्री के लिए पेश होना, बिकाऊ होना *Her books sell well abroad.* ○ *This newspaper sells over a million copies a day.* **4** [T] to make people want to buy sth लोगों के मन में कुछ ख़रीदने की चाह पैदा करना *They rely on advertising to sell their products.* ➪ **sale** noun (अर्थ सं. 1 से 4 तक के लिए) देखिए। **5** [T] **sell sth/yourself to sb** to persuade sb to accept sth; to persuade sb that you are the right person for a job, position, etc. किसी को कुछ स्वीकार करने के लिए प्रेरित करना; नौकरी आदि के लिए अपने उपयुक्त होने की बात को किसी से मनवाना *Now we have to try and sell the idea to the management.*

**PHR V** **be sold on sth** (*informal*) to be very enthusiastic about sth किसी चीज़ का दीवाना हो जाना

**sell sth off** to sell sth in order to get rid of it, often at a low price किसी वस्तु को सस्ता बेचना (उससे छुटकारा पाने के लिए) *The shops sell their remaining winter clothes off in the spring sales.*

**sell out; be sold out** (used about tickets for a concert, football game, etc.) to be all sold (संगीत समारोह, फ़ुटबॉल मैच आदि के) सारे टिकट बिक जाना *All the tickets sold out within two hours* ○ *The concert was sold out weeks ago.*

**sell out (of sth); be sold out (of sth)** to sell all of sth so that no more is/are available to be bought सारा माल बिक जाना या बेच देना *I'm afraid we've sold out of bread.*

**sell up** to sell everything you own, especially your house, your business, etc. (in order to start a new life, move to another country, etc.) (जीवन को नए सिरे से शुरू कर विदेश में बसने आदि के लिए) अपना सब कुछ (विशेषतः मकान, व्यवसाय आदि बेच देना

**seller** /ˈselə(r) ˈसेल(र्) / *noun* [C] **1** (*often in compounds*) a person or business that sells विक्रेता (व्यक्ति या कोई व्यवसाय) *a bookseller* ○ *a flower seller* **2** something that is sold, especially in the amount or way mentioned बिकने वाली वस्तु (विशेषतः निर्दिष्ट मात्रा में या प्रकार से) *This magazine is a big seller in the 25–40 age group.* ➪ **best seller** देखिए।

**selling price** *noun* [C] the price at which sth is sold विक्रय मूल्य (जिस मूल्य पर वस्तु बिके) ➪ **asking price** और **cost price** देखिए।

**Sellotape™** /ˈseləteɪp ˈसेलटेप् / (*AmE* **Scotch tape™**) *noun* [U] a type of clear tape that is sold in rolls and used for sticking things चीजें चिपकाने का पारदर्शी टेप; सेलोटेप ➪ **tape** देखिए तथा **stationery** पर चित्र भी देखिए। ▶ **sellotape** *verb* [T] सेलोटेप से वस्तुओं को चिपकाना

**selves** ➪ **self** का plural रूप

**semantic** /sɪˈmæntɪk सिˈमैन्टिक् / *adj*. connected with the meaning of words and sentences शब्दों और वाक्यों के अर्थ से संबंधित ▶ **semantically** /sɪˈmæntɪkli सिˈमैन्टिकलि / *adv*. अर्थ की दृष्टि से

**semantics** /sɪˈmæntɪks सिˈमैन्टिक्स् / *noun* [U] **1** the study of the meanings of words and phrases अर्थविज्ञान, अर्थमीमांसा; शब्दों और वाक्यांशों के अर्थ का अध्ययन **2** the meaning of words and phrases शब्दों और वाक्यांशों का अर्थ *the semantics of the language*

**semblance** /ˈsembləns ˈसेम्ब्लन्स् / *noun* [*sing*., U] (*formal*) **(a) semblance of sth** the appearance of being sth or of having a certain quality कुछ होने या किसी विशिष्ट गुण से युक्त होने का आभास

**semen** /ˈsiːmen ˈसीमेन् / *noun* [U] the liquid that is produced by the male sex organs containing the seed (**sperm**) necessary for producing babies or young (पुरुष का वीर्य) शुक्र (संतानोत्पत्ति का कारण)

**semester** /sɪˈmestə(r) सि'मेस्टर्/ *noun* [C] one of the two periods that the school or college year is divided into स्कूल या कॉलेज का अध्ययन सत्र *the first/spring semester*

**semi** /ˈsemi ˈसेमि/ *noun* [C] (*pl.* **semis** /ˈsemiz ˈसेमिज़्/) (*BrE informal*) a house that is joined to another one with a shared wall between them, forming a pair of houses (मकानों के जोड़े में) दूसरे के साथ साझी दीवार वाला मकान; जुड़वाँ मकान

**semi-** /ˈsemi ˈसेमि/ *prefix* (*used in adjectives and nouns*) half; partly अर्ध-; आंशिक *semicircular* ○ *semi-final*

**semi-arid** *adj.* (*technical*) (used about land or climate) dry; with little rain (भूमि या मौसम) शुष्क, सूखा; कम वर्षा वाला

**semicircle** /ˈsemisɜːkl ˈसेमिसक्ल्/ *noun* [C] one half of a circle; something that is arranged in this shape अर्धवृत्त; अर्धवृत्ताकार वस्तु *They sat* ***in a semicircle***. ➪ **circle** पर चित्र देखिए। ▶ **semicircular** /ˌsemiˈsɜːkjələ(r) ˌसेमिˈसक्यल(र्)/ *adj.* अर्धवृत्ताकार

**semicolon** /ˌsemiˈkəʊlən ˌसेमिˈकोलन्/ *noun* [C] a mark (;) used in writing for separating parts of a sentence or items in a list वाक्य के अंशों या सूची तालिका के मदों को अलग करने के लिए प्रयुक्त एक विराम चिह्न (;), अर्धविराम, सेमिकोलन

**semiconductor** /ˌsemikənˈdʌktə(r) ˌसेमिकन्ˈडक्टर्/ *noun* [C] (*technical*) a solid substance that allows heat or electricity to pass through it or along it in particular conditions अर्धचालक, सेमिकंडक्टर (विशिष्ट दशाओं में ताप या विद्युत का चालन करने वाला एक ठोस पदार्थ) ➪ **conductor** देखिए।

**semi-detached** *adj.* (used about a house) joined to another house with a shared wall on one side forming a pair of houses (मकानों के जोड़े में) दूसरे के साथ साझी दीवार वाला मकान; जुड़वाँ मकान

**semi-final** *noun* [C] one of the two games in a sports competition which decide which players or teams will play each other in the final अंतिम मैच से पहले का मैच, पूर्वांतिम या अंतिम-पूर्व मैच; सेमि-फ़ाइनल ➪ **quarter-final** और **final** देखिए। ▶ **semi-finalist** *noun* [C] सेमि-फ़ाइनल खेलने वाली टीम या खिलाड़ी

**seminar** /ˈsemɪnɑː(r) ˈसेमिना(र्)/ *noun* [C] **1** a class at a university, college, etc. in which a small group of students discuss or study a subject with a teacher शिक्षक और छोटे छात्रवर्ग के बीच परिसंवाद; उपकक्षा *I've got a seminar on 'Rabindranath Tagore' this morning.* **2** a meeting for business people in which working methods, etc. are taught or discussed संगोष्ठी; परिसंवाद (कार्य-प्रणालियों आदि पर चर्चा हेतु व्यवसाय से संलग्न व्यक्तियों की बैठक) *a one-day management seminar*

**semi-skilled** *adj.* (used about workers) having some special training or **qualifications**, but less than skilled people (कारीगर) अर्धकुशल (पूर्णप्रशिक्षण प्राप्त कारीगरों से कुछ कम प्रशिक्षित)

**semolina** /ˌseməˈliːnə ˌसेमˈलीना/ *noun* [U] large hard grains of wheat used for making sweet dishes and other food **(pasta)** (गेहूँ का) चोकर, दलिया, सूजी

**send** /send सेन्ड्/ *verb* [T] (*pt, pp* **sent** /sent सेन्ट्/) **1 send sth (to sb/sth); send (sb) sth** to make sth go or be taken somewhere, especially by mail, radio, etc. कहीं कुछ भेजना या भिजवाना (विशेषतः डाक, रेडियो आदि के द्वारा *to send a letter/parcel/message/fax to sb* ○ *Don't forget to send me a postcard.* **2** to tell sb to go somewhere or to do sth; to arrange for sb to go somewhere किसी को कहीं जाने के लिए या कुछ करने के लिए कहना; किसी को कहीं भिजवाना *She* ***sent*** *the children* ***to bed*** *early.* ○ *to* ***send sb to prison*** **3** to cause sb/sth to move in a particular direction, often quickly or as a reaction that cannot be prevented किसी ओर गति करने का कारण बनना (प्रायः तेज़ी से या प्रबल प्रतिक्रियावश) *I accidentally pushed the table and* ***sent*** *all the files* ***flying***. **4 send sb (to/into sth)** to make sb have a particular feeling or enter a particular state किसी के मन में कोई भाव जगाना या स्थिति-विशेष में पहुँचाना *The movement of the train* ***sent*** *me* ***to sleep***.

IDM **give/send sb your love** ➪ **love**[1] देखिए।

PHR V **send for sb/sth** to ask for sb to come to you; to ask for sth to be brought or sent to you किसी को अपने पास बुलाना; अपने लिए कोई चीज़ मँगवाना *Send for an ambulance!*

**send sth in** to send sth to a place where it will be officially dealt with कहीं कुछ विचारार्थ प्रेषित करना *I sent my application in last week.*

**send off (for sth); send away (to sb) (for sth)** to write to sb and ask for sth to be sent to you कुछ भिजवाने के लिए किसी को कहना *Let's send off for some holiday brochures.*

**send sb off** (used in a sports match) to order a player who has broken a rule to leave the field and not to return (खेल प्रतियोगिता में) नियम भंग करने वाले खिलाड़ी को मैदान से बाहर भेजा देना (लौटने की मनाही के साथ) *The referee had to send off Manoj from the field.*

**send sth off** to post sth डाक से कुछ भेजना *I'll send the information off today.*

**send sth out** 1 to send sth to a lot of different people or places बहुत से लोगों को या स्थानों पर एक ही वस्तु भेजना *We sent out the invitations two months before the wedding.* 2 to produce sth, for example light, heat, sound, etc. कुछ उत्पन्न करना (जैसे प्रकाश, ताप, ध्वनि आदि)

**send sb/sth up** (*informal*) to make sb/sth look ridiculous or silly especially by copying him/her/it in a way that is intended to be amusing किसी की नक़ल उतर कर उसकी हँसी उड़ाना (मज़ाक में)

**sender** /ˈsendə(r) ˈसेन्ड(र्)/ *noun* [C] a person who sends sth कुछ भेजने वाला व्यक्ति; प्रेषक *The sender's name appears at the top of the email.*

**senile** /ˈsi:naɪl ˈसीनाइल्/ *adj.* behaving in a confused and strange way, and unable to remember things because of old age सनकी और भुलक्कड़ (बुढ़ापे के कारण); जराजीर्ण *I think she's* ***going senile.*** ▶ **senility** /səˈnɪləti सˈनिलटि/ *noun* [U] जराजीर्णता, सठियाना

**senior[1]** /ˈsi:niə(r) ˈसीनिअ(र्)/ *adj.* 1 **senior (to sb)** having a high or higher position in a company, organization, etc. किसी कंपनी, संस्था आदि में उच्च या उच्चतर पद पर प्रतिष्ठित; वरिष्ठ, सीनियर *a senior lecturer/officer/manager* ○ *He's senior to me.* 2 (*often* **Senior**) (*abbr.* **Snr; Sr**) (*AmE*) used after the name of a man who has the same name as his son, to avoid confusion पुत्र के समान नाम वाले पिता के नाम के साथ प्रयुक्त (भ्रम से बचने के लिए) 3 (used in schools) older (स्कूलों में) आयु में बड़ा; ज्येष्ठ 4 (*AmE*) connected with the final year at high school or college स्कूल या कॉलेज में अंतिम वर्ष का (छात्र) ➪ **junior[1]** देखिए।

**senior[2]** /ˈsi:niə(r) ˈसीनिअ(र्)/ *noun* [C] 1 somebody who is older or of a higher position (than one or more other people) एक या अधिक व्यक्तियों से) आयु या पद में बड़ा *My oldest sister is* ***ten years my senior.*** 2 one of the older students at a school (स्कूल में) आयु में बड़ा छात्र 3 a student in the final year of school, college or university स्कूल, कॉलेज या विश्वविद्यालय में अंतिम वर्ष का छात्र *high school seniors* ➪ **junior[2]** देखिए।

**senior citizen** *noun* [C] an elderly person, especially sb who has retired from work बुज़ुर्ग (विशेषतः सेवानिवृत)

**seniority** /ˌsi:niˈɒrəti ˌसीनिˈऑरटि/ *noun* [U] the position or importance that a person has in a company, organization, etc. in relation to others किसी कंपनी, संस्था आदि में किसी व्यक्ति का पद या महत्त्व (दूसरों की तुलना में), किसी व्यक्ति की वरिष्ठता; सीनियॉरिटी *The names are listed below* ***in order of seniority.***

**sensation** /senˈseɪʃn सेन्ˈसेशन्/ *noun* 1 [C] a feeling that is caused by sth affecting your body or part of your body संवेदन; पूरे शरीर या अंग पर पड़े प्रभाव से उत्पन्न अनुभूति *a pleasant/unpleasant/tingling sensation* 2 [U] the ability to feel when touching or being touched स्पर्शानुभूति (स्पर्श करने या होने को अनुभव कर सकना) *For sometime after the accident he had no sensation in his legs.* 3 [C, *usually sing.*] a general feeling or impression that is difficult to explain लोगों में बड़ी उत्तेजना *I had the peculiar sensation that I was floating in the air.* 4 [C, *usually sing.*] great excitement, surprise or interest among a group of people; sb/sth that causes this excitement सनसनी (लोगों में बड़ी उत्तेजना, हैरानी या दिलचस्पी) सनसनी पैदा करने वाला व्यक्ति या वस्तु *The young Indian* ***caused a sensation*** *by beating the top player.*

**sensational** /senˈseɪʃənl सेन्ˈसेशनल्/ *adj.* 1 causing, or trying to cause, a feeling of great excitement, surprise or interest among people सनसनी खेज़ (सनसनी पैदा करने या पैदा करने की कोशिश करते हुए) *This magazine specializes in sensational stories about the rich and the famous.* 2 (*informal*) extremely good or beautiful; very exciting बहुत अच्छा या सुंदर; अति उत्तेजक ▶ **sensationally** /senˈseɪʃənəli सेन्ˈसेशनलि/ *adv.* सनसनीखेज़ ढंग से

**sense[1]** /sens सेन्स्/ *noun* 1 [U] the ability to think or act in a reasonable or sensible way; good judgement विचारपूर्वक या समझदारी से सोचने या करने की क्षमता; अच्छी परख या समझ *He* ***had the sense*** *to stop when he realized he was making a mistake.* ○ *I think there's a lot of sense in what you're saying.* ➪ **common sense** देखिए। 2 [U, *sing.*] the ability to understand sth; the ability to recognize what sth is or what its value is कुछ समझने की क्षमता; किसी चीज़ के स्वरुप या मूल्य को जानने या पहचानने की क्षमता *She seems to have lost all* ***sense of reality.*** ○ *He's got a great* ***sense of humour.*** 3 [U] **sense (in doing sth)** the reason for doing sth; purpose कुछ करने का कारण; उद्देश्य ***What's the sense*** *in making things more difficult for yourself?* 4 [U, *sing.*] a natural ability to do or produce sth well कुछ करने या बनाने की प्राकृतिक क्षमता ***business sense/dress sense*** 5 [*sing.*] a feeling or consciousness of sth किसी बात की अनुभूति या बोध या भावना ***sense of relief/sense of duty*** 6 [C] one of the five natural physical powers of sight, hearing, smell, taste and touch, that people and animals have इंद्रिय, ज्ञानेंद्रिय (मनुष्यों और पशुओं की देखने, सुनने, सूँघने, चखने और छूने की प्राकृतिक शक्ति या क्षमता) *I've got a cold and I've lost my **sense of smell**.* ○ *Dogs have an acute **sense of hearing**.* 7 [C] (used about a word, phrase, etc.) a meaning (शब्द, वाक्यांश आदि का) अर्थ; तात्पर्य *This word has two senses.*

IDM **come to your senses** to finally realize that you should do sth because it is the most sensible thing to do अंत में कुछ करने की बात समझ में आ जाना (क्योंकि वैसा करना ही बुद्धिमानी है)

**in a sense** in one particular way but not in other ways; partly एक विशेष दृष्टि से (परंतु अन्य दृष्टियों से नहीं); अंशतः *In a sense you're right, but there's more to the matter than that.*

**make sense** 1 to be possible to understand; to have a clear meaning समझ में आ सकना; स्पष्ट अर्थ देना या वाला होना *What does this sentence mean? It doesn't make sense to me.* 2 (used about an action) to be sensible or logical (किसी काम का) विवेकपूर्ण या तर्कसंगत होना *I think it would make sense to wait for a while before making a decision.*

**make sense of sth** to manage to understand sth that is not clear or is difficult to understand अस्पष्ट या दुर्बोध बात को जैसे-तैसे समझ लेना *I can't make sense of these instructions.*

**talk sense** ➪ **talk**[1] **6** देखिए।

**sense**[2] /sens सेन्स्/ *verb* [T] (*not used in the continuous tenses*) to realize or become conscious of sth; to get a feeling about sth even though you cannot see it, hear it, etc. किसी बात को अनुभव कर लेना या उसके विषय में सचेत हो जाना; कुछ जान लेना, भाँप लेना (भले ही वह दिखाई या सुनाई न दे) *I sensed that something was wrong as soon as I went in.*

NOTE यद्यपि यह क्रिया सातत्यबोधक कालों (continuous tenses) में प्रयुक्त नहीं होती तथापि इसका -ing युक्त वर्तमान कृदंत (present participle) रूप काफ़ी प्रचलित है—*Sensing a scandal, the tabloid photographers rushed to the star's hotel.*

**senseless** /ˈsensləs ˈसेन्स्लस्/ *adj.* 1 having no meaning or purpose निरर्थक या निरुद्देश्य 2 unconscious बेहोश, निश्चेतन *He was beaten senseless.*

**sensibility** /ˌsensəˈbɪləti ˌसेन्सˈबिलटि/ *noun* (*pl.* **sensibilities**) 1 [U, C] the ability to understand and experience deep feelings, for example in art, literature, etc. संवेदनशीलता; गहन भावों को समझने और अनुभव करने की क्षमता (जैसे कला, साहित्य आदि में) 2 **sensibilities** [*pl.*] a person's feelings, especially when sb is easily offended व्यक्ति की भावनाएँ (विशेषतः जल्दी बुरा मान जाने की स्थिति में); भावुकता, संवेदनशीलता

**sensible** /ˈsensəbl ˈसेन्सब्ल्/ *adj.* (used about people and their behaviour) able to make good judgements based on reason and experience; practical (व्यक्ति और उसका आचरण) तर्क और अनुभव पर आधारित निर्णय करने में समर्थ; समझदार; व्यवहार-कुशल *a sensible person/decision/precaution* ✪ विलोम **silly** या **foolish** ▶ **sensibly** /ˈsensəbli ˈसेन्सबलि/ *adv.* समझदारी से *Let's sit down and discuss the matter sensibly.*

NOTE **Sensible** और **sensitive** की तुलना कीजिए। **Sensible** का संबंध है सहज बुद्धि (समझदारी), तर्कसंगत काम और अच्छी समझ से। **Sensitive** का संबंध है भावनाओं, मनोभावों और पाँच ज्ञानेंद्रियों से।

**sensitive** /ˈsensətɪv ˈसेन्सटिव्/ *adj.* 1 **sensitive (to sth)** showing that you are conscious of and able to understand people's feelings, problems, etc. संवेदनशील; (लोगों की भावनाओं, समस्याओं आदि के प्रति सचेत और उन्हें समझने में समर्थ) *to be sensitive to sb's feelings/wishes* 2 **sensitive (about/to sth)** easily upset, offended or annoyed, especially about a particular subject तुनक-मिज़ाज, चिड़चिड़ा (जल्दी परेशान, गुस्सा या नाराज़ हो जाने वाला, विशेषतः किसी विशेष बात को लेकर) *He's very sensitive to criticism.* ✪ विलोम **insensitive** (अर्थ सं. 1 और 2 के लिए) 3 (used about a subject, a situation, etc.) needing to be dealt with carefully because it is likely to cause anger or trouble (कोई प्रसंग, स्थिति आदि) नाज़ुक (सावधानी से निपटाने योग्य, अन्यथा क्रोध या परेशानी संभावित) *This is a sensitive period in the negotiations between the two countries.* 4 **sensitive (to sth)** easily hurt or damaged; painful, especially if touched जल्दी दर्द में पीड़ाग्रस्त या क्षतिग्रस्त; तकलीफ़देह (विशेषतः छुए जाने पर) *a new cream for sensitive skin* ○ *My teeth are very sensitive to hot or cold food.* 5 (used about a scientific instrument, a piece of equipment, etc.) able to measure very small changes (कोई वैज्ञानिक उपकरण, यंत्र आदि) सूक्ष्मग्राही; ज़रा से परिवर्तन को भी माप लेने वाला ➪ **sensible** पर नोट देखिए। ▶ **sensitively** *adv.* अति सावधानी से *The investigation will need to be handled sensitively.* ▶ **sensitivity** /ˌsensəˈtɪvəti ˌसेन्सˈटिवटि/ *noun* [U] अति संवेदनशीलता, भावुकता *I think your comments showed a complete lack of sensitivity.*

**sensory** /ˈsensəri ˈसेन्सरी/ *adj.* (*usually before a noun*) (*technical*) connected with your physical senses ज्ञानेंद्रियों से संबंधित *sensory organs* ○ *sensory deprivation*

**sensual** /ˈsenʃuəl ˈसेन्शुअल्/ *adj.* connected with physical or sexual pleasure शारीरिक या यौन आनंद से संबंधित; कामुक *the sensual rhythms of Latin music* ▶ **sensuality** /ˌsenʃuˈæləti ˌसेन्शुˈऐलटि/ *noun* [U] कामुकता

**sensuous** /ˈsenʃuəs ˈसेन्शुअस्/ *adj.* giving pleasure to the mind or body through the senses मन या शरीर को इंद्रियजन्य आनंद देने वाला *the sensuous feel of pure silk* ▶ **sensuously** *adv.* इंद्रियजन्य रीति से ▶ **sensuousness** *noun* [U] इंद्रियजन्यता

**sent** ➪ **send** का past tense, past participle रूप

**sentence[1]** /ˈsentəns ˈसेन्टन्स्/ *noun* [C] **1** (*grammar*) a group of words containing a subject and a verb, that expresses a statement, a question, etc. When a sentence is written it begins with a big (**capital**) letter and ends with a full stop वाक्य, सामान्य कथन, प्रश्न आदि का व्यंजक ऐसा शब्दविन्यास जिसमें एक कर्ता हो और एक क्रिया, अंग्रेजी आदि में लिखते समय वाक्य का आरंभ बड़े अक्षर से होता है और अंत पूर्ण विराम (.) से ➪ **phrase** देखिए। **2** the punishment given by a judge to sb who has been found guilty of a crime न्यायाधीश द्वारा अपराधी को दिया गया दंड *Twenty years in prison was a very harsh sentence.*

**sentence[2]** /ˈsentəns ˈसेन्टन्स्/ *verb* [T] **sentence sb (to sth)** (used about a judge) to tell sb who has been found guilty of a crime what the punishment will be (न्यायाधीश का) अपराधी को सज़ा सुनाना *The judge sentenced her to three months in prison for shoplifting.*

**sentiment** /ˈsentɪmənt ˈसेन्टिमन्ट्/ *noun* **1** [C, U] (*often plural*) (*formal*) an attitude or opinion that is often caused or influenced by emotion मनोभाव से उत्पन्न या प्रभावित कोई मनोवृत्ति या विचार *His comments exactly expressed my sentiments.* **2** [U] feelings such as pity, romantic love, sadness, etc. that influence sb's action or behaviour (sometimes in situations where this is not appropriate) करुणा, रूमानी प्रेम, विषाद आदि भाव (जिनका व्यक्ति के कार्य या आचरण पर प्रभाव पड़ता है जो कभी-कभी प्रसंग-विशेष में अनुपयुक्त लगता है) *There's no room for sentiment in business.*

**sentimental** /ˌsentɪˈmentl ˌसेन्टिˈमेन्ट्ल्/ *adj.* **1** producing or connected with emotions such as romantic love, pity, sadness, etc. which may be too strong or not appropriate भावुकतापूर्ण (रूमानी प्रेम, करुणा, विषाद आदि को उत्पन्न करने वाला या उनसे संबंधित), जो अतिसशक्त या अनुपयुक्त हो सकता है *He is sentimental about his old car!* ○ *a sentimental love song* **2** connected with happy memories or feelings of love rather than having any financial value मधुर स्मृतियों या प्रेमानुभूतियों से संबंधित (जिसमें पैसों का महत्त्व नहीं) *The jewellery wasn't worth much but it had great **sentimental value** to me.* ▶ **sentimentality** /ˌsentɪmenˈtæləti ˌसेन्टिमेन्ˈटैलटि/ *noun* [U] भावुकता, भावप्रवणता ▶ **sentimentally** /ˌsentɪˈmentəli ˌसेन्टिˈमेन्टलि/ *adv.* भावुकता से, भावप्रवणता से

**sentinel** /ˈsentɪnəl ˈसेन्टिनल्/ *none* [C] (*literary*) = **sentry**

**sentry** /ˈsentri ˈसेन्ट्रि/ *noun* [C] (*pl.* **sentries**) a soldier who stands outside a building and guards it संतरी (किसी भवन की रक्षा हेतु बाहर खड़े सिपाही); पहरेदार

**sepal** /ˈsepl ˈसेप्ल्/ *noun* [C] (*technical*) a part of a flower, like a leaf, that lies under and supports the **petals** फूल का बाह्यदल (फूल के नीचे का पत्ता जो पंखुड़ी को सँभालता है) ➪ **calyx** देखिए तथा **flower** पर चित्र देखिए।

**separable** /ˈsepərəbl ˈसेपरब्ल्/ *adj.* able to be separated पृथकीयः जिसे पृथक किया जा सके ✪ विलोम **inseparable**

**separate[1]** /ˈseprət ˈसेप्रट्/ *adj.* **1 separate (from sth/sb)** apart; not together अलग, पृथक; न जुड़ा हुआ *You should always keep your cash and credit cards separate.* **2** different; not connected भिन्न; असंबंधित *We stayed in separate rooms in the same hotel.*

**separate[2]** /ˈsepəreɪt ˈसेप्रट्/ *verb* **1** [I, T] **separate (sb/sth) (from sb/sth)** to stop being together; to cause people or things to stop being together अलग हो जाना; व्यक्तियों या वस्तुओं का अलग कर देना *The friends separated at the airport.* ○ *I got separated from my friends in the crowd.* **2** [T] **separate sb/sth (from sb/sth)** to keep people or things apart; to be between people or things with the result that they are apart (व्यक्तियों या वस्तुओं को अलग-अलग कर देना; व्यक्तियों या वस्तुओं का अलग-अलग हो जाना *The two sides of the city are separated by the river.* **3** [I] to stop living together as a couple with your wife, husband or partner पति-पत्नी का अलग-अलग हो जाना *His parents separated when he was still a baby.*

**separated** /ˈsepəreɪtɪd ˈसेपरेटिड्/ *adj.* not living together as a couple any more अलग हो चुके (पति-पत्नी), वियुक्त दंपति *My wife and I are separated.*

**separately** /ˈseprətli ˈसेप्रट्लि/ *adv.* apart; not together अलग-अलग; मिलकर नहीं *We shall pay separately not all together?*

**separation** /ˌsepəˈreɪʃn ˌसेप्ˈरेश्न्/ *noun* **1** [C, U] the action of separating or being separated; a situation or period of being apart अलगाव, पार्थक्य (अलग करने या होने की क्रिया); अलगाव की स्थिति या अवधि **2** [C] an agreement where a couple decide not to live together any more पति-पत्नी में अब साथ-साथ न रहने का समझौता *a trial separation*

**Sept**. *abbr.* September सितंबर *2 Sept. 1920*

**sept-** /sept सेप्ट्/ *prefix* (*used in nouns, adjectives and adverbs*) seven; having seven सात; सात वाला, सप्त *septet* ○ *septennial*

**September** /sepˈtembə(r) सेप्ˈट्म्ब(र्)/ *noun* [U, C] (*abbr.* **Sept.**) the ninth month of the year, coming after August सितंबर; साल का नौवाँ महीना (अगस्त के बाद का)

> NOTE महीनों के नामों की वाक्य-प्रयोग-विधि के लिए **January** की प्रविष्टि में दी गई टिप्पणी और उदाहरण देखिए।

**septic** /ˈseptɪk ˈसेप्टिक्/ *adj.* infected with poisonous bacteria विषाक्त कीटाणुओं से संक्रामित; पूतिक, सेप्टिक *The wound **went septic**.*

**sepulchre** (*AmE* **sepulcher**) /ˈsepəlkər ˈसेपल्क(र्)/ *noun* [C] a chamber that is used as a grave. This could either be cut into rock or built of stone मक़बरा, समाधि, क़ब्र

**septicaemia** (*AmE* **septicemia**) /ˌseptɪˈsi:miə ˌसेप्टिˈसीमिआ/ *noun* [U] infection of the blood by poisonous bacteria विषाक्त कीटाणुओं से रक्तदूषण, रक्तविषाक्तता, पूतिरक्तता ✪ पर्याय **blood poisoning**

**sequel** /ˈsi:kwəl ˈसीक्वल्/ *noun* [C] **a sequel (to sth) 1** a book, film, etc. that continues the story of the one before उत्तर-कथा (पुस्तक, फ़िल्म या रचना जो पिछली कथा को आगे बढ़ाए); पश्च-कथा **2** something that happens after, or is the result of, an earlier event (पूर्व घटना की) उत्तरवर्ती स्थिति या उसका परिणाम

**sequence** /ˈsi:kwəns ˈसीक्वन्स्/ *noun* [C] **1** a number of things (actions, events, etc.) that happen or come one after another क्रम से होने या आने वाली क्रियाएं, घटनाएँ आदि; सिलसिला *Complete the following sequence 1, 4, 8, 13...* **2** [U] the order in which a number of things happen or are arranged क्रम, अनुक्रम (जिसमें घटनाएँ घटित हों या कार्यकलाप व्यवस्थित हो) *The photographs are **in sequence**.*

**sequential** /sɪˈkwenʃl सीˈक्वेन्श्ल्/ *adj.* (*formal*) following in order of time or place क्रमिक, आनुक्रमिक (समय या स्थान की दृष्टि से क्रमबद्ध) *sequential data processing* ▶ **sequentially** /-ʃəli शेलि/ *adv.* क्रम से क्रमबद्ध *data stored sequentially on the computer*

**sequin** /ˈsi:kwɪn ˈसीक्विन्/ *noun* [C] a small shiny round piece of metal or plastic that is sewn onto clothing as decoration सजावट के लिए कपड़ों पर टाँकने की सीप; कटोरी (धातु या प्लास्टिक की) ▶ **sequinned** *adj.* सीपियों से सजा

**seraph** /ˈserəf ˈसेरफ़्/ *noun* [C] (*pl.* **seraphim** or **seraphs**) an angel of the highest rank according to the Bible (बाइबल के अनुसार) देवदूत, फ़रिश्ता ➪ **cherub** देखिए।

**serene** /səˈri:n सˈरीन्/ *adj.* calm and peaceful शांत और अविक्षुब्ध या गंभीर *a serene smile* ▶ **serenely** *adv.* शांतभाव से, अविक्षुब्ध रूप से या गंभीरतापूर्वक ▶ **serenity** /səˈrenəti सˈरेनटि/ *noun* [U] शांति, गंभीरता

**serf** /sɜ:f सफ़्/ *noun* [C] (in the past) a person who was forced to live and work on land that belonged to a landowner whom they had to obey (विगत में) कृषिदास

**sergeant** /ˈsɑ:dʒənt ˈसाजन्ट्/ *noun* [C] (*abbr.* **Sgt**) **1** an officer with a low position in the army or air force थल सेना या वायुसेना में निम्नश्रेणी का अधिकारी; सार्जेंट **2** an officer with a middle position in the police force पुलिस में मध्यक्रम का अधिकारी; पुलिस सार्जेंट

**serial** /ˈsɪəriəl ˈसिअरिअल्/ *noun* [C] a story in a magazine or on television or radio that is told in a number of parts over a period of time धारावाहिक (पत्रिका, टीवी, रेडियो पर एक अवधि तक कड़ियों में प्रस्तुत कहानी) *the first part of a six-part drama serial* ➪ **series** पर नोट देखिए। ▶ **serialize** (*also* **-ise**) /-rɪəlaɪz -रिअलाइज़्/ *verb* [T] क्रमबद्ध करना, धारावाहिक निकालना

**serial number** *noun* [C] the number marked on sth to identify it and to distinguish it from other things of the same type क्रम संख्या (सूची में वस्तु के क्रम को सूचित करने वाली संख्या)

**series** /ˈsɪəri:z ˈसिअरीज़्/ *noun* [C] (*pl.* **series**) **1** a number of things that happen one after another and are of the same type or connected शृंखला, सिलसिला (क्रम से घटित होने वाली एक जैसी या संबंधित घटनाएँ) *a series of events* ○ *There has been a series of burglaries in this district recently.* **2** a number of programmes on radio or television which have the same main characters and each tell a complete story रेडियो, टीवी पर प्रस्तुत कथा-शृंखला (जिसमें कथा अपने में पूरी होती है और सबके मुख्य पात्र समान होते हैं)

> NOTE **Series** और **serial** की तुलना कीजिए। **Series** की प्रत्येक कथा दूसरे से अलग और अपने में पूरी होती है यद्यपि सबके मुख्य पात्र वही (समान) होते हैं। **Serial** में एक ही कथा सब खंडों में चलती रहती है।

**serious** /ˈsɪəriəs ˈसिअरिअस्/ *adj.* 1 bad or dangerous दुर्दशाग्रस्त; बुरी हालत या ख़तरनाक या चिंताजनक *a serious accident/illness/offence* ○ *Pollution is a very serious problem.* 2 needing to be treated as important, not just for fun गंभीरता से (न कि हलके से) लिया जाने योग्य *Don't laugh, it's a serious matter.* ○ *a serious discussion* 3 **serious (about sth/about doing sth)** (used about a person) not joking; thinking about things in a careful and sensible way (व्यक्ति) गंभीर, मज़ाकिया नहीं; सावधानी और बुद्धिमानी से मसलों पर सोचने वाला *Are you serious about starting your own business* (= are you really going to do it)? ○ *He's terribly serious. I don't think I've ever seen him laugh.* ▶ **seriousness** *noun* [U] गंभीरता

**seriously** /ˈsɪəriəsli ˈसिअरिअस्लि/ *adv.* 1 in a serious way गंभीरतापूर्वक *Three people were seriously injured in the accident.* ○ *My mother is seriously ill.* 2 used at the beginning of a sentence for showing that you are not joking or that you really mean what you are saying वाक्य के आरंभ में, प्रसंग की गंभीरता और वक्ता की सचाई प्रदर्शित करने के लिए प्रयुक्त *Seriously, I do appreciate all your help.* ○ *Seriously, you've got nothing to worry about.* 3 used for expressing surprise at what sb has said and asking if it is really true वक्ता के कथन तथा उसकी सचाई पर आश्चर्यपूर्ण प्रश्न पूछने के लिए प्रयुक्त *'I'm 40 today.' 'Seriously? You look a lot younger.'*

IDM **take sb/sth seriously** to treat sb or sth as important व्यक्ति या वस्तु को महत्त्वपूर्ण समझना *You take everything too seriously! Relax and enjoy yourself.*

**sermon** /ˈsɜːmən ˈसमन्/ *noun* [C] a speech on a religious or moral subject that is given as part of a service in church धार्मिक या नैतिक विषय पर प्रवचन (चर्च आदि में धार्मिक अनुष्ठान के अंग के रूप में)

**serpent** /ˈsɜːpənt ˈसपन्ट्/ *noun* [C] a snake, especially a large one साँप (विशेषतः बड़ा)

**serrated** /səˈreɪtɪd सˈरेटिड्/ *adj.* having a row of points in V-shapes along the edge दंदानेदार, दाँतेदार *a knife with a serrated edge*

**serum** /ˈsɪərəm ˈसिअरम्/ *noun* (*pl.* **sera** /-rə - रा/ or **serums**) 1 [U] (*medical*) the thin liquid that is left after blood has **clotted** रक्त का जलीय अंश (ख़ून जमने के बाद शेष रहा) 2 [U, C] a liquid that is taken from the blood of an animal and given to people to protect them from disease, poison, etc. सीरम (पशु के ख़ून में से लिया गया द्रव जो रोग, विष आदि के प्रभाव से रक्षा के लिए मनुष्यों के शरीर में पहुँचाया जाता है)

**servant** /ˈsɜːvənt ˈसवन्ट्/ *noun* [C] a person who is paid to work in sb's house, doing work such as cooking, cleaning, etc. नौकर (वेतन पर घर के काम करने वाला व्यक्ति) ➪ **civil servant** देखिए।

**serve** /sɜːv सव्/ *verb* 1 [T] to give food or drink to sb during a meal; to take an order and then bring food or drink to sb in a restaurant, bar, etc. भोजन परोसना; रेस्तराँ, बार आदि में ग्राहकों से आदेश लेकर खाद्य और पेय पदार्थ उन्हें पहुँचाना *Breakfast is served from 7.30 to 9.00 a.m.* 2 [T] (used about an amount of food) to be enough for a certain number of people (भोजन की विशेष मात्रा का) निश्चित संख्या के लिए लोगों के लिए पर्याप्त होना *According to the recipe, this dish serves four.* 3 [I, T] (in a shop) to take a customer's order; to give help, sell goods, etc. (दुकान पर) ग्राहक से आदेश लेना; ग्राहक की सहायता करना, उसे माल बेचना आदि *There was a long queue of people waiting to be served.* 4 [I, T] to be useful or suitable for a particular purpose उद्देश्य-विशेष के लिए उपयोगी या उपयुक्त होना *It's an old car but it will* ***serve our purpose*** *for a few months.* 5 [I, T] to perform a duty or provide a service for the public or for an organization जनता के हित में कोई काम करना या किसी संख्या को कोई सेवा उपलब्ध कराना *During the war, he served in the Army.* ○ *She became a nurse because she wanted to serve the community.* 6 [T] to spend a period of time in prison as punishment जेल में निश्चित अवधि के लिए अपराध की सज़ा काटना *He is currently* ***serving a*** *ten-year* ***sentence*** *for fraud.* 7 [I, T] (in tennis and similar sports) to start play by hitting the ball (टेनिस जैसे खेलों में) गेंद को मार कर खेल शुरू करना

IDM **first come, first served** ➪ **first**[2] देखिए।

**serve sb right** used when sth unpleasant happens to sb and you do not feel sorry for him/her because you think it is his/her own fault किसी को ग़लत काम के लिए उपयुक्त दंड मिलना *'I feel sick.' 'It serves you right for eating so much.'*

**server** /ˈsɜːvə(r) ˈसव(र्)/ *noun* [C] a computer that stores information that a number of computers can share सूचना-संचय करने वाला ऐसा कंप्यूटर जिससे अन्य अनेक कंप्यूटर भंडारित सूचना को ग्रहण करते हैं ➪ **client** देखिए।

**service**[1] /ˈsɜːvɪs ˈसविस्/ *noun* 1 [C] a system or organization that provides the public with sth that it needs; the job that an organization does जनता की आवश्यकता की पूर्ति करने वाली प्रणाली या संख्या, सेवा; संस्था द्वारा किया गया विशिष्ट काम या संस्था द्वारा उपलब्ध कराई गई सेवा *There is a regular bus* *service to the airport.* ○ *the postal service* ➪ **Civil Service** देखिए। **2** [C, U] a business whose work involves doing sth for customers but not producing goods; the work that such a service does ग्राहकों को विशिष्ट सेवा (न कि सामान) उपलब्ध कराने वाला व्यवसाय; सेवा-व्यवसाय द्वारा किया गया काम *financial/banking/insurance services* ○ *the service sector* (= the part of the economy involved in this type of business) ○ *a service industry* **3** [U] (*also* **the services**) [*pl.*] the armed forces; the army, navy or air force; the work done by the people in them सशस्त्र सेनाएँ; थलसेना, नौसेना या वायु सेना; इन सेनाओं में होने वाला काम *They both joined the services when they left school.* **4** [U, C] work done for sb; help given to sb किसी के लिए किया गया कोई काम, नौकरी; किसी को दी गई कोई सहायता, सेवा *He left the police force after thirty years' service.* **5** [U] the work or the quality of work done by sb when serving a customer ग्राहक के लिए किया गया कोई काम या ग्राहक को उपलब्ध कराई गई सेवा; काम या सेवा की गुणवत्ता *I enjoyed the meal but the service was terrible.* ○ *A 10 per cent* ***service charge*** *will be added to your bill.* **6** [C] the checks, repairs, etc. that are necessary to make sure that a machine is working properly मशीन की जाँच, मरम्मत आदि (ताकि वह सुचारु रूप से चलती रहे) *We take our car for a service every six months.* **7** [C] a religious ceremony, usually including prayers, singing, etc. धार्मिक अनुष्ठान (प्रायः प्रार्थना, भजन आदि समेत) *a funeral service* **8** [C] (in tennis and similar sports) the first hit of the ball at the start of play; a player's turn to **serve 7** (टेनिस जैसे खेलों में) खेल के आरंभ में गेंद पर पहली हिट; गेंद को मारने की खिलाड़ी की बारी

**service[2]** /ˈsɜːvɪs ˈसर्विस्/ *verb* [T] to examine and, if necessary, repair a car, machine, etc. कार, मशीन आदि की जाँच और (आवश्यकतानुसार) मरम्मत करना *All cars should be serviced at regular intervals.*

**serviceman** /ˈsɜːvɪsmən ˈसर्विस्मन्/ *noun* [C] (*pl.* **-men** /-mən -मन्/) a man who is a member of the armed forces सशस्त्र पुरुष सैनिक

**servicewoman** /ˈsɜːvɪswʊmən ˈसर्विस्वुमन्/ *noun* [C] (*pl.* **-women** /-wɪmɪn -विमिन्/) a woman who is a member of the armed forces सशस्त्र महिला सैनिक

**serviette** /ˌsɜːviˈet ˌसर्विˈएट्/ *noun* [C] a square of cloth or paper that you use when you are eating to keep your clothes clean and to clean your mouth or hands on खाने के समय प्रयुक्त नैपकिन, एक चौरस कपड़ा या काग़ज़ (कपड़े साफ़ रखने और मुँह या हाथ पोंछने के लिए) ✪ पर्याय **napkin**

**servile** /ˈsɜːvaɪl ˈसवाइल्/ *adj.* (*disapproving*) wanting too much to please sb and so obey them (अमान्य) ख़ुशामदी, चापलूस, दासोचित ▶ **servility** /sɜːˈvɪləti सˈविलटि/ *noun* [U] दासता, चापलूसी

**sesame** /ˈsesəmi ˈसेसमि/ *noun* [U] a tropical plant grown for its seeds that are used in cooking and the oil that is made from them तिल का पौधा (जिससे तिल के दाने मिलते हैं और दानों से तेल) *sesame seeds*

**session** /ˈseʃn ˈसेश्न्/ *noun* **1** [C] a period of doing a particular activity कार्य विशेष में लगी समयावधि *The whole tape was recorded in one session.* ○ *She has a session at the gym every week.* **2** [C, U] a formal meeting or series of meetings of a court of law, parliament, etc. अदालत, संसद आदि का सत्र (औपचारिक बैठक या बैठकों की शृंखला)

**set[1]** /set सेट्/ *verb* (*pres. part.* **setting**; *pt, pp* **set**) **1** [T] **to put sb/sth or to cause sb/sth** to be in a particular place or position किसी स्थान या स्थिति में किसी को रखना या रखवाना *I set the box down carefully on the floor.* **2** [T] (*often passive*) to make the action of a book, play, film, etc. take place in a particular time, situation, etc. किसी पुस्तक, नाटक, फ़िल्म आदि की कहानी को विशिष्ट समय, स्थिति, आदि में स्थापित करना *The film is set in 16th century India.* **3** [T] to cause a particular state or event; to start sth happening विशेष स्थिति या घटना को मूर्त रूप दिलवाना; किसी कार्य को मूर्त रूप देना *The new government* ***set*** *the prisoners* ***free.*** ○ *The rioters* ***set*** *a number of cars* ***on fire.*** **4** [T] to prepare or arrange sth for a particular purpose किसी चीज़ को विशेष प्रयोजन के लिए तैयार या व्यवस्थित करना *I set my alarm for 6.30 a.m.* ○ *to set the table* (= put the plates, knives, forks, etc. on it) **5** [T] to decide or arrange sth कुछ निश्चित या निर्धारित करना *Can we* ***set a limit*** *of two hours for the meeting?* ○ *They haven't* ***set the date*** *for their wedding yet.* **6** [T] to do sth good that people have to try to copy or achieve लोगों द्वारा अनुकरण या उपलब्ध करने योग्य कोई अच्छा काम करना *Try to* ***set a good example*** *to the younger children.* ○ *He has* ***set a*** *new world* ***record.*** **7** [T] to give sb a piece of work or a task किसी को कोई सामान्य या विशेष काम सौंपना *I've* ***set*** *myself* ***a target*** *of four hours' study every evening.* **8** [I] to become firm or hard मज़बूत या कड़ा हो जाना *The concrete will* ***set solid/hard*** *in just a few hours.* **9** [T] to fix a precious stone, etc. in a piece of jewellery किसी आभूषण में रत्न आदि जड़ना **10** [T] to fix a broken bone in the correct position so that it can get better टूटी हड्डी को सही स्थिति में बैठना (ताकि वह जुड़ सके) *The doctor set her broken leg.* **11** [I] (used about the sun) to go down below the horizon in the evening (सूर्य का) सायंकाल अस्त होना (क्षितिज में डूबना) ✪ विलोम **rise**

IDM **set eyes on sb/sth** to see sb/sth किसी को (स्थिर भाव से) देखना *He loved the house the moment he set eyes on it.*

**set foot (in/on sth)** to visit, enter or arrive at/in a place किसी स्थान पर जाना, प्रवेश करना या पहुँचना *No woman has ever set foot in the temple.*

**set your heart on sth; have your heart set on sth** ⇨ **heart** देखिए।

**put/set your/sb's mind at rest** ⇨ **mind¹** देखिए।

**put/set sth right** ⇨ **right¹** देखिए।

**set sail** to begin a journey by sea समुद्र यात्रा आरंभ करना *Columbus set sail for India.*

**set the scene (for sth)** ⇨ **scene** देखिए।

PHR V **set about sth** to start doing sth, especially dealing with a problem or task कोई कार्य (विशेषतः समस्यात्मक या विशिष्ट) आरंभ करना *How would you set about tackling this problem?*

**set sth aside** to keep sth to use later कुछ बचा कर रखना (बाद के लिए) *I try to set aside part of my wages every week.*

**set sb/sth back** to delay sb/sth किसी बात में विलंब करवा देना या किसी काम को पीछे कर देना *The bad weather has set our plans back six weeks.*

**set forth** (*formal*) to start a journey यात्रा आरंभ करना

**set sth forth** (*formal*) to show or tell sth to sb or to make sth known किसी व्यक्ति को कुछ दिखाना या बताना या कोई बात स्पष्टतया प्रकट करना

**set in** to arrive and stay for a period of time आ कर कुछ समय के लिए जम जाना *I'm afraid that the bad weather has set in.*

**set off** to leave on a journey यात्रा आरंभ करना *We set off at 3 o'clock this morning.*

**set sth off** to do sth which starts a reaction कुछ ऐसा करना जिसकी प्रतिक्रिया तुरंत आरंभ हो जाए *When this door is opened, it sets off an alarm.*

**set on/upon sb** to attack sb suddenly किसी पर अचानक हमला करना *He was set upon by a gang of youths on his way home.*

**set out to leave** on a journey यात्रा आरंभ करना

**set out to do sth** to decide to achieve sth कुछ प्राप्त कर लेने का निश्चय करना *He set out to prove that his theory was right.*

**set (sth) up** to start a business, organization, system, etc. किसी व्यापार, संस्था, प्रणाली आदि को स्थापित करना

**set²** /set सेट्/ *noun* [C] **1 a set (of sth)** a number of things that belong together परस्पर संबंधित वस्तुओं का समूह; सेट *a set of kitchen knives* ○ *a spare set of keys* ○ *a chess set* **2** [*with sing. or pl. verb*] a group of people who have similar interests and spend a lot of time together socially समान अभिरुचि तथा सामाजिक व्यवहार वाले लोगों का विशिष्ट वर्ग ⇨ **jet set** देखिए। **3** a piece of equipment for receiving television or radio signals टीवी या रेडियो संकेत प्राप्त करने वाला उपकरण *a television set* **4** the scenery that is made for a play or film किसी नाटक या फ़िल्म के लिए निर्मित मंच सज्जा **5** (used in games such as tennis and volleyball) a group of games forming part of a match (टेनिस और वॉलीबॉल में) एक मैच के अंतर्गत क्रीड़ा-सत्रों की शृंखला *She won **in straight sets*** (= without losing a set). **6** (*mathematics*) a group of things that have a shared quality समुच्चय (समान गुण वाली वस्तुओं या इकाइयों का समूह)

**set³** /set सेट्/ *adj.* **1** placed in a particular position विशेष स्थिति में स्थापित *deep-set eyes* ○ *Our house is quite set back from the road.* **2** fixed and not changing; firm नियत (और न बदलने वाला); पक्का, दृढ़ *There are no set hours in my job.* ○ *I'll have the set menu* (= with a fixed price and limited choice of dishes). **3** (used about a book, text, etc.) that everyone must study for an exam (पुस्तक, पठन-सामग्री आदि) परीक्षा के लिए निर्धारित *We have to study three set texts for English.* **4 set (for sth); set (to do sth)** ready, prepared or likely to do sth कुछ करने के लिए उद्यत, तैयार या संभावनायुक्त *I was all set to leave when the phone rang.* ○ *The Indian cricket team look set for victory.*

IDM **be set against sth/doing sth** to be determined that sth will not happen or that you will not do sth कोई विशेष काम न करने या होने देने पर दृढ़

**be set in your ways** to be unable to change your habits, attitudes, etc. (अपनी) आदतें, सोच आदि बदलने में असमर्थ

**be set on sth/doing sth** to be determined to do sth कोई विशेष काम करने के लिए कृतसंकल्प *She's set on a career in acting.*

**setback** /ˈsetbæk ˈसेट्बैक्/ *noun* [C] a difficulty or problem that stops you progressing as fast as you would like आघात, धक्का (इच्छानुसार तीव्रगति से प्रगति के मार्ग में बाधक कठिनाई या समस्या) *She suffered a major setback when she missed the exams through illness.*

**set square** (*AmE* **triangle**) *noun* [C] an instrument for drawing straight lines and angles, made from a flat piece of plastic or metal in the shape of a triangle with one angle of 90º समकोणक, लंब कोणक; कोनिया (प्लास्टिक या धातु का बना, एक समकोण वाले त्रिकोण की आकृति का उपकरण, सीधी रेखाएँ खींचने और कोण बनाने के लिए प्रयुक्त)

**settee** /seˈtiː सेˈटी/ *noun* [C] a long soft seat with a back and arms that more than one person can sit on बाँहों वाला एक लंबा मुलायम सोफ़ा (जिस पर एक से अधिक लोग बैठ सकते हैं); सेटि ✪ पर्याय **sofa**

**setting** /ˈsetɪŋ ˈसेटिङ्/ *noun* [C] **1** the position sth is in; the place and time in which sth happens किसी वस्तु की पृष्ठभूमि; समय और स्थान जिसमें कुछ घटित हो; वातावरण *The hotel is in a beautiful setting, close to the sea.* **2** one of the positions of the controls of a machine मशीन के नियंत्रणकारी पुरज़ों की कोई विशेष स्थिति *Cook it in the oven on a moderate setting.*

**settle** /ˈsetl ˈसेट्ल्/ *verb* **1** [I, T] to put an end to an argument or disagreement बहस या विवाद को सुलझा लेना *They settled out of court.* ○ ***We have settled our differences** now.* **2** [T] to decide or arrange sth finally किसी बात को अंतिम रूप से तय या व्यवस्थित कर देना *Everything's settled. We leave on the nine o'clock flight on Friday.* **3** [I] to go and live permanently in a new country, area, town, etc. किसी नए देश, इलाक़े, शहर आदि में जाकर बस जाना *A great many immigrants have settled in this part of Canada.* **4** [I, T] to put yourself or sb else into a comfortable position आरामदेह स्थिति में बैठ जाना या बैठा देना *I settled in front of the television for the evening.* ○ **5** [I, T] to become or to make sb/sth calm or relaxed शांत या तनावमुक्त हो जाना या कर देना *The baby wouldn't settle.* **6** [T] to pay money that you owe भुगतान करना *to settle a bill/a debt* **7** [I] to land on a surface and stop moving किसी स्थान पर आ बैठना *A flock of birds settled on the roof.*

PHR V **settle down 1** to get into a comfortable position, sitting or lying आरामदायक स्थिति में बैठना या लेटना **2** to start having a quieter way of life, especially by staying in the same place or getting married स्थिर और शांत जीवन जीने लगना (विशेषतः पुराने स्थान पर या विवाह करके) *She had a number of jobs abroad before she eventually settled down.* **3** to become calm and quiet शांत और चुप हो जाना *Settle down! It's time to start the lesson.*

**settle down to sth** to start doing sth which involves all your attention किसी काम में सारा ध्यान लगाने की शुरुआत करना *Before you settle down to your work, could I ask you something?*

**settle for sth** to accept sth that is not as good as what you wanted इच्छित से कम को भी स्वीकार कर लेना *We're going to have to settle for the second prize.*

**settle in/into sth** to start feeling comfortable in a new home, job, etc. नए मकान, नई नौकरी आदि का अभ्यस्त होने लगना *How are the children settling in at their new school?*

**settle on sth** to choose or decide sth after considering many different things काफ़ी सोच-विचार के बाद कोई चयन या निर्णय करना

**settle up (with sb)** to pay money that you owe to sb किसी का बचा भुगतान करना

**settled** /ˈsetld ˈसेट्ल्ड्/ *adj.* **1** not changing or not likely to change स्थिर *More settled weather is forecast for the next few days.* **2** comfortable; feeling that you belong (in a home, a job, a way of life, etc.) सुखी, सानंद; (घर, नौकरी, जीने के ढंग आदि से) जुड़ा हुआ अनुभव करते हुए *We feel very settled here.*

**settlement** /ˈsetlmənt ˈसेट्ल्मन्ट्/ *noun* [C, U] **1** an official agreement that ends an argument; the act of reaching an agreement विवाद का विधिमान्य समाधान; पर पहुँचने की क्रिया *a divorce settlement* ○ *the settlement of a dispute* **2** a place that a group of people have built and live in, where few or no people lived before; the process of people starting to live in a place बस्ती, उपनिवेश (लोगों के आकर बस जाने का ऐसा स्थान जहाँ पहले नगण्य आबादी थी); किसी स्थान पर लोगों के आकर बस जाने की प्रक्रिया) *There is believed to have been a prehistoric settlement on this site.* ○ *the settlement of the American West*

**settler** /ˈsetlə(r) ˈसेट्ल(र्)/ *noun* [C] a person who goes to live permanently in a place where not many people live किसी कम आबादी की बस्ती में बसने वाला व्यक्ति; आबादकार, उपनिवेशी *the first white settlers in Australia*

**seven** /ˈsevn ˈसेव्न्/ *number* **1** 7 सात (की संख्या)

> NOTE संख्याओं के वाक्य-प्रयोग के उदाहरणों के लिए **six** की प्रविष्टि देखिए।

**2** (*used to form compound adjectives*) having seven of the thing mentioned बताई गई सात वस्तुओं वाला; सात-, सप्त- *a seven-sided coin*

**seventeen** /ˌsevnˈtiːn ˌसेव्न्ˈटीन्/ *number* 17 सत्रह (की संख्या)

NOTE संख्याओं के वाक्य-प्रयोग के उदाहरणों के लिए **six** की प्रविष्टि देखिए।

**seventeenth** /ˌsevnˈtiːnθ ˌसेव्न्ˈटीन्थ्/ *det., adv.* 17th सत्रहवाँ ➪ **sixth** की प्रविष्टि के उदाहरण देखिए।

**seventh**[1] /ˈsevnθ ˈसेव्न्थ्/ *noun* [C] the $\frac{1}{7}$; one of seven equal parts of sth भिन्न $\frac{1}{7}$; (किसी का) सातवाँ हिस्सा ➪ **sixth** की प्रविष्टि के उदाहरण देखिए।

**seventh**[2] /ˈsevnθ ˈसेव्न्थ्/ *det., adv.* 7th सातवाँ ➪ **sixth** की प्रविष्टि के उदाहरण देखिए।

**seventieth** /ˈsevntiəθ ˈसेव्न्टिअथ्/ *det., adv.* 70th सत्तरवाँ ➪ **sixth** की प्रविष्टि के उदाहरण देखिए।

**seventy** /ˈsevnti ˈसेव्न्टि/ *number* 70 सत्तर (की संख्या)

NOTE संख्याओं के वाक्य-प्रयोग के उदाहरणों के लिए **sixty** की प्रविष्टि देखिए।

**sever** /ˈsevə(r) ˈसेव़(र्)/ *verb* [T] (*formal*) **1** to cut sth into two pieces; to cut sth off किसी वस्तु के दो टुकड़े करना; किसी वस्तु को काट देना *The builders accidentally severed a water pipe.* ○ *His hand was almost severed in the accident.* **2** to end a relationship or communication with sb किसी के साथ संबंध या संपर्क समाप्त करना *He has severed all links with his former friends.*

**several** /ˈsevrəl ˈसेव्रल्/ *pronoun, det.* more than two but not very many; a few दो से कुछ अधिक (बहुत अधिक नहीं), अनेक; कुछ *It took her several days to recover from the shock.* ○ *I don't think it's a good idea for several reasons.*

**severe** /sɪˈvɪə(r) सिˈव़िअ(र्)/ *adj.* **1** causing sb to suffer, be upset or have difficulties कठोर, सख़्त (जिससे व्यक्ति को तकलीफ़, परेशानी या कठिनाई हो) *Such terrible crimes deserve the severest punishment.* **2** extremely bad or serious बहुत कठिन, कष्टप्रद या गंभीर *severe financial difficulty/injuries/weather conditions* ▶ **severely** *adv.* अत्यधिक *The roof was severely damaged in the storm.* ▶ **severity** /sɪˈverəti सिˈव़ेरटि/ *noun* [U] उग्रता *I don't think you realize the severity of the problem.*

**sew** /səʊ सो/ *verb* [I, T] (*pt* **sewed**; *pp* **sewn** /səʊn सोन्/ or **sewed**) **sew (sth) (on)** to join pieces of cloth, or to join sth to cloth, using a needle and thread and forming stitches (कपड़ों को या कपड़ों के साथ किसी वस्तु को) सीना (सूई और धागे के साथ टाँके मारते हुए) *I can't sew.* ○ *A button's come off my shirt—I'll have to sew it back on.*

PHR V **sew sth up** **1** to join two things by sewing; to repair sth by sewing two things together दो चीज़ों को सी कर जोड़ना; दो चीज़ों को एक साथ सी कर सही कर देना *The surgeon sewed up the wound.* **2** to arrange sth so that it is certain to happen or be successful किसी काम के होने को निश्चित या पक्का कर देना

**sewage** /ˈsuːɪdʒ ˈसूइज्/ *noun* [U] the waste material from people's bodies that is carried away from their homes in water in large underground pipes (**sewers**) घरों से निकलकर भूमिगत नालियों में बहता मल

**sewer** /ˈsuːə(r) ˈसूअ(र्)/ *noun* [C] an underground pipe that carries human waste to a place where it can be treated मल को बहाकर मल-संसाधन केंद्र पर ले जाने वाला भूमिगत नाला

**sewing** /ˈsəʊɪŋ ˈसोइङ्/ *noun* [U] **1** using a needle and thread to make or repair things सिलाई (सूई और धागे से चीज़ें बनाने या सही करने की क्रिया) *sewing kit/a* ***sewing machine*** **2** something that is being sewn सिली जा रही वस्तु

**sewn** ➪ **sew** का past participle रूप

**sex** /seks सेक्स्/ *noun* **1** [U] the state of being either male or female लिंग (पुरुष या स्त्री होने की स्थिति) *Applications are welcome from anyone, regardless of sex or race.* ○ *Do you mind what sex your baby is?* ✪ पर्याय **gender** **2** [C] one of the two groups consisting of all male people or all female people पुरुष वर्ग या स्त्री वर्ग *the male/female sex* ○ *He's always found it difficult to get on with* ***the opposite sex*** (= women). **3** (*formal* **coitus; intercourse; sexual intercourse**) [U] the physical act in which the sexual organs of two people touch and which can result in a woman having a baby स्त्री-पुरुष सहवास या संभोग (जिसमें स्त्री का गर्भवती होना संभावित हो) *sex education in schools*

**sexism** /ˈseksɪzəm ˈसेक्सिज़म्/ *noun* [U] the unfair treatment of people, especially women, because of their sex; the attitude that causes this व्यक्तियों, विशेषतः स्त्रियों, के साथ अन्याय (उनके लिंग के कारण), लैंगिक भेदभाव; लिंगभेद की भावना ▶ **sexist** /ˈseksɪst ˈसेक्सिस्ट्/ *adj.* लिंगभेदवादी *a sexist attitude to women* ○ *sexist jokes*

**sextuplet** /ˈsekstʊplət; sekˈstjuːplət; -ˈstʌp-/ ˈसेक्स्टुप्लट्; सेक्ˈस्ट्यूप्लट्; -ˈस्टप्-/ *noun* [C] one of six children or animals that are born to one mother at the same time एक ही माँ या मादा के एक साथ जनमे छह बच्चों में से एक

**sexual** /ˈsekʃuəl ˈसेक्शुअल्/ *adj.* connected with sex लिंग संबंधी, यौन, काम-विषयक *sexual problems*

○ *a campaign for sexual equality* (= to get fair and equal treatment for both men and women) ➪ **sexy** देखिए। ▶ **sexually** /ˈsekʃəli ˈसेक्‌शलि/ *adv.* यौन दृष्टि से, काम भावना से *to be sexually attracted to sb*

**sexual intercourse** (*formal*) = **sex 3**

**sexuality** /ˌsekʃuˈæləti ˌसेक्‌शुˈऐलटि/ *noun* [U] the nature of sb's sexual activities or desires यौन क्रियाओं या इच्छाओं की प्रकृति; लैंगिकता

**sexy** /ˈseksi ˈसेक्‌सि/ *adj.* (**sexier; sexiest**) (*informal*) sexually attractive or exciting कामोद्दीपक या कामोत्तेजक *a sexy dress*

**Sgt** *abbr.* sergeant सार्जेंट

**sh** /ʃ श्/ *exclamation* used to tell sb to stop making noise शांत हो जाने या शोर न मचाने का संकेत *Sh! People are trying to study in here.*

**shabby** /ˈʃæbi ˈशैबि/ *adj.* **1** in bad condition because of having been used or worn too much बुरी हालत में (बहुत अधिक प्रयोग में आने या घिस जाने के कारण) *a shabby suit* **2** (used about people) dressed in an untidy way; wearing clothes that are in bad condition (व्यक्ति) मैला-कुचैला; फटे-पुराने वस्त्र पहने हुए **3** (used about the way that sb is treated) unfair; not generous (किसी के साथ व्यवहार) अनुचित; क्षुद्र ▶ **shabbily** /-ɪli -इलि/ *adv.* भद्दे ढंग से, फूहड़पन से *a shabbily dressed man* ○ *She felt she'd been treated shabbily by her employers.*

**shack** /ʃæk शैक्/ *noun* [C] a small building, usually made of wood or metal, that has not been built well लकड़ी या धातुखंडों से बना छोटा बेढंगा मकान; झोंपड़ा

**shackle[1]** /ˈʃækl ˈशैक्‌ल्/ *noun* [C] one of a pair of metal rings connected with a chain put around a prisoner's wrists or ankles हथकड़ी, बेड़ी

**shackle[2]** /ˈʃækl ˈशैक्‌ल्/ *verb* [T] **1** to put **shackles[1]** on sb (किसी को) हथकड़ी या बेड़ी डालना या लगाना *The prisoners were kept shackled during the trial.* **2** (*usually passive*) to prevent sb from behaving or speaking as they want किसी को अपनी इच्छा अनुसार कुछ कहने या व्यवहार करने से रोकना *She is opposed to shackling the press with privacy laws.*

**shade[1]** /ʃeɪd शेड्/ *noun* **1** [U] an area that is out of direct sunlight and is darker and cooler than areas in the sun छायादार क्षेत्र (सूर्य के प्रकाश से परे कुछ अँधेरा तथा अपेक्षाकृत ठंडा स्थान) *It was so hot that I had to go and sit* ***in the shade.*** **2** [C] something that keeps out light or makes it less bright शेड, ढक्कन (जो रोशनी को रोके या मद्धिम कर दे) *a lampshade* **3 shades** [*pl.*] (*informal*) = **sunglasses** **4** [C] **a shade (of sth)** a type of a particular colour एक विशेष प्रकार का रंग (किसी रंग की) आभा *a shade of green* **5** [C] a small difference in the form or nature of sth (किसी वस्तु के रूप या प्रकृति में) ज़रा-सा अंतर *a word with various shades of meaning* **6** [*sing.*] **a shade** a little bit ज़रा, थोड़ा

**shade[2]** /ʃeɪd शेड्/ *verb* [T] **1** to protect sth from direct light; to give shade to sth सीधे प्रकाश से किसी को बचाना; किसी वस्तु पर शेड लगाना *The sun was so bright that I had to shade my eyes.* **2 shade sth (in)** to make an area of a drawing darker, for example with a pencil (पेंसिल आदि से) किसी स्थान को धुँधला छायांकित कर देना *The trees will look more realistic once you've shaded them in.*

**shadow[1]** /ˈʃædəʊ ˈशैडो/ *noun* **1** [C] a dark shape on a surface that is caused by sth being between the light and that surface परछाई, साया (प्रकाश और सतह के बीच में किसी के आने से सतह पर बनी उसकी धुँधली आकृति) *The dog was chasing its own shadow.* ○ *The shadows lengthened as the sun went down.* ➪ **penumbra** और **umbra** देखिए। **2** [U] an area that is dark because sth prevents direct light from reaching it अँधेरा स्थान (प्रकाश के सीधे न पहुँच पाने के कारण) *His face was* ***in shadow.*** **3** [*sing.*] a very small amount of sth लेश मात्र, अल्प, थोड़ा-सा *I know without* ***a shadow of doubt*** *that he's lying.*

IDM **cast a shadow (across/over sth)** ➪ **cast[1]** देखिए।

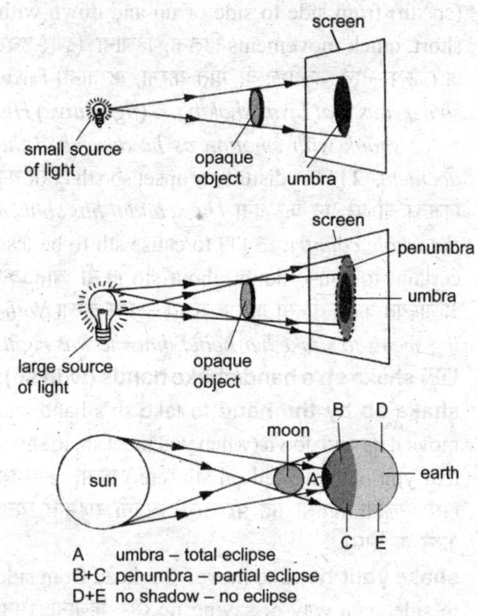


**types of shadow**

**shadow²** /ˈʃædəʊ ˈशैडो/ *verb* [T] to follow and watch sb's actions (किसी का) पीछा करना और उसकी हरकतों पर निगाह रखना *The police shadowed the suspect for three days.*

**shadowy** /ˈʃædəʊi ˈशैडोइ/ *adj.* **1** dark and full of shadows अँधेरा और छाया बहुल *a shadowy forest* **2** difficult to see because there is not much light धुँधला, अस्पष्ट (पर्याप्त प्रकाश के अभाव में जिसे देखना कठिन हो) *A shadowy figure was coming towards me.* **3** that not much is known about; mysterious अल्प-ज्ञात (जिसके विषय अधिक जानकारी न हो); रहस्यमय

**shady** /ˈʃeɪdi ˈशेडि/ *adj.* **1** giving shade; giving protection from the sun छायादार; सूर्य के प्रकाश से बचाने वाला *I found a shady spot under the trees and sat down.* **2** (*informal*) not completely honest or legal बेईमानी वाला या अवैध या ग़ैर-क़ानूनी

**shaft** /ʃɑːft शाफ़्ट्/ *noun* [C] **1** a long, narrow hole in which sth can go up and down or enter or leave कूपक (लंबा, तंग गड़हा जिसमें कोई चीज़ ऊपर-नीचे या अंदर-बाहर जा सके) *a lift shaft* ○ *a mine shaft* **2** a bar that connects parts of a machine so that power can pass between them किसी मशीन के हिस्सों को जोड़ने वाला डंडा (शक्ति-प्रवाह की सुविधा के लिए)

**shaggy** /ˈʃægi ˈशैगि/ *adj.* **1** (used about hair, material, etc.) long, thick and untidy (बाल आदि) लंबे, घने और गंदे **2** covered with long, thick, untidy hair लंबे, घने, गंदे बालों वाला *a shaggy dog*

**shake¹** /ʃeɪk शेक्/ *verb* (*pt* **shook** /ʃʊk शुक्/; *pp* **shaken** /ˈʃeɪkən ˈशेकन्/) **1** [I, T] to move (sb/sth) from side to side or up and down with short, quick movements हिलना, हिलाना (इधर-उधर और ऊपर-नीचे जल्दी-जल्दी गति करना, करवाना) *I was so nervous that I was shaking.* ○ (*figurative*) *His voice shook with emotion as he described the accident.* **2** [T] to disturb or upset sb/sth किसी को विक्षुब्ध या परेशान कर देना *The scandal has shaken the whole country.* **3** [T] to cause sth to be less certain; to cause doubt about sth किसी बात को अनिश्चित करना; किसी बात में संशय उत्पन्न करना *Nothing seems to shake her belief that she was right.*

IDM **shake sb's hand/shake hands (with sb); shake sb by the hand** to take sb's hand and move it up and down (when you meet sb, to show that you have agreed on sth, etc.) किसी के साथ हाथ मिलाना (किसी मुद्दे पर उससे अपनी सहमति व्यक्त करने के लिए)

**shake your head** to move your head from side to side, as a way of saying no सिर हिलाना (मना करने के लिए)

PHR V **shake sb/sth off** to get rid of sb/sth; to remove sth by shaking किसी से छुटकारा पाना; हिलाकर कुछ झाड़ना *I don't seem to be able to shake off this cold.* ○ *Shake the crumbs off the tablecloth.*

**shake²** /ʃeɪk शेक्/ *noun* [C] the action of shaking sth or being shaken हिलाने या हिलाए जाने की क्रिया

**shake-up** *noun* [C] a complete change in the structure or organization of sth आमूल-चूल परिवर्तन (किसी वस्तु के ढाँचे या व्यवस्था में)

**shaky** /ˈʃeɪki ˈशेकि/ *adj.* (**shakier; shakiest**) **1** shaking or feeling weak because you are frightened or ill (डर या बीमारी के कारण) काँपता हुआ या कमज़ोरी अनुभव करता हुआ **2** not firm; weak or not very good अस्थिर, डाँवाँडोल; कमज़ोर, बहुत अच्छा नहीं *The table's a bit shaky so don't put anything heavy on it.* ○ *They've had a* ***shaky start*** *to the season losing most of their games.* ► **shakily** /-ʃeɪkɪli -शेकिलि/ *adv.* अस्थिरतापूर्वक

**shale** /ʃeɪl शेल्/ *noun* [U] a type of soft stone that splits easily into thin flat layers स्लेटी पत्थर (मुलायम और आसानी से चौरस परतों में अलग-अलग हो जाने वाला)

**shall** /ʃəl; *strong form* ʃæl शल; प्रबल रूप शैल्/ *modal verb* (*negative* ) **shall not** short form **shan't** /ʃɑːnt शान्ट्/ **1** used for asking for information or advice जानकारी या सलाह माँगने के लिए प्रयुक्त *What time shall I come?* ○ *Where shall we go for our holiday?* **2** used for offering to do sth कुछ (सहायता) करने की इच्छा जतलाने के लिए प्रयुक्त *Shall I help you carry that box?* ○ *Shall we drive you home?* **3 shall we** used for suggesting that you do sth with the person or people that you are talking to किसी काम में साथी या साथियों को साथ लेने का सुझाव देने के लिए प्रयुक्त *Shall we go out for a meal this evening?*

> NOTE वृत्तिवाचक क्रियाओं (modal verbs) के बारे में अधिक जानकारी के लिए इस शब्दकोश के अंत में **Quick Grammar Reference** खंड देखिए।

**4** (*formal*) used with 'I' and 'we' in future tenses, instead of 'will' भविष्य काल के क्रिया रूपों 'I' और 'we' के साथ ('will' के स्थान पर) प्रयुक्त *I shall be very happy to see him again.* ○ *We shan't be arriving until ten o'clock.* ○ **5** (*formal*) used for saying that sth must happen or will definitely happen किसी बात के अवश्य या निश्चित रूप से घटित होने की सूचना देने वाली क्रिया, अनिवार्यता या निश्चय सूचक क्रिया *In the rules it says that a player shall be sent off for using bad language.*

**shallot** /ʃəˈlɒt शˈलॉट्/ *noun* [C] a vegetable like a small onion with a very strong taste प्याज़ की शकल की तीखे स्वाद की सब्ज़ी

**shallow** /ˈʃæləʊ ˈशैलो/ *adj.* **1** not deep; with not much distance between top and bottom छिछला, गहरा नहीं; जिसकी ऊपरी सतह और तले के बीच दूरी कम हो *The sea is very shallow here.* ○ *a shallow dish* **2** not having or showing serious or deep thought अगंभीर, उथला, ओछा (जो गंभीर या विचारशील न हो) *a shallow person/book* ✪ विलोम **deep** दोनों अर्थों का ▶ **shallowness** *noun* [U] छिछलापन, ओछापन, अगंभीरता

**sham** /ʃæm शैम्/ *noun* (*disapproving*) **1** [*sing.*] a situation, feeling, system, etc. that is not as good or true as it seems to be (अमान्य) नक़ली या बनावटी परिस्थिति, भाव या प्रणाली *The crime figures are a complete sham.* **2** (*usually sing.*) a person who pretends to be sth that they are not ढोंगी व्यक्ति **3** [U] behaviour, feelings, words, etc. that are intended to make sb/sth seem to be better than they really are व्यवहार, भावनाएँ और शब्द जो किसी व्यक्ति या वस्तु को वास्तविकता से बेहतर प्रतीत कराते हैं *Their promises turned out to be full of sham and hypocrisy.* ○ *a sham marriage* ▶ **sham** *verb* [T] (**shamming; shammed**) ढोंग करना, पाखंड करना *Is he really sick or is he just shamming?*

**shame[1]** /ʃeɪm शेम्/ *noun* **1** [U] the unpleasant feeling of guilt and embarrassment that you get when you have done sth stupid or morally wrong; the ability to have this feeling लज्जा, शर्म (मूर्खतापूर्ण या अनैतिक काम से उत्पन्न अपराध और व्याकुलता की भावना); लज्जाशीलता, शरमीलापन *She was **filled with shame** at the thought of how she had lied to her mother.* ○ *His actions have **brought shame on** his whole family.* ➪ **ashamed** adjective देखिए। **2 a shame** [*sing.*] a fact or situation that makes you feel disappointed लज्जाजनक वास्तविकता या स्थिति; खेद की बात ***It's a shame** about Anand failing his exams,* ○ ***What a shame** you have to leave so soon.*

**shame[2]** /ʃeɪm शेम्/ *verb* [T] to make sb feel shame for sth bad that he/she has done (ग़लत काम करने वाले को) शरमिंदा करना

**shameful** /ˈʃeɪmfl शेम्फ़्ल्/ *adj.* which sb should feel bad about; shocking लज्जाजनक, शर्मनाक; निंदनीय *a shameful waste of public money* ▶ **shamefully** /-fəli -फ़लि/ *adv.* शर्मनाक या लज्जाजनक तरीक़े से

**shameless** /ˈʃeɪmləs ˈशेम्लस्/ *adj.* not feeling embarrassed about doing sth bad; having no shame ढीठ (ग़लत काम करने के लिए व्याकुलता का अनुभव न करने वाला); बेशर्म, निर्लज्ज *a shameless display of greed and bad manners* ▶ **shamelessly** *adv.* बेशर्मी से, निर्लज्जतापूर्वक

**shampoo** /ʃæmˈpuː शैम्ˈपू/ *noun* **1** [C, U] a liquid that you use for washing your hair; a similar liquid for cleaning carpets, cars, etc. शैंपू (बालों को धोने के लिए प्रयुक्त तरल पदार्थ); कालीन, कार आदि को साफ़ करने का इसी प्रकार का तरल पदार्थ; शैंपू *shampoo for greasy/dry/normal hair* **2** [C] the action of washing sth with shampoo शैंपू से धोने की क्रिया ▶ **shampoo** *verb* [T] (*pres. part.* **shampooing**; *3rd person sing. pres.* **shampoos**; *pt, pp* **shampooed**) शैंपू करना

**shamrock** /ˈʃæmrɒk ˈशैम्रॉक्/ *noun* [C, U] a plant with three leaves, which is the national symbol of Ireland तीन पत्तों वाला एक पौधा, तिपतिया (आयरलैंड का राष्ट्रीय प्रतीक); शैमरॉक

**shandy** /ˈʃændi ˈशैन्डि/ *noun* [C, U] (*pl.* **shandies**) a drink that is a mixture of beer and a sweet, colourless, drink with bubbles that is not alcoholic (**lemonade**) बियर और लेमनेड (कुछ मीठा, रंगहीन, बुलबुलेदार, एलकोहल-रहित पेय) का मिश्रण पेय

**shan't** ➪ **shall not** का संक्षिप्त रूप

**shape[1]** /ʃeɪp शेप्/ *noun* **1** [C, U] the form of the outer edges or surfaces of sth; an example of sth that has a particular form शकल, आकृति (किसी वस्तु के बाहरी सिरों या सतहों का रूप); विशिष्ट आकृति वाली वस्तु का कोई उदाहरण *a round/square/rectangular shape* **2 -shaped** (*used to form compound adjectives*) having the shape mentioned बताई गई आकृति वाला *an L-shaped room* **3** [U] the physical condition of sb/sth; the good or bad state of sb/sth व्यक्ति या वस्तु की भौतिक दशा; व्यक्ति या वस्तु की अच्छी या बुरी दशा *She was **in such bad shape** (= so ill) that she had to be taken to hospital.* ○ *I go swimming regularly to keep **in shape**.* **4** [*sing.*] **the shape (of sth)** the organization, form or structure of sth किसी वस्तु का विन्यास, रूप या ढाँचा

IDM **out of shape 1** not in the usual or correct shape बिगड़ी हुई शकल में *My sweater's gone out of shape now that I've washed it.* **2** not physically fit बेडौल *You're out of shape. You should get more exercise.*

**take shape** to start to develop well ठीक से विकसित होने लगना *Plans to expand the company are beginning to take shape.*

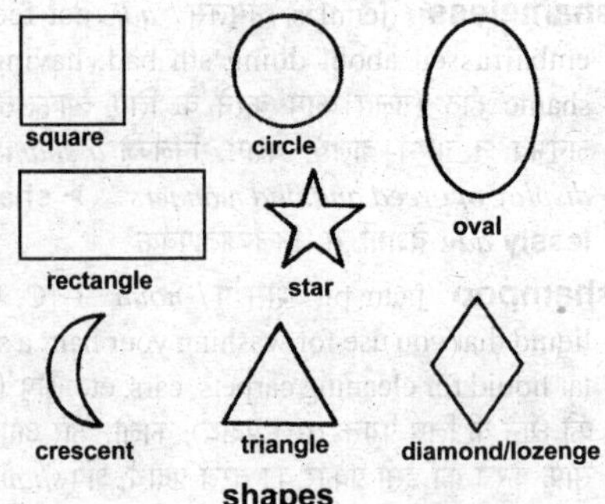

shapes

**shape²** / ʃeɪp शेप् / *verb* [T] **1 shape sth (into sth)** to make sth into a particular form किसी वस्तु को विशेष आकृति में ढालना *Shape the mixture into small balls.* **2** to influence the way in which sth develops; to cause sth to have a particular form or nature किसी वस्तु के विकास पर प्रभाव डालना; किसी वस्तु की विशिष्ट आकृति या प्रकृति निर्धारित करना *His political ideas were shaped by his upbringing.*

**shapeless** / ˈʃeɪpləs ˈशेप्लस् / *adj.* not having a clear shape बेढंगा, भद्दा *a shapeless dress*

**share¹** /ʃeə(r) शेअ(र्) / *verb* **1** [T] **share sth (out)** to divide sth between two or more people किसी वस्तु को दो या अधिक लोगों में बाँटना *We shared the pizza out between the four of us.* **2** [I, T] **share (sth) (with sb)** to have, use, do or pay sth together with another person or other people दूसरों के साथ किसी बात में हिस्सेदारी करना *I share a flat with four other people.* ○ *We share the same interests.* **3** [T] **share sth (with sb)** to tell sb about sth; to allow sb to know sth किसी को कोई बात बताना; किसी को किसी बात की जानकारी में साथी बनाना *Sometimes it helps to share your problems with others.*

**share²** / ʃeə(r) शेअ(र्) / *noun* **1** [*sing.*] **share (of sth)** a part or amount of sth that has been divided between several people किसी वस्तु का अंश या मात्रा (अनेक लोगों में विभाजित) *We each pay a share of the household bills.* ○ *I'm willing to **take my share** of the blame.* **2** [C, *usually pl.*] **share (in sth)** one of many equal parts into which the value of a company is divided, that can be sold to people who want to own part of the company कंपनी का शेयर, अंश, पत्ती (कंपनी की स्वामित्व-पूँजी के समान अंशों में से एक अंश जो ग्राहक ख़रीदता है)
**IDM the lion's share (of sth)** ➪ **lion** देखिए।
**(more than) your fair share of sth** ➪ **fair¹** देखिए।

**shareholder** / ˈʃeəhəʊldə(r) ˈशेअहोल्ड(र्) / *noun* [C] an owner of shares in a company कंपनी के शेयरों का स्वामी; शेयर-होल्डर, शेयर धारी, अंशधारी, पत्तीदार

**shark** / ʃɑːk शाक् / *noun* [C] a large, often dangerous, sea fish that has a lot of sharp teeth शार्क मछली (एक बड़ी, प्रायः ख़तरनाक, समुद्री मछली जिसकी दंतपंक्ति नोकीली और घनी होती है)

**sharp¹** / ʃɑːp शाप् / *adj.* **1** having a very thin but strong edge or point; that can cut or make a hole in sth easily तेज़ धार या नोंक वाला, धारदार या नोकदार; जो आसानी से किसी वस्तु को काट दे या उसमें छेद कर दे, पैना, तीक्ष्ण *a sharp knife/sharp teeth* ✪ विलोम **blunt** **2** (used about a change of direction or level) very great and sudden (दिशा या स्तर में परिवर्तन) अत्यधिक और आकस्मिक; तीखा, अंधा (मोड़) *a sharp rise/fall in inflation* ○ *This is a sharp bend so slow down.* **3** clear and definite स्पष्ट और निश्चित, सीमांकित *the sharp outline of the hills* ○ *a sharp contrast between the lives of the rich and the poor* **4** able to think, act, understand, see or hear quickly शीघ्रता से सोचने, काम करने, समझने, देखने या सुनने में समर्थ, तेज़, कुशाग्र बुद्धि, ज़हीन *a sharp mind* ○ *You must have sharp eyes if you can read that sign from here.* **5** (used about actions or movements) quick and sudden (कार्रवाई या हरकत) तुरंत और अचानक होने वाली *One short sharp blow was enough to end the fight.* **6** (used about words, comments, etc.) said in an angry way; intended to upset sb or be critical (भाषा, टिप्पणियाँ आदि) क्रोधपूर्ण; अपमानजनक या निंदात्मक **7** (used about pain) very strong and sudden (पीड़ा) तीव्र और आकस्मिक *a sharp pain in the chest* ✪ विलोम **dull** **8** (used about sth that affects the senses) strong; not mild or gentle, often causing an unpleasant feeling (इंद्रियों का अनुभव) तीखा, तीक्ष्ण; तेज़ (हलका या मृदु नहीं, प्रायः अरुचिकर) *a sharp taste* ○ *a sharp wind* **9** (in music) slightly higher than the correct note (संगीत में) सामान्य से उच्च स्वर में; तीव्र स्वर में *That last note was sharp. Can you sing it again?* ➪ **flat¹ 6** देखिए। ▶ **sharply** / ˈʃɑːpli ˈशापृलि / *adv.* तेज़ी से *The road bends sharply to the left.* ○ *Share prices fell sharply this morning.* ▶ **sharpness** *noun* [U] तेज़ी

**sharp²** / ʃɑːp शाप् / *adv.* **1** (used about a time) exactly, punctually (समय के लिए प्रयुक्त) ठीक, बिलकुल ठीक, सही *Be here at three o'clock sharp.* **2** turning suddenly फुरती से घूमते हुए *Go to the traffic lights and turn sharp right.* **3** (in music) slightly higher than the correct note (संगीत में) सामान्य से उच्च स्वर में; तीव्र स्वर में ➪ **flat¹ 6** देखिए।

**sharpen** / ˈʃɑːpən ˈशापन् / *verb* [I, T] to become or to make sth sharp or sharper तेज़ या अधिक तेज़ होना या करना *to sharpen a knife* ○ *The outline of the trees sharpened as it grew lighter.*

**sharpener** /ˈʃɑːpnə(r) ˈशाप्नर्/ *noun* [C] an object or a tool that is used for making sth sharp (वस्तुओं की) धार तेज़ करने वाला उपकरण; शार्पनर *a pencil/knife sharpener*

**shatter** /ˈʃætə(r) ˈशैटर्/ *verb* **1** [I, T] (used about glass, etc.) to break or make sth break into very small pieces (शीशा आदि) टुकड़े-टुकड़े हो जाना या टुकड़े-टुकड़े कर देना *I dropped the glass and it shattered on the floor.* ○ *The force of the explosion shattered the windows.* **2** [T] to destroy sth completely (किसी वस्तु को) पूर्णतया नष्ट कर देना, छिन्न-भिन्न कर देना *Her hopes were shattered by the news.*

**shattered** /ˈʃætəd ˈशैटड्/ *adj.* **1** very shocked and upset बहुत विक्षुब्ध और परेशान **2** (*informal*) very tired थककर चूर *I'm absolutely shattered.*

**shave[1]** /ʃeɪv शेव्/ *verb* [I, T] **shave (sth) (off)** to remove hair from the face or another part of the body with an extremely sharp piece of metal (**a razor**) उस्तरे से हजामत बनाना (गालों के या अन्य अंग के बाल साफ़ करना) *I cut myself shaving this morning.* ○ *When did you shave off your moustache?*

**PHR V** **shave sth off (sth)** to cut a very small amount from sth (किसी चीज़ से) थोड़ी मात्रा कम करना

**shave[2]** /ʃeɪv शेव्/ *noun* [C, *usually sing.*] the action of shaving हजामत *to have a shave* ○ *I need a shave.*

**IDM** **a close shave/thing** ➪ **close[3]** देखिए।

**shaven** /ˈʃeɪvn ˈशेव़्न्/ *adj.* having been shaved हजामत किया हुआ; सफ़ाचट *clean-shaven* (= not having a beard or moustache)

**shaver** /ˈʃeɪvə(r) ˈशेव़र्/ (*also* **electric razor**) *noun* [C] an electric tool that is used for removing hair from the face or another part of the body हजामत बनाने का (बिजली का) उपकरण; उस्तरा, रेज़र

**shawl** /ʃɔːl शॉल्/ *noun* [C] a large piece of cloth that is worn by a woman round her shoulders or head or that is put round a baby शाल; (महिलाओं द्वारा कंधों या सिर पर डालने या बच्चे को लपेटने की चादर)

**she** /ʃiː शी/ *pronoun* (*the subject of a verb*) the female person who has already been mentioned (क्रिया का कर्ता) पूर्व निर्दिष्ट स्त्री का वाचक शब्द, 'यह', 'वह' *'What does your sister do?' 'She's a dentist.'* ○ *I asked her a question but she didn't answer.*

**sheaf** /ʃiːf शीफ़्/ *noun* [C] (*pl.* **sheaves**) **1** a number of pieces of paper held or tied together (काग़ज़ों का) बंडल, पुलिंदा *She had a sheaf of documents in her hand.* **2** a bunch of corn or wheat tied together after being cut कटाई के बाद बाँधे हुए मक्की या गेहूँ के पूल या गट्ठर

**shear** /ʃɪə(r) शिअर्/ *verb* [T] (*pt* **sheared**; *pp* **shorn** /ʃɔːn शॉन्/ or **sheared**) to cut the wool off a sheep भेड़ की ऊन उतारना या काटना

**shears** /ʃɪəz शिअज़्/ *noun* [*pl.*] a tool that is like a very large pair of scissors and that is used for cutting things in the garden (बग़ीचे की घास, पौधे आदि काटने की) बड़ी कैंची, कैंचा *a pair of shears* ➪ **gardening** पर चित्र देखिए।

**sheath** /ʃiːθ शीथ़्/ *noun* [C] (*pl.* **sheaths** /ʃiːðz शीद़्ज़्/) a cover for a knife or other sharp weapon चाक़ू या पैने हथियार का खोल, आवरण, म्यान

**shed[1]** /ʃed शेड्/ *noun* [C] a small building that is used for keeping things or animals in शेड, सायबान, छप्पर (कुछ चीज़ें या पशु रखने के लिए प्रयुक्त) *a garden shed* ○ *a bicycle shed* ○ *a cattle shed*

**shed[2]** /ʃed शेड्/ *verb* [T] (*pres. part.* **shedding**; *pt, pp* **shed**) **1** to lose sth because it falls off (कुछ) गिराना, उतारना *This snake sheds its skin every year.* ○ *Autumn is coming and the trees are beginning to shed their leaves.* **2** to get rid of or remove sth that is not wanted अवांछित चीज़ से छुटकारा पाना या उसे उतार फेंकना

**IDM** **shed blood** (*written*) to kill or injure people लोगों का ख़ून बहाना (मार डालना या घायल कर देना)

**shed light on sth** to make sth clear and easy to understand किसी पर प्रकाश डालना (उसे स्पष्ट और सुबोध बनाना)

**shed tears** to cry आँसू बहाना, विलाप करना

**she'd** /ʃiːd शीड्/ ➪ **she had, she would** का संक्षिप्त रूप

**sheen** /ʃiːn शीन्/ *noun* [*sing.*] [U] a soft smooth shiny quality नर्म, चिकना और चमकदार स्वरूप; चमक *Her hair has a healthy sheen.*

**sheep** /ʃiːp शीप्/ *noun* [C] (*pl.* **sheep**) an animal that is kept on farms and used for its wool or meat भेड़ (जिसकी ऊन या मांस उपयोग किया जाता है)

**sheep**

**NOTE** नर भेड़ को **ram** कहते हैं, मादा भेड़ को **ewe** और भेड़ के बच्चे को **lamb**। भेड़ के आवाज़ करने को **bleat** कहते हैं।

**sheepdog** /ˈʃiːpdɒg ˈशीप्डॉग्/ *noun* [C] a dog that has been trained to control sheep भेड़ों की रखवाली करने वाला कुत्ता

**sheepish** /ˈʃiːpɪʃ ˈशीपिश् / *adj.* feeling or showing embarrassment because you have done sth silly बेवकूफ़ी करने के कारण शर्म-संकोच भरा; मुँहचोर *a sheepish grin* ▶ **sheepishly** *adv.* संकोचपूर्वक, मुँह चुराते हुए

**sheepskin** /ˈʃiːpskɪn ˈशीप्स्किन् / *noun* [U, C] the skin of a sheep, including the wool, from which coats, etc. are made भेड़ की खाल और ऊन (जिससे कोट आदि बनते हैं) *a sheep skin rug/jacket*

**sheer** / ʃɪə(r) शिअ(र्) / *adj.* **1** (*only before a noun*) used to emphasize the size, degree or amount of sth किसी वस्तु का आकार कोटि या मात्रा पर बल देने के लिए प्रयुक्त; महज़, निरा, सिर्फ़, केवल, मात्र *It's sheer stupidity to drink and drive.* ○ *I only agreed out of sheer desperation.* **2** very steep; almost vertical एकदम खड़ा; लगभग लंबवत *Don't walk near the edge. It's **a sheer drop** to the sea.*

**sheet** /ʃiːt शीट् / *noun* [C] **1** a large piece of material used on a bed बिस्तर (पर बिछाने) की चादर **2** a piece of paper that is used for writing, printing, etc. on काग़ज़ (लिखने, छापने आदि में प्रयुक्त) *a sheet of notepaper* ○ *Write each answer on a separate sheet.* ➪ **balance sheet** देखिए। **3** a flat, thin piece of any material, especially a square or rectangular one किसी भी वस्तु (धातु, शीशा आदि) की चद्दर, पत्तर (समतल, महीन, विशेषतः वर्गाकार या आयताकार) *a sheet of metal/glass* **4** a wide, flat area of sth किसी वस्तु की विस्तृत, समतल सतह *The road was covered with **a sheet of ice**.*

**sheet lightning** *noun* [U] **lightning** that appears as a broad area of light in the sky चद्दरी बिजली; सौदामिनी (आकाश में चादर जैसी फैली बिजली की चमक) ➪ **forked lightning** देखिए।

**sheet music** *noun* [U] music printed on separate pieces of paper rather than in a book (पुस्तक के स्थान पर) अलग-अलग काग़ज़ों पर लिखा संगीत

**sheikh** (*also* **sheik**) /ʃeɪk शेक् / *noun* [C] an Arab ruler शेख़; अरब जनजाति का मुखिया

**sheikhdom** /ˈʃeɪkdəm; ˈʃiːk- ˈशेक्डम्; ˈशीक्- / *noun* [C] an area of land ruled by a sheikh शेख़ की सलतनत

**shelf** /ʃelf शेल्फ़् / *noun* [C] (*pl.* **shelves** /ʃelvz शेल्व़्ज़् /) a long flat piece of wood, glass, etc. that is fixed to a wall or in a cupboard, used for putting things on ताक, (दीवार में जड़ा लकड़ी, शीशे आदि का फट्टा) या अलमारी का खाना (जिसके ऊपर चीज़ें रखी जाएँ); शेल्फ़ *a bookshelf*

**shell**[1] /ʃel शेल् / *noun* **1** [C, U] a hard covering that protects eggs, nuts and some animals (अंडे, गिरियों और कुछ जीवों का) बाहरी आवरण; छिलका, कोष *Some children were collecting shells on the beach.* ○ *egg shell* ➪ **mollusc** और **nut** पर चित्र देखिए। **2** [C] the walls or hard outer structure of sth किसी वस्तु की दीवारें या बाहरी कड़ा ढाँचा *The body shell of the car is made in another factory.* **3** [C] a metal container that explodes when it is fired from a large gun तोप के गोले का बाहरी खोल

IDM **come out of your shell** to become less shy and more confident when talking to other people संकोच छोड़कर आत्मविश्वास प्रदर्शित करना (दूसरों से बात करते समय)

**go, retreat, etc. into your shell** to suddenly become shy and stop talking एकाएक संकोच में पड़कर चुप-सा हो जाना

**shell**[2] /ʃel शेल् / *verb* [T] **1** to take the hard outer layer **(shell)** off a nut or other kind of food मूँगफली आदि के छिलके उतारना *to shell peas* **2** to fire metal containers **(shells)** full of explosives from a large gun तोप से गोले दाग़ना या छोड़ना

**she'll** /ʃiːl शील् / ➪ **she will** का संक्षिप्त रूप

**shellfish** /ˈʃelfɪʃ ˈशेल्फ़िश् / *noun* (*pl.* **shellfish**) **1** [C] a type of animal that lives in water and has a shell शंखमीन (शंख में रहने वाली मछली); सीपी, कवच प्राणी **2** [U] these animals eaten as food खाने की मछलियाँ

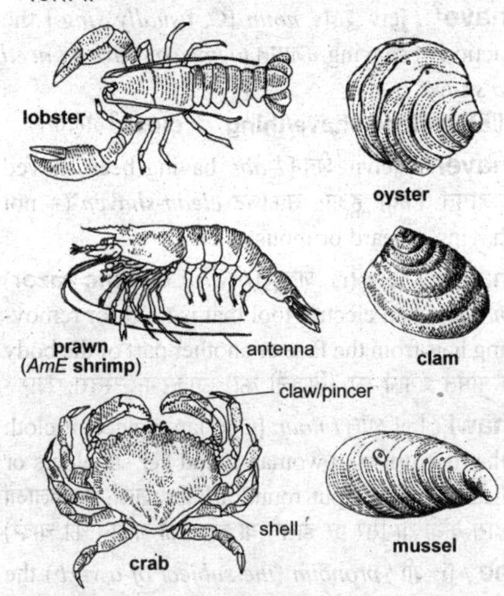


shellfish

**shelter**[1] /ˈʃeltə(r) ˈशेल्टर(र्) / *noun* **1** [U] **shelter (from sth)** protection from danger or bad weather संकट या ख़राब मौसम से सुरक्षा; शरण, पनाह *to give somebody food and shelter* ○ *We had to **take shelter** from the storm.* **2** [C] a small building that gives protection, for example from bad weather or attack (ख़राब मौसम, हमले आदि से) सुरक्षा प्रदान करने वाला स्थान; शरणस्थल, पनाह *a bus shelter* ○ *an air-raid shelter*

**shelter²** /ˈʃeltə(r) ˈशेल्ट(र्)/ *verb* **1** [I] **shelter (from sth)** to find protection or a safe place सुरक्षा पाना या सुरक्षित जगह पर पहुँचना *Let's shelter from the rain under that tree.* **2** [T] **shelter sb/sth (from sb/sth)** to protect sb/sth; to provide a safe place away from harm or danger किसी को सुरक्षा देना; (संभावित हानि या संकट से दूर) सुरक्षित स्थान उपलब्ध कराना *The trees shelter the house from the wind.*

**sheltered** /ˈʃeltəd ˈशेल्टड्/ *adj.* **1** (used about a place) protected from bad weather (स्थान) ख़राब मौसम (के प्रभाव) से सुरक्षित **2** protected from unpleasant things in your life जीवन के कटु पक्ष से सुरक्षित *We had a sheltered childhood, living in the town.*

**shelve** /ʃelv ˈशेल्व्/ *verb* [T] to decide not to continue with a plan, etc., either for a short time or permanently योजना आदि को स्थगित करना (अल्प काल के लिए अथवा स्थायी रूप से) *Plans for a new flyover have been shelved.*

**shelves** ➪ **shelf** का plural रूप

**shelving** /ˈʃelvɪŋ ˈशेल्विङ्/ *noun* [U] a set of shelves बहुत-से ताक

**shepherd¹** /ˈʃepəd ˈशेपड्/ *noun* [C] a person whose job is to look after sheep गडरिया

**shepherd²** /ˈʃepəd ˈशेपड्/ *verb* [T] to guide and look after people so that they do not get lost लोगों को रास्ता बताना और भटकने से बचाना

**sherbet** /ˈʃɜːbət ˈशबत्/ *noun* [U] **1** (*BrE*) a flavoured powder that makes bubbles when you put it in your mouth and is eaten as a sweet एक मीठा, सुगंधित पाउडर जिसके मुँह में जाते ही बुलबुले बन जाते हैं तथा जो मिठाई स्वरूप खाया जाता है **2** (*IndE*) a drink made of sweetened fruit juices diluted in water and served with ice शरबत

**sheriff** /ˈʃerɪf ˈशेरिफ़्/ *noun* [C] an officer of the law in a US county अमेरिकी काउंटि में क़ानूनी मामलों का अफ़सर; शेरिफ़

**sherry** /ˈʃeri ˈशेरि/ *noun* [C, U] (*pl.* **sherries**) a type of strong Spanish wine; a glass of this wine एक प्रकार की तेज़ स्पैनिश शराब, शेरी; गिलासभर शेरी

**she's** /ʃiːz; ʃiz शीज़्; शिज़्/ ➪ **she is, she has** का संक्षिप्त रूप

**shield¹** /ʃiːld शील्ड्/ *noun* [C] **1** (in past times) a large piece of metal or wood that soldiers carried to protect themselves धातु या लकड़ी की ढाल (प्राचीन काल में सैनिकों द्वारा आत्मरक्षा के लिए प्रयुक्त) **2 riot shield** a piece of equipment made of strong plastic, that the police use to protect themselves from angry crowds मज़बूत प्लास्टिक की ढाल (दंगा-फ़साद के समय पुलिस द्वारा आत्मरक्षा के लिए प्रयुक्त) **3** a person or thing that is used to protect sb/sth especially by forming a barrier किसी की रक्षा के लिए ढाल के समान प्रयुक्त कोई व्यक्ति या वस्तु, रक्षा कवच *The metal door acted as a shield against the explosion.* **4** an object or drawing in the shape of a shield, sometimes used as a prize in a sports competition ढाल के आकार की वस्तु या आरेख; शील्ड (कभी-कभी प्रतियोगिता में पुरस्कार के रूप में प्रयुक्त)

**shield²** /ʃiːld शील्ड्/ *verb* [T] **shield sb/sth (against/from sb/sth)** to protect sb/sth from danger or damage संकट या हानि से किसी को बचाना *I shielded my eyes from the bright light with my hand.*

**shift¹** /ʃɪft शिफ़्ट्/ *verb* [I, T] **1** to move or be moved from one position or place to another एक स्थिति या स्थान से दूसरी में (किसी को) रखना या (स्वयं) जाना; खिसकाना, खिसकना *She shifted uncomfortably in her chair.* ○ *He shifted his desk closer to the window.* **2** to change your opinion of or attitude towards sth किसी बात के प्रति अपने विचार या रुख को बदल लेना *Public attitudes towards marriage have shifted over the years.*

IDM **shift the blame/responsibility (for sth) (onto sb)** to make sb else responsible for sth you should do or for sth bad you have done अपने किए की या अपने द्वारा किए जाने योग्य काम की ज़िम्मेदारी या क़सूर दूसरे पर डालना

**shift²** /ʃɪft शिफ़्ट्/ *noun* **1** [C] **a shift (in sth)** a change in your opinion of or attitude towards sth (किसी बात के प्रति) विचार या रुख में परिवर्तन *There has been a shift in public opinion away from war.* **2** [C] (in a factory, etc.) one of the periods that the working day is divided into फ़ैक्टरी आदि की शिफ़्ट, पाली, कार्यसमय (उन अवधियों में से एक जिनमें कोई कार्यदिवस विभक्त हो) *to work* ***in shifts*** ○ *shift work/workers* ○ *day/night shift* **3** [C, *with sing. or pl. verb*] the workers who work a particular shift किसी ख़ास पाली के कर्मचारी *The night shift has/have just gone off duty.* **4** [U] one of the keys that you use for writing on a computer, etc., that allows you to write a big (**capital**) letter कंप्यूटर आदि के कुंजीपटल की एक कुंजी जिसके दबाने से बड़े अक्षर लिखे जाते हैं *the shift key*

**shifting cultivation** *noun* [U] (*technical*) a way of farming in some tropical countries in which farmers use an area of land until it cannot be used for growing plants any more, then move on to a new area of land कुछ गरम देशों में प्रचलित

स्थान-परिवर्तन-प्रधान कृषि प्रणाली (जिसमें किसान पुरानी भूमि के अनुपयोगी हो जाने के कारण खेती की ज़मीन बदलते रहते हैं)

**shifty** /ˈʃɪfti ˈशिफ़्टि/ *adj.* (used about a person or his/her appearance) giving the impression that you cannot trust him/her (व्यक्ति या उसका चेहरा) जो उसके विश्वसनीय न होने की छाप छोड़े *shifty eyes*

**shilling** /ˈʃɪlɪŋ ˈशिलिङ्/ *noun* [C] **1** the basic unit of money in some countries, for example Kenya शिलिंग (केन्या आदि में प्रचलित मुद्रा की बेसिक इकाई) **2** a British coin worth five pence that was used in past times पाँच पेंस का ब्रिटिश सिक्का (पहले प्रचलित)

**shimmer** /ˈʃɪmə(r) ˈशिम(र्)/ *verb* [I] to shine with a soft light that seems to be moving झिलमिलाना (हिलने का आभास देते हुए कोमल प्रकाश के साथ चमकना) *Moonlight shimmered on the sea.*

**shin**/ʃɪn शिन्/ *noun* [C] the front part of your leg from your knee to your foot घुटने से नीचे टखने तक पैर का अग्रभाग ➪ **body** पर चित्र देखिए।

**shin bone** = **tibia**

**shine[1]** /ʃaɪn शाइन्/ *verb* (*pt, pp* **shone** /ʃɒn शान्/) **1** [I] to send out or to send back (**reflect**) light; to be bright चमकाना या चमक बिखेरना; चमकना *I could see a light shining in the distance.* ○ *The sea shone in the light of the moon.* **2** [T] to direct a light at sb/sth किसी पर रोशनी फेंकना या डालना *The policeman shone a torch on the stranger's face.* **3** [I] **shine (at/in sth)** to be very good at a school subject, a sport, etc. पढ़ाई, खेल आदि में अच्छा होना *She has always shone at languages.*

**shine[2]** /ʃaɪn शाइन्/ *noun* [*sing.*] **1** a bright effect caused by light hitting a polished surface चमक, जगमगाहट (चमकाई गई सतह पर प्रकाश पड़ने से उत्पन्न छटा) **2** the act of polishing sth so that it shines किसी वस्तु को चमकाने की क्रिया (ताकि वह चमके)

**shingle** /ˈʃɪŋgl ˈशिङ्गल्/ *noun* [U] small pieces of stone lying in a mass on a beach (समुद्र तट पर) कंकड़ों का ढेर

**shingles** /ˈʃɪŋglz ˈशिङ्गल्ज़्/ *noun* [U] a disease that affects the long thin threads in the body that carry messages to and from the brain (**nerves**) and produces a band of painful spots on the skin कच्ची दाद (नसों की बीमारी जिसमें त्वचा पर दर्दभरे चकत्ते हो जाते हैं)

**shin pad** *noun* [C] a thick piece of material used to protect the front part of your leg from your knee to your foot (**the shin**) when playing some sports घुटने से नीचे टखने तक पैर के अग्रभाग का (कुछ खेलों में) बचाव करने वाली गद्दी; शिन पैड

**shiny** /ˈʃaɪni ˈशाइनि/ *adj.* (**shinier; shiniest**) causing a bright effect when in the sun or in light चमकदार (धूप या रोशनी में) *a shiny new car/shiny hair*

**ship[1]** /ʃɪp शिप्/ *noun* [C] a large boat used for carrying passengers or cargo by sea जहाज़, जलयान, जलपोत (समुद्र द्वारा यात्री या माल ले जाने के लिए प्रयुक्त) *to travel* ***by ship*** ○ *to launch a ship*

**ship[2]** /ʃɪp शिप्/ *verb* [T] (**shipping; shipped**) to send or carry sth by ship or by another type of transport जहाज़ या यातायात के अन्य साधन द्वारा कुछ भेजना या ले जाना

**shipbuilder** /ˈʃɪpbɪldə(r) ˈशिप्बिल्ड(र्)/ *noun* [C] a person or company who makes or builds ships जलपोत बनाने वाला व्यक्ति या कंपनी; पोतशिल्पी (व्यक्ति) या पोत निर्माता (कंपनी) ▶ **ship building** *noun* [U] जलपोत-निर्माण

**shipment** /ˈʃɪpmənt ˈशिप्मन्ट्/ *noun* **1** [U] the carrying of goods from one place to another माल को एक स्थान से दूसरे स्थान पर ले जाने का काम; लदान **2** [C] a quantity of goods that are sent from one place to another भेजे गए माल की मात्रा; पोत-लदान

**shipping** /ˈʃɪpɪŋ ˈशिपिङ्/ *noun* [U] **1** ships in general or considered as a group जलपोत या जलपोत समूह **2** the carrying of goods from one place to another माल भेजने का काम *a shipping company*

**shipshape** /ˈʃɪpʃeɪp ˈशिप्शेप्/ *adj.* (*not before a noun*) clean and neat; in good condition and ready to use स्वच्छ और साफ़; अच्छी और चालू अवस्था में

**shipwreck** /ˈʃɪprek ˈशिप्रेक्/ *noun* [C, U] an accident at sea in which a ship is destroyed by a storm, rocks, etc. and sinks समुद्र में आँधी, चट्टान से टक्कर आदि के कारण पोत के नष्ट होकर डूब जाने की दुर्घटना; पोत-भंग **NOTE** पोत-भंग के शिकार व्यक्ति या (जल) पोत के लिए शब्द **shipwrecked** है।

**shipyard** /ˈʃɪpjɑːd ˈशिप्याड्/ *noun* [C] a place where ships are repaired or built (स्थान) जहाँ जलपोतों की मरम्मत या निर्माण का काम हो; पोतशाला

**shirk** /ʃɜːk शक्/ *verb* [I, T] to avoid doing sth that is difficult or unpleasant, especially because you are too lazy कठिन या अप्रिय काम से जी चुराना (विशेषतः बहुत आलसी होने के कारण); टालना *to shirk your responsibilities*

**shirt** /ʃɜːt शट्/ *noun* [C] a piece of clothing made of cotton, etc. worn on the upper part of the body कमीज़, शर्ट (सूती आदि की)

**NOTE** सामान्यतया शर्ट के गरदन के हिस्से में **collar** होता है, लंबी या छोटी **sleeves** होती हैं, और आगे की तरफ नीचे तक **buttons** होते हैं।

**shiver** /ˈʃɪvə(r) ˈशिव़(र्)/ *verb* [I] to shake slightly, especially because you are cold or frightened ठिठुरना, काँपना (विशेषतः डर या ठंड के मारे) *shivering with cold/fright* ▶ **shiver** *noun* [C] ठिठुरन, कँपकँपी *The thought sent a shiver down my spine.*

**shoal** /ʃəʊl शोल्/ *noun* [C] a large group of fish that feed and swim together मछलियों का झुंड या गोल

**shock[1]** /ʃɒk शॉक्/ *noun* **1** [C, U] the feeling that you get when sth unpleasant happens suddenly; the situation that causes this feeling एकाएक अप्रिय घटना घट जाने से उत्पन्न मनःस्थिति, झटका, आघात, सदमा, धक्का; इस मनःस्थिति को उत्पन्न करने वाली परिस्थिति *The bad news **came as a shock** to her.* ○ *His mother is **in a state of shock**.* **2** [U] a serious medical condition of extreme weakness caused by damage to the body शरीर में चोट लगने से उत्पन्न बहुत कमज़ोरी (का रोग) *He **was in/went into shock** after the accident.* **3** [C] a violent shaking movement (caused by a crash, explosion, etc.) तेज़ झटका (टक्कर, विस्फ़ोट आदि के कारण) **4** [C] = **electric shock**

**shock[2]** /ʃɒk शॉक्/ *verb* **1** [T] to cause an unpleasant feeling of surprise in sb किसी के मन में दुखद आश्चर्य उत्पन्न करना; सदमा पहुँचाना *We were shocked by his death.* **2** [I, T] to make sb feel disgusted or offended किसी के मन में घृणा या क्रोध उत्पन्न करना *These films deliberately set out to shock.* ▶ **shocked** *adj.* आहत *a shocked expression/look*

**shock absorber** *noun* [C] a device that is fitted to each wheel of a vehicle in order to reduce the effects of travelling over rough ground, so that passengers can be more comfortable वाहन के प्रत्येक पहिए में लगा एक उपकरण जो ऊबड़-खाबड़ जगहों पर लगे धक्के सहकर यात्रियों को आराम पहुँचाता है; शॉक एबसॉर्बर

**shocking** /ˈʃɒkɪŋ ˈशॉकिङ्/ *adj.* **1** that offends or upsets people; that is morally wrong जो लोगों के मन में घृणा या क्रोध भर दे, घृणाजनक या क्रोधजनक; नैतिक दृष्टि से अनुचित *a shocking accident* ○ *shocking behaviour/news* **2** (*informal*) very bad बहुत बुरा, घटिया

**shock wave** *noun* [C] a movement of very high air pressure that is caused by an explosion, a movement of the earth's surface (**an earthquake**), etc. विस्फोट, भूकंप आदि से उत्पन्न प्रबल वायु-दाबों की गति; प्रघाती तरंग

**shod** ➪ **shoe[2]** का past tense और past participle रूप

**shoddy** /ˈʃɒdi ˈशॉडि/ *adj.* **1** made carelessly or with poor quality materials लापरवाही या घटिया माल से बना *shoddy goods* **2** dishonest or unfair बेईमानी भरा या अनुचित ▶ **shoddily** *adv.* घटियापन से

**shoe[1]** /ʃuː शू/ *noun* [C] **1** a type of covering for the foot, usually made of leather or plastic जूता (प्रायः चमड़े या प्लास्टिक का) *a pair of shoes* ○ *running shoes* **2** = **horse shoe**

IDM **in my, your, etc. place/shoes** ➪ **place[1]** देखिए।

**shoe[2]** /ʃuː शू/ *verb* [T] (*pt, pp* **shod** /ʃɒd शॉड्/) to fit a shoe on a horse घोड़े के नाल ठोकना

**shoehorn** /ˈʃuːhɔːn ˈशूहॉन्/ *noun* [C] a curved piece of plastic or metal that you use to help the back of your foot go into your shoe जूता पहनने में सहायक प्लास्टिक या धातु का मुड़ा हुआ टुकड़ा; सीगड़ा, शूहार्न

**shoelace** /ˈʃuːleɪs ˈशूलेस्/ (*AmE* **shoestring**) *noun* [C] a long thin piece of material like string used to fasten a shoe जूते का फ़ीता; तसमा *to tie/untie a shoelace* ➪ **button** पर चित्र देखिए।

**shoestring** /ˈʃuːstrɪŋ ˈशूस्ट्रिङ्/ = **shoelace**

IDM **on a shoestring** using very little money किफ़ायत से; बहुत थोड़े पैसों के सहारे *to live on a shoestring*

**shone** ➪ **shine[1]** का past tense और past participle रूप

**shoo[1]** /ʃuː शू/ *verb* [T] (*pt, pp* **shooed**) **shoo sb/sth away, off, out, etc.** to make sb/sth go away by saying 'shoo' and waving your hands 'शू' कहते और हाथ हिलाते हुए किसी को भगाना *She shooed the children out of the kitchen.*

**shoo[2]** /ʃuː शू/ *exclamation* used to tell a child or an animal to go away बच्चे या पशु को भगाने के लिए प्रयुक्त

**shook** ➪ **shake[1]** का past tense रूप

**shoot[1]** /ʃuːt शूट्/ *verb* (*pt, pp* **shot** /ʃɒt शॉट्/) **1** [I, T] **shoot (sth) (at sb/sth)** to fire a gun or another weapon बंदूक़ या कोई दूसरा अस्त्र चलाना *Don't shoot!* ○ *She shot an arrow at the target, but missed it.* **2** [T] to injure or kill sb/sth with a gun बंदूक़ से किसी को घायल करना या मार देना *The soldier was **shot dead**.* **3** [I, T] to hunt and kill birds and animals with a gun as a sport खेल-खेल में पक्षियों और पशुओं का बंदूक़ से शिकार करना *He **goes shooting** at the weekends.* ➪ **hunting** देखिए। **4** [I, T] to move somewhere quickly and suddenly; to make sth move in this way तेज़ी से और अचानक निकलना, जाना; किसी को इस तरह भेजना *The car shot past me at 100 kilometres per hour.* **5** [I] (of pain) to go very suddenly along part of your body एकदम अचानक किसी अंग में (दर्द का) उठना *The pain shot up my leg.* ○ *shooting pains in the chest* **6** [I, T] to make a film or photograph of sth फ़िल्म बनाना या किसी की फ़ोटो लेना *They shot the scene ten times.* **7** [I] **shoot (at sth)** (in football, etc.) to try to kick or hit the ball into the goal (फ़ुटबॉल आदि में) गेंद को मार कर गोल में डालने का यत्न करना *He should have shot instead of passing.* ➪ **shot** noun देखिए।

**PHR V** **shoot sb/sth down** to make sb/sth fall to the ground by shooting him/her/it गोली मार कर (किसी को) नीचे गिराना *The helicopter was shot down by a missile.*

**shoot up** to increase by a large amount; to grow very quickly बहुत अधिक बढ़ जाना; तेज़ी से बढ़ना *Prices have shot up in the past year.*

**shoot²** /ʃu:t शूट्/ *noun* [C] a new part of a plant or tree पौधे या पेड़ का नया अंश; अंकुर ➪ **flower** पर चित्र देखिए।

**shooting star** *noun* [C] a small piece of rock in space (**a meteor**) that travels very fast and burns with a bright light as it enters the earth's atmosphere उल्का खंड (अत्यंत तीव्र गति से चलता है और पृथ्वी के वातावरण में प्रवेश करने समय तेज़ रोशनी फेंकता है), टूटता हुआ तारा

shooting star

**shop¹** /ʃɒp शॉप्/ (*AmE* **store**) *noun* [C] a building or part of a building where things are bought and sold कोई इमारत या इमारत का हिस्सा जहाँ वस्तुओं का क्रय-विक्रय हो; दुकान *a cake/shoe shop* ○ *a corner shop* (= a local shop, usually at the corner of a street)

**NOTE** 'At the butcher's shop' आदि के स्थान पर **at the butcher's** आदि प्रयोग अधिक प्रचलित है।

**IDM** **talk shop** ➪ **talk¹** देखिए।

**shop²** /ʃɒp शॉप्/ *verb* [I] (**shopping; shopped**) **shop (for sth)** to go to a shop or shops in order to buy things चीज़ें ख़रीदने दुकान या दुकानों पर जाना; ख़रीदारी करना *He's shopping for some new clothes.*

**NOTE** **Shop** की अपेक्षा **go shopping** प्रयोग अधिक प्रचलित है—*We go shopping every Saturday.*

▶ **shopper** *noun* [C] ख़रीदार

**PHR V** **shop around (for sth)** to look at the price and quality of an item in different shops before you decide where to buy it किस दुकान से ख़रीदें यह तय करने से पहले चीज़ के दाम और क़िस्म या गुणवत्ता के विषय में अलग-अलग दुकानों पर पूछना

**shop assistant** (*AmE* **sales clerk; clerk**) *noun* [C] a person who works in a shop दुकान सहायक; दुकान का कर्मचारी

**shop floor** *noun* [*sing.*] (*BrE*) **1** an area of a factory where the goods are made by the workers कारख़ाने का वह हिस्सा जहाँ कर्मचारी माल तैयार करते हैं; श्रमिक कर्मशाला *to work **on the shop floor*** **2** the workers in a factory, not the managers कारख़ाने के कर्मचारी (न कि प्रबंधक-गण)

**shopkeeper** /ˈʃɒpki:pə(r) ˈशॉप्कीप(र्)/ (*AmE* **storekeeper**) *noun* [C] a person who owns or manages a small shop छोटी दुकान का मालिक या प्रबंधक; दुकानदार

**shoplifter** /ˈʃɒplɪftə(r) ˈशॉप्लिफ़्ट(र्)/ *noun* [C] a person who steals sth from a shop while pretending to be a customer (ग्राहक होने का दिखावा करते हुए) दुकान से चीज़े चुराने वाला; उठाईगीरा, उचक्का ➪ **thief** पर नोट देखिए।

**shoplifting** /ˈʃɒplɪftɪŋ ˈशॉप्लिफ़्टिङ्/ *noun* [U] the crime of stealing goods from a shop while pretending to be a customer (ग्राहक होने का दिखावा करते हुए) दुकान से सामान की चोरी (का अपराध); उठाईगीरी, उचक्कापन, छिटपुट चोरी, हथलपकी *He was arrested for shoplifting.* ➪ **lift¹ 6** देखिए।

**shopping** /ˈʃɒpɪŋ ˈशॉपिङ्/ *noun* [U] **1** the activity of going to the shops and buying things दुकानों पर जाकर चीज़ ख़रीदने की क्रिया; ख़रीदारी *We always **do the shopping** on a Friday night.* ○ *a shopping basket/bag/trolley* **2** the things that you have bought in a shop दुकान से ख़रीदी वस्तुएँ

**shopping centre** (*AmE* **shopping mall; mall**) *noun* [C] a place where there are many shops, either outside or in a covered building ऐसा स्थान जहाँ अनेक दुकानें हो (खुले में या छती हुई इमारत में); दुकान-केंद्र, विपणन-केंद्र

**shore¹** /ʃɔ:(r) शॉ(र्)/ *noun* [C, U] the land at the edge of a sea or lake समुद्र या झील का तट *The sailors went on shore* (= on land). ➪ **ashore** देखिए।

**shore²** /ʃɔ:(r) शॉ(र्)/ *verb*

**PHR V** **shore sth up 1** to support part of a building or other large structure by placing large pieces of wood or metal against or under it so that it does not fall down लकड़ी या धातु की बल्लियों से किसी भवन या बड़े ढाँचे को सहारा देना (गिरने से

बचाने के लिए) **2** to help support sth that is weak or going to fail कमजोर या शीघ्र गिर सकने वाली चीज़ को सहारा देना *The measures were aimed at shoring up the economy.*

**shorn** ➪ **shear** का past participle रूप

**short**[1] /ʃɔːt शॉट् / *adj., adv.* **1** not measuring much from one end to the other छोटा (लंबाई में) *a short line/distance/dress/hair* ○ *This essay is rather short.* ✪ विलोम **long** ➪ **shorten** verb देखिए। **2** less than the average height ठिगना, नाटा (औसत से कम लंबा) *a short, fat man* ✪ विलोम **tall** **3** not lasting a long time; brief लंबे समय तक न चलने वाला; संक्षिप्त *a short visit/film* ○ *to have a short memory* (= to only remember things that have happened recently) ✪ विलोम **long** ➪ **shorten** verb देखिए। **4 short (of/on sth)** not having enough of what is needed आवश्यक से कम *Because of illness, the team is two players short.* ○ *Good secretaries are* ***in short supply*** (= there are not enough of them). ➪ **shortage** noun देखिए। **5 suddenly** एकाएक, सहसा *She* ***stopped short*** *when she saw the accident.* **6** short for sth used as a shorter way of saying sth or as an abbreviation किसी अभिव्यक्ति या शब्द का संक्षिप्त रूप या संक्षिप्ति के संकेत के लिए प्रयुक्त *Vinnie is short for Vinayak.* **7 short (with sb)** (used about a person) speaking in an impatient and angry way to sb (व्यक्ति) किसी से भड़क कर कुछ कहते हुए ➪ **shortly** adverb देखिए।

**IDM** **cut sth/sb short** to not allow sb to finish speaking; to interrupt (किसी को) भाषण पूरा न करने देना; बीच में टोक देना, रोक देना या बाधा डालना

**fall short (of sth)** to not be enough; to not reach sth अपर्याप्त होना; कहीं तक न पहुँच पाना *The pay rise fell short of the workers' demands.*

**for short** as a short form संक्षेप में; संक्षिप्ति के रूप में, छोटे नाम के तौरपर *She's called Urmila or Urmi for short.*

**go short (of sth)** to be without enough (of sth) (किसी चीज़ की) कमी होना, किसी वस्तु का अपर्याप्त होना *He made sure his family never went short of food.*

**in the long/short term** ➪ **term**[1] देखिए।

**in short** in a few words; briefly थोड़े शब्दों में; संक्षेप में

**run short (of sth)** to have used utmost of sth so there is not much left किसी वस्तु की कमी हो जाना (अधिकतर अंश का उपयोग हो जाने के कारण) *We're running short of coffee.*

**short of sth/doing sth** apart from; except for के अतिरिक्त; को छोड़कर *Nothing short of a miracle will save the business now.*

**stop short of sth/doing sth** ➪ **stop**[1] देखिए।

**short**[2] /ʃɔːt शॉट् / *noun* [C] (*informal*) = **short circuit**

**shortage** /ˈʃɔːtɪdʒ ˈशॉटिज् / *noun* [C] a situation where there is not enough of sth किसी वस्तु की कमी या अपर्याप्तता *a food/housing/water shortage* ○ *a shortage of trained teachers*

**shortbread** /ˈʃɔːtbred ˈशॉट्ब्रेड् / *noun* [U] a sweet biscuit made with sugar, flour and butter चीनी, आटे और मक्खन से बना मीठा बिस्कुट

**short circuit** (*informal* **short**) *noun* [C] a bad electrical connection that causes a machine to stop working सदोष विद्युत संयोजन (जिसके कारण मशीन का चलना रुक जाए); लघु परिपथ, शॉर्ट-सकिट ▶ **short-circuit** *verb* [I, T] शॉर्ट-सर्कट हो जाना या कर देना *The lights short-circuited.*

**shortcoming** /ˈʃɔːtkʌmɪŋ ˈशॉट्कमिङ् / *noun* [C, *usually pl.*] a fault or weakness दोष या दुर्बलता

**short cut** *noun* [C] a quicker, easier or more direct way to get somewhere or to do sth कहीं पहुँचने या कुछ करने का शीघ्रकारी, अधिक सरल और सीधा मार्ग; सुगम उपाय, छोटा रास्ता *He* ***took a short cut*** *to school through the park.*

**shorten** /ˈʃɔːtn ˈशॉट्न् / *verb* [I, T] to become shorter or to make sth shorter छोटा हो जाना या कर देना

**shortfall** /ˈʃɔːtfɔːl ˈशॉट्फ़ॉल् / *noun* [C] **shortfall (in sth)** the amount by which sth is less than you need or expect आवश्यकता या अपेक्षा से कम (मात्रा की दृष्टि से)

**shorthand** /ˈʃɔːthænd ˈशॉट्हैन्ड् / *noun* [U] a method of writing quickly that uses signs or short forms of words संकेतों और शब्दों के संक्षिप्त रूपों की सहायता से जल्दी-जल्दी लिखने की एक प्रणाली; शीघ्रलिपि, आशुलिपि, शॉटहैंड *to write* ***in shorthand*** ○ *a shorthand typist* ➪ **longhand** देखिए।

**shortlist** /ˈʃɔːtlɪst ˈशॉर्ट्लिस्ट् / *noun* [C] [*usually sing.*] a list of the best people for a job, etc. who have been chosen from all the people who want the job किसी नौकरी के इच्छुक उम्मीदवारों में से योग्यतम व्यक्तियों की सूची; शॉर्टलिस्ट *She's one of the four people on the shortlist.* ▶ **shortlist** *verb* [T] व्यक्तियों को शॉर्टलिस्ट करना *Six candidates were shortlisted for the post.*

**short-lived** *adj.* lasting only for a short time अल्पजीवी, क्षणस्थायी

**shortly** /ˈʃɔːtli ˈशॉट्लि / *adv.* **1** soon; not long शीघ्र; अविलंब *The manager will see you shortly.* **2** in an impatient, angry way जल्दबाज़ी और गुस्से से; रूखेपन से

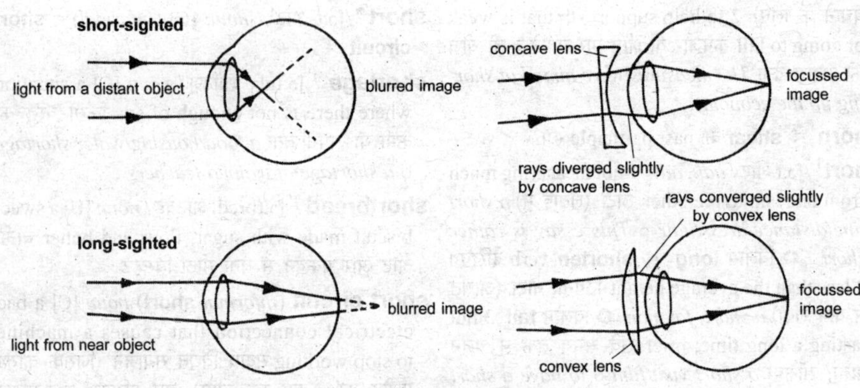


**short-sighted/long-sighted**

**shorts** /ʃɔːts शॉर्ट्स् / *noun* [*pl.*] **1** a type of short trousers ending above the knee that you wear in hot weather, while playing sports, etc. हाफ़पैंट; निकर (गरमियों में या खेलते समय पहना जाने वाला) **2** (*AmE*) = **boxer shorts**

**NOTE** याद रखिए **shorts** का प्रयोग केवल बहुवचन रूप में होता है, इसलिए 'a new short' प्रयोग ग़लत है। सही प्रयोग है—*I need to get **some new shorts**.* ○ *I need to get **a new pair of shorts**.*

**short-sighted** *adj.* **1** (*AmE* **near-sighted**) able to see things clearly only when they are very close to you केवल निकट की वस्तुओं को देखने में समर्थ; निकटदर्शी *I have to wear glasses because I'm short-sighted.* ✪ पर्याय **myopic** ✪ विलोम **long-sighted** **2** not considering what will probably happen in the future भावी को समझने में असमर्थ; अदूरदर्शी *a short-sighted attitude/policy* ▶ **short-sightedness** *noun* [U] निकट दृष्टि, अदूरदर्शिता

**short-staffed** *adj.* (used about an office, a shop, etc.) not having enough people to do the work (कोई कार्यालय, दुकान आदि) जहाँ कर्मचारियों की कमी है

**short story** *noun* [C] a piece of writing that is shorter than a novel कहानी; लघु कथा (उपन्यास से छोटी कथा-रचना)

**short-term** *adj.* lasting for a short period of time from the present अल्पकालिक; अल्पावधिक (वर्तमान से थोड़ी अवधि तक रहने वाला) *short-term plans/memory*

**short wave** *noun* [C, U] (*abbr.* **SW**) a system for sending radio signals रेडियो संकेत भेजने की एक प्रणाली; शॉर्टवेव *Short wave is a radio wave of frequency greater then 3 MHz.* ➪ **long wave** और **medium wave** देखिए।

**shot¹** /ʃɒt शॉट् / *noun* [C] **1 a shot (at sb/sth)** an act of firing a gun, etc., or the noise that this makes (बंदूक़ आदि की गोली दाग़ने की क्रिया या इस क्रिया से उत्पन्न आवाज़, बंदूक़ से निशाना या बंदूक़ का धमाका) *to **take a shot** at the target* ○ *The policeman fired **a warning shot** into the air.* **2** (in sport) the action of kicking, throwing or hitting a ball in order to score a point or a goal (खेल में) गेंद को ठोकर मारने, फेंकने या हिट करने की क्रिया (अंक बनाने या गोल करने के लिए) *Ajay scored with a low shot into the corner of the net.* ○ *Good shot!* **3** a photograph or a picture in a film फ़िल्म में कोई फ़ोटो या चित्र *I got some good shots of the runners as they crossed the line.* **4** [*usually sing.*] (*informal*) **a shot (at sth/at doing sth)** a try at doing sth; an attempt कुछ करने की कोशिश; प्रयास *Let me **have a shot** at it* (= let me try to do it). ○ *Just **give it your best shot*** (= try as hard as you can). **5** a small amount of a drug that is put into your body using a needle इंजेक्शन से शरीर में पहुँचाई गई नशीली दवा की अल्पमात्रा **6** (*often* **the shot**) a heavy metal ball that is thrown as a sport (**the shot-put**) गोला फेंक खेल में प्रयुक्त धातु का भारी गोला

**IDM** **a long shot** ➪ **long¹** देखिए।

**call the shots/tune** ➪ **call¹** देखिए।

**like a shot** (*informal*) very quickly; without stopping to think about it बहुत तेज़ी से; सोचने के लिए बिना रुके *If someone invited me on a free holiday, I'd go like a shot.*

**shot²** ➪ **shoot¹** का past tense और past pariciple रूप

**shotgun** /ˈʃɒtɡʌn ˈशॉट्गन् / *noun* [C] a long gun that is used for shooting small animals and birds छोटे पशु-पक्षियों पर गोली चलाने की लंबी बंदूक़; शॉटगन

**should** /ʃəd; *strong form* ʃʊd शड्; प्रबल रूप शुड्/ *modal verb* (*negative* **should not**; *short form* **shouldn't** /ˈʃʊdnt ˈशुड्न्ट्/) **1** (used for saying that it is right or appropriate for sb to do sth, or for sth to happen) ought to (कर्तव्य या ज़रूरत का औचित्य व्यक्त करने के लिए प्रयुक्त) चाहिए (करना, जाना आदि) *The police should do something about street crime in this area.* ○ *Children shouldn't be left on their own.* **2** used for giving or for asking for advice सलाह देने या माँगने के लिए प्रयुक्त *You should try that new restaurant.* ○ *Do you think I should phone him?* **3** used for saying that you expect sth is true or will happen किसी घटना की सचाई या घटित होने की संभावना व्यक्त करने के लिए प्रयुक्त *It's 4.30 a.m. They should be in New Delhi by now.* ○ *It should stop raining soon.* **4** (*BrE formal*) used with 'I/we' instead of 'would' in 'if' sentences, 'if' वाले वाक्यों में 'I/we' के साथ 'would' के स्थान पर प्रयुक्त *I should be most grateful if you could send me Rs 10,000.* **5** (*formal*) used after 'if' and 'in case' to refer to a possible event or situation संभावना का अर्थ व्यक्त करने के लिए 'if' और 'in case' के बाद प्रयुक्त *If you should decide to accept, please phone us.* ○ *Should you decide to accept please call us.* **6** used as the past tense of 'shall' when we report what sb says वक्ता के शब्दों को उद्धृत करने के लिए 'shall' के भूत काल के रूप में प्रयुक्त *He asked me if he should come today* (= he asked 'Shall I come today?'). **7 I should imagine, say, think, etc.** used to give opinions that you are not certain about अनिश्चित स्थितियों के विषय में अपने विचार व्यक्त करने के लिए प्रयुक्त

> **NOTE** वृत्तिवाचक क्रियाओं (modal verbs) के विषय में अधिक जानकारी के लिए इस शब्दकोश के अंत में **Quick Grammar Reference** खंड देखिए।

**shoulder¹** /ˈʃəʊldə(r) ˈशोल्ड(र्)/ *noun* **1** [C] the part of your body between your neck and the top of your arm कंधा, स्कंध *I asked him why he'd done it but he just* ***shrugged his shoulders*** (= raised his shoulders to show that he did not know or care). ➪ **body** पर चित्र देखिए। **2 -shouldered** (*used to form compound adjectives*) having the type of shoulders mentioned निर्दिष्ट प्रकार के कंधों वाला *a broad-shouldered man* **3** [C] a part of a dress, coat, etc. that covers the shoulders कोट, कमीज़ आदि का कंधा (इन कपड़ों का कंधों पर आने वाला भाग) ➪ **hard shoulder** देखिए।

**IDM a shoulder to cry on** used to describe a person who listens to your problems and understands how you feel सहानुभूतिशील व्यक्ति; हमदर्द इनसान (जो आपकी कठिनाइयों को जाने और भावना को समझे)

**have a chip on your shoulder** ➪ **chip¹** देखिए।

**rub shoulders with sb** ➪ **rub** देखिए।

**shoulder²** /ˈʃəʊldə(r) ˈशोल्ड(र्)/ *verb* [T] **1** to accept the responsibility for sth किसी बात की ज़िम्मेदारी लेना *to* ***shoulder the blame/responsibility*** *for sth* **2** to push sb/sth with your shoulder किसी को कंधे से धक्का देना

**shoulder bag** *noun* [C] a type of bag that you carry over one shoulder with a long strap कंधे पर लटकाने का थैला (जिस पर लंबा पट्टा या फ़ीता लगा हो)

**shoulder blade** *noun* [C] either of the two large flat bones on each side of your back, below your shoulders कंधे की हड्डी ✪ पर्याय **scapula** ➪ **body** पर चित्र देखिए।

**shoulder strap** *noun* [C] **1** a narrow piece of material on a dress or other piece of clothing that goes over your shoulder from the front to the back कुछ लिबासों में आगे से पीछे की ओर, कंधे के ऊपर से जाने वाला पट्टा या फ़ीता; स्ट्रैप **2** a long narrow piece of material, leather, etc. that is part of a bag so that you can carry it over your shoulder चमड़े आदि के बैग में लगा पट्टा या फ़ीता (बैग को कंधे पर लटकाने के लिए)

**shout** /ʃaʊt शाउट्/ *verb* **1** [I] **shout (at/to sb); shout out** to speak or cry out in a very loud voice ऊँची आवाज़ में बोलना या चीख़ना *The teacher shouted angrily at the boys.* ○ *to shout out in pain/excitement* **2** [T] **shout sth (at/to sb); shout sth out** to say sth in a loud voice ऊँची आवाज़ में या चीख़कर कुछ कहना *The students kept shouting out the answers, so we stopped playing in the end.* ○ *The captain shouted instructions to his team.* ➪ **scream** देखिए। ▶ **shout** *noun* [C] चीख

**PHR V shout sb down** to shout so that sb who is speaking cannot be heard ऐसे चीख़ना कि वक्ता की आवाज़ दब जाए, किसी को चीख़कर बोलने से रोकना *The speaker was shouted down by a group of protesters.*

**shove** /ʃʌv शव्/ *verb* [I, T] (*informal*) to push with a sudden, rough movement रूखेपन से ठेलना *Everybody in the crowd was* ***pushing and shoving****.* ○ *The policeman shoved the thief into the back of the police car.* ▶ **shove** *noun* [C, *usually sing.*] धक्का *to give sb/sth a shove*

**shovel** /ˈʃʌvl ˈशव्ल्/ *noun* [C] a tool used for picking up and moving earth, snow, sand, etc.

बेलचा (मिट्टी, बर्फ़, रेत आदि हटाने के लिए प्रयुक्त) ➪ **spade** देखिए तथा **gardening** पर चित्र देखिए।
▶ **shovel** *verb* [I, T] (**shovelling; shovelled** *AmE* **shoveling; shoveled**) बेलचा चलाना या बेलचे से हटाना

**show¹** /ʃəʊ शो/ *verb* (*pt* **showed;** *pp* **shown** /ʃəʊn शोन्/ or **showed**) **1** [T] **show sb/sth (to sb); show sb (sth)** to let sb see sb/sth किसी को कोई व्यक्ति या वस्तु देखने देना; दिखाना, प्रदर्शित करना *She showed me what she had bought.* ○ *She was showing signs of stress.* ○ *This white T-shirt really shows the dirt.* **2** [T] to make sth clear; to give information about sth किसी बात को स्पष्ट करना; किसी बात के विषय में जानकारी देना *Research shows that most people get too little exercise.* ○ *This graph shows how prices have gone up in the last few years.* **3** [I] to be able to be seen; to appear दिख सकना, सामने आना; प्रकट होना *I tried not to let my disappointment show.* **4** [T] to help sb to do sth by doing it yourself; to explain sth अपेक्षित काम करके दिखाना (ताकि दूसरे की सहायता हो सके); कुछ समझाना *Can you show me how to put the disk in the computer?* **5** [T] to lead sb to or round a place; to explain how to go to a place किसी को कहीं ले जाना या घुमाना; कहीं जाने का रास्ता या उपाय बताना *A guide showed us round the museum.*

**PHR V** **show (sth) off** (*informal*) to try to impress people by showing them how clever you are or by showing them sth that you are proud of अपनी चतुराई या गर्व करने योग्य वस्तु दिखाकर लोगों को प्रभावित करने का प्रयत्न करना, किसी चीज़ का दिखावा करना, किसी बात पर इतराना; इठलाना *Jai was showing off by driving his new car very fast.* ➪ **show-off** noun देखिए।

**show up** (*informal*) to arrive, especially when sb is expecting you पहुँचना (विशेषतः जब कोई प्रतीक्षा कर रहा हो) *I thought you'd never show up.*

**show (sth) up** to allow sth to be seen (किसी चीज़ को) उभार कर दिखाना *The sunlight shows up those dirty marks on the window.*

**show sb up** (*informal*) to make sb embarrassed about your behaviour or appearance अपने आचरण या शकल से किसी को विक्षुब्ध कर देना *He showed her up by shouting at the waiter.*

**show²** /ʃəʊ शो/ *noun* **1** [C] a type of entertainment performed for an audience दर्शकों के मनोरंजन के लिए प्रस्तुत कार्यक्रम *a TV comedy show* ○ *a quiz show* **2** [C, U] an occasion when a collection of things are brought together for people to look at एक अवसर जब वस्तुओं के संग्रह को लोग एक स्थान पर देखते हैं; प्रदर्शनी, नुमाइश (वस्तुओं की) *a dog show* ○ *Paintings by schoolchildren will be* ***on show*** *at Pragati Maidan next week.* **3** [C, U] something that a person does or has in order to make people believe sth that is not true झूठा दिखावा, मिथ्या प्रदर्शन *Although she disliked him, she* ***put on a show of*** *politeness.* ○ *His bravery is* ***all show*** (= he is not as brave as he pretends to be). **4** [*sing.*] an occasion when you let sb see sth किसी मनोभाव आदि सार्वजनिक अभिव्यक्ति; प्रदर्शन *a show of emotion/gratitude/temper*

**show business** (*informal* **showbiz** /ˈʃəʊbɪz ˈशोबिज़्/) *noun* [U] the business of entertaining people, in the theatre, in films, on television, etc. रंगमंच, फ़िल्म, टीवी आदि के माध्यम से लोगों का मनोरंजन करने का व्यवसाय; मनोरंजन व्यवसाय *He's been* ***in show business*** *since he was five years old.*

**showdown** /ˈʃəʊdaʊn ˈशोडाउन्/ *noun* [C] a final argument, meeting or fight at the end of a long disagreement किसी लंबे विवाद के अंत में निर्णायक बहस, बैठक, सभा या झगड़ा; शक्ति-परीक्षण *The management are preparing for a showdown with the union.*

**shower¹** /ˈʃaʊə(r) ˈशाउअ(र्)/ *noun* [C] **1** a piece of equipment that produces a spray of water that you stand under to wash; the small room or part of a room that contains a shower नल के नीचे खड़े होकर नहाते समय शरीर पर पानी छिड़कने वाला उपकरण, फुहारा, शावर; शावर युक्त स्नानघर, फुहारा-घर *The shower doesn't work.* ○ *She's in the shower.* **2** an act of washing yourself by standing under a shower फुहारे की सहायता से स्नान; फुहारा-स्नान *I'll just* ***have a quick shower.*** **3** a short period of rain बौछार (वर्षा की) ➪ **rain** और **acid rain** देखिए। **4** a lot of very small objects that fall or fly through the air together नीचे गिरने या हवा में एक साथ तैरते (किसी वस्तु के) बहुत-से छोटे-छोटे कण *a shower of sparks/broken glass*

**shower²** /ˈʃaʊə(r) ˈशाउअ(र्)/ *verb* **1** [I, T] **shower (down) on sb/sth; shower sb with sth** to cover sb/sth with a lot of small falling objects किसी पर (किसी वस्तु के) बहुत-से छोटे-छोटे कणों की बरसात-सी होना *Ash from the volcano showered down on the town.* **2** [I] to wash yourself under a shower फुहारा-स्नान करना *I came back from my run, showered and got changed.*

**showing** /ˈʃəʊɪŋ ˈशोइङ्/ *noun* **1** [C] an act of showing a film, etc. फ़िल्म आदि का प्रदर्शन *The second showing of the film begins at 8 o'clock.*

2 [*sing.*] how sb/sth behaves; how successful sb/sth is किसी का आचरण; किसी की उपलब्धि का स्तर *On its present showing, the party should win the election.*

**showjumping** /ˈʃəʊdʒʌmpɪŋ ˈशोजम्पिङ्/ *noun* [U] a competition in which a person rides a horse over a series of fences (**jumps**) घुड़सवारों की कूद-प्रदर्शन की प्रतियोगिता (जिसमें अनेक बाड़ों पर से कूदना होता है)

**shown** ➪ **show**[1] का past participle रूप

**show-off** *noun* [C] a person who tries to impress others by showing them how clever he/she is, or by showing them sth he/she is proud of अपनी चतुराई या गर्व करने योग्य वस्तु दिखाकर लोगों को प्रभावित करने में प्रयासरत व्यक्ति; दिखावा करने वाला व्यक्ति, इतराने या इठलाने वाला व्यक्ति *She's such a show-off, always boasting about how good she is at playing chess.*

**showroom** /ˈʃəʊruːm; -rʊm ˈशोरूम्; -रुम्/ *noun* [C] a type of large shop where customers can look at goods such as cars, furniture and electrical items that are on sale एक प्रकार की बड़ी दुकान जहाँ कार, फ़र्नीचर आदि वस्तुओं को ग्राहकों के प्रदर्शनार्थ रखा जाता है; शोरूम, प्रदर्शन-कक्ष

**shrank** ➪ **shrink** का past tense रूप

**shrapnel** /ˈʃræpnəl ˈश्रैप्नल्/ *noun* [U] small pieces of metal that fly around when a bomb explodes बम में से छिटकी गोलियाँ या धातु के कण

**shred**[1] /ʃred श्रेड्/ *noun* **1** [C] a small thin piece of material that has been cut or torn off किसी चीज़ का कटा या फाड़ा हुआ छोटा महीन टुकड़ा; धज्जी, कतरन *His clothes were torn to shreds by the rose bushes.* **2 a shred of sth** [*sing.*] (*in negative sentences*) a very small amount of sth लेश, कण (किसी वस्तु का) *There wasn't a shred of truth in her story.*

**shred**[2] /ʃred श्रेड्/ *verb* [T] (**shredding; shredded**) to tear or cut sth into shreds किसी वस्तु को छोटे महीन टुकड़ों में चीरना या काटना; कतरना *shredded cabbage*

**shrew** /ʃruː श्रू/ *noun* [C] **1** a small animal like a mouse with a long nose छछूँदर (लंबी नाक वाला चुहिया जैसा प्राणी) **2** (*old-fashioned*) a bad-tempered unpleasant woman बदमिज़ाज औरत

**shrewd** /ʃruːd श्रूड्/ *adj.* able to make good decisions because you understand a situation well (स्थिति को समझ लेने के कारण) उचित निर्णय करने में समर्थ; समझदार, सयाना, चतुर *a shrewd thinker/decision* ▶ **shrewdly** *adv.* सयानेपन से, चतुराई से

**shriek** /ʃriːk श्रीक्/ *verb* **1** [I] to make a short, loud, noise in a high voice चीख़ मारना *She shrieked in fright.* ○ *The children were shrieking with laughter.* **2** [T] to say sth loudly in a high voice चीख कर (कुछ) कहना या बोलना *'Stop it!' she shrieked.* ➪ **screech** देखिए। ▶ **shriek** *noun* [C] चीख़

**shrill** /ʃrɪl श्रिल्/ *adj.* (used about a sound) high and unpleasant (आवाज़) तेज़ और कानफोड़ू, अप्रिय *a shrill cry/voice*

**shrimp** /ʃrɪmp श्रिम्प्/ *noun* [C] **1** a small sea creature with a shell and a lot of legs that turns pink when you cook it झींगा मछली **NOTE Shrimps prawns** से छोटी होती हैं। **2** (*AmE*) = **prawn** ➪ **shellfish** पर चित्र देखिए।

**shrine** /ʃraɪn श्राइन्/ *noun* [C] a place that is important to a particular person or group of people for religious reasons or because it is connected with a special person विशिष्ट व्यक्ति या सामाजिक वर्ग के लिए, धार्मिक कारणों से या व्यक्ति-विशेष से संबंधित होने के कारण महत्त्वपूर्ण कोई स्थल-मंदिर, पूजास्थल, मक़बरा, समाधि

**shrink** /ʃrɪŋk श्रिङ्क्/ *verb* (*pt* **shrank** /ʃræŋk श्रैङ्क्/ or **shrunk** /ʃrʌŋk श्रङ्क्/ *pp* **shrunk**) **1** [I, T] to become smaller or make sth smaller (किसी वस्तु का) सिकुड़ जाना या किसी वस्तु को सिकोड़ देना (आकार में छोटा हो जाना या कर देना) *My T-shirt shrank in the wash.* ○ *The rate of inflation has shrunk to 4%.* **2** [I] to move back because you are frightened or shocked (डर या घृणा के कारण) पीछे हटना *We shrank back against the wall when the dog started to bark.*

**PHR V shrink from sth/doing sth** to not want to do sth because you find it unpleasant किसी काम से मुँह मोड़ लेना (बुरा लगने के कारण)

**shrink-wrapped** *adj.* covered tightly in a thin sheet of plastic महीन प्लास्टिक की पट्टी से कसकर चिपका हुआ *The books are shrink-wrapped so you can't open them in the shop.*

**shrivel** /ˈʃrɪvl ˈश्रिव्ल्/ *verb* [I, T] (**shrivelling; shrivelled** *AmE* **shriveling; shriveled**) **shrivel (sth) (up)** to become smaller, especially because of dry conditions मुरझा या सूख जाना (विशेषतः गरमी पड़ने के कारण) *The plants shrivelled up and died in the hot weather.*

**shroud**[1] /ʃraʊd श्राउड्/ *noun* [C] a cloth or sheet that is put round a dead body before it is buried कफ़न

**shroud**[2] /ʃraʊd श्राउड्/ *verb* [T] **shroud sth (in sth)** (*usually passive*) to cover or hide sth किसी वस्तु को ढकना या छिपाना

**shrub** /ʃrʌb श्रब्/ *noun* [C] a small bush झाड़ी

**shrubbery** /ˈʃrʌbəri ˈश्रबरि / *noun* [C] (*pl.* **shrubberies**) an area where a lot of small bushes have been planted झाड़-झंखाड़, झुरमुट; झाड़ियों-भरा इलाक़ा

**shrug** /ʃrʌg श्रग् / *verb* [I, T] (**shrugging; shrugged**) to lift your shoulders as a way of showing that you do not know sth or are not interested (ग़ैर-जानकारी या अरुचि जतलाने के लिए) कंधे उचकाना *'Who knows?' he said and shrugged.* ○ *'It doesn't matter to me,' he said,* ***shrugging his shoulders****.* ▶ **shrug** *noun* [C, *usually sing.*] कंधे की उचक *I asked him if he was sorry and he just answered with a shrug.*

PHR V **shrug sth off** to not allow sth to affect you in a bad way किसी बात की उपेक्षा करना (उसका कुप्रभाव न पड़ने देना) *An actor has to learn to shrug off criticism.*

**shrunk** ➪ **shrink** का past tense और past participle रूप

**shudder** /ˈʃʌdə(r) ˈशड(र्) / *verb* [I] to suddenly shake hard, especially because of an unpleasant feeling or thought थरथराना; एकाएक ज़ोर से काँपने लगना (विशेषतः अमंगल की भावना या विचार से) *Just to think about the accident makes me shudder.* ○ *The engine shuddered violently and then stopped.* ▶ **shudder** *noun* [C] थरथराहट

**shuffle¹** /ˈʃʌfl ˈशफ़ल् / *verb* **1** [I] to walk by sliding your feet along instead of lifting them off the ground पैरों को (उठाकर चलने के बजाय) घसीटते हुए चलना **2** [I, T] to move your body or feet around because you are uncomfortable or nervous शरीर या पैरों की स्थिति बदलते रहना (ऊबकर या घबराकर) *The audience were so bored that they began to shuffle in their seats.* **3** [I, T] to mix a pack of playing cards before a game ताश के पत्ते फेंटना *She shuffled the cards carefully.*

**shuffle²** /ˈʃʌfl ˈशफ़ल् / *noun* [C, *usually sing.*] **1** a way of walking without lifting your feet off the ground पैरों को घसीटकर (न कि उठाकर) चलने की क्रिया; घसीट-चाल **2** an act of shuffling cards ताश के पत्तों को फेंटने की क्रिया; फेंट

**shun** /ʃʌn शन् / *verb* [T] (**shunning; shunned**) (*written*) to avoid sb/sth; to keep away from sb/sth किसी से मुहँ मोड़ना; किसी से दूर रहना *Radha was shunned by her family when she married Rahul.*

**shunt** /ʃʌnt शन्ट् / *verb* [T] **1** to move a railway train from one track to another रेल के डिब्बे को एक पटरी से दूसरी (बग़ल की) पटरी पर ले जाना; शंट करना **2** to make sb go from one place to another किसी को एक स्थान से दूसरे पर भेज देना *He was shunted around from one hospital to another.*

**shut¹** /ʃʌt शट् / *verb* (*pres. part.* **shutting;** *pt, pp* **shut**) **1** [I, T] to make sth close; to become closed (किसी को) बंद करना; (किसी का) बंद होना *I can't shut my suitcase.* ○ *He shut his eyes and tried to go to sleep.* **2** [I, T] (used about a shop, restaurant, etc.) to stop doing business for the day; to close (दुकान, रेस्तराँ आदि का) काम करना बंद करना; बंद हो जाना या कर देना *What time do the shops shut on Saturday?* **3** [T] to prevent sb/sth from leaving a place; to close a door on sth किसी को कहीं पर बंद कर देना; किसी चीज़ पर दरवाज़ा आ जाना *She shut herself in her room and refused to come out.* ○ *Tarun shut his fingers in the door of the car.*

PHR V **shut sb/sth away** to keep sb/sth in a place where people cannot find or see him/her/it किसी को कहीं छिपाकर रखना (ताकि लोग उसे देख या उससे मिल न सकें)

**shut (sth) down** (used about a factory, etc.) to close for a long time or forever (क़ारख़ाने आदि का) लंबे समय तक बंद रहना या हमेशा के लिए बंद हो जाना *Financial problems forced the business to shut down.*

**shut sb/sth off (from sth)** to keep sb/sth apart from sth व्यक्ति या वस्तु का किसी से अपने को अलग कर लेना *He shuts himself off from the rest of the world.*

**shut sb/sth out** to keep sb/sth out व्यक्ति या वस्तु को बाहर रखना *He tried to shut out all thoughts of the accident.*

**shut (sb) up** (*informal*) **1** to stop talking; to be quiet बोलना बंद कर देना; चुप हो जाना *I wish you'd shut up!* **2** to make sb stop talking (किसी को) चुप कराना

**shut sb/sth up (in sth)** to put sb/sth somewhere and stop him/her leaving व्यक्ति या वस्तु को कहीं बंद कर देना *He was shut up in prison for nearly ten years.*

**shut²** /ʃʌt शट् / *adj.* (*not before a noun*) **1** in a closed position बंद (स्थिति में) *Make sure the door is shut properly before you leave.* NOTE याद रखिए, संज्ञा से पहले शब्द **closed** का प्रयोग तो हो सकता है परंतु **shut** का नहीं। **2** not open to the public (जनता के लिए) बंद *The restaurant was shut so we went to one round the corner.*

IDM **keep your mouth shut** ➪ **mouth¹** देखिए।

**shutter** /ˈʃʌtə(r) ˈशट(र्) / *noun* [C] **1** a wooden or metal cover that is fixed outside a window and that can be opened or shut. A shop's shutter usually slides down from the top of the shop window लकड़ी या धातु की बनी (खिड़की की) झिलमिली, शटर (जिसे खोला और बंद किया जा सकता है) (दुकान का शटर खिड़की के ऊपरी सिरे से नीचे की ओर सरक कर आता है) **2** the part at the front of a camera that opens for a very short time to let light in so that a photograph can be taken कैमरे का शटर (कैमरे का वह भाग जो रोशनी को अंदर आने देने के लिए क्षण भर के लिए खुलता है ताकि फ़ोटो लिया जा सके) ➪ **camera** पर चित्र देखिए।

**shuttle** /ˈʃʌtl ˈशट्ल्/ *noun* [C] a plane, bus or train that travels regularly between two places दो स्थानों के बीच नियमित रूप से चलने वाली रेलगाड़ी, बस या विमान; शटल

**shuttlecock** /ˈʃʌtlkɒk ˈशट्लकॉक्/ *noun* [C] (in the sport of badminton) the small, light object that is hit over the net बैडमिंटन की चिड़िया; शटलकॉक

**shy**[1] /ʃaɪ शाइ/ *adj.* **1** nervous and uncomfortable about meeting and speaking to people; showing that sb feels like this लोगों से मिलने और बात करने में घबराहट और बेचैनी अनुभव करने वाला; संकोची, शरमीला, झेंपू; संकोच दिखाने वाला *She's very shy with strangers.* ○ *a shy smile* **2 shy (of/about sth/doing sth)** frightened to do sth or to become involved in sth कुछ करने या किसी काम से जुड़ने से डरने वाला *She's not shy of telling people what she thinks.* ▸ **shyly** *adv.* संकोचपूर्वक ▸ **shyness** *noun* [U] संकोच भावना, शर्म, झेंप

**shy**[2] /ʃaɪ शाइ/ *verb* (*pres. part.* **shying;** *3rd person sing. pres.* **shies;** *pt, pp* **shied**) [I] (used about a horse) to suddenly move back or sideways in fear (घोड़े का) अचानक डर कर पीछे हटना या इधर-उधर भागना; भड़क जाना, बिदक जाना

**PHR V** **shy away from sth/from doing sth** to avoid doing sth because you are afraid डर के मारे किसी काम से हाथ खींचना

**SI** /ˌes ˈaɪ ˌएस् ˈआइ/ *abbr.* (used to describe units of measurement) International System (from French 'Système International') (माप की इकाइयों का संकेत करने के लिए प्रयुक्त) इंटरनेशनल सिस्टम *SI units* ➪ इस शब्दकोश के अंत में **Numbers** शीर्षक खंड देखिए।

**Siamese twin** /ˌsaɪəmiːz ˈtwɪn ˌसाइअमीज़् ˈट्विन्/ (*also* **conjoined twin**) *noun* [C] one of two people who are born with their bodies joined together in some way, sometimes sharing the same organs जुड़वाँ बच्चों में से कोई एक, जुड़वाँ (जन्म के समय एक जैसी शारीरिक बनावट से परस्पर जुड़े हुए और कुछ मामलों में साझे अंगों वाले दो बच्चों में से एक)

**sibling** /ˈsɪblɪŋ ˈसिबलिङ्/ *noun* [C] (*formal*) a brother or a sister (सगा) भाई या बहन **NOTE** सामान्य भाषा में **brother(s) and sister(s)** प्रयोग किया जाता है—*Have you got any brothers and sisters?*

**sic**/sɪk; siːk सिक्; सीक्/ *adv.* (written after a word that you have copied from somewhere, to show that you know that the word is wrongly spelled or wrong in some other way) बाह्य स्रोत से अपने मूल रूप में उद्धृत शब्द के आगे लिखित (यह दिखाने के लिए कि शब्द में कुछ ग़लती है और लेखक यह बात जानता है); एवमेव *In the letter to parents it said: 'The school is proud of it's [sic] record of excellence'.*

**sick**[1] /sɪk सिक्/ *adj.* **1** not well; ill स्वस्थ नहीं; बीमार *a sick child* ○ *Do you get paid for days when you're **off sick** (= from work)?*

**NOTE** ब्रिटिश अंग्रेज़ी में **be sick** का अर्थ सामान्यतया होता है वमन करना।

**2 the sick** *noun* [*pl.*] people who are ill बीमार लोग **3** feeling ill in your stomach so that you may bring up food through your mouth (**vomit**) उलटी या वमन करने की इच्छा होना *I feel sick—I think it was that fish I ate.* ○ *Don't eat any more or you'll make yourself sick.* ➪ **airsick, carsick, nausea, seasick** और **travel-sick** देखिए। **4 sick of sb/sth** feeling bored or annoyed because you have had too much of sb/sth ऊब जाना या नाराज़ हो जाना (किसी बात की अति हो जाने के कारण) *I'm sick of my job.* ○ *I'm sick of tidying up your mess!* **5 sick (at/about sth)** very annoyed or disgusted by sth किसी बात से नाराज़ या विक्षुब्ध हो जाना *He felt sick at the sight of so much waste.* **6** (*informal*) mentioning disease, suffering, death, etc. in a cruel or disgusting way रोग, कष्ट, मृत्यु आदि की निर्मम और विक्षोभकारी ढंग से चर्चा करना; संवेदन-शून्यता दिखाना *He offended every one with a sick joke about blind people.*

**IDM** **be sick** to bring up food from the stomach; vomit भोजन को वमन करना; उलटी करना

**make sb sick** to make sb very angry किसी को क्रोधित कर देना; गुस्सा दिलाना *Oh, stop complaining. You make me sick!*

**sick to death of sb/sth** feeling tired of or annoyed by sb/sth किसी के व्यवहार से निराश या नाराज़ हो जाना *I'm sick to death of his grumbling.*

**sick**[2] /sɪk सिक्/ *noun* [U] food that sb has brought up from his/her stomach; vomit वमन किया हुआ भोजन; उलटी *There was sick all over the car seat.*

**sicken** /ˈsɪkən ˈसिकन्/ *verb* [T] to make sb feel disgusted किसी को विक्षुब्ध कर देना *The sight of people* *fighting sickens me.* ▶ **sickening** *adj.* विक्षोभकारी *His head made a sickening sound as it hit the road.*

**sickle** /ˈsɪkl ˈसिकल्/ *noun* [C] a tool with a short handle and a long, curved metal part with a sharp edge (**a blade**) that is used for cutting long grass, corn, etc. हँसिया; लंबी घास, मक्का आदि काटने की दराँती ➪ **scythe** पर चित्र देखिए।

**sick leave** *noun* [U] a period spent away from work, etc. because of illness बीमारी के कारण ली गई छुट्टी; रुग्णावकाश *Mitali been off **on sick leave** since March.*

**sickle cell anaemia** *noun* [U] a serious medical condition in which the red blood cells are damaged and change shape एक गंभीर रोग जिसमें लाल रुधिर कोशिकाएँ क्षतिग्रस्त हो जाती हैं या उनकी आकृति बदल जाती है

**sickly** /ˈsɪkli ˈसिकलि/ *adj.* **1** (used about a person) weak and often ill (व्यक्ति) दुर्बल और प्रायः बीमार *a sickly child* **2** unpleasant; causing you to feel ill अरुचिकर, दूषित; बीमार-सा कर देने वाला *the sickly smell of rotten fruit*

**sickness** /ˈsɪknəs ˈसिक्नस्/ *noun* **1** [U] the state of being ill बीमारी, रोग, रुग्णावस्था *A lot of workers are absent because of sickness.* **2** [U] a feeling in your stomach that may make you bring up food through your mouth वमन करने की इच्छा; मिचली *Symptoms of the disease include sickness and diarrhoea.* **3** [C, U] a particular type of illness विशेष प्रकार की बीमारी *pills for seasickness* ➪ **sleeping sickness** देखिए।

**side¹** /saɪd साइड्/ *noun* [C] **1** one of the flat outer surfaces of sth किसी वस्तु की कोई एक समतल बाहरी सतह; पार्श्व, फलक *A cube has six sides.* **2 -sided** (*used to form compound adjectives*) having the number of sides mentioned जिसमें उतने पार्श्व हों जितने बताए गए हैं, -पक्ष वाला, -तरफ़ वाला *a six-sided coin* **3** one of the surfaces of sth except the top, bottom, front or back (सबसे ऊपर की और नीचे की, तथा आगे और पीछे की सतहों को छोड़कर) कोई एक सतह; भाग, हिस्सा *I went round to the side of the building.* ○ *The side of the car was damaged.* **4** the edge of sth, away from the middle (मध्य भाग से दूर, किसी वस्तु का) किनारा *Make sure you stay **at the side** of the road when you're cycling.* ○ *We moved **to one side** to let the doctor get past.* **5** the area to the left or right of sth; the area in front of or behind sth (किसी वस्तु के) दाएँ या बाएँ का तथा सामने या पीछे का हिस्सा, भाग *We live (on) **the other side** of the main road.* ○ *In Japan they drive on **the left-hand side** of the road.* **6** either of the two flat surfaces of sth thin (काग़ज़ आदि किसी महीन वस्तु की) कोई एक समतल सतह; तरफ़, ओर *Write on both sides of the paper.* **7** the right or the left part of your body, especially from under your arm to the top of your leg शरीर का दायाँ या बायाँ अंग (विशेषतः बाँह के नीचे से टाँग के अंत तक का), ओर, दिशा *She lay on her side.* ○ *The soldier stood with his hands by his sides.* **8** either of two or more people or groups who are fighting, playing, arguing, etc. against each other परस्पर विरोधी व्यक्तियों या समूहों में कोई एक; पक्ष, दल *The two sides agreed to stop fighting.* ○ *the winning/losing side* **9** what is said by one person or group that is different from what is said by another एक व्यक्ति या समूह का वक्तव्य जो दूसरे व्यक्ति या समूह से भिन्न हो; पक्ष, दल *I don't know whose **side of the story** to believe.* **10** your mother's or your father's family माता या पिता का परिवार, पक्ष *There is no history of illness **on** his mother's **side**.*

IDM **get on the right/wrong side of sb** to please/annoy sb किसी व्यक्ति को प्रसन्न या नाराज़ करना *He tried to get on the right side of his new boss.*

**look on the bright side** ➪ **look¹** देखिए।

**on/from all sides; on/from every side** in/from all directions सब दिशाओं में या से

**on the big, small, high, etc. side** (*informal*) slightly too big, small, high, etc. कुछ अंशतः अधिक बड़ा, छोटा, ऊँचा आदि

**on the safe side** ➪ **safe¹** देखिए।

**put sth on/to one side; leave sth on one side** to leave or keep sth so that you can use it or deal with it later (भविष्य में इस्तेमाल के लिए) कुछ छोड़ देना या बचा कर रखना *You should put some money to one side for the future.*

**side by side** next to each other; close together अग़ल-बग़ल में; पास-पास *They walked side by side along the road.*

**take sides (with sb)** to show that you support one person rather than another in an argument विवाद में किसी एक का पक्ष लेना; की तरफ़दारी करना *Parents should never take sides when their children are quarrelling.*

**side²** /saɪd साइड्/ *verb*

PHR V **side with sb (against sb)** to support sb in an argument (दूसरे के विरुद्ध) किसी का समर्थन करना या साथ देना

**sideboard** /ˈsaɪdbɔːd ˈसाइड्बॉड्/ *noun* [C] a type of low cupboard about as high as a table, that is used for storing plates, etc. in a room that is used for eating (**dining room**) भोजन कक्ष में तश्तरियों को रखने की नीची (मेज़ की ऊँचाई की) अलमारी; साइडबोर्ड

**sideburns** /ˈsaɪdbɜːnz ˈसाइड्बर्न्ज़् / *noun* [*pl.*] hair that grows down a man's face in front of his ears गलगुच्छा; पुरुष के मुहँ पर (कानों के सामने से चेहरे के नीचे तक) उगने वाले बालों का गुच्छा

**side effect** *noun* [C] **1** the unpleasant effect that a drug may have in addition to its useful effects (औषध के अनुकूल परिणाम का) सहगामी दुष्प्रभाव *Side effects of the drug include nausea and dizziness.* **2** an unexpected effect of sth that happens in addition to the intended effect (किसी वस्तु के) अभीष्ट प्रभाव के साथ होने वाला अप्रत्याशित (और अनुकूल) प्रभाव *One of the side effects when the chemical factory closed was that fish returned to the river.* ➪ **after-effect** और **effect** देखिए।

**sideline** /ˈsaɪdlaɪn ˈसाइड्लाइन् / *noun* **1** [C] something that you do in addition to your regular job, especially to earn extra money मुख्य जीविका-कार्य से अतिरिक्त (गौण) कार्य (विशेषतः कुछ अतिरिक्त धन अर्जित करने के लिए); उपजीविका, उपवेतन *He's an engineer, but he repairs cars **as a sideline**.* **2 sidelines** [*pl.*] the lines that mark the two long sides of the area used for playing sports such as football, tennis, etc.; the area behind this फ़ुटबॉल का मैदान, टेनिस का कोर्ट आदि में लंबाई की तरफ़ खिंची दो रेखाएँ, पार्श्व रेखाएँ; इन रेखाओं के पीछे का स्थान, पार्श्व-क्षेत्र

IDM **on the sidelines** not involved in an activity; not taking part in sth गतिविधि में संलिप्त नहीं, दर्शक मात्र; किसी काम में भाग न लेते हुए (केवल अवलोकन करते हुए)

**sidelong** /ˈsaɪdlɒŋ ˈसाइड्लॉङ् / *adj.* directed from the side; sideways किसी ओर से आने वाला; एक तरफ़ *a sidelong glance*

**side road** *noun* [C] a small road which joins a bigger main road अधिक बड़ी मुख्य सड़क से जुड़ने वाली छोटी सड़क; उपमार्ग

**sidestep** /ˈsaɪdstep ˈसाइड्स्टेप् / *verb* (**sidestepping; sidestepped**) **1** [T] to avoid answering a question or dealing with a problem प्रश्न का उत्तर देने या समस्या से जूझने से कतराना; टाल देना *Did you notice how she neatly sidestepped the question?* **2** [T, I] to avoid sth, for example being hit, by stepping to one side चोट खाने आदि से बचने के लिए एक तरफ़ हो जाना या एक तरफ़ होकर किसी बात (जैसे चोट खा जाना) से बचना

**side street** *noun* [C] a narrow or less important street near a main street मुख्य मार्ग के पास का तंग या छोटा मार्ग, गौण मार्ग, पतली या कम चलती गली

**sidetrack** /ˈsaɪdtræk ˈसाइड्ट्रैक् / *verb* [T] (*usually passive*) to make sb forget what he/she is doing or talking about and start doing or talking about sth less important मुख्य विषय या मुद्दे से हटकर बातें करना

**sidewalk** /ˈsaɪdwɔːk ˈसाइड्वॉक् / (*AmE*) = **pavement**

**sideways** /ˈsaɪdweɪz ˈसाइड्वेज़् / *adv., adj.* **1** to, towards or from one side एक दिशा ओर को, की या से *He jumped sideways to avoid being hit.* **2** with one of the sides at the top (किसी वस्तु को) एक तरफ़ से ऊँचा करते हुए *We'll have to turn the sofa sideways to get it through the door.*

**siding** /ˈsaɪdɪŋ ˈसाइडिङ् / *noun* [C, *usually pl.*] a short track at the side of a main railway line where trains go when they are not being used मुख्य रेल पटरी के बग़ल की छोटी लंबाई की रेल पटरी (विश्राम-अवधि में रेलगाड़ियों को खड़ा रखने के लिए), बग़ली लाइन; साइडिंग

**sidle** /ˈsaɪdl ˈसाइड्ल् / *verb* [I] **sidle up/over (to sb/sth)** to move towards sb/sth in a nervous way, as if you do not want anyone to notice you झिझकते हुए, दबकर चलना (मानो लोगों से नज़र चुराते हुए)

**siege** /siːdʒ सीज़् / *noun* [C, U] a situation in which an army surrounds a town for a long time or the police surround a building so that nobody can get in or out (सैनिकों द्वारा किसी शहर की या पुलिस द्वारा किसी इमारत की) घेराबंदी (लोगों का अंदर जाना-बाहर आना रोकने के लिए)

**siesta** /siˈestə सिˈएस्टा / *noun* [C] a short sleep or rest that people take in the afternoon, especially in hot countries दोपहर की झपकी या दोपहर का विश्राम (विशेषतः गरम देशों में); सिएस्टा

**sieve** /sɪv सिव् / *noun* [C] a type of kitchen tool that has a metal or plastic net, used for separating solids from liquids or very small pieces of food from large pieces चलनी या छलनी, छाननी, छन्ना *Pour the soup through a sieve to get rid of any lumps.* ➪ **kitchen** पर चित्र देखिए। ▶ **sieve** *verb* [T] छानना (छलनी से) *to sieve flour*

**sift** /sɪft सिफ़्ट् / *verb* **1** [T] to pass flour, sugar or a similar substance through a **sieve** in order to remove any lumps (आटा, चीनी आदि को) छानना (ढेले आदि को अलग करने के लिए) *to sift flour/sugar* **2** [I, T] **sift (through) sth** to examine sth very carefully किसी मामले की गहराई से छानबीन करना *It took weeks to sift through all the evidence.*

**sigh** /saɪ साइ / *verb* **1** [I] to let out a long, deep breath that shows you are tired, sad, disappointed, etc. आह भरना; लंबी गहरी साँस खींचना (थकान, उदासी,

निराशा आदि को प्रकट करने वाली) *She sighed with disappointment at the news.* **2** [T] to say sth with a sigh आह भरते या गहरी साँस खींचते हुए कुछ कहना *'I'm so tired,' he sighed.* **3** [I] to make a long sound like a sigh आह भरने जैसी आवाज़ करना; विलाप करना ▶ **sigh** *noun* [C] आह, लंबी, गहरी साँस

IDM **heave a sigh** ➪ **heave¹** देखिए।

**sight¹** /saɪt साइट्/ *noun* **1** [U] the ability to see दृष्टि, नजर; देखने की क्षमता *He lost his sight in the war* (= he became blind). ○ *My grandmother has very poor sight.* **2 -sighted** (*used to form compound adjectives*) able to see in the way mentioned (बताए गए ढंग से) देखने वाला, -दृष्टि युक्त *a partially sighted child* ➪ **long-sighted** और **short-sighted** देखिए। **3** [*sing.*] **the sight of sb/sth the act of seeing sb/sth** किसी को देखने की क्रिया; दृष्टि, नज़ारा *I feel ill **at the sight of** blood.* **4** [U] a position where sb/sth can be seen स्थिति जहाँ से कोई या कुछ दिख सके; दृष्टिपथ, दृष्टि *They waited until the plane was **in/within sight** and then fired.* ○ ***come into sight*** ○ ***out of sight*** **5** [C] something that you see दृश्य, नज़ारा *The burned-out building was a terrible sight.* **6 sights** [*pl.*] places of interest that are often visited by tourists (पर्यटकों के लिए) दर्शनीय स्थान *When you come to Kolkata I'll show you the sights.* **7 a sight** [*sing.*] (*informal*) a person or thing that looks strange or amusing विचित्र या मज़ेदार लगने वाला व्यक्ति या वस्तु **8** [C, *usually pl.*] the part of a gun that you look through in order to aim it बंदूक़ की मक्खी (जिसमें से देखकर निशाना साधा जाता है)

IDM **at first glance/sight** ➪ **first¹** देखिए।

**catch sight/a glimpse of sb/sth** ➪ **catch¹** देखिए।

**in sight** likely to happen or come soon शीघ्र संभावित *A peace settlement is in sight.*

**lose sight of sb/sth** ➪ **lose** देखिए।

**on sight** as soon as you see sb/sth जैसे ही कोई या कुछ दिखे; देखते ही *The soldiers were ordered to shoot the enemy on sight.*

**sight²** /saɪt साइट्/ *verb* [T] to see sb/sth, especially after looking out for him/her/it किसी को देख लेना (विशेषतः कुछ प्रयत्न के बाद)

**sighting** /ˈsaɪtɪŋ ˈसाइटिङ्/ *noun* [C] an occasion when sb/sth is seen किसी का दिख जाना *the first sighting of a new star*

**sightseeing** /ˈsaɪtsiːɪŋ ˈसाइट्सीइङ्/ *noun* [U] visiting the sights of a city, etc. as a tourist (पर्यटक के रूप में) किसी नगर आदि के दर्शनीय स्थानों की सैर *We did some sightseeing in Mumbai.*

**sightseer** /ˈsaɪtsiːə(r) ˈसाइट्सीअ(र्)/ *noun* [C] a person who visits the sights of a city, etc. as a tourist (पर्यटक के रूप में) दर्शनीय स्थानों का भ्रमण करने वाला व्यक्ति; पर्यटक, सैलानी ➪ **tourist** देखिए।

**sign¹** /saɪn साइन्/ *noun* [C] **1 sign (of sth)** something that shows that sb/sth is present, exists or may happen (किसी के विद्यमान होने, अस्तित्व में होने या घटित हो सकने का) चिह्न *The patient was **showing** some **signs** of improvement.* **2** a piece of wood, paper, etc. that has writing or a picture on it that gives you a piece of information, an instruction or a warning कुछ जानकारी; निर्देश या चेतावनी देने का संकेत (लकड़ी, काग़ज़ आदि पर लिखित रूप में या चित्र के रूप में) *a road sign* ○ *Follow the signs to Agra.* **3** a movement that you make with your head, hands or arms that has a particular meaning सिर, हाथों या बाहों को हिलाकर किया गया इशारा (विशेष अर्थ को प्रकट करने वाला) ***I made a sign** for him to follow me.* **4** a type of shape, mark or symbol that has a particular meaning विशिष्ट अर्थ युक्त एक प्रकार की आकृति, निशान या प्रतीक *mathematical signs* (+, –, ×, ÷) **5** (*also* **sign of the zodiac**) one of the twelve divisions or symbols of the **zodiac** बारह खगोल राशियों और प्रतीक चिह्नों में से कोई एक *I'm a Leo.* ○ *What sign are you?*

**sign²** /saɪn साइन्/ *verb* **1** [I, T] to write your name on a letter, document, etc. to show that you have written it or that you agree with what it says पत्र, दस्तावेज़ आदि पर हस्ताक्षर करना (यह बताने के लिए कि इसे आपने लिखा है और जो लिखा है उससे आप सहमत हैं) *I have to sign the cheque.* ○ *The two presidents signed the treaty.* ➪ **signature** noun देखिए। **2** [T] **sign sb (up)** to get sb to sign a contract to work for you किसी व्यक्ति के साथ अनुबंध करना (कि वह आपके लिए काम करे) *East Bengal have signed two new players.* **3** [I] to communicate using sign language संकेत भाषा की सहायता से संप्रेषण करना, इशारों से कहना

PHR V **sign in/out** to write your name to show you have arrived at or left a hotel, club, etc. (होटल, क्लब आदि में पहुँचने या वहाँ से जाने की सूचना के संकेत के रूप में) अपना नाम लिखना या अपने हस्ताक्षर करना

**sign up (for sth)** to agree formally to do sth कुछ करने की औपचारिक सहमति देना *I've signed up for driving classes.*

**signal** /ˈsɪɡnəl ˈसिग्नल्/ *noun* [C] **1** a sign, action or sound that sends a particular message विशेष संदेश देने वाला चिह्न, कार्य या ध्वनि; संकेत *When I give (you) the signal, run!* **2** an event, action or fact that shows that sth exists or is likely to happen

कोई घटना, कार्य या तथ्य (किसी बात के अस्तित्व या घटित होने की संभावना का सूचक) *The fall in unemployment is a clear signal that the economy is improving.* **3** a set of lights used to give information to train drivers रेलगाड़ी के ड्राइवरों को सूचना देने वाली बत्तियाँ; रेलवे सिगनल **4** a series of radio waves, etc. that are sent out or received रेडियो तरंगों आदि की शृंखला (जिन्हें प्रेषित या प्राप्त किया जाए) *a signal from a satellite* ▶ **signal** *verb* [I, T] (**signalling; signalled** *AmE* **signaling; signaled**) इशारे होना, इशारे करना *She was signalling wildly that something was wrong.*

**signatory** /ˈsɪgnətri ˈसिग्नट्रि/ *noun* [C] (*pl.* **signatories**) **signatory (to sth)** one of the people or countries that sign an agreement, etc. किसी संधि आदि पर हस्ताक्षर करने वाला व्यक्ति या देश; हस्ताक्षरकर्ता

**signature** /ˈsɪgnətʃə(r) ˈसिग्नच(र्)/ *noun* [C] a person's name, written by that person and always written in the same way व्यक्ति द्वारा लिखा (और सदा एक ही प्रकार से लिखा) गया उसका नाम; हस्ताक्षर, दस्तख़त ➪ **sign** verb देखिए।

**significance** /sɪgˈnɪfɪkəns सिग्ˈनिफ़िकन्स्/ *noun* [U] the importance or meaning of sth किसी बात का महत्त्व या अभिप्राय *Few people realized the significance of the discovery.*

**significant** /sɪgˈnɪfɪkənt सिग्ˈनिफ़िकन्ट्/ *adj.* **1** important or large enough to be noticed महत्त्वपूर्ण, काफ़ी बड़ा (इतना कि दीख जाए) *Police said that the time of the murder was extremely significant.* **2** having a particular meaning विशिष्ट अभिप्राय वाला, सार्थक *It could be significant that he took out life insurance shortly before he died.* ▶ **significantly** *adv.* सार्थक रूप से *Attitudes have changed significantly since the 1960s.*

**signify** /ˈsɪgnɪfaɪ ˈसिग्निफ़ाइ/ *verb* [T] (*pres. part.* **signifying**; *3rd person sing.* **signifies;** *pt, pp* **signified**) (*formal*) **1** to be a sign of sth; to mean किसी बात का संकेत होना; कुछ अर्थ होना *What do those lights signify?* **2** to express or indicate sth कुछ व्यक्त या सूचित करना *They signified their agreement by raising their hands.*

**sign language** *noun* [U] a language used especially by people who cannot hear or speak, using the hands to make signs instead of spoken words बधिरों या गूँगों द्वारा प्रयुक्त संकेत या इंगित भाषा (जिसमें हाथों से इशारे किए जाते हैं)

**signpost** /ˈsaɪnpəʊst ˈसाइन्पोस्ट्/ *noun* [C] a sign at the side of a road that gives information about directions and distances to towns सड़क के किनारे लगा संकेत पट (नगरों तक पहुँचने के लिए दिशाएँ और दूरियाँ बताने वाला)

**Sikh** *noun* [C] a member of one of the religions of India (**Sikhism**) that developed from Hinduism but teaches that there is only one god सिख; सिख धर्म का अनुयायी ▶ **Sikh** *adj.* सिख ▶ **Sikhism** *noun* [U] सिख मत, सिक्खी ➪ **Guru Granth Sahib** देखिए।

**silage** /ˈsaɪlɪdʒ ˈसाइलिज्/ *noun* [U] grass or other green plants that are stored without being dried and are used to feed farm animals in winter खत्ते या गड्ढे में सुरक्षित हरा चारा (सर्दियों में पशुओं के उपयोग के लिए)

**silence** /ˈsaɪləns ˈसाइलन्स्/ *noun* **1** [U] no noise or sound at all शांति, ख़ामोशी, नीरवता *There must be silence during examinations.* **2** [C, U] a period when nobody speaks or makes a noise मौन; चुप्पी या ख़ामोशी *My question was met with an awkward silence.* ○ *We ate* ***in silence.*** **3** [U] not making any comments about sth किसी विषय में कोई टिप्पणी नहीं करना, मौन, किसी से न कुछ कहना न किसी बात का जवाब देना; संप्रेषण-शून्यता की स्थिति ▶ **silence** *verb* [T] चुप करना या कराना, मौन कर देना

**silencer** /ˈsaɪlənsə(r) ˈसाइलन्स(र्)/ (*AmE* **muffler**) *noun* [C] **1** a device which is fixed to the long tube under a vehicle (**exhaust pipe**) to reduce the noise made by the engine वाहनों के नीचे लगी विशेष नली (एग्ज़ॉस्ट पाइप) जो इंजन की आवाज़ को कम कर देती है, कार आदि का साइलेंसर; आवाज़ रोक **2** the part of a gun that reduces the noise when it is fired बंदूक़, पिस्तौल या राइफ़ल का साइलेंसर

**silent** /ˈsaɪlənt ˈसाइलन्ट्/ *adj.* **1** where there is no noise; making no noise; very quiet नीरव, कोलाहलहीन; मौन, ख़ामोश; बहुत शांत *The house was empty and silent.* **2 silent (on/about sth)** refusing to speak about sth किसी विषय में बोलने को तैयार नहीं; चुप *The policeman told her she had the right to* ***remain silent.*** **3** not using spoken words मौन, सस्वर नहीं *a silent prayer/protest* **4** (of a letter) not pronounced (अक्षर या ध्वनि) अनुच्चरित *The 'b' in 'comb' is silent.* ▶ **silently** *adv.* चुपचाप, ख़ामोशी से

**silhouette** /ˌsɪluˈet ˌसिलुˈएट्/ *noun* [C] the dark solid shape of sb/sth seen against a light background हलके रंग की पृष्ठभूमि पर किसी की काली ठोस आकृति; छायाचित्र ▶ **silhouetted** *adj.* छायाचित्रित

**silica** /ˈsɪlɪkə ˈसिलिका/ *noun* [U] (*symbol* $SiO_2$) a chemical compound of silicon found in sand and in rocks such as **quartz**, used in making glass and cement काच-मणि या स्फटिक में पाया जाने वाला एक रासायनिक यौगिक (काँच और सीमेंट बनाने में प्रयुक्त); सिलिका

**silicon** /ˈsɪlɪkən ˈसिलिकन्/ *noun* [U] (*symbol* **Si**) a substance that exists as a grey solid or as a brown powder and is found in rocks and sand. It is used in making glass धूसर रंग की ठोस वस्तु या भूरे चूर्ण के रूप में चट्टानों और रेत में पाया जाने वाला पदार्थ (काँच बनाने में प्रयुक्त); सिलिकॉन

**silicon chip** *noun* [C] (*computing*) a very small piece of silicon that is used to carry a complicated electronic **circuit** कंप्यूटर के सर्कट को संचालित करने वाला सिलिकॉन का बहुत छोटा टुकड़ा; सिलिकॉन चिप, कंप्यूटर चिप

**silk** /sɪlk सिल्क्/ *noun* [U] the soft smooth cloth that is made from threads produced by an insect (**a silkworm**) रेशम का कपड़ा (रेशम के कीड़ों के बनाए तारों से निर्मित) *a silk shirt/dress*

**silkworm** /ˈsɪlkwɜːm ˈसिल्कवॉम्/ *noun* [C] a small creature with a soft body and legs (**a caterpillar**) that produces very thin thread (**silk**) रेशम का कीड़ा; रेशम कीट

**silky** /ˈsɪlki ˈसिल्कि/ *adj.* smooth, soft and shiny; like silk चिकना, कोमल और चमकदार; रेशम जैसा, रेशमी *silky hair*

**sill** /sɪl सिल्/ *noun* [C] a shelf that is at the bottom of a window, either inside or outside खिड़की के नीचे का (अंदर या बाहर का) पटरा; दासा, सिल *a window sill*

**silly** /ˈsɪli ˈसिलि/ *adj.* (**sillier; silliest**) **1** not showing thought or understanding; foolish नासमझ, नासमझी भरा; बेवकूफ़, बेवकूफ़ी भरा *a silly mistake* ○ *Don't be so silly!* ✪ विलोम **sensible** **2** appearing ridiculous, so that people will laugh हास्यास्पद लगने वाला *I'm not wearing that hat—I'd look silly in it.* ▶ **silliness** *noun* [U] नासमझी, बेवकूफ़ी

**silo** /ˈsaɪləʊ ˈसाइलो/ *noun* [C] **1** a tall tower on a farm used for storing grain, etc. मीनारनुमा ढाँचा (अनाज आदि को सुरक्षित रखने के लिए); साइलो **2** an underground place where grass or other green plants are made into a substance (**silage**) that is stored until winter to feed the farm animals (सर्दियों में पशुओं को उपयोग के लिए) हरा चारा या वनस्पतियों को सुरक्षित रखने का गड्ढा; खत्ता

**silt** /sɪlt सिल्ट्/ *noun* [U] sand, soil or mud that collects at the sides or on the bottom of a river नदी के तले या किनारों पर जमा रेत, मिट्टी या कीचड़, गाद ➪ **flood plain** पर चित्र देखिए।

**silver¹** /ˈsɪlvə(r) ˈसिल्व़(र्)/ *noun* [U] **1** (*symbol* **Ag**) a valuable grey-white metal that is used for making jewellery, coins, etc. चाँदी (एक क़ीमती धूसर-श्वेत धातु, गहने सिक्के आदि बनाने के लिए प्रयुक्त) *a silver spoon/necklace* **2** coins made from silver or sth that looks like silver चाँदी के सिक्के या चाँदी जैसा दिखने वाला **3** objects that are made of silver, for example knives, forks, spoons, dishes चाँदी की वस्तुएँ (जैस छुरियाँ, काँटे, चम्मच, तश्तरियाँ) *The thieves stole some jewellery and some valuable silver.*

IDM **every cloud has a silver lining** ➪ **cloud¹** देखिए।

**silver²** /ˈsɪlvə(r) ˈसिल्व़(र्)/ *adj.* having the colour of silver चाँदी के रंग का; रुपहला, चाँदी जैसा *a silver sports car*

**silver medal** (*also* **silver**) *noun* [C] a small flat round piece of silver that is given to the person or team that comes second in a sports competition रजत पदक; चाँदी का मेडल (जो खेल प्रतियोगिता में द्वितीय स्थान प्राप्त करने वाले को दिया जाता है) *to win a silver medal at the Asian Games* ➪ **gold medal** और **bronze medal** देखिए। ▶ **silver medallist** *noun* [C] रजत पद विजेता

**silver wedding** *noun* [C] the 25th anniversary of a wedding विवाह की रजत जयंती; पच्चीसवीं सालगिरह या वर्षगाँठ ➪ **golden wedding** और **diamond wedding** देखिए।

**silvery** /ˈsɪlvəri ˈसिल्व़रि/ *adj.* having the appearance or colour of silver चाँदी की शकल या रंग वाला; चाँदी जैसा, रुपहला *an old lady with silvery hair*

**similar** /ˈsɪmələ(r) ˈसिमिल(र्)/ *adj.* **similar (to sb/sth); similar (in sth)** like sb/sth but not exactly the same किसी के समान (परंतु पूर्णतः वही नहीं); किसी के जैसा या सदृश *Our houses are very similar in size.* ○ *Your handwriting is very similar to mine.* ✪ विलोम **different** या **dissimilar** ▶ **similarly** *adv.* वैसा ही, उस जैसा, उसी प्रकार *The plural of 'shelf' is 'shelves'. Similarly, the plural of 'wolf' is 'wolves'.*

**similarity** /ˌsɪməˈlærəti ˌसिमˈलैरटि/ *noun* (*pl.* **similarities**) **1** [U, *sing.*] **similarity (to sb/sth); similarity (in sth)** the state of being like sb/sth but not exactly the same किसी के समान या सदृश (परंतु पूर्णतः वही न) होने की स्थिति; समानता, सादृश्य *She* ***bears a*** *remarkable/striking* ***similarity*** *to her mother.* **2** [C] **a similarity (between A and B); a similarity (in/of sth)** a characteristic that people or things have which makes them similar व्यक्तियों या वस्तुओं में समानता या सादृश्य *There are some similarities between the two towns.* ○ *similarities in/of style*

**simile** /ˈsɪməli ˈसिमलि / *noun* [C, U] (*technical*) a word or phrase that compares sth to sth else, using the words 'like' or 'as', for example 'face like a mask' or 'white as snow'; the use of such words and phrases किसी अन्य वस्तु से समानता दिखाने के लिए प्रयुक्त शब्द या वाक्यांश, जैसे 'a face like mask' या 'as white as snow' में 'like' और 'as' शब्द; समानतासूचक शब्दों का प्रयोग, उपमा, अलंकार ➪ **metaphor** देखिए।

**simmer** /ˈsɪmə(r) ˈसिम(र्) / *verb* [I, T] to cook gently in a liquid that is almost boiling लगभग खौलते हुए खदबदाते द्रव में हलके-हलके पकना या पकाना

**simple** /ˈsɪmpl ˈसिम्पल् / *adj.* **1** easy to understand, do or use; not difficult or complicated समझने, करने या प्रयोग करने में आसान, सुबोध, सुकर; कठिन या जटिल नहीं, सरल *This dictionary is written in simple English.* ○ *a simple task/method/solution* **2** without decoration or unnecessary extra things; plain and basic सजावट या अनावश्यक अतिरिक्त वस्तुओं से रहित; अनलंकृत; सादा और मामूली *a simple black dress* ○ *The food is simple but perfectly cooked.* **3** used for saying that the thing you are talking about is the only thing that is important or true एक मात्र; सीधा-सादा (यह कहने के लिए प्रयुक्त कि चर्चाधीन बात ही एकमात्र महत्त्वपूर्ण या सच बात है) *I'm not going to buy it for the simple reason that* (= only because) *I haven't got enough money.* **4** (used about a person or a way of life) natural and not complicated (व्यक्ति या जीने का ढंग) स्वाभाविक; सहज *a simple life in the country* **5** not intelligent; slow to understand बुद्धिहीन; मंद बुद्धि **6** (*grammar*) used to describe the present or past tense of a verb that is formed without using another verb (**an auxiliary verb**), as in 'She loves him' and 'He arrived late.' वर्तमान या भूत काल का वह क्रियारूप जिसके साथ सहायक क्रिया नहीं आती (जैसे 'She loves him' और 'He arrived late') *the simple present/past tense*

**simplicity** /sɪmˈplɪsəti सिम्ˈप्लिसटि / *noun* [U] **1** the quality of being easy to understand, do or use सुबोधता, सुकरता (समझने, करने या प्रयुक्त करने में आसान होने का गुण) *We all admired the simplicity of the plan.* **2** the quality of having no decoration or unnecessary extra things; being natural and not complicated सजावट या अनावश्यक अतिरिक्त वस्तुओं से रहित होने का गुण; सादापन, सादगी, स्वाभाविकता और सहजता *I like the simplicity of her paintings.*

**simplify** /ˈsɪmplɪfaɪ ˈसिम्प्लिफ़ाइ / *verb* [T] (*pres. part.* **simplifying**; *3rd person sing. pres.* **simplifies**; *pt, pp* **simplified**) to make sth easier to do or understand; to make sth less complicated किसी काम या बात को सुकर या सुबोध बनाना; किसी चीज़ की जटिलता को कम करना, उसे सरल बनाना *The process of applying for visas has been simplified.* ▶ **simplification** /ˌsɪmplɪfɪˈkeɪʃn ˌसिम्प्लिफ़िˈकेश्न् / *noun* [C, U] सरलीकरण

**simplistic** /sɪmˈplɪstɪk सिम्ˈप्लिस्टिक् / *adj.* making a problem, situation, etc. seem less difficult and complicated than it really is किसी समस्या, स्थिति आदि को कम कठिन और जटिल प्रतीत कराते हुए; एकांगी

**simply** /ˈsɪmpli ˈसिम्प्लि / *adv.* **1** used to emphasize how easy or basic sth is किसी बात के आसान और प्रारंभिक या मामूली होने पर बल देने के लिए प्रयुक्त *Simply add hot water and stir.* **2** (used to emphasize an adjective) completely; absolutely (विशेषण पर बल देने के लिए प्रयुक्त) पूरी तरह से; बिलकुल, एकदम *That meal was simply excellent.* **3** in a way that makes sth easy to understand अधिक सरल तरीक़े से *Could you explain it more simply?* **4** in a simple, basic way; without decoration or unnecessary extra things सरल, प्रारंभिक तरीक़े से; बिना सजावट या अनावश्यक फ़ालतू चीज़ों के, सादगी से *They live simply, with very few luxuries.* **5** only; just केवल; मात्र, भर *The whole problem is simply a misunderstanding.*

**simulate** /ˈsɪmjuleɪt ˈसिम्युलेट् / *verb* [T] to create certain conditions that exist in real life using computers, models, etc., usually for study or training purposes कंप्यूटरों, माडलों आदि की सहायता से यथार्थ जैसी स्थितियों की सृष्टि करना (प्रायः अनुसंधान या प्रशिक्षण के प्रयोजन से); वास्तविकता का अनुरूपण करना *The astronauts trained in a machine that simulates conditions in space.* ▶ **simulation** /ˌsɪmjuˈleɪʃn ˌसिम्युˈलेश्न् / *noun* [C, U] अनुरूपण *a computer simulation of a nuclear attack*

**simultaneous** /ˌsɪmlˈteɪniəs ˌसिम्ल्ˈटेनिअस् / *adj.* happening or done at exactly the same time as sth else (दो या अधिक वस्तुओं का) ठीक एक ही समय घटित होने या किया जाने वाला; सहकालिक, समक्षणिक ▶ **simultaneously** *adv.* साथ-साथ, एक साथ, एक ही समय

**sin** /sɪn सिन् / *noun* [C, U] an action or way of behaving that is not allowed by a religion धार्मिक दृष्टि से निषिद्ध कार्य या आचरण; पाप (कर्म) *It is a sin to steal.* ▶ **sin** *verb* [I] (**sinning; sinned**) पाप करना ▶ **sinner** *noun* [C] पापी

**since** /sɪns सिन्स् / *adv., conj., prep.* **1** from a particular time in the past until a later time in the past or until now अतीत में विशिष्ट समय-बिंदु से

(अतीत में ही) बाद के किसी बिंदु तक या (वर्तमान में) अभी तक; तब से अब तक *I've been working in a bank ever since I left school.* ○ *I haven't seen him since last Tuesday.*

**NOTE** कब से कोई बात घटित हो रही है, यह अर्थ व्यक्त करने के लिए **since** और **for** दोनों का प्रयोग होता है। कुछ घटित होने की अवधि के 'आरंभ-बिंदु' की बात करनी हो तो **since** का और अवधि की 'लंबाई' की बात करनी हो तो **for** का प्रयोग होता है — *I've known her since 1997.* ○ *I've known her for three years.*

**2** at a time after a particular time in the past अतीत के विशिष्ट समय बिंदु से बाद के किसी समय में, (उस) के बाद *We were divorced two years ago and she has since married someone else.* **3** because; as क्योंकि; यद्यपि *Since they did not phone me, I'll have to phone them.*

**sincere** /sɪnˈsɪə(r) सिन्ˈसिअ(र्)/ *adj.* **1** (used about a person) really meaning or believing what you say; not pretending (व्यक्ति) अपने मन की बात करने वाला, सच्चा; दिखावटी नहीं, निश्छल *She seems so sincere.* **2** (used about a person's feelings, beliefs or behaviour) true; showing what you really mean or feel (व्यक्ति का मनोभाव, विश्वास या आचरण) सच्चा, वास्तविक; जो माने वही कहे, कहने के आशय और उसकी अभिव्यक्ति में सामंजस्य प्रदर्शित करने वाला; ईमानदार *Please accept our sincere thanks/apologies.* ✪ विलोम **insincere** ▶ **sincerely** *adv.* निष्ठापूर्वक, सच्चाई से *I am sincerely grateful to you for all your help.* ○ *Yours sincerely, ... (at the end of a formal letter)* ▶ **sincerity** /sɪnˈserəti सिन्ˈसेरटि/ *noun* [U] ईमानदारी, सच्चाई ✪ विलोम **insincerity**

**sindur** (*also* **sindoor**) *noun* [U] a red powder applied by married Indian women to the parting of the hair and sometimes on the forehead as a **bindi** सिंदूर

**sine** /saɪn साइन्/ *noun* [C] (*abbr.* **sin**) (*mathematics*) the **ratio** of the length of the side opposite one of the angles in a **right-angled** triangle to the length of the longest side ज्या, साइन ➪ **cosine** और **tangent** देखिए।

**sinew** /ˈsɪnju: ˈसिन्यू/ *noun* [C, U] a strong band of substance that joins a muscle to a bone मांसपेशियों को हड्डी से जोड़ने वाली मोटी नस; महास्नायु, महानाड़ी, कंडरा

**sinful** /ˈsɪnfl ˈसिन्फ़्ल्/ *adj.* breaking a religious law; immoral धार्मिक नियम को भंग करने वाला; पापपूर्ण, अनैतिक

**sing** /sɪŋ सिङ्/ *verb* [I, T] (*pt* **sang** /sæŋ सैङ्/; *pp* **sung** /sʌŋ सङ्/) to make musical sounds with your voice मुँह से संगीतमयी ध्वनियाँ निकालना; गाना *He sings well.* ○ *The birds were singing outside my window.* ▶ **singing** *noun* [U] गायन *singing lessons*

**singe** /sɪndʒ सिन्ज्/ *verb* [I, T] (*pres. part.* **singeing**) to burn the surface of sth slightly, usually by accident; to be burned in this way किसी वस्तु की सतह को हलका जला देना (प्रायः ग़लती से); झुलसाना; झुलसना

**singer** /ˈsɪŋə(r) ˈसिङ(र्)/ *noun* [C] a person who sings, or whose job is singing, especially in public गाने वाला या (पेशे से) गाने का (विशेषतः सभा आदि में) काम करने वाला व्यक्ति; गायक या पेशेवर गायक *a gazal singer*

**single**[1] /ˈsɪŋgl ˈसिङ्ग्ल्/ *adj.* **1** (*only before a noun*) only one केवल एक *I managed to finish the whole job in a single afternoon.* ○ **2** (*only before a noun*) used to emphasize that you are talking about each individual item of a group or series इस बात पर बल देने के लिए प्रयुक्त कि किसी समूह या शृंखला की प्रत्येक इकाई की चर्चा की जा रही है; अलग, पृथक् *He answered **every single** question correctly. Well done!* **3** not married अविवाहित, अकेला *a single man/woman* **4** (*only before a noun*) for the use of only one person केवल एक व्यक्ति के लिए *I'd like to book a single room, please.* ➪ **bed**[1] पर नोट देखिए। **5** (*also* **one-way**) (*only before a noun*) (used about a ticket or the price of a ticket) for a journey to a particular place, but not back again (टिकट या टिकट का मूल्य) एक तरफ़ का (वापसी का नहीं) *How much is the single fare to Shillong?* ➪ **return**[2] **5** देखिए।
**IDM** **in single file** ➪ **file**[1] देखिए।

**single**[2] /ˈsɪŋgl ˈसिङ्ग्ल्/ *noun* **1** [C] a ticket for a journey to a particular place, but not back again (कहीं जाने का) (केवल) एक तरफ़ का टिकट *Two singles to Goa, please.* ➪ **return**[2] **5** देखिए। **2** [C] a CD, tape, etc. that has only one song on each side; the main song on this tape or CD सीडी, टेप आदि जिसमें एक ओर केवल एक गीत हो; ऐसी सीडी या टेप पर (रिकॉर्ड किया) मुख्य गीत *Shaan's new single* ➪ **album** देखिए। **3** [C] a bedroom for one person in a hotel, etc. होटल आदि में (केवल) एक व्यक्ति के लिए शयनकक्ष ➪ **double**[3] **5** देखिए। **4 singles** [*pl.*] people who are not married and do not have a romantic relationship with sb else अविवाहित और न किसी से प्रेम संबंध रखने वाले **5 singles** [U] a game of tennis, etc. in which one player plays against one other player टेनिस आदि का एकल मैच (जिसमें दोनों तरफ़ एक-एक खिलाड़ी होता है) ➪ **doubles** देखिए।

**single**[3] /ˈsɪŋgl ˈसिङ्गल्/ *verb*

**PHR V** **single sb/sth out (for sth)** to give special attention or treatment to one person or thing from a group समूह में से किसी एक व्यक्ति या वस्तु पर विशेष ध्यान देना या उससे विशेष बरताव करना; समूह में से किसी एक को छाँटना; चुनना *She was singled out for criticism.*

**single-breasted** *adj.* (used about a jacket or a coat) having only one row of buttons that fasten in the middle (जैकेट या कोट) जिसमें मध्य से बंद किए जाने वाले बटनों की एक पंक्ति हो; इकहरे सीने वाला ➪ **double-breasted** देखिए।

**single-decker** *noun* [C] a bus with only one level एकतल्ला बस

**single-handed** *adj., adv.* on your own with nobody helping you अकेले, अपने बूते पर; बिना किसी की सहायता के

**single-minded** *adj.* having one clear aim or goal which you are determined to achieve जो (केवल) एक स्पष्ट उद्देश्य या लक्ष्य को पाने के लिए कृतसंकल्प हो; एकनिष्ठ, अनन्य ▸ **single-mindedness** *noun* [U] एकनिष्ठता, अनन्यता

**single parent** *noun* [C] a person who looks after his/her child or children without a husband, wife or partner बच्चे का अकेले पालन करने वाला पिता या माता *a single-parent family*

**singlet** /ˈsɪŋglət ˈसिङ्गलट्/ *noun* [C] a piece of clothing without sleeves, worn under or instead of a shirt, often worn by runners, etc. कमीज़ के नीचे या उसके बदले (प्रायः खिलाड़ी, धावकों द्वारा) पहना जाने वाला बिना आस्तीन का परिधान; बनियाइन, गंजी या बंडी (जैसा परिधान)

**singly** /ˈsɪŋgli ˈसिङ्गलि/ *adv.* one at a time; individually एक-एक करके; अकेले *You can buy the tapes either singly or in packs of three.*

**singular** /ˈsɪŋgjələ(r) ˈसिङ्ग्यल(र्)/ *adj.* **1** (*grammar*) in the form that is used for talking about one person or thing only (संख्या में) एक व्यक्ति या वस्तु का सूचक शब्दरूप, एकवचन या एकवचनांत (रूप) *'Table' is a singular noun; 'tables' is a plural noun.* ➪ **plural** देखिए। **2** (*written*) unusual असामान्य, असाधारण ▸ **singular** *noun* [*sing.*] (*grammar*) एकवचन रूप *The word 'clothes' has no singular.* ○ *What's the singular of 'people'?*

**singularly** /ˈsɪŋgjələli ˈसिङ्ग्यललि/ *adv.* (*formal*) very; in an unusual way अत्यधिक; असाधारण रूप से *The government has been singularly unsuccessful in its policy against terrorism.*

**sinister** /ˈsɪnɪstə(r) ˈसिनिसट(र्)/ *adj.* seeming evil or dangerous; making you feel that sth bad will happen बुरा लगने वाला या अनर्थकारी; अमंगलसूचक *There's something sinister about him. He frightens me.*

**sink**[1] /sɪŋk सिङ्क्/ *verb* (*pt* **sank** /sæŋk सैङ्क्/; *pp* **sunk** /sʌŋk सङ्क्/) **1** [I, T] to go down or make sth go down under the surface of liquid or a soft substance डूबना या (किसी वस्तु को) डुबोना (तरल या कोमल पदार्थ में) *If you throw a stone into water, it sinks.* ○ *My feet sank into the mud.* **2** [I] (used about a person) to move downwards, usually by falling or sitting down (व्यक्ति का) झुकना (प्रायः गिरते या बैठते हुए), धँसना *I sank into a chair, exhausted.* **3** [I] to get lower; to fall to a lower position or level नीचे जाना, अस्त होना; निम्नतर स्थिति या स्तर पर चला जाना, धँसना *We watched the sun sink slowly below the horizon.* **4** [I] to decrease in value, number, amount, strength, etc. (मूल्य, संख्या, मात्रा, शक्ति आदि में) कम होना; घटना

**IDM** **your heart sinks** ➪ **heart** देखिए।

**PHR V** **sink in** (used about information, an event, an experience, etc.) to be completely understood or realized (जानकारी, घटना, अनुभव आदि) का पूर्णतया समझ लिया जाना या महसूस हो जाना; दिल और दिमाग़ में घुस जाना *It took a long time for the terrible news to sink in.*

**sink in; sink into sth** (used about a liquid) to go into sth solid; to be absorbed (तरल पदार्थ का) किसी ठोस पदार्थ में समा जाना; सोख लिया जाना

**sink**[2] /sɪŋk सिङ्क्/ *noun* [C] a large open container in a kitchen, with taps to supply water, where you wash things रसोई में बरतन आदि धोने की हौज़; सिंक ➪ **washbasin** देखिए।

**sinus** /ˈsaɪnəs ˈसाइनस्/ *noun* [C] (*usually pl.*) one of the spaces in the bones of your face that are connected to your nose नाक से जुड़ी चेहरे की हड्डियों के बीच ख़ाली जगह; अस्थि-रंध्र, शिरानाल *I've got a terrible cold and my sinuses are blocked.* ○ *a sinus infection*

**sip** /sɪp सिप्/ *verb* [I, T] (**sipping**; **sipped**) to drink, taking only a very small amount of liquid into your mouth at a time थोड़ा-थोड़ा करके कोई तरल पदार्थ पीना; चुस्की भरना, घूँट-घूँट पीना *We sat in the sun, sipping lemonade.* ▸ **sip** *noun* [C] चुस्की, घूँट

**siphon** (*also* **syphon**) /ˈsaɪfn ˈसाइफ़न्/ *verb* [T] **1 siphon sth into/out of sth; siphon sth off/out** to remove a liquid from a container, often into another container, through a tube नली के द्वारा तरल पदार्थ एक पात्र से (प्रायः) दूसरे पात्र में पहुँचाना;

ख़ाली करना, द्रवनाल करना **2 siphon sth off; siphon sth (from/out of sb/sth)** to take money from a company illegally over a period of time (लंबे समय तक) कंपनी के धन की चोरी करते रहना

**sir** /sɜː(r) स(र्)/ *noun* **1** [*sing.*] used as a polite way of speaking to a man whose name you do not know, for example in a shop or restaurant, or to show respect (किसी दुकान आदि में अपरिचित अथवा अन्यत्र किसी भी व्यक्ति के लिए) विनम्रतासूचक संबोधन, श्रीमन्, श्रीमान् जी, जनाब, सर *I'm afraid we haven't got your size, sir.* ➪ **madam** देखिए। **2** [C] used at the beginning of a formal letter to a male person or male people औपचारिक पत्र में पुरुष व्यक्ति या व्यक्तियों के लिए संबोधन; श्रीमन्, सर *Dear Sir...* ○ *Dear Sirs...* ➪ **Madam** देखिए। **3** /sə(r) स(र्)/ [*sing.*] the title that is used in front of the name of a man who has received one of the highest British honours उच्चतम ब्रिटिश सम्मान-प्राप्त व्यक्ति के नाम से पहले प्रयुक्त उपाधि; सर

**siren** /ˈsaɪrən ˈसाइरन्/ *noun* [C] a device that makes a long, loud sound as a warning or signal चेतावनी या संकेत के रूप में ऊँची, लंबी आवाज़ करने वाला उपकरण; भोंपू, साइरन *an air-raid siren* ○ *Three fire engines raced past, sirens wailing.*

**sirocco** /sɪˈrɒkəʊ सिˈरॉको/ (*pl.* **siroccos**) *noun* [C] a hot wind that blows from Africa into Southern Europe अफ़्रीक़ा से दक्षिणी यूरोप की ओर बहने वाली गरम हवा; सिरॉको

**sisal** /ˈsaɪsl ˈसाइसल्/ *noun* [U] strong thin threads made from the leaves of a tropical plant and used for making rope, floor coverings, etc. उष्ण क्षेत्रों के एक पौधे के पत्तों से बने रेशे (रस्सी, फ़र्श की दरी आदि बनाने के लिए प्रयुक्त)

**sister** /ˈsɪstə(r) ˈसिस्ट(र्)/ *noun* [C] **1** a girl or woman who has the same parents as another person बहन *I've got one brother and two sisters.* ○ *We're sisters.* ➪ **half-sister** और **step sister** देखिए।

> **NOTE** अंग्रेज़ी में 'भाइयों और बहनों', दोनों का सूचक कोई सामान्य शब्द नहीं है। इस दृष्टि से **'sibling'** बहुत औपचारिक शब्द है (यद्यपि अर्थ वही है)।

**2** (*often* **Sister**) (*BrE*) a female hospital nurse in a high position (अस्पताल में) वरिष्ठ महिला नर्स; सिस्टर **3 Sister** a member of certain female religious groups; a **nun** विशिष्ट धार्मिक महिला संघ की सदस्य; (ईसाई) मठ में रहने वाली उपासिका; ईसाई नन **4** (*usually used as an adjective*) a thing that belongs to the same type or group as sth else समान प्रकार या वर्ग से संबंधित वस्तु; सह- (संस्था) *We have a sister company in Japan.* **5** (*informal*) a woman who you feel close to because she is a member of the same society, group, etc. as you (समान समाज, समूह आदि से संबंधित होने के कारण) आत्मीय लगने वाली कोई महिला; (सामाजिक दृष्टि से) बहन

**sister-in-law** *noun* [C] (*pl.* **sisters-in-law**) **1** the sister of your husband or wife पति या पत्नी की बहन; ननद या साली **2** the wife of your brother भाई की पत्नी; भाभी, भौजाई, भावज

**sit** /sɪt सिट्/ *verb* (*pres. part.* **sitting**; *pt, pp* **sat** /sæt सैट्/) **1** [I] to rest your weight on your bottom, for example in a chair बैठना, कुरसी आदि पर नितंबों के बल टिकना *We sat in the garden all afternoon.* ○ *She was sitting on the sofa, talking to her mother.* **2** [T] **sit sb (down)** to put sb into a sitting position; make sb sit down किसी को बैठने की स्थिति में रखना, बैठाना; किसी को नीचे बैठाना *He picked up his daughter and sat her down on a chair.* ○ *She sat me down and offered me a cup of tea.* **3** [I] to be in a particular place or position विशेष स्थान पर या स्थिति में होना; रखा होना या रहना *The letter sat on the table for several days before anybody opened it.* **4** [T] (*BrE*) to take an exam परीक्षा में बैठना, परीक्षा देना *If I fail, will I be able to **sit the exam** again?* **5** [I] (*formal*) (used about an official group of people) to have a meeting or series of meetings (अधिकारी वर्ग का) बैठक या बैठकें करना

**IDM** **sit on the fence** to avoid saying which side of an argument you support विवाद में किसी का पक्ष लेने से बचना

**PHRV** **sit about/around** (*informal*) to spend time doing nothing active or useful ख़ाली बैठना; बिना कोई काम की बात किए समय गुज़ारना *We just sat around chatting all afternoon.*

**sit back** to relax and not take an active part in what other people are doing आराम से बैठना (और काम में लगे लोगों के साथ हाथ न बँटाना) *Sit back and take it easy while I make dinner.*

**sit down** to lower your body into a sitting position नीचे बैठना, बैठने के लिए झुकना *He sat down in an armchair.*

**sit sth out** **1** to stay in a place and wait for sth unpleasant or boring to finish कहीं बैठकर प्रतीक्षा करना (अरुचिकर या उबाऊ कार्यक्रम के समाप्त होने तक) **2** to not take part in a dance, game, etc. नृत्य, खेल आदि में भाग न लेना

**sit through sth** to stay in your seat until sth boring or long has finished (उबाऊ या लंबे कार्यक्रम के समाप्त होने तक) अपनी सीट पर बैठे रहना

**sit up** **1** to move into a sitting position when you have been lying down or to make your back straight उठ खड़े होना (सोते से या क़मर सीधा करने के लिए) *Sit up straight and concentrate!* **2** to not go to bed although it is very late देरी होने पर भी सोने न जाना *We sat up all night talking.*

**sitar** *noun* [C] a musical instrument from India like a guitar, with a long neck and two sets of metal strings सितार (लंबा और धातु-निर्मित दो तंत्रियों वाला एक भारतीय वाद्य) ➪ पृष्ठ 789 पर चित्र देखिए।

**sitcom** /ˈsɪtkɒm ˈसिट्कॉम् / (*also* **situation comedy**) *noun* [C, U] a funny programme on television that shows the same characters in different amusing situations each week टीवी पर प्रस्तुत हास्य विनोद का साप्ताहिक कार्यक्रम, जिसमें परिस्थितियाँ भिन्न होती हैं परंतु पात्र वही रहते हैं

**site** /saɪt साइट् / *noun* [C] **1** a piece of land where a building was, is or will be situated वह स्थान जहाँ कोई इमारत खड़ी थी, है या होगी; भवन स्थल *a building/construction site* ○ *The company is looking for a site for its new offices.* **2** a place where sth has happened or that is used for sth वह स्थान जहाँ कुछ घटित हुआ या कोई काम हुआ; घटना स्थल *the site of a famous battle* **3** (*computing*) a place on the Internet where a company, an organization, a university, etc. puts information इंटरनेट पर किसी कंपनी, संस्था, विश्वविद्यालय आदि का सूचना-स्थल ➪ **website** देखिए। ▶ **site** *verb* [T] (*written*) स्थान चुनना या तय करना *They met to discuss the siting of the new school.*

**sitting** /ˈsɪtɪŋ ˈसिटिङ् / *noun* [C] **1** a period of time during which a court of law or a parliament meets and does its work न्यायालय या संसद का अधिवेशन, सत्र, बैठक (काम करने की समयावधि) **2** a time when a meal is served in a school, hotel, etc. to a number of people at the same time स्कूल, होटल आदि में सबके एक साथ भोजन करने का समय *Dinner will be in two sittings.*

**sitting room** (*BrE*) = **living room**

**situated** /ˈsɪtʃueɪtɪd ˈसिचुएटिड् / *adj.* in a particular place or position किसी विशिष्ट स्थान पर या स्थिति में; स्थित *The hotel is conveniently situated close to the beach.*

**situation** /ˌsɪtʃuˈeɪʃn ˌसिचुˈएश्न् / *noun* [C] **1** the things that are happening in a particular place or at a particular time स्थान-विशेष में या समय-विशेष पर घटित होने वाली घटनाएँ; स्थिति, दशा, हालत *Harish is **in a** difficult **situation** at the moment.* ○ *the economic/financial/political situation* **2** (*written*) the position of a building, town, etc. in relation to the area around it भवन, नगर आदि की स्थिति, अवस्थिति (आस-पास के क्षेत्र की दृष्टि से) **3** (*written*) (*old-fashioned*) a job नौकरी, जगह, स्थान *Situations Vacant* (= the part of a newspaper where jobs are advertised)

**sit-up** *noun* [C] an exercise for the stomach muscles in which you lie on your back with your legs bent, then lift the top half of your body from the floor पेट की मांस पेशियों की एक कसरत (जिसमें टाँगें मोड़कर पीठ के बल लेटते हैं और ऊपर के आधे शरीर को ऊपर की ओर उठाते हैं), (भारतीय पद्धति के) सुप्त वज्रासन जैसा व्यायाम *to **do sit-ups***

**six** /sɪks सिक्स् / *number* **1** 6 छह (की संख्या), 6 (का अंक) *The answers are on page six.* ○ *There are six of us for dinner tonight.* **2** **six-** (*in compounds*) having six of the thing mentioned छह वाली (बताई गई वस्तु); षट्- (जैसे षट्कोण) *She works a six-day week.*

> **NOTE** मापों, क़ीमतों आदि में प्रयुक्त संख्याओं के विषय में, इस शब्दकोश के अंत में, संख्याओं पर विशेष खंड देखिए।

**sixteen** /ˌsɪksˈtiːn ˌसिक्स्ˈटीन् / *number* 16 सोलह (की संख्या), 16 (का अंक)

> **NOTE** संख्याओं के वाक्य-प्रयोग के उदाहरणों के लिए **six** की प्रविष्टि देखिए।

**sixteenth** /ˌsɪksˈtiːnθ ˌसिक्स्ˈटीन्थ् / *det., adv.* 16th सोलहवाँ ➪ **sixth**[1] के उदाहरण देखिए।

**sixth**[1] /sɪksθ सिक्स्थ् / *det., adv.* 6th छठा *I've had five cups of tea already, so this is my sixth.* ○ *This is the sixth time I've tried to phone him.*

> **NOTE** मापों, क़ीमतों आदि में प्रयुक्त संख्याओं के विषय में, इस शब्दकोश के अंत में, संख्याओं पर विशेष खंड देखिए।

**sixth**[2] /sɪksθ सिक्स्थ् / *noun* [C] the fraction $\frac{1}{6}$; one of six equal parts of sth भिन्न $\frac{1}{6}$; किसी वस्तु के छह समान अंशों में से एक

**sixtieth** /ˈsɪkstiəθ ˈसिक्स्टिअथ् / *det., adv.* 60th साठवाँ, 60वाँ ➪ **sixth** के उदाहरण देखिए।

**sixty** /ˈsɪksti ˈसिक्स्टि / *number* **1** 60 साठ *There are sixty pages in the book.* ○ *He retired **at sixty**.*

> **NOTE** संख्याओं के वाक्य-प्रयोग के उदाहरणों के लिए **six** की प्रविष्टि देखिए।

**2** **the sixties** [*pl.*] the numbers, years or temperatures between 60 and 69; the 60s, 60 और 69 के बीच की संख्याएँ, वर्ष या तापमान; साठ का दशक *I don't know the exact number of members, but it's in the sixties.* ○ *My father passed out from school in the early sixties.*

**IDM in your sixties** between the age of 60 and 69, 60 से 69 के बीच की आयु ○ *in your **early/mid/** late sixties*

**NOTE** मापों, क़ीमतों आदि में प्रयुक्त संख्याओं के विषय में अधिक जानकारी के लिए, इस शब्दकोश के अंत में, संख्याओं पर विशेष खंड देखिए।

**size¹** /saɪz साइज़् / *noun* **1** [U] how big or small sth is वस्तु का आकार (वस्तु कितनी छोटी या बड़ी) *I was surprised at the size of the hotel. It was enormous!* ○ *The planet Uranus is about four times the size of Earth.*

**NOTE** सामान्य रूप से हम किसी वस्तु के आकार के बारे में पूछते हैं तो कहते हैं 'How big...?'—*How big is your house?* परंतु जब हम निश्चित नापों में निर्मित वस्तुओं के आकार के बारे में पूछते हैं तो कहते हैं 'What size...?'—***What size** shoes **do you take**?* ○ *What size are you* (= when buying clothes)*?*

**2** [C] one of a number of fixed measurements in which sth is made निर्मित वस्तुओं की निश्चित नापों में से एक *Have you got this dress **in a** bigger **size**?* ○ *What size pizza would you like? Medium or large?* **3 -sized** (*also* **-size**) (*used to form compound adjectives*) of the size mentioned बताए गए आकार का; आकार वाला *a medium-sized flat* ○ *a king-size bed*

**size²** /saɪz साइज़् / *verb*

**PHRV size sb/sth up** to form an opinion or judgement about sb/sth किसी के विषय में कोई राय बनाना या उसे आँकना

**sizeable** (*also* **sizable**) /ˈsaɪzəbl ˈसाइज़बल् quite large काफ़ी बड़ा; अच्छा-ख़ासा *a sizeable sum of money*

**sizzle** /ˈsɪzl ˈसिज़्ल् / *verb* [I] to make the sound of food frying in hot fat तलते समय कडकड़ की आवाज़ होना; कड़कड़ाना

**skate¹** /skeɪt स्केट् / *noun* [C] **1** (*also* **ice skate**) a boot with a thin sharp metal part on the bottom that is used for moving on ice बर्फ़ पर स्केटिंग (तेज़ी से फिसलने) में प्रयुक्त (विशेष) जूता जिसकी तली पर छोटे पहिए लगे होते हैं; हिम विसर्पण पादुका **2** = **roller skate** **3** a large flat sea fish that can be eaten खाने की एक बड़ी चपटी मछली

**skate²** /skeɪt स्केट् / *verb* [I] **1** (*also* **ice-skate**) to move on ice wearing special boots (**ice skates**) स्केटिंग के जूते पहन कर बर्फ़ पर स्केटिंग करना या फिसलना *Can you skate?* ○ *They skated across the frozen lake.*

**NOTE** मौज-मस्ती के लिए स्केटिंग करने के लिए **go stating** का प्रयोग होता है।

**2** = **roller skate** ▶ **skater** *noun* [C] स्केटिंग करने वाला

**skateboard** /ˈskeɪtbɔː ˈस्केट्बॉड् / *noun* [C] a short narrow board with small wheels at each end that you can stand on and ride as a sport पहिएदार छोटा तंग तख़्ता जिस पर खड़े होकर स्केटिंग की जाती है; स्केटबोर्ड ▶ **skateboarding** *noun* [U] स्केटबोर्ड लगा कर स्केटिंग करना *When we were children we used to go skateboarding in the park.*

**skating** /ˈskeɪtɪŋ ˈस्केटिङ् / *noun* [U] **1** (*also* **ice skating**) the activity or sport of moving on ice wearing special boots स्केटिंग के जूते पहनकर बर्फ़ पर स्केटिंग करने का खेल *Would you like to **go skating** this weekend?* **2** = **roller skating**

**skating rink** (*also* **ice rink; rink**) *noun* [C] a large area of ice, or a building containing a large area of ice, that is used for skating on स्केटिंग के लिए प्रयुक्त बर्फ़ का मैदान या कोई इमारत जिसमें बर्फ़ बिछी हो; स्केटिंग रिंक

**skeleton¹** /ˈskelɪtn ˈस्केलिट्न् / *noun* [C] the structure formed by all the bones in a human or animal body मानव या पशु के शरीर में हड्डियों से बना ढाँचा; कंकाल, अस्थि-पंजर *the human skeleton* ○ *a dinosaur skeleton*

**skeleton²** /ˈskelɪtn ˈस्केलिट्न् / *adj.* (used about an organization, a service, etc.) having the smallest number of people that is necessary for it to operate संचालित करने के लिए अपेक्षित कर्मचारियों की न्यूनतम संख्या वाली (संस्था, सेवा आदि)

**skeptic, skeptical, skepticism** (*AmE*) = **sceptic, sceptical, scepticism**

**sketch** /sketʃ स्केच् / *noun* [C] **1** a simple, quick drawing without many details सीमित ब्योरों वाला सरल और जल्दी में बनाया आरेख; कच्चा, ख़ाका, कच्चा नक़्शा *He drew a **rough sketch** of the new building on the back of an envelope.* **3** a short description without any details रूपरेखा; बिना ब्योरों का संक्षिप्त विवरण ▶ **sketch** *verb* [I, T] आरेख बनाना *I sat on the grass and sketched the castle.*

**sketchy** /ˈsketʃi ˈस्केचि / *adj.* not having many or enough details रूपरेखात्मक; जिसमें अधिक या प्रर्याप्त ब्योरे न हों

**skewer** /ˈskjuːə(r) ˈस्क्यूअ(र्) / *noun* [C] a long thin pointed piece of metal or wood that is pushed through pieces of meat, vegetables, etc. to hold them together while they are cooking किसी धातु या लकड़ी से लंबी पतली नुकीली चीज़, सीख़

(जिसमें गोश्त, सब्ज़ी आदि के टुकड़े फँसाकर भूने जाते हैं) ▶ **skewer** *verb* [T] सीख़ से (गोश्त, सब्ज़ी आदि) भूनना

**ski[1]** /skiː स्की / *verb* [I] (*pres. part.* **skiing**; *pt, pp* **skied**) to move over snow on skis स्की बाँधकर बर्फ़ पर चलना *They **go skiing** every year.* ▶ **ski** *adj.* स्की से संबंधित *a ski resort/instructor/slope/suit* ▶ **skiing** *noun* [U] स्की बाँधकर बर्फ़ पर चलने की क्रिया; स्कीइंग *alpine/downhill/ cross-country skiing*

**ski[2]** /skiː स्की / *noun* [C] one of a pair of long, flat, narrow pieces of wood or plastic that are fastened to boots and used for sliding over snow लकड़ी या प्लास्टिक के लंबे, चपटे तंग तख़्तों की जोड़ी में से एक जिसे जूतों से बाँधकर बर्फ़ पर फिसलते हैं; स्की *a pair of skis*

**skid** /skɪd स्किड् / *verb* [I] (**skidding; skidded**) (usually used about a vehicle) to suddenly slide forwards or sideways without any control (वाहन का) एकाएक बेक़ाबू होकर आगे की ओर या दाएँ-बाँए फिसल या रपट जाना *I skidded on a patch of ice and hit a tree.* ▶ **skid** *noun* [C] फिसलने या रपटने की क्रिया *The car went into a skid and came off the road.*

**skier** /ˈskiːə(r) ˈस्कीअ(र्) / *noun* [C] a person who skis स्कीइंग करने वाला व्यक्ति; स्कीअर *Mina's a good skier.*

**skilful** (*AmE* **skillful**) /ˈskɪlfl ˈस्किल्फ़्ल् / *adj.* **1** (used about a person) very good at doing sth (व्यक्ति) कोई काम करने में निपुण; कुशल *a skilful painter/politician* ○ *He's very skilful with his hands.* **2** done very well निपुणता के साथ किया गया; कौशलपूर्ण, दक्षतापूर्ण *skilful guitar playing* ▶ **skilfully** /-fəli -फ़लि / *adv.* निपुणतापूर्वक

**skill** /skɪl स्किल् / *noun* **1** [U] the ability to do sth well, especially because of training, practice, etc. किसी काम को अच्छे ढंग से करने की योग्यता (विशेषतः प्रशिक्षण, अभ्यास आदि के फलस्वरूप); निपुणता, कुशलता, दक्षता *It takes great skill to make such beautiful jewellery.* **2** [C] an ability that you need in order to do a job, an activity, etc. well किसी काम को अच्छे ढंग से करने के लिए अपेक्षित योग्यता; विशिष्ट योग्यता निपुणता या कुशलता *management skills*

**skilled** /skɪld स्किल्ड् / *adj.* **1** (used about a person) having skill; skilful (व्यक्ति) निपुणता रखने वाला; निपुण, कुशल, दक्ष *a skilled worker* **2** (used about work, a job etc.) needing skill or skills; done by people who have been trained (काम, नौकरी आदि) जिसमें कुशलता या कुशलताओं की अपेक्षा हो, कौशलापेक्षी; प्रशिक्षित लोगों द्वारा किया जाने वाला *a highly skilled job* ○ *Skilled work is difficult to find in this area.* ✪ विलोम **unskilled**

**skillet** /ˈskɪlɪt ˈस्किलिट् / (*AmE*) = **frying pan**

**skim** /skɪm स्किम् / *verb* (**skimming; skimmed**) **1** [T] **skim sth (off/from sth)** to remove sth from the surface of a liquid तरल पदार्थ की सतह से कुछ हटाना *to skim the cream off the milk* **2** [I, T] to move quickly over or past sth, almost touching it or touching it slightly किसी वस्तु को छूते-से या ज़रा-सा छूते हुए उसके ऊपर से या उसके पार निकल जाना *The plane flew very low, skimming the tops of the buildings.* **3** [I, T] **skim (through/over) sth** to read sth quickly in order to get the main idea, without paying attention to the details and without reading every word मुख्यभाव जानने के लिए सरसरी नज़र से कुछ पढ़ना (ब्योरों पर ध्यान न देना और न प्रत्येक शब्द पढ़ना) *I usually just skim through the newspaper in the morning.*

**skimmed milk** *noun* [U] milk from which the cream has been removed मलाई उतरा दूध, क्रीम निकला दूध; मखनिया या छूँछा दूध, सप्रेटा

**skimp** /skɪmp स्किम्प् / *verb* [I] **skimp (on sth)** to use or provide less of sth than is necessary किसी वस्तु को ज़रूरत से कम प्रयोग में लाना या उपलब्ध कराना

**skimpy** /ˈskɪmpi ˈस्किम्पि / *adj.* using or having less than is necessary; too small or few ज़रूरत से कम वाला; बहुत छोटा या कम

**skin[1]** /skɪn स्किन् / *noun* [C, U] **1** the natural outer covering of a human or animal body मनुष्य की त्वचा या पशु की खाल *to have (a) fair/dark/sensitive skin* **2 -skinned** (*used to form compound adjectives*) having the type of skin mentioned (बताए गए प्रकार की) त्वचा वाला *My sister's very dark-skinned.* **3** (*often in compounds*) the skin of a dead animal, with or without its fur, used for making things चमड़ा, चर्म (मृत पशु की बालों वाली या बाल-रहित खाल जिससे चीजें बनती हैं) *a sheepskin jacket* ○ *a bag made of crocodile skin* **4** the natural outer covering of some fruits or vegetables; the outer covering of a sausage कुछ फलों या सब्ज़ियों का छिलका; सासेज की ऊपरी परत *(a) banana/tomato skin* ➪ **rind** पर नोट देखिए। **5** the thin solid surface that can form on a liquid तरल पदार्थ पर ऊपर जमने वाली मोटी परत *A skin had formed on top of the milk.*

IDM **by the skin of your teeth** (*informal*) (used to show that sb almost failed to do sth) only just (किसी कार्य में लगभग मिली सफलता दर्शाने के लिए प्रयुक्त) बड़ी मुश्किल से *I ran into the airport and caught the plane by the skin of my teeth.*

**have a thick skin** ➪ **thick[1]** देखिए।

**skin-deep** (used about a feeling or an attitude) not as important or as strongly felt as it appears to be; superficial (मनोभाव या मनोवृत्ति) जितना सशक्त या महत्त्वपूर्ण लगे वास्तव में उतना नहीं, हलका; सतहा ऊपरी *I knew his concern about me was only skin-deep.*

**skin²** /skɪn स्किन्/ *verb* [T] (**skin<u>n</u>ing; skin<u>n</u>ed**) to remove the skin from sth (किसी से) चमड़ा उतारना या निकालना

**IDM keep your eyes peeled/skinned (for sb/sth)** ➪ **eye¹** देखिए।

**skinhead** /ˈskɪnhed ˈस्किन्हेड्/ *noun* [C] a young person with shaved or extremely short hair सिर मुँड़ा या बहुत छोटे बालों वाला लड़का

**skinny** /ˈskɪni ˈस्किनि/ *adj.* (used about a person) too thin (व्यक्ति) दुबला-पतला; सींकिया ➪ **thin** पर नोट देखिए।

**skintight** *adj.* (used about a piece of clothing) fitting very tightly and showing the shape of the body (लिबास) तंग (जिसमें से शरीर की आकृति दिखाई दे)

**skip¹** /skɪp स्किप्/ *verb* (**skip<u>p</u>ing; skip<u>p</u>ed**) **1** [I] to move along quickly and lightly in a way that is similar to dancing, with little jumps and steps, from one foot to the other उछलना-कूदना, कूद-फाँद करना *A little girl came skipping along the road.* ○ *Lambs were skipping about in the field.* **2** [I] to jump over a rope that you or two other people hold at each end, turning it round and round over the head and under the feet रस्सी कूदना या फाँदना *Some girls were skipping in the playground.* **3** [T] to not do sth that you usually do or should do नियमित गतिविधि को न करना *I got up rather late, so I skipped breakfast.* **4** [T] to miss the next thing that you would normally read, do, etc. पढ़ते, कोई काम आदि करते हुए कुछ (शब्द या वाक्य, काम) छोड़ते जाना *I accidentally skipped one of the questions in the test.*

**skip²** /skɪp स्किप्/ *noun* [C] **1** a small jumping movement उछल-कूद, कूद-फाँद **2** a large, open metal container for rubbish, often used during building work मलबा या कचरा डालने का बड़ा टोकरा या बालटी (प्रायः मकान आदि बनते समय प्रयुक्त)

**skipper** /ˈskɪpə(r) ˈस्किप(र)/ *noun* [C] (*informal*) the captain of a boat or ship, or of a sports team नाव या जलयान या खेलने वाले दल का कप्तान; स्किपर

**skipping rope** *noun* [C] a rope, often with handles at each end, that you turn over your head and then jump over, for fun or for exercise कूदने की रस्सी (प्रायः खेल या व्यायाम के प्रयोजन से)

**skirmish** /ˈskɜːmɪʃ ˈस्कमिश्/ *noun* [C] a short fight between groups of people (लोगों के बीच) झड़प

**skirt¹** /skɜːt स्कट्/ *noun* [C] **1** a piece of clothing that is worn by women and girls and that hangs down from the waist महिलाओं और लड़कियों के पहनने का एक तरह का लहँगा; घाघरा, स्कर्ट ➪ **culottes** देखिए। **2** an outer covering or protective part for the base of a vehicle or machine किसी वाहन या मशीन के आधार का रक्षक आवास *the rubber skirt around the bottom of a hovercraft* ➪ **boat** पर चित्र देखिए।

**skirt²** /skɜːt स्कट्/ *verb* [I, T] to go around the edge of sth किसी (वस्तु स्थान आदि) के किनारे-किनारे चलना; सीमांत पर चलना

**PHR V skirt round sth** to avoid talking about sth in a direct way किसी विषय पर सीधे बात करने से बचना *The manager skirted round the subject of our pay increase.*

**skirting board** /ˈskɜːtɪŋ bɔːd ˈस्कटिङ् बॉड्/ (*also* **skirting**, *AmE* **baseboard**) *noun* [C, U] a narrow piece of wood that is fixed along the bottom of the walls in a house मकान की दवारों के तले के साथ जड़ा लकड़ी का सँकरा तख़्ता

**skit** /skɪt स्किट्/ *noun* [C] a short funny performance or a piece of writing that mimics sth to show how silly it is व्यंग्य नाटक या लेख

**skittles** /ˈskɪtlz ˈस्किट्ल्ज़्/ *noun* [U] a game in which players try to knock down as many bottle-shaped objects (**skittles**) as possible by throwing or rolling a ball at them स्किटल्स का खेल (जिसमें खिलाड़ी बोतल-नुमा वस्तुओं को उन पर या की ओर गेंद फेंक या लुढ़का कर अधिक-से-अधिक संख्या में गिराने की कोशिश करता है)

**skulk** /skʌlk स्कल्क्/ *verb* [I] to stay somewhere quietly and secretly, hoping that nobody will notice you, especially because you are planning to do sth bad (यह समझते हुए कि कोई देखेगा नहीं) चुपके से और चोरी-चोरी कहीं छुपे रहना (विशेषतः बुरा काम करने की योजना बनाने के कारण)

**skull** /skʌl स्कल्/ *noun* [C] the bone structure of a human or animal head मनुष्य या पशु के सिर की अस्थि-संरचना; खोपड़ी, कपाल *She suffered a fractured skull in the fall.* ➪ **body** पर चित्र देखिए।

**sky** /skaɪ स्काइ/ *noun* [C, *usually sing.*, U] (*pl.* **skies**) the space that you can see when you look up from the earth, and where you can see the sun, moon and stars आकाश, आसमान (ज़मीन पर से ऊपर की ओर दीखने वाला स्थान जहाँ सूर्य, चंद्रमा और तारे दिखाई देते हैं) *a cloudless/clear blue sky*

**sky-high** *adj., adv.* very high बहुत ऊँचा, गगनचुंबी, आसमान की ऊँचाई पर

**skyline** /ˈskaɪlaɪn ˈस्काइलाइन्/ *noun* [C] the shape that is made by tall buildings, etc. against the sky ऊँची इमारतों आदि से आकाश पर बनी आकृति या रूपरेखा *the Manhattan skyline*

**skyscraper** /ˈskaɪskreɪpə(r) ˈस्काइस्क्रेप(र्)/ *noun* [C] an extremely tall building गगनचुंबी इमारत

**slab** /slæb स्लैब्/ *noun* [C] a thick, flat piece of sth किसी वस्तु का मोटा चपटा टुकड़ा; पटिया, स्लैब *huge concrete slabs*

**slack** /slæk स्लैक्/ *adj.* **1** loose; not tightly stretched शिथिल, ढीला; जो कसा हुआ न हो *Leave the rope slack.* **2** (used about a period of business) not busy; not having many customers (व्यापार) मंदा; जिस अवधि में ग्राहक कम हो जाएँ *Trade is very slack here in winter.* **3** not carefully or properly done सावधानी या उचित रीति से न किया हुआ; ढीला-ढाला *Slack security made terrorist attacks possible.* **4** (used about a person) not doing your work carefully or properly (व्यक्ति) लापरवाह; अपना काम सावधानी से और ठीक तरह न करने वाला *You've been rather slack about your homework lately.*

**slacken** /ˈslækən ˈस्लैकन्/ *verb* [I, T] **1** to become or make sth less tight ढीला हो जाना या कर देना *The rope slackened and he pulled his hand free.* **2 slacken (sth) (off)** to become or make sth slower or less active धीमा हो जाना या कर देना *He slackened off his pace towards the end of the race.*

**slacks** /slæks स्लैक्स्/ *noun* [*pl.*] trousers (especially not very formal ones) अनौपचारिक पतलून *a pair of slacks*

**slag¹** /slæg स्लैग्/ *verb*

**PHR V** **slag sb off** (*informal*) to say cruel or critical things about sb किसी के विषय में कटु शब्द कहना या निंदा करना

**slag²** /slæg स्लैग्/ *noun* [U] the waste material that is left after metal has been removed from rock धातु-मल, लोह-चून (चट्टान में से धातु निकाल लेने के बाद बचा कचरा या मल)

**slag heap** *noun* [C] a hill made of slag धातु-मल का ढेर

**slain** ➪ **slay** का past participle रूप

**slake** /sleɪk स्लेक्/ *verb* [T] (*literary*) **1 slake your thirst** to drink in a manner that you no longer feel thirsty प्यास बुझाना या शांत करना ✪ पर्याय **quench** **2** to satisfy a desire इच्छा की पूर्ति करना

**slalom** /ˈslɑːləm ˈस्लालम्/ *noun* [C] (in skiing, canoeing, etc.) a race along a course on which competitors have to move from side to side between poles (स्की, डोंगी-चालन आदि खेलों में) डंडों के बीच टेढ़े-मेंढ़े रास्ते से दौड़

**slam** /slæm स्लैम्/ *verb* (**slamming; slammed**) **1** [I, T] to shut or make sth shut very loudly and with great force ऊँची आवाज़ के साथ ज़ोर से दरवाज़ा बंद हो जाना या उसे बंद कर देना *I heard the front door slam.* ○ *She slammed her book shut.* **2** [T] to put sth somewhere very quickly and with great force किसी वस्तु को बहुत तेज़ी और ज़ोर से कहीं रख देना; पटक देना *He slammed the book down on the table and stormed out.* ➪ **grand slam** देखिए।

**slander** /ˈslɑːndə(r) ˈस्लान्ड(र्)/ *noun* [C, U] a spoken statement about sb that is not true and that is intended to damage the good opinion that other people have of him/her; the legal offence of making this kind of statement (किसी की) झूठी निंदा, मिथ्यापवाद (उसे बदनाम करने के लिए); झूठी निंदा या मिथ्यापवाद करने का अपराध ▶ **slander** *verb* [T] (किसी की) झूठी निंदा या मिथ्यापवाद करना ▶ **slanderous** /-dərəs -डरस्/ *adj.* मिथ्यापवादी

**slang** /slæŋ स्लैङ्/ *noun* [U] very informal words and expressions that are more common in spoken language. Slang is sometimes used only by a particular group of people (for example students, young people, criminals) and often stays in fashion for a short time. Some slang is not polite बहुत अनौपचारिक शब्द और मुहावरे जो बोलचाल की भाषा में अधिक प्रयुक्त होते हैं; अपभाषा, कभी-कभी इसे छात्र, युवा, अपराधी आदि विशिष्ट वर्ग ही इस्तेमाल करते हैं (वर्गभाषा), और यह थोड़े समय ही प्रचलन में रहती है, कुछ अपभाषाएँ अशिष्ट भी होती हैं *'Fag' is slang for 'cigarette' in British English.*

**slant¹** /slɑːnt स्लान्ट्/ *verb* **1** [I] to be at an angle, not vertical or horizontal तिरछा होना (लंबवत या क्षैतिज नहीं, खड़ी या पड़ी नहीं); तिर्यग *My handwriting slants backwards.* **2** [T] (*usually passive*) to describe information, events, etc. in a way that supports a particular group or opinion इस प्रकार से सूचना देना, घटनाओं का वर्णन आदि करना कि उससे पक्ष या विचार-विशेष की पुष्टि हो, पक्षपातपूर्ण ढंग से या तोड़-मरोड़ कर बात को पेश करना ▶ **slanting** *adj.* तिरछापन लिए हुए *She has beautiful slanting eyes.*

**slant²** /slɑːnt स्लान्ट्/ *noun* **1** [*sing.*] a position at an angle, not horizontal or vertical तिरछी स्थिति (न लंबवत, न क्षैतिज या न खड़ी, न पड़ी); ढाल *The sunlight fell on the table **at a slant**.* **2** [C] a way of thinking, writing, etc. about sth, that sees things from a particular point of view विशेष दृष्टिकोण से सोचने, लिखने आदि का ढंग; दृष्टिकोण-विशेष

**slap**[1] /slæp स्लैप्/ *verb* [T] (**slapping; slapped**) **1** to hit sb/sth with the inside of your hand when it is flat किसी को थप्पड़ मारना; तमाचा जड़ना *She* ***slapped*** *him* ***across the face***. ○ *People slapped him on the back and congratulated him on winning.* **2** to put sth onto a surface quickly and carelessly कोई वस्तु धम से पटक देना ▶ **slap** *noun* [C] तमाचा, थप्पड़ *I gave him a slap across the face.*

**slap**[2] /slæp स्लैप्/ (*also* **slap bang**) *adv.* (*informal*) used to show that sth happens accidentally at a bad time or place एकाएक बुरे वक़्त या स्थान पर कुछ घटित होने को व्यक्त करने के लिए प्रयुक्त; अचानक और भयानक रूप से *I hurried round the corner and walked slap into someone coming the other way.*

**slapdash** /ˈslæpdæʃ ˈस्लैप्डैश्/ *adj.* careless, or done quickly and carelessly लापरवाह (व्यक्ति) या जल्दबाज़ी और लापरवाही से किया गया (काम) *slapdash building methods* ○ *He's a bit slapdash about doing his homework on time.*

**slapstick** /ˈslæpstɪk ˈस्लैप्स्टिक्/ *noun* [U] a type of humour that is based on simple physical jokes, for example people falling over or hitting each other हाथ-पैर चलाने (जैसे एक-दूसरे पर गिरना या एक-दूसरे को मारना) की हरकतों पर आधारित प्रहसन; आंगिक प्रहसन, भड़ैती

**slash**[1] /slæʃ स्लैश्/ *verb* **1** [I, T] **slash (at) sb/sth** to make or try to make a long cut in sth with a violent movement ज़ोरदार झटके से किसी वस्तु को चीरना, काटना या चीरने या काटने की कोशिश करना **2** [T] to reduce an amount of money, etc. very much किसी वस्तु (से संबंधित) धन की मात्रा या क़ीमत आदि में भारी कटौती करना *The price of coffee has been slashed by 20%.*

**slash**[2] /slæʃ स्लैश्/ *noun* [C] **1** a sharp movement made with a knife, etc. in order to cut sb/sth किसी को काटने के लिए छुरी आदि से लगाया गया चीरा **2** a long narrow wound or cut गहरा सँकरा घाव या चीरा **3** (*BrE* **oblique**) the symbol (/) used to show **alternatives** for example 'lunch and/or dinner', and also to write **fractions**, as in '1/6' विकल्प-सूचक (जैसे 'lunch and/or dinner') और भिन्न संख्याएँ (जैसे '1/6') लिखने के लिए प्रयुक्त, चिह्न (/) ➪ **backslash** देखिए।

**slat** /slæt स्लैट्/ *noun* [C] one of a series of long, narrow pieces of wood, metal or plastic, used in furniture, fences etc. लकड़ी, धातु या प्लास्टिक की पट्टी (फ़र्नीचर, बाड़ आदि में प्रयुक्त)

**slate** /sleɪt स्लेट्/ *noun* **1** [U] a type of dark grey rock that can easily be split into thin flat pieces स्लेट पत्थर (गहरे राख जैसे रंग का पत्थर जिसके आसानी से चौरस टुकड़े हो जाते हैं) **2** [C] one of the thin flat pieces of slate that are used for covering roofs स्लेट का पतला टुकड़ा (छतें पाटने के लिए प्रयुक्त)

**slaughter** /ˈslɔːtə(r) ˈस्लॉट(र्)/ *verb* [T] **1** to kill an animal, usually for food पशु को मारना काटना (प्रायः खाने के लिए) **2** to kill a large number of people at one time, especially in a cruel way एक ही समय बहुत-से लोगों को मार देना (विशेषतः निर्ममतापूर्वक) *Men, women and children were slaughtered and whole villages destroyed.* ➪ **kill** पर नोट देखिए। ▶ **slaughter** *noun* [U] पशु-वध, नर-संहार

**slaughterhouse** /ˈslɔːtəhaʊs ˈस्लॉटहाउस्/ (*BrE* **abattoir**) *noun* [C] a place where animals are killed for food बूचड़ख़ाना; कट्टीघर, कसाईख़ाना (खाने के लिए पशुओं को मारने का स्थान)

**slave**[1] /sleɪv स्लेव्/ *noun* [C] (in past times) a person who was owned by another person and had to work for him/her (विगत में) ग़ुलाम, दास (ऐसा व्यक्ति जिसका मालिक कोई अन्य व्यक्ति हो और जिसे मालिक के लिए काम करना पड़े) ▶ **slavery** *noun* [U] ग़ुलामी, दासता, दास-प्रथा *the abolition of slavery in America*

**slave**[2] /sleɪv स्लेव्/ *verb* [I] **slave (away)** to work very hard बहुत मेहनत से काम करना

**slay** /sleɪ स्ले/ *verb* [T] (*pt* **slew** /sluː स्लू/; *pp* **slain** /sleɪn स्लेन्/) (*old-fashioned*) to kill violently; to murder मार डालना; हत्या कर देना

**sleazy** /ˈsliːzi ˈस्लीज़ि/ *adj.* (used about a place or a person) unpleasant and probably connected with immoral activities (स्थान या व्यक्ति) बुरा और (संभवतः) अनैतिक कार्यों से संबद्ध *a sleazy night club*

**sledge** /sledʒ स्लेज्/ (*AmE* **sled** /sled स्लेड्/) *noun* [C] a vehicle without wheels that is used for travelling on snow. Large sledges are often pulled by dogs, and smaller ones are used for going down hills, for fun or as a sport बर्फ़ पर चलने वाली बिना पहियों की गाड़ी, स्लेज/स्लेड, बर्फ़गाड़ी (बड़ी गाड़ियों को कुत्तों द्वारा खींचा जाता है और छोटी गाड़ियों में मौजमस्ती के लिए या खेल में लोग ढलान पर फिसलते हैं) ➪ **bobsleigh** और **toboggan** देखिए। ▶ **sledge** *verb* [I] बर्फ़गाड़ी से सफ़र करना

**sledgehammer** /ˈsledʒhæmə(r) ˈस्लेज्हैम(र्)/ *noun* [C] a large heavy hammer with a long handle लंबे हत्थे वाला बड़ा और भारी हथौड़ा

**sleek** /sliːk स्लीक्/ *adj.* **1** (used about hair or fur) smooth and shiny because it is healthy (बाल या फ़र) चिकना और चमकदार **2** (used about a vehicle) having an elegant, smooth shape (वाहन) रमणीक और चिकनी सतह वाला *a sleek new sports car*

**sleep**[1] /sli:p स्लीप् / *noun* **1** [U] the natural condition of rest when your eyes are closed and your mind and body are not active or conscious निद्रा, नींद *Most people need at least seven hours' sleep every night.* ○ *I couldn't* ***get to sleep*** *last night.* **2** [*sing.*] a period of sleep नींद की अवधि *You'll feel better after a good night's sleep.*

IDM **go to sleep** **1** to start sleeping सोने लगना; सो जाना, सोना *He got into bed and soon went to sleep.* **2** (used about an arm, a leg, etc.) to lose the sense of feeling in it (बाँह, टाँग आदि का) सो जाना, निश्चेतन होना

**put (an animal) to sleep** to kill an animal that is ill or injured because you want to stop it suffering बीमार या घायल पशु को मार देना (उसे तकलीफ़ से बचाने के लिए)

**sleep**[2] /sli:p स्लीप् / *verb* (*pt, pp* **slept** /slept स्लेप्ट् /) **1** [I] to rest with your eyes closed and your mind and body not active सोना; नींद आना (आँखें बंद तथा मन एवं शरीर निष्क्रिय, इस स्थिति में विश्राम करना) *I only slept for a couple of hours last night.*

> NOTE सोते हुए व्यक्ति का संकेत करने के लिए **asleep** का प्रयोग होता है—*The baby's asleep.* **Go to sleep** का अर्थ है सोने लगना (**start to sleep**) —*I was reading in bed last night, and I didn't go to sleep until about one o'clock.*

**2** [T] (used about a place) to have enough beds for a particular number of people (होटल आदि स्थान के लिए प्रयुक्त) लोगों के विरोध संख्या में लिए पर्याप्त बिस्तर या शय्याएँ होना

IDM **sleep/live rough** ⇨ **rough**[3] देखिए।

PHR V **sleep in** to sleep until later than usual in the morning because you do not have to get up सुबह देर तक सोना (कोई काम न होने के कारण) ⇨ **oversleep** देखिए।

**sleep together; sleep with sb** to have sex with sb (usually when you are not married to or living with that person) (अविवाहित या साथ रहने वाले व्यक्ति के साथ) यौन संबंध स्थापित करना

**sleeper** /ˈsli:pə(r) ˈस्लीप(र्) / *noun* [C] **1** (*with an adjective*) a person who sleeps in a particular way. If you are a light sleeper you wake up easily विशेष ढंग से सोने की आदत वाला व्यक्ति (उखड़ी नींद सोने वाला जल्दी जाग जाता है) *a light/heavy sleeper* **2** a bed on a train; a train with beds रेलगाड़ी की शायिका या सोने के लिए गद्देदार फट्टा; शायिकाओं वाली रेलगाड़ी, शयनयानों वाली रेलगाड़ी

**sleeping bag** *noun* [C] a large soft bag that you use for sleeping in when you go camping, etc. (शिविर-निवास आदि के समय) अंदर घुसकर सोने के लिए प्रयुक्त बड़ा मुलायम थैला; स्लीपिंग बैग

**sleeping car** (*also* **sleeper**) *noun* [C] a railway **carriage** with beds for people to sleep in रेलगाड़ी का शयनयान (सोने के लिए गद्दीदार फट्टों वाला डिब्बा), स्लीपर

**sleeping pill** *noun* [C] a medicine in solid form that you swallow to help you sleep नींद की गोली नींद लाने वाली दवा; स्लीपिंग पिल

**sleeping sickness** *noun* [U] a tropical disease carried by an insect (**tsetse fly**) that makes you want to go to sleep and usually causes death गरम देशों में एक कीट-विशेष के कारण होने वाला रोग जिसमें रोगी सोते रहना चाहता है (और प्रायः जिसमें मृत्यु हो जाती है), (घातक सिद्ध होने वाला); निद्रा रोग

**sleepless** /ˈsli:pləs ˈस्लीप्लस् / *adj.* (used about a period, usually the night) without sleep (अवधि, सामान्यतया रात की) जिसमें नींद न आए; निद्राहीन, विनिद्र ▸ **sleeplessness** *noun* [U] निद्राहीनता, विनिद्रता ⇨ **insomnia** देखिए।

**sleepwalk** /ˈsli:pwɔ:k ˈस्लीप्वॉक् / *verb* [I] to walk around while you are asleep नींद में चलना

**sleepy** /ˈsli:pi ˈस्लीपि / *adj.* **1** tired and ready to go to sleep उनींदा, निद्रालु (थका हुआ और सोने का इच्छुक) *These pills might make you feel a bit sleepy.* **2** (used about a place) very quiet and not having much activity (स्थान) बहुत शांत और कम सरगर्मी वाला ▸ **sleepily** *adv.* सोते-से हुए, शांतिपूर्वक

**sleet** /sli:t स्लीट् / *noun* [U] a mixture of rain and snow ओलों के साथ होने वाला वर्षा, स-हिमा वृष्टि ⇨ **weather** पर नोट देखिए।

**sleeve** /sli:v स्लीव् / *noun* [C] **1** one of the two parts of a piece of clothing that cover the arms or part of the arms (कमीज़ आदि की) आस्तीन, बाँह *a blouse with long sleeves* **2 -sleeved** (*used to form compound adjectives*) with sleeves of a particular kind (विशेष प्रकार की) आस्तीन वाला, बाहों का *a short-sleeved shirt*

**sleeveless** /ˈsli:vləs ˈस्लीव्लस् / *adj.* without sleeves बिना बाँह या आस्तीन का *a sleeveless sweater*

**sleigh** /sleɪ स्ले / *noun* [C] a vehicle without wheels that is used for travelling on snow and that is usually pulled by horses बर्फ़ पर चलने वाली बिना पहियों की गाड़ी (जिसे प्रायः घोड़े खींचते हैं), (घोड़ों वाली) बर्फ़गाड़ी ⇨ **bobsleigh** देखिए।

**slender** /ˈslendə(r) ˈस्लेन्ड(र्) / *adj.* **1** (used about a person or part of sb's body) thin in an attractive way (व्यक्ति का शरीर या शरीर का अंग) पतला; इकहरा, छरहरा *long slender fingers* **2** smaller in amount or size than you would like अभीष्ट से कम (मात्रा या आकार में); अयथेष्ट, नाकाफ़ी *My chances of winning are very slender.*

**slept** ➪ **sleep**[1] का past tense, और past participle रूप

**slew** ➪ **slay** का past tense रूप

**slice**[1] /slaɪs स्लाइस्/ *noun* [C] **1** a flat piece of food that is cut from a larger piece फाँक, कतला (खाने के बड़े टुकड़े से काटा गया छोटा टुकड़ा) *a thick/ thin slice of bread* **2** a part of sth (किसी वस्तु का) अंश, भाग *The directors have taken a large slice of the profits.*

**slice**[2] /slaɪs स्लाइस्/ *verb* **1** [T] to cut into thin flat pieces (किसी वस्तु की) फाँकें काटना; कतलें बनाना *Peel and slice the apples.* ○ *sliced bread* **2** [I, T] to cut sth easily with sth sharp किसी तेज़ धार की वस्तु (छुरी आदि) से आसानी से काटना *He sliced through the rope with a knife.* ○ *The glass sliced into her hand.* **3** [T] (in ball sports) to hit the ball on the bottom or side so that it does not travel in a straight line (गेंद वाले खेलों में) गेंद को तले पर या बग़ल से ऐसे मारना कि वह तिरछे जाए; गेंद को तिरछे उड़ाना

**slick**[1] /slɪk स्लिक्/ *adj.* **1** done smoothly and well, and seeming to be done without any effort निधि और अच्छे ढंग से तथा सहज रूप में किया गया **2** clever at persuading people but perhaps not completely honest लोगों को मनाने में चतुर (परंतु कुछ चालाकी से); सयाना, होशियार

**slick**[2] /slɪk स्लिक्/ = **oil slick**

**slide**[1] /slaɪd स्लाइड्/ *verb* (*pt, pp* **slid** /slɪd स्लिड्/) **1** [I, T] to move or make sth move smoothly along a surface किसी चीज़ का बिना अटके सरकना या उसे सरकाना *She slid along the ice.* ○ *The doors slide open automatically.* **2** [I, T] to move or make sth move quietly without being noticed (किसी का) चुपके से खिसकना या(किसी को) खिसकाना *I slid out of the room quietly.* **3** [I] (used about prices, values, etc.) to go down slowly and continuously (दामों, नैतिक मान्यताओं आदि का) धीमे-धीमे और लगातार गिरना, गिरते जाना **4** [I] to move gradually towards a worse situation पहले से ख़राब स्थिति की ओर बढ़ते जाना, स्थिति का बदतर होते जाना *The company slid into debt and eventually closed.*

**slide**[2] /slaɪd स्लाइड्/ *noun* [C] **1** a small piece of glass that you put sth on when you want to examine it under a **microscope** काँच की पट्टी; स्लाइड (जिस पर कुछ लगाकर उसकी सूक्ष्मदर्शी द्वारा जाँच की जाती है) ➪ **laboratory** पर चित्र देखिए। **2** a large toy consisting of a ladder and a long piece of metal, plastic, etc. Children climb up the ladder then slide down the other part सीढ़ी और धातु, प्लास्टिक आदि के डंडे वाला एक ढाँचा (जिसमें बच्चे सीढ़ी पर चढ़कर दूसरी ओर फिसल कर नीचे आते हैं); स्लाइड **3** a continuous slow fall, for example of prices, values, levels, etc. लगातार गिरावट (दामों, नैतिक मूल्यों, स्तर आदि की) **4** a small piece of photographic film in a plastic or cardboard frame प्लास्टिक या गत्ते के चौखटे में कसी छोटी फ़ोटो फ़िल्म; स्लाइड ➪ **transparency** देखिए।

**slide rule** *noun* [C] a long narrow instrument like a ruler, with a middle part that slides backwards and forwards, used for calculating numbers गिनती करने के लिए प्रयुक्त पैमाने जैसा लंबा सँकरा उपकरण (जिसका मध्य भाग आगे-पीछे सरकाया जाता है), परिकलन पट्टी; स्लाइड रूल

**sliding scale** *noun* [C] a system in which the rate at which sth is paid varies according to particular conditions परिस्थितियों के अनुसार बदलती भुगतान-दर प्रणाली *Fees are calculated* ***on a sliding scale*** *according to income* (= richer people pay more).

**slight** /slaɪt स्लाइट्/ *adj.* **1** very small; not important or serious बहुत छोटा; बड़ा या गंभीर नहीं, मामूली *a slight change/difference/increase/improvement* ○ *I haven't the slightest idea* (= no idea at all) *what you're talking about.* **2** (used about a person's body) thin and light (व्यक्ति का शरीर) पतला और हलका; दुबला-पतला *His slight frame is perfect for a long-distance runner.*

IDM **not in the slightest** not at all बिलकुल भी नहीं *'Are you angry with me?' 'Not in the slightest.'*

**slightly** /ˈslaɪtli ˈस्लाइट्लि/ *adv.* **1** a little थोड़ा-सा *I'm slightly older than her.* **2** a slightly built person is small and thin हलके बदन का व्यक्ति छोटा और पतला होता है

**slim**[1] /slɪm स्लिम्/ *adj.* (**slimmer; slimmest**) **1** thin in an attractive way इकहरा, छरहरा *a slim phone* ○ *a slim model* ➪ **thin** पर नोट देखिए। **2** not as big as you would like इच्छित के अनुसार नहीं, अभीष्ट से कम *Her chances of success are very slim.*

**slim**[2] /slɪm स्लिम्/ *verb* [I] (**slimming; slimmed**) to become or try to become thinner and lighter by eating less food, taking exercise, etc. अधिक पतला और हलका होना या होने का प्रयत्न करना (कम भोजन, व्यायाम आदि के द्वारा) ➪ **diet** देखिए।

**slime** /slaɪm स्लाइम्/ *noun* [U] a thick unpleasant liquid कीचड़ *The pond was covered with slime and had a horrible smell.*

**slimy** /ˈslaɪmi ˈस्लाइमि/ *adj.* **1** covered with slime चिपचिपा, कीचड़ वाला **2** (used about a person) pretending to be friendly, in a way that you do not trust or like (व्यक्ति) दोस्ती का दिखावा करने वाला (अतएव अविश्वसनीय या अप्रिय)

**sling**[1] /slɪŋ स्लिङ्/*noun* [C] **1** a piece of cloth that you put under your arm and tie around your neck to support a broken arm, wrist, etc. ज़ख़्मी हाथ, कलाई आदि को सहारा देने के लिए प्रयुक्त पट्टी (जो बाँह के नीचे से आकर गरदन से लटकती है); गल पट्टी ▶ **slinger** *noun* [C] गुलेल चलाने वाला

**sling**[2] /slɪŋ स्लिङ्/ *verb* [T] (*pt, pp* **slung**) **1** to put or throw sth somewhere in a rough or careless way रूखेपन या लापरवाही से किसी चीज़ को कहीं डाल या फेंक देना **2** to put sth into a position where it hangs loosely किसी चीज़ को ढीला-ढाला लटका देना

**slingback** /ˈslɪŋbæk ˈस्लिङ्बैक्/ *noun* [C] a woman's shoe that is open at the back with a strap around the heel महिलाओं का विशेष प्रकार का जूता (पीछे से खुला और एड़ी पर से घूमते हुए फ़ीते वाला)

**slingshot** /ˈslɪŋʃɒt ˈस्लिङ्शॉट्/ (*AmE*) = **catapult**[1]

**slink** /slɪŋk स्लिङ्क्/ *verb* [I] (*pt, pp* **slunk**) to move somewhere slowly and quietly because you do not want anyone to see you, often when you feel guilty or embarrassed चोरी-चोरी चुपके-चुपके आना-जाना (अपराध-बोध या लज्जा के कारण)

**slip**[1] /slɪp स्लिप्/ *verb* (**slipping; slipped**) **1** [I] **slip (over); slip (on sth)** to slide accidentally and fall or nearly fall अचानक फिसल कर गिर पड़ना या गिरते-गिरते बचना *She slipped over on the wet floor.* **2** [I] to slide accidentally out of the correct position or out of your hand अपने स्थान से या हाथ से किसी वस्तु का अचानक खिसक जाना *This hat's too big. It keeps slipping down over my eyes.* ○ *The glass slipped out of my hand and fell on the floor.* **3** [I] to move or go somewhere quietly, quickly, and often without being noticed चुपके से, तेज़ी से खिसक जाना (प्रायः छुपते हुए) *While everyone was dancing we slipped away and went home.* **4** [T] **slip sth (to sb); slip (sb) sth** to put sth somewhere or give sth to sb quietly and often without being noticed चुपके से कोई वस्तु सरका देना या दे देना (प्रायः छुपाकर) *She picked up the money and slipped it into her pocket.* **5** [I, T] **slip into/out of sth; slip sth on/off** to put on or take off a piece of clothing quickly and easily कपड़े को जल्दी और आसानी से पहन लेना या उतार देना *I slipped off my shoes.* **6** [I] to fall a little in value, level, etc. (मूल्य, स्तर आदि में) थोड़ी गिरावट

**IDM** **let sth slip** ➪ **let** देखिए।

**slip your mind** to be forgotten याद न रहना *I'm sorry, the meeting completely slipped my mind.*

**PHR V** **slip out** to accidentally say sth or tell sb sth मुँह से अचानक कोई बात निकल जाना *I didn't intend to tell them. It just slipped out.*

**slip up** (*informal*) to make a mistake चूक कर बैठना

**slip**[2] /slɪp स्लिप्/ *noun* [C] **1** a small mistake, usually made by being careless or not paying attention छोटी भूल (प्रायः असावधानी वश या ध्यान न देने के कारण) *to make a slip* **2** a small piece of paper काग़ज़ का छोटा टुकड़ा; परची *I made a note of her name on **a slip of paper**.* **3** an act of sliding accidentally and falling or nearly falling अचानक फिसल कर गिर पड़ने या गिरते-गिरते बच जाने की क्रिया **4** a thin piece of clothing that is worn by a woman under a dress or skirt महिलाओं द्वारा फ्रॉक या स्कर्ट के नीचे पहना जाने वाला महीन परिधान; साया, स्लिप

**IDM** **give sb the slip** (*informal*) to escape from sb who is following or trying to catch you पीछा करने या पकड़ने की कोशिश करने वाले को झाँसा देकर बच निकलना

**a slip of the tongue** something that you say that you did not mean to say ज़बान की फिसलन; अनिच्छित रूप से मुँह से निकली बात

**slipped disc** *noun* [C] a painful injury caused when one of the flat things (**discs**) between the bones in your back (**spine**) moves out of its correct position रीढ़ की हड्डी की किसी डिस्क के अपने स्थान से खिसक जाने से हुई दर्दभरी तकलीफ़; खिसका हुआ कूल्हा

**slipper** /ˈslɪpə(r) ˈस्लिप(र्)/ *noun* [C] a light soft shoe that is worn inside the house हलकी नरम चप्पल (घर में पहनने की); स्लीपर, चट्टी *a pair of slippers*

**slippery** /ˈslɪpəri ˈस्लिपरि/ (*informal* **slippy**) *adj.* (used about a surface or an object) difficult to walk on or hold because it is smooth, wet, etc. (कोई सतह या वस्तु) फिसलन भरा (चिकना, गीला आदि होने के कारण जहाँ चलना या जिसे पकड़ना कठिन हो) *a slippery floor*

**slipshod** /ˈslɪpʃɑd ˈस्लिपूशॉड्/ *adj.* done without care; doing things without care लापरवाही से किया गया; लापरवाही से करना *The work was done in a slipshod manner.* ✪ पर्याय **careless**

**slipway** /ˈslɪpweɪ ˈस्लिप्वे/ *noun* [C] a track leading down to water, on which ships are built or pulled up out of the water for repairs, or from which they are **launched** समुद्र तट से समुद्र में जाने वाला ढालू रास्ता (जहाँ जहाज़ बनते हैं, तथा पानी में उतारे या बाहर निकाले जाते हैं); जलावतरण-मंच

**slit**[1] /slɪt स्लिट्/ *noun* [C] a long narrow cut or opening चीरा, दरार (लंबा, सँकरा कटाव) या छेद *a long skirt with a slit up the back*

**slit**[2] /slɪt स्लिट्/ *verb* [T] (**slitting;** *pt, pp* **slit**) to make a long narrow cut in sth किसी वस्तु में चीरा लगाना *She slit the envelope open with a knife.*

**slither** /ˈslɪðə(r) ˈस्लिद़(र्)/ *verb* [I] to move by sliding from side to side along the ground like a snake साँप की तरह ज़मीन पर दाएँ-बाएँ फिसलते हुए चलना *I saw a snake slithering down a rock.*

**slob** /slɒb स्लॉब्/ *noun* [C] (*informal*) (used as an insult) a very lazy or untidy person (अपमान के अर्थ में प्रयुक्त) बेहद आलसी या मैला-कुचैला व्यक्ति

**slog**[1] /slɒg स्लॉग्/ *verb* [I] (**slogging; slogged**) 1 (*informal*) **slog (away) (at sth); slog (through sth)** to work hard for a long period at sth difficult or boring कठिन या उबाऊ काम को लंबे समय तक करना *I've been slogging away at this homework for hours.* 2 **slog down, up, along, etc.** to walk or move in a certain direction with a lot of effort बहुत प्रयत्न के साथ निर्धारित दिशा में चलना

**slog**[2] /slɒg स्लॉग्/ *noun* [*sing.*] a period of long, hard, boring work or a long, tiring journey देर तक चला कठिन, उबाऊ काम या लंबी, थकाऊ यात्रा

**slogan** /ˈsləʊgən ˈस्लोगन्/ *noun* [C] a short phrase that is easy to remember and that is used in politics or advertising (राजनीतिक व्यवहार या विज्ञापन की भाषा में प्रयुक्त) नारा; स्लोगन (एक छोटा वाक्यांश जिसे याद करना सरल हो) *Anti-government slogans/ an advertising slogan*

**sloop** /slu:p स्लूप्/ *noun* [C] a small sailing ship with one **mast** एक मस्तूल वाला छोटा जहाज़

**slop** /slɒp स्लॉप्/ *verb* [I, T] (**slopping; slopped**) (used about a liquid) to pour over the edge of its container; to make a liquid do this (तरल पदार्थ का) पात्र के किनारे से होकर बाहर निकलना, छलकना; तरल पदार्थ को छलकाना *He filled his glass too full and juice slopped onto the table.*

**slope** /sləʊp स्लोप्/ *noun* 1 [C] a surface or piece of land that goes up or down ढालू सतह या ज़मीन (जो ऊपर या नीचे की ओर जाए); ढाल *The village is built* ***on a slope****.* ○ *a steep/gentle slope* 2 [*sing.*] the amount that a surface is not level; the fact of not being level ढाल (ऊँची-नीची सतह) की मात्रा; ढलान (ढाल होने की स्थिति) ▶ **slope** *verb* [I] ढालू होना *The road slopes down to the river.* ○ *a sloping roof*

**sloppy** /ˈslɒpi ˈस्लॉपि/ *adj.* 1 that shows lack of care, thought or effort; untidy लापरवाह (जिसमें सावधानी, विचार या प्रयत्न की कमी हो); गंदा, बेढंगा *a sloppy worker/writer/dresser* ○ *a sloppy piece of work* 2 (used about clothes) not tight and without much shape (कपड़े) तंग और बेढंगे 3 (*BrE informal*) showing emotions in a silly embarrassing way बेवकूफ़ी और झेंपाने वाली भावुकता का प्रदर्शन करते हुए; झूठी भावुकता वाला *I can't stand sloppy love songs.* ✪ पर्याय **sentimental**

**slosh** /slɒʃ स्लॉश्/ *verb* (*informal*) 1 [I] (used about a liquid) to move around noisily inside a container (तरल पदार्थ का) पात्र में आवाज़ करते हुए घूमना 2 [T] to pour or drop liquid somewhere in a careless way तरल पदार्थ को लापरवाही से कहीं बहा देना या डाल देना

**sloshed** /slɒʃt स्लॉश्ट्/ *adj.* (*slang*) drunk पिए हुए, बदमस्त

**slot**[1] /slɒt स्लॉट्/ *noun* [C] 1 a straight narrow opening in a machine, etc. मशीन आदि में सीधा तंग छेद; झिरी *Put your money into the slot and take the ticket.* 2 a place in a list, system, organization, etc. स्थान (किसी सूची, प्रणाली, संस्था आदि में) *The single has occupied the Number One slot for the past two weeks.*

**slot**[2] /slɒt स्लॉट्/ *verb* [I, T] (**slotting; slotted**) to put sth into a particular space that is designed for it; to fit into such a space निर्धारित स्थान (झिरी आदि में) बैठाना; झिरी (आदि) में ठीक बैठ जाना *He slotted a tape into the VCR.* ○ *The video slotted in easily.*

**IDM** **fall/slot into place** ⇨ **place**[1] देखिए।

**slot machine** *noun* [C] a machine with an opening for coins that sells drinks, cigarettes, etc. or on which you can play games झिरीदार (विशेष) मशीन जिसमें सिक्के डाल कर पेय पदार्थ आदि प्राप्त किए जा सकते हैं या खेल खेले जा सकते हैं; स्लॉट मशीन

**slouch** /slaʊtʃ स्लाउच्/ *verb* [I] to sit, stand or walk in a lazy way, with your head and shoulders hanging down सुस्ती से (सिर और बाँहें लटकाते हुए) बैठना; खड़ा होना या चलना

**slovenly** /ˈslʌvnli ˈस्लव्नलि/ *adj.* (*old-fashioned*) lazy, careless and untidy सुस्त, लापरवाह और गंदा

**slow**[1] /sləʊ स्लो/ *adj., adv.* 1 moving, doing sth or happening without much speed; not fast धीमी गति से चलते, करते या घटित होते हुए, धीमा या धीमे; वेग से नहीं, मंद *Progress was slower than expected.* ○ *a slow driver/walker/reader* ✪ विलोम **fast**

> **NOTE** **Slow** का प्रयोग क्रियाविशेषण के रूप में हो सकता है परंतु इस रूप में **slowly** अधिक प्रचलित है, तथापि **slow** का प्रयोग यौगिकों या समासों में प्रायः होता है—*slow-moving traffic.* इसके दो तुलनात्मक (comparative) रूप हैं **slower** और **more slowly** और दोनों ही प्रचलित हैं—*Could you drive a bit slower/more slowly, please?*

2 **slow to do sth; slow (in/about) doing sth** not doing sth immediately जो काम को तुरंत न करें; मंदगति *She was rather slow to realize what was going on.* ○ *They've been rather slow in replying*

*to my letter!* **3** not quick to learn or understand धीमी गति से सीखने या समझने वाला; मंदबुद्धि *He's the slowest student in the class.* **4** not very busy; with little action अधिक व्यस्त नहीं, सुस्त, मंदा; निष्क्रियप्राय *Business is very slow at the moment.* **5** (*not before a noun*) (used about watches and clocks) showing a time that is earlier than the real time (हाथ की और दीवार या मेज़ की घड़ी) सुस्त पीछे चल रही *That clock is five minutes slow* (= it says it is 8.55 when the correct time is 9.00). ✪ विलोम **fast** ▶ **slowness** *noun* [U] सुस्ती, मंदता धीमापन, मंथरता

IDM **quick/slow on the uptake** ➪ **uptake** देखिए।

**slow**[2] /sləʊ स्लो / *verb* [I, T] to start to move, do sth or happen at a slower speed; to cause sth to do this (अधिक) मंद गति से चलना शुरू करना, कोई काम करना या होना; किसी से यह सब करवाना *He slowed his pace a little.*

PHR V **slow (sb/sth) down/up** to start to move, do sth or happen at a slower speed; to cause sb/sth to do this (अधिक) मंद गति से चलना शुरू करना, कोई काम करना या होना; किसी से यह सब करवाना *Can't you slow down a bit? You're driving much too fast.* ○ *These problems have slowed up the whole process.*

**slowly** /ˈsləʊli ˈस्लोलि / *adv.* at a slow speed; not quickly मंद गति से; जल्दी नहीं, धीरे-धीरे *He walked slowly along the street.*

**slow motion** *noun* [U] (in a film or on television) a method of making action appear much slower than in real life (फ़िल्म में या टीवी पर) वास्तविक से बहुत कम गति से कार्य-व्यापार को घटित होते दिखाने का तरीक़ा; स्लो मोशन *They showed the winning goal again, this time **in slow motion**.*

**slow-worm** *noun* [C] a small brownish animal with no legs, like a snake, that is found in Europe and Asia एक छोटा भूरा-सा बिना टाँगों का साँप जैसा कीट (यूरोप और एशिया में पाए जाने वाला); मदंकीट

**sludge** /slʌdʒ स्लज् / *noun* [U] a thick, soft unpleasant substance; mud गाढ़ा, नरम बदबूदार पदार्थ, तलछट; कीचड़, गंदगी

**slug** /slʌg स्लग् / *noun* [C] a small black or brown animal with a soft body and no legs, that moves slowly along the ground and eats garden plants (बिना शंख का) ज़मीन पर घूमने और वनस्पतियाँ खाने वाला घोंघा ➪ **mollusc** पर चित्र देखिए।

**sluggish** /ˈslʌgɪʃ ˈस्लगिश् / *adj.* moving or working more slowly than normal in a way that seems lazy सुस्ती भरी धीमी गति से चलने या काम करने वाला; ढीला-ढाला

**sluice** /slu:s स्लूस् / (*also* **sluice gate**) *noun* [C] a type of gate that you can open or close to control the flow of water out of or into a canal, etc. नहर के पानी को नियंत्रित करने (रोकने या खोलने के लिए प्रयुक्त विशेष प्रकार का दरवाज़ा; स्लूस गेट, जल-द्वार

**slum** /slʌm स्लम् / *noun* [C] an area of a city where living conditions are extremely bad, and where the buildings are dirty and have not been repaired for a long time शहरों में ग़रीबों की बस्ती, झुग्गी-झोंपड़ी वाला क्षेत्र; मलिन बस्ती

**slumber** /ˈslʌmbə(r) ˈस्लम्ब(र्) / *verb* [I] (*old-fashioned*) to be deeply asleep गहरी नींद सोना ▶ **slumber** *noun* [C] नींद, झपकी

**slump**[1] /slʌmp स्लम्प् / *verb* [I] **1** (used about economic activity, prices, etc.) to fall suddenly and by a large amount (आर्थिक गतिविधि, दामों आदि में) अचानक भारी गिरावट आ जाना *The newspaper's circulation has slumped by 30%.* **2** to fall or sit down suddenly when your body feels heavy and weak, usually because you are tired or ill (थक कर या कमज़ोरी के कारण) गिर पड़ना या धम से बैठ जाना

**slump**[2] /slʌmp स्लम्प् / *noun* [C] **1 a slump (in sth)** a sudden large fall in sales, prices, the value of sth, etc. (किसी चीज़ की बिक्री, क़ीमतों, मूल्यों आदि में) अचानक भारी गिरावट *a slump in house prices* **2** a period when a country's economy is doing very badly and a lot of people do not have jobs आर्थिक मंदी (आर्थिक दुरवस्था जिसमें लोगों को काम नहीं मिलता)

**slung** ➪ **sling**[2] का past tense और past participle रूप

**slunk** ➪ **slink** का past tense और past participle रूप

**slur**[1] /slɜ:(r) स्ल(र्) / *verb* [T] (**slu<u>r</u>ring; slu<u>r</u>red**) to pronounce words in a way that is not clear, often because you are drunk शब्दों का अस्पष्ट उच्चारण करना (प्रायः शराब के असर में)

**slur**[2] /slɜ:(r) स्ल(र्) / *noun* [C] **a slur (on sb/sth)** an unfair comment or an insult that could damage people's opinion of sb/sth किसी को बदनाम या लांछित करने वाले शब्द, लांछन; कलंक, निंदा

**slurp** /slɜ:p स्लप् / *verb* [I, T] (*informal*) to drink noisily आवाज़ करते हुए कुछ पीना

**slurry** /ˈslʌri ˈस्लरि / *noun* [U] a thick liquid consisting of water mixed with animal waste that farmers use on their fields to make plants grow better गोबर मिला पानी वाला (गारे जैसा) खाद्य (किसानों द्वारा उपज बढ़ाने के लिए खेतों में प्रयुक्त)

**slush** /slʌʃ स्लश् / *noun* [U] **1** snow that has been on the ground for a time and that is now a dirty mixture of ice and water बर्फ़ का कीचड़ (पानी और गंदगी मिल जाने के फलस्वरूप) **2** (*informal*) films, books, feelings, etc. that are considered to be silly because they are too romantic and emotional दयनीय फ़िल्में, पुस्तकें, मनोभाव आदि (बहुत रूमानी और भावुक होने के कारण) ▶ **slushy** *adj.* कीचड़दार, अतिरूमानी

**slush fund** *noun* [C] an amount of money that is kept to pay people illegally to do things, especially in politics ग़ैर-क़ानूनी काम (विशेषतः राजनीति में) कराने के लिए प्रयुक्त धनराशि; गंदा पैसा

**sly** /slaɪ स्लाइ / *adj.* **1** (used about a person) acting or done in a secret or dishonest way, often intending to trick people (व्यक्ति या कार्य) चोरी-छिपे या बेईमानी से काम करने वाला या किया गया, प्रायः लोगों को धोखा देने की मंशा से; कपटपूर्ण, बेईमानी भरा ✪ पर्याय **cunning** **2** (used about an action) suggesting that you know sth secret (कार्य) रहस्यपूर्ण लगने वाला *a sly smile/look* ▶ **slyly** *adv.* कपटपूर्ण

**smack** /smæk स्मैक् / *verb* [T] to hit sb with the inside of your hand when it is flat, especially as a punishment किसी के चपत लगाना (विशेषतः सज़ा के तौर पर) *I never smack my children.* ▶ **smack** *noun* [C] तमाचा, चाँटा, थप्पड़ *You're going to get a smack if you don't do as I say!*

PHR V **smack of sth** to make you think that sb/sth has an unpleasant attitude or quality किसी के अप्रिय लगने वाले सोच या विशेषता का संकेत देना

**small** /smɔːl स्मॉल् / *adj.* **1** not large in size, number, amount, etc. छोटा (आकार, संख्या, मात्रा आदि की दृष्टि से) *a small car/flat/town* ○ *a small amount of money* **2** young छोटा (बच्चा) *He has a wife and three small children.* ○ *When I was small we lived in a big old house.* **3** not important or serious; slight बड़ा या गंभीर नहीं; मामूली *Don't worry. It's only a small problem.*

> NOTE **Small** का सर्वाधिक मान्य विलोम है **big** या **large**. किसी मनोभाव या छोटेपन के अर्थ की अभिव्यक्ति के लिए **little** का प्रयोग प्रायः एक और विशेषण के साथ होता है—*a horrible little man* ○ *a lovely little girl* ○ *a nice little house.* तुलनात्मक (comparative) और उत्तमतासूचक (superlative) रूप **smaller** और **smallest** काफ़ी सामान्य हैं, तथा **'small'** का **'rather'** **'quite'** और **'very'** के साथ प्रायः प्रयोग किया जाता है—*My flat is smaller than yours.* ○ *The village is quite small.* सामान्यतया इन शब्दों के साथ **little** का प्रयोग नहीं होता, न ही इसके तुलनात्मक और उत्तमतासूचक रूप होते हैं।

▶ **small** /smɔːl स्मॉल् / *adv.* छोटे आकार में *She's painted the picture far too small.*

IDM **in a big/small way** ➪ **way**[1] देखिए।

**small ads** *noun* [*pl.*] (*BrE informal*) = **classified advertisements**

**small arms** *noun* [C, *pl.*] small light weapons that you can carry in your hands छोटे हथियार (जिन्हें हाथ में ले जा सकते हैं, जैसे पिस्तौल)

**small change** *noun* [U] coins that have a low value छोटे सिक्के; खुदरा, रेज़गारी

**smallholder** /ˈsmɔːlhəʊldə(r) ˈस्मॉल्होल्ड(र्) / *noun* [C] a person who owns or rents a small piece of land for farming छोटा किसान (थोड़ी ज़मीन का मालिक या उसे भाड़े अथवा बटाई पर लेकर खेती करने वाला)

**smallholding** /ˈsmɔːlhəʊldɪŋ ˈस्मॉल्होल्डिङ् / *noun* [C] a small piece of land that is used for farming छोटी जोत, खेती की थोड़ी ज़मीन

**the small hours** *noun* [*pl.*] the early morning hours soon after midnight आधी रात के बाद का समय; बहुत तड़के

**smallpox** /ˈsmɔːlpɒks ˈस्मॉल्पॉक्स् / *noun* [U] a serious infectious disease that causes a high temperature and leaves marks on the skin. In past times many people died from small pox चेचक (का रोग); माता (पूर्व समय में चेचक से बहुत लोग मर जाते थे)

**the small print** (*AmE* **the fine print**) *noun* [U] the important details of a legal document, contract, etc. that are usually printed in small type and are therefore easy to miss क़ानूनी दस्तावेज़; अनुबंध-पत्र आदि के महत्त्वपूर्ण ब्योरे (सामान्यतया छोटे अक्षरों में मुद्रित, अतः उनमें चूक संभावित) *Make sure you read the small print before you sign anything.*

**small-scale** *adj.* (used about an organization or activity) not large; limited in what it does (संस्था या गतिविधि) छोटा, लघु; अपने कार्यक्षेत्र तक सीमित

**small talk** *noun* [U] polite conversation, for example at a party, about unimportant things पार्टी आदि में गपशप *We had to **make small talk** for half an hour.*

**smart**[1] /smɑːt स्माट् / *adj.* **1** (*BrE*) (used about a person) having a clean and tidy appearance (व्यक्ति) साफ़-सुथरा, बना-ठना; आकर्षक *You look smart. Are you going somewhere special?* **2** (used about a piece of clothing, etc.) good enough to wear on a formal occasion (कपड़ा आदि) औपचारिक अवसरों पर पहनने योग्य *a smart suit* **3** clever; intelligent चतुर; बुद्धिमान, विवेकशील *He's not smart enough to* *be a politician.* **4** (*BrE*) fashionable and usually expensive फ़ैशनेबल और प्रायः महँगा *a smart restaurant/hotel* **5** (used about a movement or action) quick and usually done with force (कोई हरकत या कार्रवाई) तेज़ी से और प्रायः ताक़त लगा कर की गई ▸ **smartly** *adv.* आकर्षक रूप से *She's always smartly dressed.*

**smart²** /smɑːt स्माट्/ *verb* [I] **1 smart (from sth)** to feel a stinging pain in your body (शरीर में) तीखा दर्द होना **2 smart (from/over sth)** to feel upset or offended because of a criticism, failure, etc. (निंदा, विफलता आदि के कारण) परेशान या क्रोधित होना

**smart card** *noun* [C] a plastic card, for example a **credit card**, on which information can be stored in electronic form एक प्रकार का प्लास्टिक निर्मित कार्ड (जैसे क्रेडिट काडी) जिसमें इलेक्ट्रॉनिक रूप में अपेक्षित जानकारी सुरक्षित रहती है; स्मार्ट कार्ड

**smarten** /ˈsmɑːtn ˈस्माट्न्/ *verb*

**PHRV** **smarten (yourself/sb/sth) up** to make yourself/sb/sth look tidy and more attractive साफ़-सुथरा और आकर्षक दिखना

**smash¹** /smæʃ स्मैश्/ *verb* **1** [I, T] to break sth, or to be broken violently and noisily into many pieces धमाके के साथ किसी चीज़ का चूर-चूर हो जाना या उसे चूर-चूर कर देना *The glass smashed into a thousand pieces.* ○ *The police had to smash the door open.* **2** [I, T] **smash (sth) against, into, through, etc.** to move with great force in a particular direction; to hit sth very hard किसी विशेष दिशा में बहुत ज़ोर के साथ जाना; (किसी के साथ) ज़ोर से टकराना *The car smashed into a tree.* ○ *He smashed his fist through the window.* **3** [T] **smash sth (up)** to crash a vehicle, usually causing a lot of damage वाहन को टकरा देना (प्रायः उसे काफ़ी नुक़सान पहुँचाते हुए) **4** [T] (in tennis) to hit a ball that is high in the air downwards very hard over the net (टेनिस में) गेंद को दबाकर मारना (हवा में ऊँची उठी हुई गेंद को जाल के ऊपर से नीचे की ओर मारना)

**smash²** /smæʃ स्मैश्/ *noun* **1** [*sing.*] the action or the noise of sth breaking violently चूर-चूर होने की क्रिया या आवाज़ **2** [C] (in tennis, etc.) a way of hitting a ball that is high in the air downwards and very hard over the net (टेनिस में) गेंद को दबाकर मारने का ढंग; स्मैश **3** (*also* **smash hit**) [C] (*informal*) a song, play, film, etc. that is very successful अत्यंत सफल गाना, नाटक, फ़िल्म आदि

**smashing** /ˈsmæʃɪŋ ˈस्मैशिङ्/ *adj.* (*BrE informal*) extremely good; wonderful बहुत बढ़िया; कमाल का

**smattering** /ˈsmætərɪŋ ˈस्मैटरिङ्/ *noun* [U] [*sing.*] **1 a smattering of sth** a small amount of or number of sth किसी वस्तु की छोटी मात्रा या संख्या *a smattering of raindrops* **2 have a smattering of sth** a slight knowledge of something especially a language किसी के विषय में सतही ज्ञान (विशेषतः भाषा) *He only has a smattering of French.*

**smear¹** /smɪə(r) स्मिअ(र्)/ *verb* [T] **smear sth on/over sth/sb; smear sth/sb with sth** to spread a sticky substance across sth/sb किसी पर कोई चिकनी चीज़ पोतना या लगाना *Her face was smeared with blood.*

**smear²** /smɪə(r) स्मिअ(र्)/ *noun* [C] **1** a dirty mark made by spreading a substance across sth कोई चिकनी चीज़ (किसी को) लगाने से बना धब्बा; चिकनाई का दाग़ **2** something that is not true that is said or written about an important person and that is intended to damage people's opinion about him/her, especially in politics किसी बड़े आदमी को बदनाम करने के लिए किया गया झूठा प्रचार (विशेषतः राजनीति में) *He was the victim of a* ***smear campaign***.

**smell¹** /smel स्मेल्/ *verb* (*pt, pp* **smelt** /smelt स्मेल्ट्/ or **smelled** /smeld स्मेल्ड्/) **1** [I] **smell (of sth)** to have a particular smell सुगंध फैलाना; महकना *Dinner smells good!* ○ *This perfume smells of roses.* **2** [I] to have a bad smell दुर्गंध फैलाना, बदबू मारना *Your feet smell.* **3** [T] to notice or recognize sb/sth by using your nose सूँघकर (किसी का) पता लगाना या (किसी को) पहचानना *He could smell something burning.* ○ *Can you smell gas?*

> **NOTE** **Smell** या अन्य इंद्रियार्थबोधक क्रियाओं (जैसे **taste, see, hear**) का सातत्यबोधक कालों (continuous tenses) में प्रयोग नहीं होता। इसके स्थान पर **can** का प्रयोग होता है जैसे—*I can smell smoke.*

**4** [T] to put your nose near sth and breathe in so that you can discover or identify its smell पास के किसी चीज़ को सूँध कर उसकी गंध का पता लगाना या पहचान करना *I smelt the milk to see if it had gone off.* **5** [I] to be able to smell सूँध सकना *I can't smell properly because I've got a cold.*

**smell²** /smel स्मेल्/ *noun* **1** [C] the impression that you get of sth by using your nose; the thing that you smell गंध, बू; सूँधी जाने वाली वस्तु *a sweet/musty/fresh/sickly smell* ○ *a strong/faint smell of garlic* **2** [*sing.*] an unpleasant smell दुर्गंध, बदबू *Ugh! What's that smell?*

> **NOTE** दुर्गंध या बदबू का अर्थ देने वाले शब्द हैं **stink, stench** और **odour. Aroma, fragrance, perfume** और **scent** शब्दों से ख़ुशबू के अर्थ का आभास मिलता है।

3 [U] the ability to sense things with the nose सूँघ कर वस्तुओं को जानने की क्षमता; घ्राण शक्ति *Dogs have a very good* ***sense of smell.*** 4 [C] the action of putting your nose near sth to smell it सूँघने के लिए नाक को वस्तु के पास ले जाने की क्रिया *Have a smell of this milk; is it all right?*

**smelly** /ˈsmeli ˈस्मेलि/ *adj.* (*informal*) having a bad smell दुर्गंध देने वाला; बदबूदार *smelly feet*

**smelt[1]** /smelt स्मेल्ट्/ *verb* [T] to heat and melt rock containing metal (**ore**) in order to get the metal out (धातु को निकालने के लिए) कच्ची धातु को तपाना और पिघलाना

**smelt[2]** ➪ **smell** का past tense या past participle रूप

**smile[1]** /smaɪl स्माइल्/ *noun* [C] an expression on your face in which the corners of your mouth turn up, showing happiness, pleasure, etc. (चेहरे पर) मुस्कुराहट, मुस्कान (प्रसन्नता, आनंद आदि की सूचक) *to have a smile on your face* ➪ **beam, grin** और **smirk** देखिए।

**smile[2]** /smaɪl स्माइल्/ *verb* 1 [I] **smile (at sb/sth)** to make a smile appear on your face मुस्कराना *to smile sweetly/faintly/broadly* 2 [T] to say or express sth with a smile मुस्करा कर कुछ कहना या व्यक्त करना *I smiled a greeting to them.*

**smirk** /smɜːk स्मक्/ *noun* [C] an unpleasant smile which you have when you are pleased with yourself or think you are very clever भद्दी या बनावटी मुस्कुराहट (अपनी सफलता या चतुराई पर) ▶ **smirk** *verb* [I] भद्दे या बनावटी ढंग से मुस्कराना

**smith** = **blacksmith**

**smog** /smɒg स्मॉग्/ *noun* [U] dirty, poisonous air that can cover a whole city धुएँ वाला कोहरा, धूम-कोहरा (यह पूरे शहर पर भी छा जाता है)

**smoke[1]** /sməʊk स्मोक्/ *noun* 1 [U] the grey, white or black gas that you can see in the air when sth is burning (सलेटी, सफ़ेद या काला) धुआँ (किसी वस्तु के जलने से उत्पन्न) *Thick smoke poured from the chimney.* ○ *a room full of cigarette smoke* 2 [C, *usually sing.*] an action of smoking a cigarette, etc. सिगरेट आदि पीने की क्रिया

**smoke[2]** /sməʊk स्मोक्/ *verb* 1 [I, T] to breathe in smoke through a cigarette, etc. and let it out again; to use cigarettes, etc. in this way, as a habit सिगरेट आदि का कश भरना और छोड़ना; सिगरेट आदि पीना *Do you mind if I smoke?* ○ *I used to smoke twenty cigarettes a day.* 2 [I] to send out smoke धुँआ निकालना या उगलना *The oil in the pan started to smoke.* ▶ **smoker** *noun* [C] धूमपान करने वाला व्यक्ति ✪ विलोम **non-smoker** ▶ **smoking** *noun* [U] धूमपान *My doctor has advised me to give up smoking.*

**smoked** /sməʊkt स्मोक्ट्/ *adj.* (used of certain types of food) given a special taste by being hung for a period of time in smoke from wood fires धुआँरी हुई (मांस, मच्छी आदि वस्तुएँ) (इन्हें ऊपर टाँग कर नीचे से जलती लकड़ी का धुआँ दिया जाता है ताकि ये अधिक स्वादिष्ट बन सकें) *smoked salmon/ham/cheese*

**smoky** /ˈsməʊki ˈस्मोकि/ *adj.* 1 full of smoke; producing a lot of smoke धुएँ से भरा हुआ; बहुत अधिक धुआँ देने वाला *a smoky room/fire* 2 with the smell, taste or appearance of smoke धुएँ जैसी गंध या स्वाद वाला या धुएँ जैसा दिखता हुआ

**smolder** (*AmE*) = **smoulder**

**smooth[1]** /smuːð स्मूद्/ *adj.* 1 having a completely flat surface with no lumps or holes or rough areas चिकना (पूरी तरह से समतल सतह वाला, जिसमें न कोई गूमड़ या गाँठ हो न कोई छेद न ख़रदरापन) *smooth skin* ○ *a smooth piece of wood* ✪ विलोम **rough** 2 (of a liquid mixture) without lumps (तरल पदार्थ का मिश्रण, चटनी आदि) जिसमें गूमड़ न हों, अच्छी तरह मिला हुआ *Stir the sauce until it is smooth.* ✪ विलोम **lumpy** 3 without difficulties बिना किसी बाधा के; बाधारहित, निर्विघ्न, सरलता से संपन्न *The transition from the old method to the new has been very smooth.* 4 (of a journey in a car, etc.) with an even, comfortable movement (कार आदि में सफ़र) आरामदेह (जिसमें न हिचकोले लगें न धक्के) *You get a very smooth ride in this car.* ✪ विलोम **bumpy** 5 too pleasant or polite to be trusted चापलूस, चाटुकार (व्यक्ति) (अति मधुर या नम्र कि उस पर भरोसा करना कठिन हो जाए) **NOTE** यह शब्द व्यक्ति के लिए प्रयुक्त होता है और इसकी व्यंजना निंदात्मक है—*I don't like him. He's far too smooth.* ▶ **smoothness** *noun* [U] चिकनापन, अबाधता

**IDM** **take the rough with the smooth** ➪ **rough[2]** देखिए।

**smooth[2]** /smuːð स्मूद्/ *verb* [T] **smooth sth (away, back, down, out, etc.)** to move your hands in the direction mentioned over a surface to make it smooth किसी सतह को चिकना बनाना (निर्दिष्ट दिशा में हाथों को चला कर)

**smoothly** /ˈsmuːðli ˈस्मूद्लि/ *adv.* without any difficulty बिना किसी बाधा के; निर्विघ्न या अबाध रूप से *My work has been going quite smoothly.*

**smother** /ˈsmʌðə(r) ˈस्मद्र(र्)/ *verb* [T] 1 **smother sb (with sth)** to kill sb by covering his/her face so that he/she cannot breathe (कपड़े से मुँह ढकते हुए) दम घोंट कर मार डालना *She was smothered* *with a pillow.* **2 smother sth/sb in/with sth** to cover sth/sb with too much of sth किसी में ढेर सारी कोई चीज़ डाल देना, किसी में कुछ भर देना **3** to stop a feeling, etc. from being expressed किसी मनोभाव को व्यक्त न होने देना; रोकना, दबाना या छिपाना **4** to stop sth burning by covering it किसी जलती हुई वस्तु को बुझाना (उस पर कुछ डाल कर) *to smother the flames with a blanket*

**smoulder** (*AmE* **smolder**) /ˈsməʊldə(r) ˈस्मोलड(र्)/ *verb* [I] to burn slowly without a flame सुलगना (बिना लपट धीरे-धीरे जलना) *a cigarette smouldering in an ashtray*

**SMS** /ˌes em ˈes ˌएस् एम् ˈएस्/ *abbr.* Short Message (or Messaging) Service. It is a service available on most digital mobile phones and other mobile devices like palmtops, pocket PCs, etc. that permits the sending of short messages or text messages. It is also known as text messaging संक्षिप्त संदेश सेवा; डिजिटल मोबाइल फोन और अन्य मोबाइल यंत्रों जैसे पामटॉप, पॉकिट PC आदि में उपलब्ध संक्षिप्त संदेश या पाठ संदेश भेजने का प्राविधान। इसे टेक्स्ट मैसजिंग भी कहते हैं।

**smudge** /smʌdʒ स्मज्/ *verb* **1** [T] to make sth dirty or untidy by touching it किसी चीज़ को (छूकर) गंदा या मैला करना; धब्बे डालना *Leave your painting to dry or you'll smudge it.* **2** [I] to become untidy, without a clean line around it धब्बे लग जाना, (पर) धब्बे आ जाना ▶ **smudge** *noun* [C] धब्बा

**smug** /smʌg स्मग्/ *adj.* too pleased with yourself आत्मतुष्ट, दंभी (अपनी उपलब्धियों पर स्वयं ही खुश) *Don't look so smug.* **NOTE** इस शब्द की व्यंजना निंदात्मक है। ▶ **smugly** *adv.* आत्मतुष्ट भाव से, दंभ के साथ *He smiled smugly as the results were announced.* ▶ **smugness** *noun* [U] आत्मसंतोष, दंभ

**smuggle** /ˈsmʌgl ˈस्मगल्/ *verb* [T] to take things into or out of a country secretly in a way that is not allowed by the law; to take a person or a thing secretly into or out of a place माल की तस्करी करना, माल को ग़ैर-क़ानूनी ढंग से चोरी-चोरी देश के अंदर लाना या देश से बाहर ले जाना); मानव की तस्करी करना *The drugs had been smuggled through customs.* ▶ **smuggler** *noun* [C] तस्कर *a drug smuggler*

**snack** /snæk स्नैक्/ *noun* [C] food that you eat quickly between main meals जलपान *I had a snack on the train.* ▶ **snack** *verb* [I] (*informal*) **snack on sth** किसी चीज़ (फल, मिठाई आदि) का नाश्ता करना

**snack bar** *noun* [C] a type of small cafe where you can buy a small quick meal like a sandwich नाश्ता-घर, जलपान-गृह

**snag[1]** /snæg स्नैग्/ *noun* [C] a small difficulty or disadvantage that is often unexpected or hidden छोटी कठिनाई या प्रतिकूलता (प्रायः अप्रत्याशित या छिपी हुई) *His offer is very generous—are you sure there isn't a snag?*

**snag[2]** /snæg स्नैग्/ *verb* [T] (**snagging; snagged**) to catch a piece of clothing, etc. on sth sharp and tear it किसी तेज़ धार की चीज़ पर कपड़े का फँस जाना और फट जाना

**snail** /sneɪl स्नेल्/ *noun* [C] a type of animal with a soft body and no legs that is covered by a shell. Snails move very slowly घोंघा (सीपी में रहने वाला कोमल शरीर और बिना टाँगों का छोटा जीव जो धीरे-धीरे चलता है) ➪ **mollusc** पर चित्र देखिए।

**snail mail** *noun* [U] (*informal*) used by people who use email to describe the system of sending letters by ordinary post (इ-मेल के अभ्यस्त लोगों द्वारा) साधारण डाक से पत्र आदि भेजने की क्रिया का निर्देश करने के लिए प्रयुक्त शब्द (इ-मेल बनाम स्नेल मेल)

**snake[1]** /sneɪk स्नेक्/ *noun* [C] a type of long thin animal with no legs that slides along the ground by moving its body from side to side साँप, सर्प

**snake[2]** /sneɪk स्नेक्/ *verb* [I] (*written*) to move like a snake in long curves from side to side साँप की तरह चलना; सर्पण करना

**snap[1]** /snæp स्नैप्/ *verb* (**snapping; snapped**) **1** [I, T] to break or be broken suddenly, usually with a sharp noise अचानक कुछ तोड़ देना या टूट जाना (प्रायः तेज़ आवाज़ के साथ) चटकाना या चटकना, तड़काना या तड़कना *The branch snapped.* ○ *I snapped my shoelace when I was tying it.* **2** [I, T] to move or be moved into a particular position, especially with a sharp noise एक विशेष स्थिति में खिसकाना या खिसकना (विशेषतः तेज़ आवाज़ के साथ) *She snapped the bag shut and walked out.* **3** [I, T] **snap (sth) (at sb)** to speak or say sth in a quick angry way भड़क कर बोलना या कुछ कहना *Why do you always snap at me?* **4** [I] to try to bite sb/sth किसी को काटने की कोशिश करना *The dog snapped at the child's hand.* **5** [I, T] (*informal*) to take a quick photograph of sb/sth किसी का जल्दी से फ़ोटो खींचना *A tourist snapped the plane as it crashed.* **6** [I] to suddenly be unable to control your feelings any longer अचानक मनोभावों पर नियंत्रण न रह जाना *Suddenly something just snapped and I lost my temper with him.* **IDM snap your fingers** to make a sharp noise by moving your middle finger quickly against your thumb, especially when you want to attract sb's attention चुटकी बजाना (विशेषतः किसी का ध्यान खींचने के लिए)

**PHR V** **snap sth up** to buy or take sth quickly, especially because it is very cheap किसी चीज़ को लपक कर ख़रीद लेना या ले लेना (विशेषतः सस्ती होने के कारण)

**snap²** /snæp स्नैप्/ *noun* **1** [C] a sudden sharp sound of sth breaking किसी वस्तु के एकाएक टूटने से उत्पन्न तेज़ आवाज़; चिटक, चिटका, तड़क **2** (*also* **snapshot** /ˈsnæpʃɒt ˈस्नैप्शॉट्/) [C] a photograph that is taken quickly and in an informal way आनन-फ़ानन में चलते-चलते लिया गया फ़ोटो **3** [U] (*BrE*) a card game where players call out 'Snap' when two cards that are the same are put down by different players ताश का विशेष खेल (जिसमें खिलाड़ी बोलते है 'स्नैप' जब अलग-अलग खिलाड़ी एक जैसे दो पत्ते फेंकते हैं)

**snap³** /snæp स्नैप्/ *adj.* (*informal*) (*only before a noun*) done quickly and suddenly, often without any careful thought एकाएक जल्दबाज़ी से किया गया (प्रायः बिना सोचे-समझे) *a snap decision/judgement*

**snare** /sneə(r) स्नेअ(र्)/ *noun* [C] a device (**trap**) used to catch birds or small animals पक्षियों या छोटे पशुओं को फँसाने का जाल; फंदा ▶ **snare** *verb* [T] (पशु या पक्षी को) जाल में फँसाना

**snarl** /snɑːl स्नाल्/ *verb* [I, T] **snarl (sth) (at sb)** (used about an animal) to make an angry sound while showing the teeth (पशु का) दाँत चमकाते हुए गुर्राना *The dog snarled at the stranger.* ▶ **snarl** *noun* [C, *usually sing.*] गुर्राहट

**snatch¹** /snætʃ स्नैच्/ *verb* **1** [I, T] to take sth with a quick rough movement झपटा मारकर कुछ ले लेना; झपटना, छीनना *A boy snatched her handbag and ran off.* ⇨ **grab** देखिए। **2** [T] to take or get sth quickly using the only time or chance that you have उपलब्ध समय या अवसर का उपयोग करते हुए जल्दी से कुछ ले लेना या हाथ में कर लेना या प्राप्त करना *I managed to snatch some sleep on the train.*

**PHR V** **snatch at sth** एकाएक कुछ छीनने या हथियाने की कोशिश करना *The man snatched at my wallet but I didn't let go of it.*

**snatch²** /snætʃ स्नैच्/ *noun* **1** [*sing.*] a sudden movement that sb makes when trying to take hold of sth झपट्टा, झपट (किसी वस्तु को हथियाने की कोशिश में एकाएक की गई हरकत) **2** [C, *usually pl.*] a short part or period of something किसी वस्तु का छोटा अंश या छोटी अवधि *I heard snatches of conversation from the next room.*

**sneak¹** /sniːk स्नीक्/ *verb* (*pt, pp.* **sneaked;** (*informal*) *AmE* **snuck**) **1** [I] **sneak into, out of, past, etc. sth sneak in, out, away, etc.** to go very quietly in the direction mentioned, so that no one can see or hear you आँख बचाकर चुपके-चुपके चोरी-चोरी (बताई गई दिशा में) निकल जाना *The prisoner sneaked past the guards.* ○ *He sneaked out of the house to play football.* **2** [T] (*informal*) to do or take sth secretly चोरी-छिपे कुछ करना या लेना *I tried to* **sneak a look** *at the test results in the teacher's bag.*

**PHR V** **sneak up (on sb/sth)** to go near sb very quietly, especially so that you can surprise him/her चुपके-से किसी के निकट जाना (विशेषतः उसे चौंकाने के लिए); दबे पाँव

**sneak²** /sniːk स्नीक्/ *noun* [C] (*informal*) a person, especially a child, who tells sb about the bad things sb has done किसी व्यक्ति (विशेषतः बच्चे) के द्वारा किसी की बुरी बातों या ग़लतियों के विषय में (किसी को) बताना; चुगली खाना, मुख़बिरी करना **NOTE** इस शब्द की व्यंजना निंदात्मक है।

**sneaker** /ˈsniːkə(r) ˈस्नीक(र्)/ (*AmE*) = **plimsoll, trainer¹**

**sneaking** /ˈsniːkɪŋ ˈस्नीकिङ्/ *adj.* (used about feelings) not expressed; secret (भावनाएँ) अप्रकट; गुप्त *I've a sneaking suspicion that he's lying.*

**sneer** /snɪə(r) स्निअ(र्)/ *verb* [I] **sneer (at sb/sth)** to show that you have no respect for sb/sth by the expression on your face or the way that you speak मुँह बिचकाते हुए या ताना मारते हुए किसी की हँसी उड़ाना *She sneered at his attempts to speak English.* ▶ **sneer** *noun* [C] तिरस्कार भरे शब्द; उपहास

**sneeze** /sniːz स्नीज़्/ *verb* [I] to make air come out of your nose suddenly and noisily in a way that you cannot control, for example because you have a cold (ठंड आदि के कारण) छींक मारना; छींकना *Dust makes me sneeze.* ▶ **sneeze** *noun* [C] छींक

**snide** /snaɪd स्नाइड्/ *adj.* (used about an expression or comment) critical in an unpleasant way कटु निंदात्मक (शब्द या टिप्पणी)

**sniff** /snɪf स्निफ़्/ *verb* **1** [I] to breathe air in through the nose in a way that makes a sound, especially because you have a cold or you are crying नाक से साँस खींचते हुए सूँ-सूँ करना (विशेषतः ज़ुकाम या रोग़ के कारण *Stop sniffing and blow your nose.* **2** [I, T] **sniff (at) sth** to smell sth by sniffing सूँ-सूँ करके कुछ सूँघना *The dog sniffed at the bone.* ▶ **sniff** *noun* [C] सांस लेते हुए सूंघने की क्रिया *Have a sniff of this milk and tell me if it's still all right.*

**sniffle** /ˈsnɪfl ˈस्निफ़्ल्/ *verb* [I] to make noises by breathing air suddenly up your nose, especially because you have a cold or you are crying नाक से एकाएक साँस खींचते हुए सूँ-सूँ करना (विशेषतः सर्दी लगने या रोने के कारण)

**snigger** /ˈsnɪɡə(r) ˈस्निग(र्)/ *verb* [I] **snigger (at sb/sth)** to laugh quietly and secretly in an unpleasant way किसी की खिल्ली उड़ाते हुए मुहँ दबा कर चुपके से हँसना; ठी ठी करना ▶ **snigger** *noun* [C] धीमी, अप्रिय और उपहासात्मक हँसी

**snip¹** /snɪp स्निप्/ *verb* [I, T] (**snipping; snipped**) **snip (sth) (off, out, in, etc.)** to cut using scissors, with a short quick action कैंची द्वारा तेज़ी से या झटके से काटना *He sewed on the button and snipped off the ends of the cotton.* ○ *to snip a hole in sth*

**snip²** /snɪp स्निप्/ *noun* [C] **1** a small cut made with scissors कैंची से की गई छोटी कटाई; चीरा, टुक **2** (*BrE informal*) something that is much cheaper than expected बेहद सस्ती वस्तु, मिट्टी के भाव बिकने वाली वस्तु

**sniper** /ˈsnaɪpə(r) ˈस्नाइप(र्)/ *noun* [C] a person who shoots at sb from a hidden position छिपकर गोलियाँ चलाने वाला व्यक्ति; स्नाइपर

**snippet** /ˈsnɪpɪt ˈस्निपिट्/ *noun* [C] a small piece of sth, especially information or news छोटी-सी जानकारी या ख़बर

**snivel** /ˈsnɪvl ˈस्निव्ल्/ *verb* [I] (**snivelling; snivelled** *AmE* **sniveling; sniveled**) to keep crying quietly in a way that is annoying चुपचाप रोते रहना (ऐसे कि दूसरे खीझ जाएँ)

**snob** /snɒb स्नॉब्/ *noun* [C] a person who thinks he/she is better than sb of a lower social class and who admires people who have a high social position घमंडी, अकड़ू, वर्गदंभी (जो सामाजिक स्तर में छोटों से अपने को बड़ा समझे और बड़ों की तारीफ़ करे) ▶ **snobbish** *adj.* दंभपूर्ण, घमंड भरा ▶ **snobbishly** *adv.* दंभपूर्वक, घमंड से ▶ **snobbishness** *noun* [U] घमंडीपन, घमंड, दंभ

**snobbery** /ˈsnɒbəri ˈस्नॉबरि/ *noun* [U] behaviour or attitudes typical of people who think they are better than other people in society, for example because they have more money, better education, etc. दंभ, घमंड, वर्गदंभ (धन, शिक्षा आदि में बेहतर होने के कारण समाज में अपने को दूसरों से ऊँचा मानने की मनोवृत्ति या आचरण)

**snooker** /ˈsnuːkə(r) ˈस्नूक(र्)/ *noun* [U] a game in which two players try to hit a number of coloured balls into pockets at the edges of a large table using a long stick (**cue**) स्नूकर (का खेल, जिसमें दो खिलाड़ी रंग-बिरंगी गेंदों को, मेज़ के कोनों पर बनी जेबों में, लंबी छड़ी से ठेलकर, डालने की कोशिश करते हैं) *to play snooker* ➪ **billiards** और **pool** देखिए।

**snoop** /snuːp स्नूप्/ *verb* [I] **snoop (around); snoop (on sb)** to look around secretly and without permission in order to find out information, etc. ताक-झाँक करना (कुछ पता लगाने के लिए, लुक-छिप कर और बिना अनुमति के इधर-उधर देखना) *She suspected that her neighbours visited just to snoop on her.*

**snooty** /ˈsnuːti ˈस्नूटि/ *adj.* (*informal*) acting in a rude way because you think you are better than other people घमंडी, अकड़ू, दंभी, अहम्मन्य (अपने आपको दूसरों से बड़ा समझने के कारण असभ्य या रूखा व्यवहार करने वाला)

**snooze** /snuːz स्नूज़्/ *verb* [I] (*informal*) to have a short sleep, especially during the day झपकी लेना (विशेषतः दिन में) ▶ **snooze** *noun* [C, *usually sing.*] झपकी *I had a bit of a snooze on the train.* ➪ **nap** देखिए।

**snore** /snɔː(r) स्नॉ(र्)/ *verb* [I] to breathe noisily through your nose and mouth while you are asleep (सोते समय) खर्राटे भरना ▶ **snore** *noun* [C] खर्राटा *He's got the loudest snore I've ever heard.*

**snorkel** /ˈsnɔːkl ˈस्नॉकल्/ *noun* [C] a short tube that a person swimming just below the surface of the water can use to breathe through गोताख़ोर द्वारा गोता लगाते समय साँस लेने के लिए प्रयुक्त उपकरण; नली **NOTE** इस प्रकार (नली से साँस लेते हुए गोताख़ोर के) तैरने को **go snorkelling** कहते हैं।

**snort** /snɔːt स्नॉट्/ *verb* [I] **1** (used about animals) to make a noise by blowing air through the nose and mouth (पशुओं का) फुफकारना (नाक और मुँह से हवा निकालते हुए आवाज़ करना) **2** (used about people) to blow out air noisily as a way of showing that you do not like sth, or that you are impatient (व्यक्तियों का) फुफकारना (अपनी नापसंदी या अधीरता प्रकट करने के लिए) ▶ **snort** *noun* [C] फुफकार, फुँकार

**snot** /snɒt स्नॉट्/ *noun* [U] (*informal*) the liquid produced by the nose रेंट; नाक से निकलने वाला तरल पदार्थ

**snout** /snaʊt स्नाउट्/ *noun* [C] the long nose of certain animals पशुओं की थूथन; थुथनी (लंबी नाक, लंबे मुँह का आगे को निकला हुआ भाग) *a pig's snout*

**snow¹** /snəʊ स्नो/ *noun* [U] small, soft, white pieces of frozen water that fall from the sky in cold weather हिम, बर्फ़ (आकाश से गिरने वाले जमे हुए जल के छोटे, कोमल, सफ़ेद टुकड़े) *Three centimetres of snow fell during the night.* ➪ **weather** पर नोट देखिए।

**snow²** /snəʊ स्नो/ *verb* [I] (used about snow) to fall from the sky (बर्फ़ का) आकाश से गिरना; हिमपात होना *It snowed all night.*

**snowball[1]** /ˈsnəʊbɔːl ˈस्नोबॉल्/ *noun* [C] a lump of snow that is pressed into the shape of a ball and used by children for playing बर्फ़ का गोला (जिससे बच्चे खेलते हैं)

**snowball[2]** /ˈsnəʊbɔːl ˈस्नोबॉल्/ *verb* [I] to quickly grow bigger and bigger or more and more important तेज़ी से अधिकाधिक बढ़ना, फैलना या महत्त्वपूर्ण (एवं विचारणीय) हो जाना

**snowboard** /ˈsnəʊbɔːd ˈस्नोबॉड्/ *noun* [C] a type of board that you fasten to both your feet and use for moving down mountains that are covered with snow हिमाच्छादित पर्वतों पर पैरों में बाँधकर चलने के लिए प्रयुक्त, विशेष प्रकार का फट्टा; स्नोबोर्ड ➪ **skateboard** पर चित्र देखिए ▶ **snowboarding** *noun* [U] स्नोबोर्ड पहनकर बर्फ़ पर चलना *Have you ever been snowboarding?*

**snowdrift** /ˈsnəʊdrɪft ˈस्नोड्रिफ़्ट्/ *noun* [C] a deep pile of snow that has been made by the wind हवा चलने से बना हिम का बड़ा ढेर; हिमसंचय *The car got stuck in a snowdrift.*

**snowdrop** /ˈsnəʊdrɒp ˈस्नोड्रॉप्/ *noun* [C] a type of small white flower that appears at the end of winter गुलचाँदनी (का फूल जो शरद ऋतु के अंत में खिलता है)

**snowed in** *adj.* not able to leave home or travel because the snow is too deep घर में अवरुद्ध (भारी हिमपात के कारण)

**snowed under** *adj.* with more work, etc. than you can deal with क्षमता से अधिक व्यस्त (काम का बोझ लिए हुए आदि)

**snowfall** /ˈsnəʊfɔːl ˈस्नोफ़ॉल्/ *noun* **1** [C] the snow that falls on one occasion हिमपात, बर्फ़बारी *heavy snowfalls* **2** [U] the amount of snow that falls in a particular place हिमपात की मात्रा (स्थान-विशेष पर)

**snowflake** /ˈsnəʊfleɪk ˈस्नोफ़्लेक्/ *noun* [C] one of the small, soft, white pieces of frozen water that fall together as snow बर्फ़ के छोटे हलके कण; हिम-कण, हिमलव

**snowman** /ˈsnəʊmæn ˈस्नोमैन्/ *noun* [C] (*pl.* **-men** /-men -मेन्/) the figure of a person made out of snow बर्फ़ से बना आदमी का पुतला

**snowplough** (*AmE* **snowplow**) /ˈsnəʊplaʊ ˈस्नोप्लाउ/ *noun* [C] a vehicle that is used to clear snow away from roads or railways सड़कों या पटरियों पर से बर्फ़ हटाने वाली (हलयुक्त) गाड़ी; हिम-हल ➪ **plough** देखिए।

**snowy** /ˈsnəʊi ˈस्नोइ/ *adj.* with a lot of snow बर्फ़ीला, हिमाच्छादित, बर्फ़ानी *snowy weather* ○ *a snowy scene*

**Snr** (*also* **Sr**) *abbr.* (*especially AmE*) Senior सीनियर

**snub** /snʌb स्नब्/ *verb* [T] (**snubbing; snubbed**) to treat sb rudely, for example by refusing to look at or speak to him/her (किसी से) रूखा बरताव करना (जैसे, उसकी ओर नज़र न डालना या उससे बात न करना) ▶ **snub** *noun* [C] रूखा बरताव

**snuck** /snʌk स्नक्/ (*informal*) ➪ **sneak[1]** का past tense और past participle रूप

**snuff** /snʌf स्नफ़्/ *noun* [U] (especially in past times) tobacco which people breathe up into the nose in the form of a powder सूँघनी (तंबाकू का चूरा जिसे लोग सूँघते हैं) (पूर्व समय में प्रचलित)

**snuffle** /ˈsnʌfl ˈस्नफ़्ल्/ *verb* [I] (used about people and animals) to make a noise through your nose (व्यक्तियों और पशुओं का) सूँ-सूँ करना (नाक से आवाज़ करना)

**snug** /snʌg स्नग्/ *adj.* **1** warm and comfortable हलका गरम और आरामदेह *a snug little room* ○ *The children were snug in bed.* **2** fitting sb/sth closely कसा हुआ; चुस्त *Adjust the safety belt to give a snug fit.* ▶ **snugly** *adv.* चुस्ती से, आरामदेह होते हुए

**snuggle** /ˈsnʌgl ˈस्नगल्/ *verb* [I] **snuggle (up to sb); snuggle (up/down)** to get into a position that makes you feel safe, warm and comfortable, usually next to another person किसी से सटकर बैठना, छाती से लगना आदि (सुरक्षा, गरमी और आराम के अनुभव के लिए) *She snuggled up to her mother.* ○ *I snuggled down under the blanket to get warm.*

**so[1]** /səʊ सो/ *adv.* **1** used to emphasize an adjective or adverb, especially when this produces a particular result किसी विशेषण या क्रियाविशेषण पर बल देने के लिए प्रयुक्त (विशेषतः जब विशिष्ट प्रतिक्रिया का निर्देश करना हो), इतना, बहुत *She's so ill (that) she can't get out of bed.* ○ *He was driving so fast that he couldn't stop.* ➪ **such** पर नोट देखिए। **2** used in negative sentences for comparing people or things व्यक्तियों या वस्तुओं की तुलना करने के लिए निषेधवाचक वाक्यों में प्रयुक्त *She's not so clever as we thought.* **3** used in place of something that has been said already, to avoid repeating it पूर्व कथित बात को निर्दिष्ट करने के लिए प्रयुक्त (पुनः कथन से बचने के लिए) *'I failed, didn't I?' 'I'm afraid so.'*

**NOTE** औपचारिक शैली में, शब्द **do** के साथ शब्द **so** का प्रयोग करके, पूर्वकथित क्रिया-व्यापार का निर्देश किया जा सकता है—*He asked me to write to him and* ***I did so*** (= I wrote to him).

**4** (*not with verbs in the negative*) also, too भी, और भी *He's a teacher and* ***so is*** *his wife.* ○ *I like singing and* ***so does*** *Heena.* **NOTE** निषेधवाचक वाक्यों के लिए **neither** की प्रविष्टि देखिए। **5** used to show that you agree that sth is true, especially when you are surprised किसी बात पर सहमति व्यक्त करने के लिए प्रयुक्त (विशेषतः जब बात कुछ आश्चर्यजनक लगे), *'It's getting late.' 'So it is. We'd better go.'* **6** (*formal*) (used when you are showing sb sth) in this way; like this (जब किसी को कुछ दिखाने की बात हो) इस ढंग से; इस प्रकार, ऐसे *Fold the paper in two diagonally,* ***like so.***

IDM **and so on (and so forth)** used at the end of a list to show that it continues in the same way वस्तुओं की सूची के अंत में प्रयुक्त (सूची के समाप्त न होने का निर्देश करने के लिए); इत्यादि *They sell pens, pencils, paper and so on.*

**I told you so** used to tell sb that he/she should have listened to your advice किसी को यह कहने के लिए प्रयुक्त कि उन्हें आपकी सलाह मान लेनी चाहिए थी *'I missed the bus.' 'I told you so. I said you needed to leave earlier.'*

**it (just) so happens** (used to introduce a surprising fact) by chance (अचानक हो जाने वाली बात या कोई आश्चर्यजनक तथ्य बताने के लिए प्रयुक्त) संयोगवश; इत्तफ़ाक़ से, अचानक, अकस्मात *It just so happened that we were going the same way, so he gave me a lift.*

**just so** ➪ **just[1]** देखिए।

**or so** (used to show that a number, time, etc. is not exact) approximately; about (किसी संख्या, समय आदि के बिलकुल निश्चित न होने का संकेत करने के लिए प्रयुक्त) लगभग; के आस-पास *A hundred or so people came to the meeting.*

**so as to do sth** with the intention of doing sth; in order to do sth कुछ करने की मंशा से; ताकि कुछ किया जा सके

**so much for** used for saying that sth was not helpful or successful किसी बात की व्यर्थता या विफलता का संकेत करने के लिए प्रयुक्त *So much for that diet! I didn't lose any weight at all.*

**that is so** (*formal*) that is true यह सच है, बात ठीक है, बिलकुल ठीक

**so[2]** /səʊ सो/ *conj.* **1** with the result that; therefore नतीजा यह कि; नतीजतन, परिणामस्वरूप; इसलिए *She felt very tired so she went to bed early.* **2 so (that)** with the purpose that; in order that इस प्रयोजन से कि; इसलिए कि, ताकि *She wore dark glasses so (that) nobody would recognize her.* **3** used to show how one part of a story follows another कहानी में 'आगे क्या' के संकेत के लिए प्रयुक्त (कहानी के अंशों की अनुक्रमिकता बताने के लिए प्रयुक्त) *So what happened next?*

IDM **so what?** (*informal*) (showing that you think sth is not important) Who cares? तो क्या हुआ?, चिंता मत करो (किसी बात के महत्त्पूर्ण न होने का संकेत करने के लिए प्रयुक्त) *'It's late.' 'So what? We don't have to go to school tomorrow.'*

**soak** /səʊk सोक्/ *verb* **1** [I, T] to become or make sth completely wet पूरी तरह भीग जाना या भिगो देना *Leave the dishes to soak for a while.* **2** [I] **soak into/through sth; soak in** (used about a liquid) to pass into or through sth (तरल पदार्थ का) किसी वस्तु में या में से जाना; तरबतर होना *Blood had soaked through the bandage.*

PHR V **soak sth up** to take sth in (especially a liquid) सोखना (विशेषतः द्रव को), चूसना, जज़्ब करना *I soaked the water up with a cloth.*

**soaked** /səʊkt सोक्ट्/ *adj.* (*not before a noun*) extremely wet पूरी तरह भीगा हुआ; तरबतर *I got* ***soaked*** *waiting for my bus in the rain.*

**soaking** /ˈsəʊkɪŋ ˈसोकिङ्/ (*also* **soaking wet**) *adj.* extremely wet पूरी तरह भीगा हुआ; तरबतर

**so-and-so** *noun* [C] (*pl.* **so-and-sos**) (*informal*) **1** a person who is not named अमुक, फ़लाँ, ढिमाका *Imagine a Mrs So-and-so telephones. What would you say?* **2** a person that you do not like व्यक्ति जो आपको पसंद न हो; फ़लाँ-फ़लाँ, अमुक-अमुक, फ़लाना-ढिमाका *He's a bad-tempered old so-and-so.*

**soap** /səʊp सोप्/ *noun* [U] a substance that you use for washing and cleaning साबुन *He washed his hands with soap.* ○ *a bar of soap* ▶ **soapy** *adj.* साबुन जैसा; झागदार, साबुनी

**soap opera** (*informal* **soap**) *noun* [C] a story about the lives and problems of a group of people which continues several times a week on television or radio टीवी या रेडियो पर धारावाहिक रूप में प्रसारित कहानी (किसी सामाजिक वर्ग के जीवन और समस्याओं पर आधारित) ➪ **opera** देखिए।

**soar** /sɔː(r) सॉ(र्)/ *verb* [I] **1** to fly high in the air हवा में ऊँचे उड़ना **2** to rise very fast बहुत तेज़ी से बढ़ना *Prices are soaring because of inflation.*

**sob** /sɒb सॉब्/ *verb* [I] (**so<u>bb</u>ing; so<u>bb</u>ed**) to cry while taking in sudden, sharp breaths; to speak while you are crying छोटे-छोटे साँस भरते हुए रोना, सिसकना; सिसकते हुए कुछ कहना *The child was sobbing because he'd lost his toy.* ▶ **sob** *noun* [C] सिसकी *It was heartbreaking to listen to her sobs.*

**sober[1]** /ˈsəʊbə(r) ˈसोब(र्)/ *adj.* **1** (of a person) not affected by alcohol (व्यक्ति) अमत्त, न पिए हुए; सौम्य *He'd been drunk the first time he'd met her, but this time he was* ***stone-cold sober.*** **2** not funny; serious मज़ाकिया नहीं; गंभीर *a sober expression* ○ *Her death is a sober reminder of just how* *dangerous drugs can be.* **3** (of a colour) not bright or likely to be noticed (रंग) चमकीला या भड़कीला नहीं; सौम्य *a sober grey suit*

**sober²** /ˈsəʊbə(r) ˈसोब(र्)/ *verb*

**PHR V** **sober (sb) up** to become or make sb become normal again after being affected by alcohol मदिरा के प्रभाव से मुक्त हो जाना या मुक्त करना *I need a cup of black coffee to sober me up.*

**sobering** /ˈsəʊbərɪŋ ˈसोबरिङ्/ *adj.* making you feel serious सोचने के लिए विवश करने वाला *It is a* ***sobering thought*** *that over 25 million people have been killed in car accidents.*

**Soc.** *abbr.* Society सोसाइटी *Housing Soc.*

**so-called** *adj.* **1** used to show that the words you describe sb/sth with are not correct किसी के विषय में किया गया कथन सत्य या उपयुक्त नहीं यह बताने के लिए प्रयुक्त; तथाकथित *Her so-called friends only wanted her money.* **2** used to show that a special name has been given to sb/sth किसी के विशेष नाम का संकेत करने के लिए प्रयुक्त

**soccer** /ˈsɒkə(r) ˈसॉक(र्)/ (*AmE*) = **football¹**

**sociable** /ˈsəʊʃəbl ˈसोशब्ल्/ *adj.* enjoying being with other people; friendly जिसे लोगों से मिलना-जुलना अच्छा लगे; मिलनसार, प्यार-मुहब्बत वाला

**social** /ˈsəʊʃl ˈसोशल्/ *adj.* **1** connected with society and the way it is organized समाज और सामाजिक ढाँचे से संबंधित; सामाजिक, समाज-मूलक *social problems/issues/reforms* **2** concerning the position of people in society समाज में लोगों की स्थिति से संबंधित; सामाजिक *We share the same social background.* **3** connected with meeting people and enjoying yourself लोगों से मिलने और मौज-मस्ती करने से संबंधित *She has a busy* ***social life.*** ○ *Children develop their* ***social skills in*** *school.* **4** (used about animals) living in groups (पशु) समूहों में रहने वाले; यूथचर ▶ **socially** /-ʃəli -शलि/ *adv.* सामाजिक रूप से *We work together but I don't know him socially.*

**social democracy** *noun* [U, C] a political system that combines the principles of one system (**socialism**) with the greater personal freedom of another system (**democracy**); a country that has this political system of government समाजवाद और लोकतंत्र की समुचित राजनीतिक व्यवस्था, समाजवादी लोकतंत्र; समाजवादी लोकतांत्रिक देश

**social democrat** *noun* [C] समाजवादी लोकतंत्र का समर्थक

**socialism** /ˈsəʊʃəlɪzəm ˈसोशलिज़म्/ *noun* [U] the political idea that is based on the belief that all people are equal and that money and property should be equally divided समाजवाद; धन और संपत्ति के वितरण में समाज के सब सदस्यों को समान मानने की राजनीतिक विचारधारा ➪ **communism, Marxism** और **capitalism** देखिए। ▶ **socialist** *adj., noun* [C] समाजवादी *socialist beliefs/policies/writers*

**social science** *noun* [C, U] the study of people in society सामाजिक विज्ञान समाज का वैज्ञानिक अध्ययन

**social services** *noun* [*pl.*] a group of services organized by local government to help people who have money or family problems निर्धन और पारिवारिक समस्याओं से ग्रस्त लोगों के लिए स्थानीय शासन द्वारा उपलब्ध कराई गई विविध सेवाएँ; सामाजिक सेवाएँ

**social work** *noun* [U] paid work that involves giving help and advice to people living in the community who have financial or family problems वेतन लेकर किया गया समाज सेवा का काम (आर्थिक और पारिवारिक समस्याओं से ग्रस्त लोगों को सहायता और परामर्श देना); सामाजिक कार्य

**social worker** *noun* [C] a person whose job is **social work** वैतनिक सामाजिक कार्यकर्ता; वैतनिक समाज सेवक

**society** /səˈsaɪəti सˈसाइअटि/ *noun* (*pl.* **societies**) **1** [C, U] the people in a country or area, thought of as a group, who have shared customs and laws समाज (किसी देश या क्षेत्र के लोग जिन्हें एक समूह माना जाए और जिनकी प्रथाएँ और क़ानून साझे हों) *a civilized society* ○ *The role of men* ***in society*** *is changing.* **2** [C] an organization of people who share a particular interest or purpose; a club विशेष अभिरुचि या प्रयोजन की दृष्टि से समानधर्मी लोगों की संस्था; क्लब, सोसाइटी *a drama society*

**socio-** /ˈsəʊsiəʊ ˈसोसिओ/ *prefix* (*used in nouns, adjectives and adverbs*) connected with society or the study of society समाज या समाजशास्त्र से संबंधित; समाज- (जैसे समाज-भाष्यशास्त्र) *socio-economic* ○ *sociolinguistics*

**sociologist** /ˌsəʊsiˈɒlədʒɪst ˌसोसिˈऑलजिस्ट्/ *noun* [C] a student of or an expert in sociology समाजशास्त्री; समाजशास्त्र का अध्येता या विशेषज्ञ

**sociology** /ˌsəʊsiˈɒlədʒi ˌसोसिˈऑलजि/ *noun* [U] the study of human societies and social behaviour समाजशास्त्र; मानव समाजों और सामाजिक व्यवहार का अध्ययन ▶ **sociological** /ˌsəʊsiəˈlɒdʒɪkl ˌसोसिअˈलॉजिक्ल्/ *adj.* समाजशास्त्र-विषयक, समाजशास्त्रीय

**sock** /sɒk सॉक्/ *noun* [C] a piece of clothing that you wear on your foot and lower leg, inside your shoe मोज़ा, ज़ुराब *a pair of socks*

IDM **pull your socks up** (*BrE*) to start working harder or better than before पहले से अधिक मेहनत या बढ़िया करने लगना

**socket** /ˈsɒkɪt ˈसॉकिट/ *noun* [C] **1** (*also* **power point**) (*informal* **plug**) a place in a wall where a piece of electrical equipment can be connected to the electricity supply सॉकेट, प्लग (दीवार में स्थान जहाँ किसी बिजली के पुरज़े को विद्युत आपूर्ति से जोड़ा जाए) **2** a hole in a piece of electrical equipment where another piece of equipment can be connected बिजली के किसी पुरज़े में वह छेद जहाँ दूसरा पुरज़ा जोड़ा जा सके **3** a hole that sth fits into कोई छेद, विवर या कोटर जिसमें कुछ फ़िट हो जाए *your eye socket*

**soda** /ˈsəʊdə ˈसोडा/ *noun* **1** (*also* **soda water**) [U] water that has bubbles in it and is usually used for mixing with other drinks सोडा (बुलबुलेदार विशेष पानी जिसे अन्य पेयों के साथ मिलाया जा सकता है) *a whisky and soda* **2** [C] (*AmE*) = **fizzy drink** ➪ **caustic soda** देखिए।

**sodium** /ˈsəʊdiəm ˈसोडिअम्/ *noun* [U] (*symbol* **Na**) a soft silver-white metal that is found naturally only in chemical mixtures (**compounds**), such as salt सोडियम (नरम और चाँदी जैसी शुभ्र धातु जो प्राकृतिक रूप में केवल रासायनिक यौगिकों, जैसे नमक में पाई जाती है)

**sodium bicarbonate** (*also* **bicarbonate of soda; baking soda**) *noun* [U] (*symbol* **$NaHCO_3$**) a white powder that is used in baking to make cakes, etc. rise and become light सोडियम बाइ-कार्बोनेट (केक आदि को फुलाने और हलका करने के लिए प्रयुक्त एक सफ़ेद पाउडर)

**sodium carbonate** (*also* **washing soda**) *noun* [U] (*symbol* **$Na_2CO_3$**) a chemical compound in the form of white **crystals** or powder that is used in making glass, soap and paper, and for making hard water soft सोडियम कार्बोनेट (एक सफ़ेद रवेदार रासायनिक यौगिक जो काँच, साबुन, काग़ज़ आदि बनाने में तथा भारी पानी को हलका करने में प्रयुक्त होता है)

**sodium chloride** *noun* [U] (*symbol* **NaCl**) common salt (a chemical compound of **sodium** and **chlorine**) खाने का नमक, सादा नमक (सोडियम और क्लोरीन का रासायनिक यौगिक)

**sofa** /ˈsəʊfə ˈसोफ़ा/ *noun* [C] a comfortable seat with a back and arms for two or more people to sit on सोफ़ा *a sofa bed* (= a sofa that you can open out to make a bed) ✪ पर्याय **settee**

**soft** /sɒft सॉफ़्ट्/ *adj.* **1** not hard or firm कठोर या पक्का नहीं; कोमल, नरम, मुलायम *a soft bed/seat* ○ *The ground is very soft after all that rain.* ✪ विलोम **hard** **2** smooth and pleasant to touch; not rough छूने में चिकना और सुहाना लगने वाला; खुरदरा या रूखा नहीं, मसृण *soft skin/hands* ○ *a soft towel* ✪ विलोम **rough** **3** (used about sounds, voices, words, etc.) quiet or gentle; not loud or angry (ध्वनियाँ, स्वर, शब्द आदि) मंद या हलका; ऊँचा या आवेश पूर्ण नहीं, सौम्य *She spoke in a soft whisper.* ✪ विलोम **loud** या **harsh** **4** (used about light, colours etc.) gentle and pleasant (प्रकाश, रंग आदि) हलका और सुहाना *The room was decorated in soft pinks and greens.* ✪ विलोम **bright** **5** (used about people) kind and gentle, sometimes too much so (व्यक्ति) दयालु और सज्जन, कभी-कभी अत्यधिक कोमल प्रकृति का *A good manager can't afford to be too soft.* ✪ विलोम **hard** या **strict** **6** (used about water) not containing mineral salts and therefore good for washing as soap will make a lot of bubbles (जल) खनिज लवणों से रहित (और इसलिए उससे कपड़े धोना आसान); नरम ✪ विलोम **hard**
▶ **softly** *adv.* हलके से, कोमलता से *He closed the door softly behind him.* ▶ **softness** *noun* [U] कोमलता, सौम्यता, चिकनापन

IDM **have a soft spot for sb/sth** (*informal*) to have good or loving feelings towards sb/sth किसी के लिए अनुकूलता या स्नेह होना

**soft drink** *noun* [C] a cold drink that contains no alcohol (ऐलकोहल रहित) शीतल पेय

**soft drug** *noun* [C] an illegal drug, such as **cannabis**, that some people take for pleasure, that is not considered very harmful or likely to cause **addiction** भाँग जैसी ग़ैर-क़ानूनी, हलका नशीला पदार्थ (जिसे लोग केवल मज़े के लिए पीते हैं और जो अधिक हानि नहीं करता या जिसकी लत नहीं लगती) ➪ **hard drug** देखिए।

**soften** /ˈsɒfn ˈसॉफ़्न्/ *verb* **1** [I, T] to become softer or gentler; to make sb/sth softer or gentler अधिक कोमल या सौम्य हो जाना; किसी को अधिक कोमल या सौम्य बना देना *a lotion to soften the skin* **2** [T] to make sth less strong and unpleasant किसी को नरम बना देना (उग्रता और कटुता को कम कर देना) *The air bag softened the impact of the crash.*

**soft fruit** *noun* [C, U] small fruits without a large seed inside or hard skin छोटे फल (छोटे बीज या नरम छिलके वाले) *raspberries, strawberries and other soft fruits*

**soft-hearted** *adj.* kind and good at understanding other people's feelings दयालु और दूसरों की भावनाओं का सम्मान करने वाला; कोमल हृदय ✪ विलोम **hard-hearted**

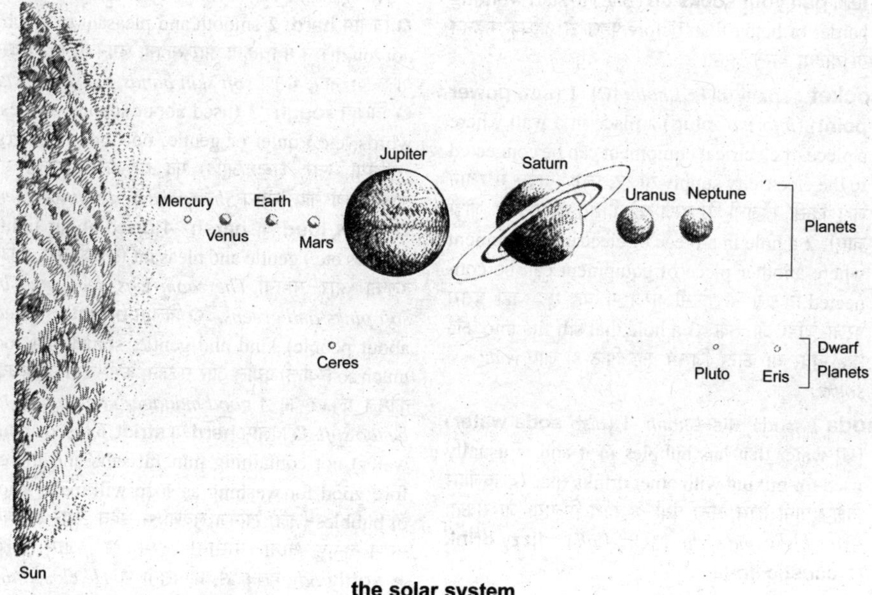


the solar system

**soft option** *noun* [C] the easier thing to do of two or more possibilities, but not the best one अधिक आसान (न कि सर्वोत्तम) विकल्प *The government has taken the soft option of agreeing to their demands.*

**soft-spoken** *adj.* having a gentle, quiet voice मृदुभाषी *He was a kind, soft-spoken man.*

**software** /ˈsɒftweə(r) ˈसॉफ़्ट्वेअ(र्)/ *noun* [U] (*computing*) the programs and other operating information used by a computer कंप्यूटर द्वारा प्रयुक्त प्रोग्राम और अन्य परिचालन संबंधी जानकारी; सॉफ़्टवेयर *There's a lot of new educational software available now.* ➪ **hardware** देखिए।

**softwood** /ˈsɒftwʊd ˈसॉफ़्ट्वुड्/ *noun* [U, C] wood that is cheap to produce and can be cut easily सस्ती और आसानी से कटने वाली लकड़ी; मृदु काष्ठ *Pine is a softwood.* ➪ **hardwood** देखिए।

**soggy** /ˈsɒgi ˈसॉगि/ *adj.* very wet and soft and so unpleasant बहुत गीली और नरम (और इसलिए परेशानी पैदा करने वाला)

**soil[1]** /sɔɪl सॉइल्/ *noun* **1** [C, U] the substance that plants, trees, etc. grow in; earth मिट्टी, धरती *poor/dry/acid/sandy soil* ➪ **ground[1]** पर नोट देखिए। **2** [U] (*written*) the land that is part of a country किसी देश की भूमि

**soil[2]** /sɔɪl सॉइल्/ *verb* [T] (*formal*) (*usually passive*) to make sth dirty मैला करना, धब्बे डालना

**solace** /ˈsɒləs ˈसॉलस्/ *noun* [U, *sing.*] (*written*) **solace (in sth)** a person or thing that makes you feel better or happier when you are sad or disappointed उदासी या निराशा के क्षणों में तसल्ली देने वाला व्यक्ति या वस्तु; सांत्वनाकारी व्यक्ति या वस्तु *to find/seek solace in sb/sth*

**solar** /ˈsəʊlə(r) ˈसोल(र्)/ *adj.* (*only before a noun*) **1** connected with the sun सूर्य से संबंधित; सौर *a solar eclipse* **2** using the sun's energy सौर ऊर्जा का प्रयोग करने संबंधी *solar heating/power* ○ *Solar panels in the roof supply the building's electricity.*

**the solar system** *noun* [*sing.*] the sun and the planets that move around it सूर्य और उसकी परिक्रमा करने वाले ग्रह; सौर प्रणाली

**solar year** *noun* [C] (*technical*) the time it takes the earth to go around the sun once, approximately 365 ¼ days पृथ्वी का सूर्य की एक बार परिक्रमा करने में लगने वाला समय (लगभग 365¼ दिन); सौर वर्ष

**sold** ➪ **sell** का past tense और past participle रूप

**solder** /ˈsəʊldə(r); ˈsɒldə(r) ˈसोल्ड(र्); ˈसॉल्ड(र्)/ *verb* [T] **solder sth (to/onto sth); solder (A and B together)** to join pieces of metal or wire together using a mixture of metals which is heated and melted राँगे से धातु या तार से परस्पर जोड़ना; राँगे से टाँका लगाना ► **solder** *noun* [U] राँगे का टाँका

**soldering iron** *noun* [C] a tool that is heated and used for joining metals and wires by **soldering** them टाँका लगाने का औज़ार; कहिया

**soldier** /ˈsəʊldʒə(r) ˈसोल्ज(र्)/ *noun* [C] a member of an army थल सेना का सदस्य; थल सैनिक *The soldiers marched past.*

**sole[1]** /səʊl सोल्/ *adj.* (*only before a noun*) **1** only; single केवल; सिर्फ़; एकमात्र *His sole interest is football.* **2** belonging to one person only; not shared केवल एक व्यक्ति का या से संबंधित; साझे का नहीं; अनन्य ▶ **solely** *adv.* केवल, एकमात्र *I agreed to come solely because of your mother.*

**sole[2]** /səʊl सोल्/ *noun* **1** [C] the bottom surface of your foot पैर का तलुआ ➪ **body** पर चित्र देखिए। **2** [C] the part of a shoe or sock that covers the bottom surface of your foot जूते या मोज़े का तल्वा (जो पैर के तलुए को ढकता है) **3** [C, U] (*pl.* **sole**) a flat sea fish that we eat खाने की चपटी समुद्री मछली; कुकुरजीभी

**solemn** /ˈsɒləm ˈसॉलम्/ *adj.* **1** (used about a person) very serious; not happy or smiling (व्यक्ति) अति गंभीर; प्रसन्न वदन या मुस्कराते हुए नहीं *Her solemn face told them that the news was bad.* **2** sincere; done or said in a formal way सत्यनिष्ठ; औपचारिक या सौम्य ढंग से किया या कहा गया *to make a solemn promise* ▶ **solemnity** /səˈlemnəti सˈलेम्नटि/ *noun* [U] सत्यनिष्ठा, गंभीरता ▶ **solemnly** *adv.* गंभीरतापूर्वक, सत्यनिष्ठापूर्वक *'I have something very important to tell you,' she began solemnly.*

**solicit** /səˈlɪsɪt सˈलिसिट्/ *verb* **1** [T] (*formal*) to ask sb for money, help, support, etc. धन, सहायता, समर्थन आदि माँगना *They tried to solicit support for the proposal.* **2** [I, T] (used about a woman who has sex for money) to go to sb, especially in a public place, and offer sex in return for money (वेश्या द्वारा) ग्राहक को पटाना (पैसे के बदले यौन-क्रिया के लिए स्वयं को पेश करना)

**solicitor** /səˈlɪsɪtə(r) सˈलिसिटर्(र्)/ *noun* [C] a lawyer whose job is to give legal advice, prepare legal documents and arrange the buying and selling of land, etc. क़ानूनी परामर्श देने, क़ानूनी दस्तावेज़ तैयार करने, ज़मीन ख़रीदवाने और बिकवाने आदि का काम करने वाला वकील; सॉलिसिटर ➪ **lawyer** पर नोट देखिए।

**solid[1]** /ˈsɒlɪd ˈसॉलिड्/ *adj.* **1** hard and firm; not in the form of liquid or gas कड़ा और पक्का; द्रव या गैस नहीं, ठोस *It was so cold that the village pond had* ***frozen solid****.* **2** having no holes or empty spaces inside; not hollow जिसके अंदरूनी भाग में छेद या खाली स्थान न हो; खोखला नहीं, घनीभूत, सघन *a solid mass of rock* **3** strong, firm and well made मज़बूत, पक्का और बनावट में सुंदर *a solid little car* ○ (*figurative*) *a solid friendship* **4** of good enough quality; that you can trust पर्याप्त गुणवत्ता युक्त, ऊँचे दर्जे का; विश्वसनीय, भरोसेमंद *The police cannot make an arrest without solid evidence.* **5** (*only before a noun*) made completely of one substance, both on the inside and outside (अंदर और बाहर दोनों तरफ़ से) पूर्णतया केवल एक वस्तु से बना हुआ; सुसंहत, ठोस *a* ***solid gold*** *chain* **6** (*spoken*) without a break or pause बिना अंतराल या रुकावट; अविच्छिन्न, निरंतर *I was so tired that I slept for twelve solid hours/twelve hours solid.* ▶ **solidity** /səˈlɪdəti सˈलिडटि/ *noun* [U] घनता, ठोसपन

**solid[2]** /ˈsɒlɪd ˈसॉलिड्/ *noun* [C] **1** a substance or object that is hard; not a liquid or gas ठोस पदार्थ या वस्तु; द्रव या गैस नहीं *Liquids become solids when frozen.* ○ *The baby is not yet on solids* (= solid food). **2** an object that has length, width and height, not a flat shape लंबाई, चौड़ाई और ऊँचाई (तीनों आयामों) वाली (न कि चौरस आकृति की) वस्तु; त्रि-आयामी वस्तु *A cube is a solid.*

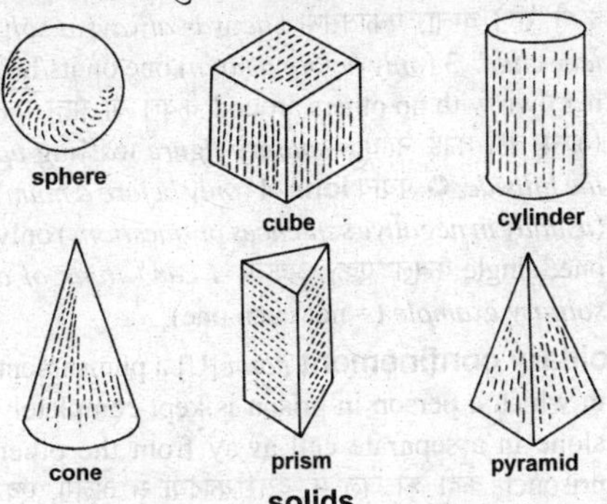

solids

**solidarity** /ˌsɒlɪˈdærəti ˌसॉलिˈडैरटि/ *noun* [U] **solidarity (with sb)** the support of one group of people for another, because they agree with their aims (उद्देश्यों की समानता के आधार पर) एक वर्ग का दूसरे वर्ग को समर्थन, दो वर्गों की एकजुटता

**solidify** /səˈlɪdɪfaɪ सˈलिडिफ़ाइ/ *verb* [I] (*pres. part.* **solidifying**; *3rd person sing. pres.* **solidifies**; *pt, pp* **solidified**) to become hard or solid कड़ा या ठोस हो जाना

**solidly** /ˈsɒlɪdli ˈसॉलिड्लि/ *adv.* **1** strongly मज़बूती से *a solidly built house* **2** without stopping बिना रुके, लगातार *It rained solidly all day.*

**soliloquy** /səˈlɪləkwi सˈलिलक्वि/ *noun* [C, U] (*pl.* **soliloquies**) a speech in a play in which a character, who is alone on the stage, speaks his/her thoughts aloud; the act of speaking thoughts aloud in this way स्वगत कथन (नाटक में, मंच पर

उपस्थित पात्र का अपने आप से ऊँचे स्वर में बात करना); स्वगत कथन की क्रिया *Hamlet's famous soliloquy, 'To be or not to be...'* ➪ **monologue** देखिए। ▶ **soliloquize** (*also* **-ise**) /səˈlɪləkwaɪz सˈलिलक्वाइज़्/ *verb* [I] स्वगत कथन करना

**solitaire** /ˌsɒlɪˈteə(r) ˌसॉलिˈटेअ(र्)/ *noun* [U] **1** a game for one person in which you remove pieces from a special board by moving other pieces over them until you have only one piece left एक व्यक्ति द्वारा खेले जाने वाला शतरंज जैसा खेल (जिसमें बोर्ड या बिसात पर मोहरे ऐसे चले जाते हैं कि काटा-काटी के बाद अंत में एक मोहरा बचता है) **2** (*AmE*) = **patience**[2] **3** [C] a single precious stone especially a diamond एक बहुमूल्य पत्थर विशेषतः हीरा *a diamond solitaire*

**solitary** /ˈsɒlətri ˈसॉलट्रि/ *adj.* **1** done alone, without other people एक व्यक्ति द्वारा अकेले किया गया (बिना साथी के) *Writing novels is a solitary occupation.* **2** (used about a person or an animal) enjoying being alone; frequently spending time alone (व्यक्ति या पशु) एकांतप्रेमी; अकेले समय-यापन करते रहने वाला, एकांतसेवी *She was always a solitary child.* **3** (*only before a noun*) one on its/his/her own with no others around केवल या मात्र एक (अन्य वहाँ कोई नहीं) *a solitary figure walking up the hillside* ✪ पर्याय **lone** **4** (*only before a noun*) (*usually in negative sentences or questions*) only one; single केवल एक; अकेला *I can't think of a solitary example* (= not even one).

**solitary confinement** *noun* [U] a punishment in which a person in prison is kept completely alone in a separate cell away from the other prisoners क़ैदी को जेल में, दूसरे क़ैदियों से अलग, एक कोठरी में पूर्णतया अकेले रखे जाने की सज़ा; एकांत क़ैद, क़ैद तनहाई

**solitude** /ˈsɒlɪtjuːd ˈसॉलिट्यूड्/ *noun* [U] the state of being alone, especially when you find this pleasant अकेलापन, एकाकीपन (विशेषतः अच्छा लगने वाला) *She longed for peace and solitude.* ➪ **loneliness** और **isolation** देखिए।

**solo**[1] /ˈsəʊləʊ ˈसोलो/ *noun* [C] (*pl.* **solos**) a piece of music for only one person to play or sing केवल एक व्यक्ति द्वारा गाई या बजाई जाने वाली संगीत-रचना; एकल संगीत-रचना ➪ **duet** देखिए। ▶ **soloist** *noun* [C] एक वादक या गायक

**solo**[2] /ˈsəʊləʊ ˈसोलो/ *adj., adv.* **1** (done) alone; by yourself एक व्यक्ति द्वारा अकेले (किया हुआ); स्वयं अकेले *a solo flight* ○ *to fly solo* **2** connected with or played as a musical solo एकल संगीत रचना से संबंधित या उसका कलाकार (गायक या वादक) *a solo artist/singer*

**solstice** /ˈsɒlstɪs ˈसोलुस्टिस्/ *noun* [C] either of the two times of the year at which the sun reaches its highest or lowest point in the sky at midday, marked by the longest and shortest days वर्ष में मध्याह्न बेला में सूर्य का उच्चतम या निम्नतम बिंदु पर पहुँचने का समय (जो वर्ष के सबसे बड़े या सबसे छोटे दिन के रूप में प्रकट होता है); अयनांत *the summer/winter solstice* ➪ **equinox** देखिए तथा **season** पर चित्र देखिए।

**soluble** /ˈsɒljəbl ˈसॉल्यबल्/ *adj.* **1 soluble (in sth)** that will dissolve in liquid तरल पदार्थ में घुल जाने वाला; घुलनशील, विलेय *These tablets are soluble in water.* **2** (*formal*) (used about a problem, etc.) that has an answer; that can be solved (समस्या, प्रश्न आदि) जिसका कोई उत्तर हो, उत्तरसापेक्ष; जिसका कोई समाधान हो; समाधेय ✪ विलोम **insoluble**

**solution** /səˈluːʃn सˈलूशन्/ *noun* **1** [C] **a solution (to sth)** a way of solving a problem, dealing with a difficult situation, etc. किसी समस्या, कठिनाई आदि से निपटने का ढंग; हल, समाधान *a solution to the problem of unemployment* **2** [C] **the solution (to sth)** the answer (to a game, competition etc.) (किसी खेल, प्रतियोगिता आदि का) हल; उत्तर *The solution to the quiz will be published next week.* **3** [C, U] (a) liquid in which sth solid has been dissolved (कोई) तरल पदार्थ जिसमें कोई ठोस पदार्थ घोला गया हो; घोल *saline solution* **4** [U] the process of dissolving a solid or gas in a liquid तरल पदार्थ में ठोस या गैस को घोलने की प्रक्रिया; विलयन *the solution of glucose in water* ➪ **erode** पर चित्र देखिए।

**solve** /sɒlv सॉल्व्/ *verb* [T] **1** to find a way of dealing with a problem or difficult situation किसी समस्या या कठिनाई को हल करना या का समाधान ढूँढ़ना *The government is trying to solve the problem of inflation.* ○ *The police have not managed to solve the crime/mystery* **2** to find the correct answer to a competition, a problem in mathematics, a series of questions, etc. किसी (क्विज़ आदि) प्रतियोगिता, गणित का प्रश्न, प्रश्नमाला आदि का सही उत्तर मालूम करना *to solve a puzzle/equation/riddle* ➪ **solution** noun देखिए तथा **soluble** adjective देखिए।

**solvent** /ˈsɒlvənt ˈसॉल्वन्ट्/ *noun* [C, U] a liquid that can dissolve another substance अन्य पदार्थ को अपने में विलीन करने वाला तरल; विलायक

**sombre** (*AmE* **somber**) /ˈsɒmbə(r) ˈसॉम्ब(र्)/ *adj.* **1** dark in colour; dull गहरे रंग का; धुँधला **2** sad and serious खिन्न और गंभीर ▶ **sombrely** *adv.* खिन्नता के साथ, धुँधलेपन से

**some** /səm; *strong form* sʌm सम्; प्रबल रूप सम्/ *det., pronoun* **1** (*before uncountable nouns and plural countable nouns*) a certain amount of or a number of (किसी वस्तु की) निश्चित या विशेष मात्रा या संख्या; कुछ राशि *We need some butter and some potatoes. I still have some money.*

NOTE निषेधवाचक और प्रश्नवाचक वाक्यों में **some** के स्थान पर **any** का प्रयोग होता है—*Do we need any butter?* ○ *I need some more money. I haven't got any.* अर्थ सं. **2** के उदाहरणों को देखिए जो प्रश्नवाचक वाक्यों में शब्द **some** का प्रयोग दर्शाते हैं।

**2** used in questions when you expect or want the answer 'yes' उन प्रश्नवाचक वाक्यों में प्रयुक्त जहाँ अनुकूल उत्तर अपेक्षित हो; कुछ, थोड़ा *Would you like some more cake?* ○ *Can I take some of this paper?* **3 some (of sb/sth)** used when you are referring to certain members of a group or certain types of a thing, but not all of them जहाँ किसी व्यक्ति समुदाय के विशिष्ट (न कि सब) सदस्यों या वस्तु के विशिष्ट (न कि सब) प्रकारों का निर्देश करना अभीष्ट हो; कुछ *Some pupils enjoy this kind of work, some don't.* ○ *Some of his books are very exciting.* **4** used with **singular countable** nouns for talking about a person or thing without saying any details (व्यक्ति या वस्तु का निश्चयात्मक संकेत करने के लिए) एकवचनांत गणनीय संज्ञाओं के साथ प्रयुक्त *I'll see you again sometime, I expect.* ○ *There must be some mistake.*

**somebody** /ˈsʌmbədi ˈसम्बडि/ (*also* **someone**) *pronoun* a person who is not known or not mentioned by name कोई (जिसके विषय में या जिसका नाम पता नहीं) *There's somebody at the door.* ○ *I think you should talk to **someone else*** (= another person) *about this problem.*

NOTE **Somebody, anybody** और **everybody** का प्रयोग एकवचनांत क्रिया के साथ होता है परंतु उनके बाद प्रायः बहुवचनांत सर्वनाम आता है (अपवाद है औपचारिक शैली जिसमें 'his/her' या 'him/her' का प्रयोग अनिवार्य है)—*Somebody has left **their** coat behind.* ○ *I'll see everybody concerned and tell **them** the news.* **Somebody** और **anybody** में वही अंतर है जो **some** और **any** में। ➪ **some** पर नोट देखिए।

**some day** (*also* **someday**) *adv.* at a time in the future that is not yet known भविष्य में कभी, किसी दिन *I hope you'll come and visit me some day.*

**somehow** /ˈsʌmhaʊ ˈसम्हाउ/ *adv.* **1** in a way that is not known or certain ऐसे ढंग से जो मालूम या निश्चित नहीं; किसी तरह से *The car's broken down but I'll get to work somehow.* ○ *Somehow we had got completely lost.* **2** for a reason you do not know or understand किसी अज्ञात या अस्पष्ट कारण से *I somehow get the feeling that I've been here before.*

**someone** /ˈsʌmwʌn ˈसम्वन्/ = **somebody**

**someplace** /ˈsʌmpleɪs ˈसम्प्लेस्/ (*AmE*) = **somewhere**

**somersault** /ˈsʌməsɔːlt ˈसमसॉल्ट्/ *noun* [C] a movement in which you roll right over with your feet going over your head कलाबाज़ी; कलैया (सिर के ऊपर से एड़ियाँ निकालते हुए कूदना)

**something** /ˈsʌmθɪŋ ˈसम्थ़िङ्/ *pronoun* **1** a thing that is not known or not named अज्ञात या अनाम या नामहीन वस्तु *I've got something in my eye.* ○ *Would you like something else* (= another thing to drink)?

NOTE **Something** और **anything** में वही अंतर है जो **some** और **any** में। ➪ **some** पर नोट देखिए।

**2** a thing that is important, useful or worth considering ऐसी बात जो महत्त्वपूर्ण, उपयोगी या विचार करने योग्य हो *There's something in what your mother says.* **3** (*informal*) used to show that a description, an amount, etc. is not exact किसी विवरण, मात्रा आदि के एकदम सही न होने की अनिश्चयात्मकता का निर्देश करने के लिए प्रयुक्त *a new comedy series aimed at **thirty-somethings*** (= people between thirty and forty years old).

IDM **or something** (*informal*) used for showing that you are not sure about what you have just said या कुछ ऐसा ही या और कुछ (अपनी ही बात के निश्चयात्मक न होने का संकेत करने के लिए प्रयुक्त) *'What's his job?' 'I think he's a plumber, or something.'*

**something like** similar to के जैसा, से मिलता-जुलता *A loganberry is something like a raspberry.*

**something to do with** connected or involved with (किसी से) संबंधित या जुड़ा हुआ *The programme's something to do with the environment.*

**sometime** (*also* **some time**) /ˈsʌmtaɪm ˈसम्टाइम्/ *adv.* at a time that you do not know exactly or have not yet decided समय जो नहीं मालूम कि ठीक-ठीक कब या जो अभी निश्चित नहीं; कभी *I'll phone you sometime this evening.* ○ *I must go and see her sometime.*

**sometimes** /ˈsʌmtaɪmz ˈसम्टाइम्ज़्/ *adv.* on some occasions; now and then कुछ मौकों पर; कभी-कभी *Sometimes I drive to work and sometimes I go by bus.* ○ *I sometimes watch television in the evenings.*

**somewhat** /ˈsʌmwɒt ˈसम्‌वॉट्/ *adv.* rather; to some degree किसी हद तक; कुछ-कुछ *We missed the train, which was somewhat unfortunate.*

**somewhere** /ˈsʌmweə(r) ˈसम्‌वेअ(र्)/ (*AmE* **someplace**) *adv.* **1** at, in, or to a place that you do not know or do not mention by name स्थान पर/में/(को) जो आपको नहीं मालूम या जिसका नाम आप नहीं बताते; कहीं *I've seen your glasses somewhere downstairs.* ○ *'Have they gone to France?' 'No, I think they've gone somewhere else* (= to another place) *this year.'*

> **NOTE** **Somewhere** और **anywhere** में वही अंतर है जो **some** और **any** में। ➪ **some** पर नोट देखिए।

**2** used when you do not know an exact time, number, etc. निश्चित समय, संख्या आदि न मालूम होने पर प्रयुक्त *Your ideal weight should probably be **somewhere around** 60 kilos.*

**son** /sʌn सन्/ *noun* [C] a male child पुत्र, बेटा, लड़का ➪ **daughter** देखिए।

**sonar** /ˈsəʊnɑː(r) ˈसोना(र्)/ *noun* [U] equipment or a system for finding objects under water using sound waves ध्वनि तरंगों की सहायता से पानी के अंदर की वस्तुओं का पता लगाने वाला उपकरण या प्रणाली; सोनार ➪ **radar** देखिए।

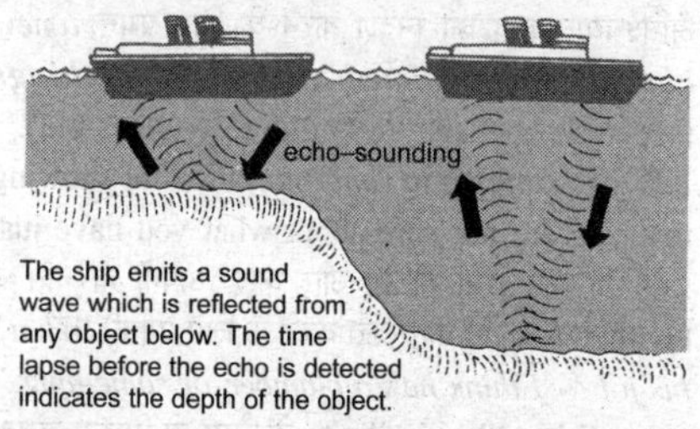


The ship emits a sound wave which is reflected from any object below. The time lapse before the echo is detected indicates the depth of the object.

**sonar**

**song** /sɒŋ सॉङ्/ *noun* **1** [C] a piece of music with words that you sing गीत, गाना, गान *a folk/love/pop song* **2** [U] songs in general; music for singing गाना (सामान्य रूप से), कोई गाना; गाने के साथ का संगीत *to burst/break into song* (= to suddenly start singing) **3** [U, C] the musical sounds that birds make पक्षियों की संगीतमय ध्वनि *bird song*

**songwriter** /ˈsɒŋraɪtə(r) ˈसॉङ्राइट(र्)/ *noun* [C] a person whose job is to write songs गाने लिखने का काम करने वाला व्यक्ति; गीतकार

**sonic** /ˈsɒnɪk ˈसॉनिक्/ *adj.* (*technical*) connected with sound waves ध्वनि तरंगों से संबंधित; ध्वनिक

**son-in-law** *noun* [C] (*pl.* **sons-in-law**) the husband of your daughter दामाद, जामाता

**sonnet** /ˈsɒnɪt ˈसॉनिट्/ *noun* [C] a poem that has 14 lines, each usually containing 10 syllables, and a fixed pattern of **rhyme** सॉनेट; (14 पंक्तियोंवाली कविता जिसमें प्रत्येक पंक्ति में प्रायः 10 अक्षर होते हैं और अंत्यानुप्रास-प्रणाली नियत होती है); चतुर्दशपदी कविता

**soon** /suːn सून्/ *adv.* **1** in a short time from now; a short time after sth else has happened अब से कुछ देर में; जल्दी, शीघ्र, कोई और बात हो जाने के कुछ देर बाद *It will soon be dark.* ○ *He left soon after me.* ○ *See you soon.* **2** early; quickly (समय से) पहले; जल्दी *Don't leave so soon. Stay for tea.*

**IDM** **as soon as** at the moment (that); when ज्यों ही; जब *Phone me as soon as you hear some news.*

**no sooner... than** (*written*) immediately when or after तुरंत तभी या बाद में *No sooner had I shut the door than I realized I'd left my keys inside.*

> **NOTE** यहाँ शब्दों के क्रम पर ध्यान दीजिए 'No sooner' के एकदम बाद क्रिया आती है और उसके बाद कर्ता।

**sooner or later** at sometime in the future; one day भविष्य में कभी, कभी-न-कभी, देर-सवेर; किसी दिन

**soot** /sʊt सुट्/ *noun* [U] black powder that comes from burning things and collects in chimneys चिमनियों में जमा कालिख (जलती चीज़ों से उत्पन्न)

**soothe** /suːð सूद्/ *verb* [T] **1** to make sb calmer or less upset; to comfort sb किसी व्यक्ति की परेशानी या विक्षोभ कम करना; किसी को आराम या राहत पहुँचाना **2** to make a part of the body or a feeling less painful शरीर के किसी अंग या मनोभाव की पीड़ा को शांत करना *The doctor gave me some skin cream to soothe the irritation.* ▶ **soothing** *adj.* शांतिदायक; आराम पहुँचाने वाला *soothing music* ○ *a soothing massage* ▶ **soothingly** *adv.* शांतिप्रद होते हुए

**sophisticated** /səˈfɪstɪkeɪtɪd सˈफ़िसिटकेटिड्/ *adj.* **1** having or showing a lot of experience of the world and social situations; knowing about fashion, culture, etc. सांसारिक और सामाजिक मामलों में अति अनुभवी; दुनियादार, सयाना; फ़ैशन, संस्कृति आदि का जानकार **2** (used about machines, systems, etc.) advanced and complicated (मशीनें, प्रणालियाँ आदि) प्रगत या उन्नत और जटिल **3** able to understand difficult or complicated things कठिन और जटिल बातों को समझने में समर्थ; सुविज्ञ, विवेकी *Voters are much more sophisticated these days.* ▶ **sophistication** /səˌfɪstɪˈkeɪʃn सˌफ़िसिटˈकेशन्/ *noun* [U] सुविज्ञता, विवेक, परिष्करण

**soppy** /ˈsɒpi ˈसॉपि/ *adj.* (*informal*) full of unnecessary emotion; silly उथली भावुकता से भरा हुआ; बेवकूफ़ *a soppy romantic film*

**soprano** /səˈprɑːnəʊ सˈप्रानो / *noun* [C] (*pl.* **sopranos** /-nəʊz -नोज़् /) the highest singing voice; a woman, girl, or boy with this voice उच्चतम स्वर; ऐसे स्वर में गाने वाला व्यक्ति

**sorcerer** /ˈsɔːsərə(r) ˈसॉसर(र्) / *noun* [C] (in stories) a man with magical powers, who is helped by evil spirits (कहानियों में) जादूगर; जादू-टोना करने वाला 'ओझा'

**sorceress** /ˈsɔːsərəs ˈसॉसरस् / *noun* [C] a female sorcerer जादूगरनी, ओझाइन

**sorcery** /ˈsɔːsəri ˈसॉसरि / *noun* [U] the art or use of magic in which the power of evil, supernatural forces or black magic is used जादू-टोना, जंतर-मंतर

**sordid** /ˈsɔːdɪd ˈसॉडिड् / *adj.* **1** unpleasant; not honest or moral अप्रिय, कुत्सित; असत्याचारी या भ्रष्ट *We discovered the truth about his sordid past.* **2** very dirty and unpleasant बहुत गंदा और दूषित

**sore[1]** /sɔː(r) सॉ(र्) / *adj.* (used about a part of the body) painful, especially when touched (शरीर का अंग) दुखता हुआ (विशेषतः छुए जाने पर) *to have a sore throat* ○ *My feet were sore from walking so far.* ▶ **soreness** *noun* [U] दुखने की स्थिति; दुखतापन *a cream to reduce soreness and swelling*

IDM **a sore point** a subject that is likely to make sb upset or angry when mentioned किसी को परेशान या क्रोधित करने वाला विषय; अप्रिय विषय

**stand/stick out like a sore thumb** to be extremely obvious, especially in a negative way किसी का बहुत उभारदार होना (ऐसे कि बुरा लगे) *A big new office block would standout like a sore thumb in the old part of town.*

**sore[2]** /sɔː(r) सॉ(र्) / *noun* [C] a painful, often red place on your body where the skin is cut or infected शरीर का दुखता, लाल पड़ चुका अंग (जहाँ पर त्वचा कट या कीटाणु-ग्रस्त हो गई हो); घाव, ज़ख़्म, फोड़ा, व्रण ➪ **cold sore** देखिए।

**sorely** /ˈsɔːli ˈसॉलि / *adv.* (*formal*) very much; seriously अत्यधिक; गंभीरता से *You'll be* ***sorely missed*** *when you leave.*

**sorrow** /ˈsɒrəʊ ˈसॉरो / *noun* (*formal*) **1** [U] a feeling of great sadness because sth bad has happened गहरी खिन्नता, दुख, उदासी (अप्रिय घटना के कारण) **2** [C] very sad event or situation अत्यंत दुखद घटना या स्थिति ▶ **sorrowful** *adj.* दुखपूर्ण, दुखी ▶ **sorrowfully** *adv.* दुखद रूप से

**sorry[1]** /ˈsɒri ˈसॉरि / *adj.* **(sorrier; sorriest) 1** (*not before a noun*) **sorry (to see, hear, etc.); sorry that...** sad or disappointed दुखी या निराश *I was sorry to hear that you've been ill.* ○ *I am sorry that we have to leave so soon.* **2** (*not before a noun*) **sorry (for/about sth); sorry (to do sth/ that...)** used for excusing yourself for sth that you have done (किए पर) क्षमा माँगने के लिए प्रयुक्त *I'm awfully sorry for spilling that coffee.* ○ *I'm sorry I've kept you all waiting.* **3** (*not before a noun*) used for politely saying 'no' to sth, disagreeing with sth or introducing bad news शिष्टतापूर्वक 'ना' कहने के लिए प्रयुक्त (मतभेद व्यक्त करते हुए या अशुभ समाचार देते हुए) *I'm sorry, I don't agree with you. I think we should accept the offer.* ○ *I'm sorry to tell you that your application has been unsuccessful.* **4** (*only before a noun*) very bad बहुत बुरा *The house was in a* ***sorry state*** *when we first moved in.*

IDM **be/feel sorry for sb** to feel sadness or pity for sb किसी के लिए दुख या करुणा अनुभव करना *I feel very sorry for the families of the victims.*

**sorry[2]** /ˈsɒri ˈसॉरि / *exclamation* **1** used for making excuses, apologizing, etc. खेद व्यक्त करने, क्षमा माँगने आदि के लिए प्रयुक्त *Sorry, I didn't see you standing behind me.* ○ *He didn't even* ***say sorry*** (= apologize)*!* **2** (used for asking sb to repeat sth that you have not heard correctly) (ठीक से न सुन पाने के कारण बात को फिर से कहने का अनुरोध करने के लिए प्रयुक्त) *'My name's Dev Mehta.' 'Sorry? Dev who?'* **3** used for correcting yourself when you have said sth wrong कुछ ग़लत कह जाने पर ग़लती सुधारने के लिए प्रयुक्त *Take the second turning, sorry, the third turning on the right.*

**sort[1]** /sɔːt सॉट् / *noun* **1** [C] **a sort of sb/sth** a type or kind प्रकार या क़िस्म *She's got* ***all sorts of*** *problems at the moment.* ○ *There were snacks —peanuts, olives,* ***that sort of thing****.* **2** [*sing.*] (*BrE*) a particular type of character; a person विशेष प्रकार का पात्र; व्यक्ति ✪ पर्याय **kind**

IDM **a sort of sth** (*informal*) a type of sth; sth that is similar to sth एक प्रकार की कोई चीज़; किसी दूसरी चीज़ जैसी कोई चीज़ *Can you hear a sort of ticking noise?*

**sort of** (*spoken*) rather; in a way किसी हद तक; एक तरह से *I'd sort of like to go, but I'm not sure.*

**sort[2]** /sɔːt सॉट् / *verb* [T] **1 sort sth (into sth)** to put things into different groups or places, according to their type, etc.; to separate things of one type from others वस्तुओं के प्रकार आदि के अनुसार उनका वर्गीकरण करना; एक प्रकार की चीज़ों को दूसरे प्रकार की चीज़ों से अलग करना *I'm just sorting these papers into the correct files.* **2** (*informal*) (*often passive*) to find an answer to a problem or difficult situation; to organize sth/sb समस्याओं या कठिनाइयों का हल ढूँढ़ना; किसी को व्यवस्थित करना *I'll have more time when I've **got things sorted** at home.*

IDM **sort sth out** 1 to find an answer to a problem; to organize sth किसी समस्या का हल ढूँढ़ना; किसी को व्यवस्थित करना *I haven't found a flat yet but I hope to sort something out soon.* 2 to tidy or organize sth चीज़ों को ठीक-ठाक या व्यवस्थित करना *The toy cupboard needs sorting out.*

**sort through sth** to look through a number of things, in order to find sth that you are looking for or to put them in order किसी विशेष वस्तु के लिए चीज़ों को टटोलना या उन्हें सुव्यवस्थित करना

**SOS** /ˌəs əʊˈes ˌएस् ओˈएस्/*noun* (*pl.* **SOSs**) 1 a signal or message that a ship or plane sends when it needs urgent help; an urgent appeal for help जल यान या वायुयान से भेजा गया संकट संदेश (सहायता के लिए); अत्यावश्यक सहायता के लिए संकट संदेश *to send an SOS*

**so-so** *adj., adv.* (*informal*) all right but not particularly good/well ठीक-सा, बस ठीक *'How are you?' 'So-so.'*

**soufflé** /ˈsuːfleɪ ˈसूफ़्ले/ *noun* [C, U] a type of food made mainly from egg whites, flour and milk, beaten together and baked until it rises अंडे की सफ़ेदी आटे और दूध को फेंट कर बना केक; सूफ़्ले

**sought** ➪ **seek** का past tense और past participle रूप

**sought after** *adj.* that people want very much, because it is of high quality or rare लोगों को बहुत पसंद (व्यक्ति या वस्तु) उच्च गुणों या दुर्लभ होने के कारण, (व्यक्ति या वस्तु) जिसके लोग दीवानें हों

**soul** /səʊl सोल्/ *noun* 1 [C] the spiritual part of a person that is believed to continue to exist after the body is dead व्यक्ति की आत्मा (जो शरीर के साथ मरती नहीं, अनश्वर है); जीवात्मा 2 [C, U] the inner part of a person containing his/her deepest thoughts and feelings व्यक्ति की अंतरात्मा, अन्तर्मन (गहनतम विचारों और भावनाओं का निवास-स्थल) *There was a feeling of restlessness deep in her soul.* ➪ **spirit** देखिए। 3 [C] (*old-fashioned*) (*used with adjectives*) a particular type of person विशेष प्रकार का व्यक्ति *She's a kind soul.* 4 [*sing.*] (*in negative statements*) a person कोई (भी) व्यक्ति *There wasn't a soul in sight* (= there was nobody). ○ *Promise me you won't tell a soul.*

IDM **heart and soul** ➪ **heart** देखिए।

**soulful** /ˈsəʊlfl ˈसोल्फ़्ल्/ *adj.* having or showing deep feeling अत्यंत भावपूर्ण; जीवंत *a soulful expression*

**soulless** /ˈsəʊlləs ˈसोल्लस्/ *adj.* without feeling, warmth or interest भावना, ऊष्मा या अभिरुचि से रहित *soulless industrial towns*

**sound**[1] /saʊnd साउन्ड्/ *noun* 1 [C, U] something that you hear or that can be heard आवाज़, ध्वनि (ऐसी चीज़ जिसे हम सुनते हैं या जो हमें सुनाई देती है) *the sound of voices* ○ *a clicking/buzzing/scratching sound* ➪ **amplitude** पर चित्र देखिए। 2 [U] what you can hear coming from a television, radio, etc. टीवी, रेडियो आदि की आवाज़ *Can you turn the sound up/down?*

IDM **by the sound of it/things** judging from what sb has said or what you have read about sb/sth किसी के अपने शब्दों या उसके विषय में दूसरों के कहे या लिखे के अनुसार उसे परखना *She must be an interesting person, by the sound of it.*

**sound**[2] /saʊnd साउन्ड्/ *verb* 1 *linking verb* (*not usually in the continuous tenses*) to give a particular impression when heard or read about; to seem (कुछ सुनकर या पढ़कर) विशेष प्रकार का प्रभाव होना; (कुछ) लगना, मालूम पड़ना, जान पड़ना *That **sounds like** a child crying.* ○ *She sounded upset and angry on the phone.*

NOTE अनौपचारिक या बोलचाल की, विशेषतः अमेरिकी, अंग्रेज़ी भाषा में 'as if' या 'as though' के स्थान पर 'like' के प्रयोग की प्रवृत्ति है, परंतु औपचारिक या लिखित ब्रिटिश अंग्रेज़ी में इसे अशुद्ध समझा जाता है।

2 **-sounding** (*used to form compound adjectives*) seeming to be of the type mentioned, from what you have heard or read (जैसा सुना या पढ़ा उससे) बताए गए प्रकार का लगनेवाला *a Marathi-sounding surname* 3 [T] to cause sth to make a sound; to give a signal by making a sound बजाना, आवाज़ उत्पन्न करना; हार्न आदि बजाकर कोई संकेत देना *A student on one of the upper floors **sounded the alarm**.* 4 [I, T] (*technical*) to measure the depth of the sea or a lake by using a line with a weight on it, or an electronic instrument समुद्र या झील की गहराई मापना (वज़न वाली डोरी या इलेक्ट्रॉनिक यंत्र की सहायता से)

PHR V **sound sb out (about sth)** to ask sb questions in order to find out what he/she thinks or intends किसी के विचार या मंशा जानने के लिए उससे प्रश्न पूछना

**sound**[3] /saʊnd साउन्ड्/ *adj.* 1 sensible; that you can depend on and that will probably give good results विवेकशील; विश्वसनीय और (संभवतः) अच्छे नतीजे देने वाला *sound advice* ○ *a sound investment*

2 healthy and strong; in good condition स्वस्थ और सशक्त; अच्छी दशा में *The structure of the bridge is basically sound.* ✪ विलोम **unsound** ▶ **soundness** *noun* [U] गंभीरता

**sound**[4] /saʊnd साउन्ड्/ *adv.*

IDM **be sound asleep** to be deeply asleep गहरी निद्रा में सोना

**the sound barrier** *noun* [*sing.*] the point at which an aircraft's speed is the same as the speed of sound विमान और ध्वनि की गति-समानता का बिंदु *to break the sound barrier* (= to travel faster than the speed of sound)

**sound effect** *noun* [C, *usually pl.*] a sound that is made artificially, for example the sound of the wind, and used in a play, film or computer game to make it more realistic कृत्रिम रूप से उत्पन्न की गई (जैसे वायु की ध्वनि) जो नाटक, फ़िल्म या कंप्यूटर गेम में वास्तविकता का प्रभाव लाती है; ध्वनि प्रभाव

**soundly** /ˈsaʊndli ˈसाउन्ड्लि/ *adv.* completely or deeply पूरी तरह से या गहराई से, अच्छी तरह *The children were sleeping soundly.*

**soundproof** /ˈsaʊndpruːf ˈसाउन्ड्प्रूफ़्/ *adj.* made so that no sound can get in or out ध्वनि-निरोधी, ध्वनिसह, साउंडप्रूफ़ *a soundproof room*

**soundtrack** /ˈsaʊndtræk ˈसाउन्ड्ट्रैक्/ *noun* [C] the recorded sound and music from a film or computer game फ़िल्म या कंप्यूटर गेम से रिकॉर्ड की गई ध्वनि और संगीत; ध्वनि पट्टी, साउन्ड ट्रैक ➪ **track** देखिए।

**soup** /suːp सूप्/ *noun* [U, C] liquid food made by cooking meat, vegetables, etc. in water गोश्त, सब्ज़ियों आदि को पानी में पका कर बनाया गया रसा; शोरबा, झोल, सूप *a tin of chicken soup*

**sour** /ˈsaʊə(r) ˈसाउअ(र्)/ *adj.* **1** having a sharp taste like that of a lemon नींबू के जैसे तीखे स्वाद वाला; खट्टा, अम्ल *This sauce is quite sour.* **2** (used especially about milk) tasting or smelling unpleasant because it is no longer fresh (विशेषतः दूध) बेस्वाद या दुर्गंध युक्त (बासी होने के कारण) *This cream has **gone sour**.* **3** (used about people) angry and unpleasant (व्यक्ति) क्रोधी और चिड़चिड़ा *a sour expression* ○ *a **sour-faced** old woman*
▶ **sour** *verb* [T] (*formal*) बिगाड़ देना, ख़राब कर देना *The disagreement over trade tariffs has soured relations between the two countries.*
▶ **sourly** *adv.* कटुता के साथ ▶ **sourness** *noun* [U] कटुता

IDM **go/turn sour** to stop being pleasant or friendly प्रिय या मित्रवत न रह जाना, ख़राब हो जाना, बिगड़ जाना *Their relationship turned sour after a few months.*

**sour grapes** pretending to not want sth that in fact you secretly want, because you cannot have it इच्छित वस्तु को न पाने पर उसके लिए अनिच्छा का दिखावा करते हुए; अंगूर खट्टे हैं

**source** /sɔːs सॉस्/ *noun* [C] a place, person or thing where sth comes or starts from or where sth is obtained स्थान, व्यक्ति या वस्तु जो किसी का उद्गम, प्रारंभ या प्राप्ति का बिंदु हो; स्रोत, उद्गम, मूल *The television is a great source of entertainment.* ○ *Police have refused to reveal the source of their information.*

**south**[1] /saʊθ साउथ्/ (*also* **the south**) *noun* [*sing.*] (*abbr.* **S**) **1** the direction that is on your right when you watch the sun rise; one of the four main directions that we give names to (**the points of the compass**) दक्षिण दिशा (सूर्य के सामने खड़े होकर दाईं और की दिशा); दिग्दर्शक यंत्र पर अंकित दक्षिण दिशा का सूचक बिंदु *warm winds from the south* ○ *Which way is south?* ○ *We live to the south of* (= further south than) *Delhi.* ➪ **compass** पर चित्र देखिए। **2 the South** the southern part of any country, city, region or the world किसी देश, नगर, क्षेत्र या विश्व का दक्षिणी भाग; दक्षिण, दक्खिन *Kerala is in the south of India.* ➪ **north, east** और **west** देखिए।

**south**[2] /saʊθ साउथ्/ *adj.*, *adv.* **1** (*also* **South**) (*only before a noun*) in the south दक्षिणी, दक्षिण में स्थित *the south coast of Tamil Nadu* **2** to or towards the south दक्षिण को या की ओर *The house faces south.* **3** (used about a wind) coming from the south (वायु) दक्षिण से आने वाली; दक्षिणी

**southbound** /ˈsaʊθbaʊnd ˈसाउथ्बाउन्ड्/ *adj.* travelling or leading towards the south दक्षिण की ओर जाने या ले जाने वाला

**south-east**[1] (**the South-East**) *noun* [*sing.*] (*abbr.* **SE**) the direction or a region that is halfway between south and east दक्षिण और पूर्व के मध्य की दिशा या क्षेत्र; दक्षिण-पूर्व ➪ **compass** पर चित्र देखिए।

**south-east**[2] *adj.*, *adv.* in, from or to the south-east of a place or country किसी स्थान या देश के दक्षिण-पूर्व में, से या को *the south-east coast of Sri Lanka*

**south-easterly** *adj.* **1** towards the south-east दक्षिण-पूर्व-अभिमुख *in a south-easterly direction* **2** (used about a wind) coming from the south-east (वायु) दक्षिण-पूर्व की ओर से आने वाली; दक्षिण-पूर्वी

**south-eastern** *adj.* (*only before a noun*) connected with the south-east of a place or country

किसी स्थान या देश के दक्षिण-पूर्व से संबंधित; दक्षिण-पूर्व *the south-eastern states of the US*

**south-eastward(s)** *adv.* towards the south-east दक्षिण-पूर्व की ओर

**southerly** /ˈsʌðəli ˈसद़लि/ *adj.* **1** to, towards or in the south दक्षिण को, की ओर या में *Keep going in a southerly direction.* **2** (used about a wind) coming from the south (वायु) दक्षिण दिशा से आगे आने वाली; दक्षिणी, दक्खिनी

**southern** (*also* **Southern**) /ˈsʌðən ˈसद़न्/ *adj.* of, in or from the south of a place कहीं से दक्षिण दिशा का, में या से; दक्षिणी *a man with a southern accent*

**southerner** (*also* **Southerner**) /ˈsʌðənə(r) ˈसद़नर(्)/ *noun* [C] a person who was born in or lives in the southern part of a country देश के दक्षिणी भाग में जन्मा या रहने वाला व्यक्ति; दक्षिणवासी, दाक्षिणात्य ✪ विलोम **northerner**

**the South Pole** *noun* [*sing.*] the point on the Earth's surface which is furthest south दक्षिण की ओर पृथ्वी का दूरतम स्थल; दक्षिणी ध्रुव ➪ **earth** पर चित्र देखिए।

**southward** /ˈsaʊθwəd ˈसाउथ्वड्/ (*also* **southwards**) *adj., adv.* towards the south दक्षिण की ओर

**south-west[1]** (*also* **the South-West**) *noun* [*sing.*] (*abbr.* **SW**) the direction or region halfway between south and west दक्षिण ओर पश्चिम के मध्य की दिशा या क्षेत्र; दक्षिण-पश्चिम ➪ **compass** पर चित्र देखिए।

**south-west[2]** *adj., adv.* in, from or to the south-west of a place or country किसी स्थान या देश के दक्षिण में, से या की ओर; दक्षिण-पश्चिमी *Our garden faces south-west.*

**south-westerly** *adj.* **1** towards the south-west दक्षिण-पश्चिम की ओर; दक्षिण-पश्चिमी *in a south-westerly direction* **2** (used about a wind) coming from the south-west (वायु) दक्षिण-पश्चिम से आने वाली; दक्षिण-पश्चिमी

**south-western** *adj.* (*only before a noun*) connected with the south-west of a place or country किसी स्थान या देश के दक्षिण-पश्चिम से संबंधित, दक्षिण-पश्चिमी

**south-westward(s)** *adv.* towards the south-west दक्षिण-पश्चिम की ओर *Follow the highway south-westward for twenty kilometres.*

**souvenir** /ˌsu:vəˈnɪə(r) ˌसूव़ˈनिअ(र्)/ *noun* [C] something that you keep to remind you of somewhere you have been on holiday or of a special event स्मृति चिह्न, निशानी (कोई वस्तु जो किसी यात्रा-स्थल या छुट्टी या विशेष कार्यक्रम की याद दिलाती रहे) *I brought back a menu as a souvenir of my trip.*

**sovereign[1]** /ˈsɒvrɪn ˈसॉव्रिन्/ *noun* [C] a king or queen शासक (राजा या रानी)

**sovereign[2]** /ˈsɒvrɪn ˈसॉव्रिन्/ *adj.* **1** (used about a country) not controlled by any other country; independent (देश) अन्य देश के अधीन नहीं; स्वतंत्र, आज़ाद **2** having the highest possible authority प्रभुसत्ता-संपन्न; संप्रभु

**sovereignty** /ˈsɒvrənti ˈसॉव्रन्टि/ *noun* [U] the power that a country has to control its own government राष्ट्र की स्वयं अपना शासन चलाने की शक्ति; संप्रभुता, प्रभु-सत्ता

**sow[1]** /saʊ सो/ *noun* [C] an adult female pig मादा सूअर ➪ **pig** पर नोट देखिए।

**sow[2]** /səʊ सो/ *verb* [T] (*pt* **sowed**; *pp* **sown** /səʊn सोन्/ or **sowed**) **sow A (in B); sow B (with A)** to plant seeds in the ground ज़मीन में बीज बोना, पौधा रोपना *to sow seeds in pots* ○ *to sow a field with wheat*

**soya** /ˈsɔɪə ˈसॉइआ/ (*AmE* **soy** /sɔɪ सॉइ/) *noun* [U] a plant on which soyabeans grow; the food obtained from those beans सोयाबीन का पौधा; सोयाबीन से बने खाद्य या पेय पदार्थ *soya flour/milk/oil*

**soyabean** (*AmE* **soybean**) *noun* [C] a type of bean that can be cooked and eaten or used to make many different kinds of food, for example flour, oil and a sort of milk एक विशेष प्रकार की फली जो खाई जाती है या जिससे अनेक प्रकार के खाद्य या पेय (जैसे आटा, तेल और एक प्रकार दूध) बनते है; सोयाबीन

**soy sauce** (*also* **soya sauce**) *noun* [U] a thin dark brown sauce that is made from soyabeans and has a salty taste, used in Chinese and Japanese cooking सोयाबीन की नमकीन चटनी (चीनी और जापानी पाक-कला में प्रयुक्त)

**spa** /spɑ: स्पा/ *noun* [C] **1** a place where mineral water comes out of the ground and where people go to drink this water because it is considered to be healthy खनिज जल वाला सोता (इस जल को स्वास्थ्यकर माना जाता है) **2** (*also* **health spa**) a place where people go to become more healthy and beautiful through regular exercices and beauty treatments हैल्थ स्पा; नियमित व्यायाम और सौंदर्य उपचार द्वारा स्वास्थ एवं सौंदर्यवर्धन का स्थल

**space[1]** /speɪs स्पेस्/ *noun* **1** [C, U] **space (for sb/sth) (to do sth)** a place or an area that is empty or not used ख़ाली या बेकार पड़ा स्थान या

इलाक़ा ➪ **room** और **place**[1] पर नोट देखिए। **2** [U] (*also* **outer space**) (*often used to form compound nouns*) the area which surrounds the planet Earth and the other planets and stars पृथ्वी और अन्य ग्रहों एवं तारों के चारों ओर का क्षेत्र; अंतरिक्ष *space travel* ○ *a spaceman/spacewoman* (= a person who travels in space) **3** [C, *usually sing.*] a period of time समय की अवधि **4** [U] time and freedom to think and do what you want इच्छानुसार सोचने और काम करने के लिए समय और स्वतंत्रता *I need some space to think.*

**space²** /speɪs स्पेस्/ *verb* [T] **space sth (out)** to arrange things so that there are empty spaces between them वस्तुओं को बीच में जगह छोड़ते हुए व्यवस्थित करना या लगाना

**spacecraft** /ˈspeɪskrɑːft ˈस्पेस्क्राफ़्ट्/ *noun* [C] (*pl.* **spacecraft**) a vehicle that travels in space अंतरिक्ष में यात्रा करने वाला-यान; अंतरिक्ष यान

**spaceship** /ˈspeɪsʃɪp ˈस्पेस्शिप्/ *noun* [C] a vehicle that travels in space, carrying people यात्रियों को लेकर अंतरिक्ष जाने वाला वाहन; अंतरिक्ष-पोत, यात्री अंतरिक्ष यान

**spacious** /ˈspeɪʃəs ˈस्पेशस्/ *adj.* having a lot of space; large in size जिसमें बहुत जगह हो; आकार में बड़ा, लंबा-चौड़ा ▶ **spaciousness** *noun* [U] लंबा-चौड़ापन, विस्तार

**spade** /speɪd स्पेड्/ *noun* **1** [C] a tool that you use for digging फावड़ा (खोदने का औज़ार) ➪ **shovel** देखिए और **gardening** पर चित्र देखिए। **2 spades** [*pl.*] the group (**suit**) of playing cards with pointed black symbols on them हुकुम के पत्ते *the king of spades* ➪ **card** पर नोट देखिए। **3** [C] one of the cards from this suit हुकुम का पत्ता *Have you got a spade?*

**spadework** /ˈspeɪdwɜːk ˈस्पेड्वक्/ *noun* [U] the hardwork that has to be done in order to prepare for sth किसी कार्य की तैयारी के लिए किया गया श्रम; आरंभिक कार्य

**spaghetti** /spəˈgeti स्पˈगेटि/ *noun* [U] a type of Italian food (**pasta**) made from flour and water that looks like long strings लंबी सींकों जैसा आटा और पानी से बना एक प्रकार का इतालवी खाद्य; पास्ता; स्पैगटि *How long does spaghetti take to cook?*

**span¹** /spæn स्पैन्/ *noun* [C] **1** the length of sth from one end to the other एक सिरे से दूसरे सिरे तक की लंबाई या दूरी *the wingspan of a bird* **2** the length of time that sth lasts or continues किसी वस्तु के रहने या बने रहने की अवधि या समयावधि *Young children have a short attention span.*

**span²** /spæn स्पैन्/ *verb* [T] (**spanning; spanned**) **1** to form a bridge over sth किसी वस्तु पर से पुल बनाना **2** to last or continue for a particular period of time निश्चित समयावधि तक रहना या बने रहना *His acting career spanned 30 years*

**spank** /spæŋk स्पैङ्क्/ *verb* [T] to hit a child on his/her bottom with an open hand as a punishment बच्चे के नितंब पर थप्पड़ मारना (सज़ा के तौर पर)

**spanner** /ˈspænə(r) ˈस्पैन(र्)/ (*AmE* **wrench**) *noun* [C] a metal tool with an end shaped for turning small metal rings (**nuts**) and pins (**bolts**) that are used for holding things together पाना, स्पैनर (क़ाबले खींचने या कसने का एक औज़ार) ➪ **adjustable spanner** देखिए और **tool** पर चित्र भी देखिए।

**spare¹** /speə(r) स्पेअ(र्)/ *adj.* **1** not needed now but kept because it may be needed in the future अतिरिक्त, बचा कर रखा हुआ (भविष्य में संभावित उपयोग के लिए) *spare tyre* ○ *a spare room* **2** not used for work ख़ाली, फ़ालतू *What do you do in your* ***spare time?*** **3** not being used; free उपयोग में नहीं; ख़ाली *There were no seats spare so we had to stand.*

▶ **spare** *noun* [C] अतिरिक्त समान *The fuse has blown. Where do you keep your spares?*

**spare²** /speə(r) स्पेअ(र्)/ *verb* [T] **1 spare sth (for sb); spare (sb) sth** to be able to give sth to sb किसी को कुछ दे सकना *I suppose I can spare you a few minutes.* **2 spare sb (from) sth/doing sth** to save sb from having an unpleasant experience किसी को अप्रिय अनुभव में से गुज़रने या परेशान होने से बचाना *You could spare yourself waiting if you book in advance.* **3 spare no effort, expense, etc.** to do sth as well as possible without limiting the money, time, etc. involved किसी काम को अच्छे-से-अच्छे ढंग से करना (पैसा, समय आदि की परवाह किए बिना) *No expense was spared at the wedding.* ○ *He spared no effort in trying to find a job.* **4 spare sb/sth (from sth)** to not hurt or damage sb/sth किसी को तकलीफ़ या चोट न पहुँचाना, तकलीफ़ या चोट से बचा लेना

**IDM to spare** more than is needed आवयकता से अधिक; अतिरिक्त *There's no time to spare. We must leave straight away.*

**spare part** *noun* [C] a part for a machine, engine, etc. that you can use to replace an old part which is damaged or broken मशीन, इंजन आदि के अतिरिक्त पुरजें (जो पुराने क्षतिग्रस्त या टूटे पुरजों के स्थान पर लगाए जा सकें)

**sparing** /ˈspeərɪŋ ˈस्पेअरिङ्/ *adj.* (*formal*) using only a little of sth; careful किसी वस्तु के अल्प अंश

का प्रयोग करते हुए; सावधानीपूर्ण *Doctors now advise only sparing use of such creams.* ▶ **sparingly** *adv.* किफ़ायत से

**spark[1]** /spɑ:k स्पाक्/ *noun* **1** [C] a very small bright piece of burning material आग की चिंगारी; स्फुलिंग, अग्निकण *A spark set fire to the carpet.* **2** [C] a flash of light that is caused by electricity बिजली से उत्पन्न प्रकाश की चमक; कौंध *A spark ignites the fuel in a car engine.* **3** [C, U] an exciting quality that sb/sth has (विशिष्ट) उत्तेजक गुण

**spark[2]** /spɑ:k स्पाक्/ *verb*

**IDM** **spark sth off** to cause sth किसी स्थिति का कारण बनना, को जन्म देना *Pradeep's comments sparked off a tremendous argument.*

**sparkle** /ˈspɑ:kl ˈस्पाक्ल्/ *verb* [I] to shine with many small points of light झिलमिलाना (छोटे-छोटे प्रकाश-बिंदुओं का चमकाना) *The river sparkled in the sunlight.* ▶ **sparkle** *noun* [C, U] झिलमिलाहट

**sparkling** /ˈspɑ:klɪŋ ˈस्पाक्लिङ्/ *adj.* **1** shining with many small points of light चमकता या झिलमिलाता हुआ; चमकदार *sparkling blue eyes* **2** (used about a drink) containing bubbles of gas (पेय पदार्थ) बुलबुलों वाला *sparkling wine/mineral water*

**spark plug** *noun* [C] a small piece of equipment in an engine that produces a bright flash of electricity (**a spark**) to make the fuel burn and start the engine इंजन को स्टार्ट करने वाला छोटा प्लग (जिसमें से बिजली की चिंगारी निकलती है और पेट्रोल या डीज़ल जलने लगता है); स्पार्क प्लग

**sparrow** /ˈspærəʊ ˈस्पैरो/ *noun* [C] a small brown and grey bird that is common in many parts of the world गौरैया

**sparse** /spɑ:s स्पास्/ *adj.* small in quantity or amount राशि या मात्रा की दृष्टि से थोड़ा, छितरा हुआ (न कि घना); झिल्लड़, विरल *a sparse crowd* ○ *He just had a few sparse hairs on his head.* ▶ **sparsely** *adv.* छितरेपन से, विरलेपन से *a sparsely populated area* ▶ **sparseness** *noun* [U] छितरापन, विरलता

**spartan** /ˈspɑ:tn ˈस्पाट्न्/ *adj.* (*formal*) very simple and not comfortable बहुत सादा और सुख-साधन रहित *spartan living conditions*

**spasm** /ˈspæzəm ˈस्पैज़म्/ *noun* [C, U] a sudden movement of a muscle that you cannot control ऐंठन, मरोड़ (मांसपेशी की एकाएक होने वाली हरकत जो नियंत्रित नहीं हो पाती); पेशी अकुंचन *He had painful muscular spasms in his leg.*

**spat** ⇨ **spit[1]** का past tense और past participle रूप

**spate** /speɪt स्पेट्/ *noun* [*sing.*] a large number or amount of sth happening at one time एक ही समय पर होने वाली घटनाओं की बड़ी संख्या या मात्रा; (घटनाओं की) बाढ़ *There has been a spate of burglaries in the area recently.*

**spatial** /ˈspeɪʃl ˈस्पेश्ल्/ *adj.* (*formal*) connected with the size or position and area of sth किसी वस्तु के आकार स्थिति और क्षेत्र से संबंधित; स्थानिक, भौगोलिक *spatial neasurements*

**spatter** /ˈspætə(r) ˈस्पैट(र्)/ *verb* [T] **spatter sb/sth (with sth); spatter sth (on sb/sth)** to cover sb/sth with small drops of sth wet किसी पर बूँदें छिड़कना, छींटे डालना

**spatula** /ˈspætʃələ ˈस्पैचला/ *noun* [C] a tool with a wide flat part used in cooking for mixing and spreading things उथला या चपटा चम्मच; स्पैचुला (जिससे बनते हुए खाद्य पदार्थ को बरतन में उलटा-पुलटा किया और फैलाया जा सकता है) ⇨ **kitchen** पर चित्र देखिए।

**speak** /spi:k स्पीक्/ *verb* (*pt* **spoke** /spəʊk स्पोक्/; *pp* **spoken** /ˈspəʊkən ˈस्पोकन्/) **1** [I] **speak (to sb) (about sb/sth); speak (of sth)** to talk or say things कुछ बोलना; कहना *I'd like to speak to the manager, please.* ○ *I was so angry I could hardly speak.*

> **NOTE** **Speak** और **talk** का अर्थ लगभग समान है, परंतु **talk** के प्रयोग में अनौपचारिकता अधिक है, इससे सूचित होता है कि दो या अधिक लोग बातचीत कर रहे हैं और **speak** से यह पता चलता है कि केवल एक व्यक्ति कुछ कह रहा है, विशेषतः औपचारिक स्थिति में—*I'd like to speak to the manager please.* ○ *We talked all night.* ○ *The head teacher spoke to the class about university courses.*

**2** [T] (*not used in the continuous tenses*) to know and be able to use a language भाषा के प्रयोग में समर्थ होना (समझना और बोलना) *Does anyone here speak Urdu?* ○ *a French-speaking guide* **3** [I] **speak (on/about sth)** to make a speech to a group of people लोगों में भाषण देना **4** [I] (*informal*) **be speaking (to sb)** *to be friendly with sb again after an argument* झगड़े के बाद फिर मित्रता हो जाना

**IDM** **be on speaking terms (with sb)** to be friendly with sb again after an argument विवादजन्य कटुता के बाद पुनः मित्रता हो जाना (और परस्पर बातचीत करने लगना) *Thankfully they are back on speaking terms again.*

**so to speak** used when you are describing sth in a way that sounds strange (अटपटी लगने वाली बात को प्रकारांतर से कहने के लिए प्रयुक्त); दूसरे शब्दों में *She turned green, so to speak, after watching* *a television programme about the environment.* **speak for itself** to be very clear so that no other explanation is needed स्वतः स्पष्ट होना (कि अतिरिक्त व्याख्या की आवश्यकता ही न हो) *The statistics speak for themselves.*

**speak/talk of the devil** ➪ **devil** देखिए।

**speak your mind** to say exactly what you think, even though you might offend sb अपने मन की बात कहना (भले ही दूसरों को बुरा लगे)

**PHR V speak for sb** to express the thoughts or opinions of sb else किसी अन्य व्यक्ति के विचार या राय प्रकट करना

**speak out (against sth)** to say publicly that you think sth is bad or wrong किसी बुरी या ग़लत लगने वाली बात के विरुद्ध खुलकर बोलना

**speak up** to speak louder ऊँचे स्वर में बोलना

**speaker** /ˈspiːkə(r) ˈस्पीक(र्)/ *noun* [C] **1** a person who makes a speech to a group of people लोगों में भाषण देने वाला व्यक्ति; वक्ता, भाषण-कर्ता *Tonight's speaker is a well-known writer and journalist.* **2** a person who speaks a particular language भाषा-विशेष को बोलने वाला व्यक्ति; विशिष्ट भाषा प्रयोक्ता *She's a fluent Russian speaker.* **3** = **loudspeaker**[1] **4 the speaker** the presiding office (= the person whose job is to control and be in charge of the discussions) in many lesgislative assemblies अध्यक्ष; चर्चा या वाद-विवाद की अध्यक्षता करने वाला व्यक्ति (विधान सभाओं आदि में) *the speaker of the Lok Sabha/Legislative Assembly*

**spear** /spɪə(r) स्पिअ(र्)/ *noun* [C] a long pole with a sharp point at one end, used for hunting or fighting भाला, बरछी, शूल

**spearhead** /ˈspɪəhed ˈस्पिअहे्ड्/ *noun* [C, *usually sing.*] a person or group that begins or leads an attack आक्रमण अभियान आरंभ करने या उसका नेतृत्व करने वाला व्यक्ति या दल; सेनामुख, अग्रणी ▶ **spearhead** *verb* [T] आक्रमण आरंभ करना, हमला बोलना या उसका नेतृत्व करना

**spearmint** /ˈspɪəmɪnt ˈस्पिअमिन्ट्/ *noun* [U] a type of leaf with a strong fresh taste that is used in sweets, etc. पुदीना *spearmint chewing gum* ➪ **peppermint** देखिए।

**special**[1] /ˈspeʃl ˈस्पे्श्ल्/ *adj.* **1** not usual or ordinary; important for some particular reason प्रायः होने वाला या साधारण नहीं, विशेष; किसी ख़ास कारण से महत्त्वपूर्ण *a special occasion* ○ *special care* **2** (*only before a noun*) for a particular purpose किसी विशेष प्रयोजन की पूर्ति करने वाला; विशिष्ट (विशेषता-युक्त) *Anil goes to a special school for the deaf.* ○ *There's a special tool for drilling.*

**special**[2] /ˈspeʃl ˈस्पे्श्ल्/ *noun* [C] something that is not of the usual or ordinary type वस्तु जो प्रायः होने वाली या साधारण कोटि की न हो; विशेष वस्तु *an all-night election special on TV* ○ *I'm going to cook one of my specials tonight.*

**specialist** /ˈspeʃəlɪst ˈस्पे्शलिस्ट्/ *noun* [C] a person with special or deep knowledge of a particular subject किसी विशेष विषय का अधिकारी विद्वान्; विशेषज्ञ *She's a specialist in diseases of cattle.* ○ *a heart specialist* ○ *specialist advice*

**speciality** /ˌspeʃiˈæləti ˌस्पे्शिˈऐलटि/ *noun* [C] (*pl.* **specialities**) (*AmE* **specialty** *pl.* **specialties**) **1** an area of study or a subject that you know a lot about (किसी व्यक्ति की) विशेषज्ञता का क्षेत्र या विषय **2** something made by a person, place, business, etc. that is very good and that he/she/it is known for कोई वस्तु जिसके लिए कोई व्यक्ति, स्थान, उद्योग आदि प्रसिद्ध हो *The cheese is a speciality of the region.*

**specialize** (*also* **-ise**) /ˈspeʃəlaɪz ˈस्पे्शलाइज़्/ *verb* [I] **specialize (in sth)** to give most of your attention to one subject, type of product, etc. विषय-विशेष, वस्तु-विशेष (के उत्पादन) आदि में विशेष योग्यता प्राप्त करना *This shop specializes in clothes for taller men.* ▶ **specialization** (*also* **-isation**) /ˌspeʃəlaɪˈzeɪʃn ˌस्पे्शलाइˈज़ेश्न्/ *noun* [U] विशेषज्ञता विशिष्टीकरण

**specialized** (*also* **-ised**) /ˈspeʃəlaɪzd ˈस्पे्शलाइज़्ड्/ *adj.* **1** to be used for a particular purpose विशेष प्रयोजन से प्रयुक्त *a specialized system* **2** having or needing deep or special knowledge of a particular subject (किसी क्षेत्र-विशेष में) विशेषज्ञता प्राप्त *We have specialized staff to help you with any problems.*

**specially** /ˈspeʃəli ˈस्पे्शलि/ (*also* **especially**) *adv.* **1** for a particular purpose or reason विशेष प्रयोजन या कारण से *I made this specially for you.* **2** particularly; very; more than usual विशेष रूप से; अत्यधिक; असाधारण या असामान्य (सामान्य से अधिक) *It's not an especially difficult exam.*

**specialty** /ˈspeʃəlti ˈस्पे्शल्टि/ = **speciality**

**species** /ˈspiːʃiːz ˈस्पीशीज़्/ *noun* [C] (*pl.* **species**) a group of plants or animals that are all the same and that can breed together एक ही प्रकार के और एक साथ प्रजनित पौधों या पशुओं का वर्ग; जाति, प्रजाति, वर्ग *This conservation group aims to protect endangered species.* ○ *a rare species of frog*

**specific** /spəˈsɪfɪk स्पˈसिफ़िक्/ *adj.* **1 specific (about sth)** detailed or exact विस्तार-युक्त विस्तृत या एकदम सही *You must give the class specific* *instructions on what they have to do.* 2 particular; not general विशेष, ख़ास; सबके लिए नहीं, निश्चित *Everyone has been given a specific job to do.* ▶ **specifically** /spəˈsɪfɪkli स्पˈसिफ़िक्लि / *adv.* विशेष रूप से *a play written specifically for radio*

**specification** /ˌspesɪfɪˈkeɪʃn ˌस्पेसिफ़िˈकेश्न् / *noun* [C, U] detailed information about how sth is or should be built or made (किसी वस्तु के विषय में या उसे बनाने के संबंध में) विस्तृत जानकारी

**specify** /ˈspesɪfaɪ ˈस्पेसिफ़ाइ / *verb* [T] (*pres. part.* **specifying;** *3rd person sing. pres.* **specifies;** *pt, pp* **specified**) to say or name sth clearly or in detail स्पष्टता या विस्तार से कुछ कहना या किसी का उल्लेख करना *The fire regulations specify the maximum number of people allowed in.*

**specimen** /ˈspesɪmən ˈस्पेसिमन् / *noun* [C] 1 an example of a particular type of thing, especially intended to be studied by experts or scientists किसी विशेष प्रकार की वस्तु का उदाहरण (विशेषतः विशेषज्ञों या वैज्ञानिकों द्वारा अध्ययन-योग्य); नमूना, निदर्श 2 a small amount of sth that is tested for medical or scientific purposes किसी वस्तु की थोड़ी मात्रा, नमूना (डॉक्टरी या वैज्ञानिक परीक्षण के लिए) *Specimens of the patient's blood were tested in the hospital laboratory.* ✪ पर्याय **sample**

**speck** /spek स्पेक् / *noun* [C] a very small spot or mark बिंदु, कण *a speck of dust/dirt*

**specs** /speks स्पेक्स् / (*informal*) = **glasses**

**spectacle** /ˈspektəkl ˈस्पेक्टक्ल् / *noun* [C] something that is impressive or shocking to look at प्रभावशाली या विक्षोभकारी दृश्य; नज़ारा

**spectacles** /ˈspektəklz ˈस्पेक्टक्ल्ज़् / (*formal*) = **glasses**

**spectacular** /spekˈtækjələ(r) स्पेक्ˈटैक्यल(र्) / *adj.* very impressive to see (देखने में) बहुत शानदार और भव्य *The view from the top of the hill is quite spectacular.* ▶ **spectacularly** *adv.* शान से, शानदार ढंग से

**spectator** /spekˈteɪtə(r) स्पेक्ˈटेट(र्) / *noun* [C] a person who is watching an event, especially a sporting event किसी कार्यक्रम (विशेषतः खेल-कूद संबंधी) का दर्शक

**spectre** (*AmE* **specter**) /ˈspektə(r) ˈस्पेक्ट(र्) / *noun* [C] 1 something unpleasant that people are afraid might happen in the future कोई आगामी संकट (जिसकी लोगों को आशंका हो) *the spectre of unemployment* 2 (*old-fashioned*) = **ghost**

**spectrum** /ˈspektrəm ˈस्पेक्ट्रम् / *noun* [C, *usually sing.*] (*pl.* **spectra** /ˈspektrə ˈस्पेक्ट्रा /) 1 the set of seven colours into which white light can be separated सात रंगों की पट्टी (जिसमें शुभ्र प्रकाश रेखा विभक्त हो सकती है); वर्णक्रम, वर्णपट, रंगावली, स्पेक्ट्रम *You can see the colours of the spectrum in a rainbow.* 2 all the possible varieties of sth किसी वस्तु के समस्त संभव भेद; संपूर्ण शृंखला *The speakers represented the whole spectrum of political opinions.*

**speculate** /ˈspekjuleɪt ˈस्पेक्युलेट् / *verb* 1 [I, T] **speculate (about/ on sth); speculate that...** to make a guess about sth (किसी के विषय में) कुछ अनुमान लगाना; अटकल लगाना *to speculate about the result of the next election* 2 [I] to buy and sell with the aim of making money but with the risk of losing it किसी चीज़ पर सट्टा लगाना (गँवाने के जोख़िम के साथ लाभ कमाने के लिए कुछ ख़रीदना और बेचना) *to speculate on the stock market* ▶ **speculation** /ˌspekjuˈleɪʃn ˌस्पेक्युˈलेश्न् / *noun* [U, C] अटकल, सट्टा ▶ **speculator** *noun* [C] अटकलबाज़, सट्टेबाज़, सटोरिया

**speculative** /ˈspekjələtɪv ˈस्पेक्यलटिव् / *adj.* 1 based on guessing without knowing all the facts; showing that you are trying to guess sth (बिना पूरी जानकारी के) अटकलबाज़ी पर आधारित; किसी के विषय में कुछ जानने की कोशिश के अंदाज़ में *a speculative look/glance* 2 (in business) done with the aim of making money but also with the risk of losing it (व्यापार में) सट्टेबाज़ी पर आधारित; आनुमानिक *speculative investment*

**sped** ➪ **speed**[2] का past tense, और past participle रूप

**speech** /spiːtʃ स्पीच् / *noun* 1 [C] a formal talk that you give to a group of people (लोगों को दिया गया) भाषण; व्याख्यान *The Chancellor is going to* ***make a speech*** *to city businessmen.* 2 [U] the ability to speak बोलने की शक्ति; वाक शक्ति *He lost the* ***power of speech*** *after the accident.* 3 [U] the particular way of speaking of a person or group of people (किसी व्यक्ति या वर्ग का) बोलने का ख़ास ढंग, भाषा *She's doing a study of children's speech.* 4 [C] a group of words that one person must say in a play नाटक में पात्र की भाषा

**speechless** /ˈspiːtʃləs ˈस्पीचलस् / *adj.* not able to speak, for example because you are shocked, angry, etc. कुछ बोलने में असमर्थ (विक्षोभ, क्रोध आदि के कारण); अवाक, मूक

**speech marks** = **quotation marks**

**speed**[1] /spiːd स्पीड् / *noun* 1 [U] fast movement गति, चाल, रफ़्तार *The bus began to* ***pick up speed*** *down the hill.* ○ *The bus was travelling* ***at speed***

*when it hit the wall.* **2** [C, U] the rate at which sb/sth moves or travels गति करने की दर

**speed²** /spiːd स्पीड्/ *verb* [I] (*pt, pp* **sped** /sped स्पेड्/) **1** to go or move very quickly बहुत वेग से गति करना *He sped round the corner on his bicycle.* **2** (*only used in the continuous tenses*) to drive a car, etc. faster than the legal speed limit वैध सीमा से अधिक गति से कार आदि चलाना *The police said she had been speeding.*

PHR V **speed (sth) up** (*pt, pp* **speeded**) to go or make sth go faster अधिक तेज़ चलना या चलाना; रफ़्तार बढ़ना या बढ़ाना *The new computer system should speed up production in the factory.*

**speedboat** /ˈspiːdbəʊt ˈस्पीड्बोट्/ *noun* [C] a small fast boat with an engine तेज़ रफ़्तार से चलने वाली इंजन-युक्त छोटी नाव; द्रुतगामी मोटर-नौका, स्पीडबोट

**speeding** /ˈspiːdɪŋ ˈस्पीडिङ्/ *noun* [U] driving a car, etc. faster than the legal speed limit वैध गति सीमा से अधिक रफ़्तार से कार आदि चलाने की क्रिया

**speed limit** *noun* [C, *usually sing.*] the highest speed that you may drive without breaking the law on a particular road गति सीमा, किसी विशेष सड़क पर कार आदि चलाने की क़ानून-सम्मत अधिकतम गति की दर *He was going way **over the speed limit**.*

**speedometer** /spiːˈdɒmɪtə(r) स्पी ˈडॉमिट(र्)/ *noun* [C] a piece of equipment in a vehicle that tells you how fast you are travelling वाहन की गति को मापने का (वाहन में लगा) यंत्र, गतिसूचक यंत्र; चालमापी, स्पीडोमीटर ➪ **car** पर चित्र देखिए।

**speedway** /ˈspiːdweɪ ˈस्पीड्वे/ *noun* [U] the sport of racing motorbikes around a track ट्रैक के चारों ओर पर मोटर-साइकिल दौड़ का खेल

**speedy** /ˈspiːdi ˈस्पीडि/ *adj.* fast; quick तेज, द्रुतगामी; शीघ्र, तत्काल *a speedy response/reply/recovery* ▶ **speedily** *adv.* तेज़ी से, शीघ्रता से ▶ **speediness** *noun* [U] तेज़ी, शीघ्रता

**spell¹** /spel स्पेल्/ *verb* (*pt, pp* **spelled** /speld स्पेल्ड्/ or **spelt** /spelt स्पेल्ट्/) **1** [I, T] to write or say the letters of a word in the correct order किसी शब्द के अक्षरों को सही क्रम में लिखना या बोलना *His name is spelt P-A-R-E-S-H.* **2** [T] (used about a set of letters) to form a particular word (अक्षरों से) विशेष शब्द बनाना *If you add an 'e' to 'car' it spells 'care'.* **3** [T] to mean sth; to have sth as a result कुछ अर्थ होना; कुछ परिणाम निकलना *Another poor harvest would **spell disaster** for the region.*

PHR V **spell sth out 1** to write or say the letters of a word or name in the correct order किसी शब्द या नाम के अक्षरों को सही क्रम में लिखना या बोलना *I have an unusual name, so I always have to spell it out to people.* **2** to express sth in a very clear and direct way किसी बात को बहुत साफ़ और सीधे ढंग से कहना; साफ़गोई करना

**spell²** /spel स्पेल्/ *noun* [C] **1** a short period of time छोटी समयावधि; दौर *a spell of cold weather* **2** (especially in stories) magic words or actions that cause sb to be in a particular state or condition (विशेषतः कहानियों में) मंत्र, जादू (जो दूसरे को मोहित या वशीभूत कर ले)

**spell check** *verb* [I, T] to use a computer program to check your writing to see if your spelling is correct शब्दों की वर्तनी की शुद्धता को जाँचने वाले कंप्यूटर प्रोग्राम का प्रयोग करना ▶ **spell check** *noun* [C] = **spellchecker**

**spellchecker** /ˈspeltʃekə(r) ˈस्पेल्चेक(र्)/ (*also* **spell check**) *noun* [C] a computer program that checks your writing to see if your spelling is correct शब्दों की वर्तनी की शुद्धता को जाँचने वाला कंप्यूटर प्रोग्राम

**spelling** /ˈspelɪŋ ˈस्पेलिङ्/ *noun* **1** [C, U] the way that letters are arranged to make a word शब्दों की रचना में वर्णों या अक्षरों का क्रम; वर्तनी, वर्णविन्यास, वर्णयोग, अक्षरी, हिज्जे *'Center' is the American spelling of 'centre'.* **2** [U] the ability to write the letters of a word correctly किसी शब्द के अक्षरों को सही क्रम में लिखने की क्षमता, शब्दों की सही वर्तनी लिखने की क्षमता *Raghu is very poor at spelling.*

**spelt** ➪ **spell¹** का past tense और past participle रूप

**spend** /spend स्पेन्ड्/ *verb* (*pt, pp* **spent** /spent स्पेन्ट्/) **1** [I, T] **spend (sth) (on sth)** to give or pay money for sth किसी वस्तु के लिए पैसा देना या भुगतान करना; ख़र्च करना *How much do you spend on food each week?* ○ *You shouldn't go on spending like that.* **2** [T] **spend sth (on sth/doing sth)** to pass time समय गुज़ारना या बिताना *I spent a whole evening writing letters.* ○ *I'm spending the weekend at my parents' house.*

**spending** /ˈspendɪŋ ˈस्पेन्डिङ्/ *noun* [U] the amount of money that is spent by a government or an organization सरकार या किसी संस्था द्वारा ख़र्च की गई धन राशि

**sperm** /spɜːm स्पम्/ *noun* **1** [C] (*pl.* **sperm** or **sperms**) a cell that is produced in the sex organs of a male and that can join with a female egg to produce young पुरुष के प्रजननांगों में बनने वाला कोशाणु (जो स्त्री के अंडे से मिलकर शिशु को जन्म देता है); शुक्राणु **2** [U] the liquid that contains sperms वीर्य, शुक्र (जिसमें शुक्राणु रहते हैं)

**spew** /spjuː स्प्यू/ *verb* [I, T] **1** to flow out quickly or to make sth flow out quickly, in large amounts तेज़ प्रवाह से बहना या प्रवाहित करना, विशेषतः बड़ी मात्रा में *The chimneys were spewing out smoke and flames.* **2 spew (sth) (up)** (*BrE, informal*) to vomit वमन करना *She spewed up all the food that she had eaten.*

**sphere** /sfɪə(r) स्फ़िअ(र्)/ *noun* [C] **1** any round object shaped like a ball गेंद के आकार की कोई गोल वस्तु; गोला ➪ **solid** पर चित्र देखिए। **2** an area of interest or activity अभिरुचि या क्रियाशीलता का क्षेत्र ▶ **spherical** /ˈsferɪkl ˈस्फ़ेरिकल्/ *adj.* गोलाकार, गेंदाकार, गोलीय

**spheroid** /ˈsfɪərɔɪd ˈस्फ़िअरॉइड्/ *noun* [C] (*technical*) a solid object that is approximately the same shape as a **sphere** गोले जैसी आकृति की कोई ठोस वस्तु; गोलाभ

**sphincter** /ˈsfɪŋktə(r) ˈस्फ़िङ्क्ट(र्)/ *noun* [C] (*technical*) a ring of muscle that surrounds an opening in the body and that can become tighter in order to close the opening (शरीर के किसी अंग के चारों ओर) गोलाकार मांसपेशी (जिसके कस जाने पर छेद बंद हो जाता है); अवरोधिनी *the anal sphincter*

**sphinx** /sfɪŋks स्फ़िङ्क्स्/ *noun* [C] an ancient Egyptian stone statue of a creature with a human head and the body of a lion lying down मिस्र में पत्थर की ऐसी प्राचीन मूर्ति जिसका सिर मानव का तथा धड़ ज़मीन पर लेटे सिंह का होता है

**spice[1]** /spaɪs स्पाइस्/ *noun* **1** [C, U] a substance, especially a powder, that is made from a plant and used to give flavour to food (मिर्च, हल्दी आदि) मसाला (भोजन का स्वाद बढ़ाने के लिए प्रयुक्त) *Pepper and paprika are two common spices.* ➪ **herb** देखिए। **2** [U] excitement and interest उत्तेजना और दिलचस्पी *to **add spice** to a situation* ▶ **spicy** *adj.* मसालेदार, चटपटा *Do you like spicy food?*

**spice[2]** /spaɪs स्पाइस्/ *verb* [T] **spice sth (up) (with sth)** **1** to add spice to food भोजन में मसाले डालना, भोजन को मसालों से चटपटा और मज़ेदार बनाना *He always spices his cooking with lots of chilli powder.* **2** to add excitement to sth किसी स्थिति को अधिक उत्तेजक (और दिलचस्प) बनाना

**spider** /ˈspaɪdə(r) ˈस्पाइड(र्)/ *noun* [C] a type of small animal like an insect with eight legs. Spiders make (**spin**) special nets (**webs**) to catch insects for food मकड़ी या मकड़ा (आठ टाँगों वाला छोटा कीट जिसके बुने जाले में कीड़े फँसते हैं और उसका भोजन बनते हैं)

**spike** /spaɪk स्पाइक्/ *noun* [C] a piece of metal, wood, etc. that has a sharp point at one end धातु, लकड़ी आदि के खंड या छड़ का नुकीला भाग; नोक

**spill** /spɪl स्पिल्/ *verb* [I, T] (*pt, pp* **spilt** /spɪlt स्पिल्ट/ or **spilled**) **1** (used especially about a liquid) to accidentally come out of a container; to make a liquid, etc. do this (तरल पदार्थ का) पात्र से एकाएक बाहर निकल आना, छलकना; तरल पदार्थ को छलकाना *The bag split, and sugar spilled everywhere.* **2** [I] **spill out, over, into, etc.** to come out of a place suddenly and go in different directions झटके से बाहर आकर इधर-उधर बिखर जाना *The train stopped and everyone spilled out.* ▶ **spill** *noun* [C] छलकाव *Many seabirds died as a result of the oil spill.*

**IDM** **spill the beans** (*informal*) to tell a person about sth that should be a secret भेद खोल देना, रहस्य को प्रकट कर देना

**spin[1]** /spɪn स्पिन्/ *verb* (**spinning**; *pt, pp* **spun** /spʌn स्पन्/) **1** [I, T] **spin (sth) (round)** to turn or to make sth turn round quickly तेज़ी से किसी चीज़ का घूमना या (को) घुमाना, किसी वस्तु का चक्कर खाना या (को) खिलाना *He spun the globe.* ○ *to spin a ball/coin/wheel* **2** [I, T] to make thread from a mass of wool, cotton, etc. ऊन, कपास आदि से धागा बनाना, ऊन, कपास आदि कातना *A spider spins a web.* **3** [T] to remove water from clothes that have just been washed by turning them round and round very fast in a machine कपड़ों को मशीन में घुमा कर निचोड़ना

**PHR V** **spin sth out** to make sth last as long as possible किसी चीज़ को जहाँ तक हो सके वहाँ तक चलाना या चालू हालत में रखना

**spin[2]** /spɪn स्पिन्/ *noun* [C, U] **1** an act of making sth spin किसी वस्तु को घुमाने की क्रिया; घुमाव, चक्रण *She **put** a lot of **spin on** the ball.* **2** (especially in politics) a way of talking publicly about a difficult situation, a mistake, etc. that makes it sound positive for you (विशेषतः राजनीति में) किसी कठिनाई आदि के विषय में जनता को सुहाने वाली बात; बहलावा

**IDM** **go/take sb for a spin** to go/take sb out in a car or other vehicle मौजमस्ती के लिए कार आदि वाहन में जाना या किसी को ले जाना

**spinach** /ˈspɪnɪtʃ; -ɪdʒ ˈस्पिनिच्; -इज्/ *noun* [U] a plant with large dark green leaves that can be cooked and eaten as a vegetable पालक (का साग)

**spinal** /ˈspaɪnl ˈस्पाइनल्/ *adj.* connected with the bones of your back (**the spine**) रीढ़-विषयक; मेरु-दंडीय

**spinal column** = **spine 1**

**spinal cord** *noun* [C] the mass of nerves inside the **spine** that connects all parts of the body to the brain मेरु-रज्जु (मेरु-दंड में स्थित शिराएँ जो शरीर के सब अंगों को मस्तिष्क से जोड़ती हैं) ➪ **body** पर चित्र देखिए।

**spindle** /ˈspɪndl ˈस्पिन्ड्ल्/*noun* [C] **1** a rod that turns in a machine, or that another part of the machine turns around धुरी **2** a thin pointed rod used for spinning wool into thread by hand तकली, तकुआ, जिससे (हाथों से) सूत काता जाता है

**spin doctor** *noun* [C] (especially in politics) a person who finds ways of talking about difficult situations, mistakes, etc. in a positive way (विशेषतः राजनीति में) किसी कठिनाई आदि के विषय में जनता को सुहाने वाली बात करने वाला व्यक्ति, बहलाने वाला राजनेता; स्पिन डॉक्टर

**spin dryer** *noun* [C] a machine that removes water from wet clothes by turning them round and round very fast गीले कपड़ों को (घुमाकर) निचोड़ने वाली मशीन ▶ **spin-dry** *verb* [T] मशीन में गीले कपड़ों को घुमाकर निचोड़ना

**spine** /spaɪn स्पाइन्/ *noun* [C] **1** the bones of the back of a person or animal मानव या पशु की रीढ़ की हड्डी ✪ पर्याय **backbone** ➪ **body** पर चित्र देखिए। **2** one of the sharp points like needles, on some plants and animals कुछ पौधों और पशुओं (की पीठ) पर काँटे *Porcupines use their spines to protect themselves.* ➪ **prickle** देखिए। **3** the narrow part of the cover of a book that you can see when it is on a shelf पुस्तक का पुट्ठा (पुस्तक का वह सँकरा हिस्सा जो पुस्तक के शेल्फ़ पर रखा होने पर सामने दीखता है, इस हिस्से में पुस्तक के पन्ने जुड़े रहते हैं)

**spineless** /ˈspaɪnləs ˈस्पाइन्लस्/ *adj.* weak and easily frightened दुर्बल और डरपोक

**spinnaker** /ˈspɪnəkə(r) ˈस्पिनक(र्)/ *noun* [C] a large extra sail on a racing **yacht** that you use when the wind is coming from behind दौड़ स्पर्धा में प्रयुक्त नौका का बड़े आकार का अतिरिक्त पाल (जो वायु का प्रवाह पीछे से होने पर दिखाई पड़ता है) ➪ **boat** पर चित्र देखिए।

**spin-off** *noun* [C] **a spin-off (from/of sth)** something unexpected and useful that develops from sth else किसी अन्य स्थिति का (दूसरी स्थिति पर) अप्रत्याशित और अनुकूल प्रभाव

**spinster** /ˈspɪnstə(r) ˈस्पिन्स्ट(र्)/ *noun* [C] (*old-fashioned*) a woman, especially an older woman, who has never been married अविवाहिता, चिर कुमारी (विशेषतः बड़ी उम्र की महिला) **NOTE** अब इस अर्थ में **single** शब्द का काफ़ी अधिक प्रचलन है और यह अविवाहित महिला और अविवाहित पुरुष, दोनों का संकेत करता है ➪ **bachelor** देखिए।

**spiral** /ˈspaɪrəl ˈस्पाइरल्/ *noun* [C] a long curved line that moves round and round away from a central point सर्पिल रेखा (केंद्र बिंदु से सर्प के रेंगने के आकार में चलती रेखा) ▶ **spiral** *adj.* चक्करदार, पेंचदार, सर्पिल *a spiral staircase* ▶ **spiral** *verb* [I] (**spiralling; spiralled** *AmE* **spiraling; spiraled**) सर्पिल गति से बढ़ना

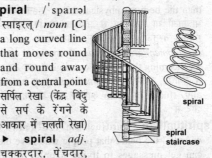

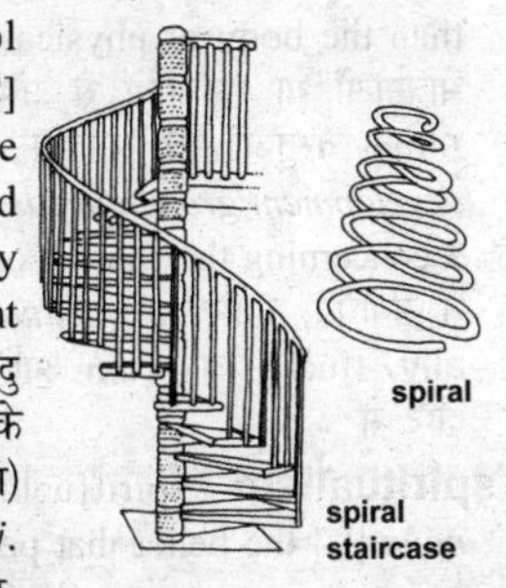


**spire** /ˈspaɪə(r) ˈस्पाइअ(र्)/ *noun* [C] a tall pointed tower on the top of a church (चर्च का) मीनार, नुकीला शिखर, लाट

**spirit¹** /ˈspɪrɪt ˈस्पिरिट्/ *noun* **1** [*sing.*] the part of a person that is not physical; your thoughts and feelings, not your body आत्मा (मानव-शरीर का अभौतिक अंश); चित (विचार और भावनाएँ, न कि शरीर) *the power of the human spirit to overcome difficulties* **2** [C] the part of a person that many people believe still exists after his/her body is dead; a ghost or a being without a body प्रेतात्मा (विश्वास के अनुसार, मानव-शरीर की मृत्यु के बाद भी विद्यमान अंग); भूत या शरीर-रहित जीव *It was believed that people could be possessed by* ***evil spirits****.* ➪ **soul** देखिए। **3** [C] the mood, attitude or state of mind of sb/sth किसी का मनोभाव, मनोवृत्ति या मनोदशा *to be* ***in high/low spirits*** (= in a happy/sad mood) **4 -spirited** (*used to form compound adjectives*) having the mood or attitude of mind mentioned यथानिर्दिष्ट मनोभाव या मनोवृत्ति वाला *a group of high-spirited teenagers* **5 spirits** [*pl.*] (*BrE*) strong alcoholic drinks, for example **whisky** and **vodka** तेज़ शराब (जैसे व्हिस्की और वोदका) **6** [U] energy, strength of mind or determination ऊर्जा; मानसिक शक्ति या दृढ़ता *The group had plenty of* ***team spirit****.* **7** [*sing.*] the typical or most important quality of sth किसी वस्तु की प्रातिनिधिक या सबसे महत्त्वपूर्ण विशेषता *The painting perfectly captures the spirit of the times.*

**spirit²** /ˈspɪrɪt ˈस्पिरिट्/ *verb*

**PHR V spirit sb/sth away/off** to take sb/sth away secretly किसी को चुपचाप उड़ा ले जाना

**spirited** /ˈspɪrɪtɪd ˈस्पिरिटिड्/ *adj.* full of energy, determination and courage ऊर्जा, दृढ़ता और साहस से पूर्ण

**spiritual** /ˈspɪrɪtʃuəl ˈस्पिरिचुअल् / *adj.* **1** concerning deep thoughts, feelings or emotions rather than the body or physical things गहन विचारों, भावनाओं या मनोभावों से संबंधित (न कि शरीर या भौतिक वस्तुओं से) आत्मिक; आध्यात्मिक *spiritual development/growth/needs* ➪ **material** देखिए। **2** concerning the Church or religion चर्च या धर्म से संबंधित; धार्मिक *a spiritual leader* ▶ **spiritually** /-tʃuəli -चुअलि / *adv.* आत्मिक, आध्यात्मिक, धार्मिक दृष्टि से

**spiritualism** /ˈspɪrɪtʃuəlɪzəm ˈस्पिरिचुअलिज़म् / *noun* [U] the belief that people who have died can get messages to living people, usually through a special person (**a medium**) प्रेतात्मवाद, प्रेतविद्या (यह धारणा कि मृत व्यक्ति जीवियों के साथ, प्रायः किसी विशिष्ट व्यक्ति माध्यम के ज़रिए, संपर्क साध सकते हैं) ▶ **spiritualist** *noun* [C] प्रेतविद्या-विशारद, प्रेतात्मवादी

**spit**[1] /spɪt स्पिट् / *verb* [I, T] (**spitting**; *pt, pp* **spat** /spæt स्पैट् /)

> **NOTE** अमेरिकी अंग्रेज़ी में **spit** भूत काल (past tense) और भूत कृदंत (past participle) रूप भी हो सकता है।

**spit (sth) (out)** to force liquid, food, etc. out from your mouth तरल पदार्थ, भोजन आदि को थूकना (बलपूर्वक बाहर निकालना) *He took one sip of the wine and spat it out.*

**spit**[2] /spɪt स्पिट् / *noun* **1** [U] (*informal*) the liquid in your mouth लार, थूक, पीक ➪ **saliva** देखिए। **2** [C] a long, thin piece of land that sticks out into the sea, a lake, etc. समुद्र, झील आदि में से बाहर को निकलता लंबा सँकरा भूखंड; भूजिह्वा **3** [C] a long thin metal stick that you put through meat to hold it when you cook it over a fire लोहे की सीख (गोश्त को भूनने के लिए जिसे गोश्त में घोंपकर पकड़े रहते हैं) *chicken roasted **on a spit***

**spite** /spaɪt स्पाइट् / *noun* [U] the desire to hurt or annoy sb किसी को हानि या कष्ट पहुँचाने की इच्छा; दुर्भावना *He stole her letters **out of spite**.* ▶ **spite** *verb* [T]

**IDM** **in spite of** used to show that sth happened although you did not expect it के होते हुए भी, के बावजूद (आशा के विपरीत कुछ घटित होने को व्यक्त करने के लिए प्रयुक्त) *In spite of all her hard work, she failed her exam.* ✪ पर्याय **despite**

**spiteful** /ˈspaɪtfl ˈस्पाइट्फ़्ल् / *adj.* behaving in a cruel or unkind way in order to hurt or upset sb द्वेषपूर्ण (किसी को अपमानित या दुखी करने के लिए निर्मम बरताव करते हुए) *He's been saying a lot of spiteful things about his ex-boss.* ▶ **spitefully** /-fəli -फ़लि / *adv.* द्वेषपूर्वक

**splash**[1] /splæʃ स्प्लैश् / *verb* [I, T] (used about a liquid) to fall or to make liquid fall noisily or fly in drops onto a person or thing किसी व्यक्ति या वस्तु पर (तरल पदार्थ के) छींटे पड़ना या डालना (शोर के साथ गिरना, गिराना या बूँदें उछलना) *Rain splashed against the windows.* ○ *The children were splashing each other with water.*

**PHR V** **splash out (on sth)** (*BrE informal*) to spend money on sth that is expensive and that you do not really need किसी महँगी और ग़ैर-ज़रूरी चीज़ पर पैसा बरबाद करना

**splash**[2] /splæʃ स्प्लैश् / *noun* [C] **1** the sound of liquid hitting sth or of sth hitting liquid छींटे उड़ने का शब्द (तरल पदार्थ और किसी वस्तु में टकराहट से उत्पन्न); छपाका, छपछप, छपाक *Pawan jumped into the pool with a big splash.* **2** a small amount of liquid that falls onto sth तरल पदार्थ की बूँद (जो किसी पर गिरे) *splashes of oil on the cooker* **3** a small bright area of colour रंग का चमकदार छींटा *Flowers add **a splash of colour** to a room.*

**splatter** /ˈsplætə(r) ˈस्प्लैट(र्) / *verb* [I, T] (used about a liquid) to fly about in large drops and hit sb/sth noisily; to throw or drop water, paint etc. on sb/sth in large drops (तरल पदार्थ की) मोटी बूँदों का उछलना और आवाज़ के साथ किसी से टकराना; किसी पर पानी की बड़ी बूँदें फेंकना या गिरना *The paint was splattered all over the floor.*

**splay** /spleɪ स्प्ले / *verb* [I, T] **splay (sth) (out)** (to cause sth) to spread out or become wide apart at one end एक सिरे को चौड़ा फैलाना या सिरे का चौड़ा फैलना *splayed fingers*

**spleen** /spli:n स्प्लीन् / *noun* **1** [C] a small organ near the stomach that controls the quality of the blood तिल्ली (पेट या आमाशय के पास छोटा अंग जिस पर रक्त का शुद्ध होना निर्भर है); प्लीहा *a ruptured spleen* **2** [U] (*written*) anger क्रोध, गुस्सा *He vented his spleen on the assembled crowd.*

**splendid** /ˈsplendɪd ˈस्प्लेन्डिड् / *adj.* **1** very good; excellent बहुत अच्छा; अत्युत्तम *What a splendid idea!* **2** very impressive बहुत शानदार *the splendid royal palace* ▶ **splendidly** *adv.* बहुत शान से

**splendour** (*AmE* **splendor**) /ˈsplendə(r) ˈस्प्लेन्ड(र्) / *noun* [U] very impressive beauty अति प्रभावशाली सौंदर्य; शान, वैभव, भव्यता

**splice** /splaɪs स्प्लाइस् /*verb* [T] **1 splice sth (together)** to join the ends of two pieces of film, tape, rope, etc. so that they form one continuous long piece फ़िल्म, टेप, रस्सी आदि के दो सिरों को जोड़कर एक लंबा अखंड भाग बनाना **2 get spliced** (*old-fashioned*) (*BrE, informal*) to get married गठबंधन करना, विवाह की गाँठ बाँधना

**splint** /splɪnt स्प्लिन्ट्/ *noun* [C] a piece of wood or metal that is tied to a broken arm or leg to keep it in the right position (बाँह या टाँग की टूटी हड्डी को सीधा रखने के लिए प्रयुक्त) (लकड़ी या धातु की) खपची; चपटी

**splinter** /ˈsplɪntə(r) ˈस्प्लिन्ट(र्)/ *noun* [C] a small thin sharp piece of wood, metal or glass that has broken off a larger piece (बड़े टुकड़े से टूटकर अलग हुआ) लकड़ी, धातु या काँच का छोटा पतला पैना टुकड़ा; किरच *I've got a splinter in my finger.* ▶ **splinter** *verb* [I, T] टुकड़ों या किरचों में टूटना या तोड़ना

**split**[1] /splɪt स्प्लिट्/ *verb* (*pres. part.* **splitting**; *pt, pp* **split**) **1** [I, T] **split (sb) (up) (into sth)** to divide or to make a group of people divide into smaller groups (लोगों के बड़े समूह या दल का छोटे समूहों या दलों में) बँट जाना, विभक्त हो जाना या उसे बाँट देना, विभक्त कर देना *Let's split into two groups.* **2** [T] **split sth (between sb/sth); split sth (with sb)** to divide or share sth किसी वस्तु को बाँटना या उसमें हिस्सा बटाना *We split the cost of the meal between the six of us.* **3** [I, T] **split (sth) (open)** to break or make sth break along a straight line किसी वस्तु का सीध में चिर या फट जाना या उसे चीर या फाड़ देना *My jeans have split.*

IDM **split the difference** (used when agreeing on a price) to agree on an amount or figure that is halfway between the two amounts or figures already mentioned किसी वस्तु के दाम पर (दो उद्धृत दामों के) बीच में समझौता या सहमति होना

**split hairs** to pay too much attention in an argument to details that are very small and not important बाल की खाल निकालना (किसी मामले के छोटे-छोटे ब्योरों पर आवश्यकता से कहीं अधिक ध्यान देना) NOTE इसकी व्यंजना सामान्यतया निंदात्मक होती है।

**split up (with sb)** to end a marriage or relationship वैवाहिक या सामाजिक संबंध को समाप्त करना, से अलग हो जाना *He's split up with his wife.*

**split**[2] /splɪt स्प्लिट्/ *noun* [C] **1** a disagreement that divides a group of people लोगों के समूह को विभक्त कर देने वाला विवाद; फूट **2** a long cut or hole in sth किसी वस्तु में दरार या छेद

**split second** *noun* [C] a very short period of time अत्यल्प समय, क्षण का अंश या क्षणांश; निमिष, पल

**splutter** /ˈsplʌtə(r) ˈस्प्लटर्(र्)/ *verb* **1** [I, T] to speak with difficulty for example because you are very angry or embarrassed (गुस्से या परेशानी में) कठिनाई से अटक-अटक कर बोलना **2** [I] to make a series of sounds like a person coughing बड़बड़ करना, बड़बड़ाना (खाँसी की-सी आवाज़ पैदा करना) ▶ **splutter** *noun* [C] बड़बड़ाहट

**spoil** /spɔɪl स्पॉइल्/ *verb* [T] (*pt, pp* **spoilt** /spɔɪlt स्पॉइल्ट्/ or **spoiled** /spɔɪld स्पॉइल्ड्/) **1** to change sth good into sth bad, unpleasant, useless, etc.; to ruin sth किसी अच्छी चीज़ का ख़राब, बेकार आदि कर देना; किसी वस्तु को बिगाड़ देना *Our holiday was spoilt by bad weather.* ○ *Eating between meals will* ***spoil** your* ***appetite***. **2** to do too much for sb, especially a child, so that you have a bad effect on his/her character किसी से (विशेषत: बच्चे से) अत्यधिक लाड़-प्यार करना (इतना कि वह बिगड़ जाए) *a spoilt child* **3 spoil sb/yourself** to do sth special or nice to make sb/yourself happy मन की ख़ुशी के लिए कोई विशेष या रुचिकर काम करना; मौज-मस्ती

**spoils** /spɔɪlz स्पॉइल्ज़्/ *noun* [*pl.*] (*written*) things that have been stolen by thieves, or taken in a war or battle चोरी का या (लड़ाई में जमा किया) लूट का माल *the spoils of war*

**spoilsport** /ˈspɔɪlspɔːt ˈस्पॉइल्स्पॉट्/ *noun* [C] (*informal*) a person who tries to stop other people enjoying themselves, for example by not taking part in an activity दूसरों का खेल बिगाड़ने वाला या दूसरों के आनंद में बाधक व्यक्ति

**spoke**[1] /spəʊk स्पोक्/ *noun* [C] one of the thin pieces of metal that connect the centre of a wheel (**the hub**) to the outside edge (**the rim**) पहिए को परिमा या रिम से जोड़ने वाली (धातु की) तीली; अर ➪ **bicycle** पर चित्र देखिए।

**spoke**[2] ➪ **speak** का past tense रूप

**spoken** ➪ **speak** का past participle रूप

**spokesman** /ˈspəʊksmən ˈस्पोक्स्मन्/ *noun* [C] (*pl.* **-men** /-mən -मन्/) a person who is chosen to speak for a group or an organization किसी समूह या संस्था का प्रवक्ता (उसकी ओर से बोलने वाला पुरुष); पुरुष-प्रवक्ता

**spokesperson** /ˈspəʊkspɜːsn ˈस्पोक्स्पसन्/ *noun* [C] (*pl.* **spokespersons** or **spokespeople** /ˈspəʊkspiːpl ˈस्पोक्स्पीपल्/) a person who is chosen to speak for a group or an organization किसी समूह या संस्था का प्रवक्ता (उसकी ओर से बोलने वाला पुरुष या महिला) NOTE **Spokesperson** को **spokesman** या **spokeswoman** पर तरजीह दी जाती है क्योंकि इसका पुरुष और महिला दोनों के लिए प्रयोग हो सकता है।

**spokeswoman** /ˈspəʊkswʊmən ˈस्पोक्सुमन्/ *noun* [C] (*pl.* **-women** /-wɪmɪn -विमिन्/) a woman who is chosen to speak for a group or organization किसी समूह या संस्था की प्रवक्ता (उसकी ओर से बोलने वाली महिला); महिला-प्रवक्ता

**sponge[1]** /spʌndʒ स्पन्ज़्/ *noun* [C, U] **1** a piece of artificial or natural material that is soft and light and full of holes and can hold water easily, used for washing yourself or cleaning sth स्पंज (नरम, हलका, छिद्रिल और पानी को अपने में रोक रखने वाला एक कृत्रिम या प्राकृतिक पदार्थ) (कुछ धोने या साफ़ करने के लिए प्रयुक्त) **2** = **sponge cake**

**sponge[2]** /spʌndʒ स्पन्ज़्/ *verb* [T] to remove or clean sth with a wet **sponge[1] 1** or cloth गीले स्पंज या कपड़े से कोई दाग़ आदि हटाना या कुछ साफ़ करना **PHRV** **sponge off sb** (*informal*) to get money, food, etc. from sb without paying or doing anything in return मुफ़्त में पैसा, खाना आदि प्राप्त करना

**sponge bag** (*also* **toilet bag**) *noun* [C] (*BrE*) a small bag in which you put soap, toothpaste, etc. (**toiletries**) when you are travelling यात्रा के दौरान साबुन आदि रखने की छोटी थैली; स्पंज-थैली

**sponge cake** (*also* **sponge**) *noun* [C, U] a light cake made with eggs, flour and sugar, and usually no fat अंडे, आटे और चीनी से बना चरबी रहित हलका केक; स्पंज-केक

**sponsor** /ˈspɒnsə(r) ˈस्पॉन्स(र्)/ *noun* [C] **1** a person or an organization that helps to pay for a special sports event, etc. (usually so that it can advertise its products) विशेष खेल स्पर्धा आदि के लिए (विज्ञापन-प्रदर्शन की सुविधा के साथ आर्थिक सहयोग करने वाला व्यक्ति या संस्था; प्रायोजक (व्यक्ति या संस्था) ➪ **patron** देखिए। **2** a person who agrees to pay money to a charity if sb else completes a particular activity (निर्धारित कार्य कर लेने पर) किसी व्यक्ति की सहायता हेतु उसे धन देने वाला व्यक्ति; समर्थक ▶ **sponsor** *verb* [T] कोई कार्यक्रम प्रायोजित करना (उसके आयोजन के लिए धन देना) *a sponsored walk to raise money for children in need* ▶ **sponsorship** *noun* [U] प्रायोजकत्व, प्रायोजकता *Many theatres depend on industry for sponsorship.*

**spontaneous** /spɒnˈteɪniəs स्पॉन्ˈटेनिअस्/ *adj.* done or happening suddenly; not planned अचानक किया गया या घटित हुआ, आकस्मिक; अनियोजित, सहज रूप से होने वाला *a spontaneous burst of applause* ▶ **spontaneously** *adv.* सहज रूप से, अकस्मात ▶ **spontaneity** /ˌspɒntəˈneɪəti ˌस्पॉन्टˈनेअटि/ *noun* [U] सहजता, आकस्मिकता

**spoof** /spu:f स्पूफ़्/ *noun* [C] an amusing copy of a film, television programme, etc. that exaggerates its typical characteristics किसी फ़िल्म, टीवी कार्यक्रम आदि की मज़ाकिया नक़ल (जिसमें मूल की निजी विशेषताओं को बढ़ा-चढ़ाकर पेश किया जाए) *It's a **spoof on** horror movies.*

**spooky** /ˈspu:ki ˈस्पूकि/ *adj.* (*informal*) strange and frightening विचित्र और डरावना *It's spooky being in the house alone at night.*

**spool** /spu:l स्पूल्/ *noun* [C] a round object which thread, film, wire, etc. is put around चरखी, फिरकी, रील (जिसके चारों ओर धागा, फ़िल्म, तार आदि लिपटे रहते हैं) ➪ **reel** देखिए।

**spoon** /spu:n स्पून्/ *noun* [C] an object with a round end and a long handle that you use for eating, mixing or serving food (छोटा या बड़ा) चम्मच, चमचा (खाने, खाने की वस्तुओं को मिश्रित करने या परोसने के लिए प्रयुक्त) *Give each person a **knife, fork and spoon**.* ➪ **kitchen** पर चित्र देखिए। ▶ **spoon** *verb* [T] चम्मच से लेना या उठाना

**spoonful** /ˈspu:nfʊl ˈस्पून्फ़ुल्/ *noun* [C] the amount that one spoon can hold चम्मच भर *Add two spoonfuls of sugar.*

**sporadic** /spəˈrædɪk स्पˈरैडिक्/ *adj.* not done or happening regularly अनियमित (रूप से किया गया या होने वाला) ▶ **sporadically** /spəˈrædɪkli स्पˈरैडिक्लि/ *adv.* अनियमित रूप से, कभी-कभी

**spore** /spɔ:(r) स्पॉ(र्)/ *noun* [C] one of the very small cells like seeds that are produced by some plants and that develop into new plants बीजाणु (कुछ पौधों के (बहुत छोटे) कोशाणु जैसे बीज जिनसे नए पौधे उत्पन्न होते हैं)

**sport** /spɔ:t स्पॉट्/ *noun* **1** [U] physical games or activity that you do for exercise or because you enjoy it खेल-कूद, क्रीड़ाएँ (व्यायाम या आनंद के लिए शारीरिक खेल या अन्य क्रियाकलाप) *Mohan **did** a lot **of sport** when he was at school.* **2** [C] a particular game or type of sport कोई विशेष खेल या विशेष प्रकार का खेल ***winter sports*** (= skiing, skating, etc.) ▶ **sporting** *adj.* खेल-कूद संबंधी *a major sporting event*

**sports car** *noun* [C] a low, fast car often with a roof that you can open स्पोर्ट्स कार (नीची, तेज़ रफ़्तार और प्रायः छत खोलने की सुविधा वाली कार)

**sportsman** /ˈspɔ:tsmən ˈस्पॉट्स्मन्/ *noun* [C] (*pl.* **-men** /-mən -मन्/) a man who does a lot of sport or who is good at sport पुरुष खिलाड़ी (खेल-कूद में ख़ूब भाग लेने वाला या खेल-कूद में अच्छा व्यक्ति) *a keen sportsman*

**sportsmanlike** /ˈspɔ:tsmənlaɪk ˈस्पॉट्स्मन्लाइक्/ *adj.* behaving in a fair, generous and polite way when you are playing a game or doing sport खेलते समय निष्पक्ष, उदार और शिष्ट आचरण वाला व्यक्ति, खेल भावना वाला व्यक्ति; सच्चा खिलाड़ी

**sportsmanship** /ˈspɔːtsmənʃɪp ˈस्पॉट्स्मनशिप् / *noun* [U] the quality of being fair, generous and polite when you are playing a game or doing sport खेलते समय निष्पक्ष, उदार और शिष्ट आचरण या गुण; खेल भावना, खिलाड़ीपन

**sportswear** /ˈspɔːtsweə(r) ˈस्पॉट्स्विअ(र्) / *noun* [U] clothes that are worn for playing sports or in informal situations खेल-कूद या अनौपचारिक अवसरों पर पहने जाने वाले कपड़े

**sportswoman** /ˈspɔːtswʊmən ˈस्पॉट्सुवुमन् / *noun* [C] (*pl.* **-women** /-wɪmɪn -विमिन् /) a woman who does a lot of sport or who is good at sport महिला खिलाड़ी (खेल कूद में ख़ूब भाग लेने वाली या खेलकूद में अच्छी महिला)

**spot**[1] /spɒt स्पॉट् / *noun* [C] 1 a small round mark on a surface किसी सतह पर छोटा गोल निशान, चित्ती *Leopards have dark spots.* ○ *a blue skirt with red spots on it* ➪ **spotted** adjective देखिए। **2** a small dirty mark on sth (किसी वस्तु पर) छोटा गंदा निशान; धब्बा, दाग़ *grease/rust spots* **3** a small red or yellow lump that appears on your skin त्वचा पर उभरा छोटा लाल या पीला गुमड़ा; दाना *Many teenagers get spots.* ➪ **spotty** adjective देखिए। **4** a particular place or area विशेष स्थान या क्षेत्र *a quiet/lonely/secluded spot* **5** [*usually sing.*] **a spot of sth** (*BrE informal*) a small amount of sth किसी चीज़ की थोड़ी मात्रा **6** = **spotlight 1**

**IDM have a soft spot for sb/sth** ➪ **soft** देखिए।

**on the spot 1** immediately तुरंत, एकदम वहीं *Neeraj was caught stealing money and was dismissed on the spot.* **2** at the place where sth happened or where sb/sth is needed घटना घटित होने या आवश्यकता वाले स्थान पर; मौक़े पर *The fire brigade were on the spot within five minutes.*

**put sb on the spot** to make sb answer a difficult question or make a difficult decision without having much time to think किसी को कठिन स्थिति में डाल देना (कठिन प्रश्न का उत्तर देने का कठिन निर्णय लेने के लिए बाध्य करना, बिना पर्याप्त समय दिए)

**spot**[2] /spɒt स्पॉट् / *verb* [T] (**spotting; spotted**) (*not used in the continuous tenses*) to see or notice sb/sth, especially suddenly or when it is not easy to do किसी को देखना या किसी पर ध्यान जाना (विशेषतः एकाएक या जब ऐसा करना सरल न हो) *I've spotted a couple of spelling mistakes.*

**NOTE** यद्यपि यह क्रिया सातत्यबोधक कालों (continuous tenses) में प्रयुक्त नहीं होती तथापि इसका '-ing' युक्त वर्तमान कृदंत (present participle) रूप काफ़ी प्रचलित है—*Spotting a familiar face in the crowd, he began to push his way towards her.*

**spot check** *noun* [C] a check that is made suddenly and without warning on a few things or people chosen from a group नमूने या निदर्श के रूप में व्यक्तियों या वस्तुओं की आकस्मिक जाँच

**spotless** /ˈspɒtləs ˈस्पॉट्लस् / *adj.* perfectly clean बेदाग़, साफ़-सुथरा

**spotlight** /ˈspɒtlaɪt ˈस्पॉट्लाइट् / *noun* 1 (*also* **spot**) [C] a lamp that can send a single ray of bright light onto a small area. Spotlights are often used in theatres सीमित स्थान को केवल एक-रेखा से आलोकित करने वाला लैंप (प्रायः रंगशालाओं में प्रयुक्त); स्पॉटलाइट, बिंदु प्रदीप **2 the spotlight** [*sing.*] the centre of public attention or interest लोगों के विशेष ध्यान पर रुचि का केंद्र; आकर्षण-केंद्र *to be **in the spotlight***

**spot on** *adj.* (*BrE informal*) (*not before a noun*) exactly right एकदम सही *Your estimate was spot on.*

**spotted** /ˈspɒtɪd ˈस्पॉटिड् / *adj.* (used about clothes, cloth, etc.) covered with round shapes of a different colour (पोशाक, कपड़ा आदि) चित्तीकार (जिस पर अलग-अलग रंगों के गोले बने हों) *a spotted blouse*

**spotty** /ˈspɒti ˈस्पॉटि / *adj.* having **spots** चकत्तेदार; चकत्तों वाला (जिसकी त्वचा पर लाल या पीले गुमड़े हों) *a spotty teenager*

**spouse** /spaʊs स्पाउस् / *noun* [C] (written) your husband or wife जीवन-साथी; पति या पत्नी

**NOTE Spouse** एक औपचारिक या प्रशासनिक शब्द है और प्रपत्रों, दस्तावेज़ों आदि में प्रयुक्त होता है।

**spout**[1] /spaʊt स्पाउट् / *noun* [C] a tube or pipe through which liquid comes out चायदानी आदि की नली या टोंटी *the spout of a teapot*

**spout**[2] /spaʊt स्पाउट् / *verb* [I, T] **1** to send out a liquid with great force; to make a liquid do this (तेज़ी से) द्रव पदार्थ की धार बहना; (तेज़ी से) द्रव पदार्थ की धार बहाना **2** (*informal*) **spout (on/off) (about sth)** to say sth, using a lot of words, in a way that is boring or annoying बकबक करना (बहुत अधिक ऐसे बोलना कि ऊब हो या बुरा लगे)

**sprain** /spreɪn स्प्रेन् / *verb* [T] to injure part of your body, especially your wrist or your **ankle** by suddenly bending or turning it कलाई या टखने का मोच खा जाना *to sprain your ankle* ► **sprain** *noun* [C] मोच

**sprang** ➪ **spring**[2] का past tense रूप

**sprawl** /sprɔːl स्प्रॉल् / *verb* [I] **1** to sit or lie with your arms and legs spread out in an untidy way पसर कर बैठना या लेटना (बेतरतीब ढंग से बाहें और टाँगें फैलाते हुए बैठना या लेटना) *People lay sprawled out in the sun.* **2** to cover a large area of land बड़े

भूक्षेत्र में फैल जाना ▶ **sprawling** *adj.* फैला हुआ, विस्तृत *the sprawling lawns in the city suburbs*

**spray[1]** /spreɪ स्प्रे/ *noun* **1** [U] liquid in very small drops that is sent through the air फुहार (किसी तरल पदार्थ की) *clouds of spray from the waves* **2** [C, U] liquid in a special container (**an aerosol**) that is forced out under pressure when you push a button दाब-व्यवस्था-युक्त विशेष फ़व्वारे से छोड़ा जाने वाला तरल पदार्थ *hairspray*

**spray[2]** /spreɪ स्प्रे/ *verb* [I, T] (used about a liquid) to be forced out of a container or sent through the air in very small drops; to send a liquid out in this way (तरल पदार्थ की) फुहार निकलना; (तरल पदार्थ की) फुहार छोड़ना *The crops are regularly sprayed with pesticide.*

**spread[1]** /spred स्प्रेड्/ *verb* (*pt, pp* **spread**) **1** [I, T] to affect a larger area or a bigger group of people; to make sth do this (किसी वस्तु का) बड़े भूक्षेत्र या लोगों की बड़ी संख्या में फैलना या (उसे) फैलाना *Rats and flies **spread disease**.* ○ *to **spread rumours** about sb* **2** [T] **spread sth (out) (on/over sth)** to open sth that has been folded so that it covers a larger area; to move things so that they cover a larger area तह लगी वस्तु को खोलकर कहीं बिछाना; वस्तुओं को ले जाकर किसी स्थान पर फैलाना *Spread the map out on the table so we can all see it!* **3** [T] **spread A on/over B; spread B with A** to cover a surface with a layer of a soft substance (मक्खन आदि) कोमल वस्तु को (ब्रेड आदि पर) लगाना; फैलाना, पोतना, चुपड़ना *to spread jam on bread* ○ *to spread bread with jam* **4** [T] to separate sth into parts and divide them between different times or people किसी वस्तु के अंश बना कर उन्हें विभिन्न समयावधियों या लोगों में बाँटना *You can spread your repayments over a period of three years.*

**PHR V** **spread (sb/yourself) out** to move away from the others in a group of people in order to cover a larger area (दूसरों से अलग होकर किसी का) बड़े इलाक़े में फैल जाना *The police spread out to search the whole area.*

**spread[2]** /spred स्प्रेड्/ *noun* **1** [U] an increase in the amount or number of sth that there is, or in the area that is affected by sth किसी वस्तु की विद्यमान मात्रा या संख्या में वृद्धि या किसी वस्तु से प्रभावित क्षेत्र का विस्तार, प्रसार या फैलाव *Dirty drinking water encourages **the spread of disease**.* **2** [C, U] a soft food that you put on bread ब्रेड पर लगाने का (क्रीम जैसा) कोमल पदार्थ *cheese spread* **3** [C] a newspaper or magazine article that covers one or more pages अख़बार या पत्रिका का पूरे पृष्ठ में या अधिक पृष्ठों तक फैला लेख *a double-page spread*

**spreadsheet** /ˈspredʃiːt ˈस्प्रेड्शीट्/ *noun* [C] (*computing*) a computer program for working with rows of numbers, used especially for doing accounts हिसाब-किताब आदि से संबंधित कंप्यूटर प्रोग्राम, इसमें पंक्ति और कालम होते हैं

**spree** /spriː स्प्री/ *noun* [C] (*informal*) a short time that you spend doing sth you enjoy, often doing too much of it आमोद-प्रमोद, ख़रीदारी आदि के (प्रायः अति तक पहुँचे) क्रियाकलाप की संक्षिप्त अवधि, रंगरलियों, ख़रीदारी आदि का दौर *to **go on a** shopping/spending **spree***

**sprig** /sprɪɡ स्प्रिग्/ *noun* [C] a small piece of a plant with leaves on it टहनी, डाली, प्रशाखा

**spring[1]** /sprɪŋ स्प्रिङ्/ *noun* **1** [C, U] the season of the year between winter and summer when the weather gets warmer and plants begin to grow वसंत ऋतु *Daffodils bloom **in spring**.* ➪ **season** पर चित्र देखिए। **2** [C] a long piece of thin metal or wire that is bent round and round. After you push or pull a spring it goes back to its original shape and size स्प्रिंग, कमानी; पत्तीदार कमानी *bed springs* **3** [C] a place where water comes up naturally from under the ground पानी का सोता, चश्मा (इसमें भूमि के नीचे से प्राकृतिक रूप से पानी आता है) *a hot spring* **4** [C] a sudden jump upwards or forwards झटके से लगाई उछाल या छलाँग

**spring[2]** /sprɪŋ स्प्रिङ्/ *verb* [I] (*pt* **sprang** /spræŋ स्प्रैङ्/; *pp* **sprung** /sprʌŋ स्प्रङ्/) **1** to jump or move quickly तेज़ी से उछलना या छलाँग मारना *to spring to your feet* (= stand up suddenly) ○ (*figurative*) *to spring to sb's defence/assistance* (= to quickly defend or help sb) **2** (used about an object) to move suddenly and violently (किसी वस्तु का) अचानक और झटके से हरकत करना *The branch sprang back and hit him in the face.* **3** to appear or come somewhere suddenly एकाएक प्रकट होना या निकल आना *Tears sprang to her eyes.* ○ *Where did you just spring from?*

**IDM** **come/spring to mind** ➪ **mind[1]** देखिए।

**PHR V** **spring from sth** (*written*) to be the result of से आना या निकलना, का परिणाम या नतीजा होना *The idea for the book sprang from an experience she had while travelling in India.*

**spring sth on sb** (*informal*) to do or say sth that sb is not expecting कोई अप्रत्याशित काम करना या बात कहना

**spring up** to appear or develop quickly or suddenly तेज़ी से या अचानक निकलना या प्रकट होना या बढ़ना या उगना

**springboard** /ˈsprɪŋbɔːd ˈस्प्रिङ्बॉड् / *noun* [C] **1** a low board that bends and that helps you jump higher, for example before you jump into a swimming pool (तरण-ताल या स्विमिंग पूल में कूदने आदि के लिए) गोता तख़्ता (आगे से झुकता हुआ नीचा तख़्ता जिससे ऊँची छलाँग लगाने में मदद मिलती है) **2 a springboard (for/to sth)** something that helps you start an activity, especially by giving you ideas किसी गतिविधि को आरंभ करने में सहायक वस्तु (विशेषतः विचारों से)

**spring-clean** *verb* [T] to clean a house, room, etc. very well, including the parts that you do not usually clean मकान, कमरे आदि (के प्रत्येक हिस्से) की अच्छी तरह से सफ़ाई करना

**spring onion** *noun* [C, U] a type of small onion with a long green central part and leaves गोली के आकार का (छोटा) प्याज; गोली प्याज़

**springtime** /ˈsprɪŋtaɪm ˈस्प्रिङ्टाइम् / *noun* [U] (written) the season of spring वसंत ऋतु

**springy** /ˈsprɪŋi ˈस्प्रिङ्इ / *adj.* going quickly back to its original shape or size after being pushed, pulled, etc. लचीला; स्प्रिंग की विशेषता वाला (धकेले, खींचे जाने आदि पर तेज़ी से अपनी शकल या नाप में लौट जाने वाला *soft springy grass*

**sprinkle** /ˈsprɪŋkl ˈस्प्रिङ्क्ल् / *verb* [T] **sprinkle A (on/onto/ over B); sprinkle B (with A)** to throw drops of liquid or small pieces of sth over a surface (कहीं पर तरल पदार्थ की बूँदें या किसी वस्तु के कण) छिड़कना, बुरकना, का छिड़काव करना *to sprinkle sugar on a cake*

**sprinkler** /ˈsprɪŋklə(r) ˈस्प्रिङ्कल(र्) / *noun* [C] a device with holes in it that sends out water in small drops. Sprinklers are used in gardens, to keep the grass green, and in buildings, to stop fires from spreading पानी छिड़काने का छिद्रीला उपकरण; फुहारा, झारा, सेंचक, स्प्रिंकलर (बग़ीचों में घास को सींचने और इमारतों में आग को फैलाने से रोकने के लिए प्रयुक्त)

**sprint** /sprɪnt स्प्रिन्ट् / *verb* [I, T] to run a short distance as fast as you can (थोड़ी दूरी) अति वेग से दौड़ना ▶ **sprint** *noun* [C] थोड़ी दूरी की तेज़ दौड़

**sprout**[1] /spraʊt स्प्राउट् / *verb* [I, T] (used about a plant) to begin to grow or to produce new leaves (पौधों का) अंकुरित होना या पत्ते उगाना आरंभ करना; पल्लवित होना *The seeds are sprouting.*

**sprout**[2] /spraʊt स्प्राउट् / *noun* [C] **1** = **Brussels sprout** **2** a new part that has grown on a plant अंकुर, कल्ला, अँखुआ

**spruce** /spruːs स्प्रूस् / *verb*

IDM **spruce (sb/yourself) up** to make sb/yourself clean and tidy स्वयं को साफ़-सुथरा बनाना

**sprung** ➪ **spring**[2] का past participle रूप

**spun** ➪ **spin**[1] का past participle रूप

**spur**[1] /spɜː(r) स्प(र्) / *noun* [C] **1** a piece of metal that a rider wears on the back of his/her boots to encourage the horse to go faster घोड़े के तेज़ दौड़ने के लिए घुड़सवार के जूतों के तले में लगा धातु का एड़ या महमेज ➪ **horse** पर चित्र देखिए। **2 a spur (to sth)** something that encourages you to do sth or that makes sth happen more quickly प्रेरक (वस्तु) (जो किसी कार्य को शीघ्रता से करने या होने को प्रेरित करे) **3** (in geography) a part of a hill that sticks out from the rest, often with lower ground around it (भूगोल में) पहाड़ी का आगे को निकला हिस्सा (जिसके चारों ओर की भूमि प्रायः नीची होती है); पर्वत-स्कंध, रिज

IDM **on the spur of the moment** without planning; suddenly बिना पूर्व योजना के; तत्काल, अकस्मात

**spur**[2] /spɜː(r) स्प(र्) / *verb* [T] (**spurring; spurred**) spur sb/sth (on/onto sth) to encourage sb or make him/her work harder or faster अधिक मेहनत या तेज़ी से काम करने के लिए (किसी को) प्रेरित या बाध्य करना *The letter spurred me into action.* ○ *We were spurred on by the positive feedback from customers.*

**spurn** /spɜːn स्पन् / *verb* [T] (*formal*) to refuse sth that sb has offered to you पेश की गई वस्तु को ठुकराना, स्वीकार न करना *to spurn an offer of friendship*

**spurt** /spɜːt स्पट् / *verb* **1** [I, T] (used about a liquid) to come out quickly with great force; to make a liquid do this (तरल पदार्थ का) तेज़ी से बहुत शक्ति के साथ बह निकलना, की धार छूटना; (तरल पदार्थ की) धार छोड़ना *Blood spurted from the wound.* **2** [I] to suddenly increase your speed or effort एकाएक रफ़्तार या कोशिश बढ़ा देना ▶ **spurt** *noun* [C] धार, फुहार

**spy**[1] /spaɪ स्पाइ / *noun* [C] (*pl.* **spies**) a person who tries to get secret information about another country, person or organization गुप्तचर, जासूस

**spy**[2] /spaɪ स्पाइ / *verb* (*pres. part.* **spying;** *3rd person sing. pres.* **spies;** *pt, pp* **spied**) **1** [I] to try to get secret information about sb/sth किसी के विषय में गुप्त जानकारी लेने का प्रयत्न करना ➪ **espionage** देखिए। **2** [T] (*formal*) to see देखना

IDM **spy on sb/sth** to watch sb/sth secretly किसी पर चुपचाप नज़र रखना, किसी की जासूसी करना, का भेद लेना *The man next door is spying on us.*

**spyhole** /ˈspaɪhəʊl ˈस्पाइहोल्/ *noun* [C] a small hole in a door for looking at the person on the other side before deciding to let him/her in दरवाज़े में बना छोटा छेद (जिसमें से दूसरी तरफ़ खड़े व्यक्ति को देखा जा सकता है)

**sq** *abbr.* 1 = **square**[2] 6 *10 sq cm* 2 **Sq.** = **square**[1] 2 *6 Wellington Sq.*

**squabble** /ˈskwɒbl ˈस्क्वॉबल्/ *verb* [I] **squabble (over/ about sth)** to argue in a noisy way about sth that is not very important छोटी-मोटी बात पर ऊँचे स्वर में झगड़ा करना ▶ **squabble** *noun* [C] छोटी-मोटी बात पर झगड़ा

**squad** /skwɒd स्क्वॉड्/ *noun* [C, *with sing. or pl. verb*] a group of people who work as a team दल के रूप में किसी विशेष काम करने वालों का समूह; दस्ता *He's a policeman with the drugs squad.*

**squadron** /ˈskwɒdrən ˈस्क्वॉड्रन्/ *noun* [C, *with sing. or pl. verb*] a group of military aircraft or ships सैन्य विमानों या पोतों का दस्ता; स्क्वाड्रन

**squalid** /ˈskwɒlɪd ˈस्क्वॉलिड्/ *adj.* very dirty, untidy and unpleasant बहुत गंदा; मैला-कुचैला और घिनौना *squalid housing conditions*

**squall** /skwɔːl स्क्वॉल्/ *noun* [C] a sudden storm with strong winds तेज़ हवाओं के साथ आँधी-तूफ़ान; झंझा-वात

**squalor** /ˈskwɒlə(r) ˈस्क्वॉल(र्)/ *noun* [U] the state of being very dirty, untidy or unpleasant घोर गंदगी; बहुत गंदा, मैला-कुचैला या घिनौना होने की स्थिति *to live* ***in squalor***

**squander** /ˈskwɒndə(r) ˈस्क्वॉन्ड(र्)/ *verb* [T] **squander sth (on sth)** to waste time, money, etc. समय, पैसा आदि बरबाद करना *He squanders his time on TV and computer games.*

**square**[1] /skweə(r) स्क्वेअ(र्)/ *noun* [C] 1 a shape that has four straight sides of the same length and four angles of 90 degrees (**right angles**) वर्ग (चार समान भुजाओं और चार समकोणों वाली आकृति) *There are 64 squares on a chess board.* ➪ **shape** पर चित्र देखिए। 2 (*also* **Square**) (*abbr.* **Sq.**) an open space in a town or city that has buildings all around it किसी कस्बे या नगर में चारों ओर भवनों से घिरा खुला इलाक़ा; चौक *Protesters gathered in the town square.* 3 the number that you get when you multiply another number by itself वर्गफल (किसी संख्या को उसी से गुणा करने पर प्राप्त संख्या) *Four is the square of two.* ➪ **squared** और **square root** देखिए।

**square**[2] /skweə(r) स्क्वेअ(र्)/ *adj., adv.* 1 having four straight sides of the same length and corners of 90° (कोई) वर्गाकार (वस्तु) (जिसकी चारों भुजाएँ और कोण समान हों) *a square tablecloth* 2 shaped like a square or forming an angle of about 90° वर्ग की शकल की या समकोण बनाती हुई-सी (कोई वस्तु) *a square face* ○ *square shoulders* 3 (*not before a noun*) not owing any money हिसाब-किताब बेबाक, चुकता या बराबर *Here is the money I owe you. Now we're (all) square.* 4 (*not before a noun*) having equal points (in a game, etc.) समान अंक प्राप्त, बराबरी पर (किसी खेल आदि में) *The teams were* ***all square*** *at half-time.* 5 fair or honest, especially in business matters निष्पक्षता या ईमानदारी का (विशेषतः व्यापारिक मामला) *a square deal* 6 (*abbr.* **sq**) used for talking about the area of sth किसी वस्तु का क्षेत्रफल बताने के लिए प्रयुक्त *If a room is 5 metres long and 4 metres wide, its area is 20 square metres.* 7 (used about sth that is square in shape) having sides of a particular length (कोई वर्गाकार वस्तु) विशेष लंबाई की भुजाओं वाली *The picture is twenty centimetres square* (= each side is twenty centimetres long). 8 (*also* **squarely**) in an obvious and direct way स्पष्ट और सीधे तौर पर ईमानदारी से या सच्चाई से *to look sb square in the eye* ○ *The blame falls squarely on her.*

**IDM** **a square meal** a good meal that makes you feel satisfied भरपेट भोजन

**square**[3] /skweə(r) स्क्वेअ(र्)/ *verb* [I, T] **square (sth) with sb/sth** to agree with sth; to make sure that sb/sth agrees with sth किसी वस्तु से संगत होना, मेल खाना; किसी के साथ पूरा ताल-मेल बैठाना या सामंजस्य स्थापित करना *Your conclusion doesn't really square with the facts.*

**PHR V** **square up (with sb)** to pay sb the money that you owe him/her किसी का उधार चुकता या बेबाक करना

**squared** /skweəd स्क्वेअड्/ *adj.* (*mathematics*) (used about a number) multiplied by itself (कोई संख्या) उसी से गुणित; वर्गकृत *Four squared is sixteen.* ➪ **square**[1] **3** और **square root** देखिए।

**square root** *noun* [C] (*mathematics*) a number that produces another particular number when it is multiplied by itself वर्गमूल (वर्गमूल को यदि वर्गमूल से गुणा किया जाए तो वह संख्या मिलती है, जिसका वह वर्गमूल है) *The square root of sixteen is four.* ➪ **square**[1] **3, squared, root** और **cube root** देखिए।

**squash**[1] /skwɒʃ स्क्वॉश्/ *verb* 1 [T] to press sth so that it is damaged, changes shape or becomes flat (को) कुचल देना (का) भुरता बना देना (किसी वस्तु को ऐसे दबाना कि वह टूट-फूट जाए, उसकी शकल बदल जाए या वह चपटी हो जाए) *The fruit at the bottom of* *the bag will* ***get squashed**.* **2** [I, T] to go into a place, or move sb/sth to a place, where there is not much space छोटी-सी जगह पर (ज़बरदस्ती) घुसकर बैठना या दूसरों को बैठाना *We all squashed into the back of the car.* **3** [T] to destroy sth because it is a problem किसी (समस्याजनक मुद्दे को) समाप्त कर देना *to squash sb's suggestion/plan/idea*

**squash[2]** /skwɒʃ स्क्वॉश्/ *noun* **1** [C, *sing.*] a lot of people in a small space भीड़-भाड़ (थोड़े-से स्थान पर बहुत-से लोग) *We can get ten people around the table, but it's* ***a bit of a squash**.* **2** [U, C] a drink that is made from fruit juice and sugar. You add water to squash before you drink it फलों के रस और चीनी से बना पेय, एक प्रकार का शरबत; स्क्वॉश (जिसमें पानी मिला कर पिया जाता है) *orange squash* **3** [U] a game for two people, played in a special room (**court**). You play squash by hitting a small rubber ball against anyone of the walls of the room एक विशेष कमरे में खेला जाने वाला दो खिलाड़ियों का खेल (जिसमें किसी दीवार पर रबड़ की गेंद को मारते हैं); स्क्वॉश का खेल *a squash racket* **4** [C, U] (*pl.* **squash**) a type of vegetable that grows on the ground with hard skin and orange flesh inside, or soft yellow or green skin and white flesh inside कुम्हड़ा

**squat[1]** /skwɒt स्क्वॉट्/ *verb* [I] (**squatting; squatted**) **1** to rest with your weight on your feet, your legs bent and your bottom just above the ground उकड़ूँ बैठना (टाँगों को मोड़कर ज़मीन से कुछ ऊपर पैरों के बल बैठना) **2** to go and live in an empty building without permission from the owner खाली मकान पर बिना मालिक से पूछे या नाजायज़, कब्ज़ा जमा लेना

**squat[2]** /skwɒt स्क्वॉट्/ *adj.* short and fat or thick छोटा और मोटा या ऊँचाई के अनुपात में अधिक चौड़ा *a squat ugly building*

**squatter** /ˈskwɒtə(r) ˈस्क्वॉट(र्)/ *noun* [C] a person who is living in an empty building without the owner's permission ख़ाली मकान पर नाजायज़ कब्ज़ा जमाने वाला व्यक्ति

**squawk** /skwɔːk स्क्वॉक्/ *verb* [I] (used especially about a bird) to make a loud unpleasant noise (पक्षी का) चीख़ मारने जैसी आवाज़ करना ▶ **squawk** *noun* [C] चीख़, चिल्लाहट

**squeak** /skwiːk स्क्वीक्/ *noun* [C] a short high noise that is not very loud चूँ चूँ (की आवाज़), चीं चीं, चरमराहट *the squeak of a mouse* ○ *a squeak of surprise* ▶ **squeak** *verb* [I, T] चीं चीं या चूँ चूँ करना ▶ **squeaky** *adj.* चीं चीं करने वाला *a squeaky floorboard* ○ *a squeaky voice*

**squeal** /skwiːl स्क्वील्/ *verb* [I, T] to make a loud high noise because of pain, fear or enjoyment (दर्द, डर या ख़ुशी के मारे) किलकारी मारना; चिल्ला उठना *The baby squealed in delight at the new toy.* ▶ **squeal** *noun* [C] किलकारी

**squeamish** /ˈskwiːmɪʃ ˈस्क्वीमिश्/ *adj.* easily upset by unpleasant sights, especially blood (ख़ून आदि के) घिनौने दृश्यों से जल्दी परेशान हो जाने वाला; सुकुमार

**squeeze[1]** /skwiːz स्क्वीज़्/ *verb* **1** [T] **squeeze sth (out); squeeze sth (from/out of sth)** to press sth hard for a particular purpose (विशेष प्रयोजन से) किसी वस्तु को कसकर दबाना *to squeeze a tube of toothpaste* **2** [I, T] **squeeze (sb/sth) into, through, etc. sth; squeeze (sb/sth) through, in, past, etc.** to force sb/sth into or through a small space थोड़ी-सी जगह में या में से किसी को ज़बरदस्ती बैठाना या निकालना *We can squeeze another person into the back of the car.*

**squeeze[2]** /skwiːz स्क्वीज़्/ *noun* **1** [C] an act of pressing sth firmly (किसी चीज़ को) कसकर दबाने की क्रिया *He gave her hand a squeeze to assure her.* **2** [C] the amount of liquid that you get from squeezing an orange, a lemon, etc. (नारंगी, नींबू आदि को) दबाकर निकाले गए रस की मात्रा *a squeeze of lemon* **3** [*sing.*] a situation where there is not much space जगह की तंगी *It was* ***a tight squeeze*** *to get everybody around the table.* **4** [C, *usually sing.*] an effort to use less money, time, etc., especially with the result that there is not enough पैसा, समय आदि के कम उपयोग का प्रयास (जिसके फलस्वरूप न्यूनता की स्थिति बन जाए)

**squelch** /skweltʃ स्क्वेल्च्/ *verb* [I] to make the sound your feet make when you are walking in deep wet mud (गाढ़े कीचड़ में चलते हुए) फच फच की आवाज़ करना

**squid** /skwɪd स्क्विड्/ *noun* [C, U] (*pl.* **squid** or **squids**) a sea animal that we eat with a long soft body and ten **tentacles** कोमल शरीर और दस स्पर्शकों वाला (खाने का) एक समुद्री जीव; समुद्रफेनी

**squiggle** /ˈskwɪgl ˈस्क्विग्ल्/ *noun* [C] (*informal*) a quickly drawn line that goes in all directions (जल्दबाज़ी में खींची गई) टेढ़ी-मेढ़ी रेखा

**squint** /skwɪnt स्क्विन्ट्/ *verb* [I] **1 squint (at sth)** to look at sth with your eyes almost closed अधखुली आँखों से (किसी को) देखना *to squint in bright sunlight* **2** to have eyes that appear to look in different directions at the same time भेंगा होना (एक ही समय में अलग-अलग दिशाओं में देखने का आभास कराना) ▶ **squint** *noun* [C] भेंगापन

**squirm** /skwɜːm स्क्वम्/ *verb* [I] to move around in your chair because you are nervous, uncomfortable, etc. (घबराहट, परेशानी आदि के कारण) छटपटाना, तड़फड़ाना (बैठे-बैठे इधर-उधर हरकत करना)

**squirrel** /ˈskwɪrəl ˈस्क्विरल्/ *noun* [C] a small red or grey animal with a long thick tail that lives in trees and eats nuts गिलहरी ➪ **rodents** पर चित्र देखिए।

**squirt** /skwɜːt स्क्वट्/ *verb* [I, T] if a liquid squirts or if you squirt it, it is suddenly forced out of sth in a particular direction (किसी विशेष दिशा में) एकाएक द्रव की धार, फुहार छूटना या छोड़ना *I cut the orange and juice squirted out.* ○ *She squirted water on the flames.* ▶ **squirt** *noun* [C] (किसी द्रव की) धार, फुहार *a squirt of lemon juice*

**Sr** *abbr.* = **Snr**

**St** *abbr.* **1** = **saint** *St Peter* **2** = **street** *20 Park St* **3 st** (*BrE*) stone; a measure of weight स्टोन; तोल की एक माप

**stab[1]** /stæb स्टैब्/ *verb* [T] (**stabbing; stabbed**) to push a knife or other pointed object into sb/sth (किसी को या में) छुरा या कोई नुकीली चीज़ भोंकना, घोंपना या घुसेड़ना *The man had been stabbed in the back.*

**stab[2]** /stæb स्टैब्/ *noun* [C] **1** an injury that was caused by a knife, etc. छुरे का घाव (छुरा आदि भोंकने से हुआ घाव) *He received stab wounds to his neck and back.* **2** a sudden sharp pain तीखा और अचानक उठा दर्द; टीस

IDM **have a stab at sth/doing sth** (*informal*) to try to do sth कुछ करने की कोशिश करना

**stabbing[1]** /ˈstæbɪŋ ˈस्टैबिङ्/ *noun* [C] an occasion when sb is injured or killed with a knife or other sharp object छुरा भोंकने की वारदात (जिसमें व्यक्ति घायल हो जाए या मर जाए)

**stabbing[2]** /ˈstæbɪŋ ˈस्टैबिङ्/ *adj.* (*only before a noun*) (used about a pain) sudden and strong (दर्द) अचानक उठा और तीखा

**stability** /stəˈbɪləti स्टˈबिलटि/ *noun* [U] the state or quality of being steady and not changing स्थिरता (स्थिर या अचल रहने की स्थिति, विशेषता या गुण) *period of stability* ○ *The ladder is slightly wider at the bottom for greater stability.* ✪ विलोम **instability** ➪ **stable** adjective देखिए।

**stabilize** (*also* **-ise**) /ˈsteɪbəlaɪz ˈस्टेबलाइज़्/ *verb* [I, T] to become or to make sth firm, steady and unlikely to change किसी वस्तु या स्थिति का बिना बदले और स्थिर रहना या उसे ऐसा बनाना *The patient's condition has stabilized.* ➪ **destabilize** देखिए।

**stable[1]** /ˈsteɪbl ˈस्टेब्ल्/ *adj.* steady, firm and unikely to change स्थिर, मज़बूत और जिसमें परिवर्तन संभावित नहीं; अनबदला *This ladder doesn't seem very stable.* ○ *The patient is* ***in a stable condition.*** ✪ विलोम **unstable** ➪ **stability** noun देखिए।

**stable[2]** /ˈsteɪbl ˈस्टेब्ल्/ *noun* [C] a building where horses are kept अस्तबल, घुड़साल

**stack[1]** /stæk स्टैक्/ *noun* [C] **1** a tidy pile of sth (किसी वस्तु का) तरीक़े से लगाया गया ढेर; अंबार, टाल *a stack of plates/books/chairs* **2** (*informal*) (*often plural*) a lot of sth बड़े परिमाण में कोई वस्तु ढेर सारी (कोई) चीज़ *I've still got stacks of work to do.* **3** (in geography) a tall thin part of a cliff that has been separated from the land and stands on its own in the sea (भूगोल में) समुद्र में (धरती से अलग होकर) अपने बूते खड़ी ऊँची पतली चट्टान

**stack[2]** /stæk स्टैक्/ *verb* [T] **stack sth (up)** to put sth into a tidy pile (किसी वस्तु की) सुव्यवस्थित ढेरी बनाना; चट्टा लगाना *Could you stack those chairs for me?*

**stacked** /stækt स्टैक्ट्/ *adj.* full of piles of things जिसमें वस्तुओं के अंबार लगे हों *The room was stacked high with books.*

**stadium** /ˈsteɪdiəm ˈस्टेडिअम्/ *noun* [C] (*pl.* **stadiums** or **stadia** /-diə -डिआ/) a large structure, usually with no roof, where people can sit and watch sport स्टेडियम (प्रायः बिना छत का, बड़ा ढाँचा जहाँ बैठकर लोग खेल देखते हैं)

**staff** /stɑːf स्टाफ़/ *noun* [C, *usually sing.*, U] **1** the group of people who work for a particular organization किसी संस्था के कार्यकर्ता या कर्मचारी; स्टाफ़ *hotel/library/medical staff* NOTE **Staff** का प्रयोग प्रायः एकवचन में होता है परंतु इसके साथ आने वाली क्रिया बहुवचन में होती है—*The staff all speak good English.* **2** (*AmE*) = **stave[1]** ▶ **staff** *verb* [T] (*usually passive*) कर्मचारी रखना *The office is staffed 24 hours a day.*

**stag** /stæg स्टैग्/ *noun* [C] the male of a **deer** (नर) हिरण

**stage[1]** /steɪdʒ स्टेज्/ *noun* **1** [C] one part of the progress or development of sth किसी वस्तु की प्रगति या विकास का एक अंश; चरण, अवस्था *We did the journey* ***in two stages.*** ○ ***At this stage*** *it's too early to say what will happen.* **2** [C] a platform in a theatre, concert hall, etc. on which actors, musicians, etc. perform रंगशाला आदि का मंच; रंगमंच **3** [*sing.*, U] the world of theatre; the profession of acting रंगमंच का क्षेत्र; अभिनय का व्यवसाय *an actor of stage and screen*

**stage**[2] /steɪdʒ स्टेज् / *verb* [T] **1** to organize a performance of a play, concert, etc. for the public नाटक, संगीत समारोह आदि का सार्वजनिक रूप से आयोजन करना **2** to organize an event किसी कार्यक्रम का आयोजन करना *They have decided to stage a 24-hour strike.*

**stage manager** *noun* [C] the person who is responsible for the stage, lights, scenery, etc. during a theatre performance मंच-व्यवस्थापक (कार्यक्रम के दौरान प्रकाश, दृश्य, सज्जा आदि की व्यवस्था करने वाला)

**stagger** /ˈstægə(r) ˈस्टैग(र्) / *verb* [I] to walk with short steps as if you could fall at any moment, for example because you are ill, drunk or carrying sth heavy (बीमार, नशे में या वज़नदार चीज़ लिए होने के कारण) लड़खड़ाना, डगमगाना (छोटे-छोटे क़दमों से गिरते-पड़ते चलना) *He staggered across the finishing line and collapsed.*

**staggered** /ˈstægəd ˈस्टैगड् / *adj.* **1** (*informal*) very surprised बहुत हैरान, अचंभित *I was absolutely staggered when I heard the news.* **2** (used about a set of times, payments, etc.) arranged so that they do not all happen at the same time (कार्यालयों के समयों, भुगतानों आदि ) अपेक्षित व्यवसाय या अंतर के साथ व्यवस्थित (न कि एक साथ संयोजित) *staggered working hours* (= when people start and finish work at different times)

**staggering** /ˈstægərɪŋ ˈस्टैगरिङ् / *adj.* that you find difficult to believe विस्मयकारी, हैरतअंगेज़ (जिस पर विश्वास करना कठिन हो) ▶ **staggeringly** *adv.* विस्मयकारी रीति से, हैरतअंगेज़ तरीक़े से

**stagnant** /ˈstægnənt ˈस्टैग्नन्ट् / *adj.* **1** (used about water) not flowing and therefore dirty and having an unpleasant smell (पानी) ठहरा हुआ, रुका हुआ (और इसलिए गंदा और बदबूदार) **2** (used about business, etc.) not active; not developing (व्यापार आदि) गतिहीन, सुस्त, मंद; विकासरुद्ध *a stagnant economy*

**stagnate** /stægˈneɪt स्टैग्ˈनेट् / *verb* [I] **1** to stop developing, changing or being active विकास परिवर्तन या गति नहीं होना, निष्क्रिय पड़ जाना *a stagnating economy* **2** (used about water) to be or become stagnant (पानी का) एक जगह रुक जाना ▶ **stagnation** /stægˈneɪʃn स्टैग्ˈनेश्न् / *noun* [U] निष्क्रियता, रुद्धता

**stag night** (*also* **stag party**) *noun* [C] a party for men only that is given for a man just before his wedding day पुरुष गोष्ठी (विवाह के दिन से ठीक पहले वर के लिए पार्टी जिसमें केवल पुरुष शामिल होते हैं) ➪ **hen party** देखिए।

**staid** /steɪd स्टेड् / *adj.* serious, old-fashioned and rather boring गंभीर, पुरानी चाल और कुछ उबाऊ क़िस्म का

**stain** /steɪn स्टेन् / *verb* [I, T] to leave a coloured mark that is difficult to remove धब्बा या दाग़ लगना (जो आसानी से साफ़ न हो सके) *Don't spill any of that tomato soup—it'll stain the carpet.* ▶ **stain** *noun* [C] दाग़, धब्बा *The blood had left a stain on his shirt.*

**stained glass** *noun* [U] pieces of coloured glass that are used in church windows, etc. (चर्च आदि की खिड़कियों में प्रयुक्त) रंगीन काँच के टुकड़े

**stainless steel** *noun* [U] a type of steel that does not **rust** स्टेनलेस स्टील (स्टील जिस पर जंग नहीं लगता) *a stainless steel pan*

**stair** /steə(r) स्टेअ(र्) / *noun* **1 stairs** [*pl.*] a series of steps inside a building that lead from one level to another (किसी इमारत के अंदर बनी) सीढ़ियाँ, ज़ीना (एक मंज़िल से दूसरी में जाने के लिए प्रयुक्त) ***a flight of stairs*** ○ ***down the stairs*** ○ ***up the stairs*** ➪ **downstairs** और **upstairs** देखिए।

> **NOTE** तुलनार्थ देखिए: **stair** और **step. Stairs** या **flights of stairs** सामान्यतया भवनों के अंदर होती हैं। **Steps** वे सीढ़ियाँ है जो प्रायः भवनों के बाहर की ओर तथा पत्थर या कंकरीट से बनी होती है।

**2** [C] one of the steps in a series inside a building (भवन के अंदर बनी) सीढ़ियों की एक सीढ़ी; सीढ़ी का तख़्ता

**staircase** /ˈsteəkeɪs ˈस्टेअकेस् / (*also* **stairway** /ˈsteəweɪ ˈस्टेअवे /) *noun* [C] a set of stairs with rails on each side that you can hold on to (दोनों ओर) रेलिंग वाला ज़ीना ➪ **escalator** देखिए तथा **spiral** पर चित्र भी देखिए।

**stake**[1] /steɪk स्टेक् / *noun* **1** [C] a wooden or metal pole with a point at one end that you push into the ground (एक ओर से नोक वाला) लकड़ी या धातु का खूँटा (ज़मीन में गाड़ने के लिए) **2** [C] a part of a company, etc. that you own, usually because you have put money into it अपने स्वामित्व वाली कंपनी आदि का एक भाग (कंपनी में पैसा लगाने के कारण), कंपनी में भागीदारी; शेयरधारिता *Foreign investors now* ***have a 20% stake in*** *the company.* **3 stakes** [*pl.*] the things that you might win or lose in a game or in a particular situation (किसी खेल या विशेष स्थिति में) दाँव पर लगाया पैसा आदि *We play cards for money, but never for very high stakes.*
**IDM at stake** in danger of being lost; at risk दाँव पर (जहाँ हार का ख़तरा है); जोख़िम में *He thought very carefully because he knew his future was at stake.*

**stake**[2] /steɪk स्टेक् / *verb* [T] **stake sth (on sth)** to put your future, etc. in danger by doing sth, because you hope that it will bring you a good result (कुछ कर के) अपने भविष्य आदि को दाँव पर

लगाना (अनुकूल फल की आशा में) *He is staking his political reputation on this issue.*

IDM **stake a/your claim (to sth)** to say that you have a right to have sth किसी चीज़ पर दावा या अधिकार जताना

PHR V **stake sth out** 1 to clearly mark an area of land that you are going to use (अपने) भूखंड की सीमा चिह्नित करना या हदबंदी करना (खूँटों आदि से घेर कर) 2 to make your position, opinion, etc. clear to everyone सबके सामने अपनी स्थिति स्पष्ट करना, अपने विचार आदि रखना *In his speech, the President staked out his position on tax reform.* 3 to watch a place secretly for a period of time (कुछ समय तक) गुप्त रीति से किसी स्थान पर निगाह रखना *The police had been staking out the house for months.*

**stalactite** /ˈstæləktaɪt ˈस्टैलक्टाइट्/ *noun* [C] (in geography) a long thin piece of rock hanging down from the roof of a **cave** (भूगोल में) किसी गुफ़ा की छत से लटका चट्टान का लंबा पतला टुकड़ा; हिमलुंबी ➪ **limestone** पर चित्र देखिए।

**stalagmite** /ˈstæləgmaɪt ˈस्टैलग्माइट्/ *noun* [C] (in geography) a thin piece of rock pointing upwards from the floor of a **cave** (भूगोल में) गुफ़ा में ज़मीन से ऊपर की ओर उठा हुआ चट्टान का पतला टुकड़ा ➪ **limestone** पर चित्र देखिए।

**stale** /steɪl स्टेल्/ *adj.* 1 (used about food or air) old and not fresh any more (खाने की वस्तु या हवा) बासी *The bread will* **go stale** *if you don't put it away.* 2 not interesting or exciting any more जो अब दिलचस्प या उत्तेजक नहीं रहा; घिसा-पिटा ➪ **fresh** देखिए।

**stalemate** /ˈsteɪlmeɪt ˈस्टेल्मेट्/ *noun* [*sing.*, U] 1 a situation in an argument in which neither side can win or make any progress गतिरोध 2 (in chess) a position in which a game ends without a winner because neither side can move (शतरंज के खेल में) हार-जीत का फैसला न हो पाने की स्थिति (मोहरों के चलना संभव न रह जाने के कारण)

**stalk[1]** /stɔːk स्टॉक्/ *noun* [C] one of the long thin parts of a plant which the flowers, leaves or fruit grow on डंठल, डंडी

**stalk[2]** /stɔːk स्टॉक्/ *verb* 1 [T] to move slowly and quietly towards an animal in order to catch or kill it लुक-छिप कर शिकार का पीछा करना *a lion stalking its prey* 2 [T] to follow a person over a period of time in a frightening or annoying way (देर तक) किसी व्यक्ति का पीछा करना (ऐसे कि वह डर या परेशान हो जाए) *The stranger had been stalking her for two years.* 3 [I] to walk in an angry way ताव से या अकड़ कर चलना

**stall[1]** /stɔːl स्टॉल्/ *noun* 1 [C] a small shop with an open front or a table with things for sale स्टॉल; छोटी दुकान (सामने से खुली या जिसमें सामान रखकर बेचने के लिए एक मेज़ लगी हो) *a market stall* ○ *a bookstall* 2 **stalls** [*pl.*] the seats nearest the front in a theatre or cinema (किसी रंगशाला या सिनेमा घर में) सबसे आगे की सीटें 3 [C, *sing.*] a situation in which a vehicle's engine suddenly stops because it is not receiving enough power पर्याप्त ऊर्जा या पेट्रोल आदि के अभाव में) वाहन के इंजन के एकाएक बंद हो जाने की स्थिति; गतिह्रास *The plane went into a stall and almost crashed.*

**stall[2]** /stɔːl स्टॉल्/ *verb* [I, T] 1 (used about a vehicle) to stop suddenly because the engine is not receiving enough power; to make a vehicle do this accidentally (पर्याप्त पेट्रोल आदि के अभाव में) वाहन के इंजन का अचानक बंद हो जाना; ग़लती से इस प्रकार इंजन को बंद कर देना *The bus often stalls on this hill.* 2 to avoid doing sth or to try to stop sth happening until a later time किसी काम को या किसी बात को होने से रोक देना (बाद में करने या होने के लिए)

**stallion** /ˈstæliən ˈस्टैलिअन्/ *noun* [C] an adult male horse, especially one that is kept for breeding वयस्क घोड़ा (विशेषतः प्रजनन क्रिया के लिए सुरक्षित) ➪ **horse** देखिए।

**stalwart** /ˈstɔːlwət ˈस्टॉल्वट्/ *adj.* always loyal to the same organization, team, etc. एक ही संस्था, टीम आदि का पक्का वफ़ादार या समर्थक *a stalwart supporter of the club* ▶ **stalwart** *noun* [C] पक्का समर्थक

**stamen** /ˈsteɪmən ˈस्टेमन्/ *noun* [C] a small thin male part in the middle of a flower that produces a fine powder (**pollen**) पुंकेसर (पुष्प के मध्य में स्थिर नर केसर, जिससे और फूल पैदा होते हैं) ➪ **flower** पर चित्र देखिए।

**stamina** /ˈstæmɪnə ˈस्टैमिना/ *noun* [U] the ability to do sth that involves a lot of physical or mental effort for a long time दम-ख़म, दम, ऊर्जस्विता (प्रचुर शारीरिक या मानसिक श्रम की अपेक्षा वाले काम को लंबे समय तक करने की क्षमता); जीवट *You need a lot of stamina to run long distances.*

**stammer** /ˈstæmə(r) ˈस्टैम(र्)/ *verb* [I, T] to speak with difficulty, repeating sounds and pausing before saying things correctly हकलाना *He stammered an apology and left quickly.* ▶ **stammer** *noun* [*sing.*] हकलाहट, हकलाने की प्रवृति *to have a stammer*

**stamp[1]** /stæmp स्टैम्प्/ *noun* [C] 1 (*formal* **postage stamp**) a small piece of paper that you stick onto a letter or package to show that you have paid for it to be posted डाक-टिकट *His hobby is collecting stamps.* **2** a small object that prints some words, a design, the date, etc. when you press it onto a surface ठप्पा, छाप, मोहर *a date stamp* **3** the mark made by stamping sth onto a surface (किसी सतह पर बना) मोहर का निशान *Have you got any visa stamps in your passport?* ○ (*figurative*) ***stamp of approval*** **4 the stamp of sth** [*usually sing.*] something that shows a particular quality or that sth was done by a particular person कोई विशिष्ट विशेषता प्रकट करने वाली वस्तु या व्यक्ति-विशेष का विशिष्ट कार्य

**stamp[2]** /stæmp स्टैम्प्/ *verb* **1** [I, T] **stamp (on sth)** to put your foot down very heavily and noisily पैर पटकना (ज़ोर से और आवाज़ करते हुए) *It was so cold that I had to stamp my feet to keep warm.* ○ *She stamped her foot in anger.* **2** [I] to walk with loud heavy steps पैर पटकते हुए चलना *She stamped around the room, shouting angrily.* **3** [T] **stamp A (on B); stamp B (with A)** to print some words, a design, the date, etc. by pressing a small object (**a stamp**) onto a surface किसी सतह पर मोहर लगाना; ठप्पा मारना *to stamp a passport* **PHR V** **stamp sth out** to put an end to sth completely किसी वस्तु को पूरी तरह से समाप्त कर देना *The police are trying to stamp out this kind of crime.*

**stamp duty** *noun* [U] a tax on some legal documents क़ानूनी दस्तावेज़ों पर लगने वाला कर; स्टाँप शुल्क

**stamped addressed envelope** (*also* **self-addressed envelope**) *noun* [C] (*abbr.* **sae**) an empty envelope with your own name and address and a stamp on it that you send to a company, etc. when you want sth sent back to you टिकट-युक्त और अपना या प्रेषक का पता लिखा लिफ़ाफ़ा

**stampede** /stæmˈpiːd स्टैम्ˈपीड्/ *noun* [C] a situation in which a large number of animals or people start running in the same direction, for example because they are frightened or excited (डर या उत्तेजना के कारण) बहुत सारे पशुओं या मनुष्यों का एक ही दिशा में भागने लगना; भगदड़ ► **stampede** *verb* [I] भगदड़ मचना या मचाना

**stance** /stæns; stɑːns स्टैन्स्; स्टान्स्/ *noun* [C, *usually sing.*] **1 stance (on sth)** the opinions that sb expresses publicly about sth किसी विषय पर सार्वजनिक रूप से व्यक्त (किसी का) दृष्टिकोण *the Prime Minister's stance on foreign affairs* **2** the position in which sb stands, especially when playing a sport खड़े होने की मुद्रा (विशेषतः कोई खेल खेलते समय)

**stand[1]** /stænd स्टैन्ड्/ *verb* [I, T] (*pt, pp* **stood** /stʊd स्टुड्/) **1** [I] to be on your feet, not sitting or lying down; to be upright खड़ा होना (न कि बैठा या लेटा होना); सीधा खड़ा रहना *to* ***stand still*** ○ *Only a few houses were left standing after the earthquake.* **2** [I] **stand (up)** to rise to your feet from another position (उठकर) खड़ा हो जाना *He stood up when I entered the room.* **3** [T] to put sb/sth in a particular place or position किसी को विशेष स्थान या स्थिति में खड़ा कर देना *We stood the mirror against the wall* **4** [I] to be or to stay in a particular position or situation किसी विशेष अवस्था या स्थिति में होना या रहना *The castle stands on a hill.* ○ *The house has stood empty for ten years.* **5** [I] (used about an offer, a decision, etc.) to stay the same as before, without being changed (प्रस्ताव, निर्णय आदि का) (बिना बदले) पहले जैसा रहना *Does your decision still stand?* **6** [I] **stand (at) sth** to be of a particular height, level, amount, etc. (किसी वस्तु की) कोई विशेष ऊँचाई, स्तर, मात्रा आदि होना *The building stands nearly 60 metres high.* **7** [I] **stand (on sth)** to have an opinion or view about sth (किसी मुद्दे पर) कोई विचार या दृष्टिकोण होना **8** [I] **stand to do sth** to be in a situation where you are likely to do sth कुछ करने की स्थिति में होना *If he has to sell the company, he stands to lose a lot of money.* **9** [I] **stand (for/as sth)** to be one of the people hoping to be chosen in an election (**a candidate**) चुनाव में उम्मीदवार होना या खड़ा होना *She's standing for the European Parliament.* **10** [T] (*in negative sentences and questions, with can/could*) to not like sb/sth at all; to hate sb/sth किसी को बिलकुल भी पसंद न करना; किसी से घृणा या नफ़रत करना *I can't stand rude behaviour.* ○ *I couldn't* ***stand the thought of*** *waiting for two hours so I went home.* ✪ पर्याय **bear** **11** [T] (*used especially with can/could*) to be able to survive difficult conditions प्रतिकूल परिस्थिति में जीवित रहना, सहन कर लेना *Camels can stand extremely hot and cold temperatures.* ✪ पर्याय **take**

**PHR V** **stand around** to stand somewhere not doing anything कहीं पर बेकार में खड़ा रहना *A lot of people were just standing around outside.*

**stand aside** to move to one side एक तरफ़ खड़ा हो जाना *People stood aside to let the police pass.*

**stand back** to move back (किसी स्थान से) पीछे हटना *The policeman told everybody to stand back.*

**stand by** **1** to be present, but do nothing in a situation (किसी अवसर पर) मात्र उपस्थित रहना (परंतु करना कुछ भी नहीं) *How can you stand by and* *let them treat their animals like that?* **2** to be ready to act कार्रवाई के लिए तैयार रहना *The police are standing by in case there's trouble.*

**stand for sth** **1** to be a short form of sth किसी (लंबे नाम आदि) का संक्षिप्त रूप होना *What does NDTV stand for?* **2** to support sth (such as an idea or opinion) (किसी मान्यता या विचार आदि को) समर्थन देना *I like everything that the party stands for.*

**stand in (for sb)** to take sb's place for a short time (थोड़े समय के लिए) किसी और के लिए काम करना, किसी का स्थानापन्न होना

**stand out** to be easily seen or noticed स्पष्ट दिखाई देना या ध्यान आकृष्ट करना, औरों से विशिष्ट होना

**stand up** to be or become vertical सीधा खड़ा होना या खड़ा हो जाना *You'll look taller if you stand up straight.*

**stand up for sb/sth** to say or do sth which shows that you support sb/sth किसी के समर्थन में कुछ कहना या करना *He always stands up for his rights.*

**stand up to sb/sth** to defend yourself against sb/sth who is stronger or more powerful अपने से अधिक सुदृढ़ या सशक्त का मुक़ाबला करना

**stand[2]** /stænd स्टैन्ड्/ *noun* [C] **1** a table or an object that holds or supports sth, often so that people can buy it or look at it वस्तु को टेकने या टिकाने का साधन (कोई मेज़ आदि) (ताकि लोग उस वस्तु को देख सकें, ख़रीद सकें); स्टैंड *a newspaper stand* **2** a large structure where people can watch sport from seats arranged in rows that are low near the front and high near the back खेल के मैदान पर दर्शकों के बैठने के लिए ढाँचा (जिसकी कतारबद्ध सीटें आगे से नीची तथा पीछे से ऊँची हों), स्टैंड, दर्शक-स्थली **3 a stand (on/against sth)** a strong effort to defend yourself or sth that you have a strong opinion about अपने बचाव या अपने पक्ष के समर्थन का सशक्त प्रयास to ***take/make a stand***

**stand-alone** *adj.* (*computing*) (used about computer machinery or programs) able to operate without any other machinery or programs (कंप्यूटर यंत्र या प्रोग्राम) अन्य यंत्र या प्रोग्राम के बिना (स्वतंत्र रूप से) कार्य करने वाला

**standard[1]** /ˈstændəd ˈस्टैन्डड्/ *noun* [C] **1** a level of quality गुणवत्ता का स्तर; मानक *This work is not **up to** your usual **standard**.* **2** a level of quality that you compare sth else with अन्य की तुलना में गुणवत्ता का स्तर ***By** Indian **standards** this is a very expensive city.* ○ *He is a brilliant player **by any standard**.* **3** [*usually pl.*] a level of behaviour that is morally acceptable (नैतिक दृष्टि से उचित) आचरण का स्तर *Many people are worried about falling standards in modern society.*

**standard[2]** /ˈstændəd ˈस्टैन्डड्/ *adj.* **1** normal or average; not special or unusual सामान्य या औसत; विशेष या असाधारण नहीं *standard sizes* **2** that people generally accept as normal and correct सामान्य और शुद्ध के रूप में साधारणतया मान्य; स्टैंडर्ड *standard English*

**standardize** (*also* **-ise**) /ˈstændədaɪz ˈस्टैन्डडाइज़्/ *verb* [T] to make things that are different the same एक दूसरे से भिन्न वस्तुओं को एक ही रूप में ढालना; मानकयुक्त या मानकीकृत करना *Safety tests on old cars have been standardized throughout Europe.* ▶ **standardization** (*also* **-isation**) /ˌstændədaɪˈzeɪʃn ˌस्टैन्डडाइˈज़ेश्न्/ *noun* [U] मानकीकरण

**standard of living** *noun* [C] a measure of how comfortable the life of a particular person or group is जीवन-स्तर (किसी व्यक्ति या समूह के जीवन के सुख-सुविधा संपन्न होने की मात्रा) *The standard of living in the cities is high.*

**standby** /ˈstændbaɪ ˈस्टैन्ड्बाइ/ *noun* **1** [C] (*pl.* **standbys**) a thing or person that can be used if needed, for example if sb/sth is not available or in an emergency किसी के उपलब्ध न होने पर या आवश्यकता के समय काम में आने वाली वस्तु या व्यक्ति; स्थानापन्न, आपाती, आपातोपयोगी, एवज़ी **2** [U] the state of being ready to do sth immediately if needed or if a ticket becomes available आपातकाल या आवश्यकता के समय के लिए (या टिकट मिलने पर) तैयार रहने की स्थिति, आपातकालीन तैयारी की स्थिति *Ambulances were **on standby** along the route of the marathon.* ○ *We were **put on standby** for the flight to Rome.* ▶ **standby** *adj.* (*only before a noun*) अवलंब, आपाती *a standby ticket/passenger*

**stand-in** *noun* [C] **1** a person who does sb's job for a short time when he/she is not available (किसी का) स्थानापन्न या एवज़ी व्यक्ति (किसी अन्य के अनुपस्थित होने पर थोड़े समय के लिए काम करने वाला व्यक्ति) **2** a person who replaces an actor in some scenes in a film, especially dangerous ones फ़िल्म में एवज़ी अभिनेता (विशेष रूप से ख़तरनाक दृश्यों के लिए)

**standing[1]** /ˈstændɪŋ ˈस्टैन्डिङ्/ *noun* [U] **1** the position that sb/sth has, or how people think of him/her/it किसी की स्थिति, हैसियत या प्रतिष्ठा *The agreement has no legal standing.* ✪ पर्याय **status** **2** the amount of time during which sth has continued to exist किसी वस्तु के आस्तित्व की अवधि

**standing[2]** /ˈstændɪŋ ˈस्टैन्डिङ्/ *adj.* that always exists; permanent जो हमेशा रहे; स्थायी

**standing order** *noun* [C] an instruction to your bank to make a regular payment to sb from your account बैंक के लिए स्थायी निर्देश खाते से किसी को नियमित भुगतान करने के लिए

**standpoint** /ˈstændpɔɪnt ˈस्टैन्ड्पॉइन्ट्/ *noun* [C] a particular way of thinking about sth (किसी विषय पर) दृष्टिकोण ✪ पर्याय **point of view**

**standstill** /ˈstændstɪl ˈस्टैन्ड्स्टिल्/ *noun* [*sing.*] a situation when there is no movement, progress or activity ठहराव, विराम (गति, प्रगति या कोई हरकत न होने की स्थिति); गतिरोध *The traffic **is at/has come to a complete standstill.***

IDM **grind to a halt/stand still** ➪ **grind**[1] देखिए।

**stank** ➪ **stink** का past tense रूप

**stanza** /ˈstænzə ˈस्टैन्ज़ा/ *noun* [C] (used about poetry) a group of lines in a repeated pattern that form a unit in some types of poem बंद, छंद, पद ✪ पर्याय **verse**

**staple** /ˈsteɪpl ˈस्टेप्ल्/ *noun* [C] a small thin piece of bent wire that you push through pieces of paper using a special tool (**stapler**) in order to fasten them together स्टेपल (विशेष औज़ार) स्टेपलर से कागज़ों को बाँधने या जोड़ने का छोटा पतला मुड़ा हुआ तार का टुकड़ा ➪ **stationery** पर चित्र देखिए।

▶ **staple** *verb* [T] स्टेपल से कागज़ों को बाँधना या जोड़ना *Staple the letter to the application form.*

▶ **stapler** *noun* [C] स्टेप्लर ➪ **stationery** पर चित्र देखिए।

**staple diet** *noun* [C, *usually sing.*] the main food that a person or animal normally eats मनुष्य या पशु का मुख्य भोजन *a staple diet of rice and fish*

**star**[1] /stɑː(r) स्टा(र्)/ *noun* **1** [C] a large ball of burning gas in outer space that you see as a small point of light in the sky at night तारा, सितारा, नक्षत्र, तारक *It was a clear night and the stars were shining brightly.* **2** [C] a shape, decoration, mark, etc. with five or six points sticking out in a regular pattern तारे जैसी कोई आकृति, सजावट की वस्तु, चिह्न आदि *I've marked the possible candidates on the list with a star.* ➪ **shape** पर चित्र देखिए। **3** [C] a mark that represents a star that is used for telling you how good sth is, especially a hotel or restaurant (होटल या रेस्तराँ की) श्रेष्ठता का सूचक तारा चिह्न; स्टार *a five-star hotel* **4** [C] a famous person in acting, music or sport अभिनय, संगीत या खेल में प्रसिद्ध व्यक्ति; स्टार (जैसे फ़िल्म स्टार, क्रिकेट स्टार) *a pop/rock/film/movie star* ○ *a football/tennis star* **5 stars** [*pl.*] = **horoscope**

**star**[2] /stɑː(r) स्टा(र्)/ *verb* (**starring; starred**) **1** [I] **star (in sth)** to be one of the main actors in a play, film, etc. किसी नाटक, फ़िल्म आदि के मुख्य अभिनेताओं में से एक होना *Aishwarya Rai is to star in a new romantic comedy.* **2** [T] to have sb as a star किसी व्यक्ति का (किसी फ़िल्म में) अभिनेता होना या अभिनय करना *The film stars Madhuri Dixit.*

**starboard** /ˈstɑːbəd ˈस्टाबड्/ *noun* [U] the side of a ship that is on the right when you are facing towards the front of it सामने के तरफ से देखने पर जहा ज़ का दाहिना भाग; दायाँ, दक्षिण पाख या पक्ष ✪ विलोम **port**

**starch** /stɑːtʃ स्टाच्/ *noun* [C, U] **1** a white substance that is found in foods such as potatoes, rice and bread स्टार्च (आलू, चावल और डबल रोटी में पाया जाने वाला श्वेत पदार्थ) **2** a substance that is used for making cloth **stiff** कलफ़, माँड

**stardom** /ˈstɑːdəm ˈस्टाडम्/ *noun* [U] the state of being a famous person in acting, music or sport अभिनय, संगीत या खेल में प्रसिद्ध होने की स्थिति; प्रसिद्धि *She **shot to stardom** in a Yash Chopra film.*

**stare** /steə(r) स्टेअ(र्)/ *verb* [I] **stare (at sb/sth)** to look at sb or sth for a long time because you are surprised, shocked, etc. (आश्चर्य, विक्षोभ आदि के कारण) किसी को देर तक देखते रहना; घूरना, टकटकी लगा कर देखना *Everybody stared at his hat.* ○ *He didn't reply, he just stared into the distance.*

**starfish** /ˈstɑːfɪʃ ˈस्टाफ़िश/ *noun* [C] (*pl.* **starfish**) a flat sea animal in the shape of a star with five or more arms तारे की शकल की मछली (जिसकी पाँच या पाँच से अधिक बाँहें होती हैं); तारामीन

**starfruit** /ˈstɑːfruːt ˈस्टाफ़्रूट्/ *noun* [C] (*pl.* **starfruit**) a green or yellow tropical fruit with a shape like a star तारे की शकल का हरा या पीला (गरम देशों में उपजने वाला) फल

**stark**[1] /stɑːk स्टाक्/ *adj.* **1** very empty and without decoration and therefore not attractive एकदम खाली या सफ़ाचट और आकर्षण-विहीन *a stark landscape* **2** unpleasant and impossible to avoid कठोर और अनिवार्य *He now faces the **stark reality** of life in prison.* **3** very different to sth in a way that is easy to see सरासर साफ़ (किसी से सरासर अलग कि स्पष्ट दिखाई दे)

**stark**[2] /stɑːk स्टाक्/ *adv.* completely; extremely पूरी तरह से; अत्यधिक *stark empty* ○ *stark raving mad*

**starlight** /ˈstɑːlaɪt ˈस्टालाइट्/ *noun* [U] the light that is sent out by stars in the sky तारों से निकलने वाला प्रकाश; नक्षत्र-प्रकाश

**starry** /ˈstɑːri ˈस्टारि / *adj.* full of stars तारों भरा *a starry night*

**start[1]** /stɑːt स्टाट् / *verb* **1** [I, T] **start (sth/to do sth/doing sth)** to begin doing sth कुछ करना आरंभ करना *We'll have to start* (= leave) *early to catch the bus.* ○ *What time do you have to* ***start work*** *in the morning?* **2** [I, T] to begin or to make sth begin to happen कोई काम आरंभ करना या करवाना *What time does the concert start?* ○ *I'd like to start the meeting now.* ➪ **begin** पर नोट देखिए। **3** [I, T] **start (sth) (up)** (used about a machine, etc.) to begin to work; to make an engine, a car, etc begin to work (किसी मशीन आदि का) चलने लगना, स्टार्ट होना; इंजन, कार आदि को चलाना शुरू करना, स्टार्ट करना *The car won't start.* ○ *He got onto his motorbike, started the engine and rode away.* **4** [I, T] **start (sth) (up)** to create a company, an organization, etc.; to begin to exist कोई कंपनी, संस्था आदि स्थापित करना; अस्तित्व में आने लगना *They've decided to start their own business.* **5** [I] to make a sudden, quick movement because you are surprised or afraid (आश्चर्य या भय से) उछल पड़ना *A loud noise outside made me start.*

**IDM get/start off on the right/wrong foot (with sb)** ➪ **foot[1]** देखिए।

**to start (off) with 1** used for giving your first reason for sth किसी बात के लिए पहला कारण बताने के लिए प्रयुक्त *'Why are you so angry?' 'Well, to start off with, you're late, and secondly you've lied to me.'* **2** in the beginning; at first आरंभ में; सबसे पहले, सर्वप्रथम

**set/start the ball rolling** ➪ **ball** देखिए।

**PHR V start off** to begin in a particular way एक विशेष ढंग से आरंभ करना *I'd like to start off by welcoming you all to Lucknow.*

**start on sth** to begin doing sth that needs to be done कोई ज़रूरी काम करना शुरू करना

**start out** to begin your life, career, etc. in a particular way that changed later अपना जीवन, व्यवसाय आदि एक विशेष ढंग से आरंभ करना (जो आगे चलकर बदल गया हो) *She started out as a teacher in Patna.*

**start over** (*AmE*) to begin again फिर से शुरू करना

**start[2]** /stɑːt स्टाट् / *noun* **1** [C, *usually sing.*] the point at which sth begins (किसी बात का) आरंभ; शुरुआत *The chairman made a short speech* ***at the start of*** *the meeting.* ○ *It was a bad idea* ***from the start.*** **2** [C, *usually sing.*] the action or process of starting कुछ आरंभ करने का कार्य या प्रक्रिया *to make a fresh start* (= do sth again in a different way) **3 the start** [*sing.*] the place where a race begins (एक) दौड़ की शुरुआत का स्थान *The athletes are now lining up at the start.* **4** [C, *usually sing.*] an amount of time or distance that you give to a weaker person at the beginning of a race, game, etc. दौड़, खेल आदि की प्रतियोगिता के शुरुआत में (दुर्बल व्यक्ति के लाभ के लिए स्वीकृत) समय या दूरी की मात्रा ➪ **head start** देखिए। **5** [C, *usually sing.*] a sudden quick movement that your body makes because you are surprised or afraid (आश्चर्य या भय के कारण) चौक जाने या उछल पड़ने की क्रिया; चौंक *She woke up* ***with a start.***

**IDM for a start** (used to emphasize your first reason for sth) (किसी बात के पहले कारण पर बल देने के लिए प्रयुक्त), पहली बात यह कि, अव्वल तो *'Why can't we go on holiday?' 'Well, for a start we can't afford it...'*

**get off to a good, bad, etc. start** to start well, badly, etc. अच्छी या बुरी शुरुआत करना

**get off to a flying start** ➪ **flying** देखिए।

**starter** /ˈstɑːtə(r) ˈस्टाट(र्) / (*AmE* **appetizer**) *noun* [C] a small amount of food that is served before the main course of a meal मुख्य भोजन के प्रारंभ में परसा गया अल्पभोजन (क्षुधावर्धक या भोजन क्रिया आरंभ होने के प्रतीक के रूप में)

**starting point** *noun* [C] **starting point (for sth) 1** an idea or a topic that you use to begin a discussion with चर्चा आरंभ करने के लिए प्रयुक्त कोई विचार या मुद्दा; चर्चा का आरंभ-बिंदु **2** the place where you begin a journey यात्रा आरंभ करने का स्थान, यात्रा का आरंभ-बिंदु

**startle** /ˈstɑːtl ˈस्टाट्ल् / *verb* [T] to surprise sb/sth in a way that slightly shocks or frightens him/her/it (किसी को) चौंका देना (थोड़ा परेशान करते या डराते हुए आश्चर्य में डाल देना) *The gunshot startled the horses.* ▶ **startled** *adj.* चौंका हुआ ▶ **startling** /ˈstɑːtlɪŋ ˈस्टाट्लिङ् / *adj.* चौंकाने वाला

**starvation** /stɑːˈveɪʃn स्टाˈव्रेश्न् / *noun* [U] suffering or death because there is not enough food भुखमरी *to die of starvation*

**starve** /stɑːv स्टाव् / *verb* [I, T] to suffer or die because you do not have enough food to eat; to make sb/sth suffer or die in this way भूखा रहने के कारण कष्ट पाना या मर जाना, भूखा मरना; किसी को भूखा रखकर कष्ट देना या मार देना, भूखा मारना *to* ***starve to death***

**IDM be starved of sth** to suffer because you are not getting enough of sth that you need किसी वस्तु के अभाव या कमी से कष्ट पाना *The children had been starved of love and affection for years.*

**be starving** (*informal*) to be extremely hungry बहुत भूखा या भुखमरा होना

**state**[1] /steɪt स्टेट्/ *noun* **1** [C] the mental, emotional or physical condition that sb/sth is in at a particular time (समय-विशेष पर किसी की मानसिक, भावनात्मक या शारीरिक दशा, अवस्था) *the state of the economy* ○ *He is in a* ***state of shock***. **2** (*also* **State**) [C] a country considered as an organized political community controlled by one government राज्य, देश (जिसे एक निश्चित शासन के अंतर्गत संगठित एक राजनीतिक समुदाय माना जाए) *India has been an independent state since 1947.* ➪ **country** पर नोट देखिए। **3 the State** [U] the government of a country किसी देश की सरकार; शासन *affairs/matters of state* ○ *a state-owned company* ○ *heads of State* (= government leaders) **4** (*also* **State**) [C] an organized political community forming part of a country प्रदेश, प्रांत, सूबा, राज्य (किसी देश के अंतर्गत कोई संगठित राजनीतिक समुदाय) *the southern States of India* ➪ **county** और **province** देखिए। **5** [U] the formal ceremonies connected with high levels of government or with the leaders of countries (शासन के उच्च स्तर पर संपन्न या विभिन्न देशों के नेताओं के लिए आयोजित) औपचारिक समारोह *The President is going on* ***a state visit*** *to China.* **6 the States** [*pl.*] (*informal*) the United States of America संयुक्त राज्य अमेरिका *We lived in the States for about five years.*

IDM **be in/get into a state** (*BrE informal*) to be or become very nervous or upset *Now don't get into a state! I'm sure everything will be all right.*

**state of affairs** a situation हालात, परिस्थिति *This state of affairs must not be allowed to continue.*

**state of mind** mental condition मनोदशा *She's in a very confused state of mind.*

**state**[2] /steɪt स्टेट्/ *verb* [T] to say or write sth, especially formally कुछ कहना या लिखना (विशेषतः औपचारिक रूप से) *Your letter states that you sent the goods on 31 March, but we have not received them.*

**stately** /ˈsteɪtli ˈस्टेट्लि/ *adj.* formal and impressive नियमित और भव्य *a stately old building*

**stately home** *noun* [C] (*BrE*) a large old house that has historical interest and can be visited by the public ऐतिहासिक महत्त्व का बड़ा प्राचीन भवन (जिसे लोग देखने आएँ)

**statement** /ˈsteɪtmənt ˈस्टेट्मन्ट्/ *noun* [C] **1** something that you say or write, especially formally कथन, प्रकथन, वक्तव्य (कही या लिखी कोई बात, विशेषतः औपचारिक रूप से) *The Prime Minister will* ***make a statement*** *about the defence cuts today.* **2** = **bank statement**

**statesman** /ˈsteɪtsmən ˈस्टेट्स्मन्/ *noun* [C] (*pl.* **-men** /-mən -मन्/) an important and experienced politician who has earned public respect राजनीतिज्ञ (लोक प्रतिष्ठा प्राप्त कोई महत्त्वपूर्ण और अनुभवी राजनीति कर्मी)

**static**[1] /ˈstætɪk ˈस्टैटिक्/ *adj.* not moving, changing or developing थमा हुआ, स्थिर (जिसमें कोई गति, परिवर्तन या विकास न हो रहा हो) *House prices are never static.*

**static**[2] /ˈstætɪk ˈस्टैटिक्/ *noun* [U] **1** sudden noises that disturb radio or television signals, caused by electricity in the atmosphere (आकाशीय विद्युत के प्रभाव से रेडियो या टीवी के प्रसारण में खलल डालने वाली) अचानक उत्पन्न आवाज़ें **2** (*also* **static electricity**) electricity that collects on a surface विद्युत जो किसी सतह पर जमा हो जाए *My hair gets full of static when I brush it.*

**station**[1] /ˈsteɪʃn ˈस्टेश्न्/ *noun* [C] **1** (*also* **railway station**) a building on a railway line where trains stop so that passengers can get on and off रेलवे स्टेशन; स्टेशन **2** (*usually in compound nouns*) a building from which buses begin and end journeys बस अड्डा, बस स्थानक **3** (*usually in compound nouns*) a building where a particular service or activity is based विशिष्ट सेवा मुहैया कराने वाला केंद्र या स्थान (जैसे दमकल केंद्र, बिजली घर आदि) *a police/fire/petrol station* ○ *a power station* **4** (*often in compound nouns*) a radio or television company and the programmes it sends out रेडियो या टीवी कार्यक्रमों को प्रसारित करने वाला प्रतिष्ठान या केंद्र *a local radio/TV station* ➪ **channel** देखिए।

**station**[2] /ˈsteɪʃn ˈस्टेश्न्/ *verb* [T] (*usually passive*) to send sb, especially members of the armed forces, to work in a place for a period of time निश्चित अवधि के लिए किसी को (विशेषतः सशस्त्र सैनिकों को) किसी स्थान पर तैनात करना

**stationary** /ˈsteɪʃənri ˈस्टेशन्रि/ *adj.* not moving खड़ा हुआ; स्थिर, गतिहीन *He crashed into the back of a stationary vehicle.*

**stationer's** /ˈsteɪʃənəz ˈस्टेशनज़्/ *noun* [*sing.*] a shop that sells writing equipment, such as paper, pens, envelopes, etc. लेखन-सामग्री (काग़ज़, क़लम, लिफ़ाफ़े आदि) बेचने की दुकान

**stationery** /ˈsteɪʃənri ˈस्टेशन्रि/ *noun* [U] writing equipment, for example pens, pencils, paper, envelopes लेखन-सामग्री (क़लम, पेंसिल, काग़ज़, लिफ़ाफ़े आदि)

**station wagon** (*AmE*) = **estate car**

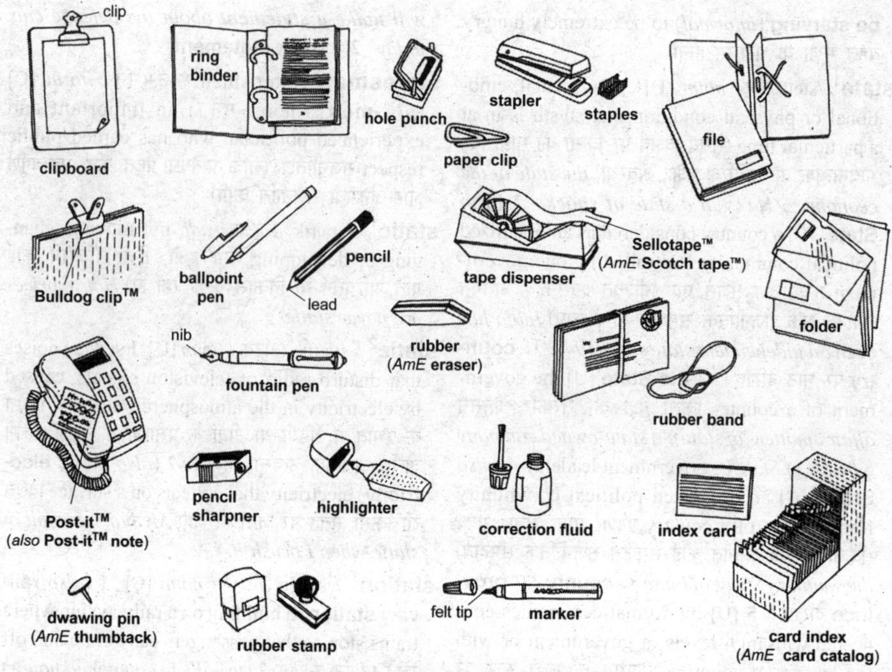


stationery

**statistics** /stəˈtɪstɪks स्टˈटिस्‌टिक्स्/ *noun* **1** [*pl.*] numbers that have been collected in order to provide information about sth (किसी स्थिति आदि के विषय में जानकारी उपलब्ध कराने के लिए संगृहीत) तथ्यात्मक संख्याएँ; आँकड़े *Statistics indicate that 90% of homes in this country have a television.* ○ *crime statistics* **2** [U] the science of collecting and studying these numbers आँकड़ों के संग्रह और अध्ययन का विज्ञान; सांख्यिकी, स्टैटिस्टिक्स ▶ **statistical** /stəˈtɪstɪkl स्टˈटिस्‌टिकल्/ *adj.* संख्यात्मक *statistical information* ▶ **statistically** /-stəˈtistɪkli स्टˈटिस्‌टिक्लि/ *adv.* संख्यात्मक दृष्टि से

**statue** /ˈstætʃuː ˈस्टैचू/ *noun* [C] a figure of a person or animal that is made of stone or metal and usually put in a public place मूर्ति, प्रतिमा (पत्थर या धातु की)

**statuette** /ˌstætʃuˈet ˌस्टैचुˈएट्/ *noun* [C] a small statue छोटी मूर्ति, लघु प्रतिमा

**stature** /ˈstætʃə(r) ˈस्टैच(र्)/ *noun* [U] (*written*) **1** the importance and respect that sb has because people have a high opinion of his/her skill or of what he/she has done योग्यता या उपलब्धि के आधार पर अर्जित महत्त्व और प्रतिष्ठा; महत्ता **2** the height of a person व्यक्ति का कद; लंबाई *He's quite small **in stature**.*

**status** /ˈsteɪtəs ˈस्टेटस/ *noun* **1** [U] the legal position of a person, group or country (व्यक्ति, वर्ग या देश की) वैधानिक स्थिति ***marital status*** ○ *They were granted refugee status.* **2** [*sing.*] your social or professional position in relation to other people सामाजिक या व्यावसायिक स्थिति या प्रतिष्ठा (दूसरों की तुलना में) *Teachers don't have a very high status in this country.* ✪ पर्याय **standing** **3** [U] a high social position उच्च सामाजिक स्थिति *The new job gave him much more status.*

**the status quo** /ˌsteɪtəs ˈkwəʊ ˌस्टेटस् ˈक्वो/ *noun* [*sing.*] the situation as it is now, or as it was before a recent change स्थिति जैसी अभी है या हाल के बदलाव से पहले थी; यथापूर्व स्थिति, यथास्थिति

**status symbol** *noun* [C] something that a person owns that shows that he/she has a high position in society and a lot of money किसी व्यक्ति के उच्च सामाजिक पद और धन संपत्ति को दर्शाने वाली कोई वस्तु (जिसका वह स्वामी हो); प्रतिष्ठा प्रतीक

**statute** /ˈstætʃuːt ˈस्टैच्यूट्/ *noun* [C] (*formal*) a law or a rule नियम या क़ानून; संविधि

**statute law** *noun* [U] (*technical*) all the written laws of a parliament, etc. संसद आदि द्वारा पारित सभी क़ानून; संविधि क़ानून ➪ **case law** और **common law** देखिए।

**statutory** /ˈstætʃətri ˈस्टैचट्रि / *adj.* (*formal*) decided by law क़ानून द्वारा निर्धारित; सांविधिक *a statutory right*

**staunch** /stɔːntʃ स्टॉन्च् / *adj.* believing in sb/sth or supporting sb/sth very strongly; loyal किसी व्यक्ति या वस्तु को ज़ोर-शोर से मानने या उसका समर्थन करने वाला; निष्ठावान, वफ़ादार, कट्टर

**stave[1]** /steɪv स्टेव् / *noun* [C] **1** a strong stick or pole मज़बूत लकड़ी या डंडा *fence staves*

**stave[2]** /steɪv स्टेव् / *verb*

**PHRV** **stave sth off** to stop sth unpleasant from happening now, although it may happen at a later time; to delay sth कुछ बुरा होने को कुछ समय के लिए रोकना; किसी काम में देर लगाना *to stave off hunger/illness/inflation/bankruptcy*

**stay[1]** /steɪ स्टे / *verb* [I] **1** to continue to be somewhere and not go away किसी स्थान पर ठहरे रहना (वहाँ से चले न जाना) *Raju stayed in bed until 11 o'clock.* ○ *Pavan's staying late at the office tonight.* **2** to continue to be in a particular state or situation without change (बिना परिवर्तन के) दशा या स्थिति विशेष में बने रहना *I can't* ***stay awake*** *any longer.*

**NOTE** **Remain** और **stay** के अर्थ (लगभग) समान हैं परंतु **remain** अधिक औपचारिक प्रयोग है।

**3** to live in a place temporarily as a visitor or guest किसी स्थान पर ठहरना (आगंतुक या अतिथि के रूप में अस्थायी रूप से रहना) *We stayed with friends in France.* ○ *Which hotel are you* ***staying at****?*

**IDM** **stay put** (*informal*) to continue in one place; to not leave एक (ही) स्थान पर जमे रहना; वहाँ से न जाना

**PHRV** **stay behind** to not leave a place after other people have gone एक स्थान पर रुके रहना (औरों के चले जाने के बाद भी) *I'll stay behind and help you wash up.*

**stay in** to be at home and not go out घर पर रहना (बाहर न जाना) *I'm going to stay in and watch TV.*

**stay on (at...)** to continue studying, working, etc. somewhere for longer than expected or after other people have left किसी स्थान पर अपना काम (पढ़ाई आदि) देर तक या लोगों के चले जाने के बाद भी जारी रखना

**stay out** to continue to be away from your house, especially late at night घर से बाहर रहना (विशेषतः रात में)

**stay up** to go to bed later than usual (सामान्य की अपेक्षा) देर से सोने जाना *I'm going to stay up to watch the late film.*

**stay[2]** /steɪ स्टे / *noun* [C] a period of time that you spend somewhere as a visitor or guest (आगंतुक या अतिथि के रूप में) कहीं पर टिकने की अवधि; वास-अवधि *Did you enjoy your stay in Goa?*

**STD** /ˌes tiː ˈdiː ˌएस् टी ˈडी / *abbr.* **1** subscriber trunk dialling; the system by which you can make long-distance telephone calls direct एसटीडी; फ़ोनकर्ता द्वारा लंबी दूरी के लिए सीधे फ़ोन मिलाने की सुविधा वाली प्रणाली **2** sexually transmitted disease यौन रोग (यौन संसर्ग से उत्पन्न रोग)

**steadfast** /ˈstedfɑːst ˈस्टेड्फ़ास्ट् / *adj.* **steadfast (in sth)** (*literary*) (*approving*) faithful and loyal; not changing in your attitudes or aims विश्वसनीय एवं निष्ठावान, वफ़ादार; (अपने लक्ष्य या रूख में) स्थिर, अडिग, अटल *steadfast loyalty* ○ *He remained steadfast in his determination to bring the criminals to justice* ▶ **steadfastly** /-li -लि /*adv.* स्थिरता से ▶ **steadfastness** *noun* [U] स्थिरता

**steady[1]** /ˈstedi ˈस्टेडि / *adj.* (**steadier; steadiest**) **1** developing, growing or happening gradually and at a regular rate नियमित गति से और क्रमशः विकसित होता, बढ़ता और घटित होता हुआ *a steady increase/decline* **2** staying the same; not changing and therefore safe स्थिर और तदेव; अपरिवर्तित और (इसलिए) सुरक्षित *a steady job/income* **3** firmly fixed, supported or balanced; not shaking or likely to fall down मज़बूती से जमा हुआ, सहारे वाला या संतुलित; हिलने या गिरने की संभावना से मुक्त या रहित *You need* ***a steady hand*** *to take good photographs.* ▶ **steadily** *adv.* नियमित गति से और क्रमशः *Unemployment has risen steadily since April 2000.*

**steady[2]** /ˈstedi ˈस्टेडि / *verb* [I, T] (*pres. part.* **steadying;** *3rd person sing. pres.* **steadies;** *pt, pp* **steadied**) to stop yourself/sb/sth from moving, shaking or falling; to stop moving, shaking or falling किसी को स्थिर करना (किसी को हिलने, काँपने या गिरने न देना); स्थिर होना (न हिलना, काँपना या गिरना) *He had to* ***steady*** *his* ***nerves/voice*** *before beginning his speech.*

**steak** /steɪk स्टेक् / *noun* [C, U] a thick flat piece of meat or fish गोश्त या मछली का मोटा चपटा टुकड़ा; टिक्का *a piece of steak* ○ *a cod/salmon steak* ⇨ **chop[2]** देखिए।

**steal** /stiːl स्टील् / *verb* (*pt* **stole** /stəʊl स्टोल् /; *pp* **stolen** /ˈstəʊlən ˈस्टोलन् /) **1** [I, T] **steal (sth) (from sb/sth)** to take sth from a person, shop, etc. without permission and without intending to return it or pay for it चुराना, चोरी करना (किसी

व्यक्ति, दुकान आदि से, बिना पूछे और लौटाने या भुगतान करने के इरादे के बिना, कोई वस्तु ले लेना *The terrorists were driving a stolen car.* ○ *We found out she had been stealing from us for years.*

NOTE वस्तुओं को चुराने के अर्थ में **steal** शब्द प्रयुक्त किया जाता है परंतु व्यक्ति या स्थान को लूटने के अर्थ में **rob** प्रयुक्त किया जाता है—*My camera has been stolen!* ○ *I've been robbed!* ○ *to rob a bank* ➪ **thief** पर नोट भी देखिए।

**2** [I] **steal away, in, out, etc.** to move somewhere secretly and quietly चोरी-चोरी और चुपके-चुपके कहीं चले जाना

**stealth** /stelθ स्टेल्थ् / *noun* [U] (*formal*) behaviour that is secret or quiet गुप्त रूप से या बिना शोरगुल के किया गया काम; चोरी, छिपाव, दुराव ▶ **stealthy** *adj.* दुरावपूर्ण, गुप्त रीति से किया गया *a stealthy approach/ movement* ▶ **stealthily** *adv.* दुरावपूर्वक, गुप्त रीति से

**steam[1]** /sti:m स्टीम् / *noun* [U] the hot gas that is produced by boiling water वाष्प, भाप (खौलते पानी से उत्पन्न गरम गैस) *Steam was rising from the coffee.*

IDM **let off steam** (*informal*) to get rid of energy or express strong feeling by behaving in a noisy or wild way अपनी (अतिरिक्त) ऊर्जा को विसर्जित करना या भावावेश को अभिव्यक्ति देना (शोरगुल मचाते या ऊधमबाजी करते हुए)

IDM **run out of steam** to gradually lose energy or enthusiasm धीरे-धीरे अपनी ऊर्जा या जोश को खोते जाना

**steam[2]** /sti:m स्टीम् / *verb* **1** [I] to send out steam भाप निकालना *a bowl of steaming hot soup* **2** [I, T] to place food over boiling water so that it cooks in the steam; to cook in this way खाद्य पदार्थ को खौलते पानी के ऊपर रख देना (भाप से पकने के लिए); खाद्य पदार्थ को भाप से पकाना *steamed vegetables/fish* ○ *Leave the potatoes to steam for 30 minutes.*

IDM **be/get steamed up** (*informal*) to be or become very angry or worried about sth किसी बात पर बहुत क्रुद्ध या चिंतित होना या हो जाना

PHR V **steam (sth) up** to cover sth or become covered with steam किसी में भाप भर देना या किसी का भाप से भर जाना *My glasses have steamed up.*

**steamer** /ˈsti:mə(r) ˈस्टीम(र्) / *noun* [C] **1** a ship that is driven by steam भाप से चलने वाला जहाज़; स्टीमर **2** a metal container with small holes in it, that is placed over a pan of boiling water in order to cook food in the steam भाप से भोजन तैयार करने वाला छेददार बर्तन (जिसे खौलते पानी पर रखा जाता है)

**steamroller** /ˈsti:mrəʊlə(r) ˈस्टीमरोल(र्) / *noun* [C] a big heavy vehicle with wide heavy wheels that is used for making the surface of a road flat सड़कें बनाने वाला भारी और बड़ा इंजन; स्टीमरोलर

**steel[1]** /sti:l स्टील् / *noun* [U] a very strong metal that is made from iron mixed with another substance (**carbon**). Steel is used for making knives, tools, machines, etc. इस्पात, फ़ौलाद, स्टील (लोहे में कार्बन मिलाकर बनाया गया मज़बूत धातु) (छुरियाँ, औज़ार, मशीनें आदि बनाने के लिए प्रयुक्त)

**steel[2]** /sti:l स्टील् / *verb* [T] **steel yourself** to prepare yourself to deal with sth difficult or unpleasant किसी कठिन या अप्रिय बात का सामना करने के लिए स्वयं को तैयार करना *Steel yourself for a shock.*

**steel wool** (*also* **wire wool**) *noun* [U] a mass of fine steel threads that you use for cleaning pots and pans, making surfaces smooth, etc. बर्तन माँजने आदि के लिए प्रयुक्त इस्पात की तारों का कुंडलीदार गोला

**steelworks** /ˈsti:lwɜ:ks ˈस्टील्वर्क्स् / *noun* [C, with *sing.* or *pl.* verb] (*pl.* **steelworks**) a factory where steel is made इस्पात का कारख़ाना (इस्पात बनाने का कारख़ाना)

**steep** /sti:p स्टीप् / *adj.* **1** (used about a hill, mountain, street, etc.) rising or falling quickly; at a sharp angle (पहाड़ी, पहाड़, सड़क आदि) बहुत अधिक चढ़ाव (उतार वाला; लगभग लंब के समान सीधा खड़ा) *I don't think I can cycle up that hill. It's too steep.* **2** (used about an increase or fall in sth) very big (किसी बात में वृद्धि या गिरावट) अत्यधिक **3** (*informal*) too expensive बहुत महँगा ▶ **steeply** *adv.* अत्यधिक *House prices have risen steeply this year.* ▶ **steepness** *noun* [U] अत्यधिकता

**steeped** /sti:pt स्टीप्ट् / *adj.* **steeped in sth** having a lot of; full of sth किसी वस्तु की अत्यधिक मात्रा वाला; पूर्णतः भरा हुआ, से ओत-प्रोत, में निमग्न *a city steeped in history*

**steeple** /ˈsti:pl ˈस्टीपूल् / *noun* [C] a tower on the roof of a church, often with a pointed top (**spire**) चर्च की मीनार का शिखर

**steer** /stɪə(r) स्टिअ(र्) / *verb* **1** [I, T] to control the direction that a vehicle is going in वाहन की गति की दिशा को नियंत्रित करना *to steer a boat/ship/bicycle/motorbike* **2** [T] to take control of a situation and try to influence the way it develops स्थिति को अपने नियंत्रण में कर उसके विकास को निर्देशित करना *She tried to steer the conversation away from the subject of money.*

**IDM keep/stay/steer clear (of sb/sth)** ➪ **clear²** देखिए।

**steering** /ˈstɪərɪŋ ˈस्टिअरिङ्/ *noun* [U] the parts of a vehicle that control the direction that it moves in वाहन की गति की दिशा को नियंत्रित करने वाले पुरज़े *a car with power steering*

**steering wheel** (*also* **wheel**) *noun* [C] the wheel that the driver turns in a vehicle to control the direction that it moves in वाहन की गति की दिशा को नियंत्रित करने वाला पहिया; स्टियरिंग व्हील ➪ **car** पर चित्र देखिए।

**stellar** /ˈstelə(r) ˈस्टेल(र्)/ *adj.* (*only before a noun*) (*technical*) connected with the stars तारों से संबंधित; तारकीय

**stem¹** /stem स्टेम्/ *noun* [C] **1** the main long thin part of a plant above the ground from which the leaves or flowers grow (पेड़-पौधों का) तना ➪ **flower** पर चित्र देखिए। **2** (*grammar*) the main part of a word onto which other parts are added शब्द का मुख्य अंश; प्रतिपादक या धातु *'Writ-' is the stem of the words 'write', 'writing', 'written' and 'writer'.*

**stem²** /stem स्टेम्/ *verb* [T] (**stemming; stemmed**) to stop sth that is increasing or spreading किसी वस्तु को बढ़ने या फैलने से रोकना; रोकथाम करना

**PHR V stem from sth** (*not used in the continuous tenses*) to be the result of sth किसी का परिणाम होना, किसी से उत्पन्न होना

> **NOTE** यद्यपि इस क्रिया का सातत्यबोधक कालों (continuous tenses) में प्रयोग नहीं होता तथापि इसका '-ing' युक्त वर्तमान कृदंत (present participle) रूप काफ़ी प्रचलित है—*He was treated for depression stemming from his domestic and business difficulties.*

**stench** /stentʃ स्टेन्च्/ *noun* [C, *sing.*] a very unpleasant smell दुर्गंध, बदबू

**stencil** /ˈstensl ˈस्टेन्सल्/ *noun* [C] a thin piece of metal, plastic or card with a design cut out of it, that you put onto a surface and paint over, so that the design is left on the surface; the pattern or design that is produced in this way धातु, प्लास्टिक या गत्ते का पतरा जिस पर डिज़ाइन कटा होता है और जिसे (डिज़ाइन को) किसी सतह पर पेंट करके उतारा जाता है, स्टेंसिल; इस प्रकार बना पैटर्न या डिज़ाइन ▶ **stencil** *verb* [T] (**stencilling; stencilled** *AmE* **stenciling; stenciled**) स्टेंसिल पर चित्रण करना

**stenographer** /stəˈnɒɡrəfə(r) स्टˈनॉग्रफ़(र्)/ (*informal* **steno**) *noun* [C] a person whose job is to write down what sb else says, using a quick system of signs or abbreviations and then to type it आशुलिपिक, स्टेनोग्राफ़र

**step¹** /step स्टेप्/ *noun* [C] **1** the action of lifting one foot and putting it down in a different place क़दम; डग *He took a step forward.* ○ *We had to* ***retrace our steps*** (= go back the way we had come). **2** one action in a series of actions that you take in order to achieve sth प्रक्रिया का चरण; सोपान *Government's reforms were* ***a step in the right direction***. **3** one of the surfaces on which you put your foot when you are going up or downstairs ज़ीने की सीढ़ी *on the top/bottom step* ➪ **stair** पर नोट देखिए।

**IDM in/out of step (with sb/sth)** moving/not moving your feet at the same time as other people when you are marching, dancing, etc. मार्च, नाच आदि में क़दम का मेल या बेमेल होना

**step by step** (used for talking about a series of actions) moving slowly and gradually from one action or stage to the next (शृंखलाबद्ध क्रियाओं के लिए प्रयुक्त) क्रमबद्ध रूप से, एक-एक करके *clear step-by-step instructions*

**take steps to do sth** to take action in order to achieve sth किसी लक्ष्य की प्राप्ति के लिए क़दम उठाना, कार्रवाई करना या उपाय करना

**watch your step** **1** to be careful about where you are walking ध्यान से चलना **2** to be careful about how you behave सोच-समझ कर या सावधानी के साथ काम या व्यवहार करना

**step²** /step स्टेप्/ *verb* [I] (**stepping; stepped**) **1** to lift one foot and put it down in a different place when you are walking क़दम रखना, डग भरना *to step forward/back* ○ **2** to move a short distance; to go somewhere थोड़ी दूर चलना या थोड़ा चलना; कहीं जाना *Could you step out of the car please, sir?* ○ *I stepped outside for a minute to get some air.*

**PHR V step down** to leave an important job or position and let sb else take your place कोई बड़ी नौकरी या पद दूसरे के लिए छोड़ना

**step in** to help sb in a difficult situation or to become involved in a dispute कठिनाई में किसी की सहायता करना या किसी झगड़े में बीच में पड़ना; हस्तक्षेप करना

**step sth up** to increase the amount, speed, etc. of sth किसी की मात्रा, गति आदि बढ़ाना *The Army has decided to step up its security arrangements.*

**step-** /step- स्टेप्- / *prefix* (*used in compound nouns*) related as a result of one parent marrying again सौतेला

**stepbrother** /ˈstepbrʌðə(r) ˈस्टेप्ब्रद्(र्) / *noun* [C] the son from an earlier marriage of sb who has married your mother or father सौतेला भाई, कठभाई ➪ **half-brother** देखिए।

**stepchild** /ˈsteptʃaɪld ˈस्टेप्चाइल्ड् / *noun* [C] (*pl.* **stepchildren**) the child from an earlier marriage of your husband or wife सौतेली संतान

**stepdaughter** /ˈstepdɔːtə(r) ˈस्टेप्डॉट(र्) / *noun* [C] the daughter from an earlier marriage of your husband or wife सौतली बेटी; कठबेटी

**stepfather** /ˈstepfɑːðə(r) ˈस्टेप्फ़ाद्(र्) / *noun* [C] the man who has married your mother when your parents are divorced or your father is dead सौतेला पिता; कठबाप

**stepladder** /ˈsteplædə(r) ˈस्टेप्लैड(र्) / *noun* [C] a short ladder with two parts, one with steps, that are joined together at the top so that it can stand on its own and be folded up when you are not using it फ़ोल्डिंग सीढ़ी (ऊपर के भाग पर जुड़ी दो हिस्सों वाली छोटी सीढ़ी, जिसमें केवल एक में डंडे होते हैं, यह बिना सहारे खड़ी हो सकती है तथा काम न होने पर फ़ोल्ड करके रखी जा सकती है)

**stepmother** /ˈstepmʌðə(r) ˈस्टेप्मद्(र्) / *noun* [C] the woman who has married your father when your parents are divorced or your mother is dead सौतेली माँ; कठमाँ

**stepney** /ˈstepni ˈस्टेप्नि /*noun* [C] (*IndE*) a spare wheel for a vehicle वाहन का अतिरिक्त पहिया; स्टेपनी

**steppe** /step स्टेप् / *noun* [C, *usually pl.*, U] a large area of land with grass but few trees, especially in south-east Europe and Siberia (लगभग वृक्षरहित) घास का बड़ा मैदान (विशेषतः दक्षिण-पूर्व यूरोप और साइबेरिया में)

**stepping stone** *noun* [C] **1** one of a line of flat stones that you can step on in order to cross a river वे चपटे पत्थर जिन पर पैर रखकर नदी को लाँघते हैं **2** something that allows you to make progress or helps you to achieve sth प्रगति या लक्ष्य-प्राप्ति में सहायक वस्तु या बात

**stepsister** /ˈstepsɪstə(r) ˈस्टेप्सिस्ट(र्) / *noun* [C] the daughter from an earlier marriage of sb who has married your mother or father सौतेली बहन; कठबहन ➪ **half-sister** देखिए।

**stepson** /ˈstepsʌn ˈस्टेप्सन् / *noun* [C] the son from an earlier marriage of your husband or wife सौतेला पुत्र; कठबेटा

**stereo** /ˈsteriəʊ ˈस्टेरिओ / (*pl.* **stereos**) *noun* **1** (*also* **stereo system**) [C] a machine that plays CDs or cassettes, or a radio that has two boxes (**speakers**) so that you hear separate sounds from each दो स्पीकरों वाला रेडियो या सीडी, कैसेट बजाने का यंत्र; स्टेरियो *a car/personal stereo* **2** [U] the system for playing recorded music, speech, etc. in which the sound is divided in two parts रिकार्ड हुआ संगीत, भाषण आदि सुनाने वाली, दो स्पीकरों वाली, प्रणाली; स्टेरियो सिस्टम *This programme is broadcast **in stereo**.* ➪ **mono** देखिए। ▶ **stereo** *adj.* दो स्पीकरों वाला, त्रि-आयामी (लंबाई, चौड़ाई, गहराई का बोध कराने वाला) *a stereo television*

**stereotype** /ˈsteriətaɪp ˈस्टेरिअटाइप् / *noun* [C] a fixed idea about a particular type of person or thing, which is often not true in reality किसी व्यक्ति या वस्तु के विषय में रूढ़ या घिसी-पिटी धारणा (जो वास्तविकता में प्रायः सच नहीं होती) ▶ **stereotype** *verb* [T] (किसी को) घिसा-पिटा रूप देना, रूढ़ स्वरूप देना *In advertisements, women are often stereotyped as housewives.*

**sterile** /ˈsteraɪl ˈस्टेराइल् / *adj.* **1** not able to produce young animals or babies प्रजनन में असमर्थ; नपुंसक, बाँझ, बंध्या **2** completely clean and free from bacteria पूर्णतया स्वच्छ और ज़ीवाणु-रहित *All equipment used during a medical operation must be sterile.* **3** not producing any useful result व्यर्थ, अर्थ-हीन, परिणाम-रहित, निष्फल *a sterile discussion/argument* ▶ **sterility** /stəˈrɪləti स्टˈरिलटि / *noun* [U] व्यर्थता, प्रजनन-असमर्थता

**sterilize** (*also* **-ise**) /ˈstərəlaɪz ˈस्टरलाइज़् / *verb* [T] **1** to make sb/sth completely clean and free from bacteria किसी वस्तु का पूर्णतया स्वच्छ और जीवाणु-रहित कर देना **2** (*usually passive*) to perform an operation on a person or an animal so that he/she/it cannot have babies शल्य-क्रिया द्वारा मनुष्य या पशु को प्रजनन में असमर्थ बनाना, बंध्या बनाना ▶ **sterilization** (*also* **-isation**) /ˌsterəlaɪˈzeɪʃn ˌस्टेरलाइˈज़ेश्न् / *noun* [U] बंध्यीकरण, जीवाणुनाशन

**sterling**[1] /ˈstɜːlɪŋ ˈस्टलिङ् / *noun* [U] the system of money that is used in Britain, that uses the pound as its basic unit ब्रिटेन में प्रचलित मुद्रा (जिसकी आधारभूत इकाई पाउंड है); स्टर्लिंग

**sterling**[2] /ˈstɜːlɪŋ ˈस्टलिङ् / *adj.* of very high quality अत्यंत उत्कृष्ट *sterling work*

**stern**[1] /stɜːn स्टन् / *adj.* very serious; not smiling कठोर, बहुत गंभीर; मुस्कान-रहित *a stern expression/warning* ▶ **sternly** *adv.* कठोरतापूर्वक

**stern**[2] /stɜːn स्टन् / *noun* [C] the back end of a ship or boat जहाज़ या नाव का पश्च भाग ➪ **bow**[2] देखिए तथा **boat** पर चित्र देखिए।

**sternum** /ˈstɜːnəm ˈस्टनम्/ *noun* [C] (*formal*) the long flat bone in the middle of your chest that the seven top pairs of curved bones (**ribs**) are connected to उरोस्थि ✪ पर्याय **breastbone** ➪ **body** पर चित्र देखिए।

**steroid** /ˈsterɔɪd ˈस्टेरॉइड्/ *noun* [C] a chemical substance produced naturally in the body. There are several different types of steroids. They can be used to treat various diseases and are also sometimes used illegally by people playing sports to improve their performance शरीर में प्राकृतिक रूप से उत्पन्न होने वाला एक रासायनिक पदार्थ, स्टेरॉयड (स्टेरॉयड अनेक प्रकार के होते हैं और इन्हें रोगों के उपचार के लिए और खिलाड़ियों द्वारा अवैध रूप से अपनी क्षमता बढ़ाने के लिए प्रयोग में लाया जाता है) ➪ **anabolic steroid** देखिए।

**stethoscope** /ˈsteθəskəʊp ˈस्टेथ़स्कोप्/ *noun* [C] the piece of equipment that a doctor uses for listening to your breathing and heart डॉक्टर द्वारा हृदय और फेफड़ों की जाँच के लिए प्रयुक्त उपकरण; स्टेथस्कोप

**stew** /stjuː स्ट्यू/ *noun* [C, U] a type of food that you make by cooking meat and/or vegetables in liquid for a long time सीझा हुआ गोश्त या सब्ज़ी (जो तरल पदार्थ में देर तक हलकी आँच में पकने से बनती है) ▶ **stew** *verb* [I, T] गोश्त या सब्ज़ी का सीझना, को सिझाना

**steward** /ˈstjuːəd ˈस्ट्यूअड्/ *noun* [C] **1** a man whose job is to look after passengers on an aircraft, a ship or a train विमान, जलयान या रेलगाड़ी में परिचारक (यात्रियों की देखभाल के लिए नियुक्त पुरुष) **2** (*BrE*) a person who helps to organize a large public event, for example a race दौड़ आदि के बड़े आयोजन में सहायक व्यक्ति

**stewardess** /ˌstjuːəˈdes; ˈstjuːə- ˌस्ट्यूअ ˈडेस्; ˈस्ट्यूअ-/ *noun* [C] **1** a woman whose job is to look after passengers on an aircraft विमान परिचारिका (विमान यात्रियों की देखभाल के लिए नियुक्त) ✪ पर्याय **air hostess** **2** a woman who looks after the passengers on a ship or train जलयान या रेलगाड़ी में परिचारिका (यात्रियों की देखभाल के लिए नियुक्त महिला)

**stick[1]** /stɪk स्टिक्/ *verb* (*pt, pp* **stuck** /stʌk स्टक्/) **1** [I, T] **stick (sth) in/into (sth)** to push a pointed object into sth; to be pushed into sth (किसी वस्तु में कोई नुकीली चीज़) चुभाना; (किसी वस्तु में) चुभाया जाना *Stick a fork into the meat to see if it's ready.* **2** [I, T] to fix sth to sth else by using a special substance (**glue**); to become fixed to sth else (गोंद आदि से एक वस्तु को दूसरी वस्तु से) चिपकाना *I stuck a stamp on an envelope.* **3** [T] (*informal*) to put sth somewhere, especially quickly or carelessly कहीं कुछ डाल देना (विशेषतः जल्दबाज़ी में या लापरवाही से) *Stick your bags in the bedroom.* ○ *Just at that moment Jai stuck his head round the door.* **4** [I] **stick (in sth)** (used about sth that can usually be moved) to become fixed in one position so that it cannot be moved (सामान्यतया मुड़ना आदि गति करने वाली वस्तु का) कहीं अटक जाना *The car was stuck in the mud.* **5** [T] (*informal*) (*often in negative sentences and questions*) to stay in a difficult or unpleasant situation कठिन या अप्रिय परिस्थिति में बने रहना, प्रतिकूल परिस्थिति को बरदाश्त करना *I can't stick this job much longer.*

**IDM** **poke/stick your nose into sth** ➪ **nose[1]** देखिए।

**stick/put your tongue out** ➪ **tongue** देखिए।

**PHR V** **stick around** (*informal*) to stay somewhere, waiting for sth to happen or for sb to arrive (कुछ घटित होने या किसी व्यक्ति की प्रतीक्षा में) किसी स्थान पर (जमे) रहना

**stick at sth** (*informal*) to continue working at sth even when it is difficult (कठिन होने पर भी) काम को जारी रखना

**stick by sb** (*informal*) to continue to give sb help and support even in difficult times (कठिनाई में भी) किसी की सहायता करते रहना

**stick out** (*informal*) to be very noticeable and easily seen (बाहर को निकला हुआ होने से) (किसी वस्तु का) बहुत साफ़ और आसानी से दिखाई देना *The new office block really sticks out from the older buildings around it.*

**stick (sth) out** to be further out than sth else; to push sth further out than sth else बाहर को निकलना; (किसी वस्तु को) बाहर की ओर निकालना *The boy's head was sticking out of the window.*

**stick it/sth out** (*informal*) to stay in a difficult or unpleasant situation until the end अंत तक कठिनाई का सामना करते रहना

**stick to sth** (*informal*) to continue with sth and not change to anything else किसी बात पर क़ायम रहना या पर डटे रहना

**stick together** (*informal*) (used about a group of people) to stay friendly and loyal to each other लोगों का एक दूसरे का मित्र और वफ़ादार बने रहना

**stick up** to point upwards ऊपर को खड़ा होना *You look funny. Your hair's sticking up!*

**stick up for yourself/sbsth** (*informal*) to support or defend yourself/sb/sth किसी को समर्थन देना या उसका बचाव करना *Don't worry. I'll stick up for you if there's any trouble.*

**stick[2]** /stɪk स्टिक्/ *noun* [C] **1** a small thin piece of wood from a tree लकड़ी का छोटा डंडा; छड़ी **2** (*BrE*) = **walking stick** **3** (in hockey and some other sports) a long thin piece of wood that you use for hitting the ball हॉकी, पोलो स्टिक आदि *a hockey stick* ➪ **bat[1] 1, club[1] 4** और **racket 3** देखिए। **4** a long thin piece of sth किसी वस्तु का लंबा पतला टुकड़ा; छड़ *a stick of celery/dynamite*

**sticker** /ˈstɪkə(r) ˈस्टिक(र्)/ *noun* [C] a piece of paper with writing or a picture on one side that you can stick onto sth चिपकने वाला काग़ज़ जिस पर कुछ लिखा हो या चित्र बना हो; स्टिकर

**stickler** /ˈstɪklə(r) ˈस्टिक्ल(र्)/ *noun* [C] **stickler (for sth)** a person who thinks that a particular quality or type of behaviour is very important and expects other people to think and behave in the same way निर्णायक या मध्यस्थ व्यक्ति जो अन्य व्यक्तियों से ऐसे विशिष्ट व्यवहार की अपेक्षा करता है जो उसे महत्त्वपूर्ण लगता है *a stickler for perfection*

**sticky** /ˈstɪki ˈस्टिकि/ *adj.* (**stickier; stickiest**) **1** used for describing a substance that easily becomes joined to things that it touches, or sth that is covered with this kind of substance सहज चिपकने वाली या चिपकौआ वस्तु; चिपचिपी वस्तु *sticky tape/sticky sweets* **2** (*informal*) (used about a situation) difficult or unpleasant (स्थिति) कठिन या अप्रिय

**stiff[1]** /stɪf स्टिफ़्/ *adj.* **1** (used about material, paper, etc.) firm and difficult to bend or move (वस्तु, काग़ज़ आदि) सख़्त, कड़ा और न झुकने या मुड़ने वाला *My new shoes feel rather stiff.* ○ *The door handle is stiff and I can't turn it.* **2** (used about parts of the body) not easy to move (शरीर के अंग) जो आसानी से मुड़ने न सकें *My arm feels really stiff after playing tennis yesterday.* **3** (used about a liquid) very thick; almost solid (द्रव) बहुत गाढ़ा; लगभग ठोस *Beat the egg whites until they are stiff.* **4** more difficult or stronger than usual सामान्य से अधिक कठिन या ज़ोरदार *a stiff breeze/wind* **5** (used about sb's behaviour) not relaxed or friendly; formal (किसी का आचरण) तनावमुक्त या मित्रवत नहीं; तकल्लुफ़ वाला **6** (used about an alcoholic drink) strong (शराब) तेज़ *a stiff whisky* ▶ **stiffness** *noun* [U] कड़ापन

**stiff[2]** /stɪf स्टिफ़/ *adv.* (*informal*) extremely अत्यधिक *to be bored/ frozen/scared/worried stiff*

**stiffen** /ˈstɪfn ˈस्टिफ़्न्/ *verb* **1** [I] (used about a person) to suddenly stop moving and hold your body very straight, usually because you are afraid or angry (व्यक्ति का) (प्रायः भय या क्रोध के कारण) अचानक रुक जाना और तनकर खड़ा हो जाना **2** [I, T] to become rigid; to make sth rigid so that it will not bend कड़ा पड़ जाना, अकड़ जाना; (किसी वस्तु को) कड़ा बना देना (कि वह मुड़ न सके)

**stiffly** /ˈstɪfli ˈस्टिफ़्लि/ *adv.* in an unfriendly formal way रूखेपन और औपचारिकता से *He smiled stiffly.*

**stifle** /ˈstaɪfl ˈस्टाइफ़्ल्/ *verb* **1** [T] to stop sth happening, developing or continuing किसी बात को होने, बढ़ने या चलते रहने से रोक देना; दबा देना *to stifle a yawn/cry/giggle* **2** [I, T] to be or to make sb unable to breathe because it is very hot and/ or there is no fresh air दम घुटना या किसी का दम घोंटना (बहुत अधिक गरमी या ताज़ी हवा न मिलने के कारण) *Rahul was almost stifled by the smoke.* ▶ **stifling** /ˈstaɪflɪŋ ˈस्टाइफ़्लिङ्/ *adj.* दमघोटू *The heat was stifling.*

**stigma** /ˈstɪgmə ˈस्टिग्मा/ *noun* **1** [C, U] bad and often unfair feelings that people in general have about a particular illness, way of behaving, etc. कलंक, लांछन, तोहमत (किसी बीमारी, किसी के बर्ताव आदि के विषय में लोगों की निंदात्मक सोच) *There is still a lot of stigma attached to being unemployed.* **2** [C] the top of the **carpel** where **pollen** is received पुष्प के गर्भकेसर का अग्रभाग; वर्तिकाग्र ➪ **flower** पर चित्र देखिए।

**still[1]** /stɪl स्टिल्/ *adv.* **1** continuing until now or until the time you are talking about and not finishing अब भी (कहीं से आरंभ होकर अब तक या बात करने तक जारी रहते हुए) *Do you still live in Delhi?* ○ *I've eaten all the food but I'm still hungry.* **2** in addition; more अभी तो (अतिरिक्त होने के अर्थ में); अधिक और *There are still ten days to go until my holiday.* **3** in spite of what has just been said तो भी, तिस पर भी (अभी कही गई बात के बावजूद) *He had a bad headache but he still went to the party.* **4** used for making a **comparative** adjective stronger तुलनात्मक विशेषण को अधिक प्रबल बनाने के लिए प्रयुक्त *It was very cold yesterday, but today it's colder still.* ○ *There was still more bad news to come.*

**still[2]** /stɪl स्टिल्/ *adj., adv.* **1** not moving बिना हरकत किए; निश्चल, स्थिर *Children find it hard to **keep/stay still** for long periods.* **2** quiet or calm हलचल-रहित या शांत *The water was perfectly still.* **3** (used about a drink) not containing gas (पेय पदार्थ) गैस-रहित; बुदबुदहीन *still mineral water* ➪ **fizzy** और **sparkling** देखिए। ▶ **stillness** *noun* [U] निश्चलता, शांति

**still**[3] /stɪl स्टिल् / *noun* [C] a single photograph that is taken from a film or video (फ़िल्म या विडियो से लिया गया) एक फ़ोटो

**stillborn** /ˈstɪlbɔːn ˈस्टिल्बॉन् / *adj.* (used about a baby) dead when it is born (शिशु) मृत पैदा हुआ; मृत जात

**stilt** /stɪlt स्टिल्ट् / *noun* [C] **1** one of two long pieces of wood, with places to rest your feet on, on which you can walk above the ground (दो में से एक) लंबा बाँस जिस पर पैर रखकर (नटबाज़ी में) व्यक्ति चलता है, पैर बाँसा; गेड़ी *Have you tried walking* ***on stilts****?* **2** one of a set of poles that support a building above the ground or water ज़मीन या पानी के ऊपर इमारत को सहारा देने वाला (अनेक खंभों में से एक) खंभा

**stilted** /ˈstɪltɪd ˈस्टिल्टिड् / *adj.* (used about a way of speaking or writing) not natural or relaxed; too formal (बोलने या लिखने का ढंग, शैली) अस्वाभाविक या असहज; अति-औपचारिक

**stimulant** /ˈstɪmjələnt ˈस्टिम्यलन्ट् / *noun* [C] a drug or medicine that makes you feel more active उत्तेजक नशीला पदार्थ या स्फूर्तिदायक औषध; उद्दीपक

**stimulate** /ˈstɪmjuleɪt ˈस्टिम्युलेट् / *verb* [T] **1** to make sth active or more active अधिक स्फूर्त या सक्रिय करना *Exercise stimulates the blood circulation.* **2** to make sb feel interested and excited about sth (किसी वस्तु को किसी के लिए) (अधिक) रोचक और उत्तेजक बना देना *The lessons don't really stimulate him.* ▶ **stimulation** /ˌstɪmjuˈleɪʃn ˌस्टिम्युˈलेशन् / *noun* [U] उत्तेजना, स्फूर्ति, प्रोत्साहन

**stimulating** /ˈstɪmjuleɪtɪŋ ˈस्टिम्युलेटिङ् / *adj.* interesting and exciting रोचक और उत्तेजक *a stimulating discussion*

**stimulus** /ˈstɪmjələs ˈस्टिम्यलस् / *noun* [C, U] (*pl.* **stimuli** /ˈstɪmjəlaɪ ˈस्टिम्यलाइ /) something that causes activity, development or interest (किसी को) सक्रिय करने, विकास की ओर ले जाने या (किसी में) रुचि बढ़ाने वाली कोई बात; उद्दीपक, प्रेरक, प्रोत्साहनकारी तत्व *Books provide children with ideas and a stimulus for play.*

**sting**[1] /stɪŋ स्टिङ् / *verb* [I, T] (*pt, pp* **stung** /stʌŋ स्टङ् /) **1** (of an insect, a plant, etc.) to prick the skin of a person or animal with a poisonous, sharp-pointed part causing sudden pain (किसी कीड़े, पौधे आदि का) किसी व्यक्ति या पशु को विषैला डंक मारना जिसके प्रभाव से व्यक्ति या पशु को एकाएक दर्द होता है *He was stung by a bee!* ○ *Be careful. Those plants sting.* **2** to make sb/sth feel a sudden, sharp pain काटने का-सा एकाएक तीखा दर्द पैदा करना *Soap stings if it gets in your eyes.* **3** to make sb feel very hurt and upset because of sth you say (कटु) बात कहकर किसी व्यक्ति को बेहद तकलीफ़ पहुँचाना या बहुत व्यथित करना

**sting**[2] /stɪŋ स्टिङ् / *noun* [C] **1** the sharp pointed part of some insects and animals that is used for pushing into the skin of a person or an animal and putting in poison (कुछ कीड़ों और जीवों का) डंक (जो शरीर को विषग्रस्त कर देता है) ➪ **insect** पर चित्र देखिए। **2** the pain that you feel when an animal or insect pushes its sting into you पशु या कीड़े के डंक लगने से हुआ दर्द; दंश *I got a wasp sting on the leg.* **3** a sharp pain that feels like a sting डंक के दर्द-सी तीखी पीड़ा

**stingy** /ˈstɪndʒi ˈस्टिन्जि /*adj.* (*informal*) not generous, unwilling to give, especially money कंजूस *Don't be stingy with friends.* ▶ **stinginess** *noun* [U] कंजूसी ➪ **miser** देखिए।

**stink** /stɪŋk स्टिङ्क् / *verb* [I] (*pt* **stank** /stæŋk स्टैङ्क् / or **stunk** /stʌŋk स्टङ्क् /; *pp* **stunk**) (*informal*) **stink (of sth) 1** to have a very strong and unpleasant smell भयंकर दुर्गंध होना, तेज़ बदबू मारना या उठना *It stinks in here—open a window!* ○ *to stink of fish* **2** to seem to be very bad, unpleasant or dishonest बहुत बुरा घिनौना या बेईमानी भरा प्रतीत होना *The whole business stinks of corruption.* ▶ **stink** *noun* [C] दुर्गंध, बदबू

**stint** /stɪnt स्टिन्ट् / *noun* [C] a fixed period of time that you spend doing sth किसी काम को करने में लगी निश्चित अवधि *He did a brief stint in the army after leaving school.*

**stipend** /ˈstaɪpend ˈस्टाइपेन्ड् /*noun* [C] (*formal*) an amount of money that is paid regularly to sb as wages or an allowance usually for some specific purpose वृत्ति, वज़ीफ़ा *She has been granted a stipend of Rs 5000 per month by the University Grants Commission (UGC) as scholarship.*

**stipulate** /ˈstɪpjuleɪt ˈस्टिप्युलेट् / *verb* [T] (*formal*) to say exactly and officially what must be done (किसी बात को) आवश्यक शर्त के रूप में प्रस्तुत करना; अनुबंध करना *The law stipulates that all schools must be inspected every three years.* ▶ **stipulation** /ˌstɪpjuˈleɪʃn ˌस्टिप्युˈलेशन् / *noun* [C, U] अनुबंध, आवश्यक शर्त

**stir**[1] /stɜː(r) स्ट(र्) / *verb* (**stirring; stirred**) **1** [T] to move a liquid, etc. round and round, using a spoon, etc. चम्मच आदि से किसी तरल पदार्थ को चलाना; विलोड़ना *She stirred her coffee with a teaspoon.* **2** [I, T] to move or make sb/sth move slightly हिलना, डोलना या किसी को हिलाना; डोलाना *She heard the baby stir in the next room.* **3** [T] to make sb feel a strong emotion किसी की भावनाओं को भड़काना *The story stirred Bratati's imagination.* ○ *a stirring speech*

PHR V **stir sth up** to cause problems, or to make people feel strong emotions परेशानियाँ पैदा करना, या लोगों की भावनाओं को भड़काना *The article stirred up a lot of anger among local residents.*

**stir²** /stɜ:(r) स्ट(र्)/ *noun* **1** [C] the action of stirring चलाने या विलोड़ित करने की क्रिया; विलोड़न *Give the soup a stir.* **2** [*sing.*] something exciting or shocking that everyone talks about उत्तेजित या भयभीत करने वाली कोई बात (जिसकी सब चर्चा करें)

**stirrup** /ˈstɪrəp ˈस्टिरप्/ *noun* [C] one of the two metal objects that you put your feet in when you are riding a horse घुड़सवार की रक़ाब (जिसमें वह पैर डालता है) ➪ **horse** पर चित्र देखिए।

**stitch¹** /stɪtʃ स्टिच्/ *noun* [C] **1** one of the small lines of thread that you can see on a piece of material after it has been sewn (सिलाई का) टाँका; तोपा **2** one of the small pieces of thread that a doctor uses to sew your skin together if you cut yourself very badly, or after an operation (डॉक्टर का लगाया) टाँका, स्टिच (कट जाने पर या शल्य-क्रिया के बाद) *How many stitches did you have in your leg?* **3** one of the small circles of wool that you put round a needle when you are knitting (बुनाई का) फंदा **4** [*usually sing.*] a sudden pain that you get in the side of your body when you are running दौड़ते हुए शरीर के पार्श्व में अचानक उठा दर्द; पार्श्वशूल, हूक, टीस

IDM **in stitches** (*informal*) laughing so much that you cannot stop हँस-हँस कर लोट-पोट हो जाना

**stitch²** /stɪtʃ स्टिच्/ *verb* [I, T] to sew सिलना या सीना, टाँके लगाना

**stock¹** /stɒk स्टॉक्/ *noun* **1** [U, C] the supply of things that a shop, etc. has for sale (दुक़ान आदि में रखा) बिक्री के लिए माल; स्टॉक *I'm afraid that book's* ***out of stock*** *at the moment.* ○ *I'll see if we have your size in stock.* **2** [C] an amount of sth that has been kept ready to be used तुरंत प्रयोग के लिए उपलब्ध वस्तुओं की मात्रा; भंडार *Food stocks in the village were very low.* **3** [C, U] a share that sb has bought in a company, or the value of a company's shares कंपनी का शेयर या शेयर-पूँजी *to invest in stocks and shares* **4** [C, U] a liquid that is made by boiling meat, bones, vegetables, etc. in water, used especially for making soups and sauces गोश्त, सब्ज़ी आदि का शोरबा (विशेषतः सूप और चटनी बनाने में प्रयुक्त)

IDM **take stock (of sth)** to think about sth very carefully before deciding what to do next (अगले क़दम के निर्णय से पहले) सावधानी से सोच-विचार करना

**stock²** /stɒk स्टॉक्/ *verb* [T] **1** (usually used about a shop) to have a supply of sth (दुकान में) माल जमा करके रखना *They stock food from all over the world.* **2** to fill a place with sth किसी स्थान को (किसी वस्तु से) भर देना *a well-stocked library*

PHR V **stock up (on/with sth)** to collect a large supply of sth for future use भविष्य के लिए सामान जमा करके रखना *to stock up with food for the winter*

**stock³** /stɒk स्टॉक्/ *adj.* (*only before a noun*) (used for describing sth that sb says) used so often that it does not have much meaning घिसा-पिटा (जवाब, आदि जिसमें कोई नई बात न हो) *He always gives the same stock answers.*

**stockbroker** /ˈstɒkbrəʊkə(r) ˈस्टॉक्ब्रोक(र्)/ (*also* **broker**) *noun* [C] a person whose job it is to buy and sell shares in companies for other people शेयर-दलाल (दूसरों के लिए कंपनी के शेयरों की ख़रीद-फ़रोख़्त करने वाला व्यक्ति)

**stock exchange** *noun* [C] **1** a place where shares in companies are bought and sold शेयर-बाज़ार (स्थान जहाँ कंपनी के शेयर ख़रीद-बेचे जाते हैं) *the Mumbai Stock Exchange* **2** (*also* **stock market**) the business or activity of buying and selling shares in companies शेयर-मार्केट (कंपनी के शेयरों का व्यापार या क्रय-विक्रय) ➪ **exchange** देखिए।

**stocking** /ˈstɒkɪŋ ˈस्टॉकिङ्/ *noun* [C] one of a pair of thin pieces of clothing that fit tightly over a woman's feet and legs लंबा मोज़ा (विशेषतः महिलाओं द्वारा प्रयुक्त) *a pair of stockings* ➪ **tights** देखिए।

**stockist** /ˈstɒkɪst ˈस्टॉकिस्ट्/ *noun* [C] a shop that sells goods made by a particular company कंपनी-विशेष द्वारा निर्मित माल को बेचने वाली दुकान; स्टॉकिस्ट (थोक) व्यापारी

**stockpile** /ˈsɒkpaɪl ˈस्टॉक्पाइल्/ *noun* [C] a large supply of sth that is kept to be used in the future if necessary (आवश्यकता होने पर भविष्य में प्रयोग के लिए सुरक्षित) किसी वस्तु का बड़ा संग्रह ▶ **stockpile** *verb* [T] बड़ी मात्रा में (किसी वस्तु का) संग्रह करना *to stockpile food/fuel*

**stocktaking** /ˈstɒkteɪkɪŋ ˈस्टॉक्टेकिङ्/ *noun* [U] the activity of counting the total supply of things that a shop or business has at a particular time समय-विशेष पर दुकान में जमा पूरे माल या स्टॉक की जाँच *They close for an hour a month to do the stocktaking.*

**stocky** /ˈstɒki ˈस्टॉकि/ *adj.* (used about a person's body) short but strong and heavy (व्यक्ति का शरीर) नाटा परंतु गठीला

**stoic** /ˈstəʊɪk ˈस्टोइक्/ (*also* **stoical** /ˈstəʊɪkl ˈस्टोइकल्/) *adj.* (*formal*) suffering pain or difficulty without complaining दुख के प्रति उदासीन; विरक्त ▶ **stoically** /ˈstəʊɪkli ˈस्टोइक्लि/ *adv.* विरक्त भाव से ▶ **stoicism** /ˈstəʊɪsɪzəm ˈस्टोइसिज़म्/ *noun* [U] विरक्ति

**stoke** /stəʊk स्टोक्/ *verb* [T] **1 stoke sth (up) (with sth)** to add fuel to a fire, etc. (भट्टी आदि में) कोयला भरना या झोंकना *to stoke up a fire with more coal* ○ *to stoke a furnace* **2 stoke sth (up)** to make people feel sth more strongly किसी प्रवृत्ति, भाव आदि को बढ़ावा देना *to stoke up anger/envy* ○ *The publicity was intended to stoke up interest in her music.*

**PHR V** **stoke up (on/with sth)** (*informal*) to eat of drink a lot of sth, especially so that you do not feel hungry later पेटभर खा-पी लेना (ताकि बाद में भूख न लगे) *Stoke up for the day on a good breakfast.*

**stole** ➪ **steal** का past tense रूप

**stolen** ➪ **steal** का past participle रूप

**stolid** /ˈstɒlɪd ˈस्टॉलिड्/ *adj.* (used about a person) showing very little emotion or excitement (व्यक्ति) भावशून्य, निर्विकार ▶ **stolidly** *adv.* निर्विकार भाव से

**stoma** /ˈstəʊmə ˈस्टोमा/ *noun* [C] (*pl.* **stomas** or **stomata** /ˈstəʊmətə ˈस्टोमटा/) (*technical*) **1** any of the very small holes in the surface of a leaf or the **stem** of a plant that allow gases to pass in and out पौधे की पत्ती या तने में गैसों के आने-जाने के लिए बहुत छोटा छिद्र; रंध्र **2** a small opening like a mouth in some simple creatures कुछ साधारण जीवों में मुख जैसा छिद्र; मुखछिद्र, मुख **3** (in medicine) a hole that is made from the surface of the body to one of the tubes inside the body (चिकित्सा कार्य में) शरीर की सतह से अंदर की किसी नली तक बनाया गया छिद्र

**stomach**[1] /ˈstʌmək ˈस्टमक्/ (*informal* **tummy**) *noun* [C] **1** the organ in your body where food goes after you have eaten it आमाशय, मेदा (पेट में भोजन एकत्र होने की थैली) *He went to the doctor with stomach pains.* ➪ **body** पर चित्र देखिए। **2** the front part of your body below your chest and above your legs पेट *She turned over onto her stomach.*

**stomach**[2] /ˈstʌmək ˈस्टमक्/ *verb* [T] (*informal*) (*usually in negative sentences and questions*) to be able to watch, listen to, accept, etc. sth that you think is unpleasant अप्रिय लगने वाली बात को सहन कर सकना *I can't stomach too much violence in films.*

**stomach-ache** *noun* [C, U] a pain in your stomach पेट-दर्द, उदर-शूल *I've got terrible stomach-ache.* ➪ **ache** पर नोट देखिए।

**stomp** /stɒmp स्टॉम्प्/ *verb* [I] (*informal*) to walk with heavy steps धम-धम करके चलना

**stone** /stəʊn स्टोन्/ *noun* **1** [U] a hard solid substance that is found in the ground पत्थर *a stone wall* ➪ **corner stone** और **foundation stone** देखिए। **2** [C] a small piece of rock पत्थर का टुकड़ा *The boy picked up a stone and threw it into the river.* **3** [C] = **precious stone** **4** [C] the hard seed inside some fruits, for example **peaches, plums, cherries and olives** गुठली (आड़ू आलूबुख़ारा, चेरी और जैतून के फल की) **5** [C] (*pl.* **stone**) a measure of weight; 6.35 kilograms. There are 14 pounds in a stone तोल की एक माप; 6.35 किलोग्राम (14 पाउंड का एक स्टोन होता है) *I weigh eleven stone two* (= 2 pounds).

**the Stone Age** *noun* [*sing.*] the very early period of human history when tools and weapons were made of stone पाषाण युग (मानव जाति के इतिहास का आरंभिक युग जब विभिन्न उपकरण और शस्त्र पाषाण या पत्थर से बनाये जाते थे)

**stoned** /stəʊnd स्टोन्ड्/ *adj.* (*slang*) not behaving or thinking normally because of drugs or alcohol (नशीली पदार्थ या शराब के प्रभाव से) बेसुध (असामान्य आचरण और सोच वाला)

**stonemason** /ˈstəʊnmeɪsn ˈस्टोन्मेसन्/ *noun* [C] a person whose job is cutting and preparing stone for buildings संगतराश (इमारतों के लिए पत्थरों को काटकर गढ़ने वाली कारीगर)

**stonework** /ˈstəʊnwɜːk ˈस्टोन्वक्/ *noun* [U] the parts of a building that are made of stone इमारत के वे भाग जहाँ पत्थर की चिनाई की गई हो

**stony** /ˈstəʊni ˈस्टोनि/ *adj.* **1** (used about the ground) having a lot of stones in it, or covered with stones (ज़मीन) पथरीली (जिसके अंदर पत्थर भरे हों या ऊपर पत्थर बिछे हों) **2** not friendly मित्रवत नहीं, पाषाण-हृदय, कठोर, संगदिल *There was a stony silence as he walked into the room.*

**stood** ➪ **stand**[1] का past tense और past participle रूप

**stool** /stuːl स्टूल्/ *noun* [C] a seat that does not have a back or arms स्टूल, तिपाई (ऐसी चौकी जिसकी न बाहें हों, न पीछे का सहारा) *a piano stool*

**stoop** /stu:p स्टूप्/ *verb* [I] to bend your head and shoulders forwards and downwards झुकना (सिर और कंधों को आगे और नीचे की ओर मोड़ना) *He had to stoop to get through the low doorway.* ▶ **stoop** *noun* [*sing.*] झुकाव, नति *to walk with a stoop*

**PHR V** **stoop to sth/doing sth** to do sth bad or wrong that you would normally not do कोई ऐसा बुरा या ग़लत काम करना जो सामान्यतया हम नहीं करते

**stop**[1] /stɒp स्टॉप्/ *verb* (**stopping**; **stopped**) **1** [I, T] to finish moving or make sth finish moving रुकना या (किसी को) रोकना (गतिमान न रहना या न रहने देना) *My watch has stopped.* ○ *Does this train stop at Kanpur?* **2** [I, T] to no longer continue or make sth not continue रुक जाना, बंद हो जाना या रोक देना या बंद कर देना *It's stopped raining now.* ○ *The bus service stops at midnight.* ○ *We tied a bandage round his arm to stop the bleeding.*

**NOTE** **Stop doing** का तात्पर्य है कि काम को बंद कर दिया गया है और वह फिर से शुरू नहीं होगा—*Stop talking and listen to me!* **Stop to do** का तात्पर्य है कि काम को प्रयोजन-विशेष से रोका गया है और (प्रयोजन सिद्धि के बाद) वह फिर से शुरू हो जाएगा—*On the way home I stopped to buy a newspaper.*

**3** [T] **stop sb/sth (from) doing sth** to make sb/sth end or finish an activity; prevent sb/sth from doing sth (किसी की) किसी हरकत को रोक देना; (किसी को) कुछ करने न देना या कुछ करने से मना कर देना *They've built a fence to stop the dog getting out.* **4** [I, T] **stop (for sth); stop (and do/to do sth)** to end an activity for a short time in order to do sth थोड़ी देर के लिए (विशेष प्रयोजन से) रुक जाना *Let's stop and look at the map.* ○ *We stopped work for half an hour to have a cup of coffee.*

**IDM** **stop at nothing** to do anything to get what you want, even if it is wrong or dangerous अभीष्ट की प्राप्ति के लिए सब कुछ करने के लिए तैयार हो जाना (भले ही वह ग़लत या ख़तरनाक हो)

**stop short of sth/doing sth** to almost do sth, but then decide not to do it at the last minute लगभग समाप्ति तक पहुँचे काम को अंतिम क्षणों में रोक देना

**PHR V** **stop off (at/in...)** to stop during a journey to do sth यात्रा के दौरान किसी प्रयोजन से रुक जाना

**stop over (at/in...)** to stay somewhere for a short time during a long journey लंबी यात्रा के दौरान थोड़े समय के लिए कहीं रुक जाना

**stop**[2] /stɒp स्टॉप्/ *noun* [C] **1** an act of stopping or state of being stopped रुकने की क्रिया या रोक दिए जाने की स्थिति; ठहराव, विराम *Our first stop will be in Rohtak.* ○ *Production at the factory will* ***come to a stop*** *at midnight tonight.* **2** the place where a bus, train, etc. stops so that people can get on and off बस, ट्रेन आदि के रुकने का स्थान (जहाँ लोग चढ़-उतर सकते हैं); बस या ट्रेन स्टॉप *a bus stop* ○ *I'm getting off at the next stop.*

**IDM** **pull out all the stops** ➪ **pull**[1] देखिए।

**put a stop to sth** to prevent sth bad or unpleasant from continuing किसी बुरी या अप्रिय स्थिति को आगे चलने न देना या रोक देना

**stopgap** /ˈstɒpgæp ˈस्टॉप्गैप्/ *noun* [C] a person or a thing that does a job for a short time until sb/sth permanent can be found (किसी काम के लिए स्थायी होने तक) अस्थायी व्यवस्था के रूप में कोई व्यक्ति या वस्तु

**stopover** /ˈstɒpəʊvə(r) ˈस्टॉप्ओव़(र्)/ *noun* [C] a short stop in a journey यात्रा के दौरान थोड़ी देर ठहरने की क्रिया; पड़ाव

**stoppage** /ˈstɒpɪdʒ ˈस्टॉपिज्/ *noun* [C] **1** a situation in which people stop working as part of a protest (विरोधस्वरूप) लोगों द्वारा काम बंद कर देने की स्थिति, काम में व्यवधान **2** (in sport) an interruption in a game for a particular reason खेल का किसी कारणवश रुक जाना, खेल में व्यवधान

**stopper** /ˈstɒpə(r) ˈस्टॉप(र्)/ *noun* [C] an object that you put into the top of a bottle in order to close it (बोतल को बंद करने के लिए) डाट; काग ➪ **Thermos** पर चित्र देखिए।

**stopwatch** /ˈstɒpwɒtʃ ˈस्टॉप्वॉच्/ *noun* [C] a watch which can be started and stopped by pressing a button, so that you can measure exactly how long sth takes विशेष घड़ी जिसे किसी घटना होने के समय को मापने के लिए आवश्यकतानुसार चलाया और बंद किया जा सकता है; स्टॉप वाच, विराम घड़ी

**storage** /ˈstɔ:rɪdʒ ˈस्टॉरिज्/ *noun* [U] the keeping of things until they are needed; the place where they are kept (आवश्यकता होने तक) वस्तुओं को संचित किए रखने की क्रिया, संग्रहण; संग्रहण-स्थल, गोदाम, भंडार *This room is being used for storage at the moment.* ➪ **cold storage** देखिए।

**store**[1] /stɔ:(r) स्टॉ(र्)/ *noun* [C] **1** a large shop स्टोर, बड़ी दुकान *a furniture store/departmental store* ➪ **chain store** देखिए। **2** (*AmE*) = **shop**[1] **1** **3** a supply of sth that you keep for future use; the place where it is kept भविष्य में उपयोग के लिए सुरक्षित सामान; भंडार, गृह *a good store of food for the winter* ○ *Police discovered a weapons store in the house.*

**IDM** **in store (for sb/sth)** going to happen in the future भविष्य में होने वाला; भावी *There's a surprise in store for you when you get home!*

**set... store by sth** to consider sth to be important किसी बात को महत्त्व देना *Nitin sets great store by his mother's opinion.*

**store**[2] /stɔ:(r) स्टॉ(र्)/ *verb* [T] to keep sth or a supply of sth for future use भविष्य के प्रयोग के लिए किसी वस्तु या वस्तु की आपूर्ति को सुरक्षित रखना *to store information on a computer*

**storekeeper** /ˈstɔ:ki:pə(r) ˈस्टॉकीप(र्)/ = **shopkeeper**

**storeroom** /ˈstɔ:ru:m; -rʊm ˈस्टॉरूम्; -रुम्/ *noun* [C] a room where things are kept until they are needed भंडारकक्ष, भंडारगृह

**storey** (*AmE* **story**) /ˈstɔ:ri ˈस्टॉरि/ *noun* [C] (*pl.* **storeys** *AmE* **stories**) one floor or level of a building (इमारत की) मंज़िल, तल्ला *The building will be five storeys high.* ○ *a multi-storey house*

**stork** /stɔ:k स्टॉक्/ *noun* [C] a large white bird with a long beak, neck and legs. Storks often make their homes (**nests**) on the top of buildngs लक़लक़; एक सारसनुमा पक्षी जो प्रायः इमारतों की छत पर अपना घोंसला बनाता है

**storm**[1] /stɔ:m स्टॉम्/ *noun* [C] very bad weather, with a lot of rain, strong winds, etc. आँधी-तूफ़ान (बहुत ख़राब मौसम जिसमें बहुत वर्षा, तेज हवाएँ आदि हों) *a hailstorm/snowstorm/sandstorm/thunderstorm*

> **NOTE** बहुत ख़राब मौसम का संकेत करने के लिए **storm** शब्द प्रयुक्त होता है। बहुत तेज़ हवा या झंझावात को **gale** कहते हैं। बहुत तेज़ हवा वाली आँधी को **hurricane** कहते हैं। चक्रवात या बवंडर (वृत्ताकार घूमती तेज़ हवा वाली आँधी) के लिए शब्द हैं— **cyclone, tornado, typhoon** या **whirlwind**. बहुत तेज़ बर्फ़ीला तूफ़ान **blizzard** कहलाता है।

**storm**[2] /stɔ:m स्टॉम्/ *verb* **1** [I] to enter or leave somewhere in a very angry and noisy way बहुत क्रोध दिखाते और लगभग चीखते हुए कहीं आना या कहीं से जाना *He threw down the book and stormed out of the room.* **2** [T] to attack a building, town, etc. suddenly and violently in order to take control of it (किसी भवन, नगर आदि पर) सहसा धावा बोलकर कब्ज़ा करने का प्रयास करना

**stormy** /ˈstɔ:mi ˈस्टॉमि/ *adj.* **1** used for talking about very bad weather, with strong winds, heavy rain, etc. तूफ़ानी, तूफ़ान वाली (ऐसे ख़राब मौसम से संबंधित जिसमें तेज़ हवा, भारी वर्षा आदि हो) *a stormy night* ○ *stormy weather* **2** involving a lot of angry argument and strong feeling क्रोध और तीव्र भावनाओं से युक्त; संकटपूर्ण *a stormy relationship*

**story** /ˈstɔ:ri ˈस्टॉरि/ *noun* [C] (*pl.* **stories**) **1 a story (about sb/sth)** a description of people and events that are not real (काल्पनिक) कथा या कहानी, क़िस्सा ***a bedtime story*** ○ *a detective/fairy/ghost/love story* **2** an account, especially a spoken one, of sth that has happened किसी घटना का विवरण (विशेषतः बोलकर दिया गया); कहानी *The police didn't believe his story.* **3** a description of true events that happened in the past अतीत की सच्ची घटनाओं का वर्णन *He's writing his life story.* **4** an article or report in a newspaper or magazine अख़बार या पत्रिका में कोई लेख या रिपोर्ट या रपट *The plane crash was the front-page story in most newspapers.* **5** (*AmE*) = **storey**

**stout** /staʊt स्टाउट्/ *adj.* **1** (used about a person) rather fat (व्यक्ति) मोटा-सा **2** strong and thick मज़बूत और मोटा *stout walking boots*

**stove** /stəʊv स्टोव्/ *noun* [C] **1** the top part of a cooker that has gas or electric rings गैस या बिजली की सिगड़ी; स्टोव, चूल्हा *He put a pan of water to boil on the stove.* **2** a closed metal box in which you burn wood, coal, etc. for heating अँगीठी, सिगड़ी *a wood-burning stove*

**stow** /stəʊ स्टो/ *verb* [T] **stow sth (away)** to put sth away in a particular place until it is needed (आवश्यकता होने तक) किसी वस्तु को कहीं रखे रहना

**straddle** /ˈstrædl ˈस्ट्रैड्ल्/ *verb* [T] **1** (used about a person) to sit or stand with your legs on each side of sb/sth (व्यक्ति का) टाँगें फैलाकर (किसी वस्तु पर) बैठना या खड़ा होना *to straddle a chair* **2** (used about a building, bridge, etc.) to cross, or exist on both sides of, a river, a road or an area of land (किसी भवन, पुल आदि का) किसी नदी, सड़क या भूखंड के आर-पार जाना या दोनों तरफ़ फैला होना

**straggle** /ˈstrægl ˈस्ट्रैग्ल्/ *verb* [I] **1** to walk, etc. more slowly than the rest of the group समूह के बाक़ी लोगों से पिछड़ जाना, अलग हो जाना, भटक जाना आदि *The children straggled along behind their parents.* **2** to grow, spread or move in an untidy way or in different directions बेढंगेपन से या इधर-उधर उग आना, फैल जाना या बिखर जाना *Her wet hair straggled across her forehead.* ▶ **straggler** *noun* [C] भटकने वाला, भटकैया ▶ **straggly** *adj.* अस्त-व्यस्त, फैला हुआ, बिखरा हुआ *long straggly hair*

**straight**[1] /streɪt स्ट्रेट्/ *adj.* **1** with no bends or curves; going in one direction only जिसमें न मोड़ हों न घुमाव; सीधा *a straight line* ○ *Keep your back straight!* **2** (*not before a noun*) in an exactly horizontal or vertical position एकदम सीधा (एकदम

खड़ी, लंबवत पड़ी या क्षैतिज दशा में) *That picture isn't straight.* **3** honest and direct ईमानदार और निष्कपट या सच्चा *Politicians never give **a straight answer**.* **4** tidy or organized as it should be साफ़-सुथरा या सुव्यवस्थित *It took ages to **put** the room **straight** after we'd decorated it.* **5** (*informal*) attracted to people of the opposite sex विपरीत लिंग के व्यक्ति के प्रति आकृष्ट; विपरीत लिंगी ➪ **heterosexual** देखिए। ✪ विलोम **gay** **6** (*informal*) used to describe a person who you think is too serious and boring अत्यधिक गंभीर और उबा ऊ लगने वाला (व्यक्ति)

IDM **get sth straight** to make sure that you understand sth completely किसी बात को पक्के तौर पर पूरी तरह से समझ लेना

**keep a straight face** to stop yourself from smiling or laughing गंभीर मुद्रा में रहना

**put/set the record straight** ➪ **record[1]** देखिए।

**straight[2]** /streɪt स्ट्रेट्/ *adv.* **1** not in a curve or at an angle; in a straight line घुमावदार, लंबवत, क्षैतिज या कोण बनाता हुआ नहीं, सीधी रेखा में, सीध में *He was looking **straight ahead**.* ○ *to sit up straight* (= with a straight back) **2** without stopping; directly बिना रुके; सीधे *I took the children straight home after school.* ○ *He joined the army straight from school.* **3** in an honest and direct way ईमानदारी से और सीधे-सीधे *Tell me straight, doctor—is it serious?*

IDM **go straight** to become honest after being a criminal अपराधी जीवन को त्याग देना

**right/straight away** ➪ **away** देखिए।

**straight out** in an honest and direct way ईमानदारी से और सीधे-सीधे *I told Asif straight out that I didn't want to see him any more.*

**straighten** /ˈstreɪtn ˈस्ट्रेट्न्/ *verb* [I, T] **straighten (sth) (up/out)** to become straight or to make sth straight सीधा हो जाना या (किसी को) सीधा कर देना *The road straightens out at the bottom of the hill.* ○ *to straighten your tie*

PHR V **straighten sth out** to remove the confusion or difficulties from a situation (किसी स्थिति के) उलझाव या कठिनाइयों को दूर करना; सुलझाना

**straighten up** to make your body straight and vertical सीधा खड़ा हो जाना

**straightforward** /ˌstreɪtˈfɔːwəd ˌस्ट्रेट्ˈफ़ॉवड्/ *adj.* **1** easy to do or understand; simple सुकर या सुबोध जिसे करना या समझना आसान हो; सरल *straightforward instructions* **2** honest and open ईमानदार और स्पष्टवादी या खुले दिल-दिमाग़ का *a straightforward person*

**strain[1]** /streɪn स्ट्रेन्/ *noun* **1** [U] pressure that is put on sth when it is pulled or pushed by a physical force (किसी भौतिक शक्ति द्वारा खींचे या धकेले जाने से किसी पर पड़ा) दबाव *Running downhill puts strain on the knees.* ○ *The rope finally broke **under the strain**.* **2** [C, U] worry or pressure caused by having too much to deal with किसी बात की अत्यधिकता (जैसे अत्यधिक परिश्रम) से उत्पन्न चिंता या दबाव *to be **under** a lot of **strain** at work* **3** [C] something that makes you feel worried and tense चिंता और तनाव उत्पन्न करने वाली वस्तु *I always find exams a terrible strain.* **4** [C, U] an injury to part of your body that is caused by using it too much मोच (शरीर के किसी अंग के अत्यधिक उपयोग से हुई क्षति) **5** [C] one type of animal, plant or disease that is slightly different from the other types पशु, पौधे या रोग का एक प्रकार जो दूसरे से थोड़ा-सा भिन्न हो; विभेद

**strain[2]** /streɪn स्ट्रेन्/ *verb* **1** [I, T] to make a great mental or physical effort to do sth किसी काम के लिए काफ़ी अधिक मानसिक या शारीरिक श्रम करना *I was straining to see what was happening.* ○ *She strained her ears* (= listened very hard) *to catch what they were saying.* **2** [T] to injure a part of your body by using it too much शरीर के किसी अंग में मोच आ जाना (उसका अत्यधिक उपयोग के कारण) *Don't read in the dark. You'll strain your eyes.* ○ *I think I have strained a muscle.* **3** [T] to put a lot of pressure on sth किसी पर अत्यधिक दबाव डालना *Money problems have strained their relationship.* **4** [T] to separate a solid and a liquid by pouring them into a special container with small holes in it छलनी से किसी चीज़ को छानना (तरल और ठोस अंशों को अलग-अलग करना) *to strain tea/vegetables/spaghetti*

**strained** /streɪnd स्ट्रेन्ड्/ *adj.* **1** not natural or friendly सहज या मैत्रीपूर्ण नहीं; तनावपूर्ण, असामान्य *Relations between the two countries are strained.* **2** worried because of having too much to deal with घोर परिश्रम के कारण थका हुआ-सा *Madhuri looked tired and strained.*

**strait** /streɪt स्ट्रेट्/ *noun* **1** [C, *usually pl.*] a narrow piece of sea that joins two larger seas दो बड़े समुद्रों को मिलाने वाला सँकरा समुद्र खंड; जल-डमरूमध्य, जल-संयोजी *the straits of Gibraltar* **2 straits** [*pl.*] a very difficult situation, especially one caused by having no money संकट की स्थिति (विशेषतः धन के अभाव से उत्पन्न) *The company is in financial straits.*

IDM **be in dire straits** ➪ **dire** देखिए।

**straitjacket** (*also* **straightjacket**) /ˈstreɪtdʒækɪt ˈस्ट्रेट्जैकिट्/ *noun* [C] a piece of clothing like a jacket with long arms which is put on people who are considered dangerous to prevent them from behaving violently लंबी आस्तीनों वाली जैकेट जैसी पोशाक जो उग्र हो रहे व्यक्ति को नियंत्रिण में लाने के लिए पहना दी जाती है; जकड़ जाना

**strand** /strænd स्ट्रैन्ड्/ *noun* [C] **1** a single piece of cotton, wool, hair, etc. कपास, ऊन आदि का एक अकेला तार या धागा, एक अकेला बाल, (एक) लड़ या लड़ी **2** one part of a story, situation or idea किसी कहानी, स्थिति या विचार का एक अंश

**stranded** /ˈstrændɪd ˈस्ट्रैन्डिड्/ *adj.* left in a place that you cannot get away from असहाय, संकटग्रस्त, बेसवारी (ऐसे स्थान पर फँसा हुआ जहाँ से निकलना मुश्किल) *We were left stranded when our car broke down in the mountains.*

**strange** /streɪndʒ स्ट्रेन्ज्/ *adj.* **1** unusual or unexpected असामान्य या अप्रत्याशित; विचित्र; अजीब *a strange noise* **2** that you have not seen, visited, met, etc. before जिसे पहले देखा, मिला, जाना आदि न हो *a strange town* ○ *strange men*

NOTE ऐसे व्यक्ति या वस्तु के लिए **strange** का प्रयोग नहीं होता जो दूसरे देश का हो। ➪ **foreign** देखिए।

▶ **strangely** *adv.* विचित्र या अजीब ढंग से *The streets were strangely quiet.* ○ *He's behaving very strangely at the moment.* ▶ **strangeness** *noun* [U] विचित्रता

**stranger** /ˈstreɪndʒə(r) ˈस्ट्रेन्ज(र्)/ *noun* [C] **1** a person that you do not know अपरिचित व्यक्ति, अजनबी *I had to ask a* ***complete stranger*** *to help me with my suitcase.*

NOTE ऐसे व्यक्ति को **stranger** नहीं कहते जो दूसरे देश का हो ➪ **foreigner** देखिए।

**2** a person who is in a place that he/she does not know किसी स्थान से अपरिचित कोई व्यक्ति *I'm a stranger to this part of the country.*

**strangle** /ˈstræŋgl ˈस्ट्रैङ्ग्ल्/ *verb* [T] **1** to kill sb by squeezing his/her neck or throat with your hands, a rope, etc. (हाथ, रस्सी आदि से) गरदन या गला घोंट कर किसी को मार देना ✪ पर्याय **throttle** ➪ **choke** देखिए। **2** to prevent sth from developing (किसी के) विकास को अवरुद्ध कर देना

**strap** /stræp स्ट्रैप्/ *noun* [C] a long narrow piece of leather, cloth, plastic, etc. that you use for carrying sth or for keeping sth in position (चमड़े, कपड़े, प्लास्टिक आदि का) पट्टा या फ़ीता (कुछ बाँध कर ले जाने या ठीक ठाक रखने के लिए प्रयुक्त) *I managed to fasten my watch strap but now I can't undo it.*

▶ **strap** *verb* [T] (**strapping; strapped**) फ़ीता बाँधना या बंधे होना *The racing driver was securely strapped into the car.*

**strata** ➪ **stratum** का plural रूप

**strategic** /strəˈtiːdʒɪk स्ट्रˈटीजिक्/ (*also* **strategical** /-dʒɪkl -जिकल्/) *adj.* **1** helping you to achieve a plan; giving you an advantage लक्ष्य की प्राप्ति में सहायक युक्तिपूर्ण; (किसी को) लाभ की स्थिति में पहुँचाते हुए, अनुकूल *They made a strategic decision to sell off part of the company.* **2** connected with a country's plans to achieve success in a war or in its defence system युद्ध में सफलता या सुरक्षा प्रणाली को कारगर बनाने की (किसी देश की) योजनाओं से संबंधित; रणनीतिक, सामरिक महत्त्व का **3** (used about bombs and other weapons) intended to be fired at the enemy's country rather than be used in battle (बम या अन्य ऐसे हथियार) शत्रु के देश पर (न कि युद्धभूमि में) आक्रमण के लिए प्रयुक्त ▶ **strategically** /strəˈtiːdʒɪkli स्ट्रˈटीजिक्लि/ *adv.* रणनीतिक दृष्टि से *The island is strategically important.*

**strategy** /ˈstrætədʒi ˈस्ट्रैटजी/ *noun* (*pl.* **strategies**) **1** [C] a plan that you use in order to achieve sth लक्ष्य प्राप्ति कराने वाली योजना, रणनीति, रण योजना **2** [U] the action of planning how to do or achieve sth कार्यनीति या लक्ष्य प्राप्ति की योजना का निर्णण *military strategy*

**stratification** /ˌstrætɪfɪˈkeɪʃn ˌस्ट्रैटिफ़िˈकेश्न्/ *noun* [U] (*technical*) the division of sth into different layers or groups विभिन्न स्तरों या वर्गों में विभाजन; स्तरीकरण या वर्गीकरण *social stratification*

**stratosphere** /ˈstrætəsfɪə(r) ˈस्ट्रैटस्फ़िअ(र्)/ *noun* [*sing.*] **the stratosphere** the layer of the earth's atmosphere between about 10 and 50 kilometres above the surface of the earth समतापमंडल ➪ **ionosphere** और **troposphere** देखिए। ▶ **stratospheric** /ˌstrætəˈsferɪk ˌस्ट्रैटˈस्फ़ेरिक्/ *adj.* समतापमंडल से संबंधित *stratospheric clouds/ozone*

**stratum** /ˈstrɑːtəm ˈस्ट्राटम्/ *noun* [C] (*pl.* **strata** /-tə -टा/) (*technical*) a layer or set of layers of rock, earth, etc. in the ground चट्टान, ज़मीन आदि की परत या परतें

**stratus** /ˈstreɪtəs; ˈstrɑːtəs ˈस्ट्रेटस्; ˈस्ट्राटस्/ *noun* [U] (*technical*) a type of cloud that forms a continuous grey sheet covering the sky स्लेटी या धूसर रंग का घना बादल; स्तरी मेघ

**straw** /strɔː स्ट्रॉ/ *noun* **1** [U] the long, straight, central parts (**stems**) of plants, for example wheat, that are dried and then used for animals to sleep on or for making baskets, covering a roof, etc. गेहूँ आदि का भूसा; पुलाल, पयाल *a straw hat* **2** [C] one piece of straw भूसे का एक तिनका **3** [C] a long plastic or paper tube that you can use for drinking through (ठंडे पेय पीने की) प्लास्टिक या काग़ज़ की लंबी नली; सींक, स्ट्रॉ, पाइप

IDM **the last/final straw** the last in a series of bad things that happen to you and that makes you decide that you cannot accept the situation any longer किसी प्रतिकूल परिस्थिति में अंतिम चोट (जिसके बाद और सहन करना संभव नहीं)

**strawberry** /ˈstrɔːbəri ˈस्ट्रॉबरि/ *noun* [C] (*pl.* **strawberries**) a small soft red fruit with small white seeds on it स्ट्रॉबेरि फल (बेर जैसा छोटे बीज वाला छोटा नरम लाल फल) *strawberries and cream* ➪ **fruit** पर चित्र देखिए।

**stray**[1] /streɪ स्ट्रे/ *verb* [I] **1** to go away from the place where you should be अपने स्थान से दूर निकल जाना; भटक जाना *The sheep had strayed onto the road.* **2** to not keep to the subject you should be thinking about or discussing (चिंतनाधीन या चर्चाधीन) विषय से हट जाना; विषयांतर करना *My thoughts strayed for a few moments.*

**stray**[2] /streɪ स्ट्रे/ *noun* [C] a dog, cat, etc. that does not have a home बेघर कुत्ता, बिल्ली आदि; आवारा या छुट्टा पशु ▶ **stray** *adj.* (*only before a noun*) आवारा, छुट्टा *a stray dog*

**streak**[1] /striːk स्ट्रीक्/ *noun* [C] **1 streak (of sth)** a thin line or mark पतली रेखा या निशान; धारी *The cat had brown fur with streaks of white in it.* **2** a part of a person's character that sometimes shows in the way he/she behaves व्यक्ति के चरित्र की कोई विशेषता जो उसके आचरण में झलकती है; प्रवृत्ति, झुकाव *Vinita is a very caring girl, but she does have a selfish streak.* **3** a continuous period of bad or good luck in a game of sport किसी खेल के मुक़ाबले में विफलता या सफलता की लगातार चलती अवधि *The team is **on a losing/winning streak** at the moment.*

**streak**[2] /striːk स्ट्रीक्/ *verb* [I] (*informal*) to run fast तेज़ दौड़ना, बड़ी तेज़ी से आना-जाना

**streaked** /striːkt स्ट्रीक्ट्/ *adj.* **streaked (with sth)** having lines of a different colour अलग रंग की धारियों वाला; धारीदार, लहरिया *black hair streaked with grey*

**stream**[1] /striːm स्ट्रीम्/ *noun* [C] **1** a small river छोटी (सँकरी) नदी *I waded across the shallow stream.* **2** the continuous movement of a liquid or gas द्रव या गैस का सतत प्रवाह या धारा *a stream of blood* **3** a continuous movement of people or things व्यक्तियों या वस्तुओं का सतत प्रवाह या ताँता *a stream of traffic* **4** a large number of things which happen one after another वस्तुओं या परिस्थितयों का ताँता लगना *a stream of letters/telephone calls/questions*

**stream**[2] /striːm स्ट्रीम्/ *verb* [I] **1** (used about a liquid, gas or light) to flow in large amounts (द्रव, गैस या प्रकाश की) धारा फूटना *Tears were streaming down his face.* ○ *Sunlight was streaming in through the windows.* **2** (used about people or things) to move somewhere in a continuous flow (व्यक्तियों या वस्तुओं का) ताँता लगना, सतत प्रवाह के रूप में कहीं पहुँचना *People were streaming out of the station.*

**streamer** /ˈstriːmə(r) ˈस्ट्रीम(र्)/ *noun* [C] a long piece of coloured paper that you use for decorating a room before a party, etc. रंगीन काग़ज़ की लंबी पट्टी; पताका, फरहरा

**streamline** /ˈstriːmlaɪn ˈस्ट्रीम्लाइन्/ *verb* [T] **1** to give a vehicle, etc. a long smooth shape so that it will move easily through air or water वाहन आदि को समतल आकृति में ढालना (ताकि वह हवा या पानी में सरलता से गति कर सके); सुप्रवाही बनाना **2** to make an organization, process, etc. work better by making it simpler किसी संस्था, प्रक्रिया आदि की जटिलता दूर कर उसकी कार्य-प्रणाली में सुधार करना ▶ **streamlined** *adj.* सरल और अधिक कारगर

**stream of consciousness** *noun* [U] a continuous flow of ideas, thoughts and feelings, as they are experienced by a person; a style of writing that expresses this without using the usual methods of description and conversation चेतना प्रवाह (किसी व्यक्ति की चेतना में कल्पनाओं, विचारों और भावनाओं का सतत प्रवाह); (लेखक द्वारा प्रयुक्त) चेतना प्रवाह की तकनीक (जिसमें वर्णन और संवाद की सामान्य पद्धतियों का प्रयोग नहीं होता)

**street** /striːt स्ट्रीट्/ *noun* [C] **1** a road in a town, village or city that has shops, houses, etc. on one or both sides मार्ग, गली, स्ट्रीट *to walk **along/down the street*** ○ ***to cross the street*** ➪ **road** पर नोट देखिए। **2 Street** (*abbr.* **St**) [*sing.*] used in the names of streets सड़कों के नाम के साथ प्रयुक्त *Parliament Street.*

IDM **the man in the street** ➪ **man**[1] देखिए।

**streets ahead (of sb/sth)** (*informal*) much better than sb/sth किसी से कहीं बेहतर

**(right) up your street** (*informal*) (used about an activity, subject, etc.) exactly right for you because you know a lot about it, like it very much, etc. (कोई क्रिया-कलाप, विषय आदि) आपके लिए एकदम सही (इसकी अच्छी जानकारी, इसमें रुचि आदि के कारण)

**strength** /streŋθ स्ट्रेङ्थ़्/ *noun* **1** [U] the quality of being physically strong; the amount of this quality that you have शारीरिक बल, शक्ति, ताक़त; किसी में शारीरिक बल या शक्ति की मात्रा *He pulled with all his strength but the rock would not move.* ○ *I didn't have the strength to walk any further.* **2** [U] the ability of an object to hold heavy weights or not to break or be damaged easily (किसी वस्तु की) भारी वज़न सँभालने, उससे न टूटने या न बिगड़ने की क्षमता; शक्ति *All our suitcases are tested for strength before they leave the factory.* **3** [U] the power and influence that sb has (किसी की) शक्ति या ताक़त और प्रभाव *China's economic strength* **4** [C] how strong a feeling or opinion is किसी भाव या मत की शक्ति **5** [C, U] a good quality or ability that sb/sth has किसी व्यक्ति या वस्तु का अच्छा गुण या सामर्थ्य *His greatest strength is his communication skills.* ○ *the strengths and weaknesses of a plan* ✪ विलोम **weakness**

IDM **at full strength** (used about a group) having all the people it needs or usually has (कोई समूह, दल) ज़रूरत के अनुसार सदस्यों की पूरी या सामान्य संख्या के साथ *Nobody is injured, so the team will be at full strength for the game.*

**below strength** (used about a group) not having the number of people it needs or usually has (कोई समूह, दल) ज़रूरत से या सामान्य से कम सदस्यों वाला

**on the strength** of as a result of information, advice, etc. (उपलब्ध) सूचना, सलाह आदि के फलस्वरूप, के अनुसार पर या के बल पर

**strengthen** /ˈstreŋθn ˈस्ट्रेङ्थ़्न्/ *verb* [I, T] to become stronger or to make sth stronger सशक्त या ताक़तवर होना या (किसी को) सशक्त या ताक़तवर बनाना *exercises to strengthen your muscles* ✪ विलोम **weaken**

**strenuous** /ˈstrenjuəs ˈस्ट्रेन्युअस्/ *adj.* needing or using a lot of effort or energy प्रयत्न साध्य या श्रमसाध्य ***strenuous exercise*** ○ ***strenuous effort***

▶ **strenuously** *adv.* प्रचुर प्रयत्न या शक्ति के साथ

**stress¹** /stres स्ट्रेस्/ *noun* **1** [C, U] worry and pressure that is caused by having too much to deal with (काम की अधिकता से उत्पन्न) चिंता और दबाव; तनाव *He's been **under** a lot of **stress** since his wife went into hospital.* ➪ **trauma** देखिए। **2** [U] **stress (on sth)** the special attention that you give to sth because you think it is important (किसी बात पर) विशेष ध्यान, बल (उसके महत्त्वपूर्ण होने के कारण) *We should **put** more **stress** on preventing crime.* **3** [C, U] **(a) stress (on sth)** the force that you put on a particular word or part of a word when you speak (शब्द या शब्दांश पर) बलाघात, बलात्मक स्वराघात (उसका उच्चारण करते हुए) *In the word 'dictionary' the stress is on the first syllable, 'dic'.* **4** [C, U] a physical force that may cause sth to bend or break भौतिक बल (भार आदि) (जो किसी को मोड़ या तोड़ दे); प्रतिबल *Heavy lorries **put** too much **stress** on this bridge.*

**stress²** /stres स्ट्रेस्/ *verb* [T] to give sth special force or attention because it is important किसी बात पर विशेष बल या ध्यान देना (उसके महत्त्वपूर्ण होने के कारण) *The minister stressed the need for a peaceful solution.* ○ *Which syllable is stressed in this word?* ✪ पर्याय **emphasize**

**stressful** /ˈstresfl ˈस्ट्रेसफ़्ल्/ *adj.* causing worry and pressure चिंता और दबाव उत्पन्न करने वाला; तनावप्रद *a stressful job*

**stress mark** *noun* [C] a mark used to show which part of a particular word or syllable is pronounced with more force than others शब्द या शब्दांश पर बलाघात-चिह्न

**stretch¹** /stretʃ स्ट्रेच्/ *verb* **1** [I, T] to pull sth so that it becomes longer or wider; to become longer or wider in this way किसी वस्तु को अधिक लंबा या चौड़ा करने के लिए खींचना; (किसी वस्तु का) खिंच कर अधिक लंबा या चौड़ा हो जाना, बढ़ जाना, तनन *The artist stretched the canvas tightly over the frame.* ○ *My T-shirt stretched when I washed it.* **2** [I, T] **stretch (sth) (out)** to push out your arms, legs, etc. as far as possible हाथ-पैर को अधिक-से अधिक पसारना या बाहर की ओर फैलाना; अँगड़ाई लेना *He switched off the alarm clock, yawned and stretched.* ○ *She stretched out her arm to take the book.* **3** [I] to cover a large area of land or a long period of time (स्थान या समय की दृष्टि से) फैला होना, दूर-दूर तक जाना *The long white beaches stretch for miles along the coast.* **4** [T] to make use of all the money, ability, time, etc. that sb has available for use उपलब्ध संपूर्ण धन, क्षमता, समय आदि का उपयोग करना *The test has been designed to really stretch students' knowledge.*

IDM **stretch your legs** to go for a walk after sitting down for a long time देर तक बैठे रहने के बाद सैर के लिए जाना

**stretch²** /stretʃ स्ट्रेच्/ *noun* [C] **1 a stretch (of sth)** an area of land or water ज़मीन या पानी का क्षेत्र *a dangerous stretch of road* **2** [*usually sing.*] the action of making the muscles in your arms, legs, back, etc. as long as possible अँगड़ाई *Stand up, everybody, and have a good stretch.*

**IDM** **at a stretch** without stopping बिना रुके, लगातार *We travelled for six hours at a stretch.*

**at full stretch** ⇨ **full**[1] देखिए।

**stretcher** /ˈstretʃə(r) ˈस्ट्रेच(र्)/ *noun* [C] a piece of cloth supported by two poles that is used for carrying a person who has been injured घायल व्यक्ति को ले जाने वाला डोला, स्ट्रेचर (दो समानांतर डंडों पर लगा कपड़ा)

**stricken** /ˈstrɪkn ˈस्ट्रिकन्/ *adj.* (*formal*) **1 stricken with (sb/sth)** seriously affected by an unpleasant feeling or disease or by a difficult situation (किसी अप्रिय भावना, रोग या कठिन परिस्थिति से) ग्रस्त *We went to the aid of the stricken boat.* **2** (*in compounds*) seriously affected by the thing mentioned -ग्रस्त *poverty-stricken families/grief-stricken widow*

**strict** /strɪkt स्ट्रिक्ट्/ *adj.* **1** not allowing people to break rules or behave badly सख़्त, कठोर (नियम भंग या ग़लत व्यवहार को सहन न करने वाला) *Samir's very strict with his children.* ○ *I went to a very strict school.* **2** that must be obeyed completely जिसका पूर्णतः पालन अपेक्षित हो *I gave her strict instructions to be home before 9 p.m.* **3** exactly correct; accurate एकदम सही; विशुद्ध, यथातथ्य *a strict interpretation of the law*

**strictly** /ˈstrɪktli ˈस्ट्रिक्ट्लि/ *adv.* in a strict way सख़्ती से, कठोरतापूर्वक *Smoking is strictly forbidden.*

**IDM** **strictly speaking** to be exactly correct or accurate एकदम सही या यथार्थ होना *Strictly speaking, the tomato is not a vegetable. It's a fruit.*

**stride**[1] /straɪd स्ट्राइड्/ *verb* [I] (*pt* **strode** /strəʊd स्ट्रोड्/ (*not used in the perfect tenses*) to walk with long steps, often because you feel very confident or determined लंबे डग भरना (आत्मविश्वास या दृढ़ संकल्प से युक्त होने के कारण) *He strode up to the house and knocked on the door.*

**stride**[2] /straɪd स्ट्राइड्/ *noun* [C] a long step एक लंबा क़दम; डग

**IDM** **get into your stride** to start to do sth in a confident way and well after an uncertain beginning (अनिश्चित शुरुआत के बाद) आत्मविश्वास के साथ और अच्छी तरह से अपना काम करने लगना, अपने काम में लग जाना

**make great strides** to make very quick progress तीव्र प्रगति करना

**take sth in your stride** to deal with a new or difficult situation easily and without worrying किसी नई या मुश्किल परिस्थिति का आसानी से और बिना चिंता किए सामना करना

**strident** /ˈstraɪdnt ˈस्ट्राइड्न्ट्/ *adj.* (used about a voice or a sound) loud and unpleasant (स्वर या ध्वनि) तीव्र और कर्णकटु; कानफोड़ू, तीक्ष्ण

**strife** /straɪf स्ट्राइफ़्/ *noun* [U] (*written*) trouble or fighting between people or groups लोगों या गुटों के बीच संघर्ष, विवाद या झगड़ा

**strike**[1] /straɪk स्ट्राइक्/ *noun* [C] **1** a period of time when people refuse to go to work, usually because they want more money or better working conditions हड़ताल *a one-day strike* ○ *Union members voted to* ***go on strike***. **2** a sudden military attack, especially by aircraft अचानक किया हमला (विशेषतः विमान द्वारा)

**strike**[2] /straɪk स्ट्राइक्/ *verb* (*pt, pp* **struck** /strʌk स्ट्रक्/) **1** [T] (*formal*) to hit sb/sth (किसी को) मारना, लगना, (किसी से) टकराना; आहनन *The stone struck her on the head.* ○ *The boat struck a rock and began to sink.* **NOTE** (इस अर्थ में) **hit** अधिक प्रचलित शब्द है—*The stone hit her on the head.* **2** [I, T] to attack and harm sb/sth suddenly किसी पर अचानक हमला कर उसे क्षति पहुँचाना *The earthquake struck Latur in 1993.* ○ *to be* ***struck by lightning*** **3** [I] to stop work as a protest (विरोधस्वरूप) हड़ताल पर जाना, काम करना बंद कर देना *The workers voted to strike for more money.* **4** [T] **strike sb (as sth)** to give sb a particular impression किसी पर विशेष तरह का प्रभाव छोड़ना *He strikes me as a very caring man.* **5** [T] (used about a thought or an idea) to come suddenly into sb's mind (किसी विचार या कल्पना का) अचानक मन में आना *It suddenly struck me that she would be the ideal person for the job.* **6** [T] to produce fire by rubbing sth, especially a match, on a surface माचिस की तीली आदि रगड़कर आग जलाना या (कुछ) जलाने के लिए माचिस की तीली रगड़ना *She struck a match and lit her cigarette.* **7** [I, T] (used about a clock) to ring a bell so that people know what time it is समय बताने के लिए घड़ी की घंटी बजना या बजाना *The clock struck eight* (= 8 o'clock). **8** [T] to discover gold, oil, etc. in the ground ज़मीन में सोना, तेल आदि का पता लगाना

**IDM** **strike a balance (between A and B)** to find a middle way between two extremes दो चरम स्थितियों के बीच का मार्ग ढूँढ़ना

**strike a bargain (with sb)** to make an agreement with sb किसी के साथ कोई समझौता करना

**within striking distance** near enough to be reached or attacked easily (कोई स्थान) बहुत नज़दीक (इतना कि आसानी से पहुँचा या उसपर हमला किया जा सके)

**PHR V** **strike back** to attack sb/sth that has attacked you किसी पर पलटवार करना
**strike up sth (with sb)** to start a conversation or friendship with sb किसी से बात छेड़ना या दोस्ती की शुरुआत करना

**striker** /ˈstraɪkə(r) ˈस्ट्राइक(र्)/ *noun* [C] **1** a person who has stopped working as a protest हड़ताली कर्मचारी **2** (in football) a player whose job is to score goals (फ़ुटबॉल में) गोल करने वाला खिलाड़ी; स्ट्राइकर

**striking** /ˈstraɪkɪŋ ˈस्ट्राइकिङ्/ *adj.* very noticeable; making a strong impression बहुत स्पष्ट; अति प्रभावशाली *There was a striking similarity between the two men.* ▶ **strikingly** *adv.* बहुत स्पष्टता से, प्रभावशाली तरीक़े से

**string¹** /strɪŋ स्ट्रिङ्/ *noun* **1** [C, U] a piece of long, strong material like very thin rope, that you use for tying things डोरी, फ़ीता, सुतली (वस्तुओं को बाँधने के लिए प्रयुक्त) *a ball/piece/length of string* ○ *The key is hanging on a string.* **2** [C] one of the pieces of thin wire, etc. that produce the sound on some musical instruments (वायलिन, गिटार आदि) वाद्यों का तार, तंत्री (जिससे स्वर उत्पन्न होते हैं) *A guitar has six strings.* ➪ पृष्ठ 789 पर चित्र देखिए। **3** [C] one of the tightly stretched pieces of **nylon,** etc. in a **racket** टेनिस और कुछ अन्य खेलों में गेंद फेंकने या लौटाने के लिए साधन रूप से प्रयुक्त रैकेट की (नाइलोन से बनी) तनी हुई डोरी **4 the strings** [*pl.*] the instruments in an orchestra that have strings वाद्य वृंद के तंत्रीयुक्त वाद्य या तंतु वाद्य **5** [C] **a string of sth** a line of things that are joined together on the same piece of thread (दानों या मनकों की) माला, लड़ी, हार *a string of beads* **6** [C] **a string of sth** a series of people, things or events that follow one after another (लोगों, वस्तुओं या घटनाओं का) ताँता, सिलसिला, शृंखला, कतार *a string of visitors* **7** [C] (*computing*) a series of letters, numbers, words, etc. (कंप्यूटर) अक्षरों, संख्याओं, शब्दों आदि की शृंखला

**IDM** **(with) no strings attached; without strings** with no special conditions बिना विशेष शर्तों के, बिना शर्त
**pull strings** ➪ **pull¹** देखिए।

**string²** /strɪŋ स्ट्रिङ्/ *verb* [T] (*pt, pp* **strung** /strʌŋ स्ट्रङ्/) **string sth (up)** to hang up a line of things with a piece of string, etc. वस्तुओं को डोरी आदि से लटका देना

**PHR V** **string sb/sth out** to make people or things form a line with spaces between each person or thing व्यक्तियों या वस्तुओं की कतार लगाना या को कतार में रखना (बीच-बीच में कुछ जगह छोड़ते हुए)
**string sth together** to put words or phrases together to make a sentence, speech, etc. शब्दों या वाक्यांशों को वाक्य, भाषण आदि में पिरोना या व्यवस्थित करना

**stringed instrument** /ˌstrɪŋd ˈɪnstrəmənt ˌस्ट्रिङ्ड् ˈइन्स्ट्रमन्ट्/ *noun* [C] any musical instrument with strings that you play with your fingers or with a **bow** तंतु वाद्य, तंत्रीयुक्त वाद्य (जिसकी तंत्रियों को उँगली या गज से बजाया जाता है)

**stringent** /ˈstrɪndʒənt ˈस्ट्रिन्जन्ट्/ *adj.* (used about a law, rule, etc.) very strict (क़ानून, नियम आदि) बहुत कठोर

**strip¹** /strɪp स्ट्रिप्/ *noun* [C] a long narrow piece of sth (क़ाग़ज़ आदि की) धज्जी, पट्टी *a strip of paper*

**strip²** /strɪp स्ट्रिप्/ *verb* (**stripping; stripped**) **1** [I, T] **strip (sth) (off)** to take off your clothes; to take off sb else's clothes अपने कपड़े उतार लेना; दूसरे के कपड़े उतार देना *The doctor asked him to strip to the waist.* ○ *He was stripped and searched at the airport by two customs officers.* **2** [T] **strip sb/sth (of sth)** to take sth away from sb/sth किसी से कोई वस्तु ले लेना, किसी वस्तु से कुछ हटा देना *They stripped the house of all its furniture.* **3** [T] **strip sth (off)** to remove sth that is covering a surface किसी सतह पर लगी वस्तु को हटा देना, निकाल देना या छील देना *to strip the paint off a door* ○ *to strip wallpaper*

**stripe** /straɪp स्ट्राइप्/ *noun* [C] a long narrow line of colour रंगीन धारी *Zebras have black and white stripes.* ▶ **striped** /straɪpt स्ट्राइप्ट्/ *adj.* रंगीन धारियों वाला; धारीदार *a red and white striped dress*

**strive** /straɪv स्ट्राइव्/ *verb* [I] (*pt* **strove** /strəʊv स्ट्रोव्/; *pp* **striven** /ˈstrɪvn ˈस्ट्रिव्न्/) (*formal*) **strive (for sth/to do sth)** to try very hard to do or get sth कठोर परिश्रम करना (कुछ करने या पाने के लिए) *to strive for perfection*

**strode** ➪ **stride¹** का past tense रूप

**stroke¹** /strəʊk स्ट्रोक्/ *noun* **1** [C] one of the movements that you make when you are writing or painting लिखते या चित्र बनाते समय (क़लम या ब्रश से) बना निशान *a brush stroke* **2** [C] one of the movements that you make when you are swimming, rowing, playing golf, etc. तैरते, नौकायन करते, गोल्फ़ आदि खेलते समय होने वाला हस्त-संचालन; स्ट्रोक *Ravi won by three strokes* (= hits of the ball in golf). **3** [C, U] (*used in compounds*) one of the styles of swimming तैरने की एक शैली *I can do backstroke and breaststroke.* ➪ **crawl** देखिए तथा **swim** पर चित्र देखिए। **4** [C] a sudden illness which attacks the brain and can leave a person unable to move part of his/her body, speak clearly, etc. पक्षाघात, फ़ालिज का दौरा, लक़वा *to **have a stroke*** 5 [*sing.*] **a stroke of sth** a sudden successful action or event एकाएक सफल हुई क्रिया या घटना *It was **a stroke of luck** finding your ring on the beach, wasn't it?*

IDM **at a/one stroke** with a single action एक ही प्रयास में

**not do a stroke (of work)** to not do any work at all कुछ भी न करना

**stroke²** /strəʊk स्ट्रोक् / *verb* [T] **1** to move your hand gently over sb/sth थपथपाना, हाथ फेरना, सहलाना *She stroked his hair affectionately.* ○ *to stroke a dog* **2** to move sth somewhere with a smooth movement किसी वस्तु को सरकाना (किसी वस्तु को धीमे से हटाकर कहीं और रखना)

**stroll** /strəʊl स्ट्रोल् / *noun* [C] a slow walk for pleasure चहलक़दमी, सैर *to **go for a stroll** along the beach* ▶ **stroll** *verb* [I] चहलक़दमी या सैर करना, टहलना

**strong** /strɒŋ स्ट्रॉङ् / *adj.* **1** (used about a person) physically powerful; able to lift or carry heavy things (व्यक्ति) शरीर से ताक़तवर, बलवान, हृष्ट-पुष्ट; वज़न उठाने या ले जाने में समर्थ *I need someone strong to help me move this bookcase.* ○ *to have strong arms/muscles* **2** (used about an object) not easily broken or damaged (वस्तु) मज़बूत, पक्का या टिकाऊ *That chair isn't strong enough for you to stand on.* **3** (used about a natural force) powerful (वायु, धूप आदि प्राकृतिक शक्ति) तीव्र, तेज़ *strong winds/currents/sunlight* **4** having a big effect on the mind, body or senses मन, शरीर या ज्ञानेंद्रियों पर प्रचुर प्रभाव डालने वाला; तेज़, गहरा *a **strong smell** of garlic* ○ *I have the **strong impression** that they don't like us.* **5** (used about opinions and beliefs) very firm; difficult to fight against (मत और मान्यता) सुदृढ़; समर्थ, ज़ोरदार (जिसका विरोध करना कठिन हो) ***strong opposition/strong support** for an idea* **6** powerful and likely to succeed मज़बूत और सक्षम *She's a strong candidate for the job.* ○ *a strong team* **7** (*used after a noun*) having a particular number of people जिसमें विशेष संख्या में व्यक्ति हों ➪ **strength** noun देखिए (सब अर्थों के लिए)। **8** used to describe the way some words are pronounced when they are emphasized. For example, the strong form of *and* is /ænd/ किसी शब्द के उच्चारण में बलयुक्त या प्रबल स्वर का संकेत करने के लिए प्रयुक्त (जैसे उच्चारण में *and* का प्रबल रूप है /ænd ऐन्ड् /) ▶ **strongly** *adv.* प्रबल रूप से *to feel very strongly about sth*

IDM **going strong** (*informal*) continuing, even after a long time बहुत लंबे समय बाद भी चलते रहना *The company was formed in 1851 and is still going strong.*

**sb's strong point** something that a person is good at (किसी व्यक्ति की) विशेष क्षमता *Maths is not my strong point.*

**stronghold** /ˈstrɒŋhəʊld ˈस्ट्रॉङ्होल्ड् / *noun* [C] **1** an area in which there is a lot of support for a particular belief or group of people especially a political party (किसी विशिष्ट धारणा, गुट या राजनीतिक दल का समर्थक) गढ़, केंद्र *a communist stronghold* **2** a castle or a place that is strongly built and difficult to attack दुर्ग, किला

**strong-minded** *adj.* having firm ideas or beliefs दृढ़ विचारों और मान्यताओं वाला; दृढ़ निश्चयी

**strontium** /ˈstrɒntiəm; ˈstrɒnʃ- ˈस्ट्रॉन्टिअम्; ˈस्ट्रॉनश्- / *noun* [U] (*symbol* **Sr**) a soft silver-white metal एक कोमल चाँदी जैसी शुभ्र धातु; स्ट्रॉन्शियम

**strove** ➪ **strive** का past tense रूप

**struck** ➪ **strike²** का past tense और past participle रूप

**structure¹** /ˈstrʌktʃə(r) ˈस्ट्रक्च(र्) / *noun* **1** [C, U] the way that the parts of sth are put together or organized बनावट, रचना *the political and social structure of a country* ○ *the grammatical structures of a language* **2** [C] a building or sth that has been built or made from a number of parts भवन या ढाँचा (अनेक खंड से रचित या निर्मित वस्तु) *The old office block had been replaced by a modern glass structure.* ▶ **structural** /ˈstrʌktʃərəl ˈस्ट्रक्चरल् / *adj.* ढाँचा-विषयक, संरचनात्मक

**structure²** /ˈstrʌktʃə(r) ˈस्ट्रक्च(र्) / *verb* [T] to arrange sth in an organized way (किसी वस्तु को) सुव्यवस्थित करना *a carefully structured English course*

**struggle¹** /ˈstrʌgl ˈस्ट्रगल् / *verb* [I] **1 struggle (with sth/for sth/to do sth)** to try very hard to do sth, especially when it is difficult कोई (विशेषतः कठिन) काम करने के लिए कठोर प्रयास करना *We struggled up the stairs with our heavy suitcases.* **2 struggle (with sb/sth); struggle (against sth)** to fight in order to prevent sth or to escape from sb संघर्ष करना (किसी बात को होने से रोकने के लिए या किसी से छुटकारा पाने के लिए) *He shouted and struggled but he couldn't get free.* ○ *He has been struggling against cancer for years.*

PHRV **struggle on** to continue to do sth although it is difficult (कठिन होते हुए भी) किसी काम को करते रहना *I felt terrible but managed to struggle on to the end of the day.*

**struggle²** /ˈstrʌgl ˈस्ट्रग्ल् / *noun* [C] **1** a fight in which sb tries to do or get sth when this is difficult संघर्ष (किसी कठिन काम को कर पाने या कठिन लक्ष्य को प्राप्त करने के लिए) *All countries should join together in the struggle against terrorism.* ○ *a struggle for independence* **2** [*usually sing.*] sth that is difficult to achieve कठिन लक्ष्य *It will be a struggle to get there on time.*

**strum** /strʌm स्ट्रम् / *verb* [I, T] (**strumming; strummed**) to play a guitar by moving your hand up and down over the strings गिटार बजाना (तारों पर ऊपर-नीचे हाथ फेरते हुए)

**strung** ➪ **string²** का past tense और past participle रूप

**strut** /strʌt स्ट्रट् / *verb* [I] (**strutting; strutted**) to walk in a proud way अकड़ कर चलना

**strychnine** /ˈstrɪkni:n ˈस्ट्रिक्नीन् / *noun* [U] a poisonous substance that can be used in very small amounts as a medicine कुचला सत, स्ट्रिकनीन (एक विषैला पदार्थ जो अत्यल्प मात्रा में औषध बनाने में प्रयुक्त होता है)

**stub** /stʌb स्टब् / *noun* [C] the short piece of a cigarette or pencil that is left after the rest of it has been used सिगरेट या पेंसिल का अंत में बचा हुआ टुकड़ा; टोंटा, टुर्रा

**stubble** /ˈstʌbl ˈस्टबल् / *noun* [U] **1** the short parts of corn, wheat, etc. that are left standing after the rest has been cut मक्का, गेहूँ आदि की फ़सल काट लिए जाने पर खेत में खड़ी नीचे की खूँटी **2** the short hairs that grow on a man's face when he has not shaved for some time (कुछ समय तक हजामत न बनने से उग आए) दाढ़ी के छोटे कड़े बाल

**stubborn** /ˈstʌbən ˈस्टबन् / *adj.* not wanting to do what other people want you to do; refusing to change your plans or decisions दूसरों की बात न मानने वाला हठी, ज़िद्दी; अपनी (बातों, योजनाओं और फैसलों) पर अड़ने वाला; अड़ियल *She's too stubborn to apologize.* ✪ पर्याय **obstinate** ➪ **pig-headed** देखिए। ▶ **stubbornly** *adv.* हठपूर्वक, अड़ते हुए *He stubbornly refused to apologize so he was sacked.* ▶ **stubbornness** *noun* [U] हठ, ज़िद, अड़ियलपन

**stuck¹** ➪ **stick²** का past tense और past participle रूप

**stuck²** /stʌk स्टक् / *adj.* **1** not able to move अटका हुआ, रुका हुआ *This drawer's stuck. I can't open it at all.* ○ *We were stuck in traffic for over two hours.* **2** not able to continue with an exercise, etc. because it is too difficult (कठिन होने के कारण) अभ्यास कार्य जारी रखने में असमर्थ *If you **get stuck**, ask your teacher for help.*

**stud** /stʌd स्टड् / *noun* **1** [C] a small piece of metal that sticks out from the rest of the surface that it is fixed to (जैकेट आदि पर) दुहरे सिरे का बटन (जो उभरा हुआ दिखाई देता है) स्टड (बटन) *a black leather jacket with studs all over it* **2** [C] a small, round, solid piece of metal that you wear through a hole in your ear or other part of the body नाक या कान की कील **3** [C] one of the pieces of plastic or metal that stick out from the bottom of football, etc. boots used an playing and that help you stand up on wet ground फ़ुटबॉल आदि के जूतों के तले में लगा प्लास्टिक या धातु की कील (जिसके सहारे गीली ज़मीन पर खड़ा हुआ जा सकता है) **4** [C, U] a number of high quality horses or other animals that are kept for breeding young animals; the place where these horses, etc. are kept बढ़िया नसल के घोड़े या अन्य पशु (प्रजनन के लिए प्रयुक्त), घोड़ा, साँड़; ऐसे घोड़ों आदि का अस्तबल, अश्व प्रजनन-शाला *a stud farm*

**studded** /ˈstʌdɪd ˈस्टडिड् / *adj.* **1** covered or decorated with studs स्टड (बटनों) वाला या उनसे सजा हुआ **2 studded (with sth)** containing a lot of sth किसी वस्तु से भरपूर *a star-studded party*

**student** /ˈstju:dnt ˈस्ट्यूडन्ट् / *noun* [C] a person who is studying at a college or university (कॉलेज या विश्वविद्यालय) का छात्र या विद्यार्थी *a fulltime/part-time student* ○ *a postgraduate/research student* ➪ **pupil, scholar, graduate** और **undergraduate** देखिए।

**studied** /ˈstʌdid ˈस्टडिड् / *adj.* (*formal*) carefully planned or done, especially when you are trying to give a particular impression सुविचारित या सम्यक रीति से किया गया (विशेषतः एक विशेष प्रकार का प्रभाव डालने की दृष्टि से)

**studio** /ˈstju:diəʊ ˈस्टूडिओ / *noun* [C] (*pl.* **studios**) **1** a room where an artist or photographer works कलाकार या फ़ोटोग्राफ़र का काम करने का कमरा; स्टूडिओ **2** a room or building where films or television programmes are made, or where music, radio programmes, etc. are recorded कमरा या भवन जहाँ फ़िल्में या टीवी कार्यक्रम तैयार किए जाते हैं, या संगीत, रेडियो कार्यक्रम आदि रिकार्ड किए जाते हैं, फ़िल्म या टीवी स्टूडियो *a film/TV/recording studio*

**studious** /ˈstju:diəs ˈस्टूडिअस् / *adj.* (used about a person) spending a lot of time studying (व्यक्ति) अध्ययन में काफ़ी अधिक समय लगाने वाला; अध्ययनशील

**studiously** /ˈstju:diəsli ˈस्टूडिअस्लि / *adv.* with great care बहुत सावधानी से

**study¹** /ˈstʌdi ˈस्टडि / *noun* (*pl.* **studies**) **1** [U] the activity of learning about sth (किसी विषय में) कुछ

सीखने का क्रिया-कलाप; अध्ययन, पढ़ाई *One hour every afternoon is left free for individual study.* ○ *Physiology is the study of how living things work.* **2 studies** [*pl.*] the subjects that you study अध्ययन के विषय *business/media/Japanese studies* **3** [C] a piece of research that examines a question or a subject in detail (किसी मुद्दे या विषय पर विस्तार से) अनुसंधान; खोजपरक अध्ययन *They are doing a study of the causes of heart disease.* **4** [C] a room in a house where you go to read, write or study (घर में) अध्ययन-कक्ष

**study²** /ˈstʌdi ˈस्टडि/ *verb* (*pres. part.* **studying**; *3rd person sing. pres.* **studies**; *pt, pp* **studied**) **1** [I, T] **study (sth/for sth)** to spend time learning about sth कुछ सीखने में समय लगाना, अध्ययन या पढ़ाई करना *to study English at university* ○ *Harish has been studying hard for his exams.* **2** [T] to look at sth very carefully किसी चीज़ को सावधानी से देखना, बारीकी से नज़र डालना *to study a map*

**stuff¹** /stʌf स्टफ़्/ *noun* [U] (*informal*) **1** used to refer to sth without using its name बिना नाम लिए किसी वस्तु का निर्देश करने के लिए प्रयुक्त; चीज़, सामान *What's that green stuff at the bottom of the bottle?* ○ *The shop was burgled and a lot of stuff was stolen.* **2** used to refer in general to things that people do, say, think, etc. लोगों के नित्य प्रति के क्रिया-कलाप (कुछ कहना, सोचना आदि) का सामान्य रूप से निर्देश करने के लिए प्रयुक्त, काम, बात *I've got lots of stuff to do tomorrow so I'm going to get up early.*

**stuff²** /stʌf स्टफ़्/ *verb* **1** [T] **stuff sth (with sth)** to fill sth with sth किसी वस्तु में कुछ भरना या डालना *The pillow was stuffed with feathers.* ○ *red peppers stuffed with paneer* **2** [T] (*informal*) **stuff sth into sth** to put sth into sth else quickly or carelessly जल्दबाज़ी में या लापरवाही से किसी वस्तु में कुछ घुसेड़ देना, ठूँस कर भर देना *He quickly stuffed a few clothes into a suitcase.* **3** [T] (*informal*) **stuff sb/yourself (with sth)** to eat too much of sth; to give sb too much to eat कोई चीज़ ठूँस-ठूँस कर खाना; ठूँस-ठूँस कर (दूसरों को) खिलाना *Rahul just sat there stuffing himself with sandwiches.* **4** [T] to fill the body of a dead bird or animal with special material so that it looks as if it is alive मृत पक्षी या पशु की खाल में विशेष पदार्थ भरना (जीवित-सा दिखाने के लिए) *They've got a stuffed crocodile in the museum.*

**stuffing** /ˈstʌfɪŋ ˈस्टफ़िङ्/ *noun* [U] **1** a mixture of small pieces of food that you put inside a chicken, vegetable, etc. before you cook it (पकाने या बनाने से पहले) चिकन, सब्ज़ी आदि में भरवाँ मसाला भरना **2** the material that you put inside cushions, soft toys, etc. गद्दियों, नरम खिलौनों आदि के अंदर डाली जाने वाली चीज़ें

**stuffy** /ˈstʌfi ˈस्टफ़ि/ *adj.* **1** (used about a room) too warm and having no fresh air (कमरा) घुटन भरा **2** (*informal*) (used about a person) formal and old-fashioned (व्यक्ति) तकल्लुफ़-प्रिय और पुरानी चाल का

**stumble** /ˈstʌmbl ˈस्टम्बल्/ *verb* [I] **1 stumble (over/on sth)** to hit your foot against sth when you are walking or running and almost fall over चलते या दौड़ते समय ठोकर खाना **2 stumble (over/through sth)** to make a mistake when you are speaking, playing music, etc. बोलने या संगीत बजाने आदि के दौरान ग़लती कर जाना *The newsreader stumbled over the name of the Russian tennis player.*

**PHR V stumble across/on sb/sth** to meet or find sb/sth by chance संयोग से किसी से भेंट हो जाना या किसी का पता लग जाना

**stumbling block** *noun* [C] something that causes trouble or a difficulty, so that you cannot achieve what you want लक्ष्यप्राप्ति के मार्ग में बाधक तत्त्व; अड़ंगा, बाधा *Money is still the stumbling block to settling the dispute.*

**stump¹** /stʌmp स्टम्प्/ *noun* [C] **1** the part that is left after sth has been cut down, broken off, etc. (पेड़ का) ठूँठ, (सिगरेट का) टोंटा *a tree stump* ➪ **erode** पर चित्र देखिए। **2 the stumps** (in cricket) a set of three upright wooden sticks that form the **wicket** (क्रिकेट में) स्टंप्स; लकड़ी के तीन ठूँठों का समुच्चय जिन्हें विकेट कहते हैं

**stump²** /stʌmp स्टम्प्/ *verb* [T] (*informal*) to cause sb to be unable to answer a question or find a solution for a problem किसी प्रश्न या समस्या का हल न ढूँढ़ पाना, किसी प्रश्न या समस्या से चकरा जाना *I was completely stumped by question 14.*

**stun** /stʌn स्टन्/ *verb* [T] (**stunning; stunned**) **1** to make a person or animal unconscious or confused, especially by hitting him/her/it on the head किसी व्यक्ति या पशु को बेहोश कर देना या चकरा देना (विशेषतः उसके सिर पर मारकर); अचेत कर देना **2** to make a person very surprised by telling him/her some unexpected news (अप्रत्याशित समाचार देकर) किसी को हक्का-बक्का कर देना *His sudden death stunned his friends and colleagues.* ► **stunned** *adj.* बेहोश, चकराया हुआ या हक्का-बक्का

**stung** ➪ **sting¹** का past tense और past participle रूप

**stunk** ➪ **stink** का past participle रूप

**stunning** /ˈstʌnɪŋ ˈस्टनिङ्/ *adj.* (*informal*) very attractive, impressive or surprising बहुत आकर्षक, प्रभावशाली या चकित कर देने वाला; अकल्पनिय *a stunning view*

**stunt**[1] /stʌnt स्टन्ट्/ *noun* [C] **1** something that you do to get people's attention लोगों का ध्यान आकृष्ट करने के लिए किया गया कोई काम *a publicity stunt* **2** a very difficult or dangerous thing that sb does to entertain people or as part of a film लोगों के मनोरंजन के लिए या फ़िल्म में किया गया कोई कठिन या ख़तरनाक काम; करतब, कलाबाज़ी, कमाल *Some actors do their own stunts, others use a stuntman.*

**stunt**[2] /stʌnt स्टन्ट्/ *verb* [T] to stop sb/sth growing or developing properly (किसी के) सम्यक विकास या वृद्धि को रोक देना *A poor diet can stunt a child's growth.*

**stuntman** /ˈstʌntmæn ˈस्टन्ट्मैन्/ *noun* [C] (*pl.* **-men** /-men -मेन्/) a person who does sth dangerous in a film in the place of an actor फ़िल्म में अभिनेता के बदले करतब, कलाबाज़ी या कमाल दिखाने वाला व्यक्ति; स्टंटमैन

**stupa** *noun* [C] a dome-shaped structure erected as a Buddhist shrine स्तूप; गुंबद के आकार का बौद्ध स्मारक

**stupendous** /stju:ˈpendəs स्ट्यूˈपेन्डस्/ *adj.* very large or impressive अति विशाल या प्रभावशाली *a stupendous achievement*

**stupid** /ˈstju:pɪd ˈस्ट्यूपिड्/ *adj.* **1** not intelligent or sensible मूर्ख, नासमझ *a stupid mistake/suggestion/question* **2** (*only before a noun*) (*informal*) used to show that you are angry or do not like sb/sth किसी के प्रति अपना क्रोध या नापसंदगी व्यक्त करने के लिए प्रयुक्त *I'm tired of hearing about his stupid car.* ▶ **stupidity** /stju:ˈpɪdəti स्ट्यूˈपिडटि/ *noun* [U] मूर्खता, नासमझी ▶ **stupidly** *adv.* मूर्खता या नासमझी से

**stupor** /ˈstju:pə(r) ˈस्ट्यूप(र्)/ *noun* [*sing.*, U] the state of being nearly unconscious or being unable to think properly लगभग बेहोशी या मानसिक जड़ता की स्थिति

**sturdy** /ˈstɜ:di ˈस्टडि/ *adj.* (**sturdier; sturdiest**) strong and healthy; that will not break easily हृष्ट-पुष्ट और स्वस्थ; जल्दी न टूटने वाला, मज़बूत, दृढ़ *sturdy legs* ○ *sturdy shoes* ▶ **sturdily** *adv.* दृढ़ता या मज़बूती से ▶ **sturdiness** *noun* [U] दृढ़ता, मज़बूती

**stutter** /ˈstʌtə(r) ˈस्टट(र्)/ *verb* [I, T] to have difficulty when you speak, so that you keep repeating the first sound of a word हकलाना ▶ **stutter** *noun* [C] हकलाहट *to have a stutter*

**sty** (*also* **stye**) /staɪ स्टाइ/ *noun* [C] (*pl.* **sties** or **styes**) **1** a painful spot on the **eyelid** पलक पर निकली फुंसी, अंजनी या गुहेरी, विलनी **2** = **pigsty**

**style** /staɪl स्टाइल्/ *noun* **1** [C, U] the way that sth is done, built, etc. रीति, शैली, विशिष्ट ढंग *a new style of architecture* ○ *The writer's style is very clear and simple.* **2** [C, U] the fashion, shape or design of sth (किसी चीज़ का) फ़ैशन, आकृति या डिज़ाइन, बनावट या बनत *We stock all the latest styles.* ○ *I like your new hairstyle.* **3** [U] the ability to do things in a way that other people admire सुरुचिपूर्ण ढंग से काम करने की क्षमता *He's got no sense of style.* **4** [C] (*technical*) the long thin part of the **carpel** that supports the **stigma** पुष्प के वर्तिकाग्र को सहारा देने वाला गर्भकेसर; वर्तिका ➪ **flower** पर चित्र देखिए।

**stylish** /ˈstaɪlɪʃ ˈस्टाइलिश्/ *adj.* fashionable and attractive फ़ैशनेबल और आकर्षक *She's a stylish dresser.*

**stylus** /ˈstaɪləs ˈस्टाइलस्/ *noun* [C] (*pl.* **styluses**) **1** a device on a **record player** that looks like a small needle and is placed on the record in order to play it ग्रामोफ़ोन की सुई; स्टाइलस **2** writing **implement**, like a small rod with a pointed end for writing on wax-covered tablets, on metal or on certain special computer screens मोम के पत्तरों, धातु या विशिष्ट कंप्यूटर स्क्रीनों पर लिखने के लिए प्रयुक्त (प्राचीन) लेखन की नुकीली क़लम

**stymie** /ˈstaɪmi ˈस्टाइमि/ *verb* [T] (*pres. part.* **stymieing** or **stymying**; *3rd person sing. pres.* **stymies**; *pt, pp* **stymied**) (*informal*) to prevent sb from doing sth that he/she has planned or wants to do; to prevent sth from happening किसी के काम में बाधा डालना, रोड़ा अटकाना; किसी बात को होने न देना ✪ पर्याय **foil**[2]

**suave** /swɑ:v स्वाव्/ *adj.* (usually used about a man) confident, elegant and polite, sometimes in a way that does not seem sincere (व्यक्ति) आत्मविश्वासी, सुरुचि संपन्न और शिष्ट, भद्र (कभी-कभी दिखावटी तौर पर)

**sub-** /sʌb सब्/ *prefix* **1** (*used in nouns and adjectives*) below; less than (से) नीचे, अध; किसी से कम, उप-/अवर-/अनु- *sub-zero temperatures* ○ *a sub lieutenant* **2** (*used in nouns and adjectives*) under (के) नीचे, आधो- *subway* ○ *submarine* **3** (*used in verbs and nouns*) making a smaller part of sth किसी वस्तु का छोटा अंश बनाते हुए, उप- *subdivide* ○ *subset*

**subconscious** /ˌsʌbˈkɒnʃəs ˌसब्ˈकॉन्शस्/ (*also* **unconscious**) *noun* [*sing.*] **the subconscious** the hidden part of your mind that can affect the way that you behave without you realizing अवचेतन मन ▶ **subconscious** *adj.* अवचेतन *the subconscious mind* ○ *Many advertisements work at a subconscious level.* ▶ **subconsciously** *adv.* अवचेतन रूप से

**subcontinent** /ˌsʌbˈkɒntɪnənt ˌसबˈकॉन्‌टिनन्ट्/ *noun* [*sing.*] a large land mass that forms part of a continent, especially the part of Asia that includes India, Pakistan and Bangladesh (भारतीय) उपमहाद्वीप (विशेष रूप से एशिया महाद्वीप का भारत-पाकिस्तान-बांग्लादेश खंड); सबकॉन्टिनेंट

**subcutaneous** /ˌsʌbkjuˈteɪniəs ˌसब्क्युˈटेनिअस्/ *adj.* (*usually before a noun*) (*technical*) under the skin त्वचा के नीचे का; अधस्त्वचीय, अवत्वक *a subcutaneous injection*

**subdivide** /ˌsʌbdɪˈvaɪd ˌसब्डिˈव़ाइड्/ *verb* [I, T] to divide or be divided into smaller parts उपविभाजित या प्रविभाजित होना या करना ▶ **subdivision** /ˈsʌbdɪvɪʒn ˈसब्डिविश़्न्/ *noun* [C, U] उपविभाजन, प्रविभाजन

**subdue** /səbˈdjuː सबˈड्यू/ *verb* [T] to defeat sb/sth or bring sb/sth under control किसी को हराना या नियंत्रण में लाना; अधीन करना, अभिभूत करना

**subdued** /səbˈdjuːd सबˈड्यूड्/ *adj.* **1** (used about a person) quieter and with less energy than usual (व्यक्ति) अभिभूत; शांत तथा सामान्य से कम उर्जा सहित **2** not very loud or bright (व्यक्ति) हारा हुआ और शांत *subdued laughter/lighting*

**subject[1]** /ˈsʌbdʒɪkt ˈसब्जिक्ट्/ *noun* [C] **1** a person or thing that is being considered, shown or talked about विचार, वर्णन या चर्चा का विषय (व्यक्ति या वस्तु) *I've tried several times to **bring up/raise the subject** of money.* **2** an area of knowledge that you study at school, university, etc. स्कूल, विश्वविद्यालय आदि में अध्ययन का विषय *My favourite subjects at school are Biology and English.* **3** (*grammar*) the person or thing that does the action described by the verb in a sentence (वाक्य में क्रिया का) कर्ता (कोई व्यक्ति या वस्तु) *In the sentence 'The cat sat on the mat', 'the cat' is the subject.* ➪ **object** देखिए। **4** a person from a particular country, especially one with a king or queen; a citizen (राजा या रानी द्वारा शासित) देश-विशेष का निवासी; प्रजा, नागरिक *a British subject*

IDM **change the subject** ➪ **change[1]** देखिए।

**subject[2]** /səbˈdʒekt सबˈजेक्ट्/ *verb*

PHR V **subject sb/sth to sth** to make sb/sth experience sth unpleasant किसी को कोई प्रतिकूल अनुभव कराना, का शिकार बनाना *He was subjected to verbal and physical abuse from the other boys.*

**subject[3]** /ˈsʌbdʒɪkt ˈसब्जिक्ट्/ *adj.* **1 subject to sth** likely to be affected by sth जिसके किसी बात से प्रभावित होने की संभावना हो, प्रभावित होने की संभावना वाला; प्रभावशील *The area is subject to regular flooding.* ○ *Smokers are more subject to heart attacks than non-smokers.* **2 subject to sth** depending on sth as a condition (शर्त के रूप में) किसी बात पर निर्भर *The plan for new housing is still subject to approval by the minister.* **3** controlled by or having to obey sb/sth किसी के द्वारा नियंत्रित या किसी के अधीन

**subjective** /səbˈdʒektɪv सबˈजेक्टिव़्/ *adj.* based on your own tastes and opinions instead of on facts (तथ्यों के स्थान पर) निजी रुचियों और विचारों पर आधारित; व्यक्तिनिष्ठ, आत्मनिष्ठ, स्वनिष्ठ ✪ विलोम **objective** ▶ **subjectively** *adv.* व्यक्तिनिष्ठता से

**subject matter** *noun* [U] the ideas or information contained in a book, speech, painting, etc. किसी ग्रंथ, भाषण, चित्रकारी आदि में निहित विचार या जानकारी विषय-वस्तु; प्रतिपाद्य

**sub judice** /ˌsʌbˈdʒuːdɪsi ˌसबˈजूडिसि/ *adj.* (*not usually before a noun*) (*law*) when something is sub judice, it is under judicial consideration and therefore is illegal for anyone to talk about it publicly विचाराधीन, न्यायाधीन; विचाराधीन केस को सार्वजनिक बनाना ग़ैर-क़ानूनी होता है

**subjugate** /ˈsʌbdʒugeɪt ˈसब्जुगेट्/ *verb* [T] (*usually passive*) (*formal*) to defeat sb/sth and make them obey you; to gain control over sb/sth किसी व्यक्ति या वस्तु को परास्त करना; किसी व्यक्ति या वस्तु का दमन करना या को अपने अधीन करना *The original inhabitants of the area were subjugated by the conquerors from Spain.* ▶ **subjugation** *noun* [U] अधीनीकरण, वशीकरण, दमन *the subjugation of women*

**subjunctive** /səbˈdʒʌŋktɪv सबˈजङ्क्टिव़्/ *noun* [*sing.*] the form of a verb in certain languages that expresses doubt, possibility, a wish, etc. संभावनार्थक क्रियारूप ▶ **subjunctive** *adj.* संभावनार्थक

**sublime** /səˈblaɪm सˈब्लाइम्/ *adj.* (*formal*) of extremely high quality that makes you admire sth very much उदात्त; अतिश्रेष्ठ और अतएव अतिप्रशंसनीय ▶ **sublimely** *adv.* उदात्त भाव से

**submarine** /ˌsʌbməˈriːn ˌसबमˈरीन्/ *noun* [C] a type of ship that can travel under the water as well as on the surface पनडुब्बी

**submerge** /səbˈmɜːdʒ सबˈमज्/ *verb* [I, T] to go or make sth go under water जलमग्न होना या करना *The fields were submerged by the floods.* ▶ **submerged** *adj.* जलमग्न, निमग्न

**submission** /səbˈmɪʃn सब्ˈमिश्न्/ *noun* **1** [U] the accepting of sb else's power or control because he/she has defeated you आत्मसमर्पण, अधीनता-स्वीकरण **2** [U, C] the action of giving a plan, document, etc. to an official organization so that it can be studied and considered; the plan, document, etc. that you send किसी सरकारी संगठन की योजना, दस्तावेज़ आदि प्रस्तुत करने की क्रिया (अध्ययन तथा विचार हेतु), प्रस्तुतीकरण; प्रस्तुत की गई योजना, दस्तावेज़ आदि

**submissive** /səbˈmɪsɪv सब्ˈमिसिव्/ *adj.* ready to obey other people and do whatever they want आज्ञाकारी, नम्र, दब्बू

**submit** /səbˈmɪt सब्ˈमिट्/ *verb* (**submitting; submitted**) **1** [T] **submit sth (to sb/sth)** to give a plan, document, etc. to an official organization so that it can be studied and considered किसी सरकारी संगठन को योजना, दस्तावेज़ आदि (अध्ययन और विचार हेतु) प्रस्तुत करना *to submit an application/complaint/claim* **2** [I] **submit (to sb/sth)** to accept sb/sth's power or control because he/she has defeated you विजेता की शक्ति या नियंत्रण को स्वीकार करना

**subordinate**[1] /səˈbɔːdɪnət सˈबॉडिनट्/ *adj.* **subordinate (to sb/sth)** having less power or authority than sb else; less important than sth else किसी के अधीन (कम शक्ति या अधिकार वाला) महत्त्व में किसी से कम या छोटा; अधीनस्थ ▶ **subordinate** *noun* [C] अधीनस्थ व्यक्ति *the relationship between superiors and their subordinates*

**subordinate**[2] /səˈbɔːdɪneɪt सˈबॉडिनेट्/ *verb* [T] to treat one person or thing as less important than another किसी व्यक्ति या वस्तु को दूसरे से कम महत्त्व का मानना; अधीनस्थ करना

**subordinate clause** *noun* [C] (*grammar*) a group of words that is not a sentence but that adds information to the main part of the sentence आश्रित या अधीन उपवाक्य (वाक्य के मुख्य अंश की सूचना में वृद्धि करने वाला शब्द-समूह जो स्वयं में वाक्य नहीं है) *In the sentence 'We left early because it was raining', 'because it was raining' is the subordinate clause.*

**subpoena** /səˈpiːnə सˈपीना/ *noun* [C] (*law*) a written order to attend a court of law to give evidence गवाही देने के लिए अदालत में उपस्थित आने का लिखित आदेश, न्यायालय-उपस्थिति आदेश; सपीना *She is appearing today under subpoena.* ▶ **subpoena** *verb* [T] (किसी को) सपीना जारी करना *The court subpoenaed her to appear as a witness.*

**subscribe** /səbˈskraɪb सब्ˈस्क्राइब्/ *verb* [I] **1 subscribe (to sth)** to pay for a newspaper or magazine to be sent to you regularly किसी अख़बार या पत्रिका का निर्धारित शुल्क देकर ग्राहक बनना **2** (*formal*) **subscribe to sth** to agree with an idea, belief, etc. किसी विचार, मान्यता का अनुमोदन करना *I don't subscribe to the view that all war is wrong.*

**subscriber** /səbˈskraɪbə(r) सब्ˈस्क्राइब(र्)/ *noun* [C] a person who pays to receive a newspaper or magazine regularly or to use a particular service अख़बार या पत्रिका या किसी सेवा का नियमित ग्राहक *subscribers to satellite and cable television*

**subscription** /səbˈskrɪpʃn सब्ˈस्क्रिप्श्न्/ *noun* [C] an amount of money that you pay, usually once a year, to receive a newspaper or magazine regularly or to belong to an organization अख़बार या पत्रिका या किसी संस्था का वार्षिक सदस्यता-शुल्क

**subsequent** /ˈsʌbsɪkwənt ˈसब्सिक्वन्ट्/ *adj.* (*formal*) (*only before a noun*) coming after or later बाद का या बाद में होने या आने वाला; परवर्ती या उत्तरवर्ती *I thought that was the end of the matter but subsequent events proved me wrong.* ▶ **subsequently** *adv.* बाद में, तदनंतर *The rumours were subsequently found to be untrue.*

**subservient** /səbˈsɜːviənt सब्ˈसविअन्ट्/ *adj.* **1 subservient (to sb/sth)** too ready to obey other people अत्यधिक आज्ञाकारी; जी-हज़ूरिया, ताबेदार **2** (*formal*) **subservient (to sth)** considered to be less important than sth else कम महत्त्वपूर्ण ▶ **subservience** *noun* [U] अति-आज्ञाकारिता, वश्यता

**subside** /səbˈsaɪd सब्ˈसाइड्/ *verb* [I] **1** to become calmer or quieter अधिक शांत या शिथिल हो जाना या मंद पड़ जाना *The storm seems to be subsiding.* **2** (used about land, a building, etc.) to sink down into the ground (भूमि, भवन आदि का) नीचे धँस जाना ▶ **subsidence** /ˈsʌbsɪdns; səbˈsaɪdns ˈसब्सिड्न्स्; सब्ˈसाइड्न्स्/ *noun* [U] धसकन, उतार, अवतलन

**subsidiary**[1] /səbˈsɪdiəri सब्ˈसिडिअरि/ *adj.* connected with sth but less important than it किसी से संबंधित परंतु उससे कम महत्त्व का; गौण

**subsidiary**[2] /səbˈsɪdiəri सब्ˈसिडिअरि/ *noun* [C] (*pl.* **subsidiaries**) a business company that belongs to and is controlled by another larger company व्यापारिक कंपनी जो बड़ी कंपनी के अंतर्गत तथा उससे नियंत्रित हो; नियंत्रित कंपनी या व्यवसाय

**subsidize** (*also* **-ise**) /ˈsʌbsɪdaɪz ˈसब्सिडाइज़्/ *verb* [T] (used about a government, etc.) to give money in order to keep the cost of a service low

(सरकार, आदि का) आर्थिक सहायता देना (सेवा की लागत में कमी लाने के लिए); इमदाद देना *Public transport should be subsidized.*

**subsidy** /ˈsʌbsədi ˈसबसिडि/ *noun* [C, U] (*pl.* **subsidies**) money that the government, etc. pays to help an organization or to keep the cost of a service low सरकार आदि द्वारा, किसी संस्था को या सेवा की लागत कम करने के लिए, दी गई आर्थिक सहायता; इमदाद, सहायकी *agricultural/state/housing subsidies*

**subsist** /səbˈsɪst सब्ˈसिस्ट्/ *verb* [I] (*formal*) **subsist (on sth)** to manage to live with very little food or money बहुत थोड़े भोजन या धन के साथ जीवन-यापन की व्यवस्था करना, ग़रीबी में जीवित भर रहना; निर्वाह करना ▶ **subsistence** *noun* [U] गुज़ारा, मात्र जीवन-निर्वाह

**subsistence crop** /səbˈsɪstəns krɒps सब्ˈसिस्टन्स् क्रॉप्स्/ *noun* [C] plants that people grow to eat or use themselves, not to sell अपने उपयोग के लिए (न कि बेचने के) लिए उगाई फ़सल; निर्वाह फ़सल ➪ **cash crop** देखिए।

**subsoil** /ˈsʌbsɔɪl ˈसबसॉइल्/ *noun* [U] (in geography) the layer of soil between the surface of the ground and the hard rock underneath it (भूगोल में) पृथ्वी की सतह और नीचे की कड़ी चट्टान के बीच की मिट्टी की परत; अवमृदा, अवभूमि ➪ **topsoil** देखिए।

**substance** /ˈsʌbstəns ˈसबस्टन्स्/ *noun* **1** [C] a solid or liquid material कोई ठोस या तरल पदार्थ *poisonous substances* **2** [U] importance, value or truth महत्त्व, मूल्य या सचाई *The commissioner's report **gives substance to** these allegations.* **3** [U] the most important or main part of sth किसी वस्तु का सर्वाधिक महत्त्वपूर्ण या मुख्य भाग; सार तत्त्व *What was the substance of his argument?*

**sub-standard** *adj.* of poor quality; not as good as usual or as it should be घटिया (गुणवत्ता में); सामान्य या अपेक्षित मानदंड से कम

**substantial** /səbˈstænʃl सब्ˈस्टैन्श्ल्/ *adj.* **1** large in amount मात्रा में बड़ा या अधिक, अच्छा-ख़ासा; प्रचुर *The storms caused substantial damage.* ○ *a substantial sum of money* **2** large or strong बड़ा या मज़बूत ✪ विलोम **insubstantial**

**substantially** /səbˈstænʃəli सब्ˈस्टैन्शलि/ *adv.* **1** very much; greatly अत्यधिक; भरपूर (मात्रा में), प्रचुर रूप से *House prices have fallen substantially.* **2** generally; in most points सामान्यतः; अधिकांशतः

**substitute** /ˈsʌbstɪtjuːt ˈसबस्टिट्यूट्/ *noun* [C] **a substitute (for sb/sth)** a person or thing that takes the place of sb/sth else किसी अन्य का स्थान लेने वाला व्यक्ति या वस्तु; स्थानापन्न व्यक्ति या वस्तु *One player was injured so the substitute was sent on to play.* ▶ **substitute** *verb* [T] **substitute sb/sth (for sb/sth)** एक के स्थान पर दूसरे का प्रयोग करना *You can substitute margarine for butter.* ▶ **substitution** /ˌsʌbstɪˈtjuːʃn ˌसबस्टिˈट्यूशन्/ *noun* [C, U] प्रतिस्थापन

**subterranean** /ˌsʌbtəˈreɪniən ˌसबटˈरेनिअन्/ *adj.* (*usually before a noun*) (*formal*) under the ground भूमिगत, भूगर्भगत (ज़मीन से नीचे), अंतः भूमिक *a subterranean cave/passage/tunnel*

**subtitle** /ˈsʌbtaɪtl ˈसबटाइट्ल्/ *noun* [C, *usually pl.*] the words at the bottom of the picture on television or at the cinema. The subtitles translate the words of a foreign film or programme or show the words that are spoken, to help people with hearing problems टीवी या सिनेमा घर में प्रदर्शित फ़िल्म में नीचे अंकित शब्दावली, जो विदेशी फ़िल्म या कार्यक्रम का अनुवाद होती है या वक्ता द्वारा कही गई बात (श्रवण विकलांग लोगों की सहायता के लिए); सब-टाइटल *a Hindi film with English subtitles* ➪ **dub 2** देखिए। ▶ **subtitle** *verb* [T] (*usually passive*) सब-टाइटलों का प्रयोग करना *a Hindi film subtitled in English*

**subtle** /ˈsʌtl ˈसट्ल्/ *adj.* **1** not very noticeable; not very strong or bright बहुत गाढ़ा या चमकदार नहीं, हलका सूक्ष्म, बारीक़ *subtle colours* ○ *I noticed a subtle difference in her.* **2** very clever; and using indirect methods to achieve sth चतुराई भरा; घुमा-फिराकर अपनी बात कहने वाला, कुछ जटिल, गूढ़ *Advertisements persuade us to buy things in very subtle ways.* ▶ **subtlety** /ˈsʌtlti ˈसट्लटि/ *noun* [C, U] (*pl.* **subtleties**) सूक्ष्मता, बारीकी, परोक्षता ▶ **subtly** /ˈsʌtli ˈसट्लि/ *adv.* चतुराई से, गूढ़ रीति से

**subtract** /səbˈtrækt सब्ˈट्रैक्ट् *verb* [T] **subtract sth (from sth)** to take one number or quantity away from another एक संख्या में से दूसरी संख्या या मात्रा घटाना *If you subtract five from nine you get four.* ✪ विलोम **add** ▶ **subtraction** /səbˈtrækʃn सब्ˈट्रैक्शन्/ *noun* [C, U] घटाने की क्रिया; घटाव

**subtropical** /ˌsʌbˈtrɒpɪkl ˌसब्ˈट्रॉपिकल्/ *adj.* (in geography) in or connected with regions that are near tropical parts of the world (भूगोल में) विश्व के उष्ण(कटिबंधीय) भागों के निकट के क्षेत्रों में स्थित या उनसे संबंधित; उपोष्ण *subtropical forests*

**suburb** /ˈsʌbɜːb ˈसबब्/ *noun* [C] an area where people live that is outside the central part of a town or city नगर के केंद्रीय भाग से बाहर का निवास-क्षेत्र; उपनगर *Most people live **in the suburbs** and work in the centre of town.* ▶ **suburban** /səˈbɜːbən सˈबबन्/ *adj.* उपनगरीय **NOTE** उपनगरों के जीवन

को बेजान-सा माना जाता है और इस दृष्टि से **suburban** कभी-कभी 'बेजान और नीरस' का अर्थ देता है। ▶ **suburbia** /səˈbɜːbiə सˈबबिआ/ *noun* [U] उपनगर-निवासियों का तौर-तरीक़ा

**subversive** /səbˈvɜːsɪv सब्ˈव़सिव़्/ *adj.* trying to destroy or damage a government, religion or political system by attacking it secretly and in an indirect way शासन, धर्म या राजनीतिक व्यवस्था पर गुप्त और परोक्ष आक्रमण द्वारा उसे विनष्ट या क्षतिग्रस्त करने का प्रयास करते हुए; विध्वसंक ▶ **subversive** *noun* [C] विध्वंसकारी गतिविधि ▶ **subversion** /səbˈvɜːʃn सब्ˈव़श्न्/ *noun* [U] विध्वंस, तोड़-फोड़, तख़्ता-पलटाव

**subvert** /səbˈvɜːt सब्ˈव़ट्/ *verb* [T] to try to destroy or damage a government, religion or political system by attacking it secretly and in an indirect way शासन, धर्म या राजनीतिक व्यवस्था पर गुप्त और परोक्ष आक्रमण द्वारा उसे विनष्ट या क्षतिग्रस्त करने का प्रयास करना; तोड़-फोड़ करना, तख़्ता पलटना

**subway** /ˈsʌbweɪ ˈसब्वे/ *noun* [C] **1** a tunnel under a busy road or railway that is for people who are walking **(pedestrians)** व्यस्त सड़क या रेलपटरी के नीचे व पैदल जाने का रास्ता; सुरंगी रास्ता, सुरंग पथ, भूमिगत पैदल पारपथ, तलमार्ग **2** (*AmE*) = **underground**[3]

**succeed** /səkˈsiːd सक्ˈसीड्/ *verb* **1** [I] **succeed (in sth/doing sth)** to manage to achieve what you want; to do well अभीष्ट को प्राप्त कर लेना; सफल होना; कामयाब होना *Our plan succeeded.* ○ *A good education will help you succeed in life.* ✪ विलोम **fail** **2** [I, T] to have a job or important position after sb else किसी अन्य के बाद कोई काम या महत्त्वपूर्ण पद प्राप्त करना, किसी का उत्तराधिकारी होना *Dr Manmohan Singh, succeeded Shri Atal Bihari Vajpayee as Prime Minister of India in 2004.*

**success** /səkˈses सक्ˈसेस्/ *noun* **1** [U] the fact that you have achieved what you want; doing well and becoming famous, rich, etc. अभीष्ट की प्राप्ति हो जाने की स्थिति; यश, धन आदि की प्राप्ति सफलता, कामयाबी *Hardwork is **the key to success**.* ○ *Her attempts to get a job for the summer have not **met with** much **success*** (= she hasn't managed to do it). **2** [C] the thing that you achieve; sth that becomes very popular वस्तु जिसकी उपलब्धि हो; वस्तु जो लोकप्रिय हो जाए *He really tried to make a success of the business.* ✪ विलोम **failure**

**successful** /səkˈsesfl सक्ˈसेसफ़्ल्/ *adj.* having achieved what you wanted; having become popular, rich, etc. सफल, अभीष्ट को उपलब्ध किए हुए; लोकप्रिय, समृद्ध आदि *a successful attempt to climb Mount Everest* ○ *a successful actor* ▶ **successfully** /-fəli -फ़लि/ *adv.* सफलतापूर्वक

**succession** /səkˈseʃn सक्ˈसेश्न्/ *noun* **1** [C] a number of people or things that follow each other in time or order; a series समय या क्रम की दृष्टि से सिलसिलेवार व्यक्ति या वस्तुएँ; अनुक्रम *a succession of events/problems/visitors* **2** [U] the right to have an important position after sb else किसी के बाद महत्त्वपूर्ण पद पर अधिकार; उत्तराधिकार

IDM **in succession** following one after another क्रमशः, उत्तरोत्तर *There have been three deaths in the family in quick succession.*

**successive** /səkˈsesiv सक्ˈसेसिव़्/ *adj.* (*only before a noun*) following immediately one after the other आनुक्रमिक, निरंतर *This was their fifth successive win.* ▶ **successively** *adv* आनुक्रमिकता से

**successor** /səkˈsesə(r) सक्ˈसेस(र्)/ *noun* [C] a person or thing that comes after sb/sth else and takes his/her/its place किसी के बाद उसका स्थान लेने वाला व्यक्ति या वस्तु; उत्तराधिकारी ➪ **predecessor** देखिए।

**succinct** /səkˈsɪŋkt सक्ˈसिङ्क्ट्/ *adj.* said clearly, in a few words स्पष्टता और संक्षेप से प्रस्तुत; सारगर्भित ▶ **succinctly** *adv.* स्पष्टतया और संक्षेप में

**succulent** /ˈsʌkjələnt ˈसकयलन्ट्/ *adj.* (used about fruit, vegetables and meat) containing a lot of juice and tasting very good (फल, सब्ज़ियाँ और गोश्त) रस से भरपूर और बहुत स्वादिष्ट; रसीला

**succumb** /səˈkʌm सˈकम्/ *verb* [I] (*formal*) **succumb (to sth)** to stop fighting against sth संघर्ष बंद कर देना, झुक जाना, हार मान लेना

**such** /sʌtʃ सच्/ *det., pronoun* **1** (used for referring to sb/sth that you mentioned earlier) of this or that type (पूर्वनिर्दिष्ट व्यक्ति या वस्तु का संकेत करने के लिए प्रयुक्त) ऐसा, वैसा, इस या उस प्रकार का *There's **no such thing**.* ○ **2** used for emphasizing the degree of sth किसी बात की मात्रा पर बल देने के लिए प्रयुक्त; इतना अधिक *such a fascinating book/such a long time.*

> NOTE **Such** का प्रयोग अकेली संज्ञा या विशेषणयुक्त संज्ञा से पहले होता है—*Sameer is such a bore!* संज्ञा रहित विशेषण से पहले **so** का प्रयोग होता है—*Don't be so boring.* इन वाक्यों के बीच तुलना कीजिए—*It was so cold we stayed at home.* ○ *It was such a cold night that we stayed at home.*

**3** used to describe the result of sth किसी बात का परिणाम का संकेत करने के लिए प्रयुक्त *The statement was worded **in such a way that it** did not upset anyone.*

**IDM** **as such** as the word is usually understood; exactly उसी रूप में (शब्द के अर्थ के अनुसार), अपने में; ठीक-ठीक *It's not a promotion as such, but it will mean more money.*

**such as** for example उदाहरणार्थ, मिसाल के तौर पर *Fatty foods such as chips are bad for you.*

**suck** /sʌk सक्/ *verb* **1** [I, T] to pull a liquid into your mouth द्रव की चुसकी लेना (मुँह में अंदर की ओर खींचना) *to suck milk up through a straw* **2** [I, T] to have sth in your mouth and keep touching it with your tongue किसी चीज़ को (मुँह में रख कर) चूसते-चाटते रहना *The boy was noisily sucking (on) a sweet.* **3** [T] to pull sth in a particular direction, using force किसी वस्तु को दिशा-विशेष में खींचना (बल का प्रयोग करते हुए) *Vacuum cleaners suck up the dirt.*

**sucker** /ˈsʌkə(r) ˈसक(र्)/ *noun* [C] **1** (*informal*) a person who believes everything that you tell him/her and who is easy to trick or persuade to do sth भोला-भाला, बुद्धू (सहज विश्वासी और जल्दी धोखे में या लोगों की बातों में आ जाने वाला) **2** a part of some plants, animals or insects that is used for helping them stick onto a surface पौधों, पशुओं या कीटों का वह अंग जिसके सहारे वह ज़मीन से चिपक जाता है; अंतर्भूस्तरी

**sucrose** /ˈsuːkrəʊz; -krəʊs ˈसूक्रोज़्; -क्रोस्/ *noun* [U] (*technical*) the form of sugar that comes from **sugar cane** or **sugar beet**, and which is used to make food sweet गन्ने या चुकंदर से बनने वाली चीनी; इक्षु शर्करा ➪ **dextrose, fructose, glucose** और **lactose** देखिए।

**suction** /ˈsʌkʃn ˈसक्शन्/ *noun* [U] the action of removing air or liquid from a space or container so that sth else can be pulled into it or so that two surfaces can stick together किसी डिब्बे या पात्र के अंदर की वायु को खींचकर बाहर निकालना (ताकि किसी अन्य वस्तु को खींचकर अंदर लाया जा सके या डिब्बे की दोनों सतहें चिपक सकें); चूषन *A vacuum cleaner works by suction.*

**sudden** /ˈsʌdn ˈसड्न्/ *adj.* done or happening quickly, or when you do not expect it जल्दबाज़ी में या अचानक किया गया या घटित हुआ; एकाएक, सहसा या आकस्मिक *a sudden decision/change* ▶ **suddenly** *adv.* एकाएक, अचानक *Suddenly, everybody started shouting.* ▶ **suddenness** *noun* [U] हड़बड़ी या जल्दबाज़ी, आकस्मिकता

**IDM** **all of a sudden** quickly and unexpectedly एकदम अचानक, तुरंत और अप्रत्याशित रूप से *All of a sudden the lights went out.*

**sudden death** a way of deciding who wins a game where the score is equal by playing one more point or game खेल में बराबर रहने पर निर्णय करने का विशेष तरीक़ा (जिसमें पहले गोल करने या अंक प्राप्त वाले दल या खिलाड़ी को विजयी माना जाता है)

**suds** /sʌdz सड्ज़्/ *noun* [*pl.*] the bubbles that you get when you mix soap and water साबुन का झाग; फेन

**sue** /suː सू/ *verb* [I, T] **sue (sb) (for sth)** to go to a court of law and ask for money from sb because he/she has done sth bad to you, or said sth bad about you (वादी द्वारा) अदालत में (किसी पर) मुक़दमा दायर करना (वादी को हुए नुक़सान का हर्जाना वसूल करने के लिए) *to sue sb for libel/breach of contract/damages*

**suede** /sweɪd स्वेड्/ *noun* [U] a type of soft leather which does not have a smooth surface and feels a little like cloth एक प्रकार का नरम चमड़ा जिसकी सतह चिकनी नहीं होती और छूने पर कपड़ा-सा लगता है; स्वेड

**suet** /ˈsuːɪt ˈसूइट्/ *noun* [U] a type of hard animal fat that is used in cooking एक प्रकार की कड़ी चरबी (भोजन बनाने में प्रयुक्त)

**suffer** /ˈsʌfə(r) ˈसफ़(र्)/ *verb* **1** [I, T] **suffer (from sth); suffer (for sth)** to experience sth unpleasant, for example pain, sadness, difficulty, etc. दर्द, विषाद, कठिनाई आदि अप्रिय बातें सहन करना; कष्ट भोगना *She often suffers from severe headaches.* ○ *Our troops suffered heavy losses.* **2** [I] to become worse in quality बदतर स्थिति में पहुँचना *My work is suffering as a result of problems at home.* ▶ **sufferer** *noun* [C] कष्टभोगी, पीड़ित *asthma sufferers* ▶ **suffering** *noun* [U] पीड़ा, कष्ट या वेदना

**suffice** /səˈfaɪs सˈफ़ाइस्/ *verb* [I] (*formal*) **1** (*not used in the continuous tense*) to be enough for sb/sth (किसी व्यक्ति या वस्तु के लिए) पर्याप्त होना *One example will suffice to illustrate the point.* **2 suffice (it) to say (that)...** used to suggest that although you could say more, what you do say will be enough to explain what you mean यह सुझाने के लिए प्रयुक्त कि अपने अभिप्राय को स्पष्ट करने के लिए कहा गया वक्तव्य पर्याप्त है

**sufficient** /səˈfɪʃnt सˈफ़िश्न्ट्/ *adj.* (*formal*) as much as is necessary; enough जितना आवश्यक हो उतना; पर्याप्त *We have sufficient oil reserves to last for three months.* ✪ विलोम **insufficient** ▶ **sufficiently** *adv.* पर्याप्त मात्रा में

**suffix** /ˈsʌfɪks ˈसफ़िक्स्/ *noun* [C] (*grammar*) a letter or group of letters that you add at the end of a word, and that changes the meaning of the word or the way it is used शब्द के अंत में लगने वाला प्रत्यय (जिससे शब्द का अर्थ या प्रयोग-विधान बदल जाता है); अनुलग्न *To form the noun from the adjective 'sad', add the suffix 'ness'*. ➪ **affix**[2] और **prefix** देखिए।

**suffocate** /ˈsʌfəkeɪt ˈसफ़केट्/ *verb* [I, T] to die because there is no air to breathe; to kill sb in this way गला घुटने से मर जाना दम घुटना; गला घोटकर (किसी को) मार देना; दम घोटना ▶ **suffocating** *adj.* दमघोटू, गला घोटू ▶ **suffocation** /ˌsʌfəˈkeɪʃn ˌसफ़ˈकेश्न्/ *noun* [U] घुटन, गला घुटने या घोटने की क्रिया

**suffrage** /ˈsʌfrɪdʒ ˈसफ़रिज्/ *noun* [U] the right to vote in political elections राजनीतिक चुनाव में मत देने का अधिकार; मताधिकार *universal suffrage* (= the right of all adults to vote) ○ *women's suffrage*

**sugar** /ˈʃʊgə(r) ˈशुग(र्)/ *noun* **1** [U] a sweet substance that you get from certain plants चीनी, शक्कर *Do you **take sugar** in tea?* **2** [C] (in a cup of tea, coffee, etc.) the amount of sugar that a small spoon can hold; a lump of sugar (चाय, काफ़ी आदि के कप में) आ सकने वाली चीनी की मात्रा, कपभर चीनी; चीनी या शक्कर का ढेला **3** [C] any of various sweet substances that are found naturally in plants, fruit, etc. अन्य पौधों, फलों आदि में प्राकृतिक रूप से उपलब्ध मधुर पदार्थ *Glucose and fructose are sugars.*

**sugar beet** (*BrE* **beet**) *noun* [U] a plant with a large round root that sugar is made from चुकंदर

**sugar cane** *noun* [U] a tall tropical plant with thick **stems** that sugar is made from गन्ना, ईख

**sugary** /ˈʃʊgəri ˈशुगरि/ *adj.* very sweet बहुत मीठा

**suggest** /səˈdʒest सˈजेस्ट्/ *verb* [T] **1 suggest sth (to sb); suggest doing sth; suggest that...** to mention a plan or an idea that you have for sb to discuss or consider (चर्चा या विचार हेतु) कोई सुझाव देना (किसी योजना या राय का उल्लेख करना) *Can anybody suggest ways of raising more money?* **2 suggest sb/sth (for/as sth)** to say that a person, thing or place is suitable (किसी प्रयोजन के लिए) किसी व्यक्ति, वस्तु या स्थान के उपयुक्त होने की बात करना या का सुझाव देना *Who would you suggest for the job?* ➪ **recommend** देखिए। **3** to say or show sth in an indirect way किसी बात को घुमा-फिरा कर कहना *Are you suggesting the accident was my fault?*

**suggestion** /səˈdʒestʃən सˈजेस्चन्/ *noun* **1** [C] a plan or idea that sb mentions for sb else to discuss and consider (चर्चा या विचार हेतु) कोई सुझाव (कोई योजना या राय) *May I **make a suggestion**?* **2** [U] putting an idea into a person's mind; giving advice about what to do किसी व्यक्ति को कोई सुझाव देने का कार्य; कोई सलाह देने का कार्य, कुछ सुझाने की क्रिया **3** [*sing.*] a slight amount or sign of sth किसी वस्तु की अल्प मात्रा या बात का हलका संकेत

**suggestive** /səˈdʒestɪv सˈजेस्टिव्/ *adj.* **1 suggestive (of sth)** making you think of sth; being a sign of sth विचारोत्तेजक (किसी बात पर विचार करने के लिए प्रेरित करने वाला); सांकेतिक (किसी स्थिति का संकेत होते हुए) *Your symptoms are more suggestive of an allergy than a virus.* **2** making you think about sex अश्लील *a suggestive dance/remark/posture* ▶ **suggestively** *adv.* सांकेतिक रूप से

**suicidal** /ˌsuːɪˈsaɪdl ˌसूइˈसाइड्ल्/ *adj.* **1** (used about a person) wanting to kill himself/herself (व्यक्ति) आत्मघाती, आत्मघातक *to be/feel suicidal* **2** likely to have a very bad result; extremely dangerous जिसका बहुत बुरा परिणाम संभावित हो; बहुत ख़तरनाक *a suicidal attempt*

**suicide** /ˈsuːɪsaɪd ˈसूइसाइड्/ *noun* [U, C] the act of killing yourself deliberately आत्महत्या करना (जान-बूझ कर अपने को मार देना) *to **commit suicide*** ○ *There have been three suicides by farmers this year.*

**suit**[1] /suːt सूट्/ *noun* [C] **1** a formal set of clothes that are made of the same material, consisting of a jacket and either trousers or a skirt औपचारिक अवसरों पर पहनने का सूट (जिसमें पैंट और कोट एक ही कपड़े से बनते हैं) *He always wears a suit and tie to work.* **2** an article of clothing or set of clothes that you wear for a particular activity विशेष क्रिया-कलाप के लिए कोई पोशाक या सूट *a tracksuit/swimsuit* **3** one of the four sets of 13 playing cards (**hearts, clubs, diamonds**) and (**spades**) that form a pack ताश के किसी एक रंग के पत्तों का सेट ➪ **card** पर नोट देखिए।

IDM **follow suit** ➪ **follow** देखिए।

**suit**[2] /suːt सूट्/ *verb* [T] (*not used in the continuous tenses*) **1** to be convenient or useful for sb/sth किसी के लिए सुविधाजनक या उपयोगी होना; सूट करना *Would Thursday at 9.30 suit you?* ○ *He will help but only when it suits him.* **2** (used about clothes, colours, etc.) to make you look attractive (कपड़ों, रंगों आदि का) किसी पर फबना या जँचना *That dress really suits you.*

**suitable** /ˈsuːtəbl ˈसूटब्ल्/ *adj.* **suitable (for sb/sth); suitable (to do sth)** right or appropriate for sb/sth (किसी के लिए) सही या उचित या उपयुक्त *The film isn't suitable for children.* ○ *I've got* *nothing suitable to wear for a wedding.* ✪ विलोम **unsuitable** ▶ **suitability** /ˌsuːtəˈbɪləti ˌसूटˈबिलटि/ *noun* [U] औचित्य, उपयुक्तता ▶ **suitably** *adv.* उचित या उपयुक्त रूप से

**suitcase** /ˈsuːtkeɪs ˈसूट्केस्/ (*also* **case**) *noun* [C] a box with a handle that you use for carrying your clothes, etc. in when you are travelling सूटकेस, बक्सा (यात्रा के दौरान कपड़े आदि ले जाने के लिए प्रयुक्त)

**suite** /swiːt स्वीट्/ *noun* [C] **1** a set of rooms, especially in a hotel (साज-सज्जा युक्त) कमरों का सेट (विशेषत: होटल में) *the honeymoon/penthouse suite* ○ *a suite of rooms/offices* ➪ **en suite** देखिए। **2** a set of two or more pieces of furniture of the same style or covered in the same material (एक ही ढंग के या एक ही कपड़े से मढ़े दो या अधिक नगों वाला) फ़र्नीचर का सेट *a three-piece suite* (= a sofa and two armchairs)

**suited** /ˈsuːtɪd ˈसूटिड्/ *adj.* **suited (for/to sb/sth)** appropriate or right for sb/sth (किसी के लिए) उपयुक्त या सही

**sulfur** (*AmE*) = **sulphur**

**sulk** /sʌlk सल्क्/ *verb* [I] to refuse to speak or smile because you want people to know that you are angry about sth रूठना, (अपना गुस्सा जतलाने के लिए न किसी से बोलना न मुसकुराना) कोप करना, कुढ़ना ▶ **sulky** *adj.* रुष्ट, नाराज़ ▶ **sulkily** /-li -लि/ *adv.* रूठते हुए, नाराज़गी के साथ

**sullen** /ˈsʌlən ˈसलन्/ *adj.* looking bad-tempered and not wanting to speak to people चिड़चिड़ा और उदासी भरा (लोगों से बोलने का अनिच्छुक); खिन्न *a sullen face/expression/glare* ▶ **sullenly** *adv.* चिड़चिड़ेपन या रूखेपन से, उदास होकर

**sulphide** (*AmE* **sulfide**) /ˈsʌlfaɪd ˈसल्फ़ाइड्/ *noun* [C, U] a compound of sulphur with another chemical element गंधक या सल्फ़र और एक अन्य रासायनिक तत्त्व का यौगिक; सल्फ़ाइड

**sulphur** (*AmE* **sulfur**) /ˈsʌlfə(r) ˈसल्फ़(र्)/ *noun* [U] (*symbol* **S**) a natural yellow substance with a strong unpleasant smell गंधक, सल्फ़र (तेज़ अप्रिय गंध वाला पीले रंग का प्राकृतिक पदार्थ)

**sulphur dioxide** (*AmE* **sulfur dioxide**) *noun* [U] (*symbol* $SO_2$) a poisonous gas with a strong smell, that is used in industry and causes air **pollution** कारख़ानों में प्रयुक्त और वायु-प्रदूषण कारी तथा तेज़ गंध वाली एक प्रकार की गैस; सल्फ़र डाइऑक्साइड

**sulphuric acid** (*AmE* **sulfuric acid**) /sʌlˌfjʊərɪkˈæsɪd सल्ˌफ़्युअरिक्ˈऐसिड्/ *noun* [U] (*symbol* $H_2SO_4$) a strong colourless acid एक तेज़ रंगहीन अम्ल; सल्फ़्यूरिक एसिड

**sultan** (*also* **Sultan**) *noun* [C] the ruler in some Muslim countries सुलतान (कुछ मुस्लिम देशों में शासक)

**sultana** /sʌlˈtɑːnə सल्ˈटाना/ *noun* [C] a dried grape with no seeds in it that is used in cooking किशमिश ➪ **raisin** देखिए।

**sultry** /ˈsʌltri ˈसल्ट्रि/ *adj.* **1** (used about the weather) hot and uncomfortable (मौसम) उमस भरा (गरम और कष्टप्रद) **2** (used about a woman) behaving in a way that makes her sexually attractive (महिला) कामोत्तेजक आचरण करने वाली; कामुक

**sum**[1] /sʌm सम्/ *noun* [C] **1** an amount of money धन की राशि *The industry has spent huge **sums of money** modernizing its equipment.* **2** [*usually sing.*] **the sum (of sth)** the amount that you get when you add two or more numbers together दो या अधिक संख्या का जोड़; योगफल *The sum of two and five is seven.* **3** a simple problem that involves calculating numbers अंकगणित का प्रश्न, सवाल *to **do sums** in your head*

**sum**[2] /sʌm सम्/ *verb* (**summing; summed**)

**PHRV** **sum (sth) up** to describe in a few words the main ideas of what sb has said or written किसी अवतरण के मुख्य भावों को संक्षेप में कहना; संक्षेप में दोहराना, समाहार करना ***To sum up**, there are three options here for you.*

**sum sb/sth up** to form an opinion about sb/sth (किसी के विषय में) राय बनाना, सम्मति स्थिर करना *He summed the situation up immediately.*

**summary**[1] /ˈsʌməri ˈसमरि/ *noun* [C] (*pl.* **summaries**) a short description of the main ideas or points of sth but without any details किसी (अवतरण) का सार-संक्षेप *A brief summary of the experiment is given at the beginning of the report.* ✪ पर्याय **précis** ▶ **summarize** (*also* **-ise**) /ˈsʌməraɪz ˈसमराइज़्/ *verb* [I, T] (किसी का) सार-संक्षेप तैयार करना; संक्षेपण करना *Could you summarize the story so far?*

**summary**[2] /ˈsʌməri ˈसमरि/ *adj.* (*formal*) done quickly and without taking time to consider whether it is the right thing to do or following the right process सरसरी तौर पर किया गया (जल्दबाज़ी में और बिना सही-ग़लत के विचार से किया गया) *a summary judgment*

**summer** /ˈsʌmə(r) ˈसम(र्)/ *noun* [C, U] one of the four seasons of the year, after spring and before autumn. Summer is the warmest season of the year ग्रीष्म ऋतु *Is it very hot here **in summer**?* ○ *a summer's day* ➪ **season** देखिए। ▶ **summery** *adj.* ग्रीष्मकालीन *summery weather* ○ *a summery dress/colour*

**summer house** *noun* [C] a small building in a park or garden where you can sit and relax in good weather पार्क या बग़ीचे में बना विश्राम भवन

**summer school** *noun* [C, U] courses that are held in the summer at a university or college (विश्वविद्यालय या कॉलेज का) ग्रीष्मकालीन अध्ययन-सत्र

**summertime** /ˈsʌmətaɪm ˈसमटाइम्/ *noun* [U] the season of summer ग्रीष्म काल, गरमियों का समय *It's busy here in the summertime.*

**summing-up** *noun* [C] (*pl.* **summings-up**) a speech in which a judge gives a short description (**summary**) of what has been said in a court of law before a decision (**verdict**) is reached निर्णय सुनाने से पहले मुक़दमे की कार्रवाई का न्यायाधीश द्वारा प्रस्तुत सार-संक्षेप

**summit** /ˈsʌmɪt ˈसमिट्/ *noun* [C] **1** the top of a mountain पर्वत का शिखर **2** an important meeting or series of meetings between the leaders of two or more countries शिखर-वार्ता (दो या अधिक देशों के शासकों के बीच विचार-विमर्श)

**summon** /ˈsʌmən ˈसमन्/ *verb* [T] **1** (*formal*) to order a person to come to a place किसी व्यक्ति को किसी स्थान पर पहुँचने का आदेश देना, किसी को बुला भेजना *The boys were summoned to the head teacher's office.* **2 summon sth (up)** to find strength, courage or some other quality that you need even though it is difficult to do so (कठिनाई के बावजूद) अपेक्षित बल, साहस या अन्य आवश्यक गुण सँजोना या बटोरना *She couldn't summon up the courage to ask her boss for leave.*

**summons** /ˈsʌmənz ˈसमन्ज़्/ *noun* [C] (*pl.* **summonses**) an order to appear in a court of law न्यायालय में उपस्थित होने का आदेश; सम्मन

**sumptuous** /ˈsʌmptʃuəs ˈसम्पचुअस्/ *adj* (*written*) very expensive and impressive; lavish अत्यंत बहुमूल्य और प्रभावशाली; भव्य

**sun**[1] /sʌn सन्/ *noun* **1 the sun** [*sing.*] the star that shines in the sky during the day and that gives the earth heat and light सूर्य, सूरज *The sun rises in the east and sets in the west.* ○ *the rays of the sun* ➪ **the solar system** पर चित्र देखिए। **2** [*sing.*, U] light and heat from the sun सूर्य का प्रकाश और ताप; धूप *Don't sit* ***in the sun*** *too long.* ○ *Too much sun can be harmful.*

IDM **catch the sun** ➪ **catch**[1] देखिए।

**sun**[2] /sʌn सन्/ *verb* [T] (**sunning; sunned**) **sun yourself** sit or lie outside when the sun is shining in order to enjoy the heat धूप सेंकना (चमकते सूर्य की गरमी का सुख पाने के लिए घर से बाहर बैठना या लेटना)

**Sun.** *abbr.* Sunday रविवार, इतवार *Sun. 5 April*

**sunbathe** /ˈsʌnbeɪð ˈसनबेद्/ *verb* [I] to take off most of your clothes and sit or lie in the sun in order to make your skin go darker (**get a tan**) धूप-स्नान (त्वचा को ताम्रवर्णी बनाने के लिए लगभग नंगे बदन धूप में बैठना या लेटना) ➪ **bathe** देखिए।

**sunbeam** /ˈsʌnbi:m ˈसनबीम्/ *noun* [C] a **ray** of sunlight सूर्य की किरण

**sunburn** /ˈsʌnbɜ:n ˈसनबन्/ *noun* [U] red painful skin caused by spending too long in the sun धूप में देर तक रहने से होने वाली झुलसन; आतपदाह, धूप-झुलस

**sunburned** /ˈsʌnbɜ:nd ˈसनबन्ड्/ (*also* **sunburnt** /ˈsʌnbɜ:nt ˈसनबन्ट्/) *adj.* **1** suffering from sunburn धूप में झुलसा **2** (used about a person or his/her skin) having an attractive brown colour from being in the sun (व्यक्ति या उसकी त्वचा) धूप-ताम्र (धूप में रहने के फलस्वरूप ताँबे जैसे रंग की त्वचा वाला)

**Sunday** /ˈsʌndeɪ; -di ˈसन्डे; -डी/ *noun* [C, U] (*abbr.* **Sun.**) the day of the week after Saturday रविवार, इतवार

> NOTE वारों के नाम हमेशा बड़े अक्षर से शुरू होते हैं। वारों के नामों के वाक्य-प्रयोग संबंधी उदाहरणों के लिए **Monday** की प्रविष्टि देखिए।

**sundial** /ˈsʌndaɪəl ˈसन्डाइअल्/ *noun* [C] a type of clock used in past times that uses the dark shape (**shadow**) caused by a pointed piece of metal being between the sun and the clock surface to show what the time is धूप-घड़ी; (पुराने ज़माने की खुले में बनी घड़ी जिसकी तीर-नुमा सूचकों की घूमती हुई छाया से समय का पता चलता रहता है)

**sundry** /ˈsʌndri ˈसन्ड्रि/ *adj.* (*only before a noun*) of various kinds that are not important enough to be named separately नानाविध, विविध

IDM **all and sundry** (*informal*) everyone हर कोई, सभी, तमाम तरह के लोग

**sunflower** /ˈsʌnflaʊə(r) ˈसन्फ़्लाउअ(र्)/ *noun* [C] a very tall plant with large yellow flowers, often grown for its seeds and their oil, which is used in cooking सूरजमुखी

**sung** ➪ **sing** का past participle रूप

**sunglasses** /ˈsʌŋglɑ:sɪz ˈसन्ग्लासिज़्/ (*also* **dark glasses**) (*informal* **shades**) *noun* [*pl.*] a pair of glasses with dark glass in them to protect your eyes from bright sunlight धूप का चश्मा, कांला चश्मा

**sunk** ➪ **sink**[1] का past participle रूप

**sunken** /ˈsʌŋkən ˈसङ्कन्/ *adj.* **1** below the water पानी में डूबा हुआ; जलमग्न *a sunken ship* **2** (used about cheeks or eyes) very far into the face as a result of illness or age (बीमारी या बुढ़ापे के कारण)

धँसी हुई (आँखें), पिचके हुए (गाल) **3** at a lower level than the surrounding area निचला (जिसका तल आसपास की सतह से नीचा हो) *a sunken bath/garden*

**sunlight** /ˈsʌnlaɪt ˈसनलाइट्/ *noun* [U] the light from the sun धूप; सूर्य का प्रकाश

**sunlit** /ˈsʌnlɪt ˈसन्लिट्/ *adj.* having bright light from the sun धूप में चमकता हुआ *a sunlit terrace*

**sunny** /ˈsʌni ˈसनि/ *adj.* (**sunnier; sunniest**) having a lot of light from the sun धूपदार (जिसमें बहुत धूप आती हो) *a sunny garden* ○ *a sunny day*

**sunrise** /ˈsʌnraɪz ˈसनराइज़्/ *noun* [U] the time when the sun comes up in the morning सूर्योदय *to get up* ***at sunrise*** ➪ **dawn** और **sunset** देखिए।

**sunset** /ˈsʌnset ˈसनसेट्/ *noun* [C, U] the time when the sun goes down in the evening सूर्यास्त *The park closes* ***at sunset***. ○ *a beautiful sunset*

**sunshine** /ˈsʌnʃaɪn ˈसन्शाइन्/ *noun* [U] heat and light from the sun धूप; सूर्य का प्रकाश और ताप *We sat down* ***in the sunshine*** *and had lunch.*

**sunspot** /ˈsʌnspɒt ˈसनस्पॉट्/ *noun* [C] a dark area that sometimes appears on the sun's surface सूर्य की सतह पर कभी-कभी दिखाई पड़ने वाला धब्बा; सूर्य-कलंक

**sunstroke** /ˈsʌnstrəʊk ˈसनस्ट्रोक्/ *noun* [U] an illness that is caused by spending too much time in very hot, strong sunlight बहुत तेज़ धूप में बहुत देर तक रहने से हुई बीमारी, धूप-आघात, सूर्य-आघात, लू लगना *Keep your head covered or you'll get sunstroke.*

**suntan** /ˈsʌntæn ˈसनटैन्/ (*also* **tan**) *noun* [C] when you have a suntan, your skin is darker than usual because you have spent time in the sun धूप-ताम्रता, धूप-कालस *to have/get a suntan* ○ *suntan oil* ▸ **suntanned** (*also* **tanned**) *adj.* धूप-ताम्र

**super** /ˈsuːpə(r) ˈसूप(र्)/ *adj.* (*informal*) **1** especially; particularly उत्कृष्ट; विशिष्ट *He's been super understanding.* **2** (*old-fashioned*) very good; wonderful बहुत बढ़िया; कमाल का *We had a super time.*

**super-** /ˈsuːpə(r) ˈसूप(र्)/ *prefix* **1** (*used in adjectives, adverbs and nouns*) extremely; more or better than normal अत्यधिक; सामान्य से अधिक या बेहतर, असाधारण, असामान्य, अति-, महा- *super-rich* ○ *superhuman* ○ *superglue* **2** (*used in nouns and verbs*) above; over शीर्षस्थ, अधि-; ऊपर, उपरि- *superstructure* ○ *superimpose*

**superb** /suːˈpɜːb सूˈपब्/ *adj.* extremely good, excellent बहुत बढ़िया, उत्कृष्ट ▸ **superbly** *adv.* उत्कृष्ट रूप से

**supercilious** /ˌsuːpəˈsɪliəs ˌसूपˈसिलिअस्/ *adj.* showing that you think that you are better than other people दंभी, मग़रूर, अवमानी *a supercilious smile* ▸ **superciliously** *adv.* दंभपूर्वक

**superconductor** /ˈsuːpəkəndʌktə(r) ˈसूपकनडक्ट(र्)/ *noun* [C] a substance which, at very low temperatures, allows electricity to flow completely freely through it सूपर कंडक्टर (एक उपकरण जिसमें से विद्युत बहुत कम तापमान में पूरी शक्ति के साथ गुज़रती है); अतिसंवाहक

**superficial** /ˌsuːpəˈfɪʃl ˌसूपˈफ़िश्ल्/ *adj.* **1** not studying or thinking about sth in a deep or complete way जिसे गहराई से या पूर्णता में न जाना या सोचा गया हो; छिछला, उथला *a superficial knowledge of the subject* **2** only on the surface, not deep सतही, गहरा नहीं, ऊपरी *a superficial wound/cut/burn* **3** (used about people) not caring about serious or important things (व्यक्ति) गंभीर या महत्त्वपूर्ण विषयों के प्रति उदासीन; अल्पज्ञ, पल्लवग्राही *He's a very superficial sort of person.* ▸ **superficiality** /ˌsuːpəˌfɪʃiˈæləti ˌसूपˌफ़िशिˈऐलटि/ *noun* [U] सतहीपन उथलापन, अल्पज्ञता ▸ **superficially** /ˌsuːpəˈfɪʃəli ˌसूपˈफ़िशलि/ *adv.* सतहीपन से, अल्पज्ञता से

**superfluous** /suːˈpɜːfluəs सूˈपफ़्लुअस्/ *adj.* more than is wanted; not needed अपेक्षित से अधिक, अतिरिक्त या फ़ालतू; अनावश्यक

**superhuman** /ˌsuːpəˈhjuːmən ˌसुपˈह्यूमन्/ *adj.* greater than is usual for human beings मानव की सामान्य क्षमता से अधिक; अतिमानवीय, अलौकिक *superhuman strength*

**superimpose** /ˌsuːpərɪmˈpəʊz ˌसूपरिम्ˈपोज़्/ *verb* [T] **superimpose sth (on sth)** to put sth on top of sth else so that what is underneath can still be seen किसी वस्तु को दूसरी वस्तु पर अध्यारोपित करना *The old street plan was superimposed on a map of the modern city.*

**superintendent** /ˌsuːpərɪnˈtendənt ˌसूपरिन्ˈटेन्डन्ट्/ *noun* [C] **1** a police officer with a high position उच्च पुलिस अधिकारी, (पुलिस) सुपरिंटेंडेंट; पुलिस-अधीक्षक *Detective Superintendent Mishra* **2** a person who looks after a large building बड़े भवन की देख-भाल करने वाला व्यक्ति; भवन-अधीक्षक

**superior**[1] /suːˈpɪəriə(r) सूˈपिअरिअ(र्)/ *adj.* **1 superior (to sb/sth)** better than usual or than sb/sth else सामान्य या अन्य से श्रेष्ठ, अधिक उत्कृष्ट *He is clearly superior to all the other candidates.* ✪ विलोम **inferior** **2 superior (to sb)** having a more important position उच्च, उच्चतर या ज्येष्ठ (अधिकारी) *a superior officer* **3** thinking that you are better than other people स्वयं को दूसरों से श्रेष्ठ समझने वाला ▶ **superiority** /suː,pɪəri'ɒrəti सू,पिअरि'ऑरटि/ *noun* [U] उच्चता, श्रेष्ठता

**superior[2]** /suː'pɪəriə(r) सू'पिअरिअ(र्)/ *noun* [C] a person of higher position उच्च अधिकारी *Report any accidents to your superior.* ✪ विलोम **inferior**

**superlative** /su'pɜːlətɪv सू'पलटिव्/ *noun* [C] the form of an adjective or adverb that expresses its highest degree विशेषणों या क्रियाविशेषणों के उत्तमतासूचक रूप *'Most beautiful', 'best' and 'fastest' are all superlatives.*

**supermarket** /'suːpəmɑːkɪt 'सूपमाकिट्/ *noun* [C] a very large shop that sells food, drink, goods used in the home, etc. सुपर मार्केट, सुपर बाज़ार (एक ही भवन में घरेलू उपयोग का सारा सामान बेचने वाली बड़ी दुकान)

**supernatural** /,suːpə'nætʃrəl ,सूप'नैच्रल्/ *adj.* **1** that cannot be explained by the laws of science विज्ञान के नियमों से जिसकी व्याख्या न की जा सके; अतिप्राकृत *a creature with supernatural powers* **2 the supernatural** *noun* [*sing.*] events, forces or powers that cannot be explained by the laws of science घटनाएँ, शक्तियाँ या योग्यताएँ जिनकी व्याख्या विज्ञान के नियमों से नहीं की जा सकती; अलौकिक या दिव्य घटनाएँ, शक्तियाँ *I don't believe in the supernatural.*

**supernova** /,suːpə'nəʊvə ,सूप'नोव़ा/ *noun* [C] (*pl.* **supernovae** /-nəʊviː -नोव़ी/ or **supernovas**) (*technical*) a star that suddenly becomes much brighter because it is exploding अधिनव-तारा, सुपरनोवा ➪ **nova** देखिए।

**superpower** /'suːpəpaʊə(r) 'सूपपाउअ(र्)/ *noun* [C] one of the countries in the world that has very great military or economic power and a lot of influence, for example the US महाशक्ति (सैन्य या आर्थिक दृष्टि से अत्यधिक शक्तिशाली या प्रभावशाली देश, जैसे संयुक्त राज्य अमेरिका) ➪ **power[1] 4** और **world power** देखिए।

**supersede** /,suːpə'siːd ,सूप'सीड्/ *verb* [T] to take the place of sb/sth which existed or was used before and which has become old-fashioned पूर्व में विद्यमान या प्रयोग में आ रही वस्तु को हटाकर उसका स्थान ले लेना; अधिक्रमण करना *Steam trains were gradually superseded by electric trains.*

**supersonic** /,suːpə'sɒnɪk ,सूप'सॉनिक्/ *adj.* faster than the speed of sound पराध्वनिक, वायुगतिकीय

**superstar** /'suːpəstɑː(r) 'सूपस्टा(र्)/ *noun* [C] a singer, film star, etc. who is very famous and popular अतिप्रसिद्ध और अतिलोकप्रिय गायक, फ़िल्म-अभिनेता आदि; सुपर स्टार

**superstition** /,suːpə'stɪʃn ,सूप'स्टिश्न्/ *noun* [C, U] a belief that cannot be explained by reason or science अंधविश्वास *According to superstition, it's unlucky to walk under a ladder.* ▶ **superstitious** /,suːpə'stɪʃəs ,सूप'स्टिशस्/ *adj.* अंधविश्वासी *I never do anything important on Friday the 13th—I'm superstitious.*

**superstore** /'suːpəstɔː(r) 'सूपस्टॉ(र्)/ *noun* [C] a very large shop that sells food or a wide variety of one particular type of goods एक ही प्रकार की वस्तु की विविध क़िस्में या खाद्य पदार्थ बेचने वाली बड़ी दुकान; सुपर स्टोर

**supervise** /'suːpəvaɪz 'सूपव़ाइज़्/ *verb* [I, T] to watch sb/sth to make sure that work is being done properly or that people are behaving correctly देखभाल करना, निगरानी करना (किए जा रहे काम की या लोगों के व्यवहार की); पर्यवेक्षण करना *Your job is to supervise the building work.* ▶ **supervision** /,suːpə'vɪʒn ,सूप'व़िश़्न्/ *noun* [U] निरीक्षण, निगरानी, पर्यवेक्षण *Children should not burst crackers without adult supervision.* ▶ **supervisor** *noun* [C] निरीक्षक

**supper** /'sʌpə(r) 'सप(र्)/ *noun* [C, U] (*old-fashioned*) the last meal of the day, either the main meal of the evening or a small meal that you eat quite late, not long before you go to bed दिन का आख़िरी भोजन (रात को सोने से पहले खाया गया शाम का मुख्य भोजन या देर में लिया गया नाश्ता)

**supple** /'sʌpl 'सप्ल्/ *adj.* that bends or moves easily; not stiff लचीला, नम्य (जो आसानी से झुकाया या हिलाया जा सके); जो कड़ा या सख़्त न हो *Children are generally far more supple than adults.* ▶ **suppleness** *noun* [U] लचीलापन, नम्यता

**supplement** /'sʌplɪmənt 'सपलिमन्ट्/ *noun* [C] something that is added to sth else अनुपूरक, परिशिष्ट, संपूरक *You have to pay a small supplement if you travel on a Saturday.* ▶ **supplement** /'sʌplɪment 'सप्लिमेन्ट्/ *verb* [T] **supplement sth (with sth)** अनुपूरित करना, कमी पूरी करना *to supplement your diet with vitamins* ▶ **supplementary** /,sʌplɪ'mentri ,सप्लि'मेन्ट्रि/ *adj.* अनुपूरक *supplementary exercises at the back of the book*

**supplier** /sə'plaɪə(r) स'प्लाइअ(र्)/ *noun* [C] a person or company that supplies goods माल मुहैया कराने वाला व्यक्ति या कंपनी; आपूर्तिकर्ता, सप्लायर

**supply[1]** /sə'plaɪ स'प्लाइ/ *verb* [T] (*pres. part.* **supplying**; *3rd person sing. pres.* **supplies**; *pt, pp* **supplied**) **supply sth (to sb); supply sb**

**(with sth)** to give or provide sth किसी वस्तु को देना या उपलब्ध कराना; मुहैया कराना, (की) आपूर्ति करना *The farmer supplies eggs to the surrounding villages.* ○ *He supplies the surrounding villages with eggs.*

**supply[2]** /sə'plaɪ स'प्लाइ/ *noun* [C] (*pl.* **supplies**) a store or amount of sth that is provided or available to be used आपूर्ति, सप्लाई *Food supplies were dropped by helicopter during floods.* ○ *In many parts of the country water is **in short supply*** (= there is not much of it).

**support[1]** /sə'pɔːt स'पॉट्/ *verb* [T] **1** to help sb by saying that you agree with him/her/it, and sometimes giving practical help such as money किसी को (सहमति के आधार पर) समर्थन देना या किसी की (धन देकर) सहायता करना *Several large companies are supporting the project.* ○ *Which political party do you support?* **2** to give sb the money he/she needs for food, clothes, etc. भोजन, कपड़ों आदि के लिए किसी को धन देना, (का) भरण-पोषण करना *Javed has to support three children from his previous marriage.* **3** to carry the weight of sb/sth किसी वस्तु को थाम रखना, (का) भार सँभालना *Large columns support the roof.* **4** to show that sth is true or correct किसी बात को सच या सही सिद्ध करना *What evidence do you have to support what you say?* **5** to have a particular sports team as your favourite अपने प्रिय क्रीड़ा-दल को प्रोत्साहित करना *Which football team do you support?*

**support[2]** /sə'pɔːt स'पॉट्/ *noun* **1** [U] **support (for sb/sth)** help and encouragement that you give to a person or thing व्यक्ति या वस्तु को सहायता और प्रोत्साहन *public support for the campaign* ○ *Surya spoke **in support of** the proposal.* **2** [C, U] something that carries the weight of sb/sth or holds sth firmly in place टेक, थूनी, सहारा *a roof support* **3** [U] money to buy food, clothes, etc. भोजन, कपड़े आदि ख़रीदने के लिए धन; जीविका *She has no job, no home and no means of support.*

IDM **moral support** ⇨ **moral[1]** देखिए।

**supporter** /sə'pɔːtə(r) स'पॉट(र्)/ *noun* [C] a person who supports a political party, sports team, etc. राजनीतिक दल, क्रीड़ा-दल आदि का समर्थक *football supporters*

**supportive** /sə'pɔːtɪv स'पॉटिव्/ *adj.* giving help or support to sb in a difficult situation कठिनाई में (किसी को) सहायता या समर्थन देते हुए *Everyone was very supportive when I lost my job.*

**suppose** /sə'pəʊz स'पोज़्/ *verb* [T] **1** to think that sth is probable किसी बात को संभावित मानना *What do you suppose could have happened?* ○ *I don't suppose that they're coming now.* **2** to pretend that sth will happen or is true किसी बात के घटित या सच होने की कल्पना करना; अटकल *Suppose you won the lottery. What would you do?* **3** used to make a suggestion, request or statement less strong किसी सुझाव, अनुरोध या वक्तव्य को कुछ घुमा-फिराकर देने के लिए प्रयुक्त *I don't suppose you'd lend me your car tonight, would you?* **4** used when you agree with sth, but are not very happy about it कुछ अनिच्छा के साथ किसी बात को मान लेने का अर्थ देने के लिए प्रयुक्त *'Can we give Anand a lift?' 'Yes, **I suppose so**, if we must.'*

IDM **be supposed to do sth** **1** to be expected to do sth or to have to do sth किसी से आशा करना कि वह कुछ करेगा या उसे करना पड़ेगा *The train was supposed to arrive ten minutes ago.* ○ **2** (*informal*) to be considered or thought to be sth किसी वस्तु को किसी रूप में समझा या माना जाना *This is supposed to be the oldest building in the city.*

**supposedly** /sə'pəʊzɪdli स'पोज़िड्लि/ *adv.* according to what many people believe अधिकतर लोगों की मान्यता या कल्पना के अनुसार

**supposing** /sə'pəʊzɪŋ स'पोज़िङ्/ *conj.* if sth happens or is true; what if मानते हुए कि; अगर ऐसा हुआ तो *Supposing the plan goes wrong, what will we do then?*

**supposition** /ˌsʌpə'zɪʃn ˌसप'ज़िश्न्/ *noun* [C, U] an idea that a person thinks is true but which has not been shown to be true अप्रमाणित, परंतु सच माना गया, विचार

**suppress** /sə'pres स'प्रेस्/ *verb* [T] **1** to stop sth by using force बल के प्रयोग से किसी को शांत कर देना; दमन करना **2** to stop sth from being seen or known किसी बात को प्रकट न होने देना, छिपा लेना *to suppress the truth* **3** to stop yourself from expressing your feelings, etc. भावनाओं आदि को व्यक्त न होने देना, दबा देना *to suppress laughter/a yawn* ▶ **suppression** /sə'preʃn स'प्रेश्न्/ *noun* [U] दमन, निग्रह

**supremacy** /suː'preməsi सू'प्रेमसि/ *noun* [U] **supremacy (over sb/sth)** the state of being the most powerful अधिकार में सर्वोच्चता की स्थिति

**supreme** /suː'priːm सू'प्रीम्/ *adj.* the highest or greatest possible सर्वोच्च या महानतम

**supremely** /suː'priːmli सू'प्रीम्लि/ *adv.* extremely अत्यंत, अत्यधिक

**Supt** *abbr.* (in the police force) Superintendent (पुलिस में) अधीक्षक, पुलिस-अधीक्षक

**surcharge** /ˈsɜːtʃɑːdʒ ˈसचाज्/ *noun* [C] an extra amount of money that you have to pay for sth किसी बात के लिए दी गई अतिरिक्त राशि; अधिकर, अधिशुल्क

**sure** /ʃɔː(r) शॉ(र्)/ *adj., adv.* **1** (*not before a noun*) having no doubt about sth; certain किसी विषय में संशयहीन; निश्चित *I'm not sure what to do next.* ○ *He was sure that he'd made the right decision.* **2** (*not before a noun*) **sure of sth; sure to do sth** that you will definitely get or do, or that will definitely happen कुछ पाने, करने या घटित होने के विषय में आश्वस्त *If you work hard you are sure to pass the exam.* ✪ विलोम **unsure** **3** that you can be certain of पक्का, संदेहरहित, निश्चित *A noise like that is a sure sign of engine trouble.* **4** (*informal*) used to say 'yes' to sb किसी अनुरोध को स्वीकृति देने के लिए प्रयुक्त *'Can I have a look at your newspaper?' 'Sure.'*

IDM **Be sure to do sth** Don't forget to do sth किसी काम को करना न भूलना; याद रखना *Be sure to write and tell me what happens.*

**for sure** without doubt निस्संदेह, बिला शक *Nobody knows for sure what happened.*

**make sure** **1** to find out whether sth is in a particular state or has been done किसी बात के विषय में आश्वस्त होना *I must go back and make sure I closed the window.* **2** to take the action that is necessary किसी बात को निश्चित रूप से करना *Make sure you are back home by 11 o'clock.*

**sure enough** as was expected आशा के अनुसार *I expected him to be early, and sure enough he arrived five minutes before the others.*

**sure of yourself** confident about your opinions, or about what you can do अपने विचारों या क्षमताओं के विषय में आश्वस्त

**sure (thing)** (*AmE informal*) yes हाँ, ज़रूर, अवश्य *'Can I borrow this book?' 'Sure thing.'*

**surely** /ˈʃɔːli ˈशॉलि/ *adv.* **1** without doubt निस्संदेह, बिला शक *This will surely cause problems.* **2** used for expressing surprise at sb else's opinions, plans, actions, etc. किसी के विचारों, कार्यक्रमों आदि पर आश्चर्य व्यक्त करने के लिए प्रयुक्त *Surely you're not going to walk home in this rain?* **3** (*AmE informal*) yes; of course हाँ; अवश्य, निश्चित रूप से

**surety** /ˈʃʊərəti; ˈʃɔːr- ˈशुअरटि; ˈशॉर-/ *noun* [C, U] (*pl.* **sureties**) (*law*) **1** money given as a promise that you will pay a debt, appear in a court of law, etc. ज़मानत *He was granted bail with a surety of Rs 10,000.* **2** a person who takes the responsibility for sb else in case they do not pay a debt, appear in a court of law, etc. किसी के कर्ज़ न चुका पाने या न्यायालय में उपस्थित न हो पाने की स्थिति में ज़िम्मेदारी लेना; प्रतिभूति

**surf¹** /sɜːf सफ़्/ *noun* [U] the white part on the top of waves in the sea समुद्री लहरों का फेन

**surf²** /sɜːf सफ़्/ *verb* [I] to stand or lie on a special board (**a surfboard**) and ride on a wave towards the beach विशेष पटरे पर खड़े होकर या लेटकर लहरों से खेलना

IDM **surf the net** to use the Internet (कंप्यूटर में) इंटरनेट पर बहुत सी साइटें खोलकर अभीष्ट साइट चुन लेना

**surface¹** /ˈsɜːfɪs ˈसफ़िस्/ *noun* **1** [C] the outside part of sth किसी वस्तु का बाहरी हिस्सा; सतह *the earth's surface* ○ *Teeth have a hard surface called enamel.* **2 the surface** [*sing.*] the top part of an area of water पानी की सतह *leaves floating on the surface of a pond* **3** [C] the flat top part of a piece of furniture, used for working on फ़र्नीचर के किसी नग का शिखरवर्ती समतल भाग *a work surface* ○ *kitchen surfaces* **4** [*sing.*] the qualities of sb/sth that you see or notice, that are not hidden किसी की दीखने या ध्यान आकृष्ट करने वाली विशेषताएँ (जो गुप्त नहीं) ***below/beneath the surface***

**surface²** /ˈsɜːfɪs ˈसफ़िस्/ *verb* **1** [I] to come up to the surface of water पानी की सतह पर आना **2** [I] to suddenly appear again or become obvious after having been hidden for a while कुछ समय तक छिपे रहने के बाद फिर से एकाएक प्रकट या स्पष्ट होना; उभरना *All the old arguments surfaced again in the discussion.* **3** (*informal*) to wake up or get up after being asleep (नींद पूरी होने पर) जाग जाना या उठ खड़ा होना **4** [T] to cover the surface of sth, especially a road or a path (सड़क या रास्ते पर) किसी वस्तु की परत चढ़ाना

**surface mail** *noun* [U] letters, packages, etc. that go by road, rail or sea, not by air सड़क, रेलगाड़ी या समुद्र के रास्ते जाने वाली डाक ➪ **airmail** देखिए।

**surfboard** /ˈsɜːfbɔːd ˈसफ़्बॉड्/ *noun* [C] a long narrow board used for the sport of riding on waves (**surfing**) लकड़ी का लंबा तंग तख़्ता जिस पर चढ़कर लहरों पर खेलते हैं; तरंग पट्टी

**surfeit** /ˈsɜːfɪt ˈसफ़िट्/ *noun* [*sing.*] (*written*) **a surfeit (of sth)** too much of sth किसी वस्तु की अत्यधिकता

**surfer** /ˈsɜːfə(r) ˈसफ़(र्)/ *noun* [C] a person who rides on waves standing on a special board (**a surfboard**) विशेष तख़्ते या तरंग पट्टी पर चढ़कर लहरों पर खेलने वाला व्यक्ति

**surfing** /ˈsɜːfɪŋ ˈसफ़िङ्/ *noun* [U] **1** the sport of riding on waves while standing on a narrow board (**a surfboard**) विशेष तख़्ते या तरंग पट्टी पर चढ़कर लहरों पर खेलने का खेल *to go surfing* **2** the activity of looking at different things on the Internet in order to find sth interesting (कंप्यूटर में) इंटरनेट पर विभिन्न प्रकार की वस्तुएँ देखते हुए कुछ रोचक को खोज निकालना

**surge** /sɜːdʒ सज्/ *noun* [C, *usually sing.*] **a surge (of/in sth) 1** a sudden strong movement in a particular direction by a large number of people or things बहुत सारे व्यक्तियों या वस्तुओं की एक विशेष दिशा में उमड़ पड़ने की क्रिया *a surge forward* ○ *a surge* (= an increase) *in the demand for electricity* **2** a sudden strong feeling आकस्मिक भावावेश ▶ **surge** *verb* [I] उमड़ पड़ना *The crowd surged forward.*

**surgeon** /ˈsɜːdʒən ˈसजन्/ *noun* [C] a doctor who performs medical operations (**surgery**) शल्य-चिकित्सक; सर्जन *a brain surgeon*

**surgery** /ˈsɜːdʒəri ˈसजरि/ *noun* (*pl.* **surgeries**) **1** [U] medical treatment in which your body is cut open so that part of it can be removed or repaired शल्य-क्रिया, शल्य-चिकित्सा, सर्जरी (शरीर के रोगग्रस्त अंग को काटकर निकाल देना या सुधार देना) *to undergo surgery* ➪ **plastic surgery** और **operation** देखिए। **2** [C, U] the place or time when a doctor or dentist sees patients डॉक्टर या दंत-चिकित्सक का परामर्श स्थल या परामर्श समय *Surgery hours are from 9.00 to 11.30.*

**surgical** /ˈsɜːdʒɪkl ˈसजिकल्/ *adj.* connected with medical operations शल्य-क्रिया संबंधी *surgical instruments* ▶ **surgically** /ˈsɜːdʒɪkli ˈसजिक्लि/ *adv.* शल्य-क्रिया की दृष्टि से

**surly** /ˈsɜːli ˈसलि/ *adj.* unfriendly and rude रूखा और उजड्ड *a surly expression*

**surmount** /səˈmaʊnt सˈमाउन्ट्/ *verb* [T] to deal successfully with a problem or difficulty समस्या या कठिनाई पर पार पाना ➪ **insurmountable** देखिए।

**surname** /ˈsɜːneɪm ˈसनेम्/ (*also* **last name**) *noun* [C] the name that you share with other people in your family कुलनाम *'What's your surname?' 'Rai.'* ➪ **name** पर नोट देखिए।

**surpass** /səˈpɑːs सˈपास्/ *verb* [T] (*formal*) to do sth better than sb/sth else or better than expected दूसरों से बेहतर या आशा से बढ़कर काम करना *The success of the film surpassed all expectations.*

**surplus** /ˈsɜːpləs ˈसप्लस्/ *noun* [C, U] an amount that is extra or more than you need ज़रूरत से अधिक या अतिरिक्त मात्रा; बेशी *the food surplus in Western Europe* ▶ **surplus** *adj.* अतिरिक्त, फ़ालतू, ज़रूरत पूरी होने के बाद बचा हुआ *They sell their surplus grain to other countries.*

**surprise[1]** /səˈpraɪz सˈप्राइज़्/ *noun* **1** [U] the feeling that you have when sth happens that you do not expect आश्चर्य, हैरानी *They looked up **in surprise** when she walked in.* **2** [C] something that you did not expect or know about आश्चर्यजनक वस्तु या घटना *The news came as a complete surprise.* ○ *a surprise visit/attack/party*

IDM **take sb by surprise** to happen or do sth when sb is not expecting it किसी को ताज्जुब में डालना, अप्रत्याशित रूप से किसी के साथ कुछ होना या करना

**surprise[2]** /səˈpraɪz सˈप्राइज़्/ *verb* [T] **1** to make sb feel surprised किसी को आश्चर्यचकित करना *It wouldn't surprise me if you get the job.* **2** to attack or find sb suddenly and unexpectedly किसी पर एकाएक या अप्रत्याशित रूप से आक्रमण करना या किसी का एकाएक या अप्रत्याशित रूप से पता लगना

**surprised** /səˈpraɪzd सˈप्राइज़्ड्/ *adj.* feeling or showing surprise आश्चर्यचकित *I was very surprised to see Tara there. I thought she was still abroad.*

**surprising** /səˈpraɪzɪŋ सˈप्राइज़िङ्/ *adj.* that causes surprise आश्चर्यजनक *It's surprising how many adults can't read or write.* ▶ **surprisingly** *adv.* आश्चर्यजनक रूप से *Surprisingly few people got the correct answer.*

**surreal** /səˈriːəl सˈरीअल्/ (*also* **surrealistic** /səˌriːəˈlɪstɪk सˌरीअˈलिस्टिक्/) *adj.* very strange; with images mixed together in a strange way like in a dream अति विचित्र; जिसमें छवियों का विचित्र मिश्रण हो (जैसे स्वप्न में) *a surreal film/painting/situation*

**surrender** /səˈrendə(r) सˈरेन्ड(र्)/ *verb* **1** [I, T] **surrender (yourself) (to sb)** to stop fighting and admit that you have lost लड़ना बंद कर अपनी हार मान लेना, आत्मसमर्पण कर देना *The hijackers eventually surrendered themselves to the police.*

✪ पर्याय **yield 2** [T] (*formal*) **surrender sb/sth (to sb)** to give sb/sth to sb else किसी को कुछ सौंप देना *The police ordered them to surrender their weapons.* ▶ **surrender** *noun* [C, U] आत्मसमर्पण

**surreptitious** /ˌsʌrəpˈtɪʃəs ˌसरप्ˈटिशस्/ *adj.* done secretly गुप्त रीति से किया गया *I had a surreptitious look at what she was writing.* ▶ **surreptitiously** *adv.* गुप्त रीति से, चोरी-छिपे

**surrogate** /ˈsʌrəgət ˈसरगट्/ *noun* [C], *adj.* (a person or thing) that takes the place of sb/sth else किसी अन्य का स्थान लेने वाला; एवज़ी (व्यक्ति या वस्तु) *a surrogate mother* (= a woman who has a baby and gives it to another woman who cannot have children)

**surround** /sə'raʊnd स'राउन्ड्/ *verb* [T] **surround sb/sth (by/with sth)** to be or go all around sb/sth किसी के चारों ओर होना या किसी को चारों ओर से घेरना *The garden is surrounded by a high wall.* ○ *Troops have surrounded the parliament building.*

**surrounding** /sə'raʊndɪŋ स'राउन्डिङ्/ *adj.* (*only before a noun*) that is near or around sth किसी के निकट या चारों ओर; आस-पास

**surroundings** /sə'raʊndɪŋz स'राउन्डिङ्ज़्/ *noun* [*pl.*] everything that is near or around you; the place where you live पास-पड़ोस, प्रतिवेश; वातावरण या परिवेश; निवास-स्थल *pleasant surroundings* ○ *animals living in their natural surroundings* (= not in zoos) ➪ **environment** देखिए।

**surveillance** /sɜː'veɪləns स'व़ेलन्स्/ *noun* [U] the careful watching of sb who may have done sth wrong (अपराधियों आदि की) निगरानी *The building is protected by surveillance cameras.*

**survey**[1] /'sɜːveɪ 'सव़े/ *noun* [C] **1** a study of the opinions, behaviour, etc. of a group of people व्यक्तियों के किसी समूह के विचारों, आचरण आदि का अध्ययन; सर्वेक्षण *to carry out/conduct/do a survey* **2** the action of examining an area of land and making a map of it किसी भूक्षेत्र की जाँच कर उसका मानचित्र बनाने का कार्य, सर्वे, भूमापन तथा मानचित्र-निर्माण **3** the action of examining a building in order to find out if it is in good condition किसी भवन की दशा की जाँच करने का कार्य; निरीक्षण

**survey**[2] /sə'veɪ स'व़े/ *verb* [T] **1** to look carefully at the whole of sth किसी वस्तु का सामान्य रूप से सावधानी के साथ अवलोकन करना *We stood at the top of the hill and surveyed the countryside.* **2** to carefully measure and make a map of an area of land सावधानी से किसी भूक्षेत्र का मापन कर मानचित्र बनाना **3** to examine a building carefully in order to find out if it is in good condition किसी भवन की दशा की सावधानी से जाँच करना

**surveyor** /sə'veɪə(r) स'व़ेअ(र्)/ *noun* [C] **1** a person whose job is to examine a building to make sure its structure is in good condition or to examine and record the details of a piece of land किसी भवन की दशा की जाँच करने या किसी भूखंड की जाँचकर उसके ब्योरे दर्ज करने वाला व्यक्ति; सर्वेयर, सर्वेक्षक, निरीक्षक ➪ **quantity surveyor** देखिए। **2** (*BrE*) an official whose job is to check that sth is accurate, of good quality, etc. वस्तु की विशुद्धता, गुणवत्ता आदि की जाँच करने वाला अधिकारी; निरीक्षक

**survive** /sə'vaɪv स'व़ाइव़्/ *verb* **1** [I, T] to continue to live or exist in or after a difficult or dangerous situation कठिन या संकटपूर्ण स्थिति में या उसके बाद जीवित या अस्तित्व में बने रहना *to survive a plane crash* ○ *Not many buildings survived the earthquake.* **2** [T] to live longer than sb/sth किसी की मृत्यु के बाद जीवित रहना ▶ **survival** /sə'vaɪvl स'व़ाइव़्ल्/ *noun* [U] जीवित या अस्तित्व में रहने की स्थिति *A heart transplant was his only chance of survival.* ▶ **survivor** *noun* [C] दुर्घटना में बच जाने वाला व्यक्ति *There were five survivors of the crash.*

**susceptible** /sə'septəbl स'सेप्टब्ल्/ *adj.* (*not before a noun*) **susceptible to sth** easily influenced, damaged or affected by sb/sth (किसी व्यक्ति से) सरलता से प्रभावित, (रोग आदि से) क्षतिग्रस्त या आक्रांत हो जानेवाला

**suspect**[1] /sə'spekt स'स्पेक्ट्/ *verb* [T] **1** to believe that sth may happen or be true, especially sth bad ऐसा मानना या विश्वास करना कि कुछ (विशेषतः अशुभ) घटित हो जाएगा या सच निकल आएगा *The situation is worse than we first suspected.* ○ *Nobody suspected that she was thinking of leaving.* ➪ **unsuspecting** देखिए। **2** to not be sure that you can trust sb or believe sth किसी पर विश्वास या किसी बात को स्वीकार करने के विषय में आश्वस्त न होना; संदेह करना *I rather suspect his motives for offering to help.* **3 suspect sb (of sth/of doing sth)** to believe that sb is guilty of sth किसी को अपराधी समझना *She strongly suspected that he was lying.* ➪ **suspicion** noun देखिए।

**suspect**[2] /'sʌspekt 'सस्पेक्ट्/ *noun* [C] a person who is thought to be guilty of a crime संदिग्ध अपराधी *The suspects are being questioned by police.*

**suspect**[3] /'sʌspekt 'सस्पेक्ट्/ *adj.* possibly not true or not to be trusted संभवतः असत्य या अविश्वसनीय *to have suspect motives* ○ *a suspect parcel* (= that may contain a bomb)

**suspend** /sə'spend स'स्पेन्ड्/ *verb* [T] **1 suspend sth (from sth) (by/on sth)** to hang sth from sth else (किसी वस्तु को किसी अन्य वस्तु से) लटकाना **2** to stop or delay sth for a time कुछ समय के लिए किसी वस्तु को रोक देना या उसके विषय में देरी लगाना; स्थगित करना *Some rail services were suspended during the strike.* **3 suspend sb (from sth)** to send sb away from his/her school, job, position, etc. for a period of time, usually as a punishment किसी को निलंबित करना (अपने पद, नौकरी आदि से कुछ समय के लिए हटा देना) (दंड के रूप में) ➪ **suspension** noun देखिए।

**suspender** /səˈspendə(r) सˈस्पेन्ड(र्)/ *noun* **1** [C, *usually pl.*] (*BrE*) a short piece of elastic that women use to hold up their **stockings** महिलाओं के लंबे मोज़े को थामने वाला फ़ीता; गेलिस **2 suspenders** [*pl.*] (*AmE*) = **brace**[1] **2**

**suspense** /səˈspens सˈस्पेन्स्/ *noun* [U] the feeling of excitement or worry that you have when you feel sth is going to happen, when you are waiting for news, etc. उत्कंठा या चिंता (आगे आने वाले समाचार, घटना आदि की प्रतीक्षा में) *Don't keep us in suspense. Tell us what happened.*

**suspension** /səˈspenʃn सˈस्पेन्शन्/ *noun* **1** [C, U] not being allowed to do your job or go to school for a period of time, usually as a punishment निलंबन (किसी को अपने पद, नौकरी आदि से कुछ समय के लिए हटाने की क्रिया) (दंड के रूप में) *suspension on full pay* **2** [U] delaying sth for a period of time कुछ समय के लिए किसी काम में देरी करने की क्रिया; विलंबन ➪ **suspend** verb देखिए। **3 the suspension** [U] the parts that are connected to the wheels of a car, etc. that make it more comfortable to ride in कार आदि वाहनों के पहियों से लगे पुरज़े (यात्री के सफ़र को आरामदेह बनाने के लिए); सस्पेंशन **4** [C, U] (*technical*) a liquid with very small pieces of solid matter floating in it; the state of such a liquid तरल पदार्थ जिसमें छोटे-छोटे ठोस-कण तैरते रहते हैं; तरल पदार्थ की तैरते ठोस-कणों से युक्त होने की स्थिति

**suspension bridge** *noun* [C] a bridge that hangs from thick steel wires that are supported by towers at each end झूला पुल (दोनों सिरों पर मीनार-नुमा ढाँचों में जड़ी इस्पात की मोटी तारों से लटकने वाला)

**suspicion** /səˈspɪʃn सˈस्पिशन्/ *noun* **1** [C, U] a feeling or belief that sth is wrong or that sb has done sth wrong संदेह, शक (यह भावना या धारणा कि दाल में कुछ काला है) *She was arrested **on suspicion of** murder.* ○ *He is **under suspicion** of being involved in drug smuggling.* **2** [C] a feeling that sth may happen or be true कुछ हो जाने या सच निकलने की आशंका *I have a suspicion that he's forgotten he invited us.* ➪ **suspect** verb देखिए।

**suspicious** /səˈspɪʃəs सˈस्पिशस्/ *adj.* **1 suspicious (of/about sb/sth)** feeling that sb has done sth wrong, dishonest or illegal जिसे किसी बात के ग़लत, अनुचित या ग़ैर-क़ानूनी होने का अहसास हो, संदेही या संशयी, संदेहग्रस्त या संशयग्रस्त *We became suspicious of his behaviour and alerted the police.* **2** that makes you feel that sth is wrong, dishonest or illegal जो (आपको) किसी बात के ग़लत, अनुचित या ग़ैर-क़ानूनी होने का अहसास कराए; संदेहास्पद, शक के घेरे में आनेवाला *The old man died **in suspicious circumstances**.* ○ *a suspicious-looking person* ▶ **suspiciously** *adv.* संदेहजनक ढंग से *to behave suspiciously*

**sustain** /səˈsteɪn सˈस्टेन्/ *verb* [T] **1** to keep sb/sth alive or healthy किसी को जीवित या स्वस्थ बनाए रखना *Oxygen sustains life.* **2** to make sth continue for a long period of time without becoming less किसी स्थिति को देर तक अपने मूल रूप में बनाए रखना; क़ायम रखना *It's hard to sustain interest for such a long time.* **3** (*formal*) to experience sth bad कटु अनुभव होना, भुगतना *to sustain damage/an injury/a defeat*

**sustainable** /səˈsteɪnəbl सˈस्टेनबल्/ *adj.* **1** involving the use of natural products and energy in a way that does not harm the environment पर्यावरण को हानि पहुँचाए बिना प्राकृतिक पदार्थों और ऊर्जा का उपयोग करते हुए *sustainable forest management* **2** that can continue or be continued for a long time जो देर तक बना रहे या क़ायम रखा जा सके ✪ विलोम **unsustainable**

**sustenance** /ˈsʌstənəns ˈसस्टनन्स्/ *noun* [U] (*formal*) **1** the food and drink that people, animals and plants need in order to live and stay healthy निर्वाह एवं संपोषण के लिए आवश्यक आहार *In some regions rice is the basis of daily sustenance.* **2 sustenance (of sth)** the process of making sth continue to exist कुछ क़ायम रखने की प्रक्रिया *Regular elections are essential for the sustenance of democracy.*

**Sutra** *noun* [U] (*IndE*) **1** a rule or a formula from Sanskrit literature, or a set of these on a particular topic like grammar, Hindu Law, philosophy, etc. सूत्र (संस्कृत साहित्य में) सत्य को दर्शाने वाला नियम या अगाध वैदिक सीख या किसी विशिष्ट विषय जैसे तत्वज्ञान, व्याकरण, हिंदू क़ानून आदि पर इनका समुच्चय *Dharmasutra* **2** a Buddhist or Jain holy text बौद्ध या जैन धर्म की धार्मिक ग्रंथ

**SW** *abbr.* **1** = **short wave** ➪ **wavelength** पर चित्र देखिए। **2** south-west(ern) दक्षिण-पश्चिम(ी) *SW Australia*

**swab** /swɒb स्वॉब्/ *noun* [C] **1** a piece of soft material used by a doctor, nurse, etc. for cleaning a place where your body has been injured or cut, or for taking a substance from your body to test it चिकित्सा में घाव आदि को साफ़ करने के लिए या जाँच के लिए प्रयुक्त मुलायम कपड़ा; फाहा, फुरेशी **2** an act of taking a substance from sb's body for testing, with a swab (जाँच के लिए) फाहे से शरीर में से कुछ निकालने की क्रिया *to take a throat swab* ▶ **swab** *verb* [T] (*pres. part.* **swabbing**; *pt, pp* **swabbed**)

**swagger** /ˈswæɡə(r) ˈस्वैग(र्)/ *verb* [I] to walk in a way that shows that you are too confident or proud अकड़कर चलना, इठलाना, इतराना ▶ **swagger** *noun* [*sing.*] अकड़

**swallow** /ˈswɒləʊ ˈस्वॉलो/ *verb* **1** [T] to make food, drink, etc. go down your throat to your stomach (खाद्य-पेय पदार्थों को) निगलना *It's easier to swallow pills if you take them with water.* **2** [I] to make a movement in your throat, often because you are afraid or surprised, etc. (भय या आश्चर्य के कारण) गले में खड़खड़ाहट होना *She swallowed hard and tried to speak, but nothing came out.* **3** [T] to accept or believe sth too easily किसी बात को बहुत जल्दी मान लेना या उसमें विश्वास कर लेना *You shouldn't swallow everything they tell you!* **4** [T] to accept an insult, etc. without complaining बिना विरोध के अपमान आदि बरदाश्त कर लेना, चुपचाप सहन कर लेना, पी जाना *I find her criticisms very hard to swallow.* **5** [T] **swallow sth (up)** to use all of sth, especially money कोई वस्तु (विशेषतः धन) सारी-की-सारी इस्तेमाल कर लेना, खा जाना *The rent swallows up most of our monthly income.* ▶ **swallow** *noun* [C] एक बार में निगली हुई वस्तु की मात्रा, ग्रास या घूँट

IDM **hard to swallow** ➪ **hard**[1] देखिए।

**swallow hole** *noun* [C] (in geography) a large hole in the ground that a river flows into, created over a long period of time by water that has fallen as rain (भूगोल में) लंबे समय तक पड़े वर्षा के पानी से ज़मीन में बना बड़ा गड्ढा (जिसमें नदी का पानी जाता है); विलय-रंध्र ➪ **limestone** पर चित्र देखिए।

**swam** ➪ **swim** का past tense रूप

**swamp**[1] /swɒmp स्वॉम्प्/ *noun* [C, U] an area of soft wet land दलदल, अनूप भूमि

**swamp**[2] /swɒmp स्वॉम्प्/ *verb* [T] **1** to cover or fill sth with water पानी से भर जाना या (किसी को) भर देना *The fishing boat was swamped by enormous waves.* **2 swamp sb/sth (with sth)** (*usually passive*) to give sb so much of sth that he/she cannot deal with it किसी चीज़ की भरमार कर देना (कि उससे निपटना मुश्किल हो जाए) *We've been swamped with applications for the job.* ✪ पर्याय **inundate**

**swan** /swɒn स्वॉन्/ *noun* [C] a large, usually white, bird with a very long neck that lives on lakes and rivers हंस (आकार में बड़ा प्रायः सफ़ेद रंग और काफ़ी लंबी नोक वाला पक्षी जो झीलों और नदियों के पास रहता है)

**swap** (*also* **swop**) /swɒp स्वॉप्/ *verb* [I, T] (**swapping; swapped**) **swap (sth) (with sb); swap A for B** to give sth for sth else; to exchange एक के बदले दूसरी चीज़ देना; (वस्तुओं का) विनिमय करना *When we finish these books shall we swap* (= you have my book and I'll have yours)*?* ▶ **swap** *noun* [*sing.*] अदल-बदल, विनिमय *Let's **do a swap**.*

IDM **change/swap places (with sb)** ➪ **place**[1] देखिए।

**swarm**[1] /swɔːm स्वॉम्/ *noun* [C] **1** a large group of insects, especially bees, moving around together एक साथ चलता-फिरता, घूमता-घामता, कीड़ों का (विशेषतः मधुमक्खियों का) बड़ा झुंड *a swarm of bees/locusts/flies* **2** a large number of people together लोगों का बड़ा झुंड; भीड़-भाड़

**swarm**[2] /swɔːm स्वॉम्/ *verb* [I] to fly or move in large numbers झुंड बनाकर उड़ना या घूमना

PHR V **swarm with sb/sth** to be too crowded or full भीड़-भाड़ वाला या भरा हुआ होना

**swash** /swɒʃ स्वॉश्/ *noun* [*sing.*] the flow of water up the beach after a wave has broken लहर उतरने के बाद पानी के तट की ओर बहने की क्रिया; हिल्लोलन, उद्धावन ➪ **backwash** देखिए तथा **wave** पर चित्र देखिए।

**swat** /swɒt स्वॉट्/ *verb* [T] (**swatting; swatted**) to hit sth, especially an insect, with sth flat किसी चपटी चीज़ (जैसे फट्टी) से किसी को (विशेषतः कीड़े को) मारना

**swathe**[1] /sweɪð स्वेद्/ (*also* **swath**) *noun* [C] (*written*) a large strip or area of sth किसी वस्तु की चौड़ी पट्टी या बड़ा टुकड़ा *a swathe of hair/fabric/sunlight*

IDM **cut a swathe through sth** (of a person fire, etc.) to pass through a particular area destroying a large part of it (व्यक्ति या आग का) किसी विशिष्ट क्षेत्र से गुज़रना प्रायः उसके विस्तृत भाग को नष्ट करते हुए

**swathe**[2] /sweɪð स्वेद्/ *verb* [T] (*usually passive*) (*written*) **swathe sb/sth (in sth)** to wrap or cover sb/sth in sth किसी वस्तु व्यक्ति या वस्तु को किसी में लपेटना या से ढकना; पट्टी बाँधना *He was lying on the hospital bed swathed in bandages.*

**sway** /sweɪ/ *verb* 1 [I] to move slowly from side to side झूमना, डोलना (धीरे-धीरे, दाएँ-बाएँ हिलना) *The trees were swaying in the wind.* **2** [T] to influence sb किसी को प्रभावित करना, अपने से सहमत कराना *Many people were swayed by his convincing arguments.*

**swear** /sweə(r) स्वेअ(र्)/ *verb* (*pt* **swore** /swɔː(r) स्वॉ(र्)/; *pp* **sworn** /swɔːn स्वॉन्/) **1** [I] **swear**

**(at sb/sth)** to use rude or bad language गाली बकना, कोसना *He hit his thumb with the hammer and swore loudly.* ➪ **curse** देखिए। **2** [I, T] **swear (to do sth); swear that...** to make a serious promise क़सम खाना, शपथ लेना *When you give evidence in court you have to swear to tell the truth.*

PHR V **swear by sth** to believe completely in the value of sth किसी के महत्त्व में पूरा विश्वास रखना

**swear sb in** (*usually passive*) to make sb say officially that he/she will accept the responsibility of a new position औपचारिक रूप से किसी पद की शपथ दिलाना (दायित्व को पूरा करने की दृष्टि से) *The President will be sworn in next week.*

**swear word** (*old-fashioned* **oath**) *noun* [C] a word that is considered rude or bad and that may offend people गाली, अपशब्द

**sweat** /swet स्वेट्/ *verb* [I] **1** to produce liquid through your skin because you are hot, ill or afraid (गरमी या डर के कारण) पसीना निकलना या पसीना आना **2 sweat (over sth)** to work hard घोर परिश्रम करना *I've been sweating over that problem all day.* ▶ **sweat** *noun* [C, U] पसीना, स्वेद, प्रस्वेद *He wiped the sweat from his forehead.* ○ *He woke up in a sweat.* ➪ **perspiration** देखिए।

IDM **work/sweat your guts out** ➪ **gut**[1] देखिए।

**sweater** /ˈswetə(r) ˈस्वेट(र्)/ *noun* [C] a warm piece of clothing with long sleeves, often made of wool, which you wear on the top half of your body (ऊन का) स्वेटर, जर्सी (पूरी बाहों की)

> NOTE **Sweater, jumper, pullover** और **jersey** इन सबका एक ही अर्थ है। ये सब ऊन या उसी प्रकार की अन्य वस्तु से बनते हैं। **Sweatshirt** प्रायः कपास से बनती है और यह अनौपचारिक अवसरों पर या खेल के दौरान पहना जा सकता है। **Cardigan** वह है जिसके बटन आगे ऊपर से नीचे तक होते हैं।

**sweatshirt** /ˈswetʃɜ:t ˈस्वेट्शट्/ *noun* [C] a warm piece of cotton clothing with long sleeves, which you wear on the top half of your body पूरी बाहों की गरम कमीज़

**sweaty** /ˈsweti ˈस्वेटि/ *adj.* **1** wet with sweat पसीने से तर *I was hot and sweaty after the match and needed a shower.* **2** causing you to sweat पसीना लाने वाला *a hot sweaty day*

**swede** /swi:d स्वीड्/ *noun* [C, U] a large, round, yellow vegetable that grows under the ground ज़मीन के नीचे उगने वाली बड़ी, गोल पीली सब्ज़ी; स्वीड

**sweep**[1] /swi:p स्वीप्/ *verb* (*pt, pp* **swept** /swept स्वेप्ट्/) **1** [I, T] to clean the floor, etc. by moving dust, dirt, etc. away with a brush झाड़ या ब्रश से फ़र्श आदि साफ़ करना *to sweep the floor* ➪ **clean**[2] पर नोट देखिए। **2** [T] to remove sth from a surface using your hand, etc. हाथ आदि से किसी वस्तु को किसी सतह से हटाना *He swept the books angrily off the table.* **3** [I, T] to move quickly and smoothly over the area or in the direction mentioned किसी इलाक़े में या बताई गई दिशा में तेज़ी से और सहज भाव से चलना *Fire swept through the building.* **4** [T] to move or push sb/sth with a lot of force काफ़ी ज़ोर के साथ अपने स्थान से हिल जाना या किसी को हिला या धकेल देना *The huge waves swept her overboard.* ○ *He was swept along by the huge crowd.* **5** [I] to move in a way that impresses or is intended to impress people लोगों पर शान जमाते हुए या शान जमाने के इरादे से चलना, अकड़ कर चलना *Five big black Mercedes swept past us.* **6** [I, T] to move over an area, especially in order to look for sth किसी इलाक़े में घूमना या विचरना (विशेषतः किसी चीज़ का पता लगाने के लिए) *The army were sweeping the fields for mines.*

PHR V **sweep (sb/sth) aside** to not allow sb/sth to affect your progress or plans अपनी प्रगति या योजनाओं पर किसी का असर न पड़ने देना, किसी (संभावित बाधाकारी तत्त्व) को एक किनारे कर देना

**sweep sth out** to remove dirt and dust from the floor of a room or building using a brush कमरे के फ़र्श या इमारत को (झाड़ू या ब्रश से) बुहारना, झाड़ना (उसकी धूल और गंदगी हटाना)

**sweep over sb** (used about a feeling) to suddenly affect sb very strongly (किसी मनोभाव से) किसी का आक्रांत हो जाना

**sweep (sth) up** to remove dirt, dust, leaves, etc. using a brush झाड़ू या ब्रश से गंदगी, धूल, पत्ते आदि हटाना

**sweep**[2] /swi:p स्वीप्/ *noun* [C] **1** [*usually sing.*] the action of moving dirt and dust from a floor or surface using a brush झाड़ू या ब्रश से फ़र्श या सतह की सफ़ाई *I'd better give the floor a sweep.* **2** a long, curving shape or movement लंबी घुमावदार शकल या गति, घुमाव या मोड़ *He showed us which way to go with a sweep of his arm.* **3** a movement over an area, especially in order to look for sth किसी क्षेत्र में विचरने की क्रिया (विशेषतः किसी चीज़ का पता लगाने के लिए) **4** = **chimney sweep**

IDM **a clean sweep** ➪ **clean**[1] देखिए।

**sweeper** /ˈswi:pə(r) ˈस्वीप(र्)/ *noun* [C] **1** a person or thing that cleans surfaces with a brush झाड़ू या ब्रश से सफ़ाई करने वाला व्यक्ति या वस्तु, सफ़ाई-कर्मचारी या सफ़ाई उपकरण *He's a road sweeper.* ○ *Do you sell carpet sweepers?* **2** (in football) the defending player who plays behind the other defending players (फ़ुटबॉल में) (आगे की) रक्षक-पंक्ति के पीछे खेलने वाला (रक्षक) खिलाड़ी; स्वीपर

**sweeping** /ˈswi:pɪŋ ˈस्वीपिङ्/ *adj.* **1** (used about statements, etc.) too general and not accurate enough (वक्तव्य आदि) अति सामान्य और पूरी तरह सही नहीं या अतिरंजित *He made a sweeping statement about all politicians being dishonest.* **2** having a great and important effect बहुत असरदार या प्रभावशाली; व्यापक *sweeping reforms*

**sweet[1]** /swi:t स्वीट्/ *adj.* **1** containing, or tasting as if it contains, a lot of sugar मधुर, मीठा (चीनी भरा), मीठा या मधुर लगने वाला *Children usually like sweet things.* ○ *This cake's too sweet.* ➪ **savoury** देखिए। **2** (used especially about children and small things) attractive (बच्चे और छोटी चीज़ें) आकर्षक, सुंदर *a sweet little kitten* ○ *Isn't that little girl sweet?* ✪ पर्याय **cute** **3** having or showing a kind character सौम्य, सदय या आत्मीयतापूर्ण, मधुर *a sweet smile* ○ *It's very sweet of you to remember my birthday!* **4** (used about a smell or a sound) pleasant भीनी (गंध) या श्रुति-मधुर (ध्वनि) ▶ **sweetness** *noun* [U] माधुर्य, मिठास

**IDM** **have a sweet tooth** to like eating sweet things मीठी चीज़ें खाना पसंद करना

**sweet[2]** /swi:t स्वीट्/ *noun* **1** [C, *usually pl.*] (*AmE* **candy** [U]) a small piece of boiled sugar, chocolate, etc., often sold in a packet (पश्चिमी देशों में प्रचलित) मिठाई कैंडी (जो चीनी, चॉकलेट आदि को उबालकर बनाई जाती है और पैकेट में बिकती है) *a sweet shop* **2** [C, U] sweet food served at the end of a meal भोजन के अंत में परसी गई मीठी चीज़ (खीर आदि) ➪ **pudding** और **dessert** देखिए।

**sweetcorn** /ˈswi:tkɔ:n ˈस्वीट्कॉन्/ (*AmE* **corn**) *noun* [U] yellow grains from a tall plant (**maize**) that taste sweet and are eaten as a vegetable मीठी मकई

**sweeten** /ˈswi:tn ˈस्वीट्न्/ *verb* [T] to make sth sweet by adding sugar, etc. किसी वस्तु को मीठा करना (उसमें चीनी आदि डालकर)

**sweetener** /ˈswi:tnə(r) ˈस्वीट्न(र्)/ *noun* [C, U] a substance used instead of sugar for making food or drink sweet खाद्य या पेय को मीठा बनाने वाला पदार्थ (चीनी का विकल्प) *artificial sweeteners*

**sweetheart** /ˈswi:thɑ:t ˈस्वीट्हाट्/ *noun* [C] **1** used when speaking to sb, especially a child, in a very friendly way दुलार में प्रयुक्त शब्द (विशेषतः बच्चे के लिए) *Do you want a drink, sweetheart?* **2** (*old-fashioned*) a boyfriend or girlfriend प्रेमी या प्रेमिका; जानेमन

**sweetly** /ˈswi:tli ˈस्वीट्लि/ *adv.* in an attractive, kind or pleasant way आकर्षक, आत्मीय या मधुर ढंग से *She smiled sweetly.* ○ *sweetly scented flowers*

**sweet potato** *noun* [C, U] a vegetable that grows under the ground and looks like a red potato, but is yellow inside and tastes sweet शकरकंद

**swell[1]** /swel स्वेल्/ *verb* (*pt* **swelled** /sweld स्वेल्ड्/; *pp* **swollen** /ˈswəʊlən ˈस्वोलन्/ or **swelled**) **1** [I, T] **swell (up)** to become or to make sth bigger, fuller or thicker (किसी का) फूलना या (किसी को) फुलाना *After the fall her ankle began to swell up.* ○ *Heavy rain had swollen the rivers.* **2** [I, T] to increase or make sth increase in number or size (संख्या या आकार में) किसी की वृद्धि होना या करना; बढ़ जाना या बढ़ा देना *The crowd swelled to 600 by the end of the evening.* **3** [I] (*written*) (used about feelings or sound) to suddenly become stronger or louder एकाएक (भावनाओं का) तीव्र हो जाना या (आवाज़ का) ऊँचा हो जाना *Hatred swelled inside him.*

**swell[2]** /swel स्वेल्/ *noun* [*sing.*] the slow movement up and down of the surface of the sea समुद्र तल का क्रमशः घटना-बढ़ना

**swelling** /ˈswelɪŋ ˈस्वेलिङ्/ *noun* **1** [C] a place on your body that is bigger or fatter than usual because of an injury or illness (चोट या बीमारी के कारण) शरीर के किसी अंग में सूजन; फुलाव, बढ़ाव, उभार *I've got a nasty swelling under my eye.* **2** [U] the process of becoming swollen सूज जाने की क्रिया; सूजन, शोध *The disease often causes swelling of the ankles and knees.*

**sweltering** /ˈsweltərɪŋ ˈस्वेल्टरिङ्/ *adj.* (*informal*) much too hot गज़ब का गरम, भीषण गरम *It was sweltering in the office today.*

**swept** ➪ **sweep[1]** का past tense और past participle रूप

**swerve** /swɜ:v स्वव्/ *verb* [I] to change direction suddenly अचानक दिशा बदल देना या मुड़ जाना *The car swerved to avoid the child.* ▶ **swerve** *noun* [C] मोड़, घुमाव, पथ-विचलन

**swift** /swɪft स्विफ़्ट्/ *adj.* happening without delay; quick द्रुत, अविलंब घटित; तेज़, शीघ्र *a swift reaction/decision/movement* ○ *a swift runner* ▶ **swiftly** *adv.* तेज़ी से, द्रुत गति से

**swill** /swɪl स्विल्/ *verb* [T] **swill sth (out/down)** to wash sth by pouring large amounts of water, etc. into, over or through it (किसी वस्तु के अंदर, ऊपर या उसमें से पानी आदि) ढेर-सा डालकर या गुज़ार कर उसे साफ़ करना

**swim** /swɪm स्विम्/ *verb* (*pres. part.* **swimming;** *pt* **swam** /swæm स्वैम्/; *pp* **swum** /swʌm स्वम्/) **1** [I, T] to move your body through water तैरना *How far can you swim?* ○ *Hundreds of tiny fish swam past.*

**NOTE** मौज-मस्ती के लिए तैरने को **go swimming** कहते हैं—*We go swimming every Saturday.* तैरने के किसी विशेष अवसर की बात हो तो **go for a swim** का प्रयोग होगा—*I went for a swim this morning.*

**2** [I] **be swimming (in/with sth)** to be covered with a lot of liquid किसी वस्तु का द्रव से भर जाना, द्रव में किसी वस्तु का तैरना *The salad was swimming in oil.* **3** [I] to seem to be moving or turning चक्कर काटता या घूमता लगना या महसूस होना *The floor began to swim before my eyes and I fainted.* **4** [I] (used about your head) to feel confused (मस्तिष्क का) उलझन में पड़ जाना; चकरा जाना *My head was swimming with so much new information.* ▶ **swim** *noun* [*sing.*] तैराई, तैराक़ी *to go for/have a swim* ▶ **swimmer** *noun* [C] तैराक *a strong/weak swimmer*

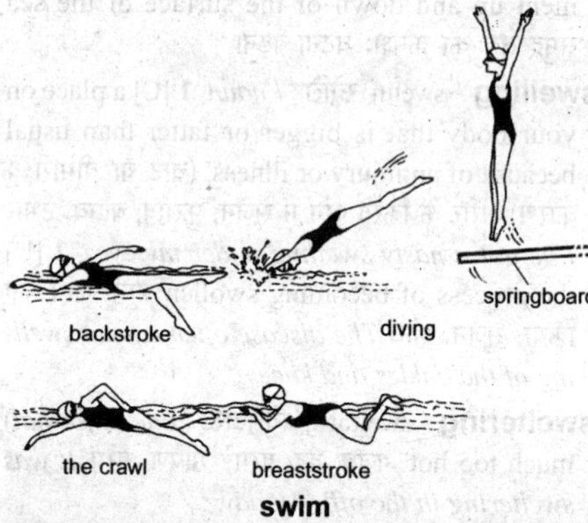

**swim**

**swimming bath** *noun* [C] (*also* **swimming baths**) [*pl.*] a public swimming pool, usually indoors सार्वजनिक तरण-ताल या स्विमिंग पूल (प्रायः भवन के अंदर)

**swimming pool** (*also* **pool**) *noun* [C] a pool that is built especially for people to swim in विशेषतः लोगों के तैरने के लिए बनाया गया तालाब, तरण-ताल; स्विमिंग पूल *an indoor/outdoor/open-air swimming pool*

**swimming trunks** *noun* [*pl.*] a piece of clothing like shorts that a man wears to go swimming पुरुषों की तैराक़ी की पोशाक (निक्कर या जाँघिये जैसी) *a pair of swimming trunks*

**swimsuit** /ˈswɪmsuːt ˈस्विम्सूट्/ (*also* **swimming costume**) *noun* [C] a piece of clothing that a woman wears to go swimming महिलाओं की तैराक़ी की पोशाक ➪ **bikini** देखिए।

**swindle** /ˈswɪndl ˈस्विन्ड्ल्/ *verb* [T] **swindle sb/sth (out of sth)** to trick sb in order to get money, etc. किसी से पैसा आदि ठगना या ऐंठ लेना ▶ **swindle** *noun* [C] ठगी, धोखेबाज़ी *a tax swindle*

**swine** /swaɪn स्वाइन्/ *noun* **1** [C] (*informal*) a very unpleasant person बेहद गंदा या बुरा आदमी **2** [*pl.*] (*old-fashioned*) pigs सूअर

**swing**[1] /swɪŋ स्विङ्/ *verb* (*pt, pp* **swung** /swʌŋ स्वङ्/) **1** [I, T] to move backwards and forwards or from side to side while hanging from sth; to make sb/sth move in this way झूलना; झुलाना *The rope was swinging from a branch.* **2** [I, T] to move or make sb/sth move in a curve गोलाई में मुड़ जाना या किसी वस्तु को मोड़ देना *The door swung open and Ravi walked in.* **3** [I] to move or change from one position or situation towards the opposite one एक दशा या स्थिति से विपरीत दशा या स्थिति में जाना या बदलना, घूम जाना *She swung round when she heard the door open.* ○ *His moods swing from one extreme to the other.* **4** [I, T] **swing (sth) (at sb/sth)** to try to hit sb/sth किसी को मारने की कोशिश करना, किसी पर घूँसा तानना

**swing**[2] /swɪŋ स्विङ्/ *noun* **1** [*sing.*] a swinging movement or rhythm झूलने की गति, लय या उतार-चढ़ाव *He took a swing at the ball.* **2** [C] a seat, a piece of rope, etc. that is hung from above so that you can swing backwards and forwards on it झूला, हिंडोला *Some children were playing on the swings.* **3** [C] a change from one position or situation towards the opposite one (झूले का) पेंग (झूले में एक दशा स्थिति से विपरीत दशा या स्थिति में जाना)

**IDM** **in full swing** ➪ **full**[1] देखिए।

**swipe** /swaɪp स्वाइप्/ *verb* **1** [I, T] (*informal*) **swipe (at) sb/sth** to hit or try to hit sb/sth by moving your arm in a curve बाँह को घुमाकर किसी को मारना या मारने की कोशिश करना *He swiped at the wasp with a newspaper but missed.* **2** [T] (*informal*) to steal sth कोई चीज़ चुरा लेना **3** [T] to pass the part of a plastic card on which information is stored through a special machine for reading it (क्रेडिट कार्ड आदि) प्लास्टिक कार्ड को विशेष मशीन में से गुज़ारना (ताकि वह कार्ड में अंकित सूचना-सामग्री को ग्रहण कर ले) स्वाइप *The receptionist swiped my credit card and handed me the slip to sign.* ▶ **swipe** *noun* [C] बाँह घुमाकर प्रहार *She took a swipe at him with her handbag.*

**swipe card** *noun* [C] a small plastic card on which information is stored which can be read by an electronic machine सूचना-सामग्री युक्त एक विशेष छोटा प्लास्टिक कार्ड (जिसमें संचित सूचना को इलेक्ट्रॉनिक मशीन ग्रहण करती है); स्वाइप कार्ड

**swirl** /swɜːl स्वल् / *verb* [I, T] to make or cause sth to make fast circular movements चक्कर खाते हुए घूमना या (किसी को) घुमाना *Her long skirt swirled round her legs as she danced.* ▶ **swirl** *noun* [C] चक्कर

**swish**[1] /swɪʃ स्विश् / *verb* [I, T] to move quickly through the air in a way that makes a soft sound; to make sth do this हवा में इस प्रकार गतिशील होना की सरसराहट की आवाज हो; किसी वस्तु से सरसराहट करना *Her dress swished as she walked past us.*

**swish**[2] /swɪʃ स्विश् / *noun* [*sing.*] the movement or soft sound made by sth moving quickly, especially through the air सरसराहट *She turned away with a swish of her skirt.*

**switch**[1] /swɪtʃ स्विच् / *noun* [C] **1** a small button or sth similar that you press up or down in order to turn on electricity बिजली का बटन या स्विच (जिसे ऊपर-नीचे दबाकर बिजली जलाई-बुझाई जाती है) *a light switch* **2** a sudden change अचानक (का) परिवर्तन *a switch in policy*

**switch**[2] /swɪtʃ स्विच् / *verb* [I, T] **1 switch (sth) (over) (to sth); switch (between A and B)** to change or be changed from one thing to another एक से दूसरी वस्तु में बदलना या बदला जाना, अदला-बदली करना या होना *The match has been switched from Saturday to Sunday.* **2 switch (sth) (with sb/ sth); switch (sth) (over/round)** to exchange positions, activities, etc. पद, क्रिया-कलाप आदि में अदल-बदल या विनिमय करना *Someone switched the signs round and everyone went the wrong way.*

**PHR V** **switch (sth) off/on** to press a switch in order to start/stop electric power बिजली जलाने या बुझाने के लिए बटन दबाना *Don't forget to switch off the cooker.*

**switch (sth) over** to change to a different television programme टीवी कार्यक्रम को बदलना

**switchboard** /ˈswɪtʃbɔːd ˈस्विच्बॉड् / *noun* [C] the place in a large company, etc. where all the telephone calls are connected किसी कंपनी के दफ़्तर में ऐसा स्थान जहाँ सारे फ़ोन कॉल आते हैं; स्विचबोर्ड

**swivel** /ˈswɪvl ˈस्विवल् / *verb* [I, T] (**swivelling; swivelled** *AmE* **swiveling; swiveled**) **swivel (sth) (round)** to turn around a central point; to make sth do this एक केंद्रीय बिंदु पर चारों ओर घूमना; किसी को इस प्रकार घुमाना *She swivelled round to face me.*

**swollen**[1] ➪ **swell**[1] का past participle रूप

**swollen**[2] /ˈswəʊlən ˈस्वोलन् / *adj.* thicker or wider than usual सूजा हुआ, फूला हुआ या उभारदार *Her leg was badly swollen after the accident.*

**swoon** /swuːn स्वून् / *verb* [I] **1 swoon (over sb)** to feel very excited, emotional, etc. about sb that you think is attractive so that you almost lose consciousness किसी व्यक्ति के प्रति (प्रायः कामुक भाव से) अत्यंत उत्तेजित या भावुक आदि होना तथा लगभग होश खो बैठना **2** (*old-fashioned*) to lose consciousness मूर्छित होना ✪ पर्याय **faint** ▶ **swoon** *noun* [*sing.*] (*old-fashioned*) to go into a swoon बेहोशी, ग़श

**swoop** /swuːp स्वूप् / *verb* [I] **1** to fly or move down suddenly झपट्टा मारना (एकाएक नीचे की ओर उड़ कर आना या गति करना) *The bird swooped down on its prey.* **2** (used especially about the police or the army) to visit or capture sb/sth without warning (विशेषतः पुलिस या सेना का) किसी पर झपटना (बिना चेतावनी दिए किसी के पास पहुँचना या उसे पकड़ लेना) *Police swooped at dawn and arrested the man.* ▶ **swoop** *noun* [C] झपट्टा **a swoop (on sb/sth)**

**swop** = **swap**

**sword** /sɔːd सॉड् / *noun* [C] a long, very sharp metal weapon, like a large knife तलवार, कटार

**swordfish** /ˈsɔːdfɪʃ ˈसॉड्फ़िश् / *noun* [C, U] (*pl.* **swordfish**) a large sea fish that you can eat, with a very long thin sharp upper jaw खाने की एक बड़ी समुद्री मछली (जिसकी ऊपरी दाढ़, तलवार जैसी, बहुत लंबी, पतली और धारदार होती है) तेगामछली

**swore** ➪ **swear** का past tense रूप

**sworn** ➪ **swear** का past participle रूप

**swot**[1] स्वॉट् /swɒt/ *verb* [I, T] (**swotting; swotted**) (*informal*) **swot (up) (for/on sth); swot sth up** to study sth very hard, especially to prepare for an exam जम कर पढ़ाई करना (विशेषतः परीक्षा की तैयारी के लिए) *She's swotting for her final exams.*

**swot**[2] /swɒt स्वॉट् / *noun* [C] (*informal*) a person who studies too hard जम कर पढ़ाई करने वाला व्यक्ति; पढ़ाकू

**swum** ➪ **swim** का past participle रूप

**swung** ➪ **swing**[1] का past tense, और past participle रूप

**sycophant** /ˈsɪkəfænt ˈसिइकफ़ैन्ट् / *noun* [C] (*formal*) (*disapproving*) a person who praises important or powerful people too much and in a way that is not sincere, especially in order to get sth from them (अमान्य) चापलूस, चाटुकार, पराश्रयी, चमचा *The leader is surrounded by sycophants.* ▶ **sycophancy** /ˈsɪkəfənsi ˈसिइकफ़न्सि / *noun* (*formal*) *disapproving* चापलूसी, चाटुकारिता, चमचेबाज़ी

**syllable** /ˈsɪləbl ˈसिलब्ल् / *noun* [C] a word or part of a word which contains one vowel sound शब्द या शब्दांश जिसमें केवल एक स्वर हो, अक्षर; सिलेबल *'Mat' has one syllable and 'mattress' has two syllables.* ○ *The stress in 'international' is on the third syllable.*

**syllabus** /ˈsɪləbəs ˈसिलबस् / *noun* [C] (*pl.* **syllabuses**) a list of subjects, etc. that are included in a course of study किसी पाठ्यक्रम में निर्धारित विषयों की सूची; पाठ्यक्रम-विवरण, पाठ्य-विवरण ➪ **curriculum** देखिए।

**symbol** /ˈsɪmbl ˈसिम्बल् / *noun* [C] **1 a symbol (of sth)** a sign, object, etc. which represents sth किसी का प्रतिनिधित्व करने वाला चिह्न, वस्तु आदि, प्रतीक *The cross is the symbol of Christianity.* **2 a symbol (for sth)** a letter, number or sign that has a particular meaning वर्ण या अक्षर, अंक या चिह्न जो किसी विशेष अर्थ को प्रकट करे; संकेत *O is the symbol for oxygen.*

**symbolic** /sɪmˈbɒlɪk सिम्ˈबॉलिक् / (*also* **symbolical** /sɪmˈbɒlɪkl सिम्ˈबॉलिकल् /) *adj.* used or seen to represent sth किसी के प्रतीक के रूप में प्रयुक्त या गृहीत, प्रतीकी, द्योतक, प्रतीकात्मक *The white dove is symbolic of peace.* ▶ **symbolically** /-bɒlɪkli -बॉलिक्लि / *adv.* प्रतीकात्मक रूप से, सांकेतिक रूप से

**symbolism** /ˈsɪmbəlɪzəm ˈसिम्बलिज़म् / *noun* [U] the use of symbols to represent things, especially in art and literature वस्तुओं का प्रतिनिधित्व करने के लिए प्रतीकों का प्रयोग (विशेषतः कला और साहित्य में); प्रतीकवाद, प्रतीकात्मकता

**symbolize** (*also* **-ise**) /ˈsɪmbəlaɪz ˈसिम्बलाइज़् / *verb* [T] to represent sth किसी का प्रतीक होना *The deepest notes in music are often used to symbolize danger or despair.*

**symmetrical** /sɪˈmetrɪkl सिˈमेट्रिकल् / (*also* **symmetric** /sɪˈmetrɪk सिˈमेट्रिक् /) *adj.* having two halves that match each other exactly in size, shape, etc. (आकार, आकृति आदि की दृष्टि से) जिसके दो अर्धांश पूर्णतया एक जैसे हों या मेल खाएँ; सममित, प्रतिसम ✪ विलोम **asymmetric** ▶ **symmetrically** /-kli -क्लि / *adv.* सममिति के साथ, सममित होकर

**symmetry** /ˈsɪmətri ˈसिमट्रि / *noun* [U] the state of having two halves that match each other exactly in size, shape, etc. (आकार, आकृति आदि की दृष्टि से) (एक वस्तु के) दो अर्धांशों का पूर्णतया एक जैसा होना या मेल खाना; सममिति, प्रतिसमता, सुडौलपन

**sympathetic** /ˌsɪmpəˈθetɪk ˌसिम्पˈथ्रेटिक् / *adj.* **1 sympathetic (to/towards sb)** showing that you understand other people's feelings, especially their problems सहानुभूतिपूर्ण, हमदर्द *When Shamma was ill, everyone was very sympathetic.*

> **NOTE** अंग्रेज़ी में **sympathetic** से 'मैत्रीपूर्ण और सुखद' का अर्थ कथित नहीं होता, इस अर्थ में उपयुक्त शब्द **nice** है—*I met Alex's sister yesterday. She's very nice.*

**2 sympathetic (to sb/sth)** being in agreement with or supporting sb/sth किसी से सहमत होते या उसे समर्थन देते हुए *I explained our ideas but she wasn't sympathetic to them.* ✪ विलोम **unsympathetic** ▶ **sympathetically** /ˌsɪmpəˈθetɪkli ˌसिम्पˈथ्रेटिक्लि / *adv.* सहानुभूतिपूर्वक, हमदर्दी के साथ

**sympathize** (*also* **-ise**) /ˈsɪmpəθaɪz ˈसिम्पथाइज़् / *verb* [I] **sympathize (with sb/sth) 1** to feel sorry for sb; to show that you understand sb's problems किसी के दुख में शरीक होना, (से) सहानुभूति होना; किसी की समस्याओं को समझना और समझ को व्यवहार में प्रकट करना *I sympathize with her, but I don't know what I can do to help.* **2** to support sb/sth किसी को स्वीकृति या समर्थन देना *I find it difficult to sympathize with his opinions.*

**sympathizer** (*also* **-iser**) /ˈsɪmpəθaɪzə(r) ˈसिम्पथाइज़(र्) / *noun* [C] a person who agrees with and supports an idea or aim किसी विचार या उद्देश्य को स्वीकृति और समर्थन देने वाला व्यक्ति; समर्थक

**sympathy** /ˈsɪmpəθi ˈसिम्पथि / *noun* (*pl.* **sympathies**) **1** [U] **sympathy (for/towards sb)** an understanding of other people's feelings, especially their problems सहानुभूति, हमदर्दी (दूसरों की भावनाओं, विशेषतः समस्याओं, की समझ) *Everyone **feels** great **sympathy** for the victims of the attack.* **2 sympathies** [*pl.*] feelings of support or agreement समर्थन या स्वीकृति के भाव

**IDM in sympathy (with sb/sth)** in agreement, showing that you support or approve of sb/sth किसी के साथ सहानुभूति (समर्थन या अनुमोदन) प्रकट करते हुए *Train drivers stopped work in sympathy with the striking bus drivers.*

**symphony** /ˈsɪmfəni ˈसिम्फ़नि / *noun* [C] (*pl.* **symphonies**) a long piece of music written for a large orchestra बड़े वाद्यवृंद के लिए तैयार की गई लंबी संगीत-रचना; सिंफ़नी

**symposium** /sɪmˈpəʊziəm सिम्ˈपोज़िअम्/ *noun* (*pl.* **symposia** or **symposiums**) **symposium (on sth)** a meeting at which experts have discussions about a particular subject; a conference विशिष्ट विषय पर विशेषज्ञों द्वारा विचार-गोष्ठी; परिचर्चा, संगोष्ठी

**symptom** /ˈsɪmptəm ˈसिम्प्टम्/ *noun* [C] **1** a change in your body that is a sign of illness रोग का चिह्न; लक्षण *The symptoms of flu include a headache, a high temperature and aches in the body.* **2** a sign (that sth bad is happening or exists) (किसी ख़राबी का) लक्षण ▶ **symptomatic** /ˌsɪmptəˈmætɪk ˌसिम्प्टˈमैटिक्/ *adj.* रोगसूचक, लक्षणात्मक

**synagogue** /ˈsɪnəgɒg ˈसिनगॉग्/ *noun* [C] a building where Jewish people go to pray or to study their religion यहूदियों का प्रार्थना-गृह या धर्मशिक्षा-स्थल; सिनगॉग

**synchronize** (*also* **-ise**) /ˈsɪŋkrənaɪz ˈसिङ्क्रनाइज़्/ *verb* [T] to make sth happen or work at the same time or speed एक ही समय में कुछ घटित होने देना या एक ही गति से कोई काम करना, दो (या अधिक) वस्तुओं या क्रियाओं का समकालिक या समान गति वाला होना *We synchronized our watches to make sure we agreed what the time was.*

**syncline** /ˈsɪŋklaɪn ˈसिङ्क्लाइन्/ *noun* [C] (*technical*) (in geology) an area of ground where layers of rock in the earth's surface have been folded into a curve that is lower in the middle than at the ends (भूविज्ञान में) भूमि का वह खंड जहाँ सतही चट्टानों की परतें मुड़कर बीच में से नीची हो जाती हैं; अभिनति ➪ **anticline** देखिए।

**syndicate** /ˈsɪndɪkət ˈसिन्डिकट्/ *noun* [C] a group of people or companies that work together in order to achieve a particular aim विशेष लक्ष्य की प्राप्ति के लिए एक साथ काम करने वाले व्यक्तियों या कंपनियों का समूह, व्यवसाय-संघ; सिंडिकेट

**syndrome** /ˈsɪndrəʊm ˈसिन्ड्रोम्/ *noun* [C] **1** a group of signs or changes in the body that are typical of an illness किसी रोग के विशिष्ट लक्षणों का समुच्चय *Down's syndrome* ○ *Acquired Immune Deficiency Syndrome* (*AIDS*) **2** a set of opinions or a way of behaving that is typical of a particular type of person, attitude or social problem विशिष्ट व्यक्ति, मनोवृति या सामाजिक समस्या की विशिष्टता की द्योतक धारणाएँ या कार्यशैली

**synonym** /ˈsɪnənɪm ˈसिननिम्/ *noun* [C] a word or phrase that has the same meaning as another word or phrase in the same language पर्यायवाची, समानार्थी शब्द *'Big' and 'large' are synonyms.* ➪ **antonym** देखिए। ▶ **synonymous** /sɪˈnɒnɪməs सिˈनॉनिमस्/ *adj.* **synonymous (with sth)** पर्याय, समानार्थक

**synopsis** /sɪˈnɒpsɪs सिˈनॉप्सिस्/ *noun* [C] (*pl.* **synopses** /-siːz सीज़्/) a **summary** of a piece of writing, a play, etc. किसी खेल, नाटक आदि का सार या संक्षेप; रूपरेखा ▶ **synoptic** /sɪˈnɒptɪk सिˈनॉप्टिक्/ *adj.* (*formal*) सारपरक, संक्षेपात्मक

**synovial** /saɪˈnəʊviəl साइˈनोविअल्/ *adj.* (*technical*) connected with a type of (**joint**) that has a piece of very thin skin (**membrane**) containing liquid between the bones, which allows the joint to move freely हड्डियों के झिल्लीदार जोड़ से संबंधित (झिल्लियों में निहित द्रव के कारण जोड़ खुलकर हिलते-डुलते हैं); संधि-स्नेहकी *a synovial joint/membrane* ➪ **arm** पर चित्र देखिए।

**syntax** /ˈsɪntæks ˈसिन्टैक्स्/ *noun* [U] the system of rules for the structure of a sentence in a language किसी भाषा के वाक्य के रचना में निहित नियमों की व्यवस्था; भाषा की वाक्य व्यवस्था

**synthesis** /ˈsɪnθəsɪs ˈसिन्थसिस्/ *noun* (*pl.* **syntheses** /-siːz -सीज़्/) **1** [U, C] **(a) synthesis (of sth)** the act of combining separate ideas, beliefs, styles, etc.; a mixture or combination of ideas, beliefs, styles, etc. भिन्न-भिन्न विचारों, धारणाओं, शैलियों आदि की समन्वित करने का कार्य, संयोजन, संश्लेषण; (भिन्न-भिन्न) विचारों, धारणाओं, शैलियों आदि का सम्मिश्रण, या समन्वय या संश्लेष *the synthesis of traditional and modern values* ○ *a synthesis of art with everyday life* **2** [U] (*technical*) the natural chemical production of a substance in animals and plants पशुओं और पौधों में किसी रासायनिक पदार्थ का प्राकृतिक रीति से उत्पादन *protein synthesis* **3** [U] (*technical*) the artificial production of a substance that is present naturally in animals and plants पशुओं और पौधों में प्राकृतिक रूप से विद्यमान (रासायनिक) पदार्थ का कृत्रिम रीति से उत्पादन *the synthesis of penicillin* **4** [U] the production of sounds, music or speech by electronic means इलेक्ट्रॉनिक उपकरणों की सहायता से ध्वनि, संगीत या मौखिक माध्यम की भाषा को उत्पन्न करने की क्रिया *digital/sound/speech synthesis*

**synthesize** (*also* **-ise**) /ˈsɪnθəsaɪz ˈसिन्थसाइज़्/ *verb* [T] **1** (*technical*) to produce a substance by artificial means किसी पदार्थ को कृत्रिम विधि से तैयार करना या बनाना **2** to produce sounds, music or speech using electronic equipment इलेक्ट्रॉनिक उपकरणों की सहायता से ध्वनि, संगीत या भाषा की मौखिक अभिव्यक्ति को उत्पन्न या व्यक्त करना **3** to combine separate ideas, beliefs, styles, etc. भिन्न-भिन्न विचारों, धारणाओं, शैलियों आदि को समन्वित या संयोजित करना

**synthesizer** (*also* **-iser**) /ˈsɪnθəsaɪzə(r) ˈसिन्थ़साइज़(र्)/ *noun* [C] an electronic musical instrument that can produce a wide variety of different sounds एक इलेक्ट्रॉनिक वाद्य जो भिन्न-भिन्न प्रकार की अनेक विध ध्वनियों को उत्पन्न करता है; सिंथसाइज़र

**synthetic** /sɪnˈθetɪk सिन्ˈथ़ेटिक्/ *adj.* made by a chemical process; not natural रासायनिक प्रक्रिया से निर्मित; कृत्रिम *synthetic materials/fibres* ▶ **synthetically** /sɪnˈθetɪkli सिन्ˈथ़ेटिक्लि/ *adv.* रासायनिक प्रक्रिया से निर्मित होकर, कृत्रिम रूप से

**syphilis** /ˈsɪfɪlɪs ˈसिफ़िलिस्/ *noun* [U] a serious disease that passes from one person to another by sexual contact गरमी, उपदंश, आतशक, (यौन-संसर्ग से उत्पन्न यौन रोग)

**syphon** = **siphon**

**syringe** /sɪˈrɪndʒ सिˈरिन्ज्/ *noun* [C] **1** a plastic or glass tube with a needle that is used for taking a small amount of blood out of the body or for putting drugs into the body प्लास्टिक या काँच से बनी सूई से युक्त एक नली; सिरिंज (इंजेक्शन लगाने के लिए प्रयुक्त) **2** a plastic or glass tube with a rubber part at the end, used for sucking up liquid and then pushing it out प्लास्टिक या काँच की पिचकारी ➪ **laboratory** पर चित्र देखिए।

**syrup** /ˈsɪrəp ˈसिरप्/ *noun* [U] a thick sweet liquid, often made by boiling sugar with water or fruit juice चाशनी, शीरा *peaches in syrup* ➪ **treacle** देखिए।

**system** /ˈsɪstəm ˈसिस्टम्/ *noun* **1** [C] a set of ideas or rules for organizing sth; a particular way of doing sth विचारों या नियमों की व्यवस्था; कुछ करने की विशिष्ट रीति; प्रणाली *We have a new computerized system in the library.* ○ *the education system.* **2** [C] a group of things or parts that work together वस्तुओं या पुरजों का समूह जो व्यवस्थित रीति से काम करता है, प्रणाली, सिस्टम *a central heating system* ○ *a transport system* **3** [C] the body of a person or animal; parts of the body that work together मनुष्य या पशु का शरीर; शरीर के अंग जो व्यवस्थित रीति से काम करते हैं, प्रणाली *the central nervous system* **4 the system** [*sing.*] (*informal*) the traditional methods and rules of a society समाज की परम्परागत प्रथाएँ और नियम, सामाजिक व्यवस्था, समाज *You can't* ***beat the system*** (= you must accept these rules).

IDM **get sth out of your system** (*informal*) to do sth to free yourself of a strong feeling or emotion तीव्र अनुभूति या मनोभाव के प्रभाव से अपने को मुक्त करना, अपना मन हलका करना

**systematic** /ˌsɪstəˈmætɪk ˌसिस्टˈमैटिक्/ *adj.* done using a fixed plan or method निश्चित योजना या विधि से किया गया; सुव्यवस्थित, योजनानुसार *a systematic search* ▶ **systematically** /-kli -क्लि/ *adv.* व्यवस्थित रीति से, योजनानुसार

**systemic** /sɪˈstemɪk; sɪˈstiːmɪk सिˈस्टेमिक्; सिˈस्टीमिक्/ *adj.* (*technical*) **1** affecting or connected with the whole of sth, especially the human body किसी वस्तु (विशेषतः मानव-शरीर) को उसकी पूर्णता में प्रभावित करते हुए उससे संबंधित, व्यवस्थात्मक या व्यवस्थापरक; सर्वांगी, दैहिक **2** systemic chemicals or drugs that are used to treat diseases in plants or animals enter the body of the plant or animal and spread to all parts of it व्यवस्थात्मक, सर्वांगी, दैहिक रसायन या औषधियाँ (जो पशुओं और पौधों के रोगोपचार के लिए प्रयुक्त होती हैं और इस प्रक्रिया में उनके सारे शरीर में फैल जाती हैं) *systemic weedkillers* ▶ **systemically** /-kli -क्लि/ *adv.* सर्वांगी या व्यवस्थात्मक रीति से

**systems analyst** *noun* [C] (*computing*) a person whose job is to look carefully at the needs of a business company or an organization and then design the best way of working and completing tasks using computer programs सिस्टम एनेलिस्ट (वह व्यक्ति जो किसी व्यापारिक कंपनी या संस्था की आवश्यकताओं का अध्ययन कर, कंप्यूटर कार्यक्रमों की सहायता से, कार्य-निष्पादन हेतु, सर्वोत्तम कार्य-प्रणाली तैयार करता है)

# T t

**T, t**[1] /ti: टी / *noun* [C, U] (*pl.* **T's**; **t's** /ti:z टीज़्/) the twentieth letter of the English alphabet अंग्रेज़ी वर्णमाला का बीसवाँ अक्षर *'Table' begins with a 'T'.*

**t**[2] (*AmE* **tn**) *abbr.* ton(s), tonne(s) टन *5t coal*

**ta** /tɑ: टा / *exclamation* (*BrE informal*) thank you धन्यवाद, शुक्रिया

**tab** /tæb टैब् / *noun* [C] **1** a small piece of cloth, metal or paper that is fixed to the edge of sth to help you open, hold or identify it किसी वस्तु को खोलने, पकड़ने या पहचानने के लिए उसके सिरे पर लगाया गया कपड़े, धातु या काग़ज़ का टुकड़ा *You open the tin by pulling the metal tab.* **2** the money that you owe for food, drink, etc. in a bar, cafe or restaurant; the bill मदिरालय, छोटे-जलपानगृह या रेस्तराँ में खाद्य, पेय आदि की देय क़ीमत; बिल

**IDM** **keep tabs on sb/sth** (*informal*) to watch sb/sth carefully; to check sth किसी पर निगाह रखना, (की) सावधानी से निगरानी करना; किसी की जाँच करना

**tabla** *noun* [C] a pair of small hand drums, one of which is slightly larger than the other, used in Indian classical music तबला ➪ पृष्ठ 789 पर चित्र देखिए।

**table** /ˈteɪbl टेब्ल् / *noun* [C] **1** a piece of furniture with a flat top supported by legs मेज़ *a dining/bedside/coffee/kitchen table*

> **NOTE** जब हम मेज़ पर चीज़ें रखते हैं तो **on the table** प्रयुक्त किया जाता है परंतु मेज़ के चारों ओर बैठने के लिए **at the table** प्रयुक्त किया जाता है।

**2** a list of facts or figures, usually arranged in rows and columns down a page तथ्यों या आकृतियों की तालिका, सारणी *Table 3 shows the results.*

**tableau** /ˈtæbləʊ ˈटैब्लो / *noun* [C] (*pl.* **tableaux** /ˈtæbləʊz ˈटैब्लोज़् /) **1** a scene showing, for example, events and people from history, that is presented by a group of actors who do not move or speak इतिहास की घटनाओं और पात्रों को दर्शाने वाला मूक-दृश्य, जो अभिनेताओं का समूह मूक-अभिनय द्वारा प्रस्तुत करता है; झाँकी *The procession included a tableau of the Battle of Panipat.* **2** a work of art showing a group of people, animals, etc. often carved out of stone कलाकृति (जन समूह, पशु समूह आदि दर्शाती हुई) विशेषतः पत्थर से तराशी हुई

**tablecloth** /ˈteɪblklɒθ ˈटेब्ल्क्लॉथ् / *noun* [C] a piece of cloth that you use for covering a table, especially when having a meal मेज़पोश

**table manners** *noun* [*pl.*] behaviour that is considered correct while you are having a meal at a table with other people दूसरे लोगों के साथ (मेज़ पर) भोजन करते समय पालन-योग्य आचार-नियम

**tablespoon** /ˈteɪblspu:n ˈटेब्ल्स्पून् / *noun* [C] **1** a large spoon used for serving or measuring food भोजन को परोसने या मापने के लिए प्रयुक्त बड़ा चम्मच **2** (*also* **tablespoonful**) the amount that a tablespoon holds बड़ा चम्मच भर (किसी वस्तु की बड़े चम्मच में आने वाली मात्रा) *Add two tablespoons of sugar.*

**tablet** /ˈtæblət ˈटैब्लट् / *noun* [C] a small amount of medicine in solid form that you swallow दवा की गोली, टिकिया ***Take** two tablets every four hours.*

**table tennis** (*informal* **ping-pong**) *noun* [U] a game with rules like tennis in which you hit a light plastic ball across a table with a small round bat टेबल टेनिस (का खेल)

**tabloid** /ˈtæblɔɪd ˈटैब्लॉइड् / *noun* [C] a newspaper with small pages, a lot of pictures and short articles छोटे आकार के पृष्ठों वाला अख़बार जिसमें ढेर सारे चित्र और छोटे लेख होते हैं, लघु समाचारपत्र; टैबलॉइड

**taboo** /təˈbu: टˈबू / *noun* [C] (*pl.* **taboos**) something that you must not say or do because it might shock, offend or make people embarrassed निषिद्ध, वर्जित शब्द या कर्म (जो लोगों के लिए आघातकारी, अपमानजनक या कष्टप्रद हो सकते हों), वर्जना(एँ); निषेध ▶ **taboo** *adj.* निषिद्ध या वर्जित *a taboo subject/word*

**tabular** /ˈtæbjələ(r) ˈटैब्यल(र्) / *adj.* (*usually before a noun*) presented or arranged in a **table** तालिका या सारणी में प्रस्तुत या व्यवस्थित; सारणीबद्ध *tabular data* ○ *The results are presented **in tabular form**.*

**tabulate** /ˈtæbjuleɪt ˈटैब्युलेट् / *verb* [T] to arrange facts or figures in columns or lists so that they can be read easily तथ्यों या आँकड़ों को तालिका या सारणी में क्रमबद्ध करना (ताकि उन्हें सरलता से पढ़ा जा सके) ▶ **tabulation** /ˌtæbjuˈleɪʃn ˌटैब्यु ˈलेश्न् / *noun* [U, C] सारणी, तालिका-निर्माण

**tacit** /ˈtæsɪt ˈटैसिट् / *adj.* (*formal*) understood but not actually said ध्वनित, व्यंजित, उपलक्षित (परोक्ष रूप से व्यक्त, न कि प्रत्यक्ष रूप से कथित) ▶ **tacitly** *adv.* सांकेतिक रूप से

**tack**[1] /tæk टैक् / *noun* **1** [*sing.*] a way of dealing with a particular situation स्थिति-विशेष से निपटने का ढंग *If people won't listen we'll have to try a* *different tack.* **2** [C] a small nail with a sharp point and a flat head चपटे माथे की छोटी नुकीली कील, (चिपटी) बिरिंजी, कटिया

**tack²** /tæk टैक्/ *verb* [T] **1** to fasten sth in place with **tacks¹ 2** किसी वस्तु पर चपटी कीलें, कटिया जड़ना या ठोकना **2** to fasten cloth together temporarily with long stitches that can be removed easily कपड़े पर कच्चे टाँके लगाना

**PHR V tack sth on (to sth)** to add sth extra on the end of sth किसी चीज़ में कुछ और जोड़ना

**tackle¹** /ˈtækl ˈटैक्ल्/ *verb* **1** [T] to make an effort to deal with a difficult situation or problem कठिन स्थिति या समस्या का हल निकालने का प्रयास करना *The government must tackle the problem of rising unemployment.* ○ **2** [I, T] (used in football, etc.) to try to take the ball from sb in the other team (फ़ुटबॉल आदि में) विरोधी दल के खिलाड़ी से गेंद छीनने का प्रयास करना **3** [T] to stop sb running away by pulling him/her down किसी (खिलाड़ी) को (गेंद लेकर) भागने से रोकना (उसे नीचे गिराकर) **4** [T] **tackle sb about sth** to speak to sb about a difficult subject विवादास्पद मुद्दे पर किसी से जूझना *I'm going to tackle him about the money he owes me.*

**tackle²** /ˈtækl ˈटैक्ल्/ *noun* **1** [C] the action of trying to get the ball from another player in football, etc. फ़ुटबॉल आदि में विरोधी खिलाड़ी से गेंद छीनने का प्रयास **2** [U] the equipment you use in some sports, especially fishing मछली पकड़ना आदि (खेलों) में प्रयुक्त साज़-सामान *fishing tackle*

**tacky** /ˈtæki ˈटैकि/ *adj.* (*informal*) **1** cheap and of poor quality and/or not in good taste सस्ता, हलका और/या फूहड़ *a shop selling tacky souvenirs* **2** (used about paint, etc.) not quite dry; sticky (पेंट आदि) जो पूरी तरह सूखा न हो; चिपचिपा

**tact** /tækt टैक्ट्/ *noun* [U] the ability to deal with people without offending or upsetting them (लोगों को अपमानित या परेशान किए बिना) व्यवहार करने की योग्यता; व्यवहार-कौशल, चतुराई *She handled the situation with great tact and diplomacy.*

**tactful** /ˈtæktfl ˈटैक्ट्फ़्ल्/ *adj.* careful not to say or do things that could offend people व्यवहार-कुशल (लोगों को नाराज़ कर सकने वाली बातें न कहने या करने वाला), चतुर ▶ **tactfully** /-fəli -फ़लि/ *adv.* व्यवहार-कौशल-पूर्वक, चतुराई से

**tactic** /ˈtæktɪk ˈटैक्टिक्/ *noun* **1** [C, *usually pl.*] the particular method you use to achieve sth कुछ प्राप्त करने के लिए अपनाया गया ख़ास तरीक़ा; दाँव-पेंच, युक्ति, चाल *We must decide what our tactics are going to be at the next meeting.* **2 tactics** [*pl.*] the skilful arrangement and use of military forces in order to win a battle युद्ध जीतने के लिए सैन्य दलों की कौशलपूर्ण व्यवस्था; रण-कौशल, रणनीति

**tactical** /ˈtæktɪkl ˈटैक्टिक्ल्/ *adj.* **1** connected with the particular method you use to achieve sth कुछ प्राप्त करने के लिए अपनाई गई युक्ति से संबंधित *a tactical error* ○ *tactical discussions/planning* **2** designed to bring a future advantage भविष्य में लाभ प्राप्ति के लिए किया या बनाया गया, योजनापूर्ण, कौशलपूर्ण *a tactical decision* ▶ **tactically** /ˈtæktɪkli ˈटैक्टिक्लि/ *adv.* योजनापूर्वक, कौशलपूर्वक

**tactless** /ˈtæktləs ˈटैक्ट्लस्/ *adj.* saying and doing things that are likely to offend and upset other people व्यवहार-कौशल-हीन (दूसरों को बुरा लग सकने वाली बातें कहने और काम करने वाला) *It was rather tactless of you to ask her how old she was.* ▶ **tactlessly** *adv.* बिना व्यवहार-कौशल के

**tadpole** /ˈtædpəʊl ˈटैड्पोल्/ *noun* [C] a young form of a **frog** when it has a large black head and a long tail बेंगची; मेंढक का बच्चा ➪ **amphibian** पर चित्र देखिए।

**tag¹** /tæg टैग्/ *noun* [C] **1** (*often used to form compound nouns*) a small piece of card, material, etc. fastened to sth to give information about it; a label किसी वस्तु के साथ बाँधा गया गत्ते आदि का टुकड़ा (उसके विषय में जानकारी देने वाला), टैग, टीका, टिकड़ा, चिप्पी; लेबल *How much is this dress? There isn't a* ***price tag*** *on it.* **2** = **question tag**

**tag²** /tæg टैग्/ *verb* [T] (**tagging; tagged**) to fasten a tag onto sb/sth किसी पर टैग, चिप्पी या लेबल लगाना

**PHR V tag along** to follow or go somewhere with sb, especially when you have not been invited किसी के पीछे हो लेना या साथ जाना (विशेषतः बिना बुलाए)

**tahr** *noun* [C] a kind of a wild goat-like animal found in the Himalayas and the Nilgiris तहर; हिमालय और नीलगिरी पहाड़ों में पाए जाने वाला पहाड़ी बकरा

**tail¹** /teɪl टेल्/ *noun* **1** [C] the part at the end of the body of an animal, bird, fish, etc. पशु, पक्षी, मछली आदि की पूँछ; दुम *The dog barked and wagged its tail.* ➪ **fish** पर चित्र देखिए। **2** [C] the back part of an aircraft, spacecraft, etc. विमान, अंतरिक्ष यान आदि का पीछे का हिस्सा ➪ **plane** पर चित्र देखिए। **3 tails** [*pl.*] a man's formal coat that is short at the front but with a long, divided piece at the back, worn especially at weddings औपचारिक अवसरों (विशेषतः विवाह) पर पुरुषों द्वारा पहना जाने वाला कोट (आगे से

छोटा और पीछे से लंबा एवं कटा हुआ) **4 tails** [*pl.*] the side of a coin that does not have the head of a person on it सिक्के का पट (वह भाग जिस पर मानव के सिर की आकृति नहीं होती) *'We'll toss a coin to decide,' said my father.* ***'Heads or tails?'*** **5** [C] (*informal*) a person who is sent to follow sb secretly to get information about him/her छिपकर किसी का पीछा करने वाला व्यक्ति (जासूसी के लिए)
IDM **make head or tail of sth** ⇨ **head**[1] देखिए।

**tail**[2] /teɪl टेल्/ *verb* [T] to follow sb closely, especially to watch where he/she goes किसी का पीछा करना (विशेषतः जानने के लिए कि वह कहाँ जाता है)
PHR V **tail away/off** to become smaller and weaker कम हो जाना, घट जाना

**tailback** /ˈteɪlbæk ˈटेल्बैक्/ *noun* [C] a long line of traffic that is moving slowly or not moving at all, because sth is blocking the road in front (आगे सड़क पर रुकावट के कारण) धीरे चलते या रुके हुए वाहनों की लंबी कतार

**tailor**[1] /ˈteɪlə(r) ˈटेल(र्)/ *noun* [C] a person whose job is to make clothes, especially for men दर्ज़ी, टेलर

**tailor**[2] /ˈteɪlə(r) ˈटेल(र्)/ *verb* [T] (*usually passive*) **1 tailor sth to/for sb/sth** to make or design sth for a particular person or purpose किसी विशेष व्यक्ति या अवसर के लिए कोई वस्तु तैयार या डिज़ाइन करना *programmes tailored to the needs of specific groups* **2** to make clothes कपड़े सीना *a well-tailored coat*

**tailorbird** *noun* [C] a small South Asian bird of the **warbler** family that stitches leaves together with fibres to hold its nest बया (पत्तों को रेशों से सिलकर घोंसला बनाने वाली दक्षिण-एशिआई चिड़िया)

**tailor-made** *adj.* **tailor-made (for sb/sth)** made for a particular person or purpose and therefore very suitable किसी विशेष व्यक्ति या अवसर के लिए बनाया गया (और अतएव बहुत उपयुक्त)

**tailplane** /ˈteɪlpleɪn ˈटेल्प्लेन्/ *noun* [C] a small horizontal wing at the back of an aircraft विमान के पिछले हिस्से में छोटा क्षैतिज, पट स्थिति में डैना ⇨ **plane** पर चित्र देखिए।

**tailwind** /ˈteɪlwɪnd ˈटेल्विन्ड्/ *noun* [C] a wind that blows from behind a moving vehicle, a runner, etc. दौड़ते हुए वाहन, धावक आदि के पीछे से चलती हवा; अनुवात, पश्च-पवन ⇨ **headwind** देखिए।

**taint** /teɪnt टेन्ट्/ *noun* [C, *usually sing.*] (*formal*) the effect of sth bad or unpleasant that spoils the quality of sb/sth किसी कुत्सित या दूषित वस्तु का दूषणकारी प्रभाव; कलंक, लांछन *the taint of corruption* ▶ **taint** *verb* [T] (*usually passive*) दूषित होना या कर दिया जाना *Her reputation was tainted by the scandal.*

**take** /teɪk टेक्/ *verb* [T] (*pt* **took** /tʊk टुक्/; *pp* **taken** /ˈteɪkən ˈटेकन्/) **1** to carry or move sb/sth; to go with sb from one place to another किसी को लेना या ले जाना; किसी के साथ कहीं जाना *Take your coat with you—it's cold.* ○ *I'm taking the children swimming this afternoon.* **2** to put your hand round sth and hold it (and move it towards you) किसी वस्तु को हाथ में लेकर पकड़ना या थामना (और अपनी ओर खींचना) *She **took** my **hand**.* **3** to remove sth from a place or a person, often without permission किसी स्थान या व्यक्ति से कोई चीज़ ले जाना (प्रायः बिना पूछे, चुपके से) *The burglars took all my jewellery.* **4** to accept or receive sth कुछ स्वीकार करना, मान लेना या प्राप्त करना, लेना *If you **take** my **advice** you'll forget all about him.* ○ ***take the blame*** ○ ***take the job*** **5** to capture a place by force; to get control of sb/sth किसी स्थान को बलपूर्वक अपने अधिकार में लेना, किसी जगह पर जबरन क़ाबिज़ होना; किसी व्यक्ति या वस्तु पर नियंत्रण स्थापित करना, (को) अपने नियंत्रण में लेना *The state will **take control of** the company.* **6** to understand sth or react to sth in a particular way किसी बात को विशेष ढंग से समझना या उसकी प्रतिक्रिया करना या उसे ग्रहण करना *I wish you would **take** things more **seriously**.* **7** to get a particular feeling from sth किसी बात से कोई विशेष अनुभव होना *He **takes** great **pleasure in** his grandchildren.* **8** to be able to deal with sth difficult or unpleasant किसी कठिन या अप्रिय स्थिति का सामना करने में समर्थ होना; झेलना *I can't take much more of this heat.* ✪ पर्याय **stand** **9** to need sth/sb किसी बात के लिए (कुछ) आवश्यक होना, (में) लगना *It took three people to move the piano.* ○ *It took a lot of courage to say that.* **10** to swallow sth किसी चीज़ को निगलना ***Take** two **tablets** four times a day.* **11** to write or record sth कुछ लिखना या रिकार्ड करना, दर्ज करना *She **took notes** during the lecture.* **12** to photograph sth किसी का फ़ोटो खींचना या लेना *I **took** some nice **photos** of the wedding.* **13** to measure sth कुछ नापना *The doctor **took** my **temperature** /pulse/blood pressure.* **14** (*not used in the continuous tenses*) to have a certain size of shoes or clothes जूतों या कपड़ों का ख़ास नाप का होना *What size shoes do you take?* **15** (*not used in the continuous tenses*) to have enough space for sb/sth (कहीं पर) किसी के लिए प्रर्याप्त स्थान होना *How many passengers can this bus take?* **16** used with nouns to say that sb is performing an action किसी कार्य को किए जाने की सूचना देने वाले संज्ञा पदों के साथ प्रयुक्त ***Take a look*** *at this article* (= look at it). ○ *We have to* ***take a decision*** (= decide). **17** to study a subject for an exam; to do an exam परीक्षा के लिए किसी विषय की पढ़ाई करना; (कोई) परीक्षा देना *I'm taking the advanced exam this summer.* **18 take sb (for sth)** to give lessons to sb किसी को (कोई विषय) पढ़ाना *Who takes you for English* (= who is your teacher)? **19** to use a form of transport; to use a particular route (कहीं जाने के लिए) किसी (विशेष) सवारी का प्रयोग करना, (कहीं के लिए) कोई (विशेष) सवारी लेना; किसी विशेष रास्ते या मार्ग से जाना *I always* ***take the train*** *to Chandigarh.* **20** (*not used in the continuous tenses*) to have or need a word to go with it in a sentence or other structure (वाक्य या अन्य संरचना में) किसी शब्द का किसी अन्य शब्द के साथ आना *The verb 'depend' takes the preposition 'on'.*

**IDM be taken with sb/sth** to find sb/sth attractive or interesting कोई व्यक्ति या वस्तु आकर्षक या रोचक लगना

**take it (that...)** (used to show that you understand sth from a situation, even though you have not been told) I imagine; I guess; I suppose (यह बताने के लिए प्रयुक्त कि परिस्थिति से कुछ विदित हुआ है; हालाँकी आपको बताया न गया हो) मुझे लगता है; मेरा विचार है *I take it that you're not coming?*

**take it from me** believe me मेरी बात पर भरोसा करो

**take a lot out of sb** to make sb very tired किसी को बेहद थका देना

**take a lot of/some doing** to need a lot of work or effort किसी काम में बहुत मेहनत या कोशिश लगना, दरकार होना या की अपेक्षा होना

> **NOTE Take** से बनने वाले अन्य मुहावरों के लिए संबंधित संज्ञाओं, विशेषणों आदि की प्रविष्टियाँ देखिए। उदाहरण के लिए **take place** की प्रविष्टि **place**[1] में मिलेगी।

**PHR V take sb aback** to surprise or shock sb किसी को अचंभित या दुखी कर देना

**take after sb** (*not used in the continuous tenses*) to look or behave like an older member of your family, especially a parent परिवार के बड़े-बूढ़े (विशेषतः माता-पिता) जैसा लगना या आचरण करना

**take sth apart** to separate sth into the different parts it is made of किसी वस्तु के अलग-अलग पुरज़े खोलना

**take sth away 1** to cause a feeling, etc. to disappear किसी मनोभाव, दर्द आदि को ग़ायब कर देना *These aspirins will take the pain away.* **2** to buy cooked food at a restaurant, etc. and carry it out to eat somewhere else, for example at home रेस्तराँ में बना भोजन (खाने के लिए) घर या अन्यत्र ले जाना ➪ **takeaway** noun देखिए।

**take sb/sth away (from sb)** to remove sb/sth किसी से कुछ ले लेना, दूर कर देना *She took the scissors away from the child.*

**take sth back 1** to return sth to the place that you got it from किसी वस्तु को वहाँ वापस ले जाना जहाँ से वह ली थी **2** to admit that sth you said was wrong अपने (अनुचित) शब्द वापस लेना

**take sth down 1** to remove a structure by separating it into the pieces it is made of हिस्से अलग कर किसी ढाँचे को ढहाना *They took the tent down and started the journey home.* **2** to write down sth that is said भाषण आदि को लिख लेना

**take sb in 1** to make sb believe sth that is not true झूठी बात में विश्वास दिला देना, किसी की बातों में आ जाना *I was completely taken in by her story.* **2** to invite sb who has no home to live with you बेसहारा को सहारा या आश्रय देना

**take sth in** to understand what you see, hear or read देखी, सुनी या पढ़ी बात को समझना *There was too much in the museum to take in at one go.*

**take off 1** (used about an aircraft) to leave the ground and start flying (विमान का) उड़ान भरना ✪ विलोम **land 2** (used about an idea, a product, etc.) to become successful or popular very quickly or suddenly (किसी विचार, उत्पादित वस्तु आदि का) बहुत जल्दी या अचानक सफल या लोकप्रिय हो जाना

**take sb off** to copy the way sb speaks or behaves in an amusing way मज़ाकिया ढंग से किसी के बोलने या काम करने के ढंग की नक़ल उतारना

**take sth off 1** to remove sth, especially clothes कोई वस्तु (विशेषतः कपड़े) निकाल देना या उतार देना *Come in and take your coat off.* **2** to have the period of time mentioned as a holiday छुट्टी पर जाना *I'm going to take a week off.*

**take sb on** to start to employ sb किसी को काम पर लगाना *The firm is taking on new staff.*

**take sth on** to accept a responsibility or decide to do sth कोई दायित्व स्वीकार या कुछ करने का निर्णय करना *He's taken on a lot of extra work.*

**take sb out** to go out with sb (for a social occasion) किसी को साथ ले जाना (सामाजिक मेल-मिलाप की दृष्टि से) *I'm taking Smita out for a meal tonight.*

**take sth out** to remove sth from inside your body शरीर के अंदर से कुछ बाहर निकालना *He's having two teeth taken out.*

**take sth out (of sth)** to remove sth from sth कहीं से कुछ बाहर निकालना *He took a notebook out of his pocket.*

**take it out on sb** to behave badly towards sb because you are angry or upset about sth, even though it is not this person's fault किसी पर अपना गुस्सा उतारना (बिना उसके क़सूर के)

**take (sth) over** to get control of sth or responsibility for sth किसी का नियंत्रण या दायित्व सँभालना *The firm is being taken over by a large company.*

**take to sb/sth** to start liking sb/sth किसी व्यक्ति या वस्तु को पसंद करने लगना

**take to sth/doing sth** to begin doing sth regularly as a habit किसी बात की आदत डाल लेना

**take sth up** to start doing sth regularly (for example as a hobby) किसी काम को नियमपूर्वक करने लगना *I've taken up yoga recently.*

**take up sth** to use or fill an amount of time or space किसी काम में समय चला जाना या किसी ख़ाली जगह को भर देना *All her time is taken up looking after the new baby.* ✪ पर्याय **occupy**

**take sb up on sth 1** to say that you disagree with sth that sb has just said, and ask him/her to explain it किसी की बात से असहमति व्यक्त करते हुए उसे (बात को) समझाने के लिए कहना *I must take you up on that last point.* **2** (*informal*) to accept an offer that sb has made किसी के प्रस्ताव को मान लेना

**take sth up with sb** to ask or complain about sth किसी विषय में कुछ पूछना या शिकायत करना *I'll take the matter up with my MP.*

**takeaway** /ˈteɪkəweɪ ˈटेकअवे/ (*AmE* **takeout; carry-out**) *noun* [C] **1** a restaurant that sells food that you can eat somewhere else कहीं और ले जाकर खाने के लिए भोजन बेचने वाला रेस्तराँ **2** the food that such a restaurant sells रेस्तराँ से ख़रीदा गया ऐसा भोजन *Let's have a takeaway.*

**take-off** *noun* [U, C] the moment when an aircraft leaves the ground and starts to fly विमान के उड़ान भरने की शुरुआत *The plane is ready for take-off.* ✪ विलोम **landing**

**takeover** /ˈteɪkəʊvə(r) ˈटेकओव़(र्)/ *noun* [C] the act of taking control of sth किसी वस्तु का नियंत्रण ग्रहण करने का कार्य *They made a takeover bid for the company.* ○ *a military takeover of the government*

**takings** /ˈteɪkɪŋz ˈटेकिङ्ज़्/ *noun* [*pl.*] the amount of money that a shop, theatre, etc. gets from selling goods, tickets, etc. दुकान, थिएटर आदि को माल, टिकट आदि बेचने से हुई आमदनी, व्यापार में प्राप्ति

**talcum powder** /ˈtælkəm paʊdə(r) ˈटैल्कम् पाउड(र्)/ (*also* **talc** /tælk टैल्क्/) *noun* [U] a soft powder which smells nice. People often put it on their skin after a bath सुगंधित कोमल पाउडर (स्नान के उपरांत शरीर पर लगाने के लिए)

**tale** /teɪl टेल्/ *noun* [C] **1** a story about events that are not real काल्पनिक कथा; क़िस्सा *fairy tales* **2** a report or description of sb/sth that may not be true कोई रिपोर्ट या विवरण (जो असत्य भी हो सकता है) *I've heard tales of people seeing ghosts in that house.*

**talent** /ˈtælənt ˈटैलन्ट्/ *noun* [C, U] **(a) talent (for sth)** a natural skill or ability प्रकृति-प्रदत्त निपुणता या योग्यता *She has a talent for painting.* ○ *His work shows great talent.* ▶ **talented** *adj.* प्रतिभा-संपन्न, प्रवीण *a talented musician*

**talk¹** /tɔːk टॉक्/ *verb* **1** [I] **talk (to/with sb) (about/of sb/sth)** to say things; to speak in order to give information or to express feelings, ideas, etc. बातचीत करना; जानकारी देने का भाव, विचार आदि व्यक्त करने के लिए बोलना, कहना या भाषण देना *I could hear them talking downstairs.* ○ *Can I talk to you for a minute?* ➪ **speak** पर नोट देखिए। **2** [I, T] to discuss sth serious or important किसी गंभीर या महत्त्वपूर्ण विषय पर चर्चा करना *Could we **talk business** after dinner?* **3** [I] to discuss people's private lives लोगों के निजी जीवन के बारे में बातें बताना *His strange lifestyle started the local people talking.* ✪ पर्याय **gossip 4** [I] to give information to sb, especially when you do not want to किसी को कुछ बताना (विशेषतः अनिच्छापूर्वक)

IDM **know what you are talking about** ➪ **know¹** देखिए।

**talk sense** to say things that are correct or sensible अकल की बातें करना *He's the only politician who talks any sense.*

**talk/speak of the devil** ➪ **devil** देखिए।

**talk shop** to talk about your work with the people you work with, outside working hours (ख़ाली समय में) अपने सहकर्मियों से काम के बारे में बात करना

PHR V **talk down to sb** to talk to sb as if he/she is less intelligent or important than you किसी को बच्चा या अपने से छोटा समझकर बात करना

**talk sb into/out of doing sth** to persuade sb to do/not to do sth किसी को कुछ करने या न करने के लिए मनाना *She tried to talk him into buying a new car.*

**talk sth over (with sb)** to discuss sth with sb, especially in order to reach an agreement or make a decision किसी से किसी मुद्दे पर विचार-विमर्श करना (विशेषतः समझौते पर पहुँचने या कोई निर्णय करने के लिए)

**talk²** /tɔːk टॉक्/ *noun* **1** [C] **a talk (with sb) (about sth)** a conversation or discussion बातचीत या चर्चा *Raman and I had a long talk about the problem.* **2 talks** [*pl.*] formal discussions between governments सरकारों के बीच औपचारिक बातचीत, वार्ता या विचार-विमर्श *arms/pay/peace talks* **3** [C] **a talk (on sth)** a formal speech on a particular subject विषय-विशेष पर औपचारिक भाषण *He's giving a talk on 'Our changing world'.* ✪ पर्याय **lecture** **4** [U] (*informal*) things that people say that are not based on facts or reality अफ़वाह *He says he's going to resign but it's just talk.* ➪ **small talk** देखिए।

**talkative** /ˈtɔːkətɪv ˈटॉकटिव़् / *adj.* liking to talk a lot बातूनी, वाचाल

**tall** /tɔːl टॉल् / *adj.* **1** (used about people or things) of more than average height; not short (व्यक्ति या वस्तुएँ) औसत से अधिक लंबा, ख़ासा लंबा; छोटा नहीं *a tall young man* ○ *a tall tree/tower/chimney* ✪ विलोम **short** **2** used to describe the height of sb/sth किसी की लंबाई का संकेत करने के लिए प्रयुक्त *How tall are you?* ○ *Rahul is taller than his brother.* ➪ **height** noun देखिए।

**NOTE** **Tall** और **high** के अर्थ समान हैं। लोगों और वृक्षों की लंबाई का संकेत करने के लिए **tall** का प्रयोग होता है—*He is six foot three inches tall.* ○ *A tall oak tree stands in the garden.* कम चौड़ाई की (संकीर्ण) वस्तुओं के लिए भी **tall** का प्रयोग होता है—*the tall sky scrapers of Manhattan.* **High** का प्रयोग तब किया जाता है जब किसी वस्तु की नाप बतानी हो—*The fence is two metres high.* या किसी वस्तु की भूतल से ऊँचाई का संकेत करना हो—*a room with high ceilings.*

**talon** /ˈtælən ˈटैलन् / *noun* [C] a long sharp curved nail on the feet of some birds, especially ones that kill other animals and birds for food (कुछ) पक्षियों का पंजा, चंगुल (जिससे वे अन्य पशु-पक्षियों का शिकार करते हैं)

**taluka** *noun* [C] an administrative unit in India below a district. It is called tehsil/tahsil in northern India भारत में जिला से निचले वर्ग का प्रशासनिक खंड; तालुक। उत्तर भारत में इसे तहसील कहते हैं

**tamarind** *noun* [U, C] **1** sticky brown acidic pulp from the pod of a tree of the pea family, used as a flavouring in Asian cookery इमली **2** the large tropical tree which yields tamarind pods इमली का पेड़

**tambourine** /ˌtæmbəˈriːn ˌटैम्बˈरीन् / *noun* [C] a musical instrument that has a circular frame covered with plastic or skin, with metal discs round the edge. To play it, you hit it or shake it with your hand डफली, खंजरी ➪ पृष्ठ 789 पर चित्र देखिए।

**tame¹** /teɪm टेम् / *adj.* **1** (used about animals or birds) not wild or afraid of people (पशु या पक्षी) घरेलू, पालतू (न कि जंगली या लोगों से डरने वाले) *The birds are so tame they will eat from your hand.* **2** boring; not interesting or exciting उबाऊ; रोचक या उत्तेजक नहीं *After the big city, you must find village life very tame.*

**tame²** /teɪm टेम् / *verb* [T] to bring sth wild under your control; to make sth tame किसी वस्तु को अपने क़ाबू में करना; किसी को पालतू बनाना

**tamper** /ˈtæmpə(r) ˈटैम्प(र्) / *verb*

**PHR V** **tamper with sth** to make changes to sth without permission, especially in order to damage it (बिना पूछे) किसी वस्तु में बदलाव करना, छेड़छाड़ करना, (विशेषत: उसे बिगाड़ने के लिए); दस्तंदाज़ी करना

**tan¹** /tæn टैन् / *noun* **1** [C] = **suntan** **2** [U] a colour between yellow and brown ताँबे जैसा रंग ▶ **tan** *adj.* ताँबे जैसे रंग का

**tan²** /tæn टैन् / *verb* [I, T] (**tanning; tanned**) (used about a person's skin) to become or make sth brown as a result of spending time in the sun (व्यक्ति की त्वचा का) धूप में देर तक बैठने के कारण ताँबे जैसा रंग हो जाना या कर देना *Do you tan easily?* ▶ **tanned** *adj.* ताँबे जैसे रंग वाला *You're looking very tanned—have you been on holiday?*

**tandem** /ˈtændəm ˈटैन्डम् / *noun* [C] a bicycle with seats for two people, one behind the other दो सीटों (एक के पीछे दूसरी) वाली साइकिल

**IDM** **in tandem (with sb/sth)** working together with sth/sb else; happening at the same time as sth else किसी अन्य के साथ मिलकर काम करते हुए; समकालिक रूप से घटित होते हुए

**tandoor** *noun* [C] a large clay oven used in the Middle East and in South Asia तंदूर ▶ **tandoori** *adj.* तंदूरी *tandoori chicken*

**tangent** /ˈtændʒənt ˈटैन्जन्ट् / *noun* [C] **1** a straight line that touches a curve but does not cross it स्पर्श रेखा (सीधी रेखा जो वृत्त रेखा को स्पर्श करती है परंतु उसे काटती नहीं) ➪ **circle** पर चित्र देखिए। **2** (*mathematics*) (*abbr.* **tan**) the **ratio** of the length of the side opposite an angle in a **right-angled** triangle to the length of the side next to it स्पर्शज्या; किसी 90° कोण वाले त्रिकोण के सामने और बग़ल वाली (विकर्ण से भिन्न) भुजाओं की लंबाइयों का अनुपात ➪ **cosine** और **sine** देखिए।

**IDM** **go off at a tangent**; (*AmE*) **go off on a tangent** to suddenly start saying or doing sth that seems to have no connection with what has gone before एकाएक असंबद्ध बातें कहने या काम करने लगना, विषयांतर या कार्यांतर कर देना

**tangerine** /ˌtændʒəˈriːn ˌटैन्जˈरीन्/ *noun* **1** [C] a fruit like a small sweet orange with a skin that is easy to take off नारंगी, संतरा जैसा फल जिसका छिलका आसानी से उतर जाए **2** [U], *adj.* (of) a deep orange colour गहरे नारंगी रंग (का)

**tangible** /ˈtændʒəbl ˈटैन्जब्ल्/ *adj.* that can be clearly seen to exist स्पष्ट और वास्तविक *There are tangible benefits in the new system.* ✪ विलोम **intangible**

**tangle** /ˈtæŋgl ˈटैङ्ग्ल्/ *noun* [C] a confused mass, especially of threads, hair, branches, etc. that cannot easily be separated from each other बालों, धागों या शाखाओं आदि की उलझी हुई गुत्थी जिसे सुलझाना मुश्किल हो *My hair's full of tangles.* ○ *This string's* ***in a tangle****.* ▶ **tangled** *adj.* उलझा हुआ *The wool was all tangled up.*

**tango** /ˈtæŋgəʊ ˈटैङ्गो/ *noun* [C] (*pl.* **tangos**) a fast South American dance with a strong rhythm, in which two people hold each other closely; a piece of music for this dance तेज़ लय और तेज़ गति वाला एक दक्षिण अमेरिकी नृत्य (जिसमें दो व्यक्ति एक दूसरे को कसकर पकड़े रहते हैं), टैंगो; टैंगो के लिए तैयार संगीत-रचना ▶ **tango** *verb* [I] (*pres. part.* **tangoing**; *pp* **tangoed**) टैंगो (नृत्य) करना

**tank** /tæŋk टैङ्क्/ *noun* [C] **1** a container for holding liquids or gas; the amount that a tank will hold तरल या गैस को सुरक्षित रखने का पात्र, टंकी, हौज़; टंकी में आने वाली (किसी वस्तु की) मात्रा *a water/fuel/petrol/fish tank* ○ *We drove there and back on one tank of petrol.* **2** a large, heavy military vehicle covered with strong metal and armed with guns, that moves on special wheels सेना का टैंक

**tanker** /ˈtæŋkə(r) ˈटैङ्क(र्)/ *noun* [C] a ship or lorry that carries oil, petrol, etc. in large amounts बड़ी मात्रा में तेल, पेट्रोल आदि ले जाने वाला जहाज़ या लॉरी; टैंकर, तेल-पोत, टैंकर-लॉरी *an oil tanker*

**tantalizing** (*also* **-ising**) /ˈtæntəlaɪzɪŋ ˈटैन्टलाइज़िङ्/ *adj.* making you want sth that you cannot have or do; tempting तरसाने वाला (सामर्थ्य से परे की वस्तु का इच्छुक बनाने वाला); ललचाने वाला *A tantalizing aroma of cooking was coming from the kitchen.* ▶ **tantalizingly** (*also* **-isingly**) *adv.* तरसाते या ललचाते हुए

**tantrum** /ˈtæntrəm ˈटैन्ट्रम्/ *noun* [C] a sudden explosion of anger, especially by a child एकाएक क्रोध का विस्फोट (विशेषतः बच्चे का); आवेश

**tap¹** /tæp टैप्/ *verb* (**tapping**; **tapped**) **1** [I, T] **tap (at/on sth); tap sb/sth (on/with sth)** to touch or hit sb/sth quickly and lightly किसी को थपकी देना या हलके-से मारना *Their feet were tapping in time to the music.* ○ *She tapped me on the shoulder.* **2** [I, T] **tap (into) sth** to make use of a source of energy, knowledge, etc. that already exists पूर्वतः विद्यमान ऊर्जा, ज्ञान आदि के स्रोत का उपयोग करना *to tap the skills of young people* **3** [T] to fit a device to sb's telephone so that his/her calls can be listened to secretly चोरी-छिपे किसी का फ़ोन सुनने के लिए (फ़ोन में) विशेष उपकरण लगाना

**tap²** /tæp टैप्/ *noun* [C] **1** (*AmE* **faucet**) a type of handle that you turn to let water, gas, etc. out of a pipe or container नल की टोंटी *Turn the hot/cold tap on/off.* **2** a light hit with your hand or fingers थपकी **3** a device that is fitted to sb's telephone so that his/her calls can be listened to secretly चोरी-छिपे फ़ोन सुनने के लिए (फ़ोन में) लगाया विशेष उपकरण

**tap dance** *noun* [C] a style of dancing in which you tap the rhythm of the music with your feet, wearing special shoes with pieces of metal on them एक प्रकार का नृत्य जिसमें (धातु जड़े विशेष जूते पहन कर) पैरों से ताल दी जाती है; टैप नृत्य ▶ **tap-dance** *verb* [I] टैप नृत्य करना

**tape¹** /teɪp टेप्/ *noun* **1** [U] a thin band of plastic material used for recording sound, pictures or information रिकॉर्डर का टेप *I've got the whole concert* ***on tape*** (= recorded). **2** [C] a cassette which is used for recording or playing music, videos, etc. संगीत, वीडियो आदि को रिकॉर्ड करने वाला कैसेट *a* ***blank tape*** (= a tape which is empty) ○ *to rewind a tape* **3** [U] a long narrow band of plastic, etc. with a sticky substance on one side that is used for sticking things together, covering electric wires, etc. चिपकाने का टेप *sticky/adhesive tape* ➪ **insulating tape** और **Sellotape** देखिए। **4** [C, U] a narrow piece of cloth that is used for tying things together or as a label वस्तुओं को बाँधने का या लेबल के रूप में प्रयुक्त फ़ीता ➪ **red tape** देखिए। **5** [C] a piece of material stretched across a race track to mark where the race finishes दौड़ के मैदान में दौड़ के अंत को चिह्नित करने वाला फ़ीता

**tape²** /teɪp टेप्/ *verb* [T] **1** to record sound, music, television programmes, etc. using a cassette कैसेट की सहायता से ध्वनि, संगीत, टीवी कार्यक्रम आदि को रिकॉर्ड करना **2 tape sth (up)** to fasten sth by sticking or tying sth with **tape¹ 3** किसी वस्तु पर टेप लगाना (टेप से चिपकाना या बाँधना)

**tape deck** *noun* [C] the part of a music system (**stereo**) on which you play cassettes or tapes स्टीरियो का वह भाग जहाँ रखकर कैसेट या टेप को बजाया जाता है; टेप डेक

**tape measure** (*also* **measuring tape**) *noun* [C] a long thin piece of plastic, cloth or metal with centimetres, etc. marked on it. It is used for measuring things प्लास्टिक, कपड़े या धातु का बना (वस्तुओं को) नापने का फ़ीता (जिस पर सेंटीमीटर आदि अंकित रहते हैं) ➪ **tape** देखिए।

**tape recorder** *noun* [C] a machine that is used for recording and playing sounds on tape टेप पर ध्वनियों को रिकॉर्ड करने और सुनाने वाली मशीन; टेप रिकॉर्डर

**tapestry** /ˈtæpəstri ˈटैपस्ट्रि / *noun* [C, U] (*pl.* **tapestries**) a piece of heavy cloth with pictures or designs sewn on it in coloured thread (परदों आदि का) भारी कपड़ा जिस पर रंगीन धागों से चित्र या डिज़ाइन सिले होते हैं, परदे आदि का बेलबूटेदार कपड़ा; टेपेस्ट्री

**tapeworm** /ˈteɪpwɜːm ˈटेप्वम् / *noun* [C] **1** a long flat creature with a soft body and no legs (**a worm**) that lives in the tube that carries food out of the stomach (**the intestines**) of humans and animals आँतों में रहने वाला एक प्रकार का कीड़ा; फ़ीता-कृमि

**tapioca** /ˌtæpiˈəʊkə ˌटैपिˈओका / [U] hard white grains obtained from a plant (**cassava plant**) often cooked with milk to make a sweet dish कसावा पौधे के कड़े सफ़ेद दाने प्रायः जिन्हें दूध में पकाकर मीठा व्यंजन बनाया जाता है ➪ **cassava** पर चित्र देखिए।

**tap water** *noun* [U] water that comes through pipes and out of taps, not water sold in bottles नल का (न कि बोतल बंद) पानी

**tar** /tɑː(r) टा(र्) / *noun* [U] **1** a thick black sticky liquid that becomes hard when it is cold. Tar is obtained from coal and is used for making roads, etc. तारकोल, अलकतरा, डामर (यह कोयले से निकलता है और सड़क आदि बनाने के काम आता है) ➪ **Tarmac** देखिए। **2** a similar substance formed by burning tobacco तंबाकू जलाने से बना (तंबाकू जैसा) पदार्थ *low-tar cigarettes*

**tarantula** /təˈræntʃələ टˈरैन्चला / *noun* [C] a large hairy spider that lives in hot countries. Some tarantulas are poisonous (गरम देशों मे पाया जाने वाला) लंबे बालों वाला बड़ा मकड़ा (कुछ मकड़े विषैले होते हैं)

**target**[1] /ˈtɑːɡɪt ˈटागिट् / *noun* [C] **1** a result that you try to achieve लक्ष्य *to be **on target*** (= making the progress we expected) ○ *a target area/audience/group* (= the particular area, audience, etc. that a product, programme, etc. is aimed at) **2** a person, place or thing that you try to hit when shooting or attacking गोली या आक्रमण का निशाना (कोई व्यक्ति, स्थान या वस्तु) *Doors and windows are **an easy target** for burglars.* **3** a person or thing that people criticize, laugh at, etc. लोगों की आलोचना, हंसी आदि का पात्र (कोई व्यक्ति या वस्तु) *The education system has been the target of heavy criticism.* **4** an object, often a round board with circles on it, that you try to hit in shooting practice शूटिंग अभ्यास का निशाना (एक ढाल, जिस पर गोले बने होते हैं) *to aim at/hit/miss a target*

**target**[2] /ˈtɑːɡɪt ˈटागिट् / *verb* [T] (*usually passive*) **target sb/sth; target sth at/on sb/sth** to try to have an effect on a particular group of people; to try to attack sb/sth समाज के विशेष वर्ग पर प्रभाव डालने का यत्न करना; किसी पर आक्रमण करने की कोशिश करना *The product is targeted at teenagers.*

**tariff** /ˈtærɪf ˈटैरिफ़् / *noun* [C] **1** a tax that has to be paid on goods coming into a country देश में आयातित सामान पर लगने वाला कर; आयात शुल्क **2** a list of prices, especially in a hotel (वस्तुओं के) मूल्यों की सूची (विशेषतः होटल में)

**Tarmac**™ /ˈtɑːmæk ˈटामैक् / *noun* **1** [U] a black material used for making the surfaces of roads तारकोल-मिश्रित रोड़ी (सड़कों की सतहें तैयार करने में प्रयुक्त) ➪ **tar** देखिए। **2 the tarmac** [*sing.*] an area covered with a Tarmac surface, especially at an airport तारकोल-मिश्रित रोड़ी वाला क्षेत्र (विशेषतः हवाई अड्डे पर)

**tarnish** /ˈtɑːnɪʃ ˈटानिश् / *verb* **1** [I, T] (used about metal, etc.) to become or to make sth less bright and shiny (धातु आदि की) चमक घट जाना या घटा देना **2** [T] to spoil the good opinion people have of sb/sth किसी की छवि बिगाड़ना

**tarpaulin** /tɑːˈpɔːlɪn टाˈपॉलिन् / *noun* [C, U] strong material that water cannot pass through, which is used for covering things to protect them from the rain तिरपाल

**tarragon** /ˈtærəɡən ˈटैरगन् / *noun* [U] a plant with leaves that have a strong taste and are used in cooking to flavour food एक पौधा जिसके पत्तों का स्वाद तीखा होता है तथा जिससे भोजन का स्वाद बढ़ता है

**tart**[1] /tɑːt टाट् / *noun* **1** [C, U] an open pie filled with sweet food such as fruit or jam फलों या मुरब्बे से भरी पेस्ट्री; टार्ट **2** [C] (*informal*) a woman who dresses or behaves in a way that people think is immoral अश्लील लगने वाले वस्त्र पहनने या अश्लील हरकतें करने वाली महिला; बाज़ारू औरत

**tart**[2] /tɑːt टाट् / *verb*

**PHRV** **tart sb/sth up** (*informal*) to decorate and improve the appearance of sb/sth किसी को सजाना और अधिक सुंदर बनाना

**tart**[3] /tɑːt टार्ट्/ *adj.* (especially in fruit) tasting unpleasantly sour (विशेषतः फल) तीखा, खट्टा या तीक्ष्ण *tart oranges*

**tartan** /ˈtɑːtn ˈटार्ट्न्/ *noun* [U, C] **1** a traditional Scottish pattern of coloured squares and lines that cross each other चारख़ाना (स्कॉटलैंड वासियों का पारंपरिक पैटर्न) **2** material made from wool with this pattern on it चारख़ाने वाला ऊनी वस्त्र आदि

**task** /tɑːsk टास्क्/ *noun* [C] a piece of work that has to be done, especially an unpleasant or difficult one नियत कार्य (विशेषतः अप्रिय या कठिन) *to perform/carry out/undertake a task*

**tassel** /ˈtæsl ˈटैस्ल्/ *noun* [C] a group of threads that are tied together at one end and hang from cushions, curtains, clothes, etc. as a decoration फुँदा, फुँदना, झब्बा (गद्दियों, परदों, कपड़ों आदि के सिरे पर सजावट के लिए बाँधा गया धागों का गुच्छा)

**taste**[1] /teɪst टेस्ट्/ *noun* **1** [*sing.*] the particular quality of different foods or drinks that allows you to recognize them when you put them in your mouth; flavour अलग-अलग खाद्यों या पेयों का अपना-अपना स्वाद; ज़ायक़ा *I don't like the taste of this coffee.* ○ *a sweet/bitter/sour/salty taste* **2** [U] the ability to recognize the flavour of food or drink खाद्यों या पेयों का ज़ायक़ा पहचानने की शक्ति *I've got such a bad cold that I seem to have lost my sense of taste.* **3** [C, *usually sing.*] **a taste (of sth)** a small amount of sth to eat or drink that you have in order to see what it is like चखने के लिए ली गई खाद्य या पेय की अल्प मात्रा *Have a taste of this cheese to see if you like it.* **4** [*sing.*] a short experience of sth किसी वस्तु का संक्षिप्त अनुभव *That was my* ***first taste*** *of success.* **5** [U] the ability to decide if things are suitable, of good quality, etc. वस्तुओं की गुणवत्ता आदि को जानने की शक्ति; आस्वादन शक्ति *He has excellent* ***taste in*** *music.* **6** [*sing.*] **a taste (for sth)** what a person likes or prefers किसी चीज़ के लिए पसंद या प्राथमिकता; रुचि *She has developed a taste for modern art.*
**IDM** **(be) in bad, poor, etc. taste** (used about sb's behaviour) (to be) unpleasant and not suitable (किसी के आचरण का) विक्षोभकारी और अनुपयुक्त होना; भद्दा होना *Some of his comments were in very bad taste.*

**taste**[2] /teɪst टेस्ट्/ *verb* **1** *linking verb* **taste (of sth)** to have a particular flavour किसी में कोई विशेष स्वाद होना *to taste sour/sweet/delicious* **2** [T] to notice or recognize the flavour of food or drink किसी खाद्य या पेय के स्वाद को जानना या पहचानना *Can you taste the garlic in this soup?* **3** [T] to try a small amount of food and drink; to test the flavour of sth (अल्प मात्रा में) खाद्य और पेय को चखना; किसी वस्तु का स्वाद चखना *Can I taste a piece of that cheese to see what it's like?*

**taste bud** *noun* [C, *usually pl.*] one of the small cells on your tongue that allow you to recognize the flavours of food and drink जिह्वा की कोशिका-विशेष (खाद्यों और पेयों के स्वाद को पहचानने में सहायक); स्वादकलिका

**tasteful** /ˈteɪstfl ˈटेस्ट्फ़्ल्/ *adj.* (used especially about clothes, furniture, decorations, etc.) attractive and well chosen (कपड़े, फ़र्नीचर, सजावटी सामान आदि) सुरुचिपूर्ण *tasteful furniture* ✪ विलोम **tasteless** ► **tastefully** /-fəli -फ़लि/ *adv.* सुरुचिपूर्वक

**tasteless** /ˈteɪstləs ˈटेस्ट्लस्/ *adj.* **1** having little or no flavour बेस्वाद; कम स्वाद वाला या स्वादहीन *This sauce is rather tasteless.* ✪ विलोम **tasty** **2** likely to offend people कुरुचिपूर्ण *His joke about the funeral was particularly tasteless.* **3** (used especially about clothes, furniture, decorations, etc.) not attractive; not well chosen (कपड़े, फ़र्नीचर, सजावटी सामान आदि) सुरुचिरहित ✪ विलोम **tasteful**

**tasty** /ˈteɪsti ˈटेस्टि/ *adj.* **(tastier; tastiest)** having a good flavour स्वादिष्ट, ज़ायक़ेदार *spaghetti with a tasty mushroom sauce*

**tattered** /ˈtætəd ˈटैटड्/ *adj.* old and torn; in bad condition फटा-पुराना, जीर्ण-शीर्ण; बुरी हालत में *a tattered coat*

**tatters** /ˈtætəz ˈटैटज़्/ *noun*
**IDM** **in tatters** badly torn or damaged; ruined बुरी तरह से फटा हुआ, चिथड़े-चिथड़े; जीर्ण अवस्था में *Her dress was in tatters.*

**tattoo** /təˈtuː टˈटू/ *noun* [C] (*pl.* **tattoos**) a picure or pattern that is marked permanently on sb's skin शरीर पर गोदे गए चित्र या पैटर्न; टैटु ► **tattoo** *verb* [T] **(tattooing; tattooed)** गोदना *She had his name tattooed on her left hand.*

**tatty** /ˈtæti ˈटैटि/ *adj.* **(tattier; tattiest)** (*informal*) in bad condition बुरी हालत में, फटा-पुराना *tatty old clothes*

**taught** ⇨ **teach** का past tense और past participle रूप

**taunt** /tɔːnt टॉन्ट्/ *verb* [T] to try to make sb angry or upset by saying unpleasant or cruel things किसी को ताना मारना, किसी पर फबती कसना ► **taunt** *noun* [C] ताना, फबती, कटाक्ष

**Taurus** /ˈtɔːrəs ˈटॉरस्/ *noun* [U] the second sign of the **zodiac**, the Bull राशिचक्र की दूसरी राशि; वृषभ

**taut** /tɔːt टॉट्/ *adj.* (used about rope, wire, etc.) stretched very tight; not loose (रस्सी, तार आदि) कसकर बाँधा गया; ढीला नहीं, कसा हुआ

**tavern** /ˈtævən ˈटैवन्/ *noun* [C] (*old-fashioned*) a pub शराबख़ाना, मदिरालय; मधुशाला

**tax** /tæks टैक्स्/ *noun* [C, U] **(a) tax (on sth)** the money that you have to pay to the government so that it can provide public services कर, टैक्स (जनसेवाओं के लिए जनता द्वारा सरकार को नियमानुसार दिया जाने वाला धन) *income tax* ▶ **tax** *verb* [T] (*usually passive*) कर लगाना *Alcohol, cigarettes and petrol are heavily taxed.*

**taxable** /ˈtæksəbl ˈटैक्सबल्/ *adj.* on which you have to pay tax जिस पर कर दिया जाना अपेक्षित हो; करदेय *taxable income*

**taxation** /tækˈseɪʃn टैक्ˈसेशन्/ *noun* [U] **1** the system by which a government takes money from people so that it can pay for public services जनसेवाओं के लिए सरकार द्वारा जनता से धन वसूलने की प्रणाली; कर-पद्धति *direct/indirect taxation* **2** the amount of money that people have to pay in tax कर के रूप में (जनता द्वारा) दिया जाने वाला धन *to increase/reduce taxation* ○ *high/low taxation*

**tax-free** *adj.* on which you do not have to pay tax कर-मुक्त

**taxi¹** /ˈtæksi ˈटैक्सि/ (*also* **taxicab** *AmE* **cab**) *noun* [C] a car with a driver whose job is to take you somewhere in exchange for money (कहीं जाने के लिए) ड्राइवर-सहित भाड़े पर मिलने वाली कार; टैक्सी *Shall we go by bus or **get/take a taxi**?*

> NOTE टैक्सी के प्रयोग के लिए देय **fare** (टैक्सी का भाड़ा) **meter** पर आ जाता है।

**taxi²** /ˈtæksi ˈटैक्सि/ *verb* [I] (used about an aircraft) to move slowly along the ground before or after flying उड़ान भरने से पहले या नीचे उतरने के बाद (विमान) का ज़मीन पर मंद गति से चलना

**taxing** /ˈtæksɪŋ ˈटैक्सिङ्/ *adj.* difficult; needing a lot of effort कठिन; जिसके लिए अत्यधिक प्रयास अपेक्षित हो, अतिश्रमसाध्य *a taxing exam*

**taxi rank** *noun* [C] a place where taxis park while they are waiting for passengers यात्रियों की प्रतीक्षा में टैक्सियों के खड़ा होने का स्थान; टैक्सी-स्टैंड

**taxonomist** /tækˈsɒnəmɪst टैक्ˈसॉनमिस्ट्/ *noun* [C] a scientist who arranges things into groups वस्तुओं का वर्गीकरण करने वाला वैज्ञानिक; वर्गिकी-विद

**taxonomy** /tækˈsɒnəmi टैक्ˈसॉनमि/ *noun* **1** [U] the scientific process of arranging things into groups वस्तुओं का वर्गीकरण करने की वैज्ञानिक प्रक्रिया; वर्गीकरण-विज्ञान, वर्गिकी **2** [C] (*pl.* **taxonomies**) one particular system of groups that things have been arranged in वस्तुओं के वर्गों की कोई एक विशिष्ट प्रणाली, कोई एक विशिष्ट वस्तु-वर्ग-व्यवस्था

**taxpayer** /ˈtækspeɪə(r) ˈटैक्स्पेअ(र्)/ *noun* [C] a person who pays tax to the government, especially on the money that he/she earns आयकर-दाता (सरकार को विशेषतः अपनी आय पर; कर देने वाला व्यक्ति)

**TB** /ˌtiː ˈbiː ˌटी ˈबी/ *abbr.* tuberculosis तपेदिक, क्षयरोग, टीबी

**tbsp** *abbr.* tablespoonful(s) चम्मचभर *Add three tbsp sugar.*

**tea** /tiː टी/ *noun* **1** [U, C] a hot drink made by pouring boiling water onto the dried leaves of the tea plant or of some other plants; a cup of this drink चाय (एक पेय के रूप में); चाय का प्याला, प्याला भर चाय *a cup/pot of tea* ○ *herb/mint/camomile tea* **2** [U] the dried leaves that are used for making tea चाय (की) पत्ती *a packet of tea* **3** [C, U] a small afternoon meal of sandwiches, cakes, etc. and tea to drink, or a cooked meal eaten at 5 or 6 o'clock (तीसरे पहर की) चाय (सैंडविच आदि के नाश्ते के साथ) या शाम (बजे 5–6 का) भोजन *The kids have their tea as soon as they get home from school.*

IDM **(not) sb's cup of tea** ⇨ **cup¹** देखिए।

**tea bag** *noun* [C] a small paper bag with tea leaves in it, that you use for making tea काग़ज़ की छोटी थैली जिसके अंदर चाय की पत्ती हो, टी बैग (चाय का पेय बनाने में प्रयुक्त)

**teach** /tiːtʃ टीच्/ *verb* (*pt, pp* **taught** /tɔːt टॉट्/) **1** [I, T] **teach sb (sth/to do sth); teach sth (to sb)** to give sb lessons or instructions so that he/she knows how to do sth किसी को कुछ करना सिखाना, (कोई विषय) पढ़ाना *Jai is teaching us how to use the computer.* ○ *He teaches English to foreign students.* **2** [T] to make sb believe sth or behave in a certain way किसी को किसी सिद्धांत या व्यवहार की शिक्षा देना *My parents taught me always to tell the truth.* **3** [T] to make sb have a bad experience so that he/she is careful not to do the thing that caused it again (किसी को) पाठ पढ़ाना या सबक़ सिखाना (ऐसा कटु अनुभव कराना कि वह दुबारा ग़लती न करे) *All the seats are taken. That'll teach you to turn up half an hour late.*

IDM **teach sb a lesson** to make sb have a bad experience so that he/she will not do the thing that caused it again किसी को पाठ पढ़ाना या सबक़ सिखाना (ऐसा कटु अनुभव कराना कि वह दुबारा ग़लती न करे)

**teacher** /ˈtiːtʃə(r) ˈटीच(र्)/ *noun* [C] a person whose job is to teach, especially in a school or college शिक्षक, अध्यापक, टीचर (विशेषतः स्कूल या कॉलेज में) *a maths/chemistry/music teacher* ➪ **head**[1] **6** देखिए।

**teaching** /ˈtiːtʃɪŋ ˈटीचिङ्/ *noun* **1** [U] the work of a teacher शिक्षक का कार्य; शिक्षण, अध्ययन *My son went into teaching and my daughter became a doctor.* ○ *teaching methods* **2** [C, *usually pl.*] ideas and beliefs that are taught by sb/sth किसी के द्वारा सिखाई गई बातें (विचार और सिद्धांत); शिक्षाएँ *the teachings of Mahatma Gandhi*

**tea cloth** (*BrE*) = **tea towel**

**teacup** /ˈtiːkʌp ˈटीकप्/ *noun* [C] a cup that you drink tea from चाय पीने का कप या प्याला

**teak** /tiːk टीक्/ *noun* [U] the strong hard wood of a tall Asian tree, used especially for making furniture सागौन की लकड़ी (विशेषतः फ़र्नीचर बनाने में प्रयुक्त)

**tea leaves** *noun* [*pl.*] the small leaves that are left in a cup after you have drunk the tea (चाय पीने के बाद) प्याले में बची चाय की पत्तियाँ

**team**[1] /tiːm टीम्/ *noun* [C] **1** a group of people who play a sport or game together against another group खिलाड़ियों का दल; टीम *a football team* ○ *Are you* ***in/on the team****?* **2** a group of people who work together एक साथ काम करने वालों का दल या टोली *a team of doctors*

> **NOTE** **Team** शब्द का एकवचन में प्रयोग होने पर साथ आने वाली क्रिया एकवचन में हो सकती है, बहुवचन में भी—*The team play/plays two matches every week.*

**team**[2] /tiːm टीम्/ *verb*

**PHR V** **team up (with sb)** to join sb in order to do sth together मिलकर काम करने के लिए किसी के साथ जुड़ना *I teamed up with Leena to plan the project.*

**teamwork** /ˈtiːmwɜːk ˈटीम्वक्/ *noun* [U] the ability of people to work together लोगों की एक साथ काम करने की क्षमता; सामूहिक कार्य क्षमता *Teamwork is a key feature of the training programme.*

**teapot** /ˈtiːpɒt ˈटीपॉट्/ *noun* [C] a container that you use for making tea in and for serving it चायदानी

**tear**[1] /tɪə(r) टिअ(र्)/ *noun* [C, *usually pl.*] a drop of water that comes from your eye when you are crying, etc. आँसू, अश्रु *I was in tears (*= crying*) at the end of the film.* ○ *The little girl* ***burst into tears*** (= suddenly started to cry).

**IDM** **shed tears** ➪ **shed**[2] देखिए।

**tear**[2] /teə(r) टेअ(र्)/ *verb* (*pt* **tore** /tɔː(r) टॉ(र्)/; *pp* **torn** /tɔːn टॉन्/) **1** [I, T] to damage sth by pulling it apart or into pieces; to become damaged in this way किसी वस्तु को चीर कर या टुकड़े-टुकड़े कर क्षति पहुँचाना; फाड़ना; चिरना, फटना *I tore a page out of my notebook.* ○ *This material doesn't tear easily.* **2** [T] to remove sth by pulling violently and quickly ज़ोर से और जल्दी से किसी वस्तु को खींच कर निकाल देना *Payal tore the poster down from the wall.* ○ *He tore the bag out of her hands.* **3** [T] to make a hole in sth by force ज़ोर लगाकर (किसी में) छेद करना **4** [I] **tear along, up, down, past, etc.** to move very quickly in a particular direction दिशा विशेष में तेज़ी से जाना *An ambulance went tearing past.*

▶ **tear** *noun* [C] दरार, चीर, फाड़ना *You've got a tear in the back of your trousers.*

**IDM** **wear and tear** ➪ **wear**[2] देखिए।

**PHR V** **tear sth apart 1** to pull sth violently into pieces ज़ोर लगाकर किसी चीज़ को फाड़ देना **2** to destroy sth completely किसी चीज़ को तहस-नहस कर देना *The country has been torn apart by the war.*

**tear yourself away (from sb/sth)** to make yourself leave sb/sth or stop doing sth किसी व्यक्ति, वस्तु या काम से अपने को अलग कर लेना

**be torn between A and B** to find it difficult to choose between two things or people दो वस्तुओं या व्यक्तियों में से किसी एक को चुनने की बाध्यता में फँस जाना

**tear sth down** (used about a building) to destroy it (किसी भवन को) गिरा देना, नष्ट कर देना *They tore down the old houses and built a shopping centre.*

**tear sth up** to pull sth into pieces, especially sth made of paper किसी वस्तु (विशेषतः कागज़ से बनी) को टुकड़े-टुकड़े कर देना *'I hate this photograph,' she said, tearing it up.*

**tearful** /ˈtɪəfl ˈटिअफ़्ल्/ *adj.* crying or nearly crying अश्रुपूरित, आँसू भर कर, रोता या रोता हुआ-सा, दुखद

**tear gas** /ˈtɪə gæs ˈटिअ गैस्/ *noun* [U] a type of gas that hurts the eyes and throat, and is used by the police, etc. to control large groups of people अश्रुगैस (पुलिस आदि बलों द्वारा भीड़ को नियंत्रित करने के लिए प्रयुक्त गैस जो आँखों और गले में चुभन पैदा करती है)

**tease** /tiːz टीज़्/ *verb* [I, T] to laugh at sb either in a friendly way or in order to upset him/her छेड़ना, चिढ़ाना (किसी की हँसी उड़ाना, मित्रता की भावना से या उसे परेशान करने के लिए) *They teased her about being fat.*

**teaspoon** /ˈtiːspuːn ˈटीस्पून्/ *noun* [C] **1** a small spoon used for putting sugar in tea, coffee, etc. छोटा चम्मच (जिससे चाय, कॉफ़ी आदि में चीनी डालते हैं)

2 (**teaspoonful** /-fʊl -फ़ुल् /) the amount that a teaspoon can hold छोटा चम्मचभर, छोटे चम्मच में आने वाली (किसी वस्तु की) मात्रा

**teat** /ti:t टीट् / *noun* [C] **1** the rubber part at the end of a baby's bottle that the baby sucks in order to get milk, etc. from the bottle बच्चे की दूध की बोतल में लगी रबर की निपिल (जिससे बच्चा दूध पीता है) **2** one of the parts of a female animal's body that the babies drink milk from मादा पशु के स्तन का अग्रभाग; चूचुक

**tea towel** (*also* **tea cloth**) *noun* [C] a small towel that is used for drying plates, knives, forks, etc. तश्तरियाँ, छुरियाँ, काँटे आदि पोंछने में प्रयुक्त छोटा तौलिया

**technical** /ˈteknɪkl ˈटेक्निकल् / *adj.* **1** connected with the practical use of machines, methods, etc. in science and industry तकनीकी (विज्ञान और उद्योग के क्षेत्र में मशीनों, कार्यविधियों आदि के व्यावहारिक उपयोग से संबंधित) *The train was delayed owing to a technical problem.* **2** connected with the skills involved in a particular activity or subject विशिष्ट क्रिया-कलाप या विषय के लिए अपेक्षित निपुणता से संबंधित तकनीकी ज्ञान की अपेक्षा वाला *This computer magazine is too technical for me.*

**technicality** /ˌteknɪˈkæləti ˌटेक्निˈकैलटि / *noun* [C] (*pl.* **technicalities**) one of the details of a particular subject or activity विशिष्ट विषय या क्रिया-कलाप का कोई ब्योरा; तकनीकी बात

**technically** /ˈteknɪkli ˈटेक्निक्लि / *adv.* **1** according to the exact meaning, facts, etc. (शब्द के) विशुद्ध अर्थ, (वस्तु संबंधी) तथ्यों आदि के अनुसार, व्यवस्था के अनुसार *Technically, you should pay by May 1st, but it doesn't matter if it's a few days late.* **2** in a way that involves detailed knowledge of the machines, etc. that are used in industry or science जिसमें उद्योग या विज्ञान के क्षेत्र में प्रयुक्त मशीनों आदि की विस्तृत जानकारी अपेक्षित हो, तकनीकी ज्ञान और व्यवहार की दृष्टि से *The country is technically not very advanced.* **3** used about sb's practical ability in a particular activity विशिष्ट गतिविधि में किसी की व्यावहारिक निपुणता का निर्देश करने के लिए प्रयुक्त; शास्त्रीय या शास्त्र-अनुमोदित दृष्टि से *He's a technically brilliant dancer.*

**technician** /tekˈnɪʃn टेक्ˈनिशन् / *noun* [C] a person whose work involves practical skills, especially in industry or science व्यावहारिक कौशलों की क्षमता वाला व्यक्ति (विशेषतः उद्योग या विज्ञान के क्षेत्र में); तकनीकी कारीगर *a laboratory technician*

**technique** /tekˈni:k ट्रेक्ˈनीक् / *noun* **1** [C] a particular way of doing sth तकनीक, प्रविधि *new techniques for teaching languages* ○ *marketing/management techniques* **2** [U] the practical skill that sb has in a particular activity कोई विशेष काम करने की व्यावहारिक निपुणता *He's a naturally talented runner, but he needs to work on his technique.*

**techno-** /ˈteknəʊ ˈट्रेक्नो / *prefix* (*used in nouns, adjectives and adverbs*) connected with technology टेक्नॉलजी या प्रौद्योगिकी से संबंधित *technophobe* (= a person who is afraid of technology)

**technology** /tekˈnɒlədʒi ट्रेक्ˈनॉलजि / *noun* [C, U] (*pl.* **technologies**) the scientific knowledge and/or equipment that is needed for a particular industry, etc. विशिष्ट उद्योग आदि के लिए अपेक्षित वैज्ञानिक जानकारी और/या उपकरण; प्रौद्योगिकी/शिल्प-विज्ञान और/या तकनीकी उपकरण *developments in computer technology* ► **technological** /ˌteknəˈlɒdʒɪkl ˌट्रेक्नˈलॉजिकल् / *adj.* प्रौद्योगिकी-विषयक *technological developments* ► **technologist** /tekˈnɒlədʒɪst ट्रेक्ˈनॉलजिस्ट् / *noun* [C] प्रौद्योगिकी-वेत्ता, शिल्प-विज्ञानी *Technologists are developing a computer that can perform surgery.*

**tectonic** /tekˈtɒnɪk ट्रेक्ˈटॉनिक् / *adj.* (in geology) connected with the structure of the earth's surface (भूविज्ञान में) पृथ्वी की सतह की संरचना से संबंधित ➪ **plate tectonics** देखिए।

**teddy** /ˈtedi ˈट्रेडि / (*also* **teddy bear**) *noun* [C] (*pl.* **teddies**) a toy for children that looks like a bear भालू जैसा दिखने वाला(बच्चों का) खिलौना

**tedious** /ˈti:diəs ˈटीडिअस् / *adj.* boring and lasting for a long time उबाऊ और (समय की दृष्टि से) लंबा *a tedious train journey*

**teem** /ti:m टीम् / *verb* [I] **teem with sth** (used about a place) to have a lot of people or things moving about in it (किसी स्थान पर) बड़ी संख्या में व्यक्तियों या वस्तुओं का चलना-फिरना *The streets were teeming with people.* ○ *river teeming with fish*

**teenage** /ˈti:neɪdʒ ˈटीनेज् / *adj.* (*only before a noun*) **1** between 13 and 19 years old किशोरावस्था का, 13 से 19 तक की आयु का *teenage children* **2** typical of or suitable for people between 13 and 19 years old, 13 से 19 तक की आयु के किशोरों के लिए उपयुक्त या विशिष्ट रूप से उनके लिए *teenage magazines/fashion*

**teenager** /ˈti:neɪdʒə(r) ˈटीनेज(र्) / *noun* [C] a person aged between 13 and 19 years old, 13 से 19 तक की आयु का किशोर *Her music is very popular with teenagers.* ➪ **adolescent** देखिए।

**teens** /ti:nz टीन्ज़् / *noun* [*pl.*] the period of a person's life between the ages of 13 and 19, 13 से 19 वर्ष तक की आयु का जीवन-काल; किशोरावस्था *to be* ***in your*** *early/late* ***teens***

**teeshirt** /ˈti:ʃɜ:t ˈटीशट् / = **T-shirt**

**teeth** ➪ **tooth** का plural रूप

**teethe** /ti:ð टीद् / *verb* [I] (*usually* **be teething**) (used about a baby) to start growing its first teeth (बच्चे के) दूध के दाँत निकलना

**teething problems** (*also* **teething troubles**) *noun* [*pl.*] the problems that can develop when a person, system, etc. is new (किसी व्यक्ति, प्रणाली आदि के लिए) नए काम में आने वाली आरंभिक समस्याएँ *We've just installed this new software and are having a few teething problems with it.*

**teetotal** /ˌti:ˈtəʊtl ˌटीˈटोटल् / *adj.* (*not before a noun*) (used about a person) never drinking alcohol (व्यक्ति) जो कभी मदिरापान नहीं करता; अमद्यप

**teetotaller** (*AmE* **teetotaler**) /ˌti:ˈtəʊtlə(r) ˌटीˈटोट्ल(र्) / *noun* [C] a person who does not drink alcohol कभी भी मदिरापान न करने वाला व्यक्ति

**TEFL** /ˈtefl ˈट्रेफ़्ल् / *abbr.* Teaching English as a Foreign Language विदेशी भाषा के रूप में अंग्रेज़ी का शिक्षण

**tel.** *abbr.* telephone (number) फ़ोन या दूरभाष(नंबर) *tel. 01865 56767*

**tele-** /ˈteli ˈटेलि / *prefix* (*used in nouns, verbs, adjectives and adverbs*) **1** over a long distance; far लंबी दूरी का; दूर *telepathy* ○ *telescopic* **2** connected with television टीवी से संबंधित *teletext* **3** done using a telephone टेलीफ़ोन द्वारा या पर किया गया *telesales*

**telecast** /ˈtelikɑ:st ˈट्रेलिकास्ट् / *noun* [C] a broadcast on television दूरदर्शन प्रसारण ▶ **telecast** *verb* [T] (*pt, pp* **telecast**) (*usually passive*) to broadcast on television दूरदर्शन पर प्रसारण करना *The event will be telecast simultaneously to nearly 200 cities around the world.*

**telecommunications** /ˌtelikə ˌmju:nɪˈkeɪʃnz ˌट्रेलिक ˌम्यूनिˈकेशन्ज़् / *noun* [*pl.*] the technology of sending signals, images and messages over long distances by radio, telephone, television, etc. दूर-संचार प्रणाली

**telegram** /ˈtelɪgræm ˈट्रेलिग्रैम् / *noun* [C] a message that is sent by a system (**telegraph**) that uses electrical signals and that is then printed and given to sb टेलीग्राफ़ प्रणाली द्वारा किसी को भेजा गया (मुद्रित) संदेश; तार, टेलीग्राम

**telegraph** /ˈtelɪgrɑ:f ˈट्रेलिग्राफ़् / *noun* [U] a method of sending messages over long distances, using wires that carry electrical signals (विद्युत-संकेतों को ले जाने वाली तारों की सहायता से) संदेशों को दूर-दूर भेजने की प्रणाली, तार-प्रेषण-प्रणाली; टेलीग्राफ़

**telegraph pole** *noun* [C] a tall wooden pole that is used for supporting telephone wires टेलीफ़ोन की तारों को टेक देने के लिए प्रयुक्त लंबा खंभा

**telemarketing** /ˈtelimɑ:kɪtɪŋ ˈटेलिमाकिटिङ् / = **telesales**

**telepathy** /təˈlepəθi टˈलेपथि/ *noun* [U] the communication of thoughts between people's minds without using speech, writing or other normal methods (मौखिक, लिखित या अन्य सामान्य संप्रेषण विधियों का प्रयोग न करते हुए) व्यक्तियों के बीच मानसिक स्तर पर संदेशों का आदान-प्रदान; दूर-संवेदन, दूर-बोध, अतींद्रिय बोध, टेलिपैथी

**telephone** /ˈtelɪfəʊn ˈट्रेलिफ़ोन् / (*informal* **phone**) *noun* **1** [U] an electrical system for talking to sb in another place by speaking into a special piece of equipment टेलीफ़ोन, फ़ोन, दूरभाष *Can I contact you* ***by telephone****?* ○ *to* ***make a phone call*** ○ ***telephone number*** **2** [C] the piece of equipment that you use when you talk to sb by telephone टेलीफ़ोन सेट, यंत्र या उपकरण *a mobile phone/a public telephone* NOTE **Telephone** की अपेक्षा **phone** अधिक प्रचलित शब्द है विशेषतः बोलचाल की स्थिति में।

NOTE जब किसी को फ़ोन किया जाता है तो सबसे पहले नंबर **dial** किया जाता है। फ़ोन **rings** (की घंटी बजती है) और सुनने वाला **answers** (उसका जवाब देता है), यदि उस समय कहीं और फ़ोन किया जा रहा है तो वह **engaged** (व्यस्त) होता है। बात समाप्त हो जाने के बाद आप (फ़ोनकर्ता) **hang up** या **put the phone down** (फ़ोन नीचे रख देते हैं)। नगर से बाहर या दूसरे देश में फ़ोन करते समय, स्थानीय फ़ोन नंबर से पहले डायल किया जाने वाला नंबर **code** कहलाता है।

▶ **telephone** (*also* **phone**) *verb* [I, T] फ़ोन करना *Seema phoned. She's going to be late.*

IDM **on the phone/telephone** ➪ **phone** देखिए।

**telephone box** (*also* **phone box**; **call box**) *noun* [C] a small covered place in a street, etc. that contains a telephone for public use सड़क आदि के किनारे लगा बक्सा जिसमें टेलीफ़ोन रखा होता है (लोगों द्वारा इस्तेमाल के लिए), फ़ोन बॉक्स

**telephone directory** (*informal* **phone book**) *noun* [C] a book that gives a list of the names, addresses and telephone numbers of the people in a particular area फ़ोन पुस्तक (क्षेत्र-विशेष के टेलीफ़ोन

धारकों के नाम, पते और फ़ोन नं. का विवरण देने वाली पुस्तक); टेलीफ़ोन निर्देशिका

**telephone exchange** (*also* **exchange**) *noun* [C] a place belonging to a telephone company where telephone lines are connected to each other टेलीफ़ोन केंद्र या एक्सचेंज

**telesales** /ˈteliseɪlz ˈटेलिसेल्ज़्/ (*also* **telemarketing**) *noun* [U] a method of selling things by telephone टेलीफ़ोन द्वारा सामान बेचने की प्रणाली *He works in telesales.*

**telescope** /ˈtelɪskəʊp ˈटेलिस्कोप्/ *noun* [C] an instrument in the shape of a tube with special pieces of glass (**lenses**) inside it. You look through it to make things that are far away appear bigger and nearer दूरबीन, दूरदर्शक ( बहुत दूर की वस्तुओं को लेंसों की सहायता से अधिक बड़ा और निकट दिखाने वाला नली के आकार का यंत्र)

**teletext** /ˈtelitekst ˈटेलिटेक्स्ट्/ *noun* [U] a service that provides news and other information in written form on television टीवी पर उपलब्ध एक सेवा जिसमें समाचार और अन्य सूचनाएँ परदे पर लिखित रूप में दिखाई देती हैं; टेली-टेक्स्ट

**televise** /ˈtelɪvaɪz ˈटेलिवाइज़्/ *verb* [T] to show sth on television टीवी पर दिखाना या प्रसारित करना *a televised concert*

**television** /ˈtelɪvɪʒn ˈटेलिविशन्/ (*also* **TV** *informal* **telly**) *noun* **1** (*also* **television set**) [C] a piece of electrical equipment in the shape of a box. It has a glass screen which shows programmes with moving pictures and sounds टीवी सेट; टेलीविज़न *to turn the television on/off* **2** [U] the programmes that are shown on a television set टीवी सेट पर प्रसारित कार्यक्रम *Pia's watching television.* **3** [U] the electrical system and business of sending out programmes so that people can watch them on their television sets टीवी कार्यक्रमों के प्रसारण की प्रणाली, प्रक्रिया या व्यापार *a television presenter/series/documentary* ○ *cable/satellite/terrestrial/digital television*

IDM **on television** being shown by television; appearing in a television programme टीवी पर (दिखाया जाने वाला); टीवी कार्यक्रम में आने वाला *What's on television tonight?*

**tell** /tel टेल्/ *verb* (*pt, pp* **told** /təʊld टोल्ड्/) **1** [T] **tell sb (sth/that...); tell sb (about sth); tell sth to sb** to give information to sb by speaking or writing कुछ बताना, जानकारी देना (बोलकर या लिखकर) *She told me her address but I've forgotten it.* ○ *to* ***tell the truth/a lie*** ➪ **say** पर नोट देखिए। **2** [T] **tell sb to do sth** to order or advise sb to do sth किसी को कुछ करने का आदेश या सलाह देना *The policewoman told us to get out of the car.* **3** [I, T] to know, see or judge (sth) correctly (किसी बात को) सही रूप में जानना, देखना या आँकना *I could tell that he had enjoyed the evening.* ○ ***You can never tell*** *what he's going to say next.* ○ *I can't* ***tell the difference between*** *Dinesh's sisters.* **4** [T] (used about a thing) to give information to sb (किसी वस्तु का) किसी को (कुछ) जानकारी देना, (किसी वस्तु से) किसी को (कुछ) जानकारी मिलना *This book will tell you all you need to know.* **5** [I] to not keep a secret भेद बताना, रहस्य खोलना *Promise you won't tell!* **6** [I] **tell (on sb/sth)** to have a noticeable effect (पर) स्पष्ट प्रभाव दिखाई पड़ना *I can't run as fast as I could—my age is beginning to tell!*

IDM **all told** with everyone or everything counted and included सबको या सब कुछ गिनाकर या मिलाकर

**(I'll) tell you what** used to introduce a suggestion कोई सुझाव पेश करने के लिए प्रयुक्त *I'll tell you what —let's ask Manoj to take us.*

**I told you (so)** (*informal*) I warned you that this would happen चेतावनी देने के लिए प्रयुक्त

**tell A and B apart** ➪ **apart** देखिए।

**tell the time** to read the time from a clock or watch घड़ी देखकर समय बताना

PHR V **tell sb off (for sth/for doing sth)** to speak to sb angrily because he/she has done sth wrong किसी पर गुस्सा करना (उसकी ग़लती के लिए) *The teacher told me off for not doing my homework.*

**tell on sb** to tell a parent, teacher, etc. about sth bad that sb has done किसी के ग़लत काम की जानकारी माता-पिता, अध्यापक आदि को देना

**telling** /ˈtelɪŋ ˈटेलिङ्/ *adj.* **1** showing, without intending to, what sb/sth is really like (बिना इरादा) किसी की वास्तविकता को दिखाने वाला *The number of homeless people is a telling comment on today's society.* **2** having a great effect असरदार, प्रभावकारी, ज़ोरदार, कारगर *That's quite a telling argument.*

**tell-tale** *adj.* giving information about sth secret or private किसी के विषय में गुप्त या निजी सूचना देने वाला; सूचक, परिचायक *He said he was fine, but there were tell-tale signs of worry on his face.*

**temp¹** /temp टेम्प्/ *noun* [C] (*informal*) a temporary employee, especially in an office, who works somewhere for a short period of time when sb else is ill or on holiday अस्थायी (एवज़ी, स्थानापन्न) कर्मचारी (विशेषतः किसी दफ़्तर में)

**temp²** *abbr.* temperature तापमान *temp 15°C*

**temper** /ˈtempə(r) ˈटेम्प(र्)/ *noun* **1** [C, U] if you have a temper you get angry very easily गुस्से वाला मिज़ाज, क्रोधी स्वभाव *You must learn to control your temper.* **2** [C] the way you are feeling at a particular time किसी विशेष क्षण में मनोदशा *It's no use talking to him when he's **in a bad temper**.* ✪ पर्याय **mood**

IDM **in a temper** feeling very angry and not controlling your behaviour बहुत गुस्से में और आत्मनियंत्रण खोते हुए

**keep/lose your temper** to stay calm/to become angry शांत रहना या क्रुद्ध हो जाना ➪ **bad-tempered** देखिए।

**temperament** /ˈtemprəmənt ˈटेम्प्रमन्ट्/ *noun* [C, U] a person's character, especially as it affects the way he/she behaves and feels व्यक्ति का स्वभाव (विशेषतः जो उसके आचरण और सोच को प्रभावित करे) *to have an artistic/a fiery/a calm temperament*

**temperamental** /ˌtemprəˈmentl ˈटेम्प्रˈमेन्ट्ल्/ *adj.* often and suddenly changing the way you behave or feel अपने आचरण या सोच को प्रायः और एकाएक बदल देने वाला; अस्थिर-चित्त

**temperate** /ˈtempərət ˈटेम्परट्/ *adj.* (used about a climate) not very hot and not very cold (मौसम) न बहुत गरम न बहुत ठंडा, बीच का

**temperature** /ˈtemprətʃə(r) ˈटेम्प्रच(र्)/ *noun* **1** [C, U] how hot or cold sth is तापमान, टेंपरेचर *Heat the oven to a temperature of 200°C.* ○ *a high/low temperature* **2** [C] how hot or cold a person's body is (मानव-शरीर का) तापमान

IDM **have a temperature** (used about a person) to be hotter than normal because you are ill (व्यक्ति को) बुख़ार होना

**take sb's temperature** to measure the temperature of sb's body with a special instrument (**a thermometer**) (थर्मामीटर से) व्यक्ति का बुख़ार मापना या टेंपरेचर लेना

**template** /ˈtempleɪt ˈटेम्प्लेट्/ *noun* [C] **1** a shape cut out of a hard material, used as a model for producing exactly the same shape many times in another material धातु आदि में कटी हुई, साँचे का काम करने वाली, आकृति (जिसकी सहायता से भिन्न वस्तु से वैसी ही आकृतियाँ बारंबार बनाई जा सकती हैं) **2** a thing that is used as a model for producing other similar examples मॉडल के रूप में प्रयुक्त कोई वस्तु (उसी प्रकार की अन्य वस्तुएँ तैयार करने के लिए प्रयुक्त) *If you need to write a lot of similar letters, set up a template on your computer.*

**temple** /ˈtempl ˈटेम्पल्/ *noun* [C] **1** a building where people pray to a god or gods मंदिर, देवालय, पूजा-स्थली *a Buddhist/Hindu temple* **2** one of the flat parts on each side of your forehead कनपटी ➪ **body** पर चित्र देखिए।

**tempo** /ˈtempəʊ ˈटेम्पो/ *noun* (*pl.* **tempos** /ˈtempəʊz ˈटेम्पोज़्/) **1** [*sing.*, U] the speed of an activity or event किसी क्रिया या गतिविधि या घटना की चाल, गति, स्पीड या रफ़्तार **2** [C, U] the speed of a piece of music किसी संगीत-रचना की गति *a fast/slow tempo* **3** [C] (in India) a three-wheeled vehicle for carrying goods (भारत में) सामान वहन करने का तिपहिया वाहन

**temporary** /ˈtemprəri ˈटेम्प्ररि/ *adj.* lasting for a short time; not permanent अल्पकालिक, अस्थायी *a temporary job* ○ *This arrangement is only temporary.* ▶ **temporarily** /ˈtemprərəli ˈटेम्प्ररलि/ *adv.* अस्थायी रूप से

**tempt** /ˈtempt ˈटेम्प्ट्/ *verb* [T] **tempt sb (into sth/into doing sth); tempt sb (to do sth)** to try to persuade or attract sb to do sth, even if it is wrong किसी कार्य को (भले ही वह ग़लत हो) करने के लिए किसी को प्रेरित या आकृष्ट करना; प्रलोभन देना, बहकाना *His dream of riches had tempted him into a life of crime.*

**temptation** /tempˈteɪʃn टेम्प्ˈटेश्न्/ *noun* **1** [U] a feeling that you want to do sth, even if you know that it is wrong किसी काम (भले ही ग़लत) को करने की चाह; प्रलोभन, लालच *I managed to **resist the temptation** to tell him what I really thought.* **2** [C] a thing that attracts you to do sth wrong or silly प्रलोभन देने वाली या ललचाने वाली वस्तु *All that money is certainly a big temptation.*

**tempting** /ˈtemptɪŋ ˈटेम्प्टिङ्/ *adj.* attractive in a way that makes you want to do or have sth प्रलोभनकारी, ललचाने वाला, लुभावना, मोहक *a tempting offer*

**ten** /ten टेन्/ *number* 10 दस (की संख्या)

NOTE संख्याओं के वाक्य-प्रयोग के उदाहरणों के लिए **six** की प्रविष्टि देखिए।

**tenacious** /təˈneɪʃəs टˈनेशस्/ *adj.* not likely to give up or let sth go; determined आसानी से हार न मानने वाला; दृढ़निश्चय ▶ **tenacity** /təˈnæsəti टˈनैसटि/ *noun* [U] दृढ़ता

**tenancy** /ˈtenənsi ˈटेनन्सि/ *noun* [C, U] (*pl.* **tenancies**) the use of a room, flat, building or piece of land, for which you pay rent to the owner कमरे, फ़्लैट, भवन या भूखंड का किराया देकर उपयोग करने का कार्य; किराएदारी, (भूखंड की) पट्टेदारी *a six-*

*month tenancy* o *It says in the tenancy agreement that you can't keep pets.*

**tenant** /ˈtenənt ˈटेनन्ट्/ *noun* [C] a person who pays money (**rent**) to the owner of a room, flat, building or piece of land so that he/she can live in it or use it कमरे, फ़्लैट, भवन या भूखंड का किराया देकर उपयोग करने वाला व्यक्ति; किराएदार, (भूखंड का) पट्टेदार, पट्टाधारी आसामी ➪ **landlady** और **landlord** देखिए।

**tend** /tend ट्रेन्ड्/ *verb* **1** [I] **tend to do sth** to usually do or be sth प्रायः कुछ करना या होना, प्रवृत्ति या झुकाव होना *There tends to be a lot of heavy traffic on that road.* o *My brother tends to talk a lot when he's nervous.* **2** [I] used for giving your opinion in a polite way नम्रतापूर्वक अपनी राय देने के लिए प्रयुक्त, (को) लगना, (का) विचार होना *I tend to think that we shouldn't interfere.* **3** [I, T] (*formal*) **tend (to) sb/sth** to look after sb/sth किसी की देखभाल करना, (पर) ध्यान देना *Paramedics tended (to) the injured.*

**tendency** /ˈtendənsi ˈटेन्डन्सि/ *noun* [C] (*pl.* **tendencies**) **a tendency (to do sth/towards sth)** something that a person or thing usually does; a way of behaving (व्यक्ति या वस्तु की) प्रवृत्ति, झुकाव, रुझान; व्यवहार करने का ढंग, आदत *They both **have a tendency** to be late for appointments.* o *The animal began to show vicious tendencies.*

**tender**[1] /ˈtendə(r) ˈटेन्ड(र्)/ *adj.* **1** kind and loving सदय और स्नेहपूर्ण; कोमल *tender words/looks* **2** (used about food) soft and easy to cut or bite; not tough (खाद्य पदार्थ) नरम और आसानी से कटने या काटे जा सकने वाले; मुलायम *The meat should be nice and tender.* **3** (used about a part of the body) painful when you touch it (शरीर का कोई अंग) छूने पर दर्द करने वाला; संवेदनशील

IDM **at a tender age; at the tender age of...** when still young and without much experience आयु और अनुभव के कम होने की स्थिति; सुकुमार, नाज़ुक *She went to live in London at the tender age of 15.* ▸ **tenderly** *adv.* कोमलता के साथ ▸ **tenderness** *noun* [U] सुकुमारता, नाज़ुकपन, कोमलता

**tender**[2] /ˈtendə(r) ˈटेन्ड(र्)/ *verb* [I, T] (*written*) to offer or give sth formally किसी वस्तु को औपचारिक रूप से प्रस्तुत करना या देना *After the scandal the Foreign Minister was forced to tender her resignation.* ▸ **tender** (*also* **bid**) *noun* [C] टेंडर, निविदा (सामान पहुँचाने का प्रस्ताव) *Several firms submitted a tender for the catering contract.*

**tendon** /ˈtendən ˈटेन्डन्/ *noun* [C] a strong, thin part inside your body that joins a muscle to a bone मांसपेशी को हड्डी से जोड़ने वाली नस; कंडरा ➪ **arm** पर चित्र देखिए।

**tendril** /ˈtendrəl ˈटेन्ड्रल्/ *noun* [C] a long thin part that grows from a climbing plant. A plant uses tendrils to fasten itself to a wall, etc. लताओं में पतले धागे या सूत का अंश (जिसके सहारे वह दीवार आदि पर चढ़ती है); तंतु, प्रतान

**tendu** (*also* **tendu leaf**) *noun* [C] the leaf of an Asian tree used to make **beedis** (in India) तेंदु के पत्ते जिनसे बीड़ी बनती है (भारत में)

**tenement** /ˈtenəmənt ˈटेनमन्ट्/ *noun* [C] a large building that is divided into small flats, especially in a poor area of a city छोटे फ़्लैटों वाली एक बड़ी इमारत (विशेषतः शहर की ग़रीब बस्ती में)

**tenet** /ˈtenɪt ˈटेनिट्/ *noun* [C] (*formal*) one of the principles or beliefs that a theory or larger set of beliefs is based on सिद्धांत या अभिमत जिस पर अन्य सिद्धांत आधारित हों *one of the basic tenets of Christianity*

**tennis** /ˈtenɪs ˈटेनिस्/ *noun* [U] a game for two or four players who hit a ball over a net using a piece of equipment (**a racket**) that is held in one hand टेनिस का खेल *to have a game of tennis* o *a tennis match*

NOTE टेनिस को **singles** (में) खेला जाता है (जिसमें आमने-सामने एक-एक खिलाड़ी होता है) और **doubles** (में) भी (जिसमें दो-दो खिलाड़ियों की दो टीमें होती हैं)।

**tenor** /ˈtenə(r) ˈटेन(र्)/ *noun* [C] a fairly high singing voice for a man; a man with this voice पुरुष (गायक) का उच्च स्वर; उच्च स्वर वाला पुरुष (गायक) *Pavarotti is a famous Italian tenor.*

**tenpin bowling** /ˌtenpɪn ˈbəʊlɪŋ ˌटेनपिन् ˈबोलिङ्/ *noun* [U] a game in which you roll a heavy ball towards ten objects (**tenpins**) and try to knock them down एक खेल जिसमें दस (बेलनाकार) खड़ी वस्तुओं को भारी गेंद के आघात से गिराया जाता है; बोलिंग

**tense**[1] /tens टेन्स्/ *adj.* **1** (used about a person) not able to relax because you are worried or nervous (चिंता या परेशानी के कारण) तनावग्रस्त (व्यक्ति) *She looked pale and tense.* **2** (used about a muscle or a part of the body) tight; not relaxed (मांसपेशी या शरीर का कोई अंग) खिंचा हुआ, कड़ा; तना हुआ **3** (used about an atmosphere or a situation) in which people feel worried and not relaxed (वातावरण या परिस्थिति) तनावभरा

**tense**[2] /tens टेन्स्/ *verb* [I, T] **tense (up)** to have muscles that have become hard and not relaxed मांसपेशियों का कड़ा पड़ जाना और तन जाना

**tense[3]** /tens टेन्स्/ *noun* [C, U] (*grammar*) a form of a verb that shows if sth happens in the past, present or future (क्रिया का) काल (भूत, वर्तमान या भविष्य में कुछ घटित होने का अर्थ देने वाला क्रियारूप)

**NOTE** क्रिया के कालों के विषय में अधिक जानकारी के लिए इस शब्दकोश के अंत में **Quick Grammar Reference** देखिए।

**tension** /ˈtenʃn ˈटेन्शन्/ *noun* **1** [U] the condition of not being able to relax because you are worried or nervous (चिंता या परेशानी के कारण) मानसिक तनाव; उत्तेजना *I could hear the tension in her voice as she spoke.* **2** [C, U] bad feeling and lack of trust between people, countries, etc. लोगों, देशों के बीच तनाव (दुर्भावना और अविश्वास) *There are signs of growing tensions between the two countries.* **3** [U] (used about a rope, muscle, etc.) the state of being stretched tight; how tightly sth is stretched (रस्सी, मांसपेशी आदि) कसा-खिंचा होने की स्थिति, कसाव, खिंचाव; कसाव या खिंचाव की मात्रा *The massage relieved the tension in my neck.*

**tent** /tent टेन्ट्/ *noun* [C] a small structure made of cloth that is held up by poles and ropes. You use a tent to sleep in when you go camping तंबू, टेंट *to put up/take down a tent*

**tentacle** /ˈtentəkl ˈटेन्टक्ल्/ *noun* [C] one of the long thin soft parts like legs that some sea animals have कुछ समुद्री जीवों का टाँग जैसा लंबा पतला कोमल अंग; स्पर्शक *An octopus has eight tentacles.* ➪ **jellyfish** पर चित्र देखिए।

**tentative** /ˈtentətɪv ˈटेन्टटिव्/ *adj.* **1** (used about plans, etc.) uncertain; not definite (योजनाएँ आदि) अनिश्चित; कच्चा, कामचलाऊ, अंतरिम **2** (used about a person or his/her behaviour) not confident about what you are saying or doing (व्यक्ति या उसका आचरण) कुछ कहने या करने में आत्मविश्वास से रहित, संकोचपूर्ण *a tentative smile/suggestion* ▶ **tentatively** *adv.* कामचलाऊ ढंग से, अस्थायी रूप से

**tenterhooks** /ˈtentəhʊks ˈटेन्टहुक्स्/ *noun* [*pl.*]

**IDM** **(be) on tenterhooks** to be in a very nervous or excited state because you are waiting to find out what is going to happen ('आगे क्या होगा' की प्रतीक्षा या चिंता में) बहुत परेशान या उत्तेजित (रहना)

**tenth[1]** /tenθ टेन्थ्/ *pronoun, det., adv.* 10th दसवाँ ➪ **sixth** के उदाहरण देखिए।

**tenth[2]** /tenθ टेन्थ्/ *noun* [C] the fraction ⅒; one of ten equal parts of sth भिन्न ⅒; किसी वस्तु का दसवाँ भाग (दस समान भागों में से एक) ➪ **sixth** के उदाहरण देखिए।

**tenuous** /ˈtenjuəs ˈटेन्युअस्/ *adj.* very weak or uncertain बहुत कमज़ोर या अनिश्चित *The connection between Mohit's story and what actually happened was tenuous.*

**tenure** /ˈtenjə(r) ˈटेन्य(र्)/ *noun* [U] a legal right to live in a place, hold a job, use land, etc. for a certain time निश्चित अवधि के लिए कहीं रहने, कोई नौकरी करने, किसी भूखंड का प्रयोग करने आदि का क़ानूनी अधिकार

**tepid** /ˈtepɪd ˈटेपिड्/ *adj.* (used about liquids) only slightly warm (द्रव) गुनगुना, हलका गरम

**Terai** *noun* (in India, Nepal and Bhutan) an area of marshy jungle near the Himalayan foothills (भारत, नेपाल तथा भूटान में) तराई; हिमालय के निचले पहाड़ी इलाक़े के दलदली जंगल

**term[1]** /tɜːm टम्/ *noun* **1** [C] a word or group of words with a particular meaning विशिष्ट अर्थ वाला कोई शब्द या शब्दावली *What exactly do you mean by the term 'racist'?* ○ *a technical term in computing* **2 terms** [*pl.*] **in terms of...; in... terms** used for showing which particular way you are thinking about sth or from which point of view की दृष्टि से, के लिहाज़ से (किसी विषय में सोचने के विशेष ढंग या दृष्टिकोण को प्रकट करने के लिए प्रयुक्त) *The flat would be ideal in terms of size, but it is very expensive.* **3 terms** [*pl.*] the conditions of an agreement समझौते की शर्तें *Both sides agreed to the peace terms.* **4** [C] a period of time into which a school or university year is divided स्कूल या विश्वविद्यालय का सत्र; शैक्षिक सत्र *the autumn/spring/summer term* ○ *an end-of-term test* **5** [C] a period of time for which sth lasts (किसी बात की) अवधि, मियाद, टर्म *The US President is now in his second term of office.*

**IDM** **be on equal terms (with sb)** ➪ **equal[1]** देखिए।

**be on good, friendly, etc. terms (with sb)** to have a friendly relationship with sb किसी के साथ दोस्ती होना

**come to terms with sth** to accept sth unpleasant or difficult किसी अप्रिय या कठिन स्थिति को स्वीकार या सहन करना

**in the long/short term** over a long/short period of time in the future दूर या निकट भविष्य में, लंबी या अल्प अवधि में

**term[2]** /tɜːm टम्/ *verb* [T] to describe sb/sth by using a particular word or expression विशिष्ट शब्द या शब्दावली की सहायता से किसी का संकेत करना; अभिहित करना *the period of history that is often termed the 'Dark Ages'*

**terminal**[1] /ˈtɜːmɪnl ˈटर्मिनल् / *adj.* (used about an illness) slowly causing death (बीमारी) (रोगी को) क्रमशः मृत्यु की ओर ले जाती हुई; लाइलाज, मरणांतक, अंतस्थ *terminal cancer* ▶ **terminally** /-nəli -नलि / *adv.* अंतिम या मरणांतक रूप से *a terminally ill patient*

**terminal**[2] /ˈtɜːmɪnl ˈटर्मिनल् / *noun* [C] **1** a large railway station, bus station or building at an airport where journeys begin and end रेल, बस का बड़ा अड्डा या हवाई अड्डे का बड़ा भवन (यात्रा का आरंभ या विराम स्थल) *the bus terminal* ○ *Which terminal are you flying from?* **2** (*computing*) the computer that one person uses for getting information from a central computer or for putting information into it टर्मिनल (कंप्यूटर) (केंद्रीय कंप्यूटर से सूचना के आदान-प्रदान के लिए प्रयुक्त कंप्यूटर)

**terminate** /ˈtɜːmɪneɪt ˈटर्मिनेट् / *verb* [I, T] (*formal*) to end or to make sth end समाप्त होना या करना *to terminate a contract/an agreement* ▶ **termination** *noun* [U] समाप्ति

**terminology** /ˌtɜːmɪˈnɒlədʒi ˌटर्मिˈनॉलजि / *noun* [U] the special words and expressions that are used in a particular profession, subject or activity पारिभाषिक शब्दावली (विशिष्ट व्यवसाय, विषय या क्रिया-कलाप में विशेष शब्द और अभिव्यक्तियाँ)

**terminus** /ˈtɜːmɪnəs ˈटर्मिनस् / *noun* [C] (*pl.* **terminuses** /-nəsɪz -नसिज़् /) the last stop or station at the end of a bus route or railway line रेल या बस का अंतिम स्टेशन

**termite** /ˈtɜːmaɪt ˈटमाइट् / *noun* [C] a small insect that lives in large groups, mainly in hot countries. Termites eat the wood of trees and buildings दीमक

**terrace** /ˈterəs ˈटेरस् / *noun* **1** [C] a flat area of stone next to a restaurant or large house where people can have meals, sit in the sun, etc. रेस्तराँ या बड़े मकान के बग़ल में फ़र्शदार जगह (जहाँ लोग खाना खाते हैं, धूप सेंकते हैं आदि); चबूतरा ➪ **patio, veranda** और **balcony** देखिए। **2** (*BrE*) [C] a line of similar houses that are all joined together परस्पर जुड़े एक जैसे मकानों की शृंखला; गृह-श्रेणी **3** [C, *usually pl.*] one of the series of steps that are cut into the side of a hill so that crops can be grown there किसी पहाड़ी के एक तरफ़ काटकर बनाए गए सीढ़ीदार खेतों की एक सीढ़ी (जिस पर फ़सलें उगाई जाती हैं) **4 terraces** [*pl.*] the wide steps that people stand on to watch a football match फ़ुटबॉल मैच के दर्शकों के लिए बनी चौड़ी सीढ़ियाँ (जिस पर खड़े होकर वे मैच देखते हैं)

**terraced** /ˈterəst ˈटेरस्ट् / *adj.* **1** (*BrE*) (used about a house) forming part of a line of similar houses that are all joined together परस्पर जुड़े एक जैसे मकानों की शृंखला का (मकान) **2** (used about a hill) having steps cut out of it so that crops can be grown there (पहाड़ी) सीढ़ीदार-खेतों वाली

**terracotta** /ˌterəˈkɒtə ˌटेराˈकॉटा / *noun* [U] red-dish-brown clay that has been baked but not covered in a shiny transparent substance (**glaze**), and is used for making pots, ornaments etc. (बरतन आभूषण आदि बनाने में प्रयुक्त) बिना पॉलिश की पक्की मिट्टी (आग में पकाई हुई लाल-भूरे रंग की); टैराकोटा

**terrain** /təˈreɪn टˈरेन् / *noun* [U] land of the type mentioned निर्दिष्ट प्रकार की भूमि *mountainous/steep/rocky terrain*

**terrestrial** / təˈrestriəl टˈरेस्ट्रिअल् / *adj.* **1** connected with the planet Earth भौमिक, स्थलीय *terrestrial life* **2** (*technical*) (of animals and plants) living on the land rather than in water or air (पशु और पौधे) स्थलजीवी, भूवासी न कि जल या वायुवासी **3** (of television and broadcasting) operating on earth rather than from a satellite (दूरदर्शन और प्रसारण प्रणाली) धरती से न कि उपग्रह से परिचालित

**terrible** /ˈterəbl ˈटेरबल् / *adj.* **1** very unpleasant; causing great shock or injury बहुत बुरा; भयानक; बहुत तकलीफ़ और चोट पहुँचाने वाला *a terrible accident* ○ *terrible news* **2** ill or very upset बीमार या बहुत परेशान *I feel terrible I'm going to be sick.* **3** very bad; of poor quality बहुत ख़राब; घटिया *a terrible hotel/book/memory/driver* **4** (*only before a noun*) used to emphasize how bad sth is किसी वस्तु के बुरी हालत में होने पर बल देने के लिए प्रयुक्त, बहुत बुरा *in terrible pain/trouble* ○ *The room was in a terrible mess.*

**terribly** /ˈterəbli ˈटेरब्लि / *adv.* **1** very अत्यधिक *I'm terribly sorry.* **2** very badly बहुत ख़राब *I played terribly.* ○ *The experiment went terribly wrong.*

**terrier** /ˈteriə(r) ˈटेरिअ(र्) / *noun* [C] a type of small dog एक छोटे कद वाली नसल का कुत्ता; टेरिअर

**terrific** /təˈrɪfɪk टˈरिफ़िक् / *adj.* **1** (*informal*) extremely nice or good; excellent बहुत बढ़िया या अच्छा; उत्कृष्ट *You're doing a terrific job!* **2** (*only before a noun*) very great बहुत ज़्यादा; प्रभूत *I've got a terrific amount of work to do.* ▶ **terrifically** /-kli -क्लि / *adv.* अत्यधिक *terrifically expensive*

**terrified** /ˈterɪfaɪd ˈटेरिफ़ाइड् / *adj.* **terrified (of sb/sth)** very afraid भयभीत *I'm absolutely terrified of snakes.*

**terrify** /ˈterɪfaɪ ˈटेरिफ़ाइ/ *verb* [T] (*pres. part.* **terrifying**; *3rd person sing. pres.* **terrifies**; *pt, pp* **terrified**) to frighten sb very much (किसी को) बहुत डरा देना, भयभीत कर देना

**territorial** /ˌterəˈtɔːriəl ˌटेरˈटॉरिअल्/ *adj.* (*only before a noun*) connected with the land or area of sea that belongs to a country किसी देश के स्वामित्व वाले भू-क्षेत्र या समुद्र-क्षेत्र से संबंधित; राज्य-क्षेत्र-विषयक

**territorial waters** *noun* [*pl.*] the parts of a sea or an ocean which are near a country's coast and are legally under its control किसी देश का तटवर्ती समुद्री क्षेत्र (जिस पर क़ानूनन उसका अधिकार होता है); सीमांतवर्ग जलक्षेत्र

**territory** /ˈterətri ˈटेरट्रि/ *noun* (*pl.* **territories**) **1** [C, U] an area of land that belongs to one country किसी देश के स्वामित्व वाला भूक्षेत्र; राज्य-क्षेत्र *to fly over enemy territory* **2** [C, U] an area that an animal has as its own किसी पशु का (विचरण) क्षेत्र **3** [U] an area of knowledge or responsibility ज्ञान-क्षेत्र या अधिकार या दायित्व-क्षेत्र *Computer programming is Leela's territory.*

**terror** /ˈterə(r) ˈटेर(र्)/ *noun* **1** [U] very great fear अत्यधिक भय; आतंक, दहशत, संत्रास *He screamed **in terror** as the rats came towards him.* **2** [C] a person or thing that makes you feel afraid आतंक या दहशत फैलाने वाला व्यक्ति या वस्तु *the terrors of the night* **3** [U] violence and the killing of ordinary people for political purposes राजनीतिक कारणों से हिंसा और आम लोगों की हत्या *a campaign of terror* **4** [C] a person or animal, especially a child, that is difficult to control उपद्रवी, दुष्ट, बेक़ाबू पशु या व्यक्ति (विशेषतः बच्चा) *Rahul's a little terror.*

**terrorism** /ˈterərɪzəm ˈटेररिज़म्/ *noun* [U] the killing of ordinary people for political purposes राजनीतिक कारणों से आम लोगों की हत्या; आतंकपूर्ण कार्रवाई, आतंकवाद, दहशतगर्दी *an act of terrorism*
► **terrorist** /ˈterərɪst ˈटेररिस्ट्/ *noun* [C], *adj.* आतंकवादी, आतंकी, दहशतगर्द

**terrorize** (*also* **-ise**) /ˈterəraɪz ˈटेरराइज़्/ *verb* [T] to make sb feel frightened by using or threatening to use violence against him/her हिंसा के प्रयोग या धमकी से किसी को डराना; आतंक, दहशत फैलाना *The gang has terrorized the neighbourhood for months.*

**terse** /tɜːs टस्/ *adj.* said in few words and in a not very friendly way संक्षिप्त और रूखा *a terse reply*

**tertiary** /ˈtɜːʃəri ˈटशरि/ *adj.* (used about education) at university or college level (शिक्षा) विश्वविद्यालय या कॉलेज स्तर की *a tertiary college*

**TESL** /ˈtesl ˈटेसल्/ *abbr.* Teaching English as a Second Language द्वितीय भाषा के रूप में अंग्रेज़ी का शिक्षण

**test**[1] /test टेस्ट्/ *noun* [C] **1** a short exam to measure sb's knowledge or skill in sth किसी विषय में किसी के ज्ञान या कौशल को मापने के लिए आयोजित लघु परीक्षा; परीक्षण, टेस्ट *We have a spelling test every Friday.* **2** a short medical examination of a part of your body शरीर के किसी अंग की डॉक्टरी जाँच *to have an eye test* **3** an experiment to find out if sth works or to find out more information about it किसी वस्तु की क्रियाशीलता या प्रभावोत्पादकता को परखने या उसके विषय में अधिक जानकारी पाने के लिए किया गया परीक्षण *to carry out/perform/do a test* **4** a situation or an event that shows how good, strong, etc. sb/sth is किसी की योग्यता, सामर्थ्य आदि को परखने वाली स्थिति या घटना

IDM **put sb/sth to the test** to do sth to find out how good, strong, etc. sb/sth is किसी की योग्यता, शक्ति आदि का परीक्षण करना

**test**[2] /test टेस्ट्/ *verb* [T] **1 test sb/sth (for sth); test sth (on sb/sth)** to try, use or examine sth carefully to find out if it is working properly or what it is like किसी वस्तु को सावधानी से आज़माना, इस्तेमाल करना या परखना (जानने के लिए कि वह कैसी है या क्या है) *These cars have all been tested for safety.* **2** to examine a part of the body to find out if it is healthy शरीर के किसी अंग की (डॉक्टरी) जाँच करना *to have your eyes tested* **3 test sb (on sth)** to examine sb's knowledge or skill in sth किसी विषय में किसी के ज्ञान या कौशल की परीक्षा करना *We're being tested on irregular verbs this morning.*

**testament** /ˈtestəmənt ˈटेस्टमन्ट्/ *noun* [C, *usually sing.*] (*written*) **a testament (to sth)** something that shows that sth exists or is true किसी बात के अस्तित्व में होने या सच होने का प्रमाण ⇨ **the New Testament** और **the Old Testament** देखिए।

**test drive** *noun* [C] an occasion when you drive a vehicle that you are thinking of buying so that you can see how well it works and if you like it (ख़रीदने से पहले) किसी वाहन को चलाने या ड्राइव करने की क्रिया (उसकी कार्यकुशलता की जाँच के लिए)
► **test-drive** *verb* [T] (ख़रीदने से पहले कार्यकुशलता की जाँच के लिए) किसी वाहन को ड्राइव करना

**testes** ⇨ **testis** का plural रूप

**testicle** /ˈtestɪkl ˈटेस्टिकल्/ *noun* [C] one of the two roundish male sex organs that produce the male cells (**sperm**) that are needed for making young पुरुष का अंडकोश (एक यौनांग जिसमें प्रजनन के लिए अपेक्षित वीर्य उत्पन्न होता है)

**testify** /ˈtestɪfaɪ ˈटेस्टिफ़ाइ/ *verb* [I, T] (*pres. part.* **testifying;** *3rd person sing. pres.* **testifies;** *pt, pp* **testified**) to make a formal statement that sth is true, especially in a court of law गवाही या साक्ष्य देना (विशेषतः न्यायालय में)

**testimony** /ˈtestɪməni ˈटेस्टिमनि/ *noun* (*pl.* **testimonies**) **1** [C, U] a formal statement that sth is true, especially one that is made in a court of law किसी बात के सच होने के पक्ष में औपचारिक वक्तव्य; गवाही या साक्ष्य (विशेषतः न्यायालय में) **2** [U, *sing.*] (*formal*) something that shows that sth else exists or is true प्रमाण, सबूत (जो किसी बात के अस्तित्व या सचाई को सामने लाए)

**testis** /ˈtestɪs ˈटेस्टिस्/ (*pl.* **testes** /-tiːz -टीज़्/) (*technical*) = **testicle**

**testosterone** /teˈstɒstərəʊn टेˈस्टॉस्टरोन्/ *noun* [U] a substance (**hormone**) produced in men's bodies that makes them develop male physical and sexual characteristics पुरुष के शरीर में उत्पन्न हॉर्मोन-विशेष जो पुरुष के विशिष्ट शारीरिक और लैंगिक गुणों का विकास करता है ➪ **oestrogen** और **progesterone** देखिए।

**test tube** *noun* [C] a thin glass tube that is used in chemical experiments काँच की परख-नली (रासायनिक परीक्षणों में प्रयुक्त) ➪ **laboratory** पर चित्र देखिए।

**tetanus** /ˈtetənəs ˈटेटनस्/ *noun* [U] a serious disease that makes your muscles, especially the muscles of your face, hard and impossible to move. It is caused by bacteria entering the body through cuts or wounds धनुष टंकार, एक गंभीर रोग जिसमें मांसपेशियाँ (विशेषतः चेहरे की) अकड़ जाती हैं, (चोट या घाव के द्वारा बैक्टीरिआ के शरीर में प्रवेश करने से यह रोग होता है)

**tether[1]** /ˈteðə(r) ˈटेद्र(र्)/ *verb* [T] to tie an animal to sth with a rope, etc. पगहे (रस्सी आदि) से पशु को बाँधना

**tether[2]** /ˈteðə(r) ˈटेद्र(र्)/ *noun* a rope chain used to tie an animal to a fixed object so as to confine it to a small area पशुओं को बाँधा गया पगहा (रस्सी आदि) **IDM** **at the end of your tether** ➪ **end[1]** देखिए।

**text[1]** /tekst टेक्स्ट्/ *noun* **1** [U] the main written part of a book, newspaper, etc. (not the pictures, notes, index, etc.) किसी पुस्तक, अख़बार का मुख्य लिखित भाग (जिसमें चित्र, टिप्पणियाँ, अनुक्रमणिका आदि शामिल नहीं); मूल पाठ **2** [C] the written form of a speech, **interview**, etc. किसी भाषण, साक्षात्कार आदि का लिखित रूप *The newspaper printed the complete text of the interview.* **3** [C] a book or a short piece of writing that people study as part of a literature or language course साहित्य या भाषा की पाठ्यपुस्तक में निर्धारित कोई पुस्तक या रचना *a set text* (= one that has to be studied for an examination)

**text[2]** /tekst टेक्स्ट्/ *verb* [T] to send sb a written message using a **mobile phone** मोबाइल फ़ोन या चल भाष पर लिखित संदेश भेजना *Text me when you reach home.*

**textbook** /ˈtekstbʊk ˈटेक्स्ट्बुक्/ *noun* [C] a book that teaches a particular subject and that is used especially in schools किसी विषय की पाठ्यपुस्तक (विशेषतः स्कूलों में) *a history textbook*

**textile** /ˈtekstaɪl ˈटेक्स्टाइल्/ *noun* [C] any cloth made in a factory कारख़ाने में बना कपड़ा; वस्त्र *cotton textiles* ○ *the textile industry*

**text message** *noun* [C] a written message that is sent from one **mobile phone** to another एक मोबाइल फ़ोन या चल भाष से दूसरे फ़ोन को भेजा गया लिखित संदेश ▶ **text messaging** *noun* [U] उक्त रीति से संदेश भेजने की क्रिया

**texture** /ˈtekstʃə(r) ˈटेक्स्च(र्)/ *noun* [C, U] the way that sth feels when you touch it किसी वस्तु के स्पर्श से हुआ विशिष्ट अनुभव *a rough/smooth/coarse/creamy texture*

**than** /ðən; *strong form* ðæn द्न्; प्रबल रूप द्रैन्/ *conj., prep.* **1** used when you are comparing two things दो वस्तुओं की तुलना के लिए प्रयुक्त से, की अपेक्षा *He's taller than me.* ○ *You speak French much better than she does/than her.* **2** used with 'more' and 'less' before numbers, expressions of time, distance, etc. संख्यावाची, समयसूचक, दूरी आदि शब्दों से पहले 'more' और 'less' के साथ प्रयुक्त *I've worked here for more than three years.* **3** used after 'would rather' to say that you prefer one thing to another एक वस्तु पर दूसरी को प्रमुखता देने के अर्थ में 'would rather' के बाद प्रयुक्त *I'd rather play tennis than football.*

**thank** /θæŋk थैङ्क्/ *verb* [T] **thank sb (for sth/for doing sth)** to tell sb that you are grateful किसी के प्रति आभार प्रकट करना, कृतज्ञता ज्ञापित करना *I'll go and thank him for offering to help.*

**NOTE** किसी का आभार जतलाने के लिए **thank you** और **thanks** दोनों का प्रयोग होता है। **Thanks** अधिक अनौपचारिक प्रयोग है—*Thank you very much for your letter.* **Thank you** और **thanks** का प्रयोग तब भी किया जा सकता है जब किसी के दिए निमंत्रण आदि को स्वीकार करना हो—*'Stay for dinner.' 'Thank you. That would be nice.'* यदि किसी वस्तु आदि को लेने से इनकार करना हो तो **no, thank you** या **no, thanks** कहा जाता है—*'Would you like some more tea?' 'No, thanks.'*

**IDM thank God/goodness/heavens** used for expressing happiness that sth unpleasant has stopped or will not happen किसी अप्रिय बात के अभी और आगे भी, घटित न होने की संभावना पर ख़ुशी प्रकट करने के लिए प्रयुक्त *Thank goodness it's stopped raining.*

**thankful** /ˈθæŋkfl ˈथैङ्क्फ़्ल्/ *adj.* **thankful (for sth/to do sth/that...)** (*not before a noun*) pleased and grateful प्रसन्न और चिंतामुक्त *I was thankful to hear that you got home safely.*

**thankfully** /ˈθæŋkfəli ˈथैङ्क्फ़लि/ *adv.* **1** used for expressing happiness that sth unpleasant did not or will not happen किसी अप्रिय बात के (अभी और बाद में) घटित न होने पर ख़ुशी प्रकट करने के लिए प्रयुक्त ✪ पर्याय **fortunately** *Thankfully, no one was injured in the accident.* **2** in a pleased or grateful way प्रसन्नता के साथ या कृतज्ञतापूर्वक *I accepted her help thankfully.*

**thankless** /ˈθæŋkləs ˈथैङ्क्लस्/ *adj.* involving hard work that other people do not notice or thank you for ऐसी मेहनत जिस पर लोगों का ध्यान नहीं जाता या वे उसके लिए एहसान नहीं मानते; व्यर्थ, बेकार, अप्रिय

**thanks** /θæŋks थैङ्क्स्/ *noun* [*pl.*] words which show that you are grateful कृतज्ञता प्रकट करने के लिए प्रयुक्त शब्द; धन्यवाद, शुक्रिया *I'd like to express my thanks to all of you for coming here today.*

**IDM thanks to sb/sth** because of sb/sth किसी व्यक्ति या वस्तु की वजह से *We're late, thanks to you!*

**a vote of thanks** ➪ **vote**[1] देखिए।

**Thanksgiving (Day)** /ˌθæŋksˈɡɪvɪŋ deɪ ˌथैङ्क्स्ˈगिविङ् डे/ *noun* [U, C] a public holiday in the US and in Canada संयुक्त राज्य अमेरिका और कनाडा का एक सार्वजनिक अवकाश; थैंक्सगिविंग(डे)

> **NOTE** **Thanksgiving Day** संयुक्त राज्य अमेरिका में नवंबर मास के चौथे गुरुवार को और कनाडा में अक्तूबर मास के दूसरे सोमवार को मनाया जाता है। यह मूल रूप में वह दिन था जब फ़सल उतरने पर लोग ईश्वर को धन्यवाद देते थे।

**thank you** *noun* [C] an expression of thanks धन्यवाद, शुक्रिया

**that** /ðæt द्रैट्/ *det., pronoun, conj., adv.* **1** (*pl.* **those** /ðəʊz द्रोज़्/) used to refer to a person or thing, especially when he/she/it is not near the person speaking वह (वक्ता से दूर स्थित किसी व्यक्ति या वस्तु का निर्देश करने के लिए प्रयुक्त) *I like that house over there.* ○ *What's that in the box?* **2** (*pl.* **those** /ðəʊz द्रोज़्/) used for talking about a person or thing already known or mentioned पूर्वज्ञात या पूर्वनिर्दिष्ट व्यक्ति या वस्तु के विषय में चर्चा के लिए प्रयुक्त *That was the year we went to Nepal, wasn't it?* ○ *Can you give me back that money I lent you last week?* **3** /ðət *strong form* ðæt द्रट्; प्रबल रूप द्रैट्/ (*used for introducing a relative clause*) the person or thing already mentioned (संबंधवाचक उपवाक्यों के शुरू में प्रयुक्त) पूर्वनिर्दिष्ट व्यक्ति या वस्तु *I'm reading the book that won the Sahitya Academy Award.*

> **NOTE** संबंधवाचक उपवाक्य (relative clause) की क्रिया के कर्म के रूप में जब **that** का प्रयोग होना हो तो प्रायः उसका लोप हो जाता है—*I want to see the doctor (that) I saw last week.* ○ *I wore the dress (that) I bought in Pune.*

**4** /ðət; *strong form* ðæt द्रट्; प्रबल रूप द्रैट्/ used after certain verbs, nouns and adjectives to introduce a new part of the sentence वाक्य में कुछ नया अंश जोड़ने के लिए कुछ निश्चित क्रियाओं, संज्ञाओं और विशेषणों के बाद प्रयुक्त *She told me that she was leaving.* ○ *I'm certain that he will come.*

> **NOTE** निम्नलिखित प्रकार के वाक्य में शब्द **that** प्रायः लुप्त रहता है—*I thought you would like it.*

**5** (*used with adjectives, adverbs*) as much as that उतना (जितना बताया गया है) *Ten kilometres? I can't walk that far.*

**IDM that is (to say)** used when you are giving more information about sb/sth किसी के विषय में अतिरिक्त जानकारी देने के लिए प्रयुक्त; यानी कि, अर्थात *I'm on holiday next week. That's to say, from Tuesday.*

**that's that** there is nothing more to say or do बस, बात ख़त्म *I'm not going and that's that.*

**thatched** /θætʃt थैच्ट्/ *adj.* (used about a building) having a roof made of dried grass (**straw**) or a similar material (मकान) फूस की छत वाला, छप्परवाला

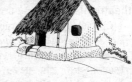

**thaw** /θɔː थॉ/ *verb* [I, T] **thaw (sth) (out)** to become or to make sth become soft or liquid again after freezing जमने के बाद किसी वस्तु का पिघलना या (किसी को) पिघलाना *Is the snow thawing?* ➪ **melt** देखिए। ► **thaw** *noun* [C, *usually sing.*] पिघलाव

**the** /ðə; ði; *strong form* ðiː द्र; द्रि प्रबल रूप द्री/ *definite article* **1** used for talking about a person or thing that is already known or that has already been mentioned पूर्वज्ञात या पूर्वनिर्दिष्ट व्यक्ति या वस्तु का उल्लेख करने के लिए प्रयुक्त (निश्चायक आर्टिकल)

*I took the children to the dentist.* ○ *We met the man who bought your house.* **2** used when there is only one of sth अपने ढंग की एकमात्र वस्तु का निर्देश करने के लिए प्रयुक्त *the sun/the moon* ○ *the World Cup* ○ *the government* **3** used with numbers and dates संख्यावाची और तिथिवाची शब्दों के साथ प्रयुक्त *This is the third time I've seen this film.* ○ *Friday the thirteenth* **4** used with adjectives to name a group of people व्यक्तियों के विशिष्ट वर्ग के सूचक विशेषणों के साथ प्रयुक्त *the Punjabis* ○ *the poor* **5** (*formal*) used with a **singular** noun when you are talking generally about sth किसी वस्तु का सामान्य रूप से उल्लेख करने वाली एकवचनांत संज्ञा के साथ प्रयुक्त *The dolphin is an intelligent animal.* **6** with units of measurement, meaning 'every' 'प्रत्येक' के अर्थ में मापन-इकाइयों के साथ प्रयुक्त *Our car does twelve kilometres to the litre.* **7** with musical instruments वाद्यों के साथ *Do you play the piano?* **8** the well-known or important one सुप्रसिद्ध या महत्त्वपूर्ण लोगों के नाम के साथ प्रयुक्त *'My best friend at school was Rahul Gandhi.' 'You mean the Rahul Gandhi?'*

NOTE इस अर्थ में 'the' का उच्चारण /ðiː द्री/ होता है।

**9 the... the...** used for saying that the way in which two things change is connected (दो) बदलने वाली वस्तुएँ किस प्रकार संबंधित हैं, यह बताने के लिए प्रयुक्त *The more you eat, the fatter you get.*

NOTE **Articles** के बारे में अधिक जानकारी के लिए इस शब्दकोश के अंत में **Quick Grammar Reference** खंड देखिए।

**theatre** (*AmE* **theater**) /ˈθɪətə(r) ˈथिअट(र्)/ *noun* **1** [C] a building where you go to see plays, shows, etc. रंगशाला, थिएटर *How often do you **go to the theatre**?* **2** [U] plays in general; drama सभी नाटक (सामान्य रूप में); ड्रामा, नाटक *He's studying modern Indian theatre.* **3** [*sing.*, U] the work of acting in or producing plays अभिनय या नाटकों का मंचन (करने का कार्य) *He's worked in (the) theatre for thirty years.* **4** [C, U] = **operating theatre**

**theatrical** /θiˈætrɪkl थिˈऐट्रिकल्/ *adj.* **1** (*only before a noun*) connected with the theatre रंगशाला-विषयक, नाटक-प्रस्तुति से संबंधित **2** (used about behaviour) dramatic and exaggerated because you want people to notice it (आचरण) नाटकीय और अतिरंजनापूर्ण (लोगों का ध्यान आकृष्ट करने के लिए)

**theft** /θeft थ़ेफ़्ट्/ *noun* [C, U] the crime of stealing sth चोरी *There have been a lot of thefts in this area recently.* ➪ **thief** पर नोट देखिए।

**their** /ðeə(r) द्रेअ(र्)/ *det.* **1** of or belonging to them उनका (उनसे संबंधित या उनके स्वामित्व वाला) *The children picked up their books and walked to the door.* **2** (*informal*) used instead of his or her, 'his' या 'her' के स्थान पर प्रयुक्त *Has everyone got their book?*

**theirs** /ðeəz द्रेअज़्/ *pronoun* of or belonging to them उनका (उनसे संबंधित या उनके स्वामित्व वाला) *Our flat isn't as big as theirs.*

**them** /ðəm; *strong form* ðem द्रम्; प्रबल रूप द्रेम्/ *pronoun* the object of a verb or preposition किसी क्रिया या पूर्वसर्ग का कर्म; उन्हें **1** the people or things mentioned earlier पूर्वनिर्दिष्ट व्यक्ति या वस्तुएँ *'I've got the keys here.' 'Oh good. Give them to me.'* ○ *We have students from several countries but **most of them** are French.* **2** (*informal*) him or her उसे या उन्हें *If anyone phones, tell them I'm busy.*

NOTE अनौपचारिक मौखिक अभिव्यक्ति की तर्ज़ पर 'them' को कभी-कभी **'em** भी लिखा जाता है।

**thematic** /θɪˈmætɪk; θiː- थिˈमैटिक्; थ़ी-/ *adj.* connected with the subject or subjects of sth किसी प्रसंग की विषय वस्तु(ओं) से संबंधित *the thematic structure of a text* ▶ **thematically** /θɪˈmætɪkli थिˈमैटिक्लि/ *adv.* विषयवस्तु या प्रतिपाद्य की दृष्टि से *The books have been grouped thematically.*

**theme** /θiːm थ़ीम्/ *noun* [C] the subject of a talk, a piece of writing or a work of art किसी वार्ता, रचना या कलाकृति का प्रतिपाद्य या विषयवस्तु *The theme of today's discussion will be 'Our changing cities'.*

**theme park** *noun* [C] a park with a lot of things to do, see, ride on, etc., which are all based on a single idea एकल कल्पना या विचार से उपजी बहुविध मनोरंजन क्रियाओं की सुविधा वाला पार्क; थीम पार्क

**themselves** /ðəmˈselvz द्रम्ˈसेल्व्ज़्/ *pronoun* **1** used when the people or things who do an action are also affected by it स्वयं, अपने आप, जब किसी क्रिया का कर्ता पर प्रभाव पड़े यह दिखाने के लिए प्रयुक्त *Hema and Esha are enjoying themselves.* ○ *People often talk to themselves when they are worried.* **2** used to emphasize 'they' शब्द 'they' पर बल देने के लिए प्रयुक्त *Did they paint the house themselves* (= or did sb else do it for them)?

IDM **(all) by themselves** **1** alone अकेले *The boys are too young to go out by themselves.* ➪ **alone** पर नोट देखिए। **2** without help बिना किसी की सहायता के *The children cooked the dinner all by themselves.*

**then** /ðen द्रेन्/ *adv.* **1** (at) that time उस समय, तब *I spoke to him on Wednesday, but I haven't seen him **since then**.* ○ *They met in 1998 and remained close friends **from then on**.* **2** next; after that अगली; उसके बाद, तत्पश्चात, तब *There was silence for a minute. Then he replied.* **3** used to show the logical result of a statement or situation किसी कथन या स्थिति का तर्कसंगत परिणाम दर्शाने के लिए प्रयुक्त *'I don't feel at all well.' 'Why don't you go to the doctor then?'* ○ *If you don't do any work then you'll fail the exam.* **4** (*spoken*) (used after words like now, okay, right, etc. to show the beginning or end of a conversation or statement) ('now, okay, right' आदि शब्दों के बाद प्रयुक्त, किसी बातचीत या वक्तव्य का आरंभ या अंत दर्शाने के लिए प्रयुक्त) *Now then, are we all ready to go?* ○ *Right then, I'll see you tomorrow.*

IDM **then/there again** ⇨ **again** देखिए।

**there and then; then and there** ⇨ **there** देखिए।

**thence** /ðens द्रेन्स्/ *adv.* (*old-fashioned*) from there वहाँ से

**theo-** /ˈθiːəʊ ˈथीओ/ *prefix* (*used in nouns, adjectives and adverbs*) connected with God or a god परमेश्वर या किसी देवता से संबंधित *theology*

**theodolite** /θiˈɒdəlaɪt थिˈऑडलाइट्/ *noun* [C] a piece of equipment that is used for measuring angles कोणों को मापने का उपकरण; कोणमापी

**theology** /θiˈɒlədʒi थिˈऑलजि/ *noun* [U] the study of religion धर्म का अध्ययन; धर्मशास्त्र ▶ **theological** /ˌθiːəˈlɒdʒɪkl ˌथीअˈलॉजिक्ल्/ *adj.* धर्मशास्त्र-विषयक, धर्मशास्त्रीय

**theorem** /ˈθɪərəm ˈथिअरम्/ *noun* [C] (*technical*) a rule or principle, especially in mathematics, that can be shown to be true सत्य सिद्ध किया जा सकने वाला नियम या सिद्धांत (विशेषतः गणित में); प्रमेय *Pythagoras' theorem*

**theoretical** /ˌθɪəˈretɪkl ˌथिअˈरेटिक्ल्/ *adj.* **1** based on ideas and principles, not on practical experience विचारों या कल्पनाओं और सिद्धांतों (न कि व्यावहारिक अनुभव) पर आधारित; सिद्धांत-प्रधान *A lot of university courses are still too theoretical these days.* **2** that may possibly exist or happen, although it is unlikely संभावित रूप से (न कि वास्तव में) सत्य; काल्पनिक *There is a theoretical possibility that the world will end tomorrow.* ⇨ **practical** देखिए। ▶ **theoretically** /ˌθɪəˈretɪkli ˌथिअˈरेटिक्लि/ *adv.* सैद्धांतिक रूप से; सिद्धांततः

**theorist** /ˈθɪərɪst ˈथिअरिस्ट्/ (*also* **theoretician** /ˌθɪərəˈtɪʃn ˌथिअरˈटिश्न्/) *noun* [C] a person who develops ideas and principles about a particular subject in order to explain why things happen or exist सिद्धांतशास्त्री, सिद्धांतकार (विषय-विशेष के संबंध में व्यवहार-परक प्रवृत्तियों पर सैद्धांतिक चिंतन करने वाला व्यक्ति)

**theory** /ˈθɪəri ˈथिअरि/ *noun* (*pl.* **theories**) **1** [C] an idea or set of ideas that tries to explain sth वास्तविकता की व्याख्या करने वाला विचार तत्व या विचार राशि; सिद्धांत *the theory about how life on earth began* **2** [U] the general idea or principles of a particular subject विषय-विशेष के आधारभूत सिद्धांत *political theory* ○ *the theory and practice of language teaching* **3** [C] an opinion or a belief that has not been shown to be true विचार या विश्वास जो प्रमाणित नहीं हो सका; परिकल्पना

IDM **in theory** as a general idea which may not be true in reality सामान्य विचार या सोच की दृष्टि से, विचार मात्र में (जो संभवतः सच न हो) *Your plan sounds fine in theory, but I don't know if it'll work in practice.*

**therapeutic** /ˌθerəˈpjuːtɪk ˌथ्रेरˈप्यूटिक्/ *adj.* **1** helping you to relax and feel better तनावमुक्त और बेहतर महसूस कराने वाला *I find listening to music very therapeutic.* **2** helping to cure an illness बीमारी ठीक करने वाला; रोगोपचारक *therapeutic drugs*

**therapy** /ˈθerəpi थ्रेरपि/ *noun* [C, U] treatment to help or cure a mental or physical illness, usually without drugs or medical operations मानसिक या शारीरिक रोगों की चिकित्सा (प्रायः बिना औषध या शल्य-क्रिया के) *to have/undergo therapy* ▶ **therapist** /ˈθerəpɪst ˈथ्रेरपिस्ट्/ *noun* [C] चिकित्सक *a speech therapist*

**there** /ðeə(r) द्रेअ(र्)/ *adv., pronoun* **1** used as the subject of 'be', 'seem', 'appear', etc. to say that sth exists किसी के अस्तित्व का संकेत करने के लिए 'be', 'seem', 'appear', आदि क्रियाओं के कर्ता के रूप में प्रयुक्त *There's a man at the door.* ○ *There seems to be a mistake here.* **2** in, at or to that place वहाँ, उस स्थान में या पर *Could you put the table there, please?* ○ *Have you been to Mumbai? We're going there next week.* **3** used for calling attention to sth किसी की ओर ध्यान आकृष्ट करने के लिए प्रयुक्त *Hello there! Can anyone hear me?* **4** at that point (in a conversation, story, etc.) उस बिंदु पर, वहाँ पर (किसी बातचीत, कहानी आदि में) *Could I interrupt you there for a minute?* **5** available if needed आवश्यकता होने पर उपलब्ध या उपस्थित *Her parents are always there if she needs help.*

IDM **be there for sb** to be available to help and support sb when he/she has a problem समस्या

होने पर सहायता और साथ देने के लिए उपलब्ध या मौजूद *Whenever I'm in trouble, my sister is always there for me.*

**then/there again** ➪ **again** देखिए।

**there and then; then and there** immediately; at that time and place तुरंत; उसी समय और उसी स्थान पर

**there you are** 1 used when you give sth to sb किसी को कुछ देने के समय प्रयुक्त *There you are. I've bought you a newspaper.* 2 used when you are explaining sth to sb किसी को कोई बात समझाने के समय प्रयुक्त *Just press the switch and there you are!*

**thereabouts** /ˌðeərəˈbaʊts ˌद्रेअरˈबाउट्स्/ (*AmE* **thereabout** /ˌðeərəˈbaʊt ˌद्रेअरˈबाउट्/) *adv.* (usually after 'or') somewhere near a number, time or place (प्रायः 'or' के बाद) (किसी संख्या, समय या स्थान) के आस-पास *There are 100 students, or thereabouts.* ○ *She lives in Shimla, or thereabouts.*

**thereafter** /ˌðeərˈɑːftə(r) ˌद्रेअर्ˈआफ़्ट(र्)/ *adv.* (*written*) after that उसके बाद; तत्पश्चात

**thereby** /ˌðeəˈbaɪ ˌद्रेअˈबाइ/ *adv.* (*written*) in that way उस रीति से, उसके संबंध में

**therefore** /ˈðeəfɔː(r) ˈद्रेअफ़ॉ(र्)/ *adv.* for that reason उस कारण से; इसलिए, अतएव *The new trains have more powerful engines and are therefore faster.* ✪ पर्याय **thus**

**therein** /ˌðeərˈɪn ˌद्रेअर्ˈइन्/ *adv.* (*written*) because of sth that has just been mentioned अभी-अभी कही बात के फलस्वरूप

**thereupon** /ˌðeərəˈpɒn ˌद्रेअरˈपॉन्/ *adv.* (*written*) immediately after that and often as the result of sth किसी बात के तुरंत बाद और प्रायः उसके फलस्वरूप

**thermal¹** /ˈθɜːml ˈथ़म्ल्/ *adj.* 1 connected with heat ऊष्मा या ताप-विषयक; तापीय, ऊष्मीय *thermal energy* 2 (used about clothes) made to keep you warm in cold weather (कपड़े) गरम *thermal underwear*

**thermal²** /ˈθɜːml ˈथ़म्ल्/ *noun* 1 **thermals** [*pl.*] clothes, especially underwear, made to keep you warm in cold weather गरम कपड़े (विशेषतया अंदर पहनने के) 2 [C] a flow of rising warm air गरम हवा का झोंका

**thermo-** /ˈθɜːməʊ ˈथ़मो/ *prefix* (*used in nouns, adjectives and adverbs*) connected with heat ताप-विषयक, तापीय *thermonuclear*

**thermometer** /θəˈmɒmɪtə(r) थ़ˈमॉमिट(र्)/ *noun* [C] an instrument for measuring temperature ज्वर या तापमान मापने का उपकरण; थर्मामीटर, तापमापी

**Thermos™** /ˈθɜːməs ˈथ़मस्/ (*also* **Thermos flask**) *noun* [C] a type of **vacuum flask** द्रव को ठंडा या गरम रखने के लिए प्रयुक्त विशेष बोतल; थर्मस बोतल, थर्मस फ़्लास्क

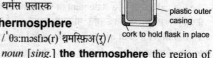

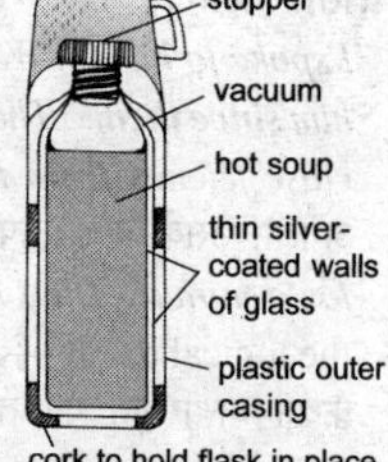


**thermosphere** /ˈθɜːməsfɪə(r) ˈथ़मस्फ़िअ(र्)/ *noun* [*sing.*] **the thermosphere** the region of the atmosphere above the **mesosphere** बाह्य वायुमंडल; यह मध्यवायुमंडल के ऊपर स्थित रहता है

**thermostat** /ˈθɜːməstæt ˈथ़मस्टैट्/ *noun* [C] a device that controls the temperature in a house or machine by switching the heat on and off as necessary आवश्यकता-नुसार मकान या मशीन के तापमान को नियंत्रित करने वाला उपकरण, ताप स्थिरक; थर्मोस्टैट

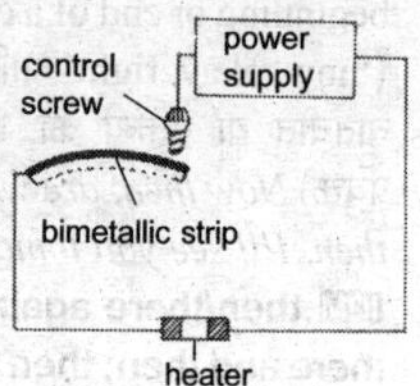


**thesaurus** /θɪˈsɔːrəs थ़िˈसॉरस्/ *noun* [C] (*pl.* **thesauruses**) a book that contains lists of words and phrases with similar meanings समानार्थी शब्दों और वाक्यांशों का कोश; पर्याय-कोश, पर्याय-शब्दकोश

**these** ➪ **this** देखिए।

**thesis** /ˈθiːsɪs ˈथ़ीसिस्/ *noun* [C] (*pl.* **theses** /ˈθiːsiːz ˈथ़ीसीज़्/) 1 a long piece of writing on a particular subject that you do as part of a university degree विषय-विशेष पर लिखा गया शोध-प्रबंध (विश्वविद्यालय की उपाधि के लिए) *He did his thesis on Indian writing in English.* ➪ **dissertation** देखिए। 2 an idea that is discussed and presented with evidence in order to show that it is true साक्ष्यों द्वारा समर्थित और प्रमाणित सिद्धांत

**they** /ðeɪ दे/ *pronoun* (*the subject of a verb*) 1 the people or things that have been mentioned क्रिया का (बहुवचनांत) कर्ता, वे पूर्वनिर्दिष्ट व्यक्ति या वस्तुएँ *We've got two children. They're both boys.* ○ *'Have you seen my keys?' 'Yes, they're on the table.'* 2 people in general or people whose identity is not known or stated सामान्यतया सभी व्यक्ति या अपरिचित व्यक्ति *They say it's going to be a mild winter.* 3 (*informal*) used instead of he or she (सर्वनाम) 'he' या 'she' के स्थान पर प्रयुक्त *Somebody phoned for you but they didn't leave their name.*

**they'd** /ðeɪd द्रेड्/ ➪ **they had, they would** का संक्षिप्त रूप

**they'll** /ðeɪl द्रेल्/ ➪ **they will** का संक्षिप्त रूप

**they're** /ðeə(r) दे्अ(र्)/ ➪ **they are** का संक्षिप्त रूप

**they've** /ðeɪv देव्/ ➪ **they have** का संक्षिप्त रूप

**thick[1]** /θɪk थिक्/ *adj.* **1** (used about sth solid) having a large distance between its opposite sides; not thin (ठोस वस्तु) मोटी या मोटा; पतला या बारीक़ से विपरीत *a thick black line* ○ *a thick coat/book/walls* **2** used for saying what the distance is between the two opposite sides of something मोटा, गहरा *The ice was six centimetres thick.* **3** having a lot of things close together घना, सघन *a thick forest* ○ *thick hair* **4** (used about a liquid) that does not flow easily (द्रव) गाढ़ा *thick cream* ○ *This paint is too thick.* **5** (used about fog, smoke, etc.) difficult to see through (कोहरा, धुआँ आदि) घना *thick fog/thick clouds of smoke* ✪ विलोम **thin** (अर्थ सं. **1, 3** और **4** के लिए) **6 thick (with sth)** containing a lot of sth/sb close together किसी व्यक्ति या वस्तु से भरा हुआ (जैसे धूल, भीड़) *The air was thick with dust.* ○ *The streets were thick with shoppers.* **7** (used about sb's accent) very strong (स्वराघात, बोलने का लहज़ा) बहुत भारी **8** (*informal*) slow to learn or understand; stupid मंदबुद्धि; मूर्ख ▶ **thick** *adv.* सघन *Snow lay thick on the ground.* ▶ **thickly** *adv.* सघनता से, मोटी परत में *Spread the butter thickly.* ○ *a thickly wooded area*

IDM **have a thick skin** to be not easily upset or worried by what people say about you मोटी चमड़ी वाला होना (लोगों की टिप्पणियों से जल्दी परेशान या चिंतित न होना)

**thick[2]** /θɪk थिक्/ *noun*

IDM **in the thick of sth** in the most active or crowded part of sth; very involved in sth किसी स्थिति के बीचोंबीच (उसके सर्वाधिक सक्रिय या सघन खंड में); किसी काम में बहुत व्यस्त या लगा हुआ

**through thick and thin** through difficult times and situations सुख-दुख में, मुसीबतों में

**thicken** /ˈθɪkən ˈथिकन्/ *verb* [I, T] to become or to make sth thicker किसी वस्तु का अधिक गाढ़ा या घना हो जाना या (उसे) कर देना

**thickness** /ˈθɪknəs ˈथिक्नस्/ *noun* [C, U] the quality of being thick or how thick sth is मोटाई गाढ़ापन, सघनता

**thick-skinned** *adj.* not easily worried or upset by what other people say about you मोटी चमड़ी वाला (लोगों की टिप्पणियों से अप्रभावित)

**thief** /θiːf थीफ़्/ *noun* [C] (*pl.* **thieves** /θiːvz थीव़्ज़्/) a person who steals things from another person चोर

> NOTE चुपके-से और बिना ख़ून-ख़राबे के चोरी करने वाले व्यक्ति के लिए **thief** एक सामान्य शब्द है। इस अपराध को **theft** कहते हैं। (प्रायः) हिंसा या धमकी की सहायता से बैंक, दुकान आदि से चोरी करने वाले को **robber** कहते हैं। प्रायः रात के समय मकान, दुकान आदि में सेंध लगाकर चोरी करने वाला **burglar** कहलाता है। खुली दुकान से चुपचाप (बिना पैसा दिए) चीजें उठा लेने वाले को **shoplifter** कहते हैं। हिंसा या धमकी की सहायता से खुले आम लूट-पाट करने वाले को **mugger** कहते हैं। **Steal** पर भी नोट देखिए।

**thigh** /θaɪ थाइ/ *noun* [C] the top part of your leg, above your knee जाँघ ➪ **body** पर चित्र देखिए।

**thigh bone** *noun* [C] the large thick bone in the top part of your leg above your knee जाँघ की हड्डी ✪ पर्याय **femur** ➪ **body** पर चित्र देखिए।

**thimble** /ˈθɪmbl ˈथिम्बल्/ *noun* [C] a small metal or plastic object that you wear on the end of your finger to protect it when you are sewing कुछ सीते समय सूई चुभने से बचाने के लिए अंगुली में पहना धातु या प्लास्टिक का छल्ला, दर्जी का छल्ला; अंगुश्ताना

**thin[1]** /θɪn थिन्/ *adj.* (**thinner; thinnest**) **1** (used about sth solid) having a small distance between the opposite sides; not thick (ठोस वस्तु) पतला; जो मोटा नहीं *a thin book/shirt* ○ *a thin slice of meat* **2** having very little fat on the body; not fat दुबला-पतला; मोटापे वाला नहीं *You need to eat more. You're too thin!*

> NOTE **Thin, skinny, slim** और **underweight** इन सबका लगभग एक ही अर्थ है। दुबले-पतले लोगों का संकेत करने के लिए **thin** सर्वाधिक प्रयुक्त शब्द है। **Slim** का प्रयोग छरहरे व्यक्तियों के लिए (जो इकहरे शरीर के कारण सुंदर लगते हैं) होता है—*You're so slim! How do you do it?* बहुत पतले और इसलिए आकर्षक न लगने वाले व्यक्ति को **skinny** कहते हैं। **Underweight** इससे कहीं अधिक औपचारिक शब्द है और ऐसे लोगों के लिए प्रयुक्त होता है जो डॉक्टर की राय में बहुत पतले (और इसलिए स्वस्थ नहीं) हैं—*The doctor says I'm underweight.*

**3** (used about a liquid) that flows easily; not thick (द्रव) पतला; जो गाढ़ा नहीं *a thin sauce* **4** (used about mist, smoke, etc.) not difficult to see through (कोहरा, धुआँ आदि) लगभग पारदर्शी; हलका **5** having only a few people or things with a lot of space between them कम छितराया हुआ; विरल *The population is rather thin in this part of the country.* ✪ विलोम **thick** (अर्थ सं. **1, 3** और **4** के लिए) ▶ **thin** *adv.* पतला, बारीक, महीन *Don't slice the onion too thin.* ▶ **thinly** *adv.* बारीकी से, विरलता से *thinly sliced bread* ○ *thinly populated areas*

**IDM thin on the ground** ➪ **ground**[1] देखिए।
**through thick and thin** ➪ **thick**[2] देखिए।
**vanish, etc. into thin air** to disappear completely पूर्णतः अदृश्य हो जाना
**wear thin** ➪ **wear**[1] देखिए।

**thin**[2] /θɪn थिन्/ *verb* [I, T] (**thinning; thinned**) **thin (sth) (out)** to become thinner or fewer in number; to make sth thinner संख्या में कम हो जाना; किसी वस्तु को अधिक पतला बनाना *The trees thin out towards the edge of the forest.* ○ *Thin the sauce by adding milk.*

**thing** /θɪŋ थिङ्/ *noun* **1** [C] an object that is not named चीज़, वस्तु *A pen is a thing you use for writing with.* ○ *I need to get a few things at the shops.* **2** [C] a quality or state कोई गुण या दशा *There is* ***no such thing*** *as a ghost* (= it does not exist). **3** [C] an action, event or statement कोई कार्य या काम, घटना, बात या वक्तव्य *A strange thing happened to me yesterday.* ○ *What a nice thing to say!* **4** [C] a fact, subject, etc. कोई तथ्य, विषय आदि *He told me a few things that I didn't know before.* **5 things** [*pl.*] clothes or tools that belong to sb or are used for a particular purpose किसी के स्वामित्व वाले या प्रयोजन-विशेष से प्रयुक्त होने वाले कपड़े या औज़ार *I'll just go and pack my things.* ○ *We keep all the cooking things in this cupboard.* **6 things** [*pl.*] the situation or conditions of your life जीवन-धारा की स्थिति या हालात *How are things with you?* **7** [C] used for expressing how you feel about a person or an animal किसी व्यक्ति या वस्तु के विषय में वक्ता की (विशेष) भावना व्यक्त करने के लिए प्रयुक्त *You've broken your finger? You poor thing!* **8 the thing** [*sing.*] exactly what is wanted or needed ठीक वह जिसकी इच्छा या आवश्यकता है *That's just the thing I was looking for!*

**IDM a close shave/thing** ➪ **close**[3] देखिए।
**be a good thing (that)** to be lucky that क़िस्मत अच्छी है कि, अच्छा हुआ कि *It's a good thing you remembered your umbrella.*
**do your own thing** to do what you want to do, independently of other people मन की बात करना (न कि दूसरों के कहे अनुसार चलना)
**first/last thing** as early/late as possible बहुत सवेरे या देर शाम *I'll telephone her first thing tomorrow morning.* ○ *I saw him last thing on Friday evening.*
**for one thing** used for introducing a reason for something एक कारण यह है कि (किसी बात का कारण बताने के लिए प्रयुक्त) *I think we should go by train. For one thing it's cheaper.*
**have a thing about sb/sth** (*informal*) to have strong feelings about sb/sth किसी व्यक्ति या वस्तु के विषय में तीव्र भावनाएँ (अरुचि आदि) होना
**to make matters/things worse** ➪ **worse** देखिए।
**take it/things easy** ➪ **easy**[2] देखिए।

**think** /θɪŋk थिङ्क्/ *verb* (*pt, pp* **thought** /θɔːt थॉट्/) **1** [I, T] **think (sth) (of/about sb/sth); think that...** to have a particular idea or opinion about sth/sb; to believe किसी व्यक्ति या वस्तु के विषय में विशेष विचार या मत रखना; (कुछ) मानना *'Do you think (that) we'll win?' 'No, I don't think so.'* ○ *What did you think of the film?* ○ *Gagan's on holiday, I think.* **2** [I] **think (about sth)** to use your mind to consider sth or to form connected ideas सोचना, विचार करना *Think before you speak.* ○ *He had to think hard* (= a lot) *about the questions.* **3** [I] **think of/about doing sth; think that...** to intend or plan to do sth कुछ करने का इरादा या योजना होना *We're thinking of buying a house.* ○ *I think I'll go for a swim.* **4** [T] to form an idea of sth; to imagine sth किसी के विषय में कोई धारणा बनाना; किसी बात की कल्पना करना ***Just think*** *what we could do with all that money!* **5** [I] **think about/of sb** to consider the feelings of sb else किसी दूसरे के विषय में सोचना, भावनाओं का ख़याल रखना *She never thinks about anyone but herself.* **6** [T] to remember sth; to have sth come into your mind किसी बात को याद करना या कोई बात याद होना; कोई बात मन में आना *Can you think where you left the keys?* **7** [T] to expect sth किसी बात की आशा करना *The job took longer than we thought.* **8** [I] to think in a particular way ख़ास ढंग से सोचना *If you want to be successful, you have to* ***think big.*** ○ *to* ***think positive*** ▸ **think** *noun* [*sing.*] सोच-विचार *I'm not sure. I'll have to* ***have a think*** *about it.*

**IDM think better of (doing) sth** to decide not to do sth; to change your mind कुछ न करने का निश्चय करना; विचार बदल लेना
**think highly, a lot, not much, etc. of sb/sth** to have a good, bad, etc. opinion of sb/sth किसी व्यक्ति या वस्तु के विषय में अच्छी, बुरी आदि राय रखना *I didn't think much of that film.*
**think the world of sb** to love and admire sb very much किसी व्यक्ति को बहुत प्यार करना और उसकी तारीफ़ करना

**PHR V think of sth** to create an idea in your imagination कोई विचार मन में आना या प्रकट करना *Who first thought of the plan?*

**think sth out** to consider carefully all the details of a plan, idea, etc. किसी योजना, विचार आदि पर पूरा सोच-विचार करना *a well-thought-out scheme*

**think sth over** to consider sth carefully किसी बात पर सावधानी से विचार करना *I'll think your offer over and let you know tomorrow.*

**think sth through** to consider every detail of sth carefully किसी बात के सब पक्षों पर सावधानी से विचार करना *He made a bad decision because he didn't think it through.*

**think sth up** to create sth in your mind; to invent मन में किसी चीज़ की कल्पना करना; कोई नई चीज़ खोजना *to think up a new advertising slogan*

**thinker** /ˈθɪŋkə(r) ˈथिङ्क(र्)/ *noun* [C] **1** a person who thinks about serious and important subjects चिंतक, विचारक **2** a person who thinks in a particular way ख़ास ढंग से सोचने वाला व्यक्ति *a quick/creative/clear thinker*

**thinking[1]** /ˈθɪŋkɪŋ ˈथिङ्किङ्/ *noun* [U] **1** using your mind to think about sth सोचने की क्रिया, सोच-विचार *We're going to have to do some quick thinking.* **2** ideas or opinions about sth किसी चीज़ के विषय में विचार या मत *This accident will make them change their thinking on safety matters.* ➪ **wishful thinking** देखिए।

**thinking[2]** /ˈθɪŋkɪŋ ˈथिङ्किङ्/ *adj.* intelligent and using your mind to think about important subjects प्रतिभाशाली और महत्त्वपूर्ण बातों पर सोच-विचार करने वाला; विचारशील

**third[1]** /θɜːd थ़र्ड्/ *det., adv.* 3rd तीसरा, तृतीय ➪ **sixth** के उदाहरण देखिए।

**third[2]** /θɜːd थ़र्ड्/ *noun* [C] **1** the fraction $\frac{1}{3}$; one of three equal parts of sth भिन्न $\frac{1}{3}$; किसी वस्तु का तीसरा हिस्सा (अन्य दो के बराबर) एक-तिहाई **2** (*BrE*) a result in final university exams, below first and second class degrees विश्वविद्यालय की अंतिम परीक्षा में तृतीय श्रेणी ➪ **sixth** के उदाहरण देखिए।

**third-degree** *adj.* (*only before a noun*) **1** (*AmE*) (used about murder) of the least serious of three kinds (हत्या) के तीन प्रकारों में सबसे हलकी (कम गंभीर) **2** (used about burns) of the most serious of three kinds, affecting the flesh under the skin and leaving permanent marks (जलने से हुए) घावों के तीन प्रकारों में सबसे गंभीर (जिसमें अंदर का मांस तक जल जाता है और पक्के दाग़ पड़ जाते हैं) ➪ **first-degree** और **second-degree** देखिए।

**thirdly** /ˈθɜːdli ˈथ़र्ड्लि/ *adv.* used to introduce the third point in a list तीसरी बात, तीसरे (किसी सूची में तीसरी वस्तु के उल्लेख के शुरू में प्रयुक्त) *We have made savings in three areas: firstly, defence; secondly, education and thirdly, health.*

**third party** *noun* [C] a person who is involved in a situation in addition to the two main people involved (किसी स्थिति में) दो मुख्य पक्षों के अतिरिक्त तीसरा पक्ष; अन्य पक्ष, तिसरैत

**the third person** *noun* [*sing.*] **1** (*grammar*) the set of pronouns and verb forms used by a speaker to refer to other people and things अन्य पुरुष (वक्ता द्वारा अन्य व्यक्तियों या वस्तुओं के निर्देश के लिए प्रयुक्त सर्वनाम और क्रियारूप) *'They are' is the third person plural of the verb 'to be'.* **2** the style of writing a novel, telling a story, etc. as the experience of sb else, using third person forms कथा-वर्णन की अन्य पुरुष शैली (जिसमें अन्य पुरुष रूपों का प्रयोग करते हुए कथाकार किसी दूसरे व्यक्ति के अनुभव का वर्णन करता है) *a book written* ***in the third person*** ➪ **the first person** और **the second person** देखिए।

**the Third World** *noun* [*sing.*] a way of referring to the poor or developing countries of Africa, Asia and Latin America अफ्रीक़ा, एशिया और दक्षिण अमेरिका के निर्धन या विकासशील देशों के लिए प्रयुक्त; तीसरी दुनिया **NOTE** इस अभिव्यक्ति को कभी-कभी अपमानजनक माना जाता है। ➪ **the First World** देखिए।

**thirst** /θɜːst थ़र्स्ट्/ *noun* **1** [U, *sing.*] the feeling that you have when you want or need a drink (पानी आदि की) प्यास *Cold tea really quenches your thirst.* ○ *to die of thirst* **2** [*sing.*] **a thirst for sth** a strong desire for sth किसी वस्तु की तीव्र इच्छा; लालसा ➪ **hunger** देखिए।

**thirsty** /ˈθɜːsti थ़र्स्टि/ *adj.* (**thirstier; thirstiest**) wanting or needing a drink प्यासा *I'm thirsty. Can I have a drink of water, please?* ➪ **hungry** देखिए।

▶ **thirstily** *adv.* प्यास के मारे या से प्रभावित होते हुए

**thirteen** /ˌθɜːˈtiːn ˌथ़र्ˈटीन्/ *number* 13 तेरह (की संख्या)

> **NOTE** संख्याओं के वाक्य-प्रयोग के उदाहरणों के लिए **six** की प्रविष्टि देखिए।

**thirteenth** /ˌθɜːˈtiːnθ ˌथ़र्ˈटीन्थ़्/ *det., adv.* 13th तेरहवाँ ➪ **sixth** के उदाहरण देखिए।

**thirtieth** /ˈθɜːtiəθ ˈथ़र्टिअथ़्/ *det., adv.* 30th तीसवाँ ➪ **sixth** के उदाहरण देखिए।

**thirty** /ˈθɜːti ˈथ़र्टि/ *number* 30 तीस (की संख्या)

> **NOTE** संख्याओं के वाक्य-प्रयोग के उदाहरणों के लिए **sixty** की प्रविष्टि देखिए।

**this** /ðɪs द़िस्/ *det., pronoun* (*pl.* **these** /ðiːz द़ीज़्/) **1** used for talking about sb/sth that is close to you in time or space यह, इस (समय या स्थान की दृष्टि से वक्ता के निकट के व्यक्ति या वस्तु का निर्देश करने के लिए प्रयुक्त) *Is this the book you asked for?* ○ *These are the letters to be filed, not those over there.* **2** used for talking about sth that was mentioned or talked about earlier पूर्वनिर्दिष्ट या पूर्वचर्चित वस्तु का उल्लेख करने के लिए प्रयुक्त *Where did you hear about this?* **3** used for introducing sb or showing sb sth किसी व्यक्ति को दूसरों से मिलाते समय या किसी को कुछ दिखाने के लिए प्रयुक्त *This is my wife, Nisha, and these are our children, Anshul and Rahul.* **4** (used with days of the week or periods of time) of today or the present week, year, etc. वर्तमान सप्ताह, वर्ष आदि या आज के दिन से संबंधित समयावधि का निर्देश करने के लिए प्रयुक्त *Are you busy this afternoon?* ○ *this Friday* (= the Friday of this week) **5** (*informal*) (used when you are telling a story) a certain (कहानी सुनाते समय प्रयुक्त) यह, इस (जिसकी कोई पहचान नहीं, वर्णित किंतु अज्ञात) *Then this woman said that she did not see me before.* ▶ **this** *adv.* इस प्रकार *The road is not usually this busy.*

IDM **this and that; this, that and the other** various things तरह-तरह की चीज़ें, यह और वह और तमाम बातें *We chatted about this and that.*

**thistle** /ˈθɪsl ˈथ़िसल्/ *noun* [C] a wild plant with purple flowers and sharp points (**prickles**) on its leaves भटकटैया का पौधा (जिसके फूल बैंगनी रंग के और पत्तियाँ काँटेदार होती हैं)

**thong** /θɒŋ/ (*AmE*) = **flip-flop**

**thorax** /ˈθɔːræks ˈथ़ॉरैक्स्/ *noun* [C] **1** (*medical*) the middle part of your body between your neck and your waist (चिकित्सा) छाती, वक्ष, सीना **2** the middle section of an insect's body, to which the legs and wings are connected कीड़े के शरीर का मध्य भाग (जिससे उसकी टाँगें और डैने जुड़े होते हैं) ➪ **abdomen** देखिए तथा **insect** पर चित्र देखिए। ▶ **thoracic** /θɔːˈræsɪk थ़ॉˈरैसिक्/ *adj.* वक्ष से संबंधित; वक्षीय

**thorn** /θɔːn थ़ॉन्/ *noun* [C] one of the hard sharp points on some plants and bushes, for example on rose bushes (कुछ पौधों और झाड़ियों पर उगा) काँटा, कंटक ➪ **flower** पर चित्र देखिए।

**thorny** /ˈθɔːni ˈथ़ॉनि/ *adj.* **1** causing difficulty or disagreement कठिनाई या असहमति पैदा करने वाला; समस्याजनक *a thorny problem/question* **2** having thorns काँटेदार

**thorough** /ˈθʌrə ˈथ़रा/ *adj.* **1** careful and complete सावधानी से और पूरी तरह किया गया; परिपूर्ण *The police made a thorough search of the house.* **2** doing things in a very careful way, making sure that you look at every detail (सब बातों पर ध्यान देते हुए) बहुत सावधानी से काम करने वाला *Anjali is slow but she is very thorough.* ▶ **thoroughness** *noun* [U] परिपूर्णता

**thoroughbred** /ˈθʌrəbred ˈथ़रब्रेड्/ *noun* [C] an animal, especially a horse, of high quality, that has parents that are both of the same type ऊँची नसल का जानवर (विशेषतः घोड़ा) ख़ालिस नसल का, जिसकी नसल में मिलावट न हो ▶ **thoroughbred** *adj.* ऊँची नसल का

**thoroughly** /ˈθʌrəli ˈथ़रलि/ *adv.* **1** in a careful and complete way सावधानी के साथ और पूरी तरह से; परिपूर्णतापूर्वक *to study a subject thoroughly* **2** completely; very much पूर्णतया, पूरा-पूरा; अत्यधिक *We thoroughly enjoyed our holiday.*

**those** ➪ **that 1, 2** का plural रूप

**though** /ðəʊ द़ो/ *conj., adv.* **1** in spite of the fact that; although किसी बात के बावजूद; यद्यपि, हालाँकि *Though he had very little money, Ajay always managed to dress smartly.* ○ *She still loved him* ***even though*** *he had treated her so badly.* **2** but परंतु, किंतु, लेकिन या मगर *I'll come as soon as I can, though I can't promise to be on time.* **3** (*informal*) however तो भी, तथापि *I quite like him. I don't like his wife, though.* ➪ **although** पर नोट देखिए।

IDM **as if** ➪ **as** देखिए।

**as though** ➪ **as** देखिए।

**thought**[1] ➪ **think** का past tense और past participle रूप

**thought**[2] /θɔːt थ़ॉट्/ *noun* **1** [C] an idea or opinion कोई विचार या मत *The thought of living alone filled her with fear.* **2** [U] the power or process of thinking सोचने की शक्ति या प्रक्रिया; चिंतन *I need to* ***give*** *this problem* ***some thought.*** **3 thoughts** [*pl.*] a person's mind and all the ideas that are in it व्यक्ति का मन और उसमें सभी विचार; भावनाएँ *anxious thoughts* ○ *She had spoken her thoughts aloud.* ○ *You are always in my thoughts.* **4** [*sing.*] a feeling of care or worry ख़याल या चिंता *They sent me flowers. What a kind thought!* **5** [U] particular ideas or a particular way of thinking विशेष विचार या सोचने का विशेष ढंग; धारणा या सोच *a change in medical thought on the subject*

IDM **deep in thought/conversation** ➪ **deep**[1] देखिए।

**a school of thought** ➪ **school** देखिए।

**second thoughts** ➪ **second**[1] देखिए।

**thoughtful** /ˈθɔːtfl ˈथॉट्फ़्ल्/ *adj.* **1** thinking deeply विचारपूर्ण *a thoughtful expression* **2** thinking about what other people want or need दूसरों की इच्छा या आवश्यकता का ध्यान रखने वाला; लिहाज़ी, विचारवान, मुरौवती *It was very thoughtful of you to send her some flowers.* ▶ **thoughtfully** /ˈθɔːtfəli ˈथॉट्फ़लि/ *adv.* विचारपूर्वक, अच्छी तरह विचार करके ▶ **thoughtfulness** *noun* [U] विचारमग्नता, ध्यानमग्नता, भरपूर सावधानी

**thoughtless** /ˈθɔːtləs ˈथॉट्लस्/ *adj.* not thinking about what other people want or need or what the result of your actions will be दूसरों की इच्छा या आवश्यकता का ध्यान न रखने वाला या अपने ऐसे व्यवहार के परिणाम के प्रति बेपरवाह; स्वार्थी या बेलिहाज़ ✪ पर्याय **inconsiderate** ▶ **thoughtlessly** *adv.* विचारशून्यता से, बेलिहाज़ होकर ▶ **thoughtlessness** *noun* [U] विचारशून्यता, बेमुरौवती

**thousand** /ˈθaʊznd ˈथाउज़न्ड्/ *number* 1000 एक हज़ार (की संख्या)

NOTE संख्या की दृष्टि से बात करनी हो तो एकवचन **thousand** का प्रयोग होता है। बहुवचन **thousands** का प्रयोग हो तो उसका अर्थ है 'बहुत सारे'—*There were over 70,000 spectators at the match.* ○ *Thousands of people attended the meeting.* संख्याओं के वाक्य-प्रयोग के उदाहरणों के लिए **six** की प्रविष्टि देखिए। संख्याओं के विषय में अधिक जानकारी के लिए इस शब्दकोश के अंत में संख्याओं पर विशेष खंड देखिए।

**thousandth**[1] /ˈθaʊznθ ˈथाउज़न्थ्/ *det.* 1000th हज़ारवाँ

**thousandth**[2] /ˈθaʊznθ ˈथाउज़न्थ्/ *noun* [C] the fraction $\frac{1}{1000}$; one of a thousand equal parts of sth भिन्न $\frac{1}{1000}$; हज़ारवाँ अंश

**thrash** /θræʃ थ्रैश्/ *verb* **1** [T] to hit sb/sth many times with a stick, etc. as a punishment (दंडस्वरूप) किसी को छड़ी से बार-बार पीटना, ख़ूब मारना (किसी की) धुनाई कर देना **2** [I, T] **thrash (sth) (about/around)** to move or make sth move wildly without any control बेतहाशा आगे बढ़ना या दौड़ना या किसी को दौड़ाना **3** [T] to defeat sb easily in a game, competition, etc. खेल, प्रतियोगिता आदि में आसानी से किसी को हरा देना

PHR V **thrash sth out** to talk about sth with sb until you reach an agreement समझौते पर पहुँचने के लिए समस्या पर विचार-विमर्श करना

**thrashing** /ˈθræʃɪŋ ˈथ्रैशिङ्/ *noun* [C] **1** the action of hitting sb/sth many times with a stick, etc. as a punishment (दंडस्वरूप) किसी की छड़ी से ख़ूब पिटाई (करने की क्रिया) **2** (*informal*) a bad defeat in a game खेल में करारी हार

**thread**[1] /θred थ्रेड्/ *noun* **1** [C, U] a long thin piece of cotton, wool, etc. that you use for sewing or making cloth (कपास, ऊन आदि का) धागा, तागा, सूत्र (कपड़े सीने या बनाने में प्रयुक्त) *a needle and thread* **2** [C] the connection between ideas, the parts of a story, etc. विचारों, कथा के अंशों आदि के बीच संबंध; विचार-सूत्र, कथा-सूत्र *I've lost the thread of this argument.*

**thread**[2] /θred थ्रेड्/ *verb* [T] **1** to put sth long and thin, especially thread, through a narrow opening or hole सूई आदि (के छेद) में धागा डालना *to thread a needle* ○ *He threaded the belt through the loops on the trousers.* **2** to join things together by putting them onto a string, etc. फूलों आदि से माला पिरोना या गूँथना

IDM **thread your way through sth** to move through sth with difficulty, going around things or people that are in your way रास्ते की बाधाओं से बचते हुए प्रयत्लपूर्वक आगे बढ़ना

**threadbare** /ˈθredbeə(r) ˈथ्रेड्बेअ(र्)/ *adj.* (used about material or clothes) old and very thin (सामान या कपड़े) फटे-पुराने और तार-तार या घिसे-पिटे

**threat** /θret थ्रेट्/ *noun* **1** [C] a warning that sb may hurt, kill or punish you if you do not do what he/she wants (इच्छित काम न करने पर) (चोट पहुँचाने या मार देने की) धमकी *to **make threats** against sb* ○ ***to carry out threat*** **2** [U, *sing.*] the possibility of trouble or danger कष्ट या संकट की आशंका *The forest is **under threat** from building developments.* **3** [C] a person or thing that may damage sth or hurt sb; something that indicates future danger व्यक्ति या वस्तु जो किसी को क्षति या चोट पहुँचा सके; भावी संकट का संकेत

**threaten** /ˈθretn ˈथ्रेट्न्/ *verb* **1** [T] **threaten sb (with sth); threaten (to do sth)** to warn that you may hurt, kill or punish sb if he/she does not do what you want (इच्छित काम न करने पर) (चोट, क्षति पहुँचाने की) धमकी देना *The boy threatened him with a knife.* ○ *She was threatened with dismissal.* **2** [I, T] to seem likely to do sth unpleasant अशुभ की आशंका होना *The wind was threatening to destroy the bridge.* ▶ **threatening** *adj.* धमकाने वाला, धमकी-भरा ▶ **threateningly** *adv.* धमकाते हुए, धमकी-भरे ढंग से

**three** /θriː थ्री/ *number* **1** 3 तीन (की संख्या) **2** (*used to form compound adjectives*) having three of the thing mentioned बताई गई तीन वस्तुओं वाला, ती-/त्रि- *a three-legged stool* ➪ **third** देखिए।

NOTE संख्याओं के वाक्य-प्रयोग के उदाहरणों के लिए **six** की प्रविष्टि देखिए।

**three-dimensional** (*also* **3-D**) *adj.* having length, width and height त्रि-आयामी (जिसके तीन आयाम–लंबाई, चौड़ाई, ऊँचाई हों); त्रिविमीय *a three-dimensional model/design*

**thresh** /θreʃ थ्रेश् / *verb* [T] to separate grains of corn, rice, etc. from the rest of the plant using a machine or, especially in the past, by hitting it with a special tool मशीन या मूसल से कूट-पीट कर अनाज को (पौधों में से) निकालना, अनाज को गाहना ▶ **threshing** *noun* [U] गाहने वाला *a threshing machine*

**threshold** /ˈθreʃhəʊld ˈथ्रेश्होल्ड् / *noun* [C] **1** the ground at the entrance to a room or building कमरे या भवन के प्रवेश द्वार पर की भूमि; दहलीज़, देहली या देहरी **2** the level at which sth starts to happen स्तर जहाँ से कोई चीज़ होनी शुरू हो, किसी घटना के घटित होने का आरंभ-बिंदु *Young children have a low boredom threshold.* **3** the time when you are just about to start sth or find sth नए काम के आरंभ या नई प्राप्ति होने की सन्निकटता (जब नया काम आरंभ होने वाला हो या नई प्राप्ति होने को हो) *We could be* ***on the threshold*** *of a scientific breakthrough.*

**threw** ➪ **throw** का past tense रूप

**thrift** /θrɪft थ्रिफ़्ट् / *noun* [U] the quality of being careful not to spend too much money फ़ज़ूल-ख़र्च न होने का गुण, कमख़र्ची, किफ़ायत, मितव्ययिता ▶ **thrifty** *adj.* कमख़र्च, किफ़ायती, किफ़ायतशार, मितव्ययी

**thrill** /θrɪl थ्रिल् / *noun* [C] a sudden strong feeling of pleasure or excitement एकाएक उत्पन्न हर्ष या उत्तेजना, रोमांच, पुलक ▶ **thrill** *verb* [T] रोमांचित या पुलकित करना *His singing thrilled the audience.* ▶ **thrilled** *adj.* रोमांचित, पुलकित *He was absolutely thrilled with my present.* ▶ **thrilling** *adj.* रोमांचकारी

**thriller** /ˈθrɪlə(r) ˈथ्रिल(र्) / *noun* [C] a play, film, book, etc. with a very exciting story, often about a crime रोमांच उत्पन्न करने वाला या सनसनीख़ेज़ नाटक, फ़िल्म आदि (प्रायः अपराध कथा पर आधारित)

**thrive** /θraɪv थ्राइव् / *verb* [I] (*pt* **thrived** or (*old-fashioned*) **throve** /θrəʊv थ्रोव् /; *pp* **thrived**) to grow or develop well सफलतापूर्वक बढ़ना या विकसित होना, फलना-फूलना ▶ **thriving** *adj.* फलता-फूलता *a thriving industry*

**throat** /θrəʊt थ्रोट् / *noun* [C] **1** the front part of your neck गला, कंठ *The attacker grabbed the man by the throat.* ➪ **body** पर चित्र देखिए। **2** the back part of your mouth and the passage down your neck through which air and food pass श्वास और आहार की नली *She got a piece of bread stuck in her throat.* ○ *I've got a sore throat.*

IDM **clear your throat** ➪ **clear**[3] देखिए।

**have/feel a lump in your throat** ➪ **lump**[1] देखिए।

**throb** /θrɒb थ्रॉब् / *verb* [I] (**throbbing; throbbed**) to make strong regular movements or noises; to beat strongly धुकधुक करना; धड़कना *Her finger throbbed with pain.* ▶ **throb** *noun* [C] धुकधुक, धड़कन

**thrombosis** /θrɒmˈbəʊsɪs थ्रॉम्ˈबोसिस् / *noun* [C, U] (*pl.* **thromboses** /-si:z -सीज़् /) a serious medical condition caused by a lump of thick blood (**clot**) forming in a tube (**blood vessel**) or in the heart हृदय या रक्त-नली में रक्त का थक्का जमने का गंभीर रोग, रक्त-जमाव; शिरावरोध

**throne** /θrəʊn थ्रोन् / *noun* **1** [C] the special chair where a king or queen sits राजा या रानी के बैठने की विशेष कुरसी; राजसिंहासन, राजगद्दी **2 the throne** [*sing.*] the position of being king or queen राजा या रानी का पद

**throng**[1] /θrɒŋ थ्रॉङ् / *noun* [C] (*written*) a large crowd of people लोगों की भारी भीड़; जमावड़ा, जनसमुदाय

**throng**[2] /θrɒŋ थ्रॉङ् / *verb* [I, T] (*written*) (used about a crowd of people) to move into or fill a particular place (भारी संख्या में) (लोगों का) किसी ओर बढ़ना या कहीं जमा हो जाना, कहीं भीड़ लगना या लगाना

**throttle**[1] /ˈθrɒtl ˈथ्रॉट्ल् / *verb* [T] to hold sb tightly by the throat and stop him/her breathing (किसी का) गला घोंटना ✪ पर्याय **strangle**

**throttle**[2] /ˈθrɒtl ˈथ्रॉट्ल् / *noun* [C] the part in a vehicle that controls the speed by controlling how much fuel goes into the engine मोटरकार का विशेष वॉल्व जो इंजन में अतिरिक्त तेल प्रवाह को नियंत्रित कर (कार की) गति कम कर देता है; थ्रॉटल

**through** /θru: थ्रू / *prep., adv.* **1** from one end or side of sth to the other (किसी वस्तु के) इस पार से उस पार; आर-पार *to look through a telescope* ○ *She cut through the rope.* ○ *to push through a crowd of people* **2** from the beginning to the end of sth (किसी के) आरंभ से अंत तक *Food supplies will not last through the winter.* ○ *We're halfway through the book.* **3** past a limit, stage or test किसी रोक, दशा या परीक्षा के पार या उसमें सफल *She didn't get through the first interview.* **4** because of; with the help of के कारण; की सहायता से *Errors were made through bad organization.* ○ *He got the* *job through his uncle.* **5** ( *AmE* **thru**) until, and including से लेकर... तक *They are staying Monday through Friday.* **6** connected by telephone टेलीफ़ोन द्वारा संपर्क में *Can you put me through to extension 5678, please?*

PHR V **be through (with sb/sth)** to have finished with sb/sth किसी व्यक्ति या वस्तु के साथ संबंध समाप्त कर देना

**throughout** /θruːˈaʊt थ्रूˈआउट्/ *adv., prep.* **1** in every part of sth सारा-का-सारा, किसी वस्तु के प्रत्येक भाग में *The house is beautifully decorated throughout.* ○ *The match can be watched live on television throughout the world.* **2** from the beginning to the end of sth (किसी वस्तु के) आरंभ से अंत तक, आद्योपांत *We didn't enjoy the holiday because it rained throughout.*

**throve** ➪ **thrive** का past tense रूप

**throw** /θrəʊ थ्रो/ *verb* (*pt,* **threw** /θruː थ्रू/; *pp* **thrown** /θrəʊn थ्रोन्/) **1** [I, T] **throw (sth) (to/at sb); throw sb sth** to send sth from your hand through the air by moving your hand or arm quickly (किसी वस्तु को) फेंकना *Throw the ball to me.* ○ *Throw me the ball.* **2** [T] to put sth somewhere quickly or carelessly जल्दबाज़ी में या लापरवाही से किसी वस्तु को कहीं डाल देना *He threw his bag down in a corner.* ○ *She threw on a sweater and ran out of the door.* **3** [T] to move your body or part of it quickly or suddenly शरीर के अंगों को तेज़ी से या झटका देकर घुमाना *She threw herself onto the bed and sobbed.* ○ *Rohit threw back his head and roared with laughter.* **4** [T] to cause sb to fall down quickly or violently जल्दबाज़ी में या झटके से किसी को नीचे गिरा देना *The bus braked and we were thrown to the floor.* **5** [T] to put sb in a particular (usually unpleasant) situation किसी को विशेष (विशेषतः अप्रिय) स्थिति में डाल देना *We were thrown into confusion by the news.* **6** [T] (*informal*) to make sb feel upset, confused or surprised किसी को परेशान कर देना, उलझन में डाल देना या चकित कर देना *The question threw me and I didn't know what to reply.* **7** [T] to send light or shade onto sth किसी पर रोशनी या छाया डालना *The tree threw a long shadow across the lawn.* ► **throw** *noun* [C] (कुछ) फेंकने की क्रिया *a throw of 97 metres*

PHR V **throw sth away 1** (*also* **throw sth out**) to get rid of rubbish or sth that you do not want कूड़ा, कचरा या अनचाही चीज़ फेंक देना *I threw his letters away.* **2** to waste or not use sth useful (कोई चीज़) बरबाद कर देना या गँवा देना *to throw away an opportunity*

**throw sth in** (*informal*) to include sth extra without increasing the price (बिना दाम बढ़ाए) किसी वस्तु के साथ कोई अतिरिक्त चीज़ दे देना

**throw sb out** to force sb to leave a place किसी को कहीं से बाहर निकाल देना

**throw sth out 1** to decide not to accept sb's idea or suggestion किसी के विचार या सुझाव को न मानने का निश्चय करना या नामंज़ूर कर देना **2** = **throw sth away 1**

**throw up** (*informal*) to vomit; to be sick वमन करना; बीमार होना

**throw sth up 1** to vomit food भोजन वमन करना **2** to produce or show sth कोई वस्तु बना देना या दिखा देना **3** to leave your job, career, studies, etc. नौकरी, पढ़ाई-लिखाई आदि छोड़ देना

**throwaway** /ˈθrəʊəweɪ ˈथ्रोअवे/ *adj.* (*only before a noun*) **1** used to describe sth that you say quickly without careful thought, sometimes in order to be funny जल्दबाज़ी में बिना सोचे-समझे कही गई बात (कभी-कभी मज़ाक में) *a throwaway line/remark/comment* **2** (used about goods, etc.) produced at a low cost and intended to be thrown away as rubbish after being used (सामान) कम लागत का, सस्ता (इस्तेमाल के बाद फेंक देने योग्य)

**thru** (*AmE*) = **through 5**

**thrust[1]** /θrʌst थ्रस्ट्/ *verb* [I, T] (*pt, pp* **thrust**) **1** to push sb/sth suddenly or violently; to move quickly and suddenly in a particular direction (किसी को) अचानक या झटके से धक्का देना; दिशा-विशेष में तेज़ी से और अचानक चल देना *The man thrust his hands deeper into his pockets.* ○ *She thrust past him and ran out of the room.* **2** to make a sudden forward movement with a knife, etc. चाकू आदि घुसेड़ना

PHR V **thrust sb/sth upon sb** to force sb to accept or deal with sb/sth किसी पर कुछ थोपना

**thrust[2]** /θrʌst थ्रस्ट्/ *noun* **1 the thrust** [*sing.*] the main part or point of an argument, policy, etc. किसी तर्क, नीति आदि का मुख्य अंश और बिंदु **2** [C] a sudden strong movement forward धक्का

**thud** /θʌd थड्/ *noun* [C] the low sound that is made when a heavy object hits sth else धम्म की आवाज़ (किसी भारी वस्तु के अन्य वस्तु से टकराने पर उत्पन्न) *Her head hit the floor with a dull thud.* ► **thud** *verb* [I] (**thudding; thudded**) धम्म की आवाज़ करना

**thug** /θʌg थग्/ *noun* [C] a violent person who may harm other people हिंसक व्यक्ति; ठग

**thumb[1]** /θʌm थम्/ *noun* [C] **1** the short thick finger at the side of each hand अँगूठा ➪ **body** पर

चित्र देखिए। **2** the part of a glove, etc. that covers your **thumb 1** दस्ताने का अँगूठा.

**IDM a rule of thumb** ➪ **rule¹** देखिए।

**stand/stick out like a sore thumb** ➪ **sore¹** देखिए।

**the thumbs up/down** a sign or an expression that shows approval/disapproval स्वीकृति या अस्वीकृति का संकेत या कथन

**under sb's thumb** (used about a person) completely controlled by sb (व्यक्ति) किसी की मुट्ठी में, पूर्णतः किसी के प्रभाव या नियंत्रण में *She's got him under her thumb.*

**thumb²** /θʌm थम्/ *verb* [I, T] **thumb (through) sth** to turn the pages of a book, etc. quickly किसी पुस्तक आदि के पन्ने जल्दी-जल्दी पलटना

**IDM thumb a lift** to hold out your thumb to cars going past, to ask sb to give you a free ride अँगूठे से इशारा कर सामने से जाते वाहन में मुफ़्त सवारी माँगना ➪ **hitch-hike** पर नोट देखिए।

**thumbtack** /ˈθʌmtæk ˈथम्‌टैक्/ (*AmE*) = **drawing pin**

**thump** /θʌmp थम्प्/ *verb* **1** [T] to hit sb/sth hard with sth, usually your closed hand (**fist**) मुट्ठी से किसी को ठोकना *Anand started coughing and Jai thumped him on the back.* **2** [I, T] to make a loud sound by hitting sth or by beating hard ज़ोर-ज़ोर से धड़कना या पीटना *His heart was thumping with excitement.* ▶ **thump** *noun* [C] आघात, धमाका

**thunder¹** /ˈθʌndə(r) ˈथन्ड(र्)/ *noun* [U] the loud noise in the sky that you can hear when there is a storm and that usually comes after a flash of light (**lightning**) आँधी के समय (बिजली चमकने के बाद उत्पन्न) कड़क, गरज, गड़गड़ाहट *a clap/crash/roll of thunder*

**thunder²** /ˈθʌndə(r) ˈथन्ड(र्)/ *verb* [I] **1** (used with it) to make a loud noise in the sky during a storm आँधी के समय आकाश में गरज या कड़क होना *The rain poured down and it started to thunder.* **2** to make a loud deep noise like thunder गरजने जैसी आवाज़ करना *Traffic thundered across the bridge.*

**thunderbolt** /ˈθʌndəbəʊlt ˈथन्डबोल्ट्/ *noun* [C] (*written*) a flash of **lightning** that comes at the same time as the noise of **thunder** and that hits sth गाज, वज्र

**thunderclap** /ˈθʌndəklæp ˈथन्डक्लैप्/ *noun* [C] a loud crash made by **thunder** बिजली की कड़क

**thunderstorm** /ˈθʌndəstɔːm ˈथन्डस्टॉम्/ *noun* [C] a storm with loud noises and flashes of light in the sky (**thunder** and **lightning**) गरज और बिजली के साथ आई आँधी, गरज-तूफ़ान, तड़ित-झंझा

**Thur.** (*also* **Thurs.**) *abbr.* Thursday गुरु(वार), बृहस्पति(वार), वीर(वार) *Thur. 26 June*

**Thursday** /ˈθɜːzdeɪ; -di ˈथ़र्ज़डे; -डि/ *noun* [C, U] (*abbr.* **Thur.; Thurs.**) the day of the week after Wednesday गुरुवार, बृहस्पतिवार या वीरवार

**NOTE** लिखते समय दिनों के नाम के शुरू में सदा बड़े अक्षर का प्रयोग होता है। इन नामों के वाक्य-प्रयोग के उदाहरणों के लिए **Monday** की प्रविष्टि देखिए।

**thus** /ðʌs दस्/ *adv.* (*formal*) **1** like this; in this way इस तरह से; इस प्रकार *Thus began the series of incidents which changed her life.* **2** because of or as a result of this इसके कारण या फलस्वरूप; इसलिए, अतएव ✪ पर्याय **therefore**

**thwart** /θwɔːt थ्वॉट्/ *verb* [T] **thwart sth; thwart sb (in sth)** to stop sb doing what he/she planned to do; to prevent sth happening किसी की योजना में अड़चन डालना; कुछ घटित होने से रोकना, कोई बात होने न देना *to thwart sb's plans/ambitions/efforts*

**thyme** /taɪm टाइम्/ *noun* [U] a plant that is used in cooking (**a herb**) and that has small leaves and a sweet smell अजवायन, बनजवायन

**thyroid** /ˈθaɪrɔɪd ˈथाइरॉइड्/ (*also* **thyroid gland**) *noun* [C] a small organ at the front of your neck that produces substances (**hormones**) that control the way in which your body grows and works अवटुग्रंथि, गलग्रंथि

**tibia** /ˈtɪbiə ˈटिबिआ/ *noun* [C] (*technical*) the inner and larger bone of the two bones in the lower part of the leg between your knee and foot टाँग के नीचे की (दो हड्डियों में से) अंदर की बड़ी हड्डी; अंतर्जंघिका, टिबिआ ✪ पर्याय **shin bone** ➪ **fibula** देखिए तथा **body** पर चित्र भी देखिए।

**tic** /tɪk टिक्/ *noun* [C] a sudden quick movement of a muscle, especially in your face or head, that you cannot control मांसपेशी (विशेषतः चेहरे या माथे की) का स्वयंभूत संकुचन; पेशी का खिंचाव *He has a nervous tic.*

**tick¹** /tɪk टिक्/ *verb* **1** [I] (used about a clock or watch) to make regular short sounds (चलती घड़ी का) टिक-टिक (आवाज़) करना **2** (*AmE* **check**) [T] to put a mark (✓) next to a name, an item on a list, etc. to show that sth has been dealt with or chosen, or that it is correct (किसी के नाम, सूची की वस्तु आदि के आगे) सही का चिह्न (✓) लगाना (मामले को निपटाया जाना, किसी चीज़ को चुनना, बात का ठीक होना दर्शाने के लिए) *Please tick the appropriate box.*

**IDM what makes sb/sth tick** the reasons why sb behaves or sth works in the way he/she/it does

किसी व्यक्ति या वस्तु के विशेष ढंग से काम करने के कारण *He has a strong interest in people and what makes them tick.*

**PHR V** **tick away/by** (used about time) to pass (समय का) बीतना

**tick sb/sth off** to put a mark (✓) next to a name an item on a list, etc. to show that sth has been done or sb has been dealt with सूची में किसी व्यक्ति या वस्तु के नाम के आगे सही का चिह्न (✓) लगाना (काम निपटाए जाने को दर्शाने के लिए)

**tick over** (*informal*) (*usually used in the continuous tenses*) **1** (used about an engine) to run slowly while the vehicle is not moving मंद गति से चलते वाहन के इंजन का घर्र-घर्र आवाज़ करना **2** to keep working slowly without producing or achieving very much मंद गति से कार्य करते रहना बिना विशेष उपलब्धि या उत्पादन के

**tick[2]** /tɪk टिक् / *noun* [C] **1** (*AmE* **check mark; check**) a mark (✓) next to an item on a list that shows that sth has been done or is correct सूची की वस्तु के आगे लगा सही का चिह्न (✓) (काम का निपटाया जाना या बात का सही होना दर्शाने के लिए) *Put a tick after each correct answer.* **2** (*also* **ticking**) the regular short sound that a watch or clock makes when it is working चलती घड़ी की टिक-टिक (की आवाज़) **3** (*BrE informal*) a moment एक क्षण, पल **4** a small animal with eight legs, like an insect, that bites humans and animals and sucks their blood किलनी, किलना (आठ टाँगों वाला कीड़ा जो मनुष्यों और पशुओं को काटता और उनका ख़ून पीता है)

**ticket** /ˈtɪkɪt ˈटिकिट् / *noun* [C] **1 a ticket (for/to sth)** a piece of paper or card that shows you have paid for a journey, or that allows you to enter a theatre, cinema, etc. (यात्रा या थिएटर आदि में प्रवेश का) टिकट *a single/return ticket to Chennai* ○ *a ticket office/machine/collector* ➪ **season ticket** देखिए। **2** a piece of paper or a label in a shop that shows the price, size, etc. of sth that is for sale दुकान में बिक्री की वस्तुओं पर लगा लेबल (वस्तु की क़ीमत, आकार आदि दर्शाने वाला) **3** an official piece of paper that you get when you have parked illegally or driven too fast telling you that you must pay money as a punishment (**a fine**) (वाहन को ग़लत पार्क करने या बहुत तेज़ चलाने पर लगे) जुरमाने का टिकट *a parking ticket*

**IDM** **just the job/ticket** ➪ **job** देखिए।

**tickle** /ˈtɪkl ˈटिक्ल् / *verb* **1** [T] to touch sb lightly with your fingers or with sth soft so that he/she laughs किसी को गुदगुदाना (ताकि वह हँस पड़े) *She tickled the baby's toes.* **2** [I, T] to produce or to have an uncomfortable feeling in a part of your body शरीर के किसी अंग को या का चुनचुनाना (खुजली और जलन-सी पैदा करना या होना) *My nose tickles/is tickling.* ○ *The woollen scarf tickled her neck.* **3** [T] (*informal*) to amuse and interest sb किसी को ख़ुश करना और (कुछ) पसंद आना *That joke really tickled me.* ▶ **tickle** *noun* [C] गुदगुदी, चुनचुनाहट

**ticklish** /ˈtɪklɪʃ ˈटिक्लिश् / *adj.* if a person is ticklish, he/she laughs when sb touches him/her in a sensitive place गुदगुदाने पर ख़ूब हँसने वाला (व्यक्ति) जिसे बहुत गुदगुदी होती है; गुदगुदिया, गुलगुलिया *Are you ticklish?*

**tidal** /ˈtaɪdl ˈटाइड्ल् / *adj.* connected with the regular rise and fall of the sea (**tides**) ज्वार-भाटा-विषयक

**tidal wave** *noun* [C] a very large wave in the sea which destroys things when it reaches the land, and is often caused by movements under the surface of the earth (**an earthquake**) ज्वार, ज्वारीय धारा (भूकंप के कारण समुद्र में उठी विशाल और विनाशकारी, लहर) **NOTE** इस अर्थ में **tsunami** अधिक तकनीकी शब्द है।

**tidbit** /ˈtɪdbɪt ˈटिड्बिट् / (*AmE*) = **titbit**

**tide[1]** /taɪd टाइड् / *noun* [C] **1** the regular change in the level of the sea caused by the moon and the sun. At **high tide** the sea is closer to the land, at **low tide** it is farther away and more of the beach can be seen चंद्रमा और सूर्य के कारण समुद्र में ज्वार-भाटा(क्रमशः लहरों का उठकर तट की ओर बढ़ना और घटकर तट से दूर जाना) *The tide is* ***coming in/going out.*** ➪ **ebb** देखिए। **2** [*usually sing.*] the way that most people think or feel about sth at a particular time समय-विशेष पर किसी विषय में लोगों की ख़ास सोच या मनोदशा *It appears that* ***the tide has turned*** *in the government's favour.*

**tide[2]** /taɪd टाइड् / *verb*

**PHR V** **tide sb over** to give sb sth to help him/her through a difficult time कठिन समय में सहायता के रूप में (किसी को कुछ) देना

**tidy[1]** /ˈtaɪdi ˈटाइडि / *adj.* (**tidier; tidiest**) **1** arranged with everything in good order ठीक-ठाक, चुस्त-दुरुस्त, सुव्यवस्थित, साफ़-सुथरा *If you keep your room tidy it is easier to find things.* **2** (used about a person) liking to keep things in good order (व्यक्ति) व्यवस्था-प्रिय, सफ़ाई-पसंद, तरतीबी, तरतीब-पसंद *Mihir is a very tidy boy.* ✪ पर्याय **neat** ✪ विलोम **untidy** ▶ **tidily** *adv.* ठीक-ठाक, सुव्यवस्थित रूप से ▶ **tidiness** *noun* [U] साफ़-सुथरापन, सुव्यवस्था

**tidy[2]** /ˈtaɪdi ˈटाइडि/ *verb* [I, T] (*pres. part.* **tidying;** *3rd person sing. pres.* **tidies;** *pt, pp* **tidied**) **tidy (sb/sth/yourself) (up)** to make sb/sth/ yourself look in order and well arranged किसी को ठीक से सजाना, ठीक-ठाक बनाना या सुव्यवस्थित करना *We must tidy this room up before the guests arrive.*

**PHR V** **tidy sth away** to put sth into the drawer, cupboard, etc. where it is kept so that it cannot be seen (अनावश्यक) वस्तुओं को कहीं और रख देना (ताकि जगह साफ़ दीखे)

**tie[1]** /taɪ टाइ/ *noun* [C] **1** (*AmE* **necktie**) a long thin piece of cloth worn round the neck, especially by men, with a knot at the front. A tie is usually worn with a shirt टाई, नेकटाई (जिसे पुरुष कमीज़ के ऊपर गले में बाँधते हैं) *a striped silk tie* ➪ **bow tie** देखिए। **2** [*usually pl.*] a strong connection between people or organizations लोगों या संस्थाओं के बीच गहरा संबंध *personal/emotional ties* ○ *family ties* **3** something that limits your freedom व्यक्ति की स्वतंत्रता को सीमित करने वाली वस्तु **4** a situation in a game or competition in which two or more teams or players get the same score किसी खेल या प्रतियोगिता में दो या अधिक टीमों, खिलाड़ियों की बराबरी पर छूटने की स्थिति; टाई *There was a tie for first place.*

**tie[2]** /taɪ टाइ/ *verb* (*pres. part.* **tying;** *3rd person sing. pres.* **ties;** *pt, pp* **tied**) **1** [T] to fasten sb/sth or fix sb/sth in position with rope, string, etc.; to make a knot in sth (रस्सी आदि से चीज़ों को परस्पर) बाँधना, कसना; किसी चीज़ में गाँठ लगाना *to tie sth in a knot* ○ *to tie your shoelaces* ✪ विलोम **untie** **2** [T] **tie sb (to sth/to doing sth)** (*usually passive*) to limit sb's freedom and make him/her unable to do everything he/she wants to किसी व्यक्ति की स्वतंत्रता को सीमित कर देना (कि वह मनचाहे काम न कर सके) *I don't want to be tied to staying in this country permanently.* **3** [I] **tie (with sb) (for sth)** to have the same number of points as another player or team at the end of a game or competition किसी खेल या प्रतियोगिता में खिलाड़ियों या टीमों का बराबरी पर छूटना, खेल का टाई हो जाना *England tied with Italy for third place.*

**IDM** **your hands are tied** ➪ **hand[1]** देखिए।

**PHR V** **tie sb/yourself down** to limit sb's/your freedom किसी की स्वतंत्रता को सीमित कर देना *Having young children really ties you down.*

**tie in (with sth)** to agree with other facts or information that you have; to match (किसी चीज़ का) पूर्व तथ्यों या जानकारी के अनुसार होना; मेल खाना *The new evidence seems to tie in with your theory.*

**tie sb/sth up** **1** to fix sb/sth in position with rope, string, etc. रस्सी, डोरी आदि से किसी को बाँधकर कहीं बंद कर देना *The dog was tied up in the back garden.* **2** (*usually passive*) to keep sb busy किसी को (किसी काम में) व्यस्त रखना, किसी का (किसी काम में) व्यस्त रहना *Mr Mitra is tied up in a meeting.*

**tier** /tɪə(r) टिअ(र्)/ *noun* [C] one of a number of levels ऊपर-नीचे की सीटों, कतारों या खानों में से कोई एक

**tiffin** /ˈtɪfɪn ˈटिफ़िन्/ *noun* [C] (*IndE*) a **snack** or light meal जलपान या हलका नाश्ता

**tiffin carrier** *noun* [C] (*IndE*) a set of circular metal containers stacked one on top of another for carrying food (भारत में) खाद्य सामग्री के लिए कई गोल डिब्बों (प्रायः एक के ऊपर एक) का पात्र; टिफ़िन कैरिअर

**tiger** /ˈtaɪɡə(r) ˈटाइग(र्)/ *noun* [C] a large wild cat that has yellow fur with black lines (**stripes**). Tigers live in parts of Asia बाघ ➪ **lion** पर चित्र देखिए।

**NOTE** बाघनी को **tigress** और बाघ के बच्चे को **cub** कहते हैं।

**tight** /taɪt टाइट्/ *adj., adv.* **1** fixed firmly in position and difficult to move or remove किसी स्थान पर कसकर बँधा हुआ (जिसका हिलना या जिसे हिलाना कठिन हो) *a tight knot* ○ *a* ***tight grip/hold*** ○ ***Hold tight*** *so that you don't fall off.*

**NOTE** भूत कृदंत (past participle) से पहले शब्द **tightly** का प्रयोग होता है (न कि **tight** का)—*The van was packed tight with boxes.* ○ *The van was tightly packed with boxes.*

**2** (used about clothes) fitting very closely in a way that is often uncomfortable (कपड़े) तंग, चुस्त (और इसलिए प्रायः असुविधाजनक) *These shoes hurt. They're too tight.* ○ *a tight-fitting skirt* ✪ विलोम **loose** **3** controlled very strictly and firmly बहुत कड़ाई और सख़्ती से नियंत्रित, बहुत कड़ा *Security is very tight at the airport.* **4** stretched or pulled hard so that it cannot be stretched further कसकर ताना हुआ *The rope was stretched tight.* **5** not having much free time or space समय या स्थान की दृष्टि से कसकर भरा हुआ; तंग *My schedule this week is very tight.* **6 -tight** (*used to form compound adjectives*) not allowing sth to get in or out अंदर आने या बाहर जाने से रोकने वाला, -रोधी (जैसे वायुरोधी, जलरोधी) *an airtight/watertight container* ▶ **tightly** *adv.* कसकर *Screw the lid on tightly.* ○ *She kept her eyes tightly closed.* ▶ **tightness** *noun* [U] कसावट, तंगी

**tighten** /ˈtaɪtn ˈटाइट्न्/ *verb* [I, T] **tighten (sth) (up)** to become or to make sth tight or tighter कसना या कस जाना या किसी वस्तु को कस देना *He tightened the screws as far as they would go.*

IDM **tighten your belt** to spend less money because you have less than usual available तंगी में गुज़ारा करना

PHR V **tighten up (on) sth** to cause sth to become stricter किसी चीज़ को अधिक कड़ा कर देना *to tighten up security/a law*

**tightrope** /ˈtaɪtrəʊp ˈटाइट्रोप्/ *noun* [C] a rope or wire that is stretched high above the ground on which people walk, especially as a form of entertainment ऊँचाई पर कसकर बँधी हुई रस्सी (जिस पर चलकर कलाबाज़ लोगों का मनोरंजन करता है), नट की रस्सी

**tights** /taɪts टाइट्स्/ (*AmE* **pantyhose**) *noun* [*pl.*] a piece of thin clothing, usually worn by women, that fits tightly from the waist over the legs and feet महिलाओं द्वारा कमर से नीचे तक पहनने की चुस्त पोशाक *a pair of tights* ➪ **stocking** देखिए।

**tilapia** /tɪˈleɪpiə; -ˈlæpiə टि ˈलेपिआ; -ˈलैपिआ/ *noun* [C] an African fish that lives in fresh water and that we can eat (लवणरहित पानी में रहने वाली) खाने की अफ़्रीक़ी मछली

**tile** /taɪl टाइल्/ *noun* [C] one of the flat, square objects that are arranged in rows to cover roofs, floors, bathroom walls, etc. पकी मिट्टी का समतल और वर्गाकार खपड़ा; टाइल (छतों, फ़र्शों, स्नानगृह की दीवारों आदि पर लगाने के लिए) ► **tile** *verb* [T] खपड़ा बिछाना या लगाना *a tiled bathroom*

**till**[1] /tɪl टिल्/ (*informal*) = **until**

**till**[2] /tɪl टिल्/ (*also* **cash register**) *noun* [C] the machine or drawer where money is kept in a shop, etc. दुकान आदि में पैसा रखने या जमा करने की मशीन या उसकी दराज़ *Please pay at the till.*

**tilt** /tɪlt टिल्ट्/ *verb* [I, T] to move, or make sth move, into a position with one end or side higher than the other एक ओर झुकना या झुकाना *The front seats of the car tilt forward.* ○ *She tilted her head to one side.* ► **tilt** *noun* [*sing.*] (एक ओर) झुकाव

**timber** /ˈtɪmbə(r) ˈटिम्ब(र्)/ *noun* **1** (*AmE* **lumber**) [U] wood that is going to be used for building इमारती काष्ठ या लकड़ी **2** [C] a large piece of wood शहतीर, लट्ठा *roof timbers*

**timbre** /ˈtæmbə(r) ˈटैम्ब(र्)/ *noun* [C] (*formal*) the quality of sound that is produced by a particular voice or musical instrument (स्वर-विशेष या वाद्य द्वारा उत्पन्न) ध्वनि का गुण; ध्वनि-स्वरूप, ध्वनि-गुणता

**time**[1] /taɪm टाइम्/ *noun* **1** [U, *sing.*] a period of minutes, hours, days, etc. समय, वक्त (मिनटों, घंटों, दिनों आदि में मापी जाने वाली अवधि) *free/spare time* ○ *I've been waiting* ***a long time***. ○ *Learning a language* ***takes time***. **2** [U, C] **time (to do sth); time (for sth)** the time in hours and minutes shown on a clock; the moment when sth happens or should happen घड़ी में दिखाया गया समय (घंटे और मिनट); समय जब कुछ घटित हो या होना चाहिए *What's the time?/What time is it?* ○ *It's time to go home.* **3** [U, *sing.*] a system for measuring time in a particular part of the world विश्व के किसी विशेष भाग में समय-मापन की प्रणाली *eleven o'clock* ***local time*** **4** [C] an occasion when you do sth or when sth happens कुछ करने या होने का समय *I phoned them three times.* ○ *I'll do it better* ***next time***. ○ ***Last time*** *I saw him, he looked ill.* **5** [C] an event or an occasion that you experience in a certain way विशेष ढंग से अनुभव करने योग्य कोई बात ***Have a good time*** *tonight.* ○ *We had a terrible time at the hospital.* **6** [C] a period in the past; a part of history अतीत का कोई समय, युग; इतिहास का कालखंड *The 19th century was a time of great industrial change.* **7** [C, U] the number of minutes, etc., taken to complete a race or an event दौड़ या किसी घटना में लगने वाला समय (मिनटों में) *What was his time in the hundred metres?*

IDM **(and) about time (too); (and) not before time** (*spoken*) used to say that sth should already have happened काम अब तक हो जाना चाहिए था, यह बताने के लिए प्रयुक्त

**ahead of your time** ➪ **ahead** देखिए।

**all the time/the whole time** during the period that sb was doing sth or that sth was happening हर समय, प्रति क्षण, सारा समय *I searched everywhere for my keys and they were in the door all the time.*

**at the same time** ➪ **same** देखिए।

**at a time** on each occasion एक बारी में, हर बार *The lift can hold six people at a time.* ○ *She ran down the stairs two at a time.*

**at one time** in the past; previously अतीत में, एक समय था कि; पहले

**at the time** at a particular moment or period in the past; then अतीत के किसी विशेष क्षण या अवधि में; उस समय, तब *I agreed at the time but later changed my mind.*

**at times** sometimes; occasionally कभी-कभी, यदा-कदा, समय-समय पर *At times I wish we'd never moved house.*

**before your time** before you were born आपके जन्म से पहले

**behind the times** not modern or fashionable पुराने ज़माने का, दक़ियानूसी, अब प्रचलन में नहीं

**bide your time** ➪ **bide** देखिए।

**buy time** ➪ **buy**[1] देखिए।

**for the time being** just for the present; not for long फ़िलहाल, इस समय; दीर्घ काल के लिए नहीं, अस्थायी रूप से

**from time to time** sometimes; not often कभी-कभी, समय-समय पर; बहुधा नहीं, यदा-कदा, बीच-बीच में

**give sb a hard time** ➪ **hard**[1] देखिए।

**have a hard time doing sth** ➪ **hard**[1] देखिए।

**have no time for sb/sth** to not like sb/sth किसी को नापसंद करना *I have no time for lazy people.*

**have the time of your life** to enjoy yourself very much भरपूर आनंद लेना, मज़े करना

**in the course of time** ➪ **course** देखिए।

**in good time** early; at the right time समय से पहले; ठीक समय पर

**in the nick of time** ➪ **nick**[1] देखिए।

**in time (for sth/to do sth)** not late; with enough time to be able to do sth देर से नहीं, समय पर; समय रहते (कुछ कर सकने के लिए) *Don't worry. We'll get to the station in time for your train.*

**It's about/high time** (*spoken*) used to say that you think sb should do sth very soon अब समय आ गया है कि (कुछ कर लिया जाए) कहने के लिए प्रयुक्त *It's about time you told him what's going on.*

**kill time, an hour, etc.** ➪ **kill**[1] देखिए।

**once upon a time** ➪ **once** देखिए।

**on time** not too late or too early; punctual न बहुत देर से और न बहुत जल्दी; निर्धारित समय पर, समयनिष्ठ *The train left the station on time.*

**one at a time** ➪ **one**[1] देखिए।

**take your time** to do sth without hurrying जल्दी न करना, आराम से काम करना

**tell the time** ➪ **tell** देखिए।

**time after time; time and (time) again** again and again; repeatedly बार-बार; पुनरावृत्त रूप से

**time²** /taɪm टाइम्/ *verb* [T] **1** (*often passive*) to arrange to do sth or arrange for sth to happen at a particular time कुछ करने की व्यवस्था करना या किसी घटना के लिए समय निश्चित करना *Their request was badly timed* (= it came at the wrong time). **2** to measure how long sb/sth takes किसी काम के लिए समय मापना (देखना कि किसी काम में कितना समय लगता है) *Try timing yourself when you write your essay.*

**time-consuming** *adj.* that takes or needs a lot of time जिसमें बहुत समय लगे, समय-साध्य

**time lag** = **lag²**

**timeless** /ˈtaɪmləs ˈटाइम्लस्/ *adj.* (*formal*) that does not seem to be changed by time or affected by changes in fashion समय गुज़रने या फ़ैशन बदलने से अप्रभावित, हमेशा क़ायम रहने वाला

**time limit** *noun* [C] a time during which sth must be done (कुछ करने की) समय की सीमा, अंतिम तिथि *We have to **set a time limit** for the work.*

**timely** /ˈtaɪmli ˈटाइम्लि/ *adj.* happening at exactly the right time एकदम ठीक समय पर होने वाला; समयोचित

**timeout** /taɪmˈaʊt टाइम्ˈआउट्/ *noun* [C] a short period of rest during a sports game खेल के दौरान विश्राम की अल्प अवधि

**timer** /ˈtaɪmə(r) ˈटाइम(र्)/ *noun* [C] a person or machine that measures time समय मापने वाला व्यक्ति या मशीन *an oven timer*

**times¹** /taɪmz टाइम्ज़्/ *prep.* used when you are multiplying one figure by another दो संख्याओं को गुणा करने में प्रयुक्त; गुणा *Three times four is twelve.*

**times²** /taɪmz टाइम्ज़्/ *noun* [*pl.*] used for comparing things (वस्तुओं की) तुलना करने के लिए प्रयुक्त *Tea is **three times as/more** expensive in England than in India.*

**timetable** /ˈtaɪmteɪbl ˈटाइम्टेब्ल्/ (*AmE* **schedule**) *noun* [C] a list that shows the times at which sth happens समय-सारणी, समय-तालिका *a bus/train/school timetable*

**timid** /ˈtɪmɪd ˈटिमिड्/ *adj.* easily frightened; shy and nervous जल्दी डर जाने वाला, भीरु; संकोची और जल्दी घबरा जाने वाला ▸ **timidity** *noun* [U] भीरुता, संकोच ▸ **timidly** *adv.* डरते-डरते, संकोचपूर्वक

**timing** /ˈtaɪmɪŋ ˈटाइमिङ्/ *noun* [U] **1** the time when sth is planned to happen कुछ करने या घटित होने के लिए निर्धारित समय; समय-निर्धारण *The manager was very careful about the timing of his announcement.* **2** the skill of doing sth at exactly the right time एकदम ठीक समय पर कुछ करने का कौशल, समय-निर्धारण का कौशल *The timing of her speech was perfect.*

**tin** /tɪn टिन्/ *noun* **1** [U] (*symbol* **Sn**) a soft silver-white metal that is often mixed with other metals टिन धातु **2** (*also* **tin can** *AmE* **can**) [C] a closed metal container in which food, paint, etc. is stored and sold; the contents of one of these containers टिन धातु से बना डिब्बा, टीन (जिसमें खाद्य पदार्थ, रंग आदि भरे जाते हैं, बिक्री के लिए); ऐसे डिब्बों में बंद सामान *a tin of peas/beans/soup* ○ *a tin of paint/varnish* **3** [C] a metal container with a lid for keeping food in खाद्य सामग्री रखने

वाला ढक्कनदार कनस्तर या डिब्बा *a biscuit/cake tin* ▶ **tinned** *adj.* डिब्बाबंद *tinned peaches/peas/soup*

**tinfoil** /ˈtɪnfɔɪl ˈटिन्फ़ॉइल् / = **foil**[1]

**tinge** /tɪndʒ टिन्ज् / *noun* [C, *usually sing.*] a small amount of a colour or a feeling किसी रंग या मनोभाव की हलकी रंगत या हलका पुट *a tinge of sadness* ▶ **tinged** *adj.* **tinged (with sth)** हलके पुट वाला, आभायुक्त *Her joy at leaving was tinged with regret.*

**tingle** /ˈtɪŋgl ˈटिङ्गल् / *verb* [I] (used about a part of the body) to feel as if a lot of small sharp points are pushing into it (व्यक्ति के शरीर के किसी अंग में) झुनझुनी चढ़ना (लगना कि कीलें-सी चुभ रही हैं) *His cheeks tingled as he came in from the cold.* ▶ **tingle** *noun* [C, *usually sing.*] झुनझुनी *a tingle of excitement/anticipation/fear*

**tinker** /ˈtɪŋkə(r) ˈटिङ्क(र्) / *verb* [I] **tinker (with sth)** to try to repair or improve sth without having the proper skill or knowledge बिना सही अभ्यास या जानकारी के किसी चीज़ की मरम्मत करने लगना; ठोका-पीटी

**tinkle** /ˈtɪŋkl ˈटिङ्कल् / *verb* [I] to make a light high ringing sound, like that of a small bell छोटी घंटी की-सी आवाज़ करना, टिनटिन या टनटन करना ▶ **tinkle** *noun* [C, *usually sing.*] टिनटिन, टनटन

**tin-opener** (*AmE* **can-opener**) *noun* [C] a tool that you use for opening a tin of food बंद डिब्बा खोलने का औज़ार ➪ **kitchen** पर चित्र देखिए।

**tinsel** /ˈtɪnsl ˈटिन्सल् / *noun* [U] long strings of shiny coloured paper, used as a decoration to hang on a Christmas tree चमकीले रंगीन काग़ज़ के लंबे फ़ीते (जिनसे क्रिसमस वृक्ष पर टाँगने की सजावटी वस्तुएँ बनती हैं)

**tint** /tɪnt टिन्ट् / *noun* [C] a shade or a small amount of a colour किसी रंग की रंगत या हलका पुट या छींटा *white paint with a pinkish tint* ▶ **tint** *verb* [T] किसी रंग का छींटा देना *tinted glasses* ○ *She had her hair tinted.*

**tiny** /ˈtaɪni ˈटाइनि / *adj.* (**tinier; tiniest**) very small बहुत छोटा; नन्हा *the baby's tiny fingers*

**tip**[1] /tɪp टिप् / *noun* [C] **1** the thin or pointed end of sth किसी वस्तु का पतला या नुकीला सिरा *the tips of your toes/fingers* ○ *the southernmost tip of India* **2 a tip (on/for sth/doing sth)** a small piece of useful advice about sth practical व्यावहारिक उपयोग की छोटी-सी सलाह *useful tips on how to save money* **3** a small amount of extra money that you give to sb who serves you, for example in a restaurant रेस्तराँ में वेटर को दी जाने वाली बख़्शीश, टिप *to leave a tip for the waiter* **4** (*also* **rubbish tip**) a place where you can take rubbish and leave it कूड़ाघर, घूरा ✪ पर्याय **dump** **5** (*informal*) a place that is very dirty or untidy बहुत गंदी, मैली-कुचैली जगह

**(have sth) on the tip of your tongue** to be sure you know sth but to be unable to remember it for the moment कोई बात लगभग (न कि पूरी तरह) याद आना

**the tip of the iceberg** only a small part of a much larger problem किसी बहुत बड़ी समस्या का सिरा-भर

**tip**[2] /tɪp टिप् / *verb* (**tipping; tipped**) **1** [I, T] **tip (sth) (up)** to move so that one side is higher than the other; to make sth move in this way (किसी चीज़ का) एक ओर उठना (उस पर बोझ आने पर); (किसी चीज़ को) एक ओर उठाना *When I stood up, the bench tipped up and the person on the other end fell off.* **2** [T] to make sth come out of a container by holding or lifting it at an angle डिब्बे को तिरछा करते या उठाते हुए उसमें से (अंदर की) चीज़ को बाहर निकालना *Tip the dirty water down the drain.* ○ *The child tipped all the toys onto the floor.* **3** [I, T] to give a **waiter,** etc. a small amount of extra money (in addition to the normal charge) to thank him/her वेटर आदि को बख़्शीश या टिप देना *She tipped the taxi driver generously.* **4** [T] **tip sb/sth (as sth/to do sth)** to think or say that sb/sth is likely to do sth (किसी की) संभावित क्रिया के विषय में भविष्यवाणी करना *He is widely tipped as the next Prime Minister.*

PHR V **tip sb off** to give sb secret information किसी को गुप्त सूचना देना

**tip (sth) up/over** to fall or turn over; to make sth do this गिरना या उलट जाना; गिराना या उलट देना *An enormous wave crashed into the little boat and it tipped over.*

**tip-off** *noun* [C] secret information that sb gives, for example to the police, about an illegal activity that is going to happen (पुलिस आदि को प्राप्त) गुप्त सूचना (संभावित अपराध के विषय में) *Acting on a tip-off, the police raided the house.*

**tiptoe**[1] /ˈtɪptəʊ ˈटिप्टो / *noun*

IDM **on tiptoe** standing or walking on the ends of your toes with your heels off the ground, in order not to make any noise or to reach sth high up (पैर के) पंजों के बल खड़ा होते या चलते हुए (ताकि शोर न हो या किसी वस्तु के ऊपर चढ़ा जा सके)

**tiptoe**[2] /ˈtɪptəʊ ˈटिप्टो / *verb* [I] to walk on your toes with your heels off the ground (पैर के) पंजों के बल चलना

**tire[1]** /ˈtaɪə(r) ˈटाइअ(र्)/ *verb* [I, T] to feel that you need to rest or sleep; to make sb feel like this आराम या नींद की ज़रूरत महसूस होना, थकावट होना, थकना; किसी को थकाना

PHRV **tire of sth/sb** to become bored or not interested in sth/sb any more ऊब जाना या किसी में दिलचस्पी खो बैठना

**tire sb/yourself out** to make sb/yourself very tired; to exhaust sb/yourself किसी को या ख़ुद को बहुत थका देना; किसी को या ख़ुद को बुरी तरह थका देना *The long walk tired us all out.*

**tire[2]** (*AmE*) = **tyre**

**tired** /ˈtaɪəd ˈटाइअड्/ *adj.* feeling that you need to rest or sleep थका हुआ, थका-माँदा, पस्त *She was tired after a hard day's work.* ○ *I was completely* ***tired out*** (= exhausted) *after all that.* ▶ **tiredness** *noun* [U] थकावट, ऊब

IDM **be tired of sb/sth/doing sth** to be bored with or annoyed by sb/sth/doing sth किसी की बातों या कामों से ऊब या गुस्सा हो जाना *I'm* ***sick and tired*** *of listening to the same thing again and again.*

**tireless** /ˈtaɪələs ˈटाइअलस्/ *adj.* putting a lot of hard work and energy into sth over a long period of time without stopping or losing interest (किसी काम के लिए) अनथक कठोर परिश्रम की क्षमता और शक्ति से भरपूर

**tiresome** /ˈtaɪəsəm ˈटाइअसम्/ *adj.* (*formal*) that makes you angry or bored; annoying खिझाऊ या उबाऊ; कष्टकर

**tiring** /ˈtaɪərɪŋ ˈटाइअरिङ्/ *adj.* making you want to rest or sleep थका देने वाला; थकाऊ *a tiring journey/job*

**tissue** /ˈtɪʃuː; ˈtɪsjuː ˈटिशू; ˈटिस्यू/ *noun* **1** [U, *pl.*] the mass of cells that form the bodies of humans, animals and plants ऊतक (मानवों, पशुओं और वनस्पतियों की शरीर की रचना करने वाला कोशिका-समूह) *muscle/brain/nerve/scar tissue* ○ *Radiation can destroy the body's tissues.* **2** [C] a thin piece of soft paper that you use to clean your nose and throw away after you have used it पतले मुलायम काग़ज़ का रूमाल (नाक आदि साफ़ करने में प्रयुक्त) *a box of tissues* **3 tissue paper** [U] thin soft paper that you use for putting around things that may break टूट सकने वाली वस्तुओं को लपेटने में प्रयुक्त मुलायम काग़ज़; टिशू पेपर

**tit** /tɪt टिट्/ *noun* [C] a small European bird that eats insects and seeds. There are several types of tit (कीड़े और अनाज के दाने खाने वाली) एक प्रकार की यूरोपीय चिड़िया (जो अनेक प्रकार की होती है)

IDM **tit for tat** something unpleasant that you do to sb because he/she has done sth to you जैसे को तैसा

**titanium** /tɪˈteɪniəm टिˈटेनिअम्/ *noun* [U] (*symbol* **Ti**) a hard silver-grey metal that is combined with other metals to make strong, light materials that do not easily **rust** टाइटेनियम धातु (एक कड़ी हलके स्लेटी रंग की धातु जो अन्य धातुओं के साथ मिलकर ज़ंगरोधी हो जाती है)

**titbit** /ˈtɪtbɪt ˈटिट्बिट्/ (*AmE* **tidbit**) *noun* [C] **1** a small but very nice piece of food चटपटे आहार का टुकड़ा **2** an interesting piece of information (छोटी लेकिन) चटपटी और मज़ेदार ख़बर

**title** /ˈtaɪtl ˈटाइट्ल्/ *noun* [C] **1** the name of a book, play, film, picture, etc. पुस्तक, नाटक, फ़िल्म, चित्र आदि का शीर्षक *I know the author's name but I can't remember the title of the book.* **2** a word that shows a person's position, profession, etc. किसी व्यक्ति के पद, व्यवसाय आदि का द्योतक शब्द, पदवी, उपाधि *'Lord', 'Doctor', 'Reverend', 'Mrs' and 'General' are all titles.* **3** the position of being the winner of a competition, especially a sports competition किसी प्रतियोगिता (विशेषतः खेल प्रतियोगिता) में विजेता का पद *Sania is playing this match to defend her title* (= to remain champion).

**titled** /ˈtaɪtld ˈटाइट्ल्ड्/ *adj.* having a word, for example 'Nawab', etc. before your name that shows that your family has an important position in society (उच्च सामाजिक प्रतिष्ठा के द्योतक) (महाराज) आदि पदवियों से अलंकृत पदवीधारी; उपाधिप्राप्त (व्यक्ति)

**title-holder** *noun* [C] the person or team who won a sports competition the last time it took place; the current champion खेल-प्रतियोगिता में गत वर्ष का विजेता व्यक्ति या दल; वर्तमान चैंपियन, इस वर्ष का विजेता

**title role** *noun* [C] the main character in a film, book, etc. whose name is the same as the title फ़िल्म, पुस्तक आदि का प्रधान पात्र जिसका नाम वही हो जो फ़िल्म आदि का है

**titration** /taɪˈtreɪʃn टाइˈट्रेश्न्/ *noun* [U] (*technical*) the process of finding out how much of a particular substance is in a liquid by measuring how much of another substance is needed to react with it किसी घोल के घटक पदार्थ की मात्रा का पता लगाना, उसके साथ प्रतिक्रिया हेतु अपेक्षित अन्य पदार्थ की मात्रा का मापन करते हुए; अनुमापन

**titter** /ˈtɪtə(r) ˈटिट(र्)/ *verb* [I] to laugh quietly, especially in an embarrassed or nervous way दबे हुए हँसना (विशेषतः खिसियाते या घबराते हुए) ▶ **titter** *noun* [C] दबी हुई हँसी

**T-junction** *noun* [C] a place where two roads join to form the shape of a T, T के आकार में दो सड़कों का मिलन-स्थल

**tn** (*AmE*) = **t²**

**TNT** /ˌtiː en ˈtiː ˌटी एन् ˈटी/ *noun* [U] a highly explosive substance एक अत्यंत विस्फोटक पदार्थ; टीएनटी

**to** /tə; *before vowels* tu; *strong form* tuː ट; स्वर ध्वनियों से पहले टु; प्रबल रूप टू/ *prep., adv.* **1** in the direction of; as far as की दिशा में, की ओर; जहाँ तक *She's going to Chennai.* ○ *Turn to the left.* **2** used to show the end or limit of a series of things or period of time (से) तक (वस्तु-शृंखला या समयावधि का अंत या सीमा दर्शाने के लिए प्रयुक्त) *from Monday to Friday* ○ *from beginning to end* **3** used to show the person or thing that receives sth कुछ पाने वाले को दर्शाने के लिए प्रयुक्त *I am very grateful to my parents.* ○ *What have you done to your hair?* **4** (nearly) touching sth; directed towards sth किसी वस्तु को (लगभग) छूते हुए; किसी वस्तु की ओर निर्देशित *They sat back to back.* ○ *She made no reference to her personal problems.* **5** reaching a particular state स्थिति-विशेष में पहुँचा हुआ *The meat was cooked to perfection.* ○ *His speech reduced her to tears* (= made her cry). **6** used to introduce the second part of a comparison जिससे तुलना की जाए उसके शुरू में प्रयुक्त *I prefer theatre to opera.* **7** (used for expressing quantity) for each unit of money, measurement, etc. मुद्रा, माप आदि की प्रत्येक इकाई में कितनी मात्रा होती है (जैसे एक रुपये में कितने पैसे होते हैं), यह बताने के लिए प्रयुक्त *How many paise are there to a rupee?* **8** (used to say what time it is) before (समय बताने के लिए) घड़ी के पूरे घंटे से पहले, कुछ बजने में बाक़ी *It's ten to three* (= ten minutes before three o'clock). **9** used to express sb's opinion or feeling about sth किसी विषय में किसी का मत या मनोभाव व्यक्त करने के लिए प्रयुक्त *To me, it was the wrong decision.* ○ *It sounded like a good idea to me.* **10** used for expressing a reaction or attitude to sth किसी विषय में किसी की प्रतिक्रिया या मनोवृत्ति व्यक्त करने के लिए प्रयुक्त *To my surprise, I saw two strangers coming out of my house.* **11** used with verbs to form the **infinitive** क्रियार्थक संज्ञा बनाने के लिए क्रिया से पहले प्रयुक्त *I want to go home now.* ○ *Don't forget to write.* **12** / tuː टू/ (used about a door) in or into a closed position (दरवाज़े को) बंद करने का अर्थ व्यक्त करने के लिए प्रयुक्त *Push the door to.*
**IDM to and fro** backwards and forwards इधर-उधर, आगे-पीछे

**toad** /təʊd टोड्/ *noun* [C] a small cold-blooded animal that has a rough skin and lives both on land and in water टोड, भेक, एक प्रकार का मेंढक (जो जल और स्थल दोनों में रहता है) ➪ **amphibian** पर चित्र देखिए।

**toadstool** /ˈtəʊdstuːl ˈटोड्स्टूल्/ *noun* [C] a type of small wild plant (**a fungus**) that is usually poisonous, with a round top and a thin supporting part छतरी के आकार का छोटा कुकुरमुत्ता (प्रायः विषैला) ➪ **mushroom** और **fungus** देखिए।

**toast** /təʊst टोस्ट्/ *noun* **1** [U] a thin piece of bread that is heated on both sides to make it brown डबलरोटी का सेंका हुआ टुकड़ा; टोस्ट *a piece/slice of toast* **2** [C] **a toast (to sb/sth)** an occasion at which a group of people wish sb happiness, success, etc., by drinking a glass of wine, etc. at the same time (प्रसन्नता, सफलता आदि की) शुभकामना का जाम पीने का उत्सव *I'd like to **propose a toast to** the bride and groom.* ➪ **drink** देखिए। ▶ **toast** *verb* [T] शुभकामना का जाम पीना

**toaster** /ˈtəʊstə(r) ˈटोस्टर्(र्)/ *noun* [C] an electrical machine for making bread turn brown by heating it on both sides डबलरोटी सेंकने का बिजली का उपकरण; टोस्टर

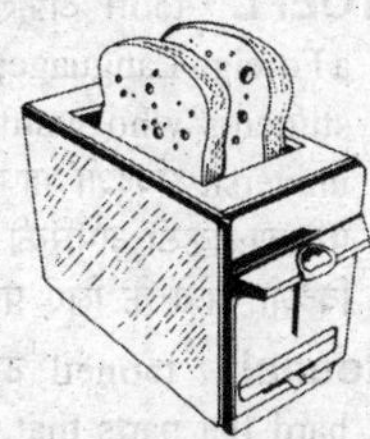

**tobacco** /təˈbækəʊ टˈबैको/ *noun* [U] the substance that people smoke in cigarettes and pipes (the dried leaves of the tobacco plant) तंबाकू

**tobacconist** /təˈbækənɪst टˈबैकनिस्ट्/ *noun* **1** [C] a person who sells cigarettes, matches, etc. सिगरेट, माचिस आदि बेचने वाला व्यक्ति; तंबाकू विक्रेता **2** (*also* **the tobacconist's**) [*sing.*] a shop where you can buy cigarettes, matches, etc. तंबाकू (सिगरेट, माचिस आदि) की दुकान

**toboggan** /təˈbɒgən टˈबॉगन्/ *noun* [C] a type of flat board with flat pieces of metal underneath, that people use for travelling down hills on snow for fun बर्फ़ पर चलने वाली छोटी गाड़ी, छोटी बर्फ़गाड़ी **NOTE** **Toboggan** एक छोटी **sledge** होती है। ➪ **bobsleigh** भी देखिए।

**today** /təˈdeɪ टˈडे/ *noun* [U], *adv.* **1** (on) this day आज के दिन, आज *Today is Monday.* ○ *School ends **a week today*** (= on this day next week). **2** (in) the present age; these days वर्तमान युग (में); इन दिनों, आजकल *Young people today have far more freedom.* ✪ विलोम **nowadays**

**toddle** /ˈtɒdl ˈटॉड्ल्/ *verb* [I] **1** to walk with short steps like a very young child नन्हे बच्चे की तरह छोटे क़दम भरते हुए चलना **2** (*informal*) to walk or go somewhere चलना या कहीं जाना

**toddler** /ˈtɒdlə(r) ˈटॉड्ल(र्)/ *noun* [C] a young child who has only just learnt to walk नन्हा बच्चा जिसने अभी चलना सीखा हो

**toddy** /ˈtɒdi ˈटॉडि/ *noun* [C, U] (in India) the fermented sap of palm trees used as a drink ताड़ी

**toe**[1] /təʊ टो/ *noun* [C] **1** one of the small parts like fingers at the end of each foot पैर की अँगुली (या अँगूठा) *the big/little toe* (= the largest/smallest toe) ➪ **body** पर चित्र देखिए। **2** the part of a sock, shoe, etc. that covers your toes ज़ुराब, जूते आदि का पंजा या ढकनी

**toe**[2] /təʊ टो/ *verb* (*pres. part.* **toeing;** *pt, pp* **toed**) IDM **toe the (party) line** to do what sb in authority tells you to do, even if you do not agree with him/her (सहमत न होते हुए भी) बड़ों की बात मानना

**TOEFL** /ˈtəʊfl ˈटोफ़्ल्/ *abbr.* Test of English as a Foreign Language; the examination for foreign students who want to study at an American university विदेशी भाषा के रूप में अंग्रेज़ी (योग्यता) का परीक्षण; किसी अमेरिकी विश्वविद्यालय में प्रवेश के इच्छुक विदेशी छात्रों के लिए परीक्षा

**toenail** /ˈtəʊneɪl ˈटोनेल्/ *noun* [C] one of the hard flat parts that cover the end of your toes पैर की अँगुली का (या अँगूठे) का नाख़ून ➪ **body** पर चित्र देखिए।

**toffee** /ˈtɒfi ˈटॉफ़ि/ *noun* [C, U] a hard sticky sweet that is made by cooking sugar and butter together टॉफ़ी (चीनी और मक्खन पकाकर बनाई गई सख़्त चिपचिपी मिठाई)

**together**[1] /təˈgeðə(r) टˈगेद्(र्)/ *adv.* **1** with or near each other एक-दूसरे के साथ या निकट; साथ-साथ *They walked home together.* ○ *Stand with your feet together.* **2** so that two or more things are mixed or joined to each other दो या अधिक वस्तुएँ सम्मिश्रित या संयुक्त *Mix the butter and sugar together.* ○ *Tie the two ends together.* **3** at the same time एक ही समय में, इकट्ठे *Don't all talk together.* IDM **get your act together** ➪ **act**[2] देखिए।

**together with** in addition to; as well as के अलावा; साथ ही *I enclose my order together with a cheque for Rs 150.*

**together**[2] /təˈgeðə(r) टˈगेद्(र्)/ *adj.* (*informal*) (used about a person) organized, capable (व्यक्ति) स्वनियंत्रित, सँभला हुआ, आत्मविश्वासपूर्ण *I'm not very together this morning.*

**togetherness** /təgeðənəs टगेद्रनस्/ *noun* [U] a feeling of friendship मैत्री की भावना

**toil** /tɔɪl टॉइल्/ *verb* [I] (*formal*) to work very hard or for a long time at sth (किसी बात के लिए) कड़ा या लंबे समय तक परिश्रम करना ▶ **toil** *noun* [U] कड़ा परिश्रम

**toilet** /ˈtɔɪlət ˈटॉइलट्/ *noun* [C] a large bowl with a seat, connected to a water pipe, that you use when you need to get rid of waste material from your body; the room containing this (मल-विसर्जन के पात्र आदि वाला) शौचस्थल; शौचगृह, शौचालय *I need* ***to go to the toilet*** (= use the toilet).

> NOTE घर में बने शौचगृह को लोग **toilet** या आम बोलचाल की भाषा में **loo** कहते हैं। **Lavatory** और **WC** औपचारिक शब्द हैं और अब प्रायः प्रचलन में नहीं हैं। सार्वजनिक शौचालयों को **Ladies** (महिलाओं के लिए) या **Gents** (पुरुषों के लिए) कहा जाता है, अमेरिकी अंग्रेज़ी में घर के शौचालय को **bathroom** कहते हैं और सार्वजनिक शौचालय को **restroom, ladies' room** या **men's room** कहते हैं।

**toilet bag** (*also* **sponge bag**) *noun* [C] a bag that you use when travelling to carry things such as soap, toothpaste, etc. (**toiletries**) यात्रा के दौरान प्रसाधन सामग्री (साबुन, मंजन आदि) ले जाने की थैली

**toilet paper** (*also* **toilet tissue**) *noun* [U] soft, thin paper that some people use to clean themselves after going to the toilet शौचक्रिया में शरीर की स्वच्छता के लिए प्रयुक्त मुलायम, पतला काग़ज़; टॉयलेट पेपर

**toiletries** /ˈtɔɪlətriz ˈटॉइलट्रिज़्/ *noun* [*pl.*] things such as soap or toothpaste that you use for washing, cleaning your teeth, etc. प्रसाधन सामग्री (साबुन, मंजन आदि)

**toilet roll** *noun* [C] a long piece of toilet paper rolled round a tube टॉयलेट पेपर का बेलनाकार बंडल

**token**[1] /ˈtəʊkən ˈटोकन्/ *noun* [C] **1** a round piece of metal, plastic, etc. that you use instead of money to operate some machines or as a form of payment धातु या प्लास्टिक का टुकड़ा; टोकन (मशीन चलाने या भुगतान के रूप में प्रयुक्त) **2** a piece of paper that you can use to buy sth of a certain value in a particular shop. Tokens are often given as presents काग़ज़ का (विशेष) टुकड़ा, टोकन (विशेष दुकान से निश्चित मूल्य की वस्तुएँ ख़रीदने के लिए प्रयुक्त) (टोकन प्रायः उपहार में दिए जाते हैं) *CD/gift token* ➪ **voucher** देखिए। **3** something that represents or is a symbol of sth किसी बात की प्रतीक कोई वस्तु; टोकन *Please accept this gift* ***as a token of*** *our gratitude.*

**token**[2] /ˈtəʊkən ˈटोकन्/ *adj.* (*only before a noun*) **1** done, chosen, etc. in a very small quantity, and only in order not to be criticized (अल्प मात्रा में और) केवल प्रतीकात्मक (ताकि आलोचना से बचा जा सके) *There is a token woman on the board of directors.* **2** small, but done or given to show that you are serious about sth and will keep a promise or an agreement अल्प मात्रा में परंतु सकारात्मक रूप से प्रतीकात्मक (वादा पूरा करने के प्रतीक के रूप में किया गया भुगतान आदि व्यवहार) *a token payment*

**told** ➪ **tell** का past tense और past participle रूप

**tolerable** /ˈtɒlərəbl ˈटॉलरबल्/ *adj.* **1** quite good, but not of the best quality काफ़ी अच्छा (परंतु सर्वोत्तम नहीं) **2** of a level that you can accept or deal with, although unpleasant or painful सहने-योग्य, सहनीय *Drugs can reduce the pain to a tolerable level.* ✪ विलोम **intolerable**

**tolerant** /ˈtɒlərənt ˈटॉलरन्ट्/ *adj.* **tolerant (of/towards sb/sth)** the ability to allow or accept sth that you do not like or agree with सहिष्णु, सहनशील (अरुचिकर या अस्वीकार्य वस्तु के प्रति) ✪ विलोम **intolerant** ▸ **tolerance** *noun* [U] **tolerance (of/for sb/sth)** सहिष्णुता, सहनशीलता *religious/racial tolerance* ✪ विलोम **intolerance**

**tolerate** /ˈtɒləreɪt ˈटॉलरेट्/ *verb* [T] **1** to allow or accept sth that you do not like or agree with सहन या बरदाश्त करना (किसी अरुचिकर या अस्वीकार्य वस्तु को), नापसंद स्थितियों को भी बने रहने देना या उनके साथ रहना *In a democracy we must tolerate opinions that are different from our own.* **2** to accept or be able to deal with sb/sth unpleasant without complaining बिना शिकायत किए अरुचिकर स्थिति का सामना करना या झेलना *The noise was more than she could tolerate.* ▸ **toleration** /ˌtɒləˈreɪʃn ˌटॉलˈरेश्न्/ *noun* = **tolerance**

**toll** /təʊl टोल्/ *noun* **1** [C] money that you pay to use a road or bridge सड़क या पुल के प्रयोग पर देय राशि, महसूल; मार्गशुल्क, राहदारी *highway tolls* ○ *a toll bridge* **2** [C, *usually sing.*] the amount of damage done or the number of people who were killed or injured by sth क्षति की मात्रा या हताहतों की संख्या *The official death toll has now reached 5000.* IDM **take a heavy toll/take its toll (on sth)** to cause great loss, damage, suffering, etc. बहुत हानि, क्षति, तकलीफ़ आदि पहुँचाना

**tom** /tɒm टॉम्/ = **tomcat**

**tomato** /təˈmɑːtəʊ टˈमाटो/ *noun* [C] (*pl.* **tomatoes**) a soft red fruit that is often eaten without being cooked in salads, or cooked as a vegetable टमाटर *tomato juice/soup/sauce* ➪ **vegetable** पर चित्र देखिए।

**tomb** /tuːm टूम्/ *noun* [C] a large place, usually built of stone under the ground, where the body of an important person is buried क़ब्र, मक़बरा या समाधि (प्रायः भूमि के अंदर और पत्थरों से बना बड़ा स्थान जहाँ किसी महापुरुष का शव दफ़न या सुरक्षित हो) *the tombs of the Nawabs* ➪ **grave** देखिए।

**tomboy** /ˈtɒmbɔɪ ˈटॉम्बॉइ/ *noun* [C] a young girl who likes the same games and activities that are traditionally considered to be for boys लड़कों जैसे खेल और क्रिया-कलाप में रुचि रखने वाली लड़की, चुलबुली या शोख़ लड़की

**tombstone** /ˈtuːmstəʊn ˈटूमस्टोन्/ *noun* [C] a large flat stone that lies on or stands at one end of a **grave** and shows the name, dates, etc. of the dead person क़ब्र या समाधि के एक किनारे ज़मीन पर लगाया या खड़ा किया गया पत्थर जिसपर दिवंगत व्यक्ति का नाम, तिथि आदि अंकित रहते हैं; समाधिशिला ➪ **gravestone** और **headstone** भी देखिए।

**tomcat** /ˈtɒmkæt ˈटॉम्कैट्/ (*also* **tom**) *noun* [C] a male cat नर बिल्ली, बिल्ला, बिलार

**tomorrow** /təˈmɒrəʊ टˈमॉरो/ *noun* [U] *adv.* **1** (on) the day after today (आने वाला) कल *Today is Friday so tomorrow is Saturday.* ○ *I'm going to bed. I've got to get up early tomorrow morning.* **2** the future भविष्य *The schoolchildren of today are tomorrow's workers.*

**tom-tom** *noun* [C] a tall narrow drum with a small head, that is played with hands टमटम

**ton** /tʌn टन्/ *noun* **1** [C] a measure of weight; 2240 pounds तोल की एक माप, टन; 2240 पाउंड NOTE **Ton** और **tonne** अलग-अलग हैं, एक ton में 1.016 tonnes होते हैं। अमेरिकी अंग्रेज़ी के ton में 2000 पाउंड होते हैं। **2 tons** [*pl.*] (*informal*) a lot ढेर सारा *I've got tons of homework to do.*

**tone[1]** /təʊn टोन्/ *noun* **1** [C, U] the quality of a sound or of sb's voice, especially expressing a particular emotion ध्वनि या किसी के स्वर का गुण (विशेषतः किसी भाव-विशेष का व्यंजक), लहज़ा, स्वर-शैली *'Do you know each other?' she asked in a casual tone of voice.* **2** [*sing.*] the general quality or style of sth किसी वस्तु की सामान्य विशेषता या शैली; रुख *The tone of the meeting was optimistic.* **3** [C] a shade of a colour (किसी रंग की), रंगत, आभा *warm tones of red and orange* **4** [C] a sound that you hear on the telephone फ़ोन पर सुनाई पड़ने वाली ध्वनि; टोन (जैसे फ़ोन व्यस्त होने की टोन) *Please speak after the tone* (= an instruction on an answering machine).

**tone²** /təʊn टोन्/ *verb* [T] **tone sth (up)** to make your muscles, skin, etc. firmer, especially by doing exercise शरीर को अधिक सुदृढ़ बनाना (विशेषतः व्यायाम के द्वारा)

**PHR V** **tone sth down** to change sth that you have said, written, etc., to make it less likely to offend अपनी (कही या लिखी) बात की तीव्रता को कम करना

**tone-deaf** *adj.* not able to sing or hear the difference between notes in music संगीत के स्वरों में अंतर को पहचानने में असमर्थ; तान-बधिर

**tongs** /tɒŋz टॉङ्ज़्/ *noun* [*pl.*] a tool that looks like a pair of scissors but that you use for holding or picking things up सँड़सी, चिमटा ➪ **laboratory** पर चित्र देखिए।

**tongue** /tʌŋ टङ्/ *noun* **1** [C] the soft part inside your mouth that you can move. You use your tongue for speaking, tasting things, etc. जीभ, जिह्वा, ज़बान ➪ **epiglottis** पर चित्र देखिए। **2** [C] (*formal*) a language भाषा *your **mother tongue***

**IDM** **on the tip of your tongue** ➪ **tip¹** देखिए।

**put/stick your tongue out** to put your tongue outside your mouth as a rude sign to sb किसी को चिढ़ाने के लिए जीभ बाहर निकालना

**a slip of the tongue** ➪ **slip²** देखिए।

**(with) tongue in cheek** done or said as a joke; not intended seriously परिहास के रूप में कुछ किया या कहा गया, झूठमूठ; जिसमें गंभीर होने का इरादा नहीं ऊपरी मन से कहा या किया गया

**tongue-tied** *adj.* not saying anything because you are shy or nervous संकोच या घबराइट के मारे एकदम चुप

**tongue-twister** *noun* [C] a phrase or sentence with many similar sounds that is difficult to say correctly when you are speaking quickly (ध्वनियों में समानता के कारण) उच्चारण की दृष्टि से कठिन पदबंध या वाक्यांश (द्रुत गति से बोलने में)

**tonic** /ˈtɒnɪk ˈटॉनिक्/ *noun* **1** (*also* **tonic water**) [U, C] a type of water with bubbles in it and a rather bitter taste that is often added to alcoholic drinks (बुलबुलेदार और कुछ कड़वा) सोडा वाटर (जो ऐल्कोहल युक्त पेयों में प्रायः मिलाया जाता है) *a gin and tonic* **2** [C, U] a medicine or sth you do that makes you feel stronger, healthier, etc., especially when you are very tired स्फूर्ति, शक्ति आदि देने वाली दवा या अन्य वस्तु; टॉनिक (विशेषतः दुर्बलता या थकावट होने पर ली जाने वाली) *A relaxing holiday is a wonderful tonic.*

**tonight** /təˈnaɪt टˈनाइट्/ *noun* [U], *adv.* (on) the evening or night of today आज (की) शाम या रात *Tonight is the last night of our holiday.* ○ *What's on TV tonight?*

**tonne** /tʌn टन्/ (*also* **metric ton**) *noun* [C] (*pl.* **tonnes** or **tonne**) a measure of weight; 1000 kilograms तोल की एक माप, टन; 1000 किलोग्राम ➪ **ton** देखिए।

**tonsil** /ˈtɒnsl ˈटॉन्सल्/ *noun* [C] one of the two soft lumps in your throat at the back of your mouth गलतुंडिका, टांसिल (गले में अंत की ओर कोमल मांसपिंड) *She had to **have her tonsils out*** (= removed in a medical operation). ➪ **epiglottis** पर चित्र देखिए।

**tonsillitis** /ˌtɒnsəˈlaɪtɪs टॉन्सˈलाइटिस्/ *noun* [U] an illness in which the tonsils become very sore and swollen गलतुंडिका-शोथ, टांसिलों में दर्द और सूजन

**too** /tuː टू/ *adv.* **1** (*used before adjectives and adverbs*) more than is good, allowed, possible, etc. अपेक्षा से अधिक *These boots are too small.* ○ *It's far too cold to go out without a coat.*

> **NOTE** ध्यान दीजिए 'It's a too long journey' प्रयोग अमान्य है। मान्य प्रयोग है—*It's too long a journey for you to make alone.*

**2** (*not with negative statements*) in addition; also इसके अतिरिक्त; भी *Red is my favourite colour but I like blue, too.* ○ *Praveen thinks you're right and I do too.*

> **NOTE** ध्यान दीजिए स्वीकारात्मक कथनों से सहमति दर्शाने के लिए उपवाक्य (clause) के अंत में too और नकारात्मक कथनों के प्रसंग में (ऐसी ही स्थिति में) **either** का प्रयोग होता है—*I like eating out and Rakesh does too.* ○ *I don't like cooking and Rakesh doesn't either.*

**3** used to add sth which makes a situation even worse स्थिति के बदतर होने को दर्शाने के लिए, प्रासंगिक शब्द के साथ प्रयुक्त *Her purse was stolen. And on her birthday too.* **4** (*usually used in negative sentences*) very बहुत *The weather is not too bad today.*

**took** ➪ **take** का past tense रूप

**tool** /tuːl टूल्/ *noun* [C] a piece of equipment such as a hammer, that you hold in your hand(s) and use to do a particular job कारीगर का औज़ार (हथौड़ा आदि) *Hammers, screwdrivers and saws are all carpenter's tools.* ○ *a tool kit* (= a set of tools in a box or a bag)

**NOTE** औज़ार (tool) वह चीज़ है जिसे सामान्यतया हाथ में पकड़ कर काम करते हैं, जैसे पाना, हथौड़ा। **Implement** बाहर की स्थिति (जैसे खेती या बाग़बानी) में उपयोग की वस्तु है। **Machine** बिजली, इंजन आदि से चलने वाली चीज़ है। तकनीकी या नाज़ुक काम जिससे किया जाए वह **instrument** है—*a dentist's instruments*. **Device** अधिक सामान्य शब्द है जो किसी विशेष काम को विशेष रूप से करने के प्रसंग में प्रयुक्त किया जाता है—*The machine has a safety device which switches the power off if there is a fault.*

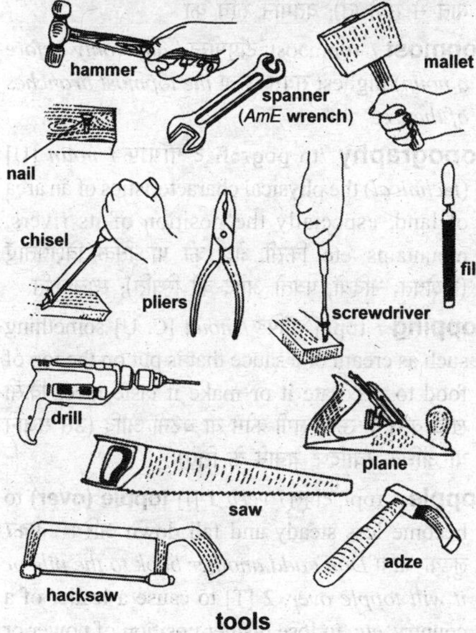

**tools**

**toolbar** /ˈtuːlbɑː(r) ˈटूलबा(र्)/ *noun* [C] a row of symbols on a computer screen that show the different things that the computer can do कंप्यूटर स्क्रीन पर बने संकेत-चित्रों की कतार (कंप्यूटर द्वारा किए जा सकने वाले कार्यों का सूचक)

**toot** /tuːt टूट्/ *noun* [C] the short high sound that a car horn makes कार हार्न या भोंपू की आवाज़ ▸ **toot** *verb* [I, T] भोंपू बजना या बजाना *Toot your horn to let them know we're here.*

**tooth** /tuːθ टूथ्/ *noun* [C] (*pl.* **teeth** /tiːθ टीथ्/) **1** one of the hard white things in your mouth that you use for biting दाँत, दंत *She's got strong teeth.*

**NOTE** खाने के बचे-खुचे टुकड़े निकालने के लिए आप दाँतों को **brush** या **clean** करते हैं। यदि दाँत **decayed** (सड़न) की दशा में पहुँच जाए तो **dentist** उसे **fill** कर सकता है या **extract/take out** (उखाड़ सकता है)। सारे दाँत निकल जाने पर आप **false teeth** या **dentures** लगा सकते हैं।

➪ **wisdom tooth** देखिए।

**2** one of the long narrow pointed parts of an object such as a comb किसी वस्तु का दाँतनुमा अंग (जैसे कंघी का दाँत)

**IDM** **by the skin of your teeth** ➪ **skin[1]** देखिए।

**gnash your teeth** ➪ **gnash** देखिए।

**grit your teeth** ➪ **grit[2]** देखिए।

**have a sweet tooth** ➪ **sweet[1]** देखिए।

**toothache** /ˈtuːθeɪk ˈटूथ्एक्/ *noun* [U, C, *usually sing.*] a pain in your tooth or teeth दाँत का दर्द; दंतशूल ➪ **ache** पर नोट देखिए।

**toothbrush** /ˈtuːθbrʌʃ ˈटूथ्ब्रश्/ *noun* [C] a small brush with a handle that you use for cleaning your teeth दाँत साफ़ करने का ब्रश; टूथब्रश

**toothpaste** /ˈtuːθpeɪst ˈटूथ्पेस्ट्/ *noun* [U] a substance that you put on your toothbrush and use for cleaning your teeth दाँत साफ़ करने वाला पेस्ट; टूथपेस्ट

**toothpick** /ˈtuːθpɪk ˈटूथ्पिक्/ *noun* [C] a short pointed piece of wood that you use for getting pieces of food out from between your teeth दाँतनी, दंतखोदनी, दंतकुरेदनी

**top[1]** /tɒp टॉप्/ *noun* **1** [C] the highest part or point of sth किसी वस्तु का उच्चतम अंग या बिंदु; चोटी, ऊपरी सिरा *The flat is **at the top of** the stairs.* ○ *Snow was falling on the mountain tops.* ✪ विलोम **foot** **2** [C] the flat upper surface of sth किसी वस्तु की समतल ऊपरी सतह *a desk/table/bench top* **3** [*sing.*] **the top (of sth)** the highest or most important position सर्वोच्च या सबसे बड़ा पद *to be at the top of your profession* **4** [C] the cover that you put onto sth in order to close it (किसी वस्तु का) ढक्कन *Put the tops back on the pens or they will dry out.*

**NOTE** **Top** या **cap** प्रायः छोटा और गोल होता है, इसे घुमा कर खोलते हैं—*a bottle top* ○ *Unscrew cap to open*. **Lid** बड़े ढक्कन को कहते हैं। इसे ऊपर उठाकर हटाया जाता है—*a saucepan lid* ○ *Put the lid back on the box.*

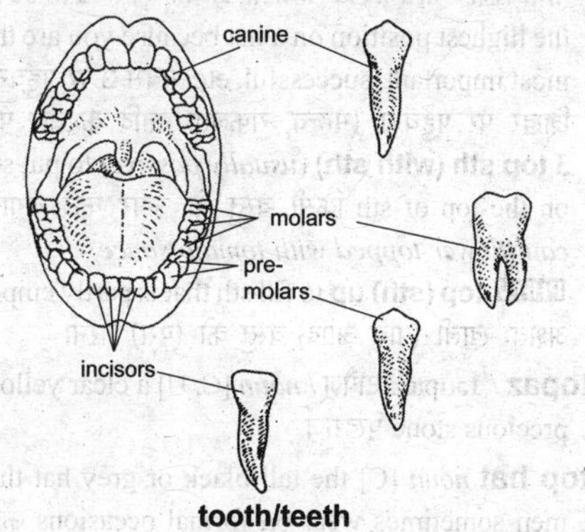

**tooth/teeth**

5 [C] a piece of clothing that you wear on the upper part of your body शरीर के ऊपरी भाग का वस्त्र; वक्षीय वस्त्र *a tracksuit/bikini/pyjama top* 6 [C] a child's toy that turns round very quickly on a point (बच्चों के खेलने का) लट्टू

**IDM at the top of your voice** as loudly as possible यथासंभव ऊँचे स्वर में, ख़ूब चिल्लाकर

**get on top of sb** (*informal*) to be too much for sb to manage or deal with (किसी काम आदि का) इतना अधिक बढ़ जाना कि सँभालना मुश्किल हो जाए, बूते से बाहर हो जाना *I've got so much work to do. It's really getting on top of me.*

**off the top of your head** (*informal*) just guessing or using your memory without preparing or thinking about sth first केवल तुक्के लगाना (बिना पहले सोचे या तैयारी किए अनुमान-भर करना या याद से कुछ करना)

**on top** 1 on or onto the highest point शिखर या चोटी पर या उस के आस-पास *a mountain with snow on top* 2 in control; in a leading position नियंत्रित, आत्मविश्वासपूर्ण; सबसे आगे *Janaki always seems to come out on top.*

**on top of sb/sth** 1 on, over or covering sb/sth else किसी अन्य पर या के ऊपर *Books were piled on top of one another.* ○ *The remote control is on top of the TV.* 2 in addition to sb/sth else अन्य बातों के अलावा *On top of everything else, the car's broken down.* 3 (*informal*) very close to sb/sth किसी के बहुत पास, पास-पास *We were all living on top of each other in that tiny flat.*

**top²** /tɒp टॉप्/ *adj.* highest in position or degree स्थिति या मात्रा आदि की दृष्टि से सबसे ऊपर; शीर्षस्थ (व्यक्ति), सर्वाधिक (अंक आदि) *the top floor* ○ *one of India's top businessmen* ○ *at top speed*

**top³** /tɒp टॉप्/ *verb* [T] (**topping; topped**) 1 to be higher or greater than a particular amount मात्रा-विशेष या निर्दिष्ट मात्रा से अधिक होना 2 to be in the highest position on a list because you are the most important, successful, etc. सबसे ऊपर पहुँचना, शिखर पर पहुँचना (महत्त्व, सफलता आदि के बल पर) 3 **top sth (with sth)** (*usually passive*) to put sth on the top of sth किसी वस्तु के ऊपर कुछ लगाना *cauliflower topped with tomato sauce*

**PHR V top (sth) up** to fill sth that is partly empty अंशतः ख़ाली (पात्र आदि) वस्तु को (पूरा) भरना

**topaz** /ˈtəʊpæz ˈटोपैज़्/ *noun* [C, U] a clear yellow precious stone पुखराज

**top hat** *noun* [C] the tall black or grey hat that men sometimes wear on formal occasions ऊँचा काला या भूरा हैट (जिसे पुरुष समारोहों में पहनते हैं), ऊँचा रेशमी हैट

**top-heavy** *adj.* heavier at the top than the bottom and likely to fall over (नीचे की अपेक्षा) जिसका ऊपरी हिस्सा भारी हो (और इसलिए जो गिर सकता है)

**topic** /ˈtɒpɪk ˈटॉपिक्/ *noun* [C] a subject that you talk, write or learn about बातचीत, लिखने या जानने का विषय, विचार-विषय

**topical** /ˈtɒpɪkl ˈटॉपिक्ल्/ *adj.* connected with sth that is happening now; that people are interested in at the present time सामयिक (इस समय होने वाली बात से संबंधित); वर्तमान रुचि का

**topmost** /ˈtɒpməʊst ˈटॉपमोस्ट्/ *adj.* (*only before a noun*) highest सबसे ऊँचा *the topmost branches of the tree*

**topography** /təˈpɒgrəfi टˈपॉग्रफ़ि/ *noun* [U] (*technical*) the physical characteristics of an area of land, especially the position of its rivers, mountains, etc. किसी क्षेत्र की प्राकृतिक विशेषताएँ (विशेषतः नदियों, पर्वतों आदि की स्थिति); स्थलाकृति

**topping** /ˈtɒpɪŋ ˈटॉपिङ्/ *noun* [C, U] something such as cream or a sauce that is put on the top of food to decorate it or make it taste nicer किसी खाद्य वस्तु के ऊपर लगी क्रीम या चटनी आदि (उसे सजाने या अधिक स्वादिष्ट बनाने के लिए)

**topple** /ˈtɒpl ˈटॉप्ल्/ *verb* 1 [I] **topple (over)** to become less steady and fall down अस्थिर होकर लुढ़क जाना *Don't add another book to the pile or it will topple over.* 2 [T] to cause a leader of a country, etc. to lose his/her position of power or authority किसी देश के नेता को सत्ता या अधिकार के पद से हटा देना

**top secret** *adj.* that must be kept very secret, especially from other governments जिसे (अन्य देशों की सरकारों से) गुप्त रखना अत्यंत आवश्यक हो, परम गुप्त

**topsoil** /ˈtɒpsɔɪl ˈटॉप्सॉइल्/ *noun* [U] (in geography) the layer of soil nearest the surface of the ground (भूगोल में) ऊपरी मिट्टी, मिट्टी की सबसे ऊपर की परत ➪ **subsoil** देखिए।

**torch** /tɔːtʃ टॉच्/ *noun* [C] 1 (*AmE* **flashlight**) a small electric light that you carry in your hand (बैटरी वाली) टार्च, चोरबत्ती 2 a long piece of wood with burning material at the end that you carry to give light मशाल *the Olympic torch*

**tore** ➪ **tear²** का past tense रूप

**torment** /ˈtɔːment ˈटॉमेन्ट्/ *noun* [U, C] great pain and suffering in your mind or body; sb/sth that causes this तीव्र मानसिक या शारीरिक वेदना; ऐसी

वेदना पहुँचाने वाला (व्यक्ति या वस्तु) *to be in* ***torment*** ▶ **torment** /tɔːˈment ˈटॉमेन्ट्/ *verb* [T] किसी को तीव्र मानसिक या शारीरिक पीड़ा पहुँचाना

**torn** ⇨ **tear²** का past participle रूप

**tornado** /tɔːˈneɪdəʊ ˈटॉनेडो/ *noun* [C] (*pl.* **tornadoes**) a violent storm with a very strong wind that blows in a circle बवंडर, तेज़ तूफ़ान, चक्रवात ⇨ **storm** पर नोट देखिए।

**torpedo** /tɔːˈpiːdəʊ टॉˈपीडो/ *noun* [C] (*pl.* **torpedoes**) a bomb, shaped like a long narrow tube, that is fired from a **submarine** and explodes when it hits another ship (दूसरे जहाज़ को नष्ट करने के लिए) पनडुब्बी से छोड़ा जाने वाला प्रक्षेपास्त्र (नलीनुमा बम); टॉरपीडो

**torque** /tɔːk टॉक्/ *noun* [U] (*technical*) a force that causes machinery, etc. to turn round (**rotate**) मशीन आदि को उसकी धुरी पर घुमाने वाली शक्ति; घूर्णन-बल *The more torque an engine has, the bigger the load it can pull in the same gear.*

**torrent** /ˈtɒrənt ˈटॉरन्ट्/ *noun* [C] a strong fast flow of sth, especially water बौछार (विशेषतः पानी की) *The rain was coming down in torrents.*

**torrential** /təˈrenʃl टˈरेन्शल्/ *adj.* (used about rain) very great in amount (वर्षा) भारी, मूसलाधार

**torsion** /ˈtɔːʃn ˈटॉश्न्/ *noun* [U] (*technical*) the action of **twisting** sth, especially one end of sth while the other end is held fixed ऐंठने या मरोड़ने की क्रिया (विशेषतः किसी एक सिरे की और अकसर जब दूसरा सिरा स्थिर हो)

**torso** /ˈtɔːsəʊ ˈटॉसो/ *noun* [C] (*pl.* **torsos**) the main part of your body, not your head, arms and legs शरीर का मुख्य भाग (सिर, बाँहों और टाँगों को छोड़कर), धड़, कबंध

**tortilla** /tɔːˈtiːə टॉˈटीआ/ *noun* [C] a type of very thin, round Mexican bread made with eggs and flour. It is usually eaten hot and filled with meat, cheese, etc. एक प्रकार की बहुत पतली, गोल, मेक्सिको की डबल रोटी (गोश्त, पनीर आदि भरकर प्रायः गरम खाई जाने वाली)

**tortoise** /ˈtɔːtəs ˈटॉटस्/ (*AmE* **turtle**) *noun* [C] a small animal with a hard shell that moves very slowly. A tortoise can pull its head and legs into its shell to protect them कछुआ, कच्छप ⇨ **reptile** पर चित्र देखिए।

**tortuous** /ˈtɔːtʃuəs ˈटॉचुअस्/ *adj.* **1** complicated, not clear and simple जटिल, उलझा हुआ (जो स्पष्ट और सरल नहीं) **2** (used about a road, etc.) with many bends (सड़क, आदि) टेढ़ी-मेढ़ी, चक्करदार

**torture** /ˈtɔːtʃə(r) ˈटॉच(र्)/ *noun* [U, C] **1** the action of causing sb great pain either as a punishment or to make him/her say or do sth (किसी को) यंत्रणा या यातना देने की क्रिया (दंडस्वरूप या आदेश के अनुसार) *His confession was extracted* ***under torture****.* **2** mental or physical suffering मानसिक या शारीरिक संताप या पीड़ा *It's torture having to sit here and listen to him complaining for hours.* ▶ **torture** *verb* [T] (किसी को) यंत्रणा या यातना देना *Most of the prisoners were tortured into making a confession.* ○ *She was tortured by the thought that the accident was her fault.* ▶ **torturer** *noun* [C] यातना देने वाला, संतापक, उत्पीड़क

**toss** /tɒs टॉस्/ *verb* **1** [T] to throw sth lightly and carelessly किसी वस्तु को हलके से और लापरवाही से फेंकना, उछालना *Bobby opened the letter and tossed the envelope into the bin.* **2** [I, T] to move, or to make sb/sth move up and down or from side to side (ऊपर-नीचे या एक ओर से दूसरी ओर) हिलना-डुलना या किसी को हिलाना-डुलाना, करवटें बदलना, हिचकोले खाना *He lay* ***tossing and turning*** *in bed, unable to sleep.* ○ *The ship was tossed about by huge waves.* **3** [T] to move your head back quickly especially to show you are annoyed or impatient सिर को झटका देना (विशेषतः क्रोध या अधीरता में) *I tried to apologize but she just* ***tossed*** *her* ***head*** *and walked away.* **4** [I, T] **toss (up) (for sth)** to throw a coin into the air in order to decide sth, by guessing which side of the coin will land facing upwards हवा में सिक्का उछालना और पहले से अनुमान कर बताना कि इसका कौन-सा पहलू गिरने के बाद ऊपर दिखाई पड़ेगा और उसके आधार पर फैसला करना; टॉस *to toss a coin* ⇨ **heads** और **tails** देखिए। ये दोनों सिक्के का दो सतहों के नाम हैं। सिक्के का कौन-सा पहलू ऊपर आएगा यह जानने के लिए सिक्का उछाल कर अटकल लगाते हुए हम कहते हैं 'heads or tails?' ▶ **toss** *noun* [C] उछाल; टॉस

IDM **win/lose the toss** to guess correctly/wrongly which side of a coin will face upwards when it lands (सिक्का उछालकर) सही या ग़लत अटकल लगाना (कि नीचे गिरने पर सिक्के का कौन-सा पहलू ऊपर आएगा) *Rahul Dravid won the toss and chose to bat first.*

**tot¹** /tɒt टॉट्/ *noun* [C] **1** (*informal*) a very small child नन्हा मुन्ना **2** (*BrE*) a small glass of a strong alcoholic drink तेज़ शराब का छोटा गिलास या की अल्प मात्रा, तेज़ शराब की घूँट

**tot²** /tɒt टॉट्/ *verb* (**totting; totted**)

PHRV **tot (sth) up** (*informal*) to add numbers together to form a total सख्याओं को जोड़कर उनका योग निकालना

**total¹** /ˈtəʊtl ˈटोट्ल्/ *adj.* being the amount after everyone or everything is counted or added together; complete सबको गिनकर या मिलाकर बनी संख्या या मात्रा; पूर्ण *What was the total number of people there?* ○ *a total failure* ○ *They ate in total silence.*

**total²** /ˈtəʊtl ˈटोट्ल्/ *noun* [C] the number that you get when you add two or more numbers or amounts together दो या अधिक संख्याओं या मात्राओं का योग ▶ **total** *verb* [T] (**totalling; totalled** *AmE* **totaling; totaled**) दो या अधिक संख्याओं या मात्राओं का योग निकालना *His debts totalled more than Rs 10,000.*

**IDM in total** when you add two or more numbers or amounts together कुल मिलाकर *The appeal raised Rs 40 lakh in total.*

**totally** /ˈtəʊtəli ˈटोटलि/ *adv.* completely पूर्णतया, पूरी तरह से *I totally agree with you.*

**totter** /ˈtɒtə(r) ˈटॉट(र्)/ *verb* [I] to stand or move in a way that is not steady, as if you are going to fall, especially because you are drunk, ill or weak (खड़े होते या चलते हुए) लड़खड़ाना (नशे में, बीमार या कमज़ोर होने के कारण)

**toucan** /ˈtuːkæn ˈटूकैन्/ *noun* [C] a tropical American bird with bright feathers and a very large beak चमकीले पंखों और बहुत लंबी चोंच वाला एक अमेरिकी पक्षी (जो गरम इलाक़ों में रहता है); टूकैन

**touch¹** /tʌtʃ टच्/ *verb* **1** [T] to put your hand or fingers onto sb/sth (किसी को) छूना, स्पर्श करना *Don't touch that plate—it's hot!* ○ *The police asked us not to touch anything.* **2** [I, T] (used about two or more things, surfaces, etc.) to be or move so close together that there is no space between them (दो या अधिक वस्तुओं, सतहों आदि का) बहुत अधिक निकट होना या आ जाना (कि छूने लगना) *This bicycle is too big. My feet don't **touch the ground**.* **3** [T] to make sb feel sad, sorry for sb, grateful, etc. किसी को उदासी, दुख, कृतज्ञता आदि भावनाओं की अनुभूति कराना, किसी के दिल को छू लेना, भाव-विह्वल या द्रवित कर देना ➪ **touched** adjective देखिए। **4** [T] (*in negative sentences*) to be as good as sb/sth in skill, quality, etc. निपुणता, गुण आदि में किसी के समान होना, किसी तक पहुँच पाना *He's a much better player than all the others. No one else can touch him.*

**IDM touch wood; knock on wood** ➪ **wood** देखिए।

**PHR V touch down** (used about an aircraft) to land (विमान का) धरती पर उतरना

**touch on/upon sth** to mention or refer to a subject for only a short time किसी विषय का अल्प मात्रा में उल्लेख या संकेत करना, स्पर्श मात्र करना

**touch²** /tʌtʃ टच्/ *noun* **1** [C, *usually sing.*] the action of putting your hands or fingers onto sb/sth (किसी को) छूने की क्रिया, स्पर्श, संस्पर्श *I felt the touch of her hand on my arm.* **2** [U] the way sth feels when you touch it स्पर्शानुभूति, स्पर्शजन्य, संवेदन *Marble is cold **to the touch**.* **3** [U] one of the five senses: the ability to feel things and know what they are like by putting your hands or fingers on them स्पर्शेंद्रिय; वस्तुओं का स्पर्श कर अनुभव करने की क्षमता *The **sense of touch** is very important to blind people.* **4** [C] a small detail that is added to improve sth गुणवत्ता में सुधार लाने वाली कोई छोटी-सी बात *The flowers in our room were **a nice touch**.* ○ *She's just **putting the finishing touches to** the cake.* **5** [*sing.*] a way or style of doing sth कुछ करने का तरीक़ा *She prefers to write her letters by hand for a more **personal touch**.* **6** [*sing.*] **a touch (of sth)** a small amount of sth किसी वस्तु की अल्प मात्रा; पुट

**IDM in/out of touch (with sb)** being/not being in contact with sb by speaking or writing to him/her (किसी के साथ) संपर्क में रहना या न रहना (उससे बातचीत या पत्रादि के माध्यम से) *During the year she was abroad, they **kept in touch** by email.*

**in/out of touch with sth** having/not having recent information about sth किसी वस्तु के विषय में अद्यतन जानकारी होना या न होना *We're out of touch with what's going on.*

**lose touch** ➪ **lose** देखिए।

**lose your touch** ➪ **lose** देखिए।

**touched** /tʌtʃt टच्ट्/ *adj.* (*not before a noun*) **touched (by sth); touched that...** made to feel sad, sorry for sb, grateful, etc. उदासी, दुख, कृतज्ञता आदि (भावों) से व्याकुल, भाव-विह्वल, द्रवित, विचलित *I was touched that he offered to help.*

**touching** /ˈtʌtʃɪŋ ˈटचिङ्/ *adj.* that makes you feel sad, sorry for sb, grateful, etc. भाव-विह्वल कर देने वाला, दिल को छू लेने वाला, हृदयस्पर्शी

**touch screen** *noun* [C] (*computing*) a computer screen which shows information when you touch it स्पर्श करने पर सूचना-सामग्री दर्शाने वाला कंप्यूटर-स्क्रीन; टच स्क्रीन

**touchy** /ˈtʌtʃi ˈटचि/ *adj.* **1 touchy (about sth)** easily upset or made angry जो जल्दी परेशान या नाराज़ हो जाए; तुनक-मिज़ाज *He's a bit touchy about his weight.* **2** (used about a subject, situation, etc.) that may easily upset people or make them angry (विषय, परिस्थिति आदि) जो लोगों की जल्दी परेशान या नाराज़ कर दे; संवेदनशील *Don't mention the exam. It's a very touchy subject.*

**tough** /tʌf टफ़्/ *adj.* **1** difficult; having or causing problems कठिन; समस्यापूर्ण या समस्या जनक *It will be a tough decision to make.* ○ *He's had **a tough time of it*** (= a lot of problems) *recently.* **2 tough (on/with sb/sth)** strict; not feeling sorry for anyone कड़ा, कठोर; किसी के प्रति नरमी न बरतने वाला *The government plans to **get tough with** people who drink and drive.* **3** strong enough to deal with difficult conditions or situations मानसिक और शारीरिक रूप से दृढ़, मज़बूत *You need to be tough to go climbing in winter.* **4** (used especially about meat) difficult to cut and eat (विशेषतः गोश्त) सख़्त, जिसे काटना और खाना मुश्किल हो **5** not easily broken, torn or cut; very strong आसानी से न टूटने, फटने या कटने वाला; बहुत मज़बूत *a tough pair of boots* **6** (*informal*) **tough (on sb)** unfortunate for sb in a way that seems unfair किसी के लिए दुर्भाग्यपूर्ण (और अन्यायपूर्ण) *It's tough on her that she lost her job.* ▶ **toughness** *noun* [U] कठोरता, दृढ़ता

**toughen** /ˈtʌfn ˈटफ़्न्/ *verb* [I, T] **toughen (sb/sth) (up)** to make sb/sth tough (किसी का) मज़बूत या सख़्त बनना या (को) बनाना

**toupee** /ˈtuːpeɪ ˈटूपे/ *noun* [C] a small section of artificial hair, worn by a man to cover an area of his head where hair no longer grows सिर के नक़ली बाल, कृत्रिम केश

**tour** /tʊə(r) टुअ(र्)/ *noun* **1** [C] **a tour (of/round/around sth)** a journey that you make for pleasure during which you visit many places उल्लास-यात्रा, मौजमस्ती के लिए विभिन्न स्थानों की यात्रा; सैर-सपाटा, पर्यटन *a sightseeing tour* ○ *a tour operator* (= a person or company that organizes tours) ➪ **travel** पर नोट देखिए। **2** [C] a short visit around a city, famous building, etc. किसी नगर, प्रसिद्ध इमारत आदि की संक्षिप्त यात्रा *a **guided tour** round Akshardham Temple* **3** [C, U] an official series of visits that singers, musicians, sports players, etc. make to different places to perform, play, etc. गायकों, संगीतकारों, खिलाड़ियों आदि द्वारा अपनी कला के प्रदर्शन के लिए विभिन्न स्थानों का आधिकारिक-दौरा, टूर *a concert/cricket tour* ▶ **tour** *verb* [I, T] (स्थानों में) घूमना, घुमाना *We toured southern India for three weeks.*

**tourism** /ˈtʊərɪzəm ˈटुअरिज़म्/ *noun* [U] the business of providing and arranging holidays and services for people who are visiting a place पर्यटन-व्यवसाय (किसी स्थान पर आने वाले पर्यटकों को निवास आदि आवश्यक सुविधाएँ उपलब्ध कराने का व्यवसाय) *The country's economy relies heavily on tourism.*

**tourist** /ˈtʊərɪst ˈटुअरिस्ट्/ *noun* [C] a person who visits a place for pleasure पर्यटक, सैलानी ➪ **sightseer** देखिए।

**tournament** /ˈtɔːnəmənt ˈटॉनमन्ट्/ *noun* [C] a competition in which many players or teams play games against each other खेल-प्रतियोगिता, टुर्नामेंट

**tourniquet** /ˈtʊənɪkeɪ ˈटुअनिके/ *noun* [C] a piece of cloth, etc. that is tied tightly around an arm or a leg to stop a cut or an injury from bleeding बाँह या टाँग के कट जाने से होने वाले रक्तस्राव को रोकने की पट्टी, रक्त-बंध

**tousled** /ˈtaʊzld ˈटाउज़्ल्ड्/ *adj.* (used about hair) untidy, often in an attractive way (बाल) बिखरे हुए, अस्त-व्यस्त (प्रायः आकर्षक प्रकार से)

**tout** /taʊt टाउट्/ *verb* **1** [T] **tout sb/sth (as sth)** to try to persuade people that sb/sth is important or valuable by praising them/it प्रशंसा द्वारा किसी व्यक्ति या वस्तु को महत्त्वपूर्ण और बहुमूल्य बताकर लोगों को फुसलाना या सहमत करना *She's being touted as the next Prime Minister.* **2** [I, T] **tout (for sth)** (*BrE*) to try to persuade people to buy certain goods or services, especially by going to them and asking them directly जन साधारण के बीच जा कर ग्राहक जुटाना (प्रायः अपने माल और सेवाओं के लिए) *unlicensed autorickshaw drivers touting for business at stations* **3** [T] (*AmE* **scalp**) to sell tickets unofficially, at a much higher price than the official price, especially outside a theatre, stadium, railway station, etc. अनाधिकारिक रूप से टिकट आदि को आधिकारिक दाम से अधिक दाम में बेचना (विशेषतः रंगमंच, स्टेडियम, स्टेशन आदि के बाहर)

**tow** /təʊ टो/ *verb* [T] to pull a car or boat behind another vehicle, using a rope or chain कार या नाव को किसी वाहन से बाँधकर खींचना *My car was towed away by the police.* ▶ **tow** *noun* [*sing.*, U]

**IDM in tow** (*informal*) following closely behind पीछे-पीछे *He arrived with his wife and five children in tow.*

**towards** /təˈwɔːdz टˈवॉड्ज़्/ (*also* **toward** /təˈwɔːd टˈवॉड्/) *prep.* **1** in the direction of sb/sth किसी की ओर खींचना *I saw Kamal walking towards the station.* ○ *a first step towards world peace* **2** near or nearer a time or date किसी समय या तारीख़ के निकट या अधिक निकट *It gets cool towards evening.* ○ *The shops get very busy towards Diwali.* **3** (used when you are talking about your feelings about sb/sth) in relation to (किसी के विषय में अपनी भावनाओं को प्रकट करते हुए प्रयुक्त) किसी के संबंध में, किसी के प्रति *What is your attitude towards this government?* **4** as part of the payment for sth किसी वस्तु के आंशिक भुगतान के रूप में *The money will* ***go towards*** *the cost of a new minibus.*

**towel** /ˈtaʊəl ˈटाउअल्/ *noun* [C] a piece of cloth or paper that you use for drying sb/sth/yourself तौलिया *a bath/hand/beach towel* ○ *kitchen/paper towels* ➪ **sanitary towel** और **tea towel** देखिए।

**towelling** (*AmE* **toweling**) /ˈtaʊəlɪŋ ˈटाउअलिङ्/ *noun* [U] a thick soft cotton cloth that is used especially for making bath towels तौलिए का कपड़ा

**tower** /ˈtaʊə(r) ˈटाउअ(र्)/ *noun* [C] a tall narrow building or part of a building such as a church or castle मीनार या किसी चर्च या किले की मीनार, टावर, बुर्ज *the Eiffel Tower* ○ *a church tower*

**tower block** *noun* [C] (*BrE*) a very tall building consisting of flats or offices ऊँचा भवन खंड (जिसमें अनेक फ़्लैट या दफ़्तर हों)

**town** /taʊn टाउन्/ *noun* **1** [C] a place with many streets and buildings. A town is larger than a village but smaller than a city क़सबा (गाँव से बड़ी और शहर से छोटी बस्ती), (लघु) नगर *After ten years away, she decided to move back to her home town* (= the town where she was born and spent her childhood). **2 the town** [*sing.*] all the people who live in a town क़सबे के समस्त निवासी *The whole town is talking about it.* **3** [U] the main part of a town, where the shops, etc. are क़सबे का मुख्य भाग या व्यापारिक केंद्र *I've got to go into town this afternoon.*

**IDM go to town (on sth)** (*informal*) to do sth with a lot of energy and enthusiasm; to spend a lot of money on sth भरपूर ताक़त और जोश से कोई काम करना; किसी चीज़ पर खुलकर ख़र्च करना

**(out) on the town** (*informal*) going to restaurants, theatres, clubs, etc., for entertainment, especially at night मनोविनोद के लिए रेस्तराँ, थिएटर, क्लब आदि में जाना (विशेषतः रात में)

**town council** *noun* [C] (*BrE*) a group of people who are responsible for the local government of a town किसी क़सबे के स्थानीय प्रशासन के लिए परिषद, (लघु) नगर-पालिका

**town hall** *noun* [C] a large building that contains the local government offices and often a large room for public meetings, concerts, etc. किसी क़सबे, स्थानीय प्रशासन का केंद्र (बना) बड़ा भवन, इसमें प्रायः कुछ बड़े कमरे या सभाभवन भी होते हैं जहाँ सार्वजनिक बैठक या मनोरंजन-कार्य आदि हो सकते हैं ➪ **hall** देखिए।

**tow truck** (*AmE*) = **breakdown truck**

**toxic** /ˈtɒksɪk ˈटॉक्सिक्/ *adj.* poisonous विषैला, ज़हरीला, विषाक्त

**toxicity** /tɒkˈsɪsəti टॉक्ˈसिसटि/ *noun* **1** [U] the quality of being poisonous; the degree to which sth is poisonous विषैलापन, विषाक्तता, ज़हरीलापन; ज़हरीलेपन या विषाक्तता की मात्रा *substances with high/low levels of toxicity* **2** [C] the effect that a poisonous substance has विषाक्त वस्तु का प्रभाव *Minor toxicities of this drug include nausea and vomiting.*

**toxicology** /ˌtɒksɪˈkɒlədʒi ˌटॉक्सिˈकॉलजि/ *noun* [U] the scientific study of poisons (विभिन्न) विषों का वैज्ञानिक अध्ययन; विष-विज्ञान ▸ **toxicological** *adj.* विष-विज्ञान-विषयक ▸ **toxicologist** *noun* [C] विष-विज्ञानी

**toxin** /ˈtɒksɪn ˈटॉक्सिन्/ *noun* [C] a poisonous substance, especially one that is produced by bacteria in plants and animals विषैला पदार्थ (विशेषतः पौधों और पशुओं के जीवाणुओं द्वारा बनाया हुआ); जीवविष

**toy**[1] /tɔɪ टॉइ/ *noun* [C] an object for a child to play with बच्चों का खिलौना *a toy car/farm/soldier* ○ *a toyshop*

**toy**[2] /tɔɪ टॉइ/ *verb*

**PHR V toy with sth** **1** to think about doing sth, perhaps not very seriously किसी बात के विषय में गंभीरता से न सोचना *She's* ***toying with the idea of*** *going abroad for a year.* **2** to move sth about without thinking about what you are doing, often because you are nervous or upset (अनजान-सी हालत में) किसी चीज़ को हिलाना-डुलाना (प्रायः घबराहट या परेशानी में) *He toyed with his food but hardly ate any of it.*

**trace**[1] /treɪs ट्रेस्/ *noun* **1** [C, U] a mark, an object or a sign that shows that sb/sth existed or happened चिह्न, कोई वस्तु या संकेत जो किसी व्यक्ति या वस्तु के अस्तित्व को या घटना के घटित होने को सूचित करे *traces of an earlier civilization* ○ *The man* ***disappeared/vanished without trace.*** **2** [C] **a trace (of sth)** a very small amount of sth किसी वस्तु की अत्यल्प मात्रा, लव, लेश *Traces of blood were found under her fingernails.*

**trace**[2] /treɪs ट्रेस्/ *verb* [T] **1 trace sb/sth (to sth)** to find out where sb/sth is by following marks, signs or other information किसी व्यक्ति या वस्तु का पता लगाना (चिह्नों, संकेतों या अन्य जानकारी की सहायता से) *The wanted man was traced to an address in Sundernagar.* **2 trace sth (back)**

**(to sth)** to find out where sth came from or what caused it; to describe the development of sth किसी वस्तु के स्रोत या मूल कारण को खोज निकालना; किसी वस्तु की विकास-यात्रा का वर्णन करना *She traced her family tree back to the 16th century.* **3** to make a copy of a map, plan, etc. by placing a piece of transparent paper (**tracing paper**) over it and drawing over the lines पारदर्शी काग़ज़ से मानचित्र आदि की नक़ल तैयार करना

**trachea** /trəˈkiːə ट्रˈकीआ / *noun* [C] (*pl.* **tracheae** /-kiːiː -कीई / or **tracheas**) (*medical*) the tube in your throat that carries air to the lungs श्वासनली ✪ पर्याय **windpipe** ➪ **body** पर चित्र देखिए।

**track¹** /træk ट्रैक् / *noun* **1** [C] a natural path or rough road लोगों के चलने से बना रास्ता, पगडंडी या ऊबड़-खाबड़ सड़क *Follow the dirt track through the wood.* **2** [C, *usually pl.*] marks that are left on the ground by a person, an animal or a moving vehicle किसी व्यक्ति, पशु या वाहन के चलने से बने निशान *The hunter followed the tracks of a deer.* ○ *tyre tracks* ➪ **print** देखिए। **3** [C, U] the two metal rails on which a train runs रेल की पटरी *The train stopped because there was a tree across the track.* **4** [C] a piece of ground, often in a circle, for people, cars, etc. to have races on मनुष्यों, कारों आदि की दौड़ का मैदान (प्रायः गोलाकार), ट्रैक *a running track* **5** [C] one song or piece of music on a cassette, CD or record कैसेट, सीडी या रिकॉर्ड पर एक (अकेला) गाना या संगीत-रचना *the first track from her latest album* ➪ **soundtrack** देखिए।

**IDM keep/lose track of sb/sth** to have/not have information about what is happening or where sb/sth is किसी घटना, व्यक्ति या वस्तु के विषय में जानकारी रखना या न रखना

**off the beaten track** ➪ **beat¹** देखिए।

**on the right/wrong track** having the right/wrong idea about sth किसी के विषय में सही या ग़लत धारणा होना *That's not the answer but you're on the right track.*

**track²** /træk ट्रैक् / *verb* [T] to follow the movements of sb/sth किसी व्यक्ति या वस्तु का पीछा करना *to track enemy planes on a radar screen*

**PHR V track sb/sth down** to find sb/sth after searching for him/her/it किसी व्यक्ति या वस्तु को खोज निकालना

**track event** *noun* [C] a sports event that consists of running round a track in a race, rather than throwing sth or jumping ट्रैक पर दौड़ने की खेल-प्रतियोगिता (न कि गोला आदि फेंकने या कूदने की) ➪ **field event** देखिए।

**track record** *noun* [*sing.*] all the past successes or failures of a person or an organization व्यक्ति या संस्था की समस्त विगत सफलताएँ या विफलताएँ

**tracksuit** /ˈtræksuːt ˈट्रैक्सूट् / *noun* [C] a warm pair of soft trousers and a matching jacket that you wear for sports practice खेल-अभ्यास के लिए प्रयुक्त गरम जोड़ा (पैंट और मेल खाती जैकेट); ट्रैकसूट

**tract** /trækt ट्रैक्ट् / *noun* [C] a system of organs or tubes in the body that are connected and that have a particular purpose विशिष्ट उद्देश्य वाले और परस्पर संबद्ध (शरीर के) अंगों और नलिकाओं की प्रणाली *the respiratory/digestive tract*

**traction** /ˈtrækʃn ˈट्रैक्श्न् / *noun* [U] **1** the action of pulling sth along a surface; the power that is used for doing this सतह पर कुछ खींचने की क्रिया, कर्षण; कर्षण में प्रयुक्त बल का प्रकार *diesel/electric/steam traction* **2** a way of treating a broken bone in the body that involves using special equipment to pull the bone gradually back into its correct place टूटी हुई हड्डी को जोड़ने का ढंग (विशेष उपकरण से हड्डी को धीमे-धीमे खींचकर अपनी जगह जमाना); अंग-कर्षण, ट्रैक्शन *He spent six weeks **in traction** after he broke his leg.* **3** the force that stops sth, for example the wheels of a vehicle, from sliding on the ground वाहन के पहियों आदि को ज़मीन पर फिसलने से रोकने वाली शक्ति, (पहियों आदि की) पकड़

**tractor** /ˈtræktə(r) ˈट्रैक्ट(र्) / *noun* [C] a large vehicle that is used on farms for pulling heavy pieces of machinery भारी मशीनें खींचने के लिए खेतों में प्रयुक्त बड़ी गाड़ी; ट्रैक्टर

**trade¹** /treɪd ट्रेड् / *noun* **1** [U] the buying or selling of goods or services between people or countries व्यापार, लेन-देन *an international trade agreement* **2** [C] a particular type of business व्यापार विशेष *the tourist/building/retail trade* **3** [C, U] a job for which you need special skill, especially with your hands विशेष (ख़ासकर हाथों की) निपुणता की अपेक्षा वाला काम, हस्तकौशल से चलने वाला व्यवसाय *Jatin is a plumber **by trade**.* ○ *to learn a trade* ➪ **work** पर नोट देखिए।

**trade²** /treɪd ट्रेड् / *verb* **1** [I] **trade (in sth) (with sb)** to buy or sell goods or services (सामान या सेवाओं का) व्यापार करना *to trade in stocks and shares* **2** [T] **trade sth (for sth)** to exchange sth for sth else एक वस्तु देकर दूसरी वस्तु लेना, वस्तु-विनिमय करना *He traded his CD player for his friend's bicycle.*

▶ **trading** *noun* [U] व्यापार

**PHR V trade sth in (for sth)** to give sth old in part payment for sth new or newer नई वस्तु के

लिए आंशिक भुगतान के रूप में पुरानी वस्तु देना *We traded in our old car for a van.*

**trade balance** = **balance of trade**

**trademark** /ˈtreɪdmɑːk ˈट्रेड्माक् / *noun* [C] (*abbr.* **TM**) a special symbol, design or name that a company puts on its products and that cannot be used by any other company व्यापार-चिह्न, मार्का, ट्रेडमार्क (किसी कंपनी द्वारा अपनी वस्तुओं के लिए प्रयुक्त विशेष चिह्न, डिज़ाइन या नाम जिसका इस्तेमाल दूसरी कंपनी नहीं कर सकती)

**trader** /ˈtreɪdə(r) ˈट्रेड(र्) / *noun* [C] a person who buys and sells things, especially goods in a market or company shares (कंपनी के शेयर या बाज़ार में माल बेचने वाला) व्यापारी

**trade secret** *noun* [C] a piece of information, for example about how a particular product is made, that is known only to the company that makes it वस्तु-विशेष की निर्माण-प्रक्रिया के विषय में निर्माता कंपनी तक सीमित जानकारी; व्यापार-रहस्य

**tradesman** /ˈtreɪdzmən ˈट्रेड्ज़्मन् / *noun* [C] (*pl.* **men** /-mən -मन् /) a person who brings goods to people's homes to sell them or who has a shop अपनी दुकान से या घर-घर जाकर सामान बेचने वाला व्यक्ति; व्यापारी, दुकानदार

**trade union** (*also* **trades union**; **union**) *noun* [C] an organization for people who all do the same type of work. Trade unions try to get better pay and working conditions for their members श्रमिक संघ, मज़दूर संगठन, ट्रेड यूनियन (एक ही प्रकार के काम करने वाले श्रमिकों का संगठन जो श्रमिकों को बेहतर वेतन आदि दिलाने का प्रयत्न करता है)

**trade wind** *noun* [C] a strong wind that blows all the time towards the **equator** and then to the west पहले भूमध्यरेखा और फिर पश्चिम की ओर बहने वाली तेज़ वायु; व्यापारिक पवन

**tradition** /trəˈdɪʃn ट्रˈडिश्न् / *noun* [C, U] a custom, belief or way of doing sth that has continued from the past to the present परंपरा (अतीत से वर्तमान तक चली आई कोई प्रथा, धारणा या कार्यशैली), परिपाटी, दस्तूर *religious/cultural/literary traditions* ▶ **traditional** /-ʃənl -शन्ल् / *adj.* परंपरागत, पारंपरिक *A sari is one of the traditional garments of India* ▶ **traditionally** /-ʃənəli -शनलि / *adv.* परंपरा के अनुसार

**traffic** /ˈtræfɪk ˈट्रैफ़िक् / *noun* [U] **1** all the vehicles that are on a road at a particular time समय-विशेष पर सड़क पर आते-जाते समस्त वाहन; यातायात, ट्रैफ़िक *heavy/light traffic* ○ *We got stuck* ***in traffic*** *and were late for the meeting.* **2** the movement of ships, aircraft, etc. जलपोतों, विमानों आदि का आना-जाना या यातायात *air traffic control* **3 traffic (in sth)** the illegal buying and selling of sth किसी वस्तु का अवैध व्यापार *the traffic in drugs/fire arms* ▶ **traffic** *verb* [I] (*pres. part.* **trafficking;** *pt, pp* **trafficked**) **traffic (in sth)** अवैध व्यापार चलना या करना *He was arrested for trafficking in drugs.* ▶ **trafficker** *noun* [C] अवैध व्यापार करने वाला, अवैध व्यापारी *a drugs trafficker*

**traffic island** (*also* **island**) *noun* [C] a higher area in the middle of the road, where you can stand and wait for the traffic to pass when you want to cross सड़क के बीच में बना (गोल) चबूतरा (जिस पर खड़े होकर सड़क पार करने के इच्छुक लोग वाहनों के गुज़र जाने की प्रतीक्षा करते हैं); यातायात चक्कर

**traffic jam** *noun* [C] a long line of cars, etc. that cannot move or that can only move very slowly सड़क पर जमा वाहनों की लंबी कतार (जो आगे नहीं बढ़ती या धीमें-धीमें बढ़ती है) *to be stuck in a traffic jam.*

**traffic light** *noun* [C, *usually pl.*] a sign with three coloured lights (**red, amber** and **green**) that is used for controlling the traffic where two or more roads meet यातायात-नियंत्रण के लिए चौराहों पर लगी तीन रंगों (लाल, कहरूबा या पीला और हरा) की बत्तियों वाली संकेत-प्रणाली, चौराहे की लालबत्ती, यातायात बत्ती

**tragedy** /ˈtrædʒədi ˈट्रैजडि / *noun* (*pl.* **tragedies**) **1** [C, U] a very sad event or situation, especially one that involves death बहुत दुखद घटना या स्थिति (विशेषतः जिसमें मृत्यु तक हो जाए) *It's a tragedy that he died so young.* **2** [C] a serious play that has a sad ending दुखांत नाटक, त्रासदी, शोकांतिका *Shakespeare's 'King Lear' is a tragedy.* ➪ **comedy** देखिए।

**tragic** /ˈtrædʒɪk ˈट्रैजिक् / *adj.* **1** that makes you very sad, especially because it involves death बहुत दुख पहुँचाने वाला, अति दुखद (मृत्यु की घटना हो जाने के कारण) *It's tragic that she lost her only child.* ○ *a tragic accident* **2** (*written*) (*only before a noun*) (used about literature) in the style of tragedy (साहित्य के लिए प्रयुक्त) त्रासदी की तर्ज़ पर, त्रासदी का-सा *a tragic actor/hero* ▶ **tragically** /-kli -क्ली / *adv.* दुखद रूप से

**trail**[1] /treɪl ट्रेल् / *noun* [C] **1** a series of marks in a long line that is left by sb/sth as he/she/it moves किसी के चलने से बनी चिह्न-रेखा *a trail of blood/footprints* **2** a track, sign or smell that is left behind and that you follow when you are hunting sb/sth पीछे छूटे निशान, संकेत या गंध (जिनके सहारे किसी का पीछा किया जाए) *The dogs ran off* ***on the trail of*** *the fox.* **3** a path through the country पगडंडी

**trail**[2] /treɪl ट्रेल् / *verb* **1** [I, T] to pull or be pulled along behind sb/sth किसी के पीछे घिसटना, खिंचना या (किसी को पीछे से) खींचना *The skirt was too long and trailed along the ground.* **2** [I] to move or walk slowly behind sb/sth else, usually because you are tired or bored किसी दूसरे के पीछे धीरे-धीरे चलना, घिसटते हुए चलना (प्रायः थक या ऊब जाने के कारण) *It was impossible to do any shopping with the kids trailing around after me.* **3** [I, T] **trail (by/in sth)** (*usually used in the continuous tenses*) to be in the process of losing a game or a competition किसी खेल या प्रतियोगिता में पिछड़ना *At half-time Liverpool were trailing by two goals to three.* **4** [I] (used about plants or sth long and thin) to grow over sth and hang downwards; to lie across a surface (पौधा या कोई लंबी और पतली वस्तु) किसी के ऊपर से होकर नीचे लटकना; किसी सतह पर एक से दूसरे छोर तक फैलना *Computer wires trailed across the floor.*

**PHR V** **trail away/off** (used about sb's voice) to gradually become quieter and then stop (किसी के स्वर का) क्रमशः मंद होते हुए शांत हो जाना

**trailer** /ˈtreɪlə(r) ˈट्रेल(र्) / *noun* [C] **1** a type of container with wheels that is pulled by a vehicle किसी वाहन द्वारा खींची जाने वाली डिब्बेदार गाड़ी, अनुयान; ट्रेलर *a car towing a trailer with a boat on it* **2** (*AmE*) = **caravan 1** **3** a series of short pieces taken from a film and used to advertise it किसी फ़िल्म का ट्रेलर (किसी फ़िल्म के विज्ञापन के लिए उससे लिए गए अंश) ➪ **clip** देखिए।

**train**[1] /treɪn ट्रेन् / *noun* [C] **1** a type of transport that is pulled by an engine along a railway line. A train is divided into sections for people (**carriages** and **coaches**) and for goods (**wagons**) रेलगाड़ी (जिसमें सवारियों के लिए डिब्बे और कोच होते हैं और माल ढोने के लिए वैगन) *a passenger/goods/freight train* ○ *a fast/slow/express train* ○ *to get on/off a train* **2** [*usually sing.*] a series of thoughts or events that are connected परस्पर संबद्ध विचारों या घटनाओं की शृंखला *A knock at the door interrupted my **train of thought**.*

**train**[2] /treɪn ट्रेन् / *verb* **1** [T] **train sb (as sth/to do sth)** to teach a person to do sth which is difficult or which needs practice किसी व्यक्ति को कठिन या अभ्यास की अपेक्षा वाला काम सिखाना, प्रशिक्षण देना *The organization trains guide dogs for the blind.* **2** [I, T] **train (as/in sth) (to do sth)** to learn how to do a job कोई काम करना सीखना (या सिखाना); प्रशिक्षण लेना (या देना) *She trained as an engineer.* ○ *He's training to be a doctor.* **3** [I, T] **train (for sth)** to prepare yourself, especially for a sports event, by practising; to help a person or an animal to do this अभ्यास करते हुए तैयारी करना (विशेषतः किसी खेल-स्पर्धा की); किसी व्यक्ति या पशु को अभ्यास कराते हुए तैयार करना (खेल-स्पर्धा में भाग लेने के लिए) *I'm training for the Olympics.* ○ *to train race horses* **4** [T] **train sth (at/on sb/sth)** to point a gun, camera, etc. at sb/sth किसी पर बंदूक़, कैमरे आदि का निशाना बाँधना या साधना ▶ **training** *noun* [U] प्रशिक्षण *to be **in training** for the Olympics*

**trainee** /ˌtreɪˈniː ˌट्रेˈनी / *noun* [C] a person who is being taught how to do a particular job प्रशिक्षणार्थी

**trainer** /ˈtreɪnə(r) ˈट्रेन(र्) / *noun* [C] **1** (*AmE* **sneaker**) [*usually pl.*] a shoe that you wear for doing sport or as informal clothing खेल के समय या घर की पोशाक के साथ पहना जाने वाला जूता **2** a person who teaches people or animals how to do a particular job or skill well, or to do a particular sport प्रशिक्षक (पशुओं को कलाबाज़ी का, व्यक्तियों को कार्य-विशेष या खेल-विशेष का प्रशिक्षण देने वाला व्यक्ति) *teacher trainers* ○ *a racehorse trainer*

**trainspotter** /ˈtreɪnspɒtə(r) ˈट्रेन्स्पॉट(र्) / *noun* [C] (*BrE*) **1** a person who collects the numbers of railway engines as a hobby शौक़ के रूप में सामने से गुजरने वाले रेल-इंजनों की संख्याओं (जो उन पर लिखी हुई होती है) को अपनी डायरी में लिखने वाला व्यक्ति **2** a person who has a boring hobby or who is interested in the details of a subject that other people find boring उबाऊ शौक़ पालने वाला या किसी विषय के दूसरों को उबाऊ लगने वाले विवरणों में रुचि रखने वाला व्यक्ति ▶ **trainspotting** *noun* [U] उबाऊ शौक़ पालने की क्रिया, रेल-इंजनों की संख्याओं का संग्रह करने की क्रिया

**trait** /treɪt ट्रेट् / *noun* [C] a quality that forms part of your character or personality किसी व्यक्ति के चरित्र या व्यक्तित्व की विशेषता

**traitor** /ˈtreɪtə(r) ˈट्रेट(र्) / *noun* [C] **a traitor (to sb/sth)** a person who is not loyal to his/her country, friends, etc. देश, मित्र आदि से गद्दारी करने वाला; देशद्रोही, मित्रद्रोही, गद्दार

**tram** /træm ट्रैम् / (*AmE* **streetcar trolley**) *noun* [C] a type of bus that works by electricity and that moves along special rails in the road ट्राम, ट्रॉली,

ट्रामगाड़ी (सड़क पर बिछी विशेष रेल-पटरियों पर बिजली से चलने वाली एक प्रकार की बस)

**tramp**[1] /træmp ट्रैम्प् / *noun* **1** [C] a person who has no home or job and who moves from place to place मारा-मारा फिरने वाला बेघर या बेकार आदमी; आवारा **2** [*sing.*] the sound of people walking with heavy or noisy steps (लोगों के भारी या आवाज़ करते क़दमों से चलते समय होने वाली) धब-धब की ध्वनि

**tramp**[2] /træmp ट्रैम्प् / *verb* [I, T] to walk with slow heavy steps, especially for a long time मंद और भारी क़दमों से चलना (विशेषतः देर तक), धब-धब करते हुए (देर तक) चलना

**trample** /ˈtræmpl ˈट्रैम्पल् / *verb* [I, T] **trample on/over sb/sth** to walk on sb/sth and damage or hurt him/her/it किसी को कुचलना; रौंदना *The boys trampled on the flowers.*

**trampoline** /ˈtræmpəliːn ˈट्रैम्पलीन् / *noun* [C] a piece of equipment for jumping up and down on, made of a piece of strong material fixed to a metal frame by springs धातु-निर्मित ढाँचे में कमानियों से जुड़ी मज़बूत चादर जिस पर (खिलाड़ी) ऊपर-नीचे उछलते हैं, उछाल-पट

**trance** /trɑːns ट्रान्स् / *noun* [C] a mental state in which you do not notice what is going on around you सुषुप्ति की अवस्था, आत्म-विस्मृति (जिसमें व्यक्ति को पता नहीं चलता कि उसके चारों ओर क्या हो रहा है) *to go/fall into a trance*

**tranquil** /ˈtræŋkwɪl ˈट्रैङ्क्विल् / *adj.* (*formal*) calm and quiet शांत और मौन

**tranquillize** (*also* **-ise;** *AmE* **tranquilize**) /ˈtræŋkwəlaɪz ˈट्रैङ्क्वलाइज़् / *verb* [T] to make a person or an animal calm or unconscious, especially by giving him/her/it a drug व्यक्ति या पशु को शांत या बेहोश करना (विशेषतः नशीली दवा देकर)

**tranquillizer** (*also* **-iser;** *AmE* **tranquilizer**) /ˈtrænkwəlaɪzə(r) ˈट्रैङ्क्वलाइज़(र्) / *noun* [C] a drug that is used for making people feel calm or to help them sleep व्यक्तियों को अपशमित या सुलाने वाली औषधी ➪ **sedative** देखिए।

**trans-** /trænz; træns ट्रैन्ज़्; ट्रैन्स् / *prefix* **1** (*used in adjectives*) across; beyond के (उस) पार; के परे *transatlantic* ○ *transcontinental* **2** (*used in verbs*) into another place or state दूसरे स्थान पर, दूसरी अवस्था में *transplant* ○ *transform*

**transaction** /trænˈzækʃn ट्रैन्ˈज़ैक्श्न् / *noun* [C] a piece of business that is done between people (लोगों के बीच) लेन-देन, सौदा *financial transactions*

**transatlantic** /ˌtrænzətˈlæntɪk ˌट्रैन् ज़ट्ˈलैन्टिक् / *adj.* to or from the other side of the Atlantic Ocean; across the Atlantic अटलांटिक सागर के उस पार की ओर या उस पार से; अटलांटिक सागर के आर-पार *a transatlantic flight/voyage*

**transcend** /trænˈsend ट्रैन्ˈसेन्ड् / *verb* [T] (*formal*) to go further than the usual limits of sth किसी वस्तु की सामान्य सीमा का अतिक्रमण करना

**transcribe** /trænˈskraɪb ट्रैन्ˈस्क्राइब् / *verb* [T] **1 transcribe sth (into sth)** to record thoughts, speech or data in a written form, or in a different written form from the original विचारों, भाषण या सामग्री को मौखिक से लिखित या मूल लिखित रूप से भिन्न लिखित रूप में रिकॉर्ड करना *Clerks transcribe everything that is said in court.* ○ *The interview was recorded and then transcribed.* **2** (*technical*) to show the sounds of speech using a special **phonetic** alphabet ध्वनिक वर्णमाला की सहायता से भाषण-ध्वनियों को लिखित रूप में प्रस्तुत करना, (का) लिप्यंकन करना ➪ **phonetic** देखिए। **3 transcribe sth (for sth)** to write a piece of music in a different form so that it can be played by another musical instrument or sung by another voice किसी संगीत रचना को भिन्न रूप में तैयार करना (अन्य वाद्य द्वारा बजाए या अन्य व्यक्ति द्वारा गाए जाने के लिए) *a piano piece transcribed for the guitar*

**transcript** /ˈtrænskrɪpt ˈट्रैन्स्क्रिप्ट् / (*also* **transcription**) *noun* [C] a written or printed copy of what sb has said भाषण आदि की लिखित या मुद्रित प्रति *a transcript of the interview/trial*

**transcription** /trænˈskrɪpʃn ट्रैन्ˈस्क्रिप्श्न् / *noun* **1** [U] the act or process of representing sth in a written or printed form किसी वस्तु को लिखित या मुद्रित रूप में प्रस्तुत करने का कार्य या प्रक्रिया; लिप्यंकन, प्रतिलेखन *errors made in transcription* ○ *phonetic transcription* **2** [C] = **transcript** *The full transcription of the interview is attached.* **3** [C] something that is represented in writing लिखित रूप में प्रस्तुत कोई वस्तु, लिप्यंकित या प्रतिलिखित अभिलेख *This dictionary gives phonetic transcriptions of all headwords.* **4** [C] a change in the written form of a piece of music so that it can be played on a different instrument or sung by a different voice किसी संगीत-रचना के लिखित रूप में परिवर्तन (अन्य वाद्य द्वारा बजाए या अन्य व्यक्ति द्वारा गाए जाने के लिए)

**transducer** /ˌtrænzˈdjuːsə(r) ˌट्रैन्ज़्ˈड्यूस(र्) / *noun* [C] (*technical*) a device for producing an electrical signal from another form of energy such as pressure ऊर्जा की भिन्न विधा (जैसे दाब) से विद्युत संकेत उत्पन्न करने वाला उपकरण; ट्रांसड्यूसर

**transfer**[1] /træns'fɜ:(r) ट्रैन्स्'फ़(र्) / *verb* (**transferring; transferred**) **1** [I, T] **transfer (sb/sth) (from...) (to...)** to move, or to make sb/sth move, from one place to another एक स्थान से दूसरे स्थान पर जाना या किसी को भेजना; स्थानांतरित होना या करना *I'd like to transfer Rs 1000 from my deposit account* (= in a bank). ○ *Transfer the data onto a disk.* **2** [T] to officially arrange for sth to belong to, or be controlled by, sb else क़ानूनी रूप से किसी वस्तु को किसी अन्य व्यक्ति के स्वामित्व या नियंत्रण में देना; हस्तांतरित करना *She transferred the property to her son.* ▶ **transferable** /-'fɜ:rəbl -'फ़रबूल् / *adj.* हस्तांतरणीय या हस्तांतरण-योग्य *This ticket is not transferable* (= may only be used by the person who bought it).

**transfer**[2] /'trænsfɜ:(r) 'ट्रैन्स्फ़(र्) / *noun* **1** [C, U] moving or being moved from one place, job or state to another किसी स्थान, नौकरी या दशा से दूसरी में जाने या भेजे जाने की क्रिया; स्थानांतरण *Pulkit is not happy here and has asked for a transfer.* **2** [U] changing to a different vehicle or route during a journey यात्रा के दौरान एक से दूसरे वाहन या मार्ग को अपनाने की क्रिया *Transfer from the airport to the hotel is included.* **3** [C] (*AmE*) a ticket that allows you to continue your journey on another bus or train (यात्री को) अन्य बस, ट्रेन द्वारा यात्रा जारी रखने का अधिकार या अनुमति देने वाला टिकट

**transform** /træns'fɔ:m ट्रैन्स्'फ़ॉर्म् / *verb* [T] **transform sb/sth (from sth) (into sth)** to change sb/sth completely, especially in a way which improves him/her/it किसी व्यक्ति या वस्तु को पूरी तरह बदल देना (विशेषतया उसमें सुधार लाते हुए), (का) रूपांतरण कर देना ▶ **transformation** /ˌtrænsfə'meɪʃn ˌट्रैन्स्फ़'मेश्न् / *noun* [C, U] रूपांतरण

**transformer** /træns'fɔ:mə(r) ट्रैन्स्'फ़ॉर्म(र्) / *noun* [C] a device for reducing or increasing the electrical force (**voltage**) that goes into a piece of electrical equipment बिजली का ट्रांसफ़ॉर्मर (किसी विद्युत उपकरण में जाने वाली विद्युत की शक्ति को घटाने या बढ़ाने वाला यंत्र) ➪ **generator** पर चित्र देखिए।

**transfusion** /træns'fju:ʒn ट्रैन्स्'फ़्यूश़्न् / *noun* [C] the action of putting new blood into a person's body instead of his/her own because he/she is ill किसी व्यक्ति को (रोग के कारण दूषित रक्त के स्थान पर) नया रक्त चढ़ाना, रक्ताधान करना *a blood transfusion*

**transistor** /træn'zɪstə(r); -'sɪst- ट्रैन्'ज़िस्ट(र्) -'सिस्ट्- / *noun* [C] a small piece of electronic equipment that is used in computers, radios, televisions, etc. ट्रांसिस्टर (कंप्यूटर, रेडियो, टीवी आदि में प्रयुक्त एक छोटा इलेक्ट्रॉनिक उपकरण)

**transit** /'trænzɪt; -'sɪt 'ट्रैन्ज़िट्; -'सिट् / *noun* [U] **1** the act of being moved or carried from one place to another एक स्थान से दूसरे स्थान पर भेजने या ले जाने की क्रिया; पारवहन *The goods had been damaged **in transit**.* **2** going through a place on the way to somewhere else कहीं अन्यत्र जाने के दौरान किसी स्थान से गुज़रने की क्रिया; पारगमन ***transit visa*** (= permission to pass through a country but not to stay there)

**transition** /træn'zɪʃn; -'sɪʃn ट्रैन्'ज़िश्न्; -'सिश्न् / *noun* [C, U] **(a) transition (from sth) (to sth)** a change from one state or form to another एक दशा या रूप से अन्य में परिवर्तन; संक्रमण, संक्रांति *the transition from childhood to adolescence* ▶ **transitional** /-ʃənl -शनूल् / *adj.* संक्रमण या संक्रांति-कालीन *a transitional stage/period*

**transition metal** (*also* **transition element**) *noun* [C] one of the group of metals in the centre of **the periodic table**. Transition metals are heavy, they melt only at high temperatures, they form coloured compounds, they can combine with another element to form more than one compound, and they often act as a **catalyst** समस्त रासायनिक तत्वों की सूची के केंद्र में स्थित अन्यतम धातु-वर्ग, ट्रांसीशन मेटल (इन धातुओं की विशेषताएँ हैं वज़न में भारी होना, ऊँचे तापमान पर ही पिघलना, रंगीन यौगिकों का निर्माण करना, अन्य तत्वों के साथ मिलकर अनेक यौगिकों की रचना करना, और उत्प्रेरक होना)

**transitive** /'trænsətɪv 'ट्रैन्सटिव् / *adj.* (*grammar*) (*used about a verb*) that has a direct object सकर्मक (क्रिया), प्रत्यक्ष कर्म वाली (क्रिया) *In this dictionary transitive verbs are marked* [T]. ✪ विलोम **intransitive**

**NOTE** सकर्मक क्रियाओं (transitive verbs) के विषय में अधिक जानकारी के लिए इस शब्दकोश के अंत में **Quick Grammar Reference** खंड देखिए।

**translate** /træns'leɪt; trænz- ट्रैनस्'लेट्; ट्रैन्ज़्- / *verb* [I, T] **translate (sth) (from sth) (into sth)** to change sth written or spoken from one language to another (एक भाषा से दूसरी भाषा में) अनुवाद करना (लिखित या मौखिक अभिव्यक्तिका) *This book has been translated from Hindi into English.* ➪ **interpret** देखिए। ▶ **translation** /træns'leɪʃn; trænz- ट्रैन्स्'लेशन्; ट्रैन्ज़्- / *noun* [C, U] अनुवाद *a word-for-word translation* ○ *an error in translation*

**translator** /træns'leɪtə(r); trænz- ट्रैन्स्'लेट(र्); ट्रैन्ज़्- / *noun* [C] a person who changes sth that has been written or spoken from one language to another अनुवादक (लिखित या मौखिक अभिव्यक्ति का) ➪ **interpreter** देखिए।

**translucent** /træns'lu:snt; trænz- ट्रैन्स्'लूसन्ट्; ट्रैन्ज़्- / *adj.* (*written*) allowing light to pass through but not transparent जिसमें से प्रकाश रेखा गुज़र सके (परंतु जो पारदर्शी न हो); पारभासक, पारभासी *The sky was a pale translucent blue.* ○ *His skin was translucent with age.* ▸ **translucence** /-sns -सन्स् / (**translucency** /-snsi -सन्सि /) *noun* [U] पारभासिकता

**transmission** /træns'mɪʃn; trænz- ट्रैन्स्'मिश्न्; ट्रैन्ज़्- / *noun* **1** [U] sending sth out or passing sth on from one person, place or thing to another एक व्यक्ति, स्थान या वस्तु से दूसरे को कुछ प्रेषित या संचारित करने की क्रिया; प्रसारण, संचारण, संप्रेषण *the transmission of television pictures by satellite* ○ *the transmission of a disease/virus* **2** [C] a television or radio programme टीवी या रेडियो का कार्यक्रम **3** [U, C] the system in a car, etc. by which power is passed from the engine to the wheels वाहन आदि में ऊर्जा बल को इंजन से पहियों तक पहुँचाने वाली प्रणाली

**transmit** /træns'mɪt; trænz- ट्रैन्स्'मिट्; ट्रैन्ज़्- / *verb* [T] (**transmitting; transmitted**) **1** to send out television or radio programmes, electronic signals, etc. टीवी या रेडियो कार्यक्रमों, विद्युत संकेतों आदि को प्रसारित करना *The match was transmitted live all over the world.* **2** to send or pass sth from one person or place to another एक व्यक्ति या स्थान से दूसरे को भेजना या पहुँचाना; संक्रमित करना *a sexually transmitted disease*

**transmitter** /træns'mɪtə(r); trænz- ट्रैन्स्'मिट(र्); ट्रैन्ज़्- / *noun* [C] a piece of equipment that sends out electronic signals, television or radio programmes, etc. विद्युत संकेतों, टीवी या रेडियो कार्यक्रमों आदि को प्रसारित करने वाला उपकरण; ट्रांसमीटर

**transparency** /træns'pærənsi ट्रैन्स्'पैरन्सि / *noun* [C] (*pl.* **transparencies**) a piece of plastic on which you can write or draw or that has a picture, etc. on it that you look at by putting it on a special machine (**projector**) and shining light through it पारदर्शी प्लास्टिक खंड जिस पर कुछ लिखा हो, आरेख या चित्र बना हो (जिसे प्रोजेक्टर पर रोशनी डालकर देखा जा सके) *a transparency for the overhead projector* ➪ **slide$^2$ 4** देखिए।

**transparent** /træns'pærənt ट्रैन्स्'पैरन्ट् / *adj.* that you can see through पारदर्शी (जिसके पार की वस्तु दिखाई दे) *Glass is transparent.* ✪ विलोम **opaque**

**transpiration** /ˌtrænspɪ'reɪʃn ˌट्रैन्स्पि'रेश्न् / *noun* [U] the process of water passing out from the surface of a plant or leaf पौधे या पत्ते की सतह पर जलकण या वाष्प प्रकट होने की प्रक्रिया; वाष्पोत्सर्जन, प्रस्वेदन

**transpire** /træn'spaɪə(r) ट्रैन्'स्पाइअ(र्) / *verb* [I] **1** (*not usually used in the progressive tenses*) to become known; to be shown to be true जानकारी में आना; सचाई का पता चलना ***It transpired that*** *the gang had had a contact inside the bank.* ○ *This story, it later transpired, was untrue.* **2** to happen घटित होना, होना *You're meeting him tomorrow? Let me know what transpires.* **3** (*technical*) when plants or leaves **transpire**, water passes out from their surface पौधों या पत्तों की सतह पर जलकण या वाष्प प्रकट होना, (का) प्रस्वेदित होना

**transplant$^1$** /træns'plɑ:nt; trænz- ट्रैन्स्'प्लान्ट्; ट्रैन्ज़्- / *verb* [T] **1** to take out an organ or other part of sb's body and put it into another person's body एक व्यक्ति के शरीर से किसी अंग को निकाल कर दूसरे के शरीर में लगाना, मानव-अंग का प्रत्यारोपण करना **2** to move a growing plant and plant it somewhere else छोटे पौधे को एक स्थान से उखाड़कर दूसरे स्थान पर लगाना, (को) प्रतिरोपित करना ➪ **graft** देखिए।

**transplant$^2$** /'trænsplɑ:nt; 'trænz- 'ट्रैन्स्प्लान्ट्; 'ट्रैन्ज़्- / *noun* [C] a medical operation in which an organ, etc. is taken out of sb's body and put into another person's body एक व्यक्ति के शरीर से किसी अंग को निकालकर दूसरे के शरीर में लगाने की शल्य-क्रिया, मानव-अंग प्रत्यारोपण (की शल्य-क्रिया) *to have a heart/liver/kidney transplant*

**transport** /'trænspɔ:t ट्रैन्स्पॉट् / (*AmE* **transportation** /ˌtrænspɔ:'teɪʃn ˌट्रैन्सपॉ'टेश्न् /) *noun* [U] **1** the action of carrying or taking people or goods from one place to another लोगों या माल को ढोना, परिवहन *road/rail/sea transport* **2** vehicles that you travel in; a method of travel सवारी के लिए वाहन; यात्रा का साधन *I travel to school by public transport.* ○ *His bike is his only* ***means of transport***. ▸ **transport** /træn'spɔ:t ट्रैन्'स्पॉट् / *verb* [T] लोगों या माल को ढोना

**transpose** /træn'spəʊz ट्रैन्'स्पोज़् / *verb* [T] (*often passive*) **1** (*formal*) to change the order of two or more things वस्तुओं के क्रम को बदलना, का क्रम-विपर्यय करना ✪ पर्याय **reverse** **2** (*formal*) to move or change sth to a different place or environment or into a different form किसी वस्तु को अन्य स्थान या वातावरण में ले जाना या अन्य रूप में परिवर्तित करना (वस्तु का) स्थानांतरण या रूपांतरण करना ✪ पर्याय **transfer** ▸ **transposition** /ˌtrænspə'zɪʃn ˌट्रैन्स्प'ज़िश्न् / *noun* [C, U] क्रम-विपर्यय, स्वरांतरण

**transverse** /'trænzvɜ:s; 'træns- 'ट्रैन्ज़्वस्; 'ट्रैन्स्- / *adj.* (*usually before a noun*) (*technical*) situated across sth आड़ा, तिरछा कटा, अनुप्रस्थ *A transverse bar joins the two posts.*

**transverse wave** *noun* [C] (*technical*) a wave that **vibrates** at an angle of 90 degrees to the direction that it is moving अपनी गति की दिशा में 90 अंश के कोण पर कंपन करने वाली लहर; अनुप्रस्थ तरंग ➪ **longitudinal wave** देखिए।

**trap[1]** /træp ट्रैप्/ *noun* [C] **1** a piece of equipment that you use for catching animals जंतुओं को पकड़ने के लिए प्रयुक्त फंदा; जाल *a mousetrap* ○ *The rabbit's leg was caught in the trap.* **2** a clever plan that is designed to trick sb किसी को फँसाने की योजना; फाँसा, छलछंद *She* ***walked straight into the trap***. **3** an unpleasant situation from which it is hard to escape अप्रिय स्थिति जिसमें से बच निकलना कठिन हो ➪ **death trap** देखिए।

**trap[2]** /træp ट्रैप्/ *verb* [T] (**trapping; trapped**) **1** (*often passive*) to keep sb in a dangerous place or a bad situation from which he/she cannot escape किसी को ख़तरनाक जगह पर या बुरी हालत में फँसा कर रखना *The door closed behind them and they were trapped.* ○ *Many people are trapped in low-paid jobs.* **2** to catch and keep or store sth किसी वस्तु को पकड़कर रोक रखना या संचित कर लेना *Special glass panels trap heat from the sun.*

**trapdoor** /ˈtræpdɔ:(r) ˈट्रैप्डॉ(र्)/ *noun* [C] a small door in a floor or ceiling फ़र्श या छत में छोटा दरवाज़ा, फ़र्श-दरवाज़ा या छतद्वार, चोर-दरवाज़ा

**trapeze** /trəˈpi:z ट्रˈपीज़्/ *noun* [C] a wooden or metal bar hanging from two ropes high above the ground, used by performers (**acrobats**) (सर्कस में) कलाबाज़ी का झूला (दो रस्सियों के सहारे हवा में लटकाना लकड़ी या धातु का डंडा, कलाबाज़ों द्वारा करतब दिखाने के लिए प्रयुक्त)

**trapezium** /trəˈpi:ziəm ट्रˈपीज़िअम्/ *noun* [C] **1** (*AmE* **trapezoid**) a flat shape with four straight sides, one pair of opposite sides being parallel and the other pair not parallel समलंबाभ चतुर्भुज (चार सीधी रेखाओं वाली आकृति जिसमें आमने-सामने की दो रेखाएँ समानांतर होती है, शेष दो नहीं) **2** (*AmE*) = **trapezoid**

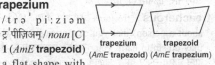

**trapezium** (*AmE* **trapezoid**) **trapezoid** (*AmE* **trapezium**)

**trapezoid** /ˈtræpəzɔɪd ˈट्रैपज़ॉइड्/ *noun* [C] **1** (*AmE* **trapezium**) a flat shape with four straight sides, none of which are parallel पूर्ण विषम चतुर्भुज (चार सीधी, परंतु असमान, रेखाओं वाली आकृति) **2** (*AmE*) = **trapezium**

**trappings** /ˈtræpɪŋz ˈट्रैपिङ्ज़्/ *noun* [*pl.*] clothes, possessions, etc. which are signs of a particular social position विशिष्ट सामाजिक स्थिति के द्योतक कपड़े, सामान आदि सामग्री साज-सामान

**trash** /træʃ ट्रैश्/ (*AmE*) = **rubbish**

**trash can** (*AmE*) = **dustbin**

**trashy** /ˈtræʃi ˈट्रैशि/ *adj.* of poor quality घटिया, रद्दी *trashy novels/clothes*

**trauma** /ˈtrɔ:mə ˈट्रॉमा/ *noun* [C, U] (an event that causes) a state of great shock or sadness गहरा आघात और खिन्नता की स्थिति (उत्पन्न करने वाली घटना) *the trauma of losing your parents* ➪ **stress** देखिए।
▶ **traumatic** /trɔ:ˈmætɪk ट्रॉˈमैटिक्/ *adj.* आघातकारी

**traumatize** (*also* **-ise**) /ˈtrɔ:mətaɪz ˈट्रॉमटाइज़्/ *verb* [T] (*usually passive*) to shock and upset sb very much, often making him/her unable to think or work normally किसी को गहरा आघात पहुँचाना (कि वह ठीक से न सोच सके न कुछ कर सके)

**travel[1]** /ˈtrævl ˈट्रैव्ल्/ *verb* (**travelling; travelled** *AmE* **traveling; traveled**) **1** [I] to go from one place to another, especially over a long distance यात्रा या सफ़र करना (विशेषतः लंबी दूरी का) *to travel to work* ○ *travelling expenses* **2** [T] to make a journey of a particular distance किसी निश्चित दूरी की यात्रा करना *They travelled 60 kilometres to come and see us.*

**IDM** **travel light** to take very few things with you when you travel केवल ज़रूरी सामान के साथ यात्रा करना

**travel[2]** /ˈtrævl ˈट्रैव्ल्/ *noun* **1** [U] the action of going from one place to another (किसी स्थान की) यात्रा, सफ़र *air/rail/space travel* ○ *a travel bag/clock/iron* (= designed to be used when travelling) **2 travels** [*pl.*] time spent travelling, especially to places that are far away दूर-दूर की यात्राएँ

**NOTE** **Travel** अगणनीय शब्द है और सामान्य रूप से किसी भी स्थान की यात्रा करने के विषय में इसका प्रयोग हो सकता है—*Foreign travel is very popular these days*. स्थान-विशेष की यात्रा के लिए **journey** शब्द का प्रयोग होता है, 'journey' लंबी हो सकती है —*journey across Canada* और छोटी भी—*the journey to work*. वृत्ताकार यात्रा या भ्रमण को **tour** कहते हैं। किसी देश, नगर, पसंदीदा स्थान आदि कहीं का भी 'tour' किया जा सकता है—*a three-week tour around Italy* ○ *a guided tour of the castle*. यात्रा-संबंधी सब मामलों (कहीं पर ठहराना, आसपास जाना और अंत में घर लौट आना) की सामूहिक बात करनी हो तो **trip** का प्रयोग होता है —*They're just back from a trip to Japan.* (परंतु निम्नलिखित प्रकार के वाक्य में 'trip' नहीं आएगा— *'How was the journey back?' 'Awful–the* *plane was delayed!*' 'Trip' छोटी हो सकती है—*a day trip* लंबी भी—*a trip round the world* या काम-धंधे, सैर-सपाटे के लिए भी—*How about a shopping trip to London this summer?* ○ *He's on a business trip to New York to meet a client.* मित्रमंडली के साथ की गई संक्षिप्त और योजनाबद्ध यात्रा **excursion** है—*The holiday includes a full-day excursion to the Red Fort.* 'Journey' 'tour' 'trip' तथा 'excursion' पर जाने की चर्चा के लिए **go on** का प्रयोग होता है—*You go on a journey/tour/trip/excursion.*

**travel agency** *noun* [C] (*pl.* **travel agencies**) a company that makes travel arrangements for people (booking tickets, flights, hotels, etc.) लोगों का यात्रा संबंधी आवश्यकताएँ (टिकट ख़रीदना, होटल तय करना आदि) पूरी करने वाली कंपनी; यात्रा एजेंसी, ट्रैवल एजेंसी

**travel agent** *noun* **1** [C] a person whose job is to make travel arrangements for people लोगों की यात्रा आवश्यकताएँ पूरी करने का काम करने वाला व्यक्ति; यात्रा एजेंट, ट्रैवल एजेंट **2 the travel agent's** [*sing.*] the shop where you can go to make travel arrangements, buy tickets, etc. यात्रा एजेंट का कार्यालय

**traveller** (*AmE* **traveler**) /ˈtrævələ(r) ˈट्रैव़ल(र्)/ *noun* [C] **1** a person who is travelling or who often travels प्रायः यात्रा करने वाला व्यक्ति; यात्री, मुसाफ़िर **2** (*BrE*) a person who travels around the country in a large vehicle and does not have a permanent home anywhere बड़े वाहन से देश में स्थान-स्थान की यात्रा करने वाला ऐसा व्यक्ति जिसका कोई स्थायी घर नहीं, मोटर वाला बेघर सैलानी ➪ **gypsy** देखिए।

**traveller's cheque** (*AmE* **traveler's check**) *noun* [C] a cheque that you can change into foreign money when you are travelling in other countries यात्री चेक (विदेशों में यात्रा के समय विदेशी मुद्रा प्राप्त करने के लिए प्रयुक्त चेक)

**travel-sick** *adj.* feeling sick or vomiting because of the movement of the vehicle you are travelling in वाहन के निरंतर हरकत में होने के कारण कुछ बीमार-सा या वमन करता हुआ (यात्री) ➪ **airsick, carsick** और **seasick** देखिए।

**travesty** /ˈtrævəsti ˈट्रैव़सटि/ *noun* [C] (*pl.* **travesties**) **travesty of sth** something that does not have the qualities or values that it should have, in a way that is often shocking or offensive विडंबना; अपेक्षित गुणवत्ता या महत्त्व का अभाव के कारण घटिया और अपमानजनक होना *This trial has proved to be a **travesty of justice**.*

**trawl**[1] /trɔːl ट्रॉल्/ *verb* [I, T] **1 trawl (through sth) (for sth/sb); trawl sth (for sth/sb)** to search through a large amount of information or a large number of people, places, etc. looking for a particular thing or person किसी ख़ास व्यक्ति या वस्तु की खोज में बहुत सारी जानकारी, बहुत-से लोगों, स्थानों आदि को छान डालना *Major companies trawl the universities for potential employees.* ○ *The police are trawling through their files for a similar case.* **2 trawl (for sth)** to fish for sth by pulling a large net with a wide opening through the water चौड़े मुँह वाले जाल को पानी में डालकर कुछ ढूँढ़ना

**trawl**[2] /trɔːl ट्रॉल्/ *noun* [C] **1** a search through a large amount of information, documents, etc. बहुत सारी जानकारी, दस्तावेज़ आदि में से की गई खोज या छान-बीन *A trawl through the newspapers yielded two possible jobs.* **2** (*also* **trawl net**) a large net with a wide opening, that is pulled along the bottom of the sea by a boat in order to catch fish समुद्र की गहाराई से मछलियाँ पकड़ने के लिए प्रयुक्त चौड़े मुँह वाला बड़ा जाल, समुद्री मछलियाँ पकड़ने का महाजाल

**trawler** /ˈtrɔːlə(r) ˈट्रॉल(र्)/ *noun* [C] a fishing boat that uses large nets that it pulls through the sea behind it मछलियाँ पकड़ने वाली नौका (जिसके पीछे जाल लगे रहते हैं), ट्रॉलर ➪ **boat** पर चित्र देखिए।

**tray** /treɪ ट्रे/ *noun* [C] **1** a flat piece of wood, plastic, metal, etc. with slightly higher edges that you use for carrying food, drink, etc. on खाद्य और पेय पदार्थों को ले जाने के लिए प्रयुक्त लकड़ी, प्लास्टिक, धातु आदि की बड़ी तश्तरी; ट्रे, किश्ती **2** a flat container with low edges in which you put papers, etc. on a desk मेज़ पर काग़ज़ आदि रखने की ट्रे (समतल और नीचे किनारों वाली)

**treacherous** /ˈtretʃərəs ˈट्रेचरस्/ *adj.* **1** (used about a person) that you cannot trust and who may do sth to harm you (व्यक्ति) विश्वासघाती और हानि पहुँचा सकने वाला; धोखेबाज़ *He was weak, cowardly and treacherous.* **2** dangerous, although seeming safe ख़तरनाक (यद्यपि दिखने में सुरक्षित)

**treachery** /ˈtretʃəri ˈट्रेचरि/ *noun* [U] the act of causing harm to sb who trusts you विश्वासघात, धोखा

**treacle** /ˈtriːkl ˈट्रीकल्/ (*AmE* **molasses**) *noun* [U] a thick, dark, sticky liquid that is made from sugar (गन्ने की) राब (गाढ़ा, काला, चिपचिपा तरल पदार्थ) ➪ **syrup** देखिए।

**tread**[1] /tred ट्रेड्/ *verb* (*pt* **trod** /trɒd ट्रॉड्/; *pp* **trodden** /ˈtrɒdn ˈट्रॉड्न्/) **1** [I] **tread (on/in/over sb/sth)** to put your foot down while you are walking (किसी चीज़ पर) चलना, पैर रखना *Don't* *tread in the puddle!* ○ *He trod on my foot and didn't even say sorry!* **2** [T] **tread sth (in/into/ down)** to press down on sth with your foot (किसी चीज़ को) कुचलना *This wine is still made by treading grapes in the traditional way.*

**tread**[2] /tred ट्रेड्/ *noun* **1** [*sing.*] the sound you make when you walk; the way you walk पैरों की आहट, पदचाप, पगध्वनि; चलने का ढंग, चाल **2** [C, U] the pattern on the surface of a tyre on a vehicle which is slightly higher than the rest of the surface टायर की गुड्डी (सतह पर की कुछ उठी हुई आकृति)

**treason** /ˈtri:zn ˈट्रीज़्न्/ *noun* [U] the criminal act of causing harm to your country, for example by helping its enemies देश से विश्वासघात, गद्दारी, देशद्रोही (उदाहरण के लिए, शत्रुओं का साथ देना) ➪ **traitor** पर नोट देखिए।

**treasure**[1] /ˈtreʒə(r) ˈट्रेश(र्)/ *noun* **1** [U] a collection of very valuable objects, for example gold, silver, jewellery, etc. सोना, चाँदी, आभूषण आदि बहुमूल्य वस्तुओं का ख़ज़ाना *to find buried treasure* **2** [C] something that is very valuable कोई बहुमूल्य वस्तु

**treasure**[2] /ˈtreʒə(r) ˈट्रेश(र्)/ *verb* [T] to consider sb/sth to be very special or valuable किसी व्यक्ति या वस्तु को बहुत ख़ास या मूल्यवान समझना *I will treasure those memories forever.*

**treasure hunt** *noun* [C] a game in which people try to find a hidden prize by following special signs (**clues**) which have been left in different places विभिन्न स्थानों पर छोड़े गए सूत्रों की सहायता से छिपा कर रखे गए पुरस्कार को ढूँढ़ निकालने का खेल

**treasurer** /ˈtreʒərə(r) ˈट्रेशर(र्)/ *noun* [C] the person who looks after the money and accounts of a club or an organization (किसी क्लब या संस्था का) ख़ज़ांची, कोषपाल

**the Treasury** /ˈtreʒəri ˈट्रेशरि/ *noun* [*sing.,with sing. or pl. verb*] the government department that controls public money राजकोष, सरकारी ख़ज़ाना

**treat**[1] /tri:t ट्रीट्/ *verb* [T] **1 treat sb/sth (with/ as/like sth)** to act or behave towards sb/sth in a particular way किसी व्यक्ति या वस्तु के प्रति विशेष ढंग से कोई कार्य करना या के साथ विशेष व्यवहार करना *You should treat older people with respect.* ○ *to treat sb badly/fairly/well* **2 treat sth as sth** to consider sth in a particular way किसी वस्तु को ख़ास ढंग से लेना *I decided to treat his comment as a joke.* **3** to deal with or discuss sth in a particular way किसी बात से विशेष ढंग से निपटना या उस पर चर्चा करना *The article treats this question in great detail.* **4 treat sb/sth (for sth)** to use medicine or medical care to try to make a sick or injured person well again किसी बीमार या घायल व्यक्ति का इलाज करना (औषधि या परिचर्या द्वारा) *The boy was treated for burns at the hospital.* **5 treat sth (with sth)** to put a chemical substance onto sth in order to protect it from damage, clean it, etc. किसी वस्तु को ख़राब होने से बचाने, साफ़ करने आदि के लिए किसी रासायनिक पदार्थ का प्रयोग करना; उपचारित करना **6 treat sb/yourself (to sth)** to pay for sth or give sb/yourself sth that is very special or enjoyable कोई विशिष्ट या आनंदप्रद वस्तु किसी के लिए ख़रीदना या किसी को देना *Chandni treated the children to an ice cream* (= she paid for them).

**treat**[2] /tri:t ट्रीट्/ *noun* [C] something special or enjoyable that you pay for or give to sb/yourself किसी के लिए ख़रीदी या किसी को दी गई विशिष्ट या आनंदप्रद वस्तु *I've brought some cream cakes as a treat.* ○ *It's a real treat for me to stay in bed late.*

**IDM trick or treat** ➪ **trick** देखिए।

**treatment** /ˈtri:tmənt ˈट्रीट्मन्ट्/ *noun* **1** [U, C] **treatment (for sth)** the use of medicine or medical care to cure an illness or injury; sth that is done to make sb feel and look good किसी बीमार या घायल व्यक्ति का इलाज (औषध या परिचर्या द्वारा) *to require hospital/medical treatment* **2** [U] the way that you behave towards sb or deal with sth किसी के प्रति व्यवहार-विशेष *The treatment of the prisoners of war was very harsh.* **3** [U, C] **treatment (for sth)** a process by which sth is cleaned, protected from damage, etc. किसी वस्तु को साफ़ करने, ख़राब होने से बचाने आदि की प्रक्रिया-विशेष; उपचार

**treaty** /ˈtri:ti ˈट्रीटि/ *noun* [C] (*pl.* **treaties**) a written agreement between two or more countries (देशों के बीच) औपचारिक संधि *to sign a peace treaty*

**treble**[1] /ˈtrebl ˈट्रेब्ल्/ *verb* [I, T] to become or to make sth three times bigger किसी वस्तु का तिगुना हो जाना या को तिगुना कर देना *Prices have trebled in the past ten years.* ▸ **treble** *det.* तिगुना *This figure is treble the number five years ago.*

**treble**[2] /ˈtrebl ˈट्रेब्ल्/ *noun* [C] **1** a high singing voice, especially that of a young boy गायक लड़के का उच्च स्वर **2** a boy who has a high singing voice उच्च स्वर से गाने वाला लड़का

**tree** /tri: ट्री/ *noun* [C] a tall plant that can live for a long time. Trees have a thick wooden central part from which branches grow वृक्ष, पेड़, दरख़्त *an oak/apple/elm tree* ➪ पृष्ठ 1270 पर चित्र देखिए।

**tree line** *noun* [*sing.*] (in geography) the level of land, for example on a mountain, above which

**trees**

trees will not grow (भूगोल में) भूमि का वह स्तर (जैसे किसी पर्वत पर) जिसके बाद वृक्ष नहीं उगते

**trek** /trek ट्रेक्/ *noun* [C] **1** a long hard walk, lasting several days or weeks, usually in the mountains (सामान्यतः) पर्वतों की लंबी कठोर पैदल यात्रा **2** (*informal*) a long walk लंबा पैदल का रास्ता *It's quite a trek to the shops.* ▶ **trek** *verb* [I] (**trekking; trekked**) लंबी पैदल यात्रा करना

**NOTE** लंबी दूरी के सैर-सपाटे के लिए **go trekking** का प्रयोग होता है।

**trellis** /ˈtrelɪs ˈट्रेलिस्/ *noun* [C] a light frame made of long thin pieces of wood that cross each other, used to support climbing plants बेलों को चढ़ने में सहारा देने वाली जाफ़री, जाली (एक दूसरे को काटती लकड़ी की फट्टियों से बनी)

**tremble** /ˈtrembl ˈट्रेम्बल्/ *verb* [I] **tremble (with sth)** to shake, for example because you are cold, frightened, etc. (ठंड, डर आदि के कारण) काँपना *She was pale and trembling with shock.* ▶ **tremble** *noun* [C] कंपन

**tremendous** /trəˈmendəs ट्रˈमेन्डस्/ *adj.* **1** very large or great बहुत बड़ा या अधिक *a tremendous amount of work* **2** (*informal*) very good बहुत अच्छा, असाधारण *It was a tremendous experience.*

**tremendously** /trəˈmendəsli ट्रˈमेन्डसलि/ *adv.* very; very much बहुत; अत्यधिक, बहुत अधिक *tremendously exciting* ○ *Prices vary tremendously from one shop to another.*

**tremor** /ˈtremə(r) ˈट्रेम(र्)/ *noun* [C] a slight shaking movement हलका कंपन *an earth tremor* (= a small earthquake) ○ *There was a tremor in his voice.*

**trench** /trentʃ ट्रेन्च्/ *noun* [C] **1** a long narrow hole dug in the ground for water to flow along पानी बहने के लिए ज़मीन में लंबी तंग नली; खाई, परिखा **2** a long deep hole dug in the ground for soldiers to hide in during enemy attacks (सैनिकों के छिपने की) खंदक (लंबा गहरा गड्ढा)

**trend** /trend ट्रेन्ड्/ *noun* [C] **a trend (towards sth)** a general change or development सामान्य प्रवृत्ति *The current trend is towards smaller families.* ○ *He always followed the latest trends in fashion.*

**IDM set a/the trend** to start a new style or fashion नया फ़ैशन शुरू करना या चलाना

**trendy** /ˈtrendi ˈट्रेन्डि/ *adj.* (**trendier; trendiest**) (*informal*) fashionable फ़ैशनेबल

**trespass** /ˈtrespəs ˈट्रेसपस्/ *verb* [I] to go onto sb's land or property without permission किसी की भूमि या (गृह) संपत्ति में अनधिकार प्रवेश करना ▶ **trespasser** *noun* [C] किसी की भू या गृह संपत्ति में अनधिकार प्रवेश करने वाला; अतिक्रमी

**tri-** /traɪ ट्राइ/ *prefix* (*used in nouns and adjectives*) three; having three तीन; तीन वाला, त्रि- *tricycle* ○ *triangular*

**trial** /ˈtraɪəl ˈट्राइअल्/ *noun* [C, U] **1** the process in a court of law where a judge, etc. listens to evidence and decides if sb is guilty of a crime or not मुक़दमा; न्यायालय में न्यायाधीश आदि के द्वारा साक्ष्यों की जाँच *a fair trial* ○ *He was* ***on trial for*** *murder.* **2** an act of testing sb/sth किसी व्यक्ति या वस्तु की जाँच *New drugs must go through extensive trials.* ○ *a* ***trial period*** *of three months*

**IDM trial and error** trying different ways of doing sth until you find the best one सर्वोत्तम प्रणाली का निश्चय होने तक विभिन्न प्रणालियों का परीक्षण; प्रयत्न-त्रुटि परीक्षा प्रणाली

**trial run** *noun* [C] an occasion when you practise doing sth in order to make sure you can do it correctly later on किसी वस्तु का नियमित व्यवहार आरंभ करने से पहले उस पर किया गया परीक्षण, आरंभिक या पूर्व परीक्षण

**triangle** /ˈtraɪæŋgl ˈट्राइऐङ्गल्/ *noun* [C] **1** a shape that has three straight sides त्रिकोण, त्रिभुज (तीन सीधे पार्श्वों वाली आकृति) *a right-angled triangle* **2** a metal musical instrument in the shape of a triangle that you play by hitting it with a metal stick त्रिभुज की आकृति वाला एक वाद्य ➪ पृष्ठ 789 पर चित्र देखिए।

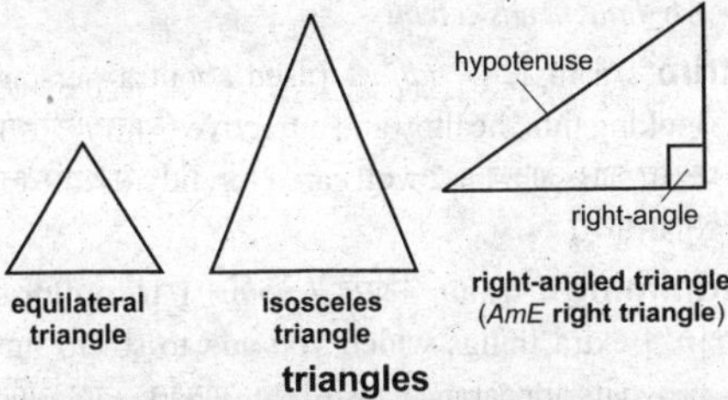


**triangles**

**triangular** /traɪˈæŋgjələ(r) ट्राइˈऐङ्ग्यल(र्)/ *adj.* shaped like a triangle त्रिकोण या त्रिभुज की आकृति का, त्रिभुजाकार या त्रिकोणीय

**tribe** /traɪb ट्राइब्/ *noun* [C] a group of people that have the same language and customs and that have a leader (**a chief**) जनजाति, क़बीला (समान भाषा और प्रथाओं वालों लोगों का समूह जिनका कोई व्यक्ति नेता होता है) *tribes living in the Andamans* ▶ **tribal** /ˈtraɪbl ˈट्राइबल्/ *adj.* जनजातीय, क़बायली *tribal art*

**tribulation** /ˌtrɪbjuˈleɪʃn ˌट्रिब्युˈलेश्न्/ *noun* [C, U] (*written*) great trouble or suffering घोर कष्ट या मुसीबत *the tribulations of modern life*

**tribunal** /traɪˈbjuːnl ट्राइˈब्यूनल्/ *noun* [C] a type of court with the authority to decide who is right in particular types of dispute or disagreement विशेष न्यायालय जो विशेष प्रकार के विवाद निपटाता है; अधिकरण न्यायाधिकरण *an industrial tribunal*

**tributary** /ˈtrɪbjətri ˈट्रिब्यट्रि/ *noun* [C] (*pl.* **tributaries**) a small river that flows into a larger river (किसी बड़ी नदी की) सहायक नदी

**tribute** /ˈtrɪbjuːt ˈट्रिब्यूट्/ *noun* **1** [C, U] **tribute (to sb)** something that you say or do to show that you respect or admire sb/sth, especially sb who has died किसी व्यक्ति या वस्तु को (विशेषतः उसकी स्मृति में) सम्मान या प्रशंसा के शब्द या कार्य; श्रद्धांजलि *A special concert was held as a tribute to the Raj Kapoor.* **2** [*sing.*] **a tribute (to sb/sth)** a sign of how good sb/sth is श्रेय की बात, श्रेष्ठ होने का संकेत *The success of the festival is a tribute to the organizers.*

IDM **pay tribute to sb/sth** ➪ **pay**[1] देखिए।

**triceps** /ˈtraɪseps ˈट्राइसेप्स्/ *noun* [C] (*pl.* **triceps**) the large muscle at the back of the top part of your arm बाँह के ऊपरी भाग के पीछे की मांसपेशी; त्रिशिरस्क ➪ **biceps** देखिए तथा **arm** पर चित्र देखिए।

**trick**[1] /trɪk ट्रिक्/ *noun* [C] **1** something that you do to make sb believe sth that is not true or a joke that you play to annoy sb चाल, दाँव-पेंच या (दूसरे को बुरा लगने वाला) मज़ाक *The thieves used a trick to get past the security guards.* **2** something that confuses you so that you see, remember, understand, etc. things in the wrong way उलझाने वाली बात (जिसके कारण ग़लती संभावित हो) *It was a* ***trick question*** (= one in which the answer looks easy, but actually is not). **3** an action that uses special skills to make people believe sth which is not true or real as a form of entertainment मनोरंजन के लिए करतब; इंद्रजाल *The magician* ***performed a trick*** *in which he made a rabbit disappear.* ○ *a card trick* **4** [*usually sing.*] a clever or the best way of doing sth कुछ करने की सूझ-बूझ वाली या सर्वोत्तम प्रणाली

IDM **do the job/trick** ➪ **job** देखिए।

**play a joke/trick on sb** ➪ **joke**[1] देखिए।

**trick or treat** (*AmE*) a tradition in which children dressed as ghosts, etc. go to people's houses on the evening of October 31st (**Hallowe'en**) and threaten to do sth bad to them if they do not give them sweets, etc. हैलोवीन पर्व (31 अक्तूबर की संध्या) पर बच्चों की शरारत (विचित्र वेश धारण कर लोगों से मिठाई आदि वसूलना) *to go trick or treating*

**trick**[2] /trɪk ट्रिक्/ *verb* [T] to make sb believe sth that is not true किसी से छल करना *I'd been tricked and I felt like a fool.* ✪ पर्याय **deceive**

IDM **trick sb into sth/doing sth** to persuade sb to do sth by making him/her believe sth that is not true किसी से चालबाज़ी से कुछ करा लेना *He tricked me into lending him money.*

**trick sb out of sth** to get sth from sb by making him/her believe sth that is not true किसी से चालबाज़ी से कुछ ले लेना *Smita was tricked out of her share of the money.*

**trickery** /ˈtrɪkəri ˈट्रिकरि/ *noun* [U] the use of dishonest methods to trick sb in order to get what you want धोखा, छल, चालबाज़ी

**trickle** /ˈtrɪkl ˈट्रिकल्/ *verb* [I] **1** (used about a liquid) to flow in a thin line (द्रव का) बूँद-बूँद टपकना *Rain drops trickled down the window.* **2** to go somewhere slowly and gradually धीमी चाल से कहीं जाना ▶ **trickle** *noun* [C, *usually sing.*] द्रव की क्षीण धारा *a trickle of water*

**tricky** /ˈtrɪki ˈट्रिकि/ *adj.* (**trickier; trickiest**) difficult to do or deal with जटिल, पेचीदा *a tricky situation*

**tricycle** /ˈtraɪsɪkl ˈट्राइसिकल्/ *noun* [C] a bicycle that has one wheel at the front and two at the back तीन पहियों वाली साइकिल

**trident** /ˈtraɪdənt ˈट्राइडन्ट्/ *noun* [C] a weapon used in the past that looks like a long pole with three sharp metal points at one of its ends त्रिशूल

**trifle** /ˈtraɪfl ˈट्राइफ़्ल्/ *noun* **1** a trifle [*sing.*] (*formal*) slightly; rather हलका-सा, ज़रा; कुछ-कुछ **2** [C] something that is of little value or importance मूल्य या महत्त्व की दृष्टि से नगण्य, तुच्छ **3** [C, U] a type of **dessert** made from cake and fruit covered with a sweet yellow sauce (**custard**) and cream एक प्रकार का मधुर पकवान (कस्टर्ड और क्रीम से लिपटा केक या फल); ट्राइफ़ल

**trifling** /ˈtraɪflɪŋ ˈट्राइफ़्लिङ्/ *adj.* very small or unimportant छोटा-सा या महत्त्वहीन, मामूली

**trigger[1]** /ˈtrɪgə(r) ˈट्रिग(र्)/ *noun* [C] **1** the part of a gun that you press to fire it (बंदूक़ का) घोड़ा *to pull the trigger* **2** the cause of a particular reaction or event, especially a bad one विशेष प्रतिक्रिया या घटना (विशेषतः बुरी) का कारण बनना

**trigger[2]** /ˈtrɪgə(r) ˈट्रिग(र्)/ *verb* [T] **trigger sth (off)** to make sth happen suddenly अचानक कुछ करवा देना, किसी (प्रतिक्रिया को एकाएक प्रवर्तित करना) *Her cigarette smoke had triggered off the fire alarm.*

**trigonometry** /ˌtrɪgəˈnɒmətri ˌट्रिगˈनॉमट्रि/ *noun* [U] the type of mathematics that deals with the relationship between the sides and angles of triangles त्रिकोणमिति (गणित की एक शाखा जिसमें त्रिकोण की भुजाओं और कोणों के बीच संबंध की व्याख्या की जाती है) ▶ **trigonometric** /ˌtrɪgənəˈmetrɪk ˌट्रिगनˈमेट्रिक्/ *adj.* त्रिकोणमितीय ▶ **trigonometrical** /-kl -क्ल्/ *adj.* त्रिकोणमिति-विषयक

**trillion** /ˈtrɪljən ˈट्रिल्यन्/ *number* one million million एक लाख करोड़/दस खरब (की संख्या)

**NOTE** संख्याओं के वाक्य-प्रयोग के उदाहरणों के लिए **six** की प्रविष्टि देखिए। संख्याओं के विषय में अधिक जानकारी के लिए इस शब्दकोश के अंत में संख्या-संबंधी विशेष खंड देखिए।

**trilogy** /ˈtrɪlədʒi ˈट्रिलजि/ *noun* [C] (*pl.* **trilogies**) a group of three novels, plays, etc. that form a set तीन संबंधित उपन्यासों, नाटकों आदि का सेट (उपन्यास-त्रयी, नाटक-त्रयी आदि)

**trim[1]** /trɪm ट्रिम्/ *verb* [T] (**trimming; trimmed**) **1** to cut a small amount off sth so that it is tidy किसी चीज़ को काँट-छाँट कर सँवारना *to trim your hair/fringe/beard* ○ *The hedge needs trimming.* **2 trim sth (off sth)** to cut sth off because you do not need it अनावश्यक अंश को काटकर निकाल देना *Trim the fat off the meat.* **3 trim sth (with sth)** to decorate the edge of sth with sth किसी वस्तु के किनारे पर कुछ (गोटा-पट्टी आदि) लगाकर उसे सजाना ▶ **trim** *noun* [C, *usually sing.*] काँट-छाँट, छँटाई *My hair needs a trim.*

**trim[2]** /trɪm ट्रिम्/ *adj.* **1** (used about a person) looking thin, healthy and attractive (व्यक्ति) छरहरा, स्वस्थ और आकर्षक **2** well cared for; tidy सुव्यवस्थित; साफ़-सुथरा

**trimming** /ˈtrɪmɪŋ ˈट्रिमिङ्/ *noun* **1 trimmings** [*pl.*] extra things which you add to sth to improve its appearance, taste, etc. आकृति, स्वाद आदि को सुधारने के लिए प्रयुक्त अतिरिक्त वस्तुएँ, सौंदर्यवर्धक, स्वादवर्धक वस्तुएँ **2** [C, U] material that you use for decorating the edge of sth सजावट का सामान, गोटा-पट्टी आदि

**trinket** /ˈtrɪŋkɪt ˈट्रिङ्किट्/ *noun* [C] a piece of jewellery or small object for decoration that is not worth much money सस्ता गहना या सजावट की छोटी-मोटी चीज़

**trio** /ˈtriːəʊ ˈट्रीओ/ *noun* (*pl.* **trios**) **1** [C, *with sing. or pl. verb*] a group of three people who play music or sing together एक साथ गाने या बजाने वालों की तिकड़ी; त्रिवादक या त्रिगायक **2** [C] a piece of music for three people to play or sing त्रिवादकों या त्रिगायकों के लिए संगीत-रचना

**trip[1]** /trɪp ट्रिप्/ *noun* [C] a journey to a place and back again, either for pleasure or for a particular purpose मौजमस्ती के लिए या प्रयोजन-विशेष कहीं की यात्रा *to* ***go on a*** *business/shopping* ***trip*** ➪ **travel** पर नोट देखिए। ▶ **tripper** *noun* [C] सैलानी, पर्यटक *Kasauli was full of* ***day trippers*** (= people on trips that last for one day) *from Chandigarh.*

**trip[2]** /trɪp ट्रिप्/ *verb* (**tripping; tripped**) **1** [I] **trip (over/up); trip (over/on sth)** to catch your foot on sth when you are walking and fall or nearly fall (चलते हुए) किसी से ठोकर खा कर गिर जाना या गिरने लगना *Don't leave your bag on the floor. Someone might trip over it.* **2** [T] **trip sb (up)** to catch sb's foot and make him/her fall or nearly fall किसी को ठोकर मार कर पूरा या लगभग गिरा देना *Leena stuck out her foot and tripped Vikram up.*

**PHR V trip (sb) up** to make a mistake; to make sb say sth that he/she did not want to say ग़लती कर देना; किसी से (उसकी) अनचाही बात निकलवा लेना *The journalist asked a difficult question to try to trip the politician up.*

**tripartite** /traɪˈpɑːtaɪt ट्राइˈपाटाइट्/ *adj.* (*formal*) having three parts or involving three people, groups, etc. त्रिपक्षीय *tripartite discussions*

**tripe** /traɪp ट्राइप्/ *noun* [U] (*informal*) something that sb says or writes that you think is nonsense or not of good quality बेकार की या घटिया बात

**triple** /ˈtrɪpl ˈट्रिप्ल्/ *adj.* (*only before a noun*) having three parts, happening three times or containing three times as much as usual त्रिपक्षीय, तिगुना या तिगुने वाला *You'll receive triple pay if you work over the New Year.* ▶ **triple** *verb* [I, T] तिगुना होना या करना

**triple jump** *noun* [*sing.*] a sporting event in which people try to jump as far forward as possible with three jumps. The first jump lands on one foot, the second on the other foot, and the third on both feet तिकड़ी कूद (पहली कूद एक पैर पर, दूसरी दूसरे पैर पर और तीसरी दोनों पैरों पर होती है)

**triplet** /ˈtrɪplət ˈट्रिप्लट्/ *noun* [C] one of three children or animals that are born to one mother at the same time एक ही माँ के एक साथ हुए तीन बच्चों में से एक ➪ **twin** देखिए।

**triplicate** /ˈtrɪplɪkət ˈट्रिप्लिकट्/ *noun* [U]

IDM **in triplicate** **1** done three times तीन बार किया गया *Each sample was tested in triplicate.* **2** with three copies (for example of an official piece of paper) that are exactly the same (किसी प्रशासनिक पत्रादि की) हूबहू प्रतियाँ तीन नक़लों में *Fill out the forms in triplicate.* ➪ **duplicate** देखिए।

**tripod** /ˈtraɪpɒd ˈट्राइपॉड्/ *noun* [C] a piece of equipment with three legs that you use for putting a camera, etc. on (कैमरा आदि ऊपर रखने की) तिपाई; त्रिपाद ➪ **laboratory** पर चित्र देखिए।

**triumph**[1] /ˈtraɪʌmf ˈट्राइअम्फ़्/ *noun* [C, U] a great success or victory; the feeling of happiness that you have because of this महान सफलता या विजय; सफलता या विजय का उल्लास *The team returned home **in triumph**.*

**triumph**[2] /ˈtraɪʌmf ˈट्राइअम्फ़्/ *verb* [I] **triumph (over sb/sth)** to achieve success; to defeat sb/sth सफलता प्राप्त करना; किसी व्यक्ति या वस्तु को हराना *India triumphed over Australia in the final.*

**triumphal** /traɪˈʌmfl ट्राइˈअम्फ़्ल्/ *adj.* (*usually before a noun*) done or made in order to celebrate a great success or victory महान सफलता या विजय को मनाने के लिए किया या बनाया गया; सफलतासूचक या विजयसूचक

**triumphant** /traɪˈʌmfənt ट्राइˈअम्फ़न्ट्/ *adj.* feeling or showing great happiness because you have won or succeeded at sth विजय या सफलता की प्राप्ति पर अत्यंत प्रसन्न; विजयोल्लसित ▶ **triumphantly** *adv.* विजयोल्लास के साथ

**trivia** /ˈtrɪviə ˈट्रिविआ/ *noun* [U] **1** unimportant matters, details or information महत्त्वहीन बातें, विवरण या जानकारी; तुच्छताएँ *He has a fantastic knowledge of cricket trivia.* **2** (*usually in compounds*) facts about many subjects that are used in a game to test people's knowledge विभिन्न विषयों के तथ्य जिससे खेल द्वारा लोगों का ज्ञान जाँचते हैं *a trivia quiz*

**trivial** /ˈtrɪviəl ˈट्रिविअल्/ *adj.* of little importance; not worth considering महत्त्वहीन, मामूली; नगण्य, तुच्छ *a trivial detail/problem* ▶ **triviality** /ˌtrɪviˈæləti ˌट्रिविˈऐलटि/ *noun* [C, U] (*pl.* **trivialities**) नगण्यता, तुच्छता, तुच्छ बात

**trivialize** (*also* **-ise**) /ˈtrɪviəlaɪz ˈट्रिविअलाइज़्/ *verb* [T] to make sth seem less important, serious, etc. than it really is किसी वस्तु का महत्त्व, गंभीरता आदि घटा देना

**trod** ➪ **tread**[1] का past tense रूप

**trodden** ➪ **tread**[1] का past participle रूप

**trolley** /ˈtrɒli ˈट्रॉलि/ *noun* [C] **1** (*AmE* **cart**) a piece of equipment on wheels that you use for carrying things सामान ढोने की हाथगाड़ी; ट्रॉली *a supermarket/shopping/luggage trolley* **2** a small table with wheels that is used for carrying or serving food and drinks (खाने-पीने का सामान ले जाने या परोसने के लिए प्रयुक्त) पहिएदार छोटी मेज़ *a tea/sweet/drinks trolley* **3** = **tram**

**trombone** /trɒmˈbəʊn ट्रॉम्ˈबोन्/ *noun* [C] a large metal (**brass**) musical instrument that you play by blowing into it and moving a long tube backwards and forwards फूँक कर बजाया जाने वाला तुरही जैसा पीतल का बाजा, पतली तुरही; ट्रॉमबोन

**troop** /tru:p ट्रूप्/ *noun* **1 troops** [*pl.*] soldiers सेना, फ़ौज **2** [C] a large group of people or animals मनुष्यों या पशुओं का बड़ा दल; टोली ▶ **troop** *verb* [I] दल, टोली बना कर आना *When the bell rang everyone trooped into the hall.*

**trophic level** /ˌtrɒfɪk ˈlevl ˌट्रॉफ़िक् ˈलेव़्ल्/ *noun* [C] each of several levels in an **ecosystem**. Each level consists of living creatures that share the same function in the **food chain** and get their food from the same source क्षेत्र-विशेष के पशुओं और पौधों की, तथा परिवेश से उनके संबंध की व्यवस्था (परिस्थिति तंत्र) के विभिन्न स्तरों में से प्रत्येक स्तर (प्रत्येक स्तर में रहने वाले समस्त प्राणियों की आहार-श्रृंखला और आहार-स्रोत समान होते हैं)

**trophy** /ˈtrəʊfi ˈट्रोफ़ि/ *noun* [C] (*pl.* **trophies**) a large silver cup, etc. that you get for winning a competition or race ट्रॉफ़ी, विजयोपहार (एक बड़ा चाँदी का प्याला आदि)

**tropic** /ˈtrɒpɪk ˈट्रॉपिक्/ *noun* **1** [C, *usually sing.*] one of the two lines around the earth that are 23° 27' north (**the Tropic of Cancer**) and south (**the Tropic of Capricorn**) of the line around the middle of the earth (**the equator**) भूमध्यरेखा के 23° 27' उत्तर या दक्षिण की निश्चित अक्षांश रेखा (उत्तर में कर्क रेखा—the Tropic of Cancer तथा दक्षिण में मकर रेखा—the Tropic of Capricorn) ➪ **earth** पर चित्र देखिए। **2 the tropics** [*pl.*] the part of the world that is between these two lines, where the climate is hot and wet इन रेखाओं के बीच का भू-प्रदेश (जहाँ जलवायु गरम और नम होती है); उष्णकटिबंध ▶ **tropical** /ˈtrɒpɪkl ˈट्रॉपिकल्/ *adj.* उष्णकटिबंधीय *tropical fruit*

**troposphere** /ˈtrɒpəsfɪə(r) ˈट्रॉपस्फ़िअ(र्)/ *noun* [*sing.*] **the troposphere** (*technical*) the lowest layer of the earth's atmosphere, between the surface of the earth and about 6 to 10 kilometres above the surface पृथ्वी के वायुमंडल (पृथ्वी की सतह से 6 से 10 किलामीटर ऊपर तक का भाग) की निम्नतम परत; क्षोभमंडल ➪ **ionosphere** और **stratosphere** देखिए तथा **mesosphere** पर चित्र देखिए।

**trot**[1] /trɒt ट्रॉट्/ *verb* (**trotting; trotted**) [I] **1** (used about a horse and its rider) to move forward at a speed that is faster than a walk (घोड़े और घुड़सवार का) दुलकी चाल-चलना (उछल-उछल कर मध्यम गति से चलना) ➪ **canter** और **gallop** देखिए। **2** (used about a person or an animal) to walk fast, taking short quick steps (व्यक्ति या पशु का) तेज़ चलना (छोटे डग भरते हुए)

**PHR V trot sth out** (*informal*) to repeat an old idea rather than thinking of sth new to say (किसी नई बात के बजाय) पुरानी बात दोहराना *to trot out the same old story*

**trot**[2] /trɒt ट्रॉट्/ *noun* [*sing.*] a speed that is faster than a walk मध्यम गति

**IDM on the trot** (*informal*) one after another; without stopping एक के बाद दूसरा; बिना रुके, निरंतर *We worked for six hours on the trot.*

**trotter** /ˈtrɒtə(r) ˈट्रॉट(र्)/ *noun* [C] a pig's foot सूअर का पैर

**trouble**[1] /ˈtrʌbl ˈट्रबल्/ *noun* **1** [U, C] **trouble (with sb/sth)** (a situation that causes) a problem, difficulty or worry समस्या, कठिनाई या चिंता (उत्पन्न करने वाली स्थिति) ***be in trouble*** ○ *I'm **having trouble** getting the car started.* ○ *financial troubles* **2** [U] extra work or effort अतिरिक्त काम या प्रयास, परेशानी *Let's eat out tonight. It will **save** you **the trouble** of cooking.* ○ *I'm sorry to **put** you **to** so much **trouble**.* **3** [C, U] a situation where people are fighting or arguing with each other झगड़ा-फ़साद, झंझट *There's often trouble in town on Saturday night after the shops have closed.* **4** [U] illness or pain बीमारी या तकलीफ़ *back/heart trouble*

**IDM ask for trouble** ➪ **ask** देखिए।

**get into trouble** to get into a situation which is dangerous or in which you may be punished किसी मुसीबत में फँस जाना

**go to a lot of trouble (to do sth)** to put a lot of work or effort into sth किसी काम में बहुत मेहनत करना *They went to a lot of trouble to make us feel welcome.*

**take trouble over/with sth; take trouble to do sth/doing sth** to do sth with care बहुत सावधानी से कोई काम करना

**take the trouble to do sth** to do sth even though it means extra work or effort काफ़ी कष्ट उठाकर कोई काम करना

**trouble**[2] /ˈtrʌbl ˈट्रबल्/ *verb* [T] **1** to make sb worried, upset, etc. किसी को चिंतित, परेशान आदि कर देना *Is there something troubling you?* **2** (*formal*) **trouble sb (for sth)** (used when you are politely asking sb for sth or to do sth) to disturb sb (नम्रतापूर्वक अनुरोध करने के लिए प्रयुक्त) किसी को कष्ट देना *Sorry to trouble you, but would you mind answering a few questions?* ✪ पर्याय **bother**

**troublemaker** /ˈtrʌblmeɪkə(r) ˈट्रबल्मेक(र्)/ *noun* [C] a person who often deliberately causes trouble मुसीबत पैदा करने वाला व्यक्ति; उपद्रवी

**troubleshoot** /ˈtrʌblʃuːt ˈट्रबल्शूट्/ *verb* [I] **1** to solve problems for an organization किसी संस्था की समस्याओं को हल करना **2** to find and correct faults in an electronic system or a machine किसी विद्युत प्रणाली या मशीन की त्रुटि को सुधारना ▶ **troubleshooter** *noun* [C] समस्या-निवारक या त्रुटि-सुधारक व्यक्ति

**troublesome** /ˈtrʌblsəm ˈट्रबल्सम्/ *adj.* causing trouble, pain, etc. over a long period of time (लंबे समय तक) कष्टकर, पीड़ादायक

**trough** /trɒf ट्रॉफ़्/ *noun* [C] **1** a long narrow container from which farm animals eat or drink (पशुओं को खिलाने या पिलाने की) नाँद, कुंड, द्रोण, द्रोणिका **2** a low area or point, between two higher areas दो ऊँचे क्षेत्रों के बीच एक नीचा क्षेत्र या बिंदु; गर्त ➪ **glacial** पर चित्र देखिए।

**trounce** /ˈtraʊns ˈट्राउन्स्/ *verb* [T] (*written*) to defeat sb completely किसी को बुरी तरह हराना, पराजित करना *Italy trounced France 6–1 in the World Cup finals.*

**trousers** /ˈtraʊzəz ˈट्राउज़ज़्/ (*AmE* **pants**) *noun* [*pl.*] a piece of clothing that covers the whole of both your legs पतलून, पैंट

NOTE **Trousers** अपने में बहुवचनांत शब्द है, अतः 'a new trouser' जैसा प्रयोग मान्य नहीं है, मान्य प्रयोग हैं—*I need some new trousers.* ○ *I need a new pair of trousers.* तथापि अन्य संज्ञा से पहले **trouser**(एकवचन) का प्रयोग ठीक है—*a trouser suit* (= a woman's suit consisting of a jacket and trousers).

**trout** /traʊt ट्राउट्/ *noun* [C, U] (*pl.* **trout**) a type of fish that lives in rivers and that we eat (नदी में रहने वाली) एक प्रकार की खाने की मछली

**trowel** /ˈtraʊəl ˈट्राउअल्/ *noun* [C] **1** a small garden tool with a short handle and a curved part for lifting plants, digging small holes, etc. माली द्वारा प्रयुक्त खुरपी जैसा औज़ार ➪ **gardening** पर चित्र देखिए। **2** a small tool with a short handle and a flat metal part used in building for spreading cement, etc. करनी, कन्नी (राज मिस्त्री द्वारा मकान बनाने में प्रयुक्त औज़ार)

**truant** /ˈtru:ənt ˈट्रूअन्ट्/ *noun* [C] a child who stays away from school without permission स्कूल से भागने वाला बच्चा, पढ़ाईचोर बालक ▶ **truancy** /-ənsi -अन्सि/ *noun* [U] पलायनशीलता

IDM **play truant;** (*AmE* **play hooky**) to stay away from school without permission स्कूल से भागे रहना, पढ़ाई चोरी

**truce** /tru:s ट्रूस्/ *noun* [C] an agreement to stop fighting for a period of time (अस्थायी) युद्धविराम ➪ **ceasefire** देखिए।

**truck** /trʌk ट्रक्/ *noun* [C] **1** (*AmE* **lorry**) ट्रक *a truck driver* **2** (*BrE*) a section of a train that is used for carrying goods or animals सामान या पशु ले जाने वाले रेलगाड़ी के डिब्बे *a cattle truck*

**trudge** /trʌdʒ ट्रज्/ *verb* [I] to walk with slow, heavy steps, for example because you are very tired थकावट के कारण धीरे-धीरे चलना

**true** /tru: ट्रू/ *adj.* **1** right or correct ठीक या सही *I didn't think the film was at all **true to life*** (= it didn't show life as it really is). ○ *Read the statements and decide if they are true or false.* ✪ विलोम **untrue** या **false** **2** real or genuine, often when this is different from how sth seems वास्तविक या प्रामाणिक *The novel was based on **a true story**.* ✪ विलोम **false** **3** having all the typical qualities of the thing mentioned जैसा बताया ठीक वैसा, सच्चा *How do you know when you have found **true love**?* **4 true (to sb/sth)** behaving as expected or as promised आशा या वायदे के अनुसार आचरण करते हुए *He was **true to his word*** (= he did what he had promised). ○ *a true friend* ➪ **truth** noun देखिए।

IDM **come true** to happen in the way you hoped or dreamed आशा या कल्पना के अनुसार घटित होना, आशा या स्वप्न का साकार होना *My dream has come true!*

**too good to be true** used to say that you cannot believe that sth/sb is as good as it/he/she seems अविश्वसनीय रूप से अच्छा

**true to form** typical; as usual व्यक्ति या वस्तु के विशेष लक्षणों वाला, अपने ढंग का; रोज़मर्रा की तरह

**true north** *noun* [U] (*technical*) north according to the earth's **axis** पृथ्वी के अक्ष के अनुसार उत्तर दिशा ➪ **magnetic north** देखिए।

**truly** /ˈtru:li ˈट्रूलि/ *adv.* **1** (used to emphasize a feeling, statement) really; completely (किसी मनोभाव और वक्तव्य पर बल देने के लिए प्रयुक्त) वस्तुतः, सचमुच; पूर्णतः, पूरी तरह से *We are truly grateful to you for your help.* **2** used to emphasize that sth is correct or accurate किसी बात के सही या यथार्थ या सुनिश्चित होने पर बल देने के लिए प्रयुक्त *I cannot truly say that I was surprised at the news.*

IDM **well and truly** ➪ **well**[1] देखिए।

**trump** /trʌmp ट्रम्प्/ *noun* [C] (in some card games) a card of the chosen set (**suit**) that has a higher value than cards of the other three sets during a particular game (ताश के कुछ खेलों में) तुरूप, रंग का पत्ता (वह पत्ता जिसे अन्य पत्तों से बड़ा मान लिया जाता है) *Spades are trumps.*

**trump card** *noun* [C] a special advantage you have over other people that you keep secret until you can surprise them with (स्पर्धा की स्थिति में) किसी को विशेष लाभ प्रदान करने वाली कोई वस्तु, क्रिया आदि (जिसका वह एकाएक प्रयोग करे), तुरूप का पत्ता, ट्रंप कार्ड *It was time for her to **play** her **trump card**.*

**trumpet**[1] /ˈtrʌmpɪt ˈट्रम्पिट्/ *noun* [C] a metal (**brass**) musical instrument that you play by blowing into it. There are three buttons on it which you press to make different notes तुरही (पीतल से बना फूँक मार कर बजाया जाने वाला बाजा, जिस पर स्वर-परिवर्तन के लिए तीन बटन लगे होते हैं) ➪ पृष्ठ 789 पर चित्र देखिए।

**trumpet**[2] /ˈtrʌmpɪt ˈट्रम्पिट्/ *verb* **1** [I] to play a trumpet तुरही बजाना **2** [T] **trumpet sth (as sth)** to talk about sth publicly in a proud or an enthusiastic way (सार्वजनिक रूप से) ढिंढोरा पीटना *to trumpet sb's achievements* **3** [I] (of a large animal, especially an elephant) to make a loud noise (स्थूल पशु, विशेषतः हाथी की) चिंघाड़

**truncate** /trʌŋˈkeɪt ट्रङ्'केट्/ *verb* [T] (*usually passive*) (*formal*) to make sth shorter, especially by cutting off the top or end किसी वस्तु को आकार में छोटा करना (विशेषतः आरंभिक या अंतिम अंश काटकर)

**truncheon** /ˈtrʌntʃən ˈट्रन्चन्/ (*BrE*) (*also* **baton**) *noun* [C] (*old-fashioned*) a short thick stick that a police officer carries as a weapon पुलिस अधिकारी द्वारा हथियार की तरह प्रयुक्त छोटी पतली छड़ी

**trundle** /ˈtrʌndl ˈट्रन्ड्ल्/ *verb* [I, T] to move, or make sth heavy move, slowly and noisily किसी भारी वस्तु का (आवाज़ करते हुए) लुढ़कना या उसे लुढ़काना *A lorry trundled down the hill.*

**trunk** /trʌŋk ट्रङ्क्/ *noun* **1** [C] the thick central part of a tree that the branches grow from वृक्ष का तना **2** [C] (*AmE*) = **boot**[1] **2** **3** [C] an elephant's long nose हाथी की सूँड़ **4 trunks** [*pl.*] = **swimming trunks** **5** [C] a large box that you use for storing or transporting things बड़ा बक्सा, ट्रंक **6** [C, *usually sing.*] the main part of your body (not including your head, arms and legs) शरीर का मध्य भाग, धड़ (जिसमें सिर, बाहें और टाँगें नहीं आती)

**trunk call** *noun* [C] (*old-fashioned*) a long distance phone call ट्रंक कॉल; लंबी दूरी की कॉल

**trunk road** *noun* [C] (*BrE*) an important main road; a highway मुख्य मार्ग; राजमार्ग

**trust**[1] /trʌst ट्रस्ट्/ *noun* **1** [U] **trust (in sb/sth)** the belief that sb is good, honest, sincere, etc. and will not try to harm or trick you किसी पर विश्वास, भरोसा (उसके भला, ईमानदार आदि होने का निश्चय) *Our marriage is based on love and trust. I should never have **put my trust in** him.* ➪ **distrust** और **mistrust** देखिए। **2** [C, U] a legal arrangement by which a person or organization looks after money and property for sb else until that person is old enough to control it ट्रस्ट, न्यास (किसी अन्य व्यक्ति की संपति की देखभाल के लिए, उसके बड़ा होने तक, की गई वैधानिक व्यवस्था)

IDM **take sth on trust** to believe what sb says without having proof that it is true कहने भर से किसी की बात को सच मान लेना *I can't prove it. You must take it on trust.*

**trust**[2] /trʌst ट्रस्ट्/ *verb* [T] **trust sb (to do sth); trust sb (with sth)** to believe that sb is good, sincere, honest, etc. and that he/she will not trick you or try to harm you किसी पर विश्वास या भरोसा करना (उसके भला, ईमानदार आदि होने के विषय में निश्चित होना) *You can't trust her with money.* ○ *I don't trust that dog. It looks dangerous.* ➪ **mistrust** और **distrust** देखिए।

IDM **Trust sb (to do sth)** (*spoken*) it is typical of sb to do sth किसी का केवल अपनी-सी करना *Trust Amisha to be late. She's never on time!*

**trustee** /trʌˈstiː ट्र'स्टी/ *noun* [C] a person who looks after money or property for sb else किसी अन्य व्यक्ति की संपति की देखभाल करने वाला व्यक्ति; ट्रस्टी, न्यासी

**trusting** /ˈtrʌstɪŋ ˈट्रस्टिङ्/ *adj.* believing that other people are good, sincere, honest, etc. दूसरों पर विश्वास करने वाला; विश्वासी

**trustworthy** /ˈtrʌstwɜːði ˈट्रस्ट्वद़्दि/ *adj.* that you can depend on to be good, sincere, honest, etc. विश्वास-योग्य, विश्वसनीय, भरोसेमंद

**truth** /truːθ ट्रूथ्/ *noun* (*pl.* **truths** /truːðz ट्रूद्ज़्/) **1 the truth** [*sing.*] what is true; the facts सत्य, सच्चाई, यथार्थता; सच्ची बातें, तथ्य *Please **tell me the truth**.* ○ ***the whole truth*** **2** [U] the state or quality of being true सत्यता, सच्चाई, असलियत, वास्तविकता *There's a lot of truth in what she says.* **3** [C] a fact or an idea that is believed by most people to be true वास्तविक तथ्य या सत्य धारणा *scientific/universal truths* ➪ **true** adjective देखिए।

**truthful** /ˈtruːθfl ˈट्रूथ्फ़ल्/ *adj.* **1 truthful (about sth)** (used about a person) who tells the truth; honest (व्यक्ति) सच्चा, सत्यवादी, सत्यनिष्ठ; ईमानदार *I don't think you're being truthful with me.* **2** (used about a statement) true or correct (वक्तव्य) सत्य या सही *a truthful account* ▶ **truthfully** /-fəli -फ़लि/ *adv.* सत्यनिष्ठापूर्वक, सचाई से

**try**[1] /traɪ ट्राइ/ *verb* (*pres. part.* **trying;** *3rd person sing. pres.* **tries;** *pt, pp* **tried**) **1** [I] **try (to do sth)** to make an effort to do sth (कुछ करने का) प्रयत्न करना *I tried to phone you but I couldn't get through.* ○ *She was **trying hard** not to laugh.*

> NOTE **Try to** की अपेक्षा **try and** अधिक अनौपचारिक है। इसका भूतकाल में प्रयोग नहीं किया जा सकता—*I'll try and get there on time.* ○ *I tried to get there on time, but I was too late.*

**2** [T] **try (doing) sth** to do, use or test sth in order to see how good or successful it is किसी चीज़ को आज़माना, परखना (कि वह कितनी अच्छी या कारगर है) *Have you ever tried raw fish?* ○ *We tried the door but it was locked.* **3** [T] **try sb (for sth)** to examine sb in a court of law in order to decide if he/she is guilty of a crime or not न्यायालय का किसी पर लगाए गए अभियोग की जाँच करना *He was tried for murder.*

IDM **try your hand at sth** to do sth such as an activity or a sport for the first time किसी काम या चीज़

पर हाथ आज़माना, किसी काम को पहली बार करके देखना **PHR V** **try sth on** to put on a piece of clothing to see if it fits you properly किसी कपड़े को पहन कर देखना (उसकी फ़िटिंग जाँचने के लिए) *Can I try these jeans on, please?*

**try sb/sth out** to test sb/sth to find out if he/she/it is good enough किसी व्यक्ति या वस्तु की (कार्य-विशेष के लिए) उपयुक्तता की जाँच करना

**try**[2] /traɪ ट्राइ/ *noun* [C] (*pl.* **tries**) an occasion when you try to do sth; an attempt कुछ करने का प्रयत्न; प्रयास, कोशिश *I don't know if I can move it by myself, but I'll* ***give it a try****.*

**trying** /ˈtraɪɪŋ ˈट्राइइङ्/ *adj.* that makes you tired or angry थकाऊ या खिजाऊ *a trying journey*

**tryst** /trɪst ट्रिस्ट्/ *noun* [C] (*literary* or *humorous*) an appointed meeting especially between lovers पूर्वनिश्चित गुप्त भेंट (प्रायः प्रेमियों की); अभिसार

**tsar** (*also* **tzar, czar**) /zɑ:(r) ज़ार(र्)/ *noun* [C] the title of the **emperor** of Russia in the past विगत में रूस के सम्राट की पदवी; ज़ार

**tsarina** (*also* **tzarina, czarina**) /zɑ:ˈri:nə ज़ाˈरीना/ *noun* [C] the title of the **empress** of Russia in the past विगत में रूस की साम्राज्ञी की पदवी; ज़ारीना

**tsetse** /ˈtetsi ˈट्रेट्सि/ (*also* **tsetse fly**) *noun* [C] an African fly that bites humans and animals and drinks their blood and can spread a serious disease (**sleeping sickness**) (मनुष्यों और पशुओं को काटने और उनका ख़ून पीने वाली) एक अफ़्रीक़ी मक्खी (जिसका शिकार 'निद्रा रोग' से ग्रस्त हो जाता है)

**T-shirt** (*also* **teeshirt**) /ˈti:ʃɜ:t ˈटीशर्ट्/ *noun* [C] a shirt with short sleeves and without buttons or a collar टी-शर्ट (आधे आस्तीन की बिना बटन या कॉलर की कमीज़)

**tsp** *abbr.* teaspoonful(s) चम्मच भर *Add 1 tsp salt.*

**T-square** *noun* [C] a plastic or metal instrument in the shape of a T for drawing or measuring **right angles** समकोण खींचने या मापने का T के आकार का प्लास्टिक या धातु खंड

**tsunami** /tsu:ˈnɑ:mi सूˈनामि/ *noun* [C] (*technical*) a very large wave in the sea which destroys things when it reaches the land, and is often caused by movements under the surface of the earth (**an earthquake**) (प्रायः समुद्र में भूकंप आने से उत्पन्न) विशाल और विनाशकारी लहर; सुनामी

> **NOTE** इसके लिए कम औपचारिक शब्द **tidal wave** है।

**tub** /tʌb टब्/ *noun* [C] **1** a large round container टब (बड़ा गोल या अंडाकार पात्र) **2** a small plastic container with a lid that is used for holding food खाद्य वस्तुएँ रखने का प्लास्टिक का छोटा ढक्कनदार पात्र *a tub of margarine/ice cream*

**tuba** /ˈtju:bə ˈट्यूबा/ *noun* [C] a large metal (**brass**) musical instrument that makes a low sound पीतल का एक बड़ा वाद्य (जिसकी आवाज़ धीमी होती है); टूबा

**tube** /tju:b ट्यूब्/ *noun* **1** [C] a long empty pipe लंबी खाली नली; ट्यूब *Blood flowed along the tube into the bottle.* ○ *the inner tube of a bicycle tyre* ➪ **test tube** देखिए। **2** [C] **a tube (of sth)** a long thin container made of soft plastic or metal with a lid at one end. Tubes are used for holding thick liquids that can be squeezed out of them मुलायम प्लास्टिक या धातु की ढक्कनदार लंबा पात्र; ट्यूब, टूथपेस्ट आदि की ट्यूब *a tube of toothpaste* **3 the tube** [*sing.*] (*BrE informal*) = **underground**[3]

**tuber** /ˈtju:bə(r) ˈट्यूब(र्)/ *noun* [C] the short thick round part of some plants, such as potatoes, which grows under the ground कंद (जैसे आलू) (जो ज़मीन के नीचे होता है)

**tuberculosis** /tju:ˌbɜ:kjuˈləʊsɪs ट्यूˌबक्युˈलोसिस्/ *noun* [U] (*abbr.* **TB**) a serious disease that affects the lungs क्षय रोग, टीबी

**tubing** /ˈtju:bɪŋ ˈट्यूबिङ्/ *noun* [U] a long piece of metal, rubber, etc. in the shape of a tube ट्यूब के आकार का लंबा धातु, रबड़ आदि का टुकड़ा ➪ **laboratory** पर चित्र देखिए।

**tuck** /tʌk टक्/ *verb* [T] **1 tuck sth in, under, round, etc. (sth)** to put or fold the ends or edges of sth into or round sth else so that it looks tidy किसी वस्तु को मोड़कर या उसकी तह बनाकर किसी अन्य वस्तु के अंदर डालना या उसके चारों ओर लपेटना (ताकि वह सँभल जाए) *Tuck your shirt in—it looks untidy like that.* **2 tuck sth (away)** to put sth into a small space, especially to hide it or to keep it safe किसी वस्तु को कहीं छिपाकर या सँभालकर रखना *The letter was tucked behind a pile of books.*

**PHR V** **tuck sth away** **1** (*only in the passive form*) to be situated in a quiet place; to be hidden शोर-गुल से दूर जगह पर स्थित होना; छिपा होना *The house was tucked away among the trees.* **2** to hide sth somewhere; to keep sth in a safe place किसी वस्तु को कहीं छिपा देना; किसी वस्तु को किसी सुरक्षित स्थान पर रख देना *He tucked his wallet away in his inside pocket.*

**tuck sb in/up** to make sb feel comfortable in bed by pulling the covers up around him/her लिहाफ़ आदि लपेटकर बिस्तर में आराम फ़रमाना

**tuck in; tuck into sth** (*BrE*) (*spoken*) to eat with pleasure मज़ा ले-ले कर खाना

**Tue.** (*also* **Tues.**) *abbr.* Tuesday मंगलवार *Tue. 9 March*

**Tuesday** /ˈtjuːzdeɪ; -di ˈट्यूज़्डे; -डि/ *noun* [C, U] (*abbr.* **Tue., Tues.**) the day of the week after Monday मंगलवार

**NOTE** लिखने में दिनों के नाम का पहला अक्षर बड़ा होता है। इन नामों के वाक्य-प्रयोग के उदाहरणों के लिए **Monday** की प्रविष्टि देखिए।

**tuft** /tʌft टफ़्ट्/ *noun* [C] a small amount of hair, grass, etc. growing together बाल, घास आदि का गुच्छा

**tug[1]** /tʌg टग्/ *verb* [I, T] (**tugging; tugged**) **tug (at/on sth)** to pull sth hard and quickly, often several times किसी वस्तु को झटके से खींचना (प्रायः अनेक बार) *The little boy tugged at his father's trouser leg.*

**tug[2]** /tʌg टग्/ *noun* [C] **1** a sudden hard pull झटका *She gave the rope a tug.* **2** (*also* **tugboat**) a small powerful boat that is used for pulling ships into a port, etc. जहाज़ों को खींचकर बंदरगाह आदि पर जाने वाली छोटी शक्तिशाली नाव, कर्षण-नौका; टगबोट ➪ **boat** पर चित्र देखिए।

**tuition** /tjuˈɪʃn ट्यूˈइश्न्/ *noun* [U] **tuition (in sth)** teaching, especially to a small group of people किसी विषय में ट्यूशन देना, उसे पढ़ाना (विशेषतः छोटे समूह को) *tuition fees/private tuition*

**tulip** /ˈtjuːlɪp ˈट्यूलिप्/ *noun* [C] a brightly coloured flower, shaped like a cup, that grows in the spring वसंत ऋतु में खिलने वाला कप के आकार का चमकदार फूल; ट्यूलिप

**tulsi** *noun* [C] a kind of basil (**herb**) cultivated in India and considered sacred by the Hindus तुलसी

**tumble** /ˈtʌmbl ˈटम्बल्/ *verb* [I] **1** to fall down suddenly but without serious injury (लड़खड़ाकर) एकाएक गिर पड़ना (बिना अधिक चोट खाए) *He tripped and tumbled all the way down the steps.* **2** to fall suddenly in value or amount क़ीमत (का) गिर जाना या मात्रा (का) घट जाना *House prices have tumbled.* **3** to move in a particular direction in an untidy way अव्यवस्थित ढंग से दिशा-विशेष में गति करना *She opened her suitcase and all her things tumbled out of it.* ▶ **tumble** *noun* [C] लड़खड़ाहट, गिरावट, अवपात

**PHR V** **tumble down** to fall down; to collapse नीचे गिर पड़ना; ढह जाना *The walls of the old house were tumbling down.*

**tumble-dryer** (*also* **tumble-drier**) *noun* [C] (*BrE*) a machine that dries clothes by moving them about in hot air गरम हवा के झोंकों से कपड़े सुखाने वाली मशीन

**tumbler** /ˈtʌmblə(r) ˈटम्ब्ल(र्)/ *noun* [C] a tall glass for drinking out of with straight sides and no handle (पानी आदि पीने का) ऊँचा गिलास (बिना मूठ का, सीधे पार्श्वों वाला)

**tummy** /ˈtʌmi ˈटमि/ *noun* [C] (*pl.* **tummies**) (*informal*) = **stomach[1]**

**tumour** (*AmE* **tumor**) /ˈtjuːmə(r) ˈट्यूम(र्)/ *noun* [C] a mass of cells that are not growing normally in the body as the result of a disease रोगाक्रांत शरीर (के किसी भाग) में ऊतकों की असामान्य वृद्धि, गाँठ, रसौली, अर्बुद, ट्यूमर *a brain tumour*

**tumultuous** /tjuːˈmʌltʃuəs ट्यूˈमल्चुअस्/ *adj.* very noisy, because people are excited कोलाहलपूर्ण, हुल्लड़-भरा (लोगों के उत्तेजित होने के कारण) *tumultuous applause*

**tuna** /ˈtjuːnə ˈट्यूना/ (*also* **tuna fish**) *noun* [C, U] (*pl.* **tuna**) a large sea fish that we eat खाने की बड़ी समुद्री मछली; ट्यूना *a tin of tuna*

**tundra** /ˈtʌndrə ˈटन्ड्रा/ *noun* [U] (in geography) the large flat Arctic regions of northern Europe, Asia and North America where no trees grow and where the soil below the surface of the ground is always frozen (भूगोल में) (यूरोप, एशिया और उत्तरी अमेरिका के) उत्तरी ध्रुव क्षेत्रों का वृक्षविहीन बर्फ़ीला विस्तृत प्रदेश; टुंड्रा

**tune[1]** /tjuːn ट्यून्/ *noun* [C, U] a series of musical notes that are sung or played to form a piece of music संगीत की कोई धुन, राग *Reena played us a tune on the piano.*

**IDM** **call the shots/tune** ➪ **call[1]** देखिए।

**change your tune** ➪ **change[1]** देखिए।

**in/out of tune** **1** at/not at the correct musical level (**pitch**) सही या ग़लत लय में, लयपूर्वक या लयहीन होकर, सुरभरा या बेसुरा *You're singing out of tune.* **2** having/not having the same opinions, interests, feelings, etc. as sb/sth विचारों, रुचियों, भावनाओं आदि की दृष्टि से एक जैसे या अलग-अलग

**tune[2]** /tjuːn ट्यून्/ *verb* **1** [T] to make small changes to the sound a musical instrument makes so that it is at the correct musical level (**pitch**) वाद्य यंत्र के सुर मिलाना (उसे) समस्वरित या ट्यून करना (स्वर की ऊँचाई के सही स्तर पर लाने के लिए उन्हें ठीक करना) *to tune a piano/guitar* **2** [T] to make small changes to an engine so that it runs well इंजन को ट्यून करना (इंजन सही ढंग से चले, इसके लिए उसे ठीक करना) **3** [T] (*usually passive*) **tune sth (in) (to sth)** to move the controls on a radio or television so that you can receive a particular station रेडियो या टीवी को ट्यून करना (स्टेशन-विशेष से जुड़ने के लिए रेडियो या टीवी सेट को व्यवस्थित करना) *The radio was tuned (in) to All India Radio.* ○ (*spoken*) ***Stay tuned for*** *the latest news.*

**PHR V** **tune in (to sth)** to listen to a radio programme or watch a television programme किसी रेडियो कार्यक्रम को सुनना या टीवी प्रसारण को देखना **tune (sth) up** to make small changes to a group of musical instruments so that they sound pleasant when played together (सितार, तबले आदि) वाद्य यंत्रों को, एक साथ बजने की दुष्टि से, समस्वरित करना, उनका सुर मिलाना

**tuneful** /ˈtju:nfl ˈट्यूनफ़्ल्/ *adj.* (used about music) pleasant to listen to (संगीत) सुनने में रुचिकर; श्रुतिमधुर

**tungsten** /ˈtʌŋstən ˈटङ्स्टन्/ *noun* [U] (*symbol* **W**) a very hard silver-grey metal, used especially in making steel and in **filaments** for **light bulbs** टंग्स्टन (एक कड़ा हलके स्लेटी रंग का धातु, इस्पात और बिजली के बल्बों के तार बनाने में प्रयुक्त) ➪ **bulb** पर चित्र देखिए।

**tunic** *noun* [C] **1** a piece of women's clothing, usually without sleeves, that is long and not tight महिलाओं की एक पोशाक (प्रायः बिना आस्तीन की, लंबी और ढीली); ट्यूनिक **2** (*BrE*) the jacket that is part of the uniform of a police officer, soldier, etc. पुलिस अफ़सर, सैनिक आदि की वरदी के साथ की जैकेट; ट्यूनिक

**tuning fork** *noun* [C] a U-shaped metal device that produces a fixed tone when struck स्वरित द्विभुज

**tunnel** /ˈtʌnl ˈटन्ल्/ *noun* [C] a passage under the ground सुरंग, भूमिगत पथ (ज़मीन के नीचे का रास्ता) *The train disappeared into a tunnel.* ▶ **tunnel** *verb* [I, T] (**tunnelling; tunnelled** *AmE* **tunneling; tunneled**) सुरंग बनना या बनाना

**turban** /ˈtɜ:bən ˈटबन्/ *noun* [C] a covering for the head worn especially by Sikh and Muslim men. A turban is made by folding a long piece of cloth around the head पगड़ी, साफ़ा

**turbine** /ˈtɜ:baɪn ˈटबाइन्/ *noun* [C] a machine or an engine that receives its power from a wheel that is turned by the pressure of water, air or gas टरबाइन (मशीन या इंजन, जो पानी, वायु, गैस के दाब से चलने वाले पहिए से संचालित होता है) *a wind turbine* ➪ **generator** पर चित्र देखिए।

**turbocharger** /ˈtɜ:bəʊtʃɑ:dʒə(r) ˈटबोचाज(र्)/ (*also* **turbo** ˈtɜ:bəʊ ˈटबो/) *noun* [C] a system in a car that sends a mixture of petrol and air into the engine at high pressure, making it more powerful टर्बो, कार इंजन की विशेष प्रणाली (जिसमें पेट्रोल और वायु का मिश्रण ऊँचे दाब पर इंजन में जाकर उसकी शक्ति को बढ़ा देता है)

**turbot** /ˈtɜ:bət ˈटबट्/ *noun* [C, U] (*pl.* **turbot** or **turbots**) a large flat European sea fish that some people eat यूरोप की एक बड़ी, चपटी समुद्री मछली (जो खाई भी जाती है); टर्बट

**turbulent** /ˈtɜ:bjələnt ˈटब्यलन्ट्/ *adj.* **1** in which there is a lot of change, disorder and disagreement, and sometimes violence विक्षोभपूर्ण, हंगामेदार **2** (used about water or air) moving in a violent way (जल या वायु) उग्र रूप से विक्षुब्ध या अशांत ▶ **turbulence** *noun* [U] विक्षोभ, अशांति, उग्र, तुमुलकारी

**turf¹** /tɜ:f टफ़्/ *noun* [U, C] (a piece of) short thick grass and the layer of soil underneath it टर्फ़, मिट्टी की परत पर लगाई गई छोटी घनी घास (का मैदान) *newly laid turf*

**turf²** /tɜ:f टफ़्/ *verb* [T] to cover ground with turf ज़मीन पर घास लगाना

**PHR V** **turf sb out (of sth)** (*BrE informal*) to force sb to leave a place किसी को कहीं से बाहर निकाल देना

**turkey** /ˈtɜ:ki ˈटकि/ *noun* [C, U] a large bird that is kept on farms. Turkeys are usually eaten at Christmas in Britain and at Thanksgiving in the US एक बड़ी चिड़िया; पीरू (इसे ब्रिटेन में क्रिसमस और अमेरिका में थैंक्स-गिविंग के पर्व पर खाया जाता है)

**IDM** **cold turkey** ➪ **cold¹** देखिए।

**turmeric** /ˈtɜ:mərɪk ˈटमरिक्/ *noun* [U] an essential spice used in South-Asian cooking usually sold in dried or powdered form. It lends a yellow colour to the food हल्दी, हरिद्रा

**turmoil** /ˈtɜ:mɔɪl ˈटमॉइल्/ *noun* [U, *sing.*] a state of great noise or confusion शोरगुल या खलबली या अनिश्चितता की स्थिति *His mind was* ***in (a) turmoil.***

**turn¹** /tɜ:n टन्/ *verb* **1** [I, T] to move or make sth move round a fixed central point (किसी वस्तु का उसके मध्य बिंदु के चारों ओर) घूमना या (को) घुमाना *She turned the key in the lock.* ○ *Turn the steering wheel to the right.* **2** [I, T] to move your body, or part of your body, so that you are facing in a different direction मुँह आदि अंग का घूम जाना या (को) घुमाना *He turned round when he heard my voice.* ○ *She* ***turned*** *her* ***back on*** *me* (= she deliberately moved her body to face away from me). **3** [I, T] to change the position of sth किसी वस्तु की स्थिति को बदल देना *I turned the box upside down.* ○ *He turned the page and started the next chapter.* **4** [T] to point or aim sth in a particular direction दिशा-विशेष की ओर (किसी वस्तु को) मोड़ना या निशाना बनाना या केंद्रित करना *She turned her attention back to the television.* **5** [I, T] to change direction when you are moving चलते-चलते मुड़ जाना या मोड़ देना, घूम जाना या घुमा देना *The car **turned the corner**.* **6** [I, T] (to cause) to become किसी की स्थिति को बदल देना, (बदल कर) कुछ (और) हो जाना *He **turned very red** when I asked him about the money.* ○ *These caterpillars will turn into butterflies.* **7** [T] (*not used in the continuous tenses*) to reach or pass a particular age or time एक निश्चित आयु और समय पर पहुँचना या पार करना *It's turned midnight.*

**NOTE** **Turn** से बनने वाले मुहावरों के लिए संबंधित संज्ञाओं, विशेषणों आदि की प्रविष्टियाँ देखिए। उदाहरण के लिए **turn a blind eye**, **blind** में मिलेगा।

**PHR V** **turn (sth) around/round** to change position or direction in order to face the opposite way, or to return the way you came पूरा घूम जाना या घुमा देना, या वापस उसी रास्ते लौटना *He turned the car around and drove off.*

**turn away** to stop looking at sb/sth किसी व्यक्ति या वस्तु से नज़र हटा लेना *She turned away in horror at the sight of the blood.*

**turn sb away** to refuse to allow a person to go into a place किसी व्यक्ति को किसी स्थान पर जाने से रोक देना

**turn back** to return the same way that you came वापस उसी रास्ते लौटना *We've come so far already, we can't turn back now.*

**turn sb/sth down** to refuse an offer, etc. or the person who makes it किसी के प्रस्ताव आदि को ठुकरा देना *He asked her to marry him, but she turned him down.*

**turn sth down** to reduce the sound or heat that sth produces किसी की आवाज़ या गरमी को कम कर देना *Turn the television down!*

**turn off (sth)** to leave one road and go on another एक सड़क छोड़कर दूसरी पर जाना, सड़क बदलना

**turn sth off** to stop the flow of electricity, water, etc. by moving a switch, tap, etc. बिजली, पानी आदि के प्रवाह को (बटन, टोंटी आदि दबा या घुमा कर) बंद कर देना *He turned the TV off.*

**turn sth on** to start the flow of electricity, water, etc. by moving a switch, tap, etc. बिजली, पानी आदि के प्रवाह को (बटन, टोंटी आदि दबा या घुमा कर) चालू कर देना *to turn the lights on*

**turn out (for sth)** to be present at an event किसी कार्यक्रम में उपस्थित होना या शिरकत करना

**turn out (to be sth)** to be in the end अंत में कुछ होना, निकलना, साबित होना *The weather turned out fine.* ○ *The house that they had promised us turned out to be a tiny flat.*

**turn sth out** to move the switch, etc. on a light or a source of heat to stop it रोशनी या(आग देने वाली) गैस आदि को बंद करने के लिए बटन आदि दबाना या घुमाना *Turn the lights out before you go to bed.*

**turn over 1** to change position so that the other side is facing out or upwards स्थिति (करवट आदि) बदलना (ऐसे कि दूसरा तल सामने या ऊपर की ओर आ जाए) *He turned over and went back to sleep.* **2** (used about an engine) to start or to continue to run (इंजन का) चालू होना या चालू रहना **3** (*BrE*) to change to another programme when you are watching television टीवी देखते समय कार्यक्रम बदल देना

**turn sth over 1** to make sth change position so that the other side is facing out or upwards किसी की स्थिति को बदल देना (ऐसे कि दूसरा तल सामने या ऊपर की ओर आ जाए), (को) पलट देना *You may now turn over your exam papers and begin.* **2** to keep thinking about sth carefully किसी बात को सावधानी से सोचते रहना *She kept turning over what he'd said in her mind.*

**turn to sb/sth** to go to sb/sth to get help, advice, etc. सहायता, सलाह आदि के लिए किसी व्यक्ति या वस्तु के पास जाना

**turn up 1** to arrive; to appear (कहीं) पहुँचना; प्रकट होना, दिखना *What time did they finally turn up?* **2** to be found, especially by chance (किसी वस्तु का) मिल जाना (विशेषतः संयोग से) *I lost my glasses a week ago and they haven't turned up yet.*

**turn sth up** to increase the sound or heat that sth produces (किसी वस्तु द्वारा उत्पन्न) आवाज़ या गरमी को बढ़ा देना *Turn the heating up—I'm cold.*

**turn²** /tɜːn टन्/ *noun* [C] **1** the action of turning sb/sth round किसी वस्तु को घुमाने की क्रिया; घुमाव *Give the screw another couple of turns to make sure it is really tight.* **2** a change of direction in a vehicle (वाहन में) दिशा-परिवर्तन *to make a **left/right turn*** ○ *a **U-turn*** **3** (*BrE* **turning**) a bend or corner in a road, river, etc. सड़क, नदी आदि पर मोड़ या कोना *Take the next turn on the left.* **4** [*usually sing.*] the time when sb in a group of people should or is allowed to do sth (कुछ करने की) बारी, मौका, क्रम *Please wait in the queue until it is your turn.* ○ *Whose turn is it to do the cleaning?* ✪ पर्याय **go** **5** an unusual or unexpected change असामान्य या अप्रत्याशित परिवर्तन *The patient's condition has **taken a turn for the worse*** (= suddenly got worse).

**IDM** **(do sb) a good turn** to do sth helpful for sb किसी की सहायता के लिए कुछ करना

**in turn** one after the other बारी-बारी से, क्रमवार *I spoke to each of the children in turn.*

**take turns (at sth)** to do sth one after the other to make sure it is fair बारी आने पर (ही) कुछ करना (ताकि नियम भंग न हो)

**the turn of the century/year** the time when a new century/year starts नई सदी या वर्ष के आरंभ का समय

**wait your turn** ➪ **wait**[1] देखिए।

**turning** /ˈtɜːnɪŋ ˈटनिङ्/ (*BrE* **turn**) *noun* [C] a place where one road leads off from another किसी सड़क पर ऐसा स्थान जहाँ से दूसरी सड़क निकले; मोड़ *We must have taken a wrong turning.*

**turning point** *noun* [C] **a turning point (in sth)** a time when an important change happens, usually a good one समय जब (किसी से) कोई बड़ा (और प्रायः अनुकूल) परिवर्तन घटित हो, (का) निर्णायक क्षण

**turnip** /ˈtɜːnɪp ˈटनिप्/ *noun* [C, U] a round white vegetable that grows under the ground शलजम (सब्ज़ी), शलग़म

**turn-off** *noun* [C] the place where a road leads away from a larger or more important road अधिक बड़ी और मुख्य सड़क पर ऐसा स्थान जहाँ से कोई और (छोटी) सड़क निकले, मुख्य सड़क पर शाखा-मार्ग का आरंभ-बिंदु *This is the turn-off for Shimla.*

**turnout** /ˈtɜːnaʊt ˈटनआउट्/ *noun* [C, *usually sing.*] the number of people who go to a meeting, sports event, etc. किसी सभा आदि में उपस्थित लोगों की संख्या, उपस्थिति, जमावड़ा

**turnover** /ˈtɜːnəʊvə(r) ˈटनओव़(र्)/ *noun* [*sing.*] **a turn over (of sth)** **1** the amount of business that a company does in a particular period of time एक निश्चित अवधि में कंपनी की कुल बिक्री *The firm has an annual turnover of Rs 100 crores.* **2** the rate at which workers leave a company and are replaced by new ones किसी कंपनी में नौकरी छोड़ने वालों के स्थान पर नई नियुक्तियों की दर, किसी कंपनी में श्रम-शक्ति परिवर्तन की दर *a high turnover of staff*

**turnstile** /ˈtɜːnstaɪl ˈटन्स्टाइल्/ *noun* [C] a metal gate that moves round in a circle when it is pushed, and allows one person at a time to enter a place घूमने वाला गेट, चक्रद्वार (घूमने वाला धातु-निर्मित गेट जिसमें से एक समय में केवल एक व्यक्ति जा सकता है)

**turntable** /ˈtɜːnteɪbl ˈटन्टेबल्/ *noun* [C] **1** the round surface on a **record player** that you place the record on to be played रिकॉर्ड प्लेयर की (घूमने वाली) गोल प्लेट (जिस पर रख कर रिकॉर्ड बजाया जाता है) **2** a large round surface that is able to move in a circle and onto which a railway engine is driven in order to turn it to go in the opposite direction रेल-इंजन की दिशा पलटने के लिए प्रयुक्त गोल घूमने वाला बड़ा मंच (जिस पर इंजन को खड़ा किया जाता है और मंच को घुमा दिया जाता है), घूमता मंच

**turpentine** /ˈtɜːpəntaɪn ˈटपन्टाइन्/ *noun* [U] a clear liquid with a strong smell that you use for removing paint or for making paint thinner तारपीन का तेल

**turquoise** /ˈtɜːkwɔɪz ˈटक्वॉइज़्/ *adj.*, *noun* **1** [C, U] a blue or greenish-blue precious stone फ़ीरोज़ा (नग) **2** [U] (of) a greenish-blue colour फ़ीरोज़ी रंग (का)

**turret** /ˈtʌrət ˈटरट्/ *noun* [C] a small tower on the top of a large building छोटा बुर्ज, कँगूरा (किंसी बड़ी इमारत के शिखर पर)

**turtle** /ˈtɜːtl ˈटट्ल्/ *noun* [C] **1** (*AmE* **sea turtle**) a reptile with a thick shell that lives in the sea समुद्री कछुआ ➪ **reptile** पर चित्र देखिए। **2** = **tortoise**

**tusk** /tʌsk टस्क्/ *noun* [C] one of the two very long pointed teeth of an elephant, etc. Tusks are made of a hard, white substance like bone (**ivory**) हाथी का (लंबा नुकीला) दाँत

**tussle** /ˈtʌsl ˈटसल्/ *noun* [C] (*informal*) **a tussle (for/over sth)** a fight, for example between two or more people who want to have the same thing एक ही वस्तु के लिए लोगों के बीच संघर्ष; हाथापाई

**tut** /tʌt टट्/ **tut-tut** *exclamation* the way of writing the sound that people make to show disapproval of sb/sth धत (अस्वीकृति या नापसंदी व्यक्त करने वाला ध्वनि-अनुकार शब्द) ▶ **tut** *verb* [I] **tutting; tutted** नापसंदी व्यक्त करना

**tutor** /ˈtjuːtə(r) ˈट्यूट(र्)/ *noun* [C] **1** a private teacher who teaches one person or a very small group (एक व्यक्ति या बहुत छोटे समूह को पढ़ाने वाला व्यक्ति) निजी शिक्षक, (प्राइवेट) ट्यूटर; अनुशिक्षक **2** a teacher who is responsible for a small group of students at school, college or university. A tutor advises students on their work or helps them if they have problems in their private life स्कूल, कॉलेज या विश्वविद्यालय में छोटे छात्र-समूह का प्रभारी शिक्षक, (छात्रों को पढ़ाई और उनकी निजी समस्याओं के मामले में परामर्श देने वाला) स्कूल, कॉलेज या विश्वविद्यालय का ट्यूटर

**tutorial** /tjuːˈtɔːriəl ट्यूˈटॉरिअल्/ *noun* [C] a lesson at a college or university for an individual student or a small group of students कॉलेज या विश्वविद्यालय में अकेले छात्र या छोटे छात्र-समूह को पढ़ाया गया पाठ; अनुशिक्षण-कक्ष

**tuxedo** /tʌkˈsiːdəʊ टक्ˈसीडो/ (*pl.* **tuxedos** /-dəʊz -डोज़्/) (*informal* **tux**) = **dinner jacket**

**TV** /ˌtiːˈviː ˌटीˈवी/ *abbr.* = **television**

**twang** /twæŋ ट्वैङ्/ *noun* [C] the sound that is made when you pull a tight piece of string, wire or elastic and then let it go suddenly तने हुए फ़ीते, तार या इलास्टिक को खींचकर छोड़ देने से उत्पन्न ध्वनि; झंकार, टंकार ▶ **twang** *verb* [I, T] झंकारना, टंकारना

**tweed** /twiːd ट्वीड्/ *noun* [U] thick woollen cloth with a rough surface used for making clothes खुरदरी-सी सतह वाला मोटा गरम कपड़ा (जिससे कोट आदि बनते हैं), ट्वीड

**tweezers** /ˈtwiːzəz ˈट्वीज़ज़्/ *noun* [*pl.*] a small tool consisting of two pieces of metal that are joined at one end. You use tweezers for picking up or pulling out very small things चिमटी (इस चिमटी से पकड़ कर बहुत छोटी चीजों को पकड़ कर हटाया जा सकता है) *a pair of tweezers*

**twelfth** /twelfθ ट्वेल्फ़्थ्/ *det., adv.* 12th बारहवाँ ➪ **sixth** के उदाहरण देखिए।

**twelve** /twelv ट्वेल्व्/ *number* 12 बारह (की संख्या) ➪ **dozen** देखिए। NOTE संख्याओं के वाक्य-प्रयोग के उदाहरणों के लिए **six** की प्रविष्टि देखिए।

**twentieth** /ˈtwentiəθ ˈट्वेन्टिअथ्/ *det., adv.* 20th बीसवाँ ➪ **sixth** के उदाहरण देखिए।

**twenty** /ˈtwenti ˈट्वेन्टि/ *number* 20 बीस (की संख्या)

NOTE संख्याओं के वाक्य-प्रयोग के उदाहरणों के लिए **sixty** की प्रविष्टि देखिए।

**twice** /twaɪs ट्वाइस्/ *adv.* two times दो बार, दो गुना *The film will be shown twice daily.* ○ *Prices have risen twice as fast in this country as in Japan.*

**twiddle** /ˈtwɪdl ˈट्विड्ल्/ *verb* [I, T] **twiddle (with) sth** to keep turning or moving sth with your fingers, often because you are nervous or bored बेचैनी या ऊब के कारण कुछ उमेठना, घुमाना

**twig** /twɪg ट्विग्/ *noun* [C] a small thin branch on a tree or bush किसी पेड़ या झाड़ी की छोटी पतली शाखा; टहनी

**twilight** /ˈtwaɪlaɪt ˈट्वाइलाइट्/ *noun* [U] the time after the sun has set and before it gets completely dark संध्या का प्रकाश, थोड़ा-थोड़ा अँधेरा, झुटपुटा ➪ **dusk** देखिए।

**twin** /twɪn ट्विन्/ *noun* [C] **1** one of two children or animals that are born to one mother at the same time जुड़वाँ बच्चों में से एक *a twin brother/sister* ○ *identical twins* ➪ **Siamese twin** और **triplet** देखिए। **2** one of a pair of things that are the same or very similar दो एक जैसी चीज़ों में से एक, जोड़े में से एक *twin engines* ○ *twin beds*

**twinge** /twɪndʒ ट्विन्ज्/ *noun* [C] **1** a sudden short pain (शरीर में) अचानक उठा दर्द; टीस *He suddenly felt a twinge in his back.* **2 a twinge (of sth)** a sudden short feeling of an unpleasant emotion मन में अचानक उत्पन्न वेदना

**twinkle** /ˈtwɪŋkl ˈट्विङ्क्ल्/ *verb* [I] **1** to shine with a light that seems to go on and off टिमटिमाना *Stars twinkled in the night sky.* **2** (used about your eyes) to look bright because you are happy (आँखों का) ख़ुशी के मारे चमकना ▶ **twinkle** *noun* [*sing.*] टिमटिमाती रोशनी, आँखों की चमक

**twin town** *noun* [C] one of two towns in different countries that have a special relationship दो भिन्न देशों के विशेष संबंध में बँधे दो शहरों में से एक; जुड़वाँ शहर

**twirl** /twɜːl ट्वर्ल्/ *verb* [I, T] **twirl (sb/sth) (around/round)** to turn round and round quickly; to make sb/sth do this तेज़ी से घूमना या चक्कर खाना; (किसी वस्तु को) तेज़ी से घुमाना या चक्कर खिलाना

**twist¹** /twɪst ट्विस्ट्/ *verb* **1** [I, T] to bend or turn sth into a particular shape, often one it does not go in naturally; to be bent in this way (सिर के बाल या कुछ) बटना, गूँथना, (टखना) मरोड़ना, ऐंठना; बटना, गुथँना, मरोड़ खा जाना, ऐंठ जाना *She twisted her long hair into a knot.* ○ *He* ***twisted*** *his* ***ankle*** *while he was playing cricket.* **2** [I, T] to turn a part of your body while the rest stays still शरीर के केवल एक अंग का घूमना या उसे घुमाना *She twisted round to see where the noise was coming from.* ○ *He kept twisting his head from side to side.* **3** [T] to turn sth around in a circle with your hand हाथ से किसी वस्तु को गोल घुमाना (चूड़ी पहनाने के ढंग से) *She twisted the ring on her finger nervously.* ○ *Most containers have twist-off caps.* **4** [I] (used about a road, etc.) to change direction often (सड़क आदि का) बार-बार मुड़ना *a narrow twisting lane* ○ *The road* ***twists and turns*** *along the coast.* **5** [I, T] **twist (sth) (round/around sth)** to put sth round another object; to be round another object (किसी वस्तु के चारों ओर कुछ) लपेटना; लिपटना *The telephone wire has* ***got twisted*** *round the table leg.* **6** [T] to change the meaning of what sb has said शब्दों के अर्थ तोड़-मरोड़ कर पेश करना *Journalists often* ***twist*** *your* ***words****.*

IDM **twist sb's arm** (*informal*) to force or persuade sb to do sth किसी की बाँह मरोड़ना (किसी को कुछ करने के लिए बाध्य करना या मनाना)

**twist²** /twɪst ट्विस्ट्/ *noun* [C] **1** the action of turning sth with your hand, or of turning part of your body (किसी वस्तु को) मरोड़ने या ऐंठने की क्रिया

*She opened the bottle cap with one twist of its neck.* **2** an unexpected change or development in a story or situation किसी कहानी या परिस्थिति में कोई अप्रत्याशित बदलाव या घटना **3** a place where a road, river, etc. bends or changes direction स्थान जहाँ सड़क, नदी आदि मुड़ती या दिशा बदलती है; मोड़, घुमाव *the **twists and turns** of the river* **4** something that has become or been bent into a particular shape ऐंठन, मरोड़ *Straighten out the wire so that there are no twists in it.*

**twit** /twɪt ट्विट्/ *noun* [C] (*informal*) a stupid person बेवकूफ़ आदमी

**twitch** /twɪtʃ ट्विच्/ *verb* [I, T] to make a quick sudden movement, often one that you cannot control; to cause sth to make a sudden movement फड़कना, झटका मारना, झटकारना; (किसी को) झटका देना, झटकारना, फड़काना *The rabbit twitched and then lay still.* ○ *He twitched his nose.* ▶ **twitch** *noun* [C] झटका, मरोड़, खिंचाव, फड़क *He has a nervous twitch.*

**twitter** /ˈtwɪtə(r) ˈट्विट(र्)/ *verb* [I] (used about birds) to make a series of short high sounds (चिड़ियों का) चहकना या चहचहाना

**two** /tu: टू/ **1** *number* 2 दो (की संख्या) ➪ **second** देखिए। **NOTE** संख्याओं के वाक्य-प्रयोग के उदाहरणों के लिए **six** की प्रविष्टि देखिए। **2 two-** (*used to form compound adjectives*) having two of the things mentioned दो की संख्या वाला, दो-/दु-/द्वि- *a two-week holiday*

**IDM be in two minds (about sth/about doing sth)** ➪ **mind**[1] देखिए।

**in two** in or into two pieces दो टुकड़े या दो टुकड़ों में *The plate fell on the floor and broke in two.*

**two-faced** *adj.* (*informal*) not sincere; not acting in a way that supports what you say or what you believe; saying different things to different people about a particular subject बेईमान, धोखेबाज़; जिसकी कथनी और करनी में अंतर हो, पाखंडी, दुरंगा; एक ही मुद्दे पर अलग-अलग लोगों को अलग-अलग बातें कहने वाला ढोंगी, बहुमुख ✪ पर्याय **hypocritical**

**two-ply** *adj.* (used about wool, wood, etc.) with two threads or thicknesses (ऊन, लकड़ी आदि) दो लड़ियों या परतों वाली, दुलड़ी( ऊन), दुरपती (लकड़ी)

**two-way** *adj.* (*usually before a noun*) **1** moving in two different directions; allowing sth to move in two different directions दो अलग दिशाओं में जाने वाला, दुतरफ़ा; जो किसी वस्तु को दो अलग दिशाओं में जाने दे *two-way traffic* **2** (used about communication between people) needing equal effort from both people or groups involved (संचार, लोगों में बातचीत) पारस्परिक (दोनों ओर से होने वाला) *Friendship is a two-way process.* **3** (used about radio equipment, etc.) used both for sending and receiving signals (रेडियो उपकरण आदि) जो संकेतों को प्राप्त करे और प्रेषित भी; द्विपथ, द्विमार्गी

**tycoon** /taɪˈku:n टाइˈकून्/ *noun* [C] a person who is very successful in business or industry and who has become rich and powerful धनी तथा शक्तिशाली व्यापारी या उद्योगपति, धनी-मानी व्यक्ति

**type**[1] /taɪp टाइप्/ *noun* **1** [C] **a type (of sth)** a group of people or things that share certain qualities and that are part of a larger group; a kind or sort समान विशेषताओं वाले व्यक्तियों या वस्तुओं का समूह (जो अपने से बड़े समूह का भाग हो); प्रकार या क़िस्म *Which type of paint should you use on metal?* ○ *You meet all types of people in this job.* **2** [C] a person of a particular kind विशेष प्रकार के गुणों का व्यक्ति *He's the careful type.* ○ *She's **not the type to** do anything silly.* ➪ **typical** देखिए। **3 -type** (*used to form compound adjectives*) having the qualities, etc. of the group, person or thing mentioned निर्दिष्ट समूह, व्यक्ति या वस्तु की विशेषताओं वाला; नमूना *a ceramic-type material* ○ *a police-type badge* **4** [U] letters that are printed or typed मुद्रण या टंकण का टाइप या अक्षर

**type**[2] /taɪp टाइप्/ *verb* [I, T] to write sth by using a **word processor** or **typewriter** टंकण, टाइप या मुद्रण करना (टाइपराइटर या वर्डप्रोसेसर की सहायता से) *to type a letter* ▶ **typing** *noun* [U] टंकण (क्रिया) *typing skills*

**typeface** /ˈtaɪpfeɪs ˈटाइपफ़ेस्/ *noun* [C] a set of letters, numbers, etc. of a particular design, used in printing टाइप-फ़ेस, मुद्री-रूप (मुद्रण-कार्य में प्रयुक्त विशेष डिज़ाइन के अक्षर, अंक आदि) *I'd like the heading to be in a different typeface from the text.*

**typewriter** /ˈtaɪpraɪtə(r) ˈटाइपराइट(र्)/ *noun* [C] a machine that you use for writing in print टाइप करने की मशीन; टाइपराइटर; टाइप-मशीन

**typewritten** /ˈtaɪprɪtn ˈटाइपरिट्न्/ *adj.* written using a typewriter or computer टाइपराइटर या कंप्यूटर की सहायता से लिखा हुआ, टंकित या कंप्यूटर-मुद्रित

**typhoid** /ˈtaɪfɔɪd ˈटाइफ़ॉइड्/ *noun* [U] a serious disease that can cause death. People get typhoid from bad food or water टाइफ़ाइड ज्वर, आंत्र-ज्वर (दूषित भोजन या जल से होने वाला रोग जो घातक भी हो सकता है)

**typhoon** /taɪˈfu:n टाइˈफ़ून्/ *noun* [C] a violent tropical storm with very strong winds प्रचंड तूफ़ान; टाइफ़ून ➪ **storm** पर नोट देखिए।

**typical** /ˈtɪpɪkl ˈटिपिक्ल्/ *adj.* **typical (of sb/sth)** **1** having or showing the usual qualities of a particular person, thing or type विशेष व्यक्ति, वस्तु या प्रकार की सामान्य विशेषताओं से युक्त, (किसी का) प्रातिनिधिक *a typical Indian village* ✪ विलोम **untypical** और **atypical** **2** behaving in the way you expect ठेठ, विशेषतासूचक *It was absolutely typical of him not to reply to my letter.*

**typically** /ˈtɪpɪkli ˈटिपिक्लि/ *adv.* **1** in a typical case; that usually happens in this way वर्गीय दृष्टि से; वर्गीय दृष्टि से होने वाला *Typically it is the girls who offer to help, not the boys.* **2** in a way that shows the usual qualities of a particular person, type or thing विशेष व्यक्ति, वस्तु या प्रकार की सामान्य विशेषताओं को प्रकट करने के ढंग से; प्रातिनिधिक रूप से *typically British humour*

**typify** /ˈtɪpɪfaɪ ˈटिपिफ़ाइ/ *verb* [T] (*pres. part.* **typifying;** *3rd person sing. pres.* **typifies;** *pt, pp* **typified**) to be a typical mark or example of sb/sth किसी व्यक्ति या वस्तु का प्रतीकी चिह्न या उदाहरण होना, का प्रतीक होना, की मिसाल होना *This film typified the Hollywood westerns of that time.*

**typist** /ˈtaɪpɪst ˈटाइपिस्ट्/ *noun* [C] a person who works in an office typing letters, etc. टंकण या टाइप करने वाला व्यक्ति; टंकक, टाइपिस्ट

**tyranny** /ˈtɪrəni ˈटिरनि/ *noun* [U] the cruel and unfair use of power by a person or small group to control a country or state जनता पर ज़ुल्म, अत्याचार (किसी व्यक्ति या समूह द्वारा किसी देश या राज्य पर अधिकार करने के लिए निर्मम और अन्यायपूर्ण बलप्रयोग) ▶ **tyrannical** /tɪˈrænɪkl टिˈरैनिक्ल्/ *adj.* अत्याचारी, ज़ालिम *a tyrannical ruler* ▶ **tyrannize** (*also* **-ise**) /ˈtɪrənaɪz ˈटिरनाइज़्/ *verb* [I, T] (पर) अत्याचार करना, ज़ुल्म करना .

**tyrant** /ˈtaɪrənt ˈटाइरन्ट्/ *noun* [C] a cruel ruler who has complete power over the people in his/her country अत्याचारी शासक, ज़ालिम हाकिम, तानाशाह ➪ **dictator** देखिए।

**tyre** (*AmE* **tire**) /ˈtaɪə(r) ˈटाइअ(र्)/ *noun* [C] the thick rubber ring that fits around the outside of a wheel (कार आदि के) पहिए का टायर ***a flat tyre*** (= a tyre with no air in it)

**tzar** = **tsar**

**tzarina** = **tsarina**

# U u

**U, u**[1] /juː यू/ *noun* [C, U] (*pl.* **U's; u's** /juːz; juːz यूज़्/) the twenty-first letter of the English alphabet अंग्रेज़ी वर्णमाला का इक्कीसवाँ अक्षर *'University' begins with a 'U'.*

**U**[2] /juː यू/ *abbr.* (used about films that are suitable for anyone, including children) universal (ऐसी फ़िल्म के लिए प्रयुक्त जिसे बच्चे और बड़े सब देख सकें), U (यूनिवर्सल)

**ubiquitous** /juːˈbɪkwɪtəs यूˈबिक्विटस्/ *adj.* (*usually before a noun*) (*formal*) seeming to be everywhere or in several places at the same time; very common एक ही समय में सर्वत्र या अनेक स्थानों पर विद्यमान लगने वाला; यत्र, तत्र, सर्वत्र दृश्यमान; बहुत आम *the ubiquitous bicycles of university towns* ○ *the ubiquitous movie star, Tom Cruise.* ▶ **ubiquitously** *adv.* सर्वव्यापिता से ▶ **ubiquity** /juːˈbɪkwəti यूˈबिक्वटि/ *noun* [U] एक ही समय में सर्वत्र विद्यमानता

**udder** /ˈʌdə(r) ˈअडर्/ *noun* [C] the part of a female cow, etc. that hangs under its body and produces milk गाय आदि के थन

**UEFA** /juˈeɪfə यूˈएफ़ा/ *abbr.* the Union of European Football Associations यूएफ़ा, यूनियन आफ़ यूरोपियन फुटबॉल एसोसिएशन (यूरोपीय फ़ुटबॉल संगठन) *the UEFA cup*

**UFO** (*also* **ufo**) /ˌjuː ef ˈəʊ ˌयू एफ़्ˈओ/ *abbr.* an unidentified flying object यूएफ़ओ, अज्ञात उड़न तश्तरी या वस्तु ➪ **flying saucer** देखिए।

**UGC** / juː dʒiːˈsiː ˌयू जीसी/ *abbr.* University Grants Commission; a central government body in India that provides funds for government-recognized universities and colleges युनिवर्सिटि ग्रांट्स कमीशन; भारत सरकार द्वारा मान्यता प्राप्त विश्वविद्यालयों एवं कॉलेजों को अनुदान देने वाली केंद्रीय समिति

**ugh** /ɜː अ/ *exclamation* used in writing to express the sound that you make when you think sth is disgusting विरक्ति, घृणा या झल्लाहट व्यक्त करने के लिए प्रयुक्त शब्द; उफ़, छिः तौबा-तौबा

**ugly** /ʌgliˈअग्लि/ *adj.* (**uglier; ugliest**) **1** unpleasant to look at or listen to; not attractive भद्दा (देखने या सुनने में); कुरूप, बदसूरत *The burn left an ugly scar on her face.* ○ *an ugly modern office block* **2** (used about a situation) dangerous or threatening (स्थिति) ख़तरनाक या भयावह ▶ **ugliness** *noun* [U] भद्दापन, कुरूपता

**UHF** /ˌjuː eɪtʃˈef ˌयू एच्ˈएफ़्/ *abbr.* ultra-high frequency; radio waves that move up and down at a particular speed and which are used to send out radio and television programmes यूएचएफ़, अति-उच्च आवृति; रेडियो और टीवी प्रसारण में प्रयुक्त विशेष गति से स्पंदन करने वाली रेडियो तरंगें ➪ **wavelength** पर चित्र देखिए।

**UHT** /ˌjuː eɪtʃˈtiː ˌयू एचˈटी/ *abbr.* ultra heat treated used about foods such as milk that are treated to last longer यूएचटी, देर तक सुरक्षित रखने के लिए उपचारित दूध आदि आहार के लिए प्रयुक्त *UHT milk*

**UK** /ˌjuː ˈkeɪ ˌयू ˈके/ *abbr.* the United Kingdom; England, Scotland, Wales and N Ireland यूके, युनाइटेड किंग्डम; इंग्लैंड, स्कॉटलैंड, वेल्स और उत्तरी आयरलैंड *a UK citizen*

**ulcer** /ˈʌlsə(r) ˈअल्सर्/ *noun* [C] a painful area on your skin or inside your body. Ulcers may produce a poisonous substance and sometimes bleed फोड़ा, व्रण, नासूर *a mouth/stomach ulcer*

**ulna** /ˈʌlnə ˈअल्ना/ *noun* [C] (*medical*) the longer bone of the two bones in the lower part of your arm between your wrist and your elbow कलाई और कोहनी के बीच बाँह के नीचे की दो में से लंबी हड्डी; अंतः प्रकोष्ठिका ➪ **radius** देखिए तथा **body** और **arm** पर चित्र देखिए।

**ulterior** /ʌlˈtɪəriə(r) अल्ˈटिअरिअर्/ *adj.* that you keep hidden or secret छिपाकर रखा गया, गूढ़ या गुप्त *Why is he suddenly being so nice to me? He must have an* ***ulterior motive.***

**ultimate**[1] /ˈʌltɪmət ˈअल्टिमट्/ *adj.* (*only before a noun*) **1** being or happening at the end; last or final अंत में होने या आने वाला; अंतिम, आख़िरी *Our ultimate goal is complete independence.* **2** the greatest, best or worst महानतम, सर्वोत्तम या निकृष्टतम, परम, चरम

**ultimate**[2] /ˈʌltɪmət ˈअल्टिमट्/ *noun* [*sing.*] (*informal*) **the ultimate (in sth)** the greatest or best सबसे बड़ा या सबसे उत्तम *This new car is the ultimate in comfort.*

**ultimately** /ˈʌltɪmətli ˈअल्टिमट्लि/ *adv.* **1** in the end अंततोगत्वा, आख़िरकार *Ultimately, the decision is yours.* **2** at the most basic level; most importantly आधारभूत रूप से, मूलतः; सर्वाधिक महत्त्वपूर्ण रूप से

**ultimatum** /ˌʌltɪˈmeɪtəm ˌअल्टिˈमेटम्/ *noun* [C] (*pl.* **ultimatums**) a final warning to sb that, if he/she does not do what you ask, you will use force or take action against him/her (आदेश न

मानने पर बल प्रयोग की) अंतिम चेतावनी *I gave him an ultimatum—either he paid his rent or he was out.*

**ultra-** /ˈʌltrə ˈअल्ट्रा/ (*in compounds*) extremely अत्यधिक, अति- *ultra-modern*

**ultrasonic** /ˌʌltrəˈsɒnɪk ˌअल्ट्राˈसॉनिक्/ *adj.* (*usually before a noun*) (used about sounds) higher than human beings can hear (ध्वनियाँ) मानव की श्रवण-क्षमता से परे की; पराश्रव्य, पराध्वनिक *ultrasonic frequencies/waves/signals*

**ultrasound** /ˈʌltrəsaʊnd ˈअल्ट्रासाउन्ड्/ *noun* **1** [U] sound that is higher than human beings can hear ऐसी ध्वनि जो मानव की श्रवण-क्षमता से परे हो; पराध्वनि **2** [U, C] a medical process that produces an image of what is inside your body शरीर के आंतरिक भाग का चित्र प्रस्तुत करने वाली डॉक्टरी प्रक्रिया; अल्ट्रासाउंड *Ultrasound showed she was expecting twins.*

**ultraviolet** /ˌʌltrəˈvaɪələt ˌअल्ट्राˈवाइअलट्/ *adj.* used about light that causes your skin to turn darker and that can be dangerous in large amounts (प्रकाश) जिससे व्यक्ति की त्वचा काली पड़ जाए और जिसकी अधिक मात्रा ख़तरनाक होती है; पराबैंगनी ➪ **infrared** देखिए तथा **wavelength** पर चित्र देखिए।

**umbilical cord** /ʌmˌbɪlɪkl ˈkɔːd अम्ˌबिलिक्ल् ˈकॉड्/ *noun* [C] the tube that connects a baby to its mother before it is born नाल, नाभि-नाड़ी, नाभि-रज्जु (गर्भस्थ शिशु को माँ से जोड़ने वाली नली)

**umbra** /ˈʌmbrə ˈअम्ब्रा/ *noun* [C] (*technical*) **1** the central part of a **shadow** where it is completely dark छाया का पूरी तरह काला मध्यभाग; प्रच्छाया **2** a completely dark area on the earth caused by the moon, or a completely dark area on the moon caused by the earth, during an **eclipse** ग्रहण के समय पृथ्वी और चंद्रमा दोनों पर पड़ने वाली एक दूसरे की गहरी छाया ➪ **penumbra** देखिए तथा **shadow** पर चित्र देखिए।

**umbrage** /ˈʌmbrɪdʒ ˈअम्ब्रिज्/ *noun* [U] a sense of slight injury or offence, often without reason क्षति या नाराज़गी का भास (प्रायः अकारणवश)

**umbrella** /ʌmˈbrelə अम्ˈब्रेला/ *noun* [C] an object that you open and hold over your head to protect yourself from the rain or from the hot sun छाता, छतरी *to put an umbrella up/down*

**umpire** /ˈʌmpaɪə(r) ˈअम्पाइअ(र्)/ *noun* [C] a person who watches a game such as tennis or cricket to make sure that the players obey the rules टेनिस या क्रिकेट में अम्पायर (वह व्यक्ति जो खेल के नियमों के पालन पर निगाह रखता है) ➪ **referee** देखिए। ▶ **umpire** *verb* [I, T] (किसी मैच में) अम्पायर होना, अम्पायर के रूप में कोई मैच खिलाना

**umpteen** /ˌʌmpˈtiːn ˌअम्प्ˈटीन्/ *pronoun, det.* (*informal*) very many; a lot बहुत बार; बहुत सारे, बहुतेरे, बहुत-से ▶ **umpteenth** /ˌʌmpˈtiːnθ ˌअम्प्ˈटीन्थ्/ *pronoun, det.* बहुत बार *For the umpteenth time—phone if you're going to be late!*

**UN** /ˌjuː ˈen ˌयू ˈएन्/ *abbr.* the United Nations (Organization) यूएन, संयुक्त राष्ट्र संघ *It's UN peace-keeping plan.*

**un-** /ʌn अन्/ *prefix* **1** (*used in adjectives, adverbs and nouns*) not; the opposite of नकारात्मक अर्थ में, अ-/अन-; के विपरीत या विरुद्ध *unable* ○ *unconsciously* *untruth* **2** used in verbs that describe the opposite of a process क्रिया से पहले विपरीत कार्य सूचक उपसर्ग *unlock/undo/unfold*

**unable** /ʌnˈeɪbl अन्ˈएब्ल्/ *adj.* unable to do sth not having the time, knowledge, skill, etc. to do sth; not able to do sth जिसके पास कोई विशेष काम करने के लिए अपेक्षित समय, ज्ञान, कौशल आदि का अभाव हो, अक्षम; कोई विशेष काम करने में असमर्थ, अशक्त *She lay there, unable to move.* ➪ **inability** noun देखिए।

**unacceptable** /ˌʌnəkˈseptəbl ˌअनक्ˈसेप्टब्ल्/ *adj.* that you cannot accept or allow जो स्वीकार्य या अनुमति देने योग्य न हो; अस्वीकार्य, अग्राह्य ✪ विलोम **acceptable** ▶ **unacceptably** /-bli -ब्लि/ *adv.* अग्राह्य रूप से

**unaccompanied** /ˌʌnəˈkʌmpənid ˌअनˈकम्पनिड्/ *adj.* alone, without sb/sth else with you अकेला, बिना किसी व्यक्ति या वस्तु को साथ लिए, बिना साथ का; असहवर्ति *Unaccompanied children are not allowed in the bar.*

**unaffected** /ˌʌnəˈfektɪd ˌअनˈफ़ेक्टिड्/ *adj.* **1** not changed by sth (किसी से) अप्रभावित **2** behaving in a natural way without trying to impress anyone (आचरण) जिसमें सहजता हो, (व्यक्ति) सहज रूप से व्यवहार करने वाला, दिखावा न करने वाला; आडंबरहीन ✪ विलोम **affected**

**unaided** /ʌnˈeɪdɪd अन्ˈएडिड्/ *adv.* without any help बिना किसी सहायता के

**unanimous** /juˈnænɪməs युˈनैनिमस्/ *adj.* **1** (used about a group of people) all agreeing about sth (व्यक्तियों का समूह) किसी बात पर एकमत *The judges were unanimous in their decision.* **2** (used about a decision, etc.) agreed by everyone (निर्णय आदि) सर्वसम्मत *The jury reached a unanimous verdict of guilty.* ▶ **unanimously** *adv.* एकमत होकर, सर्वसम्मति से

**unarmed** /ˌʌnˈɑːmd ˌअन्ˈआम्ड्/ *adj.* having no guns, knives, etc.; not armed (स्थिति) जिसमें शस्त्र का प्रयोग अपेक्षित न हो; (व्यक्ति) निःशस्त्र, निहत्था ✪ विलोम **armed**

**unashamed** /ˌʌnəˈʃeɪmd ˌअनˈशेम्ड्/ *adj.* not feeling sorry or embarrassed about sth bad that you have done निर्लज्ज, बेहया (जिसे अपने बुरे काम पर न खेद हो न लज्जा) ✪ विलोम **ashamed** ▸ **unashamedly** /-ˈʃeɪmɪdli -ˈशेमिड्लि/ *adv.* निर्लज्जता या बेहयाई से

**unassuming** /ˌʌnəˈsjuːmɪŋ ˌअनˈस्यूमिङ्/ *adj.* not wanting people to notice how good, important, etc. you are विनम्र, निरभिमानी (जो अपनी भलमनसाहट का प्रदर्शन न करे)

**unattached** /ˌʌnəˈtætʃt ˌअनˈटैच्ट्/ *adj.* **1** not connected to sb/sth else (किसी व्यक्ति या वस्तु से) असंबद्ध, असंलग्न **2** not married; without a regular partner अविवाहित; जिसका कोई नियमित साथी न हो

**unattended** /ˌʌnəˈtendɪd ˌअनˈटेन्डिड्/ *adj.* not watched or looked after जिसकी रखवाली या देखभाल न की जाए; अकेला *Do not leave children unattended.*

**unauthorized** (*also* **-ised**) /ʌnˈɔːθəraɪzd अन्ˈऑथराइज़्ड्/ *adj.* done without permission बिना अनुमति के किया गया; अनधिकृत, ग़ैर-क़ानूनी

**unavailable** /ˌʌnəˈveɪləbl ˌअनˈवेलबल्/ *adj.* (*not usually before a noun*) **unavailable (to sb/sth)** **1** that cannot be obtained जो मिल नहीं सकता; अलभ्य *Such luxury items were unavailable to ordinary people.* **2** not able or not willing to see, meet or talk to sb जो किसी को सुलभ न हो या बात करने का अनिच्छुक हो *The minister was unavailable for comment.* ✪ विलोम **available** ▸ **unavailability** /ˌʌnəˌveɪləˈbɪləti ˌअनˌवेलˈबिलटि/ *noun* [U] अलभ्यता, अनिच्छुकना

**unavoidable** /ˌʌnəˈvɔɪdəbl ˌअनˈवॉइडबल्/ *adj.* that cannot be avoided or prevented जिससे बचना या जिसे रोकना संभव न हो; अपरिहार्य, अनिवार्य ✪ विलोम **avoidable** ▸ **unavoidably** /-əbli -अबलि/ *adv.* अपरिहार्य या अनिवार्य रूप से

**unaware** /ˌʌnəˈweə(r) ˌअनˈवेअ(र्)/ *adj.* (*not before a noun*) **unaware (of sb/sth)** not knowing about or not noticing sb/sth जिसे किसी व्यक्ति या वस्तु की जानकारी न हो या कोई दिखाई न दे; अनजान, अनभिज्ञ, बेख़बर *She seemed unaware of all the trouble she had caused.* ✪ विलोम **aware**

**unawares** /ˌʌnəˈweəz ˌअनˈवेअज़्/ *adv.* by surprise; without expecting sth or being prepared for it अनजाने में; बिना आशा या तैयारी के, अकस्मात *I was **taken** completely **unawares** by his suggestion.*

**unbalanced** /ˌʌnˈbælənst ˌअन्ˈबैलन्स्ट्/ *adj.* **1** (used about a person) slightly crazy (व्यक्ति) कुछ सनकी, विक्षिप्त-सा **2** not fair to all ideas or sides of an argument (बात) असंतुलित ✪ विलोम **balanced**

**unbearable** /ʌnˈbeərəbl अन्ˈबेअरबल्/ *adj.* too unpleasant, painful, etc. for you to accept असह्य, असहनीय, बर्दाश्त से बाहर ✪ पर्याय **intolerable** ✪ विलोम **bearable** ▸ **unbearably** /-əbli -अब्लि/ *adv.* असहनीय रूप से *It was unbearably hot.*

**unbeatable** /ʌnˈbiːtəbl अन्ˈबीटबल्/ *adj.* that cannot be defeated or improved on (क़ीमत आदि) बेजोड़ (जिसकी बराबरी न की जा सके) *unbeatable prices*

**unbeaten** /ʌnˈbiːtn अन्ˈबीट्न्/ *adj.* that has not been beaten or improved on (दल आदि) अपराजित, अविजित (जो हारा न हो या जिससे बढ़कर कोई न हो)

**unbelievable** /ˌʌnbɪˈliːvəbl ˌअन्बिˈलीवबल्/ *adj.* very surprising; difficult to believe अत्यंत आश्चर्यजनक, ग़ज़ब का; अविश्वसनीय ✪ विलोम **believable** ⇨ **incredible** देखिए। ▸ **unbelievably** /-əbli -अब्लि/ *adj.* अविश्वसनीय रूप से *His work was unbelievably bad.*

**unblemished** /ʌnˈblemɪʃt अन्ˈब्लेमिश्ट्/ *adj.* not spoiled, damaged or marked in any way अदूषित, अक्षुण्ण या निष्कलंक, बेदाग़ *The new party leader has an unblemished reputation.*

**unblock** /ˌʌnˈblɒk ˌअन्ˈब्लॉक्/ *verb* [T] to clean sth, for example a pipe, by removing sth that is blocking it (पाइप आदि को) साफ़ करना, रुकावटें हटाकर खोल देना

**unborn** /ˌʌnˈbɔːn ˌअन्ˈबॉन्/ *adj.* not yet born अजन्मा (जिसका अभी जन्म नहीं हुआ)

**unbreakable** /ʌnˈbreɪkəbl अन्ˈब्रेकबल्/ *adj.* impossible to break अभाजनीय, अभंजनीय; जिसे तोड़ा न जा सके *unbreakable glasses*

**unbroken** /ʌnˈbrəʊkən अन्ˈब्रोकन्/ *adj.* **1** continuous; not interrupted सतत, निरंतर; अविच्छिन्न, अखंड *a period of unbroken silence* **2** that has not been beaten जो टूटा न हो, जिससे आगे कोई न निकला हो; अलंघित *His record for the 1500 metres remains unbroken.*

**uncalled for** /ʌnˈkɔːld fɔː(r) अन्ˈकॉल्ड् फ़ॉ(र्)/ *adj.* (used about behaviour or comments) not fair and not appropriate (आचरण या टिप्पणियाँ) अनुचित और अनुपयुक्त; अनपेक्षित *That comment was quite uncalled for.*

**uncanny** /ʌnˈkæni अन्ˈकैनि/ *adj.* very strange; that you cannot easily explain विलक्षण, हैरतंगेज़; रहस्यमय *an uncanny coincidence*

**unceasing** /ʌnˈsiːsɪŋ अन्ˈसीसिङ्/ *adj.* (*written*) continuing all the time अविच्छिन्न, सतत; अविरल *unceasing efforts* ○ *the country's history of unceasing conflict and division* ▸ **unceasingly** *adv.* लगातार, निरंतर, बिना रुके *The rain fell unceasingly.*

**uncertain** /ʌnˈsɜːtn अन्ˈसट्न्/ *adj.* **1 uncertain (about/of sth)** not sure; not able to decide अनिश्चित, संशययुक्त; निश्चय करने में असमर्थ, ढुलमुल, अनिश्चयी *She was still uncertain of his true feelings for her.* **2** not known exactly or not decided जिसकी स्पष्ट जानकारी न हो, अजाना या अनिश्चित; डाँवाँडोल *He's lost his job and his future seems very uncertain.* ✪ विलोम **certain** ▶ **uncertainly** *adv.* अनिश्चित रूप से ▶ **uncertainty** *noun* [C, U] (*pl.* **uncertainties**) अनिश्चितता, डाँवाँडोलपन *Today's decision will put an end to all the uncertainty.* ✪ विलोम **certainty**

**unchanged** /ʌnˈtʃeɪndʒd अन्ˈचेन्ज़्ड्/ *adj.* staying the same; not changed यथावत, पहले जैसा; अपरिवर्तित

**uncharacteristic** /ˌʌn ˌkærəktəˈrɪstɪk ˌअन् ˌकैरक्टˈरिस्टिक्/ *adj.* not typical or usual अस्वाभाविक (जो विशिष्ट लक्षणयुक्त या रोज़मर्रा का न हो) ✪ विलोम **characteristic** ▶ **uncharacteristically** /-kli -क्लि/ *adv.* अस्वाभाविक या अविशिष्ट रूप से

**unchecked** /ˌʌnˈtʃekt ˌअन्ˈचेक्ट्/ *adj.* if sth harmful is unchecked, it is not controlled or stopped from getting worse अनियंत्रित या अनजँचा *The rise in violent crime must not* ***go unchecked****.* ○ *The plant will soon choke ponds and waterways if* ***left unchecked****.*

**uncle** /ˈʌŋkl ˈअङ्क्ल्/ *noun* [C] the brother of your father or mother; the husband of your aunt चाचा या मामा; फूफा या मौसा *Uncle Rishi*

**unclean** /ˌʌnˈkliːn ˌअन्ˈक्लीन्/ *adj.* **1** dirty गंदा, मैला **2** considered to be bad, immoral or not pure in a religious sense, and therefore not to be touched, eaten, etc. बुरा, अनैतिक या अपवित्र (धार्मिक मत में) और अतएव छूने या खाने योग्य नहीं ✪ विलोम **clean** (अर्थ संख्या **1** और **2** के लिए)

**unclear** /ˌʌnˈklɪə(r) ˌअन्ˈक्लिअ(र्)/ *adj.* **1** not clear or definite; difficult to understand or be sure about अस्पष्ट या अनिश्चित; दुर्बोध या संशयपूर्ण *His motives are unclear.* ○ *Some of the diagrams are unclear.* **2 unclear (about sth); unclear (as to sth)** not fully understanding sth; uncertain about sth किसी बात को पूरी तरह न समझते हुए; किसी विषय में संशयग्रस्त *I'm unclear about what you want me to do.*

**uncomfortable** /ʌnˈkʌmftəbl अन्ˈकम्फ़्टब्ल्/ *adj.* **1** not pleasant to wear, sit in, lie on, etc. (पहनने, (पर) बैठने, सोने आदि में) आरामदेह नहीं असुविधाजनक, कष्टप्रद *uncomfortable shoes* **2** not able to sit, lie, etc. in a position that is pleasant बैठने, सोने आदि में परेशानी अनुभव करने वाला; बेचैन **3** feeling or causing worry or embarrassment चिंता या संकोच अनुभव या उत्पन्न करने वाला; चिंतित या संकोचपूर्ण *I felt very uncomfortable when they started arguing in front of me.* ✪ विलोम **comfortable** ▶ **uncomfortably** /-əbli -अब्लि/ *adv.* बेआरामी से, असुविधापूर्वक

**uncommon** /ʌnˈkɒmən अन्ˈकॉमन्/ *adj.* unusual असाधारण, ग़ैर-मामूली ✪ विलोम **common**

**uncompromising** /ʌnˈkɒmprəmaɪzɪŋ अन्ˈकॉम्प्रमाइज़िङ्/ *adj.* refusing to discuss or change a decision अड़ियल, हठी (अपने फ़ैसले पर क़ायम, उस पर बातचीत करने या बदलने का अनिच्छुक), हठधर्मी

**unconcerned** /ˌʌnkənˈsɜːnd ˌअन्कन्ˈसन्ड्/ *adj.* **unconcerned (about/by/with sth)** not interested in sth or not worried about it किसी बात में रुचि या चिंता से विमुख; उदासीन ✪ विलोम **concerned**

**unconditional** /ˌʌnkənˈdɪʃənl ˌअन्कन्ˈडिशन्ल्/ *adj.* without limits or conditions बिना रोक, प्रतिबंध या बिना शर्त के *an unconditional surrender* ✪ विलोम **conditional** ▶ **unconditionally** /-ʃənəli -शनलि/ *adv.* बिना रोक, बिना शर्त

**unconscious** /ʌnˈkɒnʃəs अन्ˈकॉन्शस्/ *adj.* **1** in a state that is like sleep, for example because of injury or illness (चोट या बीमारी के कारण) बेहोश, बेसुध, अचेत *He was found lying unconscious on the kitchen floor.* **2 unconscious of sb/sth** not knowing sth; not aware of sb/sth किसी बात से अनजान; किसी बात से बेख़बर **3** (used about feelings, thoughts, etc.) existing or happening without your realizing; not deliberate (भावनाएँ, विचार आदि) जिसके होने या घटित होने का अहसास न हो, सहज; जो जान-बूझ कर न किया गया; अनभिप्रेत *The article was full of unconscious humour.* ✪ विलोम **conscious** **4 the unconscious** *noun* [*sing.*] = **subconscious** ▶ **unconsciously** *adv.* बिना जाने-बूझे, सहज भाव से, अनजाने में ▶ **unconsciousness** *noun* [U] सहजता, अनभिज्ञता, बेहोशी

**uncontrollable** /ˌʌnkənˈtrəʊləbl ˌअन्कन्ˈट्रोलब्ल्/ *adj.* that you cannot control बेक़ाबू, जिसे रोका या नियंत्रित न किया जा सके; अनियंत्रणीय *I suddenly had an uncontrollable urge to laugh.* ▶ **uncontrollably** /-əbli -अब्लि/ *adv.* बेक़ाबू होकर

**uncountable** /ʌnˈkaʊntəbl अन्ˈकाउन्टब्ल्/ *adj.* (*grammar*) an uncountable noun cannot be counted and so does not have a plural. In this dictionary uncountable nouns are marked '[U]' अगणनीय (संज्ञा) (जिसे गिना न जा सके और अतएव जिसका बहुवचन न बनता हो) इस शब्दकोश में अगणनीय संज्ञाओं के लिए सूचक चिह्न '[U]' प्रयोग किया गया है ✪ विलोम **countable**

**NOTE** अगणनीय संज्ञाओं के बारे में अधिक जानकारी के लिए इस शब्दकोश के अंत में **Quick Grammar Reference** खंड देखिए।

**uncouth** /ʌnˈkuːθ अन्ˈकूथ़/ *adj.* (used about a person or his/her behaviour) rude or socially unacceptable (व्यक्ति या उसका आचरण) अशिष्ट, गँवार या जिसे समाज बुरा समझे; असभ्य

**uncover** /ʌnˈkʌvə(r) अन्ˈकव़(र्)/ *verb* [T] **1** to remove the cover from sth किसी (डिब्बे आदि) का ढक्कन खोलना; निरावरण करना, अनावृत करना ✪ विलोम **cover** **2** to find out or discover sth किसी बात का पता चलना या उसे खोज लेना; रहस्य या भेद पाना *Police 0*

**undecided** /ˌʌndɪˈsaɪdɪd ˌअन्डिˈसाइडिड्/ *adj.* **1** not having made a decision (व्यक्ति) जिसने (अभी तक) कोई निर्णय नहीं लिया; अनिश्चयी *I'm still undecided about whether to take the job or not.* **2** without any result or decision जिसका अभी कोई परिणाम नहीं निकला, परिणामहीन या जिसका निर्णय अभी नहीं हुआ; अनिर्णीत ✪ विलोम **decided**

**undemocratic** /ˌʌndeməˈkrætɪk ˌअन्डेमˈक्रैटिक्/ *adj.* against or not acting according to the principles of a system which supports equal rights for all people (**a democracy**) अलोकतांत्रिक; लोकतंत्र (सबके लिए समान अधिकार का सिद्धांत) के विरुद्ध या असंगत ✪ विलोम **democratic**

**undeniable** /ˌʌndɪˈnaɪəbl ˌअन्डिˈनाइअब्ल्/ *adj.* clear, true or certain स्पष्ट, सच या निश्चित (जिसे नकारा न जा सके); अकाट्य ▶ **undeniably** /-əbli -अब्लि/ *adv.* निश्चित या अकाट्य रूप से

**under** /ˈʌndə(r) ˈअन्ड(र्)/ *prep., adv.* **1** in or to a position that is below sth (किसी के) नीचे, नीचे से *We found him hiding under the table.* ○ *The dog crawled under the gate and ran into the road.*

**NOTE** **Under, below, beneath** और **underneath** में तुलना कीजिए। हम **under** का प्रयोग यह बताने के लिए करते हैं कि कोई वस्तु दूसरी के ठीक नीचे है, संभव है कि दोनों के बीच कुछ ख़ाली जगह हो—*The cat is asleep under the table* या एक वस्तु दूसरी का स्पर्श करे या उसे ढक ले—*I think your letter is under that book.* यह बताने के लिए कि कोई वस्तु दूसरी के नीचे स्थित है हम **below** का प्रयोग कर सकते हैं—*They live on the floor below us.* ○ *The skirt comes down to just below the knee.* यदि किसी वस्तु के एक ओर से दूसरी ओर जाने की बात करनी हो तो **under** का प्रयोग होता है (न कि **below** का)—*We swam under the bridge.* यह बताने के लिए कि कोई वस्तु दूसरी के ठीक नीचे है, औपचारिक शैली में **beneath** का प्रयोग होता है परंतु **under** ही अधिक प्रचलित है। जब हमें इस बात पर बल देना हो कि कोई वस्तु दूसरी को ढक या छिपा रही है तो हम (**under** के स्थान पर) **underneath** का प्रयोग करते हैं—*Have you looked underneath the sofa as well as behind it?*

**2** below the surface of sth; covered by sth किसी वस्तु की सतह के नीचे; किसी वस्तु से ढका हुआ या जिसके ऊपर कोई और वस्तु हो *Most of an iceberg is under the water.* ○ *He was wearing a vest under his shirt.* **3** less than a certain number; younger than a certain age किसी विशेष संख्या से कम; किसी विशेष आयु से कम आयु का *People working under 20 hours a week will pay no extra tax.* ○ *Nobody under eighteen is allowed to buy alcohol.* **4** governed or controlled by sb/sth किसी के शासन या नियंत्रण में *The country is now under martial law.* **5** according to a law, agreement, system, etc. किसी क़ानून, संधि, प्रणाली आदि के अनुसार; के अंतर्गत *Under Indian law you are innocent until you are proved guilty.* **6** experiencing a particular feeling, process or effect किसी मनोभाव, प्रक्रिया या प्रभाव में से गुज़रते हुए, के प्रभाव में; के अधीन *He was jailed for driving under the influence of alcohol.* ○ *The manager is* ***under pressure*** *to resign.* ○ *I was* ***under the impression that*** *Tarun was not very happy there.* **7** using a particular name किसी विशेष नाम से *to travel under a false name* **8** found in a particular part of a book, list, etc. किसी पुस्तक, सूची आदि के विशेष खंड में (उपलब्ध) *You'll find some information on cricket under 'team sports'.*

**under-** /ˈʌndə(r) ˈअन्ड(र्)/ *prefix* **1** (*used in nouns and adjectives*) below नीचे का, अधः, अव- *underground* ○ *undergrowth* **2** (*used in nouns*) lower in age, level or position कम आयु, स्तर या पद का, अवर-, उप- *the under-fives* ○ *an under-secretary* **3** (*used in adjectives and verbs*) not enough अपर्याप्त, न्यून-, अल्प- *undercooked food*

**underarm¹** /ˈʌndərɑːm ˈअन्डरआम्/ *adj.* **1** (*only before a noun*) connected with a person's **armpit** बग़ल या काँख से संबंधित; बग़ल या काँख का *underarm deodorant/sweating* **2** an **underarm** throw of a ball is done with the hand kept below the level of the shoulder हाथ को कंधे से नीचे रखकर फेंकी जाने वाली (गेंद)

**underarm²** /ˈʌndərɑːm ˈअन्डरआम्/ *adv.* if you throw, etc. **underarm**, you throw keeping your hand below the level of your shoulder हाथ को कंधे से नीचे रखकर कुछ फेंकते हुए

**undercarriage** /ˈʌndəkærɪdʒ ˈअन्डकैरिज़्/ (*also* **landing gear**) *noun* [C] the part of an aircraft, including the wheels, that supports it when it is landing and taking off (पहियों समेत) विमान का निचला ढाँचा; अवचक्र (जो उतरने और उड़ान भरते समय विमान को सहारा देता है) ➪ **plane** पर चित्र देखिए।

**underclothes** /ˈʌndəkləʊðz ˈअन्डक्लोद्ज़्/ *noun* [*pl.*] = **underwear**

**undercook** /ˌʌndəˈkʊk ˌअन्डˈकुक्/ *verb* [T] to not cook food for long enough भोजन को पूरा न पकाना, अधपका छोड़ देना ✪ विलोम **overcook**

**undercover** /ˌʌndəˈkʌvə(r) ˌअन्डˈकव़(र्)/ *adj.* working or happening secretly चोरी-छिपे करने या होने वाला; गुप्त *an undercover reporter/detective*

**undercurrent** /ˈʌndəkʌrənt ˈअन्डकरन्ट्/ *noun* [C] **undercurrent (of sth)** a feeling, especially a negative one, that is hidden but whose effects are felt प्रच्छन्न या गुप्त मनोभाव (विशेषतः नकारात्मक और हलके असर वाला) *I detect an undercurrent of resentment towards the new proposals.*

**undercut** /ˌʌndəˈkʌt ˌअन्डˈकट्/ *verb* [T] (*pres. part.* **undercutting;** *pt, pp* **undercut**) to sell sth at a lower price than other shops, etc. किसी वस्तु को (अन्य दुकानदारों आदि की अपेक्षा) कम दाम पर बेचना

**undercutting** /ˌʌndəˈkʌtɪŋ ˌअन्डˈकटिङ्/ *noun* [U] (in geography) the destruction by water of a softer layer of rock below a hard top layer so that after a long period of time the top layer is not supported and falls down (भूगोल में) लगातार पानी पड़ने से चट्टान की कड़ी से नीचे की परत का कट जाना (जिसके फलस्वरूप कालांतर में कड़ी परत ढह जाती है)

**underdeveloped** /ˌʌndədɪˈveləpt ˌअन्डडिˈव़ेलप्ट्/ *adj.* (used about a country, society, etc.) having few industries and a low standard of living (देश, समाज आदि) अल्पविकसित, अपूर्ण या न्यून विकसित, पिछड़ा

> **NOTE** वर्तमान में **developing country** शब्द का अधिक प्रयोग होता है।

▶ **underdevelopment** *noun* [U] अल्प, अपूर्ण या न्यून विकास; पिछड़ापन

**underdog** /ˈʌndədɒɡ ˈअन्डडॉग्/ *noun* [C] a person, team, etc. who is weaker than others, and not expected to be successful दूसरों से कमज़ोर और हारने की संभावना वाला व्यक्ति, दल आदि; गौण प्रतियोगी *Bangladesh were the underdogs, but managed to win the match by two wickets.*

**underestimate** /ˌʌndərˈestɪmeɪt ˌअन्डर्ˈएस्टिमेट्/ *verb* [T] **1** to guess that the amount, etc. of sth will be less than it really is किसी वस्तु की मात्रा आदि को वास्तविकता से कम आँकना **2** to think that sb/sth is not as strong, good, etc. as he/she/it really is किसी की शक्ति, गुणवत्ता आदि को वास्तविकता से कम समझना *Don't underestimate your opponent. He's a really good player.* ✪ विलोम **overestimate** ▶ **underestimate** /-mət -मट्/ *noun* [C] कम अंदाज़ा, न्यून प्राक्कलन

**underfoot** /ˌʌndəˈfʊt ˌअन्डˈफ़ुट्/ *adv.* under your feet; where you are walking पैरों के नीचे, पाँव तले; पैरों के नीचे की ज़मीन *It's very wet underfoot.*

**undergo** /ˌʌndəˈɡəʊ ˌअन्डˈगो/ *verb* [T] (*pt* **underwent** /-ˈwent -ˈवेन्ट्/; *pp* **undergone** /-ˈɡɒn -ˈगॉन्/) to have a difficult or unpleasant experience कठिन या अप्रिय स्थिति में से गुज़रना, कठिन या अप्रिय स्थिति को झेलना *She underwent a five-hour operation.*

**undergraduate** /ˌʌndəˈɡrædʒuət ˌअन्डˈग्रैजुअट्/ *noun* [C] a university student who has not yet taken his/her first degree विश्वविद्यालय में स्नातक कक्षा का छात्र ➪ **graduate** और **postgraduate** देखिए।

**underground[1]** /ˈʌndəɡraʊnd ˈअन्डग्राउन्ड्/ *adj.* **1** under the surface of the ground भूमि के नीचे का; भूमिगत, ज़मींदोज़ *an underground car park* **2** secret or illegal गुप्त (स्थान पर स्थित) या अवैधानिक ग़ैर-क़ानूनी *an underground radio station*

**underground[2]** /ˌʌndəˈɡraʊnd ˌअन्डˈग्राउन्ड्/ *adv.* **1** under the surface of the ground भूमिगत, ज़मींदोज़, ज़मीन के नीचे से *The cables all run underground.* **2** into a secret place गुप्त स्थान के अंदर; भूमिगत *She went underground to escape from the police.*

**underground[3]** /ˈʌndəɡraʊnd ˈअन्डग्राउन्ड्/ (*AmE* **subway**) *noun* [*sing.*] a railway system under the ground भूमिगत रेल-व्यवस्था

**undergrowth** /ˈʌndəɡrəʊθ ˈअन्डग्रोथ्/ *noun* [U] bushes and plants that grow around and under trees वृक्षों के नीचे उग आने वाली झाड़ियाँ और पौधे; झाड़-झंखाड़

**underhand** /ˌʌndəˈhænd ˌअन्डˈहैन्ड्/ *adj.* secret or not honest छिपाव-दुराव वाला, दुरावभरा या कपटभरा

**underlie** /ˌʌndəˈlaɪ ˌअन्डˈलाइ/ *verb* [T] (*pres. part.* **underlying;** *pt* **underlay** /-ˈleɪ -ˈलेन्/; *pp* **underlain** /-ˈleɪn-ˈलेन्/) (*formal*) to be the basis or cause of sth किसी वस्तु का आधार या कारण होना (का) आधारभूत होना (के) मूल में होना *It is a principle that underlies all the party's policies.*

**underline** /ˌʌndəˈlaɪn ˌअन्डˈलाइन्/ (*AmE* **underscore**) *verb* [T] **1** to draw a line under a word, etc. किसी शब्द आदि के नीचे रेखा खींचना, (को) रेखांकित करना **2** to show sth clearly or to emphasize sth

किसी बात को साफ़ तौर पर बताना या किसी बात पर बल देना *This accident underlines the need for greater care.*

**underlying** /ˌʌndəˈlaɪɪŋ ˌअन्डˈलाइइङ्/ *adj.* important but hidden महत्त्वपूर्ण परंतु गुप्त; अंतर्निहित *the underlying causes of the disaster*

**undermine** /ˌʌndəˈmaɪn ˌअन्डˈमाइन्/ *verb* [T] to make sth weaker किसी के (विशेषतः) विश्वास या आदेश देने के अधिकार की शक्ति या प्रभाव को शनैः शनैः कम करना, (उसे) क्षति पहुँचाना *The public's confidence in the government has been undermined by the crisis.*

**underneath** /ˌʌndəˈniːθ ˌअन्डˈनीथ्/ *prep., adv.* under; below के तले; के नीचे *The coin rolled underneath the chair.* ➪ **under** पर नोट देखिए।

**the underneath** /ˌʌndəˈniːθ ˌअन्डˈनीथ्/ *noun* [*sing.*] the bottom or lowest part of something (किसी वस्तु का) तला, निचला भाग *There is a lot of rust on the underneath of the car.*

**undernourished** /ˌʌndəˈnʌrɪʃt ˌअन्डˈनरिश्ट्/ *adj.* in bad health because of not having enough food or enough of the right type of food अल्पपोषित, न्यून-पोषित (पर्याप्त मात्रा में या सही प्रकार का भोजन न मिलने से दुर्बल)

**underpants** /ˈʌndəpænts ˈअन्डपैन्ट्स्/ (*BrE* **pants**) *noun* [*pl.*] a piece of clothing that men or boys wear under their trousers (पुरुषों या लड़कों की) जाँघिया

**underpass** /ˈʌndəpɑːs ˈअन्डपास्/ *noun* [C] a road or path that goes under another road, railway, etc. सड़क, रेलपटरी आदि के नीचे से निकलने वाली दूसरी सड़क या रास्ता, तलमार्ग; अंडरपास

**underpay** /ˌʌndəˈpeɪ ˌअन्डˈपे/ *verb* [T] (*pt, pp* **underpaid**) to pay sb too little किसी को बहुत (या उचित से) कम वेतन देना ✪ विलोम **overpay**

**underprivileged** /ˌʌndəˈprɪvəlɪdʒd ˌअन्डˈप्रिव़लिज्ड्/ *adj.* having less money, and fewer rights, opportunities, etc. than other people in society शोषित, अल्प अधिकार वाला (समाज के अन्य सदस्यों की अपेक्षा जिसके पास धन, अधिकार, अवसर आदि कम हों) ✪ विलोम **privileged**

**underrate** /ˌʌndəˈreɪt ˌअन्डˈरेट्/ *verb* [T] to think that sb/sth is less clever, important, good, etc. than he/she/it really is किसी को वास्तविकता से कम चतुर, बड़ा, अच्छा आदि समझना ✪ विलोम **overrate**

**underscore** /ˌʌndəˈskɔː(r) ˌअन्डˈस्कॉ(र्)/ (*AmE*) = **underline**

**undershirt** /ˈʌndəʃɜːt ˈअन्डशट्/ (*AmE*) = **vest 1**

**underside** /ˈʌndəsaɪd ˈअन्डसाइड्/ *noun* [C] the side or surface of sth that is underneath नीचे की सतह; निम्नतल ✪ पर्याय **bottom[1] 2**

**the undersigned** /ˌʌndəˈsaɪnd ˌअन्डˈसाइन्ड्/ *noun* [*pl.*] the person or people who have signed a particular legal document क़ानूनी दस्तावेज़ पर हस्ताक्षर करने वाला या वाले (व्यक्ति); अधोहस्ताक्षरी *We, the undersigned, agree to the terms and conditions mentioned in the contract.*

**understand** /ˌʌndəˈstænd ˌअन्डˈस्टैन्ड्/ *verb* (*pt, pp* **understood** /-ˈstʊd -ˈस्टुड्/) **1** [I, T] to know or realize the meaning of sth किसी बात का अर्थ समझना (उसे जानना या महसूस करना) *I'm not sure that I really understand.* ○ *Please speak more slowly. I can't understand you.* **2** [T] to know how or why sth happens or why it is important कोई क्रिया कैसे या क्यों होती है या क्यों महत्त्वपूर्ण है, इस बात की जानकारी होना *I can't understand why the engine won't start.* ○ *As far as I understand it, the changes won't affect us.* **3** [T] to know sb's character and why he/she behaves in a particular way किसी के स्वभाव या विशेष प्रकार के व्यवहार को जानना या समझना *It's easy to understand why she felt so angry.* **4** [T] (*formal*) to have heard or been told sth किसी को किसी बात की (सुनकर) जानकारी होना या किसी को कुछ बताया जाना

IDM **give sb to believe/understand (that)** ➪ **believe** देखिए।

**make yourself understood** to make your meaning clear अपना अर्थ या आशय स्पष्ट करना *I can just about make myself understood in Russian.*

**understandable** /ˌʌndəˈstændəbl ˌअन्डˈस्टैन्डब्ल्/ *adj.* that you can understand जो समझ में आ सके, बोधगम्य, सुबोध; स्वाभाविक या उचित ▶ **understandably** /-əbli -अब्लि/ *adv.* स्वाभाविक या उचित रूप से *She was understandably angry at the decision.*

**understanding[1]** /ˌʌndəˈstændɪŋ ˌअन्डˈस्टैन्डिङ्/ *noun* **1** [U, *sing.*] the knowledge that sb has of a particular subject or situation विषय या स्थिति-विशेष की जानकारी या समझ *A basic understanding of physics is necessary for this course.* ○ *He has little understanding of how computers work.* **2** [C, *usually sing.*] an informal agreement अनौपचारिक या आपसी समझौता *I'm sure we can **come to/reach an understanding** about the money I owe him.* **3** [U] the ability to know why people behave in a particular way and to forgive them if they do sth wrong or bad (ग़लती कर जाने की) दूसरों की मज़बूरी को समझने की और उन्हें माफ़ करने की

क्षमता; समझदारी **4** [U] the way in which you think sth is meant किसी बात को समझने का विशेष ढंग, किसी बात की (ख़ास) समझ *My understanding of the arrangement is that he will only phone if there is a problem.*

IDM **on the understanding that...** only if...; because it was agreed that... इस शर्त पर कि; क्योंकि यह आपस में तय हुआ था कि, आपस में तय बात के अनुसार *We let them stay in our house on the understanding that it was only for a short period.*

**understanding²** /ˌʌndəˈstændɪŋ ˌअन्डˈस्टैन्डिङ्/ *adj.* showing kind feelings towards sb; sympathetic किसी के प्रति कोमल व्यवहार वाला; (किसी से) सहानुभूति रखने वाला

**understate** /ˌʌndəˈsteɪt ˌअन्डˈस्टेट्/ *verb* [T] to say that sth is smaller or less important than it really is किसी वस्तु के आकार या महत्त्व को वास्तविकता से काफ़ी कम बताना ✪ विलोम **overstate** ▶ **understatement** *noun* [C] न्यूनोक्ति *'Is she pleased?' 'That's an understatement. She's delighted.'*

**understudy** /ˈʌndəstʌdi ˈअन्डस्टडि/ *noun* [C] (*pl.* **understudies**) an actor who learns the role of another actor and replaces him/her if he/she is ill किसी दूसरे के स्थान पर उसकी भूमिका निभाने वाला अभिनेता; स्थानापन्न अभिनेता

**undertake** /ˌʌndəˈteɪk ˌअन्डˈटेक्/ *verb* [T] (*pt* **undertook** /-ˈtʊk -ˈटुक्/; *pp* **undertaken** /-ˈteɪkən -ˈटेकन्/) **1** to decide to do sth and start doing it किसी काम को करने का निर्णय लेकर उसे आरंभ करना *The company is undertaking a major programme of modernization.* **2** to agree or promise to do sth किसी काम को करने का निर्णय लेकर उसे आरंभ करना

**undertaker** /ˈʌndəteɪkə(r) ˈअन्डटेक(र्)/ (*also* **funeral director** *AmE* **mortician**) *noun* [C] a person whose job is to prepare dead bodies to be buried and to arrange funerals अंत्येष्टिप्रबंधक (शवों के अंत्येष्टि संस्कार का प्रबंध करने वाला व्यक्ति)

**undertaking** /ˌʌndəˈteɪkɪŋ ˌअन्डˈटेकिङ्/ *noun* [C, *usually sing.*] **1** a piece of work or business उद्यम, कारोबार, व्यवसाय, उपक्रम *Buying the company would be a risky undertaking.* **2 undertaking (that.../to do sth)** a formal or legal promise to do sth (किसी काम के लिए दिया गया) औपचारिक या वैधानिक वचन

**undertone** /ˈʌndətəʊn ˈअन्डटोन्/ *noun* [C] a feeling, quality or meaning that is not expressed in a direct way परोक्ष रीति से व्यक्त भाव, गुण या अर्थ

IDM **in an undertone; in undertones** in a quiet voice मंद स्वर में

**undervalue** /ˌʌndəˈvælju: ˌअन्डˈवैल्यू/ *verb* [T] to place too low a value on sb/sth किसी वस्तु का बहुत (या उचित से) कम मूल्य आँकना या व्यक्ति का महत्त्व कम करके आँकना; अवमूल्य करना

**underwater** /ˌʌndəˈwɔ:tə(r) ˌअन्डˈवॉट(र्)/ *adj.*, *adv.* existing, happening or used below the surface of water पानी के नीचे या जल के अंदर स्थित होने वाला या प्रयोग में आने वाला; अंतर्जलीय, अघोजल *underwater exploration* ○ *an underwater camera*

**underwear** /ˈʌndəweə(r) ˈअन्डवेअ(र्)/ *noun* [U] clothing that is worn next to the skin under other clothes अंदर पहनने के कपड़े (बनियान, जाँघिया आदि) NOTE **Underclothes** का भी यही अर्थ है और यह बहुवचनांत संज्ञा है।

**underweight** /ˌʌndəˈweɪt ˌअन्डˈवेट्/ *adj.* weighing less than is normal or correct सामान्य या सही से कम वज़न का ➪ **thin** पर नोट देखिए। ✪ विलोम **overweight**

**the underworld** /ˈʌndəwɜ:ld ˈअन्डवल्ड्/ *noun* [*sing.*] people who are involved in organized crime अपराध जगत; संगठित अपराधी गिरोह

**underwrite** /ˌʌndəˈraɪt ˌअन्डˈराइट्/ *verb* [T] (*pt* **underwrote** /-ˈrəʊt -ˈरोट्/; *pp* **underwritten** /-ˈrɪtn -ˈरिट्न्/) to accept responsibility for an insurance policy by agreeing to pay if there is any damage or loss बीमा पॉलिसी के माध्यम से क्षति या हानि की पूर्ति का आर्थिक दायित्व लेना; बीमा करना ▶ **underwriter** *noun* [C] बीमाकर्त्ता

**undesirable** /ˌʌndɪˈzaɪərəbl ˌअन्डिˈज़ाइअरब्ल्/ *adj.* unpleasant or not wanted; likely to cause problems अप्रिय या अवांछित; जो समस्याएँ पैदा कर सकता हो ✪ विलोम **desirable**

**undid** ➪ **undo** का past tense रूप

**undignified** /ʌnˈdɪgnɪfaɪd अन्ˈडिग्निफ़ाइड्/ *adj.* causing you to look foolish and to lose the respect of other people अशोभन, मर्यादाहीन (आचरण) (जिसे करके आप मूर्ख लगें और लोगों की नज़र में गिर जाएँ) ✪ विलोम **dignified**

**undisputed** /ˌʌndɪˈspju:tɪd ˌअन्डिˈस्प्यूटिड्/ *adj.* **1** that cannot be questioned or shown to be false; that cannot be argued against निर्विवाद (संदेह से परे या प्रमाणित सत्य); अविवादित (विवाद या मतभेद से परे) *undisputed facts/evidence* **2** that everyone accepts or recognizes सर्वमान्य *the undisputed champion of the world*

**undisturbed** /ˌʌndɪˈstɜ:bd ˌअन्डिˈस्टब्ड्/ *adj.* **1** (*not usually before a noun*) not moved or touched by anyone or anything जिसे किसी व्यक्ति या वस्तु ने अपने स्थान से न हटाया या न छुआ, यथास्थान

या व्यवस्थित, अछूता ✪ पर्याय **untouched** 2 not interrupted by anyone बेरोकटोक 3 (*not usually before a noun*) **undisturbed (by sth)** not affected or upset by sth जो किसी बात से प्रभावित या परेशान न हो; अविक्षुब्ध ✪ पर्याय **unconcerned** *He seemed undisturbed by the news of her death.*

**undivided** /ˌʌndɪˈvaɪdɪd ˌअनुडिˈवाइडिड्/ *adj.*
**IDM get/have sb's undivided attention** to receive all sb's attention किसी बात पर किसी व्यक्ति का पूरा ध्यान लगना
**give your undivided attention (to sb/sth)** to give all your attention to sb/sth किसी व्यक्ति या वस्तु पर अपना पूरा ध्यान लगाना

**undo** /ʌnˈdu: अन्ˈडू/ *verb* [T] (*3rd person sing. pres.* **undoes;** *pt* **undid;** *pp* **undone**) 1 to open sth that was tied or fastened (बाँधी गई गाँठ या बंद किए गए बटन को) खोलना *to undo a knot/zip/button* 2 to destroy the effect of sth that has already happened किए हुए को बिगाड़ देना, व्यर्थ कर देना *His mistake has undone all our good work.*

**undone** /ʌnˈdʌn अन्ˈडन्/ *adj.* 1 open; not fastened or tied खुला हुआ; जिसे बंद नहीं किया गया या बाँधा नहीं गया *I realized that my zip was undone.* 2 not done अधूरा *I left the housework undone.*

**undoubted** /ʌnˈdaʊtɪd अन्ˈडाउटिड्/ *adj.* definite; accepted as being true निश्चित, संदेह से मुक्त; जिसे सच मान लिया गया है ▶ **undoubtedly** *adv.* निस्संदेह, निश्चित रूप से

**undress** /ʌnˈdres अन्ˈड्रेस्/ *verb* 1 [I] to take off your clothes (अपने) कपड़े उतारना **NOTE Undress** के स्थान पर **get undressed** अधिक प्रचलित है—*He got undressed and had a shower.* 2 [T] to take off sb's clothes किसी अन्य के कपड़े उतारना ✪ विलोम **dress** ▶ **undressed** *adj.* बिना कपड़े पहने; निर्वस्त्र

**undue** /ˌʌnˈdju: ˌअन्ˈड्यू/ *adj.* more than is necessary or reasonable आवश्यक या उचित मात्रा से अधिक; अत्यधिक *The police try not to use undue force when arresting a person.* ▶ **unduly** *adv.* अत्यधिक *She didn't seem unduly worried by their unexpected arrival.*

**unearth** /ʌnˈɜ:θ अन्ˈअथ्/ *verb* [T] to dig sth up out of the ground; to discover sth that was hidden खोदकर कुछ निकालना; छिपी हुई वस्तु को खोज लेना *Archaeologists have unearthed a Roman tomb.*

**unearthly** /ʌnˈɜ:θli अन्ˈअथ्लि/ *adj.* strange or frightening विचित्र या भयावह, अजीबोग़रीब या डरावना *an unearthly scream*
**IDM at an unearthly hour** (*informal*) extremely early in the morning बहुत सवेरे

**unease** /ʌnˈi:z अन्ˈईज़्/ (*also* **uneasiness**) *noun* [U] a worried or uncomfortable feeling फ़िक्र, चिंता या बैचेनी (भाव) ✪ विलोम **ease**

**uneasy** /ʌnˈi:zi अन्ˈईज़ि/ *adj.* 1 **uneasy (about sth/doing sth)** worried; not feeling relaxed or comfortable चिंतित, फ़िक्रमंद; तनावभरा या बेआराम, बैचेन 2 not settled; unlikely to last डाँवाँडोल, डगमग, अस्थिर; अस्थायी, टिकाऊ नहीं *an uneasy compromise* ▶ **uneasily** *adv.* चिंतित होकर, बेचैनी से

**uneconomic** /ˌʌni:kəˈnɒmɪk; ˌʌnek- ˌअनीकˈनॉमिक्; ˌअनेक्-/ *adj.* (used about a company, etc.) not making or likely to make a profit (कंपनी आदि) मुनाफ़ा न कमाने या न कमा सकने वाली, घाटे में जाने वाली; अलाभकर ✪ पर्याय **unprofitable** ✪ विलोम **economic**

**uneconomical** /ˌʌni:kəˈnɒmɪkl; ˌʌnek- ˌअनीकˈनॉमिकल्; ˌअनेक्-/ *adj.* wasting money, time, materials, etc. पैसा, समय, सामान आदि की बर्बादी करने वाला; किफ़ायती नहीं, अमितव्ययी, ख़र्चीला ✪ विलोम **economical** ▶ **uneconomically** /-kli -क्लि/ *adv.* अलाभकर, अमितव्ययी, या ख़र्चीले रूप से

**unemployed** /ˌʌnɪmˈplɔɪd ˌअनिम्ˈप्लॉइड्/ *adj.* 1 not able to find a job; out of work जिसके पास कोई काम-धंधा नहीं, बेकार; जिसकी नौकरी जाती रही; बेरोज़गार *She has been unemployed for over a year.* ✪ पर्याय **jobless** ✪ विलोम **employed** 2 **the unemployed** *noun* [*pl.*] people who cannot find a job बेरोज़गार लोग

**unemployment** /ˌʌnɪmˈplɔɪmənt ˌअनिम्ˈप्लॉइमन्ट्/ *noun* [U] 1 the situation of not being able to find a job बेरोज़गारी; नौकरी न मिलने की स्थिति *The number of people claiming unemployment benefit* (= money given by the state) *has gone up.* ✪ विलोम **employment** 2 the number of people who are unemployed बेरोज़गार लोगों की संख्या, बेरोज़गार *The economy is doing very badly and unemployment is rising.* ✪ पर्याय **joblessness** ➪ **dole** देखिए।

**unending** /ʌnˈendɪŋ अन्ˈएनडिङ्/ *adj.* having or seeming to have no end अंतहीन (जिसका वस्तुतः अंत न हो या लगे कि अंत नहीं)

**unequal** /ʌnˈi:kwəl अन्ˈईक्वल्/ *adj.* 1 not fair or balanced असमान, ग़ैर-बराबरी का *an unequal distribution of power* 2 different in size, amount, level, etc. आकार, मात्रा, स्तर आदि की दृष्टि से अलग ✪ विलोम **equal** ▶ **unequally** *adv.* असमानतापूर्वक

**UNESCO** (*also* **Unesco**) /ju:ˈneskəʊ यूˈनेस्को/ *abbr.* United Nations Educational, Scientific and Cultural Organization यूनेस्को; संयुक्त राष्ट्र शैक्षणिक, वैज्ञानिक, तथा सांस्कृतिक संगठन

**unethical** /ʌnˈeθɪkl अन्ˈएथिकल्/ *adj.* not morally acceptable अनैतिक, बेईमानीवाला *unethical behaviour/conduct* ✪ विलोम **ethical** ▶ **unethically** /-kli -क्लि/ *adv.* अनैतिक रूप से, बेईमानी से

**uneven** /ʌnˈiːvn अन्ˈईव्न्/ *adj.* **1** not completely smooth, level or regular छोटा-बड़ा, असमान, ऊबड़-खाबड़, खुरदरा, असमतल *The sign was painted in rather uneven letters.* ✪ विलोम **even** **2** not always of the same level or quality स्तर या गुणवत्ता की दृष्टि से असमान ▶ **unevenly** *adv.* असमान रूप से *The country's wealth is unevenly distributed.*

**unexceptional** /ˌʌnɪkˈsepʃənl ˌअनिक्ˈसेप्शनल्/ *adj.* not interesting or unusual मामूली, कुछ ख़ास नहीं या साधारण ⇨ **exceptional** देखिए।

**unexpected** /ˌʌnɪkˈspektɪd ˌअनिक्ˈस्पेक्टिड्/ *adj.* not expected and therefore causing surprise अप्रत्याशित और अतएव आश्चर्यजनक ▶ **unexpectedly** *adv.* अप्रत्याशित रूप से *I got there late because I was unexpectedly delayed.*

**unfailing** /ʌnˈfeɪlɪŋ अन्ˈफ़ेलिङ्/ *adj.* that you can depend on to always be there and always be the same विश्वसनीय, भरोसेमंद; जिसमें कोई चूक न हो *unfailing devotion/support* ○ *She fought the disease with unfailing good humour.* ▶ **unfailingly** *adv.* विश्वसनीय रूप से, बिना चूके *unfailingly loyal/polite*

**unfair** /ˌʌnˈfeə(r) ˌअन्ˈफ़ेअ(र्)/ *adj.* **1 unfair (on/to sb)** not dealing with people as they deserve; not treating each person equally जो यथायोग्य व्यवहार वाला नहीं, अन्यायपूर्ण; जिसमें लोगों को बराबर नहीं माना जाता; भेदभावपूर्ण *This law is unfair to women.* ○ *The tax is unfair on people with low incomes.* **2** not following the rules and therefore giving an advantage to one person, team, etc. नियमों को ताक पर रख कर (केवल) एक व्यक्ति, दल आदि को लाभ पहुँचाने वाला; पक्षपातपूर्ण ✪ विलोम **fair** ▶ **unfairly** *adv.* पक्षपात या भेदभाव पूर्वक ▶ **unfairness** *noun* [U] पक्षपात, भेदभाव, अन्याय

**unfaithful** /ʌnˈfeɪθfl अन्ˈफ़ेथ्फ़ल्/ *adj.* **unfaithful (to sb/sth)** having a sexual relationship with sb who is not your husband, wife or partner पति-पत्नी के संबंध में निष्ठारहित; बेवफ़ा ✪ विलोम **faithful** ▶ **unfaithfulness** *noun* [U] बेवफ़ाई, विश्वासघात

**unfamiliar** /ˌʌnfəˈmɪliə(r) ˌअनफ़ˈमिलिअ(र्)/ *adj.* **1 unfamiliar (to sb)** that you do not know well जिसे हम अच्छी तरह नहीं जानते; अपरिचित, अनजान *an unfamiliar part of town* **2 unfamiliar (with sth)** not having knowledge or experience of sth (से) अनभिज्ञ (किसी बात की जानकारी या अनुभव से रहित) *I'm unfamiliar with this author.* ✪ विलोम **familiar**

**unfashionable** /ʌnˈfæʃnəbl अन्ˈफ़ैश्नबल्/ *adj.* not popular at a particular time (अब) फ़ैशन से बाहर; अप्रचलित, लोकप्रिय नहीं *unfashionable ideas/clothes* ✪ विलोम **fashionable** ⇨ **old-fashioned** देखिए।

**unfasten** /ʌnˈfɑːsn अन्ˈफ़ास्न्/ *verb* [T] to open sth that was fastened (बंद बटन आदि को) खोलना *to unfasten a belt/button/chain/lock* ✪ पर्याय **undo** ✪ विलोम **fasten**

**unfavourable** (*AmE* **unfavorable**) /ʌnˈfeɪvərəbl अन्ˈफ़ेवरबल्/ *adj.* **1** showing that you do not like or approve of sb/sth नापसंद, अस्वीकार्य **2** not good and likely to cause problems or make sth difficult प्रतिकूल, नकारात्मक ✪ विलोम **favourable** ⇨ **adverse** भी देखिए।

**unfinished** /ʌnˈfɪnɪʃt अन्ˈफ़िनिश्ट्/ *adj.* not complete; not finished अपूर्ण; असमाप्त *We have some **unfinished business** to settle.* ○ *an unfinished drink/game/book*

**unfit** /ʌnˈfɪt अन्ˈफ़िट्/ *adj.* **1 unfit (for sth/to do sth)** not suitable or not good enough for sth अनुपयुक्त या अयोग्य *His criminal past makes him unfit to be a politician.* **2** not in good physical health, especially because you do not get enough exercise (पर्याप्त व्यायाम के अभाव में पूर्णतः) स्वस्थ नहीं; अनफ़िट ✪ विलोम **fit**

**unfold** /ʌnˈfəʊld अन्ˈफ़ोल्ड्/ *verb* [I, T] **1** to open out and become flat; to open out sth that was folded किसी वस्तु का खुलकर फैल जाना; तह लगी वस्तु को खोलना *The sofa unfolds into a spare bed.* ○ *I unfolded the letter and read it.* ✪ विलोम **fold (up)** **2** to become known, or to allow sth to become known, a little at a time थोड़ा-थोड़ा करके विदित होना या प्रकट करना

**unforeseen** /ˌʌnfɔːˈsiːn ˌअन्फ़ॉˈसीन्/ *adj.* not expected अप्रत्याशित, पूर्वतः अज्ञात, आकस्मिक *an unforeseen problem*

**unforgettable** /ˌʌnfəˈgetəbl ˌअनफ़ˈगेटबल्/ *adj.* making such a strong impression that you cannot forget it अविस्मरणीय (जो इतना गहरा प्रभाव छोड़े कि उसे भूला न जा सके)

**unforgivable** /ˌʌnfəˈgɪvəbl ˌअनफ़ˈगिवबल्/ *adj.* if sb's behaviour is unforgivable, it is so bad or unacceptable that you cannot forgive the person (बहुत बुरा या असह्य होने के कारण) क्षमा न करने योग्य; अक्षम्य (आचरण) ✪ पर्याय **inexcusable** ✪ विलोम **forgivable** ▶ **unforgivably** /-əbli -अब्लि/ *adv.* अक्षम्य रूप से

**unfortunate** /ʌnˈfɔːtʃənət अनॅफ़ॉचनट्/ *adj.* **1** not lucky (स्थिति) दुर्भाग्यपूर्ण (व्यक्ति) दुर्भाग्यशाली, अभागा ✪ विलोम **fortunate** **2** that you feel sorry about अफ़सोसनाक, खेदजनक ▸ **unfortunately** *adv.* दुर्भाग्य से *I'd like to help you but unfortunately there's nothing I can do.*

**unfounded** /ʌnˈfaʊndɪd अन्ˈफ़ाउन्डिड्/ *adj.* not based on or supported by facts जो तथ्यों पर आधारित या उनसे पुष्ट न हो; निराधार, बेबुनियाद, अपुष्ट *unfounded allegations*

**unfriendly** /ʌnˈfrendli अन्ˈफ्रेन्ड्लि/ *adj.* **unfriendly (to/towards sb)** unpleasant or not polite to sb अरुचिकर या अशिष्ट, अमित्रवत, अमैत्रीपूर्ण, रूखा ✪ विलोम **friendly**

**ungainly** /ʌnˈgeɪnli अन्ˈगेन्लि/ *adj.* moving in a way that is not smooth or elegant भोंडा, भद्दा, बेडौल

**ungrateful** /ʌnˈgreɪtfl अन्ˈग्रेट्फ़्ल्/ *adj.* not feeling or showing thanks to sb उपकार न मानने वाला; अकृतज्ञ, कृतघ्न, एहसानफ़रामोश ✪ विलोम **grateful** ▸ **ungratefully** /-fəli -फ़लि/ *adv.* कृतघ्नतापूर्वक

**unguarded** /ʌnˈgɑːdɪd अन्ˈगाडिड्/ *adj.* **1** not protected or guarded जिसके लिए बचाव या सुरक्षा की व्यवस्था न हो; अरक्षित **2** saying more than you wanted to (वाणी के प्रयोग में) असावधान, शिथिल ✪ विलोम **guarded**

**unhappily** /ʌnˈhæpɪli अन्ˈहैपिलि/ *adv.* **1** sadly दुखपूर्वक, उदास होकर **2** unfortunately दुर्भाग्य से, बदक़िस्मती से ✪ विलोम **happily**

**unhappy** /ʌnˈhæpi अन्ˈहैपि/ *adj.* (**unhappier; unhappiest**) **1 unhappy (about sth)** sad दुखी, खिन्न या उदास, दुखभरा, दुर्भाग्यपूर्ण *She's terribly unhappy about losing her job.* ○ *He had a very unhappy childhood.* **2 unhappy (about/at/with sth)** not satisfied or pleased; worried असंतुष्ट या नाराज़; दुखी, परेशान *They're unhappy at having to accept a pay cut.* ✪ विलोम **happy** ▸ **unhappiness** *noun* [U] अप्रसन्नता, नाराज़गी, दुख

**unharmed** /ʌnˈhɑːmd अन्ˈहाम्ड्/ *adj.* not injured or damaged; not harmed बिना चोट खाए या नुक़सान के; सकुशल, सही-सलामत *The hostages were released unharmed.*

**unhealthy** /ʌnˈhelθi अन्ˈहेल्थ़ि/ *adj.* **1** not having or showing good health अस्वस्थ, बीमार-सा *He looks pale and unhealthy.* **2** likely to cause illness or poor health रोग उत्पन्न कर सकने वाला या अस्वास्थ्यकर *unhealthy conditions* **3** not natural अस्वाभाविक, असामान्य *an unhealthy interest in death* ✪ विलोम **healthy**

**unheard** /ʌnˈhɜːd अन्ˈहड्/ *adj.* (*not before a noun*) not listened to or given any attention जो सुना नहीं गया अनसुना या जिस पर ध्यान नहीं दिया गया, जान-बूझ कर उपेक्षित; अनसुना *My suggestions **went unheard**.*

**unheard-of** *adj.* not known; never having happened before अज्ञात; जो पहले घटित नहीं हुआ, अभूतपूर्व, अनोखा, दृष्टांतविहीन

**unhelpful** /ʌnˈhelpfl अन्ˈहेल्प्फ़्ल्/ *adj.* not helpful or useful; not wanting to help sb असहायक, बेकार या अनुपयोगी; किसी की (भी) सहायता न करने वाला *an unhelpful response/reply* ✪ विलोम **helpful** ▸ **unhelpfully** /-fəli -फ़लि/ *adv.* असहायक रूप से

**unhurt** /ʌnˈhɜːt अन्ˈहट्/ *adj.* (*not before a noun*) not injured or harmed बिना चोट खाए, बेचोट या बिना क्षति के; अक्षत *He escaped from the crash unhurt.* ✪ पर्याय **unharmed** ✪ विलोम **hurt**

**uni-** /juːni ˈयूनि/ *prefix* (*used in nouns, adjectives and adverbs*) one; having one एक; एक वाला, एक-, इक- *uniform* ○ *unilaterally*

**UNICEF** /ˈjuːnɪsef ˈयूनिसेफ़्/ *abbr.* United Nations Children's Fund; an organization within the United Nations that helps to look after the health and education of children all over the world यूनिसेफ़; यूनाइटिड नेशन्ज़ चिल्डरन्ज़ फंड, विश्वभर के बच्चों के स्वास्थ्य और शिक्षा के काम में सहायता करने वाली संयुक्त राष्ट्र संघ की एक संस्था

**unicorn** /juːnɪkɔːn ˈयूनिकॉन्/ *noun* [C] an animal that only exists in stories, that looks like a white horse with one horn growing out of its forehead (केवल कथाओं में कल्पित) सफ़ेद रंग के घोड़े जैसा पशु जिसके माथे पर एक सींग होता है; एकशृंगी, इकसिंगा

**unidentified** /ˌʌnaɪˈdentɪfaɪd ˌअनाइˈडेन्टिफ़ाइड्/ *adj.* whose identity is not known जिसकी पहचान न हुई हो; अज्ञात *An unidentified body has been found in the river.*

**uniform¹** /ˈjuːnɪfɔːm ˈयूनिफ़ॉम्/ *noun* [C, U] the set of clothes worn at work by the members of certain organizations or groups and usually by schoolchildren एक जैसी पोशाक, वरदी (जिसे कुछ संस्थाओं या समूहों के सदस्य और अकसर स्कूली बच्चे पहनते हैं) *I didn't know he was a policeman because he wasn't **in uniform**.* ▸ **uniformed** *adj.* वरदीधारी

**uniform²** /ˈjuːnɪfɔːm ˈयूनिफ़ॉम्/ *adj.* not varying; the same in all cases or at all times जो बदलता नहीं, अविकारी, अपरिवर्ती; सब स्थितियों या समय में एक-सा, एकरूप ▸ **uniformity** /ˌjuːnɪˈfɔːməti ˌयूनिˈफ़ॉमटि/ *noun* [U] एकरूपता

**unify** /ˈjuːnɪfaɪ ˈयूनिफ़ाइ / *verb* [T] (*pres. part.* **unifying;** *3rd person sing. pres.* **unifies;** *pt, pp* **unified**) to join separate parts together to make one unit, or to make them similar to each other अलग-अलग अंशों को मिलाकर एक कर देना या उन्हें एक जैसा कर देना ▶ **unification** /ˌjuːnɪfɪˈkeɪʃn ˌयूनिफ़िˈकेश्न् / *noun* [U] एकीकरण, एकरूपीकरण

**unilateral** /ˌjuːnɪˈlætrəl ˌयूनिˈलैट्रल् / *adj.* done or made by one person who is involved in sth without the agreement of the other person or people एकपक्षीय, इकतरफ़ा (किसी उभयपक्षीय स्थिति में दूसरे पक्ष या व्यक्ति की सहमति के बिना एक पक्ष या व्यक्ति द्वारा किया गया) *a unilateral declaration of independence* ➪ **multilateral** देखिए। ▶ **unilaterally** /-rəli -रलि / *adv.* एकपक्षीय रूप से, इकतरफ़ा तौर पर

**unimportant** /ʌnɪmpɔːtnt ˌअनइम्पॉट्न्ट्/ *adj.* not important महत्त्वहीन, तुच्छ *unimportant details* ○ *They dismissed the problem as unimportant.*

**uninhabitable** /ˌʌnɪnˈhæbɪtəbl ˌअनइन्ˈहैबिटबल् / *adj.* not possible to live in जहाँ रहना संभव न हो; अनिवास्य ✪ विलोम **habitable**

**uninhabited** /ˌʌnɪnˈhæbɪtɪd ˌअनइन्ˈहैबिटिड् / *adj.* (used about a place or a building) with nobody living in it (स्थान या भवन) जहाँ कोई रहता न हो, ग़ैर-आबाद, वीरान, निर्जन ✪ विलोम **inhabited**

**uninhibited** /ˌʌnɪnˈhɪbɪtɪd ˌअनइन्ˈहिबिटिड् / *adj.* behaving in a free and natural way, without worrying what other people think of you (दूसरों की प्रतिक्रिया की चिंता किए बिना) मुक्त और सहज भाव से आचरण करने वाला; स्वच्छंद, उन्मुक्त ✪ विलोम **inhibited**

**unintelligible** /ˌʌnɪnˈtelɪdʒəbl ˌअनइन्ˈटेलिजबल् / *adj.* impossible to understand जो समझ में न आ सके; दुर्बोध ✪ विलोम **intelligible**

**uninterested** /ʌnˈɪntrəstɪd अन्ˈइनट्रस्टिड् / *adj.* **uninterested (in sb/sth)** having or showing no interest in sb/sth (किसी व्यक्ति या वस्तु में) रुचिहीन, (से) उदासीन, विमुख *She seemed uninterested in anything I had to say.* ✪ विलोम **interested** ➪ **disinterested** देखिए।

**uninteresting** /ʌnˈɪntrəstɪŋ अन्ˈइन्ट्रस्टिङ् / *adj.* boring; not interesting उबाऊ; नीरस, अरोचक, अरुचिकर *I found the novel uninteresting.* ✪ विलोम **interesting**

**union** /ˈjuːniən ˈयूनिअन् / *noun* **1** [U, *sing.*] the action of joining or the situation of being joined मिलने की क्रिया, मिलन या मिलन हो जाने की स्थिति; संयोग **2** [C] a group of states or countries that have joined together to form one country or group राज्यों या देशों का संघ, यूनियन (उनका मिलकर एक इकाई बन जाना) *the European Union* **3** = **trade union** **4** [C] an organization for a particular group of people विशेष समूह के सदस्यों का संगठन; यूनियन *the Labour Union*

**the Union Jack** *noun* [*sing.*] the national flag of the United Kingdom, with red and white crosses on a dark blue background यूनाइटेड किंगडम का राष्ट्रीय ध्वज; यूनियन जैक

**unique** /juˈniːk यूˈनीक् / *adj.* **1** not like anything else; being the only one of its type जिसके समान दूसरा नहीं, अनन्य, अद्वितीय, बेजोड़; अपनी तरह का अकेला, एकल *Shakespeare made a unique contribution to the world of literature.* **2 unique to sb/sth** connected with only one place, person or thing केवल एक स्थान, व्यक्ति या वस्तु से संबंधित *This dance is unique to this region.* **3** very unusual बहुत असाधारण; विलक्षण

**unisex** /ˈjuːnɪseks ˈयूनिसेक्स् / *adj.* designed for and used by both sexes स्त्री-पुरुष दोनों के लिए रचित या दोनों के द्वारा प्रयुक्त; एकलिंगी *unisex fashions*

**unison** /ˈjuːnɪsn ˈयूनिसन् / *noun*

IDM **in unison** saying, singing or doing the same thing at the same time as sb else एकबद्ध होकर, साथ-साथ; स्वरमेल में *'No, thank you,' they said in unison.*

**unit** /ˈjuːnɪt ˈयूनिट् / *noun* [C] **1** a single thing which is complete in itself, although it can be part of sth larger अकेली वस्तु जो अपने में पूर्ण हो यद्यपि वह अपने से बड़ी वस्तु का भाग भी हो सकती हो; इकाई *The book is divided into ten units.* **2** a fixed amount or number used as a standard of measurement माप के मानक के रूप में प्रयुक्त एक निश्चित मात्रा या संख्या; इकाई, मात्रक *a unit of currency* **3** a group of people who perform a certain function within a larger organization बड़े संस्थान के अंतर्गत विशिष्ट कार्य से संबंधित व्यक्तियों का समूह; एकांश *the intensive care unit of a hospital* **4** a small machine that performs a particular task or that is part of a larger machine छोटा यंत्र जो अपने से बड़े यंत्र का अंग हो या जो विशिष्ट कार्य करे; यूनिट *The heart of a computer is the central processing unit.* **5** a piece of furniture that fits with other pieces of furniture and has a particular use अन्य फ़र्नीचर से मेल खाता और विशेष उपयोग वाला कोई फ़र्नीचर *matching kitchen units*

**unite** /juˈnaɪt युˈनाइट्/ *verb* **1** [I, T] to join together and act in agreement; to make this happen जुड़ जाना और मिलकर काम करना; (को) जोड़ देना और मिला देना *Unless we unite, our enemies will* *defeat us.* **2** [I] **unite (in sth/in doing sth)** to join together for a particular purpose विशेष प्रयोजन से एक हो जाना *We should all unite in seeking a solution to this terrible problem.*

**united** /juˈnaɪtɪd युˈनाइटिड्/ *adj.* joined together by a common feeling or aim समान भावना या उद्देश्य से संयुक्त

**the United Kingdom** *noun [sing.]* (*abbr.* **UK**) England, Scotland, Wales and Northern Ireland युनाइटेड किंगडम (इंग्लैड, स्कॉटलैंड, वेल्स और उत्तरी आयरलैंड); यूके

**NOTE** **The UK** में इंग्लैंड, स्कॉटलैंड, वेल्स और उत्तरी आयरलैंड आते हैं परंतु आयरिश गणतंत्र एक अलग देश है। **Great Britain** में केवल इंग्लैंड, स्कॉटलैंड और वेल्स आते हैं। **The British Isles** में इंग्लैड, स्कॉटलैंड, वेल्स, उत्तरी आयरलैंड और आयरिश गणतंत्र का समावेश है।

**the United Nations** *noun [sing., with sing. or pl. verb]* (*abbr.* **UN**) the organization formed to encourage peace in the world and to deal with problems between countries संयुक्त राष्ट्र संघ

**the United States (of America)** *noun [sing., with sing. or pl. verb]* (*abbr.* **US; USA**) a large country in North America made up of 50 states and the District of Columbia संयुक्त राज्य अमेरिका (50 राज्यों और डिस्ट्रिक्ट आफ़ कोलंबिया से बना उत्तरी अमेरिका का महादेश)

**unity** /ˈjuːnəti ˈयूनटि/ *noun* [U] the situation in which people are in agreement and working together एकता, एका (ऐसी स्थिति जिसमें लोग सहमतिपूर्वक मिल-जुलकर काम करते हैं)

**universal** /ˌjuːnɪˈvɜːsl ˌयूनिˈव़सल्/ *adj.* connected with, done by or affecting everyone in the world or everyone in a particular group सार्वभौमिक; विश्व में या किसी समूह में प्रत्येक व्यक्ति से संबंधित, द्वारा किया गया या प्रभावित करने वाला; सर्विक, सार्वत्रिक ▶ **universally** /-səli -सलि/ *adv.* सार्विक रूप से

**universal indicator** *noun* [C] a substance that changes to different colours according to whether another substance that touches it is an acid or an **alkali** अम्ल या क्षार के संयोग से तदनुकूल रंग बदलने वाला पदार्थ; युनिवर्सल इंडिकेटर ➪ **pH** पर चित्र देखिए।

**the universe** /ˈjuːnɪvɜːs ˈयूनिव़स्/ *noun [sing.]* everything that exists, including the planets, stars, space, etc. सृष्टि, ब्रह्मांड (प्रत्येक वस्तु जिसका अस्तित्व है, जिसमें ग्रह, नक्षत्र, अंतरिक्ष आदि भी आते हैं)

**university** /ˌjuːnɪˈvɜːsəti ˌयूनिˈव़सटि/ *noun* [C] (*pl.* **universities**) an institution that provides the highest level of education, in which students study for degrees and in which academic research is done विश्वविद्यालय *I did History **at university**.* ○ *a university lecturer.*

**NOTE** छात्र के रूप में विश्वविद्यालय जाने का अर्थ अभीष्ट हो तो **at university** और **go to university** का प्रयोग होता है (जिसमें आर्टिकल 'a' या 'the' नहीं लगता)—*He's hoping to go to university next year.* यदि किसी अन्य प्रयोजन से विश्वविद्यालय (भवन) जाने की बात हो तो आर्टिकल 'the' का प्रयोग होता है—*I'm going to a conference at the university in July.*

**unjust** /ˌʌnˈdʒʌst ˌअन्ˈजस्ट्/ *adj.* not fair or deserved अनुचित या अन्यायपूर्ण *an unjust accusation/law/punishment* ○ *The system is corrupt and unjust.* ✪ विलोम **just** ▶ **unjustly** *adv.* अनुचित रूप से, अन्यायपूर्वक

**unkempt** /ˌʌnˈkempt ˌअन्ˈकेम्प्ट्/ *adj.* (used especially about sb's hair or general appearance) not well cared for; not tidy (बाल या आम शकल-सूरत) अस्तव्यस्त, उपेक्षित; मैला-कुचैला *greasy, unkempt hair*

**unkind** /ˌʌnˈkaɪnd ˌअन्ˈकाइन्ड्/ *adj.* unpleasant and not friendly बुरा लगने वाला और अमैत्रीपूर्ण, रूखा और निष्ठुर *That was an unkind thing to say.* ○ *The zoo was accused of being unkind to its animals.* ✪ विलोम **kind** ▶ **unkindly** *adv.* रूखेपन से, निष्ठुरतापूर्वक ▶ **unkindness** *noun* [U] रूखापन, निष्ठुरता

**unknown**[1] /ˌʌnˈnəʊn ˌअन्ˈनोन्/ *adj.* **1 unknown (to sb)** that sb does not know; without sb knowing वह बात जो किसी को मालूम न हो, अज्ञात बात; बिना (किसी को) बताए, बिना किसी की जानकारी के *Unknown to the boss, she went home early.* **2** not famous or familiar to other people जो जाना-माना या परिचित न हो, अप्रसिद्ध या अपरिचित *an unknown actress* ✪ विलोम **well known** या **famous**

**IDM** **an unknown quantity** a person or thing that you know very little about अल्पज्ञात व्यक्ति या वस्तु

**unknown**[2] /ˌʌnˈnəʊn ˌअन्ˈनोन्/ *noun* **1** (*usually* **the unknown**) *[sing.]* a place or thing that you know nothing about अज्ञात स्थान या वस्तु *a fear of the unknown* **2** [C] a person who is not well known अप्रसिद्ध व्यक्ति

**unlawful** /ʌnˈlɔːfl अन्ˈलॉफ़्ल्/ *adj.* (*formal*) not allowed by the law ग़ैर-क़ानूनी, अवैधानिक ✪ पर्याय **illegal**

**unleaded** /ˌʌnˈledɪd ˌअन्ˈलेडिड्/ *adj.* not containing lead बिना सीसे का, सीसा-रहित *unleaded petrol*

**unleash** /ʌnˈliːʃ अन्ˈलीश्/ *verb* [T] **unleash sth (on/upon sb/sth)** (*written*) to suddenly let a strong force, emotion, etc. be felt or have an effect तीव्र बल, भावना आदि के प्रवाह को उन्मुक्त कर देना या उसके असर को अनुभव कराना *The government's proposals unleashed a storm of protest in the press.*

**unleavened** /ˌʌnˈlevnd ˌअन्ˈलेव्न्ड्/ *adj.* (used about bread) made without any of the substance that makes bread rise (**yeast**) and therefore flat and heavy (डबल रोटी) बिना ख़मीर उठाए बनी (और इसलिए चपटी और भारी)

**unless** /ənˈles अन्ˈलेस्/ *conj.* if... not; except if यदि... नहीं; तब तक नहीं जब तक *I was told that unless my work improved, I would lose the job.* ○ *'Would you like a cup of coffee?' 'Not unless you've already made some.'*

**unlike** /ˌʌnˈlaɪk ˌअन्ˈलाइक्/ *adj., prep.* **1** in contrast to; different from के वैषम्य में, के विपरीत; से भिन्न *He's extremely ambitious, unlike me.* ○ *This is an exciting place to live, unlike my home town.* **2** not typical of; unusual for किसी के स्वभाव के प्रतिकूल; किसी के लिए असामान्य *It's unlike him to be so rude—he's usually very polite.*

**unlikely** /ʌnˈlaɪkli अन्ˈलाइक्लि/ *adj.* (**unlikelier; unlikeliest**) **1 unlikely (to do sth/that...)** not likely to happen; not expected; not probable असंभावित; अप्रत्याशित; असंभाव्य *I suppose she might win but I think it's very unlikely.* ○ *It's **highly unlikely** that I'll have any free time next week.* ✪ विलोम **likely** **2** difficult to believe अविश्वसनीय *an unlikely excuse* ✪ पर्याय **improbable**

**unlimited** /ʌnˈlɪmɪtɪd अन्ˈलिमिटिड्/ *adj.* without limit; as much or as great as you want असीमित, जिसकी सीमा न हो; अपरिमित, अत्यधिक, असीम ✪ विलोम **limited**

**unload** /ˌʌnˈləʊd ˌअन्ˈलोड्/ *verb* **1** [I, T] **unload (sth) (from sth)** to take things that have been transported off or out of a vehicle वाहन में लदा सामान उतारना *We unloaded the boxes from the back of the van.* **2** [I, T] (used about a vehicle) to have the things removed that have been transported (वाहन को) ख़ाली करना (उस पर लदा सामान उतार कर) *Parking here is restricted to vehicles that are loading or unloading.* ✪ विलोम **load** **3** [T] (*informal*) **unload sb/sth (on/onto sb)** to get rid of sth you do not want or to pass it to sb else अनचाही बात से पीछा छुड़ाना या उसे किसी दूसरे पर डाल देना *He shouldn't try and unload the responsibility onto you.*

**unlock** /ˌʌnˈlɒk ˌअन्ˈलॉक्/ *verb* [I, T] to open the lock on sth using a key; to be opened with a key (चाबी से) ताला खोलना; चाबी से खुलना (दरवाज़े आदि का) *I can't unlock this door.* ○ *This door won't unlock.* ✪ विलोम **lock**

**unlucky** /ʌnˈlʌki अन्ˈलकि/ *adj.* (**unluckier; unluckiest**) having or causing bad luck अभागा, बदक़िस्मत या अशुभ *They were unlucky to lose because they played so well.* ○ *Thirteen is often thought to be an unlucky number.* ✪ विलोम **lucky**
▶ **unluckily** *adv.* दुर्भाग्यवश, अभाग्यवश, बदक़िस्मती से

**unmanageable** /ʌnˈmænɪdʒəbl अन्ˈमैनिजब्ल्/ *adj.* difficult or impossible to control or deal with जिसे नियंत्रित करना या जिससे निपटना कठिन या असंभव हो; टेढ़ा, अनियंत्रणीय

**unmanned** /ˌʌnˈmænd ˌअन्ˈमैन्ड्/ *adj.* if a machine, vehicle or place is **unmanned** it does not have or need a person to control or operate it (मशीन, वाहन) जिसे चलाने वाला कोई नहीं या उसकी ज़रुरत नहीं, स्वचालित या बिना कर्मीदल का, (स्थान) मानवहीन

**unmarried** /ˌʌnˈmærid ˌअनˈमैरिड्/ *adj.* not married; single अविवाहित, कुँआरा; अकेला ✪ विलोम **married**

**unmistakable** /ˌʌnmɪˈsteɪkəbl ˌअन्मिˈस्टेकब्ल्/ *adj.* that cannot be confused with anything else; easy to recognize भ्रमरहित, स्पष्ट; आसानी से पहचाना जाने वाला *She had an unmistakable French accent.* ▶ **unmistakably** /-əbli -अब्लि/ *adv.* स्पष्ट रूप से, बिना भ्रम के

**unmoved** /ˌʌnˈmuːvd ˌअन्ˈमूव्ड्/ *adj.* not affected emotionally जिसका दिल नहीं पसीजा; अप्रभावित, अद्रवित, भावशून्य *The judge was unmoved by the boy's sad story, and sent him to jail.*

**unnatural** /ʌnˈnætʃrəl अन्ˈनैच्रल्/ *adj.* different from what is normal or expected अस्वाभाविक या अप्रत्याशित ✪ विलोम **natural** ▶ **unnaturally** /-rəli -रलि/ *adv.* अस्वाभाविक या अप्रत्याशित रूप से *It's unnaturally quiet in here.*

**unnecessary** /ˌʌnˈnesəsəri ˌअन्ˈनेससरि/ *adj.* more than is needed or acceptable ग़ैर-ज़रूरी, अनावश्यक या अनपेक्षित, व्यर्थ का *We should try to avoid all unnecessary expense.* ➪ **needless** देखिए। ✪ विलोम **necessary** ▶ **unnecessarily** /ˌʌnˈnesəsərəli; ˌʌn ˌnesəˈserəli ˌअन्ˈनेससरलि; ˌअन् ˌनेसˈसेरलि/ *adv.* अनावश्यक या अनपेक्षित रूप से *His explanation was unnecessarily complicated.*

**unnerve** /ˌʌnˈnɜːv ˌअन्ˈनव्/ *verb* [T] to make sb feel nervous or frightened or lose confidence किसी को घबराहट में डाल देना, डरा देना या हतोत्साह कर

देना *His silence unnerved us.* ▶ **unnerving** *adj.* घबराहट में डाल देने वाला; हतोत्साहकारी *an unnerving experience* ▶ **unnervingly** *adv.* घबराहट में डालते हुए, हतोत्साह करते हुए

**unnoticed** /ˌʌnˈnəʊtɪst ˌअन्ˈनोटिस्ट्/ *adj.* not noticed or seen जिस पर (किसी का) ध्यान न जाए या जो दिखाई न पड़े; अलक्षित, अनदेखा *He didn't want his hard work to go unnoticed.*

**unobtrusive** /ˌʌnəbˈtruːsɪv ˌअनब्ˈट्रूसिव्/ *adj.* avoiding being noticed; not attracting attention ध्यान में आने से बचते हुए; ध्यान आकृष्ट न करते हुए ▶ **unobtrusively** *adv.* बिना दिखे, चुपके-से, बिना (किसी का) ध्यान आकृष्ट किए *He tried to leave as unobtrusively as possible.*

**unofficial** /ˌʌnəˈfɪʃl ˌअनˈफ़िश्ल्/ *adj.* not accepted or approved by a person in authority बिना अधिकारी की स्वीकृति या अनुमोदन के; अनधिकृत, ग़ैर-सरकारी *an unofficial strike* ○ *Unofficial reports say that four people died in the explosion.* ✪ विलोम **official** ✪ पर्याय **unofficially** /-ʃəli -शलि/ *adv.* अनधिकृत रूप से, ग़ैर-सरकारी तौर पर

**unorthodox** /ʌnˈɔːθədɒks अन्ˈऑथ़डॉक्स्/ *adj.* different from what is generally accepted, usual or traditional सामान्यतया स्वीकार्य, सामान्य या परंपरागत से भिन्न; रूढ़ि-विरुद्ध, असामान्य, अपरंपरागत ✪ विलोम **orthodox**

**unpack** /ˌʌnˈpæk ˌअन्ˈपैक्/ *verb* [I, T] to take out the things that were in a bag, suitcase, etc. थैले, सूटकेस आदि को खोलना (और उसमें से सामान निकालना) *When we arrived at the hotel we unpacked and went to the beach.* ✪ विलोम **pack**

**unpaid** /ˌʌnˈpeɪd ˌअन्ˈपेड्/ *adj.* **1** not yet paid जिसका अभी भुगतान नहीं हुआ; अदत्त *an unpaid bill* **2** not receiving money for work done (व्यक्ति) अवैतनिक (बिना वेतन काम करने वाला) *an unpaid assistant* **3** (used about work) done without payment (काम) जिसके लिए धन नहीं दिया गया; अदत्तशुल्क *unpaid overtime*

**unpleasant** /ʌnˈpleznt अन्ˈप्लेज़न्ट्/ *adj.* **1** causing you to have a bad feeling; not nice अप्रीतिकर (कटु भाव उत्पन्न करने वाला); अरुचिकर *This news has come as an unpleasant surprise.* ✪ विलोम **pleasant** **2** unfriendly; not polite अमैत्रीपूर्ण, रूखा; अशिष्ट, दुर्विनीत *There's no need to be unpleasant; we can discuss this in a friendly way.* ▶ **unpleasantly** *adv.* रूखेपन से, अशिष्टतापूर्वक

**unplug** /ˌʌnˈplʌg ˌअन्ˈप्लग्/ *verb* [T] (**unplugging; unplugged**) to remove a piece of electrical equipment from the electricity supply प्लग हटाना या निकालना *Could you unplug the cassette recorder, please?* ✪ विलोम **plug sth in**

**unpopular** /ʌnˈpɒpjələ(r)अन्ˈपॉप्यल(र्)/ *adj.* **unpopular (with sb)** not liked by many people जो अधिकतर लोगों को पंसद नहीं; अलोकप्रिय *Her methods made her very unpopular with the staff.* ✪ विलोम **popular** ▶ **unpopularity** /ˌʌnˌpɒpjuˈlærəti ˌअन्ˌपॉप्युˈलैरटि/ *noun* [U] अलोकप्रियता

**unprecedented** /ʌnˈpresɪdentɪd अन्ˈप्रेसिडेन्टिड्/ *adj.* never having happened or existed before जो पहले घटित नहीं हुआ या जिसका अस्तित्व नहीं रहा; अभूतपूर्व ➪ **precedent** देखिए।

**unpredictable** /ˌʌnprɪˈdɪktəbl ˌअन्प्रिˈडिक्टब्ल्/ *adj.* **1** that cannot be predicted because it changes a lot or depends on too many different things (स्थिति) जिसके विषय में पहले से कुछ न कहा जा सके (लगातार उसमें परिवर्तन होते या अनेक बातों पर उसकी निर्भरता के कारण); अननुमेय *unpredictable weather* ○ *The result is entirely unpredictable.* **2** if a person is **unpredictable** you cannot predict how he/she will behave in a particular situation (व्यक्ति) जिसके व्यवहार का अनुमान न लगाया जा सके; बेतुका, मनमौजी ✪ विलोम **predictable** ▶ **unpredictability** /ˌʌnprɪˌdɪktəˈbɪləti ˌअन्प्रिˌडिक्टˈबिलटि/ *noun* [U] जिसका अनुमान न लगाया जा सके; अननुमेयता *the unpredictability of Delhi weather* ▶ **unpredictably** *adv.* बिना पूर्वानुमान के

**unpretentious** /ˌʌnprɪˈtenʃəs ˌअन्प्रिˈटेन्शस्/ *adj.* (*approving*) not trying to appear more special or important than you really are (मान्य) अनाडंबरी, अमहत्त्वकांक्षी ✪ विलोम **pretentious**

**unprofessional** /ˌʌnprəˈfeʃənl ˌअन्प्रˈफ़ेशनल्/ *adj.* not reaching the standard expected in a particular profession जिसके पास व्यवसाय-विशेष के लिए अपेक्षित क्षमता-स्तर नहीं; अव्यावसायिक ✪ विलोम **professional**

**unprovoked** /ˌʌnprəˈvəʊkt ˌअन्प्रˈव़ोक्ट्/ *adj.* (used especially about an attack) not caused by anything the person who is attacked has said or done (हमला) बिना किसी के भड़काए किया गया, बिना उत्तेजना; अकारण ✪ विलोम **provoked**

**unqualified** /ˌʌnˈkwɒlɪfaɪd ˌअन्ˈक्वॉलिफ़ाइड्/ *adj.* **1** not having the knowledge or not having passed the exams that you need for sth किसी काम के लिए अपेक्षित जानकारी या शैक्षिक योग्यता से रहित; अयोग्य, अनर्ह *I'm unqualified to offer an opinion on this matter.* ✪ विलोम **qualified** **2** complete; absolute पूर्ण, समग्र; परिपूर्ण, संपूर्ण *an unqualified success*

**unquestionable** /ʌnˈkwestʃənəbl अन्ˈक्वेस्‌चनबल्/ *adj.* certain; that cannot be doubted निश्चित; असंदिग्ध, निर्विवाद ✪ विलोम **questionable** ▶ **unquestionably** /-əbli -अबलि/ *adv.* निर्विवाद रूप से *She is unquestionably the most famous opera singer in the world.*

**unravel** /ʌnˈrævl अन्ˈरैवल्/ *verb* (**unravelling; unravelled** *AmE* **unraveling; unraveled**) [I, T] **1** to remove the knots from a piece of string, thread, etc.; to come unfastened in this way डोरी, धागे आदि की गाँठें सुलझाना; डोरी आदि की गाँठें सुलझना *I unravelled the tangled string and wound it into a ball.* **2** (used about a complicated story, etc.) to become or to make sth become clear (पेचीदा कहानी आदि का) स्पष्ट हो जाना या उसे स्पष्ट कर देना, (पेचीदा कहानी का) पेच सुलझना या सुलझा देना

**unreal** /ˌʌnˈrɪəl ˌअन्ˈरिअल्/ *adj.* **1** very strange and seeming more like a dream than reality अवास्तविक; बहुत विचित्र और स्वप्न जैसा *Her voice had an unreal quality about it* **2** not connected with reality असलियत से दूर; अयथार्थ *Some people have unreal expectations of marriage.*

**unrealistic** /ˌʌnrɪəˈlɪstɪk ˌअनरिअˈलिस्टिक्/ *adj.* not showing or accepting things as they are अव्यावहारिक; वास्तविकता के स्पर्श से अछूता *unrealistic expectations* ○ ***It is unrealistic to*** *expect them to be able to solve the problem immediately.* ✪ विलोम **realistic** ▶ **unrealistically** /-kli -क्लि/ *adv.* अयथार्थ रूप से, अव्यावहारिक रूप से *They're asking unrealistically high prices.*

**unreasonable** /ʌnˈriːznəbl अन्ˈरीज़नबल्/ *adj.* unfair; expecting too much अनुचित, असंगत; बहुत अधिक आशा करते हुए *I think she is being totally unreasonable.* ○ *He makes unreasonable demands on his staff.* ✪ विलोम **reasonable** ▶ **unreasonably** /-əbli -अबलि/ *adv.* असंगत रूप से

**unrelenting** /ˌʌnrɪˈlentɪŋ ˌअनरिˈलेन्टिङ्/ *adj.* continuously strong, not becoming weaker or stopping अडिग; टस से मस न होने वाला

**unreliable** /ˌʌnrɪˈlaɪəbl ˌअनरिˈलाइअबल्/ *adj.* that cannot be trusted or depended on जिस पर विश्वास या भरोसा न किया जा सके; अविश्वसनीय या ग़ैर-भरोसेमंद *Trains here are notoriously unreliable.* ○ *He's totally unreliable as a source of information.* ✪ विलोम **reliable** ▶ **unreliability** /ˌʌnrɪˌlaɪəˈbɪləti ˌअनरिˌलाइअˈबिलटि/ *noun* [U] अविश्वसनीयता *the unreliability of some statistics*

**unreserved** /ˌʌnrɪˈzɜːvd ˌअनरिˈज़र्व्ड्/ *adj.* **1** (used about seats in a theatre, etc.) not kept for the use of a particular person (सिनेमाघर की सीट आदि) अनारक्षित (व्यक्ति-विशेष के लिए निश्चित नहीं) ✪ विलोम **reserved** **2** without limit; complete अबाधा, अप्रतिबंध; संपूर्ण *The government's action received the unreserved support of all parties.* ▶ **unreservedly** /ˌʌnrɪˈzɜːvɪdli ˌअनरिˈज़र्विड्लि/ *adv.* अबाध रूप से

**unrest** /ʌnˈrest अन्ˈरेस्ट्/ *noun* [U] a situation in which people are angry or not happy and likely to protest or fight अशांति, असंतोष, उपद्रव *social unrest*

**unrivalled** (*AmE* **unrivaled**) /ʌnˈraɪvld अन्ˈराइवल्ड्/ *adj.* much better than any other of the same type जिसकी कोई सानी नहीं; बेजोड़, अप्रतिम *His knowledge of Greek theology is unrivalled.*

**unroll** /ʌnˈrəʊl अन्ˈरोल्/ *verb* [I, T] to open (sth) from a rolled position लिपटी हुई वस्तु का खुल जाना या उसे खोल देना *He unrolled the poster and stuck it on the wall.* ✪ विलोम **roll (sth) (up)**

**unruly** /ʌnˈruːli अन्ˈरूलि/ *adj.* difficult to control; without discipline बेक़ाबू, बेलगाम; अनुशासनहीन, उच्छृंखल *an unruly crowd* ▶ **unruliness** *noun* [U] उच्छृंखलता

**unsafe** /ʌnˈseɪf अन्ˈसेफ़्/ *adj.* **1** (used about a thing, a place or an activity) not safe; dangerous (वस्तु, स्थान या क्रिया-कलाप) असुरक्षित; ख़तरनाक *The roof was declared unsafe.* ○ *It was considered unsafe to release the prisoners.* **2** (used about people) in danger of being harmed (व्यक्ति) ख़तरे में, असुरक्षित *He felt unsafe and alone.* **3** (*law*) (used about a decision in a court of law) based on evidence that may be false or is not good enough (न्यायालय का निर्णय) दुर्बल साक्ष्य पर आधारित *Their convictions were declared unsafe.* ✪ विलोम **safe**

**unsaid** /ʌnˈsed अन्ˈसेड्/ *adj.* (*not before a noun*) thought but not spoken अनकहा (केवल मन में रहा) *Some things are better* ***left unsaid.***

**unsatisfactory** /ˌʌnˌsætɪsˈfæktəri ˌअन्ˌसैटिस्ˈफ़ैक्टरि/ *adj.* not acceptable; not good enough संतोषजनक नहीं; पर्याप्त नहीं ✪ पर्याय **unacceptable** ▶ **unsatisfactorily** /-tərəli -टरलि/ *adv.* असंतोषजनक रूप से

**unsaturated** /ʌnˈsætʃəreɪtɪd अन्ˈसैचरेटिड्/ *adj.* (*technical*) (used about fats in food) that are easily dealt with by the body because of their chemical structure (आहार में प्रयुक्त चरबी) जिसे शरीर आसानी से पचा ले (उसकी रासायनिक संरचना की अनुकूलता के कारण); सुपच ➪ **polyunsaturated** और **saturated** देखिए।

**unsavoury** (*AmE* **unsavory**) /ʌnˈseɪvəri अन्ˈसेव़रि / *adj.* unpleasant; not morally acceptable अप्रिय; बदनाम *His friends are all unsavoury characters.*

**unscathed** /ʌnˈskeɪðd अन्ˈस्केद्ड् / *adj.* not hurt, without injury बिना घायल हुए, बिना चोट खाए *He came out of the fight unscathed.*

**unscrew** /ˌʌnˈskruː ˌअन्ˈस्क्रू / *verb* [T] **1** to remove the screws from sth किसी वस्तु के पेच खोलना **2** to open or remove sth by turning it किसी चीज़ (जैसे ढक्कन) को घुमा कर खोलना या निकालना *Could you unscrew the top of this bottle for me?*

**unscrupulous** /ʌnˈskruːpjələs अन्ˈस्क्रूप्यलस् / *adj.* being dishonest, cruel or unfair in order to get what you want (व्यक्ति) बेईमान, निर्मम या अविवेकी (मनचाही चीज़ को पाने के लिए); अनैतिक ✪ विलोम **scrupulous**

**unseemly** /ʌnˈsiːmli अन्ˈसीम्लि / *adj. old-fashioned* or *formal*) (used about behaviour, etc.) not polite; not right in a particular situation (व्यवहार, आदि) अशोभन; स्थिति-विशेष में अनुपयुक्त

**unseen** /ˌʌnˈsiːn ˌअन्ˈसीन् / *adj.* **1** that cannot be seen जो दिखाई न पड़े, बिना दिखे; अनदेखा *unseen forces/powers* ○ *I managed to get out of the room unseen.* **2** not seen before जो पहले से न दिखे; अलक्षित *unseen dangers/difficulties*

**unselfish** /ʌnˈselfɪʃ अन्ˈसेल्फ़िश् / *adj.* if you are unselfish you care about other people's feelings and needs more than your own निःस्वार्थ ✪ पर्याय **selfless** ✪ विलोम **selfish** ▶ **unselfishly** *adv.* निःस्वार्थ भाव से

**unsettle** /ˌʌnˈsetl ˌअन्ˈसेट्ल् / *verb* [T] to make sb feel upset or worried, especially because a situation has changed किसी को परेशानी या चिंता में डाल देना, अस्थिर कर देना (विशेषतः स्थिति बदल जाने के कारण) *Changing schools might unsettle the kids.*

**unsettled** /ʌnˈsetld अन्ˈसेट्ल्ड् / *adj.* **1** (used about a situation) that may change; making people uncertain about what might happen (स्थिति) जिसमें परिवर्तन संभावित है, अस्थिर; भावी के विषय में अनिश्चित *These were difficult and unsettled times.* ○ *The weather has been very unsettled* (= it has changed a lot). **2** not calm or relaxed अशांत या तनावग्रस्त *They all felt restless and unsettled.* **3** (used about an argument, etc.) that continues without any agreement being reached (विवाद, आदि) अनसुलझा **4** (used about a bill, etc.) not yet paid (बिल, आदि) जिसका भुगतान बाक़ी है; अदत्त

**unsettling** /ʌnˈsetlɪŋ अन्ˈसेट्लिङ् / *adj.* making you feel upset, nervous or worried परेशानी; घबराहट या चिंता में डाल देने वाला

**unshaven** /ˌʌnˈʃeɪvn ˌअन्ˈशेव़्न् / *adj.* not having shaved or been shaved recently बेहजामत, जिसकी दाढ़ी अभी नहीं बनी *He looked pale and unshaven.* ○ *his unshaven face*

**unsightly** /ʌnˈsaɪtli अन्ˈसाइट्लि / *adj.* very unpleasant to look at; ugly देखने में बहुत बुरा, कुरूप; भद्दा *an unsightly new building*

**unskilled** /ˌʌnˈskɪld ˌअन्ˈस्किल्ड् / *adj.* not having or needing special skill or training जिसके पास विशेष कौशल नहीं या जिसे प्रशिक्षण की अपेक्षा नहीं; अकुशल, अदक्ष या अप्रशिक्षित *an unskilled job/worker* ✪ विलोम **skilled**

**unsolicited** /ˌʌnsəˈlɪsɪtɪd ˌअन्सˈलिसिटिड् / *adj.* not asked for जिसे माँगा न गया हो; अप्रार्थित, अयाचित *unsolicited praise/advice*

**unsound** /ˌʌnˈsaʊnd ˌअन्ˈसाउन्ड् / *adj.* **1** in poor condition; weak बुरी हालत में; कमज़ोर *The building is structurally unsound.* **2** based on wrong ideas and therefore mistaken ग़लत धारणाओं पर आधारित और इसलिए त्रुटिपूर्ण ✪ विलोम **sound**

**unspoiled** /ˌʌnˈspɔɪld ˌअन्ˈस्पाइल्ड् / (*also* **unspoilt** /ˌʌnˈspɔɪlt ˌअन्ˈस्पॉइल्ट् /) *adj.* **1** (used about a place) beautiful because it has not been changed or built on (स्थान) बिन बिगड़ा और इसलिए सुंदर (उसमें कुछ बदला नहीं या उस पर कुछ बना नहीं) **2** (used about a person) not made unpleasant, bad-tempered, etc. by being treated too well (व्यक्ति) भरपूर प्रशंसा-सत्कार के बावजूद आत्मनियंत्रित, सुशील *Despite being one of the best-known singers in the world, she has remained unspoiled.* ✪ विलोम **spoilt**

**unspoken** /ˌʌnˈspəʊkən ˌअन्ˈस्पोकन् / *adj.* (*formal*) not stated; not said in words but understood or agreed between people जिसे कहा नहीं गया, अनकहा, अकथित; जो शब्दों में व्यक्त नहीं (परंतु जिसे लोग समझते या मानते हैं); मौन *an unspoken assumption*

**unstable** /ʌnˈsteɪbl अन्ˈस्टेब्ल् / *adj.* **1** likely to fall down or move; not firmly fixed जो कभी भी गिर या हिल सकता है, अस्थिर; जो मज़बूती से स्थापित नहीं, ढुलमुल **2** likely to change or fail जो कभी भी बदल या गिर सकता है; डाँवाँडोल, अस्थिर *a period of unstable government* **3** (used about a person's moods or behaviour) likely to change suddenly or often (व्यक्ति की मनोदशा या आचरण) जो कभी भी अचानक या प्रायः बदल जाए; चंचल ✪ विलोम **stable** ➪ **instability** noun देखिए।

**unsteady** /ʌnˈstedi अन्ˈस्टेडि/ *adj.* **1** not completely in control of your movements so that you might fall ढीली पकड़ वाला (हिलने-डुलने पर पूरा नियंत्रण न होने के कारण जो कभी भी गिर सकता है), लड़खड़ाता हुआ; अस्थिर *She is still a little **unsteady on her feet** after the operation.* **2** shaking or moving in a way that is not controlled काँपता या हिलता हुआ (इसलिए बेक़ाबू), कंपायमान *an unsteady hand/voice/step* ✪ विलोम **steady** ▶ **unsteadily** /-ɪli -इलि/ *adv.* काँपते या हिलते हुए, लड़खड़ाते हुए ▶ **unsteadiness** *noun* [U] लड़खड़ाहट

**unstuck** /ˌʌnˈstʌk ˌअन्ˈस्टक्/ *adj.* no longer stuck together or stuck down उखड़ा हुआ, अलगाया हुआ *The label on the parcel had **come unstuck**.*

IDM **come unstuck** to fail badly; to be unsuccessful बुरी तरह निष्फल हो जाना; विफल हो जाना *His plan came unstuck when he realized he didn't have enough money.*

**unsuccessful** /ˌʌnsəkˈsesfl ˌअन्सक्ˈसेस्फ़्ल्/ *adj.* not successful; not achieving what you wanted to असफल, विफल; वांछित वस्तु की प्राप्ति में असमर्थ *His efforts to get a job proved unsuccessful.* ○ *They were unsuccessful in meeting their objectives for the year.* ▶ **unsuccessfully** /-fəli-फ़लि/ *adv.* असफलतापूर्वक

**unsuitable** /ʌnˈsuːtəbl अन्ˈसूटबल्/ *adj.* not right or appropriate for sb/sth (किसी व्यक्ति या वस्तु के लिए) अनुपयुक्त या जो सही न हो *This film is unsuitable for children under 12.* ✪ विलोम **suitable**

**unsure** /ˌʌnˈʃɔː(r) ˌअन्ˈशॉ(र्)/ *adj.* **1 unsure of yourself** not feeling confident about yourself अपने विषय में अनिश्चित, जिसे अपने ऊपर भरोसा न हो; आत्मविश्वासहीन *He's young and still quite unsure of himself.* **2 unsure (about/of sth)** not certain; having doubts अनिश्चितः; संदेही, संशययुक्त *I didn't argue because I was unsure of the facts.* ✪ विलोम **sure** या **certain**

**unsuspecting** /ˌʌnsəˈspektɪŋ ˌअन्सˈस्पेक्टिङ्/ *adj.* not realizing that there is danger ख़तरे से अनजान ➪ **suspect** और **suspicious** देखिए।

**unsustainable** /ˌʌnsəˈsteɪnəbl ˌअन्सस्टेनबल्/ *adj.* (*written*) that cannot be continued at the same level, rate, etc. जो (स्तर, दर आदि की दृष्टि से) अपने मूल रूप में क़ायम न रह सके ✪ विलोम **sustainable**

**unsympathetic** /ˌʌnˌsɪmpəˈθetɪk ˌअन्ˌसिम्पˈथ़ेटिक्/ *adj.* **1 unsympathetic (towards sb)** not feeling or showing any **sympathy** (किसी के प्रति) सहानुभूति न रखने या दिखाने वाला; सहानुभूतिहीन बेदर्द, कठोर **2 unsympathetic (to/towards sth)** not in agreement with sth; not supporting an idea, aim, etc. किसी बात के प्रति उपेक्षाशील; किसी धारणा, उद्देश्य आदि से असहमत *How can you trust a government that is unsympathetic to public opinion?* **3** (used about a person) not easy to like; unpleasant (व्यक्ति) जो जल्दी अच्छा न लगे; बुरा लगने वाला, अप्रिय *I found all the characters in the film unsympathetic.* ✪ विलोम **sympathetic**

**untangle** /ˌʌnˈtæŋgl ˌअन्ˈटैङ्गल्/ *verb* [T] to separate threads which have become tied together in a confused way उलझे हुए धागों को सुलझाना *The wires got mixed up and it took me ages to untangle them.*

**unthinkable** /ʌnˈθɪŋkəbl अन्ˈथ़िङ्कबल्/ *adj.* impossible to imagine or accept अविचार्य; जिसके विषय में सोचा या जिसे माना न जा सके, कल्पनातीत या अव्यावहारिक *It was unthinkable that he would never see her again.*

**unthinking** /ʌnˈθɪŋkɪŋ अन्ˈथ़िङ्किङ्/ *adj.* done, said, etc. without thinking carefully बिना सोचे-समझे किया या कहा गया; अविचारित ▶ **unthinkingly** *adv.* बिना सोचे-समझे

**untidy** /ʌnˈtaɪdi अन्ˈटाइडि/ *adj.* (**untidier; untidiest**) **1** not tidy or well arranged (वस्तु, स्थान आदि) मैला-कुचैला या अव्यवस्थित, अस्त-व्यस्त *an untidy bedroom* ○ *untidy hair* **2** (used about a person) not keeping things tidy or in good order (व्यक्ति) चीजों को साफ़-सुथरा और ढंग से न रखने वाला, लापरवाह; फूहड़ *My flatmate is so untidy!* ✪ विलोम **tidy** या **neat** ▶ **untidily** /-ɪli -इलि/ *adv.* लापरवाही से, फूहड़पन के साथ ▶ **untidiness** *noun* [U] लापरवाही, फूहड़पन

**untie** /ʌnˈtaɪ अन्ˈटाइ/ *verb* [T] (*pres. part.* **untying;** *3rd person sing. pres.* **unties;** *pt, pp* **untied**) to remove a knot; to free sb/sth that is tied by a rope, etc. गाँठ खोलना; बँधी हुई किसी चीज़ को खोलना ✪ विलोम **tie up** या **fasten**

**until** /ənˈtɪl अन्ˈटिल्/ (*also* **till**) *prep., conj.* up to the time or the event mentioned निर्दिष्ट समय या घटना के होने तक *The restaurant is open until midnight.* ○ *We won't leave until the police get here* (= we won't leave before they come).

> NOTE **Until** का प्रयोग अंग्रेज़ी भाषा की औपचारिक और अनौपचारिक दोनों शैलियों में हो सकता है। **Till** का प्रयोग अनौपचारिक अंग्रेज़ी में अधिक होता है परंतु यह वाक्य के आरंभ में प्रायः नहीं आता। यह निश्चित है कि समय के निर्देश में केवल **till/until** का प्रयोग किया जाता है। दूरी के निर्देश के लिए **as far as** का प्रयोग होता है—*I walked as far as the shops.* संख्या के निर्देश में **up to** का प्रयोग किया जाता है—*You can take up to 20 kilos of luggage.*

**untimely** /ʌnˈtaɪmli अन्ˈटाइम्लि/ *adj.* **1** happening before the normal or expected time अपेक्षित या सामान्य समय से पहले; असामयिक *an untimely death* **2** happening at a time or situation that is not suitable अनुपयुक्त समय या स्थिति में होना *Her interruption was untimely.* ✪ पर्याय **premature** ✪ पर्याय **ill-timed** ✪ विलोम **timely**

**untold** /ˌʌnˈtəʊld ˌअन्ˈटोल्ड्/ *adj.* very great; so big, etc. that you cannot count or measure it बहुत अधिक; बेइंतिहा, अपार, असीम *untold suffering*

**untouched** /ʌnˈtʌtʃt अन्ˈटच्ट्/ *adj.* (*not usually before a noun*) **1 untouched (by sth)** not affected by sth, especially sth bad or unpleasant; not damaged अप्रभावित (विशेषतः किसी ख़राब या अप्रिय स्थिति से), अपरिवर्तित, अछूता; क्षतिग्रस्त नहीं, अक्षत *The area has remained relatively untouched by commercial development.* **2** (used about food or drink) not eaten or drunk (खाद्य पदार्थ या पेय) जो झूठी नहीं की गई, बिना छुए छोड़ी गई; सुच्चा *She left her meal untouched.* **3** not changed in any way अपरिवर्तित *The final clause in the contract will be left untouched.*

**untouchable** /ʌnˈtʌtʃəbl अन्ˈटचब्ल्/ *adj.* **1** in a position where sb is unlikely to be punished or criticized अपने ओहदे के कारण अदंडनीय या अनालोचनीय *He thought he was untouchable because of his political connections.* **2** which cannot be touched or changed by other people अपरिवर्तनीय *This year's budget is untouchable.*

**untoward** /ˌʌntəˈwɔːd ˌअनूटˈवॉड्/ *adj.* (used about an event, etc.) unexpected and unpleasant (घटना आदि) अप्रत्याशित और अप्रिय *The security guard noticed **nothing untoward**.*

**untrue** /ʌnˈtruː अन्ˈट्रू/ *adj.* **1** not true; not based on facts असत्य, झूठा; जो तथ्यों पर आधारित नहीं, निराधार, बेबुनियाद *These accusations are totally untrue.* ○ *an untrue claim/statement* **2 untrue (to sb/sth)** not loyal to sb/sth जो किसी के प्रति निष्ठावान नहीं, बेवफ़ा *If he agreed to their demands, he would have to be untrue to his principles.* ✪ पर्याय **unfaithful**

**untruth** /ʌnˈtruːθ ˌअनूˈट्रूथ/ *noun* [C] (*pl.* **untruths** /-ˈtruːðz -ˈट्रूद्ज़्/) (*written*) something that is not true; a lie असत्य बात, झूठी बात; झूठ ▶ **untruthful** /-fl -फ़्ल्/ *adj.* झूठ बोलने वाला, झूठा

**untypical** /ʌnˈtɪpɪkl अन्ˈटिपिक्ल्/ *adj.* not typical or usual जो किसी का नमूना या सामान्य न हो; अनिदर्शनात्मक *an untypical example* ✪ विलोम **typical** ➪ **atypical** देखिए।

**unused¹** /ˌʌnˈjuːzd ˌअन्ˈयूज़्ड्/ *adj.* that has not been used जिसका इस्तेमाल नहीं हुआ; अप्रयुक्त

**unused²** /ʌnˈjuːst अन्ˈयूस्ट्/ *adj.* **unused to sth/to doing sth** not having any experience of sth जिस बात का अनुभव नहीं हुआ, जिसकी आदत नहीं पड़ी, (का) अनभ्यस्त *She was unused to getting such a lot of attention.*

**unusual** /ʌnˈjuːʒuəl; -ʒəl अन्ˈयूशुअल्; -श़ल्/ *adj.* **1** not expected or normal अप्रत्याशित या असामान्य *It's unusual for Juhi to be late.* ✪ विलोम **usual** **2** interesting because it is different (कुछ अलग होने से) रोचक; अनोखा, ग़ैर-मामूली *What an unusual hat!*

**unusually** /ʌnˈjuːʒuəli; -ʒəli अन्ˈयूशुअलि; -श़लि/ *adv.* **1** in a way that is not normal or typical of sb/sth असाधारण तरीक़े से, स्वभाव के विपरीत *Unusually for her, she forgot his birthday.* **2** more than is common; extremely प्रचलित से भिन्न, सामान्य से हटकर; अत्यधिक

**unveil** /ˌʌnˈveɪl ˌअन्ˈव़ेल्/ *verb* [T] to show sth new to the public for the first time सार्वजनिक रूप से किसी वस्तु को प्रथम बार प्रदर्शित करना, किसी वस्तु का अनावरण करना *The President unveiled a memorial to those who died in the war.*

**unwanted** /ˌʌnˈwɒntɪd ˌअन्ˈवॉन्टिड्/ *adj.* not wanted अवांछित, अनचाहा *an unwanted gift*

**unwarranted** /ʌnˈwɒrəntɪd अन्ˈवॉरन्टिड्/ *adj.* that is not deserved or for which there is no good reason अनुपयुक्त या अनुचित; बेजा *unwarranted criticism*

**unwelcome** /ʌnˈwelkəm अन्ˈवेल्कम्/ *adj.* not wanted अवांछित, अरुचिकर *To avoid attracting unwelcome attention he spoke quietly.* ✪ विलोम **welcome**

**unwell** /ʌnˈwel अन्ˈवेल्/ *adj.* (*not before a noun*) ill; sick अस्वस्थ; बीमार *to feel unwell*

**unwieldy** /ʌnˈwiːldi अन्ˈवील्डि/ *adj.* difficult to move or carry because it is too big, heavy, etc. भारी-भरकम, दुर्वह (बहुत बड़ा, भारी आदि होने के कारण जिसे हिलाना या ले जाना कठिन हो)

**unwilling** /ʌnˈwɪlɪŋ अन्ˈविलिङ्/ *adj.* not wanting to do sth but often forced to do it by other people (कोई विशेष काम करने का) अनिच्छुक (परंतु उसे करने पर प्रायः विवश किया गया) ✪ विलोम **willing**

**unwind** /ˌʌnˈwaɪnd ˌअन्ˈवाइन्ड्/ *verb* (*pt, pp* **unwound** /-ˈwaʊnd -ˈवाउन्ड्/) **1** [I, T] if you unwind sth or if sth unwinds, it comes away from sth that it had been put round धागे, ऊन आदि का लिपटे होने की अवस्था से खुल जाना या उसे खोल देना *The bandage had unwound.* **2** [I] (*informal*) to relax, especially after working hard आराम करना (विशेषतः कड़ी मेहनत के बाद) *After a busy day, it takes me a while to unwind.* ⇨ **wind**[3] देखिए।

**unwise** /ˌʌnˈwaɪz ˌअन्ˈवाइज़्/ *adj.* showing a lack of good judgement; foolish नासमझ, अविवेकी; मूर्ख, बेवकूफ़ *It would be unwise to tell anyone about our plan yet.* ✪ विलोम **wise** ▶ **unwisely** *adv.* नासमझी से

**unwitting** /ʌnˈwɪtɪŋ अन्ˈविटिङ्/ *adj.* not realizing sth; not intending to do sth किसी बात से अनजान; किसी काम को करने की मंशा न रखते हुए *an unwitting accomplice to the crime* ▶ **unwittingly** *adv.* अनजानेपन में

**unwrap** /ʌnˈræp अन्ˈरैप्/ *verb* [T] (**unwrapping; unwrapped**) to take off the paper, etc. that covers or protects sth किसी वस्तु पर चढ़े कागज़ आदि को हटाना

**unzip** /ˌʌnˈzɪp ˌअन्ˈज़िप्/ *verb* [I, T] (**unzipping; unzipped**) if a bag, piece of clothing, etc. unzips, or you unzip it, you open it by pulling on the device that fastens the opening (**the zip**) थैले, कपड़े आदि के ज़िप को खोलना ✪ विलोम **zip (up)**

**up**[1] /ʌp अप्/ *prep., adv.* उपर

> **NOTE** अनेक क्रियाओं के साथ **up** के संयोग से बनने वाले विशेष प्रयोगों (जैसे **pick sth up**) के लिए संबंधित क्रियाओं की प्रविष्टियाँ देखिए।

**1** at or to a high or higher level or position किसी स्तर या स्थिति पर या उसके ऊपर या अधिक ऊपर *The monkey **climbed up** the tree.* ○ *I carried her suitcase up to the third floor.* ○ ***Put** your **hand up** if you know the answer.* **2** in or into a vertical position खड़ी स्थिति में ***Stand up**, please.* ○ *Is he up* (= out of bed) *yet?* **3** used for showing an increase in sth किसी वस्तु में वृद्धि दिखाने के लिए प्रयुक्त *Prices have **gone up**.* ○ *Turn the volume up.* **4** used with verbs of closing or covering (कुछ) बंद करने या ढकने का अर्थ देने वाली क्रियाओं के साथ प्रयुक्त ***Do up** your coat. It's cold.* ○ *I found some wood to **cover up** the hole.* **5** to the place where sb/sth is उस स्थान पर जहाँ कोई (स्थित) है, के पास *A car drove up and two men got out.* **6** coming or being put together एक साथ आ जाना या हो जाना *The teacher collected up our exam papers.* ○ *Asif and Jai teamed up in the doubles competition.* **7** (used about a period of time) finished (समय की अवधि) समाप्त *Stop writing. Your time's up.* **8** into pieces टुकड़ों में, टुकड़े-टुकड़े *We chopped the old table up and used it for firewood.* ○ *She **tore up** the letter and threw it away.* **9** used for showing that an action continues until it is completed किसी क्रिया के (समाप्ति तक) जारी रहने का अर्थ व्यक्त करने के लिए प्रयुक्त ***Eat up**, children I want you to finish everything on the table.* ○ *Can you help me **clean up** the kitchen?* **10** in a particular direction दिशा-विशेष में या की ओर *I live just **up the road**.* ○ ***Move up** a little and let me sit down.* **11** in or to the north उत्तर में/की ओर *My parents have just moved **up north**.* **12** (used about computers) working; in operation (कंप्यूटर) कार्यशील अवस्था में; चलते हुए *Are the computers back up yet?* **13** (*informal*) used for showing that sth is spoiled किसी बात के बिगड़ जाने का अर्थ व्यक्त करने के लिए प्रयुक्त *I really messed up when I told the interviewer I liked sleeping.*

**IDM be up for sth** **1** to be available to be bought or chosen उपलब्ध, बिकाऊ होना या चुनाव में खड़ा होना *That house is up for sale.* ○ *How many candidates are up for election?* **2** (*informal*) to be ready to do sth and enthusiastic about doing it किसी काम के लिए जोश के साथ तैयार होना *Is anyone up for a swim?*

**be up to sb** to be sb's responsibility (किसी बात की) किसी व्यक्ति पर ज़िम्मेदारी होना *I can't take the decision. It's not up to me.*

**not up to much** (*informal*) not very good बहुत अच्छा नहीं, कुछ ख़ास नहीं *The programme wasn't up to much.*

**up against sth/sb** facing sth/sb that causes problems समस्याएँ पैदा करने वालों का सामना करना

**up and down** backwards and forwards, or rising and falling आगे पीछे या ऊपर-नीचे *He was nervously walking up and down outside the interview room.*

**up and running** (used about sth new) working well (किसी नई वस्तु का) अच्छे ढंग से काम करना, ठीक चलना

**up to sth** **1** as much/many as तक (मात्रा या संख्या की दृष्टि से) *We're expecting up to 100 people at the meeting.* **2** as far as now तक (समय की दृष्टि से) *Up to now, things have been easy.* **3** capable of sth कोई काम करने का सामर्थ्य होना या कर सकना *I don't feel up to cooking this evening. I'm too tired.* **4** doing sth secret and perhaps bad छिपाकर कोई काम (प्रायः ग़लत काम) करना *What are the children up to? Go and see.*

**what's up?** (*informal*) what's the matter? बात क्या है?

**up**[2] /ʌp अप्/ *noun*

**IDM ups and downs** the mixture of good and bad things in life or in a particular situation or relationship जीवन में उतार-चढ़ाव *Every marriage has its ups and downs.*

**up-** /ʌp अप् / *prefix* (*used in adjectives, verbs and nouns*) higher; upwards; towards the top of sth अधिक ऊँचा; ऊपर की ओर; किसी के शिखर की ओर *upland* ○ *upturned* ○ *upgrade* ○ *uphill*

**upbringing** /ˈʌpbrɪŋɪŋ ˈअप्ब्रिङ्इङ् / *noun* [*sing.*] the way a child is treated and taught how to behave by his/her parents (माता-पिता द्वारा) बच्चे का लालन-पालन और उसे सिखाना-पढ़ाना *a strict upbringing*

**update** /ˌʌpˈdeɪt ˌअप्ˈडेट् / *verb* [T] **1** to make sth more modern (किसी को) अद्यतन करना, नवीनतम स्तर तक लाना **2** to put the latest information into sth; to give sb the latest information (किसी वस्तु में) नवीनतम सूचना भरना; (किसी को) नवीनतम सूचना देना *Our database of addresses is updated regularly.* ▶ **update** /ˈʌpdeɪt ˈअप्डेट् / *noun* [C] अद्यतन स्थिति, नवीनतम जानकारी *an update on a news story* (= the latest information)

**upgrade** /ˌʌpˈgreɪd ˌअप्ˈग्रेड् / *verb* [T] to change sth so that it is of a higher standard किसी वस्तु के स्तर को उन्नत करना या का स्तरोन्नयन करना *Upgrading your computer software can be expensive.* ▶ **upgrade** /ˈʌpgreɪd ˈअप्ग्रेड् / *noun* [C] स्तरोन्नयन

**upheaval** /ʌpˈhiːvl अप्ˈहीव्ल् / *noun* [C, U] a sudden big change, especially one that causes a lot of trouble एकाएक बड़ा परिवर्तन (विशेषतः मुसीबतें पैदा करने वाला), उथल-पुथल, महापरिवर्तन

**uphill** /ˌʌpˈhɪl ˌअप्ˈहिल् / *adj., adv.* **1** going towards the top of a hill पहाड़ी पर चढ़ाते हुए ✪ विलोम **downhill** **2** needing a lot of effort बहुत कठिन; श्रमसाध्य, दुष्कर *It was an uphill struggle to find a job.*

**uphold** /ʌpˈhəʊld अप्ˈहोल्ड् / *verb* [T] (*pt, pp* **upheld** /-ˈheld -ˈहेल्ड् /) to support a decision, etc. especially when other people are against it किसी निर्णय आदि का समर्थन करना (विशेषतः उसका विरोध होने पर)

**upholstered** /ʌpˈhəʊlstəd अप्ˈहोल्स्टड् / *adj.* (used about a chair, etc.) covered with a soft thick material (कुरसी आदि) गद्दी चढ़ी हुई, गद्देदार

**upholstery** /ʌpˈhəʊlstəri अप्ˈहोल्स्टरि / *noun* [U] the thick soft materials used to cover chairs, car seats, etc. कुरसी आदि की गद्दियाँ बनाने का सामान

**upkeep** /ˈʌpkiːp ˈअप्कीप् / *noun* [U] **1** the cost or process of keeping sth in a good condition किसी वस्तु का रख-रखाव (उसे सही हालत में रखने का ख़र्च या प्रक्रिया) *The landlord pays for the upkeep of the building.* **2** the cost or process of providing children or animals with what they need to live बच्चों या पशुओं के पालन-पोषण का व्यय या प्रक्रिया

**upland** /ˈʌplənd ˈअप्लन्ड् / *noun* [C, *usually pl.*] an area of high land that is situated away from the coast तट से दूर की ऊँची भूमि या प्रदेश; अधित्यका ▶ **upland** *adj.* (*only before a noun*) ऊँची भूमि पर होने वाला, अधित्यकीय *upland agriculture*

**uplifting** /ˌʌpˈlɪftɪŋ ˌअप्ˈलिफ़्टिङ् / *adj.* producing a feeling of hope and happiness आशा और ख़ुशी देने वाला *an uplifting speech*

**upload**[1] /ˌʌpˈləʊd ˌअप्ˈलोड् / *verb* [T] (*computing*) to copy a computer file from a small computer system to a larger one कंप्यूटर फ़ाइल को अपलोड करना (छोटे कंप्यूटर से बड़े में प्रतिलिपि करना) ✪ विलोम **download**[1]

**upload**[2] /ˈʌpləʊd ˈअप्लोड् / *noun* [U] (*computing*) the act or process of copying a computer file from a small computer system to a larger one कंप्यूटर फ़ाइल को अपलोड करने (छोटे कंप्यूटर से बड़े में प्रतिलिप करने) का कार्य या प्रक्रिया ➪ **download**[2] देखिए।

**upon** /əˈpɒn अˈपॉन् / *prep.* (*formal*) = **on**

**upper** /ˈʌpə(r) ˈअप(र्) / *adj.* (*only before a noun*) in a higher position than sth else; situated above sth किसी अन्य वस्तु से अधिक ऊँचा या ऊपर का; किसी वस्तु के ऊपर स्थित; ऊपरी *He had a cut on his upper lip.* ✪ विलोम **lower** ➪ **body** पर चित्र देखिए।

IDM **get, have, etc. the upper hand** to get into a stronger position than another person; to gain control over sb का हाथ होना, किसी अन्य से अधिक सशक्त स्थिति में होना; किसी पर हावी हो जाना

**upper case** *noun* [U] letters that are written or printed in their large form; capital letters बड़े आकार में लिखे या मुद्रित अक्षर, अपर केस; बड़े अक्षर *'BBC' is written in upper case.* ✪ विलोम **lower case**

**the upper class** *noun* [*sing.*] (*also* **the upper classes**) [*pl.*] the group of people in a society who are considered to have the highest social position and who have more money and/or power than other people समाज का उच्च वर्ग *a member of the upper class/upper classes* ▶ **upper class** *adj.* उच्चवर्गीय *They're upper class.* ○ *an upper-class accent* ➪ **the middle class** और **the working class** देखिए।

**uppermost** /ˈʌpəməʊst ˈअपमोस्ट् / *adj.* in the highest or most important position उच्चतम या सर्वोच्च दशा में *Concern for her family was* ***uppermost in her mind.***

**upright** /ˈʌpraɪt ˈअप्राइट् / *adj., adv.* **1** in or into a vertical position खड़ी स्थिति में, खड़ा, सीधा *I was so tired I could hardly stay upright.* **2** honest and responsible ईमानदार और ज़िम्मेदार; खरा, सच्चा

IDM **bolt upright** ➪ **bolt**[3] देखिए।

**uprising** /ˈʌpraɪzɪŋ ˈअप्राइजिङ्/ *noun* [C] a situation in which a group of people start to fight against the people in power in their country (देश में) विद्रोह, बग़ावत (सत्ताधारी वर्ग के विरुद्ध किसी टोली द्वारा संघर्ष आरंभ कर देने की स्थिति)

**uproar** /ˈʌprɔː(r) ˈअपरॉ(र्)/ *noun* [U, *sing.*] a lot of noise, confusion, anger, etc.; an angry discussion about sth हंगामा, हुल्लड़; किसी मुद्दे पर गरमागरम बहस *The meeting ended **in uproar**.*

**uproot** /ˌʌpˈruːt ˌअपˈरूट्/ *verb* [T] to pull up a plant by the roots पौधे को जड़ से उखाड़ना *Strong winds had uprooted the tree.*

**upset**[1] /ˌʌpˈset ˌअपˈसेट्/ *verb* [T] (*pres. part.* **upsetting;** *pt, pp* **upset**) **1** to make sb worry or feel unhappy (किसी को) चिंतित या परेशान कर देना *The pictures of starving children upset her.* **2** to make sth go wrong (किसी को) गड़बड़ा देना *to upset someone's plans* **3** to knock sth over (किसी को) उलट देना *I upset a cup of tea all over the tablecloth.* **4** to make sb ill in the stomach पेट में गड़बड़ हो जाना या पेट को गड़बड़ कर देना

**upset**[2] /ˌʌpˈset ˌअप्ˈसेट्/ *adj.* **1** worried and unhappy चिंतित और परेशान *She was looking very upset about something.* **2** slightly ill हलका अस्वस्थ ***I've got an upset stomach.***

**upset**[3] /ˈʌpset ˈअप्सेट्/ *noun* **1** [C, U] a situation in which there are unexpected problems or difficulties अप्रत्याशित समस्याओं या कठिनाइयों वाली स्थिति; उलट-फेर *The company survived the recent upset in share prices.* **2** [C] a slight illness in your stomach पेट में गड़बड़ *a stomach upset* **3** [C, U] a situation that causes worry and sadness चिंता और परेशानी पैदा करने वाली स्थिति *She's had a few upsets recently.* ○ *It had been the cause of much emotional upset.*

**upshot** /ˈʌpʃɒt ˈअप्शॉट्/ *noun* [*sing.*] **the upshot (of sth)** the final result, especially of a conversation or an event अंतिम परिणाम, निष्कर्ष (विशेषतः किसी बातचीत या घटना का)

**upside down** /ˌʌpsaɪd ˈdaʊn ˌअप्साइड् ˈडाउन्/ *adv., adj.* with the top part turned to the bottom ऊपर का भाग नीचे की ओर; उलटा, औंधा *You're holding the picture upside down.*

IDM **turn sth upside down** **1** to make a place untidy when looking for sth किसी वस्तु की तलाश में चीजों को अस्तव्यस्त या तितर-बितर कर देना *I had to turn the house upside down looking for my keys.* **2** to cause large changes and confusion in a person's life किसी के जीवन में उलट-पुलट कर देना *His sudden death turned her world upside down.*

**upstairs** /ˌʌpˈsteəz ˌअप्ˈस्टेअज़्/ *adv.* to or on a higher floor of a building (भवन की) ऊपरी मंजिल पर *to **go upstairs*** ○ *She's sleeping upstairs.* ✪ विलोम **downstairs** ▶ **upstairs** /ˈʌpsteəz ˈअप्स्टेअज़्/ *adj.* ऊपरी मंजिल का, उपरला *an upstairs window* ▶ **the upstairs** *noun* [*sing.*] (*informal*) ऊपरी मंजिल *We're going to paint the upstairs.*

**upstream** /ˌʌpˈstriːm ˌअप्ˈस्ट्रीम्/ *adv., adj.* in the direction that a river flows from बहाव के विरुद्ध *He found it hard work swimming upstream.* ✪ विलोम **downstream**

**upsurge** /ˈʌpsɜːdʒ ˈअप्सज़्/ *noun* [C, *usually sing.*] **an upsurge (in sth)** a sudden increase of sth किसी चीज़ में एकाएक होने वाली वृद्धि, उमड़, लहर

**uptake** /ˈʌpteɪk ˈअप्टेक्/ *noun*

IDM **quick/slow on the uptake** quick/slow to understand the meaning of sth किसी बात को तुरंत या देर से समझने वाला *I gave him a hint but he's slow on the uptake.*

**upthrust** /ˈʌpθrʌst ˈअप्थ्रस्ट्/ *noun* [U] (*technical*) the force with which a liquid or gas pushes up against an object that is floating in it द्रव या गैस का बल जिसे वह अपने भीतर तैरती हुई वस्तु को ऊपर धकेलने में लगाता है; उत्प्लावन

**uptight** /ˌʌpˈtaɪt ˌअप्ˈटाइट्/ *adj.* (*informal*) nervous and not relaxed घबराहट में और तनावग्रस्त *He gets uptight before an exam.*

**up to date** *adj.* **1** modern आधुनिक **2** having the most recent information अद्यतन, नवीनतम जानकारी रखने वाला

**up to the minute** *adj.* having the most recent information possible एकदम अभी तक की जानकारी रखने वाला

**upturn** /ˈʌptɜːn ˈअप्टन्/ *noun* [C] **an upturn (in sth)** an improvement in sth (किसी वस्तु में) सुधार; बढ़त *an upturn in support for the government* ✪ विलोम **downturn**

**upturned** /ˌʌpˈtɜːnd ˌअप्ˈटन्ड्/ *adj.* **1** pointing upwards ऊपर की ओर को निकला हुआ *an upturned nose* **2** turned upside down औंधा किया हुआ

**upward** /ˈʌpwəd ˈअप्वड्/ *adj.* moving or directed towards a higher place ऊपर की ओर जाने वाला या निर्देशित; ऊर्ध्वाभिमुख *an upward trend in exports* (= an increase) ✪ विलोम **downward** ▶ **upward** (*also* **upwards** /-wədz -वड्ज़्/) *adv.* ऊपर की ओर

**upwards of** *prep.* more than the number mentioned (निर्दिष्ट संख्या) से अधिक *They've invited upwards of a hundred guests.*

**uranium** /juˈreɪniəm युˈरेनिअम्/ *noun* [U] (*symbol* **U**) a metal that can be used to produce nuclear energy यूरेनियम (धातु) परमाणु-ऊर्जा उत्पन्न करने में प्रयुक्त *Uranium is highly radioactive.*

**Uranus** /ˈjʊərənəs; jʊˈreɪnəs ˈयुअरनस्; युˈरेनस्/ *noun* [*sing.*] the planet that is seventh in order from the sun युरेनस (सौर मंडल में सूर्य से सातवाँ ग्रह) ➪ **the solar system** पर चित्र देखिए।

**urban** /ˈɜːbən ˈअबन्/ *adj.* connected with a town or city नगर या क़सबे से संबंधित; शहरी *urban development* ➪ **rural** देखिए।

**urbane** /ɜːˈbeɪn अˈबेन्/ *adj.* (*written*) (used especially about a man) good at knowing what to say and how to behave in social situations; appearing relaxed and confident भद्र, विनम्र, सुसभ्य; शांत और आत्मविश्वासपूर्ण लगने वाला ▶ **urbanely** *adv.* भद्रतापूर्वक, सौजन्यतापूर्वक ▶ **urbanity** /ɜːˈbænəti अˈबैनटि/ *noun* [U] भद्रता, सौजन्यता

**urbanized** (*also* **-ised**) /ˈɜːbənaɪzd ˈअबनाइज़्ड्/ *adj.* (used about an area, a country, etc.) having a lot of towns, streets, factories, etc. rather than countryside (कोई क्षेत्र, देश आदि) जिसमें बहुत-से शहर, सड़कें, कारख़ाने आदि हों; नगरीकृत, शहरीकृत ▶ **urbanization** (*also* **-isation**) /ˌɜːbənaɪˈzeɪʃn ˌअबनाइˈज़ेश्न्/ *noun* [U] नगरीकरण, शहरीकरण

**Urdu** *noun* [U] the official language of Pakistan, which is also one of the main languages of India उर्दू (पाकिस्तान की राजभाषा और भारत की एक प्रमुख भाषा)

**urea** /jʊˈriːə युˈरीआ/ *noun* [U] a colourless substance that is found especially in the liquid waste that is passed from your body when you go to the toilet (**urine**) मूत्र में पाया जाने वाला एक रंगहीन पदार्थ; यूरिया

**ureter** /juˈriːtə(r); ˈjʊərɪtə(r) युˈरीट(र्); ˈयुअरिट(र्)/ *noun* [C] (*technical*) the tube that (**urine**) passes through to get from the **kidneys** to the **bladder** मूत्र को गुर्दों से मूत्राशय तक पहुँचाने वाली नली; मूत्रवाहिनी

**urethra** /jʊˈriːθrə युˈरीथ्रा/ *noun* [C] the tube that carries liquid waste out of the body. In men and male animals male seed (**sperm**) also flows along this tube मूत्रनली (पुरुषों और नर पशुओं में शुक्राणु भी मूत्रनली से प्रवाहित होते हैं) ▶ **urethral** *adj.* मूत्रनली-विषयक

**urge**[1] /ɜːdʒ अज्/ *verb* [T] **1 urge sb (to do sth); urge sth** to advise or try hard to persuade sb to do sth किसी व्यक्ति को कुछ करने के लिए समझाना या प्रबल रूप से प्रेरित करना *I urged him to fight the decision.* ○ *Drivers are urged to take care on icy roads.* **2** to force sb/sth to go in a certain direction दिशा-विशेष में जाने के लिए (किसी व्यक्ति या वस्तु को) बाध्य करना; हाँकना *He urged his horse over the fence.*

**PHR V** **urge sb on** to encourage sb किसी व्यक्ति को प्रोत्साहित करना *The captain urged his team on.*

**urge**[2] /ɜːdʒ अज्/ *noun* [C] a strong need or desire तीव्र आवश्यकता या इच्छा *sexual/creative urges*

**urgent** /ˈɜːdʒənt ˈअजन्ट्/ *adj.* needing immediate attention जिस पर तुरंत ध्यान देना अपेक्षित है, तुरंत कार्रवाई की अपेक्षा वाला; अत्यावश्यक, बहुत ज़रूरी *an urgent message* ▶ **urgency** /-dʒənsi -जन्सि/ *noun* [U] अत्यावश्यकता *a matter of the greatest urgency* ▶ **urgently** *adv.* अत्यावश्यक रूप से *I must see you urgently.*

**urinary** /ˈjʊərɪnəri ˈयुअरिनरि/ *adj.* (*usually before a noun*) (*medical*) connected with urine or the parts of the body through which it passes मूत्र या मूत्रमार्ग विषयक

**urinate** /ˈjʊərɪneɪt ˈयुअरिनेट्/ *verb* [I] (*formal*) to pass urine from the body मूत्र-विसर्जन करना, पेशाब करना

**urine** /ˈjʊərɪn ˈयुअरिन्/ *noun* [U] the yellowish liquid that is passed from your body when you go to the toilet मूत्र, पेशाब

**URL** /ˌjuː ɑːr ˈel ˌयू आर् ˈएल्/ *abbr.* (*computing*) uniform/universal resource locator (the address of a **World Wide Web** page) यूआरएल (किसी वेबसाइट का पता)

**urn** /ɜːn अन्/ *noun* [C] **1** a special container, used especially to hold the powder (**ashes**) that is left when a dead person has been burnt (**cremated**) अस्थिकलश, भस्मकलश (मृत व्यक्ति के पार्थिव अवशेष रखने का पात्र) **2** a large metal container used for making a large quantity of tea or coffee and for keeping it hot चाय या कॉफ़ी बनाने और उसे गर्म रखने का धातु निर्मित बड़ा पात्र, बड़ी केतली

**US** /ˌjuː ˈes ˌयू ˈएस्/ *abbr.* the United States (of America) यूएस; युनाइटिड स्टेट्स ऑफ़ अमेरिका का संक्षिप्त रूप

**us** /əs; *strong form* ʌs अस्; प्रबल रूप अस्/ *pronoun* (*used as the object of a verb, or after be*) me and another person or other people; me and you (किसी क्रिया के कर्म के रूप में या **be** के बाद प्रयुक्त) हम (मैं और दूसरा या दूसरे व्यक्ति; मैं और तुम या आप) *Come with us.* ○ *Leave us alone.*

**USA** /ˌjuː es ˈeɪ ˌयू ऍस् ˈए / *abbr.* the United States of America यूएसए; द यूनाइटिड स्टेट्स ऑफ़ अमेरिका का संक्षिप्त रूप

**usable** /ˈjuːzəbl ˈयूज़बल् / *adj.* that can be used जो प्रयोग में आ सके, प्रयोगार्ह, इस्तेमाल होने के लायक़

**usage** /ˈjuːsɪdʒ ˈयूसिज् / *noun* **1** [U] the way that sth is used; the amount that sth is used किसी वस्तु का प्रयोग (प्रयुक्त होने का ढंग); प्रयुक्त हुई वस्तु की मात्रा **2** [C, U] the way that words are normally used in a language शब्दों का व्यवहार या प्रयोग (सामान्यतया भाषा में प्रयुक्त होने का ढंग) *a guide to English grammar and usage*

**use**[1] /juːz यूज़् / *verb* [T] (*pres. part.* **using;** *pt, pp* **used** /juːzd यूज़्ड् /) **1 use sth (as/for sth); use sth (to do sth)** to do sth with a machine, an object, a method, etc. for a particular purpose विशेष प्रयोजन से किसी मशीन आदि से कोई काम करना, (का) प्रयोग करना *Could I use your phone?* ○ *The building was used as a shelter for homeless people.* **2** to need or to take sth किसी चीज़ की ज़रूरत होना या उसे लेना *Don't use all the milk.* **3** to treat sb/sth in an unfair way in order to get sth that you want अपने लाभ के लिए किसी व्यक्ति या वस्तु का बेजा इस्तेमाल करना

PHR V **use sth up** to use sth until no more is left किसी वस्तु का पूरा इस्तेमाल करना

**use**[2] /juːs यूस् / *noun* **1** [U] the action of using sth or of being used किसी वस्तु का प्रयोग (किसी वस्तु को प्रयोग में लाने या उसके प्रयुक्त होने का कार्य) *The use of computers is now widespread.* ○ *She kept the money for use in an emergency.* **2** [C, U] the purpose for which sth is used किसी वस्तु के प्रयोग का प्रयोजन *This machine has many uses.* **3** [U] the ability or permission to use sth किसी वस्तु के प्रयोग की क्षमता या उसे इस्तेमाल करने देना *He lost the use of his hand after the accident.* ○ *She offered them the use of her car.* **4** [U] the advantage of sth; how useful sth is (किसी वस्तु का) लाभ, फ़ायदा; किसी वस्तु की उपयोगिता ***It's no use*** *studying for an exam at the last minute.* ○ *Will this jumper* ***be of use to*** *you or should I get rid of it?*

IDM **come into/go out of use** to start/stop being used regularly or by a lot of people किसी वस्तु का (नियमित या अनेकों द्वारा) प्रचलन शुरू होना या समाप्त हो जाना *Email came into widespread use in the 1990s.*

**make use of sth/sb** to use sth/sb in a way that will give you an advantage अपने लाभ की दृष्टि से किसी व्यक्ति या वस्तु का इस्तेमाल करना

**used** *adj.* **1** /juːzd यूज़्ड् / that has had another owner before पुराना (पहले किसी अन्य के द्वारा उपयोग में लाया गया) *a garage selling used cars* ✪ पर्याय **second-hand** **2** /juːst यूस्ट् / **used to sth/to doing sth** familiar with sth; accustomed to sth किसी वस्तु से परिचित, वाक़िफ़; किसी वस्तु का अभ्यस्त, आदि *He's used to the heat.* ○ *I'll never* ***get used to*** *getting up so early.*

**used to** /ˈjuːst tə; ˈयूस्ट् ट / (*before a vowel and in the final position* /ˈjuːst tuː ˈयूस्ट टू /) (*modal verb*) for talking about sth that happened often or continuously in the past or about a situation which existed in the past अतीत में प्रायः या निरंतर होने वाली किसी बात या अतीत की किसी स्थिति के निर्देश के लिए प्रयुक्त वृत्तिवाचक क्रिया *She used to live with her parents* (= but she doesn't now). ○ *Did you use to smoke?*

NOTE **Used to** के निषेधवाचक और प्रश्नवाचक वाक्य **did** का प्रयोग करके बनाए जाते हैं—*I didn't use to like jazz.* ○ *Did she use to be in your class?* ध्यान रहे कि निम्नलिखित प्रयोग एक दूसरे से अलग हैं—**used to** + क्रियार्थक संज्ञा जिससे केवल भूतकाल का निर्देश होता है और **be used to (doing) sth** जिससे भूत, वर्तमान और भविष्य तीनों का निर्देश हो सकता है। निम्नलिखित वाक्यों में तुलना कीजिए—*I used to live on my own* (= but now I don't). ○ *I'm used to living on my own* (= I am accustomed to it).

**useful** /ˈjuːsfl ˈयूसफ़ल् / *adj.* having some practical use; helpful उपयोगी; सहायक *a useful tool* ○ *useful advice* ▶ **usefully** /-fəli -फ़लि / *adv.* उपयोगितापूर्वक ▶ **usefulness** *noun* [U] उपयोगिता, लाभदायकता

IDM **come in useful** to be of practical help in a certain situation स्थिति-विशेष में सहायक होना *Don't throw that box away—it might come in useful for something.*

**useless** /ˈjuːsləs ˈयूसलस् / *adj.* **1** that does not work well, that does not achieve anything अनुपयोगी, बेकार (जो ठीक से काम न करे, जिससे कोई काम न सधे जो किसी काम का न हो) *This new machine is useless.* ○ *It's useless complaining/to complain—you won't get your money back.* **2** (*informal*) **useless (at sth/at doing sth)** (used about a person) weak or not successful at sth दुर्बल या किसी काम में अक्षम, निकम्मा *I'm useless at sport.* ▶ **uselessly** *adv.* व्यर्थ, बेकार, बेफ़ायदा ▶ **uselessness** *noun* [U] व्यर्थता, अनुपयोगिता

**user** /ˈjuːzə(r) ˈयूज़(र्) / *noun* [C] (*often in compounds*) a person who uses a service, machine, place, etc. किसी सेवा, मशीन, स्थान आदि का उपयोग करने वाला; उपयोगकर्ता; उपभोक्ता *users of public transport* ○ *drug users*

**user-friendly** *adj.* (used about computers, books, machines, etc.) easy to understand and use (कंप्यूटर, पुस्तकें, मशीनें आदि) जिन्हें समझना और प्रयोग करना आसान हो

**usher[1]** /ˈʌʃə(r) ˈअशर्/ *noun* [C] a person who shows people to their seats in a theatre, church, etc. प्रवेशक (वह व्यक्ति जो थिएटर, चर्च आदि में लोगों को उनका स्थान बताता है)

**usher[2]** /ˈʌʃə(r) ˈअशर्/ *verb* [T] to take or show sb where to go किसी को (अंदर) ले जाना या गंतव्य स्थान दिखाना या जगह पर पहुँचाना *I was ushered into an office.*

PHR V **usher sth in** to be the beginning of sth new or to make sth new begin किसी नई स्थिति का आरंभ-बिंदु होना या कोई नई बात शुरु करना *The agreement ushered in a new period of peace for the two countries.*

**USSR** /ˌjuː es es ˈɑː(r) ˌयू एस् एस् ˈआर्/ *abbr.* (until 1991) Union of Soviet Socialist Republics (1991 तक) यूएसएसआर; सोवियत संघ का संक्षिप्त रूप ➪ **CIS** देखिए।

**usual** /ˈjuːʒuəl; -ʒəl ˈयूशुअल्; -श़ल्/ *adj.* **usual (for sb/sth) (to do sth)** happening or used most often बहुधा होने या प्रयोग में आने वाला, हमेशा वाला *It's usual for her to work at weekends.* ○ *He got home later than usual.* ○ *I sat in my usual seat.* ✪ विलोम **unusual**

IDM **as usual** in the way that has often happened before हमेशा की तरह *Here's Dharam, late as usual!*

**usually** /ˈjuːʒuəli; -ʒəli ˈयूशुअलि; -श़लि/ *adv.* in the way that is usual; most often हमेशा के ढंग से; बहुधा, सामान्यतया *She's usually home by six.* ○ *We usually go out on Saturdays.*

**usurp** /juːˈzɜːp यूˈज़प्/ *verb* [T] (*formal*) to take sb's position and/or power without having the right to do this किसी के पद और या शक्ति को हड़प लेना ▶ **usurpation** /ˌjuːzɜːˈpeɪʃn ˌयूज़ˈपेश्न्/ *noun* [U, C] हड़प लेने की क्रिया, अनधिकार, अधिग्रहण ▶ **usurper** *noun* [C] हड़पने वाला

**utensil** /juːˈtensl यूˈटेन्स्ल्/ *noun* [C] a type of tool that is used in the home (घर में इस्तेमाल का) बरतन-भाँडा *kitchen/cooking utensils* ➪ **kitchen** पर चित्र देखिए।

**uterus** /ˈjuːtərəs ˈयूटरस्/ *noun* [C] (*pl.* **uteruses** *or, in scientific use,* **uteri** /-raɪ -राइ/) (*formal*) the part of a woman or female animal where a baby develops before it is born स्त्री या मादा पशु का गर्भाशय (वह अंग जहाँ जन्म से पूर्व शिशु या शावक पलता है) ✪ पर्याय **womb**

**utility** /juːˈtɪləti यूˈटिलटि/ *noun* (*pl.* **utilities**) **1** [C] a service provided for the public, such as a water, gas or electricity supply जनता के लिए जल, गैस या बिजली की आपूर्ति की सेवाएँ; जनोपयोगी सेवाएँ *the administration of **public utilities*** **2** [U] (*formal*) the quality of being useful उपयोगिता **3** [C] (*computing*) a program or part of a program that does a particular task विशेष कार्य को निष्पादित करने वाला कार्यक्रम या उसका अंश

**utility room** *noun* [C] a small room in some houses, often next to the kitchen, where people keep large pieces of kitchen equipment, such as a washing machine (प्रायः रसोईघर से सटा) घरेलू उपयोग के बड़े उपकरण (जैसे वाशिंग मशीन) रखने का कमरा; युटिलिटी रूम

**utilize** (*also* **-ise**) /ˈjuːtəlaɪz ˈयूटलाइज़्/ *verb* [T] (*formal*) to make use of sth किसी वस्तु को काम में लाना, (का) उपयोग करना *to utilize natural resources*

**utmost[1]** /ˈʌtməʊst ˈअट्मोस्ट्/ *adj.* (*formal*) (*only before a noun*) greatest अधिकतम, सर्वाधिक *a message **of the utmost importance***

**utmost[2]** /ˈʌtməʊst ˈअट्मोस्ट्/ *noun* [*sing.*] the greatest amount possible यथासंभव अधिकतम *Resources have been exploited **to the utmost**.* ○ *I will **do my utmost*** (= try as hard as possible) *to help.*

**Utopia** (*also* **utopia**) /juːˈtəʊpiə यूˈटोपिआ/ *noun* [C, U] a place or state that exists only in the imagination, where everything is perfect कल्पनालोक (कल्पना में बना संसार जहाँ सब कुछ आदर्श स्थिति में है), आदर्श-लोक, रामराज्य ▶ **Utopian** (*also* **utopian**) /-piən -पिअन्/ *adj.* कल्पनालोक-विषयक

**utter[1]** /ˈʌtə(r) ˈअटर्/ *adj.* (*only before a noun*) complete; total परम, पूरा, पूर्ण; निरा, पक्का, निपट *He felt an utter fool.* ▶ **utterly** *adv.* पूर्णतया *It's utterly impossible.*

**utter[2]** /ˈʌtə(r) ˈअटर्/ *verb* [T] to say sth or make a sound with your voice कुछ कहना या आवाज़ निकालना *She did not **utter a word*** (= she did not say anything) *in the meeting.* ▶ **utterance** /ˈʌtərəns ˈअटरन्स्/ *noun* [C] (*formal*) अभिव्यक्ति, कथन, उद्गार

**U-turn** *noun* [C] **1** a type of movement where a car, etc. turns round so that it goes back in the

direction it came from सड़क पर वाहन को ऐसे मोड़ना कि उसी दिशा में चलने लगे जिस दिशा से आया था, उलट-घुमाव, यू-टर्न **2** (*informal*) a sudden change from one plan or policy to a completely different or opposite one किसी योजना या नीति में अकस्मात पूर्ण परिवर्तन ➪ **about turn** देखिए।

**uvula** /ˈjuːvjələ ˈयूव्यला/ *noun* [C] (*pl.* **uvulae** /-liː -ली/) a small piece of flesh that hangs from the top of the inside of the mouth just above the throat अलिजिह्वा, काकल, कौआ, घंटी (मुँह के एकदम भीतर ठीक गले से ऊपर लकटता छोटा मांसपिंड) ➪ **body** पर चित्र देखिए।

# V v

**V, v**[1] /viː ्वी / *noun* [C, U] (*pl.* **V's; v's** /viːz व्हीज़्/) **1** the twenty-second letter of the English alphabet अँग्रेज़ी वर्णमाला का बाईसवाँ अक्षर *'Velvet' begins with a 'V'.* **2** the shape of a V, V की आकृति *a V-neck sweater*

**v**[2] *abbr.* **1** (*also* **vs**) versus; against बनाम; के विरुद्ध *India vs Pakistan* **2 V** volt(s) वोल्ट *a 9V battery* **3** verse पद्य **4** (*informal*) very बहुत *v good*

**vacancy** /ˈveɪkənsi ˈव्रेकन्सि / *noun* [C] (*pl.* **vacancies**) **1 a vacancy (for sb/sth)** a job that is available for sb to do किसी के लिए उपलब्ध कोई नौकरी; रिक्ति *We have a vacancy for a secretary in our office.* **2** a room in a hotel, etc. that is available होटल में उपलब्ध या ख़ाली कमरा *The sign outside the hotel said 'No Vacancies'.*

**vacant** /ˈveɪkənt ˈव्रेकन्ट् / *adj.* **1** (used about a house, hotel room, seat, etc.) not being used; empty (मकान, होटल का कमरा आदि) जो इस्तेमाल में नहीं आ रहा; ख़ाली **2** (used about a job in a company, etc.) that is available for sb to take (कंपनी में) नौकरी के लिए ख़ाली पद; रिक्त स्थान *the **'Situations Vacant'** page* (= the page of a newspaper where jobs are advertised) **3** showing no sign of intelligence or understanding बुद्धि या समझ न दिखाते हुए; भावशून्य *a vacant expression* ▶ **vacantly** *adv.* भावशून्य होकर *She stared at him vacantly.*

**vacate** /veɪˈkeɪt; vəˈk- व्रेˈकेट्; व्रˈक- / *verb* [T] (*formal*) to leave a building, a seat, a job, etc. so that it is available for sb else दूसरे के लिए (मकान, सीट आदि) ख़ाली करना, (अपना स्थान या पद) छोड़ना

**vacation** /vəˈkeɪʃn व्रˈकेशन् / *noun* **1** [C] any of the periods of time when universities or courts of law are closed (विश्वविद्यालय या न्यायालय में) लंबी छुट्टी; विश्रामावकाश *the Dusserah vacation* **2** [C, U] (*AmE*) (a) holiday छुट्टी, अवकाश *The boss is **on vacation**.* ➪ **holiday** पर नोट देखिए।

**vacillate** /ˈvæsəleɪt ˈवैसलेट् / *verb* [I] to keep changing your ideas or opinions about sth, especially in a way that annoys other people (विचार या मत में) दुलमुल होना, डाँवाँडोल होना, प्रायः खीजते हुए आगा-पीछा करना ✪ पर्याय **waver** ▶ **vacillation** /ˌvæsəˈleɪʃn ˌवैसˈलेशन् / *noun* [U, C] अस्थिरता, आगा-पीछा

**vaccinate** /ˈvæksɪneɪt ˈवैक्सिनेट् / *verb* [T] **vaccinate sb (against sth)** (*often passive*) to protect a person or an animal against a disease by giving him/her/it a mild form of the disease with a needle which is put under the skin (**an injection**) टीका लगाकर किसी व्यक्ति या पशु को रोग से सुरक्षित करना; टीकाकरण करना *Were you vaccinated against measles as a child?* ✪ पर्याय **immunize** और **inoculate** ▶ **vaccination** /ˌvæksɪˈneɪʃn ˌवैक्सिˈनेशन् / *noun* [C, U] टीकाकरण

**vaccine** /ˈvæksiːn ˈवैक्सीन् / *noun* [C] a mild form of a disease that is put (**injected**) into a person or an animal's blood using a needle (**an injection**) in order to protect the body against that disease टीके की दवा; वैक्सीन

**vacuole** /ˈvækjuəʊl ˈवैक्युओल् / *noun* [C] (*technical*) an empty space inside a living cell सजीव कोशिका में रिक्त स्थान; रिक्तिका

**vacuum**[1] /ˈvækjuəm ˈवैक्युअम् / *noun* [C] **1** a space that is completely empty of all substances, including air or other gases पूर्णतः रिक्त स्थान, शून्य, निर्वात *vacuum-packed foods* (= in a pack from which the air has been removed) **2** [*usually sing.*] a situation from which sth is missing or lacking किसी वस्तु की अनुपस्थिति या न्यूनता से उत्पन्न रिक्तता **3** (*informal*) = **vacuum cleaner 4** [*usually sing.*] the act of cleaning sth with a vacuum cleaner वैक्यूम क्लीनर से किसी स्थान या वस्तु की सफ़ाई *to give a room a quick vacuum*

**vacuum**[2] /ˈvækjuəm ˈवैक्युअम् / *verb* [I, T] to clean sth using a vacuum cleaner वैक्यूम क्लीनर से किसी स्थान या वस्तु की सफ़ाई करना ✪ पर्याय **hoover**

**vacuum cleaner** (*informal* **vacuum**) *noun* [C] an electric machine that cleans carpets, etc. by sucking up dirt क़ालीन आदि की (धूल सोखकर) सफ़ाई करने वाला विद्युत उपकरण; वैक्यूम क्लीनर ✪ पर्याय **Hoover**™ ➪ **cleaner** देखिए।

**vacuum flask** (*also* **flask** *AmE* **vacuum bottle**) *noun* [C] a container like a bottle with double walls with an empty space (**vacuum**) between them, used for keeping liquids hot or cold फ़्लास्क, वैक्यूम फ़्लास्क (ऐसी बोतल जिसकी दोहरी दीवारों के बीच ख़ाली जगह होती है जिससे गरम वस्तु गरम और ठंडी वस्तु ठंडी बनी रहती है) ➪ **Thermos** पर चित्र देखिए।

**vada** *noun* [C] an Indian snack made from ground lentils or mashed potatoes, that is deep fried in oil वड़ा

**vagabond** /ˈvægəbɒnd ˈवैगबॉन्ड् / *noun* [C] (*old-fashioned, disapproving*) a person without a home or a job who keeps travelling from one place to another आवारा, धुमक्कड़ व्यक्ति

**vagina** /və'dʒaɪnə व़'जाइना / *noun* [C] the passage in the body of a woman or female animal that connects the outer sex organs to the part where a baby grows (**womb**) मादा पशु या स्त्री की योनि

**vagrant** /'veɪgrənt 'व़ेग्रन्ट् / *noun* [C] a person who has no home and no job, especially one who asks people for money आवारा (बेकार और बेघर तथा दूसरों से पैसा माँगते रहने वाला व्यक्ति)

**vague** /veɪg व़ेग् / *adj.* **1** not clear or definite अस्पष्ट या अनिश्चित *He was very vague about how much money he'd spent.* ○ *a vague shape in the distance* **2** (used about a person) not thinking or understanding clearly (व्यक्ति) जिसकी सोच या समझ में स्पष्टता नहीं *She looked vague when I tried to explain.* ▶ **vagueness** *noun* [U] अस्पष्टता, अनिश्चितता

**vaguely** /'veɪgli 'व़ेगलि / *adv.* **1** in a way that is not clear; slightly साफ़ तौर से नहीं, अस्पष्ट रूप से; कुछ-कुछ, थोड़ा-थोड़ा *Her name is vaguely familiar.* **2** without thinking about what is happening बिना समझे कि क्या हो रहा है, अनिश्चय के भाव के साथ *He smiled vaguely and walked away.*

**vain** /veɪn व़ेन् / *adj.* **1** useless; failing to produce the result you want व्यर्थ, बेकार; निष्फल, बेनतीजा *She turned away* ***in a vain attempt to*** *hide her tears.* **2** (used about a person) too proud of your own appearance, abilities, etc. (व्यक्ति) अपनी अकल और शकल को लेकर घमंडी; दंभी *He's so vain—he looks in every mirror he passes.* ⇨ **vanity** noun देखिए। ▶ **vainly** *adv.* दंभ से, घमंडपूर्वक

IDM **in vain** without success बेकार में, बेफ़ायदा *The firemen tried in vain to put out the fire.*

**vale** /veɪl व़ेल् / *noun* [C] a valley घाटी, वादी *the Vale of Kashmir* NOTE स्थानवाचक शब्दों और कविता में इस शब्द का प्रयोग होता है।

**valediction** /ˌvælɪ'dɪkʃn ˌव़ैलि'डिक्शन् / *noun* [C, U] (*formal*) the act of saying goodbye, especially by making a formal speech विदाई, औपचारिक विदाई भाषण ▶ **valedictory** /ˌvælɪ'dɪktəri ˌव़ैलि'डिक्टरि / *adj.* (*usually before a noun*) विदाई भाषण संबंधी *a valedictory speech*

**valency** /'veɪlənsi 'व़ेलन्सि / *noun* [C, U] (*pl.* **valencies**) (*technical*) **1** a measurement of the power of an atom to combine with others, by the number of **hydrogen** atoms it can combine with or take the place of एक अणु की अन्य अणुओं से संयोजित होने की क्षमता; संयोजन क्षमता, संयोजकता *Carbon has a valency of 4.* **2** the number of elements that a word, especially a verb, combines with in a sentence वाक्य में किसी शब्द (विशेषतः क्रिया) के साथ संयोजित अन्य शब्दों की संख्या

**valentine** /'væləntaɪn 'व़ैलन्टाइन् / *noun* [C] **1** (*also* **valentine card**) a card that you send, usually without putting your name on it, to sb you love प्रेमी को भेजा जाने वाला कार्ड (जिस पर प्रायः प्रेषक का नाम नहीं होता), गुमनाम प्रेम-कार्ड

NOTE इस कार्ड को **St Valentine's Day** (14 फरवरी को) भेजने की परंपरा है।

**2** the person you send this card to व्यक्ति जिसे यह कार्ड भेजा जाता है, कार्ड का प्रेषिती

**valiant** /'væliənt 'व़ैलिअन्ट् / *adj.* (*formal*) full of courage and not afraid साहसी और निर्भीक ▶ **valiantly** *adv.* साहसपूर्वक

**valid** /'vælɪd 'व़ैलिड् / *adj.* **1 valid (for sth)** that is legally or officially acceptable वैधानिक या अधिकारिक रूप से मान्य; विधिमान्य *This passport is valid for one year only.* **2** based on what is logical or true; acceptable तर्कसंगत या सत्य; स्वीकार करने योग्य, मान्य *I could raise no valid objections to the plan.* ✪ विलोम **invalid** ▶ **validity** /və'lɪdəti व़'लिडटि / *noun* [U] विधिमान्यता, वैधता

**validate** /'vælɪdeɪt 'व़ैलिडेट् / *verb* [T] (*formal*) **1** to show that sth is true किसी बात को सत्य सिद्ध करना *to validate a claim/theory* ✪ विलोम **invalidate** **2** to make sth legally valid किसी बात को क़ानूनन मान्य या विधिमान्य करना *to validate a contract* ✪ विलोम **invalidate** **3** to state officially that sth is useful and of an acceptable standard किसी वस्तु की उपयोगिता और स्तरीयता को प्रमाणित करना *Check that their courses have been validated by a reputable organization.* ▶ **validation** /ˌvælɪ'deɪʃn ˌव़ैलि'डेश्न् / *noun* [U] विधिमान्यकरण

**valley** /'væli 'व़ैलि / *noun* [C] the low land between two mountains or hills, which often has a river flowing through it घाटी, वादी ⇨ **hanging valley** और **rift valley** देखिए।

**valour** (*AmE* **valor**) /'vælə(r) 'व़ैल(र्) / *noun* [U] (*written*) (*old-fashioned*) great courage and lack of fear, especially in war महान साहस और निर्भीकता (विशेषतः युद्ध में) *the soldiers' valour in battle*

**valuable** /'væljuəbl 'व़ैल्युअब्ल् / *adj.* **1** worth a lot of money बहुत महँगा, बहुमूल्य, क़ीमती *Is this ring valuable?* **2** very useful बहुत उपयोगी, बहुमूल्य, मूल्यवान *a valuable piece of information* ✪ विलोम **valueless** या **worthless** ⇨ **invaluable** देखिए।

**valuables** /'væljuəblz 'व़ैल्युअब्ल्ज़् / *noun* [*pl.*] the small things that you own that are worth a lot of money, such as jewellery, etc. (आभूषण आदि छोटी-छोटी) बहुमूल्य या क़ीमती वस्तुएँ *Please put your valuables in the hotel safe.*

**valuation** /ˌvæljuˈeɪʃn ˌवैलूयुˈएशन्/ *noun* [C] a professional judgement about how much money sth is worth किसी वस्तु का मूल्य-निर्धारण

**value¹** /ˈvælju: ˈवैल्यू/ *noun* **1** [U, C] the amount of money that sth is worth (किसी वस्तु का) मूल्य, क़ीमत *The thieves stole goods with a total value of Rs 10,000.* ○ *to go up/down in value* ➪ **face value** देखिए। **2** [U] (*BrE*) how much sth is worth compared with its price दाम के मुक़ाबले में किसी वस्तु की उपयोगिता; मूल्य, महत्त्व *The hotel was* ***good/excellent value*** (= well worth the money it cost). ○ *Package holidays give the best* ***value for money.*** **3** [U] the importance of sth किसी वस्तु का महत्त्व, उपादेयता *to be of great/little/no value to sb* ○ *This bracelet is of great* ***sentimental value*** *to me.* **4 values** [*pl.*] beliefs about what is the right and wrong way for people to behave; moral principles अच्छे और बुरे के विषय में लोगों की धारणाएँ, मूल्य; नैतिक सिद्धांत *a return to traditional values* ○ *Young people have a different* ***set of values.***

**value²** /ˈvælju: ˈवैल्यू/ *verb* [T] (*pres. part.* **valuing**) **1 value sb/sth (as sth)** to think sb/sth is very important किसी व्यक्ति या वस्तु को महत्त्वपूर्ण या मूल्यवान मानना *I really value her as a friend.* **2** (*usually passive*) **value sth (at sth)** to decide the amount of money that sth is worth किसी वस्तु की क़ीमत या मूल्य निर्धारित करना *The house was valued at Rs 750,000.*

**valueless** /ˈvælju:ləs ˈवैल्यूलस्/ *adj.* without value or use मूल्यहीन या निरुपयोगी; बेकार ✪ पर्याय **worthless** ✪ विलोम **valuable** ➪ **invaluable** देखिए।

**valve** /vælv वैल्व्/ *noun* [C] **1** a device in a pipe or tube which controls the flow of air, liquid or gas, letting it move in one direction only नल या नली का वॉल्व (एक उपकरण जो वायु, द्रव या गैस को नियंत्रित कर उसे केवल एक दिशा में जाने देता है) *a radiator valve* ○ *the valve on a bicycle tyre* ➪ **bicycle** पर चित्र देखिए। **2** a structure in your heart or in a **vein** that lets blood flow in one direction only हृदय या नस का वॉल्व (जिसके कारण रक्त का प्रवाह केवल एक दिशा में होता है) ➪ **heart** पर चित्र देखिए।

**vampire** /ˈvæmpaɪə(r) ˈवैम्पाइअ(र्)/ *noun* [C] (in horror stories) a dead person who comes out at night and drinks the blood of living people (संत्रास कथाओं में) रात के समय जीवितों का ख़ून पीने वाला भूत; रक्तपिपासु प्रेत

**van** /væn वैन्/ *noun* [C] a road vehicle that is used for transporting things माल ढोने वाली (बंद) मोटर गाड़ी; वैन NOTE **Lorry** से **van** छोटी होती है और हमेशा बंद रहती है।

**vanadium** /vəˈneɪdiəm व्ˈनेडिअम्/ *noun* [U] (*symbol* **V**) a hard grey metal, used in making special types of steel कड़ा स्लेटी या भूरा धातु (विशेष प्रकार के इस्पात बनाने में प्रयुक्त)

**vandal** /ˈvændl ˈवैन्ड्ल्/ *noun* [C] a person who damages sb else's property deliberately and for no purpose जान-बूझ कर और व्यर्थ में दूसरों की संपत्ति नष्ट करने वाला व्यक्ति; संपत्ति-विध्वंसक, बर्बर व्यक्ति ► **vandalism** /-dəlɪzəm -डलिज़म्/ *noun* [U] विध्वंसक प्रवृत्ति, बर्बरता *acts of vandalism* ► **vandalize** (*also* **-ise**) /ˈvændəlaɪz ˈवैन्डलाइज़्/ *verb* [T] (*usually passive*) जान-बूझ कर दूसरों की संपत्ति नष्ट करना *All the phone boxes in this area have been vandalized.*

**vane** /veɪn वेन्/ *noun* [C] a flat blade that is a part of the machinery in a **windmill** and is moved by wind or water पवन चक्की का फलक, पवनदिशासूचक, वातसूचक ➪ **weathervane** भी देखिए।

**vanguard** /ˈvæŋgɑ:d ˈवैन्गाड्/ *noun* [*sing.*] (*usually* **the vanguard**) **1** the leaders of a movement in society, for example in politics, art, industry, etc. (राजनीति, कला, उद्योग आदि के क्षेत्र में) आंदोलन के नेतागण; कर्णधार *The company is proud to be* ***in the vanguard of*** *scientific progress.* **2** the part of an army, etc. that is at the front when moving forward to attack the enemy युद्ध में सेना की अग्रिम की टुकड़ी; सेनामुख, हरावल

**vanilla** /vəˈnɪlə वˈनिला/ *noun* [U] a substance from a plant that is used for giving flavour to sweet food आइस्क्रीम आदि मीठे खाद्य पदार्थ को अधिक स्वादिष्ट बनाने वाला एक पदार्थ; वनीला *vanilla ice cream*

**vanish** /ˈvænɪʃ ˈवैनिश्/ *verb* [I] **1** to disappear suddenly or in a way that you cannot explain एकाएक ग़ायब हो जाना (ऐसे कि पता न चले), ओझल हो जाना *When he turned round, the two men had* ***vanished without trace.*** **2** to stop existing लुप्त हो जाना, समाप्त हो जाना, मिट जाना *This species of plant is vanishing from our countryside.*

**vanity** /ˈvænəti ˈवैनटि/ *noun* [U] the quality of being too proud of your appearance or abilities घमंड, दंभ (अपनी अकल या शकल का) ➪ **vain** adjective देखिए।

**vanquish** /ˈvæŋkwɪʃ ˈवैङ्क्विश्/ *verb* [T] (*literary*) todefeat sb completely in a contest, war, etc. (स्पर्धा या युद्ध में) परास्त करना, अभिभूत करना ✪ पर्याय **conquer**

**vantage point** /ˈvɑːntɪdʒ pɔɪnt ˈवान्टिज् पॉइन्ट्/ *noun* [C] a place from which you have a good view of sth स्थान जहाँ से कोई वस्तु अच्छी तरह दिखाई दे; अनुकूल प्रेक्षण-स्थान (*figurative*) *From our modern vantage point, we can see why the Mughal Empire collapsed.*

**vaporize** (*also* **-ise**) /ˈveɪpəraɪz ˈव्रेपराइज़्/ *verb* [I, T] (*technical*) to change into gas; to make sth change into gas किसी वस्तु का भाप बन जाना; किसी वस्तु को बदल देना, वाष्पीकृत करना ▶ **vaporization** (*also* **-isation**) /ˌveɪpəraɪˈzeɪʃn ˌव्रेपराइˈज़ेशन्/ *noun* [U] वाष्पीकरण

**vapour** (*AmE* **vapor**) /ˈveɪpə(r) ˈव्रेप(र्)/ *noun* [C, U] a mass of very small drops of liquid in the air, for example steam भाप, वाष्प *water vapour*

**variable**[1] /ˈveəriəbl ˈव्रेअरिअबल्/ *adj.* not staying the same; often changing जो यथावत न रहे; परिवर्तनशील ▶ **variability** /ˌveəriəˈbɪləti ˌव्रेअरिअˈबिलटि/ *noun* [U] परिवर्तनशील, परिवर्तनीयता

**variable**[2] /ˈveəriəbl ˈव्रेअरिअबल्/ *noun* [C] a situation, number or quantity that can vary or be varied परिवर्तित हो सकने या की जा सकने वाली स्थिति, संख्या या मात्रा; चर *With so many variables to consider, it is difficult to calculate the cost.* ○ *The temperature was kept constant throughout the experiment while pressure was a variable.*

**variance** /ˈveəriəns ˈव्रेअरिअन्स्/ *noun* [U, C] (*formal*) the amount by which sth changes or is different from sth else (किसी वस्तु में) बदलाव का (किसी वस्तु से) भिन्नता की मात्रा *variance in temperature/pay*

**IDM** **at variance (with sb/sth)** (*formal*) disagreeing with sb/sth किसी व्यक्ति या वस्तु से मतभेद रखते हुए

**variant** /ˈveəriənt ˈव्रेअरिअन्ट्/ *noun* [C] a slightly different form or type of sth किसी वस्तु का अंशतः भिन्न रूप या प्रकार

**variation** /ˌveəriˈeɪʃn ˌव्रेअरिˈएशन्/ *noun* **1** [C, U] **(a) variation (in sth)** a change or difference in the amount or level of sth किसी वस्तु की मात्रा या स्तर में परिवर्तन या भिन्नता, परिवर्तन या भिन्नता की मात्रा या स्तर *There was a lot of variation in the examination results.* ○ *There may be a slight variation in price from shop to shop.* **2** [C] **a variation (on/of sth)** a thing that is slightly different from another thing in the same general group किसी वस्तु का उसी वर्ग की अन्य वस्तु से अंशतः भिन्न रूप *All her films are just variations on a basic theme.*

**varicose vein** /ˌværɪkəʊs ˈveɪn ˌवैरिकोस् ˈव्रेन्/ *noun* [C] a **vein** especially one in the leg, which has become swollen and painful नस में (विशेषतः टाँग की नस में) सूजन और दर्द, स्फीत शिरा (नामक रोग)

**varied** /ˈveərid ˈव्रेअरिड्/ *adj.* having many different kinds of things or activities (वस्तुएँ या गतिविधियाँ) जिनमें विविधता हो; वैविध्यपूर्ण *I try to make my classes as varied as possible.*

**variety** /vəˈraɪəti व्रˈराइअटि/ *noun* (*pl.* **varieties**) **1** [*sing.*] **a variety (of sth)** a number of different types of the same thing एक ही वस्तु के विभिन्न प्रकार *There is a* ***wide variety*** *of dishes to choose from.* **2** [U] the quality of not being or doing the same all the time (वस्तुओं के होने या काम करने में) विविधता *There's so much variety in my new job. I do something different everyday!* **3** [C] **a variety (of sth)** a type of sth किसी वस्तु का प्रकार *a new variety of apple called 'Perfection'*

**various** /ˈveəriəs ˈव्रेअरिअस्/ *adj.* several different विभिन्न, विविध *I decided to leave Chennai for various reasons.*

**varnish** /ˈvɑːnɪʃ ˈवानिश्/ *noun* [U] a clear liquid that you paint onto hard surfaces, especially wood, to protect them and make them shine किसी कड़ी सतह (विशेषतः लकड़ी) को चमकाने का एक रंगहीन द्रव; वार्निश ➪ **nail varnish** देखिए। ▶ **varnish** *verb* [T] किसी वस्तु को वार्निश से चमकाना

**vary** /ˈveəri ˈव्रेअरि/ *verb* (*pres. part.* **varying;** *3rd person sing. pres.* **varies;** *pt, pp* **varied**) **1** [I] **vary (in sth)** (used about a group of similar things) to be different from each other (एक ही प्रकार की वस्तुओं के समूह का) एक-दूसरे से भिन्न होना *The hotel bedrooms vary in size from medium to very large.* **2** [I] **vary (from... to...)** to be different or to change according to the situation, etc. स्थिति आदि के अनुसार भिन्न होना या बदलना *The price of the holiday varies from Rs 500 to Rs 1200, depending on the time of year.* **3** [T] to make sth different by changing it often in some way किसी वस्तु को भिन्न बना देना (प्रायः उसे बदलकर), कुछ और बना देना, बदल देना *I try to vary my work as much as possible so I don't get bored.*

**vascular** /ˈvæskjələ(r) ˈवैस्क्यल(र्)/ *adj.* (*usually before a noun*) (*technical*) of or containing **veins** शिरा का या शिरा-संबंधी

**vase** /vɑːz वाज़्/ *noun* [C] a container that is used for holding cut flowers पुष्प-पात्र, गुलदान (पात्र जिसमें फूल काट-छाँट कर रखे जाते हैं)

**vasectomy** /vəˈsektəmi व्रˈसेक्टमि/ *noun* [C] (*pl.* **vasectomies**) (*medical*) a medical operation to stop a man being able to have children (पुरुष की) नसबंदी

**vast** /vɑːst व़ास्ट्/ *adj.* extremely big बहुत बड़ा, विशाल, विस्तृत *a vast sum of money* ○ *a vast country* ▶ **vastly** *adv.* अत्यधिक *a vastly improved traffic system*

**VAT** (*also* **Vat**) /ˌviː eɪ ˈtiː; væt ˌव़ी ए ˈटी; व़ैट्/ *abbr.* value added tax वैट; मूल्य संवर्धित कर *Prices include VAT.*

**vat** /væt व़ैट्/ *noun* [C] a large container for storing and mixing liquids, especially used in industrial processes कुंड, टंकी (प्रायः द्रवों के लिए) विशेषतः औद्योगिक प्रक्रियाओं में प्रयुक्त *a vat of whisky/distilling vats*

**vault**[1] /vɔːlt व़ॉल्ट्/ *noun* [C] **1** a room with a strong door and thick walls in a bank, etc. that is used for keeping money and other valuable things safe बैंक आदि में धन तथा अन्य क़ीमती वस्तुएँ सुरक्षित रखने का कमरा (जिसकी दीवारें मोटी और दरवाज़ा मज़बूत होता है); वॉल्ट **2** a room under a church where dead people are buried चर्च के अंतर्गत शव कोष्ठ (जिसमें शव दफ़न रहते हैं) *a family vault* **3** a high roof or ceiling in a church, etc., made from a number of arches joined together at the top चर्च की मेहराबदार छत

**vault**[2] /vɔːlt व़ॉल्ट्/ *verb* [I, T] **vault (over) sth** to jump over or onto sth in one movement, using your hands or a pole to help you (हाथ या लंबे डंडे के सहारे) एक ही बार में किसी वस्तु पर या पर से छलांग लगाना, लाँघना, फलाँगना

**VCR** /ˌviː siː ˈɑː(r) ˌव़ी सी ˈआ(र्)/ *abbr.* video cassette recorder वीसीआर, विडियो कैसेट रिकॉर्डर

**VD** /ˌviːˈdiː ˌव़ी ˈडी/ *abbr.* venereal disease यौन रोग

**VDU** /ˌviː diː ˈjuː ˌव़ी डी ˈयू/ *noun* [C] visual display unit; a screen on which you can see information from a computer वीडीयू, विशुअल डिस्प्ले यूनिट; कंप्यूटर का परदा (जिस पर सूचना-सामग्री प्रदर्शित होती है)

**veal** /viːl व़ील्/ *noun* [U] the meat from a young cow (**calf**) बछड़े का मांस

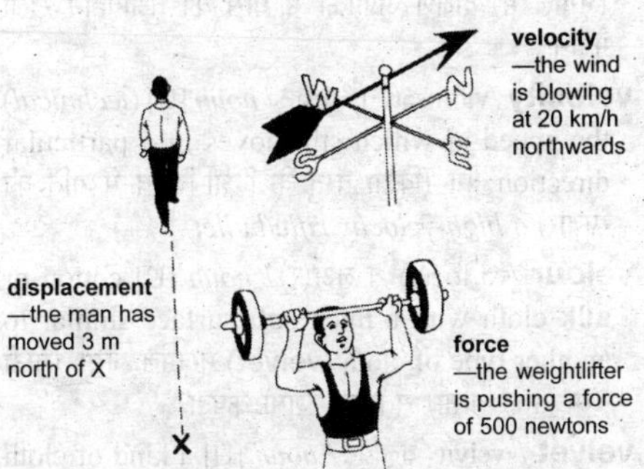
velocity
—the wind is blowing at 20 km/h northwards
displacement
—the man has moved 3 m north of X
force
—the weightlifter is pushing a force of 500 newtons
X
**examples of vectors**

**vector** /ˈvektə(r) ˈव़ेक्ट(र्)/ *noun* [C] **1** (*mathematics*) a measurement or a quantity that has both size and direction एक माप या मात्रा (जिसका आकार और दिशा दोनों होते हैं); सदिश, वेक्टर

> **NOTE** **Scalars** से आकार (विस्तार) जैसे दूरी, रफ़्तार, राशि आदि की जानकारी मिलती है। **Vectors** से विस्तार और दिशा (वेग, त्वरण, शक्ति आदि) दोनों की सूचना प्राप्त होती है।

**3** (*medical*) an insect, etc. that carries a particular disease from one living thing to another संक्रमण-क्रिया से किसी विशेष रोग का वाहक कीड़ा आदि, रोगवाहक कीट आदि *Mosquitoes are the vectors in malaria.* **3** (*technical*) the course taken by an aircraft विमान द्वारा लिया गया मार्ग; वायुमार्ग, वायुपथ

**veena** (*also* **vina**) *noun* [C] an Indian stringed instrument with four main and three **subsidiary** strings, especially used in **Carnatic music**. There are several variations of the veena वीणा (चार मुख्य और तीन अतिरिक्त तारों वाला वाद्य यंत्र) विशेषतः करनाटक संगीत में प्रयुक्त ➪ पृष्ठ 789 पर चित्र देखिए।

**veer** /vɪə(r) व़िअ(र्)/ *verb* [I] (used about vehicles) to change direction suddenly (वाहन का) अचानक मुड़ जाना *The car veered across the road and hit a tree.*

**veg**[1] /vedʒ व़ेज्/ *noun* [U] (*informal*) vegetables सब्ज़ियाँ *a fruit and veg stall*

**vegan** /ˈviːgən ˈव़ीगन्/ *noun* [C] a person who does not eat meat or any other animal products at all मांसाहार बिलकुल न करने वाला, व्यक्ति पूर्ण निरामिष भोजी, शाकाहारी व्यक्ति ➪ **vegetarian** देखिए। ▶ **vegan** *adj.* शाकाहार-संबंधी

**vegetable** /ˈvedʒtəbl ˈव़ेज्टब्ल्/ (*informal* **veg; veggie**) *noun* [C] a plant or part of a plant that we eat. Potatoes, beans and onions are vegetables सब्ज़ी, तरकारी, भाजी *vegetable soup* पृष्ठ 1316 पर चित्र देखिए।

**vegetarian** /ˌvedʒəˈteəriən ˌव़ेज ˈटेअरिअन्/ (*informal* **veggie**) *noun* [C] a person who does not eat meat or fish शाकाहारी व्यक्ति ➪ **vegan** देखिए। ▶ **vegetarian** *adj.* शाकाहार-विषयक *a vegetarian cookery book*

**vegetation** /ˌvedʒəˈteɪʃn ˌव़ेज ˈटेश्न्/ *noun* [U] (*formal*) plants in general; all the plants that are found in a particular place वनस्पति; क्षेत्र-विशेष में उगने वाले सब प्रकार के पौधे *tropical vegetation*

**veggie** /ˈvedʒi ˈव़ेजि/ *noun* [C] (*informal*) **1** = **vegetarian** **2** = **vegetable** ▶ **veggie** *adj.* शाकनिर्मित, शाकीय *a veggie burger*

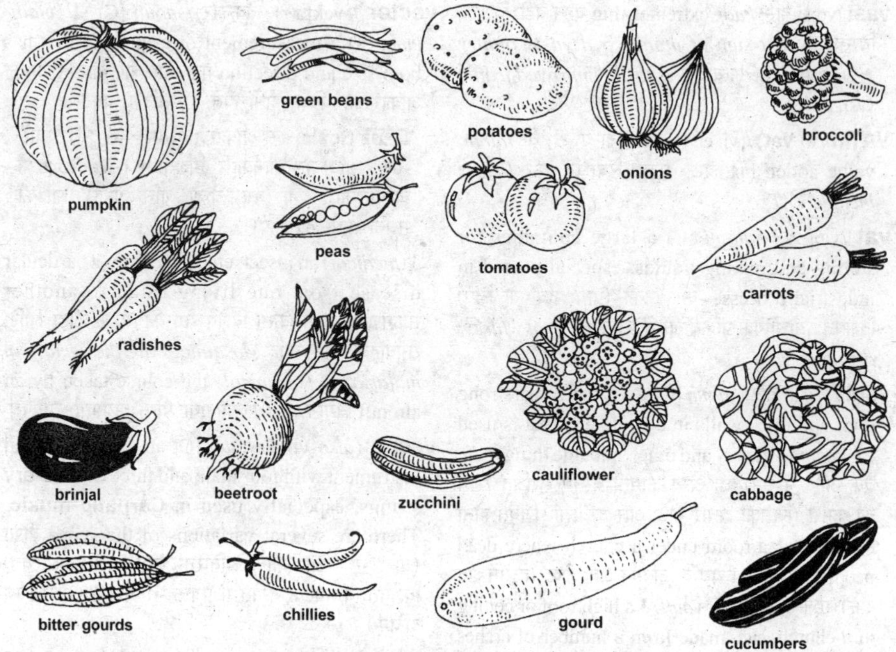


vegetables

**vehement** /ˈviːəmənt ˈवीअमन्ट्/ *adj.* showing very strong (*often negative*) feelings, especially anger (भावना, विशेषतः क्रोध की दृष्टि से) प्रचंड, उग्र *a vehement attack on the government*

**vehicle** /ˈviːəkl ˈवीअकल्/ *noun* [C] **1** something which transports people or things from place to place, especially on land, for example cars, bicycles, lorries and buses (कार, साइकिल, लॉरी, बस आदि) वाहन *Are you the owner of this vehicle?* **2** something which is used for communicating particular ideas or opinions (विशेष विचारों या धारणाओं की) अभिव्यक्ति का माध्यम *This newspaper has become a vehicle for public opinion.*

**veil** /veɪl वेल्/ *noun* [C] a piece of thin material for covering the head and face of a woman (स्त्रियों का) परदा, घूँघट, बुरक़ा *a bridal veil*

**veiled** /veɪld वेल्ड्/ *adj.* **1** not expressed directly or clearly because you do not want your meaning to be obvious अप्रत्यक्ष या अस्पष्ट *a **thinly veiled** threat/warning/criticism* **2** wearing a **veil** परदानशीन, घूँघट काढ़े हुए या घूँघट वाली; बुरक़ापोश *a veiled woman*

**vein** /veɪn वेन्/ *noun* **1** [C] one of the tubes which carry blood from all parts of your body to your heart रुधिरवाहिनी शिरा, नस ➪ **artery, jugular** और **varicose vein** देखिए। **2** [*sing.*, U] a particular style or quality विशेष शैली या गुण *After a humorous beginning, the programme continued in a more serious vein.*

**Velcro™** /ˈvelkrəʊ ˈवेल्क्रो/ *noun* [U] a material for fastening parts of clothes together. Velcro is made of a man-made material (**nylon**) and is used in small pieces, one rough and one smooth, that can stick together and be pulled apart नाइलोन से बना कपड़ों के हिस्सों को जोड़ने का विशेष धागा; वेल्क्रो (नामक) धागा ➪ **button** पर चित्र देखिए।

**veld** /velt वेल्ट्/ *noun* [U] (in geography) flat open land in South Africa with grass and no trees (भूगोल में) दक्षिण अफ़्रीका में घास का वृक्षविहीन खुला मैदान

**velocity** /vəˈlɒsəti वˈलॉसटि/ *noun* [U] (*technical*) the speed at which sth moves in a particular direction वेग (किसी वस्तु के दिशा-विशेष में गति की रफ़्तार) *a high-velocity rifle/bullet*

**velour** /vəˈlʊə(r) वˈलुअ(र्)/ *noun* [U] cotton or **silk** cloth with a thick soft surface similar to another type of cloth (**velvet**) मख़मल जैसा (मोटी नरम सतह वाला) सूती या रेशमी कपड़ा

**velvet** /ˈvelvɪt ˈवेल्विट्/ *noun* [U] a kind of cloth made of cotton or other material, with a soft thick surface on one side only मख़मल (सूत्र या अन्य सामग्री से बना एक प्रकार का कपड़ा जिसका एक पार्श्व नरम मोटी सतह की होती है) *black velvet trousers*

**vena cava** /ˌviːnə ˈkeɪvə ˌव़ीना ˈकेव़ा/ *noun* [C] (*pl.* **venae cavae** /ˌviːniː ˈkeɪviː ˌव़ीनी ˈकेव़ी/) a **vein** that takes blood without **oxygen** in it into the heart रक्त को बिना ऑक्सीजन हृदय तक पहुँचाने वाली रक्तवाहिनी शिरा ➪ **heart** पर चित्र देखिए।

**vendetta** /venˈdetə व़ेन्ˈडेटा/ *noun* [C] a serious argument or dispute between two people or groups which lasts for a long time दो व्यक्तियों या परिवारों आदि के बीच लंबा विवाद या कलह, ख़ानदानी झगड़ा; कुलवैर

**vending machine** *noun* [C] a machine from which you can buy drinks, cigarettes, etc. by putting coins in it सिक्के डालकर पेय पदार्थ, सिगरेट आदि प्राप्त करने की मशीन; वेंडिंग मशीन

**vendor** /ˈvendə(r) ˈव़ेन्ड(र्)/ *noun* [C] (*formal*) a person who is selling sth बेचने वाला व्यक्ति; विक्रेता ➪ **purchaser** देखिए।

**veneer** /vəˈnɪə(r) व़ˈनिअ(र्)/ *noun* **1** [C, U] a thin layer of wood or plastic that is stuck onto the surface of a cheaper material, especially wood, to give it a better appearance पतली परत की बढ़िया लकड़ी या प्लास्टिक जिसे मामूली लकड़ी आदि की सतह पर सजावट के लिए चिपकाया जाता है; वेनियर, मुलम्मा चढ़ाना **2** [*sing.*] (*formal*) **a veneer (of sth)** a part of sb's behaviour or of a situation which hides what it is really like underneath असली स्वभाव को ढकने वाला ऊपरी नम्रतापूर्ण आचरण *a thin veneer of politeness*

**venerate** /ˈvenəreɪt ˈव़ेनरेट्/ *verb* [T] **venerate sb/sth (as sth)** (*formal*) to have and show a lot of respect for sb/sth that is considered to be old, holy or very important किसी पुरातन, पवित्र या अत्यंत महत्त्वपूर्ण व्यक्ति या वस्तु के प्रति श्रद्धा होना और श्रद्धापूर्वक व्यवहार करना ✪ पर्याय **revere** ▶ **veneration** /ˌvenəˈreɪʃn ˌव़ेनˈरेश्न्/ *noun* [U] श्रद्धा *The relics were objects of veneration.*

**venereal disease** /vəˌnɪəriəl dɪˈziːz व़ˌनिअरिअल् डिˈज़ीज़्/ *noun* [C, U] (*abbr.* **VD**) any disease caught by having sex with a person who has it यौन-संसर्ग से उत्पन्न रोग; यौन-रोग, गुप्त रोग

**venetian blind** /vəˌniːʃn ˈblaɪnd व़ˌनीश्न् ˈब्लाइन्ड्/ *noun* [C] a covering for a window that is made of horizontal pieces of flat plastic, etc. which can be turned to let in as much light as you want झिलमिली, झिलमिल परदा (समतल प्लास्टिक की लंबी पत्तियों से बना खिड़की का परदा)

**vengeance** /ˈvendʒəns ˈव़ेन्जन्स्/ *noun* [U] (*written*) **vengeance (on sb)** the act of punishing or harming sb in return for sth bad he/she has done to you, your friends or family प्रतिशोध, बदला *He felt a terrible desire for vengeance on the people who had destroyed his career.* ➪ **revenge** देखिए।

IDM **with a vengeance** to a greater degree than is expected or usual अपेक्षा या सामान्य से अधिक मात्रा के साथ *After a week of good weather winter returned with a vengeance.*

**venison** /ˈvenɪsn ˈव़ेनिसन्/ *noun* [U] the meat from a large wild animal (**deer**) हरिण का मांस; मृगमांस

**venom** /ˈvenəm ˈव़ेनम्/ *noun* [U] **1** the poisonous liquid that some snakes, spiders, etc. produce when they bite or sting you (साँप आदि का) विष, ज़हर **2** extreme anger or hatred and a desire to hurt sb तीव्र क्रोध या घृणा और किसी को आहत करने की इच्छा *She shot him a look of pure venom.* ▶ **venomous** /ˈvenəməs ˈव़ेनमस्/ *adj.* विषैला, ज़हरीला

**vent** /vent व़ेन्ट्/ *noun* [C] an opening in the wall of a room or machine which allows air to come in, and smoke, steam or smells to go out कमरे या मशीन में बना छेद, सुराख़ (वायु के प्रवेश और धुएँ आदि के निकास के लिए) *an air vent* ○ *a heating vent*

**ventilate** /ˈventɪleɪt ˈव़ेन्टिलेट्/ *verb* [T] to allow air to move freely in and out of a room or building किसी कमरे या भवन से हवा को मुक्त रूप से आने देना *The office is badly ventilated.* ▶ **ventilation** /ˌventɪˈleɪʃn ˌव़ेन्टिˈलेश्न्/ *noun* [U] वायु का मुक्त संचार, संवातन, हवादारी *There was no ventilation in the room except for one tiny window.*

**ventilator** /ˈventɪleɪtə(r) ˈव़ेन्टिलेट(र्)/ *noun* [C] **1** a device or an opening that allows air to move freely in and out of a building, room, etc. रोशनदान, वातायन **2** a machine in a hospital that helps sb to breathe (अस्पताल में) साँस लेने में सहायक मशीन; वेंटिलेटर

**ventral** /ˈventrəl ˈव़ेन्ट्रल्/ *adj.* (*technical*) (*only before a noun*) on or connected with the underside of a fish or an animal मछली या पशु के अधस्तल उदर पर या उससे संबंधित; अधस्तलीय, उदरीय ➪ **dorsal** और **pectoral** देखिए तथा **fish** पर चित्र देखिए।

**ventricle** /ˈventrɪkl ˈव़ेन्ट्रिक्ल्/ *noun* [C] **1** either of the two lower spaces in the heart हृदय में नीचे के दो छिद्रों में से एक; निलय ➪ **heart** पर चित्र देखिए। **2** any space in the body that does not contain anything, especially one of the four main empty spaces in the brain शरीर के किसी अंग में (विशेषतः मस्तिष्क में) रिक्त स्थान; निलय

**venture[1]** /ˈventʃə(r) ˈव्रेन्च(र्)/ *noun* [C] a project which is new and possibly dangerous, because you cannot be sure that it will succeed नई और कुछ जोखिम भरी परियोजना (क्योंकि सफलता निश्चित नहीं) *a business venture*

**venture[2]** /ˈventʃə(r) ˈव्रेन्च(र्)/ *verb* [I] to do sth or go somewhere new and dangerous, when you are not sure what will happen कोई नया और जोखिम भरा काम करना या किसी नई जगह जाना (प्रायः जब यह ज्ञात न हो कि आगे क्या होगा) *He ventured out into the storm to look for the lost child.* ○ *The company has decided to venture into computer production as well as design.*

**venue** /ˈvenju: ˈव्रेन्यू/ *noun* [C] the place where people meet for an organized event, for example a concert or a sporting event स्थान जहाँ लोग आयोजित कार्यक्रम (संगीत-सभा या खेल) के लिए एकत्र हों; कार्यक्रम-स्थल

**Venus** /ˈvi:nəs ˈव्रीनस्/ *noun* [*sing.*] the planet that is second in order from the sun and nearest to the earth शुक्र ग्रह (सौरमंडल में सूर्य से दूसरा और पृथ्वी के सर्वाधिक निकट ग्रह) ➪ **solar system** पर चित्र देखिए।

**veranda** (*also* **verandah**) /vəˈrændə व़ˈरैन्डा/ (*AmE* **porch**) *noun* [C] a platform joined to the side of a house, with a roof and floor but no outside wall बरामदा ➪ **balcony, patio** और **terrace** देखिए।

**verb** /vɜ:b व़ब्/ *noun* [C] (*grammar*) a word or group of words that is used to indicate that sth happens or exists, for example **bring**, **happen**, **be**, **do** क्रिया (ऐसा शब्द या वाक्यांश जो किसी घटना के घटने या किसी वस्तु के अस्तित्व में होने का अर्थ दे, जैसे 'bring', 'happen', 'be', 'do') ➪ **phrasal verb** देखिए।

**verbal** /ˈvɜ:bl ˈव़बल्/ *adj.* (*formal*) **1** connected with words, or the use of words शब्द या शब्द प्रयोग से संबंधित; शाब्दिक *verbal skills* **2** spoken, not written मौखिक (न कि लिखित) *a verbal agreement/warning* **3** (*grammar*) connected with verbs, or the use of verbs क्रिया या क्रिया-प्रयोग से संबंधित, क्रियागत ▸ **verbally** /ˈvɜ:bəli ˈव़बलि/ *adv.* मौखिक रूप से

**verbatim** /vɜ:ˈbeɪtɪm व़ˈबेटिम्/ *adj.*, *adv.* exactly as it was spoken or written जैसा बोला या लिखा गया ठीक वैसा; शब्दशः *a verbatim report* ○ *He reported the speech verbatim.*

**verdant** /ˈvɜ:dənt ˈव़डन्ट्/ *adj.* (*literary*) (of fields, etc.) covered with green plants or grass (मैदान आदि) स्वच्छ और हरा; हरित

**verdict** /ˈvɜ:dɪkt ˈव़डिक्ट्/ *noun* [C] **1** the decision that is fmade by a specially chosen group of people (**the jury**) in a court of law, which states if a person is guilty of a crime or not न्यायालय का निर्णय (जूरी द्वारा तय किया गया) *The jury **returned a verdict** of 'not guilty'.* ○ *Has the jury **reached a verdict**?* **2 a verdict (on sb/sth)** a decision that you make or an opinion that you give after testing sth or considering sth carefully परीक्षण या गंभीर सोच विचार के बाद किया गया या व्यक्त किया गया निर्णय; अभिमत *The general verdict was that the restaurant was too expensive.*

**verge[1]** /vɜ:dʒ व़ज्/ *noun* [C] (*BrE*) the narrow piece of land at the side of a road, path, etc. that is usually covered in grass सड़क, रास्ते आदि के किनारे की घास की पट्टी

IDM **on the verge of sth/doing sth** very near to doing sth, or to sth happening कुछ करने या घटित होने के बहुत क़रीब होना *Scientists are on the verge of discovering a cure to cancer.*

**verge[2]** /vɜ:dʒ/ *verb*

PHR V **verge on sth** to be very close to an extreme state or condition किसी स्थिति या दशा की चरम अवस्था के बहुत निकट होना, कगार पर होना *What they are doing verges on the illegal.*

**verify** /ˈverɪfaɪ ˈव्रेरिफ़ाइ/ *verb* [T] (*pres. part.* **verifying;** *3rd person sing. pres.* **verifies;** *pt, pp* **verified**) (*formal*) to check or state that sth is true किसी बात की सत्यता को जाँच कर प्रमाणित करना *to verify a statement* ▸ **verification** /ˌverɪfɪˈkeɪʃn ˌव्रेरिफ़िˈकेशन्/ *noun* [U] सत्यापन

**veritable** /ˈverɪtəbl ˈव्रेरिटबल्/ *adj.* (*only before a noun*) (*formal*) a word used to emphasize that sb/sth can be compared to sb/sth else that is more exciting, more impressive, etc. वास्तविक, खरा, सच्चा (अन्य से तुलना में किसी पर बल देने के लिए प्रयुक्त *The meal was a veritable banquet.*

**vermicelli** /ˌvɜ:mɪˈtʃeli ˌव़मिˈचेलि/ *noun* [C] very fine noodle-like things used in cooking सेवई

**vermillion** /vəˈmɪlɪən व़ˈमिलिअन्/ *adj.* of a bright red colour सिंदूरी ▸ **vermillion** *noun* [U] **1** a bright red colour सिंदूरी रंग **2** (*also* **sindoor**) a kind of red-coloured powder used by married woman in India सिंदूर

**vermin** /ˈvɜ:mɪn ˈव़मिन्/ *noun* [*pl.*] small wild animals (e.g. rats) that carry disease and destroy plants and food पौधों और आहार को रोगाक्रांत कर हानि पहुँचाने वाले छोटे-छोटे जंगली जीव (जैसे चूहे)

**vernacular** /vəˈnækjələ(r) व़ˈनैक्यल(र्)/ *noun* [C] (*usually* **the vernacular**) [*sing.*] the language spoken in a particular area or by a particular group of people, especially one that is not the official or written language क्षेत्र-विशेष या वर्ग-विशेष में प्रचलित भाषा (विशेषतः जो प्रशासनिक या औपचारिक प्रयोग में नहीं आती); स्थानिक भाषा, देशी भाषा, जनभाषा

**versatile** /ˈvɜːsətaɪl ˈव़सटाइल्/ *adj.* **1** (used about an object) having many different uses (वस्तु) अनेक कामों के लिए प्रयुक्त, बहु-उद्देश्यीय, बहु-हेतुक *a versatile tool that drills, cuts or polishes* **2** (used about a person) able to do many different things (व्यक्ति) अनेक तरह के काम कर लेने वाला; बहुधंधी, बहुकर्मी, बहुमुखी प्रतिभावाला *She's so versatile! She can dance, sing, act and play the guitar!*

**verse** /vɜːs व़स्/ *noun* **1** [U] writing arranged in lines which have a definite rhythm and often finish with the same sound (**rhyme**) तुकांत रचना; पद्य *He wrote his valentine's message in verse.* **2** [C] a group of lines which form one part of a song or poem पद, छंद (पद्य का) चरण *This song has five verses.* ✪ पर्याय **stanza**

**version** /ˈvɜːʃn ˈव़श्न्/ *noun* [C] **1** a thing which has the same basic contents as sth else but which is presented in a different way (किसी वस्तु का) रूपांतर (मूल से भिन्न रूप में प्रस्तुति यद्यपि अंतर्वस्तु वही) *Have you heard the live version of this song?* **2** a person's description of sth that has happened किसी व्यक्ति द्वारा (किसी घटना का) बयान; विवरण *The two drivers gave very different versions of the accident.*

**versus** /ˈvɜːsəs ˈव़सस्/ *prep.* **1** (*abbr.* **v, vs**) used in sport for showing that two teams or people are playing against each other (खेल में) प्रतिद्वंद्वी खिलाड़ी या दलों को दर्शाने के लिए प्रयुक्त; बनाम *India versus Australia* **2** used for showing that two ideas or things that are opposite to each other, especially when you are trying to choose one of them दो विचारों या वस्तुओं के बीच चयन की दृष्टि से विरोध की स्थिति दिखाने के लिए प्रयुक्त *It's a question of quality versus price.*

**vertebra** /ˈvɜːtɪbrə ˈव़टिब्रा/ *noun* [C] (*pl.* **vertebrae** /-breɪ; -briː -ब्रे; -ब्री/) any of the small bones that are connected together to form the column of bones down the middle of your back (**spine**) रीढ़ की हड्डी की गुर्री (का एक अंश); कशेरुका ➪ **body** पर चित्र देखिए। ▶ **vertebral** *adj.* कशेरुकीय, कशेरुका-संबंधी

**vertebrate** /ˈvɜːtɪbrət ˈव़टिब्रट्/ *noun* [C] an animal, bird or fish that has a bone along its back (**a backbone**) रीढ़ की हड्डी वाला जीव (पशु, पक्षी या मछली), मेरुदंडी या कशेरुकी जीव ✪ विलोम **invertebrate**

**vertical** /ˈvɜːtɪkl ˈव़टिक्ल्/ *adj.* going straight up at an angle of 90 degrees from the ground खड़ा, सीधा, लंबवत, अनुलंब *a vertical line* ○ *The cliff was almost vertical.* ➪ **horizontal** और **perpendicular** देखिए। ▶ **vertically** /-kli -कलि/ *adv.* सीधे, खड़े, अनुलंबता से

**verve** /vɜːv व़व्/ *noun* [U, *sing.*] (*written*) energy, excitement or enthusiasm ऊर्जा, उत्तेजना या जोश *It was a performance of verve and vitality.*

**very**[1] /ˈveri ˈव़ेरि/ *adv.* (*used to emphasize an adjective or an adverb*) extremely; in a high degree अत्यधिक, बहुत; बड़ी मात्रा में *I don't like milk very much.* ○ *'Are you hungry?' 'Not very.'*

> **NOTE** उत्तमतासूचक (superlative) विशेषणों के साथ **very** का प्रयोग होता है—*very best, youngest, etc.* परंतु तुलनात्मक (comparative) विशेषणों के साथ **much** या **very much** का प्रयोग किया जाता है—*much better; very much younger.*

**very**[2] /ˈveri ˈव़ेरि/ *adj.* (*only before a noun*) **1** used to emphasize that you are talking about a particular thing or person and not about another यही, वही (न कि कोई और) (व्यक्ति-विशेष की पहचान पर बल देने के लिए प्रयुक्त) *Those were his very words.* ○ *You're the very person I wanted to talk to.* **2** extreme एकदम, बिलकुल *We climbed to the very top of the mountain.* **3** used to emphasize a noun किसी संज्ञा पर बल देने के लिए प्रयुक्त, मात्र ही *The **very thought of** the murder made her feel sick.*

**IDM** **before sb's very eyes** ➪ **eye**[1]

**vessel** /ˈvesl ˈव़ेस्ल्/ *noun* [C] **1** (written) a ship or large boat जहाज़ या बड़ी नाव **2** (*old-fashioned*) a container for liquids, for example a bottle, cup or bowl द्रव का पात्र (जैसे बोतल, प्याला या कटोरा) *ancient drinking vessels*

**vest** /vest व़ेस्ट्/ *noun* [C] **1** (*AmE* **undershirt**) a piece of clothing that you wear under your other clothes, on the top part of your body बनियान, गंजी आदि (अंदर पहनने का वस्त्र) **2** (*AmE*) = **waistcoat**

**vested interest** /ˌvestɪd ˈɪntrest ˌव़ेस्टिड् ˈइन्ट्रेस्ट्/ *noun* [C] a strong and often secret reason for doing sth that will bring you an advantage of some kind, for example more money or power निहित स्वार्थ (निजी लाभ, जैसे धन या सत्ता की प्राप्ति के लिए कुछ करने का सशक्त और प्रायः गुप्त कारण)

**vestige** /ˈvestɪdʒ ˈव़ेस्टिज्/ *noun* [C] a small part of sth that is left after the rest of it has gone किसी स्थिति का अवशेष, निशानी *the last vestige of the old system* ✪ पर्याय **trace**

**vet[1]** /vet व़ेट्/ (*formal* **veterinary surgeon** *AmE* **veterinarian**) *noun* [C] a doctor for animals पशु चिकित्सक, जानवरों का डॉक्टर *We took the cat to the vet/to the vet's.*

**vet[2]** /vet व़ेट्/ *verb* [T] (**vetting; vetted**) to do careful and secret checks before deciding if sb/sth can be accepted or not किसी व्यक्ति या वस्तु की बारीक़ी से और चुपचाप जाँच करना (उसकी उपयुक्तता के विषय में निर्णय करने से पहले) *All new employees at the Ministry of Defence are carefully vetted* (= somebody examines the details of their past lives).

**veteran** /ˈvetərən ˈव़ेटरन्/ *noun* [C] **1** a person who has served in the army, navy or air force, especially during a war अनुभवी सैनिक (विशेषतः युद्ध का अनुभव प्राप्त), पुराना सिपाही **2** a person who has very long experience of a particular job or activity (कार्य-विशेष में) दक्ष व्यक्ति (उसमें लंबा अनुभव होने के कारण), पुराना आदमी

**veterinarian** /ˌvetərɪˈneəriən ˌव़ेटरिˈनेअरिअन्/ (*AmE*) = **vet[1]**

**veterinary** /ˈvetnri ˈव़ेट्नृरि/ *adj.* connected with the medical treatment of sick or injured animals रोगी या घायल पशुओं की चिकित्सा से संबंधित; पशु चिकित्सा-विषयक *a veterinary practice* ➪ **vet** देखिए।

**veto** /ˈviːtəʊ ˈव़ीटो/ *verb* [T] (*pres. part.* **vetoing;** *3rd person sing. pres.* **vetoes;** *pt, pp* **vetoed**) to refuse to give official permission for an action or plan, when other people have agreed to it किसी कार्य या योजना को (आम सहमति के बावजूद भी) अस्वीकृत कर देना *The Prime Minister vetoed the proposal to reduce taxation.* ▶ **veto** *noun* [C, U] (*pl.* **vetoes**) अस्वीकृति, निषेध *the right of veto*

**vex** /veks व़ेक्स्/ *verb* [T] (*old-fashioned*) to annoy or to make sb feel worried खिजाना, तंग करना, विक्षुब्ध करना ▶ **vexing** *adj.* विक्षोभकारी, संतापी *a vexing question*

**vexation** /vekˈseɪʃən व़ेक्ˈसेशन्/ *noun* **1** [U] (*formal*) the feeling of being annoyed or worried उत्पीड़न, खीज या संताप की भावना **2** [C] (*old-fashioned*) sth that annoys or worries you उत्पीड़ा, खीज

**vexed** /vekst व़ेक्स्ट्/ *adj.* causing difficulty, worry, and a lot of discussion विवादग्रस्त, विवादास्पद (कठिनाई, चिंता आदि उत्पन्न करने वाला) *the vexed question of our growing prison population*

**VHF** /ˌviː eɪtʃ ˈef ˌव़ी एच् ˈएफ़्/ *abbr.* very high frequency; a band of radio waves used for sending out a high quality signal वीएचएफ, अत्युच्च आवृत्ति; उच्च गुणवत्ता के संकेत भेजने के लिए प्रयुक्त रेडियो तरंगों की परास *a VHF transmitter* ➪ **wavelength** पर चित्र देखिए।

**via** /ˈvaɪə ˈव़ाइआ/ *prep.* **1** going through a place कहीं से होकर, के मार्ग से बरास्ता *We flew from India to Australia via Bangkok.* **2** by means of sth; using sth के माध्यम से, के द्वारा; किसी की सहायता से *These pictures come to you via our satellite link.*

**viable** /ˈvaɪəbl ˈव़ाइअब्ल्/ *adj.* that can be done; that will be successful जो किया जा सके या संभव हो, व्यवहार्य; जो अपने बूते बढ़ सके, विकासक्षम, जीवनक्षम *I'm afraid your idea is just not commercially viable.* ▶ **viability** /ˌvaɪəˈbɪləti ˌव़ाइअˈबिलटि/ *noun* [U] व्यवहार्यता, विकासक्षमता, जीवनक्षमता

**viaduct** /ˈvaɪədʌkt ˈव़ाइअडक्ट्/ *noun* [C] a long, high bridge which carries a railway or road across a valley घाटी पर बना लंबा ऊँचा पुल (जिस पर से रेल की पटरी या सड़क गुज़रती है)

**via media** /ˌvaɪə ˈmiːdɪə ˌवाइआ ˈमीडिआ/ *noun* [U] (*literary*) a middle way; midway between two extremes मध्यम मार्ग; दो चरम के मध्य का मार्ग, समझौते का रास्ता

**vibrant** /ˈvaɪbrənt ˈव़ाइब्रन्ट्/ *adj.* **1** full of life and energy; exciting जीवंत और उत्साहपूर्ण; उत्तेजक *a vibrant city/atmosphere/personality* **2** (used about colours) bright and strong (रंग) चटकीला और पक्का

**vibrate** /vaɪˈbreɪt व़ाइˈब्रेट्/ *verb* [I] to make continuous very small and fast movements from side to side दोलन करना, दोलायमान होना (एक ओर से दूसरी ओर निरंतर तीव्र और संक्षिप्त गति करना) *When a guitar string vibrates it makes a sound.* ▶ **vibration** /vaɪˈbreɪʃn व़ाइˈब्रेशन्/ *noun* [C, U] दोलन, प्रदोलन, कंपन

**vicar** /ˈvɪkə(r) ˈव़िक(र्)/ *noun* [C] a priest of the Church of England. A vicar looks after a church and the people in the surrounding area (**parish**) (इंग्लैंड के चर्च में) पादरी (जो चर्च और साथ लगे क्षेत्र के निवासियों का ध्यान रखता है) ➪ **minister** देखिए।

**vicarage** /ˈvɪkərɪdʒ ˈव़िकिरिज्/ *noun* [C] the house where a vicar lives (इंग्लैंड के चर्च के) पादरी का निवास-स्थान, पादरी-निवास

**vicarious** /vɪˈkeəriəs व़िˈकेअरिअस्/ *adj.* (*only before a noun*) felt or experienced by watching or reading about sb else doing sth, rather than by doing it yourself दूसरे व्यक्ति की (न कि अपनी) उपलब्धि से प्रभावित (उसे उपलब्धि करता देखकर या उसके विषय में पढ़कर) *He got a vicarious thrill out of watching his son score the winning goal.*

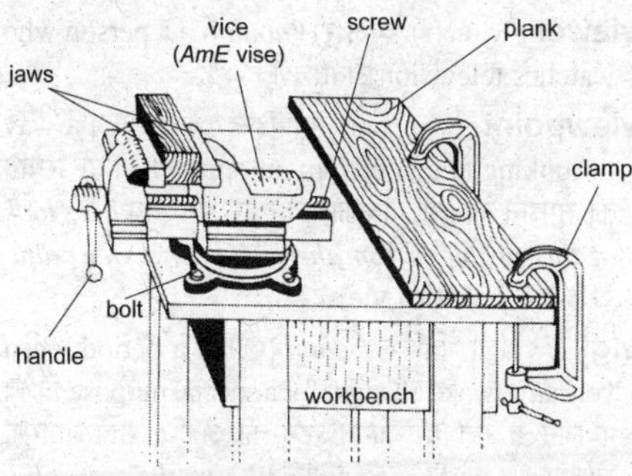


vice

**vice** /vaɪs व़ाइस्/ *noun* **1** [U] criminal activities involving sex or drugs दुराचार, अपराधी कृत्य (यौन-संबंधों या नशीले पदार्थों के सेवन से संबंधित) **2** [C] a moral weakness or bad habit नैतिक दुर्बलता पापाचार या बुरी आदत; व्यसन *Greed and envy are terrible vices.* ○ *My only vice is smoking.* ➪ **virtue** देखिए। **3** (*AmE* **vise**) [C] a tool that you use to hold a piece of wood, metal, etc. firmly while you are working on it बढ़ई का शिकंजा (*figurative*) *He held my arm in a vice-like* (= very firm) *grip.*

**vice-** /vaɪs व़ाइस्/ (*used to form compound nouns*) having a position second in importance to the position mentioned निर्दिष्ट से ठीक नीचे के पद पर आसीन, उप- *Vice-President* ○ *the vice-captain*

**vice versa** /ˌvaɪs ˈvɜːsə ˌव़ाइस् ˈव़सा/ *adv.* in the opposite way to what has just been said अभी जो कहा उससे उलटे, विपरीत क्रम से, इसके विपरीत *Anu ordered fish and Meena chicken—or was it vice versa?*

**vicinity** /vəˈsɪnəti व़ˈसिनटि/ *noun*

**IDM in the vicinity (of sth)** (*formal*) in the surrounding area पास-पड़ोस में, आस-पास के क्षेत्र में *There's no bank in the immediate vicinity.*

**vicious** /ˈvɪʃəs ˈव़िशस्/ *adj.* **1** cruel; done in order to hurt sb/sth निर्मम; कटु, द्वेषपूर्ण (व्यक्ति या वस्तु को चोट पहुँचाने के लिए किया गया) *a vicious attack* **2** (used about an animal) dangerous; likely to hurt sb (पशु) ख़तरनाक; किसी को चोट पहुँचा सकने वाला ▸ **viciously** *adv.* दुराचारिता से

**PHR V a vicious circle** a situation in which one problem leads to another and the new problem makes the first problem worse दुश्चक्र (ऐसी स्थिति जिसमें एक समस्या दूसरी को जन्म दे और फिर दूसरी समस्या पहली की स्थिति को और ख़राब कर दे)

**victim** /ˈvɪktɪm ˈव़िक्टिम्/ *noun* [C] a person or animal that is injured, killed or hurt by sb/sth किसी व्यक्ति या वस्तु द्वारा घायल किया गया, मारा या चोट पहुँचाया गया व्यक्ति या पशु, शिकार, पीड़ित या उत्पीड़ित *a murder victim* ○ *The children are often the innocent victims of a divorce.*

**victimize** (*also* **-ise**) /ˈvɪktɪmaɪz ˈव़िक्टिमाइज़्/ *verb* [T] to punish or make sb suffer unfairly किसी को दंडित करना या अनुचित रूप से सताना, शिकार बनाना ▸ **victimization** (*also* **-isation**) /ˌvɪktɪmaɪˈzeɪʃn ˌव़िक्टिमाइˈज़ेशन्/ *noun* [U] उत्पीड़न

**victor** /ˈvɪktə(r) ˈव़िक्ट(र्)/ *noun* [C] (*formal*) the person who wins a game, competition, battle, etc. विजेता, विजयी, फ़तहमंद (किसी खेल, स्पर्धा, युद्ध आदि में विजय प्राप्त करने वाला व्यक्ति)

**Victorian** /vɪkˈtɔːriən व़िक्ˈटॉरिअन्/ *adj.* **1** connected with the time of the British queen Victoria (1837–1901) ब्रिटिश महारानी विक्टोरिया (1837–1901) के शासनकाल से संबंधित, विक्टोरिया-कालीन *Victorian houses* **2** having attitudes that were typical in the time of Queen Victoria महारानी विक्टोरिया के समय में प्रचलित सोच वाला, पुराने ढंग का ▸ **Victorian** *noun* [C] विक्टोरिया-कालीन व्यक्ति

**victory** /ˈvɪktəri ˈव़िक्टरि/ *noun* [C, U] (*pl.* **victories**) success in winning a battle, game, competition, etc. युद्ध, खेल, स्पर्धा आदि में सफलता, विजय, जीत, फ़तह *Dhoni led his team to victory in the final.* ▸ **victorious** /vɪkˈtɔːriəs व़िक्ˈटॉरिअस्/ *adj.* विजयी, फ़तहमंद *the victorious team*

**IDM romp home/to victory** ➪ **romp** देखिए।

**video** /ˈvɪdiəʊ ˈव़िडिओ/ *noun* (*pl.* **videos**) **1** [U] the system of recording moving pictures and sound by using a camera, and showing them using a machine (**a video recorder**) connected to a television कैमरे से सचल चित्रों या दृश्यों और ध्वनि को रिकॉर्ड करने तथा उसे (टीवी से जुड़े) वीडियो रिकॉर्डर से प्रदर्शित करने की प्रणाली, चित्रमुद्रण या चित्र-ध्वनि, मुद्रण, वीडियो *We recorded the wedding* ***on video.*** **2 video cassette** (*also* **videotape**) [C] a tape or cassette on which you record moving pictures and sound, or on which a film or television programme has been recorded टेप या कैसेट जिस पर सचल चित्र, दृश्य और ध्वनि या फ़िल्म, टीवी कार्यक्रम रिकॉर्ड किए गए हों; वीडियो कैसेट या वीडियो टेप *Would you like to see the video we made on holiday?* ○ *to rent a video* **3** = **video recorder** ▸ **video** *verb* [T] (*3rd person sing. pres.* **videos;** *pres. part.* **videoing;** *pt, pp* **videoed**) प्रसारण हेतु दृश्य-चित्रण करना *We hired a camera to video the school play.*

**videoconferencing** /ˈvɪdiəʊkɒnfərənsɪŋ ˈव़िडियोकॉन्फ़रन्सिङ्/ *noun* [U] a system that allows people in different parts of the world to have a meeting by watching and listening to each other using video screens वीडियो-प्रक्रिया से सम्मेलन-आयोजन की प्रणाली (जिसमें विश्व के भिन्न-भिन्न भागों से व्यक्ति वीडियों-स्क्रीन की सहायता से एक-दूसरे को देखते और परस्पर बात करते हैं)

**video recorder** (*also* **video; video cassette recorder**) *noun* [C] (*abbr.* **VCR**) a machine that is connected to a television on which you can record or play back a film or television programme एक मशीन जिस पर फ़िल्म या टीवी कार्यक्रम, टीवी सेट से जोड़कर, रिकॉर्ड किया और दिखाया जा सकता है; वीडियो रिकॉर्डर

**videotape** /ˈvɪdiəʊteɪp ˈव्रिडिओटेप्/ *noun* [C] = **video 2** ▸ **videotape** *verb* [T] (*formal*) = **video** *a videotaped interview*

**view**[1] /vjuː व्यू/ *noun* **1** [C] **a view (about/on sth)** an opinion or a particular way of thinking about sth (किसी के विषय में) राय या सोचने का विशेष ढंग, विचार ***In my view***, *she has done nothing wrong.* ○ *She has* ***strong views*** *on the subject.* **2** [U] the ability to see sth or to be seen from a particular place स्थान-विशेष से किसी वस्तु को देख सकना या उसका दिखाई देना; दृष्टि, नज़र *The garden was hidden from view behind a high wall.* ○ *Just then, the sea* ***came into view***. **3** [C] what you can see from a particular place, especially beautiful natural scenery स्थान-विशेष से जो दिखाई पड़े, दृश्य (विशेषतः सुंदर प्राकृतिक दृश्य) *There are* ***breathtaking views*** *from the top of the mountain.* ○ *a room with a sea view* ➪ **scenery** पर नोट देखिए।

IDM **have, etc. sth in view** (*formal*) to have sth as a plan or idea in your mind कोई योजना या विचार मन में होना

**in full view (of sb/sth)** ➪ **full**[1] देखिए।

**in view of sth** because of sth; as a result of sth किसी बात के मद्देनज़र; किसी बात के फलस्वरूप *In view of her apology we decided to take no further action.*

**a point of view** ➪ **point**[1] देखिए।

**with a view to doing sth** (*formal*) with the aim or intention of doing sth कुछ करने के उद्देश्य या विचार से

**view**[2] /vjuː व्यू/ *verb* [T] (*formal*) **1 view sth (as sth)** to think about sth in a particular way किसी स्थिति या वस्तु के विषय में विशेष प्रकार से सोचना *She viewed holidays as a waste of time.* **2** to watch or look at sth किसी वस्तु पर ग़ौर करना या उसे देखना *Viewed from this angle, the building looks much taller than it really is.*

**viewer** /ˈvjuːə(r) ˈव्यूअ(र्)/ *noun* [C] a person who watches television टीवी दर्शक

**viewpoint** /ˈvjuːpɔɪnt ˈव्यूपॉइन्ट्/ *noun* [C] a way of looking at a situation; an opinion किसी स्थिति को समझने का ढंग, दृष्टिकोण; विचार, मत, राय *Let's look at this problem from the customer's viewpoint.* ✪ पर्याय **point of view**

**vigil** /ˈvɪdʒɪl ˈव्रिजिल्/ *noun* [C, U] a period when you stay awake all night for a special purpose विशेष प्रयोजन से रात भर जागते रहने की अवधि; रात्रि-जागरण, रतजगा *All night she* ***kept vigil*** *over the sick child.*

**vigilant** /ˈvɪdʒɪlənt ˈव्रिजिलन्ट्/ *adj.* (*formal*) careful and looking out for danger सतर्क, सावधान ▸ **vigilance** /-əns -अन्स्/ *noun* [U] सतर्कता, सावधानी

**vigilante** /ˌvɪdʒɪˈlænti ˌव्रिजिˈलैन्टि/ *noun* [C] a member of a group of people who try to prevent crime or punish criminals in a community, especially because they believe the police are not doing this सतर्कता समिति का सदस्य (पुलिस की सक्रियता के अभाव में सामाजिक अपराधों पर नियंत्रण स्वैच्छिक हेतु रूप से बनी समिति का सदस्य)

**vigour** (*AmE* **vigor**) /ˈvɪɡə(r) ˈव्रिग(र्)/ *noun* [U] strength or energy शक्ति या ऊर्जा, बल, उत्साह, जोश *After the break we started work again with renewed vigour.* ▸ **vigorous** /ˈvɪɡərəs ˈव्रिगरस्/ *adj.* ऊर्जायुक्त, ज़ोरदार, जोशभरा *vigorous exercise* ▸ **vigorously** *adv.* ज़ोरदार ढंग से, जोश के साथ

**vile** /vaɪl व्राइल्/ *adj.* very bad or unpleasant बहुत ख़राब या अप्रिय *She's in a vile mood.* ○ *a vile smell*

**villa** /ˈvɪlə ˈव्रिला/ *noun* [C] **1** a house that people rent and stay in on holiday छुट्टी बिताने के लिए किराए पर लिया गया मकान **2** a large house in the country, especially in Southern Europe देहात में बड़ा मकान, गाँव की बड़ी हवेली (विशेषतः दक्षिणी युरोप में)

**village** /ˈvɪlɪdʒ ˈव्रिलिज्/ *noun* **1** [C] a group of houses with other buildings, for example a shop, school, etc., in a country area. A village is smaller than a town गाँव, ग्राम, मौज़ा (यह क़सबे से छोटा होता है) *a small fishing village* ○ *the village shop* **2** [*sing., with sing. or pl. verb*] all the people who live in a village गाँव के सब निवासी, समुदाय के रूप में ग्रामवासी *All the village is/are taking part in the carnival.*

**villager** /ˈvɪlɪdʒə(r) ˈव्रिलिज(र्)/ *noun* [C] a person who lives in a village गाँव का रहने वाला; ग्रामवासी, ग्रामीण

**villain** /ˈvɪlən ˈव्रिलन्/ *noun* [C] **1** an evil person, especially in a book or play दुष्ट व्यक्ति (विशेषतः किसी पुस्तक या नाटक में); ख़लनायक *In most of his* *films he has played villains, but in this one he's a good guy.* ➪ **hero** देखिए। **2** (*informal*) a criminal अपराधी, गुंडा *The police caught the villains who robbed the bank.*

**villus** /ˈvɪləs ˈव़िलस् / *noun* [C] (*pl.* **villi** /ˈvɪlaɪ; -liː ˈव़िलाइ; -ली /) (*technical*) any one of the many small thin parts that stick out from some surfaces on the inside of the body (for example in the **intestine**) शरीर के अंदर के किसी भाग (जैसे आँतें) से बाहर की ओर निकलता अंकुर जैसा महीन छोटा अंश; उद्वर्ध

**vindicate** /ˈvɪndɪkeɪt ˈव़िन्डिकेट् / verb [T] (*formal*) **1** to prove that sth is true or that you were right about doing sth, especially when other people thought differently कुछ उचित ठहराना या न्यायसंगत सिद्ध करना ✪ पर्याय **justify** *Today's events partially vindicated our fears of conflict.* **2** to prove that sb is not guilty when they have been accused of doing sth wrong or illegal निर्दोष साबित करना ▸ **vindication** *noun* [U, *sing.*] औचित्य साधन, दोष-निवारण

**vindictive** /vɪnˈdɪktɪv व़िन्ˈडिक्टिव़् / *adj.* wanting or trying to hurt sb without good reason अकारण किसी को पीड़ित करने का इच्छुक या उसके लिए प्रयासरत; प्रतिकारी, अकारण-द्वेषी *a vindictive comment/person* ▸ **vindictiveness** *noun* [U] असहिष्णुता, प्रतिकारिता

**vine** /vaɪn व़ाइन् / *noun* [C] the plant that grapes grow on अंगूर की बेल

**vinegar** /ˈvɪnɪɡə(r) ˈव़िनिग(र्) / *noun* [U] a liquid with a strong sharp taste that is made from wine. Vinegar is often mixed with oil and put onto salads सिरका

**vineyard** /ˈvɪnjəd ˈव़िन्यड् / *noun* [C] a piece of land where grapes are grown अंगूर का बाग़

**vintage¹** /ˈvɪntɪdʒ ˈव़िन्टिज् / *noun* [C] the wine that was made in a particular year विशेष वर्ष में तैयार की गई (अंगूरी) शराब *1999 was an excellent vintage.*

**vintage²** /ˈvɪntɪdʒ ˈव़िन्टिज् / *adj.* (*only before a noun*) **1** vintage wine is of very good quality and has been stored for several years पुरानी शराब (इसलिए उत्कृष्ट) *vintage champagne/port/wine* **2** (used about a vehicle) made between 1917 and 1930 and admired for its style and interest (वाहन) 1917 से 1930 के बीच बनी, अपनी विशिष्ट आकृति के लिए प्रशंसित **3** typical of a period in the past and of high quality; the best work of the particular person पुराना और बढ़िया; व्यक्ति-विशेष की उत्कृटतम कृति या प्रस्तुति *a vintage performance by Ustad Bismillah Khan on the shehnai*

**vinyl** /ˈvaɪnl ˈव़ाइन्ल् / *noun* [C, U] a strong plastic that can bend easily and is used for making wall and floor covers, etc. एक प्रकार का मज़बूत लचीला प्लास्टिक जिसे दीवारों और फ़र्श पर लगाया या चिपकाया जाता है; वीनिल

**viola** /viˈəʊlə व़िˈओला / *noun* [C] a musical instrument with strings, that you hold under your chin and play with a long thin object (**a bow**) made of wood and hair वायलिन के आकार का बड़ा वाद्य, बड़ा वायलिन *A viola is like a large violin.*

**violate** /ˈvaɪəleɪt ˈव़ाइअलेट् / *verb* [T] (*formal*) **1** to break a rule, an agreement, etc. (नियम, समझौते आदि का) उल्लंघन करना *to violate a peace treaty* **2** to not respect sth; to spoil or damage sth किसी के विषय में मर्यादा का पालन न करना (का) तिरस्कार या उपेक्षा करना; किसी (स्थान आदि) को दूषित या क्षतिग्रस्त करना *to violate sb's privacy/rights* ▸ **violation** *noun* [C, U] (मर्यादा का) उल्लंघन, हनन *a violation of human rights*

**violence** /ˈvaɪələns ˈव़ाइअलन्स् / *noun* [U] **1** behaviour which harms or damages sb/sth physically किसी व्यक्ति या वस्तु को भौतिक रूप से हानि पहुँचाने वाला आचरण; हिंसा *They threatened to* ***use violence*** *if we didn't give them the money.* ○ *an* ***act of violence*** **2** great force or energy अत्यधिक शक्ति या ऊर्जा; उग्रता, प्रबलता, प्रचंडता *the violence of the storm*

**violent** /ˈvaɪələnt ˈव़ाइअलन्ट् / *adj.* **1** using physical strength to hurt or kill sb; caused by this behaviour जिसमें किसी को चोट पहुँचाने या मारने के लिए भौतिक शक्ति का प्रयोग हो, हिंसक; हिंसात्मक, हिंसापूर्ण *The demonstration started peacefully but later turned violent.* ○ *a violent death* ○ *violent crime* **2** very strong and impossible to control प्रचंड और बेक़ाबू *He has a violent temper.* ○ *a violent storm/collision* ▸ **violently** *adv.* उग्रतापूर्वक, हिंसापूर्वक *The ground shook violently and buildings collapsed in the earthquake.*

**violet** /ˈvaɪələt ˈव़ाइअलट् / *noun* **1** [C] a small plant that grows wild or in gardens and has purple or white flowers and a pleasant smell जंगलों या बग़ीचों में उगने वाला एक छोटा पौधा (जिसमें बैंगनी या सफ़ेद रंग के सुगंधित फूल खिलते हैं) **2** [U] a bluish purple colour नीलाभ बैंगनी रंग ▸ **violet** *adj.* नीलाभ बैंगनी रंग का

**violin** /ˌvaɪəˈlɪn ˌव़ाइअˈलिन् / *noun* [C] a musical instrument with strings, that you hold under your chin and play with a long thin object (**a bow**) वायलिन (वाद्य) ➪ **piano** पर नोट देखिए। **NOTE** अनौपचारिक अँग्रेज़ी में कभी-कभी **violin** को **fiddle** कहा जाता है। ➪ पृष्ठ 789 पर चित्र देखिए।

**VIP** /ˌviː aɪ ˈpiː ˌव़ी आइ ˈपी / *abbr.* (*informal*) very important person वीआईपी, बड़ी हस्ती, अत्यंत महत्त्वपूर्ण व्यक्ति *They were treated like VIPS.* ○ *give someone the VIP treatment* (= treat sb especially well)

**viper** /ˈvaɪpə(r) ˈव़ाइप(र्)/ *noun* [C] a small poisonous snake एक प्रकार का छोटा ज़हरीला साँप

**viral** ➪ **virus** देखिए।

**Vir Chakra** *noun* [C] a gallantry award presented by the Government of India for great courage and bravery on the battlefield वीर चक्र (युद्ध में अत्यंत साहस और पराक्रम के लिए भारत सरकार द्वारा प्रदत्त शौर्य अलंकरण)

**virgin[1]** /ˈvɜːdʒɪn ˈव़जिन्/ *noun* [C] a person who has never had sex कुमार या कुमारी, अक्षतवीर्य या अक्षतयोनि (पुरुष या स्त्री जिसने किसी से कभी भी यौन-संबंध स्थापित नहीं किया); कौमार्य

**virgin[2]** /ˈvɜːdʒɪn ˈव़जिन्/ *adj.* that has not yet been used, touched, damaged, etc. अभी तक अप्रयुक्त, अछूता, अक्षत आदि *virgin forest*

**virginity** /vəˈdʒɪnəti व़ˈजिनटि/ *noun* [U] the state of never having had sex कौमार्य, कुँआरापन (कभी-भी यौन-संबंध स्थापित न होने की स्थिति) *to lose your virginity*

**virgin olive oil** *noun* [U] good quality oil obtained from **olives** the first time that they are pressed उत्कृष्ठ गुणवत्ता वाला जैतून का तेल (जैतून के फलों को पहली बार में दबाकर निकाला गया)

**Virgo** /ˈvɜːɡəʊ ˈव़गो/ *noun* [U] the sixth sign of the **zodiac**, the Virgin कन्या राशि

**virile** /ˈvɪraɪl ˈव़िराइल्/ *adj.* (used about a man) strong and having great sexual energy (पुरुष) हष्ट-पुष्ट और वीर्यवान

**virility** /vəˈrɪləti व़ˈरिलटि/ *noun* [U] a man's sexual power and energy पुरुष की यौन शक्ति और ऊर्जा; पौरुष, पुरुषत्व

**virtual** /ˈvɜːtʃuəl ˈव़चुअल्/ *adj.* (*only before a noun*) **1** being almost or nearly sth लगभग या क़रीब-क़रीब *The country is in a state of virtual civil war.* **2** made to appear to exist by computer कंप्यूटर द्वारा आभासी या प्रतीयमान रूप में सृजित

**virtually** /ˈvɜːtʃuəli ˈव़चुअलि/ *adv.* **1** almost, or very nearly, so that any slight difference is not important लगभग या तक़रीबन *The building is virtually finished.* **2** (*computing*) by the use of computer programs, etc. that make sth appear to exist कंप्यूटर प्रोग्राम आदि की सहायता से (ताकि वस्तु के अस्तित्व का आभास हो जाए) *Check out our new hotel rooms virtually by visiting our website at www.rooms.com.*

**virtual reality** *noun* [U] (*computing*) images created by a computer that appear to surround the person looking at them and seem almost real आभासी या प्रतीयमान वास्तविकता (कंप्यूटर द्वारा ऐसे चित्रों का सृजन जो वास्तविक प्रतीत हों और लगे कि चित्रों को देखने वाला उनसे घिर गया है)

**virtue** /ˈvɜːtʃuː ˈव़चू/ *noun* **1** [U] behaviour which shows high moral standards उच्च नैतिकता (वाला आचरण) *to lead a life of virtue* ✪ पर्याय **goodness** **2** [C] a good quality or habit सद्गुण या सत्प्रवृत्ति *Patience is a great virtue.* ➪ **vice** देखिए। **3** [C, U] **the virtue (of sth/of being/doing sth)** an advantage or a useful quality of sth किसी वस्तु का लाभ या उपयोगी गुण *This new material* ***has the virtue*** *of being strong as well as very light.*

**IDM** **by virtue of sth** (*formal*) by means of sth or because of sth किसी के आधार पर या किसी के कारण

**virtuoso** /ˌvɜːtʃuˈəʊsəʊ ˌव़चुˈओसो/ *noun* [C] (*pl.* **virtuosos** or **virtuosi** /-siː; -ziː -सी; -ज़ी/) a person who is extremely skilful at sth, especially playing a musical instrument किसी कला में (विशेषतः वाद्य यंत्र संगीत कला में) अति दक्ष, कलाविज्ञ, कला-प्रवीण

**virtuous** /ˈvɜːtʃuəs ˈव़चुअस्/ *adj.* behaving in a morally good way सदाचारी, सद्गुणी, गुणवान

**virulent** /ˈvɪrələnt; ˈvɪrjələnt ˈव़िरलन्ट्; ˈव़िर्यलन्ट्/ *adj.* **1** (used about a poison or a disease) very strong and dangerous (विष या रोग) बहुत तीव्र, गंभीर और ख़तरनाक *a particularly virulent form of influenza* **2** (*formal*) very strong and full of anger उग्र और क्रोधपूर्ण, कटु, द्वेषपूर्ण *a virulent attack on the leader*

**virus** /ˈvaɪrəs ˈव़ाइरस्/ *noun* [C] (*pl.* **viruses**) **1** a living thing, too small to be seen without a special instrument (**microscope**), that causes disease in people, animals and plants (मनुष्यों, पशुओं और पौधों में) रोग उत्पन्न करने वाले सूक्ष्म (विषाक्त) जीवाणु, विषाणु, वाइरस *HIV, the virus that is thought to cause AIDS* ○ *to catch a virus* ➪ **bacteria** और **germ** देखिए। **2** (*computing*) instructions that are put into a computer program in order to stop it working properly and destroy information कंप्यूटर का वाइरस (कंप्यूटर प्रोग्राम में डाला गया निर्देश जिसके प्रभाव से कंप्यूटर काम करना बंद कर देता है और संचित सूचना नष्ट हो जाती है) ▶ **viral** /ˈvaɪrəl ˈव़ाइरल्/ *adj.* विषाणु-जनित, वाइरस से उत्पन्न *a viral infection*

**visa** /ˈviːzə ˈव़ीज़ा/ *noun* [C] an official mark or piece of paper that shows you are allowed to enter, leave or travel through a country वीज़ा, अन्य

देशों में आने, जाने या उसमें से गुज़रने की शासकीय अनुमति (पत्र या चिह्न के रूप में) *His passport was full of visa stamps.* ○ *a tourist/work/student visa*

**vis-à-vis** /ˌviːz ɑː ˈviː ˌव़ीज़् आ ˈव़ी/ *prep.* (*from French*) (*formal*) **1** in relation to someone or sth के संबंध में *He spoke to the Sports Minister vis-à-vis the arrangement for the World Cup.* **2** in comparison with की तुलना में, के बनाम *income vis-à-vis expenditure*

**viscous** /ˈvɪskəs ˈव़िस्कस्/ *adj.* (*technical*) (used about liquids) thick and sticky; not flowing easily (द्रव) गाढ़ा और लेसदार या चिपचिपा; जो तेज़ी से नहीं बहता ▶ **viscosity** /vɪˈskɒsəti व़िˈस्कॉसटि/ *noun* [U] गाढ़ापन, लसीलापन

**vise** (*AmE*) = **vice 3**

**visibility** /ˌvɪzəˈbɪləti ˌव़िज़ˈबिलटि/ *noun* [U] the distance that you can see in particular light or weather conditions रोशनी या मौसम की विशेष स्थिति में व्यक्ति की देख सकने वाली दूरी; दृश्यता, दृश्यता-परास *In the fog visibility was down to 50 metres.* ○ *poor/good visibility*

**visible** /ˈvɪzəbl ˈव़िज़िबल्/ *adj.* that can be seen or noticed जो दिखाई पड़े, दृश्य, दृष्टिगोचर या जिस पर ध्यान जाए, स्पष्ट, प्रकट *The church tower was visible from the other side of the valley.* ○ *a visible improvement in his work* ✪ विलोम **invisible** ▶ **visibly** /-əbli -अब्लि/ *adv.* प्रकट रूप से, साफ़ तौर पर, स्पष्ट *Rama was visibly upset.*

**vision** /ˈvɪʒn ˈव़िश़न्/ *noun* **1** [U] the ability to see; sight देखने की क्षमता; दृष्टि, नज़र *to have good/poor/normal/perfect vision* **2** [C] a picture in your imagination कल्पना में बना चित्र, मानसिक प्रतिबिंब, आकृति या मनोरूप *They have a vision of a world without weapons.* **3** [C] a dream or similar experience often connected with religion स्वप्न या स्वप्न-जैसा अनुभव (प्रायः धर्म-विषयक); दिव्य दर्शन ईश्वर दर्शन **4** [U] the ability to make great plans for the future भविष्य के लिए बड़ी योजनाएँ बनाने की क्षमता; भविष्य निरुपण *a leader of great vision* **5** [U] the picture on a television or cinema screen टीवी या सिनेमा के परदे पर चित्र *a temporary loss of vision*

**visionary** /ˈvɪʒənri ˈव़िश़नरि/ *adj.* (*pl.* **-ies**) having great plans for the future भविष्य के लिए बड़ी योजनाएँ बनाने वाला; भविष्यदर्शी *a visionary leader* ▶ **visionary** *noun* [C] (*pl.* **visionaries**) स्वप्नद्रष्टा

**visit** /ˈvɪzɪt ˈव़िज़िट्/ *verb* [I, T] to go to see a person or place for a period of time (कुछ समय के लिए) किसी व्यक्ति से मिलने जाना या कहीं पर (भ्रमण के लिए) जाना *I don't live here. I'm just visiting.* ○ *We often visit relatives at the weekend.* ▶ **visit** *noun* [C] भ्रमण, दौरा *The Prime Minister is* ***on a visit*** *to Germany.* ○ *We had* ***a flying*** (= very short) *visit from Rohit on Sunday.*

**visitor** /ˈvɪzɪtə(r) ˈव़िज़िट(र्)/ *noun* [C] a person who visits sb/sth किसी व्यक्ति से मिलने के लिए आने वाला व्यक्ति, मुलाक़ाती या कहीं पर भ्रमण के लिए जाने वाला व्यक्ति, पर्यटक या सैलानी *visitors to London from overseas*

**visor** /ˈvaɪzə(r) ˈव़ाइज़(र्)/ *noun* [C] **1** the part of a hard hat (**a helmet**) that you can pull down to protect your eyes or face हैलमेट का अग्रभाग (जिसे झुकाकर आँखों या चेहरे को ढका जाता है उन्हें बचाने के लिए); वाइज़र **2** a piece of plastic, cloth, etc. on a hat or in a car, which stops the sun shining into your eyes हैट का अग्रभाग या कार में लगा प्लास्टिक आदि का टुकड़ा (जो आँखों को धूप से बचाता है)

**vista** /ˈvɪstə ˈव़िस्टा/ *noun* [C] (*written*) **1** a beautiful view, for example of the countryside, a city, etc. (ग्रामीण अंचल, नगर आदि का) सुंदर दृश्य, मनोरम झाँकी **2** a variety of things that might happen or be possible in the future भविष्य की संभावनाएँ *This job could open up whole new vistas for her.*

**visual** /ˈvɪʒuəl ˈव़िशुअल्/ *adj.* connected with seeing दृष्टि-संबंधी, चाक्षुष, दृश्य *the visual arts* (= painting, sculpture, cinema, etc.) ▶ **visually** *adv.* दृश्य रूप से *The film is visually stunning.*

**visual aid** *noun* [C] a picture, film, map, etc. that helps a student to learn sth (चित्र, फ़िल्म, मानचित्र आदि) चाक्षुष सहायक सामग्री (कौशल या ज्ञान-अर्जन में छात्र के लिए सहायक)

**visualize** (*also* **-ise**) /ˈvɪʒuəlaɪz ˈव़िशुअलाइज़्/ *verb* [T] to imagine or have a picture in your mind of sb/sth किसी व्यक्ति या वस्तु की कल्पना करना या मन में उसका चित्र बनाना *It's hard to visualize what this place looked like before the factory was built.*

**vital** /ˈvaɪtl ˈव़ाइट्ल्/ *adj.* **1** very important or necessary बहुत महत्त्वपूर्ण या आवश्यक *Practice is vital if you want to speak a language well.* ○ *vital information* **2** full of energy; lively ऊर्जा से भरा हुआ; जीवंत, ज़िंदादिल ▶ **vitally** /ˈvaɪtəli ˈव़ाइटलि/ *adv.* अत्यधिक, सजीवता से *vitally important*

**vitality** /vaɪˈtæləti व़ाइˈटैलटि/ *noun* [U] the state of being full of energy ऊर्जामय होने की स्थिति; ऊर्जामयता, तेजस्विता

**vitamin** /ˈvɪtəmɪn ˈव़िटमिन्/ *noun* [C] one of several substances that are found in certain types of food and that are important for growth and good health विटामिन, खाद्योज (शरीर के स्वास्थ्य और वृद्धि के लिए आवश्यक तत्व, विशेष प्रकार के आहार में उपलब्ध *Oranges are rich in vitamin C.*

**vivacious** /vɪˈveɪʃəs व़िˈव़ेशस्/ *adj.* (used about a person, usually a woman) full of energy; lively and happy (व्यक्ति, प्रायः महिला) स्वस्थ, ज़िंदादिल और ख़ुशमिज़ाज

**viva voce** /ˌvaɪvəˈvəʊtsi ˌव़ाइव़ाˈव़ोचि/ (*BrE* **viva**) *noun* (*formal*) (from Latin) the oral part of an examination especially in an Indian or British university मौखिक परीक्षा (विशेषतः भारतीय तथा ब्रिटिश विश्वविद्यालयों में)

**vivid** /ˈvɪvɪd ˈव़िव़िड्/ *adj.* **1** having or producing a strong, clear picture in your mind सजीव और सुस्पष्ट (प्रभाव होने व उत्पन्न करने वाला) *vivid dreams/memories* **2** (used about light or a colour) strong and very bright (प्रकाश या रंग) तेज़ और बहुत चमकीला या चटकीला *the vivid reds and yellows of the flowers* ▶ **vividly** *adv.* सुस्पष्ट रूप से

**viviparous** /vɪˈvɪpərəs व़िˈव़िपरस्/ *adj.* (*technical*) (used about animals) that produce live babies from their bodies rather than eggs (पशु) जो सीधे (न कि अंडों के माध्यम से) जीव को जन्म देते हैं, सजीव-प्रजक, जरायुज, पिंडज ➪ **oviparous** देखिए।

**vivisection** /ˌvɪvɪˈsekʃn ˌव़िव़िˈसेक्शन्/ *noun* [U] doing scientific experiments on live animals सजीव पशुओं पर वैज्ञानिक परीक्षण करने की क्रिया; जीवोच्छेदन

**vixen** /ˈvɪksn ˈव़िक्सन्/ *noun* [C] the female of a type of reddish wild dog (**fox**) मादा लोमड़ी

**viz.** /vɪz व़िज़्/ *abbr.* (often read out as 'namely') that is to say; in other words (वाचन में प्रायः 'namely') अर्थात, कहने का तात्पर्य है कि; दूसरे शब्दों में

**vocabulary** /vəˈkæbjələri व़ˈकैब्यलरि/ *noun* (*pl.* **vocabularies**) **1** [C, U] all the words that sb knows or that are used in a particular book, subject, etc. (किसी पुस्तक, विषय आदि का) शब्दसंग्रह, शब्दावली *He has an amazing vocabulary for a five year-old.* ○ *There are many ways to increase your English vocabulary.* **2** [*sing.*] all the words in a language किसी भाषा के समान शब्द, भाषा का शब्दभंडार *New words are always coming into the vocabulary.*

**vocal** /ˈvəʊkl ˈव़ोक्ल्/ *adj.* **1** (*only before a noun*) connected with the voice कंठस्वर से संबंधित, स्वरीय **2** expressing your ideas or opinions loudly or freely अपनी धारणाओं या विचारों को ऊँचे स्वर में या खुलकर प्रकट करते हुए; मुखर *a small but vocal group of protesters*

**vocal cords** *noun* [C] the thin bands of muscle in the back of your throat that move to produce the voice स्वरतंत्रियाँ (गले के पिछले भाग में स्थित स्वर उत्पन्न करने वाली महीन माँसपेशियों की पट्टी); वाक्तंतु

**vocalist** /ˈvəʊkəlɪst ˈव़ोकलिस्ट्/ *noun* [C] a singer, especially in a band गायक (विशेषतः बैंड पार्टी में) *a lead/backing vocalist*

**vocally** /ˈvəʊkəli ˈव़ोकलि/ *adv.* **1** in a way that uses the voice मौखिक या वाचिक रूप से *to communicate vocally* **2** by speaking in a loud and confident way ऊँचे और गंभीर स्वर में *They protested vocally.*

**vocation** /vəʊˈkeɪʃn व़ोˈकेश्न्/ *noun* [C, U] a type of work or a way of life that you believe to be especially suitable for you विशेषतः अपने लिए उपयुक्त प्रतीत होने वाला व्यवसाय या जीवन बिताने का ढंग *Pankaj has finally found his vocation in life.*

**vocational** /vəʊˈkeɪʃənl व़ोˈकेशनल्/ *adj.* connected with the skills, knowledge, etc. that you need to do a particular job विशेष कार्य को करने के लिए अपेक्षित कौशल, ज्ञान आदि से संबंधित; व्यवसायिक *vocational training*

**vocative** /ˈvɒkətɪv ˈव़ॉकटिव़्/ *noun* [C] (*grammar*) (in some languages) the form of a noun, a pronoun or an adjective used when addressing a person or thing संबोधनवाचक शब्द (संज्ञा, सर्वनाम या विशेषण, व्यक्ति या वस्तु का संबोधन करने के लिए प्रयुक्त) ▶ **vocative** *adj.* संबोधक *the vocative case* ➪ **accusative, dative, genitive** और **nominative** देखिए।

**vociferous** /vəˈsɪfərəs व़ˈसिफ़रस्/ *adj.* (*formal*) expressing your opinions or feelings in a loud and confident way अपनी भावनाओं या विचारों को ज़ोरदार और गंभीर ढंग से व्यक्त करते हुए ▶ **vociferously** *adv.* चिल्लाते हुए

**vodka** /ˈvɒdkə ˈव़ॉड्का/ *noun* [C, U] a strong clear alcoholic drink originally from Russia वोदका; एक तेज़ रूसी शराब

**vogue** /vəʊg व़ोग्/ *noun* [C, U] **a vogue (for sth)** a fashion for sth (किसी बात का) फ़ैशन या प्रचलन *a vogue for large cars* ○ *That hairstyle is* ***in vogue*** *at the moment.*

**voice**[1] /vɔɪs व़ॉइस्/ *noun* **1** [C] the sounds that you make when you speak or sing; the ability to make these sounds बोलते या गाते समय निकलने वाली कंठस्वर, आवाज़, वाणी; ध्वनियाँ उत्पन्न करने की क्षमता, वाक्-शक्ति *He had a bad cold and* ***lost*** *his* ***voice*** (= could not speak for a period of time). ○ *Alan is 13 and his* ***voice is breaking*** (= becoming deep and low like a man's). **2 -voiced** (*used to form compound adjectives*) having a voice of the type mentioned निर्दिष्ट प्रकार की आवाज़ वाला *husky-voiced* **3** [*sing.*] **a voice (in sth)**

(the right to express) your ideas or opinions अपनी बात (कहने का अधिकार) *The workers want more of a voice in the running of the company.* **4** [C] a particular feeling, attitude or opinion that you have or express (किसी व्यक्ति की) विशिष्ट भावना, मनोवृत्ति या विचार *You should listen to the voice of reason and apologize.* **5** [*sing.*] (*grammar*) the form of a verb that shows if a sentence is **active** or **passive** वाच्य (विशिष्ट क्रिया रूप जिससे वाक्य का कर्ता कर्तृवाच्य या कर्मवाच्य में होना प्रकट होता है) *'Keats wrote this poem' is in the* ***active voice.*** ○ *'This poem was written by Keats' is in the* ***passive voice.***

NOTE कर्मवाच्य (passive voice) के विषय में अधिक जानकारी के लिए इस शब्दकोश के अंत में **Quick Grammar Reference** देखिए।

IDM **at the top of your voice** ⇨ **top**[1] देखिए।

**voice**[2] /vɔɪs व़ॉइस्/ *verb* [T] to express your opinions or feelings अपने विचार या भावनाएँ प्रकट करना, उन्हें अभिव्यक्ति देना *to voice complaints/criticisms*

**voice box** = **larynx**

**voicemail** /ˈvɔɪsmeɪl ˈव़ॉइस्मेल्/ *noun* [U] an electronic system which can store telephone messages, so that sb can listen to them later फ़ोन पर प्राप्त संदेशों को सुरक्षित रूप से संचित करने वाली एक प्रकार की इलेक्ट्रॉनिक प्रणाली (जिसकी सहायता से संदेशों को बाद में सुना जा सकता है); वायस-मेल

**void**[1] /vɔɪd व़ॉइड्/ *noun* [C, *usually sing.*] (*formal*) a large empty space शून्य, ख़ालीपन *Her death left a void in their lives.*

**void**[2] /vɔɪd व़ॉइड्/ *adj.* **1** (used about a ticket, contract, decision, etc.) that can no longer be accepted or used (टिकट, अनुबंध, निर्णय आदि) निष्प्रभावी, अमान्य, अवैध *The agreement was declared void.* **2** (*formal*) **void (of sth)** completely lacking sth किसी बात से पूर्णतया रहित *This book is totally void of interest for me.*

**vol.** *abbr.* **1** (*pl.* **vols.**) volume (of a book) (किसी पुस्तक का) खंड *The Complete Works of Rabindranath Tagore, Vol. 2* **2** volume मात्रा आयतन *vol. 333 ml*

**volatile** /ˈvɒlətaɪl ˈव़ॉलटाइल्/ *adj.* **1** that can change suddenly and unexpectedly (स्थिति) जो अचानक और अप्रत्याशित रूप से बदल जाए; अस्थिर, (व्यक्ति) चंचल, चुलबुला *a highly volatile situation which could easily develop into rioting* ○ *a volatile personality* **2** (used about a substance) that can easily change into a gas (पदार्थ) जो सहज ही गैस या वाष्प बन जाए; वाष्पशील ▶ **volatility** /ˌvɒləˈtɪləti ˌव़ॉलˈटिलटि/ *noun* [U] चंचलता, अस्थिरता, वाष्पशीलता

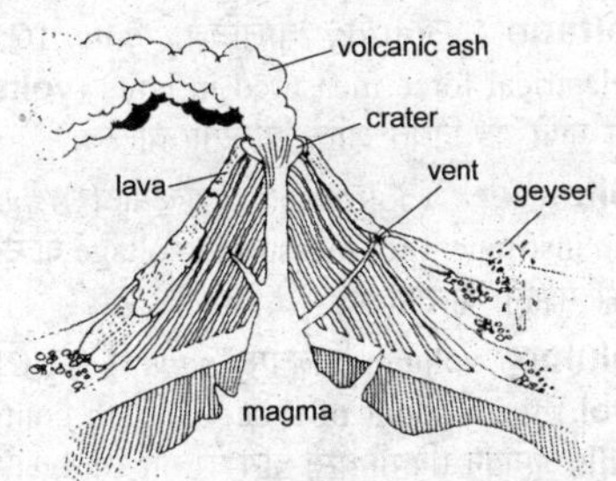


**volcano**

**volcano** /vɒlˈkeɪnəʊ व़ॉल्ˈकेनो/ *noun* [C] (*pl.* **volcanoes; volcanos**) a mountain with a hole (**crater**) at the top through which steam, hot melted rock (**lava**), fire, etc. sometimes come out ज्वालामुखी (पर्वत) *an active/dormant/extinct volcano* ○ *When did the volcano last erupt?* ▶ **volcanic** /vɒlˈkænɪk व़ॉल्ˈकैनिक्/ *adj.* ज्वालामुखी से संबंधित; ज्वालामुखीय *volcanic rock/ash*

**vole** /vəʊl व़ोल्/ *noun* [C] a small animal like a mouse or rat that lives in fields or near rivers खेतों में या नदियों के किनारे रहने वाला चूहे जैसा छोटा जीव; मूस

**volition** /vəˈlɪʃn व़ˈलिश्न्/ *noun* [U] (*formal*) the power to choose sth freely or to make your own decisions स्वतंत्र रूप से कोई काम आदि चुनने या अपने निर्णय स्वयं करने की शक्ति; चयन-क्षमता, निर्णय-क्षमता *They left entirely* ***of their own volition*** (= because they wanted to).

**volley** /ˈvɒli ˈव़ॉलि/ *noun* [C] **1** (in tennis, football, etc.) a hit or kick of the ball before it touches the ground (टेनिस, फ़ुटबॉल आदि में) (टप्पा खाने से पहले) उड़ते गेंद की मार; वॉली *a forehand/backhand volley* **2** a number of stones, bullets, etc. that are thrown or shot at the same time पत्थरों, गोलियों आदि की बौछार *The soldiers fired a volley over the heads of the crowd.* **3** a lot of questions, insults, etc. that are directed at one person very quickly, one after the other (एक व्यक्ति पर एक-के-बाद एक) प्रश्नों, अपमानजनक टिप्पणियों आदि की झड़ी *a volley of abuse* ▶ **volley** *verb* [I, T] उड़ते गेंद को मारना *Nandini volleyed the ball into the net.*

**volleyball** /ˈvɒlibɔːl ˈव़ॉलिबॉल्/ *noun* [U] a game in which two teams of six players hit a ball over a high net with their hands while trying not to let the ball touch the ground on their own side वॉलीबॉल (का खेल)

**volt** /vəʊlt व़ोल्ट्/ *noun* [C] (*abbr.* **V**) a unit for measuring electrical force वोल्ट; विद्युत शक्ति को मापने की इकाई

**voltage** /ˈvəʊltɪdʒ ˈव़ोल्टिज़् / *noun* [C, U] an electrical force measured in units (**volts**) वोल्टों से मापी गई विद्युत शक्ति; वोल्टता, वोल्टेज

**voltmeter** /ˈvəʊltmiːtə(r) ˈव़ोल्ट्मीट(र्)/ *noun* [C] an instrument for measuring voltage वोल्टेज मापने की मशीन; वोल्टमीटर

**volume** /ˈvɒljuːm ˈव़ॉल्यूम्/ *noun* **1** [U, C] (*abbr.* **vol.**) the amount of space that sth contains or fills आयतन (किसी वस्तु द्वारा घेरे गए स्थान का परिमाण) *What is the volume of this sphere?* ➪ **area 2** देखिए। **2** [C, U] the large quantity or amount of sth किसी वस्तु का बड़ा परिमाण या मात्रा *the **sheer volume** (= the large amount) of traffic on the roads* **3** [U, *sing.*] how loud a sound is आवाज़ की ऊँचाई, ध्वनि की प्रबलता *to turn the volume on a radio up/down* ○ *a low/high volume* **4** [C] (*abbr.* **vol.**) a book, especially one of a set or series अनेक खंडों वाली पुस्तक का एक खंड *That dictionary comes in three volumes.*

**voluminous** /vəˈluːmɪnəs व़ˈलूमिनस्/ *adj.* (*formal*) **1** (used about clothing) very large; having a lot of cloth (पोशाक) लंबी-चौड़ी, भारी-भरकम; जिसमें बहुत कपड़ा लगा हो *a voluminous skirt* **2** (used about a piece of writing, a book, etc.) very long and detailed (कोई कृति, पुस्तक आदि) बहुत बड़ी और विस्तृत **3** (used about a container, piece of furniture, etc.) very large (कोई पात्र, फ़र्नीचर आदि) बहुत बड़ा, बहुत स्थान घेरने वाला *a voluminous armchair*

**voluntary** /ˈvɒləntri ˈव़ॉलन्ट्रि/ *adj.* **1** done or given because you want to do it, not because you have to do it अपनी इच्छा से (न कि विवशता से) किया या दिया गया; स्वैच्छिक *He took **voluntary redundancy** and left the firm last year.* ✪ विलोम **compulsory** **2** done or working without payment बिना वेतन के किया गया या काम करते हुए; स्वयंसेवी *She does some **voluntary work** at the hospital.* **3** (used about movements of the body) that you can control (शरीर की क्रियाएँ) इच्छा से नियंत्रित ✪ विलोम **involuntary** ▶ **voluntarily** /ˈvɒləntrəli; ˌvɒlənˈterəli ˈव़ॉलन्ट्रलि; ˌव़ॉलन्ˈटेरलि / *adv.* स्वेच्छा से *She left the job voluntarily; she wasn't sacked.*

**volunteer[1]** /ˌvɒlənˈtɪə(r) ˌवॉलन्ˈटिअ(र्) / *noun* [C] **1** a person who offers or agrees to do sth without being forced or paid to do it स्वयंसेवक *Are there any volunteers to do the washing up?* **2** a person who joins the armed forces without being ordered to स्वयंसेवक सैनिक ➪ **conscript[2]** देखिए।

**volunteer[2]** /ˌvɒlənˈtɪə(r) ˌव़ॉलन्ˈटिअ(र्) / *verb* **1** [I, T] **volunteer (sth); volunteer (to do sth)** to offer sth or to do sth which you do not have to do or for which you will not be paid स्वेच्छा से सेवा समर्पित करना या कोई काम करना *They volunteered their services free.* ○ *One of my friends volunteered to take us all in his car.* **2** [I] **volunteer (for sth)** to join the armed forces without being ordered स्वेच्छा से सेना में भरती होना **3** [T] to give information, etc. or to make a comment or suggestion without being asked to बिना किसी के कहे कोई जानकारी देना या सुझाव देना *I volunteered a few helpful suggestions.*

**vomit** /ˈvɒmɪt ˈव़ॉमिट्/ *verb* [I, T] to bring food, etc. up from the stomach and out of the mouth क़ै, उलटी, वमन होना या करना NOTE दैनिक व्यवहार की ब्रिटिश अंग्रेज़ी में इस स्थिति के लिए **be sick** का प्रयोग होता है। ▶ **vomit** *noun* [C] वमन, क़ै, उलटी

**voracious** /vəˈreɪʃəs व़ˈरेशस्/ *adj.* (*written*) **1** eating or wanting large amounts of food भुक्खड़, खाऊ, पेटू, उदरपिशाच *a voracious eater* ○ *to have a **voracious appetite*** **2** wanting a lot of new information and knowledge प्रचुर मात्रा में नई जानकारी और ज्ञान प्राप्त करने का इच्छुक; ज्ञानपिपासु *a voracious reader* ▶ **voraciously** *adv.* ज्ञानपिपासा के साथ ▶ **voracity** /vəˈræsəti व़ˈरैसटि/ *noun* [U] पेटूपन, ज्ञानपिपासा

**vortex** /ˈvɔːteks ˈव़ॉटेक्स्/ *noun* [C] (*pl.* **vortexes** or **vortices** /-tɪsiːz -टिसीज़्/) a mass of air, water, etc. that turns around very fast and pulls things into its centre (पानी का) भँवर, जलावर्त, (हवा का) बवंडर, वातावर्त

**vote[1]** /vəʊt व़ोट्/ *noun* **1** [C] **a vote (for/against sb/sth)** a formal choice in an election or at a meeting, which you show by holding up your hand or writing on a piece of paper चुनाव या सभा में मतदान (किसी व्यक्ति या वस्तु के पक्ष या विपक्ष में) *The votes are still being counted.* ○ *There were 10 **votes for**, and 25 **against** the motion.* **2** [C] **a vote (on sth)** a method of deciding sth by asking people to express their choice and finding out what most people want किसी मुद्दे के पक्ष या विपक्ष में मतदान (लोगों की इच्छा जानने के लिए) *The democratic way to decide this would be to **take a vote**.* ○ *Let's **have a vote/put it to the vote**.* **3 the vote** [*sing.*] the total number of votes in an election (किसी चुनाव में हुआ) कुल मतदान *She obtained 30 per cent of the vote.* **4 the vote** [*sing.*] the legal right to vote in political elections (चुनाव में) वोट देने का अधिकार; मताधिकार *Women did not get the vote in that country until the 1920s.*

IDM **cast a/your vote** ➪ **cast[1]** देखिए।

**a vote of thanks** a short speech to thank sb, usually a guest, at a meeting, dinner, etc. (किसी सभा आदि के अंत में) धन्यवाद-ज्ञापन, धन्यवाद प्रस्ताव (प्रायः अतिथि के लिए) *The club secretary proposed a vote of thanks to the guest speaker.*

**vote**[2] /vəʊt व़ोट् / *verb* **1** [I, T] **vote (for/against sb/sth); vote (on sth); vote to do sth** to show formally a choice or opinion by marking a piece of paper or by holding up your hand (किसी के साथ या विपक्ष में) मत देना, वोट डालना *Forty-six per cent **voted in favour of*** (= for) *the proposed change.* ○ *After the debate we'll vote on the motion.* **2** [T] (*usually passive*) to choose sb for a particular position or prize स्थान या पुरस्कार-विशेष के लिए किसी व्यक्ति को चुनना *He was voted best actor at the Oscars.* ▶ **voter** *noun* [C] मतदाता, वोटर

**vouch** /vaʊtʃ व़ाउच् / *verb*

**PHR V** **vouch for sb/sth** to say that a person is honest or good or that sth is true or genuine किसी व्यक्ति के ईमानदार या भला होने का आश्वासन देना या किसी वस्तु के सही या प्रमाणिक होने का ज़िम्मा लेना *I can vouch for her ability to work hard.*

**voucher** /ˈvaʊtʃə(r) ˈव़ाउच(र्) / *noun* [C] a piece of paper that you can use instead of money to pay for all or part of sth कुछ ख़रीदने के लिए (रोकड़ के स्थान पर) प्रयुक्त परचा, वाउचर ➪ **token** देखिए।

**vouchsafe** /ˌvaʊtʃ ˈseɪf ˌव़ाउच् ˈसेफ़् / *verb* [T] (*old-fashioned* or *formal*) **1** to give or offer sth to sb or tell sth to sb, especially as a privilege कुछ कृपापूर्वक देना या कहना (विशेषतः प्राधिकार स्वरूप) *They vouchsafed his safe return from the jungle.*

**vow** /vaʊ व़ाउ / *noun* [C] a formal and serious promise (especially in a religious ceremony) प्रतिज्ञा, व्रत (विशेषतः किसी धार्मिक अनुष्ठान में) *to keep/break your **marriage vows*** ▶ **vow** *verb* [T] प्रतिज्ञा करना, क़सम खाना *We vowed never to discuss the subject again.*

**vowel** /ˈvaʊəl ˈव़ाउअल् / *noun* [C] any of the sounds represented in English by the letters a, e, i, o, or u स्वर (जैसे अँग्रेज़ी में a, e, i, o, u) ➪ **consonant** देखिए।

**voyage** /ˈvɔɪɪdʒ ˈव़ॉइइज् / *noun* [C] a long journey by sea or in space लंबी समुद्री यात्रा या अंतरिक्ष यात्रा *a voyage to Jupiter* ▶ **voyager** *noun* [C] समुद्रयात्री, अंतरिक्षयात्री

**VPP** /ˌviː piː ˈpiː ˌव़ी पी ˈपी / *abbr.* (in India and Pakistan) value payable post. The postal system in which the cost of the contents of the parcel and the postage must be paid by the receiver (भारत और पाकिस्तान में) वी पी पी; ऐसी डाक सेवा जिसमें पार्सल की सामग्री का मूल्य और डाक व्यय प्राप्तकर्त्ता भरता है

**vulgar** /ˈvʌlgə(r) ˈव़लग(र्) / *adj.* **1** not having or showing good judgement about what is attractive or appropriate; not polite or well behaved जिस व्यक्ति में किसी वस्तु के आकर्षक या उपयुक्त होने का विवेक दिखाई न पड़े, सुरुचिहीन; अशिष्ट, अभद्र *vulgar furnishings* ○ *a vulgar man/woman* **2** rude or likely to offend people अश्लील *a vulgar joke* ▶ **vulgarity** /vʌlˈgærəti व़ल्ˈगैरटि / *noun* [C, U] (*pl.* **vulgarities**) अशिष्टता, अश्लीलता, सुरुचिहीनता

**vulgar fraction** *noun* [C] (*BrE*) a **fraction** that is shown as numbers above and below a line साधारण भिन्न जैसे ¾ *and* ⅝ *are vulgar fractions.* ➪ **decimal fraction** देखिए।

**vulnerable** /ˈvʌlnərəbl ˈव़लनरबल् / *adj.* **vulnerable (to sth/sb)** weak and easy to hurt physically or emotionally दुर्बल और नाज़ुक (जिसे आसानी से शारीरिक या मानसिक आघात पहुँचाया जा सके), असुरक्षित, सुभेद्य, आघात योग्य *Poor organization left the troops vulnerable to enemy attack.* ✪ विलोम **invulnerable** ▶ **vulnerability** /ˌvʌlnərəˈbɪləti ˌव़लनरˈबिलटि / *noun* [U] दुर्बलता, नाज़ुकपन

**vulture** /ˈvʌltʃə(r) ˈव़ल्च(र्) / *noun* [C] a large bird with no feathers on its head or neck that eats dead animals गिद्ध, गीध, गृध्र

# W w

**W, w**[1] /ˈdʌblju: ˈडब्ल्यू/ *noun* [C, U] (*pl.* **W's; w's** /ˈdʌblju:z ˈडब्ल्यूज़्/) the twenty-third letter of the English alphabet अँग्रेज़ी वर्णमाला का तेईसवाँ अक्षर *'Water' begins with a 'W'.*

**W**[2] *abbr.* **1** watt(s) वाट *a 60W light bulb* **2** west(ern) पश्चिमी *W Delhi*

**wacky** (*also* **whacky**) /ˈwæki ˈवैकि/ *adj.* (*informal*) amusing or funny in a slightly crazy way मसख़रा, मज़ाकिया

**wad** /wɒd वॉड्/ *noun* [C] **1** a large number of papers, paper money, etc. folded or rolled together काग़ज़ों, नोटों आदि की गड्डी *He pulled a wad of Rs 20 notes out of his pocket.* **2** a mass of soft material that is used for blocking sth or keeping sth in place गद्दी; छेद भरने या किसी चीज़ को कहीं टिकाए रखने के लिए प्रयुक्त मुलायम सामग्री *The nurse used a wad of cotton wool to stop the bleeding.*

**waddle** /ˈwɒdl ˈवॉड्ल्/ *verb* [I] to walk with short steps, moving the weight of your body from one side to the other, like a duck बतख़ की तरह चलना (शरीर को दाएँ-बाएँ हिलाते हुए छोटे-छोटे डग भरना)

**wade** /weɪd वेड्/ *verb* [I] to walk with difficulty through fairly deep water, mud, etc. (काफ़ी गहरे पानी, कीचड़ आदि को) बड़ी मेहनत से पैदल पार करना

**PHR V** **wade through sth** to deal with or read sth that is boring and takes a long time किसी उबाऊ स्थिति का सामना करना या ऐसी चीज़ (किताब आदि) पढ़ना जिसमें लंबा समय लगे

**wadi** /ˈwɒdi ˈवॉडि/ *noun* [C] (in geography) a valley or passage in the Middle East and North Africa that is dry except when it rains (भूगोल में) वादी; नदी घाटी (मध्य पूर्व और उत्तरी अफ़्रीका में घाटी, सँकरा रास्ता या गलियारा जो बरसात को छोड़कर बाक़ी दिनों में सूखा रहता है)

**wafer** /ˈweɪfə(r) ˈवेफ़(र्)/ *noun* [C] a very thin, dry biscuit often eaten with ice cream वेफ़र; बहुत पतले प्रायः आइस्क्रीम के साथ खाए जाने वाला सूखा बिस्कुट

**waffle**[1] /ˈwɒfl ˈवॉफ़्ल्/ *noun* **1** [C] a flat cake with a pattern of squares on it that is often eaten warm with a sweet sauce (**syrup**) एक प्रकार चपटा केक जिस पर चौख़ाने बने होते हैं (प्रायः सिरप लगाकर खाया जाता है), पतली मीठी रोटी **2** [U] (*BrE informal*) language that uses a lot of words but that does not say anything important or interesting निरर्थक या निरुद्देश्य भाषा, शब्दाडंबर (ऐसी शब्दबहुल भाषा जिसमें कोई काम की बात न कही गई हो), गप, बेमतलब की बात *The last two paragraphs of your essay are just waffle.*

**waffle**[2] /ˈwɒfl ˈवॉफ़्ल्/ *verb* [I] (*BrE informal*) **waffle (on) (about sth)** to talk or write for much longer than necessary without saying anything important or interesting निरर्थक या शब्दाडंबरपूर्ण बात कहना या लिखना, गप लड़ाना

**waft** /wɒft वॉफ़्ट्/ *verb* [I, T] to move, or make sth move, gently through the air हवा में उड़ा ले जाना या बिखेरना *The smell of her perfume wafted across the room.*

**wag** /wæg वैग्/ *verb* [I, T] (**wagging; wagged**) to shake up and down or move from side to side; to make sth do this अग़ल-बग़ल या ऊपर-नीचे हिलना या (किसी वस्तु को) हिलाना *The dog wagged its tail.*

**wage**[1] /weɪdʒ वेज्/ *noun* [*sing.*] (*also* **wages;** *pl.*) the regular amount of money that you earn for a week's work वेतन, मज़दूरी (काम करने के लिए प्राप्त नियमित धनराशि) ***minimum wage*** (= the lowest wage that an employer is allowed to pay by law)

> **NOTE** एकवचनांत **wage** का प्रयोग मज़दूरी या वेतन (की धनराशि) के लिए अथवा किसी अन्य शब्द के साथ जुड़कर (जैसे 'wage packet', 'wage rise') होता है। बहुवचनांत **wages** स्वयं धनराशि का अर्थ प्रकट करता है—*I have to pay the rent out of my wages.* ➪ **pay**[2] पर नोट देखिए।

**wage**[2] /weɪdʒ वेज्/ *verb* [T] **wage sth (against/ on sb/sth)** to begin and then continue a war, battle, etc. (युद्ध, आंदोलन आदि) छेड़ना और फिर उसे जारी रखना *to wage war on your enemy*

**waggle** /ˈwægl ˈवैग्ल्/ *verb* [I, T] (*informal*) to move up and down or from side to side with quick, short movements; to make sth do this तेज़ी से ऊपर-नीचे या अग़ल-बग़ल घूमना या (किसी वस्तु को) घुमाना

**wagon** /ˈwægən ˈवैगन्/ *noun* [C] (*AmE* **freight car**) an open section of a railway train that is used for carrying goods or animals मालगाड़ी का खुला डिब्बा; वैगन

**waif** /weɪf वेफ़्/ *noun* [C] a small thin person, usually a child, who seems to have nowhere to live दुबला-पतला, छोटा बेघर व्यक्ति (प्रायः बच्चा)

**wail** /weɪl वेल्/ *verb* **1** [I, T] to cry or complain in a loud, high voice, especially because you are sad or in pain बिलख-बिलख कर रोना (दुख में या दर्द के मारे), विलाप करना **2** [I] (used about things) to make a sound like this (वस्तुओं का) विलाप की-सी ध्वनि करना *sirens wailing in the streets outside* ▶ **wail** *noun* [C] विलाप, क्रंदन, रुदन, साँय-साँय (की आवाज़)

**waist** /weɪst वेस्ट्/ *noun* [C, *usually sing.*] **1** the narrowest part around the middle of your body कमर, कटि *She put her arms around his waist.* ➪ **body** पर चित्र देखिए। **2** the part of a piece of clothing that goes round the waist पोशाक का वह भाग जो कमर के चारों ओर होता है

**waistband** /ˈweɪstbænd ˈवेस्ट्बैन्ड्/ *noun* [C] the narrow piece of material at the waist of a piece of clothing, especially trousers or a skirt कटिबंध, कमरबंद, पेटी (विशेषतः पतलून या स्कर्ट की)

**waistcoat** /ˈweɪskəʊt ˈवेस्कोट्/ (*AmE* **vest**) *noun* [C] a piece of clothing with buttons down the front and no sleeves that is often worn over a shirt and under a jacket as part of a man's suit वास्कट, फतूही (मरदाने सूट में कमीज़ और जैकेट के बीच पहनी जाने वाली आगे से बटनदार बिना आस्तीन की पोशाक)

**waistline** /ˈweɪstlaɪn ˈवेस्ट्लाइन्/ *noun* [C, *usually sing.*] **1** (used to talk about how fat or thin a person is) the measurement or size of the body around the waist (व्यक्ति की) कमर का माप, कमर का घेरा (जिससे उसका मोटापा मापा जाता है) **2** the place on a piece of clothing where your waist is पतलून आदि की कमर

**wait[1]** /weɪt वेट्/ *verb* [I] **1 wait (for sb/sth) (to do sth)** to stay in a particular place, and not do anything until sb/sth arrives or until sth happens (किसी की) प्रतीक्षा करना या इंतज़ार करना (किसी व्यक्ति के आने या किसी बात के घटित होने तक एक ही स्थान पर रुकना) *Wait here. I'll be back in a few minutes.* ○ *I'm waiting to see the doctor.*

> **NOTE** **Wait** और **expect** में तुलना कीजिए—*I was expecting him to be there at 7.30 but at 8.30 I was still waiting.* ○ *I'm waiting for the exam results but I'm not expecting to pass.* **Wait** का तात्पर्य है कि आप किसी व्यक्ति के आने या कोई बात घटित होने तक बिना कुछ और किए एक स्थान पर रुके रहते हैं—*I waited outside the theatre until they arrived.* **Expect** का अभिप्राय है कि आप किसी घटना के घटित होने की आशा में उस घटना के घटित होने तक साथ में और कुछ करते हुए अपना समय गुज़ारते हैं—*I'm expecting you to get a good grade in your exam.*

**2** to be left or delayed until a later time बाद के लिए छोड़ देना या उसमें देरी करना *Is this matter urgent or can it wait?*

**IDM** **can't wait/can hardly wait** used when you are emphasizing that sb is very excited and enthusiastic about doing sth उत्तेजना और जोश के मारे प्रतीक्षा न कर सकना, अधीर हो उठना *The kids can't wait to see their father again.*

**keep sb waiting** to make sb wait or be delayed, especially because you arrive late (स्वयं देर से आने के कारण) किसी को इंतजार कराना या उसे देरी करा देना

**wait and see** used to tell sb to be patient and to wait to find out about sth later (किसी को) (किसी बात के लिए) धैर्यपूर्वक प्रतीक्षा करने को कहने के लिए प्रयुक्त

**wait your turn** to wait until the time when you are allowed to do sth अपनी बारी की प्रतीक्षा करना

**PHR V** **wait behind** to stay in a place after others have left it (दूसरों के चले जाने तक) प्रतीक्षा करना *She waited behind after class to speak to her teacher.*

**wait in** to stay at home because you are expecting sb to come or sth to happen किसी व्यक्ति के आने की या कुछ घटित होने की आशा में प्रतीक्षा करना

**wait on sb** to serve food, drink etc. to sb, usually in a restaurant खाद्य और पेय पदार्थ परोसना (प्रायः किसी रेस्तराँ में)

**wait up (for sb)** to not go to bed because you are waiting for sb to come home किसी (के आने) की प्रतीक्षा में जागते रहना

**wait[2]** /weɪt वेट्/ *noun* [C, *usually sing.*] **a wait (for sth/sb)** a period of time when you wait प्रतीक्षा, इंतज़ार

**IDM** **lie in wait (for sb)** ➪ **lie[2]** देखिए।

**waiter** /ˈweɪtə(r) ˈवेट(र्)/ *noun* [C] a man whose job is to serve customers at their tables in a restaurant, etc. रेस्तराँ आदि में वेटर; बैरा

**waiting list** *noun* [C] a list of people who are waiting for sth, for example a service or medical treatment, that will be available in the future प्रतीक्षा सूची (किसी काम के लिए प्रतीक्षा कर रहे लोगों की सूची) *to put your name **on a waiting list***

**waiting room** *noun* [C] a room where people can sit while they are waiting, for example for a train, or to see a doctor प्रतीक्षालय; प्रतीक्षा-कक्ष (रेलगाड़ी के आने या डॉक्टर से मिलने की प्रतीक्षा करने वालों के लिए कक्ष)

**waitress** /ˈweɪtrəs ˈवेट्रस्/ *noun* [C] a woman whose job is to serve customers at their tables in a restaurant, etc. रेस्तराँ आदि में महिला वेटर

**waive** /weɪv वेव्/ *verb* [T] (*formal*) to say officially that a rule, etc. need not be obeyed; to say officially that you no longer have a right to sth किसी नियम आदि के पालन पर आग्रह न करना; किसी बात पर दावा या अधिकार छोड़ देना

**wake[1]** /weɪk वेक्/ *verb* [I, T] (*pt* **woke** /wəʊk वोक्/ ; *pp* **woken** /ˈwəʊkən ˈवोकन्/) **wake (sb) (up)** to stop sleeping; to make sb stop sleeping जागना,

जाग जाना; किसी को जगाना, जगा देना *I woke early in the morning and got straight out of bed.* ○ *Could you wake me at 7.30, please?* ➪ **awake** adjective देखिए।

**PHR V** **wake sb up** to make sb become more active or full of energy किसी को सचेत कर देना या होश में लाना

**wake up to sth** to realize sth; to notice sth किसी बात का अहसास हो जाना; किसी बात पर ध्यान चला जाना

**wake²** /weɪk वेक्/ *noun* [C] **1** an occasion before a funeral when people meet to remember the dead person, traditionally held at night to watch over the body before it is buried किसी व्यक्ति की मृत्यु पर अंतिम संस्कार से पूर्व रात्रि-जागरण **2** the track that a moving ship leaves behind on the surface of the water पानी में जहाज़ के चलने से बनी रेखा; पनरेख, अनुजल

**IDM** **in the wake of sb/sth** following or coming after sb/sth किसी बात के चलते, के परिणाम स्वरूप *The earthquake left a trail of destruction in its wake.*

**waken** /ˈweɪkən ˈवेकन्/ *verb* [I, T] (*formal, old-fashioned*) to stop sleeping or to make sb/sth stop sleeping जागना या जाग जाना या किसी को जगाना या जगा देना *She wakened from a deep sleep.*

**walk¹** /wɔːk वॉक्/ *verb* **1** [I] to move or go somewhere by putting one foot in front of the other on the ground, but without running (व्यक्ति का) चलना *He walks with a limp.* ○ *Are the shops* ***within walking distance*** (= near enough to walk to)? **2** [I] to move in this way for exercise or pleasure (व्यक्ति का) टहलना (व्यायाम के रूप में या मज़े के लिए)

> **NOTE** आनंद के लिए लंबी दूरी पैदल चलने के लिए प्रायः **go walking** का प्रयोग होता है—*We often go walking in the park in the summer.* ➪ **walk²** पर नोट देखिए।

**3** [T] to go somewhere with sb/sth on foot, especially to make sure he/she gets there safely किसी के साथ कहीं पैदल जाना (उसे सकुशल ठिकाने पर पहुँचाने के लिए) *I'll* ***walk you home*** *if you don't want to go on your own.* ○ *He walked me to my car.* **4** [T] to take a dog out for exercise कुत्ते को बाहर घुमाना *I'm just going to walk the dog.* ▶ **walker** *noun* [C] पैदल चलने वाला, पादचारी *She's a fast walker.* ○ *This area is very popular with walkers.*

**PHR V** **walk off with sth** **1** to win sth easily किसी वस्तु को सरलता से प्राप्त कर लेना *She walked off with all the prizes.* **2** to steal sth; to take sth that does not belong to you by mistake कुछ चुरा लेना; ग़लती से कुछ उठा ले जाना

**walk out (of sth)** to leave suddenly and angrily एकाएक और क्रुद्ध होकर चले जाना *She walked out of the meeting in disgust.*

**walk out on sb** (*informal*) to leave sb forever किसी को हमेशा के लिए छोड़ देना *He walked out on his wife and children after 15 years of marriage.*

**walk (all) over sb** (*informal*) **1** to treat sb badly, without considering his/her needs or feelings किसी के साथ दुर्व्यवहार करना (उसकी आवश्यकताओं या भावनाओं को बिना समझे) **2** to defeat sb completely किसी को पूरी तरह से हरा देना *He played brilliantly and walked all over his opponent.*

**walk up (to sb/sth)** to walk towards sb/sth, especially in a confident way किसी व्यक्ति या वस्तु की ओर चलकर जाना (विशेषतः आत्मविश्वास के साथ)

**walk²** /wɔːk वॉक्/ *noun* **1** [C] going somewhere on foot for pleasure, exercise, etc. कहीं पैदल चलकर जाने की क्रिया (आनंद के लिए, व्यायाम के रूप में आदि), पैदल, सैर, भ्रमण, हवाख़ोरी *I'm just going to take the dog for a walk.* ○ *The beach is five minutes' walk/ a five-minute walk from the hotel.*

> **NOTE** आनंद के लिए थोड़ी दूरी पैदल चलने (हवाख़ोरी) की बात हो तो **go for a walk** का प्रयोग होता है। यदि कई घंटे या कई दिन चलने वाली लंबी पैदल यात्रा की बात हो तो **go walking** प्रयोग किया जाता है।

**2** [C] a path or route for walking for pleasure पैदल सैर का पथ या रास्ता *From here there's a lovely walk through the woods.* **3** [*sing.*] a way or style of walking चलने का ढंग, चाल *He has a funny walk.* **4** [*sing.*] the speed of walking चलने की रफ़्तार *She slowed to a walk.*

**IDM** **a walk of life** a person's job or position in society व्यक्ति का समाज में व्यवसाय या स्थिति

**walkie-talkie** /ˌwɔːki ˈtɔːki ˌवॉकि ˈटॉकि/ *noun* [C] (*informal*) a small radio that you can carry with you to send or receive messages संदेश भेजने या प्राप्त करने का छोटा रेडियो (जिसे साथ लेकर चलते हैं), सुवाह्य रेडियो; वॉकी-टॉकी

**walking stick** (*also* **stick**) *noun* [C] a stick that you carry and use as a support to help you walk (चलते समय सहारा देने वाली) छड़ी ➪ **crutch** देखिए।

**walkover** /ˈwɔːkəʊvə(r) ˈवॉकओव़(र्)/ *noun* [C] an easy win or victory in a game or competition खेल या प्रतिस्पर्धा में आसान जीत

**wall** /wɔːl वॉल्/ *noun* [C] **1** a solid, vertical structure made of stone, brick, etc. that is built round an area of land to protect it or to divide it दीवार, दीवाल (किसी को दूसरे से अलग करने या उसकी सुरक्षा के लिए उसके चारों ओर बनाई गई) *There is a high wall all around the prison.* **2** one of the sides of a

room or building joining the ceiling and the floor छत से फ़र्श तक की किसी कमरे या इमारत की दीवार, भित्ति या भीत *He put the picture up* ***on the wall***.

IDM **up the wall** (*informal*) crazy or angry झक्की या क्रोधी *That noise is driving me up the wall.*

**wallaby** /ˈwɒləbi ˈवॉलबि/ *noun* [C] (*pl.* **wallabies**) an Australian animal that moves by jumping on its strong back legs and keeps its young in a pocket of skin (**a pouch**) on the front of the mother's body. A wallaby looks like a small **kangaroo** छोटे कँगारू जैसा एक ऑस्ट्रेलियाई पशु; वॉलबि

**walled** /wɔːld वॉल्ड्/ *adj.* surrounded by a wall दीवार से घिरा हुआ

**wallet** /ˈwɒlɪt ˈवॉलिट्/ (*AmE* **billfold**) *noun* [C] a small, flat, folding case in which you keep paper money, plastic cards, etc. मुड़ने वाला चपटा जेबी बटुआ ➪ **purse** देखिए।

**wallop** /ˈwɒləp ˈवॉलप्/ *verb* [T] (*informal*) to hit sb/sth very hard किसी को कस कर पीटना

**wallow** /ˈwɒləʊ ˈवॉलो/ *verb* [I] **wallow (in sth)** **1** (used about people and large animals) to lie and roll around in water, etc. in order to keep cool or for pleasure (मनुष्यों और बड़े पशुओं का) पानी आदि में लोटना, लोट लगाना या लोट-पोट होना (ठंडक के लिए मौज में आकर) *I spent an hour wallowing in the bath.* **2** to take great pleasure in sth (a feeling, situation, etc.) (किसी मनोभाव, स्थिति आदि में) आनंद अनुभव करना, सुख पाना *to wallow in self-pity* (= to think about your unhappiness all the time and seem to be enjoying it)

**wallpaper** /ˈwɔːlpeɪpə(r) ˈवॉलपेप(र्)/ *noun* [U] **1** paper that you stick to the walls of a room to decorate or cover them कमरे की दीवार पर (सजावट या उसे ढकने के लिए) लगाया जाने वाला काग़ज़, भित्ति-पत्र, दीवारी काग़ज़, वॉल पेपर ► **wallpaper** *verb* [I, T] वालपेपर लगना या लगाना **2** (*computing*) a picture, pattern or design that you choose to display as a background on your computer screen कंप्यूटर के स्क्रीन पर चुना हुआ चित्र, पैटर्न या रूपरेखा (प्रायः पृष्ठभूमि में); वॉलपेपर

**wall-to-wall** *adj.* (*only before a noun*) (used especially about a carpet) covering the floor of a room completely (क़ालीन) कमरे के सारे फ़र्श को ढकने वाला

**walnut** /ˈwɔːlnʌt ˈवॉलनट्/ *noun* **1** [C] a nut that we eat, with a hard brown shell that is in two halves अख़रोट (का फल) ➪ **nut** पर चित्र देखिए। **2** (*also* **walnut tree**) [C] the tree on which these nuts grow अख़रोट का पेड़ **3** [U] the wood of the walnut tree, used in making furniture अख़रोट की लकड़ी (फ़र्नीचर बनाने में प्रयुक्त)

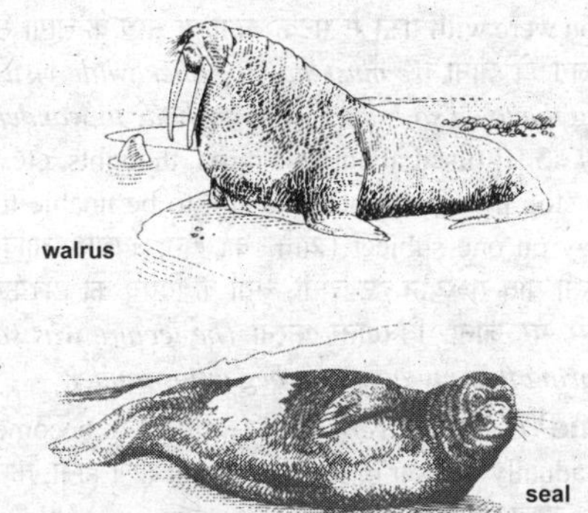


**walrus** /ˈwɔːlrəs ˈवॉलरस्/ *noun* [C] a large animal that lives in or near the sea in Arctic regions. It is similar to another sea animal (**seal**) but the walrus has two long outer teeth (**tusks**) दरियाई घोड़ा, वॉलरस (उत्तर ध्रुव के इलाक़ों में पाया जाने वाला सील मछली जैसा एक बड़ा समुद्री जानवर जिसके दो लंबे दाँत बाहर को निकले होते हैं)

**waltz[1]** /wɔːls वॉल्स्/ *noun* [C] an elegant dance that you do with a partner, to music which has a rhythm of three beats; the music for this dance तीन ताल की लय वाले संगीत की धुन पर जुगलबंदी में होने वाला एक सुंदर नृत्य, वॉल्स; वॉल्स के साथ बजने वाला संगीत *a Strauss waltz*

**waltz[2]** /wɔːls वॉल्स्/ *verb* **1** [I, T] to dance a waltz वॉल्स नृत्य करना *They waltzed around the floor.* **2** [I] (*informal*) to go somewhere in a confident way बड़े भरोसे के साथ कहीं जाना *You can't just waltz in and expect your meal to be ready for you.*

**WAN** /wæn वैन्/ *abbr.* (*computing*) wide area network (a system in which computers in different places are connected, usually over a large area) वैन; वाइड एरिया नेटवर्क (बड़े क्षेत्र में फैले हुए अलग-अलग कंप्यूटरों के परस्पर संबद्ध होने की प्रणाली ➪ **LAN** देखिए।

**wan** /wɒn वॉन्/ *adj.* looking pale and ill or tired (व्यक्ति) पीला पड़ा हुआ और बीमार या थका हुआ

**wand** /wɒnd वॉन्ड्/ *noun* [C] a thin stick that people hold when they are doing magic tricks जादूगर की छड़ी *I wish I could* ***wave a magic wand*** *and make everything better.*

**wander** /ˈwɒndə(r) ˈवॉन्ड(र्)/ *verb* **1** [I, T] to walk somewhere slowly with no particular sense of direction or purpose इधर-उधर (निष्प्रयोजन) घूमना, भटकना, मारा-मारा फिरना *We spent a pleasant day wandering around the town.* ○ *He was found in a confused state, wandering the streets.* **2** [I] **wander (away/off) (from sb/sth)** to walk away from a place where you ought to be or the people

you were with रास्ते से भटक जाना या साथ के लोगों से अलग हो जाना *We must stay together while visiting the town so I don't want anybody to wander off.* **3** [I] (used about sb's mind, thoughts, etc.) to stop paying attention to sth; to be unable to stay on one subject (व्यक्ति का मन, विचार आदि) किसी बात से ध्यान हट जाना; चर्चा के विषय को छोड़कर दूसरे पर जाना, विषयांतर करना *The lecture was so boring that my attention began to wander.*

**wane[1]** /weɪn वेन्/ *verb* [I] **1** (*written*) to become gradually weaker or less important क्षीण होना, कम हो जाना *My enthusiasm was waning rapidly.* **2** (used about the moon) to appear slightly smaller each day after being full and round (चंद्रमा) आकार में कम हो जाना, घट जाना ✪ विलोम **wax[2]**

**wane[2]** /weɪn वेन्/ *noun*

IDM **on the wane** (*written*) becoming smaller, less important or less common क्षीण होना, उतार पर होना, कमज़ोर होना

**wangle** /ˈwæŋgl ˈवैङ्ग्ल्/ *verb* [T] (*informal*) to get sth that you want by persuading sb or by having a clever plan चापलूसी से या तिकड़म रचा कर किसी से कुछ प्राप्त कर लेना, गाँठ लेना *Somehow he wangled a day off to meet me.*

**wanna** /ˈwɒnə ˈवॉना/ a way of writing 'want to' or 'want a', which is considered to be bad style, to show that sb is speaking in an informal way, 'want to' या 'want a' का अनौपचारिक लिखित रूप *I wanna go home now.* ➪ **gonna** पर नोट देखिए।

**want[1]** /wɒnt वॉन्ट्/ *verb* [T] (*not used in the continuous tenses*) **1 want sth (for sth); want (sb) to do sth; want sth (to be) done** to have a desire or a wish for sth कुछ चाहना या (किसी की) इच्छा रखना *He wants a new bike.* ○ *What do they want for breakfast?* ○ *I don't want to discuss it now.*

> NOTE **Want** और **would like** एक ही अर्थ में प्रयुक्त होते हैं परंतु 'would like' अधिक शिष्ट या परिमार्जित प्रयोग है—*'I want a drink!' screamed the child.* ○ *'Would you like some more tea, Mrs Atwal?'*

**2** (*informal*) used to say that sth needs to be done (की) ज़रुरत पड़ना, आवश्यकता होना *The house wants a new coat of paint.* **3** (*informal*) (used to give advice to sb) should or ought to (सलाह देने के लिए प्रयुक्त) चाहिए *He wants to be more careful about what he tells people.* **4** (*usually passive*) to need sb to be in a particular place or for a particular reason किसी व्यक्ति की कहीं पर या किसी काम से ज़रुरत होना, दरकार होना *She is **wanted by the police*** (= the police are looking for her because she is suspected of committing a crime). **5** to feel sexual desire for sb किसी के साथ यौन-संसर्ग की इच्छा होना

> NOTE यद्यपि इस क्रिया का सातत्यबोधक कालों (continuous tenses) में प्रयोग नहीं होता तथा इसका -ing युक्त वर्तमान कृदंत (present participle) रूप काफ़ी प्रचलित है—*She kept her head down, not wanting to attract attention.*

**want[2]** /wɒnt वॉन्ट्/ *noun* (*formal*) **1 wants** [*pl.*] sth you need or want आवश्यकता, ज़रूरत या इच्छा; चाहत *All our wants were satisfied.* **2** [*sing.*] a lack of sth (किसी चीज़ की) कमी, अभाव *He's suffering due to a want of care.*

IDM **for (the) want of sth** because of a lack of sth; because sth is not available किसी बात की कमी या अभाव के कारण; किसी की अनुपलब्धता के कारण *I took the job for want of a better offer.*

**wanting** /ˈwɒntɪŋ ˈवॉन्टिङ्/ *adj.* (*formal*) **wanting (in sth)** (*not before a noun*) **1** not having enough of sth; lacking (का) काफ़ी न होना; (की) कमी होना *The children were certainly not wanting in enthusiasm.* **2** not good enough अपर्याप्त, नाकाफ़ी, जो अपेक्षा या प्रत्याशा से कम हो *The new system **was found wanting**.*

**wanton** /ˈwɒntən ˈवॉन्टन्/ *adj.* (*formal*) (used about an action) done in order to hurt sb or damage sth for no good reason (कोई कार्य) अकारण किसी को तकलीफ़ या हानि पहुँचाने के लिए किया गया *wanton vandalism*

**WAP** /wæp वैप्/ *abbr.* wireless application protocol; a technology that connects devices such as **mobile phones** to the Internet. It consists of rules for changing Internet information so that it can be shown on a very small screen वैप; मोबाइल फ़ोनों को इंटरनेट से जोड़ने की प्रौद्योगिकी *a WAP phone*

**war** /wɔː(r) वॉ(र्)/ *noun* **1** [U, C] a state of fighting between different countries or groups within countries using armies and weapons (देशों में या देश के भीतर गुटों में) लड़ाई, युद्ध (जिसमें आवश्यकतानुसार सेना और शस्त्रों का प्रयोग हो) *The Prime Minister announced that the country was **at war**.* ○ *to **declare war on** another country* (= announce that a war has started) **2** [C, U] very aggressive competition between groups of people, companies, countries, etc. प्रबल प्रतियोगिता, कड़ी प्रतिस्पर्धा (व्यक्ति-समूहों, कंपनियों, देशों आदि में) *a price war among oil companies* **3** [U, *sing.*] **war (against/on sb/sth)** efforts to end or get rid of sth संघर्ष, लड़ाई (किसी अवांछित स्थिति की समाप्ति या उससे मुक्ति का प्रयास *We seem to be winning the war against organized crime.*

**warbler** /ˈwɔ:blə(r) ˈवॉब्ल(र्)/ *noun* [C] any of the various **species** of small birds, some of which have a musical call छोटी कूजक पक्षी प्रजाती की एक गायक पक्षी; वार्बलर

**war crime** *noun* [C] a cruel act that is committed during a war and that is against the international rules of war युद्धकालीन अपराध (ऐसे निर्मम कृत्य जो युद्ध-संबंधी अंतरराष्ट्रीय नियमों के विरुद्ध हों)

**ward**[1] /wɔ:d वॉड्/ *noun* [C] **1** a separate part or room in a hospital for patients with the same kind of medical condition (अस्पताल में) एक ही प्रकार के रोगियों के लिए पृथक विभाग या कक्ष; वॉर्ड *the maternity/psychiatric/surgical ward* **2** one of the sections into which a town is divided for elections (शहर का) वॉर्ड, हल्का (चुनावों या सामान्य प्रशासन की दृष्टि से) **3** a child who is under the protection of a court of law; a child whose parents are dead and who is cared for by another adult (**guardian**) न्यायालय या अभिभावक के संरक्षण में बालक, आश्रित, प्रतिपाल्य *The child was made a ward of court.*

**ward**[2] /wɔ:d वॉड्/ *verb*

**PHR V** **ward sb/sth off** to protect or defend yourself against danger, illness, attack, etc. किसी संकट, रोग, आक्रमण आदि से अपना बचाव करना

**warden** /ˈwɔ:dn ˈवॉड्न्/ *noun* [C] **1** a person whose job is to check that rules are obeyed or to look after the people in a particular place नियमों के पालन या स्थान-विशेष के लोगों की देखभाल पर ध्यान देने का काम करने वाला व्यक्ति; अभिरक्षक, वॉर्डन (छात्रावास का, यातायात का) *a **traffic warden*** (= a person who checks that cars are not parked in the wrong place) **2** (*AmE*) the person in charge of a prison जेल का वॉर्डन, कारापाल

**warder** /ˈwɔ:də(r) ˈवॉड(र्)/ *noun* [C] (*BrE*) a person whose job is to guard prisoners कैदियों का रक्षक, जेल का वॉर्डर, पहरेदार या चौकीदार ➪ **guard** देखिए।

**wardrobe** /ˈwɔ:drəʊb ˈवॉड्रोब्/ *noun* [C] **1** a large cupboard in which you can hang your clothes कपड़े रखने या टाँगने की अलमारी **2** a person's collection of clothes व्यक्ति के निजी कपड़ों का संग्रह *I need a new summer wardrobe.*

**ware** /weə(r) वेअ(र्)/ *noun* **1** [U] (*used in compounds*) objects made from a particular type of material or suitable for a particular use (विशेष प्रकार की सामग्री से या विशेष प्रयोग के लिए) बना माल, निर्मित वस्तुएँ *glassware* ○ *kitchenware* **2 wares** [*pl.*] (*old-fashioned*) goods offered for sale बिक्री के लिए प्रस्तुत वस्तुएँ, सौदा, माल

**warehouse** /ˈweəhaʊs ˈवेअहाउस्/ *noun* [C] a building where large quantities of goods are stored before being sent to shops मालगोदाम, गोदाम, भंडारघर

**warfare** /ˈwɔ:feə(r) ˈवॉफ़ेअ(र्)/ *noun* [U] methods of fighting a war; types of war युद्ध के तरीक़े; युद्ध के प्रकार *guerrilla warfare*

**warhead** /ˈwɔ:hed ˈवॉहेड्/ *noun* [C] the explosive part of a **missile** प्रक्षेपास्त्र का विस्फोटक से भरा भाग; स्फोटक शीर्ष

**warily, wariness** ➪ **wary** देखिए।

**warlike** /ˈwɔ:laɪk ˈवॉलाइक्/ *adj.* liking to fight or good at fighting युद्धप्रिय, लड़ाकू और जंगजू या युद्धदक्ष या रणकुशल *a warlike nation*

**warm**[1] /wɔ:m वॉम्/ *adj.* **1** having a pleasant temperature that is fairly high, between cool and hot (ठंडे और गरम के बीच का सुहावना तापमान) शरीर को भाने वाली गरमाहट से युक्त *It's quite warm in the sunshine.* ○ *I jumped up and down to keep my feet warm.* ➪ **cold**[1] पर नोट देखिए। **2** (used about clothes) preventing you from getting cold (कपड़े) ठंड से बचाने वाले, गरम *Take plenty of warm clothes.* **3** friendly, kind and pleasant मैत्रीपूर्ण, स्नेहमय और मनभावन *I was given a very warm welcome.* **4** creating a pleasant, comfortable feeling मनभावन और सुखद *warm colours* ► **the warm** *noun* [*sing.*] सुखद गरमी *It's awfully cold out here—I want to go back into the warm.* ► **warmly** *adv.* चुस्ती से, हार्दिकतापूर्वक, सुखद गरमी से *warmly dressed* ○ *She thanked him warmly for his help.*

**warm**[2] /wɔ:m वॉम्/ *verb* [I, T] **warm (sb/sth) (up)** to become or to make sb/sth become warm or warmer (सुखद रूप से) गरम हो जाना या (किसी व्यक्ति या वस्तु को) गरम कर देना *It was cold earlier but it's beginning to warm up now.* ○ *I sat in front of the fire to warm up.*

**PHR V** **warm to/towards sb** to begin to like sb that you did not like at first (जो पहले पसंद नहीं था उसे) पसंद करने लगना

**warm to sth** to become more interested in sth किसी बात में अधिक रुचि लेने लगना

**warm up** to prepare to do an activity or sport by practising gently हलके अभ्यास द्वारा किसी काम को करने या खेल खेलने की तैयारी करना *The team warmed up before the match.*

**warm-blooded** *adj.* (used about animals) having a blood temperature that does not change if the temperature of the surroundings changes (प्राणी) नियततापी (जिनके रक्त का तापमान नियत या स्थिर रहता है, परिवेश के तापमान में परिवर्तन के बावजूद) ✪ विलोम **cold-blooded**

**warm-hearted** *adj.* kind and friendly दयालु और सहृदय

**warmonger** /ˈwɔːmʌŋɡə(r) ˈवॉमङ्ग(र्)/ *noun* [C] (*formal*) a person, especially a politician or leader, who wants to start a war or encourages people to start a war युद्धलोलुप या जंगख़ोर व्यक्ति (विशेषतः राजनीतिकर्मी या नेता) ▶ **warmongering** *noun* [U] युद्धलोलुपता

**warmth** /wɔːmθ वॉम्थ़्/ *noun* [U] **1** a fairly high temperature or the effect created by this, especially when it is pleasant गरमाहट, उष्णता, ऊष्मा (विशेषतः सुखद) *She felt the warmth of the sun on her face.* **2** the quality of being kind and friendly स्नेहमयता और हार्दिकता *I was touched by the warmth of their welcome.*

**warn** /wɔːn वॉन्/ *verb* [T] **1 warn sb (of sth); warn sb (about sb/sth)** to tell sb about sth unpleasant or dangerous that exists or might happen, so that he/she can avoid it (किसी व्यक्ति को) आसन्न, विद्यमान प्रतिकूलता या ख़तरे की पूर्वसूचना देना, (से) सचेत करना (ताकि वह अपना बचाव कर सके) *When I saw the car coming I tried to warn him, but it was too late.* ○ *The government is warning the public of possible terrorist attacks.* **2 warn (sb) against doing sth; warn sb (not to do sth)** to advise sb not to do sth (किसी को किसी बात से) सावधान करना, आगाह करना *The radio warned people against going out during the storm.* ○ *I warned you not to trust him.*

**warning** /ˈwɔːnɪŋ ˈवॉनिङ्/ *noun* [C, U] something that tells you to be careful or tells you about sth, usually sth bad, before it happens (प्रायः अशुभ स्थिति से) सतर्क करने वाली बात; पूर्वसूचना, चेतावनी *Your employers can't dismiss you* ***without warning****.*

**warp** /wɔːp वॉप्/ *verb* **1** [I, T] to become bent into the wrong shape, for example as a result of getting hot or wet; to make sth become like this (आधार-प्रकार का) टेढ़ा-मेढ़ा हो जाना, बिगड़ जाना; (आकार को) टेढ़ा-मेढ़ा कर देना, बिगाड़ देना *The window frame was badly warped and wouldn't shut.* **2** [T] to influence sb so that he/she starts behaving in an unusual or shocking way किसी बात का ऐसा प्रभाव होना कि व्यक्ति का व्यवहार विकृत या असामान्य हो जाए *His experiences in the war had warped him.* ▶ **warped** *adj.* विकृत, टेढ़ा-मेढ़ा

**warpath** /ˈwɔːpɑːθ ˈवॉपाथ़्/ *noun*
IDM **(be/go) on the warpath** (*informal*) to be very angry and want to fight or punish sb क्रोध में आकर किसी से लड़ने पर उतारू हो जाना

**warrant¹** /ˈwɒrənt ˈवॉरन्ट्/ *noun* [C] an official written statement that gives sb permission to do sth (किसी काम को करने की) आधिकारिक अनुमति; वॉरंट, अधिपत्र, आज्ञापत्र *a search warrant* (= a document that allows the police to search a house)

**warrant²** /ˈwɒrənt ˈवॉरन्ट्/ *verb* [T] (*formal*) to make sth seem right or necessary; to deserve sth ऐसा आचरण करना कि कोई बात सही या आवश्यक लगे; किसी बात का पात्र होना *I don't think her behaviour warrants such criticism.*

**warranty** /ˈwɒrənti ˈवॉरन्टि/ *noun* [C, U] (*pl.* **warranties**) a written statement that you get when you buy sth, which promises to repair or replace it if it is broken or does not work किसी वस्तु को ख़रीदते समय लिखित आश्वासन कि टूट जाने या काम न करने की दशा में उसे ठीक कर या बदल दिया जाएगा; वारंटी *Fortunately my stereo is still* ***under warranty****.* ➪ **guarantee** देखिए।

**warren** /ˈwɒrən ˈवॉरन्/ = **rabbit warren**

**warrior** /ˈwɒriə(r) ˈवॉरिअ(र्)/ *noun* [C] (*old-fashioned*) a person who fights in a battle; a soldier योद्धा; सैनिक, सिपाही

**warship** /ˈwɔːʃɪp ˈवॉशिप्/ *noun* [C] a ship for use in war युद्धपोत, जंगी जहाज़

**wart** /wɔːt वॉट्/ *noun* [C] a small hard dry lump that sometimes grows on the face or body (चेहरे पर या शरीर में कहीं हो जाने वाला) मस्सा

**warthog** /ˈwɔːthɒɡ ˈवॉट्हॉग्/ *noun* [C] an African wild pig with two large outer teeth (**tusks**) and lumps on its face खाँगदार जंगली सूअर (ऐसा जंगली सूअर जिसके बाहर को निकले दो दाँत और चेहरे पर गूमड़ होते हैं)

**wartime** /ˈwɔːtaɪm ˈवॉटाइम्/ *noun* [U] a period of time during which there is a war युद्धकाल

**wary** /ˈweəri ˈवेअरि/ *adj.* **wary (of sb/sth)** careful because you are uncertain or afraid of sb/sth सावधान, सतर्क, चौकन्ना, ख़बरदार (किसी व्यक्ति या वस्तु के प्रति अनिश्चय या भय के कारण) *Since becoming famous, she has grown wary of journalists.* ▶ **warily** /-rəli -रलि/ *adv.* चौकन्नेपन से, सावधान या सतर्क होकर

**was** /wəz; *strong form* wɒz वज़्; प्रबल रूप वॉज़्/ = **be**

**wash¹** /wɒʃ वॉश्/ *verb* **1** [I, T] to clean sb/sth/yourself with water and often soap (अपनी, दूसरे की या वस्तु की) सफ़ाई करना विशेषतः पानी और साबुन से (को) धोना *to wash your hands/face/hair* ***clean*** ➪ **clean²** पर नोट देखिए। **2** [I, T] (used about water) to flow or carry sth/sb in the direction mentioned (पानी का) बहना या वस्तु या व्यक्ति को

(निर्दिष्ट दिशा में) बहाकर ले जाना *I let the waves wash over my feet.* ○ *The current washed the ball out to sea.* **3** [I] to be able to be washed without being damaged (बिना ख़राब हुए) किसी वस्तु का धुल सकना *Does this material wash well, or does the colour come out?*

IDM **wash your hands of sb/sth** to refuse to be responsible for sb/sth any longer किसी व्यक्ति या वस्तु की और अधिक ज़िम्मेदारी लेने से इनकार कर देना *They washed their hands of their son when he was sent to prison.*

PHR V **wash sb/sth away** (used about water) to carry sb/sth away (पानी का) किसी को बहा ले जाना *The floods had washed away the path.*

**wash (sth) off** to (make sth) disappear by washing धोकर (किसी चीज़ को) मिटा देना, साफ़ कर देना *The writing has washed off and now I can't read it.* ○ *Go and wash that make-up off!*

**wash out** to be removed from a material by washing किसी वस्तु पर से (धब्बे आदि का) साफ़ हो जाना, मिट जाना *These grease marks won't wash out.*

**wash sth out** to wash sth or the inside of sth in order to remove dirt किसी वस्तु को पूरी तौर पर या अंदर से धोकर साफ़ करना *I'll just wash out this bowl and then we can use it.*

**wash (sth) up** **1** (*BrE*) to wash the plates, knives, forks, etc. after a meal भोजन के बाद खाने के बरतन (तश्तरी आदि) साफ़ करना *Whose turn is it to wash up?* **2** (*AmE*) to wash your face and hands (अपना) मुँह-हाथ धोना *Go and wash up quickly and put on some clean clothes.* **3** (*often passive*) (used about water) to carry sth to land and leave it there (पानी का) किसी वस्तु को बहा कर तटपर ले आना और वहीं छोड़ देना *Police found the girl's body washed up on the beach.*

**wash²** /wɒʃ वॉश्/ *noun* **1** [C, *usually sing.*] an act of cleaning or being cleaned with water पानी से साफ़ करने, धोने या साफ़ किए जाने, धुलने की क्रिया; धुलाई, स्नान *I'd better go and **have a wash** before we go out.* **2** [*sing.*] the waves caused by the movement of a ship through water जलपोत के चलने से उत्पन्न लहरें

IDM **in the wash** (used about clothes) being washed (कपड़े) जो धुलाई में हैं या धुल रहे हैं *'Where's my red T-shirt?' 'It's in the wash.'*

**washable** /ˈwɒʃəbl ˈवॉशबल्/ *adj.* that can be washed without being damaged जो धोने पर ख़राब न हो

**washbasin** /ˈwɒʃbeɪsn ˈवॉश्बेसन्/ (*also* **basin**) *noun* [C] a large bowl for water that has taps and is fixed to a wall, in a bathroom, etc. वॉशबेसिन ➪ **sink** देखिए।

**washed out** *adj.* tired and pale थका-माँदा *They arrived looking washed out after their long journey.*

**washer** /ˈwɒʃə(r) ˈवॉश(र्)/ *noun* [C] a small flat ring made of rubber, metal or plastic placed between two surfaces to make a connection tight वॉशर, रबर, धातु या प्लास्टिक का छल्ला (जिससे दो वस्तुएँ सतह पर जुड़ कर पक्की हो जाती हैं) ➪ **bolt** पर चित्र देखिए।

**washing** /ˈwɒʃɪŋ ˈवॉशिङ्/ *noun* [U] **1** clothes that need to be washed or are being washed धुलाई के कपड़े (कपड़े जो अभी धुलने हैं या अब धुल रहे हैं) *a pile of dirty washing* **2** the act of cleaning clothes, etc. with water (पानी से) कपड़ों आदि की धुलाई *I usually **do the washing** on Mondays.*

**washing machine** *noun* [C] an electric machine for washing clothes कपड़े धोने की बिजली की मशीन; वॉशिंग मशीन

**washing powder** *noun* [U] soap in the form of powder for washing clothes कपड़े धोने का पाउडर; वॉशिंग पाउडर

**washing-up** *noun* [U] **1** the work of washing the plates, knives, forks, etc. after a meal (भोजन के बाद) खाने के बरतनों (तश्तरी आदि) की धुलाई *I'll **do the washing-up**.* **2** plates, etc. that need washing after a meal (भोजन के बाद) धुलाई के बरतन *Put the washing-up next to the sink.*

**washout** /ˈwɒʃaʊt ˈवॉश्आउट्/ *noun* [C] (*informal*) an event that is a complete failure, especially because of rain पूर्णतया विफल कार्यक्रम (विशेषतः वर्षा के कारण) पूर्णतया

**washroom** /ˈwɒʃruːm; -rʊm ˈवॉश्रूम्; -रुम्/ *noun* [C] (*AmE*) a toilet, especially in a public building शौचालय (विशेषतः सार्वजनिक भवन में); वॉशरूम

**wasn't** /ˈwɒznt ˈवॉज़न्ट्/ ➪ **be** देखिए।

**wasp** /wɒsp वॉस्प्/ *noun* [C] a small black and yellow flying insect that can sting बर्र, ततैया, भिड़ ➪ **hornet** देखिए तथा **insect** पर चित्र भी देखिए।

**wastage** /ˈweɪstɪdʒ ˈवेस्टिज्/ *noun* [U] (*formal*) using too much of sth in a careless way; the amount of sth that is wasted किसी वस्तु की बरबादी; बरबाद हुई वस्तु की मात्रा

**waste¹** /weɪst वेस्ट्/ *verb* [T] **1 waste sth (on sb/sth); waste sth (in doing sth)** to use or spend sth in a careless way or for sth that is not necessary किसी वस्तु की बरबादी करना (लापरवाही से या बिना ज़रूरत उसे इस्तेमाल या ख़र्च करना) *He wasted his time at university because he didn't work hard.* ○ *She wasted no time in decorating her new room*

(= she did it immediately). **2** (*usually passive*) to give sth to sb who does not value it किसी वस्तु की बेक़द्री करना (उसे अपात्र को देकर) *Expensive wine is wasted on me. I don't even like it.*

**waste²** /weɪst वेस्ट्/ *noun* **1** [*sing.*] **a waste (of sth)** using sth in a careless and unnecessary way (किसी वस्तु की) बरबादी *The seminar was **a waste of time**—I'd heard it all before.* **2** [U] material, food, etc. that is not needed and is therefore thrown away बेकार सामान, रद्दी माल, अपशिष्ट सामग्री *nuclear waste* ○ *A lot of household waste can be recycled and reused.* ➪ **rubbish** देखिए। **3 wastes** [*pl.*] (*formal*) large areas of land that are not lived in and not used वीरान या निर्जन इलाक़े *the wastes of the Sahara desert*

IDM **go to waste** to not be used and so thrown away and wasted बरबाद हो जाना, इस्तेमाल न होने के कारण फेंक दिया जाना *I can't bear to see good food going to waste!*

**waste³** /weɪst वेस्ट्/ *adj.* (*only before a noun*) **1** (used about land) not used or not suitable for use; not looked after (भूमि) परती या ऊसर, बंजर, अनुपजाऊ; बेकार पड़ी (हुई) *There's an area of waste ground outside the town where people dump their rubbish.* **2** no longer useful; that is thrown away बेकार, रद्दी; बाहर फेंका हुआ, उपेक्षित *waste paper* ○ *waste material*

**wasted** /ˈweɪstɪd ˈवेसटिड्/ *adj.* **1** not necessary or successful अनावश्यक या निष्फल, परिणाम-रहित, बेनतीजा *a wasted journey* **2** very thin, especially because of illness बहुत दुबला (विशेषतः बीमारी के कारण) **3** (*slang*) suffering from the effects of drugs or alcohol नशीले पदार्थों या शराब के कारण बरबाद (हो चुका)

**wasteful** /ˈweɪstfl ˈवेस्ट्फ़्ल्/ *adj.* using more of sth than necessary; causing waste फ़ज़ूलख़र्च, अपव्ययी, उड़ाऊ; ख़र्चीला

**wasteland** /ˈweɪstlænd ˈवेस्ट्लैन्ड्/ *noun* [U, C] an area of land that cannot be used or that is no longer used for building or growing things on बंजर भूमि, बेकार की ज़मीन (जिस पर न कुछ उग सकता है, न बन सकता है)

**waste-paper basket** *noun* [C] a basket, etc. in which you put paper, etc. which is to be thrown away रद्दी की टोकरी

**watch¹** /wɒtʃ वॉच्/ *verb* **1** [I, T] to look at sb/sth for a time, paying attention to what happens (किसी व्यक्ति या वस्तु को) ध्यान से देखना *I **watched in horror** as the car swerved and crashed.* ○ *I'm watching to see how you do it.* **2** [T] to take care of sth for a short time (किसी चीज़ की) रखवाली करना, चौकसी करना *Could you watch my bag for a second while I go and get a drink?* **3** [T] **watch sb/sth (for sth)** to be careful about sb/sth; to pay careful attention to sth/sb (किसी व्यक्ति या वस्तु के विषय में) सतर्क रहना; (किसी वस्तु या व्यक्ति पर) कड़ी निगाह रखना *You'd better **watch what you say** to her. She gets upset very easily.*

IDM **watch your step** ➪ **step¹** देखिए।

PHR V **watch out** to be careful because of possible danger or trouble सावधान रहना (संभावित ख़तरे या मुसीबत के कारण) *Watch out! There's a car coming.* ○ *If you don't watch out you'll lose your job.*

**watch out for sb/sth** to look carefully and be ready for sb/sth ध्यानपूर्वक सावधानी से देखना और किसी व्यक्ति या वस्तु का सामना करने के लिए तैयार रहना *Watch out for snakes if you walk through the fields.*

**watch over sb/sth** to look after or protect sb/sth किसी व्यक्ति या वस्तु की देख-भाल या रक्षा करना *For two weeks she watched over the sick child.*

**watch²** /wɒtʃ वॉच्/ *noun* **1** [C] a type of small clock that you usually wear around your wrist हाथ-घड़ी, रिस्ट-वॉच *My watch is a bit fast/slow* (= shows a time that is later/earlier than the correct time). ➪ **clock** देखिए। **2** [*sing.*, U] the action of watching sb/sth in case of possible danger or problems निगरानी, सर्तकता (संभावित ख़तरे या मुसीबत को देखते हुए) *Tour companies have to **keep a close watch on** the political situation in the region.*

**watchdog** /ˈwɒtʃdɒg ˈवॉच्डॉग्/ *noun* [C] a person or group whose job is to make sure that large companies respect people's rights बड़ी कंपनियों से लोगों के हितों की रक्षा करने में लगा व्यक्ति या व्यक्ति-समूह; हितप्रहरी *a consumer watchdog*

**watchful** /ˈwɒtʃfl ˈवॉच्फ़्ल्/ *adj.* careful to notice things जागरूक, सतर्क

**watchman** /ˈwɒtʃmən ˈवॉच्मन्/ *noun* [C] (*pl.* **watchmen** /-mən -मन्/) (*old-fashioned*) a man whose job is to guard a building, for example a bank, an office building or a factory, especially at night पहरेदार, चौकीदार ➪ **nightwatchman** देखिए।

**water¹** /ˈwɔːtə(r) ˈवॉट(र्)/ *noun* **1** [U] the clear liquid that falls as rain and is in rivers, seas and lakes पानी, जल, नीर *drinking water* ○ *tap water*

> NOTE 100° सेल्सियस पर पानी गरम किया जाए तो वह उबल जाता है (**boils**) और भाप (**steam**) बन जाता है। ठंडी वस्तु के संपर्क से भाप **condense** होकर फिर पानी बन जाता है। जब पानी को 0° सेल्सियस पर ठंडा किया जाता है वह **freeze** हो जाता है और **ice** बन जाता है।

**2** [U] a large amount of water, especially the water in a lake, river or sea जलराशि (विशेषतः झील, नदी या समुद्र की) *After the heavy rain several fields were **under water**.* **3** [U] the surface of an area of water (जलाशय आदि के) पानी की सतह *I can see my reflection in the water.* **4 waters** [*pl.*] the water in a particular sea, lake, etc. or near a particular country विशिष्ट समुद्र, झील की जलराशि या देश विशेष के निकट की जलक्षेत्र *The ship was still in Indian waters.*

IDM **keep your head above water** ➪ **head**[1] देखिए।

IDM **pass water** ➪ **pass**[1] देखिए।

**water²** /ˈwɔːtə(r) ˈवॉट(र्)/ *verb* **1** [T] to give water to plants पौधों को सींचना **2** [I] (used about the eyes or mouth) to fill with liquid आँखों से पानी निकलना या मुँह में पानी भर आना *The smoke in the room was starting to **make** my **eyes water**.* ○ *These menus will really **make** your **mouth water**.*

PHR V **water sth down** **1** to add water to a liquid in order to make it weaker किसी द्रव में पानी मिलाकर उसे पतला करना **2** to change a statement, report, etc. so that the meaning is less strong or direct किसी कथन, रिपोर्ट आदि के संदेश को कुछ कमज़ोर या परोक्ष बना देना, (उसके) समग्र प्रभाव को कम कर देना

**waterbird** /ˈwɔːtəbɜːd ˈवॉटबड्/ *noun* [C] a bird that lives near and walks or swims in water, especially rivers or lakes जल पक्षी (जल में, विशेषतः नदियों या झीलों में, तैरते रहने वाला या उनके निकट रहने वाला पक्षी) ➪ **seabird** देखिए।

**water-borne** *adj.* spread or carried by water जल से फैलने वाला, जल संक्रमित या जल से लाया गया, जलवाहित *cholera and other water-borne diseases* ➪ **airborne** देखिए।

**water buffalo** *noun* [C] a large animal of the cow family, used for pulling vehicles and farm equipment in Asia भैंसा

**watercolour** (*AmE* **watercolor**) /ˈwɔːtəkʌlə(r) ˈवॉटकल(र्)/ *noun* **1 watercolours** [*pl.*] paints that are mixed with water, not oil पानी से (न कि तेल से) मिलाकर प्रयुक्त रंग; जलरंग, वॉटरकलर **2** [C] a picture that has been painted with water colours जलरंगनिर्मित चित्र

**watercourse** /ˈwɔːtəkɔːs ˈवॉटकॉस्/ *noun* [C] (*technical*) a small river (**a stream**) or an artificial passage for water छोटी नदी या कृत्रिम जलमार्ग, छोटी नहर

**watercress** /ˈwɔːtəkres ˈवॉटक्रेस्/ *noun* [U] a type of plant with small round green leaves which have a strong taste and are often eaten in salads जलकुंभी (की जाति की लता)

**waterfall** /ˈwɔːtəfɔːl ˈवॉटफ़ॉल्/ *noun* [C] a river that falls down from a cliff, rock, etc. झरना, जलप्रपात (ऊँची खड़ी चट्टान या पहाड़ी आदि से नीचे गिरने वाली जलधारा) ➪ **glacial** पर चित्र देखिए।

**waterfront** /ˈwɔːtəfrʌnt ˈवॉटफ्रन्ट्/ *noun* [C, *usually sing.*] a part of a town or an area that is next to the sea, a river or a lake समुद्र, नदी या झील की ओर का नगर-भाग या कोई क्षेत्र, तटीय नगर-भाग या क्षेत्र

**waterhole** /ˈwɔːtəhəʊl ˈवाटहोल्/ (*also* **watering hole**) *noun* [C] a place in a hot country where animals go to drink जलगर्त; पानी का गड्ढा (गरम देशों में जानवरों के लिए पानी से भरा गड्ढा)

**watering can** *noun* [C] a container with a long tube on one side which is used for pouring water on plants हज़ारा, फौव्वारा (पौधों पर छिड़काव करने की नलदार बालटी) ➪ **gardening** पर चित्र देखिए।

**watering hole** = **waterhole**

**water lily** *noun* [C] a plant that floats on the surface of water, with large round flat leaves and white, yellow or pink flowers कुमुद (पानी पर तैरता, बड़े गोल चपटे पत्तों वाला पौधा जिसमें पीले या गुलाबी फूल खिलते हैं)

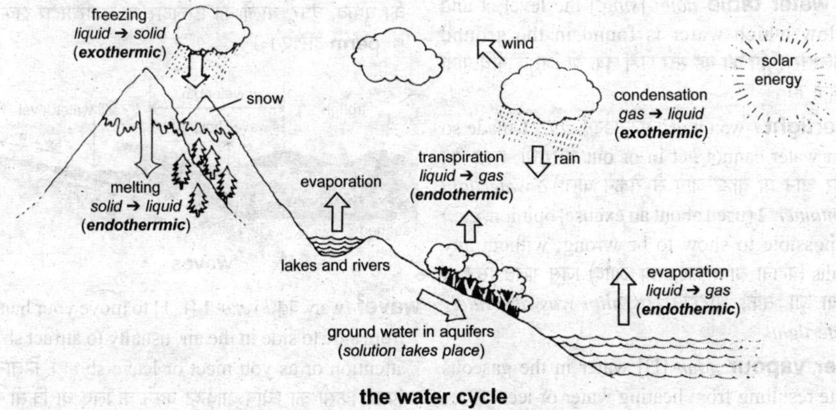


**the water cycle**

**waterlogged** /ˈwɔːtəlɒgd ˈवॉटलॉग्ड् / *adj.* **1** (used about the ground) extremely wet (मैदान) जिसमें जलभरा हो, जल-जमाव वाला *Our boots sank into the waterlogged ground.* **2** (used about a boat) full of water and likely to sink (नौका) जिसमें पानी भर गया हो और जो कभी भी डूब सकती है; जलाक्रांत

**watermark** /ˈwɔːtəmɑːk ˈवॉटमाक् / *noun* [C] a symbol or design in some types of paper, which can be seen when the paper is held against the light जलांक, जलचिह्न, वॉटरमार्क (कुछ प्रकार के काग़ज़ों में अंकित चिह्न या डिज़ाइन जो काग़ज़ को रोशनी के सामने लाने पर दीखने लगता है)

**watermelon** /ˈwɔːtəmelən ˈवॉटमेलन् / *noun* [C, U] a large, round fruit with a thick, green skin. It is pink or red inside with a lot of black seeds तरबूज़ ➪ **fruit** पर चित्र देखिए।

**waterpolo** *noun* [U] a game played by two teams of people swimming in a swimming pool. Players try to throw a ball into the other team's goal जलपोलो, वॉटर पोलो (तरण ताल या स्विमिंग पूल में दो टीमों का खेल जिसमें खिलाड़ी एक-दूसरे के गोल में गेंद फेंकने की कोशिश करते हैं)

**waterproof** /ˈwɔːtəpruːf ˈवॉटप्रूफ़् / *adj.* that does not let water go through जिसमें से होकर पानी न जा सके; जलरुद्ध, वॉटरप्रूफ़ *a waterproof jacket*

**watershed** /ˈwɔːtəʃed ˈवॉटशेड् / *noun* [C] an event or time which is important because it marks the beginning of sth new or different ऐसी घटना जो इसलिए महत्त्वपूर्ण है कि उससे स्थिति में कोई नया मोड़ आया, नव-प्रवर्तन से उत्पन्न घटना; वॉटरशेड

**waterski** /ˈwɔːtəskiː ˈवॉटस्की / *verb* [I] to move across the surface of water standing on narrow boards (**waterskis**) and being pulled by a boat एक विशेष प्रकार के स्की को बाँध कर नाव से जुड़कर पानी के स्तर पर गति करना या तैरना; वॉटरस्की

**the water table** *noun* [*sing.*] the level at and below which water is found in the ground भूजलस्तर (भूमि का वह स्तर जहाँ तक या जिसके नीचे पानी मिलता है)

**watertight** /ˈwɔːtətaɪt ˈवॉटटाइट् / *adj.* **1** made so that water cannot get in or out जलरोधी (जल को अंदर आने या बाहर जाने से रोकने वाला) *a watertight container* **2** (used about an excuse, opinion, etc.) impossible to show to be wrong; without any faults (बहाना या सफ़ाई, राय आदि) जिसे ग़लत सिद्ध न किया जा सके; त्रुटिहीन *His alibi was absolutely watertight.*

**water vapour** *noun* [U] water in the gaseous state resulting from heating water or ice वाष्प

**waterway** /ˈwɔːtəweɪ ˈवॉटवे / *noun* [C] a canal, river, etc. along which boats can travel जलमार्ग (नहर, नदी आदि जिनमें नावें चल सकें)

**watery** /ˈwɔːtəri ˈवॉटरि / *adj.* **1** containing mostly water जिसमें पानी अधिक हो; पनीला, पानी जैसा *watery soup* ○ *A watery liquid came out of the wound.* **2** weak and pale दुर्बल और निर्जीव-सा *watery sunshine* ○ *a watery smile*

**watt** /wɒt वॉट् / *noun* [C] (*abbr.* **W**) a unit of electrical power विद्युत शक्ति की इकाई; वाट *a 60-watt light bulb*

**wave¹** /weɪv वेव् / *noun* [C] **1** a line of water moving across the surface of water, especially the sea, that is higher than the rest of the surface लहर, तरंग (विशेषतः समुद्र में) *We watched the waves roll in and break on the shore.* ➪ **diffract** देखिए तथा **tidal wave** पर चित्र भी देखिए। **2** a sudden increase or spread of a feeling or type of behaviour किसी मनोभाव या आचरण का अचानक बढ़ाव या फैलाव; आवेग, लहर *There has been a wave of sympathy for the refugees.* ○ *a **crime wave*** ○ *The pain came **in waves**.* ➪ **heatwave** देखिए। **3** a large number of people or things suddenly moving or appearing somewhere लोगों या वस्तुओं की बाढ़ (एकाएक बड़ी संख्या में कहीं पर पहुँच जाना या दिखाई देने लगना) *There is normally a wave of tourists in August.* **4** a movement of sth, especially your hand, from side to side in the air किसी वस्तु (विशेषतः हाथ) को हवा में दोनों ओर हिलाने की क्रिया *With a wave of his hand, he said goodbye and left.* **5** the form that some types of energy such as sound, light, heat, etc. take when they move ध्वनि, प्रकाश, ताप आदि की तरंग *sound waves* ➪ **long wave, medium wave** और **short wave** देखिए। **6** a gentle curve in your hair बालों का घुमाव, घुँघर, बालों की छल्लेदार या लहरियादार शकल ➪ **perm** देखिए।

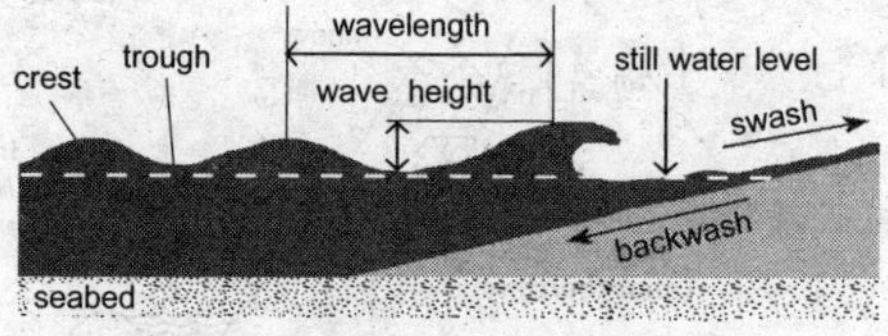


waves

**wave²** /weɪv वेव् / *verb* **1** [I, T] to move your hand from side to side in the air, usually to attract sb's attention or as you meet or leave sb हाथ हिलाना (प्रायः किसी का ध्यान आकृष्ट करने के लिए या किसी से

मुलाक़ात करते या विदा लेते समय) *I leant out of the window and waved goodbye to my friends.* **2** [T] **wave sth (at sb); wave sth (about)** to hold sth in the air and move it from side to side किसी वस्तु को हवा में लहराना *The crowd waved flags as the President came out.* ○ *She was talking excitedly and waving her arms about.* **3** [T] **wave sb/sth away, on, through, etc.** to move your hand in a particular direction to show sb/sth which way to go हाथ के संकेत से रास्ता बताना *There was a policeman in the middle of the road, waving us on.* **4** [I] to move gently up and down or from side to side ऊपर-नीचे या इधर-उधर मंद-मंद हिलना; झूमना *The branches of the trees waved gently in the breeze.*

PHR V **wave sth aside** to decide not to pay attention to sb/sth because you think he/she/it is not important किसी बात को तुच्छ मानकर ख़ारिज कर देना

**wave sb off** to wave to sb who is leaving प्रस्थान करते व्यक्ति के लिए हाथ हिलाना या हाथ हिलाकर उसे विदा करना

**waveband** /ˈweɪvbænd ˈवेव्बैन्ड्/ *noun* [C] a set of radio waves of similar length एक ही लंबाई की रेडियों तरंगों का सेट; तरंग-पट्टी, वेवबैंड

**wave-cut platform** *noun* [C] (in geography) an area of land between the cliffs and the sea which is covered by water when the sea is at its highest level (भूगोल में) ज्वार के समय ऊँची खड़ी चट्टानों और समुद्र के मध्य स्थित जल-प्लावित भूक्षेत्र

**wavelength** /ˈweɪvleŋθ ˈवेव्लेङ्थ्/ *noun* [C] **1** the distance between two sound waves दो ध्वनि-तरंगों के बीच की दूरी; वेवलेंग्थ ➪ **amplitude** पर चित्र देखिए। **2** the length of wave on which a radio station sends out its programmes तरंगदैर्घ्य, वेवलेंग्थ (तरंग की लंबाई जिस पर कोई रेडियो स्टेशन अपने कार्यक्रम प्रसारित करता है)

IDM **on the same wavelength** ➪ **same** देखिए।

**waver** /ˈweɪvə(r) ˈवेव़(र्)/ *verb* [I] **1** to become weak or uncertain, especially when making a decision or choice अनिश्चय की स्थिति में होना हिचकिचाना, आगा-पीछा करना (विशेषतः कोई निर्णय या विकल्पों में से चयन करते समय) *He never wavered in his support for her.* **2** to move in a way that is not firm or steady काँपना, डगमगाना, डाँवाँडोल होना *His hand wavered as he reached for the gun.*

**wavy** /ˈweɪvi ˈवेवि/ *adj.* having curves; not straight घुँघराला, लहरदार या लहरियादार *wavy hair* ○ *a wavy line*

**wax[1]** /wæks वैक्स्/ *noun* [U] **1** a substance made from fat or oil that melts easily and is used for making candles, polish, etc. वसा या तेल से बना पदार्थ जो जल्दी पिघल जाता है और उससे मोमबत्ती, पॉलिश आदि बनती है; मोम **2** a yellow substance that is found in your ears कान की मैल; खूँट

**wax[2]** /wæks वैक्स्/ *verb* **1** [T] to polish sth with wax मोम से (किसी वस्तु को) चमकाना **2** [T] (*often passive*) to remove hair from a part of the body using wax मोम लगाकर (शरीर के किसी अंग के) बाल साफ़ करना *to wax your legs/have your legs waxed* **3** [I] (used about the moon) to seem to get gradually bigger until its full form can be seen (चंद्रमा की) कलाओं का बढ़ना ✪ विलोम **wane**

**wax paper** (*AmE*) = **greaseproof paper**

**waxwork** /ˈwækswɜːk ˈवैक्सवक्/ *noun* [C] **1** a model of sb/sth, especially of a famous person, made of wax किसी (विशेषतः प्रसिद्ध व्यक्ति का मोम से बना पुतला, मोमी कलाकृति, मोमी प्रतिमा, मोम की मूर्ति **2 waxworks** [*sing.*] a place where wax models of famous people are shown to the public मोम की मूर्तियों का संग्रहालय

**way[1]** /weɪ वे/ *noun* **1** [C] **a way (to do sth/of doing sth)** a particular method, style or manner of doing sth कुछ करने की विशेष विधि, तरीक़ा या ढंग

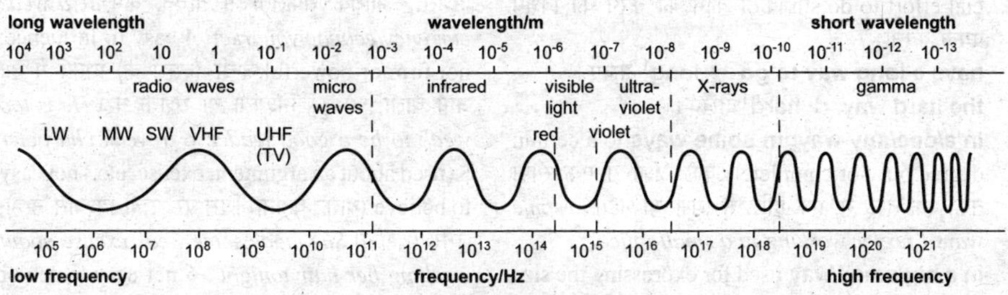

wavelength

*What is **the best way** to learn a language?* ○ *He always **does things** his **own way**.* **2** [C, *usually sing.*] the route you take to reach somewhere; the route you would take if nothing were stopping you (कहीं पहुँचने का) रास्ता, मार्ग; बिना रुके कहीं पहुँचने का रास्ता, के रास्ते में *We stopped **on the way to** Jaipur for a meal.* ○ *Can I drive you home? It's on my way.* **3** [*sing.*] a direction or position दिशा या स्थिति *Look this way!* ○ *He thought I was older than my sister but in fact it's **the other way round*** (= the opposite of what he thought). ➪ **back to front** देखिए। **4** [C] a path, road, route, etc. that you can travel along यात्रा का पथ, मार्ग, रास्ता ➪ **highway, motorway** और **railway** देखिए। **5** [*sing.*] a distance in space or time स्थान या समय की दूरी *The exams are still **a long way off**.* ○ *We came all this way to see him and he's not at home!*

IDM **be set in your ways** ➪ **set³** देखिए।

**by the way** (used for adding sth to the conversation) on a new subject (चल रही बात में कोई नई बात जोड़ने के लिए प्रयुक्त) प्रसंगवश *Oh, by the way, I saw Manoj in town yesterday.*

**change your ways** ➪ **change¹** देखिए।

**get/have your own way** to get or do what you want, although others may want sth else अपनी बात मनवाना (भले ही दूसरे सहमत न हों)

**give way** to break or fall down झुक जाना या गिर जाना *The branch of the tree suddenly gave way and he fell.*

**give way (to sb/sth)** **1** to stop or to allow sb/sth to go first किसी व्यक्ति या वस्तु के मार्ग में बाधक न बनना या उसे पहले जाने देना *Give way to traffic coming from the right.* **2** to allow sb to have what he/she wants although you did not at first agree with it (अंत में) किसी के सामने झुक जाना, उसे मनमानी करने देना *We shall not give way to the terrorists' demands.*

**go a long way** ➪ **long¹** देखिए।

**go out of your way (to do sth)** to make a special effort to do sth किसी काम को करने का विशेष प्रयत्न करना

**have a long way to go** ➪ **long¹** देखिए।

**the hard way** ➪ **hard¹** देखिए।

**in a/one/any way; in some ways** to a certain degree but not completely कुछ अंशों में एक सीमा तक, एक तरह से, एक दृष्टि से (पूर्णतया नहीं) *In some ways I prefer working in a small office.*

**in a big/small way** used for expressing the size or importance of an activity बड़े या छोटे पैमाने पर (किसी काम के आधार का महत्त्व का संकेत करने के लिए प्रयुक्त) *'Have you done any acting before?' 'Yes, but in a very small way* (= not very much).*'*

**in the way** **1** blocking the road or path रास्ते में बाधक होना, रुकावट डालना *I can't get past. There's a big lorry in the way.* **2** not needed or wanted ग़ैर-ज़रूरी या अवांछित *I felt rather in the way at my daughter's party.*

**learn the hard way** ➪ **learn** देखिए।

**no way** (*informal*) definitely not बिलकुल नहीं, यक़ीनन नहीं *'Can I borrow your car?' 'No way!'*

IDM **underway** having started and making progress आरंभ होकर आगे बढ़ना या प्रगति करना *Discussions between the two sides are now underway.*

**a/sb's way of life** the behaviour and customs that are typical of a person or group of people किसी व्यक्ति या समूह की जीवन-शैली

**way²** /weɪ वे/ *adv.* (*informal*) very far; very much बहुत दूर; बहुत अधिक *I finally found his name way down at the bottom of the list.* ○ *Mandira's got way more experience than me.*

**wayward** /ˈweɪwəd ˈवेवड्/ *adj.* (*written*) difficult to control निरंकुश, ज़िद्दी, हठी *a wayward child/animal* ▸ **waywardness** *noun* [U] निरंकुशता, ज़िद्दीपन, हठीलापन

**we** /wiː वी/ *pronoun* the subject of a verb; used for talking about the speaker and one or more other people हम (किसी क्रिया का कर्ता) *We're going to the cinema.* ○ *We are both very pleased with the house.*

**weak** /wiːk वीक्/ *adj.* **1** (used about the body) having little strength or energy; not strong (शरीर) दुर्बल, कमज़ोर, निर्बल; अशक्त *The child was weak with hunger.* ○ *Her legs felt weak.* **2** that cannot support a lot of weight; likely to break जो भारी वज़न न सँभाल सके; जो कभी भी टूट सकता हो, कमज़ोर *That bridge is too weak to take heavy traffic.* **3** not having economic success वित्तीय दृष्टि से अशस्त, आर्थिक सफलता से वंचित, कमज़ोर *a weak currency/economy/market* **4** easy to influence; not firm or powerful जल्दी (दूसरों के) प्रभाव में आ जाने वाला; जो दृढ़ निश्चयी या सशक्त नहीं *He is too weak to be a good leader.* ○ *a weak character* **5** (used about an argument, excuse, etc.) not easy to believe (युक्ति, बहाना) जिस पर जल्दी विश्वास न हो; लचर (बहाना) *She made some weak excuse about washing her hair tonight.* **6** not easy to see or hear; not definite or strong जिसे देखना या सुनना आसान न हो, कमज़ोर, क्षीण; निस्तेज, फीका *a weak*

*voice* ○ *She gave a weak smile.* **7** (used about liquids) containing a lot of water, not strong in taste (द्रव) जिसमें पानी अधिक हो और स्वाद हलका या फीका हो, पनीला और फीका या हलका *weak coffee* ○ *I like my tea quite weak.* **8 weak (at/in/on sth)** not very good at sth किसी काम में विशेष दक्ष नहीं, कम योग्यता वाला *He's weak at maths.* ○ *His maths is weak.* ○ *a weak team* ✪ विलोम **strong**

▸ **weakly** *adv.* दुर्बलता से

**weaken** /ˈwiːkən ˈवीकन्/ *verb* [I, T] **1** to become less strong; to make sb/sth less strong कमज़ोर हो जाना; (व्यक्ति या वस्तु को) कमज़ोर कर देना *The building had been weakened by the earthquake.* ✪ विलोम **strengthen** **2** to become less certain or firm about sth आग्रह छोड़ देना या कमज़ोर पड़ जाना *She eventually weakened and allowed him to stay.*

**weak form** *noun* [C] a way of pronouncing a word when it is not emphasized शब्द उच्चारणगत दुर्बल रूप, शब्द का बलाघातहीन उच्चारण

**weakness** /ˈwiːknəs ˈवीकनस्/ *noun* **1** [U] the state of being weak दुर्बलता, कमज़ोरी, निर्बलता, अशक्तता *He thought that crying was a sign of weakness.* **2** [C] a fault or lack of strength, especially in a person's character दुर्बल पक्ष, कमज़ोरी (विशेषतः व्यक्ति के चरित्र में) *It's important to know your own strengths and weaknesses.* ✪ विलोम **strength** (अर्थ सं. **1** और **2** के लिए) **3** [C, *usually sing.*] **a weakness for sth/sb** a particular and often foolish liking for sth/sb किसी व्यक्ति या वस्तु के लिए ख़ास तरह की चाहत (प्रायः बेमतलब) *I have a weakness for chocolate.*

**wealth** /welθ वेल्थ्/ *noun* **1** [U] a lot of money, property, etc. that sb owns; the state of being rich (किसी की) धन-संपत्ति, ज़मीन-जायदाद; संपन्नता, अमीरी *They were a family of enormous wealth.* ✪ पर्याय **riches** **2** [*sing.*] **a wealth of sth** a large number or amount of sth प्रचुरता, बड़ी संख्या या मात्रा *a wealth of information/experience/talent*

**wealthy** /ˈwelθi ˈवेल्थि/ *adj.* (**wealthier; wealthiest**) having a lot of money, property, etc. धनी, अमीर, संपन्न ✪ पर्याय **rich**

**wean** /wiːn वीन्/ *verb* [T] to gradually stop feeding a baby or young animal with its mother's milk and start giving it solid food (छोटे बच्चे का) धीरे-धीरे माँ का दूध छुड़ाना (और उसे ठोस आहार देना शुरू करना)

**weapon** /ˈwepən ˈवेपन्/ *noun* [C] an object which is used for fighting or for killing people, such as a gun, knife, bomb, etc. अस्त्र, शस्त्र, हथियार

**wear[1]** /weə(r) वेअ(र्)/ *verb* (*pt* **wore** /wɔː(r) वॉ(र्)/; *pp* **worn** /wɔːn वॉन्/) **1** [T] to have clothes, jewellery, etc. on your body (कपड़े, गहने आदि) पहनना, धारण करना *He was wearing a suit and tie.* ○ *I wear glasses for reading.* **2** [T] to have a certain look on your face चेहरे पर ख़ास तरह का भाव लाना, प्रकट करना, प्रदर्शित करना *His face wore a puzzled look.* **3** [I, T] to become or make sth become thinner, smoother or weaker because of being used or rubbed a lot घिस जाना, छीनना, जीर्ण हो जाना या (किसी वस्तु को) घिसा देना, जीर्ण कर देना (प्रायः अधिक इस्तेमाल या उसके रगड़ खाने के कारण) *These tyres are badly worn.* ○ *The soles of his shoes had worn smooth.* **4** [T] to make a hole, path, etc. in sth by rubbing, walking, etc. किसी वस्तु में छेद बनाना (इस्तेमाल से उसे घिसते-घिसते), कहीं पर रास्ता बनाना (उस पर चलते-चलते), आदि *I'd worn a hole in my sock.* **5** [I] to last for a long time without becoming thinner or damaged (किसी वस्तु का) बिना घिसे या ख़राब हुए देर तक चलना *This material wears well.*

**IDM** **wear thin** to have less effect because of being used too much प्रयोग की अधिकता से (किसी वस्तु के) प्रभाव में कमी आ जाना *We've heard that excuse so often that it's beginning to wear thin.*

**PHR V** **wear (sth) away** to damage sth or to make it disappear over a period of time, by using or touching it a lot; to disappear or become damaged in this way (लंबे समय तक इस्तेमाल से किसी वस्तु को) बिगाड़ देना या (बार-बार छूकर किसी निशान आदि को) ग़ायब कर देना या मिटा देना *The wind had worn the soil away.*

**wear (sth) down** to become or to make sth smaller or smoother घिसकर छोटा हो जाना या छोटा कर देना, घिस जाना या घिस डालना *The heels on these shoes have worn right down.*

**wear sb/sth down** to make sb/sth weaker by attacking, persuading, etc. (किसी व्यक्ति या वस्तु को प्रतिरोध, दबाव आदि से शिथिल कर देना *They wore him down with constant arguments until he changed his mind.*

**wear off** to become less strong or to disappear completely हलका पड़ जाना या पूर्णतया लुप्त हो जाना *The effects of the drug wore off after a few hours.*

**wear (sth) out** to become too thin or damaged to use any more; to cause sth to do this घिस जाना या ख़राब हो जाना (और काम का न रहना); किसी वस्तु को घिसा देना (और काम का न रहने देना) *Children's shoes wear out very quickly.*

**wear sb out** to make sb very tired (किसी को) बहुत थका देना *She wore herself out walking home with the heavy bags.* ➪ **worn-out** देखिए।

**wear²** /weə(r) वेअ(र्)/ *noun* [U] **1** wearing or being worn; use as clothing पहनने की क्रिया, पहनाई या पहने होने की अवस्था, पहनाव; पोशाक के रूप में *You'll need jeans and jumpers for everyday wear.* **2** (*usually in compounds*) used especially in shops to describe clothes for a particular purpose or occasion विशेष प्रयोजन से या अवसर पर पहनने के कपड़ों के लिए प्रयुक्त शब्द (विशेषतः दुकानों पर) (जैसे कैज़ुअल-विअर) *casual/evening wear* ○ *children's wear* **3** long use which damages the quality or appearance of sth लंबे इस्तेमाल से घिसावट, कट-फट (गुणवत्ता या शकल का ख़राब हो जाना) *The engine is checked regularly for signs of wear.*

IDM **wear and tear** the damage to objects, furniture, etc. that is the result of normal use सामान्य प्रयोग से वस्तुओं, फर्नीचर आदि में क्षति; टूट-फूट

**the worse for wear** ➪ **worse** देखिए।

**weary** /ˈwɪəri ˈविअरि/ *adj.* very tired, especially after you have been doing sth for a long time थका-माँदा (विशेषतः किसी काम को देर तक करते रहने के कारण) *He gave a weary smile.* ▶ **wearily** /ˈwɪərəli ˈविअरलि/ *adv.* बहुत थक कर ▶ **weariness** *noun* [U] थकान, क्लांति

**weasel** /ˈwiːzl ˈवीज़्ल्/ *noun* [C] a small wild animal with reddish-brown fur, a long thin body and short legs. Weasels eat smaller animals वीज़ल

**weather¹** /ˈweðə(r) ˈवेद(र्)/ *noun* [U] the climate at a certain place and time, how much wind, rain, sun, etc. there is and how hot or cold it is मौसम, ऋतु (किसी समय किसी स्थान का तापमापन, पवन-गति, वर्षा-मात्रा, आर्द्रता आदि) *hot/warm/sunny/fine weather* ○ *cold/wet/windy/wintry weather*

> NOTE बादलों से गिरने वाली पानी की बूँदें **rain** (वर्षा) कहलाती हैं। वर्षा जमकर **snow** (बर्फ़) बन जाती है। यह मुलायम और सफ़ेद होती है और ज़मीन पर बैठ जाती है। पूरी तरह से जमी वर्षा (की बूँदें) **hail** (ओला) कहलाती हैं। हलकी-हलकी वर्षा होना **drizzling** (बूँदाबाँदी) है, तेज वर्षा होने को **pouring** कहते हैं। **Fog** (कोहरा) वह है जो बादल-सा लगे और ज़मीन पर फैला हो, इसके कारण बहुत दूर की वस्तु देखना कठिन हो जाता है। हलके कोहरे को **mist** कहते हैं। ➪ **storm** भी देखिए।

IDM **make heavy weather of sth** ➪ **heavy** देखिए।

**under the weather** (*informal*) not very well अस्वस्थ

**weather²** /ˈweðə(r) ˈवेद्र(र्)/ *verb* **1** [I, T] to change or make sth change in appearance because of the effect of the sun, air or wind धूप, वायु या हवा के कारण रंग, शकल का बदलना या किसी का रंग या शकल बदल देना *This stone weathers to a warm pinkish-brown colour.* ➪ **erode** पर चित्र देखिए। **2** [T] to come safely through a difficult time or experience कठिन समय या अनुभव में से सही-सलामत निकल आना, को झेल लेना *Their company managed to weather the recession and recover.*

**weather-beaten** *adj.* (used especially about a person's face or skin) made rough and damaged by the sun and wind (व्यक्ति का चेहरा या त्वचा) धूप और बरसात से कठोर या विकृत मौसम की मार खाया हुआ; ऋतु-विकृत

**weather forecast** (*also* **forecast**) *noun* [C] a description of the weather that is expected for the next day or next few days मौसम या ऋतु की भविष्यवाणी ➪ **weather** देखिए।

**weathervane** /ˈweðəveɪn ˈवेद्रवेन्/ *noun* [C] a metal object on the roof of a building that turns easily in the wind and shows which direction the wind is blowing from (भवन की छत पर लगा) वायु की दिशा और गति का सूचक (मुरग़ानुमा) तीर; बादनुमा ➪ **vector** पर चित्र देखिए।

**weave** /wiːv वीव्/ *verb* [I, T] (*pt* **wove** /wəʊv वोव्/ or in sense **2 weaved**; *pp* **woven** /ˈwəʊvn ˈवोव्न्/ or in sense **2 weaved**) **1** to make cloth, etc. by passing threads under and over a set of threads that is fixed to a frame (**loom**) (कपड़ा आदि) बुनना, बुनाई करना *woven cloth* **2** to change direction often when you are moving so that you are not stopped by anything दाएँ-बाएँ चलना, टेढ़े-मेढ़े चलना *The cyclist weaved in and out of the traffic.*

**weaver** /ˈwiːvə(r) ˈवीव्र(र्)/ *noun* [C] a person whose job is weaving cloth बुनकर

**weaver-bird** *noun* [C] a small bird of tropical Africa and Asia, that builds elaborately woven nests बया, बुनकर पक्षी

**web** /web वेब्/ *noun* **1** [C] a type of fine net that a spider makes in order to catch small insects मकड़ी का जाला *A spider spins webs.* ➪ **cobweb** देखिए। **2** (*computing*) (*usually* **the Web**) [*sing.*] = **World Wide Web** *a Web browser/page*

**webbed** /webd वेब्ड्/ *adj.* (of the feet of a bird or an animal) having pieces of skin between the toes (पक्षी या पशु) जिनके पैरों के पंजे जाल जैसे चर्म से जुड़े हों, पादजाल वाले, जालपदी

**webmaster** /ˈwebmɑːstə(r) ˈवेब्मास्ट(र्)/ *noun* [C] (*computing*) a person who is responsible for particular pages of information on the **World Wide Web** वेबमास्टर, व्यक्ति जो विश्वव्यापी जाल, वर्ल्ड वाइड वेब पर (किसी प्रसंग से संबंधित) विशिष्ट सूचना के पृष्ठों की रचना करता है

**website** /ˈwebsaɪt ˈवेब्साइट्/ *noun* [C] (*computing*) a place connected to the Internet, where a company, organization, etc. puts information that can be found on the **World Wide Web** वेबसाइट इंटरनेट पर किसी कंपनी, संस्था आदि का सूचना-केंद्र (वर्ल्ड वाइड वेब—विश्वव्यापी जाल—पर उपलब्ध)

**Wed.** *abbr.* Wednesday बुधवार *Wed. 4 May*

**we'd** /wiːd वीड्/ ➪ **we had, we would** का संक्षिप्त रूप

**wedding** /ˈwedɪŋ ˈवेडिङ्/ *noun* [C] a marriage ceremony and often the meal or party that follows it (**the reception**) विवाह समारोह (संस्कार और भोज का कार्यक्रम) *I've been invited to their wedding.* ○ *a wedding dress/guest/present*

> **NOTE** **Marriage** (विवाह) शब्द का अर्थ है किसी से विवाहित होने की स्थिति। यह शब्द 'विवाह संस्कार' का अर्थ भी देता है और इस दृष्टि से **wedding** का पर्याय है। जिस पुरुष का विवाह होना है वह **bridegroom** कहलाता है और ऐसी महिला को **bride** कहा जाता है। विवाहित जीवन के 25 वर्ष पूरे होने पर **silver wedding,** 50 वर्ष पूरे होने पर **golden wedding** और 60 वर्ष पूरे होने पर **diamond wedding** मनाया जाता है।

**wedge[1]** /wedʒ वेज्/ *noun* [C] a piece of wood, etc. with one thick and one thin pointed end that you can push into a small space, for example to keep things apart फन्नी, पच्चर (V के आकार का धातु या लकड़ी का टुकड़ा जो वस्तुओं को अलग रखने के लिए उनके बीच में फँसा दिया जाता है) *The door was kept open with a wedge.*

**wedge[2]** /wedʒ वेज्/ *verb* [T] **1** to force sth apart or to prevent sth from moving by using a wedge फन्नी या पच्चर फँसा कर वस्तुओं को अलग-अलग करना, उन्हें हिलने से रोकना या एक स्थान पर जमा देना *to wedge a door open* **2** to force sth/sb to fit into a small space किसी व्यक्ति या वस्तु को तंग जगह पर घुसा देना या फँसा देना *The cupboard was wedged between the table and the door.*

**Wednesday** /ˈwenzdeɪ; -di ˈवेन्ज़्डे; -डी/ *noun* [C, U] (*abbr.* **Wed.**) the day of the week after Tuesday बुधवार

> **NOTE** दिनों के नाम लिखते समय पहला अक्षर बड़ा होता है। दिनों के नामों के वाक्य-प्रयोग के उदाहरणों के लिए **Monday** देखिए।

**weed[1]** /wiːd वीड्/ *noun* **1** [C] a wild plant that is not wanted in a garden because it prevents other plants from growing properly बग़ीचे में उग आने वाला एक हानिकर जंगली पौधा, ख़र-पतवार, अपतृण (यह दूसरे पौधों को बढ़ने नहीं देता और इसलिए उसे निकाल दिया जाता है) **2** [U] a mass of very small green plants that floats on the surface of an area of water तालाब, पोखर आदि में तैरता छोटे-छोटे हरे पौधों का गुच्छा

**weed[2]** /wiːd वीड्/ *verb* [I, T] to remove weeds from a piece of ground, etc. खेत आदि से खर-पतवार निकालना, निराई करना

**PHR V** **weed sth/sb out** to remove the things or people that you do not think are good enough अवांछित व्यक्तियों या बेकार की वस्तुओं को निकाल बाहर करना, छाँटना *He weeded out all the letters with spelling mistakes in them.*

**weedy** /ˈwiːdi ˈवीडि/ *adj.* (*informal*) small and weak छोटा, ठिगना और कमज़ोर *a small weedy man*

**week** /wiːk वीक्/ *noun* [C] **1** a period of seven days, especially from Monday to Sunday or from Sunday to Saturday सात दिनों की अवधि (विशेषत: सोमवार से शनिवार या रविवार से शनिवार तक), सप्ताह, हफ़्ता, अठवारा *We arrived **last week**.* ○ *He left two weeks ago.*

> **NOTE** ब्रिटिश अंग्रेज़ी में दो सप्ताह की अवधि (पखवाड़ा) को **fortnight** कहा जाता है।

**2** the part of the week when people go to work, etc., usually from Monday to Friday सप्ताह का वह अंश (प्राय: सोमवार से शुक्रवार तक) जिसमें लोग काम पर जाते हैं, कार्य-सप्ताह *She works hard during the week so that she can enjoy herself at the weekend.*

**IDM** **today, tomorrow, Monday, etc. week** seven days after today, tomorrow, Monday, etc. आज, कल, सोमवार आदि के एक सप्ताह बाद

**week in, week out** every week without a rest or change लगातार प्रति सप्ताह, हर हफ़्ते (बिना विश्राम या परिवर्तन के) *He's played for the same team week in, week out for 20 years.*

**a week yesterday, last Monday, etc.** seven days before yesterday, Monday, etc. कल, सोमवार आदि से एक सप्ताह पहले

**weekday** /ˈwiːkdeɪ ˈवीक्डे/ *noun* [C] any day except Saturday or Sunday शनिवार या रविवार को छोड़कर कोई दिन, कार्य-सप्ताह का कोई दिन, कार्य-दिवस *I only work on weekdays.*

**weekend** /ˌwiːkˈend ˌवीक्ˈएन्ड्/ *noun* [C] Saturday and Sunday शनिवार और रविवार; सप्ताहांत *What are you doing **at the weekend**?* ✪ पर्याय **at the weekend** (ब्रिटिश अंग्रेज़ी में) और **on the weekend** (अमेरिकी अंग्रेज़ी) में

**weekly[1]** /ˈwiːkli ˈवीक्लि/ *adj., adv.* happening or appearing once a week or every week साप्ताहिक, हफ़्तावार, प्रतिसप्ताह, हर हफ़्ते *a weekly report* ○ *We are paid weekly.*

**weekly²** /ˈwiːkli ˈवीक्लि / *noun* [C] (*pl.* **weeklies**) a newspaper or magazine that is published every week साप्ताहिक समाचार-पत्र या पत्रिका

**weep** /wiːp वीप् / *verb* [I, T] (*pt, pp* **wept** /wept वेप्ट् /) (*formal*) to let tears fall because of strong emotion; to cry आँसू बहाना, विलाप करना, रोना; ज़ोर-ज़ोर से रोना *She wept at the news of his death.*

**weigh** /weɪ वे / *verb* **1** [T] to measure how heavy sth is, especially by using a machine (**scales**) किसी वस्तु का भार मापना, वज़न करना, को तोलना (विशेषतः मशीन या तराज़ू से) *I weigh myself every week.* ○ *Can you weigh this parcel for me, please?* **2** *linking verb* to have or show a certain weight (व्यक्ति या वस्तु का ख़ास भार, वज़न होना या दिखाना *I weigh 56 kilos.* ○ *How much does this weigh?* **3** [T] **weigh sth (up)** to consider sth carefully किसी बात पर सावधानी से विचार करना *You need to weigh up your chances of success.* **4** [T] **weigh sth (against sb/sth)** to consider if one thing is better, more important, etc. than another or not (महत्त्व आदि की दृष्टि से) एक वस्तु की दूसरे से तुलना करना *We shall weigh the advantages of the plan against the risks.* **5** [I] **weigh against sb/sth** to be considered as a disadvantage when sb/sth is being judged आकलन के समय किसी बात का प्रतिकूल या बाधक होना, ख़िलाफ़ चला जाना *She didn't get the job because her lack of experience weighed against her.*

**PHR V** **weigh sb down** to make sb feel worried and sad चिंता और परेशानी महसूस करना, दब जाना *He felt weighed down by all his responsibilities.*

**weigh sb/sth down** to make it difficult for sb/sth to move (by being heavy) (वज़न के कारण) व्यक्ति या वस्तु को हिलने-डुलने में कठिनाई होना *I was weighed down by heavy shopping.*

**weigh on sb/sth** to make sb worry भार बनना, परेशान करना *The problem has been* ***weighing on my mind*** (= I have felt worried about it).

**weigh sb/sth up** to consider sb/sth carefully and form an opinion व्यक्ति या वस्तु पर सावधानी से विचार कर राय बनाना *I weighed up my chances and decided it was worth applying.*

**weight¹** /weɪt वेट् / *noun* **1** [U] how heavy sth/sb is; the fact of being heavy भार, वज़न तोल; भारी या वज़नदार होने की स्थिति *The doctor advised him to* ***lose weight*** (= become thinner and less heavy). ○ *He's* ***put on weight*** (= got fatter). **2** [C] a heavy object कोई वज़नदार या भारी वस्तु *The doctor has told me not to lift heavy weights.* **3** [C] a piece of metal that weighs a known amount that can be used to measure an amount of sth, or that can be lifted as a form of exercise तोलने का बाट या बटखरा, (भारोत्तोलन में) व्यायाम के रूप में उठाया जाने वाला वज़न *a 500-gram weight* ○ *She lifts weights in the gym.* **4** [*sing.*] something that you are worried about बोझ, भार, चिंता की बात *Telling her the truth took* ***a weight off*** *his* ***mind***.

**IDM** **carry weight** ⇨ **carry** देखिए।

**pull your weight** ⇨ **pull¹** देखिए।

**weight²** /weɪt वेट् / *verb* [T] **1 weight sth (down) (with sth)** to hold sth down with a heavy object or objects वज़नदार चीज़ बाँधकर किसी वस्तु को लटकाना *to weight down a fishing net* **2** (*usually passive*) to organize sth so that a particular person or group has an advantage/disadvantage व्यक्ति-विशेष या समूह के प्रति पक्षपातपूर्ण या भेदभावपूर्ण तरीक़े से कोई व्यवस्था करना *The system is* ***weighted in favour of/against*** *people with children.*

**weightless** /ˈweɪtləs ˈवेट्लस् / *adj.* having no weight, for example when travelling in space भारहीन (जैसे अंतरिक्ष यात्रा के दौरान) ▶ **weightlessness** *noun* [U] भारहीनता

**weightlifting** /ˈweɪtlɪftɪŋ ˈवेट्लिफ़्टिङ् / *noun* [U] the sport or activity of lifting heavy metal objects वज़नदार धातु-निर्मित वस्तुएँ उठाने का खेल या क्रिया भारोत्तोलन ▶ **weightlifter** *noun* [C] भारोत्तोलक

**weight training** *noun* [U] the activity of lifting heavy objects (**weights**) as a form of exercise भारोत्तोलन का प्रशिक्षण *I do weight training to keep fit.*

**weighty** /ˈweɪti ˈवेटि / *adj.* (**weightier; weightiest**) serious and important गंभीर और महत्त्वपूर्ण *a weighty question*

**weir** /wɪə(r) विअ(र्) / *noun* [C] a type of wall that is built across a river to stop or change the direction of the flow of water नदी के आर-पार बनी एक प्रकार की दीवार, छोटा बाँध (जल-प्रवाह को रोकने या उसकी दिशा बदलने के लिए)

**weird** /wɪəd विअड् / *adj.* strange and unusual विचित्र और असामान्य; अनोखा और अलौकिक *a weird noise/experience* ▶ **weirdly** *adv.* विचित्र रूप से, अनोखेपन के साथ

**welcome¹** /ˈwelkəm ˈवेल्कम् / *verb* [T] **1** to be friendly to sb when he/she arrives somewhere (अतिथि का) स्वागत करना, अगवानी करना *Everyone came to the door to welcome us.* **2** to be pleased to receive or accept sth कुछ प्राप्त या स्वीकार कर प्रसन्न होना, ख़ुशी से ग्रहण करना *I've no idea what to do next, so I'd welcome any suggestions.* ▶ **welcome** *noun* [C] स्वागत, अभिनंदन *Let's give a warm welcome to our next guest.*

**welcome²** /ˈwelkəm ˈवेल्कम् / *adj.* **1** received with pleasure; giving pleasure सहर्ष स्वागत; हर्षप्रद, सुखद *You're always welcome here.* ○ *welcome news* ✪ विलोम **unwelcome 2 welcome to sth/to do sth** allowed to do sth सहर्ष कुछ करने की अनुमति *You're welcome to use my bicycle.* **3** used to say that sb can have sth that you do not want yourself अपनी चीज़ किसी को स्वेच्छा से (आवश्यकता न होने के कारण) देने के लिए प्रयुक्त शब्द *Take the car if you want. You're welcome to it. It's always breaking down.* ▶ **welcome** *exclamation* आपका स्वागत; आपका अभिनंदन *Welcome to Delhi!* ○ *Welcome home!*

IDM **make sb welcome** to receive sb in a friendly way किसी का हार्दिक स्वागत करना

**you're welcome** (*spoken*) used as a polite reply when sb thanks you for sth किसी के द्वारा दिए गए धन्यवाद का विनम्र उत्तर *'Thank you for your help.' 'You're welcome.'*

**weld** /weld वेल्ड् / *verb* [I, T] to join pieces of metal by heating them and pressing them together धातु के दो खंडों को गरम कर एक साथ दबाते हुए जोड़ देना, झलाई करना; वेल्ड करना

**welfare** /ˈwelfeə(r) ˈवेल्फ़ेअ(र्) / *noun* [U] **1** the general health, happiness of a person, an animal or a group (व्यक्ति, पशु या समूह का) कुशल-क्षेम, हित, भलाई, ख़ैरियत *The doctor is concerned about the child's welfare.* **2** the help and care that is given to people who have problems with health, money, etc. (स्वास्थ्य आदि की समस्याओं से ग्रस्त व्यक्तियों की) कल्याणकारी सहायता, कल्याण-कार्य *education and welfare services*

**welfare state** *noun* [*sing.*] a system organized by a government to provide free services and money for people who have no job, who are ill, etc.; a country that has this system ज़रूरतमंद लोगों की सहायता के लिए शासन द्वारा प्रवर्तित व्यवस्था, कल्याण-व्यवस्था; कल्याणकारी राज्य

**well¹** /wel वेल् / *adv.* **(better; best) 1** in a good way भली-भाँति, संतोषजनक ढंग से *I hope your work is **going well**.* ○ *You passed your exam! **Well done!*** ✪ विलोम **badly 2** completely or fully पूरी तरह से या अच्छी तरह से *Shake the bottle well before opening.* ○ *How well do you know Hema?* **3** very much कहीं अधिक, काफ़ी ज़्यादा *They arrived home well past midnight.* ○ *This book is **well worth** reading.* **4** (*used with can, could, may or might*) probably or possibly (can, could, may या might के साथ प्रयुक्त) शायद या संभवतः *He might well be right.* **5** (*used with can, could, may or might*) with good reason (can, could, may या might के साथ प्रयुक्त) उचित कारण से, ठीक ही *'Where's Bani?' 'You may well ask (= I don't know either)!'*

IDM **as well (as sb/sth)** in addition to sb/sth के अतिरिक्त, साथ ही, भी *Can I come as well?* ○ *He's worked in Japan as well as in Italy.* ➪ **also** पर नोट देखिए।

**augur well/ill for sb/sth** ➪ **augur** देखिए।

**bode well/ill (for sb/sth)** ➪ **bode** देखिए।

**do well 1** to be successful सफल होना *Their daughter has done well at university.* **2** to be getting better after an illness बीमारी के बाद स्वास्थ्य-लाभ करना *Mr Singh is doing well after his operation.*

**do well to do sth** used to say that sth is the right and sensible thing to do यह कहने के लिए प्रयुक्त कि ऐसा या वैसा करना बुद्धिमानी होगी *He would do well to check the facts before accusing people.*

**may/might (just) as well** used for saying that sth is the best thing you can do in the situation, even though you may not want to do it परिस्थिति के अनुसार कोई ख़ास बात ही ठीक है, यह बताने के लिए प्रयुक्त (न चाहते हुए भी) *I may as well tell you the truth—you'll find out anyway.*

**mean well** ➪ **mean¹** देखिए।

**well and truly** completely पूर्णतया, पूरी तरह से, बख़ूबी *We were well and truly lost.*

**well/badly off** ➪ **off¹** देखिए।

**well²** /wel वेल् / *adj.* **(better; best)** (*not before a noun*) **1** in good health स्वस्थ, ठीक, अच्छा, चंगा, भला-चंगा *How are you? I'm very well, thanks.* ○ ***Get well soon*** (= written in a card that you send to some body who is ill). **2** in a good state ठीक-ठाक *I hope all is well with you.*

> NOTE **Well** से आरंभ होने वाले समस्त यौगिक विशेषण, जब वे क्रिया के बाद अकेले प्रयुक्त हों, हाइफ़न के 'बिना' लिखे जाते हैं, परंतु जब ये (विशेषण) संज्ञा से पहले प्रयुक्त होते हैं तो उनमें हाइफ़न लगाए जाते हैं— *She is well dressed.* ○ *a well-dressed woman.*

IDM **all very well (for sb)** (*informal*) used for showing that you are not happy or do not agree with sth किसी बात पर अपनी अप्रसन्नता या असहमति दिखाने के लिए प्रयुक्त; सब ठीक ही है (व्यंग्योक्ति) *It's all very well for her to criticize* (= it's easy for her to criticize) *but it doesn't help the situation.*

**(just) as well (to do sth)** sensible; a good idea बुद्धिमानी की बात; अच्छा ख़याल, कोई हर्ज नहीं, बुरा क्या है *It would be just as well to ask his permission.*

**it is just as well (that)** ➪ **just** देखिए।

**well³** /wel वेल्/ *exclamation* **1** used for showing surprise आश्चर्य की अभिव्यक्ति के लिए प्रयुक्त *Well, thank goodness you've arrived.* **2** used for expressing uncertainty अनिश्चय की अभिव्यक्ति, अच्छा! *'Do you like it?' 'Well, I'm not really sure.'* **3** used when you begin the next part of a story or when you are thinking about what to say next कहानी को आगे बढ़ाने या अगली बात कहने के लिए प्रयुक्त *Well, the next thing that happened was the girl vanished.* ○ *Well now, let me see what I can do for you.* **4** used to show that you are waiting for sb to say sth वक्ता से कुछ सुनने की प्रतीक्षा का भाव व्यक्त करने के लिए प्रयुक्त *Well? Are you going to tell us what happened?* **5** used to show that you want to finish a conversation बातचीत समाप्त करने की इच्छा व्यक्त करने के लिए प्रयुक्त *Well, it's been nice talking to you.* **6** (*also* **oh well**) used for showing that you know there is nothing you can do to change a situation किसी मामले में अपनी विवशता व्यक्त करने के लिए प्रयुक्त *Oh well, there's nothing we can do about it.*

**well⁴** /wel वेल्/ *noun* [C] **1** a deep hole in the ground from which water is obtained (पानी का) कुआँ, कूप *to draw water from a well* **2** = **oil well**

**well⁵** /wel वेल्/ *verb* [I] **well (out/up)** (used about a liquid) to come to the surface (द्रव का) उमड़ आना, बहने लगना *Tears welled up in her eyes*

**we'll** /wi:l वील्/ ➪ **we shall, we will** का संक्षिप्त रूप

**well balanced** *adj.* **1** (used about a person) calm and sensible (व्यक्ति) शांत और समझदार **2** (used about a meal, etc.) containing enough of the healthy types of food your body needs (आहार, आदि) जिसमें स्वास्थ्य-रक्षक या वर्धक तत्व पर्याप्त मात्रा में हों; संतुलित *a well-balanced diet*

**well behaved** *adj.* behaving in a way that most people think is correct सभ्य, सुशील, शिष्ट

**well-being** *noun* [U] a state of being healthy and happy स्वस्थ और प्रसन्न होने की स्थिति; कुशल-क्षेम, ख़ैरियत

**well done** *adj.* (used about meat, etc.) cooked for a long time (गोश्त आदि) अच्छी तरह और देर तक पकाया हुआ ➪ **rare** और **medium** देखिए।

**well dressed** *adj.* wearing attractive and fashionable clothes सुंदर और फ़ैशनेबल वस्त्र धारण किए, सुवस्त्रित, सजाधजा, बना-ठना

**well earned** *adj.* that you deserve, especially because you have been working hard जिसके आप हक़दार हैं (क्योंकि आपने बहुत मेहनत की है); सु-अर्जित *a well-earned holiday*

**well fed** *adj.* having good food regularly नियमित रूप से अच्छी ख़ुराक लेने वाला; हृष्ट-पुष्ट

**well informed** *adj.* knowing a lot about one or several subjects किसी एक या अनेक विषयों की प्रचुर जानकारी रखने वाला; बहुविज्ञ, बहुश्रुत

**wellington** /ˈwelɪŋtən ˈवेलिङ्टन्/ (*also informal* **welly** /ˈweli ˈवेलि/) *noun* [C] (*pl.* **wellingtons; wellies**) (*BrE*) one of a pair of long rubber boots that you wear to keep your feet and the lower part of your legs dry रबड़ का जूता (जिससे पैर गरम रहते हैं और टाँग के निचले हिस्सों में पसीना नहीं आता; वेलिंगटन जूता) *a pair of wellingtons*

**well kept** *adj.* looked after very carefully so that it has a tidy appearance जिसकी देख-रेख अच्छे ढंग से हो रही है ताकि वह सुंदर दीखे; सुसंरक्षित *a well-kept garden*

**well known** *adj.* known by a lot of people; famous लोगों के बीच जाना-माना; प्रसिद्ध, मशहूर, प्रतिष्ठित ✪ विलोम **unknown**

**well meaning** *adj.* (used about a person) wanting to be kind or helpful, but often not having this effect (व्यक्ति) सदाशय, भला चाहने वाला (परंतु प्रायः अभीष्ट प्रभाव से वंचित)

**well meant** *adj.* intended to be kind or helpful but not having this result नेकनीयती से किया गया, सदाशयपूर्ण (परंतु प्रायः अभीष्ट प्रभाव से वंचित)

**well read** *adj.* having read many books and therefore having a lot of knowledge बहुपठित और बहुविज्ञ

**well-to-do** *adj.* having a lot of money, property, etc. धनी-मानी, संपत्तिशाली, अमीर ✪ पर्याय **rich**

**well-wisher** *noun* [C] somebody who hopes that a person or thing will be successful शुभेच्छु, हिताभिलाषी, मंगलाकांक्षी, शुभचिंतक *She received lots of letters from well-wishers before the competition.*

**went** ➪ **go¹** का past tense रूप

**wept** ➪ **weep** का past tense और past participle रूप

**were** /wə(r) व(र्)/ ➪ **be** देखिए।

**we're** /wɪə(r) विअ(र्)/ ➪ **we are** का संक्षिप्त रूप

**west¹** /west वेस्ट्/ *noun* [*sing.*] (*abbr.* **W**) **1** (*also* **the west**) the direction you look towards in order to see the sun go down; one of the four main directions that we give names to (**the points of the compass**) पश्चिम दिशा; क़ुतुबनुमा या दिग्दर्शक पर पश्चिम दिशा दर्शाने वाला बिंदु *Which way is west?* ○ *There's a road* **to the west of** *here.* ➪ **compass** पर चित्र देखिए। **2 the west; the West** the part of any country, city, etc. that is

further to the west than other parts किसी देश, नगर आदि का पश्चिम की ओर का भाग या पश्चिमी भाग *The climate in the West is much wetter than the East.* **3 the West** [*sing.*] the countries of North America and Western Europe पश्चिमी यूरोप और उत्तरी अमेरिका के देश, पश्चिमी देश, पश्चिम ➪ **north, south** और **east** देखिए।

**west²** /west वेस्ट्/ *adj., adv.* in, to or towards the west पश्चिम में, को या की ओर *The island is twenty kilometres west of here.* ○ *to travel west*

**westbound** /ˈwestbaʊnd ˈवेस्ट्बाउन्ड्/ *adj.* travelling or leading towards the west पश्चिम की ओर जाने या ले जाने वाला; पश्चिमाभिमुख *the westbound*

**westerly** /ˈwestəli ˈवेस्टलि/ *adj.* **1** to, towards or in the west पश्चिम में, को या की ओर *in a westerly direction* **2** (used about winds) coming from the west (हवाएँ) पश्चिम की ओर से आने वाली; पश्चिमी, पछवाँ

**western** (*also* **Western**) /ˈwestən ˈवेस्टन्/ *adj.* **1** in or of the west पश्चिम में या पश्चिमी *western India* **2** from or connected with the western part of the world, especially Europe or North America विश्व के पश्चिमी भाग (विशेषतः युरोप या उत्तर अमेरिका) का या उससे संबंधित; पश्चिमी

**westerner** /ˈwestənə(r) ˈवेस्टन(र्)/ *noun* [C] a person who was born or who lives in the western part of the world, especially Europe or North America पश्चिम-निवासी (व्यक्ति) (विश्व के पश्चिमी भाग, विशेषतः युरोप या उत्तर अमेरिका में जन्मा या वहाँ रहने वाला व्यक्ति) *Westerners arriving in China usually experience culture shock.*

**westernize** (*also* **-ise**) /ˈwestənaɪz ˈवेस्टनाइज़्/ *verb* [T] (*usually passive*) to make a country or people more like Europe and North America देशों या लोगों को पाश्चात्य ढंग का बना देना, (उन्हें) पाश्चात्य रंग में रँग देना

**the West Indies** *noun* [*pl., with sing. or pl. verb*] a group of islands in the Caribbean Sea that consists of the Bahamas, the Antilles and the Leeward and Windward Islands वेस्टइंडीज़ (द्वीप समूह) (कैरिबियन सागर के किनारे स्थित द्वीपों—बहामाज़, एंटिलेस, लीवार्ड और विंडवार्ड द्वीप—का समूह) ▶ **West Indian** *noun* [C] वेस्ट इंडीज़-निवासी; वेस्ट इंडियन *The West Indians won their match against Australia.* ▶ **West Indian** *adj.* वेस्ट-इंडीज़ का या से संबंधित

**westward** /ˈwestwəd ˈवेस्ट्वड्/ *adj.* towards the west पश्चिम की ओर, पश्चिमाभिमुख; पछाँह *in a westward direction* ▶ **westward** (*also* **westwards**) *adv.* पश्चिम की ओर *to fly westwards*

**wet¹** /wet वेट्/ *adj.* (**wetter; wettest**) **1** covered in a liquid, especially water (पानी या अन्य द्रव से) गीला, तर, भीगा हुआ, आर्द्र, नम *wet clothes/hair/grass/roads* ○ *Don't **get** your feet **wet**.*

> **NOTE** **Moist** का अर्थ है हलका गीला (या नम)। **Damp** ऐसा हलका गीला या नम है जिसकी नमी बुरी लगती है—*Don't sit on the grass. It's damp.*

**2** (used about the weather, etc.) with a lot of rain (मौसम आदि) बरसाती *a wet day* **3** (used about paint, etc.) not yet dry or hard (पेंट आदि) जो अभी सूखा या कड़ा नहीं हुआ, गीला, ताज़ा लगाया हुआ *The ink is still wet.* ✪ विलोम **dry** (अर्थ सं. **1, 2** और **3** के लिए) **4** (*informal*) (used about a person) without energy or enthusiasm निस्तेज या निर्जीव ▶ **the wet** *noun* [*sing.*] बरसात, वर्षा का मौसम *Come in out of the wet* (= the rainy weather).

**IDM** **a wet blanket** (*informal*) a person who spoils other people's fun, especially because he or she refuses to take part in sth रंग में भंग करने वाला, मज़ा किरकिरा करने वाला (लोगों की मौजमस्ती में साथ न देकर)

**wet through** extremely wet बहुत गीला, तरबतर

**wet²** /wet वेट्/ *verb* [T] (*pres. part.* **wetting;** *pt, pp* **wet** or **wetted**) **1** to make sth wet (किसी वस्तु को) गीला करना, तर करना **2** (used especially of young children) to make yourself or your bed, clothes, etc. wet by **urinating** (छोटे बच्चों का) अपनें कपड़ों, बिस्तर आदि को गीला कर देना (प्रायः पेशाब करके)

**wetland** /ˈwetlənd ˈवेट्लन्ड्/ *noun* [C] (*also* **wetlands** [*pl.*]) (in geography) an area of land that is always wet (भूगोल में) दलदल

**wet suit** *noun* [C] a rubber suit that covers the whole of the body, used by people doing sports in the water or swimming under the water सारे शरीर को ढक लेने वाला रबड़ का सूट, आर्द्र सूट (इसे जलक्रीड़ाओं के खिलाड़ी या पानी के भीतर तैरने वाले पहनते हैं)

**we've** /wiːv वीव्/ ➪ **we have** का संक्षिप्त रूप

**whack** /wæk वैक्/ *verb* [T] (*informal*) to hit sb/sth hard व्यक्ति या वस्तु पर कसकर चोट करना

**whacky** = **wacky**

**whale** /weɪl वेल्/ *noun* [C] a very large animal that lives in the sea and looks like a very large fish ह्वेल मछली, तिमिंगल

**whaling** /ˈweɪlɪŋ ˈवेलिङ्/ *noun* [U] the hunting of whales ह्वेल मछली का शिकार

**wharf** /wɔ:f वॉफ़् / *noun* [C] (*pl.* **wharves** /wɔ:vz वॉव्ज़् /) a platform made of stone or wood at the side of a river where ships and boats can be tied up घाट, नावघाट, जहाज़-घाट (नदी के किनारे पत्थरों या लकड़ी से बना चबूतरा जहाँ नावें या जहाज़ बाँधे जाते हैं)

**what** /wɒt वॉट् / *det., pronoun* **1** used for asking for information about sb/sth (प्रश्न पूछने के लिए प्रयुक्त) क्या *What kind of music do you like?* ○ *She asked him what he was doing.* ➪ **which** पर नोट देखिए। **2** the thing or things that have been mentioned or said (पूर्व-वर्णित वस्तु का निर्देश करने वाला शब्द) जो *What he says is true.* ○ *I haven't got much, but you can borrow what money I have.* **3 used for emphasizing sth** (किसी बात पर बल देने के लिए प्रयुक्त) कितना? *What a kind thing to do!* **4** used to express surprise or to tell sb to say or repeat sth (आश्चर्य व्यक्त करने के लिए या बात को दुबारा कहने के लिए प्रयुक्त *'I've asked Anindita to marry me.' 'What!'*

IDM **how/what about ...?** ➪ **about²** देखिए।

**what for** for what purpose or reason किस प्रयोजन या कारण से *What's this little switch for?* ○ *What did you say that for* (= why did you say that)*?*

**what if ...?** what would happen if ...? अगर हुआ तो क्या होगा? *What if the car breaks down?*

**whatever** /wɒtˈevə(r) वॉट्ˈएव(र्)/ *det., pronoun, adv.* **1** any or every; anything or everything कोई या प्रत्येक; कोई वस्तु या प्रत्येक वस्तु कोई बात या प्रत्येक बात *You can say whatever you like.* ○ *He took whatever help he could get.* **2** used to say that it does not matter what happens or what sb does, because the result will be the same जो कुछ, जो भी, कुछ भी *I still love you, whatever you may think.* ○ *Whatever she says, she doesn't really mean it.* **3** (used for expressing surprise or worry) what (आश्चर्य या चिंता व्यक्त करने के लिए प्रयुक्त) क्या *Whatever could have happened to them?* **4** (*also* **whatsoever**) at all कुछ भी, किसी भी तरह *I've no reason whatever to doubt him.* ○ *'Any questions?' 'None whatsoever.'*

IDM **or whatever** (*informal*) or any other or others of a similar kind या इस तरह की दूसरी चीज़ या चीज़ें *You don't need to wear anything smart —jeans and a sweater or whatever.*

**whatever you do** used to emphasize that sb must not do sth (किसी काम को करने से बलपूर्वक मना करने के लिए प्रयुक्त) और चाहे जो करो *Don't touch the red switch, whatever you do.*

**wheat** /wi:t वीट् / *noun* [U] **1** a type of grain which can be made into flour गेहूँ **2** the plant which produces this grain गेहूँ का पौधा *a field of wheat* ➪ **cereal** पर चित्र देखिए।

**wheel¹** /wi:l वील् / *noun* [C] **1** one of the circular objects under a car, bicycle, etc. that turns when it moves (कार, साइकिल आदि का) पहिया, चक्का *You should to carry a spare wheel in your car.* **2** [*sing.*] = **steering wheel** *Her husband was **at the wheel*** (= he was driving) *when the accident happened.* ➪ **bicycle** पर चित्र देखिए।

**wheel²** /wi:l वील् / *verb* **1** [T] to push along an object that has wheels; to move sb about in/on a vehicle with wheels पहिएदार वस्तु को खींचना, ठेलना; पहिएदार वस्तु में या पर (बैठाकर) किसी को खींचना, ठेलना *He wheeled his bicycle up the hill.* ○ *She was wheeled back to her bed on a trolley.* **2** [I] to fly round in circles आकाश में चक्कर लगाना *Birds wheeled above the ship.* **3** [I] to turn round suddenly अचानक घूम जाना *Esha wheeled round, with a look of horror on her face.*

**wheelbarrow** /ˈwi:lbærəʊ ˈवीलबैरो / (*also* **barrow**) *noun* [C] a type of small open container with one wheel and two handles that you use outside for carrying things इकपहिया ठेला ➪ **garden** पर चित्र देखिए।

**wheelchair** /ˈwi:ltʃeə(r) ˈवील्चेअर(र्)/ *noun* [C] a chair with large wheels that a person who cannot walk can move or be pushed about in पहिए वाली कुरसी (विशेषतः विकलांग व्यक्ति के लिए)

**wheel clamp** (*BrE*) = **clamp¹ 2**

**wheeze** /wi:z वीज़् / *verb* [I] to breathe noisily, for example if you have a chest illness घरघर करते हुए साँस लेना

**when** /wen वेन् / *adv., conj.* **1** at what time कब? किस समय? *When did she arrive?* ○ *I don't know when she arrived.* **2** used for talking about the time at which sth happens or happened जब, जिस समय या वक़्त *Sunday is the day when I can relax.* ○ *He jumped up when the phone rang.*

> NOTE ध्यान दें कि यदि भविष्य की बात की जा रही हो तो **when** के बाद वर्तमान काल का प्रयोग होता है —*I'll call you when I'm ready.*

**3** since; as; considering that क्योंकि, चूंकि; जब कि; के मद्दे नज़र या का विचार करते हुए *Why do you want more money when you've got enough already?*

> NOTE **When** का प्रयोग वहाँ होता है जहाँ (हमारी सोच या जानकारी के अनुसार) किसी घटना का घटित होना निश्चित (सा) हो और **if** का वहाँ प्रयोग होता है जहाँ ऐसा होना निश्चित न हो। इन वाक्यों में तुलना

कीजिए—*I'll ask her when she comes* (= you are sure that she will come). ○ *I'll ask her if she comes* (= you are not sure whether she will come or not).

**whence** /wens वेन्स्/ *adv.* (*old-fashioned*) (from) where जहाँ (से) *They returned whence they came.*

**whenever** /wen'evə(r) वेन्'एव़(र्)/ *conj., adv.* **1** at any time; no matter when जब भी, किसी भी समय; जब चाहें तब *You can borrow my car whenever you want.* ○ *Don't worry. You can give it back the next time you see me, or whenever.* **2** (used when you are showing that you are surprised or impatient) when (आश्चर्य या अधीरता दिखाने के लिए) कब? *Whenever did you find time to do all that cooking?*

**where** /weə(r) वेअ(र्)/ *adv., conj.* **1** in or to what place or position कहाँ (से)? कौन-सी जगह (पर) या स्थिति (में)? *Where can I buy a newspaper?* ○ *I asked him where he lived.* **2** in or to the place or situation mentioned जहाँ (बताए गए स्थान या स्थिति में या पर) *We came to a village, where we stopped for lunch.* ○ ***Where** maths **is concerned**, I'm hopeless.*

**whereabouts[1]** /ˌweərə'baʊts ˌवेअर'बाउट्स्/ *adv.* where; in or near what place कहाँ?; किस जगह पर या के आस-पास? *Whereabouts did you lose your purse?*

**whereabouts[2]** /'weərəbaʊts 'वेअरबाउट्स्/ *noun* [*pl.*] the place where sb/sth is (व्यक्ति-वस्तु का) पता -ठिकाना *The whereabouts of the stolen painting are unknown.*

**whereas** /ˌweər'æz ˌवेअर्'ऐज़्/ *conj.* used for showing a fact that is different जब कि (ऐसी स्थिति दर्शाने के लिए प्रयुक्त जो भिन्न है) *He eats meat, whereas she's a vegetarian.* ✪ पर्याय **while**

**whereby** /weə'baɪ वेअ'बाइ/ *adv.* (*written*) by which; because of which जिससे, जिसके द्वारा या जिसकी सहायता से; जिसके कारण *These countries have an agreement whereby foreign visitors can have free medical care.*

**whereupon** /ˌweərə'pɒn ˌवेअर'पॉन्/ *conj.* (*written*) after which जिसके बाद *He fell asleep, whereupon she walked quietly from the room.*

**wherever** /weər'evə(r) वेअर्'एव़(र्)/ *conj., adv.* **1** in or to any place जहाँ कहीं (किसी भी स्थान में या पर) *You can sit wherever you like.* **2** everywhere, in all places that कहीं भी, जहाँ भी (सर्वत्र, सब स्थानों पर) *Wherever I go, he goes.* **3** used for showing surprise (आश्चर्य व्यक्त करने के लिए प्रयुक्त) कहाँ (से)? *Wherever did you learn to cook like that?*

IDM **or wherever** or any other place जहाँ कहीं से *The students might be from Sweden, Denmark or wherever.*

**whet** /wet वेट्/ *verb* (**whe<u>tt</u>ing; whe<u>tt</u>ed**)

IDM **whet sb's appetite** to make sb want more of sth किसी वस्तु की चाह को बढ़ाना, तेज़ करना या उद्दीप्त करना *Our short stay in Goa whetted our appetite to spend more time there.*

**whether** /'weðə(r) 'वेद्र(र्)/ *conj.* **1** (used after verbs like 'ask', 'doubt', 'know', etc.) if; ('ask', 'doubt', 'know' आदि के जैसी क्रियाओं के साथ प्रयुक्त) यदि, अगर *He asked me whether we would be coming to the party.* **2** used for expressing a choice or doubt between two or more possibilities *I can't make up my mind **whether** to go **or not**.*

NOTE अर्थ सं. **1** के लिए **whether** और **if** दोनों का प्रयोग हो सकता है। 'To' + क्रिया से पहले केवल **whether** आ सकता है—*Have you decided **whether to** accept the offer yet?* पूर्वसर्ग (preposition) के बाद भी केवल **whether** का प्रयोग हो सकता है—*the problem **of whether** to accept the offer.*

IDM **whether or not** used to say that sth will be true in either of the situations that are mentioned चाहे (कुछ) हो या न हो (सकारात्मक और नकारात्मक दोनों स्थितियों की समानता व्यक्त करने के लिए प्रयुक्त, दोनों में मुक्त विकल्प) *We shall play on Saturday whether it rains or not.* ○ *Whether or not it rains, we shall play on Saturday.*

**whey** /weɪ वे/ *noun* [U] the thin liquid that is left from sour milk after the solid parts (**curds**) have been removed छेने या दही द्वारा छोड़ा गया पानी, छेने या दही का पानी; तोड़

**which** /wɪtʃ विच्/ *det., pronoun* **1** used in questions to ask sb to be exact, when there are a number of people or things to choose from (अनेक व्यक्तियों या वस्तुओं में बिल्कुल सही को चुनने के लिए प्रयुक्त) कौन-सा? *Which hand do you write with?* ○ *She asked me which book I preferred.*

NOTE **Which** और **what** में अंतर—यदि सीमित समूह या संख्या में से बिलकुल सही व्यक्ति या वस्तु को चुनना हो तो **which** का प्रयोग होता है—*Which car is yours? The Ford or the Volvo* (= there are only two cars there)? यदि समूह या संख्या सीमित न हो तो **what** का प्रयोग होता है—*What car would you choose* (= of all the makes of car that exist), *if you could have anyone you wanted?* ○ *What is your name?*

2 used for saying exactly what thing or things you are talking about जो; जो कि (बिल्कुल सही वस्तु या वस्तुओं का निर्देश करने के लिए प्रयुक्त) *Cars which use unleaded petrol are more eco-friendly.* ○ (*formal*) *The situation* ***in which*** *he found himself was very difficult.*

**NOTE** अनौपचारिक अँग्रेज़ी में ऐसा प्रयोग होता है—*The situation* ***which*** *he found himself* ***in*** *was very difficult.* निम्नलिखित प्रकार के वाक्य में which का प्रयोग प्रायः नहीं किया जाता—*The situation he found himself in was very difficult.*

3 used for giving more information about a thing or animal (किसी वस्तु या पशु के बारे में और अधिक जानकारी देने के लिए प्रयुक्त), जो *My first car, which I bought as a student, was a Maruti 800.* **NOTE** वाक्य के उस भाग के अंत में अल्पविराम (,) लगता है जिसके बाद 'which' द्वारा प्रस्तावित वाक्य का शेष भाग आता है। 4 used for making a comment on what has just been said (कथन के पहले भाग पर टिप्पणी करने के लिए प्रयुक्त, कथन के पहले भाग को दूसरे से जोड़ने के लिए प्रयुक्त) जो, और यह बात... *We had to wait 16 hours for our plane, which was really annoying.* **NOTE** ध्यान दीजिए, 'which' से पहले अल्पविराम (,) लगा है।

**whichever** /wɪtʃˈevə(r) विच्ˈएव़(र्)/ *det., pronoun* 1 any person or thing; it does not matter which one you choose जो कोई या जो कुछ; चाहे जो जिसको चाहें लें का भाव व्यक्त करने के लिए प्रयुक्त) *You can choose whichever book you want.* 2 (used for expressing surprise) which (आश्चर्य व्यक्त करने के लिए प्रयुक्त) किसी या कोई *You're very late. Whichever way did you come?*

**whiff** /wɪf विफ़्/ *noun* [C, *usually sing.*] **a whiff (of sth)** a smell, especially one which only lasts for a short time गंध का झोंका, महक *He* ***caught a whiff*** *of her perfume.*

**while**[1] /waɪl वाइल्/ (*formal* **whilst** / waɪlst वाइल्स्ट्/) *conj.* 1 during the time that; when उस समय जब; जब *He always phones while we're having lunch.* 2 at the same time as उसी समय जब, के साथ-साथ *He always listens to the radio while he's driving to work.* 3 (*formal*) used when you are contrasting two ideas (दो स्थितियों में वैषम्य या अंतर दिखाने के लिए प्रयुक्त) जबकि *Some countries are rich, while others are extremely poor.* ✪ पर्याय **whereas**

**while**[2] /waɪl वाइल्/ *noun* [*sing.*] a (usually short) period of time समय की अवधि (प्रायः छोटी); क्षणभर *Let's sit down here for a while.*

**IDM** **once in a while** ⇨ **once** देखिए।

**worth sb's while** ⇨ **worth**[1] देखिए।

**while**[3] /waɪl वाइल्/ *verb*

**PHR V** **while sth away** to pass time in a lazy or relaxed way बेफ़िक्री से समय बिताना, मटरगश्ती करना *We whiled away the evening chatting and listening to music.*

**whim** /wɪm विम्/ *noun* [C] a sudden idea or desire to do sth (often sth that is unusual or not necessary) सनक, झक, मौज, लहर (कुछ असाधारण या अनावश्यक करने की) *We bought the house* ***on a whim.***

**whimper** /ˈwɪmpə(r) ˈविम्प(र्)/ *verb* [I] to cry softly, especially with fear or pain मंद स्वर में रोना (विशेषतः डर या दर्द के कारण), पिनपिनाना, ठुनकना, बिसूरना ▸ **whimper** *noun* [C] पिनपिनाहट, ठुनक

**whine** /waɪn वाइन्/ *verb* 1 [I, T] to complain about sth in an annoying, crying voice बुरी लगती रोती-सी आवाज़ में किसी बात की शिकायत करना *The children were whining all afternoon.* 2 [I] to make a long high unpleasant sound because you are in pain or unhappy दर्द या दुख के कारण कराहना, चीख़ना-चिल्लाना *The dog is whining to go out.* ▸ **whine** *noun* [C] कराहट

**whip**[1] /wɪp विप्/ *noun* [C] a long thin piece of leather, etc. with a handle, that is used for making animals go faster and for hitting people as a punishment कोड़ा, चाबुक, हंटर *He* ***cracked the whip*** *and the horse leapt forward.*

**whip**[2] /wɪp/ *verb* (**whipping; whipped**) 1 [T] to hit a person or an animal hard with a whip, as a punishment or to make him/her/it go faster or work harder चाबुक, कोड़े या हंटर से किसी मनुष्य या जानवर को पीटना 2 [I] (*informal*) to move quickly, suddenly or violently तेज़ी से अचानक या झटके से निकलना *She whipped round to see what had made the noise behind her.* 3 [T] to remove or pull sth quickly and suddenly तेज़ी से और अचानक किसी चीज़ को निकालना या खींचना *He whipped out a pen and made a note of the number.* 4 [T] **whip sth (up)** to mix the white part of an egg or cream until it is light and thick (क्रीम, अंडे की सफ़ेदी आदि को) फेंटना *whipped cream*

**PHR V** **whip through sth** (*informal*) to do or finish sth very quickly बहुत तेज़ी से कुछ करना या समाप्त करना

**whip sb/sth up** to deliberately try to make people excited or feel strongly about sth जान-बूझ कर लोगों को उत्तेजित करना, उकसाना या भड़काना *to whip up excitement*

**whip sth up** (*informal*) to prepare food quickly जल्दी से कोई खाने की चीज़ तैयार करना *to whip up a quick snack*

**whir** = **whirr**

**whirl¹** /wɜːl वर्ल् / *verb* [I, T] to move, or to make sb/sth move, round and round very quickly in a circle तेज़ी से चक्कर खाना या खिलाना *The dancers whirled round the room.* ○ (*figurative*) *I couldn't sleep. My mind was whirling after all the excitement.*

**whirl²** /wɜːl वर्ल् / *noun* [*sing.*] **1** the action or sound of sth moving round and round very quickly किसी वस्तु के तेज़ी से घूमते जाने की क्रिया या आवाज़; घुमाव, घूर्णन *the whirl of the helicopter's blades* **2** a state of confusion or excitement विभ्रम या उत्तेजना (की स्थिति) *My head's **in a whirl**—I'm so excited.* **3** a number of events or activities happening one after the other एक-के-बाद-एक घटने वाली घटनाएँ या क्रियाएँ; भाग-दौड़, गहमागहमी *The next few days passed in a whirl of activity.*

**IDM give sth a whirl** (*informal*) to try sth to see if you like it or can do it किसी चीज़ को आज़माना (पसंद आने या कर सकने की दृष्टि से)

**whirlpool** /ˈwɜːlpuːl ˈवर्लपूल / *noun* [C] a place in a river or the sea where currents in the water move very quickly round in a circle पानी का भँवर (नदी या समुद्र में); जलावर्त

**whirlwind** /ˈwɜːlwɪnd ˈवर्लविन्ड् / *noun* [C] a very strong circular wind that forms a tall column of air moving round and round in a circle as it travels across the land or the sea चक्रवात, बवंडर, वातावर्त ➪ **storm** पर नोट देखिए।

**whirr** (*AmE* **whir**) /wɜː(r) व(र्) / *verb* [I] to make a continuous low sound like the parts of a machine moving खरखराना (मशीन के पुरज़े के चलने की-सी आवाज़ करना) *The noise of the fan whirring kept me awake.* ▶ **whirr** (*AmE* **whir**) *noun* [C, *usually sing.*] खरखराहट

**whisk¹** /wɪsk विस्क् / *noun* [C] a tool that you use for beating eggs, cream, etc. very fast अंडे, क्रीम आदि फेंटने का (मथानी जैसा) उपकरण, फेंटनी ➪ **kitchen** पर चित्र देखिए।

**whisk²** /wɪsk विस्क् / *verb* [T] **1** to beat or mix eggs, cream, etc. very fast using a fork or a whisk (फेंटनी या काँटे से) अंडे, क्रीम आदि को फेंटना *Whisk the egg whites until stiff.* **2** to take sb/sth somewhere very quickly (व्यक्ति या वस्तु को) फुरती से कहीं ले जाना *The actor was whisked away in a black limousine.*

**whisker** /ˈwɪskə(r) ˈविस्क(र्) / *noun* [C] one of the long hairs that grow near the mouth of some animals such as a mouse, cat, etc. चूहे, बिल्ली आदि के मुँह पर का लंबा बाल; गलमुच्छा ➪ **lion** पर चित्र देखिए।

**whisky** /ˈwɪski ˈविस्कि / *noun* (*pl.* **whiskies**) **1** [U] a strong alcoholic drink that is made from grain and is sometimes drunk with water and/or ice अनाज से बनी एक तेज़ शराब; ह्विस्की *Scotch whisky* **2** [C] a glass of whisky गिलास भर ह्विस्की

**whisper** /ˈwɪspə(r) ˈविस्प (र्) / *verb* [I, T] to speak very quietly into sb's ear, so that other people cannot hear what you are saying (किसी के कान में) फुसफुसाना, खुसर-फुसर करना, कानाफूसी करना ▶ **whisper** *noun* [C] फुसफुसाहट, खुसर-फुसर, कानाफूसी *to speak **in a whisper***

**whistle¹** /ˈwɪsl ˈविसल् / *noun* [C] **1** a small metal or plastic tube that you blow into to make a long high sound or music सीटी (जिसे मुँह से फूँक कर बजाया जाता है) *The referee blew his whistle to stop the game.* **2** the sound made by blowing a whistle or by blowing air out between your lips सीटी की आवाज़ या मुँह से निकाली गई सीटी जैसी आवाज़ *United scored just moments before **the final whistle**.*

**whistle²** /ˈwɪsl ˈविसल्/ *verb* **1** [I, T] to make a musical or a high sound by forcing air out between your lips or by blowing a whistle मुँह से सीटी जैसी आवाज़ निकालना या सीटी बजाना *He whistled a tune to himself.* **2** [I] to move somewhere quickly making a sound like a whistle सीटी जैसी आवाज़ करते हुए तेज़ी से निकल जाना *A bullet whistled past his head.*

**whistle-blower** *noun* [C] a person who informs on someone engaged in illegal activities अवैध कार्य में लीन व्यक्ति के विषय में जानकारी देने वाला व्यक्ति; सूचक ▶ **whistle-blowing** *noun, adj.* अवैध कार्य सूचना या सूचक

**whistle-stop** *adj.* (*only before a noun*) visiting a lot of different places in a very short time लघु समय में भिन्न स्थानों का भ्रमण करते हुए *a whistle-stop election campaign*

**white¹** /waɪt वाइट् / *adj.* **1** of the very light colour of fresh snow or milk सफ़ेद या श्वेत रंग का (ताज़े हिंम या दुग्ध के सामन), सफ़ेद, श्वेत, चिट्टा *a white shirt* ○ *white coffee* (= with milk) **2** (used about a person) belonging to or connected with a race of people who have pale skin (व्यक्ति) सफ़ेद रंग की जाति का, गोरा, सफ़ेद चमड़ी वाला **3 white (with sth)** (used about a person) very pale because you are ill, afraid, etc. (व्यक्ति) डर या बीमारी के कारण जो बहुत पीला पड़ गया है; विवर्ण *to be white with shock/anger/fear* ○ *She went **white as a sheet** when they told her.*

**IDM black and white** ➪ **black¹** देखिए।

**white²** /waɪt वाइट्/ *noun* **1** [U] the very light colour of fresh snow or milk सफ़ेद रंग (ताज़े हिम या दुग्ध जैसा बहुत हलका रंग); धवल, शुभ्रवर्ण *She was dressed* ***in white***. **2** [C, *usually pl.*] a member of a race of people with pale skin सफ़ेद त्वचा वाली जाति का सदस्य, गोरा आदमी **3** [C, U] the part of an egg that surrounds the yellow part **(yolk)** and that becomes white when it is cooked अंडे की सफ़ेदी *Beat the whites of four eggs.* **4** [C] the white part of the eye आँख का सफ़ेद भाग; श्वेतांश

IDM **in black and white** ➪ **black²** देखिए।

**whitebait** /ˈwaɪtbeɪt ˈवाइट्बेट्/ *noun* [*pl.*] very small young fish of several types that are fried and eaten whole खाने की बहुत छोटी मछली (का एक प्रकार)

**white-collar** *adj*. (used about work) done in an office not a factory; (used about people) who work in an office दफ़्तर का काम (न कि कारख़ाने में किया गया काम); दफ़्तर का बाबू, सफ़ेदपोश इनसान ➪ **blue-collar** देखिए।

**white elephant** *noun* [*sing.*] something that you no longer need and that is not useful any more, although it cost a lot of money बहुत ख़र्चीली पर अब बेकार वस्तु; सफ़ेद हाथी

**white-hot** *adj*. (of sth burning) so hot that it looks white (वस्तु) इतनी गरम की सफ़ेद दिखे, श्वेत तप्त

**the White House** *noun* [*sing.*] **1** the large building in Washington D.C. where the US president lives and works वाशिंगटन डी. सी. में स्थित अमेरिकी राष्ट्रपति का निवास और कार्य-स्थल; ह्वाइट हाउस **2** used to refer to the US president and the other people in the government who work with him/her अमेरिकी राष्ट्रपति और उनकी सरकार में कार्यरत व्यक्ति

**white lie** *noun* [C] a lie that is not very harmful or serious, especially one that you tell because the truth would hurt sb निर्दोष झूठ, सफ़ेद झूठ (ऐसा झूठ जो बहुत हानिकर या गंभीर नहीं और सच बोलने से होने वाले कष्ट से दूसरे को बचाने के लिए बोला जाता है)

**white light** *noun* [U] ordinary light that is colourless साधारण रंगहीन प्रकाश ➪ **prism** पर चित्र देखिए।

**whitewash¹** /ˈwaɪtwɒʃ ˈवाइट्वॉश्/ *noun* [U] **1** a white liquid that you use for painting walls पुताई की गीली सफ़ेदी **2** [*sing.*] trying to hide unpleasant facts about sb/sth व्यक्ति या वस्तु के दोषों पर परदा डालने की कोशिश लीपा-पोती *The opposition claimed the report was a whitewash.*

**whitewash²** /ˈwaɪtwɒʃ ˈवाइट्वॉश्/ *verb* [T] **1** to paint whitewash onto a wall दीवार पर सफ़ेद पुताई करना **2** to try to hide sth bad or wrong that you have done अपने किए (ख़राब या ग़लत काम) पर परदा डालना

**white-water rafting** *noun* the sport of travelling down a fast rough section of a river, lake, etc. in a rubber boat रबड़ की नौका में (नदी आदि की तेज़ और अशांत जलधारा खंड में) बैठकर जाने का खेल, अशांत जलधारा क्रीड़ा

**whizz¹** (*AmE* **whiz**) /wɪz विज़्/ *verb* [I] (*informal*) to move very quickly, often making a high continuous sound सनसनाते हुए तेज़ी से निकल जाना *The racing cars went whizzing by.*

**whizz²** (*AmE* **whiz**) /wɪz विज़् / *noun* [*sing.*] (*informal*) a person who is very good and successful at sth किसी काम में माहिर (और सफल) व्यक्ति *She's a whizz at crosswords.* ○ *He's our new marketing whizz-kid* (= a young person who is very good at sth).

**WHO** /ˌdʌbljuː eɪtʃ ˈəʊ ˌडब्ल्यू एच् ˈओ/ *abbr*. World Health Organization; an international organization that tries to fight and control disease डब्ल्यूएचओ; विश्व स्वास्थ्य संगठन जो रोगों की रोकथाम के लिए कार्य करता है

**who** /huː हू/ *pronoun* **1** used in questions to ask sb's name, identity, position, etc. (व्यक्ति का नाम आदि पूछने के लिए प्रश्नसूचक वाक्यों में प्रयुक्त), कौन? *Who was on the phone?* ○ *She wondered who he was.* **2** used for saying exactly which person or what kind of person you are talking about (विशेष या विशेष प्रकार के व्यक्ति का निर्देश करने वाला शब्द), जो *The woman who I work for is very nice.*

> NOTE अंतिम दो उदाहरणों में (जहाँ who कर्म है या पूर्वसर्ग के साथ प्रयुक्त है) 'who' का प्रयोग न करने की छूट है—*That's the man I met at Rohit's party.* ○ *The woman I work for is very nice.*

**3** used for giving extra information about sb जो, जो कि (किसी व्यक्ति के विषय में अतिरिक्त जानकारी देने के लिए), जो, जो कि NOTE अतिरिक्त जानकारी से संबंधित उपवाक्य को मुख्य उपवाक्य के अंदर दोंनो ओर अलपविराम लगाते हुए, अलग पहचान दी जाती है। ➪ **whom** पर नोट देखिए।

**who'd** /huːd हूड्/ ➪ **who had, who would** का संक्षिप्त रूप

**whoever** /huːˈevə(r) हूˈएव़(र्)/ *pronoun* **1** the person or people who; any person who जो व्यक्ति या लोग; जो कोई, जो भी *I want to speak to whoever is in charge.* **2** it does not matter who जो कोई भी (इससे बहस नहीं कि वह कौन है) *I don't want to see* *anybody—whoever it is.* **3** (used for expressing surprise) who (आश्चर्य व्यक्त करने के लिए) कौन? *Whoever could have done that?*

**whole¹** /həʊl होल् / *adj.* **1** complete; full पूरा, पूर्ण; सारा-का-सारा, समग्र *I drank a whole bottle of water.* ○ *She wasn't telling me the* ***whole truth.*** **2** not broken or cut अखंड, अविकल, समूचा (जो टूटा या कटा न हो) *Snakes swallow their prey whole* (= in one piece). ➪ **wholly** adverb देखिए।

**whole²** /həʊl होल् / *noun* [*sing.*] **1** a thing that is complete or full in itself संपूर्ण, पूर्णता *Two halves make a whole.* **2 the whole of sth** all that there is of sth (कोई वस्तु) सारी-की-सारी, पूरी-की-पूरी, जितनी है सब *I spent the whole of the morning cooking.*
**IDM as a whole** as one complete thing or unit and not as separate parts समग्र रूप से, कुल मिलाकर, सब मिलाकर *This is true in India, but also in Asia as a whole.*
**on the whole** generally, but not true in every case सामान्य रूप से *On the whole I think it's a very good idea.*

**wholefood** /ˈhəʊlfuːd ˈहोलफ़ूड् / *noun* [U] **wholefoods** [*pl.*] food that is considered healthy because it does not contain artificial substances and is produced as naturally as possible स्वास्थ्यवर्धक प्राकृतिक आहार

**wholehearted** /ˌhəʊlˈhɑːtɪd ˌहोलˈहाटिड् / *adj.* complete and enthusiastic पूरा और हार्दिक, सच्चा, एकनिष्ठ, अनन्य *to give sb your wholehearted support* ▸ **wholeheartedly** *adv.* पूरे मन या उत्साह से, सच्चे हृदय से

**wholemeal** /ˈhəʊlmiːl ˈहोलमील् / (*also* **wholewheat**) *adj.* (made from) flour that contains all the grain including the outside layer (**husk**) चोकर युक्त आटे से बना *wholemeal bread/flour*

**wholesale** /ˈhəʊlseɪl ˈहोलसेल् / *adv., adj.* (*adjective only before a noun*) **1** connected with buying and selling goods in large quantities, especially in order to sell them again and make a profit थोक के भाव से, बड़ी मात्रा में; थोक *They get all their building materials wholesale.* ○ *wholesale goods/prices* ➪ **retail** देखिए। **2** (usually about sth bad) very great; on a very large scale (प्रायः कोई निंदनीय बात) बहुत अधिक, बेतहाशा, अंधाधुंध; बड़े पैमाने पर *the wholesale slaughter of wildlife*

**wholesome** /ˈhəʊlsəm ˈहोलसम् / *adj.* **1** good for your health शारीरिक स्वास्थ्य के लिए हितकर, स्वास्थ्यवर्धक, पुष्टिकर, पौष्टिक *simple wholesome food* **2** having a moral effect that is good हितकारी (नैतिक स्वास्थ्य के लिए हितकर) *clean wholesome fun*

**who'll** /huːl हूल् / ➪ **who will** का संक्षिप्त रूप

**wholly** /ˈhəʊlli ˈहोल्लि / *adv.* completely; fully पूरी तरह, पूर्णतया; सर्वथा *Gautam is not wholly to blame for the situation.*

**whom** /huːm हूम् / *pronoun* (*formal*) used instead of 'who' as the object of a verb or preposition जिसे, जिसको (पूर्वसर्ग या किसी के कर्म के रूप में 'who' के स्थान पर प्रयुक्त) *Whom did you meet there?* ○ *To whom am I speaking?*

**NOTE Who** की तुलना में **whom** काफ़ी अधिक औपचारिक प्रयोग है, जैसे यह वाक्य में—*He asked me with whom I had discussed it.* इसी के समानार्थक निम्नलिखित वाक्य में 'who' की अनौपचारिकता स्पष्ट है—*He asked me who I had discussed it with.* (ध्यान दीजिए कि इस वाक्य में पूर्वसर्ग अंत में आता है।)

**whooping cough** /ˈhuːpɪŋ kɒf ˈहूपिङ् कॉफ़् / *noun* [U] a serious disease, especially of children, which makes them cough loudly and not be able to breathe easily सूखी खाँसी, कुकुरखाँसी (यह गंभीर रोग प्रायः बच्चों को होता है और जोर से खाँसने के साथ साँस लेने में भी कष्ट होता है)

**whoops** /wʊps वूप्स् / *exclamation* used when you have, or nearly have, a small accident छोटे-मोटे हादसे पर मुहँ से सहज निकला शब्द *Whoops! I nearly dropped the cup.*

**whoosh** /wʊʃ वूश् / *noun* [C, *usually sing.*] the sudden movement and sound of air or water going past very fast सरसराहट, सनसनाहट (तेज़ी से गुज़रती हवा या पानी की फुरती भरी चाल और आवाज़) ▸ **whoosh** *verb* [I] सरसराना, सनसनाना

**who're** /ˈhuːə(r) ˈहुअ(र्) / ➪ **who are** का संक्षिप्त रूप

**who's** /huːz हूज़्/ ➪ **who is, who has** का संक्षिप्त रूप

**whose** /huːz/ *det., pronoun* **1** (used in questions to ask who sth belongs to) of whom? ('किसका है?' यह पूछने के लिए प्रश्नसूचक वाक्यों में प्रयुक्त) किसका? *Whose car is that?* ○ *Those are nice shoes—I wonder whose they are.* **2** (used to say exactly which person or thing you mean, or to give extra information about a person or thing) of whom; of which जिस (व्यक्ति) का; जिस (वस्तु) का *That's the boy whose mother I met.* ○ *My neighbours, whose house is up for sale, are moving to another city.* **NOTE** जब शब्द **'whose'** का प्रयोग वाक्य में किसी व्यक्ति या वस्तु के विषय में अधिक जानकारी देने के लिए होता है तो वाक्य के उस भाग (उपवाक्य) को अल्पविरामों द्वारा मुख्य वाक्य से भिन्न किया जाता है।

**who've** /huːv हूव् / ➪ **who have** का संक्षिप्त रूप

**why** /waɪ वाइ/ *adv.* **1** for what reason क्यों; किस कारण?, किस कारण से; किसलिए? *Why was she so late?* ○ *I wonder why they went.* **2** used for giving or talking about a reason for sth जिस लिए, जिस कारण से, यही कारण है (कारण बनाने या स्पष्टीकरण देने के लिए प्रयुक्त)

IDM **why ever** used to show that you are surprised or angry आश्चर्य या क्रोध व्यक्त करने के लिए प्रयुक्त *Why ever didn't you phone?*

**why not?** used for making or agreeing to a suggestion कोई सुझाव देने या मानने के लिए प्रयुक्त *Why not phone her tonight?* ○ *'Shall we go out tonight?' 'Yes, why not?'*

**wick** /wɪk विक्/ *noun* [C] the piece of string that burns in the middle of a candle मोमबत्ती का धागा

**wicked** /ˈwɪkɪd ˈविकिड्/ *adj.* **1** morally bad; evil चरित्रहीन, भ्रष्ट; बुरा, दुष्ट, पापी **2** (*informal*) slightly bad but in a way that is amusing and/or attractive शरारतभरा (कुछ बुरा लगने वाला मगर मज़ाकिया और मनभावन) *a wicked sense of humour* ▶ **wickedly** *adv.* दुष्टतापूर्वक ▶ **wickedness** *noun* [U] दुष्टता, चरित्रहीनता

**wicker** /ˈwɪkə(r) ˈविक(र्)/ *noun* [U] long thin sticks of wood that are used to make baskets, furniture, etc. टोकरी, फ़र्नीचर आदि बुनने के काम में आने वाली खपची या तीली

**wicket** /ˈwɪkɪt ˈविकिट्/ *noun* [C] **1** (in cricket) either of the two sets of three upright sticks with pieces of wood lying across the top (क्रिकेट में) विकेट (लकड़ी का डंडा, तीन-तीन के दो सेटों में से कोई एक) **2** the area of ground between the two wickets दोनों ओर के विकेटों के बीच की भूमि, खेल-पट्टी; विकेट

**wide¹** /waɪd वाइड्/ *adj.* **1** measuring a lot from one side to the other चौड़ा, विस्मीर्ण *The road was not wide enough for two cars to pass.* ✪ विलोम **narrow** ➪ **width** noun देखिए तथा **broad** पर नोट भी देखिए। **2** measuring a particular distance from one side to the other चौड़ा, चौड़ाई वाला *The box was only 20 centimetres wide.* **3** including a large number or variety of different people or things; covering a large area विशाल, व्यापक (जिसमें तरह-तरह के बहुत सारे लोग या चीजें हों); लंबा-चौड़ा, विस्तृत *You're the nicest person in **the whole wide world**!* ○ ***a wide range/choice/variety** of goods* **4** fully open पूरा-पूरा खुला *The children's eyes were wide with excitement.* **5** not near what you wanted to touch or hit (गेंद) स्पर्श या मार की पहुँच से बाहर; वाइड *His first serve was wide* (= the ball did not land inside the roman court). ▶ **widely** *adv.* पर्याप्त मात्रा में, दूर-दूर तक *Their opinions differ widely.*

**wide²** /waɪd वाइड्/ *adv.* as far or as much as possible; completely (यथासंभव) अधिक-से-अधिक; पूरी तरह से, पूर्णतया *It was late but she was still **wide awake**.* ○ *The front door was **wide open**.*

**widen** /ˈwaɪdn ˈवाइड्न्/ *verb* [I, T] to become wider; to make sth wider चौड़ा हो जाना; (किसी वस्तु को) चौड़ा कर देना *The road widens just up ahead.*

**wide-ranging** *adj.* covering a large area or many subjects व्यापक, विस्तृत (बड़े क्षेत्र में या अनेक विषयों तक व्याप्त) *a wide-ranging discussion*

**widespread** /ˈwaɪdspred ˈवाइड्स्प्रेड्/ *adj.* found or happening over a large area; affecting a large number of people दूर-दूर तक फैला हुआ, व्याप्त; अनेक लोगों को प्रभावित करने वाला, व्यापक *The storm has caused widespread damage.*

**widow** /ˈwɪdəʊ ˈविडो/ *noun* [C] a woman whose husband has died and who has not married again विधवा, बेवा ▶ **widowed** /ˈwɪdəʊd ˈविडोड्/ *adj.* वैधव्य को प्राप्त *She's been widowed for ten years now.*

**widower** /ˈwɪdəʊə(r) ˈविडोअ(र्)/ *noun* [C] a man whose wife has died and who has not married again विधुर (पुरुष)

**width** /wɪdθ; wɪtθ विड्थ्; विट्थ्/ *noun* **1** [C, U] the amount that sth measures from one side or edge to the other चौड़ाई (कमरे, वस्तु आदि की) *The room is eight metres **in width**.* ○ *The carpet is available in two different widths.* ➪ **wide** adjective देखिए। **2** [C] the distance from one side of a swimming pool to the other तरण-ताल की एक छोर से दूसरे छोर तक की दूरी; चौड़ाई ➪ **length** और **breadth** देखिए।

**wield** /wiːld वील्ड्/ *verb* [T] **1** to have and use power, authority, etc. शक्ति, अधिकार आदि रखना और उनका प्रयोग करना *She wields enormous power in the company.* **2** to hold and be ready to use a weapon हथियार पास रखना और उसे इस्तेमाल करने के लिए तैयार रहना *Some of the men were wielding knives.*

**wife** /waɪf वाइफ़्/ *noun* [C] (*pl.* **wives** /waɪvz वाइव्ज़्/) the woman to whom a man is married पत्नी, धर्मपत्नी, सहधर्मिणी, बीवी

**wig** /wɪg विग्/ *noun* [C] a covering made of real or false hair that you wear on your head बालों की टोपी (असली या नक़ली बालों से बनी), विग

**wiggle** /ˈwɪgl ˈविग्ल्/ *verb* [I, T] (*informal*) to move from side to side with small quick movements; to make sth do this तेज़ी से हिलना-डुलनाः तेज़ी से (किसी को) हिलाना-डुलाना *You have to wiggle your*

*hips in time to the music.* ▶ **wiggle** *noun* [C] हिलने-डुलने या हिलाने-डुलाने की क्रिया

**wiggly** /ˈwɪgli ˈविग्लि / *adj.* (of a line) having many curves in it लहरदार (रेखा)

**wild**[1] /waɪld वाइल्ड् / *adj.* **1** (used about animals or plants) living or growing in natural conditions, not looked after by people (पशु या पौधे) वन्य, जंगली (प्राकृतिक अवस्थाओं में रहने या उगने वाले) *wild animals/flowers/strawberries* **2** (used about an area of land) in its natural state; not changed by people (भूक्षेत्र या इलाक़ा) अपनी प्राकृतिक अवस्था में; जिस पर खेती-बाड़ी नहीं हुई; बीहड़ *wild moorland* **3** (used about a person or his/her behaviour or emotions) without control or discipline; slightly crazy (व्यक्ति, उसका आचरण या मनोभाव) उच्छृंखल, निरंकुश; कुछ सनकी या झक्की *The crowd **went wild** with excitement.* ○ *They let their children **run wild*** (= behave in an uncontrolled way). **4** not carefully planned; not sensible or accurate लापरवाही भरा; विवेकहीन, ग़लत या झूठा *She made **a wild guess**.* ○ *wild accusations/rumours* **5** (*informal*) **wild (about sb/sth)** *liking sb/sth very much* किसी व्यक्ति या वस्तु का दीवाना, उस पर लट्टू *I'm not wild about their new house.* **6** (used about the weather) with strong winds; stormy (मौसम) जिसमें तेज़ हवाएँ चलें; तूफ़ानी, उग्र *It was a wild night last night.* ▶ **wildly** *adv.* उच्छृंखलतापूर्वक ▶ **wildness** *noun* [U] उच्छृंखलता

**wild**[2] /waɪld वाइल्ड् / *noun* **1 the wild** [*sing.*] a natural environment that is not controlled by people (जंगल, वन) मनुष्य से अनियंत्रित प्राकृतिक क्षेत्र, (जंगल, अरण्य) *the thrill of seeing elephants **in the wild*** **2 the wilds** [*pl.*] places that are far away from towns, where few people live (शहरों से दूर) निर्जन प्रदेश *They live somewhere out in the wilds.*

**wilderness** /ˈwɪldənəs ˈविल्डनस् / *noun* [C, *usually sing.*] **1** a large area of land that has never been used for building on or for growing things उजाड़ इलाक़ा, बंजर भूमि (जहाँ न कभी कोई निर्माणकार्य हुआ न खेती) *The Antarctic is the world's last great wilderness.* **2** a place that people do not take care of or control (लोगों की उपेक्षा के कारण) उजाड़ पड़ गया इलाक़ा, घास-फूस और झाड़-झंखाड़ भरा इलाक़ा *Their garden is a wilderness.*

**wildlife** /ˈwaɪldlaɪf ˈवाइल्ड्लाइफ़् / *noun* [U] birds, plants, animals, etc. that are wild and live in a natural environment वन्य जीवन, वन्य, वनस्पति और जीवजन्तु, प्राकृतिक परिवेश में होने वाली वनस्पतियाँ या रहने वाले पशु-पक्षी

**wilful** (*AmE* **willful**) /ˈwɪlfl ˈविल्फ़्ल् / *adj.* **1** done deliberately although the person doing it knows that it is wrong जान-बूझ कर किया गया (कुकर्म) *wilful damage/neglect* **2** doing exactly what you want, no matter what other people think or say मनमानी करने वाला; ज़िद्दी, हठी, दुराग्रही *a wilful child* ▶ **wilfully** /-fəli -फ़लि / *adv.* मनमानेपन से, जान-बूझ कर

**will**[1] /wɪl विल् / *modal verb* (*short form* **'ll**; *negative* **will not**; *short form* **won't** /wəʊnt वोन्ट् /) **1** used in forming the future tenses भविष्य काल बनाने में प्रयुक्त (सहायक क्रिया) *He'll be here soon.* ○ *I'm sure you'll pass your exam.* **2** used for showing that sb is offering sth or wants to do sth, or that sth is able to do sth किसी को कुछ पेश करना या कुछ करने का इच्छुक होना या किसी वस्तु का कुछ करना *'We need some more milk.' 'I'll get it.'* ○ *My car won't start.* **3** used for asking sb to do sth (किसी के कुछ करने का) अनुरोध करने के लिए प्रयुक्त *Will you sit down, please?* **4** used for ordering sb to do sb (किसी को किसी काम का) आदेश देने के लिए प्रयुक्त *Will you all be quiet!* **5** used for saying that you think sth is probably true किसी बात की संभावना के अर्थ में प्रयुक्त *That'll be the postman at the door.* ○ *He'll have left work by now, I suppose.* **6** (*only in positive sentences*) used for talking about sth annoying that sb always or very often does (केवल स्वीकारात्मक वाक्यों में) किसी की बुरी आदतों की चर्चा के लिए प्रयुक्त

> **NOTE** इस अर्थ की अभिव्यक्ति में **will** पर अतिरिक्त बल देना होगा और इसके लघु रूप (**'ll**) का प्रयोग नहीं किया जाएगा—*He will keep interrupting me when I'm trying to work.* वृत्तिवाचक क्रियाओं (modal verbs) के विषय में अधिक जानकारी के लिए इस शब्कोश के अंत में **Quick Grammar Reference** शीर्षक खंड देखिए।

**will**[2] /wɪl विल् / *noun* **1** [C, U] the power of the mind to choose what to do; a feeling of strong determination इच्छाशक्ति; संकल्प शक्ति *Both her children have got very strong wills.* ○ *He seems to have lost **the will to live**.* **2 -willed** (*used to form compound adjectives*) having the type of will mentioned निर्दिष्ट इच्छाशक्ति वाला *a strong-willed/weak-willed person* **3** [*sing.*] what sb wants to happen in a particular situation स्थिति विशेष में किसी की विशेष इच्छा *My mother doesn't want to sell the house and I don't want to **go against** her **will**.* **4** [C] a legal document in which you write down who should have your money and property after your death वसीयतनामा, इच्छापत्र,

दिस्तापत्र, 'विल' *You really ought to **make a will**.* ○ *Granny left us some money **in her will**.*

IDM **of your own free will** ➪ **free¹** देखिए।

**will³** /wɪl विल्/ *verb* [T] to use the power of your mind to do sth or to make sth happen किसी काम के लिए इच्छाशक्ति का प्रयोग करना *He willed himself to carry on to the end of the race.*

**willing** /ˈwɪlɪŋ ˈविलिङ्/ *adj.* **1 willing (to do sth)** (*not before a noun*) happy to do sth; having no reason for not doing sth राज़ी; तैयार ***She's perfectly willing** to lend me her car.* ○ *I'm not willing to take any risks.* **2** ready or pleased to help and not needing to be persuaded; enthusiastic स्वतः इच्छुक; उत्साहित, तत्पर *a willing helper/volunteer* ✪ विलोम **unwilling** ▶ **willingly** *adv.* स्वेच्छा से, तत्परतापूर्वक ▶ **willingness** *noun* [U, *sing.*] स्वेच्छा, तत्परता

**willow** /ˈwɪləʊ ˈविलो/ (*also* **willow tree**) *noun* [C] a tree with long thin branches that hang down which grows near water बेंत, सरपत

**will power** *noun* [U] determination to do sth; strength of mind (कुछ करने का) दृढ़ संकल्प; मनोबल, अंतःशक्ति, आत्मबल *It takes a lot of will power to give up smoking.*

**willy-nilly** /ˌwɪli ˈnɪli ˌविलि ˈनिलि/ *adv.* (*informal*) **1** in a careless way without planning बिना सोचे-समझे *Don't spend your money willy-nilly.* **2** if you want to or not चाहे-अनचाहे, ज़बरदस्ती

**wilt** /wɪlt विल्ट्/ *verb* [I] (used about a plant or flower) to bend and start to die, because of heat or a lack of water (पौधे या फूल का) मुरझाना, कुम्हलाना (पानी की कमी या गरमी के कारण)

**wily** /ˈwaɪli ˈवाइलि/ *adj.* clever at getting what you want चालाक, धूर्त, चंट, काइयाँ ✪ पर्याय **cunning**

**wimp** /wɪmp विम्प्/ *noun* [C] (*informal*) a weak person who has no courage or confidence मन से कमज़ोर व्यक्ति ▶ **wimpish** *adj.* मन से कमज़ोर

**win** /wɪn विन्/ *verb* (*pres. part.* **winning;** *pt, pp* **won** /wʌn वन्/) **1** [I, T] to be the best, first or strongest in a race, game, competition, etc. जीतना, विजय प्राप्त करना (दौड़, खेल, प्रतियोगिता आदि में) *to win a game/match/championship* **2** [T] to get money, a prize, etc. as a result of success in a competition, race, etc. प्रतियोगिता में विजयी होने पर धन, पुरस्कार आदि प्राप्त करना *We won a trip to Australia.* ○ *Who won the gold medal?* **3** [T] to get sth by hard work, great effort, etc. परिश्रम, बहुत प्रयास आदि करके कुछ प्राप्त करना *Her brilliant performance won her a great deal of praise.* ○ *to win support for a plan* ▶ **win** *noun* [C] जीत, विजय *We have had two wins and a draw so far this season.* ▶ **winning** *adj.* जीतने वाला जीता हुआ, विजयी *The winning ticket is number 65.*

IDM **win/lose the toss** ➪ **toss** देखिए।

**you can't win** (*informal*) there is no way of being completely successful or of pleasing everyone आपको पूरी सफलता नहीं मिल सकती, आप सबको ख़ुश नहीं कर सकते *Whatever you do you will upset somebody. You can't win.*

PHR V **win sb over/round (to sth)** to persuade sb to support or agree with you किसी को अपनी बात मनवाना *They're against the proposal at the moment, but I'm sure we can win them over.*

**wince** /wɪns विन्स्/ *verb* [I] to make a sudden quick movement (usually with a part of your face) to show you are feeling pain or embarrassment चेहरे का ऐंठ जाना या सिकुड़ जाना (दर्द या शर्म के कारण)

**winch** /wɪntʃ विन्च्/ *noun* [C] a machine that lifts or pulls heavy objects using a thick chain, rope, etc. मोटी ज़ंजीर, रस्सी आदि से भारी वस्तुओं को उठाने या खींचने वाली मशीन; विंच मशीन ▶ **winch** *verb* [T] विंच मशीन से किसी को उठाना या खींचना *The injured climber was winched up into a helicopter.*

**wind¹** /wɪnd विन्ड्/ *noun* **1** [C, U] air that is moving across the surface of the earth हवा, वायु, वात, पवन *A **gust of wind** blew his hat off.* ○ *gale-force/strong/high winds* **2** [U] the breath that you need for doing exercise or playing a musical instrument व्यायाम करने या वाद्य यंत्र बजाने के लिए अपेक्षित श्वास, सहारा देने वाला साँस *She stopped running to get her wind back.* **3** [U] gas that is formed in your stomach पेट में बनने वाली गैस या वायु, वात, अफारा, बाय गोला *The baby cries when he has wind.* **4** [U] the group of instruments in an orchestra that you blow into to produce the sound बिगुल, तुरही आदि वाद्य (जो फूँक मारकर बजाए जाते हैं)

IDM **get wind of sth** (*informal*) to hear about sth that is secret किसी गुप्त बात की भनक लगना

**wind²** /wɪnd विन्ड्/ *verb* [T] **1** to cause sb to have difficulty in breathing साँस लेने में कठिनाई उत्पन्न करना *The punch in the stomach winded her.* **2** to help a baby get rid of painful gas in the stomach by rubbing or gently hitting its back हवा या वायु ख़ारिज करने में बच्चे की मदद करना, बच्चे का अफारा शांत करना (हलके से पीठ को ठोक कर या उस पर हाथ फेरते हुए)

**wind³** /waɪnd वाइन्ड्/ *verb* (*pt, pp* **wound** /waʊnd वाउन्ड्/) **1** [I] (used about a road, path, etc.) to have a lot of bends or curves in it (सड़क, रास्ते

आदि में) बहुत सारे घुमाव या मोड़ होना *The path winds down the cliff to the sea.* **2** [T] to put sth long round sth else several times (किसी स्थान पर पट्टी आदि को) लपेटना *She wound the bandage around his arm.* **3** [T] to make sth work or move by turning a key, handle, etc. चाबी, हैंडिल आदि घुमाकर किसी चीज़ को चलाना या हिलाना *He wound the car window down.* ○ *Wind the tape on a bit to the next song.*

**PHR V** **wind down** (about a person) to rest and relax after a period of hard work, worry, etc. कड़ी मेहनत आदि के बाद (व्यक्ति का) आराम करना और सुस्ताना ➪ **unwind** देखिए।

**wind up** to find yourself in a place or situation that you did not intend to be in (भटक कर) किसी अनचाही जगह या हालत में पहुँच जाना *We got lost and wound up in a dangerous-looking part of town.*

**wind sb up** to annoy sb until he/she becomes angry किसी को गुस्सा होने की सीमा तक तंग करना

**wind sth up** to finish, stop or close sth किसी काम को समाप्त, रोक या बंद करना

**wind chill** /ˈwɪnd tʃɪl ˈविन्ड् चिल्/ *noun* [U] the effect of low temperature combined with wind on sb/sth वायु से उत्पन्न ठंडक *Take the* ***wind-chill factor*** *into account.*

**windfall** /ˈwɪndfɔːl ˈविन्ड्फ़ॉल्/ *noun* [C] an amount of money that you win or receive unexpectedly अचानक मिला धन, अप्रत्याशित लाभ

**winding** /ˈwaɪndɪŋ ˈवाइन्डिङ्/ *adj.* with bends or curves in it घुमावदार या मोड़दार *a winding road through the hills*

**wind instrument** *noun* [C] a musical instrument that you play by blowing through it फूँक कर बजाया जाने वाला बाजा; सुषिर वाद्य

**windmill** /ˈwɪndmɪl ˈविन्ड्मिल्/ *noun* [C] a tall building or structure with long parts (**sails**) that turn in the wind. In past times windmills were used for making flour from grain, but now they are used mainly for producing electricity पवन-चक्की (पवन या वायु की शक्ति से चलने वाला ढाँचा जिससे पहले आटा पीसा जाता था और आजकल बिजली बनाई जाती है)

**window** /ˈwɪndəʊ ˈविन्डो/ *noun* [C] **1** the opening in a building, car, etc. that you can see through and that lets light in. A window usually has glass in it (इमारत, कार आदि की) खिड़की *a shop window* ○ *These windows need cleaning.* **2** (*computing*) an area inside a frame on a computer screen, that has a particular program operating in it, or shows a particular type of information कंप्यूटर की विंडो (कंप्यूटर के परदे पर एक फ्रेम के भीतर एक विशेष स्थान जहाँ कोई विशेष कार्यक्रम चलता है या विशेष प्रकार की जानकारी उपलब्ध होती है) *to create/open/close a window* **3** a time when you have not arranged to do anything and so are free to meet sb, etc. कुछ कर लेने का मौका (जब कोई और काम न हो)

**windowpane** /ˈwɪndəʊpeɪn ˈविन्डोपेन्/ *noun* [C] one piece of glass in a window खिड़की में लगा काँच का पल्ला, खिड़की का शीशा

**window-shopping** *noun* [U] looking at things in shop windows without intending to buy anything दुकान की खिड़कियों में सजी वस्तुओं को यों ही निहारना

**window sill** (*also* **window ledge**) *noun* [C] the narrow shelf at the bottom of a window, either inside or outside खिड़की के नीचे का तंग ख़ाना (अंदर या बाहर की ओर)

**windpipe** /ˈwɪndpaɪp ˈविन्ड्पाइप्/ *noun* [C] the tube that takes air from your throat to the lungs श्वासनली ✪ पर्याय **trachea** ➪ **body** पर चित्र देखिए।

**windscreen** /ˈwɪndskriːn ˈविन्ड्स्क्रीन्/ (*AmE* **windshield** /ˈwɪndʃiːld ˈविन्ड्शील्ड्/) *noun* [C] the window in the front of a vehicle कार आदि का सामने का शीशा या हवा-रोक शीशा; विंडस्क्रीन ➪ **car** पर चित्र देखिए।

**windscreen wiper** (*also* **wiper;** *AmE* **windshield wiper**) *noun* [C] one of the two moving arms (**blades**) that remove water, snow, etc. from the front window of a car (**the windscreen**) कार आदि वाहन के विंडस्क्रीन पर पड़ा पानी, बर्फ़ आदि साफ़ करने का उपकरण; वाइपर ➪ **car** पर चित्र देखिए।

**windsurf** /ˈwɪndsɜːf ˈविन्ड्सफ़्/ *verb* [I] to move over water standing on a special board with a sail पाल वाले फट्टे पर सवार या खड़ा होकर पानी पर फिसलना **NOTE** इस क्रिया के लिए प्रायः **go windsurfing** शब्द का प्रयोग होता है—*Have you ever been windsurfing?* ▶ **windsurfing** *noun* [U] पाल वाले फट्टे पर सवार या खड़ा होकर पानी पर फिसलने की क्रिया

**windsurfer** /ˈwɪndsɜːfə(r) ˈविन्ड्सफ़(र्)/ *noun* [C] **1** (*also* **sailboard**) a board with a sail that you stand on as it moves over the surface of the water, pushed by the wind पाल वाला फट्टा जिस पर व्यक्ति सवार या खड़ा होता है (हवा के धकियाने से पानी पर फिसलते हुए) **2** a person who rides on a board like this पाल वाले फट्टे पर सवार या खड़ा व्यक्ति

**windswept** /ˈwɪndswept ˈविन्ड्स्वेप्ट्/ *adj.* **1** (used about a place) that often has strong winds (स्थान) जहाँ प्रायः तेज़ हवाएँ चलती हों *a windswept coastline* **2** looking untidy because you have been in a strong wind तेज़ हवा के प्रभाव से अस्तव्यस्त (बाल, कपड़े आदि) *windswept hair*

**windward** /ˈwɪndwəd ˈविन्ड्वड्/ *adj.* on the side of a hill, building, etc. towards which the wind is blowing जिधर से हवा बह रही है उस ओर स्थित पहाड़ी या भवन का भाग; पवनभिमुख ➪ **lee** और **leeward** देखिए।

**windy** /ˈwɪndi ˈविन्डि/ *adj.* (**windier; windiest**) with a lot of wind तूफ़ानी *a windy day*

**wine** /waɪn वाइन्/ *noun* [C, U] an alcoholic drink that is made from grapes, or sometimes other fruit अंगूर की (या कभी दूसरे फल से बनी) शराब; वाइन *sweet/dry wine* ○ *German wines*

> NOTE वाइन तीन रंगों में बनती है **red, white** और **rosé**.

**wing** /wɪŋ विङ्/ *noun* **1** [C] one of the two parts that a bird, insect, etc. uses for flying पक्षी आदि का डैना, पर या पंख *The chicken ran around flapping its wings.* ➪ **insect** पर चित्र देखिए। **2** [C] one of the two long parts that stick out from the side of a plane and support it in the air विमान का पंख या डैना ➪ **plane** पर चित्र देखिए। **3** [C] a part of a building that sticks out from the main part or that was added on to the main part मुख्य भवन का बाहर को निकाला बढ़ाया गया खंड, भाग या स्कंध *the maternity wing of the hospital* **4** (*AmE* **fender**) [C] the part of the outside of a car that covers the top of the wheels कार के पहियों को ढकने वाला (कार का) हिस्सा *a wing mirror* (= fixed to the side of the car) **5** [C, *usually sing.*] a group of people in a political party that have particular beliefs or opinions राजनीतिक दल का धड़ा (जिसके सदस्यों के अपने विचार या अभिमत हों) *the right wing of the Conservative Party* ➪ **left-wing** और **right-wing** देखिए। **6** [C] (in football, etc.) the part at each side of the area where the game is played (फ़ुटबॉल आदि के) मैदान का पक्ष, बाजू या पार्श्व विंग (दोनों ओर अलग-अलग क्षेत्र जहाँ खेल खेला जाता है) *to play on the wing* **7** (also **winger**) [C] (in football, etc.) a person who plays in an attacking position at one of the sides of the field (फ़ुटबॉल आदि में) मैदान के दोनों में से एक पक्ष, बाजू या पार्श्व में आक्रमणकारी स्थिति में खेलने वाला खिलाड़ी पार्श्व खिलाड़ी; विंगर **8 the wings** [*pl.*] (in a theatre) the area at the sides of the stage where you cannot be seen by the audience (रंगशाला में) रंगमंच का पार्श्वभाग (जहाँ बैठे व्यक्ति को दर्शक देख नहीं सकते)

IDM **take sb under your wing** to take care of and help sb who has less experience than you (अपने से) छोटे को अपने संरक्षण या साये में लेना, उसे आश्रय देना

**wingspan** /ˈwɪŋspæn ˈविङ्स्पैन्/ *noun* [C] the distance between the end of one wing and the end of the other when the wings are fully stretched (विमान, पक्षी आदि का) पंख विस्तृति, पक्ष-विस्तृति (दो पंखों या पक्षों के दूरस्थ हितों के बीच का फ़ासला)

**wink** /wɪŋk विङ्क्/ *verb* [I] **wink (at sb)** to close and open one eye very quickly, usually as a signal to sb जल्दी-जल्दी पलक झपकना या आँख मिचमिचाना (प्रायः किसी को इशारे के रूप में) ➪ **blink** देखिए। ▶ **wink** *noun* [C] आँख मिचमिचाना *He smiled and gave the little girl a wink.* ○ *I didn't sleep a wink* (= not at all).

IDM **forty winks** ➪ **forty** देखिए।

**winner** /ˈwɪnə(r) ˈविन(र्)/ *noun* [C] **1** a person or animal that wins a competition, game, race, etc. (प्रतियोगिता आदि में) विजयी व्यक्ति या पशु, विजेता *The winner of the competition will be announced next week.* **2** (*informal*) something that is likely to be successful सफलता प्राप्त करने वाली बात या वस्तु *I think your idea is a winner.* **3** (in sport) a goal that wins a match, a hit that wins a point, etc. (खेल में) विजय दिलाने वाला गोल, अंक दिलाने वाला हिट आदि *Dhyan Chand scored the winner in the last minute.*

**winning** ➪ **win** देखिए।

**winnings** /ˈwɪnɪŋz ˈविनिङ्ज़्/ *noun* [*pl.*] money that sb wins in a competition, game, etc. (प्रतियोगिता, खेल आदि में) जीती हुई धनराशि, जीता माल

**winnow** /ˈwɪnəʊ ˈविनो/ *verb* [T] to blow through grain in order to remove its outer covering अनाज पछारना

PHRV **winnow sb/sth out (of sth)** (*written*) to remove people or things from a group so that only the best ones are left (व्यक्तियों या वस्तुओं को) समूह में से अलग करना ताकि केवल सर्वश्रेष्ठ बच जाएँ

**winter** /ˈwɪntə(r) ˈविन्ट(र्)/ *noun* [C, U] the coldest season of the year between autumn and spring जाड़ा, जाड़े को मौसम, शीत ऋतु, सरदी (शरद, हेमंत) *It snows a lot here* ***in winter***. ○ *a cold winter's day* ➪ **season** पर चित्र देखिए। ▶ **wintry** /ˈwɪntri ˈविन्ट्रि/ *adj.* जाड़ें का, शीतकालीन *wintry weather*

**winter sports** *noun* [*pl.*] sports which take place on snow or ice, for example **skiing** and **skating** बर्फ़ के खेल या बर्फ़ पर खेले जाने वाले खेल (जैसे स्कीइंग ओर स्केटिंग)

**wintertime** /ˈwɪntətaɪm ˈविन्टटाइम्/ *noun* [U] the period or season of winter शीतकाल या शीत ऋतु

**wipe**[1] /waɪp वाइप्/ *verb* [T] **1** to clean or dry sth by rubbing it with a cloth, etc. कपड़े आदि से साफ़ करना या पोंछना *She stopped crying and wiped her eyes with a tissue.* ○ *Could you wipe the table, please?* ➪ **clean**[2] पर नोट देखिए। **2 wipe sth**

**from/off sth; wipe sth away/off/up** to remove sth by rubbing it पोंछकर साफ़ करना, रगड़कर मिटाना पोंछ डालना *He wiped the sweat from his forehead.* ○ *Wipe up the milk you spilled.* **3 wipe sth (off) (sth)** to remove sound, information or images from sth टेप आदि से ध्वनि, सूचना-सामग्री या चित्र मिटाना *I accidentally wiped the tape.* ○ *I tried to wipe the memory from my mind.*

**PHR V** **wipe sth out** to destroy sth completely किसी वस्तु को पूर्णतया नष्ट कर देना, तहस-नहस कर देना *Whole villages were wiped out in the bombing raids.*

**wipe²** /waɪp वाइप् / *noun* [C] **1** the action of wiping पोंछने की क्रिया, सफ़ाई *He gave the table a quick wipe.* **2** a piece of paper or thin cloth that has been made wet with a special liquid and is used for cleaning sth पानी में भिगोकर साफ़ करने के लिए प्रयुक्त कागज़ या कपड़े का टुकड़ा; पोंछा, पोंछन, पोचारा *a box of baby wipes*

**wiper** /ˈwaɪpə(r) ˈवाइप(र्) / = **windscreen wiper**

**wire¹** /ˈwaɪə(r) ˈवाइअ(र्) / *noun* [C, U] **1** metal in the form of thin thread; a piece of this तार; तार का टुकड़ा *Twist those two wires together.* ○ *a wire fence* **2** a piece of wire that is used to carry electricity बिज़ली का तार, विद्युत वाली तार *telephone wires*

**wire²** /ˈwaɪə(r) ˈवाइअ(र्) / *verb* [T] **1 wire sth (up) (to sth)** to connect sth to a supply of electricity or to a piece of electrical equipment by using wires तार की सहायता से किसी वस्तु को बिजली के किसी उपकरण से जोड़ना *to wire a plug* ○ *The microphone was wired up to a loudspeaker.* **2 wire sth (to sb); wire sb sth** to send money to sb's bank account using an electronic system इलेक्ट्रॉनिक प्रणाली द्वारा बैंक खाते में पैसा जमा करना *The bank's going to wire me the money.* **3** to join two things together using wire तार से दो वस्तुओं को जोड़ना

**wire wool** = **steel wool**

**wiring** /ˈwaɪərɪŋ ˈवाइअरिङ् / *noun* [U] the system of wires that supplies electricity to rooms in a building किसी भवन के कमरों में बिजली की तारों की व्यवस्था, बिजली के तार

**wiry** /ˈwaɪəri ˈवाइअरि / *adj.* (used about a person) small and thin but strong (व्यक्ति) दुबला-पतला परंतु बलशाली

**wisdom** /ˈwɪzdəm ˈविज़्डम् / *noun* [U] the ability to make sensible decisions and judgements because of your knowledge or experience (ज्ञान या अनुभव के आधार पर) विवेकपूर्ण निर्णय लेने की क्षमता, समझदारी, बुद्धिमानी, अकलमंदी *I don't see the wisdom of this plan* (= I do not think that it is a good idea). ➪ **wise** adjective देखिए।

**wisdom tooth** *noun* [C] one of the four teeth at the back of your mouth that appear when you are about 20 years old अकलदाढ़ (लगभग बीस वर्ष की अवस्था में निकलने वाली दाढ़) ➪ **tooth** पर नोट देखिए।

**wise** /waɪz वाइज़् / *adj.* having the knowledge or experience to make good and sensible decisions and judgements बुद्धिमान समझदार या अकलमंद व्यक्ति (विवेकपूर्ण निर्णय लेने के लिए अपेक्षित ज्ञान या अनुभव से संपन्न) *a wise choice* ○ *It would be wiser to wait for a few days.* ▸ **wisely** *adv.*

**wish¹** /wɪʃ विश् / *verb* **1** [T] wish (that) (*often with a verb in the past tense*) to want sth that cannot now happen or that probably will not happen (प्रायः भूतकालिक क्रिया के साथ) किसी वस्तु की चाह रखना, किसी वस्तु को चाहना (ऐसी इच्छा रखना जो न अब पूरी हो सकती है और संभवतः न भविष्य में) *I wish I had listened more carefully.* ○ *I wish that I knew what was going to happen.*

> **NOTE** औपचारिक अंग्रेज़ी में 'I' या 'he/she' के साथ **were** का प्रयोग किया जाता है, **was** का नहीं— *I wish I were rich* ○ *She wishes she were in a different city.*

**3** [I] **wish for sth** to say to yourself that you want sth that can only happen by good luck or chance किसी वस्तु की अभिलाषा या आशा करना (ऐसी इच्छा रखना जो भाग्य से या संयोगवश ही पूरी हो सकती हो) *She wished for her mother to get better.* **3** [I, T] (*formal*) **wish (to do sth)** to want to do sth कुछ करने की चाह रखना, कुछ चाहना *I wish to make a complaint about one of the doctors.* **4** [T] to say that you hope sb will have sth किसी के लिए कोई अनुकूल कामना व्यक्त करना (शुभकामना देना आदि) *I rang him up to **wish** him **a happy birthday**.* ○ *We **wish** you **all the best** for your future career.*

**wish²** /wɪʃ विश् / *noun* **1** [C] a feeling that you want to have sth or that sth should happen इच्छा, चाह, अभिलाषा, कामना, आकांक्षा *I have no wish to see her ever again.* ○ *Doctors should respect the patient's wishes.* **2** [C] a try at making sth happen by thinking hard about it, especially in stories when it often happens by magic (किसी चीज़ की) मन्नत, मनौति, मुराद, इच्छापूर्ति कामना, वरकामना (विशेषतः कहानियों में, प्रायः जादू से पूरी होने वाली) *Throw a coin into the fountain and **make a wish**.* ○ *My wish came true* (= I got what I asked for).

**3 wishes** [*pl.*] a hope that sb will be happy or have good luck (किसी के लिए) शुभकामनाएँ *Please give your parents **my best wishes**.*

**wishful thinking** *noun* [U] ideas that are based on what you would like, not on facts ख़याली पुलाव, (मात्र) मनोरथ, कोरी आशा

**wisp** /wɪsp विस्प्/ *noun* [C] **1** a few pieces of hair that are together बालों की लट **2** a small amount of smoke धुँए का लच्छा ▸ **wispy** *adj.* लटदार, लच्छेदार

**wistful** /ˈwɪstfl ˈविस्ट्फ़्ल्/ *adj.* feeling or showing sadness because you cannot have what you want उदासी भरा, चिंतातुर, उद्विग्न (अभीष्ट वस्तु की प्राप्ति न होने से) *a wistful sigh* ▸ **wistfully** /-fəli -फ़लि/ *adv.* आतुरतापूर्वक

**wit** /wɪt विट्/ *noun* [U] **1** the ability to use words in a clever and amusing way वाग्वैदग्ध्य, वाक्चातुर्य, हाज़िरजवाबी ➪ **witty** adjective देखिए। **2 -witted** (*used to form compound adjectives*) having a particular type of intelligence विशेष प्रकार की सूझबूझ-वाला *quick-witted* ○ *slow-witted* **3** (*also* **wits** [*pl.*]) the fact of being clever; intelligence चतुराई; सूझबूझ, युक्तिकौशल *The game of chess is essentially **a battle of wits**.*

**IDM** **at your wits' end** not knowing what to do or say because you are very worried किंकर्तव्यविमूढ़, जिसकी अकल जवाब दे दे, जिसको पता न चले कि क्या करना या कहना है

**keep your wits about you** to be ready to act in a difficult situation कठिन स्थिति में भी (सूझबूझ के साथ) क्रियाशील होने के लिए तत्पर रहना

**witch** /wɪtʃ विच्/ *noun* [C] (in past times and in stories) a woman who is thought to have magic powers पूर्व समय और कहानियों में) जादूगरनी, टोनहाई या जादू-टोना करने वाली स्त्री ➪ **wizard** देखिए।

**witchcraft** /ˈwɪtʃkrɑːft ˈविच्क्राफ़्ट्/ *noun* [U] the use of magic powers, especially evil ones जादू-टोना, टोना-टोटका

**witch-hunt** *noun* [C] the activity of trying to find and punish people who hold opinions that are thought to be unacceptable or dangerous to society (समाज-हित की दृष्टि से) संदिग्ध व्यक्तियों के विरुद्ध अभियान

**with** /wɪð; wɪθ विद्/ *prep.* **1** in the company of sb/sth; in or to the same place as sb/sth (व्यक्ति या वस्तु) के पास; (व्यक्ति या वस्तु) के साथ *I live with my parents.* ○ *I talked about the problem with my tutor.* **2** having or carrying sth किसी वस्तु को साथ लिए, -वाला, -युक्त (पर स्वामित्व की विशेषता के अर्थ में) *a girl with red hair* ○ *the man with the suitcase* **3** using sth से (साधनसूचक), के द्वारा, की सहायता से *Cut it with a knife.* ○ *I did it with his help.* **4** used for saying what fills, covers, etc. sth से (कहीं कुछ भरने, डालने या लिपटाने आदि के अर्थ में) *Fill the bowl with water.* ○ *His hands were covered with oil.* **5** in competition with sb/sth; against sb/sth से, के साथ (व्यक्ति या वस्तु से स्पर्धा करते हुए); के साथ (व्यक्ति या वस्तु के विरोध में) *He's always arguing with his brother.* ○ *I usually play tennis with my sister.* **6** towards, concerning or compared with sb/sth से (व्यक्ति या वस्तु के प्रति, के विषय में या तुलना में) *Is he angry with us?* ○ *There's a problem with my visa.* **7** including sth के साथ (किसी वस्तु को शामिल करते हुए) *The price is for two people with all meals.* **8** used to say how sth happens or is done से, के साथ (कुछ करने या होने के तरीक़े के अर्थ में) *Open this parcel with care.* ○ *to greet sb with a smile* **9** because of sth; as a result of sth (किसी बात) के कारण; (किसी बात) के फलस्वरूप *We were shivering with cold.* ○ *With all the problems we've got, we're not going to finish on time.* **10** in the care of sb के पास (की सुरक्षा में या सँभाल में) *We left the keys with the neighbours.* **11** agreeing with or supporting sb/sth के साथ की तरफ़ (व्यक्ति या वस्तु के पक्ष में) *We've got everybody with us on this issue.* ✪ विलोम **against** **12** at the same time as sth के साथ-साथ (दोनों बातें एक ही समय में हों) *I can't concentrate with you watching me all the time.*

**IDM** **be with sb** to be able to follow what sb is saying किसी की बात को समझ सकना *I'm not quite with you. Say it again.*

**withdraw** /wɪðˈdrɔː विद्ˈड्रॉ/ *verb* (*pt* **withdrew** /-ˈdruː -ˈड्रू/; *pp* **withdrawn** /-ˈdrɔːn -ˈड्रॉन्/) **1** [I, T] **withdraw (sb/sth) (from sth)** to move or order sb to move back or away from a place कहीं से (पीछे या दूर) हट जाना या किसी को हटा देना *The troops withdrew from the town.* **2** [T] to remove sth or take sth away वापस लेना (प्रस्ताव या बयान) *to withdraw an offer/a statement* **3** [T] to take money out of a bank account बैंक (के खाते) से पैसा निकालना *How much would you like to withdraw?* ➪ **deposit** देखिए। **4** [I] to decide not to take part in sth (किसी काम में) भाग न लेने का फ़ैसला करना, से हट जाना *P.T. Usha withdrew from the race at the last minute.*

**withdrawal** /wɪðˈdrɔːəl विद्ˈड्रॉअल्/ *noun* **1** [C, U] moving or being moved back or away from a place कहीं से (पीछे, दूर) हटने या (किसी को) हटाने की क्रिया *the withdrawal of troops from the war zone* **2** [C] taking money out of your bank account;

the amount of money that you take out बैंक खाते से धन की निकासी, आहरण; निकाली गई, निकासी की गई या आहरित धनराशि *to **make a withdrawal*** 3 [U] the act of stopping doing sth, especially taking a drug नशा करने आदि को छोड़ देने का कार्य, नशा-त्याग *When he gave up alcohol he suffered severe **withdrawal symptoms**.*

**withdrawn** /wɪð'drɔːn विद्र'ड्रॉन्/ *adj.* (used about a person) very quiet and not wanting to talk to other people (व्यक्ति) अलग-थलग, ग़ैर-मिलनसार

**wither** /'wɪðə(r) 'विद्र(र्)/ *verb* **1** [I, T] **wither (sth) (away)** (used about plants) to become dry and die; to make a plant do this (पौधों का) मुरझा जाना, कुम्हला जाना; पौधे को सुखाकर मार देना, मुरझा देना *The plants withered in the hot sun.* **2** [I] **wither (away)** to become weaker then disappear क्षीण होते-होते समाप्त हो जाना *This type of industry will wither away in the years to come.*

**withering** /'wɪðərɪŋ 'विद्रिङ्/ *adj.* done to make sb feel silly or embarrassed किसी को मूर्ख सिद्ध करने या लज्जित करने वाला; अवज्ञापूर्ण, तिरस्कार भरा *a withering look*

**withhold** /wɪð'həʊld विद्'होल्ड्/ *verb* [T] (*pt, pp* **withheld** /-'held -'हेल्ड्/) (*formal*) **withhold sth (from sb/sth)** to refuse to give sth to sb किसी वस्तु से कोई वस्तु रोक रखना (देने से इनकार कर देना) *to withhold information from the police*

**within** /wɪ'ðɪn वि'द्रिन्/ *prep., adv.* **1** in a period not longer than a particular length of time (समयावधि की सीमा) के अंदर *I'll be back within an hour.* **2 within sth (of sth)** not further than a particular distance from sth किसी स्थान आदि से विशेष दूरी के भीतर या अंदर *The house is within a kilometre of the station.* **3** not outside the limits of sb/sth किसी व्यक्ति या वस्तु की सीमा के अंदर या भीतर *Each department must keep within its budget.* **4** (*formal*) inside sb/sth व्यक्ति या वस्तु के भीतर *The anger was still there deep within him.*

**without** /wɪ'ðaʊt वि'द्राउट्/ *prep., adv.* **1** not having or showing sth (किसी वस्तु) के बिना, के बग़ैर *Don't go out without a coat on.* ○ *He spoke without much enthusiasm.* **2** not using or being with sb/sth (किसी व्यक्ति या वस्तु) से रहित, के बिना या बग़ैर *Can you see without your glasses?* ○ *Don't leave without me.* **3** used with a verb in the *-ing* form to mean 'not' निषेध के अर्थ में क्रिया के '-ing' युक्त रूप के साथ प्रयुक्त; बिना *She left without saying goodbye.* ○ *I used her phone without her knowing.*

**withstand** /wɪð'stænd विद्'स्टैन्ड्/ *verb* [T] (*pt, pp* **withstood** /-'stʊd -'स्टुड्/) (*formal*) to be strong enough not to break, give up, be damaged, etc. सहन या बरदाश्त कर सकना *These animals can withstand very high temperatures.*

**witness** /'wɪtnəs 'विट्नस्/ *noun* [C] **1** (*also* **eyewitness**) **a witness (to sth)** a person who sees sth happen and who can tell other people about it later घटना का साक्षी; गवाह *There were two witnesses to the accident.* **2** a person who appears in a court of law to say what he/she has seen or what he/she knows about sb/sth (न्यायालय में) घटना का प्रत्यक्षदर्शी, साक्षी, चश्मदीद, गवाह *a witness for the defence/prosecution* **3** a person who sees sb sign an official document and who then signs it himself/herself सरकारी दस्तावेज़ को अनुप्रति हस्ताक्षरित करने वाला व्यक्ति (अपने सामने दूसरे के हस्ताक्षर होने के बाद स्वयं हस्ताक्षर करने वाला व्यक्ति), सत्यापित करने वाला अधिकारी

IDM **bear witness (to sth)** ➪ **bear**[2] देखिए।

**witness**[2] /'wɪtnəs 'विट्नस्/ *verb* [T] **1** to see sth happen and be able to tell other people about it later किसी घटना का गवाह या साक्षी होना *to witness a murder* **2** to see sb sign an official document and then sign it yourself सरकारी दस्तावेज़ को अनुप्रति हस्ताक्षरित करना, सत्यापित करना *to witness a will*

**witness box** (*AmE* **witness-stand**) *noun* [C] the place in a court of law where a witness stands when he/she is giving evidence कठघरा

**witty** /'wɪti 'विटि/ *adj.* (**wittier; wittiest**) clever and amusing; using words in a clever way चतुराईभरा और विनोदपूर्ण, मज़ेदार; वाक्चातुर्य प्रदर्शित करते हुए *a very witty speech* ➪ **wit** noun देखिए।

**wives** ➪ **wife** का plural रूप

**wizard** /'wɪzəd 'विज़ड्/ *noun* [C] (in stories) a man who is believed to have magic powers (कहानियों में) जादूगर, ओझा, अभिचारक, टोनहाया ➪ **witch** और **magician** देखिए।

**wk** *abbr.* (*pl.* **wks**) week सप्ताह, हफ़्ता

**wobble** /'wɒbl 'वॉबल्/ *verb* [I, T] to move from side to side in a way that is not steady; to make sb/sth do this (किसी का) लड़खड़ाना, डगमगाना, ढुलमुल होना; (किसी को) लड़खड़ा देना, ढुलमुल कर देना *Put something under the leg of the table. It's wobbling.* ○ *Stop wobbling the desk. I can't write.*

▶ **wobbly** /'wɒbli 'वॉब्लि/ *adj.* डाँवाँडोल, ढुलमुल

**woe** /wəʊ वो/ *noun* (*formal*) **1 woes** [*pl.*] the problems that sb has परेशानी, मुसीबत, संकट **2** [U] (*old-fashioned*) great unhappiness घोर कष्ट, दुख, घनी पीड़ा

**IDM woe betide sb** used as a warning that there will be trouble if sb does/does not do a particular thing कोई ख़ास बात करने या न करने पर मुसीबत में पड़ने की चेतावनी देने के लिए प्रयुक्त *Woe betide anyone who yawns while the boss is talking.*

**wok** /wɒk वॉक्/ *noun* [C] a large pan that is shaped like a bowl and used for cooking Chinese food चीनी भोजन बनाने की बड़ी कड़ाही; कड़ाह ➪ **pan** पर चित्र देखिए।

**woke** ➪ **wake¹** का past tense रूप

**woken** ➪ **wake¹** का past participle रूप

**wolf** /wʊlf वुल्फ़्/ *noun* [C] (*pl.* **wolves** /wʊlvz वुल्व़्ज़्/) a wild animal that looks like a dog and that lives and hunts in a group (**pack**) भेड़िया

**woman** /ˈwʊmən ˈवुमन्/ *noun* [C] (*pl.* **women** /ˈwɪmɪn ˈविमिन्/) **1** an adult female person स्त्री, औरत, महिला, नारी *men, women and children* **2 -woman** (*in compounds*) a woman who does a particular activity विशेष क्रिया-कलाप में संलग्न महिला *a businesswoman*

**womanhood** /ˈwʊmənhʊd ˈवुमनहुड्/ *noun* [U] the state of being a woman स्त्रीत्व, नारीत्व

**womanly** /ˈwʊmənli ˈवुमन्लि/ *adj.* having qualities considered typical of a woman स्त्रियोचित, नारीसुलभ या स्त्रीसुलभ (स्त्रियों की विशिष्ट विशेषताओं वाला)

**womb** /wu:m वूम्/ *noun* [C] the part of a woman or female animal where a baby grows before it is born स्त्री या मादापशु का गर्भाशय, बच्चेदानी, कोख ✪ पर्याय **uterus**

**won** ➪ **win** का past tense और past participle रूप

**wonder¹** /ˈwʌndə(r) ˈवन्ड(र्)/ *verb* **1** [I, T] **wonder (about sth)** to want to know sth; to ask yourself questions about sth कुछ जानना चाहना; कुछ जानने को उत्सुक होना *I wonder what the new teacher will be like.* ○ *It was something that she had been wondering about for a long time.* **2** [T] used as a polite way of asking a question or of asking sb to do sth शिष्टतापूर्वक पूछने या अनुरोध करने के लिए प्रयुक्त शब्द *I wonder if you could help me.* ○ *I was wondering if you'd like to come to dinner at our house.* **3** [I, T] **wonder (at sth)** to feel great surprise or admiration बहुत अचंभा होना या किसी को बहुत मानना, उसका आदर करना *We wondered at the speed with which he worked.* ○ *'She was very angry.' 'I don't wonder* (= I'm not surprised). *She had a right to be.'*

**wonder²** /ˈwʌndə(r) ˈवन्ड(र्)/ *noun* **1** [U] a feeling of surprise and admiration आश्चर्य और आदर का भाव *The children just stared in wonder at the acrobats.* **2** [C] something that causes you to feel surprise or admiration आश्चर्यजनक या प्रशंसनीय वस्तु *the wonders of modern technology*

**IDM do wonders (for sb/sth)** to have a very good effect on sb/sth किसी व्यक्ति या वस्तु पर (किसी बात का) चमत्कारिक प्रभाव होना *Working in Mumbai did wonders for my Marathi.*

**it's a wonder (that)...** it's surprising that... आश्चर्य की बात है कि *It's a wonder we managed to get here on time, with all the traffic.*

**no wonder** it is not surprising आश्चर्य की बात नहीं (कि) *You've been out every evening this week. No wonder you're tired.*

**wonderful** /ˈwʌndəfl ˈवन्डफ़्ल्/ *adj.* extremely good; fantastic अत्युत्तम, बहुत बढ़िया; आश्चर्यजनक, अद्भुत *What wonderful weather!* ○ *It's wonderful to see you again.* ▶ **wonderfully** /-fəli -फ़लि/ *adv.* आश्चर्यजनक रूप से

**won't** ➪ **will not** का संक्षिप्त रूप

**wood** /wʊd वुड्/ *noun* **1** [U, C] the hard substance that trees are made of लकड़ी, काठ, काष्ठ *He chopped some wood for the fire.* ○ *Pine is a soft wood.* **2** [C] (*often pl.*) an area of land that is covered with trees. A wood is smaller than a forest छोटा जंगल *a walk in the woods*

**IDM touch wood; (*AmE* knock on wood)** an expression that people use (often while touching a piece of wood) to prevent bad luck (लोक विश्वास के अनुसार) अशुभ-निवारण के लिए प्रयुक्त शब्दावली (प्रायः लकड़ी के टुकड़े का स्पर्श करते हुए) *I've been driving here for 20 years and I haven't had an accident yet—touch wood!*

**wooded** /ˈwʊdɪd ˈवुडिड्/ *adj.* (used about an area of land) having a lot of trees growing on it (कोई भूक्षेत्र) जिस पर अनेक वृक्ष लगे हों; वृक्षसंकुल

**woodcutter** /ˈwʊdkʌtə(r) ˈवुड्कट(र्)/ *noun* [C] (*old-fashioned*) a person whose job is cutting down trees लकड़हारा

**wooden** /ˈwʊdn ˈवुड्न्/ *adj.* made of wood लकड़ी का या से बना काष्ठनिर्मित

**woodland** /ˈwʊdlənd ˈवुड्लन्ड्/ *noun* [C, U] land that has a lot of trees growing on it वनस्थली (वृक्षों वाला भूक्षेत्र) *The village is surrounded by woodland.* ○ *woodland birds*

**woodpecker** /ˈwʊdpekə(r) ˈवुड्पेक(र्)/ *noun* [C] a bird with a strong beak that it uses to make holes in trees and to look for insects कठफोड़वा

**wood pulp** *noun* [U] wood that has been broken into small pieces and pressed until it is soft. It is used for making paper लकड़ी की लुगदी (काग़ज़ बनाने में प्रयुक्त)

**woodwind** /ˈwʊdwɪnd ˈवुड्विन्ड्/ *noun* [*sing., with sing. or pl. verb*] the set of musical instruments that you play by blowing into them सुषिर काष्ठ वाद्य (फूँक मार कर बजाए जाने वाले काष्ठनिर्मित वाद्य)

**woodwork** /ˈwʊdwɜːk ˈवुड्वक्/ *noun* [U] **1** the parts of a building that are made of wood such as the doors, stairs, etc. इमारत में लकड़ी का काम (दरवाज़े, सीढ़ियाँ आदि) काष्ठकर्म **2** the activity or skill of making things out of wood काष्ठशिल्प, काष्ठकला (लकड़ी से वस्तुएँ बनाना या बनाने का कौशल)

**woodworm** /ˈwʊdwɜːm ˈवुड्वम्/ *noun* **1** [C] a small, soft, fat creature, the young form of a **beetle**, that eats wood, making a lot of small holes in it घुन, घुण (लकड़ी में लगने वाला कीड़ा) **2** [U] the damage to wood caused by these creatures लकड़ी में घुन लगने से हुआ नुक़सान

**woof** /wʊf वुफ़्/ *noun* [C] (*informal*) used for describing the sound that a dog makes (**a bark**) कुत्ते के भौंकने की आवाज़

**wool** /wʊl वुल्/ *noun* [U] **1** the soft thick hair of sheep ऊन **2** thick thread or cloth that is made from wool ऊनी धागा या ऊनी कपड़ा *The sweater is 50% wool and 50% acrylic.* ➪ **cotton wool** देखिए।

**woollen** (*AmE* **woolen**) /ˈwʊlən ˈवुलन्/ *adj.* made of wool ऊन से बना, ऊनी *a warm woollen jumper*

**woolly** (*AmE* **wooly**) /ˈwʊli ˈवुलि/ *adj.* like wool or made of wool ऊन जैसा या ऊन से बना; ऊनी *The dog had a thick woolly coat.* ○ *long woolly socks*

**word[1]** /wɜːd वड्/ *noun* **1** [C] a sound or letter or group of sounds or letters that expresses a particular meaning शब्द, लफ़्ज़, पद *What does this word mean?* **2** [C] a thing that you say; a short statement or comment बात; कथन, उक्ति या टिप्पणी *Could **I have a word** with you in private?* ○ *Don't say a word about this to anyone.* **3** [*sing.*] a promise वादा, वचन, क़ौल, आश्वासन ***I give you my word** that I won't tell anyone.* ○ *You'll just have to trust him not to **go back on his word**.*

IDM **a dirty word** ➪ **dirty[1]** देखिए।

**not breathe a word (of/about sth) (to sb)** ➪ **breathe** देखिए।

**not get a word in edgeways** to not be able to interrupt when sb else is talking so that you can say sth yourself दूसरे के बोलते समय (अपनी बात कहने के लिए) उसे टोक न पाना

**have, etc. the last word** ➪ **last[1]** देखिए।

**in other words** ➪ **other** देखिए।

**lost for words** ➪ **lost[2]** देखिए।

**put in a (good) word for sb** to say sth good about sb to sb else किसी दूसरे व्यक्ति से किसी व्यक्ति की सिफ़ारिश या तारीफ़ करना *If you could put in a good word for me I might stand a better chance of getting the job.*

**take sb's word for it** to believe what sb says without any proof किसी के कथन को सत्य मान लेना (बिना प्रमाण माँगे)

**word for word** **1** repeating sth exactly शब्दशः आवृत्ति *Shama repeated word for word what he had told her.* **2** translating each word separately, not looking at the general meaning शब्द-प्रति-शब्द अनुवाद (न कि पूरे कथन के सामान्य अर्थ पर ध्यान देते हुए) *a word-for-word translation*

**word[2]** /wɜːd वड्/ *verb* [T] (*often passive*) to write or say sth using particular words विशिष्ट शब्दों में व्यक्त करना *The statement was carefully worded so that nobody would be offended by it.*

**wording** /ˈwɜːdɪŋ ˈवडिङ्/ *noun* [*sing.*] the words that you use to express sth शब्दप्रयोग, शब्दचयन और शब्दविन्यास *The wording of the contract was vague.*

**word-perfect** *adj.* able to say sth that you have learnt from memory, without making a mistake स्मृति से (बिलकुल) सही-सही कह सकने वाला, शब्दशः स्मृति पुष्ट, सुकंठस्थ

**word processing** *noun* [U] (*computing*) the use of a computer to write, store and print a piece of text कंप्यूटर की सहायता से पाठ्य, पाठ-सामग्री को लिखना, संचित करना और मुद्रित करना; शब्दसंसाधन करना *I mainly use the computer for word processing.*

**word processor** *noun* [C] a type of small computer that you can use for writing letters, reports, etc. You can correct or change what you have written before you print it out शब्दसंसाधन करने वाला कंप्यूटर (कंप्यूटर जिसमें पत्र, रिपोर्ट आदि लिखने का प्रोग्राम होता है; इसमें लिखित सामग्री को संपादित करने की सुविधा भी होती है)

**wore** ➪ **wear[1]** का past tense रूप

**work[1]** /wɜːk वक्/ *verb* **1** [I, T] **work (as sth) (for sb); work (at/on sth); work (to do sth)** to do sth which needs physical or mental effort, in order to earn money or to achieve sth काम करना (शारीरिक या मानसिक श्रम करना, धनार्जन या कुछ प्राप्त करने के लिए) *Doctors often work extremely long hours.* ○ *I hear she's working on a new novel.* **2** [T] to make yourself/sb work, especially very

hard किसी से (घोर) परिश्रम करवाना *The coach works the players very hard in training.* **3** [I, T] (used about a machine, etc.) to function; to make sth function; to operate (मशीन आदि का) काम करना, चलना; किसी को चलाना; संचालित या परिचालित करना *Our telephone hasn't been working for several days.* ○ *We still don't really understand how the brain works.* **4** [I] to have the result or effect that you want; to be successful अभीष्ट परिश्रम या प्रभाव होना; के पक्ष में जाना, को अनुकूल फल देना *Your idea sounds good but I don't think it will really work.* ○ *The heat today could work in favour of the Indian runners.* **5** [I, T] to move gradually to a new position or state अपनी जगह छोड़ देना, ढीला हो जाना धीरे-धीरे आगे बढ़ना या ऊपर चढ़ना *Engineers check the plane daily, because nuts and screws can **work loose**.* ○ *I watched the snail **work its way** up the wall.* **6** [I, T] to use materials to make a model, a picture, etc. प्रतिरूप, चित्र आदि बनाने के लिए (उपयुक्त) सामग्री का उपयोग करना *He worked the clay into the shape of a horse.* ○ *She usually works in/with oils or acrylics.*

IDM **work/perform miracles** ➪ **miracle** देखिए।

**work/sweat your guts out** ➪ **gut¹** देखिए।

**work to rule** ➪ **rule¹** देखिए।

PHR V **work out** **1** to develop or progress, especially in a good way के अनुकूल सिद्ध होना, के पक्ष में जाना *I hope things work out for you.* **2** to do physical exercises in order to keep your body fit व्यायाम करना (शरीर को चुस्त-दुरुस्त रखने के लिए) *We work out to music at my exercise class.*

**work out (at)** to come to a particular result or total after everything has been calculated कुल योग निकालना *If we divide the work between us it'll work out at about four hours each.*

**work sb out** to understand sb किसी व्यक्ति को समझाना *I've never been able to work her out.*

**work sth out** **1** to find the answer to sth; to solve sth किसी (प्रश्न) का उत्तर ढूँढना; किसी समस्या को सुलझाना; का हल निकालना *I can't work out how to do this.* **2** to calculate sth हिसाब लगाना *I worked out the total cost.* **3** to plan sth (किसी काम की) योजना बनाना *Have you worked out the route through Delhi?*

**work up to sth** to develop or progress to sth धीरे-धीरे (किसी को) किसी लक्ष्य तक पहुँचाना; आगे बढ़ाना या ले जाना *Start with 15 minutes' exercise and gradually work up to 30.*

**work sth up** to develop or improve sth with effort परिश्रमपूर्वक किसी वस्तु या स्थिति को सुधारना *I'm trying to work up the energy to go out.*

**work sb/yourself up (into sth)** to make sb/yourself become angry, excited, upset, etc. किसी को क्रोध, उत्तेजना, परेशानी आदि की स्थिति में ले आना *He had worked himself up into a state of anxiety about his interview.*

**work²** /wɜːk वक् / *noun* **1** [U] the job that you do, especially in order to earn money; the place where you do your job काम, नौकरी (विशेषतः धनार्जन के लिए); नौकरी करने की जगह, कार्य-स्थल (दफ़्तर या फ़ैक्टरी आदि) *It is very difficult to **find work** in this city.* ○ *He's been **out of work*** (= without a job) *for six months.* ○ *When do you **start work**?*

> NOTE **Work** अगणनीय संज्ञा है। कुछ संदर्भों में **job** ही सही प्रयोग है—*I've found work at the hospital.* ○ *I've got a new job at the hospital.* **Employment** का अर्थ है वेतनभोगी कर्मचारी होना और यह शब्द **work** या **job** से अधिक औपचारिक और आधिकारिक है—*Many married women are in part-time employment.* प्रपत्रों में प्रयुक्त **occupation** शब्द का अर्थ है, आप क्या हैं या क्या काम करते हैं —*Occupation: student. Occupation: bus driver.* **Profession** वह काम है जिसमें विशेष प्रशिक्षण और उच्च शिक्षा की आवश्यकता होती है—*the medical profession.* **Trade** वह काम है जो हाथों से किया जाता है और जिसमें विशेष कौशल की ज़रूरत होती है—*He's a carpenter by trade.*

**2** [U] something that requires physical or mental effort that you do in order to achieve sth (विशेष लक्ष्य को प्राप्त करने के लिए) शारीरिक या मानसिक श्रम की अपेक्षा वाली कोई वस्तु या काम *Her success is due to sheer hard work.* ○ *We hope to start work on the project next week.* **3** [U] something that you are working on or have produced बनाई वस्तु, किया हुआ काम *a piece of written work* ○ *The teacher marked their work.* **4** [C] a book, painting, piece of music, etc. (कोई) पुस्तक, पेंटिंग, संगीत-रचना आदि *the complete works of Kalidasa* **5 works** [*pl.*] the act of building or repairing sth निर्माण या मरम्मत कार्य *The roadworks are causing long traffic jams.* **6 works** [C, *with sing. or pl. verb*] (*often in compounds*) a factory फ़ैक्टरी, कारख़ाना *The steel works is/are closing down.* **7** [U] (*technical*) the use of force to produce movement गति उत्पन्न करने के लिए बल का प्रयोग

IDM **get/go/set to work (on sth)** to begin; to make a start (on sth) आरंभ करना; (किसी योजना आदि पर) काम शुरू करना

**workable** /ˈwɜːkəbl ˈवकबल् / *adj.* that can be used successfully; practical जिसे सफलतापूर्वक व्यवहार में लाया जा सके, व्यवहार्य; व्यावहारिक *a workable plan/solution*

**workaholic** /ˌwɜːkəˈhɒlɪk ˌवक ˈहॉलिक् / *noun* [C] a person who loves work and does too much of it जिस पर ख़ूब काम करने की धुन सवार हो; कार्योन्मादी, कर्मानुरागी

**workbench** /ˈwɜːkbentʃ ˈवक्‌बेन्च् / *noun* [C] a long heavy table used for doing practical jobs, working with tools, etc. (औज़ारों से होने वाले काम करने की) लंबी भारी मेज़ ➪ **vice** पर चित्र देखिए।

**workbook** /ˈwɜːkbʊk ˈवक्‌बुक् / *noun* [C] a book with questions and exercises in it that you use when you are studying sth अभ्यास-कार्य पुस्तिका (छात्रों द्वारा प्रयुक्त)

**worker** /ˈwɜːkə(r) ˈवक(र्) / *noun* [C] **1** (*often in compounds*) a person who works, especially one who does a particular kind of work कार्यकर्ता, कर्मी (विशेष प्रकार का काम करने वाला व्यक्ति) *factory/office/farm workers* ○ *skilled/manual workers* **2** a person who is employed to do physical work rather than organizing things or managing people मज़दूर, कामगार, श्रमिक *Workers' representatives will meet management today to discuss the pay dispute.* **3** a person who works in a particular way ख़ास ढंग से काम करने वाला व्यक्ति *a slow/fast worker*

**workforce** /ˈwɜːkfɔːs ˈवक्‌फ़ॉस् / *noun* [C, *with sing. or pl. verb*] **1** the total number of people who work in a company, factory, etc. कंपनी, फ़ैक्टरी आदि के कुल कर्मचारी; कर्मचारीगण **2** the total number of people in a country who are able to work (किसी देश में) काम करने के योग्य व्यक्तियों की कुल संख्या, कार्यक्षम जनसंख्या *Ten per cent of the work force is/are unemployed.*

**working** /ˈwɜːkɪŋ ˈवकिङ् / *adj.* (*only before a noun*) **1** employed; having a job कहीं नियुक्त, सेवारत; नौकरी वाला, किसी काम में लगा हुआ *the problems of childcare for working mothers* **2** connected with your job काम या नौकरी से संबंधित *He stayed with the same company for the whole of his* ***working life***. **3** good enough to be used, although it could be improved कामचलाऊ (सुधार की गुंजाइश के साथ) *We are looking for someone with* ***a working knowledge*** *of Hindi.*

**IDM** **in working order** ➪ **order**[1] देखिए।

**the working class** *noun* [*sing.*] (*also* **the working classes**) [*pl.*] the group of people in a society who do not have much money or power and who usually do physical work, especially in industry मज़दूर वर्ग या श्रमिक वर्ग, वेतनभोगी वर्ग *unemployment among the working class*
▸ **working class** *adj.* श्रमिक या वेतनभोगी (वर्ग से संबंधित) *They're working class.* ○ *a working-class family* ➪ **the middle class** और **the upper class** देखिए।

**workings** /ˈwɜːkɪŋz ˈवकिङ्ज़् / *noun* [*pl.*] the way in which a machine, an organization, etc. operates मशीन, संस्था आदि के काम करने का ढंग; कार्यप्रणाली *It's very difficult to understand the workings of the legal system.*

**workload** /ˈwɜːkləʊd ˈवक्‌लोड् / *noun* [C] the amount of work that you have to do (आपके) काम का भार या विस्तार, करणीय काम की मात्रा *She often gets home late when she has a* ***heavy workload***.

**workman** /ˈwɜːkmən ˈवक्‌मन् / *noun* [C] (*pl.* **-men** /-mən -मन् /) a man who works with his hands, especially at building or making things हाथ का कारीगर; शिल्पी

**workmanlike** /ˈwɜːkmənlaɪk ˈवक्‌मन्‌लाइक् / *adj.* done, made, etc. very well, but not original or exciting बढ़िया ढंग से किया गया, बनाया हुआ आदि (न कि मौलिक या रोचक); कारीगरीभरा, कौशलपूर्ण *The leading actor gave a workmanlike performance.*

**workmanship** /ˈwɜːkmənʃɪp ˈवक्‌मन्‌शिप् / *noun* [U] the skill with which sth is made कारीगरी, कर्म-कौशल, शिल्प

**work of art** *noun* [C] (*pl.* **works of art**) a very good painting, book, piece of music, etc. कलाकृति (श्रेष्ठ पेंटिंग, पुस्तक, संगीत-रचना आदि) ➪ **art** देखिए।

**workout** /ˈwɜːkaʊt ˈवक्‌आउट् / *noun* [C] a period of physical exercise, for example when you are training for a sport or keeping fit अभ्यास की अवधि, अभ्यासकाल *She does a twenty-minute workout every morning.*

**worksheet** /ˈwɜːkʃiːt ˈवक्‌शीट् / *noun* [C] a piece of paper with questions or exercises on it that you use when you are studying sth कार्यपत्रक (छात्रों द्वारा प्रयुक्त पत्रक जिस पर प्रश्न या अभ्यास होते हैं)

**workshop** /ˈwɜːkʃɒp ˈवक्‌शॉप् / *noun* [C] **1** a place where things are made or repaired कारख़ाना, कर्मशाला (स्थान जहाँ चीज़ें बनती हैं या उनकी मरम्मत होती है) **2** a period of discussion and practical work on a particular subject, when people share their knowledge and experience कार्यशाला, कार्यगोष्ठी (शिक्षाकर्मियों या ज्ञानकर्मियों की संवाद गोष्ठी) *a drama/writing workshop*

**workstation** /ˈwɜːksteɪʃn ˈवक्‌स्टेश्न् / *noun* [C] (*computing*) the desk and computer that a person works at; one computer that is part of a **network** डेस्क और कंप्यूटर जिस पर व्यक्ति काम करता है; कोई कंप्यूटर जो नेटवर्क का अंग हो, वर्क-स्टेशन

**worktop** /ˈwɜːktɒp ˈवक्‌टॉप् / (*also* **work surface**) *noun* [C] a flat surface in a kitchen, etc. that you use for preparing food, etc. on रसोई आदि में बना फट्टा या प्लेटफ़ार्म (जिस पर खाना बनाने आदि का काम होता है)

**work-to-rule** *noun* [*usually sing.*] a situation in which workers refuse to do any work that is not in their contracts, in order to protest about sth नियमानुसार काम (विरोधस्वरूप उठाया गया क़दम जिसमें कार्यकर्ता कोई अतिरिक्त काम नहीं करते या केवल अनुबंधित काम तक सीमित रहते हैं)

**world** /wɜːld वल्ड् / *noun* **1 the world** [*sing.*] the earth with all its countries and people विश्व, जगत, संसार, दुनिया *I took a year off work to travel* ***round the world.*** ○ *She is famous* ***all over the world.*** **2** [*sing.*] a particular part of the earth or group of countries पृथ्वी का विशेष भाग या देशों का समूह *the western world* ○ *the Third World* **3** [*sing.*] the life and activities of people; their experience लोगों का जीवन और उनके कामकाज; लोगों का अनुभव *It's time you learned something about the real world!* ○ *the modern world* **4** [C] (*often in compounds*) a particular area of activity or group of people or things क्रियाकलाप का विशिष्ट क्षेत्र या विशिष्ट कार्य करने वाले लोग या विशिष्ट वस्तुएँ *the world of sport/fashion/politics* ○ *the medical/business/animal/natural world* **5** [*sing.*] the people in the world विश्व के निवासी, संसार के लोग, मानवजाति ***The whole world*** *seemed to know the news before me!* **6** [C] a planet with life on it ग्रह जिस पर जीवन हो *Do you believe there are other worlds out there, like ours?*

IDM **do sb a/the world of good** (*informal*) to have a very good effect on sb किसी व्यक्ति का (किसी बात से) बहुत भला होना *The holiday has done her the world of good.*

**in the world** used to emphasize what you are saying अपनी बात पर बल देने के लिए प्रयुक्त *Everyone else is stressed but he doesn't seem to have a care in the world.* ○ *There's no need to rush —we've got all the time in the world.*

**the outside world** ➪ **outside**[2] देखिए।

**think the world of sb/sth** ➪ **think** देखिए।

**the World Bank** *noun* [*sing.*] an international organization that lends money to countries who are members at times when they are in danger or difficulty and need more money विश्व बैंक (संकट या कठिनाई के समय सदस्य देशों की आर्थिक सहायता करने वाला अंतरराष्ट्रीय संगठन)

**world-famous** *adj.* known all over the world विश्व प्रसिद्ध, जग-विख्यात

**worldly** /ˈwɜːldli ˈवल्ड्लि / *adj.* **1** connected with ordinary life, not with the spirit भौतिक, सांसारिक, दुनियावी (न कि आध्यात्मिक) *He left all his worldly possessions to his nephew.* **2** having a lot of experience and knowledge of life and people जीवन और लोगों के विषय में बहुत जानकारी और अनुभव रखने वाला; दुनियादार *a sophisticated and worldly man*

**world power** *noun* [C] a powerful country that has a lot of influence in international politics अंतर्राष्ट्रीय राजनीति में दबदबा रखने वाला शक्तिशाली देश; विश्वशक्ति ➪ **power**[1] **4** और **superpower** देखिए।

**world war** *noun* [C] a war that involves a lot of different countries युद्ध जिसमें बहुत-से देश उलझे हों; विश्वयुद्ध *the Second World War* ○ *World War One*

**worldwide** /ˌwɜːldˈwaɪd ˌवल्ड्ˈवाइड् / *adv.*, ˈwɜːldwaɪd ˈवल्ड्वाइड् / *adj.* (happening) in the whole world समूचे विश्व में, विश्वभर में, विश्वव्यापी *The product will be marketed worldwide.* ○ *The situation has caused worldwide concern.*

**the World Wide Web** (*also* **the Web**) *noun* [*sing.*] (*abbr.* **WWW**) the international system of computers that makes it possible for you to see information from around the world on your computer अंतर्राष्ट्रीय कंप्यूटर प्रणाली जिसकी सहायता से विश्वभर की जानकारी या सूचना-सामग्री कंप्यूटर पर उपलब्ध हो जाती है; वर्ल्ड-वाइड-वेब *a Web browser/page* ➪ **the Internet** देखिए।

**worm**[1] /wɜːm वम् / *noun* [C] **1** a small animal with a long thin body and no eyes, bones or legs कीड़ा, कृमि *an earthworm* **2 worms** [*pl.*] one or more worms that live inside a person or an animal and may cause disease मनुष्य या पशु के शरीर में रहने वाले रोग-कारक कृमि या कीड़े *He's got worms.*

**worm**[2] /wɜːm वम् / *verb* [T] **worm your way/yourself along, through, etc.** to move slowly or with difficulty in the direction mentioned निर्दिष्ट दिशा में धीमी गति या कठिनाई से चलना, कीड़े के समान रेंगते हुए चलना *I managed to worm my way through the crowd.*

PHR V **worm your way/yourself into sth** to make sb like you or trust you, in order to dishonestly gain an advantage for yourself (किसी को ठगने के लिए) उसकी पसंद बनना या उसका विश्वास जीतना

**worn** ➪ **wear**[1] का past participle of रूप

**worn-out** *adj.* **1** too old or damaged to use any more जीर्ण-शीर्ण, फटा-पुराना *My shoes are completely worn-out.* **2** extremely tired थका-माँदा, थक कर चूर *I'm absolutely worn-out. I think I'll go to bed early.* ➪ **wear** देखिए।

**worried** /ˈwʌrid ˈवरिड्/ *adj.* **worried (about sb/sth); worried (that...)** thinking that sth bad might happen or has happened (किसी आशंका से) चिंतित, फ़िक्रमंद *I'm* ***worried sick*** *about the exam.* *We were worried stiff* (= extremely worried) *that you might have had an accident.*

**worry[1]** /ˈwʌri ˈवरि/ *verb* (*pres. part.* **worrying;** *3rd person sing. pres.* **worries;** *pt, pp* **worried**) **1** [I] **worry (about sb/sth)** to think that sth bad might happen or has happened किसी दुर्घटना की आशंका से चिंतित होना, फ़िक्रमंद होना *There's nothing to worry about.* ○ *He worries if I don't phone every weekend.* **2** [T] **worry sb/yourself (about sb/sth)** to make sb/yourself think that sth bad might happen or has happened किसी दुर्घटना की आशंका से किसी को चिंता होना *What worries me is how are we going to get home?* **3** [T] **worry sb (with sth)** to disturb sb; to bother sb किसी का ध्यान बँटाना; किसी को कष्ट देना, परेशान करना *I'm sorry to worry you with my problems but I really do need some advice.*

IDM **not to worry** it is not important; it doesn't matter यह कोई बड़ी बात नहीं; इससे कोई फ़र्क नहीं पड़ता

▶ **worrying** *adj.* चिंताजनक *a worrying situation*

**worry[2]** /ˈwʌri ˈवरि/ *noun* (*pl.* **worries**) **1** [U] the state of worrying about sth (किसी बात की) चिंता, फ़िक्र *His son has caused him a lot of worry recently.* **2** [C] something that makes you worry; a problem चिंताजनक वस्तु या स्थिति; समस्या *Crime is a real worry for old people.* ○ *financial worries*

**worse** /wɜːs वस्/ *adj., adv.* (*the comparative of* **bad** *or of* **badly**) **1** not as good or as well as sth else('bad' या 'badly' का तुलनात्मक रूप) बदतर, और बुरा, और ख़राब *My exam results were* ***far/much worse*** *than I thought they would be.* **2** (*not before a noun*) more ill; less well और बीमार; जिसकी हालत या दशा अच्छी नहीं *If you* ***get any worse*** *we'll call the doctor.* ▶ **worse** *noun* बदतर [U] *The situation was already bad but there was worse to come.*

IDM **to make matters/things worse** to make a situation, problem, etc. even more difficult or dangerous than before स्थिति, समस्या आदि को और बिगाड़ देना

**none the wiser/worse** ⇨ **none[2]** देखिए।

**the worse for wear** (*informal*) damaged; not in good condition क्षतिग्रस्त; जिसकी दशा ठीक नहीं, दुर्दशाग्रस्त *This suitcase looks a bit the worse for wear.*

**worsen** /ˈwɜːsn ˈवसन्/ *verb* [I, T] to become worse or to make sth worse बदतर हो जाना या (किसी को) बदतर कर देना *Relations between the two countries have worsened.*

**worship** /ˈwɜːʃɪp ˈवशिप्/ *verb* (**worshipping; worshipped** *AmE* **worshiping; worshiped**) **1** [I, T] to pray to and show respect for God or a god (की) पूजा करना, आराधना करना (परमेश्वर या किसी देवता से विनती करना या उसके प्रति सम्मान प्रदर्शित करना) *People travel from all over the world to worship at this shrine.* **2** [T] to love or admire sb/sth very much व्यक्ति या वस्तु से अत्यधिक प्रेम करना या उसकी प्रशंसा तथा आदर करना, (को) पूजना *She worshipped her parents.* ▶ **worship** *noun* [U] पूजा, आराधना, अर्चना, इबादत *Different religions have different forms of worship.* ▶ **worshipper** *noun* [C] पूजारी, आराधक

**worst[1]** /wɜːst वस्ट्/ *adj., adv.* (*the superlative of* **bad** *or of* **badly**) the least pleasant or suitable; the least well ('bad' या 'badly' का उत्तमावस्था का रूप) सबसे बुरा या सबसे ख़राब; बदतरीन *It's been the worst winter that I can remember.* ○ *A lot of the children behaved badly but my son behaved worst of all!*

**worst[2]** /wɜːst वस्ट्/ *noun* [*sing.*] something that is as bad as it can be सबसे बुरी बात या स्थिति *My parents always expect the worst if I'm late.*

IDM **at (the) worst** if the worst happens or if you consider sb/sth in the worst way यदि सबसे बुरी बात घट जाए, यदि किसी वस्तु या व्यक्ति के विषय में सबसे बुरा सोचा जाए, बुरे से बुरा यह होगा कि *The problem doesn't look too serious. At worst we'll have to make a few small changes.*

**if the worst comes to the worst** if the worst possible situation happens यदि सबसे बुरी स्थिति आ जाए

**worth[1]** /wɜːθ वथ्/ *adj.* **1** having a particular value (in money) किसी विशेष मूल्य वाला, क़ीमत का *How much do you think that house is worth?* **2 worth doing, etc.** used as a way of recommending or advising करने (आदि) के योग्य (जैसे देखने योग्य) (सिफ़ारिश या सलाह देने के लिए प्रयुक्त) *That museum's* ***well worth*** *visiting if you have time.* ○ *The library closes in 5 minutes—it's not worth going in.*

NOTE निम्नलिखित प्रयोग भी संभव हैं—*It isn't worth repairing the car.* ○ *The car isn't worth repairing.*

**3** enjoyable or useful to do or have, even if it means extra cost, effort, etc. जिसे करना आनंदप्रद हो या जिसे लेना उपयोगी हो (भले ही उसमें धन, श्रम

आदि अधिक लगे), अधिक धन, श्रम के बावजूद भी करने या लेने योग्य *It takes a long time to walk to the top of the hill but it's worth the effort.* ○ *Don't bother cooking a big meal. It isn't* ***worth it****—we're not hungry.*

IDM **get your money's worth** ➪ **money** देखिए। **worth sb's while** helpful, useful or interesting to sb किसी व्यक्ति के लिए सहायक, उपयोगी या रोचक

**worth²** /wɜːθ वर्थ् / *noun* [U] **1** the value of sb/sth; how useful sb/sth is किसी व्यक्ति या वस्तु का महत्त्व; किसी व्यक्ति या वस्तु की उपयोगिता *She has proved her worth as a member of the team.* **2** the amount of sth that the money mentioned will buy ख़ास क़ीमत देकर प्राप्त किसी वस्तु की मात्रा *hundred rupees' worth of petrol* **3** the amount of sth that will last for the time mentioned बताई गई अवधि तक चलने वाली किसी वस्तु की मात्रा, तक का *two days' worth of food*

**worthless** /ˈwɜːθləs ˈवर्थ्लस् / *adj.* **1** having no value or use बेकार, किसी काम (या दाम) का नहीं, व्यर्थ का *It's worthless—it's only a bit of plastic!* **2** (used about a person) having bad qualities (व्यक्ति) निकम्मा ➪ **priceless, valuable** और **invaluable** देखिए।

**worthwhile** /ˌwɜːθˈwaɪl ˌवर्थ्ˈवाइल् / *adj.* enjoyable, useful or satisfying enough to be worth the cost or effort अपनी क़ीमत और (प्राप्त करने में) लगे श्रम के अनुसार आनंदप्रद, उपयोगी या संतोषजनक, लाभप्रद, सार्थक *Working for so little money just isn't worthwhile.*

**worthy** /ˈwɜːði ˈवर्दि / *adj.* (**worthier; worthiest**) **1 worthy of sth/to do sth** good enough for sth or to have sth किसी बात या वस्तु या कुछ धारण करने के योग्य *He felt he was not worthy to accept such responsibility.* **2** that should receive respect, support or attention सम्मान, समर्थन प्रशंसा पाने योग्य, माननीय, आदरणीय या प्रशंसनीय *a worthy leader* ○ *a worthy cause*

**would** /wəd; वड् *strong form* wʊd; प्रबल रूप वुड् / *modal verb* (*short form* **'d**; *negative* **would not;** *short form* **wouldn't** /ˈwʊdnt ˈवुडन्ट् /) **1** used when talking about the result of an event that you imagine काल्पनिक घटना के परिणाम के वर्णन में (प्रयुक्त) *He would be delighted if you went to see him.* ○ *I would have done more, if I'd had the time.* **2** used for asking sb politely to do sth नम्र अनुरोध में, नम्रतापूर्ण व्यवहार में प्रयुक्त *Would you come this way, please?* **3** used with 'like' or 'love' as a way of asking or saying what sb wants किसी से उसकी पसंद पूछने या अपनी पसंद बताने के लिए 'like' या 'love' के साथ प्रयुक्त ***Would you like*** *to come with us?* ○ ***I'd love*** *a piece of cake.* **4** to agree or be ready to do sth कुछ करने के लिए मान जाना या तैयार हो जाना *She just wouldn't do what I asked her.* **5** used as the past form of 'will' when you report what sb says or thinks किसी के कथन या सोच की सूचना देने के लिए 'will' के भूतकालिक रूप में प्रयुक्त (परोक्ष कथन शैली में) *They said that they would help us.* ○ *She didn't think that he would do a thing like that.* **6** used after 'wish'; शब्द 'wish' के बाद प्रयुक्त *I wish the sun would come out.* **7** used for talking about things that often happened in the past अतीत में प्रायः घटने वाली घटनाओं की चर्चा के लिए प्रयुक्त *When he was young he would often walk in these woods.* **8** used for commenting on behaviour that is typical of sb किसी के निजी ख़ास व्यवहार पर टिप्पणी करने के लिए प्रयुक्त *You would say that. You always support him.* **9** used when you are giving your opinion but are not certain that you are right कुछ अनिश्चित भाव से अपना मत व्यक्त करते हुए *I'd say she's about 40.*

NOTE वृत्तिवाचक क्रियाओं (modal verbs) के विषय में अधिक जानकारी के लिए इस शब्दकोश के अंत में **Quick Grammar Reference** शीर्षकखंड देखिए।

**would-be** *adj.* (*only before a noun*) used to describe sb who is hoping to become the type of person mentioned भावी; यथाकथित रूप से कुछ बनाने का इच्छुक *advice for would-be parents*

**wound¹** /wuːnd वून्ड् / *noun* [C] an injury to part of your body, especially a cut, often one received in fighting घाव, ज़ख़्म, क्षत *a bullet wound*

IDM **rub salt into the wound/sb's wounds** ➪ **rub** देखिए।

**wound²** /wuːnd वून्ड् / *verb* [T] (*usually passive*) **1** to injure sb's body with a weapon हथियार से किसी के अंग को चोट पहुँचाना, घायल करना *He was wounded in the leg during the war.* ➪ **hurt** पर नोट देखिए। **2** (*formal*) to hurt sb's feelings deeply किसी की भावनाओं को गहरी ठेस पहुँचाना *I was wounded by his criticism.* ▶ **wounded** /ˈwuːndɪd ˈवून्डिड् / *adj.* घायल, ज़ख़्मी *a wounded soldier* ▶ **the wounded** *noun* [*pl.*] घायल या ज़ख़्मी लोग *Paramedics tended to the wounded at the scene of the explosion.*

**wound³** ➪ **wind³** का past tense और past participle रूप

**wove** ➪ **weave** का past tense रूप

**woven** ➪ **weave** का past participle रूप

**wow** /waʊ वाउ / *exclamation* (*informal*) used for saying that you are very impressed and surprised by sth वाह-वाह (प्रशंसा और आश्चर्य व्यक्त करने के लिए प्रयुक्त अभिव्यक्ति) *Wow! What a fantastic boat!*

**WP** *abbr.* word processing; word processor शब्दसंसाधन; शब्दसंसाधक; वर्ड प्रॉसेसिंग; वर्ड प्रॉसेसर

**wrangle** /ˈræŋgl ˈरैङ्गल्/ *noun* [C] a noisy or complicated argument नोक-झोंक, कहा-सुनी वाली या पेचीदा विवाद *The company is involved in **a legal wrangle** over copyrights.* ▸ **wrangle** *verb* [I] पेचीदा विवाद में पड़ना, झगड़ा करना

**wrap** /ræp रैप्/ *verb* [T] (**wrapping; wrapped**) **1 wrap sth (up) (in sth)** to put paper or cloth around sb/sth as a cover किसी वस्तु पर काग़ज़ चढ़ाना या किसी व्यक्ति पर कपड़ा लपेटना *to wrap up a present* ○ *The baby was found wrapped in a blanket.* **2 wrap sth round/around sb/sth** to tie sth such as paper or cloth around an object or a part of the body किसी वस्तु या अंग के चारों ओर (क्रमशः) काग़ज़ या कपड़ा लपेटना या बाँधना *The man had a bandage wrapped round his head.*

**IDM be wrapped up in sth** to be very involved and interested in sb/sth किसी व्यक्ति या वस्तु से भरपूर प्रेम करना और तन्मय हो जाना, (मानो) उसमें डूब जाना *They were completely wrapped up in each other. They didn't notice I was there.*

**PHR V wrap (sb/yourself) up** to put warm clothes on sb/yourself गरम कपड़े पहनना या (किसी को) पहनाना

**wrapper** /ˈræpə(r) ˈरैप(र्)/ *noun* [C] the piece of paper or plastic which covers sth when you buy it (ख़रीदते समय) किसी चीज़ पर लपेटा गया काग़ज़ या प्लास्टिक *a sweet/chocolate wrapper*

**wrapping** /ˈræpɪŋ ˈरैपिङ्/ *noun* [C, U] paper, plastic, etc. that is used for covering sth in order to protect it किसी वस्तु पर (सुरक्षा की दृष्टि से) लपेटा गया काग़ज़, प्लास्टिक आदि *Remove the wrapping before heating the pie.*

**wrapping paper** *noun* [U] paper which is used for putting round presents उपहारों का आवरण (काग़ज़)

**wrath** /rɒθ रॉथ़्/ *noun* [U] (*written*) very great anger तीव्र रोष, तेज़ गुस्सा या क्रोधोन्माद

**wreak** /riːk रीक्/ *verb* [T] (*formal*) **wreak sth (on sb/sth)** to cause great damage or harm to sb/sth किसी व्यक्ति या वस्तु को बहुत क्षति या हानि पहुँचाना *Fierce storms **wreak havoc** at this time of year.*

**wreath** /riːθ रीथ़्/ *noun* [C] (*pl.* **wreaths** /riːðz रीद़्ज़्/) a circle of flowers and leaves, especially one that you give to the family of sb who has died (फूलों और पत्तियों का) पुष्पचक्र, मालाचक्र (विशेषतः शव पर चढ़ाई या अर्पित की गई)

**wreck** /rek रेक्/ *noun* [C] **1** a ship that has sunk or been badly damaged at sea समुद्र में मग्न या बुरी तरह क्षतिग्रस्त जहाज़ *Divers searched the wreck.* **2** a car, plane, etc. which has been badly damaged, especially in an accident (प्रायः दुर्घटना में) बुरी तरह क्षतिग्रस्त कार, विमान आदि *The car was a wreck but the lorry escaped almost without damage.* **3** [*usually sing.*] (*informal*) a person or thing that is in a very bad condition दुर्दशा को प्राप्त व्यक्ति या वस्तु *He drove so badly I was **a nervous wreck** when we got there.* ▸ **wreck** *verb* [T] बरबाद कर देना *Vandals had wrecked the school hall.* ○ *The strike wrecked all our holiday plans.*

**wreckage** /ˈrekɪdʒ ˈरेकिज्/ *noun* [U] the broken pieces of sth that has been destroyed मलबा, विनष्ट वस्तु के अवशेष *Investigators searched the wreckage of the plane for evidence.*

**wrench¹** /rentʃ रेन्च्/ *verb* [T] **1 wrench sb/sth (away, off, etc.)** to pull or turn sb/sth strongly and suddenly व्यक्ति या वस्तु को ज़ोर से और झटका देकर खींचना या मरोड़ना *They had to wrench the door off the car to get the driver out.* ○ (*figurative*) *The film was so exciting that I could hardly wrench myself away.* **2** to injure part of your body by turning it suddenly शरीर को झटके से मरोड़कर चोट खा जाना

**wrench²** /rentʃ रेन्च्/ *noun* **1** [C] a sudden, violent pull or turn तेज़ झटका या मोच *With a wrench I managed to open the door.* **2** [*sing.*] the sadness you feel because you have to leave sb/sth बिछड़ने की पीड़ा या व्यथा **3** [C] (*AmE*) = **spanner** ➪ **monkey wrench** और **adjustable spanner** देखिए तथा **tool** पर चित्र देखिए।

**wrestle** /ˈresl ˈरेस्ल्/ *verb* [I] **1 wrestle (with) sb** to fight by trying to get hold of your opponent's body and throw him/her to the ground. People wrestle as a sport (किसी से) कुश्ती लड़ना, मल्लयुद्ध करना *He managed to wrestle the man to the ground and take the knife from him.* **2 wrestle (with sth)** to try hard to deal with sth that is difficult किसी समस्या से जूझना

**wrestling** /ˈreslɪŋ ˈरेस्लिङ्/ *noun* [U] a sport in which two people fight and try to throw each other to the ground कुश्ती, मल्लयुद्ध *a wrestling match* ▸ **wrestler** *noun* [C] पहलवान, मल्ल, कुश्तीबाज़

**wretch** /retʃ रेच्/ *noun* [C] (*old-fashioned*) a poor, unhappy person ग़रीब उदास व्यक्ति, अभागा इनसान *The poor wretch was clearly starving.*

**wretched** /ˈretʃɪd ˈरेचिड्/ *adj.* **1** very unhappy बहुत दुखी, शोकसंतप्त **2** (*informal*) used for expressing anger कमीना (क्रोधावेश में प्रयुक्त) *That wretched dog has chewed up my slippers again!*

**wriggle** /ˈrɪgl ˈरिग्ल्/ *verb* [I, T] **1 wriggle (sth) (about/ around)** to move about, or to move a part of your body, with short, quick movements, especially from side to side छटपटाना, तड़पना, कुलबुलाना, टेढ़े-मेढ़े घुमाना *The baby was wriggling around on my lap.* ○ *She wriggled her fingers about in the sand.* **2** to move in the direction mentioned by making quick turning movements टेढ़े-मेढ़े घूमना, रेंगना *The worm wriggled back into the soil.*

**PHR V wriggle out of sth/doing sth** (*informal*) to avoid sth by making clever excuses तिकड़म करके बच जाना *It's your turn to wash the car—you can't wriggle out of it this time!*

**wring** /rɪŋ रिङ्/ *verb* [T] (*pt, pp* **wrung** /rʌŋ रङ्/) **wring sth (out)** to press and squeeze sth in order to remove water from it किसी वस्तु को दबाकर उसका पानी निचोड़ना

**wringing wet** *adj* extremely wet बहुत गीला

**wrinkle¹** /ˈrɪŋkl ˈरिङ्कल्/ *noun* [C] a small line in sth, especially one on the skin of your face which you get as you grow older झुर्री (विशेषतः चेहरे पर) *She's got fine wrinkles around her eyes.* ○ *Smooth out the wrinkles in the fabric.* ➪ **row** देखिए।

**wrinkle²** /ˈrɪŋkl ˈरिङ्कल्/ *verb* [I, T] **wrinkle (sth) (up)** to form small lines and folds in sth चेहरे पर या कपड़े में शिकन डालना या लाना *She wrinkled her nose at the nasty smell.* ○ *My skirt had wrinkled up on the journey.* ▶ **wrinkled** /ˈrɪŋkld ˈरिङ्कल्ड्/ *adj.* झुर्रीदार, शिकनदार

**wrist** /rɪst रिस्ट्/ *noun* [C] the narrow part at the end of your arm where it joins your hand कलाई ➪ **body** पर चित्र देखिए।

**wristwatch** /ˈrɪstwɒtʃ ˈरिस्ट्वॉच्/ *noun* [C] a watch on a strap which you wear round your arm near your hand कलाई की घड़ी, रिस्टवॉच

**writ** /rɪt रिट्/ *noun* [C] a legal order to do or not to do sth, given by a court of law न्यायालय द्वारा जारी वैधानिक आदेश; परमादेश, न्यायादेश, रिट

**write** /raɪt राइट्/ *verb* (*pt* **wrote** /rəʊt रोट्/; *pp* **written** /ˈrɪtn ˈरिट्न्/) **1** [I, T] to make words, letters, etc., especially on paper using a pen or pencil लिखना (काग़ज़ पर क़लम या पेंसिल से) *Write your name and address on the form.* **2** [T] to create a book, story, song, etc. in written form for people to read or use कोई पुस्तक, कहानी आदि लिखना, (की) रचना करना *Tolstoy wrote 'War and Peace'.* ○ *Who wrote the music for that film?* **3** [I, T] **write (sth) (to sb); write (sb) sth** to write and send a letter, etc. to sb पत्र आदि लिखकर (किसी को) भेजना *I've written a letter to my son.* ○ *I've written my son a letter.* ○ *She wrote that they were all well and would be home soon.* **4** [T] **write sth (out) (for sb)** to fill or complete a form, cheque, document, etc. with the necessary information कोई फ़ार्म, चेक, दस्तावेज आदि लिखना (उसमें आवश्यक ब्योरे भरना) *I wrote out a cheque for Rs 1000.*

**PHR V write back (to sb)** to send a reply to sb किसी को उत्तर भेजना

**write sth down** to write sth on paper, especially so that you can remember it काग़ज़ पर कुछ टाँकना (याद रखने के लिए लिख लेना)

**write in (to sb/sth) (for sth)** to write a letter to an organization, etc. to ask for sth, give an opinion, etc. किसी संस्था को पत्र लिखना (अनुरोध, सम्मति आदि के लिए)

**write off/away (to sb/sth) (for sth)** to write a letter to an organization, etc. to order sth or ask for sth कुछ मँगवाने के लिए किसी कंपनी आदि को पत्र लिखना

**write sb/sth off** to accept or decide that sb/sth will not be successful or useful किसी व्यक्ति या वस्तु को असफल या बेकार मान लेना *Don't write him off yet. He could still win.*

**write sth off** to accept that you will not get back an amount of money you have lost or spent ऋण में दी गई राशि को बट्टे खाते डालना (ऋण नहीं लौटेगा यह मानकर उसे समाप्त कर देना) *to write off a debt*

**write sth out** to write the whole of sth on paper किसी बात को पूरा-पूरा लिख डालना *Can you write out that recipe for me?*

**write sth up** to write sth in a complete and final form, often using notes that you have made किसी बात का पूरा विवरण अंतिम रूप से लिख देना (पहले तैयार नोट्स की सहायता से)

**write-off** *noun* [C] a thing, especially a vehicle, that is so badly damaged that it is not worth repairing पूर्णतः नष्ट वस्तु (विशेषतः कोई वाहन)

**writer** /ˈraɪtə(r) ˈराइट(र्)/ *noun* [C] a person who writes, especially one whose job is to write books, stories, etc. (पुस्तक आदि का) लेखक

**writhe** /raɪð राइद्/ *verb* [I] to turn and roll your body about (पीड़ा से) छटपटाना, तड़पना *She was writhing in pain.*

**writing** /ˈraɪtɪŋ ˈराइटिङ्/ *noun* **1** [U] words that have been written or printed; the way a person writes लिखित या मुद्रित शब्द; किसी व्यक्ति की लिखावट, हस्तलिपि *This card's got no writing inside. You can put your own message.* ○ *I can't read your writing, it's too small.* **2** [U] the skill or activity of writing words लेखन-कौशल या लेखन-क्रिया *He had problems with his reading and writing at*

*school.* **3** [U] the activity or job of writing books, etc. लेखन-कार्य (पुस्तकें आदि लिखने का कार्य या क्रिया) *It's difficult to earn much money from writing.* **4** [U] the books, etc. that sb has written or the style in which sb writes लिखित पुस्तक आदि या किसी व्यक्ति की लेखन-शैली *Love is a common theme in his early writing.* **5 writings** [*pl.*] a group of pieces of writing, especially by a particular person or on a particular subject (व्यक्ति-विशेष की या विषय-विशेष पर) रचनाएँ, कृतियाँ *the writings of Rabindranath Tagore*

IDM **in writing** in written form लिखित रूप में *I'll confirm the offer in writing next week.*

**writing paper** *noun* [U] paper for writing letters on पत्र लिखने का काग़ज़

**written**[1] ➪ **write** का past participle रूप

**written**[2] /ˈrɪtn ˈरिट्न् / *adj.* expressed on paper; not just spoken लिखित रूप में व्यक्त (न कि मौलिक रूप में) *a written agreement*

**wrong**[1] /rɒŋ रॉङ् / *adj., adv.* **1** not correct; in a way that is not correct अशुद्ध; ग़लत, जो सही या शुद्ध नहीं *the wrong answer* ○ *You've got the wrong number* (= on the telephone). ✪ विलोम **right** **2** not the best; not suitable ख़राब, सदोष; अनुपयुक्त *That's the wrong way to hold the bat.* ✪ विलोम **right** **3** (*not before a noun*) **wrong (with sb/sth)** causing problems or difficulties; not as it should be समस्याएँ या कठिनाइयाँ उत्पन्न करते हुए; जैसा होना चाहिए था वैसा नहीं *You look upset. Is something wrong?* ○ ***What's wrong** with the car this time?* **4 wrong (to do sth)** not morally right or honest अनैतिक या अनुचित *It's wrong to tell lies.* ○ *The man said that he had done nothing wrong.*

IDM **get on the right/wrong side of sb** ➪ **side**[1] देखिए।

**get sb wrong** (*informal*) to not understand sb किसी को ग़लत समझ लेना *Don't get me wrong! I don't dislike him.*

**go wrong 1** to make a mistake ग़लती कर जाना, से ग़लती हो जाना *I'm afraid we've gone wrong. We should have taken the other road.* **2** to stop working properly or to stop developing well काम करना बंद कर देना या ठीक से काम न करना *My computer's gone wrong and I've lost all my work.*

**get/start off on the right/wrong foot (with sb)** ➪ **foot**[1] देखिए।

**on the right/wrong track** ➪ **track**[1] देखिए।

**wrong**[2] /rɒŋ रॉङ् / *noun* **1** [U] things that are morally bad or dishonest अनैतिक या अनुचित बातें *Children quickly learn the difference between right and wrong.* **2** [C] an action or situation which is not fair ग़लत काम या बात *A terrible wrong has been done. Those men should never have gone to prison.*

IDM **in the wrong** (used about a person) having made a mistake; whose fault sth is (व्यक्ति) ग़लती पर; सदोष

**wrong**[3] /rɒŋ रॉङ् / *verb* [T] to do sth to sb which is bad or unfair किसी के प्रति ग़लत काम या अनुचित बात करना, अन्याय या अहित करना *I wronged her when I said she was lying.*

**wrong-foot** *verb* [T] (*BrE*) to put sb in a difficult or embarrassing situation by doing sth that he/she does not expect किसी व्यक्ति को (उसकी आशा के विरुद्ध) कठिनाई या परेशानी में डाल देना

**wrongful** /ˈrɒŋfl ˈरॉङ्फ़्ल् / *adj.* (*formal*) (*only before a noun*) not fair, not legal or not moral अनुचित, अवैधानिक या अनैतिक *He sued the company for wrongful dismissal.*

**wrongly** /ˈrɒŋli ˈरॉङ्लि / *adv.* in a wrong or mistaken way ग़लती से या भूल से *He was wrongly accused of stealing money.*

> NOTE क्रियाविशेषण **wrong** का प्रयोग क्रिया के या कर्म के बाद होता है (विशेषतः बातचीत में)—*He's spelt my name wrong.* क्रियाविशेषण **wrongly** का प्रयोग विशेष रूप में भूतकालिक कृदंत (past participle) या क्रिया से पहले होता है—*My name's been wrongly spelt.*

**wrote** ➪ **write** का past tense रूप

**wrought iron** /ˌrɔːt ˈaɪən ˌरॉट् ˈआइअन् / *noun* [U] a type of iron that is used for making fences, gates, etc. जंगला, दरवाज़ा आदि बनाने में प्रयुक्त एक प्रकार का लोहा, गढ़ा हुआ लोहा; पिटवाँ लोहा

**wrung** ➪ **wring** का past tense और past participle रूप

**wry** /raɪ राइ / *adj.* expressing both disappointment and amusement जिसमें निराशा के साथ विनोद का भाव भी हो *'Never mind,' she said with a wry grin. 'At least we got one vote.'* ▶ **wryly** *adv.* निराशामय विनोद भाव के साथ

**wt** *abbr.* weight भार, वज़न *net wt 500g*

**WTO** /ˌdʌbljuː tiː ˈəʊ ˌडब्ल्यू टी ˈओ / *abbr.* the World Trade Organization; an organization that encourages economic development and international **trade** डब्ल्यूटीओ; विश्व व्यापार संगठन (आर्थिक विकास और व्यापार को प्रोत्साहित करने वाली संस्था)

**WWW** /ˌdʌbljuː dʌbljuː ˈdʌbljuː ˌडब्ल्यू डब्ल्यू ˈडब्ल्यू / *abbr.* the World Wide Web डब्यू डब्ल्यू डब्ल्यू, वर्ल्ड वाइड वेब या विश्व व्यापी जाल

**X, x** /eks ऐक्स् / *noun* **1** [C, U] (*pl.* **X's; x's** /ˈeksɪz ˈएक्सीज़् /) the twenty-fourth letter of the English alphabet अंग्रेज़ी वर्णमाला का चौबीसवाँ अक्षर *'Xylophone' begins with an 'X'.* **2** [U] (*mathematics*) used to represent a number whose value is not mentioned अज्ञात मूल्य की संख्या का प्रतीक *The equation is impossible for any value of x greater than 2.* **3** [U] a person, a number, an influence, etc. that is not known or not named अज्ञात या अनाम व्यक्ति, संख्या आदि *Let's suppose X knows what Y is doing.*

NOTE रोमन अंक-पद्धति में **X** का चिह्न दस का प्रतीक है और शिक्षक लोग किसी उत्तर के ग़लत होने का संकेत करने के लिए भी इस चिह्न का प्रयोग करते हैं।

**X chromosome** *noun* [C] a part of a **chromosome** that exists in pairs in female cells and that exists by itself in male cells एक्स-गुणसूत्र, एक्स-क्रोमोसोम ➪ **Y chromosome** देखिए।

**xenon** /ˈziːnɒn; ˈzen- ˈज़ीनॉन्; ˈज़ेन्- / *noun* [U] (*symbol* **Xe**) a gas that is present in air and that is some times used in electric lamps वायु में उपस्थित एक गैस जिसका प्रयोग कभी-कभी बिजली के लैंपों में होता है; ज़ीनॉन

**xenophobia** /ˌzenəˈfəʊbiə ˌज़ेनˈफ़ोबिआ / *noun* [U] a fear or hatred of foreign people and cultures विदेशी समाज और संस्कृति के प्रति भय या घृणा का भाव, विदेशी-भीति और विदेशी-द्वेष ▶ **xenophobic** *adj.* विदेशी-भीति या द्वेष से संबंधित

**Xerox™** /ˈzɪərɒks ˈज़िअरॉक्स् / *noun* [C] **1** a machine that produces copies of letters, documents, etc. पत्र आदि की छायाप्रतियाँ तैयार करने वाली मशीन; ज़िरॉक्स **2** a copy produced by such a machine इस मशीन से निकली छायाप्रति ✪ पर्याय **photocopy** ▶ **xerox** *verb* [T] मशीन से पत्र आदि की छायाप्रतियाँ बनाना

**XL** *abbr.* extra large (size) सबसे बड़ा (आकार)

**Xmas** /ˈkrɪsməs; eksməs ˈक्रिसमस्; ˈएक्समस् / *noun* [C, U] (*informal*) (used as a short form in writing) Christmas 'क्रिसमस' का संक्षिप्त रूप लिखित भाषा में प्रयुक्त

**X-ray** *noun* [C] **1** [*usually pl.*] a kind of light that makes it possible to see inside solid objects, for example the human body, so that they can be examined and a photograph of them can be made एक्स-रे; एक्स-किरण (एक प्रकार का प्रकाश जिसकी सहायता से ठोस वस्तु जैसे मानव शरीर के अंदर के भाग को देखना, उसकी जाँच करना ओर फ़ोटो लेना संभव होता है) **2** a photograph that is made with an X-ray machine एक्स-रे मशीन से लिया गया फ़ोटो *The X-ray showed that the bone was not broken.* ➪ **ray** देखिए तथा **wavelength** पर चित्र देखिए। ▶ **X-ray** *verb* [T] एक्स-रे मशीन से किसी अंग आदि का फ़ोटो लेना *She had her chest X-rayed.*

**xylem** /ˈzaɪləm ˈज़ाइलम् / *noun* [U] (*technical*) the material in plants that carries water and food upwards from the root पौधों में पाया जाने वाला तत्व जो पानी और पोषक तत्वों की जड़ों से पत्तों तक ले जाता है; तरु तंतु ➪ **flower** पर चित्र देखिए।

**xylophone** /ˈzaɪləfəʊn ˈज़ाइलफ़ोन् / *noun* [C] a musical instrument that usually consists of two rows of wooden bars of different lengths. You play it by hitting these bars with two small hammers एक वाद्य यंत्र जिसमें लकड़ी की छोटी-बड़ी डंडियों की दो पंक्तियाँ होती हैं जिन पर दो छोटी हथौड़ियों से आघात करते हुए यंत्र को बजाया जाता है; काष्ठतरंग ➪ पृष्ठ 789 पर देखिए।

# Y y

**Y, y** /waɪ वाइज़् / *noun* **1** [C, U] (*pl.* **Y's; y's** /waɪz वाइज़् /) the twenty-fifth letter of the English alphabet अंग्रेज़ी वर्णमाला का पच्चीसवाँ अक्षर *'Yawn' begins with a 'Y'.* **2** [U] (*mathematics*) used to represent a number whose value is not mentioned अज्ञात मूल्य की संख्या का प्रतीक *Can the value of y be predicted from the value of x?* **3** [U] a person, a number, an influence, etc. that is not known or not named अज्ञात मूल्य की संख्या का प्रतीक *Let's suppose X knows what Y is doing.* ➪ **Y chromosome** देखिए।

**yacht** /jɒt यॉट् / *noun* [C] **1** a boat with sails used for pleasure जल-विहार की पाल वाली नाव, क्रीड़ा-नौका, यॉट *a yacht race* **2** a large boat with a motor, used for pleasure जल-विहार की मोटर-युक्त बड़ी नाव, केलिपोत, क्रीड़ा-नौका, यॉट ➪ **dinghy** देखिए तथा **boat** पर चित्र देखिए।

**yachting** /ˈjɒtɪŋ ˈयॉटिङ् / *noun* [U] the activity or sport of sailing or racing yachts क्रीड़ा-नौका से जल-विहार

**yachtsman** /ˈjɒtsmən ˈयॉट्स्मन् / *noun* [C] (*pl.* **-men** /-mən -मन् /) a person who sails a yacht in races or for pleasure यॉटनाविक (पुरुष)

**yachtswoman** /ˈjɒtswʊmən ˈयॉट्स्वुमन् / *noun* [C] (*pl.* **-women** /-wɪmɪn -विमिन्/) a woman who sails a yacht in races or for pleasure यॉटनाविका (स्त्री)

**yak** /jæk यैक् / *noun* [C] an animal of the cow family, with long horns and long hair, that lives in central Asia मध्य एशिया का एक गोवंशी प्राणी (जिसके सींग और बाल लंबे होते हैं), तिब्बती साँड़, सुरागाय, चमर, याक

**yam** /jæm यैम् / *noun* [C, U] the large brownish root of a tropical plant that is cooked as a vegetable घुइयाँ, रतालू, एक प्रकार की शकरकंद

**yank** /jæŋk यैङ्क् / *verb* [I, T] (*informal*) to pull sth suddenly, quickly and hard झटके के साथ खींचना (तेज़ी से और ज़ोर लगाते हुए) ▸ **yank** *noun* [C] झटका

**yap** /jæp यैप् / *verb* [I] (**yapping; yapped**) (used about dogs, especially small ones) to make short, loud noises in an excited way (कुत्ते का, विशेषतः पिल्लों का) भौंकना या चीख़ना

**yard** /jɑːd याड् / *noun* [C] **1** (*BrE*) an area outside a building, usually with a hard surface and a wall or fence around it अहाता, प्रांगण, बाड़ा (भवन के बाहर स्थित) *a school/prison yard* ➪ **courtyard** और **churchyard** देखिए। **2** (*AmE*) = **garden[1] 1** **3** (*usually in compounds*) an area, usually without a roof, used for a particular type of work or purpose प्रयोजन-विशेष या कार्य-विशेष के लिए प्रयुक्त भूक्षेत्र; यार्ड *a shipyard/boatyard* ○ *a builder's yard*

> **NOTE** ब्रिटिश अंग्रेज़ी में मकान से लगा ज़मीन का टुकड़ा **garden** (बग़ीचा) कहलाता है यदि उसमें घास, फूल आदि हों और यदि वह कंकरीट या पत्थर से बना हो तो वह **yard** कहलाता है। अमेरिकी अंग्रेज़ी में दोनों के लिए **yard** शब्द का प्रयोग होता है।

**4** (*abbr.* **yd**) a measure of length; 0.914 of a metre. There are 3 feet in a yard लंबाई की एक माप, गज़, 0.914 मीटर; एक गज़ में 3 फ़ीट होते हैं *Our house is 100 yards from the supermarket.*

**yardstick** /ˈjɑːdstɪk ˈयाड्स्टिक् / *noun* [C] a standard with which things can be compared तुलना करने का आधार, मानदंड या पैमाना *Exam results should not be the only yardstick by which pupils are judged.*

**yarn** /jɑːn यान् / *noun* **1** [U] thread (usually of wool or cotton) that has been prepared (**spun**) and is used for knitting, etc. धागा (प्रायः ऊन या सूत का) **2** [C] (*informal*) a long story that sb tells, especially one that is invented or exaggerated मनगढ़ंत क़िस्सा

**yashmak** /ˈjæʃmæk ˈयैश्मैक् / *noun* [C] a piece of material covering most of the face, worn by some Muslim women चेहरा ढकने वाला बुरक़ा, प्रायः मुस्लिम महिलाओं द्वारा प्रयुक्त; यैशमैक

**yatra** *noun* (*IndE*) a journey, a procession; a pilgrimage यात्रा, जुलूस या शोभायात्रा; तीर्थयात्रा

**yawn** /jɔːn यॉन् / *verb* [I] to open your mouth wide and breathe in deeply, especially when you are tired or bored जँभाई लेना (थकने या ऊबने पर) ▸ **yawn** *noun* [C] जँभाई *'How much longer will it take?' he said with a yawn.*

**yaws** /jɔːz यॉज़् / *noun* [U] a tropical skin disease that causes large red swellings फुंसियाँ (गरम प्रदेशों में होने वाला एक चर्म रोग); यॉज़

**Y chromosome** *noun* [C] a part of a **chromosome** that exists by itself and only in male cells वाइ-क्रोमोसोम, वाइ-गुणसूत्र ➪ **X chromosome** देखिए।

**yd** (*pl.* **yds**) *abbr.* yard, a measure of length गज़, लंबाई की एक माप

**yeah** /jeə येअ / *exclamation* (*informal*) yes हाँ

**year** /jɪə(r); jɜ:(r) यिअ(र्); य(र्) / *noun* **1** [C] (*also* **calendar year**) the period from 1 January to 31 December, 365 or 366 days divided into 12 months or 52 weeks वर्ष, साल, संवत्सर *last year/ this year/next year* ○ *Interest is paid on this account once a year.* **2** [C] any period of 12 months, measured from any date बारह महीने की अवधि (किसी भी तारीख़ से आरंभ), वर्ष *He left school just over a year ago.* ○ *In a year's time, you'll be old enough to vote.* **3** [C] a period of 12 months in connection with schools, the business world, etc. स्कूल आदि का वर्ष (बारह महीने की अवधि), शैक्षिक वर्ष, वित्तवर्ष आदि *the academic/school year* ○ *the tax/financial year* **4** [C] (used in schools, universities, etc.) the level that a particular student is at (स्कूल, विश्वविद्यालय आदि की) कक्षा, जमात, क्लास, वर्ष या साल *He was a year below me at school.* **5** [C, *usually pl.*] (used in connection with the age of sb/sth) a period of 12 months (व्यक्ति या वस्तु की आयु) वर्ष, बारह महीने की अवधि *He's ten years old today.* ○ *The company is now in its fifth year.*

NOTE *'He's ten.'* या *'He's ten years old.'* ये दोनों प्रयोग ठीक हैं परंतु *'He's ten years.'* या *'a ten-years-old boy,'* दोनों ग़लत हैं। ➪ **age** पर नोट देखिए।

**6 years** [*pl.*] a long time लंबा समय, सालों (पहले, से आदि) *It happened years ago.* ○ *I haven't seen him for years.*

IDM **all year round** for the whole year वर्ष भर, तमाम साल

**donkey's years** ➪ **donkey** देखिए।

**year after year; year in year out** every year for many years सालों-साल, बहुत सालों या वर्षों तक, हर साल या वर्ष

**yearly** /ˈjɪəli; ˈjɜ:li ˈयिअलि; ˈयलि / *adj., adv.* (happening) every year or once a year वार्षिक, सालाना (प्रति वर्ष, हर साल का, वर्ष या साल में एक बार (होने वाला) *The conference is held yearly.*

**yearn** /jɜ:n यन् / *verb* [I] (*written*) **yearn (for sb/ sth); yearn (to do sth)** to want sb/sth very much, especially sth that you cannot have (किसी दुर्लभ वस्तु के लिए) ललकना, लालायित होना, लालसा होना ▶ **yearning** *noun* [C, U] ललक, लालसा

**yeast** /ji:st यीस्ट् / *noun* [U] a substance used for making bread rise and for making beer, wine, etc. ख़मीर, यीस्ट

**yell** /jel येल् / *verb* [I, T] **yell (out) (sth); yell (sth) (at sb/sth)** to shout very loudly, often because you are angry, excited or in pain (गुस्से में, उत्तेजना या दर्द के कारण) ज़ोर से चिल्लाना, चीख़ना *She yelled out his name.* ▶ **yell** *noun* [C] चिल्लाहट, चीख़

**yellow** /ˈjeləʊ ˈयेलो / *noun* [C, U], *adj.* (of) the colour of lemons or butter पीला रंग, पीले रंग का *a pale/light yellow dress* ○ *the yellows and browns of the autumn leaves*

**yellow card** *noun* [C] (used in football) a card that is shown to a player as a warning that he/she will be sent off the field if he/she behaves badly again पीला कार्ड, येलो कार्ड (फ़ुटबॉल के खिलाड़ी को, अनुचित आचरण पर, मैदान से बाहर भेज देने की चेतावनी देने के लिए प्रयुक्त) ➪ **red card** देखिए।

**yellow fever** *noun* [U] a tropical disease that is passed from one person to another and that makes the skin turn yellow and often causes death पीत ज्वर, येलो फ़ीवर (गरम देशों में होने वाला एक छुतहा रोग जिसमें रोगी की त्वचा पीली पड़ जाती है और प्रायः मृत्यु हो जाती है)

**yellowish** /ˈjeləʊɪʃ ˈयेलोइश् / *adj.* (*also* **yellowy** /ˈjeləʊi ˈयेलोइ /) slightly yellow in colour कुछ-कुछ पीला, पीला-सा, आपीत

**the Yellow Pages™** *noun* [*pl.*] a telephone book (on yellow paper) that lists all the business companies, etc. in a certain area in sections according to the goods or services they provide पीले पृष्ठों वाली टेलीफ़ोन-डाइरेक्टरी जिसमें (क्षेत्र-विशेष की व्यापारिक कंपनियों की वर्गीकृत सूची होती है)

**yelp** /jelp येल्प् / *verb* [I] to give a sudden short cry, especially of pain चीख़ना (विशेषतः दर्द के कारण) ▶ **yelp** *noun* [C] चीख़

**yeoman** /ˈjeʊmən ˈयोमन् / *noun* [C] (*pl.* **yeomen**) **1** (in Britain, in the past) a farmer who owned the land on which he worked (विगत में, ब्रिटेन में) छोटा कृषक **2** an officer in the US navy who mainly does office work अमेरिकी नौसेना का कार्यालय अधिकारी

**yes** /jes येस् / exclamation **1** used to give a positive answer to a question, for saying that sth is true or correct or for saying that you want sth (सहमति सूचक) हाँ *'Are you having a good time?' 'Yes, thank you.'* ○ *'May I sit here?' 'Yes, of course.'* **2** used for showing you have heard sb or will do what he/she asks जी हाँ (किसी के द्वारा पुकारने पर उत्तर देने या दिए गए आदेश का पालन करने के लिए प्रयुक्त) *'Waiter!' 'Yes, madam.'* **3** used when saying that a negative statement that sb has made is not true हाँ, ठीक है (निषेधात्मक कथन

को नकारने के लिए प्रयुक्त) *'You don't care about anyone but yourself.' 'Yes I do.'* ✪ विलोम **no**
▶ **yes** *noun* [C] (*pl.* **yeses** /ˈjesɪz ˈयेसीज़्/) सहमति, हाँ में उत्तर *Was that a yes or a no?*

**yesterday** /ˈjestədeɪ; ˈjestədi ˈयेस्टडे; ˈयेस्टडि/ *adv., noun* [C, U] (on) the day before today (बीता हुआ) कल *yesterday morning/afternoon/evening* ○ *I posted the form **the day before yesterday*** (= if I am speaking on Wednesday, I posted it on Monday). ○ *Have you still got yesterday's paper?*

**yet** /jet येट्/ *adv., conj.* **1** used with negative verbs or in questions for talking about sth that has not happened but that you expect to happen अभी तक (निषेध व्यंजक क्रियाओं या प्रश्नों के साथ प्रयुक्त, प्रत्याशित बात के तब तक घटित न होने का संकेत करने के लिए) *Has it stopped raining yet?* ○ *I haven't seen that film yet.* **2** (*used with negative verbs*) now; as early as this (निषेधवाचक क्रियाओं के साथ प्रयुक्त) अब; अभी *You don't have to leave yet—your train isn't for another hour.* **3** from now until the period of time mentioned has passed अभी तो *She isn't that old; she'll live for years yet.* **4** (used especially with **may** or **might**) at sometime in the future विशेषतः 'may' या 'might' के साथ प्रयुक्त) फिर भी, आख़िर में, अंततोगत्वा, आगे चलकर *With a bit of luck, they may yet win.* **5** (*used with* superlatives) until now/until then; so far अब तक, तक अब; अभी तक *This is her best film yet.* **6** used with **comparatives** to emphasize an increase in the degree of sth (तुलनात्मक रूपों के साथ प्रयुक्त, किसी वस्तु की डिग्री में वृद्धि पर बल देने के लिए प्रयुक्त) इसके अतिरिक्त, इससे अधिक *a recent and yet more improbable theory* **7** but; in spite of that परंतु, लेकिन; के बावजूद, के होते हुए भी, तथापि, जिस पर भी, फिर भी *He seems pleasant, yet there's something about him I don't like.*

IDM **as yet** until now अभी तक, अभी भी *As yet little is known about the disease.*

**yet again** (used for expressing surprise or anger that sth happens again) once more; another time (किसी बात के दुबारा होने पर आश्चर्य या क्रोध में) एक बार फिर; एक बार और, दूसरी बार *I found out that he had lied to me yet again.*

**yet another** used for expressing surprise that there is one more of sth (किसी वस्तु की संख्या में एक और की वृद्धि पर आश्चर्य व्यक्त करने के लिए प्रयुक्त) लो, एक और *They're opening yet another fast food restaurant in the square.*

**yet to do, etc.** that has not been done and is still to do in the future जो हुआ न हो और जिसे भविष्य में करना या लेना हो *The final decision has yet to be made.*

**yew** /ju: यू/ (*also* **yew tree**) *noun* [U] a small tree with dark green leaves and small red berries; the wood of this tree एक सदाबहार वृक्ष (गहरे हरे पत्तों और छोटे लाल बेरों वाला एक छोटा पेड़); यू

**yield¹** /ji:ld यील्ड्/ *verb* **1** [T] to produce or provide crops, profits or results फ़सल या उपज, लाभ या परिणाम देना, उपलब्ध कराना *How much wheat does each field yield?* ○ *Did the experiment yield any new information?* **2** [I] **yield (to sb/sth)** (*formal*) to stop refusing to do sth or to obey sb किसी के सामने झुक जाना, किसी की बात मान लेना *The government refused to yield to the hostage takers' demands.* NOTE इस अर्थ में **give in** कम औपचारिक प्रयोग है। **3** [T] **yield sb/sth (up) (to sb/sth)** to allow sb to have control of sth that you were controlling किसी को (सत्ता आदि) सौंप देना *The army has yielded power to the rebels.* **4** [I] (*formal*) to move, bend or break because of pressure दबाव के कारण हिल, झुक या टूट जाना *The dam finally yielded under the weight of the water.* NOTE इस अर्थ में **give way** कम औपचारिक प्रयोग है। **5** [I] **yield (to sb/sth)** to allow other vehicles on a bigger road to go first (बड़ी सड़क पर) वाहनों को आगे निकलने देना *You have to yield to traffic from the left here.* NOTE इसके लिए ब्रिटिश अंग्रेज़ी में **give way** का प्रयोग होता है।

PHR V **yield to sth** (*formal*) to be replaced by sth, especially sth newer एक वस्तु (प्रायः पुरानी) के स्थान पर दूसरी (प्रायः नई) वस्तु का आ जाना *Old-fashioned methods have yielded to new technology.* NOTE इसके लिए **give way** कम औपचारिक प्रयोग है।

**yield²** /ji:ld यील्ड्/ *noun* [C] the amount that is produced उपज, उत्पादन, पैदावार *Wheat yields were down 5% this year.*

**yo** /jəʊ यो/ *exclamation* (*slang*) used by some people when they see a friend; hello मित्र के लिए अभिवादन; हेलो

**yob** /jɒb यॉब्/ *noun* [C] (*BrE slang*) a boy or young man who is rude, loud and sometimes violent or aggressive अक्खड़ बड़बोला लड़का या युवक (कभी-कभी झगड़ने पर उतारू) ➪ **lout** और **hooligan** देखिए।

**yoga** *noun* [U] **1** (Indian in origin) a system of exercises for the body that involves breath control and helps relax both your mind and body योग (श्वास-नियंत्रण तथा शारीरिक व्यायाम या कसरत

जिससे मन प्रफुल्ल या शांत रहता है) **2** a Hindu philosophy which aims to unite the self with the spirit of the universe योग; (हिंदु शास्त्र में) विश्वात्मा से स्वयं का संयोग करने का लक्ष्य

**yoghurt** (*also* **yogurt**) /ˈjɒɡət ˈयॉगट्/ *noun* [C, U] a slightly sour, thick liquid food made from milk दही, दधि *plain/banana/strawberry yoghurt*

**yoke** /jəʊk योक्/ *noun* **1** [C] a long piece of wood fixed across the necks of two animals so that they can pull heavy loads together (हल आदि का) जुआ या जूआ **2** [*sing.*] something that limits your freedom and makes your life difficult दासता, पराधीनता, गुलामी

**yolk** /jəʊk योक्/ *noun* [C, U] the yellow part in the middle of an egg अंडे की ज़रदी (पीला भाग)

**you** /jə; ju: य; यू/ *pronoun* **1** used as the subject or object of a verb, or after a preposition to refer to the person or people being spoken or written to तू, तुम, आप *You can play the guitar, can't you?* ○ *Bring your photos with you.* **2** used with a noun, adjective or phrase when calling sb sth किसी को किसी शब्द से निर्दिष्ट करते हुए संज्ञा, विशेषण या वाक्यांश के साथ प्रयुक्त *You idiot! What do you think you're doing?* **3** used for referring to people in general कोई भी व्यक्ति *The more you earn, the more tax you pay.* **NOTE** **One** का भी यही अर्थ है परंतु यह काफ़ी औपचारिक है और इसका प्रचलन कम होता जा रहा है *The more one earns, the more tax one pays.*

**you'd** /ju:d यूड्/ ➪ **you had, you would** का संक्षिप्त रूप

**you'll** /ju:l यूल्/ ➪ **you will** का संक्षिप्त रूप

**young**[1] /jʌŋ यङ्/ *adj.* (**younger** /ˈjʌŋɡə(r) ˈयङ्ग(र्)/, **youngest** /ˈjʌŋɡɪst ˈयङ्गिस्ट्/) not having lived or existed for very long; not old उम्र में छोटा *They have two young children.* ○ *My father was the youngest of eight children.* ○ *my younger brothers* ✪ विलोम **old**

**IDM** **young at heart** behaving or thinking like a young person, although you are old दिल से जवान (भले ही उम्र अधिक हो); जवाँ दिल

**young**[2] /jʌŋ यङ्/ *noun* [*pl.*] **1** young animals जानवरों के बच्चे *Swans will attack to protect their young.* **2 the young** young people considered as a group युवा वर्ग *The young of today are more ambitious than their parents.*

**youngish** /ˈjʌŋɪʃ ˈयङिश्/ *adj.* quite young बच्चा-सा या युवा-सा; ख़ासा जवान

**youngster** /ˈjʌŋstə(r) ˈयङ्स्ट(र्)/ *noun* [C] a young person छोकरा या छोकरी, बच्चा, बालक, कुमार

**your** /jə(r); jɔ:(r) य(र्); यॉ(र्)/ *det.* **1** of or belonging to the person or people being spoken to तेरा, तुम्हारा, आपका *What's your flat like?* ○ *Thanks for all your help.* **2** belonging to or connected with people in general लोगों का या लोगों से संबंधित *When your life is as busy as mine, you have little time to relax.* **3** (*informal*) used for saying that sth is well known to people in general आम लोगों का *So this is your typical English food?* **4** (*also* **Your**) used in some titles कुछ उपाधियों में प्रयुक्त *Your Highness*

**you're** /jɔ:(r); jʊə(r) यॉ(र्); युअ(र्)/ ➪ **you are** का संक्षिप्त रूप

**yours** /jɔ:z यॉज़्/ *pronoun* **1** of or belonging to you तेरा, तुम्हारा, आपका *Is this bag yours or mine?* ○ *I was talking to a friend of yours the other day.* **2 Yours** used at the end of a letter पत्र के अंत में प्रयुक्त, 'आपका', 'भवदीय' *Yours sincerely .../faithfully ...* ○ *Yours ...*

**yourself** /jɔ:ˈself; jəˈself यॉˈसेल्फ़्; यˈसेल्फ़्/ *pronoun* (*pl.* **yourselves** /-ˈselvz -ˈसेल्व़्ज़्/) **1** used when the person or people being spoken to do an action and are also affected by it तू, तुम या आप, स्वयं, खुद, ही *Be careful or you'll hurt yourself.* ○ *Here's some money. Buy yourselves a present.* ○ *You're always talking about yourself!* **2** used to emphasize sth किसी बात पर बल देने के लिए प्रयुक्त *You yourself told me there was a problem last week.* ○ *Did you repair the car yourselves* (= or did sb else do it for you)? **3** you तू, तुम, आप *'How are you?' 'Fine, thanks. And yourself?'* **4** in your normal state; healthy अपनी सामान्य स्थिति में; स्वस्थ, सेहतमंद *You don't look yourself today.*

**IDM** **(all) by yourself/yourselves** **1** alone अकेले *Do you live by yourself?* ➪ **alone** देखिए। **2** without help बिना सहायता के, अपने आप, अकेले *You can't cook dinner for ten people by yourself.*

**youth** /ju:θ यूथ़्/ *noun* (*pl.* **youths** /ju:ðz यूद्ज़्/) **1** [U] the period of your life when you are young, especially the time before a child becomes an adult किशोरावस्था, कैशोर्य, उठती जवानी *He was quite a good sportsman **in his youth**.* **2** [U] the fact or state of being young युवावस्था, यौवन, तरुणाई, जवानी *I think that her youth will be a disadvantage in this job.* **3** [C] a young person (usually a young man, and often one that you do not have a good opinion of) युवा (प्रायः युवक, कुछ उच्छृंखल) *a gang of youths* **4 the youth** [U] young people considered as a group युवा वर्ग, जवान लोग, युव जन, किशोर वर्ग *the youth of today* ➪ **age** और **old age** देखिए।

**youthful** /ˈjuːθfl ˈयूथ्फ़्ल् / *adj.* **1** typical of young people युवकोचित, जवानों जैसा *youthful enthusiasm* **2** seeming younger than you are तरुणवत, जवान-सा, यौवनसंपन्न (अपनी वास्तविक आयु से छोटा लगने वाला) *She's a youthful fifty-year-old.*

**youth hostel** *noun* [C] a cheap and simple place to stay, especially for young people, when they are travelling युवक-आवासगृह, यूथ होस्टल (परदेस में लोगों, विशेषतः युवकों, के लिए सस्ता आवासगृह)

**you've** /juːv यूव् / ➪ **you have** का संक्षिप्त रूप

**Yo Yo™** (*also* **yo-yo**) *noun* [C] (*pl.* **Yo Yos; yo-yos**) a toy which is a round piece of wood or plastic with a string round the middle. You put the string round your finger and can make the yo-yo go up and down it यो-यो नामक खिलौना (लकड़ी या प्लास्टिक का गोल खिलौना जिसके मध्य भाग में बँधी डोरी को उँगली से लपेटकर ऊपर-नीचे झुलाया जाता है)

**yr** (*pl.* **yrs**) *abbr.* year वर्ष

**yuck** /jʌk यक् / *exclamation* (*informal*) used for saying that you think sth is disgusting or very unpleasant घृणा या अरुचि व्यक्त करने के लिए प्रयुक्त, छि, उँह *It's filthy! Yuck!* ▶ **yucky** *adj.* घटिया *What a yucky colour!*

**yummy** /ˈjʌmi ˈयमि / *adj.* (*informal*) tasting very good; delicious खाने में अच्छा; स्वादिष्ट, ज़ायक़ेदार *a yummy cake*

**yuppie** (*also* **yuppy**) /ˈjʌpi ˈयपि / *noun* [C] (*pl.* **yuppies**) a successful young professional person who lives in a city, earns a lot of money and spends it on fashionable things शहरवासी सफल युवा व्यावसायिक (खूब पैसे वाला और शौक़ीन); याप्पी

# Z z

**Z, z** /zed ज़ेड्/ *noun* [C, U] (*pl.* **Z's; z's** /zedz ज़ेड्ज़्/) the twenty-sixth letter and last letter of the English alphabet अंग्रेज़ी वर्णमाला का छब्बीसवाँ और आख़िरी अक्षर *'Zero' begins with a 'Z'.*

**zany** /ˈzeɪni ˈज़ेनि/ *adj.* funny in an unusual and crazy way अजीबो-ग़रीब और सनकी *a zany comedian*

**zap** /zæp ज़ैप्/ *verb* (**zapping; zapped**) (*informal*) **1** [T] **zap sb/sth (with sth)** to destroy, hit or kill sb, usually with a gun or other weapon किसी को नष्ट कर देना, चोट पहुँचाना या मार देना (प्रायः बंदूक़ या दूसरे हथियार से) *It's a computer game where you have to zap aliens with a laser.* **2** [I, T] to change television programmes very quickly using an electronic device (**remote control**) (रिमोट कंट्रोल की सहायता से टीवी कार्यक्रमों को जल्दी-जल्दी बदलना)

**zeal** /zi:l ज़ील्/ *noun* [U] (*written*) great energy or enthusiasm अत्यधिक ऊर्जा या उत्साह *religious zeal*

**zealous** /ˈzeləs ˈज़ेलस्/ *adj.* using great energy and enthusiasm ऊर्जावान या ऊर्जापूर्ण उत्साही, उत्साहपूर्ण ▸ **zealously** *adv.* उत्साहपूर्वक

**zebra** /ˈzebrə ˈज़ेब्रा/ *noun* [C] (*pl.* **zebra** or **zebras**) an African wild animal that looks like a horse, with black and white lines (**stripes**) all over its body ज़ेबरा (घोड़े जैसा और सफ़ेद-काले धारीदार एक अफ़्रीक़ी वन्य पशु), चित्रगर्दभ

**zebra crossing** *noun* [C] (*BrE*) a place where the road is marked with black and white lines and people can cross safely because cars must stop to let them do this ज़ेबरा-पट्टी (पैदल सड़क पार करने वाले व्यक्तियों के लिए), धारीदार पैदल पारपथ (बड़ी सड़कों पर सफ़ेद-काली पट्टियाँ जो पैदल-चलने वालों को सड़क पार करने का प्रथमाधिकार देती हैं) ➪ **pedestrian crossing** देखिए।

**Zen** /zen ज़ेन्/ *noun* [U] a Japanese form of Buddhism बौद्धधर्म का जापानी रूप; ज़ेन

**Zend-Avesta** *noun* the **Zoroastrian** sacred writings, consisting of the **Avesta** (the text) and the **Zend** (the commentary) ज़ेन्द अवेस्ता (ज़रदुश्ती या पारसी धर्मग्रंथ)

**zenith** /ˈzenɪθ ˈज़ेनिथ्/ *noun* [*sing.*] (*technical*) the highest point that the sun or moon reaches in the sky, directly above you आकाश का वह बिंदु जो ठीक सिर के ऊपर हो; शिरोबिंदु, खमध्य ✪ पर्याय **peak** ✪ विलोम **nadir**

**zero** /ˈzɪərəʊ ˈज़िअरो/ *noun* **1** [C] 0, शून्य, सिफ़र (का अंग)

> **NOTE** अंकों या संख्याओं के वाक्य-प्रयोग के उदाहरणों के लिए **six** की प्रविष्टि देखिए।

**2** [U] freezing point; 0°C जमाव-बिंदु, हिमांक; 0° सेल्सियस *The temperature is likely to fall to five degrees* ***below zero*** (= –5°C). **3** [U] the lowest possible amount or level; nothing at all निम्नतम स्तर या मात्रा; कुछ भी नहीं, ज़रा भी नहीं *zero growth/inflation/profit*

> **NOTE** 0 (शून्य) अंक के ब्रिटिश अंग्रेज़ी में अनेक नाम हैं। वैज्ञानिक या तकनीकी संदर्भों में **zero** नाम सबसे अधिक प्रचलित है। खेल में, विशेषतः फ़ुटबॉल में (मौखिक अभिव्यक्ति के समय) **nil** का प्रयोग अधिक होता है। अपने से बड़ी संख्या के अंक के रूप में **0** (शून्य) के लिए **nought** शब्द प्रचलित है—*a million is one followed by six noughts.* टेलीफ़ोन या विमान की उड़ान की संख्या बताते समय शून्य अंक के लिए **O** ('ओ' स्वर, जिसका उच्चारण **oh** है) सर्वाधिक प्रचलित है।

**zero tolerance** *noun* [U] the act of following the law very strictly so that people are punished even when what they have done wrong is not very serious शून्य स्तर की सहिष्णुता, पूर्ण असहिष्णुता, क़ानून का कठोरता से पालन (छोटे-मोटे अपराधों के लिए भी ढील नहीं होना)

**zest** /zest ज़ेस्ट्/ *noun* [U, *sing.*] **zest (for sth)** a feeling of enjoyment, excitement and enthusiasm आनंद, उत्तेजना और उत्साह की भावना, ख़ुशीभरा जोश *She has a great* ***zest for life***

**zigzag** /ˈzɪgzæg ˈज़िग्ज़ैग्/ *noun* [C], *adj.* (consisting of) a line with left and right turns, like a lot of letter W's, one after the other टेढ़ा-मेढ़ा, चक्करदार, सर्पिल *The skier came down the slope in a series of zigzags.* ○ *a zigzag pattern/line* ▸ **zigzag** *verb* [I] (**zigzagging; zigzagged**) सर्पिल गति से

**zilla** *noun* [C] an administrative district in India ज़िला

**zinc** /zɪŋk ज़िङ्क्/ *noun* [U] (*symbol* **Zn**) a whitish metal, often put on the surface of iron and steel as protection against water ज़स्ता, ज़िंक (लोहे और इस्पात को ज़ंग से बचाने वाली धातु)

**zip** /zɪp ज़िप्/ (*AmE* **zipper** /ˈzɪpə(r) ˈज़िप(र्)/) *noun* [C] a device for fastening clothes, bags, etc. ज़िप (कपड़े थैले आदि के दो हिस्सों को चिपकाने या पास लाने वाली चेन) *to do up/undo a zip* ➪ **button** पर चित्र देखिए। ▸ **zip** *verb* [T] (**zipping; zipped**) **zip sth (up)** ज़िप लगाना, ज़िप से बंद करना *There was so* *much in the bag that it was difficult to zip it up.* ✪ विलोम **unzip**

**ZIP code** (*also* **zip code**) = **postcode**

**the zodiac** /ˈzəʊdiæk ˈज़ोडिऐक् / *noun* [*sing.*] a diagram of the positions of the sun, moon and planets, which is divided into twelve equal parts, each with a special name and **symbol (the signs of the zodiac)** राशिचक्र आरेख (बारह राशियों में विभाजित सूर्य, चंद्रमा और अन्य कुछ नक्षत्रों की स्थिति का आरेख जिसमें प्रत्येक राशि का विशेष नाम और चिह्न होता है)

> **NOTE** **Astrology** (फलित ज्योतिष) और जन्मकुंडली के प्रसंग में **the stars** (राशियों) का विवरण या राशि-विचार समाचार पत्रों और पत्रिकाओं में प्रकाशित किया जाता है और पाठक राशियों के अनुसार किसी के व्यक्तित्व और भविष्य का अनुमान करते हैं—*Which sign (of the zodiac) are you?*

**zone** /zəʊn ज़ोन् / *noun* [C] an area that is different from those around it for example because sth special happens there विशेष स्थिति या क्रिया से संबंधित क्षेत्र, क्षेत्र-विशेष *a war zone*

**zoo** /zu: ज़ू / *noun* [C] (*pl.* **zoos**) a park where many kinds of wild animals are kept so that people can look at them and where they are bred, studied and protected चिड़ियाघर, जंतुशाला

**zoology** /zəʊˈɒlədʒi; zuˈɒl- ज़ोˈऑलजि; ज़ुˈऑल्- / *noun* [U] the scientific study of animals जंतुविज्ञान ➪ **botany** और **biology** देखिए।

**zoological** /ˌzəʊəˈlɒdʒɪkl; ˌzu:əˈl- ˌज़ोअˈलॉजिकल्; ˌज़ूअˈल- / *adj.* ▸ **zoologist** /zəʊˈɒlədʒɪst; zuˈɒl- ज़ोˈऑलजिस्ट; ज़ुˈऑल्- / *noun* [C] जंतुविज्ञानी, जंतुशास्त्री

**zoom** /zu:m ज़ूम् / *verb* [I] to move or go somewhere very fast बहुत तेज़ी से जाना या गुज़रना

**PHR V** **zoom in (on sb/sth)** (used in photography) to give a closer view of the object/person being photographed by fixing a special device to the camera **(a zoom lens)** (फ़ोटोग्राफ़ी में) ज़ूम लैंस वाले कैमरे से वस्तु या व्यक्ति का समीपी चित्र दिखाना *The camera zoomed in on the actor's face.*

**zoom lens** *noun* [C] a device on a camera that can make an object being photographed appear gradually bigger or smaller so that it seems to be getting closer or further away ज़ूम लैंस (कैमरे के इस विशेष लैंस से व्यक्ति या वस्तुएँ धीरे-धीरे अधिक छोटी या बड़ी लगने लगती हैं और फलस्वरूप अधिक दूर या पास लगने लगती हैं)

**Zoroaster** (*also* **Zarathustra**) *noun* an ancient Persian prophet and founder of **Zoroastrianism** पुरातन ज़रदुश्त संत एवं ज़रदुश्त धर्म के संस्थापक; जॉरोएस्टर

**Zoroastrian** *noun* [C] a person who is a follower of **Zoroastrianism** पारसी या ज़रदुश्ती धर्म का अनुयायी व्यक्ति ▸ **Zoroastrian** *adj.* relating to or connected with **Zoroastrianism** पारसी या ज़रदुश्ती, ज़रदुश्त धर्म विषयक

**Zoroastrianism** *noun* [U] a religion founded in ancient Persia by **Zoroaster,** that teaches that there is one god and a continuing struggle in the world between the forces of good and evil एक ईश्वर और अच्छाई तथा बुराई के बीच निरंतर संघर्ष के विचारों को मान्यता देने वाला पारसी धर्म; ज़रदुश्त धर्म

**zucchini** /zuˈki:ni ज़ुˈकीनि / *noun* [C] (*pl.* **zucchini** or **zucchinis**) = **courgette** ➪ **vegetable** पर चित्र देखिए।

**zygote** /ˈzaɪgəʊt ˈज़ाइगोट् / *noun* [C] a cell that starts the process of forming a baby person or animal, formed by the joining together of a male and a female **gamete** पुरुष और स्त्री की कोशिकाओं के जुड़ने से बने गर्भस्थ शिशु के निर्माण की प्रक्रिया को आरंभ करने वाली कोशिका; युग्मनज

# APPENDIX 1: QUICK GRAMMAR REFERENCE

## Verbs

### The Tenses of Regular Verbs (नियमित क्रियाओं के काल)

#### The Simple Tenses (सामान्य काल)

NOTE **I, you, we** और **they** के क्रियारूप एक समान होते हैं।
**He, she** और **it** के क्रियारूप भी एक समान होते हैं।

**The present simple** (सामान्य वर्तमान)

| | | |
|---|---|---|
| I look | do I look? | I do not look (**don't look**) |
| he looks | does he look? | he does not look (**doesn't look**) |

**The simple past** (सामान्य भूत)

| | | |
|---|---|---|
| I looked | did I look? | I did not look (**didn't look**) |
| he looked | did he look? | he did not look (**didn't look**) |

**The present perfect** (पूर्ण वर्तमान)

| | | |
|---|---|---|
| I have looked (**I've looked**) | have I looked? | I have not looked (**haven't looked**) |
| he has looked (**he's looked**) | has he looked? | he has not looked (**hasn't looked**) |

**The past perfect (pluperfect)** (पूर्ण भूत)

| | | |
|---|---|---|
| I had looked (**I'd looked**) | had I looked? | I had not looked (**hadn't looked**) |
| he had looked (**he'd looked**) | had he looked? | he had not looked (**hadn't looked**) |

**The future simple** (सामान्य भविष्यत)

| | | |
|---|---|---|
| I will look (**I'll look**) | will I look? | I will not look (**won't look**) |
| he will look (**he'll look**) | will he look? | he will not look (**won't look**) |

**The future perfect** (पूर्ण भविष्यत)

| | | |
|---|---|---|
| I will have looked (**I'll have looked**) | will I have looked? | I will not have looked (**won't have looked**) |
| he will have looked (**he'll have looked**) | will he have looked? | he will not have looked (**won't have looked**) |

**The conditional** (हेतुमत)

| | | |
|---|---|---|
| I would look (**I'd look**) | would I look? | I would not look (**wouldn't look**) |
| he would look (**he'd look**) | would he look? | he would not look (**wouldn't look**) |

**The conditional perfect** (पूर्ण हेतुमत)

| | | |
|---|---|---|
| I would have looked (**would've looked**) | would I have looked? | I would not have looked (**wouldn't have looked**) |
| he would have looked (**would've looked**) | would he have looked? | he would not have looked (**wouldn't have looked**) |

## The Continuous Tenses (सातत्यबोधक काल)

**NOTE** **Continuous Tenses** (सातत्यबोधक कालों) को **progressive tenses** भी कहते हैं।
**I, you, we** और **they** के क्रियारूप समान होते हैं। जहाँ **you** का क्रियारूप भिन्न है वहाँ दिखाया गया है।
**He, she** और **it** के क्रियारूप समान होते हैं।

### The present continuous (वर्तमान सातत्यबोधक)

| | | |
|---|---|---|
| I am looking (**I'm looking**) | am I looking? | I am not looking (**I'm not looking**) |
| you are looking (**you're looking**) | are you looking? | you are not looking (**aren't looking**) |
| he is looking (**he's looking**) | is he looking? | he is not looking (**isn't looking**) |

### The past continuous (भूत सातत्यबोधक)

| | | |
|---|---|---|
| I was looking | was I looking? | I was not looking (**wasn't looking**) |
| you were looking | were you looking? | you were not looking (**weren't looking**) |
| he was looking | was he looking? | he was not looking (**wasn't looking**) |

### The present perfect continuous (वर्तमान पूर्ण सातत्यबोधक)

| | | |
|---|---|---|
| I have been looking (**I've been looking**) | have I been looking? | I have not been looking (**haven't been looking**) |
| he has been looking (**he's been looking**) | has he been looking? | he has not been looking (**hasn't been looking**) |

### The past perfect continuous (भूत पूर्ण सातत्यबोधक)

| | | |
|---|---|---|
| I had been looking (**I'd been looking**) | had I been looking? | I had not been looking (**hadn't been looking**) |
| he had been looking (**he'd been looking**) | had he been looking? | he had not been looking (**hadn't been looking**) |

### The future continuous (भविष्यत सातत्यबोधक)

| | | |
|---|---|---|
| I will be looking (**I'll be looking**) | will I be looking? | I will not be looking (**won't be looking**) |
| he will be looking (**he'll be looking**) | will he be looking? | he will not be looking (**won't be looking**) |

### The future perfect continuous (भविष्यत पूर्ण सातत्यबोधक)

| | | |
|---|---|---|
| I will have been looking (**I'll have been looking**) | will I have been looking? | I will not have been looking (**won't have been looking**) |
| he will have been looking (**he'll have been looking**) | will he have been looking? | he will not have been looking (**won't have been looking**) |

**The conditional continuous** (सातत्यबोधक हेतुमत)

| | | |
|---|---|---|
| I would be looking **(I'd be looking)** | would I be looking? | I would not be looking **(wouldn't be looking)** |
| he would be looking **(he'd be looking)** | would he be looking? | he would not be looking **(wouldn't be looking)** |

**The conditional perfect continuous** (पूर्ण सातत्यबोधक हेतुमत)

| | | |
|---|---|---|
| I would have been looking **(would've been looking)** | would I have been looking? | I would not have been looking **(wouldn't have been looking)** |
| he would have been looking **(would've been looking)** | would he have been looking? | he would not have been looking **(wouldn't have been looking)** |

# Verbs

## Talking About the Present ('वर्तमान' की बोधन-रीतियाँ)

'इस समय' हो रही क्रिया का वर्णन **present continuous** (वर्तमान सातत्यबोधक) द्वारा होता है:

—*We're just **having** breakfast.*
—*What **are** you **reading**?*
—*She **isn't listening** to me.*

**Present continuous** (वर्तमान सातत्यबोधक) का प्रयोग 'कोई क्रिया अभी तक पूरी नहीं हुई है' इसके द्योतन के लिए भी होता है, चाहे कहते समय उस क्रिया को आप कर भी नहीं रहें हैं:

—*I'**m learning** English.*
—*She's **writing** a book about snails.*

जब कोई घटना/क्रिया अकसर होती है और आप को उलझन भी उस से होती है तो आप वर्तमान सातत्यवोधक का प्रयोग शब्द **always** के साथ करते हैं:

—*He's always **asking** silly questions.*
—*They're always **coming** round here to borrow something.*

कुछ क्रियाओं के सातत्यबोधक काल नहीं प्रयुक्त होते हैं, उदाहरणार्थ **need, want, know** आदिः
➪ **promise, agree, seem, appear, understand, appreciate** प्रविष्टियों को देखिए। ये क्रियाएँ स्थिति दिखाती हैं, न कि क्रियाकार्य।

—*I **need** some new shoes.*
—*She **hates** her job.*
—*He **wants** to go home.*
—***Do** you **know** Tania Singh?*

अन्य क्रियाएँ वर्तमान सातत्यबोधक में तब प्रयुक्त होती हैं जब वे किसी क्रियाकार्य को दिखाती हैं और सामान्य वर्तमान में प्रयुक्त होती हैं, जब वे स्थिति का वर्णन करती हैं:

—*He's **tasting** the soup.*
—*The soup **tastes** salty.*
—*She's **being** difficult again.*
—*What **are** you **thinking** about?*
—*Do you **think** I should leave?*

यह बताने के लिए कि कोई स्थिति या कार्य सदैव सत्य है, आप **present simple** (सामान्य वर्तमान) का प्रयोग करते हैं:

—*Whales **are** mammals.*
—*Rice **doesn't grow** in this climate.*
—*What temperature **does** water **boil** at?*

जो क्रियाएँ नियमित रूप से होती हैं, उनके लिए आप सामान्य वर्तमान का प्रयोग करते हैं:

—*She **leaves** for school at 8 o'clock.*
—***Does** he **work** in a factory?*
—*We **don't** often **go** out for a meal.*

## Talking About the Past ('भूत' की बोधन-रीतियाँ)

अतीत में समाप्त हुए क्रियाकार्यों के बोधन में, आप **past simple** (सामान्य भूतकाल) का प्रयोग करते हैं:

*—He **got** up, **paid** the bill, and **left**.*
*—I **didn't read** the letter. I just **gave** it to Leela.*
*—What **did** you **say** to him?*

प्रायः विशिष्ट समय का उल्लेख होता है:

*—**Did** you **speak** to Anu yesterday?*

आप सामान्य भूत का प्रयोग तब भी करते हैं, जब आप उस अवस्था का वर्णन करते हैं जो कुछ समय तक तो विद्यमान या चल रही थी पर अब वह समाप्त हो गई है:

*—I **went** to school in Kolkata.*
*—**Did** she really **work** there for ten years?*
*—He **didn't grow** up in Chennai—he went there as an adult.*

अतीत में नियमित रूप से हुई घटनाओं या क्रियाकार्यों के बोधन में भी यह प्रयुक्त होता है:

*—I often **played** tennis with her.*
*—She always **won**.*
*—They never **went** to the cinema when they **lived** in the village.*

उस परिस्थिति के बोधन के लिए जो अतीत में आरंभ हुई थी और अब भी विद्यमान या चल रही है, आप **present perfect** (पूर्ण वर्तमान) का प्रयोग करते हैं:

*—I've **worked** here since 1998.*
*—I've **known** Tara for years.*

आप पूर्ण वर्तमान का प्रयोग प्रायः तब भी करते हैं, जब समय का उल्लेख नहीं है या उसका कोई महत्व नहीं है:

*—He's **written** a book.*
*—We've **bought** a new computer.*

कभी-कभी क्रियाकार्य अतीत में समाप्त हो चुका है किंतु उसका प्रभाव अब भी बना हुआ है:

*—He's **lost** his calculator* (and he still hasn't found it).

**Since** और **for** के साथ पूर्ण वर्तमान के प्रयोग पर, जहाँ वे किसी क्रियाकार्य की समय-अवधि या अभी तक बनी हुई स्थिति को दिखाते हैं, ध्यान दीजिए:

*—I've **known** about it since Christmas. How long **have** you **known**?*
*—She **hasn't bought** any new clothes for years.*

ब्रिटिश अंग्रेज़ी में पूर्ण वर्तमान का प्रायः **just, ever, already, yet** आदि शब्दों के साथ प्रयोग होता है:

*—I've just **arrived**.*
*—**Have** you ever **been** here before?*
*—He's **already packed** his suitcases.*
*—**Haven't** you **finished** yet?*

इसका प्रयोग किसी समय-अवधि में घटित क्रियाकार्य जो अभी तक जारी है का वर्णन करने के लिए भी होता है:

*—The train **has been** late three times this week.*

उस क्रियाकार्य के बोधन के लिए जो अतीत में आरंभ हुआ था और अब भी चल रहा है या जो अभी-अभी समाप्त हुआ है पर उस के परिणाम अब भी दृष्टिगोचर हैं, आप **present perfect continuous** (वर्तमान पूर्ण सातत्यबोधक) का प्रयोग करते हैं:

*—I've **been working** since eight o'clock—can I have a break now?*
*—My hands are dirty because I've **been gardening**.*
*—They **haven't been learning** English very long.*

यह बताने के लिए कि कुछ अब भी प्रगति करता जा रहा है जब कि कुछ अन्य घटित या समाप्त हो चुका है, आप **past continuous** (भूत सातत्यबोधक) का प्रयोग करते हैं:

*—It **was raining** when I left the house.*
*—**Was** he **cooking** dinner when you got home?*
*—I **wasn't wearing** a coat and I got very wet.*

वर्तमान सातत्यबोधक की तरह यह काल भी 'स्थिति' क्रियाओं के साथ नहीं प्रयुक्त हो सकता है:

*—The fresh bread **smelled** wonderful* (~~*was smelling*~~ नहीं).

यह बताने के लिए कि कुछ, अतीत में हुए किसी अन्य क्रियाकार्य के पूर्व, हो चुका है, आप **past perfect** (पूर्ण भूत) का प्रयोग करते हैं:

—*When I got to the station, the train **had left**.*
—*I **had** never **met** Raman before he came to Pune.*
—*They **had moved** into the flat three months before Jai lost his job.*

यह बताने के लिए कि किसी अन्य की तुलना में उससे भी पहले की समय-अवधी में क्रियाकार्य चलता रहा था, आप **past perfect continuous** (भूत पूर्ण सातत्यबोधक) का प्रयोग करते हैं:

—*My hands were dirty because I **had been gardening**.*
—*She **hadn't been working** at the shop very very long when they sacked her.*

## Talking About the Future ('भविष्यत' की बोधन-रीतियाँ)

उस काल को, जिसे हम भविष्यत काल कहते हैं, भविष्यत के बोधन में सामान्यता लाते हैं। किंतु **'the future'** भविष्यत के बताने की कुछ अन्य भी रीतियाँ हैं:

भावी योजना, जहाँ समय का उल्लेख है, के बोधन में आप **present continuous** (वर्तमान सातत्यबोधक) का प्रयोग करते हैं:

—*What **are** you **doing** this evening?*
—*I'**m** not **starting** my new job till next Monday.*

यह बताने के लिए कि भविष्य में आप कुछ करने का इरादा रखते हैं किंतु उसका प्रबंध अभी तक नहीं किया है, आप क्रियार्थक संज्ञा के साथ **be going to** प्रयुक्त करते हैं:

—*What **are** you **going to do** when you leave college?*
—*I'**m not going to be** as strict with my children as my parents were with me.*

बोलते समय कुछ निर्णय लिया है तो उसे बताने के लिए आप क्रियार्थक संज्ञा के साथ **will** का प्रयोग करेंगे:

—*I **can't do** this. I'**ll ask** the teacher.*
—*We'**ll have** the salad, please.*

यह बताने के लिए कि आप जानते हैं या सोचते हैं कि यह भविष्य में होगा (यद्यपि वह आप का इरादा या योजना के विषय में नहीं है) आप क्रियार्थक संज्ञा के साथ शब्द **will** का प्रयोग करते हैं:

—*It **will be** 25° tomorrow.*
—*She'**ll be** in the office on Monday.*
—***Will** he **pass** the exam, do you think?*
—*This job **won't take** long.*

**When, as soon as, before, until** आदि शब्दों के बाद भविष्य समय निर्दिष्ट करने के लिए आप **present simple** (सामान्य वर्तमान) का प्रयोग करते हैं:

—*Ring me as soon as you **hear** any news.*
—*I'll look after Jai until you **get** back.*
—*You'll recognize the street when you **see** it.*

निवेदन, वादा, प्रस्ताव आदि के लिए भी आप क्रियार्थक संज्ञा के साथ शब्द **will** का प्रयोग करते हैं:

—***Will** you **buy** some bread on your way home?*
—*We'**ll be** back early, don't worry.*
—*I'**ll help** you with your maths.*

अति निकट भविष्य को बताने के लिए आप क्रियार्थक संज्ञा के साथ **about to** का प्रयोग करते हैं:

—***Go** and ask him quickly. He's **about to go** out.*

ऐसे क्रियाकार्यों को बताने के लिए जो भविष्य में एक समय-अवधि तक जारी रहेंगे, आप **future continuous** (भविष्यत सातत्यबोधक) का प्रयोग करते हैं:

—*I'**ll be waiting** near the ticket office.*
—*I'**ll be wearing** a green hat.*
—*This time next week you'**ll be relaxing** in the sun!*

किसी से उसकी योजना या इरादा जानने के लिए आप **will be + -ing** का प्रयोग करते हैं:

—*How many nights **will** you **be staying**?*
—***Will** you **be flying** back or going by train?*

भविष्य में निर्दिष्ट समय पर समाप्त होने वाले के बोधन के लिए आप **future perfect** (पूर्ण भविष्यत) का प्रयोग करते हैं:

—*I **will have finished** this work by 3 o'clock.*
—*They'**ll have lived** here for four years in May?*

भावी योजनाएँ जिनका अधिकृत पूर्वप्रबंध हो चुका है, जैसे कि, समय सारणी या कार्यक्रम, के बोधन के लिए आप **present simple** (सामान्य वर्तमान) का प्रयोग कर सकते हैं:

—*We **leave** Kasauli at 10 and **arrive** in Chandigarh at 12.30.*
—*School **starts** on 9 January.*

## Transitive and Intransitive Verbs (सकर्मक और अकर्मक क्रियाएँ)

**[T]** क्रियाएँ जिनका प्रत्यक्ष कर्म हो सकता है **transitive verbs** (सकर्मक क्रिया) कही जाती हैं। इस शब्दकोश में वे [T] से चिह्नित हैं। क्रिया **include** की प्रविष्टि देखिए।
*—He included four new names on the list.*
यह कहना संभव नहीं है: *—He included.*

**[I]** क्रियाएँ जिनका प्रत्यक्ष कर्म नहीं हो सकता है, **intransitive verbs** (अकर्मक क्रिया) कही जाती हैं। इस शब्दकोश में वे [I] से चिह्नित हैं। **arrive** क्रिया की प्रविष्टि देखिए।
*—We arrived very late at the hotel.*
यह कहना संभव नहीं है: *—We arrived the hotel.*

**[I, T]** बहुत सी क्रियाएँ अकर्मक और सकर्मक दोनों हो सकती हैं। इस शब्दकोश में वे [I, T] से चिह्नित हैं:
*—[I] He spoke for two hours.* *—[T] Do you speak Hindi?*
*—[I] This door only locks from the outside.* *—[T] Have you locked the door?*

कुछ क्रियाओं के दो कर्म हो सकते हैं — अप्रत्यक्ष और प्रत्यक्ष। क्रिया **give** की प्रविष्टि देखिए और वहाँ दिखाई संरचना पर ध्यान दीजिए:
**—give sb sth; give sth to sb**
वाक्य में इस प्रकार आप कह सकते हैं:
*—He gave his mother the CDs.* या *He gave the CDs to his mother.*
कर्मों में कोई भी या दोनों सर्वनाम आ सकते हैं:
*—He gave her the CDs.* *—He gave them to her.*
*—He gave the CDs to her.* *—He gave her them. (informal)*
*—He gave them to his mother.*

## Conditionals (शर्तवाचक) (हेतुमत वाक्य)

**If** के साथ वाक्य 'संभावना' प्रदर्शित करते हैं। इसके तीन मुख्य भेद हैं:

1. *If I **write** my essay this afternoon, I **will have** time to go out tonight.* (= It is still morning, and it is probable that I will do this) —**if** के बाद **present tense** (वर्तमान काल) और मुख्य उपवाक्य में **future tense** (भविष्यत काल)
2. *If I **wrote** my essay this afternoon, I **would have** time to go out tonight.* (= It is still morning, but I think it is less likely that I will do this) —**if** के बाद **simple past** (सामान्य भूत) और मुख्य उपवाक्य में **conditional tense** (हेतुमत काल)
3. *If I **had written** my essay this afternoon, I **would have had** time to go out tonight.* (= It is now evening, and I haven't written my essay: it is now impossible for me to go out) —**if** के बाद **past perfect** (पूर्ण भूत) और मुख्य उपवाक्य में **conditional perfect** (पूर्ण हेतुमत काल)

**'If'** वाक्यों के कुछ अन्य भेद नीचे दिए जा रहे हैं। कोई तथ्य जो सदैव सत्य है या अतीत में सदैव सत्य था:
*—If you **mix** blue and red, you **get** purple.*
वाक्य के दोनों अंशों में **present simple** (सामान्य वर्तमान) का प्रयोग होता है।
*—If I asked her to come with us, she always **said** no.*
वाक्य के दोनों अंशों में **simple past** (सामान्य भूत) का प्रयोग होता है।

# Reported Speech (उद्धृत कथन)

## Direct Speech to Reported Speech (प्रत्यक्ष कथन से उद्धृत कथन)

जब आप किसी के कथन को **said, asked** आदि शब्दों का प्रयोग कर, उद्धृत करते हैं तो सामान्यतया काल को 'भूत' में एक चरण और पीछे ले जाते हैं:

RAJESH: 'I'm coming home.'
→ *Rajesh said he was coming home.*

'I **don't know** whether Leena **wants** to come.'
→ *He said he **didn't know** whether Leena **wanted** to come.*

'She **is thinking** of staying at home tomorrow.'
→ *He said she **was thinking** of staying at home the following day.*

'**Have** you **booked** your ticket?'
→ *He asked whether she **had booked** her ticket*

'I **finished** my exams yesterday.'
→ *He said he **had finished** his exams the day before.*

*'I'**ll ring** from the station.'*
→ *He told me he **would ring** from the station.*

Modal verbs (वृत्ति क्रियाएँ) **should, would, might, could, must,** and **ought** सामान्यतया नहीं बदलती हैं। 'We **might go** to the cinema.'
→ *They said they **might go** to the cinema.*

यदि उद्धरण करने वाली क्रिया (**say, ask**, etc.) वर्तमान या पूर्ण वर्तमान में हैं, तो वाक्य के काल सामान्यतया नहीं बदलते हैं।

BEN: I'm going home.'
→ *Ben says he's **going** home.*
*Ben's just told me he's going home.*

## Reporting Requests and Commands (निवेदन और आदेश की उद्धरण-रीति)

जब आप निवेदन या आदेश को उद्धृत करते हैं तो सामान्यतया आप **infinitive** (क्रियार्थक) संज्ञा की संरचना का प्रयोग करते हैं:

'Please will you do the dishes?'
→ *She **asked me to do** the dishes.*

'Don't touch the stove!'
→ *She **told** the children **not to touch** the stove.*

## Reporting Questions (प्रश्नों की उद्धरण-रीति)

ध्यान दीजिए कि आप हाँ/नहीं प्रश्नों के उद्धरण में शब्द **if** या **whether** का प्रयोग करते हैं:

'Are you ready?'
→ *She asked **if/whether I was ready**.*

इन वाक्यों में शब्दों का क्रम सामान्य कथन की तरह रहता है, प्रश्न की तरह नहीं:

'Did you see them?'
→ *He asked me **if I had seen** them.*

**Wh-** प्रश्नों के साथ, **wh-** शब्द उद्धृत वाक्य में विद्यमान रहता है:
'When are you leaving?'
→ *She asked me **when I was leaving**.*

## Reporting Verbs (उद्धृत करने में प्रयुक्त क्रियाएँ)

विभिन्न **reporting verbs** (उद्धृतीकरण क्रियाओं) के प्रयोग के कुछ अन्य उदाहरण नीचे दिए जा रहे हैं:

'Will you come with me?' 'All right.'
→ *She **agreed** to come with me.*

'Sorry I didn't phone you'.
→ *She **apologized** for not phoning me.*

'Did you steal the money?' 'Yes, I did.'
→ *She **admitted** (to) stealing the money.*
→ *She **admitted** that she'd stolen the money.*

'Shall we take a break now?'
→ *She **suggested** taking a break.*

'You should have a holiday.'
→ *She **advised** me to have a holiday.*

'I'm freezing!'
→ *She **complained** that she was freezing.*

## The Passive (कर्मवाच्य)

**Active** (कर्तृवाच्य) वाक्य में कर्ता (उद्देश्य) वह व्यक्ति या वस्तु है जो क्रियाकार्य का निष्पादन करता है:
*—**Masked thieves** stole a valuable painting from the museum last night.*

जब आप उसे **passive sentence** (कर्मवाच्य) में बदलते हैं तो क्रिया का कर्म कर्ता बन जाता है:
*—**A valuable painting** was stolen from the museum last night.*

कर्मवाच्य **to be** के किसी रूप और क्रिया के **past participle** (भूत कृदंत) से बनता है:
*—The painting **is valued** by experts at two million dollars.*
*—The theft **is being investigated** by the police.*
*—Other museums **have been warned** to take extra care.*
*—The painting **was kept** in a special room.*
*—The lock **had been broken** and the cameras **had been switched off**.*
*—This morning everything possible **was being done** to find the thieves.*
*—Staff at the museum **will be questioned** tomorrow.*
*—An international search **is to be started**.*
*—The theft must **have been planned** with the help of someone inside the museum.*

आप कर्मवाच्य का प्रयोग करते हैं जब आप क्रिया किसने की है यह नहीं जानते या क्रिया किसने की है यह सूचना महत्त्वपूर्ण नहीं है। यह औपचारिक लेखन में सामान्यतया मिलता है, उदाहरणार्थ, वैज्ञानिक लेखन के वाक्य:
*—The liquid was heated to 60°C and then filtered.*

यदि आप कर्ता का उल्लेख करना चाहते हैं तो वाक्य के अंत में शब्द **by** प्रयोग करते हैं:
*—The painting was stolen **by masked thieves**.*

कर्मवाच्य चुनने का एक कारण यह है कि कभी-कभी आप नवीन सूचना को वाक्य के अंत तक बलाधान की दृष्टि से सामने नहीं लाना चाहते हैं:
*—The picture was painted **by Constable**.*

द्विकर्मक क्रिया को भी कर्मवाच्य बनाया जा सकता है:
—An American millionaire gave **the museum the painting.**
*→**The museum** was given **the painting** by an American millionaire.*
—The director told the **staff the news** this morning.
*→**The staff** were told **the news** this morning by the director.*

## Modal Verbs (वृत्तिवाचक क्रियाएँ)

**Ability** (सामर्थ्य, योग्यता) — **can could be able to**

*—**Can** he swim?*
*—My brother **could** swim when he was two.*
*—I **couldn't** find my keys this morning.*
*—I **could have** run faster, but I didn't want the others to get tired.*
*—She **has** not **been able** to walk since the accident.*
*—He **was able to** speak to Anita before she left.*
*—Will people **be able to** live on the moon one day?*

➪ '**Could**' और **managed** के अंतर के लिए **could** की प्रविष्टि पर दिए टिप्पणी को देखिए।

**Possibility** (संभावना) — **could may might**

*—**Could/Might** you have lost it on the way home?*
*—She **may/might/could** be ill. I'll phone her.*
*—I **may have/might have** left my purse in the shop.*
*—Anita **might/may** know the answer.*
*—I **might/may** not go if I'm tired.*
*—He **might have** enjoyed the party if he'd gone.*

**Permission** **can could may may not must not**
(अनुज्ञा, अनुमति)

—*Can we come in?*
—*You* ***can't*** *get up until you're better.*
—***Could*** *we possibly stay at your flat?*
—*(written) Staff* ***may*** *take their break between 12 and 2.*
—*(formal)* ***May*** *I sit here?*
—*(written) Crockery* ***may not*** *be taken out of the canteen.*
—*(formal) You* ***must not*** *begin until I tell you.*

**Obligation** **ought to/should** (mild) **have (got) to/must** (strong)
(करना है, करणीय है)
—*I* ***ought to/should*** *go on a diet.*
—*I* ***ought to have/should have*** *asked her first.*
—*(written) All visitors* ***must*** *report to reception on arrival.*
—*I* ***must*** *get that report finished today.*
—*Do you* ***have to*** *write your name on the form?*
—*She* ***had to*** *throw that burnt cake away.*
—*You* ***will have to*** *wait, I'm afraid.*

**Advice** **ought to should**
(विमर्श, सलाह)
—***Ought I to/Should*** *I write and thank him?*
—*She* ***ought to/should*** *go out more often.*
—*You* ***ought to have/should have*** *gone to bed earlier.*
—*You* ***shouldn't*** *borrow the car without asking.*

**No necessity** **don't have to shouldn't have didn't need to needn't have**
(आवश्यकता-हीनता)
—*You* ***don't have to*** *pick us up; we can take a taxi.*
—*They* ***didn't have to*** *go through customs.*
—*You* ***shouldn't have*** *bothered making lunch; we could have bought a sandwich.*
—*He* ***didn't need to*** *have any fillings at the dentist's.*
—*They* ***needn't have*** *waited.*

➪ 'Didn't need to' और 'needn't have', के अंतर के लिए **need**[2] की टिप्पणी को देखिए।

**Requests** **can/will** (*informal*) **could/would** (*formal*)
(निवेदन)

—***Can*** *you pass me the dictionary?*
—***Will*** *you buy me an ice cream, Mum?*

—***Could*** *you help me with my translation?*
—***Would*** *you type this letter for me, please?*

**Offers and suggestions** **shall will**
(प्रस्ताव और सुझाव)

—***Shall*** *I do the dusting?*
—***I'll*** *take you to the airport.*
—***Shall*** *we go now?*

# Nouns

## Countable and Uncountable Nouns (गणनीय और अगणनीय संज्ञाएँ)

**[C]** गणनीय (**countable**) संज्ञाएँ एकवचन या बहुवचन हो सकती हैं:

*—a friend/two friends* *— one book/five books*

इस शब्दकोश में उन्हें [C] से चिह्नित किया गया है।

**[U]** अगणनीय (**uncountable**) संज्ञाएँ के बहुवचन रूप नहीं मिलते हैं और **a/an** के साथ उनका प्रयोग नहीं मिलता है। उनकी गिनती नहीं की जा सकती है। इस शब्दकोश में उन्हें [U] से चिह्नित किया गया है।

➪ निम्नलिखित की प्रविष्टियाँ देखिए:

**rice money water information advice furniture**

यह कहना संभव है ***some rice*** परंतु ~~***a rice***~~ या ~~***two rices***~~ नहीं।

**Importance, luck, happiness** जैसी भावार्थक संज्ञाएँ सामान्यतया अगणनीय होती हैं।

**[C, U]** कुछ संज्ञाएँ गणनीय और अगणनीय दोनों होती हैं। इस शब्दकोश में उन्हें **[C, U]** या **[U, C]** से चिह्नित किया गया है।

➪ निम्नलिखित की प्रविष्टियाँ देखिए:

**cheese coffee paper friendship**

—**[U]** *Have some cheese!*
—**[C]** *They sell a variety of cheeses.* (= types of cheese)
—**[U]** *I don't drink much coffee.*
—**[C]** *She ordered too many coffees.* (= cups of coffee)
—**[U]** *I haven't got any more paper.*
—**[C]** *Can you buy me a paper?* (= a newspaper)
—**[U]** *Friendship is more important than wealth.*
—**[C]** *None of these were lasting friendships.* (= relationships)

***[sing.]*** कुछ संज्ञाओं के केवल एकवचन रूप मिलते हैं। इस शब्दकोश में उन्हें [*sing.*] से चिह्नित किया गया है।

➪ निम्नलिखित की प्रविष्टियाँ देखिए:

**aftermath dearth brink**

इन्हें बहुवचन में प्रयुक्त नहीं किया जा सकता है। किंतु ये **a/an** या **the** के साथ प्रयुक्त हो सकते हैं:

*—in the aftermath of the earthquake*
*—There was a dearth of fresh food.*
*—We are on the brink of disaster.*

***[pl.]*** कुछ शब्द केवल बहुवचनांत (**plural**) होते हैं। इस शब्दकोश में उन्हें [*pl.*] से चिह्नित किया गया है।

➪ निम्नलिखित की प्रविष्टियाँ देखिए:

**jeans sunglasses scissors**

आप नहीं कह सकते हैं: ~~***a sunglasses***~~

इनको एकल वस्तु के रूप में बनाने के लिए आप कह सकते हैं ***a pair of:***

*—a pair of sunglasses* *—two pairs of sunglasses*

**Headphones, clothes,** and **goods** आदि शब्द केवल बहुवचन में प्रयुक्त हो सकते हैं:

*—I need to buy some new clothes.*

संज्ञाएँ जो व्यक्तियों के समूह को निर्दिष्ट करती हैं, जैसे **the poor**, बहुवचनांत होती हैं:

*—The poor are getting poorer and the rich are getting richer.*

## The Use of Articles with Nouns

### The Definite Article (निश्चायक आर्टिकल)

आप निश्चायक आर्टिकल **'the'** का प्रयोग तब करते हैं जब आप जानते या समझते हैं कि श्रोता उस व्यक्ति या वस्तु को जानते हैं जिसकी आप बात कर रहे हैं:

—*Thank you for **the** flowers* (= the ones that you brought me).
—***The** teacher said my essay was the best* (= our teacher).

आप नदियों और द्वीपसमूहों के नामों के साथ **the** का प्रयोग करते हैं:

—*Which is longer, **the** Bramhaputra or **the** Ganga?*
—*Where are **the** Seychelles?*
—*Menorca is one of **the** Balearic Islands.*

### The Indefinite Article (अनिश्चायक आर्टिकल)

आप अनिश्चायक आर्टिकल **a** (स्वर ध्वनि के पूर्व **an**), का प्रयोग तब करते हैं जब कि श्रोता यह नहीं जानता कि किस व्यक्ति या वस्तु के विषय में आप बात कर रहे हैं या आप किसी विशिष्ट वस्तु या व्यक्ति को निर्दिष्ट नहीं कर रहे हैं:

—*He's got **a** new bike.* (I haven't mentioned it before.)
—*Could you bring me **a** knife?* (Any knife will be ok.)

आप **a/an** का प्रयोग तब भी करते हैं जब आप व्यक्तियों या वस्तुओं के वर्ग या प्रकार-विशेष या समूह के संबंध में बात करते हैं जैसे आप किसी व्यक्ति के व्यावसायिक कार्य की बात कर रहे हों:

—*She's **an** accountant.*

मूल्यों, वेगों आदि में **a/an** का प्रयोग करते हैं:

—*$100 **a** day*
—*70 kilometres **an** hour*
—*50 cents **a** pack*
—*three times **a** week*

### No Article (आर्टिकल-हीनता)

जब आप 'सामान्य' के विषय में बात कर रहे हैं तो कोई आर्टिकल नहीं लगाते हैं:

—*I love flowers (all flowers).*
—*Honey is sweet (all honey).*
—*Are nurses well paid here?* (nurses in general)

अधिकांश देशों, प्रांतों, राज्यों, मार्गों आदि के साथ **the** का प्रयोग नहीं करते हैं:

—*I'm going to Paris.*
—*She's from Kanpur.*
—*They live in Shimla.*
—*a house in Park Street*
—*Lake Chilka*

या किसी व्यक्ति की उपाधि के साथ जब कि नाम का उल्लेख हो रहा है:

—*President Kennedy* **BUT** ***the** President of the United States*

➪ आर्टिकलों के प्रयोग में और अधिक सूचना के लिए निम्नलिखित की प्रविष्टियों को देखिए:
**school university college hospital prison piano**

### The Possessive with 's ('s के साथ संबंधवाचक रूप)

आप किसी शब्द या नाम के साथ **'s** को जोड़ सकते हैं जिससे दोनों का संबंध स्पष्ट होता है:

—*Amrita's job*
—*the manager's secretary*
—*my brother's computer*
—*the children's clothes*
—*the dog's basket*
—*Goa's beaches*

जहाँ शब्द बहुवचन **s** के साथ पहले से ही है, वहाँ आप उस बहुवचनांत शब्द के बाद (') चिह्न लगा देते हैं:

—*the boys' rooms*
—*the Smiths' house*

## The Use of Determiners with Nouns (संज्ञाओं के पूर्व निर्धारकों का प्रयोग)

शब्द **much** अगणनीय संज्ञाओं के पूर्व सामान्यतया नकारात्मक वाक्यों और प्रश्नों में प्रयुक्त होता है:

*—I haven't got **much** money left.*
*—Did you watch **much** television?*

सकारात्मक वाक्यों में **much** का प्रयोग अत्यंत औपचारिक है:

*—There will be **much** discussion before a decision is made.*

शब्द **many** गणनीय संज्ञाओं के पूर्व सामान्यतया नकारात्मक वाक्यों और प्रश्नों में प्रयुक्त होता है:

*—There aren't **many** tourists here in December.*
*—Are there **many** opportunities for young people?*

शब्द **many** सकारात्मक वाक्यों में **'a lot of'** से अधिक औपचारिक है:

*—**Many** people prefer to stay at home.*

**A lot of** या (अनौपचारिक) **lots of** का प्रयोग गणनीय संज्ञाओं के साथ होता है:

*—**A lot of** tourists visit the temple.*
*—I've spent **a lot of** money.*
*—He's been here **lots of** times.*
*—You need **lots of** patience to make model aircraft.*

**A little** का प्रयोग अगणनीय संज्ञाओं के साथ होता है:

*—Add **a little** vinegar.*

**A few** का प्रयोग गणनीय संज्ञाओं के साथ होता है:

*—I've got **a few** letters to write.*

**NOTE** पिछले दो उदाहरण वाक्य सकारात्मक अर्थ दर्शाते हैं। **'A'** रहित प्रयोग में **few** तथा **little** नकारात्मक अर्थ दर्शाते हैं:

—***Few*** people (= not many) *have ever seen these animals in the wild.*
—*There is now* ***little*** *hope* (= not much) *that they can win the championship.*

# Adjectives

## Comparatives and Superlatives (तुलनाद्योतक और सर्वोत्तमताद्योतक विशेषण)

निम्नलिखित अनुच्छेद को देखिए। इसमें अनेक तुलनाद्योतक और सर्वोत्तमताद्योतक विशेषण हैं:

— *Temperatures yesterday were **highest** in the south-east. The **sunniest** place was Chennai, and the **wettest** was Shillong. Tomorrow will be **cooler** than today, but in Delhi it will be a **drier** day. **Better** weather is expected for the weekend, but it will become **more changeable** again next week.*

तुलनाद्योतक और सर्वोत्तमताद्योतक के रूप इस प्रकार बनते हैं:

एक-अक्षर-समूह वाले विशेषण **-er, -est** लेते हैं:

| | | |
|---|---|---|
| **cool** | **cooler** | **coolest** |
| **high** | **higher** | **highest** |

**-e** में अंत होने वाले विशेषण **-r, -st** लेते हैं:

| | | |
|---|---|---|
| **nice** | **nicer** | **nicest** |

कुछ विशेषण अंतिम व्यंजन का द्वित्व करते हैं:

| | | |
|---|---|---|
| **wet** | **wetter** | **wettest** |
| **big** | **bigger** | **biggest** |

तीन या तीन से अधिक अक्षर-समूह वाले विशेषण **more, most** लेते हैं:

| | | |
|---|---|---|
| **changeable** | **more changeable** | **most changeable** |
| **interesting** | **more interesting** | **most interesting** |

कुछ दो अक्षर-समूह वाले विशेषण **-er, -est** लेते हैं, विशेषतया यदि उनके अंत में **-er, -y** या **-ly** हो:

**clever** **cleverer** **cleverest**

**-y** में अंत होने वाले विशेषण **-y** को **-i** में बदल देते हैं:

**sunny** **sunnier** **sunniest**
**friendly** **friendlier** **friendliest**

दो अक्षर-समूह के कुछ अन्य विशेषणों के साथ **more, most** प्रयुक्त होते हैं:

**harmful** **more harmful** **most harmful**

कुछ विशेषणों के अनियमित रूप होते हैं:

**good** **better** **best**
**bad** **worse** **worst**

## Adjectives with Nouns (संज्ञा के साथ विशेषण)

अधिकांश विशेषण, उस संज्ञा के पूर्व आते हैं जिसका वे वर्णन कर रहे हैं या श्रृंखला-क्रियाओं में संज्ञा के बाद आते हैं:

*—I need a **new** bike.*
*—This bike isn't **new**.*
*—It's an **interesting** book.*
*—She said the film sounded **interesting**.*
*—Don't wake him—he's **asleep**.*

कुछ विशेषण संज्ञा के पूर्व नहीं आ सकते हैं। **asleep** की प्रविष्टि देखिए और देखिए कि यह सूचना इस शब्दकोश में किस प्रकार दी जाती है।

आप कह सकते हैं: *Don't wake him—he's **asleep**.* पर ~~*an asleep child*~~ नहीं।

➪ निम्नलिखित की प्रविष्टियों को देखिए:

**afraid** **alive** **ashamed** **certain** **pleased**

कुछ विशेषण संज्ञा के पूर्व ही आ सकते हैं। विशेषण **chief** की प्रविष्टि देखिए और जानिए कि यह सूचना इस शब्दकोश में किस प्रकार दी जाती है:

आप कह सकते हैं: *That was the **chief** disadvantage.* पर ~~*This disadvantage was chief.*~~ ग़लत प्रयोग है।

➪ निम्नलिखित की प्रविष्टियों को देखिए:

**downright** **flagrant** **former** **main**

# Relative Clauses (संबंधवाचक उपवाक्य)

## Defining Relative Clauses (निश्चयात्मक संबंधवाचक उपवाक्य)

ये उपवाक्य अपने कथन व्यक्ति या वस्तु की पहचान या निश्चय कराते हैं:

*—Which of them is the boss?*
*—The man **who came in late** is the boss.*

**NOTE** इस प्रकार के उपवाक्य के पूर्व कोई अल्पविराम नहीं होता है।

इन उपवाक्यों में हम सर्वनाम **who, whom, that** और **which** का प्रयोग करते हैं।

जब **subject** (कर्ता) कोई व्यक्ति हो:

*—the man **who** came in late* या *the man **that** came in late*

जब **object** (कर्म) कोई व्यक्ति हो:

*—the girl **that** I saw* या *the girl I saw* या *the girl **whom** I saw (formal)*

जब **subject** (कर्ता) कोई वस्तु हो:

*—the chair **that** is in the corner* या *the chair **which** is in the corner (formal)*

जब **object** (कर्म) कोई वस्तु हो:

*—the book **that** I'm reading* या *the book I'm reading* या *the book which I'm reading (formal)*

**NOTE** शब्द **that, who** और **which** को तब प्रयुक्त नहीं किया जाता है जब वस्तु या व्यक्ति क्रिया का कर्म हो।

शब्द **whose** यह दिखा रहा है कि कोई वस्तु किसी व्यक्ति की है:

*—the woman **whose** car broke down* *—the people **whose** house was burgled*

शब्द **whose** किसी वस्तु को निर्दिष्ट करने में सामान्यतया प्रयुक्त नहीं होता है:

*— ~~the chair whose leg is broken~~* मान्य प्रयोग नहीं है।

यह इस प्रकार कहना अधिक स्वाभाविक है:

*—the chair with the broken leg*

## Non-defining Relative Clauses (अनिश्चयात्मक संबंधवाचक उपवाक्य)

ये उपवाक्य किसी व्यक्ति या किसी वस्तु के संबंध में अतिरिक्त सूचना जोड़ते हैं। यह अतिरिक्त सूचना न भी कही जाती तो भी अर्थ सही-सही निकल आता है। ये उपवाक्य मुख्य उपवाक्य से अल्पविराम (,) लगा कर पृथक्कृत किए जाते हैं:

*—The film, which was shot in Mexico, has won an Oscar.*

अनिश्चयात्मक संबंधवाचक उपवाक्यों में इन सर्वनामों का प्रयोग हो सकता है
वस्तु के लिए शब्द **which;** संबंध दर्शाने के लिए शब्द **whose**:

*—My sister, **who** is a vegetarian, ordered a cheese salad.*
*—The tickets, **which** can be bought at the station, are valid for one day.*
*—Leena, **whose** car had broken down, arrived by bus.*

# APPENDIX 2: EXPRESSIONS USING NUMBERS

| Cardinal Numbers | | Ordinal Numbers | |
|---|---|---|---|
| **1** | one | **1st** | first |
| **2** | two | **2nd** | second |
| **3** | three | **3rd** | third |
| **4** | four | **4th** | fourth |
| **5** | five | **5th** | fifth |
| **6** | six | **6th** | sixth |
| **7** | seven | **7th** | seventh |
| **8** | eight | **8th** | eighth |
| **9** | nine | **9th** | ninth |
| **10** | ten | **10th** | tenth |
| **11** | eleven | **11th** | eleventh |
| **12** | twelve | **12th** | twelfth |
| **13** | thirteen | **13th** | thirteenth |
| **14** | fourteen | **14th** | fourteenth |
| **15** | fifteen | **15th** | fifteenth |
| **16** | sixteen | **16th** | sixteenth |
| **17** | seventeen | **17th** | seventeenth |
| **18** | eighteen | **18th** | eighteenth |
| **19** | nineteen | **19th** | nineteenth |
| **20** | twenty | **20th** | twentieth |
| **21** | twenty-one | **21st** | twenty-first |
| **22** | twenty-two | **22nd** | twenty-second |
| **30** | thirty | **30th** | thirtieth |
| **40** | forty | **40th** | fortieth |
| **50** | fifty | **50th** | fiftieth |
| **60** | sixty | **60th** | sixtieth |
| **70** | seventy | **70th** | seventieth |
| **80** | eighty | **80th** | eightieth |
| **90** | ninety | **90th** | ninetieth |
| **100** | a/one hundred* | **100th** | hundredth |
| **101** | a/one hundred and one* | **101st** | hundred and first |
| **200** | two hundred | **200th** | two hundredth |
| **1000** | a/one thousand* | **1000th** | thousandth |
| **10,000** | ten thousand | **10,000th** | ten thousandth |
| **100,000** | a/one hundred thousand* | **100,000th** | hundred thousandth |
| **1,000,000** | a/one million* | **1,000,000th** | millionth |

*697 six hundred and ninety-seven*

*3402 three thousand, four hundred and two*

*80,534 eighty thousand, five hundred and thirty-four*

* **One hundred**, **one thousand** आदि का प्रयोग **a hundred**, **a thousand** के बजाए तब होता है जब एक संख्या के अर्थ पर (ना कि दो की संख्या के अर्थ पर) बल देना हो।

# APPENDIX 3: MEASUREMENTS AND SI UNITS

**Metric measures** (with approximate non-metric equivalents)

| | Metric | | | | Non-metric |
|---|---|---|---|---|---|
| **Length** | 10 millimetres (mm) | = | 1 centimetre (cm) | = | 0.394 inch |
| | 100 centimetres | = | 1 metre (m) | = | 39.4 inches/1.094 yards |
| | 1000 metres | = | 1 kilometre (km) | = | 0.6214 mile |
| **Area** | 100 square metres ($m^2$) | = | 1 are (a) | = | 0.025 acre |
| | 100 ares | = | 1 hectare (ha) | = | 2.471 acres |
| | 100 hectares | = | 1 square kilometre ($km^2$) | = | 0.386 square mile |
| **Weight** | 1000 milligrams (mg) | = | 1 gram (g) | = | 15.43 grains |
| | 1000 grams | = | 1 kilogram (kg) | = | 2.205 pounds |
| | 1000 kilograms | = | 1 tonne | = | 19.688 hundredweight |
| **Capacity** | 10 millilitres (ml) | = | 1 centilitre | = | 0.018 pint (0.021 US pint) |
| | 100 centilitres (cl) | = | 1 litre (1) | = | 1.76 pints (2.1 US pints) |
| | 10 litres | = | 1 decalitre (dal) | = | 2.2 gallons (2.63 US gallons) |

**SI Units**

| | Physical Quantity | Name | Symbol |
|---|---|---|---|
| **Base units** | length | metre | m |
| | mass | kilogram | kg |
| | time | second | s |
| | electric current | ampere | A |
| | thermodynamic temperature | kelvin | K |
| | luminous intensity | candela | cd |
| | amount of substance | mole | mol |

# APPENDIX 4: ROMAN NUMERALS

| | | | | | | | | |
|---|---|---|---|---|---|---|---|---|
| I | = | 1 | XIV | = | 14 | XC | = | 90 |
| II | = | 2 | XV | = | 15 | C | = | 100 |
| III | = | 3 | XVI | = | 16 | CC | = | 200 |
| IV | = | 4 | XVII | = | 17 | CCC | = | 300 |
| V | = | 5 | XVIII | = | 18 | CD | = | 400 |
| VI | = | 6 | XIX | = | 19 | D | = | 500 |
| VII | = | 7 | XX | = | 20 | DC | = | 600 |
| VIII | = | 8 | XXX | = | 30 | DCC | = | 700 |
| IX | = | 9 | XL | = | 40 | DCCC | = | 800 |
| X | = | 10 | L | = | 50 | CM | = | 900 |
| XI | = | 11 | LX | = | 60 | M | = | 1000 |
| XII | = | 12 | LXX | = | 70 | MM | = | 2000 |
| XIII | = | 13 | LXXX | = | 80 | | | |

# APPENDIX 5: CHEMICAL ELEMENTS

| Element | Symbol | Atomic Number | Element | Symbol | Atomic Number |
|---|---|---|---|---|---|
| actinium | Ac | 89 | mercury | Hg | 80 |
| aluminium | Al | 13 | molybdenum | Mo | 42 |
| americium | Am | 95 | neodymium | Nd | 60 |
| antimony | Sb | 51 | neon | Ne | 10 |
| argon | Ar | 18 | neptunium | Np | 93 |
| arsenic | As | 33 | nickel | Ni | 28 |
| astatine | At | 85 | niobium | Nb | 41 |
| barium | Ba | 56 | nitrogen | N | 7 |
| berkelium | Bk | 97 | nobelium | No | 102 |
| beryllium | Be | 4 | osmium | Os | 76 |
| bismuth | Bi | 83 | oxygen | O | 8 |
| boron | B | 5 | palladium | Pd | 46 |
| bromine | Br | 35 | phosphorus | P | 15 |
| cadmium | Cd | 48 | platinum | Pt | 78 |
| caesium | Cs | 55 | plutonium | Pu | 94 |
| calcium | Ca | 20 | polonium | Po | 84 |
| californium | Cf | 98 | potassium | K | 19 |
| carbon | C | 6 | praseodymium | Pr | 59 |
| cerium | Ce | 58 | promethium | Pm | 61 |
| chlorine | Cl | 17 | protactinium | Pa | 91 |
| chromium | Cr | 24 | radium | Ra | 88 |
| cobalt | Co | 27 | radon | Rn | 86 |
| copper | Cu | 29 | rhenium | Re | 75 |
| curium | Cm | 96 | rhodium | Rh | 45 |
| dysprosium | Dy | 66 | rubidium` | Rb | 37 |
| einsteinium | Es | 99 | ruthenium | Ru | 44 |
| erbium | Er | 68 | rutherfordium | Rf | 104 |
| europium | Eu | 63 | samarium | Sm | 62 |
| fermium | Fm | 100 | scandium | Sc | 21 |
| fluorine | F | 9 | selenium | Se | 34 |
| francium | Fr | 87 | silicon | Si | 14 |
| gadolinium | Gd | 64 | silver | Ag | 47 |
| gallium | Ga | 31 | sodium | Na | 11 |
| germanium | Ge | 32 | strontium | Sr | 38 |
| gold | Au | 79 | sulphur | S | 16 |
| hafnium | Hf | 72 | tantalum | Ta | 73 |
| hahnium | Ha | 105 | technetium | Tc | 43 |
| helium | He | 2 | tellurium | Te | 52 |
| holmium | Ho | 67 | terbium | Tb | 65 |
| hydrogen | H | 1 | thallium | Tl | 81 |
| indium | In | 49 | thorium | Th | 90 |
| iodine | I | 53 | thulium | Tm | 69 |
| iridium | Ir | 77 | tin | Sn | 50 |
| iron | Fe | 26 | titanium | Ti | 22 |
| krypton | Kr | 36 | tungsten | W | 74 |
| lanthanum | La | 57 | uranium | U | 92 |
| lawrencium | Lr | 103 | vanadium | V | 23 |
| lead | Pb | 82 | xenon | Xe | 54 |
| lithium | Li | 3 | ytterbium | Yb | 70 |
| lutetium | Lu | 71 | yttrium | Y | 39 |
| magnesium | Mg | 12 | zinc | Zn | 30 |
| manganese | Mn | 25 | zirconium | Zr | 40 |
| mendelevium | Md | 101 | | | |